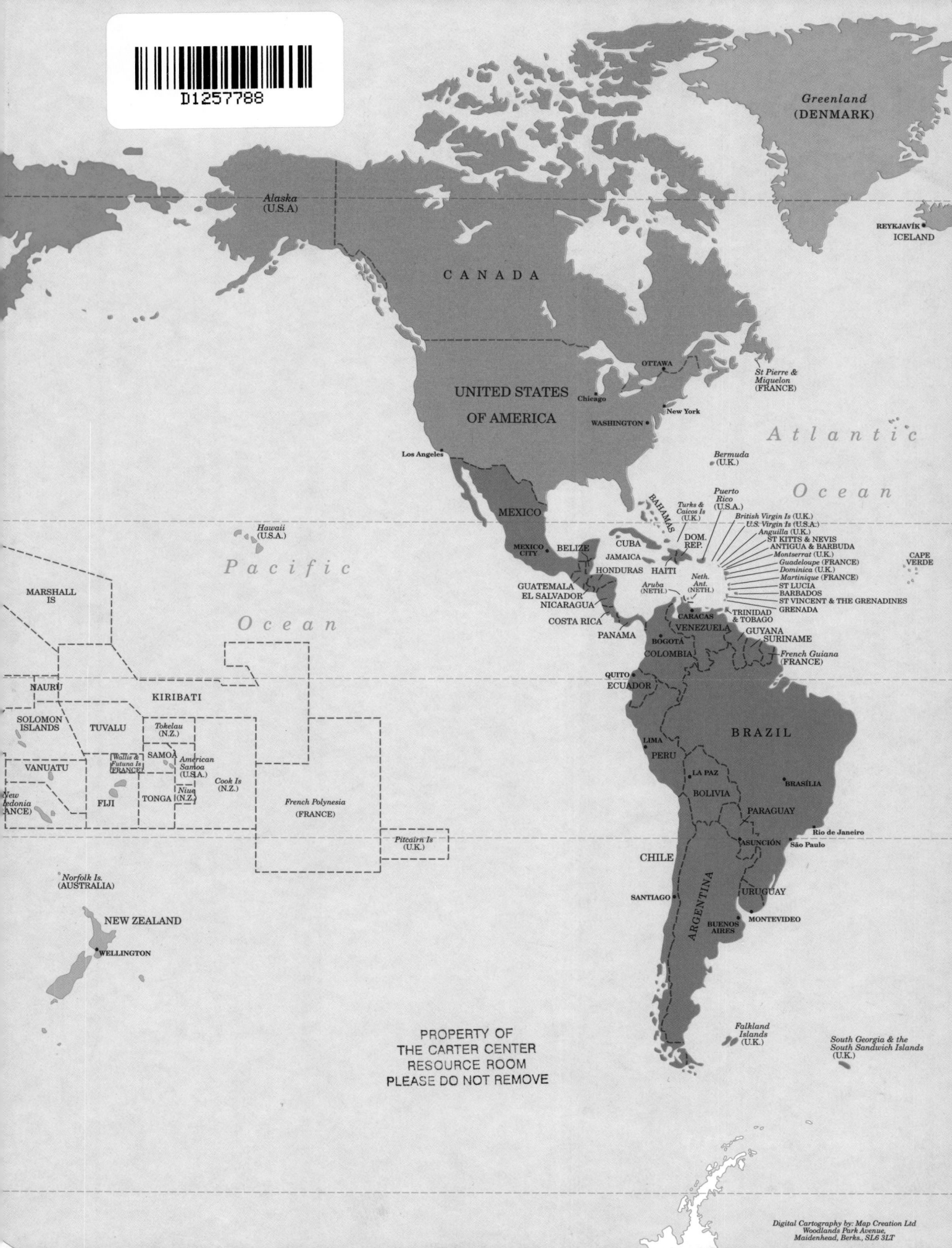

D1257788

Greenland **(DENMARK)**

REYKJAVÍK
ICELAND

Alaska (U.S.A.)

CANADA

OTTAWA

St Pierre & Miquelon (FRANCE)

A t l a n t i c

UNITED STATES OF AMERICA

Chicago
New York

WASHINGTON

O c e a n

Los Angeles

Bermuda (U.K.)

Hawaii (U.S.A.)

P a c i f i c

MEXICO

BAHAMAS

Turks & Caicos Is (U.K.)

Puerto Rico (U.S.A.)

British Virgin Is (U.K.)
U.S. Virgin Is (U.S.A.)
Anguilla (U.K.)
ST KITTS & NEVIS
ANTIGUA & BARBUDA
Montserrat (U.K.)
Guadeloupe (FRANCE)
Dominica (U.K.)
Martinique (FRANCE)
ST LUCIA
BARBADOS
ST VINCENT & THE GRENADINES
GRENADA

CAPE VERDE

MEXICO CITY
BELIZE
CUBA
JAMAICA
HAITI
DOM. REP.

O c e a n

GUATEMALA
EL SALVADOR
NICARAGUA
HONDURAS

Aruba (NETH.)
Neth. Ant. (NETH.)

MARSHALL IS

COSTA RICA

CARACAS
VENEZUELA

TRINIDAD & TOBAGO

PANAMA

BOGOTÁ

GUYANA
SURINAME

NAURU

KIRIBATI

COLOMBIA

French Guiana (FRANCE)

SOLOMON ISLANDS

TUVALU

Tokelau (N.Z.)

QUITO
ECUADOR

VANUATU

Wallis & Futuna Is (FRANCE)

SAMOA

American Samoa (U.S.A.)

Cook Is (N.Z.)

LIMA
PERU

BRAZIL

New Caledonia (FRANCE)

FIJI

TONGA

Niue (N.Z.)

French Polynesia (FRANCE)

LA PAZ

BRASÍLIA

BOLIVIA

PARAGUAY

Rio de Janeiro

Pitcairn Is (U.K.)

ASUNCIÓN
São Paulo

Norfolk Is. (AUSTRALIA)

CHILE

NEW ZEALAND

SANTIAGO

URUGUAY

WELLINGTON

ARGENTINA

BUENOS AIRES

MONTEVIDEO

Falkland Islands (U.K.)

South Georgia & the South Sandwich Islands (U.K.)

Digital Cartography by: Map Creation Ltd
Woodlands Park Avenue,
Maidenhead, Berks., SL6 3LT

Africa
South of
the Sahara
2001

Africa South of the Sahara 2001

30th Edition

EUROPA PUBLICATIONS · Taylor & Francis Group ·

First published 1971
Thirtieth Edition 2001
© Europa Publications 2000
11 New Fetter Lane, London, EC4P 4EE, England
(A member of the Taylor & Francis Group)

ISBN 1-85743-078-6
ISSN 0065-3896

Library of Congress Catalog Card Number 78-112271

Typeset by UBL International and printed by Unwin Brothers Limited
The Gresham Press
Old Woking, Surrey

FOREWORD

The thirtieth edition of AFRICA SOUTH OF THE SAHARA appears at a time of continuing transition and unrest in the sub-Saharan region. On the one hand, during the year under review major steps were taken towards the full restoration of democratic government, through the holding of elections, in Niger and Somalia, the long-standing opposition assumed power in Senegal following its victory in a free and fair general election, and peace agreements were signed in the Republic of the Congo and between Ethiopia and Eritrea. On the other hand, persistent civil strife continued in Angola, Sierra Leone and Sudan, an unexpected military coup took place in Côte d'Ivoire, and the highly-inflammatory issue of the forcible seizure and reclamation of white-owned farms in Zimbabwe resulted in serious political tension in that country. The devastating floods in Mozambique also featured strongly in the international media coverage of sub-Saharan Africa during this period. These events, together with the year's significant political and economic developments in each of the 52 states that comprise Africa south of the Sahara, are comprehensively narrated and examined. Readers' perspectives are further expanded by an evaluation of African 'Continuities and Changes' in the 'Background to the Continent' section, which also provides an in-depth examination of current Economic Trends in the region.

In addition to contributions by specialist authors, researchers and commentators, all statistical and directory material in the new edition has been extensively updated, revised and expanded. Directory information has been extended to include further e-mail and internet addresses where available. A calendar of the key political events of 1999–2000 provides a convenient rapid reference guide to the year's main developments. Extensive coverage of international organizations and research bodies active in Africa is included, together with detailed background information on the continent's major agricultural and mineral commodities.

The Editor is once again grateful to all the contributors for their articles and advice and to the numerous governments and organizations that have returned questionnaires and provided statistical and other information.

September 2000

ACKNOWLEDGEMENTS

The editors gratefully acknowledge the interest and co-operation of the many national statistical and information offices and embassies and high commissions, whose valued assistance in updating the material contained in AFRICA SOUTH OF THE SAHARA is greatly appreciated.

We acknowledge particular indebtedness for permission to reproduce material from the following publications: the United Nations' *Demographic Yearbook, Statistical Yearbook* and *Industrial Commodity Statistics Yearbook*; the United Nations Educational, Scientific and Cultural Organization's *Statistical Yearbook*; the International Labour Office's *Yearbook of Labour Statistics*; the International Monetary Fund's *International Financial Statistics* and *Government Finance*

Statistics Yearbook; the World Tourism Organization's *Yearbook of Tourism Statistics*; the Food and Agriculture Organization of the United Nations' *Production Yearbook, Yearbook of Fishery Statistics* and *Yearbook of Forest Products*; and *The Military Balance 1999–2000*, a publication of the International Institute for Strategic Studies, Arundel House, 13–15 Arundel Street, London, WC2R 3DX, England. We acknowledge *La Zone Franc* and the regular publications of the Banque centrale des états de l'Afrique de l'ouest and of the Banque des états de l'Afrique centrale as the sources of some of our financial information on francophone Africa.

The articles on St Helena, Ascension and Tristan da Cunha make use of material from *The Commonwealth Yearbook*, with the kind permission of the Stationery Office.

EXPLANATORY NOTE ON THE DIRECTORY SECTION

The Directory section of each chapter is arranged under the following headings, where they apply:

THE CONSTITUTION

THE GOVERNMENT
    HEAD OF STATE
    CABINET/COUNCIL OF MINISTERS/
    EXECUTIVE
    MINISTRY ADDRESSES

LEGISLATURE

POLITICAL ORGANIZATIONS

DIPLOMATIC REPRESENTATION

JUDICIAL SYSTEM

RELIGION

THE PRESS

PUBLISHERS

BROADCASTING AND COMMUNICATIONS

FINANCE
    CENTRAL BANK
    NATIONAL BANKS
    COMMERCIAL BANKS
    DEVELOPMENT BANKS
    MERCHANT BANKS

    SAVINGS BANKS
    INVESTMENT BANKS
    FOREIGN BANKS
    FINANCIAL INSTITUTIONS
    STOCK EXCHANGE
    INSURANCE

TRADE AND INDUSTRY
    GOVERNMENT AGENCIES
    DEVELOPMENT ORGANIZATIONS
    CHAMBERS OF COMMERCE
    INDUSTRIAL AND TRADE ASSOCIATIONS
    EMPLOYERS' ORGANIZATIONS
    UTILITIES
    MAJOR COMPANIES
    CO-OPERATIVES
    TRADE UNIONS

TRANSPORT
    RAILWAYS
    ROADS
    INLAND WATERWAYS
    SHIPPING
    CIVIL AVIATION

TOURISM

DEFENCE

EDUCATION

CONTENTS

CONTENTS

CONTENTS

CONTENTS

CONTENTS

THE CONTRIBUTORS

J. A. Allan. Professor of Geography, School of Oriental and African Studies, University of London.

L. Berry. Former Professor of Geography, University of Dar es Salaam.

E. A. Boateng. Environmental consultant and educationalist.

Sir Mervyn Brown. Former British Ambassador in Madagascar. Member, Académie Malgache.

Richard Brown. Former Dean, School of African and Asian Studies, University of Sussex at Brighton.

Marisé Castro. Researcher, Amnesty International, International Secretariat, London.

Christopher Clapham. Professor of Politics and International Relations, University of Lancaster.

John I. Clarke. Professor of Geography, University of Durham.

João Gomes Cravinho. Lecturer in International Relations, University of Coímbra.

Pierre Englebert. Political Economy and Public Policy Program, University of Southern California.

Marek Garztecki. Writer specializing in African political and economic issues.

Patrick Gilkes. Writer on Africa and the Third World for the BBC External Services.

Pierre Gourou. Professor of Geography, Université Libre de Bruxelles and Collège de France, Paris.

R. J. Harrison Church. Late Professor of Geography, London School of Economics.

David Hilling. Senior Lecturer in Geography, Royal Holloway and Bedford New College, University of London.

Edith Hodgkinson. Writer specializing in the economies of developing countries.

A. MacGregor Hutcheson. Lecturer in Geography, Aberdeen College of Education.

George Kay. Head of the Department of Geography and Recreation Studies, Staffordshire University.

B. W. Langlands. Late Professor of Geography, Makerere University College, Kampala.

Bernard Lanne. Specialist on Chad and Editor-in-Chief of *La Documentation française,* Paris.

G. C. Last. Former Adviser, Ethiopian Ministry of Education and Fine Arts.

I. M. Lewis. Professor of Anthropology, London School of Economics and Political Science.

Akin L. Mabogunje. Former Professor of Geography, University of Ibadan.

T. C. McCaskie. Lecturer in the Social History of West Africa in the Twentieth Century, Centre of West African Studies, University of Birmingham.

Hugh Macmillan. Former Professor of History, University of Transkei.

François Misser. Writer specializing in the business and economic affairs of developing countries.

Peter K. Mitchell. Honorary Senior Research Fellow, Centre of West African Studies, University of Birmingham.

W. T. W. Morgan. Senior Lecturer, Department of Geography, University of Durham.

Gregory Mthembu-Salter. Writer specializing in the political and economic affairs of African countries.

Thomas Ofcansky. Writer specializing in African political and economic issues.

J. D. Omer-Cooper. Late Professor of History, University of Otago.

Quentin Outram. Senior Lecturer in Economics, Leeds University Business School, University of Leeds.

René Pélissier. Author specializing in contemporary Spanish-speaking and Portuguese-speaking Africa.

Luisa Handem Piette. Writer specializing in African political and development issues.

Shamlal Puri. Managing Editor of *Newslink Africa*, London.

Alan Rake. Former Managing Editor of *African Business* and *New African* magazines, London.

Andrew D. Roberts. Professor of the History of Africa, School of Oriental and African Studies, University of London.

Christopher Saunders. Associate Professor and Head of the Department of History, University of Cape Town.

Markus Scheuermaier. Writer specializing in African political and economic issues.

Gerhard Seibert. Researcher, Centro de Estudos Africanos e Asiaticos, Lisbon.

Miles Smith-Morris. Writer specializing in developing countries.

Donald L. Sparks. Professor of Economics, The Citadel, Charleston, South Carolina.

David Styan. Lecturer in Politics, Birkbeck College, University of London.

Richard Synge. Writer and journalist specializing in African political and economic issues.

Virginia Thompson. Writer specializing in francophone Africa.

Linda Van Buren. Writer specializing in the business and economic affairs of African countries.

Gavin Williams. Fellow and Tutor in Politics and Sociology, St Peter's College, University of Oxford.

Geoffrey J. Williams. Former Professor of Geography, University of Zambia.

John A. Wiseman. Late Senior Lecturer in Politics, University of Newcastle.

ABBREVIATIONS

Acad.	Academician; Academy		Dr.	Drive
ACP	African, Caribbean and Pacific (States)		Dra	Doctora
ADB	African Development Bank		dwt	dead weight tons
ADF	African Development Fund			
Adm.	Admiral		E	East; Eastern; Emalangeni (Swaziland currency)
Admin.	Administration; Administrative; Administrator		€	Euro (currency)
AG	Aktiengesellschaft (limited company)		EAC	East African Community
a.i.	ad interim		EC	European Community
AIDS	acquired immunodeficiency syndrome		ECA	Economic Commission for Africa (UN)
AM	Amplitude Modulation		ECOWAS	Economic Community of West African States
Apdo	Apartado (Post Box)		ECU	European Currency Unit(s)
Apt	Apartment		Ed.(s)	Editor(s)
Ass.	Assembly		EDF	European Development Fund
Asscn	Association		edn	edition
Assoc.	Associate		EEZ	Exclusive Economic Zone
Asst	Assistant		e.g.	exempli gratia (for example)
Aug.	August		EIB	European Investment Bank
auth.	authorized		Eng.	Engineer; Engineering
Avda	Avenida (Avenue)		EPZ	Export Processing Zone
Ave	Avenue		est.	established; estimate; estimated
			etc.	etcetera
BCEAO	Banque centrale des états de l'Afrique de l'ouest		EU	European Union
Bd	Board		excl.	excluding
b/d	barrels per day		Exec.	Executive
BEAC	Banque des états de l'Afrique centrale		exhbn(s)	exhibition(s)
Bldg(s)	Building(s)		Ext.	Extension
Blvd	Boulevard			
BOAD	Banque Ouest-Africaine de développement		f.	founded
BP	Boîte Postale (Post Box)		FAO	Food and Agriculture Organization
br.(s)	branch(es)		f.a.s.	free alongside
Brig.	Brigadier		Feb.	February
			Fed.	Federation; Federal
C	Centigrade; Cedi(s) (Ghana currency)		FG	Guinea Franc
c.	circa		FIDES	Fonds d'investissement et de développement
cap.	capital			économique et social
Capt.	Captain		Flt	Flight
cc	cubic centimetre(s)		FMG	Malagasy Franc
Cdre	Commodore		fmr(ly)	former(ly)
CEMAC	Communauté économique et monétaire en		f.o.b.	free on board
	Afrique centrale		Fr	Father
Cen.	Central		Fr.	Franc(s)
CEO	Chief Executive Officer		Fri.	Friday
cf.	confer (compare)		ft	foot (feet)
CFA	Communauté financière africaine; Coopération			
	financière en Afrique centrale		g	gram(s)
Chair.	Chairman/woman		GDP	Gross Domestic Product
Cie	Compagnie		Gen.	General
c.i.f.	cost, insurance and freight		GNP	Gross National Product
C-in-C	Commander-in-Chief		Gov.	Governor
circ.	circulation		Govt	Government
cm	centimetre(s)		GPO	General Post Office
cnr	corner		grt	gross registered ton(s)
c/o	care of		GWh	gigawatt hour(s)
Co	Company; County			
Col	Colonel		ha	hectare(s)
Comm.	Commission		HIV	human immunodeficiency virus
Commdr	Commander		hl	hectolitre(s)
Commdt	Commandant		HM	His/Her Majesty
Commr	Commissioner		HQ	Headquarters
Conf.	Conference		HYV	high-yielding variety
Confed.	Confederation			
Corpn	Corporation		ibid.	ibidem (from the same source)
CP	Caixa Postal, Case Postale (Post Box)		IBRD	International Bank for Reconstruction and
Cpl	Corporal			Development (World Bank)
Cttee	Committee		IDA	International Development Association
cu	cubic		i.e.	id est (that is to say)
cwt	hundredweight		IGAD	Intergovernmental Authority on Development
			ILO	International Labour Organization/Office
Dec.	December		IMF	International Monetary Fund
Del.	Delegate		in	inch (inches)
Dem.	Democratic		Inc	Incorporated
Dep.	Deputy		incl.	include, including
dep.	deposits		Ind.	Independent
Dept	Department		Ing.	Engineer
Devt	Development		Insp.	Inspector
Dir	Director		Inst.	Institute
Div.	Division(al)		Int.	International
Dr	Doctor		Is	Islands

ISIC	International Standard Industrial Classification
Jan.	January
Jr	Junior
Jt	Joint
K	Kwacha (Malawi and Zambia currencies)
kg	kilogram(s)
km	kilometre(s)
kW	kilowatt(s)
kWh	kilowatt hour(s)
lb	pound(s)
Lda	Limitada (limited company)
Le.	Leone (Sierra Leone currency)
LNG	Liquefied natural gas
LPG	Liquefied petroleum gas
Lt	Lieutenant
Ltd	Limited
M	Maloti (Lesotho currency)
m	metre(s)
m.	million
Maj.	Major
Man.	Manager; Managing
mem.	member
Mfg	Manufacturing
mfrs	manufacturers
mg	milligram(s)
Mgr	Monseigneur, Monsignor
Mil.	Military
Mlle	Mademoiselle
mm	millimetre(s)
Mme	Madame
Mon.	Monday
MP	Member of Parliament
MSS	manuscripts
Mt	Mount
MW	megawatt(s); medium wave
MWh	megawatt hour(s)
N	North; Northern
N	Naira (Nigerian currency)
NA	National Association (banking)
n.a.	not available
Nat.	National
NCO	Non-Commissioned Officer
n.e.s.	not elsewhere specified
NGO	non-governmental organization
No.	number
Nov.	November
nr	near
nrt	net registered ton(s)
NV	Naamloze Vennootschap (limited company)
OAU	Organization of African Unity
OCAM	Organisation commune africaine et mauricienne
Oct.	October
OECD	Organisation for Economic Co-operation and Development
OIC	Organization of the Islamic Conference
OMVS	Organisation pour la mise en valeur du fleuve Sénégal
OPEC	Organization of the Petroleum Exporting Countries
opp.	opposite
Org.(s)	Organization(s)
oz	ounce(s)
P	Pula (Botswana currency)
p.	page
p.a.	per annum
Parl.	Parliament(ary)
Perm.	Permanent
PLC	Public Limited Company
PMB	Private Mail Bag
PO	Post Office
POB	Post Office Box
Pres.	President
Prin.	Principal
Prof.	Professor
Propr	Proprietor
Prov.	Province; Provincial
Pte	Private
Pty	Proprietary
p.u.	paid up
publ.(s)	publication(s); published
Publr	Publisher
Pvt.	Private
q.v.	quod vide (to which refer)
R	Rand (South African currency)
Rd	Road
regd	registered
reorg.	reorganized
Rep.	Representative
Repub.	Republic
res	reserves
retd	retired
Rev.	Reverend
Rm	Room
RMS	Royal Mail Steamer
RN	Royal Navy
Rs	Rupee(s) (Mauritius currency)
Rt	Right
S	South; Southern
SA	Société Anonyme, Sociedad Anónima (limited company); South Africa
SADC	Southern African Development Community
SARL	Sociedade Anônima de Responsabilidade Limitada (limited company)
Sat.	Saturday
SDR	Special Drawing Right(s)
Sec.	Secretary
Secr.	Secretariat
Sept.	September
Sgt	Sergeant
SITC	Standard International Trade Classification
SME	small- and medium-sized enterprises
Soc.	Society
Sq.	Square
sq	square (in measurements)
SR	Seychelles Rupee(s)
Sr	Senior
St	Street; Saint, San, Santo
Sta	Santa
Ste	Sainte
Stn	Station
Sun.	Sunday
Supt	Superintendent
tech.	technical, technology
trans.	translator, translated
Treas.	Treasurer
TV	Television
UA	Unit(s) of Account
UEE	Unidade Económica Estatal
UEMOA	Union économique et monétaire ouest-africaine
UK	United Kingdom
ul.	ulitsa (street)
UM	Ouguiya(s) (Mauritania currency)
UN	United Nations
UNCTAD	United Nations Conference on Trade and Development
UNDP	United Nations Development Programme
UNESCO	United Nations Educational, Scientific and Cultural Organization
UNHCR	United Nations High Commissioner for Refugees
UNIDO	United Nations Industrial Development Organization
Univ.	University
US(A)	United States (of America)
USSR	Union of Soviet Socialist Republics
viz.	videlicet (namely)
Vol.(s)	Volume(s)
W	West; Western
WHO	World Health Organization
WTO	World Trade Organization
yr(s)	year(s)

POLITICAL EVENTS IN AFRICA SOUTH OF THE SAHARA, 1999–2000

1999

SEPTEMBER

2 Minister of posts and telecommunications in Cameroon was replaced.

President Charles Taylor reorganized the Liberian cabinet.

Attempted coup in the Comoros.

Six-day state of emergency declared in Botswana following problems with registration of voters for forthcoming election.

6 Kenyan cabinet reshuffled and number of ministers reduced from 27 to 15.

Death of Zaccheus Chesoni, chief justice of Kenya.

7 President Laurent-Désiré Kabila made a number of senior appointments to the armed forces of the Democratic Republic of the Congo.

13 Bernard Chunga appointed director of public prosecutions in Kenya.

17 59 Zambian soldiers who took part in the failed coup against the Chiluba administration in October 1997 were found guilty of treason and sentenced to death.

22 The death sentence, pronounced in January against ex-President Traoré, his wife and his brother-in-law, was commuted to terms of life imprisonment by President Konaré of Mali.

OCTOBER

2 President Ange-Félix Patassé of the Central African Republic was re-elected in presidential election.

7 Rwandan legislature adopted motion of censure against two government ministers, who subsequently resigned.

11 Minor cabinet reorganization in Liberia.

12 President Jerry Rawlings of Ghana replaced government minister.

13 Government reshuffle announced in Burkina Faso.

14 Death of Julius Nyerere, founding president of Tanzania.

16 General election in Botswana.

20 Festus Mogae re-elected president of Botswana by national assembly.

Death of the Angolan minister of geology and mines.

21 New cabinet appointed in Botswana.

22 UN Security Council adopted a resolution establishing a peace-keeping force, the UN Mission in Sierra Leone (UNAMSIL), to supervise the implementation of the Lomé peace accord.

23 Remaining troops of the Cease-Fire Monitoring Group of the Economic Community of West African States (ECOWAS) left Liberia.

27 Mauritania established full diplomatic relations with Israel.

NOVEMBER

1 New council of ministers appointed in the Central African Republic.

2 New cabinet of national unity inaugurated in Sierra Leone by President Ahmed Tejan Kabbah.

4 President Jerry Rawlings reorganized the Ghanaian council of ministers.

Murder of former Zambian President Kenneth Kaunda's son, Maj. Wesi Kaunda.

8 Expulsions commenced of Burkinabè migrants from Côte d'Ivoire.

11 Kenyan parliament voted to remove president's power to appoint the clerk of the house.

14 Municipal elections held in Madagascar.

17 Announcement of a peace agreement in the civil war in the Republic of the Congo.

18 President Charles Taylor of Liberia appointed new chief of staff of the armed forces.

19 Ministerial reshuffle in Cape Verde.

24 In the second round of voting, Col (retd) Tandja Mamadou was elected president of Niger with 58.89% of the votes cast.

26 Kenya declares AIDS a national disaster.

28 Presidential and legislative elections held in Guinea-Bissau.

30 First day of presidential and legislative elections in Namibia (concluded on 1 December).

Establishment of the UN Mission in the Democratic Republic of the Congo (MONUC) approved by the UN Security Council.

DECEMBER

2 Appointment of Bianrifi Tarmidi as prime minister of the Comoros.

3–5 Presidential and legislative elections held in Mozambique.

6 Maj. Wanké of the Conseil de réconciliation nationale relinquished control of Niger to the transitional government, and the newly-elected Col (retd) Tandja Mamadou was subsequently sworn in to office as the new president.

13 President al-Bashir of Sudan declared a three-month state of emergency and dissolved parliament.

General strike in Burkina Faso to commemorate the anniversary of the assassination of Norbert Zongo.

14 Nagoum Yamassoum was appointed prime minister of Chad, following the resignation of Nassour Guelengdouksia Ouaidou.

15 National assembly in the Republic of the Congo granted amnesty to former rebels.

Kenyan parliament voted to form select committee to review the constitution.

20 Joseph Msika appointed second vice-president of Zimbabwe.

22 President Omar Bongo of Gabon reorganized government, reducing the number of ministers from 42 to 31.

23 Unrest began in Côte d'Ivoire, leading to a *coup d'état*.

26 Mauritania announced its withdrawal from Economic Community of West African States (ECOWAS).

President Bédié departed from Côte d'Ivoire; Brig.-Gen. Robert Guéï assumed power.

Announcement of a cease-fire between the Senegalese armed forces and the rebels of the Mouvement des forces démocratiques de la Casamance.

29 President Bongo of Gabon appointed as mediator between the authorities and the rebels in the Republic of the Congo.

31 Minor cabinet reshuffle carried out in The Gambia.

Resignation of the Sudanese government and all of the country's state governors.

2000

JANUARY

1 Botswana's vice-president and minister of presidential affairs and public administration, Lt-Gen. Seretse Ian Khama, commenced a one-year sabbatical leave from government.

4 Transitional government appointed in Côte d'Ivoire.

5 President Charles Taylor effected minor government reorganization in Liberia.

A new government was announced in Niger, following the appointment of Hama Amadou as prime minister; the opposition, however, refused the ministerial posts offered to them.

10 Government reorganization in Ghana.

11 President Pierre Buyoya of Burundi announced a minor government reorganization.

12 Kenyan parliamentary select committee on anticorruption commenced the hearing of cases.

15 Reported coup attempt in The Gambia.

16 Election of Koumba Yala as president of Guinea-Bissau.

18 President Pasteur Bizimungu of Rwanda reorganized the council of ministers.

19 Former Ugandan minister of justice, Joseph Ekemu, was imprisoned for two years for embezzlement.

24 New cabinet appointed in Sudan.

25 Appointment of Caetano Intchama as prime minister of Guinea-Bissau.

27 Referendum held in the separatist island of Nzwani in the Comoros to decide on the ratification of the Antananarivo accord.

28 Government reshuffle in Angola.

FEBRUARY

3 Electoral code modified in Burkina Faso.

4 The exiled former dictator of Chad, Hissène Habré, was indicted on charges of torture and arrested in Dakar, Senegal.

7 Peace accord signed between Djibouti government and the Front pour la restauration de l'unité et de la démocratie (FRUD).

UN Security Council voted to increase the number of UNAMSIL troops in Sierra Leone from 6,000 to 11,000.

12–13 Government-sponsored new constitution rejected in a referendum in Zimbabwe.

14 Ibrahim Boubacar Keita resigned as prime minister of Mali and a new government was subsequently announced under the premiership of Mandé Sidibé.

15 Final withdrawal of the UN peace-keeping mission, MINURCA, from the Central Africa Republic.

25 Zimbabwe's minister of transport and energy resigned over fuel crisis.

27 First round of voting in the Senegalese presidential elections held.

28 Rwandan prime minister, Pierre Célestin Rwigyema, resigned from office.

MARCH

1 New cabinet appointed in Malawi.

2 Government changes in Liberia.

9 Minor cabinet reshuffle in The Gambia.

10 Minor government reorganization in Côte d'Ivoire.

13 State of emergency in Sudan extended until the end of 2000.

18 Cabinet reshuffle in Cameroon.

19 Cabinet reorganization announced in Namibia.

Ministerial reorganization in Chad.

Abdoulaye Wade won the second round of voting in the Senegalese presidential elections.

20 A new council of ministers was formed in Rwanda, following the appointment of Bernard Makuza to the office of prime minister.

21 Attempted coup in the Comoros.

23 The Rwandan president, Pasteur Bizimungu, resigned from office.

28–29 Army mutiny quelled in Côte d'Ivoire.

APRIL

1 Abdoulaye Wade took office as president of Senegal.

3 Cabinet reshuffle in Nigeria.
New government appointed in Senegal.

5 Resignation of minister of foreign affairs and communities in São Tomé and Príncipe.

6 Zimbabwe's house of assembly narrowly approved a constitutional amendment allowing the government to seize white-owned farms without compensation.

7 and 14 Elections to the senate held in Mauritania.

10–11 Violent student unrest in The Gambia.

11 Constitutional amendment adopted in Burkina Faso, modifying the electoral law.

12 Trial opened in Guinea of opposition leader, Alpha Condé.

17 Government reshuffle in the Central African Republic.
Maj.-Gen. Paul Kagame was elected president of Rwanda by members of the transitional legislature and the government.

28 Ethiopia and Eritrea participated in unsuccessful indirect OAU-sponsored peace talks in Algiers.

MAY

2 Nigerian state governments that had earlier adopted Muslim Shari'a law agreed to revert to the national penal code.
Somali national reconciliation conference began in Arta, Djibouti.

6 Hasan at-Turabi suspended from his position as secretary-general of the Sudanese National Congress by President al-Bashir.

7 Two Kenyan government ministers replaced.

10 Cabinet reshuffle in Sudan.

12 Kenya agreed to reopen its embassy in Rwanda.
Hostilities resumed between Eritrea and Ethiopia.

14 Legislative elections held in Ethiopia.

15 Government reshuffle in São Tomé and Príncipe.

17 UN imposed 12-month arms embargo on Eritrea and Ethiopia.

President Moi of Kenya dismissed permanent secretary for education over fraud charges.

18 New government appointed in Côte d'Ivoire.

19 UN Security Council authorized further increase in the strength of UNAMSIL in Sierra Leone (to 13,000), following the abduction of some 500 peacekeeping troops by the rebel Revolutionary United Front.

25 Ethiopian troops captured key border town of Zelambessa.

28 Municipal elections held in Equatorial Guinea, which were boycotted by the opposition.

JUNE

1 Kenya ratified East African Community (EAC) Treaty.

2 Minor cabinet reorganization in Nigeria.

4 Minor cabinet reshuffle in The Gambia.

7 Major government reshuffle in Guinea.
International commission of inquiry into human rights in Togo established.

16 Minor ministerial reshuffle in Togo.

18 Ethiopia and Eritrea signed cease-fire agreement in Algiers.

20 The government of Chad signed a peace agreement with the dissident group Résistance armée contre les forces antidémocratiques, in Bénin.

22 Uganda agreed to withdraw more troops from the Democratic Republic of the Congo.

23 Liberian vice-president, Enoch Dogolea, died.

24–25 Legislative elections in Zimbabwe.

25 Municipal elections held in Guinea.

JULY

1 Ponatshego Kedikilwe resigned as Botswana's minister of education.

2 Referendum held on Mayotte to confirm the conferral of the status of collectivité départementale.
Ugandans voted to continue with 'no-party' system of rule in referendum.

4 A judge in Senegal dismissed the charges against Chadian former president Hissène Habré on the basis that he had no jurisdiction to pursue the case.

4–5 Protests by the armed forces in Côte d'Ivoire.

7 East African Community (EAC) came into force.

11 The citizens of St Helena presented their case to the UN Committee on Decolonization, for British passports and a new constitution.

12 Legislative elections in Lesotho provisionally scheduled for 26 May 2001.

15 New cabinet appointed in Zimbabwe.

22 A constitutional amendment was approved by the national assembly in Mali, including the abolition of the supreme court and the creation of a single press regulation body; however, implementation of these changes remained subject to a referendum.

23 New constitution adopted by referendum in Côte d'Ivoire.

24 New Liberian vice-president, Moses Blah, inaugurated.

30 Resignation of the prime minister of Cape Verde, Carlos Alberto Wahnon de Carvalho Veiga, and appointment of António Gualberto do Rosário as his replacement.

AUGUST

10 Mauritian parliament dissolved.

13 Somali transitional national assembly held its inaugural meeting in Djibouti.

18 Minor cabinet reshuffle announced in Malawi; new ministry of sports and culture created.

26 Signing of the Fomboni accord in the Comoros providing for greater autonomy for the three islands—Nzwani, Mwali and Njazidja.

Government of Malawi announced that local elections would take place on 21 November.

28 Power-sharing agreement signed for Burundi by 13 of 19 political groupings, convened at a summit meeting at Arusha, Tanzania.

Abdulkassim Salad Hassan inaugurated as president of Somalia.

30 Ministerial reshuffle in Chad.

31 Minor cabinet reshuffle announced in Botswana, effective from 1 September; Lt-Gen. Seretse Ian Khama to resume vice-presidency four months earlier than envisaged.

LATE INFORMATION

UNITED NATIONS PEACE-KEEPING OPERATIONS (p. 95)

On 15 September 2000 the UN Security Council authorized the deployment of a peace-keeping operation to monitor the cease-fire between Eritrea and Ethiopia. The UN Mission in Ethiopia and Eritrea (UNMEE) was to comprise up to 4,200 troops, and was to be withdrawn following the completion of the process to demarcate the two countries' disputed border.

On 20 September 2000 the UN Security Council extended the mandate of the United Nations Mission in Sierra Leone (UNAMSIL) until the end of the year.

CÔTE D'IVOIRE (p. 429)

Government Changes
(September 2000)

Minister of Defence: HONORÉ DOUTY.

Minister of State, responsible for Transport: Gen. MATHIAS DOUÉ.

Minister of Security: Gen. AUGUSTIN ASSAUD AKAWA.

Minister of Justice and Keeper of the Seals: Brig.-Gen. PASCAL YAO KONAN.

Minister of Housing and Environment: CHRISTOPHE NADO.

Minister of Youth and Sports: Naval Lt HONORÉ ZOHIN.

On 4 October 2000 Brig.-Gen. Gueï declared the imposition of a nation-wide state of emergency and curfew, which were to be in operation during 6–9 October.

ERITREA (p. 479)

Government Changes
(October 2000)

Minister of Foreign Affairs: ALI SAYYID ABDULLAH.

Minister of Trade and Industry: HAILE WOLDETENSAE.

PART ONE
Background to the Continent

REFORMING AFRICA: CONTINUITIES AND CHANGES

GAVIN WILLIAMS

PEOPLE, INSTITUTIONS AND POWER

The people and states of Africa have experienced dramatic change since colonial rulers transferred power to their African successors. Institutions of rule have been recast, whether by force or negotiation. African economies have been vulnerable to changing international markets, corrupt appropriation of limited resources, rising debts, and external direction of their policies. At the same time, political, social and economic arrangements, often of colonial origin, have continued to be reproduced in new guises. States and public institutions defend the jurisdictions within which their agents exercise authority. Both established and nascent governments face similar problems of erecting frameworks of authority and carrying out their functions with much the same organizational resources and under comparable constraints. The forms of the institutions govern the ways policies are implemented. Institutions and their agents tend to confirm the validity of their established practices. Therefore, they continue to do many of the same things, even if these are articulated in line with different policy discourses. The outcomes of their actions result from dynamic interactions among processes that may not have been foreseen, or even foreseeable. Changes are more likely to take place because existing arrangements are unsustainable than they are to conform to the plans of governments, or of international agencies.

STATES, DEVELOPMENT AND CLASS FORMATION

African nationalists sought state power as a means of transferring control of political office and economic resources from foreigners to Africans. The state would take responsibility for bringing 'development' to Africa. Nationalists mobilized political support to establish their claims to be the authentic representatives of the people. Control of the state conferred authority to rule its subjects, to exact taxes and rents from imports and exports, to receive aid and contract 'sovereign' debts, and to decide to whom to allocate public resources. The state was central to achieving the goals of nationalism and development. It was the object of the struggle for power. It became the key instrument in the continuing battle to maintain power.

Armed campaigns to take over the state have contributed to the withdrawal of colonial governments and the overthrow of repressive regimes. These sometimes opened the way to peaceful settlements. They also left legacies of political and criminal violence, and even the collapse of state authority and social order. Governments from within and beyond the continent, arms dealers, diamond buyers, and timber merchants have fuelled armed insurrections and rapacious warlords. Control of arms has secured places at the negotiating table or even presidential election.

Conquest and trade, in people and commodities, incorporated Africans into a wider global economy. The experience of colonial rule reshaped Africa and redefined state forms, social identities, gender relations, religious beliefs and class relations. Colonial powers mapped out their territories and subordinated diverse African polities to their rule. Colonial transport networks reoriented the relations of African producers and economies to the international economic systems. Colonial administrators incorporated African rulers as intermediaries within a hierarchy of chiefs. Multiple, and contested, forms of law—civil, Shari'a, and customary—sought to define relations of gender and generation and rules governing access and succession to land and property. African governments inherited the institutions through which and the boundaries within which, they exercised state authority. They took over or re-established the forms of territorial administration, the 'decentralized despotism', through which their predecessors had exercised power. Some governments have disputed, even by force of arms, the lines drawn by colonial cartographers.

The 'imagining' of African nations and ethnicities has generally taken place within and along the boundaries laid down during the 19th-century scramble for Africa. Prior to colonial rule, people's identities were defined primarily by their allegiance to a ruler or their status within a political community. Pre-colonial polities had interests in incorporating settlers and acquiring slaves to strengthen their productive and military capacities. Under colonial and post-colonial regimes, political communities were defined and defined themselves according to administrative, religious and linguistic demarcations. Their interest now lay in excluding outsiders from access to 'their' resources.

In contemporary African usage, 'tribe' or 'ethnicity' usually refers to people speaking a common language. In some cases, these have historical links to a pre-colonial polity. More commonly, they do not share a single pre-colonial identity. Their dialects were standardized into written forms of language only in the 20th century. African and Afrikaner élites fashioned new cultural identities from disparate cultural and historical materials. Ethnicities arose from the people's varied experiences of migration and urbanization, subordination and competition, religious belief and conversion. These brought African people into new relations and differentiated them in new ways. What the multiple forms of ethnicity have in common is the ways in which identities define people's access to public resources.

Christianity and Islam were established in Africa soon after their foundations. By the end of the colonial period, most Africans adhered to one of these world religions. Mission churches and Muslim foundations funded schools and hospitals. Religious beliefs and practices provided ways of making sense of a wider society and of dealing with the problems of an uncertain world. Madhist and millennial movements offered collective deliverance from oppression. Post-colonial regimes have been confronted by the stubborn resistance of believers who reject the claims of state authorities and by sects inspired by prophetic leaders. Many people have turned to charismatic religious movements to seek solutions to their private problems within a new moral and social order. Others continue to look to indigenous healers and beliefs to solve their problems. Evangelists bless the prosperity of the rich, offer hope of rewards to the many, and give solace to the poor. Successful preachers attract far greater followings than any political movements and expand their enterprises across continents.

Colonial rule subordinated African producers to the requirements of new, and often coercive, labour regimes and patterns of cultivation. The colonial economy also opened new forms of access to economic opportunities through urban employment, commercial activities and Western education. Africans engaged in new, and often multiple, class relations: as wage labourers, on docks, railways, mines and farms; as peasants or artisans producing for local or distant markets; as clerks and teachers; as traders, business people and professionals. Individuals, families and wider kin groups commonly overlap the divisions between town and country, commercial and bureaucratic activities and wage- and self-employment.

Colonial governments in Uganda and west Africa encouraged peasant production of cocoa, coffee or cotton for exports. Settler governments banned or restricted Africans from cultivating these crops or engaging in commerce. From South Africa to Kenya, 'betterment' schemes forced cultivators to separate residential, arable, grazing and woodland in the name of land use planning and soil conservation. They disrupted social networks and arable and livestock production and provoked rural resistance and support for nationalist politics.

Independent African governments spread the benefits of 'development' in the form of industrial growth, formal education, hospitals and clinics, state employment and rural development. Rises in population growth and the expansion of the cities increased demand for public services. Governments established institutional structures to bring government closer to its subjects and to draw its subjects more effectively under its control.

Several governments, following colonial precedent, have made rural people live in villages to bring development to them, to compel them to grow cotton or to 'protect' them from insurrectionary forces. Governments also expanded their activities beyond their fiscal and administrative capacities, and found themselves unable to sustain the provision of services in the face of economic crises, debt repayment and civil conflicts. Health charges raise little in revenue but reduce demand from poor people. Immunization levels have declined. Most Africans lack access to clean water. School enrolments have fallen in many countries over the last two decades; gender, class and rural-urban inequalities have tended to increase. Families are compelled to pay high costs for poor standards of state schooling. Facilities are poor, teachers are often ill-paid and uncommitted and their methods of instruction inappropriate.

Africans are vulnerable to infection from a range of endemic and epidemic diseases. HIV/AIDS transmission has proved to be particularly virulent in east and southern Africa, particularly among the economically most active sectors of the population. Additionally, many children have been orphaned and many have been born with the disease, while young girls have had to assume responsibility for the care and support of sick and elderly relatives and younger siblings. The spread of HIV is facilitated by prior infection by sexually-transmitted diseases and is linked with the incidence of tuberculosis. It spread most rapidly along transport routes and, secondarily, among migrant workers and their sex partners. Attempts to change individual behaviour have proved ineffective against the social and economic conditions encouraging unprotected sex, and the problem has been exacerbated by an attitude of fatalism, on the part of individuals and institutions, in the face of the spread of the disease, the lack of any cure, and the prohibitive costs of treating its symptoms.

Post-colonial states have been the engines of class formation. They structured people's relations to material resources and to markets, legal and illegal, in land, commodities, labour and money. In many African states, a distinctive 'political class' can be recognized. This consists of those people, usually from professional, administrative, commercial or military backgrounds, who control or aspire to control access to state offices and public resources. State presidencies and key political offices have allowed an avaricious few to acquire vast amounts of money. State favours have enabled others to accumulate capital. Many successful African capitalists owe their wealth to their ability to identify and take advantage of entrepreneurial opportunities rather than to their privileged relation to the state. They may need access to the state to pursue their business activities. Dependence on government decisions limits their capacity to pursue their collective interests, especially when these conflict with the priorities of those in power.

The expansion of education, jobs and commercial opportunities after independence augmented the middle classes. Their modest levels of prosperity and prospects for their children they attained were drastically undermined by the economic crises of the 1980s. They created a rich associational life, through which they pursue public activities and claim status and respect from their peers and communities. These organizations tend to be focused around people's communities of origin, their churches and mosques or their commercial or professional peer groups. Some are open to a wide range of members; others are exclusive or even secret.

Industrial development and state employment expanded the working class. The gender composition of the work-force varies by country, region and industry. In the textile sector, for example, women are commonly employed in Uganda, whereas young men dominate in Nigeria. Access to alternative livelihoods in the local economy strengthens the bargaining power of individual workers, and aspirations to accumulate sufficient money to leave waged work may accentuate rather than discourage labour militancy. Workers have generally embarked on strikes for economic reasons, to demand higher wages or reductions in the prices of food or petrol. The wages of industrial workers and government employees increased in the period preceding or immediately following independence. Since then, trade unions and workers have been unable to prevent their incomes falling as better placed groups claimed the lion's share of society's resources.

Governments in several countries strengthened the funding and organization of trade unions and extended the rights of workers and unions, often incorporating the latter into the ruling party, so that they could better manage industrial unrest. These reforms were of assistance to the unions in protecting their members from unemployment. When trade unions proved unable to prevent strikes, governments promoted divisions among them and arrested their leaders. In some instances, as in Uganda, employers have been allowed to dismiss workers freely, and to ignore trade unions and employment laws. Workers actions have provided a focus for popular discontent with corrupt governments and, sometimes, prompted their removal. In Zambia, following independence, and in Ghana, unions struggled to maintain their autonomy from government control. Trade unions subsequently assumed leadership of poltical coalitions opposed to authoritarian governments in Zambia and, more recently, in Zimbabwe. The Congress of South African Trade Unions (COSATU) took a leading role in the struggle against apartheid. Since 1994 COSATU has secured legislative reform through its alliance with the ruling African National Congress of South Africa (ANC), while organizing strikes in protest at unwelcome economic policy measures. Generally, trade unions have been most effective in protecting the interests of their members when they have retained their autonomy from political parties and governments.

Governments have found it difficult to persuade rural people to conform to plans for their betterment, and have often been confronted by organized local resistance. The rural populace is, however, poorly placed to act collectively to affect the composition or policies of national governments. They depend on the paltry percolation downward of benefits through layered patronage relations.

In recent years, organizations have been relabelled and new ones created under the ambiguous title of non-governmental organizations (NGO). In the 1980s, external funders promoted NGO as an alternative provider of services and saw them as independent of and opposed to authoritarian states. This allowed them to offer relatively attractive salaries, but made them dependent on foreign patronage and changing fashions among development agencies. NGO are ill-suited to take over responsibilities for public services. Most NGO seek to work with government agencies, on whose co-operation they depend for the realization of their goals and often for their access to funds. Governments have organized their own NGO and have sought to co-opt NGO and to regulate them through special legislation.

Governments in Africa, and their citizens and subjects, have re-formed the political institutions and social arrangements that they inherited from the colonial period and adapted them to their own purposes. These have tended to serve the immediate interests of those in power and exacerbated inequalities in access to power and material resources. Inherited and reformed institutions have proved ineffective in achieving many of the objectives for which they were created or providing the means by which people may agree on public goals and work together to bring them about.

DEBTS AND DEPENDENCE

African governments continue to be burdened by high debt repayments. In 1999 their total external indebtedness amounted to approximately US $230,000m. For many African countries, outlays on foreign debt-servicing exceed expenditure on health and education combined.

During the 1970s, governments in Africa (as in Eastern Europe and Latin America) borrowed money, far beyond their capacity to repay, from commercial banks, foreign governments and the World Bank. During the 1980s, they were confronted with declining prices for their primary exports and high real interest rates for their long- and short-term debts. The ensuing debt crisis both created the need, and provided the opportunity, for the introduction of structural adjustment policies (SAP) by the IMF and the World Bank.

Nkrumah borrowed heavily in the early 1960s to pay for the Volta Dam scheme and for his plans to industrialize Ghana. Zambia and Zaire (now the Democratic Republic of the Congo, DRC) mortgaged their prospective earnings from the short-lived copper boom of the early 1970s. Nigerian governments, state and federal, paid for spending from anticipated petroleum sales.

Companies, parastatal organizations and government in South Africa raised loans on the prospects of gold exports. Following the sharp rise in the world petroleum price in 1973, African governments borrowed from commercial banks at variable interest rates to meet their import bills. Many also had recourse to foreign governments to provide loans and to guarantee payments to their manufacturers by African importers.

The economic strategy of import-substituting industrialization, pursued by most African governments, increased rather than reduced this dependence. Import protection secured a market for local industries and monopolistic advantages to local and foreign investors. Industries import more in the way of machinery and other inputs than they export. The expansion of industrial production thus imposes renewed strains on the balance of payments. The import costs of industrial growth in South Africa were met by mineral exports, foreign loans and net foreign investments until the 1980s. In 1985 the fall in the gold price, exports of capital and the need to repay loans at high interest rates forced the government to devalue the rand, declare a moratorium on debt repayments and reintroduce the 'financial rand' which subsidized inward capital investments.

Some African countries were able to expand their agricultural exports rapidly after independence, thereby increasing their import capacity, government revenues and demand for industrial production. Availability of forest land and cheap migrant labour (from Burkina Faso) allowed Côte d'Ivoire to duplicate the expansion of cocoa production which had taken place in the Gold Coast (Ghana) and Nigeria earlier in the century. In Kenya, smallholders gained access to land and the opportunity to grow coffee and tea, which had largely been reserved to settlers before independence. By the 1980s, Côte d'Ivoire and Kenya could not expand the markets for their exports much further and prices were falling so that they could not sustain the level of their imports and service the debts contracted during the late 1970s.

In countries such as Ghana, Nigeria and Uganda, peasants expanded production of crops for exports during the colonial period. Colonial governments discovered the advantages of using state export monopolies to purchase agricultural produce well below the prevailing price on world markets, thereby requiring African farmers to contribute to the costs of post-war reconstruction in the United Kingdom. African politicians drew on marketing board revenues to finance development spending, political campaigns and their own business investments. When world prices fell, they maintained their revenues rather than producer prices. In the 1970s production declined and was diverted to neighbouring countries to evade the low prices paid for crops by the state marketing boards.

Governments attempted to limit inflation by maintaining the exchange rate of their currencies at unrealistic levels, and by regulating access to foreign exchange and imported goods. These policies penalized exporters and encouraged demand for imports, and consequently led to the collapse of export earnings, scarcity of imports, and a pervasive resort to smuggling and corruption. Political competition turned on the ability to dispose of government revenues and of imported goods and foreign currency, thereby intensifying contests to control state office and its perquisites.

In the 1970s the World Bank sought to repeat in Africa the seed-water-fertilizer ('green') revolution which had transformed irrigated production of grain in Asia and also to reduce Africa's high rates of population growth. However, these projects, which started not from market demand but from the supply of biochemical technologies, made little contribution to agricultural output, and resulted in increased government debt. They showed little respect for the knowledge of African farmers and for their proven capacities to expand and adapt production to meet changing market conditions—or for the varied ecologies of African countries.

By 1975 the exposure of commercial banks to 'sovereign' debts from African governments attracted the attention of the World Bank. Although the IMF provided short-term balance of payments relief and the World Bank funded long-term project loans, there was no provision for loans from public institutions to refinance debts and respond to the long-term balance of payments problems faced by African governments. This gap was filled in the 1980s by the introduction of 'structural adjustment'

loans. The IMF, with the World Bank, extended long-term programme loans to governments, arranged the rescheduling of their debts, and secured their access to commercial credit. In return, governments agreed to implement policies involving currency devaluation and liberalization of imports, foreign exchange and agricultural markets, reduction of government spending and of subsidies to parastatal bodies.

Structural Adjustment Programmes (SAP) were designed to induce governments to reform their economic policies in exchange for restructuring their debts and further access to credit. International agencies have not found it easy to enforce all the complex conditions they have laid down in their negotiations. Loans are used in a continuing process of negotiations over the adoption and implementation of economic reforms. Governments may meet some conditions but not others or go only part way to meeting set targets. The measures required to satisfy some conditions may obstruct the realization of others. Currency devaluation is the key to the successful implementation of SAP. Devaluation is also designed to encourage exports and reduce the demand for imports and is necessary to liberalize foreign exchange, imports and agricultural markets. If government spending, and the supply of money and credit are not kept firmly in check, there will be a rising demand to exchange local for foreign currency, leading either to further devaluations, or to a widening discrepancy between official and parallel exchange rates. As long as governments are reluctant to reduce arms imports and military salaries, spending on health, education, water and other services will suffer. The heaviest burden of SAP falls on wage- and salary-earners and on the poor, who cannot pass on the effects of rising prices.

The effects of SAP depend on the mechanisms adopted to implement them and on the extent to which they can be followed through. In Ghana and Nigeria, fixed exchange rates were replaced by foreign exchange auctions open to banks. The result was a proliferation of banks, which profitably recycled their foreign exchange allocations on parallel markets. Sales of government assets and allocation of mineral concessions provide lucrative opportunities for favoured beneficiaries, local or foreign. Declines in the value of the naira widened the differences between petrol prices in Nigeria and in neighbouring countries. Unpopular increases in the petrol price did not remove the discrepancy. The result of these policies was extensive smuggling, hoarding in anticipation of further price rises, and severe fuel shortages.

In Ghana and Uganda a sharp increase in official prices for cocoa and coffee, respectively, attracted trade in these crops into official channels rather than across borders. Consequently, the share of government revenue in national income, and official figures for exports and national income rose dramatically. Where few opportunities exist to grow high-value crops, SAP cannot generate such rapid increases. SAP have improved access to consumer goods and allowed a modest improvement in the utilization of industrial capacity. Manufacturers have been hit by competition from imports (including secondhand clothes) in the face of reduced trade protection, high interest rates and stagnant consumer demand. Small-scale Nigerian manufacturers sell informally branded products cheaply across the continent. Currency devaluations by one African country creates difficulties for producers in another, leading to demands to maintain or extend intra-African trade protection. Economic crisis in East Asia in the late 1990s depreciated the value of their currencies and made their exports more competitive. However, economic recovery is likely to attract more imported goods than rising exports can offset. Successful SAP depend on a sustained net inflow of foreign exchange, which may require further debt payments or profit transfers in the future.

African governments allocate a substantial proportion of their budgets and foreign exchange earnings to service debts, without making any significant impact on the principal owed. A number of governments have converted unpaid loans to grants, and some investors have bought back at a discount a certain amount of commercial debt. Refinancing and rescheduling of the debts of African governments allowed payments to decline as a proportion of exports in the 1990s but the total amounts owed continued to rise. The Highly Indebted Poor Countries (HIPC) initiative launched by the World Bank and IMF Development Committee in 1996 aimed to reduce debts to the level at which their repayments could be sustained. Debtor countries are required to meet strict macro-economic targets for three to six years to qualify. By the beginning of 2000, only two African countries, Uganda and Mozambique, had met these criteria. In 1999 the major industrial countries proposed 'faster, deeper and broader debt relief for the poorest countries that demonstrate a commitment to poverty reduction', without agreeing how it was to be funded. The IMF's macro-economic targets would be complemented by World Bank monitoring of social policies and poverty reduction programmes. These dual aims may not be easy to reconcile.

MULTI-PARTY ELECTIONS

Governments throughout Africa increasingly have to claim the legitimacy of democratic elections. During the 1980s, the contraction of resources at their disposal led those in power to appropriate ever-larger shares for themselves. This narrowed their capacity to co-opt élites and maintain a measure of public acceptance. They usually lacked the credibility to persuade workers and others to accept the imposition of SAP. Civilian and military governments alike, whether fully capitalist or of 'socialist orientation', found their authority to be under threat.

During the 1990s, most governments, willingly or reluctantly, gave their assent to multi-party elections. The state forms and political systems of different countries shaped the scope for alternation of rulers and for instituting their legal and political accountability.

In the years following independence, African rulers tended either to repress their opponents or to co-opt them into a single ruling party, or occasionally both. One-party as well as multi-party governments proved vulnerable to military coups. However, in Côte d'Ivoire, Cameroon, Kenya, Tanzania, Malawi, and Zambia, single-party governments, usually led by nationalist leaders of advancing age, maintained themselves in power for three decades. They successfully combined authoritarian rule with centralized, bureaucratic direction of policy and administration, and a regional distribution of patronage. In many other cases, politics were reduced to the unconstrained pursuit of spoils. State and private resources were plundered, public services collapsed, civic organization was undermined and ethnic conflicts fuelled. States lost their effective authority and surrendered their monopoly of the legitimate use of violence to warlords, vigilantes and their own soldiers. Patterns of 'spoils politics' are very difficult to reverse, as the extreme examples of the DRC or Sierra Leone (and less dramatic instances elsewhere) show.

President Léopold Senghor of Senegal initiated the move away from one-party politics when he licensed two opposition parties in 1974. His successor, Abdou Diouf opened elections to multi-party participation in 1981. The governing Parti socialiste, however, retained control of political patronage, the electoral machinery and the security services; it alternated between repressing political opponents and co-opting them into government. In early 2000 divisions among its leadership and loss of support from Muslim religious leaders allowed Abdoulaye Wade to defeat Diouf in the second presidential ballot. In 1989 a series of strikes in Benin against the discredited military government of President Matthieu Kérékou led in the following year to the convening of a national conference, which elected its own prime minister, Nicéphore Soglo, who went on to defeat Kérékou in presidential elections held in 1991. The pattern of national conferences, representing a multiplicity of parties and personalities, was repeated in several other francophone countries. The Benin example persuaded a number of single-party governments in other countries, such as Côte d'Ivoire in 1990, Burkina Faso in 1991 and Gabon in 1990 and 1993, to hold, and win, multi-party elections, while resisting the idea of a national conference. Several military rulers were similarly successful at the voting polls. In a few countries, such as Somalia and the DRC (then Zaire), party structures fragmented into personal cliques. More common was a tripolar division among the main parties, with no faction commanding a majority of seats. While political movements attract their support from regional and ethnic constituencies, no general inter-relation can be discerned at a regional level between ethnic demography and party systems: these are shaped by historic loyalties and political conditions specific to each country.

Membership of the Benin legislature following the 1991 elections was dispersed among 12 parties, making it difficult for President Soglo to secure a stable parliamentary majority. The costs of economic liberalization, fiscal stringency and the devaluation of the CFA franc in 1994 undermined Soglo's efforts to strengthen his political base. In 1995 opposition parties gained a clear majority in the legislative elections and, in 1996, Kérékou won the presidential election on the second ballot. A pattern of several parties, unable to form a stable coalition, proved to be a common factor in many newly-elected legislatures, leading to conflicts between presidents and legislatures or prime ministers. In Niger President Mahamane Ousmane had been elected with the support of a multi-party alliance in 1993, but could not command a majority in the national assembly, which he dissolved in the following year, having been unable to accept its choice of prime minister. This created an opportunity for Col Ibrahim Baré Maïnassara to seize power in a military coup in January 1996, and subsequently to contrive his own election to the presidency. Maïnassara was himself assassinated in 1999 and succeeded by a military junta.

In Zambia, Kenya and Malawi the rulers of one-party states were reluctant to concede to popular demands for multi-party elections. Fiscal crises and political uncertainty led governments to narrow the range of political cliques and ethnic groups among which they dispensed patronage in return for political support. This had the effect of bringing a broad range of overlapping groups into opposition. They included former members of the ruling party and government, businessmen who found themselves restricted by the government's control of economic opportunities, regional interests which were marginalized by ethnic favouritism, trade unionists and their members who were expected to bear the costs of fiscal stringency, students, consumers and citizens who had to pay higher fees and prices for fewer services, church leaders, human rights activists and political radicals. They could all look to multi-party elections as a means of gaining, or regaining, access to government.

In Zambia the Movement for Multi-party Democracy (MMD) maintained its unity, and its candidate, Frederick Chiluba, won the 1991 presidential election. In Kenya the Forum for the Restoration of Democracy split into two factions, FORD–Asili and FORD–Kenya, following the announcement by President Daniel arap Moi that multi-party elections would take place at the end of 1991. Mwai Kabaki, a former vice-president, left the ruling Kenya African National Union (KANU) to found the Democratic Party. In Malawi regional divisions between the Alliance for Democracy (AFORD) and the United Democratic Front (UDF) continued after the referendum in 1993 endorsing proposals for multi-party elections.

In power in Zambia, the MMD began to repeat many of the practices of Dr Kenneth Kaunda's United National Independence Party (UNIP) government. As did the UNIP prior to independence in 1964, the MMD achieved national support and restricted the previously dominant party to a single region of the country (the Southern province in the case of the Northern Rhodesia African National Congress in 1959, and the Eastern province in the case of UNIP). UNIP had declared a single-party state to counter defections by prominent party leaders with powerful support from their home provinces, notably the vice-president, Simon Kapwepwe. Chiluba was similarly accused of concentrating power in the executive, failing to ensure adequate representation in government for all ethnic groups, and of tolerating corruption and drugs-trafficking by senior ministers. Chiluba's vice-president, Levy Mwanawasa, resigned in 1994, citing long-standing differences with the president. As in the Kaunda period, political opponents were accused of plotting coups. The MMD, while not proscribing opposition parties, disqualified Kaunda from candidature for the presidency in the 1996 election, on the grounds that he was of Malawian origin. (Chiluba's opponents responded by asserting that his father was of Belgian Congolese origin.) Chiluba and the alliance of interests supporting the MMD won substantial victories in the presidential and legislative polls, which were boycotted by the UNIP. The rate of voter participation was low.

In Kenya President Moi, having warned that the restoration of a plural political system would exacerbate ethnic tensions, based his political strategy on fostering just such conflicts. Initially, FORD had appeared capable of recreating the consortium of social classes and diverse ethnic interests which had brought KANU to power under Jomo Kenyatta in 1962. In 1992, however, rivalries dividing the two Kikuyu and one Luo candidate prevented a Kikuyu-Luo alliance, and encouraged voters from other ethnic groups to support KANU. The elections were followed by attacks on Kikuyu farmers in the Rift Valley by Kalenjin and Masai supporters of KANU. Rather than uniting opposition, defeat encouraged new divisions. A new party, Safina ('Noah's Ark'), was established to work towards the creation of a national political consensus. The new party was refused official registration until shortly before the 1997 elections, when Moi defeated five rival candidates for the presidency, taking almost 41% of the vote.

In Malawi Bakili Muluzi defeated President Banda in presidential elections in 1994, although Muluzi's UDF did not obtain a majority in the legislature. AFORD, the third largest party, held the balance between the ruling UDF and the Malawi Congress Party (MCP), the former ruling party, and eventually gave its support to Gwandaguluwe Chakuamba, the MCP candidate, in the 1999 presidential elections. Muluzi was re-elected as president, but was again denied a legislative majority. The Zimbabwe African National Union–Patriotic Front (ZANU–PF) won elections in 1980 and 1985 on a tide of overwhelming support in the Shona-speaking areas, although its highly repressive and violent tactics failed to defeat the Zimbabwe African People's Union (ZAPU) in Matabeleland. Prime Minister Robert Mugabe incorporated ZAPU into the ruling party and became executive president in 1988. He maintained his authoritarian rule and marginalized a disparate opposition in the 1990 and 1995 elections. However, signs of effective political opposition to ZANU–PF began to emerge in 1996, following the defeat of ZANU–PF in a by-election in Harare and the formation in 1997 of the National Constituent Assembly, initiated by the Zimbabwe Council of Churches, broadened the scope and effectiveness of political debate. The decision of President Mugabe in the following year to send troops to support President Kabila of the DRC in that country's renewed civil war brought to the attention of Zimbabwe's nascent opposition the profits being derived from this conflict by key military and political figures in ZANU–PF and by their business associates – at great cost to Zimbabwean taxpayers and consumers. In 1999 the Zimbabwe Congress of Trade Unions (ZCTU) launched the Movement for Democratic Change (MDC), bringing together a disparate alliance of businesspeople, white farmers, trade unionists and academics. In February 2000, when the government failed to win a majority in the referendum on its constitutional proposals, Mugabe sought to ensure success in the 2000 elections by promising to transfer white-owned farms to so-called 'war veterans', whom he paid to attack, intimidate, abduct, and sometimes kill MDC supporters, black farm workers, white farmers, teachers, and Asians. Although Mugabe's authoritarianism had, in mid-2000, continued to be somewhat constrained by judicial decisions and by independent newspapers and civic organizations beyond the control of ZANU–PF, the political shift within Zimbabwe to unconstrained 'spoils' politics and political thuggery poses a considerable threat to the residual framework of law and civility.

In Nigeria military coups supplanted parliamentary government during 1954–66 and again during 1979–83. The military centralized the control and allocation of mineral oil revenues, encouraging conflicts between politicians for access to a share of state largesse. Generals Ibrahim Babangida (1985–93) and Sani Abacha (1993–98) personalized military rule and manipulated civilian politicians through extended transitional programmes. Babangida refused to recognize the victory of Chief Moshood Abiola in the election of June 1993 which he had organized. Abacha's sudden death in mid-1998, shortly followed by that of Chief Abiola, opened the way to a new round of elections. Gen. (retired) Olusegun Obasanjo, who had been military head of state from 1976–79, was elected president in 1999 with the support of the political and military establishments. Nigeria continues, however, to be riven by violent conflicts over the allocation of state resources, constitutional arrangements, and the rival claims of religious and ethnic groups at federal, state and local levels. Demands that Muslim-majority states adopt Shari'a law, or for changes to local government boundaries are vehicles for asserting political and econ-

omic interests. Politicians pursue spoils by legislative and violent means. Legislators fail to establish forms of political accountability or to provide ways of reconciling the conflicts they inherited from the military.

The timing, politics and outcomes of calling multi-party elections have varied considerably among African countries. In several countries, such as Benin in 1991 and 1996, Zambia in 1992, Malawi and South Africa in 1994, and Nigeria in 1999, elections provided voters with the opportunity to replace incumbent rulers. In many others, such as Senegal from 1978 to 1993, Côte d'Ivoire in 1990 and 1995, Gabon in 1993 and 1998, or Kenya in 1992 and 1997, they provided rulers with the means to perpetuate their political hegemony. Military rulers succeeded in getting themselves elected in Ghana and in Burkina Faso in 1992, and in Guinea and Guinea-Bissau in 1993. Elected governments, as in Gambia in 1994, Sierra Leone and Niger in 1997, have not been immune from military coups. The military removed President Bédié from power in Côte d'Ivoire in 2000, arguing that he was attempting unfairly to prevent Allasané Outtara from contending for the presidency. In preparing for elections, the military manipulated the political parties one against another and reinstated rules to invalidate Outtara's candidacy.

In a number of countries, such as Kenya (1992 and 1997), Burundi (1993), the Republic of the Congo (1993), the Central African Republic (1996), Sierra Leone (1996) and Zimbabwe (2000), the prospect and outcome of elections have led to political violence, often initiated by the incumbent government or the military. The 'political class', whether in opposition or in power, has been primarily concerned to retain or achieve political office and its perquisites, and to mobilize support from ethnic and regional constituencies. These interests have rarely been divided by, or particularly concerned with, issues of public policy. When there have been changes of government, the new administration has inherited the institutions and problems of the old, and may well also retain many of the political practices of its predecessor.

BEYOND APARTHEID

The election of Nelson Mandela as president of South Africa in 1994 marked the conclusion of the African struggle for national independence. As in other African states, the transfer of power from a repressive, authoritarian regime to an elected government was negotiated through national conferences preparing the way for democratically conducted elections.

During the presidency of P. W. Botha, the National Party (NP) had sought to reform the apartheid system in a manner that would ensure the retention of political power by the white community, to the exclusion of the African National Congress of South Africa (ANC) and its allies. The government persecuted its opponents both within and outside South Africa, and by the close of the 1980s had brought the military challenge of the ANC and the threat of popular insurrection under a degree of control. However, the NP was unable to formulate a longer-range solution to the country's worsening economic problems, or to its lack of internal legitimacy and international acceptability. Afrikaner intellectuals and a number of the country's leading businessmen met exiled leaders of the ANC, providing the movement with implicit recognition as the 'government-in-waiting'. However, full political reform and South Africa's rehabilitation by the international community could only proceed by releasing Mandela from detention and opening full negotiations with the ANC. For its part, the ANC came to realize that it could obtain through negotiation what it could not achieve by armed struggle.

During 1990–94, the NP government of President F. W. de Klerk retained firm control of state institutions while negotiating the terms on which it would transfer power to an ANC-led administration. Internal violence, however, escalated during this period. The struggle between mainly Zulu supporters of the Inkatha Freedom Party (IFP) and the ANC for paramountcy in KwaZulu/Natal intensified and spread to the workers' hostels and black townships of the Transvaal (now Gauteng). Extremist factions, ranging from the radical Afrikaner right wing to the black radical Pan-Africanist Congress, sought to enforce their demands by acts of sabotage and murder, while elements within the government security forces covertly supported urban terrorist outrages. The ANC was impelled to withdraw from political negotiation and resume a campaign of non-violent mass action in mid-1992 following a massacre in Boipatong, apparently by IFP activists acting in collusion with the police. When negotiations were later resumed, the ANC agreed to the formation of an interim government of national unity to follow democratic elections.

The negotiation of a new South African constitution essentially depended upon an agreement between the NP and the ANC. The closer that such an accommodation appeared, the more unacceptable it became to Chief Mangosuthu Buthelezi, the leader of the IFP, who demanded a federal, or even confederal, constitution that would ensure IFP control of KwaZulu/Natal. Buthelezi withdrew the IFP from the constitutional negotiations at a crucial juncture. However, faced with the loss of access to elective political power in KwaZulu/Natal, the IFP consented at a late stage to take part in the 1994 elections. The NP's ambition to lead a conservative coalition, capable of offering a political alternative to the ANC, was thwarted by its alienation from the IFP and a lack of other black African support.

Parties other than the ANC sought to achieve through the constitutional negotiations goals that would not be attainable through an ANC-dominated legislature. Eventually, a lengthy and much-amended draft constitution was approved by the national assembly in 1996. A number of independent commissions came into being, together with a constitutional court and a land court.

The ANC secured a decisive victory in the 1994 national elections, obtaining 62.7% of the vote for a new national assembly, while also winning legislative majorities in seven of the nine newly-delineated provinces. Assisted by support from the Coloured electorate, the NP obtained control of the Western Cape legislature, while the IFP emerged as the majority party in KwaZulu/Natal. In 1996, however, the NP, which held one of the country's two vice-presidencies, withdrew from the interim government of national unity, within which it had exercised no more than a marginal influence. At the 1999 legislative elections, the ANC received 66.4% of the vote. Each of the opposition parties remains confined to ethnic and regional bases of support, and offers no serious challenge to the ANC's dominant role in national politics. In the national assembly elected in 1999, the Democratic Party replaced the NP (now renamed the New National Party) as the official opposition and the principal party representing the interests of the white population. As in the 1994 elections, the ANC secured a clear majority in seven provincial legislatures. Thabo Mbeki, the former vice-president, succeeded Nelson Mandela as president.

The ANC and its allies have abandoned any idea of transforming the economy along socialist lines. Instead, the government is aiming to achieve the 'Africanization' of capitalism, protecting workers' rights and extending equal access to jobs and public services to the majority of the population. It has proved more expedient to build on a framework inherited from the past than to redirect policies in new directions. Government has begun to dismantle the complex structures of import controls that effectively protected manufacturing and agriculture from foreign competition, and has liberalized agricultural markets. It has increased people's access to electricity and to piped water and improved access to hospitals for mothers and children under six. It has been less successful in applying the funds allocated to the housing and land reform budgets. It lacks any coherent strategy for dealing with the spread of HIV infection, which is now increasing with alarming rapidity in South Africa. The economic opportunities offered by crime, together with the spread of privately held firearms in southern Africa during the 1980s, and the low morale and corruption within the police force have resulted in a serious escalation in the late 1990s of violent crime.

There is within South Africa an evident tension between the commitment of the ANC to non-racialism and the claims of the African majority for preferential access to the resources from which they were excluded under apartheid. The ANC has made appointments of people from all racial backgrounds to senior posts in government service, and has actively encouraged the private sector to emulate this policy. Black investors have also acquired a share in the control of major corporations in the financial, insurance and mining sectors. The ANC has itself become an extension of the patronage system of a centralized

state, devolving resources to the provinces and deploying its nominees to positions in parliament, the civil service and national and provincial administrations.

Nationalist movements throughout Africa have sought state power as a means of transferring control of political office and economic resources from foreigners to Africans, and of implementing the wider aim of bringing 'development' to Africa. Control of government enabled the ruling élite to decide to which Africans they would transfer resources. NP governments were able to reward their political supporters and punish their opponents, while extending preferential access to education, jobs and commercial opportunities to the white, and particularly Afrikaner, constituency. The ANC is also able to benefit its supporters among the new political, bureaucratic and commercial élites; it is, however, far more difficult for them to distribute resources to the majority of the population than it was for the NP to do so for the white minority.

South Africa is at the centre of the economy of the southern Africa region. Further regional economic integration requires that the Southern African Development Community (SADC) develops into a unified trading bloc with mutually convertible currencies. Ultimately this would, in effect, bring about a northwards expansion of the Southern African Customs Union (SACU) and the Rand currency zone. Governments within the region are understandably reluctant to subordinate their policies to convenience South Africa, which is concerned to protect its labour market from illegal immigrants and low-cost Zimbabwean textiles. South Africa's integration into the international economy is likely to take precedence over the gradual development of regional economic institutions. It concluded a bilateral trade agreement with the European Union in 1999. Although the countries neighbouring South Africa are no longer at risk from the military damage inflicted by the apartheid regime, they are finding that the economic policies of the new administration are not necessarily helpful to them.

INTERNATIONAL INTERVENTIONS

Throughout the Cold War period, the policies of the contending powers were shaped by their perceptions of strategic alignments, their commitments to their client states, and the scope for arms exports offered by African armies and conflicts. By the mid-1980s, the Soviet government had come to the view that it had nothing to gain from its commitments in Africa, which had become a costly impediment to *détente* with the Western bloc. Soviet and Cuban withdrawal from Africa paved the way to negotiations for an Angolan settlement, the independence of Namibia, the fall of the Mengistu regime in Ethiopia and the independence of Eritrea.

At the close of 1992 President George Bush committed US forces to lead a UN military intervention to restore civil order in Somalia. The USA withdrew in 1994, followed a year later by the remaining UN contingents, having failed either to disarm the warlords or restore stable government. The Somali experience temporarily undermined the enthusiasm of the US government for extending the 'new world order' beyond the Persian (Arabian) Gulf, and ensured that it would require the intervention of other countries to resolve the civil war in Liberia, whose existence as an independent country had been brought about by the USA.

The United Kingdom's relationship with the governments of former British colonies has tended to be one of maintaining harmonious political and economic relations with the government in power. The British government tolerated breaches of sanctions against the illegal government of Ian Smith in Rhodesia, which obtained petroleum supplies from British firms. It also resisted demands to implement economic sanctions against South Africa during the apartheid period. In 1995, following the executions of Ogoni activists by the Nigerian military regime, Britain reimposed a ban on arms exports which had supposedly been in operation since 1993. The British government joined with other international creditors in 1992 to demand improvements in human rights and a move towards political pluralism in Kenya and Malawi. This initiative followed popular demonstrations in these countries; action by their governments followed only when political stability and fiscal discipline became undermined.

France has retained close political, economic and military links with its African ex-colonies and has extended its sphere of interest to include the former Belgian possessions. The fate of governments in francophone Africa has often depended upon the willingness of the French authorities to provide troops to protect them. French military policy in Africa came under the direction of presidential appointees and the security services, whose activities were often at variance with the wishes of the French foreign ministry. France continued in the 1990s to provide troops to protect its nationals and maintain order in a number of African countries, although it did not intervene in Côte d'Ivoire in late 1999 to forestall the military overthrow of President Bédié.

France provided the tropical agricultural exports of its former colonies with privileged access to its markets. After Britain joined the European Economic Community (now the European Union—EU) in 1973, these relations became multilateral and were extended to former British colonies and to countries in the Caribbean and the Pacific under successive Lomé agreements. The EU was reluctant to extend the benefits of the Lomé agreements to South Africa's deciduous fruit exports, which compete directly with European farmers. Most of the former French colonies have continued to use the CFA franc, with its attendant benefits as a 'hard' currency. The devaluation of the CFA franc by 50% in 1994 led to sharply increased prices and consequent economic hardship throughout francophone Africa and a loss of trust in France by African leaders who had not been consulted. The future of the CFA franc, whose convertibility is guaranteed by the French government, now depends upon its relation to the euro currency unit introduced by the European Monetary Union in January 1999.

External powers continue to intervene politically when necessary to protect their interests in African countries. Their actions have frequently produced results that have accorded neither with their intentions nor their interests. International peace-keeping activities have not always succeeded in protecting civilians from harm, whether by armed militias, government troops or, indeed, the 'peace-keepers' themselves. The cost of such interventions and the uncertainties of their outcome have prompted Western governments to scale down their commitments and look to the region itself to resolve its conflicts.

AFRICAN SOLUTIONS?

Political power depends ultimately on the capacity to wield the means of coercion. Political transitions increase uncertainty. This may be resolved by the election of new, or existing, rulers to political office. Political changes may open the way to civil conflict. Insurgencies have often been initiated from and supported by neighbouring countries and expanded conflicts across borders. In many African countries, rivalries among political élites have prevented them from uniting in opposition to the resort of arms to decide struggles for power and have often aligned with armed factions or military rulers in pursuit of their sectional goals.

Wars have proved extremely costly to African people and to national economies. They have also proved highly profitable for rebel forces, and their leaders, arms manufacturers and salesmen, foreign mercenaries, and traders in diamonds, timber and ivory. Exports of natural resources sustained rebel movements and their outside promoters in Angola, Liberia, Sierra Leone and the DRC. These resources, or the promise of access to them, have also enabled governments to recruit foreign mercenaries and defray the costs of troops provided by other countries. The interest of contending armies in maintaining control both of them and of the territory from which they are extracted has made it more difficult to reach peace agreements and less likely that belligerents will abide by them.

The end of the Cold War, and the failures of UN peace-keeping missions in Somalia and Rwanda, created a need for African governments to resolve conflicts in Africa. The most visible examples were the interventions by ECOMOG, the Monitoring Group of the Economic Community of West African States (ECOWAS) in Liberia, Sierra Leone, and Guinea-Bissau. The financial and logistical difficulties experienced by the peace-keepers, the divisions among African states and the fragility of governments, dependent on outside forces, including foreign mercenaries, for their authority exposed the limitations of regional approaches to security in post-Cold War Africa. In the Horn of Africa, the Intergovernmental Authority for Development (IGAD) has as yet proved unable to resolve the civil war in Southern Sudan and Somalia.

The Organization of African Unity (OAU) has largely been displaced in the management of conflicts within and between African governments by regional institutions, such as ECOMOG. It lacks the political, financial and logistic capacity to act collectively. States directly affected by the flow of refugees, trafficking of arms and armed incursions across their borders are more likely to support regional initiatives to deal with the conflicts. However, they are also likely to support a particular faction in a conflict and thus not to be able to act as neutral arbiters. To date, the ANC government has been reluctant to commit the South African army outside the country. In 1998, however, troops from South Africa and Botswana were sent to Lesotho, following conflicts between that country's security forces and contending political factions. This intervention had the initial effect of intensifying Lesotho's internal violence, but its presence did eventually serve to open the way to political dialogue in Lesotho.

In May 1997 Laurent-Désiré Kabila arrived in Kinshasa at the head of a rebel army and declared himself president of the DRC, replacing President Mobutu Sese Seko and the name, Zaire, which Mobutu had given the country. By the middle of the following year, Kabila was in conflict with his former allies, and seven African countries had committed troops to one or other of the contending armies. Kabila's army was drawn from opponents of the central government in the Shaba (Katanga), Kasaï and Kivu regions. At its core were Tutsi militias and troops drawn from the Banyamulenge (from the DRC) and Banyarwanda (from Rwanda), with support from Burundi and Uganda, as well as from Angola, Ethiopia, Eritrea and Zimbabwe. They were provoked to take up arms by an order to the Banyamulenge to leave the country of which they claimed citizenship. This presented the Rwandan government with an opportunity to proceed against Hutu militia groups, operating among refugees in the eastern DRC and to install a sympathetic government in Kinshasa. As the rebels advanced towards the capital, Western mining interests scrambled to negotiate mineral concessions from the future government.

Kabila's accession to power followed the examples set by his principal sponsors, Uganda and Rwanda. The Front patriotique rwandais (FPR), drawn largely from exiled Tutsi, took power in Rwanda in 1994 and set up a coalition government in Kigali in the aftermath of the genocidal massacres of Tutsi and of moderate Hutu by the extremist Hutu Interahamwe militia. The presence of Belgian troops, under UN auspices, failed to halt the killings. The French government, which had supported the previous Hutu-controlled Rwandan regimes, intervened to create a 'neutral zone' in western Rwanda, protecting some Tutsi communities and facilitating the flight of Hutu refugees, and also of *genocidaires*, into the DRC. Paul Kagame, who became minister of defence and vice-president of the new Rwandan government, had served in the National Resistance Army, which Yoweri Museveni had led to power in Uganda in 1986.

Military government, together with massacres of Hutu in 1972, consolidated Tutsi political supremacy in Burundi. Pierre Buyoya relinquished the country's presidency in 1993 when he was defeated in an election by Melchior Ndadaye, who became Burundi's first Hutu president. In 1996, after a period of intense ethnic conflict, political instability and the violent deaths of both Ndadaye and his successor, Sylvestre Ntibantunganya, Buyoya resumed power in a *coup d'état*. Tutsi-dominated armed forces have since effectively controlled power in both Rwanda and Burundi.

Mobutu's government was noted for its extreme profligacy and its lack of fiscal discipline; the appropriation of the country's wealth by the president, his family and associates and its investment abroad; and for the indiscipline of its army. However, Mobutu facilitated US and South African support for the insurgent União Nacional para a Independência Total (UNITA) in its conflict with the Movimento Popular de Libertação de Angola (MPLA) government in Angola, which for its part relied on Cuban forces and Soviet-bloc arms and advisors. Mobutu was able to call on Western military support and enjoy access to funds from the International Monetary Fund (IMF) and the World Bank, despite his government's blatant failure to abide by their conditions. Only in 1991 did the IMF, the World Bank and Western governments withdraw support from his regime. In 1990 Mobutu announced plans for a transition to a multi-party government. For the following six years, he succeeded in retaining plenary powers while manipulating opposition politicians and exacerbating tensions among the various ethnic groups in Shaba, Kivu and Kasaï.

Following Mobutu's fall, Kabila assumed full executive, legislative, fiscal and military authority, pending the promulgation of a new constitution. He soon came into confrontation with politicians who had opposed Mobutu and appointed people to office from his own ethnic group or who would depend on him for their position. He multiplied security agencies and suspended the national reconstruction conference. Kabila thus emulated several aspects of his predecessor's mode of operation, while also inheriting the problems of a bankrupt country, unable to pay its foreign debts and finding it difficult to pay its soldiers and officials. He acquired funds by granting concessions to foreign mining and construction interests, and also to business associates of certain of the political leaders of his allies.

When Kabila's erstwhile Banyamulenge allies sought to remove him with Ugandan, Rwandan and Burundian support, the governments of Angola, Zimbabwe, Chad and Namibia sent troops to support his government. Divisions emerged among the rebel forces and between their sponsors in the Ugandan and Rwandan governments, whose forces came into armed conflict in Kisangani in late 1999. Subsequent attempts to secure peace agreements within the DRC have not resolved the struggle for control of territory and mineral resources in that country. Significant changes have taken place in the nature and effectiveness of governments, notably in Uganda, but, as the example of Kabila's DRC demonstrates, new governments all too easily repeat many of the patterns of the old.

A prolonged civil war in Liberia began in December 1989 when Charles Taylor led an invasion force, under the name of the National Patriotic Front of Liberia (NPFL), from Côte d'Ivoire. Taylor was initially supported by the governments of Côte d'Ivoire, Burkina Faso and Libya. The period of internal instability that followed the withdrawal of US support for the former Liberian head of state, Master-Sergeant Samuel Doe, who was deposed and murdered in 1990, facilitated Taylor's subsequent advance. Conflicts between the NPFL and the Armed Forces of Liberia, as well as other armed factions assumed an ethnic cast. In 1990 ECOWAS troops from Ghana, Nigeria, Sierra Leone, Gambia and Guinea, were sent to Liberia under the auspices of ECOMOG. Originally envisaged as a monitoring group, they established uneasy military control over Monrovia, but left Taylor in control of most of the interior and its natural resources.

Nigeria assumed the direction of ECOMOG and provided most of its arms and troops. Successive attempts to negotiate peace agreements and establish a national government failed in the face of the tensions between the Nigerian government and the NPFL, together with conflicts between political factions and the determination of Liberia's rival warlords to control territories from which they exported natural resources to finance arms purchases and maintain their armies. Under Gen. Sani Abacha, the Nigerian government eventually reached an accommodation with Charles Taylor after spending much of the previous decade trying to keep him out of power. This opened the way to Taylor's election as president in 1997. Taylor's government has repeated the autocratic practices of the Doe regime and the NPFL's abuses of human rights. The government faces severe financial difficulties in restoring Liberia's infrastructure and services and repatriating refugees. The return of refugees has led to violent ethnic clashes over land and resources. ECOMOG withdrew from Liberia in 1998.

The Liberian civil war impacted upon Sierra Leone, Côte d'Ivoire and Guinea, dispersing over 750,000 refugees into these neighbouring states. In 1991 the Revolutionary United Front (RUF), Sierra Leonean rebels allied with Taylor's NPFL,

launched attacks into Sierra Leone, whose government committed troops and airport facilities to ECOMOG's offensive against the NPFL.

The arrangements agreed by President Joseph Momoh to establish a multi-party government in Sierra Leone at the end of 1991 were interrupted by a military coup in April 1992, postponing democratic elections until 1996, when voters defied threats and attacks by the rebel Revolutionary United Front (RUF) to cast their ballots in legislative and two rounds of presidential elections. However, in May 1997, armed soldiers deposed the elected president, Ahmed Tejan Kabbah, who fled to Guinea. Kabbah's government had depended for its security on the assistance of Guinean troops, of British army-trained Gurkhas, together with privately-recruited mercenaries. The withdrawal of mercenary troops from Sierra Leone in February 1997 in accordance with the 1996 Abidjan peace agreement with the RUF (and because the government could no longer afford their services) opened the way to Kabbah's overthrow by the army, which set up an armed forces revolutionary council and allied itself with the RUF.

In March 1998 President Kabbah returned to Sierra Leone from exile in Guinea to a tumultuous welcome in Freetown. However, the restoration of the democratically elected president was neither an unqualified victory for democratic principles over military intervention nor an unqualified example of an African solution to African problems. Nor did it prove to be wholly secure. In January 1999 the Sierra Leone capital was invaded by the combined forces of the deposed military junta and the RUF, which looted the city, abducted young men and women, and maimed and killed thousands of people. Kabbah's government, which had failed to secure effective control of the country's diamond producing region, had consequently lost control of much of the north of the country. It was unable to reconstitute an effective army of its own, and had to rely on ECOMOG, and thus the Nigerian government, to restore it to power, after ECOMOG's failure to repel the attack on Freetown. In July 1999 the government finalized the terms of a power-sharing agreement with the RUF. The RUF, however, refused to relinquish its control of Sierra Leone's diamond fields, and renewed its military activities in early 2000.

No regions, and few countries, in Africa have been free of the ravages of civil wars, conflicts between African countries, dictatorial governments, and the intervention of outside powers. Political compromises—as in Zimbabwe in 1988, Mozambique in 1992, or South Africa in 1994, and armed insurgencies—as in Uganda in 1986 or Rwanda in 1994, have brought civil conflicts under some sort of control without direct intervention by powers from outside Africa. External intervention has maintained peace in the Central African Republic, but failed to resolve conflicts between the government of Guinea-Bissau and its own army in 1998. The Republic of the Congo was ravaged by rival militias until, in 1997, Angolan troops restored Denis Sassou-Nguesso, the former military ruler, to the presidency he had lost in an election in 1992. In Angola, UNITA has persistently evaded complying with successive peace agreements. Civil war continues in Sudan, as do factional and regional conflicts in Somalia and Senegal, and between Ethiopia and Eritrea. Insurgents continue to attack civilians and governments in northern Uganda, Rwanda and Burundi. In mid-2000, hostilities ceased in the border conflict between Eritrea and Ethiopia, concluding a conflict that had continued intermittently since 1998.

Neither African governments nor regional organizations have been able to bring civil or inter-state wars to peaceful conclusions. External powers have colluded with oppressive regimes and profited from arms sales and diamond purchases. They have been reluctant to act effectively or to take responsibility for outcomes when they have intervened. The United Nations has lacked the funds and arms to maintain peace, and protect civilians or even its own soldiers. Divergent aims and conflicts of interests among governments and economic interests within and outside Africa make any international co-operation to bring peace to war-torn countries difficult to achieve.

ECONOMIC TRENDS IN AFRICA SOUTH OF THE SAHARA, 2000

DONALD L. SPARKS

Sub-Saharan Africa has great diversities, yet the 51 states of the region share many common characteristics. They range significantly in terms of population, size and economic scale. Nigeria, the largest, had a population of 88.5m. at the 1991 census (although current World Bank estimates approach 118m.), while 10 other countries of the region each contain less than 1m. people. Seychelles, the smallest, has a population of 75,000. The region's total population is about 590m. Climate and topography vary greatly and include Mediterranean, tropical and semi-tropical, desert, rain forest, savannah, mountains and plains. Some countries are more intensively urbanized than others. Zambia's urban population, for example, represents almost 50.0% of the country's total, while in Burundi it is only 6.0%. Educational levels also vary greatly; for example, 54.0% of all students of secondary school age are enrolled in schools in Mauritius, followed by 52.0% in Zimbabwe, while for Rwanda the proportion is only 2.0%. Mauritius has a literacy rate of about 83.0%, while Burkina Faso's is less than 20.0%. Life expectancy also varies, from under 44 years in Guinea-Bissau, to an average for the region of 52 years. Life expectancy is falling in many countries, and in those most affected by Acquired Immunodeficiency Syndrome (AIDS), such as Zimbabwe, average life expectancy is being reduced by about 17 years. Some sub-Saharan countries, like South Africa, the Democratic Republic of the Congo (DRC) and Zimbabwe, are relatively well-endowed with natural resources, while others, such as Niger and Somalia, have few such assets. Sub-Saharan Africa contains the world's largest reserves of a number of strategic minerals, including gold, platinum, cobalt and chromium.

The economies of sub-Saharan Africa are, for the most part, small and fragile, and the region is rapidly being left behind in the global economy. The region is poor: excluding South Africa, its combined gross domestic product (GDP) is approximately US \$300,000m., less than that of the Netherlands. Sub-Saharan Africa accounts for less than 2.0% of world trade and global gross domestic product (GDP). Africa's annual GDP per caput was estimated at about \$800 in 1998, and annual income per head ranged from Ethiopia's \$100 to Seychelles' \$6,420. The region has the world's second most unequal distribution of income, after Latin America. The supply of food available per person, measured in daily caloric intake, fell from 2,140 calories in 1971 to 2,100 in the mid-1990s, increasing the number of malnourished people from 94m. to 210m., according to the FAO. About 32% of the region's children suffer from malnutrition, according to the FAO, and each day an estimated 14,000 people are infected with the Human Immunodeficiency Virus (HIV); in the late 1990s sub-Saharan Africa accounted for about 90% of AIDS-infected children world-wide. Only about one-half of the region's population has access to clean water, and only about one-third to adequate sanitation.

Given this diversity, it is accordingly difficult to draw general conclusions about the continent's economic performance as a whole during any given year. Nevertheless, some broad comparisons can be made. The region's overall economic growth rate during the previous two decades has been dismal.

While sub-Saharan Africa has recorded a 3.4% average annual growth rate in GDP since 1961, this just slightly exceeds the rate of population growth. During 1965–75, GDP per caput rose by an average of 2.6% per year, but then stagnated. Taking inflation and population growth into account, the region's real GDP per caput actually fell by 42.5% between 1980 and 1990. The region's GDP advanced by 2.2% in real terms in 1994, and by 3.2% in 1995, according to the World Bank. In 1996 sub-Saharan Africa achieved a 4.4% growth rate, well in excess of any single year during the previous two decades. The region's growth rate declined somewhat in 1997, however, to 3.0%, and declined to 2.4% in 1998. The UN has estimated that the rate of GDP growth would recover in 1999 and achieve an advance of 4.2% in 2000, followed by a rise to 4.6% in 2001. This projected

growth was attributed, in part, to 'continued appropriate macro-economic policies and to more favourable weather conditions, which stimulate farm output'. None the less, given a population increase projected at 2.6% annually, this would provide a per caput growth rate hardly exceeding 2.0%, compared with the annual rate of 7.0% viewed by the 1995 World Summit on Social Development as necessary to reduce poverty levels by one-half by 2015. Moreover, growth rates have been uneven within the region. In 1998/99 several countries, including Cameroon, Côte d'Ivoire, Ghana, Mozambique, Sudan, Tanzania and Uganda, achieved growth rates of about 5%. However, Nigeria recorded growth of only 0.5% in 1999, owing to low petroleum prices early in that year, and while South Africa's GDP rose only by 0.7% in 1998/99, this figure represented an improvement on the previous year's rate of 0.5%. Two countries, Comoros and the DRC, experienced negative growth during 1998/99.

Table 1. Gross Domestic Product Growth in Sub-Saharan Africa
(Annual percentage change in real GDP)

1982–91	1992–2000	1996	1997	1998	1999*	2000*	2001*
1.9	2.7	5.1	3.5	2.5	3.1	4.2	4.6

* Forecast.

Source: World Bank, 2000.

By virtually any economic or social indicator, sub-Saharan Africa performs less well than any other developing region. Of the 47 countries classified by the World Bank as 'least developed', 32 are in sub-Saharan Africa. In many ways sub-Saharan Africa has found itself retreating economically while other developing areas of the world are advancing strongly. The region's growth during 1960–73 was virtually indistinguishable from that of South Asia. For example, at independence in 1957, Ghana was more prosperous than the Republic of Korea, and in 1965 Indonesia's economic output approximated that of Nigeria. By 1997 Indonesia's output was eight times greater than Nigeria's, while the Republic of Korea's economy was 80 times larger than Ghana's.

Of the world's major developing areas (sub-Saharan Africa, the Middle East and North Africa, Eastern Europe, Central Asia, East Asia, South Asia and Latin America), Africa South of the Sahara has the second lowest GDP per caput growth rate (see Table 2, below), the lowest average life expectancy (at 51 years), the lowest secondary school enrolment rate (just over one-quarter of total eligible school-age children), the lowest literacy rate (about 50%), the smallest number of children immunized against childhood diseases (just under one-half), the lowest daily caloric intake, and the highest percentage of people living just under the international poverty line. By the year 2000, it was estimated, about 43.0% of the population of sub-Saharan Africa will be subsisting on incomes of less than US \$350 per year. The region also has the developing world's highest population growth rate (3.2%) and the highest rate of infant mortality (91 children out of every 1,000 die before reaching the age of five years). Of the 7m. infant deaths annually world-wide, 5m. occur in sub-Saharan Africa.

Table 2. Per Caput Gross Domestic Product in 1997
(US dollars)

Latin America/Caribbean	3,940
East Europe/Central Asia	2,310
Middle East/North Africa	2,070
East Asia	970
Sub-Saharan Africa	500
South Asia	380

Source: World Bank, 2000.

None the less, there have also been some improvements: between 1960 and 1994 life expectancy increased from 40 years to 51 years, while since the mid-1980s the proportion of the population with access to safe water has almost doubled, from 25.0% to 43.0% of the total. During the past two decades adult literacy has advanced from 27.0% to 55.0%. Between 1960 and 1996 female enrolment at secondary level rose from 8.0% to 23.0%. Over the past three decades, the infant mortality rate has fallen from 167 live births per 1,000 to 91 per 1,000.

Despite these limited improvements, almost every sub-Saharan economy declined in virtually every measurable way from the 1970s through to the mid-1990s. By 1994, per caput GDP was about 15.0% below its level a decade earlier, and per caput income was down by more than one-fifth. In some of the continent's least developed countries (LDC), such as Chad and Niger, the fall has been perhaps 30.0% or more. The poorer countries of Africa were even poorer in 1998 than they were at their independence in the 1960s.

The factors underlying Africa's parlous economic condition can be broadly categorized either as 'external' or 'internal'. The major external factors include adverse movements in the terms of trade and declines in foreign aid and foreign investment. The internal factors include poor soils, widely fluctuating and harsh climates, inadequate human and physical infrastructure, rapid urbanization and population growth, environmental degradation, ineffective government and inappropriate public policies. Unfortunately, African governments have but limited control over many of these factors, particularly the external ones.

EXTERNAL CAUSES OF ECONOMIC DECLINE

The pillars of Africa's external relationship with the Western industrialized countries are trade, aid and investment, and the declines of all three have added to the continent's poor economic performance during the past 30 years.

Trade and Regional Co-operation

Sub-Saharan Africa occupies a minor role in international trade, and accounted for only about 2.0% of the world total by 2000, compared with about 5.0% in the 1980s. One of the most serious of the external factors underlying this decline is Africa's worsening terms of trade, with declining traditional exports, both in relation to price and quantity, and increasing imports, also in volume and price. More than one-half of sub-Saharan Africa's exports generally go to the Western industrialized countries, from which the region traditionally purchases about 80% of its imports. African countries typically produce one or two major agricultural or mineral commodities for export to the industrialized countries in the West. Primary products account for approximately 80% of the region's export revenues, about the same level as during the 1960s. Poor export performances, combined with the range of problems dealt with below, have generated increased deficits in most African countries' current balance-of-payments accounts.

Table 3. Africa's Balance of Trade, 1970–96
(US dollars, '000 million)

	1970	1980	1990	1996
Exports (goods and services) .	13.6	91.7	84.4	94.4
Imports (goods and services) .	15.6	91.7	92.2	116.3
Balance	-2.0	—	-7.8	-21.9

Source: International Monetary Fund, 2000.

Price levels for the region's primary exports have been uneven. Prices for many agricultural commodities (including cocoa, palm oil, tea and tobacco) have risen since 1986, but prices for many others (coffee, sisal and sugar) have remained steady or fallen. World cotton prices fell substantially in 1998 as a consequence of increased supplies from China and lower demand from East Asian textile producers. In west Africa, Burkina Faso tripled its output of cotton during 1993–97, but its earnings from this export actually fell. World prices for petroleum, copper, gold, aluminium and a number of other metals produced in the region were in decline during 1998. Overall, the 'terms of trade' for most African states worsened between 1970 and 1981. They stabilized somewhat in the late 1980s, and by 1988 stood at about 60.0% of the 1970–73 level. The terms of trade declined

by 0.4% in 1997 and by 0.9% in 1998, before improving by 4.6% in 1999.

The purchasing power of the region's exports has fallen by 22.0% since 1987, owing primarily to the decline in world petroleum prices. The steep decline in sub-Saharan Africa's export revenues was as much attributable to falls in volume as to relative prices. Between 1970 and 1985 Africa's share of the world market for primary (non-petroleum) exports fell from 7.0% to 4.0% of the total. The maintenance of Africa's 7.0% market share would have added US $10,000m. to its overall export income. Economic advance in other areas of the world suggests that increased trade and general integration into the global economy leads to swifter growth. For example, the countries that have integrated most quickly in the past decade experienced growth about three percentage points in advance of that achieved by the slowest integrating countries. The poorest group of countries are the least able to withstand the side effects of worsening terms of trade. According to the Global Coalition for Africa, revenues from Uganda's coffee exports fell by about 50.0% between 1985 and 1990, despite a rise in volume terms. Between 1970 and 1984, the region's world market share of coffee, cotton and cocoa fell by 13.0%, 29.0% and 33.0% respectively.

The import policies of the Western industrialized countries have played a major, and often negative, role in Africa's export performance. The industrialized market economies are Africa's major trading partners. However, despite a somewhat privileged access to the European Union (EU) market, the African share of the African, Caribbean and Pacific (ACP) countries' participation in the EU market has declined relative to that of other developing countries. Notwithstanding the benefits of the Lomé Conventions, protectionism and restrictive agricultural practices, particularly in the EU and (to a lesser extent) the USA, have resulted in an over-supply of some agricultural commodities, and thus inhibited world-wide demand and weakened world prices. Tariff and non-tariff barriers to trade erected by the Western industrialized countries have discouraged value-added or semi-processed agricultural imports from African states. The World Bank has estimated that the high tariffs and anti-'dumping' regulations and other trade barriers cost sub-Saharan Africa US $20,000m. annually in lost exports. Moreover, as incomes increase in the industrialized countries, consumer demand for agricultural products does not advance proportionately (this is termed 'income inelastic demand'). Industry is increasingly turning to substitutes, such as fibre optics for copper wires in telecommunications, and to beet sugar for cane sugar. Tariffs, which are already high by world comparisons, have yet to show measurable reduction in the sub-Saharan region. Finally, as agricultural prices decline, Western consumers do not increase their consumption (this is known as 'price inelastic demand').

According to figures published by the General Agreement on Tariffs and Trade (GATT), trade among African states is low; in 1990, regional trade accounted for only about 6.0% (US $4,400m.) of Africa's export volume. Equally significant was that virtually no growth was recorded during the period 1984–90. Most African states produce similar products for export, generally primary agricultural or mineral commodities, and, as most of the value added is carried out in Western industrialized countries, there is little African demand for these products. African states themselves often discourage trade by their strongly inward-orientated, import-substitution development strategies, including overvalued exchange rates and protectionist trade policies. Their transport infrastructure is geared for export to the EU, Japan and North America, rather than to nearby countries. Tariffs have been higher than elsewhere in the world because of the limited avenues available for taxation. Because of the small size of these economies, these barriers to trade are significantly more damaging. Finally, since the landlocked countries' trade is principally with Europe, neighbouring countries are often viewed as competitive obstacles rather than potential markets. In southern Africa, for example, only 4.0% of the export trade of the 14-member Southern African Development Community (SADC) are transacted among SADC members.

The region could exploit its comparative advantage in commodity exports only if the industrialized countries agreed to support international buffer stock agreements and implement other arrangements for co-operation. African states have tried various methods of improving their trade performance, and of developing overall regional economic co-operation. There have been several attempts to form free trade areas or customs unions. Several have failed and have been abandoned, such as the colonially-imposed Central African Federation, of Zambia, Zimbabwe and Malawi, and the East African Community, comprising Kenya, Tanzania and Uganda. It should be noted, however, that in 1996 Kenya, Uganda and Tanzania established the Permanent Tripartite Commission for East African Co-operation, with the aim of eliminating tariffs and co-ordinating members' infrastructure and the development of energy resources. This was followed in 1999 by the new East African Community. Thus far the community has begun issuing common passports, made its members' currencies convertible, and declared its intention to create a customs union and common market. In early 1997 the OAU inaugurated the African Economic Community, with the eventual goal of uniting the region's existing economic organizations into a single institution similar to the EU.

One of the longest standing, and most successful, regional organizations is the Southern African Customs Union (SACU), founded in 1969 and comprising Botswana, Lesotho, Namibia, South Africa and Swaziland. SACU permits free trade among its members and provides a common external tariff. Customs revenue is generally collected by South Africa and allocated to individual members according to a formula based on members' share of total trade. In 1999 South Africa signed a wide-ranging trade pact with the EU. The Economic Commission for Africa believes that its terms will favour those local businesses which may be able to purchase imported inputs more cheaply; local businesses which may benefit competitively from acquiring new technology; and consumers and businesses for which greater access to European markets will result in lower prices. On the negative side, however, Botswana, Lesotho, Namibia and Swaziland could sustain revenue losses, while some local producers could lose domestic and regional market share to EU businesses. The trade agreement also accords EU producers greater access than neighbouring SACU countries to South African markets.

Two somewhat more recent groupings, commanding good prospects of success, are the SADC and the Economic Community of West African States (ECOWAS). ECOWAS has as its eventual goal the removal of barriers to trade, employment and movement between its 16 member states, as well as the rationalization of currency and financial payments among its members (see Part Two—Regional Organizations). This membership is drawn from francophone and lusophone as well as anglophone countries, with as much economic diversity as Nigeria and Cape Verde. Owing to the political and economic disparity of its members, it is likely to be many years before any of the above objectives are fully met. The SADC (see Part Two—Regional Organizations) was established initially as the Southern African Development Co-ordination Conference (SADCC) to provide a counter, during the era of apartheid, to South Africa's economic hegemony over the region. The SADCC did not initially seek an economic association or customs union, but rather to function as a sub-regional planning centre to rationalize development planning. Its reconstitution in 1992 as the SADC placed binding obligations on member countries with the aim of promoting economic integration towards a fully developed common market.

Another important grouping, the Franc Zone, was formed in 1948 and now comprises, together with France, 13 former French colonies, Equatorial Guinea, a former Spanish colony, and Guinea-Bissau, a former Portuguese possession (see Part Two—Regional Organizations). It operated with general success by providing a firm base of support for the members' financial and economic policies before encountering difficulties in the late 1980s. Excluding France, each of the Zone's members are small states, none with a population exceeding 15m., and most are poor. A few, such as Cameroon, the Congo Republic, Equatorial Guinea and Gabon, are heavily reliant on petroleum export revenues. The French government guarantees the convertibility of the CFA franc, and this system automatically finances mem-

bers' budgetary deficits, which aggregated at US$15m. in 1986 but had increased to $928m. by 1990.

During the early 1990s the French franc appreciated and thus made the CFA countries' exports relatively less competitive on world markets (as the value of the CFA franc also increased, its exports became more expensive). In addition, the Zone's terms of trade declined by about 45.0%, owing primarily to a fall in world commodity prices (coffee, cocoa and petroleum in particular). In 1993 per caput real income fell by 4.5% and exports declined by 3.9% in volume. In consequence of these factors, the Zone's attractiveness to potential foreign investment diminished and the outflow of capital from the CFA bloc increased. After prolonged pressure from the IMF and France to remedy the situation, in January 1994 the CFA central banks devalued the CFA franc by 50.0%. (The Comoros franc, which is aligned with the CFA franc and the French franc exchange rate, was devalued by 33.3%). This decision forestalled unilateral devaluations by individual member countries, and also set the stage for potentially closer links, eventually leading to a common market in the region. In January 1999 the French franc became one of the 11 EU currencies linked to a single currency unit, the euro (€), thus effectively pegging the CFA franc to the euro. France and the Franc Zone members have agreed to retain the existing arrangements until 2002, when the French franc will be withdrawn from circulation.

In 1994 the six members of the francophone Customs and Economic Union of Central Africa (UDEAC) advanced their move towards fuller sub-regional integration by establishing the Economic and Monetary Community of Central Africa (CEMAC). A common external tariff was implemented, while tariffs between member states continue to be lowered and non-tariff barriers have been virtually eliminated. Another noteworthy development in regional co-operation was the initial participation of 13 southern and east African and Indian Ocean states in the Cross Border Initiative (CBI), supported by the World Bank, the African Development Bank and the EU. This initiative is aimed at liberalizing the member countries' foreign exchange systems, deregulating cross-border investments and facilitating the movement of goods, services and people among the participating countries. The CBI is voluntary, and is still in its formative stages.

Foreign Debt, Aid and Investment

Three of the most obvious manifestations of external difficulties are foreign debt, declining levels of international aid and the difficulty of attracting outside investment. In 1960 the region's external debt amounted to less than US$3,000m., and the average debt-service ratio was only 2.0% of exports. During the 1970s and 1980s indebtedness advanced rapidly, from $84,000m. in 1980 to $245,300m. in 1995. In 1999 the total debt was estimated at $252,500m. Nigeria, with an external debt of about $29,000m., is the region's principal debtor. The region's aggregate ratio of debt to exports was estimated at 239.9% in 1996, down from 241.7% in 1995. However, if South Africa's exports are excluded, the ratio rises to 327.5%. The region's ratio of external debt to GDP was 78.9% in 1999. The region's debt-service to export ratios have remained fairly constant during the past few years. For example, in 1991 the ratio was 16.5%, declining to 15.0% in 1993 and to 14.5% in 1995. This compares reasonably favourably with the ratios of all developing countries: their debt-service ratios were 18.3%, 18.0% and 17.0% for the same years. Debt-service actually paid fell from 14.5% of exports in 1995 to 12.4% in 1996, the lowest ratio during that decade, and well below the 20.0% ratio of the 1980s. None the less, according to Oxfam, the region expends five times more on debt repayments than on health.

The majority of the 'most debt-distressed countries' (33 of 41) are in sub-Saharan Africa. During the past two decades there has been a continuing debate on how best to reduce poor countries' debt burdens and how to fund such reductions. In 1995 the World Bank allocated US $500m. to the Heavily Indebted Poor Countries (HIPC) Debt Initiative to help ensure that the world's poorest countries can reduce their debts to 'sustainable levels'. The HIPC guidelines require a candidate country to complete a three-year reform programme. It is then permitted a further three years to carry out further adjustments to obtain the actual debt reductions. In 1998 Uganda became the first country to obtain actual debt reduction under the initiative. By 1999 Mozambique had also qualified, although Côte d'Ivoire, Burkina Faso and Mali were expected to qualify by 2001. Pressures to change the arrangement have intensified during the past two years. In late 1999 the IMF and World Bank agreed to HIPC-2, which aims to deliver debt relief sooner than HIPC-1. Instead of waiting for up to six years to qualify, new applicants can qualify as soon as they successfully implement policies agreed to by the Bank and Fund. Eight African states will qualify for HIPC-2 by 2001. Some NGO have called for a complete cancellation of all HIPC debt, and in September 1999 the US government announced the cancellation of 100% of concessionary and commercial debt owed by HIPC candidates. Japan, the United Kingdom and the Nordic countries have also given similar undertakings.

Foreign official creditors wrote off about US $10,000m. of loans during 1989–91. These creditor countries generally converted loans to grants. Without debt relief, some countries are now paying more than their exports bring in. Indeed, by the mid-1980s and continuing through the early 1990s, as much in debt-service payments was leaving Africa as foreign aid was entering. Even under the most optimistic assumptions for economic growth, seven highly indebted countries—Burundi, Guinea-Bissau, Mozambique, São Tomé and Príncipe, Sudan, the DRC and Zambia—face an increasing scale of payments in future years to the multilateral development banks. Nevertheless, according to a recent assessment of the World Bank, African debtors and their creditors have made 'surprisingly rapid progress' in dealing with the debt issue.

The majority of the region's US $48,600m. of long-term private debt is principally owed by only a few countries: Angola, Cameroon, Côte d'Ivoire, Nigeria and South Africa. Most of this debt comprises commercial bank loans and export credits. African states owe 65.0% of their total external debt to foreign governments, of which about $46,000m. is owed to the 'Paris Club' of Western official creditors. In 1988, following the Toronto summit meeting of the G-7 countries, the 'Paris Club' began debt relief on concessionary terms to the poorest countries by cancelling up to one-third of rescheduled debt payments, or by reducing interest rates. At the same time, many creditor governments forgave some or all of the development aid owed by the poorest countries. At the 1991 London summit, the G-7 leaders agreed to increase the degree of concessionality applied to rescheduling arrangements. Following its 1994 summit in Naples, the G-7 raised the level of concessions to two-thirds on debt eligible for restructuring. Since January 1980 there have been 148 multilateral debt relief agreements between sub-Saharan African governments and official creditors. In 1996 10 countries in the region reached rescheduling agreements with the 'Paris Club'.

Africa's ability to service its debts has been impaired by severe falls in foreign exchange earnings. Additionally, after nearly two decades of annual increases in net foreign financial flows (including concessional economic assistance), during the mid-1980s these flows had levelled off and actually begun to decline. These general decreases in financial intakes from all sources are the result of fewer and smaller private-sector foreign direct investments and commercial bank lending, as well as from decreased levels of 'aid' (in real terms) from traditional Western and multilateral donors. Sub-Saharan Africa's share of official development assistance (ODA) has declined to US $12.8m. in 1996 from $14.2m. in 1992. In addition, its ODA per caput fell from $33 in 1991 to $26 in 1997. Overall, ODA to the region has decreased from 40.0% of all ODA in 1989 to about 34.0% in the late 1990s. The composition of ODA has also shifted: less is now targeted for long-term economic development and a greater proportion is being devoted to short-term emergency food aid and peace-keeping activities. Most of this decline can be ascribed to increased levels of aid to Eastern Europe and Central Asia. According to the OECD, ODA fell from $14,200m. in 1992 to $12,800m. in 1996. During 1990–95 ODA accounted for 13.3% of GDP in the low-income countries. The sub-Saharan region's major donors are members of the EU, Japan and the USA. Japan's levels of aid to sub-Saharan Africa have increased dramatically since 1980, when it provided $223m., to $1,060m. in 1996. By the mid-1990s Japan had become the leading provider of ODA to the region. In 1998 the US government proposed the enactment of an Africa Growth and Opportunity Act, under which African countries satisfying certain 'reforming' criteria would be eligible for preferential trade access and increased investment. It is a widely held view among economists that foreign aid is effective in stimulating growth in countries with sound macro-economic environments, but is ineffective, and can be detrimental, in countries with weak policy environments.

Foreign direct investment (FDI) can bring many benefits to developing countries. It contributes to capital formation, human capital development, technology transfer, increased managerial skills and market expansion. There is a strong correlation between higher FDI and economic growth. Since the late 1980s, increased levels of FDI to developing countries have generated more intense competition for new FDI. Developing countries raised their share of world FDI flows from 21.0% of the total in 1988 to 42.0% of the total in 1997. However, sub-Saharan Africa has a poor record of attracting such investment. In 1998 the region attracted less than 5.0% of the total FDI allocated to all developing countries. In 1996 FDI as a percentage of gross national product (GNP) was also low: the region showed FDI equalling 0.8% of GNP, exactly one-half the average of all developing countries. None the less, while FDI into the region (excluding South Africa), amounting to US $4,700m. in 1997, was about $100m. below the level in 1996, it represented twice the level of FDI in 1990. In 1997 South Africa led the region in attracting FDI totalling $1,710m., followed by Nigeria ($1,000m.) and Angola ($35m.). Virtually all official flows into the region were in the form of bilateral grants or loans on highly concessionary terms from multilateral creditors. Commercial bank lending increased by an estimated $4,000m. in 1996 (although South Africa alone accounted for $5,600m. of the total $5,800m. borrowed from commercial banks). Several countries followed a continuing trend in reducing their indebtedness to commercial banks in 1996. Private financial flows (comprising direct foreign investment, portfolio and other investment) have been rising since 1996, from $5,400m. in that year to $14,000m. in 1997, declining to $6,400m. in 1998 and advancing again to a forecast $13,400m. in 1999, when these investment flows represented 11.5% of those entering all regions of the developing world. The World Bank, meanwhile, has begun to offer guarantees for commercial loans to the private sector. The first of these was obtained by a group of companies in Côte d'Ivoire in 1999.

The sub-Saharan region has yet to broaden its investment base beyond energy and mining, which remain its prime attractions. And, while foreign investors are attracted by the region's vast raw materials and low-wage economies, they are fearful of internal political volatility and the uncertainty of securing the enforcement of commercial contracts. These considerations, combined with the deteriorating human and physical infrastructure, have virtually extinguished investor confidence. Investor perception is of major importance. In 1997 the World Bank conducted a survey to ascertain the level of investor confidence with regard to states' ensuring law and order, protection of property, and predictability in applying rules and policies. Sub-Saharan Africa ranked behind Asia, the Middle East, North Africa and Latin America and the Caribbean. A similar study conducted by the World Economic Forum ranked Mauritius as the most competitive country in the sub-Saharan region. The Forum's 'Competitiveness Report' (using an index of several criteria) suggested that those countries (such as Uganda, Tanzania and Mozambique) which are most serious in reforming their economic policies are also those achieving the best rates of economic growth. Countries at the bottom of the list included Angola, Nigeria, Malawi and Zimbabwe. Importantly, optimism appears to be increasing about the region in general. Investors appeared more confident about improvements in tariffs, the rule of law and access to financing.

INTERNAL CAUSES OF ECONOMIC DECLINE

Africa faces a number of 'internal' economic problems which, in the view of many analysts, outweigh the 'external' factors discussed above. According to a World Bank report in 1996, 'many countries in sub-Saharan Africa are suffering from a crisis of statehood, a crisis of capability. An urgent priority is to rebuild state effectiveness through an overhaul of public institutions, the resurrection of the rule of law, and credible checks on abuse of state power.' Indeed, the World Bank's 1989 study on sub-Saharan Africa's quest for sustainable growth suggested that 'underlying the litany of Africa's problems is a crisis of governance'.

Governance and Parastatal Organizations

Most sub-Saharan African countries achieved independence in the late 1950s and 1960s. Most of the governments quickly became one party states, with presidents who retained power for life. After independence, most newly formed African governments had three fundamental choices for the management and development of their economies, and for the encouragement of industrialization in the broadest sense. They could (i) nationalize existing entities; (ii) seek to attract private investment from abroad by offering favourable investment incentives (tax 'holidays', for example); or (iii) invest heavily in public enterprises. Most governments adopted combinations of all three, but virtually every national administration south of the Sahara opted for substantial parastatal involvement. At independence, the majority of new states had few other options open to them. By and large there was little indigenous involvement in the modern sector, and almost none in the industrial sphere.

Most of the early parastatal organizations operated in natural monopoly areas: large infrastructural projects (highways, railways and dams) and social service facilities (schools, hospitals and medical clinics). Government soon moved into areas that had previously been dominated by the private sector (or, at least, traditionally dominated by the colonial sector in most 'mixed' economies). In the early 1990s public enterprises accounted for as much as 70.0% of GDP in Malawi and 58.0% in Tanzania. The share of parastatal bodies in employment was as high as 60.0% of the labour force in Mozambique in the late 1980s, and accounted for more than one-third of employment in many other countries. In the 1980s Ghana, Mozambique, Nigeria and Tanzania each operated more than 300 parastatal bodies. This expanded use of parastatal operations ideally complemented a range of domestic economic development philosophies, such as 'scientific socialism', 'humanism', 'ujamaa' or whichever term the particular African government applied to its own mode of economic planning. During this period, many governments had justifiable concerns that the private sector could not, or would not, help to improve living conditions for the poorest citizens. Most analysts have generally considered parastatal organizations to have failed, at least in terms of economic efficiency criteria. State-owned enterprises accounted for perhaps 13.0% of the region's GDP in 1993 (compared with almost 15.0% in the late 1970s), but represented a substantially higher percentage of economic output than in any of the world's other developing regions. After independence, most African countries expanded the size of their civil service more rapidly than their economic growth justified. This expansion was designed to provide employment, and to the extent this reduced growth in the private sector, civil servants received lower and lower real wages. None the less, African élites looked to the public sector as the avenue of advancement to their careers. The region was generally slow to develop indigenous entrepreneurs. Governments became bloated and corrupt. For many, the need for better governance became critical.

Civil Strife

Social and political stability are generally associated with higher economic growth rates. Since acceding to independence, more than one-half of sub-Saharan African countries have been caught up in civil wars, uprisings, mass migrations and famine. According to the World Bank, between 1965 and 1985 the more unstable countries' average annual GDP per caput growth was 0.5%, while the region's 11 most politically stable countries achieved an average rate of 1.4%. The level of strife has, however, increased in the region. The UNHCR estimated that by 1997 some 8.1m. people in sub-Saharan Africa had been uprooted by conflict. The UN currently maintains official peace-keeping missions in the Western Sahara, Sierra Leone, Liberia, the Central African Republic, Rwanda, Burundi, Angola and Somalia. Moreover, in 2000 there was continuing warfare between Ethiopia and Eritrea, internal disorder in Somalia, and major civil unrest or civil war in the DRC, and in Southern Sudan. These conflicts now involve neighbouring countries and thus inhibit economic growth for the entire sub-continent. The

UN estimates that there are nearly 50m. land mines buried in 11 countries in the region, mostly in Angola (15m.) and in Mozambique (3m.), where land mines have so far claimed over 10,000 lives. Food production in Angola has fallen by more than 25% in recent years, and much of that decline is attributable to these mines.

Health, Population, Social Factors and Natural Environment

African states face significant problems in providing health services and education. Although both have improved since the mid-1960s, their levels remain the lowest in the world. Governments in Africa south of the Sahara expend less than 1.0% of their GDP on health care, and that care is unevenly distributed throughout many countries, with most health facilities concentrated in urban areas. According to UNICEF, a number of countries, including Angola, Ethiopia and Mozambique, spent more over many years on their military requirements than on health and education. With declining export receipts and general budget austerity, many African countries have been compelled to decrease their budgetary provisions for health. This has resulted in, for example, diminished levels of immunization. Less than one-half of Africa's population has access to clean, piped water, and some 80.0% of illness in Africa's least-developed countries (LDC) can be associated with inadequate water supplies or poor sanitation. Infant and child death rates are the world's highest.

AIDS has become the most threatening health problem in the region, and over 9m. Africans have already died from the disease. There are currently 22m. people in sub-Saharan Africa who have been infected with HIV (the virus widely believed to be the causative factor in AIDS). This figure represents about 70.0% of all known HIV infection world-wide (about 87.0% of the world's AIDS-infected children are in Africa). In addition, more than 3,800 adults are infected daily, and such is the mortality rate among the young that the average life expectancy in five African countries—Botswana, Malawi, Swaziland, Zambia and Zimbabwe—has fallen to below 40 years of age. HIV infects one in four adults in Botswana and Zimbabwe, with countries south of the Sahara accounting for the world's 21 highest rates of HIV infection among people in the 15–49 years age group. In 13 of the region's countries, HIV has infected at least 10.0% of the adult population. A 1999 Unaids report commended the prevention programmes instituted in Senegal, Tanzania and Uganda, but warned that Namibia, South Africa and other countries could reach an infection rate of 25.0% unless their governments implemented effective preventative measures. AIDS in Africa generally affects young adults (20–45 years age group) in their most economically productive years, and in Africa the educated, urban elite have been hardest hit. In fact, infection rates in urban areas are about double those of rural areas. The AIDS pandemic has created more than 10m. orphans in Africa, imposing major strains on the individual governments' ability to provide housing, health care and education. Before AIDS, one in 50 children in the region were orphans, while in some countries that rate is now one in 10. Given the size of the pandemic in several central and eastern African states, it is reasonable to expect that AIDS will curtail GDP growth in several countries during the next decade. The World Bank has expressed the view that overall growth in GDP per caput is unaffected if the country's overall infection rate remains below 5.0%. However, when the disease reaches 8.0% of the adult population, the per caput growth is 0.4% lower than it would otherwise have been. When the infection rate exceeds 25.0%, then the cost to growth is close to 1.0%. Additionally, the incidence of tuberculosis, currently the world's major infectious cause of adult deaths, had risen sharply in the recent past, claiming more than 3m. deaths world-wide in 1993. This increase has been linked to the growing AIDS incidence, as about 50.0% of tuberculosis patients are HIV-infected. In 2000 the US government approved allowing African states to develop generic AIDS vaccines without regard to US patent protections. This should reduce the costs of AIDS-combating medicines. The region is experiencing an increase in malaria. Indeed, malaria's toll is greater than that of all other tropical diseases combined. In early 2000 African leaders met in Nigeria to devise a strategy to combat malaria, which causes about 2m. deaths annually.

The disease has cost the region US $100,000m. in productivity losses during the past 35 years, according to the World Health Organization.

Until relatively recently, most African governments did not view rapid population growth or environmental degradation as matters for concern. Indeed, until quite recently most areas of the region practised what is known as 'slash and burn' agriculture, a technique which can only succeed where land is abundant. During the past decade a succession of countries, realizing that their resources cannot service such population growth, have begun to recognize the necessity for environmental protection. Some countries of Africa have the highest annual rates of population growth in the world: those of Gabon, Kenya and Côte d'Ivoire are among the developing world's highest. The sub-Saharan region's projected average annual growth rate of 3.2% for the years 1980–2000 compares with 2.9% for the period 1973–84. Sub-Saharan Africa's population has been forecast to reach 2,000m. by the year 2050, although with continued increases in HIV rates, some demographers are revising this figure significantly downward.

By 1998 about three-quarters of all African countries had family planning programmes, and some have set targets for population growth. Fertility appears to be declining in the small number of states that have established family planning services. Stemming rapid population growth in Africa is difficult because of social as well as economic factors. Most Africans live in rural areas on farms, and require large numbers of helpers. The cheapest way of obtaining such assistance is for a farmer to have more children. Because the infant mortality rate is so high (owing to poor health and nutrition), rural couples tend to want, and have, more babies. Additionally, African countries do not have organized old-age support schemes, and children are often viewed as potential providers of support for the elderly. Modern contraceptive methods, according to a recent study by the World Bank, are used by only 6.0% of couples in sub-Saharan Africa, as against 30.0% in India and 70.0% in China.

Rapid urbanization has also imposed stresses on many African economies. Africa is still very largely rural and agricultural—about 75% of all Africans dwell outside towns and cities. Nevertheless, during the past generation, urbanization has increased at an alarming pace, and it has been forecast that by the year 2025 at least one-half of the population will live in cities. More than 42.0% of all urban-dwelling sub-Saharan Africans now reside in cities of more than 500,000 population, compared with only 8% in 1960, when there were only two cities in the region with populations exceeding 500,000. Unemployment and underemployment are rampant in every major city of Africa. The population growth has put additional pressure on good agricultural and grazing lands, and on fuelwood. About 80% of the region's energy needs are supplied by fuelwood gathered by rural dwellers. In addition, population pressures add to deforestation, soil degradation and declines in agricultural output.

The informal sector has become increasingly important in the region. About 60.0% of the labour force, amounting to 40m. people, represent perhaps 20.0% of the region's total GDP. This sector has been growing at an annual rate of about 6.0% since the 1980s, according to the International Labour Organization. Perhaps most importantly, the 'hidden economy' absorbs three-quarters of new entrants into the labour market.

After initial improvements following independence, education is also declining in many sub-Saharan African countries. There has been a direct link between education and growth. Between 1960 and 1980, the African countries which had higher percentages of children enrolled in primary school also had higher economic growth rates. A further key factor is that of increased education for women, which is clearly associated with lower fertility rates. A recent study by the World Bank found that the three countries with declining fertility—Botswana, Kenya and Zimbabwe—have the highest levels of female schooling and the lowest rates of child mortality. The study also indicated that in the Sahel, where female schooling rates are lowest, both fertility rates and child mortality have remained high. With an average of 6.3 births per female, sub-Saharan Africa has the highest fertility rate in the world.

Shortly after independence, most countries of the sub-Saharan region initiated programmes aiming to establish universal primary education. By 1980 some countries had achieved this goal. Nevertheless, according to UNESCO, enrolment ratios for primary education declined during 1980–83 in 12 African countries. For sub-Saharan Africa, an estimated 88.0% of primary school-aged children were enrolled in primary schools in the mid-1990s, as against 37.0% in 1965. This compared with an enrolment rate of 91.0% for all developing countries, and almost 100.0% in Western industrialized countries. Here again, many governments have found education to be a service for which budgetary allocations may be cut back during times of fiscal crisis. African governments' emphasis on higher education at the expense of primary education has also been a negative factor for economic development. For example, average expenditures on secondary-school students per caput is some 40 times that of expenditures on primary school students as compared with a ratio of 1:16 in the Western industrialized countries. Additionally, because courses and textbooks were generally 'imported' directly from the former European colonial powers, much of the education has been inappropriate to the rural settings where most of the students live and will eventually work.

Africa's environment has been under intense pressure, especially during the past 20 years. With the increases in population discussed above, over-cultivation and over-grazing have turned vast areas into virtual wastelands. The United Nations Environment Programme (UNEP) has estimated that an area twice the size of India is under threat of desertification. During 1990–95, according to UNEP estimates, the region's woodlands were being diminished at an annual rate of 29,400 sq km. Civil wars have also contributed to environmental degradation. In the late 1980s and early 1990s civil wars have had devastating effects on the environment in such countries as Chad, Sudan, Somalia, Mozambique and Angola. In addition, the region's 5m. displaced persons have fled not only repressive political conditions, but degraded environments unable to support them economically.

Many government leaders in the past suggested that the achievement of economic growth was inconsistent with environmental protection, and that African development could only advance at the expense of its environment. It has only been in the past few years that the two goals have been recognized as not mutually exclusive. Indeed, it is now generally accepted that sustained economic growth will be impossible without adequate environmental protection. Specifically, many countries, such as Kenya, Tanzania and South Africa, will increasingly depend on tourism based on wildlife and undisturbed natural habitats. According to the World Tourism Organization, Africa attracts annually only 3.3% of the world's tourists, and absorbs less than 2.0% of tourism-generated revenue worldwide. None the less, in 1998 Africa was the fastest-growing region for international tourism; according to the World Tourism Organization, tourist visits to destinations in sub-Saharan Africa totalled 24.9m. In the late 1980s Lesotho, Madagascar and Mauritius became the first three African countries to develop national environmental action plans (NEAP). These NEAP are intended to create a framework for the better integration of environmental concerns into a country's economic development. By 1996 40 African states had begun the NEAP process, with support from a number of UN and bilateral donors. Loss of bio-diversity is also a serious problem, as many of Africa's plant and animal numbers have been extinguished. The long-term success of agriculture, the region's most important economic sector, ultimately will depend on the wise use of the environment.

Physical Infrastructure and the Structure of the Economies

For most countries in the region, physical infrastructure has generally deteriorated since the achievement of independence in the early and mid-1960s. Such essential services as roads, railways, ports and communications have been neglected, particularly in rural areas. Millions of US dollars worth of investment in transportation will be required if Africa is to take advantage of any improvement in agricultural output performances. Additional resources will also be needed if Africa's industrial sectors are to advance. African industry has expanded during the past generation, from about 25.0% of the continent's GDP in 1965 to over 30.0% by 1987. However, this contribution to GDP is lower than the LDC average. Manufacturing has not increased, because of low capacity utilization, limited trained manpower at all levels, small-scale domestic markets, inappropriate technology and poor plant design. Further, manufactured exports accounted for less of the total merchandise exports for Africa in 1987 than they did 25 years previously.

The underlying structure of sub-Saharan Africa's economies has not changed dramatically since the time of independence. In 1965 agriculture accounted for 39.0% of GDP, and industry 19.0%. By 1995 agriculture had declined to less than 30%, with industry at 34%. African goals of rapid industrialization, however, were not achieved. Manufacturing advanced rapidly in the early 1960s, but then slowed to about the same average growth rate as GDP. While petroleum output expanded more swiftly, only a few states—Angola, Cameroon, Congo, Gabon and Nigeria—benefited. By the early 1990s manufacturing represented only 11.0% of the region's economic productivity (against 9.0% in 1965). Owing to low productivity and low investment, the region's manufacturing sector's growth rate declined from 2.5% in 1997 to 2.0% in 1998. The region lacks the technology available in many other parts of the world; for example, only 16 Africans per 1,000 have telephones, as opposed to 110 per 1,000 in Latin America. The region has the lowest number of internet connections both in absolute and relative terms.

Few sub-Saharan countries have experienced rates of inflation on the scale witnessed in some parts of Latin America. During the 1980s, the rate of inflation was generally lower in countries within the Franc Zone. None the less, the sub-Saharan region experienced overall rates of inflation of 38.7% in 1993, of 54.8% in 1994 (following the devaluation of the CFA franc), and of 35.5% in 1995. However, in response to decreased inflationary pressures world-wide, as reflected in the prices of petroleum and many manufactured goods, the average rate of inflation for the sub-Saharan region was 9.2% in 1998, the lowest recorded since 1973. The region's rate of inflation was estimated at 11.0% in 1999 and was forecast to fall to 9.6% in 2000.

Many African countries' currencies appreciated in exchange rate terms during the mid-1970s. While inflation raised domestic prices, local currencies were not devalued to compensate. Thus, currencies became overvalued, meaning that their purchasing power was stronger for goods from abroad than at home, leading to increased demand for imports. Further, their export became increasingly uncompetitive in price. As their currencies became overvalued, and foreign 'hard' currencies were in short supply, many African governments had to limit or ration foreign exchange. This in turn led to 'parallel' or 'black' markets for foreign currencies. Foreign exchange overvaluation was thus a result of inflation, which in turn was generated at least in part by escalations of government budget deficits. In addition, export and import tariff revenue provides a significant portion of African government revenues, as there is little personal or corporate taxation. As trade declines, so does government revenue, thus exacerbating budget deficits.

Agriculture and Food Shortages

Unquestionably the leading factor behind the drastic declines in African economies has been the general neglect of agriculture. Agriculture accounts for about one-third of GDP for the continent as a whole, two-thirds of employment and 40.0% of export value. For virtually all African economies, the major agricultural exports consist of one or perhaps two or three primary products (cash crops such as coffee, tea, sugar, sisal, etc.) whose prices fluctuate widely from year to year on the world market. For 44 sub-Saharan African countries, their three leading agricultural exports comprise some 82.0% of their agricultural exports.

As suggested by the World Bank, 'if agriculture is in trouble, Africa is in trouble.' And agriculture has been in trouble for the past 25 years. The percentage of Africans lacking sufficient food has increased from 38.0% to 43.0%: some 41 states in the region are experiencing food deficits, with undernutrition ranging from a low of 13.0% in Swaziland to a high of 72.0% in Somalia.

During the same period, the region's food production rose by only 2.0% annually, exceeded by a population growth rate of more than 3.0% per annum. In 1996 the FAO convened a World Food Summit, where agricultural problems were discussed at the highest international levels. As Africa is the only region where the proportion of people suffering from malnutrition is rising, the summit focused special attention on the problems of the region. The World Bank disclosed that its funding for agriculture and rural development had been reduced from US \$6,000m. in 1986 to \$2,600m. in 1996, and undertook to ensure that agriculture received priority attention in its agenda in Africa. On average, agricultural growth was slower during the period 1970–90 (when it rose by 1.4% annually, about one-half the rate of population growth) than in the 1960s, when it advanced at an annual rate of 2.7%. Assisted by favourable weather, growth in agricultural output increased from 1.7% in 1997 to 3.8% in 1998.

About 180m. Africans currently suffer from chronic food insecurity, either because of insufficient local supplies, or because they cannot afford to purchase enough for their needs. Between 1980 and 1990 the region's annual imports of cereals increased from 8.5m. metric tons to 18.2m. tons. Regional production of cereals did rise in 1994, however, by 9.0%, with the agricultural sector achieving growth of 2.0% in that year. Many Africans experience transitory food insecurity owing to fluctuations in prices and production levels attending climatic difficulties and civil unrest. A smaller number, although several million, suffer from, or are at immediate risk of famine.

As discussed above, many governments have implemented economic policies that were designed to keep urban wages and living conditions high and farm prices low by maintaining the value of currencies at high, unrealistic rates of exchange. This is understandable and obvious: political power in Africa rests in the city, not in the village or countryside. This was sometimes a deliberate strategy, at other times more a result of planned rural neglect, and on many occasions such policies were endorsed by the international development community. In addition, producers were often bound by prices fixed by their governments, and at times these 'producer' prices failed to cover input costs. This resulted in farmers reducing their production for sale and reverting to subsistence agriculture.

PRESSURES FOR ECONOMIC POLICY REFORM

African governments have been coming under increasing pressure from a variety of sources to 'liberalize' their public economic policies. During the 1970s and early 1980s, the most direct pressure came from the IMF. It insisted on 'conditionality' for its support; that is, the IMF required specific policy changes, sometimes termed 'structural adjustments', usually in the area of exchange rates (i.e. devaluation), and reductions in government spending before a new loan agreement could be granted. In 1998 35 African countries had launched structural adjustment programmes (SAP) or had borrowed from the IMF to support reform policies. Additional pressures, now known as the 'Washington consensus', have come from the World Bank and USAID. Specifically, the 1981 World Bank study proposed four major and basic policy changes which it felt were critical: namely, (i) the correction of overvalued exchange rates; (ii) the improvement of price incentives for exports and agriculture; (iii) the protection of industry in a more uniform and less direct way; and (iv) the reduction of direct governmental controls. Other pressures have originated and grown internally, as more people have become increasingly dissatisfied with their declining standard of living and the poor economic performance in their own countries. During the early 1990s several countries, most notably Kenya, Madagascar, Malawi, Mauritius, Tanzania, Uganda and Zimbabwe, removed restrictions on external capital transactions. This effectively closed the gap between the official exchange rate and the 'parallel', or 'black market', rate. South Africa abolished its two-tier exchange rate system in 1995, and Angola, Zambia, Ethiopia and Sierra Leone have also unified their foreign exchange systems, making foreign trade and investment less cumbersome.

Recognizing their poor past performance, African governments are currently scaling down their involvement in parastatal organizations. The growth of parastatal companies expanded more slowly in the 1980s and early 1990s than in the 1970s. Although the number of parastatal bodies remained fairly constant during the years 1980–86, at about 3,000, more than a dozen countries have reduced the number of public enterprises. In 1987 alone, according to the World Bank, nearly

100 parastatal organizations were scheduled for transfer to the private sector. In 1995, with continued encouragement from international donors, regional governments disposed of state-owned enterprises valued at about US $544m., as against approximately $792m. in 1994. Since 1988 countries in the region have sold over $3,000m. worth of parastatal businesses. However, the lack of developed equity markets has posed an obstacle to the progress of privatization. Numerous African countries are now in the course either of reforming the institutional structures of parastatal enterprises, or providing them with greater operating autonomy. In other cases, they are being disbanded entirely. None the less, by the mid-1990s, less than one-fifth of sub-Saharan Africa's state enterprises had been transferred to the private sector, and few among these were operating in such key sectors as electricity generation, telecommunications, transport and mining. The bulk of the privatization activity—perhaps amounting to as much as two-thirds—has been restricted to only five countries: Ghana, Guinea, Mozambique, Nigeria and Senegal. Nevertheless, about 67.0% of structural adjustment programmes in the early 1990s involved public enterprise reform.

In addition to the scaling down of parastatal operations, many governments are actively seeking the participation of the private sector, both domestic and foreign. The region has experienced a dramatic growth in stock exchanges, and in the late 1990s new bourses had opened, or were soon to open, in Zambia, Malawi, Uganda, Seychelles, Sudan, Swaziland and Tanzania. With the continuing dismantlement of nationalized industries, these equity markets should gain in importance.

CURRENT OUTLOOK

Economic reforms have in general led to improved economic performance although certain sectors in most countries have experienced sharp declines. In 1994 the World Bank studied 29 countries in sub-Saharan Africa which had undertaken adjustment strategies in the 1980s. The study concluded that no African country has firmly established, in the broadest sense, a sound macro-economic policy. However, the report found that the six countries—Burkina Faso, The Gambia, Ghana, Nigeria, Tanzania and Zimbabwe—which achieved the most improvement in macro-economic policies between 1981 and 1991, also performed best in economic terms. It should be noted, however, that several of these countries were initially at such low levels of growth as to distort their actual rates of improvement. While these six countries implemented substantially improved policies, nine others achieved modest improvements, while 11 countries evidenced actual deterioration. For the six most successful states, their median rate of GDP per caput growth between 1987 and 1991 was 0.4%, and although low, it did represent a turnaround from the 1.0% annual declines during the early and mid-1980s. In contrast, the other 21 countries experienced a fall of 2.1% in median GDP per caput growth. The six best-performing countries achieved a median increase in export growth of 8.0%, while those 11 with ineffective policy reforms sustained an export decline of 0.7%. The best-performing countries achieved an advance of 6.1% in industrial growth, compared with 1.7% for the least successful 11 countries. Agricultural output advanced more rapidly (by 2.0%) in the countries which had substantially reduced their taxation of export crops, while agricultural production declined by 1.6% in countries which taxed their farmers more. The countries which devalued their currencies increased their GDP per caput growth by an average of 2.3%, while those countries with appreciating foreign exchange rates experienced growth rate declines averaging 1.7%. These conclusions were reinforced in a subsequent World Bank report.

In countries as diverse as Eritrea, Ghana, Namibia and Uganda, leaders are developing their own modes of reform. Such reform, however, must include better public administration and good governance. If African governments implement their plans for economic liberalism, encompassing generally higher agricultural producer prices, revised and realistic foreign exchange rates, together with other publicly unpopular policy measures, they will require increased outside support. By the late 1990s, economic assistance to the region was being increasingly made dependent upon economic reform, and the major donor countries of the OECD had reallocated most of their economic assistance

to countries implementing reform programmes. Additionally, the major multilateral donors were also reallocating their resources on this basis.

The OAU and the UN have launched a number of major initiatives supporting Africa's economic development. The African Priority Programme for Economic Recovery (APPER) was adopted by the OAU in 1985, followed by the UN Program of Action for African Economic Recovery and Development 1986–90 (UN–PAAERD) and the African Alternative Framework to Structural Adjustment Programs for Socio-economic Recovery and Transformation (AAF–SAP) which was proposed by the Economic Commission for Africa in 1989. This latter programme was designed to counter the effects of IMF and World Bank SAP. In 1991 the UN launched its New Agenda for the Development of Africa in the 1990s (UN–NADAF).

In 1996 the UN launched its most ambitious programme: the US $25,000m. Special Initiative on Africa (SIA), financed principally by the World Bank. The SIA will support five major sectors: (i) water: $3,000m. will be dedicated to assure sustainable water supplies for households and farms; (ii) food security: approximately $20m. will be earmarked for soil quality improvement, desertification control and assisting the role of women; (iii) governance: $1,000m. will be devoted to capacity building to help with conflict resolution; (iv) basic human needs, including education ($14,000m.) and primary health care ($6,500m.); and (v) resource mobilization, including debt relief and improved trade access. In 1997 UNCTAD established a trust fund to assist the world's 48 poorest countries (of which 34 were in sub-Saharan Africa) towards fuller integration into the world economy. About $5,000m. is being provided primarily to assist recipients to strengthen their export capabilities.

South Africa's return to the full economic community of nations has brought about and will bring significant benefits to its neighbours. Paradoxically, those with the weakest ties will probably be helped most, and those with the closest ties today will probably gain least. The potential beneficiaries include Angola and Mozambique, and probably Malawi and Tanzania. South Africa and Angola have, for example, been meeting since 1990 to negotiate terms for South Africa to purchase and refine Angolan petroleum. There will probably be little significant change for Botswana, Lesotho, Namibia or Swaziland. Their ties are so strong and extensive that it will take years to loosen them, even if there is sufficient economic rationale to do so. Except in the area of trade diversion—being able to buy from the most competitive producer in cost terms (and possibly by import-substitution)—there will be little gain for these states. Zimbabwe will also probably gain little, and may indeed prove less competitive than South Africa. Moreover, it should be stressed that South Africa under majority rule has few incentives to be unduly generous towards its smaller neighbours, and can be expected to pursue economic policies designed to strengthen its own prosperity. In a wider context, however, there can be little doubt that political developments since 1994 in South Africa will generally benefit neighbouring countries. During 1997 South Africa was involved in a number of important regional and international economic negotiations, including the Southern African Customs Area agreement, the formulation of new trading relationships with the EU, and the negotiation of a protocol creating a free trade area in the SADC by 2004.

As peace and stability come to other parts of the region, economic growth should follow. However, a recent World Bank report suggests that the 'peace dividend' does not necessarily immediately follow the resolution of civil war. The fact that such conflicts often do not end decisively means that armies are slow to demobilize, and military spending is not quickly reduced. Indeed, military spending actually increased by 40.0% in Uganda in its early years of peace after the overthrow in 1979 of Gen. Idi Amin. Moreover, the resolution of civil conflict does not necessarily translate to increased security. Demobilization often results in former military personnel resorting to banditry to survive, as witnessed in Angola, Chad and Mozambique. Economic output in these countries, according to the UN, may have fallen to only one-half of the levels that would have been achieved in conditions of internal political harmony.

Africa is a resilient continent. It has withstood drastic changes during the past three centuries and especially during the past three decades. It has moved from colonial domination to independence in less than two generations. Recent history elsewhere, particularly in Asia, suggests that the unacceptable economic deterioration of the past 30 years can be reversed. As sub-Saharan Africa moves into the third millennium its governments have begun to realize that while many economic problems were inherited, responsibility must be taken for problems that are soluble. Rather than being hostile to foreign entrepreneurs, most African governments are now actively seeking foreign business involvement. By 2000 most African governments were presenting the appearance of reform, and acknowledging the parallel between political pluralism and economic development. The combination of liberalized economic policies, together with more political openness could signal the beginning of sub-Saharan Africa's transformation towards economic recovery and sustained long-term development. Dramatic, positive political and economic changes in South Africa and in other countries, which would have seemed impossible less than a decade ago, are now widely accepted.

Despite the slower pace of GDP growth recorded in 1997 and 1998, many observers view sub-Saharan Africa's economic prospects as more favourable now than at any time during the past 20 years. A 4.0% rate of economic growth projected through to 2006 represents about double the growth rates of the preceding decade; however, per caput income (adjusted for inflation) rising at about 1.0% annually would be no higher in 2006 than

in 1982, and about 4.0% below the level of 1974. Thus, Africa's growth during the coming decade could place the region on the same footing as a generation ago. Countries which have launched structural adjustment reforms generally have outperformed those which have not put their programmes into full effect. More and more countries are 'reforming' in a determined manner. The countries of the Franc Zone, following the major reforms carried out in 1994, achieved growth of 5.0% in 1996–97. Other major 'reformers', including Ethiopia, Ghana, Tanzania and Uganda have averaged recent growth rates exceeding 4.0%. Investors who, only a few years ago, would have overlooked the region, and who might otherwise have focused their attention on Asia or Eastern Europe, may now see Africa as a viable alternative. Nevertheless, Africa's path ahead is difficult and uncertain. Pivotal questions are posed by the extent to which the region is truly committed to genuine reform. In addition, will sub-Saharan Africa continue to be marginalized, or can it find ways to better integrate into the global economy? Will the industrialized countries open their markets to competition from the region? Will the region reduce its own trade barriers and find ways to better co-operate and integrate their economies? Can the recent, positive signs of economic growth be sustained? Perhaps the new millennium will offer the region the chance finally to break the cycle of poverty and launch sub-Saharan Africa along a road to sustained recovery and growth.

EUROPEAN COLONIAL RULE IN AFRICA

RICHARD BROWN

The colonial era in Africa began with the continent's hectic partition by the European powers in the final quarter of the 19th century. It ended in circumstances of equal haste less than a century later, leaving the present states of Africa as its political legacy. However, Europe had been in direct contact with sub-Saharan Africa from the mid-15th century, following the Portuguese maritime explorations. Commercial contacts gradually became dominated by the massive and destructive trade in slaves carried on by the Portuguese, Dutch, French, British and others. In all, some 14m. Africans are estimated to have been transported to the Caribbean and the Americas or to have lost their lives as a result of the trade. Colonizing efforts were few before the 19th century, but Portugal maintained a token presence in the areas that much later were extended to become Angola and Mozambique, while the Dutch initiated European settlement from Cape Town in 1652. Elsewhere the prolonged trade contacts generated only scattered European footholds along the African coasts.

Britain was the leading trafficker in slaves in the 18th century, but after 1807, when British subjects were prohibited from further participation in the slave trade, a new era began. The subsequent campaign against the slave trade of other nations; the search for new trade products such as palm oil; the onset of geographical exploration; the outburst of Christian missionary zeal; improved communications (the telegraph and steam ships); growing knowledge of tropical medicine; and Europe's new industrial might all combined to make Africa increasingly vulnerable to European colonial encroachment. The discovery of diamonds in southern Africa in 1867, and the opening of the Suez canal two years later, further focused attention on the continent. Even before the main scramble for colonies began in the 1870s, Britain and France had been steadily increasing their commercial and political involvement in Africa.

Britain established a settlement at Freetown (Sierra Leone) as a base for freed slaves from 1808, and subsequently engaged in a series of conflicts with inland Ashanti from its outposts on the Gold Coast (Ghana), while steadily increasing its influence in the Niger delta region, in Zanzibar, and in southern Africa. In mid-century Gen. Louis Faidherbe began France's expansion into the West African interior along the River Senegal from its long-held trading settlements at the river's mouth. Simultaneously, the interests of both countries grew in Madagascar, but it was France that later annexed the island (1896). During this period of colonial expansion, France extended its penetration of West Africa from existing bases in the interior as well as from enclaves on the coast. It created, too, a second colonial fiefdom in Equatorial Africa, with its administrative base in Libreville, on the Gabon coast. The result of this strategy was the emergence of two large French colonial federations: the AOF (Afrique occidentale française, 1895) eventually included Senegal, Upper Volta (Burkina Faso), Soudan (Mali), Dahomey (Benin), Guinea, Niger, Mauritania, and Côte d'Ivoire; the AEF (Afrique equatoriale française, 1910) comprised Gabon, Middle Congo (Republic of the Congo), Oubangui Chari (Central African Republic), and Chad. Meanwhile, in West Africa, Britain extended its foothold on the Gambian coast into a protectorate, enlarged its territorial holdings in Sierra Leone, created the Gold Coast Colony (1874, later conquering Ashanti and adding territory to the north as the scramble proceeded), and sanctioned the advance of the Royal Niger Co into the heavily populated region that subsequently, as Nigeria, became Britain's most important African colony.

The quest for colonies gained momentum as other European powers entered the field. The first of these was Belgium, whose ambitious monarch, Leopold II, created the International Association for the Exploration and Civilization of Central Africa (1876) as the means of establishing and administering a vast personal empire in the Congo basin, which in 1885 was ironically designated the Congo Free State. The Association's infamous regime of exploitation led to international outrage and eventually, in 1908, to the transfer of the territory to the Belgian state.

Another late participant in the drive to colonize Africa was Germany, which had newly emerged as a major industrial power. In 1884 its chancellor, Bismarck, declared German protectorates over Togoland, Kamerun and South West Africa (Namibia). Bismarck then moved swiftly to organize the Berlin West Africa Conference (1884–85) which created a generally agreed framework for colonial expansion so as to avert any major conflict among the European powers. Shortly afterwards Bismarck added German East Africa (Tanganyika, the mainland of modern Tanzania) to Germany's colonial possessions. (After the German defeat in the First World War, the administration of these territories passed to the victors as League of Nations mandates. South Africa obtained Namibia, Tanganyika was awarded to Britain, and Ruanda-Urundi to Belgium, while Kamerun and Togoland were each partitioned between Britain and France.)

Although Britain, as the leading European economic power, would have preferred to adhere to its traditionally gradual method of empire-building, it nevertheless emerged from the scramble as the dominant colonial power, both in terms of territory and population. Apart from its West African possessions, Britain acquired substantial territorial holdings in eastern and southern Africa. The largest of these was the Sudan, a consequence of Britain's involvement in Egypt and the importance attached to the Suez canal. Egypt had been employing British soldier-administrators in its efforts to gain control of the Sudan, but in 1881 a Muslim cleric proclaimed himself the mahdi (supreme spiritual leader) and declared a *jihad* (holy war). In 1885, the mahdi's forces captured Khartoum, killing Gen. Gordon and causing outrage in Britain. The mahdist state was destroyed by Anglo-Egyptian forces led by Gen. Kitchener in 1898, just in time to forestall a parallel French expedition at Fashoda. The Sudan officially became an Anglo-Egyptian condominium, but was in effect administered as a British colony which became highly valued for its cotton production. Fertile Uganda, supposedly a key to control of the Nile valley, had been made a protectorate in 1894, and neighbouring Kenya (as British East Africa) was added by Britain the following year in order to secure access to the sea. The offshore island of Zanzibar, long a focus of British interest and commercially significant for its cloves, was formally declared a protectorate in 1890. Further to the south, missionaries played an important part in the British acquisition of the land-locked Nyasaland protectorate (Malawi) in 1891.

In the extreme south, Britain had obtained the Cape Colony by treaty at the end of the Napoleonic Wars (1814), and soon found itself in conflict both with its white settlers of mainly Dutch origin (Afrikaners, or Boers), as well as with the area's many indigenous kingdoms and chieftaincies. In 1843 the British coastal colony of Natal was founded, principally as a means of containing the Afrikaners in the interior, where they established the Orange Free State and Transvaal republics. Fatefully, these developments coincided with the discoveries of immense reserves of diamonds (1867) and gold (1886). The ensuing upheavals and an insatiable demand for 'cheap native labour', brought about the final conquest of the African peoples (most notably in the Zulu War, 1879). Acting on Britain's behalf, the mining magnate Cecil Rhodes organized from the Cape the further northward conquest and occupation of Southern Rhodesia (Zimbabwe) and Northern Rhodesia (Zambia), beginning in 1890: in 1884 Rhodes had been instrumental in Britain's acquisition of Bechuanaland (Botswana) as a protectorate, to safeguard the land route from the Cape into the interior, which had been threatened by German activity in South West Africa. Britain had also obtained Basutoland (Lesotho) in 1868, and formally established a protectorate over Swaziland in 1903. However, British claims to paramountcy throughout southern Africa were challenged by the two Afrikaner republics in the Boer War (1899–1902). Britain overcame the republics only with great difficulty, and then left the Afrikaners, who formed the main element of the privileged white minority, in political control of a newly-fashioned Union of South Africa which was then granted virtual independence (1910). Known as the high commission territories, Bechuanaland, Basutoland and Swaziland, however, remained under British rule. Subsequent South African ambitions to annex them were thwarted, and they eventually proceeded to independence in the 1960s.

Despite its economic weakness relative to the other European powers, Portugal obtained a major share of the colonial division of southern Africa. British diplomatic support helped Portugal to secure the vast colonies of Angola (including Portuguese Congo, later known as Cabinda) and Mozambique; in West Africa Portugal had long been in control of mainland (Portuguese) Guinea (now Guinea-Bissau), the Cape Verde archipelago and the islands of São Tomé and Príncipe. Spain, meanwhile, acquired the islands of Fernando Póo (Bioko) and Annobón (Pagalu), together with the mainland enclave of Río Muni, which now form the republic of Equatorial Guinea.

Some African polities themselves participated in the scramble: the kingdoms of Buganda and Ethiopia both seized opportunities to expand. Indeed, Ethiopia successfully defended itself against Italian aggression by winning a famous victory at the battle of Adowa (1896). Italy had to content itself with Eritrea and the major part of Somalia, until Mussolini's armies overran Ethiopia in 1935 (Italian occupation was ended by an Anglo-Ethiopian military expedition in 1941). Eritrea, however, was not to emerge as an independent state until 1993. Liberia, an American-inspired republic founded in 1847 and politically dominated by descendants of former slaves, remained nominally independent throughout the colonial era, but in practice became an economic dependency of US rubber-growing interests.

COLONIAL RULE

There was much resistance to the European intrusion by many of the Islamized as well as the indigenous cultures of West Africa. There were also major rebellions against the Germans in South West Africa and Tanganyika, and against the British in Southern Rhodesia; however, divisions within and between African ethnic groups, superior European weaponry and the widespread use of African troops enabled the colonial powers generally to secure control of their territorial acquisitions without great difficulty (although military operations continued in some areas until the 1920s). Boundaries were, in the main, effectively settled by 1900 or soon afterwards. Most colonies enclosed a varied assortment of societies, but many African groupings found themselves divided by the new frontiers (the Somali, for example, were split among British, French, Italian and Ethiopian administrations). Although in the long run colonialism did much to undermine previous patterns of life, its administrative policies and the development of written languages (mainly by missionaries) fostered ethnic identity, helping to replace pre-colonial cultural and political fluidity by modern tribalism. African reactions to colonialism also contributed to the growing sense of ethnic self-awareness. At the same time, members of the Western-educated indigenous élites were also exploring alternative identities based on the colonial territory (nationalism) or, indeed, on the broader concept of Pan-Africanism.

As military control gave way to civil administration, economic issues came to the fore. In the early decades of colonial rule a considerable amount of railway construction was carried out, and there was a marked development of the export-orientated economy. Colonial taxation was an important stimulus to peasant production and to wage-labour, but in the early period all colonies conscripted labour by force. In the more primitive and undeveloped colonies (as in the Portuguese territories), coercion of labour persisted into the 1960s. In much of West Africa and parts of East Africa, export production remained mainly in indigenous hands. Elsewhere, concessionary companies (as in the Belgian Congo and AEF) or white settlers (as in South Africa and Southern Rhodesia) were the major agricultural producers. White settlers, whose interests were almost invariably given priority, were also a significant force in Kenya, as well as in Northern Rhodesia, the Belgian Congo, Angola, Mozambique, Kamerun and Côte d'Ivoire. Mining was a dominant force in a number of areas. In South Africa, it provided the main impetus to the development of a strong industrial base by the late 1930s. Southern Rhodesia followed

a similar pattern, although on a smaller scale. The important copper mines of the Belgian Congo (subsequently known as Zaire and now the Democratic Republic of the Congo) were later (in the 1920s) joined by those of Northern Rhodesia. Tin in Nigeria, gold in the Gold Coast, and, later, diamonds and uranium in Namibia augmented the primary agricultural exports of these territories. Overall, the growth of a money economy did most to change African life as different areas developed new production, supplied labour, stagnated, or developed the towns which were essential to the conduct of trade and, in the late colonial period, to the growth of manufacturing in some areas additional to that already established in South Africa.

Where settlers monopolized land and resources, colonialism tended to bear harshly on traditional African life. Elsewhere, however, the direct European impact was more muted. The very small number of European colonial officials in non-settler colonies necessitated reliance on African intermediaries to sustain rule. Such administrations had to limit their interventions in African life and rely on traditional and created chiefs to carry out day-to-day administration (although often in arbitrary and non-traditional ways); but military power was never far away in the event of any breakdown in control. By the 1920s air power could be used to transport troops quickly to suppress uprisings. The British, in particular, favoured the policy of 'indirect rule', bolstering traditional authorities as subordinate allies, but often with new powers and resources unavailable to their predecessors. Britain's colonial doctrine emphasized the separateness of its colonies from the imperial power and theoretically envisaged eventual political independence. Some degree of freedom of expression was allowed (many African newspapers flourished in British West Africa), and a limited political outlet for a circumscribed few was eventually provided through the establishment of legislative councils. In contrast, the French doctrine of assimilation theoretically envisaged Africans as citizens of a greater France, but little was done to make this a reality until after the Second World War. These contrasting British and French principles were not without influence on policy, for example in the educational sphere, and they also helped to shape the later patterns of decolonization and post-colonial relationships. Whatever the theory, all colonial regimes were deeply influenced by the racist outlook which had taken hold of the European mind in the 19th century and in practice treated their colonial subjects as inferior beings.

Racial discrimination was deeply resented by the Western-educated élites. In coastal West Africa and in South Africa the existence of these élites actually pre-dated the scramble, and soon lawyers, clergy, teachers and merchants founded moderate protest associations, such as the Aborigines' Protection Society (1897) in the Gold Coast and the Native National Congress (1912), later the African National Congress, in South Africa. By the 1920s clerks and traders in Tanganyika were able to form an African Association on a territory-wide basis. In other social strata, religious associations were often the chief vehicles for African assertion. These could be traditional, Christian, Islamic or syncretic in inspiration, and often aroused mass enthusiasm to the concern of the colonial authorities. Occasionally there were violent clashes. In 1915, the Rev. John Chilembwe led an armed uprising protesting at the recruitment of Africans for service in the First World War and at conditions for tenants on European-owned estates in Nyasaland. Worker protest appeared early in towns, and on the railways and in mines. Rural protest was often about taxation (as in the 1929 riots by women in Eastern Nigeria) or commodity prices (as in the Gold Coast cocoa boycotts of the 1930s). Yet, whatever the level of discontent, prior to the Second World War the colonial grip remained unshaken.

Any complacency about the underlying state of colonial Africa had, however, already been shattered by the world economic depression beginning in 1929–30. The effects of the collapse of prices were so severe that the major European powers, Britain, France, and Belgium, began to perceive the need to provide development funds and to improve social welfare and education in their colonies if Africa's ability to export tropical products and to import finished goods was to be sustained. These ideas, however, only began to make themselves strongly felt after the

Second World War, when they were to add to the ferment of change then gathering force throughout the continent.

DECOLONIZATION

Events inside and outside Africa interacted to produce the surge towards independence after 1945. The Second World War itself provided the immediate context. The war greatly weakened the colonial powers, and brought to the fore the USA, which opposed European colonial control of Africa. African troops were enrolled to fight in Asia and the Mediterranean, returning with a deep resentment at post-war conditions and the continuing colonial subordination. The victory over fascism and the enunciation of the Atlantic Charter also encouraged thoughts of liberation within the continent. Economic change intensified as both the war and its aftermath stimulated demand, and there was a surge of African migration to the towns. Economic and social grievances multiplied, especially in relation to the inadequacy of urban facilities and lack of educational opportunities. Among peasant farmers, prices, marketing arrangements and new levels of bureaucratic interference aroused intense resentment. Because of labour migration, links between town and country were close, and provided opportunities to newly militant nationalist parties in the more developed colonies such as the Gold Coast and Côte d'Ivoire to put pressure on the colonial authorities. For the democratic European powers, the increasing African discontent raised both the moral and material costs of maintaining colonial rule. In any case, with the exception of Portugal, political control was no longer regarded as essential to the safeguarding of economic interests, particularly as capitalism was becoming increasingly internationalized and the concept of possessing colonies was beginning to appear outmoded.

In French Africa, the Second World War helped directly to set in train events which were ultimately to lead to independence. Following the German defeat of France in 1940, the AEF repudiated the Vichy government and declared its support for the 'Free French' under Gen. de Gaulle. The Brazzaville Conference convened by de Gaulle in 1944 spoke in general terms of a new deal for Africans, while the new French constitution adopted in 1946 provided for direct African elections to the French national assembly. Political parties established themselves throughout francophone Africa, although their demands were for fuller rights of citizenship within the French state rather than for independence. Attempts by the French government to thwart African political progress altogether were unsuccessful. The 1956 *loi cadre* (enabling law) introduced universal adult suffrage, but to the dismay of many nationalist politicians, the franchise was applied individually to the separate states of the two federations, so that the structures of the AOF and AEF were allowed to wither away. In 1958, de Gaulle, still attempting to salvage something of the greater France concept, organized a referendum in which only Guinea voted for full independence. By 1960, however, the remaining AOF and AEF territories, as well as Madagascar, had insisted upon receiving *de jure* independence, even if, despite outward appearances, they remained tied economically and militarily to France.

The events which ended the French empire in sub-Saharan Africa were hastened by concurrent developments in neighbouring British colonies, especially the Gold Coast. With no settler communities to placate, decolonization in British West Africa proceeded relatively smoothly, although much more rapidly than had been contemplated. Popular grievances gave a new edge to the political demands of the now sizeable educated middle classes, and Britain's cautious post-war moves towards granting internal self-government were soon perceived as inadequate even by the British themselves. When police fired on an ex-serviceman's peaceful demonstration in Accra (Gold Coast) in 1948, the resulting unrest, strikes and rural agitation led to major policy changes. Sensing the new mood, the militant nationalist, Kwame Nkrumah, formed the Convention People's Party (CPP) in 1949 with the slogan 'self-government now'. Its populist appeal enabled it in 1951 to overcome the more moderate United Gold Coast Convention party (of which Nkrumah had earlier been general secretary) in an election based on a new and more democratic constitution. Although in jail for sedition, Nkrumah was released and invited to become head of an independent government. This dramatic development, followed by the grant of independence in 1957 as Ghana (whose

boundaries also took in the former mandated territory of British Togoland), had repercussions throughout black Africa. (In fact, the Sudan had achieved independence in the previous year, when the Anglo-Egyptian condominium was brought to an end, but this had attracted little outside attention). Nkrumah sought, with some success, to intensify African revolutionary sentiment still further by organizing an African Peoples' Conference in Accra in 1958. Nigeria's progress towards independence, meanwhile, was complicated by its enormous size and colonially imposed regional structure. Rival regional and ethnic nationalisms competed, and no one party could achieve the degree of overall dominance enjoyed by the CPP in the Gold Coast. None the less a federal Nigeria became independent in 1960, followed by Sierra Leone (1961) and The Gambia (1965).

Belgium initially remained aloof from the movement towards decolonization. It appeared to believe that its relatively advanced provision for social welfare and the rapid post-war economic growth in the Belgian Congo would enable it to avoid making political concessions and to maintain the authoritarian style of government which had characterized its administration of the territory since it took over from the Belgian king. The Belgian Congo, however, could not be insulated—any more than any other part of Africa—from the anti-colonial influences at work throughout the continent. From 1955 onwards nationalist feeling spread rapidly, despite the difficulties in building effective national parties in such a huge country. Urban riots in 1959 led to a precipitate reversal in Belgian policy: at the Brussels Round Table Conference in January 1960 it was abruptly decided that independence was to follow in only six months. Not surprisingly, the disintegration of political unity and order in the country speedily followed the termination of Belgian administration. Belgian rule in the mandated territory of Ruanda-Urundi ended in 1962, and was followed by its division into the separate countries of Rwanda and Burundi.

Meanwhile, in eastern and southern Africa, Britain was also encountering difficulties in implementing decolonization. In Uganda, where its authority rested to a large extent on an alliance with the kingdom of Buganda, British policies had tended to stratify existing ethnic divisions. The deeply ingrained internal problems which preceded independence in 1962 continued to beset Uganda for the next 25 years. In contrast, however, the nationalist movement led by Julius Nyerere in Tanganyika was exceptionally united, and there was little friction prior to independence in 1961. Three years later Tanganyika united with Zanzibar (which obtained independence in 1963) as Tanzania. In Kenya, as in other colonies with significant settler minorities, the process of decolonization was troubled. In the post-war period, the settlers of Kenya sought political domination and worked to suppress emergent African nationalism. African frustrations, particularly about access to land among the Kikuyu, and growing unrest among the urban poor, led in 1952 to the declaration of a state of emergency and the violent revolt the British knew as 'Mau Mau'. This was fiercely suppressed, but only with the help of troops from Britain, a factor which helped finally to destroy the settlers' political credibility. Kenya eventually achieved independence in 1963 under the leadership of the veteran nationalist, Jomo Kenyatta. Vilified by the settlers in the 1950s as a personification of evil, Kenyatta as head of government in fact strove to protect the economic role of the settler population and to maintain good relations with Britain.

Settler interests were more obstructive further to the south. The whites of Southern Rhodesia had obtained internal self-government as early as 1923, but in 1953 the colony was allowed by Britain to become the dominant partner in a federation with Northern Rhodesia and Nyasaland. Conflict followed with African nationalists in the two northern territories, and the federation eventually collapsed in 1963 when Britain had to concede that its policy of decolonization could only effectively apply to the two northern territories whose governments it still controlled. In 1964 Nyasaland became independent as Malawi and Northern Rhodesia as Zambia. When Britain then refused white-minority rule independence to Southern Rhodesia, its settler dominated government, led by Ian Smith, unilaterally declared independence (1965). This was resisted by Britain and condemned by the United Nations, but an ineffectual campaign of economic sanctions was defeated by support for the Smith regime by neighbouring South Africa and Portugal. African nationalists eventually succeeded in organizing the guerrilla war which in the 1970s paved the way for a negotiated settlement. With Robert Mugabe as its leader, the country became independent as Zimbabwe (1980), a development which owed much to the collapse of Portuguese rule in Africa after 1974.

During the lengthy dictatorship of Dr Salazar, Portugal regarded its African colonial possessions as inalienable, and in 1951 they were declared to be overseas provinces. However, intense political repression failed to prevent the emergence of armed resistance movements in Angola (1961), Guinea-Bissau (1963) and Mozambique (1964). Most successfully in Guinea-Bissau under the leadership of Amílcar Cabral, these guerrilla movements succeeded in mobilizing rural support. Eventually, in 1974, following the military overthrow of the Portuguese

regime, progress towards internal democratization was accompanied by a determination to implement an accelerated policy of decolonization. In Angola, where the divided nationalist movement provided opportunities for external intervention on opposite sides by South African and Cuban forces, independence proved difficult to consolidate. Mozambique also suffered greatly from South Africa's policy of destabilizing its newly-independent neighbours.

During this period South Africa was itself conducting a colonial war in Namibia, which it continued to occupy in defiance of the United Nations after it had terminated the mandate in 1966. The war against the South West African People's Organisation of Namibia continued until a negotiated settlement finally led to independence in 1990, effectively concluding the colonial era in Africa.

DATES OF INDEPENDENCE OF AFRICAN COUNTRIES
IN CHRONOLOGICAL ORDER OF INDEPENDENCE—POST-WAR

Libya	24 Dec.	1951
Sudan	1 Jan.	1956
Morocco	2 March	1956
Tunisia	20 March	1956
Ghana	6 March	1957
Guinea	2 Oct.	1958
Cameroon	1 Jan.	1960
Togo	27 April	1960
Mali	20 June	1960
Senegal	20 June	1960
Madagascar	26 June	1960
The Democratic Republic of the Congo (as the Congo)	30 June	1960
Somalia	1 July	1960
Benin (as Dahomey)	1 Aug.	1960
Niger	3 Aug.	1960
Burkina Faso (as Upper Volta)	5 Aug.	1960
Côte d'Ivoire	7 Aug.	1960
Chad	11 Aug.	1960
The Central African Republic	13 Aug.	1960
The Republic of the Congo (Congo–Brazzaville)	15 Aug.	1960
Gabon	17 Aug.	1960
Nigeria	1 Oct.	1960
Mauritania	28 Nov.	1960
Sierra Leone	27 April	1961
Tanzania (as Tanganyika)	9 Dec.	1961

Rwanda	1 July	1962
Burundi	1 July	1962
Algeria	3 July	1962
Uganda	9 Oct.	1962
Zanzibar (now part of Tanzania)	10 Dec.	1963
Kenya	12 Dec.	1963
Malawi	6 July	1964
Zambia	24 Oct.	1964
The Gambia	18 Feb.	1965
Botswana	30 Sept.	1966
Lesotho	4 Oct.	1966
Mauritius	12 March	1968
Swaziland	6 Sept.	1968
Equatorial Guinea	12 Oct.	1968
Guinea-Bissau	10 Sept.	1974
Mozambique	25 June	1975
Cape Verde	5 July	1975
The Comoros	*6 July	1975
São Tomé and Príncipe	12 July	1975
Angola	11 Nov.	1975
Seychelles	29 June	1976
Djibouti	27 June	1977
Zimbabwe	18 April	1980
Namibia	21 March	1990
Eritrea	24 May	1993

* Date of unilateral declaration of independence, recognized by France (in respect of three of the four islands) in December 1975.

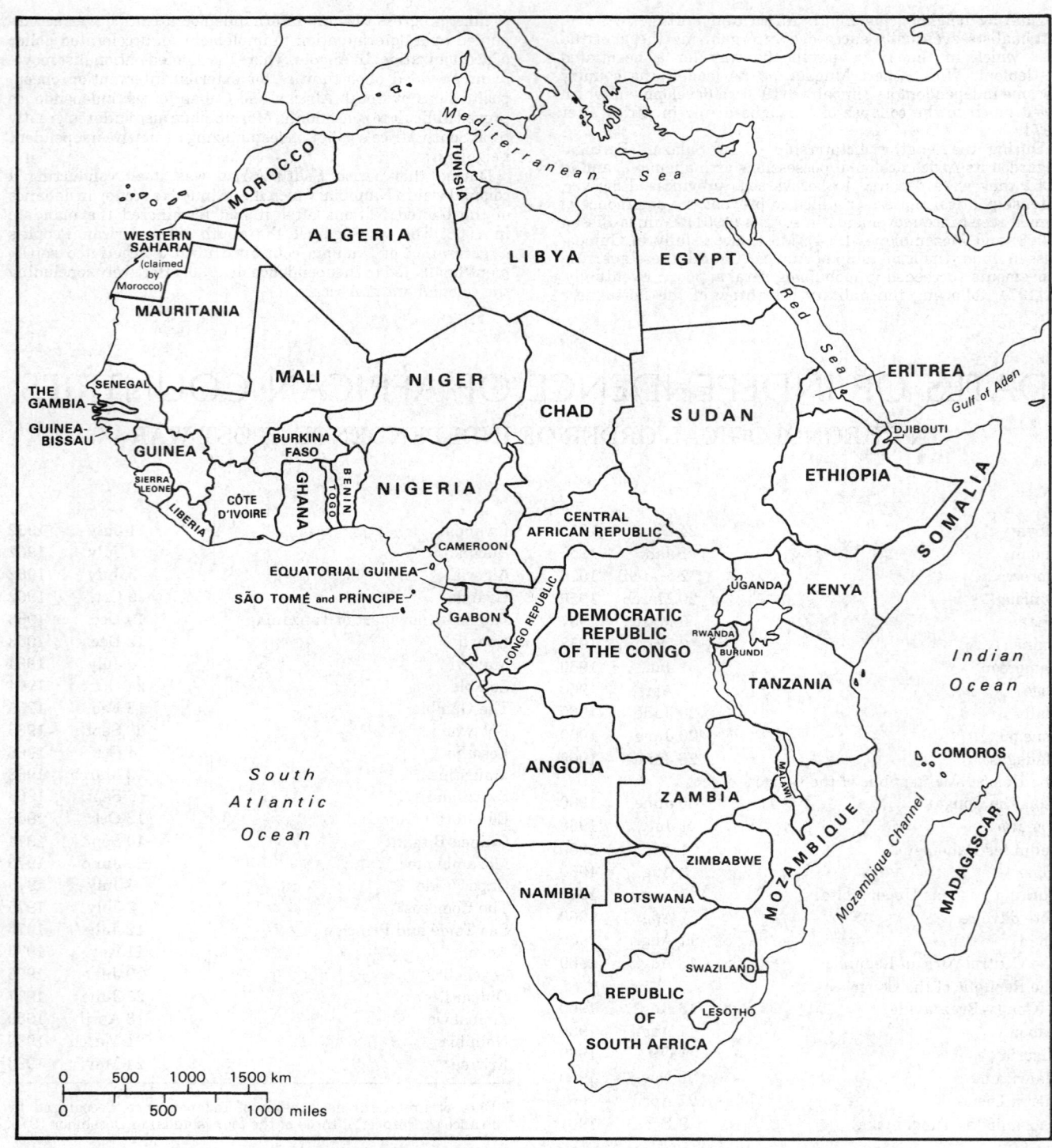

MOROCCO

TUNISIA

Mediterranean Sea

WESTERN
SAHARA
(claimed
by
Morocco)

ALGERIA

LIBYA

EGYPT

MAURITANIA

Red Sea

ERITREA

Gulf of Aden

MALI

NIGER

CHAD

SUDAN

DJIBOUTI

THE
GAMBIA

SENEGAL

GUINEA-
BISSAU

GUINEA

BURKINA
FASO

SIERRA
LEONE

CÔTE
D'IVOIRE

GHANA

BENIN

TOGO

NIGERIA

ETHIOPIA

SOMALIA

LIBERIA

CENTRAL
AFRICAN REPUBLIC

CAMEROON

EQUATORIAL GUINEA

SÃO TOMÉ and PRÍNCIPE

GABON

CONGO REPUBLIC

UGANDA

KENYA

DEMOCRATIC
REPUBLIC
OF THE CONGO

RWANDA

BURUNDI

TANZANIA

*Indian
Ocean*

*South
Atlantic
Ocean*

ANGOLA

ZAMBIA

MALAWI

COMOROS

ZIMBABWE

MOZAMBIQUE

Mozambique Channel

MADAGASCAR

NAMIBIA

BOTSWANA

SWAZILAND

REPUBLIC
OF
SOUTH AFRICA

LESOTHO

| 0 | 500 | 1000 | 1500 km |
| 0 | | 500 | 1000 miles |

Outline Political Map of Contemporary Africa

CALENDARS, TIME RECKONING, AND WEIGHTS AND MEASURES

The Islamic Calendar

The Islamic era dates from 16 July 622, which was the beginning of the Arab year in which the *Hijra* ('flight' or migration) of the prophet Muhammad (the founder of Islam), from Mecca to Medina (in modern Saudi Arabia), took place. The Islamic or *Hijri* Calendar is lunar, each year having 354 or 355 days, the extra day being intercalated 11 times every 30 years. Accordingly, the beginning of the *Hijri* year occurs earlier in the Gregorian Calendar by a few days each year. Dates are reckoned in terms of the *anno Hegirae* (AH) or year of the Hegira (*Hijra*). The Islamic year AH 1421 began on 6 April 2000.

The year is divided into the following months:

1. Muharram	30 days	7. Rajab	30 days	
2. Safar	29 ,,	8. Shaaban	29 ,,	
3. Rabia I	30 ,,	9. Ramadan	30 ,,	
4. Rabia II	29 ,,	10. Shawwal	29 ,,	
5. Jumada I	30 ,,	11. Dhu'l-Qa'da	30 ,,	
6. Jumada II	29 ,,	12. Dhu'l-Hijja	29 or 30 days	

The *Hijri* Calendar is used for religious purposes throughout the Islamic world.

PRINCIPAL ISLAMIC FESTIVALS

New Year: 1st Muharram. The first 10 days of the year are regarded as holy, especially the 10th.

Ashoura: 10th Muharram. Celebrates the first meeting of Adam and Eve after leaving Paradise, also the ending of the Flood and the death of Hussain, grandson of the prophet Muhammad. The feast is celebrated with fairs and processions.

Mouloud (Birth of Muhammad): 12th Rabia I.

Leilat al-Meiraj (Ascension of Muhammad): 27th Rajab.

Ramadan (Month of Fasting).

Id al-Fitr or **Id al-Saghir** or **Küçük Bayram** (The Small Feast): Three days beginning 1st Shawwal. This celebration follows the constraint of the Ramadan fast.

Id al-Adha or **Id al-Kabir** or **Büyük Bayram** (The Great Feast, Feast of the Sacrifice): Four days beginning on 10th Dhu'l-Hijja. The principal Islamic festival, commemorating Abraham's sacrifice and coinciding with the pilgrimage to Mecca. Celebrated by the sacrifice of a sheep, by feasting and by donations to the poor.

Islamic Year	1420		1421		1422	
New Year	17 April	1999	6 April	2000	26 March	2001
Ashoura	26 April	1999	15 April	2000	4 April	2001
Mouloud	26 June	1999	15 June	2000	4 June	2001
Leilat al-Meiraj	6 Nov.	1999	26 Oct.	2000	15 Oct.	2001
Ramadan begins . . .	9 Dec.	1999	28 Nov.	2000	17 Nov.	2001
Id al-Fitr	8 Jan.	2000	28 Dec.	2000	17 Dec.	2001
Id al-Adha	16 March	2000	6 March	2001	23 Feb.	2002

Note: Local determinations may vary by one day from those given here.

The Ethiopian Calendar

The Ethiopian Calendar is solar, and is the traditional calendar of the Ethiopian Church. New Year (1st Maskarem) usually occurs on 11 September Gregorian. The Ethiopian year 1991 began on 11 September 1998.

The year is divided into 13 months, of which 12 have 30 days each. The 13th and last month (Paguemen) has five or six days, the extra day occurring in leap years. The months are as follows:

1. Maskarem	5. Tir	10. Sene
2. Tikimit	6. Yekatit	11. Hamle
3. Hidar	7. Megabit	12. Nahasse
4. Tahsas	8. Maiza	13. Paguemen
	9. Ginbat	

The Ethiopian Calendar is used for most purposes, religious and secular, in Ethiopia.

Standard Time

One hour behind GMT	Greenwich Mean Time (GMT)	One hour ahead of GMT	Two hours ahead of GMT	Three hours ahead of GMT	Four hours ahead of GMT
Cape Verde	Ascension	Algeria	Botswana	Comoros	Mauritius
	Burkina Faso	Angola	Burundi	Djibouti	Réunion
	Côte d'Ivoire	Benin	Egypt*	Eritrea	Seychelles
	The Gambia	Cameroon	Lesotho	Ethiopia	
	Ghana	Central African	Malawi	Kenya	
	Guinea	Republic	Mozambique	Madagascar	
	Guinea-Bissau	Chad	Namibia	Mayotte	
	Liberia	Congo, Democratic	Rwanda	Somalia	
	Mali	Republic	South Africa	Tanzania	
	Mauritania	Congo, Republic	Sudan	Uganda	
	Morocco	Equatorial Guinea	Swaziland		
	St Helena	Gabon	Zambia		
	São Tomé and Príncipe	Libya	Zimbabwe		
	Senegal	Niger			
	Sierra Leone	Nigeria			
	Togo	Tunisia			
	Tristan da Cunha				

* Egypt observes summer time, the only country in Africa to do so.

Weights and Measures

Principal weights and units of measurement in common use as alternatives to the imperial and metric systems.

WEIGHT

Unit	Country	Metric equivalent	Imperial equivalent
Frasula	Ethiopia	17 kg	37.38 lb
Frazila	Tanzania (Zanzibar)	15.87 kg	35 lb
Kantar	Sudan	44.928 kg	99.05 lb
Nater	Ethiopia	450 grams	1 lb
Pound (Dutch)	South Africa	494 grams	1.09 lb
Wakiah	Tanzania (Zanzibar)	280 grams	9.88 oz
Wokiet	Ethiopia	28 grams	1 oz

LENGTH

Unit	Country	Metric equivalent	Imperial equivalent
Busa	Sudan	2.54 cm	1 in
Cubito	Somalia	55.88 cm	22 in
Foot (Cape)	South Africa	31.5 cm	12.4 in
Foot (French)	Mauritius	32.5 cm	12.8 in
Gemad	Ethiopia	100 m	328 ft
Kadam or Qadam	Sudan	30.48 cm	12 in
Kan	Ethiopia	25 km	15.5 miles
Kend	Ethiopia	40 cm–60 cm	20 in
Pouce	Mauritius	2.54 cm	1 in
Senzer	Ethiopia	20 cm	8 in

CAPACITY

Unit	Country	Metric equivalent	Imperial equivalent
Ardabb or Ardeb	Sudan	198.024 litres	45.36 gallons
Bali	South Africa	46 litres	10.119 gallons
Corde	Mauritius	3.584 cu m	128 cu ft
Gantang	South Africa	9.2 litres	2.024 gallons
Kadah	Sudan	2.063 litres	3.63 pints
Keila	Sudan	16.502 litres	3.63 gallons
Kubaya	Ethiopia	0.3 litres	0.5 pints
Kuna	Ethiopia	5 litres	1.1 gallons
Mud or Muid	South Africa	109.1 litres	24 gallons
Ratel	Sudan	0.568 litre	1 pint
Tanika	Ethiopia	20 litres	5.28 gallons

AREA

Unit	Country	Metric equivalent	Imperial equivalent
Are	Mauritius	0.01 ha	0.0247 acre
Darat or Dural	Somalia	8,000 sq m	1.98 acres
Feddan	Sudan	4,201 sq m	1.038 acres
Gasha	Ethiopia	40 ha	99 acres
Morgen	South Africa	0.857 ha	2.117 acres

Metric to Imperial Conversions

Metric units	Imperial units	To convert Metric into Imperial units, multiply by:	To convert Imperial into Metric units, multiply by:
Weight			
Gram	Ounce (Avoirdupois)	0.035274	28.3495
Kilogram (kg)	Pound (lb)	2.204623	0.453952
Metric ton	Short ton (2,000 lb)	1.102311	0.907185
	Long ton (2,240 lb)	0.984207	1.016047
	(The short ton is in general use in the USA, while the long ton is normally used in the United Kingdom and in some other countries in the Commonwealth.)		
Length			
Centimetre (cm)	Inch (in)	0.3937008	2.54
Metre (m)	Yard (=3 feet)	1.09361	0.9144
Kilometre (km)	Mile	0.62137	1.609344
Volume			
Cubic metre (cu m)	Cubic foot	35.315	0.028317
	Cubic yard	1.30795	0.764555
Capacity			
Litre	Gallon (=8 pints)	0.219969	4.54609
	Gallon (US)	0.264172	3.78541
Area			
Square metre (sq m)	Square yard	1.19599	0.836127
Hectare (ha)	Acre	2.47105	0.404686
Square kilometre (sq km)	Square mile	0.386102	2.589988

MAJOR COMMODITIES OF AFRICA

Note: For each of the commodities in this section, there are generally two statistical tables: one relating to recent levels of production, and one indicating recent trends in prices. Each production table shows estimates of output for the world and for Africa (including northern Africa, a region not covered by this volume). In addition, the table lists the main African producing countries and, for comparison, the leading producers from outside the continent. In most cases, the table referring to prices provides indexes of export prices, calculated in US dollars. The index for each commodity is based on specific price quotations for representative grades of that commodity in countries that are major traders (excluding countries of Eastern Europe and the former USSR).

Aluminium and Bauxite

Aluminium is the most abundant metallic element in the earth's crust, comprising about 8% of the total. However, it is much less widely used than steel, despite having about the same strength and only half the weight. Aluminium has important applications as a metal because of its lightness, ease of fabrication and other desirable properties. Other products of alumina (aluminium oxide) are materials in refractories, abrasives, glass manufacture, other ceramic products, catalysts and absorbers. Alumina hydrates are used for the production of aluminium chemicals, fire retardant in carpet backing, and industrial fillers in plastics and related products.

The major markets for aluminium are in transportation, building and construction, electrical machinery and equipment, consumer durables, and the packaging industry, which in the late 1990s accounted for about 20% of all aluminium use. Although the production of aluminium is energy-intensive, its light weight results in a net saving, particularly in the transportation industry. About one-quarter of aluminium output is consumed in the manufacture of transport equipment, particularly road motor vehicles and components, where the metal is increasingly being used as a substitute for steel. In the early 1990s steel substitution accounted for about 16% of world aluminium consumption, and it has been forecast that aluminium demand by the motor vehicle industry alone could more than double, to exceed 5.7m. tons in 2010, from around 2.4m. tons in 1990. Aluminium is of great value to the aerospace industry for its weight-saving characteristics and its low cost relative to alternative materials. Aluminium-lithium alloys command considerable potential for use in this sector, although the dominance of aluminium in aerospace was under challenge during the 1990s from 'composites' such as carbon-epoxy, a fusion of carbon fibres and hardened resins, whose lightness and durability can exceed that of many aluminium alloys.

World aluminium markets for finished and semi-finished aluminium products are dominated by six Western producers — Alcan (Canada), Alcoa, Reynolds, Kaiser (all USA), Pechiney (France) and algroup (Switzerland). Proposals for a merger between Alcan, algroup and Pechiney, and between Alcoa and Reynolds, were announced in August 1999. However, the proposed terms of the Pechiney-Alcan-algroup merger encountered opposition from the European Commission, on the grounds that the combined grouping could restrict market competition and adversely affect the interests of consumers. The tripartite merger plan was abandoned in April 2000, although the terms of a merger between Alcan and algroup were announced in June. The implications of the proposed amalgamation of Alcoa and Reynolds were still under consideration in mid-2000 by the European Commission and the US government. The level of dominance of these major producers has, however, been reduced in recent years by a significant geographical shift in the location of alumina and aluminium production to areas where cheap power is available, such as Australia, Brazil, Norway, Canada and Venezuela. The Gulf states of Bahrain and Dubai, with the advantage of low energy costs, also produce primary aluminium. Since the mid-1990s Russia has also become a significant force in the world aluminium market (see below), and in April 2000 the country's three principal producers announced their intention to combine into a single group representing about 75% of Russian aluminium production and approximately 10% of world output.

Bauxite is the principal aluminium ore, but nepheline syenite, kaolin, shale, anorthosite and alunite are all potential alternative sources of alumina, although not currently economic to process. Of all bauxite mined, approximately 85% is converted to alumina (Al_2O_3) for the production of aluminium metal. The developing countries, in which 70% of known bauxite reserves are located, supply 45% of the ore required. The industry is structured in three stages: bauxite mining, alumina refining and smelting. While the high degree of 'vertical integration' (i.e. the control of successive stages of production) in the industry means that a significant proportion of trade in bauxite and alumina is in the form of intra-company transfers, and the increasing tendency to site alumina refineries near to bauxite deposits has resulted in a shrinking bauxite trade, there is a growing free market in alumina, serving the needs of the increasing number of independent (i.e. non-integrated) smelters.

The alumina is separated from the ore by the Bayer process. After mining, bauxite is fed to process directly if mine-run material is adequate (as in Jamaica) or is crushed and beneficiated. Where the 'as-mined' ore presents handling problems, or weight reduction is desirable, it may be dried prior to shipment.

At the alumina plant the ore is slurried with spent-liquor directly, if the soft Caribbean type is used, or, in the case of other types, it is ball-milled to reduce it to a size which will facilitate the extraction of the alumina. The bauxite slurry is then digested with caustic soda to extract the alumina from the ore while leaving the impurities as an insoluble residue. The digest conditions depend on the aluminium minerals in the ore and the impurities. The liquor, with the dissolved alumina, is then separated from the insoluble impurities by combinations of sedimentation, decantation and filtration and the residue washed to minimize the soda losses. The clarified liquor is concentrated and the alumina precipitated by seeding with hydrate. The precipitated alumina is then filtered, washed and calcined to produce alumina. The ratio of bauxite to alumina is approximately 1.95:1.

28

The smelting of the aluminium is generally by electrolysis in molten cryolite. Because of the high consumption of electricity by this process, alumina is usually smelted in areas where low-cost electricity is available. However, most of the electricity now used in primary smelting in the Western world is generated by hydroelectricity—a renewable energy source.

The recycling of aluminium is economically (as well as environmentally) desirable, as the process uses only 5% of the electricity required to produce a similar quantity of primary aluminium. Aluminium that has been recycled from scrap currently accounts for about 40% of the total aluminium supply in the USA, and for about 30% of Western European consumption. With the added impetus of environmental concerns, considerable growth world-wide in the recycling of used beverage cans (UBC) was forecast for the 1990s. In the mid-1990s, according to aluminium industry estimates, the recycling rate of UBC amounted to at least 55% world-wide.

Total world output of primary aluminium in 1999 was estimated at 23.1m. metric tons, of which African producers accounted for almost 1.1m. tons. The USA normally accounts for about one-third of total aluminium consumption (excluding communist and former communist countries). Although it is the principal world producer, accounting for about 16% of aluminium output internationally in 1999, the USA does not produce a surplus of ingots, and limits production to satisfy its domestic requirements for fabrication, while importing the remainder from lower-cost producers elsewhere.

Guinea possesses more than one-quarter of the world's known bauxite reserves, and is the world's leading exporter of bauxite, ranking second only to Australia in terms of ore production. Bauxite and alumina exports dominate the Guinean economy, accounting for 61.4% of its external revenue in 1996. Some Guinean bauxite ore, which is of very high grade, is domestically processed into alumina, and some Guinean alumina is exported to Cameroon for refining. Cameroon has extensive bauxite deposits, estimated at some 1,200m. metric tons, but these await commercial exploitation. In 1996 Malawi began to seek international participation in the development of the country's 29m. metric tons of bauxite reserves at Mulanje. Ghana's bauxite reserves are estimated at 780m. tons. Although the country lacks an alumina refinery, it possesses a substantial aluminium smelter facility, located at Tema, which processes imported alumina. The smelter is operated by the Volta Aluminium Co (VALCO), which is 90% owned by Kaiser. However, in recent years severe drought has caused serious shortages of electricity for the VALCO smelter, and by mid-1998 only one of its five potlines was in operation. Ghana's output of primary aluminium declined from 152,000 tons in 1997 to about 56,000 tons in 1998, but recovered to an estimated 114,000 tons in 1999. However, in December 1999 VALCO received a power allocation for 2000 and 2001 that would enable the smelter to operate four potlines in those years, enough to produce about 80% of its full capacity of 200,000 tons per year. Sierra Leone has estimated bauxite reserves of 100m. tons. Exploitation of the Mkanji deposits, in the Southern province, which began in 1964, has been interrupted since early 1995 by guerrilla insurgency. In 1992 the South African aluminium producer Alusaf announced plans to construct the largest smelter complex ever to be built in the Western world, with an annual capacity of 636,000 tons. These smelters, located at Richards Bay, entered production in 1995, and the eventual full utilization of this capacity would increase total African aluminium output by a significant margin. South Africa's output of primary aluminium advanced from 195,000 tons in 1995 to 693,000 tons in 1998. Production was an estimated 687,000 tons in 1999. A major aluminium smelter project in Mozambique was formally inaugurated in 1998, although the country is not a significant producer of bauxite. The Mozal smelter, located near Maputo, represents the largest single investment project in Mozambique, with an estimated cost of about US $1,300m. The first aluminium was cast at the smelter in June 2000, six months ahead of schedule. Using alumina from Australia, Suriname and Brazil, the smelter is expected to reach its operational capacity in 2001, with an output of 250,000 tons per year, which was projected to advance to 253,000 tons per year by 2004. In Nigeria the Ikot Abasi primary aluminium smelter, with a capacity of 193,000 tons per year, entered production in late 1997, although it was operating at

only 20% of capacity in late 1998 and had to suspend its operations temporarily in June 1999, owing to lack of working capital. Nigeria's estimated output of primary aluminium was 20,000 tons in 1998 and 16,000 tons in 1999.

Although world demand for aluminium advanced by an average of 3% annually from the late 1980s until 1994, industrial recession began, in 1990, to create conditions of over-supply. Despite the implementation of capacity reductions at an annual rate of 10% by the major Western producers, stock levels began to accumulate. The supply problem was exacerbated by a rapid rise, beginning in 1991, of exports by the USSR and its successor states, which had begun to accumulate substantial stocks of aluminium as a consequence of the collapse of the Soviet arms industry. The requirements of these countries for foreign exchange to restructure their economies led to a rapid acceleration in low-cost exports of high-grade aluminium to Western markets. These sales caused considerable dislocation of the market and involved the major Western producers in heavy financial losses. Producing members of the European Community (EC, now the European Union—EU) were particularly severely affected, and in August 1993 the EC imposed quota arrangements, under which aluminium imports from the former USSR were to be cut by 50% for an initial three-month period while efforts were made to negotiate an agreement that would reduce the flow of low-price imports and achieve a reduction in aluminium stocks (by then estimated to total 4.5m. tons world-wide).

These negotiations, which involved the EC, the USA, Canada, Norway, Australia and Russia (but in which the minor producers, Brazil, the Gulf states, Venezuela and Ukraine were not invited to take part), began in October 1993. Initially, the negotiations made little progress, and in November the market price of high-grade aluminium ingots fell to an 11-year 'low'. Following further meetings in January 1994, however, a Memorandum of Understanding (MOU) was finalized, under which Russia was to 'restructure' its aluminium industry and reduce its output by 500,000 tons annually. By March the major Western aluminium producers had agreed to reduce annual production by about 1.2m. tons over a maximum period of two years. Additionally, Russia was to receive US $2,000m. in loan guarantees. The MOU provided for participants to monitor world aluminium supplies and prices on a regular basis. In March the EU quota was terminated. By July the world price had recovered by about 50% on the November 1993 level.

Production of Bauxite (crude ore, '000 metric tons)

	1997	1998*
World total (excl. USA)	122,666*	121,899
Africa	17,645*	15,656
Leading African producers		
Ghana	537	650
Guinea†	17,100*	15,000
Leading non-African producers		
Australia	44,465	44,553
Brazil	11,671	11,700
China, People's Repub.	8,000*	8,200
India	5,800*	5,700
Jamaica†	11,987	12,646
Kazakhstan	3,380*	3,400
Russia	3,350*	3,450
Suriname	3,877	4,000
Venezuela	5,084	5,100

* Estimated production.
† Dried equivalent of crude ore.
Source: US Geological Survey.

Export Price Index for Aluminium (base: 1980 = 100)

	Average	Highest month(s)	Lowest month(s)
1990	93		
1995	104		
1997	92	98 (Aug.)	87 (Dec.)
1998	77	85 (Jan.)	72 (Dec.)
1999	77	68 (Feb., March)	68 (Feb., March)

The successful operation of the MOU, combined with a strong recovery in world aluminium demand, led to the progressive reduction of stock levels and to a concurrent recovery in market prices during 1994 and 1995. Consumption in the Western industrialized countries and Japan rose by an estimated 10.3% to 17.3m. tons, representing the highest rate of annual growth since 1983. This recovery was attributed mainly to a revival in demand from the motor vehicle sector in EU countries and the USA, and to an intensified programme of public works construction in Japan. Demand for aluminium was estimated to have risen by about 13% in China, and by 7% in the less industrialized countries of the South and East Asia region. Demand in the industrialized countries advanced by 11% in 1994, and by 2.2% in 1995.

Levels of world aluminium stocks were progressively reduced during 1994, and by late 1995 it was expected that the continuing fall in stock levels could enable Western smelters to resume full capacity operation during 1996. In May 1996 stock levels were reported to have fallen to their lowest level since March 1993, and exports of aluminium from Russia, totalling 2m. tons annually, were viewed as essential to the maintenance of Western supplies. Meanwhile, progress continued to be made in arrangements under the MOU for the modernization of Russian smelters and their eventual integration into the world aluminium industry. International demand for aluminium rose by approximately 0.2% in 1995 and by 0.8% in 1996. In 1997, however, aluminium consumption by industrialized countries advanced by an estimated 5.4%. This growth in demand was satisfied by increased primary aluminium production, combined with sustained reductions in world levels of primary aluminium stocks. Demand in 1998, however, was adversely affected by the economic crisis in East Asia, and consumption of aluminium in established market economy countries (EMEC) rose by only 0.1%: the lowest growth in aluminium demand since 1982. However, consumption in the EMEC area increased by an estimated 3.9% in 1999, with demand for aluminium rising strongly in the USA and in much of Asia. Compared with 1998, growth in consumption was, however, reduced in Europe and Latin America. World-wide, the fastest-growing sector of aluminium demand in 1999 was the transport industry (the largest market for the metal), with consumption rising by about 9%. Demand was expected to remain strong in 2000, with sales of motor vehicles predicted to continue rising, while world aluminium output was forecast to increase, as additonal smelter capacity became available. Production of primary aluminium in the first six months of 2000 was about 4% above the level for the corresponding period in 1999.

In November 1993 the price of high-grade aluminium (minimum purity 99.7%) on the London Metal Exchange (LME) was quoted at US $ 1,023.5 (£691) per metric ton, its lowest level for about eight years. In July 1994 the London price of aluminium advanced to $ 1,529.5 (£981) per ton, despite a steady accumulation in LME stocks of aluminium, which rose to a series of record levels, increasing from 1.9m. tons at mid-1993 to 2.7m. tons in June 1994. In November 1994, when these holdings had declined to less than 1.9m. tons, aluminium was traded at $1,987.5 (£1,269) per ton.

In January 1995 the LME price of aluminium rose to US $2,149.5 (£1,346) per ton, its highest level since 1990. The aluminium price was reduced to $1,715.5 (£1,085) per ton in May 1995, but recovered to $1,945 (£1,219) in July. It retreated to $1,609.5 (£1,021) per ton in October. Meanwhile, on 1 May the LME's stocks of aluminium were below 1m. tons for the first time since January 1992. In October 1995 these holdings stood at 523,175 tons, their lowest level for more than four years and only 19.7% of the June 1994 peak. Thereafter, stock levels moved generally higher, reaching 970,275 tons in October 1996. During that month the London price of aluminium fell to $1,287 (£823) per ton, but later in the year it exceeded $1,500.

In March 1997 the London price of aluminium reached US $1,665.5 (£1,030) per ton. This was the highest aluminium price recorded in the first half of the year, despite a steady decline in LME stocks of the metal. After falling to less than $1,550 per ton, the London price of aluminium rose in August to $1,787.5 (£1,126). In that month, the LME's aluminium holdings were reduced to 620,475 tons, but in October they reached 744,250 tons. Stocks subsequently decreased, but at the end of December the metal's price was $1,503.5 (£914) per ton, close to its lowest for the year. The average price of aluminium on the LME in 1997 was 72.5 US cents per lb, compared with 68.3 cents per lb in 1996 and 81.9 cents per lb in 1995.

The decline in aluminium stocks continued during the early months of 1998, but this had no major impact on prices, owing partly to forecasts of long-term oversupply. In early May the LME's holdings stood at 511,225 tons, but later that month the price of aluminium fell to less than US $1,350 per ton. In June LME stocks increased to more than 550,000 tons, and in early July the price of the metal was reduced to $1,263.5 (£768) per ton. In early September the LME's holdings decreased to about 452,000 tons (their lowest level since July 1991), and the aluminium price recovered to $1,409.5 (£840) per ton. However, the market remained depressed by a reduction in demand from some consuming countries in Asia, affected by an economic downturn, and in December 1998 the London price of aluminium declined to $1,222 (£725) per ton. For the year as a whole, the average price was 61.6 US cents per lb.

During the first quarter of 1999 the aluminium market continued to be oversupplied, and in March the London price of the metal fell to US $1,139 (£708) per ton: its lowest level, in terms of US currency, since early 1994. Later that month the LME's stocks of aluminium rose to 821,650 tons. By the end of July 1999 these holdings had been reduced to 736,950 tons, and the price of aluminium had meanwhile recovered to $1,433.5 (£902) per ton. Stock levels subsequently rose, but, following the announcement in August of proposed cost-cutting mergers among major producers (see above), the aluminium price continued to increase, reaching $1,626.5 (£1,009) per ton at the end of the year. The steady rise was also attributable to a sharp increase in the price of alumina in the second half of the year. Following an explosion at (and subsequent closure of) a US alumina refinery in July, the price of the material advanced from $160 per ton in that month to $400 per ton (its highest level for 10 years) in December. However, the average LME price of aluminium for the year (61.7 US cents per lb) was almost unchanged from the 1998 level.

With alumina remaining in short supply, prices of aluminium continued to rise during the opening weeks of 2000, and in early February the London quotation reached US $1,743.5 (£1,079) per ton: its highest level for more than two years. However, the LME's stocks of the metal also increased, reaching 868,625 tons later that month. The London price of aluminium declined to $1,413 (£891) per ton in April, but recovered to $1,599 (£1,070) in July. Throughout this period there was a steady decrease in LME holdings, which were reduced to less than 700,000 tons in April, under 600,000 tons in May and below 500,000 tons in July. At the end of July aluminium stocks were 461,975 tons: only 53% of the level reached in February.

Almost all the producers of primary aluminium outside communist or former communist countries are members of the International Primary Aluminium Institute (IPAI), based in London. The IPAI's membership comprises 39 companies operating primary aluminium smelters in 24 countries, collectively representing substantially all of the Western countries' production of primary aluminium. In 1993 the International Aluminium Committee was formed to represent most of the aluminium smelters in the former USSR.

Cassava (Manioc, Tapioca, Yuca) (*Manihot esculenta*)

Cassava is a perennial woody shrub, up to 5 m in height, which is cultivated mainly for its enlarged starch-rich roots, although the young shoots and leaves of the plant are also edible. The plant can be harvested at any time from seven months to three years after planting. A native of South and Central America, cassava is now one of the most important food plants in all parts of the tropics (except at the highest altitudes), having a wide range of adaptation for rainfall (500–8,000 mm per year). Cassava is also well adapted to low-fertility soils, and grows where other crops will not. It is produced mainly on marginal agricultural land, with virtually no input of fertilizers, fungicides or insecticides.

The varieties of the plant fall into two broad groups, bitter and sweet cassava, formerly classed as two separate species, *M. utilissima* and *M. dulcis* or *aipi*. The roots of the sweet variety are usually boiled and then eaten. The roots of the bitter variety are either soaked, pounded and fermented to make a paste (such as 'fufu' in west Africa), or given an additional roasting to produce 'gari'. They can also be made into flour and starch, or dried and pelletized as animal feed.

The cassava plant contains two toxic substances, linamarin and lotaustralin, in its edible roots and leaves, which release the poison hydrocyanic acid, or cyanide, when plant tissues are damaged. Sweet varieties of cassava produce as little as 20 mg of acid per kg of fresh roots, whereas bitter varieties may produce more than 1,000 mg per kg. Although traditional methods of food preparation are effective in reducing cyanogenic content to harmless levels, if roots of bitter varieties are under-processed and the diet lacks protein and iodine (as occurs during famines and wars), cyanide poisoning can cause fatalities. Despite the disadvantages of the two toxins, some farmers prefer to cultivate the bitter varieties, possibly because the cyanide helps to protect the plant from potential pests, and possibly because the texture of certain food products made from bitter varieties is preferred to that of sweet cassavas.

Cassava, which was introduced to Africa from South America in the 16th century, is the most productive source of carbohydrates and produces more calories per unit of land than any cereal crop. Although the nutrient content of the roots consists almost entirely of starch, the leaves are high in vitamins, minerals and protein and, processed as meal or eaten as a fresh vegetable ('saka saka'), provide a useful source of nutrition in many parts of Africa, especially in the Democratic Republic of the Congo, the Congo basin, Sierra Leone, Malawi, Mozambique, Niger, Tanzania and Uganda. A plot of cassava may be left unattended in the ground for two years after maturity without deterioration of the roots, and the plant is resistant to prolonged drought, so the crop is valued as a famine reserve. The roots are highly perishable after harvest and, if not consumed immediately, must be processed (flour, starch, pellets, etc.).

While the area under cassava has expanded considerably in recent years, there is increasing concern that the rapid expansion of cassava root planting may threaten the fertility of the soil and subsequently other crops. Under cropping systems where no fertilizer is used, cassava is the last crop in the succession because of its particular adaptability to infertile soils and its high nutrient use-efficiency in yield terms (although there is now evidence to suggest that cassava yields increase with the use of fertilizer). With the exception of potassium, cassava produces more dry matter with fewer nutrients than most other food crops. Soil fertility is not threatened by cassava itself, but rather by the cultivation systems which employ it without fertilizer use.

Production of Cassava ('000 metric tons)

	1997	1998
World total	164,576*	162,249*
Africa	84,766*	90,169*
Leading African producers		
Angola	2,326†	3,211†
Benin	1,918	2,053
Cameroon	1,700*	1,500*
Congo, Dem. Repub.	16,973	17,060
Congo, Repub.	780	791
Côte d'Ivoire	1,699	1,700
Ghana	6,971	7,227
Guinea	732	812
Kenya	900*	910*
Madagascar	2,418	2,404
Mozambique	5,337	5,639
Nigeria	30,409	32,695
Tanzania	5,700	6,128
Uganda	2,291	3,204
Zambia	702†	817
Leading non-African producers		
Brazil	24,305	19,385
India	5,868	6,000*
Indonesia	15,134	14,728
Thailand	18,084	15,591

* FAO estimate.   † Unofficial figure.

As a staple source of carbohydrates in the tropics, cassava is an essential part of the diet of about 300m. people. It is culti-

vated on almost 9m. ha in Africa and provides more than one-half of the caloric requirements of about 200m. people in the continent. The area in Africa planted to cassava amounts to considerably more than one-half of the world total, and Africa's output accounts for more than 51% of world production. Most of the African crop is produced by subsistence farmers and traded domestically; only a small amount enters world trade.

Since the early 1970s African cassava production has been seriously undermined by mealybug infestation. Indigenous to South America, the mealybug (*Phenacoccus manihoti*) encountered few natural enemies in Africa, and by 1990 had infected all African cassava-growing areas, with the exceptions of Uganda and Madagascar. In 1981 the parasitic wasp *Epidinocarsis lopezi* was introduced into Nigeria from Paraguay to attack the mealybug, and by 1990 *E. lopezi* was successfully established in 25 African countries. The green spider mite (*Mononychellus tanajoa*), another threat to cassava cultivation, is also being successfully combated by the introduction of a natural enemy, the phytoseiid mite (*Typhlodromalus aripo*), which by 1997 had established a presence over 400,000 sq km in west Africa, and in 1999 was reported to have reduced the presence of the green spider mite by up to 70% in some regions. In that year the only countries remaining to be included in the programme were Angola and Liberia. Funding was being sought to extend the range of these operations into other cassava-producing regions of Africa. Another threat is African cassava leaf mosaic disease, which, like the green spider mite, deprives the plant of chlorophyll and results in low yields. A new variety of cassava, reported to be resistant to this disease, was introduced in Uganda in 1997, with the aim of restoring production in the 60,000 ha lost annually to this blight. In addition, the development of high-yielding varieties (HYV) under the aegis of the International Institute of Tropical Agriculture was being successfully conducted in Nigeria during the late 1990s. The cultivation of a new HYV, also possessing resistance to pest damage, was reported to be proceeding successfully in Ghana in 1998.

Export Price Index for Cassava (base: 1980 = 100)

	Average	Highest month(s)	Lowest month(s)
1990	78		
1995	85		
1997	68	79 (Jan.-April)	47 (Dec.)
1998	37	41 (Jan., Feb.)	35 (Sept.)
1999	36	*	*

* The monthly index remained constant at 36 throughout 1999.

In recent years there has been interest in the utilization of cassava as an industrial raw material as well as a food crop. Cassava has the potential to become a basic energy source for ethyl alcohol (ethanol), a substitute for petroleum. 'Alcogas' (a blend of cassava alcohol and petrol) can be mixed with petrol to provide motor fuel, while the high-protein residue from its production can be used for animal feed. The possibility of utilizing cassava leaves and stems (which represent about 50% of the plant and are normally discarded) as cattle-feed concentrates has also been receiving scientific attention.

During 1993 the average monthly import price of hard cassava pellets at the port of Rotterdam, in the Netherlands, declined from US $160 per metric ton in January to $120 per ton in November. The annual average was $137 per ton, compared with $183 in 1992. Prices continued downward in later years, and fell very sharply in 1998.

Chromium

Chromite is the name applied both to the mineral and to the ore containing that mineral. Chromite is the only ore from which chromium is obtained, and the terms chromite ore, chromium ore and chrome ore are used interchangeably. Chromite is used by the metallurgical, chemical and refractory industries. About 87% of total demand for chromite is from the metallurgical industry, 10% from the chemical industry and 3% from the refractory industry. For the metallurgical industry, most chromite ore is smelted in an electric arc furnace to produce ferrochromium. Within the metallurgical industry the major use of chromium is as an essential alloying element in stainless steel, which is valued for its toughness and resistance to most forms of corrosion. Chromium chemicals are used for wood preservation, dyeing, and tanning. Chrome plating is popular. Chromite is used as a refractory mineral.

Production of Chromium Ore ('000 metric tons, gross weight)

	1997	1998*
World total	13,345*	12,686
Africa	6,560*	6,300
African producers		
Madagascar	140	130
South Africa	5,740	5,500
Sudan	10*	10
Zimbabwe	670*	660
Leading non-African producers		
Albania	106*	100
Brazil	300	330
China, People's Repub.	120*	150
Finland	589	611
India	1,363	1,360
Iran	200	200
Kazakhstan	1,800	1,600
Russia	150*	130
Turkey	1,864	1,600

* Estimated production.
Source: US Geological Survey.

World reserves of chromite ore were estimated by the US Geological Survey to total about 3,700m. metric tons in 1998. More than 80% of known reserves are in South Africa, with a further 4% located in Zimbabwe and 11% in Kazakhstan. South Africa produced more than 43% of world chromite ore supplies in 1998, and is also the world's dominant ferrochromium producer, accounting for more than 44% of world ferrochromium requirements. In that year Zimbabwe accounted for about 5%. South African charge-grade, high-carbon ferrochromium (which has a chromium content of 52%–55%) has been replacing the more expensive high- and low-carbon ferrochromium (which have a chromium content of 60%–70%) since the development, during the years 1965–75, of the Argon Oxygen Decarbonizing Process, which permits the widespread use of less costly charge-grade, high-carbon ferro-chromium. South Africa's ferrochromium sector has also benefited from its access to inexpensive supplies of electrical power, and to low labour costs.

Strong demand for ferrochromium in the late 1980s, together with conditions of under-supply, generated an expansion of capacity both in South Africa and Zimbabwe. However, the potentially damaging effects of international boycotts and trade bans, and of civil disturbances, on South Africa's ferrochrome industry led, in the 1980s, to the development of new production capacity, generally close to ore deposits, in Brazil, Finland, Greece, India, Sweden and Turkey. However, the implementation of political change in South Africa after 1993 acted to consolidate its pre-eminence in international ferrochromium markets. In 1995 the People's Republic of China, a major importer of ferrochromium, acquired an interest in the Dilokong mine in northern South Africa, which has an estimated output capacity of 400,000 metric tons per year. Plans were outlined in 1996 for the construction of a charge chrome smelter, with an annual capacity of 100,000 metric tons, principally for export to Japan and China. In 1997 it was forecast that South African ferrochromium could account for 60% of world supplies by 2005.

Export Price Index for Chrome Ore (base: 1980 = 100)

	Average	Highest month(s)	Lowest month(s)
1990	144		
1995	131		
1997	217	222 (June-Dec.)	208 (Jan.-April)
1998	222	*	*
1999	222	*	*

* The monthly index remained constant at 222 from January 1998 to December 1999.

World ferrochromium supplies have exceeded demand in each year since 1990, when the resultant investment in new ferrochromium projects increased world capacity by about 15% in 1991–92. South Africa was prominent in this investment programme. Following the dissolution of the USSR in 1991, significant quantities of chromium raw materials entered the world market, and the subsequent integration of former Eastern bloc ferrochromium production exacerbated the surplus in supply, leading to rationalization measures within the industry; in South Africa, the chromite ore and ferrochromium sectors reduced their capacity by between 40%–50%. Market conditions began to improve, however, in 1994, as chromium supplies from Russia and Kazakhstan were reduced, while demand from Western stainless steel producers improved. This higher level of world demand was not sustained in 1996, with consequent reductions in ferrochromium prices. In 1997 and 1998 South Africa reinforced its pre-eminence in world chromite and ferrochromium markets. Prices of ferrochrome in early 1999 were between 32 and 37 US cents per lb: their lowest level since 1993. Oversupply of stainless steel in world markets generated supply surpluses of ferrochromium during most of 1999, although late in the year an improvement in price levels indicated a return to a balance of supply and demand.

Cobalt

Cobalt is usually mined as a by-product of another metal; in the case of African cobalt, this is principally copper, although cobalt is also produced from nickel-copper-cobalt ores in Botswana and Zimbabwe and from platinum ores in South Africa. It is rarely mined as the primary product of an ore, and is found in very weak concentration, generally 0.1%–0.5%. The ore must be crushed and ground after mining and subjected to a flotation process to obtain the concentrate. During the mid-1990s a new method of extraction, known as pressure acid leaching, was expected to increase substantially the rate of recovery of cobalt as a by-product when laterite nickel ore is treated. It was forecast that this technique, if widely applied, could eventually double existing annual cobalt output.

About 35% of cobalt production is used in the metallic form as superalloys (in gas turbine aircraft engines), hardfacing and stellite. Approximately 34% is applied to chemical uses in such industries as glass manufacture, paints and inks, rechargeable batteries and, increasingly, as catalysts in the processing of oil and petroleum feed stocks and synthetic materials. A further 10% is used in the manufacture of ceramics, 11% in magnetic alloys and 10% in the fabrication of hard metals. The USA is the world's principal consumer of cobalt.

The Democratic Republic of the Congo (DRC) possesses almost one-half of the world's identified cobalt reserves. These reserves also have the highest grade of the metal, with up to six tons of cobalt produced with every 100 tons of copper. The mining, marketing and export of cobalt from the DRC is conducted by a state monopoly, La Générale des Carrières et des Mines (GÉCAMINES). Since 1990, however, the country's cobalt output has been adversely affected by economic dislocation, caused by internal unrest, and by thefts of cobalt, which were estimated to account for between 5%–25% of the total annual

Production of Cobalt Ore (cobalt content, metric tons)

	1997	1998*
World total	27,100*	26,300
Africa	11,141*	9,662
African producers		
Botswana	334	335
Congo, Dem. Repub.	3,500*	1,500
Morocco	714	287
South Africa	450*	450
Zambia†	6,043	7,000
Zimbabwe	100*	90
Leading non-African producers		
Australia	3,000*	3,300
Brazil	400*	400
Canada	5,709	6,039
Cuba	2,082	2,200
New Caledonia	1,000*	1,000
Russia	3,300*	3,200

* Estimated production.
† Twelve months beginning 1 April of year stated.
Source: US Geological Survey.

output. However, projects by GÉCAMINES to exploit new deposits and rehabilitate existing mines in partnership with Canadian and South African interests were initiated in 1999. In 1992 the DRC (as Zaire) was overtaken by Zambia as the world's leading cobalt producer, although cobalt output in Canada advanced strongly during the 1990s and in 1993 exceeded that of Zambia. An eventual restoration of internal order within the DRC could enable the country to retrieve the levels of cobalt output of the early 1980s, when annual exports were in the range of 14,000–16,000 tons. In 1998 the DRC and Zambia jointly accounted for about 30% of world cobalt exports.

Since the early 1980s Zambia has promoted the expansion of its cobalt production in an attempt to offset declines in the country's copper output. Cobalt is extracted as a by-product by Zambia Consolidated Copper Mines (ZCCM). In the late 1990s two mining companies in South Africa were producing cobalt metal as a by-product of platinum production. In 1992 the Ugandan government initiated a project to extract cobalt, at an estimated rate of 1,000 tons per year for a period of 11 years, from waste dumps at the Kilembe copper mine, in south-western Uganda. Financing arrangements for the construction of an extraction plant, to be sited at Kasese, were finalized in 1996, and cobalt extraction operations by a Canadian company were to begin after mid-2000. Following the identification of nickel-cobalt deposits in north-western Tanzania in the early 1990s, the exploitation of cobalt reserves, estimated at 49,000 tons, was expected to begin in 2001. Reserves of cobalt identified in Côte d'Ivoire and Madagascar remained unexploited in the late 1990s.

Traditional cobalt-mining may eventually be challenged by the wide-scale retrieval of manganese nodules from the world's seabeds. It is estimated that the cobalt content of each nodule is about 0.25%, although nodules recovered from the Pacific Ocean in 1983 had a cobalt content of 2.5%. Ferro-manganese crusts, containing extractable cobalt, have been identified at relatively shallow depths within the USA's exclusive economic zones, which extend 370 km (200 nautical miles) into US coastal waters.

The Cobalt Development Institute (CDI), founded in 1982, comprises 60 members from 18 countries, consisting of consumers, processors, merchants and the seven leading producers, including the DRC and Zambia.

On the free market, the price of high-grade cobalt (minimum purity 99.8%) stood at more than US $14 per lb in early June 1993, but declined to $11.175 in November. Following reports of unrest in Zaire, the price of cobalt rose sharply in January 1994, reaching $22.75 per lb. After further fluctuations, the cobalt price increased to $28.125 per lb in October, but fell to $25.50 in December.

Another strong advance in cobalt prices occurred in early 1995, with the quotation for high-grade metal reaching US $30.40 per lb in February. The price was reduced to $27.05 per lb in April, recovered to $29.30 in May, but declined to $27.05 again in July. It advanced to $32.875 per lb in January 1996, but fell to $20.625 in August. In September the cobalt price reached $23.40 per lb.

In March 1997 the free-market price of high-grade cobalt declined to US $19 per lb, but in May, in response to the internal conflict in Zaire (now the DRC), it rose to $25.325. In June, following the establishment of the DRC, the price of cobalt eased to $22.50 per lb, although by December it had risen to $25.75. Cobalt prices subsequently declined, but the quotation for high-grade metal generally remained above $24 per lb until mid-1998. From June the price moved steadily downward, owing to increased availability and falls in demand, and in December it stood at only $12.10 per lb. Market sentiment was also affected by the continuation of regular sales of cobalt by the US government's Defense Logistics Agency (DLA). According to the CDI, deliveries of refined cobalt from the DLA's strategic stockpile in 1998 totalled 2,310 tons, accounting for 6.9% of the world's available supplies (compared with 5.8% in 1997).

The cobalt market slumped even further in January 1999, when, prior to another offering from the DLA, the price for high-grade metal declined to only US $8.40 per lb: its lowest level since the contract was introduced in June 1993. Following the announcement of proposed reductions in Russia's cobalt production, however, the metal's price rapidly recovered, reaching $19.25 per lb in February 1999. The cobalt price eased to $14.80 per lb in May, but advanced to $22.10 in June, following forecasts of declines in African production. The revival of the cobalt market was partly influenced by the conclusion, in January, of a three-year agreement granting a London-based trading company, MRG Cobalt Sales, exclusive rights to market GÉCAMINES' output of cobalt world-wide. MRG had made a similar arrangement with ZCCM in October 1998, so the new agreement gave it control of about 30% of world cobalt supplies. In the second half of 1999, however, the free-market price of cobalt moved steadily downward, and in November the quotation for high-grade metal was $14.20 per lb. The price recovered to $15.05 per lb in December. Meanwhile, in August, an Australian mining company began marketing cobalt on the internet. Another internet site for selling cobalt was established later in the year by a London-based brokerage company.

The price of high-grade cobalt rose to US $15.25 per lb in January 2000, but eased to $14.05 in February. It advanced to $16.975 per lb in early May, but slumped to $13.30 in July.

Cocoa (*Theobroma cacao*)

This tree, up to 14 m tall, originated in the tropical forests of Central and South America. The first known cocoa plantations were in southern Mexico around AD 600. Cocoa first came to Europe in the 16th century. The Spanish and Portuguese introduced cocoa into Africa—on the islands of Fernando Póo (now Bioko), in Equatorial Guinea, and São Tomé and Príncipe—at the beginning of the 19th century. At the end of the century the tree was established on the African mainland, first in Ghana and then in other west African countries.

Cocoa is now widely grown in the tropics, usually at altitudes less than 300 m above sea-level, where it needs a fairly high rainfall and good soil. The cocoa tree has a much shallower tap root than, for example, the coffee bush, making cocoa more vulnerable to dry weather. Cocoa trees can take up to four years from planting before producing sufficient fruit for harvesting. They may live to 80 years or more, although the fully productive period is usually about 20 years. The tree is highly vulnerable to pests and diseases, and it is also very sensitive to climatic changes. Its fruit is a large pod, about 15–25 cm in length, which at maturity is yellow in some varieties and red in others. The ripe pods are cut from the tree, where they grow directly out of the trunk and branches. When opened, cocoa pods disclose a mass of seeds (beans) surrounded by white mucilage. After harvesting, the beans and mucilage are scooped out and fermented. Fermentation lasts several days, allowing the flavour to develop. The mature fermented beans, dull red in colour, are then dried, ready to be bagged as raw cocoa which may be further processed or exported.

Cultivated cocoa trees may be broadly divided into three groups. All west African cocoas belong to the Amazonian Forastero group, which now accounts for more than 80% of world cocoa production. It includes the Amelonado variety, suitable for chocolate manufacturing, grown in Ghana, Côte d'Ivoire and Nigeria. Criollo cocoa is not widely grown and is used only for luxury confectionery. The third group is Trinitario, which comprises about 15% of world output and is cultivated mainly in Central America and the northern regions of South America.

Cocoa processing takes place mainly in importing countries, although processing capacity was established in west Africa during the 1960s and processed products now account for a significant part of the value of its cocoa exports. The processes include shelling, roasting and grinding the beans. Almost half of each bean after shelling consists of a fat called cocoa butter. In the manufacture of cocoa powder for use as a beverage, this fat is largely removed. Cocoa is a mildly stimulating drink, because of its caffeine content, and, unlike coffee and tea, is highly nutritional.

The most important use of cocoa is in the manufacture of chocolate, of which it is the main ingredient. About 90% of all cocoa produced is used in chocolate-making, for which extra cocoa butter is added, as well as other substances such as sugar—and milk in the case of milk chocolate. Proposals that were initially announced in December 1993 (and subsequently amended in November 1997) by the consumer countries of the European Union (EU), permitting chocolate-manufacturers in member states to add as much as 5% vegetable fats to cocoa solids and cocoa fats in the manufacture of chocolate products, have been perceived by producers as potentially damaging to the world cocoa trade. In 1998 it was estimated that the implementation of this plan could reduce world demand for cocoa beans by between 130,000–200,000 metric tons annually. In July 1999, despite protests from Belgium, which, with France, Germany, Greece, Italy, Luxembourg, the Netherlands and Spain, prohibits the manufacture or import of chocolate containing non-cocoa-butter vegetable fats, the European Commission cleared the way to the abolition of this restriction throughout the EU countries. The implementation of the new regulations took effect in May 2000.

After coffee and sugar, cocoa is the most important agricultural export commodity in international trade. Recorded world exports (excluding re-exports) of cocoa beans totalled 1,945,718 metric tons in the 12 months ending 30 September 1998. In 1998/99 export volume was estimated to have risen to 2,118,836 tons, of which African countries accounted for 1,634,680 tons. The world's leading exporters of cocoa beans in 1998/99 were Côte d'Ivoire (976,721 tons), Ghana (353,760 tons), Indonesia (319,568 tons), Nigeria (173,742 tons), Cameroon (91,761 tons) and Ecuador (48,718 tons).

The principal importers of cocoa are developed countries with market economies, which account for about 80% of cocoa imports from developing countries. Recorded world imports of cocoa beans in 1998/99 were 2,142,856 tons. The principal importing countries in that year were the USA (with 428,787 tons, representing 20% of the total), the Netherlands (338,245 tons) and the United Kingdom (243,916 tons).

Production of Cocoa Beans
('000 metric tons, year ending 30 September)

	1997/98	1998/99*
World total	2,680	2,795
Africa	1,841	1,919
Leading African producers		
Cameroon	115	124
Côte d'Ivoire	1,113	1,163
Ghana	409	398
Nigeria	165	195
Leading non-African producers		
Brazil	170	133
Colombia	45	38
Dominican Repub.	60	26
Ecuador	30	75
Indonesia	331	390
Malaysia	65	75
Mexico	35	35
Papua New Guinea	29	33

* Estimates.

Source: International Cocoa Organization.

Côte d'Ivoire, the region's dominant producer, is also the world's principal cocoa grower, accounting for more than 41% of output and 46.1% of international cocoa exports in 1998/99. Government measures, implemented in August 1999, to liberalize the country's cocoa sector included the abolition of the state cocoa board, with the consequent removal of guaranteed prices. However, in November, the impact on Ivorian cocoa-growers of sharply lower world cocoa prices (see below) prompted the government to reintroduce a minimum price mechanism and buffer stock arrangements. Since the mid-1960s, when it accounted for more than one-third of world production, Ghana's share of the world market has fallen to about 17%, owing to the neglect of the industry and to the official policy of maintaining prices payable to producers at uneconomic levels. The decline has been exacerbated by the smuggling of cocoa to neighbouring countries, where higher prices are obtainable. The spread of plant diseases, particularly black pod and swollen shoot, have also inhibited recovery. In 1992 cocoa was overtaken by gold as Ghana's main export commodity. In recent years, however, Ghana has sought to revive cocoa production through programmes of replanting and the introduction of disease-resistant varieties, together with insect spraying, and improved facilities for transport and storage. From July 1993 the Ghana Cocoa Board (COCOBOD) was deprived of its monopoly, and three trading companies were licensed to purchase cocoa direct from farmers. Although COCOBOD has retained exclusive control over Ghanaian cocoa exports, proposals were under consideration in mid-2000 for assigning it a purely advisory and regulatory role. In July 2000 Ghana and Côte d'Ivoire announced plans to co-ordinate their cocoa sales as part of a joint strategy to generate a recovery in world prices. Among the smaller African producers, cocoa exports are a significant component of the economies of Cameroon, Equatorial Guinea, São Tomé and Príncipe and Togo. Although cocoa remains Nigeria's main export crop, its significance to the economy has been eclipsed by petroleum.

World prices for cocoa are highly sensitive to changes in supply and demand, making its market position volatile. Negotiations to secure international agreement on stabilizing the cocoa industry began in 1956. Full-scale cocoa conferences, under United Nations auspices, were held in 1963, 1966 and 1967, but all proved abortive. A major difficulty was the failure to agree on a fixed minimum price. In 1972 the fourth UN Cocoa Conference took place in Geneva and resulted in the first International Cocoa Agreement (ICCA), adopted by 52 countries, although the USA, the world's principal cocoa importer, did not participate. The ICCA took formal effect in October 1973. It operated for three quota years and provided for an export quota system for producing countries, a fixed price range for cocoa beans and a buffer stock to support the agreed prices. In accordance with the ICCA, the International Cocoa Organization (ICCO), based in London, was established in 1973. In March 1999 its members comprised 18 exporting countries, accounting for more than 80% of world production and exports, excluding re-exports, of cocoa beans, and 21 importing countries, accounting for almost 70% of world imports of cocoa beans. The USA, a leading importer of cocoa, is not a member. Nor is Indonesia, whose production and exports of cocoa has expanded rapidly in recent years. The governing body of the ICCO is the International Cocoa Council (ICC), established to supervise implementation of the ICCA.

A second ICCA operated during 1979–81. It was followed by an extended agreement, which was in force in 1981–87. A fourth ICCA took effect in 1987. (For detailed information on these agreements, see *Africa South of the Sahara 1991*.) During the period of these ICCA, the effective operation of cocoa price stabilization mechanisms was frequently impeded by a number of factors, principally by crop and stock surpluses, which continued to overshadow the cocoa market in the early 1990s. In addition, the achievement of ICCA objectives was affected by the divergent views of producers and consumers, led by Côte d'Ivoire, on one side, and by the USA, on the other, as to appropriate minimum price levels. Disagreements also developed over the allocation of members' export quotas and the conduct of price support measures by means of the buffer stock (which ceased to operate during 1983–88), and subsequently over the disposal of unspent buffer stock funds. The effectiveness of financial operations under the fourth ICCA was severely curtailed by the accumulation of arrears of individual members' levy payments, notably by Côte d'Ivoire and Brazil. The fourth ICCA was extended for a two-year period from October 1990, although the suspension of the economic clauses relating to price support operations rendered the agreement ineffective in terms of exerting any influence over cocoa market prices.

Preliminary discussions on a fifth ICCA, again held under UN auspices, ended without agreement in May 1992, when consumer members, while agreeing to extend the fourth ICCA for a further year (until October 1993), refused to accept producers' proposals for the creation of an export quota system as a means of stabilizing prices, on the grounds that such arrangements would not impose sufficient limits on total production to restore equilibrium between demand and supply. Additionally, no agreement was reached on the disposition of cocoa buffer stocks, then totalling 240,000 tons. In March 1993 ICCO delegates abandoned efforts to formulate arrangements whereby prices would be stabilized by means of a stock-withholding scheme. At a further negotiating conference in July, however, terms were finally agreed for a new ICCA, to take effect from October, subject to its ratification by at least five exporting countries (accounting for at least 80% of total world exports) and by importing countries (representing at least 60% of total imports). Unlike previous commodity agreements sponsored by the UN, the fifth ICCA aimed to achieve stable prices by regulating supplies and promoting consumption, rather than through the operation of buffer stocks and export quotas.

The fifth ICCA, operating until September 1998, entered into effect in February 1994. Under the new agreement, buffer stocks totalling 233,000 tons that had accrued from the previous ICCA were to be released on the market at the rate of 51,000 tons annually over a maximum period of 4½ years, beginning in the 1993/94 crop season. At a meeting of the ICCO, held in October 1994, it was agreed that, following the completion of the stocks reduction programme, the extent of stocks held should be limited to the equivalent of three months' consumption. ICCO members also assented to a voluntary reduction in output of 75,000 tons annually, beginning in 1993/94 and terminating in 1998/99. Further measures to achieve a closer balance of production and consumption, under which the level of cocoa stocks would be maintained at 34% of world grindings during the 1996/97 crop year, were introduced by the ICCO in September 1996. The ICCA was subsequently extended until September 2001. In April 2000 the ICCO agreed to implement measures to remedy low levels of world prices (see below), which were to centre on the elimination of sub-grade cocoa in world trade: these cocoas were viewed by the ICCO as partly responsible for the downward trend in prices. In mid-July Côte d'Ivoire, Ghana, Nigeria and Cameroon disclosed that they had agreed to destroy a minimum of 250,000 tons of cocoa at the beginning of the 2000/01 crop season, with a view to assisting prices to recover and to 'improving the quality of cocoa' entering world markets.

Export Price Index for Cocoa (base: 1980 = 100)

	Average	Highest month(s)	Lowest month(s)
1990	49		
1995	55		
1997	57	61 (Oct.)	50 (Feb.)
1998	62	65 (May.)	58 (Feb., Dec.)
1999	47	58 (Jan.)	37 (Dec.)

As the table below indicates, international prices for cocoa have generally been very low in recent years. In 1992 the average of the ICCO's daily prices (based on selected quotations from the London and New York markets) was US $1,099.5 per metric ton (49.9 US cents per lb), its lowest level since 1972. The annual average price per ton subsequently rose steadily, reaching $1,456 in 1996 and $1,619 in 1997. The average rose in 1998 to $1,676 per ton, its highest level since 1987, but slumped in 1999 to $1,140 (a fall of 32.0%). In 1996 the monthly average ranged from $1,339 per ton (in March) to $1,538 (June). In 1997 it varied from $1,373 per ton (February) to $1,770 (September). The average increased in May 1998 to $1,794 per ton (its highest monthly level since February 1988), but fell in December to $1,515. In 1999 the highest monthly average was $1,455 per ton in January, and the lowest was $919 in December. The comparable figure for February 2000 was only $859 per ton: the lowest monthly average since March 1973.

On the London Commodity Exchange (LCE) the price of cocoa for short-term delivery increased from £637 (US $983) per ton in May 1993 to £1,003.5 in November, but it later retreated. In July 1994, following forecasts that the global production deficit would rise, the price reached £1,093.5 ($1,694) per ton.

In late February 1995 the London cocoa quotation for March delivery stood at £1,056.5 per ton, but in March the price was reduced to £938 (US $1,498). The downward trend continued, and in late July the LCE cocoa price was £827.5 ($1,321) per ton. Prices under short-term contracts remained below £1,000 per ton until the end of December, when the 'spot' quotation (for immediate delivery) stood at £847.5 ($1,319) per ton.

During the first quarter of 1996 London cocoa prices continued to be depressed, but in April the short-term quotation rose to more than £1,000 per ton. In May the LCE 'spot' price reached £1,104.5 (US $1,672) per ton. Cocoa prices had increased in spite of the ICCO's forecast that supply would exceed demand in 1995/96, following four consecutive years of deficits. In July 1996, however, the 'spot' quotation in London declined from £1,049 ($1,630) per ton to £924 ($1,438). In December the 'spot' price was reduced to £848.5 ($1,419) per ton.

In January and February 1997 short-term quotations for cocoa were at similarly low levels, but in March the 'spot' price

on the London market rose from £894.5 (US $1,449) per ton to £1,012.5 ($1,621) in less than two weeks. On 1 July the London 'spot' price stood at £1,143 ($1,895) per ton: its highest level, in terms of sterling, for more than nine years. Three weeks later, however, the price declined to £963 ($1,615) per ton. By late August international cocoa prices had recovered strongly, in response to fears that crops would suffer storm damage, and in early September the LCE 'spot' quotation reached £1,133.5 ($1,798) per ton, while prices for longer-term contracts were at their highest for almost a decade. Thereafter, the trend in cocoa prices was generally downward. In the first half of December, however, the London price advanced from £987 ($1,663) per ton to £1,117 ($1,824).

In February 1998 the LCE price of cocoa for short-term delivery was reduced to less than £1,000 per ton. Following political unrest in Indonesia and forecasts of an increased global supply deficit, the cocoa market rallied in the first half of May, with the London 'spot' price rising from £1,072.5 (US $1,787) per ton to £1,140 ($1,857). Meanwhile, cocoa under long-term contracts was being traded at more than £1,200 per ton. However, in late June the London price of cocoa for July delivery declined to £1,002.5 per ton. During July the 'spot' price reached £1,070 ($1,752) per ton, before easing to £1,026.5 ($1,684). London cocoa prices remained above £1,000 per ton until late September, when the 'spot' quotation fell to £970 ($1,651). Later in the year there was a steady downward trend, and in late December the price of cocoa was about £860 ($1,440) per ton.

During the early weeks of 1999 the London cocoa market remained relatively stable, but in March the 'spot' price declined to £803 (US $1,307) per ton. The slump later intensified, following forecasts of plentiful crops and a weakening in consumption trends, and by late May the London price of cocoa had fallen to only £602.5 ($962) per ton. Prices subsequently rallied, and in June, with the EU failing to resolve an impasse over common rules on chocolate products (see above), the quotation for July delivery reached £819 per ton. In July, after the EU agreed to allow chocolate manufacturers to include vegetable fats, the 'spot' price of cocoa eased to £694 ($1,089) per ton, although it later recovered to £754 ($1,194). A further decline in cocoa prices ensued, and in September the 'spot' quotation fell to £601.5 ($975) per ton. After a slight recovery, the downward trend continued. In November the London cocoa price for short-term delivery was reduced to £527.5 per ton. In December the 'spot' quotation reached £570.5 ($926) per ton, but later in the month the price retreated to £530.5 ($854): its lowest level, in terms of sterling, since 1992.

Despite the coup in Côte d'Ivoire in December 1999, the cocoa market weakened further during the opening weeks of 2000, and in late February the London price for short-term delivery stood at only £509 per ton. Meanwhile, the equivalent New York price of cocoa fell in February to only US $734 per ton: its lowest level for more than 25 years. In March the London 'spot' quotation advanced to £598.5 ($940) per ton, before easing to £549 ($874). Comparable prices in May ranged from £575.5 ($880) to £606.5 ($911) per ton, and those in July were between £582 ($881) and £599 ($907).

The Cocoa Producers' Alliance (COPAL), with headquarters in Lagos, Nigeria, whose 13 members include all the major producers except Indonesia, was formed in 1962 with the aim of preventing excessive price fluctuations by regulating the supply of cocoa. Members of COPAL account for about 82% of world cocoa production, with its seven African members providing about 53%. COPAL has acted in concert with successive ICCA.

The principal centres for cocoa-trading in the industrialized countries are the London Cocoa Terminal Market, in the United Kingdom, and the New York Coffee, Sugar and Cocoa Exchange, in the USA.

Coffee (*Coffea*)

This is an evergreen shrub or small tree, generally 5 m–10 m in height, indigenous to Asia and tropical Africa. Wild trees grow to 10 m, but cultivated shrubs are usually pruned to a maximum of 3 m. The dried seeds (beans) are roasted, ground and brewed in hot water to provide the most popular of the world's non-alcoholic beverages. Coffee is drunk in every country in the world and its consumers comprise an estimated one-third of the world's population. Although it has little nutrient value, coffee acts as a mild stimulant, owing to the presence of caffeine, an alkaloid also present in tea and cocoa.

There are about 40 species of *Coffea*, most of which grow wild in the eastern hemisphere. The species of economic importance are *C. arabica* (native to Ethiopia), which accounts for about 70%–75% of world production, and *C. canephora* (the source of robusta coffee), which accounts for all but 1% of the remainder. Arabica coffee is more aromatic but robusta, as the name implies, is a stronger plant. Coffee grows in the tropical belt, between 20°N and 20°S, and from sea-level to as much as 2,000 m above. The optimum growing conditions are found at 1,250–1,500 m above sea-level, with an average temperature of around 17°C and an average annual rainfall of 1,000–1,750 mm. Trees begin bearing fruit three to five years after planting, depending upon the variety, and give their maximum yield (up to 5 kg of fruit per year) from the sixth to the 15th year. Few shrubs remain profitable beyond 30 years.

Arabica coffee trees are grown mostly in the American tropics and supply the largest quantity and the best quality of coffee beans. In Africa and Asia arabica coffee is vulnerable in lowland areas to a serious leaf disease and consequently cultivation has been concentrated on highland areas. Some highland arabicas, such as those grown in Kenya, have a high reputation for quality.

The robusta coffee tree, grown mainly in east and west Africa, has larger leaves than arabica but the beans are generally smaller and of lower quality and price. However, robusta coffee has a higher yield than arabica as the trees are more resistant to disease. Robusta is also more suitable for the production of soluble ('instant') coffee. About 60% of African coffee is of the robusta variety. Soluble coffee accounts for more than one-fifth of world coffee consumption.

Each coffee berry, green at first but red when ripe, usually contains two beans (white in arabica, light brown in robusta) which are the commercial product of the plant. To produce the best quality arabica beans—known in the trade as 'mild' coffee—the berries are opened by a pulping machine and the beans fermented briefly in water before being dried and hulled into green coffee. Much of the crop is exported in green form. Robusta beans are generally prepared by dry-hulling. Roasting and grinding are usually undertaken in the importing countries, for economic reasons and because roasted beans rapidly lose their freshness when exposed to air.

Apart from beans, coffee produces a few minor by-products. When the coffee beans have been removed from the fruit, what remains is a wet mass of pulp and, at a later stage, the dry material of the 'hull' or fibrous sleeve that protects the beans. Coffee pulp is used as cattle feed, the fermented pulp makes a good fertilizer and coffee bean oil is an ingredient in soaps, paints and polishes.

More than one-half of the world's coffee is produced on smallholdings of less than 5 ha. In most producing countries, and especially in Africa, coffee is almost entirely an export crop, with little domestic consumption. Green coffee accounts for some 96% of all the coffee that is exported, with soluble and roasted coffee comprising the balance. Tariffs on green/raw coffee are usually low or non-existent. The USA is the largest single importer, although its volume of coffee purchases was overtaken in 1975 by the combined imports of the (then) nine countries of the European Community (EC, now the European Union—EU).

After petroleum, coffee is the major raw material in world trade, and the single most valuable agricultural export of the tropics. Arabica coffee accounts for about two-thirds of world production. Latin America (with 63.7% of estimated world output, excluding minor producers, in 1998/99) is the leading coffee-growing region. Africa, which formerly ranked second, was overtaken in 1992/93 by Asian producers. In 1998/99 African producers accounted for 14.7% of the world coffee crop, compared with 20.3% for Asian countries.

In every year during 1970–90, except in 1974 and 1984, Côte d'Ivoire was Africa's leading coffee producer, although since 1980 cocoa has overtaken coffee as its most important export crop. In the early 1990s more than three-quarters of the coffee trees in Côte d'Ivoire had passed their most productive age. A programme of extensive replanting was begun in the mid-1990s: the total area under coffee cultivation was projected to increase by 270,000 ha to 1.3m. ha by the year 2000.

Production of Green Coffee Beans
('000 bags, each of 60 kg, coffee years, ICO members only)

	1997/98	1998/99*
World total	95,923	105,225
Africa	14,360	15,462
Leading African producers		
Burundi	297	356
Cameroon	889	1,333
Congo, Dem. Repub.	789	1,000
Côte d'Ivoire	3,682	2,742
Ethiopia	2,916	2,745
Kenya	882	1,156
Madagascar	587	658
Tanzania	624	739
Togo	222	334
Uganda	2,552	3,298
Leading non-African producers		
Brazil	22,753	34,547
Colombia	12,211	10,500
Costa Rica	2,500	2,376
Ecuador	1,191	1,195
El Salvador	2,175	2,056
Guatemala	4,218	3,400
Honduras	2,564	2,196
India	4,735	4,359
Indonesia	7,758	8,366
Mexico	5,045	5,051
Nicaragua	1,084	1,073
Papua New Guinea	1,076	1,350
Peru	1,916	2,099
Thailand	1,293	993
Viet Nam	6,915	6,934

* Estimates.

Source: International Coffee Organization.

The African countries which are most dependent on coffee as a source of foreign exchange are Burundi and Uganda. Coffee sales generally account for 70%–85% of Burundi's total export revenue, and in 1997 the proportion was 88%. In Uganda coffee provided 62.5% of exports in 1996. Ethiopia is also a significant regional producer, challenging Côte d'Ivoire in output in each of the years 1991–95. Despite high domestic consumption and widespread smuggling, coffee accounted for 61.6% of Ethiopia's total export earnings in 1991, and for 70.7% in 1997/98. The coffee sector in Rwanda, which contributed more than 60% of export revenue in 1991, has been severely affected by internal unrest, and in 1994 the bulk of that year's coffee crop was lost. Rwanda's coffee output in 1997 was the smallest since 1974. Among other African countries where coffee is a major export are Cameroon, the Central African Republic, the Democratic Republic of the Congo (DRC), Kenya, Madagascar and Tanzania. Angola was formerly the world's leading exporter of robusta coffee, but production during the period 1975–95 was severely disrupted by civil conflict. In 1995 the resumption of production in three provinces produced a crop of 2,300 tons, while plans proceeded during the late 1990s for the transfer to private-sector ownership of the country's major plantations. In 1997 the government commenced the transfer of the state-controlled marketing monopoly to the private sector, and with arrangements for the sale of all state-owned coffee-producing companies. However, the full rehabilitation of Angola's coffee industry, following the political and military settlement still awaited in 2000, is expected to span many years. Plans have been announced for the initial rehabilitation of 50,000 ha of coffee estates over a five-year period to 2002, with the aim of achieving an annual coffee output of 60,000 tons.

Effective international attempts to stabilize coffee prices began in 1954, when a number of producing countries made a short-term agreement to fix export quotas. After three such agreements, a five-year International Coffee Agreement (ICA), covering both producers and consumers, and introducing a quota system, was signed in 1962. This led to the establishment in 1963 of the International Coffee Organization (ICO), with its headquarters in London. In January 2000 the ICO comprised 63 members (45 exporting countries, accounting for over 90% of world supplies, and 18 importing countries, accounting, until the withdrawal of the USA in 1993, for over 81% of world imports). Subsequent ICA were negotiated in 1968, 1976, 1983 and 1994 (see below), but the system of export quotas to stabilize prices was eventually abandoned in July 1989 (for detailed information on the 1976 and 1983 agreements, see *Africa South of the Sahara 1991*.) During each successive ICA, contention arose over the allocation of members' export quotas, the operation of price support mechanisms, and, most importantly, illicit sales by some members of surplus stocks to non-members of the ICO (notably to the USSR and to countries in Eastern Europe and the Middle East). These 'leaks' of low-price coffee, often at less than one-half of the official ICA rate, also found their way to consumer members of the ICO through free ports, depressing the general market price and making it more difficult for exporters to fulfil their quotas.

The issue of coffee export quotas became further complicated in the 1980s, as consumer tastes in the main importing market, the USA, and, to a lesser extent, in the EC moved away from the robustas exported by Brazil and the main African producers and in favour of the milder arabica coffees grown in Central America. Disagreements over a new system of quota allocations, taking account of coffee by variety, had the effect of undermining efforts in 1989 to preserve the economic provisions of the ICA, pending the negotiation of a new agreement. The ensuing deadlock between consumers and producers, as well as among the producers themselves, led in July to the collapse of the quota system and the suspension of the economic provisions of the ICA. The administrative clauses of the agreement, however, continued to operate and were subsequently extended until October 1993, pending an eventual settlement of the quota issue and the entering into force of a successor ICA.

With the abandonment of the ICA quotas, coffee prices fell sharply in world markets, and were further depressed by a substantial accumulation of coffee stocks held by consumers. The response by some Latin American producers was to seek to revive prices by imposing temporary suspensions of exports; this strategy, however, merely increased losses of coffee revenue. By early 1992 there had been general agreement among the ICO exporting members that the export quota mechanism should be revived. However, disagreements persisted over the allocation of quotas, and in April 1993 it was announced that efforts to achieve a new ICA with economic provisions had collapsed. In the following month Brazil and Colombia, the two largest coffee producers, were joined by some Central American producers in a scheme to limit their coffee production and exports in the 1993/94 coffee year. Although world consumption of coffee exceeded the level of shipments, prices were severely depressed by surpluses of coffee stocks totalling 62m. bags (each of 60 kg), with an additional 21m. bags held in reserve by consumer countries. Prices, in real terms, stood at historic 'lows'.

In September 1993 the Latin American producers announced the formation of an Association of Coffee Producing Countries (ACPC) to implement an export-withholding, or coffee retention, plan. The Inter-African Coffee Organization (IACO, see below), whose membership includes Côte d'Ivoire, Kenya and Uganda, agreed to join the Latin American producers in a new plan to withhold 20% of output whenever market prices fell below an agreed limit. With the participation of Asian producers, a 28-member ACPC was formally established. (Angola and Zaire, now the DRC, were subsequently admitted to membership.) With headquarters in London, its signatory member countries, numbering 29 in 1999, represent about two-thirds of African production and approximately 85% of coffee output world-wide.

The ACPC coffee retention plan came into operation in October 1993 and gradually generated improved prices; by April 1994 market quotations for all grades and origins of coffee had achieved their highest levels since 1989. In June and July 1994 coffee prices escalated sharply, following reports that as much as 50% of the 1995/96 Brazilian crop had been damaged by frosts. In July 1994 both Brazil and Colombia announced a temporary suspension of coffee exports. The onset of drought following the Brazilian frosts further affected prospects for its 1994/95 harvest, and ensured the maintenance of a firm tone in world coffee prices during the remainder of 1994.

The intervention of speculative activity in the coffee futures market during early 1995 led to a series of price falls, despite expectations that coffee consumption in 1995/96, at a forecast 93.4m. bags, would exceed production by about 1m. bags. In an

attempt to restore prices, the ACPC announced in March 1995 that it was to modify the price ranges of the export withholding scheme. In May the Brazilian authorities, holding coffee stocks of about 14.7m. bags, introduced new arrangements under which these stocks would be released for export only when the 20-day moving average of the ICO arabica coffee indicator rose about US $1.90 per lb. Prices, however, continued to decline, and in July Brazil joined Colombia, Costa Rica, El Salvador and Honduras in imposing a reduction of 16% in coffee exports for a one-year period. Later in the same month the ACPC collectively agreed to limit coffee shipments to 60.4m. bags from July 1995 to June 1996. This withholding measure provided for a decrease of about 6m. bags in international coffee exports during this period. In July 1997 the ACPC announced that the export withholding programme was to be replaced by arrangements for the restriction of exports of green coffee. Total exports for 1997/98 were to be restricted to 52.75m. bags. Following the withdrawal in September 1998 of Ecuador from the export restriction scheme (and subsequently from the ACPC) and the accession of India to membership in September 1999, there were 14 ratified member countries participating in the withholding arrangements. The continuing decline in world coffee prices (see below) prompted the ACPC to announce in February 2000 that it was considering the implementation of a further scheme involving the withholding of export supplies. In the following month the members indicated their intention to withdraw supplies of low-grade beans (representing about 10% of annual world exports), and in mid-May announced provisional arrangements, pending further consultations to take place in June, under which 20% of world exports would be withheld until the ICO 15-day composite price reached 95 US cents per lb (at that time the composite price stood at 69 cents per lb).

In June 1993 the members of the ICO agreed to a further extension of the ICA, to September 1994. However, the influence of the ICO, from which the USA withdrew in October 1993, was increasingly perceived as having been eclipsed by the ACPC. In 1994 the ICO agreed provisions for a new ICA, again with primarily consultative and administrative functions, to operate for a five-year period, until September 1999. In November of that year it was agreed to extend this limited ICA until September 2001. The ICO continues to favour a resumption of quota arrangements, which it views as the most effective means of preventing sharp price fluctuations.

In February 1995 five African Producers (Burundi, Kenya, Rwanda, Tanzania and Uganda) agreed to participate in coffee price guarantee contract arrangements sponsored by the Eastern and Southern Africa Trade and Development Bank under the auspices of the Common Market for Eastern and Southern Africa (COMESA). This plan seeks to promote producer price guarantees in place of stock retention schemes. The contract guarantee arrangements would indemnify producers against reductions below an agreed contract price.

Export Price Index for Coffee (base: 1980 = 100)

	Average	Highest month(s)	Lowest month(s)
1990	46		
1995	83		
1997	88	124 (May)	67 (Jan.)
1998	68	89 (Feb.)	56 (Oct.)
1999	53	62 (Dec.)	44 (Sept.)

International prices for coffee beans in the early 1990s were generally at very low levels, even in nominal terms (i.e. without taking inflation into account). On the London Commodity Exchange (LCE) the price of raw robusta coffee for short-term delivery fell in May 1992 to US $652.5 (£365) per metric ton, its lowest level, in terms of dollars, for more than 22 years. By December the London coffee price had recovered to $1,057.5 per ton (for delivery in January 1993). The LCE quotation eased to $837 (£542) per ton in January 1993, and remained within this range until August, when a sharp increase began. The coffee price advanced in September to $1,371 (£885) per ton, its highest level for the year. In April 1994 a further surge in prices began, and in May coffee was traded in London at more than $2,000 per ton for the first time since 1989. In late June 1994 there were reports from Brazil that frost had damaged the potential coffee harvest for future seasons, and the LCE quotation exceeded $3,000 per ton. In July, after further reports of frost damage to Brazilian coffee plantations, the London price reached $3,975 (£2,538) per ton. Market conditions then eased, but in September, as a drought persisted in Brazil, the LCE price of coffee increased to $4,262.5 (£2,708) per ton: its highest level since January 1986. In December 1994, following forecasts of a rise in coffee production and a fall in consumption, the London quotation for January 1995 delivery stood at $2,481.5 per ton.

The coffee market later revived, and in March 1995 the LCE price reached US $3,340 (£2,112) per ton. However, in early July coffee traded in London at $2,400 (£1,501) per ton, although later in the month, after producing countries had announced plans to limit exports, the price rose to $2,932.5 (£1,837). During September the LCE 'spot' quotation (for immediate delivery) was reduced from $2,749 (£1,770) per ton to $2,227.5 (£1,441), but in November it advanced from $2,370 (£1,501) to $2,739.5 (£1,786). Coffee for short-term delivery was traded in December at less than $2,000 per ton, while longer-term quotations were considerably lower.

In early January 1996 the 'spot' price of coffee in London stood at US $1,798 (£1,159) per ton, but later in the month it reached $2,050 (£1,360). The corresponding quotation rose to $2,146.5 (£1,401) per ton in March, but declined to $1,844.5 (£1,220) in May. The 'spot' contract in July opened at $1,730.5 (£1,112) per ton, but within four weeks the price fell to $1,487 (£956), with the easing of concern about a threat of frost damage to Brazilian coffee plantations. In November the 'spot' quotation rose to $1,571 (£934) per ton, but slumped to $1,375.5 (£819) within a week. By the end of the year the London price of coffee (for delivery in January 1997) had been reduced to $1,259 per ton.

In early January 1997 the 'spot' price for robusta coffee stood at only US $1,237 (£734) per ton, but later in the month it reached $1,597.5 (£981). The advance in the coffee market continued in February, but in March the price per ton was reduced from $1,780 (£1,109) to $1,547.5 (£960) within two weeks. In May coffee prices rose spectacularly, in response to concerns about the scarcity of supplies and fears of frost in Brazil. The London 'spot' quotation increased from $1,595 (£986) per ton to $2,502.5 (£1,526) by the end of the month. Meanwhile, on the New York market the price of arabica coffee for short-term delivery exceeded $3 per lb for the first time since 1977. However, the rally was short-lived, and in July 1997 the London price for robusta coffee declined to $1,490 (£889) per ton. In the first half of November the coffee price rose from $1,445 (£862) per ton to $1,658 (£972). During December the price for January 1998 delivery reached $1,841 per ton, but a week later it decreased to $1,657.

The coffee market rallied in January 1998, with the London 'spot' quotation rising from US $1,746.5 (£1,066) per ton to $1,841 (£1,124). Coffee prices for the corresponding contract in March ranged from $1,609 (£977) per ton to $1,787 (£1,065). Following reports of declines in the volume of coffee exports by producing countries (owing to inadequate rainfall), the upward trend in prices continued in April, with the price of robusta for short-term delivery reaching $1,992 per ton. In the first half of May there was another surge in prices (partly as a result of political unrest in Indonesia, the main coffee-producing country in Asia), with the London quotation rising from $1,881.5 (£1,129) per ton to $2,202.5 (£1,351). Later in the month, however, the price was reduced to $1,882.5 (£1,155) per ton. Coffee prices subsequently fell further, and in late July the London 'spot' contract stood at only $1,505.5 (£909) per ton, before recovering to $1,580 (£963). The quotation per ton for September delivery reached $1,699.5 at the beginning of August, having risen by $162 in a week. In September the 'spot' price advanced from $1,640 (£974) per ton to $1,765 (£1,036) a week later. In late October a further sharp rise in coffee prices began, following storm damage in Central America, and in November the London 'spot' quotation for robusta increased from $1,872.5 (£1,123) per ton to $2,142.5 (£1,278). Meanwhile, trading in other contracts continued at less than $1,800 per ton until December, when the London price of coffee (for delivery in January 1999) rose to $1,977.

Coffee prices retreated in January 1999, with the London 'spot' quotation falling from US $1,872.5 (£1,131) per ton to $1,639 (£995). During March the price was reduced from $1,795.5 (£1,111) per ton to $1,692.5 (£1,030), but recovered to $1,795 (£1,112) within a week. As before, the market for longer-term deliveries was considerably more subdued, with coffee trading mainly within a range of $1,490–$1,590 per ton. Thereafter, a generally downward trend was evident, and in May the 'spot' price declined to $1,376.5 (£850) per ton, although it reached $1,536.5 (£962) by the end of the month. The advance was short-lived, with prices for most coffee contracts standing at less than $1,400 per ton in late June. The 'spot' price in July fell to only $1,255 (£805) per ton. In August the London quotation for September 'futures', which had been only $1,282.5 per ton in July, rose to $1,407. However, the 'spot' price in September retreated from $1,323 (£825) per ton to $1,212.5 (£754). In October the price for short-term delivery was reduced to less than $1,200 per ton. The 'spot' quotation in November advanced from $1,212 (£736) per ton to $1,399.5 (£866). Prices strengthened further in December, with the London quotation for short-term delivery reaching $1,557 per ton. Meanwhile, the market for longer-term contracts was more stable, with prices remaining below $1,400 per ton. In that month the Brazilian government's forecast for the country's coffee output in the year beginning April 2000 was higher than some earlier predictions, despite fears that the crop would have been damaged by the unusually dry weather there since September 1999. For 1999 as a whole, average prices of robusta coffee declined by 18.3% from the previous year's level, while arabica prices fell by 23.2%.

In January 2000 the 'spot' price of coffee in London rose strongly towards the end of the month, increasing from US $1,401.5 (£848) per ton to $1,727.5 (£1,067) within a week. However, prices of coffee 'futures' continued to be much lower: at the end of January the quotation for March delivery was $1,073.5 per ton. In February prices of robusta coffee 'futures' were below $1,000 per ton for the first time for nearly seven years. In March the 'spot' quotation eased from $993 (£628) per ton to $944 (£593). Prices continued to weaken in April, with the quotation for short-term delivery falling to less than $900 per ton. The 'spot' price in May declined to $891.5 (£602) per ton, but recovered to $941 (£639). Another downward movement ensued, and by early July the London 'spot' quotation stood at only $807 (£532) per ton. Later that month, prices briefly recovered, owing to concerns about the possible danger of frost damage to coffee crops in Brazil. The 'spot' quotation rose to $886.5 (£585) per ton, while prices of coffee 'futures' advanced to more than $1,000. However, the fear of frost was allayed, and on the next trading day the 'spot' price of coffee in London slumped to $795 (£525) per ton: its lowest level, in terms of US currency, since September 1992.

The weakness in the market was partly attributed to the abundance of supplies, particularly from Viet Nam, which has substantially increased its production and export of coffee in recent years. By mid-2000 Viet Nam had overtaken Indonesia to become the world's leading supplier of robusta coffee and was rivalling Colombia as the second-largest coffee-producing country. Viet Nam and Mexico are the most significant producers outside the ACPC, but their representatives have supported the organization's plan for a coffee retention scheme to limit exports and thus attempt to raise international prices. The plan has also been endorsed by the Organisation africaine et malgache du café (OAMCAF), a Paris-based grouping of nine African coffee-producing countries.

The IACO was formed in 1960, with its headquarters at Abidjan in Côte d'Ivoire. In 1995 the IACO represented 25 producer countries, all of which, except Benin and Liberia, were also members of the ICO. The aim of the IACO is to study common problems and to encourage the harmonization of production.

Copper

The ores containing copper are mainly copper sulphide or copper oxide. They are mined both underground and by open-cast or surface mining. After break-up of the ore body by explosives, the lumps of ore are crushed, ground and mixed with reagents and water in the case of sulphide ores, and then subjected to a flotation process by which copper-rich minerals are extracted. The resulting concentrate, which contains about 30% copper, is then dried, smelted and cast into anode copper, which is further refined to about 99.98% purity by electrolysis (chemical decomposition by electrical action). The cathodes are then cast into convenient shapes for working or are sold as such. Oxide ores, less important than sulphides, are treated in ways rather similar to the solvent extraction process described below.

Two alternative processes of copper extraction, both now in operation in Zambia, have been developed in recent years. The first of these techniques, and as yet of minor importance in the industry, is known as 'Torco' (treatment of refractory copper ores) and is used for extracting copper from silicate ores which were previously not treatable.

The second, and relatively low-cost, technique is the solvent extraction process. This is suited to the treatment of very low-grade oxidized ores and is currently being used on both new ores and waste dumps that have accumulated over previous years from conventional copper working. The copper in the ore or waste material is dissolved in acid and the copper-bearing leach solution is then mixed with a special organic-containing chemical reagent which selectively extracts the copper. After allowing the two layers to separate, the layer containing the copper is separated from the acid leach solution. The copper is extracted from the concentrated leach solution by means of electrolysis to produce refined cathodes.

Copper is ductile, resists corrosion and is an excellent conductor of heat and electricity. Its industrial uses are mainly in the electrical industry (about 60% of copper is made into wire for use in power cables, telecommunications, domestic and industrial wiring) and the building, engineering and chemical industries. Bronzes and brasses are typical copper alloys used for both industrial and decorative purposes. There are, however, substitutes for copper in almost all of its industrial uses, and in recent years aluminium has presented a challenge in the electrical and transport industries.

The current world reserve base of copper has been estimated by the US Geological Survey at 650m. metric tons. Reserves located within the Democratic Republic of the Congo (DRC, formerly Zaire) and Zambia jointly account for about 11% of the total.

Copper production is the mainstay of Zambia's economy, and copper sales normally account for about 85% of Zambia's export earnings. Mining operations are conducted by the formerly state-owned Zambia Consolidated Copper Mines (ZCCM). Before being overtaken by Canada in 1983, Zambia ranked second only to Chile among the world's copper exporters. Zambian copper exports are virtually all in refined but unwrought form. About 43% of its sales are to European Union (EU) countries. Production of refined copper in Zambia entered a gradual decline in the mid-1980s; dwindling ore grades, high extraction costs, transport problems, shortages of foreign exchange, equipment and skilled labour, lack of maintenance and labour unrest combined to make the copper industry seem an unstable basis for the Zambian economy. However, following the country's change of government in 1991, a number of remedial measures, including the restructuring of ZCCM (whose transfer to private-sector ownership was completed in March 2000), have been carried out.

The copper industry in the DRC has become increasingly vulnerable to competition from other producers, such as Chile, which have been establishing new open-cast, low-cost mines. Increasing emphasis has been placed on efforts to increase refined production capacity, and in the late 1980s about one-half of the country's copper exports were in the form of refined copper leach cathodes and blister copper. About 70% of copper exports by the DRC are to EU countries. The mining of copper in the DRC is conducted by the state-owned minerals enterprise, La Générale des Carrières et des Mines (GÉCAMINES), which in 1998 negotiated an agreement with a consortium of foreign mining companies for the exploitation of substantial deposits of copper in the southern Kolwezi region.

South Africa is the continent's other main producer, although since the 1980s copper output has been affected by declining grades of ore, leading to mine closures and a reduction in the level of operations to about 75% of capacity. Namibia derived more than 10% of its total export revenue from copper in the late 1980s, although by 1997 this proportion had dwindled to less than 4%. Mining operations there were conducted at four mines by a South African-owned company, the Tsumeb Corpn

Production of Copper Ore (copper content, '000 metric tons)

	1997	1998*
World total	11,400*	12,200
Africa	607*	567
Leading African producers		
Congo, Dem. Repub.	40	38
South Africa	153	163
Zambia†	353	320
Leading non-African producers		
Australia	545	604
Canada	662	707
Chile	3,392	3,691
China, People's Repub.	496*	476
Indonesia	529	781
Mexico	391	385
Peru	494	521
Poland	414*	415
Russia	505*	515
USA	1,940	1,860

* Estimated production.

† Twelve months beginning 1 April of year stated.

Source: US Geological Survey.

Ltd (TCL), prior to it's liquidation in 1999, when TCL's mineral rights reverted to the Namibian government. The company's assets, which include Namibia's only copper-lead smelter complex, were, however, expected to remain in foreign ownership. In 1998 TCL had a number of new copper-mining projects in prospect: prominent among them was an Australian-promoted venture at Haib, with a production potential of more than 80,000 tons of cathode copper annually. In 1999, however, the Haib development, which would have formed the largest single mining project ever undertaken in Namibia, was suspended, pending an improvement in world copper prices. In Botswana copper and nickel are mined at Selebi-Phikwe, and high-grade copper ore deposits have also been identified in the Ghanzi area. The Sanyati copper mine in Zimbabwe, with estimated ore reserves of 5.5m. tons, entered production in 1995. Targeted output was 5,000 tons annually during the mine's expected life of eight to 10 years.

The major copper-importing countries are the countries of the EU, Japan and the USA. At the close of the 1980s, demand for copper was not being satisfied in full by current production levels, which were being affected by industrial and political unrest in some of the non-African producing countries, notably Chile, with the consequence that levels of copper stocks were declining. Production surpluses, reflecting lower levels of industrial activity in the main importing countries, occurred in the early 1990s, but were followed by supply deficits, exacerbated by low levels of copper stocks. In 1999, according to provisional figures from the International Copper Study Group (ICSG), world-wide consumption of refined copper increased by 5.4% from its 1998 level, to reach 14,178,000 metric tons, while production, including secondary output (recovery from scrap), advanced by 2.4%, to 14,370,000 tons. There was consequently a copper surplus for the year of 192,000 tons, compared with a surplus of 586,000 tons in 1998. However, identified stocks of refined copper throughout the world increased by only 93,000 tons in 1999, to total 1,455,000 tons at the end of the year. This accumulation of copper stocks tends to depress prices (see below). Provisional data from the ICSG indicate that world-wide consumption of refined copper during January–June 2000 reached 7,657,000 tons, a rise of 8.2% over the level for the corresponding half-year in 1999. Over the same period, total production (primary and secondary) was 7,308,000 tons: 3.0% higher than in January–June 1999. As a result, there was a deficit of 349,000 tons in world copper supplies for the first six months of 2000. Identified stocks of refined copper also declined, and at the end of June they stood at 1,235,000 tons.

There is no international agreement between producers and consumers governing the stabilization of supplies and prices. Although most of the world's supply of primary and secondary copper is traded directly between producers and consumers, prices quoted on the London Metal Exchange (LME) and the New York Commodity Exchange (COMEX) provide the principal price-setting mechanism for world copper trading.

Export Price Index for Copper (base: 1980 = 100)

	Average	Highest month(s)	Lowest month(s)
1990	123		
1995	135		
1997	106	122 (June)	83 (Dec.)
1998	78	83 (March, April)	69 (Dec.)
1999	75	84 (Dec.)	65 (March)

On the LME the price of Grade 'A' copper (minimum purity 99.95%) per metric ton declined from £1,563.5 (US $2,219) in February 1993 to £1,108.5 (US $1,746) in May. From 1 July 1993 the LME replaced sterling by US dollars as the basis for pricing its copper contract. In September the London copper quotation increased to $2,011.5 (£1,304) per ton, but in October, with LME stocks of copper at a 15-year 'high', the price slumped to $1,596 (£1,079). The copper price subsequently revived, with the LME quotation exceeding $1,800 per ton by the end of the year. The market remained buoyant in January 1994, although, during that month, copper stocks in LME warehouses reached 617,800 tons, their highest level since February 1978. However, stocks were quickly reduced, and the London copper price moved above $2,000 per ton in May 1994. It continued to rise, reaching $2,533.5 (£1,635) per ton in July. In December, with LME stocks of copper below 300,000 tons, the London price of the metal exceeded $3,000 per ton (a level not recorded for more than five years).

In January 1995 the London copper price reached US $3,055.5 (£1,939) per ton, but in May it fell to $2,721.5 (£1,728), although LME stocks were then less than 200,000 tons. However, in July, with copper stocks reduced to about 141,000 tons, the LME price advanced to $3,216 (£2,009) per ton, its highest level, in terms of US currency, since early 1989.

The LME's holdings of copper rose to 356,800 tons in February 1996, when the price of the metal eased to US $2,492.5 (£1,609) per ton. After increasing again, the copper price fell in April to $2,479.5 (£1,624) per ton, although in early May it recovered to $2,847.5 (£1,872). In late May and June the copper market was gravely perturbed by reports that the world's largest copper-trading company, Sumitomo Corpn of Japan, had transferred, and later dismissed, its principal trader, Yasuo Hamanaka, following revelations that he had incurred estimated losses of $1,800m. in unauthorized dealings (allegedly to maintain copper prices at artificially high levels) on international markets over a 10-year period. This news led to widespread selling of copper: in late June the LME price was reduced to $1,837.5 (£1,192) per ton, although it quickly moved above $2,000 again. In July, after LME stocks had declined to 224,100 tons, the copper price reached $2,102.5 (£1,352) per ton. The London price of copper advanced in November to $2,547.5 (£1,522) per ton, following a decline in LME stocks of the metal to 90,050 tons, their lowest level since July 1990. The copper price at the end of 1996 was $2,217 (£1,304) per ton. Meanwhile, the extent of the losses incurred in the Sumitomo scandal was revised to $2,600m. (In March 1998 a Japanese court sentenced Hamanaka to eight years' imprisonment, after he had pleaded guilty to charges of fraud and forgery.)

In January 1997 the London quotation for high-grade copper reached US $2,575.5 (£1,594) per ton, despite a steady increase in LME stocks, which rose to 222,500 tons in February. In June, with copper stocks reduced to 121,550 tons, the price of the metal reached $2,709.5 (£1,644) per ton. However, LME stocks were soon replenished, rising by 82% (to about 235,000 tons) in July and exceeding 300,000 tons in September. The LME's holdings of copper increased to more than 340,000 tons in October. By the end of that month the London price of copper had fallen below $2,000 per ton, and in late December it stood at $1,696.5 (£1,015). At the end of the year the copper price, in US currency, was 23.4% lower than it had been at the beginning. For 1997 as a whole, however, the average price per ton ($2,276) was only slightly less than in the previous year ($2,294).

The copper market remained depressed in the early weeks of 1998. In February the LME's copper stocks reached 379,325 tons (their highest level since June 1994), while the London price of the metal was reduced to US $1,601.5 (£973) per ton. The copper price recovered to $1,878 (£1,122) per ton in April. LME stocks of copper decreased to less than 247,000 tons in

July, and in that month the price advanced from $1,571 (£963) per ton to $1,756.5 (£1,058). London copper prices remained within this range until late October, when LME stocks exceeded 450,000 tons. At the end of November the COMEX price of high-grade copper for short-term delivery fell below 70 US cents per lb for the first time since 1987. In December 1998, with LME stocks amounting to about 550,000 tons, the London price of copper was reduced to $1,437.5 (£851) per ton. The average London copper price for the year was $1,653 per ton: 27% lower than in 1997 and, in real terms, the lowest annual price level since 1935. The decline in copper prices was attributed to a reduction in imports by some Asian countries, affected by severe financial and economic problems.

In late January 1999 the LME's stocks of copper surpassed the previous record of 645,300 tons, established in January 1978. In March 1999, with these holdings standing at more than 700,000 tons, the London price of copper fell to US $1,351.5 (£832) per ton: its lowest level, in terms of dollars, since 1987. In the same month the COMEX price slumped to only 61 cents per lb. Despite a continuing rise in stocks, the London copper quotation increased in May 1999 to $1,581.5 (£964) per ton, although later in the month, when the LME's holdings reached 776,375 tons, the price retreated to $1,354.5 (£845). Copper prices subsequently recovered, and in July, following reports of proposed reductions in refinery output, the London quotation reached $1,689.5 (£1,085) per ton. In August the LME's copper stocks increased to 795,375 tons, but in September the price exceeded $1,700 per ton. The advance in copper prices continued, and at the end of the year the London quotation was $1,854 (£1,150) per ton. For 1999 as a whole, however, the average London price of copper was $1,572 per ton: 4.9% lower than in 1998 and the lowest annual level, in real terms, for more than 60 years.

In January 2000 the LME's stocks of copper exceeded 800,000 tons for the first time. Nevertheless, on the same day, the London price of the metal rose to US $1,893.5 (£1,147) per ton: its highest level for more than two years. The accumulation of stocks continued, and in early March the LME's holdings reached a record 842,975 tons. The copper price was reduced to $1,619 (£1,021) per ton in April, but recovered to $1,859 (£1,228) in July. Throughout this period the LME's stocks of copper steadily declined, falling to less than 700,000 tons in April, under 600,000 tons in June and below 500,000 tons in July. At the end of July copper stocks were 487,750 tons: less than 58% of the level reached in March.

The ICSG, initially comprising 18 producing and importing countries, was formed in 1992 to compile and publish statistical information and to provide an intergovernmental forum on copper. In 1999 its membership comprised 24 countries, accounting for more than 80% of world trade in copper. The ICSG, which is based in Lisbon, Portugal, does not participate in trade or exercise any form of intervention in the market.

Cotton (*Gossypium*)

This is the name given to the hairs which grow on the epidermis of the seed of the plant genus *Gossypium*. The initial development of the cotton fibres takes place within a closed pod, called a boll, which, after a period of growth lasting about 50 days (depending upon climatic conditions), opens to reveal the familiar white tufts of cotton hair. After the seed cotton has been picked, the cotton fibre, or lint, has to be separated from the seeds by means of a mechanical process, known as ginning. Depending upon the variety and growing conditions, it takes about 3 metric tons of seed cotton to produce one ton of raw cotton fibre. After ginning, a fuzz of very short cotton hairs remains on the seed. These are called linters and may be removed and used in the manufacture of paper, cellulose-based chemicals, explosives, etc.

About one-half of the cotton produced in the world is used in the manufacture of clothing, about one-third is used for household textiles, and the remainder for numerous industrial products (tarpaulins, rubber reinforcement, abrasive backings, filters, high-quality papers, etc.).

The official cotton 'season' (for trade purposes) runs from 1 August to 31 July of the following year. Quantities are measured in both metric tons and bales; for statistical purposes, one bale of cotton is 226.8 kg (500 lb) gross or 217.7 kg (480 lb) net.

Production of Cotton Lint
('000 metric tons, excluding linters)

	1997	1998
World total	19,799*	18,511*
Africa	1,753*	1,596*
Leading African producers		
Benin	175*	150
Burkina Faso	144	136
Cameroon	75†	61†
Chad	86	103
Côte d'Ivoire	114	130
Egypt	342	230
Mali	190	218
Nigeria	90†	55†
Sudan	80*	54†
Tanzania	70	54†
Zimbabwe	101†	95
Leading non-African producers		
China, People's Repub.	4,603	4,501
India	2,635†	2,720†
Pakistan	1,562	1,495
Turkey	832	802
USA	4,092	3,030
Uzbekistan	1,080	966†

* FAO estimate.   † Unofficial figure.

The price of a particular type of cotton depends upon its availability relative to demand and upon characteristics related to yarn quality and suitability for processing. These include fibre length, fineness, cleanliness, strength and colour. The most important of these is length. Generally speaking, the length of the fibre determines the quality of the yarn produced from it, with the longer fibres being preferred for the finer, stronger and more expensive yarns.

Cotton is the world's leading textile fibre. However, with the increased use of synthetics, cotton's share in the world's total consumption of fibre declined from 50% in 1986 to an estimated 44% in 1997. About one-third of the decline in its market share is attributable to increases in the real cost of cotton relative to prices of competing fibres, and about two-thirds of the loss in market share is attributable to other factors. Expanded use of chemical fibre filament yarn (yarn that is not spun but is extruded in a continuous string) in domestic textiles, such as carpeting, accounts for much of the rest of the loss in market share for cotton. The break-up of the Council for Mutual Economic Assistance (the communist countries' trading bloc) in 1990, and of the USSR in 1991, led to substantial reductions in cotton consumption in those countries and contributed to cotton's declining share of the world market. Officially enforced limits on the use of cotton in the People's Republic of China (which accounts for about one-fifth of cotton consumption worldwide) have also made an impact on the international market.

The area devoted to cotton cultivation totalled 31m.–36m. ha between the 1950s and the early 1990s, accounting for about 4% of world cropped area. During the mid-1980s, however, world cotton consumption failed to keep pace with the growth in production, and the resultant surpluses led to a fall in prices, which had serious consequences for the many African countries that rely on cotton sales for a major portion of their export earnings. In the mid-1990s, despite improvements in world price levels, cotton cultivation came under pressure from food crop needs, and world-wide harvested areas under cotton declined from more than 35m. ha in 1995/96 to 33m. ha in 1996/97.

The leading exporters of cotton are the USA, Uzbekistan, Australia, Argentina and Greece. The countries of francophone West Africa are also significant exporters of cotton, accounting for an estimated 15% of the world market in 1997/98. Prominent among the cotton-importing countries are Russia, Japan, Indonesia, the Republic of Korea, Thailand, Italy, Taiwan, Brazil, Turkey and Germany. China, although one of the major producing countries, was the largest importer of cotton during 1994/95–1996/97, accounting for more than 10% of the world trade in cotton.

Cotton is a major source of income and employment for many developing countries, both as a primary product and, increasingly, through sales of yarn, fabrics and finished goods. Cotton is the principal commercial crop, in terms of foreign exchange earnings, in Benin, Burkina Faso, Chad, Egypt, Mali, Sudan and Togo, and is second in importance in the Central African Republic, Mozambique, Senegal and Tanzania. In the late 1990s about 80% of cotton entering the world market from sub-Saharan Africa came from the francophone countries of the CFA franc zone, in which the total area under cotton cultivation exceeded 2.4m. ha.

For many years Sudan was the largest cotton producer in sub-Saharan Africa. The industry has, however, been adversely affected by domestic difficulties resulting from climatic factors, an inflexible, government-dictated marketing policy and crop infestation by white-fly. Although cotton production, classification and marketing were reorganized in the late 1980s, and in 1990 special foreign exchange incentives were offered to producers, levels of output had yet to recover by the mid-1990s. The area under cotton cultivation in Sudan declined from 360,000 ha in the mid-1980s to 136,000 ha in the 1998/99 crop season. In 1997 overseas sales of cotton represented about 19% of the total value of Sudan's exports.

Although co-operation in cotton affairs has a long history, there have been no international agreements governing the cotton trade. Proposals in recent years to link producers and consumers in price stabilization arrangements have been opposed by the USA (the world's largest cotton exporter), and by Japan and the European Union (EU). The International Cotton Advisory Committee (ICAC), an intergovernmental body, established in 1939, with its headquarters in Washington, DC, publishes statistical and economic information and provides a forum for consultation and discussion among its 43 members.

Export Price Index for Cotton Lint (base: 1980 = 100)

	Average	Highest month(s)	Lowest month(s)
1990	93		
1995	103		
1997	82	85 (Aug.)	78 (Dec.)
1998	74	80 (July)	68 (Nov., Dec.)
1999	61	68 (Jan.)	48 (Dec.)

The British city of Liverpool is the historic centre of cotton-trading activity, and international cotton prices are still collected by organizations located in Liverpool. However, almost no US cotton has been imported through the port of Liverpool in recent years. Consumption in the textile industry in the United Kingdom has fallen to approximately 14,000 tons per year, most of which comes from Africa, Greece, Spain and Central Asia. The price for Memphis cotton, from the USA, quoted in international markets is c.i.f. North European ports, of which Bremen, in Germany, is the most important.

The average price for Memphis Territory cotton in North Europe rose to US $2,848 per metric ton in June 1995, owing to an increase in imports by the People's Republic of China, combined with declines in production in India, Turkey and Pakistan. Prices have trended down since, averaging $2,175 per ton during all of 1994/95, $2,088 in 1995/96 and $1,826 in 1996/97. The average Memphis quote c.i.f. North Europe during December 1997 fell to $1,756 per ton. The market was depressed further during the next two years.

The principal Liverpool index of cotton import prices in North Europe is based on an average of the cheapest five quotations from a selection of styles of medium-staple fibre. In 1999 the index recorded an average offering price of 53.1 US cents per lb: its lowest annual level since 1986. On a monthly basis, the average price in December 1999 was only 45.0 cents per lb. The decline in prices was attributed to the plentiful availability of cotton, with high levels of production resulting in large stocks (more than 9m. tons world-wide in recent years).

Changes in US government agricultural policies implemented in 1996, combined with reduced barriers to imports and exports of cotton in recent years in several countries, seem to be leading to a period of reduced fluctuation in cotton prices. During the 10 seasons ending in 1995/96 the average spread between the highest and lowest quotes each season for an average-quality cotton in international trade was 36%. During 1996/97 the spread between the highest and lowest quotes fell to 10%.

Major Commodities of Africa

Diamonds

The primary source of diamonds is a rock known as kimberlite, occurring in volcanic pipes which may vary in area from a few to more than 100 ha and volcanic fissures which are considerably smaller. Among the indicator minerals for kimberlite are chrome diopside, pyrope garnet, ilmenite and zircon. Few kimberlites contain diamonds and, in ore which does, the ratio of diamond to waste is about one part per 20m. There are four methods of diamond mining, of which open-cast mining is the commonest; diamonds are recovered also by underground, alluvial and off-shore mining. The diamond is separated from its ore by careful crushing and gravity concentration which maximizes the diamond's high specific gravity in a process called dense media separation. Stones are of two categories: gem qualities (used for jewellery), which are superior in terms of colour or quality; and industrial quality, about one-half of the total by weight, which are used for high-precision machining or crushed into an abrasive powder called boart.

The size of diamonds and other precious stones is measured in carats. One metric carat is equal to 0.2 gram, so one ounce avoirdupois equals 141.75 carats.

Africa is the major producing region for natural diamonds, although Australia joined the ranks of the major producers in 1983, and the Argyle diamond mine, in Western Australia, has become the world's largest producing mine and main source of industrial-grade diamonds. Output is predominantly of industrial-grade diamonds, with some lower-quality gem diamonds and a few pink diamonds. In 1998 Australian diamond output represented almost one-third of world production by volume. In 1999, however, this proportion fell to less than 27%, reflecting a sharp decline in output at Argyle, which has been undergoing enlargement to enable access to deeper ones. This project is expected to depress production further in 2000 and 2001.

In terms of value, Botswana ranks as the world's largest producer of diamonds, which are the country's principal source of export earnings, normally accounting for up to 80% of export receipts and 30%–35% of government revenues. Diamond production began in 1971, initially at the Orapa mine, which covers an area of 113 ha and is the world's second largest, after the Mwadui field in Tanzania (see below). In 1977 extraction began from a nearby mine at Letlhakane, and in 1982 a major new mine at Jwaneng entered production. Following the completion during 1998 of a major expansion programme at the Orapa mine, annual output from this source was expected to total 12m. carats annually by mid-2000. All diamond mining operations in Botswana are currently conducted by the Debswana Diamond Co (Pty), which is owned equally by the Botswana government and De Beers. Botswana's diamond production in 1999 was estimated at 21.3m. carats, compared with 19.8m. carats in 1998.

About 98% of Namibian diamonds are of gem quality, although recovery costs are high. In 1990 diamond mining commenced at Auchas, and a second mine, at Elizabeth Bay, began in 1991. The expectation that mining operations at the Oranjemund open-cast mine will cease to be economic during the early 2000s has stimulated the exploitation of Namibia's extensive deposits of 'offshore' diamonds, which in the late 1990s were estimated at up to 1,500m. carats. In 1998 'offshore' recoveries of gem-quality stones were estimated to account for more than 50% of Namibia's diamond output. Until 1993, when the government of Namibia granted marine exploration concessions to a new privately-financed venture, the Namibian Minerals Corpn (NAMCO), Consolidated Diamond Mining (CDM), a subsidiary of the De Beers group, held exclusive rights to diamond exploration and mining in Namibia. NAMCO's concession rights cover three offshore areas totalling almost 2,000 sq km, containing an estimated 80m. carats of gem-quality diamonds. Commercial recoveries began in late 1995. In 1994 the Namibian government and De Beers established the Namdeb Diamond Corpn, to which CDM's diamond operations were transferred. Namdeb is owned 50% by De Beers and 50% by the government. In April 1998 the government invited the Russian diamond corporation, Almazy Rossii-Sakha (see below), to conduct mining operations in Namibia. In the late 1990s the diamond sector accounted for about 40% of Namibia's foreign exchange revenue.

The Mwadui diamond pipe in Tanzania is the world's largest, covering an area of 146 ha. Tanzania's diamond output was

Production of Uncut Diamonds
(gem and industrial stones, million metric carats)

	1998	1999
Leading African producers		
Angola	3.0	3.6
Botswana	19.8	21.3
Central African Repub.	0.5	0.5
Congo, Dem. Repub.	25.8	22.0
Ghana	0.7	0.5
Guinea	0.3	0.6
Namibia	1.5	1.6
Sierra Leone	0.3	0.6
South Africa	10.9	9.7
Producers in other areas		
Australia	40.8	29.8
Russia	19.8	16.2
South America	1.6	1.4
Other	0.6	3.3
World total	125.8	111.1

Source: mainly Central Selling Organisation.

838,000 carats in 1971, but production later declined, owing to deterioration in diamond grades, technical engineering problems and difficulties in maintaining the mines. By the late 1980s, exports from Mwadui had effectively ceased. New prospecting agreements were signed in 1993 by the Tanzania government and the De Beers operating subsidiary managing the Mwadui mine, and also with Canadian interests, which obtained mining leases and exploration licences covering almost 9,000 sq km. Following extensive rehabilitation, operations at Mwadui recommenced in August 1995. Small-scale exports were resumed in December. During the late 1990s Tanzania's diamond output was estimated at about 100,000 carats per year.

South African diamond production was formerly conducted at five mine locations. A sixth mine, Venetia (discovered in 1980 and opened in 1992), has become the country's largest producing diamond mine, accounting for about 41% of South African output in 1998. Small-scale marine mining is conducted off the west coast.

Angola's diamond output, which totalled 2.4m. carats in 1974, subsequently fell sharply, as a result of the civil war. Official diamond production in Angola began to revive after 1990, rising from 1m. carats in 1993 to 3.8m. carats in 1996, before declining to 3.3m. carats in 1997 and to about 3.0m. carats in 1998, reflecting the continuing internal political strife, which has caused considerable disruption of official production. Angola is known to possess substantial diamondiferous deposits, occurring both in kimberlite and alluvial formations, among which particular interest has in recent years been focused on the Catoca kimberlite, 30 km west of Saurimo, in north-eastern Angola. Covering an area of more than 660 ha, its potential reserves have been estimated at up to 200m. carats, which would establish it as one of the world's largest deposits of diamonds. The initial phase of a joint Angolan–Russian mine development at Catoca commenced operations in 1998. Although a number of Canadian, Russian, South African and Brazilian entrepreneurs have carried out exploration and assessment work on other sites, subsequent technical and financial support from these sources has been suspended, pending the eventual full readmission of Angolan diamonds to official world markets (see below). A Canadian exploration company, DiamondWorks, entered commercial production in July 1997 at its initial concession at Luo, in Lunda Norte Province. A second mine, at Yetwene, also in Lunda Norte, commenced operations in mid-1998 and was expected to raise the venture's combined output of alluvial diamonds to 15,000 carats per month. Diamond-Works' Angolan mining activities at Yetwene, together with its participation in the development of new operations, was suspended in December 1999 as a result of guerrilla insurgency.

The increasing role of the world diamond trade in the financing of guerrilla insurgencies in Africa, with particular reference to Angola, Sierra Leone and the Democratic Republic of the Congo (DRC), prompted the UN Security Council in June 1998 to adopt Resolution 1173, requiring that international markets ensure that illicitly exported diamonds from these areas did not enter world trade. These 'conflict diamonds' were defined as diamonds which had been either mined or stolen by rebels in opposition to the legitimate government of a country. According to estimates by De Beers, about 3.7% of world diamond production in 1999, with a value of US $255m., could be attributed to areas (principally in Angola and Sierra Leone) under guerrilla control.

Although considerable technical difficulties exist in the identification of diamonds originating in conflict areas, De Beers, as the principal conduit for African diamond sales, implemented a range of measures to comply with the UN sanction. The company, which had in the mid-1980s discontinued purchases from Sierra Leone and Liberia (into which a large proportion of Sierra Leone's diamond output is smuggled), announced in October 1999 that it had suspended all diamond purchases in Angola, and that no diamonds of Angolan origin would be purchased by any of its offices world-wide. In order to eliminate risks that illicit Angolan diamonds might be mixed with officially marketed diamonds, De Beers subsequently suspended all purchases of diamonds originating in west and central Africa, other than those produced in its own mines, and announced that it was restricting 'outside' purchases to diamonds of Russian and Canadian origin. In March 2000 the company introduced documentation guaranteeing customers that none of its marketed diamonds emanated from conflict areas of Africa. In mid-2000 members of the 'Group of Eight' major industrial countries were preparing a new code of conduct for the diamond industry, which would prohibit its members from purchasing 'conflict diamonds'. In July the government of Sierra Leone announced the suspension of official diamond sales. Meanwhile, outlets for smuggled diamonds have continued to operate, principally in Antwerp, Mumbai (Bombay) and Tel Aviv, while illicit output from guerrilla-controlled regions of Angola is marketed under false certification provided by outlets mainly in Côte d'Ivoire, Guinea and Liberia. However, a number of other countries in the region, including Gabon, Togo, Burkina Faso and the Republic of the Congo, have been criticized by the UN for alleged complicity in the trade in 'conflict diamonds'. During mid-2000 Angola's state-controlled diamonds enterprise, the Empresa Nacional de Diamantes de Angola (ENDIAMA), was negotiating to arrange marketing facilities in Belgium for the small volume of officially mined output.

In July 2000 representatives of the two international organizations comprising diamond traders, cutters and polishers resolved to implement a certification system which would allow rough diamonds to be monitored direct from mines to trading centres. The proposed licensing regulations would require that all rough diamonds be shipped in sealed parcels which had been individually certified by authorities in exporting countries. It was announced that an international diamond council was to be established to validate these shipments; the council would also have powers to exclude from world markets any trader found to be dealing in illicit gems.

In Sierra Leone the diamond industry has long been beset by the dual problems of internal instability and widespread illicit digging and smuggling. Legal exports of diamonds have declined steadily since 1970, when 2m. carats of mainly gem-quality diamonds were exported. By the mid-1990s these sales had dwindled to negligible proportions, and in mid-2000 were officially suspended (see above). Plans exist for the eventual rehabilitation of diamond mining in the Koindu region (which had been severely hampered by guerrilla activity), together with diamond exploration in the Kono district, as well as promising initial results of exploration for offshore diamonds. However, the realization of Sierra Leone's potential for expanding this resource must await the eventual restoration of internal political stability. Similar problems exist for the diamond sector in neighbouring Liberia, whose exports averaged about 200,000 carats per year in the mid-1980s (although much of this total was attributable to stones smuggled from adjoining countries and attracted to Liberia by its currency link with the US dollar). Following the resolution of the civil war that effectively halted the country's diamond trade during 1989-96, official efforts have been made to revive the diamond sector and to suppress illegal mining and smuggling.

About 90% of output in the DRC, which is mainly derived from alluvial diamond-mining operations in Eastern Kasai, is industrial diamonds, of which the DRC (then known as Zaire) was the world's principal producer until it was overtaken by Australia in 1986. During 1993–96 the DRC's combined output of industrial and gem diamonds exceeded that of Botswana; the bulk of its production, however, is smuggled out of the country. The Société Minière de Bakwanga (MIBA), which holds the DRC diamond monopoly, cancelled its marketing agreement with De Beers in mid-1997. During 1998 MIBA announced that De Beers had been granted provisional rights to carry out an aerial exploration survey over areas adjoining the border with Angola. However, it appeared unlikely that this project would proceed in the short term, having regard to subsequent developments involving De Beers' operations in central Africa (see above). During early 2000 it emerged that senior members of the government of Zimbabwe, which has, since 1998, given significant military support to the DRC in its counter-insurgency operations, had taken substantial shareholdings in Oryx Diamonds Ltd, which was being awarded a 25-year concession in the DRC's main diamond-mining region, in an area guarded by Zimbabwean troops. In late July 2000 the DRC government granted an Israeli trading group the right to become the sole purchaser of all uncut diamonds from the DRC.

In the Central African Republic diamonds are found in alluvial deposits, mainly in the west of the country. There is, however, widespread evasion of export duties, and it has been estimated that during the 1990s upwards of 60% of total diamond production was being smuggled out of the country. In 1998 official sales of diamonds accounted for almost 43% of the republic's total export revenue. Small-scale mining for diamonds is carried out in Côte d'Ivoire, where illicit production is also widespread. The diamond sector in Ghana, which has been in decline since the 1960s, was estimated in 1993 still to contain reserves of alluvial diamond deposits sufficient for 15 years' exploitation. Among the smaller-scale African producers of diamonds are Lesotho and Swaziland. Despite the identification of numerous kimberlite pipes in the south of Zimbabwe, none have yet proved to be economic, and the country's only operating mine was closed in 1998. A geological assessment of kimberlite pipes located in Mauritania was proceeding in 1999, and the first licence to prospect for diamonds in Mozambique was granted in the same year.

In 1996 an Australian-Canadian joint venture, in which DiamondWorks (see above) has a majority interest, announced that it was to develop North America's first commercial diamond mine, at Lac de Gras, close to the Arctic Circle in the Northwest Territories of Canada. Potential output, by conventional open-pit mining, has been forecast at 3m. carats annually. A second North American mine, at Kelsey Lake in the Rocky Mountains of the USA, began operations in late 1995. Output of the mine's principally gem diamonds was expected to reach 150,000 carats annually when full production is reached.

In 1930 the major diamond producers formed The Diamond Corpn to act as the single channel through which most of the world's rough diamond production would be sold. To stabilize the market, the corporation put surplus output into reserve, to be sold at a time when conditions were favourable. The corporation is now one of a group of companies, centred in London, known as the Central Selling Organisation (CSO). Until, in-mid-2000, De Beers announced the abandonment of its monopoly of world diamond supply (see below), the CSO, acting on behalf of producers, handled about 65% of world production. The majority of diamonds produced in Africa, although not those of Ghana and Guinea, are marketed through the CSO, which has about 160 direct clients. The CSO markets the rough diamond production of De Beers Consolidated Mines Ltd. A reorganization of De Beers' interests, undertaken in 1990, placed the CSO, together with the group's diamond stocks and other non-South African based interests, under the control of a new Swiss-domiciled corporation, De Beers Centenary AG.

In 1990 De Beers Centenary entered into an arrangement with Glavalmazzoloto (the diamond monopoly operated by the former USSR), under which 95% of rough gem diamonds destined for export were to be purchased and marketed by the CSO, affording Russia a quota of 26% of all CSO sales on the world market. This agreement, which was to operate until December 1995, was continued by the successor Russian diamond corporation, Rosalmazzoloto, and subsequently by Almazy Rossii-Sakha (Alrosa). In 1992 De Beers negotiated an agreement with the Russian Autonomous Republic of Sakha (Yakutia), which occupies a large part of Siberia and accounts for approximately 98% of Russian diamond output, to market the proportion of its diamond production not procured by the central diamond authority. In January 1993 the functions of this authority were transferred to an independent body, Diamonds of Russia-Sakha. The 1990 agreement, which expired in December 1995, was extended until March 1996, when a new framework was eventually formulated for the sale of Russian diamonds. Under the revised arrangements, which were to operate for a three-year period, Alrosa obtained the right to market approximately 14% of its exports to buyers outside the CSO. The agreement aimed to achieve a substantial reduction in the volume of diamonds circumventing the CSO marketing network, while assisting Russia in its proposed establishment of a domestic diamond-cutting industry.

In August 1996, however, it was reported that further meetings were to take place between Alrosa and the CSO to discuss continuing increases in sales of Russian diamonds to purchasers outside the CSO. Meanwhile, the Argyle mine in Australia (see above), whose sales accounted for about 6% of the CSO's annual intake, announced in June that it was to terminate its marketing agreement with the CSO with effect from 1 July. For the remainder of 1996 the CSO continued to purchase Russian diamonds under the terms of the agreement that had expired in December 1995, while pursuing negotiations with ARS. However, the slow progress in finalizing new arrangements, together with the continuing 'leakage' of Russian diamonds on the open market, prompted De Beers to inform the Russian government that it was to cease purchasing diamonds under the existing arrangements with effect from the end of December 1996. Efforts to formulate new marketing arrangements remained unresolved until October 1997, when a new agreement was signed, under which the CSO was to market Russian diamonds valued at a minimum of US $550m. annually, with provision for further sales up to a maximum of $1,200m. These arrangements were to operate for a one-year period. In November 1998 a new agreement, operating until 31 December 2001, was finalized, awarding the CSO the right to market Russian diamonds with a minimum value of $550m. annually. However, in July 2000, following the announcement by De Beers that it was to cease exercising control over diamond supplies entering the world markets (see below), Alrosa, which supplies about 26% of diamonds sold through the CSO, indicated that it intended to review the terms of the 1998 agreement, with a view to obtaining enhanced financial terms.

Rough diamonds, of which there are currently more than 5,000 categories, are sold by the CSO in mixed packages 10 times each year at regular sales, known as 'sights', in London, Johannesburg and Lucerne, Switzerland. Gems account for about 20% of total sales by weight, but, it is estimated, over 90% by value. After being sold by the CSO, gem diamonds are sent to be cut and polished in preparation for jewellery manufacture. The leading cutting centres are in Antwerp, Bombay, New York and Tel Aviv, which in 1993 opened an exchange for 'raw', or uncut, diamonds, with the intention of lessening the dependence of Israeli cutters on allocations from the CSO and purchases from the small, independent diamond exchange in Antwerp. The principal markets for diamond jewellery are the USA and Japan (which account for about 60% of world consumption).

In July 2000 De Beers announced that it was to relinquish its monopoly control of world diamond sales, and would henceforth concentrate on strategies to stimulate international demand. This decision was widely ascribed to the strains imposed on the CSO by the entry into world markets of increasing quantities of diamonds mined in Australia, North America and Russia. In addition, the substantial stockpiles of diamonds maintained by De Beers required high levels of capital investment, from which no returns accrued to De Beers' shareholders.

The CSO has provided a guaranteed market to producers and, since 1930, had successfully followed a policy of stockpiling diamonds during times of recession in order to stabilize prices (which were never reduced). At the end of 1999 the value of the stockpile stood at US $3,957m., a decrease of $859m. in 12 months. Following De Beers' announcement of the termination

of its diamond sales monopoly, the CSO forecast that the value of the stock pile would fall to $2,500m. during 2001.

Diamond prices (quoted in US dollars) were increased by 15.5% in March 1989, by 5.5% in March 1990 and by 1.5% in February 1993 (mainly in respect of stones of 0.75 carat and above). In July 1995 prices for low-grade rough diamonds were reduced by 10%–15%, while prices for large stones were raised by between 2%–8%. In November prices for stones weighing 2.0 carats and above were raised by 5%, and in July 1996 prices of rough gem diamonds weighing in excess of 1.0 carat were increased by an average 7%. In September 1999 prices for low-grade rough diamonds were raised by 10%–15%. As there are so many varieties of diamond, the CSO price changes represent averages only. There are wide discrepancies in price, depending on such factors as rarity, colour and quality.

The sales turnover of US $3,417m. recorded in 1992 by the CSO represented a six-year 'low'. Sales volume advanced strongly, however, in 1993, to $4,366m., an increase of 27.8%. This recovery was, in part, attributable to reductions in producers' quotas during 1993. Sales turnover declined marginally, to about $4,250m., in 1994, owing in part to an increase of stocks in diamond-cutting centres, and despite Russian sales outside the CSO network. A rise of 6.6% in 1995 sales turnover, to $4,531m., reflected a strong level of demand for quality gem stones, particularly in the USA and Japan, which normally provide the main sources of demand for gem diamonds. Sales turnover in 1996 advanced by almost 7%, to a record $4,834m., despite the termination of marketing arrangements with the Argyle diamond mine and the impact of direct sales by Russia. In 1997, however, unfavourable economic conditions in east and south-east Asia were responsible for a fall of 4% in sales turnover, to $4,640m. CSO sales in 1998, at $3,350m., stood at their lowest level since 1987, reflecting the weakness of demand from Japan and East Asia, which traditionally account for about 40% of world diamond sales. However, sales turnover achieved a strong recovery in 1999, advancing by 57% on the 1998 total to a record $5,240m., reflecting the onset of an economic recovery in Japan and East Asia and the continuation of strong demand in the USA, which in that year overtook Japan as the principal market for gem diamonds, accounting for almost one-half of world diamond jewellery sales. In the first six months of 2000 De Beers' sales turnover rose by 44% on the corresponding period of 1999. Continuing strong demand from the US market was the major factor in this increase.

Synthetic diamonds for industrial use have been produced since the mid-1950s by a number of companies, including De Beers, using a method which simulates the intense heat present in the geological formation of diamonds. These stones, which are always very small, account for about 90% of all industrial diamond use, and have a wide variety of industrial applications. The USA, which is the main user of industrial diamonds, is also the leading producer of synthetic diamonds.

Gold

Gold minerals commonly occur in quartz and are also found in alluvial deposits and in rich thin underground veins. In South Africa gold occurs in sheets of low-grade ore (reefs) which may be at great depths below ground level. Gold is associated with silver, which is its commonest by-product. Uranium oxide is another valuable by-product, particularly in the case of South Africa. Depending upon its associations, gold is separated by cyaniding, or concentrated and smelted.

Gold, silver and platinum are customarily measured in troy weight. A troy pound (now obsolete) contains 12 ounces, each of 480 grains. One troy oz is equal to 31.1 grams (1 kg = 32.15 troy oz), compared with the avoirdupois oz of 28.3 grams.

In modern times the principal function of gold has been as bullion in reserve for bank notes issued. Since the early 1970s, however, the USA has actively sought to 'demonetize' gold and so make it simply another commodity. This objective was later adopted by the IMF, which has attempted to end the position that gold occupied for many years in the international monetary system (see below).

Gold was discovered near Johannesburg, South Africa, in 1884, and its exploitation formed the basis of the country's subsequent economic prosperity. For many years, South Africa has been the world's leading gold producer, accounting in 1999 for 21% of world gold output outside the former Eastern bloc and for almost 71% of that mined in Africa. Since the mid-1980s, however, the South African gold industry has been adversely affected by the rising costs of extracting generally declining grades of ore from ageing and increasingly marginal (low-return) mines. Additionally, the level of world gold prices has not been sufficiently high to stimulate the active exploration and development of new mines. The share of gold in South Africa's export revenue has accordingly declined in recent years, and in 1989, for the first time, the commercial profitability of South African gold production was exceeded by profits from mining activities other than gold. In 1996 South Africa's gold production fell to less than 500 tons for the first time since 1956. Output continued to fall in 1997 and 1998, although the gold-mining industry substantially reduced its costs. Production declined further in 1999, to its lowest level for 45 years.

Although South Africa remains the world's principal gold producer, the relative decline of its position in world gold markets has been accompanied by the prospect of substantial increases in output as new capacity comes into production in Australia, Brazil, Canada, Indonesia, Papua New Guinea and the USA. Following the dissolution of the USSR in 1991, the successor republics, notably Russia (which accounted for about two-thirds of Soviet output) and Uzbekistan (which contains what is reputedly the world's largest open-cast gold-mine), have assumed an increasingly significant role in international gold trading, particularly following the abolition in 1997 of Russia's state monopoly on gold purchases. However, the rate of advance of the gold-mining sector has been inhibited by a number of adverse short-term factors (which have included unpaid debts, shortages of mining equipment, transport difficulties and sharp rises in the cost of electric power). During the late 1990s, however, there was an increase in foreign financial participation in the development of gold deposits in Russia, as well as in Uzbekistan, Kazakhstan, Kyrgyzstan and Armenia. The People's Republic of China, with about 1,200 operating gold-mines in 1999, has been increasing its output of gold, although a 2% decline in production in that year was believed to represent the first set-back in the country's annual output for about 20 years.

Ghana, formerly a significant African producer of gold, has, since 1990, been reversing a long period of decline. Output doubled during 1990–92, and increased in 1993 and 1994 as a result of the continuing rehabilitation of the country's gold industry. Following a minor set-back in 1996, the country's gold output advanced each year during 1997–99. The dominant producer in Ghana is Ashanti Goldfields, which operates one of the world's largest gold-mines (with more than 20m. oz of proven reserves). The company was reopened to private-sector investment in 1994. Its output provided about 60% of the country's total gold production in 1997. Exports of gold accounted for more than 37% of Ghana's foreign revenue in 1998. Ashanti Goldfields has developed a major new mine at Bibani, which commenced production in 1997. Together with Bibani, whose output was almost doubled during its second year of operation, other gold-mining enterprises in the country, notably the Tarkwa mine operated by Goldfields Ghana, were generating further expansion in this sector in the late 1990s.

Gold was overtaken in 1980 by tobacco as Zimbabwe's major source of foreign exchange. Gold production in Mali increased substantially during 1997–99, reflecting the exploitation of deposits at Sadiola Hill, with a projected capacity of 11 tons per year. Output was forecast to increase in 2000, following the commissioning of two new mines during 1999. In 1999 gold was Mali's second most important source of export revenue, after cotton. Output in Guinea was almost doubled in 1998 with the coming on stream of its Siguiri mine, operated by Ashanti Goldfields. The Siguiri mine accounted for more than one-half of Guinea's total output of gold in 1999. Tanzania's first large-scale gold-mine began operating in November 1998. Production began in June 2000 at another Tanzanian mine, the Geita project, which is the largest producer of gold in East Africa. Although other projects were under development in the late 1990s, the sharp decline in world gold prices has led to a fall in the level of exploration activity both in Tanzania and elsewhere in Africa, which is estimated to possess about 45% of the world's recoverable gold reserves.

Production of Gold Ore (metric tons, gold content)

	1998	1999
World total*	2,540.6	2,576.2
Africa*	633.8	634.2
Leading African producers		
Ghana	73.3	78.2
Guinea	11.7	13.3
Mali	22.8	25.4
South Africa	464.4	449.5
Tanzania	5.5	9.2
Zimbabwe	27.2	29.7
Leading non-African producers		
Australia	310.1	302.8
Brazil	54.7	54.1
Canada	164.3	157.9
China, People's Repub.	160.2	156.3
Indonesia	139.1	154.5
Papua New Guinea	63.2	65.0
Peru	91.2	127.4
Russia	127.3	138.2
USA	366.0	341.9
Uzbekistan	80.4	85.8

* Estimated production.

Source: Gold Fields Mineral Services Ltd.

The supply of gold to Western countries, after allowing for central bank transactions and not including scrap, totalled 2,772 tons in 1995, including Eastern bloc sales of 102 tons and net official sales of 232 tons. In 1996, in which year sales by the former Eastern bloc ceased to be separately quantified, the world supply of gold totalled 2,879 tons. Net official sales rose to 275 tons. The world supply of gold advanced to 3,602 tons in 1997, with net official sales rising to 376 tons. In 1998, despite a rise in gold output, world supply, other than scrap, declined to 3,008 tons (including net official sales of 370 tons). However, supply from old gold scrap (mostly jewellery) reached 1,098 tons, an increase of almost 75% on the 1997 total. In 1999 the world supply of gold totalled 3,479 tons, an increase of 471 tons on the previous year. Supply from old gold scrap fell by 485 tons to 613 tons. East Asian supply from scrap declined from 633 tons in 1998 to 125 tons in 1999. The main sources of scrap in 1999 were India (82 tons) and Saudi Arabia and Yemen (67 tons).

Total world demand for gold, including the former Eastern bloc countries, which totalled 4,231 tons in 1997, declined to 4,106 tons in 1998 and to 4,092 tons in 1999. Requirements for jewellery fabrication, which accounted for 3,345 tons (79.1%) in 1997, rose to 3,151 tons (76.7%) in 1998, but declined to 3,128 tons (76.4%) in 1999. The remainder of industrial demand was absorbed mainly by medals, dentistry and the electronics industry. Of total gold fabrication in 1999 (3,722 tons), the principal consuming countries were India (18.4%), Italy (14.0%), the USA (8.7%), China (4.9%) and Japan (4.3%).

The fabrication of official coins is another important use of gold bullion, although the demand for these coins has declined since the mid-1980s. South African 'krugerrand' coins, containing exactly 1 troy oz of pure (24-carat) gold, were first issued in 1970 and held about 70% of the world market for gold bullion coins until 1985, when international sales virtually ceased, owing to the prohibition of krugerrand imports (during 1986–90) by Japan, the European Community and the USA. A number of other countries, notably Australia, Canada, Austria, Japan and the USA, entered the gold coin market and subsequently benefited from the krugerrand embargo. However, the popularity of these bullion coins in general has been declining in recent years. Following exceptional interest in 1995 in an Austrian gold coin issue, together with the minting of a US Olympic commemorative coin, underpinning a demand increase of 21.6%, the official coin sector in 1996 relapsed to its lowest level of fabrication since 1973. Production of the 'eagle' bullion coin by the US government led to a substantial revival in 1997, when coin fabrication demand rose internationally by almost 30%. The maintenance of investment interest in official coins in 1998 raised demand by 29.1%. However, demand for US and Canadian issues of coins commemorating the forthcoming millennium failed to make a significant impact on this sector in 1999, when fabrication demand advanced by only 7.0%.

As a portable real asset which is easily convertible into cash, gold is widely esteemed as a store of value. Another distinguishing feature of gold is that new production in any one year is very small in relation to existing stocks. Much of the world's gold is in private bullion stocks, held for investment purposes, or is hoarded as a 'hedge' against inflation. Private investment stocks of gold throughout the world are estimated at 15,000–20,000 tons, much of it held in East Asia and India.

During the 19th century gold was increasingly adopted as a monetary standard, with prices set by governments. In 1919 the Bank of England allowed some South African gold to be traded in London 'at the best price obtainable'. The market was suspended in 1925–31, when sterling returned to a limited form of the gold standard, and again between 1939–54. In 1934 the official price of gold was fixed at US \$35 per troy oz, and, by international agreement, all transactions in gold had to take place within narrow margins around that price. In 1960 the official gold price came under pressure from market demand. As a result, an international gold 'pool' was established in 1961 at the initiative of the USA. This 'pool' was originally a consortium of leading central banks with the object of re-straining the London price of gold in case of excessive demand. It later widened into an arrangement by which eight central banks agreed that all purchases and sales of gold should be handled by the Bank of England. However, growing private demand for gold continued to exert pressure on the official price and the gold 'pool' was ended in 1968, in favour of a two-tier price system. Central banks continued to operate the official price of \$35 per troy ounce, but private markets were permitted to deal freely in gold. However, the free market price did not rise significantly above the official price.

In August 1971 the US government announced that it would cease dealing freely in gold to maintain exchange rates for the dollar within previously agreed margins. This 'floating' of the dollar against other major currencies continued until December, when it was agreed to raise the official gold price to \$38 per oz. Gold prices on the free market rose to \$70 per oz in August 1972. In February 1973 the US dollar was devalued by a further 10%, the official gold price rising to \$42.22 per oz. Thereafter the free-market price rose even higher, reaching \$127 per oz in June 1973. In November it was announced that the two-tier system would be terminated, and from 1974 governments were permitted to value their official gold stocks at market prices.

In 1969 the IMF introduced a new unit for international monetary dealings, the special drawing right (SDR), with a value of US \$1.00, and the first allocation of SDRs was made on 1 January 1971. The SDR was linked to gold at an exchange rate of SDR 35 per troy oz. When the US dollar was devalued in December 1971 the SDR retained its gold value and a new parity with the US dollar was established. A further adjustment was made following the second dollar devaluation, in February 1973, and in July 1974 the direct link between the SDR and the US dollar was ended and the SDR was valued in terms of a weighted 'basket' of national currencies. At the same time the official gold price of SDR 35 per troy oz was retained as the IMF's basis for valuing official reserves.

In 1976 the membership of the IMF agreed on proposals for far-reaching changes in the international monetary system. These reforms, which were implemented on a gradual basis during 1977–81, included a reduction in the role of gold in the international system and the abolition of the official price of gold. (For detailed information on these arrangements, see *Africa South of the Sahara 1991*). A principal objective of the IMF plan was achieved in April 1978, when central banks were able to buy and sell gold at market prices. The physical quantity of reserve gold held by the IMF and member countries' central banks as national reserves has subsequently fallen (see below). The USA still maintains the largest national stock of gold, although the volume of its reserves has been substantially reduced in recent years. At the end of 1949 US gold reserves were 701.8m. oz, but since the beginning of the 1980s the level has been in the range of 261.4m.–264.6m. oz. At the end of 1999 the total gold reserves held by members of the IMF, excluding international financial organizations and countries not reporting, amounted to 940.5m. oz, of which the USA had 261.7m. oz (27.8%).

In June 1996 the 'Group of Seven' major industrial countries considered proposals by the United Kingdom and the USA whereby the IMF would release for sale between US \$5,000m.–\$6,000m. of its \$40,000m. gold reserves to finance debt relief for the world's poorest countries, principally in Africa. The plan, which was opposed by Germany, on the grounds that it could prompt demands for similar gold sales by its central bank, remained the subject of discussion within the IMF during 1997. During 1996 substantial amounts of gold bullion, jointly exceeding 500 metric tons, were sold by the central banks of Belgium and the Netherlands, and the Swiss National Bank announced its intention to allocate part of its gold reserves to fund a new humanitarian foundation. In July 1997 the Reserve Bank of Australia announced that it had disposed of more than two-thirds of its bullion holdings (reducing its reserves from 247 tons to 80 tons) over the previous six months. In October a Swiss government advisory group recommended the sale of more than one-half of that country's gold reserves, and in December the government of Argentina disclosed that it had sold the bulk of its gold reserves during a seven-month period earlier in the year. During 1997 loans to the market of official stocks of gold were carried out by the central banks of Germany, the Netherlands and Switzerland, and in March 1998 the central bank of Belgium disposed of one-half of its gold reserves. In December the government of Switzerland proposed constitu-tional changes, implemented in April 1999, removing the requirement for gold to support the national currency. In May the United Kingdom government announced that it intended to reduce its gold reserves by 415 tons (from 715 to 300 tons) over several years, including the offering for sale of 125 tons in the year to March 2000. The initial disposal, of 25 tons, followed in July 1999. In the previous month the 'Group of Seven' had endorsed a proposal whereby the IMF would sell about 10% of its holdings of gold to provide debt relief for 36 of the world's poorest countries. Under the plan, the proceeds of the IMF disposals would be invested and the resulting revenue used to amortize IMF loans to the designated countries. These disposals by the IMF and central banks were widely expected to depress further the level of world gold prices (see below) and caused serious concern in gold-producing countries. Nevertheless, the second auction of British gold reserves, again offering 25 tons, took place in September. Later that month the European Central Bank, in a joint statement with the central banks of Switzerland and 13 members of the European Union (Sweden, the United Kingdom and the 11 in the Eurosystem), unexpectedly announced a five-year moratorium on new sales of gold held in official reserves. However, the agreement (announced in Washington, USA, at a meeting of the IMF) allowed impending sales that had already been decided, including those of Switzer-land and the United Kingdom, to proceed, although total sales over the five-year period were not to exceed 2,000 tons. The announcement also stated that gold would remain an important element of global monetary reserves. The European agreement was generally welcomed for removing uncertainty from the gold market, although the permitted rate of sales (400 tons per year) is more than 100% greater than the average net sales by the signatory countries in 1989–98. There were also concerns that the agreement could encourage a higher level of gold sales by other countries. At the end of September 1999 the IMF confirmed that it was considering an exceptional operation involving 'off-market' sales of as much as 14m. oz (435 tons) of the organiza-tion's gold reserves to members having repayment obligations, with the purchased gold to be used to make repayments, thus returning the gold (now revalued at market prices) to the IMF. Two such sales, involving a total of about 7.7m. oz of gold, were held in December. Most of the proceeds were to be used to finance debt relief in developing countries. Meanwhile, the third British gold auction, with a further 25 tons offered, was held in November. In accordance with the European banks' September agreement, the Netherlands' central bank announced in December that it intended to sell 300 tons of gold from its reserves (about one-third of the total) over the next five years.

The fourth British gold sale took place in January 2000. Despite continuing protests from the gold industry, further disposals followed in March, May and July. As before, 25 tons were sold on each occasion. Similar auctions were planned for September and November, as part of a British programme to sell a total of 150 tons of gold in the year to March 2001. Meanwhile, in early April 2000 the Austrian National Bank revealed that it had sold 30 tons of gold from its reserves and that it planned to sell a further 60 tons (within the framework of the European agreement) by 2004. In early May 2000 Switzerland's central bank announced that it had begun to sell gold from its reserves and intended to dispose of 120 tons by the end of September, as part of a programme to reduce its gold holdings by 1,300 tons (about one-half of the total) over at least five years.

The unit of dealing in international gold markets is the 'good delivery' gold bar, weighing about 400 oz (12.5 kg). The principal centres for gold trading are London, Hong Kong and Zürich, Switzerland. The dominant markets for gold 'futures' (buying and selling for future delivery) are the New York Commodity Exchange (COMEX) and the Tokyo Commodity Exchange (TOCOM).

Gold Prices on the London Bullion Market
(afternoon 'fixes', US $ per troy oz)

	Average	Highest	Lowest
1990	383.6		
1995	384.1		
1997	331.3	366.6 (2 Jan.)	283.0 (12 Dec.)
1998	294.1	313.2 (24 April)	273.4 (28 Aug.)
1999	278.6	325.5 (5 Oct.)	252.8 (20 July)

A small group of dealers meet twice on each working day (morning and afternoon) to 'fix' the price of gold in the London Bullion Market, and the table above is based on the second of these daily 'fixes'. During any trading day, however, prices may fluctuate above or below these levels. In each of the five years 1988–92 the London price of gold bullion was lower at the year's end than at the beginning. In March 1993 the price fell to $326.1 (equivalent to £227.6 sterling) per oz, but from April there was a strong recovery in the bullion market, owing partly to speculative activity, and in late July and early August the London price exceeded $400 per oz. The gold price declined to $344 (£222) per oz in September, but ended the year at $390.75 (£264.1). The advance continued in January 1994, with the London price of gold reaching $396.5 (£266.8) per oz. The gold price fell in April to less than $370 per oz, although in June the metal was traded at more than $390 again. In early September the price per oz stood at $391.5 (then £253), and later in the month it moved higher in dollar terms, to $396 (£251). The quotation per oz fell in early November to $383.7, which, owing to the relative strength of the British currency, was equivalent to only £234. In terms of US currency, the price retreated further, standing at $376 (then £240.5) per oz in December.

In January 1995 the London gold price declined to US $373.0 (£240) per oz, but in April it advanced to $396.7 (£245). In dollar terms, the price remained within this range for the remainder of 1995, ending the year at $387 (£249) per oz. For 1995 as a whole, the margin between the highest and lowest bullion price was only about 6% of the annual average: the lowest level of price volatility in the gold market since 1968.

In January 1996, however, the gold market experienced a surge in prices, with the London quotation exceeding US $400 per oz. In February the price reached $416 (£274) per oz, its highest level, in terms of US currency, since February 1990. However, the rally was not sustained, and in early July 1996 the London gold price stood at $381 (£244) per oz. After a slight recovery, another decline in the price of bullion began in late September. The London quotation in early December was reduced to $367 (£222) per oz.

On the morning of the first day's trading in January 1997 gold was 'fixed' in London at US $367.8 (£215.7) per oz. This was only marginally above the lowest gold price recorded during 1996, but it proved to be the highest price in 1997. Later in January the London price of gold was below $350 per oz for the first time since September 1993. The price fell to $339 (£206) per ounce in February 1997, recovered to $363 (£224) in March and remained within this range until June. In early July the market was further weakened by the Australian central bank's disclosure of gold sales from its reserves (see above). A few days later the London bullion price declined to $316 (£187) per oz,

its lowest level for 12 years. A modest recovery in the gold market ensued, but later in the year, with severe economic problems affecting countries in eastern Asia, the metal's price declined further. In November, following the announcement of gold loans by European central banks (see above), the London price of gold was below $300 per oz for the first time since March 1985. The downward movement continued, and in December 1997 the gold price fell to $283 (£171) per oz, an 18-year 'low'. The price at the end of 1997 was 20.8% below its level of 12 months earlier. Compared with the previous year, the average London price in 1997 represented a decline of 14.6%: the sharpest fall since 1984. The slump in the gold price was attributed mainly to the increase in supply from sources other than mine production and old gold scrap. In 1997 the supply from these components reached 1,179 tons, more than double the 1996 total. The main agents in the mobilization of these additional gold stocks were central banks, both through net official sales and through deposits placed with commercial banks. This increase in liquidity neutralized the effects of growth in demand for gold in 1997. The use of gold (including scrap) in jewellery rose by 17.3% from the record 1996 level, mainly as a result of increased demand from India and Middle Eastern countries.

The gold market remained depressed in January 1998, with the London price of bullion falling to US $279 (£172) per oz. Despite further announcements of official sales, the gold price recovered in April to $313 (£187) per oz, but was reduced in August to $273 (£165), its lowest level for more than 19 years. The London price was above $300 per oz again in early October, following a weakening in the US currency, but declined to $286 in December. For 1998 as a whole, the average price of gold was $294 per oz, compared with $331 in 1997. The output from the world's gold-mines reached a record total in 1998, but, as in 1997, the main influence on market sentiment was the supply of above-ground stocks, including disposals by central banks and large flows of gold scrap from Asia in the first half of the year.

During the early months of 1999 the London price of gold remained generally within the range of US $280–$295 per oz, but from May, when the proposal for official British gold sales was announced (see above), the market moved steadily downward. The first of a planned series of gold auctions by the Bank of England took place in early July, when 804,000 oz (25 metric tons) were sold at $261.2 (£166.3) per oz. Two weeks later, the London price of gold slumped to $252.8 (£161.1) per oz: its lowest level, in terms of US currency, since May 1979. By the end of July 1999, as the dollar weakened, the sterling equivalent of the US currency price had fallen to only £157.8 per oz. The gold market remained depressed in August, when the London price was again below $253 per oz. In September the sterling equivalent of the dollar price was reduced to £157.0 per oz. Later that month the second Bank of England auction took place, with 804,000 oz (25 tons) of gold sold for $255.75 per oz. However, by the end of September, following the announcement by European central banks that they would limit sales of gold (see above), the metal's price had risen to more than $300 per oz, and in early October the London quotation reached $330 (almost £200): its highest level for about two years. However, the surge in prices was short-lived. In late November the third sale of official British gold reserves realized $293.5 per oz for the 25 tons on offer. In early December, following the Dutch central bank's announcement of plans as to sell gold (see above), the London price of the metal eased to $276.1 (£170.5) per oz. The gold price ended a year of extreme fluctuations at $290.8 (£180.4) per oz: 1.1% higher than its level at the end of 1998. For 1999 as a whole, however, the average London gold price was only $278.6 per oz: 5.3% below the 1998 average and the lowest annual level, in nominal terms, since 1978. In real terms (i.e. taking inflation into account), the average price of gold in 1999, measured in US dollars, was the lowest since 1972. Despite the closure of several loss-making mines, global production of gold increased in 1999, although more slowly than in 1998. However, as in other recent years, a major influence on the bullion market in 1999 was the activity of central banks, both through actual sales and lending of gold and through reports of planned disposals.

Gold prices remained relatively stable during the opening weeks of 2000, and in late January the Bank of England sold another 25-ton offering at US $289.5 per oz. However, in early February, following the announcement by a leading Canadian gold-mining group that it was suspending 'hedging' operations (forward selling of borrowed gold to protect against falling prices), the London price reached $316.6 (£198.2) per oz. The Bank of England's fifth auction of 25 tons of gold, held in March, realized $285.25 per oz. later that month the London price of the metal declined to $275.9 (£173.1) per oz. At the next sale of British gold reserves, in May, the 25 tons on offer were sold for $275.25 per oz. Later that month the London price of gold stood at $270.5 (£183.3) per oz. In July the Bank of England auctioned a further 25 tons of gold, which sold for $279.75 per oz.

The World Gold Council (WGC), founded in 1987, is an international association of gold-producing companies which aims to promote gold as a financial asset and to increase demand for the metal. The WGC, based in London, had 29 members in 2000.

Groundnut (Peanut, Monkey Nut, Earth Nut) (*Arachis hypogaea*)

This is not a true nut, although the underground pod, which contains the kernels, forms a more or less dry shell at maturity. The plant is a low-growing annual herb introduced from South America, and resembles the indigenous African Bambarra groundnut, which it now outnumbers.

Each groundnut pod contains between two and four kernels, enclosed in a reddish skin. The kernels are highly nutritious because of their high content both of protein (about 30%) and oil (40%–50%). In tropical countries the crop is grown partly for domestic consumption and partly for export. Whole nuts of selected large dessert types, with the skin removed, are eaten raw or roasted. Peanut butter is made by removing the skin and germ and grinding the roasted nuts. The most important commercial use of groundnuts is the extraction of oil. Groundnut oil is used as a cooking and salad oil, as an ingredient in margarine, and, in the case of lower-quality oil, in soap manufacture. The oil is faced with strong competition from soybean, cottonseed and sunflower oils—all produced in the USA. In the early 1990s groundnut oil was the fifth most important of soft edible oils in terms of production. During the late 1980s its position in terms of exports was ninth, accounting for only 1.5% of total world exports of food oils.

Production of Groundnuts (in shell; '000 metric tons)

	1997	1998
World total	29,457*	32,282*
Africa	7,333*	7,161*
Leading African producers		
Burkina Faso	152	215
Chad	352	471
Congo, Dem. Repub.	400	412
Côte d'Ivoire	143	136
Egypt	125†	126*
Ghana	135*	135*
Guinea	158	174
Malawi	69	108
Mali	134	144
Mozambique	126	143
Niger	114†	115*
Nigeria	2,531	2,534
Senegal	506	506*
South Africa	158	108
Sudan	1,104	800
Uganda	134	140
Zimbabwe	153†	60
Leading non-African producers		
Argentina	401	896
China, People's Repub.	9,648	11,886
India	7,457	7,450†
Indonesia	983†	988†
Myanmar	559	540
USA	1,605	1,798
Viet Nam	351	386

* FAO estimate.   † Unofficial figure.

An oilcake, used in animal feeding, is manufactured from the groundnut residue left after oil extraction. However, trade in this groundnut meal is limited by health laws in some countries,

as groundnuts can be contaminated by a mould which generates toxic and carcinogenic metabolites, the most common and most dangerous of which is aflatoxin B1. The European Community (EC, now the European Union—EU) has banned imports of oilcake and meal for use as animal feed which contain more than 0.03 mg of aflatoxin per kg. The meal can be treated with ammonia, which both eliminates the aflatoxin and enriches the cake. Groundnut shells, which are usually incinerated or simply discarded as waste, can be for converted into a low-cost organic fertilizer, which has been produced since the early 1970s.

About 80% of the world's groundnut output comes from developing countries. Groundnuts are the most important of Africa's oil seeds and form the chief export crop of Senegal and The Gambia. In 1997/98 The Gambia supplied about 1.6% of world export trade, totalling 1.2m. tons in that crop year. Except when affected by drought, Sudan and South Africa are also important suppliers, and in 1997/98 South Africa accounted for 3.3% of the world groundnut exports. Niger and Mali, formerly significant exporters, have ceased to feature in the international groundnut trade, largely as a consequence of the Sahel drought. However, measures to revive the groundnut sector in Mali, and to establish commercial production in Uganda, were proceeding in the late 1990s. Groundnut harvests in southern Africa, notably in Mozambique, South Africa and Zimbabwe, were also affected by drought during the second half of the 1980s. However, Zimbabwe subsequently planned a substantial expansion of groundnut cultivation.

African groundnut exports have been declining since the late 1970s, and most African countries grow the nut as a subsistence, particularly storage, crop. Senegal's groundnut production suffered from persistent drought, and also from marketing problems, in the early 1980s; however, subsequent output was substantially aided by government incentives to producers. These measures included the establishment of a groundnut price guarantee fund, which also had the unwelcome effect of attracting smuggled groundnut supplies from the neighbouring state of The Gambia. Since 1995, however, the minimum price guaranteed by the Senegal government has remained below prices obtainable on the 'black market', to which substantial quantities of Senegalese groundnut output have been diverted.

In recent years, as the tables below make clear, prices for groundnut oil have generally been more volatile than those for groundnuts. The average import price of groundnut oil at the port of Rotterdam, in the Netherlands, increased from US $897.3 per metric ton in 1996 to $1,010.4 per ton in 1997, but fell to $908.6 in 1998 and to $786.7 in 1999. On a monthly basis, the average price of groundnut oil per ton was reduced from $862.5 in November 1998 to $745.5 in June 1999. It recovered to $807 per ton in November, but declined to $717 in June 2000. Meanwhile, the average European import price for groundnuts was $962.0 per ton in 1996, $988.4 in 1997 and $988.8 in 1998, before falling to $834.7 in 1999. The monthly average slumped from $1,087.5 per ton in August 1998 to $817.5 in April 1999. It rose to $866 per ton in June, but stood at only $800 in August and September. The average price was $856 per ton in October and November, but fell to $786 in June 2000.

Export Price Index for Groundnuts (base: 1980 = 100)

	Average	Highest month(s)	Lowest month(s)
1990	102		
1995	92		
1997	77	82 (Nov.)	70 (Sept.)
1998	67	73 (Aug.)	58 (Dec.)
1999	57	59 (Oct.-Dec.)	55 (Feb.-April, Aug., Sept.)

Export Price Index for Groundnut Oil (base: 1980 = 100)

	Average	Highest month(s)	Lowest month(s)
1990	113		
1995	116		
1997	119	129 (July)	103 (Jan.)
1998	107	124 (Jan.)	100 (Sept., Oct.)
1999	93	98 (Jan.)	88 (May, June)

The African Groundnut Council, founded in 1964 with headquarters in Lagos, advises its member producing countries (The

Gambia, Mali, Niger, Nigeria, Senegal and Sudan) on marketing policies and, for this purpose, has a sales promotion office in Geneva, Switzerland. Western Europe, particularly France, is the principal market for African groundnuts. The market for edible groundnuts is particularly sensitive to the level of production in the USA, which provides about one-half of world import requirements.

Iron Ore

The main economic iron-ore minerals are magnetite and haematite, which are used almost exclusively to produce pig-iron and direct-reduced iron (DRI). These comprise the principal raw materials for the production of crude steel. Most iron ore is processed after mining to improve its chemical and physical characteristics and is often agglomerated by pelletizing or sintering. The transformation of the ore into pig-iron is achieved through reduction by coke in blast furnaces; the proportion of ore to pig-iron yielded is usually about 1.5 or 1.6:1. Pig-iron is used to make cast iron and wrought iron products, but most of it is converted into steel by removing most of the carbon content. In the mid-1990s processing technology was being developed in the use of high-grade ore to produce DRI, which, unlike the iron used for traditional blast furnace operations, requires no melting or refining. Particular grades of steel (e.g. stainless) are made by the addition of ferro-alloys such as chromium, nickel and manganese.

Iron is, after aluminium, the second most abundant metallic element in the earth's crust, and its ore volume production is far greater than that of any other metal. Some ores contain 70% iron, while a grade of only 25% is commercially exploitable in certain areas. As the basic feedstock for the production of steel, iron ore is a major raw material in the world economy and in international trade. Because mining the ore usually involves substantial long-term investment, about 60% of trade is conducted under long-term contracts, and the mine investments are financed with some financial participation from consumers.

Iron ore is widely distributed throughout Africa, with several countries having substantial reserves of high-grade deposits (60%–68% iron). One of the world's largest unexploited iron ore deposits (an estimated 850m. metric tons, with a metal content of 64.5%) has been located in north-east Gabon, and there are future prospects for the exploitation of ore reserves in Côte d'Ivoire and Senegal. Identified reserves in Guinea include some 350m. tons of iron ore (66.7% iron) at Mt Nimba, near the border with Liberia. The two governments have developed a joint scheme to exploit the deposits for transhipment through Liberia. Ore shipments by rail through Liberia were intended to commence in 1990, but this intention was thwarted by the civil conflict which has caused widespread dislocation of the Liberian economy. The project, which was still pending in 1998, envisaged an annual mine output of 12m. tons. The exploitation by German mining interests of iron ore reserves at Bong, which are believed to contain sufficient ore for 15 years' output at an annual production rate of 7m. tons, has also been interrupted by

internal unrest. Liberia's largest iron ore producer, the Liberian-American-Swedish Minerals Co (LAMCO), which is jointly-controlled by government and private interests, expects to be able to sustain mine production at Yekepa, in Buchanan County, until 2006. LAMCO's mining activities have been severely disrupted by civil disorder. Following the restoration of political stability in 1997, it was hoped that Liberian iron ore exports could be resumed by mid-1999.

The continent's leading producer of iron ore is South Africa. The industry is dominated by the Iron and Steel Corpn of South Africa (ISCOR), which operates 10 ore mines and four steel mills. Formerly state-owned, ISCOR was transferred to private-sector control in 1989. South African iron ore exports, particularly to Japan, have been an important source of foreign revenue since the late 1980s, despite declining world demand for steel.

Among the African producers, the country most dependent on the mineral as a source of foreign exchange is Mauritania, which has large deposits of high-grade ore (65%) in the Kédia region, near Zouérate. The Guelbs region, about 40 km to the north of Kédia, contains reserves of workable ores, estimated at 5,000m.–6,000m. tons. Although the metal content of Guelbs' ore, at 37%, is lower than at Kédia, enrichment processes are expected to produce an iron content of 67%, making it the richest in Mauritania. An enrichment plant, opened in 1984, was projected to produce 15m. tons annually by the mid-1990s. The second phase, involving a new mine at Oum Arwagen and another ore-enrichment plant, was scheduled to begin in the mid-1990s, with initial output forecast at 6m. tons per year. Preparations have also been proceeding for the exploitation of deposits at M'Haoudat, which are estimated to contain recoverable reserves of 100m. tons, and which, at a proposed production rate of 5.6m. tons annually, were expected to prove more economic, albeit more short-lived, than the Guelbs deposits. In 1996 iron ore exports accounted contributed almost 42% of Mauritania's external revenue, and accounted for more than 10% of its gross domestic product in 1998.

The exploitation of iron ore deposits in Nigeria, unofficially estimated in 1999 to exced 3,000m. tons, commenced in 1986. In 1980 deposits estimated at 20m. tons of ore (50% iron) were identified in the west of Zambia. During the late 1990s proposals were receiving consideration for the joint development by Tanzania and Malawi of ore reserves at Liganga, in Tanzania, as part of a proposed coal and steel complex. At Falémé in eastern Senegal there exist unexploited deposits of 330m. tons of high-grade ore (60% iron) and an estimated 115m. tons of lower-grade ore.

Iron ore mining in Angola has been beset by civil conflict, and ceased entirely in 1975–84. At present, output is stockpiled and the resumption of export trade in the ore depends on the eventual rehabilitation of the 520-km rail link between the mines at Cassinga and the coast. The Marampa mine in Sierra Leone has been inactive since the mid-1980s, although plans exist for the eventual resumption of operations to extract its ore deposits, which have an iron content of 69%.

Since the early 1970s world trade in iron ore has regularly exceeded 200m. metric tons (iron content) per year. In the mid-1990s the dominant exporting countries were Australia and Brazil, jointly accounting for more than 60% of iron exports world-wide. Canada, India and Ukraine are also important exporters of iron ore. The principal importers in the mid-1990s were Japan, Germany and the People's Republic of China. World iron ore reference prices are decided annually at a series of meetings between producers and purchasers (the steel industry accounts for about 95% of all iron ore consumption). The USA and the republics of the former USSR, although major steel-producing countries, rely on domestic ore production and take little part in the price negotiations. It is generally accepted that, because of its diversity in form and quality, iron ore is ill-suited to price stabilization through an international buffer stock arrangement.

The index of export prices for iron ore declined to 119 in April 2000. The two leading exporters of the mineral in 1990–97 were Brazil and Australia. Exports of iron ore and concentrates (excluding agglomerates) by these two countries were valued at about US $19.5 per metric ton in 1992, but the average price declined to $17.0 per ton in 1993 and to $15.5 per ton in 1994.

Production of Iron Ore (iron content, '000 metric tons)

	1997	1998*
World total	572,163*	560,991
Africa	30,900*	30,527
Leading African producers		
Algeria	1,100*	1,000
Egypt	1,800*	1,800
Mauritania	7,000*	7,000
South Africa	20,600*	20,400
Leading non-African producers		
Australia	97,901	96,250
Brazil	122,184	128,905
Canada†	23,857	24,880
China, People's Repub. . . .	80,400*	63,000
India	44,400	48,000
Russia	38,900*	39,700
Ukraine	29,200*	27,900
USA	40,022	39,724

* Estimated production.

† Including the metal content of by-product ore.

Source: US Geological Survey.

Export Price Index for Iron Ore (base: 1980 = 100)

	Average	Highest month(s)	Lowest month(s)
1990	124		
1995	140		
1997	141	152 (Jan.)	133 (Aug.)
1998	138	147 (Oct.)	134 (Jan.–March)
1999	133	144 (Jan.)	126 (Dec.)

The average per ton was $16.1 in 1995, $17.0 in 1996 and $17.2 in 1997.

The Association of Iron Ore Exporting Countries (known by its French initials as APEF) was established in 1975 to promote close co-operation among members, to safeguard their interests as iron ore exporters, to ensure the orderly growth of international trade in iron ore and to secure 'fair and remunerative' returns from its exploitation, processing and marketing. In 1995 the APEF, which also collects and disseminates information on iron ore from its secretariat in Geneva, Switzerland, had nine members, including Algeria, Liberia, Mauritania and Sierra Leone. The UN Conference on Trade and Development (UNCTAD) compiles statistics on iron ore production and trade, and in recent years has sought to establish a permanent international forum for discussion of the industry's problems.

Maize (Indian Corn, Mealies) (*Zea mays*)

Maize is one of the world's three principal cereal crops, with wheat and rice. Originally from America, maize has been dispersed to many parts of the world. The principal varieties are dent maize (which has large, soft, flat grains) and flint maize (which has round, hard grains). Dent maize is the predominant type world-wide but flint maize is widely grown in southern Africa. Maize may be white or yellow (there is little nutritional difference), but the former is preferred for human consumption in Africa. Maize is an annual crop, planted from seed, and matures within three to five months. It requires a warm climate and ample water supplies during the growing season. Genetically modified varieties of maize, with improved resistance to pests, are now being cultivated, particularly in the USA and Argentina.

Production of Maize ('000 metric tons)

	1998	1999*
World total	602,915	593,600
Africa	37,690	39,820
Leading African producers		
Benin	500	530
Cameroon	600	700
Congo, Dem. Repub.	1,000	1,050
Côte d'Ivoire	550	600
Egypt	6,300	6,100
Ethiopia	2,300	3,000
Ghana	850	920
Kenya	2,200	2,100
Malawi	1,650	1,750
Mozambique	950	980
Nigeria	4,950	5,000
South Africa	7,400	8,300
Tanzania	1,900	2,500
Uganda	920	800
Zambia	1,320	1,150
Zimbabwe	1,470	1,500
Leading non-African producers		
Argentina	13,200	16,000
Brazil	32,200	32,500
Canada	9,000	9,100
China, People's Repub.	133,000	125,000
France	15,200	14,900
India	10,500	10,700
Indonesia	10,100	9,100
Italy	9,000	9,000
Mexico	17,800	19,000
Romania	7,700	9,500
USA	247,900	239,700

* Provisional.

Sources: International Grains Council; FAO, *Quarterly Bulletin of Statistics*.

Maize is an important foodstuff in regions such as sub-Saharan Africa and the tropical zones of Latin America, where the climate precludes the extensive cultivation of other cereals. It is, however, inferior in nutritive value to wheat, being especially deficient in lysine, and tends to be replaced by wheat in diets, when the opportunity arises. In many African countries, the grain is ground into a meal, mixed with water, and boiled to produce a gruel or porridge. In other areas it is made into (unleavened) corn bread or breakfast cereals. Maize is also the source of an oil, which is used in cooking.

The high starch content of maize makes it highly suitable as a compound feed ingredient, especially for pigs and poultry. Animal feeding is the main use of maize in the USA, Europe and Japan, and large amounts are also used for feed in developing countries in Far East Asia, Latin America and, to some extent, in North Africa. Maize has a variety of industrial uses, including the preparation of ethyl alcohol (ethanol), which may be added to petrol to produce a blended motor fuel. Maize is also a source of dextrose and fructose, which can be used as artificial sweeteners, many times as sweet as sugar. The amounts of maize used for these purposes depend, critically, on its price to the users relative to that of petroleum, sugar and other potential raw materials. Maize cobs, previously discarded as a waste product, may be used as feedstock to produce various chemicals (e.g. acetic acid and formic acid).

In recent years world production of maize has averaged nearly 600m. tons annually. The USA is by far the largest producer, with harvests of about 240m. tons per year, except in periods of drought or excessive heat, when maize output can fall sharply: in 1995, for example, the US maize crop totalled only 187m. tons. Production in the People's Republic of China (PRC), whose output has been expanding rapidly, comprises the world's second largest, with an annual output exceeding 100m. tons. Apart from Egypt, most maize in Africa is grown south of the Sahara. The region's production averages about 33m. tons annually, and in recent years the trend has been upwards, although annual output varies according to patterns of rainfall. Maize is not grown under irrigation in most of sub-Saharan Africa, as scarce water supplies are reserved instead for higher-value export crops. Yields are therefore low. In most countries commercial farming is hindered by the lack of foreign exchange to buy essential equipment, as well as fuels and fertilizers. In addition, transport difficulties make marketing expensive and uncertain. In much of Africa maize is a subsistence crop.

The region's main producer is South Africa, which grows both white corn (for human consumption) and yellow corn (for animal feed). It was formerly an exporter of both types (except in years of severe drought), but market deregulation in 1997 altered the economic basis of commercial maize production. In the absence of government support, domestic maize is not competitive with imported maize in the feed mills of the coastal regions, with the result that sowings, particularly of yellow corn, have fallen. White corn production usually exceeds local food requirements, the surplus being exported to neighbouring food-deficit countries. Drought reduced the South African maize crop to only 7.4m. tons in 1999 but, with better conditions, an improved harvest was expected in 2000. Zimbabwe, too, is vulnerable to drought. After good harvests it exports maize, but recent crops have fallen short of rapidly-increasing domestic needs and imports have been necessary to sustain supplies. In Kenya, the influx of large numbers of refugees has added to domestic food needs, and imports of maize are now required in most seasons. In Nigeria, production averages about 5m. tons. The potential for output growth has been hindered by marketing difficulties and shortages of necessary agricultural inputs. Fertilizer supplies have improved since its procurement and distribution were privatized, but prices remain too high for many farmers to use it. Newly introduced maize varieties have improved yields. In the past, an important end-use of maize in Nigeria was for the brewing of beer, but since the ban on imports of barley and barley malt was lifted in 1998, breweries have used less maize.

One of the most notable differences between maize production in developed and developing countries is in yields. In the USA, the continual development of new hybrids and the availability of adequate fertilizer and water supplies have resulted in a substantial increase in yields, interrupted only by the occasional years of drought. In good years yields exceed 8 tons per ha; a record of 8.7 tons per ha was achieved in 1994. South Africa, Kenya and Zimbabwe usually achieve yields of at least 2 tons per ha, but in much of west and central Africa yields of 1 ton per ha are normal. Although hybrid forms of maize suited to African conditions are being developed, their adoption is hindered in many countries by low producer prices, inefficient marketing arrangements, and, above all, the inability of producers to obtain regular supplies of fertilizers at economic prices.

World trade in maize reached a record 73m. tons in 1989/90 (July–June), but subsequently declined, largely because of a fall in purchases by the former USSR. Although trade recovered to about 65m. tons annually in the mid-1990s, growth was again curtailed by economic and financial problems in Far East Asia, which had a severe impact on meat consumption in the region, and thence on its demand for animal feeds. The onset of recovery in the economies of Far East Asia, together with increased demand from North Africa and Latin America, were important factors in the increase in world maize trade to 69m. tons in 1989/99.

The pre-eminent world exporter is the USA, which typically accounts for about three-quarters of the total. Its sales reached 60m. tons in 1995/96, but subsequently declined as a result of increased competition from Argentina, the PRC and a number of countries in central and eastern Europe. US exports in the late 1990s averaged 45m. tons annually. Following deregulation, Argentine farmers expanded their maize areas and also invested in new equipment, leading to higher yields. Production in 1998 exceeded 19m. tons (almost double the level of the early 1990s). Although exports reached a record 12m. tons, farmers were disappointed with their returns, and some switched to oilseeds in the following year. Maize exports in 1998/99 totalled just under 8m. tons. The PRC was a major maize exporter in the early 1990s, and its sales increased again at the end of the decade as faltering domestic requirements could not absorb a succession of big crops. To reduce the burden of stocks, the government subsidized its export sales, which reached 7m. tons in 1997/98 before falling to 3.5m. tons in the following season. South Africa was a significant exporter in the 1980s, when annual sales, mostly of white maize, sometimes exceeded 3m. tons. Owing to smaller crop levels, exports in the second half of the 1990s averaged little more than 1m. tons per year.

The world's principal maize importer is Japan. Its purchases averaged more than 16m. tons annually in the early 1990s, but have subsequently declined, as the Japanese market has progressively opened to imports of meat. Feed users in the Republic of Korea are willing to substitute other grains, particularly feed wheat, for maize when prices are attractive, and maize imports are therefore variable, averaging about 7m. tons per year. Taiwan regularly imports about 5m. tons of maize annually, but imports by other countries in the region, particularly Indonesia, Malaysia and the Philippines, have been severely affected by the region's economic problems. In the 1980s, the USSR was a major market, but the livestock industries in the successor republics of the USSR declined sharply during the 1990s, greatly reducing feed needs. From a total of 18m. tons in 1989/90, these imports declined to 4m. tons in 1993/94 and have subsequently been less than 1m. tons annually.

Maize imports by sub-Saharan Africa vary from around 1m. tons annually in years of good crops to far higher amounts after droughts. In 1992/93, for example, these imports exceeded 8m. tons, most of which entered through South African ports, either for that country's own use or for onward transport overland to neighbouring countries.

Massive levels of carry-over stocks of maize were accumulated in the USA during the mid-1980s, reaching a high point of 124m. tons at end-August 1987. Government support programmes were successful in discouraging surplus production, but several poor harvests also contributed to the depletion of these stocks, which were reduced to only 11m. tons at the close of the 1995/96 marketing year. A succession of favourable crops in the late 1990s, together with increased competition from Argentina and the PRC, led to a substantial rebuilding of maize stocks, despite steadily rising domestic requirements for feeds, associated with the strong US economy. Carry-over stocks at the end of the 1998/99 marketing year reached 45m. tons.

Export prices of maize are mainly influenced by the level of supplies in the USA, and the intensity of competition between

Export Price Index for Maize (base: 1980 = 100)

	Average	Highest month(s)	Lowest month(s)
1990	92		
1995	80		
1997	73	77 (April)	68 (Aug.)
1998	63	69 (Jan., March)	56 (Sept.)
1999	58	60 (Jan., Sept., Oct.)	56 (July, Dec.)

the exporting countries. Record quotations were achieved in April 1996, when the price of US No. 2 Yellow Corn (f.o.b. Gulf Ports) reached US $210 per ton. It fell rapidly over the following months, to $120 per ton in November 1996, and to only $90 in the second half of 1998. Prices remained depressed in early 1999, occasionally falling below $90 per ton.

Manganese

This metal is obtained from various ores containing such minerals as hausmannite, manganite and pyrolusite. The ore is usually washed or hand-sorted and then smelted to make ferromanganese (80% manganese), in which form it is chiefly used to alloy into steel, manganese steel being particularly hard and tough. Almost 95% of manganese produced is thus used in the manufacture of steel, which, on average, consumes about 6 kg of manganese per metric ton of steel. Electrolytic manganese is used to make stainless steel and in the aluminium industry. Minor uses of manganese as oxides are in dry-cell batteries, paints and varnishes, and in ceramics and glass-making.

The current world reserve base of manganese has been estimated by the US Geological Survey at 5,000m. metric tons, of which more than three-quarters are located in South Africa and in the republics of the former USSR, principally Ukraine. Gabon, Africa's second major producer, has an estimated reserve base of 45m. tons. Until overtaken by Gabon in 1990, South Africa was, during the late 1980s, the world's leading exporter of manganese ore, exporting almost three-fifths of its mine output. Where possible, South Africa's policy has been to maximize export revenues by shipping as much as possible in processed ferro-alloy form. Export volumes of ferromanganese generally reflect world trends in steel production. The expansion by Gabon of its manganese exports was stimulated by the opening, in 1988, of a new mineral port at Owendo. In 1999 contracts were finalized for the establishment of a manganese conglomeration plant at Moanda.

Ghana, the other principal African producer, has benefited from government measures to revive manganese operations, assisted by loan finance from the World Bank. In 1991 a mine project was initiated that could establish Burkina Faso as a minor regional producer. These reserves, located at Tambao, 400 km north-west of Ouagadougou, and estimated at 19m. tons, contain an average ore content of 50% manganese. A joint venture between the government and Canadian interests to develop these resources was formed in 1995. In 1994 manganese

Production of Manganese Ore
(manganese content, '000 metric tons)

	1997	1998*
World total	7,510	7,040
Africa†‡	2,348	2,410
African producers		
Gabon†	879	966
Ghana†	149	144
South Africa†	1,320	1,300
Leading non-African producers		
Australia	1,024	729
Brazil†	828	819
China, People's Repub.	1,110	1,200
India†	680	610
Ukraine†	1,030	755

* Preliminary.

† Gross weight reported; metal content estimated.

‡ Figures represent the sum of output in the listed countries. Small quantities of manganese ore are also produced in Egypt, Morocco and Namibia.

Source: US Geological Survey.

production was resumed in Namibia after a lapse of almost 30 years. The Ofjosondu mine, 160 km north-east of Windhoek, was reactivated for production of medium-grade ore having a relatively low phosphorus content. Its initial annual output was projected at about 100,000 tons. The Democratic Republic of the Congo, once a significant source of manganese exports, has mined only on a sporadic basis since 1980, although plans to revive full operations at Kisenge, near the frontiers with Angola and Zambia, were receiving consideration in late 1997. The exploitation of manganese deposits in Angola has been interrupted by two decades of civil war.

Extensive accumulations of manganese in marine environments have been identified. The characteristic occurrences are as nodules on deep ocean floors and as crusts on seamounts at shallower depths. Both forms are oxidic and are often termed 'ferromanganese' because they generally contain iron and manganese. The main commercial interest in both types of deposit derives from the copper, nickel and cobalt contents also present, which represent large resources of these metals. Attention was focused initially on nodules, of which the Pacific Ocean encompasses the areas with the densest coverage and highest concentration of potentially economic metals. However, the exploitation of nodules has, to date, been impeded by legal, technical and economic factors.

Export Price Index for Manganese Ore (base: 1980 = 100)

	Average	Highest month(s)	Lowest month(s)
1990	243		
1995	125		
1997	127	131 (Jan., Feb.)	125 (April–Dec.)
1998	125	*	*
1999	117	125 (Jan.–March)	114 (May–Dec.)

* The monthly index remained constant at 125 throughout 1998.

The index of export prices for manganese ore remained at 114 in January, February, March and April 2000. South Africa's main producer, Samancor, reduced its export price for sales of metallurgical-grade ore to Japan by 2% in the year ending March 1999, to US $199 per metric ton of contained manganese. For the year 1999/2000 the price was further reduced, to only $181 per ton. The decreases reflected a decline in world steel production.

Most of the Western countries' manganese ore output is sold by means of annual contracts between producers and their customers, the manufacturers of steel and ferro-alloys.

Millet and Sorghum

Millet and sorghum are often grouped together in economic analyses of world cereals, not because of any affinity between the two grains—in fact they are quite dissimilar—but because in many developing countries both are subsistence crops which are little traded. Figures for the production of the individual grains should be treated only as broad estimates in most cases. Data cover only crops harvested for grain.

Data on millet relate mainly to the following: cat-tail millet (*Pennisetum glaucum* or *typhoides*), also known as bulrush millet, pearl millet or, in India and Pakistan, as 'bajra'; finger millet (*Eleusine coracana*), known in India as 'ragi'; common or bread millet (*Panicum miliaceum*), also called 'proso'; foxtail millet (*Setaria italica*), or Italian millet; and barnyard millet (*Echinochloa crusgalli*), also often called Japanese millet.

Sorghum statistics refer mainly to the several varieties of *Sorghum vulgare*, known by various names, such as great millet, Guinea corn, kafir or kafircorn (*caffrorum*), milo (in the USA and Argentina), feterita, durra, jowar, sorgo or maicillo. Other species included in the table are Sudan grass (*S. sudanense*) and Columbus grass or sorgo negro (*S. almum*). The use of grain sorghum hybrids has resulted in a considerable increase in yields in recent years.

Millet and sorghum are cultivated particularly in semi-arid areas where there is too little rainfall to sustain maize and the temperature is too high for wheat. These two cereals constitute the staple diet of people over large areas of Africa, India, the People's Republic of China (PRC) and parts of the former USSR. They are usually consumed as porridge or unleavened bread. Both grains have good nutritive value, but are less palatable

Production of Millet and Sorghum ('000 metric tons)
M = Millet; S = Sorghum.

	1998	1999*
World total: M	28,650	29,080
World total: S	62,630	64,070
Africa: M	12,540	12,200
Africa: S	19,770	20,390
Leading African producers		
Burkina Faso: M	820	830
Burkina Faso: S	1,300	1,250
Chad: M	650	620
Chad: S	250	380
Egypt: S	770	760
Ethiopia: M	300	280
Ethiopia: S	1,700	1,650
Mali: M	750	760
Mali: S	700	670
Niger: M	1,750	1,700
Niger: S	390	350
Nigeria: M	5,100	4,800
Nigeria: S	7,300	7,400
Senegal: M	441	500
South Africa: S	420	400
Sudan: M	500	800
Sudan: S	3,700	4,300
Tanzania: M	310	200
Tanzania: S	450	400
Uganda: M	630	600
Uganda: S	390	400
Leading non-African producers		
Argentina: S	3,222	3,400
Australia: S	1,664	1,263
China, People's Repub.: M	4,000	4,400
China, People's Repub.: S	4,500	4,600
India: M	10,500	10,200
India: S	10,200	10,000
Mexico: S	6,450	6,150
USA: S	13,200	15,100

* Provisional.

Source: International Grains Council.

than wheat, and tend to be replaced by the latter when circumstances permit. In many African countries sorghum is used to make beer. Sorghum is also produced and used in certain countries in the western hemisphere (particularly Argentina, Mexico and the USA), where it is used mainly as an animal feed, although the high tannin content of some varieties lowers their feeding value.

World production of both sorghum and millet has been in decline for many years, as farmers have preferred to cultivate more profitable and higher-yielding crops. Because sorghum is more drought-resistant than most cereals, it tends to be grown in marginal areas, or to be substituted at short notice for maize in dry years. World production of sorghum averages about 65m. tons annually, of which Africa accounts for about 30%. The region's major producers are Sudan, Nigeria, Ethiopia and Burkina Faso. World millet production averages just under 30m. tons annually. Sub-Saharan Africa is one of the main producing regions, accounting for about 40% of the world millet crop.

Millet and sorghum are grown largely for human consumption, but are gradually being replaced by wheat and rice, as those cereals become more widely available. Only low-grade sorghum is used for animal feed in Africa, but some is used for starch when maize is in short supply. Apart from food and animal feed requirements, sorghum is used in a number of countries in Asia and Africa for the production of beers and other alcoholic liquors.

World trade in sorghum ranges between 6m.–10m. tons per year, but has in recent years been at the lower end of this range, reflecting the small volume of exportable supplies. The principal exporters are the USA (which usually accounts for two-thirds of the total and holds the greater part of world sorghum stocks), Argentina and Australia. The PRC, South Africa, Sudan and Thailand are occasional exporters. Japan normally purchases about 2.5m. tons annually, and is thus one of the principal sorghum markets. Mexico's yearly sorghum purchases also average 2.5m. tons, but are more variable, as they depend upon the size of the domestic crop and on the relative prices of sorghum and maize. Little sorghum is imported by sub-Saharan Africa. Export prices for sorghum normally closely follow those of maize, although sorghum is generally slightly cheaper. The price of US No. 2 Yellow Sorghum (f.o.b. Gulf Ports) reached US $200 per ton in May 1996, but has since been in decline. In June 1999 it averaged $86 per ton, about $7 per ton less than the concurrent export price of maize. In June 2000 the average price of sorghum was only $80 per ton.

Very little millet enters international trade, and no reliable export price series can be established.

Oil Palm (*Elaeis guineensis*)

This tree is native to west Africa and grows wild in tropical forests along the coast of that region. The entire fruit is of use commercially; palm oil is made from its pulp, and palm kernel oil from the seed. Palm oil is a versatile product and, because of its very low acid content (4%–5%), it is almost all used in food. It is used in margarine and other edible fats; as a 'shortener' for pastry and biscuits; as an ingredient in ice cream and chocolate; and in the manufacture of soaps and detergents. Palm kernel oil, which is similar to coconut oil, is also used for making soaps and fats. The sap from the stems of the tree produces palm wine, an intoxicating beverage.

Palm oil can be produced virtually through the year once the palms have reached oil-bearing age, which takes about five years. The palms continue to bear oil for 30 years or more and the yield far exceeds that of any other oil plant, with 1 ha of oil palms producing as much oil as 6 ha of groundnuts or 10–12 ha of soybeans. However, it is an intensive crop, needing considerable investment and skilled labour.

During the 1980s palm oil accounted for more than 15% of world production of vegetable oils (second only to soybean oil), owing mainly to a substantial expansion in Malaysian output. Assisted by high levels of demand from Pakistan and the People's Republic of China, palm oil considerably increased its share of world markets for vegetable oils in the early 1990s. In the mid-1990s palm oil exports substantially exceeded those of soybean oil in international trade.

The increase in output of palm oil has posed a particular challenge to the soybean industry in the USA, which has, since the mid-1970s, been reducing its imports of palm oil. In 1988, in response to health reports that both palm and coconut oils tended to raise levels of cholesterol (a substance believed to promote arteriosclerosis in the body), several leading US food processors announced that they were to discontinue the use of these oils. The scientific validity of these reports, however, has been vigorously challenged by palm oil producers.

In Africa a large proportion of oil palms still grow in wild groves and the bulk of oil production is for local consumption. In export terms, Africa has, since 1980, accounted for less than 3% of world trade in palm oil, and in 1995 African exports comprised only 2% of the world market. Nigeria was the world's leading producer of palm oil until overtaken by Malaysia in 1971. The loss of Nigeria's market dominance was, in part, a result of civil war and the authorities' neglect to replace old, unproductive trees. Since the early 1980s, however, measures have been taken to revive palm oil output and to enhance the efficiency and capacity of associated mills and refineries. Foreign investment has been encouraged, as has the transfer of inefficiently managed state-owned plantations to private-sector ownership. A ban by the Nigerian government on palm oil imports, in force since 1986, was partially relaxed in 1990, however, as domestic output (of which an estimated 70% came from smallholder producers) was able to satisfy only two-thirds of a forecast annual demand of 900,000 tons.

In Benin, where the oil palm has traditionally been a staple crop of the national economy, oil palm plantations and natural palm groves cover more than 450,000 ha. Côte d'Ivoire is now Africa's principal palm oil exporter and the fourth largest in the world, behind Malaysia (by far the largest, accounting for about 80% of all palm oil trade), Indonesia and Singapore. However, more than one-half of Côte d'Ivoire's palms were planted in 1965–70 and have passed their peak of productivity. Management and financial difficulties during the 1990s, as well as declining world prices for palm oil, led a scaling-down of the replanting programme. However, following the revival in prices during 1997 and 1998, when Côte d'Ivoire had recourse to imports from Malaysia in order to satisfy domestic demand,

Production of Palm Kernels ('000 metric tons)

	1997	1987
World total	5,342*	5,242*
Africa	910*	907*
Leading African producers		
Cameroon	58†	58†
Congo, Dem. Repub.	66*	63*
Côte d'Ivoire	28*	28*
Ghana	35*	35*
Guinea	52*	52*
Nigeria	548*	548*
Sierra Leone	31*	31*
Leading non-African producers		
Brazil‡	135*	135*
Colombia	83†	88†
Indonesia§	1,190	1,303
Malaysia	2,638	2,428
Thailand	87†	82†

* FAO estimate. † Unofficial figure.
‡ Figures relate to babassu kernels.
§ Production on estates only.

Production of Palm Oil ('000 metric tons)

	1997	1998
World total	18,304*	18,144*
Africa	1,713*	1,781*
Leading African producers		
Angola	53*	54*
Cameroon	135†	136†
Congo, Dem. Repub.	166*	157*
Côte d'Ivoire	229	274
Ghana	100*	100*
Guinea	55*	50
Nigeria	810	845
Sierra Leone	51	51*
Leading non-African producers		
Colombia	438	483†
Indonesia‡	5,385	5,902
Malaysia	9,069	8,315
Thailand	470†	360†

* FAO estimate. † Unofficial figure.
‡ Production on estates only.

plans were announced in 1999 to increase capacity to 600,000 tons annually by 2010. The palm oil sector in Cameroon has similarly experienced delays in the implementation of replanting. The state-owned palm oil company, SOCAPALM, was to be transferred to private-sector ownership during 1998. Other African producers, notably Liberia and Ghana, also lack sufficient refinery capacity to service their palm oil output. Tanzania has received proposals for the construction by Malaysian producers of a palm oil refinery to process Malaysian crude palm oil with an initial output of 30,000 tons of edible oils annually. In 1999 a palm oil extraction mill, financed by the Netherlands, commenced production in south-east Tanzania. Uganda, which has potential to develop a palm oil sector, has received international aid to promote its establishment.

Export Price Index for Palm Oil (base: 1980 = 100)

	Average	Highest month(s)	Lowest month(s)
1990	49		
1995	107		
1997	93	99 (Feb.)	85 (July)
1998	115	120 (May, Sept.)	106 (Jan.)
1999	74	108 (Jan.)	54 (July)

Internationally, palm oil is faced with sustained competition from the other major edible lauric oils—soybean, rapeseed and sunflower oils—and these markets are subject to a complex and changing interaction of production, stocks and trade. In the longer term, prospects for palm oil exporters (particularly the higher-cost producers in sub-Saharan Africa) do not appear favourable. Technological advances in oil palm cultivation, particularly in the introduction of laboratory-produced higher-yielding varieties (HYV), may also militate against the smaller-scale producer, as, for economic and technical reasons, many HYV can be produced only on large estates, exposing smallholder cultivators to increasingly intense price pressure.

During September 1996 the import price of Malaysian palm oil in the Netherlands (c.i.f. Rotterdam) declined from US $572.5 per metric ton to $502.5 per ton. The price advanced to $585 per ton in February 1997, but fell to $467.5 in July. Subsequently the market revived, and in late December palm oil traded at $565 per ton. The upward movement continued in the early months of 1998, and in May the import price of palm oil reached $800 per ton. In June the price eased to $592.5 per ton. The Rotterdam price of palm oil stayed within this range for the remainder of 1998, ending the year at $605 per ton. For the year as a whole, the European import price averaged $671.3 per ton, compared with $545.8 in 1997. However, from January 1999 there was strong downward pressure on palm oil prices, as demand fell while supplies remained plentiful. By early August the Rotterdam import price had been reduced to only $300 per ton. The sharp fall in prices was partly due to a Chinese decision to import oilseeds rather than the oils derived from them, in an attempt to protect China's domestic processing industry. For 1999 as a whole, the European import price of palm oil averaged $436.3 per ton: 35% below the previous year's level. In February 2000 the Rotterdam price fell to $290 per ton.

Petroleum

Crude oils, from which petroleum fuel is derived, consist essentially of a wide range of hydrocarbon molecules which are separated by distillation in the refining process. Refined oil is treated in different ways to make the different varieties of fuel. More than four-fifths of total world oil supplies are used as fuel for the production of energy in the form of power or heating.

Petroleum, together with its associated mineral fuel, natural gas, is extracted both from onshore and offshore wells in many areas of the world. The dominant producing region is the Middle East, whose proven reserves in December 1998 accounted for 65.1% of known world deposits of crude petroleum and natural gas liquids. The Middle East accounted for 31.1% of world output in 1998. Africa contained 10,335m. metric tons of proven reserves (7.3% of the world total) at the end of 1998 and accounted for 10.2% of world production in that year.

From storage tanks at the oilfield wellhead, crude petroleum is conveyed, frequently by pumping for long distances through large pipelines, to coastal depots where it is either treated in a refinery or delivered into bulk storage tanks for subsequent shipment for refining overseas. In addition to pipeline transportation of crude petroleum and refined products, natural (petroleum) gas is, in some areas, also transported through networks of pipelines. Crude petroleum varies considerably in colour and viscosity, and these variations are a determinant both of price and of end-use after refining.

In the refining process, crude petroleum is heated until vaporized. The vapours are then separately condensed, according to their molecular properties, passed through airless steel tubes and pumped into the lower section of a high cylindrical tower, as a hot mixture of vapours and liquid. The heavy unvaporized liquid flows out at the base of the tower as a 'residue' from which is obtained heavy fuel and bitumen. The vapours passing upwards then undergo a series of condensation processes that produce 'distillates', which form the basis of the various petroleum products.

The most important of these products is fuel oil, composed of heavy distillates and residues, which is used to produce heating and power for industrial purposes. Products in the kerosene group have a wide number of applications, ranging from heating fuels to the powering of aviation gas turbine engines. Gasoline (petrol) products fuel internal combustion engines (used mainly in road motor vehicles), and naphtha, a gasoline distillate, is a commercial solvent that can also be processed as a feedstock. Propane and butane, the main liquefied petroleum gases, have a wide range of industrial applications and are also used for domestic heating and cooking.

Petroleum is the leading raw material in international trade. World-wide demand for this commodity totalled 71.5m. barrels per day (b/d) in 1997 and 1998. The world's 'published proven' reserves of petroleum and natural gas liquids at 31 December 1998 were estimated to total 141,730m. metric tons, equivalent to about 1,035,000m. barrels (1 metric ton is equivalent to approximately 7.3 barrels, each of 42 US gallons or 34.97 imperial gallons, i.e. 159 litres).

Nigeria's first petroleum discovery was made in the Niger delta region in 1956, and exports began in 1958. Production and exports increased steadily until output was disrupted by the outbreak of civil war in 1967. After the end of hostilities, in 1970, Nigeria's petroleum production greatly increased and it became the country's major industry. Since Libya restricted output in 1973, Nigeria has been Africa's leading petroleum-producing country. Being of low sulphur content and high quality, its petroleum is much in demand on the European market. Nigeria's proven reserves were estimated to be 3,082m. tons at 31 December 1998. A member of the Organization of the Petroleum Exporting Countries (OPEC, see below), Nigeria accounted for 7.2% of total OPEC production of 1,480m. tons in 1998. The state petroleum enterprise, the Nigerian National Petroleum Corpn (NNPC), operates refinery facilities at Kaduna, Warri, Port Harcourt and Alesa Eleme. In 1998 their total annual capacity was 21.9m. metric tons, although Nigeria occasionally has recourse to imports of refined petroleum products in order to satisfy its domestic requirements. In late 1999 Nigeria commenced exports of liquefied natural gas, while plans proceeded for the construction of a pipeline to convey natural gas from the Escravas field, in Delta State, to Benin, Ghana and Togo. In 1997 Nigeria was the world's seventh largest petroleum exporter, and in that year income from this source provided almost 98% of the country's earnings of foreign exchange. Although petroleum sales normally provide about 80% of federal government revenue, considerable official revenue is lost through illegal exports of oil to neighbouring countries, in the form of petrol, kerosene, diesel oil and fuel oil.

Angola's first petroleum discovery was made in 1955 near Luanda. However, the Cabinda province has a major offshore deposit, in production since 1968, which now forms the basis of Angola's oil industry. Output from Cabinda was briefly disrupted by the country's civil war, but has proceeded uninterruptedly since 1977, and has risen steadily since 1982. In 1997 Angola obtained almost 93% of its foreign earnings from exports by the petroleum sector, which in the mid-1990s accounted for about 80% of government revenue. In 1998 Angola's proven oil reserves were assessed at 741m. tons; however, with a number of oilfields currently under development and continuing discoveries of new deep-water petroleum fields, prospects exist for a considerable expansion in the petroleum sector, given an eventual restoration of internal order. The discovery, in 1997, of an estimated 103m. tons of recoverable offshore reserves has since been undergoing commercial evaluation. Most of Angola's output is exported in crude form, although there are plans to augment the capacity of Angola's sole refinery, at Luanda, which was 2m. tons annually in 1998, by the construction of a second refinery.

The Republic of the Congo, with proven recoverable reserves estimated at 206m. tons in 1998, entered onshore petroleum production in 1957. Subsequent expansion, however, has been in operations off shore, where major new deposits were discovered in 1992 and began to augment the country's petroleum output from 1996. Two further significant offshore discoveries were announced in 1998. A petroleum refinery at Pointe-Noire, with an annual capacity of 1m. tons in 1997, also processes some Angolan production. In neighbouring Gabon, whose recoverable reserves were estimated at 342m. tons in 1998, the exploitation of petroleum deposits began in 1956, and, as in the Congo Republic, was increased as offshore fields came into production. In 1996 sales of petroleum and petroleum products provided more than 81% of export revenue. A member of OPEC until its withdrawal from the organization in December 1996, Gabon's output accounted for only 1.4% of OPEC's total output in that year. Exports of petroleum and petroleum products dominate the Gabonese economy, however, and accounted for more than 77% of the country's foreign revenue in 1997.

Cameroon, which is virtually self-sufficient in oil and petroleum products, derived almost 32% of its export income from this source in 1998. New exploration and development projects, however, were not actively pursued during the 1990s, and the country's proven reserves (estimated at 55m. tons in 1998) were nearing exhaustion in the early 2000s. The Democratic Republic of the Congo (DRC) entered offshore petroleum production in

Production of Crude Petroleum
(estimates, '000 metric tons, including natural gas liquids)

	1997	1998*
World total	3,469,800	3,518,900
Africa	372,500	360,100
Leading African producers		
Algeria	60,200	58,900
Angola	36,500	37,500
Cameroon	6,300	5,300
Congo, Repub.	12,500	12,200
Egypt	43,800	42,900
Gabon	18,600	17,800
Libya	70,800	69,200
Nigeria	113,400	106,200
Leading non-African producers		
Canada	120,300	124,700
China, People's Repub.†	160,100	159,900
Iran	184,000	187,700
Iraq	58,100	105,300
Kuwait	105,300	107,600
Mexico	170,600	174,400
Norway	156,900	150,000
Russia	307,400	304,300
Saudi Arabia	442,100	443,200
United Arab Emirates	119,500	121,400
United Kingdom	128,000	132,600
USA	380,400	367,900
Venezuela	173,500	171,800

* Preliminary.   † Including oil from shale and coal.

Source: BP Amoco, *Statistical Review of World Energy 1999.*

1975, operating from oilfields near the Atlantic coast and at the mouth of the River Congo. These deposits became depleted at the end of the 1980s (estimates of its proven reserves fell from 13.2m. tons in 1989 to 7.6m. tons in 1990). The level of these reserves was substantially replenished during 1991, however, raising estimates to 25.6m. tons for each of the subsequent seven years. Although the DRC has an annual refinery capacity of 850,000 tons, its exceptionally heavy-grade petroleum cannot be processed locally and the DRC therefore cannot consume its own output.

Côte d'Ivoire, with estimated proven reserves of 13.7m. tons in 1998, and Benin, whose proven reserves were estimated at 1.1m. tons in that year, are among the other smaller sub-Saharan offshore producers. These were joined in 1991 by Equatorial Guinea, where the offshore Zafiro oilfield, north-west of Bioko, commenced production in late 1996. Subsequent output advanced rapidly, reaching an estimated 80,000 b/d in 1996 and contributing significantly to the country's economic growth. Equatorial Guinea's proven reserves were estimated at 1.6m. tons in 1998. Deposits of an estimated 52m.–58m. tons of petroleum have been identified off the coast of Senegal, but the development of these reserves (which are overwhelmingly of heavy oil) is not economically feasible at present. The exploitation of identified petroleum reserves of 40m.–50m. tons in south-western Chad, which had been interrupted by prolonged internal unrest, is planned by an international consortium. Output from the field, near Dobra, would be conveyed by a 1,060-km pipeline, through Cameroon, to the Atlantic coast. Finance for the project, which has provoked widespread concern about its potential for environmental damage, was approved by the World Bank in June 2000. In 1998 Sudan, a relatively minor producer with estimated proven reserves of 35.9m. tons in that year, finalized an agreement with four foreign companies to construct a 1,600-km pipeline to convey output from western Sudan to a terminal at Bachair, south of Port Sudan. The pipeline, with the capacity to carry 450,000 b/d, was inaugurated in mid-1999, and was initially expected to carry about 150,000 b/d. Commercial deposits of petroleum in Southern Sudan remain unexploited, pending the eventual resolution of internal unrest.

Among other sub-Saharan African countries where petroleum reserves are known or believed to exist, but which do not yet produce, are Guinea, Mozambique, Swaziland, Eritrea, São Tomé and Príncipe, South Africa and Tanzania. Exploration has also taken place, or is under way, in Ethiopia, Namibia, Kenya, Madagascar and Zimbabwe.

OPEC was formed in 1960 to maintain prices in the producing countries. Nigeria joined OPEC in 1971; however, Gabon, which became a full member in 1975, terminated its membership with effect from January 1997 (see above). The other African members are Algeria and Libya.

The four African members of OPEC formed the African Petroleum Producers' Association (APPA) in 1987. Angola, Benin, Cameroon, the DRC, the Republic of the Congo, Côte d'Ivoire, Egypt and Equatorial Guinea subsequently joined the association, in which Tunisia has observer status. Apart from promoting co-operation among regional producers, the APPA, which is based in Brazzaville, in the Congo Republic, co-operates with OPEC in stabilizing oil prices.

Export Price Index for Crude Petroleum (base: 1980 = 100)

	Average	Highest month(s)	Lowest month(s)
1990	69		
1995	54		
1997	58	72 (Jan.)	52 (Dec.)
1998	38	44 (Jan.)	30 (Dec.)
1995	54	77 (Dec.)	31 (Feb.)

The two leading western European producers and exporters of crude petroleum are Norway and the United Kingdom. The two countries' exports of crude petroleum earned an average of US $126 per metric ton in 1993, $118 per ton in 1994, $127 per ton in 1995, $153 per ton in 1996 and $144 per ton in 1997. Prices per barrel averaged about $20 in 1992, declined to only about $14 in late 1993, but recovered to more than $18 in mid-1994. Thereafter, international petroleum prices remained relatively stable until the early months of 1995. The price per barrel reached about $20 again in April and May 1995, but eased to $17 later in the year. In April 1996 the London price of the standard grade of North Sea petroleum for short-term delivery rose to more than $23 per barrel, following reports that stocks of petroleum in Western industrialized countries were at their lowest levels for 19 years. After another fall, the price of North Sea petroleum rose in October to more than $25 per barrel, its highest level for more than five years. The price per barrel was generally in the range of $22–$24 for the remainder of the year.

Petroleum traded at US $24–$25 per barrel in January 1997, but the short-term quotation for the standard North Sea grade fell to less than $17 in June. The price increased to more than $21 per barrel in October, in response to increased tension in the Persian (Arabian) Gulf region. However, the threat of an immediate conflict in the region subsided, and petroleum prices eased. The market was also weakened by an OPEC decision, in November, to raise the upper limit on members' production quotas, and by the severe financial and economic problems affecting many countries in eastern Asia. By the end of the year the price for North Sea petroleum had again been reduced to less than $17 per barrel.

Petroleum prices declined further in January 1998, with the standard North Sea grade trading at less than US $15 per barrel. Later in the month the price recovered to about $16.5 per barrel, but in March some grades of petroleum were trading at less than $13. Later that month three of the leading exporting countries—Saudi Arabia, Venezuela and Mexico (not an OPEC member)—agreed to reduce petroleum production, in an attempt to revive prices. In response, the price of North Sea petroleum advanced to about $15.5 per barrel. Following endorsement of the three countries' initiative by OPEC, however, there was widespread doubt that the proposals would be sufficient to have a sustained impact on prices, in view of the existence of large stocks of petroleum. Under the plan, OPEC members and five other countries (including Mexico and Norway) agreed to reduce their petroleum output between 1 April and the end of the year. The proposed reductions totalled about 1.5m. b/d (2% of world production), with Saudi Arabia making the greatest contribution (300,000 b/d). In early June, having failed to make a significant impact on international prices, the three countries that had agreed in March to restrict their production of petroleum announced further reductions in output, effective from 1 July. However, petroleum prices continued to be depressed, and in mid-June some grades sold for less than $12 per barrel. A new agreement between OPEC and other producers, concluded later that month, envisaged further reductions in output, totalling more than 1m. b/d, but this attempt to stimulate a rise in petroleum prices had little effect. The price on world markets was generally in the range of $12–$14 per barrel over the period July–October. Subsequently there was further downward pressure on petroleum prices, and in December the London quotation for the standard North Sea grade was below $10 per barrel for the first time since the introduction of the contract in 1986. For 1998 as a whole, the average price of North Sea petroleum was $13.37 per barrel, more than 30% less than in 1997 and the lowest annual level since 1976. In real terms (i.e. taking inflation into account), international prices for crude petroleum in late 1998 were at their lowest level since the 1920s.

During the early months of 1999 there was a steady recovery in the petroleum market. In March five leading producers (including Mexico) announced plans to reduce further their combined output by about 2m. b/d. Later that month an OPEC meeting agreed reductions in members' quotas totalling 1.7m. b/d (including 585,000 b/d for Saudi Arabia), to operate for 12 months from 1 April. The new quotas represented a 7% decrease from the previous levels (applicable from July 1998). At the same time, four non-members agreed voluntary cuts in production, bringing total proposed reductions in output to about 2.1m. b/d. In May the London price of North Sea petroleum rose to about US $17 per barrel. After easing somewhat, the price advanced again, reaching more than $20 per barrel in August. The upward trend continued, and in late September the price of North Sea petroleum (for November delivery) was just above $24 per barrel. After easing somewhat, prices rose again in November, when North Sea petroleum (for delivery in January 2000) was traded at more than $25 per barrel. The surge in prices followed indications that, in contrast to 1998, the previously agreed limits on output were, to a large extent, being implemented by producers and thus having an effect on stock levels. Surveys found that the rate of compliance among the 10 OPEC countries participating in the scheme to restrict production was 87% in June and July 1999, although it fell to 83% in October.

International prices for crude petroleum rose steadily during the opening weeks of 2000, with OPEC restrictions continuing to operate and stocks declining in industrial countries. In early March the London price for North Sea petroleum exceeded US $31.5 per barrel, but later in the month nine OPEC members agreed to restore production quotas to pre-March 1999 levels from 1 April 2000, representing a combined increase of about 1.7m. b/d. The London petroleum price fell in April to less than $22 per barrel, but the rise in OPEC production was insufficient to increase significantly the stocks held by major consuming countries. In June the price of North Sea petroleum rose to about $31.5 per barrel again, but later that month OPEC ministers agreed to a further rise in quotas (totalling about 700,000 b/d) from 1 July. By the end of July the North Sea petroleum price was below $27 per barrel, but in mid-August it rose to more than $32 for the first time since 1990 (when prices had surged in response to the Iraqi invasion of Kuwait).

Platinum

Platinum is one of a group of six related metals known as the platinum-group metals (PGM), which also includes palladium, rhodium, ruthenium, iridium and osmium. In nature, platinum is usually associated with the sulphides of iron, copper and nickel. Depending on the relative concentration of the PGM and copper and nickel in the deposit, platinum is either the major product or a by-product of base metal production. PGM are highly resistant to corrosion, and do not oxidize in air. They are also extremely malleable and have a high melting point, giving them a wide range of industrial uses.

Although widely employed in the petroleum refining and petrochemical sectors, the principal industrial use for platinum is in catalytic converters in motor vehicles (which reduce pollution from exhaust emissions), usually accounting for about one-third of total platinum consumption by Europe (including Eastern Europe), Japan, North America and other Western countries (an estimated 21.1%, or 1,185,000 troy ounces, in 1999). The USA, Canada, Japan, Australia, Taiwan, the Republic of Korea, the European Community (EC, now the European Union—EU) and certain Latin American countries have implemented legislation to neutralize vehicle exhaust gases, and this necessitates the fitting of catalytic converters, using platinum, rhodium and palladium, to vehicles. In 1989 the EC Council of (Environment) Ministers decided to oblige vehicle manufacturers within the Community to fit three-way catalytic converters as compulsory features in passenger cars with an engine capacity of less than 1,400 cc, effective for all new models from mid-1992 and for all new cars from January 1993. It was predicted that the new measures would reduce emissions of exhaust gases by 60%–70%. The EC Commission subsequently extended similar anti-pollution requirements to larger cars, and to heavy trucks, with effect from 1995. The resultant increase in demand for automotive emission control catalysts (autocatalysts) has generated a rising trend in the consumption of platinum, rhodium and palladium during the 1990s. In 1996 the EU announced proposals, implemented in 1998, for stricter limits on emissions, which took effect in 2000. Further restrictions on levels of emissions are due to take effect in 2005. In the USA, regulations to reduce emissions of exhaust gases by 50%–70% will require full compliance by vehicle manufacturers from 2001. The increasing use of palladium-rich catalysts, principally by US and European motor vehicle manufacturers, was reflected in a strong advance in autocatalyst demand for palladium of 970,000 oz (more than 20%) in 1999, to 5,685,000 oz (allowing for 195,000 oz in recovery from scrapped autocatalysts). Also of considerable potential significance to demand for PGM has been the development of fuel cells incorporating platinum catalysts which produce pollution-free electricity from a controlled chemical reaction between oxygen and hydrogen. The only by-products of this reaction are carbon dioxide and water, so that the fuel cell avoids environmental damage, in contrast to the disposal of radioactive waste products from nuclear plants and the production of sulphur and nitrogen oxides at coal- and oil-fired power stations. The use of these cells in power generation, assuming that their operating costs would approximate those of conventional electricity-generating plant, could substantially increase world demand for platinum and palladium.

Alloyed platinum is very heavy and hard. Platinum's white colour makes it popular for jewellery, which accounts for the other principal source of consumption (51.4%, or 2,880,000 oz, in 1999). Japan is the world's main consumer of platinum, and its jewellery industry absorbed 1,320,000 oz in 1999. Industrial and other miscellaneous applications accounted for the balance of platinum consumption; these uses include platinum for minting coins and small bars purchased as an investment, petroleum refining, production of nitric acid, glass manufacture, electrical applications and dentistry. Demand by industrial consumers, particularly in the motor vehicle industry and requirements for jewellery fabrication, raised international demand for platinum from 5,130,000 oz in 1997 to 5,370,000 oz in 1998 and to 5,600,000 oz in 1999. Supplies entering the market in 1999 declined to 4,870,000 oz from 5,400,000 oz in 1998. This decrease in supplies, which represented the lowest level in annual platinum supplies reaching the market since 1994, was brought about by a substantial fall in shipments from Russia, which could not be offset by a 6% rise in sales by South Africa.

The US Geological Survey (USGS) has estimated world reserves of PGM to be approximately 1,800m. oz, of which almost 90% are located in South Africa. Production is dominated by South Africa, which normally accounts for about three-quarters of supplies to the international market. Russia normally accounts for about 60% of the world's palladium supplies, although the country's output of the metal is believed to be less than that of South Africa. In 1997, according the estimates by the USGS, Russia exported about 140 metric tons of palladium, while its mine production was only about 62 tons. The excess in supplies was provided from accumulated Russian stockpiles, which have steadily diminished, to compensate for the continuing global production shortfall, in recent years. The size of Russia's palladium stocks has not been officially disclosed, but in 1998 it was estimated that, at current rates of depletion, they would be exhausted by 2002.

In 1991 South African technical assistance was made available to the USSR (and subsequently to Russia) for the development of its platinum industry. Russian PGM are produced mainly as by-products of coal and nickel mining (see below) in the far north of Siberia. Following the break-up of the former USSR in 1991, these operations were adversely affected by deterioration in plant and equipment, as the result of a lack of funds for essential maintenance. Production began to stabilize, however, in 1994, although it was estimated that in 1995 and 1996 about 1,000,000 oz of marketed shipments were supplied from Russian government platinum stocks. No supplies of PGM were exported by Russia during the first six months of 1997, and shipments were again interrupted during the first three months of 1998, owing to delays in authorization by the Russian government, for which the central bank acts as marketing agent. During 1999, owing to a change in Russian legislation which prevented exports by Noril'sk Nickel, the country's principal producer of PGM, most, if not all, of the 540,000 oz of platinum sold by Russia in that year were believed to come from central government stocks. Control of Noril'sk Nickel was transferred in 1995 to a bank, in preparation for full privatization. The enterprise has, however, since encountered severe financial problems and underwent further restructuring in 1998. In April 1999 Noril'sk Nickel announced plans to invest US $3,500m. during the period to 2010 in mine and infrastructural development. Canada is the third largest producer, its platinum being a by-product of its nickel production. Minor producers include the USA, Australia, Finland and Colombia. Zimbabwe, the only other African platinum producer, has significant deposits of PGM. Although operations at the Hartley platinum mine, developed by Australian interests, were suspended in June 1999, control of its assets was subsequently transferred to new ownership, and plans were proceeding in mid-2000 for the development of a new mine at Ngezi, whose output would be processed at the existing Hartley plant. Elsewhere in Africa, there are known or probable deposits of platinum in Ethiopia, Kenya and Sierra Leone. In early 1999 it was reported that significant deposits of PGM had been identified in Mongolia.

Whereas PGM are produced in Canada and Russia as by-products of copper and/or nickel production, PGM in South Africa are produced as the primary products, with nickel and copper as by-products. Another fundamental difference between the platinum deposits in South Africa and those in Russia and Canada is the ratio of platinum to palladium. In South Africa the percentage of platinum contained in PGM has, to date, exceeded that of palladium, although the ratio is expected to favour palladium in new mines being brought into production in the early 1990s (see below). In Russia, Canada and the USA there is a higher proportion of palladium than platinum.

South African production capacity was substantially increased in 1993, following the completion of a number of expansion projects which had been under development since the mid-1980s. However, the level of world platinum prices, together with rises in production costs, led to the subsequent postponement or cancellation of several of these projects and to the closure of unprofitable operations. During the mid-1990s, however, improved productivity in the platinum industry, together with the prospect of increasing demand for PGM and the continuing uncertainty of Russian exports, has encouraged South African producers to undertake a number of new expansion programmes. South Africa's platinum sales advanced from 3,680,000 oz in 1998 to 3,900,000 oz in 1999, and, with the prospect of increased productive capacity and a sustained high level of prices during the early 2000s, it has been forecast that the value of its PGM output could eventually exceed that of gold.

Prices for Platinum

(London Platinum and Palladium Market, morning and afternoon 'fixes', US$ per troy oz)

	Average	Highest	Lowest
1990	471.7		
1995	424.2		
1997	395.9	497.0 (June)	342.5 (Dec.)
1998	371.8	429.0 (April)	334.3 (Oct.)
1999	n.a.	457.0 (Nov.)	342.0 (Jan.)

For more than 17 months from mid-1994 the London price of platinum remained above US $400 per troy oz. In April 1995 the price rose to $461 (equivalent to £285 sterling) per oz, following reports that a US group had developed a new catalyst

system for motor vehicles that was claimed to reduce pollution in the atmosphere. In December, however, the platinum price fell to $398 (£256.5) per oz.

There was a revival of interest in precious metals during the early weeks of 1996, with the London price of platinum reaching US $433 (£285) per oz in February. As before, the advance was not sustained, and in June the platinum price was reduced to $389 (£251.5) per oz. The London quotation rose to $404.5 (£260) per oz in August, but declined to $367 (£219) in December.

During 1997, owing mainly to the erratic nature of supplies from Russia, the market for platinum and other PGM was characterized by extreme fluctuations in prices. At the start of the year, despite the suspension of Russian sales, the platinum market remained depressed, and in early February the London price fell to US $349.5 (£217) per oz. Later in February, however, the platinum price increased to $393.5 (£242) per oz, in response to fears of a prolonged interruption to previously plentiful supplies of Russian PGM, owing to a threatened strike at Noril'sk and to Russia's failure to settle the terms of its annual agreement to supply platinum and palladium to Japan. In May, amid continuing delays in the release of Russian platinum exports, the metal's price rose above $400 per oz. In early June the London quotation surged to $497 (£305) per oz: the highest dollar price of platinum since 1990. In July 1997, following reports that Russian sales had resumed, the platinum price eased to $396 (£235) per oz. In August, however, it rose to $457 (£281) per oz, partly in response to a surge in the palladium price (see below). By late October the London price of platinum had fallen below $400 per oz again, and in December it stood at only $342.5 (£210). The platinum market was depressed by the decline in the price of gold (to its lowest level for 18 years) and by reports that Russia was exporting large quantities of PGM to fulfil its 1997 sales quota before the end of the year. Sentiment was also influenced by the effects of economic and financial problems in several countries of eastern Asia. Platinum was perceived to be particularly vulnerable to an economic downturn in this region.

The London price of platinum advanced to US $429 (£255) per oz in April 1998 (after Russian shipments were again delayed), but declined to $345.5 (£211) in June. The platinum price rose in July to $394 (£240) per oz, but fell in October to only $334 (£200), its lowest level, in terms of US currency, for more than six years. Market sentiment was influenced by the continued Japanese recession and economic problems in other Asian countries. However, the London the price of platinum increased to $383 ($240) per oz in February 1999. Prices remained within this range until September, when the London quotation rose to more than $400 per oz. The platinum price advanced in November to $457 (£282) per oz, as uncertainty over Russian supplies continued.

A renewed surge in the early weeks of 2000 took the London price of platinum to US $573 (£357) per oz in February. The price eased in April to $470 (£297) per oz, following the resumption of Russian exports of platinum, but it rose in June to $579 (£386): its highest level since 1989. The platinum price reached $582 (£389) per oz at the end of July 2000.

Meanwhile, trends in the price of palladium have shown even greater volatility in recent years. The London price of the metal rose to US $175 per oz in April 1995, but declined to $127.5 in December. During 1996 the palladium price fluctuated between $114 and $144 per oz, with a declining trend towards the end of the year. However, as in the case of platinum, Russia (the leading supplier of palladium) suspended sales for the first six months of 1997. In response, the price of palladium advanced from $118 per oz in January to $240 in June. Following the resumption of Russian shipments in July, palladium was traded at $162 per oz. However, in August, as a result of speculative activity on the futures market in Japan, the metal's price rose to $245.5 per oz, its highest level since 1980. The London price of palladium stayed above $180 per oz for the remainder of 1997. For the year as a whole, the average price was $178.3 per oz, nearly 40% higher than in 1996. In addition to the restricted availability of supplies, the palladium market was influenced by the strong rise in demand for the metal from industrial consumers, particularly for use in vehicle catalysts (see above).

There was a further interruption to Russian sales of palladium from the beginning of 1998, leaving the market severely undersupplied. This scarcity was the main cause of another upward surge in prices. In April the London price of palladium exceeded the gold price for the first time ever and continued to advance to a succession of record levels, with a peak of US $390 per oz. In early May the palladium price eased to $321 per oz, but a week later, as Russian supplies continued to be delayed, it rose to a new record of $417, equivalent to £257 sterling. By the end of the month, however, palladium was traded at less than $300 per oz, after Russian sales resumed. In early June the price fell to $258 (£158) per oz, but in July, amid renewed concerns over Russian supplies, it increased to $347 (£210). The palladium price stayed within this range for the remainder of 1998, ending the year at $329 (£198) per oz. The average London price of palladium in 1998 was $284.2 per oz: 59% higher than in 1997.

During the early months of 1999 there was a new surge in the price of palladium, owing to uncertainty concerning Russian supplies, and in April the London quotation reached US $384 (£238) per oz. However, by early May (only two weeks later) the price had retreated to $285 (£176) per oz, following reports of a large Russian shipment of palladium. Prices in US currency remained within this range until September, when the London quotation rose to $385 (£234) per oz. The upward trend continued, with the price of palladium rising to a succession of new records, ending the year at $454 (£281) per oz.

The surge in palladium price was maintained during the opening weeks of 2000, and in February the London quotation reached US $785 (£491) per oz. In April the price of palladium eased to $554 (£350) per oz, but at the end of July it reached a new record of $822 (£549). As in the cae of platinum, the main influence on market sentiment was the delay in Russian shipments.

Rice (*Oryza*)

Rice is an annual grass belonging to the same family as (and having many similar characteristics to) small grains such as wheat, oats, rye and barley. It is principally the semi-aquatic nature of rice that distinguishes it from other grain species, and this is an important factor in determining its place of origin. In Africa and Asia, unmilled rice is referred to as 'paddy', although 'rough' rice is the common appellation in the West. After removal of the outer husk, it is called 'brown' rice. After the grain is milled to varying degrees to remove the bran layers, it is called 'milled' rice. Since rice loses 30%–40% of its weight in the milling process, most rice is traded in the milled form to save shipping expenses.

Production of Paddy Rice ('000 metric tons)

	1997	1998
World total	578,935*	567,883*
Africa	17,082*	16,138*
Leading African producers		
Côte d'Ivoire	1,287	1,223
Egypt	5,580	4,450
Guinea	716	764
Madagascar	2,558	2,447
Mali	576	589
Nigeria	3,268	3,275
Tanzania	551	811
Leading non-African producers		
Bangladesh	28,183	28,293
China, People's Repub.	200,730	191,000†
India	123,388	127,045
Indonesia	49,377	48,472
Myanmar	17,673	16,651
Thailand	23,580	22,506
Viet Nam	27,524	29,142

* FAO estimate.

† Unofficial figure. The official estimate of China's 1998 production (in '000 metric tons) is 198,713.

There are two cultivated species of rice, *Oryza sativa* and *O. glaberrima*. *O. sativa*, which originated in tropical Asia, is widely grown in tropical and semi-tropical areas, while the cultivation of *O. glaberrima* is limited to the high rainfall zone of west Africa. In Africa rice is grown mainly as a subsistence crop. Methods of cultivation differ from region to region and yields tend to be low by world standards. Rice is a staple

food in several African countries, including Madagascar and Tanzania, and especially in west African countries, where rice is a staple food of 40% of the population.

World rice production is dominated by the Asian region (which produces more than 90% of the world's total). African rice production accounts for less than 3% of total world output. As the bulk of rice production is consumed mainly in the producing countries, international trade accounts for less than 5% of world output. The market is subject to great volatility and fluctuating prices. Less than 1% of the African rice crop enters international trade and more than 90% of African rice exports come from Egypt. Africa, especially in recent years, has been a substantial net importer of rice, although the volume growth in imports has been held in check by the impact of higher world rice prices on the depleted foreign exchange reserves of many African importing countries. The major African importers include Côte d'Ivoire, Nigeria, Guinea, Sierra Leone, Senegal and Madagascar, which ranks as the world's largest rice consumer per caput. Despite the completion in 1995 of the rehabilitation of its main rice-growing areas, Madagascar has yet to achieve its goal of self-sufficiency in rice. In 1997 Madagascar had almost 1.2m. ha planted with rice. Nigeria, the largest producer in the sub-Saharan region, had about 2m. ha under rice in that year, and Côte d'Ivoire 650,000 ha.

Because rice is a relatively new crop to the region, suitable high-yielding varieties (HYV) have yet to be propagated. The development of HYV is among the activities of the 17-member West Africa Rice Development Association (WARDA), formed by the producing countries in 1970. Based in M'bé, near Bouaké, Côte d'Ivoire, WARDA maintains research centres in Nigeria, Senegal, Sierra Leone and Côte d'Ivoire, from which it conducts scientific research on crop improvement and provides technical assistance, with the aim of advancing the region towards eventual self-sufficiency in rice production.

Africa imports large quantities of rice from Thailand and the USA, the two major world exporters.

Export Price Index for Rice (base: 1980 = 100)

	Average	Highest month(s)	Lowest month(s)
1990	74		
1995	84		
1997	91	95 (Dec.)	87 (April)
1998	100	103 (Sept.)	97 (Jan.–March)
1999	93	104 (Jan.)	80 (Oct.–Dec.)

The world's leading exporter of rice in recent years has been Thailand. The average export price of Thai milled white rice increased from US $320.8 per metric ton in 1995 to $338.1 per ton in 1996, but declined to $302.5 in 1997. The price averaged $305.4 per ton in 1998, but slumped to $249.0 in 1999. On a monthly basis, the average fell from $301.7 per ton in January 1999 to $235.5 in April. The price recovered to $255.8 per ton in July, but declined to $217.0 in October. It rose to $247.0 per ton in January 2000, but fell to only $198.8 in May and to $197.9 in June. The decrease in prices was partly attributable to the plentiful supply of rice, with abundant stocks available, particularly in China and India. While world output of rice advanced in 1999/2000, the volume of trade declined, as many major importing countries, assisted by favourable weather, increased production.

Sisal (*Agave sisalana*)

Sisal, which is not indigenous to Africa, was introduced to Tanganyika (now mainland Tanzania) from Mexico at the end of the 19th century. The leaf tissue of this plant yields hard, flexible fibres which are suitable for making rope and twine, cord matting, padding and upholstery. Sisal accounts for two-thirds of world production of hard fibres, and about three-quarters of sisal consumption is for agricultural twine. World output of sisal and other hard fibres has generally declined in recent years, owing to competition from nylons and petroleum-based synthetics (in particular, polypropylene harvest twine, which is stronger than sisal and less labour-intensive to produce), although the intensity of the competition and the success of hard fibres depend on fluctuations in the price of petroleum. In 1970 Tanzania, whose sisal is generally regarded as being of the best quality, was overtaken as the world's leading pro-

Production of Sisal ('000 metric tons)

	1997	1998
World total	323*	311*
Africa	79*	81*
Leading African producers		
Kenya	28	29*
Madagascar	18	19*
Tanzania	25	26*
Leading non-African producers		
Brazil	145	116
China (incl. Taiwan)	35*	50*
Mexico	37*	37*

* FAO estimate.

ducer by Brazil. The nationalization of more than one-half of Tanzania's sisal estates in 1976, together with low prices, inefficient management and lack of equipment and spare parts, contributed to the decline of the Tanzanian crop. During the 1980s, however, the government sought to revive the industry by returning some state-owned estates to private or co-operative ownership, and in 1998 the government completed the transfer of its sisal estates and factories to a private sector consortium of European and Tanzanian entrepreneurs. However, prospects remain overshadowed by the longer-term outlook for sisal (according to FAO projections, world demand has been falling at a rate of 7% per year). Efforts are being made, however, to create new uses in such products as specialized papers and surgical bandages. With the decline of the Tanzanian sisal sector, Kenya has emerged as Brazil's main rival, although it exports only fibre, as it has no processing industry.

Although sisal producers operate a quota system, in an attempt to improve the pricing structure of the crop, the average price of sisal was in general decline between the early 1980s and the early 1990s, as relatively stable prices for petroleum allowed polypropylene to regain its competitiveness.

Export Price Index for Sisal (base: 1980 = 100)

	Average	Highest month(s)	Lowest month(s)
1990	89		
1995	91		
1997	111	115 (Jan.)	108 (March)
1998	116	119 (July–Dec.)	110 (Jan., Feb.)
1999	106	118 (Jan.)	88 (Dec.)

The average import price of ungraded East African sisal at European ports increased from US $604.6 per metric ton in 1994 to $710.4 per ton in 1995 and to $868.3 in 1996. The annual average was $777.5 per ton in 1997 and $821.3 in 1998, but fell to $695.8 in 1999. During 1998 the average price rose from $776.3 per ton in the first quarter of the year to $809.0 in the second quarter and to $850.0 in the third and fourth quarters. In 1999, however, the price declined from $787.3 per ton in the first quarter to $730.7 in the second quarter, to $649.7 in the third quarter and to only $615.3 in the fourth quarter. The index of export prices (see above) fell to 84 in February 2000, but recovered to 96 in April.

Sugar

Sugar is a sweet crystalline substance, which may be derived from the juices of various plants. Chemically, the basis of sugar is sucrose, one of a group of soluble carbohydrates which are important dietary sources of energy in the human diet. It can be obtained from trees, including the maple and certain palms, but virtually all manufactured sugar comes from two plants, sugar beet (*Beta vulgaris*) and sugar cane, a giant perennial grass of the genus *Saccharum*.

Sugar cane, found in tropical areas, grows to a height of up to 5 m. The plant is native to Polynesia, but its distribution is now widespread. It is not necessary to plant cane every season as, if the root of the plant is left in the ground, it will grow again in the following year. This practice, known as 'ratooning', may be continued for as long as three years, when yields begin to decline. Cane is ready for cutting 12–24 months after planting, depending on local conditions. Much of the world's sugar cane is still cut by hand, but rising costs are hastening the change-

over to mechanical harvesting. The cane is cut as close as possible to the ground, and the top leaves, which may be used as cattle fodder, are removed.

After cutting, the cane is loaded by hand or by machine into trucks or trailers and towed directly to a factory for processing. Sugar cane deteriorates quickly after it has been cut and should be processed as quickly as possible. At the factory the cane passes first through shredding knives or crushing rollers, which break up the hard rind and expose the inner fibre, and then to squeezing rollers, where the crushed cane is subjected to high pressure and sprayed with water. The resulting juice is heated and lime is added for clarification and the removal of impurities. The clean juice is then concentrated in evaporators. This thickened juice is next boiled in steam-heated vacuum pans until a mixture or 'massecuite' of sugar crystals and 'mother syrup' is produced. The massecuite is then spun in centrifugal machines to separate the sugar crystals (raw cane sugar) from the residual syrup (cane molasses).

The production of beet sugar follows the same process, except that the juice is extracted by osmotic diffusion. Its manufacture produces white sugar crystals which do not require further refining. In most producing countries, it is consumed domestically, although the European Union (EU), which accounts for about 15% of total world sugar production, is a net exporter of white refined sugar. Beet sugar accounts for more than one-third of world production. Production data for sugar cane and sugar beet cover generally all crops harvested, except crops grown explicitly for feed. The third table covers the production of raw sugar by the centrifugal process. In the late 1990s global output of non-centrifugal sugar (i.e. produced from sugar cane which has not undergone centrifugation) was about 14m. tons per year.

Most of the world's output of raw cane sugar is sent to refineries outside the country of origin, unless the sugar is for local consumption. Cuba, Thailand, Brazil and India are among the few cane-producers that export part of their output as refined sugar. The refining process furtherpurifies the sugar crystals and eventually results in finished products of various grades, such as granulated, icing or castor sugar. The ratio of refined to raw sugar is usually about 0.9:1.

As well as providing sugar, quantities of cane are grown in some countries for seed, feed, fresh consumption, the manufacture of alcohol and other uses. Molasses may be used as cattle feed or fermented to produce alcoholic beverages for human consumption, such as rum, a distilled spirit manufactured in Caribbean countries. Sugar cane juice may be used to produce

Production of Sugar Cane ('000 metric tons)

	1997	1998
World total	1,246,274*	1,263,191*
Africa	82,016*	84,651*
Leading African producers		
Congo, Dem. Repub.	1,726	1,731
Egypt	13,726	14,353
Ethiopia	1,600*	1,650*
Kenya	4,450*	4,900*
Madagascar	2,160	2,180
Malawi	1,750*	1,750*
Mauritius	5,787	5,781
Réunion	1,910	1,675†
South Africa‡	22,155	22,930
Sudan	5,500*	5,850*
Swaziland	3,694	3,887
Uganda	1,600*	1,550*
Zambia	1,500*	1,650*
Zimbabwe	4,651†	4,786†
Leading non-African producers		
Australia	38,633	39,531
Brazil	337,195	338,480
China, People's Repub.	78,900	83,430
Cuba	43,000*	35,000*
India	277,250	265,000
Mexico	45,220	48,895
Pakistan	41,998	53,104
Thailand	46,874	52,839

* FAO estimate.
† Unofficial figure.
‡ Cane crushed for sugar.

Production of Sugar Beets ('000 metric tons)

	1997	1998
World total	268,082*	259,392*
Africa	3,966	4,916
Leading African producers		
Egypt	1,143	1,951
Morocco	2,555	2,822
Leading non-African producers		
France	34,372	31,156
Germany	25,769	26,787
Turkey	18,553	20,000
Ukraine	17,663	15,523
USA	27,112	29,580

* FAO estimate.

ethyl alcohol (ethanol). This chemical can be mixed with petroleum derivatives to produce fuel for motor vehicles. The steep rise in the price of petroleum after 1973 made the large-scale conversion of sugar cane into alcohol economically attractive (particularly to developing nations), especially as sugar, unlike petroleum, is a renewable source of energy. Several countries developed alcohol production by this means in order to reduce petroleum imports and to support cane growers. The blended fuel used in cars is known as 'gasohol', 'alcogas' or 'green petrol'. The pioneer in this field was Brazil, which operates the largest 'gasohol' production programme in the world. During the late 1990s the use of ethanol by Brazilian motorists rapidly increased, as, despite the additional costs involved in adapting motor vehicles to ethanol consumption, the price of this fuel, which can be mixed with petrol or used in undiluted form, had fallen (owing to high levels of stocks) to less than one-half the price of petrol. In Africa, 'gasohol' plants have been planned or established in Kenya, Malawi, South Africa, Tanzania and Zambia.

After the milling of sugar, the cane has dry fibrous remnants known as bagasse, which is usually burned as fuel in sugar mills but can be pulped and used for making fibreboard, particle board and most grades of paper. As the costs of imported wood pulp have risen, cane-growing regions have turned increasingly to the manufacture of paper from bagasse. A paper mill based on this process has been established in South Africa. In view of rising energy costs, some countries (such as Mauritius) are implementing the use of bagasse as fuel for electricity production to save on foreign exchange from imports of petroleum. Another by-product, cachaza (which had formerly been discarded), is now being utilized as an animal feed.

In recent years sugar has encountered increased competition from other sweeteners, including maize-based products, such as isoglucose (a form of high-fructose corn syrup or HFCS), and chemical additives, such as saccharine, aspartame and xylitol. Aspartame (APM) was the most widely used high-intensity artificial sweetener in the early 1990s, although its market dominance under challenge during the 1990s from sucralose, which is about 600 times as sweet as sugar (compared with 200–300 times for other intense sweeteners) and is more resistant to chemical deterioration than aspartame. In the late 1980s research was being conducted in the USA to formulate means of synthesizing thaumatin, a substance derived from the fruit of a west African plant, *Thaumatoccus daniellii*, which is several thousand times as sweet as sugar. If, as has been predicted, thaumatin can be commercially produced by the year 2000, it could obtain a substantial share of the markets for both sugar and artificial sweeteners. In 1998 the US government approved the domestic marketing of sucralose, the only artificial sweetener made from sugar. Sucralose was stated to avoid many of the taste problems associated with other artificial sweeteners.

South Africa is the principal producer and exporter of sugar in sub-Saharan Africa. In the mid-1990s South Africa ranked as the world's seventh largest sugar exporter. In recent years, however, South Africa has been encountering increased competition from neighbouring countries, in particular Swaziland and Zimbabwe, whose production costs are only about one-third of those of South Africa. It has been forecast that by the end of the 1990s one-third of domestic demand in South Africa will be supplied by these sources. Swaziland is continental Africa's second largest sugar exporter. The majority of the country's

sales of sugar are to countries of the EU, under the terms of quota agreements.

Sugar is the staple product in the economies of Mauritius and Réunion, although output is vulnerable to climatic conditions, as both islands are subject to cyclones. In Mauritius, where an estimated 93% (77,000 ha) of cultivated land is devoted to sugar production, sugar sales accounted for more than 75% of the island's export revenue in 1998 (excluding exports from the Export Processing Zone). In Réunion almost one-half of the island's 63,050 ha of cultivable land is planted with sugar cane, and sales of sugar provided almost 65% of export income in 1997. The expansion of sugar output, however, has been inhibited in recent years by unfavourable weather, and by the pressure on agricultural land use from the increasing demands of road construction and housing.

The Mozambique sugar industry, formerly the country's primary source of foreign exchange, has begun to surmount the effects of many years of disruption and neglect. The resolution of internal civil conflict has made possible the rehabilitation both of cane-growing and of the country's six sugar complexes. In 1999 the Mozambique government was reported to be seeking annual export quotas to the US and EU sugar markets. However, considerable foreign aid and investment is still needed to complete the revitalization of this sector. Sugar is Malawi's third most important export commodity (after tobacco and tea), providing an estimated 7.6% of export earnings (excluding re-exports) in 1995. The development of the sugar sector in Tanzania was undergoing expansion during the 1990s, with the aim of reducing reliance on imports from Malawi and Zambia.

In Sudan one of the world's largest single sugar projects was inaugurated in 1981 at Kenana, south of Khartoum. The Kenana Sugar Co (in which the Sudan government has a 50% share), comprising an estate and processing facilities, has been instrumental in the elimination of sugar import costs, which were, until the mid-1980s, Sudan's single largest import item after petroleum. However, the subsequent imposition by the Sudan government of a regional quota distribution system has led to supply shortages and high prices, and during the 1990s the renewal of Sudan's sugar sector was further impeded by drought, inadequate investment and technical and management problems. Sugar cane grows wild throughout Nigeria, although the country's sugar industry remains largely undeveloped. However, six sugar complexes are planned, and it was hoped that self-sufficiency in sugar will be achieved by the year 2000. In the mean time, Nigeria has emerged as a significant African importer of raw sugar, importing about 980,000 tons in 1998.

The first International Sugar Agreement (ISA) was negotiated in 1958, and its economic provisions operated until 1961. A second ISA did not come into operation until 1969. It included quota arrangements and associated provisions for regulating the price of sugar traded on the open market, and established the International Sugar Organization (ISO) to administer the agreement. However, the USA and the six original members of the EC did not participate in the ISA, and, following its expiry in 1974, it was replaced by a purely administrative interim agreement, which remained operational until the finalization of a third ISA, which took effect in 1978. The new agreement's implementation was supervised by an International Sugar Council (ISC), which was empowered to establish price ranges for sugar-trading and to operate a system of quotas and special sugar stocks. Owing to the reluctance of the USA and European Community (now EU) countries (which were not a party to the agreement) to accept export controls, the ISO ultimately lost most of its power to regulate the market, and since 1984 the activities of the organization have been restricted to recording statistics and providing a forum for discussion between producers and consumers. Subsequent ISA, without effective regulatory powers, have been in operation since 1985. (For detailed information on the successive agreements, see *Africa South of the Sahara 1991*.)

Special arrangements for exports of African sugar exist in the successive Lomé Conventions, in operation since 1975, between the EU and a group of African, Caribbean and Pacific (ACP) countries, whereby a special Protocol on sugar, forming part of each Convention, requires the EU to import specified quantities of raw sugar annually from ACP countries. In June 1998,

60

Production of Centrifugal Sugar (raw value, '000 metric tons)

	1997	1998
World total	127,487*	127,642*
Africa	9,012*	8,949*
Leading African producers		
Egypt	1,230†	1,151†
Ethiopia	186†	197†
Kenya	391	489†
Malawi	195	200*
Mauritius	621	629
Morocco	406	490
Réunion	207	222†
South Africa	2,914	2,676
Sudan	604†	633†
Swaziland	476	511†
Zambia	174†	195†
Zimbabwe	602	595
Leading non-African producers		
Australia	5,732	5,778
Brazil	15,975†	19,232†
China (incl. Taiwan)	9,123†	8,859†
Cuba	4,320†	3,200†
France	5,134†	4,666†
Germany	4,045	4,054
India	14,616	14,232
Mexico	4,544	5,174
Thailand	6,098†	4,314†
USA	7,276	7,372

* FAO estimate.   † Unofficial figure.

however, the EU indicated its intention to phase out preferential sugar prices paid to ACP countries within three years.

In tandem with world output of cane and beet sugars, stock levels are an important factor in determining the prices at which sugar is traded internationally. These stocks, which were at relatively low levels in the late 1980s, increased significantly in the early 1990s, owing partly to the disruptive effects of the Gulf War on demand in the Middle East (normally a major sugar-consuming area), and also as a result of substantially increased production in Mexico and the Far East. Additionally, the output of beet sugar was expected to continue rising, as a result of substantial producers' subsidies within the EU, which, together with Australia, has been increasing the areas under sugar cane and beet. World sugar stocks were reduced in the 1993/94 trading year (September–August). However, record crops in Brazil, India and Thailand led to an increased level of sugar stocks in 1994/95. World sugar stocks continued to rise in 1995/96 and 1996/97, and advanced further in 1997/98, when world-wide consumption of raw sugar totalled about 123m. metric tons, compared with production of 126m. tons. This trend continued in 1998/99, when, according to provisional ISO data, global sugar production reached 133.2m. tons, while consumption totalled 127.8m. tons. Forecasts for 1999/2000, published in July 2000, projected another world sugar surplus, of 1.5m.–1.7m. tons.

Most of the world's sugar output is traded at fixed prices under long-term agreements. On the free market, however, sugar prices often fluctuate with extreme volatility.

Export Price Index for Sugar (base: 1980 = 100)

	Average	Highest month(s)	Lowest month(s)
1990	45		
1995	48		
1997	40	43 (Nov., Dec.)	38 (Jan., Feb.)
1998	32	41 (Jan.)	26 (Sept.)
1999	23	29 (Jan.)	20 (April, July)

In February 1992 the import price of raw cane sugar on the London market was only US $193.0 (equivalent to £107.9 sterling) per metric ton, its lowest level, in terms of US currency, for more than four years. The London price of sugar advanced to $324.9 (£211.9) per ton in May 1993, following predictions of a world sugar deficit in 1992/93. Concurrently, sugar prices in New York were at their highest levels for three years. The London sugar price declined to $237.2 (£157.9) per ton in August 1993, but increased to $370.6 (£237.4) in December 1994.

The rise in sugar prices continued in January 1995, when the London quotation for raw sugar reached US $378.1 (£243.2) per ton, its highest level, in dollar terms, since early 1990. Meanwhile, the London price of white sugar was $426.5 (£274.4) per ton, the highest quotation for four-and-a-half years. The surge in the sugar market was partly a response to forecasts of a supply deficit in the 1994/95 season. Prices later eased, and in April 1995 raw sugar was traded in London at $326.0 (£202.1) per ton. The price recovered to $373.1 (£235.6) per ton in June, but retreated to $281.5 (£179.4) in September.

During the early months of 1996 the London price of raw sugar reached about US $330 per ton. In May the price was reduced to $262.9 (£173.3) per ton, but in July it rose to $321.4 (£206.3), despite continued forecasts of a significant sugar surplus in 1995/96. The sugar price fell to $256.3 (£156.4) per ton in December.

In January 1997 the price of raw sugar declined to US $250.8 (£154.0) per ton, but in August it reached $288.5 (£179.1). In terms of US currency, the London sugar price advanced later in the year, standing at $298.5 (£178.3) per ton in December.

International sugar prices moved generally downward in the first half of 1998. In June, following forecasts that world output of raw sugar in 1997/98 would be significantly higher than in the previous crop year (leading to a further rise in surplus stocks), the London price was reduced to only US $185.0 (£113.1) per ton. In July the quotation for raw sugar recovered to $222.6 (£135.0) per ton, but in September, following forecasts of a higher surplus in 1998/99, the price fell to only $168.8 (£100.2). The sugar price stayed within this range for the remainder of 1998, ending the year at $196.9 (£118.3) per ton. For 1998 as a whole, according to the FAO, developing countries' export earnings from sugar were 22% lower than in the previous year.

In January 1999 the London price of raw sugar reached US $217.2 (£132.4) per ton, but from February the free market was affected by strong downward pressure, as sugar supplies remained plentiful. In April the London sugar price was reduced to only $127.3 (£79.0) per ton, its lowest level, in terms of US currency, since late 1986. Meanwhile, the short-term quotation in the main US sugar market declined to about 4.6 US cents per lb, also a 12-year 'low'. The slump in international sugar prices was partly a consequence of the severe economic problems affecting Russia (normally the world's leading importer of sugar) and countries in eastern Asia. The decline in demand from these areas coincided with high output, as a result of generally favourable growing conditions, in sugar-producing countries. The London price recovered to $166.2 (£105.1) per ton in June 1999, but declined to $131.4 (£84.4) in July. A renewed advance took the price to $184.3 (£111.4) per ton in October. At the end of the year the London sugar quotation stood at $162.4 (£100.8) per ton.

During the early weeks of 2000 the international sugar market was weak, and at the end of February the London price of raw sugar was reduced to US $126.5 (£80.1) per ton, its lowest level, in terms of US currency, for more than 13 years. However, there was subsequently a strong recovery in sugar prices, in response to reports of reductions in output and planting, while demand rose. At the end of July the London quotation was $264.0 (£176.3) per ton. Meanwhile, the New York price of sugar rose during that month to its highest level for more than two years.

The Group of Latin American and Caribbean Sugar Exporting Countries (GEPLACEA), with a membership of 23 Latin American and Caribbean countries, together with the Philippines, and representing about 66% of world cane production and 45% of sugar exports, complements the activities of the ISO (comprising 55 countries, including EU members, in November 1999) as a forum for co-operation and research. The USA withdrew from the ISO in 1992, following a disagreement over the formulation of members' financial contributions. The USA had previously provided about 9% of the ISO's annual budget.

Tea (*Camellia sinensis*)

Tea is a beverage made by infusing in boiling water the dried young leaves and unopened leaf-buds of the tea plant, an evergreen shrub or small tree. Black and green tea are the most common finished products. The former accounts for the bulk of the world's supply and is associated with machine manufacture and, generally, the plantation system, which guarantees an adequate supply of leaf to the factory. The latter, produced mainly in China and Japan, is grown mostly on smallholdings, and much of it is consumed locally. There are two main varieties of tea, the China and the Assam, although hybrids may be obtained, such as Darjeeling. Wherever possible, data on production and trade relate to made tea, i.e. dry, manufactured tea. Where figures have been reported in terms of green (unmanufactured) leaf, appropriate allowances have been made to convert the reported amounts to the approximate equivalent weight of made tea.

Total recorded tea exports by producing countries achieved successive records in each of the years 1983–90. World exports (excluding transactions between former Soviet republics) declined in 1991 and 1992, but increased by 13.5% in 1993. However, the total fell by 10.5% in 1994. Export volume increased again in 1995 and 1996, rising further, to 1,198,759 tons, in 1997. World tea exports reached a new record of 1,290,832 tons in 1998, but eased to 1,217,216 tons in 1999. Global production of tea reached an unprecedented level in 1998, with record crops in all the major producing countries (India, China, Kenya and Sri Lanka). In 1999, however, world output declined (from 2,962,178 tons in 1998) to an estimated 2,844,785 tons, although China and Sri Lanka again reported record crops.

India (the world's largest consumer) and Sri Lanka have traditionally been the two leading tea exporters, with approximately equal sales, but the quantity which they jointly supply has remained fairly stable (350,000 – 425,000 tons per year in 1977–96, advancing to 458,000 tons in 1997). Their joint export sales were estimated to have risen to 468,100 tons in 1998 before easing to 444,000 tons in 1999, so their share of the world tea trade has been in decline. During the 1960s these two countries together exported more than two-thirds of all the tea sold by producing countries, but in 1999 the proportion was 36.5%. From 1990 until 1995, when it was displaced by Kenya (see below), Sri Lanka ranked as the main exporting country. Exports by Sri Lanka again took primacy in 1997, when Kenya's tea sales declined sharply (see below). Sri Lanka remained the principal tea exporter in 1998, despite a strong revival in Kenyan exports, and again in 1999, although tea sales by both countries declined in the latter year. Exports from the People's Republic of China (whose sales include a large proportion of green tea) have exceeded those of India in each year since 1992. Exports of tea by African producers accounted for about one-quarter of world trade during the early 1990s, achieving successive record shipments of 330,041 tons in 1995 and 343,439 tons in 1996 before declining to 318,993 tons in 1997. Record levels of exports were again attained by African teas in 1998, with shipments totalling 386,247 tons, accounting for 29.9% of the world tea trade. African teas accounted for 29.6% of exports in 1999, despite a decline in shipments, to an estimated 359,722 tons.

Prior to its set-back in 1997, Kenya was one of the fastest-growing exporters, ranking fourth in the world during 1975–92, third in 1993, and second in 1994, when its tea exports exceeded those of China. Kenya was the principal world exporter of tea in 1995 and 1996. Conditions of severe drought during the first seven months of 1997 reduced Kenya's position to fourth in terms of world exports, but the expansion of the country's tea sales was resumed in 1998, when Kenya ranked second, after Sri Lanka, with exports of 263,402 tons, accounting for 68.1% of African tea exports and more than 20% of all tea traded internationally. In recent years the conservation of tea supplies by India to satisfy rising domestic consumption has enabled Kenya to replace India as the United Kingdom's principal supplier, providing 42% of British tea imports in 1998. Kenya's tea sales provided 19.9% of its total export receipts in 1996, making tea the country's most valuable export crop. In the late 1990s about 119,000 ha in Kenya were planted with tea.

Malawi, with about 18,800 ha under tea in 1998, is Africa's second largest producer and exporter of tea. Its exports in 1998 totalled 41,000 tons, accounting for almost 11% of all African exports. Prior to the Amin regime and the nationalization of tea plantations in 1972, neighbouring Uganda was second only to Kenya among African producers. Uganda's tea exports were negligible by the early 1980s, but, following agreements between

tea companies and the subsequent Ugandan governments, exports were resumed. There has been a sustained recovery since 1990, when sales of tea totalled only 4,760 tons. In 1994 Uganda's exports of tea comprised the country's highest annual total since 1977. Exports in subsequent years have advanced strongly, reaching 23,355 tons in 1998 and 22,100 tons in 1999. However, Uganda's role in east African tea production has come under challenge from Tanzania, whose level of exports during the 1980s ranged between 10,000–15,000 tons annually. These sales advanced significantly during the 1990s, moving from 20,511 tons in 1995 to 22,218 tons in 1998 and 21,364 tons in 1999. Zimbabwe was Africa's fifth largest exporter of tea in 1999, exporting an estimated 11,500 tons in that year (compared with a record 12,768 tons in 1989, when it ranked third among African tea-exporters). Tea has traditionally been a significant component of exports from Burundi and Rwanda: these sales were estimated at 5,500 tons and 10,872 tons, respectively, in 1999. Since 1997, Rwanda's tea industry has evidenced recovery from the disruption caused by civil unrest during 1993–96.

For many years the United Kingdom was the largest single importer of tea. However, the country's annual consumption of tea per person, which amounted to 4.55 kg in 1958, has declined in recent years, averaging 2.46 kg in 1994–96 and 1995–97, before recovering marginally, to 2.51 kg, in 1996–98. A similar trend has been observed in other developed countries, apart from the Republic of Ireland, the world's largest per caput consumer of tea, where annual consumption per person advanced from 3.17 kg in 1994–96 to 3.23 kg in 1995–97, before evidencing a slight decline, to 2.96 kg, in 1996–98. From the late 1980s consumption and imports expanded significantly in the developing countries (notably Middle East countries) and, particularly, in the USSR, which in 1989 overtook the United Kingdom as the world's principal tea importer. However, internal factors, following the break-up of the USSR in 1991, caused a sharp decline in tea imports by its successor republics; as a result, the United Kingdom regained its position as the leading tea importer in 1992. In 1993 the former Soviet republics (whose own tea production had fallen sharply) again displaced the United Kingdom as the major importer, but in 1994 the United Kingdom was again the principal importing country. Since 1995, however, imports by the former USSR have exceeded those of the United Kingdom. In 1999 the former USSR imported an estimated 184,586 tons of tea, accounting for 15.6% of the world market, followed by the United Kingdom, with 137,314 tons (11.6%), Pakistan (107,708 tons, or 9.1%) and the USA (92,865 tons, or 7.9%). Other major importers of tea in 1999 were Egypt, Japan, Iraq and Morocco.

Much of the tea traded internationally is sold by auction, principally in the exporting countries. Until declining volumes

Production of Made Tea ('000 metric tons)

	1998	1999
World total	2,962.2*	2,844.8*
Africa	445.7*	392.2*
Leading African producers		
Kenya	294.2	248.8
Malawi	40.4	38.5
Rwanda	14.9	13.0
South Africa	10.8	10.6
Tanzania	24.3	23.5
Uganda	26.4	24.7
Zimbabwe	17.8	17.0*
Leading non-African producers		
China, People's Repub.[1]	665.0	675.9
India[2]	870.4*	805.6*
Indonesia[3]	166.8*	165.4*
Japan[4]	82.6	88.5
Sri Lanka	280.7	283.8
Turkey	177.8	170.6

* Provisional.

[1] Mainly green tea (480,211 tons in 1998; 496,986 tons in 1999).
[2] Including a small quantity of green tea (8,616 tons in 1998; about 8,500 tons in 1999).
[3] Including green tea (about 38,000 tons in 1998; about 37,000 tons in 1999).
[4] All green tea.

Source: International Tea Committee, *Supplement to Annual Bulletin of Statistics 1999.*

Export Price Index for Tea (base: 1980 = 100)

	Average	Highest month(s)	Lowest month(s)
1990	127		
1995	181		
1997	237	281 (Dec.)	199 (Feb.)
1998	260	308 (Feb.)	225 (May)
1999	243	269 (Oct.)	227 (June)

brought about their termination in June 1998 (Kenya having withdrawn in 1997, and a number of other exporters, including Malawi and Tanzania, having established their own auctions), the weekly London auctions had formed the centre of the international tea trade. At the London auctions, five categories of tea were offered for sale: 'low medium' (based on a medium Malawi tea), 'medium' (based on a medium Assam and Kenyan tea), 'good medium' (representing an above-average East African tea), 'good' (referring to teas of above-average standard) and (from April 1994) 'best available'. The average price of all grades of tea sold at London auctions stood at £1,238 sterling per metric ton in 1993, but fell to £1,192 per ton in 1994 and to £1,036 per ton in 1995. The annual average price in 1995 was the lowest since 1988. The average rose to £1,135 per ton in 1996 and to £1,351 in 1997. For the first half of 1998, before the auctions ceased, the average price realized was £1,458 per ton. During 1993 the monthly average reached £1,564 per ton in January, but declined to £1,100 in June and recovered to £1,256 in November. The average was £1,102 per ton in January 1994, but rose to £1,284 in June and September. Quotations then moved generally lower, and in July 1995 the average London tea price was only £907.5 per ton, its lowest monthly level since August 1988. At one auction in September 1995 the price of 'medium' tea was reduced to only £780 per ton, its lowest level, even in nominal terms (i.e. without taking inflation into account), since 1976. The monthly average increased to £1,170.5 per ton in December 1995, but fell to £1,031 in July 1996. It moved generally higher in later months, reaching £1,528 per ton in August 1997, following reports that drought had reduced Kenya's tea crop. After easing somewhat, the average London price of tea rose in January 1998 to £1,905 per ton (its highest monthly level since March 1985), in response to news of serious flooding in eastern Africa. At one of that month's auctions the price of 'medium' tea reached £2,000 per ton, its highest level since 1985. However, the average London tea price retreated in May 1998 to £1,014 per ton. At the end of June, with the prospect of a record Kenyan crop, the quotation for 'medium' tea at the final London auction was £980 per ton. Based on country of origin, the highest-priced tea at London auctions during 1989–94 was that from Rwanda, which realized an average of £1,613 per ton in the latter year. The quantity of tea sold at these auctions declined from 43,658 tons in 1990 to 11,208 tons in 1997.

The main tea auctions in Africa are the weekly sales at Mombasa, Kenya. In contrast to London, volumes traded at the Mombasa auctions moved generally upward during the 1990s, and Mombasa is now one of the world's major centres for the international tea trade. The tea sold at Mombasa is mainly from Kenya, but smaller amounts from Tanzania, Uganda and other African producers are also traded. Total annual sales at the Mombasa auctions increased from 173,575 metric tons in 1995 to 189,800 tons in 1996. Owing to Kenya's drought, the total declined in 1997 to 166,618 tons. In 1998, however, volume rose to a record 243,566 tons (including 212,620 tons from Kenya). During the first half of 1999 sales reached 112,455 tons, compared with 131,147 tons in the corresponding period of the previous year. Meanwhile, average prices per ton in Mombasa rose from US $1,290 in 1995 to $1,420 in 1996 and to $2,000 in 1997. They eased to $1,890 per ton in 1998. On a monthly basis, the average Mombasa price of tea advanced from $1,380 per ton in July 1996 to $2,027 in May 1997. After some fluctuation, the monthly average increased to $2,817 per ton in February 1998, although it retreated to $1,544 in May. The market later rallied again, and in July 1999 'good medium' tea was traded in Mombasa at about $1,960 per ton.

An International Tea Agreement (ITA), signed in 1933 by the governments of India, Ceylon (now Sri Lanka) and the Netherlands East Indies (now Indonesia), established the International Tea Committee (ITC), based in London, as an administrative body. Although ITA operations ceased after 1955, the ITC has continued to function as a statistical and information centre. In late 1999 there were six producer/exporter members (the tea boards or associations of Kenya, Malawi, India, Indonesia, Bangladesh and Sri Lanka), four consumer members and six associate members.

In 1969 the FAO Consultative Committee on Tea was formed and an exporters' group, meeting under this committee's auspices, set export quotas in an attempt to stabilize tea prices. These quotas have applied since 1970 but are generally regarded as too liberal to have any significant effect on prices. The perishability of tea complicates the effective operation of a buffer stock, while African countries are opposed to quota arrangements and are committed to the maximum expansion of tea cultivation. India, while opposed to the revival of a formal ITA to regulate supplies and prices, has advocated greater co-operation between producers to regulate the market. The International Tea Promotion Association (ITPA), founded in 1979 and based in Nairobi, Kenya, comprises eight countries (excluding, however, India and Sri Lanka), accounting for almost one-third of the world's exports of black tea. In 1995 representatives of the tea industries of Bangladesh, China, India, Indonesia, Iran, Sri Lanka and Malawi announced their intention of forming an association of tea producers. It was hoped that Kenya would subsequently join.

Tobacco (*Nicotiana tabacum*)

Tobacco originated in South America and was used in rituals and ceremonials or as a medicine; it was smoked and chewed for centuries before its introduction into Europe in the 16th century. The generic name *Nicotiana* denotes the presence of the alkaloid nicotine in its leaves. The most important species in commercial tobacco cultivation is *N. tabacum*. Another species, *N. rustica*, is widely grown, but on a smaller scale, to yield cured leaf for snuff or simple cigarettes and cigars.

Production of Tobacco Leaves (farm sales weight, '000 metric tons)

	1997	1998
World total	8,949*	6,908*
Africa	546*	560*
Leading African producers		
Côte d'Ivoire	10*	10*
Kenya	10†	10*
Malawi	158	125
Morocco	9	11
South Africa	27	32
Tanzania	51	45*
Zimbabwe	215	260
Leading non-African producers		
Brazil	620	510
China, People's Repub.	4,251	2,364
Greece	137	137
India	599	635†
Indonesia	137	138
Italy	131	131*
Turkey	286	262
USA	811	671

* FAO estimate.   † Unofficial figure.

Commercially grown tobacco (from *N. tabacum*) can be divided into four major types—flue-cured, air-cured (including burley, cigar, light and dark), fire-cured and sun-cured (including oriental)—depending on the procedures used to dry or 'cure' the leaves. Each system imparts specific chemical and smoking characteristics to the cured leaf, although these may also be affected by other factors, such as the type of soil on which the crop is grown, the type and quantity of fertilizer applied to the crop, the cultivar used, the spacing of the crop in the field and the number of leaves left at topping (the removal of the terminal growing point). Each type is used, separately or in combination, in specific products (e.g. flue-cured in Virginia cigarettes). All types are grown in Africa.

As in other major producing areas, local research organizations in Africa have developed new cultivars with specific desirable chemical characteristics, disease-resistance properties and improved yields. The principal tobacco research centres are in

Zimbabwe, Malawi and South Africa. In recent years, efforts have been made to develop low-cost sources of tobacco in Tanzania and, more recently, in Swaziland and Mozambique.

In Zimbabwe, Malawi, South Africa and, to a lesser extent, in Zambia and Tanzania, tobacco is grown mainly as a direct-labour crop on large farms, some capable of producing as much as 250 metric tons of cured leaf per year. In other parts of Africa, however, tobacco is a smallholders' crop, with each farmer cultivating, on average, 1 or 2 ha of tobacco as well as essential food crops and, usually, other cash crops. Emphasis has been placed on improving yields by the selection of cultivars, by the increased use of fertilizers, by the reduction of crop loss (through the use of crop chemicals) and by reducing hand-labour requirements through the mechanization of land-preparation and the use of crop chemicals. Where small farmers are responsible for producing the crop, harvesting remains a manual operation, as the area under tobacco and their limited financial means preclude the adoption of mechanical harvesting devices.

The principal type of tobacco commercially cultivated in Africa is flue-cured, of which Malawi and Zimbabwe are the dominant regional producers. The tobacco sector normally accounts for about 47% of Zimbabwe's total agricultural earnings and has in recent years provided about 22% of foreign revenue. The Zimbabwean tobacco crop, of which 98% is exported, is highly regarded for its quality and flavour, and its marketability has been assisted by its relatively low tar content. Nevertheless, depressed conditions in international tobacco markets in the early 1990s were encouraging some Zimbabwean growers to switch to cotton cultivation. In 1998 tobacco sales accounted for 25% of the country's export revenues. During the 1990s Zimbabwe officially encouraged small-scale producers of burley and flue-cured tobaccos. In 1999, however, Zimbabwean tobacco plantings declined by about 8%, reflecting an accumulation in world levels of stocks held by manufacturers. In the following year, the country's tobacco sector was further overshadowed by political and agrarian unrest.

In the mid-1990s Malawi obtained up to 70% of its export revenue from the sale of its tobacco, principally the flue-cured, fire-cured and burley varieties. Malawi is the only significant African producer of burley tobacco, which accounts for about 15% of world exports. Production was limited to commercial estates, but since the early 1990s the government has encouraged its cultivation by smallholders, in order to promote a more equitable distribution of agricultural incomes. Demand for burley tobacco has been stimulated by increased manufacturers' emphasis on low-tar cigarettes. In the late 1990s Malawi tobacco growers were being encouraged to diversify into cotton cultivation.

Export Price Index for Tobacco (base: 1980 = 100)

	Average	Highest month(s)	Lowest month(s)
1990	125		
1995	132		
1997	136	139 (Dec.)	133 (Jan.)
1998	140	142 (April–Dec.)	136 (Jan.–March)
1999	141	142 (Jan.–March)	139 (April, May)

Tanzania contributes a small but significant quantity of flue-cured tobacco to the world market. Tobacco production in Nigeria is fairly static, and its flue-cured crop is entirely reserved for local consumption. Kenya has greatly increased its output of flue-cured leaf since commencing tobacco exports in 1984, and tobacco cultivation has recently been increasing in importance in Uganda, as part of a government programme to offset declining earnings from coffee. There are small but increasingly important exports of flue-cured tobacco from Sierra Leone, and small-scale Tanzanian growers are expanding their output of flue-cured tobacco. Nigeria, Malawi and South Africa account for the African crop of sun- and air-cured types of tobacco. Modest quantities of oriental tobacco are cultivated in Malawi and South Africa.

The USA is the world's principal tobacco-exporting country. The average value of US exports of unmanufactured tobacco was US $6,240 per metric ton in 1993, $6,580 per ton in 1994 and $6,673 per ton in 1995. The country's total earnings from such exports were $1,404m. in 1995. At the end of 1997 tobacco

prices in Zimbabwe, Africa's leading exporter, were 40% lower than at the start of the year.

The International Tobacco Growers' Association (ITGA), with headquarters in Portugal, was formed in 1984 by growers' groups in Argentina, Brazil, Canada, Malawi, the USA and Zimbabwe. The ITGA now includes 22 countries, accounting for more than 80% of the world's internationally traded tobacco. The ITGA provides a forum for the exchange of information among tobacco producers, conducts research and publishes studies on tobacco issues.

Uranium

Uranium occurs in a variety of ores, often in association with other minerals such as gold, phosphate and copper, and may be mined by open-cast, underground or *in situ* leach methods, depending on the circumstances. The concentration of uranium that is needed to form an economic mineral deposit varies widely, depending upon its geological setting and physical location. Average ore grades at operating uranium mines vary from 0.03% U to as high as 15% U, but are most frequently less than 1% U. South Africa produces uranium concentrates as a by-product of gold mining and copper mining, and possesses uranium conversion and enrichment facilities. Both copper mining and the exploitation of phosphates by wet (phosphoric acid-yielding) processes offer a more widespread potential for by-product uranium production.

Uranium is principally used as a fuel in nuclear reactors for the production of electricity. In 1999 435 nuclear power plants generated approximately 17% of the world's electricity. Enriched uranium is used as fuel in most nuclear power stations and in the manufacture of nuclear weapons. In the latter, however, the abandonment of East–West confrontation and the prospect of significant nuclear disarmament is likely to reverse the process, with the release of substantial quantities of uranium. In 1995 a report by the OECD's Nuclear Energy Agency and the International Atomic Energy Agency estimated that probable economic reserves of uranium (excluding those in the former Eastern bloc countries and the People's Republic of China) totalled 2.2m. tons.

Because of uranium's strategic military value, there was intense prospecting activity in the 1940s and 1950s, but the market was later depressed as government purchase programmes ceased. Uranium demand fell in the late 1960s and early 1970s, until industrialized countries responded to the 1973–74 petroleum crisis by intensifying their civil nuclear power programmes. Anticipated strong demand for rapidly expanding nuclear power further improved the uranium market until the early 1980s, when lower than expected growth in electricity consumption forced nuclear power programmes to be restricted, leaving both producers and consumers with high levels of accumulated stocks requiring liquidation. A number of mining operations were also scaled down or closed. The market was further depressed in the late 1980s, in the aftermath of the accident in 1986 at the Chernobyl nuclear plant in Ukraine (then part of the USSR). At the end of 1999 there were 29 new reactors under construction. Significant growth in nuclear power programmes was notable in the Far East, especially in the People's Republic of China, Japan, the Republic of Korea and Taiwan. Following nine consecutive years of reduced output, uranium production achieved modest advances in each year during 1995–97. The total of 33,932 tons in 1998, however, represented only about 55% of annual nuclear reactor requirements, necessitating recourse to inventories to meet a significant portion of world demand. Although uranium from dismantled nuclear weapons could satisfy some of the forecast increase in demand, there is uncertainty as to the timing and likely quantities of uranium that might come from this source. Nuclear electricity generating capacity has been forecast to grow at an annual compound rate of about 1% during the period 2000–05. Annual world demand will, according to projections by the Uranium Institute, rise to 64,000 tons by 2005, from 61,000 tons in 2000.

Canada, which accounts for about one-third of world uranium production, is expected to remain the leading producer into the 21st century. South Africa has Africa's largest identified uranium resources (estimated at 241,000 metric tons), followed by Niger (with ore reserves of about 166,000 tons), Namibia

Production of Uranium (uranium content of ores, metric tons)

	1997	1998
World total	35,692	33,932
Africa	7,974	8,186
African producers		
Gabon	472	731
Namibia	2,905	2,762
Niger	3,497	3,731
South Africa	1,100	962
Leading non-African producers		
Australia	5,520	4,885
Canada	12,029	10,924
Kazakhstan	1,000	1,250
Russia	2,000	2,000
USA	2,270	1,872
Uzbekistan	1,764	2,000

Source: Uranium Institute.

(97,000 tons) and Gabon (15,000 tons). Uranium production has been an important component of the South African mining industry since uranium extraction began in 1951, with production reaching a record 6,146 tons in 1980. Production has subsequently declined sharply, and South Africa has been supplanted by Niger as the continent's main producer. In 1997 Niger ranked as the world's third largest producer, and fourth largest exporter, of uranium. Deliveries of ore from the world's largest open-pit uranium mine, at Rössing in Namibia, began in 1976. Output exceeded its planned level in 1980, but subsequently declined, owing to a reduction in demand and increased competition from low-cost producers. The removal of sanctions against Namibian uranium, following that country's independence from South Africa in 1990, coincided with a decline in world demand.

Uranium exploration in Niger started in the 1950s, around the Aïr mountains near Agadez, with production commencing at the Arlit mine in 1971. Niger also has a uranium mine at Akouta, where production commenced in 1978, and there are several other sites awaiting development. France purchases most of Niger's uranium production, with the remainder taken by German, Japanese and Spanish customers. Like Namibia, Niger was compelled in the early 1990s to restructure and streamline its uranium operations, and output has subsequently risen. Gabon, which commenced uranium production in 1958, possesses six identified deposits containing sufficient reserves to support 30 years' output at production rates achieved during the mid-1990s. However, the depressed level of uranium prices in the late 1990s, with little prospect of recovery in the short term, prompted French interests, exploiting the deposits in conjunction with the government of Gabon, to terminate uranium-mining operations there from early 1999, leaving Namibia, Niger and South Africa as the only regional producers.

Uranium has also been found in Algeria, Botswana, the Central African Republic, Chad, the Democratic Republic of the Congo, Egypt, Guinea, Madagascar, Mali, Mauritania, Morocco, Nigeria, Somalia, Tanzania, Togo and Zambia. However, in view of conditions in the world uranium market in the mid-1990s, it was uncertain if any of these deposits would be exploited in the immediate future.

The European market price for uranium oxide reached US $8.75 per lb in October 1992, but was reduced to $8.00 per lb in November and to $7.90 in December. Market conditions remained depressed in 1993, with the price moving steadily downward to $7.00 per lb in July. It fell to $6.90 per lb in August and was maintained at that level for the remainder of the year. The price of uranium oxide was adjusted to $7.00 per lb in January 1994, and to $7.10 in July. The latter remained in effect until October, when the price was reduced to $7.00 per lb again. It was increased to $7.15 per lb in December.

From the beginning of 1995 the price of uranium oxide continued to rise. In a series of upward movements, the price per lb moved from US $7.20 in January to $10.00 in December. The price was maintained at $10.00 per lb for three months, but in March 1996 it was increased to $13.00. Further rises followed, with the price per lb advancing incrementally to $15.50 in August. The surge in prices was attributed to steady demand and to the depletion of uranium stocks. The price of $15.50 per lb was maintained until the end of September, after which the uranium market went into a steep decline. At the end of the year the price of uranium oxide stood at $14.00 per lb.

During the first half of 1997 there was a steady series of reductions in the price of uranium oxide, with low volumes of material being traded. The price per lb declined to US $13 in February, to $12 in April and to $10 at the end of June. The uranium price was reduced to $9.70 per lb in July and to $9.20 in August. It rose to $9.65 per lb in November and stayed at that level for the remainder of the year. The average uranium price on the 'spot' market (for prompt delivery) in 1997 was $12.05 per lb, compared with $15.62 in 1996.

In early 1998 the price of uranium oxide remained at $9.65 per lb. After a renewed decrease, it stood at $9.20 per lb again in May. The final quotation of the year was $8.75 per lb, but in January 1999 the price was increased to $8.85. The uranium price was maintained at this level until March, when it was reduced to $8.50 per lb. After remaining unchanged for more than three months, the price was twice reduced in July, falling to $8.20 per lb. The price of uranium remained at this level until November, when it was reduced to $7.75 per lb.

In January 2000 the price of uranium oxide stood at US $7.60 per lb. A further series of reductions followed, with the price falling to $7.50 per lb in February, to $7.40 in March and to £$7.25 in April. The uranium price declined in May to only $7.00 per lb: its lowest level since November 1994.

The Uranium Institute—the International Association for Nuclear Energy—comprises mining companies, electricity utilities and nuclear fuel processors and traders from 20 countries in Europe, North America, Asia, Africa and Australia. Founded in 1975 to promote the use of uranium for peaceful purposes, the Institute organizes meetings, conducts research, and disseminates information on uranium production and the nuclear fuel industry.

Wheat (*Triticum*)

The most common species of wheat (*T. vulgare*) includes hard, semi-hard and soft varieties which have different milling characteristics but which, in general, are suitable for bread-making. Another species, *T. durum,* is grown mainly in semi-arid areas, including north Africa and the Mediterranean. This wheat is very hard and is suitable for the manufacture of semolina. In north Africa, in addition to being used for making local bread, semolina is the basic ingredient of pasta and couscous. A third species, spelt (*T. spelta*), is also included in production figures for wheat. It is grown in very small quantities in parts of Europe and is used as animal feed.

Although a most adaptable crop, wheat does not thrive in hot and humid climates. Africa's wheat production is mainly concentrated in a narrow strip along the Mediterranean coast from Morocco to Tunisia, in the Nile valley, and in parts of South Africa. Zimbabwe, Kenya, Ethiopia and Sudan also grow limited quantities, but very little is grown in west Africa. In contrast with some developing countries of Asia, the potential of improved wheat varieties has yet to be realized in much of Africa, especially south of the Sahara. One reason is the undeveloped state of the transport systems in many countries, which hinders both the distribution of production inputs (e.g. seeds and fertilizers) and the marketing of farmers' surplus produce. Until recently, many governments have also been unwilling to pay sufficiently attractive producer prices to encourage farmers to grow wheat for marketing.

Wheat production in sub-Saharan Africa averages about 5m. tons annually. It is principally grown in the south and east of the region, often at high altitudes where conditions are less humid. South Africa is the main regional producer, but its output, which is no longer protected by tariffs from overseas imports, is tending to decline. Its annual production averages about 2m. tons. Ethiopia is the second largest regional producer, averaging about 1.5m. tons annually. Improved fertilizer inputs stimulated output in the late 1990s, although its productive potential is constrained by insecurity of land tenure and lack of good seed supplies. In some other wheat-producing countries (e.g. Tanzania and Zimbabwe) the crop is grown mainly on large commercial farms, and, with the benefit of irrigation, usually yields well. Efforts to produce wheat in tropical countries, such as the Democratic Republic of the Congo and Nigeria, have not as yet been successful.

World wheat production increased during the 1990s at an average rate of 1% a year, much less than in previous decades. The fall was largely due to the sharp decline in agricultural output in the former USSR, excluding which the trend in world production growth has been about 1.5% per year. Wheat production is highly variable from year to year. Part of the variation is due to weather conditions, particularly rainfall, in the main producing regions, but national producer-support policies are also a major influence. During the 1990s several major wheat-producing countries, including leading exporters, pursued policies of market deregulation, and began to dismantle support arrrangements for the production of particular crops. This has encouraged farmers more readily to switch between crops according to their expectation of relative market returns. After 1996, for example, when wheat was in short supply on world markets, output was stimulated in many growing areas, and a record 610m. tons was harvested in 1997. Unfavourable weather conditions in a number of countries, reduced output to 587m. tons in 1998, but, owing to low growth in consumption, exporting countries' stocks remained high, and farmers' returns fell. This discouraged plantings for the 1999 season, when production totalled only 584m. tons.

On average, 72% of world wheat production is used for human food, and between 15% and 20% for animal feed. Feed use is variable, depending on the amount of sub-standard wheat which is produced each season, and also the relationship between wheat prices and those of feed grains, especially maize. Of approximately 430m. tons of wheat consumed annually as food, developing countries account for 70%, a share which continues to increase. North Africa is an important wheat consuming region, but in sub-Saharan Africa consumption is mostly restricted to the larger towns and cities. Wheat use in the region amounts to some 12m. tons a year (2% of the world total).

Production of Wheat ('000 metric tons)

	1998	1999*
World total	586,830	583,217
Africa	18,540	15,510
Leading African producers		
Algeria	2,000	1,500
Egypt	6,100	6,300
Ethiopia	1,450	1,400
Kenya	270	300
Morocco	4,400	2,150
South Africa	1,700	1,520
Sudan	630	200
Tunisia	1,350	1,400
Zimbabwe	270	310
Leading non-African producers		
Argentina	11,500	14,700
Australia	22,100	22,800
Canada	24,100	26,900
China, People's Repub.	109,700	115,000
France	39,800	37,100
Germany	20,200	19,570
India	65,900	71,000
Pakistan	18,700	17,850
Russia	27,000	31,000
Turkey	18,500	16,500
Ukraine	14,940	13,800
United Kingdom	15,500	14,700
USA	69,400	62,700

* Provisional.

Sources: International Grains Council; FAO, *Quarterly Bulletin of Statistics*.

Wheat is the principal cereal in international trade. Amounts exported in recent years have ranged between 95m. and 100m. tons annually, of which about 10m. tons was in the form of wheat flour, 6m.–7m. tons durum wheat and semolina, up to 3m. tons of feed wheat, and the remainder wheat of bread-making quality (some of which, however, was used to make other food products, such as noodles). The main exporters are the USA (which accounts for about one-third of the total), the European Union (EU), Canada, Australia and Argentina. Developed countries were formerly the main markets, but the role of developing countries as importers has been steadily increasing, now accounting for about 80% of world trade. Africa's

imports have recently averaged about 25m. tons per year. Most of this is accounted for by North Africa, where Egypt and Algeria are regularly among the world's largest wheat importing countries. Imports by sub-Saharan Africa average about 7m. tons annually. Most countries in the region import at least small amounts (often including wheat or flour supplied as food aid) but the only markets averaging over 0.5m. tons are Nigeria, South Africa and Sudan.

A lengthy period of low international wheat prices, and heavily subsidized competition among the major exporting countries, was interrupted in 1995–96 after exporting countries' stocks had fallen to their lowest levels for 20 seasons. Prices rose to record levels, but the resultant stimulus to output led to a rapid accumulation of stocks, and by 1998 prices were again very low as competition intensified between exporting countries. Because direct export subsidies were limited under international trade agreements, much of this competition took the form of offers of credit to importing countries.

Export Price Index for Wheat (base: 1980 = 100)

	Average	Highest month(s)	Lowest month(s)
1990	82		
1995	94		
1997	84	93 (April)	76 (Dec.)
1998	69	75 (Feb., March)	61 (Aug., Sept.)
1999	64	70 (Jan.)	61 (July, Dec.)

The export price (f.o.b. Gulf ports) of US No. 2 Hard Winter, one of the most widely-traded wheat varieties, stood at around US $140 per metric ton in mid-1994. At that time, countries benefiting from export subsidies (e.g. much of North Africa) could expect to buy wheat for at least $40 per ton less. The peak, reached in April 1996, was almost $300 per ton, but by mid-1997 the price had fallen by up to 50%, to around $150 per ton. Subdued import demand, and the disposal of surpluses by a number of countries in Central and Eastern Europe, as well as by Ukraine, further depressed prices in late 1997. Markets remained subdued in 1998 and early 1999, as a consequence of high levels of export stocks and a lack of new markets. In June 1999 US Hard Winter varieties were being traded at the US Gulf at $110 per ton. At the close of 1999 the price fell to around $105 per ton, although a measure of recovery took place in the early months of 2000, in response to uncertainty regarding crop prospects in the USA, together with some revival in import demand.

Since 1949 nearly all world trade in wheat has been conducted under the auspices of successive international agreements, administered by the International Wheat Council (IWC) in London. The early agreements involved regulatory price controls and supply and purchase obligations, but such provisions became inoperable in more competitive market conditions, and were abandoned in 1972. The IWC subsequently concentrated on providing detailed market assessments to its members and encouraging them to confer on matters of mutual concern. A new Grains Trade Convention, which entered into force in July 1995, allows for improvements in the provision of information on all grains to members of the International Grains Council (IGC, the successor to the IWC), and enhances opportunities for consultations. In early 2000 the IGC had nine exporting members and 23 importing members. African members, all of which are importers, comprise Algeria, Côte d'Ivoire, Egypt, Kenya, Mauritius, Morocco, South Africa and Tunisia.

Since 1967 a series of Food Aid Conventions, linked to the successive Wheat and Grains Trade Conventions, have ensured continuity of supplies of food aid in the form of cereals to needy countries. Under the latest Convention, negotiated in 1999, the 23 donor countries have pledged to supply a minimum of some 5m. tons of food aid annually to developing countries, priority being given to least-developed countries and other low-income food-importing countries. Aid is to be provided mostly in the form of cereals, and all aid given to least-developed countries is to be in the form of grants. The Convention seeks to improve the effectiveness, and increase the impact, of food aid by improved monitoring and consultative procedures. During the late 1990s, donors' cereal shipments under the Food Aid Convention (FAC), 1995, averaged about 5m. tons per year, nearly one-third of which was sent to sub-Saharan Africa. Ethiopia, Rwanda, Angola and Mozambique were regularly among the main beneficiaries of the FAC.

ACKNOWLEDGEMENTS

We gratefully acknowledge the assistance of the following organizations in the preparation of this section:

African Groundnut Council
Association of Coffee Producing Countries
Association of Iron Ore Exporting Countries
British-American Tobacco Co
Central Selling Organisation
Centro Internacional de Agricultura Tropical
Cobalt Information Centre
Copper Development Association
De Beers
Food and Agricultural Organization of the UN
Gill & Duffus Group PLC
Gold Fields Mineral Services Ltd
Institute of Petroleum
International Cocoa Organization
International Coffee Organization
International Copper Study Group

International Cotton Advisory Committee
International Grains Council
International Institute for Cotton
International Iron and Steel Institute
International Monetary Fund
International Primary Aluminium Institute
International Rice Research Institute
International Sugar Organization
International Tea Committee
International Tobacco Growers' Association
Johnson Matthey PLC
Malaysian Oil Palm Growers' Council
United Nations Conference on Trade and Development
US Department of Energy
US Geological Survey
Uranium Institute
World Bureau of Metal Statistics

Source for Agricultural Production Tables (unless otherwise indicated): FAO, *Quarterly Bulletin of Statistics* (Rome, 1999).
Source for Export Price Indexes: UN, *Monthly Bulletin of Statistics*, issues to July 2000.

RESEARCH INSTITUTES

ASSOCIATIONS AND INSTITUTIONS STUDYING AFRICA

See also Regional Organizations in Part II

ARGENTINA

Facultad de Filosofía y Letras, Sección Interdisciplinaria de Estudios de Asia y Africa: 25 de Mayo 221, 4° piso, 1002 Buenos Aires; tel. (1) 334-7612; fax (1) 343-2733; f. 1982; multidisciplinary seminars and lectures; Dir Prof. MARÍA ELENA VELA; publs include *Temas de Africa y Asia* (2 a year).

Nigeria House: Galerías Boston, Florida 142, Local 3, 1337 Buenos Aires; tel. (1) 326-5543; fax (1) 827-3887; f. 1965; library specializing in Nigerian material and general information on Africa; Dir EMILIA MARÍA SANNAZZARI.

AUSTRALIA

Australian Institute of International Affairs: 32 Thesiger Court, Deakin, ACT 2600; tel. (2) 62822133; fax (2) 62852334; e-mail ceo@aiia.asn.au; internet www.aiia.asn.au; f. 1933; 1,800 mems; brs in all States; Pres. NEAL BLEWETT; publs include *Australian Journal of International Affairs* (3 a year).

Indian Ocean Centre for Peace Studies: University of Western Australia, Nedlands, WA 6009; tel. (8) 9380-2278; fax (8) 9380-1060; f. 1991; Contact Dr SAMINA YASMEEN; publ. *Indian Ocean Review* (quarterly).

AUSTRIA

Afro-Asiatisches Institut in Wien (Afro-Asian Institute in Vienna): 1090 Vienna, Türkenstrasse 3; tel. (1) 3105145; fax (1) 3105145-312; f. 1959; cultural and other exchanges between Austria and African and Asian countries; assistance to students from Africa and Asia; economic and social research; lectures, seminars; Pres. Rector PETRUS BSTEH; Gen. Sec. Dr BRIGETTE PROKSCH.

Österreichische Forschungsstiftung für Entwicklungshilfe (Austrian Foundation for Development Research): 1090 Vienna, Berggasse 7; tel. (1) 3174010; fax (1) 3174015; f. 1967; documentation and information on devt aid and developing countries, particularly in relation to Austria; library of 35,000 vols and 250 periodicals; publs include *Ausgewählte neue Literatur zur Entwicklungspolitik* (2 a year), *Österreichische Entwicklungspolitik* (annually).

Österreichische Gesellschaft für Aussenpolitik und Internationale Beziehungen (Austrian Society for Foreign Policy and International Relations): 1010 Vienna, Hofburg/Schweizerhof; tel. (1) 5354627; fax (1) 5322605; f. 1958; lectures, discussions; c. 400 mems; Pres. Dr WOLFGANG SCHALLENBERG; publ. *Österreichisches Jahrbuch für Internationale Politik* (annually).

Österreichisches Institut für Entwicklungshilfe und Technische Zusammenarbeit mit den Entwicklungsländern (Austrian Institute for Development Aid and Technical Co-operation with the Developing Countries): 1010 Vienna, Wipplingerstrasse 35; tel. (1) 426504; f. 1963; projects for management training; Pres Dr HANS INGLER, ERICH HOFSTETTER.

BELGIUM

Académie Royale des sciences d'outre-mer/Koninklijke Academie voor Overzeese Wetenschappen: rue Defacqz 1, Boîte 3, 1000 Brussels; tel. (2) 538-02-11; fax (2) 539-23-53; e-mail kaowarsom@skynet.be; f. 1928; the promotion of scientific knowledge of overseas areas, especially those with special devt problems; 114 mems, 86 assoc. mems, 97 corresp. mems; Perm. Sec. Prof. Y. VERHASSELT.

Afrika Instituut/Institut africain (ASDOC/CEDAF): c/o Africa Museum, Leuvensesteenweg 13, 3080 Tervuren; tel. (2) 768-19-93; fax (2) 768-19-95; e-mail esimons@africamuseum.be; f. 1970; research and documentation on African social and economic problems, with special reference to Burundi, Rwanda and the Dem. Repub. of the Congo; Dir G. DE VILLERS; publ. *Cahiers Africains–Afrika Studies* (6 a year).

Bibliothèque africaine: 19 rue des Petites Carmes, 1000 Brussels; tel. (2) 501-80-98; fax (2) 501-37-36; f. 1885; library of 500,000 vols; large collections in the fields of African history, ethnography, economics, politics; Dir M. E. DE VLEESHOUWER.

Centre international des langues, littératures et traditions d'Afrique au service du développement (CILTADE): ave des Clos 30, 1348 Louvain-la-Neuve; tel. (32) 45-06-65; fax (32) 45-56-85; e-mail nzuji@acla.ucl.ac.be; Dir Dr CLÉMENTINE MADIYA FAÏK-NZUJI.

College voor de Ontwikkelingslanden–Institute of Development Policy and Management: University of Antwerp–RUCA, Middelheimlaan 1, 2020 Antwerp; tel. (3) 218-06-60; fax (3) 218-06-66; e-mail frima@ruca.ua.ac.be; internet www.ruca.ua.ac.be/college; f. 1920; conducts postgraduate study courses; library and documentation centre; Pres. Prof. Dr D. VAN DEN BULCKE; publs research reports and papers (irregular).

Fondation pour favoriser les recherches scientifiques en Afrique: 1 rue Defacqz, BP 5, 1050 Brussels; tel. (2) 269-39-05; f. 1969 to conduct scientific research in Africa with special reference to environmental management and conservation; Dir Dr A. G. ROBYNS; publs *Exploration des Parcs nationaux, Etudes du Continent africain.*

Institut d'études du développement: Université catholique de Louvain, Dépt des sciences de la population et du développement, 1 place des Doyens, 1348 Louvain-La-Neuve; tel. (32) 47-39-35; fax (32) 47-28-05; e-mail vandenbossche@dvlp.ucl.ac.be; internet www.sped.ucl.ac.be; f. 1961; Pres. J. P. H. PEEMANS.

Institut royal des relations internationales: 13 rue de la Charité, 1210 Brussels; tel. (2) 223-41-14; fax (2) 223-41-16; e-mail irri.kiib@euronet.be; f. 1947; research in international relations, economics, law and politics; archives and library of 16,500 vols and 600 periodicals; Dir-Gen. ÉMILE MASSA; publs include *Studia Diplomatica* (bi-monthly).

Koninklijk Museum voor Midden-Afrika/Musée royal de l'Afrique centrale: Leuvensesteenweg 13, 3080 Tervuren; tel. (2) 769-52-11; fax (2) 767-02-42; internet www.africamuseum.be; f. 1897; collections of prehistory, ethnography, nature arts and crafts; geology, mineralogy, palaeontology; zoology (entomology, ornithology, mammals, reptiles, etc.); history; economics; library of 90,000 vols and 4,500 periodicals; Dir PH. MARÉCHAL; publs include *Annales du Musée royal de l'Afrique centrale.*

Société belge d'études géographiques (Belgian Society for Geographical Studies): de Croylaan 42, 3001 Heverlee (Leuven); tel. (16) 32-24-45; fax (16) 32-29-80; f. 1931; centralizes and co-ordinates geographical research in Belgium; 395 mems; Pres. Y. VERHASSELT; Sec. H. VAN DER HAEGEN; publ. *Bulletin* (2 a year).

BRAZIL

Centro de Estudos Africanos (African Studies Centre): University of São Paulo, CP 2530, 01060-970 São Paulo, SP; tel. and fax (11) 2109416; e-mail cea@edu.usp.br; f. 1969; co-ordinating unit for all depts with African interests; specialist studies in sociology, international relations and literature concerning Africa; library; Dir Prof. FERNANDO A. A. MOURÃO; publ. *África* (annually).

Centro de Estudos Afro-Asiáticos—CEAA (Afro-Asian Studies Centre): Praça Pio X 7, 9°, 20040-020, Rio de Janeiro, RJ; tel. (21) 516-7157; fax (21) 518-2798; e-mail beluce@candidomendes.br; f. 1973; instruction and seminars; library; Dir CANDIDO MENDES; publ. *Estudos Afro-Asiáticos.*

Centro de Estudos Afro-Orientais—CEAO (Afro-Oriental Studies Centre): Federal University of Bahia, Rua Augusto Viana s/n, Canela, 41170-290 Salvador-Bahia; tel. (71) 2452821;

f. 1959; African and Afro-Oriental Studies; library; Dir Prof. LUIS CÉSAR DO NASCIMENTO; publ. *Afro-Ásia* (irregular).

Centro de Estudos e Pesquisas de Cultura Yorubana (Yoruba Culture Study and Research Centre): CP 40099, CEP 20272, Rio de Janeiro, RJ; tel. (21) 2930649; instruction in Yoruba language and religion; Dir Prof. FERNANDES PORTUGAL; publs include occasional papers.

Núcleo de Estudos Afro-Asiáticos (Afro-Asian Studies Unit): State University of Londrina, CP 6001, CEP 86051-970 Londrina, PR; tel. (43) 371-4599; fax (43) 371-4679; f. 1985; seminars and lectures; Dir Prof. EDUARDO JUDAS BARROS; publ. *África Asia* (annually).

Núcleo Ibérico, Latino-Americano e Luso-Africano— NILALA (Iberian, Latin American and Luso-African Unit): University of Ijuí, Rua São Francisco 501, 98700 Ijuí, RGS; f. 1984; lectures; Dir Prof. MARÍA LUIZA DE CARVALHO ARMANDO; publ. *Cadernos Luso-Africanos* (irregular).

CANADA

Canadian Association of African Studies (CAAS): c/o J. Barry Riddell, Dept of Geography, Queen's University Kingston, ON K7L 3N6; tel. (613) 545-6037; e-mail riddell@qsilver .queensu.ca; f. 1971; publs *Canadian Journal of African Studies* (English and French), *CAAS Newsletter* (English and French).

Canadian Council for International Co-operation: 1 Nicholas St, Suite 300, Ottawa, ON K1N 7B7; tel. (613) 241-7007; fax (613) 241-5302; e-mail ccic@ccic.ca; internet www.web.net/ccic-ccci; f. 1968; information and training centre for international devt and forum for voluntary agencies; 130 mems; Pres. CAMERON CHARLEBOIS; CEO BETTY PLEWES; publs include *Newsletter* (quarterly).

Canadian Institute of International Affairs: Glendon Hall, 2275 Bayview Ave, Toronto, ON M4M 3M6; tel. (416) 487-6830; fax (416) 487-6831; e-mail mailbox@ciia.org; internet www .ciia.org; f. 1928; research in international relations; library of 8,000 vols; Chair. R. ALAN BROADBENT; Pres. and CEO BARBARA MCDOUGALL; publs include *International Journal* (quarterly), *Behind the Headlines* (quarterly).

Centre for African Studies: Dalhousie University, Halifax, NS B3H 4J5; tel. (902) 494-3814; fax (902) 494-2105; f. 1975; Dir Dr JANE L. PARPART; publs include *Dalhousie African Studies* series, *Dalhousie African Working Papers* series, *Briefing Papers on the African Crisis.*

Centre for Developing-Area Studies: McGill University, 3715 rue Peel, Montréal, QC H3A 1X1; tel. (514) 398-3507; fax (514) 398-8432; e-mail cdaspub@leacock.lan.mcgill.ca; internet www.mcgill.ca/cdas; Dir Dr R. BOYD; publs include *Labour, Capital and Society* (English and French—2 a year), discussion papers.

International Development Research Centre: POB 8500, Ottawa, ON K1G 3H9; tel. (613) 236-6163; fax (613) 238-7230; e-mail info@idrc.ca; internet www.idrc.ca; f. 1970 by the govt to support research projects designed to meet the basic needs of developing countries and to address problems associated with poverty; regional offices in Kenya, Senegal, Egypt, Singapore, Uruguay, India and South Africa; Pres. Dr MAUREEN O'NEIL; publs include *Reports* (French, Spanish and English—weekly).

PEOPLE'S REPUBLIC OF CHINA

Centre for International Studies: 22 Xianmen Dajie, POB 7411, Beijing; tel. (10) 63097083; fax (10) 63095802; f. 1982; conducts research on international relations and problems; organizes academic exchanges; Dir.-Gen. ZHANG YIJUN.

China Institute of Contemporary International Relations: 2A Wanshousi, Haidian, Beijing 100081; tel. (10) 8418640; fax (10) 8418641; f. 1980; research on international devt and peace issues; Pres. SHEN QURONG; publ. *Contemporary International Relations* (monthly).

Institute of African Studies: Siangtang University, Siangtan; tel. 24812; f. 1978.

Institute of West Asian and African Studies: Chinese Academy of Social Sciences, 3 Zhangzhizhong Rd, Beijing 100007; tel. (10) 64039171; fax (10) 64035718; e-mail iwaas@ public.fhnet.cn.net; f. 1961; research institute; 40 full-time

research fellows; library of 40,000 vols; Dir.-Gen. YANG GUANG; publ. *West Asia and Africa* (Chinese, with summary in English— 6 a year).

CZECH REPUBLIC

Ústav mezinárodních vztahů (Institute of International Relations): 118 50 Prague 1, Nerudova 3; tel. (2) 51108111; fax (2) 51108222; e-mail umv@iir.cz; internet www.czechia.com/iir; f. 1957; Dir Dr JIŘÍ ŠEDIVÝ; publs include *Mezinárodní politika / International Politics* (monthly), *Mezinárodní vztahy / International Relations* (quarterly), *Perspectives—The Central European Review of International Affairs* (in English—2 a year).

DENMARK

Center for Udviklingsforskning (Centre for Development Research): Gammel Kongevej 5, 1610 Copenhagen V; tel. 33-85-46-00; fax 33-25-81-10; e-mail cdr@cdr.dk; internet www.cdr.dk; f. 1969 to promote and undertake research in the economic, social and political problems of developing countries; library of 50,000 vols; Dir Dr POUL ENGBERG-PEDERSEN; publs include *Den Ny Verden* (quarterly), *CDR Library Papers* (irregular), *CDR Research Reports* (in English, irregular), *CDR Working Papers* (in English—irregular).

FRANCE

Académie des sciences d'outre-mer: 15 rue Lapérouse, 75116 Paris; tel. 1-47-20-87-93; fax 1-47-20-89-72; f. 1922; 275 mems, of which 200 mems are attached to sections on geography, politics and administration, law, economics and sociology, science and medicine, education; library of 60,000 vols and 2,500 periodicals; Perm. Sec. GILBERT MANGIN; publs include *Mondes et Cultures* (quarterly).

Centre d'étude d'Afrique noire: 11 allée Ausone, Domaine universitaire, 33607 Pessac; tel. 5-56-84-42-82; fax 5-56-84-43-24; e-mail info@cean.u-bordeaux.fr; internet www.cean .u-bordeaux.fr.

Centre d'études politiques et juridiques du tiers monde: Université de Paris I, 12 place du Panthéon, 75231 Paris Cedex 05; tel. 1-46-34-97-56; fax 1-46-34-97-56; e-mail cetm@ univ-paris1.fr; f. 1965; Dir Prof. JEAN-PIERRE QUÉNEUDEC.

Centre d'études et de recherches sur le développement international (CERDI): Université de Clermont-Ferrand, 65 blvd François Mitterrand, 63000 Clermont-Ferrand; tel. 4-73-43-12-00; fax 4-73-43-12-28; e-mail cerdi@u-clermont1.fr; f. 1976; Dir Prof. SYLVAINE GUILLAUMONT.

Centre de recherches africaines: 9 rue Malher, 75181 Paris Cedex 04; tel. 1-44-78-33-40; fax 1-44-78-33-33; e-mail cra@ univ-paris1.fr; an inst. of the University of Paris I; Dir JEAN BOULEGUE.

Institut français des relations internationales: 27 rue de la Procession, 75740 Paris Cedex 15; tel. 1-40-61-60-00; fax 1-40-61-60-60; e-mail accueil@ifri.org; internet www.ifri.org; f. 1979; 450 mems; library of 30,000 vols and 420 periodicals; Chair. MARCEAU LONG; Dir THIERRY DE MONTBRIAL; publs *Politique étrangère* (quarterly), *Lettre d'Information* (bi-monthly), *Ramses* (annually), *Notes de l'Ifri, Cahiers de l'Ifri.*

Institut de recherche pour le développement (IRD): 213 rue La Fayette, 75480 Paris Cedex 10; tel. 1-48-03-77-77; fax 1-48-03-08-29; internet www.ird.fr; f. 1943, reorg. 1982; self-financing; centres, missions and rep. offices in Bolivia, Brazil, Burkina Faso, Cameroon, Côte d'Ivoire, French Guiana, Guinea, Indonesia, Madagascar, Mali, Mexico, New Caledonia, Niger, Senegal and Thailand; Pres. PHILIPPE LAZAR; Dir-Gen. JEAN-PIERRE MULLER.

Musée de l'Homme: Palais de Chaillot, 17 place du Trocadéro, 75116 Paris; tel. 1-44-05-72-72; internet www.mnhn.fr; f. 1878; library of 250,000 vols (c. 30,000 on Africa), 5,000 periodicals and c. 300,000 photographic images; ethnography, physical anthropology, prehistory; also a research and education centre; Dirs Profs PIERRE ROBBE (Ethnology), SERGE TORNAY (Black Africa), ANDRÉ LANGANEY (Anthropology), HENRY DE LUMLEY (Prehistory).

Société des africanistes (CSSF): Musée de l'Homme, Palais de Chaillot, 17 place du Trocadéro, 75116 Paris; tel. 1-47-27-72-

55; e-mail africanistes@wanadoo.fr; f. 1931; 350 mems; Pres. JEAN-LOUIS BOPPE; publ. *Journal des Africanistes*.

Société française d'histoire d'outre-mer: 15 rue Catulienne, 93200 Saint-Denis; tel. and fax (Mon. and Tues. afternoons) 1-48-13-09-89; f. 1913; 500 mems; Pres. MARC MICHEL; Sec.-Gen. DANIEL LEFEUVRE; publ. *Revue française d'histoire d'outre-mer* (2 a year).

GERMANY

Deutsche Gesellschaft für Auswärtige Politik eV (German Society for Foreign Affairs): 10787 Berlin, Ramchstrasse 17/18; tel. (30) 2954231; fax (30) 2542316; e-mail dgap@compuserve .com; internet www.dgap.org; f. 1955; promotes research on problems of international politics; library of 50,000 vols; 1,600 mems; Pres. Dr WERNER LAMBY; Exec. Vice-Pres. Dr J. STABREIT; Dir Research Inst. Prof. Dr KARL KAISER; publs *Internationale Politik* (monthly), *Die Internationale Politik* (annually).

IFO–Institut für Wirtschaftsforschung (IFO–Institute for Economic Research): 81679 Munich, Poschingerstrasse 5; tel. (89) 92240; fax (89) 9224-1462; e-mail ifo@ifo.de; internet www.ifo.de; f. 1949; library of 80,000 vols; Pres. Prof. Dr HANS-WERNER SINN; publs include *Afrika-Studien, IFO-Studien zur Entwicklungsforschung, Forschungsberichte der Abteilung Entwicklungsländer*.

Informationsstelle Südliches Afrika eV (Information Centre on Southern Africa): 53227 Bonn, Königswintererstrasse 116; tel. (228) 464369; fax (228) 468177; e-mail issa@bonn.comlink .apc.org; internet www.issa-bonn.org; f. 1971; research, documentation, and information on southern Africa; publs include *Afrika Süd* (6 a year).

Institut für Afrika-Kunde (Institute of African Affairs): 20354 Hamburg, Neuer Jungfernstieg 21; tel. (40) 42834523; fax (40) 42834511; e-mail iak@uni-hamburg.de; internet www. uni-hamburg.de/IAK; f. 1963; research, documentation, information; library of 46,500 vols and 365 periodicals; Dir Dr CORD JAKOBEIT; publs include *Hamburg African Studies, Hamburger Beiträge zur Afrika-Kunde, Arbeiten aus dem Institut für Afrika-Kunde, Afrika Spectrum, Focus Afrika*.

Institut für Afrikanistik: Leipzig University, 04109 Leipzig, Burgstrasse 21; tel. (341) 9737030; fax (341) 9737048; e-mail mgrosze@rz.uni–leipzig.de; Dir Prof. Dr ROBERT KAPPEL.

HUNGARY

Magyar Tudományos Akadémia Világgazdasági Kutató Intézete (Institute for World Economics of the Hungarian Academy of Sciences): 1014 Budapest, Országház u. 30; tel. (1) 224-6760; fax (1) 224-6761; e-mail vki@vki3.vki.hu; internet www.vki.hu; f. 1965; library of 103,000 vols; Dir Prof. ANDRÁS INOTAI; publs include *Trends in World Economy* (irregular, in English), working papers (irregular, in English).

INDIA

Centre for African Studies: University of Mumbai, Vidyanagari Kalina Campus, Santacruz East, Mumbai 400 098; tel. (22) 6113091; fax (22) 6180893; Dir Dr V. S. SHETH.

Centre for Development Studies: Prasanth Nagar Rd, Ulloor, Thiruvananthapuram 695 011; tel. (471) 448881; fax (471) 447137; e-mail cdsedp@vsnl.com; f. 1971; instruction and research in disciplines relevant to economic devt; library of 125,000 vols; Dir Dr CHANDAN MUKHERJEE.

Centre for West Asian and African Studies: School of International Studies, Jawaharlal Nehru University, New Mehrauli Rd, New Delhi 110 067; tel. (11) 6107676; fax (11) 6165886; Chair. Prof. GIRIJESH PANT.

Department of African Studies: University of Delhi, Delhi 110 007; tel. (11) 7257725, Ext. 338; fax (11) 7257336; f. 1955; Head of Dept Prof. HARJINDER SINGH; publs include *Indian Journal of African Studies*.

Indian Centre for Africa: Indian Council for Cultural Relations, Azad Bhavan, Indraprastha Estate, New Delhi 110 002; tel. (11) 3319226; fax (11) 3712639; f. 1987; publ. *Africa Quarterly*.

Indian Council of World Affairs: Sapru House, Barakhamba Rd, New Delhi 110 001; tel. (11) 3317246; f. 1943; independent institution for the study of Indian and international issues; library of 127,000 vols, 490 periodicals, 2.5m. press clippings, also UN documents and microfiches; 2,480 mems; Pres. HARCHARAN SINGH JOSH; publs include *Foreign Affairs Reports* (monthly), *India Quarterly*.

Indian Society for Afro-Asian Studies: 297 Saraswati Kunj, Indraprastha Ext., Mother Dairy Rd, New Delhi 110 092; tel. (11) 2248246; fax (11) 2425698; e-mail isaas@ giasdl01.vsnl.net.in; f. 1980; conducts research and holds seminars and confs; Pres. LALIT BHASIN; Gen. Sec. Dr DHARAMPAL; publs include *Indian Review of African Affairs* (6 a year).

IRAN

Institute for Political and International Studies: Shaheed Bahonar Ave, Shaheed Aghaii Ave, POB 19395-1793, Tajrish, Teheran; tel. (21) 2571010; fax (21) 2710964; e-mail IPIS@www.dci.co.ir; internet www.Iran-IPIS.org; f. 1983; research and information on international relations, foreign policy, economics, culture and law; library of 22,000 vols; publs include *Iranian Journal of International Affairs* (quarterly).

ISRAEL

Harry S. Truman Research Institute for the Advancement of Peace: The Hebrew University of Jerusalem, Mt Scopus, Jerusalem 91905; tel. (2) 5882300; fax (2) 5828076; e-mail mstruman@mscc.huji.ac.il; f. 1965; conducts a broad range of research relating to non-Western and developing countries; Dir Prof. AMNON COHEN; Exec. Dir Dr EDY KAUFMAN.

Institute of Asian and African Studies: The Hebrew University of Jerusalem, Mt Scopus, Jerusalem 91905; tel. (2) 5883516; fax (2) 5322545; e-mail magen@hum.huji.ac.il; offers degree and postgraduate courses, covering history, social sciences and languages; Chair. Prof. STEVEN KAPLAN.

International Institute—Histadrut: Bet Berl 44905, Kfar Saba; tel. (9) 987382; f. 1958 to train leadership for trade unions, co-operatives, community orgs, women's and youth groups, etc. in developing countries; library of 35,000 vols; Chair. HAIM RAMON; Dir and Prin. Dr YEHUDAH PAZ.

Moshe Dayan Center for Middle Eastern and African Studies, Shiloah Institute: Ramat-Aviv, Tel-Aviv 69978; tel. (3) 6409100; fax (3) 6415802; e-mail dayancen@ccsg.tau.ac.il; f. 1959; Dir Dr MARTIN KRAMER; publs include *Current Contents of Periodicals on the Middle East* (6 a year), *Middle East Contemporary Survey* (annually).

ITALY

The Bologna Center, Paul H. Nitze School of Advanced International Studies, The Johns Hopkins University: Via Belmeloro 11, 40126 Bologna; tel. (51) 232185; fax (51) 228505; e-mail registrar@jhubc.it; internet www.jhubc.it; f. 1955; graduate studies in international affairs; Dir ROBERT H. EVANS; publs include *Rivista* (annually), occasional papers series.

Istituto Italiano per l'Africa e l'Oriente: Via Ulisse Aldrovandi 16, 00197 Rome; tel. (6) 3221258; fax (6) 3225348; e-mail isiao–inf@mclink.it; f. 1906; Pres. Prof. GHERARDO GNOLI; Dir-Gen. GIANCARLO GARGARUTI; publ. *Africa* (quarterly).

Istituto per gli Studi di Politica Internazionale (ISPI): Palazzo Clerici, Via Clerici 5, 20121 Milan; tel. (2) 8633131; fax (2) 8692055; f. 1933 for the promotion of the study of international relations; conducts research, documentation and training; Pres. Ambassador BORIS BIANCHERI; Man. Dir Dr GIOVANNI ROGGERO FOSSATI; publs include *Relazioni Internazionali* (6 a year).

JAPAN

Ajia Keizai Kenkyusho–IDE–JETRO (Institute of Developing Economies, Japan External Trade Organization): 3-2-2, Wakaba, Mihama-ku, Chiba-shi, Chiba 261-8545; tel. (4) 3299-9500; fax (4) 3299-9724; internet www.ide.go.jp; f. 1960; library of 500,000 vols; Chair. NOBORU HATAKEYAMA; Pres. IPPEI YAMAZAWA; publs *Ajia Keizai* (Japanese, monthly), *The Developing Economies* (English, quarterly), *Africa Report* (Japanese, bi-annually).

Institute for the Study of Languages and Cultures of Asia and Africa: Tokyo University of Foreign Studies, 4-51-21

Nishigahara, Kita-ku, Tokyo 114-8580; tel. (3) 5974-3668; fax (3) 5974-3838; e-mail editcom@aa.tufs.ac.jp; internet www.aa .tufs.ac.jp; f. 1964; library of c. 91,000 vols; Dir Prof. HIROSHI ISHII; publs *Newsletter* (3 a year), *Journal of Asian and African Studies* (2 a year).

Nihon Afurika Gakkai (Japan Asscn for African Studies): c/o Dogura and Co Ltd, 1–8 Nishihanaikecho, Koyama, Kita-ku, Kyoto 603; tel. (75) 451-4844; fax (75) 441-0436; promotes multi-disciplinary African studies; Pres. H. ODA; publs *Afurika Kenkyu* / *Journal of African Studies* (2 a year), *Kaiho* (annually).

Nihon Kokusai Mondai Kenkyusho (Japan Inst. of International Affairs): 19th Mori Bldg, 1-2-20 Toranomon, Minatu-ku, Tokyo 105; tel. (3) 3503-7261; fax (3) 3595-1755; f. 1959; Chair. YOSHIZANE IWASA; Pres. NOBUO MATSUNAGA; publs include *Kokusai Mondai* (International Affairs, monthly), *Japan Review of International Affairs* (quarterly).

MEXICO

Asociación Latinoamericana de Estudios de Asia y Africa (Latin American Asscn for Asian and African Studies): El Colegio de México, Camino al Ajusco 20, Pedregal Sta Teresa, CP 10740, Mexico DF; tel. (5) 449-3000; fax (5) 645-0464; e-mail aladaa@colmex.mx; internet www.colmex.mx/centros/ceaa/ aladaa/default.htm; f. 1976; promotes African and Asian studies in Latin America; 450 mems; Sec.-Gen. Prof. MICHIKO TANAKA; publ. newsletters and proceedings.

Centro de Estudios de Asia y Africa–CEAA (Centre for Asian and African Studies): El Colegio de México, Camino al Ajusco 20, Pedregal Sta Teresa, 01000 Alvaro Obrégon, Mexico DF; tel. (5) 449-3025; fax (5) 645-0464; internet www.colmex.mx/ centros/ceaa/default.htm; f. 1964; postgraduate studies and research; library; Dir Prof. BENJAMIN PRECIADO SOLIS; publs include *Estudios de Asia y Africa* (3 a year).

THE NETHERLANDS

Afrika-Studiecentrum: POB 9555, 2300 RB, Leiden; tel. (71) 5273372; fax (71) 5273344; e-mail asc@fsw.leidenuniv.nl; internet www.asc.leidenuniv.nl; f. 1948 to carry out research on Africa in the social sciences, and to disseminate information on African affairs; encourages the co-operation of institutions engaged in the study of Africa; Chair. E. M. A. SCHMITZ; Dir Dr G. HESSELING; publs include *African Studies Abstracts* (quarterly).

Institute of Social Studies: POB 29776, 2502 LT, The Hague; tel. (70) 4260460; fax (70) 4260799; e-mail studentoffice@iss.nl; f. 1952; postgraduate instruction, research and consultancy in devt studies; Rector Prof. H. OPSCHOOR; publs *Development and Change* (quarterly), working papers, monograph series.

Netherlands-African Business Council: 181 Bezuidenhout-seweg, POB 10, 2501 CA, The Hague; tel. (70) 3441544; fax (70) 3853531; e-mail nch@euronet.nl; f. 1946; an information bureau, contact address and documentation centre for businessmen in African countries and in the Netherlands; Chair. J. W. B. NOLST TRENITÉ; Exec. Sec. R. V. D. HALL.

Netherlands Institute for Southern Africa: Prins Hend-rikkade 33, POB 10707, 1001 ES, Amsterdam; tel. (20) 5206210; fax (20) 5206249; e-mail niza@niza.nl; internet www.niza.nl.

NORWAY

Norsk Utenrikspolitisk Institutt (Norwegian Institute of International Affairs): Grønlandsleiret 25, POB 8159 Dep, 0033 Oslo; tel. 22056500; fax 22177015; e-mail info@nupi.no; internet www.nupi.no/; f. 1959; information and research in international relations; Pres. RAKEL SURLIEN; Dir SVERRE LODGAARD; publs include *Internasjonal Politikk* (quarterly), *Forum for Development Studies* (2 a year), *NUPI Notat* and *NUPI Rapport* (research reports).

PAKISTAN

Pakistan Institute of International Affairs: Aiwan-e-Sadar Rd, POB 1447, Karachi 74200; tel. (21) 5682891; fax (21) 5686069; f. 1947 to study international affairs and to promote the study of international politics, economics and law; over 600 mems; library of c. 28,000 vols; Chair. FATEHYAB ALI KHAN; publs include *Pakistan Horizon* (quarterly).

POLAND

Departament Studiów i Planowania–MSZ (Dept of Studies and Planning, Ministry of Foreign Affairs): 00-950 Warsaw, ul. Warecka 1A; tel. (22) 8263021; fax (22) 8263026; f. 1947; library of 125,000 vols; Dir HENRYK SZLAJFER; publs include *Sprawy Międzynarodowe* (quarterly, in Polish and English), *Zbiór Dokumentów* (quarterly, in Polish, French, English and German), occasional papers (in English).

Institute of Oriental Studies, Department of African Languages and Cultures, University of Warsaw: 00-927 Warsaw, Krakowskie Przedmieście 26/28; tel. (22) 6200381, Ext. 517; fax (22) 8263683; e-mail orientuw@plearn.edu.pl; f. 1950; postgraduate studies and research in linguistics, literature, history, sociology and ethnology; Head of Dept Prof. Dr STANISŁAW PIŁASZEWICS: publ. *Studies of the Department of African Languages and Cultures*.

Instytut Krajów Rozwijających się (Institute of Developing Countries): 00-324 Warsaw, Karowa 20; tel. and fax (22) 8268547; e-mail ikr@mercury.ci.uw.edu.pl; internet www.ikr.uw .edu.pl; undergraduate and postgraduate studies; interdisciplinary research on developing countries; Dir Prof. JAN J. MILEWSKI; publs include *Africana Bulletin* (annually, in French and English), *Afryka, Azja, Ameryka Łacińska* (annually, with summaries in French and English).

PORTUGAL

Amílcar Cabral Information and Documentation Centre: Rua Pinheiro Chagas, 77-2º esq, 1050-176 Lisbon; tel. (1) 3172860; fax (1) 3172870; e-mail cidac@esoterica.pt; Pres. LUISA TEOTÓNIO PEREIRA.

Centro de Estudos Africanos (African Studies Centre): University of Coimbra, Instituto de Antropologia, Rua Arco da Traição, 3049 Coimbra; tel. (39) 829051; fax (39) 823491; e-mail areia@cygnus.ci.uc.pt; f. 1982; seminars and lectures; Dir Prof. M. L. RODRIGUES DE AREIA; publ. *Publicações do Centro de Estudos Africanos*.

Centro de Estudos Sobre África e do Desenvolvimento (Centre of African and Development Studies): Instituto Superior de Economia e Gestão, Rua Miguel Lupi 20, 1200 Lisbon; tel. (1) 3925983; fax (1) 3976271; f. 1982; e-mail cesa@iseg.ult.pt; internet www.pascal.iseg.utl.pt/~cesa; conducts research and holds seminars; publs occasional papers.

Instituto de Estudos Africanos (Institute of African Studies): Faculty of Letters, University of Lisbon, Cidade Universitária, 1669 Lisbon; literary studies and documentation centre; Dirs Prof. MANUEL FERREIRA, Prof. MANUEL VIEGAS GUERREIRO.

Instituto de Investigação Científica Tropical (Institute for Tropical Scientific Research): Ministério da Ciência e da Tecnologia, Rua Jau 47, 1300 Lisbon; f. 1883; tel. (1) 3622621; fax (1) 3631460; e-mail jacsilva@iict.pt; comprises 23 specialized research and devt centres and a documentation centre, dealing mainly with lusophone African countries; Pres. J. A. CRUZ E SILVA; publs include monographs, serials and maps.

RUSSIA

Council of Afro-Asian Studies: Afro-Aziatskiye Obshchestvo, Istoria i Sovremnost, Institut Vostokovedeniya, Institut Afriki, Rossiyskaya Akad. Nauk, 103001 Moscow, 30/1 Spiridonovka; tel. (095) 2026650; Chair. A. M. VASSILIEV; publ. *Vostok (Oriens)* (6 a year).

Institute of World Economy and International Relations: 117859 Moscow, ul. Profsoyuznaya 23; tel. (095) 1204332; fax (095) 3107027; e-mail ineir@sovam.com; f. 1956; Dir VLADEN A. MARTYNOV; publs include *Otnosheniya* (monthly).

Moscow State Institute of International Relations: 117454 Moscow, Vernadskogo pr. 76; tel. (095) 4349158; fax (095) 4349066; f. 1944; library of 718,000 vols; Rector ANATOLII V. TURKUNOV; publ. *Moscow Journal of International Law*.

Moscow State University Institute of Asian and African Studies: 103009 Moscow, Mokhovaja 11; tel. (095) 2033647; fax (095) 2036476.

SAUDI ARABIA

King Faisal Centre for Research and Islamic Studies: POB 5149, Riyadh 11543; tel. (1) 4652255; f. 1983; advances research and studies into Islamic civilization; provides grants for research and organizes symposia, lectures and confs on Islamic matters; library of over 30,000 vols and periodicals; Dir-Gen. Dr Zeid al-Husain; publ. *Newsletter*.

SOUTH AFRICA

Africa Institute of South Africa: BestMed Bldg, cnr Hamilton and Belvedere Sts, Arcadia, POB 630, Pretoria 0001; tel. (12) 328-6970; fax (12) 323-8153; e-mail (Library) amanda@ai.org.za; internet www.ai.org.za; f. 1960; undertakes research and collects and disseminates information on all aspects of continental Africa and its offshore islands, with particular focus on politics, economics and development issues; library of about 66,500 vols and periodicals; Dir Dr Eddy Maloka; publs include *Africa Insight* (quarterly).

Centre for African Studies: University of Cape Town, Faculty of Humanities, Private Bag, Rondebosch 7700; tel. (21) 650-2308; fax (21) 686-1505; internet www.uct.ac.za/depts/cas/; f. 1976; incorporates the Harry Oppenheimer Inst. for African Studies; promotes comparative study of Africa and research; offers multi-disciplinary courses at postgraduate level; Dir Prof. Brenda Cooper; publs include *Social Dynamics* (bi-annually).

Institute for Advanced Social Research: University of the Witwatersrand, 1 Jan Smuts Ave, Private Bag 3, Wits 2050, Johannesburg; tel. (11) 716-2414; fax (11) 716-8030; f. 1973; Dir Prof. Charles van Onselen.

Institute for the Study of Man in Africa (ISMA): Rm 2B17, University of the Witwatersrand Medical School, York Rd, Parktown, Johannesburg 2193; tel. (11) 717-2203; fax (11) 643-4318; e-mail 055JSK@chiron.wits.ac.za; internet www.wits.ac.za/isma; f. 1960 to perpetuate the work of the late Prof. Raymond A. Dart on the study of man in Africa, past and present; serves as a centre of anthropological and related field work; publs include the Raymond Dart series and occasional papers.

South African Institute of Race Relations: POB 31044, Braamfontein 2017; tel. (11) 403-3600; fax (11) 403-3671; e-mail sairr@milkyway.co.za; f. 1929; research, education, publishing; library; 4,313 mems, 600 affiliated bodies; Pres. Prof. Themba Sono; Dir J. Kane-Berman; publs include *Fast Facts* (monthly), *Frontiers of Freedom* (quarterly), *South Africa Survey* (annually).

SPAIN

Catedra UNESCO de Estudios Afroiberoamericanos: Vicerectorado de Relaciones Internacionales, Universidad de Alcalá, Plaza de Dan Diego s/n, 28801 Alcalá de Henares; tel. (91) 8854085; fax (91) 8854130; e-mail vrisam@uah.alcala.es; f. 1994; promotes and co-ordinates co-operation with African universities; organizes seminars, lectures and courses on African influences in Latin America; Dir Dr Luis Beltrán.

Centro de Información y Documentación Africanas–CIDAF: Gaztambide 31, 28015 Madrid; tel. (1) 915441818; fax (1) 915497789; e-mail cidaf@planalfa.es; internet www.3.planalfa.es/cidaf; f. 1979; seminars and lectures; specialized library of 16,000 vols and periodicals; Dir Fr Bartolomé Burgos Martínez; Chief Librarian Sanchez Sanz; publs include *Noticias de Africa* (monthly), *Cuadernos CIDAF*.

Colegio Mayor Universitario Nuestra Señora de Africa: Avda Ramiro de Maeztu s/n, Ciudad Universitaria, 28040 Madrid; tel. (1) 5540104; fax (1) 5540401; f. 1964; attached inst. of the Complutense Univ. of Madrid and the Spanish Ministry of Foreign Affairs; linguistic studies and cultural activities; Dir Olegario Negrín.

Mundo Negro: Arturo Soria 101; 28043 Madrid; tel. (1) 4152412; fax (1) 5192550; e-mail mundonegro@combonianos.com; internet www.combonianos.com; f. 1960; holds lectures; library and museum; Dir Fr Mariano Pérez González; publ. *Mundo Negro* (monthly).

SWEDEN

Institutet för Internationell Ekonomi (Institute for International Economic Studies): 106 91 Stockholm; tel. (8) 162000; fax (8) 161443; e-mail postmaster@iies.su.se; attached to Stockholm Univ.; Dir Prof. Torsten Persson.

Nordiska Afrikainstitutet (The Nordic Africa Institute): POB 1703, 751 47 Uppsala; tel. (18) 562200; fax (18) 562290; e-mail nai@nai.uu.se; internet www.nai.uu.se; f. 1962; documentation, information and research centre for contemporary African affairs, publication work, lectures and seminars; library of 50,000 vols and 1,000 periodicals; Dir Lennart Wohlgemuth; publs include *Current African Issues, News from the Nordic Africa Institute,* seminar proceedings, research reports, discussion papers, annual report.

Utrikespolitiska Institutet (Swedish Institute of International Affairs): Lilla Nygatan 23, POB 1253, 111 82 Stockholm; tel. (8) 234060; fax (8) 201049; e-mail siia@ui.se; f. 1938; promotes studies of international affairs; library of c. 20,000 vols and 400 periodicals; Pres. Ambassador Leif Leifland; Dir Anders Mellbourn; publs include *Världspolitikens Dagsfrågor, Världens Fakta, Internationella Studier, Länder i fickformat, Yearbook,* conference papers, research reports (in English).

SWITZERLAND

Institut universitaire d'études du développement: 24 rue Rothschild, 1211 Geneva 21; tel. (22) 9065940; fax (22) 9065953; e-mail roland.duc@iued.unize.ch; internet www.iued.ch; f. 1961; a centre of higher education and research into development problems of Africa, Latin America and Asia; conducts courses, seminars and practical work; Dir Jean-Luc Maurer; publs include *Nouveaux Cahiers de l'IUED, Annuaire Suisse-Tiers Monde, Itinéraires.*

Institut universitaire de hautes études internationales: 132 rue de Lausanne, BP 36, 1211 Geneva 21; tel. (22) 7311730; fax (22) 7384306; internet www.heiwww.unige.ch; f. 1927; a research and teaching institution studying international judicial, historical, political and economic questions; Dir. Peter Tschopp.

UNITED KINGDOM

African Studies Association of the United Kingdom: School of Oriental and African Studies, Thornhaugh St, Russell Sq., London, WC1H 0XG; tel. (20) 7898-4390; e-mail asa@soas.ac.uk; f. 1963 to advance academic studies relating to Africa by providing facilities for the interchange of information and ideas; holds inter-disciplinary confs and symposia; 350 mems; Hon. Pres. Dr J. Lonsdale; Hon. Sec. Dr N. Nelson.

African Studies Centre: Free School Lane, Cambridge, CB2 3RQ; tel. and fax (1223) 334396; e-mail african-studies@lists.cam.ac.uk; internet www.african.cam.ac.uk; attached inst. of the Univ. of Cambridge; Dir Dr Ato Quayson.

African Studies Unit: University of Leeds, Leeds, West Yorkshire, LS2 9JT; tel. (113) 2335069; e-mail african-studies@leeds.ac.uk; a liaison unit for all depts with African interests.

Catholic Institute for International Relations (CIIR): Unit 3, Canonbury Yard, 190A New North Rd, London, N1 7BJ; tel. (20) 7354-0883; fax (20) 7359-0017; e-mail ciir@ciir.org; internet www.ciir.org; f. 1940; information and analysis of socio-economic, political, church and human rights issues in the developing countries; Gen. Sec. Ian Linden; publs include specialized studies on southern Africa and EU development policy.

Centre for the Study of African Economies: Dept. of Economics, University of Oxford, Manor Rd Bldg, Manor Rd, Oxford, OX1 3UL; tel. (1865) 271084; fax (1865) 281447; e-mail csae.enquiries@economics.oxford.ac.uk; internet www.csae.ox.ac.uk; Dir Prof. J. Toye; publ. *Journal of African Economies* (3 a year).

Centre of African Studies: University of Edinburgh, Adam Ferguson Bldg, George Sq., Edinburgh, EH8 9LL, Scotland; tel. (131) 650-3878; fax (131) 650-6535; e-mail africanstudies@ed.ac.uk; f. 1962; postgraduate studies; Dir Prof. Kenneth King; publs include occasional paper series and annual conference proceedings.

Centre of West African Studies: The University of Birmingham, Edgbaston, Birmingham, B15 2TT; tel. (121) 4145128; Dir Prof. Arnold Hughes.

Development and Project Planning Centre: University of Bradford, Bradford, West Yorkshire, BD7 1DP; tel. (1274) 233980; fax (1274) 235280; internet www.brad.ac.uk/acad/dppc; f. 1969 to carry out postgraduate teaching, professional training, research and consultancy in project planning and management and devt policy and planning; an attached inst. of the Univ. of Bradford; Head of Centre Prof. JOHN WEISS; publs include discussion papers.

Institute of Commonwealth Studies: 28 Russell Sq., London, WC1B 5DS; tel. (20) 7262-8844; fax (20) 7262-8820; e-mail ics@sas.ac.uk; f. 1949; conducts postgraduate research in social sciences and recent history relating to the Commonwealth; library of 170,000 vols; Dir Prof. PAT CAPLAN.

Institute of Development Studies at the University of Sussex: Brighton, East Sussex, BN1 9RE; tel. (1273) 606261; fax (1273) 621202; e-mail ids@sussex.ac.uk; internet www.ids.ac.uk/ids/; f. 1966; Dir K. BEZANSON.

International African Institute (IAI): School of Oriental and African Studies, Thornhaugh St, London, WC1H 0XG; tel. (20) 7898-4420; fax (20) 7898-4419; e-mail iai@soas.ac.uk; internet www.oneworld.org/iai/; f. 1926 to promote the study of African peoples, their languages, cultures and social life in their traditional and modern settings; holds seminars and conducts projects; Chair. Prof. V. Y. MUDIMBE; publs include *Africa* (quarterly), *Africa Bibliography* (annually), monograph and reprint series.

International Institute for Environment and Development (IIED): 3 Endsleigh St, London, WC1H 0DD; tel. (20) 7388-2117; fax (20) 7388-2826; e-mail mailbox@iied.org; internet www.iied.org; f. 1971; resource centre promoting the sound management and sustainable use of natural resources; conducts research into drylands, forestry and land use, human settlements, sustainable agriculture, environmental economics, climate change and institutional co-operation; publ. unit in London; Exec. Dir NIGEL CROSS.

Overseas Development Institute (ODI): 111 Westminster Bridge Rd, London, SE1 7JD; tel. (20) 7922-0300; fax (20) 7922-0399; e-mail publications@odi.org.uk; internet www.odi.org.uk; f. 1960 as a research centre and forum for the discussion of development issues and problems; publishes its research findings in books and working papers; Chair. Lord CAIRNS; Dir SIMON MAXWELL; publs include *Development Policy Review* (quarterly), *Disasters* (quarterly).

Royal African Society: School of Oriental and African Studies, Thornhaugh St, Russell Sq., London, WC1H 0XG; tel. (20) 7898-4390; e-mail ras@soas.ac.uk; f. 1901; 800 mems; Chair. Sir MICHAEL MCWILLIAM; Pres. (vacant); Sec. Mrs M. L. ALLAN; publ. *African Affairs* (quarterly).

Royal Institute of International Affairs: Chatham House, 10 St James's Sq., London, SW1Y 4LE; tel. (20) 7957-5700; fax (20) 7957-5710; e-mail contact@riia.org; internet www.riia.org; f. 1920 to study international issues; c. 3,500 mems; Chair. Lord MARSHALL; Dir Dr CHRIS GAMBLE; Dir of Studies WILLIAM HOPKINSON; publs include *International Affairs* (quarterly), *The World Today* (monthly), *Chatham House Papers, Annual Report,* special papers, discussion papers, briefing papers.

School of African and Asian Studies: University of Sussex, Falmer, Brighton, East Sussex, BN1 9SJ; tel. (1273) 606755; fax (1273) 623572; e-mail s.emberton@sussex.ac.uk; internet www.susx.ac.uk/units/afras/; Dean Dr M. H. JOHNSON.

School of Development Studies: University of East Anglia, Norwich, NR4 7TJ; tel. (1603) 592807; fax (1603) 451999; e-mail dev.general@uea.ac.uk; internet www.uea.ac.uk/dev/; Dean Dr CECILE JACKSON.

School of Oriental and African Studies: Thornhaugh St, Russell Sq., London, WC1H 0XG; tel. (20) 7637-2388; fax (20) 7436-3844; e-mail study@soas.ac.uk; internet www.soas.ac.uk; f. 1916; a school of the Univ. of London; Dir Sir TIM LANKESTER; Sec. F. DABELL; 220 teachers, incl. 44 professors; 3,220 students; publs *The Bulletin, Calendar, Annual Report, Journal of African Law.*

School of Oriental and African Studies Library: Thornhaugh St, Russell Sq., London, WC1H 0XG; tel. (20) 7323-6109; fax (20) 7898-4159; e-mail libenquiry@soas.ac.uk; f. 1916; 850,000 vols and pamphlets; 4,500 current periodicals, 50,000 maps, 6,300 microforms, 2,800 MSS and private papers collections, extensive missionary archives, all covering Asian and African languages, literatures, philosophy, religions, history,

law, cultural anthropology, art and archaeology, social sciences, geography and music; Librarian KEITH WEBSTER.

UNITED STATES OF AMERICA

Africa Fund: 50 Broad St, Suite 711, New York, NY 10004-2307; tel. (212) 785-1024; fax (212) 785-1078; email africafund@igc.org; internet www.theafricafund.org; f. 1966; conducts research and issues publs on Africa; encourages positive US policies on African issues and supports African human rights and devt; Pres. Bd of Trustees TILDEN J. LEMELLE; Exec. Dir JENNIFER DAVIS; publs include *Africa Fund News* (irregular).

Africa-America Institute: 380 Lexington Ave, New York, NY 10168; tel. (212) 949-5666; fax (212) 682-6174; f. 1953; organizes training programmes and offers devt assistance; maintains reps in 21 African countries; also sponsors confs and seminars; Pres. MORA MCLEAN; Exec. Vice-Pres. STEVE MCDONALD.

African and Afro-American Studies Center: University of Texas, Jester Center A232A, Austin, TX 78705; tel. (512) 471-1784; fax (512) 471-1798; e-mail caaas@uts.cc.utexas.edu; internet www.utexas/edu/depts/caaas; f. 1969; Dir Prof. SHEILA S. WALKER; publs working papers and reprint series (irregular).

African Development Foundation: 1400 Eye St, NW, 10th Floor, Washington, DC 20005-2248; tel. (202) 673-3916; fax (202) 673-3810; e-mail info@adf.gov; internet www.adf.gov; f. 1984; an independent agency of the US federal govt; conducts community-based, self-help devt programmes in 14 sub-Saharan African countries; Pres. and CEO WILLIAM R. FORD; publs include *ADF Highlights* (annually).

African Studies and Research Program: Dept of African Studies, Howard University, Washington, DC 20059; tel. (202) 806-7115; fax (202) 806-4425; f. 1959; Chair. Dr SULAYMAN S. NYANG; publs include monographs and occasional papers.

African Studies Association of the US: c/o African Studies Asscn, Rutgers, The State University, 132 George St, New Brunswick, NJ 08901-1400; tel. (732) 932-8173; fax (732) 932-3394; internet www.africanstudies.org; f. 1957; 2,700 mems; collects information on Africa; Pres. LANSINE KABA; Dir LOREE D. JONES; publs *African Studies Review, Issue, ASA News, History in Africa.*

African Studies Center: Boston University, 270 Bay State Rd, Boston, MA 02215; tel. (617) 353-7308; fax (617) 353-4975; e-mail buasc@acs.bu.edu; internet www.bu.edu.AFR; f. 1953; research and teaching on archaeology, African languages, anthropology, economics, history, geography and political science of Africa; library of 125,000 vols and document titles, 1,000 periodicals and an extensive collection of non-current newspapers and periodicals; Dir Dr JAMES MCCANN; publs include *International Journal of African Historical Studies* (3 a year), working papers, discussion papers.

African Studies Center: Center for International Programs, Michigan State University, East Lansing, MI 48824; tel. (810) 353-1700; fax (810) 336-1209; e-mail africa@msu.edu; f. 1960; Dir Dr DAVID WILEY; offers instruction in 25 African languages; library of over 200,000 vols; publs include *African Rural and Urban Studies* (3 a year), *Northeast African Studies* (3 a year).

African Studies Program: Ohio University, 56 East Union St, Athens, OH 45701; tel. (740) 593-1834; fax (740) 593-1837; e-mail africa@intl-institute.wisc.edu; internet http://polyglot.lss.wisc.edu/afrst/asphome.html; African politics, education, economics, geography, anthropology, languages, literature, philosophy and history; Dir Prof. STEPHEN HOWARD.

African Studies Program: University of Wisconsin–Madison, 205 Ingraham Hall, 1155 Observatory Drive, Madison, WI 53706; tel. (608) 262-2380; fax (608) 265-5851; e-mail Africa@intl-institute.wisc.edu; internet www.polyglot.iss.wisc/edu/afrst/asphome; study courses; library of over 220,000 vols; Chair. Prof. JO ELLEN FAIR; publs include *News and Notes* (bi-annually), *African Economic History* (annually), occasional papers and African texts and grammars.

Africare: 440 R St, NW, Washington, DC 20001; tel. (202) 462-3614; fax (202) 387-1034; e-mail africare@africare.org; internet www.africare.org; f. 1971; supports programmes in agriculture, water resource devt, environmental man., health and emergency aid, as well as private-sector devt; Pres. C. PAYNE LUCAS; publs include *Newsletter* (2 a year).

American Committee on Africa: 50 Broad St, Suite 711, New York, NY 10004-2307; tel. (212) 785-1024; fax (212) 785-1078; e-mail acoa@igc.apc.org; internet www.prairienet.org/acas/acoa.html; f. 1953; Pres. WYATT T. WALKER; Exec. Dir JENNIFER DAVIS; publ. *ACOA Action News* (irregular).

Association of African Studies Programs: Dept of African and African–American Studies, 236 Grange Bldg, Penn State University, University Park, PA 16802; tel. (814) 863-4243; mems represent more than 40 centres of African studies at US colleges and univs; publ. *Newsletter* (2 a year).

Berkeley/Stanford Joint Center for African Studies: Bldg 240, Rm 104, Stanford University, Stanford, CA 94305-2152; tel. (650) 723-0295; fax (650) 723-8528; internet www.leland.stanford.edu/dept/AFR; f. 1979; African languages, society, culture, foreign policy and social and behavioural sciences; holds research confs; offers jt degree in African studies for students enrolled in professional schools; Co-Chair. LOUISE FORTMANN, RICHARD ROBERTS; Assoc. Dir MARTHA E. SAAVEDRA; publ. *Newsletter* (3 a year).

Brookings Institution: 1775 Massachusetts Ave, NW, Washington, DC 20036-2188; tel. (202) 797-6105; fax (202) 797-2495; e-mail brookinfo@brook.edu; internet www.brookings.org; f. 1916; research, education, and publishing in economics, govt and foreign policy; organizes confs and seminars; library of c. 75,000 vols and 700 periodicals; Pres. MICHAEL H. ARMACOST; publs include *The Brookings Review* (quarterly), *Brookings Papers on Economic Activity* (3 a year), *Brookings Trade Forum* (3 a year).

Center for African Studies: 427 Grinter Hall, University of Florida, Gainesville, FL 32611; tel. (352) 392-2183; fax (352) 392-2435; e-mail mchege@africa.ufl.edu; encourages research projects and sponsors lectures, exhbns and confs; library of 50,000 vols, 500 periodical titles, 40,000 maps; Dir MICHAEL CHEGE; publ. *African Studies Quarterly*.

Center for African Studies: University of Illinois at Urbana-Champaign, 210 International Studies Bldg, 910 South Fifth St, Champaign, IL 61820; tel. (217) 333-6335; e-mail african@uiuc.edu; internet www.afrst.uiuc.edu.

Center for International Studies: Massachusetts Institute of Technology, Bldg E38, Room 648, Cambridge, MA 02139; tel. (617) 253-8093; fax (617) 253-9330; f. 1951; Dir Dr KENNETH OYE.

Center of International Studies: Bendheim Hall, Princeton University, Princeton, NJ 08544-1022; tel. (609) 258-4851; fax (609) 258-3988; e-mail mwdoyle@wws.princeton.edu; Dir Prof. MICHAEL DOYLE.

Council on Foreign Relations, Inc: 58 East 68th St, New York, NY 10021; tel. (212) 734-9400; fax (212) 861-1789; e-mail communications@cfr.org; internet www.cfr.org; f. 1921; 3,010 mems; library of 5,000 vols, 221 periodicals, clippings files and data bases; Pres. LESLIE H. GELB; publs include *Foreign Affairs* (quarterly).

Council on Regional Studies: 5 Ivy Lane, Princeton University, Princeton, NJ 08544; tel. (609) 258-4720; f. 1961; Dir JEFFREY HERBST.

Human Rights Watch/Africa: 350 Fifth Ave, 34th Floor, New York, NY 10118-3299; tel. (212) 290-4700; fax (212) 736-1300; e-mail hrwnyc@hrw.org; internet www.humanrightswatch.org; Chair. JONATHAN FANTON.

Institute of African Affairs: Duquesne University, 600 Forbes Ave, Pittsburgh, PA 15282; tel. (412) 434-6000; fax (412) 434-5146; f. 1957; research into uncommon languages of sub-Saharan Africa; library of 9,000 vols; Dir Rev. JOSEPH L. VARGA; publ. *African Reprint Series*.

Institute of African Studies: Columbia University School of International and Public Affairs, 420 West 118th St, New York, NY 10027; tel. (212) 854-4633; fax (212) 854-4639; e-mail mm1124@columbia.edu; internet www.columbia.edu.cu/sipa/REGIONAL/IAS/index.html; Dir MAHMOOD MAMDANI.

Institute of World Affairs (IWA): 1321 Pennsylvania Ave, SE, Washington, DC 20003-2027; f. 1924; tel. (860) 544-4141; fax (860) 544-5115; e-mail info@iwa.org; internet www.iwa.org; f. 1924; conducts seminars on international issues; Pres. HRACH GREGORIAN; publ. *IWA International* (irregular).

James S. Coleman African Studies Center: University of California, Los Angeles, CA 90095-1310; tel. (310) 825-3686; fax (310) 206-2250; f. 1959; centre for co-ordination of and research on Africa in the social sciences, the arts, humanities, the sciences and public health; and for multi-disciplinary graduate training in African studies; Dir Dr EDMOND J. KELLER; publs include *African Arts* (quarterly), *Ufahamu: Journal of the African Activists Association* (3 a year), *African Studies Centre Newsletter* (2 a year).

Library of International Relations: Chicago-Kent College of Law, Illinois Institute of Technology, 565 West Adams St, Chicago, IL 60661-3691; tel. (312) 906-5600; fax (312) 906-5679; internet www.infoctr.edu; f. 1932; financed by voluntary contributions; stimulates interest and research in international problems; conducts seminars and offers special services to businesses and academic institutions; library of 520,000 items; Pres. HOKEN SEKI; Dir MICKIE A. VOGES; publ. *Newsletter* (5 a year).

Program of African and Asian Languages: Northwestern University, 356 Kresge Hall, 1859 Sheridan Rd, Evanston, IL 60208-2209; tel. (847) 491-5288; fax (847) 467-1097; f. 1973; Dir RICHARD M. LEPINE.

Program of African Studies: Northwestern University, 620 Library Place, Evanston, IL 60208-4110; tel. (847) 491-7323; fax (847) 491-3739; e-mail african-studies@nwu.edu.; f. 1948; supported by various private and govt grants for research in Africa and the USA, as well as by university; awards undergraduate minor and graduate certificate of African studies to students enrolled at Northwestern University; sponsors fellowship awards for African students pursuing doctoral studies at Northwestern University; also sponsors brief residencies for students and practitioners of the African humanities; Dir Prof. JANE I. GUYER; publs include *PAS Newsletter*, *PAS Working Paper* series, conference proceedings.

School of Advanced International Studies: Johns Hopkins University, 1740 Massachusetts Ave, NW, Washington, DC 20036-1983; tel. (202) 663-5600; fax (202) 663-5683; Dean PAUL WOLFOWITZ; Dir of African Studies I. WILLIAM ZARTMAN; publs *SAIS Studies on Africa*, *SAIS African Library*.

TransAfrica/TransAfrica Forum: 1744 R St, NW, Washington, DC 20009-2410; tel. (202) 797-2301; fax (202) 797-2382; e-mail info@transafricaforum.org; internet www.transafricaforum.org; f. 1981; Pres. RANDALL ROBINSON; publs include *TransAfrica Forum Update*.

Woodrow Wilson School of Public and International Affairs (African Studies Program): Bendheim Hall, Princeton University, Princeton, NJ 08540; tel. (609) 258-5633; fax (609) 258-5974; e-mail herbst@princeton.edu; Program Dir Prof. JEFFREY HERBST.

VATICAN CITY

Pontificio Instituto di Studi Arabi e d'Islamistica: Viale di Trastevere 89, 00153 Rome; tel. (6) 5882676; fax (6) 5882595; e-mail pisai@flashnet.it; internet www.a-vip.com/pisai/; f. 1949; library of 24,000 vols; Dir P. JUSTO LACUNZA BALDA; publs include *Encounter* (monthly), *Islamochristiana* (annually), *Etudes arabes* (annually).

The ACP–EU Courier. Commission of the European Communities, 200 rue de la Loi, 1049 Brussels, Belgium; tel. (2) 299-30-12; fax (2) 299-30-02; affairs of the African, Caribbean and Pacific countries and the European Union; English and French edns; 6 a year.

Actividade Economica de Angola. Fundo de Comercialização, CP 1338, Luanda, Angola; tel. and fax (2) 330420; f. 1935; Dir Mario Alberto Adauta de Sousa; quarterly.

AFRE (African Trade Review). German Perez Carrasco 63, 28027 Madrid, Spain; tel. (91) 367-2403; fax (91) 408-7837; e-mail ofice@editorialofice.com; Editor Ed. Arsenio Pardo Rodriguez; monthly.

Africa. Istituto Italo-Africano per l'Africa e l'Oriente, Via Ulisse Aldrovandi 16, 00197 Rome, Italy; tel. (6) 3222323; fax (6) 3225348; e-mail isiaozaf@global-italianet.it; f. 1946; Dir Prof. Gian Luigi Rossi; in English, French and Italian; quarterly.

Africa. Edinburgh University Press, 22 George Sq., Edinburgh, EH8 9LF, Scotland; tel. (131) 650-4220; fax (131) 662-0053; e-mail journals@eup.ed.ac.uk; internet www.eup.ed.ac.uk; Editor Prof. Murray Last; quarterly; also annual bibliography.

Africa Analysis. Suite 2F, Diamond House, 36–38 Hatton Garden, London, EC1N 8EB, England; tel. (20) 7404-4321; fax (20) 7404-4351; e-mail aa@africaanalysis.com; f. 1986; Editor Ahmed Rajab; fortnightly.

Africa Confidential. 73 Farringdon Rd, London, EC1M 3JQ, England; tel. (20) 7831-3511; fax (20) 7831-6778; internet www.africa-confidential.com; f. 1960; political news and analysis; Editor Patrick Smith; fortnightly.

Africa Contemporary Record. Africana Publishing Co, Holmes & Meier Publishers, Inc, 160 Broadway, East Bldg, New York, NY 10038, USA; tel. (212) 374-0100; fax (212) 374-1313; internet hmplbo@aol.com; annual documents, country surveys, special essays, indices.

Africa Development. Council for the Development of Social Science Research in Africa (CODESRIA), BP 3304, Dakar, Senegal; tel. 259822; fax 241289; e-mail codesria@sonatel.senet.net; f. 1976; in French and English; Editor Tade Akin Aina; quarterly.

Africa Economic Digest. 26–32 Whistler St, London, N5 1NH, England; tel. (20) 7359-7069; fax (20) 7359-9409; e-mail jon.ansah@which.net; f. 1980; Editor Jon Offei-Ansah; fortnightly.

Africa Energy and Mining. 142 rue Montmartre, 75002 Paris, France; tel. 1-44-88-26-10; fax 1-44-88-26-15; e-mail indigo@indigo-net.com; internet www.africaintelligence.com; f. 1983; French and English edns; Editor Francis Perrin; fortnightly.

Africa Fund News. 50 Broad St, Suite 711, New York, NY 10004-2307, USA; tel. (212) 785-1024; fax (212) 785-1078; e-mail africafund@igc.apc.org; Editor Richard Knight; irregular.

Africa Health. Vine House, Fair Green, Reach, Cambridge, CB5 0JD, England; tel. (1638) 743633; fax (1638) 743998; e-mail paul@fsg.co.uk; internet www.fsg.co.uk; f. 1978; Editor Paul Chinnock; 6 a year.

Africa Insight. Africa Institute, POB 630, Pretoria 0001, South Africa; tel. (12) 328-6970; fax (12) 323-8153; e-mail beth@ia.org.za; internet www.ai.org.za; f. 1971; Editor Elizabeth Le Roux; quarterly.

Africa International. Paris, France; tel. 1-44-93-85-95; fax 1-44-93-74-68; f. 1958; political, economic and social development in francophone Africa; Editor Marie-Roger Biloa; monthly.

Africa Quarterly. Indian Council for Cultural Relations, Azad Bhavan, Indraprastha Estate, New Delhi 110 002, India; tel. (11) 3319309; fax (11) 3318647; Editor Dr T. G. Ramamurthi.

Africa Recovery. Rm S-931, United Nations, New York, NY 10017, USA; tel. (212) 963-6857; fax (212) 963-4556; e-mail africa_recovery@un.org;internetwww.un.org/ecosocdev/geninfo/

afrec; Man. Editor Nii K. Bentsi-Enchill; in English and French; quarterly.

Africa Research Bulletin. Africa Research Ltd, c/o Blackwell Publishers, 108 Cowley Rd, Oxford, OX4 1JF, England; tel. (1865) 791100; fax (1865) 791347; e-mail jnlinfo@blackwellpublishers.co.uk; f. 1964; bulletins on political and economic topics; Editor Pita Adams; monthly.

Africa Review. Walden Publishing, 2 Market St, Saffron Walden, Essex, CB10 1HZ, England; tel. (1799) 521150; fax (1799) 524805; e-mail waldenpub@easynet.co.uk; internet www.worldinformation.com; f. 1977; Gen. Editor Tony Axon; annually.

Africa 2000. Centro Cultural Hispano-Guineano, Apdo 180, Malabo, Equatorial Guinea; tel. 27-20; f. 1985; Equato-Guinean social and cultural review; Spanish; Editor Donato Ndongo-Bidyogo; quarterly.

African Administrative Studies. Centre africain de formation et de recherche administratives pour le développement (CAFRAD), BP 310, Tangier, 90001 Morocco; fax (9) 325785; e-mail cafrad@cafrad.org; internet www.cafrad.org; English, French and Arabic; 2 a year.

African Affairs. Royal African Society, School of African and Oriental Studies, Thornhaugh St, Russell Sq., London, WC1H 0XB, England; tel. (20) 7898-4390; e-mail ras@soas.ac.uk; f. 1901; social sciences and history; Editors Prof. David Killingray, Dr Stephen Ellis; quarterly.

African Arts. James S. Coleman African Studies Center, University of California, Los Angeles, CA 90095-1310, USA; tel. (310) 825-1218; fax (310) 206-2250; e-mail afriarts@ucla.edu; Editors Donald J. Cosentino, Doran H. Ross; quarterly.

African Book Publishing Record. Bowker-Saur, Windsor Court, East Grinstead House, East Grinstead, West Sussex, RH19 1XA, England; tel. (1342) 326972; fax (1342) 336192; e-mail customerservices@bowker-saur.co.uk; internet www.bowker-saur.co.uk; f. 1975; bibliographic listings, book reviews, articles and information on book trade activities in Africa; Editor Hans M. Zell; quarterly.

African Business. 7 Coldbath Sq., London, EC1R 4LQ, England; tel. (20) 7713-7711; fax (20) 7713-7970; e-mail icpubs@dial.pipex.com; internet www.africasia.com/icpubs; f. 1966; economics, business, commerce and finance; Editor Anver Versi; monthly.

African Concord International. 26–32 Whistler St, London, N5 1NH, England; tel. (20) 7359-5335; fax (20) 7359-9173; African and international current affairs; Nigerian and international edns; Editor Soji Omotunde; weekly.

African Environment. BP 3370, Dakar, Senegal; tel. 22-42-29; f. 1975; environmental issues; English and French edns; quarterly.

African Farming and Food Processing. Alain Charles Publishing Ltd, 27 Wilfred St, London, SW1E 6PR, England; tel. (20) 7834-7676; fax (20) 7973-0076; e-mail post@alain.demon.co.uk; internet www.alaincharles.com; Editor Jonquil L. Phelan; 6 a year.

African Journal of Health Sciences. African Forum for Health Sciences, POB 54840, Nairobi, Kenya; f. 1994; tel. (2) 722541; fax (2) 720030; e-mail kemrilib@ken.healthnet.org; Editor Dr D. Koech; quarterly.

African Journal of International Affairs & Development. POB 30678, Ibadan, Nigeria; tel. and fax (2) 8104165; e-mail eduserve@skannet.com.ng; Editor Jide Owoeye; 2 a year.

African Peoples Review. 34–36 Crown St, Reading, Berks, RG1 2SE, England; tel. (1734) 391010; fax (1734) 594442; f. 1992; reviews of publications and creative arts; Editor Herbert Ekwe-Ekwe; 3 a year.

African Publishing Review. POB 3773, Harare, Zimbabwe; tel. (4) 726405; fax (4) 705106; e-mail apnet@mango.zw; internet www.africanpublishers.org; Editor Morgan Chirumiko; English and French edns; 6 a year.

African Recorder. A-126 Niti Bagh, POB 595, New Delhi 110 049, India; tel. (11) 6565405; f. 1962; news digest; Editor A. K. B. Menon; fortnightly.

African Review. Dept of Political Science and Public Administration, University of Dar es Salaam, POB 35042, Dar es Salaam, Tanzania; tel. (51) 43130; fax (51) 43395; f. 1971; Editor Charles Gasarasi; 2 a year.

African Review of Business and Technology. Alain Charles Publishing Ltd, 27 Wilfred St, London, SW1E 6PR, England; tel. (20) 7834-7676; fax (20) 7973-0076; e-mail post@alain.demon .co.uk; internet www.alaincharles.com; Editor Jonquil L. Phelan; 11 a year.

African Security Review. Institute for Security Studies, POB 1787, Brooklyn Sq. 0075, South Africa; tel. (12) 346-9500; fax (12) 346-0998; e-mail iss@iss.co.za; African security and defence issues; Editor Sarah Meek; 6 a year.

African Studies. Carfax Publishing Ltd, POB 25, Abingdon, Oxfordshire, OX14 3UE, England; tel. (1235) 401000; fax (1235) 401550; f. 1921; social and cultural studies of southern Africa; Editor C. Mather; 2 a year.

African Studies Abstracts. Bowker-Saur, Windsor Court, East Grinstead House, East Grinstead, West Sussex RH19 1XA, England; tel. (1342) 326972; fax (1342) 336192; e-mail customer .services@bowker-saur.co.uk; internet www.bowker-saur.uk; abstracting journal of the African Studies Centre, Leiden, The Netherlands; quarterly.

African Studies Review. African Studies Association, Rutgers–The State University, Douglass Campus, 132 George St, New Brunswick, NJ 08901-1400, USA; tel. (732) 932-8173; e-mail callassa@rci.rutgers.edu; internet www.africanstudies.org; Editors Ralph Faulkingham, Mitzi Goheen; 3 a year.

African Textiles. Alain Charles Publishing Co, 27 Wilfred St, London, SW1E 6PR, England; tel. (20) 7834-7676; fax (20) 7973-0076; e-mail textiles@alain.demon.co.uk; internet www .alaincharles.com; Editor Zsa Tebbit; 6 a year.

Africana Bulletin. Institute of Developing Countries, Faculty of Geography and Regional Studies, University of Warsaw, Krakowskie Przedmieście 30, 00-927 Warsaw 64, Poland; tel. (22) 8262150; fax (22) 8261965; e-mail africana@plearn.edu.pl; f. 1964; articles in English and French; Editor Dr Bogdan Stefański; annual.

Africana Marburgensia. Philipps-Universität Marburg, Fachgebiet Religionsgeschichte, Fachbereich 05, 35032 Marburg, Am Plan 3, Germany; tel. (6421) 283930; e-mail relgesch@mailer .uni-marburgide; f. 1968; religion, law, economics; in English, French and German; Editors Christoph Elsas, Reiner Mahlke, Hans H. Münkner; 2 a year.

Africanus. Unisa Press, Periodicals, POB 392, Unisa 0003, South Africa; tel. (12) 429-3111; fax (12) 429-3221; e-mail unisapress@unisa.ac.za; f. 1972; development issues; 2 a year.

Afrika. Afrika-Verlag, 85276 Pfaffenhofen, Raiffeisenstrasse 24, Germany; tel. 8441-8690; fax 8441-76582; f. 1960; edns in German and French; Editors Inga Krugman-Randolf, Ursula Bell; 6 a year.

Afrika Spectrum. Institut für Afrika-Kunde, 20354 Hamburg, Neuer Jungfernstieg 21, Germany; tel. (40) 42834523; fax (40) 42834511; e-mail iak@uni-hamburg.de; internet www.rrz .uni-hamburg.de/IAK; articles in German, English and French; 3 a year.

Afrika Süd. Informationsstelle Südliches Afrika eV, 53227 Bonn, Königswintererstrasse 116, Germany; tel. (228) 464369; fax (228) 468177; e-mail issa@bonn.comlink.apc.org; internet www.issa-bonn.org; politics, economics, social and military affairs of southern Africa and German relations with the area; 6 a year.

Afrika und Übersee, Sprachen–Kulturen. c/o Dietrich Reimer Verlag, 10969 Berlin, Zimmerstrasse 26-27, Germany; tel. (30) 25911570; fax (30) 25911577; e-mail gdornemann .drv.gmv.dvk@reimer-verlag.de; f. 1910; African linguistics and cultures; in German, English and French; Editors E. Dammann, L. Gerhardt, H. Meyer-Bahlburg, S. Uhlig, J. Zwernemann; 2 a year.

Afrique Agriculture. 6 rue du Dr Solomon, 60119 Henonville, France; tel. 1-34-35-00-26; fax 1-30-32-04-83; f. 1975; Editor Alain Zolty; monthly.

Afrique-Asie. 3 rue de Metz, 75010 Paris, France; tel. 1-40-22-06-72; fax 1-45-23-28-02; e-mail africasi@micronet.fr; internet www.afrique-asie.com; monthly.

Afrique Expansion. 17 rue d'Uzes, 75002 Paris, France; tel. 1-40-13-30-30; fax 1-40-41-94-95; building and construction; Editor Michel Levron.

Afrique Contemporaine. La Documentation française, 29–31 quai Voltaire, 75344 Paris Cedex 07, France; tel. 1-40-15-70-00; fax 1-40-15-72-30; e-mail f-gaulme@ladocfrancaise.gouv.fr; f. 1962; political, economic and sociological studies; Editor-in-Chief François Gaulme; quarterly.

Afrique Entreprise. IC Publications, 10 rue Vineuse, 75784 Paris Cedex 16, France; tel. 1-44-30-81-00; fax 1-44-30-81-11; e-mail rosenwal@wanadoo.fr; internet www.rosenwald.com; 22 a year.

Afrique Médicale. BP 1826, Dakar, Senegal; f. 1960; tel. (221) 234880; telex 1300; fax (221) 225630; f. 1960; medical review; Editor, Prof. Paul Correa; 11 a year.

Afryka, Azja, Ameryka Łacińska. Instytut Krajow Rozwijajcych Sie, 02-089 Warsaw, Zwirki i Wigury 93, Poland; tel. (2) 223051; f. 1974; in Polish, with English and French summaries; Editor Prof. Władysław Kubiak; irregular.

Annales Aequatoria. Centre Aequatoria, Maison MSC, BP 779, 3ème rue, Limete, Kinshasa 1, Democratic Republic of the Congo; e-mail vinck.aequatoria@belgacom.net; internet http://ger-www.uia.ac.be/aequatoria; f. 1980; central African culture, languages and history; Editor Honoré Vinck; annually.

Botswana Notes and Records. The Botswana Society, POB 71, Gaborone, Botswana; tel. 351500; fax 359321; e-mail botsoc@ info.bw; f. 1969; Editor Rev. Derek Jones; annually.

Bulletin of the School of Oriental and African Studies. School of Oriental and African Studies, Thornhaugh St, Russell Sq., London, WC1H 0XG, England; tel. (20) 7637-2388; fax (20) 7436-3844; e-mail eg13@soas.ac.uk; internet www.bsoas .oupjournals.org; f. 1917; 3 a year.

Business in Africa. The Club Suite, 100 Piccadilly, POB 2602, London, W1A 3NY, England; tel. (20) 7495-7969; fax (20) 7495-7966; e-mail businessinafrica@compuserve.com; internet www.businessinafrica.com; Editor Richard Paris; monthly.

CAFRAD News. Centre africain de formation et de recherche administratives pour le développement (CAFRAD), BP 310, Tangier, 90001 Morocco; fax (9) 325785; English, French and Arabic; quarterly.

Cahiers d'Etudes Africaines. Ecole des hautes études en sciences sociales, 131 blvd St-Michel, 75005 Paris, France; tel. 1-40-46-70-80; fax 1-44-07-08-89; e-mail cahiers-afr@chess.fr; f. 1960; Editor J.-L. Amselle; in French and English; quarterly.

Canadian Journal of African Studies. Canadian Association of African Studies, c/o Barry Riddell, Dept of Geography, Queen's University, Kingston, ON K7L 3N6, Canada; tel. (613) 533-6037; fax (613) 533-6122; e-mail riddellb@qsilver.queensu.ca; Editors Barry Riddell, Dennis Cordell; 3 a year.

Communications Africa. Alain Charles Publishing Ltd, 27 Wilfred St, London, SW1E 6PR, England; tel. (20) 7834-7676; fax (20) 7973-0076; e-mail commsaf@alain.demon.co.uk; internet www.alaincharles.com; f. 1991; telecommunications, broadcasting and information technology; in French and English; Editor P. Cass; 6 a year.

Development Policy Review. Overseas Development Institute, Portland House, Stag Place, London, SW1 5DP, England; tel. (20) 7393-1600; fax (20) 7393-1699; f. 1982; Editor Sheila Page; quarterly.

Development and Socio-Economic Progress. Afro-Asian People's Solidarity Organization, 89 Abdel Aziz al-Saoud St, Manial El-Roda, Cairo, Egypt; tel. (2) 845495; English, Arabic and French edns; Editor-in-Chief Nouri Abdel Razzak; quarterly.

Dokumentationsdienst Afrika. Ausgewählte neuere Literatur, Deutsches Übersee-Institut, Übersee-Dokumentation, Referat Afrika (AFDOK), 20354 Hamburg, Neuer Jungfernstieg 21, Germany; tel. (40) 42834598; fax (40) 42834512; e-mail duei-dok@uni-hamburg.de; internet www.rrz.uni-hamburg.de/ duei-dok; current bibliography; quarterly.

East Africa Journal. POB 3209, Dar es Salaam, Tanzania; tel. 724711; f. 1964; Editor B. A. Ogot; monthly.

East African Studies. Makerere Institute of Social Research, Makerere University, POB 16022, Kampala, Uganda; irregular.

Economia de Moçambique: Companhia Editoria de Moçambique, CP 81, Beira, Mozambique; Editor Antonia de Almeida.

Economic Bulletin of Ghana. Economic Society of Ghana, POB 22, Legon, Accra, Ghana; tel. (1) 775381; Editor J. C. Degraft-Johnson; quarterly.

English Studies in Africa. c/o Dept of English, University of the Witwatersrand, 1 Jan Smuts Ave, PO Wits, 2050 Johannesburg, South Africa; tel. (11) 717-4106; fax (11) 403-7309; e-mail 071vhh@muse.wits.ac.za; f. 1959; journal of the humanities; Editor Prof. V. H. Houliston; bi-annually.

Ethiopian Register. POB 159, Avon, MN 56310-0159, USA, tel. (320) 845-7770; fax (320) 845-4993; e-mail editor@ EthiopianRegister.com; internet www.EthiopianRegister.com; f. 1994; monthly.

Ethiopian Review. POB 98499, Atlanta, GA 30539, USA; tel. and fax (404) 325-8411; Editor Elias Kifle; monthly.

Heritage of Zimbabwe. History Society of Zimbabwe, POB 8268, Causeway, Zimbabwe; tel. (4) 39175; f. 1956; history of Zimbabwe and adjoining territories; Editor Michael J. Kimberley; annually.

Horn of Africa Bulletin. Life and Peace Institute, POB 1520, SE-75145 Uppsala, Sweden; tel. (18) 169500; fax (18) 693059; e-mail mats.lundstrom@life-peace.org; internet www.life-peace .org; Editor Mats Lundström; bi-monthly.

Indian Ocean Newsletter. 142 rue Montmartre, 75002 Paris, France; tel. 1-44-88-26-10; fax 1-44-88-26-15; e-mail indigo@ indigo-net.com; internet www.africaintelligence.com; f. 1981; French and English edns; Editor Francis Soler; weekly.

International African Bibliography. Bowker-Saur, Windsor Court, East Grinstead House, East Grinstead, West Sussex RH19 1XA, England; tel. (1342) 326972; fax (1342) 336192; e-mail customerservices@bowker-saur.co.uk; internet www .bowker-saur.co.uk; bibliographic listings; quarterly.

International Journal of African Historical Studies. African Studies Center, Boston University, 270 Bay State Rd, Boston, MA 02215, USA; tel. (617) 353-7306; fax (617) 353-4975; e-mail ascpub@bu.edu; f. 1968; Editor Jean Hay; 3 a year.

Jeune Afrique. Groupe Jeune Afrique, 57 bis d'Auteuil, 75016 Paris, France; tel. 1-44-30-19-60; fax 1-44-30-19-30; e-mail mail box@jeuneafrique.com; f. 1960; Editor-in-Chief Béchir ben Yahmed; weekly.

Journal of African Economies. Oxford University Press, Great Clarendon St, Oxford, OX2 6DP, England; tel. (1865) 267907; fax (1865) 267485; e-mail jnlorders@oup.co.uk; internet www.jnls/list/jafeco; f. 1992; Man. Editors Paul Collier, Jan Willem Gunning, Benno Ndulu, Ademola Oyejide; quarterly.

Journal of African History. School of Oriental and African Studies, Thornhaugh St, Russell Sq., London, WC1H 0XG, England; tel. (20) 7637-2388; fax (20) 7436-3844; e-mail louisbrennerLB2@soas.ac.uk; f. 1960; Editor Louis Brenner; 3 a year.

Journal des Africanistes. Société des Africanistes, Musée de l'Homme, Palais de Chaillot, 17 place du Trocadéro, 75116 Paris, France; tel. 1-47-27-72-55; e-mail africanistes@wanadoo.fr; f. 1931; some articles in English; 2 a year.

Journal of Asian and African Studies. Dept of Sociology, Vari Hall 2106, York University, 4700 Keele St, Downsview, ON M3J 1P3, Canada; tel. (416) 441-6343; Editor Shivu Ishwaran.

Journal of Development Studies. Frank Cass and Co Ltd, Newbury House, 890-900 Eastern Ave, Newbury Park, London, IG2 7HH, England; tel. (20) 8599-8866; fax (20) 8599-0984; e-mail info@frankcass.com; internet www.frankcass.com; f. 1964; Editors Christopher Colclough, John Harriss, Chris Milner; 6 a year.

Journal of Ethiopian Studies. Institute of Ethiopian Studies, Addis Ababa University, POB 1176, Addis Ababa, Ethiopia; tel. (1) 119469; fax (1) 552688; e-mail IES.AAU@telecom.net.et; f. 1963; social and cultural anthropology, literature, history, linguistics; Man. Editor Birhanu Teferra; 2 a year.

Journal of Imperial and Commonwealth History. Frank Cass and Co Ltd, Newbury House, 890-900 Eastern Ave, Newbury Park, London, IG2 7HH, England; tel. (20) 8599-8866; fax (20) 8599-0984; f. 1972; Editors A. J. Stockwell, Peter Burroughs; 3 a year.

Journal of Modern African Studies. Cambridge University Press, The Edinburgh Bldg, Shaftesbury Rd, Cambridge, CB2 2RU, England; tel. (1223) 312393; fax (1223) 315052; e-mail information@cup.cam.ac.uk; internet www.cup.cam.ac.uk; politics and economics; Editor Prof. Christopher Clapham; quarterly.

Journal of Peasant Studies. Frank Cass and Co Ltd, Newbury House, 890-900 Eastern Ave, Newbury Park, London, IG2 7HH, England; tel. (20) 8599-8866; fax (20) 8599-0984; e-mail info@ frankcass.com; internet www.frankcass.com; f. 1973; Editors Terry Byres, Henry Bernstein; quarterly.

Journal of Religion in Africa. Dept of Theology and Religious Studies, University of Leeds, Leeds, West Yorkshire, LS2 9JT, England; tel. (113) 2333640; fax (113) 2333654; e-mail i.lawrie @leeds.ac.uk; internet www.brill.nl; f. 1967; Editor David Maxwell; quarterly.

Journal of Southern African Studies. Centre for Development Studies, University of Leeds, Leeds, West Yorkshire, LS2 9JT, England; tel. (1482) 811227; fax (1482) 815857; e-mail cfsl@york .ac.uk; internet www.tandf.co.uk/journals; f. 1974; Editors Jocelyn Alexander, Jo Beall, Hilary Sapire; quarterly.

Journal of the Third World Spectrum: POB 44843, Washington, DC 20026-4843, USA; tel. (202) 806-7649; e-mail fshams@ fac.howard.edu; f. 1989; Editor Prof. Feraidoon Shams; 2 a year.

Leeds Africa. African Studies Unit, University of Leeds, Leeds, West Yorkshire, LS2 9JT, England; tel. (113) 2335069; e-mail african-studies@leeds.ac.uk; newsletter; 2 a year.

La Lettre d'Afrique Expansion. 17 rue d'Uzès, 75002 Paris, France; tel. 1-40-13-33-81; fax 1-40-41-94-95; f. 1984; business affairs; Editor Hassan Ziady; weekly.

La Lettre du Continent. 142 rue Montmartre, 75002 Paris, France; tel. 1-44-88-26-10; fax 1-44-88-26-15; e-mail indigo@ indigo-net.com; f. 1985; Editor Maurice Botbol; fortnightly.

Marchés Tropicaux et Méditerranéens. 190 blvd Haussmann, 75008 Paris, France; tel. 1-44-95-99-50; fax 1-49-53-90-16; e-mail moreux@club-internet.fr; f. 1945; current affairs, mainly economics; Editor Serge Marpaud; weekly.

New African. 7 Coldbath Sq., London, EC1R 4LQ, England; tel. (20) 7713-7711; fax (20) 7713-7970; e-mail icpubs@dial.pipex .com; internet www.africasia.com/icpubs; f. 1966; politics and general interest; Editor Baffour Ankomah; monthly.

Newslink Africa. 7-11 Kensington High St, London, W8 5NP, England; tel. (20) 7368-3306; fax (20) 7938-4168; e-mail 101353.1745@compuserve.com; internet www.adlinkint -newslinkafri.com; business and development issues; Editor Shamlal Puri; weekly.

Nigrizia–Il Mensile dell'Africa e del Mondo Nero. Vicolo Pozzo 1, 37129 Verona, Italy; tel. (45) 596238; fax (45) 8031455; fax (45) 8001737; e-mail nigrizia@tin.it; f. 1883; Dir Pier Maria Mazzola; monthly.

Nouveaux Cahiers de l'IUED. 24 rue Rothschild, CP 136, 1211 Geneva 21, Switzerland; tel. (22) 9065950; fax (22) 9065953; internet www.iued.ch/; Editor (vacant); 2 a year.

Nouvelles du CAFRAD. Centre africain de Formation et de Recherche administratives pour le Développement (CAFRAD), BP 310, Tangier, 90001 Morocco; fax (9) 325785; Arabic, English, French; quarterly.

Odu. A Journal of West African Studies, New Series (1969–). Obafemi Awolowo University Press, Periodicals Dept, Ile-Ife, Nigeria; tel. (36) 230284; Editor Biadun Adediren; 2 a year.

Opportunity Africa. Charles Barker Publishing, I BSMG, 56 Dean St, London, W1V 6HX, England; tel. (20) 7343-3377; fax (20) 7343-3361; e-mail oppafric@cbarker.co.uk; f. 1994; Editor Martin D. Clark; quarterly.

Optima. POB 61587, Marshalltown 2107, South Africa; tel. (11) 638-5189; fax (11) 638-3771; e-mail sspencercrooks@ angloamerican.co.za; internet www.angloamerican.co.za; f. 1951; political, economic, social, cultural and scientific aspects of South and southern African development; Editor Norman Barber; 2 a year.

Politique Africaine. Editions Karthala, 22–24 blvd Arago, 75013 Paris, France; tel. 1-43-31-15-59; fax 1-45-35-27-05; e-mail karthala@wanadoo.fr; f. 1981; political science and international relations; Editor-in-Chief Richard Banégas; quarterly.

Red Cross, Red Crescent. BP 372, 1211 Geneva 19, Switzerland; English, French and Spanish edns; tel. (22) 7304222; fax (22) 7530395; e-mail rcrc@ifrc.org; Editors Jean Milligan, Jean-François Berger; quarterly.

Research in African Literatures. Indiana University Press, 601 North Morton St, Bloomington, IN 47404, USA; tel. (812) 855-9449; fax (812) 855-8507; e-mail journals@indiana.edu/URL; internet www.iupjournals.org; Editor Abiola Irele; quarterly.

Research Review. Institute of African Studies, POB 73, University of Ghana, Legon, Ghana; tel. (21) 775512; f. 1965; Editor K. Arhin; 3 a year.

Review of African Political Economy. Taylor and Francis Ltd, POB 25, Abingdon, Oxfordshire, OX14 3UE, England; tel. (1235) 401000; fax (1235) 401550; e-mail editor@roape.org; f. 1974; Editors Jan Burgess, Chris Allen; quarterly.

Revista Internacional de Estudos Africanos. Instituto de Investigação Científica Tropical, Ministério da Ciência e da Tecnologia, Rua de Junqueira 86-1°, 1300 Lisbon, Portugal; tel. (1) 3622621; fax (1) 3631460; 2 a year.

Revue Diplomatique de l'Ocean Indien. rue H. Rabesahala, BP 46, Antsakaviro, 101 Antananarivo, Madagascar; tel. 22536; fax 34534; f. 1982; Editor Georges Ranaivasoa; quarterly.

Revue Française d'Etudes Politiques Africaines. Société Africaine d'Edition, BP 1877, Dakar, Senegal; f. 1966; political; Editors Pierre Biarnès, Philippe Decraene; monthly.

Revue Tiers Monde. 14 ave du Bois-de-l'Epine, BP 90, 91003 Evry Cedex, France; tel. 1-60-87-30-30; fax 1-60-79-20-45; e-mail revues@puf.com; f. 1960; development issues; Editor Gérard Grellet; quarterly.

SIMNOW. SIM Media Dept, 10 Huntingdale Blvd, Scarborough, ON M1W 2S5, Canada; tel. (416) 497-2424; fax (416) 497-2444; e-mail editor@sim.org; f. 1958; edns also publ. in Australia, NZ, Southern Africa, Singapore, Switzerland and UK; French, German, Italian and Chinese edns; Editorial Dir David W. Fuller; quarterly.

South Africa Survey. South African Institute of Race Relations, POB 31044, Braamfontein 2017, South Africa; tel. (11) 403-3600; fax (11) 403-3671; Dir J. S. Kane-Berman; annually.

Southern Africa Exclusive. Ludgate House, Suite 71, 107-111 Fleet St, London, EC4A 2AB, England; tel. (20) 7353-1117; fax (20) 7353-1516; f. 1992; Editor Terry Bell; monthly.

Southern Africa Monitor. 179 Queen Victoria St, London, EC4V 4DU, England; tel. (20) 7248-0468; fax (20) 7248-0467; e-mail marketing@businessmonitor.com; internet www.businessmonitor.com/southernafrica.html; f. 1996; business; Editors Paul Gamble, Nick Broughton; monthly.

Southern Africa Monthly Regional Bulletin–MRB. 112 4th St, NE, Washington, DC 20002, USA; tel. (202) 543-9050; fax (202) 543-7957; e-mail southscan@allafrica.com; f. 1992; economic and business affairs, politics; Publr David Coetzee.

Southern Africa Report. POB 261579, Excom 2023, South Africa; tel. (11) 646-8790; fax (11) 646-2596; e-mail rlouw@wn.apc.org; internet www.sareport.org.za; f. 1983; current affairs and financial newsletter; Publr and Editor Raymond Louw; 50 a year.

Southscan. 112 4th St, NE, Washington, DC 20002, USA; tel. (202) 543-9050; fax (202) 543-7957; e-mail southscan@allafrica.com; f. 1986; political and economic affairs in southern Africa; Publr David Coetzee; fortnightly.

Sudan Democratic Gazette. POB 2295, London, W14 0ND, England; tel. (20) 7602-4401; fax (20) 7602-0106; e-mail malwal@sudemgaz.demon.co.uk; f. 1990; Publr and Editor Bona Malwal.

Sudanow. POB 2651, 7 Gamhouria Ave, Khartoum, Sudan; tel. and fax (11) 77915; f. 1976.

Third World Quarterly. Dept. of Geography, Royal Holloway College, Egham, Surrey, TW20 0EX, England; fax (20) 8947-1243; e-mail sqadir@globalnet.co.uk; internet www.tandf.co.uk/journals; Editor Shahid Qadir.

Uganda Confidential. POB 9948, Kampala, Uganda; fax (41) 245580; Editors Gerald Mwaita, John Kateeba; weekly.

Vostok (Oriens). Afro-Aziatskiye Obtchestva: Istoria i Sovremenost, Institut Vostokovedeniya, Institut Afriki, Rossiyskaya Akad. Nauk, Moscow 103031, 12 Rozhdestvenka St, Russia; tel. (095) 2026650; f. 1955; text in Russian, summaries in English; Editor-in-Chief Dr V. V. Naumkin; 6 a year.

West Africa. 321 City Rd, London, EC1V 1LJ, England; tel. (20) 7837-4116; fax (20) 7278-4123; e-mail wa@westafricamagazine.co.uk; internet www.westafricamagazine.co.uk; f. 1917; Editor Adama Gaye; weekly.

West African Journal of Archaeology: c/o Dept of Archaeology, University of Ibadan, Ibadan, Nigeria; f. 1971; annually.

PART TWO
Regional Organizations

THE UNITED NATIONS IN AFRICA

Address: United Nations Plaza, New York, NY 10017, USA.

Telephone: (212) 963-1234; **fax:** (212) 963-4879; **internet:** www.un.org.

The United Nations (UN) was founded on 24 October 1945. The organization aims to maintain international peace and security, and to develop international co-operation in addressing economic, social, cultural and humanitarian problems. The principal organs of the UN are the General Assembly, the Security Council, the Economic and Social Council (ECOSOC), the International Court of Justice and the Secretariat. The General Assembly, which meets for three months each year, comprises representatives of all UN member states. The Security Council investigates disputes between member countries, and may recommend ways and means of peaceful settlement: it comprises five permanent members (the People's Republic of China, France, Russia, the United Kingdom and the USA) and 10 other members elected by the General Assembly for a two-year period. The Economic and Social Council comprises representatives of 54 member states, elected by the General Assembly for a three-year period: it promotes co-operation on economic, social, cultural and humanitarian matters, acting as a central policy-making body and co-ordinating the activities of the UN's specialized agencies. The International Court of Justice comprises 15 judges of different nationalities, elected for nine-year terms by the General Assembly and the Security Council: it adjudicates in legal disputes between UN member states.

Secretary-General of the United Nations: KOFI ANNAN (Ghana) (1997–2001).

MEMBER STATES IN AFRICA SOUTH OF THE SAHARA

(with assessments for percentage contributions to UN budget for 2000, and year of admission)

Angola	0.010	1976
Benin	0.002	1960
Botswana	0.010	1966
Burkina Faso	0.002	1960
Burundi	0.001	1962
Cameroon	0.013	1960
Cape Verde	0.002	1975
Central African Republic	0.001	1960
Chad	0.001	1960
Comoros	0.001	1975
Congo, Democratic Republic	0.007	1960
Congo, Republic	0.003	1960
Côte d'Ivoire	0.009	1960
Djibouti	0.001	1977
Equatorial Guinea	0.001	1968
Eritrea	0.001	1993
Ethiopia	0.006	1945
Gabon	0.015	1960
The Gambia	0.001	1965
Ghana	0.007	1957
Guinea	0.003	1958
Guinea-Bissau	0.001	1974
Kenya	0.007	1963
Lesotho	0.002	1966
Liberia	0.002	1945
Madagascar	0.003	1960
Malawi	0.002	1964
Mali	0.003	1960
Mauritania	0.001	1961
Mauritius	0.009	1968
Mozambique	0.001	1975
Namibia	0.007	1990
Niger	0.002	1960
Nigeria	0.032	1960
Rwanda	0.001	1962
São Tomé and Príncipe	0.001	1975
Senegal	0.006	1960
Seychelles	0.002	1976
Sierra Leone	0.001	1961
Somalia	0.001	1960
South Africa	0.366	1945
Sudan	0.007	1956
Swaziland	0.002	1968
Tanzania*	0.003	1961
Togo	0.001	1960
Uganda	0.004	1962
Zambia	0.002	1964
Zimbabwe	0.009	1980

* Tanganyika was a member of the United Nations from December 1961 and Zanzibar was a member from December 1963. From April 1964 the United Republic of Tanganyika and Zanzibar continued as a single member, changing its name to United Republic of Tanzania in November 1964.

AFRICAN PERMANENT MISSIONS TO THE UNITED NATIONS

(with Permanent Representatives—July 2000)

Angola: 125 East 73rd St, New York, NY 10021; tel. (212) 861-5656; fax (212) 861-9295; JOSÉ GONÇALVES MARTIN PATRICIO.

Benin: 4 East 73rd St, New York, NY 10021; tel. (212) 249-6014; fax (212) 734-4735; e-mail benun@undp.org; JOËL WASSI ADECHI.

Botswana: 103 East 37th St, New York, NY 10016; tel. (212) 889-2277; fax (212) 725-5061; e-mail botswana@un.int; LEGWAILA JOSEPH LEGWAILA.

Burkina Faso: 115 East 73rd St, New York, NY 10021; tel. (212) 288-7515; fax (212) 772-3562; e-mail bfaun@undp.org; MICHEL KAFANDO.

Burundi: 336 East 45th St, 12th Floor, New York, NY 10017; tel. (212) 499-0001; fax (212) 499-0006; GAMALIEL NDARUZANIYE.

Cameroon: 22 East 73rd St, New York, NY 10021; tel. (212) 794-2295; fax (212) 249-0533; MARTIN BELINGA EBOUTOU.

Cape Verde: 27 East 69th St, New York, NY 10021; tel. (212) 472-0333; fax (212) 794-1398; e-mail cpvun@undp.org; JOSÉ LUIS BARBOSA LEÃO MONTEIRO.

Central African Republic: 386 Park Ave South, Suite 1614, New York, NY 10016; tel. (212) 679-8089; fax (212) 545-8326; ANTONIO DEINDE FERNANDEZ.

Chad: 211 East 43rd St, Suite 1703, New York, NY 10017; tel. (212) 986-0980; fax (212) 986-0152; e-mail tcd@undp.org; AHMAT A. HAGGAR.

Comoros: 420 East 50th St, New York, NY 10022; tel. (212) 972-8010; fax (212) 983-4712; e-mail comun@undp.org; Chargé d'affaires a.i. MAHMOUD MOHAMED ABDOU.

Congo, Democratic Republic: 866 United Nations Plaza, Suite 511, New York, NY 10017; tel. (212) 319-8061; fax (212) 319-8232; e-mail drcun@undp.org; ANDRÉ MWAMBA KAPANGA.

Congo, Republic: 14 East 65th St, New York, NY 10021; tel. (212) 744-7840; fax (212) 744-7975; BASILE IKOUEBE.

Côte d'Ivoire: 46 East 74th St, New York, NY 10021; tel. (212) 717-5555; fax (212) 717-4492; e-mail civun@undp.org; internet www.un.int/cotedivoire; CLAUDE STANISLAS BOUAH-KAMON.

Djibouti: 866 United Nations Plaza, Suite 4011, New York, NY 10017; tel. (212) 753-3163; fax (212) 223-1276; e-mail djiboutiun@aol.com; ROBLE OLHAYE.

Equatorial Guinea: 57 Magnolia Ave, Mount Vernon, NY 10553; tel. (914) 667-6913; fax (914) 667-6838; e-mail gnq@undp.org; TEODORO BIYOGO NSUE.

Eritrea: 800 Second Ave, 18th Floor, New York, NY 10017; tel. (212) 687-3390; fax (212) 687-3138; e-mail eriun@undp.org; HAILE MENKERIOS.

Ethiopia: 866 Second Ave, 3rd Floor, New York, NY 10017; tel. (212) 421-1830; fax (212) 754-0360; e-mail ethun@undp.org; internet www.un.int/ethiopia; Dr DURI MOHAMMED.

Gabon: 18 East 41st St, 9th Floor, New York, NY 10017; tel. (212) 686-9720; fax (212) 689-5769; DENIS DANGUE RÉWAKA.

The Gambia: 800 Second Ave, Suite 400F, New York, NY 10017; tel. (212) 949-6640; fax (212) 856-9820; e-mail gambia@un.int; internet www.un.int/gambia; BABOUCARR-BLAISE ISMAILA JAGNE.

Ghana: 19 East 47th St, New York, NY 10017; tel. (212) 832-1300; fax (212) 751-6743; e-mail ghana@un.int; internet www.un.unt/ghana; NANA EFFEH-APENTENG.

Guinea: 140 East 39th St, New York, NY 10016; tel. (212) 687-8115; fax (212) 687-8248; MAHAWA BANGOURA CAMARA.

Guinea-Bissau: 211 East 43rd St, Suite 704, New York, NY 10017; tel. (212) 338-9380; fax (212) 573-6094; e-mail gnbun@undp.org; JOÃO SOARES.

Kenya: 866 United Nations Plaza, Suite 486, New York, NY 10017; tel. (212) 421-4740; fax (212) 486-1985; e-mail kenun@undp.org; PHARES MICHAEL KUINDWA.

Lesotho: 204 East 39th St, New York, NY 10016; tel. (212) 661-1690; fax (212) 682-4388; e-mail les@missions.un.org; PERCY METSING MANGOAELA.

Liberia: 820 Second Ave, 13th Floor, New York, NY 10017; tel. (212) 687-1033; fax (212) 687-1035; NEH DUKULY-TOLBERT.

Madagascar: 820 Second Ave, Suite 404, New York, NY 10017; tel. (212) 986-9491; fax (212) 986-6271; e-mail repermad@undp.org; internet www.nyrepermad.org; JEAN DELACROIX BAKONIARIVO.

Malawi: 600 Third Ave, 30th Floor, New York, NY 10016; tel. (212) 949-0180; fax (212) 599-5021; e-mail mwiun@undp.org; Prof. YUSUF MCDADLLY JUWAYEYI.

Mali: 111 East 69th St, New York, NY 10021; tel. (212) 737-4150; fax (212) 472-3778; MOCTAR OUANE.

Mauritania: 211 East 43rd St, Suite 2000, New York, NY 10017; tel. (212) 986-7963; fax (212) 986-8419; e-mail mauritania@un.int; MAHFOUDH OULD DEDDACH.

Mauritius: 211 East 43rd St, 15th Floor, New York, NY 10017; tel. (212) 949-0190; fax (212) 697-3829; e-mail twwan@undp.org; ANUND PRIYAY NEEWOOR.

Mozambique: 420 East 50th St, New York, NY 10022; tel. (212) 644-5965; fax (212) 644-5972; e-mail mozun@undp.org; internet www.un.int/mozambique; CARLOS DOS SANTOS.

Namibia: 135 East 36th St, New York, NY 10016; tel. (212) 685-2003; fax (212) 685-1561; e-mail namibia@un.int; MARTIN ANDJABA.

Niger: 417 East 50th St, New York, NY 10022; tel. (212) 421-3260; fax (212) 753-6931; OUSMANE MOUTARI.

Nigeria: 828 Second Ave, New York, NY 10017; tel. (212) 953-9130; fax (212) 697-1970; e-mail ngaun@undp.org; ARTHUR C. I. MBANEFO.

Rwanda: 124 East 39th St, New York, NY 10016; tel. (212) 679-9010; fax (212) 679-9133; e-mail rwaun@undp.org; JOSEPH W. MUTA-BOBA.

São Tomé and Príncipe: 400 Park Ave, 7th Floor, New York, NY 10022; tel. (212) 317-0533; fax (212) 317-0580; e-mail stpun@undp.org; Chargé d'affaires a.i. DOMINGOS AUGUSTO FERREIRA.

Senegal: 238 East 68th St, New York, NY 10021; tel. (212) 517-9030; fax (212) 517-3032; IBRA DEGUÈNE KA.

Seychelles: 800 Second Ave, Room 400C, New York, NY 10017; tel. (212) 972-1785; fax (212) 972-1786; e-mail seychelles@un.int; CLAUDE MOREL.

Sierra Leone: 245 East 49th St, New York, NY 10017; tel. (212) 688-1656; fax (212) 688-4924; e-mail sierraleone@un.int; IBRAHIM M'BABA KAMARA.

Somalia: 425 East 61st St, Suite 702, New York, NY 10021; tel. (212) 688-9140; fax (212) 759-0651; e-mail somun@undp.org; Chargé d'affaires a.i. FATUN MOHAMED HASSAN.

South Africa: 333 East 38th St, 9th Floor, New York, NY 10016; tel. (212) 213-5583; fax (212) 692-2498; e-mail soafun@undp.org; DUMISANA SHADRACK KUMALO.

Sudan: 655 Third Ave, Suite 500-510, New York, NY 10017; tel. (212) 573-6033; fax (212) 573-6160; e-mail sdnun@undp.org; ELFATIH MOHAMED AHMED ERWA.

Swaziland: 408 East 50th St, New York, NY 10022; tel. (212) 371-8910; fax (212) 754-2755; e-mail swaziland@un.int; CLIFFORD SIBUSISO MAMBA.

Tanzania: 205 East 42nd St, 13th Floor, New York, NY 10017; tel. (212) 972-9160; fax (212) 682-5232; e-mail tzrepny@aol.com; DAUDI NGELAUTWA MWAKAWAGO.

Togo: 112 East 40th St, New York, NY 10016; tel. (212) 490-3455; fax (212) 983-6684; e-mail togoun@undp.org; ROLAND YAO KPOTSRA.

Uganda: 336 East 45th St, New York, NY 10017; tel. (212) 949-0110; fax (212) 687-4517; e-mail ugaun@undp.org; Prof. MATIA MULAMBA SEMAKULA KIWANUKA.

Zambia: 800 Second Ave, 9th Floor, New York, NY 10017; tel. (212) 972-7200; fax (212) 972-7360; e-mail zmbun@undp.org; PETER LESA KASANDA.

Zimbabwe: 128 East 56th St, New York, NY 10022; tel. (212) 980-9511; fax (212) 308-6705; e-mail zweun@undp.org; T. J. B. JOKONYA.

Observers

Asian-African Legal Consultative Committee: 404 East 66th St, Apt 12C, New York, NY 10021; tel. (212) 734-7608; e-mail 102077.27512@compuserve.com; K. BHAGWAT-SINGH.

Commonwealth Secretariat: 800 Second Ave, 4th Floor, New York, NY 10017; tel. (212) 599-6190; fax (212) 972-3970; e-mail chogrm@aol.com.

La Francophonie: 801 Second Ave, Suite 605, New York, NY 10017; tel. (212) 867-6771; fax (212) 867-3840; e-mail francophonie @un.int; RIDHA BOUABID.

International Committee of the Red Cross: 801 Second Ave, 18th Floor, New York, NY 10017; tel. (212) 599-6021; fax (212) 599-6009; e-mail mail@icrc.delnyc.org; SYLVIE JUNOD.

International Federation of Red Cross and Red Crescent Societies: 630 Third Ave, Suite 2104, New York, NY 10017; tel. (212) 338-0161; fax (212) 338-9832; e-mail ifrcny@nygate.undp.org; ENTCHO GOSPODINOV.

Organization of African Unity: 346 East 50th St, New York, NY 10022; tel. (212) 319-5490; fax (212) 319-7135; AMADOU KÉBÉ.

Organization of the Islamic Conference: 130 East 40th St, 5th Floor, New York, NY 10016; tel. (212) 883-0140; fax (212) 883-0143; e-mail oicun@undp.org; internet www.un.int/oic; MOKHTAR LAMANI.

Several other intergovernmental organizations, including the African, Caribbean and Pacific Group of States and the African Development Bank (q.v.), have standing invitations to participate in the work of the General Assembly, but do not maintain permanent offices in New York.

Economic Commission for Africa—ECA

Address: Africa Hall, POB 3001, Addis Ababa, Ethiopia.

Telephone: (1) 515826; **fax:** (1) 512233; **e-mail:** ecainfo@un.org; **internet:** www.un.org/depts/eca.

The UN Economic Commission for Africa was founded in 1958 by a resolution of the UN Economic and Social Council (ECOSOC) to initiate and take part in measures for facilitating Africa's economic development.

MEMBERS

Algeria	Eritrea	Niger
Angola	Ethiopia	Nigeria
Benin	Gabon	Rwanda
Botswana	The Gambia	São Tomé and
Burkina Faso	Ghana	Príncipe
Burundi	Guinea	Senegal
Cameroon	Guinea-Bissau	Seychelles
Cape Verde	Kenya	Sierra Leone
Central African	Lesotho	Somalia
Republic	Liberia	South Africa
Chad	Libya	Sudan
Comoros	Madagascar	Swaziland
Congo, Democratic	Malawi	Tanzania
Republic	Mali	Togo
Congo, Republic	Mauritania	Tunisia
Côte d'Ivoire	Mauritius	Uganda
Djibouti	Morocco	Zambia
Egypt	Mozambique	Zimbabwe
Equatorial Guinea	Namibia	

Organization

(July 2000)

COMMISSION

The Commission may only act with the agreement of the government of the country concerned. It is also empowered to make recommendations on any matter within its competence directly to the government of the member or associate member concerned, to governments admitted in a consultative capacity, and to the UN Specialized Agencies. The Commission is required to submit for prior consideration by ECOSOC any of its proposals for actions that would be likely to have important effects on the international economy.

CONFERENCE OF MINISTERS

The Conference, which meets every two years, is attended by ministers responsible for economic or financial affairs, planning and development of governments of member states, and is the main deliberative body of the Commission.

The Commission's responsibility to promote concerted action for the economic and social development of Africa is vested primarily in the Conference, which considers matters of general policy and the priorities to be assigned to the Commission's programmes, considers inter-African and international economic policy, and makes recommendations to member states in connection with such matters.

OTHER POLICY-MAKING BODIES

A Conference of Ministers of Finance and a Conference of Ministers responsible for economic and social development and planning meet in alternate years to formulate policy recommendations. Each is served by a committee of experts. Five intergovernmental committees of experts attached to the Sub-regional Development Centres (see below) meet annually and report to the Commission through a Technical Preparatory Committee of the Whole, which was established in 1979 to deal with matters submitted for the consideration of the Conference.

Seven other committees meet regularly to consider issues relating to the following policy areas: women and development; development information; sustainable development; human development and civil society; industry and private sector development; natural resources and science and technology; and regional co-operation and integration.

SECRETARIAT

The Secretariat provides the services necessary for the meeting of the Conference of Ministers and the meetings of the Commission's subsidiary bodies, carries out the resolutions and implements the programmes adopted there. It comprises an Office of the Executive Secretary, the African Centre for Women and the following eight divisions: Food Security and Sustainable Development; Development Management; Development Information Services; Regional Co-operation and Integration; Programme Planning, Finance and Evaluation; Economic and Social Policy; Human Resources and System Management; Conference and General Services.

Executive Secretary: KINGSLEY Y. AMOAKO (Ghana).

SUB-REGIONAL DEVELOPMENT CENTRES

Multinational Programming and Operational Centres (MULPOCs) were established, in 1977, to implement regional development programmes. In May 1997 the Commission decided to transform the MULPOCs into Sub-regional Development Centres (SRDCs) in order to enable member states to play a more effective role in the process of African integration and to facilitate the integration efforts of the other UN agencies active in the sub-regions. In addition, the SRDCs were to act as the operational arms of ECA at national and sub-regional levels: to ensure harmony between the objectives of sub-regional and regional programmes and those defined by the Commission; to provide advisory services; to facilitate sub-regional economic co-operation, integration and development; to collect and disseminate information; to stimulate policy dialogue; and to promote gender issues. In July 1997 it was reported that ECA intended to deploy 25% of its professional personnel in the SRDCs (up from 9%) and to allocate approximately 40% of its budget to the Centres.

Central Africa: POB 836, Yaoundé, Cameroon; tel. 23-14-61; fax 23-31-85; e-mail casrdc@camnet.cm; Dir ABDOULAYE NIANG.

Eastern Africa: c/o UNDP, ave de l'Armée 12, BP 445, Kigali, Rwanda; tel. 77822; fax 76263; Dir HALIDOU OUÉDRAOGO.

North Africa: POB 316, Tangier, Morocco; tel. (9) 322346; fax (9) 340357; e-mail srdc@cybermania.net.ma; Dir S. JUGESSUR.

Southern Africa: POB 30647, Lusaka, Zambia; tel. (1) 228503; fax (1) 236949; e-mail uneca@zamnet.zm; Dir Dr ROBERT M. OKELLO.

West Africa: POB 744, Niamey, Niger; tel. 72-29-61; fax 72-28-94; Dir HENRI SOUMAH.

Activities

The Commission's activities are designed to encourage sustainable socio-economic development in Africa and to increase economic co-operation among African countries and between Africa and other parts of the world. The Secretariat is guided in its efforts by major regional strategies including the Abuja Treaty establishing the African Economic Community signed under the aegis of the Organization of African Unity and the UN New Agenda for the Development of Africa covering the period 1991–2000. ECA's main programme areas for the period 1996–2001 were based on an Agenda for Action, which was announced by the OAU Council of Ministers in March 1995 and adopted by African heads of state in June, with the stated aim of 'relaunching Africa's economic and social development'. The five overall objectives were to facilitate economic and social policy analysis and implementation; to ensure food security and sustainable development; to strengthen development management; to harness information for development; and to promote regional co-operation and integration. In all its activities ECA aimed to promote the themes of capacity-building and of fostering leadership and the empowerment of women in Africa. In May 1998 ECA's African Centre for Women inaugurated a new Fund for African Women's Development to support capacity-building activities.

DEVELOPMENT INFORMATION SYSTEMS

Until 1997 regional development information management was promoted through the Pan-African Development Information

System—PADIS (which was established in 1980 and known until 1989 as the Pan-African Documentation and Information Service). In 1997 the Development Information Services Division (DISD) was created, with responsibility for co-ordinating the implementation of the Harnessing Information Technology for Africa project (in the context of the UN system-wide Special Initiative on Africa—see p. 84) and for the implementation of the African Information Society Initiative (AISI), a framework for creating an information and communications infrastructure; for overseeing quality enhancement and dissemination of statistical databases; for improving access to information by means of enhanced library and documentation services, and output; and by strengthening geo-information systems for sustainable development. In addition, ECA encourages member governments to liberalize the telecommunications sector and stimulate imports of computers in order to enable the expansion of information technology throughout Africa.

Regional statistical development activities are managed through the Co-ordinating Committee on African Statistical Development (CASD, established in 1992). The CASD facilitates the harmonization of statistical systems and methodologies at regional and national level; establishes mechanisms for the continuous exchange of information between governments, national agencies and regional and sub-regional bodies, and all bilateral and multilateral agencies; identifies and proposes new lines of action; and informs the Conference of African Planners, Statisticians and Population and Information Specialists (PSPI) on the progress of the Addis Ababa Plan of Action for Statistical Development in the 1990s (adopted in 1992). In May 1997 five task forces were established to undertake the CASD's activities; these covered the following areas: improving e-mail connectivity; monitoring the implementation of the Addis Ababa Plan of Action; strengthening statistical training programme for Africa (STPA) centres; assisting with the formation of census and household survey data service centres in two–five pilot countries, and with the establishment of a similar regional ECA service centre; and establishing live databases, comprising core macro and sectoral statistical indicators, initially as a pilot project in two–five countries, with eventual links to a regional database facility.

ECA assists its member states in (i) population data collection and data processing; (ii) analysis of demographic data obtained from censuses or surveys; (iii) training demographers at the Regional Institute for Population Studies (RIPS) in Accra, Ghana, and at the Institut de formation et de recherche démographiques (IFORD) in Yaoundé, Cameroon; (iv) formulation of population policies and integrating population variables in development planning, through advisory missions and through the organization of national seminars on population and development; and (v) dissemination of information through its *Newsletter, Demographic Handbook for Africa,* the *African Population Studies* series and other publications. The strengthening of national population policies was an important element of ECA's objective of ensuring food security in African countries. The Ninth PSPI was held in March 1996, in Addis Ababa, Ethiopia.

DEVELOPMENT MANAGEMENT

ECA aims to assist governments, public corporations, universities and the private sector in improving their financial management; strengthening policy-making and analytical capacities; adopting measures to redress skill shortages; enhancing human resources development and utilization; and promoting social development through programmes focusing on youth, people with disabilities and the elderly. The Secretariat organizes training workshops, seminars and conferences at national, subregional and regional levels for ministers, public administrators and senior policy-makers, as well as for private and non-governmental organizations. ECA aims to increase the participation of women in economic development and incorporates this objective into its administrative activities and work programmes.

Following the failure to implement many of the proposals under the UN Industrial Development Decade for Africa (IDDA, 1980–90) and the UN Programme of Action for African Economic Recovery and Development (1986–90), a second IDDA was adopted by the Conference of African Ministers of Industry in July 1991. The main objectives of the second IDDA included the consolidation and rehabilitation of existing industries, the expansion of new investments, and the promotion of small-scale industries and technological capabilities. In June 1996 a conference, organized by ECA, was held in Accra, Ghana, with the aim of reviving private investment in Africa in order to stimulate the private sector and promote future economic development. In October 1999 the first African Development Forum (ADF) was held in Addis Ababa, Ethiopia. The ADF process was initiated by ECA to formulate an agenda for effective, sustainable development in African countries through dialogue and partnership between governments, academics, the private sector, donor agencies etc. It was intended that the process would focus towards an annual meeting concerned with a specific development issue. The first Forum was convened on the theme 'The Challenge to Africa of Globalization and the Information Age'.

It reviewed the AISI (see above) and formulated country action plans and work programmes for 2000. The four issues addressed were: strengthening Africa's information infrastructure; Africa and the information economy; information and communication technologies for improved governance; and democratizing access to the information society. The second ADF, scheduled to be convened in October 2000 at Addis Ababa, on the theme 'AIDS: the Greatest Leadership Challenge', was to address the impact of the human immunodeficiency virus (HIV) and acquired immunodeficiency syndrome (AIDS) on Africa. The conference aimed to evaluate action undertaken hitherto in the areas of prevention and care; to analyse the consequences of HIV and AIDS for the economic development of the continent as well as for the social and defence sectors; to agree a framework for emergency action to manage the crisis; to identify future country action plans, priority programmes for implementation and arrangements for monitoring subsequent progress; and to assess the imposition on resources that an intensified and sustained initiative to control the epidemic would represent for African governments and international partners.

In 1997 ECA hosted the first of a series of meetings on good governance, in the context of the UN system-wide Special Initiative on Africa. The second African Governance Forum (AGF II) was held in Accra, Ghana, in June 1998. The Forum focused on accountability and transparency, which participants agreed were essential elements in promoting development in Africa and should involve commitment from both governments and civil organizations. AGF III was convened in June 1999 in Bamako, Mali, to consider issues relating to conflict prevention, management and governance.

ECONOMIC AND SOCIAL POLICY

The Economic and Social Policy division concentrates on the following areas: economic policy analysis, trade and debt, social policy and poverty analysis, and the co-ordination and monitoring of special issues and programmes. Monitoring economic and social trends in the African region and studying the development problems concerning it are among the fundamental tasks of the Commission, while the special issues programme updates legislative bodies regarding the progress made in the implementation of initiatives affecting the continent. Every year the Commission publishes the *Survey of Economic and Social Conditions in Africa* and the *Economic Report on Africa*.

The Commission gives assistance to governments in general economic analysis, fiscal, financial and monetary management, trade liberalization, regional integration and planning. The ECA's work on economic planning has been broadened in recent years, in order to give more emphasis to macro-economic management in a mixed economy approach: a project is being undertaken to develop short-term forecasting and policy models to support economic management. The Commission has also undertaken a major study of the informal sector in African countries. Special assistance is given to least-developed, land-locked and island countries which have a much lower income level than other countries and which are faced with heavier constraints. Studies are also undertaken to assist longer-term planning.

In May 1994 ECA ministers of economic and social development and of planning, meeting in Addis Ababa, adopted a *Framework Agenda for Building and Utilizing Critical Capacities in Africa*. The agenda aimed to identify new priority areas to stimulate development by, for example, strengthening management structures, a more efficient use of a country's physical infrastructure and by expanding processing or manufacturing facilities.

ECA aims to strengthen African participation in international negotiations. To this end, assistance has been provided to member states in the ongoing multilateral trade negotiations under the World Trade Organization; in the annual conferences of the IMF and the World Bank; in negotiations with the EU; and in meetings related to economic co-operation among developing countries. Studies have been prepared on problems and prospects likely to arise for the African region from the implementation of the Common Fund for Commodities and the Generalized System of Trade Preferences (both supervised by UNCTAD); the impacts of exchange-rate fluctuations on the economies of African countries; and on the long-term implications of different debt arrangements for African economies. ECA assists individual member states by undertaking studies on domestic trade, expansion of intra-African trade, trans-national corporations, integration of women in trade and development, and strengthening the capacities of state-trading organizations. ECA encourages the diversification of production, the liberalization of cross-border trade and the expansion of domestic trade structures, within regional economic groupings, in order to promote intra-African trade. ECA also helps to organize regional and 'All-Africa' trade fairs.

In March/April 1997 the Conference of African Ministers of Finance, meeting in Addis Ababa, reviewed a new initiative of the World Bank and IMF to assist the world's 41 most heavily indebted poor countries, of which 33 were identified as being in sub-Saharan Africa. While the Conference recognized the importance of the involvement of multilateral institutions in assisting African economies to achieve a sustainable level of development, it criticized aspects of the structural adjustment programmes imposed by the institutions and advocated more flexible criteria to determine eligibility for the new initiative.

In 1997, with regard to social policy, ECA focused upon improving the socio-economic prospects of women through the promotion of social and legal equality, increasing opportunities for entering higher education and monitoring the prevalence of poverty.

FOOD SECURITY AND SUSTAINABLE DEVELOPMENT

In the early 1990s reports were compiled on the development, implementation and sound management of environmental programmes at national, sub-regional and regional levels. ECA members adopted a common African position for the UN Conference on Environment and Development, held in June 1992. In 1995 ECA published its first comprehensive report and statistical survey of human development issues in African countries. The *Human Development in Africa Report*, which was to be published every two years, aimed to demonstrate levels of development attained, particularly in the education and child health sectors, to identify areas of concern and to encourage further action by policy-makers and development experts. In 1997 ECA was actively involved in the promotion of food security in African countries and the study of the relationship between population, food security, the environment and sustainable development.

PROGRAMME PLANNING, FINANCE AND EVALUATION

ECA provides guidance in the formulation of policies towards the achievement of Africa's development objectives to the policy-making organs of the UN and OAU. It contributes to the work of the General Assembly and other specialized agencies by providing an African perspective in the preparation of development strategies. In March 1996 the UN announced a system-wide Special Initiative on Africa to mobilize resources and to implement a series of political and economic development objectives over a 10-year period. ECA's Executive Secretary is the Co-Chair, with the Administrator of the UNDP, of the Steering Committee for the Initiative.

REGIONAL CO-OPERATION AND INTEGRATION

The Regional Co-operation and Integration Division administers the transport and communications and mineral and energy sectors, in addition to its activities concerning the Sub-regional Development Centres (SRDCs—see above), the integrated development of transboundary water resources, and facilitating and enhancing the process of regional economic integration.

ECA was appointed lead agency for the second United Nations Transport and Communications Decade in Africa (UNTACDA II), covering the period 1991–2000. The principal aim of UNTACDA II was the establishment of an efficient, integrated transport and communications system in Africa. The specific objectives of the programme included: (i) the removal of physical and non-physical barriers to intra-African trade and travel, and improvement in the road transport sector; (ii) improvement in the efficiency and financial viability of railways; (iii) development of Africa's shipping capacity and improvement in the performance of Africa's ports; (iv) development of integrated transport systems for each lake and river basin; (v) improvement of integration of all modes of transport in order to carry cargo in one chain of transport smoothly; (vi) integration of African airlines, and restructuring of civil aviation and airport management authorities; (vii) improvement in the quality and availability of transport in urban areas; (viii) development of integrated regional telecommunications networks; (ix) development of broadcasting services, with the aim of supporting socio-economic development; and (x) expansion of Africa's postal network. ECA is the co-ordinator, with the World Bank, of a regional Road Maintenance Initiative, which was launched in 1988. By early 1996 13 African countries were receiving assistance under the initiative, which sought to encourage a partnership between the public and private sectors to manage and maintain road infrastructure more efficiently and thus to improve country-wide communications and transportation activities. The third African road safety congress was held in April 1997, in Pretoria, South Africa. The congress, which was jointly organized by ECA and the OECD, aimed to increase awareness of the need to adopt an integrated approach to road safety problems. During 1998/99 transport activities included consideration of a new African air transport policy, workshops on port restructuring, and regional and country analyses of transport trends and reforms.

The Fourth Regional Conference on the Development and Utilization of Mineral Resources in Africa, held in March 1991, adopted an action plan that included the formulation of national mineral exploitation policies; and the promotion of the gemstone industry, small-scale mining and the iron and steel industry. ECA supports the Southern African Mineral Resources Development Centre in Dar-es-Salaam, Tanzania, and the Central African Mineral Development Centre in Brazzaville, Republic of the Congo, which provide advisory and laboratory services to their respective member states.

ECA's Energy Programme provides assistance to member states in the development of indigenous energy resources and the formulation of energy policies to extricate member states from continued energy crises. In 1997 ECA strengthened co-operation with the World Energy Council and agreed to help implement the Council's African Energy Programme.

ECA assists member states in the assessment and use of water resources and the development of river and lake basins common to more than one country. ECA encourages co-operation between countries with regard to water issues and collaborates with other UN agencies and regional organizations to promote technical and economic co-operation in this area. A meeting of chief executives of river and lake basin organizations in Africa was scheduled to be held, under ECA auspices, in July 1999. ECA has been particularly active in efforts to promote the integrated development of the water resources of the Zambezi river basin and of Lake Victoria.

In all of its activities ECA aims to strengthen institutional capacities in order to support the process of regional integration, and aims to assist countries to implement existing co-operative agreements, for example by promoting the harmonization of macroeconomic and taxation policies and the removal of non-tariff barriers to trade.

Finance

For the two-year period 2000–01 ECA's regular budget, an appropriation from the UN budget, was an estimated US $78.5m.

Publications

Africa in Figures.

African Statistical Yearbook.

African Women's Report (annually).

Compendium of Intra-African and Related Foreign Trade Statistics.

Economic Report on Africa (annually).

Directory of African Statisticians (every 2 years).

ECA Development Policy Review.

ECA Environment Newsletter (3 a year).

FCANews (monthly).

Focus on African Industry (2 a year).

GenderNet (annually).

Human Development in Africa Report (every 2 years).

Human Rights Education.

People First (2 a year).

Population of Africa: Data and Statistics.

Report of the Executive Secretary (every 2 years).

Survey of Economic and Social Conditions in Africa (annually).

Country reports, policy and discussion papers, reports of conferences and meetings, training series, working paper series.

United Nations Development Programme—UNDP

Address: One United Nations Plaza, New York, NY 10017, USA.
Telephone: (212) 906-5315; **fax:** (212) 906-5364; **e-mail:** hq@undp .org; **internet:** www.undp.org.

The Programme was established in 1965 by the UN General Assembly. Its central mission is to help countries to eradicate poverty and achieve a sustainable level of human development.

Organization

(July 2000)

UNDP is responsible to the UN General Assembly, to which it reports through the UN Economic and Social Council.

EXECUTIVE BOARD

The 36-member Executive Board is responsible for providing intergovernmental support to and supervision of the activities of UNDP and the UN Population Fund (UNFPA, of which UNDP is the governing body).

SECRETARIAT

Offices and divisions at the Secretariat include: Planning and Resource Management; Development Policy Resources and External Affairs; Evaluation, Audit and Performance Review; and the Office of the Human Development Report. Five regional bureaux, all at the Secretariat in New York, cover: Africa; Asia and the Pacific; the Arab states; Latin America and the Caribbean; and Europe and the Commonwealth of Independent States.

Administrator: MARK MALLOCH BROWN (United Kingdom).

Assistant Administrator and Director, Regional Bureau for Africa: ABDOULIE JANNEH.

COUNTRY OFFICES

In almost every country receiving UNDP assistance there is an office, headed by the UNDP Resident Representative, who co-ordinates all UN technical assistance, advises the Government on formulating the country programme, ensures that field activities are carried out, and acts as the leader of the UN team of experts working in the country. Resident Representatives are normally designated as co-ordinators for all UN operational development activities; the offices function as the primary presence of the UN in most developing countries.

OFFICES OF UNDP REPRESENTATIVES IN AFRICA SOUTH OF THE SAHARA

Angola: Rua Major Kanhangulo 197, CP 910, Luanda; tel. (2) 334986; fax (2) 335609; e-mail fo.ang@undp.org.

Benin: Lot 3, Zone Residentielle, BP 506, Cotonou; tel. 31-30-45; fax 31-57-86; e-mail fo.ben@undp.org.

Botswana: Barclays House, Khama Crescent, POB 54, Gaborone; tel. 351680; fax 356093; e-mail fo.bwa@undp.org.

Burkina Faso: Immeuble SONAR, Quartier Ex-Koulouba, Secteur 4, 01 BP 575, Ouagadougou 01; tel. (3) 30-67-65; fax (3) 31-04-70; e-mail fo.bfa@undp.org.

Burundi: 3 rue du Marché, BP 1490, Bujumbura; tel. (2) 223135; fax (2) 225850; e-mail fo.bdi@undp.org.

Cameroon: Immeuble Balanos, rue Giscard d'Estaing, BP 836, Yaoundé; tel. 22-50-35; fax 22-43-69; e-mail fo.cmr@undp.org; internet www.un.cm/pnud.

Cape Verde: Casa Moeda, Avda Andrade Corvo, CP 62, Praia; tel. 61-57-40; fax 62-13-52; e-mail fo.cpv@undp.org.

Central African Republic: ave de l'Indépendance, BP 872, Bangui; tel. 61-19-77; fax 61-17-32; e-mail fo.caf@undp.org.

Chad: ave Colonel D'Ornano, BP 906, N'Djamena; tel. 51-41-00; fax 51-63-30; e-mail fo.chd@undp.org.

Comoros: Hamramba, BP 648, Moroni; tel. 73-15-58; fax 73-15-77; e-mail fo.coi@undp.org..

Congo, Democratic Republic: Immeuble Royal, blvd du 30 juin, BP 7248, Kinshasa; tel. (12) 33431; fax (871) 1503261.

Congo, Republic: ave du Maréchal Foch, BP 465, Brazzaville; tel. 83-59-53; fax 83-39-87; e-mail fo.cog@undp.org.

Côte d'Ivoire: angle rue Gourgas et ave Marchand, Abidjan-Plateau, 01 BP 1747, Abidjan 01; tel. 21-29-95; fax 21-13-67; e-mail fo.civa@undp.org.

Djibouti: blvd Maréchal Joffre, Plâteau du Serpent, BP 2001, Djibouti; tel. 354354; fax 350587; e-mail pnud@intnet.dj; internet www.undp.org.dj.

Equatorial Guinea: Esquina Calle de Kenia con Calle Rey Boncoro, CP 399, Malabo; tel. (9) 3269; fax (871) 383-138168; e-mail fo.gnq@undp.org.

Eritrea: 5 Andinet St (Airport Rd), POB 5366, Asmara; tel. (1) 151143; fax (1) 151081; e-mail fo.eri@undp.org.

Ethiopia: Africa Hall, Old ECA Bldg, 7th Floor, Menelik II Ave, POB 5580, Addis Ababa; tel. (1) 511025; fax (1) 515177; e-mail fo.eth@undp.org.

Gabon: Immeuble Africa No 1, blvd Triomphal Omar Bongo, entre Ministère des Affaires Etrangères et Hypermarché Mbolo, BP 2183, Libreville; tel. 74-52-35; fax 74-34-99; e-mail fo.gab@undp.org.

The Gambia: ave Ann Marie Javouhey, POB 553, Banjul; tel. (2) 28722; fax (2) 28921; e-mail fo.gmb@undp.org.

Ghana: Ring Rd Dual Carriage, nr Police HQ, POB 1423, Accra; tel. (21) 777831; fax (21) 773899; e-mail fo.gha@undp.org.

Guinea: Immeuble Union, ave de la République, BP 222, Conakry; tel. 41-36-22; fax 41-24-85; e-mail fo.gin@undp.org.

Guinea-Bissau: Rua Rui Djassi, 72 A/B, POB 1011, Bissau; tel. 201368; fax 201753; e-mail fo.gnb@undp.org.

Kenya: Kenyatta International Conference Center, Harambee Ave, POB 30218, Nairobi; tel. (2) 228776; fax (2) 211226; e-mail fo.ken@undp.org.

Lesotho: cnr Hilton and Nightingale Rds, POB 301, Maseru 100; tel. 313944; fax 310042; e-mail fo.les@undp.org.

Liberia: Daher Apt, UN Drive, Mamba Point, POB 10-0274, Monrovia 10; tel. 226188; fax (874) 150-5746; e-mail fo.lbr@undp.org.

Madagascar: rue Rainitovo, Antsahavola, BP 1348, Antananarivo 10147; tel. (2) 21907; fax (2) 33315; e-mail undpmag@dts.mag.

Malawi: Plot No 7, Area 40, POB 30135, Lilongwe 3; tel. 782278; fax 783637; e-mail fo.mwi@undp.org.

Mali: Immeuble Me Hamaciré N'Douré, Badalabougou-Est, BP 120, Bamako; tel. 22-20-52; fax 22-62-98; e-mail fo.mli@undp.org; internet www.undp.org/fomli.

Mauritania: Lot K, Lots No. 159–161, BP 620, Nouakchott; tel. (2) 56900; fax (2) 52616; e-mail fo.mrt@undp.org.

Mauritius: Anglo-Mauritius House, Intendance St, POB 253, Port Louis; tel. 208-8691; fax 208-4871; e-mail 100075.3612@ compuserve.com.

Mozambique: Avda Kenneth Kaunda, 921/931, POB 4595, Maputo; tel. (1) 491475; fax (1) 491691; e-mail fo.moz@undp.org.

Namibia: Sanlam Centre, 154 Independence St, Private Bag 13329, Windhoek 9000; tel. (61) 229220; fax (61) 229084; e-mail fo.nam@ undp.org.

Niger: Maison de l'Afrique, BP 11207, Niamey; tel. 72-34-90; fax 72-36-30; e-mail fo.ner@undp.org.

Nigeria: 11 Oyinkan Abayomi Drive, Ikoyi, POB 2075, Lagos; tel. (1) 269-1722; fax (1) 269-3397; e-mail fo.nga@undp.org.

Rwanda: ave de l'Armée 12, BP 445, Kigali; tel. 77822; fax 76263; e-mail fo.rwa@undp.org.

São Tomé and Príncipe: Avda das Naçoes Unidas, CP 109, São Tomé; tel. 21123; fax 22198; e-mail fo.stp@undp.org; internet www.uns.st/undp.note.htm.

Senegal: Immeuble Faycal, 19 rue Parchappe, BP 154, Dakar; tel. 823-60-12; fax 823-55-00; e-mail fo.sen@undp.org.

Seychelles: covered by office in Mauritius.

Sierra Leone: United Nations House, 43 Siaka Stevens St, POB 1011, Freetown; tel. (22) 225346; fax (22) 228720; e-mail fo.sle@ undp.org.

Somalia: covered by office in Kenya.

South Africa: Metropark Bldg, 9th and 10th Floors, 351 Schoeman St, POB 6541, Pretoria 0001; tel. (12) 320-4360; fax (12) 320-4353; e-mail fo.zaf@undp.org.

Sudan: House No 7, Block 5, R.F.E., Gama'a Ave, POB 913, Khartoum; tel. (11) 783755; fax (11) 773128; e-mail fo.sdn@undp.org.

Swaziland: SRIC Bldg, Gilfillan St, Mbabane; tel. 42305; fax 45341; e-mail fo.swz@undp.org.

Tanzania: Matasalamat Mansions, 2nd Floor, Zanaki St, POB 9182, Dar es Salaam; tel. (51) 113270; fax (51) 113272; e-mail fo.tza@undp.org.

Togo: 40 ave des Nations Unies, 1e étage, BP 911, Lomé; tel. 21-20-22; fax 21-16-41; e-mail fo.tgo@undp.org.

Uganda: UN House, 15 Clement Hill Rd, POB 7184, Kampala; tel. (41) 233440; fax (41) 244801; e-mail fo.uga@undp.org.

Zambia: Plot No. 11867, Alick Nkhata Ave, Longacres, POB 31966, Lusaka; tel. (1) 254417; fax (1) 253805; e-mail fo.zmb@undp.org.

Zimbabwe: Takura House, 9th Floor, 67-69 Union Ave, POB 4775, Harare; tel. (4) 792681; fax (4) 728695; e-mail fo.zwe@undp.org.

Activities

As the world's largest source of grant technical assistance in developing countries, UNDP works with more than 150 governments and 40 international agencies in efforts to eradicate poverty and to achieve faster economic growth and better standards of living throughout the world. Most of the work is undertaken in the field by the various United Nations agencies, or by the government of the country concerned. UNDP is committed to allocating some 87% of its core resources to low-income countries with an annual income per caput of less than US $750, while 60% of resources are allocated to the world's least-developed countries.

Assistance is mostly non-monetary, comprising the provision of experts' services, consultancies, equipment, and fellowships for advanced study abroad. In 1996 35% of spending on projects was for the services of experts, 25% was for subcontracts, 18% was for equipment and 16% was for training; the remainder was for other costs, such as technical support. Most UNDP projects incorporate training for local workers. Developing countries themselves provide 50% or more of the total project costs in terms of personnel, facilities, equipment and supplies. In 1996 UNDP expenditure on projects in Africa amounted to US $256.5m., or 21% of the total field programme expenditure.

In June 1994 the Executive Board adopted a programme for change which focused on UNDP's role in achieving sustainable human development, an approach to economic growth that encompasses individual well-being and choice, equitable distribution of the benefits of development and conservation of the environment. Within this framework there were to be the following priority objectives: poverty elimination; sustainable livelihoods; good governance; environmental regeneration; and the advancement and empowerment of women. The allocation of UNDP programming resources has subsequently reflected this agenda, with 26% of funding directed towards poverty eradication and livelihoods for the poor, 25% to capacity-building and governance, 24% to projects concerned with the environment and food security, and 23% to public resources management for sustainable human development (with 2% for other activities).

In 1994 the Executive Board also determined that UNDP should assume a more active and integrative role within the UN development system. This approach has been implemented by UNDP Resident Representatives, who aim to co-ordinate UN policies to achieve sustainable human development, in consultation with other agencies, in particular UNEP, FAO and UNHCR. UNDP has subsequently allocated more resources to training and skill-sharing programmes in order to promote this co-ordinating role. In late 1997 the UNDP Administrator was appointed to chair a UN Development Group, which was established as part of a series of structural reform measures initiated by the UN Secretary-General and which aimed to strengthen collaboration between some 20 UN funds, programmes and other development bodies. UNDP's leading role within the process of UN reform was also reflected in its own internal reform process, 'UNDP 2001', which was scheduled for completion in 2000.

Approximately one-quarter of UNDP programme resources support national efforts to ensure efficient governance and to build effective relations between the state, the private sector and civil society, which are essential to achieving sustainable development. UNDP undertakes assessment missions to help ensure free and fair elections and works to promote human rights, an accountable and competent public sector, a competent judicial system and decentralized government and decision making. Within the context of the UN Special Initiative on Africa (see below), UNDP supports the Africa Governance Forum which convenes annually to consider aspects of governance and development. In July 1997 UNDP organized an International Conference on Governance for Sustainable Growth and Equity, which was held in New York, USA, and attended by more than 1,000 representatives of national and local authorities and the business and non-governmental sectors. At the Conference UNDP initiated a four-year programme to promote activities and to encourage new approaches in support of good governance.

Within UNDP's framework of urban development activities the Local Initiative Facility for Urban Environment (LIFE) undertakes small-scale environmental projects in low-income communities, in collaboration with local authorities and community-based groups. Other initiatives include the Urban Management Programme and the Public-Private Partnerships Programme for the Urban Environment which aimed to generate funds, promote research and support new technologies to enhance sustainable environments in urban areas. In November 1996 UNDP initiated a process of collaboration between city authorities world-wide to promote implementation of the commitments made at the 1995 Copenhagen summit for social development (see below) and to help to combat aspects of poverty and other urban problems, such as poor housing, transport, the management of waste disposal, water supply and sanitation. The first Forum of the so-called World Alliance of Cities Against Poverty was convened in October 1998, in Lyon, France. The second Forum took place in April 2000 in Geneva, Switzerland. UNDP supports the development of national programmes that emphasize the sustainable management of natural resources, for example through its Sustainable Energy Initiative, which promotes more efficient use of energy resources and the introduction of renewable alternatives to conventional fuels. UNDP is also concerned with forest management, the aquatic environment and sustainable agriculture and food security. Its 'Africa 2000' networks support small-scale agricultural projects, such as irrigation schemes, to help eradicate poverty and promote environmentally sustainable development.

UNDP aims to help governments to reassess their development priorities and to design initiatives for sustainable development at a country-specific level. UNDP country offices support the formulation of national human development reports (NHDRs), which aim to facilitate activities such as policy-making, the allocation of resources, and monitoring progress towards poverty eradication and sustainable development. In 1998 NHDRs were produced for 20

African countries (Angola, Benin, Burkina Faso, Cameroon, Cape Verde, Comoros, Ethiopia, Gabon, Lesotho, Malawi, Mali, Mauritania, Mozambique, Namibia, Nigeria, Niger, South Africa, Uganda, Zambia and Zimbabwe). In addition, the preparation of Advisory Notes and Country Co-operation Frameworks help to highlight country-specific aspects of poverty eradication and national strategic priorities. In January 1998 the Executive Board adopted eight guiding principles relating to sustainable human development that were to be implemented by all country offices, in order to ensure a focus to UNDP activities. A network of Sub-regional Resource Facilities (SURFs) has been established to strengthen and co-ordinate UNDP's technical assistance services. UNDP is a co-sponsor, jointly with WHO, the World Bank, UNDCP, UNICEF, UNESCO and UNFPA, of a Joint UN Programme on HIV and AIDS, which became operational on 1 January 1996. UNDP supports the Africa Project Development Facility (APDF) which is administered by the International Finance Corporation (q.v.), and which aims to encourage private investment in the region, and is a co-sponsor, with the World Bank and African Development Bank of the African Capacity Building Initiative (q.v.), which aims to strengthen economic management in African countries. UNDP also has responsibility for co-ordinating activities following global UN conferences. In March 1995 government representatives attending the World Summit for Social Development, which was held in Copenhagen, Denmark, adopted the Copenhagen Declaration and a Programme of Action, which included initiatives to promote the eradication of poverty, to increase and reallocate official development assistance to basic social programmes and to promote equal access to education. With particular reference to UNDP, the Programme of Action advocated that UNDP support the implementation of social development programmes, co-ordinate these efforts through its field offices and organize efforts on the part of the UN system to stimulate capacity-building at local, national and regional levels. By 1998 a multi-donor Poverty Strategies Initiative, introduced following the Summit, was being implemented in more than 80 countries. Other activities were directed towards strengthening the private sectors in developing countries, in particular through the provision of financing for micro-enterprises, and creating the capacity for sound economic management and good governance. A Special Session of the UN General Assembly to review implementation of the Summit's objectives was convened in June 2000. Following the UN Fourth World Conference on Women, held in Beijing, People's Republic of China, in September 1995, UNDP led inter-agency efforts to ensure the full participation of women in all economic, political and professional activities and assisted with further situation analysis and training activities. UNDP also created a Gender in Development Office to ensure that women participate more fully in UNDP-sponsored activities. In June 2000 a Special Session of the UN General Assembly was convened to review the conference, entitled Women 2000: Gender Equality, Development and Peace for the 21st Century (Beijing + 5). UNDP played an important role, at both national and international levels, in preparing for the second UN Conference on Human Settlements (Habitat II), which was held in Istanbul, Turkey, in June 1996. At the conference UNDP announced the establishment of a new facility, which was designed to promote private-sector investment in urban infrastructure. The facility was to be allocated initial resources of US $10m., with the aim of generating a total of $1,000m. from private sources for this sector.

In January 1996 UNDP organized a regional conference, held in Ouagadougou, Burkina Faso, and attended by its Resident Representatives, the ministers of economy and finance of 45 African countries, as well as representatives of other regional organizations, in order to review UNDP's development activities in Africa and to consider a new UN initiative for the region. UNDP's Africa regional bureau presented its three-year programme, for the period 1997–99, which was to concentrate on the enhancement of governance in African countries, strengthening their capacities for economic management, furthering regional trade and economic integration and development of the private sector, in particular at the grass-roots level. In March 1996 the UN Secretary-General inaugurated the Special Initiative on Africa, which was envisaged as a collaborative effort between the principal UN bodies and major regional organizations to secure a set of development objectives for Africa. The cost of the initiative was estimated at US $25,000m. over a 10-year period. UNDP's Africa bureau was initially to provide a secretariat for the programme, while UNDP's mandated involvement was in the areas of conflict prevention, strengthening democracy and enhancing public management in African countries. The other priorities of the Initiative were to achieve improvements in basic education, health and hygiene, food and water security and the expansion of South-South co-operation.

In the mid-1990s UNDP expanded its role in countries in crisis and with special circumstances, working in collaboration with other UN agencies to bridge relief and development efforts. In particular, UNDP was concerned to achieve reconciliation, reintegration and reconstruction in affected countries, as well as to support emergency interventions and manage the delivery of programme aid. During 1996–97 special development initiatives to promote peace and national recovery were undertaken in more than 32 countries, including the demobilization and reintegration of soldiers in Angola and Mali; environmental rehabilitation to resettle displaced populations in the Horn of Africa; and government capacity-building for programme planning and monitoring in Rwanda. UNDP has established a mine action unit within its Emergency Response Division, in order to strengthen national de-mining capabilities. In December 1996 UNDP launched the Civilian Reconstruction Teams programme, creating some 5,000 jobs for former combatants in Liberia to work on the rehabilitation of the country's infrastructure. During 1996 UNDP organized successful meetings of donor governments, multilateral institutions and private sector organizations, which generated funding commitments of US $900m. for the Republic of the Congo, $617m. for rehabilitation and development programmes in Rwanda, and $231m. for Sierra Leone. In early 1998 the UNDP Administrator visited several countries in central Africa in his capacity as Chairman of a UN Task Force on Relief, Reconstruction and Development in the Great Lakes.

Since 1990 UNDP has published an annual *Human Development Report* incorporating a Human Development Index, which ranks countries in terms of human development, using three key indicators: life expectancy, adult literacy and basic income required for a decent standard of living. In 1997 a Human Poverty Index and a Gender-related Development Index, which assesses gender equality on the basis of life expectancy, education and income, were introduced into the Report for the first time. In 1996 UNDP implemented its first corporate communications and advocacy strategy, which aimed to generate public awareness of the activities of the UN system, to promote debate on development issues and to mobilize resources by increasing public and donor appreciation of UNDP. A series of national and regional workshops was held, while media activities focused on the publication of the annual *Human Development Report* and the International Day for the Eradication of Poverty, held each year on 17 October. UNDP aims to use the developments in information technology to advance its communications strategy and to disseminate guide-lines and technical support throughout its country office network. UNDP's Africa regional bureau co-ordinates the Internet Initiative for Africa—IIA, which aims to provide member countries with access to information and expertise; to facilitate policy-makiing at national level; to assist with the establishment of national information infrastructures; to encourage the involvement of African experts in the development of internet infrastructures, policies, regulations and services; and, through the utilization of information technology, to promote regional development. UNDP's Bureau for Development Policy operates the Information Technology for Development Programme, which, jointly with the IIA and the South Africa country office, has undertaken to support a pilot project in that country to promote the benefits of information and communications technologies for sustainable human development and poverty alleviation programmes.

In October 1999 UNDP, in collaboration with an international communications company, Cisco Systems, organized NetAid, a series of international concerts held to improve awareness of Third World poverty, and broadcast live on the internet. A proportion of the proceeds and donations generated by the initiative was to be used to assist the poorest African nations.

Finance

UNDP is financed by the voluntary contributions of members of the United Nations and the Programme's participating agencies as well as by cost-sharing by recipient governments and third-party donors. In 1998 total voluntary contributions amounted to US $1,600m. In that year core expenditure on field programme activities totalled $1,211.0m.

Publications

Annual Report.

Choices (quarterly).

Global Public Goods: International Co-operation in the 21st Century.

Human Development Report (annually).

Discussion and working papers series.

Associated Funds and Programmes

UNDP is the central funding, planning and co-ordinating body for technical co-operation within the UN. Associated funds and programmes, financed separately by means of voluntary contributions, provide specific services through the UNDP network. Total expenditure of these funds and programmes amounted to an estimated US $263.3m. in 1996.

CAPACITY 21

UNDP initiated Capacity 21 at the UN Conference on Environment and Development, which was held in June 1992, to support developing countries in preparing and implementing policies for sustainable development. Capacity 21 promotes new approaches to development, through national development strategies, community-based management and training programmes. During 1998 programmes funded by Capacity 21 were being undertaken in 52 countries.

GLOBAL ENVIRONMENT FACILITY—GEF

The GEF, which is managed jointly by UNDP, the World Bank and UNEP, began operations in 1991, with funding of US $1,500m. over a three-year period. Its aim is to support projects for the prevention of climate change, conserving biological diversity, protecting international waters, and reducing the depletion of the ozone layer in the atmosphere. UNDP is responsible for capacity-building, targeted research, pre-investment activities and technical assistance. UNDP also administers the Small Grants Programme of the GEF, which supports community-based activities by local non-governmental organizations. During the initial phase of the GEF, in the period 1991–94, $242.5m. in funding was approved for 55 UNDP projects. In 1994 representatives of 34 countries agreed to provide $2,000m. to replenish GEF funds. In 1998 36 donor countries pledged $2,750m. for a renewed replenishment of GEF funds.

UNITED NATIONS CAPITAL DEVELOPMENT FUND—UNCDF

The Fund was established in 1966 and became fully operational in 1974. It invests in poor communities in least-developed countries by providing economic and social infrastructure, credit for both agricultural and small-scale entrepreneurial activities, and local development funds which encourage people's participation as well as that of local government in the planning and implementation of projects. UNCDF aims to promote the interests of women in community projects and to enhance their earning capacities. By 1999 56 countries had received UNCDF assistance, including 32 African nations. In 1998 UNCDF nominated 15 countries (including Benin, Burkina Faso, Ethiopia, Guinea, Malawi, Mali, Mozambique, Senegal, Tanzania and Uganda) in which to concentrate subsequent programmes. A Special Unit for Microfinance (SUM) was established in 1997 as a joint UNDP/UNCDF operation, to facilitate co-ordination between microcredit initiatives of the UN, and to support UNDP's MicroStart initiative. SUM was fully integrated into UNCDF in 1999. In May 1996 stable funding for the Fund was pledged by eight donors for a three-year period. UNCDF's annual programming budget amounts to some US $40m.

Executive-Secretary: POUL GROSEN.

UNITED NATIONS DEVELOPMENT FUND FOR WOMEN— UNIFEM

UNIFEM is the UN's lead agency in addressing the issues relating to women in development and promoting the rights of women worldwide. The Fund provides direct financial and technical support to enable low-income women in developing countries to increase earnings, gain access to labour-saving technologies and otherwise improve the quality of their lives. It also funds activities that include women in decision-making related to mainstream development projects. In 1998 UNIFEM approved 64 new projects and continued to support some 90 ongoing programmes in more than 100 nations. UNIFEM has supported the preparation of national reports in 30 countries and used the priorities identified in these reports and in other regional initiatives to formulate a Women's Development Agenda for the 21st century. Through these efforts, UNIFEM played an active role in the preparation for the UN Fourth World Conference on Women, which was held in Beijing, People's Republic of China, in September 1995. In June 2000 UNIFEM participated in a Special Session of the UN General Assembly convened to review the conference, entitled Women 2000: Gender Equality, Development and Peace for the 21st Century (Beijing + 5). Programme expenditure in 1998 amounted to US $18.3m.

Director: NOELEEN HEYZER (Singapore).

OFFICE TO COMBAT DESERTIFICATION AND DROUGHT—UNSO

The Office was established following the conclusion, in October 1994, of the UN Convention to Combat Desertification in Those Countries Experiencing Serious Drought and/or Desertification, Particularly in Africa. It replaced the former UN Sudano–Sahelian Office (UNSO), while retaining the same acronym. UNSO is responsible for UNDP's role in desertification control and dryland management. Special emphasis is given to strengthening the environmental planning and management capacities of national institutions. During 1998 UNSO, in collaboration with other international partners, supported the implementation of the UN Convention in 55 designated countries.

Director: PHILIP DOBIE.

Regional Office in West and Central Africa: Ave de la Résistance du 17 Mai, Immeuble de la Caisse Générale de Péréquation, Secteur 4, 01 BP 366, Ouagadougou 01, Burkina Faso; tel. 30-63-35; fax 31-05-81; e-mail unso@cenatrin.bf.

UNITED NATIONS VOLUNTEERS—UNV

The United Nations Volunteers is an important source of middle-level skills for the UN development system, supplied at modest cost, particularly in the least-developed countries. Volunteers expand the scope of UNDP project activities by supplementing the work of international and host-country experts and by extending the influence of projects to local community levels. The UN Short-term Advisory Programme, which is the private-sector development branch of UNV, has increasingly focused its attention on countries in the process of economic transition. In addition to development activities, UNV has been increasingly involved in areas such as election and human-rights monitoring, peace-building and community-based programmes concerned with environmental management and protection.

Since 1994 UNV has administered UNDP's Transfer of Knowledge Through Expatriate Nationals (TOKTEN) programme, which was initiated in 1977 to enable specialists and professionals from developing countries to contribute to development efforts in their countries of origin through short-term technical assignments.

At 31 May 2000 2,942 UNVs were serving in 127 countries. The total number of people who had served under the initiative amounted to 20,642 at 31 December 1999.

Executive Co-ordinator: SHARON CAPELING-ALAKIJA.

United Nations Environment Programme—UNEP

Address: POB 30552, Nairobi, Kenya.
Telephone: (2) 624283; **fax:** (2) 623928; **e-mail:** ainfo@unep.org; **internet:** www.unep.org.

The United Nations Environment Programme was established in 1972 by the UN General Assembly, following recommendations of the 1972 UN Conference on the Human Environment, in Stockholm, Sweden, to encourage international co-operation in matters relating to the human environment.

Organization

(July 2000)

GOVERNING COUNCIL

The main functions of the Governing Council, which meets every two years, are to promote international co-operation in the area of the environment and to provide general policy guide-lines for the direction and co-ordination of environmental programmes within the UN system. It comprises representatives of 58 states, elected by the UN General Assembly, for four-year terms, on a regional basis. The Council is assisted in its work by a Committee of Permanent Representatives.

HIGH-LEVEL COMMITTEE OF MINISTERS AND OFFICIALS IN CHARGE OF THE ENVIRONMENT

The Committee was established by the Governing Council in April 1997, with a mandate to consider the international environmental agenda and to make recommendations to the Council on reform and policy issues. In addition, the Committee, comprising 36 elected members, was to provide guidance and advice to the Executive Director, to enhance UNEP's collaboration and co-operation with other multilateral bodies and to help to mobilize financial resources for UNEP.

SECRETARIAT

The Secretariat serves as a focal point for environmental action within the UN system.

Executive Director: Dr KLAUS TÖPFER (Germany).

OTHER OFFICES

Convention on International Trade in Endangered Species of Wild Fauna and Flora (CITES): 15 chemin des Anémones, 1219 Châtelaine, Geneva, Switzerland; tel. (22) 9178139; fax (22) 7973417; e-mail cites@unep.ch; internet www.cites.org; Sec.-Gen. WILLEM WOUTER WIJNSTEKERS; Regional Co-ordinator for Africa JOHN N. KUNDAELI.

Global Programme of Action for the Protection of the Marine Environment from Land-based Activities: POB 16227, 2500 The Hague, The Netherlands; tel. (70) 4114460; fax (70) 3456648; e-mail gpa@unep.nl; Co-ordinator VEERLE VANDEWEERD.

Regional Co-ordinating Unit for the Eastern African Seas Programme: POB 487, Victoria, Mahé, Seychelles; e-mail uneprcu@seychelles.net.

Secretariat of the Basel Convention: 15 chemin des Anémones, 1219 Châtelaine, Geneva, Switzerland; tel. (22) 9799111; fax (22) 7973454; e-mail sbc@unep.ch; internet www.basel.int; Officer-in-Charge PER BAKKEN.

Secretariat of the Convention on Biological Diversity: World Trade Centre, 393 St Jacques St West, Suite 300, Montréal, QC HR7 1N9, Canada; tel. (514) 288-2220; fax (514) 288-6588; e-mail secretariat@biodiv.org; internet www.biodiv.org; Exec. Sec. Dr HAM-DALLAH ZEDAN (acting).

Secretariat of the Multilateral Fund for the Implementation of the Montreal Protocol: 1800 ave Collège McGill, 27e étage, Montréal, QC H3A 3J6, Canada; tel. (514) 282-1122; fax (514) 282-0068; e-mail secretariat@unmfs.org; Chief Dr OMAR EL-ARINI.

UNEP Chemicals: 11–13 chemin des Anémones, 1219 Châtelaine, Geneva, Switzerland; tel. (22) 9178111; fax (22) 7973460; e-mail jwillis@unep.ch; internet www.chem.unep.ch; Dir JAMES B. WILLIS.

UNEP Division of Technology, Industry and Economics: Tour Mirabeau, 39–43 Quai André Citroën, 75739 Paris Cedex 15, France; tel. 1-44-37-14-50; fax 1-44-37-14-74; e-mail unepie@unep.fr; internet www.unepie.org; Dir JACQUELINE ALOISI DE LARDEREL.

UNEP International Environmental Technology Centre: 2-110 Ryokuchi koen, Tsurumi-ku, Osaka 538-0036, Japan; tel. (6) 6915-4581; fax (6) 6915-0304; e-mail ietc@unep.or.jp; internet www.unep.or.jp; Dir STEVE HALLS.

UNEP Ozone Secretariat: POB 30552, Nairobi, Kenya; tel. (2) 623885; fax (2) 623913; e-mail ozoneinfo@unep.org; internet www.unep.org/ozone; Exec. Sec. K. MADHAVA SARMA.

UNEP Secretariat for the UN Scientific Committee on the Effects of Atomic Radiation: Vienna International Centre, Wagramerstrasse 5, 1400 Vienna, Austria; tel. (1) 26060-4330; fax (1) 26060-5902; e-mail burton.bennett@unvienna.un.or.at; Sec. B. G. BENNETT.

UNEP/CMS (Convention on the Conservation of Migratory Species of Wild Animals) **Secretariat:** Martin-Luther-King-Str 8, 53175 Bonn, Germany; tel. (228) 8152401; fax (228) 8152449; e-mail cms@unep.de; internet www.wcmc.org.uk/cms; Exec. Sec. ARNULF MÜLLER-HELMBRECHT.

Activities

UNEP aims to maintain a constant watch on the changing state of the environment; to analyse the trends; to assess the problems using a wide range of data and techniques; and to promote projects leading to environmentally sound development. It plays a catalytic and co-ordinating role within and beyond the UN system. Many UNEP projects are implemented in co-operation with other UN agencies, particularly UNDP, the World Bank group, FAO, UNESCO and WHO. About 45 intergovernmental organizations outside the UN system and 60 international non-governmental organizations have official observer status on UNEP's Governing Council, and, through the Environment Liaison Centre in Nairobi, UNEP is linked to more than 6,000 non-governmental bodies concerned with the environment.

In February 1997 the Governing Council, at its 19th session, adopted a ministerial declaration (the Nairobi Declaration) on UNEP's future role and mandate, which recognized the organization as the principal UN body working in the field of the environment and as the leading global environmental authority, setting and overseeing the international environmental agenda. In June a Special Session of the UN General Assembly, referred to as the 'Earth Summit + 5', was convened to review the state of the environment and progress achieved in implementing the objectives of the UN Conference on Environment and Development (UNCED), held in Rio de Janeiro, Brazil, in June 1992. The meeting adopted a Programme for Further Implementation of Agenda 21 (a programme of activities to promote sustainable development, adopted by UNCED) in order to intensify efforts in areas such as energy, freshwater resources and technology transfer. The meeting confirmed UNEP's essential role in advancing the Programme and as a global authority

promoting a coherent legal and political approach to the environmental challenges of sustainable development. An extensive process of restructuring and realignment of functions was subsequently initiated by UNEP, and a new organizational structure reflecting the decisions of the Nairobi Declaration was implemented during 1999.

ENVIRONMENTAL ASSESSMENT AND EARLY WARNING

The Nairobi Declaration resolved that the strengthening of UNEP's information, monitoring and assessment capabilities was a crucial element of the organization's restructuring, in order to help establish priorities for international, national and regional action, and to ensure the efficient and accurate dissemination of emerging environmental trends and emergencies.

UNEP has developed an extensive network of collaborating centres to assist in its analysis of the state of the global environment. The outcome of its work, the first Global Environment Outlook (GEO-I), was published in January 1997. A second process of global assessment resulted in the publication of GEO-II in September 1999. UNEP has initiated a major Global International Waters Assessment to consider all aspects of the world's water-related issues, in particular problems of shared transboundary waters, and of future sustainable management of water resources. UNEP is also a sponsoring agency of the Joint Group of Experts on the Scientific Aspects of Marine Environmental Pollution and contributes to the preparation of reports on the state of the marine environment and on the impact of land-based activities on that environment. In November 1995 UNEP published a Global Biodiversity Assessment, which was the first comprehensive study of biological resources throughout the world.

UNEP's environmental information network includes the Global Resource Information Database (GRID), which converts collected data into information usable by decision-makers. The INFOTERRA programme facilitates the exchange of environmental information through an extensive network of national 'focal points'. By the end of 1998 178 countries were participating in the network. UNEP promotes public access to environmental information, as well as participation in environmental concerns, through the INFOTERRA initiative. UNEP aims to establish in every developing region an Environment and Natural Resource Information Network (ENRIN) in order to make available technical advice and manage environmental information and data for improved decision-making and action-planning in countries most in need of assistance. UNEP aims to integrate all its information resources in order to improve access to information and to promote the international exchange of information. This was to be achieved through the design and implementation of UNEPNET, which was to operate throughout the UN system and be fully accessible through the world-wide information networks. In addition, by late 1998, 15 so-called Mercure satellite systems were operational world-wide, linking UNEP offices and partner agencies.

UNEP's information, monitoring and assessment structures also serve to enhance early-warning capabilities and to provide accurate information during an environmental emergency. In 1997 and 1998 UNEP organized a series of meetings to assess the environmental damage resulting from forest fires in Indonesia and to consider measures to respond effectively to further incidents. In April 1998 an international meeting, convened under UNEP auspices in Geneva, Switzerland, approved US $10m. to finance an immediate package of measures aimed at extinguishing the most dangerous fires, preventing others from spreading and improving Indonesia's firefighting capabilities. UNEP was also concerned with other 'man-made' fires, in particular in Brazil where an extensive conflagration was threatening an indigenous reserve and a number of endangered species.

POLICY DEVELOPMENT AND LAW

UNEP aims to promote the development of policy tools and guidelines in order to achieve the sustainable management of the world environment. At a national level it assists governments to develop and implement appropriate environmental instruments and aims to co-ordinate policy initiatives. Training workshops in various aspects of environmental law and its applications are conducted. UNEP supports the development of new legal, economic and other policy instruments to improve the effectiveness of existing environmental agreements.

UNEP was instrumental in the drafting of a Convention on Biological Diversity (CBD) to preserve the immense variety of plant and animal species, in particular those threatened with extinction. The Convention entered into force at the end of 1993; by mid-1998 174 countries were parties to the CBD. UNEP supports co-operation for biodiversity assessment and management in selected developing regions and for the development of strategies for the conservation and sustainable exploitation of individual threatened species (e.g. the Global Tiger Action Plan). UNEP also provides assistance for the preparation of individual country studies and strategies to strengthen national biodiversity management and research. In 1996 an *ad hoc* working group on biosafety was established to negotiate the conclusion of a protocol to the CBD to regulate international trade in living modified organisms (including genetically modified—GM—seeds and crops and pharmaceutical derivatives), in order to reduce any potential adverse effects on biodiversity and human health. An extraordinary session of the conference of parties to the CBD was convened in Cartagena, Colombia, in February 1999, to consider the provisional text formulated by the group and, if approved, to adopt its legally-binding provisions. The meeting, however, was suspended, owing to outstanding differences between the main producer countries and developing nations regarding the implications of the protocol on principles of free trade. An agreement on the so-called Cartagena Protocol was finally concluded at a meeting of parties to the CBD, held in Montreal, Canada, in January 2000. The Protocol permitted countries to ban imports of GM products if there were outstanding safety concerns, and provided for greater transparency in the description of products containing GM organisms, through a limited labelling system.

In October 1994 87 countries, meeting under UN auspices, signed a Convention to Combat Desertification (see UNSO, p. 88), which aimed to provide a legal framework to counter the degradation of drylands. An estimated 75% of all drylands have suffered some land degradation, affecting approximately 1,000m. people in 110 countries. A second conference of the parties to the Convention was held in Dakar, Senegal, in December 1998. UNEP continues to support the implementation of the Convention, as part of its efforts to protect land resources. UNEP also aims to improve the assessment of dryland degradation and desertification in co-operation with governments and other international bodies, as well as identifying the causes of degradation and measures to overcome these.

UNEP estimates that one-third of the world's population will suffer chronic water shortages by 2025, owing to rising demand for drinking water as a result of growing populations, decreasing quality of water because of pollution, and increasing requirements of industries and agriculture. UNEP provides scientific, technical and administrative support to facilitate the implementation and co-ordination of regional seas conventions and plans of action. UNEP promotes international co-operation in the management of river basins and coastal areas and for the development of tools and guidelines to achieve the sustainable management of freshwater and coastal resources. In particular, UNEP aims to control land-based activities, principally pollution, which affect freshwater resources, marine biodiversity and the coastal ecosystems of small-island developing states. In November 1995 110 governments adopted a Global Programme of Action for the Protection of the Marine Environment from Land-based Activities. UNEP aims to develop a similar global instrument to ensure the integrated management of freshwater resources, in order to address current and future needs.

In 1996 UNEP, in collaboration with FAO, began to work towards promoting and formulating a legally-binding international convention on prior informed consent (PIC) for hazardous chemicals and pesticides in international trade, extending a voluntary PIC procedure of information exchange undertaken by more than 100 governments since 1991. The Convention was adopted at a conference held in Rotterdam, the Netherlands, in September 1998, and was to enter into force on being ratified by 50 signatory states. It aimed to reduce risks to human health and the environment by restricting the production, export and use of hazardous substances and enhancing information exchange procedures.

In conjunction with UNCHS (Habitat), UNDP, the World Bank and other regional organizations and institutions, UNEP promotes environmental concerns in urban planning and management through the Sustainable Cities Programme, as well as regional workshops concerned with urban pollution and the impact of transportation systems. In January 1994 UNEP inaugurated an International Environmental Technology Centre (IETC), with offices in Osaka and Shiga, Japan, in order to strengthen the capabilities of developing countries and countries with economies in transition to promote environmentally-sound management of cities and freshwater reservoirs through technology co-operation and partnerships.

UNEP has played a key role in global efforts to combat risks to the ozone layer, resultant climatic changes and atmospheric pollution. UNEP worked in collaboration with the World Meteorological Organization to formulate a Framework Convention on Climate Change, with the aim of reducing the emission of gases that have a warming effect on the atmosphere, and has remained an active participant in the ongoing process to review and enforce its implementation (see WMO, p. 114, for further details). UNEP was the lead agency in formulating the 1987 Montreal Protocol to the Vienna Convention for the Protection of the Ozone Layer (1985), which provided for a 50% reduction in the production of chlorofluorocarbons (CFCs) by 2000. An amendment to the Protocol was adopted in 1990, which required complete cessation of the production of CFCs by 2000 in industrialized countries and by 2010 in developing countries; these deadlines were advanced to 1996 and 2006, respectively, in November 1992. In 1997 the ninth Conference of the Parties to the Vienna Convention adopted a further amendment which aimed to introduce a licensing system for all controlled substances.

A Multilateral Fund for the Implementation of the Montreal Protocol was established in June 1990 to promote the use of suitable technologies and the transfer of technologies to developing countries. UNEP, UNDP, the World Bank and UNIDO are the sponsors of the Fund, which by early 1997 had financed 1,800 projects in 106 developing countries at a cost of US \$565m. In November 1996 the Fund was replenished, with commitments totalling \$540m. for the three-year period 1997–99.

POLICY IMPLEMENTATION

UNEP's Division of Environmental Policy Implementation incorporates two main functions: technical co-operation and response to environmental emergencies.

With the UN Office for the Co-ordination of Humanitarian Assistance, UNEP has established an Environmental Emergencies Unit to mobilize and co-ordinate international assistance and expertise to countries facing disasters. It undertakes initial assessments of the situation, as well as post-conflict analysis, as required. During 1998 the Unit provided assistance to Armenia and Georgia, following extensive flooding, to Chile, to combat acute river pollution, to Madagascar, following a serious chemical fire, to Moldova, threatened with underground water pollution, and to Somalia, to investigate an alleged dumping of hazardous substances. Other major environmental emergencies occurred during that year as a result of the floods and heavy rain in Bangladesh, the People's Republic of China, Mexico and parts of East Africa, and as the result of drought caused by the El Niño weather phenomenon in Brazil, Cuba and Indonesia. In mid-1999 UNEP established a Balkan Task Force to assess the environmental impact of NATO's aerial offensive against the Federal Republic of Yugoslavia.

UNEP, together with UNDP and the World Bank, is an implementing agency of the Global Environment Facility (GEF, see p. 88), which was established in 1991 as a mechanism for international co-operation in projects concerned with biological diversity, climate change, international waters and depletion of the ozone layer. UNEP services the Scientific and Technical Advisory Panel, which was established to provide expert advice on GEF programmes and operational strategies.

TECHNOLOGY, INDUSTRY AND ECONOMICS

The use of inappropriate industrial technologies and the widespread adoption of unsustainable production and consumption patterns have been identified as being inefficient in the use of renewable resources and wasteful, in particular in the use of energy and water. UNEP aims to encourage governments and the private sector to develop and adopt policies and practices that are cleaner and safer, make efficient use of natural resources, incorporate environmental costs, ensure the environmentally sound management of chemicals, and reduce pollution and risks to human health and the environment. In collaboration with other organizations and agencies UNEP works to define and formulate international guide-lines and agreements to address these issues. UNEP also promotes the transfer of appropriate technologies and organizes conferences and training workshops to provide sustainable production practices. Relevant information is disseminated through the International Cleaner Production Information Clearing House. UNEP, together with UNIDO, has established eight National Cleaner Production Centres to promote a preventive approach to industrial pollution control. In May 1999 representatives of some 33 countries signed an International Declaration on Cleaner Production, launched by UNEP in 1998, with a commitment to implement cleaner and more sustainable production methods and to monitor results.

UNEP provides institutional servicing to the Basel Convention on the Control of Transboundary Movements of Hazardous Wastes and their Disposal, which was adopted in 1989 with the aim of preventing the disposal of wastes from industrialized countries in countries that have no processing facilities. In March 1994 the second meeting of parties to the Convention agreed to ban exportation of hazardous wastes between OECD and non-OECD countries by the end of 1997. The amendment of the Convention required ratification by three-quarters of signatory states before it could enter into effect, and was not achieved by December 1997. The fourth full meeting of parties to the Convention, held in February 1998, attempted to clarify the classification and listing of hazardous wastes, which was expected to stimulate further ratifications. In December 1999 132 states adopted a Protocol to the Convention to address issues relating to liability and compensation for damages from waste exports. The governments also agreed to establish a multilateral fund to finance immediate clean-up operations following any environmental accident.

The UNEP Chemicals office was established to promote the sound management of hazardous substances, central to which was the International Register of Potentially Toxic Chemicals (IRPTC). UNEP aims to facilitate access to data on chemicals and hazardous wastes, in order to assess and control health and environmental risks, by using the IRPTC as a clearing house facility of relevant information and by publishing information and technical reports on the impact of the use of chemicals.

UNEP's OzonAction Programme works to promote information exchange, training and technological awareness. Its objective is to strengthen the capacity of governments and industry in developing countries to undertake measures towards the cost-effective phasing-out of ozone-depleting substances. UNEP also encourages the development of alternative and renewable sources of energy. To achieve this, UNEP is supporting the establishment of a network of centres to research and exchange information of environmentally-sound energy technology resources.

REGIONAL CO-OPERATION AND REPRESENTATION

UNEP maintains six regional offices. These work to initiate and promote UNEP objectives and to ensure that all programme formulation and delivery meets the specific needs of countries and regions. They also provide a focal point for building national, sub-regional and regional partnership and enhancing local participation in UNEP initiatives. Following UNEP's reorganization a co-ordination office was established at headquarters to promote regional policy integration, to co-ordinate programme planning, and to provide necessary services to the regional offices.

UNEP provides administrative support to several regional conventions, for example the Lusaka Agreement on Co-operative Enforcement Operations Directed at Illegal Trade in Wild Flora and Fauna, which entered into force in December 1996 having been concluded under UNEP auspices in order to strengthen the implementation of the Convention on Biological Diversity and the Convention on International Trade in Endangered Species (CITES) in Eastern and Central Africa. UNEP also organizes conferences, workshops and seminars at national and regional levels, and may extend advisory services or technical assistance to individual governments.

CONVENTIONS

UNEP aims to develop and promote international environmental legislation in order to pursue an integrated response to global environmental issues, to enhance collaboration among existing convention secretariats, and to co-ordinate support to implement the work programmes of international instruments.

UNEP has been an active participant in the formulation of several major conventions (see above). The Division of Environmental Conventions is mandated to assist the Division of Policy Development and Law in the formulation of new agreements or protocols to existing conventions. Following the successful adoption of the Rotterdam Convention in September 1998, UNEP is working to formulate a multilateral agreement to reduce and ultimately eliminate the manufacture and use of Persistent Organic Pollutants (POPs), which are considered to be a major global environmental hazard. UNEP sponsored the first meeting of an Intergovernmental Negotiating Committee on POPs, which was held in Montreal, Canada, in June 1998. An agreement on POPs was expected to be ready for signature in 2000.

UNEP has been designated to provide secretariat functions to a number of global and regional environmental conventions (see above for list of offices).

COMMUNICATION AND PUBLIC INFORMATION

UNEP's public education campaigns and outreach programmes promote community involvement in environmental issues. Further communication of environmental concerns is undertaken through the media, an information centre service and special promotional events, including World Environment Day, photograph competitions and the awarding of the Sasakawa Prize to recognize distinguished service to the environment by individuals and groups. In 1996 UNEP initiated a Global Environment Citizenship Programme to promote acknowledgment of the environmental responsibilities of all sectors of society.

Finance

UNEP derives its finances from the regular budget of the United Nations and from voluntary contributions to the Environment Fund. In February 1999 the Governing Council authorized a budget of US $120m. for the two-year period 2000–01, of which $100m. was for programme activities, $14.4m. for management and administration, and $5m. for fund programme reserves.

Publications

Annual Report.
APELL Newsletter (2 a year).
Cleaner Production Newsletter (2 a year).
Climate Change Bulletin (quarterly).
Connect (UNESCO-UNEP newsletter on environmental degradation, quarterly).
Desertification Control Bulletin (2 a year).
EarthViews (quarterly).
Environment Forum (quarterly).
Environmental Law Bulletin (2 a year).
Financial Services Initiative (2 a year).
GEF News (quarterly).
GPA Newsletter.
IETC Insight (3 a year).
Industry and Environment Review (quarterly).
Leave it to Us (children's magazine, 2 a year).
Managing Hazardous Waste (2 a year).
Our Planet (quarterly).
OzonAction Newsletter (quarterly).
Report of the Executive Director (every 2 years).
Tierramerica (4–6 a year).
Tourism Focus (2 a year).
UNEP Chemicals Newsletters (2 a year).
UNEP Update (monthly).
World Atlas of Desertification.
Studies, reports, legal texts, technical guide-lines, etc.

United Nations High Commissioner for Refugees— UNHCR

Address: CP 2500, 1211 Geneva 2 dépôt, Switzerland.
Telephone: (22) 7398111; **fax:** (22) 7319546; **internet:** www.unhcr.ch/.

The Office of the High Commissioner was established in 1951 to provide international protection for refugees and to seek durable solutions to their problems.

Organization
(July 2000)

HIGH COMMISSIONER

The High Commissioner is elected by the United Nations General Assembly on the nomination of the Secretary-General, and is responsible to the General Assembly and to the UN Economic and Social Council (ECOSOC).

High Commissioner: SADAKO OGATA (Japan).

Deputy High Commissioner: FREDERICK BARTON (USA).

EXECUTIVE COMMITTEE

The Executive Committee of the High Commissioner's Programme, established by ECOSOC, gives the High Commissioner policy directives in respect of material assistance programmes and advice in the field of international protection. In addition, it oversees UNHCR's general policies and use of funds. The Committee, which comprises representatives from 53 states (both members and non-members of the UN), meets once a year.

ADMINISTRATION

Headquarters include the Executive Office, comprising the offices of the High Commissioner, the Deputy High Commissioner and the Assistant High Commissioner. There are separate offices for the Inspector General, the Special Envoy in the former Yugoslavia, and the Director of the UNHCR liaison office in New York. The other principal administrative units are the Division of Communication and Information, the Department of International Protection, the

Division of Resource Management, and the Department of Operations, which is responsible for the five regional bureaux covering Africa; Asia and the Pacific; Europe; the Americas and the Caribbean; and Central Asia, South-West Asia, North Africa and the Middle East. At July 1999 there were 274 UNHCR field offices in 120 countries. At that time UNHCR employed 5,155 people, including short-term staff, of whom 4,265 (or 83%) were working in the field.

Activities

The competence of the High Commissioner extends to any person who, owing to well-founded fear of being persecuted for reasons of race, religion, nationality or political opinion, is outside the country of his or her nationality and is unable or, owing to such fear or for reasons other than personal convenience, remains unwilling to accept the protection of that country; or who, not having a nationality and being outside the country of former habitual residence, is unable or, owing to such fear or for reasons other than personal convenience, is unwilling to return to it. Refugees who are assisted by other United Nations agencies, or who have rights or obligations as nationals of their country of residence, are outside the mandate of UNHCR.

In recent years there was a significant shift in UNHCR's focus of activities. Increasingly, UNHCR is called upon to support people who have been displaced within their own country (i.e. with similar needs to those of refugees but who have not crossed an international border) or those threatened with displacement as a result of armed conflict. Operations involving internally displaced persons (IDPs) may be undertaken only at the request of the UN Secretary-General or the General Assembly and with the consent of the country concerned. In addition, UNHCR is providing greater support to refugees who have returned to their country of origin, to assist their reintegration, and is working to enable the local community to support the returnees.

INTERNATIONAL PROTECTION

As laid down in the Statute of the Office, one of the two primary functions of UNHCR is to extend international protection to refugees. In the exercise of this function UNHCR seeks to ensure that refugees and asylum-seekers are protected against *refoulement* (forcible return), that they receive asylum, and that they are treated according to internationally recognized standards. UNHCR pursues these objectives by a variety of means which include promoting the conclusion and ratification by states of international conventions for the protection of refugees, particularly the 1951 UN Convention relating to the Status of Refugees, extended by a Protocol adopted in 1967 (a total of 139 states had acceded to either or both of these instruments by July 2000). The Convention defines the rights and duties of refugees and contains provisions dealing with a variety of matters which affect their day-to-day lives. UNHCR has also continued to encourage further accessions to the 1969 OAU Convention Governing the Specific Aspects of Refuge Problems in Africa (to which 42 states were party at March 1995). UNHCR has given close attention to the problems of military attacks against refugee camps and settlements in southern Africa and elsewhere, in the hope of formulating a set of internationally recognised principles to ensure the safety of refugees.

ASSISTANCE ACTIVITIES

UNHCR assistance activities are divided into General Programmes, which include a Programme Reserve, a General Allocation for Voluntary Repatriation and an Emergency Fund, and Special Programmes. The latter are undertaken at the request of the UN General Assembly, the Secretary-General of the UN or member states, in response to a particular crisis.

The first phase of an assistance operation uses UNHCR's capacity of emergency preparedness and response. This enables UNHCR to address the immediate needs of refugees at short notice, for example, by employing specially trained emergency teams and maintaining stockpiles of basic equipment, medical aid and materials. A significant proportion of UNHCR expenditure is allocated to the next phase of an operation, providing 'care and maintenance' in stable refugee circumstances. This assistance can take various forms, including the provision of food, shelter, medical care and essential supplies. Also often covered are basic services, including education and counselling.

As far as possible, assistance is geared towards the identification and implementation of durable solutions to refugee problems—this being the second statutory responsibility of UNHCR. Such solutions generally take one of three forms: voluntary repatriation, local integration or resettlement in another country. Where voluntary repatriation is feasible, the Office assists refugees to overcome obstacles preventing their return to their country of origin. This may be done through negotiations with governments involved, or

by providing funds for the physical movement of refugees or for the rehabilitation of returnees once back in their own country. When voluntary repatriation is not feasible, efforts are made to assist refugees to integrate locally and to become self-supporting in their countries of asylum. In cases where resettlement through emigration is the only viable solution, UNHCR negotiates with governments in an endeavour to obtain suitable resettlement opportunities, to encourage liberalization of admission criteria and to draw up special immigration schemes. During 1998 21,210 refugees were resettled under UNHCR auspices.

In the early 1990s UNHCR aimed to consolidate efforts to integrate certain priorities into its programme planning and implementation, as a standard discipline in all phases of assistance. The considerations include awareness of specific problems confronting refugee women, the needs of refugee children, the environmental impact of refugee programmes and long-term development objectives. In an effort to improve the effectiveness of its programmes UNHCR has initiated a process of delegating authority, as well as responsibility for operational budgets, to its regional and field representatives, increasing flexibility and accountability. In 1995 a new Inspection and Evaluation Service was established in order to strengthen UNHCR's capacity to review operational effectiveness and efficiency.

REGIONAL ASSISTANCE

During the 1990s UNHCR provided assistance to refugee populations in many parts of the continent where civil conflict, violations of human rights, drought, famine or environmental degradation had forced people to flee their countries. The majority of African refugees and returnees are located in countries that are themselves suffering major economic problems and are thus unable to provide the basic requirements of the uprooted people. Furthermore, UNHCR has often failed to receive adequate international financial support to implement effective relief programmes. At 1 January 2000 there were an estimated 6.2m. people of concern to UNHCR in Africa (of a world-wide total of 22.3m.), of whom 3.5m. were refugees, 1.7m. internally displaced, and 0.9m. recent returnees.

The Horn of Africa, afflicted by famine, separatist violence and ethnic conflict, has experienced large-scale population movements in recent years. In 1992 UNHCR initiated a repatriation programme for the massive Somali and Ethiopian refugee populations in Kenya, which included assistance with reconstruction projects and the provision of food to returnees and displaced persons. The implementation by UNHCR of community-based projects, for example seed distribution, the establishment of a women's bakery co-operative and support for a brick production initiative, served as important instruments of assistance and of bringing stability to areas of returnee settlements. However, the continuing instability in north-western Somalia prevented a completion of the repatriation process. From October 1997 severe flooding in southern areas of Somalia further hindered the repatriation of refugees. None the less, UNHCR and the authorities in north-western Somalia agreed to proceed with the repatriation process, with the aim of facilitating the speedy return of 100,000 Somalis, and to initiate projects to aid their reintegration. During 1998 an estimated 48,100 Somali refugees were repatriated from Ethiopia under UNHCR auspices. Some spontaneous repatriation also took place, leaving a total Somali refugee population of 480,800, of whom 249,200 were in Ethiopia and 174,000 were in Kenya. At 31 December 1998 Ethiopia was still hosting some 262,000 refugees, while Kenya was sheltering 238,200. By November 1997 UNHCR estimated that some 600,000 Ethiopians had repatriated, either by spontaneous or organized movements. The voluntary repatriation operation of the estimated 50,000 Ethiopians remaining in Sudan was concluded in mid-1998. With effect from 1 March 2000 UNHCR withdrew the automatic refugee status of Ethiopians who left their country before 1991. From late 1999 until March 2000 transportation and rehabilitation assistance were offered to those concerned who wished to repatriate.

From 1992 some 500,000 Eritreans took refuge in Sudan as a result of separatist conflicts; however, by 1995 an estimated 125,000 had returned spontaneously, in particular following Eritrea's accession to independence in May 1993. A UNHCR repatriation programme to assist the remaining refugees, which had been delayed for various political, security and funding considerations, was initiated in November 1994. However, its implementation was hindered by a shortfall in donor funding and by differences between the Eritrean and Sudanese Governments. At the end of 1998 Sudan still hosted a total of 391,500 refugees, including 342,300 from Eritrea and 35,600 from Ethiopia. Renewed conflict between Eritrea and Ethiopia, which commenced in 1998, had, by mid-1999, resulted in the displacement of some 350,000 Eritreans and 300,000 Ethiopians. In mid-2000, following an escalation of the conflict in May, UNHCR reported that some 95,000 Eritreans had sought refuge in Sudan, while smaller numbers had fled to Djibouti and Yemen. Consequently, an operation to repatriate 160,000 long-term Eritrean refugees in Sudan (scheduled to commence in May) had been postponed. Following the conclusion of a peace agreement between Eritrea and Ethiopia in June, UNHCR initiated an operation to repatriate the most recent wave of Eritrean refugees from Sudan. At 31 December 1998 some 374,000 Sudanese remained as refugees, mainly in the Central African Republic, Uganda, Kenya, the Democratic Republic of the Congo and Ethiopia, owing to continuing civil unrest in southern Sudan. The Ugandan Government, hosting an estimated 189,800 of these refugees, has provided new resettlement sites and has supported refugee efforts to construct homes and cultivate crops in order to achieve some degree of self-sufficiency.

In West Africa the refugee population increased by one-third during 1992 and the first half of 1993, with the addition of new refugees fleeing Togo, Liberia and Senegal. In accordance with a peace agreement, signed in July 1993, UNHCR was responsible for the repatriation of Liberian refugees who had fled to Guinea, Côte d'Ivoire and Sierra Leone during the civil conflict. UNHCR also began to provide emergency relief to the displaced population within the country. Persisting political insecurity prevented any solution to the refugee problem, and in mid-1996 UNHCR suspended its preparatory activities for a large-scale repatriation and reintegration operation of Liberian refugees, owing to an escalation in hostilities. At February 1997 the Liberian refugee population in West Africa totalled 758,000; however, the prospect of a peaceful settlement in Liberia, with preparations under way for a general election to be conducted in July, prompted a movement of refugees returning home, and in April UNHCR initiated an organized repatriation of Liberian refugees from Ghana. By the end of 1997 the Liberian refugee population had declined to 486,700, of whom 243,000 were located in Guinea and 207,000 in Côte d'Ivoire. The return of refugees and other displaced persons was expected to accelerate during 1998 following the establishment of a democratically-elected government and the consolidation of the peace settlement. In the event the process was hindered slightly by logistical difficulties and the persisting volatility of some border regions. In April UNHCR operations in northern Liberia were temporarily suspended as a result of attacks by anti-government militia and clashes between rebel and government forces which prompted 6,000 Liberians to flee to Guinea. During the year UNHCR assisted a total of 75,700 Liberian refugees to return home and organized quick impact projects to facilitate their reintegration. By the end of that year there were some 251,400 recently returned Liberian refugees of concern to UNHCR. At the end of 1999 there were still some 207,000 Liberian refugees, of whom 100,000 were in Côte d'Ivoire and 107,000 in Guinea. A further 215,000 Liberians were estimated to have returned without assistance.

Further large-scale population displacement in West Africa followed an escalation of violence in Sierra Leone in early 1995. By December 1996 there were 120,000 Sierra Leonean refugees in Liberia and 248,827 in Guinea, while a further 654,600 internally displaced Sierra Leoneans were of concern to UNHCR. The repatriation of Sierra Leonean refugees from Liberia was initiated in February 1997. However, the programme was suspended in May, owing to renewed political violence, which forced UNHCR staff to evacuate the country, and the seizure of power by military forces. Thousands of people fled to other parts of the country, as well as to neighbouring countries to escape the hostilities. Following the intervention of the ECOMOG multinational force (see ECOWAS p.128) and the conclusion of a peace agreement in October, residents of the Sierra Leone capital, Freetown, who had been displaced by the conflict, began to return. In February 1998 ECOMOG troops took control of Freetown from the rebel military forces, and in the following month the elected President, Ahmed Tejan Kabbah, was reinstated as Head of State. None the less, during the first half of the year an estimated 210,000 Sierra Leoneans crossed the border into Guinea and 40,000 into Liberia, owing to ongoing violence in the northern and eastern regions of the country and severe food shortages. At 31 December 1998 there were some 297,200 Sierra Leonean refugees in Guinea and 103,000 in Liberia. There were also 198,400 recently returned refugees in Sierra Leone of concern to UNHCR and an estimated displaced population of 670,000. In early 1999 anti-government forces again advanced on Freetown, prompting heavy fighting with ECOMOG troops and the displacement of thousands more civilians. In February a reported 200,000 people fled the town of Kenema in south-eastern Sierra Leone following attacks by rebel militia. In May a cease-fire agreement was concluded between the Government and opposition forces, and a formal peace accord was signed in early July. By November, however, UNHCR noted that few Sierra Leonean refugees had repatriated, owing to persisting security concerns. A resumption of hostilities in May 2000 was expected to delay the planned repatriation of nearly 77,000 Sierra Leonean refugees from Guinea during that year (a further 150,000 had been scheduled to return from Guinea in 2001).

In June 1998 UNHCR expressed concern at the outbreak of fighting in Guinea-Bissau, which had prompted the majority of the capital's population of some 300,000 people to flee into the surrounding countryside and generated concern for the safety of the estimated 15,000 Senegalese refugees who had been based in camps in Guinea-Bissau since 1992. UNHCR staff attempted to monitor the movements of the population, and, despite the border between Guinea and Guinea-Bissau officially being declared closed, estimated that some 12,000 people crossed into the neighbouring country during June 1998. A cease-fire was agreed between the conflicting forces in August; however there was renewed conflict in October prompting further population displacement. UNHCR staff attempted to distribute mosquito nets and other non-food supplies to the displaced population, but, along with other humanitarian personnel, they were repeatedly obliged to evacuate the country owing to the ongoing violence. A peace accord was concluded in November. In early 1999 UNHCR began preparations to implement a repatriation programme and continued to provide assistance to some 150,000 IDPs.

In early 1994 some 40,000 Tuareg nomads, who had fled from northern Mali into Burkina Faso, received protection and material assistance from two newly-established UNHCR field offices. During 1995 large numbers of the Malian refugee population (totalling some 175,000) returned spontaneously from camps in Mauritania, Burkina Faso and Algeria, owing to favourable political developments in Mali. An organized repatriation of the remaining refugees was initiated in 1996. In November UNHCR signed an agreement with the Malian and Nigerien Governments establishing the conditions of repatriation of 25,000 Tuareg refugees living in Niger. By 31 December 1998 almost all Malian refugees in the region had repatriated, and there were 61,400 recently returned refugees of concern to UNHCR.

Since 1993 the Great Lakes region of central Africa has experienced massive population displacement, causing immense operational challenges and demands on the resources of international humanitarian and relief agencies. In October of that year a military coup in Burundi prompted some 580,000 people to flee into Rwanda and Tanzania, although many had returned by early 1994. By May 1994, however, an estimated 860,000 people from Burundi and Rwanda had fled to neighbouring states (following a resurgence of ethnic violence in both countries), including 250,000 mainly Rwandan Tutsi refugees who entered Tanzania over a 24-hour period in late April in the most rapid mass exodus ever witnessed by UNHCR. In May UNHCR began an immediate operation to airlift emergency supplies to the refugees. For the first time in an emergency operation UNHCR organized support to be rendered in the form of eight defined 'service packages', for example, to provide domestic fuel, road servicing and security or sanitation facilities. Despite overcrowding in camps and a high incidence of cholera and dysentery (particularly in camps in eastern Zaire, where many thousands of Rwandan Hutus had sought refuge following the establishment of a new Government in July) large numbers of refugees refused to accept UNHCR-assisted repatriation, owing to fears of reprisal ethnic killings. In September reports of mass ethnic violence in Rwanda, which were disputed by some UN agencies, continued to disrupt UNHCR's policy of repatriation and to prompt returnees to cross the border back into Zaire. Security in the refugee camps, which was undermined by the presence of military and political elements of the former Rwandan government regime, remained an outstanding concern for UNHCR. Efforts to restore law and order and to prevent the intimidation of refugees, by introducing more security personnel into the camps, were initiated by UNHCR, in co-operation with the Tanzanian and Zairean authorities. A resurgence of violence in Burundi, in February 1995, provoked further mass population movements. However, in March the Tanzanian authorities, reportedly frustrated at the lack of international assistance for the refugees and the environmental degradation resulting from the camps, closed Tanzania's border with Burundi, thus preventing the admission into the country of some 100,000 Rwandan Hutu refugees who were fleeing camps in Burundi. While persisting disturbances in Rwanda disrupted UNHCR's repatriation programme, in April Rwandan government troops employed intimidation tactics to force some 90,000 internally displaced Hutus to leave a heavily-populated camp in the south-west of the country; other small camps were closed. In August the Zairean Government initiated a programme of forcible repatriation of the estimated 1m. Rwandan and 70,000 Burundian Hutu refugees remaining in the country, which prompted as many as 100,000 refugees to flee the camps into the surrounding countryside. Following widespread international condemnation of the forcible repatriation and expressions of concern for the welfare of the remaining refugees, the Zairean Government suspended the programme, having first received an assurance that UNHCR would assume responsibility for the repatriation of all the refugees by the end of 1995 (although in December the Zairean Government accepted that its deadline could not be achieved). In September Rwanda agreed to strengthen its reception facilities and to provide greater security and protection for returnees, in collaboration with UNHCR, in order to prepare for any large-scale repatriation. UNHCR, meanwhile, expanded its information campaign, to promote the return of refugees, and enhanced its facilities at official border entry points. In December UNHCR negotiated an agreement between the Rwandan and Tanzanian authorities concerning the repatriation of the estimated 500,000 Rwandans remaining in camps in Tanzania. UNHCR agreed to establish a separate camp in north-west Tanzania in order to accommodate elements of the refugee population that might disrupt the repatriation programme. The repatriation of Rwandan refugees from all host countries was affected by reports of reprisals against Hutu returnees by the Tutsi-dominated Government in Rwanda. In February 1996 the Zairean Government renewed its efforts to accelerate the repatriation process, owing to concerns that the camps were becoming permanent settlements and that they were being used to train and rearm a Hutu militia. In July the Burundian Government forcibly repatriated 15,000 Rwandan refugees, having announced the closure of all remaining refugee camps. The repatriation programme was condemned by UNHCR and was suspended by the country's new military authorities, but only after many more thousands of refugees had been obliged to return to Rwanda and up to 30,000 had fled to Tanzania.

In October 1996 an escalation of hostilities between Zairean government forces, accused by Rwanda of arming the Hutu *Interahamwe* militia, and Zairean (Banyamulenge) Tutsis, who had been the focus of increasingly violent assaults, resulted in an extreme humanitarian crisis. Some 250,000 refugees fled 12 camps in the east of the country, including 90,000 Burundians who returned home. An estimated 500,000 refugees regrouped in Muganga camp, west of Goma, with insufficient relief assistance, following the temporary evacuation of international aid workers. UNHCR appealed to all Rwandan Hutu refugees to return home, and issued assurances of the presence of human rights observers in Rwanda to enhance their security. In mid-November, with the apparent withdrawal of *Interahamwe* forces and the advance of the Tutsi-dominated Alliance des forces démocratiques pour la libération du Congo–Zaïre (AFDL), an estimated 600,000 refugees unexpectedly returned to Rwanda; however, concern remained on the part of the international community for the substantial number of Rwandan Hutu refugees at large in eastern Zaire. Further mass movement of Rwandan refugee populations occurred in December, owing to the threat of forcible repatriation by the Tanzanian Government, which had announced its intention of closing all camps by the end of the year. UNHCR initiated a repatriation programme; however, 200,000 refugees, unwilling to return to Rwanda, fled their camps. The majority of the refugees were later identified by the Tanzanian national army and escorted to the Rwandan border. By the end of December some 483,000 refugees had returned to Rwanda from Tanzania.

In February 1997 violence in Zaire escalated, which prompted some 56,000 Zaireans to flee into Tanzania and disrupted the distribution of essential humanitarian supplies to refugees remaining in Zaire. An estimated 170,000 refugees abandoned their temporary encampment at Tingi-Tingi, fearing attacks by the advancing AFDL forces. About 75,000 reassembled at Ubundu, south of Kisangani, while the fate of the other refugees remained uncertain. In March and April continued reports of attacks on refugee camps by AFDL forces and local Zaireans, resulted in large numbers of people fleeing into the surrounding countryside, with the consequent deaths of many of the most vulnerable members of the refugee population from disease and starvation. At the end of April the leader of the AFDL, Laurent-Désiré Kabila, ordered the repatriation of all Rwandan Hutu refugees by the UN within 60 days. Emergency air and land operations to evacuate some 185,000 refugees who had regrouped into temporary settlements were initiated a few days later. The repatriation process, however, was hindered by administrative and logistical difficulties and lack of co-operation on the part of the AFDL forces. By June an estimated 215,000 Rwandans were still missing or dispersed throughout the former Zaire (renamed the Democratic Republic of the Congo—DRC—by the AFDL in May). In the following months relations between the Kabila Government and UNHCR deteriorated as a result of several incidences of forcible repatriations of refugees to Rwanda and reports that the authorities were hindering a UN investigation into alleged abuses of human rights, committed against the Rwandan Hutu refugees by AFDL forces. In August an agreement was concluded to provide for the voluntary repatriation of some 75,000 refugees from the DRC remaining in Tanzania, under UNHCR supervision. The repatriation of the estimated 260,000 Burundians remaining in Tanzania was hindered in early 1998 by an escalation of violence, which destabilized areas of return for both refugees and internally displaced persons. In December 1997 a tripartite agreement was signed to provide for the organized repatriation of the remaining former Zairean refugees in Rwanda, with both Governments agreeing to observe strict conditions of security for the refugees on both sides of the border. Meanwhile, an estimated 40,000 refugees from the Republic of the Congo fled to the DRC in mid-1997, following the outbreak of civil conflict. In December a memorandum of understanding was signed by representatives of the two Governments and of UNHCR, providing for their immediate repatriation. UNHCR's concerns in the Great Lakes region in 1998 were to ensure the security of returning refugee populations and to assist their reintegr-

ation and national reconciliation. UNCHR also resolved to work, in co-operation with UNDP and WFP, to rehabilitate areas previously inhabited by refugees in countries of asylum and undertook to repair roads, bridges and other essential transport infrastructure, improve water and sanitation facilities, and strengthen the education sector. However, the political stability of the region remained uncertain. In August fighting between rebel and government forces again broke out in the DRC, which forced UNHCR temporarily to evacuate and prompted substantial numbers of people to flee to neighbouring countries. At 31 December the major populations of concern to UNHCR in the Great Lakes region were as follows: 231,800 returned refugees, and a further 625,000 IDPs, in Rwanda; 240,300 refugees, and some 111,300 recently returned refugees, in the DRC; 100,000 IDPs in Burundi, as well as 114,600 returned refugees; and a refugee population of 543,900 remaining in Tanzania.

From late 1998 intense fighting in the Republic of the Congo disrupted UNHCR humanitarian efforts in that country, causing 20,000 Congolese immediately to seek refuge in the DRC and leaving some 200,000 people displaced southwest of the capital, Brazzaville. Of these, 40,000 subsequently also fled to the DRC. UNHCR launched a repatriation operation in April 1999. However, fighting continued, and in July more than 12,000 Congolese refugees fled to Gabon. Following the agreement of a cease-fire in the Republic of the Congo in December it was expected that the refugee population would be repatriated. In July some 14,000 refugees from the DRC crossed into the Central African Republic, bringing the total number of refugees since the resumption of conflict in the DRC in August 1998 to some 100,000 (the majority of whom were in Tanzania), while a further 100,000 people were thought to have been displaced. In August 1999 the security situation in Burundi deteriorated, and there were reports of a steady flow of Burundians fleeing to camps in Tanzania. In October UNHCR, along with other agencies, suspended its non-essential operations in Burundi as a result of the deaths of two UN personnel.

In 1994 continuing civil conflict in Angola caused some 370,000 people to leave their home areas. Prior to the signing of a peace settlement in November, UNHCR provided assistance to 112,000 internally displaced Angolans and returnees, although military activities, which hindered accessibility, undermined the effectiveness of the assistance programme. In mid-1995, following a consolidation of the peace process in Angola, UNHCR appealed for US $44m. to support the voluntary repatriation of some 300,000 Angolan refugees over a two-and-a-half-year operation. By June 1996 implementation of the repatriation programme was delayed, reportedly owing to poor accommodation and other facilities for returnees, limited progress in confining and disarming opposition troops and the continued hazard of land-mines throughout the country. During 1997 an estimated 53,000 Angolans voluntarily returned from the DRC and Zambia, bringing the total returnees to some 130,000 since mid-1995. In November 1997 UNHCR resolved to implement an operation to provide for the repatriation and reintegration of 240,000 Angolan refugees by June 1999. UNHCR allocated $15.7m. to support the repatriation process and other activities in Angola, including strengthening the country's road infrastructure, monitoring areas of return, reintegration projects and promoting links with other development programmes. In May 1998, however, the security situation in Angola deteriorated, and at the end of June UNHCR declared a temporary suspension of the repatriation operation. The renewed violence also resulted in further population displacement: by the end of 1998 at least 90,000 people had been displaced within Angola and 40,000 had fled to the DRC. At that time the total Angolan refugee population amounted to some 315,900, while there were 75,800 recently returned Angolan refugees of concern to UNHCR. Heavy fighting in central Angola in early 1999 resulted in massive population displacement in and around the city of Huambo, and, by April, a further 21,500 refugees had arrived in the DRC. From October 1999 a new influx of Angolan refugees, numbering more than 40,000, arrived in the DRC; some 26,000 Angolans also crossed into Zambia, and 5,000 into Namibia. In early 2000 UNHCR resolved to expand its operations in Angola with a view to providing emergency humanitarian assistance to Angolan IDPs (estimated at that time to exceed 1.5m.).

CO-OPERATION WITH OTHER ORGANIZATIONS

UNHCR works closely with other UN agencies, intergovernmental organizations and non-governmental organizations (NGOs) to increase the scope and effectiveness of its emergency operations. Within the UN system UNHCR co-operates, principally, with the World Food Programme in the distribution of food aid, UNICEF and the World Health Organization in the provision of family welfare and child immunization programmes and with the UN Development Programme in development-related activities and in the preparation of guide-lines for the continuum of emergency assistance to development programmes. UNHCR also has a close working relationship with the International Committee of the Red Cross and the International Organization for Migration. In 1999 UNHCR worked with

513 NGOs as 'implementing partners', enabling UNHCR to broaden the use of its resources, as well as to benefit from local knowledge and skills, while maintaining a co-ordinating role in the provision of assistance. In 1998 UNHCR established a joint secretariat, with the Organization of African Unity, to prepare for a ministerial meeting of refugees, returnees and IDPs, which was held in Khartoum, Sudan, in December.

TRAINING

During 1995 three emergency management training programmes were organized by UNHCR, including one in Ghana for English-speaking countries in West Africa. A programme workshop covering French-speaking countries in West Africa was scheduled to be held during 1996, while an emergency training workshop incorporating the countries in the Horn of Africa and East Africa was conducted early in that year in Addis Ababa, Ethiopia. The workshops aimed to formulate guide-lines and a co-ordinated strategy for response to an emergency situation. Other training activities conducted in the region during 1995 and 1996 were concerned with the registration and identification of refugees, enhancing 'people-oriented planning', the dissemination of information through the electronic media, security awareness, and stress management.

In June 1996 UNHCR launched an Education Fund for African Refugees to provide scholarships for refugee students at secondary level.

Finance

Prior to 2000 UNHCR's activities were designated as General Programmes and Special Programmes, and were financed separately. With effect from January 2000 these were unified under a single annual programme budget. Of the US $933.5m. approved for 2000, $100.2m. was allocated to the Great Lakes programme, $91.2nm. to the operation in the Horn of Africa and $69.2m. to that in West and Central Africa. Any further requirements identified following the approval of the annual programme budget were to be managed in the form of supplementary programmes, to be funded by separate appeals. (For example, in 2000 supplementary programmes were subsequently announced to support the repatriation and reintegration of Sierra Leonean refugees, and to provide emergency humanitarian assistance to IDPs in Angola.)

Publications

Refugees (quarterly, in English, French, German, Italian, Japanese and Spanish).
UNHCR Handbook for Emergencies.
Refugee Survey Quarterly.
The State of the World's Refugees (every 2 years).

United Nations Peace-keeping Operations

Address: Department of Peace-keeping Operations, Room S-3727-B, United Nations, New York, NY 10017, USA.

Telephone: (212) 963-8079; **fax:** (212) 963-9222; **internet:** www.un.org/Depts/dpko/.

United Nations peace-keeping operations have been conceived as instruments of conflict control. The UN has used these operations in various conflicts, with the consent of the parties involved, to maintain international peace and security, without prejudice to the positions or claims of parties, in order to facilitate the search for political settlements through peaceful means such as mediation and the good offices of the Secretary-General. Each operation has been established with a specific mandate, which requires periodic review by the Security Council. United Nations peace-keeping operations fall into two categories: peace-keeping forces and observer missions.

Peace-keeping forces are composed of contingents of military and civilian personnel, made available by member states. These forces assist in preventing the recurrence of fighting, restoring and maintaining peace, and promoting a return to normal conditions. To this end, peace-keeping forces are authorized as necessary to undertake negotiations, persuasion, observation and fact-finding. They run patrols and interpose physically between the opposing parties. Peace-keeping forces are permitted to use their weapons only in self-defence.

Military observer missions are composed of officers (usually unarmed), who are made available, on the Secretary-General's request, by member states. A mission's function is to observe and report to the Secretary-General (who in turn informs the UN Security Council) on the maintenance of a cease-fire, to investigate violations and to do what it can to improve the situation.

Peace-keeping forces and observer missions must at all times maintain complete impartiality and avoid any action that might affect the claims or positions of the parties.

The UN's peace-keeping operations are financed by assessed contributions from member states (with the exception of two operations, which are ongoing and financed by the regular budget of the UN). During the 1990s a significant expansion in the UN's peace-keeping activities has been accompanied by a perpetual financial crisis within the organization, as a result of the increased financial burden and some member states delaying payment. At the end of 1999 unpaid contributions to peace-keeping accounts totalled US $1,482m.

UNITED NATIONS MISSION IN SIERRA LEONE—UNAMSIL

Headquarters: Freetown, Sierra Leone.
Special Representative of the UN Secretary-General and Chief of Mission: OLUYEMI ADENIJI (Nigeria).
Commander: Maj.-Gen. VIJAY KUMAR JETLEY (India).

In July 1998 the Security Council established a UN observer mission in Sierra Leone (UNOMSIL) to monitor the military and security situation in that country following the restoration of a democratically-elected government. UNOMSIL was authorized to oversee the disarmament and demobilization of former combatants, as well as the voluntary disarmament of members of the civilian defence force, and to assist in monitoring respect for international humanitarian law. The Special Representative, with the civilian component of the mission, was authorized to advise the Sierra Leonean authorities on police practice, training and reform, and to help to address the country's human rights needs. UNOMSIL was to work closely with forces of the Economic Community for West African States (ECOWAS) in promoting peace and national reconciliation. In January 1999, following a sudden escalation of hostilities, the UN Security Council extended the mandate of UNOMSIL for a further two months, although it acknowledged that several UNOMSIL military observers, together with civilian support staff, would withdraw to Conakry, Guinea, until the security situation improved. In March the Security Council condemned the ongoing violation of human rights in Sierra Leone and urged all neighbouring countries to prevent the cross-border supply of armaments to anti-government forces. None the less, the Council extended the mission's mandate until mid-June and, subsequently, until mid-December. In August the Security Council authorized a provisional expansion of UNOMSIL of up to 210 military observers, in order to support the implementation of a peace agreement which had been signed by the parties to the Sierra Leone conflict in July, in Lomé, Togo. In October the Council authorized the establishment of the UN Mission in Sierra Leone (UNAMSIL), comprising up to 6,000 military personnel, to help to consolidate peace in that country. UNAMSIL was mandated to co-operate with the Sierra Leonean Government and all other parties to enforce the cease-fire accord and Lomé peace agreement, to implement a plan for the disarmament and demobilization of all former combatants, and to facilitate the delivery of humanitarian assistance. The Mission was to assume responsibility for all civilian, political and military components of UNOMSIL, the mandate of which was terminated with immediate effect. In February 2000 the Council expanded UNAMSIL's mandate to include the provision of security at key locations and government installations, assistance to the Sierra Leone law enforcement authorities, and the safekeeping and subsequent disposal of military equipment collected from former combatants. The Council also enlarged the Mission's authorized strength from 6,000 to 11,100 military personnel. During early 2000, in contravention of the Lomé agreement, Sierra Leone rebels repeatedly obstructed the implementation of the disarmament and demobilization plan. In May, following an attack on a contingent of UNAMSIL troops in the previous month, rebels killed several Mission personnel and captured and detained a large number of others (reportedly as many as 500); these were all released later in the month. In response to the breakdown in security the United Kingdom deployed a force in Sierra Leone in early May, with a mandate to evacuate British nationals; the presence of the British troops was also regarded, however, as a deterrent to any escalation in rebel activities pending the arrival of UNAMSIL reinforcements. In mid-May the Security Council approved a further increase in the Mission's authorized strength, providing for a total of 13,000 military personnel. In mid-July UNAMSIL mounted a successful operation to release 233 of its personnel, who had been surrounded by rebels in eastern Sierra Leone since the end of May.

At 26 July 2000 UNAMSIL comprised 12,180 troops and 260 military observers, assisted by 34 civilian police and some 334 international and local civilian personnel. The Mission's budget amounted to US $504.4m. for the period until 30 June 2001.

UNITED NATIONS MISSION IN THE DEMOCRATIC REPUBLIC OF THE CONGO—MONUC

Headquarters: Kinshasa, Democratic Republic of the Congo.
Special Representative of the UN Secretary-General and Chief of Mission: KAMEL MORJANE (Tunisia).
Commander: Maj.-Gen. MOUNTAGA DIALLO (Senegal).

In August 1999 the UN Security Council authorized the deployment of up to 90 military liaison personnel to support implementation of a cease-fire agreement for the Democratic Republic of the Congo (DRC) which had been signed in Lusaka, Zambia, in July. Technical officers were also to be dispatched to Namibia, Rwanda, Uganda and Zimbabwe, all signatories of the Lusaka accord, to assess the security of any future UN presence in the sub-region. The Security Council approved the establishment of MONUC in late November. With an initial mandate until 1 March 2000, the mission was to continue to establish contacts with all signatories to the cease-fire agreement and to liaise with the newly-established Joint Military Commission in the DRC in order to uphold implementation of the agreement. MONOC was also mandated to plan for the observation of the cease-fire and disengagement of forces, to facilitate the delivery of humanitarian assistance, and to report on local security conditions. MONUC was to comprise liaison and technical assessment officers, as well as other multidisciplinary personnel, previously authorized by the Council; however, the Council requested that up to 500 military observers be equipped ready for deployment pending further recommendations on the security situation in the DRC by the UN Secretary-General. In February 2000 the Security Council extended MONUC's mandate to the end of August and authorized the expansion of the Mission.

At 30 June 2000 MONUC comprised 258 military observers, assisted by 279 international and local civilian personnel. The proposed budget for the Mission amounted to US $141.3m. for the period until 30 June 2001.

Food and Agriculture Organization—FAO

Address: Viale delle Terme di Caracalla, 00100 Rome, Italy.
Telephone: (06) 57051; **fax:** (06) 5705-3152; **e-mail:** telex-room@-fao.org; **internet:** www.fao.org.

FAO, the first specialized agency of the UN to be founded after World War II, was established in Québec, Canada, in October 1945. The Organization combats malnutrition and hunger, and serves as a co-ordinating agency for development programmes in the whole range of food and agriculture, including forestry and fisheries. It helps developing countries to promote educational and training facilities and the creation of appropriate institutions.

Organization

(July 2000)

CONFERENCE

The governing body is the FAO Conference of member nations. It meets every two years, formulates policy, determines the Organization's programme and budget on a biennial basis, and elects new members. It also elects the Director-General of the Secretariat and the Independent Chairman of the Council. Every second year, FAO also holds conferences in each of its five regions (the Near East, Asia and the Pacific, Africa, Latin America and the Caribbean, and Europe).

COUNCIL

The FAO Council is composed of representatives of 49 member nations, elected by the Conference for staggered three-year terms. It is the interim governing body of FAO between sessions of the Conference. The most important standing Committees of the Council are: the Finance and Programme Committees, the Committee on Commodity Problems, the Committee on Fisheries, the Committee on Agriculture and the Committee on Forestry.

SECRETARIAT

The total number of staff at FAO headquarters in September 1999 was 2,278, of whom 67 were associate experts, while staff in field, regional and country offices numbered 1,865, including 132 associate experts. Work is supervised by the following Departments: Administration and Finance; General Affairs and Information; Economic and Social Policy; Agriculture; Forestry; Fisheries; Sustainable Development; and Technical Co-operation.

Director-General: JACQUES DIOUF (Senegal).

REGIONAL OFFICES

Regional Office for Africa: UN Agency Bldg, North Maxwell Rd, POB 1628, Accra, Ghana; tel. (21) 666851; fax (21) 668427; e-mail fao-raf@fao.org; Regional Rep. BAMBIDELE F. DADA.

Sub-regional Office for Southern and Eastern Africa: POB 3730, Harare, Zimbabwe; tel. (4) 791407; fax (4) 703497; e-mail fao-safr-registry@field.fao.org; Subregional Rep. VICTORIA SEKITOLEKO.

Activities

FAO aims to raise levels of nutrition and standards of living, by improving the production and distribution of food and other commodities derived from farms, fisheries and forests. FAO provides technical information, advice and assistance by disseminating information; acting as a neutral forum for discussion of food and agricultural issues; advising governments on policy and planning; and developing capacity directly in the field.

In November 1998 the FAO Conference identified the following areas of activity as FAO priorities for 2000–01; the Special Programme for Food Security; transboundary animal and plant pests and diseases; forestry; the Codex Alimentarius code on food standards; and strengthing the Technical Co-operation Programme (which funds 12% of FAO's field programme expenditure); and the implementation of a Programme Against African Trypanosomiasis. In October 1997 FAO organized its first televised fund-raising event, 'TeleFood', broadcast to an estimated 500m. viewers in some 70 countries. The initiative has subsequently been organized on an annual basis in order to raise public awareness of the problems of hunger and malnutrition. Since 1997 public donations to TeleFood have totalled more than US $4m., financing some 476 'grass-roots' projects in nearly 100 countries. The projects provided tools, seeds and other essential supplies directly to small-scale farmers, and were especially aimed at helping women. In November 1996 FAO organized the World Food Summit, which was held in Rome and was attended by heads of state and senior government representatives of 186 countries. Participants approved the Rome Declaration on World Food Security and the World Food Summit Plan of Action, with the aim of halving the number of people afflicted by undernutrition, at that time estimated to total 828m. world-wide, no later than 2015.

FAO's total field programme expenditure for 1998 was US $278m., compared with $260m. spent in 1997. An estimated 33% of field projects were in Africa, 22% in Asia and the Pacific, 12% in the Near East, 10% in Latin America and the Caribbean, 4% in Europe, and 19% were inter-regional or global.

AGRICULTURE

FAO's Field Programme provides training and technical assistance to enable small farmers to increase production, by a number of methods, including improved seeds and fertilizer use, soil conservation and reafforestation, better water resource management techniques, upgrading storage facilities, and improvements in processing and marketing. FAO promotes the production of under-exploited traditional food crops, such as cassava, yams, breadfruit, sweet potato and plantains. During the 1980s FAO developed 'wheatless bread', which can be made using cassava, sorghum or millet flour, and is intended to reduce dependence on imports of wheat. Governments are advised on the conservation of genetic resources, on improving the supply of seeds and on crop protection: animal and plant gene banks are maintained. In June 1996 representatives of more than 150 governments attending a conference in Leipzig, Germany, organized by FAO, adopted a Global Plan of Action to conserve and improve the use of plant genetic resources, in order to enhance food security throughout the world. The Plan included measures to strengthen the development of plant varieties and to promote the use and availability of local varieties and locally-adapted crops to farmers, in particular following a natural disaster, war or civil conflict.

Plant protection, weed control, and animal health programmes form an important part of FAO's work as farming methods become more intensive, and pests more resistant to control methods. In 1985 the FAO Conference approved an International Code of Conduct on the Distribution and Use of Pesticides and in 1989 the Conference adopted an additional clause concerning 'Prior Informed Consent' (PIC), whereby international shipments of newly banned or restricted pesticides should not proceed without the agreement of importing countries. In mid-1996 FAO, in collaboration with UNEP, publicized a new initiative which aimed to increase awareness of, and to promote international action on, obsolete and hazardous stocks of pesticides remaining throughout the world. In September 1998 a new legally-binding treaty on the PIC procedure for trade in hazardous chemicals and pesticides was adopted at an international conference held in Rotterdam, the Netherlands. The so-called Rotterdam Convention required that hazardous chemicals and pesticides banned or severely restricted in at least two countries should not be exported unless explicitly agreed by the importing country. It also identified certain pesticide formulations as too dangerous to be used by farmers in developing countries, and incorporated an obligation that countries halt national production of those hazardous compounds. The treaty was to enter into force on being ratified by 50 signatory states. FAO was co-operating with UNEP to provide an interim secretariat for the Convention. In July 1999 a conference on the Rotterdam Convention, held in Rome, established an Interim Chemical Review Committee with responsibility for recommending the inclusion of chemicals or pesticide formulations in the PIC procedure. By September the treaty had been signed by 60 states. A central concept of FAO's plant protection programme is the Integrated Pest Management (IPM) strategy, which was initiated in 1988 in order to reduce over-reliance on pesticides. IPM principles include biological control methods, such as the introduction of natural predators to avert pests, crop rotation and the use of pest-resistant crop varieties. FAO's Joint Division with the International Atomic Energy Agency (IAEA), tests controlled-release formulas of pesticides and herbicides that can limit the amount of agrochemicals needed to protect crops. The Joint FAO-IAEA Division is engaged in exploring biotechnologies and in developing non-toxic fertilizers (especially those that are locally available) and improved strains of food crops (especially from indigenous varieties). FAO's plant nutrition activities aim to promote nutrient management, such as the Integrated Plant Nutritions Systems (IPNS), which are based on the recycling of nutrients through crop production and the efficient use of mineral fertilizers.

An Emergency Prevention System for Transboundary Animal and Plant Pests and Diseases (EMPRES) was established in 1994 to strengthen FAO's activities in the prevention, control and, where possible, eradication of highly contagious diseases and pests. EMPRES's initial priorities were locusts and rinderpest. During 1994 EMPRES published guide-lines on all aspects of desert locust monitoring, commissioned an evaluation of recent control efforts and prepared a concept paper on desert locust management. FAO has assumed responsibility for technical leadership and co-ordination of the Global Rinderpest Eradication Campaign, which aims to eradicate the disease, endemic in areas of the Horn of Africa, by 2010. In early 1997 EMPRES was involved in intensive surveillance activities in east Africa, following a serious outbreak of rinderpest in eastern and southern Kenya and the border region of Tanzania. In March 1995 FAO initiated an emergency programme to combat bovine pleuro-pneumonia, a disease which had affected livestock in Tanzania and was a potential threat to a further three million cattle in southern Africa, in particular in Zambia and Malawi. The programme included widespread livestock vaccination and restrictions on cattle movement. Following an incidence of African swine fever in Côte d'Ivoire in April 1996, FAO initiated a long-term epidemio-surveillance programme with the Ivorian authorities. An outbreak of the disease in Côte d'Ivoire in 1997 was contained with the assistance of EMPRES. African swine fever control programmes have been established in Benin, Nigeria and Togo. In November 1997 FAO initiated a Programme Against African Trypanosomiasis, which aimed to counter the disease affecting cattle in almost one-third of Africa. In the late 1990s EMPRES programmes to combat desert locust plagues were initiated in Djibouti, Eritrea and Ethiopia.

FISHERIES

FAO's Fisheries Department consists of a multi-disciplinary body of experts who are involved in every aspect of fisheries development from coastal surveys, improved production, processing and storage, to the compilation of statistics, development of computer databases, improvement of fishing gear, institution building and training. In March 1995 a ministerial meeting of fisheries adopted a Rome Consensus on World Fisheries, which identified a need for immediate action to eliminate overfishing and to rebuild and enhance depleted fish stocks. In November the FAO Conference adopted a Code of Conduct for Responsible Fishing, which incorporated many global fisheries and aquaculture issues (including fisheries resource conservation and development, fish catches, seafood and fish processing, commercialization, trade and research) to promote the sustainable development of the sector. FAO promotes aquaculture as a valuable source of animal protein, and as an income-generating activity for rural communities. In 1996/97 FAO participated in 21 technical consultations on the management of marine resources, strengthened work on aquatic genetic resources and conducted studies to monitor the impact of 'El Niño', a periodic warming of the tropical Pacific Ocean, on aquaculture in Latin America and Africa. In February 1999 the FAO Committee on Fisheries adopted new international measures, within the framework of the Code of Conduct, in order to reduce over-exploitation of the world's fish resources, as well as plans of action for the conservation and management of sharks and the reduction in the incidental catch of seabirds in longline fisheries. The voluntary measures were endorsed at a ministerial meeting, held in March and attended by representatives of some 126 countries, which issued a declaration to promote the implementation of the Code of Conduct and to achieve sustainable management of fisheries and aquaculture. In October a new Sustainable Fisheries Livelihoods Programme was initiated to assist 24 African countries to implement the Code of Conduct and to promote small-scale artisanal fishing projects.

FORESTRY

FAO focuses on the contribution of forestry to food security, on effective and responsible forest management and on maintaining a balance between the economic, ecological and social benefits of forest resources. The Organization has helped to develop national forestry programmes and to promote the sustainable development of all types of forest. FAO's Forests, Trees and People Programme promotes the sustainable management of tree and forest resources, based on local knowledge and management practices, in order to improve the livelihoods of rural people in developing countries. In sub-Saharan Africa the Programme is implemented in collaboration with organizations and institutions in Benin, Burkina Faso, Cameroon, Ethiopia, Kenya, Mali, Niger, Senegal, Tanzania and Uganda. A draft strategic plan for the sustainable management of trees and forests was formulated in 1997, the main objectives of which were to maintain the environmental diversity of forests, to realise the economic potential of forests and trees within a sustainable framework, and to establish broad social networks of interested parties to manage and develop forest environments. A series of meetings of the regional forestry commission was held during 1998 to consider the plan.

PROCESSING AND MARKETING

An estimated 20% of all food harvested is lost before it can be consumed. FAO helps reduce immediate post-harvest losses, with the introduction of improved processing methods and storage systems. It also advises on the distribution and marketing of agricultural produce and on the selection and preparation of foods for optimum nutrition. A Centre for Agricultural Marketing Training in Eastern and Southern Africa has been established with FAO assistance in Harare, Zimbabwe, to serve Kenya, Malawi, Tanzania and Zimbabwe. FAO continues to favour the elimination of export subsidies and related discriminatory practices, in particular those which create unfavourable trading conditions for developing countries dependent on agricultural products as their main source of foreign income. By late 1997 FAO had organized 18 regional workshops and 44 national projects in order to help member states to implement new World Trade Organization regulations, in particular with regard to agricultural policy, intellectual property rights, sanitary and phytosanitary measures, technical barriers to trade and the international standards of the Codex Alimentarius, and to consider the impact on member states of the ministerial decision concerning the possible negative effects of the reform programme on least-developed and net-food importing developing countries. FAO evaluates new market trends and helps to develop improved plant and animal quarantine procedures. In November 1997 the FAO Conference adopted new guide-lines on surveillance and on export certification systems in order to harmonize plant quarantine standards. In August 1999 FAO announced the establishment of a new forum, PhAction, to promote post-harvest research and the development of effective post-harvest services and infrastructure.

ENVIRONMENT

At the UN Conference on Environment and Development, held in Rio de Janeiro, Brazil, in June 1992, FAO participated in several working parties and supported the adoption of Agenda 21, a programme of activities to promote sustainable development. FAO was subsequently designated as the UN agency responsible for the chapters of Agenda 21 concerned with water resources, forests, fragile mountain ecosystems and sustainable agriculture and rural development.

NUTRITION

In December 1992 an International Conference on Nutrition was held in Rome, administered jointly by FAO and WHO. The Conference approved a World Declaration on Nutrition and a Plan of Action, aimed at promoting efforts to combat malnutrition as a development priority. Since the conference, more than 100 countries have formulated national plans of action for nutrition, many of which were based on existing development plans such as comprehensive food security initiatives, national poverty alleviation programmes and action plans to attain the targets set by the World Summit for Children in September 1990.

FOOD SECURITY

FAO's food security policy aims to encourage the production of adequate food supplies, to maximize stability in the flow of supplies, and to ensure access on the part of those who need them. FAO's Special Programme for Food Security (SPFS) was initiated in 1994 to assist target countries, i.e. low-income countries with a food deficit, to increase food production and productivity as rapidly as possible. This was to be achieved primarily through the widespread adoption by farmers of available improved production technologies, with emphasis on areas of high potential. In December 1999 83 countries were categorized as 'low-income food-deficit', of which 42 were in Africa, while the Programme was engaged in projects in 54 countries. A budget of US $10m. was allocated to the Programme for the two year period 1998–99. FAO was actively involved in the formulation of a Plan of Action on food security, adopted at the World Food Summit in November 1996, and was to be responsible for monitoring and promoting its implementation. In March 1999, FAO signed agreements with both the International Fund for Agricultural Development (IFAD, q.v.) and the World Food Programme (WFP, q.v.), which aimed to increase co-operation within the framework of the SPFS. The Programme promotes South-South co-operation to improve food security and the exchange of knowledge and experience. By mid-1999 10 bilateral co-operation agreements were in force, for example, between Viet Nam and Senegal, and India and Eritrea.

FAO's Global Information and Early Warning System (GIEWS), which became operational in 1975, monitors the crop and food outlook at global and national levels in order to detect emerging food supply difficulties and disasters and to ensure rapid intervention in countries experiencing food supply shortages. It publishes regular reports on the weather conditions and crop prospects in sub-Saharan Africa and in the Sahel region and issues special alerts which describe the situation in countries or sub-regions experiencing food difficulties and recommends an appropriate international response. In October 1999 FAO published the first *State of Food Insecurity in the World*, based on data compiled by a new Food Insecurity and Vulnerability Information and Mapping Systems programme.

FAO INVESTMENT CENTRE

The Investment Centre was established in 1964 to help countries prepare viable investment projects that would attract external financing. The Centre focuses its evaluation of projects on two fundamental concerns: the promotion of sustainable activities for land management, forestry development and environmental protection, and the alleviation of rural poverty. In 1998 44 projects were approved, representing a total investment of some US $3,000m.

EMERGENCY RELIEF

FAO works to rehabilitate agricultural production following natural and man-made disasters by providing emergency seed, tools, and technical and other assistance. In 1997 more than 60 countries suffered the effects of heavy flooding or severe drought, caused wholly or partially by the El Niño weather phenomenon. FAO attempted to help assess the damage to agricultural systems, to provide rehabilitation assistance and to initiate efforts to strengthen the resistance of agricultural sectors against future weather anomalies. In 1998 FAO was concerned at the possible effects of a converse climatic occurrence, 'La Niña', caused by upswelling of cold water in areas of the Pacific Ocean. By 30 November FAO's Special Relief Operations Service had undertaken 96 new projects in 45 countries, at a cost of US $93.3m. New projects approved in 1999 included the provision of seeds and agricultural tools to displaced and returning populations in Burundi, to those affected by conflict in the Democratic Republic of the Congo, Guinea-Bissau and Liberia, to refugees living in Tanzania, to rural populations affected by flooding in Djibouti, and also to those combating drought in Burundi, Eritrea and Ethiopia; surveillance and control of Rift Valley Fever in Mauritania; and a regional programme to help prevent and control outbreaks of locust and grasshoppers throughout Africa. Jointly with the United Nations, FAO is responsible for WFP (see below), which provides emergency food supplies and food aid in support of development projects.

INFORMATION

FAO functions as an information centre, collecting, analysing, interpreting and disseminating information through various media, including an extensive interest site. It issues regular statistical reports, commodity studies, and technical manuals in local languages (see list of publications below). Other materials produced by the FAO include information booklets, reference papers, reports of meetings, training manuals and audiovisuals.

FAO compiles and co-ordinates an extensive range of international databases on agriculture, fisheries, forestry, food and statistics, the most important of these being AGRIS (the International Information System for the Agricultural Sciences and Technology) and CARIS (the Current Agricultural Research Information System). Statistical databases include GLOBEFISH databank and electronic library, FISHDAB (the Fisheries Statistical Database), FORIS (Forest Resources Information System), and GIS (the Geographical Information System). In addition, AGROSTAT PC has been designed to provide access to updated figures in six agriculture-related topics via personal computer. In 1996 FAO established a World Agricultural Information Centre (WAICENT), which offers wide access to agricultural data through the internet.

FAO Regional Commissions

African Commission on Agricultural Statistics: c/o FAO Regional Office for Africa, POB 1628, Accra, Ghana; f. 1961 to advise member countries on the development and standardization of food and agricultural statistics. Mems: 37 states.

African Forestry and Wildlife Commission: Via delle Terme di Caracalla, 00100 Rome, Italy; f. 1959 to advise on the formulation of forest policy and to review and co-ordinate its implementation on a regional level; to exchange information and advise on technical problems. Mems: 42 states.

Commission on African Animal Trypanosomiasis: Via delle Terme di Caracalla, 00100 Rome, Italy; f. 1979 to develop and implement programmes to combat this pathogen. Mems: 39 states.

Joint FAO/WHO/OAU Regional Food and Nutrition Commission for Africa: c/o FAO Regional Office for Africa, POB 1628, Accra, Ghana; f. 1962 to provide liaison in matters concerning food and nutrition, and to review food and nutritional problems in Africa. Mems: 43 states.

Finance

FAO's Regular Programme, which is financed by contributions from member governments, covers the cost of the FAO's Secretariat, its Technical Co-operation Programme (TCP) and part of the cost of several special action programmes. The budget for the two years 2000–01 amounted to US $650m. Much of FAO's Field Programme is funded from extra-budgetary sources. The single largest contributor is the United Nations Development Programme (UNDP), which in 1998 accounted for $33m., or 12% of total Field Programme expenditures. More important are the trust funds that come mainly from donor countries and international financing institutions. In 1998 they totalled $208m., or 75% of Field Programme expenditure. FAO's contribution under the TCP (FAO's regular budgetary funds for the Field Programme) was $34m., or 12% of expenditure in that year, while the contribution under the Special Programme for Food Security was $3m., or some 1% of the total $278m.

World Food Programme—WFP

Address: Via Cesare Giulio Viola 68, Parco dei Medici, 00148 Rome, Italy.

Telephone: (06) 6513-1; **fax:** (06) 6590-632; **e-mail:** wfpinfo @wfp.org; **internet:** www.wfp.org.

WFP, which became operational in 1963, is the principal food aid agency of the UN. It aims to eradicate chronic undernourishment by assisting social development and human growth, and to alleviate acute hunger by providing emergency relief following natural or man-made humanitarian disasters. Priority is given to vulnerable groups, such as children and pregnant women. During 1999 WFP food assistance benefitted some 89m. people world-wide, of whom 19m. received aid through development projects, 29m. were refugees, returnees or internally displaced, while 41m. were victims of natural disasters. Total food deliveries amounted to 3.4m. metric tons in 82 countries.

Through its development activities WFP aims to alleviate poverty in developing countries by promoting self-reliant families and communities. Food is supplied, for example, as an incentive in labour-intensive projects which provide employment and strengthen self-help capacity. WFP supports activities to boost agricultural production, to rehabilitate and improve local infrastructure, particularly transport systems, and to encourage education, training and health programmes. Some WFP projects are intended to alleviate the effects of structural adjustment programmes (particularly programmes which involve reductions in public expenditure and in subsidies for basic foods). During 1999 WFP supported 146 development projects, for which operational expenditures totalled an estimated US $246.5m.

In the early 1990s there was a substantial shift in the balance between emergency and development assistance provided by WFP, owing to the growing needs of victims of drought and other natural disasters, refugees and displaced persons. WFP maintains strategic stores of food and logistics equipment in Nairobi, Kenya, and Pisa, Italy, to enable it to respond effectively to emergency situations. WFP also administers field units in Ethiopia, Malawi, Senegal, Sudan, Tanzania and Zambia, which undertake vulnerability analysis and mapping to help identify regions and communities at risk from food shortages. In 1998 WFP organized its largest ever delivery of food aid by air, in order to reach some 1.8m. people in southern Sudan affected by famine resulting from poor harvests, fighting and floods. A special task force was established in July to co-ordinate the humanitarian operation. In 1999 the main focus of WFP's relief activities continued to be sub-Saharan Africa. The main populations of concern throughout 1999 were those in Angola, the Great Lakes region and Sierra Leone, affected by civil conflict, and in the Horn of Africa, affected by extreme climatic conditions and renewed conflict. In early 2000 emergency operations approved included the delivery of relief aid to populations affected by flooding in Mozambique and by drought in east Africa, and the provision of assistance to war-affected populations, including Eritreans displaced by the border conflict with Ethiopia and those displaced by the ongoing unrest in the Democratic Republic of the Congo.

Following a comprehensive evaluation of its activities, WFP is increasingly focused on linking its relief and development activities to provide a continuum between short-term relief and longer-term rehabilitation and development. In order to achieve this objective, WFP aims to integrate elements that strengthen disaster mitigation into development projects, including soil conservation, reafforestation, irrigation infrastructure and transport construction and rehabilitation and to promote capacity-building elements within relief operations, e.g. training, income-generating activities and environmental protection measures. In 1999 WFP approved 23 new 'protracted refugee and displaced persons operations', where the emphasis was on fostering stability, rehabilitation and long-term development after an emergency. In all these operations, which are undertaken in collaboration with UNHCR and other international agencies, WFP is responsible for mobilizing basic food commodities and for related transport, handling and storage costs. In 1998 expenditure on these operations in sub-Saharan Africa amounted to US $167.5m., or 26% of total expenditure in the region.

WFP Executive Director: CATHERINE A. BERTINI (USA).

FAO Publications

Animal Health Yearbook.
Commodity Review and Outlook (annually).
Environment and Energy Bulletin.
Fertilizer Yearbook.
Food Crops and Shortages (6 a year).
Food Outlook (5 a year).
Plant Protection Bulletin (quarterly).
Production Yearbook (in English, French and Spanish).
Quarterly Bulletin of Statistics.
The State of Food and Agriculture (annually).
The State of World Fisheries and Aquaculture (annually).
The State of the World's Forests (every two years).
Technical Co-operation Among Developing Countries Newsletter (in English only).
Trade Yearbook.
Unasylva (quarterly).
Yearbook of Fishery Statistics (in English, French and Spanish).
Yearbook of Forest Products (in English, French and Spanish).
World Animal Review (quarterly).
World Watch List for Domestic Animal Diversity.
Commodity reviews; studies; manuals.

International Bank for Reconstruction and Development—IBRD—and International Development Association—IDA (World Bank)

Address: 1818 H St, NW, Washington, DC 20433, USA.

Telephone: (202) 477-1234; **fax:** (202) 477-6391; **e-mail:** pic@worldbank.org; **internet:** www.worldbank.org/.

The IBRD was established on 27 December 1945. Initially it was concerned with post-war reconstruction in Europe; since then its aim has been to assist the economic development of member nations by making loans where private capital is not available on reasonable terms to finance productive investments. Loans are made either direct to governments, or to private enterprises with the guarantee of their governments. The World Bank, as it is commonly known, comprises the IBRD and the International Development Association (IDA), which was founded in 1960. The affiliated group of institutions, comprising the IBRD, IDA, the International Finance Corporation (IFC, q.v.), the Multilateral Investment Guarantee Agency (MIGA, q.v.) and the International Centre for Settlement of Investment Disputes (ICSID, see below), is now referred to as the World Bank Group. Only members of the International Monetary Fund (IMF, q.v.) may be considered for membership in the Bank. Subscriptions to the capital stock of the Bank are based on each member's quota in the IMF, which is designed to reflect the country's relative economic strength. Voting rights are related to shareholdings.

Organization

(July 2000)

Officers and staff of the IBRD serve concurrently as officers and staff in the IDA. The World Bank has offices in New York, Paris, Brussels, London and Tokyo; regional missions in Nairobi (for eastern Africa) and Abidjan (for western Africa); and resident missions in more than 70 countries.

BOARD OF GOVERNORS

The Board of Governors consists of one Governor appointed by each member nation. Typically, a Governor is the country's finance minister, central bank governor, or a minister or an official of comparable rank. The Board normally meets once a year.

EXECUTIVE DIRECTORS

The general operations of the World Bank are conducted by a Board of 24 Executive Directors. Five Directors are appointed by the five members having the largest number of shares of capital stock, and the rest are elected by the Governors representing the other members. The President of the Bank is Chairman of the Board.

OFFICERS

President and Chairman of Executive Directors: JAMES D. WOLFENSOHN (USA).

Vice-Presidents, Africa Regional Office: CALLISTO E. MADAVO, JEAN-LOUIS SARBIB.

REGIONAL OFFICES

Regional Mission in Eastern Africa: POB 30577, Nairobi; Hill Park Bldg, Upper Hill, Nairobi, Kenya; tel. (2) 260441; fax (2) 260380; Chief HAROLD E. WACKMAN.

Regional Mission in Western Africa: Booker Washington/Jacques Aka Cocody, BP 1850, Abidjan 01, Côte d'Ivoire; tel. 44-32-44; fax 44-16-87; Chief SHIGEO KATSU.

Activities

FINANCIAL OPERATIONS

The World Bank's primary objectives are the achievement of sustainable economic growth, and the reduction of poverty in developing countries. In mid-1994 the World Bank Group published a review of its role and activities and identified the following five major development issues on which it intended to focus in the future: the pursuit of economic reforms; investment in people, in particular through education, health, nutrition and family-planning programmes; the protection of the environment; stimulation of the private sector; and reorientation of government, in order to enhance the private sector by reforming and strengthening the public sector. The Bank compiles country-specific assessments and formulates country assistance strategies (CASs) to review and guide the Bank's country programmes. Since August 1998 the Bank has published CASs, with the approval of the governments concerned. In 1989/90 systematic 'screening' of all new projects was introduced, in order to assess their environmental impact. The Bank also supports individual countries to prepare and implement national environmental action plans (NEAPs) and to strengthen their institutional capacity for environmental planning and management.

IBRD loans are usually for a period of 20 years or less. Loans are made to governments, or must be guaranteed by the government concerned. IDA assistance is aimed at the poorer developing countries (i.e. mainly those with a GNP per caput of less than US $761, in 1998 dollars, in 1998/99) and the majority of the countries of sub-Saharan Africa are eligible to receive it. Under IDA lending conditions, credits can be extended to countries whose balance of payments could not sustain the burden of repayment required for IBRD loans. Terms are more favourable than those provided by the IBRD; credits are for a period of 35–40 years, with a 'grace' period of 10 years, and carry no interest charges.

The IBRD's capital is derived from members' subscriptions to capital shares, the calculation of which is based on their quotas in the IMF. At 30 June 1999 the total subscribed capital of the IBRD was US $188,220m., of which the paid-in portion was $11,395m. (6.1%); the remainder is subject to call if required. Most of the IBRD's lendable funds come from its borrowing in world capital markets, and also from its retained earnings and the flow of repayments on its loans. Bank loans carry a variable interest rate, rather than a rate fixed at the time of borrowing.

IDA's development resources, consisting of members' subscriptions and supplementary resources (additional subscriptions and contributions) are replenished periodically by contributions from the more affluent member countries. In March 1996 representatives of more than 30 donor countries concluded negotiations for the 11th replenishment of IDA funds (and for a one-year interim fund), to finance the period July 1996–June 1999. New contributions over the three-year period were to amount to US $11,000m., while total funds available for lending, including past donor contributions, repayments of IDA credits and the World Bank's contributions, were to amount to $22,000m. In November 1998 representatives of 39 donor countries agreed to provide $11,600m. for the 12th replenishment of IDA funds, enabling total lending to amount to an estimated $20,500m. in the period July 1999–June 2002. The new IDA-12 resources were to be directed towards the following objectives: investing in people; promoting good governance; promoting broad-based growth; and protecting the environment.

During the year ending 30 June 1999 61 operations were approved for Africa south of the Sahara amounting to US $2,068.5m. (7.1% of World Bank assistance in that year), of which $5.0m. was in the form of an IBRD loan and $2,063.5m. in IDA credits.

The Bank's poverty reduction strategy for Africa, where an estimated 45% of the population are affected by poverty, involves projects that aim to alleviate the adverse effects of structural adjustment programmes; that assist governments to assess and monitor poverty; and that increase food security. In December 1996 a special task force recommended that the Bank revise its lending strategy to emphasize poverty reduction objectives and strengthen systematic monitoring of the poverty situation in all sub-Saharan African countries receiving World Bank assistance. During 1996/97 the Bank established a Capacity Building Technical Group within the African regional offices to enhance the Bank's effectiveness in working with local partners in the development of human and institutional capacities. Additionally, the Bank established a Poverty Sector Board, within a new Poverty Reduction and Economic Management network, to direct the implementation of the Bank's poverty reduction strategy. In March 1996 a new programme to co-ordinate development efforts in Africa was announced by the UN Secretary-General. The World Bank was to facilitate the mobilization of the estimated US $25,000m. required to achieve the objectives of the Special Initiative on Africa over a 10-year period. In addition, the Bank was to provide technical assistance to enable countries to devise economic plans (in particular following a period of civil conflict), agricultural development programmes and a common strategy for African countries to strengthen the management capacities of the public sector. In July the Bank established a 'war-to-peace' transition team in order to respond effectively to countries needing assistance for post-conflict economic and social reconstruction. In March 1997 the Executive Board approved the 'Strategic Compact', providing for a programme of reforms, to be implemented over a period of 30 months, to increase the effectiveness of the Bank in achieving its central objective of poverty reduction. The reforms, which aimed to increase the proportion of projects rated as satisfactory in development terms from 66% to 75%, included greater decentralization of decision-making, enhancing the administration of loans, and improving access to information and co-ordination of Bank activities through a knowledge management system comprising four thematic networks: the Human Development Network; the Environmentally and Socially Sustainable Development Network; the Finance, Private Sector and Infrastructure Development Network; and the Poverty Reduction and Economic Management Network. In 1998/99 the Bank's Executive Directors endorsed a Comprehensive Development Framework (CDF) to effect a new approach to development assistance based on partnerships and country responsibility, with an emphasis on the interdependence of the social, structural, human, governmental, economic and environmental elements of development. The Framework, which aimed to enhance the overall effectiveness of development assistance, was formulated after a series of consultative meetings, organized by the Bank and attended by representatives of governments, donor agencies, financial institutions, non-governmental organizations, the private sector and academics. By May 2000 13 countries were implementing pilot projects based on the CDF concept, including Côte d'Ivoire, Eritrea, Ethiopia, Ghana and Uganda.

In July 1985 a Special Facility for sub-Saharan Africa became effective for a three-year period, with funds of US $1,250m., to finance structural adjustment, sectoral reform programmes and rehabilitation. A 'Special Programme of Assistance' (SPA) for sub-Saharan Africa, available from 1988, aimed to increase concessional lending to heavily-indebted and impoverished African countries, mainly by the co-ordination of international aid contributions and to co-financing mechanisms. Only IDA member countries implementing a policy adjustment programme, with a debt-service ration of more than 30%, were to be eligible for SPA funds. In 1991 the African Capacity Building Foundation was established by the World Bank, the African Development Bank and UNDP, with the aim of encouraging indigenous research and managerial capabilities, by supporting or creating institutions for training, research and analysis.

In September 1996 the World Bank/IMF Development Committee endorsed a joint initiative to assist heavily indebted poor countries (HIPCs) to reduce their debt burden to a sustainable level, in order to make more resources available for poverty reduction and economic growth. A new Trust Fund was established by the World Bank in November to finance the initiative, consisting of an initial allocation of US $500m. from the IBRD surplus and other contributions from multilateral creditors. It was to be administered by IDA. Of the 41 HIPCs identified by the Bank, 33 were in sub-Saharan Africa. In the majority of cases a sustainable level of debt was targetted at 200%–250% of the net present value (NPV) of the debt in relation to total annual exports. Other countries with a lower debt-to-export ratio were to be eligible for assistance under the initiative providing that their export earnings were more than 40% of GDP and government revenue at least 20% of GDP. All countries had to have implemented extensive programmes of economic and social reform for at least three years before being considered eligible for assistance, and for a total of at least six years before receiving any assistance. In April 1997 the World Bank and the IMF announced that Uganda was to be the first beneficiary of the HIPC initiative, enabling the Ugandan Government to reduce its external debt by some 20%, or an estimated $338m. The Bank's approved loan of $160m. was to be disbursed in April 1998, conditional on the contribution by other official creditors and multinational institutions of their share of debt relief and on Uganda's pursuing its programme of economic and social development reforms. In September 1997 assistance valued at $115m. in NPV terms (as at the 'completion point' of the process to ensure eligibility to receive debt relief) was approved for Burkina Faso, subject to the same conditions as for Uganda. Also in September an agreement under the initiative was approved for Bolivia, while a package of assistance was approved for Guyana in December. In March 1998 Côte d'Ivoire qualified for assistance to reduce its external debt by $345m., of which the Bank was to contribute $91m., and in April an agreement was approved for Mozambique totalling $1,442m. in assistance (increased to $1,716m., with $381m. from the Bank, when Mozambique reached completion point in June 1999). In September 1998 assistance totalling $128m. was approved for Mali. At 30 June 1999 a total of $3,355m. of debt relief in NPV terms had been agreed under the initiative, of which the Bank's share was $801m.

WORLD BANK OPERATIONS IN AFRICA SOUTH OF THE SAHARA

IBRD Loan Approved, 1 July 1997–30 June 1998
(US $ million)

Country	Purpose	Amount
Gabon . . .	Pilot infrastructure works	5.0
Total		5.0

IDA Credits Approved, 1 July 1998–30 June 1999
(US $ million)

Country	Purpose	Amount
Benin . . .	Decentralized city management I project	25.5
Burkina Faso .	Pilot private irrigation development project	5.2
	Economic management reform support operation	15.0
Cameroon .	Structural adjustment credit III	13.1
	National agricultural extension and research programme support project	15.1
Cape Verde .	Education and training consolidation and modernization project	6.0
	Social sector development project	16.1
	Energy and water sector reform and development project	17.5
	Privatization and regulatory capacity building project	9.0
Chad . . .	Structural adjustment credit III	30.0
	Health and safe motherhood project supplement	10.9
Côte d'Ivoire .	Transport sector adjustment/ investment programme	25.6
	National agricultural services support II project	50.0
Djibouti. . .	Ex-combatants reintegration pilot project	2.7
	Social development and public works	14.8
Ethiopia .	Health centre development programme	100.0
Gambia. . .	Poverty alleviation and capacity-building project	15.0
	Education sector III project	20.0
Ghana . . .	National functional literacy programme	32.0
	Community-based poverty reduction project	5.0
	Economic reform support operation credit II	180.0
	Public-sector management reform project	14.3
	Trade and investment gateway project	50.5
Guinea . . .	Urban development III project	18.0
	Village communities support programme project	22.0
	Population and reproductive health project	11.3
Kenya . . .	Pre-service teacher education project	4.1
	El Niño emergency project	40.0
Lesotho. . .	Education sector development II project	21.0
Madagascar. .	Structural adjustment credit II	100.0
	Microfinance project	16.4
	Social fund III project	15.0
Malawi . . .	Road maintenance and rehabilitation project	30.0
	Fiscal restructuring and deregulation programme II technical assistance project	92.0
	Second social action fund project	66.0
	Population and family planning project	5.0
Mali . . .	Health sector development programme	40.0
Mauritania . .	Telecommunications and postal sector reform project	10.8
	Mining sector capacity building project	15.0
	Nutrition, food security, and social mobilization investment project	4.9
	Public resource management project	0.1
Mozambique .	Agriculture sector public expenditure programme project	30.0
	Education sector strategic programme project	71.0
	National water development project I	75.0
Niger . . .	Public finance reform credit	64.0
	Privatization and regulatory reform technical assistance project	18.6
Rwanda. . .	Economic recovery credit	75.0
	Community reintegration and development project	5.0
Senegal. . .	Second transport sector project	90.0
	Agricultural services and producer organizations project	27.4
Tanzania . .	Tax administration project	40.0
Togo . . .	Pilot social fund project	5.0
Uganda. . .	Road development programme phase I project	91.0
	Financial markets assistance project	13.0
	Nakivubo Channel rehabilitation project	22.4
	Agricultural research and training II project	26.0
	Institutional capacity-building for protected areas management and sustainable use project	12.4
Zambia . . .	Public-sector reform and export promotion credit	2.8
	Public-sector reform and export promotion credit	170.0
	Basic education subsector investment programme support project	40.0
Total		2,063.5

Source: *World Bank Annual Report 1999.*

In early 1999 the World Bank and IMF initiated a comprehensive review of the HIPC initiative. By April meetings of the Group of Seven industrialized nations (G-7) and of the governing bodies of the Bank and IMF indicated a consensus that the scheme needed to be amended and strengthened, in order to allow more countries to benefit from the initiative, to accelerate the process by which a country may qualify for assistance, and to enhance the effectiveness of debt relief. In June the G-7 and Russia (the G-8), meeting in Cologne, Germany, agreed to increase contributions to the HIPC Trust Fund and to cancel substantial amounts of outstanding debt, and proposed more flexible terms for eligibility. In September the Bank and IMF reached an agreement on an enhanced HIPC scheme, with further revenue to be generated through the revaluation of a percentage of IMF gold reserves. In February 2000 Mauritania qualified for assistance totalling $622m. (in NPV terms) under the enhanced HIPC. Assistance was approved for Senegal in June, amounting to $450m., and for Benin in July ($265m.). In February 2000 additional assistance for Uganda, amounting to nearly $700m., was approved under the enhanced HIPC initiative. Mozambique

qualified for an additional $254m. in June, and in July additional debt relief, amounting to $229m., was approved for Burkina Faso.

TECHNICAL ASSISTANCE

The provision of technical assistance to member countries is a major component of Bank activities. The economic sector and project analysis undertaken by the Bank in the normal course of its operations is the vehicle for considerable technical assistance. In addition, project loans and credits may include funds designated specifically for feasibility studies, resource surveys, management or planning advice, and training. In 1975 a Project Preparation Facility (PPF) was established to provide cash advances to prepare projects that may be financed by the Bank. In 1992 the Bank established an Institutional Development Fund (IDF) to provide rapid, small-scale financial assistance, to a maximum value of US $500,000, for capacity-building proposals.

ECONOMIC RESEARCH AND STUDIES

In the 1990s the World Bank's research, conducted by its own research staff, was increasingly concerned with providing information to reinforce the Bank's expanding advisory role to developing countries. Consequently the principal areas of current research focus on issues such as maintaining sustainable growth while protecting the environment and the poorest sectors of society, encouraging the development of the private sector, and reducing and decentralizing government activities. The Bank chairs the Consultative Group on International Agricultural Research (CGIAR), which was formed in 1971 to raise financial support for research on improving crops and animal production in developing countries. The Group supports 16 research centres.

CO-OPERATION WITH OTHER ORGANIZATIONS

The World Bank co-operates closely with other UN bodies through consultations, meetings, and joint activities, particularly in response to the economic crisis in Africa south of the Sahara, where co-operation with UNDP and WHO is especially important. It collaborates with the IMF in implementing economic adjustment programmes in developing countries. The Bank holds regular consultations with the European Community and OECD on development issues, and the Bank-NGO Committee provides an annual forum for discussion with non-governmental organizations (NGOs). The Bank chairs meetings of donor governments and organizations for the co-ordination of aid to particular countries. The Bank also conducts co-financing and aid co-ordination projects with official aid agencies, export credit institutions and commercial banks. In April 1997 the World Bank signed a co-operation agreement with the World Trade Organization, in order to co-ordinate efforts to integrate developing countries into the global economy. In 1997/98 the Bank co-operated with the Southern African Development Community (SADC) to harmonize payment systems.

The World Bank administers the Global Environment Facility (GEF), which was established in 1990, in conjunction with UNDP and UNEP. The aim of the GEF, which became operational in 1991 for an initial three-year period,was to assist developing countries in implementing policies that benefit the global environment. In March 1994 34 countries participating in the Facility agreed to restructure and replenish the GEF, pledging funds totalling US $2,000m., which were to enable the GEF to act as the financial mechanism for the conventions on climate changes and biological diversity that were signed at the UN Conference on Environment and Development in June 1992. In November 1997 36 donor countries agreed to provide $2,750m. for a further replenishment of GEF funds; this second replenishment was approved by the Bank's Executive Board in July 1998. At 30 June a total of 338 GEF projects had been approved, receiving nearly $2,400m. in funding, and covering the following areas: biodiversity; climate change; the phase-out of ozone-depleting substances; and international waters. During 1998/99 60 major and 30 medium-sized projects were approved.

In June 1995 the World Bank joined other international donors (including regional development banks, other UN bodies, Canada, France, the Netherlands and the USA) in establishing a Consultative Group to Assist the Poorest (CGAP), which was to channel funds to the most needy through grass-roots agencies. An initial credit of approximately US $200m. was committed by the donors. The Bank manages the CGAP Secretariat, which is responsible for the administration of external funding and for the evaluation and approval of project financing. In addition, the CGAP provides training and information services on microfinance for policy-makers and practitioners.

EVALUATION

The World Bank's Operations Evaluation Department studies and publishes the results of projects after a loan has been fully disbursed, so as to identify problems and possible improvements in future activities. Internal auditing is also carried out, to monitor the effectiveness of the Bank's operations and management.

In September 1993 the Bank's Board of Executive Directors agreed to establish an Independent Inspection Panel, consistent with the Bank's objective of improving project implementation and account-ability. The Panel, which became operational in September 1994, was to conduct independent investigations and report on complaints concerning the design, appraisal and implementation of development projects supported by the Bank.

IBRD INSTITUTIONS

World Bank Institute—WBI: founded in March 1999 by merger of the Bank's Learning and Leadership Centre, previously responsible for internal staff training, and the Economic Development Institute (EDI), which had been established in 1955 to train government officials concerned with development programmes and policies. The new Institute aimed to emphasize the Bank's priority areas through the provision of training courses and seminars relating to poverty, crisis response, good governance and anti-corruption strategies. The Institute was also to take the lead in co-ordinating a process of consultation and dialogue with researchers and other representatives of civil society to examine poverty for a forthcoming *World Development Report*. Activities of the Institute in 1998/99 included a new training programme for public officials responsible for financial sector supervision and the establishment of a World Bank Learning Network. Under the EDI a World Links for Development programme was initiated to connect schools in developing countries with partner establishments in industrialized nations via the internet. Dir VINOD THOMAS (India).

International Centre for Settlement of Investment Disputes—ICSID: founded in 1966 under the Convention of the Settlement of Investment Disputes between States and Nationals of Other States. The Convention was designed to encourage the growth of private foreign investment for economic development, by creating the possibility, always subject to the consent of both parties, for a Contracting State and a foreign investor who is a national of another Contracting State to settle any legal dispute that might arise out of such an investment by conciliation and/or arbitration before an impartial, international forum. The governing body of the Centre is its Administrative Council, composed of one representative of each Contracting State, all of whom have equal voting power. The President of the World Bank is (*ex officio*) the non-voting Chairman of the Administrative Council.

At March 2000 131 states had ratified the Convention to become ICSID Contracting States. In late 1999 the number of cases registered with the Centre totalled 67. Sec.-Gen. KO-YUNG TUNG (Japan).

Publications

Abstracts of Current Studies: The World Bank Research Program (annually).

Annual Report on Operations Evaluation.

Annual Report on Portfolio Performance.

Global Development Finance (annually, also on CD Rom).

Global Economic Prospects and Developing Countries (annually).

ICSID Annual Report.

News from ICSID (2 a year).

Research News (quarterly).

Staff Working Papers.

Transition (every 2 months).

Trends in Developing Economies (annually).

World Bank Annual Report.

World Bank Atlas (annually).

World Bank Economic Review (3 a year).

The World Bank and the Environment (annually).

World Bank Research Observer (2 a year).

World Development Indicators (annually, also on CD Rom).

World Development Report (annually).

World Tables (annually).

International Finance Corporation—IFC

Address: 2121 Pennsylvania Ave, NW, Washington, DC 20433, USA.

Telephone: (202) 473-1234; **fax:** (202) 974-4384; **e-mail:** information@ifc.org; **internet:** www.ifc.org/.

IFC was founded in 1956 as an affiliate of the World Bank to encourage the growth of productive private enterprise in its member countries, particularly in the less-developed areas.

Organization

(July 2000)

IFC is a separate legal entity in the World Bank Group. Executive Directors of the World Bank also serve as Directors of IFC. The President of the World Bank is, *ex officio*, Chairman of the IFC Board of Directors, which has appointed him President of IFC. Subject to his overall supervision, the day-to-day operations of IFC are conducted by its staff under the direction of the Executive Vice-President.

PRINCIPAL OFFICERS

President: JAMES D. WOLFENSOHN (USA).

Executive Vice-President: PETER L. WOICKE (Germany).

REGIONAL MISSIONS

East Africa: PO Box 30577, Hill Park Bldg, Upper Hill Rd, Nairobi, Kenya; tel. (2) 720349; fax (2) 260383; Regional Rep. MICHAEL HOOPER.

Southern Africa: 101 Union Ave, 7th Floor, POB 2960, Harare, Zimbabwe; tel. (4) 794868; fax (4) 793805; Regional Rep. MICHAEL TILLER.

West and Central Africa: angle rues Booker Washington/Jacques Aka Cocody, BP 1850, Abidjan 01, Côte d'Ivoire; tel. 44-32-44; fax 44-44-83; Regional Rep. LUCIANO BORIN.

Activities

IFC provides financial support and advice for private sector ventures and projects, and assists governments to create conditions that stimulate the flow of domestic and foreign private savings and investment. Increasingly IFC has worked to mobilize additional capital from other financial institutions. In all its activities IFC is guided by three major principles:

(i) The catalytic principle. IFC should seek above all to be a catalyst in helping private investors and markets to make good investments.

(ii) The business principle. IFC should function like a business in partnership with the private sector and take the same commercial risks, so that its funds, although backed by public sources, are transferred under market disciplines.

(iii) The principle of the special contribution. IFC should participate in an investment only when it makes a special contribution that supplements or complements the role of market operators.

IFC's authorized capital is US $2,450.0m. The World Bank is the principal source of borrowed funds, but IFC also borrows from private capital markets. At 30 June 1999 paid-in capital was $2,349.8m. In that financial year project financing approved amounted to $5,280m. for 255 projects, compared with $5,910m. for 308 projects in the previous year. Of the total approved, $3,505m. was for IFC's own account, while $1,775m. was used in loan syndications and underwriting of securities issues and investment funds by more than 100 participant banks and institutional investors. Generally, the IFC limits its financing to 5%–15% of the total cost of a project, but may take up to a 35% stake in a venture (although never as a majority shareholder).

In 1998/99 IFC approved financing for 80 projects (including those under the Africa Enterprise Fund—see below) in 26 countries in sub-Saharan Africa. These included projects concerned with the education sector in Côte d'Ivoire, The Gambia, Guinea and Senegal; the banking and financial sectors in Côte d'Ivoire, Kenya and South Africa; microfinance, equipment-leasing and printing and publishing services in Mali; food-processing and cement production in Senegal; sugar-processing in Mozambique; and tourism and agribusiness in Tanzania.

In April 1989 IFC (with UNDP and the African Development Bank—ADB) initiated the African Management Services Company (AMSCo): its aim is to help find qualified senior executives from around the world to work with African companies, assist in the training of local managers, and provide supporting services. At 31 December 1998 AMSCo had management training contracts with 67 companies in 23 countries. The IFC's Africa Enterprise Fund (AEF), which began operations in 1988, provides financial assistance to small and medium-sized enterprises, typically in the tourism, agribusiness and small-scale manufacturing sectors. In 1998/99 AEF financed 39 projects in 16 countries at a total cost of US $31.1m. In 1995 IFC initiated Enterprise Support Services for Africa (ESSA) in order to provide post-investment operational advice, including the development and strengthening of management information systems and technical capacity, to small- and medium-sized enterprises in the sub-Saharan region. ESSA commenced operation, on a pilot basis, in Ghana, in March 1996. In 1998/99 ESSA was expanded to be available throughout sub-Saharan Africa as part of the APDF (see below). During 1996/97 IFC inaugurated a three year pilot programme, 'Extending IFC's Reach', which aimed to encourage private investment in 16 countries and regions (expanded to 20 in 1998/99) where adverse political conditions had previously limited IFC intervention. IFC has expanded its field-based activities in those countries in order to enhance local knowledge, strengthen relationships with government authorities and local businesses and improve access to IFC products and services. By 30 June 1999 IFC had approved 160 projects in 'Outreach' countries, at a cost of some $1,000m.

IFC provides advisory services, particularly in connection with privatization and corporate restructuring, private infrastructure, and the development of capital markets. Under the Technical Assistance Trust Funds Program (TATF), established in 1988, IFC manages resources contributed by various governments and agencies to provide finance for feasibility studies, project identification studies and other types of technical assistance relating to project preparation. By 30 June 1999 the TATF had mobilized US $98m. through 34 trust funds. Some 153 new technical assistance projects were approved in 1998/99.

The Foreign Investment Advisory Service (FIAS), established in 1986, is operated jointly by IFC and the IBRD, and provides advice to governments on attracting foreign investment. During 1998/99 FIAS undertook projects and assignments in 33 countries at the request of governments.

AFRICA PROJECT DEVELOPMENT FACILITY (APDF)

APDF was established by IFC, UNDP and the ADB in 1986, with additional funding by 15 industrialized countries, to provide technical assistance to entrepreneurs in sub-Saharan Africa. IFC acts as the executing agency responsible for managing the facility, while the ADB is its regional sponsor (UNDP having withdrawn from the project in May 1996). The Facility advises entrepreneurs seeking to start businesses or expand existing ones, and helps them identify and prepare viable projects. APDF does not finance projects, but assists entrepreneurs in obtaining debt and equity financing and identifying business partners, both foreign and domestic. Typically, projects assisted by APDF are small, with costs ranging from US $250,000 to $7m. During the year to 31 December 1998 APDF assisted the funding of 38 projects, which were estimated to have created or secured 4,286 jobs. The projects were implemented in 12 countries.

East Africa: International House, 6th Floor, Mama Ngina St, POB 46534, Nairobi, Kenya; tel. (2) 217370; telex 25303; fax (2) 339121; Regional Man. MISHEK NGATUNGA.

Southern Africa: Southampton House, 5th Floor, 68-70 Union Ave, Box UA 400, Harare, Zimbabwe; tel. (4) 701232; fax (4) 701231; Regional Man. JESPER KJAER.

Western and Central Africa: Immeuble CCIA, 17e étage, 01 BP 8669, Abidjan 01, Côte d'Ivoire; tel. 21-96-97; fax 21-61-51; e-mail hrabarijohn@ifc.org; Regional Man. HENRI E. RABARIJOHN.

Publications

Annual Report.

Emerging Stock Markets Factbook (annually).

Global Agribusiness (series of industry reports).

Impact (quarterly).

Lessons of Experience series.

Results on the Ground (series).

Discussion papers, technical reports and study series.

Multilateral Investment Guarantee Agency—MIGA

Address: 1818 H Street, NW, Washington, DC 20433, USA.
Telephone: (202) 477-1234; **fax:** (202) 477-6391; **internet:** www.miga.org/.
MIGA was founded in 1988 as an affiliate of the World Bank, to encourage the flow of investments for productive purposes among its member countries, especially developing countries, through the mitigation of non-commercial barriers to investment (especially political risk).

Organization

(July 2000)

MIGA is legally and financially separate from the World Bank. It is supervised by a Council of Governors (comprising one Governor and one Alternate of each member country) and an elected Board of Directors (of no less than 12 members).
President: JAMES D. WOLFENSOHN (USA).
Executive Vice-President: MOTOMICHI IKAWA (Japan).

Activities

The convention establishing MIGA took effect in April 1988. Authorized capital was US $1,082m. In April 1998 MIGA's Board of Directors approved an increase in MIGA's capital base. A grant of $150m. was transferred from the IBRD as part of the package, while the capital increase (totalling $700m. callable capital and $150m. paid-in capital) was approved by MIGA's Council of Governors in April 1999.

MIGA's purpose is to guarantee eligible investments against losses resulting from non-commercial risks, under four main categories:

transfer risk resulting from host government restrictions on currency conversion and transfer;

risk of loss resulting from legislative or administrative actions of the host government;

repudiation by the host government of contracts with investors in cases in which the investor has no access to a competent forum;

the risk of armed conflict and civil unrest.

Before guaranteeing any investment, MIGA must ensure that it is commercially viable, contributes to the development process and is not harmful to the environment. During the fiscal year 1998/99 MIGA and IFC appointed the first Compliance Advisor and Ombudsman to consider the concerns of local communities directly affected by MIGA or IFC sponsored projects.

During the year ending 30 June 1999 MIGA issued 72 investment insurance contracts in 29 countries with a value of US $1,310m. The amount of direct investment associated with the contracts totalled approximately $5,200m.

MIGA also provides policy and advisory services to promote foreign investment in developing countries and in transitional economies, and to disseminate information on investment opportunities. Since 1993 MIGA has organized an annual conference to promote investment in the mining sector in Africa. In October 1995 MIGA established a new network on investment opportunities, to connect investment promotion agencies (IPAs) throughout the world. The so-called IPA*net* aimed to encourage further investments among developing countries, to provide access to comprehensive information on investment laws and conditions and to strengthen communications between governmental, business and financial associations and investors. A new version of IPA*net* was launched in 1997. In June 1998 MIGA initiated a new internet-based facility, 'PrivatizationLink', to provide information on investment opportunities resulting from the privatization of industries in emerging economies.

Publications

Annual Report.
MIGA News (quarterly).

International Fund for Agricultural Development—IFAD

Address: Via del Serafico 107, 00142 Rome, Italy.
Telephone: (06) 54591; **fax:** (06) 5043463; **e-mail:** ifad@ifad.org; **internet:** www.ifad.org.
IFAD was established in 1977, following a decision by the 1974 UN World Food Conference, with a mandate to combat hunger and eradicate poverty on a sustainable basis in the low-income, food-deficit regions of the world. Funding operations began in January 1978.

Organization

(July 2000)

GOVERNING COUNCIL

Each member state is represented in the Governing Council by a Governor and an Alternate. Sessions are held annually, with special sessions convened as required. The Governing Council elects the President of the Fund (who also chairs the Executive Board) by a two-thirds majority for a four-year term. The President is eligible for re-election.

EXECUTIVE BOARD

The Board consists of 18 members and 18 alternates, elected by the Governing Council, who serve a three year term. The Executive Board is responsible for the conduct and general operation of IFAD and approves loans and grants for projects; it holds three regular sessions each year.

Following agreement on the fourth replenishment of the Fund's resources in February 1997, the governance structure of the Fund was amended. Former Category I countries (i.e. industrialized donor countries) were reclassified as List A countries and were awarded

a greater share of the 1,800 votes in the Governing Council and Executive Board, in order to reflect their financial contributions to the Fund. Former Category II countries (petroleum-exporting developing donor countries) were reclassified as List B countries, while recipient developing countries, formally Category III countries, were termed as List C countries, and divided into three regional Sub-Lists. Where previously each category was ensured equal representation on the Executive Board, the new allocation of seats was as follows: eight List A countries, four List B, and two of each Sub-List C group of countries.

President and Chairman of Executive Board: FAWZI HAMAD AL-SULTAN (Kuwait).
Vice-President: JOHN WESTLEY (USA).

Activities

The Fund's objective is to mobilize additional resources to be made available on concessionary terms for agricultural development in developing member states. IFAD provides financing primarily for projects and programmes specifically designed to introduce, expand or improve food production systems and to strengthen related policies, services and institutions within the framework of national priorities and strategies. In allocating resources IFAD is guided by: the need to increase food production in the poorest food-deficit countries; the potential for increasing food production in other developing countries; and the importance of improving the nutrition, health and education of the poorest people in developing countries i.e. small-scale farmers, artisanal fishermen, nomadic pastoralists, indigenous populations, rural women, and the rural landless. All projects emphasize the participation of beneficiaries in development initiatives, both at the local and national level.

PROJECTS IN AFRICA SOUTH OF THE SAHARA APPROVED IN 1999

Country	Purpose	Loan amount (SDRm.*)
Burkina Faso	Rural microenterprise support project	7.0
Burundi . .	Rural recovery and development programme	14.8
Cameroon. .	National microfinance programme support project	8.1
Cape Verde .	Rural poverty alleviation programme	7.0
Ghana . .	Upper-East Region land conservation and smallholder rehabilitation project–phase II	8.3
Guinea .	Programme for participatory rural development in Haute-Guinée	10.2
Mauritius. .	Rural diversification programme	8.2
Mozambique	PAMA support project	16.6
Nigeria . .	Roots and tubers expension programme	16.7
Senegal . .	National rural infrastructure project	5.4
Sudan. . .	North Kordofan rural development project	7.8
Tanzania . .	Participatory irrigation development programme	12.6
Uganda . .	Area-based agricultural modernization programme	9.6
Zambia . .	Forest resource management project	9.2
. . . .	Smallholder enterprise and marketing programme	11.6
Total		153.1

* The average value of the SDR—Special Drawing Right—in 1999 was US $1.3673.

IFAD is empowered to make both grants and loans. Grants are limited to 7.5% of the resources committed in any one financial year. Loans are available on highly concessionary, intermediate or ordinary terms. In 1999 most of the loans approved for sub-Saharan Africa were awarded on highly concessionary terms, i.e. with no interest charges (although bearing an annual service charge of 0.75%) and a repayment period of 40 years, including a 10-year grace period. To avoid duplication of work, the administration of loans, for the purpose of disbursements and supervision of project implementation, is entrusted to competent international financial institutions, with the Fund retaining an active interest. During 1999 IFAD provided financing for 57.2% of the costs of projects approved during that year, while the remainder was contributed by external donors, multilateral institutions and the recipient countries.

IFAD's development projects usually include a number of components, such as infrastructure (e.g. improvement of water supplies, small-scale irrigation and road construction); input supply (e.g. improved seeds, fertilizers and pesticides); institutional support (e.g. research, training and extension services); and producer incentives (e.g. pricing and marketing improvements). IFAD also attempts to enable the landless to acquire income-generating assets: by increasing the provision of credit for the rural poor, it seeks to free them from dependence on the capital market and to generate productive activities. The Fund supports projects that are concerned with environmental conservation, in an effort to alleviate poverty that results from the deterioration of natural resources. The Fund extends environmental assessment grants to review the environmental consequences of projects under preparation.

IFAD is a leading repository of knowledge, resources and expertise in the field of rural hunger and poverty alleviation. During 1995 a team established to review IFAD's activities focused on IFAD's role as an innovator, emphasizing the importance of pioneering practices and strategies that can be replicated, and of making its knowledge available to relevant agencies and governments. Through its technical assistance grants, IFAD aims to promote research and capacity-building in the agricultural sector, as well as the development of technologies to increase production and alleviate rural poverty. IFAD has supported the research on accelerated diffusion of rice technology, conducted by the West Africa Rice Development Association (WARDA, q.v.) and efforts to identify the technological and socio-economic aspects to sericulture- and apiculture-based farming practices in rural Africa, undertaken by the International Centre for Insect Physiology and Ecology (ICIPE). In 1995 IFAD's Executive Board approved financing for the second phase of its Agricultural Management Training Programme for Africa. In 1998 IFAD approved a grant to establish an internet-based network to promote the exchange of information and experience among 30 IFAD-sponsored projects and 15 partner institutions in West and Central Africa.

In 1986 IFAD inaugurated a Special Programme for sub-Saharan African Countries Affected by Drought and Desertification (SPA) in response to the critical failure of agricultural and economic systems during a severe drought in the region in the mid-1980s. The SPA aims to improve sustainable food-crop production through soil and water conservation (with emphasis on traditional techniques), small-scale irrigation and local forestry development. In the second phase of the Programme, which began in 1992, the SPA extended its lending criteria to cover off-farm activities and to promote economic diversification. At the same time the number of countries eligible for assistance increased from 22 to 27. In September 1995 the Executive Board decided the SPA would be terminated and its resources be integrated into the regular programmes as of 1 January 1996. At that time a total of 47 projects had been approved under the SPA (including 12 financed jointly under the SPA and the regular programme), costing some US $377.2m., since 1986.

During 1999 IFAD approved lending for seven projects in the Western and Central African region and seven in Eastern and Southern Africa, involving loans amounting to US $85.7m. (or 19.8% of total lending in that year) and $112.7m. (26.0%) respectively. In that year lending was also approved for a project in Sudan, which IFAD classifies as part of its Near East and Northern Africa subregion.

In October 1997 IFAD was appointed to administer the Global Mechanism of the Convention to Combat Desertification in those Countries Experiencing Drought and Desertification, Particularly in Africa, which entered into force in December 1996. The Mechanism was envisaged as a means of mobilizing and channelling resources for implementation of the Convention. A series of collaborative institutional arrangements were to be concluded between IFAD, UNDP and the World Bank in order to facilitate the effective functioning of the Mechanism.

In February 1998 IFAD inaugurated a new Trust Fund to complement the multilateral debt initiative for Heavily Indebted Poor Countries (HIPCs—see World Bank p. 100). The Fund was intended to assist IFAD's poorest members deemed to be eligible under the initiative to channel resources from debt repayments to communities in need. Also in 1998 IFAD's Executive Board endorsed a policy framework for the Fund's role in providing development assistance in post-conflict situations, with the aim of achieving a continuum from emergency relief to a secure basis from which to pursue sustainable development. At the end of that year IFAD was involved in a project to address problems resulting from civil conflict in Angola and to assist the rehabilitation of returning refugees in Rwanda. During 1999–2000 IFAD was conducting a detailed study of rural poverty, the conclusions and recommendations of which were to be issued in December 2000, as the *Rural Poverty Report 2000*.

Finance

IFAD's programme of work for 1999 envisaged loans and grants totalling US $472.8m., while the provisional budget for administrative expenses amounted to US $55.0m.

Publications

Annual Report.

IFAD Update (2 a year).

Staff Working Papers (series).

The State of World Rural Poverty.

International Monetary Fund—IMF

Address: 700 19th St, NW, Washington, DC 20431, USA.
Telephone: (202) 623-7430; **fax:** (202) 623-6220; **internet:** www.imf.org.

The IMF was established at the same time as the World Bank (IBRD) in 1945, to promote international monetary co-operation, to facilitate the expansion and balanced growth of international trade and to promote stability in foreign exchange.

Organization

(July 2000)

BOARD OF GOVERNORS

The highest authority of the Fund is exercised by the Board of Governors, on which each member country is represented by a Governor and an Alternate Governor. The Board normally meets annually. The International Monetary and Financial Committee (formerly the Interim Committee) meets twice a year. The voting power of each country is related to its quota in the Fund.

BOARD OF EXECUTIVE DIRECTORS

The 24-member Board of Executive Directors is responsible for the day-to-day operations of the Fund. The USA, the United Kingdom, Germany, France and Japan each appoint one Executive Director, while 16 of the remainder are elected by groups of member countries sharing similar interests; there is also one Executive Director each from the People's Republic of China, Russia and Saudi Arabia.

OFFICERS

Managing Director: HORST KÖHLER (Germany).
First Deputy Managing Director: STANLEY FISCHER (USA).
Deputy Managing Director: SHIGEMITSU SUGISAKI (Japan); EDUARDO ANINAT (Chile).
Director, African Department: G. E. GONOWE.

Activities

The purposes of the IMF, as defined in the Articles of Agreement, are:
(i) To promote international monetary co-operation through a permanent institution which provides the machinery for consultation and collaboration on monetary problems;
(ii) To facilitate the expansion and balanced growth of international trade, and to contribute thereby to the promotion and maintenance of high levels of employment and real income and to the development of members' productive resources;
(iii) To promote exchange stability, to maintain orderly exchange arrangements among members, and to avoid competitive exchange depreciation;
(iv) To assist in the establishment of a multilateral system of payments in respect of current transactions between members and in the elimination of foreign exchange restrictions which hamper the growth of trade;
(v) To give confidence to members by making the general resources of the Fund temporarily available to them, under adequate safeguards, thus providing them with the opportunity to correct maladjustments in their balance of payments, without resorting to measures destructive of national or international prosperity; and
(vi) In accordance with the above, to shorten the duration of and lessen the degree of disequilibrium in the international balances of payments of members.

In joining the Fund, each country agrees to co-operate with the above objectives, and the Fund monitors members' compliance by holding an annual consultation with each country, in order to survey the country's exchange rate policies and determine its need for assistance.

In accordance with its objective of facilitating the expansion of international trade, the IMF encourages its members to accept the obligations of Article VIII, Sections two, three and four, of the IMF Articles of Agreement. Members that accept Article VIII undertake to refrain from imposing restrictions on the making of payments and transfers for current international transactions and from engaging in discriminatory currency arrangements or multiple currency practices without IMF approval. By the end of 1999 148 members had accepted Article VIII status.

RESOURCES

Members' subscriptions form the basic resource of the IMF. They are supplemented by borrowing. Under the General Arrangements to Borrow (GAB), established in 1962, the 'Group of Ten' industrialized nations (Belgium, Canada, France, Germany, Italy, Japan, the Netherlands, Sweden, the United Kingdom and the USA) and Switzerland (which became a member of the IMF in 1992, but which had been a full participant in the GAB from 1984) undertake to lend the Fund up to SDR 17,000m. in their own currencies, so as to help fulfill the balance-of-payments requirements of any member of the group, or to meet requests to the Fund from countries with balance-of-payments problems that could threaten the stability of the international monetary system. In May 1996 GAB participants concluded an agreement in principle to expand the resources available for borrowing to SDR 34,000m., by securing the support of other countries with the financial capacity to support the international monetary system. The so-called New Arrangements to Borrow (NAB) was approved by the Executive Board in January 1997; it was to enter into force, for an initial five-year period, as soon as the five largest potential creditors (of the anticipated 25 member countries and institutions participating in NAB) had approved the initiative and the total credit arrangement of participants endorsing the scheme had reached at least SDR 28,900m. While the GAB credit arrangement was to remain in effect, the NAB was expected to be the first facility to be activated in the event of the Fund's requiring supplementary resources. In July 1998 the GAB was activated for the first time in more than 20 years in order to provide funds totalling US $6,300m. in support of an IMF emergency assistance package for Russia (the first time the GAB had been used for a non-participant). The NAB became effective in November, and was used for the first time as part of an extensive programme of support for Brazil, which was adopted by the IMF in early December.

DRAWING ARRANGEMENTS

Exchange transactions within the Fund take the form of members' purchases (i.e. drawings) from the Fund of the currencies of other members for the equivalent amounts of their own currencies. Fund resources are available to eligible members on an essentially short-term and revolving basis to provide members with temporary assistance to contribute to the solution of their payments problems. Before making a purchase, a member must show that its balance of payments or reserve position make the purchase necessary. Apart from this requirement, reserve tranche purchases (i.e. purchases that do not bring the Fund's holdings of the member's currency to a level above its quota) are permitted unconditionally.

With further purchases, however, the Fund's policy of 'conditionality' means that a member requesting assistance must agree to adjust its economic policies, as stipulated by the IMF. All requests other than for use of the reserve tranche are examined by the Executive Board to determine whether the proposed use would be consistent with the Fund's policies, and a member must discuss its proposed adjustment programme (including fiscal, monetary, exchange and trade policies) with IMF staff. Purchases outside the reserve tranche are made in four credit tranches, each equivalent to 25% of the member's quota; a member must reverse the transaction by repurchasing its own currency (with SDR or currencies specified by the Fund) within a specified time. A credit tranche purchase is usually made under a 'stand-by arrangement' with the Fund, or under the extended Fund facility. A stand-by arrangement is normally of one or two years' duration, and the amount is made available in instalments, subject to the member's observance of 'performance criteria'; repurchases must be made within three-and-a-quarter to five years. An extended arrangement is normally of three years' duration, and the member must submit detailed economic programmes and progress reports for each year; repurchases must be made within four-and-a-half to 10 years. A member whose payments imbalance is large in relation to its quota may make use of temporary facilities established by the Fund using borrowed resources, namely the 'enlarged access policy' established in 1981, which helps to finance stand-by and extended arrangements for such a member, up to a limit of between 90% and 110% of the member's quota annually. In October 1994 the Executive Board agreed to increase, for three years, the annual access limit under IMF regular tranche drawings, stand-by arrangements and extended Fund facility credits from 68% to 100% of a member's quota with the cumulative access limit remaining at 300% of quota. The arrangements were extended, on a temporary basis, in November 1997.

In addition, special-purpose arrangements have been introduced, all of which are subject to the member's co-operation with the Fund to find an appropriate solution to its difficulties. The buffer stock financing facility (BSFF), established in 1969 in order to enable members to pay their contributions to the buffer stocks which are intended to stabilize primary commodity markets, was abolished in

MEMBERSHIP AND QUOTAS IN AFRICA SOUTH OF THE SAHARA (million SDR)*

Country	July 2000
Angola	286.3
Benin	61.9
Botswana	63.0
Burkina Faso	60.2
Burundi	77.0
Cameroon	185.7
Cape Verde	9.6
Central African Republic	55.7
Chad	56.0
Comoros	8.9
Congo, Democratic Republic†	(533.0) 291.0
Congo, Republic	84.6
Côte d'Ivoire	325.2
Djibouti	15.9
Equatorial Guinea	32.6
Eritrea	15.9
Ethiopia	133.7
Gabon	154.3
The Gambia	31.1
Ghana	369.0
Guinea	107.1
Guinea-Bissau	14.2
Kenya	271.4
Lesotho	34.9
Liberia†	(129.2) 71.3
Madagascar	122.2
Malawi	69.4
Mali	93.3
Mauritania	64.4
Mauritius	101.6
Mozambique	113.6
Namibia	136.5
Niger	65.8
Nigeria	1,753.2
Rwanda	80.1
São Tomé and Príncipe	7.4
Senegal	161.8
Seychelles	8.8
Sierra Leone	103.7
Somalia†	(81.7) 44.2
South Africa	1,868.5
Sudan†	(315.1) 169.7
Swaziland	50.7
Tanzania	198.9
Togo	73.4
Uganda	180.5
Zambia	489.1
Zimbabwe	353.4

* The Special Drawing Right (SDR) was introduced in 1970 as a substitute for gold in international payments, and is intended eventually to become the principal reserve asset in the international monetary system. Its value (which was US $1.3192 at 30 April 2000 and averaged $1.3673 in 1999) is based on the currencies of the five largest exporting countries. Each member is assigned a quota related to its national income, monetary reserves, trade balance and other economic indicators; the quota approximately determines a member's voting power and the amount of foreign exchange it may purchase from the Fund. A member's subscription is equal to its quota. Under the Ninth General Review of Quotas, which was completed in June 1990, an increase of about 50% in total quotas (from SDR 90,035m. to SDR 135,200m.) was authorized. The increase entered into effect in November 1992. The Tenth General Review of Quotas was concluded, in December 1994, with no further increase of quotas. In February 1998 the Board of Governors adopted a resolution in support of an increase, under the Eleventh General Review, of some 45% in total quotas, subject to approval by member states constituting 85% of total quotas (as at December 1997). Sufficient consent had been granted by January 1999 to enable the overall increase in quotas to enter into effect. All members were then granted until 30 July to consent to the higher quotas. At July 2000 total quotas in the Fund amounted to SDR 210,251.4m.

† At July 2000 these members had overdue obligations and were therefore ineligible to consent to any increase in their quotas. The figures listed are those determined under the Eighth General Review while the figures in parentheses are the proposed Eleventh General Review quotas.

January 2000, having last been used in 1984. In August 1988 the Fund established the compensatory and contingency financing facility (CCFF), which replaced and expanded a previous facility. The CCFF provides compensation to members whose export earnings are reduced owing to circumstances beyond their control, or who are affected by excess costs of cereal imports. In January 2000 the Executive Board resolved to eliminate the contingency component, which provided financing to help members maintain their efforts at economic adjustment even when affected by a sharp increase in interest rates or other externally-derived difficulties. In December 1997 the Executive Board established a new Supplemental Reserve Facility (SRF) to provide short-term assistance to members experiencing exceptional balance-of-payments difficulties resulting from a sudden loss of market confidence. Repayments were to be made within one to one-and-a-half years of the purchase, unless otherwise extended by the Board. In April 1999 an additional facility was established, for a two-year period, to provide short-term financing on similar terms to the SRF in order to prevent more stable economies being affected by adverse international financial developments and to maintain investor confidence. Under the Contingent Credit Lines (CCL) member countries were to have access to up to 500% of their quota, subject to meeting various economic criteria stipulated by the Fund.

The structural adjustment facility (SAF) was established in 1986 to support medium-term macroeconomic adjustment and structural reforms in low-income developing countries on concessional terms. Following the adoption of the enlarged enhanced structural adjustment facility (ESAF—see below) it was agreed that no further resources would be made available for SAF arrangements. However, an exceptional SAF arrangement was approved during 1993/94 for Sierra Leone and resources were retained for a previously agreed arrangement for Zambia.

The ESAF, established in 1987, was to provide new resources to assist the adjustment efforts of, in particular, heavily indebted countries. Eligible members must develop a three-year adjustment programme (with assistance given jointly by staff of the Fund and of the World Bank) to strengthen the balance-of-payments situation and foster sustainable economic growth. ESAF loans carry an interest rate of 0.5% per year and are repayable within 10 years, including a five-and-a-half-year grace period. Maximum access is set at 190% (255% in exceptional circumstances) of the member's quota. Originally 34 African countries were eligible for ESAF loans; in April 1992 Angola, Côte d'Ivoire, Nigeria and Zimbabwe were granted eligibility for the first time. In February 1994 a new period of operations of the ESAF became effective, following an agreement to enlarge the ESAF Trust (the funding source for ESAF arrangements). The terms and conditions of the new facility remained the same as those of the original ESAF, but the list of countries eligible for assistance was enlarged by six, of which Cameroon was the only African country, to 78 (subsequently extended to 80). In January 1995 Eritrea became the 79th member eligible for ESAF assistance. The new commitment period for

NEW ESAF ARRANGEMENTS AGREED FOR COUNTRIES IN AFRICA SOUTH OF THE SAHARA

1 May 1997–30 April 1998	
Country	Loan (million SDR)
Cameroon	162.12
Côte d'Ivoire	285.84
Senegal	107.01
Uganda	100.43

1 May 1998–30 April 1999	
Country	Loan (million SDR)
Central African Republic	49.44
The Gambia	20.61
Rwanda	71.40
Zambia	254.45

PURCHASES OF CURRENCIES AND SPECIAL DRAWING RIGHTS FROM THE IMF BY MEMBERS IN AFRICA SOUTH OF THE SAHARA

1 May 1997–30 April 1998		1 May 1998–30 April 1999	
Member	Total purchases (million SDR)	Member	Total purchases (million SDR)
Djibouti	1.1	Zimbabwe	39.2
Gabon	16.5		

lending from the ESAF Trust was to expire on 31 December 1996, while disbursements were to be made until 31 December 1999. In September 1996 the Interim Committee of the Board of Governors endorsed measures to finance the ESAF for a further five-year (2000–2004) period, after which the facility was to become self-sustaining. The interim period of the ESAF was to be funded mainly from bilateral contributions, but drawing on the Fund's additional resources as necessary. At 30 April 1999 35 ESAF arrangements were in effect, with commitments amounting to SDR 4,186m. In 1998/99 ESAF disbursements amounted to SDR 998m. Cumulative SAF and ESAF disbursements to the end of April 1998 totalled SDR 8,145m. In September 1999 it was announced that the successor facility to the ESAF was to be a Poverty Reduction and Growth Facility, with greater emphasis on poverty reduction as a key element of growth-orientated economic strategies.

The ESAF was to support, through long-maturity loans and grants, IMF participation in a joint initiative, with the World Bank, to provide exceptional assistance to heavily indebted poor countries (HIPCs), in order to help them to achieve a sustainable level of debt management. Of the 41 HIPCs identified under the initiative, 33 were in sub-Saharan Africa. The initiative was formally approved at the September 1996 meeting of the Interim Committee, having received the support of the 'Paris Club' of official creditors which agreed to increase the relief on official debt from 67% to 80%. (see World Bank, p. 100). An ESAF-HIPC trust was established in February 1997, through which the IMF was to channel resources for the HIPC initiative and interim operations.

In April 1997 the World Bank and the IMF announced that Uganda was to be the first beneficiary of the initiative. The IMF's share of the anticipated debt relief of US $338m. was to total $69m., effective from April 1998 (i.e. the 'completion point' of the process to assess eligibility for debt relief). In September 1997 assistance was approved for Bolivia and Burkina Faso under the HIPC initiative and in December Guyana was deemed to be eligible. By the end of 1998 debt reduction commitments had been approved for Côte d'Ivoire, Mali and Mozambique. In early 1999 the IMF and World Bank initiated a comprehensive review of the HIPC scheme, in order to consider modifications of the initiative and to strengthen the link between debt relief and poverty reduction. A consensus emerged among the financial institutions and leading industrialized nations to enhance the scheme, in order to make it available to more countries, and to accelerate the process of providing debt relief. In September the IMF Board of Governors expressed its commitment to undertaking an off-market transaction of a percentage of the Fund's gold reserves (i.e. a sale, at market prices, to central banks of member countries with repayment obligations to the Fund, which were then to be made in gold), as part of the funding arrangements of the enhanced HIPC scheme. In that month IMF assistance under the scheme in net present value terms amounted to $305m. of a total of $3,355m. of assistance committed, which had a nominal debt relief value of $6,770m. By July 2000 debt relief arrangements under the enhanced HIPC had been approved for Benin, Mauritania and Senegal, while agreements on additional assistance under the enhanced initiative had been reached for Burkina Faso, Mozambique and Uganda.

SURVEILLANCE

Under its Articles of Agreement, the Fund is mandated to oversee the effective functioning of the international monetary system and to review the policies of individual member countries to ensure the stability of the exchange rate system. The Fund's main tools of surveillance are regular consultations with member countries conducted in accordance with Article IV of the Articles of Agreement, which cover fiscal and monetary policies, balance of payments and external debt developments, as well as policies that affect the economic performance of a country, such as the labour market, social and environmental issues and good governance, and aspects of the country's capital accounts, and finance and banking sectors. In addition, World Economic Outlook discussions are held, normally twice a year, by the Executive Board to assess policy implications from a multilateral perspective and to monitor global developments. The rapid decline in the value of the Mexican peso in late 1994 and the financial crisis in Asia, which became apparent in mid-1997, focused attention on the importance of IMF surveillance of the

economies and financial policies of member states and prompted the Fund to enhance the effectiveness of its surveillance and to encourage the full and timely provision of data by member countries in order to maintain fiscal transparency. In April 1996 the IMF established the Special Data Dissemination Standard, which was intended to improve access to reliable economic statistical information for member countries that draw, or are seeking, access to international capital markets. In March 1999 the IMF undertook to strengthen the Standard by the introduction of a new reserves data template. By July 2000 47 countries had subscribed to the Standard. In March 1997 the Executive Board agreed to develop a General Data Dissemination System (GDDS), to encourage all member countries to improve the production and dissemination of core economic data. The operational phase of the GDDS commenced in May 2000. In April 1997, in an effort to improve the value of surveillance by means of increased transparency, the Executive Board agreed to the voluntary release of Press Information Notices, following each member's Article IV consultation with the Board. In March 2000 the Executive Board adopted a strengthened framework to safeguard the use of IMF resources. All member countries making use of Fund resources were to be required to publish annual central bank statements audited in accordance with internationally accepted standards. It was also agreed that any instance of intentional misreporting of information by a member country should be publicized. In the following month the Executive Board approved the establishment of an independent evaluation office.

TECHNICAL ASSISTANCE

Technical assistance is provided by special missions or resident representatives who advise members on every aspect of economic management. Assistance is provided by the IMF's various specialized departments and is becoming an increasingly important aspect of the Fund's relationship with its member countries. In particular, the expansion of the Fund's technical assistance activities during the early 1990s resulted from the increase in countries undergoing economic and systemic transformations. The IMF Institute, founded in 1964, trains officials from member countries in financial analysis and policy, balance-of-payments methodology and public finance; it also gives assistance to national and regional training centres. In May 1999 the Institute, in collaboration with the Bank of Mauritius, organized a high-level seminar on structural adjustment in sub-Saharan Africa. Participants reviewed economic progress achieved, as well as the experience of different countries, and considered measures to ensure more rapid and sustainable growth in the future, for example good governance and trade liberalization. In January the IMF, in co-operation with the African Development Bank and the World Bank, announced the establishment of a Joint Africa Institute, in Abidjan, Côte d'Ivoire, which was to provide training to officials from the region in economic policy and management, as well as in other development and governance issues, from late 1999.

Publications

Annual Report.
Balance of Payments Statistics Yearbook.
Direction of Trade Statistics (quarterly and annually).
Finance and Development (quarterly, published jointly with the World Bank).
Government Finance Statistics Yearbook.
IMF Economic Reviews (3 a year).
IMF Survey (2 a month).
International Capital Markets: Developments, Prospects and Key Policy Issues.
International Financial Statistics (monthly and annually).
Joint BIS-IMF-OECD-World Bank Statistics on External Debt (quarterly).
Staff Papers (quarterly).
World Economic Outlook (2 a year).
Occasional papers, books and pamphlets.

World Health Organization—WHO

Address: ave Appia, 1211 Geneva 27, Switzerland.
Telephone: (22) 7912111; **fax:** (22) 7910746; **e-mail:** info@who.ch;
internet: www.who.int.

WHO was established in 1948 as the central agency directing international health work.

Organization

(July 2000)

WORLD HEALTH ASSEMBLY

The Assembly meets annually in Geneva; it is responsible for policy making, and the biennial programme and budget; it appoints the Director-General, admits new members and reviews budget contributions.

EXECUTIVE BOARD

The Board is composed of 32 health experts designated by, but not representing, their governments; they serve for three years, and the World Health Assembly elects 10 or 11 member states each year to the Board. It meets at least twice a year to review the Director-General's programme, which it forwards to the Assembly with any recommendations that seem necessary. It advises on questions referred to it by the Assembly and is responsible for putting into effect the decisions and policies of the Assembly. It is also empowered to take emergency measures in case of epidemics or disasters.

SECRETARIAT

Director-General: Dr GRO HARLEM BRUNDTLAND (Norway).
Executive Directors: Dr JULIO J. FRENK (Mexico), Dr DAVID L. HEYMANN (USA), ANN KERN (Australia), Dr POONAM KHETRAPAL SINGH (India), Dr SOUAD LYAGOUBI-OUAHCHI (Tunisia), Dr DAVID NABARRO (United Kingdom), Dr OLIVE SHISANA (South Africa), Dr YASUHIRO SUZUKI (Japan), Dr DEREK YACH (South Africa).

REGIONAL OFFICES

Regional Office in Africa: (temporary address) Parirenyatwa Hospital, Mazoe St, POB BE 773, Belvedere, Harare, Zimbabwe; tel. (4) 4707493; fax (4) 4790146; e-mail regafro@whoafr.org; internet www.whoafr.org; Dir Dr EBRAHIM MALICK SAMBA (The Gambia).

Sub-regional offices were established in Bamako, Mali, and Harare, Zimbabwe, in 1985.

Activities

WHO's objective is stated in the constitution as 'the attainment by all peoples of the highest possible level of health'.

It acts as the central authority directing international health work, and establishes relations with professional groups and government health authorities on that basis.

It supports, on request from member states, programmes to promote health, prevent and control health problems, control or eradicate disease, train health workers best suited to local needs and strengthen national health systems. Aid is provided in emergencies and natural disasters.

A global programme of collaborative research and exchange of scientific information is carried out in co-operation with about 1,000 leading national institutions. Particular stress is laid on the widespread communicable diseases of the tropics, and the countries directly concerned are assisted in developing their research capabilities.

It keeps diseases and other health problems under constant surveillance, promotes the exchange of information, formulates health regulations for international travel, and sets standards for the quality control of drugs, vaccines and other substances affecting health.

It collects and disseminates health data and carries out statistical analyses and comparative studies in such diseases as cancer, heart disease and mental illness.

It promotes improved environmental conditions, including housing, sanitation and working conditions. All available information on effects on human health of the pollutants in the environment is critically reviewed and published.

Co-operation among scientists and professional groups is encouraged, and WHO may propose international conventions and agreements. It assists in developing an informed public opinion on matters of health.

Strengthening of the national health services has been one of WHO's primary tasks in Africa south of the Sahara. Integrated health systems are being developed to provide services related to medical care, rehabilitation, family health, communicable disease control, environmental health, health education, and health statistics. By providing educators and fellowships and by organizing training courses, support is given to national programmes aimed at preparing health workers best suited to local needs and resources. Specialists and advisory services are provided to assist in planning the health sector, which in most African countries forms an integral part of the overall plan for socio-economic development.

In May 1981 the World Health Assembly adopted a Global Strategy in support of 'Health for all by the year 2000', which aimed to ensure that all citizens of the world attain a level of health that will permit them to lead a socially and economically productive life. Primary health care was considered to be the key to 'Health for all', with the following as minimum requirements:

Safe water in the home or within 15 minutes' walking distance, and adequate sanitary facilities in the home or immediate vicinity;

Immunization against diphtheria, pertussis, tetanus, poliomyelitis, measles and tuberculosis;

Local health care, including availability of at least 20 essential drugs, within one hour's travel; and

Trained personnel to attend childbirth, and to care for pregnant mothers and children up to at least one year old.

In May 1998 the World Health Assembly agreed that a new global strategy should be effected, through regional and national health policies. The so-called 'Health for all in the 21st century' initiative was to build on the primary health care approach of the 'Health for all' strategy, but was to strengthen the emphasis on quality of life, equity in health, and access to health services.

In July 1998 Dr Gro Harlem Brundtland officially took office as the new Director-General of WHO. She immediately announced an extensive reform of the organization, including restructuring the WHO technical programmes into nine groups or 'clusters', each headed by an Executive Director (see above). The groups were established within the framework of the following four main areas of activity: Combating ill health, incorporating Communicable Diseases and Non-communicable Diseases; Building healthy populations and communities, comprising the groups Health Systems and Community Health, Sustainable Development and Healthy Environments and Social Change and Mental Health; Sustained health, including the groups Health Technology and Pharmaceuticals, and Evidence and Information for Policy; and Internal support—reaching out, comprising External Affairs and Governing Bodies, and General Management.

COMMUNICABLE DISEASES

The Communicable Diseases group works to reduce the impact of infectious diseases world-wide through surveillance and response; prevention and control; eradication and elimination; and research and development. The group seeks to strengthen global monitoring of important communicable disease problems and to increase the organization's capacity to provide an effective response to those problems. WHO also aims to reduce the impact of other communicable diseases through intensive, routine, prevention and control and, where possible, through the elimination or eradication of specific infections.

One of WHO's major achievements was the eradication of smallpox. Following a massive international campaign of vaccination and surveillance, begun in 1958 and intensified in 1967, the last case was detected in 1977 and the eradication of the disease was declared in 1980. In May 1996 the World Health Assembly resolved that, pending a final endorsement, all remaining stocks of the smallpox virus were to be destroyed on 30 June 1999, although 500,000 doses of smallpox vaccine were to remain, along with a supply of the smallpox vaccine seed virus, in order to ensure that a further supply of the vaccine could be made available if required. In May 1999, however, the Assembly authorized a temporary retention of stocks of the virus until 2002. In 1988 the World Health Assembly declared its commitment to the eradication of poliomyelitis by 2000 and launched the Global Polio Eradication Initiative. (The certification date for the global eradication of polio was subsequently revised to 2005.) In 1996 WHO, UNICEF, Rotary International and other national and international partners initiated a campaign to 'kick polio out of Africa' through the immunization of more than 100m. children in 46 countries over a three-year period. By the end of 1999 the number of reported polio cases world-wide had declined to some 6,000, from 35,000 in 1988 (the actual number of cases in 1988 was estimated at around 350,000). A severe outbreak of the disease in Angola in early 1999 prompted renewed international support for the conduct of National Immunization Days, which, in Angola, had a target coverage of 3.3m. children. During that year 'days of tranquillity' were encouraged in the conflict-affected Democratic Republic of the Congo (DRC), to coincide with National Immunization Days. In 2000 six of WHO's 10 global priority countries for the eradication of polio were in Africa: Angola, the DRC, Ethiopia, Nigeria, Somalia and Sudan.

The objective of providing immunization for all children by 1990 was adopted by the World Health Assembly in 1977. Six diseases (measles, whooping cough, tetanus, poliomyelitis, tuberculosis and diphtheria) became the target of the Expanded Programme on Immunization (EPI), in which WHO, UNICEF and many other organizations collaborated. As a result of massive international and national efforts, the global immunization coverage increased from 20% in the early 1980s to the targeted rate of 80% by the end of 1990. This coverage signified that more than 100m. children in the developing world under the age of one had been successfully vaccinated against the targeted diseases, the lives of about 3m. children had been saved every year, and 500,000 annual cases of paralysis as a result of polio had been prevented. In 1992 the Assembly resolved to reach a new target of 90% immunization coverage with the six EPI vaccines, to introduce hepatitis B as a seventh vaccine and to introduce the yellow fever vaccine in areas where it occurs endemically.

As a result of the reform of WHO implemented from mid-1998, the former Division of Control of Tropical Diseases was integrated into the Communicable Diseases cluster, providing active support for planning and implementing control programmes (based on global strategies for integrated tropical disease control) at regional, sub-regional and national levels. It assists with the mobilization of resources for disease control where needed, and the co-ordination of national and international participation. The group also promotes research and training that are directly relevant to control needs, and promotes the monitoring and evaluation of control measures. WHO's Special Programme for Research and Training in Tropical Diseases, sponsored jointly by WHO, UNDP and the World Bank, was established in 1975, and comprises a world-wide network of about 5,000 scientists working on the development of vaccines, new drugs, diagnostic kits, preventive measures, and applied field research on practical community issues affecting the target diseases. The programme aims to strengthen research institutions in developing countries, and to encourage participation by scientists from the countries most affected by tropical diseases.

The Onchocerciasis Control Programme in West Africa (OCP) was initiated in 1974 to eliminate onchocerciasis, which can cause blindness, as a major public health problem and an impediment to socio-economic development in 11 countries of the region. In January 1996 a new initiative, the African Programme for Onchocerciasis Control (APOC), covering 19 countries outside West Africa, became operational, with funding co-ordinated by the World Bank and with WHO as the executing agency. In December 1994 WHO announced that the OCP was to be terminated in 2002, by which time it was estimated that 40m. people would have been protected from the disease and 600,000 people prevented from blindness. In May 1999 WHO reported that the Programme, based in Ouagadougou, Burkina Faso, was to be transformed into a Multi-disease Surveillance Centre. In January 1998 a new 20-year programme to eliminate lymphatic filariasis was initiated, with substantial funding and support from public and private bodies.

A Ministerial Conference on Malaria, organized by WHO in October 1992, adopted a global strategy specifying requirements for effective control of the disease, which kills an estimated 1m. people every year and affects a further 300m.–500m. Some 90% of all cases occur in sub-Saharan Africa. WHO assists countries where malaria is endemic to prepare national plans of action for malaria control in accordance with WHO's Global Malaria Control Strategy, which emphasized strengthening local capabilities, for example through training, for effective health control. In July 1998 WHO declared the control of malaria a priority concern, and in October formally launched the 'Roll Back Malaria' programme, in conjunction with UNICEF, the World Bank and UNDP. Emphasis was to be placed on strengthening local health systems and on the promotion of inexpensive preventative measures, including the use of bednets treated with insecticides (which were proven to be effective in trials in Burkina Faso, The Gambia, Ghana and Kenya). WHO, with a number of private and public partners, also supports the development of more effective anti-malaria drugs and vaccines through the 'Medicines for Malaria' venture. A new 'African Initiative for Malaria Control in the 21st Century', aims to reduce the prevalence of malaria in 42 African countries by as much as 50% by 2010.

In July 1994 WHO, together with the Sasakawa Memorial Health Foundation, organized an international conference on the elimination of leprosy. The conference adopted a declaration on their commitment to the elimination of leprosy (the reduction of the prevalence of leprosy to less than one case per 10,000 population) by 2000 and WHO established a Special Programme devoted to this

objective. In September 1998 WHO announced that the use of a combination of three drugs (known as multi-drug therapy—MDT) had resulted in a reduction in the number of leprosy cases world-wide from 10m.–12m. in 1988, to 1.15m. in 1997. Moreover, in April 1999 WHO announced that the number of countries having more than one case of leprosy per 10,000 had declined from 122 in 1985 to 28. In November 1999 WHO launched a new initiative, in collaboration with several governments and a major pharmaceutical company, to eradicate leprosy by the end of 2005. In July 1998 the Director-General of WHO and representatives of more than 20 countries, meeting in Yamoussoukro, Côte d'Ivoire, signed a declaration on the control of another emerging mycobacterial disease, Buruli ulcer.

In 1995 WHO established a Global Tuberculosis Programme to address the emerging challenges of the TB epidemic. According to WHO estimates, around 2m. people die from the disease each year, prompting WHO to declare TB a global emergency. WHO provides technical support to all member countries, with special attention being given to those with high TB prevalence, to establish effective national tuberculosis control programmes. WHO's strategy for TB control includes the use of DOTS (directly observed treatment, short-course), standardized treatment guide-lines, and result accountability through routine evaluation of treatment outcomes. Simultaneously, WHO is encouraging research with the aim of further disseminating DOTS, adapting DOTS for wider use, developing new tools for prevention, diagnosis and treatment, and containing new threats such as the HIV/TB co-epidemic. Nevertheless, by late 1998 WHO estimated that there were still 8m. new cases of TB occurring world-wide each year. In March 1999 WHO announced the launch of a new initiative, 'Stop TB', in co-operation with the World Bank, the US Government and a coalition of non-governmental organizations, which aimed to promote DOTS to ensure its use in 85% of cases by 2005, compared with some 16% in the late 1990s. In 1999 WHO identified Kenya and Tanzania among several countries successfully controlling TB through the use of DOTS.

NON-COMMUNICABLE DISEASES

The Non-communicable Diseases group comprises three departments responsible for the surveillance, prevention and management of uninfectious diseases (such as those arising from an unhealthy diet).

'Inter-Health', a programme to combat non-communicable diseases, was initiated in 1990, with the particular aim of preventing an increase in the incidence of such diseases in developing countries. WHO's programmes for diabetes mellitus, chronic rheumatic diseases and asthma assist with the development of national programmes, based upon goals and targets for the improvement of early detection, care and reduction of long-term complications. They also monitor the global epidemiological situation and co-ordinate multinational research activities concerned with the prevention and care of non-communicable diseases. In mid-1998 WHO adopted a resolution on measures to be taken to combat these diseases, the prevalence of which was anticipated to increase, particularly in developing countries, owing to rising life expectancy and changes in lifestyles. For example, between 1995 and 2025 the number of adults affected by diabetes was projected to increase from 135m. to 300m. In February 1999 WHO initiated a new programme, 'Vision 2020: the Right to Sight', which aimed to eliminate avoidable blindness (estimated to be as much as 80% of all cases) by 2020. Blindness was otherwise predicted to increase by as much as twofold, owing to the increased longevity of the global population.

HEALTH SYSTEMS AND COMMUNITY HEALTH

During 1998 WHO integrated its programmes relating to the health and development of children and adolescents, reproductive health and research, women's health, and health systems within the Health Systems and Community Health group. The group's aim is to improve access to sustainable health care for all by strengthening health systems and fostering individual, family and community development. Activities include newborn care; child health, including promoting and protecting the health and development of the child through such approaches as promotion of breast-feeding and use of the mother-baby package, as well as care of the sick child, including diarrhoeal and acute respiratory disease control and support to women and children in difficult circumstances; the promotion of safe motherhood and maternal health; adolescent health, including the promotion and development of young people and the prevention of specific health problems; women, health and development, including addressing issues of gender, sexual violence, and harmful traditional practices; and human reproduction, including research related to contraceptive technologies and effective methods. In addition, WHO aimed to provide technical leadership and co-ordination on reproductive health and to support countries in their efforts to ensure that people: experience healthy sexual development and maturation; have the capacity for healthy, equitable and responsible relationships; can achieve their reproductive intentions safely and healthily; avoid illnesses, diseases and injury related to sexuality and reproduction; and receive appropriate counselling, care and rehabilitation for diseases and conditions related to sexuality and reproduction.

WHO's Division of Diarrhoeal and Acute Respiratory Disease Control encourages national programmes aimed at reducing the estimated 3.5m. yearly childhood deaths as a result of diarrhoea, particularly through the use of oral rehydration therapy and preventive measures. The Division is also seeking to reduce deaths from pneumonia in infants through the use of a simple case-management strategy involving the recognition of danger signs and treatment with an appropriate antibiotic. In September 1997 WHO, in collaboration with UNICEF, formally launched a programme advocating the Integrated Management of Childhood Illness (IMCI), following successful regional trials in more than 20 developing countries during 1996–97. IMCI recognizes that pneumonia, diarrhoea, measles, malaria and malnutrition cause some 70% of the 11m. childhood deaths each year, and recommends screening sick children for all five conditions, in order to enable health workers to reach a more accurate diagnosis than may be achieved from the results of a single assessment.

In December 1995 WHO's Global Programme on AIDS, which began in 1987, was concluded and, on 1 January 1996, a Joint UN Programme on HIV/AIDS (UNAIDS) became operational. It is sponsored jointly by WHO, the World Bank, UNICEF, UNDCP, UNDP, UNESCO and UNFPA. WHO established an Office of HIV/AIDS and Sexually-Transmitted Diseases in order to ensure continuity of its global response to the problem, which included support for national control and education plans, improving the safety of blood supplies and improving the care and support of AIDS patients. In addition, the Office was to liaise with UNAIDS and to make available WHO's research and technical expertise. In December 1999 an estimated 33.6m. adults and children world-wide were living with HIV/AIDS; of these, 5.6m. were estimated to have been newly infected during that year. Some 95% of those known to be living with HIV/AIDS were living in developing countries. By the end of 1999 an estimated 16m. people world-wide had died as a result of HIV/AIDS-related illnesses.

SUSTAINABLE DEVELOPMENT AND HEALTHY ENVIRONMENTS

The Sustainable Development and Healthy Environment group comprises four departments that concentrate on: health in sustainable development; nutrition for health and development; protection of the human environment; and emergency and humanitarian action.

The group seeks to monitor the advantages and disadvantages for health, nutrition, environment and development arising from the process of globalization; to integrate the issue of health into poverty reduction programmes; and to promote human rights and equality. Adequate and safe food and nutrition is a priority programme area. An estimated 780m. world-wide cannot meet basic needs for energy and protein, more than 2,000m. people lack essential vitamins and minerals, and 170m. children are estimated to be malnourished.

WHO collaborates with FAO, WFP, UNICEF and other UN agencies in pursuing its objectives relating to nutrition and food safety. In December 1992 an International Conference on Nutrition, co-sponsored by FAO and WHO, adopted a World Declaration on Nutrition and a Plan of Action designed to make the fight against malnutrition a development priority. In pursuing the objectives of the Declaration WHO promotes the elaboration and implementation of national plans of action for nutrition and aims to identify and support countries with high levels of malnutrition, which includes protein energy deficiencies, and deficiencies of iron, vitamin A and iodine. A strategy of universal salt iodization was launched in 1993 (iodine deficiency causes mental handicap.) In collaboration with other international agencies, WHO is implementing a comprehensive strategy for promoting appropriate infant, young-child and maternal nutrition, and for dealing effectively with nutritional emergencies in large populations. Areas of emphasis include promoting health-care practices that enhance successful breast-feeding; appropriate complementary feeding; refining the use and interpretation of body measurements for assessing nutritional status; relevant information, education and training; and action to give effect to the International Code of Marketing of Breast-milk Substitutes. WHO's Food Safety Programme aims to eliminate risks, such as biological or chemical contaminants in foods which are a major cause of diarrhoea and malnutrition in children. WHO, together with FAO, establishes food standards (through the work of the Codex Alimentarius Commission) and evaluates food additives, pesticide residues and other contaminants and their implications for health. The Programme provides expert advice on such issues as food-borne pathogens (e.g. listeria), production methods (e.g. aquaculture) and food biotechnology (e.g. genetic modification).

WHO's Programme for the Promotion of Environmental Health undertakes a wide range of initiatives to tackle the increasing threats to health and well-being from a changing environment, especially in relation to air pollution, water quality, sanitation, protection against radiation, management of hazardous waste, chemical safety and housing hygiene. The major part of WHO's technical co-operation in environmental health in developing countries is concerned with community water supply and sanitation. In sub-Saharan Africa, where conditions are considered to be the worst in the world, WHO estimated that, at early 1996, more than half of all people in the region were lacking safe drinking water, and some 70% were living without adequate sanitation, contributing to the problems of endemic malnutrition and diarrhoeal diseases. In October 1998 representatives of 46 African governments convened in Harare, Zimbabwe, to review implementation of the African 2000 initiative on water supply and sanitation, which was adopted in 1993 to strengthen local capacities for the development of safe and effective water supply and sanitation facilities. In order to contribute to the solution of environmental health problems associated with the rapid urbanization of cities in the developing world, the Programme was promoting globally in the 1990s the Healthy City approach that had been initiated in Europe. WHO is also working with other agencies to consider the implications on human health of global climate change.

Through its Division of Emergency and Humanitarian Action, WHO acts as the 'health arm' of disaster relief undertaken by the UN system. Its emergency preparedness activities include co-ordination, policy making and planning, awareness-building, technical advice, training, publication of standards and guide-lines, and research. Its emergency relief activities include organizational support, the provision of emergency drugs and supplies, and conducting technical emergency assessment missions. The Division's objective is to build the capacity of disaster-vulnerable member states to reduce the adverse health consequences of disasters. In responding to emergency situations, WHO always tries to develop projects and activities that will assist the national authorities concerned in rebuilding or strengthening their own capacity to handle the impact of such situations. In early 1999 WHO organized emergency medical teams to respond to an extreme outbreak of haemorrhagic fever in the Democratic Republic of the Congo. WHO collaborated with local personnel in the provision of essential treatment and distribution of medical supplies, and instituted surveillance and health education schemes.

SOCIAL CHANGE AND MENTAL HEALTH

The Social Change and Mental Health group comprises four departments: Health Promotion; Disability, Injury Prevention and Rehabilitation; Mental Health; and Substance Abuse. The group works to assess the impact of injuries, violence and sensory impairments on health, and formulates guide-lines and protocols for the prevention and management of mental problems. WHO promotes decentralized and community-based health programmes and is concerned with the challenge of population ageing and encouraging healthy lifestyles and self-care. Several projects have been undertaken by WHO regional and country offices in collaboration with other relevant organizations, including: the Global School Health Initiative, to bridge the sectors of health and education and to promote the health of school-age children; the Global Strategy for Occupational Health, to promote the health of the working population and the control of occupational health risks; Community-based Rehabilitation, which aimed to provide a more enabling environment for people with disabilities; and a communication strategy to provide training and support for health communications personnel and initiatives. In September 1997 WHO announced that three new regional networks for the development of health promoting schools—covering central Africa, South-East Asia and part of the Western Pacific—were to be established, within the context of the Global School Health Initiative.

The Substance Abuse department is concerned with problems of alcohol, drugs and other substance abuse. Within its Programme on Substance Abuse (PSA), which was established in 1990 in response to the global increase in substance abuse, WHO provides technical support to assist countries in formulating policies with regard to the prevention and reduction of the health and social effects of psychoactive substance abuse. PSA's sphere of activity includes epidemiological surveillance and risk assessment, advocacy and the dissemination of information, strengthening national and regional prevention and health promotion techniques and strategies, the development of cost-effective treatment and rehabilitation approaches, and also encompasses regulatory activities as required under the international drugs-control treaties in force.

The Tobacco or Health Programme, which was incorporated into the PSA in May 1994, aims to reduce the use of tobacco, by educating tobacco-users and preventing young people from adopting the habit. In 1996 WHO published its first report on the tobacco situation world-wide. According to WHO, about one-third of the world's population aged over 15 years smoke tobacco, which causes approximately 3.5m. deaths each year (through lung cancer, heart disease, chronic bronchitis and other effects). In 1998 the 'Tobacco Free Initiative', a major global anti-smoking campaign, was established. In May 1999 the World Health Assembly endorsed the formulation of a Framework Convention on Tobacco Control to help to combat the increase in tobacco use and production, and to regulate aspects of the tobacco industry.

HEALTH TECHNOLOGY AND PHARMACEUTICALS

WHO's Health Technology and Pharmaceuticals group comprises the following three departments: Essential Drugs and Other Medicines; Vaccines and Other Biologicals; and Blood Safety and Clinical Technology. Accordingly, the group promotes the development and effective use of drugs and vaccines, as well as the appropriate use of traditional medicines, the self-sufficiency of immunization programmes, and world-wide co-operation on blood safety.

In January 1999 the Executive Board adopted a resolution on WHO's Revised Drug Strategy, which placed emphasis on the inequalities of access to pharmaceuticals, and also covered specific aspects of drugs policy, quality assurance, drug promotion, drug donation, independent drug information and rational drug use. Plans of action involving co-operation with member states and other international organizations were to be developed in order to monitor and analyse the pharmaceutical and public health implications of international agreements, including trade agreements.

In September 1991 the Children's Vaccine Initiative (CVI) was launched, jointly sponsored by the Rockefeller Foundation, UNDP, UNICEF, WHO and the World Bank, to facilitate the development and provision of children's vaccines. The CVI has as its ultimate goal the development of a single oral immunization shortly after birth that will protect against all major childhood diseases. In 1998 the CVI reported that 4m. children die each year of diseases for which there are existing, common vaccines. In 1999 WHO, UNICEF, the World Bank and a number of public- and private-sector partners formed the Global Alliance for Vaccines and Immunization (GAVI), which aimed to expand the provision of existing vaccines and to accelerate the development and introduction of new vaccines and technologies, with the goal of protecting children of all nationalities and from all socio-economic backgrounds against vaccine-preventable diseases.

Finance

WHO's regular budget is provided by assessment of member states and associate members. An additional fund for specific projects is provided by voluntary contributions from members and other sources. Funds are received from the UNDP for particular projects and from UNFPA for population programmes. A regular budget of $842.65m. was proposed for the 2000–01 biennium, of which $176.82m. (21%) was for Africa.

Publications

Bulletin of WHO (monthly).
Environmental Health Criteria.
International Digest of Health Legislation (quarterly).
International Statistical Classification of Diseases and Related Health Problems, Tenth Revision, 1992–94.
Weekly Epidemiological Record.
WHO Drug Information (quarterly).
World Health Statistics Annual.
Series of technical reports.

Other UN Organizations Active in Africa

INTERNATIONAL CRIMINAL TRIBUNAL FOR RWANDA

Address: Arusha International Centre, POB 6016, Arusha, Tanzania.

Telephone: (57) 4207; **fax:** (57) 4000; **internet:** www.ictr.org.

In November 1994 the UN Security Council adopted Resolution 955, establishing an International Criminal Tribunal for Rwanda (ICTR) to prosecute persons responsible for genocide and other serious violations of humanitarian law that had been committed in Rwanda and by Rwandans in neighbouring states. The Tribunal comprises three three-member trial chambers and one appeals chamber with five additional judges. Its temporal jurisdiction is limited to the period 1 January to 31 December 1994. The first plenary session of the Tribunal was held in The Hague, Netherlands, in June 1995; formal proceedings at its permanent headquarters in Arusha, Tanzania, were initiated in November. The first trial of persons charged by the Tribunal commenced in January 1997, and sentences were imposed in July. In September 1998 the former Rwandan Prime Minister, Jean Kambanda, and a former mayor of Taba, Jean-Paul Akayesu, both Hutu extremists, were found guilty of genocide and crimes against humanity; Kambanda subsequently became the first person ever to be sentenced under the 1948 Convention on the Prevention and Punishment of the Crime of Genocide. By October 1999 a total of 48 people had been indicted by the ICTR, of whom 38 were being detained in custody. Seven people had been sentenced by the Tribunal at April 2000.

President of the ICTR: NAVANETHEM PILLAY (South Africa).

OFFICE FOR THE CO-ORDINATION OF HUMANITARIAN AFFAIRS

Address: United Nations Plaza, New York, NY 10017, USA.

Telephone: (212) 963-1234; **fax:** (212) 963-9489; **e-mail:** ochany@un.org; **internet:** www.reliefweb.int/dha-ol.

The Office was established in January 1998 as part of the UN Secretariat, with a mandate to co-ordinate international humanitarian assistance and to provide policy and other advice on humanitarian issues. It administers the Humanitarian Early Warning System, as well as Integrated Regional Information Networks to monitor the situation in different countries and a Disaster Response System.

Under Secretary-General for Humanitarian Affairs and Emergency Relief Co-ordinator: SERGIO VIEIRA DE MELLO (Brazil).

OFFICE FOR DRUG CONTROL AND CRIME PREVENTION—ODCCP

Address: Vienna International Centre, POB 500, 1400 Vienna, Austria.

Telephone: (1) 26060-4266; **fax:** (1) 26060-5866; **internet:** odccp.org.

The Office was established on 1 November 1997 to strengthen the UN's integrated approach to issues relating to drug control, crime prevention and international terrorism. It comprises two principal components: the United Nations International Drug Control Programme (UNDCP) and the Centre for International Crime Prevention, both headed by the ODCCP Executive Director.

Executive Director: PINO ARLACCHI (Italy).

OFFICE OF THE UNITED NATIONS HIGH COMMISSIONER FOR HUMAN RIGHTS

Address: Palais des Nations, 1211 Geneva 10, Switzerland.

Telephone: (22) 9171873; **fax:** (22) 9170245; **e-mail:** scrt.hchr@unog.ch; **internet:** www.unhchr.ch.

The Office is a body of the UN Secretariat and is the focal point for UN human rights activities. Since September 1997 it has incorporated the Centre for Human Rights. The High Commissioner is the UN official with principal responsibility for UN human rights activities.

High Commissioner: MARY ROBINSON (Ireland).

UNITED NATIONS CENTRE FOR HUMAN SETTLEMENTS—UNCHS (Habitat)

Address: POB 30030, Nairobi, Kenya.

Telephone: (2) 621234; **fax:** (2) 624266; **e-mail:** habitat@unchs.org; **internet:** www.unchs.org.

The Centre was established in 1978 to service the inter-governmental Commission on Human Settlements, and to serve as a focus for human settlements activities in the UN system.

Executive Director: Dr KLAUS TÖPFER (Germany) (acting).

UNITED NATIONS CHILDREN'S FUND—UNICEF

Address: 3 United Nations Plaza, New York, NY 10017, USA.

Telephone: (212) 326-7000; **fax:** (212) 888-7465; **e-mail:** webmaster@unicef.org; **internet:** www.unicef.org.

UNICEF was established in 1946 by the UN General Assembly as the UN International Children's Emergency Fund, to meet the emergency needs of children in post-war Europe and China. In 1950 its mandate was changed to emphasize programmes giving long-term benefits to children everywhere, particularly those in developing countries who are in the greatest need.

Executive Director: CAROL BELLAMY (USA).

Regional Office for Eastern and Southern Africa: POB 44145, Nairobi, Kenya; tel. (2) 621234; fax (2) 622678; e-mail nairobiro@unicef.org.

Regional Office for West and Central Africa: BP 443, Abidjan 04, Côte d'Ivoire; tel. 213131; fax 227607; e-mail wcaro@unicef.org.

UNITED NATIONS CONFERENCE ON TRADE AND DEVELOPMENT—UNCTAD

Address: Palais des Nations, 1211 Geneva 10, Switzerland.

Telephone: (22) 9071234; **fax:** (22) 9070057; **e-mail:** ers@unctad.org; **internet:** www.unctad.org.

UNCTAD was established in 1964. Its role is to promote international trade, particularly that of developing countries, with a view to accelerating economic development. UNCTAD is the principal organ of the UN General Assembly concerned with trade and development, and is the focal point within the UN system for integrated activities relating trade, finance, technology, investment and sustainable development.

Secretary-General: RUBENS RICÚPERO (Brazil).

UNITED NATIONS POPULATION FUND—UNFPA

Address: 220 East 42nd St, New York, NY 10017, USA.

Telephone: (212) 297-5020; **fax:** (212) 557-6416; **internet:** www.unfpa.org.

Created in 1967 as the Trust Fund for Population Activities, the UN Fund for Population Activities (UNFPA) was established as a Fund of the UN General Assembly in 1972 and was made a subsidiary organ of the UN General Assembly in 1979, with the UNDP Governing Council designated as its governing body. In 1987 UNFPA's name was changed to the United Nations Population Fund (retaining the same acronym).

Executive Director: Dr NAFIS SADIK (Pakistan).

UN Specialized Agencies

INTERNATIONAL ATOMIC ENERGY AGENCY—IAEA

Address: Wagramerstrasse 5, Postfach 100, 1400 Vienna, Austria.

Telephone: (1) 26000; **fax:** (1) 26007; **e-mail:** official.mail@iaea.org; **internet:** www.iaea.or.at/.

The Agency was founded in 1957 with the aim of enlarging the contribution of atomic energy to peace, health and prosperity throughout the world, through technical co-operation (assisting research on and practical application of atomic energy for peaceful uses) and safeguards (ensuring that materials and services provided by the Agency are not used for any military purpose).

Director-General: Dr MOHAMMAD EL-BARADEI (Egypt).

INTERNATIONAL CIVIL AVIATION ORGANIZATION—ICAO

Address: 999 rue Université, Montréal, QC H5C 5H7, Canada.

Telephone: (514) 954-8219; **fax:** (514) 954-6077; **e-mail:** icaohq@icao.org; **internet:** www.icao.int.

ICAO was founded in 1947 to develop the techniques of international air navigation and to help in the planning and improvement of international air transport. It is based on the Convention on International Civil Aviation, signed in Chicago, in 1944.

Secretary-General: RENATO CLAUDIO COSTA PEREIRA (Brazil).

Regional Office for Eastern and Southern Africa: POB 46294, Nairobi, Kenya; tel. 2333930; fax 2520199.

Regional Office for Western and Central Africa: BP 2356, Dakar, Senegal; tel. 823-54-52; fax 823-69-26.

INTERNATIONAL LABOUR ORGANIZATION—ILO

Address: 4 route des Morillons, 1211 Geneva 22, Switzerland.

Telephone: (22) 7996111; **fax:** (22) 7998577; **internet:** www.ilo.org.

ILO was founded in 1919 to work for social justice as a basis for lasting peace. It carries out this mandate by promoting decent living standards, satisfactory conditions of work and pay and adequate employment opportunities. Methods of action include the creation of international labour standards; the provision of technical co-operation services; and research and publications on social and labour matters.

Director-General: JUAN O. SOMAVÍA (Chile).

Regional Office for Africa: 01 BP 3960, Abidjan 01, Côte d'Ivoire; tel. 32-27-16.

INTERNATIONAL MARITIME ORGANIZATION—IMO

Address: 4 Albert Embankment, London, SE1 7SR, United Kingdom.

Telephone: (20) 7735-7611; **fax:** (20) 7587-3210; **e-mail:** info@imo.org; **internet:** www.imo.org.

The Inter-Governmental Maritime Consultative Organization (IMCO) began operations in 1959, as a specialized agency of the UN to facilitate co-operation among governments on technical matters affecting international shipping. Its main functions are the achievement of safe and efficient navigation, and the control of pollution caused by ships and craft operating in the marine environment. IMCO became IMO in 1982.

Secretary-General: WILLIAM A. O'NEIL (Canada).

INTERNATIONAL TELECOMMUNICATION UNION—ITU

Address: Place des Nations, 1211 Geneva 20, Switzerland.

Telephone: (22) 7305111; **fax:** (22) 7337256. **e-mail:** itumail@itu.int; **internet:** www.itu.int.

Founded in 1865, ITU became a specialized agency of the UN in 1947. It acts to encourage world co-operation in the use of telecommunication, to promote technical development and to harmonize national policies in the field. Since 1986 ITU has organized an Africa Telecom Forum, held every four years to promote the development of the telecommunications industry in the region.

Secretary-General: YOSHIO UTSUMI (Japan).

UNITED NATIONS EDUCATIONAL, SCIENTIFIC AND CULTURAL ORGANIZATION—UNESCO

Address: 7 place de Fontenoy, 75352 Paris, France.

Telephone: 1-45-68-10-00; **fax:** 1-45-67-16-90; **internet:** www.unesco.org.

UNESCO was established in 1946 'for the purpose of advancing, through the educational, scientific and cultural relations of the peoples of the world, the objectives of international peace and the common welfare of mankind'. UNESCO's main programme activities are concerned with education, science, social sciences, culture and communication, information and informatics. UNESCO is leading a five-year project, concerned with 'communications for peace-building', within the framework of the system-wide Special Initiative on Africa.

Director-General: FEDERICO MAYOR (Spain).

Regional Office for Education in Africa: BP 3311, Dakar, Senegal; tel. 823-50-82; fax 823-83-93; e-mail uhdak@unesco.org.

Regional Office for Science and Technology for Africa: POB 30592, Nairobi, Kenya; tel. (2) 621234; fax (2) 215991; e-mail nairobi@unesco.org.

UNITED NATIONS INDUSTRIAL DEVELOPMENT ORGANIZATION—UNIDO

Address: Vienna International Centre, POB 300, 1400 Vienna, Austria.

Telephone: (1) 260260; **fax:** (1) 2692669; **e-mail:** unido-pinfo@unido.org; **internet:** www.unido.org.

UNIDO began operations in 1967. It aims to promote sustainable and socially equitable industrial development in developing countries and in countries with economies in transition; encourages industrial partnerships between governments and the private sector and acts as a worldwide forum for industrial development; provides technical co-operation services.

Director-General: CARLOS ALFREDO MAGARIÑOS (Argentina).

UNIVERSAL POSTAL UNION—UPU

Address: Case postale, 3000 Berne 15, Switzerland.

Telephone: (31) 3503111; **fax:** (31) 3503110; e-mail info@upu.int; **internet:** www.upu.int.

The General Postal Union was founded by the Treaty of Berne (1874), begining operations in July 1875. Three years later its name was changed to the Universal Postal Union. In 1948 UPU became a specialized agency of the UN. It aims to develop and unify the international postal service, to study problems and to provide training.

Director-General: THOMAS E. LEAVEY (USA).

WORLD INTELLECTUAL PROPERTY ORGANIZATION—WIPO

Address: 34 chemin des Colombettes, 1211 Geneva 20, Switzerland.
Telephone: (22) 3389111; **fax:** (22) 7335428; **e-mail:** wipo.mail@wipo.int; **internet:** www.wipo.int.

WIPO was established in 1970. It became a specialized agency of the UN in 1974 concerned with the protection of intellectual property (e.g. industrial and technical patents and literary copyrights) throughout the world. WIPO formulates and administers treaties embodying international norms and standards of intellectual property, establishes model laws, and facilitates applications for the protection of inventions, trademarks etc. WIPO provides legal and technical assistance to developing countries and countries with economies in transition and advises countries on obligations under the World Trade Organization's agreement on Trade-Related Aspects of Intellectual Property Rights (TRIPS).

Director-General: Dr KAMIL IDRIS (Sudan).

WORLD METEOROLOGICAL ORGANIZATION—WMO

Address: 7 bis ave de la Paix, 1211 Geneva 2, Switzerland.
Telephone: (22) 7308111; **fax:** (22) 7308181; **e-mail:** ipa@gateway.wmo.ch; **internet:** www.wmo.ch.

WMO started its activities in 1951, aiming to improve the exchange of information in the fields of meteorology, climatology and operational hydrology, and its applications.

Secretary-General: Prof. G. O. P. OBASI (Nigeria).

Regional Office for Africa: BP 605, Bujumbura, Burundi; tel. (2) 25237; fax (2) 22990.

United Nations Information Centres

Burkina Faso: BP 135, ave Georges Konseiga, Secteur no 4, Ouagadougou; tel. (3) 306076; fax (3) 311322; e-mail cinu.oui@fasonet.bf. (Also covers Chad, Mali and Niger.)

Burundi: BP 2160, 117 ave de la Révolution, Bujumbura; tel. (2) 225018; fax (2) 241798; e-mail unicbuj@binf.com.

Cameroon: Immeuble Kamden, rue Joseph Clère, BP 836, Yaoundé; tel. 22-50-43; fax 23-51-73; e-mail unic@camnet.com. (Also covers the Central African Republic and Gabon.)

Congo, Democratic Republic: Bâtiment Deuxième République, blvd du 30 juin, BP 7248, Kinshasa; tel. (12) 33431; fax (871) 150-3261; e-mail amisi.ramazani@undp.org.

Congo, Republic: ave Foch, Case ORTF 15, BNP 13210, Brazzaville; tel. 814447; fax 812744.

Eritrea: 5 Andinet St (Airport Rd), POB 5366, Asmara; tel. (1) 182166; fax (1) 181081; e-mail fo.eri@undp.org.

Ethiopia: Africa Hall, POB 3001, Addis Ababa; tel. (1) 515826; fax (1) 510365.

Ghana: Gamel Abdul Nasser/Liberia Rds, POB 2239, Accra; tel. (21) 666851; fax (21) 665578; e-mail unicar@ncs.com.gh. (Also covers Sierra Leone.)

Kenya: United Nations Office, POB 30552, Gigiri, Nairobi; tel. (2) 333930; fax (2) 623927. (Also covers Seychelles and Uganda.)

Lesotho: Letsie Rd, Food Aid Compound, behind Hotel Victoria, POB 301, Maseru 100; tel. 312496; fax 310042; e-mail fo.lso@undp.org.

Madagascar: 22 rue Rainitovo, Antasahavola, BP 1348, Antananarivo; tel. (2) 24115; fax (2) 33315.

Namibia: Private Bag 13351, 372 Independence Ave, Windhoek; tel. (61) 233034; fax (61) 233036; e-mail unic@un.na.

Nigeria: POB 1068, 17 Kingsway Rd, Ikoyi, Lagos; tel. (1) 269-4886; fax (1) 269-1934; e-mail uniclag@unic.org.ng.

Senegal: Immeuble UNESCO, 12 ave Roume, BP 154, Dakar; tel. 823-30-70; fax 822-26-79; e-mail loum@sonatel.senet.net. (Also covers Cape Verde, Côte d'Ivoire, The Gambia, Guinea, Guinea-Bissau and Mauritania.)

South Africa: POB 12677, Metro Park Bldg, 351 Schoeman St, Pretoria; tel. (12) 320-1110; fax (12) 320-1122; e-mail unic@un.org.za.

Sudan: United Nations Compound, Gamma'a Ave, POB 913, Khartoum; tel. (11) 777816; fax (871) 151-6741. (Also covers Somalia.)

Tanzania: Old Boma Bldg, Marogoro Rd/Sokoine Drive, POB 9224, Dar es Salaam; tel. (51) 112923; fax (51) 113272; e-mail fo.tza@undp.org.

Togo: 107 blvd de 13 janvier, BP 911, Lomé; tel. and fax 212306. (Also covers Benin.)

Zambia: POB 32905, Lusaka 10101; tel. (1) 228487; fax (1) 222958; e-mail unic@zamnet.zam. (Also covers Botswana, Malawi and Swaziland.)

Zimbabwe: Zimre Centre, 3rd Floor, L. Takawira St/Union Ave, POB 4408, Harare; tel. (4) 79-15-21; fax (4) 75-04-76.

AFRICAN DEVELOPMENT BANK—ADB

Address: rue Joseph Anoma, 01 BP 1387, Abidjan 01, Côte d'Ivoire.
Telephone: 20-20-44-44; **fax:** 20-20-40-06; **e-mail:** comuadb@ afdb.org; **internet:** www.afdb.org.

Established in 1964, the Bank began operations in July 1966, with the aim of financing economic and social development in African countries.

AFRICAN MEMBERS

Algeria	Equatorial Guinea	Namibia
Angola	Eritrea	Niger
Benin	Ethiopia	Nigeria
Botswana	Gabon	Rwanda
Burkina Faso	The Gambia	São Tomé and
Burundi	Ghana	Príncipe
Cameroon	Guinea	Senegal
Cape Verde	Guinea-Bissau	Seychelles
Central African	Kenya	Sierra Leone
Republic	Lesotho	Somalia
Chad	Liberia	South Africa
Comoros	Libya	Sudan
Congo,	Madagascar	Swaziland
Democratic	Malawi	Tanzania
Republic	Mali	Togo
Congo, Republic	Mauritania	Tunisia
Côte d'Ivoire	Mauritius	Uganda
Djibouti	Morocco	Zambia
Egypt	Mozambique	Zimbabwe

There are also 24 non-African members.

Organization

(July 2000)

BOARD OF GOVERNORS

The highest policy-making body of the Bank. Each member country nominates one Governor, usually its Minister of Finance and Economic Affairs, and an alternate Governor or the Governor of its Central Bank. The Board meets once a year. It elects the Board of Directors and the President.

BOARD OF DIRECTORS

The Board consists of 18 members (of whom six are non-African), elected by the Board of Governors for a term of three years, renewable once; it is responsible for the general operations of the Bank. The Board meets on a weekly basis.

OFFICERS

The President is responsible for the organization and the day-to-day operations of the Bank under guidance of the Board of Directors. The President is elected for a five-year term and serves as the Chairman of the Board of Directors. Three Vice-Presidents are responsible for Operations, Finance and Planning, and Corporate Management.

The Bank's operational activities are divided into five regional departments (for northern, southern, eastern, western and central Africa), departments for central operations and for the private sector, and units for co-operation and for environment and sustainable development.

Executive President and Chairman of Board of Directors: OMAR KABBAJ (Morocco).

Vice-President (Finance and Planning): AHMED M. F. BAHGAT (Egypt).

Vice-President (Administration and Corporate Management): CHANEL BOUCHER (Canada).

Vice-President (Operations): CYRIL ENWEZE (Nigeria).

Secretary-General: PHILIBERT AFRIKA (Rwanda).

FINANCIAL STRUCTURE

The ADB Group of development financing institutions comprises the African Development Fund (ADF) and the Nigeria Trust Fund (NTF), which provide concessional loans, and the African Development Bank itself. The group uses a unit of account (UA), which, at 31 July 2000, was valued at US $1.3134.

The capital stock of the Bank was at first exclusively open for subscription by African countries, with each member's subscription consisting of an equal number of paid-up and callable shares. In 1978, however, the Governors agreed to open the capital stock of the Bank to subscription by non-regional states on the basis of

nine principles aimed at maintaining the African character of the institution. The decision was finally ratified in May 1982, and the participation of non-regional countries became effective on 30 December. It was agreed that African members should still hold two-thirds of the share capital, that all loan operations should be restricted to African members, and that the Bank's President should always be an African national. In May 1998 the Board of Governors approved an increase in capital of 35%, and resolved that the non-African members' share of the capital be increased from 33.3% to 40%. In 1998 the ADB's authorized capital was US $21,810m. At the end of 1998 subscribed capital was $22,375m. (of which the paid-up portion was $2,765m.).

Activities

At the end of 1998 total loan and grant approvals by the ADB Group since the beginning of its operations amounted to US $34,584m. Of that amount agriculture received the largest proportion of assistance (23.1%), while public utilities received 21.0%, transport 16.3%, industry 15.8%, multi-sector activities 13.7%, and social projects 10.1%. In 1998 the group approved 133 loans and grants amounting to $1,742m.

A new credit policy, adopted in May 1995, effectively disqualified 39 low-income regional members, deemed to be non-creditworthy, from receiving non-concessional ADB financing, in an attempt to reduce the accumulation of arrears. The ADB Group estimated that its capital requirements for the period 1997–2001 would amount to US $46,500m. to allow for greater flexibility in its lending. During 1996 the Bank supported international efforts to address the problem of heavily indebted poor countries (HIPCs), and agreed to participate in a six-year initiative which aimed to encourage economic prospects in those countries while reducing outstanding debt and preventing its recurrence (see World Bank, p. 100). The ADB's initial contribution to the HIPC initiative, approved in April 1997, was an amount up to UA 230m., to be generated over the period 1997–2003. In September 1997 the Bank approved an initial UA 133m. to establish a Supplementary Financing Mechanism, which aimed to assist countries eligible for ADF funds to meet interest payments on outstanding Bank debt.

The ADB contributed funds for the establishment in 1986 of the Africa Project Development Facility, which assists the private sector in Africa by providing advisory services and finance for entrepreneurs: it is managed by the International Finance Corporation (IFC—see p. 103). In 1989 the ADB, in co-ordination with IFC and UNDP, created the African Management Services Company (AMSCo) which provides management support and training to private companies in Africa.

The Bank also provides technical assistance to regional member countries in the form of experts' services, pre-investment feasibility studies, and staff training; much of this assistance is financed through bilateral aid funds contributed by non-African member states. The Bank's African Development Institute provides training for officials of regional member countries in order to enhance the management of Bank-financed projects and, more broadly, to strengthen national capacities for promoting sustainable development. In 1990 the ADB established the African Business Round Table (ABR), which is composed of the chief executives of Africa's leading corporations. The ABR aims to strengthen Africa's private sector, promote intra-African trade and investment, and attract foreign investment to Africa. The ABR is chaired by the ADB's Executive President. At its fourth annual meeting, held in Arusha, Tanzania, in March 1994, the ABR resolved to establish an African Investment Bank, in co-operation with the ADB, which was to provide financial services to African companies. In November 1999 a Joint Africa Institute, which had been established by the Bank, the World Bank and the IMF, was formally inaugurated in Abidjan, Côte d'Ivoire. The Institute aimed to enhance training opportunities in economic policy and management and to strengthen capacity-building in the region.

In 1990 a Memorandum of Understanding for the Reinforcement of Co-operation between the Organization of African Unity (OAU—q.v.), the UN's Economic Commission for Africa (q.v.) and the ADB was signed by the three organizations. A joint secretariat supports co-operation activities between the organizations.

AFRICAN DEVELOPMENT BANK (ADB)

The Bank makes loans at a variable rate of interest, which is adjusted twice a year (the rate was 7.39% per year at December 1997), plus a commitment fee of 0.75%. Loan approvals amounted to US $931.9m. for 18 loans in 1998. Since October 1997 new fixed and floating rate loans have also been made available.

Group Loan and Grant Approvals by Country
(millions of UA)

Country	1997	1998	Cumulative total*
Algeria	—	156.71	1,493.21
Angola	—	—	294.14
Benin	19.33	—	265.26
Botswana	—	—	324.93
Burkina Faso	32.76	16.37	294.89
Burundi	—	8.59	275.96
Cameroon	29.40	21.46	555.40
Cape Verde	8.47	3.00	148.09
Central African Republic	—	—	139.39
Chad	37.22	12.41	272.54
Comoros	—	—	64.74
Congo, Democratic Republic	—	—	936.20
Congo, Republic	—	—	277.83
Côte d'Ivoire	6.07	81.09	998.88
Djibouti	—	7.05	90.95
Egypt	44.47	35.44	1,434.69
Equatorial Guinea	—	2.20	67.19
Eritrea	22.49	1.07	37.59
Ethiopia	28.00	118.66	1,044.27
Gabon	19.81	17.11	596.81
Gambia	11.03	0.76	169.75
Ghana	58.00	16.30	571.31
Guinea	29.94	0.85	457.18
Guinea Bissau	18.50	—	157.26
Kenya	1.10	25.69	510.79
Lesotho	0.80	13.30	259.80
Liberia	—	—	153.25
Madagascar	34.61	26.61	375.41
Malawi	39.08	46.07	485.51
Mali	61.13	1.40	389.47
Mauritania	4.02	2.18	240.24
Mauritius	9.30	—	151.95
Morocco	151.48	227.20	2,690.48
Mozambique	76.00	30.10	598.96
Namibia	—	28.11	55.03
Niger	0.70	46.08	210.50
Nigeria	—	—	1,902.87
Rwanda	1.50	46.64	278.41
São Tomé and Príncipe	1.88	—	89.58
Senegal	20.00	11.09	409.14
Seychelles	8.36	—	82.40
Sierra Leone	12.15	—	158.75
Somalia	—	—	150.40
South Africa	114.20	—	114.20
Sudan	—	—	349.80
Swaziland	—	—	188.93
Tanzania	108.16	19.43	607.06
Togo	12.20	1.20	158.50
Tunisia	168.46	104.67	2,156.58
Uganda	27.77	34.33	541.20
Zambia	17.78	1.87	538.78
Zimbabwe	80.57	—	607.92
Total	1,316.74	1,165.04	25,424.38

* Since the initial operation of the three institutions (1967 for ADB, 1974 for ADF and 1976 for NTF).

AFRICAN DEVELOPMENT FUND (ADF)

The Fund commenced operations in 1974. It grants interest-free loans to low-income African countries for projects with repayment over 50 years (including a 10-year grace period) and with a service charge of 0.75% per annum. Grants for project feasibility studies are made to the poorest countries.

In 1987 donor countries agreed on a fifth replenishment of the Fund's resources, amounting to US $2,800m. for 1988–90. In future 85% of available resources was to be reserved for the poorest countries (those with annual GDP per caput of less than $510, at 1985 prices). In 1991 a sixth replenishment of the Fund's resources amounting to $3,340m. was approved for 1991–93. Negotiations for the seventh replenishment of the Fund's resources commenced in May 1993. However, in May 1994, donor countries withheld any new funds owing to dissatisfaction with the Bank's governance. In May 1996, following the implementation of various institutional reforms to strengthen the Bank's financial management and deci-sion-making capabilities and to reduce its administrative costs, an agreement was concluded on the seventh replenishment of the ADF. Donor countries pledged some $2,690m. for the period 1996–98. An additional allocation of $420m. was endorsed at a special donors' meeting held in Osaka, Japan, in June. The ADF aimed to offer concessional assistance to 42 African countries over the period

Summary of Bank Group Activities (US $ million)

	1997	1998	Cumulative total*
ADB loans			
Number	21	18	772
Amount approved	798.50	931.92	21,864.60
Disbursements	927.23	618.96	14,862.21
ADF loans and grants			
Number	91	115	1,404
Amount approved	1,081.53	810.49	12,399.02
Disbursements	646.07	623.88	8,235.53
NTF loans			
Number	—	—	58
Amount approved	—	—	320.27
Disbursements	4.86	6.73	217.24
Group total			
Number	112	133	2,234
Amount approved	1,880.03	1,742.41	34,583.89
Disbursements	1,578.16	1,249.58	23,314.99

* Since the initial operations of the three institutions (1967 for ADB, 1974 for ADF and 1976 for NTF).

Source: *Annual Report 1998*.

Group Loan and Grant Approvals by Sector, 1996–97
(millions of UA)

Sector	1996	%	1997	%
Agriculture	72.45	13.0	165.11	12.5
Transport	110.34	19.8	181.12	13.8
Public utilities	75.60	13.5	133.62	10.1
Industry	117.16	21.0	229.18	17.4
Social	23.80	4.3	178.38	13.5
Multisector	159.19	28.5	429.30	32.6
Total	558.54	100.0	1,316.74	100.0

1996–98. In January 1999 negotiations on the eighth replenishment of the Fund were concluded with an agreement to provide additional resources amounting to $3,437m. The replenishment was approved by the Board of Governors in May.

In 1998 115 ADF loans and grants were approved amounting to US $810m.

NIGERIA TRUST FUND (NTF)

The Agreement establishing the Nigeria Trust Fund was signed in February 1976 by the Bank and the Government of Nigeria. The Fund is administered by the Bank and its loans are granted for up to 25 years, including grace periods of up to five years, and carry 0.75% commitment charges and 4% interest charges. The loans are intended to provide financing for projects in co-operation with other lending institutions. The Fund also aims to promote the private sector and trade between African countries by providing information on African and international financial institutions able to finance African trade.

In 1996 the fund approved one loan amounting to US $8.63m., bringing the total amount committed since operations began to $320.27m. for 58 loans. There were no NTF loan approvals in 1997 and 1998.

ASSOCIATED INSTITUTIONS

The ADB actively participated in the establishment of five associated institutions:

Africa Reinsurance Corporation—Africa-Re: Reinsurance House, 46 Marina, PMB 12765, Lagos, Nigeria; tel. (1) 2663323; fax (1) 2668802; e-mail africare@hyperia.com; f. 1977; started operations in 1978; its purpose is to foster the development of the insurance and reinsurance industry in Africa and to promote the growth of national and regional underwriting capacities; auth. cap. US $50m., of which the ADB holds 10%. There are 12 directors, one appointed by the Bank. Mems: 41 countries, the ADB, and some 90 insurance and reinsurance cos. Man. Dir BAKARY KAMARA.

African Export-Import Bank—Afreximbank: POB 404 Gezira, Cairo 11568; World Trade Centre Bldg, 1191 Corniche el-Nil, Cairo 11221, Egypt; tel. (2) 5780282; fax (2) 5780277; e-mail mail@ afreximbank.com; internet www.afreximbank.com; f. 1993; aims to increase the volume of African exports and to expand intra-African trade by financing exporters and importers directly and indirectly through trade finance institutions, such as commercial banks; auth. cap. US $750m.; paid-up cap. $145.4m. (Dec. 1998). Pres. CHRISTO-PHER C. EDORDU; Exec. Vice-Pres. JEAN-LOUIS EKRA. Publ. *Annual Report*.

Association of African Development Finance Institutions—AADFI: c/o ADB, 01 BP 1387, Abidjan 01, Côte d'Ivoire; tel. 20-40-90; fax 22-73-44; e-mail adfi@africaonline.co.ci; f. 1975; aims to promote co-operation among financial institutions in the region in matters relating to economic and social development, research, project design, financing and the exchange of information. Mems: 92 in 43 African and non-African countries. Pres. GERSHOM MUMBA; Sec.-Gen. Dr MAGATTE WADE.

Shelter-Afrique (Société pour l'habitat et le logement territorial en Afrique): Longonot Rd, POB 41479, Nairobi, Kenya; tel. (2) 722305; fax (2) 722024; e-mail info@shelter.co.ke; f. 1982 to finance housing in ADB mem. countries. Share cap. is US $300m., held by 40 African countries, the ADB, Africa-Re and the Commonwealth Development Corpn; Chair. Paul M. N'KOUE-N'KONGO; Man. Dir P. M'BAYE.

Société Internationale Financière pour les Investissements et le Développement en Afrique—SIFIDA: 22 rue François-Perréard, BP 310, 1225 Chêne-Bourg/Geneva, Switzerland; tel. (22) 8692000; fax (22) 8692001; e-mail headoffice@sifida.com; internet www.sifida.com; f. 1970 by 120 financial and industrial institutions, including the ADB and the IFC. Following a restructuring at the end of 1995, the main shareholders are the Banque Nationale de Paris (BNP), SFOM (itself owned by BNP and Dresdner Bank) and the six banking affiliates of BNP/SFOM in West and Central Africa. SIFIDA is active in the fields of project and trade finance in Africa and also provides financial advisory services, notably in the context of privatizations and debt conversion; auth. cap. US $75m., subscribed cap. $12.5m. Chair. VIVIEN LÉVY-GARBOUA; Man. Dir PHILIPPE SÉCHAUD. Publ. *African Banking Directory* (annually).

Publications

Annual Report.

ADB Today (every 2 months).

African Development Report (annually).

African Development Review.

Basic Information (annually).

Economic Research Papers.

Quarterly Operational Summary.

Statistical Handbook (annually).

Summaries of operations in each member country and various background documents.

COMMON MARKET FOR EASTERN AND SOUTHERN AFRICA—COMESA

Address: COMESA Centre, Ben Bella Rd, POB 30051, 10101 Lusaka, Zambia.

Telephone: (1) 229726; **fax:** (1) 225107; **e-mail:** comesa@comesa.zm; **internet:** www.comesa.int.

COMESA was formally inaugurated in 1994 as a successor to the Preferential Trade Area for Eastern and Southern Africa (PTA), which was established in 1981.

MEMBERS

Angola	Mauritius
Burundi	Namibia
Comoros	Rwanda
Congo, Democratic Republic	Seychelles
Djibouti	Sudan
Egypt	Swaziland
Eritrea	Tanzania*
Ethiopia	Uganda
Kenya	Zambia
Madagascar	Zimbabwe
Malawi	

* In July 1999 announced intention to withdraw membership.

Organization

(July 2000)

AUTHORITY

The Authority of the Common Market is the supreme policy organ of COMESA, comprising heads of state or of government of member countries. The inaugural meeting of the Authority took place in Lilongwe, Malawi, in December 1994. The fifth summit meeting was held in Grand Baie, Mauritius, in May 2000.

COUNCIL OF MINISTERS

Each member government appoints a minister to participate in the Council. The Council monitors COMESA activities, including supervision of the Secretariat, recommends policy direction and development, and reports to the Authority.

A Committee of Governors of Central Banks advises the Authority and the Council of Ministers on monetary and financial matters.

COURT OF JUSTICE

The COMESA treaty envisaged the establishment of a sub-regional Court of Justice, to replace the former PTA Tribunal, with authority to settle disputes between member states and to adjudicate on matters concerning the interpretation of the treaty. In June 1998 COMESA heads of state announced the appointment of seven judges to serve in the Court.

President: JOSEPHAT KANYWANYI (Tanzania).

SECRETARIAT

In 1998 the administrative structure of COMESA was undergoing a process of restructuring, according to which the existing 12 divisional areas were to be consolidated into the following four divisions: Trade, customs and monetary affairs; Investment promotion and private sector development; Infrastructure development; and Information.

Secretary-General: J. E. O. (ERASTUS) MWENCHA (Kenya).

Activities

The COMESA treaty was signed by member states of the PTA in November 1993 and was scheduled to come into effect on being ratified by 10 countries. COMESA formally succeeded the PTA in December 1994 (by which time it had received 12 ratifications), with the aim of strengthening the process of regional economic integration that had been initiated under the PTA, in order to help member states achieve sustainable economic growth.

COMESA aims to establish a free-trade area by 31 October 2000, requiring full liberalization of trading practices, including the elimination of non-tariff barriers, to ensure the free movement of goods, services and capital within the Common Market. In April 1997 COMESA heads of state agreed that a common external tariff would be implemented by 2004, to strengthen the establishment of a regional customs union, with a zero tariff on products originating from within the Common Market. COMESA aimed to formulate a common investment procedure to promote domestic, cross-border and direct foreign investment by ensuring the free movement of capital, services and labour. In May 1999 14 countries were reported to have reduced tariff rates on goods originating within the Common Market by 60%–90%. During that month heads of state agreed to establish a Free Trade Area Committee, comprising representatives of the Democratic Republic of the Congo, Egypt, Kenya, Malawi, Mauritius, Uganda, Zambia and Zimbabwe, to facilitate and co-ordinate preparations for the establishment of the free-trade zone.

The PTA aimed to facilitate intra-regional trade by establishing a clearing house to deal with credit arrangements and balance of payments issues. The clearing house became operational in February 1984 using the unit of account of the PTA (UAPTA) as its currency. (The UAPTA was valued at the rate of the IMF special drawing rights.) The clearing house, based in Harare, Zimbabwe, remained an integral part of the COMESA infrastructure, although its role was diminished by the liberalization of foreign exchange markets in the majority of member countries. In April 1997 the Authority endorsed a proposal to replace UAPTA with a COMESA dollar (CMD), to be equivalent to the value of the US currency. An Automated System of Customs Data (ASYCUDA) has been established to facilitate customs administration in all COMESA member states. Through support for capacity-building activities and the establishment of other specialized institutions (see below) COMESA aims to reinforce its objectives of regional integration.

Preparations for the establishment of a COMESA Telecommunications Company were under way in 2000.

Co-operation programmes have been implemented by COMESA in the industrial, agricultural, energy and transport and communications sectors. A regional food security programme aimed to ensure adequate food supplies at all times. In 1997 COMESA Heads of State advocated that the food sector be supported by the immediate implementation of an irrigation action plan for the region. The organization also supports the establishment of common agricultural standards and phytosanitary regulations throughout the region in order to stimulate trade in food crops. Other initiatives include a road customs declaration document, a regional customs bond guarantee scheme, third party motor vehicle insurance scheme and travellers cheques in the UAPTA unit of currency. A Trade Information Network, established under the PTA to disseminate information on the production and marketing of goods manufactured and traded in the region, was scheduled to be transformed into the COMESA Information Network (COMNET). The first meeting of representatives of business communities in COMESA countries was held in November 1997, and the first COMESA trade fair was held in Nairobi, Kenya, in May 1999. The first COMESA economic forum was held in Cairo, Egypt in February 2000.

Since its establishment there have been concerns on the part of member states, as well as other regional non-member countries, in particular South Africa, of adverse rivalry between COMESA and the Southern African Development Community (SADC, q.v.) and of a duplication of roles. In December 1996 and January 1997 respectively, Lesotho and Mozambique suspended their membership of COMESA and announced their intention to withdraw from the organization owing to concerns that their continued participation in COMESA was incompatible with their SADC membership. Lesotho subsequently terminated its membership. In July 1999 Tanzania declared its intention to withdraw from COMESA, reportedly in opposition to further proposed tariff reductions.

COMESA INSTITUTIONS

COMESA Association of Commercial Banks: 101 Union Ave, POB 2940, Harare, Zimbabwe; tel. (4) 793911; fax (4) 730819; aims to strengthen co-operation between banks in the region; organizes training activities; conducts studies to harmonize banking laws and operations. Mems: commercial banking orgs in Burundi, Kenya, Malawi, Sudan, Tanzania, Uganda.

COMESA Leather and Leather Products Institute—LLPI: POB 5538, Addis Ababa, Ethiopia; tel (1) 510361; fax (1) 615755; e-mail comesa.llpi@telecom.net.et; internet www.leathernet.com/comesa/llpi; f. 1990 as the PTA Leather Institute. Mems: Govts of 17 COMESA mem. states; Dir Dr ROBERT ARUNGA.

COMESA Metallurgical Technology Centre: c/o 101 Union Ave, Harare, Zimbabwe; tel. (1) 793911; fax (1) 730819; conducts research, testing and evaluation of raw materials, training and the exchange of appropriate technologies in order to promote the local mineral resources sectors.

Compagnie de réassurance de la Zone d'échanges préférentiels—ZEP-RE (PTA Reinsurance Co): Anniversary Towers, University Way, POB 42769, Nairobi, Kenya; tel. (2) 212792; fax (2) 224102; e-mail zep-re@africaonline.co.ke; f. 1992 (began operations on 1 January 1993); provides local reinsurance services and training to personnel in the insurance industry; auth. cap. CMD 27.3m.; Man. Dir S. M. LUBASI.

Eastern and Southern African Trade and Development Bank: NSSF Bldg, 23rd Floor, Bishop's Rd, POB 48596, Nairobi, Kenya; tel. (2) 712260; fax (2) 711510; e-mail infoserv@ptabank.co.ke; internet www.ptabank.co.ke; f. 1983 as PTA Development Bank; aims to mobilize resources and finance COMESA activities to foster regional integration; promotes investment and co-financing within the region; shareholders 16 COMESA mem. states and the African Development Bank; cap. p.u. SDR 63.7m. (Dec. 1998); Pres. Dr MICHAEL GONDWE (acting).

Federation of National Associations of Women in Business — FEMCOM: c/o COMESA Secretariat; f. 1993 to provide links between female business executives throughout the region and to promote greater awareness of relevant issues at policy level. FEMCOM was to be supported by a Revolving Fund for Women in Business.

Finance

COMESA is financed by member states. Its administrative budget for 1996 amounted to US $4m. In April 1997 COMESA heads of state concluded that the organization's activities were being undermined by lack of resources, and determined to expel countries which fail to pay membership dues over a five-year period.

Publications

Annual Report of the Council of Ministers.

Asycuda Newsletter.

COMESA Journal.

COMESA Trade Directory (annually).

COMESA Trade Information Newsletter (monthly).

Demand/supply surveys, catalogues and reports.

THE COMMONWEALTH

Address: Commonwealth Secretariat, Marlborough House, Pall Mall, London, SW1Y 5HX, United Kingdom.

Telephone: (20) 7839-3411; **fax:** (20) 7930-0827; **e-mail:** info@commonwealth.int; **internet:** www.thecommonwealth.org.

The Commonwealth is a voluntary association of 54 independent states, comprising nearly one-quarter of the world's population. It includes the United Kingdom and most of its former dependencies, and former dependencies of Australia and New Zealand (themselves Commonwealth countries). All Commonwealth countries accept Queen Elizabeth II as the symbol of the free association of the independent member nations and as such the Head of the Commonwealth.

MEMBERS IN AFRICA SOUTH OF THE SAHARA

Botswana	Mauritius	Swaziland
Camerooon	Mozambique	Tanzania
The Gambia	Namibia	Uganda
Ghana	Nigeria	Zambia
Kenya	Seychelles	Zimbabwe
Lesotho	Sierra Leone	
Malawi	South Africa	

Dependencies

British Indian Ocean Territory
St Helena
  Ascension
  Tristan da Cunha

Organization

(July 2000)

The Commonwealth is not a federation: there is no central government nor are there any rigid contractual obligations such as bind members of the United Nations.

The Commonwealth has no written constitution but its members subscribe to the ideals of the Declaration of Commonwealth Principles (see below) unanimously approved by a meeting of heads of government in Singapore in 1971. Members also approved the 1977 statement on apartheid in sport (the Gleneagles Agreement); the 1979 Lusaka Declaration on Racism and Racial Prejudice (see below); the 1981 Melbourne Declaration on relations between developed and developing countries; the 1983 New Delhi Statement on Economic Action; the 1983 Goa Declaration on International Security; the 1985 Nassau Declaration on World Order; the Commonwealth Accord on Southern Africa (1985); the 1987 Vancouver Declaration on World Trade; the Okanagan Statement and Programme of Action on Southern Africa (1987); the Langkawi Declaration on the Environment (1989); the Kuala Lumpur Statement on Southern Africa (1989); the Harare Commonwealth Declaration (1991) (see below); the Ottawa Declaration on Women and Structural Adjustment (1991); the Limassol Statement on the Uruguay Round of multilateral trade negotiations (1993); the Millbrook Commonwealth Action Programme on the Harare Declaration (1995); and the Edinburgh Commonwealth Economic Declaration (1997).

MEETINGS OF HEADS OF GOVERNMENT

Meetings are private and informal and operate not by voting but by consensus. The emphasis is on consultation and exchange of views for co-operation. A communiqué is issued at the end of every meeting. Meetings are held every two years in different capitals in the Commonwealth. The 1999 meeting was held in Durban, South Africa, in November, and the 2001 meeting was to be held in Australia.

OTHER CONSULTATIONS

Meetings at ministerial and official level are also held regularly. Since 1959 finance ministers have met in a Commonwealth country in the week prior to the annual meetings of the IMF and the World Bank. Meetings on education, legal, women's and youth affairs are held at ministerial level every three years. Ministers of health hold annual meetings, with major meetings every three years, and ministers of agriculture meet every two years. Ministers of trade, labour and employment, industry, science and the environment also hold periodic meetings.

Senior officials—cabinet secretaries, permanent secretaries to heads of government and others—meet regularly in the year between meetings of heads of government to provide continuity and to exchange views on various developments.

COMMONWEALTH SECRETARIAT

The Secretariat, established by Commonwealth heads of government in 1965, operates as an international organization at the service of all Commonwealth countries. It organizes consultations between governments and runs programmes of co-operation. Meetings of heads of government, ministers and senior officials decide these programmes and provide overall direction.

The Secretariat is headed by a secretary-general (elected by heads of government), assisted by three deputy secretaries-general. One deputy is responsible for political affairs, one for economic and social affairs, and one for development co-operation (including the Commonwealth Fund for Technical Co-operation—see below). The Secretariat comprises 12 Divisions in the fields of political affairs; legal and constitutional affairs; information and public affairs; administration; economic affairs; human resource development; gender and youth affairs; science and technology; economic and legal advisory services; export and industrial development; management and training services; and general technical assistance services. It also includes a non-governmental organizations desk and a unit for strategic planning and evaluation.

Secretary-General: DONALD (DON) C. MCKINNON (New Zealand).

Deputy Secretary-General (Political): KRISHNAN SRINIVASAN (India).

Deputy Secretary-General (Economic and Social): Dame VERONICA SUTHERLAND (United Kingdom).

Deputy Secretary-General (Development Co-operation): (vacant).

Activities

INTERNATIONAL AFFAIRS

In October 1991 heads of government, meeting in Harare, Zimbabwe, issued the Harare Commonwealth Declaration, in which they reaffirmed their commitment to the Commonwealth Principles declared in 1971, and stressed the need to promote sustainable development and the alleviation of poverty. The Declaration placed emphasis on the promotion of democracy and respect for human rights and resolved to strengthen the Commonwealth's capacity to assist countries in entrenching democratic practices. The meeting also welcomed the political reforms introduced by the South African Government to end the system of apartheid and urged all South African political parties to commence negotiations on a new constitution as soon as possible. The meeting endorsed measures on the phased removal of punitive measures against South Africa. 'People-to-people' sanctions (including consular and visa restrictions, cultural and scientific boycotts and restrictions on tourism promotion) were removed immediately, with economic sanctions to remain in place until a constitution for a new democratic, non-racial state had been agreed. A sports boycott, first imposed in 1977, would continue to be repealed on a sport-by-sport basis, as each sport in South Africa became integrated and non-racial. The embargo on the supply of armaments would remain in place until a post-apartheid, democratic regime had been firmly established in South Africa. In December a group of six eminent Commonwealth citizens was dispatched to observe multi-party negotiations on the future of South Africa and to assist the process where possible. In October 1992, in a fresh attempt to assist the South African peace process, a Commonwealth team of 18 observers was sent to monitor political violence in the country. A second phase of the Commonwealth

Mission to South Africa (COMSA) began in February 1993, comprising 10 observers with backgrounds in policing, the law, politics and public life. COMSA issued a report in May in which it urged a concerted effort to build a culture of political tolerance in South Africa. In a report on its third phase, issued in December, COMSA appealed strongly to all political parties to participate in the transitional arrangements leading to democratic elections. In October the Commonwealth heads of government, meeting in Limassol, Cyprus, agreed that a democratic and non-racial South Africa would be invited to join the organization. They endorsed the removal of all economic sanctions against South Africa, but agreed to retain the arms embargo until a post-apartheid, democratic government had been established.

In November 1995 Commonwealth heads of government, convened in New Zealand, formulated and adopted the Millbrook Commonwealth Action Programme on the Harare Declaration, to promote adherence by member countries to the fundamental principles of democracy and human rights (as proclaimed in the 1991 Declaration). The Programme incorporated a framework of measures to be pursued in support of democratic processes and institutions, and actions to be taken in response to violations of the Harare Declaration principles, in particular the unlawful removal of a democratically-elected government. A Commonwealth Ministerial Action Group on the Harare Declaration (CMAG) was to be established to implement this process and to assist the member country involved to comply with the Harare principles. On the basis of this Programme, the leaders suspended Nigeria from the Commonwealth with immediate effect, following the execution by that country's military Government of nine environmental and human rights protesters and a series of other violations of human rights. The meeting determined to expel Nigeria from the Commonwealth if no 'demonstrable progress' had been made towards the establishment of a democratic authority by the time of the next summit meeting. In addition, the Programme formulated measures to promote sustainable development in member countries, which was considered to be an important element in sustaining democracy, and to facilitate consensus-building within the international community. Earlier in the meeting a statement was issued declaring the 'overwhelming majority' of Commonwealth governments to be opposed to nuclear-testing programmes being undertaken in the South Pacific region. However, in view of events in Nigeria, the issue of nuclear testing and disagreement among member countries did not assume the significance anticipated.

In December 1995 CMAG convened for its inaugural meeting in London. The Group, comprising the ministers of foreign affairs of Canada, Ghana, Jamaica, Malaysia, New Zealand, South Africa, the United Kingdom and Zimbabwe, commenced by considering efforts to restore democratic government in the three Commonwealth countries under military regimes, i.e. The Gambia, Nigeria and Sierra Leone. At the second meeting of the Group, in April 1996, ministers commended the conduct of presidential and parliamentary elections in Sierra Leone and the announcement by The Gambia's military leaders to proceed with a transition to civilian rule. In June a three-member CMAG delegation visited The Gambia to reaffirm Commonwealth support of the transition process in that country and to identify possible areas of further Commonwealth assistance. In August the Gambian authorities issued a decree removing the ban on political activities and parties, although shortly afterwards prohibited certain parties and candidates involved in political life prior to the military take-over from contesting the elections. CMAG recommended that in such circumstances there should be no Commonwealth observers sent to either the presidential or parliamentary elections, which were held in September 1996 and January 1997 respectively. Following the restoration of a civilian Government in early 1997, CMAG requested the Commonwealth Secretary-General to extend technical assistance to The Gambia in order to consolidate the democratic transition process. In April 1996 it was noted that the human rights situation in Nigeria had continued to deteriorate. CMAG, having pursued unsuccessful efforts to initiate dialogue with the Nigerian authorities, outlined a series of punitive and restrictive measures (including visa restrictions on members of the administration, a cessation of sporting contacts and an embargo on the export of armaments) that it would recommend for collective Commonwealth action in order to exert further pressure for reform in Nigeria. Following a meeting of a high-level delegation of the Nigerian Government and CMAG in June, the Group agreed to postpone the implementation of the sanctions, pending progress on the dialogue. (Canada, however, determined, unilaterally, to impose the measures with immediate effect; the United Kingdom did so in accordance with a decision of the European Union to implement limited sanctions against Nigeria.) A proposed CMAG mission to Nigeria was postponed in August, owing to restrictions imposed by the military authorities on access to political detainees and other civilian activists in that country. In September the Group agreed to proceed with the visit and to delay further a decision on the implementation of sanction measures. CMAG, without the participation of the representative of the Canadian Government, undertook its ministerial mission in November. In July 1997 the Group reiterated the Commonwealth Secretary-General's condemnation of a military coup in Sierra Leone in May, and decided to suspend that country's participation in meetings of the Commonwealth pending the restoration of a democratic government.

In October 1997 Commonwealth heads of government, meeting in Edinburgh, the United Kingdom, endorsed CMAG's recommendation that the imposition of sanctions against Nigeria be held in abeyance pending the scheduled completion of a transition programme towards democracy by October 1998. It was also agreed that CMAG be formally constituted as a permanent organ to investigate abuses of human rights throughout the Commonwealth. Jamaica and South Africa were to be replaced as members of CMAG by Barbados and Botswana, respectively.

In March 1998 CMAG, at its ninth meeting, commended the efforts of the Economic Community of West African States in restoring the democratically-elected Government of President Ahmed Tejan Kabbah in Sierra Leone, and agreed to remove all restrictions on Sierra Leone's participation in Commonwealth activities. Later in that month, a representative mission of CMAG visited Sierra Leone to express its support for Kabbah's administration and to consider the country's needs in its process of reconstruction. At the CMAG meeting held in October members agreed that Sierra Leone should no longer be considered under the Group's mandate; however, they urged the Secretary-General to continue to assist that country in the process of national reconciliation and to facilitate negotiations with opposition forces to ensure a lasting cease-fire.

In April 1998 the Nigerian military leader, Gen. Sani Abacha, confirmed his intention to conduct a presidential election in August, but indicated that, following an agreement with other political organizations, he was to be the sole candidate. In June, however, Abacha died suddenly. His successor, Gen. Abdulsalam Abubakar, immediately released several prominent political prisoners, and in early July agreed to meet with the Secretaries-General of the UN and the Commonwealth to discuss the release of the imprisoned opposition leader, Chief Moshood Abiola. Abubakar also confirmed his intention to abide by the programme for transition to civilian rule by October. In mid-July, however, shortly before he was to have been liberated, Abiola died. The Commonwealth Secretary-General subsequently endorsed a new transition programme, which provided for the election of a civilian leader in May 1999. In October 1998 CMAG, convened for its 10th formal meeting, acknowledged Abubakar's efforts towards restoring a democratic government and recommended that member states begin to remove sanctions against Nigeria and that it resume participation in certain Commonwealth activities. The Commonwealth Secretary-General subsequently announced a programme of technical assistance to support Nigeria in the planning and conduct of democratic elections. Staff teams from the Commonwealth Secretariat observed local government, and state and governorship elections, held in December and in January 1999, respectively. A 23-member Commonwealth Observer Group was also dispatched to Nigeria to participate in international and local efforts to monitor the preparations and conduct of legislative and presidential elections, held in late February. While the Group reported several deficiencies and irregularities in the conduct of the polling, it confirmed that, in general, the conditions had existed for free and fair elections and that the elections were a legitimate basis for the transition of power to a democratic, civilian government. In April CMAG voted to readmit Nigeria to full membership on 29 May, upon the installation of the new civilian administration.

In 1999 the Commonwealth Secretary-General appointed a Special Envoy to broker an agreement in order to end a civil dispute in Honiara, Solomon Islands. An accord was signed in late June, and it was envisaged that the Commonwealth would monitor its implementation. In October a Commonwealth Multinational Police Peace Monitoring Group was stationed in Solomon Islands; this was superseded by a Commonwealth Multinational Police Assistance Force in January 2000. Also in June 1999 an agreement was concluded between opposing political groups in Zanzibar, having been facilitated by the good offices of the Secretary-General; by mid-2000, however, this had not been fully implemented.

In mid-October 1999 a special meeting of CMAG was convened to consider the overthrow of the democratically-elected Government in Pakistan in a military coup. The meeting condemned the action as a violation of Commonwealth principles and urged the new authorities to declare a timetable for the return to democratic rule. CMAG also resolved to send a four-member delegation, comprising the ministers of foreign affairs of Barbados, Canada, Ghana and Malaysia, to discuss this future course of action with the military regime. Pakistan was suspended from participation in meetings of the Commonwealth with immediate effect. The suspension, pending the restoration of a democratic government, was endorsed by heads of government, meeting in November, who requested that CMAG keep the situation in Pakistan under review. At the meeting, held in Durban, South Africa, CMAG was reconstituted to comprise the

ministers of foreign affairs of Australia, Bangladesh, Barbados, Botswana, Canada, Malaysia, Nigeria and the United Kingdom. It was agreed that no country would serve for more than two consecutive two-year terms. CMAG was requested to remain actively involved in the post-conflict development and rehabilitation of Sierra Leone and the process of consolidating peace. It was also urged to monitor persistent violations of the Harare Declaration principles in all countries. Its future mandate was to be considered by a Commonwealth High Level Group, which was established by heads of government to review the role and activities of the Commonwealth.

In June 2000, following the overthrow in May of the Fijian Government by a group of armed civilians, and the subsequent illegal detention of members of the elected administration, CMAG suspended Fiji's participation in meetings of the Commonwealth pending the restoration of democratic rule. In June CMAG also determined to send a Commonwealth mission to Solomon Islands, whose Prime Minister had been seized by armed militants; the mission was mandated to mediate negotiations between the opposing parties, to convey the Commonwealth's concern and to offer assistance.

Political Affairs Division: assists consultation among member governments on international and Commonwealth matters of common interest. In association with host governments, it organizes the meetings of heads of government and senior officials. The Division services committees and special groups set up by heads of government dealing with political matters. The Secretariat has observer status at the United Nations, and the Division manages a joint office in New York to enable small states, which would otherwise be unable to afford facilities there, to maintain a presence at the United Nations. The Division monitors political developments in the Commonwealth and international progress in such matters as disarmament, the concerns of small states, dismantling of apartheid and the Law of the Sea. It also undertakes research on matters of common interest to member governments, and reports back to them. The Division is involved in diplomatic training and consular co-operation.

In 1990 Commonwealth heads of government mandated the Division to support the promotion of democracy by monitoring the preparations for and conduct of parliamentary, presidential or other elections in member countries at the request of national governments. In March 1998 the Commonwealth undertook its first joint mission with La Francophonie, to observe elections in Seychelles. In the same month representatives of the Commonwealth Secretary-General were present at elections held in Vanuatu. In May an observer mission was dispatched to monitor the electoral process in Lesotho. Further observer missions were undertaken in Nigeria, in February 1999, in Antigua and Barbuda, in March, and in Malawi and South Africa, in June. In June 2000 an observer group was sent to monitor legislative elections in Zimbabwe.

A new expert group on good governance and the elimination of corruption in economic management convened for its first meeting in May 1998. In November 1999 Commonwealth heads of government endorsed a Framework for Principles for Promoting Good Governance and Combating Corruption, which had been drafted by the group.

LAW

Legal and Constitutional Affairs Division: promotes and facilitates co-operation and the exchange of information among member governments on legal matters. It administers, jointly with the Commonwealth of Learning, a distance training programme for legislative draftsmen and assists governments to reform national laws to meet the obligations of international conventions. The Division organizes the triennial meeting of ministers, Attorneys General and senior ministry officials concerned with the legal systems in Commonwealth countries. It has also initiated four Commonwealth schemes for co-operation on extradition, the protection of material cultural heritage, mutual assistance in criminal matters and the transfer of convicted offenders within the Commonwealth. It liaises with the Commonwealth Magistrates' and Judges' Association, the Commonwealth Legal Education Association, the Commonwealth Lawyers' Association (with which it helps to prepare the triennial Commonwealth Law Conference for the practising profession), the Commonwealth Association of Legislative Counsel, and with other international non-governmental organizations. The Division provides in-house legal advice for the Secretariat. The quarterly *Commonwealth Law Bulletin* reports on legal developments in and beyond the Commonwealth.

The Division's Commercial Crime Unit assists member countries to combat financial and organized crime, in particular transborder criminal activities, and promotes the exchange of information regarding national and international efforts to combat serious commercial crime through a quarterly publication, *Commonwealth Legal Assistance News,* and the *Crimewatch* bulletin. A Human Rights Unit aims to assist governments to strengthen national institutions and other mechanisms for the protection for human rights. It also organizes training workshops and promotes the exchange of relevant information among member countries.

ECONOMIC CO-OPERATION

In October 1997 Commonwealth heads of government, meeting in Edinburgh, the United Kingdom, signed an Economic Declaration that focused on issues relating to global trade, investment and development and committed all member countries to free-market economic principles. The Declaration also incorporated a provision for the establishment of a Trade and Investment Access Facility within the Secretariat in order to assist developing member states in the process of international trade liberalization and promote intra-Commonwealth trade.

In May 1998 the Commonwealth Secretary-General appealed to the Group of Eight industrialized nations to accelerate and expand the initiative to ease the debt burden of the most heavily indebted poor countries (HIPCs) (see World Bank and IMF). However, the Group failed to endorse the so-called 'Mauritius Mandate', adopted by Commonwealth finance ministers, meeting in Mauritius, in September 1997, which stipulated that by 2000 all eligible HIPCs should have in progress measures to reduce their external debt. In October 1998 Commonwealth finance ministers, convened in Ottawa, Canada, reiterated their appeal to international financial institutions to accelerate the HIPC initiative. The meeting also issued a Commonwealth Statement on the global economic crisis and endorsed several proposals to help to counter the difficulties experienced by several countries. These measures included a mechanism to enable countries to suspend payments on all short-term financial obligations at a time of emergency without defaulting, assistance to governments to attract private capital and to manage capital market volatility, and the development of international codes of conduct regarding financial and monetary policies and corporate governance. In March 1999 the Commonwealth Secretariat hosted a joint IMF-World Bank conference to review the HIPC scheme and initiate a process of reform. In November 1999 Commonwealth heads of government, meeting in South Africa, declared their support for measures undertaken by the World Bank and IMF to enhance the HIPC initiative. At the end of an informal retreat the leaders adopted the Fancourt Commonwealth Declaration on Globalization and People-Centred Development, which emphasized the need for a more equitable spread of wealth generated by the process of globalization, and expressed a renewed commitment to the elimination of all forms of discrimination, the promotion of people-centred development and capacity-building, and efforts to ensure developing countries benefit from future multilateral trade liberalization measures.

In October 1998 ministers of finance agreed to establish a Commonwealth Y2K (Year 2000) Preparedness facility to help countries to deal with the technical difficulties resulting from the millennium date change.

Economic Affairs Division: organizes and services the annual meetings of Commonwealth ministers of finance and the ministerial group on small states and assists in servicing the biennial meetings of heads of government and periodic meetings of environment ministers. It engages in research and analysis on economic issues of interest to member governments and organizes seminars and conferences of government officials and experts. The Division undertook a major programme of technical assistance to enable developing Commonwealth countries to participate in the Uruguay Round of multilateral trade negotiations and has assisted the African, Caribbean and Pacific (ACP) group of countries in their trade negotiations with the European Union. It continues to help developing countries to strengthen their links with international capital markets and foreign investors. The Division also services groups of experts on economic affairs that have been commissioned by governments to report on, among other things, protectionism; obstacles to the North-South negotiating process; reform of the international financial and trading system; the debt crisis; management of technological change; the special needs of small states; the impact of change on the development process; environmental issues; women and structural adjustment; and youth unemployment. The Division co-ordinates the Secretariat's environmental work and manages the Iwokrama International Rainforest Programme.

The Division played a catalytic role in the establishment of a Commonwealth Equity Fund, initiated in September 1990, to allow developing member countries to improve their access to private institutional investment, and promoted a Caribbean Investment Fund. The Division supported the establishment of a Commonwealth Private Investment Initiative (CPII) to mobilize capital, on a regional basis, for investment in newly-privatized companies and in small and medium-sized businesses in the private sector. The first regional fund under the CPII was launched in July 1996. The Commonwealth Africa Investment Fund (Comafin), was to be managed by the United Kingdom's official development institution, the Commonwealth Development Corporation, to assist businesses

in 19 countries in sub-Saharan Africa, with initial resources of US $63.5m. In August 1997 a fund for the Pacific Islands was launched, with an initial capital of $15.0m. A $200m. South Asia Regional Fund was established at the Heads of Government Meeting in October. In October 1998 a fund for the Caribbean states was inaugurated, at a meeting of Commonwealth finance ministers.

HUMAN RESOURCES

Human Resource Development Division: consists of two departments concerned with education and health. The Division co-operates with member countries in devising strategies for human resource development.

The **Education Department** arranges specialist seminars, workshops and co-operative projects, and commissions studies in areas identified by ministers of education, whose three-yearly meetings it also services. Its present areas of emphasis include improving the quality of and access to basic education; strengthening the culture of science, technology and mathematics education in formal and non-formal areas of education; improving the quality of management in institutions of higher learning and basic education; improving the performance of teachers; strengthening examination assessment systems; and promoting the movement of students between Commonwealth countries. The Department also promotes multi-sectoral strategies to be incorporated in the development of human resources. Emphasis is placed on ensuring a gender balance, the appropriate use of technology, promoting good governance, addressing the problems of scale particular to smaller member countries, and encouraging collaboration between governments, the private sector and other non-governmental organizations.

The **Health Department** organizes ministerial, technical and expert group meetings and workshops, to promote co-operation on health matters, and the exchange of health information and expertise. The Department commissions relevant studies and provides professional and technical advice to member countries and to the Secretariat. It also supports the work of regional health organizations and promotes health for all people in Commonwealth countries.

Gender and Youth Affairs Division: consists of the Gender Affairs Department and the Commonwealth Youth Affairs Department.

The **Gender Affairs Department** is responsible for the implementation of the 1995 Commonwealth Plan of Action on Gender and Development, which was endorsed by the Heads of Government in order to achieve gender equality in the Commonwealth. The main objective of the Plan is to ensure that gender is incorporated into all policies, programmes, structures and procedures of member states and of the Commonwealth Secretariat. The Department is also addressing specific concerns such as the integration of gender issues into national budgetary processes, increasing the participation of women in politics and conflict prevention and resolution, and the promotion of human rights, including the elimination of violence against women and girls.

The **Youth Affairs Department** administers the Commonwealth Youth Programme (CYP), funded through separate voluntary contributions from governments, which seeks to promote the involvement of young people in the economic and social development of their countries. The CYP was awarded a budget of £2.1m. for 1998/99. It provides policy advice for governments and operates regional training programmes for youth workers and policy-makers through its centres in Africa, Asia, the Caribbean and the Pacific. It conducts a Youth Study Fellowship scheme, a Youth Project Fund, a Youth Exchange Programme (in the Caribbean), and a Youth Service Awards Scheme, holds conferences and seminars, carries out research and disseminates information. In May 1995 a Commonwealth Youth Credit Initiative was launched, in order to provide funds, training and advice to young entrepreneurs. In May 1998 a Commonwealth ministerial meeting, held in Kuala Lumpur, Malaysia, approved a new Plan of Action on Youth Empowerment to the Year 2005, which was to be presented to the 1999 meeting of heads of government.

SCIENCE

Science and Technology Division: is partially funded and governed by the Commonwealth Science Council, consisting of 35 member governments, which aims to enhance the scientific and technological capabilities of member countries, through co-operative research, training and the exchange of information. Current priority areas of work are concerned with the promotion of sustainable development and cover biological diversity and genetic resources, water resources, and renewable energy.

TECHNICAL CO-OPERATION

Commonwealth Fund for Technical Co-operation (CFTC): f. 1971 to facilitate the exchange of skills between member countries and to promote economic and social development. It is administered by the Commonwealth Secretariat and financed by voluntary subscriptions from member governments. The CFTC responds to requests from member governments for technical assistance, such as the provision of experts for short- or medium-term projects, advice on economic or legal matters, in particular in the areas of natural resources management and public-sector reform, and training programmes. The CFTC also administers the Langkawi awards for the study of environmental issues, which is funded by the Canadian Government. The CFTC budget for 1998/99 amounted to £20.5m. During 1995–97 more than 9,000 nationals from 49 Commonwealth developing countries trained under CFTC programmes, while more than 700 experts and consultants were assigned to projects in 45 countries. During that time CFTC also assisted six countries to define their maritime boundaries, 17 countries to develop their mineral and petroleum resources and undertook 84 export-promotion programmes.

CFTC activities are implemented by the following divisions:

Economic and Legal Advisory Services Division: serves as an in-house consultancy, offering advice to governments on macro-economic and financial management, capital market and private-sector development, debt management, the development of natural resources, and the negotiation of maritime boundaries and fisheries access agreements;

Export and Industrial Development Division: advises on all aspects of export marketing and the development of tourism, industry, small businesses and enterprises. Includes an Agricultural Development Unit, which provides technical assistance in agriculture and renewable resources;

General Technical Assistance Services Division: provides short- and long-term experts in all fields of development;

Management and Training Services Division: provides integrated packages of consultancy and training to enhance skills in areas such as public sector reform and the restructuring of enterprises, and arranges specific country and overseas training programmes.

The Secretariat also includes an Administration Division, a Strategic Planning and Evaluation Unit, and an Information and Public Affairs Division, which produces information publications, and radio and television programmes, about Commonwealth co-operation and consultation activities.

Finance

The Secretariat's budget for 1998/99 was £10.5m. Member governments meet the cost of the Secretariat through subscriptions on a scale related to income and population.

Publications

Commonwealth Currents (quarterly).
Commonwealth Declarations 1971–91.
Commonwealth Organisations (directory).
The Commonwealth Today.
In Common (quarterly newsletter of the Youth Programme).
International Development Policies (quarterly).
Link In to Gender and Development (2 a year).
Notes on the Commonwealth (series of reference leaflets).
Report of the Commonwealth Secretary-General (every 2 years).
The Commonwealth Yearbook.
Numerous reports, studies and papers (catalogue available).

Commonwealth Organizations

(In the United Kingdom, unless otherwise stated.)

PRINCIPAL BODIES

Commonwealth Foundation: Marlborough House, Pall Mall, London, SW1Y 5HY; tel. (20) 7930-3783; fax (20) 7839-8157; e-mail geninfo@commonwealth.int; internet www.commonwealth foundation.com; f. 1966; intergovernmental body promoting people-to-people interaction, and collaboration within the non-governmental sector of the Commonwealth; supports non-governmental organizations, professional associations and Commonwealth arts and culture. Awards an annual Commonwealth Writers' Prize. Funds are provided by Commonwealth govts. Chair. DONALD O. MILLS (Jamaica); Dir COLIN BELL (United Kingdom). Publ. *Common Path* (quarterly).

The Commonwealth of Learning (COL): 1285 West Broadway, Suite 600, Vancouver, BC V6H 3X8, Canada; tel. (604) 775-8200; fax (604) 775-8210; e-mail info@col.org; internet www.col.org; f. 1987 by Commonwealth Heads of Government to promote the devt and

sharing of distance education and open learning resources, including materials, expertise and technologies, throughout the Commonwealth and in other countries; implements and assists with national and regional educational programmes; acts as consultant to international agencies and national governments; conducts seminars and studies on specific educational needs. COL is financed by Commonwealth governments on a voluntary basis. Pres. Dato' Prof. GAJARAJ DHANARAJAN (Malaysia). Publs *Connections, EdTech News*.

The following represents a selection of other Commonwealth organizations:

AGRICULTURE AND FORESTRY

Commonwealth Forestry Association: c/o Oxford Forestry Institute, South Parks Rd, Oxford, OX1 3RB; tel. (1865) 271037; fax (1865) 275074; e-mail cfa_ox@hotmail.com; f. 1921; produces, collects and circulates information relating to world forestry and promotes good management, use and conservation of forests and forest lands throughout the world. Mems: 900. Chair. Dr J. S. MAINI. Publs *International Forestry Review* (quarterly), *Commonwealth Forestry News* (quarterly), *Commonwealth Forestry Handbook* (irregular).

Standing Committee on Commonwealth Forestry: Forestry Commission, 231 Corstorphine Rd, Edinburgh, EH12 7AT; tel. (131) 314-6137; fax (131) 334-0442; e-mail libby.jones@forestry .gov.uk; f. 1923 to provide continuity between Confs, and to provide a forum for discussion on any forestry matters of common interest to mem. govts which may be brought to the Cttee's notice by any member country or organization; 54 mems. 1997 Conference: Victoria Falls, Zimbabwe; 2001 Conference: Perth, Australia. Sec. LIBBY JONES. Publ. *Newsletter* (quarterly).

COMMONWEALTH STUDIES

Institute of Commonwealth Studies: 28 Russell Sq., London, WC1B 5DS; tel. (20) 7862-8844; fax (20) 7862-8820; e-mail ics@sas .ac.uk; internet www.sas.ac.uk/commonwealthstudies/; f. 1949 to promote advanced study of the Commonwealth; provides a library and meeting place for postgraduate students and academic staff engaged in research in this field; offers postgraduate teaching. Dir Prof. PAT CAPLAN. Publs *Annual Report, Collected Seminar Papers, Newsletter, Theses in Progress in Commonwealth Studies.*

COMMUNICATIONS

Commonwealth Telecommunications Organization: Clareville House, 26–27 Oxendon St, London, SW1Y 4EL; tel. (20) 7930-5516; fax (20) 7930-4248; e-mail info@cto.int; f. 1967; aims to enhance the development of telecommunications in Commonwealth countries and contribute to the communications infrastructure required for economic and social devt, through a devt and training programme. Exec. Dir Dr DAVID SOUTER. Publ. *CTO Briefing* (3 a year).

EDUCATION AND CULTURE

Association of Commonwealth Universities (ACU): John Foster House, 36 Gordon Sq., London, WC1H 0PF; tel. (20) 7387-8572; fax (20) 7387-2655; e-mail info@acu.ac.uk; internet www.acu .ac.uk; f. 1913; organizes major meetings of Commonwealth universities and their representatives; publishes factual information about Commonwealth universities and access to them; acts as a liaison office and general information centre and provides a recruitment advertising and publicity service; hosts a management consultancy service; supplies secretariats for the Commonwealth Scholarship Comm., the Marshall Aid Commemoration Comm. and the Commonwealth Universities Study Abroad Consortium; administers various other fellowship and scholarship programmes. Mems: 486 universities in 36 Commonwealth countries or regions. Sec.-Gen. Prof. MICHAEL GIBBONS. Publs include: *Commonwealth Universities Yearbook, ACU Bulletin of Current Documentation* (5 a year), *ACU: Aims and Functions* (annually), *Report of the Council of the ACU* (annually), *Awards for University Teachers and Research Workers, Awards for Postgraduate Study at Commonwealth Universities, Awards for First Degree Study at Commonwealth Universities, Awards for University Administrators and Librarians, Who's Who of Executive Heads: Vice-Chancellors, Presidents, Principals and Rectors,* Student Information Papers (study abroad series).

Commonwealth Association for Education in Journalism and Communication—CAEJC: c/o Faculty of Law, University of Western Ontario, London, ON N6A 3K7, Canada; tel. (519) 6613348; fax (519) 6613790; e-mail caejc@julian.uwo.ca; f. 1985; aims to foster high standards of journalism and communication education and research in Commonwealth countries and to promote co-operation among institutions and professions. c. 700 mems in 32 Commonwealth countries. Pres. Prof. SYED ARABI IDID (Malaysia); Sec. Prof. ROBERT MARTIN (Canada). Publ. *CAEJAC Journal* (annually).

Commonwealth Association of Science, Technology and Mathematics Educators—CASTME: c/o Education Dept, Human

Resource Development Division, Commonwealth Secretariat, Marlborough House, Pall Mall, London, SW1Y 5HX; tel. (20) 7747-6282; fax (20) 7747-6287; f. 1974; special emphasis is given to the social significance of education in these subjects. Organizes an Awards Scheme to promote effective teaching and learning in these subjects, and biennial regional seminars. Pres. Sir HERMANN BONDI; Hon. Sec. Dr VED GOEL. Publ. *CASTME Journal* (quarterly).

Commonwealth Council for Educational Administration and Management: c/o International Educational Leadership Centre, School of Management, Lincoln University Campus, Brayford Pool, Lincoln, LN6 7TS; tel. (1522) 886071; fax (1522) 886023; e-mail athody@lincoln.ac.uk; f. 1970; aims to foster quality in professional development and links among educational administrators; holds nat. and regional confs, as well as visits and seminars. Mems: 24 affiliated groups representing 3,000 persons. Pres. Prof. ANGELA THODY; Sec. GERALDINE BRISTOW. Publs *Managing Education Matters* (2 a year), *International Studies in Educational Administration* (2 a year).

Commonwealth Institute: 230 Kensington High St, London, W8 6NQ; tel. (20) 7603-4535; fax (20) 7602-7374; e-mail info@commonwealth.org.uk; internet www.commonwealth.org.uk; f. 1893 as the Imperial Institute; restructured as an independent pan-Commonwealth agency Jan. 2000; governed by a Bd of Trustees elected by the Bd of Governors; Commonwealth High Commissioners to the United Kingdom act as ex-officio Governors; the Inst. houses a Commonwealth Resource and Literature Library and a Conference and Events Centre; supplies educational resource materials and training throughout the United Kingdom; provides internet services to the Commonwealth; operates as an arts and conference centre, running a Commonwealth-based cultural programme; a new five-year strategic plan, entitled 'Commonwealth 21', was inaugurated in 1998. Chair. DAVID A. THOMPSON; Chief Exec. DAVID FRENCH. Publ. *Annual Review*.

League for the Exchange of Commonwealth Teachers: 7 Lion Yard, Tremadoc Rd, London, SW4 7NQ; tel. (20) 7498-1101; fax (20) 7720-5403; e-mail lectcom_exchange@compuserve.com; internet www.lect.org.uk; f. 1901; promotes educational exchanges between teachers in Australia, the Bahamas, Barbados, Bermuda, Canada, Guyana, India, Jamaica, Kenya, Malawi, New Zealand, Pakistan, South Africa and Trinidad and Tobago. Dir ANNA TOMLINSON. Publs *Annual Report, Exchange Teacher* (annually).

HEALTH

Commonwealth Medical Association: BMA House, Tavistock Sq., London, WC1H 9JP; tel. (20) 7383-6095; fax (20) 7383-6195; e-mail com_med_assn@compuserve.com; internet www.coma.co.za; f. 1962 for the exchange of information; provision of tech. co-operation and advice; formulation and maintenance of a code of ethics; provision of continuing medical education; devt and promotion of health education programmes; and liaison with WHO and the UN on health issues; meetings of its Council are held every three years. Mems: medical asscns in Commonwealth countries. Sec. Dr J. D. J. HAVARD. Publ. *CommonHealth* (quarterly).

Commonwealth Pharmaceutical Association: 1 Lambeth High St, London, SE1 7JN; tel. (20) 7820-3399 ext. 303; fax (20) 7582-3401; e-mail eharden@rpsgb.org.uk; f. 1970 to promote the interests of pharmaceutical sciences and the profession of pharmacy in the Commonwealth; to maintain high professional standards, encourage links between members and the creation of nat. asscns; and to facilitate the dissemination of information. Holds confs (every four years) and regional meetings. Mems: 39 pharmaceutical asscns. Sec. PHILIP E. GREEN. Publ. *Quarterly Newsletter*.

Commonwealth Society for the Deaf: 34 Buckingham Palace Rd, London, SW1W 0RE; tel. (20) 7233-5700; fax (20) 7233-5800; e-mail sound.seekers@btinternet.com; internet www.sound-seekers.org.uk; promotes the health, education and general welfare of the deaf in developing Commonwealth countries; encourages and assists the development of educational facilities, the training of teachers of the deaf, and the provision of support for parents of deaf children; organizes visits by volunteer specialists to developing countries; provides audiological equipment and organizes the training of audiological maintenance technicians; conducts research into the causes and prevention of deafness. CEO Brig. J. A. DAVIS. Publ. *Annual Report*.

Sight Savers International (Royal Commonwealth Society for the Blind): Grosvenor Hall, Bolnore Rd, Haywards Heath, West Sussex, RH16 4BX; tel. (1444) 446600; fax (1444) 446688; e-mail information@sightsaversint.org.uk; internet www.sightsavers.org.uk; f. 1950 to prevent blindness and restore sight in developing countries, and to provide education and community-based training for incurably blind people; operates in collaboration with local partners, with high priority given to training local staff; Chair. DAVID THOMPSON; Dir RICHARD PORTER. Publ. *Horizons* (newsletter, 3 a year).

INFORMATION AND THE MEDIA

Commonwealth Broadcasting Association: 17 Fleet St, London, EC4Y 1AA; tel. (20) 7583-5550; fax (20) 7583-5549; e-mail cba@cba.org.uk; internet www.oneworld.org/cba; f. 1945; gen. confs are held every two years. Mems: 100 in 57 countries. Sec.-Gen. ELIZABETH SMITH. Publs *Commonwealth Broadcaster* (quarterly), *Commonwealth Broadcaster Directory* (annually).

Commonwealth Institute: see under Education.

Commonwealth Journalists Association: 17 Nottingham St, London, W1M 3RD; tel. (20) 7486-3844; fax (20) 7486-3822; f. 1978 to promote co-operation between journalists in Commonwealth countries, organize training facilities and confs, and foster understanding among Commonwealth peoples. Pres. MURRAY BURT; Exec. Dir LAWRIE BREEN.

Commonwealth Press Union (Asscn of Commonwealth Newspapers, News Agencies and Periodicals): 17 Fleet St, London, EC4Y 1AA; tel. (20) 7583-7733; fax (20) 7583-6868; e-mail 106156.3331@compuserve.com; f. 1950; promotes the welfare of the Commonwealth press; provides training for journalists and organizes biennial confs. Mems: c. 1,000 newspapers, news agencies, periodicals in 42 Commonwealth countries. Dir ROBIN MACKICHAN. Publs *CPU News, Annual Report*.

LAW

Commonwealth Lawyers' Association: c/o The Law Society, 114 Chancery Lane, London, WC2A 1PL; tel. (20) 7320-5772; fax (20) 7831-0057; e-mail cla@lawsociety.org.uk; internet www.commonwealthlawyers.com; f. 1983 (fmrly the Commonwealth Legal Bureau); seeks to maintain and promote the rule of law throughout the Commonwealth, by ensuring that the people of the Commonwealth are served by an independent and efficient legal profession; upholds professional standards and promotes the availability of legal services; assists in organizing the triennial Commonwealth law confs. Pres. (1999–2001) CYRUS DAS; Exec. Sec. HELEN POTTS. Publs *The Commonwealth Lawyer, Clarion*.

Commonwealth Legal Advisory Service: c/o British Institute of International and Comparative Law, Charles Clore House, 17 Russell Sq., London, WC1B 5JP; tel. (20) 7862-5151; fax (20) 7862-5152; e-mail info@biicl.org; financed by the British Institute and by contributions from Commonwealth govts; provides research facilities for Commonwealth govts and law reform commissions.

Commonwealth Legal Education Association: c/o Legal and Constitutional Affairs Division, Commonwealth Secretariat, Marlborough House, Pall Mall, London, SW1Y 5HX; tel. (20) 7747-6415; fax (20) 7747-6406; e-mail clea@commonwealth.int; internet www.clea.com.uk; f. 1971 to promote contacts and exchanges and to provide information regarding legal education. Gen. Sec. JOHN HATCHARD. Publs *Commonwealth Legal Education Association Newsletter* (3 a year), *Directory of Commonwealth Law Schools* (every 2 years).

Commonwealth Magistrates' and Judges' Association: Uganda House, 58/59 Trafalgar Sq., London, WC2N 5DX; tel. (20) 7976-1007; fax (20) 7976-2395; e-mail info@cmja.org; internet www.cmja.org; f. 1970 to advance the administration of the law by promoting the independence of the judiciary, to further education in law and crime prevention and to disseminate information; confs and study tours; corporate membership for asscns of the judiciary or courts of limited jurisdiction; assoc. membership for individuals. Pres. DAVID ARMATI; Sec.-Gen. Dr KAREN BREWER. Publ. *Commonwealth Judicial Journal* (2 a year).

PARLIAMENTARY AFFAIRS

Commonwealth Parliamentary Association: Westminster House, Suite 700, 7 Millbank, London, SW1P 3JA; tel. (20) 7799-1460; fax (20) 7222-6073; e-mail hq.sec@comparlhq.org.uk; internet www.comparlhq.org.uk; f. 1911 to promote understanding and co-operation between Commonwealth parliamentarians; organization: Exec. Cttee of 32 MPs responsible to annual Gen. Assembly; 155 brs throughout the Commonwealth; holds annual Commonwealth Parliamentary Confs and seminars; also regional confs and seminars; Sec.-Gen. ARTHUR DONAHOE. Publ. *The Parliamentarian* (quarterly).

PROFESSIONAL AND INDUSTRIAL RELATIONS

Commonwealth Association of Architects: 66 Portland Pl., London, W1N 4AD; tel. (20) 7490-3024; fax (20) 7253-2592; e-mail caa@gharchitects.demon.co.uk; internet www.archexchange.org; f. 1964; an asscn of 38 socs of architects in various Commonwealth countries. Objects: to facilitate the reciprocal recognition of professional qualifications; to provide a clearing house for information on architectural practice, and to encourage collaboration. Plenary confs every three years; regional confs are also held. Exec. Dir TONY GODWIN. Publs *Handbook, Objectives and Procedures: CAA Schools Visiting Boards, Architectural Education in the Commonwealth* (annotated bibliography of research), *CAA Newsnet* (2 a year), a survey and list of schools of architecture.

Commonwealth Association for Public Administration and Management—CAPAM: 1075 Bay St, Suite 402, Toronto, ON M5S 2B1, Canada; tel. (416) 920-3337; fax (416) 920-6574; e-mail capam@capam.ca; internet www.comnet.mt/capam/; f. 1994; aims to promote sound management of the public sector in Commonwealth countries and to assist those countries undergoing political or financial reforms. An international awards programme to reward innovation within the public sector was introduced in 1997, and was to be awarded every 2 years. Pres. Dr ZOLA SKWEYIYA (South Africa); Exec. Dir ART STEVENSON (Canada).

Commonwealth Trade Union Council: Congress House, 23–28 Great Russell St, London, WC1B 3LS; tel. (20) 7631-0728; fax (20) 7436-0301; e-mail info@commonwealthtuc.org; internet www .commonwealthtuc.org; f. 1979; links trade union national centres (representing more than 30m. trade union mems) throughout the Commonwealth; promotes the application of democratic principles and core labour standards, works closely with other international trade union orgs. Dir ANNIE WATSON. Publ. *Annual Report.*

SCIENCE AND TECHNOLOGY

Commonwealth Engineers' Council: c/o Institution of Civil Engineers, One Great George St, London, SW1P 3AA; tel. (20) 7222-7722; fax (20) 7222-7500; e-mail international@ice.org.uk; f. 1946; the Council meets every two years to provide an opportunity for engineering institutions of Commonwealth countries to exchange views on collaboration; there is a standing cttee on engineering education and training; organizes seminars on related topics. Sec. J. A. WHITWELL.

Commonwealth Geological Surveys Consultative Group: c/o Commonwealth Science Council, CSC Earth Sciences Programme, Marlborough House, Pall Mall, London, SW1Y 5HX; tel. (20) 7839-3411; fax (20) 7839-6174; e-mail comsci@gn.apc.org; f. 1948 to promote collaboration in geological, geochemical, geophysical and remote sensing techniques and the exchange of information. Geological Programme Officer Dr SIYAN MALOMO; Publ. *Earth Sciences Newsletter.*

SPORT

Commonwealth Games Federation: Walkden House, 3–10 Melton St, London, NW1 2EB; tel. (20) 7383-5596; fax (20) 7383-5506; e-mail commonwealthgamesfederation@btinternet .com; internet www.commonwealthgames-fed.org; the Games were first held in 1930 and are now held every four years; participation is limited to competitors representing the mem. countries of the Commonwealth; to be held in Manchester, United Kingdom, in 2002. Mems: 72 affiliated bodies. Pres. HRH The Earl of WESSEX; Chair. MICHAEL FENNELL.

YOUTH

Commonwealth Youth Exchange Council: 7 Lion Yard, Tremadoc Rd, London, SW4 7NQ; tel. (20) 7498-6151; fax (20) 7720-5403; e-mail mail@cyec.demon.co.uk; f. 1970; promotes contact between groups of young people of the United Kingdom and other Commonwealth countries by means of educational exchange visits, provides information for organizers and allocates grants; 224 mem. orgs. Dir V. S. G. CRAGGS. Publs *Contact* (handbook), *Exchange* (newsletter), *Safety and Welfare* (guide-lines for Commonwealth Youth Exchange groups).

Duke of Edinburgh's Award International Association: Award House, 7-11 St Matthew St, London, SW1P 2JT; tel. (20) 7222-4242; fax (20) 7222-4141; e-mail sect@intaward.org; internet www .intaward.org; f. 1956; offers a programme of leisure activities for young people, comprising Service, Expeditions, Physical Recreation, and Skills; operates in more than 90 countries (not confined to the Commonwealth). International Sec.-Gen. PAUL ARENGO-JONES. Publs *Award World* (2 a year), *Annual Report*, handbooks and guides.

MISCELLANEOUS

British Commonwealth Ex-Services League: 48 Pall Mall, London, SW1Y 5JG; tel. (20) 7973-7263; fax (20) 7973-7308; links the ex-service orgs in the Commonwealth, assists ex-servicemen of the Crown and their dependants who are resident abroad; holds triennial confs. Grand Pres. HRH The Duke of EDINBURGH; Sec.-Gen. Lt-Col S. POPE. Publ. *Annual Report.*

Commonwealth Countries League: 14 Thistleworth Close, Isleworth, Middlesex, TW7 4QQ; tel. (20) 8737-3572; fax (20) 8568-2495; f. 1925 to secure equal opportunities and status between men and women in the Commonwealth, to act as a link between Commonwealth women's orgs, and to promote and finance secondary education of disadvantaged girls of high ability in their own countries, through the CCL Educational Fund; holds meetings with speakers and an annual Conf., organizes the annual Commonwealth Fair for fund-raising; individual mems and affiliated socs in the Commonwealth. Sec.-Gen. SHEILA O'REILLY. Publ. *CCL Newsletter* (3 a year).

Commonwealth War Graves Commission: 2 Marlow Rd, Maidenhead, Berks, SL6 7DX; tel. (1628) 634221; fax (1628) 771208; e-mail general.enq@cwgc.org; internet www.cwgc.org; f. 1917 (as Imperial War Graves Commission); responsible for the commemoration in perpetuity of the 1.7m. members of the Commonwealth Forces who died during the wars of 1914–18 and 1939–45; provides for the marking and maintenance of war graves and memorials at some 23,000 locations in 150 countries. Mems: Australia, Canada, India, New Zealand, South Africa, United Kingdom. Pres. HRH The Duke of KENT; Dir-Gen. R. KELLAWAY (from Sept. 2000).

Joint Commonwealth Societies' Council: c/o Royal Commonwealth Society, 18 Northumberland Ave, London, WC2N 5BJ; tel. (20) 7930-6733; fax (20) 7930-9705; e-mail jcsc@rcsint .org; internet www.rcsint.org; f. 1947; provides a forum for the exchange of information regarding activities of mem. orgs which promote understanding among countries of the Commonwealth; co-ordinates the distribution of the Commonwealth Day message by Queen Elizabeth, organizes the observance of the Commonwealth Day and produces educational materials relating to the occasion; mems: 16 unofficial Commonwealth orgs and four official bodies. Chair. Sir PETER MARSHALL; Sec. GWENDOLYN WHITE.

Royal Commonwealth Society: 18 Northumberland Ave, London, WC2N 5BJ; tel. (20) 7930-6733; fax (20) 7930-9705; e-mail info@rcsint.org; internet www.rcsint.org; f. 1868; to promote international understanding of the Commonwealth and its people; organizes meetings and seminars on topical issues, and cultural and social events; library housed by Cambridge University Library. Chair. Sir MICHAEL MCWILLIAM; Dir PETER LUFF. Publs *Annual Report, Newsletter* (3 a year), conference reports.

Royal Over-Seas League: Over-Seas House, Park Place, St James's St, London, SW1A 1LR; tel. (20) 7408-0214; fax (20) 7499-6738; f. 1910 to promote friendship and understanding in the Commonwealth; club houses in London and Edinburgh; membership is open to all British subjects and Commonwealth citizens. Chair. Sir GEOFFREY ELLERTON; Dir-Gen. ROBERT F. NEWELL. Publ. *Overseas* (quarterly).

The Victoria League for Commonwealth Friendship: 55 Leinster Sq., London, W2 4PW; tel. (20) 7243-2633; fax (20) 7229-2994; f. 1901; aims to further personal friendship among Commonwealth peoples and to provide hospitality for visitors; maintains Student House, providing accommodation for students from Commonwealth countries; has brs elsewhere in the UK and abroad. Pres. HRH Princess MARGARET, Countess of SNOWDON; Chair. COLIN WEBBER; Gen. Sec. JOHN ALLAN. Publ. *Annual Report.*

Declaration of Commonwealth Principles

(Agreed by the Commonwealth Heads of Government Meeting at Singapore, 22 January 1971.)

The Commonwealth of Nations is a voluntary association of independent sovereign states, each responsible for its own policies, consulting and co-operating in the common interests of their peoples and in the promotion of international understanding and world peace.

Members of the Commonwealth come from territories in the six continents and five oceans, include peoples of different races, languages and religions, and display every stage of economic development from poor developing nations to wealthy industrialized nations. They encompass a rich variety of cultures, traditions and institutions.

Membership of the Commonwealth is compatible with the freedom of member-governments to be non-aligned or to belong to any other grouping, association or alliance. Within this diversity all members of the Commonwealth hold certain principles in common. It is by pursuing these principles that the Commonwealth can continue to influence international society for the benefit of mankind.

We believe that international peace and order are essential to the security and prosperity of mankind; we therefore support the United Nations and seek to strengthen its influence for peace in the world, and its efforts to remove the causes of tension between nations.

We believe in the liberty of the individual, in equal rights for all citizens regardless of race, colour, creed or political belief, and in their inalienable right to participate by means of free and democratic political processes in framing the society in which they live. We therefore strive to promote in each of our countries those representative institutions and guarantees for personal freedom under the law that are our common heritage.

We recognize racial prejudice as a dangerous sickness threatening the healthy development of the human race and racial discrimination as an unmitigated evil of society. Each of us will vigorously combat this evil within our own nation.

No country will afford to regimes which practise racial discrimination assistance which in its own judgment directly contributes to the pursuit or consolidation of this evil policy. We oppose all forms of colonial domination and racial oppression and are committed to the principles of human dignity and equality.

We will therefore use all our efforts to foster human equality and dignity everywhere, and to further the principles of self-determination and non-racialism.

We believe that the wide disparities in wealth now existing between different sections of mankind are too great to be tolerated. They also create world tensions. Our aim is their progressive removal. We therefore seek to use our efforts to overcome poverty, ignorance and disease, in raising standards of life and achieving a more equitable international society.

To this end our aim is to achieve the freest possible flow of international trade on terms fair and equitable to all, taking into account the special requirements of the developing countries, and to encourage the flow of adequate resources, including governmental and private resources, to the developing countries, bearing in mind the importance of doing this in a true spirit of partnership and of establishing for this purpose in the developing countries conditions which are conducive to sustained investment and growth.

We believe that international co-operation is essential to remove the causes of war, promote tolerance, combat injustice, and secure development among the peoples of the world. We are convinced that the Commonwealth is one of the most fruitful associations for these purposes.

In pursuing these principles the members of the Commonwealth believe that they can provide a constructive example of the multi-national approach which is vital to peace and progress in the modern world. The association is based on consultation, discussion and co-operation.

In rejecting coercion as an instrument of policy they recognize that the security of each member state from external aggression is a matter of concern to all members. It provides many channels for continuing exchanges of knowledge and views on professional, cultural, economic, legal and political issues among member states.

These relationships we intend to foster and extend, for we believe that our multi-national association can expand human understanding and understanding among nations, assist in the elimination of discrimination based on differences of race, colour or creed, maintain and strengthen personal liberty, contribute to the enrichment of life for all, and provide a powerful influence for peace among nations.

The Lusaka Declaration on Racism and Racial Prejudice

The Declaration, adopted by Heads of Government in 1979, includes the following statements:

United in our desire to rid the world of the evils of racism and racial prejudice, we proclaim our faith in the inherent dignity and worth of the human person and declare that:

(i) the peoples of the Commonwealth have the right to live freely in dignity and equality, without any distinction or exclusion based on race, colour, sex, descent, or national or ethnic origin;

(ii) while everyone is free to retain diversity in his or her culture and lifestyle this diversity does not justify the perpetuation of racial prejudice or racially discriminatory practices;

(iii) everyone has the right to equality before the law and equal justice under the law; and

(iv) everyone has the right to effective remedies and protection against any form of discrimination based on the grounds of race, colour, sex, descent, or national or ethnic origin.

We reject as inhuman and intolerable all policies designed to perpetuate apartheid, racial segregation or other policies based on theories that racial groups are or may be inherently superior or inferior.

We reaffirm that it is the duty of all the peoples of the Commonwealth to work together for the total eradication of the infamous policy of apartheid which is internationally recognized as a crime against the conscience and dignity of mankind and the very existence of which is an affront to humanity.

We agree that everyone has the right to protection against acts of incitement to racial hatred and discrimination, whether committed by individuals, groups or other organizations. . . .

Inspired by the principles of freedom and equality which characterise our association, we accept the solemn duty of working together to eliminate racism and racial prejudice. This duty involves the acceptance of the principle that positive measures may be required to advance the elimination of racism, including assistance to those struggling to rid themselves and their environment of the practice.

Being aware that legislation alone cannot eliminate racism and racial prejudice, we endorse the need to initiate public information and education policies designed to promote understanding, tolerance, respect and friendship among peoples and racial groups. . . .

We note that racism and racial prejudice, wherever they occur, are significant factors contributing to tension between nations and thus inhibit peaceful progress and development. We believe that the goal of the eradication of racism stands as a critical priority for governments of the Commonwealth committed as they are to the promotion of the ideals of peaceful and happy lives for their people.

Harare Commonwealth Declaration

The following are the major points of the Declaration adopted by Heads of Government at the meeting held in Harare, Zimbabwe, in 1991:

Having reaffirmed the principles to which the Commonwealth is committed, and reviewed the problems and challenges which the world, and the Commonwealth as part of it, face, we pledge the Commonwealth and our countries to work with renewed vigour, concentrating especially in the following areas: the protection and promotion of the fundamental political values of the Commonwealth; equality for women, so that they may exercise their full and equal rights; provision of universal access to education for the population of our countries; continuing action to bring about the end of apartheid and the establishment of a free, democratic, non-racial and prosperous South Africa; the promotion of sustainable development and the alleviation of poverty in the countries of the Commonwealth; extending the benefits of development within a framework of respect for human rights; the protection of the environment through respect for the principles of sustainable development which we enunciated at Langkawi; action to combat drugs trafficking and abuse and communicable diseases; help for small Commonwealth states in tackling their particular economic and security problems; and support of the United Nations and other international institutions in the world's search for peace, disarmament and effective arms control; and in the promotion of international consensus on major global political, economic and social issues.

To give weight and effectiveness to our commitments we intend to focus and improve Commonwealth co-operation in these areas. This would include strengthening the capacity of the Commonwealth to respond to requests from members for assistance in entrenching the practices of democracy, accountable administration and the rule of law.

In reaffirming the principles of the Commonwealth and in committing ourselves to pursue them in policy and action in response to the challenges of the 1990s, in areas where we believe that the Commonwealth has a distinctive contribution to offer, we the Heads of Government express our determination to renew and enhance the value and importance of the Commonwealth as an institution which can and should strengthen and enrich the lives not only of its own members and their peoples but also of the wider community of peoples of which they are a part.

ECONOMIC COMMUNITY OF WEST AFRICAN STATES—ECOWAS

Address: ECOWAS Secretariat and Conference Centre, 60 Yakubu Gowon Crescent, Asokoro, Abuja, Nigeria.

Telephone and fax: (9) 2347648; **e-mail:** info@ecowas.net; **internet:** www.ecowas.net.

The Treaty of Lagos, establishing ECOWAS, was signed in May 1975 by 15 states, with the object of promoting trade, co-operation and self-reliance in West Africa. Outstanding protocols bringing certain key features of the Treaty into effect were ratified in November 1976. Cape Verde joined in 1977. A revised ECOWAS treaty, designed to accelerate economic integration and to increase political co-operation, was signed in July 1993.

MEMBERS

Benin	Guinea	Niger
Burkina Faso	Guinea-Bissau	Nigeria
Cape Verde	Liberia	Senegal
Côte d'Ivoire	Mali	Sierra Leone
The Gambia	Mauritania*	Togo
Ghana		

*Mauritania announced its intention to withdraw from ECOWAS in December 1999.

Organization

(July 2000)

AUTHORITY OF HEADS OF STATE AND GOVERNMENT

The Authority is the supreme decision-making organ of the Community, with responsibility for its general development and realization of its objectives. The Chairman is drawn from the member states in turn. In August 1997 ECOWAS heads of state decided that the Authority (previously convened on an annual basis) should meet twice each year to enhance monitoring and co-ordination of the Community's activities.

COUNCIL OF MINISTERS

The Council consists of two representatives from each country; a chairman is drawn from each country in turn. It meets twice a year, and is responsible for the running of the Community.

EXECUTIVE SECRETARIAT

The Executive Secretary is elected for a four-year term, which may be renewed once only.

Executive Secretary: Lansana Kouyaté (Guinea).

SPECIALIZED TECHNICAL COMMISSIONS

There are eight commissions, comprising representatives of each member state, which prepare Community projects and programmes in the following areas:

  (i) Food and Agriculture;

 (ii) Industry, Science and Technology, and Energy;

 (iii) Environment and Natural Resources;

 (iv) Transport, Communications, and Tourism;

  (v) Trade, Customs, Taxation, Statistics, and Money and Payments;

 (vi) Political, Judicial and Legal Affairs, Regional Security, and Integration;

(vii) Human Resources, Information, and Social and Cultural Affairs; and

(viii) Administration and Finance.

ECOWAS FUND FOR CO-OPERATION, COMPENSATION AND DEVELOPMENT

Address: BP 2704, blvd du 13 Janvier, Lomé, Togo.

Telephone and fax: 216864.

The Fund is administered by a Board of Directors. The chief executive of the Fund is the Managing Director, who holds office for a renewable term of four years. There is a staff of 100. The authorized cap. of the Fund is US $500m.; paid-up cap. totalled $66.5m. at Dec. 1997. In 1988 agreements were reached with the African Development Bank and the Islamic Development Bank on the co-financing of projects and joint training of staff. Efforts have been initiated to enhance the Fund's financial resources, by opening its capital to non-regional participants. At a summit of ECOWAS heads of state and government in December 1999 it was announced that the Fund was to be converted into an Investment and Development Bank, which was to have two divisions, a Regional Investment Bank and a Regional Development Fund.

Managing Director: Drabo D. Barthelamy (acting).

Activities

ECOWAS aims to promote co-operation and development in economic, social and cultural activity, particularly in the fields for which specialized technical commissions (see above) are appointed, to raise the standard of living of the people of the member countries, increase and maintain economic stability, improve relations among member countries and contribute to the progress and development of Africa.

The treaty provides for compensation for states whose import duties are reduced through trade liberalization and contains a clause permitting safeguard measures in favour of any country affected by economic disturbances through the application of the treaty.

The treaty also contains a commitment to abolish all obstacles to the free movement of people, services and capital, and to promote: harmonization of agricultural policies; common projects in marketing, research and the agriculturally based industries; joint development of economic and industrial policies and elimination of disparities in levels of development; and common monetary policies.

Lack of success in many of ECOWAS' aims has been attributed to the existence of numerous other intergovernmental organizations in the region (in particular the Union économique et monétaire ouest-africaine, which replaced the francophone Communauté économique de l'Afrique de l'ouest in 1994, q.v.) and to some member governments' lack of commitment, shown by their reluctance to implement policies at the national level, their failure to provide the agreed financial resources, and the absence of national links with the Secretariat. During the 1990s ECOWAS' activities were increasingly dominated by its efforts to secure peace in Liberia, and later in Sierra Leone (see below). At a summit meeting in December 1999 ECOWAS heads of state appealed to external development partners for assistance with the implementation of their ongoing programme to establish a single monetary zone (see below).

A revised treaty for the Community was drawn up by an ECOWAS Committee of Eminent Persons in 1991–92, and was signed at the ECOWAS summit conference that took place in Cotonou, Benin, in July 1993. The treaty, which was to extend economic and political co-operation among member states, designates the achievement of a common market and a single currency as economic objectives, while in the political sphere it envisages the establishment of a West African Parliament, an economic and social council and an ECOWAS Court of Justice to replace the existing Tribunal and enforce Community decisions. The treaty also formally assigned the Community with the responsibility of preventing and settling regional conflicts. At the summit meeting, held in Abuja, Nigeria, in August 1994, ECOWAS heads of state and government signed a protocol agreement for the establishment of a regional parliament; however, no timetable was specified for this to be achieved. The meeting also adopted a Convention on Extradition of non-political offenders. At the end of July 1995 the new ECOWAS treaty was reported to have entered into effect, having received the required number of ratifications. A draft protocol providing for the creation of a mechanism for the prevention, management and settlement of conflicts, and for the maintenance of peace in the region, was approved by ECOWAS heads of state and government in December 1999.

TRADE AND MONETARY UNION

Elimination of tariffs and other obstructions to trade among member states, and the establishment of a common external tariff, were planned over a transitional period of 15 years. At the 1978 Conference of Heads of State and Government it was decided that from May 1979 no member state might increase its customs tariff on goods from another member. This was regarded as the first step towards the abolition of customs duties within the Community. During the first two years import duties on intra-community trade were to be maintained, and then eliminated in phases over the next eight years. Quotas and other restrictions of equivalent effect were to be abolished in the first 10 years. In the remaining five years all differences between external customs tariffs were to be abolished.

In 1980 ECOWAS heads of state and government decided to establish a free-trade area for unprocessed agricultural products and handicrafts from May 1981. Tariffs on industrial products made by specified community enterprises were also to be abolished from that date, but implementation was delayed by difficulties in defining the enterprises. From 1 January 1990 tariffs were eliminated on 25 listed items manufactured in ECOWAS member states. Over the ensuing decade, tariffs on other industrial products were to be eliminated as follows: the 'most-developed' countries of ECOWAS (Côte d'Ivoire, Ghana, Nigeria and Senegal) were to abolish tariffs on 'priority' products within four years and on 'non-priority' products within six years; the second group (Benin, Guinea, Liberia, Sierra Leone and Togo) were to abolish tariffs on 'priority' products within six years, and on 'non-priority' products within eight years; and the 'least-developed' members (Burkina Faso, Cape Verde, The Gambia, Guinea-Bissau, Mali, Mauritania and Niger) were to abolish tariffs on 'priority' products within eight years and on 'non-priority' products within 10 years. By 1997 an estimated 400 industrial goods had been approved under the trade liberalization scheme.

In 1990 ECOWAS heads of state and government agreed to adopt measures that would create a single monetary zone and remove barriers to trade in goods that originated in the Community. ECOWAS regards monetary union as necessary to encourage investment in the region, since it would greatly facilitate capital transactions with foreign countries. In September 1992 it was announced that, as part of efforts to enhance monetary co-operation and financial harmonization in the region, the West African Clearing House was to be restructured as the West African Monetary Agency (WAMA, see p. 153). As a specialized agency of ECOWAS, WAMA was to be responsible for administering an ECOWAS exchange rate system (EERS) and for establishing the single monetary zone. A credit guarantee scheme and travellers' cheque system were to be established in association with the EERS. The agreement founding WAMA was signed by the Governors of the central banks of ECOWAS member states, meeting in Banjul, The Gambia, in March 1996. In July the Authority agreed to impose a common value-added tax (VAT) on consumer goods, in order to rationalize indirect taxation and to stimulate greater intra-Community trade. In August 1997 ECOWAS heads of state and government appointed an *ad hoc* monitoring committee to promote and oversee the implementation of trade liberalization measures and the establishment of a single monetary zone by 2000. (This deadline was subsequently revised to 1 January 2004.) The meeting also authorized the introduction of the regional travellers' cheque scheme. In March 1998 senior customs officials of ECOWAS countries agreed to harmonize customs policies and administrations, in order to facilitate intra-Community trade, and to pursue the objective of establishing a common external tariff by 2000. (This deadline was subsequently advanced to 1 January 2001.) In October 1998 the travellers' cheque scheme was formally inaugurated at a meeting of ECOWAS heads of state. The cheques were to be issued by WAMA in denominations of a West African Unit of Account and convertible into each local currency at the rate of one Special Drawing Right (SDR—see IMF p. 107). The cheques entered into circulation on 1 July 1999.

In December 1992 ECOWAS ministers agreed on the institutionalization of an ECOWAS trade fair, in order to promote trade liberalization and intra-Community trade. The first trade fair, which was held in Dakar, Senegal in May/June 1995, was attended by some 400 private businesses from the 16 member states. A second trade fair was staged in Accra, Ghana, in March 1999.

TRAVEL, TRANSPORT AND COMMUNICATIONS

In 1979 ECOWAS heads of state signed a Protocol relating to free circulation of the region's citizens and to rights of residence and establishment of commercial enterprises. The first provision (the right of entry without a visa) came into force in 1980. The second provision, allowing unlimited rights of residence, was signed in 1986 (although Nigeria indicated that unskilled workers and certain categories of professionals would not be allowed to stay for an indefinite period) and came into force in 1989. The third provision, concerning the right to establish a commercial enterprise in another member state was signed in 1990. In July 1992 the ECOWAS Authority formulated a Minimum Agenda for Action for the implementation of Community agreements regarding the free movement of goods and people, for example the removal of non-tariff barriers, the simplification of customs and transit procedures and a reduction in the number of control posts on international roads. By mid-1996 the ECOWAS summit meeting observed that few measures had been adopted by member states to implement the Minimum Agenda, and emphasized that it remained a central element of the Community's integration process. In April 1997 the Gambian and Senegalese finance and trade officials concluded an agreement on measures to facilitate the export of goods via Senegal to neighbouring countries, in accordance with ECOWAS protocols relating to inter-state road transit arrangements. A Brown Card scheme, providing a recognized third-party liability insurance throughout the region, was operational in 1998. At its so-called Jubilee summit, held in May 2000,

ECOWAS endorsed the initiation of a process to establish a regional passport. During mid-2000 the regional grouping announced the impending inauguration of its own airline, ECOAIR.

In August 1996 the initial phase of a programme to improve regional telecommunications was reported to have been completed. Some US $35m. had been granted for project financing in eight ECOWAS countries. A second phase of the programme (INTELCOM II), which aimed to modernize and expand the region's telecommunications services, was initiated by ECOWAS heads of state in August 1997.

A programme for the development of an integrated regional road network was adopted in 1980. Under the programme, two major trans-regional roads were to be completed: the Trans-Coastal Highway, linking Lagos, Nigeria, with Nouackchott, Mauritania (4,767 km); and the Trans-Sahelian Highway, linking Dakar, Senegal, with N'Djamena, Chad (4,633 km). By mid-1998 about 83% of the trans-coastal route was complete, and about 87% of the trans-Sahelian route.

ECONOMIC AND INDUSTRIAL DEVELOPMENT

In November 1984 ECOWAS heads of state and government approved the establishment of a private regional investment bank, to be known as Ecobank Transnational Inc. The bank, which was based in Lomé, Togo, opened in March 1988. ECOWAS has a 10% share in the bank. By mid-1999 Ecobank affiliates were operating in Benin, Burkina Faso, Côte d'Ivoire, Ghana, Mali, Nigeria and Togo. At that time plans were underway to commence operations in Guinea, Liberia, Niger and Senegal.

The West African Industrial Forum, sponsored by ECOWAS, is held every two years to promote regional industrial investment. The Secretariat is formulating a West African Industrial Master Plan. The first phase involved the compilation of an inventory of industrial enterprises, while the second phase was to comprise study of important industrial sub-sectors, prior to the drawing up of the Master Plan.

In September 1995 Nigeria, Ghana, Togo and Benin resolved to develop a gas pipeline to connect Nigerian gas supplies to the other countries. In August 1999 the participating countries, together with two petroleum companies operating in Nigeria, signed an agreement on the financing and construction of the pipeline, which was expected to become operational in 2002. During 1997 a Community initiative to connect the electricity supply networks throughout the region was under consideration.

In August 1997 the Authority of Heads of State and Government urged all member states to co-ordinate their long-term development programmes in order to formulate common objectives and to encourage greater economic growth in the region as a whole.

REGIONAL SECURITY

In 1990 a Standing Mediation Committee was formed to mediate disputes between member states. Member states reaffirmed their commitment to refrain from aggression against one another at a summit conference in 1991. The revised ECOWAS treaty, signed in July 1993, incorporates a separate provision for regional security, requiring member states to work towards the maintenance of peace, stability and security.

In December 1997 an extraordinary meeting of ECOWAS heads of state and government was convened in Lomé, Togo, to consider the future stability and security of the region. It was agreed that a permanent mechanism be established for conflict prevention and the maintenance of peace. ECOWAS leaders also reaffirmed their commitment to pursuing dialogue to prevent conflicts, co-operating in the early deployment of peace-keeping forces and implementing measures to counter trans-border crime and the illegal trafficking of armaments and drugs. At the meeting ECOWAS leaders acknowledged ECOMOG's role in restoring constitutional order in Liberia and expressed their appreciation of the force's current efforts in Sierra Leone (see below). In March 1998 ECOWAS ministers of foreign affairs, meeting in Yamoussoukro, Côte d'Ivoire, resolved that ECOMOG should become the region's permanent peace-keeping force, and upheld the decision of heads of state regarding the establishment of a new body, which should be used to observe, analyse and monitor the security situation in the West African region. Ministers agreed to undertake a redefinition of the command structure within the organization in order to strengthen decision-making and the legal status of the ECOMOG force.

In July 1998 ECOWAS ministers of defence and of security adopted a draft mechanism for conflict management, peace-keeping and security, which provided for ECOWAS intervention in the internal affairs of member states, where a conflict or military uprising threatened the region's security. In October the ECOWAS Authority resolved to establish a Committee of Mediation and Security. The meeting also agreed to implement a three-year ban on the import, export or manufacture of small armaments in order to enhance the security of the sub-region. In addition, the meeting issued a declaration on the control and prevention of drug abuse and agreed to allocate US $150,000 to establish an Eco-Drug Fund to finance regional activities in countering substance abuse.

At a summit meeting held in December 1999 at Lomé, Togo, ECOWAS heads of state and government approved a draft protocol to the organization's treaty, providing for the establishment of a permanent mechanism for the prevention, management and settlement of conflicts and the maintenance of peace in the region, as envisaged at their conference in December 1997.

Peace-keeping operations

In August 1990 an ECOWAS Cease-fire Monitoring Group (ECOMOG—initially comprising about 4,000 troops from The Gambia, Ghana, Guinea, Nigeria and Sierra Leone) was dispatched to Liberia in an attempt to enforce a cease-fire between conflicting factions there, to restore public order, and to establish an interim government, until elections could be held. In November a temporary cease-fire was agreed by the protagonists in Liberia, and an interim president was installed by ECOMOG. Following the signature of a new cease-fire agreement a national conference, organized by ECOWAS in March 1991, established a temporary government, pending elections to be held in early 1992. In June 1991 ECOWAS established a committee (initially comprising representatives of five member states, later expanded to nine) to co-ordinate the peace negotiations. In September, at a meeting in Yamoussoukro, Côte d'Ivoire, held under the aegis of the ECOWAS committee, two of the rival factions in Liberia agreed to encamp their troops in designated areas and to disarm under ECOMOG supervision. During the period preceding the proposed elections, ECOMOG was to occupy Liberian air and sea ports, and create a 'buffer zone' along the country's border with Sierra Leone. By September 1992, however, ECOMOG had been unable either to effect the disarmament of two of the principal military factions, the National Patriotic Front of Liberia (NPFL) and the United Liberation Movement of Liberia for Democracy (ULIMO), or to occupy positions in substantial areas of the country, as a result of resistance on the part of the NPFL. The proposed elections were consequently postponed indefinitely.

In October 1992 ECOMOG began offensive action against NPFL positions, with a campaign of aerial bombardment. In November ECOWAS imposed a land, sea and air blockade on the NPFL's territory, in response to the Front's refusal to comply with the Yamoussoukro accord of October 1991. In April 1993 ECOMOG announced that the disarmament of ULIMO had been completed, amid widespread accusations that ECOMOG had supported ULIMO against the NPFL, and was no longer a neutral force. An ECOWAS-brokered cease-fire agreement was signed in Cotonou, Benin, in July, and took effect on 1 August. In September a 300-member UN observer mission (UNOMIL) was established in Liberia to work alongside ECOMOG in monitoring the process of disarming troops, as well as to verify the impartiality of ECOMOG.

In September 1994 leaders of the country's main military factions, having negotiated with representatives of ECOWAS, the Organization of African Unity (OAU, q.v.) and the UN, signed an amendment to the Cotonou Agreement in Akosombo, Ghana. The accord provided for a new five-member Council of State, in the context of a cease-fire, as a replacement to the expired interim executive authority, and established a new timetable for democratic elections. In early 1995 negotiations to secure a peace settlement, conducted under ECOWAS auspices, collapsed, owing to disagreement on the composition of a new Council of State. In May, in an attempt to ease the political deadlock, ECOWAS heads of state and of government met leaders of the six main warring factions. Under continuing pressure from the international community, the leaders of the Liberian factions signed a new peace accord, in Abuja, Nigeria, in August. This political development led to renewed efforts on the part of ECOWAS countries to strengthen ECOMOG, and by October Burkina Faso, Nigeria, Ghana and Guinea had pledged troop contributions to increase the force strength from 7,268 to 12,000. In accordance with the peace agreement, ECOMOG forces, with UNOMIL, were to be deployed throughout Liberia and along its borders to prevent the flow of arms into the country and to monitor the disarmament of the warring parties. In December an attack on ECOMOG troops, by a dissident ULIMO faction (ULIMO–J), disrupted the deployment of the multinational forces and the disarmament process, which was scheduled to commence in mid-January 1996. At least 16 members of the peace-keeping force were killed in the fighting that ensued. Clashes between ECOMOG and the ULIMO–J forces continued in the west of the country in late December 1995 and early January 1996, during which time 130 Nigerian members of ECOMOG were held hostage. In April, following a series of violations of the cease-fire, serious hostilities erupted in the Liberian capital, Monrovia, between government forces and dissident troops. An initial agreement to end the fighting, negotiated under ECOWAS auspices, was unsuccessful; however, it secured the release of several civilians and soldiers who had been taken hostage during the civil disruption. Later in April a further cease-fire agreement was concluded, under the aegis of the US Government, the UN and ECOWAS. In May ministers of foreign

affairs of the countries constituting the ECOWAS Committee of Nine advocated that all armed factions be withdrawn from Monrovia and that ECOMOG troops be deployed throughout the capital in order to re-establish the city's 'safe-haven' status. According to the Committee's demands, all property, armaments and equipment seized unlawfully from civilians, ECOMOG and other international organizations during the fighting were to be returned, while efforts to disarm the warring factions and to pursue the restoration of democracy in the country were to be resumed. At the end of May the deployment of ECOMOG troops was initiated. In August a new cease-fire accord was signed by the leaders of the principal factions in Liberia, which envisaged the completion of the disarmament process by the end of January 1997, with elections to be held in May. The disarmament process began in November 1996, and by the end of January 1997 ECOMOG confirmed that 23,000 of the targeted 30,000–35,000 soldiers had been disarmed (the original estimate of 60,000 troops having been revised, disputed by both faction leaders and ECOMOG officials once movement between factions was taken into account). The deadline for disarmament was extended by seven days, during which time a further 1,500 soldiers were reported to have been disarmed. However, vigilante attacks by remaining armed faction fighters continued and were condemned by the ECOMOG commander. In February, at the end of a meeting of the Committee of Nine, it was announced that presidential and legislative elections would be held on 30 May (later revised to 19 July). ECOMOG was to withdraw from Liberia six months after the election date, until which time it had proposed to offer security for the incoming government and to provide training for a new unified Liberian army. The Committee also agreed, in consultation with the Council of State, to replace the existing Electoral Commission with a new Commission comprising seven members, to reflect all aspects of Liberian society. The Chairman would be selected from among the seven, in consultation with ECOWAS, which along with the UN and the OAU, would act as a 'technical adviser' to the Commission. ECOMOG deployed additional troops, who were joined by other international observers in ensuring that the elections were conducted in the necessary conditions of security. In early August several ECOWAS leaders celebrated the democratic transition of power in Liberia at the inauguration of Charles Taylor (formerly leader of the NPFL) as the newly-elected President. Later in that month ECOWAS heads of state agreed that the ECOMOG force in Liberia was to be reconstituted and would henceforth assist in the process of national reconstruction, including the restructuring of the armed and security forces, and the maintenance of security; it was further envisaged that ECOMOG's mandate (officially due to expire on 2 February 1998) would be extended in agreement with the Liberian Government. A Status of Forces Agreement, which defined ECOMOG's post-conflict responsibilities (i.e. capacity-building and maintenance of security) and imposed conditions on the peace-keeping forces remaining in the country, was signed by the Liberian Government and ECOWAS in June 1998. Relations with the Taylor administration, however, deteriorated, owing to accusations that ECOMOG was providing assistance to opposition groupings. The tense political situation, therefore, and the need for greater resources in Sierra Leone, resulted in ECOMOG transferring its headquarters from Monrovia to Freetown in Sierra Leone. The transfer was reported to have been completed by October, with just two ECOMOG battalions remaining in Liberia. The ECOMOG mission in Liberia was effectively terminated in October 1999 when the final declared stocks of rebel armaments were destroyed. In August a regional meeting was convened, under ECOWAS auspices, to attempt to defuse escalating tensions between Liberia and Guinea following an incursion into northern Liberia by Guinean rebel forces earlier in that month. In September representatives of eight member countries determined to establish a monitoring body to supervise the border region between Guinea, Liberia and Sierra Leone.

In May 1997 the democratically elected Sierra Leonean leader, President Ahmed Tejan Kabbah, was overthrown by a military coup involving officers of the national army and Revolutionary United Front (RUF) rebels. Nigerian forces based in Sierra Leone as part of a bilateral defence pact attempted to restore constitutional order. Their numbers were strengthened by the arrival of more than 700 Nigerian soldiers and two naval vessels which had been serving under the ECOMOG mandate in neighbouring Liberia. At the end of June ECOWAS ministers of foreign affairs, convened in Conakry, Guinea, agreed to pursue the objective of restoring a democratic government in Sierra Leone through dialogue and the imposition of economic sanctions. In July a four-member ministerial committee, comprising Côte d'Ivoire, Ghana, Guinea and Nigeria, together with representatives of the OAU, negotiated an agreement with the so-called Armed Forces Revolutionary Council (AFRC) in Sierra Leone to establish an immediate cease-fire and to pursue efforts towards the restoration of constitutional order. In August ECOWAS heads of state reaffirmed the Community's condemnation of the removal of President Kabbah and officially endorsed a series of punitive measures against the AFRC authorities in order to accelerate the restoration of democratic government. The meeting mandated

ECOMOG to maintain and monitor the cease-fire and to prevent all goods, excepting essential humanitarian supplies, from entering that country. It was also agreed that the committee on Sierra Leone include Liberia and be convened at the level of heads of state. In October the UN Security Council imposed an embargo on the sale or supply of armaments to Sierra Leone and authorized ECOWAS to ensure implementation of these measures. In September ECOMOG forces fired on container ships in the port of Freetown, which were suspected of violating the economic embargo. Clashes occurred between ECOMOG troops and AFRC/RUF soldiers, in particular around the area of Freetown's international airport which had been seized by ECOMOG; further ECOMOG air attacks against commercial and military targets were also conducted, with the aim of upholding the international sanctions and in self-defence. Despite the escalation in hostilities, the Committee of Five pursued negotiations with the military authorities, and at the end of October both sides signed a peace agreement, in Conakry, Guinea, providing for an immediate end to all fighting and the reinstatement of Kabbah's Government by April 1998; all combatants were to be disarmed and demobilized under the supervision of a disarmament committee comprising representatives of ECOMOG, the military authorities and local forces loyal to President Kabbah. In November 1997, however, the peace process was undermined by reports that ECOMOG forces had violated the cease-fire agreement following a series of air raids on Freetown, which ECOMOG claimed to have been in retaliation for attacks by AFRC/RUF-operated anti-aircraft equipment, and a demand by the AFRC authorities that the Nigerian contingent of ECOMOG leave the country. In mid-February 1998, following a series of offensive attacks against forces loyal to the military authorities, ECOMOG assumed control of Freetown and arrested several members of the AFRC/RUC regime. Some 50 AFRC officials were arrested by troops serving under ECOMOG on arrival at James Spriggs Payne Airport in Liberia, prompting protests from the Liberian Government at the Nigerian military intervention. An 11-member supervisory task force, which included the ECOMOG Commander, was established in Sierra Leone to maintain order, pending Kabbah's return from exile. ECOMOG troops subsequently also monitored the removal of the embargo against the use of the airport and port facilities in Freetown. Kabbah returned to Sierra Leone in March and installed a new administration. It was agreed that ECOMOG forces were to remain in the country in order to ensure the full restoration of peace and security, to assist in the restructuring of the armed forces and to help to resolve the problems of the substantial numbers of refugees and internally displaced persons. In early May ECOWAS Chiefs of Staff, meeting in Accra, Ghana, urged member states to provide more troops and logistical support to strengthen the ECOMOG force in Sierra Leone (at that time numbering some 10,000 troops), which was still involved in ongoing clashes with remaining rebel soldiers in eastern regions of the country. In July the UN established an Observer Mission in Sierra Leone (UNOMSIL), whose officers were to monitor the cease-fire, mainly in areas secured by ECOMOG troops. In October ECOMOG transferred its headquarters to Freetown, in order, partly, to reinforce its presence in the country. In January 1999 rebel soldiers attacked the capital and engaged in heavy fighting with ECOMOG forces, amid reports that the Liberian Government was supporting the rebels. Nigeria dispatched several thousand additional troops to counter the rebel advance and to secure the border with Liberia. In February, however, once ECOMOG had regained control of Freetown, the Nigerian Government expressed its desire to withdraw all its troops from the peace-keeping force by May, owing to financial restraints. Efforts to negotiate a peace settlement were initiated, with the Chairman of ECOWAS at that time, President Gnassingbe Eyadéma of Togo, actively involved in mediation between the opposing groups, despite persisting reports of fighting between ECOMOG and rebel soldiers in areas east of the capital. A cease-fire agreement was concluded in May, and a political settlement was signed, by Kabbah and the RUF leader, in Lomé, Togo, in July. ECOMOG's mandate in Sierra Leone was adapted to support the consolidation of peace in that country and national reconstruction. In October UNOMSIL was replaced by the UN Mission in Sierra Leone (UNAMSIL), which was to assist with the implementation of the Lomé accord and to assume some of the functions then being performed by ECOMOG, including the provision of security at Lungi international airport and at other key installations, buildings and government institutions in the Freetown area. In consequence the ECOMOG contingent was withdrawn in April 2000. However, following a resurgence of RUF violence in April and May, when as many as 500 members of UNAMSIL were captured by the rebels, ECOWAS heads of government agreed to reinforce the UN peace-keeping operation with some 3,000 regional troops.

In July 1998 ECOWAS ministers of defence and of foreign affairs met to consider the political unrest in Guinea-Bissau, following an unsuccessful attempt by rebel soldiers, in June, to overthrow the Government of President João Vieira, and urged both sides to co-operate in negotiating a settlement. An ECOWAS Committee of Seven on Guinea-Bissau (comprising the ministers of foreign affairs of Burkina Faso, Côte d'Ivoire, The Gambia, Ghana, Guinea, Nigeria and Senegal) was established and met for the first time in August. In late August, following mediation by ECOWAS representatives and a contact group of the Comunidade dos Países de Língua Portuguesa (CPLP, q.v.), which had secured an initial cease-fire, an agreement was signed by the conflicting parties providing for an end to hostilities, the reopening of the international airport to facilitate the provision of humanitarian supplies, and for independent supervision of the cease-fire agreement. ECOWAS subsequently held discussions with the CPLP in order to co-ordinate efforts to secure peace in Guinea-Bissau. In late October ECOWAS heads of state endorsed the deployment of ECOMOG forces in Guinea-Bissau. On 1 November the two sides in the dispute, meeting in Abuja, Nigeria, signed a peace accord under ECOWAS auspices, which reinforced the August cease-fire and incorporated an agreement to establish a government of national unity. ECOMOG forces were to replace all foreign troops, mainly Senegalese, currently in Guinea-Bissau, supervise the security of the border region between those two countries, and enable humanitarian organizations to have free access to those needing assistance. In addition ECOMOG was to be responsible for monitoring the conduct of presidential and legislative elections, scheduled to be held in 1999. In early February President Vieira and the rebel leader Gen. Manè signed a cease-fire accord, under ECOWAS auspices. A new Government of National Unity was established later in that month and an ECOMOG Interposition Force began to be dispatched to Guinea-Bissau. In early May, however, President Vieira was ousted by the rebel forces. Meeting later in that month, in Lomé, Togo, ECOWAS ministers of foreign affairs, condemned the overthrow of Vieira. They resolved to withdraw the ECOMOG contingent, at that time numbering 600 troops from Benin, Gabon, Niger and Togo, owing to the political developments and lack of finances. By early June all ECOMOG troops had left Guinea-Bissau.

ENVIRONMENTAL PROTECTION

ECOWAS promotes implementation of the UN Convention on Desertification Control and supports programmes initiated at national and sub-regional level within the framework of the treaty. Together with the Permanent Inter-State Committee on Drought Control in the Sahel (CILSS, q.v.). ECOWAS has been designated as a project leader for implementing the Convention in West Africa. Other environmental initiatives include a regional meteorological project to enhance meteorological activities and applications, and in particular to contribute to food security and natural resource management in the sub-region. ECOWAS pilot schemes have formed the basis of integrated control projects for the control of floating weeds in five water basins in West Africa, which had hindered the development of the local fishery sectors. A rural water supply programme aims to ensure adequate water for rural dwellers in order to improve their living standards. The first phase of the project focused on schemes to develop village and pastoral water points in Burkina Faso, Guinea, Mali, Niger and Senegal, with funds from various multilateral donors.

AGRICULTURE AND FISHING

An Agricultural Development Strategy was adopted in 1982, aiming at sub-regional self-sufficiency by the year 2000. The strategy included plans for selecting seeds and cattle species, and called for solidarity among member states during international commodity negotiations. A transhumance certification scheme, to facilitate the monitoring of animal movement and animal health surveillance and protection in the sub-region, was under preparation in 1997.

In November 1995 an agro-industrial forum, jointly organized by ECOWAS and the European Union, was held in Dakar, Senegal. The forum aimed to facilitate co-operation between companies in the two regions, to develop the agro-industrial sector in West Africa and to promote business opportunities.

SOCIAL PROGRAMME

Four organizations have been established within ECOWAS by the Executive Secretariat: the Organization of Trade Unions of West Africa, which held its first meeting in 1984; the West African Youth Association; the West African Universities' Association; and the West Africa Women's Association (whose statutes were approved by a meeting of ministers of social affairs in May 1987). Regional sports competitions are held annually. In 1987 ECOWAS member states agreed to establish a West African Health Organization by merger of the existing West African Health Community (q.v.) and the Organization for Co-ordination and Co-operation in the Struggle against Endemic Diseases; however, in 2000 this process was still ongoing.

INFORMATION AND MEDIA

In March 1990 ECOWAS ministers of information formulated a policy on the dissemination of information about ECOWAS throughout the region and the appraisal of attitudes of its population towards the Community. The ministers established a new information commission. In November 1991 a conference on press communication and African integration, organized by ECOWAS, recommended the creation of an ECOWAS press card, judicial safeguards to protect journalists, training programmes for journalists and the establishment of a regional documentation centre and data bank. In November 1994 the commission of social and cultural affairs, meeting in Lagos, Nigeria, endorsed a series of measures to promote west African integration. These included special radio, television and newspaper features, sporting events and other competitions or rallies.

Finance

ECOWAS is financed by contributions from member states, although there is a poor record of punctual payment of dues, which has hampered the work of the Secretariat. Arrears in contributions to the Secretariat were reported to total US \$42m. at October 1998. Under the revised treaty, ECOWAS was to receive revenue from a community tax, based on the total value of imports from member countries. In July 1996 the summit meeting approved a protocol on a community levy, providing for the imposition of a 0.5% tax on the value of imports from a third country. Member states were requested to ratify the protocol, in order to enable its application with effect from 1 January 1997. In August 1997 the Authority of Heads of State and Government determined that the community levy should replace budgetary contributions as the organization's principal source of finance. By October 1998 only five member states had ratified the protocol.

The 1998 budget amounted to approximately US \$10m.

Publications

Annual Report.
Contact.
ECOWAS National Accounts.
ECOWAS News.
West African Bulletin.

EUROPEAN UNION—ACP PARTNERSHIP

The European Union (EU) as a whole provides emergency humanitarian assistance for developing and other non-EU countries, amounting to ECU 517m. in 1998, including ECU 76m., for operations in the Great Lakes region of Africa (mainly to assist refugees and displaced persons), ECU 36.8m. for Sudan and ECU 18m. for Angola. From 1976–February 2000, however, the principal means of co-operation between the Community and developing countries was the Lomé Convention, concluded by the EU and African, Caribbean and Pacific (ACP) states. The First Lomé Convention (Lomé I), which came into force on 1 April 1976, replaced the Yaoundé Conventions and the Arusha Agreement, and was designed to provide a new framework of co-operation, taking into account the varying needs of developing countries. Lomé II was concluded at Lomé, Togo, in October 1979, and came into force on 1 January 1981. Lomé III was signed in December 1984, and came into force on 1 March 1985 (trade provisions) and 1 May 1986 (aid). The Fourth Lomé Convention, which had a 10-year commitment period, was signed in December 1989: its trade provisions entered into force on 1 March 1990, and the remainder followed in September 1991. In February 2000 negotiations on a successor arrangement to the Lomé Convention, initiated in September 1998, were concluded. The new partnership accord was signed by ACP and EU Heads of State and Government in Cotonou, Benin, in June 2000, and was to enter into force following ratification by the European Parliament and by the ACP national legislatures.

Organization

ACP–EU INSTITUTIONS

Council of Ministers: one minister from each signatory state; one co-chairman from each of the two groups; meets annually.

Committee of Ambassadors: one ambassador from each signatory state; chairmanship alternates between the two groups; meets at least every six months.

Joint Assembly: EU and ACP are equally represented; attended by parliamentary delegates from each of the ACP countries and an equal number of members of the European Parliament; one co-chairman from each group; meets twice a year.

Centre for the Development of Industry—CDI: 52 ave Herrmann Debroux, 1160 Brussels, Belgium; tel. (2) 679-18-11; fax (2) 675-26-03; e-mail director@cdi.be; internet www.cdi.be; f. 1977 to encourage investment in the ACP states by providing contacts and advice, holding promotion meetings, and helping to finance feasibility studies; Dir SURENDRA SHARMA.

Technical Centre for Agricultural and Rural Co-operation: Postbus 380, 6700 AJ Wageningen, Netherlands; tel. (317) 467100; fax (317) 460067; f. 1983 to provide ACP states with better access to information, research, training and innovations in agricultural development and extension; Dir Dr R. D. COOKE.

ACP INSTITUTIONS

ACP Council of Ministers.

ACP Committee of Ambassadors.

ACP Secretariat: ACP House, 451 ave Georges Henri, 1200 Brussels, Belgium; tel. (2) 743-06-00; fax (2) 735-55-73; e-mail info@ acpsec.org; internet www.oneworld.org/acpsec; Sec.-Gen. JEAN-ROBERT GOULONGANA (Gabon).

DELEGATIONS AND OFFICES OF THE EUROPEAN COMMISSION IN AFRICA SOUTH OF THE SAHARA

Angola: Rua Rainha Jinga 6, CP 6, Luanda; tel. (2) 303038; fax (2) 392531.

Benin: ave de Clozel, 01 BP 910, Cotonou; tel. 31-26-84; fax 31-53-28.

Botswana: North Ring Rd, POB 1253, Gaborone; tel. 314455; fax 313626.

Burkina Faso: BP 352, Ouagadougou; tel. 30-37-85; fax 30-89-66.

Burundi: ave du 13 octobre, BP 103, Bujumbura; tel. (2) 23426; fax (2) 24612.

Cameroon: 105 rue 1770, quartier Bastos, BP 847, Yaoundé; tel. 20-13-87; fax 20-21-49.

Cape Verde: Achada de Santo António, CP 122, Praia, Santiago; tel. 62-13-92; fax 62-13-91.

Central African Republic: rue de Flandre, BP 1298, Bangui; tel. 61-30-53; fax 61-65-35.

Chad: route de Farcha, BP 552, N'Djamena; tel. 52-89-77; fax 52-71-05.

Comoros: blvd de la Corniche, BP 559, Moroni; tel. (73) 2306; fax (73) 2494.

Congo, Democratic Republic: 71 ave Lemera, BP 2000, Kinshasa; tel. (871) 685053336; fax (871) 685053337; e-mail endelrdc@ic.cd.

Congo, Republic: ave Lyautey, opposite Embassy of Italy, BP 2149, Brazzaville; tel. (871) 761480259; fax (871) 761480261.

Côte d'Ivoire: 18 rue de Dr Crozet, BP 1821, Abidjan 01; tel. 21-24-28; fax 21-40-89.

Djibouti: 11 blvd de Maréchal Joffre, BP 2477, Djibouti; tel. 352615; fax 350036.

Eritrea: 1 Gainer St, POB 5710, Asmara; tel. (1) 126566; fax (1) 126578.

Ethiopia: POB 5570, Addis Ababa; tel. (1) 612511; fax (1) 612877.

Gabon: Bas de Gué-Gué, BP 321, Libreville; tel. 73-22-50; fax 73-65-54.

Gambia: 10 Tenth St South, POB 512, Fajara; tel. 495146; fax 497848.

Ghana: The Round House, 81 Cantonments Rd, Accra; POB 9505, Kotoka International Airport, Accra; tel. (21) 774202; fax (21) 774154; e-mail delcomgh@ghana.com.

Guinea: Corniche Sud, Madina Dispensaire, BP 730, Conakry; tel. 46-49-42; fax 46-18-74; e-mail delce.gui@eti-bull.net.

Guinea-Bissau: Bairro da Penha, CP 359, 1113 Bissau; tel. 251027; fax 251044.

Kenya: Union Insurance Bldg, Ragati Rd, POB 45119, Nairobi; tel. (2) 713020; fax (2) 716487.

Lesotho: 167 Constitution Rd, POB MS 518, Maseru; tel. 313726; fax 310193.

Liberia: EC Aid Co-ordination Office, UN Drive, Mamba Point, Monrovia; tel. 266273; fax 266274.

Madagascar: Immeuble Ny Havana, BP 746, Antananarivo 101; tel. (20) 2224216; fax (20) 2264562; e-mail delcemad@dts.mg.

Malawi: Europa House, POB 30102, Capital City, Lilongwe 3; tel. 783199; fax 783534.

Mali: ave de l'OUA, Badalabougou est, BP 115, Bamako; tel. 22-23-56; fax 22-36-70; e-mail endelmli@cefib.com.

Mauritania: Ilot V, Lot 24, BP 213, Nouakchott; tel. 527-24; fax 535-24.

Mauritius: James Court, 8th Floor, Bâtiment St, POB 1148, Port Louis; tel. 211-6295; fax 211-6624; e-mail europe@bow.intnet.mu.

Mozambique: Avda do Zimbabwe 1214, CP 1306, Maputo; tel. (1) 490266; fax (1) 491866.

Namibia: Sanlam Bldg, 4th Floor, 154 Independence Ave, 9000 Windhoek; tel. (61) 220099; fax (61) 235135; e-mail eudelnam@iwwn.com.na.

Niger: BP 10388, Niamey; tel. 73-23-60; fax 73-23-22.

Nigeria: Knorr House, Ozumba Mbadiwe Ave, opp. 1004 Flats, Victoria Island, PMB 12767, Lagos; tel. (1) 2617852; fax (1) 2617248; e-mail ecnig@infoweb.abs.net.

Rwanda: 14 ave Député Kamuzinzi, BP 515, Kigali; tel. 75586; fax 74313.

São Tomé and Príncipe: CP 132, São Tomé; tel. 21780; fax 22683.

Senegal: 12 ave Albert Sarraut, BP 3345, Dakar; tel. 823-13-14; fax 823-68-85.

Seychelles: POB 530, Victoria, Mahé; tel. 323940; fax 323890.

Sierra Leone: Wesley House, 4 George St, POB 1399, Freetown; tel. (22) 223975; fax (22) 225212.

Somalia: EC Somalia Unit, Union Insurance House, 1st Floor, Ragati Rd, Nairobi, Kenya; tel. (2) 712830; fax (2) 710997.

Sudan: AAAID Bldg, 3rd Floor, Osman Digna Ave, POB 2363, Khartoum; tel. (11) 775054; fax (11) 775393.

Swaziland: Lilunga House, 4th Floor, Gilfillan St, Mbabane; tel. 42908; fax 46729.

Tanzania: 38 Mirambo St, POB 9514, Dar es Salaam; tel. (51) 117473; fax (51) 113277.

Togo: 37 ave Nicolas Grunitzky, BP 1657, Lomé; tel. 21-36-62; fax 21-13-00.

Uganda: Rwenzori House, 5th Floor, 1 Lumumba Ave, POB 5244, Kampala; tel. (41) 233303; fax (41) 233708; e-mail ecdelug@imul.com.

Zambia: Plot 4899, Los Angeles Blvd, POB 34871, Lusaka; tel. (1) 250711; fax (1) 250906; e-mail deczam@zamnet.zm.

Zimbabwe: Construction House, 6th Floor, 110 Leopold Takawira St, POB 4252, Harare; tel. (4) 707120; fax (4) 725360.

Activities

Under the first Lomé Convention (Lomé I), the Community committed 3,052.4m. European Currency Units (ECU) for aid and investment in developing countries, through the European Development Fund (EDF) and the European Investment Bank (EIB). Provision was made for over 99% of ACP (mainly agricultural) exports to enter the EC market duty free, while certain products which compete directly with Community agriculture, such as sugar, were given preferential treatment but not free access. The Stabex (Stabilization of Export Earnings) scheme was designed to help developing countries to withstand fluctuations in the price of their agricultural products, by paying compensation for reduced export earnings.

The second Lomé Convention envisaged Community expenditure of ECU 5,530m.; it extended some of the provisions of Lomé I, and introduced new fields of co-operation. One of the most important innovations was a scheme, Sysmin, similar to Stabex, to safeguard exports of minerals. Lomé III provided a total of ECU 8,500m. (about US $6,000m. at 30 January 1985) in assistance to the ACP states over the five years from March 1985, representing little or no increase, in real terms, over the amount provided by Lomé II.

Under the fourth Lomé Convention the financial protocol for 1990–95 made commitments of ECU 12,000m. (US $13,700m.), of which ECU 10,800m. was from the EDF (including ECU 1,500m. for Stabex and ECU 480m. for Sysmin) and ECU 1,200m. from the EIB. Under Lomé IV the obligation of most of the ACP states to contribute to the replenishment of Stabex resources, including the repayment of transfers made under the first three Conventions, was removed. In addition, special loans made to ACP member countries were to be cancelled, except in the case of profit-orientated businesses. Other innovations included the provision of assistance for structural adjustment programmes, measures to avoid increasing the recipient countries' indebtedness (e.g. by providing Stabex and

Sysmin assistance in the form of grants, rather than loans), and increased support for the private sector, environmental protection, and control of growth in population. In March 1997 the Commission proposed the provision of debt relief assistance worth ECU 25m. per year for the period 1997–2000 to the 11 heavily indebted poor countries (as identified by the World Bank and IMF) which form part of the ACP Group. This funding would support international efforts to reduce outstanding debt and encourage economic prospects. In September 1993 the Community announced plans to revise and strengthen its relations with the ACP countries under the Lomé Convention. A mid-term review of the Lomé IV Convention was initiated in May 1994, amid concern on the part of ACP signatory states regarding the future of the Convention. In February 1995 a joint EU-ACP ministerial council, which was scheduled to conclude the negotiations, was adjourned, owing to significant disagreement among EU member states concerning reimbursement of the EDF for the period 1995–2000. In June 1995 EU heads of government reached an agreement, which was subsequently endorsed by an EU-ACP ministerial group. The accord was to provide ECU 14,625m. for the second phase of the Lomé IV Convention, of which ECU 12,967m. was to be allocated from the EDF and ECU 1,658m. for loans from the EIB. Agreement was also reached on revision of the country-of-origin rules for manufactured goods; expansion of the preferential system of trade for ACP products; a new protocol on the sustainable management of forest resources; and a joint declaration on support for the banana industry. The revised Convention was signed in November, in Mauritius. The new agreement included a reference to the observance of human rights and respect for democracy and the rule of law as essential elements of the preferential trading arrangement accorded under the Convention. Financial resources were to be made available to support institutional and administrative reforms to strengthen these principles in contracting states. The revised Convention formally entered into force on 1 June 1998 having been ratified by all 15 EU member states.

On 1 July 1993 the European Community (EC, as the EU was previously entitled) introduced a regime concerning the import of bananas into the Community, that was designed to protect the banana industries of ACP countries (mostly in the Caribbean), which were threatened by cheaper bananas produced by countries in Latin America. The new regime, which was opposed by the low-cost producing countries and by Germany (the largest EU consumer of bananas), placed an annual quota of 2m. metric tons of bananas imported from Latin America, which would incur a uniform duty of 20%, while imports above this level were to be subject to a tariff of ECU 850 per ton. In February 1994 a dispute panel of the General Agreement on Tariffs and Trade (GATT) upheld a complaint brought by five Latin American countries that the EU import regime, which reserved 30% of its market for production of member states and ACP countries, was in contravention of free-trade principles. An agreement was reached in March under which the EU increased the quota for Latin American banana imports to 2.1m. tons from October 1994 and 2.2m. tons in 1995. In February 1996 the USA, supported by four Latin American countries, submitted a formal complaint about the import regime to the World Trade Organization (WTO). The final ruling of the WTO, issued in May 1997, concluded that the EU banana import regime violated 19 free-trade regulations. The EU appealed against the ruling; however, in September the WTO endorsed the original verdict. None the less, the allocation of preferential tariffs to ACP producers, covered by a waiver since late 1994, was upheld. In October 1997 the EU agreed to amend its banana import regime to comply with the WTO ruling. An arbitration report issued in January 1998 compelled the EU to implement changes to the regime by 1 January 1999. In June 1998 EU ministers responsible for agriculture approved a reform of the import regime, providing for two separate quota systems, granting Latin American producers greater access to the European market, with a quota of 2.53m. tons (at a tariff of ECU 75 per ton), while ACP countries would have a quota of 857,000 tons (tariff-free). The US Government, however, continued to dispute the import regime, and in April 1999 the WTO confirmed that the EU had failed to conform to WTO provisions.

In November 1997 the first summit meeting of heads of state of ACP countries was held, in Libreville, Gabon. The principal issues under consideration at the meeting were the strategic challenges confronting the ACP group of countries and, in particular, relations with the EU beyond 2000, when Lomé IV was scheduled to expire. The summit mandated ACP ministers of finance and of trade and industry to organize a series of regular meetings in order to strengthen co-ordination within the grouping. In May 1998 ACP ministers of trade and industry agreed further to co-operate in the formulation of policies to promote intra-ACP trade and to establish a common position with regard to future relations with the EU, multilateral trade negotiations under the WTO and other discussions at an international level.

Formal negotiations on the conclusion of a successor agreement to the Lomé Convention were initiated on 30 September 1998. In mid-1998 EU ministers of foreign affairs had approved a request by the Cuban Government to participate in the negotiations with observer status. The negotiations were concluded in February 2000, and the new partnership accord was signed by ACP and EU Heads of State and Government in June 2000 in Cotonou, Benin. The so-called Cotonou Agreement (which was to enter into effect following ratification by the European Parliament and by the ACP national legislatures, and was to cover the period 2000–20) comprised the following main elements: increased political co-operation; the enhanced participation of civil society in ACP–EC partnership affairs; a strong focus on the reduction of poverty (addressing the economic and technical marginalization of developing nations was a primary concern); a new framework for economic and trade co-operation, see below; and a reform of the existing structures for financial co-operation. Under the provisions of the new accord the EU and ACP countries were to negotiate free-trade arrangements (replacing the previous non-reciprocal trade preferences) with the most developed ACP countries during 2000–08; these would be structured around a system of free trade zones—FTZs. An assessment to be conducted in 2004 would identify those mid-ranking ACP nations also capable of entering into such free-trade deals. Meanwhile, the 41 least-developed ACP nations were to benefit from an EU initiative to allow free access for most of their products by 2005. The preferential agreements currently in force would be retained initially (phase I), in view of a waiver granted by the WTO; thereafter ACP—EU trade was to be gradually liberalized over a period of 12—15 years (phase II). It was envisaged that Stabex and Sysmin would be eliminated gradually.

THE FRANC ZONE

Address: Direction Générale des Services Etrangers (Service de la Zone Franc), Banque de France, 39 rue Croix-des-Petits-Champs, 75049, Paris Cédex 01, France.
Telephone: 1-42-92-31-46; **fax:** 1-42-92-39-88.

MEMBERS

Benin	Equatorial Guinea
Burkina Faso	French Republic*
Cameroon	Gabon
Central African Republic	Guinea-Bissau
Chad	Mali
The Comoros	Niger
Republic of the Congo	Senegal
Côte d'Ivoire	Togo

* Metropolitan France, Mayotte, St Pierre and Miquelon and the Overseas Departments and Territories.

The Franc Zone embraces all those countries and groups of countries whose currencies are linked with the French franc at a fixed rate of exchange and who agree to hold their reserves mainly in the form of French francs and to effect their exchange on the Paris market. Each of these countries or groups of countries has its own central issuing bank and its currency is freely convertible into French francs. This monetary union is based on agreements concluded between France and each country or group of countries.

Apart from Guinea and Mauritania, all of the countries that formerly comprised French West and Equatorial Africa are members of the Franc Zone. The former West and Equatorial African territories are still grouped within the currency areas that existed before independence, each group having its own currency issued by a central bank.

A number of states left the Franc Zone during the period 1958–73: Guinea, Tunisia, Morocco, Algeria, Mauritania and Madagascar.

The Comoros, formerly a French Overseas Territory, did not join the Franc Zone following its unilateral declaration of independence in 1975. However, francs CFA were used as the currency of the new state and the Institut d'émission des Comores continued to function as a Franc Zone organization. In 1976 the Comoros formally assumed membership. In July 1981 the Banque centrale des Comores replaced the Institut d'émission des Comores, establishing its own currency, the Comoros franc. The island of Mayotte, however, has remained under French administration as an Overseas Collectivité Territoriale, using the French franc as its unit of currency.

Equatorial Guinea, a former Spanish possession, joined the Franc Zone in January 1985, and Guinea-Bissau, a former Portuguese territory, joined in May 1997.

During the late 1980s and early 1990s the economies of the African Franc Zone countries were adversely affected by increasing foreign debt and by a decline in the prices paid for their principal export commodities. The French Government, however, refused to devalue the franc CFA, as recommended by the IMF. In 1990 the Franc Zone governments agreed to develop economic union, with integrated public finances and common commercial legislation. In April 1992, at a meeting of Franc Zone ministers, a treaty was signed on the insurance industry whereby a regulatory body for the industry was to be established: the Conférence Intrafricaine des Marchés d'Assurances (CIMA). Under the treaty, which was to be effective from 31 December 1992, a council of Franc Zone ministers responsible for the insurance industry was also to be established with its secretariat in Libreville, Gabon. (A code of conduct for members of CIMA came into effect in early 1995.) At the meeting held in April 1992 ministers also agreed that a further council of ministers was to be created with the task of monitoring the social security systems in Franc Zone countries. A programme drawn up by Franc Zone finance ministers concerning the harmonization of commercial legislation in member states through the establishment of l'Organisation pour l'Harmonisation du Droit des Affaires en Afrique (OHADA), was approved by the Franco-African summit in October. A treaty to align corporate and investment regulations was signed by 11 member countries at the annual meeting with France in October 1993. Devaluations of the franc CFA and the Comoros franc were agreed by CFA central banks in January 1994 (see below). Following the devaluation the CFA countries embarked on programmes of economic adjustment, including restrictive fiscal and wage policies and other monetary, structural and social measures, designed to stimulate growth and to ensure eligibility for development assistance from international financial institutions. France established a special development fund of FFr 300m. to alleviate the immediate social consequences of the devaluation, and announced substantial debt cancellations. In April the French Government announced assistance amounting to FFr 10,000m. over three years to Franc Zone countries undertaking structural adjustment programmes. The IMF, which had strongly advocated a devaluation of the franc CFA, and the World Bank approved immediate soft-credit loans, technical assistance and cancellations or rescheduling of debts. In June 1994 heads of state (or representatives) of African Franc Zone countries convened in Libreville, Gabon, to review the effects of the currency realignment. The final communiqué of the meeting urged further international support for the countries' economic development efforts. In April 1995 Franc Zone finance ministers, meeting in Paris, recognized the positive impact of the devaluation on agricultural export sectors, in particular in west African countries, though central African countries, it was noted, were still afflicted by serious economic difficulties. In September the Franc Zone member countries and the French Government agreed to establish a research and training institution, Afristat, which was to support national statistical organizations in order to strengthen economic management capabilities in participating states. In April 1997 finance ministers met to review the economies of member states. Capital entries (private investment and public development aid) along with tax and wage policies and an increase in exports were found to have contributed to economic growth. Improvements were continuing within a programme supported by the IMF and the World Bank, though ministers stated that economic development efforts were not sufficiently supported by the private sector, with the average rate of investment remaining at 10% of GDP. The adoption of a charter to encourage private investors was discussed, but postponed pending an investigation into proposals made by UEMOA and CEMAC. The co-operation agreement permitting Guinea-Bissau's membership of the Franc Zone, to come into effect on 2 May, was also signed. In the same month delegates from OHADA met donors in Guinea-Bissau, aiming to raise funds worth US $50m. over a 12-year period, to allow them to train commercial court judges, provide information for businesses and cover administration costs. In April 1998 the annual meeting of finance ministers was dominated by discussions regarding the future of the Franc Zone and possible currency devaluations resulting from the introduction of a European single currency, the euro, within the framework of a European economic and monetary union, in which France was scheduled to participate when it entered into effect on 1 January 1999. In July 1998 the European Commission recommended that all convertibility arrangements concluded between France and the Franc Zone countries be preserved after the introduction of the euro, and that member countries maintain the fixed parity of the franc CFA (and of the Comoros franc). These arrangements consequently remained in effect after 1 January 1999.

EXCHANGE REGULATIONS

Currencies of the Franc Zone are freely convertible into the French franc at a fixed rate, through 'operations accounts' established by agreements concluded between the French Treasury and the individual issuing banks. It is backed fully by the French Treasury, which also provides the issuing banks with overdraft facilities.

The monetary reserves of the CFA countries are normally held in French francs in the French Treasury. However, the Banque centrale des états de l'Afrique de l'ouest (BCEAO) and the Banque des états de l'Afrique centrale (BEAC) are authorized to hold up to 35% of their foreign exchange holdings in currencies other than the franc. Exchange is effected on the Paris market. Part of the reserves earned by richer members can be used to offset the deficits incurred by poorer countries.

Regulations drawn up in 1967 provided for the free convertibility of currency with that of countries outside the Franc Zone. Restrictions were removed on the import and export of CFA banknotes, although some capital transfers are subject to approval by the governments concerned.

When the French Government instituted exchange control to protect the French franc in May 1968, other Franc Zone countries were obliged to take similar action in order to maintain free convertibility within the Franc Zone. The franc CFA was devalued following devaluation of the French franc in August 1969. Since March 1973 the French authorities have ceased to maintain the franc-US dollar rate within previously agreed margins, and, as a result, the value of the franc CFA has fluctuated on foreign exchange markets in line with the French franc.

In August 1993, as a result of the financial turmoil regarding the European exchange rate mechanism and the continuing weakness of the French franc, the BCEAO and the BEAC decided to suspend repurchasing of francs CFA outside the Franc Zone. Effectively this signified the withdrawal of guaranteed convertibility of the franc CFA with the French franc. In January 1994 the franc CFA was devalued by 50%, and the Comoros franc by 33.3%.

CURRENCIES OF THE FRANC ZONE

French franc (= 100 centimes): used in Metropolitan France, in the Overseas Departments of Guadeloupe, French Guiana, Martinique, Réunion, and in the Overseas Collectivités Territoriales of Mayotte and St Pierre and Miquelon.

1 franc CFA = 1 French centime. CFA stands for Communauté financière africaine in the West African area and for Coopération financière en Afrique centrale in the Central African area. Used in the monetary areas of West and Central Africa respectively.

1 Comoros franc = 1.333 French centimes (1 French franc = 75 Comoros francs). Used in the Comoros, where it replaced the franc CFA in 1981.

1 franc CFP = 5.5 French centimes. CFP stands for Comptoirs français du Pacifique. Used in New Caledonia, French Polynesia and the Wallis and Futuna Islands.

WEST AFRICA

Union économique et monétaire ouest-africaine—UEMOA: BP 543, Ouagadougou, Burkina Faso; tel. 31-88-73; fax 31-88-72; e-mail commission@uemoa.bf; internet www.uemoa.bf; f. 1994; replaced the Communauté économique de l'Afrique de l'ouest–CEAO; promotes regional monetary and economic convergence, and aims to improve regional trade by facilitating the movement of labour and capital between member states. The first meeting of heads of state of UEMOA member countries, held in May 1996 in Ouagadougou, agreed to establish a customs union with effect from 1 January 1998. A preferential tariff scheme, eliminating duties on most local products and reducing by 30% import duties on many Community-produced industrial goods, became operational on 1 July 1996; in addition, from 1 July, a community solidarity tax of 0.5% was imposed on all goods from third countries sold within the Community, in order to strengthen UEMOA's capacity to promote economic integration. (This was increased to 1% in December 1999.) In June 1997 the second meeting of UEMOA heads of state and government agreed to reduce import duties on industrial products originating in the Community by a further 30%. The meeting also confirmed that Côte d'Ivoire's stock exchange was to be transformed into a regional institution serving the UEMOA sub-region, in order to further economic integration (see below). At the meeting UEMOA heads of state adopted a declaration on peace and security in the region. In November UEMOA ministers of finance, meeting in extraordinary session, agreed to postpone the establishment of a customs union until 1 January 2000. On that date internal tariffs were eliminated on all local products (including industrial goods) and a joint external tariff system, reportedly in five bands of between 0% and 20%, was imposed on goods deriving from outside the customs union. Guinea-Bissau was excluded from the arrangement owing to its unstable political situation. In March 1998 an inter-parliamentary committee, recognized as the predecessor of a

UEMOA legislature, was inaugurated in Mali. In August 1999 the committee adopted a draft treaty on the establishment of a UEMOA parliament, which was scheduled to become operational in 2000, comprising 10 representatives from each member state. Mems: Benin, Burkina Faso, Côte d'Ivoire, Guinea-Bissau, Mali, Niger, Senegal and Togo. Chair. Gen. GNASSINGBE EYADÉMA (Togo).

Union monétaire ouest-africaine—UMOA (West African Monetary Union): established by Treaty of November 1973, entered into force 1974; in 1990 the UMOA Banking Commission was established, which is responsible for supervising the activities of banks and financial institutions in the region, with the authority to prohibit the operation of a banking institution. UMOA constitutes an integral part of UEMOA.

Banque centrale des états de l'Afrique de l'ouest—BCEAO: ave Abdoulaye Fadiga, BP 3108, Dakar, Senegal; tel. 839-05-00; fax 823-93-35; e-mail akangni@bceao.int; internet www.bceao.int; f. 1962; central bank of issue for the mems of UEMOA; cap. and res 806,919m. francs CFA (Dec. 1998). Mems: Benin, Burkina Faso, Côte d'Ivoire, Guinea Bissau, Mali, Niger, Senegal and Togo. Gov. CHARLES KONAN BANNY (Côte d'Ivoire); Sec.-Gen. MICHEL K. KLOUSSEH (Togo). Publs *Annual Report, Notes d'Information et Statistiques* (monthly), *Annuaire des banques, Bilan des banques et établissements financiers* (annually).

Banque ouest-africaine de développement—BOAD: 68 ave de la Libération, BP 1172, Lomé, Togo; tel. 21-42-44; fax 21-52-67; e-mail boadsiege@boad.org; internet www.boad.org; f. 1973 to promote the balanced development of mem. states and the economic integration of West Africa; cap. 27,435m. francs CFA (Dec. 1998). A Guarantee Fund for Private Investment in west Africa, established jtly by BOAD and the European Investment Bank, was inaugurated in Dec. 1994. The Fund, which had an initial cap. of 8,615.5m. francs CFA, aimed to guarantee medium- and long-term credits to private sector businesses in the region. Mems: Benin, Burkina Faso, Côte d'Ivoire, Guinea-Bissau, Mali, Niger, Senegal, Togo. Chair. BONI YAYI (Benin); Vice-Chair. ALPHA TOURÉ. Publs *Rapport Annuel, BOAD-INFO* (quarterly).

Bourse Régionale des Valeurs Mobilières—BRVM: 18 ave Joseph Anoma, BP 3802, Abidjan 01, Côte d'Ivoire; tel. 32-66-85; fax 32-66-84; f. 1998; Pres. LAMASEH ALEXIS LOOKY; Man. KOKOU GOZAN (acting).

CENTRAL AFRICA

Communauté économique et monétaire de l'Afrique centrale—CEMAC: BP 969, Bangui, Central African Republic; tel. and fax 61-21-35; e-mail sgudeac@intnet.cf; internet www.socatel.intnet.cf/accueil1.html; f. 1998; formally inaugurated as the successor to the Union douanière et économique de l'Afrique centrale (UDEAC, f. 1966) at a meeting of heads of state held in Malabo, Equatorial Guinea, in June 1999; aims to promote the process of sub-regional integration within the framework of an economic union and a monetary union; CEMAC was also to comprise a parliament and sub-regional tribunal. UDEAC established a common external tariff for imports from other countries and administered a common code for investment policy and a Solidarity Fund to counteract regional disparities of wealth and economic development. Mems: Cameroon, Central African Republic, Chad, Republic of the Congo, Equatorial Guinea, Gabon. Sec.-Gen. THOMAS DAKAYI KAMGA (Cameroon).

At a summit meeting in December 1981, UDEAC leaders agreed in principle to form an economic community of Central African states (Communauté économique des états d'Afrique centrale–CEEAC, to include UDEAC members and Burundi, Rwanda, São Tomé and Príncipe and Zaire (now Democratic Republic of the Congo). CEEAC (q.v.) began operations in 1985.

Banque de développement des états de l'Afrique centrale—BDEAC: place du Gouvernement, BP 1177, Brazzaville, Republic of the Congo; tel. 81-18-85; fax 81-18-80; f. 1975; cap. 20,095m. francs CFA (June 1998); shareholders: Cameroon, Central African Republic, Chad, Republic of the Congo, Gabon, Equatorial Guinea, ADB, BEAC, France, Germany and Kuwait; Dir-Gen. EMMANUEL DOKOUNA.

Banque des états de l'Afrique centrale—BEAC: ave Mgr François Xavier Vogt, BP 1917, Yaoundé, Cameroon; tel. 23-40-30; fax 23-33-29; f. 1973 as the central bank of issue of Cameroon, the Central African Republic, Chad, Republic of the Congo, Equatorial Guinea and Gabon; a monetary market, incorporating all national financial institutions of the BEAC countries, came into effect on 1 July 1994; cap. 45,000m. francs CFA (Dec. 1998). Gov. JEAN-FÉLIX MAMALEPOT. Publs *Rapport annuel, Etudes et statistiques* (monthly).

CENTRAL ISSUING BANKS

Banque centrale des Comores: place de France, BP 405, Moroni, Comoros; tel. (73) 1002; fax (73) 0349; f. 1981; cap. 1,100m. Comoros francs (Dec. 1997); Gov. SAÏD AHMED SAÏD ALI.

Banque centrale des états de l'Afrique de l'ouest: see above.

Banque des états de l'Afrique centrale: see above.

Banque de France: 39 rue Croix-des-Petits-Champs, BP 140-01, 75049 Paris, France; tel. 1-42-92-42-92; fax 1-42-96-04-23; f. 1800; bank of issue for Metropolitan France; Gov. JEAN-CLAUDE TRICHET; Dep. Govs DENIS FERMAN, HERVÉ HANNOUN.

Institut d'émission des départements d'outre-mer—IEDOM: 5 rue Roland Barthes, 75598 Paris Cédex 12, France; tel. 1-53-44-41-41; issuing authority for the French Overseas Departments and the French Overseas Collectivités Territoriales of St Pierre and Miquelon, and Mayotte; Pres. DENIS FERMAN; Dir-Gen. ANTOINE POUIL-LIEUTE; Dir GILLES AUDREN.

Institut d'émission d'outre-mer—IEOM: 5 rue Roland Barthes, 75598 Paris Cédex 12, France; tel. 1-53-44-41-41; issuing authority for the French Overseas Territories; Pres. DENIS FERMAN; Dir-Gen. ANTOINE POUILLIEUTE; Dir GILLES AUDREN.

FRENCH ECONOMIC AID

France's connection with the African Franc Zone countries involves not only monetary arrangements, but also includes comprehensive French assistance in the forms of budget support, foreign aid, technical assistance and subsidies on commodity exports.

Official French financial aid and technical assistance to developing countries is administered by the following agencies:

Agence française de développement—AFD: 5 rue Roland Barthes, 75598 Paris Cédex 12, France; tel. 1-53-44-31-31; fax 1-44-87-99-39; internet www.afd.fr/; f. 1941; fmrly the Caisse française de développement—CFD; French development bank which lends money to member states and former member states of the Franc Zone and several other states, and executes the financial operations of the FAC (see below). Following the devaluation of the franc CFA in January 1994, the French Government cancelled some 25,000m. French francs in debt arrears owed by member states to the CFD. The CFD established a Special Fund for Development and the Exceptional Facility for Short-term Financing to help alleviate the immediate difficulties resulting from the devaluation. A total of FFr 4,600m. of financial assistance was awarded to Franc Zone countries in 1994. In early 1994 the CFD made available funds totalling 2,420m. francs CFA to assist the establishment of CEMAC (see above). Serves as the secretariat for the Fonds français pour l'environnement mondial (f. 1994). Dir-Gen. ANTOINE POUILLIEUTE.

Fonds d'aide et de coopération—FAC: 20 rue Monsieur, 75007 Paris, France; tel. 1-53-69-00-00; fax 1-53-69-43-82; in 1959 FAC took over from FIDES (Fonds d'investissement pour le développement économique et social) the administration of subsidies and loans from the French Government to the former French African states. FAC is administered by the Ministry of Co-operation, which allocates budgetary funds to it.

INTERGOVERNMENTAL AUTHORITY ON DEVELOPMENT—IGAD

Address: BP 2653, Djibouti.

Telephone: 354050; **fax:** 356994; **e-mail:** igad@intnet.dj.

The Intergovernmental Authority on Development (IGAD) was established in 1996 to supersede the Intergovernmental Authority on Drought and Development (IGADD), founded in 1986 to co-ordinate measures to combat the effects of drought and desertification and attain regional food security.

MEMBERS

Djibouti	Kenya	Sudan
Eritrea	Somalia	Uganda
Ethiopia		

Organization

(August 2000)

ASSEMBLY

The Assembly, consisting of heads of state and of government of member states, is the supreme policy-making organ of the Authority. It holds a summit meeting at least once a year. The sixth Assembly meeting of heads of state and of government was held in Djibouti in March 1998.

Chairman: ISMAEL OMAR GELLEH (Djibouti).

COUNCIL OF MINISTERS

The Council of Ministers is composed of the minister of foreign affairs and one other minister from each member state. It meets at least twice a year and approves the work programme and the annual budget of the Secretariat.

COMMITTEE OF AMBASSADORS

The Committee of Ambassadors comprises the ambassadors or plenipotentiaries of member states to Djibouti. It convenes as regularly as required to advise and assist the Executive Secretary concerning the interpretation of policies and guide-lines and the realization of the annual work programme.

SECRETARIAT

The Secretariat, the executive body of IGAD, is headed by the Executive Secretary, who is appointed by the Assembly for a term of four years, renewable once. In addition to the Office of the Executive Secretary, the Secretariat comprises the following three divisions: Agriculture and Environment; Economic Co-operation; and Political and Humanitarian Affairs.

Executive Secretary: ATALLAH HAMAD AL-BASHIR (Sudan).

Activities

IGADD was established in 1986 by Djibouti, Ethiopia, Kenya, Somalia, Sudan and Uganda, to combat the effects of aridity and desertification, as a result of the severe drought and famine that had affected the Horn of Africa during the early 1980s. Eritrea became a member of IGADD in September 1993, following its proclamation as an independent state. In April 1995, at an extraordinary summit meeting held in Addis Ababa, Ethiopia, heads of state and of government resolved to reorganize and expand the Authority. In March 1996 IGAD was endorsed to supersede IGADD, at a second extraordinary summit meeting of heads of state and of government, held in Nairobi, Kenya. The meeting led to the adoption of an agreement for a new organizational structure and the approval of an extended mandate to co-ordinate and harmonize policy in the areas of economic co-operation and political and humanitarian affairs, in addition to its existing responsibilities for food security and environmental protection.

IGAD aims to achieve regional co-operation and economic integration. To facilitate this IGAD assists the governments of member states to maximize resources and co-ordinates efforts to initiate and implement regional development programmes and projects. In this context, IGAD promotes the harmonization of policies relating to agriculture and natural resources, communications, customs, trade and transport; the implementation of programmes in the fields of social sciences, research, science and technology; and effective participation in the global economy.

FOOD SECURITY AND ENVIRONMENTAL PROTECTION

IGAD seeks to achieve regional food security, the sustainable development of natural resources and environmental protection, and to encourage and assist member states in their efforts to combat the consequences of drought and other natural and man-made disasters. The region suffers from recurrent droughts, which severely impede crop and livestock production. Natural and man-made disasters increase the strain on resources, resulting in annual food deficits. About 80% of the IGAD sub-region is classified as arid or semi-arid, and some 40% of the region is unproductive, owing to severe environmental degradation. Priority areas of activity to improve food security and preserve natural resources during 1997–2001 included: the introduction of remote-sensing services; a Marketing Information System and a Regional Integrated Information System; the establishment of training and credit schemes for fishermen; research into the sustainable production of drought-resistant, high-yielding crop varieties; transboundary livestock disease control and vaccine production; the control of environmental pollution; the promotion of alternative sources of energy in the home; the management of integrated water resources; the promotion of community-based land husbandry; training programmes in grain marketing; and the implementation of the International Convention to Combat Desertification.

ECONOMIC CO-OPERATION

The Economic Co-operation division concentrates on the development of a co-ordinated infrastructure for the region, in particular in the areas of transport and communications, to promote foreign, cross-border and domestic trade and investment opportunities. IGAD seeks to harmonize national transport and trade policy and thereby facilitate the free movement of people, goods and services. The improvements to infrastructure also aim to facilitate more timely interventions to conflicts, disasters and emergencies in the sub-region. Projects to be undertaken by the end of 2001 included: the construction of missing segments of the Trans-African Highway and the Pan African Telecommunications Network; the removal of barriers to trade and communications; improvements to ports and inland container terminals; and the modernization of railway telecommunications services.

POLITICAL AND HUMANITARIAN AFFAIRS

The field of political and humanitarian affairs focuses on conflict prevention, management and resolution through dialogue. The division's primary aim is to restore peace and stability to member countries affected by conflict, in order that resources may be diverted for development purposes. In the late 1990s efforts were being undertaken to strengthen capacity for conflict prevention and to relieve humanitarian crises. In September 1995 negotiations between the Sudanese Government and opposition leaders were initiated, under the auspices of IGAD, with the aim of resolving the conflict in southern Sudan; these were reconvened periodically during 1996–mid-2000. A peace initiative on Somalia has also been formed under a mandate from IGAD and the Organization of African Unity (OAU). IGAD has supported efforts by the OAU to mediate a settlement of the conflict between Eritrea and Ethiopia, which commenced in mid-1998.

Publications

Annual Report.

IGAD News (2 a year).

Proceedings of the Summit of Heads of State and Government.

Reports of the Council of Ministers' Meetings.

ISLAMIC DEVELOPMENT BANK

Address: POB 5925, Jeddah 21432, Saudi Arabia.

Telephone: (2) 6361400; **fax:** (2) 6366871; **e-mail:** archives@isdb.org.sa; **internet:** www.isdb.org.

The Bank is an international financial institution that was established following a conference of Ministers of Finance of member countries of the Organization of the Islamic Conference (OIC, q.v.), held in Jeddah in December 1973. Its aim is to encourage the economic development and social progress of member countries and of Muslim communities in non-member countries, in accordance with the principles of the Islamic *Shari'a* (sacred law). The Bank formally opened in October 1975.

MEMBERS

There are 53 members.

Organization

(August 2000)

BOARD OF GOVERNORS

Each member country is represented by a governor, usually its Minister of Finance, and an alternate. The Board of Governors is the supreme authority of the Bank, and meets annually.

BOARD OF EXECUTIVE DIRECTORS

The Board consists of 14 members, seven of whom are appointed by the seven largest subscribers to the capital stock of the Bank; the remaining seven are elected by Governors representing the other subscribers. Members of the Board of Executive Directors are elected for three-year terms. The Board is responsible for the direction of the general operations of the Bank.

President of the Bank and Chairman of the Board of Executive Directors: Dr AHMED MOHAMED ALI.

Bank Secretary: Dr ABD AR-RAHIM OMRANA.

REGIONAL OFFICES

Kazakhstan: c/o Director, External Aid Co-ordination Dept, 93–95 Ablay-Khan Ave, 480091 Almaty; tel. (3272) 62-18-68; fax (3272) 69-61-52; Dir ZHANKYN KAKIMZKANOVA.

Malaysia: Level 11, Front Wing, Bank Industri, Jalan Sultan Ismail, POB 13671, 50818 Kuala Lumpur; tel. (3) 2946627; fax (3) 2946626; Dir Dr MUHAMMAD SIDDIK.

Morocco: 177 Ave John Kennedy, Souissi 10105, POB 5003, Rabat; tel. (7) 757191; fax (7) 775726; Dir Dr MARWAN SEIFUDDIN.

FINANCIAL STRUCTURE

The authorized capital of the Bank is 6,000m. Islamic Dinars (divided into 600,000 shares, having a value of 10,000 Islamic Dinars each). The Islamic Dinar (ID) is the Bank's unit of account and is equivalent to the value of one Special Drawing Right of the IMF (SDR 1 = US $1.32002 at 31 May 2000).

Subscribed capital amounts to ID 4,000m.

Activities

The Bank adheres to the Islamic principle forbidding usury, and does not grant loans or credits for interest. Instead, its methods of project financing are: provision of interest-free loans (with a service fee), mainly for infrastructural projects which are expected to have a marked impact on long-term socio-economic development; provision of technical assistance (e.g. for feasibility studies); equity participation in industrial and agricultural projects; leasing operations, involving the leasing of equipment such as ships, and instalment sale financing; and profit-sharing operations. Funds not immediately needed for projects are used for foreign trade financing. Under the Import Trade Financing Operations (ITFO) scheme, funds are used for importing commodities for development purposes (i.e. raw materials and intermediate industrial goods, rather than consumer goods), with priority given to the import of goods from other member countries (see table). The Longer-term Trade Financing Scheme (LTTFS) was introduced in 1987/88 to provide financing for the export of non-traditional and capital goods. During AH 1419 the LTTFS was renamed the Export Financing Scheme (EFS). In

SUBSCRIPTIONS (million Islamic Dinars, as at December 1998)

Afghanistan	. .	5.00	Maldives	. .	2.50
Albania	. .	2.50	Mali	. .	4.92
Algeria	. .	124.26	Mauritania	. .	4.92
Azerbaijan	. .	4.92	Morocco	. .	24.81
Bahrain	. .	7.00	Mozambique	. .	2.50
Bangladesh	. .	49.29	Niger	. .	12.41
Benin	. .	4.92	Oman	. .	13.78
Brunei	. .	12.41	Pakistan	. .	124.26
Burkina Faso	. .	12.41	Palestine	. .	9.85
Cameroon	. .	12.41	Qatar	. .	49.23
Chad	. .	4.92	Saudi Arabia	. .	997.17
Comoros	. .	2.50	Senegal	. .	12.42
Djibouti	. .	2.50	Sierra Leone	. .	2.50
Egypt	. .	49.23	Somalia	. .	2.50
Gabon	. .	14.77	Sudan	. .	19.69
The Gambia	. .	2.50	Suriname	. .	2.50
Guinea	. .	12.41	Syria	. .	5.00
Guinea-Bissau	. .	2.50	Tajikistan	. .	2.50
Indonesia	. .	124.26	Togo	. .	2.50
Iran	. .	349.97	Tunisia	. .	9.85
Iraq	. .	13.05	Turkey	. .	315.47
Jordan	. .	19.89	Turkmenistan	. .	2.50
Kazakhstan	. .	2.50	Uganda	. .	12.41
Kuwait	. .	496.64	United Arab		
Kyrgyzstan	. .	2.50	Emirates	. .	283.03
Lebanon	. .	4.92	Yemen	. .	24.81
Libya	. .	400.00	**Total**	. .	3,763.77
Malaysia	. .	79.56			

Operations approved, Islamic year 1419 (8 May 1998–16 April 1999)

Type of operation	Number of operations	Total amount (million Islamic Dinars)
Ordinary operations	98	525.28
Project financing	69	519.39
Technical assistance	29	5.90
Trade financing operations*	65	766.45
Waqf Fund operations	49	7.97
Total†	**212**	**1,299.70**

* Including ITFO, the EFS, the Islamic Bank's Portfolio and the UIF.
† Excluding cancelled operations.

addition, the Special Assistance Waqf Fund (which was established with effect from 7 May 1997, formerly the Special Assistance Account) provides emergency aid and other assistance, with particular emphasis on education in Islamic communities in non-member countries. A Special Account for least-developed member countries aims to assist these countries by providing loans on concessionary terms. Loans financed by this Account are charged an annual service fee of 0.75%, compared with 2.5% for ordinary loans, and have a repayment period of 25–30 years, compared with 15–25 years.

By 16 April 1999 the Bank had approved a total of ID 4,306.61m. for project financing and technical assistance, a total of ID 10,606.58m. for foreign trade financing, and ID 378.92m. for special assistance operations, excluding amounts for cancelled operations. During the Islamic year 1419 (8 May 1998 to 16 April 1999) the Bank approved a total of ID 1,299.70m., for 212 operations.

The Bank approved 37 loans in the year ending 16 April 1999, amounting to ID 159.05m. (compared with 31 loans, totalling

Project financing and technical assistance by sector, Islamic year 1419*

Sector	Number of Operations	Amount (million Islamic Dinars)	%
Agriculture and agro-industry	24	76.72	14.6
Industry and mining	3	33.09	6.3
Transport and communications	14	67.61	12.9
Public utilities	20	155.58	29.9
Social sectors	24	109.12	20.8
Other*	13	83.16	15.8
Total†	**98**	**525.28**	**100.0**

* Mainly approved amounts for Islamic banks.
† Excluding cancelled operations.

ID 133.90m., in the previous year). These loans supported projects concerned with infrastructural improvements, for example of roads, canals, sewerage, water-supply and rural electrification, the construction of schools and health centres, and agricultural developments.

During AH 1419 the Bank approved 29 technical assistance operations for 19 countries (as well as three regional projects) in the form of grants and loans, amounting to ID 5.90m.

Import trade financing approved during the Islamic year 1419 amounted to ID 629.78m. for 36 operations in 11 member countries. By the end of that year cumulative import trade financing amounted to ID 8,851.44m., of which 38.1% was for imports of crude petroleum, 27.1% for intermediate industrial goods, 8.0% for vegetable oil and 5.8% for refined petroleum products. Export financing approved under the EFS amounted to ID 47.99m. for 15 operations in eight countries in AH 1419. In the same year the Bank's Portfolio for Investment and Development, established in AH 1407 (1986–87), approved 17 operations amounting to US $321m. (or approximately

ID 218.56m.). Since its introduction, the Portfolio has approved net financing operations amounting to $1,817m.

During AH 1419 the Bank approved 49 special assistance operations, amounting to ID 7.97m., providing assistance primarily in the education sector, as well as emergency relief; of the total financing, 27 operations provided for Muslim communities in 18 non-member countries.

The Bank's scholarships programme sponsored 459 students from seven member and 30 non-member countries during the year to 16 April 1999. The Merit Scholarship Programme, initiated in AH 1412 (1991–92), aims to develop scientific, technological and research capacities in member countries through advanced studies and/or research. By AH 1419 (1998–99) 134 scholars from 38 member countries had been placed in academic centres of excellence in Australia, Europe and the USA under the programme; a further 15 scholarships were awarded in AH 1420. In December 1997 the Board of Executive Directors approved a new scholarship programme designed specifically to assist scholars from least-developed member countries to study for a masters degree in science and technology. Some 20 scholarships were allocated in AH 1419, and it was expected that a total of 190 would be awarded by AH 1423. The Bank's Programme for Technical Co-operation aims to mobilize technical capabilities among member countries and to promote the exchange of expertise, experience and skills through expert missions, training, seminars and workshops. During AH 1419 96 projects were implemented under the programme. The Bank also undertakes the distribution of meat sacrificed by Muslim pilgrims: in AH 1419 meat from approximately 469,150 animals was distributed to the needy in 24 countries.

During the year ending 16 April 1999 the Bank's disbursements totalled ID 535m., bringing the total cumulative disbursements since the Bank began operations to ID 10,139m.

The Bank's Unit Investment Fund (UIF) became operational in 1990, with the aim of mobilizing additional resources and providing a profitable channel for investments conforming to *Shari'a*. The initial issue of the UIF was US $100m., which has subsequently been increased to $325m. The Fund finances mainly private-sector industrial projects in middle-income countries. The UIF also finances short-term trade financing operations: four were approved in AH 1419, amounting to $17.60m. In October 1998 the Bank announced the establishment of a new fund to invest in infrastructure projects in member states. The Bank committed $250m. to the fund, which was to comprise $1,000m. equity capital and a $500m. Islamic financing facility. In September 1999 the Bank's Board of Executive Directors approved the establishment of an Islamic Corporation for the Development of the Private Sector, which was scheduled to commence operations in 2000.

SUBSIDIARY ORGANS

Islamic Corporation for the Insurance of Investment and Export Credit—ICIEC: POB 15722, Jeddah 21454, Saudi Arabia; tel. (2) 6445666; fax (2) 6379504; e-mail idb.iciec@mail.oicisnet.org; internet www.isdb.org; f. 1994; aims to promote trade and the flow of investments among member countries of the OIC through the provision of export credit and investment insurance services; auth. cap. ID 100m., subscribed cap. ID 91.2m. (April 1999). Man. Dr ABDEL RAHMAN A. TAHA. Mems: 23 OIC member states.

Islamic Research and Training Institute: POB 9201, Jeddah 21413, Saudi Arabia; tel. (2) 6361400; fax (2) 6378927; internet www.irti.org; f. 1982 to undertake research enabling economic, financial and banking activities to conform to Islamic law, and to provide training for staff involved in development activities in the Bank's member countries. The Institute also organizes seminars and workshops, and holds training courses aimed at furthering the expertise of government and financial officials in Islamic developing countries. Dir Dr MABID ALI AL-JARHI. Publs *Annual Report, Journal of Islamic Economic Studies*, various research studies, monographs, reports.

Publication

Annual Report.

ORGANIZATION OF AFRICAN UNITY—OAU

Address: POB 3243, Addis Ababa, Ethiopia.
Telephone: (1) 517700; **fax:** (1) 513036.
The Organization was founded in 1963 to promote unity and solidarity among African states.

FORMATION

There were various attempts at establishing an inter-African organization before the OAU Charter was drawn up. In November 1958 Ghana and Guinea (later joined by Mali) drafted a Charter which was to form the basis of a Union of African States. In January 1961 a conference was held at Casablanca, attended by the heads of state of Ghana, Guinea, Mali, Morocco, and representatives of Libya and of the provisional government of the Algerian Republic (GPRA). Tunisia, Nigeria, Liberia and Togo declined the invitation to attend. An African Charter was adopted and it was decided to set up an African Military Command and an African Common Market.

Between October 1960 and March 1961 three conferences were held by French-speaking African countries, at Abidjan, Brazzaville and Yaoundé. None of the 12 countries which attended these meetings had been present at the Casablanca Conference. These conferences led eventually to the signing in September 1961, at Tananarive, of a charter establishing the Union africaine et malgache, later the Organisation commune africaine et mauricienne (OCAM).

In May 1961 a conference was held at Monrovia, Liberia, attended by the heads of state or representatives of 19 countries: Cameroon, Central African Republic, Chad, Congo Republic (ex-French), Côte d'Ivoire, Dahomey, Ethiopia, Gabon, Liberia, Madagascar, Mauritania, Niger, Nigeria, Senegal, Sierra Leone, Somalia, Togo, Tunisia and Upper Volta. They met again (with the exception of Tunisia and with the addition of the ex-Belgian Congo Republic) in January 1962 at Lagos, Nigeria, and set up a permanent secretariat and a standing committee of finance ministers, and accepted a draft charter for an Organization of Inter-African and Malagasy States.

It was the Conference of Addis Ababa, held in 1963, which finally brought together African states despite the regional, political and linguistic differences which divided them. The foreign ministers of 32 African states attended the Preparatory Meeting held in May: Algeria, Burundi, Cameroon, Central African Republic, Chad, Congo (Brazzaville) (now Republic of the Congo), Congo (Léopoldville) (now Democratic Republic of the Congo), Côte d'Ivoire, Dahomey (now Benin), Ethiopia, Gabon, Ghana, Guinea, Liberia, Libya, Madagascar, Mali, Mauritania, Morocco, Niger, Nigeria, Rwanda, Senegal, Sierra Leone, Somalia, Sudan, Tanganyika (now Tanzania), Togo, Tunisia, Uganda, the United Arab Republic (Egypt) and Upper Volta (now Burkina Faso).

The topics discussed by the meeting were: (i) creation of the Organization of African States; (ii) co-operation among African states in the following fields: economic and social; education, culture and science; collective defence; (iii) decolonization; (iv) apartheid and racial discrimination; (v) effects of economic grouping on the economic development of Africa; (vi) disarmament; (vii) creation of a Permanent Conciliation Commission; and (viii) Africa and the United Nations.

The Heads of State Conference which opened on 23 May drew up the Charter of the Organization of African Unity, which was then signed by the heads of 30 states on 25 May 1963. The Charter was essentially functional and reflected a compromise between the concept of a loose association of states favoured by the Monrovia Group and the federal idea supported by the Casablanca Group, and in particular by Ghana.

Organization

(August 2000)

ASSEMBLY OF HEADS OF STATE

The Assembly of Heads of State and Government meets annually to co-ordinate policies of African states. Resolutions are passed by a two-thirds majority, procedural matters by a simple majority. A chairman is elected at each meeting from among the members, to hold office for one year.
Chairman (1999/2000): ABDELAZIZ BOUTEFLIKA (Algeria).

COUNCIL OF MINISTERS

Consists of ministers of foreign affairs and others and meets twice a year, with provision for extraordinary sessions. Each session elects its own Chairman. Prepares meetings of, and is responsible to, the Assembly of Heads of State.

MEMBERS*

Algeria	Eritrea	Nigeria
Angola	Ethiopia	Rwanda
Benin	Gabon	São Tomé and
Botswana	The Gambia	Príncipe
Burkina Faso	Ghana	Senegal
Burundi	Guinea	Seychelles
Cameroon	Guinea-Bissau	Sierra Leone
Cape Verde	Kenya	Somalia
Central African	Lesotho	South Africa
Republic	Liberia	Sudan
Chad	Libya	Swaziland
The Comoros	Madagascar	Tanzania
Congo, Democratic	Malawi	Togo
Republic†	Mali	Tunisia
Congo, Republic	Mauritania	Uganda
Côte d'Ivoire	Mauritius	Zambia
Djibouti	Mozambique	Zimbabwe
Egypt	Namibia	
Equatorial Guinea	Niger	

* The Sahrawi Arab Democratic Republic (SADR–Western Sahara) was admitted to the OAU in February 1982, following recognition by 26 of the 50 members, but its membership was disputed by Morocco and other states which claimed that a two-thirds majority was needed to admit a state whose existence was in question. Morocco withdrew from the OAU with effect from November 1985.
† Known as Zaire between 1971 and 1997.

GENERAL SECRETARIAT

The permanent headquarters of the organization. It carries out functions assigned to it in the Charter of the OAU and by other agreements and treaties made between member states. Departments: Political; Finance; Education, Science, Culture and Social Affairs; Economic Development and Co-operation; Administration and Conferences. The Secretary-General is elected for a four-year term by the Assembly of Heads of State.
Secretary-General: SALIM AHMED SALIM (Tanzania).

ARBITRATION COMMISSION

Commission of Mediation, Conciliation and Arbitration: Addis Ababa; f. 1964; consists of 21 members elected by the Assembly of Heads of State for a five-year term; no state may have more than one member; has a Bureau consisting of a President and two Vice-Presidents, who shall not be eligible for re-election. Its task is to hear and settle disputes between member states by peaceful means.

SPECIALIZED COMMISSIONS

There are specialized commissions for economic, social, transport and communications affairs; education, science, culture and health; defence; human rights; and labour.

Finance

Member states contribute in accordance with their United Nations assessment. No member state is assessed for an amount exceeding 20% of the yearly regular budget of the Organization. The budget for 2000–01 was US $29m. At March 1999 member states owed some $45m. in outstanding contributions. By March 2000 the following countries had their voting rights in the Organization suspended owing to outstanding arrears: Central African Republic, Comoros, Guinea, Guinea-Bissau, Liberia, São Tomé and Príncipe, and Seychelles.

Principal Events, 1989–2000

1989

Jan.   A meeting on apartheid, organized by the OAU, resulted in the formation of an African Anti-Apartheid Committee.

May   The OAU Chairman undertook a mission of mediation between the governments of Mauritania and Senegal, following ethnic conflict between the citizens of the two countries.

July   The Assembly of Heads of State discussed the Namibian independence process, and urged that the UN should ensure that the forthcoming elections there would be fairly conducted. They reiterated requests that an international conference on Africa's substantial external debt should be held.

Sept.– Dec.
The newly-elected OAU Secretary-General, Salim Ahmed Salim, attempted to mediate in the dispute between Mauritania and Senegal. In November a mediation committee, comprising representatives of six countries, visited Mauritania and Senegal.

1990

March
A monitoring group was formed by the OAU to report on events in South Africa. The OAU urged the international community to continue imposing economic sanctions on South Africa.

July
The Assembly of Heads of State reviewed the implications for Africa of recent socio-economic and political changes in Eastern Europe, and of the European Community's progress towards monetary and political union.

1991

June
The Assembly of Heads of State signed the treaty on the creation of an African Economic Community (AEC). The treaty was to enter into force after ratification by two-thirds of OAU member states. The Community was to be established by 2025, beginning with a five-year stage during which measures would be taken to strengthen existing economic groupings. The meeting also established a committee of heads of state to assist national reconciliation in Ethiopia; and gave a mandate to the OAU Secretary-General to undertake a mission to assist in restoring political stability in Somalia.

1992

Feb.– March
The OAU was involved, together with the UN and the Organization of the Islamic Conference (OIC, q.v.), in mediation between the warring factions in Mogadishu, Somalia. The OAU subsequently continued to assist in efforts to achieve a peace settlement in Somalia.

May
An OAU mission was dispatched to South Africa to monitor the continued violence in that country.

June– July
Proposals were advanced at the Assembly of Heads of State, held in Dakar, Senegal, for a mechanism to be established within the OAU for 'conflict management, prevention and resolution'. These proposals were accepted in principle, but operational details were to be elaborated at a later stage.

Oct.
The *Ad Hoc* Committee on Southern Africa met in Gaborone, Botswana, to discuss a report compiled by a team of OAU experts on practical steps to be taken towards the democratization of South Africa. Plans to send a mission to monitor the Mozambican peace accord were announced.

1993

Feb.
A session of the Council of Ministers discussed the OAU's serious financial crisis. The meeting agreed to allocate US $250,000 to the creation of a conflict prevention bureau, and a further $250,000 for the purposes of monitoring elections.

May
A Pan-African Conference on Reparations for the suffering caused by colonialism in Africa, organized by the OAU together with the Nigerian Government, was held in Abuja. The Conference appealed to those countries which had benefited from the colonization of Africa and the use of Africans as slaves (particularly European countries and the USA) to make reparations to Africans and their descendants, either in the form of capital transfers, or cancellation of debt.

June
Eritrea was admitted as the 52nd member of the OAU. The 29th Assembly of Heads of State resolved to establish a mechanism for conflict prevention and resolution. The mechanism's primary objective was to be anticipation and prevention of conflict. In cases where conflicts had already occurred, the OAU was to undertake peace-making and peace-building activities, including the deployment of civilian or military monitoring missions. However, in the case of a conflict seriously degenerating, assistance would be sought from the United Nations.

July
A seminar on the AEC was held in Addis Ababa, Ethiopia, concerned with the popularization of the treaty establishing the Community. Lack of resources emerged as one of the main barriers to the actual creation of the Community.

Sept.
The OAU announced the immediate removal of economic sanctions against South Africa, following the approval by

that country's Parliament of a bill to establish a transitional executive council prior to the democratic elections, scheduled to be conducted in April 1994.

Oct.
The OAU Secretary-General condemned an attempted military coup in Burundi, in which the President and six Cabinet ministers were killed, and the subsequent civil unrest.

Nov.
A summit conference of African ministers of foreign affairs, conducted in Addis Ababa, resolved to establish a 200-member OAU protection and observation mission to Burundi, and appealed for international financial and material support to assist the mission. The ministers approved the principles for the establishment of a mechanism for conflict prevention, management and resolution. The meeting suggested that 5% of the OAU budget, but not less than US $1m., be allocated for an OAU Peace Fund to finance the mechanism, and that $0.5m. be made available for 1993.

Dec.
A meeting of 11 African Heads of State approved the establishment of the Peace Fund and called for contributions from the international community. A draft statement of the mechanism for conflict prevention, management and resolution, issued by the OAU Secretary-General, expressed support for the efforts to resolve the conflict in Somalia and emphasized the need to promote national reconciliation.

1994

Feb.
The Council of Ministers reaffirmed its support for the results of elections in Burundi, which were conducted in 1993, and endorsed the establishment of an OAU mission to promote dialogue and national reconciliation in that country. The Council condemned anti-government forces for the escalation of violence in Angola.

April
The OAU mission to South Africa participated as observers of the electoral process. An OAU delegation visited Nigeria and Cameroon to investigate the border dispute between the two countries.

May
South Africa was admitted as the 53rd member of the OAU.

June
Consultations with each of the conflicting parties in Rwanda were conducted by the OAU. The Assembly of Heads of State, meeting in Tunis, approved a code of conduct for inter-African relations, in order to strengthen political consultation and co-operation for the promotion of security and stability in the region. Nine countries were nominated to serve on the central committee (organ) of the mechanism for conflict prevention, management and resolution. The military component of the OAU mission in Burundi was now deployed in that country, and its mandate was extended until mid-September. (The mission was subsequently granted three-monthly extensions of its mandate.)

Nov.
The Secretary-General, noting the Organization's serious financial situation, warned that most activities of the regular budget for 1994/95 would have to be suspended. Certain sanctions were to be imposed on any country that had not paid its contribution in full by 1 June 1995.

1995

March
An extraordinary session of the Council of Ministers, held in Cairo, Egypt, adopted an Agenda for Action, which aimed to stimulate African economic and social development. The document emphasized the importance of peace, democratic government and stability in achieving development targets. It also assessed Africa's role in the world economy and the need for structural reforms of countries' economies, in particular in view of agreements reached under the GATT Uruguay Round of trade negotiations. The OAU, together with representatives of the UN and the Commonwealth Secretariat, dispatched a special mission to Sierra Leone, in order to assess means of facilitating the peace process in that country.

April
A meeting of the conflict mechanism's central organ, held in Tunis, Tunisia, reviewed OAU peace initiatives. The meeting urged OAU member states to offer humanitarian aid to consolidate the peace process in Angola and for further OAU assistance for the rehabilitation and reconstruction of Somalia. A seminar, organized jointly by the OAU and the International Committee of the Red Cross, assembled military and civil experts in Yaoundé, Cameroon, to discuss the issue of land-mines.

May
An 81-member OAU observer group was deployed to monitor a general election in Ethiopia. The group confirmed that the electoral process had been 'free and fair'.

June   At the 31st Assembly of Heads of State, held in Addis Ababa, Ethiopia, the Secretary-General observed that the OAU's peace-keeping role had been severely affected by the failure of member states to pay their contributions. Sanctions were to be imposed on those countries which had failed to pay 25% of their arrears by the end of June. (Liberia and Somalia were exempted from this deadline.) The meeting endorsed a proposal to establish a conflict management centre, provisionally in Cairo, Egypt, to strengthen the OAU's role in conflict prevention. The situation in warring African countries was discussed, as well as the problem of large-scale refugee and displaced populations in the region. In addition, member states urged the international community to end the application of sanctions against Libya.

Sept.   An extraordinary meeting of the conflict mechanism's central organ condemned the attempted assassination of Egypt's President Mubarak prior to the Heads of State meeting in June. The committee censured Sudan for protecting the alleged perpetrators of the attack and for supporting other terrorist elements in the country.

Oct.   OAU observers monitored the conduct of elections in Zanzibar and attempted to mediate between the parties when the vote failed to secure a decisive result.

Nov.   A 50-member OAU observer group was deployed to monitor elections in Algeria, as part of an international team.

1996

Feb.   The Council of Ministers reiterated the OAU's readiness to promote and support dialogue and reconciliation in Burundi. However, the meeting did not support military intervention in that country, despite a UN report proposing international co-operation with the OAU to establish a stand-by force for Burundi.

March   The UN Secretary-General launched a system-wide Special Initiative on Africa, which was based on the development objectives outlined in the OAU Agenda for Action (see above). Funds were to be allocated under the Initiative to strengthen the OAU's capacity for conflict prevention, management and resolution.

May–   The OAU assisted the International Peace Academy to
June   conduct a meeting of international organizations, in Cape Town, South Africa, to promote the OAU's conflict mechanism, under the theme of 'Civil Society and Conflict Management in Africa'.

July   The 32nd Assembly of Heads of State agreed to support a plan, formulated earlier that month by the Governments of Tanzania, Uganda and Ethiopia, to send troops to Burundi in a peace-keeping capacity. The Assembly requested logistical and financial support from the international community for the initiative. In a separate declaration OAU leaders expressed their support for Boutros Boutros-Ghali's candidacy for a second term as the UN Secretary-General. The endorsement was opposed by the President of Rwanda, Pasteur Bizimungu, who condemned the lack of UN protection afforded to his country during the civil unrest in 1994. At the end of July, following a military coup in Burundi, the OAU endorsed a decision of seven east and central African states to impose economic sanctions against the new regime.

Oct.   The OAU Secretary-General cautiously endorsed a US proposal to establish an African military force for the protection of civilian populations in areas of conflict. A regional committee of the OAU declared its support for the continuation of the economic embargo against Burundi.

Nov.   An OAU delegation, meeting with the heads of state of eight African countries in Nairobi, Kenya, supported the establishment of an international humanitarian force, to be sent to Zaire (although this was never deployed).

Dec.   The OAU President, in an attempt to overcome the impasse reached regarding the election of a new UN Secretary-General (owing to US opposition to Boutros-Ghali), confirmed that African nations should propose alternative candidates for the position.

1997

Jan.   The UN and the OAU appointed Muhamed Sahnoun as a joint Special Representative for the Great Lakes Region.

Feb.   The 65th session of the Council of Ministers, meeting in Libya, expressed its support of that country in the face of sanctions imposed upon it by the international community. The OAU welcomed the newly-elected Secretary-General of the UN, the Ghanaian, Kofi Annan. The situation in Zaire was discussed and an extraordinary summit of the

OAU's conflict management mechanism was scheduled for March. Further donations to the OAU Peace Fund were requested.

March   A special summit of the OAU Organ on conflict prevention, management and resolution, which was attended by delegations from both the Zairean Government and the rebel AFDL forces, called for an immediate cease-fire and concluded a provisional agreement for negotiations between the two sides based on a five-point plan that had been formulated by Sahnoun and approved by the UN Security Council in February.

June   The Assembly of Heads of State, meeting in Harare, Zimbabwe, condemned the military coup in Sierra Leone, which took place in May, and endorsed the intervention of ECOMOG troops in order to restore a democratic government in that country. The OAU stated that future coups in the continent would not be tolerated, and the importance of universal human rights to be established across Africa was reiterated throughout the meeting. The first meeting between ministers of the OAU and the European Union was held in New York, USA. The inaugural meeting of the African Economic Community took place.

July   The UNDP donated US $3m. to the OAU conflict management mechanism. An OAU observer group was deployed to monitor elections in Liberia.

Aug.   The OAU appointed a special envoy to the Comoros, Pierre Yere, following a declaration of independence by separatists on the islands of Nzwani and Mwali.

Oct.   Chiefs of Defence Staff, meeting in Harare, Zimbabwe, proposed a series of measures to strengthen the capacity of African countries to lead peace-keeping missions in the region, which included the establishment of operations, training and early-warning units.

Nov.   A group of OAU military observers was reported to have been dispatched to the Comoros.

Dec.   The OAU organized an international conference, held in Addis Ababa, Ethiopia, which aimed to resolve the dispute between the Comoran Government and the secessionists and to initiate a process of political dialogue. In a separate meeting OAU ministers of justice adopted a protocol approving the creation of a permanent African court of human rights (based on the African Charter of Human and People's Rights, signed in 1981).

1998

Feb.   The OAU concluded an agreement with La Francophonie (q.v.) to co-operate in economic and cultural areas.

March   The OAU declared its support for ECOWAS efforts in restoring President Ahmed Tejan Kabbah to power in Sierra Leone. A nine-member OAU ministerial mission visited the Comoros in an attempt to further a peaceful solution to the dispute; however, it was prevented from conducting discussions with the separatist leaders in Nzwani.

June   Fighting between Eritrea and Ethiopia dominated discussions at the 34th Assembly of Heads of State, held in Burkina Faso. It was agreed to send a delegation to attempt to resolve the dispute. The Assembly also considered economic issues affecting the region, and resolved to disregard certain economic and humanitarian sanctions imposed against Libya, owing to that country's refusal to release two people suspected of the bombing of a US aircraft over the United Kingdom in 1988. The OAU leaders reiterated their support for the proposal of the Libyan authorities that the suspects be tried in a neutral venue. The OAU agreed to establish a seven-member International Panel of Eminent Personalities to examine all aspects of the genocide that occurred in Rwanda in 1994; a special trust fund was to be established to finance its activities. (The Panel met for the first time in October.)

July   An OAU delegation conducted discussions with the Eritrean and Ethiopian authorities in an attempt to conclude a peace settlement. The OAU Secretary-General also expressed support for efforts to negotiate a settlement between the conflicting parties in Guinea-Bissau.

Aug.   The OAU expressed its concern at the escalating violence in the Democratic Republic of the Congo (DRC), in particular the involvement of armed forces from other countries in the region, and resolved to send a mission to negotiate a cease-fire. An OAU ministerial committee (comprising representatives of Burkina Faso, Djibouti and Zimbabwe) pursued efforts to negotiate an accord between Eritrea and Ethiopia. The proposed OAU framework agreement was based on a US-Rwandan peace plan, presented to both sides in June, and included implementation of an immediate cease-fire, the initiation of peace discussions and recognition of the positions prior to the start of hostilities in May. At the end of August delegates of the SADC held talks at OAU headquarters, and urged an immediate cease-fire by all sides in the Congolese conflict.

Sept. The OAU Secretary-General supported a request of the Sudanese Government for an international commission of inquiry to be established to examine the US airstrike on a pharmaceutical plant in Khartoum, in retaliation to terrorist bombing incidents in August.

Nov. A meeting of the OAU mediation committee on the Eritrean/Ethiopian dispute was held in Ouagadougou.

Dec. A special meeting of the conflict resolution mechanism, at the level of heads of state, was held to pursue a peace settlement in the DRC. The ongoing Eritrean-Ethiopian dispute and the unstable security situation in Angola were also considered. A Special OAU Ministerial Meeting on Refugees, Returnees and Internally Displaced Persons was convened, in Khartoum; the meeting urged member states to implement efforts to mitigate problems associated with the mass movement of populations, and to promote humanitarian assistance efforts.

1999

Feb. A high-level OAU delegation, including the Chairman and Secretary-General, replaced the previous ministerial committee on a visit to Eritrea, following that country's refusal to negotiate with a representative of Djibouti. In early February an OAU delegation conducted talks with representatives of the Nzwani separatist factions and the Government of the Comoros; however, the negotiations failed to conclude an agreement on a political settlement to the conflict or on the establishment of an OAU peace-keeping mission.

March An OAU mission visited the authorities in Ethiopia and Eritrea to pursue efforts towards settling the conflict. The Chairman of the OAU cancelled a special summit meeting on African conflict scheduled to take place at the end of March, owing to controversy over the extension of invitations to rebel leaders from those countries affected by civil conflict. A meeting of the Council of Ministers appointed the President of Zambia, Frederick Chiluba, to co-ordinate efforts to resolve the conflict in the DRC. The meeting also imposed sanctions against eight countries that had failed to pay their annual contributions to the Organization for two years. The sanctions denied nationals from those countries the right to vote or to work at the OAU offices, which resulted in a substantial reduction in personnel at OAU headquarters.

April The first OAU conference on human rights, at ministerial level, was convened in Mauritius. An inter-island conference was held, under OAU auspices, in Antananarivo, Madagascar, to conclude arrangements for a new political union in the Comoros. At the end of the month, however, the Government of the Comoros was removed by army officers following renewed unrest. The OAU condemned the coup, but urged the Nzwani representatives to sign the agreed framework.

May The OAU announced the withdrawal of the military component of its observer mission in the Comoros. A new round of talks with the heads of government of Eritrea and Ethiopia was initiated to provide for a cessation of hostilities.

July The summit meeting, held in Algiers, was concerned with the economic development of Africa and prospects for greater integration, as well as ongoing conflicts in the region. The meeting requested the Secretary-General to send a fact-finding mission to Somalia to assess its post-conflict needs. The OAU also appointed a senior Algerian army general to chair a Joint Military Commission in the DRC, which was to be established according to the terms of a peace accord signed earlier in July. Heads of state declared that the Organization would not recognize any authority in a member state which assumed power illegally. An African convention for the prevention and combating of terrorism was signed, which included provisions for the exchange of information to help counter terrorism and for signatory states to refrain from granting asylum to terrorists. The meeting also declared that 2000 was to be the Year of Peace, Security and Solidarity in Africa.

Sept. An extraordinary summit meeting was convened in Sirte, Libya, at the request of the Libyan leader Col al-Qaddafi, in order to promote African unity and to demonstrate African solidarity with Libya. The meeting determined to establish an African Union, based on the principles and objectives of the OAU. A new charter was to be adopted by 2001. In addition, heads of state declared their commitment to accelerating the establishment of regional institutions, including an African parliament, court of justice, and central bank, as well as the implementation of an economic and monetary union. The Ethiopian Government rejected the final technical arrangements for implementation of the framework peace plan, which had been approved by Eritrea in August, on the grounds that they did not ensure the return of disputed territories to their status prior to the start of the conflict.

Oct. A conference on Industrial Partnerships and Investment in Africa was held in Dakar, Senegal, jointly organized by OAU with UNIDO, the ECA, the African Development Bank, and the Alliance for Africa's Industrialization.

Dec. The OAU Chairman, President Bouteflika of Algeria, urged the removal of UN sanctions against Libya. The OAU condemned the military's seizure of power in Côte d'Ivoire.

2000

Feb. The OAU imposed economic sanctions against the Nzwani separatists in the Comoros, including the immobilization of their overseas assets, and urged the co-operation of OAU members in implementing these. The OAU dispatched a special envoy to mediate between Eritrea and Ethiopia; the Ethiopian adminstration reiterated its dissatisfaction with the technical arrangements (deemed no longer negotiable by the OAU) for the framework peace plan, which in other respects it was prepared to approve.

March An OAU conference unanimously approved a peace plan for Somalia that had been drafted in late 1999 by the Djibouti President (and IGAD Chairman), Ismael Omar Gelleh. Further punitive measures were imposed against the Nzwani separatists in the Comoros, including the suspension of telephone communications, and restrictions on oil deliveries and on sea and air traffic.

April The OAU participated in an EU–Africa summit, held in Cairo, Egypt.

May In early May an initiative by the OAU's special envoy to mediate indirect communications ('proximity talks') between Eritrea and Ethiopia failed, and was followed by a serious escalation of their conflict. The OAU urged an immediate cessation of hostilities and commitment from both sides to pursuing a peaceful resolution. Indirect negotiations, mediated by the OAU and envoys of the EU and USA, resumed in late May.

June The OAU, EU and USA continue to mediate proximity talks between Eritrea and Ethiopia, culminating, in mid-June, in the conclusion of a cease-fire agreement, which was formalized at Algiers. The Algiers accord stipulated the immediate cessation of hostilities and withdrawal by both sides to the positions that had been held prior to the commencement of the conflict. Meanwhile, a UN peace-keeping force was to be deployed to supervise the disputed border area. Subsequently negotiations were to be convened on the implementation of the OAU framework agreement.

July At the annual summit meeting, held at Lomé, Togo, OAU Heads of State signed a draft treaty on the establishment of the African Union, which was to enter into force following ratification by two-thirds of member states' governments. It was envisaged that the African Union would be inaugurated, and would thereby replace the OAU, one year after the endorsement of the draft treaty. At the end of July the OAU announced that it was to send observers to the Horn of Africa to monitor the implementation of the Algiers cease-fire accord.

Specialized Agencies

African Accounting Council: POB 11223, Kinshasa, Democratic Republic of the Congo; tel. (12) 33567; f. 1979; provides assistance to institutions in member countries on standardization of accounting; promotes education, further training and research in accountancy and related areas of study. Publ. *Information and Liaison Bulletin* (every two months).

African Bureau for Educational Sciences: 29 ave de la Justice, BP 1764, Kinshasa I, Democratic Republic of the Congo; tel. (12) 22006; f. 1973 to conduct educational research. Publs *Bulletin d'Information* (quarterly), *Revue africaine des sciences de l'éducation* (2 a year), *Répertoire africain des institutions de recherche* (annually).

African Civil Aviation Commission—AFCAC: 15 blvd de la République, BP 2356, Dakar, Senegal; tel. 839-93-93; fax 823-26-61;

e-mail cafac@telecomplus.sn; internet www.afcac-cafac.sn; f. 1969 to encourage co-operation in all civil aviation activities; promotes co-ordination and better utilization and development of African air transport systems and the standardization of aircraft, flight equipment and training programmes for pilots and mechanics; organizes working groups and seminars, and compiles statistics. Pres. Capt. SHETTIMA ABBA GANA (Nigeria); Sec. A. CHEIFFOU (acting).

Pan-African News Agency—PANA: BP 4650, Dakar, Senegal; tel. 824-14-10; fax 824-13-90; internet www.africanews.org/PANA; regional headquarters in Khartoum, Sudan; Lusaka, Zambia; Kinshasa, Democratic Republic of the Congo; Lagos, Nigeria; Tripoli, Libya; began operations in May 1983; receives information from national news agencies and circulates news in English and French. Following financial problems, plans to restructure the agency at a cost of US $4.7m., in order to allow shares to be held by the private sector, were announced in June 1997. Capital was to be increased by 25,000 shares, while the agency was to be renamed PANA Presse. Co-ordinator BABACAR FALL. Publ. *PANA Review*.

Pan-African Postal Union—PAPU: POB 6026, Arusha, Tanzania; tel. (27) 2508603; fax (27) 2503913; e-mail papu@habari.co.tz; f. 1980 to extend members' co-operation in the improvement of postal services. Sec.-Gen. JILANI BEN HADDADA. Publ. *PAPU Bulletin*.

Pan-African Railways Union: BP 687, Kinshasa, Democratic Republic of the Congo; tel. (12) 23861; f. 1972 to standardize, expand, co-ordinate and improve members' railway services; the ultimate aim is to link all systems; main organs: Gen. Assembly, Exec. Bd, Gen. Secr., five tech. cttees. Mems in 30 African countries.

Pan-African Telecommunications Union: POB 7248, Kinshasa, Democratic Republic of the Congo; f. 1977; co-ordinates devt of telecommunications networks and services in Africa.

Supreme Council for Sports in Africa: BP 1363, Yaoundé, Cameroon; tel. and fax 23-95-80; Sec.-Gen. Dr AWOTURE ELEYAE (Nigeria). Publs *SCSA News* (6 a year), *African Sports Movement Directory* (annually).

ORGANIZATION OF THE ISLAMIC CONFERENCE—OIC

Address: Kilo 6, Mecca Rd, POB 178, Jeddah 21411, Saudi Arabia.

Telephone: (2) 680-0800; **fax:** (2) 687-3568.

The Organization was formally established in May 1971, when its Secretariat became operational, following a summit meeting of Muslim heads of state at Rabat, Morocco, in September 1969, and the Islamic Foreign Ministers' Conference in Jeddah in March 1970, and in Karachi, Pakistan, in December 1970.

MEMBERS

Afghanistan	Indonesia	Palestine
Albania	Iran	Qatar
Algeria	Iraq	Saudi Arabia
Azerbaijan	Jordan	Senegal
Bahrain	Kazakhstan	Sierra Leone
Bangladesh	Kuwait	Somalia
Benin	Kyrgyzstan	Sudan
Brunei	Lebanon	Suriname
Burkina Faso	Libya	Syria
Cameroon	Malaysia	Tajikistan
Chad	Maldives	Togo
The Comoros	Mali	Tunisia
Djibouti	Mauritania	Turkey
Egypt	Morocco	Turkmenistan
Gabon	Mozambique	Uganda
The Gambia	Niger	United Arab
Guinea	Nigeria*	Emirates
Guinea-Bissau	Oman	Uzbekistan
Guyana	Pakistan	Yemen

* Nigeria renounced its membership of the OIC in May 1991; however, the OIC has not formally recognized this decision.
Note: Observer status has been granted to Bosnia and Herzegovina, the Central African Republic, Côte d'Ivoire, Thailand, the Muslim community of the 'Turkish Republic of Northern Cyprus', the Moro National Liberation Front (MNLF) of the southern Philippines, the United Nations, the Non-Aligned Movement, the League of Arab States, the Organization of African Unity, the Economic Co-operation Organization, the Union of the Arab Maghreb and the Co-operation Council for the Arab States of the Gulf.

Organization

(August 2000)

SUMMIT CONFERENCES

The supreme body of the Organization is the Conference of Heads of State, which met in 1969 at Rabat, Morocco, in 1974 at Lahore, Pakistan, and in January 1981 at Mecca, Saudi Arabia, when it was decided that summit conferences would be held every three years in future. Eighth Conference: Teheran, Iran, December 1997. The ninth Conference was to be held in Doha, Qatar, in 2000.

CONFERENCE OF MINISTERS OF FOREIGN AFFAIRS

Conferences take place annually, to consider the means for implementing the general policy of the Organization, although they may also be convened for extraordinary sessions.

SECRETARIAT

The executive organ of the Organization, headed by a Secretary-General (who is elected by the Conference of Ministers of Foreign Affairs for a four-year term, renewable only once) and four Assistant Secretaries-General (similarly appointed).

Secretary-General: AZEDDINE LARAKI (Morocco) (until Dec. 2000), ABDELOUAHED BELKEZIZ (Morocco) (designate).

At the summit conference in January 1981 it was decided that an International Islamic Court of Justice should be established to adjudicate in disputes between Muslim countries. Experts met in January 1983 to draw up a constitution for the court; however, by 1999 it was not yet in operation.

SPECIALIZED COMMITTEES

Al-Quds Committee: f. 1975 to implement the resolutions of the Islamic Conference on the status of Jerusalem (Al-Quds); it meets at the level of foreign ministers; maintains the Al-Quds Fund; Chair. King MUHAMMAD VI of Morocco.

Standing Committee for Economic and Commercial Co-operation (COMCEC): f. 1981; Chair. SÜLEYMAN DEMIREL (Pres. of Turkey).

Standing Committee for Information and Cultural Affairs (COMIAC): f. 1981.

Standing Committee for Scientific and Technological Co-operation (COMSTECH): f. 1981; Chair. MOHAMMAD RAFIQ TARAR (Pres. of Pakistan).

Islamic Commission for Economic, Cultural and Social Affairs: f. 1976.

Permanent Finance Committee.

Other committees comprise the Committee of Islamic Solidarity with the Peoples of the Sahel, the Six-Member Committee on the Situation of Muslims in the Philippines, the Six-Member Committee on Palestine, the *ad hoc* Committee on Afghanistan, the OIC contact group on Bosnia and Herzegovina (with an expanded mandate to include Kosovo and Metohija, Yugoslavia), and the OIC contact group on Jammu and Kashmir.

Activities

The Organization's aims, as proclaimed in the Charter that was adopted in 1972, are:

(i) To promote Islamic solidarity among member states;

(ii) To consolidate co-operation among member states in the economic, social, cultural, scientific and other vital fields, and to arrange consultations among member states belonging to international organizations;

(iii) To endeavour to eliminate racial segregation and discrimination and to eradicate colonialism in all its forms;

(iv) To take necessary measures to support international peace and security founded on justice;

(v) To co-ordinate all efforts for the safeguard of the Holy Places and support of the struggle of the people of Palestine, and help them to regain their rights and liberate their land;

(vi) To strengthen the struggle of all Muslim people with a view to safeguarding their dignity, independence and national rights; and

(vii) To create a suitable atmosphere for the promotion of co-operation and understanding among member states and other countries.

The first summit conference of Islamic leaders (representing 24 states) took place in 1969 following the burning of the Al Aqsa Mosque in Jerusalem. At this conference it was decided that Islamic governments should 'consult together with a view to promoting close co-operation and mutual assistance in the economic, scientific, cultural and spiritual fields, inspired by the immortal teachings of Islam'. Thereafter the foreign ministers of the countries concerned met annually, and adopted the Charter of the Organization of the Islamic Conference in 1972.

At the second Islamic summit conference (Lahore, Pakistan, 1974), the Islamic Solidarity Fund was established, together with a committee of representatives which later evolved into the Islamic Commission for Economic, Cultural and Social Affairs. Subsequently, numerous other subsidiary bodies have been set up (see below).

ECONOMIC CO-OPERATION

A general agreement for economic, technical and commercial co-operation came into force in 1981, providing for the establishment of joint investment projects and trade co-ordination. This was followed by an agreement on promotion, protection and guarantee of investments among member states. A plan of action to strengthen economic co-operation was adopted at the third Islamic summit conference in 1981, aiming to promote collective self-reliance and the development of joint ventures in all sectors. In May 1993 the OIC committee for economic and commercial co-operation, meeting in İstanbul, agreed to review and update the 1981 plan of action.

A meeting of ministers of industry was held in February 1982, and agreed to promote industrial co-operation, including joint ventures in agricultural machinery, engineering and other basic industries. The fifth summit conference, held in 1987, approved proposals for joint development of modern technology, and for improving scientific and technical skills in the less developed Islamic countries. In December 1988 it was announced that a committee of experts, established by the OIC, was to draw up a 10-year programme of assistance to developing countries (mainly in Africa) in science and technology.

CULTURAL CO-OPERATION

The Organization supports education in Muslim communities throughout the world, and was instrumental in the establishment of Islamic universities in Niger and Uganda (see below). It organizes seminars on various aspects of Islam, and encourages dialogue with the other monotheistic religions. Support is given to publications on Islam both in Muslim and Western countries.

HUMANITARIAN ASSISTANCE

Assistance is given to Muslim communities affected by wars and natural disasters, in co-operation with UN organizations, particularly UNHCR. The countries of the Sahel region (Burkina Faso, Cape Verde, Chad, The Gambia, Guinea, Guinea-Bissau, Mali, Mauritania, Niger and Senegal) receive particular attention as victims of drought. In April 1993 member states pledged US $80m. in emergency assistance for Muslims affected by the war in Bosnia and Herzegovina (see below for details of subsequent assistance). In April 1999 the OIC resolved to send humanitarian aid to assist the displaced ethnic Albanian population of Kosovo and Metohija, in southern Serbia.

POLITICAL CO-OPERATION

Since its inception the OIC has called for vacation of Arab territories by Israel, recognition of the rights of Palestinians and of the Palestine Liberation Organization (PLO) as their sole legitimate representative, and the restoration of Jerusalem to Arab rule. The 1981 summit conference called for a *jihad* (holy war—though not necessarily in a military sense) 'for the liberation of Jerusalem and the occupied territories'; this was to include an Islamic economic boycott of Israel. In 1982 Islamic ministers of foreign affairs decided to establish Islamic offices for boycotting Israel and for military co-operation with the PLO. The 1984 summit conference agreed to reinstate Egypt (suspended following the peace treaty signed with Israel in 1979) as a member of the OIC, although the resolution was opposed by seven states.

The fifth summit conference, held in January 1987, discussed the continuing Iran–Iraq war, and agreed that the Islamic Peace Committee should attempt to prevent the sale of military equipment to the parties in the conflict. The conference also discussed the conflicts in Chad and Lebanon, and requested the holding of a United Nations conference to define international terrorism, as opposed to legitimate fighting for freedom.

In August 1990 a majority of ministers of foreign affairs condemned Iraq's recent invasion of Kuwait, and demanded the withdrawal of Iraqi forces. In August 1991 the Conference of Ministers of Foreign Affairs obstructed Iraq's attempt to propose a resolution demanding the repeal of economic sanctions against the country. The sixth summit conference, held in Senegal in December 1991, reflected the divisions in the Arab world that resulted from Iraq's invasion of Kuwait and the ensuing war. Twelve heads of state did not attend, reportedly to register protest at the presence of Jordan and the PLO at the conference, both of which had given support to Iraq. Disagreement also arose between the PLO and the majority of other OIC members when a proposal was adopted to cease the OIC's support for the PLO's *jihad* in the Arab territories occupied by Israel, in an attempt to further the Middle East peace negotiations.

In August 1992 the UN General Assembly approved a non-binding resolution, introduced by the OIC, that requested the UN Security Council to take increased action, including the use of force, in order to defend the non-Serbian population of Bosnia and Herzegovina (some 43% of Bosnians being Muslims) from Serbian aggression, and to restore its 'territorial integrity'. The OIC Conference of Ministers of Foreign Affairs, which was held in Jeddah, Saudi Arabia, in December, demanded anew that the UN Security Council take all necessary measures against Serbia and Montenegro, including military intervention, in accordance with Article 42 of the UN Charter, in order to protect the Bosnian Muslims. In February 1993 the OIC appealed to the Security Council to remove the embargo on armaments to Bosnia and Herzegovina with regard to the Bosnian Muslims, to allow them to defend themselves from the Bosnian Serbs, who were far better armed.

A report by an OIC fact-finding mission, which in February 1993 visited Azad Kashmir while investigating allegations of repression of the largely Muslim population of the Indian state of Jammu and Kashmir by the Indian armed forces, was presented to the 1993 Conference. The meeting urged member states to take the necessary measures to persuade India to cease the 'massive human rights violations' in Jammu and Kashmir and to allow the Indian Kashmiris to 'exercise their inalienable right to self-determination'. In September 1994 ministers of foreign affairs, meeting in Islamabad, Pakistan, urged the Indian Government to grant permission for an OIC fact-finding mission, and for other human rights groups, to visit Jammu and Kashmir (which it had continually refused to do) and to refrain from human rights violations of the Kashmiri people. The ministers agreed to establish a contact group on Jammu and Kashmir, which was to provide a mechanism for promoting international awareness of the situation in that region and for seeking a peaceful solution to the dispute. In December OIC heads of state approved a resolution condemning reported human rights abuses by Indian security forces in Kashmir.

In July 1994 the OIC Secretary-General visited Afghanistan and proposed the establishment of a preparatory mechanism to promote national reconciliation in that country. In mid-1995 Saudi Arabia, acting as a representative of the OIC, pursued a peace initiative for Afghanistan and issued an invitation for leaders of the different factions to hold negotiations in Jeddah.

A special ministerial meeting on Bosnia and Herzegovina was held in July 1993, at which seven OIC countries committed themselves to making available up to 17,000 troops to serve in the UN Protection Force in the former Yugoslavia (UNPROFOR). The meeting also decided to dispatch immediately a ministerial mission to persuade influential governments to support the OIC's demands for the removal of the arms embargo on Bosnian Muslims and the convening of a restructured international conference to bring about a political solution to the conflict. At the end of September 1994 ministers of foreign affairs of nine countries constituting the OIC contact group on Bosnia and Herzegovina, meeting in New York, resolved to prepare an assessment document on the issue, and to establish an alliance with its Western counterpart (comprising France, Germany, Russia, the United Kingdom and the USA). The two groups met in Geneva, Switzerland, in January 1995. In December 1994 OIC heads of state, convened in Morocco, proclaimed that the UN arms embargo on Bosnia and Herzegovina could not be applied to the Muslim authorities of that Republic. The Conference also resolved to review economic relations between OIC member states and any country that supported Serbian activities. An aid fund was established, to which member states were requested to contribute between

US $500,000 and US $5m., in order to provide further humanitarian and economic assistance to Bosnian Muslims. In relation to wider concerns the conference adopted a Code of Conduct for Combating International Terrorism, in an attempt to control Muslim extremist groups. The code commits states to ensuring that militant groups do not use their territory for planning or executing terrorist activity against other states, in addition to states refraining from direct support or participation in acts of terrorism. In a further resolution the OIC supported the decision by Iraq to recognize Kuwait, but advocated that Iraq comply with all UN Security Council decisions.

In July 1995 the OIC contact group on Bosnia and Herzegovina (at that time comprising Egypt, Iran, Malaysia, Morocco, Pakistan, Saudi Arabia, Senegal and Turkey), meeting in Geneva, declared the UN arms embargo against Bosnia and Herzegovina to be 'invalid'. Several Governments subsequently announced their willingness officially to supply weapons and other military assistance to the Bosnian Muslim forces. In September a meeting of all OIC ministers of defence and foreign affairs endorsed the establishment of an 'assistance mobilization group' which was to supply military, economic, legal and other assistance to Bosnia and Herzegovina. In a joint declaration the ministers also demanded the return of all territory seized by Bosnian Serb forces, the continued NATO bombing of Serb military targets, and that the city of Sarajevo be preserved under a Muslim-led Bosnian Government. In November the OIC Secretary-General endorsed the peace accord for the former Yugoslavia, which was concluded, in Dayton, USA, by leaders of all the conflicting factions, and reaffirmed the commitment of Islamic states to participate in efforts to implement the accord. In the following month the OIC Conference of Ministers of Foreign Affairs, convened in Conakry, Guinea, requested the full support of the international community to reconstruct Bosnia and Herzegovina through humanitarian aid as well as economic and technical co-operation. Ministers declared that Palestine and the establishment of fully-autonomous Palestinian control of Jerusalem were issues of central importance for the Muslim world. The Conference urged the removal of all aspects of occupation and the cessation of the construction of Israeli settlements in the occupied territories. In addition, the final statement of the meeting condemned Armenian aggression against Azerbaijan, registered concern at the persisting civil conflict in Afghanistan, demanded the elimination of all weapons of mass destruction and pledged support for Libya (affected by the US trade embargo).

In December 1996 OIC ministers of foreign affairs, meeting in Jakarta, Indonesia, urged the international community to apply pressure on Israel in order to ensure its implementation of the terms of the Middle East peace process. The ministers reaffirmed the importance of ensuring that the provisions of the Dayton Peace Agreement for the former Yugoslavia were fully implemented, called for a peaceful settlement of the Kashmir issue, demanded that Iraq fulfil its obligations for the establishment of security, peace and stability in the region and proposed that an international conference on peace and national reconciliation in Somalia be convened. The ministers elected a new Secretary-General, Azeddine Laraki, who confirmed that the organization would continue to develop its role as an international mediator. In March 1997, at an extraordinary summit held in Pakistan, OIC heads of state and of government reiterated the organization's objective of increasing international pressure on Israel to ensure the full implementation of the terms of the Middle East peace process. An 'Islamabad Declaration' was also adopted, which pledged to increase co-operation between members of the OIC. In June the OIC condemned the decision by the US House of Representatives to recognize Jerusalem as the Israeli capital. The Secretary-General of the OIC issued a statement rejecting the US decision as counter to the role of the USA as sponsor of the Middle East peace plan. In December OIC heads of state attended the eighth summit conference, held in Iran. The Teheran Declaration, issued at the end of the conference, demanded the 'liberation' of the Israeli-occupied territories and the creation of an autonomous Palestinian state. The conference also appealed for a cessation of the conflicts in Afghanistan, and between Armenia and Azerbaijan. It was requested that the UN sanctions against Libya be removed and that the US legislation threatening sanctions against foreign companies investing in certain countries (including Iran and Libya), introduced in July 1996, be dismissed as invalid. In addition, the Declaration encouraged the increased participation of women in OIC activities.

In early 1998 the OIC appealed for an end to the threat of US-led military action against Iraq arising from a dispute regarding access granted to international weapons inspectors. The crisis was averted by an agreement concluded between the Iraqi authorities and the UN Secretary-General in February. In March OIC ministers of foreign affairs, meeting in Doha, Qatar, requested an end to the international sanctions against Iraq. Additionally, the ministers urged all states to end the process of restoring normal trading and diplomatic relations with Israel until that country withdraws from the occupied territories and permits the establishment of an independent Palestinian state.

In April 1998 the OIC, jointly with the UN, sponsored new peace negotiations between the main disputing factions in Afghanistan, which were conducted in Islamabad, Pakistan. In early May, however, the talks collapsed and were postponed indefinitely. In September the Secretaries-General of the OIC and UN agreed to establish a joint mission to counter the deteriorating security situation along the Afghan-Iranian border, following the large-scale deployment of Taliban troops in the region and consequent military manoeuvres by the Iranian authorities. They also reiterated the need to proceed with negotiations to conclude a peaceful settlement in Afghanistan.

In December 1998 the OIC appealed for a diplomatic solution to the tensions arising from Iraq's withdrawal of co-operation with UN weapons inspectors, and criticized subsequent military airstrikes, led by the USA, as having been conducted without renewed UN authority.

In early April 1999 ministers of foreign affairs of the countries comprising OIC's Contact Group met to consider the crisis in Kosovo. The meeting condemned Serbian atrocities being committed against the local Albanian population and urged the provision of international assistance for the thousands of people displaced by the conflict. The Group resolved to establish a committee to co-ordinate relief aid provided by member states. The ministers also expressed their willingness to help to formulate a peaceful settlement and to participate in any subsequent implementation force.

SUBSIDIARY ORGANS

International Commission for the Preservation of Islamic Cultural Heritage (ICPICH): POB 24, 80692 Beşiktaş, İstanbul, Turkey; tel. (212) 2591742; fax (212) 2584365; e-mail ircica@superonline.com; internet www.ircica.hypermart.net/ircica.html; f. 1982. Sec. Prof. Dr EKMELEDDİN İHSANOĞLU (Turkey). Publ. *Newsletter* (3 a year).

Islamic Centre for the Development of Trade: Complexe Commercial des Habous, ave des FAR, BP 13545, Casablanca, Morocco; tel. (2) 314974; fax (2) 310110; e-mail icdt@icdt.org; internet www.icdt.org; f. 1983 to encourage regular commercial contacts, harmonize policies and promote investments among OIC mems. Dir BADRE EDDINE ALLALI. Publs *Tijaris: International and Inter-Islamic Trade Magazine* (quarterly), *Inter-Islamic Trade Report* (annually).

Islamic Institute of Technology (IIT): GPO Box 3003, Board Bazar, Gazipur 1704, Dhaka, Bangladesh; tel. (2) 980-0960; fax (2) 980-0970; e-mail dg@iit.bangla.net; internet www.iitoicdhaka.edu; f. 1981 to develop human resources in OIC mem. states, with special reference to engineering, technology, tech. and vocational education and research; 224 staff and 1,000 students; library of 23,000 vols. Dir-Gen. Prof. Dr M. ANWAR HOSSAIN. Publs *News Bulletin* (annually), annual calendar and announcement for admission, reports, human resources development series.

Islamic Jurisprudence Academy: Jeddah, Saudi Arabia; f. 1982. Sec.-Gen. Sheikh MOHAMED HABIB BELKHOJAH.

Islamic Solidarity Fund: c/o OIC Secretariat, POB 178, Jeddah 21411, Saudi Arabia; tel. (2) 680-0800; fax (2) 687-3568; f. 1974 to meet the needs of Islamic communities by providing emergency aid and the finance to build mosques, Islamic centres, hospitals, schools and universities. Chair. Sheikh NASIR ABDULLAH BIN HAMDAN; Exec. Dir ABDULLAH HERSI.

Islamic University of Niger: BP 11507, Niamey, Niger; tel. 723903; fax 733796; f. 1984; provides courses of study in *Shari'a* (Islamic law) and Arabic language and literature; also offers courses in pedagogy and teacher training; receives grants from Islamic Solidarity Fund and contributions from OIC member states. Rector Prof. ABDELALI OUDHRIRI.

Islamic University in Uganda: POB 2555, Mbale, Uganda; tel. (45) 33502; fax (45) 34452; e-mail iuiu@info.com.co.ug; Kampala Liaison Office: POB 7689, Kampala; tel. (41) 236874; fax (41) 254576; f. 1988 to meet the educational needs of Muslim populations in English-speaking African countries; mainly financed by OIC. Principal Officer Prof. MAHDI ADAMU.

Research Centre for Islamic History, Art and Culture (IRCICA): POB 24, Beşiktaş 80692, İstanbul, Turkey; tel. (212) 2591742; fax (212) 2584365; e-mail ircica@superonline.com; internet www.ircica.hypermart.net/ircica.html; f. 1980; library of 50,000 vols. Dir-Gen. Prof. Dr EKMELEDDİN İHSANOĞLU. Publs *Newsletter* (3 a year), monographical studies.

Statistical, Economic and Social Research and Training Centre for the Islamic Countries: Attar Sok 4, GOP 06700, Ankara, Turkey; tel. (312) 4686172; fax (312) 4673458; e-mail sesrtcic@tr-net.net.tr; f. 1978. Dir-Gen. ERDINÇ ERDÜN.

SPECIALIZED INSTITUTIONS

International Islamic News Agency (IINA): King Khalid Palace, Madinah Rd, POB 5054, Jeddah, Saudi Arabia; tel. (2) 665-8561; fax (2) 665-9358; e-mail iina@ogertel.com; internet www.islamicnews.org; f. 1972. Dir-Gen. ABDULWAHAB KASHIF.

Islamic Educational, Scientific and Cultural Organization (ISESCO): Ave Attine, Hay Ryad, BP 2275, Rabat 10104, Morocco; tel. (7) 772433; fax (7) 777459; e-mail cid@isesco.org.ma; internet www.isesco.org.ma; f. 1982. Dir-Gen. Dr ABDULAZIZ BIN OTHMAN AL-TWAIJRI. Publs *ISESCO Newsletter* (quarterly), *Islam Today* (2 a year), *ISESCO Triennial*.

Islamic States Broadcasting Organization (ISBO): POB 6351, Jeddah 21442, Saudi Arabia; tel. (2) 672-1121; fax (2) 672-2600; f. 1975. Sec.-Gen. HUSSEIN AL-ASKARY.

AFFILIATED INSTITUTIONS

International Association of Islamic Banks (IAIB): King Abdul-aziz St, Queen's Bldg, 23rd Floor, Al-Balad Dist, POB 23425, Jeddah 21426, Saudi Arabia; tel. (2) 643-1276; fax (2) 644-7239; f. 1977 to link financial institutions operating on Islamic banking principles; activities include training and research; mems: 192 banks and other financial institutions in 34 countries. Sec.-Gen. SAMIR A. SHAIKH.

Islamic Chamber of Commerce and Industry: POB 3831, Clifton, Karachi 75600, Pakistan; tel. (21) 5874756; fax (21) 5870765; e-mail icci@icci-oic.org; internet www.icci.org.pk/islamic/main.html;

f. 1979 to promote trade and industry among member states; comprises nat. chambers or feds of chambers of commerce and industry. Sec.-Gen. AQEEL AHMAD AL-JASSEM.

Islamic Committee for the International Crescent: c/o OIC, Kilo 6, Mecca Rd, POB 178, Jeddah 21411, Saudi Arabia; tel. (2) 680-0800; fax (2) 687-3568; f. 1979 to attempt to alleviate the suffering caused by natural disasters and war. Sec.-Gen. Dr AHMAD ABDALLAH CHERIF.

Islamic Solidarity Sports Federation: POB 6040, Riyadh 11442, Saudi Arabia; tel. and fax (1) 482-2145; f. 1981. Sec.-Gen. Dr MOHAMMAD SALEH GAZDAR.

Organization of Islamic Capitals and Cities—OICC: POB 13621, Jeddah 21414, Saudi Arabia; tel. (2) 698-1953; fax (2) 698-1053; e-mail oiccorg@icc.net.sa; f. 1980 to promote and develop co-operation among OICC mems, to preserve their character and heritage, to implement planning guide-lines for the growth of Islamic cities and to upgrade standards of public services and utilities in those cities. Sec.-Gen. OMAR ABDULLAH KADI.

Organization of the Islamic Shipowners' Association: POB 14900, Jeddah 21434, Saudi Arabia; tel. (2) 663-7882; fax (2) 660-4920; internet www.icdt.org/oisa.htm; f. 1981 to promote co-operation among maritime cos in Islamic countries. In 1998 mems approved the establishment of a new commercial venture, the Bakkah Shipping Company, to enhance sea transport in the region. Sec.-Gen. Dr ABDULLATIF A. SULTAN.

SOUTHERN AFRICAN DEVELOPMENT COMMUNITY—SADC

Address: SADC Bldg, Private Bag 0095, Gaborone, Botswana.

Telephone: 351863; **fax:** 372848; **e-mail:** sadcsec@sadc.int; **internet:** www.sadc.int.

The first Southern African Development Co-ordination Conference (SADCC) was held at Arusha, Tanzania, in July 1979, to harmonize development plans and to reduce the region's economic dependence on South Africa. On 17 August 1992 the 10 member countries of the SADCC signed a treaty establishing the Southern African Development Community (SADC), which replaced the SADCC. The treaty places binding obligations on member countries, with the aim of promoting economic integration towards a fully developed common market. A tribunal was to be established to arbitrate in the case of disputes between member states arising from the treaty. By September 1993 all of the member states had ratified the treaty; it came into effect on 5 October.

MEMBERS

Angola	Malawi	South Africa
Botswana	Mauritius	Swaziland
Congo, Democratic	Mozambique	Tanzania
Republic	Namibia	Zambia
Lesotho	Seychelles	Zimbabwe

Organization

(August 2000)

SUMMIT MEETING

The meeting is held at least once a year and is attended by heads of state and government or their representatives. It is the supreme policy-making organ of the SADC and is responsible for the appointment of the Executive Secretary.

COUNCIL OF MINISTERS

Representatives of SADC member countries at ministerial level meet at least once a year. In addition, special meetings of sectoral committees of ministers are held to co-ordinate regional policy in a particular field by, for example, ministers of energy and ministers of transport.

STANDING COMMITTEE OF OFFICIALS

The Committee, comprising senior officials, usually from the ministry responsible for economic planning or finance, acts as the technical advisory body to the Council. It meets at least once a year. Members of the Committee also act as a national contact point for matters relating to SADC.

SECRETARIAT

Executive Secretary a.i.: PAKEREESAMY ('PREGA') RAMSAMY (Mauritius).

SECTORAL CO-ORDINATION OFFICES

Each member state has a responsibility to promote and co-ordinate regional policies and programmes in specific areas on behalf of the organization as a whole. Accordingly, the Sectoral Co-ordinating Units are part of national governments and administered by the civil service of that country. Sectoral Commissions and Centres are regional institutions, which are established and supported by all member states.

Agricultural Research and Training: Private Bag 0033, Gaborone, Botswana; tel. 328780; fax 328965; e-mail dar@info.bw; Dir Dr L. M. MAZHANI.

Culture, Information and Sport: Avda Francisco Orlando Magumbwe 780, 10th Floor, POB 1154, Maputo, Mozambique; tel. (1) 497944; fax (1) 497943; e-mail sacis@sadc.uem.mz; Dir RENATO MATUSSE.

Employment and Labour: POB 31969, Lusaka, Zambia; tel. (1) 251719; fax (1) 252095; Dir C. J. CHANDA.

Energy: rua Gil Vicente No. 2, CP 2876, Luanda, Angola; tel. (2) 345288; fax (2) 343003; e-mail sadc_elec@ebonet.net; internet www.ebonet.net/sadc; Dir ANTONIO HENRIQUE DA SILVA.

Environment and Land Management: Ministry of Agriculture and Co-operatives, POB 24, Maseru 100, Lesotho; tel. 323561; fax 310349; Dir BATAUNG LELEKA.

Finance and Investment: Private Bag X115, Pretoria, 0001, South Africa; tel. (12) 3155653; fax (12) 3219580; Dir SECHOCHA MAKHOALIBE.

Food, Agriculture and Natural Resources: 43 Robson Manyika Ave, POB 4046, Harare, Zimbabwe; tel. (4) 736051; telex 22440; fax (4) 795345; e-mail fstau@fanr-sadc.org.zw; Dir REGINALD MUGWARA.

Human Resources Development: Ministry of Public Service and Information, POB 5873, Mbabane, Swaziland; tel. 4046344; fax 4046407; e-mail sadchrd@realnet.co.sz; Dir ENNET NKAMBULE.

Industry and Trade: POB 9491, Dar es Salaam, Tanzania; tel. (51) 31455; fax (51) 46919; Dir ABRAHIM PALLANGYO.

Inland Fisheries, Wildlife and Forestry: Ministry of Forestry, Fisheries and Environmental Affairs, Private Bag 350, Lilongwe 3, Malawi; tel. 782600; fax 780260; Dir D. KAMBAUWA.

Livestock Production and Animal Disease Control: Private Bag 0032, Gaborone, Botswana; tel. 350620; fax 303744; Dir M. FANI-KISO.

Marine Fisheries and Resources: Private Bag 13355, Windhoek, Namibia; tel. (61) 2053911; fax (61) 235269; Dir Z. A. ISHITILE.

Mining: Ministry of Mines and Mineral Development, Chilufya Mulenga Rd, POB 31969, 10101 Lusaka, Zambia; tel. (1) 254043; fax (1) 252095; e-mail sadc-mcu@zamnet.zm; internet www.sadc mining.org.zm; Dir C. J. CHANDA.

Southern African Centre for Co-operation in Agricultural Research (SACCAR): Private Bag 00108, Gaborone, Botswana; tel. 328847; fax 328806; Dir K. MOLAPONG.

Southern African Transport and Communications Commission (SATCC): CP 2677, Maputo, Mozambique; tel. (1) 420214; fax (1) 420213; e-mail director@satcc.org; internet www.satcc.org; Dir E. H. MSOLOMBA.

Tourism: c/o Ministry of Tourism and Leisure, Air Mauritius Centre, Level 12, Pres. J. F. Kennedy St, Port Louis, Mauritius; tel. 210-1329; fax 208-6776; e-mail mot@intnet.mu; Dir SUSY EDUARD.

Water: c/o Ministry of Natural Resources, POB 426, Maseru 100, Lesotho; tel. 323163; fax 310250.

Activities

In July 1979 the first Southern African Development Co-ordination Conference was attended by delegations from Angola, Botswana, Mozambique, Tanzania and Zambia, with representatives from donor governments and international agencies. In April 1980 a regional economic summit conference was held in Lusaka, Zambia, and the Lusaka Declaration, a statement of strategy entitled 'Southern Africa: Towards Economic Liberation', was approved, together with a programme of action allotting specific studies and tasks to member governments (see list of co-ordinating offices, above). The members aimed to reduce their dependence on South Africa for rail and air links and port facilities, imports of raw materials and manufactured goods, and the supply of electric power. In 1985, however, an SADCC report noted that since 1980 the region had become still more dependent on South Africa for its trade outlets, and the 1986 summit meeting, although it recommended the adoption of economic sanctions against South Africa, failed to establish a timetable for doing so.

In January 1992 a meeting of the SADCC Council of Ministers approved proposals to transform the organization (by then expanded to include Lesotho, Malawi, Namibia and Swaziland) into a fully integrated economic community, and in mid-August the treaty establishing the SADC (see above) was signed. South Africa became a member of the SADC in August 1994, thus strengthening the objective of regional co-operation and economic integration. Mauritius became a member in August 1995. In September 1997 SADC heads of state agreed to admit the Democratic Republic of the Congo and Seychelles as members of the Community.

A possible merger between the SADC and the Preferential Trade Area for Eastern and Southern African States (PTA), which consisted of all the members of the SADC apart from Botswana and had similar aims of enhancing economic co-operation, was rejected by the SADC's Executive Secretary in January 1993. He denied that the two organizations were duplicating each other's work, as had been suggested. In August 1994 SADC heads of state, meeting in Gaborone, Botswana, advocated that, in order to minimize any duplication of activities, the PTA be divided into two sections: a southern region, incorporating all SADC members, and a northern region. It was emphasized that there would not be a merger between the two groupings. However, concerns of regional rivalry with the PTA's successor, the Common Market for Eastern and Southern Africa (COMESA, q.v.), persisted. In August 1996 an SADC–COMESA ministerial meeting advocated the continued separate functioning of the two organizations.

In September 1994 the first meeting of ministers of foreign affairs of the SADC and the European Union (EU) was held in Berlin, Germany. The two sides agreed to establish working groups to promote closer trade, political, regional and economic co-operation. In particular, a declaration issued from the meeting specified joint objectives, including a reduction of exports of weapons to southern Africa and of the arms trade within the region, promotion of investment in the region's manufacturing sector and support for democracy at all levels. A consultative meeting between representatives of the SADC and EU was held in February 1995, in Lilongwe, Malawi, at which both groupings resolved to strengthen security in the southern African region. The meeting proposed initiating mechanisms to prevent conflicts and to maintain peace, and agreed to organize a conference to address the problems of drugs-trafficking and cross-border crime in the region. A second SADC–EU ministerial meeting, held in Namibia in October 1996, endorsed a Regional Indicative Programme to enhance co-operation between the two organizations over the next five years. The third ministerial meeting took place in Vienna, Austria, in November 1998. In September 1999 the SADC signed a co-operation agreement with the US Government, which incorporated measures to promote US investment in the region,

and commitments to support HIV/AIDS assessment and prevention programmes, and to assist member states to develop environmental protection capabilities.

In April 1997 the SADC announced the establishment of a Parliamentary Forum to promote democracy, human rights and good governance throughout the region. Membership was to be open to national parliaments of all SADC countries, and was to offer fair representation for women. Representatives were to serve for a period of five years. The Parliamentary Forum, with its headquarters in Windhoek, Namibia, was to receive funds from member parliaments, governments and charitable and international organizations. In September SADC heads of state endorsed the establishment of the Forum as an autonomous institution.

REGIONAL SECURITY

In November 1994 SADC ministers of defence, meeting in Arusha, Tanzania, approved the establishment of a regional rapid-deployment peace-keeping force, which could be used to contain regional conflicts or civil unrest in member states. In April 1997 a training programme was held, which aimed to inform troops from nine SADC countries of UN peace-keeping doctrines, procedures and strategies. The exercise took place in Zimbabwe at a cost of US $900,000, provided by the British Government and the Zimbabwe National Army. A peace-keeping exercise involving 4,000 troops was held in South Africa, in April 1999. An SADC Mine Action Committee has been established to monitor and co-ordinate the process of removing anti-personnel land devices from countries in the region.

In June 1996 SADC heads of state and government, meeting in Gaborone, Botswana, inaugurated a new Organ on Politics, Defence and Security, which was expected to enhance co-ordination of national policies and activities in these areas. The objectives of the body were, *inter alia*, to safeguard the people and development of the region against instability arising from civil disorder, inter-state conflict and external aggression; to undertake conflict prevention, management and resolution activities, by mediating in inter-state and intra-state disputes and conflicts, pre-empting conflicts through an early-warning system and using diplomacy and peace-keeping to achieve sustainable peace; to promote the development of a common foreign policy, in areas of mutual interest, and the evolution of common political institutions; to develop close co-operation between the police and security services of the region; and to encourage the observance of universal human rights, as provided for in the charters of the UN and OAU. The summit meeting elected the Zimbabwean President, Robert Mugabe, to chair the Organ. The Zambian President, Frederick Chiluba, failed to attend the meeting, owing to his Government's concern that the new body was empowered to interfere in the country's internal affairs. In October the Organ convened, at summit level, to consider measures to promote the peace process in Angola; however, there were disagreements within SADC regarding the future status of the security Organ either as an integrated part of the community (favoured by South Africa) or as a more autonomous body (supported by Zimbabwe). In March 1998 the Presidents of Malawi, Mozambique and Namibia were charged by SADC leaders to undertake a review of the issue.

In August 1998 the Zimbabwean Government convened a meeting of the heads of state of seven SADC member states to discuss the escalation of civil conflict in the Democratic Republic of the Congo (DRC) and the threat to regional security, with Rwanda and Uganda reportedly having sent troops to assist anti-government forces. Later in that month ministers of defence and defence officials of several SADC countries declared their support for an initiative of the Zimbabwean Government to send military assistance to the forces loyal to President Kabila in the DRC. South Africa, which did not attend the meeting, rejected any military intervention under SADC auspices and insisted that the organization would pursue a diplomatic initiative. Zimbabwe, Angola and Namibia proceeded to send troops and logistical support to counter rebel Congolese forces. The Presidents of those countries failed to attend an emergency meeting of heads of state, convened by President Mandela of South Africa, which called for an immediate cease-fire and presented a 10-point-peace plan. A further emergency meeting, held in early September and attended by all SADC leaders, agreed to pursue negotiations for a peaceful settlement of the conflict. Some unity within the grouping was restored by Mandela's endorsement of the objective of supporting Kabila as the legitimate leader in the DRC. Furthermore, at the annual SADC summit meeting, held in Mauritius, it was agreed that discussion of the report on the security Organ, scheduled to have been presented to the conference, would be deferred to a specially convened summit meeting (although no date was agreed). Talks attended by Angola, the DRC, Namibia, Rwanda, Uganda, Zambia and Zimbabwe, conducted in mid-September, in Victoria Falls, agreed in principle on a cease-fire in the DRC but failed to conclude a detailed peace accord. Fighting continued to escalate, and in October Zimbabwe, Angola and Namibia resolved to send reinforcements to counter the advancing rebel forces. Meanwhile, in September representatives of the SADC attempted to mediate between government and opposition parties in Lesotho amidst a deteriorating security situation in that country. At the end of the month, following an attempt by the Lesotho military to seize power, South Africa, together with Botswana, sent troops into Lesotho to restore civil order. The operation was declared to have been conducted under SADC auspices, however it prompted widespread criticism owing to the troops' involvement in heavy fighting with opposition forces. A committee was established by SADC to secure a cease-fire in Lesotho. Also at the end of September SADC chiefs of staff agreed that the Community would assist the Angolan Government to eliminate the UNITA movement, owing to its adverse impact on the region's security. In mid-October an SADC ministerial team, comprising representatives of South Africa, Botswana, Mozambique and Zimbabwe, negotiated an accord between the opposing sides in Lesotho providing for the conduct of democratic elections. The withdrawal of foreign troops from Lesotho was initiated at the end of April 1999, and was reported to have been completed by mid-May.

During the first half of 1999 Zambia's President Chiluba pursued efforts, under SADC auspices, to negotiate a political solution to the conflict in the DRC. Troops from the region, in particular from Angola and Zimbabwe, remained actively involved in the struggle to uphold Kabila's administration. SADC ministers of defence and of foreign affairs convened in Lusaka, in late June, in order to secure a cease-fire agreement. An accord was finally signed in July between Kabila, leaders of the rebel forces and foreign allies of both sides. All foreign troops were to be withdrawn within nine months according to a schedule to be drawn up by the UN, OAU and a Joint Military Commission. In mid-2000, however, outbreaks of fighting were continuing in the DRC.

TRANSPORT AND COMMUNICATIONS

At the SADC's inception transport was seen as the most important area to be developed, on the grounds that, as the Lusaka Declaration noted, without the establishment of an adequate regional transport and communications system, other areas of co-operation become impractical. Priority was to be given to the improvement of road and railway services into Mozambique, so that the landlocked countries of the region could transport their goods through Mozambican ports instead of South African ones. The Southern African Transport and Communications Commission (SATCC) was established, in Maputo, Mozambique, in order to undertake SADC's activities in this sector. The successful distribution of emergency supplies in 1992/93, following a severe drought in the region, was reliant on improvements made to the region's infrastructure. The facilities of 12 ports in southern Africa, including South Africa, were used to import some 11.5m. metric tons of drought-related commodities, and the SADC co-ordinated six transport corridors to ensure unobstructed movement of food and other supplies. During 1995 the SATCC undertook a study of regional transport and communications to provide a comprehensive framework and strategy for future courses of action. A task force was also established to identify measures to simplify procedures at border crossings throughout southern Africa. In 1996 the SATCC Road Network Management and Financing Task Force was established.

In 1996/97 174 of the SADC's 407 development projects were in the transport and communications sector, amounting to US $6,474.4m., or 80% of total project financing. These projects aimed to address missing links and over-stretched sections of the regional network, as well as to improve efficiency, operational co-ordination and human resource development, such as management training projects. Other sectoral objectives were to ensure the compatibility of technical systems within the region and to promote the harmonization of regulations relating to intra-regional traffic and trade. In 1997 Namibia announced plans, supported by the SADC, to establish a rail link with Angola in order to form a trade route similar to that created in Mozambique, on the western side of southern Africa. In March 1998 the final stage of the trans-Kalahari highway, linking ports on the east and west coasts of southern Africa, was officially opened. In July 1999 a 317-km rail link between Bulawayo, Zimbabwe, and the border town of Beitbridge, administered by the SADC as its first build-operate-transfer project, was opened.

The SADC promotes greater co-operation in the civil aviation sector, in order to improve efficiency and to reverse a steady decline in the region's airline industries. Within the telecommunications sector efforts have been made to increase the capacity of direct exchange lines and international subscriber dialling (ISD) services. In January 1997 the Southern African Telecommunications Regional Authority (SATRA), a regulatory authority, was established. An SADC Expedited Mail Service operates in the postal services sector. The SATCC's Technical Unit oversees the region's meteorological services and issues a regular *Drought-Watch for Southern Africa* bulletin, a monthly *Drought Overview* bulletin and forewarnings of impending natural disasters.

FOOD, AGRICULTURE AND NATURAL RESOURCES

The food, agriculture and natural resources sector covers eight sub-sectors: agricultural research and training; inland fisheries; forestry; wildlife; marine fisheries and resources; food security; livestock production and animal disease control; and environment and land management. The importance of this sector is evident in the fact that, according to SADC figures, agriculture contributes one-third of the region's GNP, accounts for 26% of total earnings of foreign exchange and employs some 80% of the labour force. The sector's principal objectives are regional food security, agricultural development and natural resource development.

The Southern African Centre for Co-operation in Agricultural Research (SACCAR), was established in Gaborone, Botswana, in 1985. It aims to strengthen national agricultural research systems, in order to improve management, increase productivity, promote the development and transfer of technology to assist local farmers, and improve training. Examples of activity include: a sorghum and millet improvement programme; a land and water management research programme; a root crop research network; agroforestry research, implemented in Malawi, Tanzania, Zambia and Zimbabwe; and a grain legume improvement programme, comprising separate research units for groundnuts, beans and cowpeas. The SADC's Plant Genetic Resources Centre was established in 1988, near Lusaka, Zambia, to collect, conserve and utilize indigenous and exotic plant genetic resources and to develop appropriate management practices.

The sub-sector for livestock production and animal disease control aims to improve breeding methods in the region through the Management of Farm Animal Genetic Research Programme. It also seeks to control diseases such as contagious bovine pleuro-pneumonia, foot and mouth disease and heartwater through diagnosis, monitoring and vaccination programmes. An *Animal Health Mortality Bulletin* is published, as is a monthly *Animal Disease Situation Bulletin*, which alerts member states to outbreaks of disease in the region.

The sector aims to promote inland and marine fisheries as an important, sustainable source of animal protein. Marine fisheries are also considered to be a potential source of income of foreign exchange. In May 1993 the first formal meeting of SADC ministers of marine fisheries convened in Namibia, and it was agreed to hold annual meetings. In April 1997 it was agreed that Namibia would co-ordinate the establishment of inspectorates to monitor and control marine fisheries in the region for a period of five years. The development of fresh water fisheries is focused on aquaculture projects, and their integration into rural community activities. The environment and land management sub-sector is concerned with sustainability as an essential quality of development. It aims to protect and improve the health, environment and livelihoods of people living in the southern African region; to preserve the natural heritage and biodiversity of the region; and to support regional economic development on a sustainable basis. The sector also focuses on capacity-building, training, regional co-operation and the exchange of information in all areas related to the environment and land management. It administers an SADC Environmental Exchange Network, which was established in 1995, and the Community's Land Degradation and Desertification Control Programme. The sector also undertakes projects for the conservation and sustainable development of forestry and wildlife.

Under the food security programme, the Harare-based Regional Early Warning System aims to anticipate and prevent food shortages through the provision of information relating to the food security situation in member states. As a result of the drought crisis experience, SADC member states have agreed to inform the food security sector of their food and non-food requirements on a regular basis, in order to assess the needs of the region as a whole. A regional food reserve project was also to be developed.

WATER

Following the severe drought in the region in 1991/92, the need for water resource development became a priority. The water sector was established as a separate administrative unit in August 1996, although the terms of reference of the sector were only formally approved by the Council, meeting in Windhoek, Namibia, in February 1997. The sector aims to promote the equitable distribution and effective management of water resources, in order to address the concern that many SADC member countries may be affected by future droughts and water scarcity. In April a workshop was held in Swaziland concerning the implementation of a new SADC Protocol on Shared Watercourse Systems. The involvement of the private sector in the region's water policies was under consideration at the Round Table Conference on Integrated Water Resources Development in October 1998.

ENERGY

Areas of activity in the energy sector include: joint petroleum exploration, training programmes for the petroleum sector and studies for strategic fuel storage facilities; promotion of the use of coal; development of hydroelectric power and the co-ordination of SADC generation and transmission capacities; new and renewable sources of energy, including pilot projects in solar energy; assessment of the environmental and socio-economic impact of wood-fuel scarcity and relevant education programmes; and energy conservation. In July 1995 SADC energy ministers approved the establishment of a Southern African Power Pool, whereby all member states were to be linked into a single electricity grid. (Several grids are already integrated and others are being rehabilitated.) At the same time, ministers endorsed a Protocol to promote greater co-operation in energy development within the SADC. On receiving final approval and signature by member states, the Protocol was to replace the energy sector with an Energy Commission, responsible for 'demand-side' management, pricing, ensuring private-sector involvement and competition, training and research, collecting information, etc. The sector administers a joint SADC Petroleum Exploration Programme. In September 1997 heads of state endorsed an Energy Action Plan to proceed with the implementation of co-operative policies and strategies in four key areas of energy: trade, information exchange, training and organizational capacity-building, and investment and financing. A technical unit of the Energy Commission was to be responsible for implementation of the Action Plan.

TRADE, INDUSTRY AND MINING

Under the treaty establishing the SADC, efforts were to be undertaken to achieve regional economic integration. The trade and industry sector aims to facilitate this by the creation of an enabling investment and trade environment in SADC countries, the establishment of a single regional market, by progressively removing barriers to the movement of goods, services and people, and the promotion of cross-border investment. The sector supports programmes for industrial research and development and standardization and quality assurance. A sector of finance and investment has been established to mobilize industrial investment resources and to co-ordinate economic policies and the development of the financial sector. During 1995 work continued on the preparation of two Protocols on trade co-operation and finance and investment, which were to provide the legal framework for integration. In August 1996 SADC member states (except Angola) signed a Protocol providing for the establishment of a free-trade area, through the gradual elimination of tariff barriers over an eight-year period, at a summit meeting held in Lesotho. By May 2000 the Protocol had been ratified by 10 member countries. In accordance with a revised schedule, announced in that month, it was envisaged that the regional free-trade area would be launched in September and that all intra-SADC trade tariffs would be removed by 2012 (with about 85% to be withdrawn by 2008). In September 1999 representatives of the private sector in SADC member states, meeting in Mauritius, agreed to establish an Association of SADC Chambers of Commerce.

In January 1992 a five-year strategy for the promotion of mining in the region was approved, with the principal objective of stimulating local and foreign investment in the sector to maximize benefits from the region's mineral resources. In December 1994 the SADC held a mining forum, jointly with the EU, in Lusaka, Zambia, with the aim of demonstrating to potential investors and promoters the possibilities of mining exploration in the region. A second mining investment forum was held in Lusaka in December 1998. Other objectives of the mining sector are the improvement of industry training, increasing the contribution of small-scale mining, reducing the illicit trade in gemstones and gold, increasing co-operation in mineral exploration and processing, and minimizing the adverse impact of mining operations on the environment. At the summit meeting, held in September 1997, SADC heads of state signed a Protocol providing for the harmonization of policies and programmes relating to the development and exploitation of mineral resources in the region.

HUMAN RESOURCES DEVELOPMENT

The SADC helps to supply the region's requirements in skilled manpower by providing training in the following categories: high-level managerial personnel; agricultural managers; high- and medium-level technicians; artisans; and instructors. The Technical Committee on Accreditation and Certification aims to harmonize and strengthen the education and training systems in the SADC through initiatives such as the standardization of curricula and examinations. The sector also aims to determine active labour market information systems and institutions in the region, improve education policy analysis and formulation, and address issues of teaching and learning materials in the region. It administers an Intra-regional Skills Development Programme. The sector has initiated a programme of distance education to enable greater access to education, and operates the SADC's scholarship and training awards programme. In September 1997 heads of state, meeting in Blantyre, Malawi, endorsed the establishment of a Gender Department within the Secretariat to promote the advancement and education of women. At the same time representatives of all member countries (except Angola) signed a Protocol on Education and Training, which was to provide a legal framework for co-operation in this sector.

EMPLOYMENT AND LABOUR

The sector was founded in 1996, and is co-ordinated by Zambia. It seeks to promote employment and harmonize legislation concerning labour and social protection. Its activities include: the implementation of International Labour Standards, the improvement of health and safety standards in the workplace, combating child labour and the establishment of a statistical database for employment and labour issues.

CULTURE, SPORT AND INFORMATION

A culture and information sector was established in 1990, and is co-ordinated by Mozambique. Following the ratification of the treaty establishing the Community, the sector was expected to emphasize regional socio-cultural development as part of the process of greater integration. The SADC Press Trust was established, in Harare, Zimbabwe, to disseminate information about the SADC and to articulate the concerns and priorities of the region. Public education initiatives have commenced to encourage the involvement of people in the process of regional integration and development, as well as to promote democratic and human rights' values. In 1998 a new project—'Information 21'—was to be implemented under the sector, in collaboration with the SADC secretariat and the Southern African Research and Documentation Centre (q.v.), which aimed to promote community-building and greater participation in decision-making at all levels of government. Efforts to harmonize legislation in order to prevent breaches of copyright were underway in early 1999. A four-year programme, entitled the SADC Festival on Arts and Culture, was initiated in 1994. Events included a theatre festival, held in Maputo, Mozambique, in June 1997, a visual arts and crafts regional exposition, in Namibia, in April 1998, and a dance festival in Mauritius in 1999.

TOURISM

The sector aims to promote tourism within the context of national and regional socio-economic development objectives. It comprises four components: tourism product development; tourism marketing and research; tourism services; and human resources development and training. The SADC has promoted tourism for the region at trade fairs in Europe, and has initiated a project to provide a range of promotional material and a regional tourism directory. By September 1993 a project to design a standard grading classification system for tourist accommodation in the region was completed, with the assistance of the World Tourism Organization, and the Council approved its implementation. A new five-year development strategy for tourism in the region was initiated in 1995, the key element of which was the establishment of a new tourism body, to be administered jointly by SADC officials and private-sector operators. The Regional Tourism Organization for Southern Africa (RETOSA) was to assist member states to formulate tourism promotion policies and strategies. A legal charter for the establishment of RETOSA was signed by ministers of tourism in September 1997. During 1999 a feasibility study on the development of the Upper Zambezi basin as a site for eco-tourism was initiated.

FINANCE AND INVESTMENT

In July 1998 a Banking Association was officially constituted by representatives of SADC member states. The Association was to establish international banking standards and regional payments systems, organize training and harmonize banking legislation in the region. In April 1999 governors of SADC central banks determined to strengthen and harmonize banking procedures and technology in order to facilitate the financial integration of the region. Efforts to harmonize stock exchanges in the region were also initiated in 1999.

Finance

The SADC's administrative budget for 1998, approved by the Council in February, amounted to US $12.5m., financed mainly by contributions from member states. At February 1998 members owed some $4.5m. in unpaid arrears.

SADC PROJECT FINANCING BY SECTOR (July 1996/97)

Sector	Number of projects	Total cost (US $ million)	Funding secured (US $ million)*
Culture and information . .	7	15.90	4.95
Energy.	48	924.67	627.14
Food, agriculture and natural resources	83	573.91	320.21
Agricultural research and training	14	120.44	77.16
Inland fisheries	8	44.91	26.12
Food security	11	71.21	22.35
Forestry	15	125.94	46.71
Wildlife	11	94.30	81.99
Livestock production and animal disease control . .	11	96.27	59.24
Environment and land management . . .	7	18.99	5.93
Marine fisheries and resources	6	1.85	0.71
Finance and investment . .	10	1.92	0.37
Human resources development.	16	44.76	16.27
Industry and trade. . . .	19	20.01	10.45
Mining.	36	18.51	10.15
Tourism	11	4.96	2.95
Transport and communications.	174	6,474.40	2,991.70
Water	3	11.05	9.75
Total	407	8,090.09	3,993.95

* Includes both local and foreign resources.

Publications

SACCAR Newsletter (quarterly).

SADC Annual Report.

SADC Energy Bulletin.

SADC Today (six a year)

SATCC Bulletin (quarterly).

SKILLS.

SPLASH.

OTHER REGIONAL ORGANIZATIONS

These organizations are arranged under the following categories:

Agriculture, Food, Forestry and Fisheries
Arts and Culture
Commodities
Development and Economic Co-operation
Economics and Finance
Education

Government and Politics
Industrial and Professional Relations
Law
Medicine and Public Health
Press, Radio and Telecommunications
Religion

Science and Technology
Social Sciences, Social Welfare and Human Rights
Trade and Industry
Transport and Tourism

AGRICULTURE, FOOD, FORESTRY AND FISHERIES

African Feed Resources Network–AFRNET: c/o International Livestock Research Institute (ILRI), POB 30709, Nairobi, Kenya; tel. (2) 630743; fax (2) 631499; e-mail ilri@cgiar.org; f. 1991 by merger of two African livestock fodder and one animal nutrition research networks; aims to assist farmers in finding effective ways to feed their livestock; Co-ordinator Dr JEAN NDIKUMAMA. Publ. *AFRNET Newsletter* (quarterly).

African Timber Organization: BP 1077, Libreville, Gabon; tel. 73-29-28; fax 734030; f. 1976 to enable mems to study and co-ordinate ways of ensuring the optimum utilization and conservation of their forests. Mems: Angola, Cameroon, Central African Repub., Dem. Repub. of the Congo, Repub. of the Congo, Côte d'Ivoire, Equatorial Guinea, Gabon, Ghana, Liberia, Nigeria, São Tomé and Príncipe, Tanzania. Tech. Dir PHILEMON SELEBANGUE; Sec.-Gen. MOHAMMED LAWAL GARBA. Publs *ATO-Information* (quarterly), *Annual Report*, *International Magazine of African Timber* (2 a year).

Association for the Advancement of Agricultural Science in Africa–AAASA: POB 30087, Addis Ababa, Ethiopia; tel. (1) 44-3536; f. 1968 to promote the development and application of agricultural sciences and the exchange of ideas; to encourage Africans to enter training; holds several seminars each year in different African countries. Mems: individual agricultural scientists, research insts in 63 countries. Sec.-Gen. Prof. M. EL-FOULQ (acting). Publs *Journal* (2 a year), *Newsletter* (quarterly).

CAB International (CABI): Wallingford, Oxon, OX10 8DE, United Kingdom; tel. (1491) 832111; fax (1491) 833508; e-mail cabi@cabi.org; internet www.cabi.org; f. 1929 as the Imperial Agricultural Bureaux (later Commonwealth Agricultural Bureaux); current name adopted in 1985; intergovernmental organization which aims to improve human welfare world-wide through the generation, dissemination and application of scientific knowledge in support of sustainable development. It places particular emphasis on forestry, human health and the management of natural resources, with priority given to the needs of developing countries. CABI compiles and publishes extensive information (in a variety of print and electronic forms) on aspects of agriculture, forestry, veterinary medicine, the environment and natural resources, Third World rural development, leisure, recreation and tourism, human nutrition, and human health. Maintains regional centres in Kenya, Malaysia, Pakistan, Switzerland and Trinidad and Tobago. Mems: 40 countries. Dir-Gen. DENIS BRIGHT.

CABI Bioscience: Bakeham Lane, Egham, Surrey, TW20 9TY, United Kingdom; tel. (1784) 470111; fax (1784) 470909; e-mail bioscience@cabi.org; f. 1998 by integration of the capabilities and resources of the following four CABI scientific institutions: International Institute of Biological Control; International Institute of Entomology; International Institute of Parasitology; International Mycological Institute; undertakes research, training, capacity-building and institutional development in the three general sectors of biological pest management, biodiversity and biosystematics, and environment.

Desert Locust Control Organization for Eastern Africa: POB 30023, Nairobi, Kenya; tel. (2) 501704; fax (2) 505137; f. 1962 to promote effective control of desert locust in the region and to conduct research into the locust's environment and behaviour; conducts pesticides residue analysis; assists mem. states in the monitoring and extermination of other migratory pests such as the quelea-quelea (grain-eating birds), the army worm and the tsetse fly; bases at Asmara (Eritrea), Dire Dawa (Ethiopia), Mogadishu and Hargeisa (Somalia), Nairobi (Kenya), Khartoum (Sudan), Arusha (Tanzania), Kampala (Uganda) and Djibouti. Mems: Djibouti, Eritrea, Ethiopia, Kenya, Somalia, Sudan, Tanzania and Uganda. Dir Dr KARRAR; Co-ordinator C. K. MUINAMIA. Publs *Desert Locust Situation Reports* (monthly), *Annual Report*, technical reports.

International Crops Research Institute for the Semi-Arid Tropics (ICRISAT) Sahelian Centre: BP 12404, Niamey, Niger; tel. 72-25-29; fax 73-43-29; e-mail icrisatsc@cgnet.com; ICRISAT f. 1972 with headquarters in India. Aims to help improve food security, reduce poverty and protect the environment in the semi-arid tropics through international agricultural research; research is based on development objectives, with emphasis on genetic resources, natural resource management and the specific socio-economic resources of the semi-arid tropics; research at the Sahelian Centre focuses on the improvement of pearl millet, the generation of improved resource management technologies (in collaboration with national programmes) and socio-economic studies related to input markets. The Sahelian Centre hosts the Sahelian Programme of the ILRI (see below), the West and Central African Millet Research Network, and the Initiative on Desert Margins of the Consultative Group on International Agricultural Research (q.v.).

International Institute of Tropical Agriculture—IITA: Oyo Rd, PMB 5320, Ibadan, Nigeria; tel. (2) 2412626; fax (2) 241-2221; e-mail iita@cgiar.org; internet www.cgiar.org/iita; f. 1967; principal financing arranged by the Consultative Group on International Agricultural Research (CGIAR, q.v.), an informal group of donor countries, development banks, foundations and agencies. Three main research programmes: crop improvement (chiefly cassava, maize, plantain/banana, yam and soybean); plant health management; and resource and crop management. The international co-operation programme comprises large-scale research projects with nat. programmes and a training programme for scientists and technicians in tropical agriculture. The information services programme produces publs on research results and an extensive library of 75,000 vols and maintains database of records; it also administers six agro-ecological research stations. Dir-Gen. Dr LUKAS BRADER. Publs *Annual Report*, *IITA Research*.

International Livestock Research Institute—ILRI: POB 30709, Nairobi, Kenya; tel. (2) 630743; fax (2) 631499; e-mail ilri kenya@cgiar.org; internet www.cgiar.org/ilri; f. 1995, to replace the International Laboratory for Research on Animal Diseases and the International Livestock Centre for Africa; conducts laboratory and field research on animal health (in particular, animal trypanosomiasis and theileriosis), the conservation of genetic resources, production systems analysis, natural resource management, livestock policy analysis and strengthening national research capacities; undertakes training programmes for scientists and technicians; specialized science library. Dir Dr HANK FITZHUGH. Publs *Annual Report*, *Annual Scientific Report*, *Livestock Research for Development Newsletter* (2 a year).

International Red Locust Control Organization for Central and Southern Africa: POB 240252, Ndola, Zambia; tel. (2) 615684; fax (2) 614285; e-mail locust@zamnet.zm; f. 1971; controls locusts in eastern, central and southern Africa, and assists in the control of African army-worm and quelea-quelea. Mems: eight countries. Dir E. K. BYARUHANGA. Publs *Annual Report*, *Monthly Report* and scientific reports.

International Scientific Council for Trypanosomiasis Research and Control: c/o OAU Interafrican Bureau for Animal Resources, POB 30786, Nairobi, Kenya; tel. (2) 338544; fax (2) 332046; e-mail parcibar@africaonline.co.ke; f. 1949 to review the work on tsetse and trypanosomiasis problems carried out by organizations and workers concerned in laboratories and in the field; to stimulate further research and discussion and to promote co-ordination between research workers and organizations in the different countries in Africa, and to provide a regular opportunity for the discussion of particular problems and for the exposition of new experiments and discoveries. Sec. Dr SOLOMON H. MARIAM.

Joint Organization for Control of Desert Locust and Bird Pests (Organisation commune de lutte antiacridienne et de lutte antiaviaire—OCLALAV): route des Pères Maristes, BP 1066, Dakar, Senegal; tel. 832-32-80; fax 832-04-87; f. 1965 to eradicate the desert locust and grain-eating birds, in particular the quelea-quelea, and to sponsor related research projects. Mems: Benin, Burkina Faso, Cameroon, Chad, Côte d'Ivoire, The Gambia, Mali, Mauritania, Niger, Senegal. Dir-Gen. ABDULLAHI OULD SOUEID AHMED. Publ. *Bulletin* (monthly).

ARTS AND CULTURE

Afro-Asian Writers' Association: 'Al Ahram', Al Gala's St, Cairo, Egypt; tel. (2) 5747011; fax (2) 5747023; f. 1958. Mems: writers' orgs in 51 countries. Sec.-Gen. LOTFI EL-KHOLY. Publs *Lotus Magazine of Afro-Asian Writings* (quarterly in English, French and Arabic), *Afro-Asian Literature Series* (in English, French and Arabic).

Pan-African Writers' Association—PAWA: Accra, Ghana; f. 1989; awards the African Prize for Literature; in 1993 launched a

US $10m. fund to encourage African writers; organizes an International African Writers' Day. Sec.-Gen. ATUKWEI OKAI (Ghana).

Society of African Culture (Société africaine de culture): 25 bis rue des Ecoles, 75005 Paris, France; tel. 1-43-54-15-88; fax 1-43-25-96-67; f. 1956 to create unity and friendship among black scholars in Africa, the Caribbean, Europe and America for the encouragement of their own cultures. Mems from 45 countries. Pres. AIMÉ CÉSAIRE; Sec.-Gen. CHRISTIANE YANDÉ DIOP. Publ. *La Revue Présence Africaine* (2 a year).

COMMODITIES

African Groundnut Council: Trade Fair Complex, Badagry Expressway Km 15, POB 3025, Marina, Lagos, Nigeria; tel. (1) 887811; fax (1) 880982; f. 1964 to advise producing countries on marketing policies; administers compensation fund. Mems: The Gambia, Mali, Niger, Nigeria, Senegal, Sudan. Chair. Alhaji MOHAMMED ABBAS (Nigeria); Exec. Sec. Alhaji MOUR MAMADOU SAMB (Senegal). Publs *Groundnut Review*, *Newsletter* (French and English).

African Oil Palm Development Association–AFOPDA: 15 BP 341, Abidjan 15, Côte d'Ivoire; tel. 25-15-18; fax 25-47-00; f. 1985; seeks to increase production of and investment in palm oil. Mems: Benin, Cameroon, Dem. Repub. of the Congo, Côte d'Ivoire, Ghana, Guinea, Nigeria, Togo. Exec. Sec. BAUDELAIRE SOUROU.

African Petroleum Producers' Association–APPA: BP 1097, Brazzaville, Repub. of the Congo; tel. 83-64-38; fax 83-67-99; f. 1987 by African petroleum-producing countries to reinforce co-operation among regional producers and to stabilize prices; council of ministers responsible for the hydrocarbons sector of each country meets twice a year. Mems: Algeria, Angola, Benin, Cameroon, Dem. Repub. of the Congo, Repub. of the Congo, Côte d'Ivoire, Egypt, Equatorial Guinea, Gabon, Nigeria. Presidency rotates. Publ. *APPA Bulletin* (2 a year).

Association of Coffee Producing Countries–ACPC: 7–10 Old Park Lane, Suite B, 5th Floor, London, W1Y 3LJ, United Kingdom; tel. (20) 7493-4790; fax (20) 7355-1698; f. 1998; aims to co-ordinate policies of coffee production and to co-ordinate the efforts of producer countries to achieve stability in the world coffee market. Mems: 29 African, Asian and Latin American countries. Pres. RUBENS BARBOSA; Sec.-Gen. ROBÉRIO OLIVEIRA SILVA.

Cocoa Producers' Alliance: Western House, 8–10 Broad St, POB 1718, Lagos, Nigeria; tel. (1) 2635574; fax (1) 2635684; f. 1962 to exchange scientific and tech. information; to discuss problems of mutual concern to producers; to ensure adequate supplies at remunerative prices; to promote consumption. Mems: Brazil, Cameroon, Côte d'Ivoire, Dominican Republic, Ecuador, Gabon, Ghana, Malaysia, Nigeria, São Tomé and Príncipe, Togo and Trinidad and Tobago. Sec.-Gen. DJEUMO SILAS KAMGA.

Inter-African Coffee Organization–IACO: BP V210, Abidjan, Côte d'Ivoire; tel. 20-21-61-31; fax 20-21-62-12; e-mail oiac-iaco@aviso.ci; f. 1960 to adopt a united policy on the marketing of coffee. General Assembly meets annually; Bd of Dirs holds quarterly meetings to direct policy; the financial contribution of mem. countries is based on the volume of their exports; mem. countries account for about 97% of African coffee exports. Aims to foster greater collaboration in research techniques, in particular through the establishment of the African Coffee Research Network, and improve quality of exports. Mems: Angola, Benin, Burundi, Cameroon, Central African Repub., Dem. Repub. of the Congo, Repub. of the Congo, Côte d'Ivoire, Equatorial Guinea, Ethiopia, Gabon, Ghana, Guinea, Kenya, Liberia, Madagascar, Malawi, Nigeria, Rwanda, Sierra Leone, Tanzania, Togo, Uganda, Zambia and Zimbabwe. Chair. Dr ISRAEL KIBIRIGE-SEBUNYA (Uganda); Sec.-Gen. JOSEFA LEONEL CORREIA SACKO (Angola).

International Cocoa Organization–ICCO: 22 Berners St, London, W1P 3DB, United Kingdom; tel. (20) 7637-3211; fax (20) 7631-0114; e-mail exec.dir@icco.org; internet http://www.icco.org; f. 1973 under the first International Cocoa Agreement, 1972 (renewed in 1975, 1980, 1986; the fifth ICA entered into force in Feb. 1994 and was extended for a further 2 years from 1 Oct. 1999). ICCO supervises the implementation of the agreement, and provides member governments with conference facilities and up-to-date information on the world cocoa economy and the operation of the agreement. Mems: 18 exporting countries which account for about three-quarters of world cocoa exports, and 21 importing countries which account for about 55% of world cocoa imports. (The USA is not a member.) Council Chair. (1999/2000) D. P. D. VAN RAPPARD (Netherlands); Exec. Dir EDOUARD KOUAMÉ (Côte d'Ivoire). Publs *Quarterly Bulletin of Cocoa Statistics*, *Annual Report*, *The World Cocoa Directory*, *Cocoa Newsletter*, *The World Cocoa Market to the Year 2000*.

International Coffee Organization: 22 Berners St, London, W1P 4DD, United Kingdom; tel. (20) 7580-8591; fax (20) 7580-6129; e-mail info@ico.org; internet http://www.icoffee.org; f. 1963 under the International Coffee Agreement, 1962, which was renegotiated in 1968, 1976, 1983 and 1994; aims to achieve a reasonable balance between supply and demand on a basis which will assure adequate supplies at fair prices to consumers and expanding markets at remunerative prices to producers; system of export quotas, to stabilize prices, was abandoned in July 1989. Mems: 44 exporting countries and 18 importing countries, and the European Community. Exec. Dir CELSIUS A. LODDER (Brazil).

International Grains Council: 1 Canada Sq., Canary Wharf, London, E14 5AE, United Kingdom; tel. (20) 7513-1122; fax (20) 7513-0630; e-mail igc-fac@igc.org.uk; internet www.igc.org.uk; f. 1949 as International Wheat Council, present name adopted in 1995; responsible for the admin. of the Grains Trade Convention of the International Grains Agreement, 1995; aims to further international co-operation in all aspects of trade in grains, to promote international trade in grains, and to secure the freest possible flow of this trade in the interests of mems, particularly developing mem. countries; and to contribute to the stability of the international grain market; acts as forum for consultations between mems, and provides comprehensive information on the international grain market and factors affecting it. Mems: 31 countries and the EU. Exec. Dir. G. DENIS. Publs *World Grain Statistics* (annually). *Wheat and Coarse Grain Shipments* (annually), *Report for the Fiscal Year* (annually), *Grain Market Report* (monthly).

International Sugar Organization: 1 Canada Sq., Canary Wharf, London, E14 5AA, United Kingdom; tel. (20) 7513-1144; fax (20) 7513-1146; e-mail exdir@isosugar.org; internet www.isosugar.org; administers the International Sugar Agreement (1992); the agreement does not include measures for stabilizing markets. Mems: 56 countries. Exec. Dir Dr P. BARON. Publs *Sugar Year Book*, *Monthly Statistical Bulletin*, *Market Report and Press Summary*, *Quarterly Market Review*, seminar proceedings.

International Tea Committee Ltd: Sir John Lyon House, 5 High Timber St, London, EC4V 3NH, United Kingdom; tel. (20) 7248-4672; fax (20) 7329-6955; e-mail inteacom@globalnet.co.uk; f. 1933 to administer the International Tea Agreement; now serves as a statistical and information centre; in 1979 membership was extended to include consuming countries. Producer Mems: national tea boards or asscns of Bangladesh, India, Indonesia, Japan, Kenya, Malawi, Sri Lanka, Zimbabwe; Consumer Mems: United Kingdom Tea Asscn, Tea Asscn of the USA Inc., Comité Européen du Thé and the Tea Council of Canada; Assoc. Mems: Netherlands and UK ministries of agriculture, Cameroon Development Corpn. Chair. M. J. BUNSTON; Consultant and Sec. PETER ABEL. Publs *Annual Bulletin of Statistics*, *Monthly Statistical Summary*.

International Tea Promotion Association: c/o Tea Board of Kenya, POB 20064, Nairobi, Kenya; tel. (2) 220241; fax (2) 331650; f. 1979. Mems: Bangladesh, Indonesia, Kenya, Malawi, Mauritius, Mozambique, Tanzania, and Uganda, accounting for about 35% of world exports of black tea. Chair. GEORGE M. KIMANI; Liaison Officer NGOIMA WA MWAURA. Publ. *International Tea Journal* (2 a year).

International Tobacco Growers' Association: Apdo 5, 6001 Castelo Branco, Portugal; tel. (72) 325901; fax (72) 325906; e-mail itga@mail.telepac.pt; internet www.tobaccoleaf.org; f. 1984 to provide a forum for the exchange of information of concern to tobacco producers and to provide information relating to tobacco production; mems collectively produce more than 80% of the world's internationally traded tobacco. Mems: 23 countries. Chair. RICHARD TATE (Zimbabwe); Exec. Dir Dr ANTONIO ABRUNHOSA (Portugal). Publs *Tobacco Courier* (quarterly), *Tobacco Briefing*.

International Tropical Timber Organization–ITTO: International Organizations Center, 5th Floor, Pacifico-Yokohama, 1-1-1, Minato-Mirai, Nishi-ku, Yokohama 220, Japan; tel. (45) 223-1110; fax (45) 223-1111; e-mail itto@mail.itto-unet.ocn.ne.jp; internet www.itto.or.jp; f. 1985 under the International Tropical Timber Agreement 1983; a new treaty, ITTA 1994, entered into force in 1997; aims to promote the conservation of tropical forest resources through sustainable management; conducts research and development in marketing and economics, and reafforestation and forest management; and provides a forum for consultation and co-operation between producers and consumers, as well as non-governmental orgs; facilitates progress towards the 'Year 2000' objective (by which year all trade in tropical timber is to be derived from sustainably managed resources) through the Bali Partnership Fund. Mems: 26 producing and 26 consuming countries, and the EU. Exec. Dir FREEZAILAH BIN CHE YEOM (Malaysia). Publs *Annual Review*, *Market Information Service* (every 2 weeks), *Tropical Forest Update* (quarterly).

West Africa Rice Development Association–WARDA: 01 BP 2551, Bouaké 01, Côte d'Ivoire; tel. 31-63-45-14; fax 31-63-47-14; e-mail warda@cgiar.org; internet http://www.cgiar.org/warda; f. 1971; aims to contribute to food security and poverty eradication in poor rural and urban populations, particularly in West and Central Africa, through research, partnerships, capacity-strengthening and policy support on rice-based systems, and in ways that promote sustainable agricultural development based on environmentally-sound management of natural resources; maintains research stations in Côte d'Ivoire, Nigeria and Senegal; major research projects undertaken through four continuing programmes: the Rainfed Rice Programme, Policy Support Programme, Systems Development and Technology Transfer Programme (based in M'be, Côte d'Ivoire) and the Irrigated Rice Programme (based in St Louis, Senegal); WARDA is a member of the network of agricultural research centres supported by the Consultative Group on International Agricultural Research (CGIAR, q.v.) and collaborates with the national agricultural research systems of member states, academic institutions, international donors and other organizations world-wide; revenue US \$10.3m. (1998). Mems: Benin, Burkina Faso, Cameroon, Chad, Côte d'Ivoire, The Gambia, Ghana, Guinea, Guinea-Bissau, Liberia, Mali, Mauritania, Niger, Nigeria, Senegal, Sierra Leone, Togo. Dir-Gen. KANAYO NWANZE (Nigeria). Publs *Annual Report, Directory of Rice Scientists in West Africa, Current Contents at WARDA* (monthly), *Program Report, Advances in Rice Research*, reprint series, proceedings, leaflets.

DEVELOPMENT AND ECONOMIC CO-OPERATION

African Capacity Building Foundation: POB 1562, Harare, Zimbabwe; tel. (4) 702931; fax (4) 702915; e-mail root@acbf.co.zw; f. 1991 by the World Bank, UNDP, the African Development Bank, bilateral donors and African Governments; assists African countries to develop and strengthen institutional and human capacity in economic policy analysis and development management. Assists 30 institutions in 20 countries. Exec. Sec. ABEL L. THOAHLANE.

Afro-Asian Rural Development Organization–AARDO: Plot No. 2, State Guest Houses Complex, nr Telephone Exchange, Chanakyapuri, New Delhi 110021, India; tel. (11) 4100475; fax (11) 4672045; e-mail aardohq@nde.vsnl.net.in; internet www.aardo.org; f. 1962 to act as a catalyst for co-operative restructuring of rural life in Africa and Asia and to explore, collectively, opportunities for co-ordination of efforts to promote welfare and eradicate malnutrition, disease, illiteracy and poverty among rural people. Activities include collaborative research on development issues; training; assistance in forming orgs of farmers and other rural people; the exchange of information; international confs and seminars; and awarding 100 individual training fellowships at nine insts in Egypt, India, Japan, the Repub. of Korea, Malaysia and Taiwan. Mems: 12 African, 14 Asian, and one African assoc. Sec.-Gen. Dr BAHAR MUNIP. Publs *Afro-Asian Journal of Rural Development, Annual Report, Rural Reconstruction* (2 a year), *AARDO Newsletter* (2 a year), conference and committee reports.

Agence de la Francophonie: 13 quai André Citroën, 75015 Paris, France; tel. 1-44-37-33-00; fax 1-45-79-14-98; internet www.francophonie.org; f. 1970 as l'Agence de coopération culturelle et technique; promotes co-operation among French-speaking countries in the areas of education, culture, science and technology; implements decisions of the Sommet francophone (q.v.); tech. and financial assistance has been given to projects in every mem. country, mainly to aid rural people. Mems: 47 countries, mainly African; Gen. Dir ROGER DEHAYBE (Belgium). Publs *Journal de l'Agence de la Francophonie* (monthly).

Arab Bank for Economic Development in Africa (Banque arabe pour le développement économique en Afrique—BADEA): Sayed Abdar-Rahman el-Mahdi St, POB 2640, Khartoum, Sudan; tel. (11) 773646; fax (11) 770600; e-mail badeadev@sudanmail .net; f. 1973 by Arab League; provides loans and grants to sub-Saharan African countries to finance development projects; paid-up cap. US \$1,145.8m. (Dec. 1998). During 1998 the Bank approved loans and grants totalling \$104.95m., and tech. assistance for feasibility studies and institutional support amounting to \$4.99m. By the end of 1998 total financial operations approved since funding activities began in 1975 totalled \$1840.40m. Chair. AHMAD ABDALLAH AL-AKEIL (Saudi Arabia); Dir-Gen. MEDHAT SAMI LOTFY (Egypt). Publs *Annual Report, Co-operation for Development* (quarterly), Studies on Afro-Arab co-operation.

Centre africain de formation et de recherches administratives pour le développement–CAFRAD (African Training and Research Centre in Administration for Development): ave Mohamed V, BP 310, Tangier, 90001 Morocco; fax (9) 325785; e-mail cafrad@cafrad.org; internet www.cafrad.com; f. 1964 by agreement between Morocco and UNESCO; undertakes research into administrative problems in Africa, documentation of results, provision of a consultative service for govts and orgs; holds frequent seminars; aided by nat. and international orgs. Mems: 33 African countries. Pres. M. EL HOUSSINE AZIZ; Dir-Gen. Dr TIJJANI MUHAMMAD BANDE (acting). Publs include *Cahiers Africains d'Administration Publique* (4 a year), *African Administrative Studies* (2 a year), *CAFRAD News* (4 a year, in English, French and Arabic), *Collection: Etudes et Documents, Répertoire des Consultants.*

Centre on Integrated Rural Development for Africa–CIRDAfrica: POB 6115, Arusha, Tanzania; tel. (57) 2576;

fax (57) 8532; f. 1979 (operational 1982) to promote integrated rural development through a network of nat. institutions; to improve the production, income and living conditions of small-scale farmers and other rural groups; to provide tech. support; and to foster the exchange of ideas and experience; financed by mem. states and donor agencies. Mems: 17 African countries. Dir Dr ABDELMONEIM M. ELSHEIKH. Publ. *CIRDAfrica Rural Tribune* (2 a year).

Club du Sahel (Club of the Sahel): c/o OECD, 2 rue André Pascal, 75775 Paris, France; tel. 1-45-24-89-87; fax 1-45-24-90-31; e-mail sahel.contact@oecd.org; internet www.oecd.org/sah; f. 1976; an informal forum of donor countries and mem. states of the Permanent Inter-State Committee on Drought Control in the Sahel—CILSS (q.v.), for promoting the co-ordination of long-term policies and programmes in key devt sectors and improved methods of aid delivery in the nine mem. countries of the CILSS; formed by the CILSS in assocn with the OECD mem. countries active in the region. The Club collects information, conducts studies and helps to mobilize resources for the devt of the Sahel region in agriculture, environment, decentralization and local devt and regional integration.

Communauté économique des états de l'Afrique centrale–CEEAC (Economic Community of Central African States): BP 2112, Libreville, Gabon; tel. 73-35-47; f. 1983; operational since 1985; aims to promote co-operation between member states by abolishing trade restrictions, establishing a common external customs tariff, linking commercial banks, and setting up a development fund, over a period of 12 years; budget (1998) US \$1.8m. Mems: Angola, Burundi, Central African Repub., Chad, Dem. Repub. of the Congo, the Repub. of the Congo, Equatorial Guinea, Gabon, Rwanda, São Tomé and Príncipe. Sec.-Gen. LOUIS-SYLVAIN GOMA (Democratic Republic of the Congo).

Communauté économique des pays des Grands Lacs—CEPGL (Economic Community of the Great Lakes Countries): BP 58, Gisenyi, Rwanda; tel. 40228; fax 40785; f. 1976; main organs: annual conf. of heads of state, council of ministers, perm. exec. secr., consultative comm., security comm., three specialized tech. comms. There are three specialized agencies: the Banque de développement des états des Grands Lacs (BDEGL, BP 3355, Goma, Dem. Repub. of the Congo); the Organisation de la CEPGL pour l'Energie (BP 1912, Bujumbura, Burundi); the Institut de Recherche Agronomique et Zoologique (BP 91, Gitega, Burundi); and four jt enterprises, producing electric power, glass bottles, cement and hoes. Secr. budget (1999): 1,353m. francs CFA. Mems: Dem. Repub. of the Congo, Burundi, Rwanda. Publs *Grands Lacs* (quarterly review), *Journal* (annually).

Community of the Sahel-Saharan States (Communauté des Etats du Sahel et du Sahara–COMESSA): Tripoli, Libya; f. 1997; aims to strengthen co-operation between signatory states; established a jt commission with the OAU, in 1998, to support mediation in the conflicts between Eritrea and Ethiopia. Mems: Burkina Faso, Chad, Djibouti, Egypt, Eritrea, the Gambia, Libya, Mali, Niger, Senegal, Sudan, Tunisia. Sec.-Gen. ALMADANI AL-AZHARI (Libya).

Conseil de l'Entente (Entente Council): 01 BP 3734, Abidjan 01, Côte d'Ivoire; tel. 33-28-35; fax 33-11-49; f. 1959; aims to promote economic development in the region. The Council's Mutual Aid and Loan Guarantee Fund (Fonds d'Entraide et de Garantie des Emprunts) finances development projects, including agricultural projects, vocational training centres, research into new sources of energy and building of hotels to encourage tourism. A Convention of Assistance and Co-operation was signed February 1996. Holds annual summit: 1999 in Yamoussoukro, in May. Fund budget (1999): 15,000m. francs CFA. Mems: Benin, Burkina Faso, Côte d'Ivoire, Niger, Togo. Admin. Sec.-Gen. PAUL KOUAMÉ. Publ *Rapport d'activité* (annually).

Communauté économique du bétail et de la viande du Conseil de l'Entente (Livestock and Meat Economic Community of the Entente Council): 01 BP 638, Ouagadougou, Burkina Faso; tel. 30-62-67; fax 30-62-68; e-mail cebv@cenatrin.bf; internet www.cenatrin.bf/cebv; f. 1970 to promote the production, processing and marketing of livestock and meat; negotiates between mems and with third countries on tech. and financial co-operation and co-ordinated legislation; attempts to co-ordinate measures to combat drought and cattle disease. Mems: states belonging to the Conseil de l'Entente. Exec. Sec. Dr ELIE LADIKPO.

Gambia River Basin Development Organization (Organisation pour la mise en valeur du fleuve Gambie—OMVG): 13 passage Leblanc, BP 2353, Dakar, Senegal; tel. 822-31-59; fax 822-59-26; e-mail omvg@telecomplus.sn; f. 1978 by Senegal and The Gambia; Guinea joined in 1981 and Guinea-Bissau in 1983. Plans include the interconnection of the national electricity transmission grid of mem. states and the construction of four hydroelectric dams; a natural resources management project, and the completion of a hydraulic devt plan of the river; maintains documentation centre. Administrative budget (1998): 160m. francs CFA. Exec. Sec. MAMADOU NASSIROU DIALLO.

Indian Ocean Commission–IOC: Q4, ave Sir Guy Forget, BP 7, Quatre Bornes, Mauritius; tel. 425-9564; fax 425-2709; e-mail coi@intnet.mu; internet www.coi.intnet.mu; f. 1982 to promote regional co-operation, particularly in economic devt; prin. projects under way in the early 1990s (at a cost of 11.6m. francs CFA) comprised tuna-fishing and regional tourism devt and the protection and management of environmental resources, reinforcement of meteorological services; with assistance principally from the European Union, UN Environment Programme and World Bank; tariff reduction is also envisaged. Perm. tech. cttees cover: tuna-fishing; regional industrial co-operation; regional commerce; tourism; environment; maritime transport; handicrafts; education, telecommunication and culture; sports. The IOC organizes an annual regional trade fair (1994: Madagascar). Mems: Comoros, France (representing the French Overseas Department of Réunion), Madagascar, Mauritius and Seychelles. Sec.-Gen. CAABI E. MOHAMED.

Indian Ocean Rim Association for Regional Co-operation–IOR-ARC: Sorèze House, 14 Angus Rd, Vacoas, Mauritius; tel. 698-3979; fax 697-5390; e-mail iorarchq@intnet.mu; the first intergovernmental meeting of countries in the region to promote an Indian Ocean Rim initiative was convened in March 1995; charter to establish the Asscn signed at a ministerial meeting in March 1997; aims to promote regional economic co-operation through trade, investment, infrastructure, tourism, science and technology. Mems: Australia, Bangladesh, India, Iran, Indonesia, Kenya, Madagascar, Malaysia, Mauritius, Mozambique, Oman, Seychelles, Singapore, South Africa, Sri Lanka, Tanzania, Thailand, United Arab Emirates and Yemen. Chair. Dr LEONARDO SIMAO (Mozambique); Sec.-Gen. KAILASH RUHEE (Mauritius).

Lake Chad Basin Commission–LCBC: BP 727, N'Djamena, Chad; tel. 52-41-45; fax 51-41-37; e-mail lcbc@intnet.td; f. 1964; aims to promote co-operation in developing the Lake Chad region; to regulate and control the use of water and other natural resources in the basin; and to examine complaints and promote the settlement of disputes. Maintains relations with donor agencies and other international orgs in order to attract financial and tech. assistance. During 1988–92 a border demarcation exercise concerning all mem. states was conducted; a work programme, adopted by heads of state in March 1994, emphasized protection and sound environmental management and development of Lake Chad and incorporated 36 projects relating to water resources, agriculture, forestry, biodiversity management, livestock and fishery developments within the basin; a new eight-year management programme was formulated by the LCBC and Global Environment Fund in 1997, which included proposals for the establishment of information networks, the control of environmental contaminants, the protection of flood-plains and the initiation of studies on intra- and inter-basin water transfer. Budget 400m. francs CFA. Mems: Cameroon, Central African Repub., Chad, Niger, Nigeria. Exec. Sec. BOBBOI JAURO ABUBAKAR.

Liptako-Gourma Integrated Development Authority (Autorité de développement intégré de la région du Liptako-Gourma): BP 619, ave M. Thevenond, Ouagadougou, Burkina Faso; tel. 30-61-48; f. 1972; scope of activities includes water infrastructure, telecommunications and construction of roads and railways; in 1986 undertook study on development of water resources in the basin of the Niger river (for hydroelectricity and irrigation). Budget (1996) 400m. francs CFA. Mems: Burkina Faso, Mali, Niger. Dir-Gen. GISANGA DEMBÉLÉ (Mali).

Mano River Union: Mail Bag 133, Freetown, Sierra Leone; tel. (22) 226883; f. 1973 to establish a customs and economic union between mem. states, in order to accelerate development by means of integration. A common external tariff was instituted in April 1977; intra-union free trade was officially introduced on 1 May 1981, as the first stage in progress towards a customs union. An industrial development unit was set up in 1980 to identify projects and encourage investment. Construction of the Monrovia–Freetown–Monrovia highway was partially completed by 1991, and other road projects were also being undertaken in 1991. The Union was inactive for three years until mid-1994, owing to disagreements regarding funding. In January 1995 a Mano River Union Centre for Peace and Development was established, which was to be temporarily based in London, the United Kingdom. The Centre aimed to provide a permanent mechanism for conflict prevention and resolution, monitoring of human rights violations and to promote sustainable peace and development in the region following a peaceful resolution of the civil conflicts. Decisions are taken at meetings of a joint ministerial council. Mems: Guinea, Liberia, Sierra Leone. Dir Dr KABINEH KOROMAH (Sierra Leone).

Niger Basin Authority (Autorité du bassin du Niger): BP 729, Niamey, Niger; tel. 72-31-02; fax 73-53-10; f. 1964 to harmonize national programmes concerned with the River Niger Basin and to execute an integrated development plan; activities comprise: statistics; navigation regulation; hydrological forecasting; environmental control; infrastructure and agro-pastoral devt; and arranging assistance for these projects. Mems: Benin, Burkina Faso, Cameroon, Chad, Côte d'Ivoire, Guinea, Mali, Niger, Nigeria. Exec. Sec. OTHMAN MUSTAPHA (Nigeria). Publs *Bulletin, Bibliographical Index.*

Organization for the Development of the Senegal River (Organisation pour la mise en valeur du fleuve Sénégal—OMVS): 46 rue Carnot, BP 3152, Dakar, Senegal; tel. 823-45-30; fax 823-47-62; e-mail omvs.sphc@telecomplus.sn; f. 1972 to use the Senegal river for hydroelectricity, irrigation and navigation. The Djama dam in Senegal (completed in 1986) provides a barrage to prevent salt water from moving upstream, and the Manantali dam in Mali (completed in 1988) is intended to provide a reservoir for irrigation of about 375,000 ha of land and (eventually) for production of hydroelectricity and provision of year-round navigation for ocean-going vessels. In 1997 two companies were formed to manage the dams: Société de Gestion de l'Energie de Manantali (SOGEM) and Société de Gestion et d'Exploitation du Barrage de Djama (SOGED). Work began in 1997 on a hydroelectric power station on the Senegal River, for which international donors provided US $440m. for the project, which was expected to be operational by 2001. Mems: Mali, Mauritania, Senegal; Guinea has held observer status since 1987; Chair. MAAOUYA OULD SID'AHMED TAYA.

Organization for the Management and Development of the Kagera River Basin (Organisation pour l'aménagement et le développement du bassin de la rivière Kagera): BP 297, Kigali, Rwanda; tel. (7) 84665; fax (7) 82172; f. 1978; envisages jt devt and management of resources, incl. the construction of a 61.5-MW hydroelectric dam at Rusomo Falls, on the Rwanda-Tanzania border, a 2,000-km railway network between the four mem. countries, road construction (914 km) and a telecommunications network between mem. states (financed by US $16m. from the ADB). Budget (1992): $2m. Mems: Burundi, Rwanda, Tanzania, Uganda. Exec. Sec. JEAN-BOSCO BALINDA.

Pan-African Institute for Development—PAID: BP 4056, Douala, Cameroon; tel. 42-10-61; fax 42-43-35; f. 1964 to train people from African countries (48 countries in 1998), involved with devt at grassroots, intermediate and senior levels; emphasis in education is given to: devt management and financing; agriculture and rural devt; gender and devt; promotion of small and medium-sized enterprises; training policies and systems; environment, health and community devt; research, support and consultancy services; and specialized training. Four regional insts in Africa, two anglophone (BP 133, Buéa, Cameroon; POB 80448, Kabwe, Zambia), two francophone (BP 4078, Douala, Cameroon; BP 1756, Ouagadougou, Burkina Faso). Sec.-Gen. FAYA KONDIANO. Publs *Newsletter* (2 a year), *PAID Report* (quarterly), *Annual Progress Report.*

Permanent Inter-State Committee on Drought Control in the Sahel (Comité permanent inter-états de lutte contre la sécheresse dans le Sahel–CILSS): BP 7049, Ouagadougou, Burkina Faso; tel. 30-67-58; fax 30-67-57; e-mail cilss@fasonet.bf; f. 1973; works in co-operation with the UN Office to Combat Desertification and Drought (UNSO, q.v.); aims to combat the effects of chronic drought in the Sahel region, where the deficit in grain production was estimated at 1.7m. metric tons for 1988, by improving irrigation and food production, halting deforestation and creating food reserves. Maintains Institut du Sahel at Bamako (Mali) and centre at Niamey (Niger). Budget (2000): 9,506.1m. francs CFA, of which 10,200m. francs CFA to be provided by donors and 318.5m. francs CFA by member states. Mems: Burkina Faso, Cape Verde, Chad, The Gambia, Guinea-Bissau, Mali, Mauritania, Niger, Senegal. Exec. Sec. CISSÉ MARIAM K. SIDIBE. Publ. *Reflets Sahéliens* (quarterly).

Permanent Tripartite Commission for East African Co-operation: International Conference Centre, Arusha, Tanzania; tel. (57) 4253; fax (57) 4255; e-mail eac@cybernet.co.tz; internet home .turiga.com/eac; f. 1993 by agreement between the heads of state of Kenya, Tanzania and Uganda to promote greater regional co-operation (previously pursued under the East African Community; f. 1967, dissolved 1977); agreement to establish a secretariat was signed in Nov. 1994; initial areas for co-operation were to be trade and industry, security, immigration, transport and communications, and promotion of investment; further objectives were the elimination of trade barriers, strengthening regional infrastructure and ensuring the free movement of people and capital within the grouping. Secretariat inaugurated in March 1996. A treaty on further political and economic integration (providing for the formal establishment of the Community) was signed in November 1999. Exec. Sec. FRANCIS KIRIMI MUTHAURA.

United Nations African Institute for Economic Development and Planning (Institut africain de développement économique et de planification—IDEP): BP 3186, Dakar, Senegal; tel. 823-10-20; fax 822-29-64; e-mail idep@idep.sn; internet www.un.org/Depts/eca/idep; f. 1963 by ECA (q.v.) to train economic development planners, conduct research and provide advisory services; has library of books, journals and documents. Dir Dr JEGGAN C. SENGHOR.

ECONOMICS AND FINANCE

African Centre for Monetary Studies (Centre africain d'études monétaires—CAEM): 15 blvd Franklin Roosevelt, BP 4128, Dakar, Senegal; tel. 821-93-80; fax 822-73-43; e-mail caem@syfed .refer.sn; f. 1978 as an organ of the Association of African Central

Banks (AACB, see below) as a result of a decision by the OAU Heads of State and Government; aims to promote better understanding of banking and monetary matters; to study monetary problems of African countries and their effect on international monetary devts; seeks to enable African countries to co-ordinate strategies in international monetary affairs. Mems: all mems of AACB. Dir. MAMADOU SIDIBE (acting). Publs *Financial Journal* (2 a year), *Annual Report*.

African Insurance Organization: BP 5860, Douala, Cameroon; tel. 42-47-58; fax 43-20-08; e-mail aio@sprynet.com; internet www .africaninsurance.org; f. 1972 to promote the expansion of the insurance and reinsurance industry in Africa, and to increase regional co-operation; has established African insurance 'pools' for aviation, petroleum and fire risks; holds annual conference (2000: Abuja, Nigeria), periodic seminars and workshops, and arranges meetings for reinsurers, brokers, consultants and regulators in Africa; is developing insurance software for small and medium-sized African insurance markets. The AIO has established the African Insurance Educators' Agency, the Asscn of African Insurance Brokers and the Asscn of African Insurance Supervisory Authorities. Mems: insurers, reinsurers, brokers and supervisory authorities in 42 African countries. Sec.-Gen. YOSEPH ASEFFA.

Association of African Central Banks (Association des Banques Centrales Africaines—ABCA): 15 blvd Franklin Roosevelt, BP 4128, Dakar, Senegal; tel. 821-93-80; fax 822-73-43; f. 1968 to promote co-operation among mem. central banks in monetary and banking policy, and to provide a forum for views and information on matters of interest to monetary and financial stability on the African continent. Mems: 36 African central banks, representing 47 countries. Chair. Dr PAUL A. OGWUMA (Nigeria).

Association of African Tax Administrators: POB 13255, Yaoundé, Cameroon; tel. 22-41-57; fax 22-41-51; f. 1980 to promote co-operation among African countries in the fields of taxation policy, legislation and admin. Mems: 20 states. Chair. JAMES A. H. SCOTT; Sec.-Gen. OWONA PASCAL-BAYLON.

East African Development Bank: 4 Nile Ave, POB 7128, Kampala, Uganda; tel. (41) 230021; fax (41) 259763; f. 1967 by the fmr East African Community, to promote devt within Kenya, Tanzania and Uganda, which each hold 25.78% of the equity capital; the remaining equity is held by the African Devt Bank and other institutional investors; cap. SDR 25.4m. (Dec. 1995). Dir-Gen. F. R. TIBEITA.

Fonds Africain de Garantie et de Co-opération Economique— FAGACE (African Guarantee and Economic Co-operation Fund): BP 2045, Cotonou, Benin; tel. 300376; fax 300284; commenced operations in 1981; guarantees loans for devt projects, provides loans and grants for specific operations and supports nat. and regional enterprises. Cap. 7,750m. francs CFA. Mems: Benin, Burkina Faso, Central African Repub., Côte d'Ivoire, Mali, Niger, Rwanda, Senegal, Togo. Dir-Gen. SOULEYMANE GADO.

Union africaine des banques pour le développement: BP 2045, Cotonou, Benin; tel. 30-15-00; fax 30-02-84; f. 1962 to promote devt through exchanges, training and co-operation by regional banks. Mems: national or central banks of 12 countries. Exec. Sec. KOUANVI TIGOUE (Togo).

West African Bankers' Association: 11-13 Ecowas St, PMBag 1012, Freetown, Sierra Leone; fax (22) 229024; f. 1981; aims to strengthen links between banks in West Africa, to enable exchange of information, and to contribute to regional economic development; holds annual general assembly. Mems: 135 commercial banks in 14 countries. Sec.-Gen. PHILIP A. LATILO. Publ. *West African Banking Almanac*.

West African Monetary Agency: 11-13 ECOWAS St, PMBag 218, Freetown, Sierra Leone; tel. (22) 224485; fax (22) 223943; e-mail wama@sierratel.sl; f. 1975 (as West African Clearing House), began operating in 1976; administers payments among its 10 mem. central banks in order to promote the use of local currencies for sub-regional trade and monetary co-operation, thus effecting savings in mems' foreign reserves; administers ECOWAS travellers' cheques scheme. Mems: Banque centrale des états de l'Afrique de l'ouest (serving Benin, Burkina Faso, Côte d'Ivoire, Guinea Bissau, Mali, Niger, Senegal and Togo: see under Franc Zone) and the central banks of Cape Verde, The Gambia, Ghana, Guinea, Liberia, Mauritania, Nigeria and Sierra Leone. Dir-Gen. ANTOINE M. F. NDIAYE (Senegal). Publ. *Annual Report*.

EDUCATION

African Association for Literacy and Adult Education: Finance House, 6th Floor, Loita St, POB 50768, Nairobi, Kenya; tel. (2) 222391; fax (2) 340849; f. 1984, combining the fmr African Adult Education Assen and the AFROLIT Society (both f. 1968); aims to promote adult education and literacy in Africa, to study the problems involved, and to allow the exchange of information; programmes are developed and implemented by 'networks' of educators; holds assembly every three years. Mems: 28 nat. education asscns and 300 institutions in 33 countries. Chair. (vacant). Publs. *The Spider Newsletter* (quarterly,

French and English), *Regional Conference Report* (every 3 years), *Journal* (2 a year).

Association for the Development of Education in Africa: c/o International Institute for Educational Planning, 7-9 rue Eugène Delacroix, 75116 Paris, France; tel. 1-45-03-37-96; fax 1-45-03-39-65; e-mail adea@iiep.unesco.org; internet www.adea.org/; f. 1988 as Donors to African Education, adopted present name in 1995; aims to enhance collaboration in the support of African education; undertakes research, advocacy and capacity-building in areas of education in sub-Saharan Africa through working groups comprising representatives of donor countries and African ministries of education. Exec. Sec. RICHARD SACK.

Association of African Universities (Association des universités africaines): POB 5744, Accra North, Ghana; tel. (21) 774495; fax (21) 774821; f. 1967 to promote exchanges, contacts and co-operation between African university institutions; to study and make known educational and related needs in Africa, and to co-ordinate arrangements to meet these needs, to collect, classify and disseminate information on higher education and research, particularly in Africa. Mems: 132 univs in 39 African countries. Sec.-Gen. Prof. NARCISO MATOS (Mozambique). Publs include *Newsletter* (3 a year), *Handbook of African Universities* (every 2 years).

International Association for the Development of Documentation, Libraries and Archives in Africa: BP 375, Dakar, Senegal; tel. 824-09-54; f. 1957 to organize and develop documentation and archives in all African countries. Sec.-Gen. ZACHEUS SUNDAY ALI (Nigeria); Perm. Sec. EMMANUEL K. W. DADZIE (Togo).

International Congress of African Studies: c/o International African Institute, Thornhaugh St, London, WC1H 0XG, United Kingdom; tel. (20) 7898-4420; fax (20) 7898-4419; f. 1962 to encourage co-operation and research in African studies; Congress convened approx. every five years (1990: in Khartoum, Sudan). Publ. *Proceedings*.

West African Examinations Council—WAEC (Conseil des examens de l'Afrique orientale): POB 125, Accra, Ghana; tel. (21) 221511; fax (21) 222905; e-mail waechqrs@africaonline.com.gh; internet www.africaonline.com.gh/waec; f. 1952; administers prescribed examinations in mem. countries; aims to harmonize examinations procedures and standards. Offices in each mem. country and in London, the United Kingdom. Mems: The Gambia, Ghana, Liberia, Nigeria, Sierra Leone. Chair. Dr YAHAYA HAMZA; Registrar Dr SYLVIA AWO MANSAH BOYE.

GOVERNMENT AND POLITICS

Accord de Non-agression et d'Assistance en Matière de Défence—ANAD (Non-Aggression and Defence Aid Agreement): 08 BP 2065, Abidjan 08, Côte d'Ivoire; tel. 20-21-88-33; fax 20-33-86-13; e-mail colpape@aviso.ci; f. 1997 to serve as a framework for sub-regional co-operation in conflict prevention and resolution; adopted a draft protocol for the establishment of a regional peace-keeping force and a fund to promote peace and security in April 1999. Mems: Benin, Burkina Faso, Côte d'Ivoire, Mali, Mauritania, Niger, Senegal, Togo. Sec.-Gen. Col. PAPA KHALILOU FALL.

African Association for Public Administration and Management: POB 48677, Nairobi, Kenya; tel. (2) 52-19-44; fax (2) 52-18-45; e-mail aapam@africaonline.co.ke; f. 1971 to provide senior officials with a forum for the exchange of ideas and experience, to promote the study of professional techniques and encourage research in particular African admin. problems. Mems: 500 individual, 50 corporate. Pres. Dr ROBERT DODOO; Sec.-Gen. Dr IJUKA KABUMBA. Publs *Newsletter* (quarterly), *African Journal of Public Administration and Management*, annual seminar reports.

Afro-Asian Peoples' Solidarity Organization—AAPSO: 89 Abdel Aziz Al-Saoud St, POB 11559-61 Manial El-Roda, Cairo, Egypt; tel. (2) 3636081; fax (2) 3637361; e-mail aapso@idsc.gov.eg; f. 1958; acts among and for the peoples of Africa and Asia in their struggle for genuine independence, sovereignty, socio-economic devt, peace and disarmament. Mems: 82 nat. cttees from African and Asian countries, and 10 European orgs as assoc. mems. Pres. Dr MORAD GHALEB; Sec.-Gen. NOURI AR-RAZZAK HUSSEIN (Iraq). Publs *Solidarity Bulletin*, (monthly), *Development and Socio-Economic Progress* (quarterly, in Arabic, English and French), *Human Rights Newsletter* (6 a year).

Comunidade dos Países de Língua Portuguesa (Community of Portuguese-Speaking Countries): rua S. Caetano 32, 1200 Lisbon, Portugal; tel. (1) 392-8560; fax (1) 392-8588; f. July 1996; aims to promote close political, economic, diplomatic and cultural links between Portuguese-speaking countries and to strengthen the influence of the Lusophone commonwealth within the international community; undertook efforts in mid-1998 to negotiate a cease-fire in Guinea-Bissau. In May 1999 ministers of defence resolved to establish a CPLP peace-keeping force. Mems: Angola, Brazil, Cape Verde, Guinea-Bissau, Mozambique, Portugal and São Tomé and Príncipe. Exec. Sec. MARCOLINO MOCO (Angola).

La Francophonie: c/o Agence de la francophonie, 13 quai André Citroën, 75015 Paris, France; tel. 1-44-37-33-00; fax 1-45-79-14-98; internet http://www.francophonie.org; political grouping of French-speaking countries; conference of heads of state convened every two years to promote co-operation throughout the French-speaking world (1997: Hanoi, Viet Nam). Mems: Govts of 49 countries. Sec.-Gen. BOUTROS BOUTROS-GHALI (Egypt).

Gulf of Guinea Commission (Commission de Golfe de Guinée—CGG): f. Nov. 1999 to promote co-operation among member countries and the peaceful and sustainable development of natural resources in the sub-region. Mems: Angola, Cameroon, the Repub. of the Congo, Equatorial Guinea, Gabon, Nigeria, Sao Tomé and Príncipe.

Pan-African Youth Movement: BP 72, Didouch Morad, 16000 Algiers, Algeria; tel. and fax (2) 912543; f. 1962; promotes participation of African youth in socio-economic and political devt; organizes confs, seminars and festivals. Mems: over 60 orgs and independence movements in African countries. Publ. *MPJ News* (quarterly).

Union of African Parliaments: BP V314, Abidjan 01, Côte d'Ivoire; tel. 21-37-57; fax 22-20-87; f. 1976; holds annual conf. Mems: 31 states. Sec.-Gen. HENRI ADOU SESS.

INDUSTRIAL AND PROFESSIONAL RELATIONS

International Confederation of Free Trade Unions—African Regional Organization (ICFTU—AFRO): POB 67273, Ambank House, 14th Floor, University Way, Nairobi, Kenya; tel. (2) 221357; fax (2) 215072; e-mail icftuafro@formnet.com; f. 1957. Mems: 5m. workers in 36 African countries; Gen. Sec. ANDREW KAILEMBO (Tanzania).

Organisation of African Trade Union Unity—OATUU: POB M386, Accra, Ghana; tel. 772574; fax 772621; f. 1973 as a single continental trade union org, independent of international trade union organizations; has affiliates from all African trade unions. Congress, composed of four delegates from all affiliated trade union centres, meets at least every four years as supreme policy-making body; General Council, composed of one representative from all affiliated trade unions, meets annually to implement Congress decisions and to approve annual budget. Mems: trade union movements in 52 independent African countries. Sec.-Gen. HASSAN SUNMONU (Nigeria). Publ. *Voice of African Workers*.

Pan-African Employers' Confederation: c/o Federation of Kenya Employers, POB 48311, Nairobi, Kenya; tel. (2) 721929; fax (2) 721990; f. 1986 to link African employers' orgs, and to represent them at the UN, the International Labour Organization and the OAU. Pres. HEDI JILIANI (Tunisia); Sec.-Gen. TOM DIJU OWUOR (Kenya).

LAW

African Bar Association: 29/31 Obafemi Awolowo Way, Ikeja-Lagos, Nigeria (temporary address); tel. (1) 4936907; fax (1) 7752202; f. 1972; aims to uphold the rule of law, to maintain the independence of the judiciary, and to improve legal services. Pres. PETER ALA ADJETY (Ghana); Sec.-Gen. FEMI FALANA (Nigeria).

African Society of International and Comparative Law: Kairaba Ave, Private Bag 520, Banjul, The Gambia; tel. 375476; fax 375469; f. 1986; promotes public education on law and civil liberties; aims to provide a legal aid and advice system in each African country, and to facilitate the exchange of information on civil liberties in Africa; seeks to promote the Rule of Law by the publ. of legal texts and org. of confs. Pres. MOHAMMED BEDJAOUI; Sec. EMILE YAKPO. Publs *African Journal of International and Comparative Law* (quarterly in French and English), *Reportings of the Annual Conferences of the African Society of International and Comparative Law* (annually in French and English), *Report of the African Commission on Human and People's Rights* (biennially in French, English and Arabic).

Asian-African Legal Consultative Committee: E-66, Vasant Marg, Vasant Vihar, New Delhi 110057, India; tel. (11) 6152251; fax (11) 6152041; e-mail aalcc@vsnl.com; internet www.aalcc.org; f. 1956 to consider legal problems referred to it by mem. countries and to be a forum for Afro-Asian co-operation in international law and economic relations; provides background material for confs, prepares standard/model contract forms suited to the needs of the region; promotes arbitration as a means of settling international commercial disputes; trains officers of mem. states; has perm. UN observer status. Mems: 45 states. Sec.-Gen. Dr WAFIK ZAHER KAMIL (Egypt).

Inter-African Union of Lawyers: 12 rue du Prince Moulay Abdullah, Casablanca, Morocco; tel. (2) 271017; fax (2) 204686; f. 1980; holds congress every three years. Pres. ABDELAZIZ BENZAKOUR (Morocco); Sec.-Gen. FRANÇOIS XAVIER AGONDJO-OKAWE (Gabon). Publ. *L'avocat africain* (2 a year).

MEDICINE AND PUBLIC HEALTH

International Federation of Red Cross and Red Crescent Societies—IFRC: 17 chemin des Crêts, Petit-Saconnex, CP 372, 1211 Geneva 19, Switzerland; tel. (22) 7304222; fax (22) 7330395; e-mail secretariat@ifrc.org; internet www.ifrc.org; f. 1919 to prevent and alleviate human suffering, and to promote humanitarian activities by nat. Red Cross and Red Crescent socs; conducts relief operations for refugees and victims of disasters, co-ordinates relief supplies and assists in disaster prevention; Pres. Dr ASTRID NØKLEBYE HEIBERG (Norway); Sec.-Gen. DIDIER CHERPITEL (France). Publs *Annual Report, Red Cross Red Crescent* (quarterly), *Weekly News, World Disasters Report, Emergency Appeal*.

Médecins sans frontières: rue de la Tourelle, 1040 Brussels, Belgium; tel. (2) 280-18-81; fax (2) 280-01-73; f. 1971; undertakes emergency humanitarian missions, provides medical treatment in refugee camps, and supports long-term field operations in countries with inadequate health facilities. Publs *Annual Report, MSF International Newsletter*.

Organisation panafricaine de lutte contre le SIDA—OPALS: 15/21 rue de L'Ecole de Médecine, 75006 Paris, France; tel. 1-43-26-72-28; fax 1-43-29-70-93; f. 1988; disseminates information relating to the treatment and prevention of AIDS; provides training of medical personnel; promotes co-operation between African medical centres and specialized centres in the USA and Europe. Publ. *OPALS Liaison*.

Organization for Co-ordination and Co-operation in the Struggle against Endemic Diseases (Organisation de coordination et de coopération pour la lutte contre les grandes endémies—OCCGE): 01 BP 153, Bobo-Dioulasso 01, Burkina Faso; tel. 97-01-55; fax 97-00-99; e-mail sg@pegase.occge.bf; f. 1960; conducts research, provides training and maintains a documentation centre and computer information system; in 1990 announced intention to merge with anglophone West African Health Community (q.v.) to form West African Health Organization. Mems: Govts of Benin, Burkina Faso, Côte d'Ivoire, Mali, Mauritania, Niger, Senegal, Togo. Sec.-Gen. Prof. ABDOULAYE RHALY. Publs *OCCGE Info* (3 a year), *Rapport annuel, Bulletin Bibliographique* (quarterly). Centres of the OCCGE are:

Centre de recherches sur les méningites et les schistosomiases: BP 10887, Niamey, Niger; tel. 75-20-45; fax 75-31-80; e-mail chippaux@ird.ne; internet www.ird.ne/cermes; f. 1979; Dir Dr J.-P. CHIPPAUX.

Centre Muraz: 01 BP 153, Bobo-Dioulasso 01, Burkina Faso; tel. 97-01-02; fax 97-04-57; e-mail direction.muraz@fasonet.bf; multi-disciplinary medical research centre with special interest in biology and epidemiology of tropical diseases and training of health workers. Dir Prof. PHILIPPE VANDEPERRE.

Institut Marchoux: BP 251, Bamako, Mali; tel. 22-51-31; fax 22-28-45; f. 1935; research and training on leprosy. Dir Prof. MAMADOU HAMET CISSE.

Institut d'ophtalmologie tropicale africaine—IOTA: BP 248, Bamako, Mali; tel. 22-34-21; fax 22-51-86; e-mail dirista@iotaoccge.org; f. 1952; undertakes training, research and specialized care in ophthalmology. Dir Dr AUZEMERY.

Institut Pierre Richet: 01 BP 1500, Côte d'Ivoire; tel. 63-37-46; fax 63-27-38; e-mail carneval@bouake2.orstom.ci; research on yellow fever and arbovirus, simulium chemical control, rice-field and malaria; administers a geographical information system; Dir Dr PIERRE CARNEVALE.

Office de recherches sur l'alimentation et la nutrition africaine—ORANA: BP 2098, Dakar, Senegal; tel. 822-58-92; f. 1956. Dir Dr A. M. NDIAYE.

Offices are also based in Cotonou, Benin (entomology), Lomé, Togo (nutrition), Nouakchott, Mauritania (tuberculosis), and Bafoulabé, Mali (leprosy).

Organization for Co-ordination of the Control of Endemic Diseases in Central Africa (Organisation de coordination pour la lutte contre les endémies en Afrique centrale—OCEAC): BP 288, Yaoundé, Cameroon; tel. 23-22-32; fax 23-00-61; e-mail oceac@camnet.cm; f. 1965 to standardize methods of fighting endemic diseases, to co-ordinate national action, and to negotiate programmes of assistance on a regional scale. Mems: Cameroon, Central African Repub., Chad, Repub. of the Congo, Equatorial Guinea, Gabon. Pres. L. ESSO (Cameroon); Sec.-Gen. Dr BILONGO MANENE. Publs *Rapport Final des Conférences Techniques* (every 2 years), *Rapport annuel, Bulletin de liaison et de documentation* (quarterly), *EPI–Notes OCEAC* (quarterly).

West African Health Community: PMB 2023, Yaba, Lagos, Nigeria; tel. and fax (1) 862324; f. 1972 to promote higher medical and allied professional education, disseminate tech. health information, establish special agencies and programmes and collaborate with other medical orgs in mem. states and elsewhere; Ministers of Health meet annually. Three specialized agencies have been formed: the West African Postgraduate Medical College, the West African Pharmaceutical Federation and the West African College of Nursing. Mems: The Gambia, Ghana, Liberia, Nigeria and Sierra Leone; in 1990 announced intention to merge with francophone Organization for Co-ordination and Co-operation in the Struggle against Endemic Diseases (q.v.) to form the West African Health Organization, covering all the mem. states of ECOWAS (subject to ratification by mem. states). Exec. Dir Dr KABBA T. JOINER. Publ. *West African Journal of Medicine*, *West African Journal of Nursing*, *West African Pharmacy Journal*.

PRESS, RADIO AND TELECOMMUNICATIONS

African Postal and Telecommunications Union: Republic of the Congo; f. 1961 to improve postal and telecommunication services between mem. administrations; consists of three Commissions: Post and Financial Services, Telecommunications, Administrative and Budget Affairs. Mems: Benin, Burkina Faso, Central African Repub., Chad, Repub. of the Congo, Côte d'Ivoire, Mali, Mauritania, Niger, Rwanda, Senegal, Togo. Sec.-Gen. MAHMOUDOU SAMOURA.

Regional African Satellite Communications System– RASCOM: c/o International Telecommunication Union, place des Nations, 1211 Geneva 20, Switzerland; tel. (22) 7305111; fax (22) 7337256; f. 1992 to launch Africa's first satellite into space within five years. Mems: 42 countries.

Southern African Broadcasting Association–SABA: 19 Pettenkoffer St, Windhoek West, POB 50576, Bachbrecht, Windhoek, Namibia; tel. (61) 291-2117; fax (61) 255-166; e-mail musukuma@iafrica.com.ne; internet www.cctproductions.co.uk/saba; f. 1993; promotes quality public broadcasting; facilitates training of broadcasters at all levels; co-ordinates broadcasting activities in the SADC region; organizes radio news exchange service; produces television and radio programmes. Mems: corpns in more than 20 countries. Sec.-Gen. JOHN J. MUSUKUMA.

Union of National Radio and Television Organizations of Africa–URTNA (Union des radiodiffusions et télévisions nationales d'Afrique): BP 3237, 101 rue Carnot, Dakar, Senegal; tel. 821-59-70; fax 822-51-13; e-mail urtnadkr@telecomplus.sn; f. 1962; co-ordinates radio and television services, including monitoring and frequency allocation, the exchange of information and coverage of national and international events, among African countries; maintains programme exchange centre (Nairobi, Kenya), tech. centre (Bamako, Mali) and a centre for rural radio studies (Ouagadougou, Burkina Faso); AFRO-VISION co-ordinating centre for the exchange of television news in Algiers, Algeria. Budget (1993): US $1.8m. There are 49 active, two supplementary active and nine assoc. mem. orgs. Sec.-Gen. EFOE ADODO MENSAH (Togo). Publs *URTNA Review* (2 a year in English and French).

West African Journalists' Association: BP 849, 20 rue Mohammad V, Dakar, Senegal; tel. 822-36-25; fax 822-17-61; e-mail sysop@endakak.gn.apc.org; f. 1986; defends journalists and the freedom of the press, and promotes links between journalists' asscns. Mems: journalists' asscns in the mem. states of ECOWAS.

RELIGION

All Africa Conference of Churches: POB 14205, Waiyaki Way, Nairobi, Kenya; tel. (2) 441483; fax (2) 443241; e-mail aacc-secretariat@maf.org; f. 1958; promotes co-operation and fellowship among Protestant, Orthodox and independent Churches and Christian Councils in Africa; 1997 Assembly: Addis Ababa, Ethiopia. Mems: 147 churches and associated councils in 39 African countries. Pres. Very Rev. Prof. KWESI DICKSON (Ghana); Gen. Sec. Canon CLEMENT JANDA (Uganda). Publs *ACLCA News, Tam Tam*.

SCIENCE AND TECHNOLOGY

African Organization of Cartography and Remote Sensing: BP 102, 16040 Hussein Dey, Algiers, Algeria; tel. (2) 23-17-17; fax (2) 23-33-39; f. 1988 by amalgamation of African Association of Cartography and African Council for Remote Sensing; aims to encourage the development of cartography and of remote-sensing by satellites; organizes confs and other meetings, promotes establishment of training inst; maintains regional training centres in Burkina Faso, Kenya, Nigeria and Tunisia. Mems: national cartographic institutions of 24 countries. Sec.-Gen. UNIS MUFTAH.

African Regional Centre for Technology: Immeuble FAHD, 17e étage, blvd Djily Mbaye, BP 2435, Dakar, Senegal; tel. 823-77-12; fax 823-77-13; f. 1980 to encourage the devt of indigenous tech. and to improve the terms of access to imported tech.; assists the establishment of nat. centres. Dir Dr OUSMANE KANE. Publs include *African Technodevelopment, Alert Africa, Infonet*.

Association for the Taxonomic Study of Tropical African Flora: National Botanic Garden of Belgium, Domein van Bouchout, B-1860 Meise, Belgium; tel. (2) 260-09-28; fax (2) 260-09-45; e-mail rammeloo@br.fgov.be; f. 1950 to facilitate co-operation and liaison between botanists engaged in the study of the flora of tropical Africa; maintains a library. Mems: c. 800 botanists in 63 countries. Sec.-Gen. Prof. J. RAMMELOO. Publs *AETFAT Bulletin* (annually), *Proceedings*.

Inter-African Committee for Hydraulic Studies (Comité interafricain d'études hydrauliques–CIEH): 01 BP 369, Ouagadougou, Burkina Faso; tel. 30-71-12; fax 36-24-41; f. 1960 to ensure co-operation in hydrology, hydrogeology, climatology, urban sanitation and other water sciences; co-ordination of research and other projects. Mems: 14 African countries. Sec.-Gen. AMADOU CISSÉ. Publs scientific and technical research studies, *Bulletin de liaison technique* (quarterly).

Pan-African Union of Science and Technology: BP 2339, Brazzaville, Republic of the Congo; tel. 83-22-65; fax 83-21-85; f. 1987 to promote the use of science and tech. in furthering the devt of Africa; membership open to any scientific or tech. inst. or asscn in Africa. Pres. Prof. EDWARD AYENSU (Ghana); Sec.-Gen. Prof. LÉVY MAKANY.

Regional Centre for Services in Surveying, Mapping and Remote Sensing: POB 18118, Nairobi, Kenya; tel. (2) 803320; fax (2) 802767; e-mail rcssmrs@unep.org; f. 1975 to provide services in the professional techniques of map-making and the application of satellite and remote sensing data in resource analysis and devt planning; undertakes training and research and provides advisory services to African govts. Mems: 15 signatory and eight non-signatory states. Dir-Gen. Prof. SIMON NDYETABULA.

Regional Centre for Training in Aerospace Surveys (RECTAS): PMB 5545, Ile-Ife, Nigeria; tel. (36) 230050; fax (36) 230481; f. 1972 to provide training, research and advisory services in aerial surveying; administered by the ECA (q.v.). Mems: Benin, Burkina Faso, Cameroon, Ghana, Mali, Niger, Nigeria, Senegal. Dir J. A. OGUNLAMI. Publ. *RECTAS Newsletter* (annually).

Scientific, Technical and Research Commission–STRC: Nigerian Ports Authority Bldg, PMB 2359, Marina, Lagos, Nigeria; tel. (1) 2633430; fax (1) 2636093; e-mail oaustrc@rcl.nig.com; f. 1965 to succeed the Commission for Technical Co-operation in Africa (f. 1954). Supervises the Inter-African Bureau for Animal Resources (Nairobi, Kenya), the Inter-African Bureau for Soils (Lagos, Nigeria) and the Inter-African Phytosanitary Commission (Yaoundé, Cameroon) and several joint research projects. The Commission provides training in agricultural man., and conducts pest control programmes. Exec. Sec. Dr ROBERT N. MSHANA.

United Nations University Institute for Natural Resources in Africa (UNU/INRA): ISSER Bldg Complex, Nasia Rd, University of Ghana, Legon; Private Mail Bag, Kotoka International Airport, Accra, Ghana; tel. (21) 500396; fax (21) 500792; e-mail unuinra@ghana.com; internet www.unu.edu/inra; f. 1986 as a research and training centre of the United Nations University (Tokyo, Japan); operational since 1990; aims at human resource development and institutional capacity building through co-ordination with African universities and research institutes in advanced research, training and dissemination of knowledge and information on the conservation and management of Africa's natural resources and their rational utilization for sustainable devt. Dir. Prof. A. UZO MOKWUNYE. INRA has a mineral resources unit (MRU) at the University of Zambia in Lusaka. MRU Co-ordinator Dr GLASSWELL NKONDE.

SOCIAL SCIENCES, SOCIAL WELFARE AND HUMAN RIGHTS

African Centre for Applied Research and Training in Social Development–ACARTSOD: Africa Centre, Wahda Quarter, Zawia Rd, POB 80606, Tripoli, Libya; tel. (21) 4835103; fax (21) 4835066; e-mail fituri_acartsod@hotmail.com; f. 1977 under the jt auspices of the ECA and OAU to promote and co-ordinate applied research and training in social devt, and to assist in formulating nat. development strategies. Head Dr AHMED SAID FITURI.

African Commission on Human and People's Rights: Kairaba Ave, POB 673, Banjul, The Gambia; tel. 392962; fax 390764; f. 1987; meets twice a year in March and Oct.; the Commission comprises 11 members. Its mandate is to monitor compliance with the African Charter on Human and People's Rights (ratified in 1986), and it investigates claims of human rights abuses perpetrated by states that have ratified the Charter. Claims may be brought by other African states, the victims themselves, or by a third party. Sec. GERMAIN BARICAKO (Burundi).

African Social and Environmental Studies Programme: Nairobi, Kenya; f. 1968; develops and disseminates educational material on social environmental studies, and education for all in eastern and southern Africa. Mems: 18 African countries. Chair. Prof. WILLIAM SEMTEZA KAJUBI; Exec. Dir Prof. PETER MUYANDA MUTEBI. Publs *African Social Studies Forum* (2 a year), teaching guides.

Council for the Development of Social Science Research in Africa–CODESRIA: ave Cheikh Anta Diop, Angle Canal IV, BP 3304, Dakar, Senegal; tel. 825-98-22; fax 824-12-89; e-mail codesria@sonatel.senet.net; f. 1973; promotes research, provides confs, working groups and information services. Mems: research insts and university faculties in African countries. Exec. Sec. ACHILLE MBEMBE. Publs *Africa Development/Afrique et Développement* (quarterly), *CODESRIA Bulletin* (quarterly), *Index of African Social Science Periodical Articles* (annually).

Southern African Research and Documentation Centre–SARDC: POB 5690, Harare, Zimbabwe; tel. (4) 738695; fax (4) 738693; e-mail sardc@sardc.net; f. 1987; aims to enhance and disseminate information on political, economic, cultural and social developments in southern Africa; Exec. Dir PHYLLIS JOHNSON.

Third World Forum: 39 Dokki St, POB 43, Orman, Cairo, Egypt; f. 1973 to link social scientists and others from the developing countries, to discuss alternative devt policies and encourage research. Regional offices in Mexico, Senegal and Sri Lanka. Mems: individuals in more than 50 countries. Chair. ISMAIL-SABRI ABDALLA. Publ. *TWF Newsletter*.

TRADE AND INDUSTRY

African Regional Industrial Property Organization–ARIPO: POB 4228, Harare, Zimbabwe; tel. (4) 794338; fax (4) 704025; e-mail aripo@harare.iafrica.com; f. 1976 to grant patents, register industrial designs and marks and to promote devt and harmonization of laws concerning industrial property. Mems: Botswana, The Gambia, Ghana, Kenya, Lesotho, Malawi, Sierra Leone, Somalia, Sudan, Swaziland, Tanzania, Uganda, Zambia and Zimbabwe. Dir.-Gen. MZONDI H. CHIRAMBO.

African Regional Organization for Standardization: POB 57363, Nairobi, Kenya; tel. (2) 224561; fax (2) 218792; e-mail arso@nbnet.co.ke; internet www.nbnet.co.ke/test/arso; f.1977 to promote standardization, quality control, certification and metrology in the continent, to formulate regional standards to promote the exchange of information on standards, tech. regulations and related subjects and to co-ordinate participation in international standardization activities. Mems: 24 states. Sec.-Gen. Dr A. O. OYEJOLA. Publs *News Bulletin* (2 a year), *ARSO Catalogue of Regional Standards* (annually).

Association of African Trade Promotion Organizations–AATPO: Pavillon International, BP 23, Tangier, Morocco; tel. (9) 324465; fax (9) 943779; e-mail aoapc@mtds.com; f. 1974 under the auspices of the ECA and OAU to encourage regular trade contact between African states and to assist in the harmonization of their commercial policies in order to promote intra-African trade. Mems: 26 states. Sec.-Gen. Prof. ADEYINKA W. ORIMALADE. Publs include *FLASH: African Trade* (monthly), *Directory of Trade Promotion Institutions in Africa*, *Directory of State Trading Organizations*, *Directory of Exporters and Importers of Food Products in Africa*, *Calendar of Major Trade Events in Africa*, *African Trade Perspective* (on individual countries).

Federation of African Chambers of Commerce: c/o ECA, POB 3001, Addis Ababa, Ethiopia; tel. (1) 517200; fax (1) 514416; f. 1983. Dir Dr B. W. MUTHAUKA.

Organization of the Petroleum Exporting Countries–OPEC: 1020 Vienna, Obere Donaustrasse 93, Austria; tel. (1) 211-12-0; telex 134474; fax (1) 214-98-27; e-mail prid@opec.org; internet www.opec.org; f. 1960 to unify and co-ordinate members' petroleum policies and to safeguard their interests generally: holds regular confs of mem. countries to set prices and production levels; conducts research in energy studies, economics and finance; provides data services and news agency covering petroleum and energy issues. Mems: Algeria, Indonesia, Iran, Iraq, Kuwait, Libya, Nigeria, Qatar, Saudi Arabia, United Arab Emirates, Venezuela. Sec.-Gen. Dr. RILWANU LUKMAN (Nigeria). Publs *OPEC Bulletin* (monthly), *OPEC Review* (quarterly), *Annual Report*, *Annual Statistical Bulletin*, *Monthly Oil Market Report*.

OPEC Fund for International Development: Postfach 995, 1011 Vienna, Austria; tel. (1) 515-64-0; fax (1) 513-92-38; e-mail info@opecfund.org; internet www.opecfund.org; f. 1976 by mem. countries of OPEC, to provide financial co-operation and assistance for developing countries; in 1999 commitments amounted to US \$320.5m.; 53% of project loans approved in 1999 was for countries in Africa south of the Sahara. Dir-Gen. Y. SEYYID ABDULAI (Nigeria). Publs *Annual Report*, *OPEC Fund Newsletter* (3 a year).

Southern African Customs Union: no permanent headquarters; f. 1969; provides common pool of customs, excise and sales duties, according to the relative volume of trade and production in each country; goods are traded within the union free of duty and quotas, subject to certain protective measures for less developed mems; the South African rand is legal tender in Lesotho and Swaziland. The Customs Union Commission meets annually in each of the mems' capital cities in turn. Mems: Botswana, Lesotho, Namibia, South Africa, Swaziland.

Southern and Eastern African Mineral Centre—SEAMIC: POB 9573, Dar es Salaam, Tanzania; tel. (51) 650321; fax (51) 650319; e-mail seamic@cats-net.com; internet www.seamic.org; f. 1977 to promote socio-economic and environmentally responsible mineral sector development in the region; sponsored by ECA (q.v.); provides advisory and consultancy services in exploration geology, geophysics, geochemistry, mining and mineral processing; organizes training courses; operates specialized laboratory services. Mems: Angola, Comoros, Ethiopia, Mozambique, Tanzania, Uganda. Dir A. M. A. PEDRO.

Union of African Water Suppliers: 01 BP 1843, Abidjan 01, Côte d'Ivoire; tel. 24-14-43; fax 24-26-29; e-mail uadewup@africaonline.co.ci; f. 1980; facilitates co-operation between public and private bodies concerned with water supply and sewage management in Africa; promotes the study of economic, technical and scientific matters relating to the industry; congress held every two years (2000 congress scheduled to be held in Durban, South Africa). Mems in 32 countries.

Union of Producers, Conveyors and Distributors of Electric Power in Africa–UPDEA: 01 BP 1345, Abidjan 01, Côte d'Ivoire; tel. 32-64-33; fax 33-12-10; f. 1970 to study tech. matters and to promote efficient devt of enterprises in this sector; operates training school in Côte d'Ivoire. Mems: 22 nat. electricity authorities in Africa. Sec.-Gen. LIONEL KELLER. Publs *AFRIQUELEC* (periodical), technical papers.

TRANSPORT AND TOURISM

African Airlines Association: POB 20116, Nairobi, Kenya; tel. (2) 503655; fax (2) 604966; e-mail afraa@africaonline.co.ke; f. 1968 to give African air cos expert advice in tech., financial, juridical and market matters; to improve communications in Africa; to represent African airlines; and to develop manpower resources; published first continent-wide timetable in 1988. Mems: 34 nat. carriers. Pres. (2000) BISRAT NIGATU (Ethiopia).

Agency for the Safety of Air Navigation in Africa and Madagascar–ASECNA (Agence pour la sécurité de la navigation aérienne en Afrique et Madagascar): BP 8132, Dakar, Senegal; tel. 820-07-80; fax 820-06-00; f. 1959; organizes air-traffic communications in mem. states; co-ordinates meteorological forecasts; provides training for air-traffic controllers, meteorologists and airport fire-fighters. ASECNA is under the authority of a cttee comprising Ministers of Civil Aviation of mem. states. Mems: Benin, Burkina Faso, Cameroon, Central African Repub., Chad, Repub. of the Congo, Côte d'Ivoire, France, Gabon, Madagascar, Mali, Mauritania, Niger, Senegal, Togo. Dir-Gen. OUSMANE ISSOUFOU OUBANDAWAKI (Niger).

Southern African Regional Tourism Council: POB 564 Blantyre, Malawi; tel. 624888; fax 634339; f. 1973 for the devt and marketing of tourism in southern African countries. Mems: public and private representatives in 22 countries world-wide.

INDEX OF REGIONAL ORGANIZATIONS

(Main references only)

PART THREE
Country Surveys

ANGOLA

Physical and Social Geography

RENÉ PÉLISSIER

PHYSICAL FEATURES

The Republic of Angola, covering an area of 1,246,700 sq km (481,354 sq miles), is the largest Portuguese-speaking state in Africa. It is composed of 18 provinces, one of which, Cabinda (formerly known as Portuguese Congo), is separated from the others by the oceanic outlet of the Democratic Republic of the Congo (DRC, formerly Zaire) and the delta of the River Congo. On its landward side Cabinda is surrounded by the DRC and the Republic of the Congo. Greater Angola is bordered to the north and east by the DRC, to the east by Zambia and to the south by Namibia. Excluding the Cabinda exclave, Angola extends 1,277 km from the northern to the southern border, and 1,236 km from the mouth of the Cunene river to the Zambian border.

Two-thirds of Angola is a plateau. The average elevation is 1,050–1,350 m above sea-level, with higher ranges and massifs reaching above 2,000 m. The highest point of Angola is Mt Moco (2,620 m) in the Huambo province. Through the central part of the inland plateau runs the watershed of Angola's rivers. The coastal plain on the Atlantic is separated from this plateau by a sub-plateau zone which varies in breadth from about 160 km in the north to between 25–40 km in the centre and south. The Namib desert occupies the coastal plain at a considerable height above Namibe. Towards the Cuango (Kwango) basin, in the Zaire province, a sedimentary hollow forms the Cassange depression, in which cotton is cultivated. The north-western section of the Angolan plateau has jungle-covered mountains which are suitable for the cultivation of coffee. The Mayombe range in Cabinda is covered by equatorial jungle.

Except for the Cuanza (Kwanza) river, which is navigable up to Dondo (193 km upstream), Angolan rivers do not provide easy access to the interior from the coast. On the other hand, they are harnessed for the production of electricity and for irrigation. The main rivers are, above the Cuanza, the Chiloango (Cabinda), the Congo, the M'bridge, the Loge, the Dange and the Bengo. The Cassai (Kasai), Cuilo (Kwilu) and Cuango rivers are known more for their importance to the DRC than for their upper reaches in Angola, although many tributaries of the Kasai intersect the Angolan plateau, exposing rich deposits of alluvial diamonds in the Lunda provinces.

Angola has a tropical climate, locally tempered by altitude. The Benguela current, along the coast, influences and reduces rainfall in that part of the country which is arid or semi-arid. The interior uplands in the Bié, Huambo and Huíla provinces enjoy an equable climate. On the other hand, along the Cuanza river, in the north-west and north-east, and in the eastern and southern provinces, high temperatures and heavy seasonal rainfall discouraged European colonization wherever there were no economic incentives, such as coffee in the provinces of Zaire and Uíge, and diamonds in Lunda.

POPULATION

Angola is an underpopulated country, with only 5,646,166 inhabitants enumerated at the 1970 census, when the popula-tion density was 4.5 persons per sq km. By mid-1997, when the population was officially estimated at 12,240,000, the density had risen to 9.8 persons per sq km. Angola is overwhelmingly rural and has considerable ethnic diversity, although all indigenous groups, of which the Ovimbundu and Mbundu are the most numerous, are of Bantu stock. An important characteristic of the population is its youth, as 45% are under 15 years old and only 5% are over 60. According to UN estimates, the average life expectancy at birth in 1990–95 was 46.5 years. In 1990–98 Angola's population increased at an average annual rate of 3.8%.

Since the onset of civil strife in the mid-1970s, Angola has experienced considerable economic dislocation, accompanied by a widespread regrouping of African populations, brought about by insecurity and massacres. There has also been general movement from cities to rural areas. In the late 1980s less than 25% of the population were believed to be residing in urban centres of more than 2,000 inhabitants. The population is predominantly engaged in food-crop farming and, in the south, in cattle-raising. Only in areas where coffee, cotton and maize are cultivated are Africans engaged to any extent in commercial agriculture. Almost three-quarters of the economically active population were employed in the agricultural sector in 1997. Since the mid-1980s, government-controlled towns and villages have, over large parts of the country, co-existed with regroupings of guerrilla-controlled populations sheltered in shifting villages: this has applied mostly to the south-east, east and north-east. Serious food shortages and periods of famine have periodically beset central and southern Angola during the years of post-independence strife. The war has also created problems of 'internal' refugees (estimated to number up to 1.2m. people), while in the late 1980s it was estimated that more than 500,000 Angolans had fled to neighbouring countries.

The population of the capital, Luanda (which was 480,613 at the 1970 census), was estimated to have risen to 1.3m. by 1986. Outside the capital, most urban centres are operating at a reduced level, some having been partially destroyed or looted. Benguela and Lobito (the outlet of the Benguela railway, which has been effectively out of operation since 1975) have felt the impact of war, and Lobito harbour is still suffering from the disruption of traffic with the DRC and Zambia. It was expected that the rehabilitation of the Lobito corridor, which will benefit both cities, would be expedited following the eventual restoration of a unified central administration. Huambo, formerly an important centre for rail traffic to the eastern regions, and to the DRC and Zambia, and for road traffic to Luanda and Namibia, should again become a focal point of economic activity. Other centres, such as Namibe, Lubango, Kuito and Luena, have also suffered from the war and local disorder. The city of Cabinda has benefited from the exploitation of offshore petroleum resources, while pioneer towns such as Menongue and Saurimo may eventually assume new importance as regional centres.

Recent History

MAREK GARZTECKI

Based on an earlier article by João Gomes Cravinho

INDEPENDENCE AND CIVIL WAR

The period preceding its independence in 1975 bestowed the former Portuguese colony of Angola with four competing nationalist movements, none of which was able to assert its supremacy over the others. They comprised the Movimento Popular de Libertação de Angola (MPLA), the Frente Nacional de Libertação de Angola (FNLA), the União Nacional para a Independência Total de Angola (UNITA) and the Frente para a Libertação do Enclave de Cabinda (FLEC). The divisions between the groups stemmed from a combination of factors, including the ethnic and social origins of their respective leaderships, their ideologies and the concomitant international patronage that they received.

The MPLA, a successor to the oldest Angolan anti-colonialist movement, the Partido da Luta Unida dos Africanos de Angola, was considered to be dominated by the Mbundu people, who inhabited (and continue to inhabit) the area around the capital, Luanda. Although it aimed to represent all Angolans, the MPLA's programme primarily reflected the views of the urban intellectuals, mostly *assimilados* (the Europeanized Africans granted Portuguese citizenship) and *mestiços* (people of mixed African and European descent), as personified by its first leader, Mário de Andrade. From its inception in 1956, the MPLA displayed a strong leftist orientation as well as links with the Portuguese Communist Party. These proclivities led to substantial material support from the countries of the Soviet bloc. Being most exposed, because of its urban base, to Portuguese anti-nationalist repression, the MPLA was significantly bolstered by the appointment, as president of the movement, in 1974 of Dr Agostinho Neto, an *assimilado* Mbundu and former political prisoner.

As the name of the FNLA's predecessor, the União das Populações do Norte de Angola, indicates, the movement was established in 1962 initially to represent the interests of the Bakongo people living in the north of Angola. Although it later abandoned the phrase 'do Norte', the organization continued to retain strong links with the Bakongo of Zaire (now the Democratic Republic of the Congo—DRC), which were cemented by family ties between its leader, Holden Roberto, and the Zairean leader, Mobutu Sese Seko. Largely as a result of Mobutu's high standing among Western powers, the FNLA was able to secure US assistance, which increased as the days of the Portuguese colonial empire were coming to an end. Following an anti-Portuguese uprising, the FNLA formed an Angolan government-in-exile, the Governo Revolucionário de Angola no Exílio (GRAE).

The third major nationalist movement, UNITA, was formed in 1966, following the defection from the FNLA/GRAE of representatives of the Ovimbundu people, led by Jonas Savimbi. The most numerous among the Angolan tribes, the Ovimbundu populate mainly the rural areas of the country's central Bie plateau. More traditional in their cultural outlook, most Ovimbundu leaders retained their African names, unlike their more urban MPLA counterparts who usually adopted Portuguese ones. With the two superpowers of the USSR and the USA already committed to other Angolan nationalist movements, UNITA turned for support to the People's Republic of China. As well as the receipt of arms deliveries and direct military training from China, UNITA also embraced the Maoist military doctrine and party-political structure.

The smallest of the Angolan nationalist movements, FLEC, never actually aspired to broaden its appeal beyond its regional base in the Cabinda enclave. Its secessionist programme precluded alliances with any of the other movements, as they all supported, at least in theory, Angola's territorial integrity. FLEC's key personalities included António Eduardo Sozinho, representing the Mayombe ethnic minority, and Henriques N'zita Tiago.

Each organization had a military wing, in the case of the MPLA entitled the Forças Armadas Populares de Libertação de Angola (FAPLA) and in the FNLA's case the Exército de Libertação Nacional de Angola (ELNA), all of which engaged in armed struggle against Portuguese colonial rule. The differences between the movements as well as within them, however, seriously restricted their effectiveness. Angola's progress towards independence was substantially bolstered by the *coup d'état* in Portugal in April 1974, itself a product of popular dissatisfaction with colonial wars in Africa. Fighting between the nationalists and the Portuguese army, which had been ongoing since the early 1960s, ceased and all the nationalist organizations were permitted to operate legally. On 10 January 1975 at a meeting in Alvor, Portugal, an agreement was reached between the representatives of the MPLA, UNITA, the FNLA and the Portuguese government, establishing the date for Angola's independence as 11 November 1975, and allowing for the formation of a transitional Angolan government. Headed by a Portuguese high commissioner, the 'government of national unity' consisted principally of representatives of the MPLA, UNITA and the FNLA, to the exclusion not only of FLEC but of some smaller groups as well. The new administration also disregarded the interests of the white population of Angola, which numbered some 335,000 at the time. By mid-1975 the fragile governing coalition had started to disintegrate, falling victim to serious internal differences as well as to the growing superpower rivalry in which the Angolans played the role of proxies. The pro-Western FNLA, seen at the time as the strongest of the three nationalist movements, was the recipient of a US $300,000-grant from the USA, and also benefited from a covert mercenary recruitment campaign directed by the US Central Intelligence Agency (CIA). In response, the USSR provided the MPLA forces with substantial military aid, which was followed by the clandestine arrival of Cuban military instructors in Angola. In early June heavy fighting broke out between MPLA and FNLA forces in Luanda, and rapidly spread to other major towns. By the end of that month the FNLA had been ejected from the capital, while the MPLA had been forced out of the northern provinces of Uige and Zaire, with UNITA drawn into the conflict on the side of the FNLA. The pro-MPLA stance of the Portuguese administration helped to tilt the balance further between the movements. When the transitional government in Luanda collapsed in August, the positions vacated by the FNLA and UNITA were allocated to the MPLA nominees. By early October more Cuban military personnel, estimated at between 1,100 and 1,500 combat troops, had arrived, helping the MPLA to gain control of 12 of the country's 16 provincial capitals. Meanwhile, in August South African forces entered Angola, in support of the FNLA-UNITA alliance, and occupied the Ruacana hydroelectric complex on the boundary Cunene River. This was followed, on 23 October, by an invasion of more than 3,000 South African-led troops, which rapidly advanced to within 100 km of Luanda. The South African intervention prompted an immediate massive inflow of Soviet arms and Cuban troops. It also resulted in a significant decline in international support for the FNLA and UNITA, especially among their former African backers, weary of the MPLA's overtly pro-communist stance.

Angolan independence was declared, as originally planned, on 11 November 1975; however, the country found itself divided by two competing administrations. While the MPLA declared the creation of the People's Republic of Angola in Luanda, with Dr Agostinho Neto as president of the newly-independent state, the FNLA and UNITA proclaimed the establishment of the Democratic People's Republic of Angola in Huambo (formerly Nova Lisboa), the country's second largest city. By the beginning of 1976 the MPLA had gained the upper hand, bolstered by the support of some 10,000 Cuban troops and an estimated US $200m. worth of Soviet arms. By the end of February the forces of the FNLA and its mercenaries in northern Angola had been decisively defeated, and in the following month South African troops, under international pressure, withdrew into Namibia and UNITA was forced out of Huambo.

Despite its military success, the MPLA government faced considerable difficulties. Angola's infrastructure had been damaged by the war, the administration had ceased to function and the economy had collapsed. The exodus of the Portuguese population, who represented a significant proportion of the skilled work-force, as well as the massive internal displacement of the remaining population served only to worsen the situation. The MPLA itself had come under severe strain from factionalism and internal dissension, exacerbated by an increasingly orthodox communist stance adopted by the dominant grouping led by Dr Agostinho Neto. At a plenum of its central committee in October 1976, the MPLA formally adopted Marxism-Leninism. The transformation was completed in December 1977, when the first congress expanded the name of the movement to MPLA—Partido do Trabalho (Party of Labour) (MPLA—PT), and proclaimed it a vanguard party of the working classes. The internal opposition to the Neto group included the Active Revolt faction, which comprised several intellectuals and more senior MPLA leaders, including the movement's first president, Mario de Andrade, as well as the so-called *Nitistas* faction, led by the minister of the interior, Nito Alves, and central committee member, Fernando José Franca van Dúnem. *Nitistas* considered the government's economic policies too moderate and denounced the perceived over-representation of whites and *mesticos* in the leadership. A bloody power struggle ensued in May 1977, during which *Nitistas* was responsible for the deaths of a number of senior government leaders. Nitistas were, however, defeated, following the intervention in support of Neto's faction of Cuban troops stationed in Angola. A thorough purge of the MPLA—PT followed, during which the party lost more than two-thirds of its membership.

The cornerstone of Angolan foreign policy after 1976 was a close relationship with the Soviet bloc countries, although the MPLA—PT regime consistently denied that it was a communist client state. In October 1976 the Angolan government signed a Treaty of Friendship and Co-operation with the USSR, which gave the latter the right to use Angolan airports and harbours for military purposes. The government also attempted to improve its relations with Angola's immediate neighbours. As a result, Zambia undertook to expel UNITA forces operating from its territory. Relations with Zaire (now the Democratic Republic of Congo, DRC), however, remained tense, and deteriorated during 1977, following two incursions from Angola into Zaire's Shaba (Katanga) province by forces of the Zairean anti-Mobutu Front National pour la Libération du Congo. As a result of Western pressure, the Mobutu and MPLA—PT governments eventually agreed in 1978 not to support each other's opponents. The expulsion from Zaire in 1979 of the leaders of the FNLA and FLEC strengthened the international position of the MPLA—PT regime.

The United Kingdom opened an embassy in Luanda in 1977. Relations between Angola and Portugal remained under strain until 1978, when the two countries resolved most of their remaining differences. Full diplomatic relations with France and the Federal Republic of Germany were established in 1979. Angola also became an active member of the alliance of the 'front-line states', which opposed the apartheid regime in power in South Africa. The African National Congress (ANC) and the South-West Africa People's Organisation (SWAPO) both opened offices in Luanda. SWAPO, fighting for the independence of South African-occupied Namibia was allowed to establish bases on territory controlled by the MPLA—PT. These factors, combined with increasingly open South African support for UNITA, led to increasing confrontation between the MPLA—PT and South Africa.

As a result of the party's new Marxist-Leninist programme, but also in response to the economic crisis caused by the war and the emigration of skilled Portuguese workers, the MPLA—PT introduced a policy of state interventionism and wide-scale nationalization. The damage to the agricultural sector, which employed about 75% of the economically active population, was aggravated by the ongoing 'hit-and-run' operations of UNITA in rural areas. Although Angola, once a food exporter, was forced to rely increasingly on imports, the overall economic position of the MPLA—PT regime improved following discoveries of petroleum reserves in the area under its control. In an attempt to attract foreign capital to the sector, legislation offering substantial investment incentives was introduced. Increasingly, the interests of multinational petroleum companies also started to influence the attitudes of Western governments towards Luanda.

Substantial political changes, starting in December 1978, cemented the ascendancy of Dr Agostinho Neto and those loyal to him. The posts of prime minister and deputy prime minister were abolished in that month, giving Neto direct control over the government, while the ethnic composition of the MPLA—PT political bureau was significantly altered by the appointment of several non-Mbundu members. Improved party cohesion allowed the smooth transfer of power (as leader of the MPLA—PT and state president) to José Eduardo dos Santos following Neto's death in Septmber 1979. Despite his Soviet education, and the opposition of the more dogmatic MPLA—PT 'old guard' dos Santos continued to pursue the more pragmatic economic policies of his predecessor. He also promoted a number of moderate and more Western-orientated ministers to the party's central committee.

CONFLICT WITH SOUTH AFRICA AND THE RESURGENCE OF UNITA

On the military front, the Angolan government was coming under increasing threat from the UNITA guerrilla campaign and South African military incursions. UNITA was able to revive its activities because of the tenacity and high discipline of its forces, strengthened by regular purges of dissenters, and the continued loyalty of its traditional, primarily Ovimbundu constituency. Savimbi, was able to capitalize on the fact that neither the MPLA—PT nor the Luanda government had a single Ovimbundu in a position of leadership. Following the precepts of his Maoist teachers, Savimbi always considered the rural areas to be UNITA's natural environment. He also made a point of operating from within Angolan territory, unlike the exiled leaders of the FNLA.

A key element to UNITA's survival, however, was the South African military and logistical support that it received. The South African government in Pretoria felt threatened by the continuing presence of a large number of Cuban forces in Angola and resented the MPLA—PT's backing of SWAPO. The South African Defence Forces (SADF) established support bases for UNITA in Cuando-Cubango province, while the South African air force provided air cover for Savimbi's headquarters in Jamba. From the late 1970s the SADF regularly launched minor incursions into Angola in pursuit of SWAPO guerrillas, culminating in a violent raid on a Namibian refugee camp at Cassinga in May 1978. The most significant act of military escalation was 'Operation Protea' in August 1981, in which several thousand SADF troops advanced some 120 km into Angola. From the early 1980s an undeclared war between South Africa and Angola was in full force.

Armed incursions by South Africa were accompanied by an escalation in the activities of UNITA, which assumed a more prominent military role, expanding its operations in eastern Angola while the government deployed its main forces in the west against 'Operation Protea'. Throughout 1982 and 1983 the SADF and UNITA together intensified their activities in Angola, with the South Africans occupying large sections of Cunene province, while UNITA launched attacks on a wide variety of targets. In August 1983 the conflict sharply escalated when a large UNITA force captured the strategic town of Cangamba in Moxico province, with the aid of intense aerial bombardment by the South African air force. This type of operation was increasingly difficult to justify as a 'hot-pursuit' action against SWAPO, and was clearly aimed at destabilizing the MPLA—PT government.

To counter the threat, the Angolan government continued to diversify its international contacts, establishing formal relations with the People's Republic of China in 1983 and closer links with the European Community (EC, now the European Union—EU). The petroleum industry, the country's economic mainstay, continued to prosper. At least 50% of the government's revenue from the petroleum sector was spent on defence and security, including the procurement of increasingly sophisticated military equipment. In July 1983 regional military councils were established in all areas affected by the fighting, concentrating all state power in the hands of military officers, directly responsible to the president. This increased the efficiency of FAPLA, which now constituted the country's official armed forces.

In January 1984 South Africa offered to withdraw its troops in exchange for Angola's restraining SWAPO's activities. This proposal, which was formulated in February and known as the Lusaka Accord, was conditional on South Africa granting independence to Namibia, in accordance with the UN Security Council's Resolution 435. Following the signing of the Lusaka Accord, the SADF officially withdrew from Angola in April 1985. The following month, however, a unit of its special forces was captured while engaged in operations against petroleum installations in Cabinda. The SADF's 'hot-pursuit' incursions into Angola were resumed in June 1985.

The ebbs and flows of the conflict reflected internal factors as much as the wider context of superpower rivalry. The USA, while negotiating the Lusaka Accord, also attempted to weaken the USSR and Cuba, the principal supporters of the MPLA—PT government. US views converged with those of the South African government, that the SADF's withdrawal from Angola and the creation of an independent Namibia should be linked to a legally-binding, complete withdrawal of Cuban troops from Angola. The advent of a new Republican administration in the USA, led by Ronald Reagan, in 1980 led to a reversal in US policy towards UNITA. The US government's belief that the Angolan government should be sufficiently weakened in order to force the Cubans' departure, brought about a period of rapidly increasing US military support for UNITA. In January 1986 during a visit to the USA, which included a well-publicized meeting with President Reagan, Savimbi was treated in a manner befitting a head of state. UNITA's efforts to achieve a similar degree of recognition in Europe, however, proved largely unsuccessful. The Angolan government initially tried to apply pressure on the US government, lodging a complaint in April with the UN secretary-general requesting that the role of the USA as primary mediator in Namibian independence negotiations be terminated. In August, however, the Angolan government approached the US administration directly, with a view to improving relations. These overtures proved to be largely unsuccessful.

UNITA's efforts to boost its international profile continued with an offer, made in March 1987, to allow non-military traffic to operate on the Benguela railway. Providing the shortest link for Zambia and the Zairean province of Shaba to the sea, the railway had been closed since 1977 as a result of persistent sabotage by UNITA. However, the sincerity of UNITA's offer was put into question in June 1987, when it renewed its attacks on the line.

In April 1987 representatives of the MPLA—PT administration and the US government resumed efforts to solve the interlinked issues of Namibian independence and the withdrawal of third-party forces from Angola. Negotiations were held, without much success, until July and were then resumed in January 1988. The readiness of the MPLA—PT to establish good relations with the USA was reflected in the change in direction of the party's economic policy, indicated in August by Angola's application for membership of the International Monetary Fund (IMF).

In October 1987 South Africa admitted, for the first time, that it was maintaining a 'limited presence' inside Angola, and in the following month it confirmed that it was providing military support to UNITA, and had engaged in direct military action against Soviet and Cuban forces stationed there. South Africa's intensification of aggression against Angola was widely condemned and in late November the UN Security Council demanded the unconditional withdrawal of South African troops from Angola within two weeks. Despite agreeing to comply with this demand, South Africa nevertheless continued its military incursions into Angola. These were matched by a massive escalation of UNITA operations in the countryside, which led to the displacement of hundreds of thousands of peasants and caused a dramatic decline in food production.

TOWARDS A REGIONAL ACCORD

Continuous military activity throughout 1987 and 1988 provided the background to various efforts to end the conflict, including a meeting in Luanda between representatives of Angola, Cuba and the USA in March 1988, as well as separate negotiations between South Africa and UNITA, and the USA and the USSR. In May 1988 Cuba and Angola held 'exploratory talks' with South Africa in London, with the USA as mediator. In the mean time the security situation worsened considerably as both sides tried to strengthen their bargaining position. UNITA, which was excluded from the London meeting and subsequent consultations, initiated a diplomatic campaign in major Western capitals to advance its terms for an Angolan settlement.

On 22 December 1988 the participants in the negotiations met in New York, where a bilateral agreement was signed by Angola and Cuba, and a tripartite accord by Angola, Cuba and South Africa. Under these agreements, 1 April 1989 was designated as the date of the implementation of the Namibian independence process, which was to culminate in elections to a constituent assembly from 1 November. In addition, Cuba undertook to complete a phased withdrawal of its estimated 50,000 troops from Angola by July 1991. Angola, Cuba and South Africa were to establish a joint commission, in which the USA and the USSR would be present as observers. All prisoners of war were to be exchanged and the signatories of the tripartie accord were to refrain from supporting forces intent on undermining each other's governments. The latter clause necessitated both the curtailment of South African aid to UNITA and the departure from Angola of an estimated 6,000 members of the ANC. In accordance with the agreements, the UN Security Council authorized the creation of a UN Angola Verification Mission (UNAVEM) to monitor the redeployment and withdrawal of Cuban troops. UNAVEM commenced operations in January 1989 with a mandate for a period of 31 months.

The New York accords ended South African involvement in Angolan affairs, but failed to resolve the internal conflict in Angola. The MPLA—PT government continued to reject UNITA's appeals for a cease-fire, instead offering the rebel organization, in early February 1989, a 12-month amnesty, in an atttempt to reassimilate defectors from UNITA into society. However, UNITA, reiterating its own aim of negotiating a settlement with the government that would lay the foundations for a multi-party democracy in Angola, responded by launching a major offensive against FAPLA targets. In March, following a statement by President dos Santos declaring his willingness to find a resolution to the conflict, Savimbi announced UNITA's intention to honour a unilateral moratorium on offensive military operations until mid-July to facilitate outside mediation. Savimbi also offered to exclude himself from any peace negotiations, in an attempt to make them more acceptable to the dos Santos government.

In June 1989, however, both Savimbi and dos Santos attended a conference in Gbadolite, Zaire, organized by President Mobutu, where they agreed to hold direct negotiations and eventually signed a cease-fire accord. A commission to monitor the implementation of the peace agreement was established, including the presidents of the Congo Republic, Gabon and Zaire. The full terms of the accord were not, however, made public at that time and it soon became clear that these were interpreted differently by each party. Claims by the Angolan government that Savimbi had agreed to go into temporary exile and that members of UNITA were to be absorbed into existing MPLA—PT-run institutions and to respect the official constitution were strongly denied by the rebels. Within one week each side had accused the other of violating the cease-fire. In late August Savimbi announced a resumption of hostilities.

In September 1989, after boycotting a conference in Kinshasa, Zaire, at which the Gbadolite Accord had been redrafted, Savimbi announced a series of counter-proposals, envisaging the creation of an African peace-keeping force to supervise a renewed cease-fire, and the commencement of direct negotiations between UNITA and the MPLA—PT government. A series of talks between the two sides, some of which were mediated by Mobutu, took place between the two sides, some of which were mediated by Mobutu, took place between October 1989 and early 1991. In mid-January 1990 Cuba temporarily suspended its troop withdrawal, following an attack by UNITA which resulted in the deaths of four Cuban soldiers. From February to May the Mavinga area in the south-eastern Cuando-Cubango province became the focus of intense military activity.

THE ESTORIL PEACE AGREEMENT

The MPLA—PT government and UNITA both made significant political concessions during 1990. In May UNITA recognized dos Santos as head of state, and in October it accepted the MPLA—PT government as an interim administration, pending elections. At an historic meeting of the MPLA—PT central committee in late June and early July, the country's evolution towards a multi-party political system, which had long been one of UNITA's principal demands, was finally accepted. Further reforms, including the replacement of the party's Marxist-Leninist ideology with a commitment to 'democratic socialism', the introduction of a market economy, the legalization of political parties, the transformation of the army from a party to a state institution, and a revision of the constitution were formally approved at the MPLA—PT congress in December. The legalization of political parties, which was passed by the People's Assembly in March 1991, paved the way for the final round of talks between UNITA and the government. On 1 May 1991 a peace agreement was signed by the two sides in Estoril, Portugal. The agreement provided for a cease-fire from midnight on 15 May, which was to be monitored by a joint political and military committee comprising representatives from the MPLA—PT, UNITA, the UN, Portugal, the USA and the USSR. Immediately following the cease-fire, the provision of aid from abroad to the warring parties was to cease and a new national army was to be established, composed of equal numbers of FAPLA and UNITA soldiers. Free and democratic elections were to be held by the end of 1992, and refugees and exiles were to be allowed to return to Angola.

The legalization of opposition parties in March 1991 prompted the emergence of numerous political groups. Among the most influential of these were the Associação Cívica Angolana, which was expected to deflect votes from the MPLA—PT and the Forum Democrático Angolano, which was considered a rival to UNITA for electoral support. The legislation stipulated that political parties must enjoy support in at least 14 of Angola's 18 provinces, in order to discourage the emergence of ethnically-based political movements. This measure effectively exluded the Cabinda-based FLEC from the democratic process.

Implementation of the Estoril peace accord was subject to considerable delay in its initial stages. At the end of September 1991 Savimbi returned to Luanda for the first time since the civil war began in 1975, and UNITA headquarters were transferred to the capital from Jamba in October 1991. Despite the appointment of Gen. João Baptista de Matos, commander of FAPLA's ground troops, and Gen. Abilo Kamalata 'Numa', commander of UNITA's northern front, as joint supreme commanders of the united armed forces in January 1992, concerns were expressed following reports of the declining number of government and UNITA troops in the confinement areas and the reoccupation of territory by rebel forces. The demobilized soldiers from both armies were blamed for rising levels of criminal activity. By the end of March it was reported that 94% of UNITA's forces and 64% of FAPLA's had gathered at assembly points. There were reports, however, that both sides planned to keep some forces in reserve, and that the demobilization process and the creation of a unified national army could fall behind schedule.

Multi-party Politics and the 1992 Elections

Evidence of serious divisions within UNITA became apparent in early March 1992, with the announcement that two leading members, Gen. Miguel N'Zau Puna and Gen. Tony da Costa Fernandes, had resigned. It was alleged by UNITA that both men supported the secession of Cabinda (the petroleum-producing exclave) from Angola. After having denounced Savimbi's dictatorial tendencies and claimed that he was maintaining substantial clandestine troops near the Namibian border, Puna and Fernandes formed a 'Democratic Breakaway Tendency' to attract UNITA dissidents. This added to persistent reports of bloody purges and 'disappearances' of Savimbi's opponents or rivals within UNITA. Amongst those who 'disappeared' were UNITA's former chief of staff, Waldemar Chindondo, and Sav-

imbi's former business representative, Jorge Ornelas Sangumba.

The Partido Renovador Democrático, regarded as the third largest of the 30 or more political parties that had been formed since the introduction of a multi-party system, held its first congress in late April 1992, and immediately afterwards divided into two factions. At an extraordinary congress of the MPLA—PT, held in early May, delegates voted to readmit a number of prominent ex-dissidents, and removed the suffix 'Partido do Trabalho' from the party's official name.

In August 1992 a constitutional revision took effect, removing the remants of the country's former Marxist ideology, and deleting the worlds 'People's' and 'Popular' from the constitution and from the names of offical institutions. The name of the country was changed from the People's Republic of Angola to the Republic of Angola.

On 27 September 1992 FAPLA and the UNITA forces were formally disbanded, and the new 50,000-strong national army, the Forças Armadas de Angola (FAA), was officially established. From the very beginning the process of its creation proved to be arduous and prone to delays. Tens of thousands of government troops were reported to be awaiting demobilization or to have abandoned confinement areas, owing to poor conditions and non-payment of wages. It also became apparent that only a small percentage of UNITA forces had been demobilized, and that Savimbi could still call on a heavily-armed and disciplined force. UNITA had deliberately slowed the process of demobilizing its soldiers, in protest at the formation of a new government paramilitary unit, the 'emergency police', recruited from the MPLA's own special forces.

Increased tension and outbreaks of violence prior to the general elections seriously threatened to disrupt the electoral process. Nevertheless, presidential and legislative elections took place, as scheduled, on 29–30 September 1992, with dos Santos, Savimbi, and the FNLA president, Holden Roberto, among the 12 registered presidential candidates. Despite fears of violence and intimidation, the level of participation was high, averaging almost 90% of the electorate. Only in Cabinda, where FLEC had urged its supporters to boycott the election, was a low turn-out reported. International observers judged the conduct of the elections to have been free and fair. This assessment was, however, questioned by Savimbi, when the preliminary results indicated that the MPLA had obtained a majority of seats in the new national assembly. He demanded the suspension of the official announcement of the results and an inquiry into the alleged electoral irregularities. On 5 October UNITA withdrew from the FAA. According to the official election results, published on 17 October, dos Santos received 49.57% of the total votes cast in the presidential election, just short of the 50% required to avoid a second round against Savimbi, who secured 40.07%. In the legislative elections the MPLA won 129 of the 220 seats in the national assembly, compared with 70 for UNITA. Ten other parties won between one and six seats each. UNITA's share of the total vote was 34.1%, compared with the MPLA's 53.7%. Savimbi, who had withdrawn to the UNITA-dominated province of Huambo, had agreed to participate in a second round of presidential elections on the condition that it be monitored by the UN. The government, on the other hand, insisted that the election should not take place until UNITA had conformed to the rules of the Estoril peace agreement by transferring its troops to assembly points and by returning to the FAA.

RESUMPTION OF CIVIL STRIFE

Following the announcement of the official election results, violence erupted between MPLA and UNITA supporters in various cities, including Luanda and Huambo, and by October 1992 hostilities had spread throughout the country. While the MPLA accused UNITA of renewing the hostilities and rearming the majority of its soldiers, government supporters conducted an effective hunt for opposition supporters in towns under its control. As a result, some 1,000 people were killed, including a number of senior UNITA officials.

During November and December 1992 there was growing international pressure on both sides in the renewed conflict to cease hostilities and comply with the terms of the Estoril peace agreement. This included visits to Angola by the UN under-secretary-general for peace-keeping operations, Marrack Goulding, and by the US deputy assistant secretary of state for African affairs, Jeffrey Davidow. While the second round of the presidential elections was postponed indefinitely, the newly-elected national assembly convened on 26 November. It elected as its president an MPLA veteran and former prime minister, Fernando José França van-Dúnem. The 70 elected UNITA parliamentarians refused to take their seats, claiming that to convene the assembly in the absence of an elected state president was illegal. This, however, did not prevent dos Santos from nominating the secretary-general of the MPLA, Marcolino José Carlos Moco, as the new prime minister. The majority of the posts in Moco's council of ministers were assigned to members of the MPLA, with four smaller parties also represented. UNITA was allocated one ministerial and four deputy ministerial posts, despite the fact that outside the capital Savimbi's forces were again engaged in full combat with government troops.

The situation in Angola throughout 1993 and 1994 was characterized by continuous efforts by the UN to broker a permanent peace accord between the government and UNITA. Meanwhile, civil war in which both sides claimed military gains and suffered heavy losses, continued. Initially UNITA made considerable military gains, as the FAA was in the process of being established following the mass desertions of former FAPLA conscripts. Already in control of most of the Angolan countryside, UNITA laid siege to and captured a number of major cities, including Huambo and Kuito. Eventually the FAA repulsed the UNITA forces and retook most of the towns, but at the cost of heavy casualties. During the two-month battle of Huambo alone some 10,000 people were thought to have died. Vast tracts of the country were made uninhabitable and thousands were seriously injured as a result of the large-scale laying of land-mines, which were also a factor in the internal displacement of more than 2m. Angolans. In June 1993 the UN secretary-general's special representative in Angola, Margaret Anstee, estimated the cost of urgent humanitarian aid required in Angola to be in excess of US $227m. Diplomatic moves to end the hostilities included unsuccessful talks in Addis Ababa, Ethiopia, convened by the UN in January 1993, abortive talks in Abidjan, Côte d'Ivoire, in April–May, and finally lengthy negotiations in Lusaka, Zambia, which commenced in early 1994. Gradually, a view was formed among the international observers that the principal reason for the failure of negotiations laid with UNITA and its leader. Savimbi was accused of continuously raising new conditions and objections to procedures that had already been agreed upon. Although stalling on peace negotiations often helped UNITA to preserve some military gains, it also resulted in the erosion of international support for the rebel movement. In mid-May 1993 the USA announced its decision to recognize the Angolan government, and in the same month South Africa reopened its representative office in Luanda (diplomatic relations between Angola and South Africa were upgraded to ambassadorial level in June). In August the United Kingdom lifted its embargo on arms deliveries to the government, which had been in force since 1975. The government's case was helped by the advent of the administration of President Bill Clinton in the USA, which did not share the pro-UNITA sympathies of its predecessors. The end of the white apartheid regime in South Africa and the rise to power of the ANC also increased UNITA's isolation.

The UNAVEM Missions and Attempts at *Rapprochement*

In order to apply pressure on UNITA the UN imposed a number of sanctions on the rebels, including an embargo on the sales of arms and petroleum, the 'freezing' of UNITA's foreign assets, and the expulsion of its representatives from Western capitals. To monitor compliance with the agreed peace measures, the UN also established UNAVEM II in 1993. By appearing to concede, from time to time, to the UN's key demands, UNITA was able to postpone the introduction of sanctions for almost three years. A lack of adequate co-operation from the Angolan government as well as from UNITA, however, severely limited the effectiveness of UNAVEM II. A peace accord, which had been agreed upon by the combatants on 31 October 1994, during the talks in Lusaka, was formally signed on 20 November by UNITA's secretary-general, Eugénio Antonio Ngolo Manuvakola, and the government's minister of foreign affairs, Dr Venâncio da Silva Moura. The chief of general staff of the FAA, Gen. João Baptista

de Matos, and his UNITA counterpart, Gen. Arlindo Chenda Isaac Pena 'Ben-Ben', meeting in Chipipa, in Huambo province, in January 1995, agreed to the immediate cessation of hostilities and the disengagement of troops. Despite these undertakings hostilities persisted.

In early February 1995 the UN Security Council adopted Resolution 976 creating UNAVEM III. The new mission was to comprise a military peace-keeping force of some 7,000 troops, in addition to 350 military observers, 260 police observers and some 350 civilian staff. Its deployment, however, was conditional on the cessation of hostilities and the disengagement of government and UNITA forces. A critical report to the UN Security Council by the UN secretary-general, Dr Boutros Boutros-Ghali, published in March 1995 accused UNITA and the government of a lack of good will in implementing the peace process. As a result of mediation by the UN secretary-general's special representative in Angola, Alioune Blondin Beye, Savimbi and dos Santos met in early May in Lusaka for direct talks. Addressing dos Santos as president of Angola, Savimbi officially accepted dos Santos' election as head of state and pledged his full co-operation in national reconstruction. Dos Santos requested that Savimbi nominate immediately the UNITA appointees to a new government of national unity. Savimbi was also offered one of two vice-presidential posts that were to be created. In the following months UNAVEM III was able to confirm that recorded cease-fire violations had decreased by approximately 50% between July and September.

In late September 1995 the government signed a four-month cease-fire agreement with FLEC—Renovada (FLEC—R), a breakaway faction of the main FLEC separatist movement in Cabinda province. It was anticipated that the agreement, which followed an offensive by FLEC—R on Cabinda City in the previous month, would facilitate negotiations between the government and all factions of FLEC over terms for a pact of national reconciliation.

The cantonment of UNITA forces officially began in late November 1995. However, continued hostilities were reported that month, including confrontations in the diamond-producing areas of the north-east and in the Cabinda enclave. In early December, following concerted military operations by government forces aimed at occupying UNITA-controlled territory in Zaire province, Savimbi suspended the confinement of his troops. In an effort to rebuild foundering confidence in the peace process, dos Santos ordered the withdrawal of government troops from positions seized in Zaire province. He also cancelled the government's contract with Executive Outcomes, a South African company ostensibly providing military advisers to give logistical support to the FAA, but condemned by UNITA as mercenaries in active service, in direct contravention of the Lusaka Accord, which forbids mercenary support for either side.

In March 1996, at discussions held in Libreville, Gabon, dos Santos and Savimbi agreed on terms for the establishment of a government of national unity and reconciliation, in accordance with the provisions of the Lusaka Accord. Savimbi presented a proposal listing UNITA's governmental nominees. However, he made their participation conditional on the inclusion of other opposition parties in the government, most notably the president of the FNLA, Holden Roberto. In May Savimbi introduced further conditions, such as the retention under UNITA control of the country's diamond-producing areas in north-eastern Angola.

In mid-May 1996 the government and one of the Cabinda secessionist faction, FLEC—Forças Armadas Cabindesas (FLEC—FAC), signed an agreement outlining the terms of a cease-fire. However, following renewed fighting later that month between government troops and the secessionists, the leader of FLEC—FAC, Henrique N'zita Tiago, declared that a definitive cease-fire would only follow the withdrawal of the FAA from Cabinda.

In mid-1996 public protest at deteriorating economic conditions and at the high level of corruption within the state apparatus placed increasing political pressure on dos Santos, who responded in early June with the replacement of Moco as prime minister by the president of the national assembly and former prime minister, Fernando José França van-Dúnem. In addition, the governor of the Banco Nacional de Angola was dismissed. A new government was sworn in on 8 June, with only four changes to the previous administration. Meanwhile the UNITA leadership was still delaying the full integration of its military forces into the FAA, pending agreement between the two sides over the special status to be accorded to Savimbi, following his earlier rejection of the vice-presidency.

In March 1997 UN officials reported the involvement of both government and UNITA troops in the civil war in Zaire. UNITA, which relied on Zaire as a conduit for exporting diamonds and importing arms, was reported to have sent some 2,000 troops to support its ally and maintain supply lines, while the Angolan government supported the rebels of Laurent-Désiré Kabila. The subsequent capture of Kamina, a Zairian military base of considerable strategic importance to UNITA, by Kabila's forces was believed to have ended any possibility of Savimbi resuming military action against the Angolan government and consequently appeared to remove any remaining obstacles to UNITA fully implementing the Lusaka Accord.

In early April 1997 an agreement was reached to confer on Savimbi the special status of official 'leader of the opposition'. Following the arrival of the full contingent of UNITA deputies and government nominees in Luanda, on April 11 the new government of national unity and reconciliation was inaugurated. The ceremony, attended by 13 foreign heads of state, was conducted in the absence of Savimbi, who had expressed fears for his personal security. UNITA received four ministerial posts, including that of geology and mines, and seven deputy ministerial posts. A further 10 minor political parties were represented in the 87-member government.

In May 1997, following the prompt recognition by Luanda of the Democratic Republic of the Congo (DRC, as Zaire was renamed) and its new government (reflecting the satisfaction of the MPLA at Kabila's victory), the FAA launched an offensive against the UNITA-controlled provinces of Lunda-Sul and Lunda-Norte. UNITA claimed that the FAA was contravening the Lusaka Accord by attempting forcibly to restore its control over the areas. Savimbi reiterated that UNITA would not relinquish control of these diamond-producing regions, which industry sources estimated to have earned UNITA some US $2,000m. since 1992.

Collapse of the Peace Process

On 30 June 1997 the UN Security Council voted unanimously to approve the secretary-general's recommendations that UNAVEM III be disbanded and replaced by a scaled-down operation, the United Nations Observer Mission in Angola (MONUA), with a seven-month mandate to oversee the implementation of the remaining tasks of the Lusaka Accord.

In October 1997 the Angolan government provided decisive military support to the ex-president of the Republic of the Congo, Gen. Denis Sassou-Nguesso, in his military coup against the elected government of President Pascal Lissouba. Angola's involvement was reported to have been prompted by Lissouba's support for FLEC and UNITA forces, which had freely operated from bases in the Congo Republic. Shortly after the installation of the Sassou-Nguesso government, the Angolan administration's continuing efforts to isolate UNITA were furthered by dos Santos at a summit meeting, held in Angola, attended by the presidents of the Congo Republic, the DRC, Angola and Gabon. The meeting served to underline Angola's rapid rise to a position of great influence in the region, in contrast to the dwindling support for UNITA. The Angolan government subsequently issued a warning to Zambia that it would not tolerate the use of its territory as a conduit for arms to UNITA, and threatened Zambia with military intervention.

On 31 October 1992 the UN Security Council finally ordered the implementation of additional sanctions against UNITA, on the grounds that the movement had failed to meet its obligations by the 30 October deadline, as set out under the terms of the peace process. In January 1998 UNITA formally transferred the important Cuango valley diamond mines in Lunda-Norte province to government control. In that month a new schedule was agreed for the implementation of the Lusaka protocol. However, despite repeated assurances to the UN and other international representatives that he would transfer UNITA headquarters to Luanda, Savimbi remained in the UNITA stronghold of Andulo in central Angola at mid-1998. On 31 August the government suspended UNITA's government and parliamentary representatives from office.

On 2 September 1998 a group of five UNITA moderates, who were based in the capital and led by the suspended minister of hotels and tourism, Jorge Alicerces Valentim, issued a manifesto announcing the suspension of Savimbi and the introduction of an interim UNITA leadership, pending a general congress of the party. However, the group, which styled itself UNITA—Renovada (UNITA—R), commanded very limited support among UNITA's leaders in Luanda, while UNITA's secretary-general dismissed the group as irrelevant. Conversely, the government welcomed the development, quickly recognizing the faction and reappointing its supporters to the executive. Following this recognition some senior UNITA figures, among them the movement's chief representative in the joint commission, Isaias Samakuva, left Luanda.

In mid-September 1998 dos Santos announced that his government had ceased dialogue with Savimbi and recognized UNITA—R as the sole and legitimate representative of the movement in negotiations concerning the implementation of the Lusaka peace process. He justified his decision by the fact that the leadership of UNITA—R included the movement's former secretary-general, Euginio Manuvakola, who was the signatory to the Lusaka Accord on behalf of Savimbi. In addition, dos Santos was supported in his decision by the Southern Africa Development Community (SADC), which passed a resolution denouncing Savimbi and recognizing the new group. However, while UNITA—R pledged to implement the Lusaka Peace Accord, observers questioned its ability to influence UNITA members outside of the capital. The UN Security Council continued to seek the resumption of talks between dos Santos and Savimbi as the only solution to the conflict.

In October 1998 the national assembly revoked Savimbi's special status. In that month UNITA—R failed to impose its candidate to lead the UNITA parliamentary group when Abdel Chivukuvuku was overwhelmingly re-elected as its chairman. While no longer claiming allegiance to Savimbi, Chivukuvuku also opposed UNITA—R, and emerged as the informal leader of another faction of UNITA.

The ruling MPLA also succumbed to increasing factional divisions. At its fourth congress in December 1998 dos Santos strengthened his continuing tenure of the party presidency by having his close ally João Manuel Gonçalves Lourenço elected as secretary-general of the MPLA. On the other hand, several senior figures, including former prime ministers Moco, van-Dúnem and Lopo do Nascimento, were removed from the enlarged central committee. This group of veteran MPLA leaders, the *collosi*, began to express growing opposition to the policies of the dos Santos faction, the members of which were referred to as *futungistas* (from the name of the presidential palace, Futungo de Belas). At the end of January 1999 dos Santos reorganized the government, assuming the responsibilities of prime minister, a post he abolished, in line with the constitution, for an 'exceptional period' in order to conduct the war. The reorganization also saw the return to government of Gen. Kundi Paihama as minister of defence. In the same month UNITA—R held its first congress, in Luanda, at which Euginio Manuvakola was elected leader.

The political reshuffles in Luanda were conducted while the military situation within the country worsened dramatically. In addition, following an uprising against Kabila's regime in the DRC in the latter half of 1998, the Angolan government dispatched some 5,000 troops to support its ally in Kinshasa. In early December, at the onset of the dry season, the FAA began its annual offensive against UNITA positions. This followed the established pattern whereby UNITA would gain the upper hand in the wet season, which favoured guerrilla tactics, while the FAA, relying more on heavy armoury and set-piece battles, would try to reverse the situation in the dry season. Government intelligence sources failed to detect that Savimbi's representatives had been selling substantial amounts of diamonds from the mines under their control throughout 1998, and spending the proceeds on substantial arms purchases. FAA generals consequently were surprised to discover that UNITA soldiers were armed, for the first time, with tanks, armoured personnel carriers, and multiple rocket launchers.

Weakened by military reverses, the government accused the UN of failing to monitor UNITA's military preparation. By the beginning of 1999 there was a growing realization that the

UN Angolan operations over the previous four years, despite expenditure of US $1,500m., had proved unsuccessful. On 26 February the UN Security Council voted unanimously to end MONUA's mandate and withdraw its operatives from Angola by 20 March. The move was widely condemned by various non-governmental organizations (NGOs), which claimed that it would hamper their humanitarian efforts to assist the vast numbers of Angolan victims of war. The UN decided, however, to tighten further its sanctions regime against UNITA, following the appointment of Canadian diplomat, Robert Fowler, as chairman of the UN Sanctions Committee. A UN report, which was prepared by Fowler's 10-strong group of experts, after several weeks of investigation, and was published in June, generated some controversy. For the first time the Committee did not shy from 'naming and shaming' those contravening sanctions, listing, amongst others, the presidents of Togo and Burkina Faso as being involved in the trading of arms for UNITA-mined diamonds. The ensuing furore forced the international diamond-buying cartel De Beers to announce a policy of purchasing only legitimately mined gems. The Angolan government, for its part, also attempted to stem the flow of illegal diamonds by introducing a strict regime of stone certification.

Using the revenue from the rapidly increasing number of petroleum concessions, the government decided to attempt to buy its way out of the military stalemate. It secured 'up-front' payments for several years' worth of petroleum production, in deals described as 'mortgaging the future'. One such deal, brokered by the Swiss petroleum trader Glencore, was reported to be worth US $900m., while the total investment in military hardware was estimated to amount to almost $1,500m. It became obvious that dos Santos believed that only a decisive military victory would curb UNITA's activities and bring peace to Angola. This view also seemed to be shared by major international powers. By the end of 1999 Western diplomats, the British in particular, were claiming that the Angolan government should be allowed to conclude the conflict on its own terms, and only then could the country's humanitarian, political and economic issues be addressed. It was widely believed that such views were being fostered by the British, French and US petroleum companies competing for a stage in Angola's fast-growing petroleum sector.

In the second half of 1999, backed by superior air power and intelligence, the FAA made considerable military gains against UNITA. There were also reports of the government using private air surveillance companies, in clear breach of the Lusaka protocols. By the end of October the UNITA headquarters in Bailundo and the military base in Andulo had fallen to government forces, reportedly with heavy losses of military and logistical equipment on the part of UNITA. The latter's defeat was believed to have been partly as a result of anti-Savimbi dissent within its own ranks. The removal and demotion of several experienced UNITA stalwarts such as Gen. Altino Sapalalo 'Bock' and Gen. Abilio Kamalata 'Numa', combined with the promotion of loyal younger, but inexperienced, commanders, who were unable or unwilling to report to headquarters, contributed to Savimbi's

tactical mistakes. By January 2000 UNITA was pronounced, not for the first time, to be finished as a substantial fighting force. The FAA's tactics seemed to be based on attempts to split UNITA into small, isolated units and to negotiate individually their surrender rather than engaging in yet further peace talks with Savimbi. The fall of Bailundo, which is the traditional seat of the principal Ovimbundu *regulos* (tribal kings), significantly weakened Savimbi's claim to represent Angola's largest ethnic group. It also boosted the position of Luanda-based Abel Chivukuvuku, himself a scion of an Ovimbundu *regulo*. Chivukuvuku's appeal across partly-political lines and his skills as a politician, which were clearly illustrated by his parliamentary performances, marked him out as a credible challenger not only to Savimbi but also to dos Santos himself.

In March 2000 another UN report was published, criticizing the leaders of a number of African countries, as well as individuals in Belgium and Bulgaria, for the alleged violation of sanctions that had been imposed in UNITA following the discovery of the trade in illegally-mined diamonds. In response, the Angolan government announced the creation of a state-owned company, which, it was hoped, would centralize and regulate the country's diamond trade.

By early July 2000 the Angolan government claimed that it controlled 92% of the country's 157 districts. The conventional war against Savimbi, according to the official spokesman, Domingos Culolo, was over. Yet even the FAA commander Gen. dos Matos cautioned against easy triumphalism, as UNITA still retained sufficient capacity to mount long-term 'hit-and-run' guerrilla operations. It was widely believed that without a workable final accord between dos Santos and Savimbi there was little chance of concluding Angola's civil war.

At the end of June 2000 it was alleged that secret talks had taken place between the Angolan government and UNITA representatives. These were apparently prompted by a conference on the possible means of achieving peace in Angola, organized by the Mozambican Higher Institute of International Relations in Maputo. The conference was attended by the Angolan deputy minister of foreign affairs, George Chicoti, by Eugenio Manuvakola from UNITA—R and by Abel Chivukuvu. Unofficially, the conference was also reported to have been attended by the MPLA's head of foreign relations, Paulo Jorge, and his UNITA counterpart, Isaias Samakuva. Dos Santos' speech in Caixito on 19 June had also hinted at the possibility of a reconciliation with Savimbi.

In mid-2000 the view from the presidential palace in Luanda seemed to be that UNITA, weakened militarily and split into three factions, should not pose a serious political threat, even if allowed to operate unhampered as a purely political party. As part of this strategy, the government decided to hold a long-delayed general election, hoping to repeat its earlier victory at the ballot box. The creation of a 'Front for Change', however, incorporating 17 minor political parties, as well as the formation of a growing church-based independent peace movement, appeared to indicate the presence of an increasingly vociferous opposition, which was committed to ending the war and holding free and fair elections.

Economy

JOHN HUGHES

Revised for this edition by MAREK GARZTECKI

INTRODUCTION

Prior to independence in 1975, Angola enjoyed a high-output economy, with a rapidly expanding manufacturing sector, near self-sufficiency in agriculture, with crop surpluses for export, and abundant natural resources, such as petroleum and iron ore. The petroleum sector has continued to prosper, but almost all other sectors of the economy are operating at a fraction of pre-independence levels. The civil war that began in 1975 disrupted output, made transport and distribution increasingly difficult and led to the displacement of a large part of the population. Resources were diverted towards defence; in the late 1980s annual defence spending absorbed as much as 48% of the government's total budget expenditure, and following the resumption of hostilities in 1992, the purchase of arms was estimated to have surpassed the levels of the 1980s, with some analysts estimating government expenditure on arms (including unofficial spending) to amount to some 89% of total expenditure.

Assessments of output are uncertain, although, according to estimates by the UN, Angola's gross domestic product (GDP) increased, in real terms, by an average of 3.1% per year in 1980–85, and by 0.9% per year in 1985–95. According to the IMF, GDP increased, in real terms, by an estimated 6.6% in 1997, before decreasing by 1.5% in 1998, and rising again, by 4.0%, in 1999. These figures should be regarded with great caution, however, and it must be remembered that the economy has experienced severe disruption since 1975. Petroleum has become the mainstay of the economy, accounting for an estimated 90% of export earnings in 1997. Mining, of which petroleum is by far the largest component, provided an estimated 45.6% of GDP in 1998. It is estimated, however, that some 70% of the economically active population are dependent on the depressed agricultural sector.

Following independence, the government implemented economic policies based on its Marxist-Leninist ideology. During 1987, however, President dos Santos announced that the government intended to implement major reforms of the economy, aimed at reducing reliance on the state sector, and increasing productivity, purchasing power and consumption levels. In August 1987 dos Santos announced that Angola would seek membership of the International Monetary Fund (IMF) in order to take advantage of Western financial assistance for a programme of economic reform. This economic and financial restructuring programme, the Saneamento Económico e Financeiro (SEF), was instituted on 1 January 1988. The main elements included: a restructuring of state enterprises, allowing for much greater managerial and financial autonomy; redeployment of civil servants to more productive enterprises; improvements in the supply and distribution systems; and more price incentives for smaller enterprises. External financial support was needed for the success of the programme, and the government actively encouraged joint ventures between foreign and Angolan enterprises. In 1988 the government introduced a new law relating to foreign investment, offering tax concessions and permitting the repatriation of profits. Angola was admitted to the IMF in September 1989, thus enhancing prospects for a rescheduling of payments on Angola's external debt, which was estimated at US $12,173m. at the end of 1998, of which $10,616m. was medium- and long-term public debt. In 1999, however, total external debt decreased to $11,900m. In 1997 the cost of debt-servicing was equivalent to 15.9% of the value of exports of goods and services. In September 1990 the kwanza was replaced, at par, by a new kwanza. With effect from October 1990, the new kwanza was devalued by more than 50%, with the exchange rate adjusted to US $1 = 60 new kwanza. Despite intense popular opposition to this measure, a further devaluation took place in March 1991. In late October 1990 the central committee of the ruling MPLA–PT proposed the introduction of a market economy. In April 1991 the government announced that 100 companies which were nationalized after independence would be returned to their original owners, and that some state-owned enterprises, including the national airline and the state diamond company, Empresa Nacional de Diamantes de Angola (ENDIAMA), would transfer up to 49% of their equity to the private sector.

A programme of radical economic reforms was announced in November 1991, as part of the government's commitment to move towards a market economy. The measures included: a 33.3% devaluation of the currency, bringing the exchange rate of US $1 = 90 new kwanza; reductions in personal income taxes and consumer taxes; the abolition of price 'ceilings' on all except a few basic commodities; salary increases for public-sector workers, to compensate for the withdrawal of ration cards, and a national minimum wage of 12,000 kwanza per month. A further 50% devaluation, with the exchange rate adjusted to US $1 = 180 new kwanza, was announced in December, followed by a devaluation of 67% (to US $1 = 550 new kwanza) in April 1992. A heavy devaluation of the currency, to US $1 = 7,000 new kwanza, was announced on 1 February 1993. This measure, which brought the official exchange rate closer to the 'black market' rate of approximately 10,000 new kwanza per US dollar, was unfavourably received by the legislature and the local business community. In late February the minister of finance and the governor of the central bank were dismissed, on the grounds that they had exceeded their powers in authorizing the devaluation. In mid-April the exchange rate was adjusted to US $1 = 4,000 new kwanza.

The state budget for 1993 envisaged expenditure of 1,300,000m. new kwanza and included subsidies of some 150,000m. new kwanza for a fund to assist in mitigating the effects of sharply rising unemployment. A tripling of the budgetary deficit in the previous year, due to unplanned (largely military) spending, had contributed to a rise in inflation to an annual rate of some 500%. In conjunction with the budget statement, the government announced an emergency programme to combat inflation and the effects of devaluation.

In October 1993 the new kwanza was devalued by 39.5% to US $1 = 6,500 new kwanza, compared with a free market rate of US $1 = 50,000 new kwanza. A series of devaluations of the currency followed, taking the official rate to US $1 = 35,000 new kwanza at the end of March 1994, when it compared with a free market rate of US $1 = 135,000 new kwanza. In April the government introduced a new method of fixing exchange rates through agreement between the central bank and the commercial banks, with the effect that the currency underwent an effective devaluation, decreasing to US $1 = 68,297 kwanza in that month. The new policy sought to provide for an end to the system of multiple exchange rates.

The main feature of the 1994 state budget, which totalled the equivalent of US $1,700m., was a policy to guarantee the prices of basic commodities, although defence remained the sector with the largest allocation of funds. Successive devaluations of the currency between April and December resulted in an exchange rate of US $1 = 1,320,000 new kwanza at 30 December 1994. In January 1995 the currency underwent a further devaluation of 63%. The creation of a 'readjusted' kwanza, with a value equivalent to 1,000 new kwanza, was approved in June, and the new currency entered circulation in the following month.

The state budget for 1995 envisaged expenditure of 4,793,863,326.3m. new kwanza and estimated revenue of 3,880,103,863.2m. new kwanza.

The erosion of the value of the currency continued throughout 1995 and early 1996. In March 1996 the readjusted kwanza underwent a devaluation of some 80%, to US $1 = 31,784 readjusted kwanza. By June the rate had declined further, to US $1 = 55,000 readjusted kwanza, while the free market rate stood at about US $1 = 240,000 readjusted kwanza.

The state budget for 1996 envisaged expenditure of 178,000,000m. readjusted kwanza. In July the government introduced a reform programme known as *Nova Vida* ('New Life') which resulted in lowering the inflation rate by about 13% per month and decreasing the differential between the official and parallel exchange rates to around 10%.

The 1997 state budget and economic and social plan focused on restoring economic and financial stability and promoting economic production. Some 38% of the US $890m. budget was allocated to state operating costs while the remainder was to be spent on economic reconstruction and stabilization programmes, including plans to reduce foreign debt, programmes for the promotion of rural trade, health, education, agricultural development and the stabilization of the diamond mining sector. The budget also sought to support private sector development through fiscal, customs and financial incentives for productive investment.

During 1996 and 1997 the banking sector exhibited signs of revival. In September 1996 the central bank ceased all commercial activities in order to focus on the monetary system, limiting itself to the role of a central bank. The Banco de Crédito Comercial e Industrial assumed the commercial responsibilities of the central bank. In 1997 various foreign investors declared an interest in the privatization of the Banco de Comércio e Indústria, which was founded in 1991 in order to support international business activities in Angola.

The state budget for 1998, approved in February 1998, envisaged expenditure of 1,348,205,000m. readjusted kwanza. A considerable decline in international petroleum prices, to as little as US $10 per barrel, in 1998 resulted in a shortfall of some $1,000m. in budget revenue that year. In June the government was forced to cut budgetary expenditure by one-quarter, while pressure on the state sector was intensified further by an increase in defence spending. Several sizeable petroleum deposits were discovered in 1998 and early 1999. Although revenue from these would not be realized in time to ease the current budgetary deficit the government was due to receive some $800m. in signature bonuses from foreign petroleum companies in return for licences to operate in three ultra-deep-water petroleum blocks.

The currency stabilized somewhat during 1998 and 1999; the free market rate stood at US $1 = 257,000 readjusted kwanza in May 1998. By March 1999, however, the value of the currency had deteriorated considerably, with the free market rate standing at US $1 = 1,480,000 readjusted kwanza.

The state budget for 1999, approved in March 1999, gave priority to defence and security while recommending austerity and the streamlining of public expenditure as well as introducing measures designed to increase revenue from non-petroleum sectors. The budget projected real GDP growth of 1% and an annual inflation rate of 95%. It also provided for the creation of an inter-bank foreign currency market, and the establishment of mechanisms to permit more realistic interest rates with the intention of gradually reducing the gap between the official and the informal foreign exchange rates to no more than 10% in 1999.

Seen as a key element in the liberalization of the Angolan financial system, the dual exchange rate was abolished in May 1999, despite strong opposition from powerful elements in the presidency, who had previously benefited from access to foreign exchange at artificially cheap rates. Banking transactions were liberalized, allowing commercial banks to trade amongst themselves in US dollars, thus creating an interbank money market. The governor of the Banco Nacional de Angola (BNA) announced his intention to raise interest rates, in an attempt to inject more liquidity into the banking system. Following this decision, the Banco Totta e Açores reopened previously closed branches and the Banco Africano de Investimentos announced plans for further expansion.

In September 1999 plans to reduce public expenditure were announced, and in November the tax revenue collection system was significantly improved. In December a new currency, the kwanza, replaced the readjusted kwanza at a rate of 1 kwanza = 1,000,000 readjusted kwanza. Following the establishment of free floating exchange rates, the rate for the new kwanza was set at US $1 = 5.5 kwanza. On 12 January 2000 the government abolished the much-criticized policy of recording foreign exchange transactions in the petroleum sector as 'off-budget' items and requiring all transactions to be registered with the BNA.

The annual rate of inflation averaged 1,650.1% in 1996, 147.7% in 1997, 134.8% in 1998 and 329% in 1999.

Talks between the government and the IMF continued in mid-1999 regarding the provision of an enhanced structural adjustment facility, which would ensure funding of US $75m. to be made available over a period of three years, approval of which was expected to facilitate further bilateral and multilateral assistance and a restructuring of the country's external debt. Doubts over the government's resolve in implementing the necessary reforms prompted the World Bank to suspend all further loans to Angola. However, the government's new reform programme helped to initiate a new round of negotiations with the IMF towards the end of the year. On 3 April 2000 an agreement with the IMF provided for the implementation of a staff-monitored programme (SMP) for a nine-month period; however, no new disbursements of funds were agreed upon. The agreed action plan included a list of economic reforms and a timetable for their implementation. The reforms included a commitment to greater budget transparency, a consistent policy for dealing with external debt, as well as the progressive elimination of subsidies, tax exemptions, import licences, extra-budgetary expenditure and unauthorized payments by the central bank. In the light of Angola's poor track record in implementing previously-agreed economic reforms, and considering the well-entrenched opposition to such measures, notably from certain sections of the ruling Movimento Popular de Libertação de Angola (MPLA), there was considerable scepticism regarding the chances of success of such an ambitious programme. If successfully implemented, however, it was hoped that it could lead to a poverty reduction and growth facility (PRGF) either in late 2000 or early 2001.

The state budget for 2000, approved on 28 January 2000, continued the reformist course. Measures included the proposed reduction of the rate of inflation to 87%, the retention of the floating exchange rate, while aiming to maintain a minimum rate of US $1 = 9.26 kwanza. Total revenue was forecast at 19,900m. kwanza, equivalent to a 53% increase in real terms. The government also pledged to remove fuel prices subsidies, and the long-delayed privatization programme was to be restarted. The projected GDP growth of 3.5% was thought to underestimate the Angolan economy's potential for growth. However, a US $150m.-economic and social development programme, intended to provide loans to local businesses, was criticized for conflicting with the government's generally interventionist policies. It was also feared that the 1,400% rise in fuel prices, following the abolition of subsidies, would drive inflation well beyond the target rate.

MAJOR CROPS

Only about 3% of Angola's total area is cultivated as arable or permanent crop land. Reliable statistics have not yet revealed the true magnitude of the deterioration of modern agriculture caused by the departure of Portuguese settlers in 1974–75. The main cash crop is coffee. Prior to independence, annual production of green coffee was more than 200,000 metric tons, with the USA as the main export customer. In the mid-1970s Angola was the second largest African coffee producer and the world's main supplier of robusta coffee, cultivated mainly in the Uíge, Cuanza-Norte, Cuanza-Sul and Luanda provinces. Coffee was cultivated on a variety of Portuguese plantations, ranging from substantial commercial holdings, employing thousands of labourers, down to family plantations with only a score of workers, where the owner combined agriculture with minor trade with local Africans. However, the subsequent departure of the Portuguese, neglect of the plantations (which were nationalized following independence), drought, insufficient transport, excessive bureaucracy and the continuing armed conflict have all contributed to the decline, reducing production to about one-fiftieth of pre-independence levels. Output was estimated at about 5,000 tons in 1993, declining to just 1,560 tons in 1994, before increasing to 2,880 tons in 1995, to 4,140 tons in 1996 and to an estimated 6,000 tons in 1997. The impact of the decline in agricultural production has been aggravated by reductions in world prices for robusta coffee, following the collapse in 1989 of the International Coffee Organization's export quota systems, by increasing competition from Asian producers of robusta and by a shift in Western consumer demand to arabica varieties. Export earnings from coffee fell from US $80m. in 1984 to an estimated $4.6m. in 1997. In 1983 the government established the Empresa de Rebenefício e Exportação do Café de Angola (CAFANGOL), a state-controlled coffee-processing and trading organization. Plans to privatize CAFANGOL, together with the state-owned coffee plantations, were announced in 1991, and commenced in 1997. Foreign investment in the plantations has been sought, but overall foreign ownership was being limited to between 30%–40%. According to government estimates issued in 1995, about $20m. would be required for the rehabilitation of 60,000 ha of family plantations and 30,000 ha of private estates. However, the potential revenue from coffee production was estimated to be as high as $15m. per annum. In early 2000 a $8m.-pilot scheme to revive coffee production was proposed. Financed by the International Coffee Organization (ICO), with the support of the UN Common Fund for Commodities (CFC), it intended to resettle up to a thousand coffee-producing families in the Amboim area of the Cuanza-Sul province.

Sisal exports reached 66,719 metric tons in 1974, when Angola was Africa's second most important producer. Production has since fallen sharply; according to FAO estimates, output amounted to only 1,000 tons per year during the period 1987–98. In the intervening years the crop was adversely affected by a slump in world prices and by the transition from private ownership to state enterprise. The main producing regions were the Benguela plateau, Huíla, Cuanza-Norte and Malanje provinces. Maize formerly ranked fifth or sixth among Angola's agricultural exports, with a harvest of 700,000 tons in 1973. However, by 1975 the country's output of cereals was declining, and from that year Angola has been a recipient of food aid. Maize output was reduced to some 300,000 tons in 1980, and had fallen further, to an estimated 250,000 tons, in 1985. Output increased to 300,000 tons in 1987, falling to 180,000 tons in 1990, before rising again, to an estimated 369,000 tons in 1992. The resumption of hostilities led to a renewed decline in production, with output of 274,000 tons in 1993 and 201,000 tons in 1994, increasing slightly to 235,000 tons in 1995. By 1996 maize production had increased to 398,000 tons, although it declined slightly to 370,000 tons in 1997 before rising again, to 505,000 tons in 1998. The escalation in fighting in 1999 caused production levels to fall by an estimated 15% that year, compared with 1998.

Cotton was formerly one of the most promising products of Angola, and was both a concessionary and an African cultivation. At independence, the main areas of cultivation were the Baixa de Cassange, in the Malanje province, and the region east of Luanda. Organized planters in the Cuanza-Sul province were responsible for a large increase in mechanized production, and an increasing part of production was processed in Angola by three textile mills. The breakdown of activities in most European-owned plantations reduced production of seed (unginned) cotton from 104,000 metric tons in 1974 to an estimated 33,000 tons annually during the 1980s, according to the FAO. Advisers from the USSR were unable to revive this activity and, for the first time in Angola's history, cotton was imported in 1983. The first exports of cotton since independence resumed on a small scale in 1995. Total cotton production was estimated at 12,000 tons in 1998.

Prior to independence, sugar production was controlled by three Portuguese companies, and output of raw sugar was about 85,000 tons per year from annual sugar cane production of just under 1m. tons. Following independence, the main sugar cane plantations were reorganized as workers' co-operatives, with Cuban management and assistance. Production of raw sugar subsequently declined sharply, and nearly all sugar for domestic consumption is imported. The withdrawal of Cuban personnel by mid-1991 led to further deterioration in the sector, with sugar cane production declining to 220,000 metric tons per annum between 1993–95. The annual cane harvest stood at an estimated 330,000 tons in 1998. In mid-1998 the Angolan government was seeking private-sector investment for a US $67m.-project to rehabilitate sugar production in Dombe Grande, near the southern port of Benguela. The terms of reference for a public tender were expected to be prepared by

the end of 2000. The government planned to rehabilitate the sugar-cane plantations before their eventual privatization.

Cassava is the main Angolan crop in terms of volume produced, and is the staple food of the majority of the population. Production was an estimated 3.2m. metric tons in 1998, and most of the crop is consumed domestically, with no transaction above the local market level. The cultivation of bananas is being increased in the lower reaches of the rivers north of Luanda and of the Cuvo river. Estimated output was 295,000 tons in 1998.

OTHER CROPS

Exports of palm oil totalled 4,410 metric tons in 1973. From the 1980s onwards estimated annual production was 12,000 tons of palm kernels and 40,000 tons of palm oil, rising to an estimated 16,000 tons of palm kernels and 52,000 tons of palm oil in 1997. Tobacco grows well on the formerly white-owned farms in the central and southern provinces of Benguela, Huíla and Namibe, with an estimated output of 3,900 tons in 1997. Other commodities (such as rice, millet, sorghum, beans, tropical and temperate fruit, cocoa and groundnuts) are testimony to the agricultural potential of Angola, provided that investment capital and expertise can be deployed for this sector.

Because of its large area and variety of climate, Angola is one of the most promising agricultural countries of southern Africa. However, owing to civil unrest, transport problems, the lack of proper marketing facilities and incentives, and drought, shortages have been prevalent and famine has been a frequent occurrence. By early 1984 malnutrition affected some 15% of Luanda's population, and physical survival had become the prime objective of more than 50% of Angola's rural population. By early 1991 it was estimated that food shortages threatened 1.8m. people. In recent years less than one-half of the country's cereal requirements have been produced locally, and high levels of cereal imports have been required. According to the UN Special Relief Programme for Angola, the cereal deficit for 1990 was 565,000 metric tons. Some 236,000 tons of cereals were not covered by commercial imports, and were therefore required as food aid. The resumption of the civil war in late 1992 represented a considerable reverse to efforts to effect a recovery in agricultural production. By February 1993 the UN World Food Programme (WFP) was warning that as many as 3m. people were threatened with hunger and disease, with harvests in many areas destroyed or disrupted by the hostilities. In April the WFP appealed for 350,000 tons of emergency food supplies for nearly 2m. Angolans. Those in need of assistance included 344,000 people displaced from their homes, 122,000 former refugees who had returned from Zambia and Zaire, and 256,000 affected by drought in the south-western provinces of Huíla, Cunene and Namibe. In 1994 there was an estimated shortfall on the country's maize requirements of 1.3m. tons. As the consequence of the resumption of the war in late 1998, by April 1999 some 780,000 people had fled their homes. This depopulation of the countryside resulted in crops being left unharvested and in a wide-spread failure to replant. The Early Warning Unit of the SADC's Food Security Organ stated that the country's maize harvest was likely to be reduced by one-quarter, and estimated that Angola would need to import 322,000 tons of maize, 16,000 tons of wheat and 76,000 tons of rice in 1999. The cereal import requirements for 2000 were estimated at 505,000 tons, and with only 325,000 tons being imported commercially, the remaining 180,000 tons would have to be provided as food aid.

One of the most serious impediments to increasing the level of agricultural production is the vast number of anti-personnel mines which remain concealed about the countryside as a result of the war. It is estimated that there are some 10m. unexploded mines in Angola, and around 70,000 civilians have suffered casualties necessitating the amputation of limbs as a result of accidentally detonating mines; this is the highest proportion of casualties among the civilian population of any country in the world. UNICEF, UNHCR and other international organizations have joined forces with UNAVEM in conducting demining operations and in supporting the UNAVEM Central Mine Action Training School, established to instruct demobilized soldiers from both the government and UNITA forces. Efforts to demine the country were stalled in 1998 as programmes were suspended owing to the resumption of hostilities. With both the government and UNITA laying new mines the prospects of agricultural revival deteriorated considerably.

LIVESTOCK, FORESTRY AND FISHERIES

Livestock raising is concentrated in southern and central Angola, owing to the prevalence of the tsetse fly and the poor quality of the natural pastures in the north of the country. Some two-thirds of all cattle are found in Huíla province alone. The modern ranching sector, established by the Portuguese, was nationalized following independence, and has subsequently been adversely affected by civil war and drought. Meat shortages are prevalent in all cities, and imports of meat are indispensable. In 1973 Angola had only about 4.4m. head of cattle, 2m. goats, 1.4m. pigs and 350,000 sheep. In 1998 cattle numbers were estimated by the FAO at 3.5m., pigs at 810,000, sheep at 245,000 and goats at 1.45m. (These figures appear to be inflated: the full extent of damage to the livestock industry in the civil war may not have been taken into account.)

Angola possesses important forestry resources, especially in the Cabinda, Moxico, Luanda and Kwanza-Norte provinces. Cabinda, in particular, has some valuable indigenous species, such as African sandalwood, rosewood and ebony. Softwood plantations of eucalyptus and cypress are used for fuel and grow along the Benguela railway and near Benguela, where they are used for wood pulp and paper manufacture. Exports of timber, however, ceased at independence. As in other sectors, output of logs fell sharply after independence, from over 550,000 cu m in 1973 to 39,750 cu m in 1981. Although this activity was especially sensitive to guerrilla actions, output of logs recovered to 116,000 cu m in 1984, and to 134,000 cu m in 1985. However, production was estimated at only 66,000 cu m per annum between 1990–97.

Fisheries are mainly in and off Namibe, Tombua and Benguela. However, of a total of 263 Angolan trawlers in 1981, only 87 were operational, owing to lack of maintenance. In that year the government formed a fisheries enterprise, in an attempt to restore the industry, and Angola was granted a loan of US $10m. from the Arab Bank for Economic Development in Africa (BADEA) for the rehabilitation of fishing facilities. A further grant of ECU 6.76m. was made to the fishing sector by the EC in 1984. Foreign trawlers operate off the coast and have significantly depleted the fish reserves in Angolan waters. In February 1988 the USSR agreed to strengthen co-operation in the fisheries sector, with the possibility of the establishment of a joint fisheries venture and the construction of a fishing port in Namibe province. The Swedish government has spent US $100m. on programmes for technical vocational training and research into different marine species, providing training for some 1,700 people in various branches of the fishing industry. The total catch declined from an average annual of 450,000 metric tons in the early 1970s to 191,000 tons in 1985. According to FAO figures, the total catch was 72,200 tons in 1997.

MINERALS

Angola is believed to be one of the richest countries in mineral reserves of southern Africa. Two minerals, petroleum and diamonds, are of paramount importance to the Angolan economy, and Angola is the second largest exporter of hydrocarbons in sub-Saharan Africa, after Nigeria.

Angola's kimberlite pipes, first discovered in 1911, are believed to rank among the world's five richest deposits of embedded diamonds. Since 1986, full control of this sector has been exercised by the state enterprise, ENDIAMA, which instigated a new national diamond policy, whereby mining was to be divided into blocks, to be exploited under production-sharing agreements with foreign concessionaires. Angola's total output of diamonds was 2.4m. carats in 1974, falling to about 300,000 carats in 1976, following independence. Annual production remained below 1m. carats until 1989, when it achieved 1.3m. carats. Output in 1996 was estimated at 3.8m. carats, although production in 1997 decreased to 3.3m. carats. Official sales of diamonds, which until 1996 were subject to a marketing agreement between ENDIAMA and the De Beers group (see below), earned US $190m. in 1991 and $250m. in 1992, but declined to $63m. in 1993. However, figures of diamond output are deceptive, since a significant proportion (perhaps one-half)

of the real production has been mined and smuggled by UNITA, whose leader, Dr Jonas Savimbi, has admitted that his movement has derived a significant share of its resources from the diamond-producing area, which remained partially under his control during the civil war. Following the resumption of the civil war in late 1992, diamond mining areas again came under UNITA control. Losses incurred by ENDIAMA due to illegal excavation and smuggling (mainly into Zaire) in 1994 were estimated at between $300m.–$500m. In November 1996 ENDIAMA granted permission for UNITA representatives to begin negotiations with foreign corporations concerning the exploration and mining of diamond reserves in areas under *de facto* UNITA control. At the same time ENDIAMA announced plans to increase diamond production, over a period of three to four years, to more than 2m. carats per year. According to the ministry of geology and mines, Angola's formal mineral sector produced diamonds amounting to some 432,170 carats in 1997. It was estimated that output of the informal sector amounted to a further 882,000 carats in that year. In 1998 revenue from diamond production was estimated at $480m., although of this only $180m. was generated by the formal sector. In event of peace it was estimated that annual diamond production could increase rapidly, to about 7m. carats, within three years.

In December 1987 Angola and the USSR signed a co-operation agreement, covering the mining of diamonds and quartz. De Beers Consolidated Mines lost exclusive marketing rights over ENDIAMA diamonds in 1985; however, in May 1989 ENDIAMA and De Beers signed a 'declaration of intent' to enter into co-operation in diamond prospecting, mining and marketing, and in 1991 an agreement was signed to market all production from the Cuango area through De Beers' Central Selling Organisation (CSO). This agreement lapsed in 1996, although the CSO has continued to purchase Angolan diamonds from other sources. De Beers, meanwhile, has remained active in exploration both for alluvial and kimberlite diamonds in five areas of the country, and other South African, Canadian, Brazilian, Portuguese and Russian interests are also currently involved in exploration activities. In conjunction with ENDIAMA, a Russian diamond corporation, Almazy Rossii-Sakha, has opened a processing mill at the Catoca diamond field in north-eastern Angola. Covering an area of more than 660 ha, the Catoca kimberlite has been estimated to contain potential diamond reserves of up to 200m. carats, which would establish it as one of the world's largest deposits of diamonds. Catoca entered its initial phase of production in 1998.

In September 1995 the government introduced a programme aimed at curbing the activities of the many thousands of illegal diamond prospectors and traders operating in areas under its control. In early 1995 ENDIAMA and De Beers reached an agreement providing the latter with a prospecting contract which committed it to an investment of US $40m. in the short term, increasing to $500m. in the medium term, provided that peace was sustained. The objective was to increase output to around 4m.–5m. carats per annum, and to end illegal prospecting. Under the terms of this agreement, De Beers began prospecting in the area of Mavinga, Cuando-Cubango province, in May 1997. However, De Beers has experienced difficulties in gaining access to the sites, owing to the security situation. UNITA was also party to an agreement signed between ENDIAMA and a Brazilian company, Odebrecht, for a vast diamond concession in the Lunda provinces. By mid-1997 UNITA had come under increasing pressure to reach a definitive profit-sharing agreement covering the mining areas still under its control. Following the fall, in May, of UNITA's ally, Mobutu Sese Seko of Zaire, the government launched several military offensives against UNITA-controlled mines, recovering about 10% of UNITA's productive areas. Meanwhile, UNITA set up its own legal mining company, Sociedade Geral das Minas, which was awarded two prospecting concessions in May, one in Cuando-Cubango province, the other near the central town of Andulo. UNITA was also offered a share in a consortium comprising Ashton Mining (Australia), Odebrecht (Brazil) and ENDIAMA, which has been awarded the extremely important Cuango Valley concession. However, negotiations broke down and UNITA was left without a stake in the Cuango Valley. The fall, in October, of another of UNITA's allies, Pascal Lissouba of the Republic of the Congo, made unofficial mineral production increasingly difficult for UNITA as lines of transport for equipment and buyers were cut off. In 1998 UNITA's diamond mining income was estimated to have declined to some $200,000.

The Canadian mining company DiamondWorks entered commercial production in its alluvial diamond concessions in the province of Lunda-Norte in mid-1997. Two further investments were announced for Lunda-Norte in March 1997: the Namibian Minerals Corpn announced plans to invest US $2.5m. to develop three diamond concessions; and the Canadian company Southern Era Resources announced that it would invest $5m. over the next five years in the development of a major kimberlite pipe. Another Canadian company, Pure Gold Minerals Inc, announced in mid-1998 that it was negotiating for a concession on the Chicapa River in Lunda-Norte.

Despite the resumption of full-scale hostilities between the government and UNITA in 1999, foreign interest and levels of investment in the diamond industry remained high. In May a number of senior staff and the director-general of ENDIAMA were dismissed by the government and replaced by a military lawyer, Gen. Agostinho Dias Gaspar. In October heavy fighting led to the temporary closure of the Luzamba mines in the Cuango valley. The role played by the illicit diamond trade in perpetuating the civil war in Angola was highlighted in a high profile campaign launched by the London-based organization Global Witness. The resultant publicity forced De Beers to announce, in October, that it would only purchase diamonds bearing government certificates of origin. However, it was alleged that the certification system was open to widespread abuse, with a number of government officials believed to have colluded with UNITA and illegal traders by issuing them with certificates. The government subsequently announced its decision to produce new certificates that were more difficult to tamper with. In early 2000 a complete restructuring of the industry was initiated with the creation of a new state diamond company, Sociedade de Comercialização de Diamantes (Sodiam). The role of ENDIAMA was reduced to that of a prospecting company, retaining its joint ventures with foreign producers. All marketing was transferred to the newly-created Angolan Selling Corporation (Ascorp), in which Sodiam held a 51% interest. All existing marketing licences were terminated and operators were given 30 days to sign agreements with Ascorp. It was also announced that prospecting licences were to be reduced in size to an estimated 3,000 sq km.

Pressure on the diamond industry was intensified following the publication, in March 2000, of a report by the UN sanctions committee 'naming and shaming' the presidents of Togo and Burkina Faso, as well as Belgian, Bulgarian and Ukrainian officials, accusing them of involvement in the illicit diamond trade and of providing military assistance to UNITA. As a result, the diamond high council in Antwerp in the Netherlands entered into an origin-verification agreement with the Angolan government. Moreover, De Beers announced a complete restructuring of its own operations. These measures created considerable uncertainty among those foreign companies active in diamond prospecting in Angola; the arbitrary manner in which the government had abrogated their existing contracts was severely criticized. In addition, the reduction in the area of land covered by prospecting licences was seen as highly impractical in the case of alluvial, rapidly depleting mines. However, by mid-2000 several new diamond fields had been explored and the government expressed hope that official production would increase.

The petroleum industry is the principal economic mainstay of the government, with petroleum extraction, refining and distribution constituting Angola's most important economic activity. Hydrocarbons generally accounted for more than 90% of total exports in the mid-1980s. The petroleum sector accounts for about 80% of state revenues. In 1998 the petroleum sector accounted for 44.9% of GDP. Estimates of proven recoverable reserves of crude petroleum, which stood at 5,409m. barrels in 1997, had almost doubled by April 2000, when production averaged 845,000 barrels per day (b/d).

In 1955 a Belgian-owned company, Petrofina, discovered petroleum in the Cuanza valley. A petroleum company, Fina Petróleos de Angola (PETRANGOL), was subsequently established, under the joint ownership of the Angola government and Petrofina interests. PETRANGOL constructed a refinery in the suburbs of Luanda. The greatest impetus to expansion came from the Cabinda Gulf Oil Co (Cabgoc), which discovered petroleum offshore at Cabinda in 1966. In 1976 a national oil company, the Sociedade Nacional de Combustíveis de Angola (SONANGOL), was established to manage all fuel production and distribution. In 1978 SONANGOL was authorized to acquire a 51% interest in all petroleum companies operating in Angola, although the management of operations was to remain under the control of foreign companies. In the late 1970s the government initiated a campaign to attract foreign oil companies. In 1978–79 SONANGOL divided the Angolan coast, excluding Cabinda, into 13 exploration blocks, which were leased to foreign companies under production-sharing agreements. Although Cabgoc's Cabinda offshore fields (which are operated by the US Chevron Corpn) remain the core of the Angolan petroleum industry (accounting for about two-thirds of total output), production is buoyant at other concessions, held by Agip, Elf Aquitaine, Conoco and Texaco. In addition SONANGOL itself operates a production block in association with Petrobrás Internacional (BRASPETRO) of Brazil and Petrofina. In 1992 Elf took a 10% interest in Cabgoc, reducing SONANGOL's share to 41%, with Chevron holding 39.2% and Agip 9.8%. Onshore, Petrofina remained the operator. SONANGOL took a 51% interest in Petrofina's original Cuanza valley operations, including the Luanda refinery, whose capacity meets most domestic requirements. SONANGOL also had a 51% interest in an onshore venture by Petrofina in the River Congo estuary area, in which Texaco held a 16.33% share. Onshore production in 1991 was estimated at 30,000 b/d; however, with recoverable petroleum reserves almost exhausted and activities vulnerable to UNITA attack, production declined and in 1993 Petrofina suspended onshore operations near the port of Soyo, in northern Angola near the Zaire border. Production was resumed, however, in February 1996, when an output of 5,000 b/d was quickly restored.

Despite the uncertain security situation in the Cabinda enclave, exploration licences for three onshore blocks were awarded in October 1992. The principal operators for the three concessions, Cabinda North, Central and South, were to be Occidental of the USA, British Petroleum and Petrofina respectively. In 1994 Chevron announced the discovery of four new offshore fields. It estimated that production would increase from 320,000 b/d in 1994 to 390,000 b/d in 1995 as the development of deep-water areas continued under its five-year programme. In 1995 Chevron announced a US $5,100m. capital and exploration expenditure programme for that year, an increase of 5% on 1994. In 1997 Chevron announced its intention to invest $700m. a year until 2000 and envisaged increasing its output to 600,000 b/d. In late 1994 Texaco announced a five-year investment programme for petroleum exploration and production totalling $600m.; the programme aimed to increase Texaco's output in the country by 50%. In September 1996 SONANGOL signed new production sharing agreements with six international petroleum companies: Shell Exploration Angola, Amoco Angola, Eagle (Nigeria), Petro Inett Corpn (South Africa), Mobil and Texaco.

Output of petroleum expanded rapidly during the 1980s, averaging 155,000 b/d in late 1982 and rising steadily, reaching 549,000 b/d in 1992. Following a small decline in 1993, production again increased consistently, reaching an estimated 715,000 b/d in 1997. In April 1997 Chevron announced the discovery of a further new oilfield off the coast of Cabinda which was thought capable of producing an additional 20,000 b/d. In May, following another significant deep-water discovery, production began in the remote North N'Dola oilfield, which was expected to yield up to 20,000 b/d by the end of 1997. In August Elf Aquitane announced the discovery of one of Africa's largest ever petroleum fields, with estimated reserves of 3,500m. barrels, off the Angolan coast. In that year the law governing the exploitation of petroleum was under revision with a view to facilitating further foreign investment. In 1998 Exxon announced a large petroleum discovery in Block 15. Of the three wells found in this block two were expected to produce 10,000 b/d; the block's total reserves were estimated at 1,000m. barrels. A deposit discovered in Block 14, in the Benguela well off the coast of Cabinda, was being exploited by SONANGOL in collaboration with Cabinda Gulf Oil, Agip, Total and Petrogal. Preliminary tests indicated reserves of more than 20,000 b/d. In October the discovery in the same block of a major petroleum well, with an estimated production of 10,000 b/d, was announced. The principal operators were to be Total, Agip, Chevron and Petrogal. Another large find, at Dikanza in Block 15, has a predicted output of 4,400 b/d. Oil companies continued to make substantial discoveries throughout 1999. In September Exxon announced a discovery at Xicomba, in Block 15, with an estimated production of 1,435 b/d. This followed the company's earlier discovery at Chocalho, which tested at 4,500 b/d. Also in September, Elf announced a find in Block 17, named Orquidea-1, and in October, Cravo-1, with a tested rate of 12,800 b/d. In May 2000 Elf announced a further discovery, Jasmim, with a test rate of 10,800 b/d. Production from the deep-water Kuito petroleum field commenced in December 1999, reaching 50,000 b/d in January 2000.

National output of crude petroleum was projected to increase from 800,000 b/d in 1998 to 1m. b/d by late 2001. In August 1999 the Angolan minister of petroleum, José Botelho de Vasconcelos, predicted that output would reach 1.4m. b/d in 2003.

The major portion of Angola's petroleum is exported to the USA in its crude form (397,000 b/d during 1997), although the 30-year-old Luanda refinery processes around 35,000 b/d of crude petroleum. The government announced in April 1998 that it intended to invest US $10m. to upgrade and increase the capacity of the Luanda refinery to 60,000 b/d. There are also plans to construct a new refinery, capable of processing 150,000–200,000 b/d at Lobito or Benguela. Although financial support was offered by the People's Republic of China, experts questioned whether the project would be commercially viable. The government announced its intention to commence the production of liquefied natural gas (LNG), from a plant in Luanda, by 2004.

Angola's export earnings from petroleum increased after 1982, following the rise in production, and reached US $1,191m. in 1985. With the sharp fall in the price of petroleum, export earnings declined to $1,140m. in the following year, but recovered to $2,100m. in 1987, $2,250m. in 1988, $2,700m. in 1989 and—helped by increased production and a period of higher prices, due to the Gulf crisis—an estimated $3,580m. in 1990. In 1991 petroleum export earnings stood at $3,217m., increasing to $3,556m. in 1992 before declining to $2,813m. in 1993 and then recovering to $3,425m. in 1995 and $4,651m. in 1996. In 1997 estimated earnings from petroleum exports stood at $4,507m., decreasing to $3,158m. in 1998. As Angola is not a member of OPEC, the country is not constrained by production quotas, enabling it to stabilize the value of its petroleum exports during the late 1980s, when world prices remained depressed, by increasing output.

Iron mining began in 1956 and production averaged 700,000–800,000 metric tons annually in the 1960s from mines in the Huambo and Bié provinces. However, the Cassinga mines in the Huíla province, which have proven reserves of more than 1,000m. tons of high-grade haematite, were the decisive factor in increasing production. A railway spur was built to link the mines with the Namibe–Menongue railway, and a new harbour built to the north of Namibe. Ore output was about 6m. tons (60%–65% iron) in 1973. However, in 1975 the Cassinga mines were partially destroyed in the fighting, and they have since remained inoperative. In 1981 a state-owned iron company, Empresa Nacional de Ferro de Angola (FERRANGOL), was created. In May 1998 the government announced its intention to rehabilitate the Cassinga mines, reiterating its intentions in mid-2000. Angola holds considerable ore production stockpiles, which await the eventual rehabilitation of rail links to the coast.

Other minerals abound. Reserves of copper have been identified in the Uíge province, and other deposits are known to exist in the Namibe, Huíla and Moxico provinces. Important deposits of feldspar have been found in the southern province of Huíla. Manganese ore was mined in the Malanje province, with 4,682 metric tons exported in 1973. Unexploited reserves of phosphate rock exist in the Zaire and Cabinda provinces, and deposits of uranium have been found along the border with Namibia. In 1991 a new secretariat of geology and mines was established to co-ordinate mining activity and to formulate mineral policy in preparation for the restoration of civil order. In 1998 the government announced its intention to promote investment for the extraction of other minerals, including platinum, manganese, copper, phosphates and gold.

POWER

Angola's power potential exceeds its needs. Most of Angola's energy output is of hydroelectric origin, and there is an impressive dam on the Cuanza at Cambambe, constructed and operated by a Brazilian company, which produced 370.7m. kWh in 1972, and whose generating capacity stood at 450MW in 1989. Luanda's industries are the main beneficiaries of Cambambe power. In 1996 a US $64m.-project was under way to renovate the transmission lines from Cambambe to Luanda, with funding of $35.5m. from the World Bank and $20m. from the African Development Bank. A 520-MW power station is being constructed at Kapunda, on the Cuanza river, with assistance from Brazilian and former Soviet contractors. The US $2,000m.-project, described by the World Bank as the key to Angola's post-war reconstruction, would increase the country's generating capacity by almost 100%. The first two Russian-built turbines were scheduled to be installed in 1993, but in early 1992 the project's future appeared to be in some doubt, pending agreement on the repayment of Angola's military debt to the former Soviet Union. An attack on the dam site by UNITA in November 1992 was reported to have caused damage amounting to $40m., delaying completion by as much as one year. In February 2000 it was reported that work at Kapunda was to be resumed, following the rescheduling of the $100m. debt owed to the Russian engineering company. The project, however, still remained vulnerable to possible UNITA attacks. Further south, Lobito and Benguela were provided with electricity by two privately-owned dams, the Lomaum and the Biópio, both on the Catumbela river. Production exceeded 206m. kWh in 1973. Destruction of the Lomaum dam reportedly reduced the power resources of Lobito and Benguela. In late 1987 it was announced that a Portuguese banking consortium was providing $11m. towards the first stage of a scheme to rehabilitate the Lomaum dam, and earlier in the year the Portuguese government granted a credit of $140m. towards the scheme. However, there has been no further progress in the rehabilitation of this dam. Still further south, the Matala dam serves Lubango, Namibe and Cassinga. However, this project is only a very small part of the grandiose Angolan-Namibian scheme for damming the Cunene river, thus providing Namibia, which is deficient in power and water, with cheap electricity and a permanent water supply. The Gove dam, in the Huambo course of the Cunene river, was completed with South African capital but was destroyed during the war. The construction of a major power station at the Ruacaná Falls, where the Cunene river reaches the Namibian border, has been impeded by the military and political instability in the region, although the first stage became operational in 1977. The potential annual output of the scheme is provisionally assessed at 1,000m. kWh. In October 1991 Angola and Namibia agreed to pursue feasibility studies for construction of a hydroelectric dam on the Cunene, although its location was contested by the two governments, and heavily opposed by environmental campaigners. Since 1977 there have been no significant additions to Angola's power generating capacity, although demand for power is still growing. Erratic power supplies have forced some foreign companies to install their own power plants. The fragmentation of the market into several independent producers, as well as the absence of a national grid, have exacerbated the situation. Only two-thirds of the 290-MW of installed hydroelectric capacity, and 53% of the 235-MW thermal capacity is currently operational. A five-year US $640m.-plan for the rehabilitation of the generation and distribution networks, including the provision of $211m. in funding for their expansion, was expected to be implemented following the cessation of hostilities.

INDUSTRY

Angola's industrial activity is centred on construction materials, petroleum refining, food processing, textiles, equipment for the petroleum industry, steel, chemicals, electrical goods and vehicle assembly. Output from Angola's industrial sector has dwindled to a fraction of pre-independence levels. Following the withdrawal of Portuguese owners, many enterprises were brought under state control and ownership, and by the mid-1980s about 80% of the industrial work-force was employed in state-owned companies. Under the SEF, introduced in January 1988 (see above), legislation was to be reformed, granting state enterprises autonomous control of management. The continuing civil unrest, shortages of raw materials, unreliability of power supplies and disruption of the transport infrastructure have all since contributed to the sharp reduction in industrial output. Official figures showed manufacturing output in 1985 to be only 54% of its 1973 level, and the sector suffered more in the ensuing three years, when a decline in earnings from petroleum exports, caused by the sharp fall in the price of petroleum, reduced the supply of foreign exchange needed for industrial raw materials and imports of capital goods. However, the allocation of foreign exchange for this purpose was more than doubled in 1990.

Angola's manufacturing sector has considerable potential, in view of the country's abundance of raw materials, such as petroleum and iron ore. During 1962–70, manufacturing output expanded at an average rate of 19% per year. The food-processing, brewing and tobacco industries were the most developed. The textile industry flourished after the ban on the creation of industries competing against metropolitan manufacturers was repealed in 1966. Cotton is the principal fibre used, and in 1973 textile industries occupied second place in Angola. In 1979 French industrialists built a new textile complex at Lobito, with a capacity of 16m. metres of cloth per year, and a second was planned in Luanda, with a capacity of 18m. metres per year. In 1987 production of textile fabrics was equivalent to only one-third of its 1973 level. A steel plant, built in Luanda in 1972–73, was reopened in 1984. Production of steel bars was 6,589 metric tons in 1986, compared with 26,572 tons in 1973.

Most branches of the manufacturing sector continued to contract during the 1980s. However, there are a few exceptions to the general depressed state of the sector. A yard for the construction of oil equipment was built at Ambriz in 1984/85. In mid-1987 a loan was approved by the African Development Bank for the construction of three pharmaceutical plants, and construction work on one of these commenced in February 1989. In September 1987 the government signed a contract with a Dutch company for the import and assembly of trucks at a plant in Luanda. In 1988 a new foreign investment code was introduced, which aimed to increase the rights of foreign companies regarding operation, transfer of profits, taxation, etc., while, in return, foreign investors were expected to expand transfer of technical and managerial skills to Angolan industrial personnel. Under the new code, however, many sectors remained closed to foreign investment: these included the postal and telecommunications sectors, the news media, air transport and shipping, defence and security and state banking. The approval in April 1994 of a US export credit guarantee protocol, under which US investors were to be insured against political upheaval and have access to loans, was expected to stimulate investment from the USA. In mid-1994 the government introduced legislative proposals for new regulations regarding foreign investment and privatization aimed at attracting foreign capital, increasing private investment in national economic activity and reducing state participation.

After independence, activity in the building trade effectively ceased, except for the reconstruction of some of the 130 bridges destroyed in the conflict (by 1978 more than 60 had been rebuilt). Major housing programmes have been initiated in large cities. Acute shortages of building materials have limited construction, for the most part, to shanty buildings, resulting in unzoned urban growth. However, the construction sector has been helped by the rehabilitation of the main cement works, operated by the Empresa de Cimento de Angola (CIMANGOLA), in Luanda, and the sector is expected to benefit greatly from the Kapunda dam project. Nova Cimangola, a cement company formed as a public-private partnership with a Norwegian firm, increased production from 182,000 metric tons in 1995 to 356,000 tons in 1999.

In January 2000 a Coca-Cola bottling plant, created as a US $36m.-joint venture between the Angolan government and Indol International (a subsidiary of South African Breweries) began production at Bom Jesus, some 60 km from Luanda. In May of that year a Chinese company announced a $7.2m. investment in a motorcycle assembly plant in Angola. There were also signs of recovery in the textile industry, with the reopening of a factory in Luanda producing uniforms for the Angolan armed forces. The Angolan industrial development plan for 1998–2000 envisaged expenditure of $195m. to establish 100 industrial companies, creating some 10,000 jobs. A further $140m. was to be spent on the food processing industry. Plans were also published for the transfer to private ownership of one-quarter of state-owned industrial companies.

TRANSPORT AND TRADE

Angola's colonial administration made a considerable effort to improve the communications network, and in 1974 there were 8,317 km of tarred roads in a total road network of 72,323 km. It is now theoretically possible to drive on tarred roads from Quimbele (Uíge province) to the Namibian border, and from Luanda to Lumbala (Moxico province), close to the Zambian frontier. Bus transportation was fairly developed following independence, carrying some 22.4m. passengers in 1978, but has since suffered from shortages of imported spare parts. In 1997 Angola had 72,626 km of roads, of which about 25% were paved. However, since the early 1980s guerrilla warfare has dramatically curtailed most road transportation. A substantial programme of road and bridge rehabilitation was announced by president dos Santos in January 2000.

Railways serve a dual purpose, to open the interior and to provide export channels for Zambia and the land-locked province of Katanga (Shaba) in the Democratic Republic of the Congo (formerly Zaire), which export large volumes of minerals. Hence, all railway lines run towards the coast. The Luanda railway, chiefly for local goods traffic and passengers, was the only line functioning with a degree of regularity during the late 1980s, albeit at a low level of activity, transporting only 63,000 metric tons of freight in 1985. In mid-1999 the Luanda railway remained closed between Dondo and Malanje due to the destruction by UNITA of bridges prior to the signing of the May 1991 peace agreement. The Namibe railway, in the south, was assuming a new importance as a carrier of iron ore from Cassinga before the security situation resulted in the closure of the mines. This railway transported 196,000 tons of freight in 1985. The Benguela railway was of international importance and was the strategic outlet for exports of copper and zinc from Zaire and Zambia, bypassing South Africa and providing the most direct link to the west coast. However, UNITA guerrilla attacks caused the suspension of all cross-border traffic after 1975. In April 1987 a declaration of intent to restore these services was signed by the governments of Angola, Zambia and Zaire. For the most part the domestic Lobito–Huambo section of the railway was maintained in operation, although at a reduced level; it transported 262,000 tons of freight along the coastal tracks during 1985. The Amboim railway was of local importance, but is not currently operational. The volume of freight handled on Angolan railways was 9,272,883 tons in 1973, but the annual total had declined to 443,200 tons by 1990.

Internal air transport is well developed, with a network of good airports and rural landing strips, and has become the only moderately safe means of transportation, owing to the insecurity on road and rail routes: 198,667 passengers were carried by air in 1973, with the total increasing to 927,000 in 1985, but falling to 553,000 in 1995 before increasing to 585,000 in 1996. Plans were announced in June 2000 to provide a direct link between Luanda and London, served by British Airways. Angola's main harbours are Lobito, Luanda and Namibe. Cabinda has become the principal loading port, with 7,552,652 tons (mostly petroleum) handled in 1973. In 1985 Lobito handled 522,000 tons of cargo, compared with 2.5m. tons in 1973; Luanda handled more than 942,000 tons in 1985, compared with 2.3m. tons in 1973. Namibe's traffic declined from 6,379,000 tons in 1973 to 171,000 tons in 1985. As the country exports very little except petroleum, unloaded goods account for about 85% of traffic south of Cabinda. Passenger traffic is now almost negligible. A state-owned shipping company is in operation.

In 1988 an emergency programme was launched to rehabilitate the transport infrastructure. Under the programme, which was to cost a total of US $340m., $142m. was allocated to the rehabilitation of roads and $121m. to the rehabilitation of the Luanda and Namibe railways. The programme was also to include work on the ports of Luanda and Namibe, and on Saurino and Luena airports. In February 1992 a Portuguese consortium, led by the state railway authority (Caminhos de Ferro de Portugal), signed an $11.5m. agreement to repair port and railway installations that had been damaged during the civil war. In 1995 the cost of rehabilitating the Namibe railway and corresponding port facilities was estimated at $272m. In 1997 the state-owned road construction and maintenance company, the Instituto de Estradas de Angola, declared that 80% of the country's road network was in disrepair and estimated the total cost of rebuilding roads and bridges destroyed during the civil conflict at $4,000m.

In January 1989 international donors pledged most of the US $94m. required to finance the first phase of a 10-year programme initiated by the Southern African Development Co-ordination Conference (SADCC, now the Southern African Development Community—SADC) for the development of the Lobito corridor: the programme was to include the rehabilitation of the ports of Lobito and Benguela, while the rehabilitation of the Benguela railway (see above) was also to come under its auspices. An emergency plan to restore services on the Benguela railway between Lobito and Kuito was announced, following the May 1991 cease-fire between the government and UNITA. Estimated to cost $17m., the project aimed to restore full services to Kuito by 1995. Discussions were to be held with the World Bank in late 1992 on rehabilitation of the line from Kuito to the Zaire border, following the completion of a new study of the Lobito corridor. The World Bank subsequently released $21m. in funds for the redevelopment of the Benguela railway. In 1997 an Italian company, Tor di Vale, began a $450m.-programme of repairs to the Benguela railway. Minimum repairs allowing the resumption of freight traffic were expected to take three years to complete, to be followed by further modernization including the reconstruction of 22 passenger stations. Finance for the project was to come from the harvest and export of 37,000 ha of eucalyptus plantations belonging to the Benguela Railway Co, which were expected to generate revenue of as much as $500m. The plan, which was suspended due to renewed hostilities, was partially reviewed in early 2000, and envisaged the rehabilitation of the railway to Cubal, east of Benguela. In April 1997 work was completed on the reconstruction of the 180 km rail link between Luanda and Dondo, in Cuanza-Norte province, which had been closed for seven years owing to the hostilities. Rehabilitation of the rail link between Dondo and Malanje was proceeding in 1999.

Angola's telephone communications network, which was badly damaged during the years of war, was due to benefit from considerable investment in the late 1990s. After inter-state communications were re-established with Menongue in March 1997, only three provincial capitals remained without inter-state communications: namely, Ndalatando, Mbanza-Kongo and Malanje. The first step in Angola Telecom's plans for improving and extending services is the recovery of some US $18m. in service payments owed by government agencies. The next step will be to begin an $80m. infrastructure investment plan, focusing initially on the cities of Luanda and Benguela. Angola Telecom's infrastructure investment aims for compatibility with Africa One, the $1,600m. fibre-optic cable system that will serve the African continent. A $7m.-extension to Luanda's digital telephone network, financed by the Japanese government, was being constructed by early 2000. A $6.5m. Norwegian-financed project to digitalize the telephone network in Benguela and double its capacity to 12,000 lines, was completed in June 1999.

It is estimated that more than one-half of the country's food requirements are now imported, and Angola survives as a result of external purchases and assistance, mostly from Western Europe and the UN organizations. In February 1998 the UN launched its 1998 Consolidated Inter-Agency Appeal for Angola, seeking US $91m. mainly for humanitarian needs. The 1999 Appeal called for $66m. aimed at short-term emergency needs. Of this the World Food Programme was to receive $31m. and UNICEF $15m. The principal exported commodities in 1997 were: mineral fuels and lubricants (an estimated 92.5%); diamonds (an estimated 6.9%). In that year the total value of exports was an estimated $5,008m. and the value of imports was an estimated $2,477m., leaving a trade surplus of an estimated $2,530m. There was a deficit of an estimated $866m. on the current account of the balance of payments in that year. In 1997 the USA remained Angola's principal customer (taking 63.6% of total exports), followed by the People's Republic of China (12.9%) and Belgium-Luxembourg (6.0%). The main sources of imports in that year were Portugal (20.6%), South Africa (14.1%), the USA (13.2%) and Spain (8.2%). Economic relations with Portugal have developed renewed momentum since the conclusion of the Estoril peace agreement in 1991. In February 1992 Portugal agreed to lend $325m. to enable Angola to import Portuguese goods. At the same time, it was agreed that Portugal would increase its purchases of petroleum from Angola, and that four Portuguese banks were to open branches in Angola.

Angola's inclusion in the African, Caribbean and Pacific group of signatories of the third and fourth Lomé Conventions should, in addition to making more funds available from the European Community (EC, now the European Union—EU), increase both the range and volume of its trading operations. Angola participates fully in the SADC, and has special responsibility for the co-ordination of energy development and conservation. In January 1999 Angola became a member of the Communauté économique des états de l'Afrique centrale (CEEAC).

Statistical Survey

Source (unless otherwise stated): Instituto Nacional de Estatística, Luanda.

Area and Population

AREA, POPULATION AND DENSITY

Area (sq km)	1,246,700*
Population (census results)	
30 December 1960	4,480,719
15 December 1970	
Males	2,943,974
Females	2,702,192
Total	5,646,166
Population (official estimates at mid-year)†	
1995	11,559,000
1996	11,895,000
1997	12,240,000
Density (per sq km) at mid-1997	9.8

* 481,354 sq miles.

† Population figures are projected from the 1970 census. In mid-1996, according to a nation-wide survey, the population was an estimated 15,300,000.

DISTRIBUTION OF POPULATION BY PROVINCE
(provisional estimates, mid-1995)

	Area (sq km)	Population	Density (per sq km)
Luanda	2,418	2,002,000	828.0
Huambo	34,274	1,687,000	49.2
Bié	70,314	1,246,000	17.7
Malanje	87,246	975,000	11.2
Huíla	75,002	948,000	12.6
Uíge	58,698	948,000	16.2
Benguela	31,788	702,000	22.1
Cuanza-Sul	55,660	688,000	12.4
Cuanza-Norte	24,110	412,000	17.1
Moxico	223,023	349,000	1.6
Lunda-Norte	102,783	311,000	3.0
Zaire	40,130	247,000	6.2
Cunene	88,342	245,000	2.8
Cabinda	7,270	185,000	25.4
Bengo	31,371	184,000	5.9
Lunda-Sul	56,985	160,000	2.8
Cuando-Cubango	199,049	137,000	0.7
Namibe	58,137	135,000	2.3
Total	1,246,600	11,561,000	9.3

PRINCIPAL TOWNS (population at 1970 census)

Luanda (capital) .	480,613*	Benguela . .	40,996
Huambo (Nova		Lubango (Sá da	
Lisboa) . .	61,885	Bandeira) . .	31,674
Lobito . . .	59,258	Malanje . . .	31,559

* 1982 estimate: 1,200,000.

Source: Direcção dos Serviços de Estatística, Luanda.

BIRTHS AND DEATHS (UN estimates, annual averages)

	1980–85	1985–90	1990–95
Birth rate (per 1,000) . . .	50.8	51.3	50.8
Death rate (per 1,000) . . .	22.8	21.3	19.2

Expectation of life (UN estimates, years at birth, 1990–95): 46.5 (males 44.9; females 48.1).

Source: UN, *World Population Prospects: The 1998 Revision.*

ECONOMICALLY ACTIVE POPULATION
(estimates, '000 persons, 1991)

	Males	Females	Total
Agriculture, etc.	1,518	1,374	2,892
Industry	405	33	438
Services	644	192	836
Total labour force . . .	2,567	1,599	4,166

Source: UN Economic Commission for Africa, *African Statistical Yearbook.*

Mid-1998 (estimates in '000): Agriculture, etc. 4,028; Total (incl. others) 5,564. Source: FAO, *Production Yearbook.*

Agriculture

PRINCIPAL CROPS ('000 metric tons)

	1996	1997	1998
Wheat*	5*	5*	6
Rice (paddy)*	25	25	26
Maize†	398	370	505
Millet and sorghum†	102	62	89
Potatoes*	33	31	33
Sweet potatoes*	200	195	198
Cassava (Manioc)	2,500*	2,326†	3,211†
Dry beans†	55	66	86
Groundnuts (in shell)* . . .	23	22	23
Sunflower seed*	11	10	11
Cottonseed†	8	8	8
Cotton (lint)†	4	4	4
Palm kernels*	16	16	16
Palm oil*	54	53	54
Vegetables*	263	256	263
Citrus fruit*	82	80	82
Pineapples*	38	36	38
Bananas*	295	295	295
Other fruits*	31	30	31
Sugar cane*	290	310	330
Coffee (green)	4†	5†	6*
Tobacco (leaves)	4†	4†	4*
Sisal*	1	1	1

* FAO estimate(s).   † Unofficial figure(s).

Source: FAO, *Production Yearbook.*

LIVESTOCK ('000 head, year ending September)

	1996	1997	1998
Cattle	3,309	3,556†	3,500*
Pigs*	810	820	810
Sheep*	245	250	245
Goats*	1,470	1,480	1,450

Poultry (million): 7* in 1996; 7* in 1997; 7* in 1998.

* FAO estimate(s).   † Unofficial figure.

Source: FAO, *Production Yearbook.*

LIVESTOCK PRODUCTS (FAO estimates, '000 metric tons)

	1996	1997	1998
Beef and veal	58	61	60
Goat meat	4	4	4
Pig meat	22	23	22
Poultry meat	7	7	7
Other meat	8	8	9
Cows' milk	162	175	172
Cheese	1	1	1
Poultry eggs	4	4	4
Honey	23	23	22
Cattle hides	9	9	9

Source: FAO, *Production Yearbook.*

Forestry

ROUNDWOOD REMOVALS
('000 cubic metres, excluding bark)

	1995	1996	1997
Sawlogs, veneer logs and logs for sleepers*	66	66	66
Other industrial wood . . .	910	941	974
Fuel wood	5,893	6,057	6,229
Total	6,869	7,064	7,269

* Annual output assumed to be unchanged since 1990.

Source: FAO, *Yearbook of Forest Products.*

SAWNWOOD PRODUCTION
('000 cubic metres, including railway sleepers)

	1995	1996	1997
Total	5	5	5

Source: FAO, *Yearbook of Forest Products.*

Fishing

('000 metric tons, live weight)

	1995	1996	1997
Freshwater fishes . . .	6.0	6.0	6.0
Cunene horse mackerel . .	25.3	19.8	35.8
Sardinellas	34.2	17.5	21.0
Other marine fishes (incl. unspecified) . . .	27.2	28.8	9.4
Total fish . . .	92.7	72.1	72.2
Crustaceans and molluscs . .	1.1	0.8	0.0
Total catch	93.8	72.8	72.2

Source: FAO, *Yearbook of Fishery Statistics.*

Mining

('000 metric tons, unless otherwise indicated)

	1994	1995	1996
Crude petroleum . . .	27,193	32,132	34,777
Natural gas (petajoules)* .	7	7	7
Salt (unrefined)*† . .	30	30	30
Diamonds ('000 carats):†			
Industrial	30	300	400*
Gem	270	2,700	3,600*
Gypsum (crude)† . . .	50	50	50*

* Estimate(s).
† Data from the US Bureau of Mines.

Source: UN, *Industrial Commodity Statistics Yearbook.*

1997 ('000 metric tons): Crude petroleum 35,341 (Source: UN, *Monthly Bulletin of Statistics*).

Industry

SELECTED PRODUCTS
('000 metric tons, unless otherwise indicated)

	1994	1995	1996
Raw sugar*	20	20	25
Plywood ('000 cubic metres)*† .	10	10	10
Chemical wood pulp*† .	15	15	15
Jet fuels†	160	158	160
Motor spirit (petrol)† . .	105	108	110
Kerosene†	50	50	55
Distillate fuel oils† . .	320	315	320
Residual fuel oils† . .	640	630	635
Cement†‡	300	300	n.a.
Crude steel†	9	9	9‡
Electric energy (million kWh)†	1,865	1,870	1,885

* Data from the FAO.
† Estimates.
‡ Data from the US Bureau of Mines.

Source: UN, *Industrial Commodity Statistics Yearbook.*

Finance

CURRENCY AND EXCHANGE RATES

Monetary Units
100 lwei = 1 readjusted kwanza.

Sterling, Dollar and Euro Equivalents (28 April 2000)
£1 sterling = 10,529,729 readjusted kwanza;
US $1 = 6,714,960 readjusted kwanza;
€1 = 6,100,541 readjusted kwanza;
100,000,000 readjusted kwanza = £9.497 = $14.892 = €16.392.

Average Exchange Rate (readjusted kwanza per US $)

1997	229,040
1998	392,824
1999	2,790,706

Note: An official exchange rate of US $1 = 29.62 kwanza was introduced in 1976 and remained in force until September 1990. In that month the kwanza was replaced, at par, by the new kwanza. At the same time, it was announced that the currency was to be devalued by more than 50%, with the exchange rate adjusted to US $1 = 60 new kwanza, with effect from 1 October 1990. This rate remained in force until 18 November 1991, when a basic rate of US $1 = 90 new kwanza was established. The currency underwent further devaluation, by 50% in December 1991, and by more than 67% on 15 April 1992, when a basic rate of US $1 = 550 new kwanza was established. In February 1993 the currency was again devalued, when a basic rate of US $1 = 7,000 new kwanza was established. In April 1993 this was adjusted to US $1 = 4,000 new kwanza, and in October to US $1 = 6,500 new kwanza, a devaluation of 38.5%. Following a series of four devaluations in February and March 1994, a rate of US $1 = 35,000 new kwanza was established in late March. In April 1994 the introduction of a new method of setting exchange rates resulted in an effective devaluation, to US $1 = 68,297 new kwanza, and provided for an end to the system of multiple exchange rates. Further substantial devaluations followed, and in July 1995 a 'readjusted' kwanza, equivalent to 1,000 new kwanza, was introduced. The currency, however, continued to depreciate. Between July 1997 and June 1998 a fixed official rate of US $1 = 262,376 readjusted kwanza was in operation. In May 1999 the Central Bank announced its decision to abolish the existing dual currency exchange rate system. On 1 December 1999 the readjusted kwanza was replaced by a new currency, the kwanza, equivalent to 1m. readjusted kwanza. The former currency was to remain in circulation until 31 May 2000.

BUDGET ('000 million readjusted kwanza)

Revenue	1995	1996	1997*
Tax revenue .	4,074.0	374,404	496,528
Income tax	2,843.7	246,033	271,592
Petroleum corporate tax .	1,508.1	106,459	195,286
Petroleum transaction tax	1,236.7	132,524	51,704
Tax on goods and services	935.0	105,499	171,169
Petroleum sector .	835.3	96,580	143,955
Diamond sector .	2.2	1,887	—
Taxes on foreign trade .	201.0	16,086	33,830
Other taxes	94.3	6,786	19,937
Stamp tax	83.8	5,890	14,145
Non-tax revenue .	41.5	1,856	141,387
Total	4,115.6	376,260	637,915

* Estimates.

Expenditure*	1995	1996	1997†
General public services	1,513	64,628	173,598
Defence and public order .	2,469	162,354	355,565
Peace process	39	3,666	6,097
Education	399	21,546	48,346
Health	450	13,909	30,740
Social security, welfare and housing	247	9,968	51,470
Economic affairs and services .	523	39,385	85,192
Interest payments	1,483	97,391	97,247
Total (incl. others)	7,863	463,867	980,319

* Including adjustments for unrecorded transactions. The data include lending minus repayments.
† Estimates.
Source: IMF, *Angola: Statistical Annex* (April 1999).

INTERNATIONAL RESERVES (US $ million at 31 December)

	1997	1998	1999
IMF special drawing rights .	0.16	0.17	0.18
Foreign exchange	396.27	203.29	495.93
Total	396.43	203.46	496.10

Source: IMF, *International Financial Statistics*.

MONEY SUPPLY ('000 million readjusted kwanza at 31 December)

	1997	1998	1999
Currency outside banks .	101,619	165,686	650,450
Demand deposits at banking institutions	93,292	106,583	510,630
Total (incl. others) .	194,910	272,432	1,161,080

Source: IMF, *International Financial Statistics*.

COST OF LIVING

(Consumer Price Index for Luanda at December; base: 1994 average = 100)

	1995	1996	1997
Food	10,425	170,984	318,793
Clothing	19,152	307,789	420,558
Rent, fuel and light .	10,295	257,809	4,572,341
All items (incl. others) .	11,642	203,768	504,818

Source: IMF, *Angola: Statistical Annex* (April 1999).

All items (Consumer Price Index for Luanda; annual averages; base: 1995 = 100): 25,327.3 in 1998; 97,799.1 in 1999 (Source: IMF, *International Financial Statistics*).

NATIONAL ACCOUNTS
Composition of the Gross National Product (US $ million)

	1987	1988	1989
Gross domestic product (GDP) at factor cost .	6,482	6,877	7,682
Indirect taxes	94	95	117
Less Subsidies .	189	122	93
GDP in purchasers' values	6,386	6,850	7,706
Net factor income from abroad .	−402	−938	−1,079
Gross national product	5,984	5,912	6,627

Gross Domestic Product by Economic Activity
('000 million readjusted kwanza at current prices)

	1996	1997	1998*
Agriculture, forestry and fishing	62,113.5	166,032.7	300,921.4
Mining	518,629.4	908,348.6	1,073,894.4
Processing industry	28,789.1	76,700.3	141,397.2
Electricity and water	289.4	772.1	1,451.8
Construction	25,911.4	71,344.4	131,649.4
Trade .	125,472.9	282,933.0	433,953.7
Other services .	68,741.5	197,306.7	270,915.9
Sub-total .	829,947.5	1,703,437.7	2,354,183.9
Import duties	15,931.6	33,829.7	35,250.7
GDP in purchasers' values	845,878.8	1,737,267.4	2,389,434.6

* Provisional figures.

BALANCE OF PAYMENTS (US $ million)

	1995	1996	1997*
Exports of goods f.o.b. .	3,723	5,095	5,008
Imports of goods f.o.b. .	−1,852	−2,040	−2,477
Trade balance .	1,871	3,055	2,530
Services (net) .			
Interest payments (net) . }	−2,864	−3,378	−3,397
Unrequited transfers (net) .			
Current balance .	−994	−323	−866
Direct investment (net) .	303	588	492
Other long-term capital (net) .	−729	−306	267
Short-term capital (net) .	221	−208	−669
Net errors and omissions .	−20	31	−30
Overall balance .	−1,218	−218	−806

* Estimates.
Source: IMF, *Angola: Statistical Annex* (April 1999).

External Trade

SELECTED COMMODITIES

Imports (million kwanza)	1983	1984	1985
Animal products .	1,315	1,226	1,084
Vegetable products .	2,158	3,099	2,284
Fats and oils .	946	1,006	1,196
Food and beverages .	2,400	1,949	1,892
Industrial chemical products .	1,859	1,419	1,702
Plastic materials .	431	704	454
Paper products .	376	380	411
Textiles .	1,612	1,816	1,451
Base metals .	1,985	3,730	2,385
Electrical equipment .	3,296	2,879	2,571
Transport equipment .	2,762	2,240	3,123
Total (incl. others) .	20,197	21,370	19,694

Total Imports (million kwanza): 18,691 in 1986; 13,372 in 1987; 29,845 in 1988; 34,392 in 1989 (Source: UN, *Monthly Bulletin of Statistics*).

Exports (US $ million)	1995	1996	1997*
Crude petroleum. . . .	3,425	4,651	4,507
Refined petroleum products . .	96	130	123
Diamonds . . .	168	267	348
Total (incl. others) . . .	3,723	5,095	5,008

* Estimates.

Source: IMF, *Angola: Statistical Annex* (April 1999).

PRINCIPAL TRADING PARTNERS (US $ million)

Imports c.i.f.	1987	1988	1989
Belgium-Luxembourg . . .	17.9	22.9	99.9
Brazil	55.8	119.2	104.0
France	63.3	8.8	114.1
German Dem. Repub. . .	35.2	34.7	41.9
Germany, Fed. Repub. . .	51.0	149.0	178.4
Italy	19.0	19.3	35.2
Japan	8.1	39.7	34.5
Netherlands	20.6	148.3	160.5
Portugal.	51.4	171.4	206.8
Spain	4.8	53.2	55.6
United Arab Emirates . .	70.5	25.1	23.1
United Kingdom	9.1	26.7	32.9
Total (incl. others) . . .	442.6	987.9	1,139.6

Total Imports (US $ million): 1,139.5 in 1990; 457.9 in 1991; 728.7 in 1992.

Exports f.o.b.	1990	1991	1992
Austria	62.8	—	—
Belgium-Luxembourg . .	231.9	45.9	106.0
Brazil	80.0	210.2	46.0
Canada	28.1	37.1	—
Chile	76.7	22.2	—
China, People's Repub. . .	—	—	63.0
France	456.3	290.4	300.0
Germany	40.4	21.0	—
Gibraltar	72.8	12.5	—
Italy	143.9	82.6	37.0
Netherlands	414.0	206.2	167.1
Portugal.	88.8	87.8	75.5
Singapore	—	—	49.0
Spain	2.5	40.5	50.1
United Kingdom	21.5	144.3	316.0
USA	2,067.6	2,094.6	2,460.0
Yugoslavia	—	62.2	—
Total (incl. others) . . .	3,910.3	3,409.7	3,697.5

Source: UN, *International Trade Statistics Yearbook.*

Transport

GOODS TRANSPORT ('000 metric tons)

	1988	1989	1990
Road	1,056.7	690.1	867.3
Railway	580.9	510.3	443.2
Water	780.8	608.6	812.1
Air	24.6	10.5	28.3
Total	2,443.0	1,819.5	2,150.9

Sources: Instituto Nacional de Estatística; Ministério de Transporte e Comunicações.

PASSENGER TRANSPORT ('000 journeys)

	1988	1989	1990
Road	12,699.2	32,658.7	48,796.1
Railway	6,659.7	6,951.2	6,455.8
Water	151.8	163.2	223.8
Air	608.9	618.4	615.9
Total	20,119.6	40,391.5	56,091.6

Sources: Instituto Nacional de Estatística; Ministério de Transporte e Comunicações, Luanda.

ROAD TRAFFIC (estimates, motor vehicles in use at 31 December)

	1994	1995	1996
Passenger cars	180,000	197,000	207,000
Lorries and vans . . .	32,340	26,000	25,000
Total	212,340	223,000	232,000

Source: IRF, *World Road Statistics.*

SHIPPING

Merchant Fleet (registered at 31 December)

	1996	1997	1998
Number of vessels . . .	113	109	123
Total displacement (grt) . .	81,856	68,031	73,907

Source: Lloyd's Register of Shipping, *World Fleet Statistics.*

International Sea-borne Freight Traffic (estimates, '000 metric tons)

	1989	1990	1991
Goods loaded	19,980	21,102	23,288
Goods unloaded	1,235	1,242	1,261

Source: UN Economic Commission for Africa, *African Statistical Yearbook.*

CIVIL AVIATION (traffic on scheduled services)

	1994	1995	1996
Kilometres flown (million) . .	13	8	8
Passengers carried ('000) . .	519	553	585
Passenger-km (million) . .	1,594	833	880
Total ton-km (million) . .	197	133	141

Source: UN, *Statistical Yearbook.*

Tourism

FOREIGN TOURIST ARRIVALS

Country of origin	1995	1996	1997
Belgium	938	943	4,151
Brazil	1,038	1,732	2,175
Congo, Republic . . .	429	467	1,054
France	1,413	1,726	5,553
Italy	93	425	1,839
Namibia	118	356	1,703
Portugal.	3,357	6,927	14,282
South Africa	700	1,545	8,067
Total (incl. others) . . .	9,546	20,978	45,139

Tourism receipts (US $ million): 10 in 1995; 9 in 1996; 9 in 1997.

Source: World Tourism Organization, *Yearbook of Tourism Statistics.*

Communications Media

	1994	1995	1996
Radio receivers ('000 in use) . .	320	370	600
Television receivers ('000 in use) .	70	80	100
Telephones ('000 main lines in use)	55*	60*	52
Mobile cellular telephones			
(subscribers)	1,824	1,994	3,298
Daily newspapers			
Number	4	5	5
Average circulation ('000 copies)	117	122	128

* Provisional figure.

Book production: 47 titles (books 35, pamphlets 12) and 419,000 copies (books 338,000, pamphlets 81,000) in 1985; 14 titles (all books) and 130,000 copies in 1986; 22 titles (all books) in 1995.

1997 ('000 in use): Radio receivers 630; Television receivers 150.

Sources: UNESCO, *Statistical Yearbook*; UN, *Statistical Yearbook*.

Education

(1991/92)

	Teachers	Pupils
Pre-primary	n.a.	214,867
Primary	31,062*	989,443
Secondary:		
general	5,138†	196,099
teacher training	280‡	10,772
vocational	286†	12,116
Higher	787	6,331

* Figure for school year 1990/91.
† Figure for school year 1989/90.
‡ Figure for school year 1987/88.

Source: mainly UNESCO, *Statistical Yearbook*.

Directory

The Constitution

The MPLA regime adopted an independence Constitution for Angola in November 1975. It was amended in October 1976, September 1980, March 1991, April and August 1992, and November 1996. The main provisions of the Constitution, as amended, are summarized below:

BASIC PRINCIPLES

The Republic of Angola shall be a sovereign and independent state whose prime objective shall be to build a free and democratic society of peace, justice and social progress. It shall be a democratic state based on the rule of law, founded on national unity, the dignity of human beings, pluralism of expression and political organization, respecting and guaranteeing the basic rights and freedoms of persons, whether as individuals or as members of organized social groups. Sovereignty shall be vested in the people, which shall exercise political power through periodic universal suffrage.

The Republic of Angola shall be a unitary and indivisible state. Economic, social and cultural solidarity shall be promoted between all the Republic's regions for the common development of the entire nation and the elimination of regionalism and tribalism.

Religion

The Republic shall be a secular state and there shall be complete separation of the State and religious institutions. All religions shall be respected.

The Economy

The economic system shall be based on the coexistence of diverse forms of property—public, private, mixed, co-operative and family— and all shall enjoy equal protection. The State shall protect foreign investment and foreign property, in accordance with the law. The fiscal system shall aim to satisfy the economic, social and administrative needs of the State and to ensure a fair distribution of income and wealth. Taxes may be created and abolished only by law, which shall determine applicability, rates, tax benefits and guarantees for taxpayers.

Education

The Republic shall vigorously combat illiteracy and obscurantism and shall promote the development of education and of a true national culture.

FUNDAMENTAL RIGHTS AND DUTIES

The State shall respect and protect the human person and human dignity. All citizens shall be equal before the law. They shall be subject to the same duties, without any distinction based on colour, race, ethnic group, sex, place of birth, religion, level of education, or economic or social status.

All citizens aged 18 years and over, other than those legally deprived of political and civil rights, shall have the right and duty to take an active part in public life, to vote and be elected to any state organ, and to discharge their mandates with full dedication to the cause of the Angolan nation. The law shall establish limitations in respect of non-political allegiance of soldiers on active service, judges and police forces, as well as the electoral incapacity of soldiers on active service and police forces.

Freedom of expression, of assembly, of demonstration, of association and of all other forms of expression shall be guaranteed. Groupings whose aims or activities are contrary to the constitutional order and penal laws, or that, even indirectly, pursue political objectives through organizations of a military, paramilitary or militarized nature shall be forbidden. Every citizen has the right to a defence if accused of a crime. Individual freedoms are guaranteed. Freedom of conscience and belief shall be inviolable. Work shall be the right and duty of all citizens. The State shall promote measures necessary to ensure the right of citizens to medical and health care, as well as assistance in childhood, motherhood, disability, old age, etc. It shall also promote access to education, culture and sports for all citizens.

STATE ORGANS

President of the Republic

The President of the Republic shall be the Head of State, Head of Government and Commander-in-Chief of the Angolan armed forces. The President of the Republic shall be elected directly by a secret universal ballot and shall have the following powers:

to appoint and dismiss the Prime Minister, Ministers and other government officials determined by law;

to appoint the judges of the Supreme Court;

to preside over the Council of Ministers;

to declare war and make peace, following authorization by the National Assembly;

to sign, promulgate and publish the laws of the National Assembly, government decrees and statutory decrees;

to preside over the National Defence Council;

to decree a state of siege or state of emergency;

to announce the holding of general elections;

to issue pardons and commute sentences;

to perform all other duties provided for in the Constitution.

National Assembly

The National Assembly is the supreme state legislative body, to which the Government is responsible. The National Assembly shall be composed of 223 deputies, elected for a term of four years. The National Assembly shall convene in ordinary session twice yearly and in special session on the initiative of the President of the National Assembly, the Standing Commission of the National Assembly or of no less than one-third of its deputies. The Standing Commission shall be the organ of the National Assembly that represents and assumes its powers between sessions.

Government

The Government shall comprise the President of the Republic, the ministers and the secretaries of state, and other members whom the law shall indicate, and shall have the following functions:

to organize and direct the implementation of state domestic and foreign policy, in accordance with decision of the National Assembly and its Standing Commission;

to ensure national defence, the maintenance of internal order and security, and the protection of the rights of citizens;

to prepare the draft National Plan and General State Budget for approval by the National Assembly, and to organize, direct and control their execution;

The Council of Ministers shall be answerable to the National Assembly. In the exercise of its powers, the Council of Ministers shall issue decrees and resolutions.

Judiciary

The organization, composition and competence of the courts shall be established by law. Judges shall be independent in the discharge of their functions.

Local State Organs

The organs of state power at provincial level shall be the Provincial Assemblies and their executive bodies. The Provincial Assemblies shall work in close co-operation with social organizations and rely on the initiative and broad participation of citizens. The Provincial Assemblies shall elect commissions of deputies to perform permanent or specific tasks. The executive organs of Provincial Assemblies shall be the Provincial Governments, which shall be led by the Provincial Governors. The Provincial Governors shall be answerable to the President of the Republic, the Council of Ministers and the Provincial Assemblies.

National Defence

The State shall ensure national defence. The National Defence Council shall be presided over by the President of the Republic, and its composition shall be determined by law. The Angolan armed forces, as a state institution, shall be permanent, regular and non-partisan. Defence of the country shall be the right and the highest indeclinable duty of every citizen. Military service shall be compulsory. The forms in which it is fulfilled shall be defined by the law.

Note: In accordance with the terms of the Lusaka peace accord of November 1994, in April 1997 a new Government of National Unity and Reconciliation was inaugurated in which UNITA held four portfolios. In November 1996 the National Assembly adopted a constitutional revision extending the parliamentary mandate, which was due to expire that month, for a period of between two and four years in order to allow for the establishment of suitable conditions for the conduct of elections.

The Government

HEAD OF STATE

President: José Eduardo dos Santos (assumed office 21 September 1979).

COUNCIL OF MINISTERS
(August 2000)

Prime Minister: José Eduardo dos Santos.

Minister of Defence: Gen. Kundi Paihama.

Minister of the Interior: Fernando da Piedade Dias dos Santos.

Minister of Foreign Affairs: João Bernardo de Miranda.

Minister of Territorial Administration: Fernando Faustino Muteka.

Minister of Finance: Joaquim Duarte da Costa David.

Minister of Economic Planning: Ana Dias Lourenço.

Minister of Petroleum: José Botelho de Vasconcelos.

Minister of Industry: Albina Faria de Assis Pereira Africano.

Minister of Agriculture and Rural Development: Gilberto Buta Lutukuta.

Minister of Fisheries and Environment: Maria de Fátima Monteiro Jardim.

Minister of Geology and Mines: Manuel António Africano.

Minister of Public Works and Housing: António Henriques da Silva.

Minister of Transport: André Luís Brandão.

Minister of Trade: Victorino Domingos Hossi.

Minister of Health: Albertina Júlia Hamukuaya.

Minister of Education and Culture: António Burity da Silva Neto.

Minister of Social Welfare: Albino Malungo.

Minister of Youth and Sports: José Marcos Barrica.

Minister of Justice: Dr Paulo Tchipilica.

Minister of Public Administration, Employment and Social Security: Dr António Domingos Pitra Costa Neto.

Minister of Social Communication: Dr Pedro Hendrik Vaal Neto.

Minister of Science and Technology: João Baptista Nganda Gina.

Minister of Post and Telecommunications: Licínio Tavares Ribeiro.

Minister of Family and the Promotion of Women: Cândida Celeste da Silva.

Minister of War Veterans: Pedro José van-Dúnem.

Minister of Hotels and Tourism: Jorge Alicerces Valentim.

Minister of Energy and Water: Luis Filipe da Silva.

Secretaries of State with Independent Charge

Secretary of State for Coffee: Gilberto Buta Lutukuta.

Secretary of State for Environment: Manuel David Mendes.

MINISTRIES

All Ministries are located in Luanda.

Ministry of Agriculture and Rural Development: Avda Norton de Matos 2, Luanda.

Ministry of Defence: Rua Silva Carvalho ex Quartel General, Luanda.

Ministry of Education and Culture: Avda Comandante Jika, CP 1281, Luanda; tel. (2) 321592; fax (2) 321592.

Ministry of Finance: Avda 4 de Fevereiro, Luanda; tel. (2) 344628.

Ministry of Fisheries and Environment: Avda 4 de Fevereiro 25, Predio Atlântico, Luanda; tel. (2) 392782.

Ministry of Foreign Affairs: Avda Comandante Jika, Luanda.

Ministry of Geology and Mines: CP 1260, Luanda; tel. (2) 322766; fax (2) 321655.

Ministry of Health: Rua Diogo Cão, Luanda.

Ministry of the Interior: Avda 4 de Fevereiro, Luanda.

Ministry of Justice: Largo do Palácio, Luanda.

Ministry of Petroleum: Avda 4 de Fevereiro 105, CP 1279, Luanda; tel. (2) 337448.

Ministry of Public Administration, Employment and Social Security: Rua 17 de Setembro 32, CP 1986, Luanda; tel. (2) 339656; fax (2) 339054.

Ministry of Social Communication: Avda Comandante Válodia, CP 2608, Luanda; tel. (2) 343495.

Ministry of Trade: Largo Kinaxixi 14, Luanda; tel. (2) 344525.

Ministry of Transport and Communications: Avda 4 de Fevereiro 42, CP 1250-C, Luanda; tel. (2) 370061.

PROVINCIAL GOVERNORS*

Bengo: Ezelino Mendes.

Benguela: Dumilde das Chagas Simões Rangel.

Bié: Luís Paulino dos Santos.

Cabinda: José Amaro Tati.

Cuando-Cubango: Manuel Gama.

Cuanza-Norte: Manuel Pedro Pacavira.

Cuanza-Sul: Francisco Higino Lopes Carneiro.

Cunene: Pedro Mutinde.

Huambo: Paulo Kassoma.

Huíla: Francisco José Ramos da Cruz.

Luanda: José Aníbal Lopes Rocha.

Lunda-Norte: Manuel Francisco Gomes Maiato.

Lunda-Sul: Francisco Sozinho Chiubsa.

Malanje: Flavio Fernandes.

Moxico: João Ernesto dos Santos (Liberdade).

Namibe: Salomeo José Lueto Sirimbimbe.

Uíge: Cordero Ernesto Zacundomba.

Zaire: Ludi Kissassunda.

*All Governors are ex-officio members of the Government.

President and Legislature

PRESIDENT*

Presidential Election, 29 and 30 September 1992

	Votes	% of votes
José Eduardo dos Santos (MPLA) . .	1,953,335	49.57
Dr Jonas Malheiro Savimbi (UNITA). .	1,579,298	40.07
António Alberto Neto (PDA) . . .	85,249	2.16
Holden Roberto (FNLA)	83,135	2.11
Honorato Lando (PDLA)	75,789	1.92
Luís dos Passos (PRD)	59,121	1.47
Bengui Pedro João (PSD)	38,243	0.97
Simão Cacete (FPD)	26,385	0.67
Daniel Júlio Chipenda (Independent) .	20,646	0.52
Anália de Victória Pereira (PLD) . .	11,475	0.29
Rui de Victória Pereira (PRA) . .	9,208	0.23
Total	**3,940,884**	**100.00**

NATIONAL ASSEMBLY

President: Roberto de Almeida.

Legislative Election, 29 and 30 September 1992

	Votes	% of votes	Seats†
MPLA	2,124,126	53.74	129
UNITA	1,347,636	34.10	70
FNLA	94,742	2.40	5
PLD	94,269	2.39	3
PRS	89,875	2.27	6
PRD	35,293	0.89	1
AD Coalition	34,166	0.86	1
PSD	33,088	0.84	1
PAJOCA	13,924	0.35	1
FDA	12,038	0.30	1
PDP–ANA	10,620	0.27	1
PNDA	10,281	0.26	1
CNDA	10,237	0.26	—
PSDA	19,217	0.26	—
PAI	9,007	0.23	—
PDLA	8,025	0.20	—
PDA	8,014	0.20	—
PRA	6,719	0.17	—
Total	**3,952,277**	**100.00**	**220**

* Under the terms of the electoral law, a second round of presidential elections was required to take place in order to determine which of the two leading candidates from the first round would be elected. However, a resumption of hostilities between UNITA and government forces prevented a second round of presidential elections from taking place. The electoral process was to resume only when the provisions of the Estoril peace agreement, concluded in May 1991, had been fulfilled. However, provision in the Lusaka peace accord of November 1994 for the second round of presidential elections was not pursued.

† According to the Constitution, the total number of seats in the National Assembly is 223. On the decision of the National Electoral Council, however, elections to fill three seats reserved for Angolans resident abroad were abandoned.

Political Organizations

Aliança Democrática de Angola: Leader Simba da Costa.

Angolan Alliance and Hamista Party.

Angolan Democratic Coalition (AD Coalition): Pres. Evidor Quiela (acting).

Angolan Democratic Confederation: f. 1994; Chair. Gaspar Neto.

Angolan Democratic Unification: Leader Eduardo Milton Sivi.

Associação Cívica Angolana (ACA): f. 1990; Leader Joaquim Pinto de Andrade.

Centro Democrático Social (CDS): Pres. Mateus José; Sec.-Gen. Delfina Francisco Capciel.

Christian Democratic Convention: Leader Gaspar Neto.

Democratic Civilian Opposition: f. 1994; opposition alliance including:

Convenção Nacional Democrata de Angola (CNDA): Leader Paulino Pinto João.

Frente Nacional de Libertação de Angola (FNLA): internet www.fnla.org; f. 1962; Pres. Lucas Ngonda.

Frente para a Democracia (FPD): Leader Nelso Pestana; Sec.-Gen. Filomeno Vieira Lopes.

Movimento de Defesa dos Interesses de Angola—Partido de Consciência Nacional: Leader Isidoro Klala.

National Ecological Party of Angola: Leader Sukawa Dizi-zeko Ricardo.

National Union for Democracy: Leader Sebastião Rogerio Suzama.

Partido Renovador Social (PRS): Pres. Eduardo Kwangana.

Party of Solidarity and the Conscience of Angola: Leader Fernando Dombassi Quiesse.

Fórum Democrático Angolano (FDA): Leader Jorge Rebelo Pinto Chicoti.

Frente de Libertação do Enclave de Cabinda (FLEC): f. 1963; comprises several factions, claiming total forces of c. 5,000 guerrillas, seeking the secession of Cabinda province; mem. groups include:

Frente Democrática de Cabinda (FDC): Leader Francisco Xavier Lubota.

Frente de Libertação do Enclave de Cabinda–Forças Armadas Cabindesas (FLEC–FAC): Chair. Henrique Tiago N'Zita; Chief-of-Staff (FAC) Commdr Estanislau Miguel Bomba.

Frente de Libertação do Enclave de Cabinda–Renovada (FLEC–R): Pres. António Bento Bembe; Sec.-Gen. Arturo Chibasa.

Movimento Amplo para a Democracia: Leader Francisco Viana.

Movimento Popular de Libertação de Angola (MPLA) (People's Movement for the Liberation of Angola): Luanda; f. 1956; in 1961–74 conducted guerrilla operations against Portuguese rule; governing party since 1975; known as Movimento Popular de Libertação de Angola–Partido do Trabalho (MPLA–PT) (People's Movement for the Liberation of Angola–Workers' Party) 1977–92; in Dec. 1990 replaced Marxist-Leninist ideology with commitment to 'democratic socialism'; Chair. José Eduardo dos Santos; Sec.-Gen. João Manuel Gonçalves Lourenço.

Movimento de Unidade Democrática para a Reconstrução (Mudar): Leader Manuel dos Santos Lima.

National Union for the Light of Democracy and Development of Angola: Pres. Miguel Muendo; Sec.-Gen. Domingos Chizela.

Partido de Aliança de Juventude, Operários e Camponêses de Angola (PAJOCA) (Angolan Youth, Workers' and Peasants' Alliance Party): Leader Miguel João Sebastião.

Partido para a Aliança Popular: Leader Campos Neto.

Partido Angolano Independente (PAI): Leader Adriano Parreira.

Partido Democrático Angolano (PDA): Leader António Alberto Neto.

Partido Liberal Democrata (PLD): Leader Anália de Victória Pereira.

Partido Nacional Democrata de Angola (PNDA): Sec.-Gen. Pedro João António.

Partido Reformador de Angola (PRA): Leader Rui de Victória Pereira.

Partido Renovador Democrático (PRD): Leader Luís dos Passos.

Partido Republicano Conservador de Angola (PRCA): Leader Martinho Mateus.

Partido Social Democrata (PSD): Leader Bengui Pedro João.

Partido do Trabalho de Angola (PTA): Leader Agostinho Paldo.

Patriotic Front: f. 1995; opposition alliance including:

Partido Angolano Liberal (PAL): Leader Manuel Francisco Lulo (acting).

Partido Democrático Liberal de Angola (PDLA): Leader Honorato Lando.

Partido Democrático para o Progresso–Aliança Nacional de Angola (PDP–ANA): Leader Mfufumpinga Nlandu Victor.

Partido Social Democrata de Angola (PSDA): Leader André Milton Kilandonoco.

Peaceful Democratic Party of Angola: Leader António Kunzo-lako.

Unangola: Leader André Franco de Sousa.

União Nacional para a Independência Total de Angola (UNITA): internet www.unita.org; f. 1966 to secure independence from Portugal; later received Portuguese support to oppose the MPLA; UNITA and the Frente Nacional de Libertação de Angola conducted guerrilla campaign against the MPLA Govt with aid from some Western countries, 1975–76; supported by South Africa until 1984 and in 1987–88, and by USA after 1986; obtained legal status in March 1998; support drawn mainly from Ovimbundu ethnic group; Pres. Dr JONAS MALHEIRO SAVIMBI; Sec.-Gen. PAULO LUKAMBA 'GATO'.

UNITA—Renovada: f. 1998; splinter group claiming to be legitimate leadership of UNITA and recognized as such by MPLA, although commanding minority support among UNITA mems; Leader EUGINIO MANUVAKOLA.

United Front for the Salvation of Angola: Leader JOSÉ AUGUSTO DA SILVA COELHO.

Vofangola: Leader LOMBY ZUENDOKI.

Diplomatic Representation

EMBASSIES IN ANGOLA

Algeria: Luanda; Ambassador: HANAFI OUSSEDIK.

Belgium: Avda 4 de Fevereiro 93, CP 1203, Luanda; tel. (2) 336437; fax (2) 336438; e-mail luanda@diplobel.org; Ambassador: MICHEL VANTROYEN.

Brazil: Rua Houari Boumedienne 132, CP 5428, Luanda; tel. (2) 344848; Ambassador: PAULO DYRCEU PINHEIRO.

Bulgaria: Rua Fernão Mendes Pinto 35, CP 2260, Luanda; tel. (2) 321010; Chargé d'affaires a.i.: LILO TOCHEV.

Cape Verde: Rua Alexandre Peres 29, Luanda; tel. (2) 333211; Ambassador: JOSÉ LUÍS JESUS.

China, People's Republic: Rua Houari Boumedienne 196, Luanda; tel. (2) 344185; Ambassador: XIAO SIJIN.

Congo, Democratic Republic: Rua Cesario Verde 24, Luanda; tel. (2) 361953; Ambassador: MUNDINDI DIDI KILENGO.

Congo, Republic: Rua 4 de Fevereiro 3, Luanda; Ambassador: ANATOLE KHONDO.

Côte d'Ivoire: Rua Karl Marx 43, Luanda; tel. (2) 333992; fax (2) 333997; Ambassador: ETIENNE MIEZAN EZO.

Cuba: Rua Che Guevara 42, Bairro Ingombotas, Luanda; tel. (2) 339165; Ambassador: JUAN B. PUJOL-SÁNCHEZ.

Egypt: Rua Comandante Stona 247, Luanda; tel. (2) 321590; Ambassador: ANWAR DAKROURY.

France: Rua Reverendo Pedro Agostinho Neto 31–33, Luanda; tel. (2) 334335; fax (2) 391949; Ambassador: ANDRÉ CIRA.

Gabon: Avda 4 de Fevereiro 95, Luanda; tel. (2) 372614; Ambassador: RAPHAËL NKASSA-NZOGHO.

Germany: Avda 4 de Fevereiro 120, CP 1295, Luanda; tel. (2) 334516; fax (2) 334516; Ambassador: Dr HENDRIK DANE.

Ghana: Rua Cirilo da Conceição e Silva 5, CP 1012, Luanda; tel. (2) 339222; fax (2) 338235; Ambassador: SIMON S. PULI.

Guinea: Luanda.

Holy See: Rua Luther King 123, CP 1030, Luanda (Apostolic Delegation); tel. (2) 336289; fax (2) 332378; Apostolic Delegate: Most Rev. ALDO CAVALLI, Titular Archbishop of Vibo Valentia.

Hungary: Rua Comandante Stona 226-228, Luanda; tel. (2) 32313; fax (2) 322448; Ambassador: Dr GÁBOR TÓTH.

India: Prédio dos Armazens Carrapas 81, 1°, D, CP 6040, Luanda; tel. (2) 345398; fax (2) 342061; Ambassador: BALDEV RAJ GHULIANI.

Italy: Edif. Rua dos Enganos 1, CP 6220, Luanda; tel. (2) 393533; fax (2) 333743; e-mail embitaly@ebonet.net; Ambassador: PAOLA SANNELLA.

Korea, Democratic People's Republic: Rua Cabral Moncada 116–120, CP 599, Luanda; tel. (2) 395575; fax (2) 332813; Ambassador: HYON SOK.

Morocco: Largo 4 de Fevereiro 3, Luanda; tel. (2) 338847.

Mozambique: Luanda; tel. (2) 330811; Ambassador: M. SALESSIO.

Namibia: Rua dos Cocqueiros, CP 953, Luanda; tel. (2) 395483; fax (2) 339234; e-mail embnam@netangola.com.

Netherlands: Edif. Secil, Avda 4 de Fevereiro 42, CP 3624, Luanda; tel. (2) 333540; fax (2) 333699; e-mail lua@gg.lua.minbuza.nl; Ambassador: H. KROON.

Nigeria: Rua Houari Boumedienne 120, CP 479, Luanda; tel. (2) 340084; Ambassador: AGWOM GOKIR GOTIP.

Poland: Rua Comandante N'zaji 21–23, CP 1340, Luanda; tel. (2) 323086; Ambassador: JAN BOJKO.

Portugal: Rua Karl Marx 50, CP 1346, Luanda; tel. (2) 333027; Ambassador: RAMALHO ORTIGÃO.

Romania: Ramalho Ortigão 30, Alvalade, Luanda; tel. and fax (2) 321076; Ambassador: MARIN ILIESCU.

Russia: Rua Houari Boumedienne 170, CP 3141, Luanda; tel. (2) 345028; Ambassador: YURII KAPRALOV.

São Tomé and Príncipe: Rua Armindo de Andrade 173–175, Luanda; tel. (2) 345677; Ambassador: ARIOSTO CASTELO DAVID.

Slovakia: Rua Amílcar Cabral 5, CP 2691, Luanda; tel. (2) 334456.

South Africa: Rua Manuel Fernandes Caldeira 6B, CP 6212 Luanda; tel. (2) 397391; fax (2) 339126; Ambassador: R. J. M. MAMPANE.

Spain: Avda 4 de Fevereiro 95, 1°, CP 3061, Luanda; tel. (2) 391187; fax (2) 391188; Ambassador: ALVARO IRANZO.

Sweden: Rua Garcia Neto 9, Luanda; tel. (2) 340424; Ambassador: LENA SUND.

Switzerland: Avda 4 de Fevereiro 129, 2°, CP 3163, Luanda; tel. (2) 338314; fax (2) 336878; Chargé d'affaires a.i.: ARNOLDO LARDI.

Tanzania: Rua Joaquim Kapango 57–63, Luanda; tel. (2) 330536.

United Kingdom: Rua Diogo Cão 4, CP 1244, Luanda; tel. (2) 392991; fax (2) 333331; Ambassador: CAROLINE ELMES.

USA: Rua Houari Boumedienne 32, Miramar, CP 6468, Luanda; tel. (2) 347028; fax (2) 346924; Ambassador: JOSEPH SULLIVAN.

Viet Nam: Rua Comandante N'zaji 66–68, CP 75, Luanda; tel. (2) 323388; Ambassador: NGUYEN HUY LOI.

Yugoslavia: Rua Comandante N'zaji 25–27, Luanda; tel. (2) 321421; fax (2) 321724; Chargé d'affaires a.i.: BRANKO MARKOVIĆ.

Zambia: Rua Rei Katyavala 106–108, CP 1496, Luanda; tel. (2) 331145; Ambassador: BONIFACE ZULU.

Zimbabwe: Edif. do Ministério de Transportes e Comunicações, Avda 4 de Fevereiro 42, CP 428, Luanda; tel. (2) 310125; fax (2) 311528; Ambassador: B. G. CHIDYAUSIKU.

Judicial System

There is a Supreme Court and Court of Appeal in Luanda. There are also civil, criminal and military courts.

Chief Justice of the Supreme Court: JOÃO FELIZARDO.

Religion

Much of the population follows traditional African beliefs, although a majority profess to be Christians, mainly Roman Catholics.

CHRISTIANITY

Conselho de Igrejas Cristãs em Angola (Council of Christian Churches in Angola): Rua Amílcar Cabral 182, 1° andar, CP 1659, Luanda; tel. (2) 330415; fax (2) 393746; f. 1977; 14 mem. churches; five assoc. mems; one observer; Pres. Rev. ALVARO RODRIGUES; Gen. Sec. Rev. AUGUSTO CHIPESSE.

Protestant Churches

Evangelical Congregational Church in Angola (Igreja Evangélica Congregacional em Angola): CP 551, Huambo; tel. 3087; 100,000 mems; Gen. Sec. Rev. JÚLIO FRANCISCO.

Evangelical Pentecostal Church of Angola (Missão Evangélica Pentecostal de Angola): CP 219, Porto Amboim; 13,600 mems; Sec. Rev. JOSÉ DOMINGOS CAETANO.

United Evangelical Church of Angola (Igreja Evangélica Unida de Angola): CP 122, Uíge; 11,000 mems; Gen. Sec. Rev. A. L. DOMINGOS.

Other active denominations include the African Apostolic Church, the Church of Apostolic Faith in Angola, the Church of Our Lord Jesus Christ in the World, the Evangelical Baptist Church, the Evangelical Church in Angola, the Evangelical Church of the Apostles of Jerusalem, the Evangelical Reformed Church of Angola, the Kimbanguist Church in Angola and the United Methodist Church.

The Roman Catholic Church

Angola comprises three archdioceses and 12 dioceses. At 31 December 1998 an estimated 43.5% of the total population were adherents.

Bishops' Conference: Conferência Episcopal de Angola e São Tomé, CP 87, Luanda; tel. (2) 343686; fax (2) 345504; f. 1967; Pres. Most Rev. ZACARIAS KAMWENHO, Archbishop of Lubango.

Archbishop of Huambo: Most Rev. FRANCISCO VITI, Arcebispado, CP 10, Huambo; tel. 20130.

Archbishop of Luanda: Cardinal ALEXANDRE DO NASCIMENTO, Arcebispado, Largo do Palácio, CP 87, 1230-C, Luanda; tel. (2) 331481; fax (2) 334433; e-mail arquidiocese@snet.co.ao.

Archbishop of Lubango: Most Rev. ZACARIAS KAMWENHO, Arcebispado, CP 231, Lubango; tel. 20405; fax 23547.

The Press

The press was nationalized in 1976.

DAILIES

Diário da República: CP 1306, Luanda; official govt bulletin.

O Jornal de Angola: Rua Rainha Ginga 18–24, CP 1312, Luanda; tel. (2) 338947; fax (2) 333342; f. 1923; Dir-Gen. LUÍS FERNANDO; mornings and Sun.; circ. 41,000.

Newspapers are also published in several regional towns.

PERIODICALS

Actual: Luanda; weekly; Editor JOAQUIM ALVES.

Agora: Luanda; weekly; Dir ANGUEAR DOS SANTOS.

Angola Norte: CP 97, Malanje; weekly.

A Célula: Luanda; political journal of MPLA; monthly.

Comércio Externo: Rua da Missão 81, CP 6375, Luanda; tel. (2) 334060; fax (2) 392216; f. 1993 as *Comércio Actualidade*; Editor VICTOR ALEIXO.

Correio da Semana: Rua Rainha Ginga 18–24, CP 1213, Luanda; tel. (2) 331623; fax (2) 333342; f. 1992; owned by *O Jornal de Angola*; weekly; Editor-in-Chief MANUEL DIONISIO.

Eme: Rua Ho Chi Minh, Luanda; tel. (2) 321130; f. 1996; MPLA publ.

Folha 8: Rua Conselheiro Julio de Vilhena 24, 5° andar, Luanda; tel. (2) 391943; fax (2) 392289; two a week; Dir WILLIAM TONET.

Horizonte: Rua da Samba 144, 1° andar, Luanda.

Jornal de Benguela: CP 17, Benguela; two a week.

Lavra & Oficina: CP 2767-C, Luanda; tel. (2) 322155; f. 1975; journal of the Union of Angolan Writers; monthly; circ. 5,000.

Militar: Luanda; f. 1993; Editor-in-Chief CARMO NETO.

Noticias de Angola: Calçada G. Ferreira, Luanda; weekly.

Novembro: CP 3947, Luanda; tel. (2) 331660; monthly; Dir ROBERTO DE ALMEIDA.

O Planalto: CP 96, Huambo; two a week.

Tempos Novos: Avda Combatentes 244, 2° andar, CP 16088, Luanda; tel. (2) 349534; fax (2) 349534.

A Voz do Povo: Rua João de Deus 99-103, Vila Alice, Luanda.

A Voz do Trabalhador: Avda 4 de Fevereiro 210, CP 28, Luanda; journal of União Nacional de Trabalhadores Angolanos (National Union of Angolan Workers); monthly.

NEWS AGENCIES

ANGOP: Rua Rei Katiavala 120, CP 2181, Luanda; tel. (2) 391525; fax (2) 391537; Dir-Gen. and Editor-in-Chief AVELINO MIGUEL.

Foreign Bureaux

Agence France-Presse (AFP): Prédio Mutamba, CP 2357, Luanda; tel. (2) 334939; Bureau Chief MANUELA TEIXEIRA.

Allgemeiner Deutscher Nachrichtendienst (ADN) (Germany): CP 3193, Luanda; Correspondent GUDRUN GROSS.

Informatsionnoye Telegrafnoye Agentstvo Rossii—Telegrafnoye Agentstvo Suverennykh Stran (ITAR—TASS) (Russia): Rua Marechal Tito 75, CP 3209, Luanda; tel. (2) 342524; Correspondent VLADIMIR BORISOVICH BUYANOV.

Inter Press Service (IPS) (Italy): c/o Centro de Imprensa Anibal de Melo, Rua Cequeira Lukoki 124, Luanda; tel. (2) 334895; fax: (2) 393445; Correspondent CHRIS SIMPSON.

Prensa Latina (Cuba): Rua D. Miguel de Melo 92-2, Luanda; tel. (2) 336804; Chief Correspondent LUÍS MANUEL SÁEZ.

Reuters (UK): c/o Centro de Imprensa Anibal de Melo, Rua Cequeira Lukoki 124, Luanda; tel. (2) 334895; fax (2) 393445; Correspondent CRISTINA MULLER.

Rossiyskoye Informatsionnoye Agentstvo—Novosti (RIA—Novosti) (Russia): Luanda; Chief Officer VLADISLAV Z. KOMAROV.

Xinhua (New China) News Agency (People's Republic of China): Rua Karl Marx 57-3, andar E, Bairro das Ingombotas, Zona 4, Luanda; tel. (2) 332415; Correspondent ZHAO XIAOZHONG.

Publishers

Empresa Distribuidora Livreira (EDIL), UEE: Rua da Missão 107, CP 1245, Luanda; tel. (2) 334034.

Neográfica, SARL: CP 6518, Luanda; publrs of *Novembro*.

Nova Editorial Angolana, SARL: CP 1225, Luanda; f. 1935; general and educational; Man. Dir POMBO FERNANDES.

Offsetográfica Gráfica Industrial Lda: CP 911, Benguela; tel. 32568; f. 1966; Man. FERNANDO MARTINS.

Government Publishing House

Imprensa Nacional, UEE: CP 1306, Luanda; f. 1845; Gen. Man. Dr ANTÓNIO DUARTE DE ALMEIDA E CARMO.

Broadcasting and Communications

TELECOMMUNICATIONS

Angola Telecom: Rua I Congresso 26, CP 625, Luanda; tel. (2) 331032; fax (2) 395446; international telecommunications.

BROADCASTING

Radio

Rádio Nacional de Angola: Rua Comandante Jika, CP 1329, Luanda; tel. (2) 323172; fax (2) 324647; broadcasts in Portuguese, English, French, Spanish and vernacular languages (Chokwe, Kikongo, Kimbundu, Kwanyama, Fiote, Ngangela, Luvale, Songu, Umbundu); Dir-Gen. MANUEL RABELAIS.

Luanda Antena Comercial (LAC): Praceta Luther King 5, Luanda; tel. (2) 396229; e-mail lac@ebonet.net.

Rádio Eclésia: Rua Comandante Bula 118, CP 3579, Luanda; tel. (2) 343041; fax (2) 343093; e-mail reclesia@ebonet.net; Dir-Gen. D. BENEDITO ROBERTO.

Television

Televisão Popular de Angola (TPA): Rua Ho Chi Minh, CP 2604, Luanda; tel. (2) 320025; fax (2) 391091; f. 1975; state-controlled; Man. Dir CARLOS CUNHA.

Finance

(cap. = capital; res = reserves; dep. = deposits; m. = million; brs = branches; amounts in old kwanza, unless otherwise indicated)

BANKING

All banks were nationalized in 1975. In 1995 the Government authorized the formation of private banks.

Central Bank

Banco Nacional de Angola: Avda 4 de Fevereiro 151, CP 1298, Luanda; tel. (2) 332633; fax (2) 390579; e-mail bnagab@ebonet; internet www.ebonet.net/bna; f. 1976; bank of issue; cap. and res 7,657m.; dep. 111,975m. (1983); Gov. AGUINALDO JAIME.

Commercial Banks

Banco de Poupança e Crédito (BPC): Largo Saydi Mingas, CP 1343, Luanda; tel. (2) 393790; fax (2) 393790; 100% state-owned; cap. 10,000m. (Dec. 1992); Chair. AMILCAR S. AZEVEDO SILVA; brs throughout Angola.

Caixa de Crédito Agro-Pecuario e Pescas (CCAPP): Rua Rainha Ginga 83; tel. (2) 392749; fax (2) 392225; f. 1991; assumed commercial operations of Banco Nacional de Angola in 1996.

Development Bank

Banco de Comércio e Indústria SARL: Avda 4 de Fevereiro 85, CP 1395, Luanda; tel. (2) 333684; fax (2) 334924; e-mail oscarn@ebonet.net; f. 1991; 91% state-owned; provides loans to businesses in all sectors; cap. and res 10,810.4m. readjusted kwanza (1998); Chair. PEDRO MAIANGALA PUNA; 2 brs.

Investment Bank

Banco Africano de Investimentos SARL (BAI): Rua Rainha Ginga 34, Luanda; tel. (2) 335749; fax (2) 335486; f. 1996; 37.5% interest owned by Angolan shareholders; Pres. AGUINALDO JAIME.

Foreign Banks

Banco Espírito Santo e Comercial de Lisboa SA: 5-3°, Rua Cirilo da Conceição Silva, CP 1471, Luanda; tel. (2) 392287; fax (2) 391484; Rep. JOSÉ RIBEIRO DA SILVA.

Banco de Fomento e Exterior SA: Agencia da Missão, Luanda; tel. (2) 394275; fax (2) 397090; Man. TERESA MATEUS.

Banco Português do Atlântico: Largo Rainha Ginga 6–8, CP 5726, Luanda; tel. (2) 397946; fax (2) 397397.

Banco Totta e Açores SA: Avda 4 de Fevereiro 99, CP 1231, Luanda; tel. (2) 336440; fax (2) 333233; e-mail totta-ang@edonet.net; Gen. Man. Dr MÁRIO NELSON MAXIMINO.

INSURANCE

Empresa Nacional de Seguros e Resseguros de Angola (ENSA), UEE: Avda 4 de Fevereiro 93, CP 5778, Luanda; tel. (2) 332991; fax 332946; f. 1978.

Trade and Industry

SUPERVISORY BODY

National Supplies Commission: Luanda; f. 1977 to combat sabotage and negligence.

CHAMBERS OF COMMERCE

Angolan Chamber of Commerce and Industry: Largo do Kinaxixi 14, 1° andar, CP 92, Luanda; tel. (2) 344506; fax (2) 344629; Pres. ANTÓNIO JOÃO DOS SANTOS.

Associação Comercial de Luanda: Edifício Palácio de Comércio, 1° andar, CP 1275, Luanda; tel. (2) 322453.

STATE TRADING ORGANIZATIONS

Angomédica, UEE: Rua do Sanatório, Bairro Palanca, CP 2698, Luanda; tel. (2) 363765; fax (2) 362336; f. 1981 to import pharmaceutical goods; Gen. Dir Dr FÁTIMA SAIUNDO.

Direcção dos Serviços de Comércio (Dept of Trade): Largo Diogo Cão, CP 1337, Luanda; f. 1970; brs throughout Angola.

Epmel, UEE: Rua Karl Marx 35–37, Luanda; tel. (2) 330943; industrial agricultural machinery.

Exportang, UEE: Rua dos Enganos 1A, CP 1000, Luanda; tel. (2) 332363; co-ordinates exports.

Importang, UEE: Calçada do Município 10, CP 1003, Luanda; tel. (2) 337994; f. 1977; co-ordinates majority of imports; Dir-Gen. SIMÃO DIOGO DA CRUZ.

Maquimport, UEE: Rua Rainha Ginga 152, CP 2975, Luanda; tel. (2) 339044; f. 1981 to import office equipment.

Mecanang, UEE: Rua dos Enganos, 1°–7° andar, CP 1347, Luanda; tel. (2) 390644; f. 1981 to import agricultural and construction machinery, tools and spare parts.

STATE INDUSTRIAL ENTERPRISES

Companhia do Açúcar de Angola: Rua Direita 77, Luanda; production of sugar.

Companhia Geral dos Algodões de Angola (COTONANG): Avda da Boavista, Luanda; production of cotton textiles.

Empresa Abastecimento Técnico Material (EMATEC), UEE: Largo Rainha Ginga 3, CP 2952, Luanda; tel. (2) 338891; technical and material suppliers to the Ministry of Defence.

Empresa Açucareira Centro (OSUKA), UEE: Estrada Principal do Lobito, CP 37, Catumbela; tel. 24681; sugar industry.

Empresa Açucareira Norte (ACUNOR), UEE: Rua Robert Shilds, Caxito, Bengo; tel. 71720; sugar production.

Empresa Angolana de Embalagens (METANGOL), UEE: Rua Estrada do Cacuaco, CP 151, Luanda; tel. (2) 370680; production of non-specified metal goods.

Empresa de Cimento de Angola (CIMANGOLA), UEE: Avda 4 de Fevereiro 42, Luanda; tel. (2) 371190; f. 1954; 69% state-owned; cement production; exports to several African countries.

Empresa de Construção de Edificações (CONSTROI), UEE: Rua Alexandre Peres, CP 2566, Luanda; tel. (2) 333930; construction.

Empresa de Pesca de Angola (PESCANGOLA), UEE: Luanda; f. 1981; state fishing enterprise, responsible to Ministry of Fisheries and Environment.

Empresa de Rebenefício e Exportação do Café de Angola (CAFANGOL), UEE: Rua Robert Shields 4/6, CP 342, Luanda; tel. (2) 337916; fax (2) 334742; e-mail cafango@arrobasnet.co.ao; f. 1983; nat. coffee-processing and trade org; proposed transfer to private sector announced in 1991; Dir-Gen. ALVARO FARIA.

Empresa de Tecidos de Angola (TEXTANG), UEE: Rua N'gola Kiluanji-Kazenga, CP 5404, Luanda; tel. (2) 381134; production of textiles.

Empresa Nacional de Cimento (ENCIME), UEE: CP 157, Lobito; tel. (711) 2325; cement production.

Empresa Nacional de Comercialização e Distribuição de Produtos Agrícolas (ENCODIPA): Luanda; central marketing agency for agricultural produce; numerous brs throughout Angola.

Empresa Nacional de Diamantes de Angola (ENDIAMA), UEE: Rua Major Kanhangulo 100, CP 1247, Luanda; tel. (2) 392336; fax (2) 337276; f. 1981 as the sole diamond-mining concession; commenced operations 1986; Dir-Gen. AUGUSTO PAULINO ALMEIDA NETO.

Empresa Nacional de Ferro de Angola (FERRANGOL): Rua João de Barros 26, CP 2692, Luanda; tel. (2) 373800; iron production; Dir ARMANDO DE SOUSA (MACHADINHO).

Empresa Nacional de Manutenção (MANUTECNICA), UEE: Rua 7, Avda do Cazenga 10, CP 3508, Luanda; tel. (2) 383646; assembly of machines and specialized equipment for industry.

Empresa Texteis de Angola (ENTEX), UEE: Avda Comandante Kima Kienda, CP 5720, Luanda; tel. (2) 336182; weaving and tissue finishing.

Geotécnica Unidad Económica Estatal: Rua Angola Kilmanse 389/393, Luanda; tel. (2) 382730; fax (2) 382730; f. 1978 for surveying and excavation; Man. P. M. M. ELVINO Jnr; 500 employees.

Siderurgia Nacional, UEE: CP Zona Industrial do Forel das Lagostas, Luanda; tel. (2) 373028; f. 1963, nationalized 1980; steelworks and rolling mill plant.

Sociedade Nacional de Combustíveis de Angola (SONANGOL): Rua I Congresso do MPLA, CP 1318, Luanda; tel. (2) 331690; fax 391782; f. 1976 for exploration, production and refining of crude petroleum, and marketing and distribution of petroleum products; sole concessionary in Angola, supervises on- and offshore operations of foreign petroleum cos; holds majority interest in jt ventures with Cabinda Gulf Oil Co (Cabgoc), Fina Petróleos de Angola and Texaco Petróleos de Angola; Man. Dir JOAQUIM DAVID.

Sociedade Unificada de Tabacos de Angola, Lda (SUT): Rua Deolinda Rodrigues 530/537, CP 1263, Luanda; tel. (2) 391630; fax (2) 362138; f. 1919; tobacco products; Gen. Man. Dr MANUEL LAMAS.

UTILITIES

Electricity

Empresa Nacional de Construções Eléctricas (ENCEL), UEE: Rua Comandante Che Guevara 185/7, Luanda; tel. (2) 391630; fax (2) 331411; e-mail encel.dg@netangola.com; f. 1982.

Empresa Nacional de Electricidade (ENE), UEE: Edifício Geominas, 6°–7° andar, CP 772, Luanda; tel. (2) 321529; fax (2) 323382; e-mail enedg@netangola.com; f. 1980; production and distribution of electricity; Dir-Gen. Eng. MARIO FERNANDO PONTES MOREIRA FONTES.

MAJOR COMPANIES

Cabinda Gulf Oil Co (Cabgoc): CP 2950, Luanda; tel. (2) 392646; wholly-owned subsidiary of Chevron Corpn (USA): undertakes exploration and production of petroleum in Cabinda province, in asscn with SONANGOL, which holds a 51% interest in these jt ventures; other partners incl. Elf Petroleum (Angola) (10%) and Agip Angola Ltd (9.8%); Dir M. PUCKETT.

Fina Petróleos de Angola SARL: CP 1320, Luanda; tel. (2) 336855; fax (2) 391031; e-mail carlos.alves@fpa.ebonet.net; f. 1958 for exploration, production and refining of petroleum and natural gas; operates Luanda petroleum refinery, Petrangol, with capacity of 40,000 b/d; also operates Quinfuquena terminal; 64.1% owned by TotalFina SA (France); Gen. Man. CARLOS ALVES; 553 employees.

TRADE UNIONS

Angolan General Independent and Free Trade Union Confederation: Chair. MANUEL DIFUILA.

União Nacional de Trabalhadores Angolanos (UNTA) (National Union of Angolan Workers): Avda 4 de Fevereiro 210, CP 28, Luanda; tel. (2) 334670; fax (2) 393590; f. 1960; Pres. MANUEL DIOGO DA SILVA NETO; Gen. Sec. MANUEL AUGUSTO VIAGE; 600,000 mems.

Transport

The transport infrastructure has been severely dislocated by the civil war.

RAILWAYS

The total length of track operated was 2,952 km in 1987. There are plans to extend the Namibe line beyond Menongue and to construct north–south rail links.

Caminhos de Ferro de Angola: Avda 4 de Fevereiro 42, CP 1250-C, Luanda; tel. (2) 339794; fax (2) 339976; f. 1975; nat. network operating four fmrly independent systems covering 2,952 track-km; Nat. Dir R. M. DA CONCEIÇÃO JUNIOR.

Amboim Railway: Porto Amboim; f. 1922; 123 track-km; Dir A. GUIA.

Benguela Railway (Companhia do Caminho de Ferro de Benguela): Rua Praça 11 Novembro 3, CP 32, Lobito; tel. (711) 22645; fax (711) 22865; f. 1903, line completed 1928; owned 90% by Tank Consolidated Investments (a subsidiary of Société Générale de Belgique), 10% by Govt of Angola; line carrying passenger and freight traffic from the port of Lobito across Angola, via Huambo and Luena, to the border of the Democratic Republic of the Congo (fmrly Zaire) where it connects with that country's railway system, which, in turn, links with Zambia Railways, thus providing the shortest west coast route for central African trade; 1,394 track-km; guerrilla operations by UNITA suspended all international traffic from 1975, with only irregular services from Lobito to Huambo being operated; a declaration of intent to reopen the cross-border lines was signed in 1987 by Angola, Zambia and Zaire, and the rehabilitation of the railway was a priority of a 10-year programme, planned by the SADCC (now SADC), to develop the 'Lobito corridor'; In 1997 an Italian company, Tor di Vale, began a US $450m.-programme of repairs to the railway. Minimum repairs allowing the resumption of freight traffic were expected to take three years to complete, to be followed by further modernization, including the reconstruction of 22 passenger stations; Dir-Gen. DANIEL QUIPAXE.

Luanda Railway (Empresa de Caminho de Ferro de Luanda, UEE): CP 1250-C, Luanda; tel. (2) 370061; f. 1886; serves an iron, cotton and sisal-producing region between Luanda and Malanje; reconstruction of Luanda-Dondo rail link completed 1997, rehabilitation of Dondo-Malanje section proceeding in 1999; 536 track-km; Man. A. ALVARO AGANTE.

Namibe Railway: CP 130, Lubango; f. 1905; main line from Namibe to Menongue, via Lubango; br. lines to Chibia and iron ore mines at Cassinga; 899 track-km; Gen. Man. J. SALVADOR.

ROADS

In 1996 Angola had 72,626 km of roads, of which 7,955 km were main roads and 15,571 km were secondary roads. About 25% of roads were paved. In 1997 the state-owned road construction and maintenance company, the Instituto de Estradas de Angola, reported that 80% of the country's road network was in disrepair and that the cost of rebuilding the roads and bridges damaged during the civil conflict would total some US $4,000m.

SHIPPING

The main harbours are at Lobito, Luanda and Namibe; the commercial port of Porto Amboim, in Cuanza-Sul province, has been closed for repairs since 1984. The expansion of port facilities in Cabinda was due to begin in late 1995 and was expected to be completed within two years. In 1983 a regular shipping service began to operate between Luanda and Maputo (Mozambique). Under the emergency transport programme launched in 1988, refurbishment work was to be undertaken on the ports of Luanda and Namibe. The first phase of a 10-year SADCC (now SADC) programme to develop the 'Lobito corridor', for which funds were pledged in January 1989, was to include the rehabilitation of the ports of Lobito and Benguela.

Angonave—Linhas Marítimas de Angola, UEE: Rua Serqueira 31, CP 5953, Luanda; tel. (2) 330144; shipping line; Dir-Gen. FRANCISCO VENÂNCIO.

Cabotang—Cabotagem Nacional Angolana, UEE: Avda 4 de Fevereiro 83A, Luanda; tel. (2) 373133; operates off the coasts of Angola and Mozambique; Dir-Gen. JOÃO OCTAVIO VAN-DÚNEM.

Empresa Portuária do Lobito, UEE: Avda da Independência, CP 16, Lobito; tel. (711) 2710; long-distance sea transport; Gen. Man. JOSÉ CARLOS GOMES.

Empresa Portuária de Moçâmedes—Namibe, UEE: Rua Pedro Benje 10A and 10C, CP 49, Namibe; tel. (64) 60643; long-distance sea transport; Dir HUMBERTO DE ATAIDE DIAS.

Secil Marítima SARL, UEE: Avda 4 de Fevereiro 42, 1° andar, CP 5910, Luanda; tel. (2) 335230.

CIVIL AVIATION

Air Nacoia: Rua Comandante Che Guevara 67, 1° andar, Luanda; tel. and fax (2) 395477; f. 1993; Pres. SALVADOR SILVA.

TAAG—Linhas Aéreas de Angola: Rua da Missão 123, CP 79, Luanda; tel. (2) 332485; fax (2) 393548; f. 1939; internal scheduled passenger and cargo services, and services from Luanda to destinations within Africa and to Europe, South America and the Caribbean; Chair. JÚLIO SAMPAIO ALMEIDA; Dir-Gen. ABEL ANTÓNIO LOPES.

Angola Air Charter: Aeroporto Internacional 4 de Fevereiro, CP 5433, Luanda; tel. (2) 350559; fax (2) 392229; f. 1992; subsidiary of TAAG.

Transafrik International: Rua Joaquim Kapango, CP 2839, Luanda; tel. (2) 352141; fax (2) 351723; f. 1986; operates contract cargo services mainly within Africa; Man. Dir ERICH F. KOCH; Gen. Man. PIMENTAL ARAUJO.

Tourism

National Tourist Agency: Palácio de Vidro, CP 1240, Luanda; tel. (2) 372750.

Defence

In December 1990 the governing party, the Movimento Popular de Libertação de Angola—Partido do Trabalho (MPLA—PT), agreed to terminate its direct link with the armed forces. In accordance with the peace agreement concluded by the government and the União Nacional para a Independência Total de Angola (UNITA) in May 1991 (see Recent History), a new 50,000-strong national army, the Forças Armadas de Angola (FAA), was to be established, comprising equal numbers of government forces, the Forças Armadas Populares de Libertação de Angola (FAPLA), and UNITA soldiers. The formation of the FAA was to coincide with the holding of a general election in late September 1992. Pending the general election, a cease-fire between FAPLA and UNITA forces, which commenced in mid-May 1991, was monitored by a joint political and military commission, comprising representatives of the MPLA—PT, UNITA, the UN, Portugal, the USA and the USSR. This commission was to oversee the withdrawal of FAPLA and UNITA forces to specific confinement areas, to await demobilization. Although not all troops had entered the confinement areas, demobilization began in late March 1992. Military advisers from Portugal, France and the United Kingdom were to assist with the formation of the new national army. However, the demobilization process and the formation of the FAA fell behind schedule and were only partially completed by the end of September and the holding of the general election. Following the election, UNITA withdrew its troops from the FAA, alleging electoral fraud on the part of the MPLA, and hostilities resumed. Following the signing of the Lusaka peace accord in November 1994, preparations for the confinement and demobilization of troops, and the integration of the UNITA contingent into the FAA, resumed. In mid-1995 agreement was reached between the government and UNITA on the enlargement of the FAA to comprise a total of 90,000 troops, and discussions began concerning the potential formation of a fourth, non-combatant branch of the FAA, which would engage in public works projects. The internment of UNITA forces began in November 1995. In March 1996 agreement was reached that the unified FAA would include 26,300 UNITA troops. The process of selecting UNITA troops for integration into the FAA began in June. In December the UN Angola Verification Mission (UNAVEM III) expressed concern that, of a total of 70,336 UNITA troops registered at confinement areas, some 15,705 had deserted. In mid-1997 the government estimated that UNITA maintained a residual force numbering some 25,000–30,000 troops, while UNITA claimed to have a force of only 2,963 'police'. In March 1998 UNITA issued a declaration announcing the complete demobilization of its forces. However, some military sources believed that, despite this declaration, UNITA retained a force of some 15,000 troops and substantial quantities of heavy weaponry. Evidence of the existence of a large and well-armed UNITA force became apparent with the escalation of hostilities in Angola in late 1998.

In August 1999 the FAA had an estimated total strength of 112,500: army 100,000, navy 1,500 and air force 11,000. In addition, there was a paramilitary force numbering an estimated 15,000. By May 1998 some 11,000 UNITA soldiers had been integrated into the FAA. However, the integration process was abandoned following the resumption of hostilities between the government and UNITA in December 1998.

Defence Expenditure: Budgeted at US $574m. for 1999.

Chief of General Staff of the Armed Forces: Gen. JOÃO BAPTISTA DE MATOS.

Education

Education is officially compulsory for eight years, between seven and 15 years of age, and is provided free of charge by the government. Primary education begins at the age of six and lasts for four years. Secondary education, beginning at the age of 10, lasts for up to seven years, comprising a first cycle of four years and a second of three years. As a proportion of the school-age population, the total enrolment at primary and secondary schools was 45% in 1991. Enrolment at primary schools stood at 989,443 in 1991/92, and that at secondary schools (including students receiving vocational instruction and teacher training) totalled 218,987. There is one university, at Luanda, with 6,331 students in 1991/92. In 1991 the government approved legislation permitting the foundation of private educational establishments.

At independence the adult illiteracy rate was over 85%, and Angola's independent economic development continues to be hampered by the widespread lack of basic skills. A national literacy campaign was launched in 1976, and the average rate of adult illiteracy in 1990 was estimated by UNESCO to be 58.3% (males 44.4%, females 71.5%). The 1997 budget allocated an estimated 48,346,000m. readjusted kwanza (4.9% of total expenditure) to education.

Bibliography

Africa Watch. *Angola: Violations of the Laws of War on Both Sides.* London, Human Rights Watch, 1989.

Andresen Guimarães, F. *The Origins of the Angolan Civil War: Foreign Intervention and Domestic Political Conflict, 1961–1976.* London, Macmillan, and New York, St Martin's Press, 1997.

Anstee, M. *Orphan of the Cold War: The Inside Story of the Collapse of the Angolan Peace Process.* London, Macmillan, and New York, St Martin's Press, 1996.

Bhagavan, M. R. *Angola's Political Economy: 1975–1985.* Uppsala, Scandinavian Institute of African Studies, 1986.

Birmingham, D. *Frontline Nationalism in Angola and Mozambique.* London, Currey; Trenton, NJ, Africa World Press, 1992.

Bridgland, F. *Jonas Savimbi: A Key to Africa.* Edinburgh, Mainstream, 1986.

Brittain, V. *Death of Dignity.* London, Pluto Press, 1998.

Broadhead, S. H. *Historical Dictionary of Angola.* 3rd Edn. Metuchen, NJ, Scarecrow Press, 1992.

Cann, J. P. *Counter-insurgency in Africa: The Portuguese Way of War 1961–1974.* Greenwood Press, Westport, CT, 1997.

Clarence-Smith, G. *The Third Portuguese Empire.* Manchester, Manchester University Press, 1985.

Conçalves, J. *Economics and Politics of the Angolan Conflict: The Transition Re-Negotiated.* Bellville, South Africa, Centre for Southern Africa Studies, University of the Western Cape, 1995.

Crocker, C. A. *High Noon in Southern Africa: Making Peace in a Rough Neighbourhood.* New York, W. W. Norton, 1992.

Davidson, B. *In the Eye of the Storm: Angola's People.* London, Longman, 1972.

Ekwe-Ekwe, H. *Conflict and Intervention in Africa: Nigeria, Angola and Zaire.* London, Macmillan, 1990.

Estermann, C. *Ethnographie du sud-ouest de l'Angola.* 2 vols. Paris, Académie des Sciences d'Outre-mer, 1984.

Hart, K., and Lewis, J. (Eds). *Why Angola Matters.* London, James Currey Publishers, 1995.

Heimer, F.-W. *The Decolonisation Conflict in Angola, 1974–1976.* Geneva, Institut Universitaire des Hautes Etudes, 1979.

Henderson, L. W. *Angola: Five Centuries of Conflict.* Ithaca, NY, Cornell University Press, 1979.

Hodges, T. *Angola to 2000: Prospects For Recovery.* London, Economist Intelligence Unit, 1993.

Konczacki, Z. A., Parpart, J. L., and Shaw, T. M. (Eds). *Studies in the Economic History of Southern Africa.* Vol. I. London, Cass, 1990.

MacQueen, N. *The Decolonization of Portuguese Africa: Metropolitan Revolution and the Dissolution of Empire.* Harlow, Longman, 1997.

McCormick, S. H. *The Angolan Economy: Prospects for Growth in a Postwar Environment.* Washington DC, CSIS, 1994.

Maier, K. *Angola: Promises and Lies.* London, SERIF, 1996.

Marcum, J. *The Angolan Revolution.* 2 vols. Cambridge, MA, MIT Press, 1969, 1978 (new edn).

Martin, J. W. *A Political History of the Civil War in Angola, 1974–90.* New Brunswick, NJ, Transaction Publishers, 1992.

Martin, P. M. *Historical Dictionary of Angola.* London, 1980.

Minter, W. (Ed). *Operation Timber: Pages From the Savimbi Dossier.* New Jersey, Africa World Press, 1988.

Apartheid's Contras: An Inquiry into the Roots of War in Angola and Mozambique. London, Zed Press, 1994.

Mohanty, S. *Political Development and Ethnic Indentity in Africa: a Study of Angola since 1960.* London, Sangham, 1992.

Núñez, B. *Dictionary of Portuguese-African Civilization.* Vol. I. London, Hans Zell, 1995.

Pélissier, R. *Explorar: Voyages en Angola.* Orgeval, Editions Pélissier, 1980.

La Colonie du Minotaure. Orgeval, Editions Pélissier.

Roque, F. *A Economia de Angola.* Lisbon, Bertrand, 1991.

Sogge, D. *Sustainable Peace: Angola's Recovery.* Harare, Southern African Resource and Documentation Centre, 1992.

Somerville, K. *Angola: Politics, Economics and Society.* London, Frances Pinter; Boulder, CO, Lynne Riener, 1986.

Spikes, D. *Angola and the Politics of Intervention.* Jefferson, NC, McFarland Publishers, 1993.

Steenkamp, W. *South Africa's Border War, 1966–1989.* Gibraltar, Ashanti Publishers, 1989.

Tredten, I. *Angola: Struggle for Peace and Reconstruction.* Boulder, CO, Westview Press, 1997.

United Nations. *The United Nations and the Situation in Angola, May 1991–February 1995.* New York, United Nations, 1995.

Venter, A. J. *War in Angola.* Hong Kong, Concord Publications, 1992.

Vincenti, S. *Angola e Africa do Sul.* Luanda, Eclicas do Autor, 1994.

Virmani, K. K. (Ed.). *Angola and the Super Powers.* Delhi, University of Delhi, 1989.

Wheeler, D. L., and Pélissier, R. *Angola.* London, Greenwood Press, 1978.

Wolfers, M., and Bergerol, J. *Angola in the Front Line.* London, Zed Press, 1983.

World Bank. *Angola: An Introductory Economic Review.* Washington, DC, International Bank for Reconstruction and Development, 1990.

Wright, G. *Destruction of a Nation: United States Policy towards Angola since 1945.* London, Pluto Press, 1997.

BENIN

Physical and Social Geography

R. J. HARRISON CHURCH

The Republic of Benin, bordered on the east by Nigeria, on the west by Togo and to the north by Burkina Faso and Niger, covers an area of 112,622 sq km (43,484 sq miles). From a coastline of some 100 km on the Gulf of Guinea, the republic extends inland about 650 km to the Niger river. The population was 4,915,555 at the census of February 1992, rising to 5,816,488 at mid-1998 (according to official estimates—giving an average population density of 51.6 inhabitants per sq km). The population of Cotonou, the political capital and major port, was estimated at 750,000 in 1994, and that of Porto-Novo, the official capital, at 200,000.

The coast is a straight sand-bar, pounded by heavy surf on the seaward side and backed by one or more lagoons and former shorelines on the landward side. Rivers flow into these lagoons, Lakes Ahémé and Nokoué being estuaries of two rivers whose seaward exits are obstructed by the sand-bar. A lagoon waterway is navigable for barges to Lagos, in Nigeria.

North of Lake Nokoué the Ouémé river has a wide marshy delta, with considerable agricultural potential. Elsewhere the lagoons are backed northward by the Terre de Barre, a fertile and intensively farmed region of clay soils. North again is the seasonally flooded Lama swamp. Beyond are areas comparable with the Terre de Barre, and the realm of the pre-colonial kingdom of Dahomey.

Most of the rest of the country is underlain by Pre-Cambrian rocks, with occasional bare domes, laterite cappings on level surfaces, and poor soils. In the north-west are the Atacora mountains, whose soils, although less poor, are much eroded. On the northern borders are Primary and other sandstones, extremely infertile and short of water.

Deposits of low-grade iron ores, chromium, rutile, phosphates, kaolin and gold occur in the north of the country. There is a small oilfield, offshore from Cotonou, at Sémé. Reserves of natural gas, estimated to total 4,000m. cu m, were being evaluated in the mid-1990s. Limestone and marble are currently mined.

Southern Benin has an equatorial climate, most typical along the coast, although with a low rainfall of some 1,300 mm. Away from the coast the dry months increase until a tropical climate prevails over the northern half of the country. There a dry season alternates with a wet one, the latter being of seven months in the centre and four months in the north; the rainfall nevertheless averages 1,300 mm per year.

In the colonial period the Fon and Yoruba of the south enjoyed educational advantages and were prominent in administration throughout French West Africa. After independence many were expelled to Benin, where there is great unemployment or under-employment of literates. The northern peoples, such as the Somba and Bariba, are less Westernized.

Recent History

PIERRE ENGLEBERT

Revised for this edition by the Editor

INDEPENDENCE AND ARMY RULE

Benin (then Dahomey) became a self-governing republic within the French Community in December 1958 and an independent state on 1 August 1960. Political life in the republic was extremely unstable following independence, as regionally-based interests contended for power. Hubert Maga, the republic's first president, was deposed in October 1963 by an army coup d'état, and successive army-supported regimes, none of which succeeded in resolving regional rivalries, governed the country for the ensuing decade.

In October 1972 Maj. (later Brig.-Gen.) Mathieu Kérékou, a northerner, seized power. Marxism-Leninism was introduced as the national ideology, and banking, insurance and the principal industrial sectors were nationalized. In 1975 the country was renamed the People's Republic of Benin. By the early 1980s, however, a more pragmatic approach to Benin's economic needs began to supplant the government's socialist philosophy. Western private investment was encouraged, and the government undertook a reform of the largely corrupt and inefficient parastatal sector. The worsening internal economy prompted Benin to move increasingly towards the Western bloc and the IMF. By the mid-1980s France had replaced the USSR as the principal supplier of military equipment, while also remaining predominant in trade, development assistance and other forms of co-operation. Financial support was also obtained from some of the more conservative African countries, including Côte d'Ivoire, Cameroon and Gabon. Benin's economic problems, however, exacerbated social tensions and ethnic rivalries, necessi-

tating a strengthened internal security network. Kérékou left the army in January 1987 to become a civilian head of state, and made efforts to restore equilibrium in both north-south and military-civilian representation. However, ensuing tensions between the government and the army culminated in an attempted coup d'état, apparently instigated by disaffected southerners, in March 1988. There was a further attempt to overthrow the government in June, while Kérékou was attending a regional conference in neighbouring Togo.

'CIVILIAN COUP'

A period of repression in the aftermath of the coup attempts, in conjunction with popular dissatisfaction at IMF-stipulated austerity measures, engendered an atmosphere of increased social tension and instability. In early 1989 public-sector workers took strike action in protest against protracted delays in the payment of salaries, while students boycotted classes, demanding the disbursement of delayed grants and scholarships. There was, moreover, evidence of corruption within the government and in the banking sector, as well as allegations that the government had agreed to accept shipments of hazardous waste from Western countries. None the less, at legislative elections in June 1989, a single list of 206 candidates was approved by almost 90% of the votes cast. In August the legislature, the Assemblée nationale révolutionnaire (ANR) re-elected Kérékou to the presidency for a further five-year term. Several new ministers, in a government that comprised relatively fewer military officers and members of the sole authorized party, the Parti de la révolution populaire du Bénin (PRPB), were known to have expressed support for multi-party politics. In August the government announced a partial payment of salaries owed to public-sector employees. In the same month an amnesty was announced for some 200 dissidents.

Although academic staff and students agreed to resume classes in October 1989, persistent social and political diffi-culties—including the decision by the sole official labour organization, the Union nationale des syndicats des travailleurs du Bénin (UNSTB), to sever its links with the PRPB—continued to undermine Kérékou's authority. In December, as the gov-ernment's failure to pay the salaries of public-sector employees caused further disruption, the Kérékou regime yielded to de-mands made by the Beninois population and by the country's external creditors (notably France), announcing the abandon-ment of Marxism-Leninism as the state ideology. Benin's external creditors subsequently agreed to a partial funding of outstanding salaries.

Almost 500 delegates attended a national conference of the 'active forces of the nation', which took place in Cotonou in February 1990. The conference declared itself sovereign and voted to abolish the existing structure of government and its institutions. Pending national elections to a new legislature, the functions of the ANR were to be assumed by an interim Haut conseil de la république (HCR), which was to include the principal opposition leaders. The president of the republic was for the first time to be elected by universal suffrage, with a five-year mandate, renewable only once. The conference designated Nicéphore Soglo, a former official of the World Bank, as interim prime minister. Kérékou was obliged to relinquish the defence portfolio to Soglo, and also to accept the conference's resolution to change the country's name to the Republic of Benin. In March 1990 an amnesty was announced for all dissidents, and a human rights commission was established. In the same month the HCR was inaugurated, and Soglo named his transitional, civilian government. In May the military prefects of Benin's six prov-inces were replaced by civilians, and in June the transitional government undertook an extensive restructuring of the armed forces. In August legislation was promulgated to permit the registration of political parties. Restrictions on the press were relaxed, and independent journals flourished.

Benin was thus the first sub-Saharan African country to experience a 'civilian coup': a single-party regime, dominated by the armed forces, which had assumed power following a *coup d'état*, was obliged by popular pressure to accept a return to multi-party democracy.

A draft constitution was submitted to a national referendum in December 1990. Voters were asked to choose between two versions of the constitution, one of which incorporated a clause stipulating upper and lower age-limits for presidential candi-dates (thereby automatically disqualifying several ex-presi-dents). In all, 95.8% of those who voted gave their assent to one or other of the versions, with 79.7% of voters endorsing the age-restrictions.

Some 24 political parties participated in the legislative elec-tion, which took place in February 1991. No party or group of parties won an overall majority of the 64 seats in the national assembly, although a pro-Soglo alliance secured the greatest number of seats (12) in the new legislature. (The successor party to the PRPB, the Union des forces du progrès, failed to win any seats.) The first round of the presidential election, on 10 March, was contested by 13 candidates. The distribution of votes between the two leading candidates largely reflected regional ethnic divisions: Soglo, who secured 36.2% of the total, received his greatest support in the south of the country, while Kérékou, who was reported to have the support of more than 80% of voters in the north, took 27.3% of the overall vote. Soglo and Kérékou proceeded to a second round of voting, which was conducted in March amid allegations of electoral fraud and the intimidation of supporters of the rival candidates. Despite continuing support for Kérékou in the north, Soglo (supported by most of the candidates eliminated at the first round) was elected president, securing 67.7% of the total votes cast. Before its dissolution, in late March, the HCR granted Kérékou immunity from any legal proceedings arising from his years in power.

THE SOGLO PRESIDENCY, 1991–96

Soglo was inaugurated as president on 4 April 1991. He subse-quently relinquished the defence portfolio to his brother-in-law, Désiré Vieyra. In July the leader of the Parti du renouveau démocratique (PRD), Adrien Houngbédji, who had also con-tested the presidency earlier in the year, was elected speaker of the national assembly.

The Soglo administration intensified efforts at economic liber-alization, and also began criminal proceedings against corrupt former state officials (among them former close associates of Kérékou). During 1991–92, none the less, civil servants, resenting that salary arrears accumulated in the final years of the Kérékou regime remained unpaid, undertook intermittent industrial action.

In May 1992 several soldiers were arrested near the presiden-tial palace in Cotonou, accused of plotting a coup. Among those detained was Capt. Pascal Tawes, a former deputy commander of Kérékou's (now-disbanded) presidential guard. Tawes and some of his associates subsequently escaped from custody, and in August gained control of an army base in the north. The rebellion collapsed when the government dispatched élite para-troops to recover the captured base: one rebel was killed and about 45 mutineers were detained, although Tawes himself evaded arrest. In September 1994 Tawes and 15 others were sentenced *in absentia* to life imprisonment with hard labour, convicted of plotting to overthrow the government.

Coalition Alliances

Although broad groupings of parties evolved, the absence of a majority party or coalition in the national assembly tended to delay the passage of legislation, a situation exacerbated by the legislature's apparent determination to assert its independence from the executive, most notably in areas of economic policy. However, the president's position was strengthened by the formation in June 1992 of Le Renouveau, a pro-Soglo majority group comprising 34 deputies from 10 parliamentary parties.

Despite the existence of legislation guaranteeing press freedom, libel proceedings were instigated during 1992–93 against journalists who had criticized Soglo and his associates. None the less, Soglo sought to consolidate popular support for his administration, and made particular efforts to develop contacts in the north. He also displayed a conciliatory attitude towards practitioners of traditional *vodoun* religious rites, which had been discouraged under the Kérékou regime. Social unrest persisted in Cotonou, however, with government proposals for a 10% reduction in civil servants' salaries (in accordance with the economic adjustment programme) provoking a three-day strike in February 1993.

In March 1993 more than 100 prisoners escaped from deten-tion in the south-western town of Ouidah; among them were several soldiers who were suspected of involvement in the pre-vious year's alleged coup plot. The subsequent dismissal of the armed forces chief of staff and of other senior members of the security forces prompted the resignation of the government minister responsible for defence, who protested that Soglo had acted unconstitutionally by making new appointments without consulting him. In September Soglo announced a reorganization of the government. In October Soglo lost his majority support in the national assembly when 15 members of Le Renouveau, including the group's chairman, withdrew from the coalition, alleging that the president was consistently excluding the legis-lature from the decision-making process. In July, meanwhile, Soglo had aligned himself with the (Parti de la) Renaissance du Bénin (RB), formed by his wife, Rosine, in 1992; he was ap-pointed leader of the RB in July 1994.

Social unrest was exacerbated by the 50% devaluation, in January 1994, of the CFA franc. Following several weeks of severe labour unrest, in March the government announced salary increases of 10% for all state employees, as well as the reintroduction of housing allowances (abolished in 1986) and an end to an eight-year 'freeze' on promotions within the civil service. In July 1994 the national assembly approved increases in wages and student grants that exceeded those envisaged in the government's draft budget. Stating that an imbalanced budget was not only unconstitutional, but would also cause the loss of funding and debt relief already agreed with external creditors, Soglo announced that he was to impose the government's draft budget by decree. The national assembly referred the matter for adjudication by the constitutional court, which effectively ruled that presidential recourse to the relevant article of the constitution was discretionary, and could not therefore be subject to legal control. The payment of salary arrears from 1983–91 began in November 1994.

Electoral Tensions

Preparations for elections to the national assembly, scheduled for February 1995, were the cause of further friction between the executive and legislature. In November 1994 parliament voted to establish an independent Commission électorale nationale autonome (CENA) to oversee the elections: the creation of such a body, which Soglo was known to oppose, was subsequently approved by the constitutional court. Soglo also opposed the planned increase in the number of parliamentary deputies from 64 to 83. Organizational difficulties twice necessitated the postponement of the legislative elections, which finally took place on 28 March. Some 31 political organizations had been authorized to participate, and a total of 5,580 candidates contested seats in the enlarged legislature. Although observers concluded that the elections had generally been conducted fairly, irregularities were apparent in several constituencies in Atlantique province, in the south, and in the Bourgou region in the north. Provisional results indicated that, although the RB had won the largest number of seats in the legislature, opposition parties were likely, in alliance, to outnumber the president's supporters. Of the opposition parties, Houngbédji's PRD emerged as the strongest, while supporters of ex-president Kérékou, mainly representing the Front d'action pour le renouveau et le développement–Alafia (FARD–Alafia), enjoyed particular success in the north, although Kérékou himself had not actively campaigned in the elections. In mid-April the constitutional court annulled the results of voting for nine seats in Cotonou (part of the Atlantique province) and for four seats in the Bourgou region. Following by-elections in May, the RB held 20 seats in the national assembly, and other supporters of Soglo a total of 13. Opposition parties held, in all, 49 seats, the most prominent being the PRD, with 19 seats, and FARD–Alafia, with 10. Bruno Amoussou, the leader of the opposition Parti social-démocrate, was elected speaker of the legislature. A new government was announced in late June.

From October 1995 rumours circulated of a coup plot and of attempts to sabotage a conference of heads of state and government of the Conseil permanent de la francophonie, which was due to take place in Cotonou in December. Although the government denied suggestions that a destabilization plot had been discovered, it was confirmed that members of the military had been among several people arrested in security operations. Tensions escalated in November, following a rocket attack on the newly-built conference centre at which the francophone summit was to take place. It was subsequently announced that one person had been killed and several arrested, and that munitions stolen during a raid on the Ouidah barracks in early 1994 had been recovered, as part of operations to apprehend the perpetrators of the rocket attack.

Presidential Candidacies

Despite Kérékou's effective withdrawal from active politics following his defeat in 1991, the success of his supporters at the 1995 parliamentary elections prompted speculation that he might again contest the presidency in 1996. While Soglo's economic policies had earned him the respect of the international financial community, there was disquiet within Benin that strong growth had been achieved at the expense of social concerns; moreover, criticism was increasingly levelled at what was termed the regime's 'authoritarian drift' and alleged nepotism. Tribute was paid, meanwhile, to what was regarded as Kérékou's dignified acceptance of the decisions of the 1990 national conference and of his 1991 electoral defeat. By the time Kérékou officially announced, in January 1996, that he was again to contest the presidency, promising greater emphasis on social issues, it was widely accepted that his would be the most powerful challenge to a second Soglo presidency.

Renewed institutional conflict followed the national assembly's decision, in late December 1995, to delay ratification of the third phase of the country's structural adjustment programme,

a particularly contentious element of which was the planned restructuring of the state company responsible for the distribution of petroleum products. The legislature rejected a revised programme twice during January 1996, and also rejected the draft budget for 1996, prompting Soglo to announce that, in the national interest, he was to implement the budget and adjustment programme by decree.

The first round of the presidential election, on 3 March 1996, was contested by seven candidates. As had been expected, Soglo and Kérékou emerged as the leading candidates, although Soglo's supporters alleged widespread vote-rigging. More than one-fifth of the votes cast were subsequently invalidated by the constitutional court prior to the announcement of the official results. Soglo secured 35.7% of the valid votes and Kérékou 33.9%, followed by Houngbédji (19.7%) and Amoussou (7.8%). The rate of participation by voters was high, at 86.9%. Most of the defeated candidates quickly expressed their support for Kérékou, among them Houngbédji (who had in 1975 been sentenced to death *in absentia* for his part in a plot to overthrow Kérékou's military regime). A government decision to delay the second round of voting by four days, to 21 March (owing to the late proclamation of the results of the first poll), was overturned by the constitutional court following an appeal by Kérékou's supporters, and the vote took place on 18 March.

Prior to the official announcement of the second-round results, a gun attack was reported on the home of a member of the constitutional court. (Earlier in the month members of the court had received intimidatory letters, signed by 'southerners in rebellion', accusing them of plotting against democracy.) On 24 March 1996 the constitutional court proclaimed that Kérékou had received the support of 52.5% of voters. Some 78.1% of those eligible had voted, and less than 3% of the votes had been invalidated. Soglo, who continued to claim victory, announced that he was contesting the outcome on several counts. A statement issued by the constitutional court in late March, denouncing pressure brought to bear on its members by Soglo and his associates, was rejected by Soglo's aides as a deliberate attempt to tarnish the president's reputation. International monitors, meanwhile, stated that any irregularities in the conduct of voting in no way affected the overall credibility of the result. On 1 April the court announced that it had rejected all appeals against the outcome of the election, and accordingly confirmed Kérékou's victory; Soglo conceded defeat the following day.

THE RETURN OF KÉRÉKOU

At his inauguration, on 4 April 1996, Kérékou undertook to strive for national reconciliation. Having sought authorization by the constitutional court for the appointment of a prime minister (provision for such a post is not stipulated in the constitution), he named Houngbédji as premier in a government that included representatives of eight parties that had supported his presidential campaign; Kérékou assumed personal responsibility for defence. The government's stated priorities were to be to strengthen the rule of law, and to promote economic revival and social development. Despite Kérékou's campaign pledges to halt privatization, a new funding arrangement was approved by the IMF in August.

A national economic conference took place in mid-December 1996, with the aim of identifying, and ensuring consensus regarding, Benin's economic aims. The six-day meeting was attended by some 500 delegates from all sectors, including representatives of commerce, industry, trade unions and political organizations, together with observers from the IMF and the World Bank. Addressing the conference, Kérékou expressed his belief that the further development of the private sector was essential to Benin's future economic prosperity. He also emphasized his commitment to eliminating corruption in all areas of public life.

In early 1997 measures permitting the private ownership of radio and television stations received parliamentary approval. The first licences were issued by the Haut autorité de l'audiovisuel et de la communication in November. In early August, meanwhile, a new law on territorial administration was endorsed by the national assembly, whereby Benin was to be divided into 12 administrative departments.

In early September 1997 the national assembly approved an amnesty benefiting, most notably, some 30 members of the military and civilians implicated in the events of late 1995. The amnesty, which embraced all acts seeking to undermine state security, together with what were termed election and media crimes committed between January 1990 and June 1996, provoked protests by the RB, which warned that the measure would excerbate 'ethno-regionalist' divisions (the majority of those amnestied were northerners) and tensions and indiscipline within the army. The law was promulgated by Kérékou shortly afterwards, and one of its principal beneficiaries, Pascal Tawes, returned to Benin at the end of September 1997. In mid-October, however, the constitutional court invalidated the amnesty legislation, on the grounds that the government had discussed the draft law without first consulting the supreme court, whose involvement in the formulation of such legislation the constitutional court deemed obligatory.

The government was obliged to revise its budgetary provisions for 1998 in late 1997, after the national assembly rejected proposals to end automatic promotions within the civil service. The proposed emphasis on promotions according to merit had prompted strike action by state employees during previous weeks. From mid-February 1998 a series of general strikes, involving some 37,000 civil servants who were demanding payment of salary arrears which had accumulated since 1992, as well as improved working and living conditions, caused considerable disruption in many sectors. At the beginning of March 1998 agreement was reached on the payment of arrears valued by the government at 5,000m. francs CFA, and on efforts to preserve jobs in privatized enterprises. In early May Kérékou met with trade union leaders, after civil servants announced their intention to resume strike action in protest at the state's failure to honour its commitment to pay arrears. The crisis in the public sector assumed wider political dimensions as Kérékou undertook personally to address the issue of salary arrears, and invited the trade unions to nominate a new minister responsible for the civil service, for inclusion in a new government whose appointment was imminent. (A general strike none the less proceeded in mid-May.) Houngbédji resigned, and announced the withdrawal of the PRD from the government. Mediation by a delegation led by the Togolese prime minister failed to resolve differences between Kérékou and Houngbédji, who was reportedly concerned that the likely composition of the new government would result in a loss of influence for himself and his party; the outgoing prime minister had, moreover, intimated his dissatisfaction at having been largely excluded from the drafting of the 1998 budget, and had demanded that his prerogatives be clearly defined. Kérékou named his government in mid-May. There was no prime minister, the most senior member being Pierre Otcho (formerly responsible for foreign affairs and co-operation), as minister-delegate to the presidency, in charge of defence and relations with the institutions. Only three ministers retained their previous positions, with some 13 new ministers being appointed. Despite Kérékou's stated intention of redistributing portfolios to the satisfaction of some 20 parties that had supported his election in 1996, the new government, which included representatives of seven parties, was calculated to command the support of just 27 members of the national assembly. Further conflict between the executive and legislature thus appeared inevitable.

Legislative Elections

In early September 1998 the Assemblée nationale approved legislation providing for the establishment of a new permanent secretariat (Secrétariat administratif permanent–SAP) for the national election committee, the CENA. The SAP was to prepare electoral material, to manage the voter register and to advise the members of the CENA. The CENA, however, declared that it would not be able fully to collaborate with the SAP, as the SAP was to be directly responsible to the president, which the CENA felt would compromise its independence. From mid-February 1999 the CENA organized extensive programmes throughout Benin to ensure the correct conduct of the legislative elections scheduled for 28 March 1999. Single ballot papers were introduced, featuring party symbols, in order to simplify the voting process.

Campaigning for the elections was marred by some civil disturbances, and by three days of industrial action by workers at the state radio and television broadcasting company. In early March 1999 irregularities were discovered in the registration of voters in Cotonou and Porto-Novo. Six people were sentenced to prison terms for forging and selling voters' cards and for registering false names on voter registers. A further 40 people were also arrested and charged with electoral offences.

In early March 1999 it was announced that the legislative elections were to be postponed by two days, as the earlier date had coincided with Muslim and Christian holy days. On 30 March 1999 some 2,900 candidates from 35 parties and alliances contested the 83 seats in the national assembly. The 200 international observers monitoring the elections reported that the elections had been conducted peacefully and democratically. The opposition parties won a narrow victory in the elections, taking 42 seats, while the pro-Kérékou parties won 41. Voting was divided on clear regional lines: the RB of ex-president Soglo won 27 seats, principally in Cotonou, and in the centre and south of Benin, while parties supporting the president performed strongly in the north and in the west. The CENA estimated the rate of participation at over 70%. Soglo himself did not stand in the elections, although his wife was expected to continue as the party's parliamentary leader. The opposition was swift to reassure observers that it intended to co-operate with the president and to seek consensus where possible. Former prime minister Adrien Houngbédji was elected president of the national assembly.

In June 1999 Kérékou carried out a minor cabinet reshuffle, reportedly in order to strengthen his support in the national assembly by increasing the number of parties represented in the council of ministers from seven to 10. The council was increased in size from 18 to 19 members.

In July 1999 the commission of inquiry into corruption in Benin, established by Kérékou in 1996, announced its findings. The commission, which had investigated 167 suspected cases of corruption, disclosed that more than 70,000m. francs CFA had been embezzled between April 1996 and April 1999. In the same month the government established by decree a code of ethics, which aimed to curb corruption by excluding those convicted of corruption from public office, and by obliging the disclosure of all payments made during tendering for state projects.

In early October 1999 an estimated 20,000 people attended a demonstration in Lokosso, in the north-west, against perceived weaknesses in Benin's judicial system. The rally was organized by vigilante groups, who were reported to have been responsible for the execution of over 100 alleged criminals in the previous two months. The government, while critical of the vigilantes' actions, expressed its understanding of their frustration and refrained from suggesting that action would be taken against them. However, following criticism from human rights groups, the government dispatched troops to the north-west in order to restore order in the region. In the following weeks local groups handed over some 150 suspected criminals to the armed forces. Further disturbances were, however, reported in Lokosso in November following a judge's decision to release without charge a suspect arrested by a local group and accused of banditry.

In late October 1999 an estimated 32,000 civil servants undertook a three-day general strike after negotiations between public-sector unions and the government failed to reach agreement on the payment of salary arrears and the abolition of a new system of promotions according to merit. The government, while stating that it 'deplored' the strike action, offered to pursue further negotiations with the unions. In early November, however, some unions began further industrial action, claiming that offers made by the government were not satisfactory. Agreement was subsequently reached on the creation of a bipartisan commission to investigate a new system of remuneration and promotion for the civil service, and on the payment of salary arrears. None the less, one trade union federation, the Centrale des organisations syndicales indépendantes, resumed strike action the following week, demanding the immediate implementation of the terms of the agreement.

In January 2000 the president was obliged to impose the budget for 2000 by decree, after the opposition in the national assembly had rejected its provisions. It was widely believed that the opposition, which claimed to have noted procedural irregularities in the preparation of the budget, intended to call attention to the limited nature of support for Kérékou in the national assembly in advance of the presidential elections, scheduled for 2001. In the same month members of the armed forces demonstrated in Cotonou in order to complain that they had not received the bonus payments due to them for their service in West African peace-keeping missions; the government later admitted that sums of money due to the troops involved had in fact been misappropriated by senior military figures. Kérékou subsequently announced that he suspected that the armed forces and certain opposition parties were preparing a *coup d'état*. The opposition, which rejected the accusation, challenged the president to produce evidence of his claims, and, in its turn, accused the government of conspiring to assassinate ex-president Soglo prior to the presidential elections due to take place in 2001.

In late June 2000 one of Benin's principal trade union federations, the Centrale syndicale autonome du Bénin, undertook a 48-hour strike in order to protest at the rapid escalation of the cost of petrol (rises of up to 77% had been announced earlier in the month), and to call for improvements in salaries and social welfare in order to offset the increases. Popular discontent at the rises continued to escalate, and in early July an estimated 10,000 people attended a public demonstration in Cotonou, organized by Benin's six trade union federations. The government later announced that funds would be made available for social measures to compensate those affected by the price rise. The trade union federations, however, rejected the government's proposals as inadequate, and called for further protest demonstrations in mid-July.

EXTERNAL AFFAIRS

Benin's international standing was enhanced following the introduction of democratic reforms, and the success of the Soglo regime's economic liberalization measures in promoting strong growth earned the respect of the international financial community. Soglo's relations with France were generally close, and

France provided significant financial support for the construction of Cotonou's new conference centre, in preparation for the 1995 summit meeting of the Conseil permanent de la francophonie.

Following Kérékou's election to the presidency in March 1996, there was initial uncertainty regarding his government's likely conduct of external political and economic relations. While he had undoubtedly abandoned his former commitment to Marxist economic theory, Kérékou's campaign pledges to halt privatization and devote increased resources to social and welfare projects raised doubts as to the future conduct of relations with the IMF (which stipulated continued spending restraint as a precondition for assistance) and thus with other creditors. None the less, the conclusion of the new agreement with the IMF in August indicated a pragmatic approach to international economic relations. France was swift to acknowledge the legitimacy of Kérékou's election. During an official visit to that country in October, Kérékou asked for French assistance in transferring the economic capital from Cotonou to the administrative capital, Porto-Novo.

The new regime has also sought to foster close regional relations. In April 1998 Benin was one of eight countries to participate in the 'Cohésion Kompienga '98' military exercises (conducted as part of efforts to train regional armies in peace-keeping and humanitarian assistance operations). Benin subsequently contributed some 140 troops to the peace-keeping operations in Guinea-Bissau undertaken by the ECOWAS Cease-fire Monitoring Group (ECOMOG), although it withdrew its force in June 1999 following the *coup d'état* in Guinea-Bissau. Benin maintains generally good relations with neighbouring countries, although in mid-2000 a long-term dispute between Benin and Niger over the ownership of various small islands in the Niger River, erupted once more after Nigerien soldiers reportedly sabotaged the construction of a Beninois administrative building on Lété Island. A meeting between representatives of the two governments failed to resolve the dispute, which was subsequently referred to the Organization of African Unity for arbitration.

Economy

EDITH HODGKINSON

The dominant characteristics of the economy of Benin are its dualism and its dependence on Nigeria. There is an official, documented sector covering government and relatively modern industry and agriculture, and an unofficial, largely unrecorded sector consisting of basic food production and cross-border trade with Nigeria. Changes in the rate of economic growth are largely determined by trends in Nigeria. Overall economic growth has been slow, with the annual increase in Benin's gross domestic product (GDP) averaging only 2.0%, in real terms, in 1980–90. During this period the performance of the Beninois economy fluctuated fairly widely. Beginning in 1985 Benin suffered a period of economic depression, caused by the closure of the border with Nigeria (which was in force between April 1984 and March 1986), the economic recession in Nigeria, and the decline in international prices for Benin's major export commodities, cotton and petroleum, while the strengthening of the CFA franc in relation to the US dollar reduced the proceeds from these commodities in local currency terms. The 1990s saw an improvement in economic performance, with GDP growth averaging 4.6% per year in 1992–99. This owed much to good harvests in almost every year, but a significant contribution was also made by the complete reversal in economic policy in 1990–91 under the new civilian regime, which aimed to enhance the role of the private sector and to reduce government participation in production. The structural reform programme undertaken by the administration of Nicéphore Soglo was supported by the significant rescheduling of debt that was agreed by bilateral official creditors in December 1991 (see below) and an Enhanced Structural Adjustment Facility (ESAF) at the IMF for the period 1993–95.

However, the context for the programme was fundamentally modified by the devaluation, by 50%, of the CFA franc in January 1994. This had severe short-term costs, in the form of a sudden increase in the rate of inflation which the government was not fully able to counter by the imposition of price controls. Inflation accelerated from near zero in 1993 to an average of 37.4% in 1994. Moreover, the domestic manufacturing sector, which is heavily dependent on foreign supplies of raw materials and intermediates, was adversely affected by the overnight doubling of import costs. None the less, the devaluation had some positive effects—stimulating export growth (since producers of export goods, in particular agricultural commodities, obtain more in local currency terms) and demand for local products, notably foodstuffs. With increased inflows of foreign aid to allow the maintenance of imports that are essential for the economy's expansion, in conjunction with particularly good cotton crops, GDP growth was increasing during the mid-1990s. However, the reduction in household income that devaluation entailed—even if the erosion lessened as average inflation fell below double figures in 1996—alienated popular support for the Soglo regime, and it was the urban areas (traditionally a stronghold for the president) that bore the brunt of the adjustment. Devaluation thus had a high political cost, which was paid by President Soglo when he was defeated in the 1996 election. Contrary to some expectations, the new Kérékou administration has not reverted to the Marxist economic policies of the past. Liberalization is now well entrenched in many sectors, and, in view of the country's dependence on foreign assistance and the need to generate sustainable, long-term growth so as to fulfil its promises of improved living standards and more jobs, the government maintained a co-operative relationship with the IMF. Within months of Kérékou taking power, the terms were agreed for an ESAF to replace that which had expired in the final months of the Soglo regime. The programme the funding supports aimed to achieve a steady improvement in economic growth, to 6.2% in 1999, with inflation in the low single digits and both fiscal and current-account deficits falling as a ratio of GDP. Whereas the record in the first year of the programme was satisfactory (GDP growth reached 5.7% in 1997), economic growth slowed in the second year, to 4.4%, because of severe shortfalls in electricity supply as drought hit capacity at the Akosombo dam in Ghana. At the same time, inadequate petroleum supplies from Nigeria pushed up the price of oil, and hence inflation (to an estimated average 5.6%). It was, however, the government's slow progress in implementing two major requirements, privatization and a retrenchment in the public sector payroll, which caused the IMF to suspend disbursements in the course of 1998. The facility was resumed in January 1999, after the government agreed to abolish the automatic yearly pay rise for the civil service and to push through the sale of a number of major state enterprises (see below). While the restoration of power supply allowed GDP growth to pick up once more in 1999, at 5% the rate was still below the programme target, owing to the fall in the international price for cotton, the main export commodity.

POPULATION AND EMPLOYMENT

Despite its relative lack of urbanization in previous decades, Benin has for some time had a high standard of education; the existence of a large élite—for whom employment cannot easily be found in an underdeveloped, slowly-growing economy—was at the root of Benin's unstable political situation in the years after independence. Another contributory factor, again exacerbated by the unsatisfactory economic situation, is the rift between three clearly-defined regions: Parakou and the north, Abomey and the centre-south, and the narrow coastal zone around Cotonou (the main port) and Porto-Novo (the official capital). Almost three-quarters of the country's inhabitants—the population was estimated to total 6.24m. at mid-1999—reside in the southern regions, giving a population density there of more than 120 per sq km—one of the highest in western Africa. Recent years have seen a pronounced movement to the towns. About 40% of inhabitants are urban, around double the level in 1990, and the population of Cotonou is now well above the 533,000 registered at the 1992 census. While agriculture, livestock and fishing engage around half of the work-force, the public sector has also been a significant source of employment, accounting for about one-half of wage and salary earners. This proportion will have been declining under the privatization and fiscal stabilization programmes implemented by the Soglo administration and continued by its successor.

AGRICULTURE

The economy is mainly dependent on the agricultural sector, which accounts for around two-fifths of GDP and more than half of the working population. Output of the major food crops has been rising strongly since the drought of 1981–83, reflecting both improved climatic conditions and a transfer of emphasis from cash crops to the cultivation of staple foods, and Benin is self-sufficient in basic foods. In 1997/98 output of cassava was 1,918,000 metric tons, yams 1,407,000, maize 701,000 and millet and sorghum 147,000 tons. Production of non-traditional food crops—notably rice (to substitute for imports), tomatoes, beans and onions—has also risen.

In the past the major cash crop was oil palm, which remains the principal tree crop. Output of palm products, which was formerly based on natural plantations covering 400,000 ha, benefited in the 1970s from intensive cultivation on some 30,000 ha of industrial plantations, partly financed by French aid. Production of palm kernels was estimated at 70,000 tons in 1976, and palm oil at more than 23,000 tons. However, output subsequently fell, owing to low producer prices and the overvalued CFA franc, and total marketed production of palm oil and palm kernel oil was down to an average of only about 10,000 tons per year by the early 1990s. The figure for marketed production is distorted by the incidence of smuggling from Nigeria (in order to secure payment in the 'hard currency' CFA franc, rather than in the unstable naira).

By far the most valuable commercial crop is cotton, the production of which expanded rapidly in the 1980s, and which now accounts for over half of recorded export earnings. Benin's annual output of unginned (seed) cotton increased from 9,000 tons in 1966/67 to 50,000 tons in 1972/73, as cultivation was established in the northern areas, supported by funds from the World Bank. Output declined in subsequent years, to an annual average of around 14,000 tons in the late 1970s and early 1980s. The overall decline in cotton production was partly the result of the departure of a French cotton company and partly the result of poor marketing organization and smuggling to neighbouring countries, because of low producer prices locally. However, with new investment in this sector, output tripled in the mid-1980s, reaching 131,262 tons in 1986/87. With an expansion in the area under cultivation, output levels continued to increase in the early 1990s, and, boosted by the increase in producer prices following the currency's devaluation, production reached a record 385,000 tons in 1997/98. Output has since fallen, however, owing to management problems at the cotton-marketing board and weaker international prices. Production was down to 325,000 tons in 1998/99, far below the target of 400,000 tons for that year. Production recovered in 1999/2000 to 380,000 tons, the vast majority of which was sold at a price above the international average, and an official production target of 400,000 tons was set for 2000/01.

Whereas cotton is grown mainly in the north, other cash crops are produced in the south, where there are two rainy seasons. These include coffee, cocoa, groundnuts and shea-nuts (karité nuts). Marketed production of cocoa and coffee tends to vary widely, since most of the recorded production is normally not from Benin but originates in Nigeria. Recorded production of cash crops has been in decline because official purchase prices did not keep pace with the rise in the cost of living, prompting farmers to switch to subsistence food crops, or to sell their output outside official channels, on the local 'black market' or across the border in Nigeria. This situation has to some extent been remedied by the 1994 devaluation, whose doubling of the local-currency value of foreign earnings has benefited producers.

Exploitation of timber resources (mainly for fuel) is still limited, though rising, with annual roundwood removals increasing from 2.05m. cu m in 1970 to an estimated 6.0m. cu m in 1995. A reafforestation programme, which was inaugurated in 1985 to counter desertification, is concentrating on fast-growing species around populated areas. Livestock farming is practised in its traditional form in the north. In 1998 cattle herds numbered 1.4m., sheep and goats 1.6m., and pigs (kept mainly in the south) 580,000. Food supply is also supplemented by fishing (according to the FAO, the total annual catch has, in recent years, averaged some 43,000 tons). The more advanced sector of fishing should grow rapidly as new investment comes into effect: two deep-sea fishing boats have been bought for the national fishing company. Meanwhile, the traditional sector is in decline, owing to salination of the lagoons from the development of the port of Cotonou.

MINING AND POWER

Although phosphates, kaolin, chromium, rutile, gold and iron ore have been located in the north, the only minerals so far exploited are limestone, marble, petroleum and natural gas. Production of petroleum in Benin began in the Sémé oilfield, 15 km offshore from Cotonou, in 1982, with initial output averaging 4,000 barrels per day (b/d). Production reached a peak of 9,000 b/d in 1985, with the entry into operation of a third well and of water-injection facilities; five new wells were also drilled. However, the transfer of the service contracts from the Norwegian developer in 1985 failed to realize the expected increase in output, and production was reduced to 3,000 b/d by mid-1988. New investment in remedial work and an enhanced recovery programme backed by funds from the International Development Association (IDA) only temporarily pushed output above 3,000 b/d, and by 1996 it was reduced to 1,500 b/d. With the international price for petroleum weak, production ceased at the end of 1998. In October 1999, however, Zetah Oil signed a contract to rehabilitate the oilfield.

Electricity supply (332m. kWh in 1997) comes largely from the Akosombo hydroelectric dam in Ghana, as operations at the 62 MW installation on the frontier with Togo at Nangbeto, on the River Mono, which began in 1988, have tended to be sporadic. A second dam, with 104 MW capacity, is under construction at Adjarala, with the aim of achieving self-sufficiency in power for both Benin and Togo.

MANUFACTURING

Manufacturing activity is still small-scale and, apart from the construction materials industry, is confined to the processing of primary products for export (cotton ginning, oil palm processing), or import substitution of simple consumer goods. The sector accounted for an estimated 9% of GDP in the late 1990s. Cotton processing has been the most important activity since the late 1980s, after additional ginning plants came into operation, including three new ginneries in a joint venture between the cotton marketing agency, the Société nationale pour la promotion agricole (SONAPRA) and a French company in 1995/96. With capacity at 462,000 tons, the entire national crop can now be processed domestically. In addition, other agricultural processing plants—for maize, cashew-nuts and vegetables—have been rehabilitated to supply the stronger domestic and foreign markets. By contrast oil palm processing, previously a major industry, has been in decline for over two decades. Its processing capacity, of 215,000 tons, is grossly underutilized. The sector is now being restructured, with aid from the World Bank, with a view to privatization.

Two joint ventures with Nigeria came into operation in the early 1980s, but proved unprofitable. The cement plant at Onigbolo began production in 1982. Plans to sell one-half of the scheduled annual output of 600,000 tons to Nigeria failed to materialize, because of the downturn in its economy and overcapacity in cement production in west Africa. The plant has been operating at only about one-half of its capacity. Meanwhile, the other joint venture with Nigeria, a sugar complex at Savé, with an annual capacity of 45,000 tons, operated only intermittently, and at a small fraction of capacity, following its commissioning in 1983. With world sugar prices much lower than the project's production costs, the complex was unprofitable, and it ceased operation in 1991. These two projects are among those that the Soglo government aimed to dispose of as part of its privatization programme. This represented a complete reversal of the policies pursued by Kérékou's military regime in its early years: during the 1970s there had been an increasing emphasis on state participation in industry, exemplified by the nationalization of a number of private enterprises. However, the worsening in budget finances, as the economy contracted, forced the government to reconsider the desirability of maintaining the parastatal organizations (which cover a wide range of services as well as products). Through the privatization, rehabilitation or liquidation of these organizations, the number of parastatals was reduced from a high point of 120 to only 15 by the end of the Soglo regime. The process had slowed, however, as it became increasingly difficult to attract offers at acceptable prices. Meanwhile, the debts accumulated at the Onigbolo cement plant and the Savé sugar complex delayed the privatization agreed in principle by the two governments. The future of the whole privatization programme was thrown into doubt by the outcome of the 1996 presidential election. The new Kérékou administration initially expressed its opposition to any further disposals of state assets, essentially because of the job losses this often entails, but one of the commitments made by the new regime to secure another ESAF was a continuation of the privatization programme. It was the slow progress on this pledge that caused the IMF to suspend fund releases under the ESAF in 1998. The conditions attached to their resumption in 1999 included the long-planned privatization of the petroleum company, the Société nationale de commercialisation des produits pétroliers (SONACOP) and the textile enterprise, Société industrielle des textiles (SITEX), and the liberalization of the telecommunications and cotton sectors. A 55% stake in SONACOP has been sold, and the management of the two loss-making joint ventures with Nigeria was leased out to overseas investors in 1999. A French group has a five-year lease on the cement plant, to prepare it for privatization, while a Mauritian company is to rehabilitate the Savé complex.

TRANSPORT INFRASTRUCTURE

The country's transport infrastructure is comparatively good. Most internal transportation uses the country's road network: the classified road network totals some 7,500 km, about one-fifth of which is paved. A number of major road construction schemes, including the upgrading of the 222-km Dassa–Parakou link of the Cotonou–Niger highway, have been implemented, with financial support from the European Community (now European Union—EU), the African Development Bank and the Arab Bank for Economic Development in Africa. By the construction of new roads and the upgrading of existing routes, it is hoped to develop the country's status as an entrepôt for regional trade. Current plans include the construction of a road from Savalou (in the centre of the country) to Djougou (in the north-east), which would improve communications with Burkina Faso and Mali; external finance has been obtained. Feeder roads are also being built for the marketing of agricultural products. Benin's foreign earnings benefit from the transit trade from Niger via the 579-km Benin–Niger railway. There have long been plans to extend the line from Parakou to Niamey, but, given the country's economic circumstances and strained budget resources, the project's implementation is now only a remote possibility. France provided the funding for a programme, undertaken in 1987–91, to rehabilitate rolling stock and to overhaul 440 km of track between Cotonou and Parakou, as well as to restructure the rail company's finances. In 1995 the network handled 388,000 tons of goods. The port of Cotonou handles 2m.–2.5m. tons of freight a year, of which around 300,000 tons is transit trade with Niger and Burkina Faso. The port was operating well below capacity in the 1980s, but it has benefited in recent years from US $4m. in investment by the Danish company, Maersk Line, in container facilities. The company began operations at the port in May 1998, thus ending the state company's monopoly on container trade (which had reached 739,000 tons in 1997). The port's oil-handling capacity was increased by around 60% in November 1999 with the opening of a new terminal.

FINANCE

For over a decade now successive governments have been struggling to reduce the chronic deficit on its budget. Government finances had come under pressure in the mid-1980s as the result of the impact on revenues of economic recession in Nigeria and of the temporary closure of the border (customs duties account for the greater part of budgetary revenue), while spending was inflated by the cost of operating the parastatal companies. After the budget deficit had reached a peak of 7.3% of GDP in 1986, a wide-ranging austerity programme was implemented in 1987, with the aim of reducing current expenditure. Public enterprises were transferred to private ownership, liquidated or rehabilitated, and public-sector salaries were initially 'frozen' (in 1987) and subsequently reduced (in 1988). Further retrenchment was planned for 1989, with reductions both in personnel and salaries in the civil service, together with measures to improve the collection of taxes. However, the political turmoil of late 1989 and early 1990 meant that revenue from taxation virtually ceased, and it was the accumulation of salary arrears that precipitated the downfall of the Kérékou regime. The budget deficit surged to 10.7% of GDP in 1989. The Soglo administration succeeded in reducing the deficit to 4.7% by 1993. This was due to several factors: higher revenues (as the rate of economic growth improved, and port trade was displaced from Togo to Benin), privatization (which both generates immediate funds and, in the case of loss-making operations, relieves a drain on budget resources), and a reduction in interest payments (as a result of the rescheduling of foreign debt by the 'Paris Club' of official creditors in 1991). The devaluation of the CFA franc put pressure on the spending side of the budget, as the government was obliged to concede an overall increase of 21% in public-sector salaries, to compensate for the surge in consumer prices, while interest payments on the external debt doubled in local currency terms. Consequently, the deficit again rose to 7.4% of GDP in 1994. Although the deficit rose again in 1995, to 7.7% of GDP, there were some significant structural improvements, with a higher proportion of total spending going to the capital programme and a lower proportion to salaries, as the public-sector payroll was reduced. The combination of a higher deficit and higher capital spending was maintained through 1996 and 1997. The deficit was then pulled down sharply once more, from 4.2% of GDP in 1997 (52,600m. francs CFA) to only 1.6% of GDP, at 19,600m. francs CFA in 1998. This reduction was almost entirely due to the fall in spending, with capital outgoings down by a fifth because of delays in the disbursement of external grants (the main source of funding) and current spending growth held to 12%, despite a continuing rise in the wage bill. The 1999 budget envisaged an upturn in the deficit, to 100,200m. francs CFA, stemming from a 45% rise in total spending, based on the expectation of a recovery in external funding after the IMF agreed to resume lending under the 1996 ESAF. The budget for 2000 set a much less marked rise in spending, of 12.8%, but as this was still higher than the planned increase in revenue, the deficit was expected to rise once more, to 124,500m. francs CFA.

Benin's fiscal difficulties were compounded by the breakdown of the entire state banking system in 1988–89, when the Banque Commerciale du Bénin (the country's sole commercial bank, created in 1974 following the nationalization of all banks) collapsed as a result of protracted mismanagement and corruption, and the Banque Béninoise de Développement and the Caisse Nationale de Crédit Agricole were wound up. An important component of the structural adjustment programme adopted in 1989 was the rehabilitation of the banking system. The state's monopoly over the sector has been ended, and new, foreign-owned banks have been established.

FOREIGN TRADE AND PAYMENTS

Benin has traditionally maintained a very substantial external trade deficit, with import spending usually some 50% more than the level of export receipts. During the 1980s export earnings were adversely affected by the recession in Nigeria, the closure of the border between the two countries during 1984–86, the impact of drought upon palm products, cocoa and coffee in 1981–83, and the decline in international cotton prices in 1986 and 1987 (cotton being the leading export). Despite a good recovery in exports in the early 1990s, the gap between exports and imports remained massive because the resumption of economic growth prompted an increase in the level of imports. By 1993 the trade gap was US $168m. The sharp depreciation of the currency in the following year only temporarily narrowed this gap because the decline in import spending was immediately made up as economic growth gathered momentum. By 1995 the trade deficit was at a new record level of $203m. Fluctuations continued throughout subsequent years, reflecting the impact on export earnings of trends in cotton prices, and the impact on the cost of imports of the international price of petroleum. By 1998–99 the imbalance was averaging around $170m.

The deficit on merchandise trade has historically been partly covered by remittances from Beninois overseas, which were estimated at US $100m. in the early 1990s, but which have since fallen to an estimated annual average of $60m.–$70m. A more significant offset is the inflow of aid. Disbursements of development aid by non-communist countries and agencies, which averaged some US $84m. per year in the early 1980s, increased in the second half of that decade, to reach $285m. in 1990, boosted by French aid for the restructuring of the banking sector. Aid inflows increased between 1991 and 1993, in support of the new democratic regime, and averaged a net $251m. per year in 1994–98. In the 1970s loans from governments and multilateral agencies accounted for the major part of the external public debt ($158.4m. out of $192.2m. at the end of 1979), as Benin's radical economic policies tended to deter

foreign private capital. Commercial borrowing then increased sharply in the early 1980s, to finance the oil development programme, and at the end of 1987 42% of the long-term debt was owed to private creditors. The situation was reversed again as a result of the 1989 debt-relief agreement (see below), and at the end of 1997 virtually all of Benin's medium- and long-term debt was owed to official creditors (multilateral and bilateral). Throughout the whole decade around 80% of this debt was on concessional terms.

Variations in the terms of the foreign debt have had a marked effect on the burden of debt service. Payments on the external public debt in 1979 had amounted to only 5.1% of total earnings from exports of goods and services in that year. This very manageable ratio deteriorated markedly with the rise in borrowing from private sources, at much higher interest rates, which caused debt-servicing payments to increase more than 10-fold by 1986, when they reached US $62m. (equivalent to 13.6% of export earnings). However, even this represented only one-half of the debt-servicing payments due in that year, and arrears on both debt principal and interest accumulated to more than $400m. by the end of 1988. After a structural reform programme was agreed with the IMF, and a three-year structural adjustment facility awarded in June 1989, the 'Paris Club' agreed to the rescheduling of $193m. in debt. Further relief was accorded in December 1991, when the 'Paris Club', recognizing the efforts of the new government to resolve the country's public-financing difficulties, undertook to reduce the debt-service burden by one-half. Creditors would either cancel 30% of outstanding debt, reschedule the balance over 23 years (including six years' grace), or reduce interest rates so as to halve the net payments. There was a further rescheduling, on similar terms, in June 1993, after the IMF accorded Benin access to the ESAF. These concessions relieved pressure on government finances at a time when the economic adjustment programme would otherwise have had even greater consequences for employment and income within the country.

The devaluation of the CFA franc in January 1994 greatly increased the burden on the Beninois economy of servicing foreign debt (the value of which had thereby doubled in local currency terms). Supplementary assistance was therefore arranged (for the entire Franc Zone in Africa) by the IMF, the World Bank and the EU, and France accorded debt waivers. In the case of Benin, 600m. French francs (equivalent to US $109m.) was cancelled with immediate effect. However, the increase in borrowing, particularly from multilateral institutions (which is not eligible for rescheduling), had pushed Benin's debt to $1,614m. by the end of 1995. The ESAF extended to the new administration in August 1996 opened the way to a fourth round of debt rescheduling by the country's bilateral official creditors. About $208m. in non-concessional debt was restructured on the highly concessionary 'Naples' terms. Under these terms, creditors either write off two-thirds of the liability (both principal and interest) and reschedule the balance over 23 years at market rates, or they reduce interest rates, with repayment over 33 years (effectively reducing the debt by two-thirds). By the end of 1996 the debt had declined to $1,594m., equivalent to 74% of GNP—a far more manageable level than the 109% registered in 1994—while the debt-service ratio was a comfortable 7.3% in 1996. The fall in export earnings in 1997 resulted in a slight deterioration in the debt-service ratio, to 9.1%, but Benin's foreign debt is considered sustainable and despite the economy remaining very vulnerable to climatic and external factors, Benin is not considered eligible for the Heavily Indebted Poor Countries (HIPC) initiative at the World Bank.

Statistical Survey

Source (unless otherwise stated): Institut National de la Statistique et de l'Analyse Economique, Ministère du Plan, de la Restructuration Economique et de la Promotion de l'Emploi, BP 342, Cotonou; tel. 30-00-30; fax 30-16-60; e-mail ddarig@planben.intnet.bj; internet planben.intnet.bj.

Area and Population

AREA, POPULATION AND DENSITY

Area (sq km)	112,622*
Population (census results)	
20–30 March 1979	
Total	3,331,210
15–29 February 1992	
Males	2,390,336
Females	2,525,219
Total	4,915,555
Population (official estimates at mid-year)	
1996	5,592,000
1997	5,646,987
1998	5,816,488
Density (per sq km) at mid-1998	51.6

* 43,484 sq miles.

ETHNIC GROUPS

1992 census (percentages): Fon 42.2; Adja 15.6; Yoruba 12.1; Bariba 8.6; Otamari 6.1; Peulh 6.1; Yoa-Lokpa 3.8; Dendi 2.8; Others 2.7.

POPULATION BY PROVINCE (1992 census)

Atakora	649,308
Atlantique	1,066,373
Borgou	827,925
Mono	676,377
Ouémé	876,574
Zou	818,998
Total	4,915,555

Note: Legislation was approved in August 1997 whereby Benin was reorganized into 12 administrative departments: Alibori, Atacora, Atlantique, Borgou, Colline, Donga, Couffo, Littoral, Mono, Ouémé, Plateau, Zou.

PRINCIPAL TOWNS (official estimates, 1994)

Cotonou . . .	750,000	Djougou . . .	132,000
Porto-Novo (capital) .	200,000	Parakou . . .	120,000

Source: La Zone Franc, *Rapport Annuel 1997*.

BIRTHS AND DEATHS (UN estimates, annual averages)

	1980–85	1985–90	1990–95
Birth rate (per 1,000) . . .	51.4	49.0	44.2
Death rate (per 1,000) . . .	17.7	16.2	14.4

Expectation of life (UN estimates, years at birth, 1990–95): 52.5 (males 50.7; females 54.5).
Source: UN, *World Population Prospects: The 1998 Revision*.

1998 (official estimates at mid-year): Birth rate (per 1,000) 45.82; Death rate (per 1,000) 12.77; Expectation of life (years at birth) 53.61.

ECONOMICALLY ACTIVE POPULATION
(persons aged 10 years and over, 1992 census)

	Males	Females	Total
Agriculture, hunting, forestry and fishing	780,469	367,277	1,147,746
Mining and quarrying . . .	609	52	661
Manufacturing	93,157	67,249	160,406
Electricity, gas and water . .	1,152	24	1,176
Construction.	50,959	696	51,655
Trade, restaurants and hotels .	36,672	395,829	432,501
Transport, storage and communications . . .	52,228	609	52,837
Finance, insurance, real estate and business services . . .	2,705	401	3,106
Community, social and personal services	126,122	38,422	164,544
Activities not adequately defined .	25,579	12,917	38,496
Total employed . . .	1,169,652	883,476	2,053,128
Unemployed	26,475	5,843	32,318
Total labour force	1,196,127	889,319	2,085,446

Source: ILO, *Yearbook of Labour Statistics*.

Mid-1998 (estimates in '000): Agriculture, etc. 1,472; Total 2,631 (Source: FAO, *Production Yearbook*).

Agriculture

PRINCIPAL CROPS ('000 metric tons)

	1996	1997	1998*
Rice (paddy)	22	27	27
Maize	504	514	514
Millet	29	28†	28
Sorghum	112	120	120
Sweet potatoes	68	57	57
Cassava (Manioc) . . .	1,452	1,625*	1,625
Yams	1,346	1,408	1,408
Taro (Coco yam)	3*	4	4
Dry beans	59	74	74
Groundnuts (in shell). . .	84	102	102
Cottonseed	252	220*	220
Cotton (lint)	166	175*	175
Coconuts	20†	20*	20
Palm kernels*	16	14	14
Tomatoes	72	121	121
Chillies and peppers (green)* . .	12	12	12
Other vegetables* . . .	155	146	146
Oranges*	12	12	12
Mangoes*	12	12	12
Bananas.	13†	13*	13
Pineapples*	3	3	3
Other fruit*	109	108	108

* FAO estimate(s).   † Unofficial figure.
Source: FAO, *Production Yearbook*.

LIVESTOCK ('000 head, year ending September)

	1996	1997	1998*
Horses*	6	6	6
Asses*	1	1	1
Cattle	1,350	1,400*	1,400
Pigs	584	580*	580
Sheep	601	605*	605
Goats	1,013	1,020*	1,020

Poultry (million): 25† in 1996; 27* in 1997; 27* in 1998.

* FAO estimate(s).   † Unofficial figure.

Source: FAO, *Production Yearbook*.

LIVESTOCK PRODUCTS (FAO estimates, '000 metric tons)

	1996	1997	1998
Beef and veal	18	18	18
Mutton and lamb . . .	3	3	3
Goat meat	4	4	4
Pig meat	8	8	7
Poultry meat	28	30	33
Other meat	5	5	5
Cows' milk	20	20	20
Goats' milk	7	7	7
Poultry eggs	18	20	20
Cattle hides	3	3	3
Goatskins	1	1	1

Source: FAO, *Production Yearbook*.

Forestry

ROUNDWOOD REMOVALS
('000 cubic metres, excl. bark)

	1995	1996	1997
Sawlogs, veneer logs and logs for sleepers	50	50	50
Other industrial wood . . .	271	278	286
Fuel wood	5,580	5,742	5,901
Total	5,901	6,070	6,237

Source: FAO, *Yearbook of Forest Products*.

SAWNWOOD PRODUCTION
('000 cubic metres, incl. railway sleepers)

	1995	1996	1997
Total (all broadleaved) . .	24	24	24

Source: FAO, *Yearbook of Forest Products*.

Fishing

('000 metric tons, live weight)

	1995	1996*	1997*
Tilapias	11.7	10.7	10.3
Black catfishes	1.3	1.2	1.1
Torpedo-shaped catfishes . .	2.3	2.1	2.0
Freshwater gobies . . .	0.9	0.8	0.8
Other freshwater fishes . .	10.4	9.4	9.1
Groupers and seabasses* . .	1.3	1.6	2.2
Threadfins and tasselfishes* .	1.0	1.1	1.5
Sardinellas*	1.4	1.6	2.2
Bonga shad	2.0	1.8	1.7
Other marine fishes* . . .	4.2	4.6	5.8
Total fish*	36.6	34.9	36.7
Freshwater crustaceans . .	4.7	4.3	4.1
Marine crustaceans* . . .	3.2	3.0	2.9
Total catch	44.4	42.2	43.8

* FAO estimate(s).

Note: Figures exclude catches by Beninois canoes operating from outside the country.

Source: FAO, *Yearbook of Fishery Statistics*.

Mining

('000 barrels)

	1996	1997	1998
Crude petroleum . . .	552.1	455.1	355.9

Source: Banque centrale des états de l'Afrique de l'ouest.

Industry

SELECTED PRODUCTS ('000 metric tons, unless otherwise indicated)

	1993	1994	1995
Salted, dried or smoked fish* . .	2.0	2.0	2.0
Cement†	380	380	380
Electric energy (million kWh)‡ . .	5	6	6

* Data from FAO.

† Data from the US Bureau of Mines.

‡ Provisional or estimated figures.

Source: UN, *Industrial Commodity Statistics Yearbook*.

Palm oil and palm kernel oil ('000 metric tons): 10.8 in 1993; 10.3 in 1994; 5.4 in 1995; 7.4 in 1996; 6.6 in 1997 (Source: IMF, *Benin: Selected Issues and Statistical Appendix*, September 1998).

Finance

CURRENCY AND EXCHANGE RATES

Monetary Units

100 centimes = 1 franc de la Communauté financière africaine (CFA).

Sterling, Dollar and Euro Equivalents (28 April 2000)

£1 sterling = 1,132.20 francs CFA;

US $1 = 722.02 francs CFA;

€1 = 655.96 francs CFA;

10,000 francs CFA = £8.832 = $13.850 = €15.245.

Average Exchange Rate (francs CFA per US $)

1997   583.67

1998   589.95

1999   615.70

Note: An exchange rate of 1 French franc = 50 francs CFA, established in 1948, remained in force until January 1994, when the CFA franc was devalued by 50%, with the exchange rate adjusted to 1 French franc = 100 francs CFA. This relationship to French currency remained in effect with the introduction of the euro on 1 January 1999. From that date, accordingly, a fixed exchange rate of €1 = 655.957 francs CFA has been in operation.

BUDGET ('000 million francs CFA)

Revenue			1996	1997	1998
Tax revenue .	.	.	142.6	158.8	182.4
Direct taxation	.	.	46.3	42.7	49.6
Indirect taxation	.	.	96.3	116.1	n.a.
Taxes on goods and services	.		26.0	33.4	n.a.
Import duties	.	.	70.3	82.7	91.3
Non-tax revenue .	.	.	29.3	23.1	28.6
Total	.	.	171.9	181.9	211.0

Expenditure*			1996	1997	1998
Current expenditure .	.	.	147.9	151.4	150.6
Salaries .	.	.	58.2	62.0	64.1
Social security payments	.	.	16.9	16.2	n.a.
Interest due .	.	.	27.3	21.1	19.1
Domestic debt	.	.	3.2	2.7	2.6
External debt	.	.	24.1	18.4	16.5
Other current expenditure	.	.	45.5	52.1	n.a.
Capital expenditure .	.	.	71.8	83.6	80.0
Internal financing .	.	.	7.3	11.9	15.0
External financing .	.	.	64.5	71.7	65.0
Total	.	.	219.7	235.0	230.6

* Excluding net lending ('000 million francs CFA): 0.7 in 1996; −0.7 in 1997; 2.8 in 1998.

Source: Banque centrale des états de l'Afrique de l'ouest.

1999 (draft budget, '000 million francs CFA): Revenue 235.0; Expenditure 335.2.
2000 (draft budget, '000 million francs CFA): Revenue 251.3; Expenditure 375.8.

INTERNATIONAL RESERVES (US $ million at 31 December)

			1997	1998	1999
Gold*	.	.	3.4	3.3	3.3
IMF special drawing rights	.		0.1	0.1	0.2
Reserve position in IMF	.	.	2.9	3.1	3.0
Foreign exchange	.	.	250.1	258.4	396.4
Total	.	.	256.5	264.9	402.9

* Valued at market-related prices.

Source: IMF, *International Financial Statistics*.

MONEY SUPPLY ('000 million francs CFA at 31 December)

			1997	1998	1999
Currency outside banks	.	.	80.8	70.4	162.3
Demand deposit at deposit money banks .			107.5	108.4	104.5
Checking deposits at post office	.		4.4	4.7	5.1
Total money (incl. others) .		.	193.4	184.2	272.9

Source: IMF, *International Financial Statistics*.

COST OF LIVING
(Consumer price index; base: 1995 = 100)

			1997	1998	1999
All items	.	.	108.6	114.8	115.2

Source: IMF, *International Financial Statistics*.

NATIONAL ACCOUNTS
('000 million francs CFA at current prices)

Expenditure on the Gross Domestic Product

	1997	1998	1999
Government final consumption expenditure	113.8	119.6	125.6
Private final consumption expenditure	1,017.2	1,099.4	1,177.1
Increase in stocks . . .	6.2	6.8	7.3
Gross fixed capital formation . .	223.1	242.0	271.5
Total domestic expenditure .	1,360.3	1,467.8	1,581.5
Exports of goods and services .	337.2	367.8	403.8
Less Imports of goods and services .	447.7	474.8	511.8
GDP in purchasers' values .	1,249.8	1,360.6	1,473.6

Source: IMF, *International Financial Statistics*.

Gross Domestic Product by Economic Activity

	1996	1997	1998*
Agriculture, livestock, forestry, hunting and fishing . .	425.4	479.8	541.1
Mining	4.9 }	109.4	117.7
Manufacturing and handicrafts .	93.4 }		
Water, gas and electricity .	8.2	10.1	10.1
Construction and public works .	48.6	54.6	58.5
Trade and hotels	205.6	222.5	245.3
Transport and communications .	82.7	87.8	94.1
Financial services . . .	111.2	115.7	128.1
Other services	82.3	86.7	89.1
GDP at factor cost . . .	1,062.2	1,166.6	1,284.0
Indirect taxes, *less* subsidies .	67.3	83.2	88.7
GDP in purchasers' values .	1,129.5	1,249.8	1,372.7

* Provisional figures.

Source: Banque centrale des états de l'Afrique de l'ouest.

BALANCE OF PAYMENTS ('000 million francs CFA)

	1996	1997	1998*
Exports of goods f.o.b. . .	269.9	247.5	227.5
Imports of goods f.o.b. . . .	−286.3	−336.7	−326.4
Trade balance	−16.4	−89.2	−98.9
Services and other income (net) .	−42.8	−44.5	−43.9
Balance on goods, services and income	−59.1	−133.7	−142.8
Private unrequited transfers (net)	32.1	38.2	44.5
Public unrequited transfers (net) .	62.9	55.0	44.1
Current balance . . .	35.8	−40.5	−54.2
Long-term capital (net) . . .	−17.7	13.5	36.8
Short-term capital (net) . . .	0.8	68.7	5.9
Net errors and omissions . . .	3.2	3.9	—
Overall balance . . .	22.1	45.6	−11.5

* Provisional figures.

Source: Banque centrale des états de l'Afrique de l'ouest.

External Trade

PRINCIPAL COMMODITIES (million francs CFA)

Imports c.i.f.*	1988	1989	1990
Food products . . .	25,743	12,814	17,863
Food products of animal origin .	2,856	2,040	1,300
Food products of plant origin . .	19,655	8,579	15,020
Rice	13,523	4,753	9,110
Wheat . . .	2,170	1,769	3,562
Processed foodstuffs . .	3,222	2,195	1,543
Beverages and tobacco .	4,643	4,688	5,268
Alcoholic beverages . . .	1,863	1,199	2,241
Manufactured tobacco products .	2,760	3,482	2,983
Energy products . . .	13,343	10,113	10,393
Refined petroleum products . .	9,355	5,795	6,158
Other raw materials (inedible) .	4,500	2,449	2,410
Machinery and transport			
equipment	13,302	9,593	7,860
Non-electrical machinery . . .	5,478	3,486	n.a.
Electrical machinery . . .	4,239	2,251	n.a.
Road transport equipment . . .	3,454	3,812	n.a.
Other industrial products . .	34,774	25,036	28,026
Chemical products . . .	7,726	4,710	7,235
Fertilizers . . .	866	3	1,533
Miscellaneous manufactured articles	27,048	20,326	20,791
Cotton yarn and fabrics . .	14,988	11,160	7,715
Total (incl. others) . . .	97,257	66,132	72,192

* Excluding imports for re-export.

Source: Banque centrale des états de l'Afrique de l'ouest.

Exports f.o.b.*†	1995	1996	1997‡
Crude petroleum	4,700	5,200	5,000
Cottonseed	8,500	4,800	6,500
Cotton (ginned)	86,400	107,600	112,700
Palm and palm-kernel oil . .	3,200	900	1,200
Total (incl. others) . . .	117,300	134,300	142,100

* Excluding re-exports: 85,000 in 1995; 81,700 in 1996; 89,000 in 1997‡.
† Figures rounded to the nearest '000.
‡ Estimate(s).

Source: IMF, *Benin: Selected Issues and Statistical Appendix* (September 1998).

PRINCIPAL TRADING PARTNERS (US $ '000)

Imports c.i.f.	1993	1994	1995
China, People's Repub. . .	33,151	17,730	20,420
Côte d'Ivoire	10,138	12,506	23,353
France (incl. Monaco) . .	148,499	111,522	225,347
Germany	16,798	21,588	22,758
Japan	33,844	24,772	28,637
Netherlands	52,046	22,749	31,125
Senegal	8,988	5,675	21,596
Thailand	99,249	69,562	64,459
United Kingdom . . .	15,502	14,265	21,833
USA	24,175	18,519	31,755
Total (incl. others) . . .	571,719	431,558	647,065

Exports f.o.b.	1993	1994	1995
Brazil	10,662	31,162	32,914
China, People's Repub. . .	13,298	966	4,147
France (incl. Monaco) . .	5,953	11,586	4,578
India	7,199	3,635	10,597
Indonesia	2,579	7,138	7,258
Italy	13,476	7,141	7,064
Morocco	63,923	15,091	16,801
Nigeria	5,873	11,654	4,336
Portugal	9,230	17,868	24,242
Southern African Customs Union*	5,199	2,500	4,291
Thailand	3,390	4,806	8,419
Total (incl. others) . . .	181,589	163,260	164,955

* Comprising Botswana, Lesotho, Namibia, South Africa and Swaziland.

Source: UN, *International Trade Statistics Yearbook*.

Transport

RAILWAYS (traffic)

	1995	1996	1997
Passenger-km (million) . . .	116.0	117.0	121.8
Freight ton-km (million) . . .	388.4	269.7	311.4

Source: IMF, *Benin—Selected Issues and Statistical Appendix* (September 1998).

ROAD TRAFFIC (motor vehicles in use)

	1994	1995	1996
Passenger cars	26,507	30,346	37,772
Buses and coaches . . .	353	405	504
Lorries and vans . . .	5,301	6,069	7,554
Road tractors	2,192	2,404	2,620
Motor cycles and mopeds . . .	220,800	235,400	250,000

Source: IRF, *World Road Statistics*.

SHIPPING
Merchant Fleet (registered at 31 December)

	1996	1997	1998
Number of vessels	7	8	6
Total displacement ('000 grt) . .	1.0	1.2	0.9

Source: Lloyd's Register of Shipping, *World Fleet Statistics*.

International Sea-borne Freight Traffic
(at Cotonou, including goods in transit, '000 metric tons)

	1996	1997	1998
Goods loaded	423.9	370.3	379.0
Goods unloaded	1,795.8	1,877.9	2,004.6

Source: Banque centrale des états de l'Afrique de l'ouest.

CIVIL AVIATION (traffic on scheduled services)*

	1994	1995	1996
Kilometres flown (million) . .	2	3	3
Passengers carried ('000) . .	69	74	75
Passenger-km (million) . . .	215	223	225
Total ton-km (million) . . .	34	36	37

* Including an apportionment of the traffic of Air Afrique.

Source: UN, *Statistical Yearbook*.

Tourism

	1995	1996	1997
Tourist arrivals ('000) . . .	138	143	148
Tourism receipts (US $ million) .	27	29	31

Source: World Tourism Organization, *Yearbook of Tourism Statistics*.

Communications Media

	1994	1995	1996
Radio receivers ('000 in use) . .	480	500	600
Television receivers ('000 in use) .	30	32	50
Telephones ('000 main lines in use)	24	28	33
Telefax stations (number in use) .	600	800	1,064
Mobile cellular telephones			
(subscribers)	n.a.	1,050	2,587
Daily newspapers			
Number	1	1	1
Average circulation ('000 copies)	1	3	12
Non-daily newspapers			
Number	n.a.	10	4
Average circulation ('000 copies)	n.a.	51	66
Book production*			
Titles	84	n.a.	n.a.
Copies ('000)	42	n.a.	n.a.

* First editions.

1997: Radio receivers ('000 in use) 620; Television receivers ('000 in use) 60.

Sources: UNESCO, *Statistical Yearbook*; UN, *Statistical Yearbook*.

Education

(1996/97)

	Institu-tions	Teach-ers	Students		
			Males	Females	Total
Pre-primary . .	283*	622	9,106	8,335	17,441
Primary . . .	3,088*	13,957	492,826	286,503	779,329
Secondary					
General . .	145§	5,352	102,011	44,124	146,135
Vocational§ . .	14	283	3,553	1,320	4,873
Higher . . .	9	962‡	11,398†	2,657†	14,055†

*1995/96.   †1996.   ‡1995.   §1993/94.

Source: mainly UNESCO, *Statistical Yearbook*.

Directory

The Constitution

A new Constitution was approved in a national referendum on 2 December 1990.

The Constitution of the Republic of Benin guarantees the basic rights and freedoms of citizens. The functions of the principal organs of state are delineated therein.

The President of the Republic, who is Head of State and Head of Government, is directly elected, by universal adult suffrage, for a period of five years, renewable only once. The President appoints government members, who are responsible to the Head of State. The legislature is the 83-member Assemblée nationale, which is elected, also by direct universal suffrage, for a period of four years.

The Constitution upholds the principle of an independent judiciary. The Constitutional Court, the Economic and Social Council and Higher Audiovisual and Communications Authority are intended to counterbalance executive authority.

The Government

HEAD OF STATE

President: Gen. (retd) MATHIEU KÉRÉKOU (took office 4 April 1996).

COUNCIL OF MINISTERS
(August 2000)

President: Gen. (retd) MATHIEU KÉRÉKOU.

Minister of State in charge of Co-ordinating Government Action, Planning, Development and Promotion of Employment: BRUNO AMOUSSOU.

Minister-delegate at the Presidency, in charge of National Defence: PIERRE OTCHO.

Minister of the Interior, Security and Local Government: DANIEL TAWÉMA.

Minister of Foreign Affairs and Co-operation: ANTOINE KOLA-WOLE IDJI.

Minister of Justice, Legislation and Human Rights: JOSEPH GNONLONFOUN.

Minister of Finance and the Economy: ABDOULAYE BIO TCHANE.

Minister of Relations with the Institutions, Civil Society and Benin Nationals Abroad: SYLVAIN ADEKPEDJOU AKINDES.

Minister of the Civil Service, Labour and Administrative Reform: OUSMANE BATOKO.

Minister of Rural Development: THÉOPHILE NATA.

Minister of Trade, Handicrafts and Tourism: SÉVÉRIN ADJOVI.

Minister of Mining, Energy and Water: FÉLIX ESSOU.

Minister of Public Works and Transport: JOSEPH SOUROU ATTIN.

Minister of the Environment, Housing and Urban Development: LUC-MARIE CONSTANT GNACADJA.

Minister of Youth, Sports and Recreation: VALENTIN ADITI HOUDE.

Minister of Culture and Communication, Spokesman for the Government: GASTON ZOSSOU.

Minister of Education and Scientific Research: DAMIEN ZINSOU ALAHASSA.

Minister of Industry and Small and Medium-Sized Enterprises: PIERRE JOHN IGUE.

Minister of Public Health: MARINA D'ALMEIDA MASSOUGBODJI.

Minister of Social and Family Affairs: RAMATOU BABA MOUSSA.

MINISTRIES

Office of the President: BP 1288, Cotonou; tel. 30-02-28.

Ministry of the Civil Service, Labour and Administrative Reform: BP 907, Cotonou; tel. 31-26-18.

Ministry of Culture and Communication: BP 120, Cotonou; fax. 31-59-31.

Ministry of Education and Scientific Research: BP 348, Cotonou; tel. 30-06-81; fax 30-18-48.

Ministry of the Environment, Housing and Urban Development: 01 BP 3621, Cotonou; tel. 31-55-96; fax 31-50-81.

Ministry of Finance and the Economy: BP 302, Cotonou; tel. 30-10-20; fax 31-58-98.

Ministry of Foreign Affairs and Co-operation: BP 318, Cotonou; tel. 30-04-00.

Ministry of Industry and Small and Medium-sized Enterprises: BP 363, Cotonou; tel. 30-16-46.

Ministry of the Interior, Security and Local Government: BP 925, Cotonou; tel. 30-10-06.

Ministry of Justice, Legislation and Human Rights: BP 967, Cotonou; tel. 31-31-46; fax 31-34-48.

Ministry of Mining, Energy and Water: 04 BP 1412, Cotonou; tel. 31-41-19; fax 31-35-46.

Ministry of National Defence: BP 2493, Cotonou; tel. 30-08-90.

Ministry of Planning, Economic Restructuring and Employment Promotion: BP 342, Cotonou; tel. 30-05-41; internet planben .intnet.bj.

Ministry of Public Health: BP 882, Cotonou; tel. 33-08-70.

Ministry of Public Works and Transport: BP 351, Cotonou; tel. 31-56-96.

Ministry of Rural Development: 03 BP 2900, Cotonou; tel. 30-19-55; fax 30-03-26.

Ministry of Social and Family Affairs: Cotonou.

Ministry of Trade, Handicrafts and Tourism: Cotonou.

Ministry of Youth, Sports and Recreation: 03 BP 2103, Cotonou; tel. 31-46-00.

President and Legislature

PRESIDENT

Presidential Election, First Ballot, 3 March 1996

Candidate									% of votes
NICÉPHORE SOGLO	.	.	.	.	.	.	.	.	35.69
MATHIEU KÉRÉKOU	.	.	.	.	.	.	.	.	33.94
ADRIEN HOUNGBÉDJI	.	.	.	.	.	.	.	.	19.71
BRUNO AMOUSSOU	.	.	.	.	.	.	.	.	7.76
PASCAL FANTONDJI	.	.	.	.	.	.	.	.	1.08
LÉANDRE DJAGOUE	.	.	.	.	.	.	.	.	0.92
JACQUES LIONEL AGBO	.	.	.	.	.	.	.	.	0.90
Total	.	.	.	.	.	.	.	.	**100.00**

Second Ballot, 18 March 1996

Candidate					Votes	% of votes
MATHIEU KÉRÉKOU	.	.	.	.	999,453	52.49
NICÉPHORE SOGLO	.	.	.	.	904,626	47.51
Total	.	.	.	.	**1,904,079**	**100.00**

ASSEMBLÉE NATIONALE

President: ADRIEN HOUNGBÉDJI (PSD).

Elections, 30 March 1999

Party									Seats
RB	.	.	.	.	.	.	.	.	27
PRD	.	.	.	.	.	.	.	.	11
FARD—Alafia	.	.	.	.	.	.	.	.	10
PSD	.	.	.	.	.	.	.	.	9
MADEP	.	.	.	.	.	.	.	.	6
Alliance Etoile	.	.	.	.	.	.	.	.	4
Alliance IPD	.	.	.	.	.	.	.	.	4
CAR—DUNYA	.	.	.	.	.	.	.	.	3
MERCI	.	.	.	.	.	.	.	.	2
Alliance RPR—UNSD	.	.	.	.	.	.	.	.	1
Alliance SURU	.	.	.	.	.	.	.	.	1
PDB	.	.	.	.	.	.	.	.	1
PN Ensemble	.	.	.	.	.	.	.	.	1
PS	.	.	.	.	.	.	.	.	1
RDP	.	.	.	.	.	.	.	.	1
RUND	.	.	.	.	.	.	.	.	1
Total	.	.	.	.	.	.	.	.	**83**

Advisory Councils

Cour Constitutionnelle: (see Judicial System, below).

Conseil Economique et Social (ECOSOC): Cotonou; f. 1994; 30 mems, representing the executive, legislature and 'all sections of the nation'; reviews all legislation relating to economic and social affairs; competent to advise on proposed economic and social legislation, as well as to recommend economic and social reforms; Pres. RAPHIOU TOUKOUROU.

Political Organizations

The registration of political parties commenced in August 1990. In late 1999 there were 116 registered parties. The following 35 parties and coalitions contested the March 1999 legislative election:

The **Alliance étoile**; the **Alliance fraternité**; the **Alliance pour la démocratie et le progrès (ADP):** Leader ADEKPEDJOU S. AKINDES; the **Alliance des patriotes**; the **Alliance impulsion pour le progrès et la démocratie (Alliance IPD)**; the **Alliance pour le progrès (Alliance APP)**; eight mem. parties: Leader EMILE DERLIN ZINSOU: the **Alliance rassemblement pour la république—Union nationale pour la solidarité et le développement (Alliance RPR—UNSD)**; the **Alliance républicaine**; the **Alliance SURU**; four mem. parties: Leader GADO GUIRIGISSIOU; the **Alliance union pour le développement économique et social (Alliance UDES)**; the **Congrès africain pour le renouveau—DUNYA (CAR—DUNYA)**; the **Congrès du peuple pour le progrès (CPP)**; the **Front d'action pour le renouveau, la démocratie et le développement—Alafia (FARD—Alafia):** Leader SAKA KINA; the **Front pour la république (FPR)**; the **Mouvement africain pour la démocratie et le progrès (MADEP):** Leader SEFOU FAG-

BOHOUN; the **Mouvement africain pour le progrès (MAP)**; the **Mouvement pour l'engagement et le réveil des citoyens (MERCI)**; five mem. parties; **Notre cause commune (NCC):** Leader FRANÇOIS ODJO TANKPINON; the **Parti africain pour la rédemption et l'indépendance (PARI)**; the **Parti communiste du Bénin (PCB):** Leader PASCAL FANTONDJI; the **Parti démocratique du Bénin (PDB)**; the **Parti national campagne pour la moralité et la démocratie (PN CMD)**; the **Parti national 'ensemble' (PN Ensemble)**; the **Parti du renouveau démocratique (PRD):** Leader ADRIEN HOUNGBÉDJI; the **Parti du salut (PS)**; the **Parti social démocrate (PSD):** Leader BRUNO AMOUSSOU; the **Parti social démocrate—Bélier (PSD—Bélier)**; the **Parti socialiste du Bénin (PSB)**; the **Rassemblement pour la démocratie et le panafricanisme (RDP)**; the **Rassemblement pour l'unité nationale et la démocratie (RUND)**; the **Rassemblement national pour la démocratie (RND)**; the **Renaissance du Bénin (RB):** Leader NICÉPHORE SOGLO; the **Union pour la patrie et le travail (UPT)**; the **Union républicaine du peuple (URP)**; the **Union pour le triomphe de la république (UTR)**.

The **Coalition des forces démocratiques** (Pres. GATIEN HOUNGBÉDJI) is an alliance of parties and organizations supporting President Kérékou.

Diplomatic Representation

EMBASSIES IN BENIN

China, People's Republic: 2 blvd de France, 01 BP 196, Cotonou; tel. 30-12-92; fax 30-08-41; Ambassador: CHUNLAI DUAN.

Congo, Democratic Republic: Carré 221, Ayélawadjè, Derrière la maison du Peuple d'Akpakpa à côté de l'école Ronsard, Cotonou; tel. 30-00-01; Chargé d'affaires: NDOMPETELO DEKA.

Cuba: ave de la Marina, face Hôtel du Port, 01 BP 948, Cotonou; tel. and fax 31-52-97; Ambassador: FERNANDO PRATS MARI.

Denmark: Lot P7, Les Cocotiers, 04 BP 1223, Cotonou; tel. 30-38-62; fax 30-38-60; e-mail ambdan@bow.intnet.bj; Chargé d'affaires: JOHNNY FLENTØ.

Egypt: route de l'Aéroport, Lot G26, BP 1215, Cotonou; tel. 30-08-42; fax 30-14-25; Ambassador: MOHAMED MAHMOUD NAGUIB.

France: ave Jean-Paul II, BP 966, Cotonou; tel. 30-02-25; fax 30-15-47; e-mail ambafrance@serv.eit.bj; internet www.eit.bj/ambafrance-benin; Ambassador: (vacant).

Germany: 7 ave Jean-Paul II, 01 BP 504, Recette Principale, Cotonou; tel. 31-29-68; fax 31-29-62; Ambassador: VOLKER SEITZ.

Ghana: route de l'Aéroport, Lot F, Les Cocotiers, BP 488, Cotonou; tel. 30-07-46; fax 30-03-45; Ambassador: AGYOGBE ACHAAB.

Libya: Les Cocotiers, BP 405, Cotonou; tel. 30-04-52; Ambassador: TOUFIK ASHOUR ADAM.

Netherlands: ave Jean-Paul II, 08 BP 0783, Cotonou; tel. 30-41-52; fax 30-41-50; e-mail nlgovcot@intnet.bj; Chargé d'affaires: SASKIA N. BAKKER.

Niger: derrière l'Hôtel de la Plage, BP 352, Cotonou; tel. 31-56-65; Ambassador: MAHAMAN BACHIR ZADAA.

Nigeria: blvd de France–Marina, BP 2019, Cotonou; tel. 30-11-42; Chargé d'affaires a.i.: M. S. ADOLI.

Russia: BP 2013, Cotonou; tel. 31-28-34; fax 31-28-35; Ambassador: YURII TCHEPIK.

USA: rue Caporal Anani Bernard, BP 2012, Cotonou; tel. 30-06-50; fax 30-19-74; e-mail usis.cotonou@bow.intnet.bj; Ambassador: PAMELA E. BRIDGEWATER.

Judicial System

The Constitution of December 1990 establishes the judiciary as an organ of state whose authority acts as a counterbalance to that of the executive and of the legislature.

Cour Constitutionnelle: BP 2050, Cotonou; tel. 31-16-10; fax 31-37-12; f. 1990, inaug. 1993; seven mems (four appointed by the Assemblée nationale, three by the President of the Republic); exercises highest jurisdiction in constitutional affairs; determines the constitutionality of legislation, oversees and proclaims results of national elections and referendums, responsible for protection of individual and public rights and obligations, charged with regulating functions of organs of state and authorities; Pres. CONCEPTIA OUINSOU; Sec.-Gen. JEAN-BAPTISTE MONSI.

Haute Cour de Justice: comprises the members of the Cour constitutionnelle (other than its President), six deputies of the Assemblée nationale and the President of the Cour suprême; competent to try the President of the Republic and members of the Government in cases of high treason, crimes committed in, or at the time of, the exercise of their functions, and of plotting against state security.

Cour Suprême: highest juridical authority in administrative and judicial affairs and in matters of public accounts; competent in disputes relating to local elections; advises the executive on jurisdiction and administrative affairs; comprises a President (appointed by the President of the Republic, after consultation with the President of the Assemblée nationale, senior magistrates and jurists), presidents of the component chambers and counsellors.

Religion

At the time of the 1992 census it was estimated that some 35% of the population held animist beliefs; another 35% were Christians (mainly Roman Catholics) and the remainder were mostly Muslims. Religious and spiritual cults, which were discouraged under Kérékou's military regime, re-emerged as a prominent force in Beninois society during the early 1990s.

CHRISTIANITY
The Roman Catholic Church

Benin comprises two archdioceses and eight dioceses. At 31 December 1998 there were an estimated 1.3m. Roman Catholics (about 21.4% of the population), mainly in the south of the country.

Bishops' Conference: Conférence Episcopale du Bénin, Archevêché, BP 491, Cotonou; tel. 31-31-45; fax 30-07-07; Pres. Rt Rev. LUCIEN MONSI-AGBOKA, Bishop of Abomey.

Archbishop of Cotonou: Most Rev. NESTOR ASSOGBA, Archevêché, 01 BP 491, Cotonou; tel. 30-01-45; fax 30-07-07; e-mail cotonou@cef.fr; internet evry.cefm.net/evry/cotonou/index.html.

Archbishop of Parakou: Most Rev. FIDÈLE AGBATCHI, Archevêché, BP 75, Parakou; tel. 61-02-54; fax 61-01-99.

Protestant Church

There are an estimated 257 Protestant mission centres in Benin.

Eglise protestante méthodiste en République du Bénin: 54 ave Mgr Steinmetz, BP 34, Cotonou; tel. 31-11-42; fax 31-25-20; f. 1843; Pres. Rev. Dr MOÏSE SAGBOHAN; Sec. Rev. MATHIEU D. OLODO; 95,827 mems (1996).

VODOUN

The origins of the traditional *vodoun* religion can be traced to the 14th century. Its influence is particularly strong in Latin America and the Caribbean, owing to the shipment of slaves from the West African region to the Americas in the 18th and 19th centuries.

Grand conseil de la religion vodoun du Bénin: Ouidah; Supreme Chief DAAGBO HOUNON HOUNAN.

The Press

DAILIES

L'Aurore: Face Clinique Boni, Akpakpa, 05 BP 464, Cotonou; tel. 33-70-43; Dir PATRICK ADJAMONSI.

Bénin-Presse Info: 01 BP 72, Cotonou; tel. 31-26-55; Dir YAOVI HOUNKPONOU; Chief Editor AMÈGNIHOUÉ HOUNDJI.

Le Citoyen: Akpakpa, 06 BP 723, Cotonou; tel. and fax 33-59-33, e-mail lecitoyen@intnet.bj; Dir LÉON BRATHIER; Editor-in-Chief PHILIPPE D'ALMEIDA.

La Cloche: Carré 2248, Zogbo, 07 BP 65, Cotonou; tel. 30-56-04; e-mail lacloche@h2com.com; Dir VINCENT METONNOU; Chief Editor GASPARD C. KODJO.

La Dépêche du Soir: Carré 555, Akpakpa, 03 BP 1100, Cotonou; tel. 33-51-53; Dir EUSÈBE SOTON.

Les Echos du Jour: Akpakpa, 08 BP 718, Cotonou; tel. 33-18-33; fax 33-17-06; e-mail echos@intnet.bj; independent; Dir MAURICE CHABI; Editor-in-Chief GERMAIN ADELAKOUN.

Le Journal: Cotonou; f. 1999; independent; Chief Editor LUC AIMÉ DANSOU.

Liberté: Carré 1094, Wologuèdè, 03 BP 3555; tel. 32-55-19; Dir SYLVESTE FOHOUNGO.

Le Matin: Carré 8/16, Guinkomey, Cotonou; tel. 31-30-80; fax 31-10-81; f. 1994; independent; Dir MOÏSE DATO; Editor-in-Chief PIERRE MATCHOUDO.

Le Matinal: 06 BP 1989, Cotonou; tel. 31-49-20; fax 31-49-19; Dir CHARLES TOKO; Editor-in-Chief AGAPIT N. MAFORIKAN.

Le Matinal Sport: 06 BP 1989, Cotonou; tel. 31-49-20; fax 31-49-19.

La Nation: Cadjèhoun, 01 BP 1210, Cotonou; tel. 30-02-99; fax 30-34-63; e-mail lanation@elodia.intnet.bj; internet elodia.intnet.bj/nation.htm; f. 1990; official newspaper; Dir INNOCENT M. ADJAHO; Editor-in-Chief ALFRED AHOUNOU.

L'Oeil du Peuple: rue PTT, Gbégamey, Carré 743, 08 BP 0131; tel. 30-22-07; Dir CÉLESTIN ABISSI.

Le Point au Quotidien: 322 rue du Renouveau, 05 BP 934, Cotonou; tel. 32-50-55; fax 32-25-31; independent; Dir VINCENT FOLY; Editor-in-Chief CÉLESTIN AKPOVO.

Le Progrès: 05 BP 708, Cotonou; Dir EDOUARD LOKO; Chief Editors SEPTIME TOLLI, MAURILLE GNANSOUNOU.

PERIODICALS

Africa Visages: BP 2297, Porto-Novo; tel. 22-40-25; fax 21-25-25; fortnightly; Dir ERICK HOUNTONDJI.

L'Autre Gazette: 02 BP 1537, Cotonou; tel. 32-59-97; e-mail collegi@beninweb.org; fmrly Le Collégien; 2 a month; Dir WILFRIDO AYIBATIN; circ. 2,500.

L'Avenir: 02 BP 8143, Cotonou; tel. 30-29-70; fortnightly; Dir FIRMIN GANGBE.

Bénin Info: 06 BP 590, Cotonou; tel. 32-52-64; fortnightly; Dir ROMAIN TOI.

Bénin Santé: 06 BP 1905, Cotonou, tel. 33-26-38; fax 33-18-23; bi-monthly.

Le Continental: BP 4419, Cotonou; Dir ARNAULD HOUNDETE.

La Croix du Bénin: 01 BP 105, Cotonou; tel. and fax 32-11-19; f. 1946; fortnightly; Roman Catholic; Dir BARTHÉLEMY ASSOGBA CAKPO.

Le Démocrate: Carré 637, Gbégamey, BP 1538, Cotonou; tel. 30-52-27.

L'Enjeu: 04 BP 0454, Cotonou; tel. 30-47-18; Dir MATHURIN ASSOGBA.

L'Essor: Carré 497, Jéricho, 06 BP 1182, Cotonou; tel. 32-43-13; monthly; Dir JEAN-BAPTISTE HOUNKONNOU.

Exécutif Info: 04 BP 1379, Cotonou; tel. 30-08-13; fax 30-33-15; monthly; Editor-in-Chief FRÉJUS BOCCO.

Le Forum de la Semaine: 04 BP 0301, Cotonou; tel. 30-26-23; weekly; Dir FRANCK AGBANGLAN.

La Gazette du Golfe: Immeuble La Gazette du Golfe, Carré 902 E Sikècodji, 03 BP 1624, Cotonou; tel. 32-42-08; fax 32-52-26; e-mail gazettedugolfe@serv.eit.bj; internet www.eit.bj/gazettedugolfe.htm; f. 1987; weekly; Dir ISMAËL Y. SOUMANOU; Editor MARCUS BONI TEIGA; circ. 18,000 (nat. edn), 5,000 (international edn).

Le Gongonneur: 04 BP 1432, Cotonou; e-mail dahoun@yahoo.com; Dir MATHIAS C. SOSSOU; Editor-in-Chief IBRAHIM IMOROU.

Initiatives: 01 BP 2093, Cotonou; tel. 31-44-47; quarterly; Dir THÉOPHILE CAPO-CHICHI.

Journal Officiel de la République du Bénin: BP 59, Porto-Novo; tel. 21-39-77; f. 1890; official govt bulletin; fortnightly; Dir AFIZE D. ADAMON.

Labari: BP 816, Parakou; tel. and fax 61-09-10; f. 1997; weekly; Dir DRAMANE AMITOURE; circ. 3,000.

Le Label: 03 BP 3190, Cotonou; tel. 30-04-72; weekly; Dir GASPARD KODJO; Chief Editor YVES AGONDANOU.

Les Lumières de l'Islam: 08 BP 0430, Cotonou; tel. 31-34-59.

Le Messager du Jeudi: 01 BP 4419, Cotonou; tel. 30-04-37; fax 30-03-21; weekly.

Nouvelle Vision: BP 73, Abomey-Calavi; Dir CLÉMENT AHOSSI.

Le Pélican: 03 BP 0432, Cotonou; tel. 30-33-97; monthly; Dir OSCAR S. GBAGUIDI.

Le Perroquet: Carré 478, 03 BP 0880, Cotonou; tel. 32-18-54; f. 1996; 2 a month; independent; news and analysis; Dir DAMIEN P. HOUESSOU; Chief Editor ADRIEN HOUNKOUÉ; circ. 2,500.

Préférence Magazine: Carré 2202, 08 BP 0185, Cotonou; sporting and cultural; monthly.

La Pyramide: BP 2560, Cotonou; tel. 33-38-33; monthly; Dir CHRISTOPHE HODONOU.

Le Recadaire: 02 BP 308, Cotonou; tel. 22-60-11; e-mail lerecadaire@yahoo.com; Dir GUTEMBERT HOUNKANRIN.

La Région: Carré 1439, Akpakpa centre, 05 BP 708, Cotonou; tel. 30-20-09; monthly; Dir AGAPIT N. MAFORIKAN.

La Sirène: Carré 357, Sènadé, 01 BP 122, Cotonou; tel. 33-40-17; Dir ETIENNE HOUSSOU.

Le Soleil: 02 BP 8187, Cotonou; tel. 31-11-99; fax 30-61-56-49; weekly; Dir EDGARD KAHO.

Le Tam-Tam-Express: BP 2302, Cotonou; tel. 30-12-05; fax 30-39-75; f. 1988; fortnightly; Dir DENIS HODONOU; circ. 8,000.

Le Télégramme: 06 BP 1519, Cotonou; tel. 33-04-18; fortnightly; Dir ETIENNE HOUESSOU; Chief Editor RAYMOND MONOKE.

La Tribune de l'Economie: ave du Général de Gaulle, 01 BP 31, Cotonou; tel. 31-20-81; fax 31-22-99; monthly; published by Chambre de Commerce et d'Industrie du Bénin; Dir WASSI MOUFTAOU.

Press Association

Union des Journalistes de la Presse Privée du Bénin (UJPB): Cotonou; association of independent journalists.

NEWS AGENCIES

Agence Bénin-Presse (ABP): BP 72, Cotonou; tel. 31-26-55; fax 31-12-26; e-mail abpben@bow.intnet.bj; f. 1961; national news agency; section of the Ministry of Culture and Communication; Dir YAOVI R. HOUNKPONOU.

Foreign Bureaux

Agence France-Presse (AFP): 06 BP 1382, Cotonou; tel. 33-51-32; fax 33-39-23; Correspondent VIRGILE C. AHISSOU.

Associated Press (USA) and Reuters (UK) are also represented in Benin.

Publishers

Les Editions de l'ACACIA: 06 BP 1978, Cotonou; tel. and fax 31-49-40; f. 1997; fmrly Les Editions du Flamboyant; Man. OSCAR DE SOUZA.

Graphitec: 04 BP 825, Cotonou; tel. and fax 30-46-04; e-mail padonou@bow.intnet.bj.

Government Publishing House

Office National de Presse et d'Imprimerie (ONPI): BP 1210, Cotonou; tel. 30-02-99; fax 30-11-52; f. 1975; Dir-Gen. INNOCENT ADJAHO.

Broadcasting and Communications

TELECOMMUNICATIONS

Office des Postes et des Télécommunications (OPT): Cotonou; tel. 31-20-45; fax 31-38-43; internet www.opt.bj; f. 1890; state-owned; Dir-Gen. BARTHÉLEMY AGNAN.

Libercom: Villa Fadoul 4, Cotonou; tel. 30-54-84; fax 30-54-85; f. 2000; mobile cellular telephone operator initially operating solely in Cotonou; jt venture between the OPT and Titan Africa; 3,300 subscribers.

Three mobile cellular telephone operators (Belgolaise, Spacetel-Bénin and Télécel Bénin) were awaiting interconnection with the OPT network in mid-2000.

BROADCASTING

Regulatory Authority

Since 1997 the HAAC has issued licences to private radio and television stations.

Haute Autorité de l'Audiovisuel et de la Communication (HAAC): Cotonou; f. in accordance with the 1990 Constitution to act as the highest authority for the media; Pres. RENÉ M. DOSSA.

Radio

Office de Radiodiffusion et de Télévision du Bénin (ORTB): 01 BP 366, Cotonou; tel. 30-10-96; fax 30-04-48; state-owned; radio programmes broadcast from Cotonou and Parakou in French, English and 18 local languages; Dir-Gen. JEAN N'TCHA; Dir of Radio PELU C. DIOGO.

> **Atlantic FM:** 01 BP 366, Cotonou; tel. 30-30-41; Dir JOSEPH OGOUNCHI.

> **Radio Cotonou:** 01 BP 306, Cotonou; tel. 30-04-81; Dir PELU CHRISTOPHE DIOGO.

> **Radio Régionale de Parakou:** BP 128, Parakou; tel. 61-07-73; Dir DIEUDONNÉ METOZOUNVÉ.

Ahémé FM: Centre Africa OBOTA, Possotomè; Promoter RUFIN GODJO.

CAPP FM: 06 BP 2076, Cotonou; tel. 31-08-10; Promoter JERÔME CARLOS.

Gerddes FM: 01 BP 1258, Cotonou; tel. 33-43-33; Man. ALEXANDRE DURAND.

Golfe FM: 03 BP 1624, Cotonou; tel. 32-42-08; fax 32-52-26; e-mail golfefm@serv.eit.bj; internet www.eit.bj/golfefm.htm; Promoter ISMAËL SOUMANOU.

Radio Iléma: 01 BP 3609, Cotonou; tel. 32-46-67; fax 53-01-37; Promoter FRANÇOIS SOUROU OKIOH.

Radio Immaculée Conception: BP 49, Cotonou; tel. 37-10-23; operated by the Roman Catholic Church of Benin; Promoter Mgr ISADORE DE SOUZA.

Radio Maranatha: 03 BP 4113, Cotonou; tel. 32-53-23; operated by the Conseil des Eglises Protestantes évangéliques du Bénin; promoter Rev. ROMAIN ZANNOU.

Noon-Sina FM: BP 04, Bembèrèkè; Man. ALI ZATO.

Radio Solidarité FM: BP 135, Djougou; tel. 80-01-95; fax 80-15-63; Promoter DAOUDA TAKPARA.

Radio Star: 04 BP 0553, Cotonou; tel. 32-53-22; Promoter MARCELLIN Y. ATINDEGLA.

Radio Tokpa: Carré 233, 01 BP 2445, Cotonou; tel. 31-45-32; Man. GUY KPAKPO.

La Voix de la Lama: BP 21, Porto Novo; tel. 31-11-61; Promoter SÉRAPHINE DADY.

La Voix de l'Islam: 08 BP 134, Cotonou; tel. 31-11-34; operated by the Communauté musulmane de Zongo; Man. El Hadj MAMAN YARO.

Radio Wêkê: 03 BP 2753, Cotonou; tel. 33-13-82; Promoter SOULÉ ISSA BADAROU.

Benin also receives broadcasts from Africa No. 1, BBC World Service and Radio France International.

Television

ORTB: (see radio); Dir of Television MAMA SOUMAÏLA.

ATVS: BP 7101, Cotonou; tel. 31-43-19; owned by African Television System-Sobiex; Promoter JACOB AKINOCHO.

La Chaîne 2 (LC2): 05 BP 427, Cotonou; tel. 33-47-49; fax 33-46-76; e-mail lc2@intnet.bj; commenced broadcasts 1997; Promoter CHRISTIAN LAGNIDÉ.

Telco: 01 BP 1241, Cotonou; tel. 31-37-72; e-mail telco@serv.eit.bj; internet www.eit.bj/telco.htm; relays five international channels; Promoter JOSEPH JÉBARA.

TV+ International: 01 BP 2376, Cotonou; tel. 31-53-54; Promoter CLAUDE KARAM.

Finance

(cap. = capital; res = reserves; m. = million; br. = branch; amounts in francs CFA)

BANKING

Central Bank

Banque Centrale des Etats de l'Afrique de l'Ouest (BCEAO): ave Jean-Paul II, BP 325, Cotonou; tel. 31-24-66; fax 31-24-65; e-mail akangni@bceao.int; internet www.bceao.int; HQ in Dakar, Senegal; f. 1962; bank of issue for the mem. states of the Union économique et monétaire ouest-africaine (UEMOA, comprising Benin, Burkina Faso, Côte d'Ivoire, Guinea-Bissau, Mali, Niger, Senegal and Togo); cap. and res 806,918m., total assets 4,084,464m. (Dec. 1998); Gov. CHARLES KONAN BANNY; Dir in Benin IDRISS LYASSOU DAOUDA; br. at Parakou.

Commercial Banks

Bank of Africa—Bénin: ave Jean-Paul II, 08 BP 0879, Cotonou; tel. 31-32-28; fax 31-31-17; e-mail boa.benin@firstnet.bj; f. 1990; 28% owned by African Financial Holding; cap. and res 11,047m., total assets 129,335m. (Dec. 1998); Pres. FRANÇOIS TANKPINOU; Man. Dir RENÉ FORMEY DE SAINT-LOUVENT.

Banque Internationale du Bénin (BIBE): carrefour des Trois Banques, ave Giran, 03 BP 2098, Jéricho, Cotonou; tel. 31-55-49; fax 31-23-65; e-mail bibe@intnet.bj; f. 1989; owned by Nigerian commercial interests; cap. 3,000m., total assets 46,223m. (Dec. 1998); Pres. Chief ARTHUR C. I. MBANEFO; Man. Dir OLADÉLÉ R. ADEBOLU; 4 brs.

Continental Bank—Bénin: ave Jean-Paul II, carrefour des Trois Banques, 01 BP 2020, Cotonou; tel. 31-24-24; fax 31-51-77; e-mail contibk@intnet.bj; internet www.ad-net.fr/cbb/index.htm; f. 1995 to assume activities of Crédit Lyonnais Bénin; 25% state-owned; cap. and res 4,647m., total assets 38,421m. (Dec. 1998); Pres. WASSI MOUFTAOU; Man. Dir MICHEL SABATH D'ALMEIDA.

Ecobank—Bénin SA: rue du Gouverneur Bayol, 01 BP 1280, Cotonou; tel. 31-40-33; fax 31-33-85; e-mail ecobank@bow.intnet.bj; internet www.ecobank.com; f. 1989; 84% owned by Ecobank Transnational Inc (operating under the auspices of the Economic Community of West African States); cap. and res 3,452m., total assets 84,086m. (Dec. 1998); Pres. GILBERT MEDJE; Gen. Man. M. F. SOSSAH; 1 br.

Financial Bank Bénin (FBB): Immeuble Adjibi, rue du Commandant Decoeur, 01 BP 2700, Cotonou; tel. 31-31-00; fax 31-31-02; e-mail financial@ment.fr; f. 1988; 85% owned by Financial BC (Switzerland); cap. and res 2,392m., total assets 45,002m. (Dec. 1998); Pres. and Man. Dir RÉMY BAYSSET; 8 brs.

Savings Bank

Caisse Nationale d'Epargne: Cadjèhoun, route Inter-Etat Cotonou-Lomé, Cotonou; tel. 30-18-35; fax 31-38-43; state-owned; cap. and res 736m., total assets 15,738m. (Dec. 1997); Pres. MARCELLIN DOSSOU KPANOU; Dir ANDRÉ H. AFFEDJOU.

Credit Institutions

Crédit du Bénin: 08 BP 0936, Cotonou; tel. 31-30-02; fax 31-37-01; Man. Dir GILBERT HOUNKPAIN.

Crédit Promotion Bénin: 03 BP 1672, Cotonou; tel. 31-31-44; fax 31-31-66; wholly owned by private investors; cap. 150m., total assets 409m. (Dec. 1998); Pres. BERNARD ADIKPETO; Man. Dir DÉNIS OBA CHABI.

Equipbail Bénin: blvd Jean-Paul II, 08 BP 0690, Cotonou; tel. 31-11-45; fax 31-31-17; 49% owned by Bank of Africa—Bénin; cap. and res 486m., total assets 3,041m. (Dec. 1998); Pres. PAUL DERREUMAUX; Man. Dir CLAUDE D'ALMEIDA.

Financial Institution

Caisse Autonome d'Amortissement du Bénin: BP 59, Cotonou; tel. 31-47-81; fax 31-53-56; manages state funds; Man. Dir IBRAHIM PEDRO-BONI.

STOCK EXCHANGE

Bourse Régionale des Valeurs Mobilières (BRVM): Immeuble Chambre de Commerce et d'Industrie du Bénin, ave Charles de Gaulle, 01 BP 2985, Cotonou; tel. 31-21-26; fax 31-20-77; f. 1998; national branch of BRVM (regional stock exchange based in Abidjan, Côte d'Ivoire, serving the member states of UEMOA); Man. in Benin YVETTE GNIGLA.

INSURANCE

A&C Benin SA: Cotonou; internet elodia.intnet.bj/acb/index .htm; all branches; Dir Gen. JUSTIN HERBERT AGBOTON.

Gras Savoye Benin: Immeuble Goussanou, rue du Rev. Père Colineau, BP 294, Cotonou; tel. 31-24-34; fax 31-25-32; Man. YVES MEHOU-LOKO.

Société Nationale d'Assurances et de Réassurances (SONAR): BP 2030, Cotonou; tel. 30-16-49; fax 30-09-84; parastatal co; Pres. S. ATTOLOU.

Union Béninoise d'Assurance-Vie: Cotonou; f. 1994; cap. 400m.; 51% owned by Union Africaine Vie (Côte d'Ivoire).

Trade and Industry

GOVERNMENT AGENCIES

Centre Béninois de la Recherche Scientifique et Technique (CBRST): 03 BP 1665, Cotonou; tel. 32-12-63; fax 30-14-66; internet www.refer.org/benin_ct/rec/cbrst/cbrst.htm; f. 1986 to promote scientific and technical research.

Centre Béninois du Commerce Extérieur: Place du Souvenir, BP 1254, Cotonou; tel. 30-13-20; fax 30-04-36; f. 1988; provides information to export cos.

Centre de Promotion pour l'Emploi, la Petite et Moyenne Entreprise (CEPEPE): Face à la Mairie de Xlacondji, BP 2093, Cotonou; tel. 31-44-47; fax 31-59-50; promotes business and employment.

Institut National de Recherches Agricoles du Bénin (INRAB): Cotonou; fax 30-37-70; internet www.refer.org/benin_ct/rec/inrab/inrab.htm; f. 1992; undertakes research into agricultural improvements; publicizes advances in agriculture.

Office Béninois de Recherches Géologiques et Minières (OBRGM): Ministère des mines, de l'energie et de l'hydraulique, 01 BP 249, Cotonou; tel. 31-03-09; fax 31-41-20; e-mail obrgm@ artsbobo.bj; f. 1996 as govt agency responsible for mining policy, exploitation and research; Dir-Gen. ALIOU MORIBA DJIBRIL.

Office National d'Appui à la Sécurité Alimentaire (ONASA): 06 BP 2544, Cotonou; tel. 33-15-02; fax 33-02-93; f. 1992; distribution of cereals; state-owned; Pres. IMAROU SALÉ; Dir-Gen. MOUSSA ASSOUMA.

Office National du Bois (ONAB): BP 1238, Recette Principale, Cotonou; tel. 33-16-32; fax 33-19-56; f. 1983; forest development and management, manufacture and marketing of wood products; transfer of industrial activities to private ownership pending; Man. Dir PASCAL PATINVOH.

DEVELOPMENT ORGANIZATIONS

Agence Française de Développement (AFD): blvd Jean-Paul II, BP 38, Cotonou; tel. 31-35-80; fax 31-20-18; fmrly Caisse Française de Développement; Dir HENRI PHILIPPE DE CLERCQ.

Mission de Coopération et d'Action Culturelle (Mission Française d'Aide et de Coopération): BP 476, Cotonou; tel. 30-08-24; administers bilateral aid from France according to the co-operation agreement of 1975; Dir BERNARD HADJADJ.

CHAMBER OF COMMERCE

Chambre de Commerce et d'Industrie du Bénin (CCIB): ave du Général de Gaulle, 01 BP 31, Cotonou; tel. 31-20-81; fax 31-32-99; e-mail albert.tevoedjre@planben.intnet.bj; internet planben .intnet.bj/pne/ccib.htm; Pres. WASSI MOUFTAOU; Sec.-Gen. N. A. VIAD-ENOU; brs at Parakou, Abomey and Porto-Novo.

EMPLOYERS' ORGANIZATIONS

Association des Syndicats du Bénin (ASYNBA): Cotonou; Pres. PIERRE FOURN.

Fondation de l'Entrepreneurship du Bénin (FEB): Place du Québec, 08 BP 1155, Cotonou; tel. 31-35-37; fax 31-37-26; e-mail fonda@intnet.bj; internet elodia.intnet.bj/feb.htm; non profit-making org.; encourages the devt of the private sector and of small and medium-sized businesses.

Groupement Interprofessionnel des Entreprises du Bénin (GIBA): BP 6, Cotonou; Pres. A. JEUKENS.

Organisation Nationale des Employeurs du Bénin (ONEB): BP 41, Cotonou; tel. 33-13-00; fax 31-39-50.

Syndicat des Commerçants Importateurs et Exportateurs du Bénin: BP 6, Cotonou; Pres. M. BENCHIMOL.

Syndicat Interprofessionnel des Entreprises Industrielles du Bénin: Cotonou; Pres. M. DOUCET.

Syndicat National des Commerçants et Industriels Africains du Bénin (SYNACIB): BP 367, Cotonou; Pres. URBAIN DA SILVA.

UTILITIES

Electricity and Water

Communauté Electrique du Bénin (CEB): BP 385, Cotonou; f. 1968 as a jt venture between Benin and Togo to exploit energy resources in the two countries.

Société Béninoise d'Electricité et d'Eau (SBEE): BP 123, Cotonou; tel. 31-21-45; fax 31-50-28; f. 1973; state-owned; production and distribution of electricity and water; Man. Dir GODEFROY CHEKETE.

MAJOR COMPANIES

The following are among the largest companies in terms of either capital investment or employment.

Bio-Benin: 04 BP 1227, Cotonou; tel. 30-16-81; fax 30-12-76; f. 1982; cap. 300m. francs CFA; mfrs and wholesalers of pharmaceutical preparations; Dir ALI ASSANI.

Centrale de l'Automobile et de Materiel Industriel (CAMIN): BP 2636, Cotonou; tel. 33-12-56; fax 33-12-55; f. 1986; import and export of motor vehicle components and parts; Chair. and Man. Dir YESSOUFOU RÉMY GAUDENS.

CFAO Bénin: ave Pierre Delorme, BP 7, Cotonou; tel. 31-34-61; fax 31-34-63; f. 1973; cap. 963.4m. francs CFA; import-export co, mfrs of bicycles and mopeds; Pres. and Man. Dir EMMANUEL KOUTON.

CIMBENIN SA: 01 BP 1124, Cotonou; tel. 30-03-30; fax 33-02-45; e-mail cimdg@bow.intnet.bj; f. 1991; cap. 1,950m. francs CFA; mfrs of cement and wholesalers of bldg materials; 48.7% owned by Scancem International, Norway; Man. Dir OLA ORA.

Complexe Textile du Bénin SA (COTEB): BP 231, Parakou; tel. 61-09-49; fax 61-11-99; production of textiles and garments; Dir-Gen. D. LENAERTS.

Grands Moulins du Bénin (GMB): Zone Industrielle d'Akpakpa, BP 949, Cotonou; tel. 33-08-17; f. 1971; cap. 438m. francs CFA; Lebanese shareholders hold majority interest; wheat-milling; Man. Dir GILBERT CHAGOURY-RAMEZ.

Groupe la Tour: Carrefour de l'Eglise, Sacré-Coeur, Akpakpa, 01 BP 3900, Cotonou; tel. 33-47-56; fax 33-55-97; e-mail tour@serv .eit.bj; internet www.eit.bj/latour.htm; construction materials.

Société Béninoise de Brasserie (SOBEBRA): route de Porto-Novo, BP 135, Cotonou; tel. 33-10-61; fax 33-01-48; f. 1957, nationalized 1975–91 (as Société Nationale de Boissons); cap. 3,200m. francs CFA; production and marketing of beer, soft drinks and ice; Pres. BARNABÉ BIDOUZO; Man. Dir ANDRÉ FONTANA.

Société Béninoise de Sidérurgie (SBS): Cotonou; f. 1989; operates a wire and steel mill; Chair. JOHN MOORE.

Société Béninoise des Tabacs et Allumettes du Bénin (SOBETA): BP 07, Ouidah; tel. 34-13-04; fax 34-13-23; f. 1984 as Manufacture de Cigarettes et d'Allumettes de Ouidah; owned by Rothmans International PLC (UK); mfrs of tobacco products and matches; Pres. SÉFOU FAGBOHOUN; Man. Dir ERIC PACITTI.

Société Béninoise de Textiles (SOBETEX): BP 208, Cotonou; tel. 33-09-16; f. 1968; cap. 500m. francs CFA; 49% state-owned; bleaching, printing and dyeing of imported fabrics; Pres. FRANÇOIS VRINAT; Man. Dir ALBERT CHAMBOST.

Société de Commerce d'Automobile et de Réprésentation SA (SOCAR Bénin): PK3, route de Porto-Novo, BP 6, Cotonou; tel. 33-11-83; fax 33-11-84; wholesale trade in motor vehicles and spare parts; Dir-Gen. JEAN-FRANÇOIS MEUNIER.

Société des Ciments du Bénin: Plakonji Ancien Wharf, BP 448, Cotonou; tel. 31-37-83; produces and distributes cement; owned by Almida Group.

Société des Ciments d'Onigbolo (SCO): Onigbolo; f. 1975; cap. 10,000m. francs CFA; 51% state-owned; managed by the SCB Lafarge group (France); produces and markets cement; Pres JUSTIN GNIDEHOU; Man. Dir JEAN-MARIE OCTAVE ROKO.

Société des Huileries du Bénin (SHB): Bohicon; processes cotton seed for cooking oil.

Société Nationale de Brasseries 'La Béninoise': BP 135, Cotonou; brewery; fmrly Brasseries du Dahomey.

Société Nationale de Commercialisation des Produits Pétroliers (SONACOP): ave d'Ornano, BP 245, Cotonou; tel. 31-22-90; f. 1974; cap. 1,500m. francs CFA; 75% state-owned; 25% govt stake transferred to private ownership in 1997, further privatization pending; imports and distributes petroleum products; Pres. PATRICE NADJO; Man. Dir EDMOND-PIERRE AMOUSSOU.

Société Nationale pour l'Industrie des Corps Gras (SONICOG): BP 312, Cotonou; tel. 33-07-01; fax 33-15-20; f. 1962; state-owned; processes shea-nuts (karité nuts), palm kernels and cottonseed; Man. Dir JOSEPH GABIN DOSSOU.

Société Nationale pour la Promotion Agricole (SONAPRA): BP 933, Cotonou; tel. 33-08-20; fax 33-19-48; f. 1983; state-owned; manages five cotton-ginning plants and one fertilizer plant; distributes fertilizers and markets agricultural products; Pres. IMOROU SALLEY; Man. Dir CLAUDE D'ALMEDIA.

TRADE UNIONS

In mid-2000 there were six trade union federations active in Benin:

Centrale des Organisations Syndicales Indépendantes (COSI): Cotonou; principally active in the health and education sectors; Sec.-Gen. JOSÉ DE SOUZA.

Centrale Syndicale Autonome du Bénin (CSA—Bénin): Cotonou; principally active in private-sector enterprises; Sec.-Gen. GUILLAUME ATTIGBÉ.

Centrale Syndicale des Travailleurs du Bénin (CSTB): Cotonou; actively opposes privatization and the influence of the international financial community; linked to the Parti Communiste du Bénin; Sec.-Gen. GASTON AZOUA.

Centrale Syndicale Unie des Travailleurs du Bénin (CSUB): Cotonou; f. 1999.

Confédération Générale des Travailleurs du Bénin (CGTB): Cotonou; principally active in public administration; Sec.-Gen. PASCAL TODJINOU.

Union Nationale des Syndicats de Travailleurs du Bénin (UNSTB): 1 blvd Saint-Michel, BP 69, Cotonou; tel. and fax 30-36-13; principally active in public administration; sole officially-recognized trade union 1974–90; Sec.-Gen. LAWANI AMINOU.

Transport

In 1996 the World Bank approved a credit of US $40m., to be issued through the International Development Association, in support of a major programme of investment in Benin's transport network. The integrated programme aimed to enhance Benin's status as an entrepôt for regional trade, and also to boost domestic employment and, by improving the infrastructure and reducing transport costs, agricultural and manufacturing output.

RAILWAYS

In 1997 the network handled 311,400 metric tons of goods. Plans for a 650-km extension, linking Parakou to Niamey (Niger), via Gaya, were postponed in the late 1980s, owing to lack of finance. In January 1999 the line between Cotonou and Porto-Novo was re-opened after nine years of closure.

Organisation Commune Bénin-Niger des Chemins de Fer et des Transports (OCBN): BP 16, Cotonou; tel. 31-33-80; fax 31-41-50; f. 1959; 50% owned by Govt of Benin, 50% by Govt of Niger; total of 579 track-km; main line runs for 438 km from Cotonou to Parakou in the interior; br. line runs westward via Ouidah to Segborouê (34 km); also line of 107 km from Cotonou via Porto-Novo to Pobé (near the Nigerian border); Man. Dir ISAAC ENIDÉ KILANYOSSI.

ROADS

In 1996 there were 6,787 km of roads, including 10 km of motorway, 3,425 km of main roads and 3,352 km of secondary roads. About one-fifth of the network was paved.

AGETRAC: BP 1933, Cotonou; tel. 31-32-22; e-mail agetrac@leland.bj; f. 1967; goods transportation and warehousing.

Compagnie de Transit et de Consignation du Bénin (CTCB

Express): route de l'Aéroport, BP 7079, Cotonou; f. 1986; Pres. SOULÉMAN KOURA ZOUMAROU.

SHIPPING

The main port is at Cotonou. In 1998 the port handled some 2,383,600 metric tons of goods.

Port Autonome de Cotonou: BP 927, Cotonou; tel. 31-28-90; fax 31-28-91; e-mail pac@leland.bj; f. 1965; state-owned port authority; Dir-Gen. FERDINAND ASSOGBA-DOGNON.

Association pour la Défense des Intérêts du Port de Cotonou (AIPC) (Communauté Portuaire du Bénin): Port Autonome de Cotonou; tel. 31-17-26; fax 31-28-91; f. 1993; promotes, develops and co-ordinates of port activities at Cotonou; Pres. ISSA BADAROU-SOULÉ; Sec.-Gen. CAMILLE MÉDÉGAN.

Compagnie Béninoise de Navigation Maritime (COBENAM): Place Ganhi, 01 BP 2032, Cotonou; tel. 31-32-87; fax 31-09-78; f. 1974; 51% state-owned, 49% by Govt of Algeria; Pres. ABDEL KADER ALLAL; Man. Dir COCOU THÉOPHILE HOUNKPONOU.

Maersk Line: BP 2826, Cotonou; tel. 31-43-30; Danish co.

SDV Bénin: route du Collège de l'Union, Akpakpa, Cotonou; tel. 33-11-78; fax 33-06-11; e-mail sdvbenin@bow.intnet.bj; f. 1986; Pres. J. F. MIGNONNEAU; Dir-Gen. R. PH. RANJARD.

Société Béninoise d'Entreprises Maritimes: blvd de France, Zone Portuaire, BP 1733, Cotonou; tel. 31-21-19; fax 31-59-26; warehousing, storage and transportation.

Société Béninoise des Manutentions Portuaires (SOBEMAP): place des Martyrs, BP 35, Cotonou; tel. 31-39-83; state-owned; Pres. GEORGES SEKLOKA; Man. Dir THÉODORE AHOUMÉNOU AHOUASSOU.

Société Béninoise Maritime (SOBEMAR): Carré 8, Cruintomé, 08 BP 0956, Cotonou; tel. 31-50-26; fax 31-52-51; e-mail sobemarn@intnet.bj.

CIVIL AVIATION

The international airport at Cotonou (Cotonou-Cadjehoun) has a 2.4-km runway, and there are secondary airports at Parakou, Natitingou, Kandi and Abomey.

Air Afrique: ave du Gouverneur Ballot, BP 200, Cotonou; tel. 31-21-07; fax 31-53-41; see the chapter on Côte d'Ivoire; Dir in Benin JOSEPH KANZA.

Bénin Inter-Régional: Cotonou; f. 1991 as a jt venture by private Beninois interests and Aeroflot (then the state airline of the USSR); operates domestic and regional flights.

Tourism

Benin's rich cultural diversity and its national parks and game reserves are the principal tourist attractions. About 148,000 tourists visited Benin in 1997, when receipts from tourism were estimated at US $31m.

Conseil National du Tourisme: Cotonou; f. 1993.

Defence

In August 1999 the Beninois Armed Forces numbered an estimated 4,800 active personnel (land army 4,500, navy about 150, air force 150). Paramilitary forces comprised a 2,500-strong gendarmerie. Military service is by selective conscription, and lasts for 18 months.

Defence Expenditure: Budgeted at 21,000m. francs CFA in 1999.

Chief of Defence Staff: Col GANDONOU KODJA.

Chief of Staff of the Army: Col FERNAND AMOUSSOU.

Chief of Staff of the Navy: Lt-Col PROSPER TIANDO.

Chief of Staff of the Air Force: Col TAFFA ADAMS.

Education

The Constitution of Benin obliges the state to make a quality compulsory primary education available to all children. All public primary and secondary schools in Benin finance themselves through school fees. Primary education begins at six years of age and lasts for six years. Secondary education, beginning at 12 years of age, lasts for up to seven years, comprising a first cycle of four years and a second of three years. In 1996 62% of children in the relevant age-group were enrolled at primary schools (78% of boys; 46% of girls). Enrolment at secondary schools in that year was equivalent to only 17% of the appropriate age-group (23% of boys; 10% of girls). In the 1990s the Government sought to extend the provision of education.

In 1993 girls in rural areas were exempted from school fees, and in 1999 the Government created a 500m. francs CFA fund to increase female enrolment. Higher education facilities include the University of Benin, founded at Cotonou in 1970. In 1996 the number of students enrolled at tertiary institutions totalled 14,055. At the time of the 1992 census the average rate of adult illiteracy was 72.5% (males 59.9%; females 83.2%); UNESCO estimated an adult illiteracy rate of 62.5% (males 47.8%; females 76.4%) in 2000. The 1995 budget allocated 31,074m. francs CFA to the education sector (equivalent to 15.2% of total government expenditure).

Bibliography

Adamon, A. D. *Renouvea démocratique au Bénin: La Conférence nationale des forces vives et la période de transition.* Paris, L'Harmattan, 1995.

Adekounte, F. L. *Entreprises publiques Béninoises: La Descente aux Enfers.* Cotonou, Les Éditions du Flamboyant, 1996.

Allen, C., Radu, M. S., and Somerville, K., (Eds). *Benin, The Congo, Burkina Faso: Economics, Politics and Society.* New York and London, Pinter Publishers, Marxist Regimes Series, 1989.

Campbell, W. D. *The Emergent Independent Press in Benin and Côte d'Ivoire.* Westport, CT, Praeger Publishers, 1998.

Cornevin, R. *La République populaire du Bénin, des Origines dahoméennes à nos jours.* Paris, Académie des Sciences d'Outre-mer, 1984.

Le Dahomey. Paris, Presses universitaires de France, 1965.

Histoire du Dahomey. Paris, Berger-Levrault, 1962; new edn as *Histoire du Bénin.* Paris, Maisonneuve et Larose.

Decalo, S. *Historical Dictionary of Benin.* Metuchen, NJ, Scarecrow Press, 1995.

Dunn, J. (Ed.). *West African States: Failure and Promise.* Cambridge University Press, 1978.

Eades, J. S., and Allen, C. *Benin.* Oxford, Clio, 1996.

Egharevba, J. *A Short History of Benin (1900–1933).* Oxford, ABC, Ibadan University Press, 1991.

Garcia, L. *Le royaume du Dahomé face à la pénétration coloniale.* Paris, Éditions Karthala, 1988.

Harrison Church, R. J. *West Africa.* 8th Edn. London, Longman, 1979.

Heilbrunn, J. R. *Markets, Profits and Power: The Politics of Business in Benin and Togo.* Bordeaux, Centre d'étude d'Afrique noire, 1996.

Manning, P. *Slavery, Colonialism and Economic Growth in Dahomey, 1640–1960.* Cambridge, Cambridge University Press, 1982.

Ogbemudia, S. O. *Years of Challenge.* Oxford, Heinemann Educational Books (Nigeria), 1991.

Onibon, Y. O. *Les Femmes Béninoises: De l'étalage a la conquête du marché international.* Paris, Université de Paris, 1995.

Peffer-Engels, J. *Benin.* Danbury, CT, Franklin Watts, 1997.

Rimmer, D. *The Economies of West Africa.* London, Weidenfeld and Nicolson, 1984.

Van Ufford, P. Q. *Trade and Traders: The Making of the Cattle Market in Benin.* Amsterdam, Thela Thesis, 1999.

World Trade Organization. *Republic of Benin 1997.* Geneva, World Trade Organization, 1998.

BOTSWANA

Physical and Social Geography

A. MacGREGOR HUTCHESON

PHYSICAL FEATURES

The Republic of Botswana is a land-locked country, bordered by Namibia to the west and north, by the latter's Caprivi Strip to the north, by Zimbabwe to the north-east, and by South Africa to the south and south-east. Botswana occupies 581,730 sq km (224,607 sq miles) of the downwarped Kalahari Basin of the great southern African plateau, which has here an average altitude of 900 m above sea-level. Gentle undulations to flat surfaces, consisting of Kalahari sands overlying Archean rocks, are characteristic of most of the country but the east is more hilly and broken. Most of southern Botswana is without surface drainage and, apart from the bordering Limpopo and Chobe rivers, the rest of the country's drainage is interior and does not reach the sea. Flowing into the north-west from the Angolan highlands, the perennial Okavango river is Botswana's major system. The Okavango drains into a depression in the plateau, 145 km from the border, to form the Okavango swamps and the ephemeral Lake Ngami. From this vast marsh covering 16,000 sq km there is a seasonal flow of water eastwards along the Botletle river 260 km to Lake Xau and thence into the Makarakari salt pan. Most of the water brought into Botswana by the Okavango is lost through evaporation and transpiration in the swamps.

The Kalahari Desert dominates southern and western Botswana. From the near-desert conditions of the extreme south-west with an average annual rainfall around 130 mm, there is a gradual increase in precipitation towards the north (635 mm) and east (380–500 mm). There is an associated transition in the natural vegetation from the sparse thornveld of the Kalahari Desert to the dry woodland savannah of the north and east, and the infertile sands give way eastwards to better soils developed on granitic and sedimentary rocks.

POPULATION AND RESOURCES

The eastern strip, the best-endowed and most developed region of Botswana, possesses about 80% of the population, which was officially estimated to be 1,572,000 in mid-August 1998. Seven of the eight Batswana tribes, and most of the Europeans and Asians, are concentrated in the east. A substantial number of Batswana (the figure is unrecorded but estimated to be at least 50,000) are employed in South Africa, many of them (an estimated 12,746 in 1995) in mining. The absence of these workers helps to ease pressure on resources and contributes to the country's income through deferred pay and remittances sent home to their families. However, as a result of the rapid population growth, and since a large proportion of the population is less than 15 years of age, there is a pressing need for improvements in agricultural productivity and in other sectors of the economy to provide work for the growing number of young people who are entering the labour market.

Shortage of water, resulting from the low annual rainfall and aggravated by considerable fluctuations in the monthly distribution and total seasonal rainfall, is the main hindrance to the development of Botswana's natural resources, although a number of projects have improved water supply to the main centres of economic activity. Limitations imposed by rainfall make much of the country more suitable for the rearing of livestock, especially cattle, but it has been estimated that in eastern Botswana 4.45m. ha are suitable for cultivation, of which only about 10% is actually cultivated. Although in the east the irrigation potential is limited, the Okavango-Chobe swamps offer substantial scope for irrigation (as much as an estimated 600,000 ha).

In recent years Botswana's economic base has been considerably widened. Exploitable deposits of diamonds (of which Botswana is the world's largest producer by value), gold, silver, uranium, copper, nickel, coal, manganese, asbestos, common salt, potash, soda ash and sodium sulphate have been identified, and some of these minerals are currently being mined. In particular, the major developments of diamond mining at Orapa, Letlhakane and Jwaneng, and copper-nickel mining focused on Selebi-Phikwe, with their attendant infrastructural improvements, are assisting in the diversification of the predominantly agricultural economy.

Recent History

CHRISTOPHER SAUNDERS

Based on an earlier article by RICHARD BROWN

The political history of the Republic of Botswana (known as Bechuanaland prior to independence in 1966) has been influenced by three main factors: the country's geographical position, adjoining the formerly white-ruled South Africa, Namibia and Zimbabwe; the absence of a significant indigenous nationalist movement prior to independence; and the strong allegiances among the country's eight principal tribal groups.

In 1885 the British government declared Bechuanaland a protectorate, at the request of local rulers who wished to deter encroachment by Boers from the Transvaal. It was the British government's intention that Bechuanaland would eventually join the Union of South Africa, but this was resolutely opposed by the indigenous population.

In 1960 the Bechuanaland People's Party (BPP) was founded, maintaining close links with the African National Congress of South Africa (ANC). The BPP soon split into two factions, which later became the Botswana Independence Party (BIP) and the more important Botswana People's Party (BPP). In 1961 Seretse (later Sir Seretse) Khama, the former heir to the chieftainship of the important Bamangwato tribe (who had been forced to renounce the chieftainship in 1956, by pressure from the British, South African and Southern Rhodesian governments, after he had married a white woman), gained a seat on the legislative council, and was also appointed to the territory's executive council. In 1962 Khama formed the Bechuanaland Democratic Party (BDP). Many white settlers also gave their support to the BDP, in preference to the more radical BPP. In the territory's first direct legislative election under universal adult suffrage, held in 1965, the BDP won 28 of the 31 seats. Khama duly became prime minister. Independence followed on 30 September 1966, when Bechuanaland became the Republic of Botswana, with Khama as president.

During the years following independence, the BDP (restyled the Botswana Democratic Party) was challenged by the BPP (particularly in urban areas) and by a new Marxist-orientated party, the Botswana National Front (BNF). The BDP nevertheless retained by far the largest legislative majority.

Following the unilateral declaration of independence by Rhodesia (now Zimbabwe) in 1965, Khama, while opposing the illegal regime was unable to implement effective economic sanctions against Rhodesia, owing to Botswana's dependence on the Rhodesian-owned railways for its economic survival. During the 1970s Botswana supported the nationalist Patriotic Front in Rhodesia, and allowed sanctuary and passage for nationalist guerrillas, although they were not permitted to establish military bases in Botswana. Zimbabwe's achievement of internationally recognized independence in April 1980 brought considerable economic benefits to Botswana. Botswana was a founder member of the Southern African Development Co-ordination Conference (SADCC), formed in 1979, with the aim of encouraging regional development and reducing members' economic dependence on South Africa. (The SADCC was superseded by the Southern African Development Community—SADC in 1992.)

THE MASIRE PRESIDENCY, 1980–98

Following his death in July 1980, Khama was succeeded as president by his vice-president, Dr Quett (later Sir Quett) Ketumile Masire, a founder of the BDP. Masire had previously served for several years as minister of finance and development planning, and had occupied an important role in the country's economic development.

Masire's presidency was renewed in September 1984, when, in a general election to the national assembly, the BDP again won a decisive victory. Although the BDP's success in the parliamentary elections consolidated its position, discontent at the country's high level of unemployment was reflected in the outcome of local elections held concurrently, in which the BDP lost control of all the town councils except that of Selebi-Phikwe. The BDP's strength was further undermined by the defection, in 1985, of two prominent party members to the BNF.

Tension between the BDP and the BNF intensified in early 1987. In May some members of the BDP alleged that youthful elements within the BNF were being trained in insurgency techniques by Libya and the USSR. The government, however, dissociated itself from these allegations. In September 1987 a referendum was held on constitutional amendments concerning the electoral system; a large majority reportedly voted in favour of endorsing the reforms, although the BNF boycotted the referendum.

At parliamentary elections held in October 1989, the BDP strengthened its position by winning 31 of the 34 elective seats, receiving 65% of all votes cast. The BNF, weakened by internal dissension, won only three seats, although it obtained 27% of the total votes. As in 1984, the BNF challenged the results in a number of constituencies. The BPP lost its only seat, and four other parties also failed to secure representation. In October the new national assembly elected Masire for a third term as president. He subsequently threatened that his government would take action against workers involved in illegal strikes, as a measure to suppress widespread unrest among bank employees, mineworkers and primary school teachers.

In 1990 the BNF and the BPP formed an electoral alliance, agreeing to nominate a single candidate in each constituency at future elections. However, the BNF candidate failed to win a by-election at Mochudi in June, and a claim by some BNF leaders that the party had become a national liberation movement disrupted the harmony of the opposition coalition. Masire, following a legal challenge by the BNF of the Mochudi by-election, accused the opposition parties of bringing Botswana's democratic system into disrepute by persistently challenging election results. In late 1991 the government dismissed some 12,000 public-sector workers, who had taken strike action in support of demands for wage increases.

In early March 1992 the vice-president, Peter Mmusi, and the minister of agriculture, Daniel Kwelagobe, resigned, having been implicated by a commission of inquiry in a corruption scandal involving the illegal transfer of land. Festus Mogae, the minister of finance and development planning, was appointed

vice-president and also allocated the portfolio of local government and lands; a new minister of agriculture was also appointed. In June Mmusi and Kwelagobe were suspended from the central committee of the BDP, but were re-elected at the party's congress in July 1993. As leaders of one of the two main factions into which the BDP was increasingly divided, Mmusi and Kwelagobe opposed the government's economic liberalization policy, and sought to overturn the findings of the commission on illegal land dealings. A corruption scandal in 1993, involving the Botswana Housing Corpn, led to the resignation of two other government ministers. The government's reputation was also undermined by the revelation that seven ministers were among the debtors of the National Development Bank, which was found to be in financial difficulties. Uncertainty about the future leadership of the BDP and the president's silence on this matter added to the divisions within the ruling party both before and after the general election, held in October 1994. (In July 1995 Ponatshego Kedikilwe, the minister of presidential affairs and public administration, was appointed chairman of the BDP—a post which had remained vacant since the death of Mmusi in October 1994.)

Meanwhile, the BNF's demands, made in May 1993, for the appointment of an independent electoral commission and for the reduction of the voting age (to 18 years) were rejected by the government. In spite of this, the BNF abandoned its threat to boycott elections and sought, instead, to mobilize popular support on the issues of government corruption and the recession in Botswana's economy. The success of this strategy was demonstrated when the party fared unexpectedly well in the general election of 15 October 1994, winning 37.7% of votes and increasing its representation to 13 of the 40 elective seats. The BNF attracted strong support in urban areas, and for the first time an opposition party emerged from an election in a position to offer a serious challenge to the ruling party. The BDP, however, with 53.1% of the vote, retained its dominance in rural constituencies, winning a total of 26 of the elective seats. The election was conducted peacefully, with over 70% of the electorate turning out to vote. Only three ministers (including Mogae) retained their portfolios in the new cabinet. The national assembly re-elected Masire to the presidency, on 17 October. One week later four additional deputies were elected to the national assembly, including two new cabinet ministers. The new cabinet included Kwelagobe as minister of works, transport and communications. (Kwelagobe had been acquitted by the high court of charges relating to the corruption allegations made in 1992.)

The months following the election were marked by sporadic unrest, triggered by the release of three people who had been detained in connection with the ritual killing of a schoolgirl, but also reflecting a more generalized social and political discontent. Rioting, which had begun in Mochudi, north of Gaborone, in late January 1995, spread to the capital in mid-February, when demonstrators (mainly students and unemployed youths) were prevented by the security forces from entering the parliament buildings; the protesters subsequently erected barricades outside the university. Three days of violent clashes and looting followed, during which one person was killed. The BNF denied government allegations that it had promoted the unrest, which it claimed to be a reaction to the country's high rate of unemployment and other social problems. The government rejected allegations of excessive violence by the security forces in their suppression of the demonstrations.

A number of amendments to the constitution, which had been proposed during 1995–96, were adopted in August and September 1997. On 6 August the national assembly formally approved revisions restricting the presidential mandate to two terms of office and providing for the automatic succession to the presidency of the vice-president, in the event of the death or resignation of the president. Further amendments approved by the national assembly, reforming aspects of the electoral system, were endorsed in a national referendum on 5 September. The reforms reduced the age of eligibility to vote from 21 to 18 years and provided for the introduction of votes for Batswana resident abroad, and for the establishment of an independent electoral commission; opposition parties had hitherto been critical of the prevailing system, whereby the election supervisor was an appointee of the president's office. According to official figures, only 16.7% of the electorate participated in the referendum; the low turnout was attributed to a certain degree of apathy among voters, given the consensus of all the political parties on the need for reform, and to the requirement that votes be cast in the constituencies at which voters had registered for the 1994 general election. In November 1997 Masire announced that he was to retire from politics in March 1998.

THE MOGAE PRESIDENCY

The ceremony held on 31 March 1998 to commemorate Masire's retirement was attended by a number of foreign dignitaries, including President Clinton of the USA, who was on his first visit to southern Africa. On the following day Festus Mogae was inaugurated as president and subsequently appointed a new cabinet, in which the only new minister was Lt-Gen. Seretse Ian Khama, son of Botswana's first president (the late Sir Seretse Khama) and hitherto commander of the Botswana Defence Force (BDF). Ian Khama received the portfolio of presidential affairs and public administration, and was later designated as Mogae's vice-president, subject to his election to the national assembly. Kedikilwe, who had been favoured for the vice-presidency by certain prominent members of the BDP leadership, was appointed minister of finance and development planning. Khama was elected to the national assembly in July, and was sworn in as vice-president.

Meanwhile, hostility between Kenneth Koma, the leader of the BNF, and his deputy, Michael Dingake, had led to a split in the party. At the BNF's annual congress in April 1998 relations deteriorated over the issue of dissident members who had been expelled from the party. Koma, supported by the dissidents, ordered the expulsion from the party of central committee members. His actions were upheld by the party's constitution, and ultimately on appeal by the high court. In June members of the dissolved central committee formed the Botswana Congress Party (BCP), which was declared the official opposition in mid-July, after 11 of the BNF's 13 deputies decided to join the new party. Discontent within the BDP focused in part on the conduct of its primary elections to select candidates for the general election, which gave rise to allegations of favouritism. Concern about corruption also persisted within the party.

In early September 1999 Mogae declared a six-day state of emergency in order to facilitate the resolution of a registration problem which threatened to disenfranchise 15% of eligible voters. Divisions within the opposition parties enabled the ruling party to win a decisive victory on 16 October in the general election. Of the 459,000 Batswana who registered as voters, some 77% participated in the polls. The ruling BDP won all but seven of the 40 seats, with the BNF securing six seats, and the BCP only one, with Dingake, its leader, defeated in Gaborone. While the BDP regained five of the seats taken by the BNF in 1994, the BNF, which fielded 38 candidates, recovered seats it had lost to the BCP in mid-1998, performing well in the urban centres, particularly Gaborone, Lobatse and Kgatleng. Opposition leaders claimed that the BDP had identified itself with the state during the electoral campaign, and blamed the ruling party for the high rate of unemployment, the growing inequalities between rich and poor, and for failing to take the necessary action to arrest the spread of AIDS; by the end of 1999 the UN estimated that 35.8% of adults (aged between 15 and 49 years) were infected with HIV. Meanwhile, the BDP presented itself as the party of stability, offering the prospect of continued economic prosperity. Following the announcement of the election results, the opposition complained that it had not had sufficient funds to mount an effective campaign against the BDP, which, it claimed, had received substantial funding from the private sector. Mogae was re-elected to the presidency by the national assembly on 20 October and announced the formation of a new cabinet on the following day.

In December 1999 Mogae provoked outrage among the opposition parties, and tension within the ruling party, when he granted Vice-President Khama an unprecedented one-year sabbatical leave, effective from 1 January 2000. In July 2000 Kedikilwe resigned as minister of education, a position he had held since October 1999. Khama resumed his duties as vice-president in September 2000, and a minor cabinet reshuffle was effected.

EXTERNAL RELATIONS

During the 1980s, relations with South Africa remained strained, and Botswana was not immune to South Africa's general destabilizing pressures on its black-ruled neighbours. Revelations in mid-1980 that the South African armed forces had been recruiting Basarwa (Bushmen) from Botswana to serve in Namibia against guerrillas of the South West Africa People's Organisation of Namibia (SWAPO) caused alarm, and President Masire promised that the government would conduct an investigation. During 1981 tensions developed with South Africa over the supply of Soviet military equipment for the BDF. Masire defended the purchases on financial grounds and reiterated Botswana's adherence to its policy of non-alignment, stating that the instructors who accompanied the weapons had all left the country. By expanding the capabilities of the BDF, Botswana sought to achieve a more extensive and effective surveillance of its borders, thereby preventing insurgents from crossing into South Africa, and so removing any South African excuse for mounting punitive raids into Botswana. At the same time, it remained Botswana's policy to accommodate South African refugees, while not allowing them to use the country as a base for attacks on South Africa.

Several incidents, including, in April 1982, an exchange of fire over the border between Botswana and South African troops, led to increased tensions. In May 1984 Masire accused South Africa of attempting to coerce Botswana into signing a non-aggression pact similar to that negotiated by the Pretoria government with Lesotho. The president claimed that South Africa had hinted that, if Botswana refused to sign, it might position troops along the frontier between the two countries and cause disruptions of cross-border traffic. However, in late February 1985 South Africa reportedly abandoned its insistence that Botswana sign a formal joint security pact. Relations deteriorated once again in June, following a raid on alleged ANC bases in Gaborone by South African forces, in which at least 15 people were killed.

In early 1986 the United Kingdom and the USA pledged military aid to help Botswana to deter South African attacks and terrorist infiltration. In February Botswana's government reiterated its undertaking that the country was not to be used as a base for attacks by terrorists, and in March ANC representatives were expelled. The improvement in relations was short-lived: in May 1986, in conjunction with attacks on Zambia and Zimbabwe, South African troops launched land and air attacks on targets near Gaborone, causing one death. South Africa again claimed that its action was aimed at ANC bases. Although Botswana fully sympathized with the renewed international condemnation of apartheid, the vulnerability of the country's position, both geographically and economically, prevented the government from committing itself to the imposition of economic sanctions against South Africa, which was recommended by the SADCC in August.

With the approach of the South African general election in May 1987, tension increased as South Africa warned Botswana and other 'front-line' states that it would launch attacks against them in order to pre-empt disruption of the election by the ANC. Such an attack was alleged to have taken place in April, when four people were killed in a bomb explosion in Gaborone. In March 1988 South Africa openly admitted responsibility for a commando raid on a house in Gaborone, in which four alleged members of the ANC were killed. In June Masire announced the capture of two members of a South African defence force unit which had allegedly opened fire on Botswana security forces while engaged in a commando raid. South Africa claimed that the unit had been on an intelligence mission. South African armed incursions continued in subsequent months, and in March 1989 nine South Africans were expelled from Botswana for 'security reasons'. The relaxation of the political climate within South Africa from 1990 onwards, however, led to a gradual improvement in relations between the two countries. Full diplomatic relations were established in June 1994; and the two countries worked closely together in the SADC.

When the prime minister of Lesotho sought the help of neighbouring countries to quell internal instability in his country in September 1998, only South Africa and Botswana responded. South Africa agreed to assist militarily, as did Botswana, thus allowing the external intervention to assume the form of a regional intervention by the SADC. The initial deployment of South African troops met with resistance from elements within the Lesotho army, so that the few hundred Botswana forces who followed the South Africans into Lesotho became part of a major peace-keeping mission. There was some debate within Botswana itself over the role of its troops in Lesotho, and in May 1999 all the remaining SADC forces were withdrawn, bringing Operation Boleas to an end. A group of instructors from Botswana and South Africa remained in Lesotho until May 2000 in an advisory and training capacity. In another area of co-operation with South Africa, a bilateral agreement was signed in April 1999 on the administrative merger of South Africa's Kalahari Gemsbok Park and Botswana's Gemsbok Park, to create a substantial wildlife and nature reserve. The Kgalagadi Transfrontier Park was officially opened in May 2000 by President Mogae and President Thabo Mbeki of South Africa.

Relations between Botswana and Zimbabwe (whose ideologies are far apart) have been correct rather than friendly. Although Masire made an official visit to Harare in 1982, tension subsequently increased as a large number of former guerrillas of the Zimbabwe African People's Union (ZAPU), supporters of Joshua Nkomo (viewed as insurgents by the Zimbabwe government), crossed the border and entered refugee camps. A sharp deterioration in Botswana-Zimbabwe relations occurred in March 1983, when, with serious unrest in Zimbabwe's Matabeleland province, Nkomo fled to Botswana. Zimbabwe had already claimed that Botswana was providing a base for pro-Nkomo insurgents. To the considerable relief of the Botswana government, Nkomo left for London after only a few days in the country.

The presence of Zimbabwean refugees in Botswana persistently beset relations between the two countries throughout the 1980s. In 1983 allegations that armed dissidents from Zimbabwe were being sheltered among the 3,000–4,000 Zimbabwean refugees encamped in Botswana led the Botswana government to agree to impose stricter controls on the refugees. In May 1983 Botswana and Zimbabwe established full diplomatic relations. In August Robert Mugabe, the prime minister (later president) of Zimbabwe, visited Botswana for discussions, and it was announced that a joint trade agreement was being drafted. However, the recurrence of incidents on the Botswana–Zimbabwe border between members of the BDF and armed men wearing Zimbabwean military uniforms created further tension, and led to security talks between the two countries in late 1983. In July 1984 the Zimbabwe government stated that Botswana had repatriated more than 1,200 Zimbabwean refugees, including more than 300 alleged guerrillas. However, following the July 1985 general election in Zimbabwe, a new influx of refugees threatened to disrupt relations once again. In May 1988 Masire expressed confidence that the remaining Zimbabwean exiles would return to their country voluntarily as a result of an apparent improvement in the political climate in Zimbabwe. At the end of April 1989 the Botswana government announced that refugee status for Zimbabwean nationals in the country was to be revoked, and by September almost all Zimbabwean refugees were reported to have left Botswana. In the mid-1990s, however, the government expressed concern at the growing number of illegal immigrants in the country, the majority of whom were from Zimbabwe; of more than 40,000 illegal immigrants repatriated during 1995, more than 14,000 were Zimbabwean. Relations between the two countries were again strained in early 2000 as instability in Zimbabwe increased. Mogae expressed his commitment to respect for private property rights, described developments in Zimbabwe as 'regrettable', and attempted, by diplomatic means, to moderate Mugabe's excesses.

Following the achievement of independence by Namibia in March 1990, presidential visits were exchanged by Botswana and Namibia and steps were taken to ensure bilateral co-operation. However, in 1992 a border dispute developed between the two countries regarding their rival territorial claims over a small island (Sedudu-Kasikili) in the Chobe river. In early 1995 Botswana and Namibia agreed to present the case for arbitration at the International Court of Justice (ICJ); and in February 1996 the two countries signed an agreement committing themselves in advance to the court's eventual judgement. Meanwhile,

Namibia appealed to Botswana to remove its troops—stated by the Botswana authorities to be anti-poaching patrols—and national flag from the island. In the following month it was announced that Botswana and Namibia were to establish joint sub-committees at posts along the frontier in order to control illegal border crossings and smuggling. None the less, what were perceived as attempts by Botswana to extend the role and capabilities of its armed forces (most notably the completion of a new air base in 1995 and efforts during 1996–97 to procure military tanks) remained a source of friction between the two countries, although Botswana emphasized that a principal aim of such expansion was to enable its military to fulfil a wider regional and international peace-keeping role. Namibia's decision to construct a pipeline to take water from the Okavango river created further tension in 1996. (The river feeds the Okavango delta, an important habitat for Botswana's varied wildlife.) In early 1997 it was reported that Namibia had been angered by Botswana's erection of a fence along Namibia's Caprivi Strip, which separates the two countries to the north; Botswana insisted, however, that the fence was simply a measure to control the spread of livestock diseases. In January 1998 an emergency meeting of the Botswana–Namibia joint commission on defence and security was held to discuss ownership of another island (Situngu) in the Chobe river, following allegations by Namibia that the BDF had occupied the island and was stealing crops planted by Namibian farmers resident there. Representatives from both countries recommended that a joint technical commission be set up to demarcate the joint border; discussions regarding its establishment took place in mid-May. In March 1999 both Botswana and Namibia confirmed that they would accept the judgement of the ICJ on the Sedudu-Kasikili island issue. In December the ICJ awarded the island to Botswana, as widely expected. The two countries subsequently established a joint commission to investigate other demarcation disputes along the Chobe river.

In late 1998 relations between the two countries were further strained by the arrival of numbers of refugees in Botswana from the Caprivi Strip in Namibia. These included Mishake Muyongo, who had been suspended as president of the opposition Democratic Turnhalle Alliance in August, and other leading Caprivians who had been campaigning for the secession of their region from Namibia. Other refugees followed, claiming intimidation and harassment by the Namibian army, and by early 1999 more than 2,000 had taken up residence in a camp near Gaborone. Demands by Namibia for their extradition were refused by Mogae, although it was agreed by the two governments in March 1999 that prominent dissidents among the refugees would be allowed to leave Botswana for another country, and that an amnesty was to be extended to other refugees returning to Namibia. A formal agreement to this effect was signed in May under the auspices of the UNHCR, after which Muyongo and two others were granted asylum in Denmark. In early 2000 the eventual fate of more than 1,000 refugees still resident in Botswana remained uncertain.

During 1996–98 the Botswana government provoked international criticism with its attempts to relocate Baswara (San) people from their ancestral lands within the Central Kalahari Game Reserve to a new settlement outside the reserve. The San claimed that harsh measures were being employed in furtherance of this aim, including the cutting off of water supplies and threats of military enforcement. Protest on the issue subsequently receded, and on a visit to the USA in April 1999 to promote investment, Mogae laid stress on Botswana's favourable record in the field of human rights.

Botswana is a member of the OAU, the UN and the Commonwealth. From October 1997 it participated in a Commonwealth Ministerial Action Group which investigated human rights abuses in member states with military governments and worked to restore democratic civilian rule in Nigeria. In December 1999 former President Masire assumed the role of facilitator in efforts to achieve peace in the Democratic Republic of the Congo. Botswana's principled stand over apartheid, its enviable political stability and democratic record, and its reputation for moderation of approach, have given the country a minor but effective voice in many international deliberations.

Economy

LINDA VAN BUREN

Diamonds have transformed the Botswana economy, providing a level of stability that is rare in Africa. Diamonds contribute about one-third of the country's gross domestic product (GDP) and earn some 70% of its export revenue. Yet at independence, in 1966, Botswana was one of the 20 poorest countries in the world, with minimal infrastructural development and a predominantly subsistence economy. Government revenues were critically dependent on foreign aid and on the remittances of Batswana males employed in South Africa. The average life expectancy at birth was 50 years. Dominated by a few large-scale, mainly expatriate, farms, the commercial livestock sector was the principal component of GDP and export earnings. During the 1980s, however, Botswana's economic performance exceeded that of all other non-petroleum-producing countries in Africa. GDP rose, in real terms, by an average of 10.3% per year in 1980–90, giving Botswana one of the world's highest economic growth rates, and by an average of 4.8% yearly in 1990–99. This exceptional record was caused in part by the rapid expansion of the beef industry, although the principal factor was the discovery and development of valuable mineral resources, especially diamonds. Apart from transforming the export base, the growth of the mining sector has also helped to stimulate and finance the development of Botswana's infrastructure, manufacturing sector and social services. In the 1990s Botswana became an 'upper middle-income' country under World Bank definitions and, unusually for an African country, a net contributor to Bank funds. The infant-mortality rate declined from 71.0 per 1,000 live births in 1981 to 42.0 in 1997, and the average life expectancy rose to 61.0 years in the late 1980s, before AIDS began taking its toll.

The rise in the mineral sector is reflected in changes in the economic structure after 1966. The contribution of agriculture to GDP fell dramatically, exacerbated by prolonged periods of drought during 1981–87, from almost 40% of the total at independence to an average of 3.9% in 1990/91–1998/99. The contribution of mining increased from nil to an average of 35.5% during 1990/91–1998/99, having reached an exceptional 50.1% in 1988/89. The mining sector's output increased by 57% in 1999. Growth in manufacturing, transport and communications, and financial and social services was also impressive, if less dramatic. A similar situation has prevailed in exports, with beef sales falling from over 90% of merchandise earnings in 1966 to less than 3% in 1996. Visible export earnings from diamonds rose from nil in 1966 to 67.0% in 1998.

Growth based on such narrow foundations is vulnerable and difficult to sustain in the long term. The sixth National Development Plan (NDP) of 1984/85–1989/90 was predicated on a substantial diminution in GDP growth rates, to an average of 4.8% per year. However, this figure proved to be overly pessimistic; GDP increased, in real terms, at an average annual rate of 11.7% over the plan period. An important contributory factor was a rapid increase in government expenditure, which cannot be sustained indefinitely. The seventh NDP, covering the period 1990/91–1996/97, aimed to increase earnings from the mining sector sufficiently to support a doubling of government expenditure and envisaged an expanded role for the private sector in economic development. In 1993 the government scaled down the targets of the seventh NDP and identified a shortage of skilled manpower as being the major constraint on faster progress. Economic performance was adversely affected during the early 1990s by the international economic recession, and real GDP declined by 0.1% in 1992/93, falling below the rate of population growth for the first time since independence. The recovery of the diamond market in late 1993 was the principal cause of a return to positive GDP growth in 1993/94, at 4.2%. A mining downturn reduced GDP growth to 2.5% in 1994/95, but a subsequent upturn in the sector lifted GDP growth to 6.6% in 1995/96, a level which was sustained in 1996/97, at 7.1%, and in 1997/98, at 8.3%. The government estimate for GDP growth in 1998/99 was a more modest 4.2%. Real GDP per

caput, expressed in constant 1985/86 prices, increased by 4.5%, from P3,428 in 1995/96 to P3,584 in 1996/97, and by 5.7%, to P3,787, in 1997/98. These figures are based on an assumed population growth rate of 2.5% per annum. Forecasts for future rises in GDP per caput reflect a slowdown in population growth, estimated by the UN at 1.9% per annum in 1995–2000 and projected at 1.2% per annum in 2000–2005, as well as continued positive GDP growth. The eighth NDP, covering the period 1997/98–2002/03, was introduced with the theme 'Sustainable Economic Diversification', and forecast annual economic growth of 4.2% per annum, a figure that was exceeded in the first year of the plan. Emphasis was placed on encouraging the growth of the private sector and on intensifying diversification efforts. During the same period, under a scheme called 'Vision 2016', the people of Botswana were invited to participate in the debate on development issues that affect their future.

AGRICULTURE

Botswana's agricultural sector employed some 44.8% of the economically active population in 1998, according to FAO estimates. Composed partly of semi-desert and partly of a savannah area with highly erratic rainfall and relatively poor soils, the country is more suited to grazing than to arable production; only about 5% of Botswana's land is arable. During the 1990s attempts were made to compensate for this shortage of arable land by developing the country's irrigation potential, but agriculture remained dominated by the livestock sector generally, and by the cattle industry in particular. The raising of cattle was the main economic activity of rural Botswana in 1998, and contributed over 80% of agricultural output in that year. Agricultural GDP declined by an average of 1.2% per year in 1990/91–1998/99, and by 1998/99 the sector contributed just 2.9% of GDP. Nevertheless, the improved management of the agriculture sector is seen as a government priority, especially because of its key role in providing employment. In June 1998 the government commissioned a consultancy to formulate a National Master Plan for Agricultural Development (NAMPAD), aimed at boosting productivity and at guiding investment in such a way as to protect the country's fragile rangelands, now at risk from overgrazing. The scheme focused on diversification into such areas as horticulture, forestry, game farming and bee keeping. The 2000/2001 national budget allocated P5m. to fund pilot projects under the NAMPAD, including demonstration dairy and vegetable farms and a strategy for reusing waste water for irrigation in this normally dry country.

The national cattle herd increased dramatically after independence, from 1.4m. head in 1965 to a peak of almost 3m. head in 1981, stimulated by improved beef export prices, the expansion of available grazing through the drilling of new boreholes, and the establishment of effective disease control, based on a system of cordon fences and vaccination, which kept most of the country free of foot-and-mouth disease after 1981. The cordon system opened up the lucrative market within the European Union (EU), which offered preferential terms and handsome price subsidies (in Botswana's case, a 92% levy rebate, with a quota of 18,910 metric tons of beef per annum) to Lomé Convention signatories able to satisfy the stringent disease-control criteria, but it also involved the government in international controversy over the impact of the cordon system on wildlife. The criticism was intensified by the fact that the economic benefit of beef exports largely accrued to the 5% of households which were estimated to own more than one-half of the national herd, with about one-fifth of the total held by 360 large-scale commercial farms. Approximately 50% of rural households neither owned nor had access to cattle. In 1999 the Ministry of Agriculture initiated a computerized cattle-identification and -tracing system in order to comply with an EU directive, issued in 1997 in response to the bovine spongiform encephalopathy (BSE) crisis in the European beef market, which required that all cattle slaughtered and exported to EU countries be traced to the farm on which they were born. By February 2000 the system had not yet been implemented, and the national budget allocated P11m. towards the establishment of a compliant cattle-origin database.

The Botswana Meat Commission (BMC) is responsible for slaughtering cattle and is capable of handling the high levels of throughput which occur in times of drought, although in the absence of drought conditions, when owners are replenishing their herds, the BMC has excess capacity. The Commission slaughtered 162,000 head of cattle in 1997/98, up 28% from the 127,000 head killed in 1996/97. The BMC abattoirs at Lobatse and Francistown operated at just 62% of capacity in 1997/98. The Commission also has an abattoir at Maun.

The General Agreement on Tariffs and Trade (GATT), renegotiated in December 1993 and renamed the World Trade Organization (WTO), proposed to end the beef subsidies from the EU enjoyed by Botswana and other eligible countries under the beef protocol of the Lomé Convention, although the WTO did agree to a waiver until the year 2000. The gradual elimination of beef quotas is expected to have a delayed effect, as they have been underused by most eligible countries. A new electrified cordon fence was installed south of the West Caprivi National Park near the border with Namibia in May 1998. An outbreak of animal sleeping sickness, known in Botswana as *nagana*, occurred in Ngamiland and Okavango, in the north of the country, in October 1999, and 21 head of cattle were reported to have died by May 2000. Meanwhile, heavy rains and flooding hampered the spraying of insecticides. An earlier outbreak of cattle lung disease was contained.

In contrast to the cattle sector, sheep and goat numbers have withstood the periodic droughts reasonably well. Predominantly a subsistence-sector resource, the national herd of sheep and goats increased from 776,000 head in 1982 to 2.45m. head in 1998. The main commercial development other than beef has been in urban poultry farming. Efforts have also been made to improve the availability of eggs and chickens in rural areas, and to improve local production of milk and fish. Diversification efforts have focused on ostrich farming and fish farming, and on improving the infrastructure for the marketing of fresh milk. Ostrich farming has become a promising new industry, with a view to marketing this low-cholesterol red meat in European markets.

In the arable sector, as in beef, commercial farmers provide a disproportionate share of crop production: official figures indicate that just 100 commercial farms accounted for 37% of total output of sorghum, maize, millet, beans and pulses in 1995. Of the 85% of small-scale farms producing crops, almost one-third covered less than 3 ha, and only 6.8% covered more than the 10 ha minimum necessary for household self-sufficiency, even in years of adequate rains. As a result, two-thirds of rural households were reported to depend for as much as 40% of their income on members employed in the formal, predominantly commercial, agricultural sector. In 1992 a commission of inquiry uncovered widespread corruption in the sale and distribution of land. In February 1997 a new fresh-produce horticultural market was opened in Lobatse, and a similar facility was planned for Francistown.

As a result of the 1991/92 drought (the worst of the 20th century), the total area planted with food crops was reduced by 70%–80%; even prior to this decline, however, the government had abandoned its former aim of achieving national self-sufficiency in cereals. In accordance with the seventh NDP, shortfalls in cereal production were to be offset by imports, and efforts were made to improve household incomes, in order to reduce reliance on subsidies. In 1993 Botswana imported some 133,000 metric tons of cereals. An official drought was declared for the fourth consecutive year in April 1995, when the output of both maize and sorghum declined sharply. The government allocated P131m. for the drought-relief programme in the year to 30 June 1996. Good rains in late 1995 and early 1996 led the government to announce that drought relief in 1996/97 should be rendered unnecessary. Rains in the 1996/97 growing season were good enough to augment cereal production, but imports of 140,000 tons of maize, 90,000 tons of wheat, 40,000 tons of sorghum and 13,000 tons of rice were still required. In comparison, in 1998 Botswana produced 7,000 tons of sorghum, traditionally the staple crop, as well as 1,000 tons of maize, 1,000 tons of millet

and 500 tons of wheat. In early 2000 even this dry country did not escape the heavy floods of southern Africa. While the world's media focused on the huge floodplain of Mozambique, 160,000 Batswana lost their homes, and five people lost their lives. Controversially, the government announced that there would be no state compensation to help rebuild private homes.

In the mid-1980s land under irrigation totalled only 1,000 ha, the majority consisting of privately-owned farms producing primarily cotton, citrus fruits and tobacco. Botswana is considered to have substantial irrigation potential, particularly in the Okavango Delta and Chobe areas. In view of the unique and fragile nature of the Okavango, especially, there are also significant possible environmental risks in realizing this potential, which became the subject of considerable study in the mid-1990s. Some experimentation, utilizing flood-recession irrigation, was initiated at Molapo, on the eastern fringe of the Okavango. Pending the final outcome of environmental studies, it was planned to proceed with a scheme, costing P180m., to develop 5,000–10,000 ha of high-yielding crops by improving water- and crop-management systems. Other projects were also being studied under the government's 'accelerated water-resource development programme'.

MINERALS AND MINING

In 1996 Botswana was Africa's third-largest mineral producer by value, but it was not until after independence 30 years earlier that the country was found to possess abundant reserves of diamonds, coal, copper-nickel, soda ash, potash and sodium sulphate. Substantial deposits of salts and plutonium, as well as smaller reserves of gold, silver and a variety of industrial minerals, were also identified. In real terms, the GDP of the mining sector increased at an average rate of 2.3% per year between 1990/91 and 1998/99, with growth of 9.9% recorded in 1995/96. Growth slowed to 5.8% in 1996/97, owing to a decline in the output of copper-nickel, but reached 9.5% in 1997/98. Mining GDP decreased by 4.4% in 1998/99. Revenue from diamond exports fell by 21%, from P7,675.3m. in 1997 to P6,060.6m. in 1998, owing to a decline in sales volume resulting from the Asian economic crisis. However, as the economies of the Far East, not least Japan, proved to be more resilient than had been expected, so did Botswana's mineral exports to those countries. The value of Botswana's diamond exports reached P9,812.8m. in 1999, an increase of 62% over 1998. Meanwhile, the Asian economic crisis led to sharp falls in international prices for copper and nickel, although these too recovered in the second half of 1999.

Large-scale mineral exploitation began in 1971, when the Orapa diamond mine began production, and Botswana proceeded to develop a relatively diverse mining sector, with three major diamond mines, coal exploitation and copper-nickel production, as well as the mining of gold, industrial minerals and semiprecious stones. The diamond mines are owned and operated by the Debswana Diamond Co (Pty), a joint venture owned equally by the Botswana government and De Beers Consolidated Mines of South Africa. De Beers began diamond exploration in 1955, but it was not until 1969 that the 117-ha Orapa kimberlite pipe, the world's second-largest in terms of size, was discovered. Mining at Orapa, which commenced in 1971, was followed in 1977 by the inauguration of production at the adjacent Letlhakane pipe, and in 1982 a major new mine at Jwaneng, 125 km west of Gaborone, was brought into production. A 20% expansion at Jwaneng in 1995 was credited with raising GDP by a full percentage point. This expansion of plant capacity, known as Jwaneng Fourth Stream, was followed by a further expansion at Orapa, at a cost of P1,400m., which commenced in 1997. Known firstly as Orapa Fourth Stream, and subsequently as Orapa 2000, this investment included an additional treatment plant and was expected to double Orapa's annual output from 6m. carats to 11.9m. carats annually. Despite the depressed global demand at the time, the government confirmed in February 1999 that the Orapa expansion would proceed on schedule, and indeed, President Mogae formally opened Orapa 2000 in May 2000. In 1999 Debswana was the world's largest producer of diamonds by value. Although all current diamond-mining operations are carried out by Debswana, a number of other companies have become involved in diamond exploration, carrying out extensive ground surveys.

Four kimberlite pipes reportedly have been located under the desert sands. Continuous operation at Jwaneng began in 1997, with production increasing from six days a week to seven, despite earlier objections by trade unions.

Since the mid-1980s the diamond industry has continued to strengthen its role as the mainstay of Botswana's vigorous economic performance. In 1987 Debswana sold its stockpile to De Beers. The sale, valued at some US $600m., formed part of an agreement giving Debswana a 5.27% shareholding in De Beers. For the government, this arrangement provided an effective 2.6% equity interest, entitling it to appoint two directors both to the main De Beers board and to that of its London-based diamond-trading subsidiary, in reflection of Botswana's increasing importance in production by the group. For the Botswana government, the agreement was not only a long-term investment but also a means of gaining access to decision-making in the diamond market. By 1997 diamonds accounted for an estimated 70% of Botswana's exports, more than 45% of government revenue and some 30% of GDP. The government in the mid-1990s also encouraged the development of two diamond-cutting and -polishing ventures. Debswana employed a work-force of more than 6,000 workers in 1997, with the Orapa Fourth Stream expected to create a further 1,500 jobs during construction and 300 permanent jobs upon completion.

Production of copper-nickel matte at Selebi-Phikwe began in 1974, and output rose steadily, reaching some 50,000 metric tons per year by the late 1980s. However, the value of sales of matte per ton declined consistently during the 1980s, owing to depressed international prices for nickel and copper. These low prices created acute financial problems for the operating company, Bamangwato Concessions Ltd (BCL), and for its parent group, Botswana Roan Selection Trust, in which the Botswana government held 15%, with Anglo American Corpn of South Africa and Amax Corpn of the USA holding the remainder. To address these problems, a programme of financial restructurings and debt-reschedulings was undertaken. A resurgence of prices for base metals after mid-1987 improved BCL's financial position, safeguarding the jobs of its work-force of 5,000, enabling the company to contribute up to 10% of Botswana's total export earnings and allowing it to bring on stream two new copper-nickel mines, including the high-grade Selebi North mine, with a view to reaching full capacity of about 1,500 metric tons of ore per day by mid-1990. Nevertheless, another slump in international copper prices in 1993 rendered BCL unable to cover its operating costs. The government subsequently warned that BCL would need a substantial level of new capital investment, together with stringent restraints on wages, if the mine were to survive as a viable operation. Copper export earnings fell to US $99m. in 1994. The other copper-nickel mine—at Selkirk, east of Francistown—was brought into production at the end of 1988 by a consortium of Swiss and British investors. At full capacity, output was expected to reach 60,000 tons of high-grade ore per year; BCL was to undertake refining of the output on a toll basis. There were also plans to develop the adjacent, and larger, Phoenix deposit. BCL's smelter was refurbished in 1995. Under the Lomé Convention, the company benefited from Sysmin compensation amounting to ECU 33.8m. in 1996 and to the equivalent of P51.7m. in 1998. The 1998 crisis, a direct result of the economic turmoil in the Far East, rendered BCL unable to meet its operating costs in that year, and the government extended an emergency loan of P132m. to keep the company solvent and maintain employment; P10m. of the loan was repaid in 1999.

Plans to exploit Botswana's coal reserves have been restricted by the low level of international prices and by the great distance to major coal markets. Some 17,000m. metric tons of steam coal suitable for power-plant use have been identified in the east, and coal is extracted at the Morupule colliery, whose output rose from 579,400 tons in 1987 to 901,500 tons in 1992. Most of the coal is for electricity generation to service the mining industry and the soda ash plant at Sua Pan. The government has also encouraged domestic coal use, in order to conserve fuel wood. In 1998 imports of mineral fuels accounted for 5.4% of the value of total imports.

Following independence, several attempts were made to exploit brine deposits at Sua Pan, in central Botswana, by establishing a soda-ash and salt plant. Soda ash is used in the production of glass, paper, steel and detergents. In 1986 South African interests began talks with the Botswana government for a joint venture, Soda Ash Botswana (Pty) Ltd, to build a plant at Sua Pan, with forecast annual output of some 300,000 metric tons of soda ash and 650,000 tons of salt. The success of the project always depended on the sale of the soda ash to South Africa. Agreement to undertake the project was completed in 1988, and production began, on schedule, in early 1991. However, output of 63,154 tons of soda ash in 1991 was considerably below expectations, owing initially to technical problems, and subsequently to a lack of demand and increased competition in the South African market, and remained at a level well below profitable operation. Soda Ash Botswana was liquidated in May 1995 and was succeeded later that year by Botswana Ash (Pty) Ltd (Botash), 50% of which is owned by the Botswana government, 14% by Anglo American Corpn, 14% by De Beers and 14% by African Explosives and Chemical Industries, with the remaining 8% held by a consortium of banks. Despite being relieved of a heavy debt burden, Botash's problems continued; floods in 1996 once again halted production. However, the company achieved a 69.1% rise in production in the first quarter of 1997, compared to the same period of 1996. In June 1999 the project achieved its highest-ever monthly production level for salt, at 32,300 tons, and in September soda-ash output reached a peak of 25,779 tons, up from 16,900 tons in September 1998. Nevertheless, while Botash has had considerable success in overcoming production problems, the fact remains that the target market for the scheme's output, South Africa, has never exhibited demand as strong as was envisaged in the planning stages.

Botswana's dependence on South African support to implement the soda-ash project raised domestic and regional concern that the government was increasing the country's vulnerability to political pressure from its neighbour. Similar concerns surrounded exploration work on plutonium deposits carried out in southern Botswana by two South African firms, Gold Fields of South Africa (GFSA) and Southern Prospecting. GFSA held three prospecting licences, through its Gold Fields of Botswana subsidiary, for a 3,000 sq km concession north of the Molopo river, adjacent to its existing concession in South Africa's Bushveld igneous complex, which contains substantial reserves of platinum and chromium. Botswana's reserves are, however, thought to be of lower grade and far less substantial, and in 1992 platinum exploration in the Molopo area was suspended.

For many years, gold has been mined, on a small scale, in Botswana. In 1987 a joint venture, Shashe Mines, was formed by the Botswana government and private US and Canadian interests to explore gold deposits at Map Nora near Francistown; exploitation of the mineral commenced in 1989. Botswana's total output of gold reached 67 kg in 1989, but had dwindled to only 40 kg annually by the early 1990s. The Bonanza gold mine in Tati Schist, 40 km from Francistown, has proven reserves of 2,040 metric tons, with a gold content of 14.8 grams per ton, in association with silver and other minerals. Kudu Mining also operates the Rainbow gold mine, some 60 km from Francistown.

MANUFACTURING AND CONSTRUCTION

The GDP of the manufacturing sector grew by an average of 10.1% per year in 1985/86–1994/95, and by 5.1% per year in 1995/96–1998/99. The largest factor inhibiting growth has been the small size of the Botswana market, at 1.5m. people, coupled with trade barriers restricting Botswana-based manufacturers from operating in neighbouring, larger markets. Manufacturers exporting to Zimbabwe were particularly concerned in 2000 about that country's ability to settle payments for goods from Botswana. However, in the late 1990s the percentage of Botswana's exports that went to Zimbabwe had been declining anyway and by 2000 represented only about 10% of total exports excluding diamonds. Botswana's weak infrastructure, which once was cited as a deterrent, is now being significantly improved, but import dependence and a shortage of skilled manpower remain. The government is addressing the skills shortage, with some success, through concerted efforts to improve education and training. Import dependence remains a problem, however; the percentage of value added to some products in Botswana is used by neighbouring states as an excuse to maintain trade barriers. Nevertheless, as the labour force becomes more skilled, there will be greater potential for higher proportions of value to be added. In 1997 the government launched a three-year 'local procurement programme', aimed at obtaining more of the central government's purchases from local suppliers. Botswana has created an enabling environment that is highly favourable to enterprises manufacturing a wide range of products. Those sub-sectors showing the most rapid growth during the mid-1990s were textiles, beverages, chemicals, paper, metals, plastics, vegetable oils and electrical products. A new vehicle-assembly plant, the Motor Co of Botswana, began constructing cars from kits from the South Korean company Hyundai in 1998, producing 4,000 units by the end of the year. However, the Motor Co of Botswana was subsequently placed under provisional liquidation by its creditors, both local and foreign, including the Botswana Development Corpn. The company later collapsed, owing the government P21.5m. in customs duties. At the same plant, assembly of two models of passenger cars from Volvo of Sweden began in early 1999. Volvo envisaged the assembly of several thousand cars a year at the Gaborone plant for export to markets both in the region and extending to Australia. Botswana reduced the rate of company tax from 35% to 15% in the 1995/96 budget in order to encourage the manufacturing sector, and extended the tax to a broader range of companies in the 1999/2000 budget. The government has maintained a stable monetary policy, keeping control of inflation and ensuring the availability of foreign exchange and the ease of international remittances.

It is the manufacturing sector which is seen, in the end, as the primary stimulus for job creation, which is often cited as the Botswana economy's most serious challenge. Past performance shows that the sector does hold considerable job-creation potential. Formal employment in manufacturing stood at 4,400 jobs in 1978, with more than one-third of those posts at the parastatal BMC; by 1991 the sector had created six times as many jobs and was employing 27,548 people, while the BMC's proportion had dropped to 14%. In 1996 29,530 people were engaged in the manufacturing sector. The sector's strong performance can be attributed to a number of government policies, based on its Financial Assistance Policy (FAP), inaugurated in 1982, which provided a wide range of subsidies to potential entrepreneurs, particularly in the small-scale sector, and a highly attractive foreign investment code. The government's current diversification programme also places priority on the country's need to develop manufacturing. Since 1970 the parastatal Botswana Development Corpn (BDC) has supported more than 100 enterprises, including companies involved in brewing, sugar packaging, furniture making, clothing manufacture, tourism, milling and concrete products. In 1984 the BDC embarked on a programme of divestment, establishing the Setshaba Investment Trust Co as a vehicle for offering shares in its subsidiaries to the public. During 1982–97 the sale of 45 enterprises generated substantial proceeds. In 1995/96 the BDC sold 50% of its remaining share in Setshaba. A reorganization of the BDC was followed by a cash injection of P72m. in the 1999/2000 budget to enable it, among other things, to construct more factory shells for small manufacturing enterprises. The Botswana Export Development and Investment Authority was established in the late 1990s to promote exports of the country's manufactured goods.

The construction sector developed rapidly during the 1980s, particularly from 1988/89, when the sector registered growth of 30%. In the early 1990s, however, growth in the sector slowed, reflecting both the general downturn in economic performance and the management crisis at the Botswana Housing Corpn (see Recent History). From July 1995 the government increased the wage rate from P4.50 to P6.00 per day for workers on the 'drought labour-intensive public works programme'. More than 12 road-construction projects were allocated funding in the 1999/2000 budget, followed by a further seven in the 2000/2001 budget.

ENERGY AND WATER DEVELOPMENT

Rapid growth in the economy and in the population resulted in an equally rapid expansion in the demand for energy and water. The Botswana Power Corpn (BPC) has been implementing a continuing programme of capacity expansion, of which a major project was the Morupule power station. Using coal mined at

Morupule, the station became the focus of a new national grid system linking the existing northern and southern networks, based on the Selebi-Phikwe and Gaborone power stations, with six 30-MW units in operation. A project to link Botswana into the Zambian and Zimbabwean grids was completed in 1991, and in the late 1990s, as part of a major expansion into other areas of southern Africa by South Africa's Eskom, a 400-kilovolt transmission line linking Bulawayo in Zimbabwe to Matimba in South Africa was to run across Botswana. Apart from the further work at Morupule, the main short-term focus of the electricity programme was the extension of the rural catchment area of the national grid, with the aim of conserving fuel wood and reducing oil demand. The BPC, following the political changes in South Africa in 1994, undertook a major shift in its policy from self-sufficiency to the supplementation of local supply through imports, in order to take advantage of the cheaper power available south of the border. In so doing, the BPC was able to reduce its tariffs by 10% in October 1995. The BPC's previous controversially high connection charges were also reduced. In rural collective schemes, consumers who once had to save up to pay 40% of the cost of connection now had to pay only 10% in advance. For major consumers, the 100% deposit fell to 25%. In 1996/97 the BPC was able to declare a financial dividend and became the third parastatal enterprise, after the BDC and the Botswana Telecommunications Corpn, to achieve profitability. Although oil imports have not imposed nearly as heavy a burden on foreign exchange in Botswana as they have in many other African countries, they accounted for some 7.5% of total imports in 1998. Between April 1997 and February 1999 28 villages were electrified, and a further 70 villages were to be connected to the national grid in 1999 and 2000.

For an arid country such as Botswana, the provision of water is a formidable challenge. Outside the remote Okavango and Chobe areas, the country has only minimal surface water supplies, and 80% of the national demand is met from groundwater sources, with livestock the largest single user, consuming about one-third, followed by mining, urban areas, and rural areas and villages. Although not fully assessed, groundwater supplies are not expected to exceed 4,000m. cu m per year, and intense competition for water resources has emerged in the main urban and mining areas in the east, leading to the postponement of plans for the development of industrial sites, particularly in Gaborone. The situation has been further exacerbated by recurrent drought. Aid from overseas is currently being used to develop water resources. In addition, an 'accelerated water resource development programme' initiated in 1989, sought to provide more dams, in an attempt to fulfil the projected requirements of the 1990s. Now part of the Botswana National Water Master Plan, the Nordic-assisted North South Carrier Water Project proposed the construction (at a cost of US $350m.) of a dam on the Motlontse river, transfer pipelines, four pumping stations and a water-treatment plant, all of which were to enhance the water supply in the capital and in adjacent districts of eastern Botswana. Problems encountered in the laying of glass-reinforced piping led to delays, however, and the target completion date of January 1999 was not met, although the project was expected to be commissioned by mid-2000. Construction of the Letsibogo Dam was at an advanced stage in early 1999, and was reported to be 18% full at 31 January of that year. By February 2000, Letsibogo was 82% full, while the Shashe Dam was overflowing, after some of the heaviest rains in the country's history.

A government project to provide water for the southern Okavango region was suspended in early 1991, following pressure from local and international environmentalists. However, Namibia announced plans in 1996 to pump 20m. cu m of water from the Okavango river, a project which has also been severely criticized by environmentalists. The Okavango river empties into a land-locked delta in Botswana, and any removal upstream of large amounts of water would severely alter the fragile ecology of this unique habitat, which is rich in wildlife.

FOREIGN TRADE AND BALANCE OF PAYMENTS

Diamonds have been Botswana's principal export by value since the mid-1970s, accounting for as much as 88% of total earnings and for more than 40% of government revenue in some years.

Other exports include vehicles and parts, copper-nickel matte, textiles and meat and meat products. Botswana's principal imports are vehicles and transport equipment, machinery and electrical equipment, food, beverages and tobacco, metals and related products, chemical and rubber products, and textiles and footwear. The United Kingdom is generally the principal client, purchasing some two-thirds of all exports, mainly diamonds consigned to the London-based Central Selling Organisation. Other major clients include the countries of the Southern African Customs Union (SACU), principally South Africa, with some 15%, followed by continental Europe. Botswana's main supplier is SACU, mainly South Africa, which provides some 70% of all imports.

Merchandise exports f.o.b. increased by 43% in 1999, primarily owing to improved sales of diamonds and, to a lesser extent, of other minerals, while imports grew by a more modest 11%, resulting in a significant improvement in the visible trade surplus. Invisibles, on the other hand, registered a deficit of P1,000m. in 1999, while the financial account ended with a deficit of P182m. Nevertheless, strong export performance boosted the surpluses both on the current account and on the overall balance of payments, which reached P1,685m., equivalent to about 7% of GDP. These positive figures are not unusual; Botswana has generally enjoyed a secure balance-of-payments position since 1976. Net transfers, including Botswana's share of revenue from SACU, and capital inflows of private investment and foreign aid, have usually more than offset the continuing deficit on the invisible trade account. The most obvious effect of Botswana's generally strong balance-of-payments position has been the increase in official reserves of foreign exchange. These were sufficient to cover 5.5 months of imports in 1980; in comparison, foreign reserves stood at US$6,100m. in December 1999, enough to cover 28 months of imports of goods and services. Although this figure was slightly lower than the 29 months of cover accumulated in 1998, it still represented by far the longest forward reach in the world. The government regards the high level of reserves as essential to sustain Botswana's future economic development as diamond earnings level out, with no single source of export revenue to replace them. The rapid escalation in reserves after 1985 was paralleled, however, by increasing criticism of the government's concern with long-term financial security. According to critics, the government's conservative fiscal policies were depressing productive investment, particularly by the private sector, and were subsequently hindering job creation.

Botswana operates an open economy, with combined import and export values exceeding GDP, making both the domestic economy and the external account vulnerable to fluctuations in the terms of trade and exchange rates. The government has maintained a flexible, trade-orientated exchange-rate policy since the pula was established in 1976 as the national currency. It was initially tied to the US dollar, but the appreciation of the South African rand against the dollar forced several revaluations in the following four years, in order to contain import costs and domestic inflation. In June 1980 the pula was linked to a trade-weighted 'basket' of currencies, in order to minimize such disruptions. After 1982 the relationship between the US dollar and the South African rand began to reverse, while the pula strengthened in relation to the rand as the annual rate of domestic inflation fell from 12.7% in 1982 to 5.5% in late 1984, considerably below the South African rate. The result was a series of trade-orientated devaluations during 1982-85. From the early 1980s onwards, Botswana's exchange controls have been liberal by African standards, and more liberal than those of South Africa. In January 1995 a major liberalization of controls was introduced by the Bank of Botswana (the central bank). Following these relaxations, the Bank of Botswana monitored foreign-currency transactions closely to assess the effects of the reforms. They were found to be sufficiently favourable to foreshadow further liberalizations for 1996. A number of companies reported that the reforms significantly reduced their commercial overheads in Botswana. The exchange rate of the pula depreciated by 14.5% against the US dollar during the year to 31 December 1998, but appreciated by 3.1% against the South African rand. Domestic inflation averaged 11.4% per year in 1988-95 but then began to decline, from 10.5% in 1995 to 10.1% in 1996, 8.7% in 1997, 6.5% in 1998 and 7.2% in 1999.

At April 2000 the annualized rate of inflation was 7.0%, compared to 6.4% in March. Nevertheless, for an economy as open as Botswana's, even in a year of considerable global upheaval such as 1998, the rate of inflation has remained remarkably stable. In February 2000 the minister of finance and development emphasized the need to restrain inflation in order to avoid loss of competitiveness of the pula, particularly with respect to overseas markets, given the abolition of all exchange controls.

Botswana's balance-of-payments situation has also been helped by its low debt burden. The country's total external debt at the end of 1998 was US $548.2m., a sum which could be paid off completely out of the country's foreign reserves 10 times over. Total disbursements of loans from foreign sources was only $20.0m. in 1998. The cost of servicing Botswana's external debt in that year was $78.6m. A full year of Botswana's debt-servicing costs could be more than covered by one month's export earnings.

GOVERNMENT FINANCE

At independence about one-half of Botswana's public expenditure was financed directly by the government of the United Kingdom. This extreme level of reliance on external support was altered by Botswana's accession to SACU in 1969, and the country had become financially independent of the United Kingdom by 1972/73. From 1977/78 until 1982/83 customs revenue constituted the principal component of government income, but since then this source has been overtaken by mineral revenue, which in 1997/98 accounted for 57.3% of total revenue excluding grants, compared with 14.5% for customs revenue. In the outturn, 1999/2000 budget total revenues and grants of P11,922m. were 13.8% higher than had been envisaged. Although a budgetary deficit of P400m. had been forecast for 1999, revised estimates indicated a surplus of P510m. For 2000/2001 total revenues and grants were forecast at P11,777m., against total expenditure and net lending of P11,730m. Of the spending total, P8,188m. was for recurrent expenditure, P3,434m. was for development expenditure and P168m. was allocated to the Financial Assistance Policy.

EMPLOYMENT AND WAGES

Botswana's annual population growth rate peaked in 1981, at 4.7%, and then slowed thereafter. In its 1998 revision of world population prospects, the UN disclosed that in the early 1990s 91% of all AIDS deaths in the world occurred in just 34 developing countries, of which 29 were in Africa, with the most adversely affected country being Botswana, where one in every four adults was infected by HIV. The average life expectancy in Botswana, according to the UN, would have been 67 years in 1995-2000 in the absence of HIV/AIDS, but instead was estimated at 47 years for the same period; furthermore, it is expected to fall to 41 years in 2000-2005. The UN's population-growth forecasts for Botswana have also been revised downward, to 1.9% per annum in 1995-2000 and to 1.2% per annum in 2000-2005. Botswana's high fertility rate, nevertheless, will counteract the effects of HIV and AIDS, and the UN forecasts that the country's population will still double between 1995 and 2050. The impact of the HIV/AIDS epidemic on the country's economy will certainly be significant. On the one hand, a slower growth rate will mean that the challenge to create jobs for school leavers will not be quite so difficult, but on the other hand, companies often point to a shortage of skills as a major constraint on investment, and government resources spent on training a skilled labour force will be diluted, if one in four people trained has a shorter working life.

During the 1980s Botswana experienced rapid urbanization; of the total population, only 18.2% lived in urban areas in 1981, whereas 45.7% lived in urban areas by 1991. The rate of urban drift slowed somewhat during the 1990s and had reached only 48.2% by 1996. The unemployment rate rose from 10.2% in 1981 to 14% in 1991 and to 21.2% in 1994, before declining slightly to 19.6% in 1998. In September 1999 255,618 Batswana were in formal-sector employment, up 5.8% from the 241,662 in September 1998. Between September 1998 and September 1999 general government employment grew by 3.2%, from 101,955 to 105,248, while employment in the private and parastatal sector increased by 7.6%, from 139,707 to 150,370. This increase exceeds the downwardly revised overall rate of population growth, but the challenge of finding jobs for the still high number of school leavers entering the labour market each year remains a priority. Whereas 57% of those in formal-sector employment worked in the private sector in March 1997, more than one-half of the 12,200 jobs created in the following 12 months were in the public sector. The number of Batswana working in South African mines, which stood at a record 25,500 in 1976, had fallen to 12,464 by 1997, and because priority in mine employment was being given to South African citizens, that figure was unlikely to rise. The informal sector, engaged mainly in wholesale and retail trade and in light manufacturing, comprised some 57,240 workers in 1998, of whom about 42% were self-employed.

The government in 2000 was studying the informal sector with some intensity, in view of its job-creation potential. Job creation had long been a stated priority in government planning, and the eighth NDP was no exception, placing emphasis on economic diversification as a means of generating employment and reducing poverty. The plan also embraced external-sector liberalization, the rationalization of public-sector activities through restructuring and downsizing, and privatization. The focus of government activity was on infrastructural development and on the development of human resources as a means of supporting the private sector, which was to carry the hope of job creation. However, workers who were already in employment were exerting upward pressure on wage rates in 1998, at the same time restricting companies' ability to create new jobs. Efforts were being made to link pay rises to increased productivity, as the only way to resolve the issue.

Statistical Survey

Source (unless otherwise stated): Central Statistics Office, Private Bag 0024, Gaborone; tel. 352200; fax 352201.

Area and Population

AREA, POPULATION AND DENSITY

Area (sq km)	581,730*
Population (census results)	
16 August 1981.	941,027†
21 August 1991	
Males	634,400
Females	692,396
Total	1,326,796
Population (official estimates at 19 August)	
1996	1,495,993
1997	1,533,393
1998	1,572,000
Density (per sq km) at August 1998	2.7

* 224,607 sq miles.
† Excluding 42,069 citizens absent from the country during enumeration.

POPULATION BY ADMINISTRATIVE DISTRICT
(August 1997 estimates)

Barolong	. . .	19,837	Lobatse . . .	29,872
Central	. . .	457,349	Ngamiland. . .	62,403
Chobe .	. . .	16,845	Ngwaketse. . .	143,370
Francistown	. .	88,195	North-East . .	47,312
Gaborone	. . .	183,487	Okavango . . .	41,687
Ghanzi	. . .	27,099	Orapa . . .	10,244
Jwaneng	. .	14,866	Selebi-Phikwe .	45,651
Kgalagadi	. . .	34,537	South-East . .	54,091
Kgatleng	. . .	63,712	Sowa	3,154
Kweneng	. . .	189,672		

PRINCIPAL TOWNS (estimated population, August 1988)

Gaborone (capital)	.	110,973	Kanye . . .	26,300
Francistown	. .	49,396	Mahalapye . .	26,239
Selebi-Phikwe	.	46,490	Lobatse . . .	25,689
Molepolole	. .	29,212	Maun . . .	18,470
Serowe	. .	28,267	Ramotswa . .	17,961
Mochudi	. .	26,320		

August 1991 (census results): Gaborone 133,468; Francistown 65,244; Selebi-Phikwe 39,772; Lobatse 26,052.

BIRTHS AND DEATHS (UN estimates, annual averages)

	1980–85	1985–90	1990–95
Birth rate (per 1,000) . . .	44.1	40.2	36.8
Death rate (per 1,000) . . .	9.5	7.7	8.0

Expectation of life (UN estimates, years at birth, 1990–95): 61.2 (males 59.5; females 62.9).

Source: UN, *World Population Prospects: The 1998 Revision.*

ECONOMICALLY ACTIVE POPULATION*
(sample survey, persons aged 12 years and over, year ending August 1996)

	Males	Females	Total
Agriculture, hunting, forestry and fishing	37,050	16,729	53,779
Mining and quarrying . . .	12,754	2,379	15,133
Manufacturing	14,157	15,373	29,530
Electricity, gas and water supply .	2,633	172	2,805
Construction	28,096	12,929	41,025
Wholesale and retail trade; repair of motor vehicles, motorcycles and personal and household goods	19,526	24,615	44,141
Hotels and restaurants . . .	2,524	7,491	10,015
Transport, storage and communications	5,778	1,937	7,715
Financial intermediation . . .	1,781	2,315	4,096
Real estate, renting and business services	5,766	1,875	7,641
Public administration and defence; compulsory social security	37,928	22,029	59,957
Education	12,377	20,854	33,231
Health and social work . . .	2,096	7,280	9,376
Other community, social and personal service activities . .	4,330	2,977	7,307
Private households with employed persons	1,957	16,997	18,954
Extra-territorial organizations and bodies	197	27	224
Activities not adequately defined .	351	125	476
Total employed	189,301	156,104	345,405
Unemployed	45,461	49,067	94,528
Total labour force . . .	234,762	205,171	439,933

* Excluding members of the armed forces and those not actively seeking work.

Source: Labour Statistics Unit, Central Statistics Office.

Mid-1998 (estimates, '000 persons): Agriculture, etc. 309; Total labour force 689. (Source: FAO, *Production Yearbook*).

Agriculture

PRINCIPAL CROPS ('000 metric tons)

	1996	1997	1998
Wheat*	1	1	1
Maize	23†	12	1†
Millet*	4	2	1
Sorghum	55*	17	7*
Roots and tubers*	9	10	10
Pulses*	16	15	12
Cottonseed*	2	2	1
Cotton (lint)*	1	1	1
Vegetables*	17	16	15
Fruit*	12	11	8

* FAO estimate(s).   † Unofficial figure.
Source: FAO, *Production Yearbook*.

LIVESTOCK (FAO estimates, '000 head, year ending September)

	1996	1997	1998
Cattle	2,400	2,420	2,330
Horses	32	33	33
Asses	232	235	238
Sheep	240	250	240
Goats	1,850	1,870	1,820
Pigs	3	4	4

Poultry (FAO estimates, million): 2 in 1996; 2 in 1997; 2 in 1998.
Source: FAO, *Production Yearbook*.

LIVESTOCK PRODUCTS (FAO estimates, '000 metric tons)

	1996	1997	1998
Beef and veal	44	46	40
Goat meat	5	5	5
Poultry meat	7	7	7
Other meat	11	11	11
Cows' milk	102	102	98
Goats' milk	3	3	3
Cheese	2	2	2
Butter and ghee	1	1	1
Hen eggs	1	2	2
Cattle hides	6	6	5

Source: FAO, *Production Yearbook*.

Forestry

ROUNDWOOD REMOVALS ('000 cubic metres, excl. bark)

	1995	1996	1997
Industrial wood	96	98	100
Fuel wood	1,450	1,484	1,518
Total	1,546	1,582	1,618

Source: FAO, *Yearbook of Forest Products*.

Fishing

(FAO estimates, metric tons, live weight)

	1995	1996	1997
Total catch (freshwater fishes)	2,000	2,100	2,000

Source: FAO, *Yearbook of Fishery Statistics*.

Mining

(metric tons, unless otherwise indicated)

	1996	1997	1998
Diamonds ('000 carats)	17,707	20,121	19,773
Copper*	20,979	18,350	19,432
Nickel*	17,461	14,996	15,593
Cobalt*	405	348	352
Soda ash	119,137	199,990	195,500
Salt	93,886	184,533	214,700
Coal	763,000	776,917	928,100
Clay (cu metres)	81,900	73,700	82,500
Crushed stone (cu metres)	845,526	1,091,877	997,244

* Figures refer to the metal content of ores.
Source: *Mining Journal*.

Industry

SELECTED PRODUCTS

	1994	1995	1996
Beer ('000 hectolitres)	1,305	1,366	1,351
Soft drinks ('000 hectolitres)	278	293	308
Electric energy (million kWh)	1,088	1,070*	n.a.

* Provisional or estimated figure.
Source: UN, *Industrial Commodity Statistics Yearbook*.

Finance

CURRENCY AND EXCHANGE RATES
Monetary Units
100 thebe = 1 pula (P).

Sterling, Dollar and Euro Equivalents (28 April 2000)
£1 sterling = 7.940 pula;
US $1 = 5.063 pula;
€1 = 4.600 pula;
100 pula = £12.59 = $19.75 = €21.74.

Average Exchange Rate (pula per US $)
1997   3.6508
1998   4.2259
1999   4.6244

BUDGET (million pula, year ending 31 March)

Revenue*	1996/97	1997/98	1998/99†
Taxation	5,198.5	6,766.1	5,636.5
Mineral revenues	3,640.1	4,681.1	3,186.6
Customs pool revenues	896.2	1,186.1	1,261.3
Non-mineral income tax	385.0	537.4	739.3
General sales tax	248.4	327.9	400.5
Other current revenue	2,113.3	1,401.8	1,900.3
Interest	235.4	257.1	208.6
Other property income	1,740.3	984.5	1,252.9
Fees, charges, etc.	111.6	133.5	378.0
Sales of fixed assets and land	26.0	32.5	60.8
Total	7,311.8	8,167.9	7,536.8

* Excluding grants received (million pula): 83.0 in 1996/97; 112.1 in 1997/98; 137.7 in 1998/99.
† Provisional figures.

Expenditure*	1996/97	1997/98	1998/99
General services (incl. defence) .	1,633.3	2,027.9	2,608.4
Education	1,518.0	1,786.2	2,275.7
Health	299.2	411.2	468.4
Housing, urban and regional development	503.3	554.9	669.7
Food and social welfare programme	65.1	160.2	320.9
Other community and social services	96.0	131.4	270.4
Economic services	1,533.3	1,796.8	1,679.8
Agriculture, forestry and fishing	513.3	379.2	440.0
Mining	64.4	58.5	201.2
Electricity and water supply .	332.1	704.4	451.1
Roads	276.0	321.8	390.9
Interest on public debt . .	91.4	86.2	94.6
Deficit grants to local authorities .	472.1	567.5	706.0
Other grants	72.0	102.0	108.0
Total	**6,283.4**	**7,624.3**	**9,201.9**

* Figures refer to recurrent and development expenditure, excluding net lending (million pula): −191.1 in 1996/97; −218.1 in 1997/98; −134.3 in 1998/99.

Source: Bank of Botswana, Gaborone.

INTERNATIONAL RESERVES (US $ million at 31 December)

	1997	1998	1999
IMF special drawing rights . .	40.96	45.63	38.50
Reserve position in IMF . . .	24.46	38.87	31.00
Foreign exchange . . .	5,675.00	5,940.67	6,229.21
Total	**5,740.42**	**6,025.17**	**6,298.72**

Source: IMF, *International Financial Statistics.*

MONEY SUPPLY (million pula at 31 December)

	1997	1998	1999
Currency outside banks . . .	276	353	404
Demand deposits at commercial banks	762	1,160	1,371
Total money	**1,038**	**1,513**	**1,775**

Source: IMF, *International Financial Statistics.*

COST OF LIVING (Consumer Price Index; base: 1990 = 100)

	1995	1996	1997
Food (incl. beverages) . .	182.9	207.0	228.3
Clothing (incl. footwear) . .	198.0	219.1	239.9
All items (incl. others) . .	**181.4**	**199.8**	**217.2**

Source: ILO, *Yearbook of Labour Statistics.*

1998: Food 242.3; All items 231.4 (Source: UN, *Monthly Bulletin of Statistics*).

NATIONAL ACCOUNTS
(million pula at current prices, year ending 30 June)
National Income and Product

	1985/86	1986/87	1987/88
Compensation of employees . .	700.7	849.6	1,051.6
Operating surplus	1,216.7	1,312.3	1,936.3
Domestic factor incomes . .	**1,917.4**	**2,161.9**	**2,987.9**
Consumption of fixed capital . .	349.8	432.4	575.6
Gross domestic product (GDP) at factor cost . . .	**2,267.2**	**2,594.3**	**3,563.5**
Indirect taxes	160.4	226.2	251.2
Less Subsidies	7.0	10.7	19.1
GDP in purchasers' values .	**2,420.6**	**2,809.8**	**3,795.6**
Factor income received from abroad	173.0	225.9	308.7
Less Factor income paid abroad .	495.8	477.9	773.8
Gross national product . .	**2,097.8**	**2,557.8**	**3,330.5**
Less Consumption of fixed capital .	349.8	432.4	575.6
National income in market prices	**1,748.0**	**2,125.4**	**2,754.9**
Other current transfers from abroad	141.5	123.2	115.1
Less Other current transfers paid abroad . . .	68.5	78.6	233.3
National disposable income .	**1,821.0**	**2,169.9**	**2,636.7**

Source: UN, *National Accounts Statistics.*

Expenditure on the Gross Domestic Product (provisional figures)

	1996/97	1997/98	1998/99
Government final consumption expenditure . . .	4,908.1	5,812.2	6,705.7
Private final consumption expenditure . . .	5,410.5	6,587.8	8,673.2
Increase in stocks . . .	−162.5	699.5	1,730.8
Gross fixed capital formation . .	4,176.5	5,047.1	6,433.8
Total domestic expenditure .	**14,332.6**	**18,146.6**	**23,543.4**
Exports of goods and services .	9,988.0	11,359.7	9,863.9
Less Imports of goods and services	6,834.9	9,143.2	10,148.5
GDP in purchasers' values .	**17,485.7**	**20,363.1**	**23,258.9**
GDP at constant 1993/94 prices	**12,838.4**	**13,868.6**	**14,451.0**

Source: Bank of Botswana, Gaborone.

Gross Domestic Product by Economic Activity (provisional figures)

	1996/97	1997/98	1998/99
Agriculture, hunting, forestry and fishing	602.7	635.3	644.2
Mining and quarrying . . .	6,469.1	7,682.2	8,148.8
Manufacturing	866.1	988.2	1,093.6
Water and electricity . . .	316.0	366.3	440.8
Construction	1,016.5	1,152.7	1,382.3
Trade, restaurants and hotels .	3,019.6	3,527.6	2,750.6
Transport	686.5	791.5	946.6
Finance, insurance and business services	1,816.1	2,068.6	2,438.9
Government services	2,490.3	2,969.6	3,722.1
Social and personal services . .	682.0	785.7	911.3
Sub-total	**17,964.9**	**20,967.7**	**22,479.2**
Customs duties*	—	—	1,419.2
Less Imputed bank service charge .	462.1	539.3	639.6
GDP in purchasers' values . .	**17,502.9**	**20,428.3**	**23,258.8**

* Prior to 1998/99 customs duties were not separated from the various sectors of economic activity.

Source: Bank of Botswana, Gaborone.

BALANCE OF PAYMENTS (US $ million)

	1996	1997	1998
Exports of goods f.o.b.	2,217.5	2,819.8	2,060.6
Imports of goods f.o.b.	−1,467.7	−1,924.4	−1,983.1
Trade balance	749.8	895.4	77.5
Exports of services	163.0	210.2	255.3
Imports of services	−343.6	−440.7	−522.4
Balance on goods and services	569.2	664.9	−189.6
Other income received	501.7	622.1	622.7
Other income paid	−754.8	−766.9	−503.1
Balance on goods, services and income	316.1	520.1	70.0
Current transfers received	355.4	456.8	460.9
Current transfers paid	−176.6	−255.5	−220.8
Current balance	495.0	721.5	170.1
Capital account (net)	6.2	16.9	31.8
Direct investment abroad	1.1	−4.1	−3.5
Direct investment from abroad	71.2	100.1	95.3
Portfolio investment assets	−35.5	−43.9	−37.6
Portfolio investment liabilities	31.0	10.8	−14.1
Other investment assets	−95.6	−166.5	−310.8
Other investment liabilities	70.3	109.3	68.2
Net errors and omissions	−32.9	−108.9	63.0
Overall balance	510.7	635.1	62.6

Source: IMF, *International Financial Statistics*.

External Trade

PRINCIPAL COMMODITIES (US $ million)

Imports c.i.f.	1996	1997	1998
Food, beverages and tobacco	292	297	306
Fuels	110	127	125
Chemicals and rubber products	176	205	211
Wood and paper products	126	140	144
Textiles and footwear	129	146	150
Metals and metal products	152	241	249
Machinery and electrical equipment	278	398	410
Vehicles and transport equipment	243	452	465
Total (incl. others)	1,727	2,260	2,326

Exports f.o.b.	1996	1997	1998
Meat and meat products	62	63	79
Diamonds	1,721	2,095	1,477
Copper-nickel matte	134	127	61
Textiles	59	68	39
Vehicles and parts	345	324	331
Total (incl. others)	2,449	2,846	2,206

Source: IMF, *Botswana: Selected Issues and Statistical Appendix* (Nov. 1999).

PRINCIPAL TRADING PARTNERS (million pula)

Imports c.i.f.	1996	1997	1998*
SACU†	4,474	5,982	6,972
Zimbabwe	329	368	418
United Kingdom	147	163	161
Other Europe	241	580	915
Korea, Repub.	250	785	699
USA	74	89	152
Total (incl. others)	5,735	8,256	9,839

Exports f.o.b.	1996	1997	1998*
SACU†	1,490	1,485	1,333
Zimbabwe	251	383	343
Other Africa	51	114	102
United Kingdom	4,424	5,840	5,240
Other Europe	1,827	2,444	2,193
USA	78	102	91
Total (incl. others)	8,142	10,391	9,324

* Estimates.

† Southern African Customs Union, of which Botswana is a member; also including Lesotho, Namibia, South Africa and Swaziland.

Source: IMF, *Botswana: Selected Issues and Statistical Appendix* (Nov. 1999).

Transport

RAILWAYS (traffic)

	1996/97	1997/98	1998/99
Number of passengers ('000)	574	494	360
Passenger-km (million)	96	94	89
Freight ('000 metric tons)	1,967	2,568	2,812
Freight net ton-km (million)	795	1,111	1,282

Source: Botswana Railways.

ROAD TRAFFIC (vehicles registered at 31 December)

	1993	1994	1995
Passenger cars	26,320	27,058	30,517
Lorries and vans	51,352	57,235	59,710
Others	16,938	17,153	17,448
Total	94,610	101,446	107,675

CIVIL AVIATION (traffic on scheduled services)

	1994	1995	1996
Kilometres flown (million)	2	2	2
Passengers carried ('000)	101	100	104
Passenger-km (million)	58	53	51
Total ton-km (million)	6	5	5

Source: UN, *Statistical Yearbook*.

Tourism

FOREIGN TOURIST ARRIVALS (incl. same-day visitors)*

Country of origin	1995	1996	1997
South Africa	491,000	545,306	561,375
United Kingdom and Ireland	41,810	42,275	43,520
Zambia	32,162	34,975	36,006
Zimbabwe	337,697	336,889	346,817
Total (incl. others)	1,020,000	1,052,000	1,083,000

* Figures refer to arrivals at frontiers of visitors from abroad.

Receipts from tourism (US $ million): 162 in 1995; 181 in 1996; 184 in 1997.

Source: World Tourism Organization, *Yearbook of Tourism Statistics*.

Communications Media

	1994	1995	1996
Radio receivers ('000 in use) . .	180	190	230
Television receivers ('000 in use) .	24	27	29
Daily newspapers:			
Number	1	1	1
Average circulation ('000 copies)	35	45	40
Non-daily newspapers:			
Number	n.a.	5	3
Average circulation ('000 copies)	n.a.	79	51

Book production (first editions only, 1991): 158 titles, including 61 pamphlets.

Other periodicals (1992): 14 titles (average circulation 177,000 copies).

1997: Radio receivers ('000 in use) 237; Television receivers ('000 in use) 31.

Source: UNESCO, *Statistical Yearbook*.

Telephones ('000 main lines in use, year ending 31 March): 50 in 1994/95; 60 in 1995/96; 72 in 1996/97 (Source: UN, *Statistical Yearbook*).

Telefax stations (estimated number in use, year ending 31 March): 2,100 in 1994/95; 3,149 in 1995/96; 3,413 in 1996/97 (Source: UN, *Statistical Yearbook*).

Education

(1998)

	Institutions	Teachers	Students
Primary	721	11,617	323,348
Secondary	272	7,977	143,503
Brigades*	31	492	4,022
Teacher training . . .	4	207	1,056
Technical education . . .	15	524	5,917
Colleges of education . . .	2	170	1,257
Agricultural college . . .	1	87†	392†
University	1	507‡	8,598

* Semi-autonomous units providing craft and practical training.

† 1997 figure.

‡ 1994 figure.

Source: Ministry of Education, Gaborone.

Directory

The Constitution

The Constitution of the Republic of Botswana took effect at independence on 30 September 1966; it was amended in August and September 1997.

EXECUTIVE

President

Executive power lies with the President of Botswana, who is also Commander-in-Chief of the armed forces. Election for the office of President is linked with the election of members of the National Assembly. The President is restricted to two terms of office. Presidential candidates must be over 30 years of age and receive at least 1,000 nominations. If there is more than one candidate for the Presidency, each candidate for office in the Assembly must declare support for a presidential candidate. The candidate for President who commands the votes of more than one-half of the elected members of the Assembly will be declared President. In the event of the death or resignation of the President, the Vice-President will automatically assume the Presidency. The President, who is an *ex-officio* member of the National Assembly, holds office for the duration of Parliament. The President chooses four members of the National Assembly.

Cabinet

There is also a Vice-President, whose office is ministerial. The Vice-President is appointed by the President and deputizes in the absence of the President. The Cabinet consists of the President, the Vice-President and other Ministers, including Assistant Ministers, appointed by the President. The Cabinet is responsible to the National Assembly.

LEGISLATURE

Legislative power is vested in Parliament, consisting of the President and the National Assembly, acting after consultation in certain cases with the House of Chiefs. The President may withhold assent to a Bill passed by the National Assembly. If the same Bill is again presented after six months, the President is required to assent to it or to dissolve Parliament within 21 days.

House of Chiefs

The House of Chiefs comprises the Chiefs of the eight principal tribes of Botswana as *ex-officio* members, four members elected by sub-chiefs from their own number, and three members elected by the other 12 members of the House. Bills and motions relating to chieftaincy matters and alterations of the Constitution must be referred to the House, which may also deliberate and make representations on any matter.

National Assembly

The National Assembly consists of 40 members directly elected by universal adult suffrage, together with four members who are elected by the National Assembly from a list of candidates submitted by the President; the President and the Attorney-General are also *ex-officio* members of the Assembly. The life of the Assembly is five years.

The Constitution contains a code of human rights, enforceable by the High Court.

The Government

HEAD OF STATE

President: Festus G. Mogae (took office 1 April 1998; sworn in 20 October 1999).

Vice-President: Lt-Gen. Seretse Ian Khama (sworn in 13 July 1998).

CABINET

(September 2000)

President: Festus G. Mogae.

Vice-President: Lt-Gen. Seretse Ian Khama.

Minister of Presidential Affairs and Public Administration: Thebe Mogami.

Minister of Health: Joy Phumaphi.

Minister of Agriculture: Johnnie Swartz.

Minister of Foreign Affairs: Lt-Gen. Mompati Merafhe.

Minister of Minerals, Energy and Water Affairs: Boometswe Mokgothu.

Minister of Commerce and Industry: Tebelelo Seretse.

Minister of Local Government: Margaret Nasha.

Minister of Works, Transport and Communications: David Magang.

Minister of Finance and Development Planning: Baledzi Gaolathe.

Minister of Education: George Kgoroba.

Minister of Labour and Home Affairs: Daniel Kwelagobe.

Minister of Lands and Housing: Jacob Nkate.

In addition, there are four Assistant Ministers.

MINISTRIES

Office of the President: Private Bag 001, Gaborone; tel. 350800; fax 312525.

Ministry of Agriculture: Private Bag 003, Gaborone; tel. 350603; fax 356027.

Ministry of Commerce and Industry: Private Bag 004, Gaborone; tel. 3601200; fax 371538.

Ministry of Education: Private Bag 005, Gaborone; tel. 3655400; fax 3655458.

Ministry of Finance and Development Planning: Private Bag 008, Gaborone; tel. 350100; fax 356086; e-mail kbaleseng@gov.bw.

Ministry of Foreign Affairs: Private Bag 00368, Gaborone; tel. 3600700; fax 313366.

Ministry of Health: Private Bag 0038, Gaborone; tel. 352000; fax 353100; e-mail lmanthe@gov.bw.

Ministry of Labour and Home Affairs: Private Bag 002, Gaborone; tel. 611100; fax 313584.

Ministry of Lands and Housing: Private Bag 006, Gaborone; tel. 354100; fax 352382.

Ministry of Local Government: Private Bag 006, Gaborone; tel. 354100; fax 352091.

Ministry of Minerals, Energy and Water Affairs: Khama Crescent, Private Bag 0018, Gaborone; tel. 3656600; fax 372738.

Ministry of Presidential Affairs and Public Administration: Private Bag 001, Gaborone; tel. 350800.

Ministry of Works, Transport and Communications: Private Bag 007, Gaborone; tel. 358500; and fax 313303.

Legislature

HOUSE OF CHIEFS

The House has a total of 15 members.

Chairman: Chief TAWANA II.

NATIONAL ASSEMBLY

Speaker: RAY MATLAPENG MOLOMO.

General Election, 16 October 1999

Party	Votes	%	Seats
Botswana Democratic Party	192,598	57.2	33
Botswana National Front	87,457	26.0	6
Botswana Congress Party	40,096	11.9	1
Botswana Alliance Movement	15,805	4.7	—
Others	1,026	0.3	—
Total	336,982	100.0	40*

* The President and the Attorney-General are also *ex-officio* members of the National Assembly.

Political Organizations

Botswana Alliance Movement (BAM): Private Bag BO 210, Gaborone; tel. 313476; fax 314634; f. 1998 as an alliance of three opposition parties to contest the 1999 general election; Botswana People's Party withdrew in July 2000; Leader LEPETU SETSHWAELO.

    Independence Freedom Party (IFP): POB 3, Maun; f. by merger of Botswana Freedom Party and Botswana Independence Party; Pres. MOTSAMAI K. MPHO.

    United Action Party (UAP): Private Bag BO 210, Gaborone; f. 1998; Leader LEPETU SETSHWAELO.

Botswana Congress Party (BCP): POB 2918, Gaborone; tel. and fax 581805; f. 1998, following a split in the Botswana National Front; Leader MICHAEL DINGAKE.

Botswana Democratic Party (BDP): POB 28, Tsholetsa House, Gaborone; tel. 352564; fax 313911; e-mail domkrag@info.bw; f. 1962; Pres. FESTUS G. MOGAE; Chair. PONATSHEGO KEDIKILWE; Sec.-Gen. DANIEL K. KWELAGOBE.

Botswana Labour Party: POB 140, Mahalopye; f. 1989; Pres. LENYELETSE KOMA.

Botswana National Front (BNF): POB 1720, Gaborone; tel. 351789; fax 584970; f. 1966; Pres. Dr KENNETH KOMA; Sec.-Gen. Dr BADZIYILI NFILA.

Botswana People's Party (BPP): POB 484, Francistown; f. 1960; Pres. MOTLATSI MOLAPISI; Chair. JOSEPH MOGOTLE; Sec.-Gen. KOPANO CHINGAPANE.

Botswana Progressive Union (BPU): POB 328, Nkange; f. 1982; Leader G. KAELO.

Botswana Workers' Front (BWF): POB 597, Jweneng; tel. 380420; f. 1993; Leader M. M. AKANYANG.

MELS Movement of Botswana: POB 501818, Gaborone; tel. and fax 306005; f. 1993; Leader T. JOINA.

Social Democratic Party (SDP): POB 201818, Gaborone; tel. 356516; f. 1994; Leader Ms O. MARUMO.

United Socialist Party (USP): POB 233, Lobatse; f. 1994; Leader N. MODUBULE.

Diplomatic Representation

EMBASSIES AND HIGH COMMISSIONS IN BOTSWANA

Angola: 5131 Kopanyo House, Nelson Mandela Rd, Private Bag BR 111, Gaborone; tel. 300204; fax 375089; Ambassador: EVARISTO DOMINGOS KIMBA.

China, People's Republic: 3096 North Ring Rd, POB 1031, Gaborone; tel. 352209; fax 300156; Ambassador: BAO SHUSHENG.

Germany: Professional House, Broadhurst, Segodithsane Way, POB 315, Gaborone; tel. 353143; fax 353038; Ambassador: Dr IRENE HINRICHSEN.

India: 5375 President's Dr., Private Bag 249, Gaborone; tel. 372676; fax 374636; e-mail hicomind@global.bw; High Commissioner: RAJEET MITTER.

Libya: POB 180, Plot 8851 (Government Enclave), Gaborone; tel. 352481; Ambassador: JUMA MOHAMED JUBAIL.

Namibia: POB 987, 2nd Floor, Debswana House, Gaborone; tel. 302181; fax 302248; e-mail nhc.gabs@info.bw; High Commissioner: Dr JOSEPH HOEBEB.

Nigeria: POB 274, The Mall, Gaborone; tel. 313561; fax 313738; High Commissioner: Ms HARRISON-OBAFEMI.

Russia: Plot 4711 Tawana Close, POB 81, Gaborone; tel. 353389; fax 352930; e-mail embarus@info.bw; Ambassador: VALERII A. KALUGIN.

South Africa: Private Bag 00402, Kopanyo House, Plot 5131, Nelson Mandela Dr., Gaborone; tel. 304800; fax 305501; High Commissioner: (vacant).

Sweden: Development House, Private Bag 0017, Gaborone; tel. 353912; fax 353942; e-mail swembgab@global.co.za; Ambassador: CHRISTINA REHLEN.

United Kingdom: Private Bag 0023, Gaborone; tel. 352841; fax 356105; e-mail british@bc.bw; internet www.british.global.bw; High Commissioner: JOHN WILDE.

USA: POB 90, Gaborone; tel. 353982; fax 356947; Ambassador: Dr JOHN E. LANGE.

Zambia: POB 362, Gaborone; tel. 351951; fax 353952; High Commissioner: J. PHIRI.

Zimbabwe: Plot 8850, POB 1232, Gaborone; tel. 314495; fax 305863; High Commissioner: (vacant).

Judicial System

There is a High Court at Lobatse and a branch at Francistown, and Magistrates' Courts in each district. Appeals lie to the Court of Appeal of Botswana. The Chief Justice and the President of the Court of Appeal are appointed by the President.

High Court: Private Bag 1, Lobatse; tel. 330396; fax 332317.

Chief Justice: JULIAN NGANUNU.

President of the Court of Appeal: A. N. E. AMISSAH.

Justices of Appeal: T. A. AGUDA, W. H. R. SCHREINER, J. STEYN, P. H. TEBBUTT, W. COWIE, G. G. HOEXTER, W. ALLANBRIDGE.

Puisne Judges: I. R. ABOAGYE, J. B. GITTINGS, M. DIBOTELO, M. GAEFELE, J. Z. MASOJANE, I. K. B. LESETEDI (acting).

Registrar and Master: W. G. GRANTE.

Office of the Attorney-General: Private Bag 009, Gaborone; tel. 354700; fax 357089.

Attorney-General: PHANDU SKELEMANI.

Religion

The majority of the population hold animist beliefs; an estimated 30% are thought to be Christians. There are Islamic mosques in Gaborone and Lobatse. The Bahá'í Faith is also represented.

CHRISTIANITY

Lekgotla la Sekeresete la Botswana (Botswana Christian Council): POB 355, Gaborone; tel. 351981; f. 1966; comprises 34 churches and organizations; Pres. Rev. K. F. MOKOBIJ; Gen. Sec. DAVID J. MODIEGA.

The Anglican Communion

Anglicans are adherents of the Church of the Province of Central Africa, comprising 12 dioceses and covering Botswana, Malawi, Zambia and Zimbabwe. The Province was established in 1955, and the diocese of Botswana was formed in 1972.

Archbishop of the Province of Central Africa and Bishop of Botswana: Most Rev. WALTER PAUL KHOTSO MAKHULU, POB 769, Gaborone; fax 313015; e-mail acenter@info.bw.

Protestant Churches

African Methodist Episcopal Church: POB 141, Lobatse; Rev. L. M. MBULAWA.

Evangelical Lutheran Church in Botswana: POB 1976, Gaborone; tel. 352227; fax 313966; Bishop Rev. PHILIP ROBINSON; 16,305 mems.

Evangelical Lutheran Church in Southern Africa (Botswana Diocese): POB 400, Gaborone; tel. 353976; Bishop Rev. M. NTUPING.

Methodist Church in Botswana: POB 260, Gaborone; Dist. Supt Rev. Z. S. M. MOSAI.

United Congregational Church of Southern Africa (Synod of Botswana): POB 1263, Gaborone; tel. 352491; Synod status since 1980; Chair. Rev. D. T. MAPITSE; Sec. Rev. M. P. P. DIBEELA; 24,000 mems.

Other denominations active in Botswana include the Church of God in Christ, the Dutch Reformed Church, the United Methodist Church and the Seventh-day Adventists.

The Roman Catholic Church

Botswana comprises one diocese and an apostolic vicariate. The metropolitan see is Bloemfontein, South Africa. The church was established in Botswana in 1928, and had an estimated 76,587 adherents (some 5.5% of the total population) in the country at 31 December 1998. The Bishop participates in the Southern African Catholic Bishops' Conference, currently based in Pretoria, South Africa.

Bishop of Gaborone: Rt Rev. BONIFACE TSHOSA SETLALEKGOSI, POB 218, Bishop's House, Gaborone; tel. 312958; fax 356970.

Vicar Apostolic of Francistown: Rt Rev. FRANKLYN NUBUASAH.

The Press

DAILY NEWSPAPER

Dikgang tsa Gompieno (Daily News): Private Bag 0060, Gaborone; tel. 352541; f. 1964; publ. by Dept of Information and Broadcasting; Setswana and English; Mon.–Fri.; Editor L. LESHAGA; circ. 50,000.

PERIODICALS

Agrinews: Private Bag 003, Gaborone; f. 1971; monthly; agriculture and rural development; circ. 6,000.

Botswana Advertiser: POB 130, 5647 Nakedi Rd, Broadhurst, Gaborone; tel. 312844; weekly.

The Botswana Gazette: POB 1605, Gaborone; tel. 312833; fax 372283; weekly; circ. 16,000; Publisher CLARA OLSEN.

Botswana Guardian: POB 1641, Gaborone; tel. 308408; fax 308457; e-mail guardsun@info.bw; f. 1982; weekly; Editor OUTSA MOKONE; circ. 20,792.

Business and Financial Times: POB 402396, Gaborone; tel. 586397; fax 561700; e-mail bftimes@info.bw.

Government Gazette: Private Bag 0081, Gaborone; tel. 314441; fax 312001; weekly.

Kutlwano: Private Bag 0060, Gaborone; tel. 352541; monthly; Setswana and English; publ. by Dept of Information and Broadcasting; circ. 24,000.

The Midweek Sun: POB 1641, Gaborone; tel. 308408; fax 308457; e-mail guardsun@info.bw; f. 1989; weekly; Editor MIKE MOTHIBI; circ. 18,108.

Mmegi/The Reporter: Private Bag BR50, Gaborone; tel. 374784; fax 305508; e-mail mmegi@info.bw; internet www.mmegi.bw; f. 1984; weekly; Setswana and English; publ. by Dikgang Publishing Co; Man. Editor TITUS MBUYA; circ. 24,000.

Motswana Woman: 686 Botswana Rd, Gaborone; tel. 375362; fax 375378; monthly; women's interests; circ. 4,000.

Northern Advertiser: POB 402, Francistown; tel. 212265; fax 213769; e-mail rsfish@global.bw; f. 1985; weekly; advertisements, local interest, sport; Editor GRACE FISH; circ. 5,500.

The Zebra's Voice: Private Bag 00114, National Museum, Independence Ave, Gaborone; tel. 374616; f. 1982; quarterly; cultural affairs; circ. 7,000.

NEWS AGENCIES

Botswana Press Agency (BOPA): Private Bag 0060, Gaborone; tel. 313601; f. 1981.

Foreign Bureaux

Deutsche Presse-Agentur (Germany) and **Reuters** (UK) are represented in Botswana.

Publishers

A.C. Braby (Botswana) (Pty) Ltd: POB 1549, Gaborone; tel. 371444; fax 373462; telephone directories.

The Botswana Society: POB 71, Gaborone; tel. 351500; fax 359321; f. 1968; archaeology, arts, history, law, sciences.

Department of Information and Broadcasting: Private Bag 0060, Gaborone; tel. 352541; fax 357138.

Heinemann Educational Botswana (Pty) Ltd: POB 10103, Gaborone; tel. 372305; fax 371832; Man. Dir LESEDI SEITEI.

Longman Botswana (Pty) Ltd: POB 1083, Lobatse Rd, Gaborone; tel. 313969; fax 322682; e-mail joe@info.bw; f. 1981; educational; Man. Dir J. K. CHALASHIKA.

Macmillan Botswana Publishing Co (Pty) Ltd: POB 1155, Gaborone; tel. 314379; fax 374326; Gen. Man. W. UITERWIJK.

Magnum Press (Pty) Ltd: Gaborone; tel. 372852; fax 374558.

Morula Press: Business School of Botswana, POB 402492, Gaborone; tel. 353499; fax 304809; f. 1994; business, law.

Printing and Publishing Co (Botswana) (Pty) Ltd: POB 130, 5647 Nakedi Rd, Broadhurst, Gaborone; tel. 312844.

Sygma Publishing: POB 753, Gaborone; tel. 372532; fax 372531; e-mail sygma@info.bw.

Government Publishing House

Department of Government Printing and Publishing Services: Private Bag 0081, Gaborone; tel. 314441; fax 312001.

Broadcasting and Communications

TELECOMMUNICATIONS

In early 1998 two companies were granted licences to operate mobile cellular telephone networks.

Botswana Telecommunications Authority (BTA): Private Bag 00495, Gaborone; tel. 357755; fax 357976; e-mail bta@info.bw; f. 1996; Chair. C. M. LEKAUKAU.

Botswana Telecommunications Corporation: POB 700, Gaborone; tel. 358411; fax 352777; e-mail jramutsh@btc.bw; internet www.btc.bw; f. 1980; state-owned; Chair. A. V. LIONJANGA; CEO M. T. CURRY.

BROADCASTING

Department of Information and Broadcasting: Private Bag 0060, Gaborone; Dir TED MAKGEKENENE.

Radio

Radio Botswana: Private Bag 0060, Gaborone; tel. 352541; fax 357138; e-mail rbeng@info.bw; broadcasts in Setswana and English; govt-owned; f. 1965; Dir TED MAKGEKENENE; Chief Eng. HABUJI SOSOME.

Radio Botswana II: Private Bag 0060, Gaborone; tel. 352541; fax 371588; f. 1992; commercial service.

Yarona FM: Gaborone; f. 1999; independent; Gen. Man. MORAKI MOKGASANA.

Television

Botswana Television: Department of Information & Broadcasting, Private Bag 0060, Gaborone; tel. 300050; fax 300051; e-mail simon.higman@btv.bw; govt-funded national TV service; broadcasts commenced in July 2000; Gen. Man. SIMON HIGMAN.

TV Association of Botswana: Gaborone; relays SABC-TV and BOP-TV programmes from South Africa.

Finance

(cap. = capital; res = reserves; dep. = deposits; m. = million; brs = branches; amounts in pula)

BANKING

Central Bank

Bank of Botswana: POB 712, Private Bag 154, Plot 1863, Khama Crescent, Gaborone; tel. 360600; fax 301100; e-mail rakhudme@bob.bw; f. 1975; bank of issue; cap. 25m., res 3,176m., dep. 22,436.3m. (Dec. 1998); Gov. LINAH MOHOHLO.

Commercial Banks

Barclays Bank of Botswana Ltd: POB 478, Barclays House, 6th Floor, Plot 8842, Khama Crescent, Gaborone; tel. 352041; fax 353699; f. 1975; 74.9% owned by Barclays Bank PLC (UK); cap. and res 157.0m., total assets 1,768.7m. (Dec. 1997); Chair. C. TIBONE; Man. Dir C. LOWE; 48 brs, etc.

First National Bank of Botswana Ltd: POB 1552, Finance House, 5th Floor, Plot 8843, Khama Crescent, Gaborone; tel. 311669; fax 306130; e-mail jchibuye@fnb.co.za; f. 1991; 70% owned by First National Bank Holdings Botswana Ltd; cap. and res 172.7m., dep. 1,487.5m. (June 1999); Chair. H. C. L. HERMANS; Man. Dir J. K. MACASKILL; 11 brs.

Stanbic Bank Botswana Ltd: Private Bag 00168, Travaglini House, Plot 1271, Old Lobatse Rd, Gaborone; tel. 301600; fax 300171; f. 1992 by merger; subsidiary of Standard Bank Investment Corpn Africa Holdings Ltd; cap. and res 54.3m., dep 571.6m. (March 1999); Chair. J. N. LEGGETT; Man. Dir W. L. V. PRICE; 4 brs.

Standard Chartered Bank Botswana Ltd: POB 496, Standard House, 5th Floor, Plots 1124–1127, The Mall, Gaborone; tel. 353111; fax 372933; internet www.standardcharteredbank.com; f. 1975; 75% owned by Standard Chartered Holdings (Africa) BV, Amsterdam; cap. and res 109.9m. (Dec. 1997), dep. 881.7m. (Dec. 1995); Chair. P. L. STEENKAMP; Man. Dir D. N. T. KUWANA; 15 brs.

Other Banks

Botswana Savings Bank: POB 1150, Gaborone; tel. 312555; fax 352608; e-mail bsb@info.bw; cap. and res 47.8m. (March 1999); Chair. F. MODISE; Man. Dir E. B. MATHE.

Investec Bank: Gaborone; f. 1998; merchant bank; Man. Dir KUMBULANI MUNAMTI.

National Development Bank: POB 225, Development House, Queens Rd, Gaborone; tel. 352801; fax 374446; f. 1964; cap. and res 94.8m. (March 1998), dep. 51.3m. (March 1997); priority given to agricultural credit for Botswana farmers, and co-operative credit and loans for local business ventures; Chair. F. MODISE; Gen. Man. J. HOWELL; 5 brs.

STOCK EXCHANGE

Botswana Stock Exchange: Private Bag 00417, 4th Floor, Finance House, Khama Crescent, Gaborone; tel. 374078; fax 374079; e-mail stockex@ncs.com.gh; f. 1989; commenced formal functions of a stock exchange in 1995; Chair. LOUIS NCHINDO; CEO R. MCCAMMON.

INSURANCE

Botswana Co-operative Insurance Co Ltd: POB 199, Gaborone; tel. and fax 313654; Man. Dir PHILIP MAKGALEMELE.

Botswana Eagle Insurance Co Ltd: POB 1221, 501 Botsalano House, Gaborone; tel. 319910; fax 319911; Gen. Man. JOHN MAIN.

Botswana Insurance Holdings: POB 336, Gaborone; tel. 351791; fax 306386; Chair. W. A. JACK; Man. Dir J. A. BURDIDGE.

Botswana Life: Private Bag 00296, Gaborone; tel. 351791; fax 305884; e-mail blil@lifeinsurance.bw.

Mutual and Federal Insurance Co of Botswana Ltd: Private Bag 00347, Gaborone; tel. 303333; fax 303400; Gen. Man. JEAN WALKIN.

Sedgwick James Insurance Brokers (Pty) Ltd: POB 103, Plot 730, The Mall, Botswana Rd, Gaborone; tel. 314241; fax 373120.

Tshireletso Insurance Brokers: POB 1967, Gaborone; tel. 357064; fax 371558.

Trade and Industry

GOVERNMENT AGENCIES

Botswana Housing Corporation: POB 412, Gaborone; tel. 3605102; fax 314101; f. 1971; e-mail bhc@info.bw; provides housing for central govt and local authority needs and assists with private-sector housing schemes; Gen. Man. E. M. MAPHANYANE; 950 employees.

Department of Food Resources: POB 96, Gaborone; tel. 354124. 1982; procurement, storage and distribution of food commodities under the Drought Relief Programme; Admin. Officer M. S. SEHLULANE.

Department of Town and Regional Planning: Private Bag 0042, Gaborone; tel. 351935; e-mail infoterra@info.bw; f. 1972; responsible for physical planning matters throughout the country, including formulation of national physical planning policy; prepares devt plans for settlements and regions and provides physical planning advice to govt and local authorities as well as private bodies.

DEVELOPMENT ORGANIZATIONS

Botswana Development Corporation Ltd: Private Bag 160, Moedi, Plot 50380, Gaborone International Showgrounds, off Machel Drive, Gaborone; tel. 351811; fax 303105; e-mail bdc@bdc.bw; f. 1970; Chair. O. K. MATAMBO; Man. Dir. M. O. MOLEFANE.

Botswana Enterprise Development Unit (BEDU): Plot No. 1269, Lobatse Rd, POB 0014, Gaborone; f. 1974; promotes industrialization and rural devt; Dir J. LINDFORS.

Botswana Export Development and Investment Authority (BEDIA): BIC House, 4th Floor, The Main Mall, POB 3122, Gaborone; tel. 581931; fax 581941; f. 1998; promotes and facilitates local and foreign investment.

Department of Trade and Investment Promotion (TIPA), Ministry of Commerce and Industry: Private Bag 00367, Gaborone; tel. 351790; fax 305375; e-mail tipa@info.bw; internet www.tipa.bw; promotes industrial and commercial investment, diversification and expansion; offers consultancy, liaison and information services; participates in overseas trade fairs and trade and investment missions; Dir D. TSHEKO.

Financial Services Co of Botswana (Pty) Ltd: POB 1129, Finance House, Khama Crescent, Gaborone; tel. 351363; fax 357815; f. 1974; hire purchase, mortgages, industrial leasing and debt factoring; Chair. M. E. HOPKINS; Man. Dir R. A. PAWSON.

Integrated Field Services: Private Bag 004, Ministry of Commerce and Industry, Gaborone; tel. 353024; fax 371539; promotes industrialization and rural development; Dir B. T. TIBONE.

CHAMBER OF COMMERCE

Botswana National Chamber of Commerce and Industry: POB 20344, Gaborone; tel. 52677.

INDUSTRIAL AND TRADE ASSOCIATIONS

Botswana Agricultural Marketing Board (BAMB): Private Bag 0053, 1227 Haile Selassie Rd, Gaborone; tel. 351341; fax 352926; Chair. the Perm. Sec., Ministry of Agriculture; Gen. Man. S. B. TAUKOBONG.

Botswana Meat Commission (BMC): Private Bag 4, Lobatse; tel. 330321; fax 330504; e-mail bmc_gm_finance@info.bw; f. 1966; slaughter of livestock, export of hides and skins, carcasses, frozen and chilled boneless beef; operates tannery and beef products cannery; Chair. Dr MARTIN M. MANNATHOKO; CEO O. K. NIELSEN.

EMPLOYERS' ORGANIZATION

Botswana Confederation of Commerce, Industry and Manpower (BOCCIM): POB 432, BOCCIM House, Gaborone; f. 1971; Chair. D. N. MOROKA; Dir MODIRI J. MBAAKANYI; 1,478 affiliated mems.

UTILITIES

Electricity

Botswana Power Corporation: POB 48, Motlakase House, Macheng Way, Gaborone; tel. 3603000; fax 308674; f. 1971; operates power stations at Selebi-Phikwe (capacity 65 MW) and Moropule (132 MW); Chair. the Dep. Perm. Sec., Ministry of Minerals, Energy and Water Affairs; CEO KETANE SITHOLE.

Water

Department of Water Affairs: Gaborone; provides public water supplies for rural areas.

Water Utilities Corporation: Private Bag 00276, Gaborone; tel. 3604400; fax 373852; e-mail metsi@wuc.bw; f. 1970; 100% state-owned; supplies water to main urban centres; Chair. the Perm. Sec., Ministry of Minerals, Energy and Water Affairs; Chief Exec. B. MPHO.

MAJOR COMPANIES

The following are among the leading companies in Botswana in terms of capital investment and employment.

Bata Shoe Company Botswana Ltd: POB 1882, Gaborone; tel. 324575; fax 561182; e-mail bata@info.bw; manufactures footwear; Man. Dir P. JAKUBEC.

Botswana RST Ltd (Botrest): POB 3, Selebi-Phikwe; tel. 810211; fax 810441; f. 1967 as Botswana Roan Selection Trust Ltd; holding co with 85% shareholding in copper-nickel producers, BCL Ltd; Chair. Dr D. J. HUDSON; Man. Dir Dr B. V. STEWART.

BP Botswana (Pty) Ltd: Box 183, Gaborone; tel. 351077; fax 312836; petroleum exploration and production; Man. Dir D. M. MOROKA.

Debswana Diamond Co (Pty) Ltd: Debswana House, The Mall, POB 329, Gaborone; tel. 351131; fax 356110; e-mail jmatome@debswana.bw; sole diamond-mining interest in Botswana; owned equally by De Beers Centenary AG and the Botswana Govt; Chair. N. F. OPPENHEIMER; Man. Dir LOUIS NCHINDO.

Gold Fields Botswana (Pty) Ltd: Barclays House, 4th Floor, Khama Crescent, POB 271, Gaborone; holds prospecting licences covering an area of 4,986 sq km.

Northern Textile Mills (Pty) Ltd: POB 1508, Francistown; tel. 214773; fax 214947; e-mail nortex@global.co.za; manufactures household textiles; Chair. B. M. DISELE; Man. Dir M. JOSH.

Sechaba Brewery Holdings Ltd: POB 438, Gaborone; tel. 371598; fax 371594; Chair. EDWARD KOMANYANE; CEO COLZA MOLEBATSI KOPI.

Sefalana Holding Co Ltd: Private Bag 0080, Gaborone; tel. 313661; fax 307613; e-mail jenny.m@sefalana.bw; manufactures animal feed, mills wheat, maize and sorghum; Man. Dir B. A. FROH-LICH.

CO-OPERATIVES

Department of Co-operative Development: POB 86, Gaborone; f. 1964; promotes marketing and supply, consumer, dairy, horticultural and fisheries co-operatives, thrift and loan societies, credit societies, a co-operative union and a co-operative bank.

Botswana Co-operative Union: Gaborone. 1970; Dir AARON RAMO-SAKO.

TRADE UNIONS

Botswana Federation of Trade Unions: POB 440, Gaborone; tel. and fax 352534; f. 1977; Gen. Sec. MARANYANE KEBITSANG.

Affiliated Unions

Air Botswana Employees' Union: POB 92, Gaborone; Gen. Sec. DANIEL MOTSUMI.

Barclays Management Staff Union: POB 478, Gaborone; Gen. Sec. TEFO LIONJANGA.

BCL Senior Staff Union: POB 383, Selebi-Phikwe; Gen. Sec. KABELO MATTHEWS.

Botswana Agricultural Marketing Board Workers' Union: Private Bag 0053, Gaborone; Gen. Sec. M. E. SEMATHANE.

Botswana Bank Employees' Union: POB 111, Gaborone; Gen. Sec. KEOLOPILE GABORONE.

Botswana Beverages and Allied Workers' Union: POB 41358, Gaborone; Gen. Sec. S. SENWELO.

Botswana Brigade Teachers' Union: Private Bag 007, Molepolole; Gen. Sec. SADIKE KGOKONG.

Botswana Commercial and General Workers' Union: Gaborone; Gen. Sec. KEDIRETSE MPETANG.

Botswana Construction Workers' Union: POB 1508, Gaborone; Gen. Sec. JOSHUA KESIILWE.

Botswana Diamond Sorters-Valuators' Union: POB 1186, Gaborone; Gen. Sec. FELIX T. LESETEDI.

Botswana Housing Corporation Staff Union: POB 412, Gaborone; Gen. Sec. GORATA DINGALO.

Botswana Meat Industry Workers' Union: POB 181, Lobatse; Gen. Sec. JOHNSON BOJOSI.

Botswana Mining Workers' Union: Gaborone; Gen. Sec. BALEKA-MANG S. GANASIANE.

Botswana Postal Services Workers' Union: POB 87, Gaborone; Gen. Sec. AARON MOSWEU.

Botswana Power Corporation Workers' Union: Private Bag 0053, Gaborone; Gen. Sec. MOLEFE MODISE.

Botswana Railways and Artisan Employees' Union: POB 1486, Gaborone; Gen. Sec. PATRICK MAGOWE.

Botswana Railways Senior Staff Union: Mahalapye; Gen. Sec. LENTSWE LETSWELETSE.

Botswana Railways Workers' Union: POB 181, Gaborone; Gen. Sec. ERNEST T. G. MOHUTSIWA.

Botswana Telecommunications Employees' Union: Gaborone; Gen. Sec. SEDIBANA ROBERT.

Botswana Vaccine Institute Staff Union: Private Bag 0031, Gaborone; Gen. Sec. ELLIOT MODISE.

Central Bank Union: POB 712, Gaborone; Gen. Sec. GODFREY NGIDI.

National Amalgamated Local and Central Government, Parastatal, Statutory Body and Manual Workers' Union: POB 374, Gaborone; Gen. Sec. DICKSON KELATLHEGETSWE.

National Development Bank Employees' Union: POB 225, Gaborone; Sec.-Gen. MATSHEDISO FOLOGANG.

Non-Academic Staff Union: Private Bag 0022, Gaborone; Gen. Sec. ISAAC THOTHE.

Transport

RAILWAYS

The 960-km railway line from Mafikeng, South Africa, to Bulawayo, Zimbabwe, passes through Botswana and has been operated by Botswana Railways (BR) since 1987. In 1997 there were 888 km of 1,067-mm-gauge track within Botswana, including three branches serving the Selebi-Phikwe mining complex (56 km), the Morupule colliery (16 km) and the Sua Pan soda-ash deposits (175 km). BR derives 85%–90% of its earnings from freight traffic, although pas-senger services do operate between Gaborone and Francistown, and Lobatse and Bulawayo. Through its links with Spoornet, which operates the South African railways system and the National Railways of Zimbabwe, BR provides connections with Namibia and Swaziland to the south, and an unbroken rail link to Zambia, the Democratic Republic of the Congo, Angola, Mozambique, Tanzania and Malawi to the north.

Botswana Railways (BR): Private Bag 52, Mahalapye; tel. 411375; fax 411385; e-mail botrail@info.bw; f. 1987; Gen. Man. C. B. BOTANA.

ROADS

In 1996 there were 18,482 km of roads, including 4,350 km of main roads, and 4,566 km of secondary roads; some 23.5% of the road network was bituminized (including a main road from Gaborone, via Francistown, to Kazungula, where the borders of Botswana, Namibia, Zambia and Zimbabwe meet). The construction of a 340-km road between Nata and Maun is currently under way. Construction of the 600-km Trans-Kalahari Highway, from Jwaneng to the port of Walvis Bay on the Namibian coast, commenced in 1990 and was completed in 1998. A car-ferry service operates from Kazungula across the Zambezi river into Zambia.

Roads Department: Private Bag 0026, Gaborone; tel. 55515; responsible for national road network; responsible to the Ministry of Works, Transport and Communications.

CIVIL AVIATION

The main international airport is at Gaborone. Two other major airports are located at Kasane and Maun in northern Botswana. There are also airfiels at Francistown and Selebi-Phikwe, and there are numerous airstrips throughout the country. Scheduled services of Air Botswana are supplemented by an active charter and business sector.

Air Botswana: POB 92, Sir Seretse Khama Airport, Gaborone; tel. 352812; fax 375408; f. 1972; govt-owned; transfer to private sector to be completed by mid-2001; domestic services and regional services to countries in eastern and southern Africa.

Tourism

There are five game reserves and three national parks, including Chobe, near Victoria Falls, on the Zambia–Zimbabwe border. Efforts to expand the tourism industry include plans for the construction of new hotels and the rehabilitation of existing hotel facilities. In 1997 tourist arrivals (including same-day visitors) totalled 1,083,000 and receipts from tourism amounted to US $184m.

Department of Tourism: Ministry of Commerce and Industry, Private Bag 0047, Standard House, 2nd Floor, Main Mall, Gaborone; tel. 353024; fax 308675; e-mail botswanatourism@gov.bw; internet www.botswana-tourism.gov.bw; f. 1994; Dir GAYLARD KOMBANI.

Department of Wildlife and National Parks: POB 131, Gaborone; tel. 371405; fax 312354; e-mail dwnpbots@global.bw; Dir. S. MODISE.

Hotel and Tourism Association of Botswana: Gaborone; Dir MODISA MOTHOAGAE.

Defence

Military service is voluntary. Botswana established a permanent defence force in 1977. In August 1999 the total strength of the Botswana Defence Force was some 9,000, comprising an army of 8,500 and an air force of 500. In addition, there was a paramilitary police force of 1,000. There are plans to enlarge the strength of the army to 10,000 men.

Defence Expenditure: Budgeted at P869m. in 1998/99.

Defence Force Commander: Lt-Gen. MATSHWENYEGO FISCHER.

Education

Although education is not compulsory, enrolment ratios are high. Primary education, which is provided free of charge, begins at seven years of age and lasts for up to seven years. Secondary education, beginning at the age of 13, lasts for a further five years, comprising a first cycle of three years and a second of two years. As a proportion of the school-age population, the total enrolment at primary and secondary schools increased from 52% in 1975 to the equivalent of 91% (boys 90%; girls 93%) in 1996.

Enrolment at primary schools in 1997 included 96.7% of children in the relevant age-group (boys 95.7%; girls 97.7%), while the comparable ratio for secondary enrolment was 53.3% (boys 51.0%; girls 55.5%). The government aims to provide universal access to

10 years of basic education. Botswana has the highest teacher-pupil ratio in Africa, but continues to rely heavily on expatriate secondary school teachers. In 1999 tertiary education was provided by 30 technical and vocational training centres, including health institutes, four teacher-training colleges, two further education colleges and a university.

According to estimates by UNESCO, the average rate of adult illiteracy in 1995 was 27.3% (males 30.0%; females 24.9%). Education was allocated some 15.5% of total projected expenditure under the National Development Plan for 1998–2003. Expenditure on education by the central government in 1998/99 totalled P2,275.7m. (representing 24.7% of total expenditure by the central government).

Bibliography

Amanze, J. N. (Ed.). *African Christianity in Botswana*. Gweru, Mambo Press, 1998.

Bhuiyan, M. N. (Ed.). *Selected Papers on the Botswana Economy*. Gaborone, Bank of Botswana, 1987.

Botswana Society. *Settlement in Botswana*. London, Heinemann Educational, 1982.

Chipasula, J. C., and Miti, K. *Botswana in Southern Africa*. Delhi, Ajanta, 1989.

Colclough, C., and McCarthy, S. *The Political Economy of Botswana: A Study of Growth and Distribution*. London, Oxford University Press, 1980.

Dale, R. *Botswana's Search for Autonomy in Southern Africa*. Westport, CT, Greenwood Press, 1995.

Du Toit, P. *State Building and Democracy in Southern Africa: Botswana, Zimbabwe and South Africa*. Washington, DC, US Institute of Peace Press, 1995.

Good, K. *Realizing Democracy in Botswana, Namibia and South Africa*. Pretoria, Africa Institute, 1997.

Hailey, Lord. *The Republic of South Africa and the High Commission Territories*. London, Oxford University Press, 1963.

Hartland-Thunberg, P. *Botswana: An African Growth Economy*. Boulder, CO, Westview Press, 1978.

Harvey, C. (Ed.). *Papers on the Economy of Botswana*. London, Heinemann Educational, 1981.

    Banking Policy in Botswana: Orthodox but Untypical. Brighton, Institute of Development Studies, 1996.

Harvey, C., and Lewis, S. R. *Policy Choice and Development Performance in Botswana*. Basingstoke, Macmillan, 1990.

Hayward, M. F. *Elections in Independent Africa*. Boulder, CO, Westview Press, 1987.

Jackson, A. *Botswana, 1939–1945*. Oxford, Clarendon Press, 1999.

Konzacki, Z.A., Parpart, J. L., and Shaw, T. M. (Eds). *Studies in the Economic History of Southern Africa*. Vol. 1. London, Cass, 1990.

Landau, P. S. *The Realm of the Word: Language, Gender and Christianity in a Southern African Kingdom*. London, James Currey Publishers, 1996.

Lipton, M. *Employment and Labour Use in Botswana*. Gaborone, Botswana Government Printer, 1978.

Mazonde, I. N. *Ranching and Enterprise in Eastern Botswana: A Case Study of Black and White Farmers*. London, Edinburgh University Press, 1994.

    Women and Food Security in Rural Botswana. Arlington, W1, 1998.

Mogalakwe, M. *The State and Organised Labour in Botswana*. Aldershot, Ashgate, 1997.

Molomo, M. G., and Mokopakgosi, B. T. *Multi-Party Democracy in Botswana*. Harare, SAPES Trust, 1991.

Morton, F., et al. *Historical Dictionary of Botswana*. 2nd Edn, Methuen, NJ, Scarecrow Press, 1989.

Oommen, M. A., et al. *Botswana Economy since Independence*. New Delhi, Tate/McGraw-Hill, 1983.

Parson, J. D. *Botswana: Liberal Democracy and Labour Reserve in Southern Africa*. Aldershot, Gower Publishers, Boulder CO, Westview Press, 1984.

Peters, P. E. *Dividing the Commons: Politics, Policy and Culture in Botswana*. London, University Press of Virginia, 1994.

Picard, L. A. *The Politics of Development in Botswana: A Model For Success*. Boulder, CO, Lynne Rienner Publishers, 1987.

Picard, L. A. (Ed.). *The Evolution of Modern Botswana*. London, Rex Collings, 1988.

    Politics and Rural Development in Southern Africa: The Evolution of Modern Botswana. London, Rex Collings, 1985.

Rakner, L. *Botswana: 30 Years of Economic Growth, Democracy and Aid*. Bergen, CMI, 1996.

Sallein, J. S. (Ed.), et al. *Aspects of the Botswana Economy*. Oxford, James Curry Publishers, 1998.

Seidman, J. *In Our Own Image*. Gaborone Foundation for Education with Production 1990.

Seisa, S., and Youngman, F. (Eds). *Education For All in Botswana*. Gaborone, Macmillan Botswana, 1995.

Stedman, S. J. *Botswana: The Political Economy of Democratic Development*. Boulder, CO, Lynne Rienner Publishers, 1993.

Tlou, T., and Campbell, A. *History of Botswana*. Gaborone, Macmillan Botswana, 1984.

Tlou, T., et al. *Seretse Khama, 1921–1980*. Johannesburg, Macmillan, 1995.

Wiseman, J. *Botswana*. Oxford, ABC Clio, 1992.

THE BRITISH INDIAN OCEAN TERRITORY (BIOT)

The British Indian Ocean Territory (BIOT) was formed in November 1965, through the amalgamation of the former Seychelles islands of Aldabra, Desroches and Farquhar with the Chagos Archipelago, a group of islands 1,930 km north-east of Mauritius, and previously administered by the governor of Mauritius. Aldabra, Desroches and Farquhar were ceded to Seychelles when that country was granted independence in June 1976. Since then BIOT has comprised only the Chagos Archipelago, including the coral atoll Diego Garcia, with a total land area of 60 sq km (23 sq miles), together with a surrounding area of some 54,400 sq km (21,000 sq miles) of ocean.

BIOT was established to meet British and US defence requirements in the Indian Ocean. Previously, the principal economic function of the islands was the production of copra: the islands, together with the coconut plantations, were owned by a private company. The copra industry, however, went into decline after the Second World War, and, following the purchase of the islands by the British crown in 1967, the plantations ceased to operate and the inhabitants were offered the choice of resettlement in Mauritius or in Seychelles. The majority (which numbered about 1,200) went to Mauritius, the resettlement taking place during 1969–73, prior to the construction of the military facility. Mauritius subsequently campaigned for the immediate return of the Territory, and received support from the Organization of African Unity and from India. The election victory of the left-wing Mouvement Militant Mauricien in 1982 led to an intensification of these demands. Mauritius supported the former island population in a protracted dispute with the United Kingdom over compensation for those displaced, which ended in 1982 when the British government agreed to an *ex gratia* payment of £4m. In early 1984, however, it was reported that people who had been displaced from Diego Garcia were seeking US $6m. from the US Government to finance their resettlement in Mauritius. The US administration declined to accept any financial responsibility for the population. In March 1999 a former resident of BIOT obtained leave from the high court in London to seek a judicial review of the validity of the Immigration Ordinance of 1971 under which the islanders were removed from BIOT, and which continues to prevent them from resettling in the Territory; a review was instigated in July 2000. Later in March 1999, it was disclosed that the displaced islanders and their families, now estimated to number up to 4,000, were not to be included in the offer of full British citizenship, with the right of abode in the United Kingdom, that was to be extended to residents of other United Kingdom Overseas Territories by legislation pending in the British parliament.

A 1966 agreement between the United Kingdom and the USA provides for BIOT to be used by both countries over an initial period of 50 years, with the option of extending this for a further 20 years. The United Kingdom undertook to cede the Chagos Archipelago to Mauritius when it was no longer required for defence purposes. Originally the US military presence was limited to a communications centre on Diego Garcia. In 1972, however, construction of a naval support facility was begun, apparently in response to the expansion of the Soviet maritime presence in the Indian Ocean. This plan was expanded in 1974, the agreement being formalized by an 'exchange

of notes' in 1976, and again following Soviet military intervention in Afghanistan in December 1979. Facilities on Diego Garcia include a communications centre, a runway with a length of 3,650 m, anchorage, refuelling and various ancillary services. During the 1980s the US government undertook a programme of expansion and improvement of the naval support facility which was to include a space-tracking station. In August 1987 the US navy began to use Diego Garcia as a facility for minesweeping helicopters taking part in operations in the Persian (Arabian) Gulf. Following Iraq's invasion of Kuwait in August 1990, Diego Garcia was used as a base for US B-52 aircraft, which were deployed in the Gulf region. Runway facilities on Diego Garcia were again used in September 1996 and December 1998 as a base for US support aircraft during US missile attacks on Iraq.

In January 1988 Mauritius renewed its campaign to regain sovereignty over the Chagos Archipelago, and reiterated its support for a 'zone of peace' in the Indian Ocean. In November 1989, following an incident in which a military aircraft belonging to the US air force accidentally bombed a US naval vessel near Diego Garcia, a demonstration was held outside the US embassy in Mauritius, demanding the withdrawal of foreign military forces from the area. The Mauritius government announced that it would draw the attention of the UN Security Council to the dangers that it perceived in the execution of US military air exercises. However, the US assistant secretary of state for african affairs reiterated during an official visit to Mauritius, in the same month, that the USA would maintain its military presence in the Indian Ocean.

In January 1994 arrangements were agreed for the establishment of a joint British-Mauritius fisheries commission to promote and co-ordinate conservation and scientific research within the territorial waters of Mauritius and BIOT. In May the Mauritius government ministers of foreign affairs and fisheries paid a two-day official visit to the Chagos Archipelago.

The civil administration of BIOT is the responsibility of a non-resident commissioner in the Foreign and Commonwealth Office in London, represented on Diego Garcia by a Royal Naval commander and a small British naval presence. A chief justice, a senior magistrate and a principal legal adviser (who performs the functions of an attorney-general) are resident in the United Kingdom.

Land Area: about 60 sq km.

Population: There are no permanent inhabitants. In 1998 there were about 3,100 US and British military personnel stationed in the Territory.

Currency: The US dollar is used.

Commissioner: JOHN WHITE, Head of Overseas Territories Dept, Foreign and Commonwealth Office, King Charles St, London, SW1A 2AH, United Kingdom; tel. (20) 7270-3000.

Administrator: LOUISE SAVILL, Overseas Territories Dept, Foreign and Commonwealth Office, King Charles St, London, SW1A 2AH, United Kingdom; tel. (20) 7270-3000.

Commissioner's Representative: Commdr PETER LEWIS, RN, Diego Garcia, c/o BFPO Ships.

BURKINA FASO

Physical and Social Geography

R. J. HARRISON CHURCH

Like Niger and Mali, Burkina Faso (formerly the Republic of Upper Volta) is a land-locked state of west Africa and is situated north of Côte d'Ivoire, Ghana and Togo. Burkina has an area of 274,200 sq km (105,870 sq miles). The December 1996 census recorded a total population of 10,312,609, giving an average density of 38 inhabitants per sq km. According to UN estimates, the population had risen to 10,683,000 at mid-1998. In recent years there has been large-scale emigration to neighbouring Côte d'Ivoire and Ghana by people seeking work on farms, in industries and the service trades, although economic difficulties in these host countries have prompted the return of large numbers of migrant workers to Burkina. The main ethnic groups are the Mossi in the north, the Bobo in the south-west, and the Gourma in the east respectively. Along the northern border are the semi-nomadic Fulani, who are also present in the east of the country.

Towards the south-western border with Mali there are Primary sandstones, terminating eastward in the Banfora escarpment. As in Guinea, Mali and Ghana, where there are also great expanses of these rocks, their residual soils are poor and water percolates deeply within them. Although most of the rest of the country is underlain by granite, gneisses and schists, there is much loose sand or bare laterite; consequently, there are extensive infertile areas. Moreover, annual rainfall is only some 635–1,145 mm, and comes in a rainy season of at the most five months. Water is scarce except by the rivers or in the Gourma swampy area; by the former the simulium fly, whose bite leads to blindness, has been the target of extensive eradication projects, while in the latter the tsetse, a fly which can cause sleeping-sickness, is found. Given the grim physical environment, the density of population in the north-central Mossi area is remarkable. The area is, in fact, one of the oldest indigenous kingdoms of west Africa, dating back to the 11th century. Islam first penetrated the area during the 14th–16th centuries. At the end of the 18th century it was adopted by some local rulers, notably the leader of the Mossi, but traditional religious practices among the population remained strong. Islam's expansion was facilitated by the circumstances of French rule but more than one-half of the population retain their traditional beliefs.

Burkina Faso has valuable deposits of gold, manganese and zinc, industrial exploitation of which is in progress or is planned. Reserves of silver, nickel, lead, phosphates and vanadium have also been identified.

Recent History

PIERRE ENGLEBERT

Revised for this edition by the Editor

Burkina Faso (then Upper Volta) became a self-governing republic within the French Community in December 1958. Full independence followed on 5 August 1960, with Maurice Yaméogo, the leader of the Union démocratique voltaïque (UDV), as president of the new republic. Support for the UDV was centred on the Mossi, the country's dominant ethnic group, comprising about 50% of the population.

Yaméogo's administration was autocratic in style. Opposition parties were banned, and popular support for the government receded as the country's economic condition worsened. In January 1966 Yaméogo was deposed in an army coup, led by Lt-Col Sangoulé Lamizana. An elected civilian administration was permitted to take office in December 1970, although effective power remained with the army. Further elections took place in May 1978, but all political parties except the UDV, the Union nationale pour la défense de la démocratie (UNDD), led by Herman Yaméogo, the son of the country's first president, and Prof. Joseph Ki-Zerbo's Union progressiste voltaïque (UPV) were suppressed. For much of the 1970s Upper Volta was ravaged by the Sahelian drought, which disrupted the economy and caused severe food shortages in rural areas.

ARMY REGIMES, 1980–87

In November 1980, following a period of renewed economic difficulty and popular unrest, Lamizana was overthrown in a bloodless *coup d'état* led by Col Saye Zerbo, who formed a governing Comité militaire de redressement pour le progrès national (CMRPN) and imposed a total ban on political activity. By early 1982, serious rifts had become evident within the CMRPN, and in November Zerbo and the CMRPN were supplanted by a military Conseil du salut du peuple (CSP), led by Surgeon-Maj. Jean-Baptiste Ouédraogo. Capt. Thomas Sankara, who had resigned from the CMRPN in the previous April, was appointed prime minister.

It became increasingly apparent, however, that Ouédraogo was presiding over a divided regime, as the compromise between traditionalists in the army and the radicals (led by Sankara) degenerated into open conflict in May 1983, when Ouédraogo ordered the arrest of Sankara and his supporters in the CSP. Members of Sankara's commando unit, led by Capt. Blaise Compaoré, mutinied; the rebellion spread, and in August Sankara deposed Ouédraogo in a military coup. Sankara installed a Conseil national de la révolution (CNR) and formed a new government, with himself as head of state and Compaoré as minister of state at the presidency. The CNR also attracted support from a previously clandestine left-wing civilian group, the Ligue patriotique pour le développement (LIPAD).

The CNR swiftly reorganized the country's public administration, deprived traditional chiefs of their privileges and influence, and installed 'revolutionary people's tribunals' to try former public officials charged with corruption. The army was purged of 'reactionary' elements, and civilian Comités pour la défense de la révolution (CDR) were established throughout the country to implement government policy. To symbolize the political changes that were taking place, and as an expression of 'decolonization', in August 1984 Sankara renamed the country Burkina Faso ('Land of the Incorruptible Men'). The momentum for change was maintained by a thorough reform of the judicial and education systems, and through economic austerity measures. The regime's links with LIPAD were progressively abandoned, and Sankara's revolution was now generally seen to be less identified with Marxist forces, and as seeking to accommodate a wider cross-section of society.

A long-standing dispute with Mali over the Agacher strip, a well-irrigated and reputedly mineral-rich border region, erupted into armed conflict in December 1985. During six days of fighting, Mali, with its superior forces and armaments, inflicted considerable damage inside Burkinabè territory. The regional defence grouping, Accord de non-agression et d'assistance en matière de défense, negotiated a cease-fire and dispatched peace-keeping forces, and in January 1986 Sankara and President Traoré of Mali agreed to withdraw their troops from the disputed area, and diplomatic relations were resumed after a break of 12 years. In December the International Court of Justice, to which the dispute had been referred in 1983, ruled that the disputed territory be divided equally, with Burkina obtaining sovereignty over the eastern district of Beli.

During 1987 divisions between Sankara and the other leaders of the CNR, Compaoré, a minister of state, Boukary Lingani, the minister of defence, and Capt. Henri Zongo, the minister of economic development, became increasingly evident. In particular, Compaoré opposed Sankara's attitude to the trade unions, which was exemplified, in May, by the renewed imprisonment of Soumane Touré, a prominent activist in LIPAD. Divisions were equally apparent between two of the semi-official political organizations participating in the CNR: the generally pro-Sankara Union des luttes communistes reconstruite (ULCR) and the Union des communistes burkinabè (UCB), which was closely associated with Compaoré. A split in the ULCR undermined Sankara's principal base of civilian support, and forced him to dismiss two of the three ULCR ministers in August. A proposal by Sankara that a single party be formed to embrace all existing political organizations (in an attempt to forestall his further marginalization in the CNR) was vehemently opposed by his former allies. On 15 October a commando unit loyal to Compaoré opened fire on Sankara, killing him and 13 of his associates. A Front populaire (FP) was proclaimed as successor to the CNR, and Compaoré, the chairman of the FP, became head of state. Sankara was denounced as a traitor and a renegade, and many of his relatives and former ministers were arrested.

THE FRONT POPULAIRE

While the FP pledged a continuation of the CNR's revolutionary process, a new phase, to be known as 'rectification', was announced. This concept embraced both economic liberalization (including attempts to foster private enterprise, as well as the instigation of negotiations for financial assistance with the IMF and the World Bank) and the removal from positions of influence of Sankara loyalists. The CDR were abolished in March 1988 and replaced by Comités révolutionnaires; however, attempts at recruitment to these attracted little popular interest. In April 1989 the formation was announced of a new political grouping, the Organisation pour la démocratie populaire/Mouvement du travail (ODP/MT), under the leadership of the former head of the UCB, Clément Oumarou Ouédraogo. Prominent members of groups that had refused to affiliate to the ODP/MT were swiftly removed from political office, while Ouédraogo was appointed to the newly-created government post of minister-delegate to the co-ordinating committee of the FP.

The remaining 'orthodox' elements of the 1983 revolution were eliminated in September 1989, when Zongo and Boukary Lingani were summarily executed, together with two others, following the alleged discovery of a coup plot. Compaoré subsequently assumed the defence and security portfolio. None the less, the continuing 'revolutionary' dogma of the ODP/MT, in contrast with Compaoré's increasingly moderate orientation, remained a potential source of instability within the FP, and in December it was announced that a further conspiracy had been uncovered.

The first congress of the FP, convened in March 1990, was attended by representatives of seven political organizations. Delegates appointed a commission to draft a new constitution that would define a process of 'democratization'. In April Clément Oumarou Ouédraogo, accused of having deviated from the political doctrine of the ODP/MT, was dismissed from its

leadership and subsequently removed from the government. Roch Marc-Christian Kaboré, whose political orientation was closer to that of Compaoré, assumed both the leadership of the ODP/MT and the post of secretary for political affairs within the FP's executive committee. Kaboré was promoted to the rank of minister of state in September.

The constitutional commission was not accorded plenary powers, suggesting that the FP intended to exercise close supervision over the process of democratization. The first draft of the constitution, published in October 1990, provided for a multi-party political system in what was to be designated the fourth republic. Among the main provisions of the final document was a clause denying legitimacy to any regime that might take power as the result of a *coup d'état*. In March 1991 a congress of the ODP/MT adopted Compaoré as the party's official candidate to contest the forthcoming presidential election, and at the same time replaced its Marxist-Leninist ideology with a commitment to policies of free enterprise. In April an official amnesty was proclaimed for the alleged perpetrators of the December 1989 coup attempt; the rehabilitation was announced, in May 1991, of Maurice Yaméogo, and an appeal was made to political exiles to return to Burkina. In June plans were announced for the construction of a memorial honouring Sankara, and in August Compaoré declared an amnesty for all political 'crimes' committed since independence.

THE FOURTH REPUBLIC

The draft constitution was submitted for approval in a national referendum on 2 June 1991, and was endorsed by 93% of those who voted (reportedly one-half of the electorate). The constitution took effect on 11 June, whereupon the functions of the (restructured) FP were separated from the organs of state. The council of ministers was also dissolved and a transitional administration appointed. Compaoré remained head of state on an interim basis, pending a presidential election. The most senior member of the new cabinet was Kaboré (as minister of state, in charge of the co-ordination of government action), and its composition was notable for the appointment of a civilian as minister of popular defence and security. Many political parties criticized the dominant role of the ODP/MT, and several nominated government members declined to accept their appointments. A reorganized government, appointed in July, included several opposition figures, among them Herman Yaméogo. (Yaméogo, himself now a presidential candidate, had been appointed to the FP in March 1990, only to be expelled three months later.)

Compaoré's refusal to accede to persistent opposition demands that a sovereign national conference be convened in advance of the presidential and legislative elections was a source of considerable political tension. In August 1991 Yaméogo and two other members of his Alliance pour la démocratie et la fédération (ADF) resigned their government posts, in protest against proposed electoral procedures. In the following month opposition parties established a Coordination des forces démocratiques (CFD), to which about 20 political organizations had affiliated by the end of the year. The seven remaining opposition members resigned from the transitional government later in September. In October, furthermore, five CFD representatives who had previously declared their intention to contest the presidency withdrew their candidatures. Compaoré (who had resigned his army commission in order to contest the presidency as a civilian) was thus the sole candidate in the presidential election, which took place, as scheduled, on 1 December 1991. He secured the support of 90.4% of those who voted, but an appeal by the CFD for a boycott of the poll had been widely heeded, and an abstention rate of 74.7% was recorded.

Shortly after the election Clément Oumarou Ouédraogo was assassinated while leaving a CFD meeting. Although the government and the ODP/MT condemned the attack, opposition leaders accused the Compaoré administration of seeking to eliminate political figures who held evidence of its earlier misdeeds. Two days after Ouédraogo's death the government announced the indefinite postponement of the legislative elections. (The CFD had for some weeks been advocating a boycott of the elections to the new legislature, and few parties had registered their intention to submit candidates. Compaoré was sworn in as president of the fourth republic on 24 December 1991. In

January 1992 the rehabilitation was announced of some 4,000 people who had been punished for political or trade union activity since 1983. In a further attempt to restore a national consensus, Compaoré proposed a 'national reconciliation forum', embracing diverse political and social groups, to discuss the democratic process, human rights and development issues. The agenda of the reconciliation forum (which was convened in February 1992 and attended by some 380 delegates) was, however, very limited, and the conference was suspended within two weeks. In late February, none the less, the government was reorganized again to include Herman Yaméogo and three other opposition members.

In all, 27 parties contested the elections to the Assemblée des députés populaires (ADP), which finally took place on 24 May 1992. Although international observers declared that the poll had been conducted in a satisfactory manner, Compaoré's opponents alleged widespread malpractice. The ODP/MT won 78 of the new legislature's 107 seats; Pierre Tapsoba's Convention nationale des patriotes progressistes–Parti social-démocrate (CNPP–PSD) obtained 12 seats, while the ADF secured four. An abstention rate of 64.8% was recorded. The ADP was inaugurated on 15 June. Compaoré appointed a young economist, Youssouf Ouédraogo, to the premiership; the new government included representatives of seven political organizations, although the ODP/MT retained control of most strategic ministries. The ODP/MT's predominance in the legislature was further enhanced following a split in the CNPP–PSD in May 1993, as a result of which six of the party's parliamentary members joined Joseph Ki-Zerbo's newly-formed Parti pour la démocratie et le progrès (PDP).

In December 1992 the government, trade unions and representatives of the private sector began a series of negotiations, with a view to defining a 'social charter'. During late 1992 and early 1993, none the less, there was evidence of social tensions, mainly linked to the government's adoption of austerity measures (in the context of its structural adjustment programme), with some labour unrest and disruption in the education sector. A 'freeze' in public-sector salaries, in force since 1987, was ended in January 1993. In April the Confédération générale du travail burkinabè (CGTB) withdrew from the 'social charter' negotiations, protesting at the government's dilatory attitude towards addressing workers' grievances.

Following the 50% devaluation of the CFA franc, in January 1994, the government introduced emergency measures in an attempt to offset the immediate adverse effects of the currency's depreciation. However, trade unions denounced such measures as inadequate, demanding compensatory salary increases of 40%–50%. Negotiations between the government and trade unions failed to reach a compromise, and in March Youssouf Ouédraogo resigned. Roch Marc-Christian Kaboré, the minister of state with responsibility for relations with the organs of state, was subsequently appointed prime minister; his administration, dominated by the ODP/MT and its associates, included a new minister of the economy, finance and planning. Herman Yaméogo was designated minister of state, with responsibility for African integration and solidarity. The new government upheld Compaoré's desire to enforce austerity measures necessitated by the devaluation and the structural adjustment programme. A dialogue was sought with trade union leaders, but proposed salary increases of 6%–10%, as well as other concessions designed to mitigate the effects of the removal of temporary price controls, failed to prevent a three-day general strike by members of the CGTB in April.

At municipal elections in February 1995 the ODP/MT won control of 26 of the country's 33 major towns. Representatives of 19 parties contested the elections (some opposition parties had refused to participate, protesting at what they claimed to be inadequate preparations for the elections). Fewer than 10% of those eligible were reported to have registered to vote. In August Ernest Nongma Ouédraogo, the secretary-general of the Bloc socialiste burkinabè (BSB), was convicted of insulting the head of state and sentenced to six months' imprisonment: in an article published in an independent journal, *L'Observateur Paalga*, Ouédraogo, a Sankara loyalist, had alleged that Compaoré had fraudulently amassed a personal fortune.

Members were appointed to Burkina's second legislative chamber, the 178-member chamber of representatives, in December 1995. According to the 1991 constitution, this body, to be composed of what were termed the 'active forces of the nation', was to function in an advisory capacity; all members were to be nominated for a three-year term.

In early February 1996 Kadré Désiré Ouédraogo, hitherto deputy governor of the Banque centrale des états de l'Afrique de l'ouest, was appointed to succeed Kaboré as prime minister. Kaboré was designated special adviser to the presidency and also first vice-president of a new, pro-Compaoré political party, the Congrès pour la démocratie et le progrès (CDP). The CDP, termed a social-democratic party, grouped the ODP/MT and some 10 other parties (among them the CNPP–PSD); its president was a long-time ally of Compaoré, Arsène Bognessan Yè, the president of the ADP and the former head of the ODP/MT.

The new prime minister claimed no party political affiliation. He stated that his government's priority would be to strengthen and revitalize economic development, with particular emphasis on the agro-pastoral sector, employment, the stable management of public finances and on environmental protection. Ouédraogo assumed personal responsibility for the economy and finance in a government reshuffle in early September 1996.

In October 1996 the government confirmed newspaper reports of the arrest of several members of the presidential security services. It emerged that those detained (numbering about 25) were close associates of Chief Warrant Officer Hyacinthe Kafando, hitherto responsible for the head of state's security, who had been ordered to return from a period of training in Morocco but who was reportedly seeking asylum at the French embassy in Abidjan, Côte d'Ivoire. Rumours circulated, in particular, of animosity between Kafando and Capt. Gilbert Diendéré, Compaoré's personal chief of staff, and it was also reported that the recent closure of the élite commando training centre from which members of the presidential guard were recruited had been a source of dissatisfaction within the service. The government denied press speculation that a coup attempt had been foiled, emphasizing that there was no 'political connotation' to the arrests. Representatives of the national human rights organization, the Mouvement burkinabè des droits de l'homme et du peuple (MBDHP), visited the detainees, and subsequently confirmed that two relations of Kafando (one a civilian) were among those arrested. The MBDHP was, meanwhile, informed by Diendéré that Kafando had left the French embassy in Abidjan, and that his whereabouts were unknown.

Constitutional amendments and a new electoral code were approved by the ADP in January 1997: among the changes were the removal of restrictions on the renewal of the presidential mandate (hitherto renewable only once), as well as an increase (with effect from the forthcoming elections) in the number of parliamentary seats to 111. The number of administrative provinces was also increased from 30 to 45. Symbolizing Burkina's departure from its revolutionary past, the national motto, hitherto 'fatherland or death, we shall conquer', was changed to 'unity, progress, justice', and parts of the national anthem were modified. (Similarly, in October the country's militaristic coat of arms was replaced with one reflecting the country's historical and agricultural traditions.) In February the ADP approved proposals for a national commission for the organization of elections. However, since the compilation and revision of voters' lists were to remain under the control of the ministry of territorial administration and security, the new commission was denounced as non-independent by opposition groups.

The general election to the enlarged ADP took place on 11 May 1997, contested by some 569 candidates from 13 political parties. As had been expected, the CDP won a resounding victory. In mid-May the supreme court annulled the results of voting for four seats, all of which had been won by the CDP; these were retained by the party at a further round of voting in the relevant constituencies in mid-June. The CDP, with a total of 101 seats, thus preserved its overwhelming majority in the legislature. The opposition was represented by the PDP, with six seats, and the Rassemblement démocratique africain, which returned two deputies. The ADF also retained two seats. A new government, again led by Kadré Désiré Ouédraogo, was appointed in mid-June, with Tertius Zongo as minister of the economy and finance. Herman Yaméogo left the cabinet, while

Arsène Bognessan Yè was named minister of state at the presidency of the republic.

Legislation adopted by the ADP in late October 1997 regarding rights of assembly and public procession was denounced by opposition parties and trade unions as a severe curtailment of public freedoms. Further controversy was provoked by the announcement that, from the end of the year, private radio stations in Burkina would no longer be permitted to relay foreign radio broadcasts. In early December there was a strike by civil servants in protest at the likely effects of the government's privatization programme and new civil service regulations favouring contract employment. (Legislation regulating the civil service and employment was endorsed by the ADP in late April 1998.)

In early April 1998, following consultations with pro-government and opposition parties, the council of ministers adopted legislation providing for the establishment of an independent electoral body: the 26-member Commission électorale nationale indépendante (CENI) was to comprise six representatives of the majority (i.e. the CDP and its allies), together with six opposition representatives, the remainder being representatives of civic society. In February 10 opposition parties had formed a Front uni pour la démocratie et la république (FUDR), in preparation for the presidential election scheduled for November. The CENI was inaugurated in mid-July. Shortly beforehand, however, the FUDR had announced that it was to boycott the presidential election, stating that the measures in place were no guarantee of transparency at the poll.

Political Instability

As the presidential election approached, there was some dispute among opposition parties regarding participation in the poll. Several key figures, including Joseph Ki-Zerbo and Herman Yaméogo (the latter now leading the Alliance pour la démocratie et la fédération–Rassemblement démocratique africain), refused to participate. Compaoré, who was seeking a renewed mandate, was challenged by Ram Ouédraogo, leader of the ecologist Union des verts pour le développement du Burkina, and Frédéric Guirma, representing the Front de refus du rassemblement démocratique africain. Despite opposition demands that the elections be postponed, voting proceeded, as scheduled, on 18 November 1998 in an atmosphere of calm. The opposition denounced the elections as fraudulent, but international monitors and national observers pronounced themselves satisfied with the conduct of the campaign (although the latter expressed some concerns, mainly regarding the compilation of voters' lists and the distribution of ballot cards). Turn-out by voters, at 56.1%, was appreciably higher than at the 1991 presidential elections, despite opposition calls for a boycott. The provisional results, issued by the CENI on 18 November 1998, confirmed a decisive victory for Compaoré, with 87.53% of the valid votes cast; Ram Ouédraogo took 6.61%, and Guirma 5.86%. A new government, again headed by Kadré Désiré Ouédraogo, was appointed in January 1999.

On 13 December 1998 Norbert Zongo, a popular investigative journalist and managing editor of the newspaper, *L'Indépendant*, was found murdered, along with three colleagues. Zongo had frequently criticized Compaoré, and had been investigating the death of David Ouédraogo, a chauffeur who had allegedly been tortured to death by members of the presidential guard for having stolen money from his employer, François Compaoré, the president's brother. A combined opposition group, the Collectif d'organisations démocratiques de masse et de partis politiques, was subsequently formed to demand a full investigation of the matter. In early January 1999, in response to demonstrations, during which the opposition leader Joseph Ki-Zerbo was arrested, the minister for security, Yéro Boly, announced the formation of an independent commission of inquiry. The Collectif refused to participate in the commission, despite Boly's assurances that it would be impartial, and students subsequently boycotted classes in Ouagadougou, while a protest march took place in Bobo-Dioulasso. Later in the month the Collectif called a three-day strike to demand further investigation into the murder.

In February 1999 President Compaoré met opposition leaders to seek a resolution of the political *impasse* caused by Zongo's murder. A meeting in the following month between the prime

minister and representatives of the Collectif failed to allay public discontent, and in late March and mid-April further demonstrations and protests took place in Ouagadougou. During April an international committee was also formed to request that the government reopen investigations into the circumstances surrounding the death of ex-president Sankara.

In early May 1999 the commission of inquiry submitted its final report, in which it suggested that members of the presidential bodyguard implicated in the death of David Ouédraogo were also responsible for the murders of Zongo and his colleagues. The announcement of the commission's findings was followed by unrest and student demonstrations in Ouagadougou. The only foreign member of the commission of inquiry, Robert Ménard, the head of the international press freedom group, Reporters sans frontières, was subsequently detained in his hotel and deported. In mid-May three prominent members of the opposition, including Halidou Ouédraogo, the chairman of the Collectif, and Herman Yaméogo of the ADF–RDA, were arrested by the security forces. They were accused of having repeated Ménard's criticisms of the presidential guard, of having incited vandalism and of having plotted a *coup d'état*. Ouédraogo and Yaméogo were both briefly detained.

In late May 1999 Compaoré announced that the judge investigating the Zongo case would be given every facility in his attempts to prosecute those involved in the murders. Compaoré also announced the reorganization of the presidential guard, an amnesty for those arrested in the recent student protests, the reopening of the educational establishments closed during the unrest, and state compensation for the families of David Ouédraogo, Norbert Zongo and their associates. The Collectif welcomed these measures, but alleged that government influence was being brought to bear on the judiciary, and in early June called for a general strike to protest the absence of legal action against the murder suspects.

In early June 1999 Compaoré established a college of elders, composed of former Burkinabè heads of state, religious and ethnic leaders, and respected citizens. The college was to work towards national reconciliation and to investigate unpunished political crimes from 1960 onwards. In mid-June the college ordered the arrest of three members of the presidential guard, accused of the murder of David Ouédraogo, and further implicated in the murder of Zongo. Compaoré subsequently called for a reform of the judicial system in order to improve its efficiency and ensure that it did not endanger political cohesion in Burkina. In late June, however, state electricity workers observed a 24-hour strike in protest at the alleged murder of one of their colleagues by the security forces, and several days later a two-day general strike took place to protest against low wages, the privatization of parastatal enterprises and alleged human rights abuses by the government. In mid-July unarmed soldiers and junior officers, who were demanding the payment of outstanding allowances, briefly blocked the entrances to the ministry of defence, the headquarters of the armed forces and the principal army barracks in Ouagadougou. The protest was abandoned after Compaoré announced that the troops' demands would be met. Trade unions organized a further two-day general strike in mid-August.

The college of elders published its report in early August 1999. Its main recommendations were that a government of national unity should be formed as well as a 'commission of truth and justice' to oversee the transition to a truly plural political system and to investigate unresolved political murders, including that of former president Sankara. The college also suggested that an amnesty should be granted to those implicated during the commission's investigations, and that compensation be paid to the families of victims. The college further recommended the creation of a commission to investigate certain clauses of the constitution and to formulate rules governing political parties; also that Compaoré should not seek re-election and that fresh legislative elections should be held. The college's report, which was praised by Compaoré, was, however, criticized by the opposition, who rejected the proposed amnesty and the need for Compaoré to assent to the proposed reforms.

In September 1999 the prime minister began negotiations with the leaders of the major political parties in order to identify the key objectives of any government of national unity. Most political leaders indicated, however, that they would not participate in any such government until legal proceedings were expedited against those suspected of the murders of Ouédraogo and Zongo. Consequently, only two opposition figures were included in the new council of ministers announced in mid-October.

In November 1999 a demonstration by students in Ouagadougou demanded the reinstatement of pupils expelled from their secondary schools for having participated in protests against the assassination of Zongo; further demonstrations took place in December. Meanwhile health workers undertook industrial action in order to demand improved wages. In the same month there was also much criticism of the government's handling of the enforced repatriation of Burkinabè citizens from Côte d'Ivoire (see below).

At the end of October 1999 in accordance with the recommendations of the college of elders, two advisory commissions were created, one of which was to examine certain clauses of the constitution and to formulate rules governing political parties, while the other was to promote national reconciliation. Despite official assurances that the commissions' findings would be binding, many opposition parties refused to participate in the commissions, which were inaugurated in November, claiming that debate would be restricted and that their conclusions would carry little weight. Shortly afterwards, the Collectif organized a series of mass demonstrations intended to mark the first anniversary of the murder of Zongo. In early December it was announced that several important figures in the Collectif had been detained by the police and accused of 'inciting revolt and sedition in the army' by publishing a joint letter in *Le Pays* urging the security forces to guarantee the security of protesters and to reject the 'terrorist tactics' of the authorities. A court subsequently dismissed the case against the men.

In early January 2000 Compaoré offered to bring forward the legislative elections scheduled for 2002, in the hope of resolving the political crisis. Many opposition leaders, however, rejected Compaoré's proposal, suggesting that the establishment of a political solution and the prosecution of suspects in the Ouédraogo and Zongo cases should precede the elections. In the same month a court in Ouagadougou declared itself unable to hear a case brought by the widow of former president Sankara, whereby she accused unknown persons of attempting to conceal the murder of her husband by claiming on his death certificate that he had died of natural causes. The court suggested that a military court should hear the case; however, lawyers for Mme Sankara announced that they intended to bring the case before the supreme court.

In late January 2000 the ruling CDP organized a public demonstration in favour of the proposals of the advisory commission on political reform, which had recommended the modification of the electoral code and the reform of the judiciary and the constitution. In particular, the commission recommended that presidents should not serve more than two successive presidential terms. The Assemblée nationale subsequently voted to revise the electoral code and to accord greater powers to the independent electoral commission, and therefore to postpone the municipal elections scheduled for late February in order to allow the implementation of the revisions. The opposition, however, criticized what they perceived to be the limited nature of the reforms, and expressed their continued determination to boycott any elections until the Ouédraogo and Zongo cases were fully resolved.

In late February 2000 the advisory commission on national reconciliation published its report, which called for the prosecution of those suspected of involvement in the embezzlement of public funds and in so-called political killings. The report also recommended that victims of political violence or their relations should receive an official apology, compensation and a guarantee regarding their future security. The commission also called for greater freedom of speech and of assembly, the resolution of legal proceedings in the Ouédraogo and Zongo cases, the strengthening of the freedom of the press, the introduction of an amnesty law, and the construction of a monument to former president Sankara. The commission's final recommendation was that a further commission should be established in order to monitor the implementation of its recommendations.

In April 2000 a demonstration in Ouagadougou, held in order to demand the resolution of the Zongo case, resulted in violent clashes between student demonstrators and the security forces.

The opposition subsequently called for a three-day general strike and a series of demonstrations in order to protest at the intervention of the security forces. Halidou Ouédraogo, the chairman of the Collectif, and 38 other activists were briefly detained on charges of endangering public order, and the government also announced the temporary closure of all schools and universities in Ouagadougou and Bobo-Dioulasso. The government subsequently sought to defuse the tension with the announcement later in the month that it was to encourage the return to Burkina Faso of political exiles, and that it was to undertake the construction of a mausoleum for ex-president Sankara.

In late April 2000 the Assemblée nationale adopted legislation revising the electoral code; under the new regulations, which also introduced proportional representation, 91 deputies would be elected from a regional list, while 21 would be elected from a national list. The new law also reduced the presidential mandate from seven to five years renewable only once. However, the opposition, while broadly welcoming the reforms, noted that, as the new limits were not be to introduced until the next election, it would be possible for Compaoré to stand again in 2005 and 2010. A new law regulating opposition parties was also introduced, which defined the rights, in particular regarding public funding, and the responsibilities of opposition parties. In the same month Herman Yaméogo was expelled from the Groupe du 14 février opposition group for having criticized the group's policy of not co-operating with the government on reform until the Ouédraogo and Zongo cases had been resolved.

In early May 2000 the government announced that the postponed municipal elections would be held on 30 July. Several opposition parties, however, criticized the date as unfeasible in view of the political climate and called for the Ouédraogoa and Zongo cases to be resolved prior to the elections. In late May Compaoré held a meeting with Halidou Ouédraogo and other members of the Collectif, in order to discuss the process of reform. However, the death in late May of a police officer, Abdoulaye Semde Juge, who had been implicated in attempts to conceal the murder of David Ouédraogo, was widely viewed as suspicious by the opposition, and in late June the Collectif refused to meet Compaoré, who they accused of having reneged on agreements reached at their previous meeting. The opposition continued to reject the proposed date for the municipal election, and in mid-July the chairman of the independent electoral commission also called for the postponement of the elections by at least one month in order to give the commission time to resolve difficulties in the compilation of voter registers and the distribution of voter cards.

FOREIGN RELATIONS

During the 1990s Compaoré gained considerable respect as a regional mediator. Some regional and Western governments have, none the less, expressed concern at Compaoré's role in the Liberian conflict, and later in the conflicts in Sierra Leone and Angola.

Following the escalation of the civil conflict in Liberia after early 1990, Burkina's relations with some members of the Economic Community of West African States (ECOWAS) deteriorated as a result of the Compaoré government's open support for Charles Taylor's rebel National Patriotic Front of Liberia (NPFL) and refusal to contribute troops to the ECOWAS force (ECOMOG) that was sent to Liberia in mid-1990. Allegations that Burkina was aiding the NPFL persisted, and in November 1992 the US government temporarily severed diplomatic links with Burkina owing to Burkina's alleged role in transporting arms from Libya to the NPFL. Shortly afterwards, however, Compaoré expressed willingness in principle to contribute a military contingent to ECOMOG on condition that its role be confined to that of a neutral peace-keeping body. Allegations of Burkinabè support for the NPFL persisted, but in September 1995, following the signing of a new peace agreement in Abuja, Nigeria, the Compaoré administration, stating that it regarded the new accord as more 'credible' than previous peace settlements for Liberia, announced that Burkina would contribute troops to ECOMOG. In February 1997 Burkinabè troops assisted in the preparations for the forthcoming elections in Liberia; members of the Burkinabè military subsequently remained in Liberia to assist in training new armed forces.

In May 1998 the government of Burkina vehemently denied allegations (made by Sierra Leonean refugees entering Guinea) that Burkinabè forces were assisting anti-government fighters in Sierra Leone. In early 1999 accusations were made by President Kabbah of Sierra Leone, by the Nigerian government and by the international press that Burkina and Liberia were co-operating to provide support to the rebels in Sierra Leone and to supply them with arms. The Burkinabè government continued to deny its involvement. In early 2000 a report to the UN Security Council accused Burkina Faso of having supplied weapons to the rebels in Sierra Leone in exchange for diamonds on several occasions. It was also alleged that Burkina Faso had supplied weapons to Liberia and to Angolan rebel groups, despite international embargoes on the supply of weapons to those countries. The report, which further accused Compaoré of having conducted personal negotiations with the Angolan rebel leader Jonas Savimbi, was strenuously denied by the Burkinabè government, which stated that the external policy of Burkina Faso was entirely motivated by a desire to establish peace in the region.

In early November 1999 a dispute over land rights between Burkinabè settlers in the south-west of Côte d'Ivoire and the indigenous minority Krou population, which caused two deaths, led to the violent and systematic expulsion from the region of several hundred Burkinabè plantation workers by militant Krou. Several deaths were reported, and it was estimated that between 9,000 and 12,000 expatriates had returned to Burkina in subsequent weeks. In late November the Burkinabè minister of foreign affairs, Yossouf Ouédraogo, visited Côte d'Ivoire in order to discuss the expulsions with the Ivorian authorities. The two governments emphasized, however, that the problem was a local one and that relations between the two countries remained cordial. Following the *coup d'état* in Côte d'Ivoire in December 1999, the military authorities assured the government of Burkina that the expulsions would cease and that measures would be taken in order to allow workers to return.

In December 1988 Compaoré attended the Franco-African summit, held in Morocco (the first occasion on which the country had been represented since 1983); subsequent meetings of this bloc have also been attended. Compaoré's first official visit to France, in June 1993, was widely interpreted as a recognition by the French authorities of his legitimacy following the installation of elected organs of state. Burkina swiftly forged close relations with Jacques Chirac following his election to the French presidency in May 1995, and contacts have remained frequent. The 19th Franco-African summit took place in Ouagadougou in December 1996. Compaoré subsequently participated in a regional mediation effort, conceived at the meeting, to resolve the political crisis in the Central African Republic (CAR). The ADP authorized the contribution of a Burkinabè military contingent to the surveillance mission for the CAR in February 1997, and a Burkinabè force remained in the CAR as part of the UN peace-keeping force which succeeded the regional mission in April 1998.

In regional affairs, Burkina has been active in efforts to establish a regional crisis intervention force, and in April 1998 Burkina was one of eight regional countries to participate in the 'Cohésion Kompienga '98' military exercises. The 34th assembly of heads of state and government of the OAU took place in Ouagadougou in June; Compaoré, as incoming chairman, subsequently played an active role in mediation initiatives in the dispute between Eritrea and Ethiopia. In early March 1999 the Burkinabè government was obliged to cancel plans to hold an extraordinary summit of the OAU later in the month. It had been hoped that the summit would contribute to peace initiatives in Angola, Sierra Leone and the Democratic Republic of the Congo. However, the governments of Angola and Sierra Leone expressed their strong opposition to Burkina's policy of inviting representatives of rebel factions to the summit, accusing Compaoré of seeking to legitimize the rebel groups. Burkina subsequently announced that the quorum necessary to hold an extraordinary summit had not been achieved.

Relations with Libya have generally been strong in the 10 years of the Compaoré regime; Burkina was, notably, a founder member of the Libyan-sponsored commission of Sahelian and Saharan states (COMESSA), established in Tripoli in 1997, and in April 1999 Compaoré attended the first COMESSA summit held in Syrte, Libya.

Economy

EDITH HODGKINSON

A land-locked country in the savannah lands of the west African Sahel, Burkina Faso has been continually challenged in its efforts to ensure the survival of its agricultural and pastoral economy, and has only limited prospects for modernization, whether through industrialization or the expansion of external trade. The population (estimated at 10.68m. in mid-1998) is largely rural, depending on traditional farming methods for subsistence and receiving modest earnings from the sale of cash crops, fruit, vegetables, livestock or firewood. The climate is arid, and the rivers mostly seasonal, so supplies of water can run low during the long dry period, and the economy is very vulnerable to weather conditions.

Burkina is also highly dependent on the maintenance of good economic and political relations with its six neighbours. Large numbers of Burkinabè work in Côte d'Ivoire, some seasonally and some permanently. There is also seasonal migration to Ghana. In all, an estimated 2m. Burkinabè work abroad. This migration of workers reinforces Burkina's commercial contacts with its southern neighbours, where many consumer goods are purchased for resale in Burkina, and their remittances also contribute substantially to the national balance of payments, helping to offset the country's chronic trade deficit.

Manufacturing activity is restricted to small units, established principally in Bobo-Dioulasso and, to a lesser extent, in the capital, Ouagadougou. It takes the form of import substitution and the processing of local agricultural commodities, and, apart from cotton ginning, the manufacturing sector makes little contribution to exports. Small-scale artisanal production serves regional and tourist markets, with the active informal sector representing an important source of jobs and income. Burkina's mineral resources are only just beginning to be exploited on a significant basis, and there is considerable optimism regarding the country's deposits of gold (which has been mined in small quantities for centuries), zinc and manganese.

The economy's dependence on agriculture—and hence the weather—and on workers' remittances means that its performance can fluctuate widely from year to year. However, whereas in the late 1980s and early 1990s growth in gross domestic product (GDP) on average only just kept pace with the increase in population, since 1995 the rate of expansion has improved, with a peak of 6.1% in 1996 and an average 5.3% a year in 1995–99. The improvement can be attributed to the structural adjustment programme initiated in 1991, and to the enhancement of export earnings generated by the 50% devaluation of the CFA franc in January 1994. The related strong growth of the cotton sector has also contributed. The economy, however, remains small, so that, with gross national product (GNP) per head estimated by the World Bank at only US $240 in 1998 (about one-third of the level in neighbouring Côte d'Ivoire), Burkina remains one of the world's poorest countries: on the UNDP human development index, Burkina ranked 172nd of 175 countries in 1997, mainly because of its very poor health and education indicators.

Reversing the nationalization policy pursued by the Sankara regime in 1983–87, a major aspect of the structural adjustment now being implemented is a divestment programme designed to enhance the role of the private sector. Although the programme has attracted some interest from both domestic and foreign private investors, the domestic private sector is itself limited in size and influence—having had little opportunity to develop in a previously state-controlled environment—while foreign investors have in general been reluctant to locate in African members of the Franc Zone, especially prior to the currency devaluation. Burkina's best prospects for modernization and economic growth would appear to lie in the development of the mining sector, small-scale, resource-based manufacturing, increased exports of horticultural products to Europe and in a modest expansion of the tourism industry.

AGRICULTURE

Agriculture and livestock—which accounts for around one-third of Burkina's GDP, and provides a livelihood for 80%–90% of the population—is largely at subsistence level. In those years when conditions are favourable, the country rebuilds its food stocks to last through periods of unfavourable climatic conditions, when severe shortages have been experienced. In all years poor transport and storage facilities serve to reduce the supply that is effectively available. Inadequate rain in 1997/98 resulted in the lowest cereals crop of the decade, at only 2,273,000 tons. The return to good rainfall in 1998/99 brought an increase in the total cereals crop to a record 2,657,000 tons. Despite subsequent decreases in the production of millet and sorghum in 1999/2000, increased production of maize and rice contributed to a record cereal crop in that year of 2,699,900 tons. None the less, it was announced that, despite the overall increase in 1999/2000, some regions had in fact suffered decreases in cereal production, while a slight decline in the production of vegetable crops was recorded throughout the country.

Burkina's cash crops were formerly the surplus of subsistence cultivation, mainly shea-nuts (karité nuts), marketed production of which was 75,700 tons in 1995/96, and sesame seeds (7,800 tons). In the past decade, however, there has been considerable government investment in cotton, groundnuts, sugar, cashew nuts and market gardening, with financial aid from, among others, the European Development Fund. The most important cash crop (and principal source of export earnings—66% of the total in 1998, according to official estimates) is cotton, output of which more than doubled in the decade to 1985. The sector received a strong boost from the higher local-currency prices paid to producers after the devaluation of the CFA franc in January 1994 and as the result of the more favourable international market. Consequently output, which was down to 117,000 tons in 1993/94, had risen to 170,000 tons by 1995/96. A major investment programme for the cotton sector, announced in 1996, aims to increase output by the state-owned processing and marketing company, Société burkinabè des fibres textiles (SOFITEX), to 345,000 tons within five years, through the modernization of facilities and an expansion in the area cultivated. This programme, together with good rains and the construction of rural feeder roads, allowed an even more marked rise in production, to 214,000 tons in 1996/97 and, despite less favourable weather, to 338,000 tons in 1997/98, as farmers responded to an accelerated payments schedule. The following year saw a fall, however, to an estimated 310,000 tons owing to parasite infestation and, apparently, some shift out of cotton to cereals production, reversing a well-established trend.

It was the switch to cotton production which brought a reduction in output of groundnuts during the 1980s. However, there was a good recovery in the 1990s: marketed production increased from an average of 132,000 tons per year in 1989/90–1990/91 to 231,000 tons in 1997/98. Output of sugar, which began in 1974/75, has recently amounted to 30,000–40,000 tons (refined) annually.

The livestock sector (including livestock and livestock products, hides and skins) accounts for about one-sixth of the country's export earnings—and significantly more if unrecorded shipments are taken into account. Stock-rearing is practised by the semi-nomadic Fulani in the thinly-populated area of the north and east, although a large-scale programme is redeveloping livestock production in the west of the country. A west African regional development project, supported by the FAO, for those areas affected by trypanosomiasis (sleeping-sickness), includes Burkina Faso. In 1998 there were an estimated 4.5m. cattle, 6.2m. sheep and 7.9m. goats. Livestock exports were boosted by the currency devaluation: numbers exported increased from 295,700 (including 101,600 cattle) in 1993 to 417,300 (173,000 cattle) in 1994, with Côte d'Ivoire constituting the principal market. They subsequently edged down slightly, to 412,200 (147,600 cattle) in 1996, but remain well above pre-devaluation levels. The small fish catch (some 8,000 tons per year, according to the FAO) is consumed locally. Timber production is insignificant, despite the large area under forest (almost one-quarter of the total); however, foreign agencies are now funding timber development projects in the Kompienga and Bagré dam regions.

MINING AND POWER

A priority of the Compaoré administration is the exploitation of Burkina's mineral resources, which include gold, manganese, zinc and silver. Industrial gold-mining output, mainly at Poura in western-central Burkina, reached a peak of 3,572 kg in 1990, but declined steadily thereafter, owing to production difficulties at Poura, to 1,275 kg in 1994. To bring in new capital to enhance production at this mine, where reserves are estimated at 25,000–27,000 kg, and as part of the wider programme to attract foreign investment in mining, the government privatized the company involved in its development, the Société de recherche et d'exploitations minières du Burkina (SOREMIB). Sahelian Goldfields of Canada, which took over the rehabilitation work at Poura in late 1995, bought a 90% stake, forming a new company, Société aurifère du Sahel, which reopened the mine in October 1998. The new company planned to invest 3,000m. francs CFA over four years and had an output target of 4,000 kg per year. The liberalization of the mining code in 1996–97 and the boost of currency devaluation combined to attract other mining companies, from Australia and South Africa, including BHP and Randgold Resources. Significant quantities of gold are also produced on an artisanal basis (an estimated average of 2.5 tons per year in 1995–97), with much escaping documentation and smuggled out of the country. Gold is now Burkina's third largest source of export revenue (after cotton and livestock). The prospects for the sector, however, suffered from the sharp decline in the price of gold in 1999, which caused the closure of the Poura mine in August of that year and a considerable retrenchment of prospecting activity.

Trial exploitation of manganese deposits at Tambao, in the north-east, was begun by Interstar of Canada during 1993. The deposits are estimated at 19m. tons of ore, containing 51% manganese, and the aim was to produce 30,000–80,000 tons per year in the initial phase of development. However, the project is hampered by the lack of a rail connection to the port of Abidjan, in Côte d'Ivoire. The government's railway extension project has been completed between Ouagadougou and Kaya, but this is more than 200 km short of the mining area, a distance which in the first phase will be served by road transport. Output has been significantly less than expected, at only 324 tons a year in 1994–95, and the Burkinabè government is seeking to cancel the contract with Interstar.

The potential for zinc mining operations at Perkoa (in central Burkina), which would be well served by the existing railway through Koudougou, was investigated in the early 1990s by Boliden International of Sweden. Proven reserves of some 7m. tons of ore have been identified. However, transport difficulties and low world prices prompted the company to abandon the project. It has since had several different owners, with a South African company, Metorex, acquiring the joint venture set up to develop the mine, Billitan Burkina Faso, in September 1999. Burkina's other mineral resources include titanium, vanadium, nickel, bauxite, lead and phosphates, although none of these is considered to be commercially viable at present. A more immediate development prospect is for the quarrying of limestone deposits at Tin Hrassan, near Tambao, which can be developed for cement production.

Electricity generating capacity is being considerably expanded. The bulk of output is thermal (149m. kWh out of a total 243m. in 1998), with the remainder largely provided by two hydroelectric stations, on the Kompienga and Bagré rivers, with a combined capacity of 31 MW. Work on a 12 MW scheme at Diébougou began in 1998, with 70% of the 35,000m. francs CFA cost financed by Hydro Afrique, a consortium of South African companies. In addition, agreement was reached in the same year for a 30 MW facility, Ouaga III, at the Kossodo industrial zone, to be built and run by an affiliate of the Aga Khan's Economic Development Fund. There are also plans for electricity interconnection with Côte d'Ivoire and Ghana; France and the European Investment Bank (EIB) are to finance the cost (21,100m. francs CFA) of the latter scheme. Although it is not proposed to sell off the state-owned power utility as part of the divestment programme, the government plans to end its monopoly on production and distribution, in order to stimulate more private investment in this sector.

MANUFACTURING

Manufacturing activity is still rudimentary but has been expanding over the long term, with its share of GDP increasing from 8% in 1960 to some 20% in the 1990s. Growth has been modest because of the small size of the domestic market, the lack of indigenous raw materials, and shortages of finance and management skills. Before the 1994 devaluation the sector was suffering from competition from imported (often smuggled) products from countries outside the Franc Zone, and in every year in 1991–94 industrial production declined. The much higher local cost of imports since devaluation contributed to some recovery in the sector in the second half of the 1990s. However, the introduction at the beginning of 2000 of duty-free trade in industrial goods within the regional grouping, the Union économique et monétaire ouest-africain (UEMOA, see p. 133), will bring stiffer competition, which most local manufacturers are not well placed to counter. Production takes the form of agricultural processing (in particular, cotton, leather and sugar) and the substitution of consumer goods imports. The first industrial plant of any significance was the textile plant at Koudougou, which entered production in 1970. Cotton-ginning capacity was increased in 1989 with the expansion of the SOFITEX complex in Bobo-Dioulasso; further expansion is taking place (see above).

During the period of political revolution under Sankara, the Société des brasseries du Burkina Faso (BRAKINA) brewery operation was one of the few major industries to retain a substantial private holding. By contrast, the Compaoré regime has implemented an extensive divestment programme, aiming to reduce the government's equity in industrial concerns to a maximum of 25%. In line with this, part of the state's holding in the Société industrielle du Faso, which produces motor cycles and bicycles (important methods of transport in this predominantly rural country), was sold to private Burkinabè interests in 1993. Under the first phase of the privatization programme (1994–96) 22 parastatals were identified for sale, and all but three were subsequently disposed of. Legislation was adopted in 1994 authorizing the privatization of a further 19 organizations, among them the Caisse de stabilisation des prix des produits agricoles du Burkina, the Société Sucrière de la Comoé (SOSUCO) and the Société Faso-Fani textiles concern. Progress on these privatizations has been inhibited by their political sensitivity, and above all by the likely consequences for jobs: SOSUCO ranks second only to the government as a source of employment. When a 52% stake in the sugar complex was finally sold in July 1998, the new owner, a consortium headed by an Aga Khan affiliate, pledged to retain all the permanent workforce.

TRANSPORT INFRASTRUCTURE

Overall the transport network is relatively poor, although it has received considerable new investment in recent years. An important transport artery is the railway line from the border with Côte d'Ivoire through Bobo-Dioulasso, Koudougou and Ouagadougou to Kaya. However, the track, vehicles and services have been in need of maintenance and further investment. The extension of the main line to Tambao is dependent upon the provision of external financing (see above). Following the withdrawal, in 1987, of Côte d'Ivoire from the joint rail partnership, Burkina and Côte d'Ivoire established separate rail companies, and in 1993 issued a joint tender for the transfer to private ownership of services on the line. SITARAIL, a consortium of French, Belgian, Ivorian and Burkinabè interests, assumed management of operations in 1995. Financing for the attendant investment programme was provided by the International Development Asscn, the Caisse française de développement, the EIB, the West African Development Bank and the

Belgian government. Classified roads are estimated at 13,200 km, but only 1,800 km are tarred. World Bank funds are supporting the rehabilitation of the road network, while seven African and Arab organizations pledged funds in 1997 for the paving of two major roads to the borders with Ghana and Côte d'Ivoire. The runways of the country's two international airports (at Ouagadougou and Bobo-Dioulasso) were extended during the 1980s to accommodate large cargo aircraft; infrastructure at Ouagadougou airport is being updated, with financial assistance from France.

FINANCE

Since the early 1970s, when expenditure was held down and small budget surpluses were achieved, there has been a history of fiscal deficit, which is attributable mainly to the economy's very low taxable capacity. During the early 1980s the government attempted to narrow the deficit by restricting expenditure, particularly on development. There was a noticeable change in direction in 1985, when spending was forecast to rise by one-fifth, as development expenditure more than doubled, reflecting work on the Kompienga and Bagré dams and on the Tambao rail link. The budget deficit was, none the less, almost eliminated, as the Sankara government introduced new taxes. There were further increases in taxation in both 1986 and 1987; however, the budget deficit rose dramatically, reaching the equivalent of about 13% of GDP in 1987, as a result of even higher increases in government current and capital outlays.

The Compaoré government initially relaxed the unpopular austerity measures that had been introduced under Sankara. None the less, the structural adjustment programme for 1991–93, agreed with the World Bank and the IMF, again made rigorous control of government finances a priority. The programme included measures to widen the tax base and reform customs duties, while aiming to stabilize expenditure on wages and channel funds into such areas as primary education and health. However, the government was unable to achieve the improvement it sought, owing to the stagnation of the economy in 1992–93, with the result that, despite the introduction of value-added tax (VAT) in 1993, the overall deficit (excluding grants) was some 72,900m. francs CFA in that year, equivalent to 9.2% of GDP.

Reducing the budget deficit remained the aim under the terms of the Enhanced Structural Adjustment Facility accorded in 1993 and again in 1996 (for 1996–98). In 1994, under pressure on expenditure as a result of the currency devaluation and additions to the state payroll, the budget deficit reached 11.3% of GDP. However, some progress was subsequently made, through controls on current spending (which fell in both 1995 and 1996) and enhanced revenue from taxation, including higher VAT rates from September 1996. The deficit in that year narrowed to 8.9% of GDP, but election pressures on the spending side pushed the imbalance to 10.2% in 1997. The deficit was only reduced by a single percentage point in 1998. Some of the strain on government finances is now being eased as the divestment of loss-making state enterprises continues and those remaining in public hands (such as telecommunications) are restructured. However, neither the Burkinabè government nor its creditors expect to eliminate the dependence on external grants to support the government's capital spending programme. The prospect of declining aid inflows caused budget spending on capital projects to be cut in 1999, while the loss of customs revenue under the new regional tariff structure in 2000 required total planned budget spending to be reduced by 1% in that year.

FOREIGN TRADE AND PAYMENTS

Burkina suffers a chronic and substantial trade deficit. Its export capacity is highly vulnerable to weather conditions and trends in international prices for cotton, while the import bill reflects a range of factors: the domestic food balance, international prices for petroleum and the level of investment spending, both public and private. Annual fluctuations in the size of the deficit have therefore been substantial. Over time it has tended to rise in nominal terms, registering a peak of US $367m. in 1993 (calculated in balance-of-payments terms, which exclude the cost of transportation—a significant item for this remote, land-locked country). Coverage by export earnings of the import bill rarely exceeded one-half. The immediate impact of the devaluation of the CFA franc in 1994 was a 27% fall in import spending in US dollar terms, while receipts from exports declined by only 5% (representing an 87% rise in CFA franc values). The trade deficit consequently fell to only $129m. (in payments terms), while import cover improved to almost two-thirds. The trade gap widened in subsequent years, as demand for imports revived, and averaged $280m. per year in 1995–98, although the level of import cover improved slightly.

The merchandise deficit thus represents a large outflow on the current account, compounded by the substantial debt represented by transport costs. It is in part—and in some years wholly—offset by remittances from emigrants and aid inflows. Workers' remittances fluctuate in response to economic conditions in host countries, and have not yet regained the peak of US $187m. registered in 1988. In 1994–98 these inflows averaged $99m. per year, with the decline in part reflecting the depreciation in the currencies of host countries against the dollar.

Meanwhile, net inflows of official development assistance from OECD and OPEC countries and multilateral institutions averaged US $423m. per year in 1990–98, with grants (which appear on the current account of the balance of payments) averaging $329m. By far the major source of bilateral aid is France; Germany, the Netherlands, and Denmark are also important donors. Given this significant inflow of concessionary funds, Burkina's external debt has remained comparatively low and its debt-service burden moderate. At the end of 1990 the external debt, at $834m., was equivalent to only 30% of GNP, with 71% on concessionary terms, while the debt-servicing ratio (payments of principal and interest as a proportion of total foreign earnings) was only 6.8% in the same year. Although most of the relatively marked rise in foreign debt in the following three years (to

$1,117m. at the end of 1993) was on concessionary terms, bringing the proportion to 82% of total indebtedness, Burkina still had difficulties in meeting debt-servicing payments. Consequently, the country's bilateral creditors agreed, in 1991 and again in 1993, to rescheduling. Further concessions were made after the devaluation of the CFA franc, which had the effect of doubling the external debt denominated in local currency. The application of so-called Naples terms to $70m. in non-concessionary debt (which effectively annul two-thirds of the liability) was agreed in June 1996; in the same month France cancelled 60,300m. francs CFA in concessional debt. The share of bilateral debt has thus fallen, leaving 77% of debt owed to multilateral institutions in 1997 and therefore not open to rescheduling or cancellation. Therefore, while the country's debt ratios are theoretically not excessive—with total debt at the end of 1997, at $1,297m., equivalent to 54.3% of GNP and debt-service at 11.8%—in practice, given the fragility of the economy, Burkina has very limited scope to increase its call on foreign funds other than on extremely concessionary terms. None the less, in recognition of its commitment to structural adjustment and a debt burden classified as 'unsustainable' because of the dependence on workers' remittances, Burkina was deemed eligible for debt-reduction under the terms of the Heavily Indebted Poor Countries (HIPC) initiative, introduced by the World Bank and the IMF in 1997. Burkina Faso subsequently also qualified for assistance under the IMF-sponsored Poverty Reduction and Growth Facility, and in July 2000 the IMF and World Bank agreed debt-reduction arrangements with Burkina Faso valued at US $700m. It was estimated that the overall reduction in the country's debt-servicing obligations would thereby be reduced by around one-half in subsequent years, allowing, it was hoped, increased government expenditure on social development.

Statistical Survey

Source (except where otherwise stated): Institut National de la Statistique et de la Démographie, 555 blvd de la Révolution, 01 BP 374, Ouagadougou 01; tel. 32-49-76; fax 31-07-60.

Area and Population

AREA, POPULATION AND DENSITY

Area (sq km)	274,200*
Population (census results)	
10–20 December 1985	7,964,705
December 1996	
Males	4,970,882
Females	5,341,727
Total	10,312,609
Population (official estimate at mid-year)	
1998	10,683,000
Density (per sq km) at mid-1998	38.9

* 105,870 sq miles.

POPULATION BY PROVINCE (at 1985 census)

Province	Population	Capital
Bam	162,575	Kongoussi
Bazèga	303,941	Kombissiri
Bougouriba	220,895	Diébougou
Boulougou	402,236	Tenkodogo
Boulkiemdé	365,223	Koudougou
Comoé	249,967	Banfora
Ganzourgou	195,452	Zorgo
Gnagna	229,152	Bogandé
Gourma	294,235	Fada-Ngourma
Houet	581,722	Bobo-Dioulasso
Kadiogo	459,826	Ouagadougou
Kénédougou	139,973	Orodara
Kossi	332,960	Nounga

Province — *continued*	Population	Capital
Kouritenga	198,486	Koupéla
Mouhoun	288,735	Dédougou
Nahouri	105,509	Pô
Namentenga	198,890	Boulsa
Oubritenga	304,265	Ziniaré
Oudalan	106,194	Gorom-Gorom
Passoré	223,830	Yako
Poni	235,480	Gaoua
Sangouié	217,277	Réo
Sanmatenga	367,724	Kaya
Séno	228,875	Dori
Sissili	244,919	Léo
Soum	186,812	Djibo
Sourou	268,108	Tougan
Tapoa	158,859	Diapaga
Yatenga	536,578	Ouahigouya
Zoundwéogo	156,007	Manga
Total	**7,964,705**	

Sources: UN, *Demographic Yearbook*; Secrétariat du Comité Monétaire de la Zone Franc, *La Zone Franc—Rapport 1994*.

Note: In early 1997 the number of provinces was increased from 30 to 45.

PRINCIPAL TOWNS (population at 1985 census)

Ouagadougou (capital)	441,514	Ouahigouya . . .	38,902
Bobo-Dioulasso . . .	228,668	Banfora	35,319
Koudougou . . .	51,926	Kaya	25,814

1993 (official estimates, '000): Ouagadougou 690; Bobo-Dioulasso 300; Koudougou 105.

Source: Secrétariat du Comité Monétaire de la Zone Franc, *Rapport Annuel*.

BIRTHS AND DEATHS (UN estimates, annual averages)

	1980–85	1985–90	1990–95
Birth rate (per 1,000) . . .	50.1	48.9	47.7
Death rate (per 1,000) . . .	20.1	18.9	18.9

Expectation of life (UN estimates, years at birth, 1990–95): 45.0 (males 44.1; females 46.1).

Source: UN, *World Population Prospects: The 1998 Revision.*

ECONOMICALLY ACTIVE POPULATION
(sample survey, persons aged 10 years and over, 1991)

	Males	Females	Total
Agriculture, hunting, forestry and fishing	2,162,759	2,131,025	4,293,784
Mining and quarrying . .	2,286	304	2,590
Manufacturing	26,996	24,698	51,694
Electricity, gas and water . .	3,038	806	3,844
Construction	10,988	28	11,016
Trade, restaurants and hotels. .	48,117	72,197	120,314
Transport, storage and communications . . .	14,620	421	15,041
Finance, insurance, real estate and business services . .	1,650	425	2,075
Community, social and personal services	84,136	27,420	111,556
Activities not adequately defined .	8,355	9,105	17,460
Total employed . . .	2,362,945	2,266,429	4,629,374
Unemployed . . .	38,515	11,304	49,819
Total labour force . . .	2,401,460	2,277,733	4,679,193

Source: ILO, *Yearbook of Labour Statistics.*

Mid-1998 (estimates in '000): Agriculture, etc. 5,177; Total 5,612 (Source: FAO, *Production Yearbook*).

Agriculture

PRINCIPAL CROPS ('000 metric tons)

	1996	1997	1998†
Maize	294*	220	220
Millet	811*	604	604
Sorghum	1,254*	943	943
Rice (paddy)	95†	90	90
Sweet potatoes† . . .	20	16	20
Yams†	40	36	36
Other roots and tubers† . .	10	11	11
Tomatoes† . . .	30	30	30
Other vegetables† . .	224	224	224
Fruit†	73	73	73
Pulses†	62	66	66
Groundnuts (in shell) . .	230‡	152	152
Cottonseed . . .	130†	196	196
Cotton (lint) . . .	88*	144	144
Sesame seed† . . .	5	8	8
Tobacco (leaves)† . .	1	1	1
Sugar cane†	400	400	400

* Unofficial figure.   † FAO estimate(s).

Source: FAO, *Production Yearbook.*

LIVESTOCK ('000 head, year ending September)

	1996	1997	1998*
Cattle	4,433	4,522	4,522
Sheep	5,950*	6,207	6,207
Goats	7,550*	7,914	7,914
Pigs	575	587	587
Horses*	24	25	25
Asses*	465	475	475
Camels*	14	14	14

Poultry (million): 20* in 1996; 21 in 1997; 21* in 1998.

* FAO estimate(s).

Source: FAO, *Production Yearbook.*

LIVESTOCK PRODUCTS (FAO estimates unless otherwise indicated, '000 metric tons)

	1996	1997	1998
Beef and veal	47	50	50
Mutton and lamb . . .	12	13	13
Goat meat	21	22	23
Pig meat	7	8	8
Poultry meat	22	23	24
Other meat	9	7	7
Cows' milk	121	157*	160*
Goats' milk	21	52	52
Butter	1	1	1
Hen eggs	17	17	17
Cattle hides	8	8	7
Sheepskins	3	3	3
Goatskins	5	6	6

* Official figure.

Source: FAO, *Production Yearbook.*

Forestry

ROUNDWOOD REMOVALS
('000 cubic metres, excluding bark)

	1995	1996	1997
Sawlogs, veneer logs and logs for sleepers	1	1	1
Other industrial wood . .	460	473	486
Fuel wood	9,731	10,011	10,297
Total	10,192	10,485	10,784

Source: FAO, *Yearbook of Forest Products.*

SAWNWOOD PRODUCTION ('000 cubic metres)

	1995	1996	1997
Total (all broadleaved) . . .	2	2	2

Source: FAO, *Yearbook of Forest Products.*

Fishing

('000 metric tons, live weight)

	1995	1996	1997
Total catch	8.0	8.0	8.0

Source: FAO, *Yearbook of Fishery Statistics.*

Mining

	1996	1997	1998
Gold (kilograms)	1,063	1,088	1,091

Source: IMF, *Burkina Faso: Statistical Annex* (July 1999).

Industry

SELECTED PRODUCTS

	1996	1997	1998
Edible oils (metric tons)	4,590	14,475	13,269
Shea (karité) butter (metric tons)	0	0	316
Flour (metric tons)	30,265	33,669	31,511
Pasta (metric tons)	869	870	117
Sugar (metric tons)	30,310	30,906	32,330
Beer ('000 hl)	435	460	371
Soft drinks ('000 hl)	142	168	144
Cigarettes (million packets)	46	60	55
Printed fabric ('000 sq metres)	5,098	4,141	2,828
Soap (metric tons)	6,872	11,580	9,229
Matches (cartons)	3,351	6,234	7,504
Bicycles (units)	33,158	36,030	34,289
Mopeds (units)	10,694	17,283	14,876
Tyres ('000)	462	480	205
Inner tubes ('000)	2,245	2,604	1,267
Electric energy ('000 kWh)	273,530	305,531	n.a.

Source: IMF, *Burkina Faso: Statistical Annex* (July 1999).

Finance

CURRENCY AND EXCHANGE RATES

Monetary Units
100 centimes = 1 franc de la Communauté financière africaine (CFA).

Sterling, Dollar and Euro Equivalents (28 April 2000)
£1 sterling = 1,132.20 francs CFA;
US $1 = 722.02 francs CFA;
€1 = 655.96 francs CFA;
10,000 francs CFA = £8.832 = $13.850 = €15.245.

Average Exchange Rate (francs CFA per US $)
1997   583.67
1998   589.95
1999   615.70

Note: An exchange rate of 1 French franc = 50 francs CFA, established in 1948, remained in force until January 1994, when the CFA franc was devalued by 50%, with the exchange rate adjusted to 1 French franc = 100 francs CFA. This relationship to French currency remained in effect with the introduction of the euro in January 1999. From that date, accordingly, a fixed exchange rate of €1 = 655.957 francs CFA has been in operation.

BUDGET ('000 million francs CFA)

Revenue	1996	1997	1998
Current revenue	160.0	181.3	199.2
Tax revenue	149.0	167.4	183.9
Income and profits	39.5	39.8	43.6
Domestic goods and services	59.9	72.3	82.4
International trade	45.2	50.0	52.2
Other tax revenue	4.5	5.3	5.7
Non-tax revenue	11.0	13.9	15.4
Capital revenue	0.0	0.1	0.2
Total	160.0	181.5	199.4

Expenditure and net lending	1996	1997	1998
Domestic expenditure and net lending	150.1	177.8	205.1
Wages and salaries	64.7	67.7	72.0
Goods and services	27.0	28.0	34.6
Interest payments	11.5	11.7	12.7
Current transfers	31.7	33.1	38.7
Budgetary contribution to investment	16.9	39.7	47.6
Net lending*	−1.7	−2.5	−0.6
Foreign-financed government investment	125.2	135.0	132.6
Restructuring operations	1.6	10.5	2.4
Total	276.8	323.3	340.1

* Including proceeds from privatization, which are excluded from revenue and are treated as a deduction from expenditure.

Source: IMF, *Burkina Faso: Statistical Annex* (July 1999).

INTERNATIONAL RESERVES (US $ million at 31 December)

	1997	1998	1999
Gold*	3.4	3.3	3.3
IMF special drawing rights	2.2	0.8	0.7
Reserve position in IMF	9.7	10.2	9.9
Foreign exchange	332.9	362.4	284.4
Total	348.2	376.7	298.3

* Valued at market-related prices.

Source: IMF, *International Financial Statistics*.

MONEY SUPPLY ('000 million francs CFA at 31 December)

	1997	1998	1999
Currency outside banks	170.1	165.0	142.5
Demand deposits at deposit money banks*	90.7	89.5	107.7
Checking deposits at post office	2.1	2.3	2.3
Total money (incl. others)	268.9	261.9	256.9

* Excluding the deposits of public establishments of an administrative or social nature.

Source: IMF, *International Financial Statistics*.

COST OF LIVING (Consumer Price Index for African households in Ouagadougou; base: 1995 = 100)

	1997	1998	1999
All items	108.6	114.2	112.9

Source: IMF, *International Financial Statistics*.

NATIONAL ACCOUNTS
(estimates, '000 million francs CFA at current prices)

Expenditure on the Gross Domestic Product

	1996	1997	1998
Government final consumption expenditure	170.4	172.3	191.4
Private final consumption expenditure	1,030.2	1,091.2	1,161.0
Increase in stocks	8.8	−11.3	—
Gross fixed capital formation	318.5	367.0	389.2
Total domestic expenditure	1,527.9	1,619.2	1,741.6
Exports of goods and services	141.4	155.8	212.7
Less Imports of goods and services	371.0	385.0	431.5
GDP in purchasers' values	1,298.3	1,390.0	1,522.8
GDP at constant 1985 prices	908.4	951.6	1,010.5

Source: IMF, *Burkina Faso: Statistical Annex* (July 1999).

Gross Domestic Product by Economic Activity

	1996	1997	1998
Agriculture, livestock, forestry and fishing	425.9	415.7	460.0
Mining	232.7	266.2	307.7
Manufacturing			
Electricity, gas and water	10.5	11.5	12.4
Construction and public works	65.2	74.0	79.3
Trade	156.8	175.6	189.5
Transport and communications	49.9	55.9	60.3
Non-marketable services	130.9	138.3	146.5
Other services	151.7	169.9	183.3
Sub-total	1,223.6	1,306.8	1,438.8
Import taxes and duties	74.7	83.3	84.0
GDP in purchasers' values	1,298.3	1,390.0	1,522.8

Source: IMF, *Burkina Faso: Statistical Annex* (July 1999).

BALANCE OF PAYMENTS ('000 million francs CFA)

	1996	1997	1998*
Exports of goods f.o.b. . . .	119.0	133.6	182.4
Imports of goods f.o.b. . . .	−287.8	−297.7	−335.0
Trade balance	**−168.8**	**−164.1**	**−152.6**
Services and other income (net)	−64.7	−72.9	−75.6
Balance on goods, services and income	**−233.5**	**−237.0**	**−228.2**
Private unrequited transfers (net)	45.2	47.2	45.0
Public unrequited transfers (net)	147.0	140.0	135.3
Current balance	**−41.2**	**−49.8**	**−47.9**
Long-term capital (net) . . .	34.2	24.5	44.8
Short-term capital (net) . . .	8.3	7.3	−11.0
Net errors and omissions . . .	−2.0	−2.4	−7.6
Overall balance	**−0.7**	**−20.5**	**−21.7**

* Provisional figures.

Source: Banque centrale des états de l'Afrique de l'ouest.

External Trade

PRINCIPAL COMMODITIES (estimates, '000 million francs CFA)

Imports f.o.b.	1996	1997	1998
Food products	43.9	41.3	45.0
Petroleum products . . .	37.6	40.1	40.0
Capital equipment . . .	86.8	90.4	90.0
Raw materials . . .	21.5	23.4	30.0
Total (incl. others) . . .	**288.0**	**297.7**	**335.0**

Exports f.o.b.	1996	1997	1998
Livestock and livestock products	33.0	27.1	27.1
Live animals	17.5	14.6	14.6
Hides and skins . . .	13.7	11.1	10.9
Cotton	49.6	74.6	120.9
Gold	9.0	9.0	9.0
Total (incl. others) . . .	**119.0**	**133.7**	**182.4**

Source: Banque centrale des états de l'Afrique de l'ouest in IMF, *Burkina Faso: Statistical Annex* (July 1999).

PRINCIPAL TRADING PARTNERS ('000 million francs CFA)*

Imports c.i.f.	1995	1996	1997
Belgium-Luxembourg . . .	9.9	9.0	7.6
China, People's Repub. . . .	4.0	3.5	3.5
Côte d'Ivoire	34.9	51.3	58.1
France	58.2	81.9	88.5
Germany	7.7	13.3	8.4
Ghana	2.7	2.7	3.0
India	—	12.0	3.2
Italy	6.3	13.2	12.2
Japan	15.7	17.3	17.0
Netherlands	8.2	5.8	10.1
Nigeria	13.3	13.8	8.4
Pakistan	0.7	2.9	6.8
Senegal	2.8	2.1	4.8
Taiwan	1.7	2.5	1.2
Togo	2.5	3.0	4.4
United Kingdom	3.9	5.9	4.1
USA	18.0	12.6	13.4
Total (incl. others)	**227.2**	**301.8**	**309.3**

Exports f.o.b.	1996	1997	1998
Colombia	—	—	1.3
Côte d'Ivoire	16.4	11.2	11.7
France	12.3	13.5	16.7
Ghana	2.2	2.7	3.7
Hong Kong	2.0	0.9	0.7
Indonesia	—	23.2	7.1
Italy	6.8	2.9	3.0
Japan	2.6	0.1	1.1
Mali	0.4	1.1	1.3
Niger	0.7	1.1	1.5
Taiwan	1.4	0.8	4.1
Togo	2.6	3.5	3.6
United Kingdom	0.2	1.3	0.9
USA	0.2	0.3	1.8
Total (incl. others) . . .	**80.1**	**96.5**	**106.9**

* Figures refer to recorded trade only.

Source: Banque centrale des états de l'Afrique de l'ouest in IMF, *Burkina Faso: Statistical Annex* (July 1999).

Transport

RAILWAYS (freight traffic, '000 metric tons)

	1995	1996*	1997*
Domestic	2	n.a.	n.a.
International	183	386	513

* Estimates.

Source: IMF, *Burkina Faso: Statistical Annex* (July 1999).

Passenger-km (million, 1993): 403 (Source: UN Economic Commission for Africa, *African Statistical Yearbook*).

ROAD TRAFFIC (motor vehicles in use)

	1994	1995	1996*
Passenger cars	32,224	35,460	38,220
Buses and coaches . . .	1,939	2,237	2,460
Lorries and vans	14,439	14,985	15,520
Road tractors	2,087	2,251	2,400
Motor cycles and mopeds . . .	97,900	100,591	105,000

* Estimates.

Source: IRF, *World Road Statistics*.

CIVIL AVIATION (traffic on scheduled services)*

	1994	1995	1996
Kilometres flown (million) . .	3	3	4
Passengers carried ('000) . .	130	137	138
Passenger-km (million) . . .	247	256	258
Total ton-km (million) . . .	37	40	40

* Including an apportionment of the traffic of Air Afrique.

Source: UN, *Statistical Yearbook*.

Tourism

FOREIGN VISITORS BY COUNTRY OF ORIGIN*

	1996	1997	1998
Côte d'Ivoire .	14,381	15,172	12,906
France .	29,972	31,621	45,136
Germany .	4,661	4,918	4,810
Mali .	8,143	8,591	5,774
Niger .	4,990	5,265	5,629
Senegal .	5,190	5,476	4,545
Togo .	4,329	4,567	4,223
USA .	3,854	4,066	5,310
Total (incl. others) .	131,113	138,364	160,284

* Arrivals at hotels and similar establishments.

Receipts from tourism ('000 million francs CFA) 13.2 in 1996; 17.6 in 1997; 25.1 in 1998.

Source: Direction du Tourisme et de l'Hôtellerie: *Statistiques du Tourisme (Année 1994–1998).*

Communications Media

	1994	1995	1996
Radio receivers ('000 in use) .	280	290	350
Television receivers ('000 in use) .	57	60	90
Telephones ('000 main lines in use)	26	30	34
Mobile cellular telephones			
(subscribers) .	n.a.	n.a.	169
Daily newspapers			
Number .	4	3	4
Average circulation ('000 copies)	16	15	14
Non-daily newspapers			
Number .	n.a.	9	n.a.
Average circulation ('000 copies)	n.a.	42	n.a.
Book production*			
Titles .	4	17	12
Copies ('000) .	n.a.	37	14

* All first editions.

1997: Radio receivers ('000 in use) 370; Television receivers ('000 in use) 100.

Sources: UNESCO, *Statistical Yearbook*; UN, *Statistical Yearbook.*

Education

(1995/96)

	Institu-tions	Teachers	Students		
			Males	Females	Total
Primary .	3,568	14,037	426,869	275,335	702,204
Secondary					
General .	252	4,162	89,609	47,648	137,257
Vocational* .	41	731	4,890	4,703	9,539
Tertiary .	9	632†	7,245	2,286	9,531

* Including teacher training.

† Teachers at the Universities of Ouagadougou and Bobo-Dioulasso.

Pre-primary (1996/97): Institutions 141; Teachers 423; Students 17,005 (Males 8,347; Females 8,658).

Pre-primary (1997/98): Institutions 147; Teachers 441; Students 18,045 (Males 8,921; Females 9,124).

Tertiary (1996/97): Teachers 352; Students 8,911 (Males 6,889; Females 2,022).

Sources: Ministère de l'Enseignement de Base et de l'Alphabétisation, Ouagadougou; UNESCO, *Statistical Yearbook.*

Directory

The Constitution

The present Constitution was approved in a national referendum on 2 June 1991, and was formally adopted on 11 June. The following are its main provisions:

The Constitution of the 'revolutionary, democratic, unitary and secular' Fourth Republic of Burkina Faso guarantees the collective and individual political and social rights of Burkinabè citizens, and delineates the powers of the executive, legislature and judiciary.

Executive power is vested in the President, who is Head of State, and in the Government, which is appointed by the President upon the recommendation of the Prime Minister. The President is elected, by universal suffrage, for a seven-year term; as amended in January 1997, there are no restrictions on the renewal of the presidential mandate. Under proposals introduced in April 2000 the Presidential mandate was to be reduced to five years, renewable only once.

Legislative power is exercised by the multi-party Assemblée nationale (Assemblée des députés du peuple until a constitutional amendment in January 1997). Deputies are elected, by universal suffrage, for a five-year term. An increase in the number of deputies, from 107 to 111, was provided for by constitutional amendment in January 1997. Under proposals introduced in April 2000 91 members of the Assemblée nationale would be elected from regional lists, while 21 would be elected from a national list. Both elections would be conducted under the rules of proportional representation. The President is empowered to appoint a Prime Minister; however, the Assemblée nationale has the right to veto any such appointment. The second chamber of the Parlement is the consultative Chambre des représentants, comprising 178 members, nominated from among the 'active forces of the nation' for a three-year term of office.

Both the Government and the Assemblée nationale may initiate legislation.

The judiciary is independent. Judges are accountable to a Higher Council, under the chairmanship of the Head of State.

The Constitution also makes provision for a Conseil économique et sociale, for a Conseil supérieur de l'information, and for a national ombudsman.

The Constitution denies legitimacy to any regime that might take power as the result of a *coup d'état.*

The Government

HEAD OF STATE

President: BLAISE COMPAORÉ (assumed power as Chairman of the Front populaire 15 October 1987; elected President 1 December 1991; re-elected 15 November 1998).

COUNCIL OF MINISTERS
(August 2000)

President: BLAISE COMPAORÉ.

Prime Minister: KADRÉ DÉSIRÉ OUÉDRAOGO.

Minister of State, Minister of the Environment and Water Resources: ARSÈNE BOGNESSAN YÈ.

Minister of State, Minister of Foreign Affairs: YOUSSOUF OUÉD-RAOGO.

Minister of State without Portfolio: RAM OUÉDRAOGO.

Minister in charge of Presidential Affairs: PIERRE JOSEPH EMMANUEL TAPSOBA.

Minister of the Economy and Finance, Spokesperson for the Government: TERTIUS ZONGO.

Minister of Defence: ALBERT DÉ MILLOGO.

Minister of Justice and Keeper of the Seals: BOUREIMA BADINI.

Minister of Territorial Administration and Security: YÉRO BOLY.

Minister of Agriculture: ISSA MARTIN BIKIENGA.

Minister of Trade, Industry and Crafts: ABDOULAYE ABDOUL-KADER CISSÉ.

Minister of Energy and Mines: ELIE OUÉDRAOGO.

Minister of Secondary and Higher Education and Scientific Research: CHRISTOPHE DABIRÉ.

Minister of Primary Education and Mass Literacy: BAWORO SEYDOU SANOU.

Minister of Infrastructure, Housing and Town Planning: HIPPOLYTE LINGANI.

Minister of the Civil Service and Institutional Development: PARAMANGA ERNEST YONLI.

Minister of Employment, Labour and Social Security: SANNÉ MOHAMED TOPAN.

Minister of Regional Integration: BERNADETTE SANOU.

Minister in charge of Relations with Parliament: CYRIL GOUNGOUNGA.

Minister of Culture and Arts: MAHAMOUDOU OUÉDRAOGO.

Minister of Communications: KILIMITÉ THÉODORE IHEN.

Minister of Health: ALAIN LUDOVIC TOU.

Minister of Transport and Tourism: BÉDOUMA ALAIN YODA.

Minister of Social Welfare and the Family: NAYABTIGUNGU CONGO-KABORÉ.

Minister of Animal Resources: ALASSANE SÉRÉ.

Minister of Youth and Sports: RENÉ EMILE KABORÉ.

Minister for the Promotion of Women: GISÈLE GUIGMA.

There are, in addition, six ministers-delegate responsible for the Budget, Economic Development, the Environment, Security, Housing and Town Planning and the Promotion of Employment. There are also three Secretaries of State responsible for Telecommunications, Energy and Youth.

MINISTRIES

Office of the President: 03 BP 7030, Ouagadougou 03; tel. 30-66-30; fax 31-49-26; internet www.primature.gov.bf.

Office of the Prime Minister: 03 BP 7027, Ouagadougou 03; tel. 32-48-89; fax 31-47-61; internet www.primature.gov.bf.

Ministry of Agriculture: 03 BP 7005, Ouagadougou 03; tel. 32-49-63.

Ministry of Animal Resources: 03 BP 7026, Ouagadougou 03; tel. 32-46-51; fax 31-84-75.

Ministry of the Civil Service and Institutional Development: 03 BP 7006, Ouagadougou 03; tel. 32-40-10.

Ministry of Communications: 03 BP 7045, Ouagadougou 03; tel. 32-48-86; fax 31-55-99.

Ministry of Culture and Arts: 03 BP 7045, Ouagadougou 03; tel. 32-48-86; fax 31-55-99.

Ministry of Defence: 01 BP 496, Ouagadougou 01; tel. 30-72-14; fax 31-36-10.

Ministry of the Economy and Finance: 03 BP 7012, Ouagadougou 03; tel. 30-69-98; fax 31-27-15; e-mail finances@cenatrin.bf; internet www.finances.gov.bf.

Ministry of Employment, Labour and Social Security: 03 BP 7016, Ouagadougou 03; tel. 30-09-60; fax 31-88-01.

Ministry of Energy and Mines: 01 BP 644, Ouagadougou 01; tel. 31-84-29; fax 31-84-30.

Ministry of the Environment and Water Resources: 565 rue Agostino Neto, Secteur 4, Koulouba, 03 BP 7044, Ouagadougou 03; tel. 32-40-74; fax 31-46-05; e-mail diallo@ouaga.orstom.bf; internet www.ohraoc.orstom.bf/htmlf/partnat/mee.

Ministry of Foreign Affairs: 03 BP 7038, Ouagadougou 03; tel. 32-47-34; fax 30-87-92; e-mail mam@cenatrin.bf.

Ministry of Health: 03 BP 7009, Ouagadougou 03; tel. 32-41-71.

Ministry of Infrastructure, Housing and Town Planning: 03 BP 7011, Ouagadougou 03; tel. 32-49-54; fax 31-84-08.

Ministry of Justice: 01 BP 526, Ouagadougou 01; tel. 32-48-33.

Ministry of Primary Education and Mass Literacy: 03 BP 7032, Ouagadougou 03; tel. 32-48-70; fax 30-80-86.

Ministry of Regional Integration: 01 BP 06, Ouagadougou 01; tel. 32-48-33; fax 31-41-90.

Ministry of Secondary and Higher Education and Scientific Research: 03 BP 7047, Ouagadougou 03; tel. 32-48-68; fax 31-41-41.

Ministry of Social Welfare and the Family: 01 BP 515, Ouagadougou 01; tel. 30-68-75; fax 31-67-37.

Ministry of Territorial Administration and Security: 03 BP 7034, Ouagadougou 03; tel. 32-47-83; fax 30-84-17.

Ministry of Trade, Industry and Crafts: 01 BP 514, Ouagadougou 01; tel. 32-47-86; fax 32-48-28.

Ministry of Transport and Tourism: 03 BP 7048, Ouagadougou 03; tel. 30-62-11.

Ministry of Women's Promotion: Ouagadougou.

Ministry of Youth and Sports: 03 BP 7035, Ouagadougou 03; tel. 32-47-86.

President and Legislature

PRESIDENT

Presidential Election, 15 November 1998

Candidate	Votes	% of votes
BLAISE COMPAORÉ	1,996,151	87.53
RAM OUÉDRAOGO	150,793	6.61
FRÉDÉRIC GUIRMA	133,552	5.86
Total	2,280,496*	100.00

* There were, in addition, 89,458 blank votes.

PARLEMENT

Assemblée Nationale

President: MÉLÉGUÉ MAURICE TRAORÉ.

General Election, 11 May 1997

Party	Seats
Congrès pour la démocratie et le progrès (CDP) . .	101*
Parti pour la démocratie et le progrès (PDP) . . .	6
Alliance pour la démocratie et la fédération (ADF). .	2
Rassemblement démocratique africain (RDA) . . .	2
Total	111

* This total includes the results of voting in four constituencies won by the CDP at a further round of voting on 18 June, after the Supreme Court annulled the previous results.

Chambre des Représentants

President: MOUSSA SANOGO.

The second chamber comprises 178 members, nominated from among the 'active forces of the nation' for a three-year term. The Chambre des Représentants, which has advisory functions, was inaugurated in December 1995.

Advisory Council

Conseil Economique et Social: 01 BP 6162, Ouagadougou 01; tel. 32-40-90; fax 31-06-54; f. 1985 as Conseil Révolutionnaire Economique et Social, present name adopted in 1992; 90 mems; Pres. JULIETTE BONKOUGOU-YAMÉOGO.

Political Organizations

There were 27 political parties officially registered in March 2000. The following are amongst the most important:

Alliance pour la démocratie et la fédération—Rassemblement démocratique africain (ADF—RDA): 01 BP 2061 Ouagadougou 01; tel. 31-15-15; f. 1990 as Alliance pour la démocratie et la fédération, absorbed faction of Rassemblement démocratique africain in 1998; Pres. Me HERMAN YAMÉOGO.

Congrès pour la démocratie et le progrès (CDP): Ouagadougou; tel. 31-80-18; e-mail cdp@cenatrin.bf; internet www.cdp.bf; f. 1996, by merger of more than 10 parties, to succeed the Organisation pour la démocratie populaire/Mouvement du travail as the prin. political org. supporting Pres. Compaoré; social democratic; Exec. Sec. ROCH MARC-CHRISTIAN KABORÉ.

Convention des partis sankaristes (CPS): Ouagadougou; tel. 35-74-11; f. 1999, by merger of four parties; promotes the policies of former president Sankara; Pres. ERNEST NONGMA OUÉDRAOGO.

Mouvement pour la tolérance et le progrès (MTP): Ouagadougou; tel. 31-85-11; Leader NAYABTIGUNGOU CONGO KABORÉ.

Parti pour la démocratie et le progrès (PDP): BP 606, Ouagadougou; tel. 31-16-46; f. 1993, expanded in 1996 to include three other parties; Pres. JOSEPH KI-ZERBO.

Rassemblement démocratique africain (RDA): Ouagadougou; pre-independence party; self-styled Front de refus du Rassemblement démocratique africain represented by FRÉDÉRIC GUIRMA at 1998 presidential election; Leader GÉRARD KANGO OUÉDRAOGO.

Les Verts du Burkina: Ouagadougou; tel. 36-39-08; ecologist party; Leader RAM OUÉDRAOGO.

The **Groupe du 14 février (G-14f)**, an alliance of some eight opposition parties including the PDP and the ADF—RDA, boycotted the 1998 presidential election.

Diplomatic Representation

EMBASSIES IN BURKINA FASO

Algeria: 01 BP 3893, Ouagadougou 01; tel. 30-64-01; Ambassador: AHCENE BOUKHELFA.

Belgium: Ouagadougou; tel. 31-21-64; Ambassador: JACQUES HENIN.

Canada: 01 BP 548, Ouagadougou 01; tel. 31-18-94; fax 31-18-00; e-mail ouaga@dfait-maeci.gc.ca; Ambassador: JULES SAVARIA.

China (Taiwan): 01 BP 5563, Ouagadougou 01; tel. 31-61-95; fax 31-61-97; Ambassador: SAINTING KUNG.

Côte d'Ivoire: 01 BP 20, Ouagadougou 01; tel. 31-82-28; fax 31-82-30; Ambassador: VALAMA GEORGES BAKAYOKO.

Cuba: 01 BP 3422, Ouagadougou 06; tel. 30-64-91; Chargé d'affaires a.i.: JOSÉ LUIS NORIEGA SÁNCHEZ.

Denmark: rue Agostino Neto, 01 BP 1760, Ouagadougou 01; tel. 31-31-92; fax 31-31-89; e-mail ouaamb@ouaamb.dk; Ambasssador: STIG BARLYNG.

Egypt: Zone du Conseil de L'Entente, Secteur 4, 03 BP 3893, Ouagadougou 03; tel. 30-66-39; Ambassador: Dr MOHAMED SAID ABDEL HAMID.

France: 33 rue Yalgado Ouedraogo, 01 BP 504, Ouagadougou 01; tel. 30-67-74; fax 31-41-66; e-mail ambassade.france@cenatrin.bf; internet www.france-burkina.bf; Ambassador: MAURICE PORTICHE.

Germany: BP 600, Ouagadougou 01; tel. 30-67-31; fax 31-39-91; e-mail amb.allemagne@fasonet.bf; Ambassador: Dr HELMUT RAU.

Ghana: 22 ave d'Oubritenga, 01 BP 212, Ouagadougou 01; tel. 30-76-35; Ambassador: BAFFOUR ASSASIE-GYIMAH.

India: 167 rue Joseph Badoua, BP 6648, Ouagadougou; tel. 31-43-67; Chargé d'affaires a.i.: MOHAN LAL.

Libya: 01 BP 1601, Ouagadougou 01; tel. 30-67-53; fax 31-34-70.

Mali: 01 BP 1911, Ouagadougou 01; tel. 38-19-22; Chargé d'affaires a.i.: DIARRA DAOUDA.

Netherlands: 415 ave du Dr Kwamé N'Krumah, 01 BP 1302, Ouagadougou 01; tel. 30-61-34; fax 30-76-95; Ambassador: ALPHONS J. M. G. HENNEKENS.

Nigeria: 01 BP 132, Ouagadougou 01; tel. 36-30-15; Ambassador: Alhaji BABA AHMAD JIDDA.

Senegal: Ouagadougou; tel. 31-14-18; Ambassador: CHEIKH SYLLA.

USA: 01 BP 35, Ouagadougou 01; tel. 30-67-23; fax 30-38-90; Ambassador: JIMMY J. KOLKER.

Judicial System

The Constitution provides for the independence of the judiciary. Judges are to be accountable to a Higher Council, under the chairmanship of the President of the Republic.

Supreme Court: 01 BP 5577, Ouagadougou 01; tel. 31-08-35; fax 31-08-96; Pres. SAMBO ANTOINE KOMI.

Religion

The Constitution provides for freedom of religion, and the Government respects this right in practice. The country is a secular state. Islam, Christianity, and traditional religions operate freely without government interference. More than 50% of the population follow animist beliefs.

ISLAM

An estimated 30% of the population are Muslims.

CHRISTIANITY
The Roman Catholic Church

Burkina comprises one archdiocese and ten dioceses. At 31 December 1998 Roman Catholics comprised an estimated 10.5% of the total population.

Bishops' Conference: Conférence des Evêques de Burkina Faso et du Niger, BP 1195, Ouagadougou; tel. 30-60-26; f. 1966, legally recognized 1978; Pres. Rt Rev. JEAN-BAPTISTE SOMÉ, Bishop of Diébougou.

Archbishop of Ouagadougou: Most Rev. JEAN-MARIE UNTAANI COMPAORÉ, Archevêché, 01 BP 1472, Ouagadougou 01; tel. 30-67-04; fax 30-72-75; e-mail untaani@fasonet.bf.

Protestant Churches

At 31 December 1986 there were an estimated 106,467 adherents.

The Press

Direction de la presse écrite: Ouagadougou; govt body responsible for press direction.

DAILIES

L'Express du Faso: Ouagadougou; privately-owned.

Le Journal du Soir: 02 BP 5468, Ouagadougou 02; tel. 31-59-20; fax 31-59-22; Dir ISSA TAPSOBA; Editor NOEL OUANZA LIEHOUN; circ. 3,000.

L'Observateur Paalga (New Observer): 01 BP 584, Ouagadougou 01; tel. 33-27-05; fax 31-45-79; e-mail lobs@fasonet.bf; internet www.lobservateur.bf; f. 1974; also a Sunday edn; Dir EDOUARD OUÉDRAOGO; circ. 8,000.

Le Pays: 01 BP 4577, Ouagadougou 01; tel. 31-35-46; fax 31-45-50; f. 1991; privately-owned; Dir BOUREIMA SIGUE; circ. 5,000.

Sidwaya Quotidien (Daily Truth): 5 rue du Marché, 01 BP 507, Ouagadougou 01; tel. 30-63-07; fax 31-03-62; e-mail sidwayas@mcc.gov.bf; internet www.sidwaya.bf; f. 1984; state-owned; Editor-in-Chief ISSAKA SOURWEMA; circ. 3,000.

24 Heures: Ouagadougou; privately-owned.

PERIODICALS

Bendré: Ouagadougou; weekly; Dir CHERIFF SY.

Le Berger: Zone commerciale, ave Binger, Bobo-Dioulasso; f. 1992; weekly; Dir KOULIGA BLAISE YAMÉOGO.

Bulletin de l'Agence d'Information du Burkina: 01 BP 2507, Ouagadougou 01; tel. 30-70-52; fax 30-70-56; 2 a week; Editor-in-Chief JAMES DABIRÉ; circ. 200.

La Clef: Ouagadougou; tel. 31-38-27; f. 1992; weekly; Dir KY SATURNIN; circ. 6,000.

Fitla: 5 rue du Marché, 01 BP 507, Ouagadougou 01; tel. 30-63-07; fax 31-03-62; f. 2000.

L'Hébdomadaire: Ouagadougou; tel. 31-47-62; e-mail hebdcom@fasonet.bf; internet www.fasonet.bf/hebdo; f. 1999; weekly on Fridays; Dir ZÉPHIRIN KPODA; Editor- in-Chief DJIBRIL TOURÉ.

L'Indépendant: 01 BP 4809, Ouagadougou 01; tel. 30-74-93; fax 31-44-58; f. 1993; weekly.

L'Intrus Toujours: 01 BP 2009, Ouagadougou 01; f. 1985; weekly; satirical; Dir JEAN HUBERT BAZIÉ; circ. 10,000.

Le Journal du Jeudi: 01 BP 4707, Ouagadougou 01; tel. 31-41-08; fax 31-38-74; e-mail jj@fasonet.bf; internet altern.org/journaldujeudi; f. 1991; weekly; Dir BOUBACAR DIALLO; circ. 9,000.

Le Matin: BP 339, Bobo-Dioulasso; tel. 97-16-93; f. 1992; weekly; Dir DOFINITA FLAURENT BONZI.

Nekr Wagati: Ouagadougou; six a year; Dir SIMON COMPAORÉ.

La Nouvelle Tribune: Ouagadougou; weekly; Dir KYALBABOUÉ BAYILI.

L'Opinion: 01 BP 6459, Ouagadougou 01; tel. 30-89-48; fax 30-89-47; e-mail zedcom@fasonet.bf; internet www.zedcom.bf/actualite/actualite.htm; weekly; Editor ISSAKA LINGANI.

L'Ouragan: 06 BP 9276, Ouagadougou 06; weekly; Dir LOHÉ ISSA KONATÉ; circ. 4,000.

Regard: 01 BP 4707, Ouagadougou 01; tel. 31-16-70; fax 31-57-47; weekly; Dir CHRIS VALÉA; Editor PATRICK ILBOUDO; circ. 4,000.

San Finna: Ouagadougou 01; privately-owned; weekly; Editor-in-Chief PAULIN YAMÉOGO; circ. 3,000.

Sidwaya Hebdo: 5 rue du Marché, 01 BP 507, Ouagadougou 01; tel. 30-63-07; fax 31-03-62; e-mail sidwayas@mcc-gov.bf; internet www.sidwaya.bf; f. 1997; weekly.

Sidwaya Magazine: 5 rue du Marché, 01 BP 507, Ouagadougou 01; tel. 30-63-07; fax 31-03-62; e-mail sidwayas@mcc.gov.bf; internet www.sidwaya.bf; f. 1989; state-owned; monthly; Editor-in-Chief BONIFACE COULIBALY; circ. 2,500.

Le Tam Tam: 01 BP 6660, Ouagadougou 01; tel. 30-70-01; f. 1992; weekly; Dir ZANGA OUATTARA; Editor ZONGO BOUREIMA; circ. 3,500.

Yeelen (Light): Ouagadougou; monthly; pro-Govt.

NEWS AGENCIES

Agence d'Information du Burkina (AIB): 03 BP 2507, Ouagadougou 03; tel. 32-46-39; fax 32-46-40; e-mail aib.redaction@mcc.gov.fc; internet www.aib.bf; f. 1964; fmrly Agence Voltaïque de Presse; state-controlled; Dir JAMES DABIRÉ.

Foreign Bureaux

Agence France-Presse (AFP): BP 391, Ouagadougou; tel. 33-56-56.

Reuters (UK) is also represented in Burkina Faso.

PRESS ASSOCIATION

Association des Journalistes du Burkina: 01 BP 507, Ouagadougou 01; tel. 31-01-14; fax 31-62-03; e-mail cnpress@fasonet.bf; also operates a Press centre; Pres. JEAN-CLAUDE MÉDA.

Publishers

Presses Africaines SA: BP 1471, Ouagadougou; tel. 33-43-07; general fiction, religion, primary and secondary textbooks; Man. Dir A. WININGA.

Société Nationale d'Edition et de Presse (SONEPRESS): BP 810, Ouagadougou; f. 1972; general, periodicals; Pres. MARTIAL OUÉDRAOGO.

Government Publishing House

Imprimerie Nationale du Burkina Faso (INBF): route de l'Hôpital Yalgado, BP 7040, Ouagadougou; tel. 33-52-92; f. 1963; Dir LATY SOULEYMANE TRAORÉ.

Broadcasting and Communications

TELECOMMUNICATIONS

The introduction of a regulatory framework for the telecommunications industry is ongoing and the increased liberalization of the sector is expected.

Office National des Télécommunications (ONATEL): ave Nelson Mandela, 01 BP 10000, Ouagadougou 01; tel. 33-40-01; fax 31-03-31; e-mail webmaster@onatel.bf; internet www.onatel.bf; partial privatization pending; Dir-Gen. JACQUES LOUARI.

Telecel-Faso: Ouagadougou; f. 2000; mobile cellular telephone operator; subsid. of Telecel International, South Africa; operates in Ouagadougou and Bobo-Dioulasso.

In mid-2000 the authorities were considering the application for a mobile cellular telephone licence of Mobile System International Cellular Investments Holding (MSI/CI).

BROADCASTING
Regulatory Authority

Conseil Supérieur de l'Information (CSI): 290 ave Ho Chi Minh, 01 BP 6618, Ouagadougou 01; tel. 30-11-24; fax 30-11-33; internet www.primature.gov.bf/republic/acc_csi.htm; f. 1995; Pres. ADAMA FOFANA.

Radio

Twelve state-owned radio stations and 30 private radio stations operated in Burkina Faso in mid-2000.

Radiodiffusion Nationale du Burkina: 03 BP 7029, Ouagadougou 03; tel. 32-40-55; fax 31-04-41; f. 1959; state radio service; operates nationally; Dir RODRIGUE BARRY.

Canal Arc-en-Ciel: Ouagadougou; state-owned; tel. 32-41-41; br. at Bobo-Dioulasso.

Radio CEDICOM Fréquence Espoir: Dédougou; religious broadcaster.

Radio ABGA (Radio Energie): Ouagadougou; operates five stations nationally; tel. 31-61-69.

Radio Bobo-Dioulasso: BP 392, Bobo-Dioulasso; tel. 97-14-13; daily programmes in French and vernacular languages; regional broadcaster; Dir of Programmes SITA KAM.

Radio Evangile: Ouagadougou; three stations at Ouagadougou; Bobo-Dioulasso and Ouahigouya; religious broadcaster; tel. 34-08-38.

Radio Gaoua: Gaoua; state-owned regional broadcaster.

Radio Horizon FM: 01 BP 2714, Ouagadougou 01; tel. 31-28-58; fax 31-39-34; private commercial station; broadcasts in French, English and eight vernacular languages; operates eight stations nationally; Dir MOUSTAPHA LAABLI THIOMBIANO.

Radio Maria: Ouagadougou; religious broadcaster; tel. 31-70-70; br. at Koupéla.

Radio Palabre: Kougoudou; community broadcaster; tel. 44-00-81.

Radio Toamba: Fada N'Gourma; religious broadcaster; tel. 77-02-33.

Radio Vive le Paysan: Saponé; community broadcaster; tel. 40-56-21.

Radio la Voix du Paysan: Ouahigouya; community broadcaster.

Television

Télévision Nationale du Burkina: 29 blvd de la Révolution, 01 BP 2530, Ouagadougou 01; tel. 31-83-53; fax 32-48-09; e-mail tnb@mcc.gov.bf; internet www.tnb.bf; f. 1963; Dir ALINE KOALA.

Télévision Canal Viim Koéga: Ouagadougou; private broadcaster.

Télévision Multi Media: Ouagadougou; commercial broadcaster.

Finance

(cap. = capital; res = reserves; m. = million; brs = branches; amounts in francs CFA)

BANKING
Central Bank

Banque Centrale des Etats de l'Afrique de l'Ouest (BCEAO): ave Gamel-Abdel-Nasser, BP 356, Ouagadougou; tel. 30-60-15; fax 31-01-22; e-mail akangni@bceao.int; internet www.bceao.int; HQ in Dakar, Senegal; f. 1962; bank of issue for the mem. states of the Union économique et monétaire ouest-africaine (UEMOA, comprising Benin, Burkina Faso, Côte d'Ivoire, Guinea-Bissau, Mali, Niger, Senegal and Togo); cap. and res 806,918m., total assets 4,084,464m. (December 1998); Gov. CHARLES KONAN BANNY; Dir in Burkina Faso CÉLESTIN KOUKA ZALLE; br. in Bobo-Dioulasso.

Other Banks

Bank of Africa—Burkina (BOA—Burkina): ave de la Résistance du 17 mai, 01 BP 1319, Ouagadougou 01; tel. 30-88-70; fax 30-88-74; e-mail boadg@fasonet.bf; f. 1998; cap. 1,250m., total assets 6,333m. (Dec. 1998); Pres. LASSINÉ DIAWARA; Man. Dir PHILIPPE IYADAUDY.

Banque Commerciale du Burkina (BCB): ave Nelson Mandela, 01 BP 1336, Ouagadougou 01; tel. 30-79-00; fax 31-06-28; e-mail bcb@fasonet.bf; f. 1988; 50% owned by Libyan Arab Foreign Bank, 25% state-owned, cap. and res 2,102m., total assets 11,987m. (Dec. 1998); Pres. IBRAHIMA OUATTARA; Man. Dir HAMMUDA MAHMUD.

Banque Internationale du Burkina (BIB): ave Dimdolobsom, 01 BP 362, Ouagadougou 01; tel. 30-61-69; fax 31-00-94; e-mail bib.ouaga@fasonet.bf; f. 1974; 25% owned by Banque Belgolaise SA (Belgium), 23% state-owned; cap. and res 9,688m., total assets 112,281m. (Dec. 1998); Pres. and Man. Dir GASPARD OUÉDRAOGO; 21 brs.

Banque Internationale pour le Commerce, l'Industrie et l'Agriculture du Burkina (BICIA—B): ave Dr Kwamé N'Krumah, 01 BP 08, Ouagadougou 01; tel. 30-62-26; fax 31-19-55; e-mail biciadg@fasonet.bf; f. 1973; 25% state-owned; cap. and res 7,463m., total assets 136,756m. (Dec. 1998); Pres. AMADOU TRAORÉ; Dir-Gen. AMADÉ OUÉDRAOGO; 11 brs.

Caisse Nationale de Crédit Agricole du Burkina (CNCA—B): 2 ave Gamal-Abdel-Nasser, 01 BP 1644, Ouagadougou 01; tel. 30-24-88; fax 31-43-52; e-mail cncabf@cenatrin.bf; f. 1979; 26% state-owned; cap. and res 9,829m., total assets 39,549m. (Dec. 1997); Pres. ANGÈLE SOUDRE; Man. Dir CÉLESTIN KOUKA ZALLE; 4 brs.

Ecobank—Burkina SA: 633 rue Maurice Bishop, 01 BP 145, Ouagadougou 01; tel. 31-89-75; fax 31-89-81; e-mail ecobank@ecobank.com; f. 1997; 48% owned by Ecobank Transnational Inc, 12% by Ecobank Benin, 12% by Ecobank Togo; cap. and res. 1,575m., total assets 22,452m.; Pres. PAUL BALKOUMA; Man. Dir OLAYEMI ALAMU AKAPO.

Société Générale des Banques du Burkina (SGBB): 4 rue du Marché, 01 BP 585, Ouagadougou 01; tel. 30-60-34; fax 31-05-61; f. 1998 by restructuring of Banque pour le Financement du Commerce et des Investissements du Burkina; cap. and res 2,100m., total assets 34,078m. (Dec. 1998); Pres. and Man. Dir EMILE PARÉ.

Credit Institutions

Burkina Bail SA: Immeuble CGP, 1ère étage BIB CGB, Ouagadougou 01; tel. and fax 30-69-87; 52% owned by BIB; cap. 500m.

Société Burkinabè de Financement (SOBFI): Immeuble Nassa, 1242 ave Dr Kwamé N'Krumah, 10 BP 13876, Ouagadougou 10;

tel. 31-80-04; fax 33-71-62; e-mail sobfi@fasonet.bf; cap. 300m., total assets 397m. (Dec. 1998); Pres. M. DIACK; Man. Dir M. GUILLEMOT.

Bankers' Association

Association Professionnelle des Banques et Etablissements Financiers (APBEF): Ouagadougou; Pres. HAMADÉ OUÉDRAOGO.

STOCK EXCHANGE

Bourse Régionale des Valeurs Mobilières (BRVM): s/c Chambre de Commerce, d'Industrie et d'Artisanat du Burkina, 180/220 rue 3-119, 01 BP 502, Ouagadougou 01; tel. 30-87-73; fax 30-87-19; f. 1998; national branch of BRVM (regional stock exchange based in Abidjan, Côte d'Ivoire, serving the member states of UEMOA); Man. LÉOPOLD OUÉDRAOGO.

INSURANCE

Fonci-Assurances (FONCIAS): ave Léo Frobénius, 01 BP 398, Ouagadougou 01; tel. 30-62-04; fax 31-01-53; f. 1978; 51% owned by Athena Afrique (France), 20% state-owned; cap. 140m.; Pres. El Hadj OUMAROU KANAZOÉ; Man. Dir GÉRARD G. MANTOUX.

Société Nationale d'Assurances et de Réassurances (SONAR): 01 BP 406, Ouagadougou 01; tel. 33-46-66; fax 30-89-75; e-mail sonar@cenatrin.bf; f. 1973; 25% state-owned; cap. 240m.; Man. Dir ANDRÉ BAYALA.

Union des Assurances du Burkina (UAB): 08 BP 11041, Ouagadougou 08; tel. 31-26-15; fax 31-26-20; f. 1991; 20% owned by l'Union Africaine—IARD (Côte d'Ivoire); cap. 270m.; Man. Dir J. V. ALFRED YARÉOGO.

Trade and Industry

GOVERNMENT AGENCIES

Bureau des Mines et de la Géologie du Burkina (BUMIGEB): 01 BP 601, Ouagadougou 01; tel. 30-01-94; fax 30-01-87; f. 1978, restructured 1997; research into geological and mineral resources; Pres. S. KY; Man. Dir JEAN-LÉONARD COMPAORÉ.

Caisse de Stabilisation des Prix des Produits Agricoles du Burkina (CSPPAB): 01 BP 1453, Ouagadougou 01; tel. 30-62-17; fax 31-06-14; f. 1964; responsible for purchase and marketing of shea-nuts (karité nuts), sesame seeds, cashew nuts and groundnuts; transfer pending to private ownership; Admin. DIANGO CHARLY HEBIE (acting); br. at Bobo-Dioulasso, representation at Boromo, Fada N'Gourma and Gaoua.

Comptoir Burkinabè des Métaux Précieux (CBMP): Ouagadougou; promotes gold sector, liaises with artisanal producers.

Office National d'Aménagement des Terroirs (ONAT): 01 BP 524, Ouagadougou 01; tel. 30-61-10; fax 30-61-12; f. 1974; fmrly Autorité des Aménagements des Vallées des Voltas; integrated rural development, including economic and social planning; Man. Dir ZACHARIE OUÉDRAOGO.

Office National des Barrages et des Aménagements Hydroagricoles (ONBAH): 03 BP 7056, Ouagadougou 03, tel. 30-89-82; fax 31-04-26; e-mail onbah@cenatrin.bf; f. 1976; control and development of water for agricultural use, construction of dams, water and soil conservation; state-owned; Dir-Gen. AÏZO TINDANO.

Office National du Commerce Extérieur (ONAC): ave Léo Frobénius, 01 BP 389, Ouagadougou 01; tel. 31-13-00; fax 31-14-69; f. 1974; promotes and supervises external trade; Man. Dir SÉRIBA OUATTARA (acting).

DEVELOPMENT ORGANIZATIONS

Agence Française de Développement (AFD): 52 ave de la Nation, 01 BP 529, Ouagadougou 01; tel. 30-60-92; fax 30-19-66; e-mail afd@cenatrin.bf; fmrly Caisse Française de Développement; Dir M. GLEIZES.

Association Française des Volontaires du Progrès (AFVP): 01 BP 947, Ouagadougou 01; tel. 30-70-43; supports unofficial small business.

Bureau d'Appui aux Micro Entreprises (BAME): BP 610, Bobo-Dioulasso; tel. 97-16-28; fax 97-21-76; supports small business.

Cellule d'Appui à la Petite et Moyenne Entreprise d'Ouagadougou (CAPEO): 01 BP 6443, Ouagadougou 01; tel. 31-37-62; supports small and medium-sized enterprises, in particular those owned by women.

Fondation pour la Promotion de l'Entreprise et de l'Emploi (FEE): 01 BP 6466, Ouagadougou 01; tel. 31-27-90; promotes private enterprise.

Promotion du Développement Industriel, Artisanal et Agricole (PRODIA): 01 BP 2344, Ouagadougou; tel. 30-26-29; fax 34-23-80; supports small business.

CHAMBER OF COMMERCE

Chambre de Commerce, d'Industrie et d'Artisanat du Burkina: 180/220 rue 3-119, 01 BP 502, Ouagadougou 01; tel. 30-61-14; fax 30-61-16; e-mail ccia-bf@cenatrin.bf; internet www.ccia.bf; f. 1948; Pres. El Hadj OUMAROU KANAZOÉ; brs in Bobo-Dioulasso, Koupèla and Ouahigouya.

EMPLOYERS' ORGANIZATIONS

Association Femmes Solidaritées (AFS): 01 BP 1749, Ouagadougou 01; tel. 30-01-50; association of female employers.

Conseil National du Patronat Burkinabè: 02 BP 660, Ouagadougou 02; tel. 31-29-24; fax 30-25-21; Pres. BRUNO ILBOUDO.

Groupement Professionnel des Industriels: BP 810, Ouagadougou; tel. 30-28-19; f. 1974; Pres. MARTIAL OUÉDRAOGO.

Syndicat des Commerçants Importateurs et Exportateurs (SCIMPEX): 01 BP 552, Ouagadougou 01; tel. 31-18-70; fax 31-30-36; e-mail scimpex@cenatrin.bf; Pres. OLE KAM.

UTILITIES

Electricity

Société Générale de Travaux et de Constructions Electriques (SOGETEL): Zone Industrielle, Quartier S.O. Gounghin, 01 BP 429, Ouagadougou 01; tel. 30-23-45; fax 34-25-70; e-mail sogetel@cenatrin.bf/sogetel; internet www.cenatrin.bf/sogetel; transport and distribution of electricity; installation of electrical apparatus.

Société Nationale Burkinabè d'Electricité (SONABEL): ave Nelson Mandela, 01 BP 54, Ouagadougou 01; tel. 30-61-00; fax 31-03-40; f. 1954; state-owned; production and distribution of electricity; Dir-Gen. EUGÈNE MEDA.

Water

Office National de l'Eau et de l'Assainissement (ONEA): 01 BP 170, Ouagadougou 01; tel. 30-60-73; fax 30-33-60; f. 1977; storage, purification and distribution of water; Dir ALY CONGO.

CO-OPERATIVES

Société de Commercialisation du Burkina 'Faso Yaar': ave du Loudun, Ouagadougou; tel. 30-61-28; f. 1967; 99% state-owned; transfer pending to private ownership; import-export and domestic trade; Pres. Minister of Trade, Industry and Crafts.

Union des Coopératives Agricoles et Maraîchères du Burkina (UCOBAM): 01 BP 277, Ouagadougou 01; tel. 30-65-27; fax 30-65-28; e-mail ucobam@cenatrin.bf; f. 1968; comprises 8 regional co-perative unions (20,000 mems); production and marketing of fruit, vegetables, jams and conserves.

MAJOR COMPANIES

The following are some of the largest companies in terms of either capital investment or employment.

Burkina Moto: 01 BP 8171, Ouagadougou 01; tel. 30-61-27; fax 30-84-96; f. 1985; import and distribution of bicycles, motorcycles and tyres; private co; Pres. and Dir-Gen. APPOLINAIRE T. CAMPAORÉ.

Caisse Générale de Péréquation (CGP): 01 BP 2513, Ouagadougou 01; tel. 31-31-58; fax 31-19-80; f. 1978; import, storage and wholesale trade in rice; state-owned; Dir-Gen. GILBERT SEDGO.

Centre National d'Equipement Agricole (CNEA): 03 BP 7240, Ouagadougou 03; tel. 34-03-54; fax 34-03-54; f. 1983; manufacture and sale of agricultural equipment; state-owned; Dir-Gen. BARRÉ E. KAFANDO.

La Cimenterie du Burkina (CIMAT): 01 BP 1930, Ouagadougou 01; tel. 30-59-21; fax 30-59-23; cap. 2,103m. francs CFA; cement production, clinker crushing; Man. Dir DIDIER BONHOMME; 194 employees.

Compagnie Burkinabè pour la Transformation des Métaux (CBTM): BP 235, Bobo-Dioulasso; tel. 97-03-93; f. 1973; cap. 120m. francs CFA; mfrs of aluminium household goods; Pres. SIDI MADATALI; Man. Dir JEAN-PIERRE JOYEUX; 54 employees (Sept. 1997).

Compagnie des Mines d'Or de Kieré (COMIDOK): Kiéré; f. 1993; exploitation and exploration of gold deposits.

Compagnie Minière de Tambao (COMITAM): 01 BP 12, Ouagadougou 01; tel. 30-67-47; fax 31-27-58; f. 1975; cap. 200m. francs CFA; 65% owned by Interstar Mining Group Inc (Canada), 35% state-owned; restructuring pending; exploitation of manganese deposits at Tambao; Pres. S. DONALD MOORE; Man. Dir K. H. E. REICHER.

Comptoir Burkinabè de Papier: 01 BP 1338, Ouagadougou 01; tel. 30-87-41; fax 31-37-06; f. 1989; paper producer; private co; Pres. and Dir-Gen. JOSEPH BAAKLINI.

Elf Oil Burkina SA: 01 BP 21, Ouagadougou 01; tel. 30-63-19; fax 31-05-46; petroleum distribution; Dir-Gen. ROBERT DION.

Etablissement Tiko-Tamou: 08 BP 11244, Ouagadougou 08; tel. 31-37-73; fax 31-78-61; fax. 1986; mfrs of traditional woven clothing, handicrafts and musical instruments; private co; Pres. and Dir-Gen. SATA TAMINI.

Grands Moulins du Burkina (GMB): BP 64, Banfora; tel. 88-00-57; fax 88-00-88; f. 1970; cap. 865m. francs CFA; flour-millers and mfrs of animal feed; Man. Dir ISSA BRUNO BICABA; 127 employees (Sept. 1997).

Groupe Aliz: Secteur Industrie, BP 2069, Ouagadougou; tel. 31-47-24; processing and export of animal hides and skins; 2m. hides and skins processed, 600,000 raw hides exported annually; Pres. and Dir-Gen. ALIZÉTA OUEDRAOGO.

Manufacture Burkinabè de Cigarettes (MABUCIG): BP 94, Bobo-Dioulasso; tel. 97-01-22; fax 97-21-62; f. 1966; cap. 935m. francs CFA; cigarette production of 1,000 metric tons per year; Pres. PIERRE IMBERT; Man. Dir MICHEL BLONDE; 158 employees (Sept. 1997).

Shell Burkina Faso: 01 BP 569, Ouagadougou 01; tel. 30-22-06; fax 31-22-46; f. 1976; marketing and distribution of petroleum products; Dir-Gen. DOMINIQUE KONATE.

Société Africaine de Pneumatiques (SAP): BP 389, Bobo-Dioulasso; tel. 97-03-86; fax 97-11-18; e-mail sap@fasonet.bf; f. 1972; cap. 980m. francs CFA; tyres and inner tubes; Pres. and Man. Dir K. LAZARE SORE; 250 employees (1999).

Société des Brasseries du Burkina Faso (BRAKINA): 01 BP 519, Ouagadougou 01; tel. 35-61-35; fax 35-60-22; f. 1960; cap. 2,530m. francs CFA; brewers and mfrs of soft-drinks and ice; Pres. JEAN-CLAUDE PALU; Man. Dir JEAN-MARIE GROSBOIS.

Société Burkinabè des Fibres Textiles (SOFITEX): 01 BP 147, Bobo-Dioulasso 01; tel. 97-00-24; fax 97-00-23; f. 1979; cap. 4,400m. francs CFA; 65% state-owned; development and processing of cotton and other fibrous plants; offers technical and financial support to growers; Pres. MARIE-BLANCHE BADO; Man. Dir CÉLESTIN TIENDRÉ-BÉOGO; 1,168 employees (Sept. 1997).

Société Burkinabè de Manufacture de Cuir (SBMC): BP 7033, Ouagadougou; tel. 30-11-00; fax 36-16-56; f. 1985; cap. 113m. francs CFA; leather tanning and processing; Dir-Gen. BARNABE SAM; 127 employees (Sept. 1997).

Société de Construction et de Gestion Immobilière du Burkina (SOCOGIB): BP 148, Ouagadougou; tel. 30-01-97; f. 1961; cap. 1,843m. francs CFA; 36% state-owned; housing development; Man. Dir ANATOLE BELEMSAGHA.

Société de Fabrication des Piles du Faso (SOFAPIL): Zone Industrielle, BP 266, Bobo-Dioulasso; tel. 98-04-97; fax 98-21-54; f. 1971; cap. 683m. francs CFA; mfrs of batteries; Pres. SALIF OUÉDRAOGO; Man. Dir PATRICK LEYDET.

Société Faso-Fani: BP 105, Koudougou; tel. 44-01-33; fax 44-01-26; f. 1965 as Société Voltaïque des Textiles; cap. 1,064m. francs CFA; 56% state-owned; transfer pending to private ownership; weaving, spinning, dyeing and printing of textiles; Man. Dir PATRICE YOGO; 510 employees (Sept. 1997).

Société des Fruits et Légumes du Faso: BP 136, Ouagadougou, tel. 30-65-26; fax 31-11-51; f. 1987; export of fruit and vegetables; 25% state-owned; Pres. ISMAEL OUÉDRAOGO.

Société Industrielle du Faso (SIFA): BP 358, Bobo-Dioulasso; tel. 97-10-25; cap. 1,122m. francs CFA; affiliate of Cie française de l'Afrique Occidentale; mfrs of motor cycles and bicycles; 158 employees (Sept. 1997).

Société Nationale Burkinabè d'Hydrocarbures (SONABHY): 01 BP 4394, Ouagadougou 01; tel. 30-20-02; fax 30-37-10; f. 1985; import, transport and distribution of refined hydrocarbons; state-owned; Man. Dir JEAN-HUBERT YAMÉOGO.

Société Nationale d'Exploitation et de Distribution Cinématographique du Burkina (SONACIB): BP 206, Ouagadougou; tel. 33-55-04; cap. 128m. francs CFA; 95% state-owned; Man. JUSTIN KAREMBEGA.

Société Nouvelle Huilerie et Savonnerie CITEC (SN CITEC): 01 BP 1300, Bobo-Dioulasso 01; tel. 97-25-50; fax 97-27-01; cap. 3,445m. francs CFA; production of groundnut oil; mfrs of shea (karité) butter, soap and animal feed; Pres. GUY SOMÉ; Man. Dir FULGENCE TOE.

Société des Plastiques du Faso (FASOPLAST): Zone Industrielle de Gounghin, 01 BP 534, Ouagadougou 01; tel. 30-20-76; fax 34-20-67; f. 1986; cap. 681m. francs CFA; mfrs of plastics; Man. Dir MAMADY SANOH; 150 employees.

Société de Recherches et d'Exploitations Minières du Burkina (SOREMIB): BP 5562, Ouagadougou; tel. 30-62-35; f. 1961, restructured 1996; cap. 4,000m. francs CFA; 60% state-owned; mineral exploration and exploitation; Pres. DIEUDONNÉ YAMÉOGO; Man. Dir JOSEPH OUÉDRAOGO.

Société Sucrière de la Comoé (SOSUCO): BP 13, Banfora; tel. 88-00-18; fax 88-04-38; f. 1969; fmrly Société Sucrière du Burkina Faso; cap. 6,031m. francs CFA; privatized in 1998; sugar refining; Man. Dir FULGENCE TOE.

Total Burkina: 01 BP 359, Ouagadougou 01; tel. 36-19-31; fax 36-15-42; f. 1976; petroleum distribution; Dir-Gen. KHIERRY CORTALE; br. at Bobo-Dioulasso.

TRADE UNIONS

There are more than 20 autonomous trade unions. The five trade union syndicates are:

Confédération Générale du Travail Burkinabè (CGTB): Ouagadougou; f. 1988; confed. of several autonomous trade unions; Sec.-Gen. TOLE SAGNON.

Confédération Nationale des Travailleurs Burkinabè (CNTB): BP 445, Ouagadougou; f. 1972; Leader of Governing Directorate ABDOULAYE BÂ.

Confédération Syndicale Burkinabè (CSB): Ouagadougou; f. 1974; mainly public service unions; Sec.-Gen. YACINTHE OUÉDRAOGO.

Organisation Nationale des Syndicats Libres (ONSL): BP 99, Ouagadougou; f. 1960; 6,000 mems.

Union Syndicale des Travailleurs Burkinabè (USTB): BP 381, Ouagadougou; f. 1958; Sec.-Gen. BONIFACE SOMDAH; 35,000 mems in 45 affiliated orgs.

Transport

RAILWAY

At the end of 1991 there were some 622 km of track in Burkina Faso. A 105-km extension from Donsin to Ouagadougou was inaugurated in December of that year. Plans exist for the construction of an extension to the manganese deposits at Tambao. Responsibility for operations on the railway line linking Abidjan (Côte d'Ivoire) and Kaya, via Ouagadougou, was transferred to SITARAIL (a consortium of French, Belgian, Ivorian and Burkinabè interests) in 1995.

SITARAIL—Transport Ferroviaire de Personnes et de Marchandises: 01 BP 1192, Ouagadougou 01; tel. 30-60-50; fax 30-85-21; national branch of SITARAIL (based in Abidjan, Côte d'Ivoire); Rep. in Burkina S. YAMÉOGO.

Société de Gestion du Patrimoine Ferroviaire du Burkina (SOPAFER—B): 01 BP 192, Ouagadougou 01; tel. 31-35-99; fax 31-35-94; railway network services; Dir-Gen. OUMAR ZONGO.

ROADS

In 1996 there were an estimated 12,100 km of roads, including 5,720 km of main roads and 3,030 km of secondary roads; about 16% of the road network was paved in 1995. A major aim of current road projects is to improve transport links with other countries of the region. In 1999 a US $37m. project was begun to upgrade the road linking Ouagadougou with the Ghanaian border via the more isolated southern provinces.

Burkina Transit: 01 BP 1947, Ouagadougou 01; tel. 30-79-88; fax 31-05-15; passenger transport.

Interafricaine de Transport et de Transit (IATT): 04 BP 8242, Ouagadougou 04; tel. 30-25-12; fax 30-37-04.

Régie Nationale des Transports en Commun (RNTC X9): Ouagadougou 01; tel. 30-42-96; f. 1984; urban, national and international public transport co; Dir FRANÇOIS KONSEIBO.

Société Africaine de Transit (SAT): 01 BP 4249, Ouagadougou 01; tel. 31-09-16.

Société Africaine de Transports Routiers (SATR): 01 BP 5298, Ouagadougou 01; tel. 34-08-62.

Société Nationale du Transit du Burkina (SNTB): 474 ave Bishop, 01 BP 1192, Ouagadougou 01; tel. 30-60-54; fax 30-85-21; f. 1977; road haulage and warehousing; Dir-Gen. SEYDOU DIAKITÉ.

CIVIL AVIATION

There are international airports at Ouagadougou and Bobo-Dioulasso, 49 small airfields and 13 private airstrips. Ouagadougou airport handled an estimated 176,400 passengers and 7,000 metric tons of freight in 1997.

Air Afrique: BP 141, Ouagadougou; tel. 30-60-20; see under Côte d'Ivoire.

Air Burkina: ave Loudun, 01 BP 1459, Ouagadougou 01; tel. 30-76-76; fax 31-48-80; f. 1967 as Air Volta; 25% state-owned; operates domestic and regional services; Man. Dir MATHIEU BOUDA.

Air Inter-Burkina: Ouagadougou; f. 1994; operates domestic passenger and postal services.

Tourism

Burkina Faso, which possesses some 2.8m. hectares of nature reserves, is considered to provide some of the best opportunities to observe wild animals in West Africa. Some big game hunting is also permitted. Several important cultural events are also held in Burkina Faso: the biennial pan-African film festival is held in Ouagadougou, as is the biennial international exhibition of handicrafts, while Bobo-Dioulasso hosts the biennial week of national culture. In 1998 there were 160,284 foreign visitors (28.2% of whom were from France), and receipts from tourism were estimated at 25.1m. francs CFA.

Association des Hôteliers et Restaurateurs du Burkina Faso (Association of Hotel and Restaurant Owners): 02 BP 5044, Ouagadougou 02; fax 34-29-41; e-mail ahrbf@ahrbf.com; internet www.ahrbf.com; f. 1980.

Direction du Tourisme et de l'Hôtellerie: 01 BP 624, Ouagadougou 01; tel. 30-63-96; Dir JEAN-PIERRE SIMPORE.

Office National du Tourisme Burkinabè: BP 1318, Ouagadougou; tel. 3-19-59; fax 31-44-34; Dir-Gen. ISIDORE NABALOUM.

Defence

National service is voluntary, and lasts for two years on a part-time basis. In August 1999 the armed forces numbered 10,000 (army 5,600, air force 200, paramilitary gendarmerie 4,200). There was also a 'security company' of 250 and a part-time people's militia of 45,000.

Defence Expenditure: Estimated at 46,000m. francs CFA in 1999.

Chief of the General Staff of the Armed Forces and Chief of Staff of the Army: Col KWAMÉ LOUGUÉ.

Education

Education is provided free of charge, and is officially compulsory for six years between the ages of seven and 14. Primary education begins at seven years of age and lasts for six years. Secondary education, beginning at the age of 13, lasts for a further seven years, comprising a first cycle of four years and a second of three years. In 1995 primary enrolment included only 40% of children in the relevant age-group (males 48%; females 31%). Secondary enrolment in 1993/94 included only 7% of the appropriate age-group (males 9%; females 5%). There are universities at Ouagadougou and at Bobo-Dioulasso. In total, 8,911 students were enrolled at tertiary institutions in Burkina Faso in 1996/97. A rural radio service has been established to further general and technical education in rural areas. In 2000, according to UNESCO estimates, adult illiteracy averaged 77.0% (males 66.8%; females 86.9%). Central government expenditure on education in 1994 was 36,315m. francs CFA, representing some 11.1% of total government spending in that year).

Bibliography

Allen, C., Radu, M. S., and Somerville, K. (Eds). *Benin, The Congo, Burkina Faso: Economics, Politics and Society.* New York and London, Pinter Publishers, 1989.

Anderson, S. (Ed. and Trans.). *Thomas Sankara Speaks: The Burkina Faso Revolution 1983–87.* New York and London, Pathfinder Press, 1988.

Andrimirado, S. *Sankara le rebelle.* Paris, Jeune Afrique Livres, 1987.

Il s'appelait Sankara: Chronique d'une mort violente. Paris, Jeune Afrique Livres, 1988.

Cruise O'Brien, D. B., Dunn, J., and Rathbone, R. (Eds). *Contemporary West African States.* Cambridge, Cambridge University Press, 1989.

Duval, M. *Un totalitarisme sans état—essai d'anthropologie politique à partir d'un village burkinabè.* Paris, L'Harmattan, 1985.

Emerging Markets Investment Center. *Burkina Faso Investment and Business Guide.* 2nd. Edn. USA, International Business Publications.

Englebert, P. *Burkina Faso: Unsteady Statehood in West Africa.* Boulder, CO, Westview Press, 1996.

Guion, J. R. *Blaise Compaoré: Réalisme et intégrité.* Paris, Mondes en devenir, 1991.

Guissou, B. *Burkina Faso, un espoir en Afrique.* Paris, L'Harmattan, 1995.

Harrison Church, R. J. *West Africa.* 8th Edn. London, Longman, 1979.

Kayeba-Muase, C. *Syndicalisme et démocratie en Afrique noire. L'expérience de Burkina.* Paris, Editions Karthala, 1989.

Koulansouonthe Pale, F.O. et al. *Aspects du développement économique dans un pays enclave: Burkina Faso.* Talence, Centre de Recherche sur le Transport et la Logistique, 1998.

Labazée, P. *Entreprises et entrepreneurs du Burkina Faso.* Paris, Editions Karthala, 1988.

Lachaud, J.-P. *Pauvreté, vulnerabilité et marché du travail au Burkina Faso.* Pessac, Université de Bordeaux, 1997.

Martens, L. *Sankara, Compaoré et la révolution Burkinabè,* EPO, Antwerp, 1989.

Meijenfeldt, R. von, Santiso, C., Otayek, R. *La démocratie au Burkina Faso.* Stockholm, International Institute for Democracy and Electoral Assistance, 1998.

Obinwa Nnaji, B. *Blaise Compaoré: The Architect of Burkina Faso Revolution.* Ibadan, Spectrum Books, 1989.

Rimmer, D. *The Economies of West Africa.* London, Weidenfeld and Nicolson, 1984.

Rupley, L., Miles, D., and McFarland, D. M. *Historical Dictionary of Burkina Faso.* 2nd Edn. Metuchen, NJ, Scarecrow Press, 1998.

Savadogo, K., and Wetta, C. *The Impact of Self-Imposed Adjustment: The Case of Burkina Faso 1983–1989.* Florence, Spedale degli Innocenti, 1991.

Savonnet-Guyot, C. *Etat et sociétés au Burkina: essai sur le politique africain.* Paris, Editions Karthala, 1986.

Somé, V. *Thomas Sankara, L'espoir assassiné.* Paris, L'Harmattan, 1990.

Ye, B. A. *Profil politique de la Haute Volta coloniale et néo-coloniale ou les origines du Burkina Faso révolutionnaire.* Ouagadougou, Imprimerie Nouvelle du Centre, 1986.

Zagré, P. *Les Politiques économiques du Burkina Faso, une tradition d'ajustement structurel.* Paris, Editions Karthala, 1994.

Ziegler, J. *Sankara, Un nouveau pouvoir africain.* Lausanne, Pierre-Marcel Favre/ABC, 1986.

BURUNDI

Physical and Social Geography

The Republic of Burundi, like its neighbour Rwanda, is exceptionally small in area, comprising 27,834 sq km (10,747 sq miles), but with a relatively large population of 6,300,000 (official estimate for mid-1998). The result is a high density of 226.3 persons per sq km. The principal towns are the capital, Bujumbura (population 235,440 at the 1990 census), and Gitega (population 15,943 in 1978).

Burundi is bordered by Rwanda to the north, by the Democratic Republic of the Congo (DRC) to the west and by Tanzania to the south and east. The natural divide between Burundi and the DRC is formed by Lake Tanganyika and the Ruzizi river on the floor of the western rift-valley system. To the east, the land rises sharply to elevations of around 1,800 m above sea-level in a range that stretches north into the much higher, and volcanic, mountains of Rwanda. Away from the edge of the rift valley,

elevations are lower, and most of Burundi consists of plateaux of 1,400–1,800 m. Here the average temperature is 20°C and annual rainfall 1,200 mm. In the valley the temperature averages 23°C, while rainfall is much lower at 750 mm.

Population has concentrated on the fertile, volcanic soils at 1,500–1,800 m above sea-level, away from the arid and hot floor and margins of the rift valley. The consequent pressure on the land, together with recurrent outbreaks of intense internal unrest, has resulted in extensive migration, mainly to Tanzania, the DRC and Uganda. The ethnic composition of the population is much the same as that of Rwanda: about 85% Hutu, 14% Tutsi and less than 1% Twa, pygmoid hunters. Historically, the kingdoms of Urundi and Ruanda had a strong adversarial tradition, and rivalry between the successor republics remains strong.

Recent History

GREGORY MTHEMBU-SALTER

Unlike most African states, Burundi and its northern neighbour Rwanda were not artificial creations of colonial rule. On their incorporation into German East Africa in 1899, they had been organized kingdoms for centuries, belatedly forced to open their borders to European intrusion. When, in 1916, Belgium occupied Ruanda-Urundi (as the League of Nations mandated territory encompassing both Rwanda and Burundi was designated), it continued the system of 'indirect rule' operated by the Germans. This choice of colonial policy had a particular impact, since an ethnic minority, the Tutsi (comprising about 14% of the population), had long been dominant over the majority Hutu (85%) and a pygmoid group, the Twa (1%). Unlike the situation in Rwanda, however, the potential for conflict between Hutu and Tutsi was contained by the existence of the ganwa, an intermediate princely class between the mwami (king) and the populace. The mwami and ganwa were Tutsi, standing apart from the Tutsi masses, who, in turn, comprised two main groups, the Banyaruguru and the Bahima. Relations between the ordinary Tutsi and the Hutu were on an equal footing, and intermarriage was common.

To fulfil the criteria imposed by the UN Trusteeship Council after 1948, the Belgian administration moved towards some degree of democratization. Two main parties came to the fore. The Union pour le progrès national (UPRONA), led by Prince Louis Rwagasore (the eldest son of the mwami), was a progressive nationalist movement. The rival Parti démocrate chrétien (PDC) was more conservative and maintained cordial links with the Belgian administration. At legislative elections held in September 1961, prior to the granting of internal self-government in January 1962, UPRONA won 58 of the 64 seats in the new national assembly. Rwagasore, who became prime minister after the elections, was assassinated in October 1961 by agents of the PDC. His death proved a crucial event in the subsequent history of Burundi; the absence of his unifying influence resulted in the division of UPRONA and to the emergence of open conflict between Hutu and Tutsi.

MICOMBERO AND BAGAZA

UPRONA was unable to contain the ethnic tensions that followed the attainment of independence on 1 July 1962. In order

to consolidate his own position, the mwami, Mwambutsa IV, sought to ensure a balance of ethnic interests in government. Four governments held office during 1963–65, each comprising almost equal proportions of Hutu and Tutsi. Tensions were exacerbated when the Hutu prime minister, Pierre Ngendandumwe, was assassinated in January 1965, only a week after taking office. The ensuing political crisis was resolved by a decisive Hutu victory at parliamentary elections held in May. Mwambutsa nevertheless appointed a Tutsi prince as the new prime minister. Incensed by this and by other actions taken by the mwami, a faction of the Hutu-dominated gendarmerie attempted to seize power in October. The repression of this abortive coup was extremely violent: virtually the entire Hutu political establishment was massacred, together with thousands of rurally-based Hutu who had supported the revolt.

In July 1966 Mwambutsa was deposed by his son, who took the title of Ntare V. He appointed Capt. (later Lt-Gen.) Michel Micombero as prime minister. In November Ntare was himself deposed by Micombero, who declared Burundi a republic. Subsequent purges of Hutu officers and politicians further consolidated Tutsi supremacy. Following an abortive coup attempt in April 1972, massacres of unprecedented magnitude and brutality were carried out. An estimated 100,000–200,000 Hutu were killed, and a further 200,000 fled the country, mainly to Zaire (now the Democratic Republic of the Congo, DRC), Tanzania and Rwanda. All Hutu elements were eliminated from the armed forces.

In November 1976 Col Jean-Baptiste Bagaza seized power in a bloodless coup. Although the army remained a significant force, attempts were made by the Bagaza regime to increase democratic participation in government. The first legislative elections under universal adult suffrage were held in October 1982, and in August 1984 Bagaza, as sole candidate, was elected head of state, for the first time by direct suffrage.

During the period 1984–87 there was a sharp deterioration in the government's observance of human rights. This was particularly marked in relation to religious freedom, and led Bagaza's regime into intense conflict with several Christian denominations. The number of political prisoners, which rose considerably during this period, included critics of government restrictions on religious activities, as well as people suspected of involvement in Hutu opposition groups. Many detainees were reported to have been subjected to torture. This intensification of authoritarian rule led to strained relations with a number of donor countries, which sought to bring pressure on Bagaza by withholding development aid.

THE BUYOYA REGIME, 1987-93

In September 1987, during a visit abroad, Bagaza was deposed by an army-led coup, instigated by Maj. Pierre Buyoya, a close associate who accused the former president of corruption and formed a 31–member Military Committee for National Salvation (CMSN). UPRONA was dissolved and the 1981 constitution was suspended. On 2 October Buyoya was sworn in as president, at the head of a new government. Bagaza subsequently went into exile in Libya.

Apart from its adoption of a more liberal approach to the issue of religious freedoms, the new regime did not differ significantly from that of Bagaza. It remained dependent upon the support of a small Tutsi-Hima élite, prevalent in the army, the civil service, the judiciary and educational institutions. Although Buyoya emphasized a desire for *rapprochement* and released hundreds of political prisoners, it was clear that the major problem facing the new leadership, as had been the case with Bagaza's regime, was the claim by the Hutu majority for fuller participation in public life.

Hutu-Tutsi Tensions

In August 1988 groups of Hutu, claiming Tutsi provocation, slaughtered hundreds of Tutsi in the northern towns of Ntega and Marangara. The Tutsi-dominated army was immediately dispatched to the region to restore order, and in the subsequent week, large-scale tribal massacres, similar to those of 1972, occurred. More than 60,000 refugees, mainly Hutu, fled to neighbouring Rwanda, as the death toll rose to an estimated 20,000. In the aftermath of the killings, a group of Hutu intellectuals were arrested for protesting against the army's actions and for demanding the establishment of an independent inquiry into the massacres. In October 1988, however, Buyoya announced changes to the council of ministers, including the appointment of a Hutu, Adrien Sibomana, to the post of prime minister. Significantly, the council comprised an equal number of Tutsi and Hutu representatives. In the same month a commission for national unity (again comprising an equal number of Tutsi and Hutu) was established to investigate the massacres and to make recommendations for national reconciliation.

During the first half of 1989 there were several attempted coups by hard-line Tutsi activists and by supporters of ex-president Bagaza. Following the publication, in April, of the report of the commission for national unity, Buyoya announced plans to combat all forms of discrimination against the Hutu and to introduce new regulations to ensure equal opportunities in education, employment and in the armed forces. Inter-ethnic tensions continued to fester, however, and in August 1991 the detention, by security forces, of several suspected members of the Parti de libération du peuple Hutu (PALIPEHUTU), the principal Hutu opposition party, for alleged 'incitement to massacre', was denounced by the human rights organization Amnesty International. In November violent confrontations occurred in Bujumbura and the north and north-west of the country. In January 1992 the minister of the interior stated that order had been restored and announced an official total of 551 deaths resulting from the November disturbances. Unofficial sources, however, estimated that as many as 3,000 had been murdered, many of them Hutus killed by government security forces in reprisal attacks. In late April 1992 further violent disturbances were reported along the border with Rwanda. The government attributed responsibility for the unrest to an insurgency by PALIPEHUTU activists, whom they alleged had been trained and armed in Rwanda. Despite a bilateral undertaking, agreed in August 1992, to implement increased border security and to co-operate more fully in attempts to repatriate refugees, border tension persisted into late 1992 and early 1993.

Constitutional Transition

In April 1990 the commission for national unity produced a draft charter, which, as with the 1989 report, was submitted to extensive national debate. Public discussion, however, was closely directed and monitored by UPRONA, and did little to satisfy the demands of internal (clandestine) and external opposition groups. Political tensions were renewed in August, when the exiled leader of PALIPEHUTU died in prison in Tanzania, and the leader of a smaller dissident group was killed in a motor accident in Rwanda. Opponents of UPRONA alleged that both men had been assassinated by agents of Buyoya. Later in the same month, army barracks at Mabanda, in southern Burundi, were attacked by an armed group of exiled Hutu who had crossed the frontier from Tanzania.

In December 1990 UPRONA disbanded the CMSN and transferred its functions to an 80-member central committee of UPRONA, with a Hutu, Nicolas Mayugi, as its secretary-general. The draft charter on national unity, approved at a referendum in February 1991 by an electoral margin of 89.2% to 10.2%, was rejected by PALIPEHUTU and other opposition groups. Later in the same month the implementation of a cabinet reshuffle, whereby Hutus were appointed to 12 of the 23 government portfolios, was viewed with scepticism by political opponents. In March a commission was established to prepare a report on the 'democratization' of national institutions and political structures, in preparation for the drafting of a new constitution.

In September 1991 Buyoya presented the report of the constitutional commission on 'national democratization'. Among its recommendations were the establishment of a parliamentary forum to operate in conjunction with a presidential system of government, a renewable five-year presidential mandate, the introduction of proportional representation, freedom of the press, guarantees of human rights, and a system of 'controlled multi-partyism' whereby political groupings seeking legal recognition would be required to comply with certain requirements, including acceptance of the charter on national unity.

In February 1992 the government announced that a referendum was to be held on 9 March to ascertain support for the constitutional reform proposals. It was stated that electoral endorsement of the draft constitution would be followed by legislative elections, and by a presidential poll in 1993. A swiftly suppressed coup attempt, only days before the referendum, failed to disrupt the proceedings, and the proposals received the support of more than 90% of voters. The new constitution was promulgated on 13 March. At the beginning of April, in an extensive ministerial reshuffle, seven ministers left the government, and Hutus were appointed to 15 of the 25 portfolios. In April Buyoya approved legislation relating to the creation of new political parties in accordance with the provisions of the new constitution. The legislation required new political parties to demonstrate impartiality with regard to ethnic or regional origin, gender and religion, and to support national unity. By October eight political parties had received legal recognition. Later in that month, the president announced the creation of the National Electoral Preparatory Commission (NEPC), a 33-member body comprising representatives of the eight recognized political parties, together with administrative, judicial, religious and military officials. The NEPC, which was responsible for co-ordinating the process of democratization, met for the first time at the end of November. Earlier that month Buyoya had rejected the demands of five political parties to participate in a transitional government to oversee preparations for the forthcoming legislative elections. In response, however, the president announced the creation of a national consultative commission on democratization, to function in a purely advisory capacity. By early December 1992 Buyoya had appointed a new 12-member technical commission, charged with drafting an electoral code and a communal law.

In February 1993 Buyoya announced that presidential and legislative elections would take place in June, with elections for local government officials to follow in November. The presidential poll, conducted on 1 June, was won, with 64.8% of votes cast, by Melchior Ndadaye, the candidate of the Front pour la démocratie au Burundi (FRODEBU), with the support of the Rassemblement du peuple burundien (RPB), the Parti du peuple (PP) and the Parti liberal (PL). Buyoya, the UPRONA candidate, received 32.4% of the votes, with support from the Rassemblement pour la démocratie et le développement économique et social (RADDES) and the Parti social démocrate (PSD). Legislative elections for 81 seats in the new legislative body were held on 29 June. Once again, FRODEBU emerged as the leading party, with 71% of the votes and 65 of the 81 seats in the new legislature. UPRONA, with 21.4% of the votes, secured the remaining 16 seats. The Parti de réconciliation du peuple (PRP), the PP, the RADDES and the PRB all failed to attract the minimum 5% of votes needed for representation in the legislature. The elections, however, were followed in early July by an attempted coup by army officers, which was swiftly suppressed. Ndadaye assumed the presidency on 10 July, thus becoming Burundi's first ever Hutu head of state. A new 23-member council of ministers was subsequently announced. The new prime minister, Sylvie Kinigi, was one of seven newly-appointed Tutsi ministers.

NDADAYE, NTARYAMIRA AND THE RESURGENCE OF ETHNIC UNREST

On 21 October 1993 more than 100 army paratroopers overwhelmed supporters of the government, and occupied the presidential palace and the headquarters of the national broadcasting company. Several prominent Hutu politicians and officials, including President Ndadaye, were detained and subsequently killed by the insurgents, who later proclaimed François Ngeze, one of the few prominent Hutu members of UPRONA, and a minister in the government of ex-president Buyoya, as head of a National Committee for Public Salvation (CPSN). While members of the government sought refuge abroad and in the offices of foreign diplomatic missions in Bujumbura, the armed forces declared a state of emergency, closing national borders and the capital's airport. However, immediate and unanimous international condemnation of the coup, together with the scale and ferocity of renewed inter-ethnic massacres, undermined support for the insurgents from within the armed forces, and precipitated the collapse of the CPSN, which was disbanded on 25 October. The prime minister, Sylvie Kinigi, who had earlier refused to accept the insurgents' offer of surrender in exchange for amnesty, remained in hiding, and urged the international community to send an international force to Burundi to protect the civilian government. Communications were restored on 27 October, and on the following day the UN confirmed that the government had reassumed control of the country. Ngeze and 10 coup leaders were placed under arrest, although about 40 other insurgents were thought to have fled to Zaire. In early December a commission of judicial inquiry was created to investigate the insurgency.

Meanwhile, in early November 1993 several members of the government, including the prime minister, had left the French embassy (where they had remained throughout the uprising) with a small escort of French troops; and on 8 November Kinigi convened a meeting of the surviving government ministers in an attempt to address the humanitarian crisis arising from the massacre and displacement of thousands of Burundians (see below) provoked by the failed coup. On the same day the constitutional court officially recognized the presidential vacancy resulting from the murder of both Ndadaye and his constitutional successor, Giles Bimazubute, the speaker of the national assembly, and directed that presidential powers should pass to the council of ministers, acting in a collegiate capacity, pending fresh presidential elections, to be conducted within three months. However, the minister of external relations and co-operation, Sylvestre Ntibantunganya (who had succeeded Ndadaye as leader of FRODEBU), rejected these arrangements, asserting that elections should await the resolution of internal security difficulties and the initiation of a comprehensive programme for the repatriation of refugees. Ntibantunganya was subsequently elected speaker of the national assembly, and relinquished the foreign affairs portfolio, which was assumed by Jean-Marie Ngendahayo, minister of communications and government spokesman.

In early January 1994 the FRODEBU deputies in the national assembly approved a draft amendment to the constitution, whereby henceforth a president of the republic could be elected by the national assembly, in the event of a presidential vacancy having been recognized by the constitutional court. UPRONA deputies, who had boycotted the vote, challenged the constitutionality of the amendment, and expressed concern that such a procedure represented election by indirect suffrage, in direct contravention of the terms of the constitution. Although the continued boycott of the national assembly by UPRONA deputies, together with procedural impediments to the immediate ratification of the amendment, forced the postponement, on 10 January, of an attempt by FRODEBU deputies to elect their presidential candidate, the minister of agriculture and livestock, Cyprien Ntaryamira. However, three days later, following the successful negotiation of a political truce with opposition parties, Ntaryamira was elected president by the national assembly (with 78 of the 79 votes cast), and assumed office on 5 February. Anatole Kanyenkiko, of UPRONA, was appointed prime minister while the composition of a new multi-party council of ministers was finally agreed in mid-February.

In November 1993, following repeated requests by the government for an international contribution to the protection of government ministers in Burundi, the OAU agreed to the deployment of a 200-strong protection force (MIPROBU), to be composed of civilian and military personnel, for a period of six months. In December opposition parties, including UPRONA and the RADDES, organized demonstrations in protest at the arrival of the military contingent of 180, scheduled for late January 1994, claiming that Burundi's sovereignty and territorial integrity were being compromised.

On 11 February 1994 an international commission of inquiry, established by a number of human rights organizations, concluded that a majority of members of the armed forces had been directly or indirectly involved in the October coup attempt. It was estimated that 25,000–50,000 Burundians had died as a result of the violence arising from the insurrection.

During February 1994 ethnic tension mounted as extremist factions of both Hutu and Tutsi groups attempted to establish territorial strongholds within the country. Reports that both sides had amassed considerable supplies of armaments aroused fears of a severe escalation of the conflict. (The minister of the interior, Léonard Nyangoma, claimed that the armed forces had been distributing weapons to Tutsi extremists since 1973, whereas Burundian Hutu refugees in Rwanda were thought to have received arms and military training from the Rwandan armed forces and the Hutu extremist Interahamwe militia operating in Rwanda.) Fighting in the capital in early February resulted in the deaths of around 100 Burundians, prompting a delay in the deployment of MIPROBU. (In mid-March the government persuaded the OAU to reduce the MIPROBU military contingent from 180 to 47.) Attempts by the armed forces to disable Hutu strongholds in and around the capital resulted in the imposition of a *de facto* curfew in Bujumbura in late March, exaggerating existing divisions between FRODEBU's moderate faction, led by Ntaryamira (who, anxious to maintain cordial relations with the armed forces, advocated a programme of forced disarmament of militia groups on both sides), and Nyangoma's hardline faction, which opposed further military action against the militias. However, Ntaryamira's insistence that several senior army personnel and the chief of the national gendarmerie should be replaced for having failed to address the security crisis, and that the armed forces should not overlook its own ranks in the enforcement of the pacification programme, provoked sections of the security forces to embark on a campaign of violent destruction in the capital, resulting in dozens of civilian deaths.

POLITICAL MANOEUVRES AND COALITION GOVERNMENT

On 6 April 1994, returning from a regional summit meeting in Dar es Salaam, Tanzania, Ntaryamira was killed (together with the ministers of development, planning and reconstruction, and communications) when the aircraft of Rwandan President Juvénal Habyarimana, in which the Burundi delegation was travelling, was brought down by a rocket attack above Kigali airport, and crashed on landing. (Habyarimana, who was also killed in the crash, was widely acknowledged to have been the intended victim of the attack.) In contrast to the violent political and tribal chaos which erupted in Rwanda in the aftermath of the death of Habyarimana, Burundians responded positively to appeals for calm issued by Sylvestre Ntibantunganya, the speaker of the national assembly, who, on 8 April, was confirmed (in accordance with the constitution) as interim president for a three-month period, following which a presidential election would be held. Ntibantunganya's statesmanship was immediately tested by several army dissidents, who attempted to organize a coup but were swiftly apprehended by loyalist troops on 25 April.

Meanwhile, sporadic violent exchanges between Hutu extremist rebels and factions of the armed forces continued to claim casualties, including the attorney-general. In late April the president issued an ultimatum to the warring militias, that all illegal arms should be surrendered by 1 May. Following unsuccessful attempts to negotiate the disarmament of the Kamenge 'people's army', the armed forces were authorized to bombard the district with mortar shells, forcing the withdrawal and surrender of many of the rebels. Relations between the government and the armed forces improved considerably as a result, prompting the president to indicate that the contentious reform of the armed forces would not be achieved through the imposition of ethnic quotas. The government and the military were further reconciled following a statement, issued by the prime minister in early May, that Nyangoma had forfeited his position in the council of ministers, having failed to return from government business abroad. During May UPRONA elected a Hutu, Charles Mukasi, as its new leader. In the same month, ex-president Bagaza resumed political activity, at the head of a new party, the Parti pour le redressement national (PARENA).

Having discounted the possibility of organizing a general election, owing to security considerations, in June 1994 all major political parties engaged in lengthy negotiations to establish a procedure for the restoration of an elected presidency. The mandate of the interim president was extended for three months by the constitutional court in July, and by the end of August it had been decided that a new president would be elected by a broadly representative commission, with a composition yet to be decided. A new agreement on power-sharing, in addition to a tentative agreement concluded in mid-July, was announced on 10 September. This convention of government, which detailed the terms of government for a four-year transitional period (including the allocation of 45% of cabinet posts to opposition parties), was incorporated into the constitution on 22 September. The convention also provided for the creation of a national security council (formally inaugurated on 10 October) to address the national security crisis. On 30 September the convention elected Ntibantunganya to the presidency from a list of six candidates including Charles Mukasi, the UPRONA leader. Ntibantunganya's appointment was endorsed immediately by the national assembly, and he was formally inaugurated on 1 October 1994. Anatole Kanyenkiko was reappointed as prime minister on 3 October, and two days later a coalition government was formed, with a composition reflecting the terms of the September convention.

In December 1994 UPRONA announced its intention to withdraw from the coalition government and from the legislature, following the election earlier that month of Jean Minani (a prominent FRODEBU member) to the post of speaker of the national assembly. UPRONA members accused Minani of having incited Hutu attacks against Tutsis in the aftermath of the October 1993 attempted coup. In early January 1995 the political crisis was averted by agreement on a compromise FRODEBU candidate, Léonce Ngendakumana. Minani subsequently assumed the FRODEBU party leadership, and by mid-January UPRONA had declared its willingness to rejoin the government. Later in the month, however, Kanyenkiko resisted attempts by the UPRONA leadership to expel him from the party for having failed to comply with party demands for the withdrawal from the government of all party members over the Minani affair. Two UPRONA ministers were subsequently dismissed from the council of ministers, in apparent retaliation, prompting the UPRONA leader, Mukasi, to demand the resignation of the prime minister, and to declare an indefinite general strike in support of this demand, in mid-February. Increased political opposition to Kanyenkiko forced the prime minister to acknowledge that he no longer enjoyed the necessary mandate to continue in office, and on 22 February Antoine Nduwayo, a UPRONA candidate selected in consultation with other opposition parties, amid allegations of extremist Tutsi militia intimidation, was appointed prime minister by presidential decree. A new coalition council of ministers was announced on 1 March, but political stability was undermined immediately by the

murder, in early March, of the Hutu minister of energy and mines, Ernest Kabushemeye.

Ethnic tension persisted in the second half of 1994, exacerbated by the scale and proximity of the violence in Rwanda (see above), and by the presence in Burundi of an estimated 200,000 Rwandan Hutu refugees, who had fled the advancing FPR in Rwanda. While nationwide civil confrontation was largely contained in Burundi, ethnically-motivated atrocities became a daily occurrence in parts of the country (several prominent politicians and government officials were murdered), resulting in the imposition of a partial curfew in the capital in December. Fears that the security crisis in Burundi would develop into civil war were agitated, in late 1994, by reports that the allegedly 30,000-strong Force pour la défense de la démocratie (FDD), the armed wing of Nyangoma's extremist Conseil national pour la défense de la démocratie (CNDD), were making preparations for an armed struggle against the armed forces in Burundi. In early November the national security council had urged all political and civilian groups to dissociate themselves from Nyangoma, who was believed to be co-ordinating party activities from Zaire. An escalation in the scale and frequency of incidents of politically- and ethnically-motivated violence during 1995 prompted renewed concern that the security crisis would precipitate genocide similar to that witnessed in Rwanda during 1994. Government-sponsored military initiatives were concentrated in Hutu-dominated suburbs of Bujumbura and in the northeast, where an aggressive campaign was waged against the alleged insurgent activities of PALIPEHUTU members, resulting in the deaths of hundreds of Hutu civilians. The government accused Hutu extremist militiamen of conducting an intimidating and violent programme of recruitment of Hutu males in the region.

In May 1995 humanitarian organizations suspended their activities in Burundi for one week to draw international attention to the security situation and the increasingly dangerous position of relief workers in the area. Anti-insurgency operations were intensified in June in several suburbs of the capital, where an estimated 2,000 heavily-armed troops sought to apprehend members of the FDD. It was reported that as many as 130 civilians were killed (many of them women and children) in the ensuing hostilities, which also forced thousands of Hutus to flee into the surrounding countryside. (In October the armed forces claimed to have destroyed the FDD headquarters.) Also in June, a report published by Amnesty International claimed that national security forces in Burundi had collaborated with extremist Tutsi factions in the murder of thousands of Hutus since 1993. A number of increased security measures, announced by the president in the same month, included restrictions on a number of civil liberties and the regrouping of many communes into administrative sectors to be administered jointly by civilian and military personnel. A request by the president to be granted the power to rule by decree until the next legislative session, scheduled for October 1995, was subsequently rejected by the national assembly which considered such a move to be incompatible with the spirit of the convention of government.

In late June 1995 the minister of state in charge of external relations and co-operation, Jean-Marie Ngendahayo, announced his resignation, in expression of his dissatisfaction at the government's inability to guarantee the safety and basic rights of the population. Later in the month, a meeting of the OAU, convened in Addis Ababa, Ethiopia, concluded that some degree of military intervention in Burundi would be necessary should ethnic violence continue to escalate. (In April the Burundian government had declined an OAU offer of military intervention in favour of increasing the number of MIPROBU personnel to 67.) In early July Paul Munyembari was appointed to the external relations portfolio. Vedaste Ngendanganya was appointed minister of posts and telecommunications in early September, in place of Innocent Nimpagariste, who had resigned from the post in August amid concern for his safety, following a number of unsuccessful assassination attempts. Further changes to the council of ministers were announced in October, in response to a division within the governing coalition arising from remarks made by prominent members of the government (most notably the UPRONA minister of the interior, Gabriel Sinarinzi), which were highly critical of the attitude to the country's security crisis demonstrated by the US ambassador to Burundi. Sinarinzi was among seven ministers replaced in the reshuffle. In September 1995 the UN secretary-general, Dr Boutros Boutros-Ghali, announced the composition of a UN-sponsored, five-member commission of inquiry into events leading to the assassination of President Ndadaye in October 1993.

ETHNIC CONFRONTATION

By early 1996 reports of atrocities perpetrated against both Hutu and Tutsi civilians by rogue elements of the Tutsi-led armed forces (including militias known as the 'Sans Echecs'), and by extremist Hutu rebel groups had become almost commonplace in rural areas. It was estimated that the capital had been effectively purged of any significant Hutu presence by the end of 1995. In late December the UN secretary-general had petitioned the Security Council to sanction some form of international military intervention in Burundi to address rapidly worsening security conditions, and in February these efforts were renewed following a UN report on human rights which concluded that no discernible improvement had been made in the protection of human rights since mid-1995 and that a state of near civil war existed in many areas of the country. However, the Burundian government (and the weight of Tutsi political opinion in Burundi) remained fiercely opposed to a foreign military presence and persuaded the UN Security Council that a negotiated settlement to the conflict was still attainable. Reports delivered by representatives of the US Agency for International Development and the Humanitarian Office of the European Union (EU) following an official visit to Burundi, undertaken in early April, were severely critical of the administration's failure to reconcile the country's various ethnic and political interests within government, and expressed doubts that effective power-sharing could be achieved within the terms of the 1994 convention of government and under the leadership of a Tutsi premier with considerable executive power. The USA and the EU announced the immediate suspension of aid to Burundi.

Despite an undertaking by President Ntibantunganya in late April 1996 that a human rights commission was to be established and a comprehensive reform of the security forces and the judiciary was to be carried out, violence continued to escalate, prompting the suspension of French military co-operation with Burundi at the end of May. (Aid workers reported a number of atrocities perpetrated by units of the armed forces against Hutu civilians — including separate incidents in which some 235 villagers in Buhoro and an estimated 375 villagers in Kivyuka were massacred — during May.) In early June the International Committee of the Red Cross (ICRC) suspended all activities in Burundi following the murder of three ICRC employees in the north-west of the country. Other aid agencies announced that future operations would be restricted to the capital. All ICRC staff were subsequently withdrawn from Burundi.

At a meeting of the member nations of the Economic Community of the Great Lakes Countries, convened in Cairo, Egypt in November 1995 at the request of the UN secretary-general, the presidents of Burundi, Rwanda, Uganda and Zaire, and a Tanzanian presidential representative, announced a subregional initiative for a negotiated peace in Burundi, involving mediation by eminent African statesmen, including (most prominently) the former president of Tanzania, Julius Nyerere. Nyerere's role as principal mediator in the conflict was endorsed at a meeting between representatives of more than 20 African states and European and UN diplomats in Addis Ababa at the end of February 1996. Representatives of some 13 political parties (including FRODEBU and UPRONA) participated in inter-party discussions conducted in Mwanza, Tanzania, with Nyerere as mediator, in April. A second round of discussions, scheduled for May, was subsequently postponed. While a reluctance to further interrupt the work of the current legislative session in Burundi was offered as an official explanation for the stalling of negotiations, unofficial reports indicated that UPRONA representatives had objected to the possible participation of the CNDD. A second round of talks was conducted in Mwanza in early June, again with mediation by Nyerere, but political polarization appeared to have been intensified by the talks. Mukasi, representing UPRONA and an informal coalition of seven smaller, predominantly Tutsi parties (the Rassemblement unitaire),

accused FRODEBU deputies of seeking to abrogate the convention of government, a charge which was strenuously denied by FRODEBU spokesmen following the talks. At a conference of regional powers in Arusha, Tanzania, in late June 1996, the Burundian president and prime minister requested foreign intervention to protect politicians, civil servants and crucial installations. By early July a regional technical commission to examine the request for 'security assistance' (comprising regional defence ministers, but not representatives of the Burundian armed forces) had convened in Arusha and had reached preliminary agreement, with the support of the UN, for an intervention force to be composed of units of the Ugandan and Tanzanian armed forces and police officers from Kenya. Meanwhile, significant differences of interpretation, with regard to the purpose and mandate of such a force, had emerged between Ntibantunganya and Nduwayo (who suggested that the president was attempting to neutralize the country's military capability). At a mass rally of Tutsi-dominated opposition parties, organized in the capital on 5 July, the prime minister joined other political leaders, including Mukasi, in rejecting foreign military intervention and criticizing Ntibantunganya's alleged encouragement of external interference in domestic affairs. Some days later, however, full endorsement of the Arusha proposal for intervention was recorded by member nations of the OAU at a summit meeting convened in Yaoundé, Cameroon.

Political and ethnic tensions intensified still further when reports of a massacre of more than 300 Tutsi civilians at Bugendana, allegedly committed by Hutu extremists including heavily-armed Rwandan Hutu refugees, emerged just hours after the UN accused the Burundian authorities of collaborating with the Rwandan administration in a new initiative of (mainly enforced) repatriation of Rwandan refugees in Burundi (see below). While FRODEBU members made un urgent appeal for foreign military intervention to contain the increasingly violent civil and military reaction to these events, ex-president Bagaza urged civil resistance to foreign intervention and advocated a general strike in the capital, which was partially observed. Meanwhile students (with the support of the political opposition) began a second week of protests against regional military intervention, and demonstrated in support of demands for the removal of the country's leadership. On 23 July 1996 Ntibantunganya was forced to abandon an attempt to attend the funeral of the victims of the Bugendana massacre following the pelting with missiles of the presidential helicopter by enraged mourners. On the following day, amid strong indications that UPRONA intended to join a number of smaller opposition parties that had already withdrawn from the convention of government, Ntibantunganya sought refuge in the US embassy. Several government ministers and the speaker of the national assembly withdrew to the German embassy compound, while the FRODEBU chairman, Jean Minani, fled the country.

THE RETURN OF BUYOYA

On 25 July 1996, in a bloodless military coup, the armed forces were extensively deployed in the capital. An announcement made by the minister of national defence, Lt-Col Firmin Sinzoyiheba, criticized the failure of the administration to safeguard national security and announced the suspension of the national assembly and all political activity, the imposition of a nationwide curfew and the closure of national borders and the airport at Bujumbura. Former president Buyoya was declared to be the new interim president of a transitional republic. In an address to the nation, delivered on the same day, Buyoya defined his immediate aim as the restoration of peace and national security, and sought to reassure former ministers and government officials that their safety would be guaranteed by the new regime. While Ntibantunganya conveyed his refusal to relinquish office, Nduwayo immediately resigned. In response to widespread condemnation of the coup, Buyoya announced that a largely civilian, broadly-based government of national unity would be promptly installed, and that future negotiations with all Hutu groups would be considered. The forced repatriation of Rwandan Hutu refugees was halted immediately. Despite the appointment of Pascal-Firmin Ndimira, a Hutu member of UPRONA, as prime minister, and an urgent attempt by Buyoya to obtain support from East African countries, a summit meeting of regional powers, convened in Arusha on 31 July, declared its intention to impose severe economic sanctions against the new regime, failing the immediate restoration of constitutional government. Western countries, which had until this point strongly supported regional initiatives in Burundi, were unwilling to carry out the imposition of sanctions. In early August the composition of a new 23-member, multi-ethnic cabinet was announced. In mid-August Buyoya announced that an expanded transitional national assembly, incorporating existing elected deputies, would be inaugurated during September for a three-year period. A consultative council of elders was also to be established to oversee a period of broad political debate, during which time formal political activity would remain proscribed. Meanwhile, reports emerged that the armed forces were launching indiscriminate attacks against Hutus (thousands had been killed since the coup) in an attempt to safeguard rural and border regions for Tutsi communities, and Hutu militia were also indiscriminately attacking Tutsi civilians. In mid-August, following the publication of a report by the UN on events preceding the 1993 coup, Buyoya dismissed the army chief-of-staff, Col Jean Bikomagu, and the commander of the *gendarmerie,* Col Pascal Simbanduko, both of whom were found by the UN to be involved in plotting the coup.

In the months following August 1996, military action in eastern Zaire, temporarily destroyed most of the FDD operations in the area, and prompted the repatriation of at least 30,000 Burundians. Most militia activists appear to have crossed into Tanzania, from where they have since made frequent incursions into Burundi's southern provinces, attacking both military targets and unarmed civilians.

The shift in the balance of power in eastern Zaire weakened the regional sanctions initiative, and enabled some Burundian exports to be transported via Goma and a limited amount of imports from east Africa to enter Burundi. However, the bulk of Burundi's trade passes through countries which were party to the sanctions agreement, prior to its suspension in January 1999, and the availability of the same range of products in Burundi as before the embargo (albeit at higher prices for some of them), demonstrated widespread violations of sanctions by these countries. In August 1996 Buyoya met Nyerere in Tanzania, in an unsuccessful attempt to obtain a relaxation of the sanctions. In the following month the Regional Sanctions Coordinating Committee (RSCC) held its first meeting, at which it agreed to ease restrictions on the importation of emergency relief supplies; however, it emphasized that economic sanctions would remain in force until the national assembly was restored, political parties legalized and unconditional negotiations opened with Hutu militias, including the FDD.

On 12 September 1996 Buyoya announced that political parties that made a 'positive contribution' to national life would be permitted to operate. The powers of the national assembly were restored, with the proviso that it could not dismiss the government. Exiled members of the national assembly were invited to return to the country. The response of the NSCC was to invite Buyoya to a meeting of regional heads of state, but as a factional leader and not as president. Neither Buyoya nor Nyangoma, who was also approached by the RSCC, attended the conference. No further concessions were forthcoming from the RSCC, which imposed a deadline of 31 October for the commencement of negotiations between the Burundi government and Hutu militias. Buyoya informed the RSCC that he was unwilling to enter into negotiations until economic sanctions were eased. The RSCC granted further exemptions for aid agencies in October 1996, and in December there were further discussions in Arusha, at which Nyerere unsuccessfully sought to bring together the government, FRODEBU, the CNDD and UPRONA. A further meeting of the regional heads of state also took place, at which it was agreed to retain economic sanctions pending the opening of negotiations by the contending forces.

Towards the end of 1996, the government instituted a policy of 'regroupment' in a number of provinces. This involved the transfer of the population of villages in areas affected by violence to guarded camps from which agricultural activity had to be carried out under military supervision, thus severely curtailing the country's agricultural production. Most of the villagers affected were Hutu, the majority of rural Tutsi having been in 'displacement' camps for some time.

Successive reports by the UN, published in December and in January 1997, alleged widespread human rights abuses, carried out both by Hutu militias and the army. The reports were rejected by the government, with the threat to expel UN human rights observers if their 'unfounded' allegations continued. In January legal proceedings were commenced against the speaker of the national assembly, Leonce Ngendakumana, for his alleged complicity in massacres of Tutsi people following the October 1993 coup; the charges were dismissed in March 1998, owing to lack of evidence.

By February 1997, when Buyoya declared his willingness to negotiate prior to the lifting of economic sanctions, most major commodities were widely available in Burundi, with sufficient supplies of fuel entering the country from illicit suppliers in Tanzania and Rwanda. The economic embargo had, however, led to increased unemployment, particularly in the capital, and had thus been the cause of a general decline in living standards.

Most members of the national executive of PARENA were taken into custody in mid-March 1997, following an allegation by Buyoya that the security forces had uncovered a coup conspiracy. Ex-president Bagaza, the party leader, was placed under house arrest until February 1998, when he was released by a military court.

A further meeting of regional heads of state was convened in mid-April at Arusha; on this occasion, Buyoya was invited to attend as president rather than faction leader. Recognizing the effective collapse of the sanctions policy, the heads of state agreed to permit the import of most goods, although imports of fuel remained at the discretion of the aid agencies; the export of goods through countries participating in the sanctions programme was to remain prohibited. The CNDD, which initially denounced the relaxation of sanctions, subsequently abandoned its objections and intensified its armed attacks.

It was disclosed by Buyoya in May 1997 that contacts had taken place in Rome, Italy, between the government and the CNDD, but that no substantive peace negotiations were immediately contemplated. This announcement prompted violent protests by university students (who are almost exclusively Tutsi), and was denounced by the UPRONA leadership, although some sections of the party expressed cautious support for a peace initiative. The UPRONA leadership later complained of police and army harassment, and in late July the Rome talks were suspended.

Fighting betweeen the army and Hutu militias spread across a number of provinces in July and August 1997; most of the casualties were unarmed civilians. Reports also emerged of clashes beteen the FDD and PALIPEHUTU at that time, particularly in Bubanza province. Tension increased on the border with Tanzania; the Burundian government blamed armed incursions by Hutu militias based in refugee camps in Tanzania. The Burundian government has repeatedly accused the Tanzanian authorities of complicity in these attacks; Tanzania has consistently denied this claim and has accused Burundi of attempting to deflect international opinion from the internal nature of the conflict. The UN agreed to send a fact-finding mission to the border area during November; in late September and October there were clashes between Tanzanian and Burundian troops stationed on the border.

At a meeting of regional foreign ministers, held in Kampala, Uganda, on 15 August 1997, it was decided to maintain the trade embargo on Burundi despite vigorous appeals from the Burundian government to lift the sanctions. The Burundian government accused Tanzania of influencing other countries to continue the embargo, and it subsequently withdrew from all-party talks, organized by Nyerere, that took place in Arusha in late August.

On 6 December 1997 FRODEBU re-elected Jean Minani as its president. On 8 December the Burundian government imposed a six-month suspension on FRODEBU on the grounds that Minani was not resident in Burundi and that he was in 'open conflict' with the government. Later the same day, however, the government rescinded the suspension and subsequently referred the matter to the supreme court.

By the end of 1997 the Burundian courts had handed down 220 death sentences to those found guilty of committing genocide in 1993. The trial of those accused of involvement in the 1993 coup attempt, and of assassinating President Ndadaye and six others, however, was subject to repeated adjournments, and verdicts were not delivered until May 1999. Five soldiers were sentenced to death and a number of others received prison terms; however, Hutu political parties expressed concern that all the senior officers implicated in the coup attempt, including Bikomagu, were acquitted.

In a large-scale rebel attack on 1 January 1998, at least 1,000 guerrillas, thought to include Rwandan militia, attacked a military camp and village close to Bujumbura airport. They made significant advances but retreated before a sizeable army counter-attack; more than 250 people were reported to have been killed, including many Hutu civilians. On 2 January Astère Girukwigomba was appointed finance minister, following the resignation of Gérard Niyibigira on the grounds of ill health. At the end of the month the minister of defence, Firmin Sinzoyiheba, was killed in a helicopter crash; he was replaced by Alfred Nkurunziza, Buyoya's chief military adviser.

On 21 February 1998 a meeting of regional heads of state in Kampala again decided to maintain sanctions, despite earlier indications from some governments that the sanctions would be lifted. Meanwhile, few incidents had been reported on the Tanzanian border since the beginning of the year, and on 12 March tripartite talks held by Burundi, Tanzania and the UNHCR further eased tensions; the UNHCR proposed the policing of Burundian refugee camps to ensure that no military activity took place. Although security levels slowly improved in most of the country, in March armed attacks intensified in Bujumbura Rural province, and left some 20,000 people homeless. Signs of divisions in the CNDD–FDD also began to appear, culminating in the suspension of Nyangoma on 8 May and his replacement with the FDD chief of staff, Jean-Bosco Ndayikengurukiye. (Nyangoma subsequently headed a faction of the CNDD.)

In March 1998 the government initiated negotiations with the national assembly concerning the expiry of FRODEBU's electoral mandate at the end of June. FRODEBU demanded a return to the 1992 constitution, while the government proposed a continuation of the terms of office introduced by Buyoya after the July 1996 coup. A compromise was eventually reached, which Buyoya described as a new partnership between the government and the national assembly. The partnership exacerbated division within FRODEBU, and was also denounced by the CNDD, which maintained that the Arusha arrangements comprised the only legitimate negotiating forum. On 6 June 1998 the transitional constitution, which combined elements of both the 1992 constitution and the 1996 decree-law adopted by Buyoya after the July coup, was promulgated. Under this constitution, the national assembly was expanded from 81 to 121 members, the size of the council of ministers was reduced, and two vice-presidential posts were created. On 11 June 1998 Buyoya was sworn in as head of state, and two days later a new council of ministers was announced, in which 14 new appointments were made. The total number of ministerial portfolios was reduced from 24 to 22. On 15–21 June the government attended all-party talks in Arusha, under the chairmanship of Nyerere, at which all the participating delegations agreed to hold further talks on 20 July and to suspend hostilities at that date. However, both the government and the FDD immediately distanced themselves from the agreement, thus undermining its effectiveness. It was also decided to establish a number of commissions to examine each of the key issues in the Burundian conflict. The second round of talks in July made little progress and was dominated by procedural debate and lengthy presentations from each of the delegations. Following the July talks, Burundi's main donors called for a review of the regional sanctions policy in order to encourage progress at the talks.

On 8 October 1998 Charles Mukasi, an opponent of the Arusha negotiations, was replaced as UPRONA president by the minister of information and government spokesman, Luc Rukingama. Further talks were held in Arusha in October. Despite a lack of funds which forced an early end to the talks, three of the planned commissions were successfully constituted. The three commissions were to examine the nature of the Burundian conflict, democracy and good governance, and peace and security, respectively, and convened in mid-December to prepare for talks in Arusha in January 1999. The remaining commissions, when constituted, were to examine the rehabilitation of refugees and economic development, transitional institutions, and the guarantees for the implementation of the eventual peace agreement.

The FDD and other militia groups continued their attacks in Burundi throughout 1998 and early 1999, particularly on camps for the internally displaced. The majority of reported incidents took place in Bujumbura Rural and Makamba provinces, and their intensity increased prior to each round of talks in Arusha.

In late 1998 Burundian security forces increased their involvement in the civil war in the DRC (their presence there had been initially denied) and by May 1999 at least 3,000 troops were believed to be deployed there. Their activities focused on the destruction of FDD camps in the eastern DRC. Since the outbreak in August 1998 of the insurgency in the DRC, the FDD has increased its presence there, lending military support to the DRC government, while at the same time utilizing the disturbed conditions within the DRC as an opportunity to regroup and rearm (although its political leadership insists that it still supports the Arusha process). The DRC government has objected to the presence of Burundian troops in the DRC and in May 1999 threatened to launch an attack on Bujumbura. Burundi, however, asserted that the presence of its troops in the DRC was necessary to confront the security threat posed by FDD forces, and that it would respond to any attack on its territory.

A fourth round of talks was held at Arusha in January 1999, with the CNDD–FDD again officially excluded despite speculation that means might be found to include it more formally. Discussions about economic reconstruction dominated the talks, which concluded on 31 January. A meeting of regional heads of state on 21–23 January 1999 resulted in the suspension of the economic embargo. It was hoped that this measure would strengthen the Arusha peace process. The decision was welcomed both within Burundi and abroad, although the CNDD dismissed it as premature. In mid-February Burundi's minister of external relations and co-operation, Sévérin Ntahomvukiye, visited Tanzania, where he met the Tanzanian minister of foreign affairs and international co-operation, Lt-Col Jakaya Kikwete, to discuss relations between the two countries. It was agreed to establish a tripartite commission to include representatives from Burundi and Tanzania and the UN High Commissioner for Refugees to investigate alleged incursions into Burundi from Tanzania by armed militia groups. The commission was scheduled to convene in late March but this meeting was subsequently cancelled without explanation by the Tanzanian government. Buyoya met the Tanzanian president, Benjamin Mkapa, in May for further discussions on this matter. Relations, however, remain tense.

The Arusha commissions continued their work in mid-March 1999. Progress was, however, slow and the Arusha process received continued criticism from the Burundian government and the internal wing of FRODEBU for being cumbersome and not conducive to agreement. On 18 March the FRODEBU secretary-general, Augustin Nzojibwami, suspended former president Ntibantunganya from the executive committee, along with other senior members, for alleged ethnicism and ill discipline. However, the FRODEBU president, Jean Minani, ordered Nzojibwami's expulsion from the party (although Nzojibwami has refused to recognize the expulsion). In June a split emerged within FRODEBU, creating separate factions centred around Minani and Nzojibwami. Several government ministers were among those to join Nzojibwami's supporters.

President Pasteur Bizimungu of Rwanda arrived in Burundi for a three-day visit on April 17 1999, the first head of state to do so since the 1996 coup. Bizimungu and Buyoya issued a joint statement at the end of the visit pledging that Rwanda and Burundi would co-operate in the fight against genocidal forces in the region.

In early May 1999 seven predominantly Hutu parties, including the CNDD and the external wing of FRODEBU, met in Moshi, Tanzania, in order to negotiate a common position prior to the commissions convening in mid-May. By this time a fourth commission, to examine the rehabilitation of refugees and economic development, had been constituted. During the meetings of the commissions the parties assumed a joint stance on a number of issues and became known as the Moshi group. The Burundian government and the internal wing of FRODEBU condemned the alliance for allegedly encouraging ethnic polariz-ation while Nyerere supported it, arguing that it facilitated the talks by minimizing differences. In response to the formation of the Moshi group, eight predominantly Tutsi parties present at the Arusha talks also formed a negotiating bloc (known as G8). Delegations representing UPRONA, the government and the national assembly remained outside the two blocs. At the end of May Buyoya proposed a 10-year political transition for Burundi, including plans for the establishment of a senate, and for the national assembly to be enlarged. Buyoya proposed that he rule for five years and a FRODEBU appointee for the remaining five years. The proposals were rejected by all external Burundian political forces.

On 3 June 1999 the national assembly adopted a new penal code, which came into force in January 2000. The code provided for the early intervention of defence lawyers, prohibited torture, arbitrary arrest and prolonged detention without trial. Around 8,000 of Burundi's estimated 10,000 prisoners had not been to trial, although the prosecutor-general, Gerard Ngendabanka, ensured the release of several hundred of these by the end of 1999.

Commission meetings in Arusha resumed in early July 1999 for a fifth round, but made little progress, exhausting hopes that the formation of three blocs would facilitate negotiations. The fifth round of negotiations was eventually concluded, earlier than anticipated, on 17 July by Nyerere, who attributed the failure of the discussions to the Burundian government. The government, in return, blamed Nyerere for the continued ab-sence of the CNDD–FDD, and a faction of PALIPEHUTU's armed wing, the Forces nationales de libération (FNL). In late July, in response to growing concerns about corruption within the government, Buyoya replaced the minister of commerce, industry and tourism.

A sixth round of discussions at Arusha was due to begin in September 1999, but was postponed because of Nyerere's ill health. Nyerere subsequently died in London on 14 October. Nyerere's death resulted in the suspension of the Arusha pro-cess, despite the main negotiating parties reporting good pro-gress at a meeting in the Tanzanian capital, Dar es Salaam, in early September, and reaching a degree of consensus on the integration of rebel forces into the military and Buyoya's transi-tion programme.

In early October 1999 a new political alliance, known as Convergence pour la paix et la réconciliation (CNPR), was formed. This brought together UPRONA, the internal wing of FRODEBU and most of the minor Tutsi parties that had previously been in G8. In response, in early December, the Alliance nationale pour le changement (ANAC) was constituted, primarily consisting of the external wing of FRODEBU and PARENA. The CNPR and ANAC, both of which included Hutu and Tutsi political parties, effectively ended the Moshi, G8 and government negotiating blocs of May 1999.

The CNDD–FDD and FNL intensified their attacks on Bujum-bura in August and September 1999. In early August militia attacked Kanyosha, near the capital. A counter-insurgency oper-ation by the armed forces resulted in hundreds of civilian casualties, according to Amnesty International, although the armed forces admitted to only about 11 militia deaths. Hutu militia attacked Bujumbura's Musega and Mutanga suburbs in late August, killing at least 50 people. The government res-ponded by intensifying regroupment in Bujumbura Rural prov-ince, and by mid-September a further 200,000 civilians had been gathered into camps.

Buyoya visited the South African president, Thabo Mbeki, in Pretoria in late August 1999, requesting that South Africa play an active role in the peace process. In early December, regional heads of state, meeting in Arusha, unanimously selected the former South African president, Nelson Mandela, as the new Burundi mediator. The appointment received international sup-port as well as the endorsement of the Burundi government. Militia representatives were more cautious, having previously accused the South African government of bias in the conflict.

Immediately after his appointment, Mandela called for the inclusion of Hutu militia leaders in the peace process. Mandela made his first official visit to Arusha in mid-January 2000, when he told participants that they were responsible for massacres in Burundi and should show greater urgency in compromising to

reach a solution acceptable to all participants in the peace process. Mandela subsequently attended a meeting about Burundi at the UN Security Council. The meeting condemned the government's regroupment policy, but resolved to encourage donors to resume substantial assistance to Burundi. A general strike in Bujumbura in January in support of higher wages and against corruption revealed increasing popular dissatisfaction with the government, despite a major reorganization earlier that month in which the minister of finance and minister of defence were replaced.

Mandale attended his first round of Arusha discussions, the seventh of the process, in February 2000. Mandela caused a stir among delegates by criticizing Tutsi domination of Burundi's public life and urging equal representation of Hutus and Tutsi in the armed forces, while also referring to Hutu rebel attacks on civilians as 'terrorism'. Mandela criticized Buyoya for his imprisonment of political opponents, and denounced 'regroup-ment', describing the camps as unfit for human habitation. After the discussions, the Burundian government swiftly reassured the armed forces that it would not allow the imposition of ethnic quotas in the military. Mandela met senior army commanders and the minister of defence, Col Cyrille Ndayirukiye, in Johan-nesburg in mid-March, and afterwards praised them for their realistic stance. Mandela also met the leadership of the CNDD–FDD and the FNL.

At the next Arusha round of negotiations, which commenced on 27 March 2000, talks focused on the issue of army integration, despite the continued absence of the CNDD–FDD and FNL. The discussions concluded with the distribution of a draft accord to delegations for their consideration. Meanwhile, fierce fighting was reported during March and April in provinces bordering Tanzania, as well as skirmishes on the outskirts of Bujumbura. The fighting continued in May, particularly in Makamba, res-ulting in thousands of new displacements and refugees. Two committees, one charged with examining good governance and democracy, and the other with the implementation of the peace agreement, were convened during April. The good governance committee, despite agreement on most issues, remained at an impasse on electoral arrangements and transition government modalities. The peace agreement implementation committee became deadlocked over foreign military assistance with the transition. As previously, predominantly Hutu parties dem-anded external assistance, while the government and mainly Tutsi parties (with the notable exception of PARENA) remained opposed. The implementation committee met again in late May, and reported good progress on the issue.

Mandela arrived in Burundi for the first time in late April 2000 for a brief visit that had been preceded by increased violence, particularly near Bujumbura. In late May Mandela met with senior army commanders and militia leaders in Johan-nesburg, although the CNDD–FDD declined to participate. Mandela met with Buyoya in Johannesburg in early June, and subsequently announced that Buyoya had agreed to ensure equal Hutu–Tutsi representation in the army and had guar-anteed the closure by the end of the month of Burundi's regroup-ment camps. Mandela visited Burundi again in mid-June, meeting senior politicians, prominent members of civil society, and visiting regroupment camps and prisons. Later that month the vice-president of the CNDD, Christian Sendegeya, left the CNDD–FDD and created a breakaway faction.

In early July 2000 it was announced that the CNDD–FDD had agreed for the first time to attend a further round of peace discussions, under the mediation of Mandela, which was to commence on 19 July. The revised peace accord was presented to Mandela by a team of mediators prior to the peace discussions; the draft agreement reportedly stipulated the terms for the creation of a transitional government, the integration of former Hutu rebels into the armed forces, and the establishment of an electoral system,which would ensure power-sharing between the Tutsi and Hutu. Mandela announced that, although a number of issues remained outstanding, the discussions were expected to result in an endorsement of the peace plan, and that the agree-ment would be formally signed on 28 August. The Arusha summit meeting, which was attended by the heads of state of Zambia, Ethiopia, Uganda, Kenya and Rwanda, was convened on 19 July as scheduled. Discussions were subsequently adjourned to allow delegates time to consider the revised draft of the peace accord. However, the CNDD–FDD demanded the release of political prisoners, the dissolution of regroupment camps and further negotiations with the armed forces, as a precondition to the movement's disarmament and acceptance of the peace accord, whereas the government insisted that the rebels cease hostilities prior to the signing of the agreement. (The FNL had again failed to attend the discussions.) Meanwhile, further hostilities were reported in eastern Burundi, near the border with Tanzania. On 28 August the power-sharing agreement was signed by the government, the armed forces, seven Hutu political associations and seven Tutsi parties. The further three Tutsi groups which had attended the Arusha meeting agreed in mid-September to sign the accord at cease-fire discussions, scheduled to take place in Nairobi, Kenya, on 20 September. (However, it was unclear whether the FNL would attend these negotiations.)

REFUGEE AND AID CONCERNS

The cross-border movement of vast numbers of refugees, provoked by regional ethnic and political violence, remains an important factor in relations with Rwanda, Tanzania and the DRC. In October and November 1993, following an abortive coup by factions of the Tutsi-dominated armed forces (see above), ethnic violence erupted on a massive scale throughout the country, claiming an estimated 50,000 lives and leaving an estimated 800,000 displaced persons, including 500,000 who had fled into neighbouring Tanzania, Rwanda and Zaire. Following the Rwandan genocide and the subsequent victory by the Front patriotique rwandais (FPR), thousands of Rwandan

Hutus sought refuge in Burundi; most of the Burundian refugees in Rwanda were repatriated at that time. Large-scale efforts at repatriating Rwandan refugees were successful, and during 1995 and 1996 most of the Rwandan refugees returned to Rwanda. Estimates compiled by the UN in June 1997 suggested that over 600,000 Burundians, more than 10% of the population, were internally displaced, including at least 275,00 who had been 'regrouped'. A number of the 'displacement' camps have subsequently been dismantled and more than 100,000 people have been allowed to return to their homes. Regroupment, however, intensified in particular after a series of rebel attacks against the capital in late 1999. By mid-2000 at least 350,000 people were regrouped, despite widespread international condemnation (see above). The government pledged to dismantle most of the camps in April 2000, but failed to do so; in June Buyoya repeated his commitment to close the camps. In mid-November 1997 armed forces of the DRC, believed to have been assisted by Rwandan and Burundian soldiers, expelled refugees from the eastern DRC. These expulsions included most of the Burundian émigrés. Burundian refugee numbers in Tanzania have fluctuated over the years, but have not been less than 200,000 since the early 1970s. Of the 473,800 Burundian refugees in Tanzania at the end of 1998, about 200,000 were not assisted by the UNHCR. In the first half of 2000 the latest in a long series of refugee emigrations towards Tanzania took place, at its peak reaching over 1,000 a day, although some of these latest arrivals subsequently returned home. In mid-2000 all but an estimated 20,000 of Burundi's 370,000 refugees were resident in Tanzania.

Economy

FRANÇOIS MISSER

In terms of average income, Burundi is one of the poorest countries in the world, and its economic performance is heavily dependent on the international price of coffee. In 1998, according to estimates by the World Bank, Burundi's gross national product (GNP), measured at average 1996–98 prices, was US $911m., equivalent to $140 per head. During 1990–98, in the context of a high rate of population growth (2.6% annually), GNP per head decreased, in real terms, at an average annual rate of 6.4%. However, overall GNP declined dramatically in 1993, owing to a decline in international coffee prices and the civil disturbances arising from the assassination of President Melchior Ndadaye. The recovery of coffee markets in 1994, however, failed to reverse the economy's downward trend, and a decline in all sectors contributed to a 16.7% reduction in per-caput GNP. Overall, gross domestic product (GDP) increased, in real terms, at an average rate of 7.1% per year during 1965–80, and by an average of 4.4% per year in 1980–90. In 1990–98 real GDP decreased at an average annual rate of 3.3%. Owing to the combination of declining coffee prices, chronic shortages of fuel and manufacturing components and the effects of the drought, only a slight increase in GDP was estimated in 1999. According to Burundian government estimates, by February 1996 more than 60% of the population were living in conditions of extreme poverty, compared with 30% before October 1993. Other social indicators, such as primary school enrolment, also deteriorated during this period and the rate of childhood malnutrition doubled, to 12%. The annual rate of inflation averaged 7.6% in 1980–90 and increased to an average annual rate of 15.2% in 1990–98. The rate averaged 19.4% in 1995, and in 1996 rose to 26.4%, largely as a result of a more than three-fold increase in petroleum prices, owing to the trade embargo imposed by neighbouring countries from mid-1996 to January 1999. The inflation rate for 1998 was 12.5%, but increased to 20% in 1999, according to government estimates.

Burundi is among the 30 African states designated by the fourth Lomé Convention as least developed and therefore qualifying for special treatment under that Convention's scheme to stabilize export earnings (Stabex) for products sold to the European Union (EU). At mid-1998 Burundi had a population

density of 226.3 persons per sq km, one of the highest in mainland Africa. Burundi's population density has been subject to significant fluctuation since mid-1993 as a result of the cross-border movement of vast numbers of refugees. Large numbers of Burundians have also been relocated under government plans aimed at removing them from areas of conflict. In April 1997 UN officials reported that this large-scale movement, combined with the shortage of food aid had led to widespread childhood malnutrition in the 'regroupment' camps. This in turn provoked more cross-border movement as did the attacks against Burundian refugee camps in Zaire by Zairean rebels and Rwandan troops in October 1996. In April 1997 the neighbouring states partially lifted the embargo to allow for the import of food aid. However, administrative obstacles resulted in insufficient supplies entering the country. Serious flooding also prevented about two-thirds of the food aid from reaching its destination, and by the end of 1998 some 350,000 people remained dependent on food aid for their survival. In 1999 increased insecurity further disrupted agricultural activities.

AGRICULTURE AND TRADE

At mid-1998 an estimated 90.6% of the labour force were engaged in agriculture (including forestry and fishing), mainly at subsistence level, and the sector provided about 53% of GDP in that year. During 1980–90 agricultural GDP increased, in real terms, by an average of 3.1% per year. During 1990–98 it declined by 90.6% per year. Burundi's dominant cash crop is coffee. However, the overwhelming dependence on coffee, which provided 87.7% of total export earnings in 1997, has had an adverse effect on the balance of payments in times of declining international coffee prices. The Stabex scheme, introduced in 1975 under the first Lomé Convention and retained in the three subsequent Conventions, has helped to ease this difficulty. Additionally, in the early 1990s the government acted to attract private-sector investment in the coffee industry. The state monopoly on coffee exports was relaxed, and a restructuring of the two factories that process Burundi's entire coffee crop was undertaken. By 1991 the value of exports of coffee had improved to US $74m. However, a depression in international coffee prices and a reduction in the volume of production as a result of civil unrest reduced revenues to just $36m. in 1993. A spectacular recovery in international prices prompted a significant rise in the value of coffee exports, with revenue exceeding $93m. in 1994, and $80m. in 1995. In 1996, however, as a result of the trade embargo imposed on Burundi, revenue declined to $25m. In 1997 coffee exporters managed to break the embargo, by shipping production through Lake Tanganyika via Zambia, and by airlifting the remainder via Angola and the Republic of the Congo. As a result, export revenue for coffee more than tripled in that year, to $77m. The improvement in the international price of coffee resulted in a similar level of revenue in 1998, despite a declining crop caused by a shortage of fertilizers and the age of the plantations. However, the lower price of coffee in 1999 (78.4 cents per lb, compared with 114.5 cents per lb in 1998) resulted in a decline in export revenue, to $43m.

Despite civil and political disturbances during 1993 and 1994, the mid-year crop amounted to 29,526 metric tons (a 42% increase in production compared to the previous mid-year crop), owing to favourable climatic conditions. From mid-1994, however, the military operations of extremist guerrilla groups, based principally in Zaire (now the Democratic Republic of the Congo, DRC), and the military response to such incursions, by the Burundian army, created a climate of extreme insecurity, which was reflected in a 13.1% decrease in the mid-year crop for 1995 (24,773 metric tons). The mid-1996 crop also decreased, to 22,600 metric tons, due to the destruction of eight washing stations and the increased insecurity. According to the central bank, just over one-half of this total was exported before the embargo came into force. The mid-1997 crop again showed a small decline, to 20,300 metric tons, which the central bank attributed to the continued insecurity and the trade embargo. Coffee traders did, however, manage to export the entire crop, mostly through Zambia. (Despite the embargo, the remainder of the 1996 crop had been exported by air, with the assistance of private airlines.) In 1998 output continued to decrease, to 16,000 metric tons, although a slight increase, to 20,000 metric tons, was forecast for 1999, owing to the rehabilitation of several washing stations. A programme was initiated at that time to renovate the country's coffee plantations, to include replacement planting of some coffee trees, although these were not expected to become productive for several years. Following a report from the international medical relief charity Médecins sans frontières in January 1997 that 50% of Burundian child mortality was caused by malnutrition, some restrictions on medicine and food aid ended in April.

Burundi's total export earnings amounted to US $104m. in 1995 and $119m. in 1994 (owing to improved international coffee prices), compared with $62m. in 1993. In 1996, as a result of the trade embargo, total export earnings decreased to $40m., although in 1997, owing to improved international coffee prices and Burundi's ability to break the embargo, earnings increased to $87m. Total export earnings declined to $64m. in 1998, and to $55m. in 1999. The principal exports are coffee, tea, and raw hides and skins. In 1999 the government established an exports promotion fund of 1,000m. Burundian francs to assist in the marketing efforts of Burundian exporting companies. Meanwhile, the cost of imports declined to $205m. in 1993, only to increase again, to $224m. in 1994 and $234m. in 1995. In 1996, as a result of the embargo, the cost of imports fell to $123m., decreasing slightly to $122m. in 1997. The cost of imports increased to $157m. in 1998, but declined to $118m. in 1999. The principal imports are refined petroleum products (including gasoline and gas oils), general industrial machinery, road vehicles, basic metal manufactures, cereals and cereal preparations (especially malt) and non-metallic mineral manufactures (especially cement). Imports greatly decreased in 1996, as a result of the embargo imposed by neighbouring countries, but it was not entirely effective, as products were still being smuggled in from Tanzania and Rwanda. In 1997 imports from the rest of Africa increased to 1995 levels, with Kenya, Zambia, South Africa, Zimbabwe and Rwanda significantly increasing exports to Burundi, although imports from Tanzania and the DRC decreased. The EU countries (in particular Belgium-Luxembourg, France and Germany), together with the USA, Kenya and Japan, are Burundi's main trading partners.

The credibility of a free export zone, established in 1992, was seriously undermined in August 1993, when the new administration withdrew the financial advantages being offered to Affimet, a Belgian gold dealer and refiner, under the scheme, having calculated that the company's use of the zone was depriving the state of US $12m. per year in taxes. In 1994, however, these advantages were once again extended to the company. An estimated 9.6 metric tons of gold were exported from Burundi in 1994. Almost 80% of this total was believed to have originated in Zaire, with the remainder proceeding from Tanzania and Uganda, and only an insignificant share mined locally. In 1999 Affimet exported an estimated 3 tons of gold. Import statistics from the Belgian office of foreign trade suggest that in 1992 Burundi exported precious stones and metals worth 1,100m. Belgian francs to Belgium. In 1993 the value of these exports increased to 1,500m. Belgian francs, declining to 784m. Belgian francs (around US $23m.) in 1994. However, despite official claims that such transactions involve 'goods in transit', the failure of official export statistics in Burundi to reflect the importance of the trade in gold has prompted concern as to the accuracy of official export figures in general. As a result of the embargo, the trade in gold fell considerably from the end of July 1996. This prompted Affimet to consider other locations for a gold refining plant, in Rwanda or the DRC. In January 1999, however, the government signed an agreement allowing Affimet to purchase, process and export all precious and semi-precious minerals from Burundi. In February 1999 the US-based court for the settlement of disputes related to investment eventually ruled that the Burundian government reimburse $3m. to Affimet. This amount represented a deposit by Affimet corresponding to taxes and royalties, which the Belgian company should not have paid, according to the initial free export zone agreement. After the authorities failed to reimburse this amount by the deadline of 1 April 1999, Affimet decided to seize Burundi's bank assets in Belgium by the end of that year. The measure initially included not only accounts of the Burundian state, but also those of the Central Bank of Burundi in Belgium. Central Bank lawyers succeeded in ending the measure in March 2000. Meanwhile, the Burundian ministry of commerce ordered the closure of Affimet, together with an 'offshore' bank and an airline owned by the same Belgian gold trader in Burundi. The dispute obstructed attempts by the Burundian government to attract other foreign companies to develop a free export zone in the country.

Officially, tea is now Burundi's second most important export commodity, and had steadily increased its share of export earnings until the recovery of international coffee prices in late 1993. Exports of tea accounted for 12.6% of total export earnings in 1993, compared with 5.3% in 1985. In 1994 and 1995, however, export revenues from tea represented 11.6% and 8.6% of total exports, respectively. Exports of tea fell again in 1996, amounting to 1,640m. Burundian francs, although they increased in 1997, to 3,176m. Burundian francs, and in 1998, to 4,912m. Burundian francs, representing 17.1% of the value of total export earnings in that year. In 1999 tea exports increased again to 6,133m. Burundian francs, representing 19.8% of total export earnings. During the early 1990s five tea plantations underwent development and expansion, with financial assistance from the Caisse française de développement and the European Development Fund (EDF). The 1994 crop of 6,862 metric tons represented a 24.3% increase compared with the output of 5,520 metric tons for 1993. A further 1.7% increase in production (to 6,982 metric tons) was recorded in 1995. However, in 1996 production fell to 5,716 metric tons, owing to the destruction of the Teza tea factory and a further decrease, to 4,169 metric tons, was recorded for the 1997 crop. In 1998 an increase in tea production, to 6,500 tons, was recorded, largely owing to the reconstruction of the Teza tea factory. The end of the regional trade embargo which had increased export costs, in January 1999, and a price rise from 33 to 45 Burundian francs per kg by the Office du Thé du Burundi (OTB) parastatal in that year was expected to encourage producers for the 2000 season.

In 1987 cotton became a significant export, accounting for 5.7% of total export receipts. Production subsequently declined sharply, following heavy rains which destroyed some 600 ha of plantations. In 1993 revenue from cotton exports accounted for just 5% of total export earnings and in 1994 production declined to 4,915 metric tons, almost one-half of that for 1993. Production continued to decline in 1995, to 4,593 metric tons, and this trend continued in 1996, with a decline to 2,605 metric tons owing to worker migration as a result of violent confrontation between the armed forces and guerrilla troops on the Imbo plain. Mainly grown in the plain of Ruzizi, the cotton crop was traditionally nearly all sold to Belgium, although cotton exports ceased in 1996 as a result of the declining crop. Output continued to decline in 1997, to 2,381 metric tons, although a slight recovery, to 3,300 tons, was achieved in 1998. However, output again declined, to 2,300 metric tons in 1999, owing to insufficient producer prices, and to the effects of a drought.

Burundi has obtained foreign assistance for the development of other crops. On the Imbo plain, land is being reclaimed for the cultivation of cotton and rice in an integrated rural development scheme which is assisted by the UN Development Programme and the FAO. However, rice development projects have also been disrupted by fighting in the region and many fields have been abandoned, road maintenance has deteriorated and pumping stations have been sabotaged. The extent of the security crisis has also inclined the majority of aid workers from bilateral and multilateral agencies to leave the country or to remain in the capital. Plans to establish an integrated sugar scheme in the south-east of the Mosso region, with finance provided mainly by the African Development Bank, the OPEC Fund and the Arab Bank for Economic Development in Africa (BADEA), are proceeding. Plantations of sugar cane have been established on the Mosso plain, near Bujumbura, in association with a refinery, which was projected to meet 90% of Burundi's demand for sugar by the early 1990s, with further potential for exports. However, both civil unrest and the inadequate size of the cultivated areas have prevented Burundi from becoming self-sufficient in cane. Bananas, sweet potatoes, cassava, pulses and maize are other important, but mainly subsistence, crops.

Although potentially self-sufficient in food production, recent civil disturbances have tended to disrupt the country's infrastructure and have prevented supplies from reaching urban centres. In September 1994 there was an estimated food deficit of 200,000 metric tons. In addition, large-scale illicit trade in staple products and sugar from Burundi to the neighbouring countries results from various factors, particularly in the case of rice (of which production reached 40,000 tons in 1999). One factor is the significant difference between the official and the parallel rate of the Burundian franc to the dollar. Another incentive for such smuggling is the difference between the fixed price paid to the peasants by the rice estate parastatal, which produces about a third of the country's production in the Imbo plain, and the consumer price in Bujumbura, which was three times higher by the end of 1999.

The development of livestock is hindered by the social system, which encourages the maintenance of cattle herds that are both too large and too little exploited. However, the sale of hides has increased, and in the early 1990s was among the most valuable source of export earnings (641m. Burundian francs in 1994). However, as with other sub-sectors, livestock-rearing has been adversely affected by civil unrest, and in 1995 and early 1996 cattle rustlers removed entire herds (some cattle were used by rebel groups to explode mines around army barracks). Export revenue declined as a result, to 215.9m. Burundian francs in 1996, to 44.8m. Burundian francs in 1997, and to US $32.1m. in 1998. However, revenue from the export of hides again increased, to $76.8m., in 1999. The shortage of veterinary products, as a consequence of the embargo, contributed to the spread of a foot-and-mouth disease epidemic in the east of the country in March–June 1999. Some fishing is practised in the waters of Lake Tanganyika, but this activity was banned by the government in April 1996 following reports that the lake was being used as a transit point by extremist insurgents from Zaire and Tanzania. In 1998, however, as security on the lake improved, the resumption of fishing was authorized.

MINERALS

Small quantities of bastnaesite and cassiterite have been exploited by the Karongo Mining Co (SOMIKA). In 1995 the government was considering extending the financial advantages of the free-trade zone to a private company seeking to export cassiterite; in that year 171 metric tons of cassiterite were exported through Bujumbura port. No exports were recorded for 1996 or 1997 and in 1998 only 23 metric tons of cassiterite were exported; in 1999, however, exports increased to 90 metric tons. Burundi also exported 83 metric tons of niobium ore in 1995, but exports of niobium had declined to only 14 tons by 1999. Tungsten and columbo-tantalite are mined in small quantities. A small amount of alluvial gold is also produced but production could increase significantly if a project to exploit the Muyinga reserves, estimated at 60 metric tons of gold ore, associating the Canadian corporation, AMTEC, and the government-owned Burundi Mining Corpn (BUMINCO), proves successful. In March 1999 the Preferential Trade Area Bank agreed to disburse a US $297,500 loan to allow BUMINCO to purchase equipment for a gold processing plant (which was to have a monthly capacity of 10 kg), pending completion of a feasibility study on an industrial project at Masaka. Initial prospecting on the Masaka site by BUMINCO was completed in May 1999, and further exploration commenced during the same month on sites at Rugomero and Butihinda. Important deposits of vanadium (estimated at some 14m. metric tons) and uranium are being surveyed. Petroleum has been detected beneath Lake Tanganyika and in the Ruzizi valley, for which test drillings were carried out in the late 1980s by US petroleum interests, in association with the Burundian government. In 1973 a UN survey discovered large nickel deposits, then estimated at 5% of world reserves, near Musongati. Subsequent surveys estimated Burundi's nickel deposits to be about 300m. metric tons. In March 1999 an agreement was signed between the Burundian government and the Australian company Andover Resources for the exploitation of the Musongati deposits. Andover Resources was to complete a feasibility study to assess the economic viability of the project, which envisaged the construction of a plant with an annual capacity of 45,000 metric tons of nickel by 2002, at a total estimated cost of US $700m.; the project was also to include the construction of employee housing, of a 35 MW power station and of rail or road access to the plant. In 1999 Andover Resources (which became a subsidiary of the Canadian enterprise, Argosy Minerals Inc.) obtained concessions on further deposits at Nyabikere and Waga. In May 2000, however, Andover Resources, declared that it was unable to proceed with the Musongati project, owing to instability in the region. An evaluation of the economic feasibility of exploiting identified deposits of phosphate rock in the Matongo region was under way in 1991. (With estimated reserves of 15m. metric tons, Burundi has the potential to fulfil the demands of the domestic market for inputs.) Sufficient reserves of carbonatite (7.3m. metric tons) to satisfy the domestic demand for cement have also been identified, near Gatara; Burundi is currently wholly dependent on imports of cement. However, the continuing deterioration of the security situation in 1995 and 1996 deterred foreign companies from bringing these projects to fruition.

INDUSTRY AND TRANSPORT

There is little industrial activity in Burundi, apart from the processing of agricultural products, e.g. cotton, coffee, tea and vegetable oil extraction, and small-scale wood mills. Industry, comprising mining, manufacturing, construction and utilities, provided an estimated 17.0% of GDP in 1997. During 1980–90 industrial GDP increased at an average annual rate of 4.5%. However, as a result of civil unrest, the sector's GDP decreased by an average of 8.4% per year in 1990–97. Problems with the electricity supply, due to sabotage, and a lack of imported raw materials owing to the economic embargo continued to depress Burundi's GDP in 1996. Although the electricity supply improved in 1997, the continued shortage of raw materials resulted in a decrease of 4.9% in the industrial GDP in that year. However, increased electricity production in 1998, combined with a less vigilant implementation of the embargo by neighbouring states, contributed to a 3.1% rise in industrial GDP in that year. Only 2.3% of the working population were employed in industrial activities in 1979, and this ratio had not increased by 1992. Manufacturing GDP increased, in real terms, at an average annual rate of 5.7% in 1980–90, but fell by 9.9% per year in 1990–97; the sector accounted for some 12% of GDP in 1994 and 6% of exports in 1995. By the mid-1980s several small enterprises, including glass, cement, footwear, insecticide factories, a flour mill and a brewery, had been established. (The Brarudi brewery, 60%-owned by Heineken and 40%-owned by the government of Burundi, was reported to have provided almost 40% of total government tax receipts in 1996.) A textile industry was also developed, with aid from the People's Republic of China, which exported fabrics to the neighbouring states of Rwanda and Zaire until the end of 1995 when, as with most industry in Bujumbura, the plant was closed temporarily after the sabotage of electricity pylons which left the capital without electric power for several weeks. However, the government demonstrated its determination to keep the sector operational and the installations were repaired and placed in the custody of the army; textile production increased by 11% in 1997 and by a further 42% in 1998. A further increase of 15.7% was recorded in 1999, as a result of growing demand from neighbouring Rwanda, in conjunction with the much faster depreciation of the Burundian franc. However, the decrease of domestic cotton production forced the main company, the Complexe textile de Bujumbura to rely mainly on imports. In October 1999 it signed a contract for the import of 1,000 metric tons of cotton from Malawi. One sign of recovery was the company's rapidly increasing turnover, from 2,469m. Burundian francs in 1997, to 3,669m. francs in 1998, and to 5,516m. francs in 1999. Otherwise, except for textiles, pharmaceutical products, matches and cigarettes, the output of most industries suffered a further decline in 1999. The production of beer and soft drinks fell by 5% and 11.5% respectively in 1999, to 984m. litres and 126m. litres. In January 1996, as a safeguard against similar inconveniences in the future, the government purchased a US $3.5m. thermal power station, comprising four generators with a total capacity of 5.2 MW. Burundi remains, however, a net importer of electricity, with domestic production of 98.3m. kWh in 1999, compared with a total consumption of 146.9m. kWh.

During 1994, within the framework of the Preferential Trade Area for Eastern and Southern African States, Burundi and Zimbabwe initiated a series of trade negotiations at which Burundi hoped to secure greater access to the textile market in Zimbabwe in exchange for a commitment from the Burundian government to purchase 50% of its malt requirements from Zimbabwe. (Almost all of the malt used in breweries in Burundi is currently imported from Europe.)

The International Development Association (IDA) is helping to finance a long-term programme to develop basic forestry services, and to promote tree-planting to supply wood for fuel, building-poles and timber. The project will benefit an estimated 60,000 rural families. The Irish Peat Development Authority has been assisting Burundi to exploit peat bogs as an alternative fuel source. An estimated 12,000 metric tons of peat were extracted in 1992.

Industrial development is hampered by Burundi's distance from the sea (about 1,400 km to Dar es Salaam and 2,000 km to Mombasa), which means that only manufactures capable of absorbing the high costs of transport can be developed.

The network of roads is dense, but few of the 14,480 km of routes are made up with asphalt, and these are the roads that connect Bujumbura with Gitega, Kayanza and Nyanza-Lac. In 1992 the government revealed that 600 km of roads had been rehabilitated during the previous three years, and announced a four-year programme of future road improvements covering a further 1,000 km. A new crossing of the Ruzizi river, the Bridge of Concord (Burundi's longest bridge), was inaugurated in early 1992. However, recent improvements to Tanzania's road network, the reopening in 1994 of the Rwanda-Uganda border (facilitating road access to Mombasa) and competition between Burundian private road transport concerns and Tanzanian railways for the movement of goods from Burundi, have all contributed to a reduction in transportation costs.

Lake Tanganyika (about 8% of which is the sovereign responsibility of Burundi) is a crucial component in Burundi's transport system, since most of the country's external trade is conducted along the lake between Bujumbura and Tanzania and the DRC. This trade became more difficult in 1996 due to the embargo and also to guerrilla attacks on shipping. Traffic at the port of Bujumbura decreased from 211,900 metric tons in 1995 to 97,200 metric tons in 1996; it recovered slightly in 1997, to 99,000 metric tons. However, traffic at the port increased to 151,900 metric tons in 1998, and to 167,100 tons in 1999, as a result of measures taken by the government to curb guerrilla activity on the lake combined with efforts to find an alternative trade route through Zambia to the ports of Durban, South Africa, and Dar es Salaam, Tanzania. Plans to construct a railway linking Burundi with Uganda, Rwanda and Tanzania were announced in 1987. The proposed line would connect with the Kigoma–Dar es Salaam line in Tanzania, substantially improving Burundi's isolated trade position. However, the civil unrest in Burundi has since caused these plans to be postponed. There is an international airport at Bujumbura. The trade embargo resulted in a decrease in passenger traffic from 48,768 in 1996 to 15,628 in 1997. Passenger traffic increased to 31,151 in 1998 as a result of the violation of the embargo by regional airlines. Freight traffic increased from 3,571 metric tons in 1996 to 25,891 metric tons in 1997. However, freight traffic fell to 10,830 metric tons in 1998, and to 3,626 metric tons in 1999, largely owing to the resumption of traffic at the port of Bujumbura and on Lake Tanganyika. Following the suspension of sanctions in January 1999, several regional airlines resumed flights to Burundi.

FOREIGN AID AND DEVELOPMENT PLANNING

Burundi is severely dependent on foreign assistance, not only for capital projects but also for budgetary support. Before early 1996 the main bilateral donors of aid and technical assistance were Belgium, France, Japan and Germany. The multilateral agencies, such as the IDA and the EDF, have been involved in schemes to increase Burundi's production of coffee, and BADEA has also been a substantial source of development loans. Burundi has also been a considerable beneficiary of aid from the European Union (EU) through the Lomé Conventions. The main focus of EU development aid has been the rural sector, while Stabex transfers have been of pivotal importance to the coffee, tea and cotton industries. Under the current Lomé agreement, which operates until 2000, the EDF allocated ECU 126m. for projects in Burundi during the period 1990–95, of which ECU 112m. was in grants and the balance in venture capital. However, the lack of regional security had prompted many donors (who had already withdrawn aid workers to the capital and even to their own countries) to 'freeze' disbursements and to stall projects. Although Belgium released the first tranche of a 180m. Belgian franc aid package for primary health care and education projects in December 1998, EU development ministers stated at that time that the full resumption of aid was dependent on the successful conclusion of the Arusha talks. A meeting of donors, scheduled for June 1999, was to examine Burundi's reconstruction plans, but did not take place, owing to the continuing instability in the country. A World Bank mission in November 1998 had considered possible reconstruction measures including increased support for community-based services, employment generation schemes, protection of social expenditure and agricultural rehabilitation programmes. Burundi joined the Multilateral Investment Guarantee Agency in March 1998. In 1999 the World Bank was financing three projects in Burundi totalling commitments of US $40m. in the sectors of health, population, social welfare and infrastructure (rural water supplies). The projects were restructured in that year to promote community-level activities. In April 2000 the World Bank approved a $35m.-credit to help Burundi stabilize its economy. This emergency project aimed to assist the government in preparing an environment for economic recovery and restoring essential social services to support peace and reconciliation negotiations. It was also to finance the recovery of the private sector, rehabilitation in health, education and agricultural infrastructure, and to improve economic productivity for conflict-affected private businesses. The World Bank also intends to prepare three additional projects in 2001 with a total commitment of $63m., concerning employment generation, transport rehabilitation and a leverage insurance facility for trade as guarantees for foreign investment. In June 2000, an EU rehabilitation programme of €48m. was to finance schools, housing and water supply projects, to provide credit for small and medium-sized enterprises and communities, and also to support livestock-rearing, and the production and the distribution of seeds to farmers. Out of this total, €3m. were allocated to finance the creation of jobs for demobilized combatants.

In 1977 Burundi, Rwanda and Tanzania established the Organization for the Management and Development of the Kagera River Basin, which was formed to continue projects started in 1971 to develop irrigation, electric power, navigation and mining in the basin. The Kagera river basin project, combined with a hydroelectric power station already completed at Mugere and another, of 18 MW, at Rwegura, which was inaugurated in 1986 and was expected to provide about one-third of Burundi's electricity requirements, should eventually free Burundi from dependence on electricity from outside sources, mainly the DRC. Eventual self-sufficiency in power should also promote mineral production. Despite sabotage at the Rwegura station in early 1998, electricity production increased from 84.2m. kWh in 1997 to 109.4m. kWh in 1998, but fell to 98.3m. kWh in 1999. Burundi remains dependent on outside sources for its power supply; in 1999 total consumption exceeded domestic production by 33%.

In 1976 Burundi, Rwanda and Zaire established the Economic Community of the Great Lakes Countries (CEPGL). The energy directorate of CEPGL was established in Bujumbura in 1981, and a large joint hydroelectric scheme to benefit the three member-countries (the Ruzizi II project) was commissioned in 1987. In 1996 and 1997, however, the systematic sabotage of the high-power line from the Ruzizi power station interrupted the electricity supply, and, owing to continued export shortfalls, the government has been forced to restrict infrastructural investment, raising the question of whether Burundi can make a significant contribution to regional integration schemes. In 1985 Burundi became a full member of the Preferential Trade Area for Eastern and Southern African States (superseded in 1993 by the Common Market for Eastern and Southern Africa—COMESA).

In July 1986 a structural adjustment programme (SAP) was agreed with the IMF and the World Bank as a counter to Burundi's over-reliance on coffee export earnings, and to address the decline in economic growth and the rapid increase in external indebtedness. By 1990, however, few of the programme's specific objectives had been achieved. Burundi remained dependent upon foreign resources to finance its external account deficits, no significant diversification of its productive base had taken place, and coffee remained the dominant export commodity. Despite a series of currency devaluations in the late 1980s, the Burundian franc was devalued by a further 15% in August 1991, and in November the World Bank agreed to extend the SAP arrangements. The currency's direct link with the SDR ended in May 1992, since when the value of the Burundian franc has been determined in relation to a 'basket' of the currencies of the country's principal trading partners. An open general licensing system (OGL) was also introduced in May 1992 to liberalize current account transactions, a measure designed to facilitate imports, stimulate diversification of exports and to promote non-traditional exports. An export-processing zone was established in 1993, but operations are currently suspended (except for the processing of gold) owing to political and civil instability.

World Bank forecasts of economic growth for 1993 and the following years were undermined by increased internal instability in late 1993 and early 1994, and by the financial burden of repatriating and accommodating the resulting refugees and displaced persons. By 1994, according to IMF estimates, the annual rate of inflation had risen to 14.7%, and GDP decreased by 3.7% in that year. Inflation continued to increase, reaching 19.4% in 1995, 26.4% in 1996 and 31.1% in 1997, reflecting food shortages and a rapid expansion in money supply, whereas real GDP declined by 7.3% in 1995, and by 8.4% in 1996. GDP increased by an estimated 0.4% in 1997 and by 4.8% in 1998. In 1995 and 1996 the budgetary deficit was estimated to be equivalent to 9.3% of GDP, compared with 8.7% of GDP in 1994,

although this figure was slightly lower than had been predicted, largely owing to the government's appropriation of the surplus of the Coffee Stabilization Fund. In 1997 the budget deficit amounted to 6.6% of GDP. The successful implementation of plans to privatize one-half of all public enterprises and establish private management contracts for the remainder, by the end of 1995, proved unattainable, given the unrest in the country, and by mid-1996 54 enterprises remained under state ownership and management. In 1998 the telecommunications sector was liberalized. (By February 2000 three operators were competing for the mobile cellular telephone market.) In November 1999 the government-owned Société Hôtelière et Touristique du Burundi launched an offer for the purchase of the Source du Nil Hôtel, the largest in Bujumbura. Foreign debt remains a major cause of economic concern. Burundi's external debt at the end of 1997 was US $1,066m., of which $1,022m. was long-term public debt. In 1998 external debt represented the equivalent of 118% of the country's GDP. By the end of 1997 more than three-quarters of Burundi's outstanding debt was owed to multilateral organizations and was not reschedulable. In 1997 the cost of debt-servicing was equivalent to 49.5% of revenue from exports of goods and services. In 1998 the radio declined to 36.9%. Since 1995 Burundi has accumulated arrears to bilateral creditors at a rate of about $10m. per year. By April 2000 the financial crisis in the country was such that currency reserves were the equivalent of only two months of imports.

Burundi's structural adjustment programme (SAP) was interrupted by political and civil instability and was terminated in June 1995. Despite the introduction of adjustments, including a new labour code, a new banking law and central bank statutes, the promotion of exports, a duty drawback scheme and transport subsidies for exports, the government failed to reduce the role of the state in the economy and to redirect public resources to support development or improve the efficiency, transparency and accountability of public sector management. Military expenditure and subsidies for inefficient parastatals remained high and, in the view of the Bretton Woods institutions, adequate state divestment was not achieved. During 1985–95 military expenditure increased from 3.0% to 4.4% of GDP, and from 20.8% to 24.8% of the budget, while the size of the armed forces rose from some 9,000 to 22,000. In early 2000 a report submitted by the ministry of finance revealed that embezzlement and fraud at the expense of the Burundian parastatals amounted to 10,860m. Burundian francs.

Major economic reconstruction is needed. In late 1994 it was reported that production of food staples had declined by 20%, the financial sector was in crisis with unpaid debts amounting to 514m. Burundian francs, and rehabilitation of the education infrastructure was expected to cost some 550m. Burundian francs. While assistance from the international donor community resumed in mid-1995 with a US $21.3m. loan from the IDA for the reconstruction of the health infrastructure, in September 1994 a meeting of potential donors, conducted in Paris under the auspices of the World Bank, had insisted that national reconciliation and the respect of human rights and democracy would be preconditions to the resumption of a comprehensive programme of financial assistance for Burundi. The World Bank identified a number of key areas with potential for economic growth, given a swift resolution of the security crisis. These included improvements in productivity of traditional crops, the introduction of new export crops (flowers, fruits, vegetables, medicines and ornamental plants), artisanal mining (cassiterite, gold, columbo-tantalite), light manufacturing, industrial mining and the services sector. However, political and civil instability continued to deteriorate during 1995. Development projects outside of the capital became increasingly difficult to implement and foreign financial assistance dwindled while public investment declined by more than 50%.

Statistical Survey

Area and Population

AREA, POPULATION AND DENSITY

Area (sq km)	27,834*
Population (census results)†	
15–16 August 1979	4,028,420
16–30 August 1990	
Males	2,473,599
Females	2,665,474
Total	5,139,073
Population (official estimates at mid-year)	
1996	6,088,000
1997	6,194,000
1998	6,300,000
Density (per sq km) at mid-1998	226.3

* 10,747 sq miles.
† Excluding adjustment for underenumeration.

PRINCIPAL TOWNS

Bujumbura (capital), population 235,440 (census result, August 1990); Gitega 15,943 (1978).

Source: Banque de la République du Burundi.

BIRTHS AND DEATHS (UN estimates, annual averages)

	1980–85	1985–90	1990–95
Birth rate (per 1,000) . . .	46.2	46.7	46.2
Death rate (per 1,000) . .	17.9	18.1	21.5

Expectation of life (UN estimates, years at birth, 1990–95): 41.6 (males 40.1; females 43.0).

Source: UN, *World Population Prospects: The 1998 Revision.*

ECONOMICALLY ACTIVE POPULATION*
(persons aged 10 years and over, 1990 census)

	Males	Females	Total
Agriculture, hunting, forestry and fishing	1,153,890	1,420,553	2,574,443
Mining and quarrying . .	1,146	39	1,185
Manufacturing	24,120	9,747	33,867
Electricity, gas and water. .	1,847	74	1,921
Construction.	19,447	290	19,737
Trade, restaurants and hotels. .	19,667	6,155	25,822
Transport, storage and communications . . .	8,193	311	8,504
Financing, insurance, real estate and business services . .	1,387	618	2,005
Community, social and personal services	68,905	16,286	85,191
Activities not adequately defined .	8,653	4,617	13,270
Total labour force	1,307,255	1,458,690	2,765,945

* Figures exclude persons seeking work for the first time, totalling 13,832 (males 9,608; females 4,224).

Source: UN, *Demographic Yearbook.*

Mid-1998 (estimates in '000): Agriculture, etc. 3,132; Total 3,458 (Source: FAO, *Production Yearbook*).

Agriculture

PRINCIPAL CROPS ('000 metric tons)

	1996	1997	1998
Wheat	9*	10*	10
Rice (paddy)	42*	65*	41
Maize	144*	145*	132
Millet	11*	17*	11
Sorghum	66*	68*	67
Potatoes	42*	49*	23
Sweet potatoes . . .	670*	681*	590
Cassava (Manioc) . .	549*	603*	622
Yams	8*	11*	11
Taro (Coco yam) . . .	95*	105*	76
Dry beans	288*	271*	275
Dry peas	36*	37*	36
Groundnuts (in shell) . .	10†	11†	9*
Cottonseed	2*	1*	2
Palm kernels† . . .	2	2	2
Vegetables and melons† . .	215	220	215
Sugar cane	158†	178†	190
Bananas and plantains . .	1,544*	1,543*	1,399
Other fruits (excl. melons) .	85	86	85
Coffee (green)	25	20*	17
Tea (made)	6	4	6
Cotton (lint)	1	1*	1*

* Unofficial figure.   † FAO estimate(s).

Source: FAO, *Production Yearbook.*

LIVESTOCK ('000 head, year ending September)

	1996	1997	1998
Cattle	449*	311*	346
Pigs.	75†	70†	73
Sheep†	320	310	320
Goats†	900	890	900

Poultry (million): 5† in 1996; 4† in 1997; 5 in 1998.

* Unofficial figure.   † FAO estimate(s).

Source: FAO, *Production Yearbook.*

LIVESTOCK PRODUCTS (FAO estimates, '000 metric tons)

	1996	1997	1998
Beef and veal	13	9	10
Mutton and lamb . . .	1	1	1
Goat meat	3	3	3
Pig meat	5	4	4
Poultry meat	6	6	6
Cows' milk	35	24	27
Sheep's milk	1	1	1
Goats' milk	9	9	9
Poultry eggs	3	3	3
Cattle hides	3	2	2
Goatskins	1	1	1

Source: FAO, *Production Yearbook.*

Forestry

ROUNDWOOD REMOVALS ('000 cubic metres, excl. bark)

	1995	1996	1997
Sawlogs, veneer logs and logs for sleepers	43	33	33
Other industrial wood	72	10	10
Fuel wood	4,616	4,734	4,866
Total	4,731	4,777	4,909

Source: FAO, *Yearbook of Forest Products.*

SAWNWOOD PRODUCTION ('000 cubic metres, incl. railway sleepers)

	1995	1996	1997
Coniferous (softwood)	21	7	7*
Broadleaved (hardwood)	22	26	26*
Total	43	33	33

* FAO estimate.

Source: FAO, *Yearbook of Forest Products.*

Fishing

('000 metric tons, live weight)

	1995	1996	1997
Dagaas	18.2	1.5	17.9
Freshwater perches	2.9	1.2	2.4
Total catch (incl. others)	21.1	3.0	20.3

Source: FAO, *Yearbook of Fishery Statistics.*

Mining

	1994	1995	1996
Gold (kilograms)*†	20	10	10
Tin ore (metric tons)*†	10	0	0
Kaolin ('000 metric tons)*†	5	1	1
Peat ('000 metric tons)*	10	10	10

* Data from US Bureau of Mines.
† Estimate(s). Figures for gold and tin refer to the metal content of ores.

Source: UN, *Industrial Commodity Statistics Yearbook.*

Industry

SELECTED PRODUCTS ('000 metric tons, unless otherwise indicated)

	1995	1996	1997*
Flour	0.5	0.4	n.a.
Beer ('000 hectolitres)	1,404.2	1,227.9	1,161.2
Soft drinks ('000 hectolitres)	219.7	179.1	146.6
Cottonseed oil ('000 hectolitres)	211.5	234.6	199.7
Sugar	15.3	17.8	19.6
Paint	0.5	0.4	0.4
Insecticides	2.4	2.4	2.4
Soap	5.6	3.4	2.8
Bottles	3.7	2.5	2.1
Blankets ('000)	137.7	116.2	21.7
Footwear ('000 pairs)	10.0	n.a.	n.a.
Fibro-cement products	0.6	0.2	0.7
Steel rods	0.3	0.1	0.1
Batteries ('000 cartons)†	n.a.	14.5	n.a.
Electric energy (million kWh)	97.2	99.3	87.8

* Estimates.
† Cartons of 240 batteries.

Source: IMF, *Burundi: Statistical Annex* (February 1999).

Finance

CURRENCY AND EXCHANGE RATES

Monetary Units
100 centimes = 1 Burundian franc.

Sterling, Dollar and Euro Equivalents (28 April 2000)
£1 sterling = 1,054.9 francs;
US $1 = 672.7 francs;
€1 = 611.1 francs;
10,000 Burundian francs = £9.480 = $14.865 = €16.363.

Average Exchange Rate (Burundian francs per US dollar)
1997   352.35
1998   447.77
1999   563.56

BUDGET (million Burundian francs)*

Revenue†	1997	1998	1999
Tax revenue	42,880	61,554	66,627
Taxes on income and profits	10,322	13,139	15,122
Social security contributions	3,731	4,281	5,357
Domestic taxes on goods and services	20,744	25,305	31,640
Transaction tax	7,281	11,435	12,643
Excise tax	13,155	13,870	18,997
Taxes on international trade	7,229	18,829	14,508
Import duties	6,527	10,726	11,022
Export tax	702	4,562	28
Entrepreneurial and property income	1,920	3,106	3,071
Other current revenue	1,345	1,610	2,238
Capital revenue	108	64	111
Total	46,253	66,334	72,047

Expenditure‡	1997	1998	1999
General public services	18,154	20,513	25,122
Defence	21,100	23,325	24,564
Public order and safety	1,344	2,153	2,502
Education	11,204	14,080	15,990
Health	2,085	2,421	2,271
Social security and welfare	4,718	6,510	2,401
Recreational, cultural and religious affairs and services	334	286	345
Economic affairs and services	n.a.	3,062	3,721
Fuel and energy	n.a.	232	543
Agriculture, forestry, fishing and hunting	n.a.	1,499	1,941
Mining, manufacturing and construction	n.a.	995	1,068
Transport and communications	n.a.	336	169
Other purposes	n.a.	25,711	28,265
Interest payments	6,071	6,844	9,507
Total	80,800	98,061	105,181
Current	58,207	74,082	80,966
Capital	12,322	23,979	24,215
Adjustment to total expenditure	10,271	—	—

* Figures refer to the consolidated operations of the central Government, comprising the general budget, social security funds and extrabudgetary accounts (covering transactions undertaken through foreign borrowing arrangements and grants not recorded in treasury accounts). The data exclude the operations of other central government units with individual budgets.
† Excluding grants received.
‡ Excluding lending minus repayments.

Source: IMF, *Government Finance Statistics Yearbook.*

CENTRAL BANK RESERVES (US $ million at 31 December)

	1997	1998	1999
Gold*	4.99	4.95	5.00
IMF special drawing rights	0.06	0.09	0.10
Reserve position in IMF	7.91	8.25	8.04
Foreign exchange	105.07	57.18	39.84
Total	118.03	70.47	52.98

* Valued at market-related prices.

Source: IMF, *International Financial Statistics.*

MONEY SUPPLY (million Burundian francs at 31 December)

	1997	1998	1999
Currency outside banks . .	23,693	24,180	32,087
Deposits at central bank . .	749	860	710
Demand deposits at commercial banks	22,235	22,180	34,296
Demand deposits at other monetary institutions . . .	1,527	1,595	2,200
Total money	48,203	48,816	69,293

Source: IMF, *International Financial Statistics*.

COST OF LIVING
(Consumer Price Index for Bujumbura; base: January 1991 = 100)

	1995	1996	1997
Food	160.4	199.0	268.7
Clothing	157.0	199.3	308.7
Housing, heating and light . .	148.0	192.1	235.4
Transport	102.0	176.4	229.1
All items (incl. others) .	153.0	193.4	253.6

Source: IMF, *Burundi: Statistical Annex* (February 1999).
All items (base: 1995 = 100): 186.5 in 1998; 192.8 in 1999 (Source: IMF, *International Financial Statistics*).

NATIONAL ACCOUNTS (million Burundian francs at current prices)
Composition of the Gross National Product

	1997	1998	1999
GDP in purchasers' values .	431,037	506,305	552,037
Net factor income from abroad .	−4,416	−3,699	−4,902
Gross national product .	426,621	502,606	547,135

Source: IMF, *International Financial Statistics*.

Expenditure on the Gross Domestic Product

	1997	1998	1999
Government final consumption expenditure . . .	34,474	47,400	51,000
Private final consumption expenditure . . .	297,563	389,268	413,900
Increase in stocks . . .	5,205	−10,529	−991
Gross fixed capital formation .	21,976	24,000	34,314
Total domestic expenditure	361,812	450,139	498,223
Exports of goods and services .	33,760	32,019	31,185
Less Imports of goods and services	−49,473	−77,775	−71,177
Statistical discrepancy . .	84,938	101,922	93,806
GDP in purchasers' values .	431,037	506,305	552,037
GDP at constant 1980 prices	105,512	110,249	n.a.

Source: IMF, *International Financial Statistics*.

Gross Domestic Product by Economic Activity (estimates)

	1995	1996	1997
Agriculture, hunting, forestry and fishing	105,035	136,018	163,354
Mining and quarrying . . } Electricity, gas and water . . }	1,296	1,487	2,432
Manufacturing*	26,344	22,682	29,592
Construction	14,339	13,970	19,193
Trade, restaurants and hotels .	12,957	10,884	13,165
Transport, storage and communications . . .	10,440	12,598	13,593
Government services . . .	41,728	43,706	57,757
Other services	5,998	6,837	7,347
GDP at factor cost . . .	218,137	248,182	306,432
Indirect taxes, *less* subsidies .	31,728	24,400	30,900
GDP in purchasers' values .	249,865	272,582	337,332

* Including handicrafts (million francs): 5,709 in 1995; 6,182 in 1996; 9,302 in 1997.

Source: IMF, *Burundi: Statistical Annex* (February 1999).

BALANCE OF PAYMENTS (US $ million)

	1995	1996	1997
Exports of goods f.o.b. . .	112.5	40.1	87.3
Imports of goods f.o.b. . .	−175.6	−100.0	−97.9
Trade balance	−63.1	−59.9	−10.6
Exports of services . . .	16.4	10.5	8.7
Imports of services . . .	−101.2	−38.4	−41.3
Balance on goods and services	−147.8	−87.7	−43.3
Other income received . .	10.4	6.4	4.3
Other income paid . . .	−22.9	−20.4	−16.8
Balance on goods, services and income	−160.3	−101.6	−55.8
Current transfers received .	154.7	62.5	61.3
Current transfers paid . .	−2.1	−1.1	−1.6
Current balance . . .	−7.8	−40.3	4.0
Capital account (net) . . .	−0.8	−0.3	−0.1
Direct investment abroad . .	−0.6	—	—
Direct investment from abroad .	2.0	—	—
Other investment assets . .	8.2	6.6	15.4
Other investment liabilities .	11.4	7.6	−1.4
Net errors and omissions . .	24.2	−8.9	−7.1
Overall balance . . .	36.7	−35.3	10.8

Source: IMF, *International Financial Statistics*.

External Trade

PRINCIPAL COMMODITIES (distribution by SITC, US $ '000)

Imports c.i.f.	1991	1992	1993
Food and live animals . .	22,675	19,706	20,312
Cereals and cereal preparations .	14,424	12,520	13,341
Wheat meal and flour of wheat and meslin . .	6,453	3,904	3,859
Flour of wheat or meslin . .	6,445	3,835	3,859
Cereal preparations, etc. . .	6,447	7,116	7,480
Malt (incl. malt flour) .	6,290	6,962	7,365
Crude materials (inedible) except fuels . . .	8,081	4,915	5,478
Mineral fuels, lubricants, etc. .	31,183	27,992	25,387
Petroleum, petroleum products, etc.	31,044	27,888	25,346
Refined petroleum products .	29,603	27,248	24,538
Motor spirit (gasoline) and other light oils. . .	12,511	10,570	8,630
Gas oils	9,893	8,966	7,993

Imports c.i.f. — *continued*	1991	1992	1993
Chemicals and related products	33,890	32,475	28,807
Medicinal and pharmaceutical products	10,289	11,554	8,523
Manufactured fertilizers . .	3,228	4,865	4,562
Artificial resins, plastic materials, etc.	4,774	4,721	5,401
Disinfectants, insecticides, fungicides, weed-killers, etc., for retail sale	5,809	3,581	2,785
Insecticides	5,713	3,451	2,635
Basic manufactures . .	52,433	48,948	42,868
Rubber manufactures . .	6,641	5,383	7,077
Rubber tyres, tubes, etc.	5,334	4,059	5,215
Paper, paperboard and manufactures	6,062	5,777	5,556
Non-metallic mineral manufactures . . .	13,512	12,898	9,445
Lime, cement, etc. . .	11,093	10,896	7,145
Cement	10,481	10,226	6,820
Machinery and transport equipment . . .	70,144	63,206	43,603
General industrial machinery, equipment and parts . .	29,926	23,147	20,484
Electrical machinery, apparatus and appliances . . .	12,351	14,437	3,894
Road vehicles and parts (excl. tyres, engines and electrical parts)	26,388	23,999	18,265
Passenger motor cars (excl. buses)	9,687	8,202	5,350
Motor vehicles for the transport of goods or materials . .	9,557	7,530	5,984
Parts and accessories for cars, buses, lorries, etc. . .	4,326	5,543	4,194
Miscellaneous manufactured articles . . .	12,105	16,798	8,188
Photographic apparatus, optical goods, watches and clocks .	6,725	10,154	4,182
Special transactions and commodities not classified according to kind . .	14,291	13,406	19,877
Total (incl. others) . . .	247,087	229,508	204,525

Source: UN, *International Trade Statistics Yearbook.*

1994 (US $ million): *Imports c.i.f.:* Capital goods 80.9; Intermediate goods 55.3 (Petroleum products 29.0); Consumption goods 87.4 (Food 30.0); Total 223.6.
1995 (US $ million): *Imports c.i.f.:* Capital goods 87.6; Intermediate goods 62.4 (Petroleum products 26.6); Consumption goods 82.9 (Food 28.8); Total 232.9.
1996 (US $ million): *Imports c.i.f.:* Capital goods 48.5; Intermediate goods 38.1 (Petroleum products 18.2); Consumption goods 36.8 (Food 10.9); Total 123.4.
1997 (estimates, US $ million): *Imports c.i.f.:* Capital goods 45.3; Intermediate goods 33.3 (Petroleum products 13.8); Consumption goods 44.1 (Food 11.2); Total 122.7.
Source (for 1994, 1995, 1996 and 1997): IMF, *Burundi: Statistical Annex* (February 1999).

Exports f.o.b.	1997	1998	1999
Food and live animals . .	86,094	62,933	53,761
Coffee, tea, cocoa and spices .	85,583	62,015	52,836
Coffee (incl. husks and skins)	76,567	51,048	41,953
Tea	9,015	10,967	10,883
Beverages and tobacco. .	36	177	75
Crude materials (inedible) except fuels . .	127	72	136
Raw hides, skins and furskins	127	72	136
Special transactions and commodities not classified according to kind . .	897	945	984
Total (incl. others) . . .	87,320	63,950	54,956

Source: Banque de la République du Burundi.

PRINCIPAL TRADING PARTNERS

Imports c.i.f. (US $ '000)	1997	1998	1999
Belgium	22,358	30,254	19,851
China, People's Repub. . .	2,812	6,403	3,961
France	11,645	14,217	5,980
Germany	8,042	9,585	5,901
Iran.	900	250	181
Italy	4,220	4,811	3,423
Japan	7,567	5,989	3,677
Kenya	5,305	8,784	6,199
Korea, Repub. . . .	768	1,120	875
Netherlands	5,234	4,656	2,246
Tanzania	3,057	3,113	5,118
United Arab Emirates . .	5,445	5,224	3,909
United Kingdom . . .	2,041	2,314	2,511
USA	2,281	2,339	2,557
Zambia	6,761	12,530	6,734
Zimbabwe	2,806	1,562	2,208
Total (incl. others) . . .	122,745	156,944	117,658

Exports (million Burundian Francs)	1997	1998	1999
Belgium-Luxembourg . .	4,929.3	2,624.8	995.5
France	37.3	17.8	358.1
Germany	6,579.5	2,968.8	1,520.9
Italy	72.0	32.1	38.4
United Kingdom . . .	8,305.7	8,125.9	10,278.9
Total (incl. others) . . .	30,767.2	28,634.8	30,970.8

Source: Banque de la République du Burundi.

Transport

ROAD TRAFFIC (estimates, '000 motor vehicles in use)

	1992	1993	1994
Passenger cars	17.5	18.5	17.5
Commercial vehicles . . .	11.8	12.3	10.2

Source: UN, *Statistical Yearbook.*

LAKE TRAFFIC (Bujumbura—'000 metric tons)

	1997	1998	1999
Goods:			
Arrivals	70.9	123.1	142.5
Departures	28.1	28.1	28.2

Source: Banque de la République du Burundi.

CIVIL AVIATION (traffic on scheduled services)

	1994	1995	1996
Passengers carried ('000) . .	9	9	9
Passenger-km (million) . . .	2	2	2

Source: UN, *Statistical Yearbook.*

Tourism

TOURIST ARRIVALS BY REGION*

	1996	1997	1998
Africa	13,004	5,011	7,394
Americas	1,660	639	1,092
Asia.	2,213	852	1,218
Europe	10,514	4,051	5,700
Total	27,391	10,553	15,404

* Including Burundian nationals residing abroad.
Tourism receipts (US $ million): 1 in 1995; 1 in 1996; 1 in 1997.
Source: World Tourism Organization, *Yearbook of Tourism Statistics.*

Communications Media

	1995	1996	1997
Radio receivers ('000 in use) . .	410	425	440
Television receivers ('000 in use) .	12	20	25
Telephones ('000 main lines in use)	17	15	n.a.
Telefax stations (number in use) .	2,000	3,000	4,000
Mobile cellular telephones			
(subscribers)	500	525	n.a.
Daily newspapers:			
Number	1	1	n.a.
Circulation ('000 copies) . .	20	20	n.a.

Sources: UNESCO, *Statistical Yearbook,* and UN, *Statistical Yearbook.*

Education

(1992/93, unless otherwise indicated)

	Teachers	Students		
		Males	Females	Total
Pre-primary*	49	1,220	1,161	2,381
Primary	10,400	358,180	292,906	651,086
Secondary:				
General . . . . }	2,060 {	28,706	17,675	46,381
Teacher-training . . . }		1,237	1,233	2,470
Vocational	502	4,170	2,692	6,862
Higher	556	3,129	1,127	4,256

* Figures refer to 1988/89.

Primary (1995/96): Institutions 1,501; Teachers 10,316; Students 518,144 (males 283,516; females 234,628).

Source: UNESCO, *Statistical Yearbook.*

1996 (students): *Primary* 453,746; *Secondary (General)* 56,887; *Secondary (Teacher-training and Vocational)* 5,712; *Higher* 4,379 (Source: IMF, *Burundi: Statistical Annex* (February 1999)).

Directory

The Constitution

The Constitution was promulgated on 13 March 1992 and provided for the establishment of a plural political system. The Constitution seeks to guarantee human rights and basic freedoms for all citizens, together with the freedom of the press. Executive powers are vested in the President, who (under normal circumstances—see below) is elected directly, by universal adult suffrage, for a five-year term, renewable only once. Statutory power is shared with the Prime Minister, who appoints a Council of Ministers. Legislative power is exercised by a National Assembly, whose members are elected directly, by universal adult suffrage, for a five-year renewable mandate. In September 1994 a Convention of Government was agreed among the country's major political parties. The Convention, which defines the terms of government for a four-year transitional period, provides for the establishment of a National Security Council whose members include the President, the Prime Minister and the Ministers of State with responsibility for External Affairs, Interior and Public Security, and National Defence. The Convention was incorporated into the Constitution on 22 September 1994. However, the Convention disintegrated in July 1996, prompting the military coup which returned Maj. Pierre Buyoya to power.

On 6 June 1998 a Transitional Constitution was promulgated. It combined elements of the 1992 Constitution and the terms of office introduced by Buyoya in 1996, and provided for the enlargement of the National Assembly from 81 to 121 seats and the creation of two vice-presidencies to replace the post of Prime Minister.

The Government

HEAD OF STATE

President: Maj. PIERRE BUYOYA (assumed power 25 July 1996).

COUNCIL OF MINISTERS
(July 2000)

Vice-President responsible for Political and Administrative Affairs: FRÉDÉRIQUE BAVUGINYUMVIRA.

Vice-President responsible for Economic and Social Affairs: MATHIAS SINAMENYE.

Minister of External Relations and Co-operation: SÉVÉRIN NTAHOMVUKIYE.

Minister of the Interior and Public Security: Col ASCENSION TWAGIRAMUNGU.

Minister of Justice: TÉRENCE SINUNGURUZA.

Minister of National Defence: Col CYRILLE NDAYIRUKIYE.

Minister of Development, Planning and Reconstruction: LÉON NIMBONA.

Minister of Communal Development and Handicrafts: DENIS NSHIMIRIMANA.

Minister of Relocation and Resettlement of Displaced and Repatriated Persons: PASCAL NKURUNZIZA.

Minister of the Peace Process: AMBROISE NIYONSABA.

Minister of Territorial Development and the Environment: JEAN-PACIFIQUE NSENGIYUMVA.

Minister of Agriculture and Livestock: SALVATOR NTIHABOSE.

Minister of Labour, the Public Service and Professional Training: EMMANUEL TUNGAMWESE.

Minister of Finance: CHARLES NIHANGAZA.

Minister of Commerce, Industry and Tourism: JOSEPH NTANYOTORA.

Minister of Education: PROSPER MPAWENAYO.

Minister of Social Action and Women's Affairs: ROMAINE NDORIMANA.

Minister of Culture, Youth and Sport: GÉRARD NYAMWIZA.

Minister of Public Health: Dr STANISLAS NTAHOBARI.

Minister of Information and Government Spokesman: Dr LUC RUKINGAMA.

Minister of Public Works and Housing: GASPARD NTIRAMPEBA.

Minister of Transport, Posts and Telecommunications: CYPRIEN MBONIGABA.

Minister of Energy and Mines: BERNARD BARANDEREKA.

Minister of Human Rights, Institutional Reforms and Relations with the National Assembly: EUGÈNE NINDORERA.

There are also two Secretaries of State.

MINISTRIES

Office of the President: Bujumbura; tel. 226063.

Ministry of Agriculture and Livestock: Bujumbura; tel. 222087.

Ministry of Commerce, Industry and Tourism: BP 492, Bujumbura; tel. 225330; fax 225595.

Ministry of Communal Development: Bujumbura.

Ministry of Culture, Youth and Sport: Bujumbura; tel. 226822.

Ministry of Development, Planning and Reconstruction: BP 1830, Bujumbura; tel. 223988.

Ministry of Education: Bujumbura.

Ministry of Energy and Mines: BP 745, Bujumbura; tel. 225909; fax 223337.

Ministry of External Relations and Co-operation: Bujumbura; tel. 222150.

Ministry of Finance: BP 1830, Bujumbura; tel. 225142; fax 223128.

Ministry of Human Rights, Institutional Reforms and Relations with the National Assembly: Bujumbura.

Ministry of Information: BP 2870, Bujumbura.

Ministry of the Interior and Public Security: Bujumbura.

Ministry of Justice: Bujumbura; tel. 222148.

Ministry of Labour, the Public Service and Professional Training: BP 1480, Bujumbura; tel. 223514; fax 228715.

Ministry of National Defence: Bujumbura.

Ministry of the Peace Process: Bujumbura.

Ministry of Public Health: Bujumbura.

Ministry of Public Works and Housing: BP 1860, Bujumbura; tel. 226841; fax 226840.

Ministry of Relocation and Resettlement of Displaced and Repatriated Persons: Bujumbura.

Ministry of Social Action and Women's Affairs: Bujumbura; tel. 225039.

Ministry of Territorial Development and the Environment: Bujumbura.

Ministry of Transport, Posts and Telecommunications: BP 2000, Bujumbura; tel. 222923; fax 226900.

President and Legislature

PRESIDENT

Following the assassination of President Melchior Ndadaye and his constitutional successor in October 1993, a constitutional amendment was adopted whereby a successor was to be elected by the National Assembly. On 13 January 1994 Cyprien Ntaryamira, a member of FRODEBU, was elected President by 78 of the 79 votes cast by the National Assembly. Following Ntaryamira's death in April 1994, the Speaker of the National Assembly, Sylvestre Ntibantunganya, assumed the presidency for an interim, three-month period (subsequently extended for a further three months), in accordance with the Constitution. Ntibantunganya was subsequently appointed to the presidency for a four-year transitional term, by broad consensus in accordance with the Convention of Government adopted in September 1994. In July 1996 Ntibantunganya was deposed by a military coup and replaced by Maj. Pierre Buyoya.

NATIONAL ASSEMBLY*

Speaker: LÉONCE NGENDAKUMANA (FRODEBU).

Legislative Elections, 29 June 1993

Party					Votes cast	% of votes cast	Seats
FRODEBU	.	.	.	.	1,532,107	71.04	65
UPRONA.	.	.	.	.	462,324	21.44	16
RPB .	.	.	.	.	35,932	1.67	—
PRP .	.	.	.	.	29,966	1.39	—
RADDES .	.	.	.	.	26,631	1.23	—
PP .	.	.	.	.	24,372	1.13	—
Independents.	.	.	.	.	853	0.04	—
Invalid votes .	.	.	.	.	44,474	2.06	—
Total.	.	.	.	.	2,156,659	100.00	81

* The National Assembly was suspended following the July 1996 coup, but was reconvened in October. Under the Transitional Constitution promulgated in June 1998, the membership of the National Assembly was enlarged from 81 to 121 members in order to incorporate representatives of smaller parties and the civilian population. The composition of the new National Assembly, which was inaugurated on 18 July, was as follows: FRODEBU controlled 65 seats, UPRONA 16, other political parties 13 seats (although four remained vacant, owing to internal party problems) and civilians 27 seats.

Political Organizations

Political parties are required to demonstrate firm commitment to national unity, and impartiality with regard to ethnic or regional origin, gender and religion, in order to receive legal recognition.

Alliance burundaise-africaine pour le salut (ABASA): Bujumbura.

Alliance nationale pour les droits et le développement economique (ANADDE): Bujumbura; f. 1992.

Alliance nationale pour le changement (ANAC): f. 1999 with the aim of restoring political order, comprising the following political parties, together with two members of the national assembly, and the former prime minister, Anatole Kanyenkiko.

Front pour la démocratie au Burundi (FRODEBU): Bujumbura; f. 1992; split in June 1999; Chair. JEAN MINANI; Sec.-Gen. AUGUSTIN NZOJIBWAMI.

Parti du peuple (PP): Bujumbura; f. 1992; Leader SHADRAK NIYONKURU.

Parti pour le redressement national (PARENA): Bujumbura; f. 1994; Leader JEAN-BAPTISTE BAGAZA.

Rassemblement du peuple burundien (RPB): Bujumbura; f. 1992; Leader PHILIPPE NZOGBO.

Solidarité pour la défénce des minorités (SOJEDEM): Bujumbura.

AV–Intware (Alliance of the Brave): Bujumbura.

Convergence nationale pour la paix et la réconciliation (CNPR): Bujumbura; f. Oct. 1999; alliance comprising Union pour le progrès national, a faction of Front pour la démocratie au Burundi and several Tutsi parties; Pres. AUGUSTIN NZOJIBWAMI.

Forum démocratique (FODE): Bujumbura; f. Nov. 1999; Leader DEOGRATIAS BABURIFATO.

Inkinzo y'Ijambo Ry'abarundi (Inkinzo) (Guarantor of Freedom of Speech in Burundi): Bujumbura; f. 1993; Pres. Dr ALPHONSE RUGAMBARARA.

Parti indépendant des travailleurs (PIT): Bujumbura.

Parti libéral (PL): Bujumbura; f. 1992; Sec.-Gen. JOSEPH NTIDENDEREZA.

Parti de réconciliation du peuple (PRP): Bujumbura; f. 1992.

Parti social démocrate (PSD): Bujumbura; f. 1993.

Rassemblement pour la démocratie et le développement économique et social (RADDES): Bujumbura; f. 1992; Chair. JOSEPH NZENZIMANA.

Union pour le progrès national (UPRONA): BP 1810, Bujumbura; tel. 225028; f. 1958; following the 1961 elections, the numerous small parties which had been defeated merged with UPRONA, which became the sole legal political party in 1966; party activities were suspended following the coup of Sept. 1987, but resumed in 1989; Chair. CHARLES MUKASI; in Oct. 1999 moderate mems of the cen. cttee who opposed Mukasi's rejection of the Arusha talks elected Dr LUC RUKINGAMA as a rival Chair.

The exclusion of political organizations advocating 'tribalism, divisionalism or violence' and the requirement that party leaderships be equally representative of Hutu and Tutsi ethnic groups have been opposed by some externally-based opposition parties. These include the **Parti de libération du peuple hutu (PALIPEHUTU**, f. 1980 and based in Tanzania), which seeks to advance the interests of the Hutu ethnic group. An armed dissident wing of PALIPE-HUTU, known as the **Force nationale de libération (FNL)**, led by KABORA KHOSSAN, is based in southern Rwanda. Another grouping representing the interests of Hutu extremists, the **Conseil national pour la défense de la démocratie (CNDD)** is led by LÉONARD NYANGOMA, who was in exile in Zaire (now the Democratic Republic of the Congo) prior to Tutsi-led rebellion of 1996–97. The 30,000-strong armed wing of the CNDD, the **Force pour la défence de la démocratie (FDD)**, rebelled against the political leadership of the CNDD in 1998 and was led by its Commander-in-Chief, JEAN-BOSCO NDAYIKENGURUKIYE.

Diplomatic Representation

EMBASSIES IN BURUNDI

Belgium: 9 ave de l'Industrie, BP 1920, Bujumbura; tel. 223676; Ambassador: JAN MOUTON.

China, People's Republic: BP 2550, Bujumbura; tel. 224307; Ambassador: SHI TONGNING.

Egypt: 31 ave de la Liberté, BP 1520, Bujumbura; tel. 223161; Ambassador: MUHAMMAD MOUSA.

France: 60 ave de l'UPRONA, BP 1740, Bujumbura; tel. 226767; fax 227443; Ambassador: CHRISTIAN DAZIANO.

Germany: 22 rue 18 septembre, BP 480, Bujumbura; tel. 226412; Ambassador: Dr BERND MORAST.

Holy See: 46 chaussée Prince Louis-Rwagasore, BP 1068, Bujumbura (Apostolic Nunciature); tel. 222326; fax 223176; Apostolic Nuncio: Most Rev. EMIL PAUL TSCHERRIG, Titular Archbishop of Voli.

Korea, Democratic People's Republic: BP 1620, Bujumbura; tel. 222881; Ambassador: PAE SOK JUN.

Russia: 78 blvd de l'UPRONA, BP 1034, Bujumbura; tel. 226098; fax 222984; Ambassador: IGOR S. LIAKIN-FROLOV.

Rwanda: 24 ave du Zaïre, BP 400, Bujumbura; tel. 223140; Ambassador: SYLVESTRE UWIBAJIJE.

Tanzania: BP 1653, Bujumbura; Ambassador: ANTHONY NYAKYI.

USA: ave des Etats-Unis, BP 1720, Bujumbura; tel. 223454; fax 222926; Ambassador: Mary Carlin Yates.

Judicial System

Constitutional Court: Bujumbura.

Supreme Court: BP 1460, Bujumbura; tel. 222571; fax 222148. Court of final instance; four divisions: ordinary, cassation, constitutional and administrative.

Courts of Appeal: Bujumbura, Gitega and Ngozi.

Tribunals of First Instance: There are 17 provincial tribunals and 123 smaller resident tribunals in other areas.

Tribunal of Trade: Bujumbura.

Tribunals of Labour: Bujumbura and Gitega.

Administrative Courts: Bujumbura and Gitega.

Religion

More than 65% of the population are Christians, the majority of whom (an estimated 61%) are Roman Catholics. Anglicans number about 60,000. There are about 200,000 other Protestant adherents, of whom about 160,000 are Pentecostalists. Fewer than 40% of the population adhere to traditional beliefs, which include the worship of the God 'Imana'. About 1% of the population are Muslims. The Bahá'í Faith is also active in Burundi.

CHRISTIANITY

Conseil National des Eglises protestantes du Burundi (CNEB): BP 17, Bujumbura; tel. 224216; fax 227941; f. 1970; five mem. churches; Pres. Rt. Rev. Jean Nduwayo (Anglican Bishop of Gitega); Gen. Sec. Rev. Osias Habingabwa.

The Anglican Communion

The Church of the Province of Burundi, established in 1992, comprises five dioceses.

Archbishop of Burundi and Bishop of Buye: Most Rev. Samuel Ndayisenga, BP 94, Ngozi; fax 302317.

Provincial Secretary: (vacant), BP 2098, Bujumbura.

The Roman Catholic Church

Burundi comprises one archdiocese and six dioceses. At 31 December 1998 there were an estimated 3,763,923 adherents, equivalent to 62.6% of the total population.

Bishops' Conference: Conférence des Evêques Catholiques du Burundi, 5 blvd de l'UPRONA, BP 1390, Bujumbura; tel. 223263; fax 223270; e-mail cecab@cbinf.com; f. 1980; Pres. Most Rev. Simon Ntamwana, Archbishop of Gitega.

Archbishop of Gitega: Most Rev. Simon Ntamwana, Archevêché, BP 118, Gitega; tel. 402160; fax 402620.

Other Christian Churches

Union of Baptist Churches of Burundi: Rubura, DS 117, Bujumbura 1; Pres. Paul Baruhenamwo.

Other denominations active in the country include the Evangelical Christian Brotherhood of Burundi, the Free Methodist Church of Burundi and the United Methodist Church of Burundi.

BAHÁ'Í FAITH

National Spiritual Assembly: BP 1578, Bujumbura.

The Press

NEWSPAPERS

Burundi chrétien: BP 232, Bujumbura; Roman Catholic weekly; French.

Le Renouveau du Burundi: Ministry of Information, BP 2870, Bujumbura; f. 1978; publ. by UPRONA; daily; French; circ. 20,000; Dir Jean Nzeyimana.

Ubumwe: BP 1400, Bujumbura; tel. 223929; f. 1971; weekly; Kirundi; circ. 20,000.

PERIODICALS

Au Coeur de l'Afrique: Association des conférences des ordinaires du Rwanda et Burundi, BP 1390, Bujumbura; fax 223027; e-mail cnid@cbinf.com; bimonthly; education; circ. 1,000.

Bulletin économique et financier: BP 482, Bujumbura; bi-monthly.

Bulletin mensuel: Banque de la République du Burundi, Service des études, BP 705, Bujumbura; tel. 225142; monthly.

Bulletin officiel du Burundi: Bujumbura; monthly.

Le Burundi en Images: BP 1400, Bujumbura; f. 1979; monthly.

Culture et Sociétés: BP 1400, Bujumbura; f. 1978; quarterly.

Ndongozi Y'uburundi: Catholic Mission, BP 690, Bujumbura; tel. 222762; fax 228907; fortnightly; Kirundi.

Revue administration et juridique: Association d'études administratives et juridiques du Burundi, BP 1613, Bujumbura; quarterly; French.

PRESS ASSOCIATION

Burundian Association of Journalists (BAJ): Bujumbura; Pres. François Sendazirasa.

NEWS AGENCY

Agence burundaise de Presse (ABP): ave Nicolas Mayugi, BP 2870, Bujumbura; tel. 225793; fax (2) 22282; e-mail abp@cbinf.com; internet cni.cbinf.com/abp.htm; publ. daily bulletin.

Publishers

BURSTA: BP 1908, Bujumbura; tel. 231796; fax 232842; f. 1986; Dir Richard Kashirahamwe.

Editions Intore: 14 ave Patrice Emery Lumumba, BP 2524, Bujumbura; tel. 223499; f. 1992; philosophy, history, journalism, literature, social sciences; Dir Dr André Birabuza.

GRAVIMPORT: BP 156, Bujumbura; tel. 222285; fax 226953.

IMPARUDI: ave du 18 septembre 3, BP 3010, Bujumbura; tel. 223125; fax 222572; f. 1982; Dir Théoneste Mutambuka.

Imprimerie la Licorne: 29 ave de la Mission, BP 2942, Bujumbura; tel. 223503; fax 227225; f. 1991.

Imprimerie MAHI: BP 673, Bujumbura.

MICROBU: BP 645, Bujumbura.

Imprimerie Moderne: BP 2555, Bujumbura.

Imprimerie du Parti: BP 1810, Bujumbura.

Les Presses Lavigerie: 5 ave de l'UPRONA, BP 1640, Bujumbura; tel. 222368; fax 220318.

Régie de Productions Pédagogiques: BP 3118, Bujumbura; tel. 226111; fax 222631; f. 1984; school textbooks; Dir Léonard Bizongwako.

SASCO: BP 204, Bujumbura.

Government Publishing House

Imprimerie nationale du Burundi (INABU): BP 991, Bujumbura; tel. 224046; fax 225399; f. 1978; Dir Nicolas Nijimbere.

Broadcasting and Communications

TELECOMMUNICATIONS

Direction générale des transports, postes et télécommunications: BP 2390, Bujumbura; tel. 225422; fax 226900; govt telecommunications authority; Dir-Gen. Apollinaire Ndayizeye.

Office nationale des télécommunications (ONATEL): BP 60, Bujumbura; tel. 223196; fax 226917; service provider; privatization pending; Dir-Gen. Lt-Col Nestor Misigaro.

Téléphonie Cellulaire du Burundi (TELECEL): Bujumbura; 40% govt-owned; mobile telephone service provider.

BROADCASTING

Radio

Radio Umwizero/Radio Hope: BP 5314, Bujumbura; tel. 217068; e-mail umwizero@cbinf.com; f. 1996; EU-funded, private station promoting national reconciliation, peace and development projects; broadcasts nine hours daily in Kirundi, Swahili and French; Dir. Hubert Vieille.

Voix de la Révolution/La Radiodiffusion et Télévision Nationale du Burundi (RTNB): BP 1900, Bujumbura; tel. 223742; fax 226547; e-mail rtnb@cbinf.com; f. 1960; govt-controlled; daily radio broadcasts in Kirundi, Swahili, French and English; Dir-Gen. Innocent Muhozi; Dir (Radio) Emmanuel Nzeyimana; Dir (Television) David Hicuburumai.

Television

Voix de la Révolution/La Radiodiffusion et Télévision Nationale du Burundi (RTNB): BP 1900, Bujumbura; tel. 223742; fax 226547; f. 1960; govt-controlled; television service in Kirundi, Swahili, French and English; Dir (Television) Clément Kirahagazwi.

Finance

(cap. = capital; res = reserves; dep. = deposits; m. = million;
brs = branches; amounts in Burundian francs)

BANKING

Central Bank

Banque de la République du Burundi (BRB): BP 705, Bujumbura; tel. 225142; fax 223128; f. 1964 as Banque du Royaume du Burundi; state-owned; bank of issue; cap. and res 14,378.3m., dep. 10,473.9m. (Dec. 1997); Gov. GRÉGOIRE BANYIYEZAKO; Vice-Gov. CYPRIEN SINZOBAHAMVYA; 2 brs.

Commercial Banks

Banque Burundaise pour le Commerce et l'Investissement SARL (BBCI): blvd du Peuple Murundi, BP 2320, Bujumbura; tel. 223328; fax 223339; f. 1988; cap. and res 507.4m., total assets 3,451.0m. (Dec. 1998); Pres. ZACHARIE GASABANYA; Vice-Pres. CLÔTILDE NIZIGAMA.

Banque Commerciale du Burundi SARL (BANCOBU): 84 chaussée Prince Louis-Rwagasore, BP 990, Bujumbura; tel. 222317; fax 221018; e-mail bancobu@cbinf.com; f. 1988 by merger; cap. and res 2,914.6m., total assets 27,155.4m. (Sept. 1999); Pres. N. BARUTWANAYO; Dir-Gen. LIBÈRE NDABAKWAJE; 6 brs.

Banque de Commerce et de Développement (BCD): ave de Grèce, BP 2020, Bujumbura;; tel. 210950; fax 210952; e-mail bcd@cbinf.com; f. 1999; cap. and res 1,016.0m., total assets 5,024.7m. (June 1999); Pres. FRANÇOIS BUTOKE; Man. Dir ANTOINE NDUWAYO.

Banque de Crédit de Bujumbura SMei: ave Patrice Emery Lumumba, BP 300, Bujumbura; tel. 222091; fax 223007; f. 1964; cap. and res 3,282.4m., total assets 22,546.8m. (Dec. 1998); Pres. CHARLES NIHANGAZA; Man. ATHANASE GAHUNGU; 6 brs.

Banque de Gestion et de Financement: 1 blvd de la Liberté, BP 1035, Bujumbura; tel. 221352; fax 221351; e-mail bgf@cbinf.com; f. 1992; cap. and res 760.1m., total assets 3,847.8m. (Dec. 1998); Pres. DIDACE NZOHABONAYO; Dir-Gen. MATHIAS NDIKUMANA.

Banque Populaire du Burundi (BPB): 10 ave du 18 Septembre, BP 1780, Bujumbura; tel. 221257; fax 221256; e-mail bpb@cbinf.com; internet www.cbinf.com; f. 1992; cap. and res 685.4m., total assets 5,328.3m. (Dec. 1998); Pres. THÉODORE KAMWENUBUSA; Dir-Gen. D. BUKOBERO.

Interbank Burundi SARL: 15 ave de l'Industrie, BP 2970, Bujumbura; tel. 220629; fax 220461; e-mail interb@cbinf.com; cap. and res 1,623.6m., total assets 14,545.7m. (Dec. 1997); Pres. GEORGES COUCOULIS.

Development Bank

Banque Nationale pour le Développement Economique SARL (BNDE): 3 ave du Marché, BP 1620, Bujumbura; tel. 222888; fax 223775; e-mail bnde@cbinf.com; f. 1966; cap. and res 2,112m., total assets 12,533m. (Dec. 1998); Pres. and Dir-Gen. GASPARD SINDIYIGAYA; Gen. Sec. FRANÇOIS BARWENDERE.

Co-operative Bank

Banque Coopérative d'Epargne et de Crédit Mutuel (BCM): BP 1340, Bujumbura; operating licence granted in April 1995; Vice-Pres. JULIEN MUSARAGANY.

INSURANCE

Burundi Insurance Corporation (BICOR): BP 2377, Bujumbura.

Société d'Assurances du Burundi (SOCABU): 14–18 rue de l'Amitié, BP 2440, Bujumbura; tel. 226520; fax 226803; e-mail socabu@cbinf.com; f. 1977; partly state-owned; cap. 180m.; Dir-Gen. (Admin.) SÉRAPHINE RUVAHAFI.

Société Générale d'Assurances et de Réassurance (SOGEAR): BP 2432, Bujumbura; tel. 222345; fax 229338; f. 1991; Pres. BENOIT NDORIMANA; Dir-Gen. L. SAUSSEZ.

Union Commerciale d'Assurances et de Réassurance (UCAR): BP 3012, Bujumbura; tel. 223638; fax 223695; f. 1986; cap. 150m.; Chair. Lt-Col EDOUARD NZAMBIMANA; Man. Dir HENRY TARMO.

Trade and Industry

GOVERNMENT AGENCIES

Agences de Promotion des Echanges Extérieurs (APEE): Bujumbura; promotes and supervises foreign exchanges.

Office des Cultures Industrielles du Burundi (Office du Café du Burundi) (OCIBU): BP 450, Bujumbura; tel. 224017; fax 225532; e-mail ocibu3@cbinf.com; f. 1964; supervises coffee plantations and coffee exports; Dir-Gen. BARTHÉLÉMY NIYIKIZA.

Office du Thé du Burundi (OTB): 52 blvd de l'UPRONA, Bujumbura; tel. 224228; fax 224657; f. 1979 supervises production and marketing of tea; Man. Dir SALVATORE NIMUBONA.

Office National du Commerce (ONC): Bujumbura; f. 1973; supervises international commercial operations between the Govt of Burundi and other states or private orgs; also organizes the import of essential materials; subsidiary offices in each province.

Office National du Logement (ONL): BP 2480, Bujumbura; tel. 226074; f. 1974 to supervise housing construction.

DEVELOPMENT ORGANIZATIONS

Compagnie de Gérance du Coton (COGERCO): BP 2571, Bujumbura; tel. 222208; fax 224370; e-mail cogerco@cbinf.com; f. 1947; promotion and development of cotton industry; Pres. SÉBASTIEN NDAVIZEYE; Dir FRANÇOIS KABURA.

Fonds de Développement Communal (FDC): Bujumbura; funds local development.

Institut des Sciences Agronomiques du Burundi (ISABU): BP 795, Bujumbura; tel. 223390; fax 225798; e-mail isabu@cni.cbinf.com.; f. 1962 for the scientific development of agriculture and livestock.

Office National de la Tourbe (ONATOUR): BP 2360, Bujumbura; tel. 226480; fax 226709; f. 1977 to promote the exploitation of peat deposits.

Société d'Exploitation du Quinquina du Burundi (SOKINABU): 16 blvd Mwezi Gisabo, BP 1783, Bujumbura; tel. 223469; f. 1975 to develop and exploit cinchona trees, the source of quinine; Dir RAPHAËL REMEZO.

Société de Financement et Développement de l'Habitat Urbain (SOFIDHAR): Bujumbura; urban development.

Société Régionale de Développement de l'IMBO (SRDI): Bujumbura; promotes development of IMBO region.

Société Régionale de Développement de Kayanza (SRD KAYANZA): Kayanza; promotes development of Kayanza region.

Société Régionale de Développement de Kirimiro (SRD KIRIMIRO): Bujumbura; promotes development of Kirimiro region.

Société Régionale de Développement de Kirundo (SRD KIRUNDO): Bujumbura; promotes development of Kirundo region.

Société Régionale de Développement de Mumirwa (SRD MUMIRWA): Bujumbura; promotes development of Mumirwa region.

Société Régionale de Développement de Rumonge (SRD RUMONGE): Bujumbura; promotes development of Rumonge region.

Société Sucrière du Mosso (SOSUMO): BP 835, Bujumbura; tel. 275002; fax 275004; e-mail sosumo@cbinf.com; f. 1982 to develop and manage sugar cane plantations; Pres. PHILIPPE NIYONGABO; Dir-Gen. (Admin.) ALEXI RWAGATORE.
.

CHAMBER OF COMMERCE

Chambre de Commerce, d'Industrie, d'Agriculture et d'Artisanat du Burundi: BP 313, Bujumbura; tel. 222280; fax 227895; f. 1923; Pres. DIDACE NZOHABONAYO; Sec.-Gen. CYRILLE SINGEJEJE; 130 mems.

UTILITIES

Régie de Distribution d'Eau et d'Electricité (REGIDESCO): Bujumbura; state-owned distributor of water and electricity services.

MAJOR COMPANY

Complexe Textile de Bujumbura (COTEBU): BP 2899, Bujumbura; tel. 231900; fax 231750; textile mfrs; Dirs JEAN KABURA, DÉO NDABANEZE, ANICET NDAYISABA.

TRADE UNIONS

Confédération des Syndicats du Burundi (COSIBU): Bujumbura; Chair. CHARLES NDAMIRAWE.

Union des Travailleurs du Burundi (UTB): BP 1340, Bujumbura; tel. 223884; f. 1967 by merger of all existing unions; closely allied with UPRONA; sole authorized trade union prior to 1994, with 18 affiliated nat. professional feds; Sec.-Gen. MARIUS RURAHENYE.

Transport

RAILWAYS

There are no railways in Burundi. Plans have been under consideration since 1987 for the construction of a line passing through Uganda, Rwanda and Burundi, to connect with the Kigoma–Dar es Salaam line in Tanzania. This rail link would relieve Burundi's isolated trade position.

ROADS

The road network is very dense and in 1996 there was a total of 14,480 km of roads, of which 1,950 km were national highways and 2,530 km secondary roads. A new crossing of the Ruzizi River, the Bridge of Concord (Burundi's longest bridge), was opened in early 1992.

Office des Transports en Commun (OTRACO): Bujumbura; 100% govt-owned; operates public transport.

INLAND WATERWAYS

Bujumbura is the principal port for both passenger and freight traffic on Lake Tanganyika, and the greater part of Burundi's external trade is dependent on the shipping services between Bujumbura and lake ports in Tanzania, Zambia and the Democratic Republic of the Congo.

Exploitation du Port de Bujumbura (EPB): Bujumbura; 43% state-owned; controls Bujumbura port.

CIVIL AVIATION

The international airport at Bujumbura is equipped to take large jet-engined aircraft.

Air Burundi: 40 ave du Commerce, BP 2460, Bujumbura; tel. 224609; fax 223452; f. 1971 as Société de Transports Aériens du Burundi; state-owned; operates charter and scheduled passenger services to destinations throughout central Africa; CEO Maj. ISAAC GAFURERO.

Tourism

Tourism is relatively undeveloped. The annual total of tourist arrivals declined from 125,000 in 1991 (with receipts amounting to US $4m.) to only 10,553 in 1997 (receipts $1m.); total arrivals recovered somewhat, however, to reach 15,404 in 1998.

Office National du Tourisme (ONT): 2 ave des Euphorbes, BP 902, Bujumbura; tel. 224208; fax 229390; f. 1972; responsible for the promotion and supervision of tourism; Dir HERMENEGILDE NIMBONA (acting).

Defence

The total armed strength in August 1999 was 45,500, comprising an army of an estimated 40,000 (including an air wing of 200), and a paramilitary force of 5,500 gendarmes (including a 50-strong marine police force).

Defence Expenditure: Budgeted at 24,564m. Burundian francs for 1999.

Chief of Staff of the Army: Lt-Col VINCENT NIYUNGEKO.

Chief of Staff of the Gendarmerie: Col. GEORGES MUKURAKO.

Education

Education is provided free of charge. Kirundi is the language of instruction in primary schools, while French is used in secondary schools. Primary education, which is officially compulsory, begins at seven years of age and lasts for six years. Secondary education, which is not compulsory, begins at the age of 13 and lasts for up to seven years, comprising a first cycle of four years and a second of three years. In 1995 the total enrolment at primary schools included 51% of students in the relevant age-group (males 55%; females 46%). Enrolment at primary schools increased from 175,856 in 1980 to 453,746 in 1996. Enrolment at secondary schools, including pupils receiving vocational instruction and teacher training, rose from 19,013 in 1980 to 62,599 in 1996. In 1995 the total enrolment at secondary schools included 7% of students in the relevant age-group (males 9%; females 5%). There is one university, in Bujumbura, with 2,749 students in 1988/89. In 1996 there were 4,379 students in higher education. According to UNESCO estimates, the average rate of illiteracy among the population aged 15 years and over was 64.7% (Males 50.7%; females 77.5%) in 1995. Expenditure on education was budgeted at 15,990m. Burundian francs (15.2% of total government spending) in 1999.

Bibliography

Chrétien, J.-P. 'La société du Burundi: Des mythes aux réalités', in *Revue Française d'Etudes Politiques Africaines,* July-August 1979, Nos. 163–4, pp. 94–118.

Histoire rurale de l'Afrique des Grands Lacs. Paris, Editions Karthala.

Chrétien, J.-P., Guichaoua, A., and Le Jeune, G. *La crise d'août 1988 au Burundi.* Paris, Editions Karthala.

Eggas, E. *Historical Dictionary of Burundi.* 2nd Edn. Metuchen, NJ, Scarecrow Press, 1997.

Gahama, J. *Le Burundi sous administration belge.* Paris, Editions Karthala, 1983.

Guichaoua, A. (Ed.). *Les crises politiques au Burundi et au Rwanda (1993–1994).* Paris, Editions Karthala, 1995.

Guillet, C., and Ndayishinguje, P. *Légendes historiques du Burundi.* Paris, Editions Karthala, 1987.

Hausner, K.-H., and Jezic, B. *Rwanda et Burundi.* Bonn, Kurt Schroeder, 1968.

Lambert, M. Y. *Enquête démographique Burundi* (1970–1971). Bujumbura, Ministère du Plan, 1972.

Lemarchand, R. *Rwanda and Burundi.* London, Pall Mall, 1970.

Selective Genocide in Burundi. 1974.

African Kingships in Perspective. 1974.

Ethnocide as Discourse and Practice. Woodrow Wilson Center Press and Cambridge University Press, 1994.

Burundi: Ethnic Conflict and Genocide. Cambridge, Cambridge University Press, 1996.

Mpozagara, G. *La République du Burundi.* Paris, Berger-Levrault, 1971.

Mworoha, E. *Histoire du Burundi.* Paris, Hatier, 1987.

Nsanzé, T. *Le Burundi au carrefour de l'Afrique.* Brussels, Remarques africaines, 1970.

L'Edification de la République du Burundi. Brussels, 1970.

Ntahombaye, P. *Des noms et des hommes. Aspects du nom au Burundi.* Paris, Editions Karthala, 1983.

République du Burundi. *Plan quinquennal de développement économique et social du Burundi (1978–82).* Bujumbura.

Reyntjens, F. *Burundi 1972–1988. Continuité et changement.* Brussels, Centre d'étude et de documentation africaines (CEDAF–ASDOC), 1989.

United States Committee for Refugees. *From Coup to Coup: Thirty Years of Death, Fear and Displacement in Burundi.* Washington, DC, USCR, 1996.

University of Burundi. *Questions sur la paysannerie au Burundi. Actes de la table ronde: Sciences sociales, humaines et développement rural.* Bujumbura, 1985.

Vasina, J. *La légende du passé, traditions orales du Burundi.* Tervuren, Musée royale de l'Afrique centrale, 1972.

Weinstein, W. *Historical Dictionary of Burundi.* Metuchen, NJ, Scarecrow Press, 1976.

World Bank. *Farming Systems in Africa: The Great Lakes Highlands of Zaire, Rwanda and Burundi.* Washington, DC, International Bank for Reconstruction and Development, 1984.

CAMEROON

Physical and Social Geography

JOHN I. CLARKE

PHYSICAL FEATURES

The Republic of Cameroon covers an area of 475,442 sq km (183,569 sq miles), and contains exceptionally diverse physical environments. The country occupies a fairly central position within the African continent, with the additional advantage of a 200-km coastline. Its environmental diversity arises from various factors, including the country's position astride the volcanic belt along the hinge between west and central Africa, together with its intermediate location between the great basins of the Congo, the Niger and Lake Chad, its latitudinal extent between 2° and 13°N, its altitudinal range from sea-level to more than 4,000 m, and its spread from coastal mangrove swamp to remote continental interior.

In the south and centre of the country a large undulating and broken plateau surface of granites, schists and gneisses rises northwards away from the Congo basin to the Adamawa plateau (900–1,520 m above sea-level). North of the steep Adamawa escarpment, which effectively divides northern from southern Cameroon, lies the basin of the Benue river, a tributary of the Niger, which is floored by sedimentary rocks, interspersed with inselbergs and buttes. In the west of the country a long line of rounded volcanic mountains and hills extends from Mt Cameroun (4,095 m), the highest mountain in west and central Africa, north-eastwards along the former boundary between East and West Cameroon and then along the Nigerian border. Volcanic soils derived from these mountains are more fertile than most others in the country and have permitted much higher rural population densities than elsewhere.

Cameroon has a marked south-north gradation of climates, from a seasonal equatorial climate in the south (with two rainy seasons and two moderately dry seasons of unequal length), to southern savannah and savannah climates (with one dry and one wet season), to a hotter drier climate of the Sahel type in the far north. Rainfall thus varies from more than 5,000 mm in the south-west to around 610 mm near Lake Chad. Corresponding to this climatic zonation is a south-north gradation of vegetal landscapes: dense rain forest, Guinea savannah, Sudan savannah and thorn steppe, while Mt Cameroun incorporates a vertical series of sharply divided vegetation zones.

POPULATION

The population of Cameroon was enumerated at 10,493,655 at the census of April 1987, and was officially estimated to have risen to 14,859,000 in mid-1999, giving an average density of 31.3 inhabitants per sq km. Population growth has been rapid (an average rate of 3.2% per year in 1990–98) and the composition and distribution are extremely diverse. In the southern forest regions Bantu peoples predominate, although there are also pygmy groups in some of the more remote areas. North of the Bantu tribes live many semi-Bantu peoples including the ubiquitous Bamiléké. Further north the diversity increases, with Sudanese Negroes, Hamitic Fulani (or Foulbe) and Arab Choa.

The distribution of population is uneven, with concentrations in the west, the south-central region and the Sudan savannah zone of the north. An important religious and social divide lies across the country. While the peoples of the south and west have been profoundly influenced by Christianity and by the European introduction of an externally orientated colonial-type economy, the peoples of the north are either Muslim or animist and have largely retained their traditional modes of life. Consequently, the population of the south and west is much more developed, economically and socially, than that of the north, although the government has made efforts to reduce this regional disparity.

One aspect of this disparity is the southern location of the capital, Yaoundé (estimated population 1,372,800 in 1999), and the main port of Douala (1,448,300), as well as most of the other towns. Much of their growth results from rural-urban migration; many of the migrants come from overcrowded mountain massifs in the west, and the Bamiléké constitute more than one-third of the inhabitants of Douala. Nevertheless, about two-thirds of all Cameroonians remain rural village-dwellers.

One other major contrast in the social geography of Cameroon is between anglophone north-west and south-west Cameroon, with less than one-tenth of the area and just over one-fifth of the population, and the much larger, more populous francophone area of former East Cameroon. The contrasting influences of British and French rule remain evident in education, commerce, law and elsewhere, although unification of the civil services since 1972, official bilingualism and the integration of transport networks and economies have helped to reduce the disparities between the two zones.

Recent History

PIERRE ENGLEBERT

Revised for this edition by the Editor

The German protectorate of Kamerun, of which the Republic of Cameroon was formerly a part, was established in 1884. In 1916 the German administration was overthrown by combined French-British-Belgian military operations during the First World War and in 1919 the territory was divided into British and French spheres of influence. In 1922 both zones became subject to mandates of the League of Nations, which allocated four-fifths of the territory to French administration as French Cameroun, and the other one-fifth, comprising two long, non-contiguous areas along the eastern Nigerian border, to British administration as the Northern and Southern Cameroons.

In 1946 the mandates were converted into UN trust territories, still under their respective French and British administrations. However, growing anti-colonial sentiment made it difficult for France and Britain to resist the UN Charter's promise of eventual self-determination for all inhabitants of trust territories. In 1957 French Cameroun became an autonomous state within the French Community, and on 1 January 1960 proceeded to full independence as the Republic of Cameroon. Ahmadou Ahidjo, the leader of the Union camerounaise, who had served as prime minister since 1958, was elected as the country's first president.

In the British Cameroons, which was attached for administrative purposes to neighbouring Nigeria, a UN-supervised plebiscite was held in February 1961 in both parts of the trust territory. Voters in the Southern Cameroons opted for union with the Republic of Cameroon (which took place on 1 October), while northern Cameroon voters chose to merge with Nigeria (becoming the province of Sardauna). The new Federal Republic of Cameroon thus comprised two states: the former French zone became East Cameroon, while the former British portion became West Cameroon. Ahidjo assumed the presidency of the federation. In June 1972 the country was officially renamed the United Republic of Cameroon. The sole legal party, the Union nationale camerounaise (UNC) assumed full supervision of Cameroon's organized political and social affairs. In its foreign policy, the UNC government adopted a non-aligned stance and sought to reduce its dependence on France and the Western bloc.

Despite dissatisfaction in some quarters with the single-party system and discontent among English-speaking politicians about their relatively low representation in government, Ahidjo and the UNC retained popular support in subsequent single-list elections. However, an increase in activity by clandestine opposition groups dissatisfied with Ahidjo's autocratic rule began to emerge in the late 1970s, notably in the English-speaking south-western region of the country. In April 1980, however, Ahidjo was again re-elected as sole candidate for a further five-year term.

THE BIYA PRESIDENCY

In November 1982 Ahidjo resigned on the grounds of ill-health, and transferred the presidency to Paul Biya, the country's prime minister since 1975. Ahidjo, however, retained the chairmanship of the UNC. By mid-1983 divisions between Ahidjo and Biya had become evident, and in August Biya announced the discovery of a plot to overthrow the government. Two close associates of Ahidjo were arrested and later in that month Ahidjo passed the chairmanship of the UNC to Biya and left the country, dying in exile in 1989. In January 1984 Biya was re-elected president, as sole candidate, and the country's original official name, the Republic of Cameroon, was subsequently restored.

Reassertion of Presidential Power

An unsuccessful attempt by an army faction to overthrow the government in April 1984 temporarily destabilized the Biya regime. In the following months, however, Biya moved decisively to reassert his control. Members of the government whose loyalty to Biya remained in doubt were gradually removed from office, and most of the major public enterprises experienced a change of leadership. In March 1985 the UNC was renamed the Rassemblement démocratique du peuple camerounais (RDPC).

From January to March 1986 elections took place for members of RDPC bodies on all levels; the choice of candidates presented for election indicated that a measure of democratization was beginning to emerge; new candidates were elected to more than 50% of the posts, with the proportion rising to 70% at the lower levels of office. The gradual appointment to the administration, often to posts in the parastatal corporations, of a number of the formerly influential functionaries of the Ahidjo period also indicated Biya's increasing confidence in the stability of his regime.

Elections to the national assembly were held in April 1988, together with a presidential election (brought forward from January 1989 for reasons of economy). Voters in the legislative elections were presented with a choice of RDPC-approved candidates; however, the abstention rate was estimated at 9.9% (compared with 0.8% at the previous general election, in May 1983). Biya, the sole candidate for the presidency, obtained 98.75% of the votes cast. In May 1988 Biya dismissed 24 ministers and several ministries were merged or abolished. In subsequent months the president's relations with the press became increasingly strained, and journalists who were critical of the government were detained. The ensuing appointment of a reputable journalist as minister of information was intended to reduce tensions between the government and the media. In a government reorganization in April 1989, an additional secretary of state for finance was appointed to assist in negotiations for the rescheduling of Cameroon's external debt, following the adoption of an IMF-approved structural adjustment programme (see Economy).

Opposition and the Pro-Democracy Movement

In February 1990 a number of people were arrested and tried for subversion, as a result of their alleged involvement in an unofficial opposition organization, the Social Democratic Front (SDF). Twelve of the 18 defendants were imprisoned. Later that month, in an apparent attempt to strengthen national unity in the aftermath of the convictions, it was announced that an estimated 100 prisoners who had been detained following the April 1984 coup attempt were to be released.

Biya continued to oppose the establishment of a multi-party system, stating that such a fundamental political change would undermine attempts to resolve the prevailing economic crisis. From March 1990 a series of demonstrations in support of the RDPC took place. In May six deaths were reported, after security forces violently suppressed a demonstration organized by the SDF, which took place in Bamenda (in the English-speaking north-west of the country) and was attended by at least 20,000 people. The SDF, led by John Fru Ndi, received the support of many prominent writers and lawyers (and was alleged by the government to be receiving financial support from Nigeria).

In late June 1990 a congress of the RDPC re-elected Biya as president of the party and carried out a major reorganization of the central committee. In response to continued civil unrest, Biya stated that the future adoption of a multi-party system was envisaged, and subsequently announced a series of reforms, including the abolition of laws governing subversion, the relaxation of restraints on the press, and the reform of legislation prohibiting political associations. In the same month a committee was established to formulate legislation on human rights. In August several political prisoners were released. In early September Biya effected an extensive reorganization of the cabinet, and created a new ministry to oversee the country's programme for economic stabilization. Later in September the vice-president of the RDPC resigned, in protest at alleged corruption and violations of human rights by the government.

In December 1990 the national assembly approved a constitutional amendment providing for the establishment of a multi-party system. Under the new arrangements, the government was required to grant (or refuse) registration within three months to any political association seeking legal recognition. In addition, registered parties were to receive state support during election campaigns. However, the recruitment of party activists on a regional or ethnic basis and the financing of political parties from external sources was prohibited. A large number of political associations subsequently emerged.

During 1991 pressure for political reform intensified. In January anti-government demonstrators protested at Biya's failure (despite previous undertakings) to grant an amnesty to prisoners implicated in the April 1984 coup attempt. In the same month the trial of two journalists, who had published an article critical of Biya in an independent periodical, provoked violent rioting. Meanwhile, opposition leaders renewed their demands for the convening of a national conference to formulate a timetable for multi-party elections. In April 1991 Biya's continued opposition to the holding of such a conference provoked a series of demonstrations and widespread riots, which were violently suppressed by security forces; by the end of that month more than 100 people were reported to have been killed. Later in April in response to increasing pressure for constitutional reform, the national assembly formally granted a general amnesty to all political prisoners, and reintroduced the post of prime minister. Sadou Hayatou, hitherto secretary-general to the presidency, was appointed to the position. Hayatou subsequently formed a 32-member transitional government, which principally comprised members of the former cabinet.

In late April 1991 a newly-established alliance of 11 leading opposition groups, the National Co-ordination Committee of Opposition Parties (NCCOP), demanded an unconditional amnesty for all political prisoners (the existing arrangements for an amnesty excluded an estimated 400 political prisoners jailed ostensibly for non-political offences), and the convening of a national conference before 10 May. In early May the University of Yaoundé was closed, after security forces suppressed demonstrations by students. The continuing reluctance of the government to set a date for the national conference prompted the NCCOP to initiate a campaign of civil disobedience, initially comprising one-day strikes and demonstrations. Opposition leaders also demanded the resignation of Hayatou and his cabinet as a precondition to multi-party elections. Later that month seven of Cameroon's 10 provinces were placed under military rule, and in June the government prohibited meetings of opposition parties. In June the NCCOP intensified the campaign of civil disobedience, and orchestrated a general strike, which halted economic activity in most towns. In an attempt to end the campaign, the government prohibited opposition gatherings, and, following continued civil disturbances, banned the NCCOP, whose leaders declared that the campaign of civil disobedience was to continue. (However, the effect of the general strike declined in subsequent months.) In September several opposition leaders were temporarily detained, following further violent demonstrations, together with several hundred protestors.

In October 1991 Biya announced that legislative elections were to take place in February 1992, and that a prime minister was to be appointed from the party that secured a majority in the national assembly. He also invited opposition leaders to meet Hayatou to discuss the proposed establishment of a new electoral code. Tripartite negotiations between the government, the opposition parties and independent officials commenced at the end of October, but were delayed by procedural disputes, brought about by opposition demands that the scope of the discussions be extended to include a review of the constitution. In mid-November, however, the government and about 40 of the 47 registered opposition parties signed an agreement providing for the establishment of a 10-member committee to draft constitutional reforms. The opposition pledged to suspend the campaign of civil disobedience, while the government agreed to end the ban on opposition meetings and to release all prisoners who had been arrested during the demonstrations earlier that year. However, several parties within the NCCOP, including the SDF, subsequently rejected the agreement, resulting in further division within the opposition. Later in November the government revoked the ban on opposition gatherings, and, in December, ended the military rule which had been imposed in seven of the provinces. In the same month the national assembly approved a new electoral code.

In January 1992 the government announced that legislative elections would be held on 1 March, following demands from opposition leaders that elections be postponed in order to allow additional time for preparation. However, a number of opposition groups, including two of the four principal parties, the SDF and the Union démocratique du Cameroun (UDC), refused to participate in the elections, claiming that the scheduled date was too early and that the electoral code was biased in favour of the RDPC.

In February 1992 the opposition parties that had not accepted the tripartite agreement in November 1991 formed a political coalition, the Alliance pour le redressement du Cameroun (ARC), which was to boycott the elections. Later in February the former prime minister, Bello Bouba Maigari, was elected as chairman of one of the principal opposition movements, the Union nationale pour la démocratie et le progrès (UNDP), which announced that it would take part in the elections.

At the legislative elections on 1 March 1992, which were contested by 32 political parties, the RDPC won 88 of the 180 seats in the national assembly; the UNDP secured 68 seats, the Union des populations camerounaises (UPC) 18, and the Mouvement pour la défense de la République (MDR) six seats. An estimated 61% of registered voters took part in the elections, although the proportion was only 10% in regions affected by the general strike. Following discussions between Biya and the leader of the MDR, Dakole Daissala, after the elections, the RDPC formed an alliance with the MDR, thereby securing an absolute majority in the national assembly. Biya subsequently appointed Joseph-Charles Doumbu as secretary-general of the RDPC, replacing Ebénézer Njoh Mouelle, who had lost his seat in the legislative elections. Later in March a francophone member of the RDPC, Djibril Cavaye Yeguie, was elected as president of the national assembly. On 9 April Biya announced a new cabinet, which retained the majority of ministers from the previous administration. Five members of the MDR, including Dakole Daissala, also received portfolios. Simon Achidi Achu, an anglophone member of the

RDPC who had served in the Ahidjo administration, was appointed as prime minister.

In August 1992 Biya announced that the forthcoming presidential election, due to take place in May 1993, was to be brought forward to that October. This measure was widely believed to benefit the government, following the failure of a large number of opposition supporters to register earlier that year, as a result of the SDF boycott of the legislative elections. Later in August 1992 the minister of the civil service and administrative reform, who had been relieved of certain duties after his discovery of financial malpractice within the civil service, left the government. In September three independent publications, including *Le Messager,* were banned. Later that month the government introduced legislation regulating the election of the president, which prohibited political parties from forming electoral alliances, and stipulated that, contrary to the system in operation in most other francophone African countries, the election was to comprise a single round of voting. Following protracted political negotiations, two of the seven opposition candidates withdrew in favour of the leader of the SDF, John Fru Ndi, who received the endorsement of the ARC alliance.

At the presidential election, which took place on 11 October 1992, Biya was re-elected by 39.9% of votes cast, while Fru Ndi secured 35.9%, and Maigari, the candidate of the UNDP, 19.2% of the vote. However, Fru Ndi disputed the official results, and claimed that he had won the election. A number of protest demonstrations ensued, particularly in the North-West Province and in Douala. Later in October, however, the supreme court ruled against a petition by Fru Ndi to invalidate the election results, despite confirmation from a US monitoring organization that it had detected widespread electoral irregularities. At the end of October, in response to continued unrest, the government placed Fru Ndi and a number of his supporters under house arrest, and placed the North-West Province under a state of emergency for a period of three months.

Pressure for Constitutional Reform

Biya was inaugurated for a third term as president in November 1992. Although he undertook to carry out further constitutional reforms, international criticism of the government increased, resulting in the suspension of economic aid by the USA and Germany in protest at the government's suppression of opposition activity and the continued enforcement of the state of emergency. At the end of November Biya appointed a new cabinet, which included, for the first time, representatives of the UPC, the UNDP and the Parti national du progrès (PNP). In December order was restored in the North-West Province, and at the end of that month, the state of emergency was lifted. In January 1993 the government granted an amnesty to a number of political prisoners, who had been arrested in October 1992.

In March 1993 the Union pour le changement, an alliance of opposition parties, which included the SDF, co-ordinated a campaign of demonstrations and a boycott of French consumer goods (in protest at the French government's continuing support for Biya), to reinforce demands that a new presidential election take place. The government accused the Union pour le changement of attempting to incite civil disorder in order to destabilize the country. In the same month, however, in response to international pressure, the government announced that a national debate on constitutional reform was to take place by the end of May. In early April, following SDF demands that a revised constitution be submitted for approval at a national referendum by a stipulated date, Fru Ndi stated that he was to convene a national conference to determine the political future of Cameroon. In the same month a meeting organized by the Cameroon Anglophone Movement (CAM), which took place in Buéa, the capital of the South-West Province, issued demands for the restoration of a federal system of government, as a counter to the dominance of the French-speaking section of the population in the country. (The SDF, however, opposed the proposed establishment of a federal state.)

Following a meeting with the French president, François Mitterrand, in May 1993, Biya announced that the planned debate on the revision of the constitution was to take place in early June. Instead of the envisaged national conference, however, a technical commission was established to prepare recommendations based on proposals from all sectors of the population. Later in

May the government published draft constitutional amendments, which provided for a democratic system of government, including the establishment of an upper legislative chamber, a council of supreme judiciary affairs, a council of state, and a high authority to govern the civil service. The constitutional provisions also limited the tenure of the president to two five-year terms of office. Elections were to comprise two rounds of voting (a system more favourable to the opposition). The draft legislation retained a unitary state, but, in recognition of demands by supporters of federalism, introduced a more decentralized system of government. The constitutional proposals were subject to amendment, following the recommendations of the technical commission. However, three representatives of the English-speaking community subsequently resigned from the technical commission, in protest at the government's alleged control of the constitutional debate.

At a party congress, which took place in July 1993, the SDF adopted a draft constitution that provided for a decentralized federal state. At the end of August a two-day strike, which was organized by the SDF as part of its anti-government campaign, failed to attract the support of other prominent opposition parties, and was only partially observed. In September a number of opposition activists were arrested, in an effort by the government to pre-empt further strikes. Later that month, however, the Union pour le changement announced plans to organize a new series of demonstrations in support of its demands. In early November security forces prevented Fru Ndi from conducting a press conference in Yaoundé, and about 30 SDF members were arrested; Fru Ndi briefly took refuge at the Netherlands embassy. The SDF detainees were subsequently released, following representations by the French government.

In February 1994 six principal opposition parties (excluding the SDF) formed an electoral coalition, the Front démocratique et patriotique, to contest municipal elections which were due to take place later that year. In April the authorities banned a conference by supporters of the CAM, which, nevertheless, took place at Bamenda. In July, in accordance with the government's aim of promoting economic recovery, a new ministry with responsibility for the economy and finance was created as part of an extensive reconstruction of the cabinet. At the end of that month about eight people were killed in clashes in the northern town of Maroua, following agitation within the UNDP, which subsequently led to a split in the party, over the decision by its vice-chairman, Hamadou Moustapha, to accept a cabinet portfolio without obtaining the party's prior consent.

In September 1994 it was reported that a former prominent member of the security forces had confessed to conspiring to assassinate Biya at a public ceremony in May. Later that month an informal alliance of 16 opposition movements, the Front des alliés pour le changement (FAC), was established under the leadership of Fru Ndi (effectively replacing the Union pour le changement); the FAC criticized alleged human rights violations on the part of the authorities, together with the indefinite postponement of the municipal elections and the proposed transfer of state-owned enterprises to the private sector. Two of the most prominent opposition parties, the UNDP and the UDC refused to join the alliance, however, on the grounds that it was dominated by the SDF. In October the SDF organized a one-day strike, which was observed principally in anglophone regions. In early November Biya announced that discussions on the revision of the constitution were to resume, following the establishment of a 'consultative constitutional review committee' and that the municipal elections were to take place in 1995. Later that month the SDF accused the French ambassador in Yaoundé of discrediting the movement at meetings with traditional leaders. Also in November UNDP deputies boycotted parliamentary sessions in support of demands for the release of a number of party members who had been detained following the factional clashes in July.

Constitutional discussions began in mid-December 1994, but were boycotted by the opposition, which objected to limitations in the agenda of the debate; the UDC (the only opposition movement to attend the discussions) withdrew after two days. In early 1995, however, revised constitutional amendments were submitted to Biya for consideration. In February the leader of the Mouvement pour la démocratie et le progrès, Samuel Eboua, was elected president of the FAC, replacing Fru Ndi. In the same month the UNDP expelled Moustapha and another member of government from the party; Moustapha subsequently established a breakaway faction. In April Biya announced the creation of 64 new local government districts, in preparation for the forthcoming municipal elections. Following reports of division within the SDF, seven members of the executive committee were refused admission to the party congress, which took place in May; a breakaway group, the Social Democratic Movement, was subsequently formed under the leadership of the former secretary-general of the SDF, Siga Asanga.

In early July 1995 members of a newly-emerged anglophone organization, the Southern Cameroons National Council (SCNC, which demanded that the former portion of the British Cameroons that had amalgamated with the republic of Cameroon in 1961 be granted autonomy), staged a demonstration in Bamenda, subsequently clashing with security forces. Later that month English-speaking representatives of the government criticized the demands for the establishment of an anglophone republic (which would be known as Southern Cameroons); the SCNC apparently intended to proclaim formally the independence of Southern Cameroons on 1 October 1996, following the adoption of a separate constitution for the new republic. In early August the SCNC was prohibited from staging a demonstration. In the same month representatives of anglophone movements, including the SCNC and the CAM, officially presented their demands for the establishment of an independent republic of Southern Cameroons at the UN, and urged the international community to assist in resolving the issue in order to avert civil conflict in Cameroon; the organizations claimed that the plebiscite of 1961, whereby the former southern portion of British Cameroons had voted to merge with the Republic of Cameroon on terms of equal status, had been rendered invalid by subsequent francophone domination.

In October 1995 a special congress of the RDPC re-elected Biya as leader of the party for a further term of five years. Meanwhile, Cameroon's pending application for membership of the Commonwealth (see below) prompted further controversy; opposition movements urged the Commonwealth to refuse admission to Cameroon on the grounds that no progress had been achieved with regard to Commonwealth stipulations on human rights and the democratic process, while the SCNC submitted a rival application for membership on behalf of the proposed independent republic of Southern Cameroons. (Nevertheless, following a visit by Commonwealth officials in mid-1995, Cameroon was admitted to the organization in November.) In the same month Biya announced that the municipal elections were to take place in January 1996 (although both opposition movements and parties belonging to the government coalition had demanded that the elections be preceded by constitutional reform and the establishment of an independent electoral commission). In December 1995 the national assembly formally adopted the revised constitutional amendments, submitted by Biya earlier that month, which increased the presidential mandate from five to seven years (while restricting the maximum tenure of office to two terms).

Some 38 political parties participated in the municipal elections, which took place relatively quietly in January 1996 (although the SDF had urged its supporters to disrupt voting in constituencies where the movement had been refused authorization to present candidates). The RDPC (which was the only party to contest the elections in 45 constituencies) retained about 55% of the 336 local government areas, while the SDF secured 27%, principally in the west of the country. In March the SDF and the UNDP (which had also achieved some success in the municipal elections, principally in the north) urged a campaign of civil disobedience in protest at the government's appointment by decree of representatives to replace the elected mayors in principal towns. Later in March the supreme court annulled the results of municipal elections in two constituencies, which had been secured by the RDPC, owing to alleged irregularities. In the same month eight UNDP activists were imprisoned for their involvement in an attack on the vehicle of a UNDP deputy minister in July 1994 (during violence that had been prompted by the factional division within the party). In April the government imposed a total ban on all media reports of the SDF and UNDP campaign of civil disobedience.

In May 1996, following increasing division within the UPC apparently resulting from its lack of success in the municipal elections, the secretary-general, Augustin Frédéric Kodock (who held the ministerial portfolio of agriculture), was dismissed from the party, and subsequently formed a breakaway faction. In the same month a two-day general strike, organized by the SDF and the UNDP in protest at the appointment of the government delegates in towns, was principally observed in western and northern regions, where the parties received popular support. The two parties announced a further general strike in June, which was, however, supported only in the west of the country.

In August 1996 Fru Ndi criticized SCNC activists for urging supporters of anglophone movements to boycott the registration process for the forthcoming elections. (A number of SDF members were believed to also belong to the SCNC.) In September Biya appointed Peter Mafany Musonge, hitherto the manager of the Cameroon Development Corpn, to the office of prime minister, replacing Achidi Achu; the cabinet was subsequently reorganized. In October the editor of *Le Messager*, Pius Njawe, and another journalist were imprisoned, after publishing material critical of Biya. (Following an appeal by Njawe, however, the supreme court ordered his release in November.) In December Biya was nominated by an RDPC congress as the party candidate in the presidential election (which was due to take place in October 1997). At the end of January 1997 the government announced that the legislative elections, which had been scheduled to take place in early March, were to be postponed owing to organizational difficulties, following opposition complaints that its supporters had been allowed insufficient time for registration. (However, Biya's failure to extend the mandate of the incumbent national assembly, which expired in early March, subsequently prompted criticism from opposition deputies.) Also in January Fru Ndi stated that the opposition would not stage demonstrations in support of demands that the government establish an independent electoral commission, in order to avert unrest prior to the elections. At the end of March, however, about 10 people, including three police officers, were killed when unidentified armed groups staged attacks against government and security buildings in Bamenda and other towns in the North-West Province; a curfew was imposed in the province and a number of people were subsequently detained in connection with the violence, which was generally attributed to members of the SCNC. In April the government announced that the legislative elections were to take place on 17 May.

In May 1997 about five people were killed in pre-election violence, which prompted the imposition of increased security measures, including the closure of the country's borders. The government ordered an inquiry into clashes which took place in the northern town of Rey Bouba between supporters of a UNDP candidate and followers of the local traditional leader (an RDPC member). The legislative elections, which were contested on 17 May by 46 political parties, were monitored by a Commonwealth observer mission; the poll was extended in parts of northern Cameroon, where voting had been delayed as a result of logistical difficulties. The announcement later that month of provisional election results (which attributed a large majority of seats to the RDPC) prompted claims from the opposition parties of widespread electoral malpractice. (The Commonwealth observer group also expressed general dissatisfaction with the election process.) Three people were killed in clashes between RDPC and SDF members in the South-West Province, where the election result was disputed by the two parties. In early June the supreme court (which had rejected most opposition appeals against RDPC victories) announced the official election results: the RDPC had secured 109 of the 180 seats in the legislature, while the SDF had obtained 43, the UNDP 13 and the UDC five seats; the Mouvement pour la jeunesse du Cameroun (MLJC), the UPC and the MDR obtained one seat each. On 3 August further polls were conducted in seven constituencies, where the results had been annulled, owing to alleged irregularities; the RDPC won all of the seats, thus increasing its level of representation in the national assembly to 116 seats. In mid-June the SDF announced that it had abandoned its earlier decision to boycott the national assembly.

In July 1997 it was reported that the former minister of public health, Titus Edzoa, who in April had resigned from the cabinet in order to contest the presidential election later that year, had been arrested and charged with embezzlement. Supporters of Edzoa claimed, however, that the leading RDPC politician was being detained in a 'torture centre'. In September it was announced that the presidential election would be held on 12

October. In mid-September Biya was officially selected as the RDPC presidential candidate. The leader of the MDP, Samuel Eboua, had announced his candidacy in the forthcoming election in July. In September, shortly after the announcement of the date of the election, the three major opposition parties, the SDF, UNDP and UDC, announced their intention to boycott all elections, including the imminent presidential election, in protest at the absence of any independent electoral commission; Hubert Kamgang's Union du peuple africain (UPA) also subsequently joined the boycott. A meeting planned for 7 October by the leaders of the parties involved in the boycott, at which they intended to explain the reasons for their actions, was banned by the authorities in Yaoundé.

The presidential election, held on 12 October 1997, was contested by seven candidates. While official sources asserted that a record 81.4% of the electorate participated in the election, opposition leaders claimed that, in fact, the abstention rate was higher than 80%, and denounced the poll as an 'electoral masquerade'. As anticipated, Biya was re-elected, obtaining a reported 92.6% of the votes cast. Of the other candidates, Henri Hogbe Nlend of the UPC secured 2.5% of the vote, while Samuel Eboua of the MDP won 2.4%. On 3 November Biya was formally inaugurated, beginning, in accordance with the revised constitution, a seven-year term in presidential office. However, the announcement of the new cabinet was not made until 7 December, following Biya's reappointment of Musonge as prime minister. As a result of negotiations between the RDPC and elements of the opposition following the election in October, the new government included members from four of Cameroon's approximately 150 political parties; the RDPC retained 45 of the 50 ministerial posts. Among the non-RDPC appointees included in the cabinet was Bello Bouba Maigari of the UNDP (unexpectedly appointed senior minister in charge of industrial and commercial development), one of several prominent figures to have boycotted the election in October; two other members of the UNDP were also appointed to the new government. Henri Hogbe Nlend was appointed minister of scientific and technical research. A number of perceived supporters of Edzoa were dismissed from the government. It was reported that, prior to the announcement of the new cabinet, Musonge had attempted, on behalf of the ruling RDPC, to persuade the SDF to enter into a coalition government, but that the SDF had declined to do so. Further negotiations between the RDPC and the SDF began in January 1998; on 15 February, however, following the failure of talks between the RDPC and the SDF (reportedly over the issue of the establishment of an independent national electoral commission), the SDF and the UDC announced their intention to form a common front of opposition.

On 24 December 1997 the journalist and editor, Pius Njawe, was arrested and charged with propagating false information, following the publication in his newspaper, *Le Messager*, of an article which suggested that Biya was in poor health. Njawe was subsequently fined and sentenced to two years' imprisonment (reduced on appeal to one year). Njawe subsequently received a presidential pardon and was released in October 1998.

In early February 1998 an estimated 10 people were killed in ethnic clashes between the Balikumbat and Bafanji communities in north-western Cameroon. Further violence broke out between the two communities a little over a month later, during which a number of people were injured and at least one was killed.

In July 1998 10 of the 43 SFD parliamentary deputies resigned from the party, in protest at the perceived tribalism and authoritarianism of its leadership. In October the SDF expelled its first national vice president, Soulaimane Mahamad, following the latter's criticism of Fru Ndi's authoritarian style of leadership. In January 1999, however, Fru Ndi announced that he was willing to engage in direct dialogue with President Biya. It was, however, alleged that Fru Ndi had announced this radical change of policy in the hope of securing a favourable verdict in his prosecution on charges of defaming a former SDF official, Basile Kamndoum. (In April Fru Ndi was found guilty, and was fined and given a three-year suspended sentence.) At the SDF party conference in April Fru Ndi was re-elected party leader by an overwhelming majority of delegates, despite accusations made by his opponent, Christian Tabessing, that he had presided over the disintegration of the SDF as a political force. The conference also voted not to enter into dialogue with the government until an independent electoral commission had been established. It also resolved to improve internal party discipline.

Meanwhile, in September 1998 it was reported that, following attacks on police premises, more than 40 anglophone Cameroonians, who were alleged to be secessionists campaigning for the independence of Southern Cameroon, were being detained without trial and tortured in Yaoundé. The opposition suggested, however, that the raids had been staged by government agents as a pretext for further suppression of demands for increased decentralization. In January 1999 the opposition condemned the government for the alleged marginalization of the anglophone minority, noting that only three of the 2,000 soldiers recently recruited by the armed forces were English-speaking. The trial of the alleged anglophone secessionists (the majority of whom had been arrested in 1997) began in June 1999. The defendants claimed that confessions that they were members of the separatist SCNC had been extracted under torture and threats of summary execution. The human rights organization Amnesty International later claimed that, prior to the start of the trial, several of the detainees had died in prison either because of torture or lack of medical care. In late August the accused formally denied all the charges against them, although several individuals admitted to being members of a cultural association linked to the SCNC. In October three of the defendants were sentenced to life imprisonment, others received lengthy prison sentences, while 29 were acquitted. Amnesty International and the United Nations Human Rights Committee both subsequently criticized Cameroon for its alleged failure to protect and to respect fundamental human rights.

In September 1999 Mounchipou Seydou was dismissed from his post as minister of posts and telecommunications and was subsequently arrested on charges of embezzlement of public funds. The government convened a meeting in November of the national commission on corruption (which had met only infrequently since its creation in 1997), at which senior government officials outlined strategies to combat corruption in their areas of responsibility. There was a cabinet reshuffle in March 2000, which was widely interpreted as a response to an escalation in urban crime (several foreign diplomats, including the ambassadors of the USA and the Netherlands had been attacked). All ministers linked to security matters were involved in the reshuffle, most notably the minister of territorial administration, Samson Ename, who was replaced by Ferdinand Kougou Edima, a former governor.

In late March 1999 247 people were left homeless when earth tremors and lava flows, caused by an eruption of Mt Cameroon, destroyed villages in South-West Province. The eruptions continued into early April, and gas masks were distributed to the population to avoid a repetition of a similar disaster in 1986, when 1,746 people died after a sudden discharge of toxic volcanic gases. In mid-April 1999 Biya visited the area and promised state assistance and compensation to those affected by the eruptions.

REGIONAL CONCERNS

During 1989–93 President Biya actively sought Cameroon's admission to the Commonwealth, which, following the government's agreement to comply with certain democratic conditions, was approved in 1993. Its membership took effect in November 1995. Apart from a border dispute with Nigeria, relations with neighbouring countries are generally harmonious.

The Bakassi Dispute

In June 1991 the Nigerian government claimed that Cameroon had annexed nine Nigerian fishing settlements, following a long-standing border dispute, based on a 1913 agreement between Germany and the United Kingdom that ceded the Bakassi peninsula in the Gulf of Guinea (then a region of strategic significance) to Cameroon. Subsequent attempts to negotiate the dispute achieved little progress, and further incursions by Cameroon were reported in November. In early January 1994 it was reported that members of the Cameroonian security forces had entered Nigeria and raided villages, killing several Nigerian nationals. Nigeria subsequently occupied the two nom-

inally Cameroonian islands of Diamant and Jabane in the Gulf of Guinea. Cameroon also dispatched troops to the region, although the two countries agreed to resume efforts to achieve a resolution of the dispute. In February the Cameroon government announced that it was to submit the matter to adjudication by the UN Security Council, the Organization of African Unity (OAU) and the International Court of Justice (ICJ). However, subsequent clashes between Nigerian and Cameroonian forces in the disputed region prompted fears of a full-scale conflict. Shortly afterwards, a French diplomatic and military mission arrived in Cameroon, in response to a request for military assistance from the Cameroon government under the bilateral defence agreement. In late March, following further negotiations between Cameroon and Nigeria, the Nigerian government proposed that a referendum be held to decide the future status of the contested areas. This was rejected by the Cameroon government. In the same month the OAU urged the withdrawal of troops from the disputed region; however Cameroon failed to obtain an official condemnation of Nigeria, and both governments indicated dissatisfaction with the resolution. In May two members of the Nigerian armed forces were killed in further clashes in the region. Later that month negotiations between the two nations, which were mediated by the Togolese government, resumed in Yaoundé. In September 10 members of the Cameroonian armed forces were killed in further confrontations.

In February 1996 renewed hostilities between Nigerian and Cameroonian forces in the Bakassi peninsula resulted in several casualties. Later that month, however, Cameroon and Nigeria agreed to refrain from further military action, and delegations from the two countries resumed discussions, with mediation by the Togolese president, in an attempt to resolve the dispute. In March the ICJ ruled that Cameroon had failed to provide sufficient evidence to substantiate its contention that Nigeria had instigated the border dispute, and ordered both nations to cease military operations in the region, to withdraw troops to former positions, and to co-operate with a UN investigative mission, which was to be dispatched to the area. In April, however, clashes continued, with each government accusing the other of initiating the attacks. Claims by Nigeria that the Cameroonian forces were supported by troops from France were denied by the French government. Diplomatic efforts to avoid further conflict increased; in May a delegation from Cameroon visited Nigeria, while the Nigerian president accepted an invitation to attend an OAU summit meeting (which was convened in Yaoundé in July). However, tension between the two countries increased prior to the OAU summit meeting, after the Nigerian government accused Cameroon of reinforcing its contingent in the Bakassi peninsula. In September both governments assured the UN investigative mission of their commitment to a peaceful settlement of the dispute. In December, however, the Nigerian authorities claimed that Cameroonian troops had resumed attacks in the region. In May 1997 the Cameroon government denied further Nigerian claims that it had initiated attacks. In the same month the UN requested that the Togolese government continue efforts to mediate in the dispute.

Renewed fighting between Cameroonian and Nigerian forces was reported in early December 1997. In late February 1998 seven Cameroonian soldiers were reportedly killed by the Nigerian forces when violence again flared between the two sides. It was suggested in the Cameroonian press that the violence represented an attempt on the part of the Nigerian authorities to influence the March hearings of the Bakassi dispute at the ICJ; a Nigerian military spokesman, however, denied that an attack had taken place. Accusations made in early February by the Nigerian authorities that Cameroon was massing troops close to the border in preparation for the launching of an attack were denied by the Cameroon government.

In March 1998, at the preliminary ICJ hearing on the dispute, Nigeria argued that the ICJ lacked jurisdiction in the matter. In June, however, the ICJ declared itself competent to examine the dispute; the final ruling was not expected for several months. In September Nigeria moved more troops and equipment into the peninsular in response to reports, denied by the authorities in Yaoundé, that Cameroon had massed troops in the area. In October further contention arose when Nigeria alleged that Cameroon had awarded a Canadian company a concession to prospect for petroleum in the disputed area. Cameroon insisted that the concession had been granted for three areas, none of which was in the Bakassi peninsula.

From late 1998 relations between the two countries began to improve, and in November 1998 the International Committee of the Red Cross organized a prisoner exchange between the two sides, in which 87 Cameroonians and 124 Nigerians were released. In April 1999 the president-elect of Nigeria, Gen. Obasanjo, visited Cameroon, the first such visit since the beginning of the border conflict in 1994, and in May 1999 the outgoing

Nigerian head of state, Gen. Abdulsalami Abubakar, held further talks with Biya in Yaoundé. The two countries were reported to have agreed to resolve the dispute 'in a fraternal way'. It was announced, however, that the proceedings before the ICJ were to continue, and in late May Nigeria filed its legal defence. In July the ICJ ruled that it would allow counter-claims from Nigeria relating to the apportioning of responsibility for border incidents; the counter-claims were to be examined alongside Cameroonian complaints.

Economy

EDITH HODGKINSON

From independence until the mid-1980s Cameroon's record was one of strengthening, diversified economic growth. This was based on a flourishing agricultural sector, with a range of export and food crops (food self-sufficiency was attained relatively early), and the development of petroleum from the late 1970s, and was underpinned by the moderate, centrist economic policies pursued by successive governments. In the first half of the 1980s economic growth averaged 7%–8% annually (more than double the annual average in the previous two decades).

The situation deteriorated sharply, however, after the steep decline in the international price for petroleum in 1986, although the effects were initially limited by the government's policy of drawing on accumulated revenue from sales of petroleum in order to sustain the level of investment expenditure and imports. Nevertheless, owing to sustained weakness in international prices for petroleum and for the country's major cash crops, these funds were depleted by the end of the decade, and the Biya government was obliged to introduce austerity programmes, involving reductions in both current and capital expenditure. Consequently, the economy contracted sharply, with the rate of decline in real gross domestic product (GDP) reaching 10.4% in the year ending 30 June 1988, but easing to about 2% per year in 1988/89 and 1989/90. In this situation, and with the support of loans from the World Bank, the African Development Bank (ADB) and France, Cameroon undertook an extensive, five-year programme of economic restructuring in 1989/90. This entailed the reform of the country's parastatal organizations (through the liquidation of unprofitable enterprises and the transfer to private ownership of others) and of the cumbersome and inefficient administrative structure. Specifically, the role of the national agricultural marketing board, the Office national de commercialisation des produits de base (ONCPB), was reduced, and responsibility for marketing was gradually transferred to the private sector. The implementation of reforms was, however, held back by political instability and the widespread corruption within the civil service. Thus GDP continued to decline by an average of about 4% per year between 1990/91 and 1993/94.

Economic decline was arrested by the devaluation of the CFA franc in January 1994, which doubled the local currency value of petroleum and other commodity exports, stimulating an increase in supply. Stronger prices for agricultural commodities on the international market provided further assistance. GDP rose by 3.3% in 1994/95, and growth was maintained at 4%–5% per year throughout the following four years, representing a steady improvement in per caput income. The economy's dependence on export crops has intensified, owing to the adverse effects on the manufacturing and services sectors of the sharp reduction in real income following devaluation, and the stagnation in petroleum output in the 1990s. Cameroon's prospects for sustained recovery in the long term are therefore reliant on continuing structural reform, to improve resource allocation and to ensure the maintenance of debt-relief on its substantial external debt.

AGRICULTURE

Although the contribution of agriculture, forestry and fishing to Cameroon's GDP declined as the petroleum sector developed, from 32% in the year 1978/79 to 21% in 1984/85, it has gained ground once more as oil output has contracted, registering a

two-fifths share in the late 1990s. Its dominance in employment is even more marked, with the sector accounting for two-thirds of the labour force in the same year. Small-scale farmers dominate agricultural export production with the exception of rubber and palm oil. By contrast, timber production remains the sphere of large foreign firms, despite efforts to enhance Cameroonian participation.

The sector is well-diversified, reflecting the country's varied ecology. Coffee is cultivated on some 400,000 ha, predominantly in the west and south. Nine-tenths of the coffee crop is robusta. Output has fluctuated widely in recent years, in response to climatic and vegetative circumstances and trends in producer prices. Thus, the dramatic reduction in the robusta price in 1989/90 prompted a decline in its production from 121,857 metric tons in 1988/89 to 76,000 tons. After recovering in subsequent years, it fell to a low of 48,000 tons in 1992/93. Output of cocoa, grown on around 350,000 ha, demonstrated a similar decline since the producer price was reduced in 1989/90. Both coffee and cocoa yields suffered as a result of the failure of replanting programmes to keep pace with the ageing of plantations. The liberalization of marketing and the abandonment of the producer price system, as well as the impact of devaluation, resulted in a recovery in output by the late 1990s. Production of coffee rose in most years, to reach 110,000 tons by 1998/99—around a tenth below its peak in 1988/89. Cocoa's improvement has been more marked, with the crop at a record 148,000 tons in 1998/99. Cameroon thus remains a significant world producer of cocoa, ranking sixth in recent years. Structural change has had an even more pronounced impact in the banana sector,-where output had declined from more than 100,000 tons in the early 1960s to about two-thirds of this level in the early 1980s. Following a major restructuring of the sector, which began in the late 1980s, and the transfer to the private sector of the state-owned enterprise, Organisation camerounaise de banane, output has increased sharply, reaching an average of 240,000 tons per year in 1995/96–1997/98. Bananas are therefore a leading agricultural export. The sector's prospects have dimmed somewhat since the ruling by the World Trade Organization in 1997 (upheld on appeal) against the banana quota scheme operated by the European Union (EU), of which Cameroon is a beneficiary.

Cotton production, which is concentrated in the north, recovered from the drought of the late 1970s and early 1980s, and reached a record 165,400 metric tons of unginned (seed) cotton in 1988/89. Production declined in subsequent years, in response to weaker world prices. Devaluation, which permitted a 44% increase in the producer price for the 1994/95 crop, gave a big boost to output, which rose in each year to reach 237,000 tons in 1997/98. Output of palm oil was averaging 100,000 tons per year in the mid-1990s; however, the product is not competitive on world markets, and production was down to an estimated 76,000 tons in 1997/98. Rubber, in contrast, has good prospects, with yields competing with those of the major Asian producers. After a decline in the early 1990s, output exceeded the previous high of 1989/90, at 55,500 tons in 1994/95, and was estimated at 87,000 tons in 1996/97.

Cameroon's food production has been advancing at a higher rate than population growth, and the country is generally self-sufficient. In 1997/98 output of millet and sorghum reached 371,000 metric tons, while maize production amounted to some

789,000 tons. The annual harvest of paddy rice, which is grown under both traditional and modern methods, had increased from only 15,000 tons in 1979/80 to 107,400 tons in 1984/85, reflecting the government's priority of achieving self-sufficiency in this cereal. Output has since fluctuated fairly widely, mainly in response to drought, and was down to an average 55,000 tons a year in the late 1990s. Nevertheless the long-term target for annual rice production remains 280,000 tons. Commercial production of sugar began in 1966 and averaged some 55,000 tons per year in the mid-1990s. Livestock, mainly raised by traditional methods, makes a significant contribution to the food supply. In mid-1998 the national herds were assessed by the government at 4.8m. cattle, 5.6m. sheep and goats, and 1.2m. pigs, while commercial poultry farms had an estimated 31m. birds. The development of the fisheries industry has been constrained by the relatively small area available for exploitation (because of boundary disputes and the presence of the offshore island of Bioko, part of Equatorial Guinea) and the poor level of fish stocks in these waters. In 1997 the total catch was estimated at some 89,000 tons by the FAO, with industrial fishing accounting for less than one-tenth of the total.

Almost half of the country is covered by forest, but an inadequate transport system has impeded the development of this sector, and only around one third of the area has been exploited. Devaluation has been a spur to output, which has risen from 2.4m. cu m in the early 1990s to an estimated 3.6m. cu m in 1997/98. Logs and lumber are a significant export, earning US $127m. in 1997/98—representing 11% of total export receipts. The government has tried to increase the value added in this sector, with a law introduced in 1993 requiring 70% of timber production to be locally processed, and from July 1999 the export of logs was banned. However, corruption (particularly in the award of forestry concessions) has undermined such regulations, and there is considerable concern about the environmental impact of inadequately controlled and unsustainably rapid exploitation.

MINING AND POWER

In 1976 Elf, the French petroleum company, established a commercial oilfield in shallow water near the Nigerian border, and four fields came on stream in 1977–78. Production of crude petroleum reached a peak of 9.16m. metric tons in 1985, but then declined in each subsequent year, to 5.2m. tons in 1995/96. A recovery was recorded, in response to improved incentives for the development of marginal fields, to 5.9m. tons in 1997/98. However, output declined in 1998/99, in part owing to the sharp fall in world prices, to 5.5m. tons. With total recoverable oil reserves estimated at 263m. barrels at the beginning of 1998, equivalent to 6–7 years' output, Cameroon would cease to be a significant exporter of oil early in the next decade. A consortium involving the US company, Exxon, Petronas of Malaysia and Chevron of the USA, plans to construct a 1,000-km pipeline to transport oil from the Doba basin in southern Chad to the southern Cameroonian port of Kribi. Royalties from the pipeline, which was scheduled to be operational by the year 2000, were expected partially to offset the decline in direct revenue from petroleum; the project, however, raised concerns amongst campaigners for the protection of the environment, and production from the Doba field is not expected to start before 2005. In June 2000, the World Bank approved a loan of US $39.5m. to Chad and $53.4m. to Cameroon to support the construction of the pipeline. Natural gas reserves, officially estimated at over 200,000m. cu m, are still unexploited, although feasibility studies have begun on developing the Sanaga Sud offshore gasfield to fuel a power plant.

Two major bauxite deposits, at Minim Martap (900m. metric tons) and Ngoundal (200m. tons), have also yet to be exploited, although their development would enable the Edéa smelter, which was dependent on imports of bauxite from Guinea, to be supplied locally. Deposits of iron ore near Kribi also remain unexploited, and uranium reserves totalling up to 10,000 tons have been identified, but not developed, owing to low international prices. There is potential for gold mining, but so far all operations remain small-scale. Extensive limestone deposits near Garoua supply clinker and cement plants.

Hydroelectricity meets 98% of the country's electricity demand: heavy industry is the major consumer, with the

aluminium plant taking nearly 50% of the total generation. The chief installations are at Edéa (total capacity 263 MW) and at Song-Loulou (total capacity 384 MW). These stations supply the network linking Yaoundé, Edéa, Douala and the west. The other major network supplies the north and draws principally on the 72-MW hydroelectric station at Lagdo. There is considerable, still unharnessed, potential on the Sanaga river.

MANUFACTURING

Manufacturing accounts for only around one-tenth of GDP. The sector is dominated by the processing of raw materials, and the assembly of imported raw materials and components. It is therefore not deeply integrated into the economic structure and has limited linkage effects. Efforts to deepen linkages with a number of projects initiated at the beginning of the 1980s were not generally successful. An integrated pulp and paper mill was developed at Edéa but was in operation for only five years, closing down in 1986 after suffering heavy losses. A petroleum refinery began production at Cap Limboh in 1981. Its initial annual capacity was increased to 2m. tons, but output declined to 883,000 tons, owing to competition from illicit imports from Nigeria. Although an industrial free zone, which offers concessions for energy-intensive operations, was established on 300 ha in Douala in 1991, interest remained limited, owing to the country's economic and political crisis. Local manufacturing in general has been adversely affected by the widespread illicit trade in Nigerian goods, resulting from the strong CFA franc; the currency devaluation of 1994 provided only a temporary respite.

The bulk of manufacturing industry is of post-independence origin. The government gave priority to industrial development aimed at national and regional markets as a means of accelerating growth. To this end, extensive tax and financing incentives were made available, while the state took substantial shareholdings in major ventures, held through the Société nationale d'investissement du Cameroun (SNI). The economic crisis in the 1980s prompted a reversal in government policies, with a programme for the privatization of state-owned companies and a tightening up or liquidation of those running at a loss. However, resistance from adversely affected interests meant that little progress was made until late 1990, when 15 companies were transferred to the private sector. Other parastatal enterprises were liquidated, and those remaining under the aegis of the state, such as the electricity corporation, SONEL, were obliged to sign performance contracts with the government as part of the overall structural adjustment programme. Privatization continued in subsequent years, although the programme was constantly behind target, owing, in part, to the poor financial situation of the enterprises. Following renewed pressure from its multilateral creditors, the government has expanded the programme since mid-1994; and by early 2000 some major disposals had been effected; the shipping line, the rubber producer, the state railway and the sugar and palm oil companies. Still pending were the water and electricity utilities, as well as the largest single state enterprise, the Cameroon Development Corpn, which has interests in rubber, palm oil, bananas and tea.

TRANSPORT

The transport infrastructure overall suffers from inadequate investment and maintenance. The rail network, totalling some 1,104 km, forms the most important component. The main line is the 885-km 'Transcameroon', from Douala to Ngaoundéré. There are plans to connect the line with the proposed new port at Grand Batanga (see below) and, in the long term, to construct a 1,000 km-line from Kribi to the Central African Republic (CAR).

The road network totals some 49,300 km, of which an estimated 4,100 km are paved. Roads in the north have been improved to give access to the Ngaoundéré rail-head, and there are long-term plans to upgrade the east-west road linking Nigeria with the CAR. In recent years, however, development has been impeded by the economic crisis.

Cameroon has seaports at Douala-Bonabéri, Kribi and Limbe-Tiko (although the latter is now almost completely unuseable), and a river port at Garoua. Total traffic handled by Doula-Bonabéri in 1997/98 was 5.5m. tons, accounting for nearly all port activity. Feasibility studies have been conducted for deep-water ports at Cap Limboh (near Limbe and the oil refinery) and Grand Batanga, south of the existing port handling wood and minerals at Kribi. The latter is dependent on the exploitation of the offshore gas reserve and iron ore reserves, neither of which seems likely in the near future.

The poor state of the road network has encouraged the development of internal air travel and of small domestic airports. Cameroon Airlines—75% owned by the government and 25% by Air France, but scheduled for privatization—has provided domestic flights and services to Africa and Europe since Cameroon's withdrawal from Air Afrique in 1971. There are international airports at Douala, Garoua and Yaoundé.

FINANCE

Revenue from petroleum production profoundly changed the country's fiscal position, and allowed a rapid rise in both current and capital spending during the early 1980s. The situation was transformed by the collapse of international oil prices in 1986, which led to diminished petroleum royalties, and was followed by a general contraction in the economy and—in the early 1990s—a politically motivated refusal to pay taxes. Although the impact of lower oil revenues was initially cushioned by drawing on the accumulated oil revenue held in an extrabudgetary account, by 1990/91 the fiscal deficit had risen to the equivalent of 13.4% of GDP. To secure the agreement of international creditors to restructure its foreign debt, the burden of which had risen because of falling oil export earnings, and to provide new capital funding, the government had to impose tight controls on spending at the same time as it expanded its tax take. Its record was initially very patchy, with the deficit trimmed to 6.3% of GDP by 1992/93, then increased to 9.2% in 1993/94, but performance has since improved, to within the range 1%–2% (after grants) in 1995/96–1997/98. This was due to a sharp pruning in the salary bill, which was particularly marked in 1993/94 when it fell by a quarter because of early retirements and a freeze on recruitment, and a steady improvement in non-oil tax receipts, notably through the restoration in 1994/95 of export taxes on agro-industrial products (made feasible by the currency's devaluation) and an increase and extension of the sales tax. The privatization or liquidation of parastatal companies also contributed to reducing the fiscal imbalance, and the government was aiming to keep the overall budget deficit to below 3% of GDP in 1999/2000 and 2000/01, with revenue increased by the introduction of value-added tax in 1999 and by other measures to broaden the tax base.

The financial sector is relatively sophisticated; however, the economic crisis of the late 1980s affected the sector rapidly and severely, as the government withdrew its reserves with the commercial banks and private companies supplying the public sector suffered from accumulating arrears. By mid-1987 most commercial banks were technically insolvent. An important element of the structural adjustment programme was a restructuring of the financial sector, with banks being liquidated or, in a few cases, merging. The Banque internationale pour le commerce et l'industrie du Cameroun was closed down in 1996 and its assets transferred to a new bank, under French management, which was scheduled for privatization by mid-2000. The commercial banking sector had returned to profit by mid-1997, and later in that year two new commercial banks opened up, the Commercial Bank of Cameroon and Citicorp of Cameroon.

FOREIGN TRADE AND AID

The emergence of petroleum as a leading export in the late 1970s (crude oil accounted for 55% of export earnings in 1985) resulted in a considerable and growing surplus on foreign trade, despite significant increases in the level of import spending.

Although petroleum earnings declined sharply in the late 1980s, trade remained in substantial surplus, sustained by earnings from agricultural exports. However, export coverage of imports narrowed from the 200% recorded in 1985 to an average of 140% by the late 1990s.

The high level of earnings from the petroleum sector during the early 1980s enabled development expenditure to be financed without a substantial increase in the foreign debt. Servicing of the foreign debt was thus manageable, representing about 15% of export earnings in most years during the first half of the decade. From 1986, however, there was a marked deterioration, owing to the sharp decline in revenue from the petroleum sector, while debt rose by over a quarter in that year. The combination of increasing debt and slowing export growth resulted in a debt-servicing ratio of 31% by 1988, which was clearly unsustainable. The current account of the balance of payments showed the strain, with the endemic deficit rising to a record US $893m. in 1987. Consequently, in May 1989, following the negotiation of agreements with the IMF on stand-by and compensatory credits, and in the context of continuing budgetary restraint, Cameroon obtained rescheduling over a period of 10 years of $435m. in liabilities to official creditors in the 'Paris Club'. The debt-servicing ratio was consequently reduced to 16.3% in 1989, and remained at around this level for the following three years. However, this rate represented debt service paid—not that falling due. With arrears steadily building up, another, more sizeable ($922m.) rescheduling of 'Paris Club' debt was negotiated in 1992. As the January 1994 devaluation of the CFA franc doubled overnight the local currency value of the foreign debt, special debt relief measures were agreed, with another rescheduling (of $1,240m.) and the write-off by France of $534m.

With foreign debt inexorably rising (by the end of 1995 it stood at US $9,346m., equivalent to 126% of GNP) and the urgent necessity of holding down payments, Cameroon has been obliged to maintain good relations with the IMF and World Bank, to ensure continuing accommodation by its bilateral official creditors. Relations have, however, proved difficult and disbursements have repeatedly been suspended as the government was deemed not to have complied with performance criteria. Thus IMF support accorded in the wake of the 1994 currency devaluation was suspended within three months. A standby credit, agreed with the IMF in September 1995, was rapidly converted to a non-disbursing IMF-monitored programme, and a concomitant 'Paris Club' rescheduling agreement suspended. In August 1997, however, with the new government under Peter Mafany Musonge showing convincing commitment to structural reform, the IMF extended a $220m. enhanced structural adjustment facility (ESAF), which paved the way for a major new debt rescheduling deal in October with the 'Paris Club' under 'Naples' terms and valued at some $2,000m. over a three-year period. As a result Cameroon cleared all its arrears on previously deferred debt to 'Paris Club' creditors and was up to date on non-rescheduled debt. While the external debt continued to rise, to $9,763m. by the end of 1997, still in excess of total GNP in that year, the debt service ratio was down to a more manageable 12.9%. The current-account deficit, meanwhile, was estimated to have fallen below $100m. in 1997/98.

Against this background Cameroon looked to a recovery in inflows of development assistance, which had been falling in most years since 1994, when they had reached a peak of US $730.3m. (net of repayment) after the currency devaluation had made Cameroon—formerly a middle-income country—eligible for multilateral funds on concessional terms. In 1998 net inflows were $423.6m. However, the return to sustained economic growth, on the basis of its diversified economy, will ease Cameroon's relatively limited dependence on foreign aid.

Statistical Survey

Source (unless otherwise stated): Direction de la Prévision, Ministère de l'Economie et des Finances, BP 18, Yaoundé; tel. 23-40-40; fax 23-21-50.

Area and Population

AREA, POPULATION AND DENSITY

Area (sq km)	475,442*
Population (census results)	
9 April 1976†	7,663,246
9 April 1987	
Males	5,162,878
Females	5,330,777
Total	10,493,655
Population (official estimates at mid-year)	
1997	14,044,000
1998	14,439,000
1999	14,859,000
Density (per sq km) at mid-1999 . . .	31.3

* 183,569 sq miles.
† Including an adjustment for underenumeration, estimated at 7.4%. The enumerated total was 7,090,115.

PROVINCES (population at 1987 census)

	Urban	Rural	Total
Centre	877,481	774,119	1,651,600
Littoral	1,093,323	259,510	1,352,833
West	431,337	908,454	1,339,791
South-West	258,940	579,102	838,042
North-West	271,114	966,234	1,237,348
North	234,572	597,593	832,165
East	152,787	364,411	517,198
South	104,023	269,775	373,798
Adamaoua	178,644	316,541	495,185
Far North	366,698	1,488,997	1,855,695
Total	3,968,919	6,524,736	10,493,655

PRINCIPAL TOWNS (population at 1987 census)

Douala . . .	810,000	Bamenda . . .	110,000
Yaoundé (capital) .	649,000	Nkongsamba . .	85,420
Garoua . . .	142,000	Kumba . . .	70,112
Maroua . . .	123,000	Limbé . . .	44,561
Bafoussam. . .	113,000		

1999 (estimated population, '000): Douala 1,448.3; Yaoundé 1,372.8 (Source: MINPAT, *Indicateurs démographiques sur le Cameroun*).

BIRTHS AND DEATHS (official estimates, annual averages)

	1987–92	1993–97	1998–2000
Birth rate (per 1,000). . . .	41.7	39.7	38.2
Death rate (per 1,000) . .	12.8	11.4	10.1

Expectation of life (official estimates, years at birth, 1998–2000): 59.0 (males 56.7; females 61.3).

Source: MINPAT, *Indicateurs démographiques sur le Cameroun*.

ECONOMICALLY ACTIVE POPULATION
(official estimates, persons aged six years and over, mid-1985)

	Males	Females	Total
Agriculture, hunting, forestry and fishing	1,574,946	1,325,925	2,900,871
Mining and quarrying . .	1,693	100	1,793
Manufacturing	137,671	36,827	174,498
Electricity, gas and water . .	3,373	149	3,522
Construction	65,666	1,018	66,684
Trade, restaurants and hotels .	115,269	38,745	154,014
Transport, storage and communications . .	50,664	1,024	51,688
Financing, insurance, real estate and business services .	7,447	562	8,009
Community, social and personal services . .	255,076	37,846	292,922
Activities not adequately defined .	18,515	17,444	35,959
Total in employment . . .	2,230,320	1,459,640	3,689,960
Unemployed	180,016	47,659	227,675
Total labour force . . .	2,410,336	1,507,299	3,917,635

Source: ILO, *Yearbook of Labour Statistics*.

Mid-1998 (estimates in '000): Agriculture, etc. 3,585; Total labour force 5,816 (Source: FAO, *Production Yearbook*).

Agriculture

PRINCIPAL CROPS ('000 metric tons)

	1996	1997	1998
Rice (paddy)	54	55†	55†
Maize	750	600†	600†
Millet	71	71†	71†
Sorghum	439	400*	500*
Potatoes	35	35†	35†
Sweet potatoes† . . .	250	250	220
Cassava (Manioc)† . . .	1,700	1,700	1,500
Yams†	130	130	130
Other roots and tubers . .	600	600†	550†
Dry beans†	95	91	91
Groundnuts (in shell). . .	171	90*	170*
Sesame seed† . . .	16	16	16
Cottonseed	72*	48*	80†
Palm kernels* . . .	62	58	58
Tomatoes	60	60†	60†
Onions (dry)	20	20†	20†
Other vegetables . . .	413	423†	433†
Sugar cane†	1,350	1,350	1,350
Avocados†	45	45	45
Pineapples	48	48†	48†
Bananas	986	986†	986†
Plantains†	1,000	1,030	1,030
Other fruit	105	105†	105†
Coffee (green)	53	92*	102*
Cocoa beans	126	127*	130*
Tea (made)	4	4†	4†
Tobacco (leaves) . . .	2	2†	2†
Cotton lint	79	75*	61*
Natural rubber	53	54†	54†

* Unofficial figure(s).   † FAO estimate(s).

Source: FAO, *Production Yearbook*.

LIVESTOCK (FAO estimates, '000 head, year ending September)

	1996	1997	1998
Horses	15	15	15
Asses	36	36	36
Cattle	5,500	5,700	5,900
Pigs	1,410	1,410	1,410
Sheep	3,800	3,800	3,800
Goats	3,800	3,800	3,800

Poultry (FAO estimates, million): 20 in 1996; 20 in 1997; 20 in 1998.

Source: FAO, *Production Yearbook.*

LIVESTOCK PRODUCTS (FAO estimates, '000 metric tons)

	1996	1997	1998
Beef and veal	85	88	90
Mutton and lamb	16	16	16
Goat meat	14	14	14
Pig meat	18	18	18
Poultry meat	20	20	20
Other meat	47	46	46
Cows' milk	125	125	125
Sheep's milk	17	17	17
Goats' milk	42	42	42
Poultry eggs	13	13	13
Honey	3	3	3
Cattle hides	12	13	13
Sheepskins	3	3	3
Goatskins	1	1	1

Source: FAO, *Production Yearbook.*

Forestry

ROUNDWOOD REMOVALS ('000 cubic metres, excl. bark)

	1995	1996	1997
Sawlogs, veneer logs and logs for sleepers	2,447	2,447	2,447
Other industrial wood	889	913	939
Fuel wood	12,335	12,648	12,970
Total	15,671	16,008	16,356

Source: FAO, *Yearbook of Forest Products.*

SAWNWOOD PRODUCTION
(FAO estimates, '000 cubic metres, incl. railway sleepers)

	1995	1996	1997
Total (all broadleaved)	1,400	1,400	1,400

Source: FAO, *Yearbook of Forest Products.*

Fishing

('000 metric tons, live weight)

	1995	1996	1997*
Freshwater fishes*	21.0	23.0	25.0
Croakers and drums	10.8	10.5	10.5
Threadfins and tasselfishes	2.2	2.0	2.0
Sardinellas	24.0	24.0	24.0
Bonga shad	24.0	24.0	24.0
Other marine fishes (incl. unspecified)	3.2	3.0	3.1
Total fish*	85.2	86.5	88.5
Crustaceans and molluscs	0.5	0.5	0.5
Total catch*	85.7	87.0	89.0

* FAO estimates.

Source: FAO, *Yearbook of Fishery Statistics.*

Mining

	1994	1995	1996
Crude petroleum ('000 metric tons)	5,809	5,080*	n.a.
Tin ore (metric tons)†	2	2	1
Gold (kilograms)†	560	1,000	1,000

* Estimate.

† Estimates of metal content (data from the US Bureau of Mines).

Source: UN, *Industrial Commodity Statistics Yearbook.*

Crude petroleum (estimate, million barrels): 43.8 in 1998/99 (Source: Société Nationale des Hydrocarbures).

Industry

SELECTED PRODUCTS ('000 metric tons, unless otherwise indicated)

	1993	1994	1995
Palm oil*	123	125	130
Raw sugar*	57	58	48
Veneer sheets ('000 cu metres)	31	31	31
Plywood ('000 cu metres)	43	43	43
Paper and paperboard	5	5	5
Aviation gasoline†	14	14	15
Jet fuels†	9	9	10
Motor spirit (petrol)	414	296	298†
Kerosene	203†	245	243†
Gas-diesel (distillate fuel) oil	283†	287	288†
Residual fuel oils†	130	135	153
Lubricating oils†	27	28	38
Petroleum bitumen (asphalt)†	9	10	10
Liquefied petroleum gas†	21	20	21
Cement	620‡	620‡	522
Aluminium (unwrought)	86.5§	81.1§	71.4
Electric energy (million kWh)†	2,731	2,740	2,746

1996 ('000 metric tons, unless otherwise indicated): Palm oil* 161; Raw sugar* 50 (unofficial figure); Veneer sheets ('000 cu metres) 31; Plywood ('000 cu metres) 43; Paper and paperboard 5; Aluminium (unwrought) 82.3§.
1997 ('000 metric tons): Palm oil* 135 (unofficial estimate); Raw sugar* 50 (unofficial figure).
1998 ('000 metric tons): Palm oil* 160 (FAO estimate); Raw sugar* 54 (unofficial figure).

* Data from the FAO.

† Provisional or estimated figure(s).

‡ Data from the US Bureau of Mines.

§ Data from *World Metal Statistics* (London).

Sources: UN, *Industrial Commodity Statistics Yearbook*; FAO, *Production Yearbook.*

Finance

CURRENCY AND EXCHANGE RATES

Monetary Units
100 centimes = 1 franc de la Coopération financière en Afrique central (CFA).

Sterling, Dollar and Euro Equivalents (28 April 2000)
£1 sterling = 1,132.20 francs CFA;
US $1 = 722.02 francs CFA;
€1 = 655.96 francs CFA;
10,000 francs CFA = £8.832 = $13.850 = €15.245.

Average Exchange Rate (francs CFA per US $)
1997   583.67
1998   589.95
1999   615.70

Note: An exchange rate of 1 French franc = 50 francs CFA, established in 1948, remained in force until January 1994, when the CFA franc was devalued by 50%, with the exchange rate adjusted to 1 French franc = 100 francs CFA. This relationship to French currency remained in effect with the introduction of the euro on 1 January 1999. From that date, accordingly, a fixed exchange rate of €1 = 655.957 francs CFA has been in operation.

BUDGET ('000 million francs CFA, year ending 30 June)

Revenue	1995/96	1996/97	1997/98
Oil revenue	142.8	204.3	204.4
National oil company's contributions . . .	108.9	187.3	165.8
Profit taxes	33.9	17.0	38.6
Non-oil revenue . . .	512.2	563.8	630.4
Tax revenue	450.1	486.7	563.8
Taxes on income and profits .	65.1	101.2	114.6
Individual income taxes .	35.5	35.0	44.3
Wages and salaries .	18.4	17.6	22.7
Progressive surcharge .	17.1	17.4	21.6
Profit taxes	29.5	35.0	44.7
Taxes on goods and services .	209.0	200.0	248.0
Domestic taxes . . .	128.5	100.1	144.0
Turnover taxes . .	90.4	83.5	96.7
Excise taxes . . .	17.6	16.6	21.7
Taxes collected by customs .	80.5	99.9	104.0
Turnover taxes . .	63.5	73.4	102.8
Excise taxes . . .	1.4	1.2	1.2
Excise tax on petroleum products	50.0	58.1	58.4
Taxes on international trade .	126.0	127.4	142.8
Import duties . . .	72.1	75.1	94.4
Export duties . . .	51.2	47.6	43.1
Non-tax revenue . . .	62.1	77.1	66.6
Privatization proceeds . .	1.4	22.4	1.0
Total	**655.0**	**768.1**	**834.8**

Expenditure*	1994/95	1995/96	1996/97
General government services . .	72.9	52.9	60.1
Defence	57.9	57.8	57.3
Public order and justice . .	2.9	29.8	46.9
Education	78.2	95.2	93.6
Health	21.0	23.9	30.1
Social security . . .	2.7	3.3	4.0
Housing and community affairs .	9.9	7.1	11.1
Recreational and cultural affairs .	5.3	5.7	7.2
Economic affairs and services .	415.3	458.0	482.8
Energy and mining . . .	2.2	2.4	3.0
Agriculture, forestry and fishing	26.1	29.2	41.2
Public works, transport and communications . . .	37.5	35.7	48.7
Other economic services . .	349.5	390.7	389.9
Interest on public debt . .	262.0	302.0	299.0
Total	**666.0**	**733.9**	**793.0**
Current	618.6	690.5	718.6
Capital	47.4	43.5	74.4

* Excluding adjustment for changes in payments arrears.

1997/98 ('000 million francs CFA, year ending 30 June): Total expenditure 936.9 (Current 783.6, Capital 153.3.)

Sources: IMF, *Cameroon: Statistical Appendix* (March 1998); IMF, *Cameroon: Selected Issues and Statistical Appendix* (May 1999).

INTERNATIONAL RESERVES
(US $ million, excluding gold, at 31 December)

	1996	1997	1998
Gold*	11.04	8.72	8.61
IMF special drawing rights . .	0.16	—	0.02
Reserve position in IMF .	0.53	0.55	0.63
Foreign exchange . . .	2.08	0.31	0.64
Total	**13.81**	**9.58**	**9.90**

* Valued at market-related prices.
Source: IMF, *International Financial Statistics*.

MONEY SUPPLY ('000 million francs CFA at 31 December)

	1997	1998	1999
Currency outside banks . .	180.28	205.76	237.40
Demand deposits at deposit money banks	237.72	271.06	294.49
Total money (incl. others) . .	**423.90**	**485.29**	**537.73**

Source: IMF, *International Financial Statistics*.

COST OF LIVING
(Consumer Price Index for Africans in Yaoundé; base: 1995 = 100)

	1996	1997	1998
All items	104.7	106.3	105.9

Source: IMF, *International Financial Statistics*.

NATIONAL ACCOUNTS
('000 million francs CFA at current prices, year ending 30 June)
National Income and Product

	1986/87	1987/88	1988/89
Compensation of employees .	1,142.4	1,091.2	1,055.1
Operating surplus . . .	2,197.7	2,003.0	1,934.5
Domestic factor incomes .	**3,340.1**	**3,094.3**	**2,989.7**
Consumption of fixed capital . .	190.8	232.6	230.4
Gross domestic product (GDP) at factor cost	**3,530.9**	**3,326.9**	**3,220.1**
Indirect taxes	430.2	337.9	299.3
Less Subsidies	39.2	20.2	6.3
GDP in purchasers' values . .	**3,921.9**	**3,644.5**	**3,513.0**
Factor income received from abroad	5.3	3.4	−121.0
Less Factor income paid abroad .	88.1	103.5	
Gross national product . .	**3,839.1**	**3,544.5**	**3,392.0**
Less Consumption of fixed capital .	190.8	232.6	230.4
National income in market prices	**3,648.4**	**3,311.9**	**3,161.6**
Other current transfers received from abroad	13.1	8.9	−60.0
Less Other current transfers paid abroad	57.0	82.8	
National disposable income .	**3,604.5**	**3,238.0**	**3,101.6**

Source: UN, *National Accounts Statistics*.

Expenditure on the Gross Domestic Product

	1995/96	1996/97	1997/98*
Government final consumption expenditure	386.0	405.8	480.4
Private final consumption expenditure	3,313.6	3,510.8	3,701.3
Gross capital formation . .	702.0	798.0	963.6
Total domestic expenditure .	**4,401.6**	**4,714.6**	**5,145.3**
Exports of goods and services . .	1,106.0	1,322.1	1,405.3
Less Imports of goods and services	937.0	1,104.4	1,310.6
GDP in purchasers' values . .	**4,570.7**	**4,932.3**	**5,240.0**
GDP at constant 1989/90 prices	**3,204.0**	**3,367.4**	**3,537.5**

* Estimates.
Source: IMF, *Cameroon: Selected Issues and Statistical Appendix* (May 1999).

Gross Domestic Product by Economic Activity

	1995/96	1996/97	1997/98*
Agriculture, hunting, forestry and fishing	1,835.9	2,018.0	2,158.9
Mining and quarrying . . .	333.5	315.4	288.4
Manufacturing	452.9	506.5	544.8
Electricity, gas and water . .	73.4	75.4	78.4
Construction	146.7	162.6	188.7
Services	1,600.2	1,716.3	1,828.9
GDP at factor cost . . .	**4,442.6**	**4,794.2**	**5,088.1**
Indirect taxes, *less* subsidies . .	128.1	138.1	151.9
GDP in purchasers' values . .	**4,570.7**	**4,932.3**	**5,240.0**

* Estimates.
Source: IMF, *Cameroon: Selected Issues and Statistical Appendix* (May 1999).

CAMEROON

CAMEROON

CAMEROON

BALANCE OF PAYMENTS (million francs CFA, year ending 30 June)

	1995/96	1996/97	1997/98*
Exports of goods f.o.b.	883,800	1,065,000	1,124,400
Imports of goods f.o.b.	−602,400	−729,000	−827,400
Trade balance	281,300	336,100	297,000
Services and other income (net)	−408,400	−448,000	−484,800
Balance on goods, services and income	−127,100	−111,900	−187,800
Transfers (net)	17,200	46,800	55,200
Current balance	−109,800	−65,100	−132,600
Long-term capital (net)	−217,600	−191,300	−27,400
Short-term capital (net)	300	−3,200	−42,900
Net errors and omissions	900	5,600	—
Overall balance	−326,300	−254,000	−203,000

* Estimates.

Source: IMF, *Cameroon: Selected Issues and Statistical Appendix* (May 1999).

External Trade

PRINCIPAL COMMODITIES
(million francs CFA, year ending 30 June)

Imports c.i.f.	1995/96	1996/97	1997/98*
Food, beverages and tobacco	52,400	64,200	79,900
Energy and lubricants	6,500	13,800	11,000
Animal and vegetable raw materials	20,400	23,900	35,400
Mineral and other raw materials	60,800	111,000	108,700
Semi-finished goods	103,500	117,900	123,500
Transportation equipment	50,100	77,300	116,000
Agricultural equipment	1,500	1,400	1,600
Industrial equipment	74,500	91,800	99,300
Household consumption	69,100	74,400	87,700
Enterprise consumption	125,800	132,600	142,400
Total	564,600	708,300	805,500

* Estimates.

Exports f.o.b.	1995/96	1996/97	1997/98*
Petroleum and petroleum products	286,400	401,900	356,300
Cocoa beans	103,500	111,000	150,200
Cocoa products	20,500	21,800	29,400
Coffee (robusta)	81,500	81,600	104,200
Coffee (arabica)	13,300	20,500	24,200
Raw cotton	40,400	72,500	78,000
Sawlogs, veneer logs, etc.	91,300	125,900	126,600
Aluminium	69,800	70,900	80,800
Total (incl. others)	883,500	1,064,600	1,124,400

* Estimates.

Source: IMF, *Cameroon: Selected Issues and Statistical Appendix* (May 1999).

PRINCIPAL TRADING PARTNERS (million francs CFA)

Imports c.i.f.	1996	1997
Belgium-Luxembourg	29,710	37,217
China, People's Repub.	7,646	12,345
Côte d'Ivoire	7,636	30,298
Equatorial Guinea	20,680	19,841
France (incl. Monaco)	166,996	193,863
Germany	44,913	54,844
Guinea	15,400	23,369
Italy	22,736	32,776
Japan	30,578	43,138
Netherlands	17,178	23,008
Nigeria	58,817	56,817
Spain	10,908	14,504
United Kingdom	18,169	22,148
USA	52,439	66,033
Total (incl. others)	627,424	793,930

Statistical Survey

Exports f.o.b.	1996	1997
Belgium-Luxembourg	19,912	25,997
China, People's Repub.	15,768	37,156
Equatorial Guinea	16,145	14,230
France (incl. Monaco)	153,934	158,839
Gabon	16,377	25,835
Germany	15,983	23,241
Italy	183,258	291,700
Korea, Repub.	9,171	18,482
Netherlands	92,233	75,858
Philippines	4,748	14,658
Portugal	14,172	19,400
Spain	192,295	192,775
Taiwan	10,591	34,453
United Kingdom	15,603	18,890
Total (incl. others)	904,869	1,084,509

Transport

RAILWAYS (traffic, year ending 30 June)

	1990/91	1991/92	1992/93
Freight ton-km (million)	679	613	653
Passenger-km (million)	530	445	352

Source: UN, *Statistical Yearbook*.

ROAD TRAFFIC (estimates, motor vehicles in use at 31 December)

	1994	1995	1996
Passenger cars	89,000	93,000	98,000
Goods vehicles	57,000	60,000	64,350

Source: International Road Federation, *World Road Statistics*.

SHIPPING

Merchant Fleet (registered at 31 December)

	1996	1997	1998
Number of vessels	50	48	58
Total displacement ('000 grt)	36.7	11.4	12.9

Source: Lloyd's Register of Shipping.

International Sea-borne Freight Traffic
(freight traffic at Douala, '000 metric tons)

	1995	1996	1997
Goods loaded	1,841	1,967	2,385
Goods unloaded	2,317	2,211	2,497

Source: Banque des états de l'Afrique centrale, *Etudes et Statistiques*.

CIVIL AVIATION (traffic on scheduled services)

	1994	1995	1996
Kilometres flown (million)	5	7	7
Passengers carried ('000)	295	345	362
Passenger-km (million)	436	615	649
Total ton-km (million)	64	94	100

Source: UN, *Statistical Yearbook*.

283

Tourism

FOREIGN VISITORS BY COUNTRY OF ORIGIN*

	1995	1996	1997
Belgium	2,562	2,597	3,696
Canada	2,650	2,687	2,763
France	35,612	36,096	35,626
Germany	6,211	6,296	6,659
Italy	4,237	4,295	3,083
Switzerland	2,516	2,550	5,443
United Kingdom	3,798	3,849	4,106
USA	4,974	5,041	11,317
Total (incl. others)	99,749	101,106	132,839

* Arrivals at hotels and similar establishments.

Receipts from tourism (US $ million): 36 in 1995; 38 in 1996; 39 in 1997.

Source: World Tourism Organization, *Yearbook of Tourism Statistics*.

Communications Media

	1994	1995	1996
Radio receivers ('000 in use)	1,900	2,000	2,200
Television receivers ('000 in use)	309	320	400
Telephones ('000 main lines in use)	58	66	71
Mobile cellular telephones:			
(subscribers)	1,600	2,800	2,200
Daily newspapers:			
Number	1	2	2
Average circulation ('000)	50	85	91
Non-daily newspapers:			
Number	n.a.	n.a.	7
Average circulation ('000)	n.a.	n.a.	152

1997 ('000 in use): Radio receivers 2,270; Television receivers 450.

Mobile cellular telephones (subscribers, July 1999): 4,800.

Sources: mainly UNESCO, *Statistical Yearbook*; UN, *Statistical Yearbook*.

Education

(1996/97, unless otherwise indicated)

	Institutions	Teachers	Students
Pre-primary	1,109	4,545	87,318
Primary	8,514	39,384	1,921,186
Secondary			
General*	700	19,148	484,461
Vocational*	324	7,245	108,519
Universities	6	761†	42,199

* 1995/96 figure.

† 1990/91 figure.

Sources: UNESCO, *Statistical Yearbook*; *Annuaire statistique du Cameroun*.

Directory

The Constitution*

The Republic of Cameroon is a multi-party state. The main provisions of the 1972 Constitution, as amended, are summarized below:

The Constitution declares that the human being, without distinction as to race, religion, sex or belief, possesses inalienable and sacred rights. It affirms its attachment to the fundamental freedoms embodied in the Universal Declaration of Human Rights and the UN Charter. The State guarantees to all citizens of either sex the rights and freedoms set out in the preamble of the Constitution.

SOVEREIGNTY

1. The Republic of Cameroon shall be one and indivisible, democratic, secular and dedicated to social service. It shall ensure the equality before the law of all its citizens. Provisions that the official languages be French and English, for the motto, flag, national anthem and seal, that the capital be Yaoundé.

2–3. Sovereignty shall be vested in the people who shall exercise it either through the President of the Republic and the members returned by it to the National Assembly or by means of referendum. Elections are by universal suffrage, direct or indirect, by every citizen aged 21 or over in a secret ballot. Political parties or groups may take part in elections subject to the law and the principles of democracy and of national sovereignty and unity.

4. State authority shall be exercised by the President of the Republic and the National Assembly.

THE PRESIDENT OF THE REPUBLIC

5. The President of the Republic, as Head of State and Head of the Government, shall be responsible for the conduct of the affairs of the Republic. He shall define national policy and may charge the members of the Government with the implementation of this policy in certain spheres.

6–7. Candidates for the office of President must hold civic and political rights, be at least 35 years old and have resided in Cameroon for a minimum of 12 consecutive months, and may not hold any other elective office or professional activity. The President is elected for seven years, by a majority of votes cast by the people, and may serve a maximum of two terms. Provisions are made for the continuity of office in the case of the President's resignation.

8–9. The Ministers and Vice-Ministers are appointed by the President to whom they are responsible, and they may hold no other appointment. The President is also head of the armed forces, he negotiates and ratifies treaties, may exercise clemency after consultation with the Higher Judicial Council, promulgates and is responsible for the enforcement of laws, is responsible for internal and external security, makes civil and military appointments, provides for necessary administrative services.

10. The President, by reference to the Supreme Court, ensures that all laws passed are constitutional.

11. Provisions whereby the President may declare a state of emergency or state of siege.

THE NATIONAL ASSEMBLY

12. The National Assembly shall be renewed every five years, though it may at the instance of the President of the Republic legislate to extend or shorten its term of office. It shall be composed of 180 members elected by universal suffrage.

13–14. Laws shall normally be passed by a simple majority of those present, but if a bill is read a second time at the request of the President of the Republic a majority of the National Assembly as a whole is required.

15–16. The National Assembly shall meet twice a year, each session to last not more than 30 days; in one session it shall approve the budget. It may be recalled to an extraordinary session of not more than 15 days.

17–18. Elections and suitability of candidates and sitting members shall be governed by law.

RELATIONS BETWEEN THE EXECUTIVE AND THE LEGISLATURE

19. Bills may be introduced either by the President of the Republic or by any member of the National Assembly.

20. Reserved to the legislature are: the fundamental rights and duties of the citizen; the law of persons and property; the political, administrative and judicial system in respect of elections to the National Assembly, general regulation of national defence, authorization of penalties and criminal and civil procedure etc., and the organization of the local authorities; currency, the budget, dues and taxes, legislation on public property; economic and social policy; the education system.

21. The National Assembly may empower the President of the Republic to legislate by way of ordinance for a limited period and for given purposes.

22–26. Other matters of procedure, including the right of the President of the Republic to address the Assembly and of the Ministers and Vice-Ministers to take part in debates.

27–29. The composition and conduct of the Assembly's programme of business. Provisions whereby the Assembly may inquire into governmental activity. The obligation of the President of the Republic to promulgate laws, which shall be published in both languages of the Republic.

30. Provisions whereby the President of the Republic, after consultation with the National Assembly, may submit to referendum certain reform bills liable to have profound repercussions on the future of the nation and national institutions.

THE JUDICIARY

31. Justice is administered in the name of the people. The President of the Republic shall ensure the independence of the judiciary and shall make appointments with the assistance of the Higher Judicial Council.

THE SUPREME COURT

32–33. The Supreme Court has powers to uphold the Constitution in such cases as the death or incapacity of the President and the admissibility of laws, to give final judgments on appeals on the Judgment of the Court of Appeal and to decide complaints against administrative acts. It may be assisted by experts appointed by the President of the Republic.

IMPEACHMENT

34. There shall be a Court of Impeachment with jurisdiction to try the President of the Republic for high treason and the Ministers and Vice-Ministers for conspiracy against the security of the State.

THE ECONOMIC AND SOCIAL COUNCIL

35. There shall be an Economic and Social Council, regulated by the law.

AMENDMENT OF THE CONSTITUTION

36–37. Bills to amend the Constitution may be introduced either by the President of the Republic or the National Assembly. The President may decide to submit any amendment to the people by way of a referendum. No procedure to amend the Constitution may be accepted if it tends to impair the republican character, unity or territorial integrity of the State, or the democratic principles by which the Republic is governed.

* In December 1995 the National Assembly formally adopted constitutional amendments that provided for a democratic system of government, with the establishment of an upper legislative chamber (to be known as the Senate), a Council of Supreme Judiciary Affairs, a Council of State, and a Civil Service High Authority, and restricted the power vested in the President, who was to serve a maximum of two seven-year terms. The restoration of decentralized local government areas was also envisaged.

The Government

HEAD OF STATE

President: PAUL BIYA (took office 6 November 1982; elected 14 January 1984; re-elected 24 April 1988, 11 October 1992 and 12 October 1997).

CABINET
(August 2000)

A coalition of the Rassemblement démocratique du peuple camerounais (RDPC), the Union nationale pour la démocratie et le progrès (UNDP), the Union des populations camerounaises (UPC), and the Nouvelle convention (NC). With the exception of those specified, all cabinet members belong to the RDPC.

Prime Minister: PETER MAFANY MUSONGE.

Ministers of State

Minister of State, Delegate at the Presidency in charge of Defence: AMADOUA ALI.

Minister of State in charge of External Relations: AUGUSTIN KONTCHOU KOUEMEGNI.

Minister of State in charge of Culture: FERDINAND LÉOPOLD OYONO.

Minister of State in charge of Industrial and Commercial Development: BELLO BOUBA MAIGARI (UNDP).

Minister of State in charge of Economy and Finance: EDOUARD AKAME MFOUMOU.

Minister of State in charge of National Education: JOSEPH OWONA.

Ministers

Minister of Justice, Keeper of the Seals: ROBERT MBELLA MBAPPÉ.

Minister of Territorial Administration: FERDINAND KOUNGOU EDIMA.

Minister of Scientific and Technical Research: HENRI HOGBE NLEND (UPC).

Minister of Youth and Sports: BIDOUNG MKPATT.

Minister of Public Health: LAURENT ESSO.

Minister of Agriculture: TEREVET ZACHARIE.

Minister of the Environment and Forestry: SYLVESTRE NAAH ONDOUA.

Minister of Town Planning and Housing: BOUBARY YÉRIMA HALILOU.

Minister of Urban Affairs: CLAUDE JOSEPH MBAFOU.

Minister of Higher Education: JEAN-MARIE ATANGANA MEBARA.

Minister of Tourism: PIERRE HELLE (UNDP).

Minister of Public Service and Administrative Reform: RENÉ ZE NGUELE.

Minister of Communication: JACQUES FAME NDONGO.

Minister of Social Affairs: MARIE MADELEINE FOUDA.

Minister of Women's Affairs: JULIENNE NGO NSOM.

Minister of Public Investments and Regional Development: MARTIN OKOUDA.

Minister of Public Works: JÉRÔME ETAH.

Minister of Transport: JOSEPH TSANGA ABANDA.

Minister of Employment, Labour and Social Welfare: PIUS ONDOUA.

Minister of Mines, Water Resources and Energy: Dr YVES MBELE.

Minister of Livestock, Fisheries and Animal Industries: Dr HAMADJOUDA HAJOUDJI.

Minister of Posts and Telecommunications: ISAAC NJIEMOUN.

Ministers responsible for Special Duties at the Presidency: PETER ABETY, JUSTIN NDIORO, RAFAËL ONAMBÉLÉ, BABA HAMADOU, ELVIS NGOLE NGOLE.

Ministers Delegate

Minister Delegate at the Presidency in charge of Relations with the Assemblies and with the Economic and Social Council: GRÉGOIRE OWONA.

Minister Delegate at the Presidency in charge of the Supreme State Audit: LUCY GWANMESIA.

Minister Delegate at the Ministry of External Relations in charge of Relations with the Commonwealth: JOSEPH NDION NGUTE.

Minister Delegate at the Ministry of External Relations in charge of Relations with the Islamic World: ADOUM GARGOUM.

Minister Delegate at the Ministry of Economy and Finance in charge of the Budget: ROGER MELINGUI.

Minister Delegate at the Ministry of Economy and Finance in charge of the Stabilization Plan: JEAN-MARIE GANKOU.

Secretaries of State

Secretary of State for Territorial Administration in charge of Prisons Administration: ADAMA MODI BAKARI.

Secretary of State for Agriculture: ABOUBAKARY ABDOULAYE.

Secretary of State for Defence in charge of Gendarmerie: RÉMY ZE MEKA.

Secretary of State for Industrial and Commercial Development: EDMOND MOUAMPÉA MBIO.

First Secretary of State for National Education: JOSEPH YUNGA TEGHEN.

Second Secretary of State for National Education: HAMAN ADAMA.

Secretary of State for Public Investments and Regional Development: SHEY JOHN YEMBE.

Secretary of State for Posts and Telecommunications: DENIS OUMAROU.

Secretary of State for Public Health: ALIM HAYATOU.

Secretary of State for Transport: Dr NANA ABOUBAKAR DJALLOH (UNDP).

Secretary of State for Public Works: EMMANUEL BONDE.

Secretary of State for Town Planning and Housing in charge of Lands: TSALA MESSI.

Other officials with the rank of Minister

Secretary-General of the Presidency: YAYA MARAFA HAMIDOU.

Assistant Secretary-General of the Presidency: EPHRAIM INONI.

Assistant Secretary-General of the Presidency: RENÉ OWONA.

Director of the Cabinet of the President of the Republic: NGO'O MEBE.

MINISTRIES

Correspondence to ministries not holding post boxes should generally be addressed c/o the Central Post Office, Yaoundé.

Office of the President: Palais de l'Unité, Yaoundé; tel. 23-40-25; internet www.camnet.cm/celcom/homepr.htm.

Office of the Prime Minister: Yaoundé; tel. 23-80-05; fax 23-57-35; e-mail spm@spm.gov.cm; internet www.spm.gov.cm.

Ministry of Agriculture: Yaoundé; tel. 23-40-85.

Ministry of Animal Breeding, Fisheries and Animal Industry: Yaoundé; tel. 22-33-11.

Ministry of City Affairs: Yaoundé.

Ministry of Communication: BP 1588, Yaoundé; tel. 23-34-04.

Ministry of Culture: Yaoundé; tel. 22-65-79; fax 23-30-22.

Ministry of Defence: Yaoundé; tel. 23-40-55.

Ministry of Economy and Finance: BP 18, Yaoundé; tel. and fax 23-20-99; internet www.camnet.cm/investir/minfi/.

Ministry of Education: Yaoundé; tel. 23-40-50.

Ministry of Employment, Labour and Social Welfare: Yaoundé; tel. 22-01-86; fax 23-18-20.

Ministry of the Environment and Forest: Yaoundé; tel. 22-14-54.

Ministry of External Relations: Yaoundé; tel. 22-01-33; fax 20-25-91.

Ministry of Higher Education: 2 ave du 20 Mai, BP 1457, Yaoundé; tel. 22-17-70; fax 22-97-24; e-mail aowono@wycdc.uninet.cm; internet uycdc.uninet.cm/apage.html.

Ministry of Industrial and Commercial Development: Yaoundé; tel. 23-23-88; fax 22-27-04; e-mail mindic@camnet.cm; internet www.camnet.cm/investir/mindic.

Ministry of Justice: Yaoundé; tel. 22-01-97; fax 23-59-61.

Ministry of Mines, Water Resources and Energy: Yaoundé; tel. 23-34-04; fax 22-34-00; e-mail minmee@camnet.cm; internet www.camnet.cm/investir/minmee.

Ministry of Posts and Telecommunications: Yaoundé; tel. 23-06-15; fax 23-31-59.

Ministry of Public Health: Yaoundé; tel. 22-29-01.

Ministry of Public Investments and Regional Planning: Yaoundé.

Ministry of the Public Service and Administrative Reform: Yaoundé; tel. 22-03-56; fax 23-08-00.

Ministry of Public Works: Yaoundé; tel. 22-19-16; fax 22-01-56.

Ministry of Scientific and Technical Research: Yaoundé.

Ministry of Social Affairs and of Women's Affairs: Yaoundé; tel. 22-41-48.

Ministry of Territorial Administration: Yaoundé; tel. 23-40-90.

Ministry of Tourism: BP 266, Yaoundé; tel. 22-44-11; fax 22-12-95; e-mail mintour@camnet.cm; internet www.camnet.cm/mintour/tourisme.

Ministry of Town Planning and Housing: Yaoundé; tel. 23-22-82.

Ministry of Transport: Yaoundé; tel. 22-87-09; fax 23-45-20; e-mail mintrans@camnet.cm; internet www.camnet.cm/investir/transport.

Ministry of Youth and Sports: Yaoundé; tel. 23-32-57; internet www.camnet.cm/minjes3/accueil.htm.

President and Legislature

PRESIDENT

Election, 12 October 1997

Candidate	Votes	% of votes
PAUL BIYA (RDPC)	3,167,820	92.57
HENRI HOGBE NLEND (UPC)	85,693	2.50
SAMUEL EBOUA (MDP)	83,506	2.44
ALBERT DZONGANG (PPD)	40,814	1.19
JOACHIM TABI OWONO (AMEC)	15,817	0.46
ANTOINE DEMANNU (RDPF)	15,490	0.45
GUSTAVE ESSAKA (DIC)	12,915	0.38
Total*	3,422,055	100.00

* Excluding invalid votes.

NATIONAL ASSEMBLY

President: DJIBRIL CAVAYÉ YEGUIE.

General Election, 17 May 1997

Party	Seats
Rassemblement démocratique du peuple camerounais	109
Social Democratic Front	43
Union nationale pour la démocratie et le progrès	13
Union démocratique du Cameroun	5
Mouvement pour la défense de la République	1
Mouvement pour la jeunesse du Cameroun	1
Union des populations camerounaises (K)	1
Total*	180

* On 3 August 1997 further elections took place in seven constituencies, where the results had been annulled; all the seats were won by the RDPC.

Political Organizations

In mid-2000 there were approximately 150 active political parties, of which the most important are listed below:

Action for Meritocracy and Equal Opportunity Party (AMEC): Leader JOACHIM TABI OWONO.

Alliance pour la démocratie et le développement (ADD): Sec.-Gen. GARGA HAMAN ADJI.

Alliance démocratique pour le progrès du Cameroun (ADPC): Garoua; f. 1991.

Alliance pour le progrès et l'émancipation des dépossédés (APED): Yaoundé; f. 1991; Leader BOHIN BOHIN.

Alliance pour le redressement du Cameroun (ARC): f. 1992 by a number of opposition movements.

Association social-démocrate du Cameroun (ASDC): Maroua; f. 1991.

Cameroon Anglophone Movement (CAM): advocates a federal system of govt.

Congrès panafricain du Cameroun (CPC): Douala; f. 1991.

Convention libérale (CL): f. 1991; Leader PIERRE-FLAMBEAU NGAYAP.

Démocratie intégrale au Cameroun (DIC): Douala; f. 1991; Leader GUSTAVE ESSAKA.

Front des alliés pour le changement (FAC): Douala; f. 1994; alliance of 16 opposition movements; Leader SAMUEL EBOUA.

Front démocratique et patriotique (FDP): f. 1994; alliance of six opposition parties.

Liberal Democratic Alliance (LDA): Buéa; Pres. HENRI FOSSUNG.

Mouvement pour la démocratie et le progrès (MDP): f. 1992; Leader SAMUEL EBOUA.

Mouvement pour la défense de la République (MDR): f. 1991; Leader DAKOLE DAISSALA.

Mouvement pour la jeunesse du Cameroun (MLJC): Leader MARCEL YONDO.

Mouvement social pour la nouvelle démocratie (MSND): Leader YONDO BLACK.

Nouvelle convention (NC): Yaoundé.

Parti des démocrates camerounais (PDC): Yaoundé; f. 1991; Leader Louis-Tobie Mbida.

Parti libéral-democrate (PLD): f. 1991; Leader Njoh Litumbe.

Parti populaire pour le développement (PPD): f. 1997.

Parti républicain du peuple camerounais (PRPC): Bertoua; f. 1991; Leader Ateba Ngoua.

Parti socialiste camerounais (PSC): Leader Jean-Pierre Dembele.

Parti socialiste démocratique (PSD): Douala; f. 1991; Leader Ernest Koum Bin Biltik.

Parti socialiste démocratique du Cameroun (PSDC): Leader Jean Michel Tekam.

Rassemblement démocratique du peuple camerounais (RDPC): BP 867, Yaoundé; tel. 23-27-40. 1966 as Union nationale camerounaise by merger of the Union camerounaise, the Kamerun National Democratic Party and four opposition parties; adopted present name in 1985; sole legal party 1972–90; Pres. Paul Biya; Sec.-Gen. Joseph-Charles Doumba.

Rassemblement démocratique du peuple sans frontières (RDPF): f. 1997.

Social Democratic Front (SDF): Bamenda; f. 1990; e-mail webmaster@sdfparty.org; internet www.sdfparty.org; Chair. John Fru Ndi; Sec.-Gen. Prof. Tazoacha Asonganyi.

Social Democratic Movement (SDM): f. 1995; breakaway faction of the Social Democratic Front; Leader Siga Asanga.

Southern Cameroons National Council (SCNC): f. 1995; supports the establishment of an independent republic in anglophone Cameroon; Chair. Sam Ekontang Elad.

Union démocratique du Cameroun (UDC): f. 1991; Leader Adamou Ndam Njoya.

Union des forces démocratiques du Cameroun (UFDC): Yaoundé; f. 1991; Leader Victorin Hameni Bieleu.

Union nationale pour la démocratie et le progrès (UNDP): f. 1991; split in 1995; Chair. Bello Bouba Maigari.

Union des populations camerounaises (UPC): Douala; f. 1948; split into two main factions in 1996: UPC (N), led by Ndeh Ntumazah, and UPC (K), led by Augustin Frédéric Kodock.

Diplomatic Representation

EMBASSIES AND HIGH COMMISSIONS IN CAMEROON

Algeria: Yaoundé; tel. 21-53-51; fax 21-53-54; Ambassador: M'Hamed Achache.

Belgium: BP 816, Yaoundé; tel. 20-67-47; fax 20-05-21; Ambassador: Baudouin Vanderhulst.

Brazil: BP 348, Yaoundé; tel. 21-45-67; fax 21-19-57; Chargé d'affaires a.i.: Sergio Couri Elias.

Canada: Immeuble Stamatiades, BP 572, Yaoundé; tel. 23-02-03; fax 22-10-90; High Commissioner: Claude Baillargeon.

Central African Republic: BP 396, Yaoundé; tel. and fax 20-51-55; Ambassador: Jean Poloko.

Chad: BP 506, Yaoundé; tel. and fax 21-06-24; Ambassador: Homsala Ouangmotching.

China, People's Republic: BP 1307, Yaoundé; tel. 21-00-83; fax 21-43-95; Ambassador: Zhu Yourong.

Congo, Democratic Republic: BP 632, Yaoundé; tel. 22-51-03; Ambassador: (vacant).

Congo, Republic: BP 1422, Yaoundé; tel. 21-24-58; Ambassador: Marcel Makome.

Egypt: BP 809, Yaoundé; tel. 20-39-22; fax 20-26-47; Ambassador: Nofal Ibrahim el-Sayed.

Equatorial Guinea: BP 277, Yaoundé; tel. and fax 21-14-04; Ambassador: Santiago Eneme Ovono.

France: Plateau Atémengué, BP 1631, Yaoundé; tel. 23-40-13; fax 23-50-43; e-mail ambafrancecam@camnet.cm; Ambassador: Jean-Paul Véziant.

Gabon: BP 4130, Yaoundé; tel. 20-29-66; fax 21-02-24; Ambassador: Pépin Mongockodji.

Germany: rue Charles de Gaulle, BP 1160, Yaoundé; tel. 20-05-66; fax 20-73-13; Ambassador: Jürgen Dröge.

Greece: BP 82, Yaoundé; tel. and fax 20-39-36; Ambassador: Athanassios Camilos.

Holy See: rue du Vatican, BP 210, Yaoundé (Apostolic Nunciature); tel. 20-04-75; fax 20-75-13; Apostolic Pro-Nuncio: Most Rev. Félix del Blanco Prieto, Titular Archbishop of Vannida.

Israel: BP 5934, Yaoundé; tel. 20-16-44; fax 21-08-23; Ambassador: (vacant).

Italy: Quartier Bastos, BP 827, Yaoundé; tel. 20-33-76; fax 21-52-50; e-mail ambyaounde@gcnet.com; Ambassador: Francesco Lanata.

Japan: Bastos-Ekoudou, Yaoundé; tel. 20-62-02; Ambassador: Takeru Sasaguchi.

Korea, Republic: BP 301, Yaoundé; tel. 21-32-23; fax 20-17-25; Ambassador: Dae-Taek Lim.

Liberia: Ekoudou, Quartier Bastos, BP 1185, Yaoundé; tel. 21-12-96; fax 20-97-81; Ambassador: Carlton Alexwyn Karpeh.

Libya: Quartier Bastos, POB 1980, Yaoundé; tel. 22-41-38.

Morocco: BP 1629, Yaoundé; tel. 20-50-92; fax 20-37-93; Ambassador: Mohamed Benomar.

Nigeria: BP 448, Yaoundé; tel. 22-34-55; High Commissioner: Mahmud George Bello.

Romania: Quartier Bastos, BP 6212, Yaoundé; tel. and fax 21-39-86; Chargé d'affaires a.i.: Ion Mogos.

Russia: BP 488, Yaoundé; tel. 20-17-14; fax 20-78-91; Ambassador: Yevgenii Utkin.

Saudi Arabia: BP 1602, Yaoundé; tel. 21-26-75; fax 20-66-89; Ambassador: Abdulaziz Fahd ar-Rebdi.

Spain: BP 877, Yaoundé; tel. 20-35-43; fax 20-64-91; Ambassador: José Javier Nagore San Martín.

Tunisia: rue de Rotary, BP 6074, Yaoundé; tel. 20-33-68; fax 21-05-07; Chargé d'affaires a.i.: Mohamed Amiri.

United Kingdom: ave Winston Churchill, BP 547, Yaoundé; tel. 22-05-45; fax 22-01-48; High Commissioner: Peter Boon.

USA: rue Nachtigal, BP 817, Yaoundé; tel. 23-40-14; fax 23-07-53; Ambassador: Charles H. Twining.

Judicial System

Supreme Court: Yaoundé; tel. 22-01-64; fax 22-05-76; consists of a president, nine titular and substitute judges, a procureur général, an avocat général, deputies to the procureur général, a registrar and clerks.

President: Alexandre Dipanda Mouelle.

High Court of Justice: Yaoundé; consists of 9 titular judges and 6 substitute judges, all elected by the National Assembly.

Attorney-General: Rissouck A. Moullong.

Religion

It is estimated that 53% of the population are Christians (mainly Roman Catholics), 25% adhere to traditional religious beliefs and 22% are Muslims.

CHRISTIANITY
Protestant Churches

There are about 1m. Protestants in Cameroon, with about 3,000 church and mission workers, and four theological schools.

Fédération des Eglises et missions évangéliques du Cameroun (FEMEC): BP 491, Yaoundé; tel. 22-30-78; f. 1968; 10 mem. churches; Pres. Rev. Dr Jean Kotto (Evangelical Church of Cameroon); Admin. Sec. Rev. Dr Grégoire Ambadiang de Mendeng (Presbyterian Church of Cameroon).

Eglise évangélique du Cameroun (Evangelical Church of Cameroon): BP 89, Douala; tel. 42-36-11; fax 42-40-11; f. 1957; 500,000 mems (1992); Pres. Rev. Charles E. Njike; Sec. Rev. Hans Edjenguele.

Eglise presbytérienne camerounaise (Presbyterian Church of Cameroon): BP 519, Yaoundé; tel. 32-42-36; independent since 1957; comprises four synods and 16 presbyteries; 200,000 mems (1985); Gen. Sec. Rev. Grégoire Ambadiang de Mendeng.

Eglise protestante africaine (African Protestant Church): BP 26, Lolodorf; f. 1934; 8,400 mems (1985); Dir-Gen. Rev. Marnia Woungly-Massaga.

Presbyterian Church in Cameroon: BP 19, Buéa; tel. 32-23-36; 250,000 mems (1990); 211 ministers; Moderator Rev. Henry Anye Awasom.

Union des Eglises baptistes au Cameroun (Union of Baptist Churches of Cameroon): BP 6007, New Bell, Douala; tel. 42-41-06; autonomous since 1957; 37,000 mems (1985); Gen. Sec. Rev. Emmanuel Mbenda.

Other Protestant churches active in Cameroon include the Cameroon Baptist Church, the Cameroon Baptist Convention, the Church of the Lutheran Brethren of Cameroon, the Evangelical Lutheran Church of Cameroon, the Presbyterian Church in West Cameroon and the Union of Evangelical Churches of North Cameroon.

The Roman Catholic Church

Cameroon comprises five archdioceses and 18 dioceses. At 31 December 1998 adherents represented some 23.6% of the total population. There are several active missionary orders, and four major seminaries for African priests.

Bishops' Conference: Conférence Episcopale Nationale du Cameroun, BP 1963, Yaoundé; tel. 31-15-92; fax 31-29-77; e-mail basc@rctmail.net; f. 1989; Pres. Rt Rev. ANDRÉ WOUKING, Bishop of Bafoussam; Sec.-Gen. Fr PATRICK LAFON.

Archbishop of Bamenda: Most Rev. PAUL VERDZEKOV, Archbishop's House, BP 82, Bamenda; tel. 36-12-41; fax 36-34-87; e-mail abpbda@compuserve.com.

Archbishop of Bertoua: Most Rev. LAMBERTUS JOHANNES VAN HEYGEN, Archevêché, BP 40, Bertoua; tel. 24-17-48; fax 24-25-85.

Archbishop of Douala: Cardinal CHRISTIAN WIYGHAN TUMI, Archevêché, BP 179, Douala; tel. 42-37-14; fax 42-18-37.

Archbishop of Garoua: Most Rev. ANTOINE NTALOU, Archevêché, BP 272, Garoua; tel. 27-13-53; fax 27-29-42.

Archbishop of Yaoundé: Most Rev. ANDRÉ WOUKING, Archevêché, BP 185, Yaoundé; tel. 22-24-89; fax 23-50-58; e-mail procure.yde@rctmail.net.

BAHÁ'Í FAITH

National Spiritual Assembly: BP 145, Limbe; tel. 33-21-46; mems in 1,744 localities.

The Press

Restrictions on the press have operated since 1966.

DAILIES

Cameroon Tribune: BP 1218, Yaoundé; tel. 30-36-89; fax 30-43-62; e-mail camtrib@gcnet.cm; internet www.gcnet.cm/camtrib; f. 1974; govt-controlled; French and English; Dir PAUL C. NDEMBIYEMBE; Editor-in-Chief EBOKEM FOMENKY; circ. 20,000.

Politiks Matinal: Yaoundé; f. 1999; independent; French; circ. 10,000.

Le Quotidien: BP 13088, Douala; tel. 39-11-89; fax 39-18-19; French.

PERIODICALS

Affaires Légales: BP 3681, Douala; tel. 42-58-38; fax 43-22-59; monthly; legal periodical.

Afrique en Dossiers: BP 1715; Yaoundé; f. 1970; French and English; Dir EBONGUE SOELLE.

Cameroon Outlook: BP 124, Limbe; f. 1969; 3 a week; independent; English; Editor JEROME F. GWELLEM; circ. 20,000.

Cameroon Panorama: BP 46, Buéa; tel. 32-22-40; f. 1962; monthly; English; Roman Catholic; Editor Sister MERCY HORGAN; circ. 1,500.

Cameroon Post: Yaoundé; weekly; independent; English; Publr PADDY MBAWA; Editor JULIUS WAMEY; circ. 50,000.

Cameroon Review: BP 408, Limbe; monthly; Editor-in-Chief JEROME F. GWELLEM; circ. 70,000.

Cameroon Times: BP 408, Limbe; f. 1960; weekly; English; Editor-in-Chief JEROME F. GWELLEM; circ. 12,000.

Challenge Hebdo: BP 1388, Douala; weekly; Editor BENJAMIN ZEBAZE.

Le Combattant: Yaoundé; weekly; independent; Editor BENYIMBE JOSEPH; circ. 21,000.

Courrier Sportif du Bénin: BP 17, Douala; weekly; Dir HENRI JONG.

Dikalo: BP 4320, Douala; tel. 37-00-32; fax 37-19-06; independent; 2 a week; French; Dir EMMANUEL NOUBISSIE NGANKAM.

L'Effort Camerounais: BP 15231, Douala; tel. 43-27-26; fax 43-18-37; weekly; Catholic.

L'Expression: BP 15333, Douala; tel. 43-22-27; fax 43-26-69; e-mail expression@cybernum.com; 3 times a week.

La Gazette: BP 5485, Douala; 2 a week; Editor ABODEL KARIMOU; circ. 35,000.

The Herald: BP 3659, Yaoundé; tel. 31-55-22; fax 31-81-61; 3 a week; English; Dir Dr BONIFACE FORBIN; circ. 8,000.

Al Houda: BP 1638, Yaoundé; quarterly; Islamic cultural review.

L'Indépendant Hebdo: Yaoundé; Chief Editor EVARISTE MENOUNGA.

Le Jeune Observateur: Yaoundé; f. 1991; Editor JULES KOUM.

Journal Officiel de la République du Cameroun: BP 1603, Yaoundé; tel. 23-12-77; fortnightly; official govt notices; circ. 4,000.

Le Messager: 266 blvd de la Liberté, BP 5925, Douala; tel. 42-04-39; fax 42-02-14; e-mail lemessager@camnet.cm; internet www .wagne.net/gmessager; f. 1979; 3 a week; independent; Man. Editor PIUS N. NJAWE; circ. 39,000.

Le Messager Popoli: 266 blvd de la Liberté, BP 5925, Douala; tel. 42-04-39; fax 42-02-14; f. 1993; 2 a week; independent; Man. Editor PIUS N. NJAWE; circ. 24,000.

The Messenger: BP 15043, Douala; English edn of *Le Messager*; Editor HILARY FOKUM.

Mutations: BP 12348, Yaoundé; tel. 22-51-04; fax 22-51-04; e-mail mutations@cybernum.com; 2 a week; French.

Nleb Ensemble: Imprimerie Saint-Paul, BP 763, Yaoundé; tel. 23-97-73; fax 23-50-58; f. 1935; fortnightly; Ewondo; Dir Most Rev. JEAN ZOA; Editor JOSEPH BEFE ATEBA; circ. 6,000.

La Nouvelle Expression: BP 15333, Douala; independent; 3 a week; French; Man. Editor SÉVERIN TCHOUNKOU.

Presbyterian Newsletter: BP 19, Buéa; quarterly.

Que Savoir: BP 1986, Douala; monthly; industry, commerce and tourism.

Recherches et Études Camerounaises: BP 193, Yaoundé; monthly; publ. by Office National de Recherches Scientifiques du Cameroun.

La Révélation: Yaoundé; Dir BOSCO TCHOUBET.

Le Serment: Yaoundé; newspaper; Editor-in-Chief ANSELME MBALLA.

Le Serviteur: BP 1405, Yaoundé; monthly; Protestant; Dir Pastor DANIEL AKO'O; circ. 3,000.

Le Travailleur/The Worker: BP 1610, Yaoundé; tel. 22-33-15; f. 1972; monthly; French and English; journal of Organisation Syndicale des Travailleurs du Cameroun/Cameroon Trade Union Congress; Sec.-Gen. LOUIS SOMBES; circ. 10,000.

L'Unité: BP 867, Yaoundé; weekly; French and English.

Weekly Post: Obili, Yaoundé; Publr Chief BISONG ETAHOBEN.

NEWS AGENCIES

CamNews: c/o SOPECAM, BP 1218, Yaoundé; tel. 30-38-30; fax 30-43-62; Dir JEAN NGANDJEU.

Foreign Bureaux

Xinhua (New China) News Agency (People's Republic of China): ave Joseph Omgba, BP 1583, Yaoundé; tel. 20-25-72; Chief Correspondent SUN XINGWEN.

Agence France-Presse (France), Reuters (UK) and ITAR—TASS (Russia) are also represented.

Publishers

Editions Buma Kor: BP 727, Yaoundé; tel. 23-13-30; fax 23-07-68; f. 1977; general, children's, educational and Christian; English and French; Man. Dir B. D. BUMA KOR.

Editions Clé: BP 1501, Yaoundé; tel. 22-35-54; fax 23-27-09; e-mail cle@a_vip.com; f. 1963; African and Christian literature and studies; school textbooks; medicine and science; general non-fiction; Gen. Man. COMLAN PROSPER DEH.

Editions Le Flambeau: BP 113, Yaoundé; tel. 22-36-72; f. 1977; general; Man. Dir JOSEPH NDZIE.

Editions Semences Africaines: BP 5329, Yaoundé-Nlongkak; tel. 22-40-58; f. 1974; fiction, history, religion, textbooks; Man. Dir PHILIPPE-LOUIS OMBEDE.

New Times Publishing House: Presbook Compound, BP 408, Limbe; tel. 33-32-17; f. 1983; publishing and book trade reference; Dir and Editor-in-Chief J. F. GWELLEM.

Government Publishing Houses

Centre d'Edition et de Production pour l'Enseignement et la Recherche (CEPER): BP 808, Yaoundé; tel. 22-13-23. 1967; transfer pending to private ownership; general non-fiction, science and technology, tertiary, secondary and primary textbooks; Man. Dir JEAN CLAUDE FOUTH.

Imprimerie Nationale: BP 1603, Yaoundé; tel. 23-12-77; scheduled for transfer to private ownership; Dir AMADOU VAMOULKE.

Société de Presse et d'Editions du Cameroun (SOPECAM): BP 1218, Yaoundé; tel. 30-40-12; fax 30-43-62; f. 1977; under the supervision of the Ministry of Communication; Dir-Gen. PAUL CÉLESTIN NDEMBIYEMBE; Man. Editor PIERRE ESSAMA ESSOMBA.

Broadcasting and Communications

TELECOMMUNICATIONS

A Telecommunications Regulation Agency was established in early 1999.

Cameroon Telecommunications (CAMTEL): BP 1571, Yaoundé; tel. 23-40-65; fax 23-03-03; e-mail camtel@camnet.cm; internet www.camnet.cm; f. 1999 by merger of INTELCAM and the Dept of Telecommunications; 51% privatization pending; Pres. NFON VICTOR MUKETE; Dir-Gen. EMMANUEL NGUIAMBA NLOUTSIRI.

CAMTEL Mobile: BP 1571, Yaoundé; f. 1999; mobile cellular telephone operator; 95% state-owned; privatization pending; Pres. NGOLLE PHILIP NGWESSE; Dir-Gen. PATIENCE EBOUMBOU.

Société Camerounaise de Mobiles: Yaoundé; f. 1999; mobile cellular telephone operator; operates in Yaoundé, Douala and Bafoussam; 100% owned by France Câbles et Radio; Dir-Gen. JEAN-PAUL GANDET.

BROADCASTING
Radio

Office de Radiodiffusion-Télévision Camerounaise (CRTV): BP 1634, Yaoundé; tel. 21-40-88; fax 20-43-40; internet www.ditof.cm/crtv; f. 1987 by merger; broadcasts in French and English; Pres. HENRI BANDOLO; Dir-Gen. Prof. GERVAIS MENDOZE.

Radio Bertoua: BP 260, Bertoua; tel. 24-14-45.

Radio Buéa: POB 86, Buéa; tel. 32-26-15; programmes in English, French and 15 vernacular languages; Man. PETERSON CHIA YUH; Head of Station GIDEON MULU TAKA.

Radio Douala: BP 986, Douala; tel. 42-60-60; programmes in French, English, Douala, Bassa, Ewondo, Bakoko and Bamiléké; Dir BRUNO DJEM; Head of Station LINUS ONANA MVONDO.

Radio Garoua: BP 103, Garoua; tel. 27-11-67; programmes in French, Hausa, English, Foulfouldé, Arabic and Choa; Dir BELLO MALGANA; Head of Station MOUSSA EPOPA.

Radio Ngaoundéré: BP 135, Ngaoundéré; tel. 25-21-48.

Radio Yaoundé: BP 1634, Yaoundé; tel. 20-25-02.

There are also provincial radio stations at Abong Mbang, Bafoussam, Bamenda, Ebolowa and Maroua.

Television

Television programmes from France were broadcast by the Office de Radiodiffusion-Télévision Camerounaise from early 1990.

Office de Radiodiffusion-Télévision Camerounaise (CRTV): see Radio.

Finance

(cap. = capital; res = reserves; dep. = deposits; m. = million; brs = branches; amounts in francs CFA)

BANKING
Central Bank

Banque des Etats de l'Afrique Centrale (BEAC): rue du Dr Jamot, BP 1917, Yaoundé; tel. 23-40-30; fax 23-33-29; f. 1973; bank of issue for mem. states of the Communauté économique et monétaire de l'Afrique centrale (CEMAC, fmrly Union douanière et économique de l'Afrique centrale) Cameroon, the Central African Repub., Chad, the Repub. of the Congo, Equatorial Guinea and Gabon); cap. and res 210,014m., total assets 1,303,226m. (June 1999); Gov. JEAN-FÉLIX MAMALEPOT; Dir in Cameroon SADOU HAYATOU; 5 brs in Cameroon.

Commercial Banks

Amity Bank Cameroon SA: Commercial Ave, BP 2171, Bamenda; tel. 36-36-51; fax 36-36-59; e-mail amibac@camnet.cm; internet www.afrika.com/amity-bank; f. 1990; cap. and res 1,106m., total assets 19,071m. (June 1999); Pres. LAWRENCE LOWEH TASHA, Vice-Pres. Prof. VICTOR ANOMAH NGU; 4 brs.

Banque Internationale pour le Commerce et l'Industrie du Cameroun SA: ave du Général de Gaulle, BP 4070, Douala; tel. 23-40-07; fax 42-41-16; f. 1962; 51% owned by Banque Populaire de France; cap. 3,000m. (March 1997); Pres. RAYMOND MALOUMA; Dir-Gen. SADOU HAYATOU; 34 brs.

Citibank N.A. Cameroon: 96 rue Flatters, Bonanjo, BP 4571, Douala; tel. 42-42-72; fax 42-40-74; f. 1997; Dir-Gen. LOUIS ADANDE; Asst Dir-Gen. OSMAN EL TOUM.

Commercial Bank of Cameroon: BP 4004, Douala; tel. 42-02-02; fax 43-38-00; e-mail cbcbank@camnet.cm; f. 1997; cap. and res 1,450.1m., total assets 41,602.1m. (March 1999); Pres. VICTOR FOTSO; Dir-Gen. JEAN LOUIS CHAPUIS.

Highland Corporation Bank SA: Immeuble Hotel Hilton, blvd du 20 mai, BP 10039, Yaoundé; tel. 23-92-87; fax 23-92-91; e-mail hicobk@camnet.cm; f. 1995; 100% privately owned; cap. 600m. (Dec. 1996); Exec. Pres. PAUL ATANGA NJI; Asst Dir-Gen. JOHANES MBATI.

Société Commerciale de Banque—Crédit Lyonnais Cameroun (SCB—CLC): 220 ave Monseigneur Vogt, BP 700, Yaoundé; tel. 23-40-05; fax 22-41-32; e-mail andré.roggemans@camnet.cm; f. 1989; 35% state-owned; cap. and res 12,817.5m., total assets 185,237.7m. (June 1998); Pres. MARTIN OKOUDA; Dir-Gen. BERNARD FOURNIER; 18 brs.

Société Générale de Banques au Cameroun (SGBC): 10 rue Joss, BP 4042, Douala; tel. 42-70-10; fax 42-71-32; e-mail sgbcdla@camnet.cm; f. 1963; 25.6% state-owned; cap. and res 8,035.6m., total assets 219,187.3m. (June 1998); Pres. AHMADOU MOULIOM NJIFENDJOU; Dir-Gen. GASTON NGUENTI; 26 brs.

Standard Chartered Bank Cameroon SA: blvd de la Liberté, BP 1784, Douala; tel. 42-36-12; fax 42-27-89; internet www.standardchartered.com/cm/index.html; f. 1980 as Boston Bank Cameroon; 34% state-owned; cap. 3,500m., total assets 85,256m. (Dec. 1997); Pres. EPHRAIM INONI; Man. Dir JOHN SPINK TAYLOR; 3 brs.

Development Banks

Banque de Développement des États de l'Afrique Centrale: (see Franc Zone, p. 201).

Crédit Foncier du Cameroun (CFC): 484 blvd du 20 mai 1972, BP 1531, Yaoundé; tel. 23-52-15; fax 23-52-21; f. 1977; 70% owned by Banque des Etats de l'Afrique Centrale; cap. and res 7,913.1m., total assets 77,963.7m. (June 1997); provides assistance for low-cost housing; Pres. GEORGES NGANGO; Dir-Gen. SYLVESTRE NAAH ONDOA.

Société Nationale d'Investissement du Cameroun (SNI): place de la Poste, BP 423, Yaoundé; tel. 22-44-22; fax 23-13-32; f. 1964; state-owned investment and credit agency; cap. and res 12,510.2m., total assets 37,392.9m. (June 1995); Pres. VICTOR AYISSI MVODO; Dir-Gen. ESTHER BELIBI DANG.

Financial Institutions

Caisse Autonome d'Amortissement du Cameroun: BP 7167, Yaoundé; tel. 22-22-26; fax 22-01-29; f. 1985; e-mail camtis@camnet.cm; cap. 5,000m. (1998); Dir-Gen. DANIEL LAMERE NJANKOUO.

Caisse Commune d'Epargne et d'Investissement (CCEI): place de l'Indépendance, BP 11834, Yaoundé; tel. 23-30-68; fax 22-17-85; cap. and res 7,400m., total assets 76,700m. (June 1998); Pres. Dr PAUL KANMOGNE FOKAM; Dir-Gen. BONIFACE KACYEM.

Fonds d'Aide et de Garantie des Crédits aux Petites et Moyennes Entreprises (FOGAPE): BP 1591, Yaoundé; tel. 23-38-59; fax 22-32-74; f. 1984; cap. 1,000m. (Oct. 1997); Pres. JOSEPH HENGA; Vice-Pres. ARMAND FIRMIN MVONDO.

Société Camerounaise de Crédit Automobile (SOCCA): rue du Roi Albert, BP 554, Douala; tel. 42-74-78; fax 42-12-19; cap. and res 2,059.6m., total assets 15,239.6m. (June 1998); Pres. VALENTIN MOUYOMBON; Dir-Gen. PHILIPPE DE LAPLAGNOLLE.

Société Camerounaise de Crédit-Bail (SOCABAIL): rue du Roi Albert, BP 554, Douala; tel. 42-74-78; fax 42-12-19; cap. and res 1,347.8m., total assets 5,059.6m. (June 1998); Pres. ALAIN GUYON.

INSURANCE

Activa Assurances: Douala; f. 1999; all branches except life insurance; cap. 400m.; 66% owned by Cameroonian investors, 33% by Ivorian investors; Chair. JEAN DIAGOU; Gen. Man. RICHARD LOWE.

Assurances Mutuelles Agricoles du Cameroun (AMACAM): BP 962, Yaoundé; tel. 22-49-66; f. 1965; cap. 100m.; state-owned; privatization pending; Pres. SAMUEL NGBWA NGUELE; Dir-Gen. LUC CLAUDE NANFA.

Caisse Nationale de Réassurances (CNR): ave Foch, BP 4180, Yaoundé; tel. 22-37-99; fax 23-36-80; f. 1965; all classes of reinsurance; cap. 1,000m.; state-owned; scheduled for transfer to private ownership by 2000; Pres. JEAN KEUTCHA; Man. Dir ANTOINE NTSIMI.

Compagnie Camerounaise d'Assurances et de Réassurances (CCAR): 11 rue Franqueville, BP 4068, Douala; tel. 42-31-59; fax 42-64-53; f. 1974; cap. 499.5m.; Pres. YVETTE CHASSAGNE; Dir Gen. CHRISTIAN LE GOFF.

Compagnie Nationale d'Assurances (CNA): BP 12125, Douala; tel. 42-44-46; fax 42-47-27; f. 1986; all classes of insurance; cap. 600m.; Chair. THÉODORE EBOBO; Man. Dir. PROTAIS AYANGMA AMANG.

General and Equitable Assurance Cameroon Ltd (GEACAM): 56 blvd de la Liberté, BP 426, Douala; tel. 42-59-85; fax 42-71-03; cap. 300m.; Pres. V. A. NGU; Man. Dir J. CHEBAUT.

Société Camerounaise d'Assurances et de Réassurances (SOCAR): 1450 blvd de la Liberté, BP 280, Douala; tel. 42-55-84; fax 42-13-35; f. 1973; cap. 800m.; state-owned; scheduled for transfer to private ownership by 2000; Chair. J. YONTA; Man. Dir R. BIOUELE.

Société Nouvelle d'Assurances du Cameroun (SNAC): rue Manga Bell, BP 105, Douala; tel. and fax 42-92-03. 1974; all classes of insurance; cap. 700m.; Dir-Gen. JEAN CHEBAUT.

Trade and Industry
GOVERNMENT AGENCY

Economic and Social Council: BP 1058, Yaoundé; tel. 23-24-74; advises the Govt on economic and social problems; comprises 150 mems and a perm. secr.; mems serve a five-year term; Pres. Luc Ayang; Sec.-Gen. François Eyok.

DEVELOPMENT ORGANIZATIONS

Caisse Française de Développement (CFD): BP 46, Yaoundé; tel. 22-23-24; fax 23-57-07; Dir Dominique Dordain.

Cameroon Development Corporation (CAMDEV): Bota, Limbe; tel. 33-22-51; fax 43-17-40; f. 1947, reorg. 1982; cap. 15,626m. francs CFA; state-owned; statutory corpn established to acquire and develop plantations of tropical crops for local and export markets; operates two oil mills, seven banana-packing stations, three tea and seven rubber factories; owned by Del Monte, USA; Chair. Nerius Namaso Mbile; Gen. Man. Njallu Quan.

Direction Générale des Grands Travaux du Cameroon (DGTC): BP 6604, Yaoundé; tel. 22-18-03; fax 22-13-00; f. 1988; commissioning, implementation and supervision of public works contracts; Chair. Jean Fouman Akame; Man. Dir Michel Kowalzick.

Hévéa-Cameroun (HEVECAM): BP 1298, Douala and BP 174, Kribi; tel. 42-75-64. 1975; cap. 16,518m. francs CFA; state-owned; development of 15,000 ha rubber plantation; 4,500 employees; transferred to private ownership in 1997; Pres. Nyokwedi Malonga; Man. Dir Paul de Kippeleyr.

Mission d'Aménagement et d'Equipement des Terrains Urbains et Ruraux (MAETUR): BP 1248, Yaoundé; tel. 22-31-13. 1977; Pres. Léopold Ferdinand Oyono; Dir-Gen. André Mama Fouda.

Mission de Développement de la Province du Nord-Ouest (MIDENO): BP 442, Bamenda; Dir Andrew Waindim Ndonyi.

Mission Française de Coopération et d'Action Culturelle: BP 1616, Yaoundé; tel. 22-44-43; fax 22-33-96; administers bilateral aid from France; Dir Jean Boulogne.

Office Céréalier dans la Province du Nord: BP 298, Garoua; tel. 27-14-38. 1975 to combat effects of drought in northern Cameroon and stabilize cereal prices; Pres. Alhadji Mahamat; Dir-Gen. Gilbert Gourlemond.

Société de Développement du Cacao (SODECAO): BP 1651, Yaoundé; tel. 30-45-44; fax 30-33-95; f. 1974, reorg. 1980; cap. 425m. francs CFA; development of cocoa, coffee and food crop production in the Littoral, Centre, East and South provinces; Pres. Joseph-Charles Doumba; Dir-Gen. Joseph Ingwat II.

Société de Développement de l'Elevage (SODEVA): BP 50, Kousseri; cap. 50m. francs CFA; Dir Alhadji Oumarou Bakary.

Société de Développement et d'Exploitation des Productions Animales (SODEPA): BP 1410, Yaoundé; tel. 22-24-28; f. 1974; cap. 375m. francs CFA; development of livestock and livestock products; Man. Dir Etienne Enguelguele.

Société de Développement de la Haute-Vallée du Noun (UNVDA): BP 25, N'Dop, North-West Province, f. 1970; cap. 1,380m. francs CFA; rice, maize and soya bean cultivation; Dir-Gen. Samuel Bawe Chi Wanki.

Société d'Expansion et de Modernisation de la Riziculture de Yagoua (SEMRY): BP 46, Yagoua; tel. 29-62-13. 1971; cap. 4,580m. francs CFA; commercialization of rice products and expansion of rice-growing in areas where irrigation is possible; Pres. Albert Ekono; Dir-Gen. Limangana Tori.

Société Immobilière du Cameroun (SIC): BP 387, Yaoundé; tel. 23-34-11; fax 22-51-19; f. 1952; cap. 1,000m. francs CFA; housing construction and development; Pres. Enoch Kwayeb; Dir-Gen. Gilles-Roger Belinga.

CHAMBERS OF COMMERCE

Chambre d'Agriculture, d'Elevage et des Forêts du Cameroun: Parc Repiquet, BP 287, Yaoundé; tel. 23-14-96. 1955; 120 mems; Pres. Philémon Adjibolo; Sec.-Gen. Solomon Nfor Gwei; other chambers at Yaoundé, Ebolowa, Bertoua, Douala, Ngaoundéré, Garoua, Maroua, Buéa, Bumenda and Bafoussam.

Chambre de Commerce, d'Industrie et des Mines du Cameroun (CCIM): rue de Chambre de Commerce, BP 4011, Douala; tel. 42-68-55; fax 42-55-96; internet www.g77tin.org/ccimhp.html; f. 1921; also at BP 36, Yaoundé; BP 211, Limbe; BP 59, Garoua; BP 944, Bafoussam; BP 551, Bamenda; 138 mems; Pres. Pierre Tchanque; Sec.-Gen. Saïdou Abdoulaye Bobboy.

EMPLOYERS' ORGANIZATIONS

Groupement des Femmes d'Affaires du Cameroun (GFAC): BP 1940, Douala; tel. 42-4-64; Pres. Françoise Foning.

Groupement Interpatronal du Cameroun (GICAM): ave Konrad Adenauer, BP 1134, Yaoundé; tel. 20-27-22; fax 20-96-94; also at BP 829, Douala; tel. and fax 42-31-41; f. 1957; Pres. André Siaka; Sec.-Gen. Francis Sanzouango.

Syndicat des Commerçants Importateurs-Exportateurs du Cameroun (SCIEC): 16 rue Quillien, BP 562, Douala; tel. 42-03-04; Sec.-Gen. G. Toscano.

Syndicat des Industriels du Cameroun (SYNDUSTRICAM): 17 blvd de Liberté, BP 673, Douala; tel. 42-30-58; fax 42-56-16; f. 1953; Pres. Samuel Kondo Ebellé.

Syndicat des Producteurs et Exportateurs de Bois du Cameroun: BP 570, Yaoundé; tel. 20-27-22; fax 20-96-94; Pres. Carlo Oriani.

Syndicat Professionnel des Entreprises du Bâtiment, des Travaux Publics et des Activités Annexes: BP 1134, Yaoundé; also at BP 660, Douala; tel. and fax 20-27-22; Pres. (vacant).

Syndicats Professionnels Forestiers et Activités connexes du Cameroun: BP 100, Douala.

Union des Syndicats Professionnels du Cameroun (USPC): BP 829, Douala; Pres. Moukoko Kingue.

West Cameroon Employers' Association (WCEA): BP 97, Tiko.

UTILITIES

Electricity

Société Nationale d'Electricité du Cameroun (SONEL): BP 4077, 63 ave de Gaulle, Douala; tel. 42-54-44; fax 42-22-47; f. 1974; 93.1% state owned; scheduled for transfer to the private sector by 2000; CEO Jean Fouman Akame; Dir-Gen. Marcel Niat Nji-Fenji.

Water

Société Nationale des Eaux du Cameroun (SNEC): BP 157, Douala; tel. 42-87-11; f. 1967; 73% state owned; scheduled for transfer to the private sector by 2000; Pres. Amadou Ali; Dir-Gen. Clément Obouh Fegue.

MAJOR COMPANIES

The following are some of the largest companies in terms of either capital investment or employment:

ALUCAM, Camerounaise de l'Aluminium: BP 54, Edéa; tel. 46-43-11; fax 42-74-74; f. 1954; cap. 17,388m. francs CFA; 39% state-owned; manufacture of aluminium by electrolysis using imported alumina; Pres. Maurice Laparra; Man. Dir M. Malong.

British American Tobacco Cameroun (BAT Cameroun): BP 94, Yaoundé; tel. 21-08-75; fax 20-04-00; f. 1946; cap. 2,394.8m. francs CFA; 99.5% owned by British American Tobacco; manufacture of cigarettes; Chair. and Man. Dir Richard Howe.

Cameroon Sugar Co, Inc (CAMSUCO): BP 1462, Yaoundé; tel. 23-09-56; f. 1975; cap. 10,691m. francs CFA; sugar plantations, refining and marketing; transferred to private ownership in 1999; Pres. Salomon Elogo Metomo; Gen. Man. Joseph Zambo.

Céramiques Industrielles du Cameroun (CERICAM): BP 2033, Douala; tel. 42-37-71. 1969; cap. 1,200m. francs CFA; 20% state-owned; production of ceramic tiles, enamelled mosaics, etc.; Dir-Gen. Michelangelo Balducci.

Cimenteries du Cameroun (CIMENCAM): BP 1323, Douala; tel. 39-11-19; fax 39-09-84; e-mail sat.cim@camnet.cm; f. 1965; cap. 5,600m. francs CFA; cement works at Figuil and clinker-crushing plant at Douala-Bonabéri; Pres. Adama Modi; Dir-Gen. Jean Jung.

Contreplaqués du Cameroun (COCAM): BP 154, Mbalmayo; tel. 28-11-20; fax 28-14-20; f. 1966; cap. 2,489m. francs CFA; 89% state-owned, of which 49% by Société nationale d'investissement du Cameroun; development of forest resources, production of plywood and slatted panels; Pres. Patrice Mandeng; Dir-Gen. Raymond Vincent Atagana Abena.

Cotonnière Industrielle du Cameroun (CICAM): BP 7012, Douala-Bassa; tel. 40-62-15; fax 40-86-75; f. 1965; cap. 2,137m. francs CFA; factory for bleaching, printing and dyeing of cotton at Douala; Pres. Esther Dang; Dir-Gen. Michel Viallet; 1,000 employees.

Dumez Camindustrie: BP 3476, Douala; tel. 42-79-24. 1982; cap. 1,250m. francs CFA; mfrs of construction materials; Pres. André Kamel.

Les Grandes Huileries Camerounaises: Zone Industrielle de Bassa, Douala; f. 1982; cap. 1,400m. francs CFA; 50% state-owned; Pres. Alhadji Bachirou; Man. Dir Eric Jacobsen.

Guinness Cameroun SA: BP 1213, Douala; tel. 40-27-58; fax 40-71-82; f. 1967; cap. 6,410m. francs CFA; production and marketing of beers; Man. Dir B. Johnson; 927 employees.

Nouvelles Brasseries Africaines (NOBRA): BP 2280, Douala; tel. 42-85-03. 1979; cap. 7,000m. francs CFA; mfrs of soft drinks; Pres. Pierre Tchanque; Dir-Gen. Anders Andersen.

Société Africaine Forestière et Agricole du Cameroun (SAFACAM): BP 100, Douala; tel. 42-97-58; fax 42-75-12; f. 1897; cap. 1,820m. francs CFA; plantation of natural rubber and production of rubber and latex; rubber and palm plantations at Dizangué; Pres. Jacques Rouland; Man. Dir Gilbert Sujet; 1,900 employees.

Société Anonyme des Brasseries du Cameroun (SABC): BP 4036, Douala; tel. 42-91-33; fax 42-79-45; f. 1948; cap. 11,084m.

francs CFA; production of beer and soft drinks; Dir Gen. ANDRÉ SIAKA; 1,414 employees.

Société Bernabe Cameroun SARL: BP 529, Douala; tel. 42-96-22; fax 42-50-33; f. 1950; cap. 1,276m. francs CFA; mfrs of metal goods, hardware and construction materials; Pres. ANDRÉ NICOLAS; Man. Dir GÉRARD BOUYER.

Société Camerounaise des Dépôts Pétroliers (SCDP): rue de la Cité Chardy, BP 2271, Douala; tel. 40-54-45; fax 40-47-96; f. 1978; cap. 3,500m. francs CFA; storage and distribution of Cameroon petroleum; Pres. BERNARD MOUDIO; Dir JEAN-BAPTISTE NGUINI EFFA.

Société Camerounaise de Fabrication de Piles Electriques (PILCAM): BP 1916, Douala; tel. 42-26-28. 1970; cap. 1,472m. francs CFA; Pres. VICTOR FOTSO; Dir ANDRÉ FONTANA; 745 employees.

Société Camerounaise de Métallurgie (SCDM): BP 706, Douala; tel. 42-42-56; fax 42-01-85; f. 1984; cap. 1,475m. francs CFA; steel processors and mfrs of metal products; Man. Dir ALAIN GILBERT-DESVALLONS.

Société Camerounaise de Palmeraies (SOCAPALM): blvd Leclerc, BP 691, Douala; tel. 42-81-38. 1968; cap. 9,470m. francs CFA; 68.1% state-owned; management of palm plantations and production of palm oil and manufactured products; scheduled for transfer to private ownership by 2000; Chair. JEAN-BAPTISTE YONKEU; Gen. Man. ROBERT MBELLA MBAPPE.

Société Camerounaise de Sacherie (SCS): Zone Industrielle de Bassa, BP 398, Douala; tel. 42-31-04. 1971; cap. 2,075m. francs CFA; 39% owned by ONCPB; production of sacks; Pres. GUILLAUME NSEKE; Dir THOMAS DAKAYI KAMGA.

Société Camerounaise des Tabacs (SCT): rue Joseph-Clerc, BP 29, Yaoundé; tel. 22-14-88. 1964; cap. 1,750m. francs CFA; tobacco cultivation and curing; Pres. PHILÉMON ADJIBOLO; Man. Dir LUCIEN KINGUE EBONGUE.

Société Camerounaise de Transformation de l'Aluminium (SOCATRAL): BP 291, Edéa; tel. 46-40-24; fax 46-47-74; f. 1960; cap. 750m. francs CFA; 49% owned by ALUCAM (q.v.); production of corrugated sheets, aluminium strips and rolled discs; Pres. M. CHARDON; Dir-Gen. M. NDIORO.

Société Camerounaise de Verrerie (SOCAVER): BP 1456, Douala; tel. 40-05-06; fax 40-64-03; f. 1966; cap. 1,100m. francs CFA; 47% owned by SABC (q.v.); mfrs of glassware; Pres. MICHEL PALU; Man. Dir CHRISTIAN BOULON.

Société de Développement du Coton au Cameroun (SODE-COTON): BP 302, Garoua; tel. 27-10-80; fax 27-20-68; f. 1974; cap. 4,529m. francs CFA; 70% state-owned; cotton ginning and production of cottonseed oil; scheduled for transfer to private ownership by 2000; Pres. GOUNOKO HAOUNAYE; Man. Dir MOHAMED IYA.

Société ELF de Recherches et d'Exploitation des Pétroles du Cameroun (ELF–SEREPCA): 83 blvd de la Liberté, BP 2214, Douala-Bassa; tel. 42-17-85; fax 42-13-66; f. 1951; cap. 1,000m. francs CFA; 20% state-owned; prospecting and exploitation of off-shore petroleum; Pres. JEAN LOUIS VERMEULEN; Dir-Gen. MICHEL CHARLES.

Société Forestière et Industrielle de Belabo (SOFIBEL): BP 1762, Yaoundé; tel. 23-26-57. 1975; cap. 1,902m. francs CFA; 39% state-owned; sawmill; mfrs of plywood; Pres. SADOU DAOUDOU; Man. Dir DENIS KEEDI ATOK.

Société Générale des Travaux Métalliques (GETRAM): Douala; tel. 42-80-68; fax 42-77-61; f. 1980; cap. 1,200m. francs CFA; Pres. BERNARD MOUNDIO; Dir-Gen. OLIVIER BOUYGUES.

Société Industrielle Camerounaise des Cacaos (SIC CACAOS): BP 570, Douala; tel. 40-37-95. 1949; cap. 1,147.5m. francs CFA; production of cocoa and cocoa butter; Pres. JEAN-MARC DIEUDONNÉ OYONO; Man. Dir YVES SCHMUCK.

Société Industrielle des Tabacs du Cameroun (SITABAC): BP 1105, Douala; tel. 42-49-19; fax 42-59-49; e-mail sitabac@camnet.cm; cap. 4,556.6m. francs CFA; manufacture and sale of cigarettes; Pres. and Dir-Gen. JAMES ONOBIONO.

La Société les Minotiers du Cameroun: BP 785, Douala; tel. 37-75-01; fax 37-17-61; f. 1986; cap. 1,010m. francs CFA; flour mill; Pres. BABA AHMADOU; Dir-Gen. ANDRÉ NGANDEU.

Société Nationale des Hydrocarbures (SNH): BP 955, Yaoundé; tel. 20-19-10; fax 20-46-51; f. 1980; cap. 8,000m. francs CFA; national petroleum co; Pres. MARAFA HAMIDOU YAYA; Dir-Gen. ADOLPHE MOUDIKI.

Société Nationale de Raffinage (SONARA): BP 365, Cap Limboh, Limbé; tel. 42-38-15; fax 42-34-44; f. 1976; cap. 17,800m. francs CFA; 66% state-owned; establishment and operation of petroleum refinery at Cap Limboh; Chair. JOHN EBONG NGOLE; Gen. Man. BERNARD EDING; 548 employees.

Société de Palmeraies de la Ferme Suisse (SPFS): BP 06, Edéa-Ongué; tel. 42-34-18. 1976; cap. 1,525m. francs CFA; cultivation of products for industrial processing, operates factory for processing

palm oil and palm kernels; Pres. and Man. Dir PHILIPPE PIECHAUD; Man. YVON LE FLOCH (acting).

Société Shell du Cameroun: BP 4082, Douala; tel. 42-24-15; fax 42-60-31; f. 1954; cap. 1,600m. francs CFA; import and distribution of petroleum products; Pres. and Dir-Gen. OLIVIER DE TINGUY.

Société Sucrière du Cameroun (SOSUCAM): BP 857, Yaoundé; tel. 22-07-99. 1965; cap. 2,500m. francs CFA; 24% state-owned; sugar refinery at M'bandjock; Man. Dir. LOUIS YINDA.

Société Textile du Cameroun pour le Linge de Maison (SOL-ICAM): BP 2413, Douala; tel. 42-97-20. 1979; cap. 3,000m. francs CFA; textile complex; Pres. SIMON NGANNYON; Dir-Gen. MICHEL VIALLET.

Total Cameroun: rue de la Cité Chardy, BP 4048, Douala; tel. 42-63-41. 1947; cap. 1,646m. francs CFA; exploration for, exploitation and distribution of petroleum reserves; Pres. J. GOUBEAU; Dir P. THIBAUD.

PRINCIPAL CO-OPERATIVE ORGANIZATIONS

Centre National de Développement des Entreprises Coopératives (CENADEC): Yaoundé; f. 1970; promotes and organizes the co-operative movement; bureaux at BP 43, Kumba and BP 26, Bamenda; Dir JACQUES SANGUE.

Union Centrale des Coopératives Agricoles de l'Ouest (UCCAO): ave Samuel Wonko, BP 1002, Bafoussam; tel. 44-14-39; fax 44-11-01; f. 1957; marketing of cocoa and coffee; 110,000 mems; Pres. VICTOR GNIMPIEBA; Dir-Gen. PIERRE NZEFA TSACHOUA.

West Cameroon Co-operative Association Ltd: BP 135, Kumba; founded as cen. financing body of the co-operative movement; provides short-term credits and agricultural services to mem. socs; policy-making body for the co-operative movement in West Cameroon; 142 mem. unions and socs representing c. 45,000 mems; Pres. Chief T. E. NJEA.

TRADE UNION FEDERATION

Confederation of Cameroon Trade Unions (CCTU): BP 1610, Yaoundé; tel. 22-33-15; f. 1985; fmrly the Union National des Travailleurs du Cameroun (UNTC); Pres. EMMANUEL BAKOD; Sec.-Gen. LOUIS SOMBES.

Transport

RAILWAYS

There are some 1,104 km of track—the West Line running from Douala to Nkongsamba (166 km) with a branch line leading south-west from Mbanga to Kumba (29 km), and the Transcameroon railway which runs from Douala to Ngaoundéré (885 km), with a branch line from Ngoumou to Mbalmayo (30 km).

Cameroon Railways (CAMRAIL): Gare Centrale de Bessengue, blvd de la Réunification, BP 766, Douala; tel. 40-60-45; fax 40-82-52; f. 1999; Pres. ETIENNE GIROS; Dir-Gen. PATRICK CLAES.

Office du Chemin de Fer Transcamerounais: BP 625, Yaoundé; tel. 22-44-33; supervises the laying of new railway lines and improvements to existing lines, and undertakes relevant research; Dir-Gen. LUC TOWA FOTSO.

ROADS

In 1999 there were an estimated 49,300 km of roads, of which about 4,100 km were paved.

SHIPPING

There are seaports at Kribi and Limbé-Tiko, a river port at Garoua, and an estuary port at Douala-Bonabéri, the principal port and main outlet, which has 2,510 m of quays and a minimum depth of 5.8 m in the channels and 8.5 m at the quays. In 1997 the port handled 4,882,000 metric tons of cargo. Total handling capacity is 7m. metric tons annually. Plans are under way to increase the annual capacity of the container terminal. There are also plans to modernize Limbé–Tiko and to promote it internationally.

Office National des Ports/National Ports Authority: Centre des Affaires Maritimes, 18 rue Joffre, BP 4002, Douala; tel. 42-01-33; fax 42-67-97; e-mail onpc@camnet.cm; internet www.camnet .cm/investir/transport/onpc; f. 1971; Chair. JOSEPH TSANGA ABANDA (Minister of Transport); Gen. Man. TCHOUTA MOUSSA.

Cameroon Shipping Lines SA (CAMSHIP): Centre des Affaires Maritimes, 18 rue Joffre, BP 4054, Douala; tel. 42-00-38; fax 42-21-81; f. 1975; scheduled for transfer to private-sector ownership by 2000; 6 vessels trading with western Europe, USA, Far East and Africa; Chair. FRANÇOIS SENGAT KUO; Man. Dir RENÉ MBAYEN.

Camafrica Liner Co: Centre des Affaires Maritimes, 18 rue Joffre, BP 4045, Douala; operates 4 cargo vessels trading between West Africa and Europe.

Compagnie Maritime Camerounaise SA (CMC): Douala.

Conseil National des Chargeurs du Cameroun (CNCC): BP 1588, Douala; tel. 42-32-06; fax 42-89-01; f. 1986; promotion of the maritime sector; Gen. Man. EMMANUEL EDOU.

Delmas Cameroun: rue Kitchener, BP 263, Douala; tel. 42-47-50; fax 42-88-51; f. 1977; Pres. JEAN-GUY LE FLOCH; Dir-Gen. DANY CHUTAUX.

Société Africaine de Transit et d'Affrètement (SATA): Douala; tel. 42-82-09. 1950; Man. Dir RAYMOND PARIZOT.

Société Agence Maritime de l'Ouest Africain Cameroun (SAMOA): 5 blvd de la Liberté, BP 1127, Douala; tel. 42-16-80. 1953; shipping agents; Dir JEAN PERRIER.

Société Camerounaise de Manutention et d'Acconage (SOCAMAC): BP 284, Douala; tel. 42-40-51. 1976; freight handling; Pres. MOHAMADOU TALBA; Dir-Gen. HARRY J. GHOOS.

Société Camerounaise de Transport et d'Affrètement (SCTA): BP 974, Douala; tel. 42-17-24. 1951; Pres. JACQUES VIAULT; Dir-Gen. GONTRAN FRAUCIEL.

Société Ouest-Africaine d'Entreprises Maritimes—Cameroun (SOAEM—Cameroun): 5 blvd de la Liberté, BP 4057, Douala; tel. 42-52-69; fax 42-05-18; f. 1959; Pres. JACQUES COLOMBANI; Man. Dir JEAN-LOUIS GRECIET.

Société de Transports Urbains du Cameroun (SOTUC): BP 1697, Yaoundé; tel. 21-38-07; fax 20-77-84; f. 1973; 58% owned by Société Nationale d'Investissement du Cameroun; operates urban transport services in Yaoundé and Douala; Dir-Gen. MARCEL YONDO; Mans JEAN-VICTOR OUM (Yaoundé), GABRIEL VASSEUR (Douala).

SOCOPAO (Cameroun): BP 215, Douala; tel. 42-64-64. 1951; shipping agents; Pres. VINCENT BOLLORE; Man. Dir E. DUPUY.

Transcap Cameroun: BP 4059, Douala; tel. 42-72-14. 1960; Pres. RENÉ DUPRAZ; Man. Dir MICHEL BARDOU.

CIVIL AVIATION

There are international airports at Douala, Garoua and Yaoundé; there are, in addition, 11 domestic airports, as well as a number of secondary airfields.

Aéroports du Cameroun (ADC): Aéroport de Douala; f. 1999; manages major airports; 35% owned by Aéroports de Paris, 29% state-owned.

Air Affaires Afrique: BP 1325, Douala; tel. 42-29-77; fax 42-99-03; f. 1978; regional and domestic charter passenger services; CEO BYRON BYRON-EXARCOS.

Cameroon Airlines (CAMAIR): 3 ave du Général de Gaulle, BP 4092, Douala; tel. 42-25-25; fax 42-34-59; f. 1971; domestic flights

and services to Africa and Europe; privatization pending; Chair. JÉRÔME EMILIEN ABONDO; CEO CYRILLE ETOUNDI ATANGANA.

Tourism

Tourists are attracted by Cameroon's cultural diversity and by its national parks, game reserves and sandy beaches. In 1997 an estimated 132,839 tourists visited Cameroon. In that year receipts from tourism totalled some US $39m.

Ministère du Tourisme: BP 266, Yaoundé; tel. 22-44-11; fax 22-12-95; e-mail mintour@camnet.cm; internet www.camnet.cm/mintour/tourisme.

Defence

In August 1999 Cameroon's armed forces totalled 22,100 men, including 9,000 in paramilitary forces. The army numbered 11,500, the navy about 1,300 and the air force 300. Cameroon has a bilateral defence agreement with France.

Defence Expenditure: Estimated at 150,000m. francs CFA in 1998.

Commander-in-Chief of the Armed Forces: PAUL BIYA.

Education

Since independence, Cameroon has achieved one of the highest rates of school attendance in Africa, but provision of educational facilities varies according to region. Education, which is bilingual, is provided by the government, missionary societies and private concerns. Education in state schools is available free of charge, and the government provides financial assistance for other schools.

Primary education begins at six years of age. It lasts for six years in Eastern Cameroon (where it is officially compulsory), and for seven years in Western Cameroon. Secondary education, beginning at the age of 12 or 13, lasts for a further seven years, comprising two cycles of four years and three years in Eastern Cameroon, and two years in Western Cameroon. In 1994 primary enrolment was equivalent to 88% of children in the appropriate age-group (males 93%; females 84%), while secondary enrolment in that year was equivalent to only 27% (males 32%; females 22%). In 1995, according to estimates by UNESCO, the average rate of adult illiteracy was 30.7% (males 22.8%; females 38.4%). The State University at Yaoundé, which was established in 1962, has been decentralized, and consists of five regional campuses, each devoted to a different field of study. Expenditure on education by the central government in 1996/97 was an estimated 93,600m. francs CFA (11.8% of total spending).

Bibliography

Asuagbor, G. O. *Democratization and Modernization in a Multilingual Cameroon.* Edwin Mellin Press, 1998.

Bandolo, H. *La flamme et la fumée.* Yaoundé, Editions SOPECAM, 1988.

Bayart, J.-F. *L'état au Cameroun.* Paris, Presses de la Fondation Nationale des Sciences Politiques, 1985.

Belinga, E. *Cameroun: La Révolution pacifique du 20 mai.* Yaoundé, 1976.

Beti, M. *Lutte ouverte aux camerounais.* Rouen, Editions des Peuples Noirs, 1986.

Biya, P. *Communal Liberalism.* London, Macmillan, 1987.

Biyita bi Essam, J.-P. *Cameroun: Complots et Bruits de Bottes.* Paris, Harmattan, 1984.

Bjornson, R. *The African Quest for Freedom and Identity: Cameroonian Writing and the National Experience.* Bloomington, Indiana University Press, 1994.

Bouchaud, J. *La Côte du Cameroun dans l'histoire et la cartographie des origines à l'annexation allemande.* Yaoundé, Centre IFAN, 1952.

Burnham, P. *The Politics of Cultural Differences in Northern Cameroon.* Edinburgh, Edinburgh University Press, 1996.

Cruise O'Brien, D. B., Dunn, J., and Rathbone, R. *Contemporary West African States.* Cambridge University Press, 1989.

De Lancey, M. W. *Cameroon: Dependence and Independence.* Boulder, CO, Westview Press, 1989.

De Lancey, M. W., and Schrader, P.J. *Cameroon.* Oxford, Clio, 1986.

Donnat, G. *Afin que nul l'oublie.* Paris, Editions L'Harmattan, 1986.

Epale, S. J. *Plantations and Development in Western Cameroon 1875-1975: A Study in Agrarian Capitalism.* New York, Vantage Press, 1985.

Eyinga, A. *Introduction à la politique camerounaise.* Paris, Harmattan, 1984.

Gabriel, R. *L'Administration publique camerounaise.* Paris, Librairie Générale de Droit et de Jurisprudence, 1986.

Gaillard, P. *Le Cameroun.* Paris, Editions L'Harmattan, 1989.

Goheen, M. *Men Own the Fields, Women Own the Crops: Gender and Power in the Cameroon Grassfields.* Madison, University of Wisconsin Press, 1996.

Hugon, P. *Analyse du sous-développement en Afrique noire: L'example de l'économie du Cameroun.* Paris, Presses Universitaires de France, 1968.

Joseph, R. A. *Radical Nationalism in Cameroon.* London, Oxford University Press, 1977.

Koenig, E. L., Chia, E., and Povey, J. (Eds). *A Socio-Linquistic Profile of Urban Centers in Cameroon.* Los Angeles, UCLA (Crossroads Press), 1983.

Konings, P. *Labour Resistance in Cameroon.* London, James Currey Publishers, 1993.

Gender and Class in the Tea Estates of Cameroon. Brookfield, VT, Ashgate Publishing, 1996.

Le Vine, V. T., and Nye, R.P. *Historical Dictionary of the Republic of Cameroon.* 2nd Edn. Metuchen, NJ., Scarecrow Press, 1990.

Manga, E. J. *The African Economic Dilemma: The Case of Cameroon.* Lanham, MD, University Press of America, 1998.

Marc, A. *La Politique économique de l'état britannique dans la région du sud-Cameroun, 1920–1960.* Paris, 1985.

Mbembe, J. A. *Ruben Um Nyobe: Le Problème national kamerunais.* Paris, Editions L'Harmattan, 1984.

Mehler, A. *Kamerun in der Ära Biya: Bedingungen, erste Schritte und Blockaden einer demokratischen Transition.* Hamburg, Institut für Afrika-Kunde, 1993. (Hamburger Beiträge zur Afrika-Kunde; 42).

Ndongko, W.A., and ViveKananda, F. *Economic Development of Cameroon.* Stockholm, Bethany Books, 1990.

Ngoh, V.J. *Cameroon 1884-1985: A Hundred Years of History.* Yaoundé, Imprimerie Nationale, 1988.

Ngongo, L. *Histoire des forces religieuses au Cameroun.* Paris, Editions Karthala, 1982.

Ngwa, J.A. *A New Geography of Cameroon.* 2nd Edn, London, Longman, 1979.

Previtali, S. *Le Cameroun par les ponts et par les routes.* Paris, Editions Karthala, 1988.

Schatzberg, M. G., and Zartman, W. *The Political Economy of Cameroon.* New York, Praeger, 1986.

Stoecker, H. (Ed.). *German Imperialism in Africa.* London, Hurst Humanities, 1986.

Takougang, J., and Krieger, M. H. *African State and Society in the 1990s: Cameroon's Political Crossroads.* Boulder, CO, Westview Press, 1998.

Weiss, L. T. *Migrants nigérians, la diaspora dans le sud-ouest du Cameroun.* Paris, Editions L'Harmattan, 1998.

Zeltner, J.-C., and Torneux, H. *L'arabe dans le bassin du Tchad.* Paris, Editions Karthala, 1986.

CAPE VERDE

Physical and Social Geography
RENÉ PÉLISSIER

Revised for this edition by MARKUS SCHEUERMAIER

The island Republic of Cape Verde, comprising 10 islands, of which nine are inhabited, and five islets, lies in the Atlantic Ocean, about 500 km west of Dakar, Senegal. The archipelago comprises the windward islands of Santo Antão (754 sq km), São Vicente (228 sq km), Santa Luzia (34 sq km), São Nicolau (342 sq km), Boa Vista (622 sq km), and Sal (215 sq km) to the north, while to the south lie the leeward islands of Maio (267 sq km), Santiago (992 sq km), Fogo (477 sq km) and Brava (65 sq km).

The total area is 4,033 sq km (1,557 sq miles) and the administrative capital is Praia (population estimated at 117,026 in 1999) on Santiago Island. The other main centre of population is Mindelo (São Vicente), with an estimated 73,197 inhabitants in 1999, which is the principal port and, with Praia, the economic centre of the archipelago. The 1990 census recorded a total population of 341,491 (84.7 inhabitants per sq km). According to government estimates, the population numbered 439,600 at mid-2000. Santiago is the most populous of the inhabited islands, with an estimated population of 237,671 in 2000, followed by São Vicente (73,197), Santo Antão (49,885) and Fogo (37,582). Santa Luzia has no permanent inhabitants.

Except for the low-lying islands of Sal, Boa Vista and Maio, the archipelago is mountainous, craggy and deeply indented by erosion and volcanic activity. The highest point is Mt Fogo (2,829 m), an active volcano. Located in the semi-arid belt, the islands have an anaemic hydrography, and suffer from chronic shortages of rainfall, which, combined with high temperatures (yearly average 22°–26° C at Praia), cause intense periodic droughts which have an economically devastating effect on the islands and necessitate heavy dependence on international food aid, which provides most of Cape Verde's food requirements. A desalination plant in São Vicente serves the needs of Mindelo, which is otherwise without drinkable water.

Ethnically, about 71% of the inhabitants are of mixed descent, except on Santiago, where the majority is of pure African stock. Whites represent about 1% of the population. The two official languages are Portuguese and Crioulo, a creole Portuguese, which is influenced by African vocabulary, syntax and pronunciation. Illiteracy is still widespread. In 1990 the average life expectancy at birth was 63.5 years for men and 71.3 years for women.

Since independence, a significant number of islanders have emigrated, principally to the USA, the Netherlands, Italy and Portugal, where Cape Verdeans have replaced Portuguese migrants to other countries of the European Union. At least 700,000 Cape Verdeans live outside the country, and their remittances provide an important source of development capital.

Recent History
JONATHAN GREPNE

Revised for this edition by MARKUS SCHEUERMAIER

The Cape Verde islands were colonized by Portugal in the 15th century. In the movement during the 1950s for independence from Portuguese rule, Cape Verde aligned itself with the mainland territory of Portuguese Guinea (now Guinea-Bissau) in a unified nationalist movement, the Partido Africano da Independência do Guiné e Cabo Verde (PAIGC). At Guinea-Bissau's independence in September 1974, however, the PAIGC leadership in Cape Verde decided to pursue its claims separately, rather than to seek an immediate federation with Guinea-Bissau, with which there were few unifying factors other than a common colonial heritage. In December 1974 the Portuguese government and representatives of the islands' PAIGC formed a transitional administration, from which members of other political parties were excluded. Elections to a national people's assembly took place in June 1975, with independence, as the Republic of Cape Verde, following on 5 July. Aristides Pereira, the secretary-general of the PAIGC, became the republic's first president. Gen. Pedro Verona Rodrigues Pires was appointed prime minister, with effective control of government. In 1980 the PAIGC was constitutionally established as the sole legal party, and in November of the same year prospects of unification with Guinea-Bissau were extinguished when Luis Cabral, the president of Guinea-Bissau (and himself a Cape Verdean), was removed in a *coup d'état*. In 1981 the Cape Verdean branch of the PAIGC renamed itself the Partido Africano da Independência de Cabo Verde (PAICV).

POST-INDEPENDENCE CHALLENGES

Cape Verde's political affairs have long been secondary to the islands' struggle for physical survival amid geographical and economic pressures. Substantial infusions of foreign aid (from the European Union (EU), the USA and, until the late 1980s, the former Eastern bloc countries) have been augmented by remittances from Cape Verdeans resident overseas (whose numbers greatly exceed those living in the country). Owing to the rugged terrain of most of the islands, only some 10% of the land area is suitable for farming, and this hindrance is exacerbated by the country's constant vulnerability to drought. During the 1980s an ambitious programme of dike-construction and tree-planting was implemented, to enhance the islands' capacity for water-retention. In 1985 the government made the promotion of birth control a priority, and in 1987 the national assembly approved legislation to legalize abortion, despite concerted opposition by the Roman Catholic Church.

Although Cape Verde was, until September 1990, a one-party state (see below), government policies were generally pragmatic and sensitive, and in the mid-1980s non-PAICV members began to take an increasingly prominent role in public and political life. Central control of the economy was eased, to allow a greater degree of private economic initiative, and in 1989 the government introduced legislation to encourage Cape Verdeans abroad to become involved in the process of development.

Moves towards a relaxation of the PAICV's political monopoly began to emerge in early 1990, as Cape Verde became affected both by political changes in west Africa and by those overtaking the Eastern bloc. In February 1990, in an apparent response to increasing pressure from church and academic circles, the PAICV announced the convening of an emergency congress to discuss the possible abolition of the constitutional provision which guaranteed its political monopoly. Two months later, a newly-formed opposition group, the Movimento para a Democracia (MPD), issued a manifesto in Paris, France, which demanded the immediate introduction of a multi-party system. Pereira subsequently announced that the next presidential election, which was planned for December 1990, would be held, for the first time, on the basis of universal adult suffrage.

The tempo of opposition activity on the islands increased in May 1990, with the presentation of a petition to the president of the national people's assembly, appealing for an immediate introduction of a multi-party system. Later in the month, Pereira announced that he would retire as secretary-general of the PAICV at the party congress in July, in preparation for his own political campaigning in a future multi-party system. At the first public meeting of the MPD, held in Praia in June, the movement's co-ordinator, Carlos Veiga, stated that the MPD was prepared to negotiate with the PAICV for a transition to political plurality. The party was also to seek immediate constitutional reform, the disbanding of the political police, the separation of the army from the PAICV and multi-party legislative elections to precede the presidential election.

Some of the opposition's demands were met in the following month. In July 1990 Pereira announced that legislative elections would be held on a multi-party basis before the end of the year. In September Cape Verde officially became a multi-party state, with the approval by the national people's assembly of the constitutional amendment abolishing the PAICV's monopoly of power. No limit was placed on the number of parties that could be registered, although it was stipulated that they should not be based on religious affiliation or purely regional interests. Legislative elections were scheduled for January 1991, with the presidential election to follow before the end of February. Although the MPD duly obtained registration, an application made by the União Caboverdiana Independente e Democrática (UCID), led by John Wahnon, was rejected. The UCID, founded in 1974 and subsequently active mainly abroad (particularly among Cape Verdeans resident in the USA, Portugal and the Netherlands), subsequently announced that it was to co-operate with the MPD in the forthcoming elections. The MPD held its first congress in Praia in November 1990, at which Veiga was elected party chairman. The MPD subsequently declared its support for the candidacy of António Manuel Mascarenhas Gomes Monteiro, a former supreme court judge, in the forthcoming presidential election. In November Pereira confirmed that he would seek re-election as president.

VEIGA AND THE SECOND REPUBLIC

The legislative elections held in January 1991 resulted in a clear victory for the MPD, which secured 56 of the 79 seats in the national assembly. The PAICV held the remaining 23 seats. The PAICV government resigned, and the party declared its intention to adopt a constructive role in parliamentary opposition. In late January Veiga was sworn in as prime minister at the head of an interim government, pending the result of the presidential election. This took place in February, and resulted in a decisive victory for Mascarenhas, who secured 73.5% of the votes cast. Mascarenhas took office in March, and a new government was formed in April. In his initial statements of the new government's policies, Veiga promised to limit public spending, through the restructuring and privatization of cumbersome state enterprises, and to improve the poor living conditions which affect the majority of the population. Cape Verde would maintain a non-aligned foreign policy. In the economic sphere, Veiga cited fishing, tourism and service industries as areas of priority for development.

The first multi-party local elections, held in December 1991, brought another decisive victory for the MPD, which gained control of 10 of the 14 local councils, including that of the capital, Praia. The PAICV secured control of three councils, and an independent group, which was supported by the UCID, won control of one council.

In January 1992 Veiga restructured the cabinet and created four new ministries including that for public administration and parliamentary affairs; the minister appointed to the portfolio was responsible both for creating an efficient and cost-effective civil service and for enhancing the role and influence of the national assembly. A new constitution, enshrining the democratic basis of the 'Second Republic', took effect in September, when a new national flag and emblem were adopted.

In a further reorganization of the council of ministers, in March 1993, a new ministry, of economic co-ordination, was created incorporating the ministries of economy and of finance and planning.

At its annual national congress in August 1993 the PAICV elected Aristides Lima to the post of secretary-general of the party, replacing Pires who was appointed to the newly created post of party president. The development during 1993 of dissent within the MPD prompted Veiga to announce that a special convention of the party would take place in February 1994. In December 1993 the minister for health, Rui Alberto Figueiredo Soares, left the government, and in the same month the minister of justice and labour, Eurico Correia Monteiro, was dismissed following his announcement that he would seek the leadership of the MPD at the forthcoming convention. The minister of public administration and parliamentary affairs, Alfredo Gonçalves Teixeira, was also dismissed.

At the party convention held in February 1994, Veiga was re-elected to the MPD presidency. However, increasing internal dissent prompted about 15 senior members of the party, led by Eurico Monteiro and a former minister of foreign affairs, Jorge Carlos Almeida Fonseca, to leave the MPD and form a new opposition group, the Partido da Convergência Democrática (PCD).

In March 1994 Veiga again reshuffled the council of ministers, replacing the ministers of justice and of health and creating a new ministry, of employment, youth and social promotion. In May a motion of confidence in the government was debated by the legislature. It was carried in the government's favour by a narrow margin of 41 votes to 38.

In December 1994 Veiga extensively restructured the cabinet, reducing the number of ministerial portfolios to 11 and that of secretaryships to three. The ministry of tourism, industry and commerce was dissolved and its functions transferred to the ministry of economic co-ordination. The ministries of culture and communications, cabinet affairs, and public administration and parliamentary affairs were also abolished. The ministry of fisheries, agriculture and rural activity was divided into two separate ministries, of agriculture and of the sea.

At legislative elections held in December 1995 the MPD obtained an absolute majority, taking 50 seats in a smaller national assembly (reduced from 79 seats to 72 under legislation approved in 1994); the PAICV gained 21 seats and the PCD won the remaining seat. Two other parties, the UCID and the Partido Socialista Democrático (PSD), attracted little support, placing their continued existence in question. At local elections which took place in January 1996 the MPD won control of eight of the islands' 16 municipal councils, while the PAICV secured four, with the remainder gained by independents. At the presidential election which followed in February, Mascarenhas was re-elected unopposed. However, despite appeals for the electorate to demonstrate its support for Mascarenhas' second term of office, the turnout of voters was low, at only 45%. Veiga, meanwhile, expressed his intention to continue the policies of liberal economic and social reform of his previous term in office, and to introduce further constitutional amendments in 1997.

In March 1996 Veiga announced a further reorganization of the cabinet. The ministry of employment, youth and social promotion was disbanded, and the minister responsible for that portfolio was appointed assistant minister to the prime minister, with responsibility for public administration, labour, employment and training, social communication, youth and sports. New ministers were appointed to portfolios of foreign affairs and communities, education, science and culture, and justice and internal administration, and the number of secretaryships was increased from three to seven. In April the minister of infrastructure and transport was replaced. In June 1997 the assistant minister to the prime minister assumed the additional portfolio of social promotion.

At the annual party congress of the PAICV, held in September 1997, Gen. Pedro Verona Rodrigues Pires, prime minister during 1975–91 and secretary-general of the party during 1990–93, was elected leader of the PAICV. Pires, an advocate of traditional left-wing policies, defeated José Maria Neves, who represented the reformist and centrist policies favoured by some of the younger party membership.

In May 1998 Veiga reshuffled the council of ministers, creating several new ministries and appointing the minister of economic co-ordination, António Gualberto do Rosário, to the newly-created post of deputy prime minister. In March 1999 Veiga confirmed speculation that he would not seek re-election as the chairman of the MPD at the next party convention, and would withdraw in order that another party member could be elected to lead the party. Do Rosário and the mayor of Praia, Jacinto Santos, subsequently announced their candidacies for the chairmanship of the MPD, and thus the premiership. The contest escalated into a bitter leadership battle that seriously weakened the ruling party. In November 1999 Veiga sought to regain control of the MPD by dismissing the minister of education, science, youth and sports, José Luís Livramento, the minister of justice, Simão Gomes Monteiro, as well as the secretary of state for decentralization, César Barbosa de Almeida, who were considered to be close associates of Santos. However, this move failed to prevent substantial losses in the municipal elections held in February 2000. The MPD retained eight out of a possible 17 local councils, but lost the capital, Praia, to the PAICV, which re-emerged as a credible political force. Following the resignation of Pedro Pires, who announced his candidacy for the presidential election, the PAICV elected José Maria Neves as the new president of the party in late June 2000. At the fifth convention of the MPD, held in early July, do Rosário was elected chairman of the party. In late July Veiga announced his resignation from the premiership and declared his intention to contest the forthcoming presidential election, which was due to take place in February 2001; do Rosário was immediately appointed prime minister.

External Affairs and Foreign Aid

Since taking office in 1991, the MPD government has successfully sought to extend Cape Verde's range of international contacts, with special emphasis on potential new sources of development aid: substantial assistance has been received from both Israel and the Gulf states. The MPD government has extended the scope of Cape Verde's diplomatic contacts, establishing embassies in South Africa and Sweden, as well as diplomatic presences in Hong Kong, Macau, Singapore, Spain, the United Kingdom and the USA. Promotional trips overseas by the president and the prime minister have included visits to Angola, Belgium, Brazil, Hong Kong, Luxembourg, Macau, the Netherlands, the People's Republic of China, France, Germany, Italy, Portugal, Senegal, Singapore, Switzerland and the USA. Cape Verde has particularly good relations with Portugal, exemplified by official visits made by the then Portuguese prime minister, Aníbal Cavaco Silva, who visited Cape Verde in November 1994 to promote trade and investment in the islands, and by the president of Portugal, Jorge Sampaio, in May 1996. In February 1997 the Portuguese prime minister, António Guterres, made an official trip to Cape Verde accompanied by several of his ministers and a large delegation of Portuguese business representatives. The presidents of the autonomous regions of the Canary Islands (Spain), the Azores (Portugal) and Madeira (Portugal) made official visits to Cape Verde in 1998 and 1999 supported by delegations of local business representatives. Protocols were signed with these neighbouring archipelagos aimed at promoting co-operation, particularly in the fields of fishing, education and transport, as well as creating further incentives for investment in Cape Verde. The country, which remains militarily non-aligned, has also maintained particularly close relations with Brazil, and with other former lusophone African colonies—Angola, Guinea-Bissau, Mozambique and São Tomé and Príncipe, known collectively, with Cape Verde, as the Países Africanos da Língua Oficial Portuguesa (PALOP). Cape Verde is regularly represented at meetings of PALOP, whose principal aid donors include the EU, the IMF, the World Bank and the African Development Bank. In July 1996 a 'lusophone commonwealth', known as the Comunidade dos Países de Língua Portuguesa (CPLP), comprising the five PALOP countries together with Portugal and Brazil, was formed with the intention of benefiting each member state through joint co-operation on technical, cultural and social matters. The second CPLP summit was held in November 1998 in Praia. In December 1996 Cape Verde became a full member of the Sommet francophone, a francophone commonwealth comprising the world's French-speaking countries, from which it derives membership of the Agence de coopération culturelle et technique, an agency which promotes cultural and technical co-operation among francophone countries. (Cape Verde had been an observer at annual meetings of the Sommet francophone since 1977.) Cape Verde is a member of the Organization of African Unity (OAU), the Economic Community of West African States (ECOWAS), the UN, and is a signatory to the Lomé Convention, which promotes co-operation between the EU and African, Caribbean and Pacific (ACP) countries.

Economy

JONATHAN GREPNE

Revised for this edition by MARKUS SCHEUERMAIER

According to the revised national accounts, published in 1999, Cape Verde's gross domestic product (GDP) in 1998 was US $496m., equivalent to $1,200 per head. Cape Verde's GDP per head is greater than that of the other four former Portuguese African colonies combined, and thus Cape Verde is the only lusophone African nation within the World Bank's lower middle-income bracket. However, according to the World Bank, 14% of the population are classified as very poor and a further 30% as poor, so that poverty remains the dominant theme in this largely subsistence economy. In 1999 unemployment was estimated to affect about 26% of the labour force, with a further 26% underemployed.

Despite the country's physical disadvantages, the economy has grown fairly steadily since independence in 1975, benefiting from the considerable provision of official aid, on very favourable terms, and the substantial remittances of Cape Verdean emigrés, whose number is almost double that of those actually living on the islands. Cape Verde's GDP increased, in real terms, at an average annual rate of 7.0% in 1975–82, 4.3% in 1986–91, and 5.0% in 1991–98. In comparison, the population has increased by an average of 2.2% per year since 1990. Real GDP growth fell from 7.5% in 1995 to 3.5% in 1996, before increasing to 5.2% in 1997 and to 5.0% in 1998. Real GDP growth of 8.0% was recorded in 1999. The annual rate of inflation has averaged 6.5% since 1991. Average annual inflation fell from 8.4% in 1995 to 6.0% in 1996, before increasing again to 8.6% in 1997. It declined to 4.3% in 1998 and to 4.0% in 1999.

AGRICULTURE AND FISHERIES

The Cape Verde archipelago is situated in the Sahelian climatic zone and thus suffers from severe periodic droughts. Only some 10% (39,000 ha) of Cape Verde's total surface area is cultivable (one-half of this is on Santiago), with cultivation actually taking place on 34,000 ha, of which only 3,000 ha are irrigated. In the absence of the necessary infrastructure to combat the effects of droughts, Cape Verde has not been able to achieve self-sufficiency in food production. As a result, agriculture (including forestry and fishing) contributed just 12.1% of GDP in 1998, although the sector is an important source of employment, employing 24.4% of the economically active population in 1998. About 54% of farms on cultivated land are smaller than 1 ha and fewer than 3% exceed 5 ha. In the late 1970s the Partido Africano da Independência de Cabo Verde (PAICV) government nationalized a few large irrigated properties, mainly banana plantations (predominantly white-owned), and in 1981 it enacted an agrarian reform law to distribute to their peasant cultivators landholdings over 5 ha (1 ha if irrigated) that were not directly farmed by their owners. However, in 1993, the Movimento para a Democracia (MPD) government revoked the agrarian reform law, which had been widely condemned by farmers, who perceived it as an attempt by the former PAICV regime to exercise further control over them.

On average, only about 12.5% of Cape Verde's annual food requirements are grown on the islands, with the remainder having to be imported. International food aid has been required since independence in 1975. A 10-year drought eased in 1978, but in 1979, 1981 and 1983 the drought was so severe that almost all crops were lost. In 1984 heavy rainfall caused catastrophic floods, which were followed by drought in 1985, 1986, 1989, 1990, 1991 and 1994. In 1996 the worst drought for nearly 50 years again resulted in an almost total loss of crops, and there were further droughts in 1997 and 1998.

The amount of international food aid required has fluctuated according to the extent of each drought. In 1986 and 1987 these requirements amounted to 70,000 metric tons and 56,000 tons respectively, but were reduced to 28,000 tons in 1988 and 1989, following two years of good harvests. In 1992 65,000 tons of cereal were imported, of which 58,000 tons were anticipated food aid and only 7,000 tons were commercial imports. In January 1995 Cape Verde appealed for further emergency food aid following a particularly poor harvest in the previous year. In 1996, following an exceptionally severe drought, the appeal for emergency food aid included a request for some 82,000 tons of cereal. Further emergency food aid was requested following the drought of 1997 and 1998. In August 1997 the EU (European Union, formerly the European Community—EC) agreed to grant financial credits to the Cape Verde treasury to purchase its food requirements rather than delivering the produce itself.

A reafforestation plan has been put into effect with assistance from the FAO. Some 12m. drought-resistant trees (American acacias) were planted during 1978–86, and the government aimed to continue planting 3m. trees annually to reduce soil erosion and increase groundwater levels. A five-year programme of soil conservation began in 1990, with the aim of planting a further 2m. trees on three islands. In 1991 some 16% of the total surface area of the archipelago was forested. Estimates suggest that the total potentially exploitable groundwater and surface water resources of Cape Verde are around 150m. cubic metres per year; enough to irrigate around 8,600 ha, compared with the present area under irrigation of around 3,000 ha. About 7,200 rainwater dikes have been built, and well-sinking is a high priority in the government's programme, which aims to irrigate a further 5,600 ha by the end of the century. Since 1994 a new, more efficient system of irrigation has been adopted. This system is expected to be introduced at an average of 50 ha per year, to cover 300 ha by the year 2000. At that point the water saved is expected to be sufficient to irrigate a further 150 ha.

Santiago is the main agricultural producer (contributing about 50% of total production), followed by Santo Antão, Fogo and São Nicolau. Cash crops, such as bananas (production 6,000 tons in 1998, according to FAO estimates), arabica coffee, groundnuts, castor beans and pineapples, are encouraged, but poor inter-island communications, low educational attainment, the shortage of government funds, the lack of suitable available land and adverse climatic conditions militate against the development of a thriving agriculture. Cape Verde's food crops are maize, beans, cassava and sweet potatoes, supplemented (wherever soils, terrain and rainfall permit) with bananas, vegetables, sugar cane, fruits, etc. The main staples are beans and maize, which are intercropped. As the result of drought and damage by locusts, production of maize declined from 16,000 metric tons in 1988/89 to 2,500 tons in 1991, before increasing to 5,000 tons

in 1992, and to 12,000 tons in 1993, but declining to 6,000 tons in 1994 following another year of drought. Maize output improved to 10,000 tons, owing to better rainfall levels, in 1995, but was estimated to be almost negligible following severe droughts in 1996 and 1998. Cape Verde's overall cereal requirement was 110,000 tons in 1998. More than one-half of Cape Verde's total irrigated land is under sugar cane (production totalled 13,000 tons in 1998, according to FAO estimates), most of which is used in the production of a popular alcoholic beverage for local consumption. The government is seeking to reallocate this land to staple and cash crops by encouraging the manufacture (and future export) of an alternative liquor using imported molasses.

The islands' only significant crop export is bananas (2,054 metric tons in 1992, and 864 tons in 1993). These were mainly shipped to Portugal, with a small amount going to Germany. However, strict quality restrictions imposed by the EU on banana imports from ACP countries in 1994 halted almost all banana exports from Cape Verde to the EU. The EU granted funding of US $700,000 in 1995 and a further $390,000 in 1996 towards the improvement of banana production, packaging and delivery in order that Cape Verdean bananas may meet the quality requirements. Cape Verde has a 4,800 ton banana quota with the EU which, if fulfilled, could produce valuable export earnings. Banana exports recommenced in 1998 with Germany importing 100 tons; this figure was scheduled to increase significantly in years to come. A rather exotic commodity, locally known as *purgueira (Jatropha curcas),* which grows wild, is also exported (for soap-making). In the past Cape Verde exported coffee, castor beans and tomatoes, but only in minimal quantities, owing to the prevailing climatic conditions.

Livestock herds have been reduced to one-quarter, or even one-tenth, of their pre-drought level, but are slowly recovering. In 1998, according to FAO estimates, about 22,000 cattle, 110,000 goats, 9,000 sheep and 636,000 pigs were raised for food and milk. Following the poor rains in 1990, the government announced emergency measures to maintain stocks of cattle fodder. In early 1998 an outbreak of African swine fever threatened severely to reduce pork production on the islands; by 1999 the outbreak appeared to be under control. About 14,000 horses, asses and mules provide the main form of transport in rural areas.

Fishing offers great development potential, and modern appliances and boats are being slowly introduced to the sector. Fishing exports consist primarily of tuna and lobster. In the long term Cape Verde should be able to reduce its dependency on high levels of food aid by developing its fishing resources. Cape Verde's exclusive economic zone comprises 734,265 sq km and contains one of the last significantly underused fishing grounds in the world. However, fishing remains very much a small-scale industry, employing about 7,000 local fishermen in 1993, representing some 6% of the economically active population. The sector is still largely in the hands of artisanal fishermen who catch only a small percentage of the total sustainable yield, estimated at about 45,000 metric tons per year. Productivity is low for both artisanal and commercial fishermen, who together contribute no more than 4% of GDP. This is mainly the result of inadequate training, the lack of modern equipment and technology, and the shortage of available finance. Of some 1,400 fishing boats only around 40% are motorized, and of some 95 larger vessels used for industrial fishing, only 64 are fully operational. The MPD government, which has privatized the state-owned fishing company, the Empresa Caboverdiana de Pescas (PESCAVE), aims to encourage private entrepreneurs by means of credit facilities, training and research. A fishing agreement was signed with the EC for the first time in 1990. The agreement initially operated for three years and was subsequently renewed for a further two-year period, establishing quotas for catches by boats from EC countries in Cape Verdean waters, in exchange for which the EC agreed to pay Cape Verde US $1.2m. per year, in addition to the revenue from the sale of fishing licences. In August 1997 the EU signed a three-year fishing agreement with Cape Verde, providing Spanish, French and Portuguese vessels with a licence to catch 5,000 tons of tuna fish annually in Cape Verdean waters. In 1994 the European Investment Bank granted a loan of $2.5m. to help finance the construction of an anchovy canning plant in Mindelo by an

Italo-Spanish consortium, Fishpackers Lda, which announced in 1996 its intention to open another factory, which will can mackerel and tuna, caught in Cape Verdean waters, for export, principally to Europe and the USA. Annual fishing catches increased from 8,500 tons in 1995 to 10,000 tons in 1997. The government aimed to increase annual production of canned fish products to 1,400 tons by 1997. Exports of fish and shellfish amounted to $181,000 in 1998. In March 1999 the government announced an emergency plan to assist fishermen who had suffered a decline of some 40% in their overall catch owing to changes in local water temperatures that had led to the disappearance of certain types of fish, particularly tuna.

TRANSPORT AND TOURISM

Cape Verde is strategically located between Africa, Europe and America. International maritime and air transport, including transhipment, have been identified as an important source of foreign exchange by both the PAICV and MPD governments. The main port of the islands is Porto Grande at Mindelo on São Vicente, where a new ship-building and repair yard was opened in 1983. Work was completed in 1997 on a US $13.2m.-project to increase capacity and modernize the container storage terminal at Porto Grande to contend with an increase in trade from local light industrial activities. The port of Praia was recently completely modernized to handle 550,000 metric tons of cargo per year and offers refrigerator and container storage. New quays and port facilities were opened on Maio and Boa Vista islands during 1997, at a cost of $10.5m. A new port was also opened in June 1999 on Fogo, with funding of DM 14m. from Germany; a new port was expected to be completed by the end of 2000 on Brava. In January 1997 the government formed two companies in strategic partnership with a US ship manufacturer and operator, Skaarup, and with local investors; Seainvest builds and charters cargo vessels, while CS Line leases the same vessels to operate shipping services to Europe. Under this venture two new vessels were being built during 1997 at a total cost of $24m. In 1988 the Cape Verdean government rejected an offer of $65m. from a consortium of Western industrialized countries, including the USA and Australia, to dispose of their toxic waste in Cape Verdean waters.

The Amílcar Cabral international airport on Sal Island has a throughput capacity of 1m. passengers per year and can accommodate aircraft of up to 50 metric tons. A new terminal for international traffic was constructed in 1991 with a loan of US $8m. from Portugal, and work began in May 1998 to upgrade the domestic and international flights terminals. Further improvements were implemented in 1998/99 at a cost of $15m. The airport's facilities have been used as a strategic refuelling point, chiefly by South African Airways (SAA) and Aeroflot (Russia), as well as a number of cargo transportation airlines. During 1987–91 Cape Verde suffered a loss of about $6m. in revenue as a result of the curtailment by the US government of flights by SAA to the USA. These transatlantic flights, which had previously comprised 90% of air traffic through Sal, declined from 38 to only six per month. However, following the repeal of US sanctions in late 1991, South African air traffic was resumed. In 1993 other African countries, located on a more direct flight path, ended their ban on SAA flights, thus substantially reducing the importance of Sal as a refuelling point. In early 1996, nevertheless, SAA announced that it would be increasing the number of its flights from Johannesburg and New York using Sal as a stop-over from four to seven per week between July and November. In 1994 some 300,000 passengers passed through the airport, when cargo lines, principally between Europe and South America, accounted for around 30% of all landings. Annual passenger numbers were expected to increase to some 400,000 before the end of 2000. The national airline, Transportes Aéreos de Cabo Verde (TACV), operates a regular inter-island service as well as scheduled international flights to Amsterdam (the Netherlands), Banjul, Bissau, Bologna (Italy), Boston (USA), Conakry, Dakar, Las Palmas (Spain), Lisbon, Madrid (Spain), Milan (Italy), Munich (Germany), Paris (France) and Vienna (Austria). A new international airport is under construction at Praia, funded by the African Development Bank ($22.5m.), and is due for completion in 2000. The airport is designed to accommodate Airbus 310 aircraft and will be able to receive flights from Europe and the USA. Work began in 1998, with

financing of $7m. from France, to upgrade the airport on São Vicente to international capacity. Plans were also being prepared for the construction of an international airport on Boa Vista.

Tourism has been identified as the area with the most potential for economic development. Cape Verde benefits from its proximity to the European market, enjoys a favourable climate for most of the year, and offers white sandy beaches and some spectacular mountain scenery. At present the industry contributes only around 3.5% of GDP, but legislation, introduced since 1991, has aimed to provide increased incentives and guarantees to investors. Tourism has been the sector to gain the greatest benefit from foreign investment, and several new hotel developments began operating in 1996 on Sal, Santiago, São Vicente and Boa Vista. The successful development of tourism on Santiago is envisaged with the opening of the new international airport at Praia. British and Portuguese investors plan to develop a luxury hotel resort at the Baia de São Francisco, with construction expected to begin in 2000. Currently there are nine hotels of international standard on Sal, three on Boa Vista, three on São Vicente and nine on Santiago. In 1998 around 52,000 tourists visited Cape Verde, mainly from Italy, Portugal, Germany, Austria, France, the Netherlands, Belgium and Spain. This increased to 67,000 in 1999. In 1997 earnings from tourism totalled US $15m. It was estimated that tourist numbers would increase to 65,000 in 1999, with earnings of $20m. envisaged. Foreign investment totalling some $60m. was expected to increase the number of hotel beds from 2,500 in mid-1997 to 4,850 during 1999/2000.

MANUFACTURING

The industrial sector remains largely undeveloped, accounting for 18.5% of GDP in 1998; 9.7% in industry and energy and 8.8% in construction. Manufacturing consists primarily of fish canning, clothing, footwear, rum distilling and bottling plants, and employed about 6% of the total labour force in 1995. In 1995 Cape Verde had around 120 small- and medium-sized industrial enterprises, mostly privately-owned. The larger enterprises were mainly formed under the PAICV government and have, since 1991, been privatized, restructured, liquidated or identified for future privatization. In October 1993 the free-zone enterprise law was enacted permitting enterprises producing goods and services exclusively for export to benefit from exemptions on tax and customs duties for a period of 10 years. The law also applied to new firms specializing in transhipment. It was intended that the new legislation would attract foreign investment and promote the expansion of Cape Verde's industrial exports. Further incentives to foreign investment in the manufacturing sector are the country's geographical location, available work-force, low wage costs and beneficial trade agreements with the countries of the Economic Community of West African States (ECOWAS), as well as the EU and the USA. In the first three years since the introduction of the free-zone enterprise law, the manufacturing sector attracted some US $35m. in foreign investment, most of which originated from Portugal; Confecções Porto Grande, established in Mindelo on São Vicente in 1995 by Portuguese investors, produces clothing for export to Europe, while footwear manufacturer Growela, another example of Portuguese investment, manufactures uppers for footwear for export directly to the United Kingdom. In 1999 there were eight manufacturing companies operating in Cape Verde that had been established by foreign investors under the new free-zone enterprise law. Legislation enacted in 1999 provided for the transformation of industrial parks at Mindelo and Praia into free trade zones and for the establishment of a further free trade zone on Sal island. Mining is of little significance, representing less than 1% of GDP in 1993, with pozzolana, a volcanic ash used in cement manufacture (10,000 metric tons per year in 1981–90, according to estimates by the US Bureau of Mines and the UN), and salt (an estimated 1,000 tons in 1996) being the main products. A consortium led by a Portuguese enterprise, CIMPOR, announced in 1995 that it was to establish a company on Maio for the manufacture of cement, involving a total investment of some $45m., to date the largest individual foreign investment project proposed in Cape Verde. The plant, in which a Chinese cement producer and local investors will have a stake, is to open in 2000, with an annual capacity of 200,000 tons. This will supply the domestic market and save the government some $8m. a year on cement imports necessary for public investment projects.

AID AND INVESTMENT

Government policy in recent years has sought to attract private foreign investment, particularly towards the tourism, fishing and light manufacturing sectors. In 1989 legislation was introduced to open the economy to private external investment, but this was limited to the Cape Verdean emigrant community. In 1991 the World Bank provided a loan of US $8m. for a programme to promote foreign investment. In that year the Centro de Promoção Turística, do Investimento Externo e das Exportações (PROMEX), a body under partial government control and funded by the US Agency for International Development (USAID), was established to promote exports and foreign investment in Cape Verde. In 1993 an external investment law opened the economy to all foreign investment. A free-zone enterprise law (see above) was also passed in that year. Industrial parks at Praia and Mindelo were constructed with funding from the EU. On completion of the new international airport at Praia the smaller existing airport is to be transformed into an international trade fair centre. Between 1992 and 1998 Cape Verde attracted some $82m. in foreign investment, creating about 2,000 new jobs. Some 60% of all foreign investment was in the manufacturing sector, mostly originating from Portugal. However, since 1996 an increasing proportion of foreign investment, principally from Italy, has been in the tourism sector. In 1997 Italy and Spain both signed agreements with Cape Verde designed to facilitate investment and promote co-operation in the development of the tourism infrastructure. The main area for public investment, accounting for about one-third of total government expenditure, is that of infrastructure, in particular telecommunications, port and airport facilities, roads, and the provision of water and electricity. In 1995 40% of the state telecommunications company, Cabo Verde Telecom (CVT), was sold to Portugal Telecom International for $20m. In 1997–98 a further 50% of CVT was divested. Some $90m. had been pledged for investment, principally by the Portuguese company, before the year 2000 to modernize and expand the current network from 21,500 to 55,000 subscribers (in 1999 there were 42,592 subscribers). In 1995 Austria and the OPEC Development Fund granted financing of $12m. for the installation of a fibre optic telecommunication line linking Santiago, Sal, São Nicolau and São Vicente. The line, which began operating in mid-1997, offers on-line data communications and video-conferencing and will eventually be linked to a transatlantic network. CVT has also introduced a mobile telephone network and provision for Internet services. Improved telecommunications will, potentially, enable the government to transform Cape Verde into an offshore banking centre. In 1997 investors from the USA, Saudi Arabia and Pakistan founded an international ship registration agency in Mindelo, establishing the Cape Verdean flag as a 'flag of convenience.'

Foreign aid is indispensable to Cape Verde, which receives one of the highest levels of aid per caput in the world (US $270 in 1997). According to the Organisation for Economic Co-operation and Development, total official development assistance reached $117.9m. in 1993, $121.4m. in 1994, $112.4m. in 1995, $120.3m. in 1996 and $109.6m. in 1997. Grants account for 88% of international aid, and loans for the remainder. In 1997 bilateral aid totalled $68.0m. The principal donors were Portugal ($12.4m.), Germany ($11.1m.), the Netherlands ($9.4m.), the USA ($8.0m.) and France ($5.4m.). In that year, of the $42.0m. in multilateral aid, the EU provided $22.1m., the World Food Programme $3.0m., the African Development Fund (ADF) $3.8m. and the International Development Association (IDA) $8.2m. Cape Verde receives aid from the EU under the Lomé Conventions, and was allocated $28.1m. for its 1986–90 development programme, $38m. for 1991–95, and $42.2m. for 1996–2000.

The EU aid programme is primarily directed at improving the provision of water, electricity and sanitation, particularly in Praia and Mindelo. In 1993 the EU granted US $6m. for a project to provide a network of water pipelines connecting suburban water wells and a reservoir to Praia by the end of 1999. A more comprehensive government scheme estimated to cost some $82m., to be funded by major foreign donors, was announced in 1993. The project aimed to provide access to drinking water for the entire population by 2005. In 1995 Israeli technology was being used to install desalination units in Praia, with finance provided by the EU. In 1994 a project funded by the EU ($6m.), to provide wind-powered electricity generators at Praia, Mindelo and on Sal island was completed. On average the new generators provide about 10% of local residential electricity requirements. In early 1993 the European Investment Bank agreed to lend more than $6m. towards the extension of the power plant at Mindelo.

In 1995 the IDA approved a credit of US $11.5m. for a programme aimed at achieving 100% enrolment in primary education by 1999. The project also included plans to adapt vocational training to the requirements of the local employment market. In 1996 the IDA approved a credit of $11.4m., of which $5.6m. was allocated to PROMEX for the period 1996–98 and $4.6m. was for a vocational training programme designed to modernize the management of financial institutions. In May 1999 the IDA approved a credit of $22.2m. to support the National Development Plan for 1997–2001 (see below). Of the total $16m. was for poverty alleviation, principally sanitation, water and electricity provision; other principal areas of funding were education and vocational training for local and central government employees.

In August 1992 the IDA agreed to provide a US $4.7m. loan to finance technical assistance in preparation for privatization and private-sector economic development programmes. A further $10m. was provided by the World Bank in 1998 for the second phase of the programme which was due for completion by the end of 2001. By mid-1997 the government had divested 90% of the fuel retailer Empresa Nacional de Combustíveis and 100% of Hotel-Mar (a hotel holding company). Several public companies have been liquidated and others have been restructured or undergone partial privatization. The government was to sell all its shares in the public sector, held within 25 companies, by 2002; only the post office and the air traffic control and airport handling firm, ASA, would remain under state control. The Banco Comercial do Atlântico, the Caixa Económica de Cabo Verde, Garantia (insurance) and Promotora (venture capital) were fully or partially privatized in 1999–2000. In April 1999 the government established agencies to regulate the operation of certain newly-privatized businesses; the multi-sectoral regulation agency was to regulate transport, aviation, communication, water, electricity and the environment, while the national agency for security of food provision would ensure that food imports were adequately distributed following the privatization of the Empresa Pública de Abastecimento. Legislation was approved in 1997 providing tax incentives for investors and companies trading in the Praia Stock Exchange, which opened in early April 1998.

TRADE, FINANCE AND PLANNING

Cape Verde's principal merchandise exports are canned tuna and mackerel, frozen fish, lobster and manufactured textile goods (mainly clothing and footwear). Small amounts of salt and pozzolana are exported. Large scale exports of bananas, interrupted in 1994 owing to quality restrictions imposed by the EU, resumed in 1998. Exports of processed fish and light-manufactured goods are expected to increase substantially in the future as new freezing and canning plants come into operation, as well as free trade zones at Praia and Mindelo. Merchandise exports increased from US $11.4m. in 1992 to some $43.2m. in 1997, but declined to $32.7m. in 1998. Cape Verde traditionally operates a substantial trade deficit which stems from the need to import some 85% of its food requirements (although most of this is provided free under aid schemes), as well as manufactured goods, fuel and other essential goods. Since 1991 imports have risen significantly, thus widening the trade deficit further. This has resulted in part from the MPD government's open market policies; notably, the liberalization of previous restrictions on almost all imported goods, and the introduction of measures enabling local firms to borrow from domestic banks in order to purchase imported materials. In 1992 the trade deficit stood at $157.1m., with exports covering around 6.8% of imports. However, the deficit increased to $217.1m. in 1995, when exports covered 7.1% of imports. In 1996 and 1997 the government imposed import restrictions and tariffs on certain non-essential goods in order to reduce the trade deficit. In 1996 the deficit declined to $183.6m., with exports covering 11.5% of imports, and in 1997 the deficit was reduced further to $171.9m., with exports covering 20.1% of imports. The deficit increased again, however, to $185.6m. in 1998, owing mainly to a fall in exports. In recent years Portugal has significantly increased its trading with Cape Verde. In 1989 Portugal exported goods worth $34m. (32% of imports) to Cape Verde, but the value of these transactions reached about $107m. (49.8% of imports) in 1997. Other important sources of imports in 1997 were France (8.7%), the Netherlands (5.1%), and the United Kingdom (3.6%). Portugal is also the principal market for exports, accounting for an estimated 45% of the total in 1997. Of income from the export of goods and services, the latter typically accounted for some 90% of the total between 1989 and 1994, providing average annual receipts of $50m. In 1995 exports of services provided revenue of almost $75m. It was envisaged that export earnings from the services sector would increase significantly in the near future, particularly from tourism, transhipment and the refuelling and servicing of aircraft belonging to foreign airlines.

In July 1993 the first commercial bank was established, the Banco Comercial do Atlântico (BCA). Despite the fact that its capital was raised solely from state funds provided by the Banco de Cabo Verde, the BCA enjoyed relative independence from the central bank and has a high degree of autonomy in its administration and management. The state's shares in BCA were sold in 1999 to a consortium led by the Portuguese Caixa Geral de Depósitos (CGD). The Banco de Cabo Verde now functions solely as a central bank. The state's shares in the Caixa Económica de Cabo Verde, which specializes in real estate banking services, were sold in early 2000 to a consortium led by the Portuguese Caixa Económica Montepio Geral. New legislation introduced in 1993 provides for the creation of financial institutions to offer loans and credit to small- and medium-sized entrepreneurs. Four Portuguese banks have established representation in Cape Verde: Banco Totta e Açores (BTA) opened a branch in Praia in December 1995, Banco Nacional Ultramarino and Banco Mello opened offices in Praia during 1996, and in 1998 the CGD opened branches in Praia and Mindelo. Banco Interatlântico, a subsidiary of CGD, was established in 1999. The establishment of these foreign banks in Cape Verde was expected to raise the level of available credit lines through Portugal, and subsequently the level of investment and imports from that country. Cape Verde's first venture capital company, Promotora, began operating in July 1997 and will support the development of the private sector by offering local businessmen an opportunity to enter into joint ventures with foreign partners. Promotora was sold to CGD in 1999.

A fourth National Development Plan (NDP), adopted in 1997, set out the government's plans for social and economic development up to 2001. The plan, which was the outcome of close collaboration between the government, the United Nations Development Programme and Cape Verde's international aid donors, comprises four principal programmes: poverty alleviation (allocated some US $60m.); health promotion; a 12-year programme to improve sanitation in Praia (to cost some $65m.); and economic reform (to include an acceleration of the privatiza-

tion programme and new measures to encourage foreign investment). According to the fourth NDP, real GDP growth per head was expected to average some 3% per year in 1998–2001, with the annual rate of inflation expected to average 3.5% during the same period.

A point worth noting is the low level of Cape Verde's debt-servicing costs, which the budget-conscious government has kept to a minimum. Cape Verde's total external debt at the end of 1998 was US $243.7m., of which $237.3m. was long-term debt. As a proportion of the value of exports of goods and services, the debt-service ratio was 9.9% in that year. Public domestic debt, however, increased from about $40m. in 1992 to $180m. at the end of 1997, despite a government commitment to reduce the budget deficit. At a meeting of Cape Verde's development partners in late 1997 the government announced that the servicing of the national debt was the greatest constraint on its ability to finance Cape Verde's economic development. In addition to supporting the NDP, Cape Verde's international donors agreed to provide $100m. for a scheme to ameliorate the burden of national debt. The government was to contribute a further $80m. in revenue from the accelerated privatization programme. The total of $180m. was to be deposited in an offshore trust fund from which 95% of the interest earned would be used to repay the national debt, with the remainder placed in a special development fund. However, contributions to the fund from both domestic and external sources were below initial expectations and the debt-conversion operation only commenced in 1999.

In December 1997 the national assembly approved the annual state budget for 1998,which included budget projections for 1999 and 2000. The three-year budget plan, which envisaged a balanced budget for each year, was adopted to demonstrate the government's commitment to fulfilling its spending obligations under the NDP. Total government expenditure for 1998 was projected at 20,500m. Cape Verde escudos and that for 1999 at 20,800m. escudos. Spending on social areas such as education, social security, health, housing and sanitation was to comprise 40.4% of total budgetary expenditure in 1999, while spending on public administration and defence was to remain low at around 15% and 2%, respectively. A voluntary redundancy scheme, introduced in 1993 to reduce the size of the civil service, was to be continued and improved under the NDP's economic reform programme. Revenue from fiscal sources was to be increased following the broadening of the scope of liability for income tax and modernization of the tax collection system.

In March 1998 Cape Verde and Portugal signed an agreement providing for their respective currencies to become linked through a fixed exchange rate. The linking of the two currencies in July 1998 not only transformed the Cape Verde escudo into a convertible currency, thus encouraging foreign investment and trade, but established a firm monetary link to the single European currency following its introduction in January 1999. Under the terms of the agreement, Portugal agreed to underwrite the link with some US $50m. to augment Cape Verde's foreign currency reserves. Furthermore, the new development was expected to encourage trade with west African countries in the CFA franc zone, which is linked through the French franc to the single European currency.

Statistical Survey

Source (unless otherwise stated): Statistical Service, Banco de Cabo Verde, Avda Amílcar Cabral, Santiago; tel. 61-31-53.

AREA AND POPULATION

Area: 4,033 sq km (1,557 sq miles).

Population: 295,703 (males 135,695; females 160,008) at census of 2 June 1980; 341,491 (males 161,494; females 179,997) at census of 23 June 1990; 439,600 (official estimate) at mid-2000. *By island* (official estimates, mid-2000): Boa Vista 3,515, Brava 6,319, Fogo 37,582, Maio 6,236, Sal 11,593, Santo Antão 49,885, São Nicolau 13,602, Santiago 237,671, São Vicente 73,197.

Density (mid-2000): 109.0 per sq. km.

Principal Town: Cidade de Praia (capital), population 61,644 at 1990 census; 117,026 in 1999 (official estimate).

Births, Marriages and Deaths (1998, provisional): Registered live births 15,460 (birth rate 37.1 per 1,000); Registered marriages (1994) 1,200 (marriage rate 3.2 per 1,000); Registered deaths (1995) 3,439 (death rate 8.9 per 1,000). Source: UN, *Demographic Yearbook* and *Population and Vital Statistics Report*.

Expectation of Life (years at birth, 1990): Males 63.53; Females 71.33. Source: UN, *Demographic Yearbook*.

Economically Active Population (persons aged 10 years and over, 1990 census): Agriculture, hunting, forestry and fishing 29,876; Mining and quarrying 410; Manufacturing 5,520; Electricity, gas and water 883; Construction 22,722; Trade, restaurants and hotels 12,747; Transport, storage and communications 6,138; Financing, insurance, real estate and business services 821; Community, social and personal services 17,358; Activities not adequately defined 24,090; Total labour force 120,565 (males 75,786; females 44,779), including 31,049 unemployed persons (males 19,712; females 11,337). Source: International Labour Office, *Yearbook of Labour Statistics.*

AGRICULTURE, ETC.

Principal Crops (FAO estimates, '000 metric tons, 1998): Maize 11; Potatoes 2; Sweet potatoes 4; Cassava 3; Pulses 3; Coconuts 5; Cabbages 6; Tomatoes 5; Onions (dry) 2; Green beans 2; Other vegetables 2; Sugar cane 13; Mangoes 5; Bananas 6; Other fruits 4. Source: FAO, *Production Yearbook.*

Livestock (FAO estimates,'000 head, year ending September 1998): Cattle 22; Pigs 636; Sheep 9; Goats 110; Asses 14. Source: FAO, *Production Yearbook.*

Livestock Products (FAO estimates, '000 metric tons, 1998): Pig meat 8; Other meat 2; Cows' milk 6; Goats' milk 5. Source: FAO, *Production Yearbook.*

Fishing ('000 metric tons, live weight): Total catch 8.5 in 1995; 9.3 in 1996; 10.0 in 1997. Source: FAO, *Yearbook of Fishery Statistics.*

MINING

Production (metric tons): Salt (unrefined) 1,000 (1996 estimate, Source: US Bureau of Mines—Washington, DC); Pozzolana 10,000 (1990, Source: UN Economic Commission for Africa, *African Statistical Yearbook*).

INDUSTRY

Production (metric tons, unless otherwise indicated, 1998): Biscuits 348 (1990 figure); Bread 5,628 (1995 figure); Canned tuna 337 (1995 figure); Frozen fish 900 (FAO estimate, 1995 figure); Flour 65,916; Beer 4,234,560 litres; Soft drinks 922,714 litres (1996 figure); Cigarettes and tobacco 43 kg (1996 figure); Paint 628,243 kg (1996 figure); Footwear 670,676 pairs (1996 figure); Soap 1,722,114 kg (1996 figure); Electric energy 39m. kWh. (estimate, 1995 figure). Sources: UN, *Industrial Commodity Statistics Yearbook;* IMF, *Cape Verde: Recent Economic Developments* (July 1999).

FINANCE

Currency and Exchange Rates: 100 centavos = 1 Cape Verde escudo; 1,000 escudos are known as a conto. *Sterling, Dollar and Euro Equivalents* (31 March 2000): £1 sterling = 178.276 escudos; US $1 = 111.765 escudos; €1 = 106.769 escudos; 1,000 Cape Verde escudos = £5.609 = $8.947 = €9.366. *Average Exchange Rate* (escudos per US dollar): 93.177 in 1997; 98.158 in 1998; 102.700 in 1999.

Budget (preliminary, million escudos, 1998): *Revenue:* Taxation 8,409 (Taxes on income and profits 3,068, Municipal taxes 68, Taxes on international trade 4,906, Stamp and liquor tax 435); Other revenue 3,247 (Licences and miscellaneous fees 382, Property income 428, Transfers 256, Reimbursement of debt principal by public enterprises 1,292, Sales of fixed assets and services 264, Autonomous revenue 495); Total 11,656, excl. external grants (5,241) and domestic capital participation (64). *Expenditure:* Recurrent 10,718 (Wages and salaries 4,894, Goods and services 350, Interest on public debt 1,893, Subsidies and transfers 2,672, Other current 710, Autonomous 200); Capital 8,319 (Foreign financing 7,355, Domestic resources 964); Total 19,037. Source: IMF, *Cape Verde: Recent Economic Developments* (July 1999).

International Reserves (US $ million at 31 December 1999): IMF special drawing rights 0.02; Foreign exchange 60.37; Total 60.39. Source: IMF, *International Financial Statistics.*

Money Supply (million escudos at 31 December 1999): Currency outside banks 6,026.1; Demand deposits at commercial banks 12,216.4; Total money 18,332.6. Source: IMF, *International Financial Statistics.*

Cost of Living (Consumer Price Index for Praia; base: 1995 = 100): 106 in 1996; 115 in 1997; 120 in 1998. Source: IMF, *International Financial Statistics.*

Expenditure on the Gross Domestic Product (estimates, million escudos at current prices, 1998): Government final consumption expenditure 11,317; Private final consumption expenditure 33,327; Gross capital formation 19,580; *Total domestic expenditure* 64,224;

Exports of goods and services 12,139; *Less* Imports of goods and services 27,696; *GDP in purchasers' values* 48,667. Source: IMF, *Cape Verde: Recent Economic Developments* (July 1999).

Gross Domestic Product by Economic Activity (estimates, million escudos at current prices, 1998): Agriculture, forestry and livestock 5,212; Fishing 740; Industry and energy 4,711; Construction 4,304; Commerce 7,571; Hotels 1,669; Transport and communications 8,575; Banks and insurance 2,605; Housing 3,099; Public service 6,577; Other services 3,315; New industries 289; *GDP at market prices* 48,667. Source: IMF, *Cape Verde: Recent Economic Developments* (July 1999).

Balance of Payments (US $ million, 1998): Exports of goods f.o.b. 32.69; Imports of goods f.o.b. –218.33; *Trade balance* –185.64; Exports of services 86.45; Imports of services –90.57; *Balance on goods and services* –189.76; Other income received 2.51; Other income paid –8.07; *Balance on goods, services and income* –195.32; Current transfers received 142.46; Current transfers paid –5.15; *Current balance* –58.00; Capital account (net) 19.01; Direct investment from abroad 9.04; Other investment assets –22.44; Other investment liabilities 50.39; Net errors and omissions 12.77; *Overall balance* 10.76. Source: IMF, *International Financial Statistics.*

EXTERNAL TRADE

Total Trade (million escudos): *Imports c.i.f.:* 19,335 in 1996; 21,936 in 1997; 22,395 in 1998. *Exports f.o.b.*:* 1,039 in 1996; 1,294 in 1997; 1,024 in 1998.

* Figures exclude stores and bunkers for ships (million escudos): 1,402 in 1996; 2,449 in 1997; 1,678 in 1998.

Source: IMF, *Cape Verde: Recent Economic Developments* (July 1999).

Principal Commodities (million escudos, 1998): *Imports c.i.f.:* Live animals and animal products 1,025 (Milk 616); Vegetable products 2,472 (Maize 599, Rice 625); Edible oils and fats 1,079; Food and beverage products 3,222 (Sugar 665); Mineral products 1,949 (Cement 815, Diesel oil 483); Chemical products 1,375; Plastics and rubber 798; Wood products 518; Paper and paper products 558; Textiles 560; Stone and glass products 721; Metal and metal products 1,632; Machines and electrical equipment 3,887; Transportation material 1,510; Total (incl. others) 22,395. *Exports f.o.b.:* Fish 105; Crustaceans 76; Footwear (incl. parts) 609; Clothing 193; Total (incl. others)* 1,024. * Excluding stores and bunkers for ships (million escudos): 1,678. Source: IMF, *Cape Verde: Recent Economic Developments* (July 1999).

Principal Trading Partners (US $ million, 1995): *Imports c.i.f.:* Belgium and Luxembourg 21.1; Brazil 10.9; Côte d'Ivoire 3.4; Denmark 2.7; France 10.0; Germany 10.2; Israel 3.9; Italy 3.5; Japan 12.8; Netherlands 20.0; Portugal 100.4; Romania 3.2; Spain 4.4; Sweden 5.9; United Kingdom 5.3; USA 8.2; Viet Nam 2.7; Total (incl. others) 252.4. *Exports f.o.b.:* France 0.2; Netherlands 0.1; Portugal 7.4; Seychelles 0.5; Spain 0.6; USA 0.1; Total (incl. others) 8.9. Source: UN, *International Trade Statistics Yearbook.*

TRANSPORT

Road Traffic (motor vehicles in use, estimates, December, 1996): Passenger cars 3,280; Lorries and vans 820. Source: IRF, *World Road Statistics.*

Shipping: Merchant fleet (registered at 31 December 1998): Number of vessels 37, total displacement ('000 grt) 19.9 (Source: Lloyd's Register of Shipping, *World Fleet Statistics*); International freight traffic (estimates, '000 metric tons, 1993): Goods loaded 144, goods unloaded 299 (Source: UN Economic Commission for Africa, *African Statistical Yearbook*).

Civil Aviation (traffic on scheduled services, 1996): Kilometres flown 3,000,000; passengers carried 129,000; passenger-km 188,000,000; total ton-km 18,000,000. Source: UN, *Statistical Yearbook.*

TOURISM

Tourist Arrivals: 37,000 in 1996; 45,000 in 1997; 52,000 in 1998.

Tourist Arrivals by Country of Residence: (1997): France 4,762, Germany 5,560, Italy 13,750, Portugal 13,762; Total (incl. others) 45,000. Source: World Tourism Organization, *Yearbook of Tourism Statistics.*

1999: 67,000 tourist arrivals. Source: Centro de Promoção Turística, do Investimento Externo e das Exportações (PROMEX).

Tourism Receipts (US $ million): 10 in 1995; 11 in 1996; 15 in 1997.

COMMUNICATIONS MEDIA

Radio Receivers* (1997): 73,000 in use.

Television Receivers* (1997): 2,000 in use.

Telephones (1995): 21,500 in use. Source: Cabo Verde Telecom.

Telefax Stations† (1996): 1,000 in use.

Non-daily Newspapers* (1996): 4 titles (average circulation 20,000 copies).

Book Production* (1989): 10 titles.

* Source: UNESCO, *Statistical Yearbook*.

† Source: UN, *Statistical Yearbook*.

EDUCATION

Pre-primary (1986/87): 58 schools; 136 teachers; 4,523 pupils.

Primary (1997/98): 370 schools (1990/91); 3,219 teachers; 91,777 pupils.

Total Secondary (1997/98): 1,372 teachers; 31,602 pupils.

  General Secondary (1993/94): 438 teachers; 11,808 pupils.

  Teacher Training: 25 teachers (1987/88); 889 pupils (1993/94).

  Vocational Schools (1993/94): 94 teachers; 1,400 pupils.

Source: UNESCO, *Statistical Yearbook*.

Directory

The Constitution

A new constitution of the Republic of Cape Verde ('the Second Republic') came into force on 25 September 1992. The constitution defines Cape Verde as a sovereign, unitary and democratic republic, guaranteeing respect for human dignity and recognizing the inviolable and inalienable rights of man as a fundament of humanity, peace and justice. It recognizes the equality of all citizens before the law, without distinction of social origin, social condition, economic status, race, sex, religion, political convictions or ideologies and promises transparency for all citizens in the practising of fundamental liberties. The constitution gives assent to popular will, and has a fundamental objective in the realization of economic, political, social and cultural democracy and the construction of a society which is free, just and in solidarity.

The head of state is the president of the republic, who is elected by universal adult suffrage and must obtain two-thirds of the votes cast to win in the first round of the election. If no candidate secures the requisite majority, a new election is held within 21 days and contested by the two candidates who received the highest number of votes in the first round. Voting is conducted by secret ballot. Legislative power is vested in the national assembly, which is also elected by universal adult suffrage. The Prime Minister is nominated by the national assembly, to which he is responsible. On the recommendation of the prime minister, the president appoints the council of ministers, whose members must be elected deputies of the national assembly. There are 17 local government councils, elected by universal suffrage for a period of five years.

A constitutional revision, adopted in July 1999, gave the president the right to dissolve the national assembly, established a constitutional court (tribunal de constituçâo), created a new advisory chamber (conselho económico e social), and adopted *Crioulo* as the country's second official language.

The Government

HEAD OF STATE

President: ANTÓNIO MANUEL MASCARENHAS GOMES MONTEIRO (took office 22 March 1991; re-elected 18 February 1996).

COUNCIL OF MINISTERS
(August 2000)

Prime Minister and Minister of Economic Co-ordination: Dr ANTÓNIO GUALBERTO DO ROSÁRIO.

Minister of Finance: Dr JOSÉ ULISSES DE PINA CORREIA E SILVA.

Minister of Foreign Affairs and Communities: Dr RUI ALBERTO DE FIGUEIREDO SOARES.

Minister of Tourism, Transport and the Sea: Dra MARIA HELENA NOBRE DE MORAIS SEMEDO.

Minister of Commerce, Industry and Energy: Eng. ALEXANDRE DIAS MONTEIRO.

Minister of Education, Science, Youth and Sports and of Infrastructure and Housing: Eng. ANTÓNIO JOAQUIM ROCHA MENDES FERNANDES.

Minister of Employment, Training and Social Integration: Dra ORLANDA MARIA DUARTE SANTOS FERREIRA.

Minister of Culture and Social Communication: Dr ANTÓNIO JORGE DELGADO.

Minister of Health: Dr JOÃO BAPTISTA FERREIRA MEDINA.

Minister of Agriculture, Food and the Environment: Dr JOSÉ ANTÓNIO PINTO MONTEIRO.

Minister of Justice and Internal Administration: JANUÁRIA TAVARES SILVA MOREIRA DA COSTA.

Minister in the Office of the President of the Council of Ministers: Dr ORLANDO PEREIRA DIAS.

Assistant Minister to the President of the Council of Ministers and Minister of Defence: Dr ÚLPIO NAPOLEÃO FERNANDES.

Secretary of State for Communities: D. MARLEY DE MENESSES BARBOSA VICENTE.

Secretary of State for Public Administration: Dra PAULA ALMEIDA.

Secretary of State for the Fight Against Poverty: Dra MANUELA SILVA GOMES.

Secretary of State for Education, Science, Youth and Sport: Dra FILOMENA DELGADO.

Secretary of State Assistant to the Prime Minister: Eng. MÁRIO FERNANDES.

MINISTRIES

Office of the President: Presidência da República, Plateau, Praia, Santiago; tel. 61-65-66.

Office of the Prime Minister: Palácio do Governo, Várzea, CP 16, Praia, Santiago; tel. 61-05-13; fax 61-30-99.

Ministry of Agriculture, Food and the Environment: Ponta Belém, Praia, Santiago; tel. 61-57-13; fax 61-40-54.

Ministry of Commerce, Industry and Energy: Praia, Santiago; tel. 61-31-42.

Ministry of Culture and Social Communication: Praia, Santiago; tel. 61-16-10.

Ministry of Economic Co-ordination: 107 Avda Amílcar Cabral, CP 30, Praia, Santiago; tel. 61-56-98; fax 61-38-97.

Ministry of Education, Science, Youth and Sports: Palácio do Governo, Várzea, CP 111, Praia, Santiago; tel. 61-02-11; fax 61-56-75; internet www.gov.cv/contacto.

Ministry of Employment, Training and Social Integration: Plateau, Praia, Santiago; tel. 61-16-16.

Ministry of Finance: 107 Avda Amílcar Cabral, CP 30, Praia, Santiago; tel. 61-43-50.

Ministry of Foreign Affairs and Communities: Praça Dr Lorena, Praia, Santiago; tel. 61-57-27; fax 61-39-52.

Ministry of Health: Palácio do Governo, Várzea, Praia, Santiago; tel. 61-05-01.

Ministry of Infrastructure and Housing: Ponta Belém, Praia, Santiago; tel. 61-56-99; fax 61-56-99.

Ministry of Justice and Internal Administration: Rua Serpa Pinto, Praia, Santiago; tel. 62-32-62; fax 61-56-78.

Ministry of National Defence: Palácio do Governo, Várzea, Praia, Santiago; tel. 61-03-44; fax 61-05-15.

Ministry of Tourism, Transport and the Sea: Palácio do Governo, Várzea, Praia, Santiago; tel. 61-17-70; fax 61-17-70.

President and Legislature

PRESIDENT

At a presidential election held on 18 February 1996 the incumbent President, ANTÓNIO MANUEL MASCARENHAS GOMES MONTEIRO, as the sole candidate, was duly re-elected. Presidential elections were scheduled to be held in February 2001.

Elections to the national assembly were scheduled to be held in December 2000.

Legislative Election, 17 December 1995

Party	Votes	% of votes	Seats
Movimento para a Democracia (MPD)	93,249	61.3	50
Partido Africano da Independência de Cabo Verde (PAICV) . . .	45,263	29.8	21
Partido da Convergência Democrática (PCD) . .	10,211	6.7	1
Other parties	3,399	2.2	—
Total	152,122	100.0	72

Political Organizations

Movimento para a Democracia (MPD): Achada Santo António, CP 90A, Praia, Santiago; tel. 61-40-82; fax 61-41-22; f. 1990; advocates administrative decentralization; governing party since Jan. 1991; Chair. ANTÓNIO GUALBERTO DO ROSÁRIO.

Partido Africano da Independência de Cabo Verde (PAICV): Avda Amílcar Cabral, CP 22, Praia, Santiago; tel. 61-27-20; fax 61-14-10; internet www.paicv.org; f. 1956 as the Partido Africano da Independência do Guiné e Cabo Verde (PAIGC); name changed in 1981, following the 1980 coup in Guinea-Bissau; sole authorized political party 1975–90; Chair. JOSÉ MARIA NEVES; Sec.-Gen. ARISTIDES LIMA.

Partido da Convergência Democrática (PCD): Praia, Santiago; f. 1994 by fmr mems of the MPD; Pres. Dr EURICO CORREIA MONTEIRO.

Partido Socialista Democrático (PSD): Praia, Santiago; f. 1992; Sec.-Gen. JOÃO ALÉM.

Partido de Trabalho e Solidariedade: Praia, Santiago; f. 1998; Leader ONESIMO SILVEIRA.

União Caboverdiana Independente e Democrática (UCID): Praia, Santiago; f. 1974 by emigrants opposed to the PAICV; obtained legal recognition in 1991; Pres. CELSO CELESTINO.

Diplomatic Representation

EMBASSIES IN CAPE VERDE

Angola: Praia, Santiago; Ambassador: CÉSAR A. KILUANGE.

Brazil: Chã de Areia, CP 93, Praia, Santiago; tel. 61-56-07; fax 61-56-09; Ambassador: ROMEO ZERO.

China, People's Republic: Achada de Santo António, Praia, Santiago; tel. 61-55-86; Ambassador: LIAO QIPING.

Cuba: Prainha, Praia, Santiago; tel. 61-55-97; fax 61-55-90; Ambassador: PABLO REIS DOMINGUES.

France: CP 192, Praia, Santiago; tel. 61-55-89; fax 61-55-90; Ambassador: ANDRÉ BARBE.

Portugal: Achada de Santo António, CP 160, Praia, Santiago; tel. 61-56-02; fax 61-40-58; Ambassador: RUI QUARTIN SANTOS.

Russia: Achada de Santo António, CP 31, Praia, Santiago; tel. 62-27-39; fax 62-27-38; Ambassador: VLADIMIR E. PETUKHOV.

Senegal: Prainha, Praia, Santiago; tel. 61-56-21; Ambassador: SILCARNEYI GUEYE.

USA: Rua Hoji Ya Yenna 81, CP 201, Praia, Santiago; tel. 61-56-16; fax 61-13-55; Ambassador: MICHAEL METELITS.

Judicial System

Tribunal de Constitução: f. 1999; the supreme court.

Supremo Tribunal de Justiça: Rua Cesário de Lacerda, CP 117, Praia, Santiago; tel. 61-58-10; fax 61-17-51; established 1975; the highest court.

President: Dr OSCAR GOMES.

Attorney-General: Dr HENRIQUE MONTEIRO.

Religion

CHRISTIANITY

At 31 December 1998 there were an estimated 432,424 adherents of the Roman Catholic Church, representing 95.7% of the total population. Protestant churches, among which the Church of the Nazarene is prominent, represent about 1% of the population.

The Roman Catholic Church

Cape Verde comprises the single diocese of Santiago de Cabo Verde, directly responsible to the Holy See. The Bishop participates in the Episcopal Conference of Senegal, Mauritania, Cape Verde and Guinea-Bissau, currently based in Senegal.

Bishop of Santiago de Cabo Verde: Rt Rev. PAULINO DO LIVRAMENTO ÉVORA, Avda Amílcar Cabral, Largo 5 de Outubro, CP 46, Praia, Santiago; tel. 61-11-19; fax 61-45-99.

The Anglican Communion

Cape Verde forms part of the diocese of The Gambia, within the Church of the Province of West Africa. The Bishop is resident in Banjul, The Gambia.

The Press

Agaviva: Mindelo, São Vicente; tel. 31-21-21; f. 1991; monthly; Editor GERMANO ALMEIDA; circ. 4,000.

Boletim Informativo: CP 126, Praia, Santiago; f. 1976; weekly; publ. by the Ministry of Foreign Affairs; circ. 1,500.

Boletim Oficial da República de Cabo Verde: Imprensa Nacional, CP 113, Praia, Santiago; tel. 61-41-50; weekly; official announcements.

O Cidadão: Praça Dr António Aurélio Gonçalves 2, CP 669, Mindelo, São Vicente; tel. 32-50-24; fax 32-50-22; e-mail ocidadao@mail.cvtelecom.cv; Editor JOSÉ MÁRIO CORREIA.

Contacto: CP 89C, Praia, Santiago; tel. 61-57-52; fax 61-14-42; f. 1993; quarterly; economic bulletin publ. by Centro de Promoção Turística, do Investimento Externo e das Exportações (PROMEX); circ. 1,500.

Horizonte: Achada de Santo António, CP 40, Praia, Santiago; tel. 62-24-47; fax 62-33-30; e-mail infopress@cvtelecom.cv; f. 1999; weekly; pro-government; Editor FERNANDO MONTEIRO; circ. 5,000.

Perspectiva: Achada de Santo António, CP 89C, Praia, Santiago; tel. 62-27-41; fax 62-27-37; f. 1995; annual; economic bulletin publ. by Centro de Promoção Turística, do Investimento Externo e das Exportações (PROMEX); Editor Dr AGUINALDO MARÇAL; circ. 5,000.

Raízes: CP 98, Praia, Santiago; tel. 319; f. 1977; quarterly; cultural review; Editor ARNALDO FRANÇA; circ. 1,500.

A Semana: CP 36C, Avda Cidade de Lisboa, Praia, Santiago; tel. 61-39-50; fax 61-52-91; e-mail asemana@mail.cvtelecom.cv; weekly; independent; Editor FILOMENA SILVA; circ. 5,000.

Terra Nova: CP 166, São Vicente; tel. 32-24-42; fax 32-14-75; e-mail terranova@cabonet.cv; f. 1975; monthly; Roman Catholic; Editor P. ANTÓNIO FIDALGO BARROS; circ. 3,000.

NEWS AGENCIES

Cabopress: Achada de Santo António, CP 40/A, Praia, Santiago; tel. 62-30-21; fax 62-30-23; f. 1988.

Foreign Bureaux

Agence France-Presse (AFP): CP 26/118 Praia, Santiago; tel. 61-38-89; Rep. FÁTIMA AZEVEDO.

Agência Portuguesa de Notícias (LUSA): Prainha, Praia, Santiago; tel. 61-35-19.

Inter Press Service (IPS) (Italy): CP 14, Mindelo, São Vicente; tel. 31-45-50; Rep. JUAN A. COLOMA.

Publisher

Government Publishing House

Imprensa Nacional: CP 113, Praia, Santiago; tel. 61-42-09; Admin. JOÃO DE PINA.

Broadcasting and Communications

TELECOMMUNICATIONS

Cabo Verde Telecom: CP 220, Varzea, Praia, Santiago; tel. 61-55-79; e-mail cvtelecom@mail.cvtelecom.cv; internet www.cvtelecom.cv; f. 1995; Chief Exec. ANTÓNIO PIRES CORREIA.

BROADCASTING

Rádio Televisão de Cabo Verde (RTC): Praça Albuquerque, CP 26, Praia, Santiago; tel. 61-57-55; fax 61-57-54; govt-controlled; five radio transmitters and five solar relay radio transmitters; FM transmission only; radio broadcasts in Portuguese and Creole for 18 hours daily; one television transmitter and seven relay television transmitters; television broadcasts in Portuguese and Creole for eight hours daily with co-operation of RTPI (Portugal); Dir MANUELA FONSECA SOARES.

Praia FM: Rua Justino Lopes 1, CP 276-C, Praia, Santiago; tel. 61-63-56; fax 61-63-57; e-mail gccomunicacoes@mail.cvtelecom.cv; Dir. GIORDANO CUSTÓDIO.

Rádio Comercial: Achada Santo António, Prédio Gomes Irmãos 3c, Santiago; tel. 62-31-56; fax 62-24-13; e-mail multimedia.rc@cvtelecom.cv; Dir. CARLOS FILIPE GONÇALVES.

Rádio Educativa de Cabo Verde: Achada de Santo António, Praia, Santiago; tel. 61-11-61.

Rádio Nova—Emissora Cristã/Cabo Verde: CP 426, Mindelo, São Vicente; tel. 32-20-83; fax 32-14-75; Dir ANTONIO FIDALGO BARROS.

Voz de São Vicente: CP 29, Mindelo, São Vicente; fax 31-10-06; f. 1974; govt-controlled; Dir JOSÉ FONSECA SOARES.

Finance

(cap. = capital; res = reserves; dep. = deposits; m. = million; †brs = branches; amounts in Cape Verde escudos)

BANKING

Central Bank

Banco de Cabo Verde (BCV): 117 Avda Amílcar Cabral, CP 101, Praia, Santiago; tel. 60-70-00; fax 61-19-14; f. 1976; bank of issue; cap. and res 3,169m., dep. 5,143m. (Dec. 1998); Gov. OLAVO CORREIA.

Other Banks

Banco Comercial do Atlântico (BCA): Avda Amílcar Cabral, CP 214, Praia, Santiago; tel. 61-30-93; fax 61-31-00; f. 1993; main commercial bank; cap. 3,402m. (1998); Gen. Man. AMÉLIA FIGUEIREDO; 17 brs.

Banco Interatlântico (Caixa Geral de Depósitos) (Portugal): Avda Cidade de Lisboa, CP 131A, Varzea, Praia, Santiago; tel. 61-38-29; fax 61-47-52; Pres. Dr. ANTÓNIO MIGUEL ORNELAS AFONSO.

Banco Mello Comercial (Portugal): Avda Amílcar Cabral 84, CP 33, Plateau, Praia, Santiago; tel. 61-72-50; fax 61-72-51.

Banco Nacional Ultramarino: Edifício Socotril, Avda Cidade de Lisboa, Varzea, Praia, Santiago; tel. 61-42-32; fax 61-42-53.

Banco Totta e Açores (BTA) (Portugal): Rua Roberto Silva, CP 593, Praia, Santiago; tel. 61-16-62; fax 61-40-06; cap. 330m. (Dec. 1998); Gen. Man. RODRIGO NASCIMENTO; 1 br.

Caixa de Crédito Rural: Praia, Santiago; f. 1995; rural credit bank.

Caixa Económica de Cabo Verde (CECV): Avda Cidade de Lisboa, CP 193, Praia, Santiago; tel. 61-55-61; fax 61-55-60; f. 1928; commercial bank; cap. 1,332m. (Dec. 1998).

The **Fundo de Solidariedade Nacional** is the main savings institution; the **Fundo de Desenvolvimento Nacional** channels public investment resources; and the **Instituto Caboverdiano** administers international aid.

STOCK EXCHANGE

Bolsa de Valores de Cabo Verde: Achada de Santo António, CP 115-A, Praia, Santiago; tel. 60-30-30; fax 60-30-35; e-mail bcv@mail.cvtelecom.cv; f. 1998.

INSURANCE

Companhia Caboverdiana de Seguros (IMPAR): Avda Amílcar Cabral, CP 469, Praia, Santiago; tel. 61-14-05; fax 61-37-65; f. 1991; Pres. Dr CORSINO FORTES.

Garantia Companhia de Seguros: CP 138, Praia, Santiago; tel. 61-35-32; fax 61-25-55; f. 1991.

Trade and Industry

GOVERNMENT AGENCIES

Centro de Promoção Turística, do Investimento Externo e das Exportações (PROMEX): CP 89c, Achada de Santo António, Praia, Santiago; tel. 62-27-41; fax 62-27-37; f. 1990; promotes tourism, foreign investment and exports; Pres. Dr PEDRO BARROS.

Gabinete de Apoio à Reestruturação do Sector Empresarial do Estado (GARSEE; Cabo Verde Privatization): Praia, Santiago; tel. 61-47-48; fax 61-23-34; e-mail cvprivatization@mail.cvtelecom.cv; internet http://cvprivatization.org; bureau in charge of planning and supervising restructuring and divestment of public enterprises; Project Dir: Dr SÉRGIO CENTEIO.

DEVELOPMENT ORGANIZATION

Instituto Nacional de Investigação e Desenvolvimento Agrário: CP 84, Praia, Santiago; tel. 71-11-47; fax 71-11-33; e-mail inida@mail.cvtelecom.cv; f. 1979; under the supervision of the Ministry of Agriculture, Food and the Environment; research and training on agricultural issues.

CHAMBERS OF COMMERCE

Associação Comercial Industrial e Agrícola de Barlavento (ACIAB): CP 62, Mindelo, São Vicente; tel. 31-32-81; fax 32-36-58; f. 1918.

Associação Comercial de Sotavento (ACAS): Rua Serpa Pinto 23, 1°, CP 78, Praia, Santiago; tel. 61-29-91; fax 61-29-64; e-mail acs@milton.cvtelecom.cv.

STATE INDUSTRIAL ENTERPRISES

Correios de Cabo Verde, SARL: CP 92, Praia, Santiago; tel. 61-10-49; fax 61-34-78.

Empresa de Comercialização de Produtos do Mar-INTERBASE, EP: CP 59, Mindelo, São Vicente; tel. 32-66-89; fax 32-66-91; e-mail interbase-sv@mail.cvtelecom.sv; supervises marketing of seafood; shipping agency and ship chandler; Man. Dir CARLOS ALBERTO RAMOS FARIA.

Empresa Nacional de Conservação e Reparação de Equipamentos (SONACOR): Praia, Santiago; tel. 61-25-57.

Empresa Nacional de Produtos Farmacêuticos (EMPROFAC): CP 59, Praia, Santiago; tel. 62-78-95; fax 62-78-99; f. 1979; state monopoly of pharmaceuticals and medical imports.

UTILITIES

Electricity and Water

Empresa de Electricidade e Água (ELECTRA): 10 Avda Baltazar Lopes Silva, CP 137, Mindelo, São Vicente; tel. 32-44-48; fax 32-44-46; e-mail dg-electra@mail.cvtelecom.cv; f. 1982; Chair. MARTINHO CRISTOGOMO RAMOS.

MAJOR COMPANIES

Companhia da Pozolana de Cabo Verde: Porto Novo, Ilha de Santo Antão; pozzolan industry.

Companhia dos Tabacos de Cabo Verde, SARL: CP 67, São Vicente; tel. 314400; manufacture of tobacco and tobacco products.

Companhia Fomento de Cabo Verde: Santa Maria, Ilha do Sal; salt industry.

Empresa de Abastecimento (EMPA): CP 107, Praia, Santiago; tel. 63-39-69; fax 63-39-22; e-mail empa@mail.cvtelecom.cv; f. 1975; provisioning enterprise, supervising imports, exports and domestic distribution; 40% state-owned, 60% owned by private company; Dir-Gen. NASOLINO SILVA DOS SANTOS; 830 employees.

Empresa Nacional de Combustíveis, EP (ENACOL): CP 1, Mindelo, São Vicente; tel. 31-31-49; fax 31-48-73; f. 1979; sales 1,592m. escudos (1994); supervises import and distribution of petroleum; Dir Dr MÁRIO A. RODRIGUES.

Salins du Cap Vert: Pedra Lume, Ilha do Sal; salt industry.

SOCAL: Sociedade Industrial de Calçado, SARL: CP 92, Mindelo, São Vicente; tel. 31-50-59; fax 31-20-61; industrial shoe factory.

CO-OPERATIVES

Instituto Nacional das Cooperativas: Fazenda, CP 218, Praia, Santiago; tel. 61-41-12; fax 61-39-59; central co-operative organization.

TRADE UNIONS

Confederação Cabo-Verdiana dos Sindicatos Livres (CCSL): Rua Dr Júlio Abreu, Praia, Santiago; tel. 61-63-19; Sec.-Gen. JOSÉ MANUEL VAZ.

Sindicato da Indústria, Agricultura e Pesca (SIAP): Plateau, Praia, Santiago; tel. 61-63-19.

Sindicato dos Transportes, Comunicações e Turismo (STCT): Praia, Santiago; tel. 61-63-38.

União Nacional dos Trabalhadores de Cabo Verde—Central Sindical (UNTC—CS): Estrada do Aeroporto, Praia, Santiago; tel. 61-43-05; fax 61-36-29; f. 1978; Chair. JÚLIO ASCENSÃO SILVA.

Transport

ROADS

In 1996 there were an estimated 1,100 km of roads, of which 858 km were paved.

SHIPPING

Cargo-passenger ships call regularly at Porto Grande, Mindelo, on São Vicente, and Praia, on Santiago. In 1993 plans were announced for the upgrading of Porto Grande, and for the re-establishment of the port of Vale dos Cavaleiros, on Fogo island. There are small ports on the other inhabited islands.

Comissão de Gestão dos Transportes Marítimos de Cabo Verde: CP 153, São Vicente; tel. 31-49-79; fax 31-20-55.

Empresa Nacional de Administração dos Portos, EP (ENAPOR): Avda Marginal, CP 82, Mindelo, São Vicente; tel. 31-44-14; fax 31-46-61; f. 1982; Chair. and Man. Dir. MANUEL VICENTE A. SILVA; 499 employees.

Companhia Cabo-Verdiana de Transportes Marítimos: CP 150, Praia, Santiago; tel. 61-22-84; fax 61-60-95.

Companhia Nacional de Navegação Arca Verde: Rua 5 de Julho, CP 41, Praia, Santiago; tel. 61-10-60; fax 61-54-96; f. 1975.

Companhia de Navegação Estrela Negra: Avda 5 de Julho 17, CP 91, São Vicente; tel. 31-54-23; fax 31-53-82.

Companhia Portuguesa de Transportes Marítimos: Agent in Santiago: João Benoliel de Carvalho, Lda, CP 56, Praia, Santiago.

CS Line: Praia, Santiago.

Linhas Marítimas Caboverdianas (LINMAC): Dr João Battista Ferreira Medina, CP 357, Praia, Santiago; tel. 61-43-52; fax 61-37-15; Man. ESTHER SPENCER.

Mare Verde: Mindelo, São Vicente.

Seage Agência de Navegação de Cabo Verde: Avda Cidade de Lisboa, CP 232, Praia, Santiago; tel. 61-57-58; fax 61-25-24; Chair. CÉSAR MANUEL SEMEDO LOPES.

CIVIL AVIATION

The Amílcar Cabral international airport, at Espargos, on Sal island, can accommodate aircraft of up to 50 tons and 1m. passengers per year. The airport's facilities were expanded during the 1990s. A second international airport, under construction on Santiago, capable of accommodating long-range aircraft, was due for completion in 2000. There is also a small airport on each of the other inhabited islands. Work was begun in 1998 to upgrade the airport on São Vicente to international capacity. Plans were also under way for the construction of an international airport on Boa Vista.

Empresa Nacional de Aeroportos e Segurança Aérea, EP (ASA): Aeroporto Amílcar Cabral, CP 58, Ilha do Sal; tel. 41-13-94; fax 41-15-70; e-mail asacv@mail.cvtelecom.cv; airports and aircraft security; Pres. VALDEMAR CORREIA; 344 employees.

CABOVIMO: 32 Avda Unidade Guiné-Cabo Verde, Praia, Santiago; tel. 61-33-14; fax 61-55-59; f. 1992; internal flights; Gen. Man. JORGE DANIEL SPENCER LIMA.

Transportes Aéreos de Cabo Verde (TACV): Avda Amílcar Cabral, CP 1, Praia, Santiago; tel. 61-58-13; fax 61-35-85; e-mail cv.airline@milton.cvtelecom.cv; internet www.tacv.com; f. 1958; internal services connecting the nine inhabited islands; also operates regional services to Senegal, Guinea, the Gambia and Guinea-Bissau, and long-distance services to Europe and the USA; Dir ALFREDO CARVALHO.

Tourism

The islands of Santiago, Santo Antão, Fogo and Brava offer attractive mountain scenery. There are extensive beaches on the islands of Santiago, Sal, Boa Vista and Maio. There are nine hotels on Sal, three on Boa Vista, three on São Vicente, and nine on Santiago. Some 52,000 tourists visited Cape Verde during 1998, mainly from Italy, Portugal, Germany, Austria, France, the Netherlands, Belgium and Spain. In 1999 an estimated 67,000 tourists visited Cape Verde. In 1997 tourism receipts totalled US $15m. The sector is undergoing rapid expansion, with tourist arrivals projected to increase to about 400,000 annually by 2008.

Centro de Promocão Turística, do Investimento Externo e das Exportações (PROMEX): CP 89c, Achada de Santo António, Praia, Santiago; tel. 62-27-36; fax 62-27-37; f. 1990; promotes tourism, foreign investment and exports; Dir of Tourism AIDA DUARTE SILVA.

Defence

The armed forces numbered about 1,100 (army 1,000, air force less than 100) in August 1999. There is also a police force, the Police for Public Order, which is organized by the local municipal councils. National service is by selective conscription.

Defence Expenditure: Budgeted at 508m. Cape Verde escudos (US $5.4m.) in 1999.

Education

Primary education, beginning at seven years of age and lasting for six years, comprises a first cycle of four years, which is compulsory, and a second cycle of two years. Secondary education, beginning at 13 years of age, is also divided into two cycles, the first comprising a three-year general course, the second a three-year pre-university course. There are three teacher-training units and two industrial and commercial schools of further education. In 1997 the total enrolment at primary and secondary schools was equivalent to 103% of all school-age children. In 1986/87 there were 4,523 children enrolled at pre-primary schools. In 1997/98 91,777 pupils attended primary schools, and in 1993/94 11,808 attended general secondary schools. Primary enrolment in 1997 was equivalent to 148% of children in the relevant age-group, while secondary enrolment was equivalent to 55% of children in the relevant age-group. In 1996/97 there were 1,660 Cape Verdean students studying at overseas universities. A university was to be established in Praia in 1998 with assistance from Portugal. In 1995, according to estimates by UNESCO, the average rate of illiteracy among the population aged 15 years and over was 30.6% (males 19.3%; females 39.3%).

Bibliography

A.G.U. *Cabo Verde*. Lisbon, 1966.

Amaral, I. d. *Santiago de Cabo Verde*. Lisbon, 1964.

Cabral, N. E. *Le Moulin et le Pilon, les îles du Cap-Vert*. Paris, 1980.

Cann, J. P. *Counter-insurgency in Africa: The Portuguese Way of War 1961–1974*. Greenwood Press, Newport, CT, 1997.

Cape Verde Government Publication. *República de Cabo Verde: 5 Anos de Independência (1975–80)*. Lisbon, 1980.

Carreira, A. *Cabo Verde, Formação e Extinção de uma Sociedade Escravocrata*. Bissau, 1972.

 Migrações nas Ilhas de Cabo Verde. Lisbon, Universidade Nova, 1977.

 Cabo Verde: Classes sociais, estructura familiar, migrações. Lisbon, Ulmeiro, 1977.

 The People of the Cape Verde Islands: Exploitation and Emigration (trans. and edited by C. Fyfe). London, Hurst, and Hamden, CT, Archon Books, 1983.

Davidson, B. *No Fist is Big Enough to Hide the Sky: The Liberation of Guinea-Bissau and Cape Verde*. 2nd Edn. London, Zed Press, 1984.

 The Fortunate Isles: A Study of Cape Verde. London, Hutchinson, and Trenton, NJ, World Press, 1989.

de Pina, M.-P. *Les îles du Cap-Vert*. Paris, Karthala, 1987.

Foy, C. *Cape Verde: Politics, Economics and Society*. London, Pinter Publishers, Marxist Regimes Series, 1988.

Langworthy, M., and Finan, T. J. *Waiting for Rain: Agriculture and Ecological Imbalance in Cape Verde*. Boulder, CO, Lynne Rienner, 1997.

Lesourd, M. *État et société aux îles du Cap Vert*. Paris, Karthala, 1995.

Lima, A. *Reforma Política em Cabo Verde: do Paternalismo à Modernização do Estado*. Praia, 1992.

Lobban, R. *Historical Dictionary of Cape Verde*. 3rd Edn. Metuchen, NJ, Scarecrow Press, 1995.

 Cape Verde: Crioulo Colony to Independent Nation. Boulder, CO, Westview Press, 1995.

May, S. *Tourismus in der Dritten Welt: Das Beispiel Kapverde*. Frankfurt am Main, Campus Verlag, 1985.

Meintel, D. *Race, Culture and Portuguese Colonialism in Cabo Verde*. Syracuse, NY, Syracuse University Press, 1985.

Núñez, B. *Dictionary of Portuguese-African Civilization*. Vol. I. London, Hans Zell, 1995.

Promex–Centre for Export and Investment Promotion, *Cape Verde–Guide for Investors*. Praia, 1994.

World Bank Report. *Poverty in Cape Verde–A Summary Assessment and a Strategy for its Alleviation*. Africa Region, 1994.

THE CENTRAL AFRICAN REPUBLIC

Physical and Social Geography

DAVID HILLING

Bordered to the north by Chad, to the east by Sudan, to the south by the Republic of the Congo and the Democratic Republic of the Congo, and to the west by Cameroon, the Central African Republic forms a geographic link between the Sudano-Sahelian zone and the Congo basin. The country consists mainly of plateau surfaces at 600–900 m above sea-level, which provide the watershed between drainage northwards to Lake Chad and southwards to the Oubangui/Congo river system. There are numerous rivers, and during the main rainy season (July–October) much of the south-east of the country becomes inaccessible as a result of extensive inundation. The Oubangui river to the south of Bangui provides near-year-round commercial navigation and is the main outlet for external trade. However, development of the country is inhibited by its land-locked location and the great distance (1,815 km) to the sea by way of the fluvial route from Bangui to Brazzaville, in the Republic of the Congo, and thence by rail to Pointe-Noire.

The Central African Republic covers an area of 622,984 sq km (240,535 sq miles). At the census of December 1988 the population was 2,463,616. According to UN estimates, the popul-

ation numbered 3,485,000 in mid-1998, giving an average density of 5.6 inhabitants per sq km. The greatest concentration of population is in the western part of the country; large areas in the east are virtually uninhabited. Of the country's numerous ethnic groups, the Banda and Baya jointly comprise more than 50% of the population. Sango, a lingua franca, has been adopted as the national language.

Only in the south-west of the country is the rainfall sufficient (1,250 mm) to sustain a forest vegetation. The south-western Lobaye region is a source of coffee (the main cash crop), cocoa, rubber, palm produce and timber. Cotton, also an important cash crop, is cultivated in a belt beyond the forest. This area could benefit substantially from a proposed rail link with the Transcameroon railway.

Alluvial deposits of diamonds occur widely and are exploited, but uranium is potentially of much greater economic importance. The exploitation of ore-rich deposits at Bakouma, 480 km east of Bangui, which has been inhibited by inadequate access routes and by technical problems, awaits a sustained recovery in the present level of world uranium prices.

Recent History

PIERRE ENGLEBERT

Revised for this edition by the Editor

The former French territory of Oubangui-Chari became the Central African Republic (CAR) on achieving internal self-government in 1958. David Dacko became the republic's first president at independence on 13 August 1960. The ruling Mouvement d'évolution sociale de l'Afrique noire (MESAN) was declared the sole legal party in December 1962. In December 1965–January 1966 Dacko's cousin, Col Jean-Bédel Bokassa, the c-in-c of the armed forces, seized power in a *coup d'état*. Bokassa, whose regime, until its collapse in 1979, became increasingly despotic, inefficient and corrupt, encountered little open opposition within the country, although several external opposition groups were formed, including the Mouvement pour la libération du peuple centrafricain (MLPC), led by Ange-Félix Patassé (who had been dismissed as prime minister in 1978 and had fled to France). In July 1979 these groups formed a common front. In September Bokassa, who was absent in Libya, was deposed in a bloodless coup by Dacko, supported by a contingent of French troops flown in from Gabon. A multi-party system was restored in February 1981 and a presidential election followed in March. Dacko was elected with 50% of the votes cast, while his main opponent, Patassé, received 38%. Political opposition to Dacko increased during 1981; legislative elections were cancelled, and opposition parties were suppressed. Under increasing political pressure and deprived of French support by the change of government in Paris, Dacko was persuaded to transfer power to a military government. In September Gen. André Kolingba, the army chief of staff, was declared head of state.

KOLINGBA'S RULE, 1981–93

Kolingba imposed a total ban on political activity, and disenchantment with the military regime rapidly became evident. In March 1982 an unsuccessful coup attempt was staged by Patassé, who subsequently took refuge in the French embassy. A crisis in the two countries' relations followed when the French,

despite consistent support for the Kolingba administration, insisted that Patassé be granted safe passage to exile in Togo. Kolingba, whose regime relied on French economic support, had little option but to comply. In August Abel Goumba, the leader of the opposition Front patriotique oubanguien–Parti du travail (FPO–PT), was arrested, with another leading member of the party, on charges of plotting against the government. Following intense but discreet French pressure, they were released in September 1983, together with some of those detained following the 1982 coup attempt. Other members of the FPO–PT, meanwhile, had appointed a new leadership which was committed to armed struggle. The two other political parties fell into a similar state of fragmentation: part of the membership of the MLPC rejected the leadership of Patassé; and sections of the Mouvement centrafricain pour la libération nationale (MCLN) rejected their leader, Dr Iddi Lala. Some elements of the three parties agreed in August 1983 to form a united front, named the Parti révolutionnaire centrafricain. The government appeared to be less alarmed by this development, however, than by Bokassa's attempt, in November, to return from exile. However, the Côte d'Ivoire government instead expelled him to France, where he was reluctantly allowed to take up residence.

In early 1984 several civilian politicians, including Goumba and Henri Maidou, a former vice-president, were arrested for violating the ban on political parties. At a trial held in July, sentences of up to 10 years' imprisonment were passed on those implicated in the 1982 coup attempt. Some of these were reduced by Kolingba in December 1984, when both Goumba and Maidou were also released. In July 1986 the MLPC and the FPO–PT announced the formation of a Front uni (FU), which was to campaign for a democratic system of government.

In September 1985 Kolingba formed a new administration, in which civilians were not only appointed ministers for the first time since the military take-over, but also received the majority of portfolios. Nevertheless, military personnel retained the major posts. At a referendum held in November 1986 some 91.17% of voters granted a further six-year mandate to Kolingba as president and approved a draft constitution which provided for wide-ranging powers for the head of state, with the legislature occupying a mainly advisory role. In December a government reshuffle took place, in which Kolingba assumed the defence portfolio. In February 1987, at the constitutive assembly of the Rassemblement démocratique centrafricain (RDC), the sole political party stipulated in the new constitution, a clear separation was defined between party and state, and membership of the party was made voluntary. In July the country's first legislative elections for 20 years took place. These were, however, boycotted by the FU; consequently all 142 candidates contesting the 52 seats in the national assembly were RDC nominees.

In October 1986, with the economy under scrutiny from the IMF and moves towards an ostensibly more democratic regime in progress, the government was highly embarrassed when Bokassa suddenly returned to the CAR. He was arrested and placed on public trial, and in June 1987 was convicted of four of the 14 charges brought against him, and condemned to death. In February 1988 the sentence was commuted to imprisonment for life and was subsequently reduced to 10 years' imprisonment. Bokassa was released from prison in 1993 and died in November 1996.

Following the Bokassa trial, Kolingba resumed his earlier attempts at democratization and national reconciliation. The first municipal elections were held in May 1988, at which voters were offered a choice of RDC-approved candidates. A government reshuffle followed in July. Kolingba sought a *rapprochement* with former opponents of his regime by inviting Brig.-Gen. (later Gen.) François Bozize, an instigator of the 1982 coup attempt, to return from exile. (Bozize chose to remain in Benin, where he had founded an opposition movement, the Rassemblement populaire pour la reconstruction de la Centrafrique.) In addition, Kolingba appointed Maidou to an influential banking position. Members of Patassé's MLPC were also rehabilitated during 1988, although Patassé himself remained in exile in Togo. However, in July 1989 12 opponents of the Kolingba regime, including members of the FPO–PT and Bozize, were arrested in Benin, and subsequently extradited to the CAR and imprisoned.

In May 1990 the RDC ruled that the establishment of a multi-party system in the CAR would be 'incompatible' with the country's political and economic development. However, this ruling was immediately contested in the form of a petition for a national conference on the future of the country, signed by 253 prominent citizens. The petition claimed that society in the CAR was 'corrupted by tribal discrimination, nepotism, fraud and injustice'. In October rioting occurred in Bangui, following an attempt by the police to disperse a public meeting of opposition supporters; several people were detained, including Dacko, Maidou and Goumba.

From late 1990 the government's unpopularity intensified, owing to the implementation of further economic austerity measures. Public servants were unpaid for several months in 1990, and in December the trade union movement, the Union syndicale des travailleurs de la Centrafrique (USTC), appealed for a general strike. The RDC eventually agreed to pay the workers one-quarter of the arrears owed to them, as well as promising to re-establish the post of prime minister and to undertake a fundamental review of the constitution. In March 1991 most of those who had been detained after the riots of October 1990 were released. The new post of prime minister was created in March 1991, with Edouard Franck, a former minister of state at the presidency, as the first occupant.

During April–July 1991 sporadic strikes plagued the government, as the political opposition conducted its operations from within the USTC. In early July, following the arrests of at least 10 union leaders on charges of convening an illegal political assembly, the government finally agreed to the restoration of a multi-party system. Kolingba conceded that the reforms were being made to meet the wishes of the international donor community. However, public meetings remained illegal, opposition parties were prevented access to the state-controlled media and civil service unions were banned by decree until the end of

October. In early August the USTC called a brief general strike in protest at the arrests of its leaders, and at the suppression of civil service unions. In August Kolingba relinquished the presidency of the RDC.

At the end of October 1991 the Kolingba administration agreed to convene a national debate, comprising representatives of the government and opposition movements. In December Kolingba pardoned Bozize for his involvement in the attempted coup of March 1982.

In August 1992 Kolingba opened the 'grand national debate'. Boycotted by the main opposition grouping, the Concertation des forces démocratiques (CFD), which was prepared only to participate in a multi-party national conference with sovereign powers, and by the Roman Catholic Church, the debate was dominated by pro-Kolingba nominees from the RDC and local government. The opening session coincided with the killing of a leading member of the CFD by the security forces during an anti-government protest: this incident provoked condemnation from Amnesty International and the US ambassador.

At the end of August 1992, the national assembly approved legislation in accordance with decisions taken by the grand national debate: constitutional amendments provided for the strict separation of executive, legislative and judicial powers and Kolingba was granted temporary powers to rule by decree pending the election of a multi-party legislature. Concurrent legislative and presidential elections commenced in October, but were suspended by decree of the president (himself a candidate at the presidential election) and subsequently annulled by the supreme court, owing to alleged electoral irregularities. Three other candidates (ex-president David Dacko, former premier Ange-Félix Patassé and Enoch Derant Lakoué, the leader of the Parti social-démocrate—PSD) supported the annullment, although it was opposed by Dr Abel Goumba, the CFD candidate and leader of the Front patriotique pour le progrès (FPP). The CFD eventually accepted the postponement, suggesting that the elections should be restaged in February 1993. All sides accepted this proposal, and Kolingba appointed Gen. Timothée Malendoma as prime minister of a transitional government. Malendoma's Forum civique had broken ranks with the CFD by participating in the grand national debate, but Malendoma nevertheless retained the support of the opposition, having been one of the founders of the campaign for democracy. However, the CFD chose not to participate in his government.

In January 1993 Malendoma was dismissed after complaining that Kolingba had curtailed his powers as prime minister. The elections were again postponed, and in May the new prime minister, Enoch Durant Lakoué, announced that polling would take place in October. However, after strong opposition protest and severe pressure from the French government, Kolingba brought the elections forward to August. At the first round of the presidential election on 22 August, Patassé received 37.31% of the votes cast, followed by Goumba with 21.68%, and Dacko with 20.1%. Kolingba received just 12.1%. At the elections to the legislature, held concurrently, of the 31 seats won outright, 15 were secured by the MLPC (led by Patassé), four seats by supporters of Dacko, four by the RDC and eight by smaller parties, some of which were grouped in the CFD. Kolingba initially sought to prevent the publication of the first-round results by issuing decrees which modified the electoral code and altered the composition of the supreme court. However, strong pressure from France, including the threat to suspend all forms of bilateral co-operation, forced him to reverse his decision.

DEMOCRATIC TRANSITION

Patassé won the second round of the ballot on 19 September 1993, receiving 52.47% of votes cast (Goumba received 45.62%), and was declared president by the supreme court on 27 September. After the second round of voting for seats in the national assembly the MLPC held a total of 34 seats (nine seats short of an absolute majority), the RDC had 13 seats, the FPP and Parti libéral-démocrate (PLD) had seven seats each, and the Alliance pour la démocratie et le progrès (ADP) and supporters of Dacko, had six seats each. The remaining 12 seats were shared among seven minor parties and independents.

Patassé was sworn in as president on 22 October 1993. In his inaugural address he stressed that his administration would aim to promote the decentralization of government. He also pledged to address the outstanding problem of unpaid salaries for civil servants. In late October Patassé appointed Jean-Luc Mandaba, a former minister of health under Kolingba and vice-president of the MLPC, as prime minister. After appointing a 19-member cabinet at the end of October, which included three ministers from the outgoing administration, Mandaba emphasized the primacy of economic policy in his reform programme. In addition to the MLPC, the new government included representatives of the PLD, the ADP and supporters of David Dacko, giving the coalition government a working majority of 53 seats in the national assembly.

In December 1993 Dacko launched a new party, the Mouvement pour la démocratie et le développement (MDD). In March 1994, following the arrest for seditious activities of two senior members of the RDC, ex-president Kolingba was deprived of his army rank.

In December 1994 a draft constitution was approved by 82% of voters in a national referendum. The new constitution, which was duly adopted in January 1995, included provisions empowering the president to nominate senior military, civil service and judicial officials, and requiring the prime minister to implement policies decided by the president. In addition, provision was made for the creation of directly-elected regional assemblies and for the establishment of an advisory state council, which was to deliberate on administrative issues. Several groups in the governing coalition (notably the MDD) expressed concern at the powers afforded to the president.

In April 1995 Mandaba resigned as prime minister, pre-empting a threatened vote of no confidence in his government (initiated by his own party), following accusations against the administration of corruption and incompetence. On the following day Patassé appointed Gabriel Koyambounou, a former civil servant, as the new prime minister. Koyambounou subsequently nominated a new cabinet, with an enlarged membership.

At the end of August 1995 supporters of Kolingba's RDC staged a peaceful demonstration in protest at perceived abuses of power by the government, including the imposition of a two-year term of imprisonment on the editor of the RDC newspaper, who had been convicted of treason following the publication of an article which criticized the head of state. In December several opposition movements (including the ADP and MDD, but excluding the RDC) united to form the Conseil démocratique des partis politiques de l'opposition (CODEPO), which aimed to campaign against alleged corruption and political and economic mismanagement by the Patassé regime.

ARMY DISCONTENT

In the mid-1990s the government repeatedly failed to pay the salaries of public-sector employees and members of the security forces, prompting frequent strikes and mounting political unrest. In mid-April 1996 CODEPO staged an anti-government rally in Bangui. Shortly afterwards part of the national army mutinied in the capital and demanded the immediate settlement of all salary arrears. Patassé promised that part of the overdue salaries would be paid and that the mutineers would not be subject to prosecution. Faced with the presence of French troops (the Eléments français d'assistance opérationelle—EFAO) in Bangui, with a mandate to secure the safety of foreign nationals and (in accordance with a bilateral military accord) to protect the presidential palace and other key installations, the rebellion swiftly collapsed. About nine people, including civilians, were reported to have died in the uprising. In late April Patassé appointed a new chief of staff of the armed forces, Col Maurice Regonessa, and banned all public demonstrations. In mid-May, however, discontent again resurfaced and CODEPO organized another rally in Bangui, at which it demanded the resignation of the government. Patassé defended the record of his administration by blaming the country's economic crisis on his predecessors. Soon afterwards, in an attempt to tighten his hold on power, the president ordered that control of the national armoury should be transferred from the regular army to the traditionally loyal presidential guard. However, adverse reaction to this move within the ranks of the armed forces rapidly escalated into a second, more determined insurrection. Once again EFAO troops were deployed to protect the Patassé administration; some 500 reinforcements were brought in from Chad and Gabon to consolidate the resident French military presence

(numbering 1,400). Five hostages were taken by the mutineers, including Col Regonessa, together with a cabinet minister and the president of the national assembly. After five days of fierce fighting between dissident and loyalist troops, the French forces intervened to suppress the rebellion. France's military action (which allegedly resulted in civilian deaths) prompted intense scrutiny of the role of the former colonial power, and precipitated large pro- and anti-French demonstrations in Bangui. In all, 11 soliders and 32 civilians were reported to have been killed in the second army mutiny. Following extended negotiations between the mutineers and government representatives, the two sides eventually signed an accord, providing for an amnesty for the rebels (who were to return to barracks under EFAO guard), the immediate release of hostages, and the installation of a new government of national unity. The political opposition now became active in the debate, rejecting the proposed government of national unity and demanding instead a transitional government leading to fresh legislative and presidential elections. The opposition also requested a revision of the constitution to transfer some executive powers from the president to the prime minister.

In early June 1996 a protocol was signed by the government and the opposition, which provided for the establishment of a government of national unity under the leadership of a civilian prime minister with no official party ties. Although the constitution was not to be amended to alter the balance of power between the president and the prime minister, Patassé agreed to permit 'some room for manoeuvre'. Meanwhile, France agreed to assist the CAR authorities with the payment of salary arrears still owed to public-sector employees and members of the security forces. (Nevertheless, many arrears remained unpaid by late 1997.) Following the publication of the protocol, Koyambounou's government resigned. Jean-Paul Ngoupandé, hitherto ambassador to France and with no official political affiliation (although previously secretary-general of the RDC in the late 1980s), was appointed as the new prime minister; Ngoupandé immediately nominated a new cabinet. National co-operation, however, remained elusive. CODEPO, dissatisfied with the level of its representation in the council of ministers, immediately withdrew from the government of national unity. Moreover, it was reported that there was a growing animosity between Patassé and Ngoupandé, with the former refusing to transfer any effective power to the latter.

At a conference on national defence held in late August and early September 1996, several resolutions were adopted regarding restructuring and improving conditions within the army. In late October, however, it was reported that troops who had been involved in the insurrections of April and May were refusing to be transferred from their barracks in the capital to a more remote location; Patassé insisted that their departure would take place none the less. However, in mid-November a further mutiny erupted among these troops, shortly after the withdrawal from CODEPO of four opposition parties, including the ADP and the MDD. A substantial part of Bangui was occupied by the rebels, and a number of hostages were taken. The latest uprising appeared to have a strong tribal and political motivation: the mutineers, who were demanding the resignation of Patassé, belonged to the Yakoma ethnic group of Kolingba. EFAO troops were deployed once again, ostensibly to maintain order and protect foreign residents; however, by guarding key installations and government buildings they also effectively prevented the overthrow of the Patassé administration. More than 100 people were killed in the unrest during late November and early December, including a former (Yakoma) cabinet minister under Kolingba, who was abducted and murdered, allegedly by troops loyal to the government.

In December 1996 the presidents of Burkina Faso, Chad, Gabon and Mali negotiated a 15-day truce, which was supervised by the former transitional president of Mali, Brig.-Gen. Amadou Toumani Touré; a one-month extension to the cease-fire was subsequently agreed. In January 1997, following the killing of two French soldiers in Bangui (reportedly by mutineers), EFAO troops retaliated by killing at least 10 members of the rebel forces; French military involvement in the CAR was condemned by prominent opposition parties, including the ADP, the MDD and the RDC, which also sought (without success) to initiate a parliamentary vote to bring impeachment proceedings against

Patassé. Subsequent to the renewal of violence, Touré again came to Bangui as mediator and assisted in the establishment of a cross-party committee of consultation and dialogue. The 'Bangui accords', drawn up by this committee, were signed towards the end of January; these, as well as offering an amnesty to the mutineers, agreed upon the formation of a new government of national unity and on the replacement of the EFAO troops patrolling Bangui by peace-keeping forces from African nations. The opposition at first threatened to boycott the new government, voicing its discontent with the appointment at the end of January of Michel Gbezera-Bria (a close associate of Patassé and hitherto the minister of foreign affairs) as prime minister. However, with the creation of new ministerial posts for opposition politicians, a 'Government of Action' (which did not include Ngoupandé) was formed in mid-February; soon afterwards, Gen. Bozize replaced Regonessa as chief of staff of the armed forces.

MISAB AND MINURCA

During February 1997 responsibility for peace-keeping operations was transferred from the EFAO to forces of the newly-formed Mission interafricaine de surveillance des accords de Bangui (MISAB), comprising some 700 soldiers from Burkina Faso, Chad, Gabon, Mali, Senegal and Togo (with logistical support from 50 French military personnel). MISAB soldiers were also to assist in disarming the former mutineers; however, when in late March they attempted to do so, fighting broke out in which some 20 MISAB soldiers were killed. A spokesman for the rebels, Capt. Anicet Saulet, claimed that the lack of representation of the former mutineers in the new government constituted a breach of the 'Bangui accords'; following a meeting between Saulet and Patassé in early April, the council of ministers was expanded to include two military officers as representatives of the rebels. Later in that month several hundred of the former mutineers attended a ceremony marking their reintegration into the regular armed forces.

In mid-April 1997 a dusk-to-dawn curfew was imposed on Bangui, following serious escalations in violent crime, much of which was allegedly perpetrated by groups of former mutineers. In early May, following the deaths in police custody of three former rebels suspected of criminal activities, members of the G11 (a grouping of 11 opposition parties, including the ADP, the FPP, the MDD and the RDC), as well as the two representatives of the former mutineers, suspended participation in the government.

In late June 1997 violent clashes erupted once again between MISAB forces and former mutineers. In response to several attacks on the French embassy by the rebels, several hundred EFAO troops were redeployed on the streets of Bangui, and MISAB forces launched a major offensive in the capital, capturing most of the rebel-controlled districts. This assault led to the arrest of more than 80 former mutineers, but also to some 100 deaths, both of soldiers and of civilians, while numerous homes and business premises were destroyed. Soon afterwards some 500 demonstrators gathered outside the French embassy in protest at alleged human rights abuses by MISAB troops; MISAB officials claimed that criminals were impersonating their soldiers in order to perpetrate atrocities. On the same day Touré arrived once again in Bangui in his capacity as chairman of MISAB, and negotiated a four-day truce, which took effect at the end of June, followed by a 10-day cease-fire agreement, signed at the beginning of July: all of the former mutineers were to be reintegrated into the regular armed forces, and their safety and that of the people living in the districts under their control was guaranteed; the rebels, for their part, were to relinquish their weaponry.

Towards the end of July 1997 many of the people who had been held in custody in relation to the previous month's violence were released by the authorities, and the curfew in Bangui was eased, while it was reported that almost all of the former mutineers had rejoined the regular armed forces. In early September the nine representatives of opposition parties in the council of ministers resumed their vacant posts. Shortly afterwards students who held a demonstration in Bangui in protest at the alleged non-payment of their grants were dispersed by the security forces. In October an amnesty for the return of

weapons was extended, as several thousand firearms had apparently not yet been surrendered.

In July 1997 France announced its intention to withdraw its troops from the CAR by April 1998; the first troops left the country in October 1997. France campaigned vigorously for the formation of a United Nations (UN) force to replace MISAB, which was heavily dependent on French logistical support, but the proposal encountered initial resistance from the USA. A National Reconciliation Conference held in Bangui in February 1998 led to the signing on 5 March of a National Reconciliation Pact by Patassé, and 40 representatives of all the country's political and social groups. The accord was countersigned by Brig.-Gen. Touré and witnessed by many other African heads of state. The pact restated the main provisions of the Bangui Accords and of the political protocol of June 1996. It provided for military and political restructuring implemented by a civilian prime minister supported by all the country's social and political groups. The powers and position of the president were, however, guaranteed, and presidential elections were scheduled for late 1999.

The signature of the pact facilitated the authorization later in March 1998 by the UN Security Council of the establishment of a peace-keeping mission, the UN Mission in the Central African Republic (MINURCA) to replace MISAB. MINURCA comprised 1,345 troops from Benin, Burkina Faso, Canada, Chad, Côte d'Ivoire, Egypt, France, Gabon, Mali, Portugal, Senegal and Togo, and was granted a mandate to remain in the country for an initial period of three months. The UN secretary-general, Kofi Annan, recommended in his report, submitted in February, that the mission should extend for two to three months after the completion of legislative elections, while Patassé urged the retention of the peace-keeping force to ensure the smooth conduct of the presidential elections. MINURCA's initial mandate was to maintain security and stability around Bangui, to supervise the final disposition of weapons retrieved under the disarmament programme, to assist in efforts to train a national police force, and to provide advice and technical assistance for the legislative elections. The mission was subsequently extended until the end of February 1999 in order to support and verify the legislative elections.

There was substantial support for the new political solution and, significantly, when in April 1998 the principal trade union, the Union syndicale des travailleurs de la centrafrique, called for a 48-hour general strike to protest against outstanding pay arrears, their action received little support. However, preparations for the legislative elections were marked by disagreement between the government and the G11 group of opposition parties. In May the G11 rejected the government's appointment of Michel Adama-Tamboux, a former president of the national assembly, as chairman of the independent electoral commission (CEMI), as he had not been first selected by the members of the commission. When the authorities announced in August that the elections were being postponed owing to the difficulties of registering rural voters, the opposition parties claimed there was little political will for the elections in government circles, and in September public demonstrations took place to protest against the indefinite postponement of the legislative elections and the subsequent extension of the term of office of deputies.

The first round of elections to the newly reorganized national assembly finally took place on 22 November and 13 December 1998. A reportedly large number of the 1,403,952 registered voters (of a population of 3,342,501) participated in the elections, which were contested by 29 parties. Parties loyal to Patassé (the so-called Mouvance présidentielle) won 47 of the seats and secured the co-operation of seven independent candidates. The opposition won 55 of the assembly's 109 seats; however, the defection, amidst allegations of bribery, of a newly-elected PSD deputy, Dieudonné Koudoufara, gave the Mouvance présidentielle a majority in the assembly. The opposition called for Koudoufara's resignation, and the opening of the assembly was delayed. Prior to its opening in early January 1999, 10 opposition ministers resigned from the government in protest at what they termed the Mouvance présidentielle's disregard for the results of the election. Only three opposition ministers attended the opening ceremony, and MINURCA soldiers were deployed to protect deputies from protesters gathered outside. The news that Patassé had called on a close associate, the nominally independent former minister of finance, Anicet Georges Dologuélé, to form a new government, provoked public demonstrations, and caused the opposition formally to withdraw from the chamber (the boycott lasted until March). Dologuélé subsequently announced the composition of a council of ministers, which included members of the opposition MDD, despite an opposition agreement not to accept posts in the new government. The MDD leadership subsequently ordered its members to resign their posts; however, Armand Sama, the nominated minister of town planning, housing and public buildings, defied the MDD leadership in order to retain his post. In March two PSD deputies resigned from the party, announcing their intention to retain their seats as independents.

In February 1999 the UN Security Council extended MINURCA's mandate until mid-November 1999 in order that it might assist in the preparations and conduct of the presidential elections, although it was agreed that the force would gradually be reduced after the successful conclusion of the elections with the aim of withdrawing all troops prior to the end of MINURCA's mandate. The Security Council expressed its concern at the political tension caused by the disputed legislative elections, and reminded the government that it had undertaken to implement reform, particularly of the economy and of the armed forces. France was said to have opposed an extension of the mandate, and in the same month French troops withdrew from the CAR. They were replaced within MINURCA by a further Egyptian force. In April the contingent from Côte d'Ivoire also withdrew from MINURCA.

In April 1999 the UN secretary-general, Kofi Annan, called on all factions in the CAR to co-operate in preparations for the presidential elections scheduled for 29 August and 19 September. In particular, Annan criticized delays in the appointment of the independent electoral commission (CEMI). The 27 members of the CEMI were sworn in in May, after agreement was finally reached. In late June the FODEM appointed Charles Massi as its candidate, and in early July the PUN selected Jean-Paul Ngoupandé, although Ngoupandé indicated that he still hoped that negotiations with other members of the opposition grouping, the Union des forces acquises à la paix (UFAP), would lead to the appointment of a single opposition candidate. President Patassé announced that he intended to seek re-election, and Fidèle N'Gouandjika, the president of the CAR's martial arts association, also announced his intention to stand as an independent candidate. The final date for the declaration of candidacy was set at 28 July, and by that date 10 candidates had registered. In the same month MINURCA supervised the destruction in Bangui of hundreds of weapons collected under the disarmament programme. In early August a 45-member body was established, at the request of bilateral creditors and the UN, in order to supervise the activities of the CEMI. It comprised members of both opposition and pro-Patassé parties, and was intended to ensure transparency in the conduct of the election. In mid-August the UFAP requested that voting be postponed until late September because of the delay in the appointment of the CEMI. Patassé later announced that the election would be postponed until 12 September. In the event, the election was not held until 19 September, owing to organizational problems. The voting procedure was conducted in a peaceful manner and international observers reported that, despite some attempts at fraud by a number of individuals, no widespread irregularities had been discovered. On 2 October the constitutional court announced that Patassé had won 517,993 votes, equivalent to 51.6% of the total votes cast, and had, therefore, by attaining more than 50% of the vote, been re-elected president without the need for a second round of voting. Patassé's nearest rivals were Kolingba, who won 194,486 votes (19.4%), Dacko, who received 111,886 votes (11.2%), and Goumba, who obtained 60,778 votes (6.1%). The nine defeated candidates subsequently demanded the annulment of the election results, which they claimed had been manipulated; however, they asked their supporters to remain calm, and on 22 October Patassé was sworn in as president for a further six-year term. In early November the recently-reappointed Prime Minister Dologuélé announced the formation of a new council of ministers, which included members of parties loyal to Patassé as well as independents, three opposition representatives and two members of the armed forces. In late November the govern-

ment stated that its main priorities were to improve human development in the CAR and to combat poverty; particular emphasis was also laid on the restructuring of the public sector and of the armed forces.

In late November 1999 it was reported that several members of the MLPC, who were allegedly dissatisfied at the party's level of representation in the council of ministers, had threatened to assassinate Patassé; security was consequently reinforced at the presidential residence. In the same month a MINURCA unit successfully disabled two bombs, which were discovered near the ministry of foreign affairs and francophone affairs. It remained unclear whether the bombs had been lying there, undiscovered, since the 1997 mutinies. At the end of the month, accounts that armed insurgents had erected barricades in the streets of Kembe and the neighbouring town of Bimbi led the authorities to dispatch troops and police reinforcements to the region to restore order and to initiate a judical enquiry into the recent events.

In October 1999 Kofi Annan requested the UN Security Council to authorize the gradual withdrawal of MINURCA from the CAR over a three-month period following the end of its mandate on 15 November. Annan stressed the important role of MINURCA in guaranteeing stability in the post-electoral period, while he also noted that a delayed withdrawal would enable MINURCA units to complete a training course for local police recruits. In December the UN announced proposals to establish a Bureau de soutien à la consolidation de la paix en Centrafrique (BONUCA), in Bangui, the role of which would be to monitor developments in the CAR in the areas of politics, socio-economics, human rights and security issues, as well as to facilitate dialogue among politicians. BONUCA began its operation on the same day of the final withdrawal of MINURCA, 15 February 2000, with a mandate for a one-year period.

In April 2000 there was a ministerial reshuffle, which included the appointment of Antoine Grothe as the new minister of justice to replace Denis Wangao Kizmalé, who was transferred to the ministry of the civil service and employment. In the same month the Dologuélé government was subject to a vote of 'no confidence', which was proposed by the opposition, in the assemblée nationale. Forty deputies voted for the motion, 58 against and four abstained. The government survived and remained in office.

EXTERNAL RELATIONS

The CAR's relations with France, the former colonial power, have remained important. France is still the principal source of foreign aid, and French advisers oversee the CAR's security services. For many years France maintained a military presence in the CAR, which was regarded as a vital element of its strategy in the region, notably with regard to Chad. However, in accordance with a foreign policy decision by France during the late 1990s to disengage forces from its former African colonies, the French military presence in the CAR was substantially reduced during October 1997–April 1998, leaving only 300 troops to assist with the international peace-keeping operation. France withdrew its contingent from the international force in February 1999 and they were replaced by Egyptian troops.

In July 2000 France agreed to lend the CAR 1,950m. francs CFA over a three-year period to help finance projects to aid the education system, the development of the cotton sector and internal security.

In May 1997 the CAR recognized the administration of President Laurent Kabila in the neighbouring Democratic Republic of the Congo (DRC, formerly Zaire). In the same month the CAR and the DRC signed a mutual assistance pact, which provided for permanent consultation on internal security and defence. The pact also sought to guarantee border security; however during mid-1997 armed soldiers of the former Zairean army were reported to be fleeing troops loyal to Kabila and crossing the Oubangui river into the CAR. In May 1998 the CAR and the DRC signed a further joint defence pact. In June 1998 a small number of DRC soldiers crossed into the CAR following a dispute with local fishermen, who had been protesting about harassment and extortion by Kabila's troops. Their action provoked a minor skirmish with CAR border guards. In January 1999 some 5,000 Congolese civilians crossed the Oubangui to escape the fighting between government troops and the rebel soldiers occupying the northern part of the DRC. Although the CAR has not formally ratified the treaty of mutual assistance with the DRC, in January the authorities permitted DRC troops to enter CAR territory in order to try to halt the rebel advance in the north. In early July, following significant rebel advances, an estimated 13,000 Congolese refugees, including some military personnel, crossed into the CAR, prompting fears of a humanitarian disaster. In mid-August the regional office of the UN High Commissioner for Refugees estimated that the CAR was sheltering about 54,000 refugees from the DRC, Chad and Sudan.

The continuing conflict in the Republic of the Congo has also proved a destabilizing factor in the region. In February 1999, during an official visit to Brazzaville, President Patassé offered his services as a mediator, and in June it was announced that Patassé had been invited by the two sides in the conflict to act in this role. The government in Brazzaville later denied that any such invitation had been extended, and repudiated the suggestion that it was to negotiate with the rebel militias.

In July 1991 the CAR established diplomatic relations with Taiwan, and those with the People's Republic of China were suspended. In January 1998, despite significant financial assistance from Taiwan, the CAR again changed its allegiance in favour of the People's Republic of China. In June 1999 Patassé made an official visit to Beijing.

In February 1994 the Patassé administration sponsored peace negotiations in Bangui between the government of Chad and rebel factions. At the end of 1994 the CAR and Chad agreed to establish a bilateral security structure to ensure mutual border security. In 1994 the CAR also became the fifth member of the Lake Chad Basin Commission. Attacks on Chadian nationals resident in Bangui and on the Chadian contingent of the MISAB forces in late 1996 and early 1997 (carried out apparently by members of the security forces and of the general public, as well as by mutineers), led the Chadian government to issue a *communiqué* in March 1997 warning that further incidences of such aggression would not be tolerated. In June 1999 President Patassé issued an apology to the people of Chad, following disturbances in Bangui in which five Chadian nationals were killed and several more injured. In August the CAR government agreed to pay compensation to the families of the victims. None the less, in December it was reported that some 1,500 Chadian refugees were preparing to leave the CAR, allegedly owing to fears for their security following the scheduled departure of MINURCA forces.

In May 1997 it was reported that considerable numbers of Rwandan Hutus (many of whom had previously served in that country's army when it was implicated in acts of genocide) were seeking asylum in the CAR. In November 1998 it was reported that hundreds of the refugees had departed the country for the DRC, after the CAR government had accused them of violating CAR laws.

The CAR maintains good relations with Nigeria, and in June 1999 a bilateral trade agreement was signed. In April 1999 a treaty of friendship and co-operation was signed with Togo. Patassé also expressed his appreciation of the work of Togolese peace-keeping forces in the CAR. The CAR is a close ally of Libya, and in April 1999 joined the Libyan-sponsored Community of Sahel and Saharan States (COMESSA).

Economy

EDITH HODGKINSON

While the economy of the Central African Republic (CAR) is constrained by the country's landlocked location and its small population, it has a good primary resource base, notably diamonds and rainforest timber, and relatively diversified agriculture. The record since independence has, however, been patchy. Under the first government of President Dacko (to 1965) the economy stagnated, as cotton output fell. In 1966 the new military government, under Jean-Bédel Bokassa, introduced measures to revive agricultural production and to encourage rural development. These measures had some considerable success up to 1970; however, during the early 1970s economic stagnation and recession recurred, and these problems became increasingly severe during the three years of the 'Central African Empire' (1976–79). The country's economic plight was a prime factor in the military take-over in 1981. The new government under General Kolingba immediately negotiated a standby credit from the International Monetary Fund (IMF), paving the way for a rescheduling of the country's debt. However the austerity programme that the government was required to implement, involving steep cuts in budget spending, generated such severe political strains that the Kolingba government temporarily reneged on its budgetary promises in 1983. But it could not hold out for long, and the IMF-approved programme was soon reinstated. A significant step forward was the three-year structural adjustment facility agreed with the IMF in 1987. The programme this supported aimed to liberalize the economy, to foster private enterprise and to improve public finances, primarily through policies of retrenchment in the civil service and the liquidation or privatization of parastatal organizations. Considerable progress was made along these lines, and real growth in gross domestic product (GDP) was a steady 2% per year in 1988–90. A second structural adjustment programme was agreed in 1990.

By the early 1990s, however, the overvaluation of the CFA franc was having a markedly adverse effect on the economy, depressing the coffee and cotton sectors and stimulating a high level of diamond smuggling. After stagnating in 1991, gross domestic product (GDP) declined by 2.5% in 1992 and 2.6% in 1993. In 1994 the 50% devaluation of the CFA franc gave a major immediate boost to coffee and cotton exports, accelerating GDP growth to 4.9% in 1994 and 6.4% in 1995. However, the newly installed Patassé government procrastinated on the implementation of the reforms necessary to secure an enhanced structural adjustment facility (ESAF) from the IMF, thereby failing to take advantage of the willingness of the CAR's major aid donors to increase funding and to reduce the debt burden. Corruption and financial mismanagement, including the failure to pay arrears on public sector and military salaries, caused the army mutinies of 1996, and contributed to the 1.5% fall in GDP in that year. The economy subsequently recovered strongly, with GDP growth reaching 5.1% in 1997 and 5.5% in 1998. In June 1998, conscious of the political need to deliver regular growth and to guarantee the payment of salaries in the public sector, the Patassé government accepted IMF conditions for an ESAF, valued at US $66m.; the CAR was thus the last Franc Zone country to secure this facility in the wake of the devaluation of the CFA franc.

The new programme, which covered the period to 2000, emphasized the implementation of privatizations (including the petroleum distribution company and the two main commercial banks) and the enhancement of government revenue, rather than cuts in spending, to create a modest fall in the budget deficit. The target for GDP was to maintain the growth rate registered in 1997–98. Progress in the first 12 months was good, with GDP growth estimated at 5.6% in 1999, movement on privatization of the two major commercial banks as well as the petroleum distribution company, and strong growth in tax revenues. The IMF consequently delivered a positive verdict at its mid-term review in July 1999. The prospect of this programme being maintained was greatly enhanced in October 1999 when, after his re-election, President Patassé reappointed his reformist prime minister.

AGRICULTURE

Agriculture, forestry and fishing dominate the economy, contributing over 50% of GDP (in 1997 the figure was 51.1%) and employing close to 80% of the working population. Agriculture is concentrated in the tropical rain-forest area of the south-west and the savannah lands in the central region and north-west. Output of the major food crops (cassava, maize, millet, sorghum, groundnuts and rice) was rising in the late 1990s, as the government put greater emphasis on this sector in its regional development programmes. As a result the CAR is now broadly self-sufficient in basic foods. At the same time agricultural diversification has been promoted, mainly to substitute imports. A palm oil complex is in operation at Bossongo, with an oil mill with an annual capacity of 7,500 tons, servicing 2,500 ha of plantations, and a sugar refinery at Ouaka, supplied from 1,300 ha of new plantations. The government has also encouraged the cultivation of vegetables for export to the European market: peppers and green beans are cultivated in an area within easy reach of the country's international airport at Bangui.

Coffee used to be the CAR's major export crop, but it has been superseded by cotton in recent years, and accounted for only 6% of recorded export earnings in 1998. Formerly produced on large, European-owned plantations, it is now the domain of smallholders. The crop is cultivated mainly in the south-western and central-southern regions of the country, and more than 90% is of the *robusta* variety. The Agence de développement de la zone caféière (ADECAF) is the parastatal organization responsible for the purchase, transportation and marketing of this commodity. Production levels vary widely, influenced by both weather and world prices, reaching 16,600 tons in 1992/93, falling to only 6,080 tons in 1997/98, and then recovering to an estimated 10,500 tons in 1998/99.

Cotton, the country's leading export crop, is also cultivated by smallholders. The sector has had a chequered history since the mid-1980s, with the government responding to the fall in world prices in 1986 (and World Bank pressure) by cutting back subsidies to cotton farmers and closing down three of the country's seven cotton-ginning complexes. The sector increasingly suffered from the overvaluation of the CFA franc, which kept producer prices low, while the government was unable to maintain its subsidy payments. By 1992/93 the crop was down to 7,000 tons, a quarter of the average in the 1980s. Boosted by much higher prices since the 1994 currency devaluation, the area under cultivation has risen by a third since the beginning of the decade, and the crop was at a record 46,000 tons in 1996/97, when cotton gins were operating at full capacity. Although the sector subsequently encountered difficulties, with high input costs and unfavourable weather conditions depressing output to 38,000 tons in 1998/99, the long-term outlook for the CAR's cotton crop is favourable, particularly as it is less vulnerable to drought than some other crops.

For decades now efforts have been made to develop the livestock industry, and the number of cattle has increased substantially, despite the problems provided by droughts, the limitations of available fodder and the prevalence of the tsetse fly. Efforts are being made to improve marketing, and to encourage the sedentary raising of cattle to allow for treatment against disease. The herd has also grown as a result of migration from Chad and Sudan. In 1998 there were an estimated 3.0m. head of cattle and 2.3m. goats. Nevertheless, domestic meat production fails to satisfy demand.

The CAR's large forest resources (an estimated 102,000 sq. km of tropical rain-forest) are at present under-exploited commercially, largely as a result of a lack of adequate roads and low-cost means of transportation to the coast. Only about 10% of the forest area is accessible to river transport. In addition, large areas are held as private hunting reserves. Nevertheless, timber exploitation expanded considerably from the late 1960s, following the formation of new companies geared to export and the establishment of new sawmills. Fellings of industrial roundwood reached a peak of 846,000 cu m in 1974, but fell back sharply in subsequent years, owing partly to low water levels on the traditional transport route along the Congo river. Moreover, the rise in the value of the CFA franc in relation to the currencies of the major Asian producers reduced the price competitiveness of the CAR product. Log production declined to 168,000 cu m in 1993, but had surged to 601,400 cu m by 1998 and was forecast at 681,000 cu m in 1999. In 1998 timber accounted for 16% of recorded export earnings, in third place, just behind cotton. The government is trying to raise the value added of wood exports, but a ban on saw log exports imposed

in 1995 proved impractical and the requirement was relaxed in 1996 to give companies more time to invest in processing plants.

MINING

The contribution of mining to GDP is undoubtedly considerably greater than the 3.6% estimated by the IMF for 1997, since between one-half and two-thirds of the output of diamonds—the leading mineral—is thought to be smuggled out of the country and so escapes the official record. Diamonds are found in alluvial deposits, mainly in the south-west and west of the country. Until 1960 production was controlled by expatriate companies but by 1970 individual African prospectors had taken over the whole of production. The decline in recorded output, from a peak of 609,000 carats in 1968 to an average of 466,000 carats per year in 1995–98, is partly attributable to increased smuggling, a concomitant of which has been a decline in the quality of officially traded stones. In the mid-1980s the government attempted to discourage smuggling by increasing customs surveillance and by reducing the relatively high export tax. Subsequently there was some improvement in recorded diamond exports, but this proved short-lived. The government aims to encourage the development of local cutting and polishing industries; by the end of the 1990s, however, there was still only one diamond cutting centre, and exports of diamonds remained almost entirely in uncut form. They were valued at US $35m. in 1998, representing 44% of total export earnings.

Gold is also mined, although production levels have fluctuated sharply, from a peak of 538 kg in 1980 to 98 kg in 1995. The government plans to establish a gold-processing plant. Uranium has been discovered near Bakouma, 480 km east of Bangui. Reserves are estimated at 20,000 tons, with a concentration ratio of some 50%. The weakening in international prices for uranium has obstructed development of the deposits, which would also necessitate the construction of a road from Bakouma to the border with Cameroon. Reserves of iron ore, copper, tin, lignite and limestone have also been located, although the inadequacy of the country's transport infrastructure has deterred mining companies from attempting their commercial exploitation.

MANUFACTURING AND POWER

Manufacturing is based on the processing of primary products and is relatively little developed, contributing an estimated 8.1% of GDP in 1997. The destruction wrought by successive mutinies in Bangui in 1996–97 severely damaged the sector, which registered a contraction of one-fifth in its contribution to GDP over the two years. The country's second largest employer, the Société Centrafricaine de Cigarettes, ceased production in 1996, following the destruction of its premises, and a total of more than 3,000 jobs were lost.

Following independence, the textile and leather industries constituted the chief manufacturing sector. A textile complex, undertaking spinning, weaving and dyeing, which formed the CAR's largest single manufacturing enterprise, and which had been taken over by the state when it was near liquidation, was closed down in 1980. Despite funding from the European Investment Bank and the French government to rehabilitate the project, at a capacity of 4.4m. metres of cloth per year, the complex has never functioned satisfactorily.

The main source of power supply (102.8m. kWh in 1995) is hydroelectric, at the two stations at the M'Bali falls. Plans are under way to construct a new hydroelectric plant at Kembe. A significant strand of the government's current privatization programme is the divestment of its holdings in the state power utility (ENERCA) and the petroleum distribution company (PETROCA). The latter was privatized in 1999, with the network taken over by Elf and Total of France and Shell, while ENERCA's power distribution division was put out to tender in early 2000.

TRANSPORT

The transport infrastructure is underdeveloped and a major constraint on the country's economic development. There is an extensive network of roads (24,000 km in 1996), but only about 2% of the system is paved. The road network has suffered serious deterioration, owing to lack of maintenance, due to the government's budget crisis. However, international development organizations and bilateral donors have extended funds for road rehabilitation projects. The CAR section of the Transafrican highway from Lagos to Mombasa was completed in 1984, providing a link with Cameroon. There is no railway, but there are long-standing plans to extend the Transcameroon line to Bangui and also to link the CAR with the rail systems in Sudan and Gabon. For the foreseeable future any development in the land transport network will be in the form of roads rather than rail. A much larger volume of freight is carried by river; of a total of 7,000 km of inland waterways, some 2,800 km are navigable, most importantly the Oubangui river south of Bangui, which is the country's main outlet for external trade, and the Sangha and Lobaye rivers. Port facilities are being improved, with assistance from France and the European Union.

The principal route for the import and export trade has traditionally been the trans-equatorial route, which involves 1,800 km by river from Bangui to Brazzaville, in the Republic of the Congo, and then rail from Brazzaville to Pointe-Noire. However, instability in the Republic of the Congo since 1997 has led to periodic suspension of this service. River traffic has therefore declined, as importers and exporters have turned to the new land route through Cameroon, although the outlet via Pointe Noire remains important for timber shipments.

There is an international airport at Bangui–M'Poko, and there are also 37 small airports. Internal services are, however, irregular and dependent on the availability of fuel.

PUBLIC FINANCE

The CAR's fiscal position has been extremely weak, with a narrow tax base which is vulnerable to adverse trends in international prices for coffee and cotton and prone to erosion as a result of smuggling, while bearing the burden of losses incurred by the parastatal organizations and of personnel expenditure for the cumbersome civil service. Consequently, substantial deficits have been frequently incurred. As part of its agreement with the IMF, the government implemented measures in 1982 to reduce the numbers of the 27,000-strong civil service and to cut the salaries of those remaining by 28%. This had only limited effect, reducing the deficit by one-tenth in 1983 to 7,500m. francs CFA, equivalent to around 3% of GDP, and only after grant aid from France was included. More rigorous implementation of budgetary austerity measures brought the budget to near balance by 1985, but the very fitful pace of economic reform in subsequent years meant that the deficit rose to 36,000m. francs CFA in 1994 (7% of GDP; excluding grants the deficit was almost twice as high). The deficit before grants was brought down slightly in 1995 only through the non-payment of salaries.

The resulting unrest and political insecurity damaged the domestic revenue base in 1996–97, but the programme agreed with the IMF in 1998 envisaged a rise of 55% in tax revenue as economic activity in Bangui resumed and as the result of a drive to collect more customs and diamond levies. This ambitious target was not quite achieved, but the 38.5% rise in revenue permitted a narrowing of the budget deficit in 1998. The aim is to reduce the imbalance to 4.6% of GDP in 2000.

FOREIGN TRADE AND THE BALANCE OF PAYMENTS

The CAR's foreign trade accounts have historically shown a persistent, if relatively modest, deficit. While imports tended to increase, export receipts fluctuated widely, in response to trends in international prices for diamonds, coffee, timber and cotton. The impact of the 1994 devaluation of the CFA franc, notably on exports of cotton, has been a significant factor in pushing the trade account into a marginal surplus since 1996 (at an average of US $34m. per year in 1996–98, according to the IMF). Since a large proportion of diamond exports are thought to be unrecorded, the true balance is likely to have been considerably better, at close to $100m. per year.

However, with a large net outflow on services, reflecting transport costs stemming from the country's landlocked position, the CAR has recorded a persistent deficit on the current account of the balance of payments, estimated at an average US $63m. per year in 1995–98. This imbalance has been relatively high (equivalent to 6% of GDP) despite substantial inflows of aid in grant form. In 1994–98 grants from members of the OECD's Development Assistance Committee averaged $136m. per year. France has been the leading single source throughout, accounting for almost one-half of these inflows.

The deficit on the current account has largely been covered by borrowing from governments and multilateral institutions, since the CAR has not proved very attractive to foreign private investors (other than in the diamond sector). The total external debt has consequently been rising over a long period, reaching a peak of US $946m. in 1995. It had, however, eased to $885m. by the end of 1997 and to $774m. at the close of 1998. In 1997 96% of the total external debt was owed to official creditors and 90% was on concessionary terms. The high proportion of concessionary debt ensured, however, that despite total debt in 1998 being equivalent to 75% of GNP (a high ratio), the debt service ratio (expenditure on interest and repayment as a proportion of total foreign earnings) was a modest 5.2%, a much lower percentage than in many other countries in the region. The proportion of debt that is on concessionary terms and owed to official sources does, however, underline the need for the CAR to maintain its compliance with IMF-approved policies.

Statistical Survey

Source (unless otherwise stated): Division des Statistiques et des Etudes Economiques, Ministère de l'Economie, du Plan et de la Coopération Internationale, Bangui.

Area and Population

AREA, POPULATION AND DENSITY

Area (sq km)	622,984*
Population (census results)	
8 December 1975	2,054,610
8 December 1988	
Males	1,210,734
Females	1,252,882
Total	2,463,616
Population (UN estimate at mid-year)	
1998	3,485,000
Density (per sq km) at mid-1998	5.6

* 240,535 sq miles.

PRINCIPAL TOWNS (population, 1988 census)

Bangui (capital) . .	451,690	Bambari . . .	38,633
Berbérati . . .	41,891	Bossangoa . . .	31,502
Bouar	39,676	Carnot	31,324

1996: Bangui 524,000 (estimate).

BIRTHS AND DEATHS (UN estimates, annual averages)

	1980–85	1985–90	1990–95
Birth rate (per 1,000).	42.4	42.1	39.6
Death rate (per 1,000)	18.5	17.9	17.4

Source: UN, *World Population Prospects: The 1998 Revision*.

1994: Registered live births 124,707 (birth rate 41.6 per 1,000); Registered deaths 50,063 (death rate 16.7 per 1,000) (Source: UN, *Population and Vital Statistics Report*).

Expectation of life (UN estimates, years at birth, 1990–95): 47.5 (males 45.9; females 49.3) (Source: UN, *World Population Prospects: The 1998 Revision*).

ECONOMICALLY ACTIVE POPULATION
(persons aged 6 years and over, 1988 census)

	Males	Females	Total
Agriculture, hunting, forestry and fishing	417,630	463,007	880,637
Mining and quarrying	11,823	586	12,409
Manufacturing	16,096	1,250	17,346
Electricity, gas and water	751	58	809
Construction	5,583	49	5,632
Trade, restaurants and hotels	37,435	54,563	91,998
Transport, storage and communications	6,601	150	6,751
Financing, insurance, real estate and business services	505	147	652
Community, social and personal services	61,764	8,537	70,301
Activities not adequately defined	7,042	4,627	11,669
Total employed	565,230	532,974	1,098,204
Unemployed.	66,624	22,144	88,768
Total labour force	631,854	555,118	1,186,972

Source: International Labour Office, *Yearbook of Labour Statistics*.

Mid-1998 (estimates in '000): Agriculture, etc. 1,238; Total labour force 1,665 (Source: FAO, *Production Yearbook*).

Agriculture

PRINCIPAL CROPS ('000 metric tons)

	1996	1997	1998
Rice (paddy).	15	17	17*
Maize	76	82	82*
Millet	12*	12†	10*
Sorghum	35	38	38*
Cassava (Manioc)	526	579	579*
Yams*	340	340	360
Taro (Coco yam)*	90	90	100
Pulses*	28	28	28
Groundnuts (in shell)	91	97	100†
Sesame seed	31	32	32*
Cottonseed*	21	26	22
Palm kernels*	5	5	5
Pumpkins, squash and gourds	17†	18	18*
Other vegetables (incl. melons)	55	57	57*
Sugar cane	79	80*	80*
Oranges*	20	22	22
Mangoes*	9	9	9
Pineapples*	13	13	13
Bananas*	105	110	110
Plantains*	78	80	80
Other fruits (excl. melons)*	10	11	11
Coffee (green)	18	15	14†
Cotton (lint)	18	22	19†

* FAO estimate(s).   † Unofficial figure.

Source: FAO, *Production Yearbook*.

LIVESTOCK ('000 head, year ending September)

	1996	1997	1998*
Cattle	2,861	2,926	2,992
Goats	2,093	2,213	2,339
Sheep	181	191	201
Pigs.	571	596	622

Poultry (million): 4 in 1996; 4* in 1997; 4* in 1998.

* Unofficial figure(s).

Source: FAO, *Production Yearbook*.

LIVESTOCK PRODUCTS ('000 metric tons)

	1996	1997	1998
Beef and veal†	61	50	51
Mutton and lamb*	1	1	1
Goat meat	7	8	8*
Pig meat	11	12	12*
Poultry meat	3	3	3†
Other meat*.	9	7	7
Cows' milk	58	60*	60*
Cattle hides (fresh)*	8	7	8
Goatskins (fresh)*	1	1	1
Hen eggs*	1	1	1
Honey*	11	11	11

* FAO estimate(s).   † Unofficial figure(s).

Source: FAO, *Production Yearbook*.

Forestry

ROUNDWOOD REMOVALS ('000 cubic metres, excluding bark)

	1995	1996	1997
Sawlogs, veneer logs and logs for sleepers	326	305	461
Other industrial wood	284	290	296
Fuel wood	3,000	2,804	2,915
Total	3,610	3,399	3,672

Source: FAO, *Yearbook of Forest Products*.

SAWNWOOD PRODUCTION
('000 cubic metres, including railway sleepers)

	1995	1996	1997
Total (all broadleaved)	70	61	72

Source: FAO, *Yearbook of Forest Products*.

Fishing

(FAO estimates, '000 metric tons, live weight)

	1995	1996	1997
Total catch (freshwater fish).	12.9	12.7	12.5

Source: FAO, *Yearbook of Fishery Statistics*.

Mining

	1996	1997	1998
Gold (kg, metal content of ore)	38.7	35.1	23.8
Diamonds ('000 carats)	487.4	486.8	419.8

Source: Banque des Etats de l'Afrique Centrale, *Etudes et Statistiques*.

Industry

SELECTED PRODUCTS

	1995	1996	1997*
Beer ('000 hectolitres) . .	268.9	156.4	130.2
Soft drinks and syrups ('000 hectolitres)	52.8	60.6	42.1
Cigarettes (million packets) . .	18.6	7.8	n.a.
Palm oil ('000 metric tons) . .	3.2	2.3	2.5
Plywood ('000 cubic metres) . .	2.4	1.5	1.4
Motor cycles (number) . .	338	n.a.	n.a.
Bicycles (number) . . .	647	n.a.	n.a.
Electric energy (million kWh) .	101.4	98.7	100.7

* Figures are provisional.

Source: IMF, *Central African Republic: Statistical Annex* (September 1998).

Raw sugar (FAO estimates, '000 metric tons): 10 in 1995; 10 in 1996; 11 in 1997; 11 in 1998 (Source: mainly FAO, *Production Yearbook*).

Finance

CURRENCY AND EXCHANGE RATES

Monetary Units
100 centimes = 1 franc de la Coopération financière en Afrique centrale (CFA).

Sterling, Dollar and Euro Equivalents (28 April 2000)
£1 sterling = 1,132.20 francs CFA;
US $1 = 722.02 francs CFA;
€1 = 655.96 francs CFA;
10,000 francs CFA = £8.832 = $13.850 = €15.245.

Average Exchange Rate (francs CFA per US $)
1997   583.67
1998   589.95
1999   615.70

Note: The exchange rate of 1 French franc = 50 francs CFA, established in 1948, remained in force until January 1994, when the CFA franc was devalued by 50%, with the exchange rate adjusted to 1 French franc = 100 francs CFA. This relationship to French currency remained in effect with the introduction of the euro on 1 January 1999. From that date, accordingly, a fixed exchange rate of €1 = 655.957 francs CFA has been in operation.

BUDGET (million francs CFA)

Revenue	1995	1996	1997*
Tax revenue	49,300	32,900	42,400
Taxes on income and profits .	10,600	8,100	8,700
Domestic taxes on goods and services	16,800	11,900	16,500
Taxes on international trade	21,900	12,900	17,100
Import duties and taxes .	17,900	9,700	15,400
Other receipts	2,200	300	2,600
Total	51,500	33,200	45,000

Expenditure	1995	1996	1997*
Current expenditure . . .	57,400	47,400	52,200†
Wages and salaries. . .	26,000	25,300	26,600
Other goods and services .	11,500	7,600	10,200
Transfers and subsidies .	7,200	4,100	3,800
Interest payments . . .	12,800	10,500	7,900
Capital expenditure . . .	57,900	13,200	30,700
Sub-total	115,300	60,600	82,900
Adjustment for payments arrears‡	−25,700	22,800	−21,300
Total	89,600	83,400	61,600

* Estimates.

† Including extrabudgetary expenditure (million francs CFA): 3,600.

‡ Minus sign indicates an increase in arrears.

Source: IMF, *Central African Republic: Statistical Annex* (September 1998).

INTERNATIONAL RESERVES (US $ million at 31 December)

	1996	1997	1998
Gold*	4.10	3.24	3.20
IMF special drawing rights . .	0.01	—	0.01
Reserve position in IMF . . .	0.14	0.13	0.13
Foreign exchange	232.09	178.43	145.56
Total	236.34	181.80	148.90

* National valuation.

Source: IMF, *International Financial Statistics*.

MONEY SUPPLY ('000 million francs CFA at 31 December)

	1997	1998	1999
Currency outside banks . .	92.96	75.25	81.12
Demand deposits at commercial and development banks . .	14.22	12.33	17.53
Total money	107.19	87.58	98.64

Source: IMF, *International Financial Statistics*.

COST OF LIVING
(Consumer Price Index for Bangui; base: 1981 = 100)

	1995	1996	1997
Food	179.9	193.2	188.1
Fuel and light	151.5	153.4	161.7
Clothing.	238.7	223.5	252.6
All items (incl. others)* . .	187.5	195.7	196.8

* Excluding rent.

Source: IMF, *Central African Republic: Statistical Annex* (September 1998).

NATIONAL ACCOUNTS
(IMF estimates, million francs CFA at current prices)

Expenditure on the Gross Domestic Product

	1995	1996	1997
Government final consumption expenditure	73,700	41,700	55,300
Private final consumption expenditure	453,100	41,700	55,300
Increase in stocks } Gross fixed capital formation . }	83,500	19,100	53,400
Total domestic expenditure .	610,300	596,900	608,400
Exports of goods and services .	114,200	97,400	124,100
Less Imports of goods and services	155,100	117,700	137,800
GDP in purchasers' values .	569,400	556,600	594,600
GDP at constant 1985 prices	403,100	397,200	417,600

Source: IMF, *Central African Republic: Statistical Annex* (September 1998).

Gross Domestic Product by Economic Activity

	1995	1996	1997
Agriculture, hunting, forestry and fishing	257,600	277,800	303,700
Mining and quarrying . .	23,000	21,900	21,600
Manufacturing . . .	55,400	53,100	48,000
Electricity, gas and water .	5,000	5,000	4,800
Construction	30,100	23,800	26,600
Trade, restaurants and hotels	72,200	77,500	79,900
Transport, storage and communications . . .	13,900	14,400	14,700
Other private services . .	25,900	27,600	27,800
Government services . . .	47,700	30,800	33,800
GDP at factor cost . . .	530,700	531,800	561,000
Indirect taxes	38,700	24,800	33,600
GDP in purchasers' values .	569,400	556,600	594,600

Source: IMF, *Central African Republic: Statistical Annex* (September 1998).

BALANCE OF PAYMENTS ('000 million francs CFA)

	1995	1996	1997*
Exports of goods	89.3	74.5	101.2
Imports of goods	−89.2	−60.6	−74.2
Trade balance	0.1	13.9	27.0
Services and other income (net)	−51.3	−39.6	−47.0
Balance on goods, services and income	−51.2	−25.7	−20.0
Private unrequited transfers (net)	−5.4	−5.1	−5.8
Public unrequited transfers (net)	51.9	25.2	29.4
Current balance	−4.7	−5.6	3.6
Long-term capital (net) . .	5.3	−5.4	−11.8
Short-term capital (net) . . .	3.1	7.8	−5.8
Net errors and omissions . .	−8.4	−4.7	−8.9
Overall balance . . .	−4.7	−7.9	−22.9

* Estimates.

Source: La Zone Franc, *Rapport Annuel 1997*.

External Trade

PRINCIPAL COMMODITIES (distribution by SITC, US $'000)

Imports c.i.f.	1994	1995	1996
Food and live animals . .	24,635	27,587	12,585
Cereals and cereal preparations	17,183	15,010	5,915
Flour of wheat or meslin .	13,990	7,999	3,442
Beverages and tobacco . .	14,238	12,128	8,977
Tobacco and tobacco manufactures	12,216	9,244	6,709
Unmanufactured tobacco and tobacco refuse . . .	4,417	8,510	3,632
Cigarettes	7,799	734	3,077
Crude materials (inedible) except fuels	10,353	27,184	25,177
Cork and wood . . .	97	2,466	4,365
Coniferous sawlogs and veneer logs	90	1,921	3,901
Textile fibres (excl. wool tops) and waste	9,361	22,443	19,132
Cotton	7,951	20,547	17,501
Mineral fuels, lubricants, etc.	11,606	23,063	14,594
Petroleum, petroleum products, etc.	11,374	22,755	14,550
Refined petroleum products .	11,223	22,715	14,447
Motor spirit (gasoline) and other light oils. . .	3,223	8,364	4,756
Kerosene and other medium oils	3,948	4,239	2,973
Gas oils (distillate fuels) .	2,242	7,651	4,809
Chemicals and related products	25,037	20,721	14,056
Medicinal and pharmaceutical products . . .	16,759	9,522	6,416
Medicaments . . .	15,912	8,300	5,960
Disinfectants, insecticides, fungicides, etc. . . .	2,824	3,760	4,039
Basic manufactures . .	21,404	29,201	19,118
Paper, paperboard and manufactures . . .	3,483	4,169	3,970
Non-ferrous metals . .	4,685	3,548	1,812
Aluminium and aluminium alloys	4,393	3,204	1,210
Plates, sheets and strip . .	3,985	2,575	1,066

Imports c.i.f. — *continued*	1994	1995	1996
Machinery and transport equipment . . .	36,668	112,122	67,289
Power-generating machinery and equipment . . .	1,424	3,897	3,704
Machinery specialized for particular industries . .	2,809	26,240	7,912
Civil engineering and contractors' plant and equipment . . .	876	23,753	4,939
Construction and mining machinery . . .	460	20,437	3,685
Self-propelled bulldozers, angledozers and levellers.	366	14,872	472
General industrial machinery, equipment and parts . .	5,969	9,441	5,042
Telecommunications and sound equipment . . .	3,131	12,119	4,777
Television and radio transmitters, etc. . .	983	6,170	2,496
Other electrical machinery, apparatus, etc. . .	4,120	5,494	4,180
Road vehicles and parts* . .	16,456	49,770	33,043
Passenger motor cars (excl. buses)	2,948	8,935	5,473
Motor vehicles for goods transport and special purposes	4,847	17,160	13,314
Goods vehicles (lorries and trucks)	4,500	11,006	11,387
Special-purpose motor lorries and vans . . .	347	6,154	1,927
Public-service passenger motor vehicles (buses, etc.) . .	1,071	5,987	2,815
Parts and accessories for cars, buses, lorries, etc.* . .	4,204	9,836	7,056
Other transport equipment* . .	557	1,963	5,771
Aircraft, associated equipment and parts* . . .	548	1,791	5,771
Miscellaneous manufactured articles	7,040	12,019	10,386
Printed matter . . .	1,544	2,582	3,890
Armoured fighting vehicles, arms of war and ammunition	17	6	7,152
Tanks and other armoured fighting vehicles, motorized, and parts	—	—	6,830
Total (incl. others) . . .	154,162	265,499	179,942

* Excluding tyres, engines and electrical parts.

Exports f.o.b.	1994	1995	1996
Food and live animals . . .	2,605	4,142	1,295
Coffee, tea, cocoa and spices . .	2,054	3,109	872
Coffee and coffee substitutes	2,049	3,103	872
Unroasted coffee, husks and skins	2,049	3,103	872
Crude materials (inedible) except fuels . . .	42,858	59,829	57,334
Cork and wood	1,299	2,790	4,756
Coniferous sawlogs and veneer logs	142	1,736	3,883
Textile fibres (excl. wool tops) and waste	7,531	20,351	22,379
Cotton	7,528	20,309	22,379
Crude fertilizers and crude minerals (excl. coal, petroleum and precious stones) . . .	33,545	35,998	29,437
Industrial diamonds (sorted)	33,545	35,998	29,435
Basic manufactures . . .	31,114	41,776	40,107
Non-metallic mineral manufactures . . .	30,839	39,887	39,725
Diamonds (excl. sorted industrial diamonds), unmounted . . .	30,836	39,880	39,715
Sorted non-industrial diamonds, rough or simply worked . . .	29,877	39,812	39,663
Machinery and transport equipment . . .	2,239	10,543	8,663
Road vehicles and parts* . .	2,008	9,259	7,119
Public-service passenger motor vehicles (buses, etc.) . .	74	3,277	823
Parts and accessories for cars, buses, lorries, etc.* . .	1,237	3,351	4,141
Armoured fighting vehicles, arms of war and ammunition	692	—	6,992
Tanks and other armoured fighting vehicles, motorized, and parts	—	—	6,829
Total (incl. others)	81,451	119,522	115,128

* Excluding tyres, engines and electrical parts.

Source: UN, *International Trade Statistics Yearbook*.

PRINCIPAL TRADING PARTNERS (US $'000)*

Imports c.i.f.	1994	1995	1996
Belgium-Luxembourg . . .	2,675	6,589	2,805
Cameroon	8,448	12,880	7,103
Congo, Dem. Repub. . . .	1,386	1,841	1,938
Congo, Repub. . . .	18,047	4,738	3,371
France (incl. Monaco) . .	59,149	90,739	71,137
Germany	3,213	7,626	2,792
Italy	1,332	2,921	1,674
Japan	8,586	52,303	15,676
Netherlands	1,685	2,815	1,845
United Kingdom . . .	1,437	1,563	3,148
USA	2,447	4,871	2,971
Total (incl. others) . . .	154,162	265,499	179,942

Exports f.o.b.	1994	1995	1996
Belgium-Luxembourg . . .	64,906	75,487	69,192
Cameroon	226	1,825	1,184
Congo, Dem. Repub. . . .	437	1,917	1,904
Congo, Repub. . . .	1,012	1,374	850
France (incl. Monaco) . .	9,862	30,207	35,556
Spain	1,154	4	—
United Kingdom . . .	270	2,069	3,996
Total (incl. others) . . .	81,451	119,522	115,128

* Imports by country of production; exports by country of consumption.

Source: UN, *International Trade Statistics Yearbook*.

Transport

ROAD TRAFFIC (motor vehicles in use)

	1993	1994	1995
Passenger cars . . .	10,400	11,900	8,900
Commercial vehicles . . .	2,400	2,800	3,500

Source: UN, *Statistical Yearbook*.

INLAND WATERWAYS TRAFFIC—INTERNATIONAL SHIPPING (metric tons)

	1996	1997	1998
Freight unloaded at Bangui . .	60,311	56,206	57,513
Freight loaded at Bangui . . .	5,348	5,907	12,524
Total	63,659	62,113	70,037

Source: Banque des Etats de l'Afrique Centrale, *Etudes et Statistiques*.

CIVIL AVIATION (traffic on scheduled services)*

	1994	1995	1996
Kilometres flown (million) . .	2	3	3
Passengers carried ('000) . . .	69	74	75
Passenger-km (million) . . .	215	223	225
Total ton-km (million) . . .	34	36	37

* Including an apportionment of the traffic of Air Afrique.

Source: UN, *Statistical Yearbook*.

Tourism

	1995	1996	1997
Tourist arrivals ('000) . .	26	21	17
Tourism receipts (US $ million) .	5	5	5

Source: World Tourism Organization, *Yearbook of Tourism Statistics*.

Communications Media

	1994	1995	1996
Radio receivers ('000 in use) . .	235	245	280
Television receivers ('000 in use) .	16	16	15
Telephones ('000 main lines in use)	7	8	10
Telefax stations (number in use) .	103	136	222
Mobile cellular telephones (subscribers) . .	n.a.	44	471
Daily newspapers			
Number	1	1	3
Average circulation ('000 copies)	2	2	6

Non-daily newspapers (1995): 1 (estimated circulation 2,000 copies).

Sources: UNESCO, *Statistical Yearbook;* UN, *Statistical Yearbook*.

Education

(1990/91, unless otherwise indicated)

	Schools	Teachers	Pupils
Pre-primary	162	572*	15,734
Primary	930	4,004	308,409
Secondary			
General	46†	1,005 {	46,989
Vocational	n.a.		1,862
Higher	n.a.	136	2,823

* 1987/88 figure.

† State-funded general secondary schools.

1991/92: Primary pupils 277,961; General secondary pupils 42,263; Vocational secondary pupils 1,477; University teachers 139; University students 2,923.

Source: UNESCO, *Statistical Yearbook*.

Directory

The Constitution

A new Constitution was adopted on 7 January 1995, following approval by a national referendum held on 28 December 1994. It replaced the 1986 Constitution and all subsequent amendments. The new Constitution provided for decentralization, through the election of regional assemblies by direct universal adult suffrage, and the establishment of a Constitutional Court (whose officials were to be appointed by the President), and it redefined the separation of sovereign and executive powers between the President and the Prime Minister.

THE PRESIDENCY

The President of the Republic is Head of State and Commander-in-Chief of the national armed forces. The President is elected for a six-year term by direct universal suffrage and may serve for a maximum of two consecutive terms*. Election of the President is determined by an absolute majority of votes cast. If such is not obtained at the first ballot, a second ballot is to take place, contested by the two candidates gaining the largest number of votes in the first ballot. The election of the new President is to take place not less than 20 days and not more than 40 days before the expiration of the mandate of the President in office. However, the President may choose to hold a referendum to determine whether or not his mandate is to be renewed. Should the electorate reject the proposal, the President is to resign and a new presidential election is to be held two weeks after the publication of the results of the referendum. The Presidency is to become vacant only in the event of the President's death, resignation, condemnation by the High Court of Justice or permanent physical incapacitation, as certified by a Special Committee comprising the presidents of the Assemblée nationale, the Economic and Regional Council and the Supreme Court (see below). The election of a new President must take place not less than 20 days and not more than 40 days following the occurrence of a vacancy, during which time the president of the Assemblée nationale is to act as interim President, with limited powers.

The President appoints the Prime Minister, who presides over the Council of Ministers. The President promulgates laws adopted by the Assemblée nationale or by the Congress and has the power to dissolve the Assemblée nationale, in which event legislative elections must take place not less than 20 and not more than 40 days following its dissolution.

PARLIAMENT

This is composed of the Assemblée nationale, the Economic and Regional Council and the State Council, which, when sitting together, are to be known as the Congress. The primary function of the Congress is to pass organic laws in implementation of the Constitution, whenever these are not submitted to a referendum.

Assemblée nationale

The Assemblée nationale is composed of 109 deputies elected by direct universal suffrage for a five-year term. Its president is designated by, and from within, its bureau. Legislation may be introduced either by the President of the Republic or by a consensus of one-third of the members of the Assemblée. Provisions are made for the rendering inadmissible of any law providing for the execution of projects carrying a financial cost to the State which exceeds their potential value. The Assemblée nationale holds two ordinary sessions per year of 60 days each, at the summons of the President of the Republic, who may also summon it to hold extraordinary sessions with a pre-determined agenda. Sessions of the Assemblée nationale are opened and closed by presidential decree.

The Economic and Regional Council

The Economic and Regional Council is composed of representatives from the principal sectors of economic and social activity. One-half of its members are appointed by the President, and the remaining half are elected by the Assemblée nationale on the nomination of that body's president. It acts as an advisory body in all legislative proposals of an economic and social nature.

The State Council

The State Council is an advisory body which deliberates on administrative matters that are referred to it by the president of the Assemblée nationale.

The Congress

The Congress has the same president and bureau as the Assemblée nationale. An absolute majority of its members is needed to pass organic laws, as well as laws pertaining to the amendment of the Constitution which have not been submitted to a referendum. It defines development priorities and may meet, at the summons of the President, to ratify treaties or to declare a state of war.

* A special clause was incorporated in the 1995 Constitution, whereby the incumbent President, Ange-Félix Patassé, was to be permitted to remain in office, if re-elected, for three consecutive terms.

The Government

HEAD OF STATE

President: ANGE-FÉLIX PATASSÉ (elected 19 September 1993; re-elected 19 September 1999).

COUNCIL OF MINISTERS
(August 2000)

A coalition comprising members of the Mouvement pour la libération du peuple centrafricain (MLPC), the Convention nationale (CN), the Parti libéral-démocrate (PLD), the Parti pour l'union nationale (PUN), the Parti social-démocrate (PSD), the Mouvement pour la démocratie et le développement (MDD), independents (Ind.) and members of the armed forces.

Prime Minister, Minister of the Economy, Finance, Planning and International Co-operation: ANICET GEORGES DOLOGUÉLÉ (Ind.).

Minister of Foreign Affairs and Francophone Affairs: MARCEL METEFARA (MLPC).

Minister of Defence, Restructuring of the Armed Forces and Former Combattants: JEAN-JACQUES DEMAFOUTH (MLPC).

Minister of Justice, Keeper of the Seals: ANTOINE GROTHE.

Minister of Internal Affairs: MAURICE REGONESSA.*

Minister of Education: ELOI ANGUIMATE (CN).

Minister of Higher Education and Scientific Research: TIMO-LÉON MBAIKOUA (MLPC).

Minister of Trade and Industry and the Promotion of the Private Sector: JEAN-BAPTISTE KOYASSAMBIA (Ind.).

Minister of Mining and Energy: ANDRÉ LATOU (MLPC).

Minister of Agriculture and Livestock: GABRIEL DOTE BADEKARA.

Minister of Transport and Civil Aviation: DÉSIRÉ PENDEMOU (MLPC).

Minister of the Civil Service and Employment: DENIS WANGAO KIZMALÉ.*

Minister of Social Affairs, Family Affairs and the Handicapped: RACHEL DEA NAMBONA (MLPC).

Minister of Posts and Telecommunications: JEAN BRUNO VICKOS (PUN).

Minister of Youth and Sports: BERNARD YORO (PLD).

Minister of Communication: FRANCIS ALBERT OUAKANGA (MLPC).

Minister of the Environment, Water Resources, Forestry, Hunting and Fisheries: DANIEL EMERY DÉDÉ (PLD).

Minister of Tourism: NATHALIE CONSTANCE GOUNEBANA (PLD).

Minister of Equipment, Territorial Administration and Urban Planning: JOSEPH KALITÉ.

Minister of Housing and Public Works: ANDRÉ NALKÉ.

Minister of Public Health and Population: RICHARD LAKOUÉ (Ind.).

Minister for the Promotion of Civic Culture and Parliamentary Relations: AGBA OTIKPO ME ZODE (Ind.).

Minister in charge of Presidential Affairs: MICHEL GBEZERA-BRIA (Ind.).

Minister-delegate for Relations with the Arab World: BELLO MAMADOU (Ind.).

Minister-delegate of Finance responsible for the Budget: THÉODORE DABANGA (Ind.).

Minister-delegate of the Economy, Planning and International Co-operation: JACOB MBAÏTADJIM (Ind.).

* Member of the armed forces.

MINISTRIES

Office of the President: Palais de la Renaissance, Bangui; tel. 61-46-63; internet www.socatel.cf/patasse.htm.

318

Ministry of Agriculture and Livestock: Bangui; tel. 61-28-00.

Ministry of the Civil Service and Employment: Bangui; tel. 61-01-44.

Ministry of Defence, Restructuring of the Armed Forces and Former Combattants: Bangui; tel. 61-46-11.

Ministry of the Economy, Finance, Planning and International Co-operation: BP 912, Bangui; tel. 61-70-55; fax 61-63-98.

Ministry of Education: BP 791, Bangui.

Ministry of Foreign Affairs and Francophone Affairs: Bangui; tel. 61-35-55; fax 61-20-76.

Ministry of Justice: Bangui; tel. 61-16-44.

Ministry of Mining and Energy: Bangui; tel. 61-20-54; fax 61-60-76.

Ministry of Posts and Telecommunications: BP 940, Bangui; fax 61-68-59.

Ministry of Public Health and Population: Bangui; tel. 61-29-01.

Ministry of Transport and Civil Aviation: BP 941, Bangui; tel. 61-23-07; fax 61-15-52.

President and Legislature

PRESIDENT

Presidential Election, 19 September 1999

Candidate	% of votes
Ange-Félix Patassé (MLPC)	51.6
Gen. André Kolingba (RDC)	19.4
David Dacko (MDD)	11.2
Abel Goumba (FPP)	6.1
Henri Pouzère (Independent)	4.1
Jean-Paul Ngoupandé (PUN)	3.1
Enoch Derant Lakoué (PSD)	1.3
Charles Massi (Independent)	1.3
Fidèle Ngouandjika (Independent)	0.9
Joseph Abossolo (Independent)	0.8
Total	**100.00**

ASSEMBLÉE NATIONALE

President: Luc-Apollinaire Dondon-Konamabayé.

General Election, 22 November and 13 December 1998

	Seats
MLPC	47
RDC	20
MDD	8
FPP	7
PSD	6*
ADP	5
PUN	3
PLD	2
FODEM	2
FC	1
UPR	1
Independents	7
Total	**109**

* In December 1998 one member of the PSD left the party, declaring his intention to support the parties loyal to the President. In March 1999 two further PSD representatives left the parliamentary party to vote as independents.

Political Organizations

Alliance pour la démocratie et le progrès (ADP): Bangui; f. 1991; progressive; Leader François Pehoua; Nat. Sec. Tchapka Brédé.

Conseil démocratique des partis politiques de l'opposition (CODEPO): Bangui; f. 1995; political alliance led by Auguste Boukanga; comprises the following parties:

    Mouvement démocratique pour la renaissance et l'évolution de la République Centrafricaine (MDRERC): Bangui; Chair. Joseph Bendounga; Sec.-Gen. Léon Sebou.

    Parti républicain centrafricain (PRC): Bangui.

Convention nationale (CN): Bangui; f. 1991; Leader David Galiambo.

Forum civique (FC): Bangui; Leader Gen. Timothée Malendoma.

Forum démocratique pour la modernité (FODEM): Bangui; f. 1998; Pres. Charles Massi.

Front patriotique pour le progrès (FPP): BP 259, Bangui; tel. 61-52-23; fax 61-10-93; f. 1972; aims to promote political education and debate; Leader Prof. Abel Goumba.

G11: Bangui; f. 1997; alliance of 11 opposition parties led by Prof. Abel Goumba; prin. mems: ADP, FPP, MDD and RDC.

Mouvement d'évolution sociale de l'Afrique noire (MESAN): Bangui; f. 1949; comprises two factions, led respectively by Prosper Lavodrama and Joseph Ngbangadibo.

Mouvement pour la démocratie et le développement (MDD): Bangui; f. 1993; aims to safeguard national unity and the equitable distribution of national wealth; Leader David Dacko.

Mouvement pour la démocratie, l'indépendance et le progrès social (MDI–PS): BP 1404, Bangui; tel. 61-18-21; e-mail mdicentrafrique@chez.com; internet www.chez.com/mdicentrafrique; Sec. Gen. Daniel Nditifei Boysembe.

Mouvement pour la libération du peuple centrafricain (MLPC): Bangui; f. 1979; leading party in govt since Oct. 1993; Pres. Ange-Félix Patassé; Vice-Pres. Jean-Luc Mandaba.

Parti libéral-démocrate (PLD): Bangui; Leader Nestor Kombo-Naguemon.

Parti social-démocrate (PSD): BP 543, Bangui; tel.61-59-02; fax 61-58-44; Leader Enoch Derant Lakoué.

Parti pour l'union nationale (PUN): Bangui; Leader Jean-Paul Ngoupandé.

Rassemblement démocratique centrafricain (RDC): BP 503, Bangui; tel. 61-53-75; f. 1987; sole legal political party 1987–91; Leader Gen. André Kolingba.

Rassemblement populaire pour la reconstruction de la Centrafrique (RPRC): Bangui; Leader Gen. François Bozize.

Union des forces acquises à la paix (UFAP): Bangui; f. 1998; opposition alliance, including political parties, trade unions and human rights orgs; weakened by withdrawals in Nov. 1999; Pres. Paul Bellét.

Union nationale démocratique du peuple centrafricain (UNDPC): Bangui; f. 1998; Islamic fundamentalist; based in south-east CAR; Leader Mahamat Saleh.

Diplomatic Representation

EMBASSIES IN THE CENTRAL AFRICAN REPUBLIC

Cameroon: rue du Languedoc, BP 935, Bangui; tel. 61-18-57; fax 61-16-87; Chargé d'affaires a.i.: Gilbert Noula.

Chad: ave Valérie Giscard d'Estaing, BP 461, Bangui; tel. 61-46-77; Ambassador: Hassan-Michel Djangdeï (recalled June 2000).

China, People's Republic of: Bangui; tel. 61-36-28; fax 61-37-41; Chargé d'affaires: Cui Yongquian.

Congo, Democratic Republic: BP 989, Bangui; tel. 61-33-44; Ambassador: Embe Isea Mbambe.

Congo, Republic: BP 1414, Bangui; tel. 61-18-77; fax 61-03-09; Chargé d'affaires a.i.: Antoine Delica.

Egypt: BP 1422, Bangui; tel. 61-46-88; fax 61-35-45; Ambassador: Sameh Samy Darwiche.

France: blvd du Général de Gaulle, BP 884, Bangui; tel. 61-30-00; fax 61-74-04; Ambassador: Gildas Le Lidec.

Gabon: BP 1570, Bangui; tel. 61-29-97; Ambassador: François de Paule Moulengui.

Germany: ave G. A. Nasser, BP 901, Bangui; tel. 61-07-46; fax 61-19-89; Ambassador: Reinhard Buchholz.

Holy See: ave Boganda, BP 1447, Bangui; tel. 61-26-54; fax 61-03-71; e-mail nonrca@intnet.cf; Apostolic Nuncio: Most Rev. Diego Causero, Titular Archbishop of Meta.

Japan: ave Barthélemy Boganda, BP 1367, Bangui; tel. 61-16-10; fax 61-06-68; e-mail japonamb@intnet.cf; Ambassador: Yoichi Hayashi.

Libya: Bangui; tel. 61-46-62; fax 61-12-79; Head of Mission: (vacant).

Nigeria: ave des Martyrs, BP 1010, Bangui; tel. 61-40-97; fax 61-12-79; Chargé d'affaires a.i.: Ayodele J. Bakare.

Russia: rue Fourreau-lamy, BP1405, Bangui; tel. 61-03-11; Ambassador: Boris Krasnikov.

Sudan: ave de l'Indépendance, BP 1351, Bangui; tel. 61-38-21; Ambassador: Tijani Salih Fadayl.

USA: ave David Dacko, BP 924, Bangui; tel. 61-02-00; fax 61-44-94; Ambassador: Robert C. Perry.

Judicial System

Supreme Court: BP 926, Bangui; tel. 61-41-33; highest judicial organ; acts as a Court of Cassation in civil and penal cases and as Court of Appeal in administrative cases; comprises four chambers: constitutional, judicial, administrative and financial.

President of the Supreme Court: EDOUARD FRANCK.

There is also a Court of Appeal, a Criminal Court, 16 tribunaux de grande instance, 37 tribunaux d'instance, six labour tribunals and a permanent military tribunal. A High Court of Justice was established under the 1986 Constitution, with jurisdiction in all cases of crimes against state security, including high treason by the President of the Republic.

In August 1992 constitutional amendments were introduced which provided for the strict separation of executive, legislative and judicial powers.

The 1995 Constitution established a Constitutional Court, the judges of which are appointed by the President.

Religion

It is estimated that 24% of the population hold animist beliefs, 50% are Christians (25% Roman Catholic, 25% Protestant) and 15% are Muslims. There is no official state religion.

CHRISTIANITY

The Roman Catholic Church

The Central African Republic comprises one archdiocese and seven dioceses. There were an estimated 708,808 adherents at 31 December 1998.

Bishops' Conference: Conférence Episcopale Centrafricaine, BP 1518, Bangui; tel. 50-24-84; f. 1982; Pres. Rt Rev. PAULIN POMODIMO, Bishop of Bossangoa.

Archbishop of Bangui: Most Rev. JOACHIM N'DAYEN, Archevêché, BP 1518, Bangui; tel. 61-31-48; fax 61-46-92; e-mail cent_afr@intnet.cf.

Protestant Church

Eglise Protestante de Bangui: Bangui.

The Press

The independent press is higly regulated. Independent publications must hold a trading licence and prove their status as a commercial enterprise. They must also have proof that they fulfil taxation requirements. There is little press activity outside Bangui.

DAILIES

Le Citoyen: BP 974, Bangui; tel. 61-89-16; independent; Publr MAKA GBOSSOKOTTO; circ. 3,000.

Le Novateur: BP 913, Bangui; tel. 61-48-84; fax 61-87-03; e-mail ccea-ln@intnet.cf; independent; Publr MARCEL MOKWAPI; circ. 750.

PERIODICALS

Bangui Match: Bangui; monthly.

Le Courrier Rural: BP 850, Bangui; publ. by Chambre d'Agriculture.

Le Delit d'Opinion: Bangui; independent.

Demain le Monde: BP 650, Bangui; tel. 61-23-15; f. 1985; fortnightly; independent; Editor-in-Chief NGANAM NÖEL.

Journal Officiel de la République Centrafricaine: BP 739, Bangui; f. 1974; fortnightly; economic data; Dir-Gen. GABRIEL AGBA.

Nations Nouvelles: BP 965, Bangui; publ. by Organisation Commune Africaine et Mauricienne; politics and current affairs.

Le Peuple: BP 569, Bangui; tel. 61-76-34; f. 1995; weekly; Editor-in-Chief VERMOND TCHENDO.

Le Progrès: BP 154, Bangui; tel. 61-70-26; f. 1991; monthly; Editor-in-Chief BELIBANGA CLÉMENT; circ. 2,000.

Le Rassemblement: Bangui; organ of the RDC; Editor-in-Chief MATHIAS GONEVO REAPOGO.

La Tortue Déchainée: Bangui; independent; satirical; Publr MAKA GBOSSOKOTTO.

PRESS ASSOCIATION

Groupement des Editeurs de la Presse privée indépendante de Centrafrique (GEPAIC): Bangui; Pres. MAKA GBOSSOKOTO.

NEWS AGENCIES

Agence Centrafricaine de Presse (ACAP): BP 40, Bangui; tel. 61-10-88; f. 1974; Gen. Man. VICTOR DETO TETEYA.

Informatsionnoye Telegrafnoye Agentstvo Rossii—Telegrafnoye Agentstvo Suverennykh Stran (ITAR—TASS) (Russia) and Agence France-Presse are represented in the CAR.

Publisher

Government Publishing House

Imprimerie Centrafricaine: BP 329, Bangui; tel. 61-00-33; f. 1974; Dir-Gen. PIERRE SALAMATE-KOILET.

Broadcasting and Communications

TELECOMMUNICATIONS

Société Centrafricaine de Télécommunications (SOCATEL): BP 939, Bangui; tel. 61-74-69; fax 61-44-49; e-mail postmaster@intnet.cf; internet www.socatel.intnet.cf; f. 1990; 60% state-owned; 40% owned by France Cables et Radio.

CARATEL Entreprises: BP 2439, Bangui; tel. 61-44-10; fax 61-44-49; e-mail telecomp@intnet.cf; internet www.socatel.intnet.cf/carat.html; mobile cellular telephone operator.

BROADCASTING

Radiodiffusion-Télévision Centrafricaine: BP 940, Bangui; tel. 61-25-88; f. 1958 as Radiodiffusion Nationale Centrafricaine; govt-controlled; broadcasts in French and Sango; Man. Dir PAUL SERVICE.

Radio Rurale: community stations operating in Bouar, Nola, Berbérati and Bambari.

Finance

(cap. = capital; res = reserves; dep. = deposits; m. = million; amounts in francs CFA)

BANKING

Central Bank

Banque des Etats de l'Afrique Centrale (BEAC): BP 851, Bangui; tel. 61-24-00; fax 61-19-95; HQ in Yaoundé, Cameroon; f. 1973; bank of issue for mem. states of the Communauté économique et monétaire de l'Afrique centrale (CEMAC, fmrly Union douanière et économique de l'Afrique centrale), comprising Cameroon, the Central African Repub., Chad, the Repub. of the Congo, Equatorial Guinea and Gabon); cap. and res 210,014m., total assets 1,303,226m. (June 1999); Gov. JEAN-FÉLIX MAMALEPOT; Dir in CAR JONAS YOLOGAZA.

Commercial Banks

Banque Internationale pour le Centrafrique (BICA): place de la République, BP 910, Bangui; tel. 61-00-42; fax 61-61-36; e-mail bica@intnet.cf; internet www.socatel.intnet.cf/bica.html; f. 1946; present name adopted 1996; 35% owned by Banque Belgolaise SA, Brussels, 15% by group of African investors (COFIPA), 40.4% by private citizens, 9.6% by Govt; cap. and res 497.1m., dep. 17,352.6m. (Dec. 1998); Pres. BABA MARTIN; Dir-Gen. JEAN-PAUL LE CALM; 1 br.

Banque Populaire Maroco-Centrafricaine (BPMC): rue Guerillot, BP 844, Bangui; tel. 61-12-90; fax 61-62-30; f. 1991; 50% owned by Banque Centrale Populaire (Morocco), 12.5% owned by Banque Marocaine du Commerce Extérieur, 50% owned by Banque Centrale Populaire du Maroc and 37.5% state-owned; cap. and res 5,622.2m., total assets 6,353.7m. (Dec. 1998); Pres. ABDALLAH EL MAAGOUFI; Dir-Gen. MOHAMED BENZIANI.

Union Bancaire en Afrique Centrale SA (UBAC): rue de Brazza, BP 59, Bangui; tel. 61-29-90; fax 61-34-54; e-mail rcubac@intnet.cf; internet www.socatel.intnet.cf/ubac.html; f. 1962; state-owned; 49% privatization pending; cap. and res 728m., total assets 22,753m. (Dec. 1998); Pres. JEAN-SERGE WAFIO; Gen. Man. ETIENNE DJIMARIM; 1 br.

Development Bank

Banque de Developpement des Etats de l'Afrique Centrale: (see Franc Zone, p. 201).

Investment Bank

Banque Centrafricaine d'Investissement (BCI): Bangui; tel. 61-00-64; f. 1976; 34.8% state-owned; cap. 1,000m.; Pres. ALPHONSE KONGOLO; Man. Dir GÉRARD SAMBO.

Financial Institutions

Caisse Autonome d'Amortissement de la République Centrafricaine: Bangui; fax 61-21-82; management of state funds; Dir-Gen. JOSEPH PINGAMA.

Caisse Nationale d'Epargne (CNE): Office national des postes et de l'épargne, Bangui; tel. 61-22-96; fax 61-78-80; Pres. JUSTIN SALAMATE; Dir-Gen. AMBROISE DAOUDA; Man. RAPHAÏL OLONGA.

Bankers' Association
Association Professionnelle des Banques: Bangui.

Development Agencies

Agence Française de Développement: rue de la Moyenne corniche, BP 817, Bangui; tel. 61-03-06; fax 61-22-40; e-mail afd@intnet.cf; administers economic aid and finances specific development projects; Man. JEAN-FRANÇOIS VAVASSEUR.

Mission Française de Coopération et d'Action Culturelle: BP 934, Bangui; tel. 61-63-34; fax 61-28-24; administers bilateral aid from France; Dir HERVÉ CRONEL.

INSURANCE

Agence Centrafricaine d'Assurances (ACA): BP 512, Bangui; tel. 61-06-23; f. 1956; Dir Mme R. CERBELLAUD.

Assureurs Conseils Centrafricains Faugère et Jutheau: rue de la Kouanga, BP 743, Bangui; tel. 61-19-33; fax 61-44-70; f. 1968; Dir JEAN CLAUDE ROY.

Entreprise d'Etat d'Assurances et de Réassurances (SIRIRI): Bangui; tel. 61-36-55; f. 1972; Pres. EMMANUEL DOKOUNA; Dir-Gen. JEAN-MARIE YOLLOT.

Legendre, A. & Cie: rue de la Victoire, BP 896, Bangui; Pres. and Dir-Gen. ANDRÉ LEGENDRE.

Union Centrafricaine d'Assurances et de Réassurances: BP 343, Bangui; tel. 61-36-66; fax 61-33-40.

Trade and Industry

DEVELOPMENT ORGANIZATION

Société Centrafricaine de Développement Agricole (SOCADA): ave David Dacko, BP 997, Bangui; tel. 61-30-33; f. 1964; reorg. 1980; 75% state-owned, 25% Cie Française pour le Développement des Fibres Textiles (France); purchasing, transport and marketing of cotton, cotton-ginning, production of cottonseed oil and groundnut oil; Pres. MAURICE METHOT.

INDUSTRIAL AND TRADE ASSOCIATIONS

Agence de Développement de la Zone Caféière (ADECAF): BP 1935, Bangui; tel. 61-47-30; coffee producers' asscn; assists coffee marketing co-operatives; Dir-Gen. J. J. NIMIZIAMBI.

Agence Nationale pour le Développement de l'Élevage (ANDE): BP 1509, Bangui; tel. 61-69-60; fax 61-50-83; assists with development of livestock.

Caisse de Stabilisation et de Pérequation des Produits Agricoles (CAISTAB): BP 76, Bangui; tel. 61-08-00; supervises marketing and pricing of agricultural produce; Dir-Gen. M. BOUNANDELE-KOUMBA.

Fédération Nationale des Éleveurs Centrafricains (FNEC): ave des Martyrs, BP 588, Bangui; tel. 61-23-97; fax 61-47-24.

Office National des Forêts (ONF): BP 915, Bangui; tel. 61-38-27; f. 1969; reafforestation, development of forest resources; Dir-Gen. C. D. SONGUET.

CHAMBERS OF COMMERCE

Chambre d'Agriculture, d'Elevage, des Eaux, Forêts, Chasses, Pêches et Tourisme: BP 850, Bangui; tel. 61-09-33; f. 1964; Pres. FRANÇOIS T. BEYÉLÉ; Sec.-Gen. MOÏSE DENISSIO.

Chambre de Commerce, d'Industrie, des Mines et de l'Artisanat (CCIMA): BP 813, Bangui; tel. 61-16-68; fax 61-35-70; Pres. RIGOBERT YOMBO; Sec. GERTRUDE ZOUTA-YAMANDJA.

EMPLOYERS' ORGANIZATION

Union Nationale du Patronat Centrafricain (UNPC): Bangui; Pres. RIGOBERT YOMBO.

UTILITIES
Electricity

Société Energie de Centrafrique (ENERCA): ave de l'Indépendance, BP 880, Bangui; tel. 61-20-22; f. 1967; state-owned; privatization pending; production and distribution of electric energy.

Water

Société Nationale des Eaux (SNE): BP 1838, Bangui; tel. 61-20-28; f. 1975; state-owned co responsible for supply, treatment and distribution of water; Dir-Gen. FRANÇOIS FARRA-FROND.

MAJOR COMPANIES

The following are among the largest companies in terms of either capital investment or employment.

Alpha Robusta Café: BP 320, Bangui; fax 61-44-49; internet www.socatel.intnet.cf/banga.htm; purchase and distribution of coffee; Man. CHRISTELIN BANGANDOZOU.

Bata SA Centrafricaine: Bangui; tel. 61-45-79; f. 1969; cap. 150m. francs CFA; footwear mfrs; Dir VICTOR DE RYCKE.

Centrafrique-Roumano-Bois (CAROMBOIS): BP 1159, Bangui; f. 1974; cap. 673m. francs CFA; 60% owned by FOREXIM (Romania); Dir-Gen. VICTOR IONESCU; 306 employees.

COLALU: rue Chavannes, BP 1326, Bangui; tel. 61-20-42; f. 1969; cap. 69m. francs CFA; 57% owned by ALUCAM (Cameroon); mfrs of household articles and sheet aluminium; Pres. CLAUDE MILLET; Dir-Gen. M. KAPPES.

Compagnie Industrielle d'Ouvrages en Textiles (CIOT): BP 190, Bangui; tel. 61-36-22; f. 1949; cap. 250m. francs CFA; mfrs of clothing and hosiery; Dir-Gen. MICHEL ROBERT.

Comptoir National du Diamant (CND): blvd B. Boganela, Bangui; tel. 61-07-02; f. 1964; 50% state-owned, 50% owned by Diamond Distributors (USA); mining and marketing of diamonds; Dir-Gen. M. VASSOS.

Entreprise Forestière des Bois Africains Centrafrique (EFBACA): BP 205, Bangui; tel. 61-25-33; f. 1969; cap. 259m. francs CFA; 12% state-owned; exploitation of forests and wood processing; Pres. VICTOR BALET; Dir JEAN QUENNOZ.

Huilerie Savonnerie Centrafricaine (HUSACA): BP 1020, Bangui; tel. 61-58-54; fax 61-68-11; mfrs of soap, edible oil and animal feed; Dir B. ABDALLAH.

Industrie Centrafricaine du Textile (ICAT): BP 981, Bangui; tel. 61-40-00; f. 1965; cap. 586m. francs CFA; state-owned; textile complex; Man. Dir M. NGOUNDOUKOUA.

Industries Forestières de Batalimo (IFB): BP 517, Bangui; f. 1970; cap. 100m. francs CFA; Dir JACQUES GADEN.

Manufacture Centrafricaine de Cigares (MANUCACIG): Bangui; tel. 61-23-14; f. 1976; cap. 163m. francs CFA; 13% state-owned; processes locally-grown tobacco leaf; capacity: 10m. cigars per annum; Pres. ALBERT GOFFI; Dir JEAN-MARIE DECOURCHELLE; 130 employees.

Motte-Cordonnier-Afrique (MOCAF): BP 806, Bangui; tel. 61-04-77; f. 1951; cap. 1,123m. francs CFA; production of beer, soft drinks and ice; Pres. BERTRAND MOTTE; Dir-Gen. PHILIPPE MAGNAVAL.

Société Centrafricaine de Cigarettes (SOCACIG): BP 728, Bangui; tel. 61-03-00; fax 61-51-30; f. 1970; cap. 698.4m. francs CFA; cigarette mfrs; Pres. PIERRE IMBERT; Dir in Bangui ALAIN PERREARD.

Société Centrafricaine des Cuirs (CENTRA-CUIRS): Bangui; f. 1975; cap. 75m. francs CFA; 20% state-owned; mfrs of leather goods.

Société Centrafricaine de Déroulage (SCAD): BP 1607, Bangui; tel. 61-18-05; fax 61-56-60; f. 1972; cap. 700m. francs CFA; exploitation of forests, mfrs of plywood; also operates a sawmill; Dir-Gen. J. KAMACH; 392 employees.

Société Centrafricaine du Diamant (SODIAM): BP 1016, Bangui; tel. 61-03-79; cap. 100m. francs CFA; export of diamonds; Dir DIMITRI ANAGNOSTELLIS.

Société Centrafricaine d'Exploitation Forestière et Industrielle (SOCEFI): BP 3, M'Bata-Bangui; f. 1947, nationalized 1974; cap. 880m. francs CFA; operates a sawmill; also timber exporters and mfrs of prefabricated dwellings; Man. Dir PIERRE OPANZOYEN.

Société Centrafricaine des Gaz Industriels (SOCAGI): blvd du Général de Gaulle, BP 905, Bangui; tel. 61-19-11; f. 1965; cap. 53m. francs CFA; manufacture and sale of industrial and medical gases; Pres. and Dir-Gen. PAUL LALAGUE.

Société Centrafricaine des Palmiers (CENTRAPALM): BP 1355, Bangui; tel. 61-49-40; fax 61-38-75; f. 1975; state-owned; production and marketing of palm oil; operates the Bossongoa agro-industrial complex; Pres. MATHIEU-FRANCIS NGANAWARA; Gen. Man. Dr JOËL BEASSEM.

Société Cotonnière Centrafricaine (SOCOCA): BP 154, Bangui-Lakouanga; tel. 61-06-85; fax 61-06-17; plant at Bossangoa; cotton producer.

Société de Gestion des Sucreries Centrafricaines (SOGESCA): ave Boganda, km 4, BP 1370, Bangui; sugar producer; factory at Ouaka.

Société d'Exploitation et d'Industrialisation Forestière en RCA (SLOVENIA-BOIS): BP 1571, Bangui; tel. 61-44-35; f. 1970; cap. 250m. francs CFA; partly Slovenian-owned; sawmill; Dir FRANC BENKOVIĆ.

Société Industrielle Centrafricaine (SICA): BP 1325, Bangui; tel. 61-44-99; f. 1967; cap. 200m. francs CFA; sawmill at M'baiki in the Lobaye area, annual capacity 18,000 cu m; Dir CHARLES SYLVAIN.

Société Industrielle Forestière en Afrique Centrale (SIFAC): BP 156, Bangui; f. 1970; cap. 95m. francs CFA; sawmill and joinery; Dir JACQUES GADEN.

Société Pétrolière de Centrafrique (PETROCA): BP 724, Bangui; tel. 61-23-67; 75% state-owned, operated by Total; imports and markets petroleum and gas products; Dir-Gen. DOGONE JIBE.

Société de Plantations d'Hévéas et de Caféiers (SPHC): BP 1384, Bangui; f. 1974; cap. 160m. francs CFA; rubber and coffee plantations.

Total Centrafricaine de Gestion (TOCAGES): BP 724, Bangui; tel. 61-05-88; f. 1950; cap. 200m. francs CFA; 51% state-owned; storage, retailing and transport of petroleum products; Dir CHRISTIAN-DIMANCHE SONGUET.

TRADE UNIONS

There are five officially recognized trade union federations, including:

Organization of Free Public-Sector Unions: Bangui.

Union Syndicale des Travailleurs de la Centrafrique (USTC): Bangui; affiliated with the International Confed. of Free Trade Unions; Sec.-Gen. THÉOPHILE SONNY KOLLE.

Transport

RAILWAYS

There are no railways at present. There are long-term plans to connect Bangui to the Transcameroon railway. A line linking Sudan's Darfur region with the CAR's Vakaga province has also been proposed.

ROADS

In 1996 there were an estimated 24,000 km of roads, including 4,280 km of main roads and 3,910 km of secondary roads. Only about 1.8% of the total network is paved. Eight main routes serve Bangui, and those that are surfaced are toll roads. Both the total road length and the condition of the roads are inadequate for current requirements. In 1997 the European Union provided 32,500m. francs CFA to improve infrastructure in the CAR. In September a vast road improvement scheme was launched, concentrating initially on roads to the south and north-west of Bangui. The CAR is linked with Cameroon by the Transafrican Lagos–Mombasa highway. Roads are frequently impassable in the rainy season (May to October).

Bureau d'Affrètement Routier Centrafricain (BARC): BP 523, Bangui; tel. 61-20-55; fax 61-37-44; Dir-Gen. J. M. LAGUEREMA-YADINGUIN.

Compagnie Nationale des Transports Routiers (CNTR): Bangui; tel. 61-46-44; state-owned; Dir-Gen. GEORGES YABADA.

INLAND WATERWAYS

There are some 2,800 km of navigable waterways along two main water courses. The first, formed by the Congo river and its tributary the Oubangui, can accommodate convoys of barges (of up to 800 metric tons load) between Bangui and Brazzaville and Pointe-Noire in the Republic of the Congo, except during the dry season, when the route is impassable. The second is the river Sangha, also a tributary of the Congo, on which traffic is again seasonal. There are two ports, at Bangui and Salo, on the rivers Oubangui and Sangha respectively. Bangui port has a handling capacity of 350,000 tons, with 350 m of wharfs and 24,000 sq m of warehousing. Efforts are being made to develop the Sangha upstream from Salo to increase

the transportation of timber from this area, and to develop Nola as a timber port.

Agence Centrafricaine des Communications Fluviales (ACCF): BP 822, Bangui; tel. 61-31-10; f. 1969; state-owned; supervises development of inland waterways transport system; Man. Dir JUSTIN NDJAPOU.

Société Centrafricaine de Transports Fluviaux (SOCATRAF): BP 1445, Bangui; tel. and fax 61-43-15; f. 1980; 51%-owned by ACCF; Man. Dir FRANÇOIS TOUSSAINT.

CIVIL AVIATION

The international airport is at Bangui-M'Poko. There are also 37 small airports for internal services.

Agence pour la sécurité de la navigation aérienne en Afrique et Madagascar (ASECNA): BP 828, Bangui; tel. 61-33-80; fax 61-49-18.

Air Afrique: BP 875, Bangui; tel. 60-47-00; fax 61-44-29; see under Côte d'Ivoire; Dir in Bangui ALBERT BAGNERES.

Centrafrican Airlines (CAL): Aéroport Bangui-M'Poko; f. 1999; privately-owned; internal flights.

Mondial Air Fret (MAF): BP 1883, Bangui; tel. 61-14-58; fax 61-62-62; f. 1998; Dir THÉOPHILE SONNY COLE.

Tourism

Although tourism remains relatively undeveloped, the Central African Republic possesses considerable scenic attractions in its waterfalls, forests and wildlife. Tourist arrivals were estimated at 17,000 in 1997, compared with only 1,599 in 1990. In 1997 receipts from tourism were estimated at US $5m.

Office National Centrafricain du Tourisme (OCATOUR): BP 655, Bangui; tel. 61-45-66.

Defence

In August 1999 the armed forces numbered about 2,650 men (army 2,500; air force 150), with a further 2,300 men in paramilitary forces. Military service is selective and lasts for two years. In April 1998 the UN Mission to the Central African Republic (MINURCA) commenced peace-keeping operations in the country; MINURCA completed its gradual withdrawal on 15 February 2000.

Defence Expenditure: Estimated at 28,000m. francs CFA in 1999.

Chief of Staff of the Armed Forces: Gen. FRANÇOIS BOZIZE.

Education

Education is officially compulsory for eight years between six and 14 years of age. Primary education begins at the age of six and lasts for six years. Secondary education begins at the age of 12 and lasts for up to seven years, comprising a first cycle of four years and a second of three years. In 1991 enrolment at primary schools was equivalent to an estimated 57% of children in the relevant age-group (69% of boys; 45% of girls), while secondary enrolment was equivalent to only 10% (boys 15%; girls 6%). According to estimates by UNESCO, the adult illiteracy rate in 1995 averaged 60.3% (males 46.4%; females 72.8%). Current expenditure by the ministry of education in 1995 totalled 8,820m. francs CFA, equivalent to 1.6% of gross national product. The provision of state-funded education was severely disrupted during the 1990s, owing to the inadequacy of financial resources.

Bibliography

Bigo, D. *Pouvoir et obéissance en Centrafrique.* Paris, Editions Karthala, 1989.

Brégeon, J.-N. *Administrateurs en Oubangui-Chari.* Paris, Editions Denoël, 1998.

Carter, G. M. (Ed.). *National Unity and Regionalism in Eight African States.* Ithaca, NY, Cornell University Press, 1966.

de Dreux Brezé, J. *Le Problème du regroupement en Afrique équatoriale.* Paris, Librairie Gale de Droit et de Jurisprudence, 1968.

Emerging Markets Investment Center. *Central African Republic Investment and Business Guide.* 2nd Edn. USA, International Business Publications, 1998.

   Central African Republic Investment and Business Opportunities Yearbook. USA, International Business Publications, 1998.

Hance, W. A. 'Middle Africa from Chad to Congo (Brazzaville)', in *The Geography of Modern Africa.* New York and London, Columbia University Press, 1964.

Kalck, P. *Central African Republic (World Bibliographical Series).* Paris, Abc-Clio, 1993.

   Histoire de la République Centrafricaine. Paris, Berger Levrault, 1977.

Ngoupandé, J.-P. *Chronique de la crise centrafricaine 1996–1997: Le syndrome barracuda.* Paris, l'Harmattan, 1997.

O'Toole, T. *The Central African Republic. The Continent's Hidden Heart.* Boulder, CO, Westview Press, 1986.

   Historical Dictionary of the Central African Republic. 2nd Edn. Metuchen, NJ, Scarecrow Press, 1992.

Robson, P. 'Economic Integration in Equatorial Africa', in *Economic Integration in Africa.* London, Allen and Unwin, 1968.

UDEAC. *Bulletin des statistiques générales de l'UDEAC.* Bangui, Secrétariat-Général de l'UDEAC, 1976.

Zoctizoum, Y. *Histoire de la République Centrafricaine,* 2 vols. Paris, l'Harmattan, 1984.

CHAD

Physical and Social Geography
DAVID HILLING

The Republic of Chad is bordered to the north by Libya, to the south by the Central African Republic, to the west by Niger and Cameroon and to the east by Sudan. The northernmost of the four independent states which emerged from French Equatorial Africa, Chad is, with an area of 1,284,000 sq km (495,800 sq miles), the largest in terms of size and population (6,279,931 at the census of April 1993). Traditionally a focal point for equatorial and Saharan trade routes, the country's vast size, land-locked location and great distance from the coast create problems for economic development.

The relief is relatively simple. From 240 m in the Lake Chad depression in the south-west, the land rises northwards through the Guéra massif at 1,800 m to the mountainous Saharan region of Tibesti at 3,350 m. Eastwards, heights of 1,500 m are attained in the Ouaddai massif. In the south the watershed area between the Chari and Congo rivers is of subdued relief and only slight elevation. The only rivers of importance, both for irrigation and seasonal navigation, are the Chari and Logone, which traverse the south-west of the country and join at N'Djamena, before flowing into Lake Chad.

Extending across more than 16° of latitude, Chad has three well-defined zones of climate, natural vegetation and associated economic activity. The southern third of the country has annual rainfall in excess of 744 mm (increasing to 1,200 mm in the extreme south), and has a savannah woodland vegetation. This is the country's principal agricultural zone, providing the two main cash crops, cotton and groundnuts, and a variety of local food crops (especially rice). Northwards, with rainfall of 250–500 mm per year, there is a more open grassland, where there is emphasis on pastoral activity, limited cultivation of groundnuts and local grains, and some collection of gum arabic. This marginal Sahel zone was adversely affected by drought during most of the 1970s and 1980s, and the cattle herds were greatly reduced in number. The northern third of the country has negligible rainfall and a sparse scrub vegetation, which grades north into pure desert with little apparent economic potential, although the 'Aozou strip', a region of 114,000 sq km in the extreme north, is believed to contain significant reserves of uranium and other minerals. Substantial petroleum reserves in the Doba Basin, in the south of the country, and also at Sedigi were being developed in the late 1990s. There was also believed to be considerable potential for the commercial exploitation of gold, particularly at Mayo-Kebbi, in the south of the country.

Chad's total population is relatively small in relation to its large area, and is markedly concentrated in the southern half of the country. Religious and ethnic tensions between the people of the north and south have traditionally dominated the history of Chad. The population of the north is predominantly Islamic, of a nomadic or semi-nomadic character, and is largely engaged in farming and in breeding livestock. Rivalry between ethnic groups is strong. By contrast, the inhabitants of the south are settled farmers, who largely follow animist beliefs. The Sara tribes, some 10 ethnic groups with related languages and cultural links, comprise a large section of the population of the south. Since the end of the Second World War, the population of the south has inclined towards a more Westernized culture; the rate of literacy has increased rapidly, and Christian churches have attracted a number of adherents. The population of the north, however, forms a traditional, Islamic society, and is largely unaffected by modern education. The state is secular and exercises neutrality in relation to religious affiliations. French and Arabic are the official languages. Karembou, Ouadi, Teda, Daza, Djonkor are the principal vernaculars.

Recent History
BERNARD LANNE
Revised for this edition by the Editor

Formerly part of French Equatorial Africa, Chad became an autonomous republic within the French Community in November 1958. François Tombalbaye, a southerner and leader of the Parti progressiste tchadien (PPT), was elected prime minister in March 1959. Chad proceeded to independence on 11 August 1960, with Tombalbaye as president. However, the Saharan territory of the north, Borkou-Ennedi-Tibesti (BET), remained under French military administration until 1964. In 1963 the PPT was declared the sole legal party. Its political monopoly was opposed by certain northern politicians. Mismanagement and corruption on the part of government officials intensified this discontent, and in 1965 a serious rebellion broke out, focused mainly in the north. The Front de libération nationale du Tchad (FROLINAT), formed in Sudan in 1966, later assumed leadership of the revolt. In August 1968 French troops intervened in support of the government.

Despite various initiatives by the government to satisfy the political aspirations of FROLINAT supporters, the rebellion in the north of the country continued. As a result of the French military intervention, however, the rebellion was contained (although FROLINAT remained undefeated), and in 1972 the French reinforcements left the country. Libya, which maintained a claim to sovereignty over the 'Aozou strip' in northern Chad, provided support to FROLINAT. Following a deterioration in relations between Chad and France, Tombalbaye signed a pact of friendship with Libya in 1972; Libya, however, continued to provide military assistance to FROLINAT, and in 1973 annexed the 'Aozou strip'.

In April 1975 Tombalbaye was killed in a military coup promoted by army officers originating from the south. Gen. Félix Malloum, former army chief-of-staff who had been imprisoned since 1973 on conspiracy charges, assumed power. Although the new government sought national reconciliation, a number of rebel groups, including FROLINAT, remained in opposition. However, divisions subsequently emerged within FROLINAT, whose leader, Hissène Habré, an opponent of the Libyan annexation of the 'Aozou strip', was replaced by Goukouni Oueddei. (Habré continued, however, to lead a faction within FROLINAT.) The Libyan government meanwhile increased military aid to FROLINAT, which launched renewed offensives during 1977 and 1978, and overran large areas of territory. The government successfully sought French assistance to halt the advance of FROLINAT.

CIVIL CONFLICT AND LIBYAN INTERVENTION

In August 1978 Malloum appointed Habré to the post of prime minister, at the head of a civilian government. However, relations between Malloum and Habré soon deteriorated, and in February 1979 fighting broke out in N'Djamena, the capital, between government forces (Forces armées tchadiennes, FAT) and Habré's troops, the Forces armées du nord (FAN). With the tacit support of France, the FAN seized control of N'Djamena, while the rebel faction led by Goukouni (the Forces armées populaires, FAP), gained territory in the north. In March Malloum resigned and fled the country, after appointing the former commander of the gendarmerie, Lt-Col (later Gen.) Wadal Abdelkader Kamougué, as his successor.

In April 1979 a provisional government (Gouvernement d'union nationale de transition, GUNT) was formed by FROLINAT, the FAN, the Mouvement populaire pour la libération du Tchad (MPLT), and the FAT. The leader of the MPLT, Lol Mahamat Choua, was appointed president, while Goukouni and Habré took ministerial portfolios. However, the southern factions rejected the authority of the new government, and a committee, under the presidency of Kamougué, was established at Moundou to govern the south. Attempts by the GUNT to dislodge Kamougué's forces failed, and the provisional government became increasingly isolated. In August a second GUNT was organized under the presidency of Goukouni, with Kamougué as vice-president. However, the fragmentation of the northern factions increased, while Goukouni's authority was undermined by continued disagreement with Habré.

In March 1980 fighting between the FAP and the FAN resumed in N'Djamena, and in the following month Habré was dismissed from the provisional government. In accordance with the French government's stated policy of neutrality, its troops were withdrawn from Chad in May. In June, without the prior consent of the GUNT, a treaty of friendship and co-operation was signed in Tripoli between Libya and a representative of Goukouni. In October Libyan forces intervened in the hostilities, resulting in the defeat of Habré and the retreat of the FAN from N'Djamena by the end of that year. A 15,000-strong Libyan contingent subsequently entered the country.

In January 1981, to the intense disapproval of France, Goukouni signed a further agreement with Libya which provided for a gradual political union of the two countries. In April Libyan troops intervened in skirmishes between members of Goukouni's FAP and the Conseil démocratique révolutionnaire (CDR), one of the breakaway factions of FROLINAT, at Abéché, resulting in numerous casualties. In November Libyan forces were withdrawn, and at the behest of France the Organization of African Unity (OAU) sent a peace-keeping force to Chad. In February 1982 the OAU proposed that a cease-fire be declared later that month, with elections under its supervision to take place before 30 June. The OAU plan, which effectively comprised a political victory for the FAN, was rejected by Goukouni, and hostilities intensified. The FAN continued to advance, and finally captured N'Djamena in early June. Goukouni fled the country, and the coalition of factions that constituted the GUNT began to fragment.

HABRÉ IN POWER, 1982–90

In mid-June 1982, following the capture of N'Djamena, the formation of a provisional council of state, with Habré as head of state, was announced. By the end of that month the OAU force had withdrawn from Chad, and in October Habré was inaugurated as president. A new government was formed, in which southerners held a large proportion of ministerial portfolios. However, Goukouni's troops regained control of the greater part of the BET, with Libyan support, and in October Goukouni announced the formation of a rival 'government of national salvation' at Bardaï. Habré's government, however, obtained international recognition, occupying Chad's seat at the UN and gaining the support of the majority of African states. By early 1983 tribal differences in the north had caused divisions within the FAN. In January of that year a number of members of Kamougué's FAT joined the FAN to form the Forces armées nationales tchadiennes (FANT).

In March 1983 negotiations took place between Habré and the Libyan government; however, Habré rejected Libyan demands for the recognition of Chad's Islamic character and of the annexation of the 'Aozou strip', and the signing of a treaty of alliance. By early July Goukouni's rebel troops, with assistance from Libya, had occupied the entire BET region, subsequently advancing to Abéché. Appeals by Habré for aid were initially ignored by the French government. However, following further advances by the FANT and Goukouni's forces (with Libyan air support), France acceded to pressure from francophone African heads of state, and dispatched some 3,000 troops to Chad, who imposed an 'interdiction line' from Salal to Arada, preventing Goukouni's troops and their Libyan allies from advancing further south; by mid-September all fighting between the Chadian factions had ceased.

Political and Military Initiatives

During early 1984 it became increasingly evident that Habré needed to regain support in southern Chad in order to consolidate political power. In June Habré replaced the FROLINAT–FAN grouping with a new official party, the Union nationale pour l'indépendance et la révolution (UNIR). Six of the 15 members of UNIR's executive bureau were southerners, but former FAN officials maintained a prominent role in the new party. In a government reshuffle, which took place in July, one-half of the ministerial posts (including the foreign affairs portfolio) were allocated to southerners.

In late August 1984 a guerrilla commando force, known as the *commandos rouges*, or *codos*, led by Col Alphonse Kotiga Guerina, suspended negotiations with the government and resumed hostilities. The entire region of southern Chad, apart from Mayo-Kebbi, returned to civil war. The subsequent suppression of the rebellion by government forces effectively intensified religious and ethnic rivalries, and negated any political advantages gained by the formation of UNIR. In November, following offers of financial remuneration by Habré, some 1,200 *codos* joined government forces; by the end of the year hostilities had ceased.

Meanwhile, increasing dissension among anti-Habré forces emerged, resulting in the formation by GUNT factions of new 'splinter groups' and an anti-Goukouni movement. At a meeting of GUNT factions in August 1985 a Conseil suprême de la révolution (CSR), comprising seven anti-government groupings, under the presidency of Goukouni, was formed. Later that year, however, several former opposition factions declared support for the Habré regime, including the Front démocratique du Tchad (FDT) and the Comité d'action et de concertation (CAC–CDR), which had broken away from the pro-Goukouni CDR.

In September 1984 France and Libya agreed to the simultaneous withdrawal of their forces in Chad. The evacuation of French forces was completed in early November, but Libyan troops remained, in contravention of the agreement. Following unsuccessful representations to Libya, the French government stated that it would not enforce Libyan withdrawal from northern Chad, but would intervene if Libyan forces advanced towards N'Djamena. President François Mitterrand recognized Chad's claim to the 'Aozou strip', while criticizing Habré for jeopardizing national unity in favour of territorial gain.

From October 1985 Libya began to reinforce its military presence in the north of Chad, assembling an estimated 4,000 troops. In November Mitterrand reiterated that France would respond to any Libyan military action in Chad. In February 1986, however, GUNT forces initiated Libyan-supported attacks on government positions to the south of the 16th parallel. The offensive was repelled by the FANT, and Habré appealed to France for increased military aid. Shortly afterwards French military aircraft, operating from the Central African Republic (CAR), bombed a Libyan-built airstrip at Ouadi Doum, northeast of Faya-Largeau. A retaliatory air attack on N'Djamena airport caused minor damage. France subsequently established an air strike force at N'Djamena to counteract any further Libyan attack (an intervention designated 'Opération Epervier'), while the USA provided supplementary military aid to Habré's forces. Further incursions across the interdiction line in March were repelled by FANT ground forces. Later that month hostilities ceased temporarily, following the capture by government forces of a rebel base at Chicha.

Recapture of the North

In March 1986 Habré appointed several former opponents to the council of ministers. Meanwhile, divisions within the GUNT increased; Goukouni's refusal to attend OAU-convened reconciliation talks prompted the resignation in June of the vice-president of the GUNT, Col Kamougué, who transferred his support to Habré in February 1987 and joined the government in August of that year. In August 1986 Acheikh Ibn Oumar's CDR withdrew its support for Goukouni, leaving the latter virtually isolated. Later that month there were clashes between FAP and CDR troops in the Tibesti region. By October Goukouni had indicated his willingness to negotiate with Habré, amid indications that the FAP had decided to join Habré's FANT. Goukouni was subsequently wounded in Tripoli during an alleged attempt at abduction by Libyan troops, and in mid-November, with Libyan support, Oumar assumed the presidency of a reconstituted GUNT coalition, comprising seven of the original 11 factions, including the Mouvement révolutionnaire du peuple (MRP), formerly led by Kamougué.

In December 1986 clashes took place in the Tibesti region between Libyan forces and the now pro-Habré FAP. In January 1987 FANT troops recaptured a number of strategic targets in the north of the country. Following a Libyan offensive on the southern town of Arada, France launched a retaliatory air attack against Ouadi Doum; in March Ouadi Doum was recaptured by the FANT. Libyan forces subsequently began to retreat, evacuating Faya-Largeau, and by May Habré's troops had regained control of northern Chad, with Libya occupying only the Aozou region. In August the FANT seized control of the town of Aozou, the region's administrative centre, but later had to withdraw to positions in Tibesti, following a series of Libyan air attacks on Chadian targets. In September Habré's forces entered south-eastern Libya, where they attacked and occupied the military base of Maaten-es-Sarra. A Libyan military aircraft was subsequently shot down over N'Djamena by French fire, and French positions at Abéché were bombed. (In protest at this offensive, the French government suspended supplies of arms to Chad until December.) In September an OAU-brokered cease-fire took effect. However, the Chadian government claimed that Libyan aircraft continued to infringe Chadian airspace, and that members of a Libyan-supported 'Islamic Legion' had clashed with members of the FANT near the border with Sudan. There was also a considerable reinforcement of the Libyan bases in the Aozou region and at Toummo (on the Niger–Libya border). Military engagements took place in November 1987, near Goz Beïda, and in March 1988, to the east of Ennedi.

Reconciliation with Libya

A meeting between the heads of state of Chad and Libya, under the aegis of an OAU *ad hoc* committee (established in 1977 to debate the question of the sovereignty of the Aozou region) was scheduled for May 1988. Shortly before the summit it was announced that the Libyan leader, Col Qaddafi (who had repeatedly boycotted meetings of the *ad hoc* committee) would not be attending. However, the Libyan government subsequently announced its willingness to recognize the Habré régime, invited Habré and Goukouni to meet in Libya for discussions concerning reconciliation, and offered to provide financial aid for the reconstruction of bombed towns in northern Chad. Habré reacted with caution to Libyan proposals, but in early June announced that his government was prepared to restore diplomatic relations with Libya, which had been suspended in 1982. Following discussions between the ministers of foreign affairs of the two countries, which took place in Gabon in July 1988, both Chad and Libya agreed, in principle, to the restoration of diplomatic relations, although the issues of the fate of Libyan prisoners of war in Chad, the disputed sovereignty of the Aozou region and the future security of common borders remained to be resolved. In October, following mediation by Togo, Chad and Libya issued a joint communiqué expressing their willingness to seek a peaceful solution to the territorial dispute, and to co-operate with the OAU *ad hoc* committee. The cease-fire was reaffirmed,

diplomatic relations were resumed, and the two countries exchanged ambassadors in November.

Although a Libyan delegation attended the second UNIR congress in November 1988, relations between the two countries remained uneasy. Chad continued to accuse Libya of repeated violations of the cease-fire agreement, and in December there were reports of clashes between Chadian and pro-Libyan forces near the border with Sudan. Relations between the two countries deteriorated further in mid-1989, when Habré accused Col Qaddafi of collusion with the Sudanese government in preparing a military attack against Chad. Subsequent negotiations between Habré and Col Qaddafi were inconclusive, owing to Habré's rejection of proposals made by President Chadli of Algeria entailing the withdrawal of the 'Epervier' force from Chad. At the end of August, however, Chad and Libya signed a draft agreement for the peaceful resolution of the dispute: if a political settlement was not achieved within one year, the issue would be submitted to arbitration by the International Court of Justice (ICJ). Provision was made for all armed forces to be withdrawn from the Aozou region, under OAU supervision, and for the release of all prisoners of war. Both countries reaffirmed their commitment to the principles of the September 1987 cease-fire agreement, and declared a policy of mutual non-interference in each other's internal affairs. In September, however, the first session of a Chad-Libya joint commission, which was to oversee the implementation of the agreement, broke down over arrangements for the release of Libyan prisoners of war. Later that year the agreement was further undermined by the resumption of hostilities between the FANT and pro-Libyan forces along Chad's border with Sudan.

In March 1990 Deby and his supporters, the Forces patriotiques du salut (subsequently known as the Mouvement patriotique du salut, MPS), launched an invasion of eastern Chad from bases in Sudan. France dispatched military equipment and personnel to reinforce 'Opération Epervier' at Abéché: although the French contingent did not participate in the military engagements, its presence undoubtedly induced the rebel forces to retreat. In late March discussions in Gabon between Oumar and Libyan officials were undermined by a statement issued by the Chadian government, alleging Libyan and Sudanese support for the MPS; the accusations were denied by the leaders of both countries. In May the fifth session of the Chad-Libya joint commission was compromised by the seizure, by Chadian forces, of 10 Libyan vehicles on Sudanese territory; Libya subsequently protested to the UN and the OAU at this offensive against what were claimed to be civilian vehicles. In July the Chadian government alleged that Libya and Sudan were massing forces in Sudan's Darfur region, in preparation for a major offensive against Chad. In late August, none the less, shortly before the agreed deadline for a settlement, apparently successful negotiations between Habré and Col Qaddafi took place in Morocco. Both governments subsequently agreed to refer the territorial dispute for adjudication by the ICJ.

Internal Tensions

In July 1987, meanwhile, reconciliation talks between Habré and Goukouni (the latter now resident in Algiers) ended in failure. Following a ministerial reshuffle in August, both Kamougué and the former leader of the *codos,* Col Kotiga Guerina, joined the government. In February 1988 a number of former opposition parties, including the FAP and the CAC–CDR, merged with UNIR. In March the GUNT was reconstituted under Goukouni, following a dispute with Acheikh Ibn Oumar regarding the leadership. In November, following the conclusion of a peace agreement in Iraq, forces led by Oumar declared support for Habré, and subsequently returned to Chad. In January 1989 it was announced that the GUNT was willing to resume negotiations with the Habré government.

Despite a semblance of unity, which was exemplified in March 1989 by the appointment of Oumar as minister of foreign affairs, political tensions persisted. In early April the minister of the interior and territorial administration, Ibrahim Mahamat Itno, was arrested, following the discovery of an alleged plot to overthrow the Habré government. The c-in-c of the armed forces, Hassan Djamous, and his predecessor in that post, Idriss Deby (who were both implicated in the conspiracy), fled to Sudan with their supporters. FANT troops were dispatched to quell the mutiny, during which Djamous was killed. Meanwhile, Deby escaped to Libya (with Sudanese assistance), and in June formed a new opposition movement, the 'Action du 1 avril', based in Sudan. In July the unity of the GUNT was undermined when a number of factions announced their withdrawal from the coalition.

In July 1988 a presidential decree established a committee to formulate a new constitution. Its proposals were submitted to Habré in June 1989, and a draft document was approved in a national referendum on 10 December (reportedly receiving the support of 99.94% of votes cast). The new constitution, promulgated on 20 December, confirmed Habré as president for a further seven-year term, upheld the principle of a single party state, and provided for the creation of a legislative national assembly, which was to be elected, with a five-year mandate, by direct universal suffrage. At legislative elections in July 1990, 436 candidates contested 123 seats; the electoral turn-out was 56%. A number of prominent members of UNIR failed to secure seats in the new legislature.

DEBY TAKES POWER

On 10 November 1990 forces led by Deby, which were believed to number some 2,000, again invaded Chad from Sudan, and launched an attack on positions held by Chadian government forces at Tiné, north-east of Abéché. The governments of Libya and Sudan again denied involvement in the offensive. The FANT initially forced the rebels to retreat to Sudan; however, attacks were soon resumed, and by mid-November the MPS was reported to have captured Tiné. Despite an appeal by Habré to the French government for military assistance, the 'Opération Epervier' contingent, which had been reinforced to protect French interests in the region, took no part in the military engagements. The MPS continued to consolidate its position in eastern Chad, and many FANT units reportedly transferred their allegiance to Deby. Negotiations concerning the sovereignty of the Aozou region, scheduled for late November, were suspended by Col Qaddafi, who claimed that recent Chadian allegations of Libyan involvement in the rebel invasion had undermined conditions for the discussions. Although the US government declared its full support for Habré, France maintained its policy of non-intervention in Chad's internal affairs. (It was widely believed that France's lack of support for the incumbent regime reflected Habré's failure to initiate a transition towards multi-party democracy.)

On 30 November 1990 Habré, together with members of his family and of the council of ministers, fled the country, after the MPS had seized control of Abéché. Deby arrived in N'Djamena two days later, and declared his commitment to the creation of a democratic multi-party political system. The national assembly was dissolved, the constitution was suspended and a provisional council of state was formed, with Deby as interim head of state. The new 33-member council of state mainly comprised members of the MPS and allied parties; however, Acheikh Ibn Oumar was appointed special adviser to the head of state. A number of political organizations that had opposed Habré subsequently declared their support for the MPS. Goukouni Oueddei indicated his willingness to open political negotiations with the new government, despite persistent reports that he was massing forces in northern Chad. Following the publication of a report, compiled by the MPS, accusing Habré of violations of human rights and of corruption, Deby sought Habré's extradition from Senegal (where he had been granted political asylum). Later in December the government announced that the FANT was to be restructured as a smaller army, designated the Armées nationales tchadiennes (ANT), and that a national gendarmerie was to replace the military police.

Following the accession to power of the MPS, it was announced that aid and co-operation agreements between France and the Habré government would be honoured, and that new accords would be formulated. The USA, however, refused to extend formal recognition to the new regime, on the grounds of Deby's allegedly close links with Libya, although it affirmed its commitment to existing aid agreements. The Libyan and Sudanese governments declared support for the new regime, and undertook not to allow forces hostile to Deby to operate on their territory. A visit to Libya by Deby in February 1991 consolidated

relations between the two countries. The issue of sovereignty over the Aozou region remained under consideration by the ICJ.

On 1 March 1991 a national charter, drafted by the executive committee of the MPS, was adopted for a 30-month transitional period, at the end of which a referendum was to be held to determine Chad's constitutional future. The charter confirmed Deby's appointment as president, head of state and chairman of the MPS, and required the government to institute measures to prepare for the implementation of a multi-party system. Under the terms of the charter, a new council of ministers and a 31-member legislative council of the republic were to replace the provisional council of state. On 4 March Deby was formally inaugurated as president. The council of state was dissolved, and the former president of the national assembly, Dr Jean Alingue Bawoyeu, was appointed prime minister in a new government.

POLITICAL REFORM

In May 1991 Deby announced that a national conference, scheduled for May 1992, would prepare a new constitution to provide for the introduction of a multi-party system, and would be followed by legislative elections. Constitutional amendments permitting the registration of opposition movements would enter into force in January 1992. Goukouni, who visited Chad (from Algeria) for the first time in nine years, subsequently met Deby to discuss the proposals for the introduction of a pluralist system. In October the council of ministers adopted the recommendations of an *ad hoc* commission regarding the authorization of political parties. Under the new legislation, each party was required to have a minimum of 30 founder members, three each from 10 of Chad's 14 prefectures; the formation of parties on an ethnic or regional basis was prohibited. However, the MPS was exempted from the conditions of registration, and opposition groups denounced the legislation as biased in its favour.

OPPOSITION TO THE DEBY GOVERNMENT

In September 1991 rebels attacked military garrisons in Tibesti, in northern Chad, killing 50 people. Deby alleged that the offensive was instigated from Niger by Habré-loyalist troops who had fled in December 1990. In October troops attacked an arsenal at N'Djamena airport in an attempt to seize power; some 40 people were killed in the ensuing fighting. Several officials, including the minister of the interior, Maldoum Bada Abbas, were arrested on charges connected with the incident. Although the government asserted that Abbas had been motivated by personal ambition, there was speculation that the coup attempt had been provoked by discontent within his ethnic group, the Hadjerai, who were under-represented in government. France reaffirmed its support for the MPS, and announced that the 'Opération Epervier' contingent would be reinforced by an additional 300 troops. Following the coup attempt, the Chadian government abrogated a co-operation agreement with Libya that Abbas had negotiated in September, on the grounds that the sovereignty of the Aozou region remained in dispute.

In late December 1991 some 3,000 troops loyal to Habré attacked several towns in the region of Lake Chad. The rebels were reported to be members of the Mouvement pour la démocratie et le développement (MDD), an opposition group based in Libya, led by Goukouni Guët. By early January 1992 the rebels had captured the towns of Liwa and Bol, and were advancing towards N'Djamena; government forces, in their counter-offensive, suffered heavy losses. The French government dispatched some 450 troops to reinforce the 'Opération Epervier' force (which numbered about 1,100), ostensibly to protect French citizens in the area. Shortly afterwards the government claimed that the rebels had been defeated, and that the ANT had recaptured Liwa and Bol. A number of prominent members of the opposition and former ministers of the Habré government were subsequently arrested, and there were reports of summary executions. The French government condemned such violations of human rights, and warned that its continued support for Deby was dependent on the implementation of political reforms. Later in January the government reaffirmed its commitment to the process of democratization, and declared an amnesty for political prisoners. Maldoum Bada Abbas was among those released, and in the following month he was appointed as president of a new provisional council of the republic. However, there were reports that ethnic factions within the ANT continued acts of persecution in the capital, particularly targeting southerners.

In February 1992 government forces suppressed an alleged coup attempt, when a group of disaffected soldiers, styling themselves the Comité de sursaut national pour la paix et la démocratie (CSNPD), attacked a police station in N'Djamena. In March four French citizens stated to have been involved in the incident were expelled from Chad. In early April the French government announced that the role of 'Opération Epervier' as a defensive strike force was to cease, although French troops were to remain in the country to assist in the restructuring of the ANT. This change in policy was widely interpreted as a warning to Deby to end the human rights violations perpetrated against opponents of the government, and to continue with the implementation of democratic reform. In the same month the MDD claimed that more than 40 of its members, including Goukouni Guët, had been arrested in Nigeria in February, extradited to Chad, and subsequently imprisoned or executed. Later in April soldiers mainly belonging to the Zaghawa ethnic group surrounded the presidential palace in protest at government plans to demilitarize N'Djamena and to reduce the size of the ANT, in which the Zaghawa perceived themselves as under-represented. After mediation by the minister of state for public works and transport, Abbas Koti (himself a Zaghawa), the troops withdrew.

In May 1992 the national conference was postponed, on the grounds that the preparatory commission had not completed its work. In late May Joseph Yodoyman, a member of the Alliance nationale pour la démocratie et le développement (ANDD), replaced Bawoyeu as prime minister. Deby formed a new council of ministers, which included, for the first time, five members of the opposition. However, it was reported that several opposition leaders had refused to join the government, and the influence of southerners in the council of ministers was also reduced.

In late May 1992 MDD rebels launched a further attack in the region of Lake Chad, against which government forces subsequently counter-attacked from Nigerian territory. In mid-June an agreement between the government and the CSNPD provided for the release of detained members of the group. Later that month the government announced that it had pre-empted a coup attempt, led by Abbas Koti. Shortly afterwards members of the pro-Koti Conseil national de redressement du Tchad (CNRT), attacked government forces in the region of Lake Chad; fighting was also reported at Chicha, near Faya-Largeau. At the end of June representatives of the government and the MDD, meeting in Libreville, Gabon, signed an agreement envisaging cessation of hostilities and the immediate release of detained MDD activists. In July, however, government forces were reported to have launched renewed attacks against MDD troops in the region of Lake Chad. In the following month clashes between CSNPD forces and government troops were reported in Doba, in southern Chad. In September, none the less, the government signed further peace agreements with the MDD, the CSNPD and an opposition movement based in Sudan, the Front national du Tchad (FNT).

In July 1992 the trade union federation, the Union syndicale du Tchad (UST), organized a series of strikes, in protest at government plans to reduce salaries and to increase taxes. Later that month Yodoyman was expelled from the ANDD for allegedly failing to support the process of democratic reform. Shortly afterwards the minister of the civil service and labour, Nabia Ndali (a member of the ANDD), resigned from the government. In early August three representatives of human rights organizations serving in the government, including a member of the Ligue tchadienne des droits de l'homme (LTDH), also resigned, in protest at the conduct of security forces in N'Djamena. In October the UST organized a one-month general strike, demanding higher salaries in the public sector and the convening of the national conference. Two former opposition members resigned their ministerial portfolios, to protest at the subsequent ban imposed by the government on the activities of the UST. In mid-October, in response to increasing public pressure, the government announced that the national conference would take place in January 1993. In November a number of UST activists were arrested after the general strike was extended for a further

month. Later in November the government ended the ban on the UST, but suspended civil servants who continued to observe the general strike. In January 1993 the government withdrew the sanctions that had been imposed on a number of civil servants, and the general strike effectively ended.

Meanwhile, in October 1992 the MDD was reported to have begun a renewed offensive against government forces in the Lake Chad region; at the end of that month the MDD officially declared the peace agreement, signed in September, to be invalid, alleging that the government had received armaments from Libya and was preparing to resume hostilities. In December further clashes between government forces and members of the MDD were reported in the Lake Chad region.

CIVIL TENSION AND TRANSITION

The national conference was convened in January 1993, attended by some 800 delegates (representing, among others, the institutions of state and 30 political organizations, together with trade unions and professional associations). However, arguments swiftly emerged regarding attempts to confer sovereign status on the conference. Progress was also impeded by controversy over demands for the extension of the use of Arabic for official communications. In April 1993 the conference finally adopted a transitional charter, elected Dr Fidèle Moungar, hitherto minister of national and higher education, to be prime minister, and established a 57-member interim legislature, the Conseil supérieur de la transition (CST). The leader of the Rassemblement pour la démocratie et le progrès (RDP), ex-president Choua, was elected chairman of the CST. It was agreed that Deby was to remain in office as head of state and c-in-c of the armed forces for a period of one year (with provision for one extension), while a transitional government, under the supervision of the CST, was to implement economic, political and social programmes drafted by the conference; multi-party elections were to take place at the end of this period. Moungar's government retained only four members of the former council of ministers, and included representatives of a number of opposition parties. (The membership of the transitional government was almost halved in June.)

Meanwhile, in January 1993 it was reported that CSNPD forces had attacked government troops at Gore, in the south. Later in January troops loyal to Habré attempted a coup while Deby was visiting France. In February government troops, in conflict with the MDD in the region of Lake Chad, clashed with members of the Nigerien armed forces after attacking rebel bases in Niger. In the same month, following renewed military engagements between government troops and the CSNPD in southern Chad, opposition groups claimed that members of the ANT had massacred civilians in the region of Gore. By March some 15,000 civilians had fled from southern Chad to the CAR, to escape alleged atrocities by government forces. In the same month it was reported that Koti (who had been arrested in Cameroon in December 1992) had escaped from detention.

In May 1993, following a report by a commission of inquiry, the transitional government confirmed that members of the ANT had perpetrated massacres of civilians in southern Chad earlier that year, apparently in reprisal for hostilities initiated by the CSNPD. Moungar stated that officials implicated in the violence had been arrested, that military units in the region were to be replaced, and that a judicial investigation was to take place. In the same month Deby dissolved the government intelligence service, which had attracted criticism from opposition and human rights groups. Later in May a human rights organization, Tchad non-violence, withdrew its representative from the CST, in protest at the violence perpetrated by members of the ANT, and at the alleged failure of the government to observe the decisions of the national conference. In June the CST refused to ratify a co-operation agreement that had been signed with Libya in November 1992, in view of the outstanding issue of the sovereignty of the Aozou region (which was to be reviewed by the ICJ later that month).

Widespread concern at the increasing incidence of violent crime intensified following the assassination in mid-1993 of the director of the soldiers' reintegration committee by troops in N'Djamena. In an attempt to restore civil order, the transitional government implemented a number of new security measures, and in early July announced that the ANT and the security forces were to be reorganized. Violent crime persisted throughout the country, however, and in July opposition parties organized a one-day general strike, in protest at the continuing civil disorder.

In August 1993 some 82 civilians were killed in the Ouaddai region, apparently as a result of ethnic clashes. Shortly afterwards it was reported that some 41 people had been killed when a demonstration by residents of N'Djamena (originating from Ouaddai), in protest at the massacre, was violently suppressed by the republican guard. The CST accused the government of exceeding its powers by deploying the republican guard to disperse the demonstration, and by imposing a national curfew in response to the unrest. In mid-August Koti (who had denied allegations by the government that CNRT troops had been responsible for the massacre in Ouaddai) returned to Chad, after a peace agreement was reached by the CNRT and the Chadian authorities. In September, despite efforts by the government to allay discontent in the south, the CSNPD threatened to impede plans to exploit petroleum reserves in the region of Doba—considered essential to future prospects of economic development—unless the government met its demands for the establishment of a federal state. In mid-October Koti signed a further agreement with the government, whereby the CNRT was to be granted legal status as a political party and its forces were to be integrated into the ANT. However, Koti was subsequently killed by security forces while allegedly resisting arrest on charges of involvement in a conspiracy to overthrow the government. The CNRT rejected claims by the authorities that documents, signed by Koti, detailing plans for an armed coup had been discovered, and announced that operations against government forces would be resumed.

KOUMAKOYE AND OPPOSITION PRESSURE

Increasing disagreement between Deby and Moungar concerning government policy culminated, in October 1993, in the approval by the CST of a motion expressing 'no confidence' in the Moungar administration, apparently initiated by supporters of Deby. Moungar subsequently resigned and his government was dissolved. In November the CST elected Delwa Kassire Koumakoye, hitherto minister of justice, as prime minister, and a new transitional government, which retained 10 members of the former administration, was appointed. In December an 'institutional committee' was established to prepare a draft constitution, an electoral code and legislation governing the registration of political organizations; the committee, which included representatives of the transitional organs and several political parties, was to submit recommendations within a period of two months. However, industrial action by teachers and other public sector workers, in protest at the government's failure to pay salary arrears, resumed, and in January 1994 the government banned an opposition demonstration and threatened to implement sanctions against striking civil servants.

Meanwhile, activity by what had come to be known as 'politico-military' groups continued. The MDD and the Union nationale pour la démocratie et le socialisme announced in January 1994 that they were to unite against government forces, while members of the FNT, who apparently were to have been integrated into the army following a peace agreement, attacked a military garrison at Abéché. (It was subsequently reported that more than 200 people had been killed in ensuing clashes between the FNT and government forces.) Also in January the authorities in Cameroon claimed that members of the CNRT, who were allegedly planning an attack on N'Djamena, had killed members of the Cameroonian security forces in the north of that country. In March there were clashes between government and CSNPD forces in southern Chad, after a cease-fire agreement, mediated by the CAR in the previous month, failed to secure a lasting peace.

THE RETURN OF THE AOZOU REGION

In February 1994 the ICJ ruled in favour of Chad in the dispute over the sovereignty of the Aozou region, thereby upholding the provisions of a treaty that had been signed in 1955 by the governments of France and Libya. Later that month, however, Chad claimed that Libya had deployed additional troops in the region. In April Libya agreed to commence the withdrawal of troops from the region, in an operation that was to be monitored

by UN observers and officials from both countries. At the end of May Libya and Chad issued a joint statement confirming that the withdrawal of Libyan troops had been completed as scheduled. In the following month the two governments signed a co-operation agreement.

CONSTITUTIONAL PROPOSALS

In March 1994 the institutional committee presented recommendations for a draft constitution, including provisions for the election of a president for a term of five years, the installation of a bicameral legislature and a constitutional court, and the establishment of a decentralized administrative structure. In April the CST extended the transitional period for one year, on the grounds that the government had achieved little progress in the preparation of democratic elections. A new electoral timetable was adopted, whereby the government was obliged to provide funds for the organization of the elections and reach an agreement with the UST in order to end industrial unrest. Further preparatory measures, to be adopted by June, included the adoption of an electoral code, the establishment of a national reconciliation council to negotiate a peace settlement with rebel movements, and the appointment of electoral and human rights commissions. The constitutional recommendations were to be submitted for approval at a national referendum in December, to be followed by legislative elections in January 1995 and a presidential election in March.

Government efforts to negotiate a settlement with the UST were, however, impeded by further strike action by public sector workers at the end of April 1994, in support of demands for an increase in salaries in compensation for the 50% devaluation of the CFA franc three months earlier. A presidential decree issued at the beginning of May declared the strike illegal, but industrial action continued. Also in May, despite apparent opposition from Deby, the government established a 12-member national reconciliation council, which was to initiate negotiations with the politico-military opposition. Later that month Deby announced an extensive government reorganization. However, one of the newly-appointed ministers, Salomon Ngarbaye Tombalbaye, son of Chad's first president and leader of the Mouvement pour la démocratie et le socialisme du Tchad, refused to serve in the government, citing its continued failure to address social and economic hardship. In July the government and the UST negotiated a settlement providing for a limited increase in salaries and the payment of arrears.

TRANSITIONAL POLITICS

In August 1994, following the resumption of negotiations between the Chadian authorities and the CSNPD (with mediation by the CAR, which had prohibited the CSNPD from conducting military activities from its territory after peace talks failed in March), the two sides signed a cease-fire agreement, providing for the recognition of the CSNPD as a legal political organization, and the integration of its forces into the ANT; implementation of the agreement was to be supervised by a committee comprising representatives of the UN and the governments of the CAR, France and Gabon. Later in August, however, it was reported that government troops had killed some 26 civilians in southern Chad, in reprisal for attacks by members of another rebel faction, the Forces armées pour la République fédérale (FARF).

In September 1994 it was reported that the minister of mines and energy, Lt-Col Mahamat Garfa (who had recently been dismissed as chief of army staff), had fled N'Djamena with substantial government funds, and, together with some 600 members of the ANT, had joined CNRT forces in eastern Chad. In October Choua (who had previously been twice re-elected as chairman of the CST) was replaced by a member of the MPS, Mahamat Bachar Ghadaia. Choua subsequently accused the government of perpetrating violations of human rights, including the assassination of two prominent members of the RDP, after several RDP activists were arrested apparently on the grounds that they were supporters of the MDD. Also in October the government and the FNT negotiated a peace agreement, which was, however, subsequently repudiated by the leader of the FNT. In the following month a number of former members of the CSNPD were integrated into the ANT.

Deby officially announced in November 1994 that the process of democratic transition would be completed on 9 April 1995, following presidential and legislative elections. In December 1994 Deby proclaimed a general amnesty for political prisoners and, excluding Habré, opposition members in exile. Although a number of political detainees were subsequently released, the LTDH continued to accuse Deby of violations of human rights—specifically reprisals undertaken by the ANT for rebel activity. In January 1995 the CST adopted a new electoral code, and an independent national electoral commission was established. Later in January the CST approved the draft constitution, which had been amended in accordance with recommendations reached by consensus at a national conference in August 1994.

In February and early March 1995 the government conducted a population census, to enable revision of the electoral register; following reports of widespread irregularities, however, opposition parties accused the MPS of attempted electoral malpractice and demanded that a new census be organized. At the end of March the CST extended the transitional period for a further year, and amended the national charter to the effect that the incumbent prime minister was henceforth prohibited from contesting the forthcoming presidential election or from belonging to a political party. These measures attracted strong criticism from opposition parties, which subsequently sought a legal challenge to the validity of the extension of the transitional period. In April the CST voted to remove Koumakoye as prime minister, after criticizing him for the government's lack of progress in the organization of democratic elections. Although Koumakoye rejected the attempt to dismiss him as unconstitutional, the CST elected Djimasta Koibla, a prominent member of Jean Alingue Bawoyeu's Union pour la démocratie et la République (UDR), as prime minister. A new transitional government was subsequently formed, in which, despite the CSNPD's condemnation of the extension of the transitional period, the group's leader, Col Moïse Nedji Kette, joined the cabinet as minister of the environment and tourism. In the same month the results of the population census were annulled by the court of appeal on grounds of procedural irregularities. In May the national electoral commission scheduled the constitutional referendum for November; the presidential election was to take place in February 1996, with legislative elections to follow, in two rounds, in April and May.

In May 1995 Amnesty International and the LTDH claimed that members of the ANT had perpetrated human rights' violations against civilians in retaliation for rebel attacks. In June members of the armed forces raided the premises of an independent newspaper, *N'Djamena-Hebdo*, which had published an article critical of the ANT. Deby subsequently announced an inquiry into the incident, in response to widespread protests. Later that month the authorities banned a demonstration planned by the opposition in protest at the government's continued failure to adopt democratic conditions. In July a unilateral government declaration of a national cease-fire was received with caution by the rebel movements.

In August 1995 the chairman and other members of the executive bureau of the CST resigned, following accusations of the misappropriation of funds. At the end of the month security forces raided the home of Saleh Kebzabo, the leader of the opposition Union nationale pour le développement et le renouveau (UNDR). The Concertation des partis politiques (CPP), an informal opposition alliance to which the UNDR belonged, announced that its members were to suspend participation in the CST and the national reconciliation council, and demanded the resignation of the head of security forces. In September Kebzabo was arrested and charged with endangering state security by associating with rebel groups, prompting further protests from the CPP. (He was released on bail later that month.)

In November 1995 Deby announced that Gabon was to sponsor reconciliation discussions, to be convened in December between the government and political organizations and armed opposition groups. Later that month the government and the MDD signed a peace agreement providing for a cease-fire, an exchange of prisoners and the integration of a number of MDD troops into the ANT. Also in November the independent national electoral commission promulgated a further timetable whereby a constitutional referendum was to take place in March 1996,

followed by a presidential election in June and legislative elections later that year. A further population census (conducted with financial assistance from France and the European Union—EU) commenced in December 1995.

The reconciliation discussions were convened in Franceville, Gabon, in January 1996, with mediation by the governments of Gabon, the CAR and Niger. However, a number of delegates from the politico-military groups immediately objected that Deby had failed to invite representatives from all the opposition organizations to the negotiations, and demanded his resignation. In March, following protracted negotiations, the government and 13 opposition parties signed an agreement providing for the imposition of a cease-fire and the establishment of a special security force to maintain order during the electoral period. It was reported, however, that the majority of armed movements had rejected the agreement.

PRESIDENTIAL AND LEGISLATIVE ELECTIONS

The conclusion of the Franceville agreement allowed the electoral timetable to proceed as rescheduled. However, a number of opposition groups, particularly the southern-based organizations that supported the adoption of a federal system of government, urged their members to reject the draft constitution (which enshrined a unitary state) at the national referendum. Despite consequent opposition from the south of the country, the new constitution was adopted by 63.5% of votes cast at the referendum, which took place on 31 March 1996.

By April 1996 15 presidential candidates, including Deby, had emerged; a further five potential candidates (including Moungar) had been rejected on the grounds that they had failed to meet electoral regulations concerning residency in the country. Koumakoye, who in March had been jailed for three months for the illegal possession of arms, was released shortly before the election. In the first round of voting, which took place on 2 June, Deby secured 43.8% of votes cast, with Wadal Abdelkader Kamougué (contesting the election on behalf of the Union pour le renouveau et la démocratie—URD) taking 12.4% and Kebzabo (for the UNDR) 8.5%. Opposition parties claimed that the French government had supported efforts by the Chad authorities to perpetrate electoral fraud, and the majority of the candidates who had been eliminated urged a boycott of the second round. However, Kebzabo announced his support for Deby. In early July the government suspended the activities of the UST, after it attempted to organize a boycott of the election.

The second round of the presidential election, contested by Deby and Kamougué, took place on 3 July 1996: according to official results, Deby was elected by 69.1% of votes cast. He was officially inaugurated as president on 8 August, and subsequently reappointed Koibla to the office of prime minister. Later that month Koibla announced the formation of a new government, which included several opposition members, notably Kebzabo (who, in exchange for his support for Deby in the second round, received the foreign affairs portfolio). The ban on the UST was revoked at the end of July.

In August 1996 the CNRT merged with another dissident faction, the Front d'action pour l'installation de la démocratie au Tchad, to form the Congrès pour le renouveau et la démocratie. Later that month the government and elements of the FARF signed a peace agreement, providing for the imposition of a cease-fire and an amnesty for members of the faction, which was to be reconstituted as a legal political organization, the Front patriotique pour la démocratie. In September the Front national du Tchad renové (FNTR) threatened to abandon plans for peace negotiations with the Chadian authorities, after claiming that government forces had launched attacks against FNTR positions in eastern Chad. The government and a faction of the MDD signed a peace agreement in Niger later that month, envisaging a cease-fire and an amnesty; a further peace accord was signed in December with a separate MDD faction. In October Deby announced that he had dispatched an adviser to meet representatives of other dissident factions, in an effort to initiate peace negotiations.

In October 1996 Amnesty International published a report accusing France of complicity in violations of human rights in Chad; the allegations were denied by the French government. Deby, while apparently conceding that problems existed, insisted that French training of Chadian troops had, in fact, improved human rights. In January 1997 several human rights organizations, including the LTDH, severely criticized a decree sanctioning the summary execution of alleged criminals, which had resulted in dozens of shootings since its promulgation in November 1996. The decree was finally revoked as a result of international pressure, including a condemnation of Chad by the EU for serious violations of human rights.

Meanwhile, in October 1996 France announced that, as a result of Chad's improved relations with neighbouring states, the mission of the 'Epervier' force was to be redefined, but with no reduction in the number of troops deployed. In December Deby participated in efforts to mediate in the political crisis in the CAR, and in early 1997 Chadian troops joined the regional surveillance mission in that country. Chadian forces remained in the CAR as part of the UN peace-keeping mission that began operations in April 1998.

Legislative voting was again delayed, and eventually took place on 5 January and 23 February 1997. A total of 658 candidates representing some 49 political parties contested the 125 national assembly seats. Voting was reported to have been conducted relatively peacefully, however, a number of opposition activists, including two RDP candidates, were arrested for disrupting the electoral process in N'Djamena. During March preliminary results for a number of constituencies were challenged by both the MPS and opposition parties. Later that month the court of appeal announced the final results, allocating a further eight seats to the MPS, which thus secured an absolute majority with a total of 63 seats, while the URD won 29 seats, the UNDR 15, and the UDR four. The national assembly was installed on 4 April, and in early May Kamougué was elected president of the national assembly by a large majority, following an accord between his party, the URD, the MPS and the UNDR. Later that month Nassour Guelengdouksia Ouaidou (hitherto secretary-general at the president's office) was appointed prime minister. His government included representatives of several parties, although the MPS retained the most senior ministerial portfolios. Kebzabo was redesignated minister of state for public works, transport, housing and town planning.

In April 1997 the transitional government and the FARF signed a peace agreement, providing for the cessation of all hostilities between the ANT and the FARF, a general amnesty for FARF members, the integration of its civilian and armed members into the state apparatus, and the legalization of the movement as a political party. In May the incoming administration was reported to have negotiated a peace agreement with the FAP (the military wing of Goukouni's FROLINAT). In August formation of a new opposition group, the Résistance armée contre les forces antidémocratiques (RAFAD), was announced in Nigeria; the stated aim of the group was the forcible removal of the Deby government. (However, in June 2000 RAFAD signed a peace agreement with the government during a general amnesty.) At the end of August 1997 the leaders of 21 opposition parties denounced the continuing presence of French troops in Chad as a reinforcement of the Deby regime.

INSURGENCY PROBLEMS

In October 1997, following a meeting in N'Djamena of representatives of the government, the FNT, the FNTR and the Mouvement pour la justice sociale et la démocratie, the government extended a general amnesty to members of the three groups; agreement was also reached on measures to reintegrate members of these 'politico-military' groups, which were to be legalized as political parties, and for the return of refugees associated with them. In the same month the government announced plans for the establishment of a rapid intervention force, directly accountable to the president, within the Chadian army. At the end of October clashes erupted in Moundou, in Logone Occidental prefecture, between members of the ANT and the FARF. According to official figures, 42 FARF rebels, 52 civilians and four members of the ANT were killed. The FARF accused the government of reneging on commitments made under the terms of the April peace agreement, notably concerning the integration of fighters into the regular armed forces. However, the government reaffirmed its commitment to the pursuit of peace, and undertook to expedite the reintegration of rebel forces. Tension between the army and the FARF rebels remained high, and several civilians were reported to have been killed in

clashes in Logone Occidental at the end of November. In late December clashes were also reported to have occurred in the Lake Chad area between government troops and elements of the MDD, bringing to an end a period of relative peace in the region.

Deby implemented an extensive reorganization of the government in early January 1998. Nassour Ouaidou was reappointed prime minister, while Kebzabo was redesignated minister of state, with responsibility for mines, energy and petroleum.

In early February 1998 four French nationals were taken hostage in Moyen-Chari prefecture by the insurgent Union des forces démocratiques (UFD). The hostages were released unharmed following an operation by the security forces in which 11 rebels were reported killed and 19 others captured. French 'Epervier' forces were mobilized in support of the Chadian security forces, although the military attaché at the French embassy in N'Djamena, said to be an associate of the UFD leader, Dr Mahamout Nahour, was declared *persona non grata* by the Chadian authorities after Nahour demanded only to negotiate with him.

The restoration of peace, particularly in the south, was regarded as imperative as efforts continued to secure external funding for the development of petroleum resources. In early March 1998 it was revealed that discreet talks had been taking place since January between Kamougué and the FARF leader, Laokein Barde: the petroleum-rich Logone region, a centre for FARF activities, was a political stronghold of Kamougué's URD. During that month, however, there was a renewed outbreak of violence in southern Chad. In a statement released that month the government acknowledged the recent occurrence of serious violence in the southern part of the country, for which it held the FARF responsible, disclosing that about 50 people, including 30 members of the security forces, had been killed in the region at the beginning of March. This acknowledgement of the recent violence was viewed by some observers as an attempt to reduce the impact of a report by Amnesty International, which contained allegations of the summary execution by the security forces of at least 100 civilians in southern Chad. In late March the FNTR, demanding the withdrawal of French troops and petroleum companies from Chad, claimed responsibility for the kidnapping of eight Europeans. (All had been released by the end of the month.)

A warrant was issued in March 1998 for the arrest of Laokein Barde. None the less, contacts between the FARF and Kamougué were maintained, and in early May a new peace accord was signed by the government and the FARF chief of general staff. (Reports later in the year stated that Barde had been presumed dead since April.) The accord provided for an immediate cease-fire in Logone Oriental and Logone Occidental prefectures, a general amnesty for FARF rebels and sympathizers and the withdrawal of élite elements of the nomadic and national security guards from southern Chad; the accord renewed the provision included in the agreement of April 1997 for the transformation of the FARF into a political party and the integration of its forces into the Chadian army.

Kebzabo was dismissed from the government, together with two other members of the UNDR, in mid-May 1998. Further government reshuffles took place in mid-July, in which the secretary-general of the MPS, Mahamat Saleh Ahmat, was appointed as a minister of state, and in late October.

In mid-February 1998 the editor-in-chief of *N'Djamena Hebdo*, Dieudonné Djonabaye, received a two-year suspended prison sentence, having been convicted of libelling the head of state. In late March Djonabaye was reportedly detained and severely beaten by security forces while attempting (in his capacity as correspondent for Radio France Internationale) to visit the headquarters of the 'Epervier' force; he was released reportedly after intervention by French military representatives. In July Ngarledjy Yorongar, the sole representative of the Front des forces d'action pour la République in the national assembly, was sentenced to three years' imprisonment. A southerner who had been an outspoken critic of provisions for the exploitation of petroleum in southern Chad, Yorongar had claimed that the national assembly president had received payment of 1,500m. francs CFA from a French petroleum company, and had also alleged that Deby and his family were mismanaging the country's oil resources. (The editor-in-chief and a correspondent of the independent journal that had published the allegations, *l'Observateur*, were each fined and given suspended prison sentences.) In late March and early April, meanwhile, security forces intervened to prevent gatherings of Koumakoye's Rassemblement national pour la démocratie et le progrès, planned to demand the restoration of democracy and a halt to massacres of civilians in the south.

In September 1998 a faction of the MDD issued a communiqué asserting that it had ousted Moussa Medella Mahamat as its leader, with the aim of engaging in peace talks with the government. However, Medella denounced this rallying to the government, and condemned the Chadian regime for seeking to recruit its opponents, rather than creating a true framework for dialogue. The MDD leader further condemned a joint offensive against its militants by security forces in Chad, Niger and Nigeria. (In April 1999 the MDD stated that almost 50 bodies discovered in a mass grave near Lake Chad were probably those of activists expelled from neighbouring countries during this operation.) In late November 1998 Goukouni Oueddei appealed from Algiers for a general mobilization against the Deby regime. At the end of the month, however, the FARF—now reportedly led by Dienambaye Barde, the brother of Laokein Barde—had rallied to the MPS 'in order to preserve peace and strengthen democratic gains'.

From late 1998 reports emerged of a rebellion in the Tibesti region of northern Chad by the Mouvement pour la démocratie et la justice au Tchad (MDJT), led by Youssouf Togoimi, who had been dismissed as minister of defence in June 1997. The government did not acknowledge the existence of any dissident movement in Tibesti until March 1999—and even then asserted that Togoimi was leading a group of only some 30 Toubou rebels. The authorities confirmed that military reinforcements had been deployed to prevent infiltration by Toubou sympathizers from neighbouring countries, and acknowledged that the ANT had suffered some losses in actions against the rebels. However, claims by the MDJT to be in control of much of the north of the country were categorically denied. In late March, amid unconfirmed reports that some 300 people had been killed or injured in the Tibesti region since October 1998, it was revealed that a 3,000-strong élite military force had been deployed to counter the MDJT. In April 1999 the MDJT, the MDD and Acheikh Ibn Oumar's CDR announced that they were to join forces to end what they termed the 'bloody drift' of the past decade. In late June FROLINAT stated that it was giving political and logistical support to the MDJT. In an interview with the Paris-based *Jeune Afrique*, published in June, Togoimi asserted that the MDJT had taken control of several oases and military posts in the extreme north, as well as access roads to the Tibesti mountains, and would have reached N'Djamena by the end of the year. The former defence minister stated that there could be no question of negotiating with Deby, and denounced the incumbent regime as authoritarian and corrupt. Togoimi further claimed that there had been dozens of arrests and summary executions since mid-1997. Claims by the MDJT in mid-July 1999 to have killed 77 soldiers in an ambush in the Tibesti mountains were denied by the government. In August it was reported that a senior ANT officer had defected to the MDJT. Meanwhile, Deby dispatched a group of negotiators to the north, in an effort to establish contacts with the rebels. In late October Togoimi expressed for the first time his willingness to meet the presidential envoys. In early November, however, the MDJT, the MDD and the CDR alleged that the Chadian government had acquired what were termed 'dirty weapons', such as chemicals to poison wells, from countries of the former communist bloc, in order to 'decimate' the population of Tibesti. In a communiqué issued later in November, furthermore, the MDJT claimed to have defeated ANT forces in Aozou, killing 80 and capturing 47 (a further 42 ANT troops were said to have defected to the rebellion). The MDJT asserted that its victory followed heavy fighting precipitated by an ambush by ANT forces who had allegedly used the cover of civilian negotiators in order to access MDJT positions. During the first half of 2000 claims made by the MDJT of further military successes around the strongholds of Yebibon, Guizinti and Bardai were dismissed or diminished by the government. In February 2000 the government admitted that its mediation mission to the north, led by the former prime minister Djimasta Koibla, had proved fruitless.

Meanwhile, in July 1999 Medella returned to N'Djamena, following the signing in Khartoum, Sudan, of a reconciliation accord with the Deby regime. MDD dissidents, however, denounced Medella, and the leadershp of the movement was assumed by Issa Faki Mahamat and Gaileth Gatoul Bourkoumandah. At the end of September the MDD alleged that joint forces from Chad, Niger and Nigeria were waging a 'campaign of terror' in the region of Lake Chad against suspected opposition sympathizers. In February 2000 it was reported that the former armed wing of the MDD had renamed itself the Mouvement pour l'unité et la République (MUR), under the leadership of Bourkoumandah. It was alleged that the MUR had subsequently allied itself with the MDJT and the CDR.

Ouaidou resigned as prime minister in mid-December 1999. He was replaced by Nagoum Yamassoum, whose new government included five UNDR members, among them Saleh Kebzabo as minister of state, with responsibility for agriculture. Kebzabo retained this position in an extensive ministerial reshuffle carried out at the end of August 2000.

Meanwhile, in early 1998 it was reported that Chad was to seek the extradition from Senegal of former President Habré, with a view to his prosecution in relation to human rights abuses and in connection with the embezzlement of state funds. A committee of inquiry, established by the Deby regime, had held Habré's 'political police' responsible for the deaths of some 40,000 people; the deposed president was also alleged to have taken some 7,000m. francs CFA in state funds when he fled the country in 1990. In early February 2000, following a ruling by a Senegalese court that he could be tried for alleged crimes committed in Chad under his leadership, Habré was charged with complicity in acts of torture and barbarity, and placed under house arrest. The charges were rejected in July, however, on the basis that Senegal lacked the appropriate penal procedure to process such an international case; implications of political interference were subsequently made.

EXTERNAL RELATIONS

Relations with France appeared uneasy in the first half of 1998, particularly following the expulsion of the French military attaché, accused of maintaining dangerous contacts with the opposition (i.e. Nahour and the UFD). In May Deby denounced what he termed the 'neo-imperialism' of the international media and human rights groups, accusing the West of imposing multiparty politics on Africa. (Kamougué openly distanced himself from Deby's remarks, asserting that the head of state was guarantor of the constitution and thus of the pluralist system that it enshrined.) In June 30 agents of the French Direction générale de la sécurité extérieure, who had apparently been operating as Deby's protection agents, were dismissed. Deby none the less met with President Jacques Chirac during a visit to France in the following month, and in September the French army chief of staff visited Chad in an effort to ease tensions. In late 1998 the French minister of defence indicated the possibility of a new defence accord with Chad, in place of existing agreements governing military co-operation and assistance. It was generally believed that France, which had undertaken a comprehensive restructuring of its armed forces, regarded the maintenance of its military presence in Chad as a priority, given the country's proximity to potential conflict zones in central Africa, and also, notably, to Libya.

During the late 1990s Chad forged increasingly close relations with its neighbours, particularly Libya. Chad was a founder member of the Community of the Sahel-Saharan States (COMESSA), established in Tripoli in 1997. Deby and members of his administration made several visits to Libya in 1997–2000; some of these visits were made by air prior to the ending of the UN embargo on air links with Libya in April 1999. In May 1998 the Libyan leader, Col Muammar al-Qaddafi, made what was reported as his first visit to Chad since 1981.

Chad dispatched troops to the CAR in early 1997, as part of a regional surveillance mission, and Chadian forces remained in the CAR as part of the UN peace-keeping mission (MINURCA) that began operations in April 1998.

In late September 1998 it was confirmed that Chadian troops had been dispatched to the Democratic Republic of the Congo (DRC, q.v.) in support of President Laurent-Désiré Kabila. The Chadian authorities asserted that the military had intervened to assist in the restoration of peace and recovery of territorial integrity in the DRC. It was denied, furthermore, that Libya was lending logistical support for the Chadian intervention. There was, however, considerable domestic opposition to Chad's involvement in the DRC. Following discussion of the conflict in the DRC at a summit meeting held under the auspices of COMESSA in Sirte, Libya, in April 1999, it was announced that Chad was to withdraw its troops from the DRC: the Chadian military began its departure in late May. Figures released by Chad's ministry of defence in June 1999 specified that 2,227

troops had been dispatched to the DRC in September 1998; the number of deaths within the Chadian contingent was confirmed as 105. Chad stated that it was holding 119 prisoners of war, among them 27 Ugandans and 10 Rwandans, and that Uganda was holding six Chadians. (Rwanda, notably, denied that any of its nationals was being held by Chad.) An exchange of prisoners was to take place under the auspices of the International Committee of the Red Cross. Meanwhile, the Chadian government denied that its decision to withdraw from the DRC reflected concern at the security situation in the Tibesti region.

Economy

EDITH HODGKINSON

Revised for this edition by the Editor

Chad is one of the poorest and least developed countries of continental Africa, and its geographical isolation, climate and meagre natural resources have resulted in an economy of very narrow range. The agricultural sector has traditionally dominated the economy, accounting for some 40% of Chad's gross domestic product (GDP) and four-fifths of the labour force. Virtually all of the country's limited industrial and commercial production facilities are located in or close to N'Djamena, the capital. Much economic activity is illicit, and very few statistics are published. There are hardly any all-weather roads and no railways. The country is land-locked and its major economic centres are situated 1,400–2,800 km from the sea. Its structural problems of economic development, immense in any circumstances, have been rendered still more acute by civil conflict and by drought. Consequently, for most of the period since independence, the authorities have had to focus on 'crisis management' rather than on the pursuit of a longer-term economic strategy. In any event, policies formulated in N'Djamena have tended to have limited impact in the remote hinterland of the centre and north and also in large parts of the disaffected south.

The country's recent economic performance has thus been poor. GDP contracted by one-quarter in 1977–81, recovered slightly overall in the 1980s (with wide fluctuations from year to year) and then declined by nearly one-fifth in 1989-1993. The 50% devaluation of the CFA franc in January 1994 stimulated the economy, benefiting both cotton and livestock production, and GDP increased by 10.2% in that year. The rate of growth slowed sharply to 0.9% in 1995, before increasing to 3.7% in 1996 and 4.1% in 1997 as a result of higher cotton prices and increased output, and despite drought in the latter year. The return of favourable rains in 1998, and consequent increase in food output, was a principal factor contributing to real GDP growth of some 7.0% in that year (notably achieved in spite of a decline in seed cotton production, as well as chronic fuel shortages and a consequent energy crisis). The IMF, supporting the government's reform programme under its enhanced structural adjustment facility (ESAF), projected growth of just 1.2% in 1999, as food production stabilized and output of ginned cotton declined to reflect the previous year's reduced cotton crop. While economic performance remains vulnerable to climatic conditions, and to world prices for a single commodity, the planned construction of a pipeline linking the oilfields in southern Chad to the Cameroonian port of Kribi should give a new impetus to economic growth, and offers the prospect of considerably higher income in the early years of the new century. Meanwhile, gross national product (GNP) per head, at US $230 in 1998, remains among the lowest in the world.

AGRICULTURE

The main area of crop production is situated in the south of the country, with cattle production prevailing in the more arid northern zones. In the extreme north camel- and sheep-rearing and date orchards are predominant. Subsistence agriculture accounts for three-quarters of annual crop production. The principal food crops are sorghum, millet and groundnuts. Cassava, rice, dates and maize are also grown for domestic consump-

tion. After declining dramatically to a 20-year low of 289,800 metric tons in 1984/85 as a consequence of drought resulting in a severe famine, cereal production recovered during the following decade, owing to generally adequate rainfall, to reach 1,059,000 tons in 1994/95. This was broadly sufficient to meet the country's annual requirement. Output declined to 907,300 tons in 1995/96, and, further, to 877,738 tons in 1996/97. The poor harvest in the latter year was in large part attributable to inadequate rainfall in the Sahelian region, exacerbated by bird damage and a reduction of the area cultivated to the profit of cotton, and resulted in a cereals deficit of some 200,000 tons. Favourable rains, in conjunction with increased planting and measures to counter pests, contributed to cereal production of 985,000 tons in 1997/98 and 1,296,000 tons in 1998/99. Some progress has been made in the cultivation of rice by modern methods. Rural development schemes, which have been implemented in southern Chad, with assistance from France, the European Union (EU), Canada and the World Bank, aim to increase production of cereals and livestock. However, major problems remain in the area of distribution and marketing, which have resulted in some localized scarcity.

Cotton is the dominant crop and principal export commodity. Production has been widely encouraged since the 1920s, and cotton was grown on some 336,000 ha in 1998/99, in the south of the country. Annual yields fluctuate widely, mainly reflecting rainfall patterns. Owing to civil conflict in the south in late 1984 and early 1985, and the decline in international prices for cotton in the following years, production declined to 89,500 metric tons in 1986/87, contributing to the substantial losses already incurred by the marketing monopoly, the Société cotonnière du Tchad (COTONTCHAD), largely as a result of mismanagement and corruption. This agency, which is presently 75% state-owned, is responsible for the provision of inputs and the purchasing, transportation, ginning and marketing of the crop, and the manufacture of cottonseed oil. In response to the near bankruptcy of COTONTCHAD in 1986, the country's donors contributed funds for its restructuring. The programme involved the closure of half of the cotton-ginning mills and the elimination of the subsidies on fertilizers and pesticides for farmers. Following the introduction of new pricing policies to provide greater incentives for production, seed cotton output increased to 174,516 tons in 1991/92. There was a sharp decline in output in the following two years, with only 94,943 tons recorded in 1993/94, as international prices weakened. However, the devaluation of the CFA franc in January 1994 was followed by a 50% increase in the producer price, which generated an immediate increase in output, to 156,756 tons in 1994/95. With world cotton prices rising strongly, producer prices were increased in each of the following two years, prompting more extensive planting and increased use of inputs. Additionally boosted by advantageous climatic conditions, marketed production of seed cotton reached an all-time record level of 261,292 tons in 1997/98; however, output declined to 220,000 tons in 1998/99. The IMF and World Bank regard the restructuring of COTONTCHAD as a priority, but there is considerable domestic opposition to the dismantling of the monopoly. A financial rehabilitation plan with regard to the state monopoly body was under way in 2000, including the appointment of a Controller General.

Gum arabic, which is harvested from traditional plantations in the north, is a minor export product. Output has been adversely affected by drought and the unstable political situation: in the late 1980s annual production averaged 200 metric tons (compared with the record level of 1,100 tons produced in 1969). As with cotton, currency devaluation stimulated exports, which were reported to have quadrupled in value, to $26m., in 1994. However, there has been little increase in levels of output in recent years (with annual growth rate averaging about 5%), as international prices remain low.

Livestock production has a significant role in the Chadian economy, accounting for 12% of GDP, and engaging about 40% of the labour force. It generally yields more in terms of cash income than the cotton industry, but much of this is not officially registered. Cattle raising is concentrated in the central part of the country, but as a result of drought cattle have moved southwards into the mainly-crop producing prefectures of Moyen-Chari and Mayo-Kebbi. Livestock is often exported illicitly, without payment of taxes, mainly to Nigeria where it is sold or bartered for consumer goods. In 1998, according to FAO estimates, there were some 5.58m. cattle and 7.40m. sheep and goats. In the long term there is considerable potential for livestock production in Chad, but its realization would require the upgrading of the herds and improvements in marketing arrangements. A large slaughterhouse has been constructed near N'Djamena, intended as the centre of an export-orientated meat industry: output was 18,351 metric tons in 1997. The abattoir was privatized in 1998. Fishing was an important economic activity in the Lake Chad region, but effectively ceased during the drought period in the early 1980s. However, the sector subsequently recovered; in 1997, according to data published by FAO, the total catch amounted to 85,000 metric tons.

MINING, MANUFACTURING AND POWER

Exploitation of proven deposits of petroleum has been inhibited by the high cost of importing plant and machinery long distances with poor or non-existent transport facilities. In response to the increase in the international price of petroleum during the 1970s, petroleum extraction began in the Sedigi region, to the north of Lake Chad, in 1977. However, output was very modest—about 1,500 barrels per day (b/d) in 1979/80—and the operation was subsequently suspended because of the precarious security situation. In 1988 an agreement was signed with a consortium led by Exxon, Shell and Chevron, for the establishment of a petroleum refinery to exploit the reserves in the Sedigi region, estimated at 70m. tons. (In 1992 Elf Aquitaine replaced Chevron in the consortium.) The project was abandoned in 1993, but in the same year exploration in the Doba Basin (in southern Chad) revealed reserves of petroleum now estimated at some 1,000m. barrels. The consortium of Exxon (through its affiliate Esso Exploration and Production Chad, Inc), Shell (Société Shell Tchadienne de Recherche et d'Exploitation) and Elf (Elf Hydrocarbures Tchad) planned to develop 300 wells and install a processing facility, and begin production from 2001: peak production, at a rate of 225,000 b/d, was expected within one year, with output projected over some 30 years. An agreement was signed in 1995 with the governments of Chad and Cameroon for the construction and operation of a 1,050-km pipeline to transport petroleum to the Cameroon port of Kribi. However, in November 1999, both Elf and Shell announced that they were to withdraw progressively from the project. By June 2000 the consortium consisted of Exxon Mobil (40%), Petronas of Malaysia (35%) and Chevron (25%). In that month the World Bank committed itself to providing a US $39.5m.-loan to Chad towards the project, a further $300m. was to be raised through a syndicated loan from private banks. The cost of the project was estimated to be $1,500m. for Chad and $3,700m. overall. Following a stipulation by the World Bank, the government adopted legislation whereby 80% of state revenue from the petroleum sector would be allotted to the development of educa-

tion, health and infrastructure. Nevertheless, environmental and human rights organizations expressed strong objections to the project. Meanwhile, a protocol between the government of Chad and Exxon, Shell and Elf, signed in November 1996, also provided for the development of the Sedigi field, with the construction of a pipeline to supply a refinery in the capital to commence in 2000. Total development costs were estimated at $80m.

Natron, found in pans on the northern edge of Lake Chad, is the only mineral of importance currently exploited in Chad. It is used as salt, for human and animal consumption, in the preservation of meats and hides and in soap production, and has been exported to Nigeria via the Logone river from N'Djamena. Alluvial gold and materials for the construction industry are also extracted. There is believed to be considerable potential for the further exploitation of gold deposits, particularly in the Mayo-Kebbi region, and for the development of bauxite and uranium reserves.

Manufacturing (which contributed 12.4% of GDP in 1998) is centred in N'Djamena and Moundou, and is mainly devoted to the processing of agricultural products. The processing of cotton is the principal industry; however, the importance of this sector declined during the 1980s, with the closure of one-half of COTONTCHAD's ginning mills (by the late 1980s annual ginning capacity was only 120,000 metric tons, compared with 184,000 tons at the beginning of the decade). The recovery in cotton production during the mid-1990s prompted COTONTCHAD to increase capacity at its eight mills in 1996/97. Meanwhile, production by the Sarh-based Société textile du Tchad, suspended in 1992 (principally as illicit imports from Nigeria had made domestic output of cotton thread and cloth uncompetitive), resumed in response to the positive effects of devaluation. The restructuring of COTONTCHAD, long promoted by the Bretton Woods institutions, appeared closer in 1999, with the separation of the oil and soap activities from the company under consideration. The transfer to majority private ownership of the Société sucrière du Tchad (SONASUT) was completed in April 2000, while the sale of the Abattoir frigorifique de Farcha, the state-owned slaughterhouse, had been completed earlier. There is a wide range of small-scale enterprises operating outside the recorded sector, including crafts and the production of agricultural implements, which make a significant contribution to employment and overall production.

Electricity in Chad is generated by two oil-powered plants operated by a public corporation, Société tchadienne d'eau et d'électricité (STEE); installed capacity is 29 MW. The annual output of electricity increased rapidly until the mid-1970s, but has since stagnated, as a result of the difficulties in importing petroleum. The utility has also been severely affected by persistent non-payment of bills, notably by other public sector enterprises. The project to refine petroleum from Sedigi domestically would significantly reduce Chad's dependence on imported fuel for the generation of electricity. An explosion at a Nigerian refinery in early 1998 resulted in a severe shortage in petroleum imports to Chad and the consequent major disruption of the electricity supply, which remained largely unresolved in mid-2000. Negotiations on the privatization of the STEE were initiated in late 1999, and France granted Chad a loan of US $4.8m. to aid the process in July 2000.

TRANSPORT

Transportation within Chad is inadequate and expensive. Communications with the outside world are difficult, slow and costly because of the great distance from the sea, the character of the trade, and poor facilities in neighbouring countries. The total length of the road network in 1996 was an estimated 33,400 km, but only some 500 km are paved. Transport limitations are a major obstacle to the country's economic development, and efforts are being made to improve the internal transport system (with help from the World Bank, the European Development Fund (EDF) and the USA), including the rehabilitation and construction of an ancillary road network as part of rural development in the south. The IMF has also overseen preparations for the privatization of the national road maintenance company, the Société Générale d'Entreprise Routière, in 2000. Some 250 km of tarred road between Abéché and N'Djamena has been completed, in a project funded by French aid, and the construction of a road linking N'Djamena to Mao is also under way. Transport infrastructural improvements in adjacent countries, especially in Cameroon, were expected to benefit Chad. The EU is contributing funds to the construction of a road linking Sarh and Léré, on the Cameroon border, and of a 400-km highway linking Moundou and Ngaoundéré, in northern Cameroon. A new land transport agreement was signed by the two countries in early 1999. Plans to extend the Transcameroon railway from Ngaoundéré to Sarh, in southern Chad, have, however, been postponed indefinitely. Inland waterways are significant, with 2,000 km of the Chari and Logone rivers navigable in all seasons. The international airport at N'Djamena is served by Air Afrique, in which Chad is a participant, and there are regular services to Sudan and northern Nigeria.

PUBLIC FINANCE

Economic decline and civil strife have exacerbated Chad's severe public-finance difficulties, which can be relieved only by substantial contributions from both international agencies and the country's allies, notably France and the USA. There is a deep and chronic deficit on the budget because of the low level of tax revenue, which is normally sufficient to cover only one-third of spending. Foreign aid has therefore been required to maintain basic government services. Since the mid-1980s, with the support of the IMF, the World Bank and the major bilateral donors, the government has attempted to increase revenue receipts (through increased taxes on petroleum products and luxury goods) and to reduce spending (for example, on subsidies for cotton production and on civil service employment). An austerity budget was announced in 1992, with a programme to restructure the civil service and to transfer a number of banks and state-owned enterprises to the private sector. Despite such efforts, however, the deficit (on a commitment basis, including grants) was 35,517m. francs CFA in 1993, equivalent to 12.2% of GDP. An important factor contributing to the continuing deficit was that of low revenues, depressed by falling customs receipts (the principal source of revenue) largely as the result of an increase in illicit trade across the Nigerian and Cameroonian borders. Revenue losses from illicit trade with Nigeria eased somewhat after the devaluation of the CFA franc in January 1994. In March of that year the government introduced a structural adjustment programme, supported by credits from the IMF and World Bank, which aimed to reduce the deficit on the primary budget (the balance before interest payments) from 6% in 1994 to 2.25% in 1995 and to produce a modest surplus of 1.25% by 1998. The funds from the World Bank were to be used, in part, for severance payments in the reduction in members of the armed forces. Only limited progress was made in 1994 and 1995, because any improvement in customs collection is difficult to achieve, while spending was under pressure from the sharp inflationary impact of devaluation. The government's economic programme, backed by an enhanced structural adjustment facility extended by the IMF in September 1995, again laid emphasis on improving revenue collection, and also included the introduction of a single turnover tax, effective from the beginning of 1997. Spending was to be controlled through reform of the large state enterprises (in cotton, sugar and electricity), including the sale of state equity, retrenchment in the civil service and a further reduction in the number of military personnel. A degree of progress was made in 1996, when domestic revenue increased by one-third (at current prices). However, in the same year current spending also increased (by almost 20%); the budget deficit thus increased once more, to 41,625m. francs CFA, from 31,802m. francs CFA in 1995. Excluding grants, the deficit in 1996 amounted to 92,242m. francs CFA. The shortfall stabilized at this level in 1997, as a 5.9% increase in spending was more than offset by an increase of 14.8% in budgetary receipts. Public finances continued to improve in 1998, although the adverse impact on the economy of the energy crisis meant that revenue, while 11% higher than in 1997 (as customs operations became more efficient), was, at 7.7% of GDP, 1.3% below the budgeted target. Current expenditure increased by less than 3%, with spending on non-priority sectors reduced by 20%, and efforts were strengthened to restrict the public-sector payroll. Spending on education and health was, none the less, increased

by some 30%. The overall deficit, excluding grants, was equivalent to 7.9% of GDP, compared with 10.2% in 1997 and continued to decrease in 1999 and the first half of 2000. A value-added tax was introduced in January 2000 and was expected to encourage further economic growth.

FOREIGN TRADE, AID AND PAYMENTS

While exports and imports have fluctuated widely as a result of the civil war, Chad's foreign trade has, almost without exception, shown a very large deficit, owing to the low level of production in the economy and the high cost of transport. The principal imports are food products (accounting for 19% of the cost of total imports in 1995) and petroleum. Cotton is the principal export commodity (contributing 66% of total export earnings in 1997), followed by meat and live animals (17%). In the late 1980s the decline in international prices for cotton resulted in a significant reduction in export revenue, while imports increased sharply, resulting in a substantial rise in the trade deficit to 35,000m. francs CFA in 1987, more than the total value of exports in that year. The subsequent rise in output of cotton and the improvement in international prices generated an increase in export earnings, and the trade deficit remained between 16,000m. and 20,000m. francs CFA for most of the early 1990s. The devaluation of the CFA franc in 1994 failed to reduce the imbalance in that year—the deficit was 16,150m. francs CFA—because, while export earnings more than doubled in CFA franc terms, import spending rose by almost the same rate as a result of the economy's high dependence on imports. The strong performance of cotton exports did, however, produce a modest surplus on foreign trade in 1995, of 15,880m. francs CFA, although the balance reverted to deficit in 1996. Exports increased by some 18.9% in 1997, largely as a result of a 34.3% increase in exports of cotton; however, the deficit in that year widened to 22,100m. francs CFA, as import spending rose by 19.6%—largely reflecting initial spending relating to the Doba scheme. The development of the Doba and Sedigi petroleum fields, and related public works and infrastructural projects, was expected to entail continued high levels of import spending into the next decade. The current account has been persistently in deficit, however, owing to the very high outflows on services, largely reflecting transport costs.

To offset the deficit Chad has relied heavily on foreign assistance, which has also been needed to fund basic budgetary requirements and any development expenditure, as well as the episodes of military activity. France has remained the principal supplier of aid, including direct budgetary assistance (60% of the bilateral aid disbursed in 1992–96 was of French origin). EU and other multilateral agencies and, more recently, Arab countries also provide substantial help, principally for agricultural and infrastructure projects. Net inflows of aid funds increased during the second half of the 1980s, to US $317m. in 1990, subsequently declining, prior to a dramatic rise in multilateral aid following the currency devaluation. Net multilateral aid is now greater than bilateral inflows, accounting for $180m. in 1996 out of a total of $305m. A large proportion of this aid is in the form of grants (71% in 1994–96). Aid inflows totalled $225m. in 1997.

Most of Chad's borrowing has been from government and other official sources, on highly concessionary terms. Consequently, while external debt has increased significantly, from US $284m. in 1980 to $1,091m. at the end of 1998, debt-servicing has remained relatively low, equivalent to 10.6% of earnings from exports of goods and services in the latter year, helped by good cotton export earnings. This modest level has also been due to failure to pay liabilities as they fall due (arrears on repayment were $30m. at the end of 1997), as well as debt relief accorded by France. The CFA franc's devaluation—which represented an immediate increase in the cost of debt-servicing—was followed by the cancellation of Chad's official debt to France. Moreover, in February 1995 Chad was granted enhanced relief on its debt to official bilateral creditors under the 'Naples terms' (which apply to countries with a high debt-to-export ratio or particularly low GNP per head). However, as the greater part of Chad's foreign debt is to multilateral institutions (73% of the total at the end of 1997), and hence not eligible for debt relief, there is little scope for a reduction in the already low burden of debt service. Also, while petroleum development holds out the prospect of much improved foreign earnings in the next decade, this and other efforts to develop the economy could be affected by political developments. Meanwhile, the reconstruction task remains substantial.

Statistical Survey

Source (unless otherwise stated): Direction de la Statistique, des Etudes Economiques et Démographiques, BP 453, N'Djamena.

Area and Population

AREA, POPULATION AND DENSITY

Area (sq km)	
Land	1,259,200
Inland waters	24,800
Total	1,284,000*
Population (sample survey)	
December 1963–August 1964 . . .	3,254,000†
Population (census result)	
8 April 1993‡	
Males	2,950,415
Females	3,208,577
Total	6,158,992
Population (official estimate at mid-year)	
1994	6,214,000§
Density (per sq km) at mid-1994	4.9§

* 495,800 sq miles.
† Including areas not covered by the survey.
‡ Figures are provisional. The revised total, including an adjustment for underenumeration (estimated at 1.4%), is 6,279,931.
§ Not revised to take account of the 1993 census result (see above).

PREFECTURES (official estimates, mid-1988)

	Area (sq km)	Population	Density (per sq km)
Batha	88,800	431,000	4.9
Biltine	46,850	216,000	4.6
Borkou-Ennedi-Tibesti (BET) .	600,350	109,000	0.2
Chari-Baguirmi . . .	82,910	844,000	10.2
Guera	58,950	254,000	4.3
Kanem	114,520	245,000	2.1
Lac	22,320	165,000	7.4
Logone Occidental . . .	8,695	365,000	42.0
Logone Oriental . . .	28,035	377,000	13.4
Mayo-Kebbi . . .	30,105	852,000	28.3
Moyen Chari . . .	45,180	646,000	14.3
Ouaddaï	76,240	422,000	5.5
Salamat	63,000	131,000	2.1
Tandjilé	18,045	371,000	20.6
Total	1,284,000	5,428,000	4.2

Note: As a result of administrative reform, Chad's former prefectures have been replaced by the following departments: Assongha (capital Adre), Bahr el Gazal (Moussoro), Bahr Koh (Sarh), Baguirmi (Massenya), Batha Est (Oum-Hadjer), Batha Ouest (Ati), Biltine (Biltine), Bourkou (Faya), Dababa (Bokoro), Ennedi (Fada), Guéra (Mongo), Hadjer Lamis (Massaguet), Kabia (Gonou Gaya), Kanem (Mao), Lac (Bol), Lac Iro (Kyabe), Logone Occidental (Moundou), Logone Oriental (Doba), Mandoul (Koumra), Mayo-Dala (Pala), Mayo Boneye (Bongor), Monts de Lam (Mbaibokoum), Ouaddaï (Abéché), Salamat (Am-Timan), Sila (Goz-Beida), Tandjilé Est (Lai), Tandjilé Ouest (Kélo), Tibesti (Bardai).

PRINCIPAL TOWNS (officially-estimated population in 1988)

N'Djamena (capital) .	594,000	Moundou . . .	102,000
Sarh	113,400	Abéché . . .	83,000

BIRTHS AND DEATHS (UN estimates, annual averages)

	1980–85	1985–90	1990–95
Birth rate (per 1,000) . . .	49.1	47.7	46.7
Death rate (per 1,000) . .	22.4	20.5	19.3

Expectation of life (UN estimates, years at birth, 1990–95): 45.9 (males 44.4; females 47.5).

Source: UN, *World Population Prospects: The 1998 Revision.*

ECONOMICALLY ACTIVE POPULATION
(ILO estimates, '000 persons at mid-1980)

	Males	Females	Total
Agriculture, etc.	1,043	318	1,361
Industry.	72	4	76
Services	154	44	197
Total labour force . . .	1,269	366	1,635

Source: ILO, *Economically Active Population Estimates and Projections, 1950–2025.*

1993 census (persons aged six years and over): Total labour force 2,719,443 (males 1,416,449; females 1,302,994) (Source: ILO, *Yearbook of Labour Statistics*).

Mid-1998 (estimates in '000): Agriculture, etc. 2,604; Total 3,382 (Source: FAO, *Production Yearbook*).

Agriculture

PRINCIPAL CROPS ('000 metric tons)

	1996	1997	1998
Wheat	1	4	1
Rice (paddy) . . .	98	112	100
Maize	75	99	173
Millet	258	248	366
Sorghum . . .	453	521	637
Other cereals . .	90	93	92
Potatoes* . . .	8	8	8
Sweet potatoes . .	58	60*	65*
Cassava (Manioc) . .	268	250*	275
Yams*	240	240	240
Taro (Coco yam)* . .	38	38	38
Dry beans . . .	21	24	53
Other pulses . . .	20	20	20
Groundnuts (in shell) .	305	352	471
Sesame seed . . .	13	26	15
Cottonseed . . .	125*	120	146
Cotton (lint) . . .	86	86	103
Dry onions* . . .	14	14	14
Other vegetables* . .	88	87	87
Dates*	18	18	18
Mangoes* . . .	32	32	32
Other fruit* . . .	60	65	65
Sugar cane . . .	330	330*	280*

* FAO estimate(s).

Source: FAO, *Production Yearbook.*

LIVESTOCK ('000 head, year ending September)

	1996	1997	1998
Cattle	4,860	5,451	5,582
Goats	3,918	4,824	4,968
Sheep	2,317	2,361	2,432
Pigs	18*	19*	23†
Horses	224*	228*	228†
Asses	275*	280*	280†
Camels	632	677*	677†

Poultry (million)†: 5 in 1996; 5 in 1997; 5 in 1998.

* Unofficial figure.   † FAO estimate(s).

Source: FAO, *Production Yearbook*.

LIVESTOCK PRODUCTS (FAO estimates, '000 metric tons)

	1996	1997	1998
Beef and veal	38	39	40
Mutton and lamb	12	12	12
Goat meat	13	13	14
Poultry meat	4	4	5
Other meat	5	6	4
Cows' milk	123	123	123
Sheep's milk	10	10	10
Goats' milk	22	23	23
Poultry eggs	4	4	4
Cattle hides	6	6	6
Sheepskins	2	2	2
Goatskins	2	2	2

Source: FAO, *Production Yearbook*.

Forestry

ROUNDWOOD REMOVALS ('000 cubic metres, excl. bark)

	1995	1996	1997
Sawlogs, veneer logs and logs for sleepers	14	14	14
Other industrial wood	634	652	671
Fuel wood	3,864	3,977	4,091
Total	4,512	4,643	4,776

Source: FAO, *Yearbook of Forest Products*.

SAWNWOOD PRODUCTION ('000 cubic metres, incl. railway sleepers)

	1995	1996	1997
Total (all broadleaved)	2	2	2*

* FAO estimate.

Source: FAO, *Yearbook of Forest Products*.

Fishing

('000 metric tons, live weight)

	1995	1996	1997
Total catch (freshwater fishes)	90.0	100.0	85.0

Source: FAO, *Yearbook of Fishery Statistics*.

Industry

SELECTED PRODUCTS

	1996	1997	1998
Edible oil ('000 hectolitres)	114.1	156.1	160.0
Sugar ('000 metric tons)	35.0	33.0	29.0
Beer ('000 hectolitres)	118.2	123.0	135.0
Cigarettes (million)	700	780	860
Woven cotton fabrics (million metres)	0.8	1.0	1.1
Electric energy (million kWh)	92.1	81.2	74.9

Source: IMF, *Chad—Recent Economic Developments* (May 1999).

Finance

CURRENCY AND EXCHANGE RATES

Monetary Units
100 centimes = 1 franc de la Coopération financière en Afrique centrale (CFA).

Sterling, Dollar and Euro Equivalents (28 April 2000)
£1 sterling = 1,132.20 francs CFA;
US $1 = 722.02 francs CFA;
€1 = 655.96 francs CFA;
10,000 francs CFA = £8.832 = $13.850 = €15.245.

Average Exchange Rate (francs CFA per US $)
1997   583.67
1998   589.95
1999   615.70

Note: An exchange rate of 1 French franc = 50 francs CFA, established in 1948, remained in force until January 1994, when the CFA franc was devalued by 50%, with the exchange rate adjusted to 1 French franc = 100 francs CFA. This relationship to French currency remained in effect with the introduction of the euro on 1 January 1999. From that date, accordingly, a fixed exchange rate of €1 = 655.957 francs CFA has been in operation.

BUDGET ('000 million francs CFA)

Revenue*	1996	1997	1998†
Tax revenue	53.0	61.3	69.8
Taxes on income and profits	21.5	21.6	22.6
Companies	11.9	9.7	10.7
Individuals	8.5	10.8	10.6
Employers' payroll tax	1.1	1.0	1.4
Taxes on goods and services	11.1	17.0	14.4
Turnover tax	6.5	10.8	8.5
Tax on petroleum products	2.9	3.4	3.5
Taxes on international trade	18.6	20.7	27.4
Import taxes	17.0	18.7	25.7
Export taxes	0.9	1.4	1.3
Other tax revenues	1.9	2.1	5.4
Other revenue	6.5	7.1	6.5
Property income	0.4	1.3	1.3
Total	59.6	68.4	76.2

Expenditure‡			1996	1997	1998†
Current expenditure	.	.	77.2	73.5	75.4
Primary current expenditure		.	64.4	61.3	65.7
Wages and salaries	.	.	30.8	30.8	31.5
Materials and supplies	.	.	17.1	14.6	16.1
Transfers	.	.	3.9	6.1	8.6
Defence	.	.	12.7	9.7	9.5
Salaries	.	.	10.7	8.4	8.3
Elections	.	.	3.8	0.3	0.0
Interest	.	.	8.4	8.5	8.9
External	.	.	7.1	7.0	7.5
Investment expenditure	.	.	74.6	85.4	78.4
Foreign-financed	.	.	74.0	81.4	73.3
Total	.	.	151.8	158.9	153.8

* Excluding grants received ('000 million francs CFA): 50.6 in 1996; 56.4 in 1997; 50.9 (provisional) in 1998.
† Preliminary figures.
‡ Excluding adjustment for payments arrears.
Source: IMF, *Chad: Recent Economic Developments* (May 1999).

INTERNATIONAL RESERVES (US $ million at 31 December)

			1997	1998	1999
Gold*	.	.	n.a.	3.20	n.a.
IMF special drawing rights	.	.	0.01	0.01	0.03
Reserve position in IMF	.	.	0.38	0.40	0.39
Foreign exchange	.	.	135.44	119.68	94.60
Total	.	.	n.a.	123.29	n.a.

* Valued at market-related prices.
Source: IMF, *International Financial Statistics*.

MONEY SUPPLY ('000 million francs CFA at 31 December)

	1997	1998	1999
Currency outside banks .	78.81	73.62	68.25
Demand deposits at commercial and development banks	27.11	25.38	27.80
Total money (incl. others) .	108.47	99.75	96.67

Source: IMF, *International Financial Statistics*.

COST OF LIVING (Consumer Price Index for African households in N'Djamena; base: 1995 = 100)

	1997	1998	1999
All items . . .	118.7	133.1	124.1

Source: IMF, *International Financial Statistics*.

NATIONAL ACCOUNTS
('000 million francs CFA at current prices)
Expenditure on the Gross Domestic Product

	1996	1997	1998
Government final consumption expenditure . . .	100.4	97.0	94.1
Private final consumption expenditure . . .	752.9	803.9	887.8
Increase in stocks . . .	13.0	16.8	5.0
Gross fixed capital formation .	98.8	128.0	144.6
Total domestic expenditure .	965.2	1,045.7	1,131.5
Exports of goods and services .	144.7	155.7	180.5
Less Imports of goods and services .	279.2	313.5	327.8
GDP in purchasers' values .	830.7	887.9	984.2

Gross Domestic Product by Economic Activity

			1996	1997	1998
Agriculture*	.	.	285.0	306.1	348.6
Mining and quarrying†	.	.	23.5	25.8	28.1
Electricity, gas and water.	.		5.4	5.5	5.4
Manufacturing	.	.	92.5	110.6	117.8
Construction	.	.	13.8	14.4	15.4
Wholesale and retail trade, restaurants and hotels . . }			204.2	214.2	239.9
Transport and communications					
Public administration	.	.	98.6	95.0	104.7
Other services	.	.	85.2	91.0	92.1
GDP at factor cost .	.	.	808.2	862.6	951.9
Indirect taxes, *less* subsidies .	.		22.5	25.3	32.3
GDP in purchasers' values .	.		830.7	887.9	984.2

* Excluding fishing.   † Including fishing.
Source: IMF, *Chad: Recent Economic Developments* (May 1999).

BALANCE OF PAYMENTS ('000 million francs CFA)

			1996	1997	1998
Exports of goods f.o.b.	.	.	113.1	123.2	145.3
Imports of goods f.o.b.	.	.	−148.0	−165.5	−175.0
Trade balance .	.	.	−34.9	−42.3	−29.7
Exports of services	.	.	31.6	32.5	35.2
Imports of services	.	.	−131.2	−148.0	−152.8
Balance on goods and services			−134.4	−157.8	−147.2
Other income (net)	.	.	−16.6	−17.0	−17.9
Balance on goods, services and income	.	.	−151.0	−174.8	−165.1
Current transfers (net)	.	.	50.0	41.6	43.5
Current balance	.	.	−101.0	−133.2	−121.6
Capital account	.	.	36.4	36.1	28.4
Direct investment (net)	.	.	7.6	9.2	15.8
Other investment (net)	.	.	64.1	75.4	81.9
Net errors and omissions .	.	.	13.7	6.3	−9.6
Overall balance	.	.	20.7	−6.2	−5.1

Source: IMF, *Chad: Recent Economic Developments* (May 1999).

External Trade

PRINCIPAL COMMODITIES

Imports c.i.f. (US $'000)	1995
Food and live animals	41,182
Cereals and cereal preparations	16,028
Rice (semi- or wholly-milled) . . .	4,589
Wheat and meslin (unmilled) . . .	8,945
Sugar, sugar preparations and honey . . .	17,078
Sugar and honey	16,970
Refined sugars, etc.. . . .	16,825
Beverages and tobacco	7,175
Beverages	4,526
Mineral fuels, lubricants, etc.	38,592
Petroleum, petroleum products, etc.	38,574
Refined petroleum products	38,551
Motor spirit (gasoline) and other light oils .	6,490
Kerosene and other medium oils . .	8,456
Gas oils	23,318
Chemicals and related products	15,507
Medicinal and pharmaceutical products . . .	7,789
Medicaments (incl. veterinary medicaments) .	6,351
Basic manufactures	26,190
Non-metallic mineral manufactures	7,654
Lime, cement and fabricated construction materials .	6,394
Cement	6,247
Metal manufactures	8,804

Imports c.i.f. (US $'000) — *continued*	1995
Machinery and transport equipment . . .	51,246
General industrial machinery, equipment and parts . .	8,175
Telecommunications and sound recording and reproducing	
equipment and parts . .	4,572
Telecommunications equipment and parts . . .	4,375
Road vehicles (incl. air-cushion vehicles) and parts* .	17,873
Motor vehicles for the transport of goods or materials,	
etc. . .	4,444
Lorries and trucks	4,338
Parts and accessories for cars, lorries, buses, etc.* . .	8,253
Miscellaneous manufactured articles . . .	27,335
Professional, scientific and controlling instruments and	
apparatus	5,073
Printed matter	13,565
Postage stamps, banknotes, etc.	11,622
Total (incl. others)	215,171

* Excluding tyres, engines and electrical parts.

Source: UN, *International Trade Statistics Yearbook*.

Exports (million francs CFA)	1983
Live cattle	49.5
Meat	23.5
Fish	2.0
Oil-cake	8.1
Natron	8.1
Gums and resins	0.4
Hides and skins	16.6
Raw cotton	3,753.7
Total (incl. others)	4,120.0

Total exports (million francs CFA): 27,781 in 1985; 34,145 in 1986; 32,892 in 1987; 42,900 in 1988; 49,570 in 1989; 51,202 in 1990; 54,600 in 1991; 48,250 in 1992; 37,330 in 1993; 82,160 in 1994; 125,600 in 1995; 117,230 in 1996; 138,100 in 1997. (Source: Banque des Etats de l'Afrique Centrale).

Cotton exports ('000 million francs CFA): 26.8 in 1991; 25.3 in 1992.

PRINCIPAL TRADING PARTNERS

Imports c.i.f. (US $'000)	1995
Belgium-Luxembourg	4,771
Cameroon	33,911
Central African Repub.	3,010
China, People's Repub.	6,251
France	88,887
Germany	2,988
Italy	6,452
Japan	5,121
Malaysia	2,234
Netherlands	2,843
Nigeria	25,269
Spain	3,402
USA	13,966
Total (incl. others)	215,171

Source: UN, *International Trade Statistics Yearbook*.

Exports (million francs CFA)	1984	1985	1986
Cameroon	929	1,711	2,661
Central African Repub. . .	64	1,219	321
France	6,950	1,432	1,774
Nigeria	113	1,981	425
Sudan	8	47	101
Congo, Democratic Repub. . .	125	5	n.a.
Total (incl. others) . . .	8,231	6,446	5,374

Transport

ROAD TRAFFIC (motor vehicles in use at 31 December)

	1994	1995*	1996*
Passenger cars . . .	8,720	9,700	10,560
Buses and coaches . . .	708	760	820
Lorries and vans	12,650	13,720	14,550
Tractors . . .	1,413	1,500	1,580
Motorcycles and mopeds . .	1,855	2,730	3,640

* Estimates.

Source: International Road Federation, *World Road Statistics*.

CIVIL AVIATION (traffic on scheduled services*)

	1994	1995	1996
Kilometres flown (million) . .	2	3	3
Passengers carried ('000) . .	86	92	93
Passengers-km (million) . .	222	231	233
Total ton-km (million) . .	35	37	37

* Including an apportionment of the traffic of Air Afrique.

Source: UN, *Statistical Yearbook*.

Tourism

	1996	1997	1998
Tourist arrivals ('000) . . .	8	9	11
Tourism receipts (US $ million)	10	n.a.	n.a.

Source: World Tourism Organization, *Yearbook of Tourism Statistics*.

Communications Media

	1994	1995	1996
Radio receivers ('000 in use) . .	1,520	1,570	1,620
Television receivers ('000 in use) .	9	9	9
Telephones ('000 main lines in use) .	5	5	6
Telefax stations (number in use) .	140	174	175
Daily newspapers:			
Number	1	1	1
Average circulation ('000 copies)	2	2	2
Non-daily newspapers:			
Number	n.a.	2	n.a.
Average circulation ('000 copies)	n.a.	10	n.a.

1997 ('000 in use): Radio receivers 1,670; Television receivers 10.

Sources: UNESCO, *Statistical Yearbook*; UN *Statistical Yearbook*.

Education

(1996/97, unless otherwise indicated)

	Insti-tutions	Teachers	Students Males	Students Females	Students Total
Pre-primary* . .	24	67	938	735	1,673
Primary . . .	2,660†	10,151	447,685	233,224	680,909
Secondary:					
General . .	153†	2,598	77,622	19,389	97,011
Teacher training .	6†	46	360	265	625
Vocational . .	12†	148	1,506	647	2,153
University-level† . .	n.a.	288	2,868‡	406‡	3,274‡

* 1994/95 figures; public education only.

† 1995/96 figures.

‡ Provisional figure.

Source: mainly UNESCO, *Statistical Yearbook*.

Directory

The Constitution

The Constitution of the Republic of Chad, which was adopted by national referendum on 31 March 1996, enshrines a unitary state. The President is elected for a term of five years by direct universal adult suffrage, and is restricted to a maximum of two terms in office. The Prime Minister, who is appointed by the President, nominates the Council of Ministers. The bicameral legislature includes a 125-member Assemblée nationale, which is elected by direct universal adult suffrage for a term of four years. Provision is also made for an upper legislative chamber, the Sénat, with one-third of members renewed every two years. The Constitution provides for an independent judicial system, with a High Court of Justice, and the establishment of a Constitutional Court and a High Council for Communication.

The Government

HEAD OF STATE

President and Commander-in-Chief of the Armed Forces: IDRISS DEBY (assumed office 4 December 1990; elected President 3 August 1996).

COUNCIL OF MINISTERS
(August 2000)

Prime Minister: NAGOUM YAMASSOUM.

Minister of State, Minister of Agriculture: SALEH KEBZABO.

Minister of the Economy, Territorial Development and Co-operation: AHMAT LAMINE ALI.

Minister of Foreign Affairs and Co-operation: MAHAMAT SALEH ANNADIF.

Minister of Mines, Energy and Petroleum: MOCTAR MOUSSA.

Minister of Finance: MAHAMAT ALI HASSANE.

Minister of National Defence and Reintegration: WEIDING ASSI-ASSOUE.

Minister of the Interior, Security and Decentralization: ABDERAHMANE MOUSSA.

Minister of Justice, Keeper of the Seals: MAHAMAT HAMAT ALABO.

Minister of Livestock: MAHAMAT NOURI.

Minister of Public Health: NADJO ABDELKERIM.

Minister of Higher Education: LAOUKISSAM NISSALA.

Minister of National Education: ABDERAHIM BREME HAMID.

Minister of Industrial and Commercial Development and Crafts: SALIBOU GARBA.

Minister of Communications, Delegate to the Parliament, Spokesperson for the Government: MAHAMAT LOANI.

Minister of Social Welfare and the Family: FATIME KIMTO.

Minister of the Environment and Water Resources: OUMAR BOUKAR KADJALAMI.

Minister of Tourism Development: ABBA KOI DJOUASSAB.

Minister of Civil Service, Labour, Employment Promotion and Modernization: ROUTOUANG YOMA GOLOM.

Minister of Public Works, Transport, Housing and Town Planning: BICHARA CHÉRIF DAOUSSA.

Minister of Posts and Telecommunications: MOUADJIDIBAYE TITINGAR.

Minister of Culture, Youth and Sports: MAHAMAT AHMAT CHOUKOU.

Minister, Secretary-General of the Government, in charge of Relations with Parliament: DAVID HOUDEINGAR.

MINISTRIES

All of the ministries are located in N'Djamena.

Office of the President: N'Djamena; tel. 51-44-37.

Ministry of Agriculture: BP 441, N'Djamena; tel. 52-21-48; fax 52-51-19.

Ministry of the Civil Service, Labour, Employment Promotion and Modernization: BP 437, N'Djamena; tel. and fax 52-21-98.

Ministry of Communications: BP 154, N'Djamena; tel. 51-41-64; fax 51-60-94.

Ministry of Culture, Youth and Sports: N'Djamena.

Ministry of Finance and the Economy: BP 144, N'Djamena; tel. 52-21-61; fax 52-49-08.

Ministry of Foreign Affairs and Co-operation: N'Djamena; tel. 51-50-82.

Ministry of Industrial and Commercial Development and Crafts: BP 458, N'Djamena; tel. 52-30-49; fax 52-27-33.

Ministry of Justice: N'Djamena; tel. 51-56-56.

Ministry of Livestock: N'Djamena; tel. 51-59-07.

Ministry of Mines, Energy and Petroleum: BP 94, N'Djamena; tel. 51-56-03; fax 52-25-65.

Ministry of National Defence: N'Djamena; tel. 51-58-89.

Ministry of Posts and Telecommunications: BP 154, N'Djamena; tel. 51-41-64; fax 51-28-35.

Ministry of Public Health: N'Djamena; tel. 51-39-60.

Ministry of Public Works, Transport, Housing and Town Planning: BP 436, N'Djamena; tel. 51-20-96.

President and Legislature

PRESIDENT

In a first round of voting, which took place on 2 June 1996, none of the 15 candidates secured the requisite 50% of total votes cast. A second round of voting took place on 3 July: the incumbent, President IDRISS DEBY, was elected by 69.1% of the votes, while the other candidate, Gen. WADAL ABDELKADER KAMOUGUÉ, received 30.9%.

ASSEMBLÉE NATIONALE

President: Gen. WADAL ABDELKADER KAMOUGUÉ.

General Election, 5 January and 23 February 1997

Party	Seats
Mouvement patriotique du salut	65
Union pour le renouveau et la démocratie	29
Union nationale pour le développement et le renouveau	15
Union pour la démocratie et la République	4
Parti pour la liberté et le développement	3
Rassemblement pour la démocratie et le progrès	3
Other opposition parties	6
Total	**125**

Note: The Constitution also makes provision for an upper house of the legislature, the Sénat.

Political Organizations

Legislation permitting the operation of political associations, subject to official registration, took effect in October 1991. In late 1999 there were about 60 active political organizations, of which the most important are listed below.

Action pour l'unité et le socialisme (ACTUS): N'Djamena; f. 1992; Leader Dr FIDÈLE MOUNGAR.

Alliance nationale pour la démocratie et le développement (ANDD): BP 4066, N'Djamena; tel. 51-46-72; f. 1992; Leader SALIBOU GARBA.

Comité de sursaut national pour la paix et la démocratie (CSNPD): fmr dissident faction; obtained legal recognition in Sept. 1994; Leader (vacant).

Concertation nationale pour la démocratie sociale (CNDS): N'Djamena; Leader ADOUM MOUSSA SEIF.

Front des forces d'action pour la République (FAR): Leader NGARLEDJY YORONGAR (sentenced to three years' imprisonment in July 1998).

Mouvement patriotique du salut (MPS): N'Djamena; f. 1990 as a coalition of several opposition movements; other opposition groups joined during the Nov. 1990 offensive against the regime of Hissène Habré, and following the movement's accession to power in Dec. 1990; Chair. MALDOM BADA ABBAS; Sec.-Gen. MAHAMAT SALEH AHMAT.

Mouvement pour la démocratie et le socialisme du Tchad (MDST): N'Djamena; Leader Dr SALOMON NGARBAYE TOMBALBAYE.

Parti pour la liberté et le développement (PLD): N'Djamena; f. 1993; Leader IBN OUMAR MAHAMAT SALEH.

Rassemblement pour la démocratie et le progrès (RDP): N'Djamena; f. 1992; Leader LOL MAHAMAT CHOUA.

Rassemblement pour le développement et le progrès: f. 1992; Leader MAMADOU BISSO.

Rassemblement national pour la démocratie et le progrès (RNDP): N'Djamena; f. 1992; Pres. KASSIRE DELWA KOUMAKOYE.

Union pour la démocratie et la République (UDR): N'Djamena; f. 1992; Leader Dr JEAN ALINGUE BAWOYEU.

Union nationale pour le développement et le renouveau (UNDR): Leader SALEH KEBZABO.

Union pour le renouveau et la démocratie (URD): BP 92, N'Djamena; tel. 51-44-23; fax 51-41-87; f. 1992; Leader Gen. WADAL ABDELKADER KAMOUGUÉ.

A number of unregistered dissident groups (some based abroad) are also active. These 'politico-military' organizations include the **Conseil démocratique révolutionnaire (CDR)**, led by ACHEIKH IBN OUMAR; the **Front de libération nationale du Tchad (FROLINAT)**, based in Algeria and led by GOUKOUNI OUEDDEI; the **Front national du Tchad (FNT)**, based in Sudan and led by Dr FARIS BACHAR; the **Front national du Tchad renové (FNTR)**, led by AHMAT YACOUB; the **Mouvement pour la démocratie et le développement (MDD)**, led by ISSA FAKI MAHAMAT; the **Mouvement pour la démocratie et la justice au Tchad (MDJT)**, led by YOUSSOUF TOGOIMI; the **Mouvement pour l'unité et la République (MUR;** f. 2000 as a breakaway faction of the MDD), led by GAILETH GATOUL BOURKOUMANDAH; the **Résistance armée contre les forces antidémocratiques (RAFAD)**, based in northern Nigeria, under the chairmanship of ADOUM MOUSSA SEIF; and the **Union des forces démocratiques (UFD)**, led by Dr MAHAMAT NAHOUR.

Under the terms of a peace agreement signed by the Chadian Government and the **Forces armées pour la République fédérale (FARF)** in April 1997 (the terms of which were renewed in May 1998), the FARF was to cease armed activities and was to be legalized as a political organization. The FARF, reportedly under the leadership of DIENAMBAYE BARDE, rallied to the MPS in November 1998. The former MDD leader, MOUSSA MEDELLA MAHAMAT, signed a reconciliation document, on behalf of the movement, with the government in July 1999, but the accord was denounced by the present MDD leadership.

Diplomatic Representation

EMBASSIES IN CHAD

Algeria: N'Djamena; tel. 51-38-15; Ambassador: MOHAMED CHELLALI KHOURI.

Central African Republic: BP 115, N'Djamena; tel. 51-32-06; Ambassador: DAVID NGUINDO.

Congo, Democratic Republic: ave du 20 août, BP 910, N'Djamena; tel. 51-59-35; Ambassador: (vacant).

Egypt: BP 1094, N'Djamena; tel. 51-36-60; Ambassador: AZIZ M. NOUR EL-DIN.

France: BP 431, N'Djamena; tel. 52-25-75; fax 52-28-55; e-mail amba-france@intnet.td; internet www.tit.td/amba-france; Ambassador: JACQUES COURBIN.

Germany: ave Félix Eboué, BP 893, N'Djamena; tel. 51-62-02; fax 51-48-00; Chargé d'affaires a.i.: DIETER FREUND.

Holy See: BP 490, N'Djamena; tel. 52-31-15; fax 52-38-27; Apostolic Nuncio: Most Rev. JOSEPH CHENNOTH, Titular Archbishop of Milevi.

Libya: N'Djamena; Sec. of People's Bureau: GHAYTH SALIM.

Nigeria: 35 ave Charles de Gaulle, BP 752, N'Djamena; tel. 51-24-98; Chargé d'affaires a.i.: A. M. ALIYU BIU.

Sudan: BP 45, N'Djamena; tel. 51-34-97; Ambassador: TAHA MAKKAWI.

USA: ave Félix Eboué, BP 413, N'Djamena; tel. 51-70-09; fax 51-56-54; e-mail usis@intnet.td; internet usembassy.state.gov/posts/cd1/wwwhm001.html; Ambassador: CHRISTOPHER GOLDTHWAITE.

Judicial System

The highest judicial authority is the Supreme Court. There is also a Constitutional Council, with final jurisdiction in matters of state. The legal structure also comprises the Court of Appeal, and Magistrate and Criminal Courts. Under the terms of the Constitution adopted in 1996, a High Court of Justice was to be established.

President of the Supreme Court: AHMAT BATCHIRET.

President of the Constitutional Council: NAGOUM YAMASSOUM.

Religion

It is estimated that some 50% of the population are Muslims and about 30% Christians. Most of the remainder follow animist beliefs.

ISLAM

Conseil Suprème des Affaires Islamiques: POB 1101, N'Djamena; tel. 51-81-80; fax 52-58-84.

Head of the Islamic Community: Imam MOUSSA IBRAHIM.

CHRISTIANITY

The Roman Catholic Church

Chad comprises one archdiocese and six dioceses. At 31 December 1998 Roman Catholics numbered an estimated 463,103 (about 6.8% of the total population).

Bishops' Conference: Conférence Episcopale du Tchad, BP 456, N'Djamena; tel. 51-44-43; fax 51-28-60; f. 1991; Pres. Most Rev. CHARLES VANDAME, Archbishop of N'Djamena.

Archbishop of N'Djamena: Most Rev. CHARLES VANDAME, Archevêché, BP 456, N'Djamena; tel. 51-74-44; fax 52-50-51; e-mail diocndja@intnet.td.

Protestant Churches

Entente des Eglises et Missions Evangéliques au Tchad: BP 2006, N'Djamena; tel. and fax 51-53-93; an asscn of churches and missions working in Chad; includes Assemblées Chrétiennes au Tchad (ACT), Eglise Evangélique des Frères au Tchad (EEFT), Eglise Evangélique au Tchad (EET), Eglise Fraternelle Luthérienne au Tchad (EFLT); also five assoc. mems.

BAHÁ'Í FAITH

National Spiritual Assembly: BP 181, N'Djamena; tel. 51-47-05; mems in 1,125 localities.

The Press

Al-Watan: BP 407, N'Djamena; tel. 51-57-96; weekly; Editor-in-Chief MOUSSA NDORKOÏ.

Bulletin Mensuel de Statistiques du Tchad: BP 453, N'Djamena; monthly.

Comnat: BP 731, N'Djamena; tel. 51-46-75; fax 51-46-71; quarterly; publ. by Commission Nationale Tchadienne for UNESCO.

Contact: N'Djamena; f. 1989; current affairs; Dir KOULAMALO SOURADJ.

Info-Tchad: BP 670, N'Djamena; tel. 51-58-67; news bulletin issued by Agence Tchadienne de Presse; daily; French.

Informations Economiques: BP 458, N'Djamena; publ. by the Chambre de Commerce, d'Agriculture et d'Industrie; weekly.

N'Djamena Hebdo: BP 760, N'Djamena; tel. 51-53-14; fax 52-14-98; weekly; Arabic and French; Editor-in-Chief DIEUDONNÉ DJONABAYE.

L'Observateur: N'Djamena; fortnightly; Editor-in-Chief SINGA GALI KOUMBA.

Le Progrès: N'Djamena; daily.

NEWS AGENCIES

Agence Tchadienne de Presse (ATP): BP 670, N'Djamena; tel. 51-58-67.

Foreign Bureaux

Agence France-Presse (AFP): N'Djamena; tel. 51-54-71; Correspondent ALDOM NADJI TITO.

Publisher

Government Publishing House: BP 453, N'Djamena.

Broadcasting and Communications

TELECOMMUNICATIONS

Office Nationale des Postes et des Télécommunications (ONPT): BP 154, N'Djamena; tel. 52-14-28; fax 51-28-35; state-owned; Dir-Gen. ALHOKI BLAMKAKOU.

The ONPT was to be reorganized into two structures, the **Société des Télécommunications du Tchad (SOTE—TCHAD)** and the **Société Tchadienne des Postes et de l'Epargne (STPE)**, prior to the privatization of the telecommunications sector. A tender was issued in late 1998 for a licence to operate the country's first cellular telephone network.

Société des Télécommunications Internationales du Tchad (TIT): BP 1132, N'Djamena; tel. 51-57-82; fax 51-50-66; internet www.tit.td; f. 1976; 52% state-owned; Man. Dir MAHAMAT S. ANNADIF.

BROADCASTING
Radio

Radiodiffusion Nationale Tchadienne: BP 892, N'Djamena; tel. 51-60-71; state-controlled; programmes in French, Arabic and eight vernacular languages; there are four transmitters; Dir KHAMIS TOGOÏ.

Radio Abéché: BP 36, Abéché; tel. 69-81-49; Dir DIMANANGAR DJAINTA.

Radio Moundou: BP 122, Moundou; tel. 69-13-22; daily programmes in French, Sara and Arabic; Dir DIMANANGAR DJAINTA.

Radio Sarh: BP 270, Sarh; tel. 68-13-61; daily programmes in French, Sara and Arabic; Dir BIANA FOUDA NACTOUANDI.

Television

Télé-Chad: Commission for Information and Culture, BP 748, N'Djamena; tel. 52-29-23; fax 52-51-63; state-controlled; broadcasts c. 12 hours per week in French and Arabic; Dir HOURMADJI HOUSSA DOUMGOR.

Finance

(cap. = capital; res = reserves; m. = million; br. = branch; amounts in francs CFA)

BANKING
Central Bank

Banque des Etats de l'Afrique Centrale (BEAC): BP 50, N'Djamena; tel. 52-41-76; fax 52-44-87; HQ in Yaoundé, Cameroon; f. 1973; bank of issue for mem. states of the Communauté économique et monétaire de l'Afrique centrale (CEMAC, fmrly Union douanière et économique de l'Afrique centrale), comprising Cameroon, the Central African Repub., Chad, the Repub. of the Congo, Equatorial Guinea and Gabon); cap. and res 218,644m., total assets 1,303,372m. (June 1998); Gov. JEAN-FÉLIX MAMALEPOT; Dir in Chad MAHAMAD AMINE BEN BARKA; 2 brs.

Other Banks

Banque de Développement du Tchad (BDT): rue Capitaine Ohrel, BP 19, N'Djamena; tel. 52-28-29; fax 52-33-18; e-mail exp.bdt@intnet.td; f. 1962; 25.9% state-owned; transfer to private ownership pending; cap. and res 3,386m., total assets 13,536m. (Dec. 1998); Pres. MAHAMAT AHMAT SALEH; Dir-Gen. ABDESSIT MAHAMAT.

Banque Internationale pour l'Afrique au Tchad: ave Charles de Gaulle, BP 87, N'Djamena; tel. 51-43-14; fax 51-23-45; f. 1980; fmrly Banque Meridien BIAO Tchad; Dir-Gen. GILLES D'HALLUIN.

Financial Bank Tchad: ave Charles de Gaulle, BP 804; tel. 52-33-89; fax 52-29-05; e-mail fbt@intnet.td; f. 1992; 97.9% owned by Financial BC SA (Switzerland); cap. and res 1,000m., total assets 9,675m. (Dec. 1998); Pres. RÉMY BAYSSET; Dir-Gen. PIERRE LECLAIRE.

Société Générale Tchadienne de Banque (SGBT): 2–6 rue Robert Lévy, BP 461, N'Djamena; tel. 52-28-76; fax 52-37-13; f. 1963; fmrly Banque Tchadienne de Crédit et de Dépôtes; 30% owned by Société Générale, SA (France), 20% state-owned, cap. and res 2,189m., total assets 33,233m. (Dec. 1998); Pres. and Dir-Gen. CHEMI KOGRIMI; br. at Moundou.

Bankers' Organizations

Association Professionnelle des Banques au Tchad: 2–6 rue Robert Lévy, BP 461, N'Djamena; tel. 52-41-90; fax 52-17-13; Pres. CHEMI KOGRIMI.

Conseil National de Crédit: N'Djamena; f. 1965 to formulate a national credit policy and to organize the banking profession.

INSURANCE

Assureurs Conseils Tchadiens Cécar & Jutheau: BP 139, N'Djamena; tel. 52-21-15; fax 52-35-39; e-mail biliou.alikeke@intnet.td; Dir BILIOU ALI-KEKE.

Société de Représentation d'Assurances et de Réassurances Africaines (SORARAF): N'Djamena; Dir Mme FOURNIER.

Société Tchadienne d'Assurances et de Réassurances (STAR): BP 914, N'Djamena; tel. 51-56-77; Dir PHILIPPE SABIT.

Trade and Industry

DEVELOPMENT ORGANIZATIONS

Agence Française de Développement: BP 478, N'Djamena; tel. 51-40-71; fax 51-28-31; fmrly Caisse Française de Développement; Dir JACBIE BATHANY.

Mission Française de Coopération et d'Action Culturelle: BP 898, N'Djamena; tel. 52-42-87; fax 52-44-38; administers bilateral aid from France; Dir EDOUARD LAPORTE.

Office National de Développement Rural (ONDR): BP 896, N'Djamena; tel. 51-48-64; f. 1968; Dir MICKAEL DJIBRAEL.

Société pour le Développement de la Région du Lac (SODELAC): BP 782, N'Djamena; tel. 51-35-03; f. 1967; cap. 180m. francs CFA; Pres. CHERIF ABDELWAHAB; Dir-Gen. MAHAMAT MOCTAR ALI.

CHAMBER OF COMMERCE

Chambre Consulaire: BP 458, N'Djamena; tel. 51-52-64; f. 1938; Pres. ELIE ROMBA; Sec.-Gen. SALEH MAHAMAT RAHMA; brs at Sarh, Moundou, Bol and Abéché.

TRADE ASSOCIATIONS

Office National des Céréales (ONC): BP 21, N'Djamena; tel. 51-37-31; f. 1978; production and marketing of cereals; Dir YBRAHIM MAHAMAT TIDEI; 11 regional offices.

Société Nationale de Commercialisation du Tchad (SONACOT): N'Djamena; f. 1965; cap. 150m. francs CFA; 76% state-owned; nat. marketing, distribution and import-export co; Man. Dir MARBROUCK NATROUD.

UTILITIES
Electricity and Water

Société Tchadienne d'Eau et d'Electricité (STEE): 11 rue du Colonel Largeau, BP 44, N'Djamena; tel. 51-28-81; fax 51-21-34; f. 1968; state-owned; transfer to private ownership pending; production and distribution of electricity and water; Pres. GOMON MAWATA WAKAG; Dir-Gen. ISMAEL MAHAMAT ADOUM.

MAJOR COMPANIES

The following are some of the largest private and state-owned companies in terms of capital investment or employment.

Abattoir Frigorifique de Farcha (AFF): Farcha; privatized 1998; industrial slaughterhouse for meat industry.

Boissons et Glacières du Tchad (BGT): BP 656, N'Djamena; tel. 51-31-71; fax 51-24-77; f. 1972; cap. 110m. francs CFA; production of mineral water, Coca-Cola, squashes and ice; Pres. MARCEL ILLE; Dir GASTON BONLEUX.

Brasseries du Logone: ave du Gouverneur Général Félix Eboué, BP 170, Moundou; f. 1962; cap. 800m. francs CFA; brewery; Man. Dir BRUNO DELORME; 145 employees.

Grande Bijouterie du Tchad (LA): BP 1233, N'Djamena; tel. 51-31-16; fax 51-58-84; sale of gold and diamond jewellery.

Les Grands Moulins du Tchad: BP 173, N'Djamena; f. 1963; cap. 158.25m. francs CFA; milling of flour; mfrs of pasta, biscuits and cattle feed; Pres. EMILE MIMRAN; Man. Dir in N'Djamena JEAN-PAUL BAILLEUX.

Manufacture de Cigarettes du Tchad: BP 572, N'Djamena; tel. 51-21-45; fax 51-20-43; f. 1968; cap. 340m. francs CFA; 15% state-owned; mfrs of cigarettes at Moundou; Pres. PIERRE IMBERT; Man. Dir XAVIER LAMBERT.

Shell Tchad: route de Farcha, BP 110, N'Djamena; tel. 51-24-90; fax 51-22-67; f. 1971; cap. 205m. francs CFA; Pres. DAVID LAWSON LOUGHMAN; Dir-Gen. JEAN-RENÉ MBIANDJEU.

Société Cotonnière du Tchad (COTONTCHAD): rue du Capitaine d'Abzac, BP 1116, N'Djamena; tel. 52-41-26; fax 52-31-71; f. 1971; cap. 4,256m. francs CFA; 75% state-owned; buying, ginning and marketing of cotton; owns eight cotton gins and one cottonseed oil mill; restructuring and divestment of some operations in progress; Pres. NGARNAYAL MBAILEMDANA; Dir-Gen. IBRAHIM MALLOUM.

Société d'Étude et d'Exploitation de la Raffinerie du Tchad (SEERAT): BP 467, N'Djamena; tel. 52-80-70; fax 52-71-08; construction of pipelines and petroleum refineries; Chair. YOUSSOUF MAINA.

Société Nationale Sucrière du Tchad (SONASUT): BP 37, N'Djamena; tel. 51-32-70; fax 51-28-12; f. 1963, 53% state-owned; cap. 5,871m. francs CFA; transfer to majority private ownership pending; refining of sugar; mfrs of lump sugar and confectionery; Pres. YOUSSOUF SIDI SOUGOUNI; Dir-Gen. NOUSSA KADAM.

Société Textile du Tchad (STT): BP 238, Sarh; f. 1966, operations suspended 1992–94; textiles complex.

TRADE UNIONS

Union Syndicale du Tchad (UST): BP 1143, N'Djamena; tel. 51-42-75; f. 1988 by merger; Pres. DOMBAL DJIMBAGUE; Sec.-Gen. DJIBRINE ASSALI HAMDALLAH.

Groupement Professionnel de Transport Routier Tchadien: BP 326, N'Djamena; tel. 51-43-55.

Union des Transportateurs Tchadiens: BP 529, N'Djamena; tel. 51-45-27.

CHAD

Directory, Bibliography

Transport

RAILWAYS

There are no railways in Chad. In 1962 the Governments of Chad and Cameroon signed an agreement to extend the Transcameroon railway from Ngaoundéré to Sarh, a distance of 500 km. Although the Transcameroon reached Ngaoundéré in 1974, its proposed extension into Chad remains indefinitely postponed.

ROADS

The total length of the road network in 1996 was an estimated 33,400 km, of which 7,880 km were principal roads and 5,380 km were secondary roads. There are also some 20,000 km of tracks suitable for motor traffic during the October–July dry season. The European Union is contributing to the construction of a highway connecting N'Djamena with Sarh and Léré, on the Cameroon border, and of a 400-km highway linking Moundou and Ngaoundéré.

Coopérative des Transportateurs Tchadiens (CTT): BP 336, N'Djamena; tel. 51-43-55; road haulage; Pres. SALEH KHALIFA; brs at Sarh, Moundou, Bangui (CAR), Douala and Ngaoundéré (Cameroon).

Société Générale d'Entreprise Routière (SGER): BP 175, N'Djamena; tel. and fax 51-55-12; devt and maintenance of roads; transfer to private ownership pending in 2000.

INLAND WATERWAYS

The Chari and Logone rivers, which converge to the south of N'Djamena, are navigable. These waterways connect Sarh with N'Djamena on the Chari and Bongor and Moundou with N'Djamena on the Logone.

CIVIL AVIATION

The international airport is at N'Djamena. There are also more than 40 smaller airfields.

Air Afrique: BP 466, N'Djamena; tel. 51-40-20; see under Côte d'Ivoire.

Air Tchad: 27 ave du Président Tombalbaye, BP 168, N'Djamena; tel. 51-50-90; f. 1966; 98% govt-owned; liquidation pending; international charters and domestic passenger, freight and charter services; Chair. DJIBANGAR MADJIREBAYE; Man. Dir MAHAMAT NOURI.

Tourism

Chad's potential attractions for tourists include a variety of scenery from the dense forests of the south to the deserts of the north. Receipts from tourism in 1996 totalled an estimated US $10m. A total of 11,249 tourists visited Chad in 1998, compared with about 9,000 in 1997.

Defence

In August 1996 the Armée nationale tchadienne (ANT) was estimated to number 30,350 (army approximately 25,000, air force 350, Republican Guard 5,000). In addition, there was a 4,500-strong gendarmerie. In September of that year it was announced that the army was to be restructured and the number of troops reduced, with financial support from the World Bank and the French government; in April 1997 it was announced that the army had been reduced in size from 30,000 to about 20,000 soldiers. Military service is by conscription. Under defence agreements with France, the army receives technical and other aid: in mid-2000 there were an estimated 900 French troops deployed in Chad.

Defence Expenditure: Budgeted at an estimated 29,000m. francs CFA in 1999.

Commander-in-Chief of the Armed Forces: Pres. IDRISS DEBY.

Chief of Army Staff: Gen. GOUAR LASSOU.

Chief of Naval Staff: Lt MORNADJI MBAISSANEBE.

Chief of Air Force: (vacant).

Education

Education is officially compulsory for six years between six and 12 years of age. Primary education begins at the age of six and lasts for six years. Secondary education, from the age of 12, lasts for a further seven years, comprising a first cycle of four years and a second cycle of three years. In 1996 primary enrolment was equivalent to 57% of children in the relevant age-group (76% of boys; 39% of girls). The rate of secondary enrolment in the same year was equivalent to only 9% of the appropriate age-group (15% of boys; 4% of girls). The Université du Tchad was opened at N'Djamena in 1971. In addition, there are several technical colleges. Total central government expenditure on education (excluding foreign-financed investment) in 1996 was 32,196m. francs CFA (21.2% of total government expenditure). According to estimates by UNESCO, the average rate of adult illiteracy was 51.8% (males 37.8%; females 65.2%) in 1995.

Bibliography

Azevedo, M. J. *Roots of Violence: A History of War in Chad.* Amsterdam, Gordon and Breach, 1998.

Azevedo, M. J., and Naadozie, E. U. *Chad: A Nation in Search of its Future.* Boulder, CO, Westview Press, 1998.

Buijtenhuijs, R. *Le Frolinat et les révoltes populaires du Tchad (1965–1976).* The Hague, 1978.

    Le Frolinat et les guerres civiles du Tchad (1977–1984). Paris, Editions Karthala, 1987.

Burr, M., and Collins, R. O. *Africa's Thirty Years' War: Libya, Chad and the Sudan 1963–1993.* Boulder, CO, Westview Press, 1999.

Collelo, T. (Ed.). *Chad: A Country Study.* Washington, DC, Federal Research Division, US Library of Congress, 1990.

Cruise O'Brien, D. B., Dunn, J., and Rathbone, R. (Eds). *Contemporary West African States.* Cambridge, Cambridge University Press, 1989.

Decalo, S. *Historical Dictionary of Chad.* 3rd Edn. Metuchen, NJ, Scarecrow Press, 1997.

Desjardins, T. *Avec les otages du Tchad.* Paris, 1975.

Foltz, W. J. 'Chad's Third Republic: Strengths, Problems and Prospects', in *CSIS Africa Notes*, Briefing Paper No. 77. Washington, DC, Center for Strategic and International Studies, 1987.

Hugo, P. *Le Tchad.* Paris, Nouvelles Editions Latines, 1965.

Lanne, B. *Tchad-Libye. La querelle des frontières.* Paris, Editions Karthala, 1982.

Le Cornec, J. *Histoire politique du Tchad de 1900 à 1962.* Paris, Librairie générale de Droit et Jurisprudence, 1963.

Le Rouvreur, A. *Sahariens et Sahéliens du Tchad.* Paris, Berger-Levrault, 1962.

Magnant, J.-P. (Ed.). *L'Islam au Tchad.* Talence Cedex, IEP, 1992.

Mbaïosso, A. *L'éducation au Tchad.* Paris, Editions Karthala, 1990.

Nebardoum, D. *Le labyrinthe de l'instabilité politique au Tchad.* Paris, L'Harmattan, 1998.

N'Gangbet, M. *Peut-on encore sauver le Tchad?* Paris, Editions Karthala, 1984.

N'Gansop, G.-J. *Tchad: Vingt ans de crise.* Paris, Harmattan, 1986.

Nolutshungu, S. C. *Limits of Anarchy: Intervention and State Formation in Chad.* Virginia, University Press of Virginia, 1996.

Sikes, S. *Lake Chad.* London, 1972.

Whiteman, K. *Chad.* London, Minority Rights Group (Report No. 80), 1988.

Zeltner, J.-C., and Tourneux, H. *L'arabe dans le bassin du Tchad.* Paris, Editions Karthala, 1986.

343

THE COMOROS*

Physical and Social Geography

R. J. HARRISON CHURCH

The Comoro Islands, an archipelago of four small islands, together with numerous islets and coral reefs, lie between the east African coast and the north-western coast of Madagascar. The four islands cover a total land area of only 2,236 sq km (863 sq miles) and are scattered along a NW–SE axis, a distance of 300 km separating the towns of Moroni in the west and Dzaoudzi in the east. The French names for the islands, Grande-Comore (on which the capital, Moroni, is situated), Anjouan, Mohéli and Mayotte were changed in May 1977 to Njazidja, Nzwani, Mwali and Mahoré respectively, although the former names are still widely used. The islands are volcanic in structure, and Mt Karthala (rising to 2,440 m above sea-level) on Njazidja is still active; its last significant eruption was in 1991. Climate, rainfall and vegetation all vary greatly from island to island. There are similar divergences in soil characteristics, although in this instance natural causes have been reinforced by human actions, notably in deforestation and exhaustion of the soil.

The ethnic composition of the population (officially enumerated at 446,817, excluding Mayotte, at the census of September 1991) is complex. The first settlers were probably Melano-Polynesian peoples who came to the islands from the Far East by the sixth century AD. Immigrants from the coast of Africa, Indonesia, Madagascar and Persia, as well as Arabs, had all arrived by about 1600, when the Comoros were becoming established as a port of call on European trade routes to India and the Indonesian archipelago. The Portuguese, the Dutch and the French further enriched the ethnic pattern, the latter introducing into the islands Chinese (who have since left) and Indians. In Mayotte and Mwali Arabic features are less evident, mainly because the two islands were settled by immigrants from the African coast and Madagascar. In fact, while Arab characteristics are strong in the islands generally, in particular in the coastal towns, the African is predominant in the territory as a whole. Islam is the prevalent religion of the islands. The official languages are Comorian (a mixture of Swahili and Arabic), French and Arabic. The average population density (excluding Mayotte) was 240 inhabitants per sq km at the census of September 1991, and has since been increasing rapidly in conjunction with growing pressure on the available land.

Recent History

Revised for this edition by the Editor

The Comoros, acquired as a French possession during 1841–1909, became a French Overseas Territory in 1947. Internal autonomy was granted in 1961, although substantial powers were retained by France. At a referendum held in December 1974, there was a 96% vote in favour of independence. This was strongly opposed, however, by the island of Mayotte (Mahoré), which sought the status of a French overseas department. France sought to persuade the Comoran government to draft a constitution for the islands which would allow a large measure of decentralization and thus satisfy the population of Mayotte. It was also proposed by France that any constitutional proposals should be ratified by referendum in each island separately before independence could be granted. These proposals were rejected by the Comoran chamber of deputies, and on 6 July 1975 the chamber approved a unilateral declaration of independence, and designated Ahmed Abdallah, the president of the government council, as president of the republic. Although France made no attempt to intervene, it retained control of Mayotte.

In August 1975 Abdallah was removed from office and replaced by Prince Saïd Mohammed Jaffar, who favoured a more conciliatory policy towards Mayotte. Jaffar was replaced as president in January 1976 by Ali Soilih. In February Mayotte voted overwhelmingly to retain its links with France. (For further information on Mayotte, see p. 000.)

Preparations for the 1976 referendum in Mayotte were accompanied by a deterioration in relations between France and the Comoros: the Comoran government nationalized all French administrative property and expelled French officials. On 31 December 1975 France formally recognized the independence of Grande-Comore (Njazidja), Anjouan (Nzwani) and Mohéli (Mwali), but all relations between the two governments, together with aid and technical assistance programmes, were effectively suspended.

The Soilih regime initiated a revolutionary programme, blending Maoist and Islamic philosophies, aimed at creating an economically self-sufficient and ideologically progressive state. The excesses of Soilih's methods aroused widespread resentment among traditional elements of society, and his programme of reform seriously undermined the economy.

ABDALLAH IN POWER, 1978–89

In May 1978 Soilih was overthrown and subsequently killed in a *coup d'état*, carried out by a small mercenary force led by a French national, Col Robert Denard, on behalf of the exiled ex-president, Ahmed Abdallah. Power was assumed by a 'politico-military directory', with Abdallah at its head. The new administration pledged to implement democratic reforms and to restore good relations with members of the Arab League and with France. French economic, cultural and military co-operation was duly resumed, and additional assistance was also forthcoming from Arab countries (including Saudi Arabia, Kuwait and Iraq), the European Community (EC, now the European Union—EU) and the African Development Fund. A new constitution approved by referendum in October 1978 was followed by presidential and legislative elections. Abdallah was elected president for a six-year term. However, despite the constitutional guarantee of free activity of all political parties, the federal assembly established the Union comorienne pour le progrès (Udzima) as the sole legal party for a period of 12 years from 1982. A number of unofficial opposition groups, which were based mainly in France, were established.

---

* Most of the information contained in this chapter relates to the whole Comoran archipelago, which the Comoros claims as its national territory and has styled 'The Federal Islamic Republic of the Comoros'. The island of Mayotte, however, is administered by France as an Overseas Collectivité Territoriale, and is treated separately at the end of this chapter (p. 358).

344

Abdallah's regime pursued an increasingly authoritarian course as the 1980s proceeded. Power was progressively centralized, reducing the role of the governors of the four islands, and the federal government became responsible for controlling the islands' economic resources. Amnesty International and other groups expressed concern at reports of the alleged ill-treatment of political detainees; reports of an attempt to overthrow Abdallah were officially denied in 1981. Government programmes for economic revival were beset by official corruption and financial mismanagement.

At a presidential election, which took place in September 1984, Abdallah, as sole candidate, was re-elected for a further six-year term by 99.4% of votes cast. Despite appeals by opposition groups for voters to boycott the election, some 98% of the electorate participated. In January 1985, following the adoption of constitutional amendments, the post of prime minister was abolished, and Abdallah assumed the powers of head of government. In March an attempt by members of the presidential guard to depose Abdallah (who was absent on a private visit to France) was thwarted. In November 17 people, including Moustoifa Saïd Cheikh, the secretary-general of the Front démocratique (FD), a banned opposition movement, were sentenced to forced labour for life and 50 others were imprisoned for their part in the coup attempt. In December, however, 30 political prisoners, many of whom were members of the FD, were granted amnesty, and in May 1986 a further 15 detainees were released.

In February 1987 the government announced that elections to the federal assembly would take place in March. Although Abdallah had indicated that all political groups would be permitted to participate, opposition candidates were allowed to contest seats only on Njazidja, where they obtained more than 35% of votes cast; Udzima retained full control of the legislature. In July 1987 Abdallah reinstated all the civil servants who had been dismissed or suspended following the coup attempt in 1985, in an apparent effort to gain favour with the traditional Comoran élite, which dominated the civil service. In November 1987, during Abdallah's absence in France, the Comoran authorities suppressed an attempted coup by a left-wing group.

In mid-1987 it was reported that Abdallah intended to secure a third elected term as president, following the expiry of his mandate in 1990, and that the constitution, which limited presidential tenure to two six-year terms, was to be revised accordingly. In November 1989 the constitutional amendment permitting Abdallah to serve a third six-year term as president was approved by 92.5% of votes cast in a popular referendum. However, this result was challenged by the president's opponents, and violent demonstrations ensued.

Mercenary Intervention

On the night of 26–27 November 1989 Abdallah was assassinated by members of the presidential guard (which included a number of European advisers), under the command of Col Denard. As stipulated in the constitution, the president of the supreme court, Saïd Mohamed Djohar, took office as interim head of state, pending a presidential election. Denard and his supporters however, staged a pre-emptive *coup d'état*, in which 27 members of the security forces were reportedly killed. This seizure of power by Denard prompted immediate international condemnation. Despite denials by Denard of any complicity in Abdallah's death, France and South Africa suspended aid to the islands. France despatched a naval task force to Mayotte, with the stated aim of evacuating French citizens from the Comoros. In mid-December Denard agreed to withdraw peacefully from the islands, and, following the arrival of French paratroops in Moroni, was flown to South Africa with 25 other mercenaries. It was subsequently agreed that a French military presence would remain on the islands for up to two years in order to train local security forces. (In May 1999 Denard stood trial in France and was acquitted of Abdallah's assassination.)

THE DJOHAR PRESIDENCY, 1990–95

At the end of December 1989 the main political groups agreed to form a provisional government of national unity. A general amnesty was extended to all political prisoners, and an inquiry was initiated into the death of President Abdallah. In January 1990 demonstrations were staged in protest at the postponement of the presidential election, due to be held that month, until

February. The election duly took place on 18 February, but voting was abandoned, amid opposition allegations of widespread fraud. Balloting eventually took place on 4 and 11 March; after an inconclusive first round, Djohar, who was supported by Udzima, obtained 55.3% of the total votes cast, while Mohamed Taki, the leader of the Union nationale pour la démocratie aux Comores (UNDC), secured 44.7% of the vote. In late March Djohar appointed a new government, which included two of his minor opponents in the presidential election: Prince Saïd Ali Kemal, a grandson of the last sultan of the Comoros and the founder of the opposition Islands' Fraternity and Unity Party (CHUMA), and Ali Mroudjae, a former prime minister and the leader of the Parti comorien pour la démocratie et le progrès (PCDP). In April Djohar accused Taki, who was temporarily abroad, of attempting to destabilize the government, and threatened reprisals against him. In the same month Djohar announced plans for the formal constitutional restoration of a multi-party political system, and indicated that extensive economic reforms were to be undertaken.

On 18–19 August 1990 a coup was attempted by armed rebels, who attacked various French installations on Njazidja. Two Comorans who were detained in connection with the plot were alleged to be supporters of the UNDC. The revolt was apparently organized by a small group of European mercenaries, who intended to bring about Djohar's downfall through the enforced removal of French forces from the islands. In September the minister of the interior and administrative reform, Ibrahim Halidi, was dismissed for his alleged involvement in the conspiracy, and more than 20 people were detained in connection with the insurgency. It was reported in October that the leader of the conspirators, Max Veillard, had been killed by Comoran security forces.

A ministerial reshuffle, which took place in October 1990, was followed by a period of dissension within the leadership of Udzima. By December an unofficial contest for the chairmanship of the party had emerged between the minister of foreign affairs, Mtara Maecha, and two former ministers from the Abdallah administration, Saïd Ahmed Saïd Ali (Sharif) and Omar Tamou.

In March 1991 the government announced that a conference, comprising three representatives of each political association, was to be convened to discuss constitutional reform. The conference took place in May, but several principal opposition parties, which objected to arrangements whereby Djohar reserved the right to modify the conference's recommendations, refused to attend. However, the conference presented draft constitutional amendments, which were to be submitted for endorsement by a national referendum.

On 3 August 1991 the president of the supreme court, Ibrahim Ahmed Halidi, announced the dismissal of Djohar, on the grounds of negligence, with the support of the court, and proclaimed himself interim president. Opposition leaders declared that the seizure of power was justified by the constitution. Djohar responded by ordering the arrests of Halidi and several other members of the supreme court, and imposing a state of emergency, which remained in force until early September. In August the government banned all public demonstrations, following violent clashes between pro-government demonstrators and members of the opposition.

Djohar subsequently formed a new coalition government, which included two members of the FD. In an attempt to appease increasing discontent on the island of Mwali, which had repeatedly demanded greater autonomy, two members of Mwalian opposition groups were appointed to the government. However, the two dominant parties in the coalition, Udzima and the PCDP, objected to the ministerial changes, and accused Djohar of attempting to reduce their influence. Shortly afterwards the PCDP and Udzima left the government.

In November 1991 Udzima denounced the proposed constitutional amendments and joined the opposition. Opposition leaders demanded the dissolution of the federal assembly, which they declared to be unlawfully constituted, on the grounds that it had been elected under the former one-party system, and the formation of a government of national unity. Later in November, however, Djohar reached an agreement with the principal opposition leaders, including Taki, to initiate a process of national reconciliation, which would include the formation of a government of national unity and the convening of a new constitutional conference. The agreement also recognized the legitimacy of Djohar's election as president.

In January 1992 a new transitional government of national unity was formed, under the leadership of Taki, who was designated as its 'co-ordinator'. Later in January a national conference, comprising both representatives of political associations supporting Djohar and of opposition parties, was convened to draft a new constitution, which was subsequently to be submitted for approval by public referendum. However, the conference was boycotted by representatives of Mwali (which in late 1991 had announced plans to conduct its own referendum on self-determination). In April 1992 the conference submitted a number of constitutional reform proposals.

In May 1992 18 opposition parties demanded the resignation of Djohar's son-in-law, Mohamed M'Changama, as minister of finance, following allegations of irregularities in negotiating government contracts. Djohar subsequently redesignated Taki as prime minister and formed a new interim cabinet, in which, however, M'Changama retained his portfolio. The constitutional referendum was postponed from late May until 7 June, when, despite concerted opposition by eight parties, led by Udzima and the FD, the reform proposals were accepted by 74.25% of those voting. The new constitutional provisions, which limited presidential tenure to a maximum of two five-year terms, also provided for a bicameral legislature, comprising a federal assembly, together with a 15-member senate, comprising five representatives from each island to be chosen by an electoral college. Elections at national and local level were to take place later in 1992. In early July Djohar dismissed Taki from the cabinet, on the grounds that he had allegedly appointed a former associate of Col Denard to a financial advisory post in the government. Later that month a new government was formed.

In mid-1992 social and economic conditions on the Comoros deteriorated, following renewed strikes in protest at economic austerity measures undertaken by the government in conjunction with the IMF and World Bank. In early September Djohar announced that legislative elections were to begin in late October, but opposition parties claimed that the schedule provided insufficient time for preparation, and threatened to boycott the elections. Later that month a demonstration, organized by Udzima, the UNDC and the FD, in support of demands for Djohar's resignation, was forcibly suppressed.

In late September 1992, during a visit by Djohar to Paris, a coup attempt was mounted by disaffected members of the armed forces, who seized the radio station at Moroni and announced that the government had been overthrown. A number of the rebels, including two sons of ex-president Abdallah were subsequently detained, and, in October, were charged with involvement in the insurgency. In mid-October rebel troops, led by a former member of Abdallah's presidential guard, attacked the military garrison of Kandani, in an attempt to release the detainees. Shortly afterwards, government forces attacked the rebels at Mbeni, to the north-east of Moroni; fighting was also reported on Nzwani. Later in October a demonstration was staged in protest at the French government's support of Djohar. By the end of October some 25 people had been killed in clashes between rebels and government troops in Moroni.

In October 1992 Djohar agreed to postpone the legislative elections until late November, although opposition parties demanded a further delay, and Udzima and the UNDC maintained their electoral boycott. The first round of the elections, which took place on 22 November, was marred by widespread violence and electoral irregularities. Several of the 21 political parties that had contested the election demanded that the results be declared invalid, and joined the boycott implemented by Udzima and the UNDC. Results in six constituencies were subsequently annulled, while the second round of voting, on 29 November, took place in only 34 of the 42 constituencies. Following partial elections on 13 and 30 December, reports indicated that candidates supporting the president, including seven members of the Union des démocrates pour le développement (UDD), had secured a narrow majority in the federal assembly. The leader of the UDD, Ibrahim Abdérémane Halidi, was appointed prime minister on 1 January 1993, and formed a new council of ministers. Later in January, in response to pressure from the Mwalian deputies in the federal assembly, one of their number, Amir Attoumane, was elected speaker. Shortly after the new

government took office, political tensions began to emerge between Djohar and Halidi, while the parties supporting Djohar, which commanded a majority in the federal assembly, fragmented into three dissenting factions. A cabinet reshuffle in late February failed to resolve these divisions.

In April 1993 nine people, including the two sons of ex-president Abdallah and two prominent members of Udzima, were convicted on charges of complicity in the coup attempt in September 1992, and sentenced to death. After domestic and international pressure the sentences were commuted. In May 1993 the government announced that local government elections were to take place in September. Later in May eight supporters of M'Changama, allied with a number of opposition deputies, proposed a motion of censure against the government (apparently with the tacit support of Djohar), challenging Halidi's competence as prime minister. Following the approval of the motion by 23 of the 42 deputies in the federal assembly, Djohar replaced Halidi with an associate of M'Changama, Saïd Ali Mohamed. Mohamed subsequently formed a new council of ministers, which, however, received the support of only 13 of the 42 members of the federal assembly. In mid-June 19 parliamentary deputies affiliated to Halidi, who had established an informal alliance, known as the Rassemblement pour le triomphe et la démocratie, proposed a motion of censure against the new government, on the grounds that the prime minister had not been appointed from a party that commanded a majority in the federal assembly. However, Djohar declared the motion unconstitutional, dissolved the federal assembly, and announced legislative elections. Shortly afterwards, he appointed a former presidential adviser, Ahmed Ben Cheikh Attoumane, as prime minister. A new council of ministers was subsequently formed (although two of the newly-appointed ministers immediately resigned).

Following the dissolution of the federal assembly, opposition parties declared Djohar unfit to hold office, in view of the increasing political confusion, and demanded that legislative elections take place within the period of 40 days stipulated in the constitution. In early July, however, Djohar announced that the elections were to be postponed until October, and requested that the 24 registered political parties form themselves into three main groupings. Despite pressure from the French government, Djohar failed to honour earlier pledges to grant amnesties to those imprisoned following the coup attempt in September 1992. Later in July 1993 opposition parties organized a widely-observed one-day general strike as a prelude to a campaign of civil disobedience designed to force Djohar to bring forward the legislative elections or to resign. Opposition members who had allegedly participated in the campaign of civil disobedience were temporarily detained.

In early September 1993 a number of opposition movements, led by Udzima and the UNDC, established an informal electoral alliance, known as the Union pour la République et le progrès. The FD, the PCDP, CHUMA and the Mouvement pour la démocratie et le progrès (MDP) also announced that they would present joint candidates. Later in September Djohar postponed the legislative elections until November, officially on the grounds that the government had inadequate resources to conduct them.

Having failed to obtain party political support for an electoral alliance, (owing to hostility towards M'Changama) Djohar announced in October 1993 the formation of a new party, the Rassemblement pour la démocratie et le renouveau (RDR), mainly comprising supporters of M'Changama and including several prominent members of the government. Later that month 16 political parties, including several organizations that supported Djohar, threatened to boycott the elections unless the government repealed legislation that redrew constituency boundaries and appointed a new electoral commission. Opposition supporters subsequently prevented government candidates from convening political gatherings. In November the legislative elections were rescheduled for 12 and 19 December, and local government elections were postponed indefinitely. Later in November Djohar reshuffled the council of ministers, and established a new electoral commission, in compliance with the demands of the opposition.

In the first round of the legislative elections, which took place on 12 December 1993, four opposition candidates secured seats in the federal assembly, apparently provoking official concern. However, in the second round of polling, it was reported that three people had been killed in violent incidents on Nzwani, where the authorities had taken over supervision of the polling stations. The electoral commission subsequently invalidated results in eight constituencies. Partial elections later took place in these constituencies and at Moroni, where the second round of voting had been postponed at the demand of two government candidates; however, opposition candidates refused to participate on the grounds that voting was again to be conducted under government supervision rather than that of the electoral commission. The RDR consequently secured all 10 contested seats in the partial elections, and 22 seats in total, thereby gaining a narrow majority in the federal assembly. In early January 1994 Djohar appointed the secretary-general of the RDR, Mohamed Abdou Madi, as prime minister. The new council of ministers included several supporters of M'Changama, who was elected speaker of the federal assembly.

Following the installation of the new government, 12 prominent opposition parties adopted a joint resolution claiming that the RDR had obtained power illegally, and established a new alliance, known as the Forum pour le redressement national (FRN), led by Djoussouf. Later in January 1994 three opposition leaders, including Djoussouf, were temporarily prevented from leaving the Comoros. In February security forces seized the transmitters of a private radio station, owned by Udzima, which had broadcast independent news coverage. In March the Comoros protested to the French government, after a French periodical published an article claiming that M'Changama was implicated in a number of fraudulent business transactions. At a religious ceremony later that month, attended by Djohar, a former bodyguard of an RDR candidate was arrested by the security forces and stated to be in possession of a firearm. A former governor of Njazidja and member of the FRN, Mohamed Abdérémane, was subsequently arrested and temporarily detained, on suspicion of involvement in an assassination attempt against Djohar. Djoussouf and Mroudjae (who was also a prominent member of the FRN) were also questioned.

In April 1994 pressure increased from both the Comoran opposition and the French government in favour of an amnesty for political prisoners. In the same month disagreements emerged between M'Changama and Abdou Madi over the appointments of a number of senior officials. At the end of May teachers initiated strike action (which was later joined by health workers) in support of higher salaries and the reorganization of the public sector. In early June a motion of censure against Abdou Madi, proposed by supporters of the FRN in the federal assembly, was rejected. In mid-June five people were killed on Mwali, following an opposition demonstration in support of the strike, which was violently suppressed by the security forces.

An agreement by the government to sell the state-owned airline, Air Comores, to an international financier, known as Rowland Ashley, was rescinded in June 1994, following protests from both opposition and government supporters in the federal assembly. As a compromise, Ashley's privately-owned company was granted management of the airline's operations. In August, however, Ashley's credentials were shown to be fraudulent; he subsequently alleged that prominent members of the government had accepted bribes in connection with the proposed sale. Later that month the political management committee of the RDR, which was headed by M'Changama, criticized Abdou Madi's involvement in the affair.

In early September 1994 public-sector workers carried out further strikes; union officials refused to enter into negotiations with the authorities while Abdou Madi's government remained in power. In mid-September the government suspended the salaries of workers joining the general strike. In the same month the French national airline, Air France, threatened to suspend flights to the Comoros, in protest at debts incurred by Air Comores under Ashley's management. Despite previous expressions of support for Abdou Madi, in October Djohar dismissed him as prime minister (apparently over the Air Comores affair), and appointed Halifa Houmadi to the post. The resultant new council of ministers included only two members of the former administration.

In December 1994 Djohar denied a request by the federal assembly to grant amnesty to political prisoners who had been implicated in the coup attempt in September 1992. In January 1995 public-sector workers suspended strike action, after the government agreed to a number of union demands. In the same month Djohar condemned a decision by the French government to reimpose visa requirements for Comoran nationals entering Mayotte; the French authorities were responding to concerns over illegal economic migration by Comorans. Threats were reportedly issued against French residents. Later in January divisions emerged within the RDR, after the party chairman and secretary-general (Abdou Madi) both criticized the government's failure to contain the hostility towards French citizens. At an RDR congress in early February the two officials were removed from the party, and Houmadi took over the chairmanship. In the same month the government announced that elections to the regional councils would take place in April, to be followed by the establishment of a senate and a constitutional council (in accordance with the terms of the constitution). The opposition, however, accused Djohar of resorting to unconstitutional tactics and electoral manipulation. In March Djohar announced that forthcoming elections to the regional councils were to be rescheduled for July 1996, ostensibly for financial reasons.

In April 1995 reports emerged of disagreements between Djohar and Houmadi, following accusations by Houmadi of financial corruption by Djohar and M'Changama. Djohar subsequently replaced Houmadi as prime minister with a former minister of finance, Mohamed Caabi El Yachroutu, who brought with him a reputation as a reformist, technocratic administrator, with good relations with the IMF and World Bank. A 13-member cabinet, including only five members of the previous administration, was formed. In May three former prime ministers, Mohamed, Abdou Madi and Houmadi, urged the removal of M'Changama (who, they claimed, exerted undue influence over Djohar) and the dissolution of the federal assembly. In July further tension developed within the cabinet over an agreement whereby Air Comores was to be jointly managed by an airline based in the United Arab Emirates, Menon Airways: M'Changama and the minister of transport and tourism, Ahmed Saïd Issilame, claimed that the agreement was technically invalid, having been signed by Djohar before legislation providing for the privatization of Air Comores had been approved in the federal assembly. Meanwhile, it was feared that the further postponement of elections to the regional councils would delay the presidential election. To facilitate the organization of the presidential poll, the government introduced minor constitutional amendments, including the relaxation of regulations governing the registration of political candidates and a provision allowing the prime minister to act as interim head of state. At the end of July Djohar removed Issilame and a further three associates of M'Changama from the council of ministers.

INVASION, INTERVENTION AND INTERIM GOVERNMENT

In late September 1995 about 30 European mercenaries, led by Denard, invaded Njazidja, seized control of the garrison at Kandani and captured Djohar. The mercenaries, who were joined by about 300 members of the Comoran armed forces, released a number of prisoners (including those detained for involvement in the September 1992 coup attempt), and installed a former associate of Denard, Capt. Ayouba Combo, as a leader of a transitional military committee. The French government denounced the coup and suspended economic aid to the Comoros, but initially refused to intervene, despite requests for assistance from El Yachroutu, who had taken refuge in the French embassy. In early October Combo announced that he had transferred authority to Mohamed Taki and the leader of CHUMA, Saïd Ali Kemal (both of whom had welcomed the coup), as joint civilian presidents, apparently in an attempt to avert military action by the French government. The FRN, however, rejected the new leadership and entered into negotiations with El Yachroutu. Following a further appeal for intervention from El Yachroutu, who invoked a defence co-operation agreement that had been negotiated in 1978, some 900 French military personnel landed on the Comoros. Shortly afterwards, Denard and his associates, together with the disaffected members of the Comoran armed forces, surrendered to the French troops. (The mercenaries were subsequently placed under arrest and deported to France.)

Following the French military intervention, El Yachroutu declared himself interim president in accordance with the constitution and announced the formation of a government of national unity, which included members of the constituent parties of the FRN. Djohar (who had been transported to Réunion by the French in order to receive medical treatment) rejected El Yachroutu's assumption of power and announced the reappointment of Saïd Ali Mohamed as prime minister. Later in October 1995 a national reconciliation conference agreed that El Yachroutu would remain interim president, pending the forthcoming election, which was provisionally scheduled for early 1996. The interim administration, which was supported by the armed forces, refused to recognize Djohar's appointments and announced that he would be prohibited from re-entering the country. At the end of October 1995 El Yachroutu granted an amnesty to all Comorans involved in the coup attempt and appointed representatives of the UNDC and Udzima (which had supported the coup) to the new council of ministers. In early November both governments simultaneously convened cabinet meetings and held rival political rallies in the capital, and it was reported that separatist movements had become active on Nzwani and Mwali. Representatives of the OAU, who visited the Comoros and Réunion in mid-November in an effort to resolve the situation, unofficially advised their organization that only El Yachroutu's administration was capable of governing. It was also widely believed that the French government had tacitly encouraged Djohar's removal from power. Later in November, however, supporters of Djohar, including M'Changama, organized a political gathering to demand the resignation of El Yachroutu's administration. Meanwhile, political leaders on Mwali rejected the authority of both rival governments, urged a campaign of civil disobedience and established a 'citizens' committee' to govern the island; discontent with the central administration also emerged on Nzwani.

THE TAKI PRESIDENCY, 1996–98

In December 1995 a decision by El Yachroutu's government to schedule the presidential election for the end of January 1996 was opposed by a number of political leaders (including Taki, Kemal and M'Changama), who demanded a postponement until March, ostensibly on the grounds that the stipulated date would coincide with the Islamic festival of Ramadan. In January 1996 the government agreed to reschedule the presidential election for March. Later that month Djohar returned to the Comoros, after apparently signing an agreement stipulating that he would retain only symbolic presidential powers.

In the first round of the presidential election, which took place on 6 March 1996, Taki and the leader of the MDP, Abbas Djoussouf, secured the highest number of votes; it was subsequently reported that 12 of the 13 unsuccessful candidates had transferred their support to Taki in the second round of the election. Taki was duly elected to the presidency on 16 March, obtaining 64% of the vote. International observers, including delegates from the UN and OAU, were satisfied with the electoral process; officials reported that 62% of the electorate had participated in the second round. The new head of state was sworn in on 25 March. Taki appointed a new council of ministers, headed by Tadjidine Ben Saïd Massoundi, which included five of the presidential candidates who had given him their support in the second round of the election.

In early April 1996 Taki dissolved the federal assembly and announced that legislative elections would take place on 6 October, despite the constitutional requirement that elections be held within a period of 40 days following a dissolution. New governors, all belonging to the UNDC, were appointed to each of the three islands. In mid-June, during a visit to France, discussions took place between Taki and the French president, Jacques Chirac. Taki requested financial aid to enable him to liquidate the wage arrears owed to civil servants, and confirmed his wish for French troops to remain on the Comoros. It was subsequently announced that Chirac had agreed to these requests and, in addition, had offered French assistance in the reorganization of public finance, education, public health and the judicial system.

In a government reorganization in late August 1996, Saïd Ali Kemal and a representative of the Forces pour l'action

républicaine were dismissed, following their parties' refusal to disband in order to join the single pro-presidential party that Taki intended to establish. A consultative committee on the constitution, established in September, considered requests from Taki for the reinforcement of presidential powers, including the president's right to choose governors for each island, and an end to the two-term limit on presidential office. Other proposals included a more visibly Islamist orientation of the state, with the names of Allah and the Prophet Muhammad to be inscribed on the national flag. Taki also promised to reinstate Islamic Shari'a law (public executions for murder were instituted in September). The constitutional committee was boycotted by the FRN and other opposition parties. The referendum on the constitutional reforms, held on 20 October, attracted a reported 64% turnout, 85% of whom voted in favour of the new constitution. Legislative elections were postponed until 1 December. Meanwhile, Taki had succeeded in building a single-party ruling group to back his presidency. On 5 October delegates from the UNDC, RDR, Udzima, and 20 other pro-government parties merged, as the Rassemblement national pour le développement (RND). This prompted Abbas Djoussouf and other anti-Taki politicians to form the Collectif de l'opposition and announce, on 13 November, a boycott of the legislative elections. On 30 November a number of government opponents, including former prime ministers Ali Mroudjae and Mohamed Abdou Madi, were arrested on arson charges, as the boycott campaign continued. They were released on 2 December. Results from the polls held on 1 December gave the RND 32 seats out of a total of 43 in the federal assembly. There were widespread reports of irregularities. The second round awarded a further four seats to the RND, giving it 36 seats, with the Islamist Front national pour la justice obtaining three seats, and independent candidates four.

Following the elections, the prime minister, Tadjidine Ben Saïd Massoundi, resigned. A new government was appointed on 27 December 1996, under Ahmed Abdou. It included such veteran politicians as Ibrahim Halidi and Mouazoir Abdallah. The government quickly came into conflict with opposition politicians and public servants. On 1 January 1997 workers went on strike in protest against salary arrears of up to 10 months. Opposition politicians, including Djoussouf, were detained on several occasions in January, and 30 people were injured during a demonstration in Moroni late in the month when strikers clashed with the security forces. There was further unrest and isolated incidents of arson in February. Meanwhile, tensions rose further on Nzwani and Mwali. On Nzwani there were serious clashes between workers and the security forces in mid-March, as up to 3,000 people erected barricades in the streets of the main town, Mutsamudu. Up to four people were reported to have been killed. Taki replaced the senior members of the Nzwani island administration and carried out a minor cabinet reshuffle. By that time, informal contacts had been taking place with Djoussouf and other opposition leaders and in May it was reported that, in an attempt to resolve the crisis, Taki and Djoussouf had agreed to establish a joint commission to define terms for a proposed accord on the participation of the FRN in formulating national policy.

Separatist Problems

During July 1997 two people were killed on Nzwani in skirmishes between the security forces and separatist demonstrators. The unrest rapidly escalated into a full-scale movement for secession on Nzwani and Mwali, which was aggravated by the government's unsuccessful attempts to subdue separatists on Nzwani, who had declared their intention to seek a return to French sovereignty. The relative economic wealth of neighbouring Mayotte as a French overseas collectivité territoriale was thought to have influenced popular feeling on Nzwani. Several separatist movements had emerged, notably the Mouvement populaire anjouanais, whose leader, Abdallah Ibrahim, was chosen to chair a 'political directorate' on Nzwani. On 3 August 1997 the 'political directorate' unilaterally declared Nzwani's secession from the Comoros; Ibrahim was subsequently elected as president of a 13-member 'politico-administrative co-ordination', which included Abdou Madi, a former prime minister during Djohar's presidency, as spokesperson. Meanwhile, separatist activity on Mwali intensified, and on 11

August secessionists declared the island's independence and appointed their own government.

The OAU proposed inter-Comoran dialogue to defuse the situation, but President Taki, influenced by extremists in the Moroni administration, despatched a force of at least 200 men to invade Nzwani on 2–3 September. Barricades were erected in Mutsamudu and an unknown number of people, reportedly far more than 100, were killed as the invasion failed to suppress the insurrection, after two days of heavy fighting. This failure prompted the dissolution of Ahmed Abdou's government; Taki assumed absolute power for a three-week period, and then named a transitional commission, which excluded those who had advocated the invasion plan.

Underlying much of the unrest were attempts by Taki to centralize the administration of the archipelago; this was seen on Nzwani and Mwali as a bid for political and administrative supremacy on Njazidja. At this stage the OAU and the UN became increasingly involved with the unfolding crisis, with the secretary-general of the OAU, Salim Ahmed Salim, urging all parties to work towards a negotiated solution. A reconciliation conference was scheduled for the end of October 1997, at the OAU's headquarters in Addis Ababa, Ethiopia. Ibrahim held a referendum on Nzwani's secession on 26 October, despite the objections of the Moroni government and the misgivings of some separatists, notably Abdou Madi; the reported result was 99.9% in favour of independence. France continued to reject absolutely demands for Nzwani to be reincorporated into the former colonial power as a collectivité territoriale. Meanwhile, efforts by the president to open channels of dialogue with Djoussouf, leader of the FRN, met with little success.

As Taki steadily lost his remaining support on Njazidja, amid administrative paralysis and economic decline, the crisis continued in deadlock for the remainder of 1997. A separatist government was appointed by the secessionists on Nzwani in October, further inflaming inter-island relations. Opposition parties in Moroni demanded that Taki be removed, declared that they would participate in the formation of a government of national unity only if separatists from Nzwani and Mwali were involved, and insisted that the dispute had to be resolved under the aegis of the OAU. In early December Taki named a new council of ministers, under Nourdine Bourhane (originally from Mayotte, but educated on Nzwani), although the transitional commission appointed in September remained in existence. The inter-Comoran reconciliation conference that had been scheduled for October finally took place in December; a peace agreement between Nzwani and Moroni was signed under OAU auspices, but its provisions were never fully implemented.

Factional disputes were reported on Nzwani in early 1998; in February Abdou Madi, who had fled the island after the referendum of October 1997, returned in an unsuccessful attempt to mount resistance to the separatists, reportedly with the support of both Taki and the OAU. A referendum on a separatist constitution was carried by a reported 99.5% of votes cast on Nzwani in late February 1998. In March Ibrahim appointed a new government. A plan for an OAU peace-keeping force was rejected on Nzwani, as Taki appeared to be modifying the government's previous uncompromising stance. In an effort to establish dialogue with the opposition, Taki named a three-member committee of political veterans in mid-May to examine the problem. At the end of the month the council of ministers was reshuffled in favour of moderates, and the president succeeded in bringing Abdou Madi back into government, although overtures to the Moroni opposition were unsuccessful, as they again demanded that Taki step down. As government employees' salaries remained unpaid, political unrest spread in Moroni itself, and more ominously within the army. Two days of anti-government rioting in the capital resulted in at least three deaths in mid-May. In August Taki carried out a minor reshuffle of the council of ministers.

In July 1998, as social unrest on Nzwani escalated, a dispute over the future aims of the secessionist movement led to the dismissal of the island's government, provoking violent clashes between islanders loyal to Ibrahim, who favoured independence within the framework of an association of the Comoran islands, and supporters of the outgoing prime minister, Chamassi Saïd Omar, who continued to advocate re-attachment to France. It was subsequently reported that Ahmed Mohamed Hazi, a former

Comoran army chief of staff and ally of Omar, had failed in an attempt to depose Ibrahim.

Meanwhile, as social and economic conditions deteriorated further, with salaries still unpaid and strike action ongoing, Taki visited a number of countries, including Mozambique, South Africa and the United Kingdom, to seek assistance in resolving the crisis. In August 1998 the government provisionally suspended transport links with both Nzwani and Mayotte. France later refused the government's request for a suspension of links between Mayotte and Nzwani, thus worsening the already fragile relations between the two countries. As industrial action continued into September, it was reported that the government had banned news broadcasts by privately-owned radio and television stations.

In October 1998, in a renewed effort to find a solution to the Comoran crisis, the OAU suggested that a meeting be held in South Africa between Taki and Ibrahim, and also encouraged dialogue between Taki and opposition leaders. At subsequent meetings with Djoussouf and the leadership of his own party, Taki proposed the establishment of a government of public salvation, an idea opposed by many members of the RND and several government ministers.

INTERIM GOVERNMENT AND ARMY COUP

On 6 November 1998 President Taki died unexpectedly. It was stated that he had suffered a heart attack, although several senior officials expressed serious doubts about the actual circumstances of the president's death. Tadjidine Ben Saïd Massoundi, the Nzwanian president of the high council of the republic and a former prime minister (March–December 1996), was designated acting president, in accordance with the constitution, pending an election, which would be held after 30–90 days. Massoundi immediately revoked the ban on the movement of people and goods to Nzwani and, despite the continued opposition of several government ministers, proceeded with Taki's project for the formation of a government of public salvation. Djoussouf, the main opposition leader, was subsequently appointed prime minister, to head a council of ministers composed of members of the FRN and the RND. Divisions within the RND over its participation in the new government led to a split in the party. In late January 1999 Massoundi extended his presidential mandate, which was soon to expire, pending a resolution of the crisis dividing the islands. In February an agreement was signed by the acting president and political parties opposed to the FRN-RND government, which provided for the formation of a new government to be supported by up to three technical commissions. However, the FRN refused to participate in the agreement, declaring its intention to remain in power until a Comoran inter-island conference had been held.

Meanwhile, renewed tension within the separatist administration on Nzwani intensified in December 1998, provoking eight days of armed clashes between rival militias, which led to at least 60 deaths before a cease-fire agreement was signed. In January 1999 Ibrahim agreed to transfer some of his powers to a five-member 'politico-administrative directorate', as meetings commenced between the rival separatist factions. No consensus was achieved in the following months, however, and, when Ibrahim replaced the directorate with a 'committee of national security' in March, the new administration was immediately rejected by rival leaders. In February the UN World Food Programme undertook a two-month emergency operation to distribute provisions to some 18,000 people who had been displaced by severe fighting in Mutsamudu in late 1998. Resistance to the ruling administration in Moroni increased in March 1999, when opposition leaders organized a protest meeting, during which they strongly denounced Massoundi; six people were later injured during clashes with the security forces after demonstrators, demanding the dismissal of Njazidja's governor, attempted to occupy his official residence.

On 19–23 April 1999 an OAU-sponsored inter-island conference was held in Antananarivo, Madagascar. An accord was reached whereby the federal state would become a union within one year, with the presidency rotating among the three islands. However, the delegates from Nzwani failed to sign the agreement, insisting on the need for consultation prior to a full endorsement. Several days of rioting followed in Moroni, as demonstrators protested against Nzwani's refusal to ratify the accord, reportedly forcing more than 1,000 Nzwanians from their homes before order was restored.

On 30 April 1999 the chief of staff of the Comoran armed forces, Col Assoumani Azzali, seized power in a bloodless coup, deposing Massoundi and dissolving the government, the federal assembly and all other constitutional institutions. Having sought to justify his actions on the grounds that the authorities had failed to take the political measures necessary to control the security situation in the Comoros, Azzali promulgated a new constitutional charter in which he proclaimed himself head of state and of government, and c-in-c of the armed forces. Full legislative functions were also vested in Azzali, who undertook to relinquish power following the creation of the new institutions provided for in the Antananarivo accord. The appointment of a state committee (composed of six members from Njazidja, four from Mwali and two from Nzwani) was followed by that of a state council, which was to supervise the activities of the state committee and comprised eight civilians and 11 army officers. The OAU, which had not been represented at Azzali's inauguration (although the UN had sent representatives), condemned the coup, withdrew its military observers from the Comoros and urged the international community not to recognize the new regime. It was also reported that Djoussouf had withdrawn his party, the MDP, from the FRN.

At the beginning of June 1999 Azzali created five technical commissions which were charged with directing the implementation of the Antananarivo accord. An electoral commission was established, while the other commissions were to oversee various projects, including the drafting of new constitutions for the union and the islands and the preparation of a donors' conference. However, despite an undertaking by Azzali to transfer power to a civilian government within a year, domestic discontent with the new administration increased, as the main political parties boycotted a meeting at which they were to have nominated representatives to serve on the new commissions. Furthermore, France and the USA were reported to have suspended all military co-operation with the republic.

In mid-June 1999 Lt-Col Abdérémane Saïd Abeid, who had previously occupied the role of national mediator on Nzwani, formed a government of national unity on the island, appointing himself as 'co-ordinator'. The disarmament of Nzwani militia and the ratification of the Antananarivo agreement were identified as priorities for the new government. Relations between Njazidja and Nzwani appeared to be improving to some extent in early July, when Azzali and Abeid met on Mwali and agreed to further talks. The meeting represented the most senior-level contact between the islands since the secessions of August 1997. In mid-July 1999 Azzali was reported to have attended the OAU summit of heads of state in Algeria, despite the opposition of several members and the organization's earlier condemnation of the new Comoran regime. In mid-August elections to establish a 25-member national assembly on Nzwani were held. No official results were released, but reports indicated that the most staunch separatists won the majority of seats. In the same month the OAU secretary-general's newly-appointed special envoy for the Comoros, Francisco Caetano José Madeira, visited the islands in an attempt to persuade the separatists on Nzwani to sign the Antananarivo accord. By the end of August the growing divisions between Njazidja and Nzwani became more apparent when Azzali refused to allow 500 Nzwanian secondary-school students to sit an exam on Njazidja. Furthermore, several senior civil servants from Nzwani were dismissed from their jobs in Moroni and many more were threatened with transfers back to their island. In mid-September the Nzwani executive council announced its decision not to sign the Antananarivo peace agreement; Abeid stated that the signature of the accord would not be in accordance with the aspirations of the island's population. In late October Madeira once again visited the Comoros in an attempt to convince the separatists to sign the Antananarivo peace agreement. The separatist leaders, however, refused to relent, citing their fear of social unrest if they signed the agreement. In response, Madeira suggested that an OAU peace-keeping force be dispatched to Nzwani to prevent possible trouble; this offer led the separatist leaders to request

further time to reconsider their position. In December the OAU adopted a tougher stance towards the Nzwani separatists by threatening the imposition of sanctions on the island should its leaders not have signed the peace accord by 1 February 2000. In retaliation, Abeid announced that a referendum would be held on Nzwani on 23 January 2000 regarding the signature of the Antananarivo accord. According to the separatist authorities of Nzwani, the results of the referendum revealed an overwhelming majority (94.47%) in favour of full independence for the island; the OAU, however, announced that it did not recognize the outcome of the ballot, following allegations of intimidation and repression of those in favour of reconciliation. In February 2000 the ministers of the interior, finance and transport indefinitely suspended the movement of sea freight to and from Nzwani. Telephone communications as well as all air and sea links were subsequently suspended and banks were closed, following sanctions recommendations by the OAU. Meanwhile, following a series of meetings between Azzali and a number of political parties from all three islands regarding the establishment of a more representative and decentralized government in Moroni, the state committee underwent an extensive reorganization in early December 1999, including the appointment of a new prime minister, namely Bianrifi Tarmidi (from Mwali). Although Mwali was well represented in the new executive, only one Nzwani minister was appointed.

It was reported in March 2000 that army units, led by Capt. Abderamane Ahmed Abdallah (the son of the former President Ahmed Abdallah), attempted, unsuccessfully, to overthrow Azzali. Abdallah was subsequently arrested. In April of that year demonstrations were organized by a number of political parties in protest at Azzali's failure to transfer the country to civilian rule by 14 April, as promised by him following the April 1999 coup (see above). Azzali later claimed that the conditions set by him for the holding of elections, namely the signing of the Antananarivo accord by Nzwani separatists, had not been met.

In May 2000 the OAU announced that the possibility of lifting the sanctions against Nzwani separatists was also connected to the return to constitutional order on the Comoros; it advocated the restoration of the October 1996 constitution, the return of Tadjidine Ben Saïd Massoundi as head of state, as well as the appointment of an interim government and prime minister. The following month an OAU delegation, led by Madeira, arrived in Moroni in an attempt to revive peace talks. However, Abeid reiterated his rejection of the Antananarivo accord. In response, the OAU announced the possibility of armed intervention on Nzwani. This was rejected at the OAU summit, held in July; however, it was agreed that a total maritime blockade of Nzwani would be established. In late July Azzali announced that a new draft constitution was shortly to be presented to the state committee for approval, in an attempt to satisfy the aspirations of those sections of the population demanding a return to constitutional order.

On 26 August 2000 an agreement, known as the Fomboni accord, was signed by Azzali and Abeid. The accord provided for the drawing up of a new constitution, which would grant Nzwani, Njazidja and Mwali considerable control over their own affairs. However, the central government would maintain jurisdiction over foreign affairs, external defence, currency, nationality and religion. There was to be a one-year transition period, following which the constitutional amendments were to be submitted to a referendum vote. However, the accord was severely criticized by the OAU on the grounds that it contravened the terms of the Antananarivo accord.

EXTERNAL RELATIONS

Diplomatic relations between the Comoros and France, suspended in December 1975, were restored in July 1978; in November of that year the two countries signed agreements on military and economic co-operation, apparently deferring any decision on the future of Mayotte. In subsequent years, however, member countries of the UN general assembly repeatedly voted in favour of a resolution affirming the Comoros' sovereignty over Mayotte, with only France dissenting. Following Djohar's accession to power, diplomatic relations were established with the USA in June 1990. In September of that year the Comoros and South Africa signed a bilateral agreement providing for a series of South African loans towards the development of infrastructure in the Comoros. In September 1993 the League of Arab States (Arab League) accepted an application for membership from the Comoros. In November 1994 the government signed an agreement with Israel that provided for the establishment of diplomatic relations betwen the two countries, prompting protests from the Arab League and from Islamic leaders in the Comoros. Djohar subsequently announced that the implementation of the agreement was to be postponed, pending a satisfactory resolution to the conflict in the Middle East. During his presidency Taki cultivated closer relations with the president of Gabon, Omar Bongo, and with the People's Republic of China. In mid-1999, following the military coup headed by Col Azzali, France and the USA suspended all military co-operation with the Comoros.

Economy

Revised for this edition by the Editor

The Comoros, with few natural resources, a chronic shortage of cultivable land, a narrow base of agricultural crops and a high density of population, is among the poorest countries of sub-Saharan Africa, and is highly dependent on external trade and assistance. In 1998, according to estimates by the World Bank, the gross national product (GNP) of the Comoros (excluding Mayotte), measured at average 1996–98 prices, was US $197m., equivalent to $370 per head. During 1990–98, it was estimated, GNP per head declined, in real terms, at an average annual rate of 3.1%. Over the same period, the population increased by an average of 2.9% per year. The Comoros' gross domestic product (GDP) declined, in real terms, at an average annual rate of 0.7% in 1990–96, according to the IMF; real GDP declined by 3.9% in 1995, and by 0.4% in 1996. It was officially estimated that GDP declined by 0.1% in 1997, but increased, according to provisional figures, by more than 1% in 1998.

Agriculture is the dominant economic activity in the Comoros (contributing 40.6% of GDP in 1998 and employing about 74.4% of the labour force in that year). At the census of September 1991, despite large-scale emigration to neighbouring countries, overall population density was 240 inhabitants per sq km (excluding Mayotte), with a density of 445.6 on the island of Nzwani (Anjouan). The problem of overpopulation on the three independent islands has worsened since the break with Mayotte, which has the largest area of unexploited cultivable land in the archipelago. Settlers from Nzwani and Njazidja (Grande-Comore) have been compelled to leave Mayotte and return to their already overpopulated native islands, where the potential for agricultural development is extremely limited. Demographic pressure was considered to be one of the main causes of the attempted secession by Nzwani and Mwali (Mohéli) in 1997.

Local subsistence farming, using primitive implements and techniques, is inadequate to maintain the population. Yields are very poor, storage facilities lacking, and much of the best land is reserved for export cash-crop production. Cassava, taro, rice, maize, pulses, coconuts and bananas are also cultivated. Almost all meat and vegetables are imported, as is most of the rice consumed on the islands.

The major export crops are vanilla, ylang-ylang and cloves. Prices for vanilla, of which the islands traditionally have been one of the world's largest producers (with average outputs of 180–200 tons per year), have been affected in recent years by competition from low-cost producers, notably Indonesia, and by synthetic substitutes. In 1998 exports of vanilla totalled 132.1 metric tons, a decline of 18.4% from the previous year; unit prices also fell sharply. France accounts for about one-third of the Comoros' vanilla exports. The world clove market has virtually collapsed since the mid-1980s. Export levels have fluctuated considerably since the early 1990s: while 2,755 tons of cloves were exported in 1994, exports of only 483 tons were recorded in 1995, recovering to 822 tons in 1996 and to 1,582.8 tons in 1997. During the 1990s prices remained depressed, falling to as low as US $0.30 per kg. However, as a result of the political instability in Indonesia (the main producer of cloves), prices increased substantially in late 1999. The Comoros is the world's main supplier of ylang-ylang, for which prices have been favourable until recently. Ageing plantations and inadequate processing equipment, however, have prevented this export from achieving its full potential, and output declined from 72 metric tons in 1989 to 43 tons in 1997, but increased to 67 tons in 1998. Shortfalls in foreign exchange revenue from these three commodities have been met by funds, under the Stabex (Stabilization of Export Earnings) scheme provided for in the Lomé Conventions. Agronomists argue that major investment is required in the essences sector, although it is difficult to see from where this will come. According to the IMF, agricultural GDP declined at an average annual rate of 0.7% in 1990–96; it declined by 1.2% in 1995, and by 0.4% in 1996.

Fishing is practised on a small scale, with a total catch of about 14,300 metric tons in 1998, according to estimates by the Banque Centrale des Comores. According to recent studies, the Comoros has a potential annual catch of 25,000–30,000 tons of tuna, which could provide the basis for a processing industry. The Comoros' fishing industry has received substantial aid from Japan. In October 1987 the Comoros and the European Community (EC, now the European Union—EU) signed a fishing agreement which permitted 40 tuna-fishing vessels from EC countries to operate in Comoran waters for three years and allowed the implementation of a scientific programme; the agreement was renewed in early 1995, with effect until July 1997.

The manufacturing sector contributed 3.8% of GDP in 1998. The sector consists primarily of the processing of vanilla and essential oils, and a few factories supplying the domestic market. According to the IMF, manufacturing GDP declined at an average annual rate of 0.5% in 1990–96; it declined by 14.2% in 1995, and by 0.4% in 1996, as political instability intensified.

The Comoros has a fragile tourist industry. In 1991 16,942 tourists visited the islands (compared with 7,627 in 1990). In 1993 the number of tourists increased to 23,671, while receipts from tourism totalled 4,000m. Comoros francs. The devaluation of the Comoros franc by 33% (in relation to the French franc) in January 1994 was thought to have improved the sector's competitiveness, and receipts increased considerably, mostly due to the change in the exchange rate; the number of tourists increased to 27,061 in that year. However, unrest in the wake of the attempted mercenary coup of September 1995, followed by political instability resulting from the unilateral secession of Nzwani and Mwali in August 1997, have inhibited subsequent growth. Furthermore, in mid-1999 the South African authorities advised tourists not to visit the Comoros, following the military *coup d'état* in April (see Recent History). This had a particularly adverse effect on tourism and, according to official figures, the decrease in the number of tourists visiting the archipelago led to a loss of revenue of 200m. Comoros francs in the first half of 1999. In 1998 there were 28,840 tourist arrivals, and receipts from tourism totalled US $26m. in 1997. The majority of tourists are from France and South Africa.

Economic development in the Comoros is impeded by poor infrastructure, an increasingly erratic power and water supply, a very limited road system and a lack of reliable transportation between the islands and with the outside world. In the early 1990s, however, EC funds facilitated the construction of a port at Fomboni, on Mwali, to improve shipping access to the island, and the expansion of the road network on all three islands. The country's air carrier, Air Comores, has been inactive since privatization arrangements collapsed in 1994 (see below). Charter operations have taken its place, providing long-haul air links with Dubai, Paris and Johannesburg, although there have been constant problems in maintaining a regular service. There were reports in mid-2000 that Air Comores was to be relaunched as a private company under the name Comoros

Air International. However, discussions between the potential private owners and the Comoran government ended, following a number of disagreements between the two parties.

France represents the main source of economic support (see below), while the other member states of the EU, Japan (see above), Saudi Arabia, Kuwait and the United Arab Emirates also provide financial assistance. Development priorities during the 1980s included increasing food and energy production and improving the transport infrastructure; substantial amounts of project finance were pledged by foreign donors, with a highly variable degree of success. French budgetary aid played a vital role in the late 1980s and early 1990s. In 1990 the French government cancelled Comoran debt totalling 229m. French francs, and waived repayment of a state loan of a further 9m. French francs. In 1991 the Comoros government received substantial budgetary aid from France, which facilitated the repayment of about $14m. of debt arrears owed to the African Development Bank (ADB), allowing the resumption of suspended disbursements. Following the devaluation of the Comoros franc in January 1994, the French government agreed to cancel outstanding debt arrears. French aid in 1994 allowed the repayment of arrears owed to the ADB, as a precondition to the resumption of credit from that organization. French aid to the Comoros reached an estimated 168.9m. French francs in 1996. At the end of 1994, however, France suspended budgetary assistance (which had totalled 24m. French francs in 1994), in response to the Comoran government's failure to agree a structural adjustment programme with the IMF and the World Bank, but later agreed to continue to provide aid for projects in the social sector and education. Finance in the latter area was also to be forthcoming from the United Nations Development Programme, the World Bank and UNICEF. In May 1997, following the agreement of a six-month surveillance programme with the IMF (see below), the French government sent a number of technical advisers to assist with financial administration in the Comoros, although little lasting progress had been made by the end of the year.

The Comoros' foreign trade accounts have shown a persistent deficit; imports have tended to increase, while export receipts have fluctuated widely, in response to trends in international prices for vanilla, cloves and ylang-ylang. Although both the trade and current-account balances strengthened in the late 1980s, in 1990 the visible trade deficit increased to US $27.3m., and there was a deficit of $9.3m. on the current account of the balance of payments. The trade gap widened to reach $36.8m. in 1992, giving a current-account deficit of $14.2m. There was a modest improvement in 1993, largely due to compressed demand for imports, but exports collapsed to around $11m. in 1994 and 1995, leading to trade deficits of $34.2m. and $42.2m. respectively. The situation worsened in 1996 as world markets for the Comoros' principal exports weakened further. Merchandise exports collapsed to less than $5m., resulting in a trade deficit of $32m. and import cover of 11% (it had been 18% in 1995). In 1997 there was a visible trade deficit of 16,064m. Comoros francs, and there was a deficit of 2,601.5m. Comoros francs on the current account of the balance of payments. The central bank credited an increase in private transfers for this improvement. Principal export destinations in 1999 were France, Germany and the USA. The main source of imports was France, followed by South Africa and Réunion. Vanilla and ylang-ylang accounted for virtually all exports; imports were dominated by rice, petroleum products and meat. Government figures, released in September 1999, showed a 21% decline in the value of exports in the first half of 1999, compared with the previous year. Despite this decline, the trade deficit narrowed over the six-month period, owing to a decrease in the cost of imports.

Although budgetary reforms in 1990 had some success, domestic and external arrears remained high. In 1991 the budgetary deficit increased to the equivalent of 20% of GDP (compared with a level of 18% of GDP in 1990). As a result, the government suffered difficulties in meeting wage and other payment obligations. In 1993 the budget (after external grants) was in surplus by 1,924m. Comoros francs, but the following years saw heavy deficits: of 5,940m. Comoros francs in 1994, 6,359m. Comoros francs in 1995, 4,761m. Comoros francs in 1996, and 5,493m. Comoros francs in 1998. Wages and salaries

expanded well beyond target in 1996, to 8,285m. Comoros francs. The annual rate of inflation, averaged 4.6% during 1990–98. The rate rose to 25.3% in 1994, following the 33.3% devaluation of the Comoros franc, but slowed to 5.5% in 1995, to 2.4% in 1996 and to 1.6% in 1997. Consumer prices increased by an annual average of 1.8% in 1998.

At the end of 1998 the Comoros' external public debt totalled US $203.1m. (of which $188.1m. was long-term public debt), while the cost of debt-servicing was equivalent to 1.5% of the value of exports of goods and services, due to the highly concessionary nature of the debt and accumulated interest arrears. Following negotiations with the IMF, a three-year structural adjustment programme for the period 1991–93 was agreed, providing facilities totalling almost $135m., whereby the Comoros government undertook to diversify exports, reduce public expenditure, promote export-orientated industries and transfer state-owned enterprises to private-sector ownership. Measures subsequently implemented under the programme included the abolition of levies on export crops, the liberalization of imports of a number of commodities, the initiation of environmental projects to control soil erosion (particularly on Nzwani), the 'privatization' of a number of state-owned hotels, the liquidation of the state-owned meat-marketing company, the Société comorienne des viandes (SOCOVIA), and the dismissal of a number of civil servants. However, the restructure of the public sector prompted widespread strikes, which caused severe economic disruption. In 1992 it appeared that insufficient progress had been achieved under the programme, and in September of that year it was announced that IMF and World Bank delegations were to visit the Comoros to discuss new reform objectives. In early 1993 the World Bank and IMF agreed to continue disbursements, following the approval of government plans, which included further privatization measures and reductions in civil service personnel. However, the continuing volubility of internal political conditions impeded the implementation of the structural adjustment programme, and, despite some success in reducing fiscal imbalances, economic prospects have remained unfavourable.

In January 1994 the devaluation of the Comoros franc led to a sharp increase in the price of imported goods, prompting strike action in the education and health sectors in support of higher salaries. In March, however, following the adoption of an economic reform programme for the period 1994–96, the IMF approved a one-year structural adjustment facility, equivalent to US $1.9m., while the World Bank also agreed to further credit. The programme laid emphasis on the continuation of the restructuring of the public sector and the reduction of price controls; the government aimed to achieve economic growth of 4%, to restrict the rate of inflation to 4%, and to reduce the current-account deficit (excluding official transfers) to less than 15% of GDP by 1996. In 1995–97, however, plans to privatize state-owned enterprises such as the national airline, Air Comores, and the public utilities enterprise, Electricité et Eau des Comores (EEDC), in conjunction with the structural adjustment programme were impeded by inter-government dissension. At the end of 1995 it was announced that Air Comores was to be liquidated, with a view to establishing a new airline, but by early 1998 plans had still not been finalized and French air carriers had withdrawn from the Moroni route. By mid-1997 it had been agreed that EEDC would pass into private management by the French company SOGEA, with finance provided by the Caisse française de développement (CFD, now the Agence française de développement). This project, involving 41m. French francs in CFD aid, was repeatedly delayed, owing to Comoran political infighting and French concerns regarding technical details. For much of 1997 there was no network electricity supply on the islands.

In mid-1995, in response to a further deterioration in the fiscal situation, the government introduced a number of measures to limit budgetary expenditure under a public finance recovery programme, including tax increases and a reduction in civil servants' salaries. However, political instability continued to impede economic progress; following a coup attempt in September (see Recent History), a new interim government initiated emergency financial measures, which included the payment of debts outstanding to the World Bank in order to qualify for agreements with international institutions. In early 1996 the government failed to adopt a budget for that year, and interim financial procedures were instigated, with the resultant confusion contributing to a further decline in the economy. In April the World Bank outlined measures that needed to be taken by the Comoros to improve the economy: greater control of the wage bill, a reduction in public-sector staff, increased customs and fiscal revenues and the privatization of state-owned companies. In February 1997 an IMF-supervised six-month surveillance programme was agreed. The government hoped that this would lead to the approval of an enhanced structural adjustment facility, but the programme was soon beset by problems, firstly over politically-motivated dismissals in the customs service, and then over disorganization in the vital power sector. By July the IMF was warning that insufficient progress had been made, especially where privatization and salary payments were concerned. Following a six-month extension of the monitoring programme, in February 1998 the IMF again concluded that the Comoros had failed to meet its economic objectives. In August increasing arrears on loan repayments led the World Bank to suspend the disbursement of funds to the Comoros. In early 1999 the European Union (EU) suspended all aid to the islands. The intensification of political instability, following the seizure of power by the military in April (see Recent History), had a particularly adverse effect on maritime trade and on tourism. In January 2000, following the required repayment of arrears by the Comoran authorities, the World Bank resumed the disbursement of funds to the Comoros (the EU was expected to follow suit). Furthermore, in March a joint delegation of the World Bank and the IMF suggested measures to reduce the Comoros' state deficit. Measures included cuts in government spending and the possibility of a reduction of, or moratorium on, the Comoran foreign debt. In early 2000 the Comoran authorities reduced customs duties by 80% on products from member countries of the Indian Ocean Commission (IOC), as part of moves to comply with the integrated regional programme for trade development. However, it was feared that this would lead to a substantial shortfall in customs revenue, which usually represents up to three-quarters of the state budget. In February of that year the ministers of the interior, finance and transport indefinitely suspended the movement of sea freight to and from Nzwani. Moreover, in March the Organization of African Unity (OAU) suspended telephone communications and restricted petroleum deliveries by sea and air. It was subsequently reported that there were serious fuel shortages on the island and that petroleum prices had dramatically increased.

Statistical Survey

Source (unless otherwise stated): Ministry of Finance, the Budget and the Economy, BP 324, Moroni; tel. (73) 2767.
Note: Unless otherwise indicated, figures in this Statistical Survey exclude data for Mayotte.

AREA AND POPULATION

Area: 1,862 sq km (719 sq miles). *By island:* Njazidja (Grande-Comore) 1,146 sq km, Nzwani (Anjouan) 424 sq km, Mwali (Mohéli) 290 sq km.

Population: 335,150 (males 167,089; females 168,061), excluding Mayotte (estimated population 50,740), at census of 15 September 1980; 484,000 (official estimate), including Mayotte, at 31 December 1986; 446,817 (males 221,152; females 225,665), excluding Mayotte, at census of 15 September 1991. *By island* (1991 census): Njazidja (Grande-Comore) 233,533, Nzwani (Anjouan) 188,953, Mwali (Mohéli) 24,331.

Density (per sq km, 1991 census): 240.0 (Njazidja 203.8; Nzwani 445.6; Mwali 83.9).

Principal Towns (population at 1980 census): Moroni (capital) 17,267; Mutsamudu 13,000; Fomboni 5,400.

Births and Deaths (including figures for Mayotte, UN estimates): Average annual birth rate 48.5 per 1,000 in 1980–85, 42.4 per 1,000 in 1985–90, 38.2 per 1,000 in 1990–95; average annual death rate 13.8 per 1,000 in 1980–85, 11.9 per 1,000 in 1985–90, 10.2 per 1,000 in 1990–95. Source: UN, *World Population Prospects: The 1998 Revision.*

Expectation of Life (UN estimates, years at birth, including Mayotte, 1990–95): 57.2 (males 55.4; females 59.2). Source: UN, *World Population Prospects: The 1998 Revision.*

Economically Active Population (ILO estimates, '000 persons at mid-1980, including figures for Mayotte): Agriculture, forestry and fishing 150; Industry 10; Services 20; Total 181 (males 104, females 77). Source: ILO, *Economically Active Population Estimates and Projections, 1950–2025.*

1991 census (persons aged 12 years and over, excluding Mayotte): Total labour force 126,510 (males 88,034; females 38,476). Source: UN, *Demographic Yearbook.*

AGRICULTURE, ETC.

Principal Crops (estimates, '000 metric tons, unless otherwise indicated, 1998): Rice (paddy) 2.9; Maize 4.0; Potatoes 1.0; Cassava (Manioc) 51.9; Taro 8.7; Other tubers 5.3; Pulses 0.2; Groundnuts 0.2; Coconuts (million) 75; Tomatoes 0.5; Other vegetables 5.6; Bananas 58.9; Other fruits 3.3; Vanilla (dried, metric tons) 180; Clove buds (metric tons) 1,700; Ylang-ylang essence (metric tons) 67. Source: Banque Centrale des Comores, *Rapport Annuel.*

Livestock (FAO estimates, '000 head, year ending September 1998): Asses 5, Cattle 50, Sheep 20, Goats 128. Source: FAO, *Production Yearbook.*

Livestock Products (estimates, metric tons, unless otherwise indicated, 1998): Beef and veal 950; Mutton, lamb and goat meat 170; Poultry meat 210; Milk ('000 litres) 970; Eggs ('000) 4,700. Source: Banque Centrale des Comores, *Rapport Annuel.*

Fishing (FAO estimates, '000 metric tons, live weight): Total catch 13.2 in 1995; 13.0 in 1996; 12.5 in 1997. Source: FAO, *Yearbook of Fishery Statistics.*

1998 ('000 metric tons): Total catch 14.3. Source: Banque Centrale des Comores, *Rapport Annuel.*

INDUSTRY

Electric Energy (million kWh): 30.9 in 1996; 12.3 in 1997; 28.5 in 1998. Source: Banque Centrale des Comores, *Rapport Annuel.*

FINANCE

Currency and Exchange Rates: 100 centimes = 1 Comoros franc. *Sterling, Dollar and Euro Equivalents* (28 April 2000): £1 sterling = 849.15 Comoros francs; US $1 = 541.52 Comoros francs; €1 = 491.97 Comoros francs; 1,000 Comoros francs = £1.178 = $1.847 = €2.033. *Average Exchange Rate* (Comoros francs per US $): 437.75 in 1997; 442.46 in 1998; 461.77 in 1999. Note: The Comoros franc was introduced in 1981, replacing (at par) the CFA franc. The fixed link to French currency was retained, with the exchange rate set at 1 French franc = 50 Comoros francs. This remained in effect until January 1994, when the Comoros franc was devalued by 33.3%, with the exchange rate adjusted to 1 French franc = 75 Comoros francs. This relationship to French currency remained in effect with the introduction of the euro on 1 January 1999. From that date, accordingly, a fixed exchange rate of €1 = 491.968 Comoros francs has been in operation.

Budget (provisional, million Comoros francs, 1998): *Revenue:* Tax revenue 9,172; Other revenue 959; Total 10,131, excluding grants received (7,144). *Expenditure:* Budgetary current expenditure 12,683 (Wages and salaries 7,100; Goods and services 4,100; Transfers 561; Interest payments 922); Current expenditure under technical assistance programmes 4,658; Budgetary capital expenditure 360; Capital expenditure financed with external resources 5,067; Total 22,768. Source: Banque Centrale des Comores, *Rapport Annuel.*

International Reserves (US $ million at 31 December 1999): Gold n.a.; IMF special drawing rights 0.16; Reserve position in IMF 0.74; Foreign exchange 36.24; Total 37.15. Source: IMF, *International Financial Statistics.*

Money Supply (million Comoros francs at 31 December 1999): Currency outside deposit money banks 6,310; Demand deposits at deposit money banks 4,386; Total money (incl. others) 11,662. Source: IMF, *International Financial Statistics*.

Cost of Living (Consumer Price Index; base: 1993 = 100): All items 135 in 1996; 137 in 1997; 139 in 1998. Source: Banque Centrale des Comores, *Rapport Annuel*.

Expenditure on the Gross Domestic Product (million Comoros francs at current prices, 1996): Government final consumption expenditure 12,434; Private final consumption expenditure 74,366; Increase in stocks 104; Gross fixed capital formation 15,333; *Total domestic expenditure* 102,237; Exports of goods and services 16,204; *Less* Imports of goods and services 36,594; *GDP in purchasers' values* 81,847. Source: IMF, *Comoros—Statistical Annex* (November 1997).

Gross Domestic Product by Economic Activity (million Comoros francs at current prices, 1998, provisional figures): Agriculture, hunting, forestry and fishing 35,387; Manufacturing 3,276; Electricity, gas and water 1,299; Construction 5,179; Trade, restaurants and hotels 21,864; Transport and communications 4,457; Finance, insurance, real estate and business services 3,034; Government services 12,196; Other services 426; *Sub-total* 87,116; *Less* Imputed bank service charge 1,448; *GDP in purchasers' values* 85,668. Source: Banque Centrale des Comores, *Rapport Annuel*.

Balance of Payments (US $ million, 1995): Exports of goods f.o.b. 11.32; Imports of goods f.o.b. -53.50; *Trade balance* -42.18; Exports of services 34.51; Imports of services -49.85; *Balance on goods and services* -57.53; Other income received 3.40; Other income paid -2.39; *Balance on goods, services and income* -56.51; Current transfers received 41.06; Current transfers paid -3.50; *Current balance* -18.96; Direct investment from abroad 0.89; Other investment assets -1.83; Other investment liabilities 11.81; Net errors and omissions -1.77; *Overall balance* -9.86. Source: IMF, *International Financial Statistics*.

EXTERNAL TRADE

Principal Commodities (million Comoros francs, 1998): *Imports c.i.f.*: Rice 3,184; Meat and fish 1,786; Flour 597; Sugar 699; Dairy products 639; Petroleum products 2,253; Cement 1,131; Vehicles 2,459; Iron and steel 794; Total (incl. others) 22,241. *Exports f.o.b.*: Vanilla 1,058; Ylang-ylang 566; Total (incl. others) 1,967. Note: Figures for exports exclude shipments of cloves from Nzwani (Anjouan). Source: Banque Centrale des Comores, *Rapport Annuel*.

Principal Trading Partners (US $'000, 1995): *Imports*: France 20,040; India 10,834; Saudi Arabia 5,887; Total (incl. others) 62,625. *Exports*: France 4,150; Germany 913; USA 3,222; Total (incl. others) 11,361. Source: UN, *International Trade Statistics Yearbook*.

1996 (percentage of trade): *Imports*: Belgium/Luxembourg 2.0%; France 41.6%; Germany 1.2%; Kenya 7.0%; Madagascar 1.4%; Mauritius 1.2%; Pakistan 8.2%; Réunion 2.9%; Romania 1.5%; Saudi Arabia 3.2%; Singapore 1.7%; South Africa 7.0%; Switzerland 1.1%; Viet Nam 6.1%. *Exports*: France 48.9%; Germany 13.6%; Nether-

lands 2.3%; USA 11.8%. Source: IMF, *Comoros—Statistical Annex* (November 1997).

1999 (percentage of trade): *Imports*: France 32.0%; South Africa 8.0%; Réunion 8.0%; Kenya 6.0%; United Arab Emirates 6.0%. *Exports*: USA 26.8%; France 25.4%; Germany 12.2%; Singapore 8.6%.

TRANSPORT

Road Traffic (estimates, motor vehicles in use, 1996): Passenger cars 9,100; Lorries and vans 4,950. Source: International Road Federation, *World Road Statistics*.

International Shipping (estimated sea-borne freight traffic, '000 metric tons, 1991): Goods loaded 12; Goods unloaded 107. Source: UN Economic Commission for Africa, *African Statistical Yearbook*.

Civil Aviation (traffic on scheduled services, 1996): Passengers carried ('000) 27; Passenger-km (million) 3. Source: UN, *Statistical Yearbook*.

TOURISM

Tourist Arrivals: 23,775 in 1996; 26,219 in 1997; 28,840 in 1998. Source: Banque Centrale des Comores, *Rapport Annuel*.

Tourist Arrivals by Country (1997): France 7,870, Germany 729, Madagascar 877, Réunion 1,728, South Africa 9,452, United Kingdom 1,016; Total (incl. others) 26,219.

Receipts from Tourism (US $ million): 21 in 1995; 23 in 1996; 26 in 1997. Source: World Tourism Organization, *Yearbook of Tourism Statistics*.

COMMUNICATIONS MEDIA

Radio Receivers (1997): 90,000 in use. Source: UNESCO, *Statistical Yearbook*.

Television Receivers (1997): 1,000 in use. Source: UNESCO, *Statistical Yearbook*.

Telephones (1998): 6,226 main lines in use. Source: Banque Centrale des Comores, *Rapport Annuel*.

Telefax Stations (1996): 100 in use. Source: UN, *Statistical Yearbook*.

EDUCATION

Pre-primary (1980/81): 600 teachers; 17,778 pupils.

Primary (1995/96): 327 schools; 1,508 teachers (public education only); 78,527 pupils.

Secondary: Teachers: general education 591 (1995/96, public education only); teacher training 11 (1991/92); vocational 31 (1986/87). Pupils: general education 21,192 (1995/96); teacher training 37 (1993/94); vocational 126 (1993/94).

Higher: 32 teachers (1989/90); 348 pupils (1995/96).

Source: UNESCO, *Statistical Yearbook*.

Directory

The Constitution

On 6 May 1999, following the coup of 30 April, Col Assoumani Azzali promulgated a new constitutional charter, pending the introduction of new constitutional arrangements which were to take effect within one year. According to the charter, Col Azzali is the Head of State and leader of a State Committee and the Armed Forces, and holds full legislative and executive power. Prior to their revocation, the following constitutional provisions had been in effect since their approval by referendum on 20 October 1996.

PREAMBLE

The preamble affirms the will of the Comoran people to derive from the state religion, Islam, inspiration for the principles and laws that the State and its institutions govern, to adhere to the principles laid down by the Charters of the UN, the Organization of African Unity and the Organization of the Islamic Conference and by the Treaty of the League of Arab States, and to guarantee the rights of all citizens, without discrimination, in accordance with the UN Declaration of Human Rights and the African Charter of Human Rights.

GENERAL PROVISIONS

The Comoros archipelago constitutes a federal Islamic republic. Sovereignty belongs to the people, and is exercised through their elected representatives or by the process of referendum. There is universal secret suffrage, which can be direct or indirect, for all citizens who are over the age of 18 and in full possession of their civil and political rights. Political parties and groups operate freely, respecting national sovereignty, democracy and territorial integrity. However, political parties which are not represented by at least two deputies from each island, as a result of the first legislative election to follow the adoption of the Constitution, will be dissolved, unless those parties merge with others which are legitimately represented in the Federal Assembly. If only one political party has representation in the Federal Assembly, the party which has obtained the second highest number of votes will continue to operate freely. Only political parties and groups active throughout the Republic may participate in national elections. Political parties must be democratic both in their internal structure and their activities.

PRESIDENT OF THE REPUBLIC

The President is the Head of State and is elected by direct universal suffrage for a six-year term, which is renewable for an unrestricted number of mandates. He is also Head of the Armed Forces and ensures the legitimate functioning of public powers and the continuation of the State. He is the guarantor of national independence, the unity of the Republic, the autonomy of the islands, territorial integrity and adherence to international agreements. Candidates for the presidency must be aged between 40 and 75 years, of Comoran nationality by birth, and resident in the archipelago for at least 12 consecutive months prior to elections. The President presides over the Council of Ministers. He is empowered to ask the Federal Assembly to reconsider a Bill. The President can, having consulted with the Prime Minister and the Presidents of the Federal Assembly and the High Council of the Republic in writing, dissolve the Federal Assembly. The President determines and implements the Republic's foreign policy.

THE GOVERNMENT

The President appoints the Prime Minister, and on his recommendations, the other members of the Government. Under the authority of the President of the Republic, the Council of Ministers determines and implements domestic policy.

LEGISLATIVE POWER

Legislative power is vested in the Federal Assembly, which represents the Comoran nation. Deputies in the Federal Assembly are elected for five years by direct suffrage. Legislative elections take place between 30 and 90 days after the expiry of the mandate of the incumbent Federal Assembly. The electoral law dictates the number of members of the Federal Assembly, but there is a minimum of five deputies from each island. The deputies elect the President of the Federal Assembly at the beginning of their mandate. The Federal Assembly sits for two sessions each year and, if necessary, for extraordinary sessions. Matters covered by federal legislation include constitutional institutions, defence, posts and telecommunications, transport, civil and penal law, public finance, external trade, federal taxation, long-term economic planning, education and health.

JUDICIAL POWER

Judicial power is independent of executive and legislative power. The President is the guarantor of the independence of the judicial system and chairs the Higher Council of the Magistracy (Conseil Supérieur de la Magistrature), of which the Minister of Justice is Vice-President.

HIGH COUNCIL OF THE REPUBLIC

The High Council of the Republic considers constitutional matters and the control of public finance, and acts as a High Court of Justice. It has a renewable mandate of seven years and is composed of four members appointed by the President, three members elected by the Federal Assembly and one member elected by the Council of each island. The High Council oversees and proclaims the results of presidential and legislative elections and referendums.

COUNCIL OF THE ULÉMAS

The Council of the Ulémas offers opinions on projects for laws, ordinances and decrees. The President of the Republic, the Prime Minister, the President of the Federal Assembly, the Presidents of the Councils and the Governors of the islands may consult the Council of the Ulémas on any religious issue. The Council of the Ulémas may submit recommendations to the Federal Assembly, the Government or the Governors of the islands if it considers legislation to be in contravention of the principles of Islam.

ISLAND INSTITUTIONS

While respecting the unity of the Republic, each island is an autonomous territorial entity which freely controls its own administration through a Governor and a Council. The Governor of each island is appointed by the President of the Republic, from three candidates proposed by the Council of the island. The Council of each island is composed of the mayors of the communes and sits for not more than 15 days at a time, in March and December, and, if necessary, for extraordinary sessions. The Council is responsible for such matters as the budget of the island, taxes, culture, health, primary education and the environment.

REVISION OF THE CONSTITUTION

The power to initiate constitutional revision is vested in the President of the Republic. However, one-third of the members of the Federal Assembly may propose amendments to the President. Constitutional revision must be approved by a majority of two-thirds of the deputies in the Federal Assembly, and is subject to approval by national referendum. However, the President of the Republic may decide to promulgate a constitutional project, without submitting it to a referendum, if it has been adopted at a congress of deputies and the councillors of the islands, by a majority of two-thirds. The Republican and Islamic nature of the State cannot be revised.

The Government

HEAD OF STATE

Head of State and Minister of Defence: Col ASSOUMANI AZZALI (assumed power 30 April 1999, inaugurated 6 May 1999).

STATE COMMITTEE
(August 2000)

Head of State and Minister of Defence: Col ASSOUMANI AZZALI.

Prime Minister: BIANRIFI TARMIDI.

Minister of Finance, the Budget and Planning: SOUNDI ABDOU TOUBOU.

Minister of the Interior and the Implementation of Institutions: MOHAMED ABDOU SOIMADOU.

Minister of Justice and Islamic Affairs: ABDOULBAR YOUSSOUF.

Minister of Production and the Environment: CHARIF ABDALLAH.

Minister of National Education, Professional and Vocational Training, and Francophone Affairs: MOINAECHA YAHAYA CHEIKH.

Minister of Foreign Affairs and Co-operation: SOUEFOU MOHAMED ELAMINE.

Minister of Public Health, Population and the Status of Women: MIAHAILI MISTOIHI.

Minister of Civil Service, Employment and Labour: MILISSANI HAMDIYA.

Minister of the Economy, Trade, Industry and Crafts: ASSOUMANY ABOUDOU.

Minister of Information, Youth and Sports: Capt. AHMED SIDI.

Minister of Tourism, Transport, and Posts and Telecommunications: SAÏD DHOIFIR BOUNOU.

Minister of Facilities and Energy: DJAFFAR M'MADI.

Governor of National Defence: AHMADI MADI (BOLERO).

MINISTRIES

Office of the Head of State: BP 521, Moroni; tel. (74) 4814; fax (74) 4829.

Ministry of the Civil Service, Employment and Labour: Moroni; tel. (74) 4277.

Ministry of Defence: Moroni; tel. (74) 4862.

Ministry of the Economy, Trade, Industry and Crafts: Moroni; tel. (74) 4235.

Ministry of Facilities and Energy: Moroni.

Ministry of Finance, the Budget and Planning: BP 324, Moroni; tel. (74) 4145; fax (74) 4140.

Ministry of Foreign Affairs and Co-operation: BP 482, Moroni; tel. (74) 4100; fax (74) 4111.

Ministry of Information, Youth and Sports: BP 421, Moroni.

Ministry of the Interior and the Implementation of Institutions: BP 520, Moroni; tel. (74) 4666.

Ministry of Justice and Islamic Affairs: Moroni; tel. (74) 4200.

Ministry of National Education, Professional and Vocational Training, and Francophone Affairs: BP 421, Moroni; tel. (74) 4185; fax (74) 4180.

Ministry of Production and the Environment: Moroni.

Ministry of Public Health, Population and the Status of Women: Moroni.

Ministry of Tourism, Transport and Posts and Telecommunications: Moroni; tel. (73) 2098.

President and Legislature

PRESIDENT

In the first round of voting, which took place on 6 March 1996, none of the 15 candidates received 50% of the total votes cast. A second round of voting took place on 16 March, when voters chose between the two leading candidates. MOHAMED TAKI ABDOULKARIM received 64.3% of the votes, while ABBAS DJOUSSOUF obtained 35.7%. Following the death of MOHAMED TAKI ABDOULKARIM on 6 November 1998, TADJIDINE BEN SAÏD MASSOUNDI was designated acting President, pending the holding of an election. Col ASSOUMANI AZZALI was sworn in as Head of State on 6 May 1999, having seized power in a military coup on 30 April.

ASSEMBLÉE FÉDÉRALE

Following the coup of 30 April 1999, the Federal Assembly (Assemblée Fédérale) was dissolved.

Political Organizations

CHUMA (Islands' Fraternity and Unity Party): Moroni; Leader Prince SAÏD ALI KEMAL.

Comité de suivi et d'orientation pour l'autonomie de Mohéli.

Forces pour l'action républicaine (FAR): Leader Maj. ABDU-RAZAKU ABDULHAMID.

Forum pour le redressement national (FRN): f. 1994; alliance of 12 parties; Leader ABBAS DJOUSSOUF.

Front démocratique (FD): BP 758, Moroni; tel. (73) 3603; e-mail idriss@snpt.km; f. 1982; Leader MOUSTOIFA SAÏD CHEIKH.

Front national pour la justice (FNJ): Islamic fundamentalist orientation; Leader AHMED ABDALLAH MOHAMED.

Front populaire comorien (FPC): Mwali; Leader MOHAMED HAS-SANALY.

Groupe d'initiative pour le redressement du mouvement anjouanais (GIRMA): f. 1999; separatist group on Nzwani (Anjouan); Leader AHMED CHARIKAN.

Mkoutrouo: principal separatist group on Mwali (Mohéli); Leader SAÏD MOHAMED SOUEF.

Mouvement des citoyens pour la République (MCR): f. 1998; Leader MAHAMOUD MRADABI.

Mouvement mohélien pour l'égalité des îles: f.1995.

Mouvement populaire anjouanais (MPA): f. 1997 by merger of Organisation pour l'indépendance d'Anjouan and Mouvement séparatiste anjouanais; principal separatist movement on Nzwani (Anjouan).

Mouvement pour la démocratie et le progrès (MDP): Moroni; founder-mem. of the FRN (see above); Leader ABBAS DJOUSSOUF.

Mouvement pour la rénovation et l'action démocratique (MOURAD): Moroni; f. 1990; aims to promote economic and financial rehabilitation; Leader ABDOY ISSA.

Nguzo: Moroni; Leader TAKI MBOREHA.

Parti comorien pour la démocratie et le progrès (PCDP): Route Djivani, BP 179, Moroni; tel. (73) 1733; fax (73) 0650; Leader ALI MROUDJAE.

Parti républicain des Comores: f. 1998; Leader MOHAMED M'CHANGAMA; Sec.-Gen. AHAMADA MADI.

Parti socialiste des Comores (PASOCO): POB 720, Moroni; tel. (73) 1328; Leader ALI IDAROUSSE.

Parti du salut national (PSN): f. 1993; breakaway faction of PCDP; Islamic orientation; Leader SAÏD ALI MOHAMED.

Rassemblement national pour le développement (RND): f. 1996 by 24 parties supporting President Taki; Chair. ALI BAZI SELIM; Sec. Gen. ABDOULHAMID AFFRAITANE.

Diplomatic Representation

EMBASSIES IN THE COMOROS

China, People's Republic: BP 442, Moroni; tel. (73) 2721; fax (73) 2866; Ambassador: XU DAIJIE.

France: blvd de Strasbourg, BP 465, Moroni; tel. (73) 0753; fax (73) 1727; Ambassador: JEAN PIERRE LAJAUNIE.

Korea, Democratic People's Republic: Moroni; Ambassador: KIM RYONG YONG.

Libya: BP 1787, Moroni; tel. (73) 2819.

Mauritius: Moroni.

Seychelles: Moroni.

Judicial System

Under the terms of the Constitution of October 1996, the President is the guarantor of the independence of the judicial system, and chairs the Higher Council of the Magistracy (Conseil Supérieur de la Magistrature), of which the Minister of Justice is Vice-President. The High Council of the Republic, which comprises four members appointed by the President, three members elected by the Federal Assembly and one member elected by the Council of each island, acts as a High Court of Justice. The judicial system was to be reorganized under new constitutional arrangements under consideration in mid-1999.

Religion

The majority of the population are Muslims. At 31 December 1998 there were an estimated 2,000 adherents of the Roman Catholic Church, equivalent to 0.3% of the total population.

CHRISTIANITY
The Roman Catholic Church

Office of Apostolic Administrator of the Comoros: Mission Catholique, BP 46, Moroni; tel. (73) 0570; fax (73) 0503; Apostolic Pro-Admin. Fr JAN SZPILKA.

The Press

Al Watwany: Nagoudjou, BP 984, Moroni; tel. (73) 2861; f. 1985; weekly; state-owned; Dir-Gen. MOHAMED IBRAHIM; Editor-in-Chief (vacant); circ. 1,500.

L'Archipel: Moroni; f. 1988; weekly; independent; Publrs ABOUBACAR MCHANGAMA, SAINDOU KAMAL; circ. 300.

La Tribune de Moroni: Moroni; monthly.

NEWS AGENCIES

Agence Comores Presse (ACP): Moroni.

Foreign Bureau

Agence France-Presse (AFP): BP 1327, Moroni. ABOUBACAR MICH-ANGAMA.

Broadcasting and Communications

TELECOMMUNICATIONS

Société Nationale des Postes et des Télécommunications: BP 5000, Moroni; tel. (73) 0610; fax (73) 1079; operates post and telecommunications services; Dir-Gen. SAÏD ABASSE DAHLANI.

RADIO

Transmissions to the Comoros from Radio France Internationale commenced in early 1994. By 1998 a number of privately-owned radio stations were broadcasting in the Comoros.

Radio-Comoro: BP 452, Moroni; tel. (73) 2531; fax (73) 0303; govt-controlled; domestic programmes in Comoran and French; international broadcasts in Swahili, Arabic and French; Dir-Gen. ISMAIL IBOUROI; Tech. Dir ABDULLAH RADJAB.

Finance

BANKING

(cap. = capital; res = reserves; dep. = deposits; m. = million; brs = branches; amounts in Comoros francs)

Central Bank

Banque Centrale des Comores: place de France, BP 405, Moroni; tel. (73) 1814; fax (73) 0349; f. 1981; bank of issue; cap. and res 8,550m., dep. 5,970m. (Dec. 1997); Pres. MOHAMED HALIFA; Gov. SAÏD AHMED SAÏD ALI.

Commercial Bank

Banque pour l'Industrie et le Commerce—Comores (BIC): place de France, BP 175, Moroni; tel. (73) 0243; fax (73) 1229; e-mail bic@snpt.km; f. 1990; 51% owned by Banque Nationale de Paris Intercontinentale; 34% state-owned; cap. and res 1,817.6m., total assets 14,435.3m. (Dec. 1998); Pres. MRADABI MAHAMOUD; Dir-Gen. GUY CAZENAVE; 6 brs.

Development Bank

Banque de Développement des Comores: place de France, BP 298, Moroni; tel. (73) 0818; fax (73) 0397; f. 1982; provides loans, guarantees and equity participation for small- and medium-scale projects; 50% state-owned; cap. and res 1,477.1m., total assets 3,728.5m. (Dec. 1998); Pres. MZE CHEI OUBEIDI; Gen. Man. SAÏD ABDIL-LAHI.

Trade and Industry

GOVERNMENT AGENCIES

Office National du Commerce: Moroni; state-operated agency for the promotion and development of domestic and external trade.

Société de Développement de la Pêche Artisanale des Comores (SODEPAC): Moroni; state-operated agency overseeing fisheries development programme.

DEVELOPMENT ORGANIZATIONS

CEFADER: a rural design, co-ordination and support centre, with brs on each island.

Mission de Coopération et d'Action Culturelle: BP 85, Moroni; tel. (73) 0391; fax (73) 1274; f. 1978; centre for administering bilateral aid from France; Dir JEAN-FRANCIS GOSPODAROWICZ.

CHAMBER OF COMMERCE

Chambre de Commerce, d'Industrie et d'Agriculture: BP 763, Moroni; privatized in 1995.

EMPLOYERS' ORGANIZATION

Club d'Actions des Promoteurs Economiques: Moroni; f. 1999; Head SAID HASSANE DINI.

UTILITIES

Comorienne de l'Eau et de l'Electricité (CEE): BP 1762, Moroni; tel. (73) 3130; fax (73) 2359; fmrly Electricité et Eau des Comores; state-controlled enterprise responsible for the production and distribution of electricity and water; transferred to private management in 1997; Dir-Gen. DENIS BAILLARD.

STATE-OWNED ENTERPRISE

Société Comorienne des Hydrocarbures (SCH): POB 28, Moroni; tel. (73) 0486; fax (73) 1883; imports petroleum products; transfer to private management pending; Gen. Man. MAHAMOUD MRADABI.

TRADE UNION

Union des Syndicats Autonomes des Travailleurs des Comores: BP 1199, Moroni; tel. and fax (73) 5143; f. 1996; Sec.-Gen. IBOUROI ALI TABIBOU.

Transport

ROADS

In 1996 there were an estimated 900 km of classified roads, of which 440 km were principal roads and 230 km secondary roads. About 76.5% of the network was paved in 1995.

SHIPPING

The port of Mutsamudu, on Njazidja, can accommodate vessels of up to 11 m draught. Goods from Europe are routed via Madagascar, and coastal vessels connect the Comoros with the east coast of Africa. The development of the port of Moroni, with support from the European Community (EC, now European Union), was completed in mid-1991. In 1993 the EC pledged US $4m. to finance the construction of a port at Fomboni, on Mwali, to improve shipping access to the island.

Société Comorienne de Navigation: Moroni; services to Madagascar.

CIVIL AVIATION

The international airport is at Moroni-Hahaya on Njazidja. Each of the three other islands has a small airfield. At the end of 1995 it was announced that Air Comores, the national airline, was to be liquidated. In October 1999 Yemen Airways (Yemenia), following negotiations with the Comoran government, was granted the status of the national airline of the Comoros and the use of the Comoran air traffic rights between Moroni and Paris, France.

Comores Aviation: Moroni; f. 1999; twice-weekly charter flights between Moroni and Mayotte; Dir JEAN MARC HEINTZ.

Tourism

The principal tourist attractions are the beaches, underwater fishing and mountain scenery. In 1991 hotel capacity increased from 112 to 294 rooms, following the implementation of a number of hotel development projects, which resulted in a considerable increase in tourism receipts that year. In 1997 there were 26,219 tourist arrivals by air in the Comoros, and receipts from tourism totalled US $26m.; tourist arrivals increased to 28,840 in 1998.

Société Comorienne de Tourisme et d'Hôtellerie (COMOTEL): Itsandra Hotel, Njazidja; tel. (73) 2365; national tourist agency: Dir-Gen. SITTI ATTOMANE.

Defence

The national army, the Force comorienne de défense (FCD), comprised about 1,500 men in mid-1997. In December 1996 an agreement was ratified with France, which provided for the permanent presence of a French military contingent in the Comoros. Following the military coup in April 1999, France suspended all military co-operation with the Comoros.

Defence Expenditure: Estimated at US $3m. in 1994.

Commander-in-Chief of the Comoran Armed Forces: Col ASSOUMANI AZZALI.

Education

Education is officially compulsory for nine years between seven and 16 years of age. Primary education begins at the age of seven and lasts for six years. Secondary education, beginning at 13 years of age, lasts for a further seven years, comprising a first cycle of four years and a second of three years. In 1995 enrolment at primary schools was equivalent to 75% of children in the relevant age-group. Children may also receive a basic education through traditional Koranic schools, which are staffed by Comoran teachers. In 1995 enrolment at secondary schools was equivalent to 21% of children in the relevant age-group (males 24%; females 19%). Expenditure by the central government on education in 1995 was 3,381m. Comoros francs, representing 21.1% of current expenditure. In 1995, according to estimates by UNESCO, the average rate of adult illiteracy was 45.0% (males 37.5%, females 52.4%).

MAYOTTE

Since the Comoros unilaterally declared independence in July 1975, Mayotte (Mahoré) has been administered separately by France. The independent Comoran state claims Mayotte as part of its territory and officially represents it in international organizations, including the UN. In December 1976, following a referendum in April (in which the population voted to renounce the status of an overseas territory), France introduced the special status of *collectivité territoriale* for the island. The French government is represented on Mayotte by an appointed prefect. There is a general council, with 19 members, who are elected by universal adult suffrage. Mayotte has one representative in the national assembly in Paris, and one in the senate.

Following the coup in the Comoros in May 1978, Mayotte rejected the new government's proposal that it should rejoin the other islands under a federal system, and reaffirmed its intention of remaining linked to France. The main political party on Mayotte, the Mouvement populaire mahorais (MPM), seeks full departmental status for the island, but France has been reluctant to grant this, in view of Mayotte's underdeveloped condition. In December 1979 the French national assembly approved legislation to prolong Mayotte's special status for another five years, during which period a referendum was to be conducted on the island. In October 1984, however, the national assembly further extended Mayotte's status, and the referendum on the island's future was postponed indefinitely. The UN general assembly has adopted several resolutions reaffirming the sovereignty of the Comoros over the island, and urging France to reach an agreement with the Comoran government as soon as possible. The Organization of African Unity (OAU) has endorsed this view.

Following elections to the French national assembly in March 1986, Henry Jean-Baptiste, representing an alliance of the Centre des démocrates sociaux (CDS) and the Union pour la démocratie française (UDF), was elected as deputy for Mayotte. In October Jacques Chirac became the first French prime minister to visit Mayotte, where he assured the islanders that they would remain French citizens for as long as they wished. However, relations between the MPM and the French government rapidly deteriorated following the Franco-African summit in November 1987, when Chirac expressed his reservations to the Comoran president concerning the elevation of Mayotte to the status of a full overseas department (despite his announcement, in early 1986, that he endorsed the MPM's aim to upgrade the status of Mayotte.)

In the first round of the 1988 French presidential election, which took place on 24 April, the islanders demonstrated their response to Chirac's stance on Mayotte's constitutional future by favouring the candidacy of Raymond Barre to that of Chirac. The second round of the election, held on 10 May, was contested by Chirac and François Mitterrand, the incumbent president and candidate of the Parti socialiste (PS); a substantial proportion of votes on Mayotte was transferred to Mitterrand, who received 50.3% of votes cast on Mayotte, defeating Chirac. At elections to the French national assembly, which took place in June, Jean-Baptiste retained his seat. (Later that month he joined the newly-formed centrist group in the French national assembly, the Union du centre.) In elections to the general council in September and October, the MPM retained a majority of seats.

In November 1989 the general council demanded that the French government introduce measures to curb immigration to Mayotte from neighbouring islands, particularly from the Comoros. In January 1990 pressure by a group from the town of Mamoudzou resulted in increasing tension over the presence of Comoran refugees on the island. Later that month there was a demonstration in protest against illegal immigration to the island. A paramilitary organization, 'Caiman' (which demanded the expulsion of illegal immigrants), was subsequently formed. In May the Comoran president, Saïd Mohamed Djohar, undertook to pursue peaceful dialogue to resolve the question of Mayotte's sovereignty, and issued a formal appeal to France to review the island's status. Mayotte was used as a strategic

military base in late 1990, in preparation for French participation in multinational operations during the 1991 Gulf War.

In late June 1991 a demonstration was held on the adjacent islet of Pamandzi, in protest at the relocation of a number of people as a result of the expansion of the airfield. Unrest among young people on Pamandzi escalated in early July; the mayor fled after demonstrators attempted to set fire to the town hall. Clashes took place between demonstrators and security forces, and the prefect requested that police reinforcements be dispatched from Réunion to restore order. An organization of young people, the Association des jeunes pour le développement de Pamandzi (AJDP), accused the mayor of maladministration and demanded his resignation. The demonstrations, which threatened to destabilize the MPM, were generally viewed as a manifestation of general discontent among young people on Mayotte (who comprised about 60% of the population). Later in July five members of the AJDP, who had taken part in the demonstration at the airfield in June, received prison sentences.

In June 1992 increasing tension resulted in further attacks against Comoran immigrants resident in Mayotte. In early September representatives of the MPM met the French prime minister, Pierre Bérégovoy, to request the reintroduction of entry visas in order to restrict immigration from the Comoros. Later that month the MPM organized a boycott (which was widely observed) of Mayotte's participation in the French referendum on the Treaty on European Union, in protest at the French government's refusal to introduce entry visas. In December legal proceedings were taken against the prefect of Mayotte, Jean-Paul Costes, and a number of other prominent officials, in connection with the deaths of several people in domestic fires that had been caused by poor quality fuel imported from Bahrain. In February 1993 a general strike, staged in support of wage increases, culminated in violent rioting; security forces were subsequently dispatched from Réunion and mainland France to restore order. At the end of February Costes was replaced as prefect by Jean-Jacques Debacq.

At elections to the French national assembly, which took place in March 1993, Jean-Baptiste was returned by 53.4% of votes cast, while Mansour Kamardine, the secretary-general of the local branch of the right-wing French mainland party, the Rassemblement pour la Républic (RPR), obtained 44.3% of the vote. Kamardine subsequently accused Jean-Baptiste of illegally claiming the support of an electoral alliance of the RPR and the UDF, known as the Union pour la France (UPF), by forging the signatures of the secretary-general of the RPR and his UDF counterpart on a document. However, Jean-Baptiste denied the allegations, and, in turn, began legal proceedings against Kamardine for alleged forgery and defamation. Elections to the general council (which was enlarged from 17 to 19 members) took place in March 1994; the MPM secured 12 seats, the local branch of the RPR four seats, and independent candidates three seats. During an official visit to Mayotte in November, the French prime minister, Edouard Balladur, announced the reintroduction of entry visas as a requirement for Comoran nationals and the adoption of a number of security measures, in an effort to reduce illegal immigration. He also indicated that a referendum to determine the future of Mayotte would be conducted by the year 2000. In the first round of the French presidential election, which took place in April 1995, Balladur received the highest number of votes on Mayotte (although Chirac subsequently won the election).

Following a further coup attempt in September 1995 by mercenaries in the Comoros, the French government dispatched additional troops to Mayotte, prior to carrying out a military intervention. In elections to the French senate held in that month, the incumbent MPM representative, Marcel Henry, was returned by a large majority. During a visit to Mayotte in October, the French secretary of state for overseas departments and territories pledged that a referendum on the future status of the island would be conducted by 1999. In October 1996 he confirmed that two commissions, operating from Paris and Dzaoudzi, were preparing a consultation document, which would be presented in late 1997, and announced that the proposed referendum would take place before the end of the decade.

Partial elections to fill nine seats in the general council were held in March 1997; the MPM secured three seats (losing two that it had previously held), the local branch of the RPR won three seats, the local PS one seat, and independent right-wing candidates two seats. In elections to the French national assembly Jean-Baptiste, representing the UDF/Force démocrate (FD, formerly the CDS) alliance, defeated Kamardine, securing 51.7% of votes cast in the second round of voting, which took place in June.

In July 1997 the relative prosperity of Mayotte was thought to have prompted separatist movements on the Comoron islands of Nzwani and Mwali to demand the restoration of French rule, and subsequently to declare their independence in August. In September, following an unsuccessful military intervention, mounted by the Comoron government in an attempt to quell the insurrection, many of those injured in the fighting were taken to Mayotte for medical treatment. Illegal immigration from the Comoros has continued to be a major concern for the authorities on Mayotte; during January–February 1997 some 6,000 Comorans were expelled from the island, with many more agreeing to leave voluntarily. In December 1998 demonstrators protested against the influx of refugees fleeing the fighting on Nzwani.

Meanwhile, uncertainty remained over the future status of Mayotte. In April 1998 one of the commissions charged with examining the issue submitted its report, which concluded that the present status of collectivité territoriale was no longer appropriate, but did not advocate an alternative. In May the MPM declared its support for an adapted form of departmental administration, and urged the French authorities to decide on a date for a referendum. In July Pierre Bayle succeeded Philippe Boisadam as prefect of Mayotte. Two rounds of preparatory talks on the island's constitutional future took place in December 1998 between local political organizations and senior French government officials; a project was drafted which addressed various options, although no consensus was reached. Further talks expected to take place in February 1999 were suspended, apparently owing to France's concerns over the continuing political instability in the Comoros, particularly as French sovereignty over Mayotte remains unrecognized by the UN and the OAU. In the following months Jean-Baptiste and Younoussa Bamana, the president of the general council, increased pressure on the government in Paris to organize a referendum by the end of 1999. In August, following negotiations between the French secretary of state for overseas departments and territories, Jean-Jack Queyranne, and island representatives, Mayotte members of the RPR and the PS as well as the leader of the MPM, Bamana, signed a draft document providing for the transformation of Mayotte into a *collectivité départementale*, if approved at a referendum. However, both Henry and Jean-Baptiste rejected the document. The two politicians subsequently announced their departure from the MPM and formed a new political party entitled the Mouvement Départementaliste Mahorais (MDM), whilst reiterating their demands that Mayotte be granted full overseas department status. Following the approval of Mayotte's proposed new status by the general council (by 14 votes to five) and the municipal councils, an accord to this effect was signed by Queyranne and political representatives of Mayotte on 27 January 2000. On 2 July a referendum was held, in which the population of Mayotte voted overwhelmingly in favour of the January accord, granting Mayotte the status of *collectivité départementale* for a period of 10 years. A bill

confirming Mayotte's new status, was expected to be presented to the French parliament before the end of 2000.

Mayotte's gross domestic product (GDP) per head was estimated at 4,050 French francs in 1991. Between the censuses of 1991 and 1997 the population of Mayotte increased at an average annual rate of 5.7%. The economy of Mayotte is based mainly on agriculture. In 1997 18.6% of the employed labour force were engaged in this sector. Rice, cassava and maize are cultivated for domestic consumption, and vanilla, ylang-ylang (an ingredient of perfume), coffee and copra are the main export products. Industry (which is dominated by the construction sector) engaged 21.5% of the employed population in 1997. There are no mineral resources on the island. Imports of mineral products comprised 5.0%, and metals 10.3% of the cost of total imports in 1997. Services engaged 59.8% of the employed population in 1997. The annual total of tourist arrivals (excluding cruise-ship passengers) increased from 6,700 in 1995 to 21,000 in 1999. Receipts from tourism in 1999 totalled 50m. francs.

In 1997 France was the principal source of imports (accounting for 60% of the total), and the principal market for exports (68%). Other major trading partners were South Africa and Réunion. Owing to its reliance on imports, Mayotte operates a substantial trade deficit, which totalled 896m. French francs in 1998. In 1997 the principal imports were foodstuffs (22.8%), machinery and transport equipment (32.7%) and metals (10.3%). The main exports in 1997 were oil of ylang-ylang, transport equipment and foodstuffs. In that year falling prices and increased competition on international markets led to a significant decline in exports of vanilla (usually one of Mayotte's principal exports). In 1986 Mayotte's external assets totalled 203.8m. francs. In 1997 Mayotte's total budget revenue was estimated at 1,022.4m. francs, while total expenditure was estimated at 964.2m. francs. Official debt totalled 435.7m. francs at 31 December 1995. The rate of inflation in the year to December 1997 was 2.1%. Some 41.2% of the labour force were unemployed in 1997. As Mayotte's labour force has continued to increase, mostly owing to a high birth rate and continued illegal immigration, youth unemployment has caused particular concern. In 1997 37.8% of the unemployed population were under 25 years of age.

In 1995 the Caisse française de développement (now the Agence française de développement), granted a loan of 80m. French francs, as part of a 153m. francs programme, to further develop infrastructure on the island. Substantial aid from France during the period 1987–92 was designed to stimulate the development of tourism on the island through the construction of a deep-water port at Longoni and the expansion of the airfield at Dzaoudzi. Mayotte's remote location, however, remains an obstacle to the development of tourism. In 1994 it was reported that the value of exports had declined, owing, in part, to strong regional competition in the agricultural sector, in conjunction with an increase in the cost of labour on the island. In April 1995 an economic and social programme was agreed with the French government for the period 1995–99. Later in that year Mayotte received credit from France to finance further investment in infrastructure, particularly in the road network. The adjustment of the minimum wage, which increased by 10.3% in 1994, sustained economic activity, resulting in higher consumer spending and imports. In 1996 construction began on a plant to produce Coca-Cola products in the industrial zone around Longoni; construction costs were estimated at 16m.–18m. francs.

The principal towns are the capital, Dzaoudzi (estimated population 8,300 in 1991), Mamoudzou and Pamandzi-Labattoir. France is responsible for the defence of the island: in August 1999 there were 2,850 French troops stationed on Mayotte and Réunion.

Statistical Survey

Source (unless otherwise indicated): Institut National de la Statistique et des Etudes Economiques; 51 hauts des Jardins du Collège, BP 1362, 97600 Mamoudzou.

AREA AND POPULATION

Area: 374 sq km (144 sq miles).

Population: 67,167 (census of August 1985); 94,410 (census of August 1991); 131,368 (males 66,600; females 64,768) at census of August 1997; 142,000 (official estimate) at 1 January 1998. *Principal towns* (population of communes at 1997 census): Dzaoudzi (capital) 10,792, Mamoudzou 32,733, Koungou 10,165.

Density (1 January 1998): 379.7 per sq km.

Births and Deaths (1997): Registered live births 5,326 (birth rate 40.6 per 1,000); Death rate 5.6 per 1,000.

Economically Active Population (persons aged betweeen 15 and 64 years, census of August 1997): Agriculture and fishing 4,672; Electricity, gas and water 399; Industry 1,164; Construction and engineering 3,843; Wholesale and retail trade 2,717; Transport and telecommunications 1,563; Other marketable services 1,530; Finance and insurance 97; Other non-marketable services 9,108; Total employed 25,093 (males 18,200, females 6,893); Persons on compulsory military service 143 (males 139, females 4); Unemployed 17,660 (males 8,982, females 8,678); Total labour force 42,896 (males 27,321, females 15,575).

AGRICULTURE, ETC.

Livestock (1995): Cattle 15,000; Sheep 2,700; Goats 23,000.

Fishing (metric tons, live weight): Total catch 646 in 1995; 1,217 in 1996; 1,531 in 1997. Source: FAO, *Yearbook of Fishery Statistics.*

FINANCE

Currency and Exchange Rates: 100 centimes = 1 French franc. *Sterling, Dollar and Euro Equivalents* (28 April 2000): £1 sterling = 11.3220 francs; US \$ 7.2202 francs; € = 6.5596 francs; 1,000 French francs = £88.32 = \$138.50 = €152.45. *Average Exchange Rate* (French francs per US dollar): 5.8367 in 1997; 5.8995 in 1998; 6.1570 in 1999. Since the introduction of the euro, with French participation, on 1 January 1999, a fixed exchange rate of €1 = 6.55957 francs has been in operation.

Budget (million French francs, 1997): Total revenue 1,022.4 (current 783.7, capital 238.7); Total expenditure 964.2 (current 725.4, capital 238.7).

Money Supply (million French francs at 31 December 1997): Currency outside banks 789; Demand deposits 266; Total money 1,055.

Cost of Living (Consumer Price Index; base: December 1996 = 100). 102.1 in December 1997.

EXTERNAL TRADE

Total Trade (million French francs): *Imports:* 915 in 1998. *Exports:* 19 in 1998.

Principal Commodities (million French francs, 1997): *Imports:* Foodstuffs 188.1 (Beef and veal 19.2, Poultry and rabbit meat 26.4, Rice 33.6); Mineral products 41.0 (Hydraulic cements 31.4); Chemicals and related products 63.1 (Medicinal and pharmaceutical products 21.6); Plastic materials, ethers and resins 29.1; Wood, charcoal and wickerwork 25.5 (Sawnwood 16.2); Paper-making material, paper and paper products 20.8; Textiles 22.9; Base metals and metal products 84.6; Electrical machinery, apparatus and appliances 168.5; Transport equipment 101.1 (Passenger motor cars 44.3, Road motor vehicles for goods transport 25.2); Optical and photographic apparatus 21.4; Miscellaneous goods 20.1; Total (incl. others) 823.4. *Exports:* Foodstuffs 2.4 (Vanilla 0.8); Chemicals and related products 5.8 (Ylang-ylang 5.6); Paper-making materials, paper and paper products 1.5; Base metals and metal products 1.9; Electrical machinery, apparatus and appliances 2.2; Transport equipment 4.6 (Passenger motor cars 1.0, Road motor vehicles for goods transport 1.9); Total (incl. others) 20.2.

Principal Trading Partners (percentage of trade, 1997): *Imports:* France 60%; South Africa 8%. *Exports:* France 68%; Réunion 7%.

TRANSPORT

Road Traffic (1998): Motor vehicles in use 8,213.

Shipping: *Traffic* (metric tons, 1998): Goods unloaded 21,102; Goods loaded 8,165.

Civil Aviation (1998): *Passenger arrivals:* 42,260; *Passenger departures:* 45,774; *Freight carried:* 1,012 metric tons.

TOURISM

Visitor Arrivals (excluding cruise-ship passengers): 9,500 in 1997; 11,400 in 1998; 21,000 in 1999.

Tourism Receipts (million French francs): 50 in 1999.

COMMUNICATIONS MEDIA

Telephones (1997): 9,314 subscribers.

EDUCATION

Pre-primary (1997): 42 schools; 5,663 pupils.
Primary (1997): 99 schools; 24,681 pupils.
General Secondary (1997): 14 schools; 10,616 pupils.
Vocational and Technical (1997): 2 institutions; 1,449 students.

Directory

The Constitution

Under the status of *collectivité territoriale*, which was adopted in December 1976, Mayotte has an elected general council, comprising 19 members, which assists the prefect in the administration of the island. On 2 July 2000 a referendum was held on Mayotte, in which the population overwhelmingly approved the proposed transformation of the island into a *collectivité départementale*.

The Government

Représentation du Gouvernement, 97610 Dzaoudzi; tel. 60-10-54; fax 60-18-50.
(August 2000)

Prefect: Pierre Bayle.
Secretary-General: Jean-Pierre Laflaquière.
Deputy to the French National Assembly: Henry Jean-Baptiste (MDM).
Representative to the French Senate: Marcel Henry (MDM).

GOVERNMENT DEPARTMENTS

Department of Agriculture and Forestry: 15 rue Mariazé, 97600 Mamoudzou; tel. 61-12-13; fax 61-10-31.

Department of Education: rue du collège, 97600 Mamoudzou; tel. 61-10-24; fax 61-09-87.

Department of Health and Social Security: rue de l'Hôpital, 96700 Mamoudzou; tel. 61-12-25; fax 60-19-56.

Department of Work, Employment and Training: 4 place du Mariage, 97600 Mamoudzou; tel. 61-16-57; fax 61-03-37.

Department of Youth and Sports: rue Mariage, BP 248, 97600 Mamoudzou; tel. 61-16-60; fax 61-01-26.

CONSEIL GÉNÉRAL

Conseil Général, 8 rue de l'Hôpital, 97600 Mamoudzou; tel. 61-12-33; fax 61-10-18.

The general council comprises 19 members. At elections in March 1994, the Mouvement Populaire Mahorais (MPM) secured 12 seats, the Fédération de Mayotte du Rassemblement pour la République four seats, and independent candidates three seats. As a result of by-elections held in March 1997, the MPM holds eight seats, the

Fédération de Mayotte du Rassemblement pour la République five seats, independent right-wing candidates five seats, and the Parti Socialiste one seat.

President of the General Council: YOUNOUSSA BAMANA.

Political Organizations

Fédération de Mayotte du Rassemblement pour la République: 97610 Dzaoudzi; local branch of the French (Gaullist) Rassemblement pour la République (RPR); Sec.-Gen. MANSOUR KAMARDINE.

Mouvement Départementaliste Mahorais (MDM): 97610 Dzaoudzi; f. 1999 by former members of the MPM; seeks full overseas departmental status for Mayotte; Leader HENRY JEAN-BAPTISTE.

Mouvement Populaire Mahorais (MPM): 97610 Dzaoudzi; seeks departmental status for Mayotte; Leader YOUNOUSSA BAMANA.

Parti pour le Rassemblement Démocratique des Mahorais (PRDM): 97610 Dzaoudzi; f. 1978; seeks unification with the Federal Islamic Republic of the Comoros; Leader DAROUÈCHE MAOULIDA.

Parti Socialiste: Dzaoudzi; local branch of the French party of the same name; Leader IBRAHIM ABUBACAR.

Judicial System

Tribunal Supérieur d'Appel: 97600 Mamoudzou, tel. 61-12-65; fax 61-19-63; Pres. JEAN-BAPTISTE FLORI; Prosecutor JEAN-LOUIS BEC.

Procureur de la République: PATRICK BROSSIER.

Tribunal de Première Instance: Pres. ARLETTE MEALLONNIER-DUGUE.

Religion

Muslims comprise about 98% of the population. Most of the remainder are Christians, mainly Roman Catholics.

CHRISTIANITY
The Roman Catholic Church

Mayotte is within the jurisdiction of the Apostolic Administrator of the Comoros.

Office of the Apostolic Administrator: BP 1012, 97600 Mamoudzou; tel. and fax 61-11-53.

The Press

L'Insulaire: Immeuble Villa Bourhani, rue du Collège, BP 88, 97600 Mamoudzou; tel. 61-37-85; fax 61-37-86; weekly.

Le Kwezi: BP 5, 97600 Mamoudzou; tel. 61-30-00; fax 61-19-91; e-mail kwezi@wanadoo.fr; f. 1996; biweekly; Dir ZAÏDOU BAMANA; Editor-in-Chief LAURENT CANAVATE.

Broadcasting and Communications
RADIO AND TELEVISION

Société Nationale de Radio-Télévision Française d'Outre-mer (RFO): BP 103, 97610 Dzaoudzi; tel. 60-10-17; fax 60-18-52; e-mail jrv@wanadoo.fr; internet www.rfo.fr; f. 1977; govt-owned; radio broadcasts in French and Mahorian; television transmissions began in 1986; plans for a satellite service were announced in 1998; Pres. ANDRÉ-MICHEL BESSE; Dir-Gen. GEROGES CHOW-TOUN.

Finance
BANKS

Issuing Authority

Institut d'Emission des Départements d'Outre-mer: BP 500, 97600 Mamoudzou; tel. 61-10-38; fax 61-05-02.

Commercial Bank

Banque Française Commerciale Océan Indien: BP 322, 97600 Mamoudzou; tel. 61-10-91; fax 61-17-40; br. at Dzaoudzi.

Transport
ROADS

In 1984 the main road network totalled approximately 93 km, of which 72 km were bituminized. There were 137 km of local roads, of which 40 km were tarred, and 54 km of minor tracks (unusable during the rainy season).

SHIPPING

Coastal shipping is provided by locally-owned small craft. There is a deep-water port at Longoni.

CIVIL AVIATION

There is an airfield at Dzaoudzi, serving four-times weekly commercial flights to Réunion, twice-weekly services to Madagascar, Njazidja, Nzwani and Mwali, and a weekly service to Kenya. A direct service to Paris, expected to commence in 1999, was postponed, owing to the inadequacy of facilities at the island's airfield.

Tourism

Tropical scenery provides the main tourist attraction. In 1999 the island had six hotels, providing 118 rooms, five guest houses and eight apartments and lodges. Excluding cruise-ship passengers, Mayotte received 21,000 visitors in 1999, and tourism receipts totalled 50m. French francs in that year.

Comité du Tourisme de Mayotte: rue de la Pompe, BP 1169, 97600 Mamoudzou; tel. 61-09-09; fax 61-03-46; e-mail comite-du-tourisme-mayotte@wanadoo.fr; internet www.mayotte-island.com.

Bibliography

Bourde, A. 'The Comoro Islands: Problems of a Microcosm', in *Journal of Modern African Studies*, No. 3, 1965.

Cornu, H. *Paris et Bourbon, La politique française dans l'Océan indien*. Paris, Académie des Sciences d'Outre-mer, 1984.

Dubins, B. 'The Comoro Islands: A Bibliographical Essay', in *African Studies Bulletin*, No. 12, 1969.

Mantoux, T. 'Notes socio-économiques sur l'archipel des Comores', in *Revue française d'études politiques africaines*, No. 100, 1974.

Marquardt, W. *Seychellen, Komoren und Maskarenen*. Munich, 1976.

Newitt, M. *The Comoros Islands: Struggle against Dependency in the Indian Ocean*. Aldershot, Gower, 1985.

Perri, P. *Les nouveaux mercenaires*. Paris, L'Harmattan, 1994.

Salesse, Y. *Mayotte: L'illusion de la France, propositions pour une décolonisation*. Paris, L'Harmattan, 1995.

Weinberg, S. *Last of the Pirates: The Search for Bob Denard*. London, Jonathan Cape, 1994.

World Bank. *Comoros: Current Economic Situation and Prospects*. Washington, DC, International Bank for Reconstruction and Development, 1983.

THE DEMOCRATIC REPUBLIC OF THE CONGO

Physical and Social Geography

PIERRE GOUROU

PHYSICAL FEATURES

Covering an area of 2,344,885 sq km (905,365 sq miles), the Democratic Republic of the Congo (DRC, formerly Zaire) is bordered by the Republic of the Congo to the north-west, by the Central African Republic and Sudan to the north, by Uganda, Rwanda, Burundi and Tanzania to the east, and by Zambia and Angola to the south. There is a short coastline at the outlet of the River Congo. The DRC is, after Sudan, the largest country of sub-Saharan Africa. Despite its vast size, it lacks any particularly noteworthy points of relief, affording it a considerable natural advantage. Lying across the Equator, the DRC has an equatorial climate in the whole of the central region. Average temperatures range from 26°C in the coastal and basin areas to 18°C in the mountainous regions. Rainfall is plentiful in all seasons. In the north (Uele) the winter of the northern hemisphere is a dry season; in Katanga (formerly Shaba) in the south, the winter of the southern hemisphere is dry. The only arid region (less than 800 mm of rain per annum) is an extremely small area on the bank of the lower Congo.

The basin of the River Congo forms the country's dominant geographical feature. This basin had a deep tectonic origin; the continental shelf of Africa had given way to form an immense hollow, which drew towards it the waters from the north (Ubangi), from the east (Uele, Arruwimi), and from the south (Lualaba—that is the upper branch of the River Congo, Kasaï, Kwango). The crystalline continental shelf levels out at the periphery into plateaux in Katanga and the Congo-Nile ridge. The most broken-up parts of this periphery can be found in the west, in Bas-Congo, where the river cuts the folds of a Pre-Cambrian chain by a 'powerful breach', and above all in the east. Here, as a result of the volcanic overflow from the Virunga, they are varied by an upheaval of the rift valleys (where Lakes Tanganyika, Kivu, Edward and Albert are located).

The climate is generally conducive to agriculture and wood-forestry. Evergreen equatorial forest covers approximately 1m. sq km in the equatorial and sub-equatorial regions. In the north as in the south of this evergreen forest, tropical vegetation appears, with many trees that lose their leaves in the dry season. Vast stretches from the north to the south are, probably as a result of frequent fires, covered by sparse forest land, where trees grow alongside grasses (biombo from east Africa), and savannah dotted with shrubs.

The natural resources of the DRC are immense: its climate is favourable to profitable agriculture; the forests, if rationally exploited, could yield excellent results; the abundance of water should eventually be useful to industry and agriculture; and finally, there is considerable mineral wealth. The network of waterways is naturally navigable. The River Congo carries the second largest volume of water in the world. With the average flow to the mouth being 40,000 cu m per second, there are enormous possibilities for power generation, some of which are being realized at Inga. Indeed, the hydroelectric resources are considerable in the whole of the Congo basin.

The major exports of the DRC derive from the exploitation of its mineral resources. Copper is mined in upper Katanga, as are other metals—tin, silver, uranium, cobalt, manganese and tungsten. Diamonds are found in Kasaï, and tin, columbite, etc. in the east, around Maniema. In addition, many other mineral resources (such as iron ore and bauxite) await exploitation.

POPULATION

The DRC's population comprises numerous ethnic groups, which the external boundaries separate. The Kongo people are divided between the DRC, the Republic of the Congo, and Angola; the Zande between the DRC and Sudan; the Chokwe between the DRC and Angola; the Bemba between the DRC and Zambia; and the Alur between the DRC and Uganda. Even within its frontiers, the ethnic and linguistic geography of the DRC is highly diverse. The most numerous people are the Kongo; the people of Kwangu-Kwilu, who are related to them; the Mongo with their many subdivisions, who inhabit the Great Forest; the Luba, with their related groups the Lulua and Songe; the Bwaka; and the Zande. The majority speak Bantu languages, of which there is a great diversity. However, the north of the DRC belongs linguistically to Sudan. The extreme linguistic variety of the DRC is maintained to some extent by the ability of the people to speak several languages, by the existence of 'intermediary' languages (a Kongo dialect, a Luba dialect, Swahili and Lingala) and by the use of French.

According to UN estimates, the country's population at mid-year was 37,363,000 in 1990, increasing to 45,421,000 in 1995, to 46,772,000 in 1996, to 47,987,000 in 1997, and to 49,139,000 in 1998.

About 80% of the DRC's inhabitants reside in rural areas. The average density of population is low (estimated by the UN to be 21.0 per sq km at mid-1998), and the population is unevenly distributed. The population density in the Great Forest is only about one-half of the national average, with stretches of several tens of thousands of sq km virtually deserted, although this is not because the area cannot accommodate more people. However, it is clear that the population (with the exception of some pygmies) cannot increase in density as long as the forest is preserved. Indeed, certain areas belonging to the forest belt but partly cleared for cultivation, although they have no particular natural advantages, have higher than average densities. At the northern edge of the Great Forest the population density increases up to 20 people per sq km, and is then reduced to one or two in the extreme north of the country. Certain parts of Mayombé (Bas-Congo) have 100 people per sq km, but the south of the republic is sparsely populated (between 1–3 people per sq km). The capital, Kinshasa, had 2,653,558 inhabitants at the 1984 census and is the principal urban centre. Other major centres of population are Lubumbashi, with 543,268 inhabitants at the 1984 census; Mbuji-Mayi (423,363); Kananga (290,898) and Kisangani (282,650).

Recent History

GREGORY MTHEMBU-SALTER

Belgian interest in the area now comprising the Democratic Republic of the Congo (DRC, formerly Zaire) dates from 1876, when the Association internationale du Congo, under the control of King Léopold II of Belgium, began to establish a chain of trading stations along the River Congo. Economic exploitation of the territory expanded rapidly with the increasing demand for wild rubber, following the development of rubber tyres. However, the methods used in the collection of rubber frequently involved the infliction of atrocities on the indigenous population, and in 1908, as a result of British and US diplomatic pressure, responsibility for the administration of the territory was transferred from the king to the Belgian government, and the Congo became a Belgian colony.

As African political activity was not encouraged, radical Africans organized in 'cultural associations', which included the Alliance des Ba-Kongo (ABAKO), led by Joseph Kasavubu. Following a violent demonstration organized by ABAKO in January 1959, the Belgian government, alarmed at the prospect of involvement in a prolonged colonial war, adopted a course aimed at accelerated independence for the territory. While Belgium favoured the creation of a unitary state, based on the centralized pattern of the colonial system, the ABAKO and most other Congolese political groups were ethnically based, and (with the exception of Patrice Lumumba's Mouvement national congolais, MNC) preferred a federal structure. The constitutional arrangements that eventually emerged represented a compromise, affirming the unitary character of the state, but allowing each province to have its own government and legislature, and equal representation in a national senate.

THE FIRST REPUBLIC

The independence of the Republic of the Congo was proclaimed on 30 June 1960. Kasavubu became president and Lumumba prime minister. Five days later the armed forces mutinied. Their demands were partly satisfied by the replacement of the Belgian chief of staff by Col (later Marshal) Joseph-Désiré Mobutu who was aligned with Lumumba's MNC. Belgian troops intervened to protect their nationals, and at the same time the provinces of Katanga (subsequently Shaba) and South Kasaï resolved to secede. Lumumba requested help from the United Nations. Disagreement over Lumumba's response to the secession led to his dismissal by Kasavubu in September. This was challenged by Lumumba, who asked the legislature to remove Kasavubu. The political deadlock was resolved by the intervention of the armed forces. In September Col Mobutu assumed control of the country, ruling with the assistance of a collège des commissaires généraux (CCG). The CCG governed the Congo for one year, but failed to establish control of the north-eastern region, where some of Lumumba's former ministers had established a rival government in Stanleyville (later Kisangani).

Mobutu restored power to President Kasavubu in February 1961. A few days later Lumumba was murdered. The forceful reactions to this development by African governments and the UN prompted negotiations between Kasavubu and the MNC, and in August a new government was formed, with Cyrille Adoula as prime minister. The new administration received the support of most political groups (with the exception of Katanga separatists, led by Moïse Tshombe), and it was hoped that it would progressively re-establish national unity. A new constitution entered into force on 1 August 1964, establishing a presidential system of government and a federalist structure.

Meanwhile, the movement for the secession of Katanga had collapsed in January 1963, when its leader, Tshombe, went into exile. During early 1964 rebellions broke out in the Kwilu region and in southern Kivu and northern Katanga provinces. Within a few months the rebels had established their capital at Stanleyville (Kisangani). In July Kasavubu invited Tshombe to become interim prime minister, pending legislative elections. In the following month the country was renamed the Democratic

Republic of the Congo. In early 1965 the rebellion was defeated by the army, assisted by Belgian troops and by mercenaries.

In March and April 1965 the Tshombe government organized legislative elections. The coalition led by Tshombe, the Convention nationale congolaise (CONACO), won 122 of the 167 seats in the chamber of deputies. However, an opposition bloc, the Front démocratique congolais, soon emerged, and a political deadlock ensued. At this point the army, led by Mobutu, again intervened, and on 24 November 1965 Mobutu assumed full executive powers and declared himself the head of the 'Second Republic'.

'PRESIDENTIALISM' AND THE PARTY-STATE

Moving swiftly to consolidate his power, Mobutu imposed a five-year ban on party politics, and in 1966 founded the Mouvement populaire de la révolution (MPR) to facilitate the concentration of power in the hands of the president, who became the sole legislator and the head of government. The number of provinces was successively reduced, from 21 to eight, and provincial institutions were supplanted by appointed governors, who were responsible to the president. Kasavubu and Tshombe both left political life: both men died in 1969, while a number of former ministers, accused of plotting against Mobutu, were executed in June of that year. In June of that year a new constitution was approved by referendum, establishing a presidential regime, with a new legislature to be elected at a date to be determined by the president. The constitution provided for a maximum of two legally-authorized political parties, but the claims of existing political groups to official recognition were ignored. The constitution was amended so that the government, the legislature and the judiciary all became institutions of the MPR, and all citizens automatically became party members. By 1970 Mobutu had eliminated all potential opposition. In October 1971 the country was renamed the Republic of Zaire. In 1972 the president took the name Mobutu Sese Seko Kuku Ngbendu Wa Za Banga, as part of a national policy of 'authenticity'.

From the 1960s onwards one of the rival factions fighting for independence in the neighbouring Portuguese colony of Angola, the Frente Nacional de Libertação de Angola (FNLA), was permitted to maintain guerrilla bases and refugee camps along the border in Bas-Zaïre province. However, in 1976, after a rival faction, the Movimento Popular de Libertação de Angola (MPLA) had won the struggle for decolonization, there was an apparent reconciliation between Mobutu and President Neto of Angola. It was agreed that Angolan refugees in Zaire would be repatriated, and that Angola would return to Zaire several thousand Katangese soldiers, who had been members of Tshombe's forces at the time of the secession of Katanga. In March 1977 some of the latter, distrusting Mobutu's promises of an amnesty, invaded the Zairean province of Shaba (as Katanga had been renamed) from Angola, receiving support from many of the disaffected inhabitants. Mobutu obtained military assistance from France and Morocco, and by May the 'First Shaba War' was over. Subsequent retribution by the army against those who had failed to support the government after the 1977 invasion caused resentment, and this helped to provoke the 'Second Shaba War': in early May 1978 several thousand men, originating from Angola, crossed the Zambian border and entered Shaba, occupying Kolwezi, a major mining centre. French paratroops intervened to assist the Zairean forces in recapturing the town, and in June a Pan-African peace-keeping force arrived in Shaba, remaining there for more than a year.

THE ONSET OF OPPOSITION

During 1982 opponents of Zaire's one-party system of government attempted to establish a new party, the Union pour la démocratie et le progrès social (UDPS). Mobutu responded to this challenge by imprisoning 13 of its supporters in the national legislative council. In October, however, Nguza Karl-I-Bond, formerly a close political associate of Mobutu, emerged as the spokesman for a new coalition of opposition exile groups, the Front congolais pour le rétablissement de la démocratie (FCD).

In May 1983, following the publication of a highly critical report on Zaire by the human rights organization, Amnesty International, Mobutu offered an amnesty to all political exiles who returned to Zaire by 30 June. A number of exiles accepted the offer, but a substantial opposition movement remained active in Belgium. Internal opposition to Mobutu's regime continued to manifest itself during 1984, when a rebel force briefly occupied the town of Moba, in Shaba province. Zaire accused Belgium of harbouring the groups responsible for these insurgencies, and claimed that the rebels had crossed into Zaire from neighbouring Tanzania. However, the main opposition groups in Belgium denied any involvement in the occupation of Moba, and suggested that mutinous Zairean troops had been responsible.

Ministerial reshuffles in February, April and July 1985, and a further round of changes in the structure of the MPR (separating party and governmental functions), reinforced Mobutu's personal position. In July 1985 the return from exile of Nguza Karl-I-Bond (who was appointed ambassador to the USA in July 1986, a post which he held until March 1988), and the lifting of restrictions on seven members of the banned UDPS under the terms of another amnesty for political opponents, appeared to provide further evidence of the president's confidence in his position. The post of first state commissioner was abolished in late 1985, but was revived in January 1987, and allocated to Mabi Mulumba, previously state commissioner for finance. In March 1988 Mobutu again installed a new government, replacing Mabi Mulumba with Sambwa Pida Nbagui as first state commissioner. In November, in the fourth ministerial reshuffle of the year, Mobutu replaced about one-third of the members of the national executive council and reinstated Kengo Wa Dondo as first state commissioner.

In March 1986 Amnesty International published a further report condemning Zaire for abuses of human rights, specifically accusing the Mobutu regime of the illegal arrest, torture or murder of UDPS supporters in 1985. In October 1986 Mobutu responded to the allegations in the report by appointing a state commissioner for citizens' rights, and announcing the disbandment of the military state security agency.

Regional and municipal elections were held in May and June 1987, but the results were annulled because of alleged electoral malpractice. The elections were rescheduled for March 1988, but were subsequently postponed until March 1989, for 'budgetary reasons' and to ensure their conduct in a democratic and harmonious manner. Elections to the national legislative council took place in September 1987. In the same month several opposition groups announced that they had united to form a government-in-exile.

In June 1987 several members of the UDPS, including Etienne Tshisekedi Wa Mulumba (its secretary-general and a former minister of the interior), availed themselves of an amnesty offered by Mobutu. In October four other former UDPS leaders were admitted to the central committee of the MPR, and other reconciled opponents of the government were appointed to senior posts in state-owned enterprises. In January 1988, however, Tshisekedi was arrested after he attempted to organize an unauthorized public meeting, and subsequently placed under house arrest. In April he was rearrested after advocating a boycott of the partial legislative elections scheduled to take place in Kinshasa on 10 April. In September Tshisekedi withdrew from political activity, although this did not prevent his arrest in March 1989 for alleged involvement in student disturbances which broke out in Kinshasa and Lubumbashi at the end of February, in which an estimated 37 people were killed.

In February 1990 the UDPS organized demonstrations in Kinshasa and three other towns to commemorate the 29th anniversary of the assassination of Lumumba. Further unrest followed in April, when students staged protests in Kinshasa to demand larger study grants and the removal of Mobutu from power. In what was seen by many observers as an attempt to defuse the growing tension, Mobutu announced in late April that a multi-party political system, initially comprising three parties (including the MPR), would be introduced after a transitional period of one year. At the same time Mobutu declared

the inauguration of the 'Third Republic' and announced his resignation as chairman of the MPR and state commissioner for national defence. However, he retained the office of president. The national executive council was dissolved, and Prof. Lunda Bululu, the secretary-general of the Economic Community of Central African States (CEEAC) and formerly a legal adviser to Mobutu, replaced Kengo Wa Dondo as first state commissioner.

In early May 1990 a new transitional government was formed. Mobutu announced that a special commission would draft a new constitution by the end of April 1991, and that presidential elections would be held before December of that year, with legislative elections to follow in 1992. He also announced the imminent 'depoliticization of the armed forces, the gendarmerie, the civil guard, the security services and the administration in general'. In late April 1990 Tshisekedi was released from house arrest.

Further unrest occurred in early May 1990, when students at Lubumbashi University staged anti-government demonstrations. It was reported that between 50–150 students were massacred by members of the presidential guard, acting on Mobutu's orders. Strong condemnation was voiced by many humanitarian organizations, and the Belgian government announced the immediate suspension of all official bilateral assistance to Zaire. After some procrastination and strenuous denial of the reports, Mobutu authorized an official parliamentary inquiry, as a result of which a provincial governor and other senior local officials were arrested and charged with having organized the killing of one student and the injury of 13 others. However, Mobutu refused to allow an independent international board of inquiry to enter Zaire, despite Belgium's insistence, to investigate the case further.

As part of the continuing process of political reform, in late June 1990 the legislature adopted amendments to the constitution, whereby presidential control over the national executive council and over foreign policy was ended. At the same time the establishment of independent trade unions was authorized. In early October Mobutu announced that a full multi-party political system would be established, and in November the necessary enabling legislation was adopted. In the same month, however, the USA announced that it was to terminate all military and economic aid to Zaire. This development followed renewed allegations of abuses of human rights in Zaire, and also reflected speculation that for many years Mobutu had been systematically misappropriating foreign economic aid. Popular unrest re-emerged in late 1990: in November an anti-government rally in Kinshasa, organized by the UDPS, was violently suppressed, and in the following months anti-government demonstrations took place in Kinshasa and Matadi. There was further unrest in February 1991 when hundreds of thousands of workers, civil servants and public service employees held a three-day general strike to protest against working and living conditions and to demand the resignation of the government. Later in the same month 20,000 people attended an anti-government rally, in Kinshasa, organized by the UDPS.

NATIONAL CONFERENCE

The announcement of a timetable for the restoration of multi-party politics led to a proliferation of political parties. Prominent among these was the Union des fédéralistes et républicains indépendants (UFERI), led by Nguza Karl-I-Bond. In March 1991 a new and enlarged transitional government was appointed, in which Lunda Bululu was replaced as first state commissioner by Prof. Mulumba Lukoji, an economist who had served in previous administrations. Several minor political parties were represented in the transitional government, although more influential opposition parties refused to participate. In April Mobutu announced that a national conference would convene at the end of the month, at which members of the government and opposition organizations would discuss the drafting of a new constitution, which would then be submitted for approval in a national referendum. The response of the major opposition parties was to reject the call for a national conference unless Mobutu relinquished power. Widespread anti-government demonstrations followed this announcement, and in mid-April 42 people were reported to have been killed and many others wounded when security forces opened fire on demonstrators in the town of Mbuji-Mayi, in central Zaire. Mobutu reacted to these developments initially by suspending and then reconvening the national conference for 31 July.

In response to these initiatives, three of the more influential opposition parties, the Parti démocrate et social chrétien (PDSC), the UDPS and the UFERI, formed the Union sacrée de l'opposition radicale (USOR), which urged a general boycott of the national conference. By the end of July 1991 the USOR had expanded to include 130 parties. It then decided that its growing influence and the weakening of Mobutu's power justified its participation in the national conference. On 22 July Mobutu requested the resignation of the Lukoji administration, and under increasing pressure from the USOR, offered the premiership to Tshisekedi of the UDPS. However, this overture was rejected by Tshisekedi, under pressure from his party, and Lukoji's government was reinstated.

The national conference opened on 7 August 1991, with 2,850 delegates, including 900 representing opposition political parties. The opposition delegates, however, immediately threatened to withdraw unless its demands were met in full. The election of Isaac Kalonji Mutambay, a protestant pastor, as president of the conference was rejected by the opposition delegates, and by late September the conference, from which representatives of the influential Roman Catholic Church had withdrawn, had become overshadowed by a worsening internal crisis.

On 2 September 1991 violent clashes took place between opposition supporters and the security forces, with heavy casualties. The demonstrations represented growing popular frustration with the national conference, massive inflation and aggravated hardship. By late September the disorders had developed into widespread rioting and looting, which was initiated by the military and then spread to the civilian population. Massive destruction of properties and business premises took place and a large number of deaths were reported. French and Belgian troops were dispatched, ostensibly to evacuate foreigners, and suppressed the rioting.

In the wake of these riots France, Belgium and the USA put pressure on Mobutu to appoint a new government, as a result of which Tshisekedi returned as first state commissioner on 2 October 1991. However, he remained in this post for only 12 days, when he was dismissed by Mobutu and a 'government of crisis' sworn in: Tshisekedi's departure had been hastened by his refusal to swear an oath of allegiance to the president, and by his public denunciation of Mobutu as a 'human monster'. Four posts in the 'government of crisis' were awarded to the MPR. Bernardin Mungul Diaka, the leader of the Rassemblement démocratique pour la République (RDR), was appointed first state commissioner. Although the RDR was part of the USOR, Mungul Diaka had formerly been a close political associate of Mobutu.

It rapidly became evident that the 'government of crisis' lacked acceptance both within Zaire and among the Western powers. A new initiative was undertaken by President Diouf of Senegal to break the impasse. Diouf's proposals committed both Mobutu and opposition supporters to the convening of a sovereign national conference, which would have legislative power, and a first state commissioner drawn from the opposition. With an agreement signed on 22 November 1991, a new government was sworn in on 28 November, with Nguza Karl-I-Bond, the leader of the UFERI, as first state commissioner. Various political factions were present in this government, but the USOR was largely excluded and key portfolios retained by Mobutu's allies, who received eight ministerial posts, including defence and security, external relations and international co-operation. The national conference was resumed in December under the presidency of the Roman Catholic archbishop of Kisangani, Laurent Monsengwo Pasinya. Joseph Ileo (also known as Ileo Nsongo Amba), who had been prime minister in 1960–61 and was now the leader of the PDSC, was chosen as vice-president.

Serious divisions soon arose within the national conference. The UFERI, once a central force within the USOR, became instrumental in setting up a new political coalition, the Alliance of Patriotic Forces, grouping 30 political parties which declared themselves opposed to 'extremist measures' in obtaining political reform. Nguza Karl-I-Bond, following consultations with Mobutu, suspended the national conference in January 1992, citing its cost and its alleged responsibility for exacerbating ethnic tensions. Violence soon followed; on 14 January the

Rassemblement des démocrates libéraux (RDL), which had close links with the UFERI, claimed that seven of its supporters had been killed in clashes with another political party in Kasaï Oriental (a stronghold of the USOR). Similarly Nguza Karl-I-Bond announced eight deaths following clashes between the Lunda (his ethnic group) and the Luba (Tshisekedi's ethnic group). Nguza Karl-I-Bond proposed that each party should only have one representative at the national conference from any ethnic group. Mobutu endorsed this view, accusing the conference of being unrepresentative, and asserting that 45% of the delegates originated from the two Kasaï provinces.

During January and February 1992 violence intensified as the USOR and Christian churches attempted to mobilize demonstrations against the suspension of the conference. On 16 February over 30 people were killed by security forces in mass protests in Kinshasa. These incidents further impaired Mobutu's international standing with France, Belgium and the USA, leading to pressure from donor countries for the national conference to be reinstated, and to a further suspension of aid. On 22–23 January troops briefly seized the national radio station, urging the removal of the government and resumption of the national conference. A number of strikes broke out in February demanding both better wages and resumption of the political conference. At the end of March, two government ministers resigned in protest at government policies.

Increasingly isolated and under pressure at home and abroad, Mobutu, against the wishes of Nguza Karl-I-Bond, agreed to reconvene the conference on 6 April 1992. On 17 April the conference declared itself 'sovereign', with power to take binding legislative and executive decisions, thus undermining the role of the government. In return for accepting this ruling, Mobutu was permitted by the conference to remain as head of state. The main role of the conference was now to define a draft constitution, which would be put to a referendum, and to establish a timetable for legislative and presidential elections. In June a special commission was set up to examine arrangements for a transitional multi-party government. In the same month it was announced that a transitional government would take office in July, and that an electoral college was to be formed.

As the conference began debating the choice of a first state commissioner, in mid-June 1992, Mobutu warned that the conference had the power only to draw up a draft constitution, not to adopt it, and threatened to 'call the conference to order', as he had done in the past. However, by late July Mobutu appeared to have conceded to the conference's demands. On 23 July it was announced that it had been mutually agreed that the conference would elect a transitional first state commissioner, who would appoint a government. It was reported that Mobutu had also agreed to the establishment of a high council of the republic, to oversee the implementation of the conference's decisions, and to place the gendarmerie and civil guard under the control of the transitional government. Mobutu, however, was to retain control of the army.

On 15 August 1992 the conference overwhelmingly elected Tshisekedi as the transitional prime minister, replacing Nguza Karl-I-Bond, who had not stood for re-election. The conference granted Tshisekedi a 24-month mandate, pending the promulgation of a new constitution which would curtail the powers of the president. On 30 August Tshisekedi, whose election was widely welcomed as a victory for pro-democratic forces, appointed a 'transitional government of national union' which included opponents of Mobutu.

The political interests of Tshisekedi and Mobutu clashed almost immediately, following an announcement by the president of his intention to promote the adoption of a 'semi-presidential constitution', in opposition to the parliamentary system favoured by the conference. In October 1992 attacks on opposition leaders and the offices of newspapers critical of Mobutu became increasingly frequent in Kinshasa, while Shaba was beset by ethnic violence. On 14 November the national conference (without the participation of Mobutu's supporters) adopted a draft constitution providing for the establishment of a 'Federal Republic of the Congo', the introduction of a bicameral legislature and the election, by universal suffrage, of a non-executive president to fulfil largely ceremonial functions. (Executive and military power was to be exercised by the prime minister.) The draft document was vigorously opposed by Mobutu who, having failed to persuade Tshisekedi to reorganize his government in order to accommodate the president's own supporters, unsuccessfully attempted in early December to declare the Tshisekedi government dissolved.

HIGH COUNCIL OF THE REPUBLIC

On 6 December 1992 the national conference dissolved itself and was succeeded by a 453-member high council of the republic (HCR), retaining Archbishop Monsengwo as its president. As the supreme interim executive and legislative authority, the HCR was empowered to amend and adopt the new constitution and to organize legislative and presidential elections. Monsengwo announced that the report of a special commission, established by the conference in order to examine allegations of corruption brought against the president and his associates, would be considered by the high council. In response to this effective seizure of his powers, Mobutu ordered the suspension of the HCR and the government, and decreed that civil servants should usurp ministers in the supervision of government ministries (a demand which they refused). Attempts by the presidential guard to obstruct the convening of the high council ended following the organization of a public demonstration in Kinshasa, organized by the HCR, in protest at the actions of the armed forces. The HCR received the support of the USA, Belgium and France, in its declaration of Tshisekedi as head of Zaire's government.

In mid-January 1993 the HCR declared Mobutu to be guilty of treason and threatened impeachment proceedings unless he recognized the legitimacy of the transitional government. A brief general strike and campaign of civil disobedience, organized by the USOR, resulted in five fatalities and numerous injuries. At the end of the month several units of the army rioted in protest at an attempt by the president to pay them with discredited banknotes. Order was eventually restored, but only after the deaths of some 65 people (including the French ambassador to Zaire), and the intervention of French troops.

Rival Governments

In early March 1993, in an attempt to reassert his political authority, Mobutu convened a special 'conclave' of political forces to debate the country's future. The HCR and the USOR declined to participate. In mid-March the 'conclave' appointed Faustin Birindwa, a former UDPS member and adviser to Tshisekedi, as prime minister, charged with the formation of a 'government of national salvation'. Mobutu also reconvened the dormant national assembly as a rival to the HCR. In early April Birindwa appointed a cabinet which included Nguza Karl-I-Bond (as first deputy prime minister in charge of defence), and three members of the USOR, who were immediately expelled from that organization. While the Birindwa administration was denied official recognition by Belgium, France, the USA and the European Union (EU), Tshisekedi became increasingly frustrated at the impotence of his own government and increasing internal instability (during April the army embarked upon a campaign of intimidation of opposition members, while tribal warfare re-emerged in Shaba and also erupted in the northeastern province of Kivu), and sought the intervention of the UN. In July the secretary-general of the UN appointed Lakhdar Brahimi, a former minister of foreign affairs in Algeria, as his special envoy to Zaire and mediator there. Meanwhile, in late June, six of Birindwa's ministers, all former activists in the USOR, had announced the formation of the Union sacrée rénovée (USR), claiming that the USOR had abandoned its original political objectives in the pursuit of radical policies. Mobutu was widely perceived to be fostering divisions in the opposition through the extensive use of his personal patronage: he had direct access to much of the country's capital and assets. A series of pre-negotiations, conducted during August between representatives of the 'conclave', the USOR and the HCR, failed to conclude a significant initiative for future consensus. In early September, in response to a declaration made by Mobutu scheduling a constitutional referendum for October and presidential elections for December, Tshisekedi announced the formation of a new opposition grouping, the Forces démocratiques de Congo-Kinshasa. The new party, led by Tshisekedi, was to take no part in any future negotiations with the presidential

'conclave', and accepted the exclusive right of the HCR to formulate electoral arrangements.

In late September 1993, following almost three weeks of negotiations, an agreement was reached between representatives of Mobutu and the principal opposition groups, providing for the adoption of a single constitutional text for the transitional period, which would be subject to approval by a national referendum. Under the provisions of the agreement, transitional institutions would include the president of the republic, a reorganized transitional parliament, together with the transitional government and the national judiciary. As already agreed, the organization of presidential and legislative elections would provide for the establishment of a new republic in January 1995. During October 1993, however, attempts to finalize the terms of the agreement were complicated by the insistence of Tshisekedi's supporters that he should continue in the office of prime minister, despite the objections of Mobutu's representatives that Tshisekedi's mandate, proceeding from the national conference, had been superseded by the September agreement. The opposing positions of the principal political parties (largely polarized as the supporters of Tshisekedi in the USOR and the pro-Mobutu Forces politiques du conclave, FPC) became more firmly entrenched during the closing weeks of 1993.

In December 1993, at a rally in Kolwezi attended by Nguza Karl-I-Bond, the governor of Shaba declared the autonomy of the province (reverting to the name of Katanga). While Nguza Karl-I-Bond denied that his presence had in any way endorsed the declaration, the (separatist) UFERI welcomed the development and encouraged provincial political committees to pursue the establishment of greater regional autonomy. Mobutu's subdued response to the Shaba declaration was attributed to his reluctance to engender further political opposition during negotiations that might dictate his political future.

EMERGENCE OF THE HCR–PT

An ultimatum, issued to all political parties by Mobutu in early January 1994, in an attempt to end the political impasse, led to an agreement to form a government of national reconciliation, signed by all major constituent parties of the FPC and the USOR (with the notable exception of Tshisekedi's UDPS). Encouraged by the unexpected level of political support for the initiative, on 14 January Mobutu announced the dissolution of the HCR and the national legislative council, the dismissal of the Birindwa government, and a contest for the premiership between two contestants, Tshisekedi and Molumba Lukoji, to be decided by a transitional legislature (to be known as the haut conseil de la république–parlement de transition, HCR–PT) within 15 days of its inauguration, provisionally scheduled for 17 January. Despite widespread opposition condemnation of Mobutu's procedural circumvention of the authority of the HCR, and a well-supported 24-hour strike organized in Kinshasa, the HCR–PT was convened on 23 January under the presidency of Archbishop Monsengwo. The HCR–PT immediately rejected Mobutu's procedure for the selection of a new prime minister, but its subsequent attempts to formulate a new procedure were frustrated by the increasingly divergent interests of the member parties of the USOR, and by Tshisekedi's insistence of his legitimate claim to the office.

On 8 April 1994 the HCR–PT endorsed a new transitional constitution act, reiterating the provisions of previous accords for the organization of a constitutional referendum and presidential and legislative elections, and defining the functions of and relationship between the president of the republic, the transitional government and the HCR–PT, during a 15-month transitional period. The government, to be accountable to the HCR–PT, was to assume some relinquished powers of the president, including the control of the central bank and the security forces and the nomination of candidates for senior posts in the civil service. A new prime minister was to be appointed from opposition candidates, to be nominated within 10 days of the president's promulgation of the act. Despite the initial indignation of Tshisekedi's supporters at the declaration of a prime-ministerial vacancy that they did not recognize, by late April Tshisekedi was reported to have agreed to be considered for the post. Widening divisions within the USOR frustrated attempts to unite the opposition behind Tshisekedi as sole candidate, prompting the expulsion, in May, of 10 dissident parties from the USOR (including the Union pour la république et la démocratie–URD, whose members occupied several ministerial posts in the transitional government).

In June 1994 the HCR–PT ratified the candidature of seven opposition representatives for the premiership, rejecting that of Tshisekedi on the grounds that he had described his position as 'prime minister awaiting rehabilitation', rather than candidate for the office. On 14 June it was reported that Léon Kengo Wa Dondo, described as a moderate opposition leader, had been elected prime minister by 322 votes to 133 in the HCR–PT. However, Kengo Wa Dondo's election was immediately rejected as void, under the terms of the April constitution act, by opposition spokesmen and by the president of the HCR–PT (who refused to endorse the actions of the legislature). A new transitional government, announced on 6 July, was similarly rejected by the radical opposition, despite the offer of two cabinet posts to the UDPS. On 11 July, during a motion of confidence, the government received overwhelming support from the HCR–PT. The new prime minister swiftly sought to restore the confidence of the international donor community by committing the new administration to the implementation of political change and economic adjustment. In mid-1994 the international standing of the new government was further enhanced by its support for French and US initiatives to address the humanitarian crisis presented by the flight to Zaire of more than 2m. Rwandan refugees seeking to escape the violent aftermath of the death of President Habyarimana.

In October 1994 an expanded radical opposition grouping (the Union sacrée de l'opposition radicale et ses alliés, USORAL) resumed its participation in the HCR–PT, having boycotted proceedings since the election of Kengo Wa Dondo in June. By early November a reformist wing of the UDPS, led by Joseph Ruhana Mirindi, had agreed to join the government, and the subsequent reallocation of portfolios included the appointment of two ministers and two deputy ministers who were (or had previously been) members of the UDPS.

Despite the adoption, in May 1995, of the electoral law establishing the national electoral commission, a lack of government funds and the logistical problems presented by the presence in Zaire of as many as 2.5m. refugees forced the extension of the 15-month period of transitional government beyond the 9 July deadline. In late June political consensus was achieved between the FPC and the USORAL, resulting in the HCR–PT's adoption of a constitutional amendment (approved by Mobutu) whereby the period of national transition was to be extended by two years. On 1 July deputies from both groups had voted to relieve Archbishop Monsengwo of the presidency of the transitional legislature, prompting concern that the concerted political strength of the FPC and the USORAL would be sufficient to remove the prime minister. Meanwhile, Monsengwo's protest at the unconstitutional nature of his dismissal received cautious support from the French and Belgian governments. Further political manoeuvring in July suggested that the FPC and the radical opposition were seeking to replace Kengo Wa Dondo with Tshisekedi. Mobutu, however, made no apparent effort to resolve the crisis, prompting suggestions that such political divisions could only serve to strengthen his own position. In late July, however, Kengo Wa Dondo announced a reallocation of cabinet portfolios which appeared to consolidate his own position and to restore, to some extent, the confidence of the international community in the stability of his administration.

Meanwhile, opposition frustration at the government's failure to finalize an electoral timetable continued to escalate. In late July 1995, at an anti-government demonstration organized in the capital, some 2,000 supporters of the Parti lumumbiste unifié (PALU, an organization which supports the aims of the late prime minister, Patrice Lumumba) clashed with the security forces, resulting in the deaths of nine civilians and one police officer. A subsequent protest in Kinshasa, organized by the USORAL in early August, denounced international endorsement of the prime minister and urged his removal. The demonstration, which was conducted peacefully, was attended by an estimated 5,000 of Tshisekedi's supporters. In early December opposition groups voiced a unanimous rejection of a government offer to participate in a national coalition government, and reiterated their demands for the prompt announcement of a timetable for multi-party elections. At the end of

December the HCR–PT formalized the establishment of the national electoral commission (NEC), to be composed of 44 members (22 from both of the major political groupings), under the chairmanship of Bayona Bameya, a close political associate of Mobutu. A comprehensive reorganization of the cabinet was effected in late February 1996, and in early April the NEC was formally installed.

In mid-April 1996 it was announced that a referendum on a new constitution in December would be followed by presidential, legislative, regional and municipal elections in 1997. However, neither the elections nor the referendum took place, as the security situation in the country rapidly worsened (see below). A draft of the new constitution, which provided for a federal state with a semi-presidential parliamentary system of government, was adopted by the government in late May, and by the HCR–PT in October. Meanwhile, by late 1995 tensions within the UDPS appeared to be intensifying, with support divided between Tshisekedi and the USORAL president, Frédéric Kibassa Maliba. Divisions were exacerbated in April 1996 by Tshisekedi's attempt to expel 60 prominent members who refused to support his demands for his return to the premiership prior to the organization of elections. In early May a meeting of representatives of some 215 opposition interests within the USORAL voted to remove Tshisekedi from the leadership. Kibassa Maliba was re-elected to the USORAL presidency. Supporters of Tshisekedi within the UDPS, however, pressed demands that he replace Kengo Wa Dondo as prime minister.

A delay in the electoral timetable was announced in July 1996. In that month Nguza Karl-I-Bond, who had been in poor health since 1993, returned to active politics, with his resumption of the chairmanship of the FPC. In August 1996 it was announced that Mobutu had left for Switzerland to receive treatment for a serious form of cancer.

THE FALL OF MOBUTU

Mobutu's illness (which necessitated a four-month stay in Europe), combined with the political and military legacy of the 1994 Rwandan refugee crisis, proved to be the turning-point in his rule. Kengo Wa Dondo's government was left to confront a rapid escalation of violence in the eastern provinces of North and South Kivu. Rwandan Hutu militiamen and former soldiers who had fled their own country in 1994, fearing Tutsi retribution, had been allowed to mingle freely with civilian refugees, and had turned the refugee camps into bases for rearmament. From mid-1996 Rwandan Hutu militias actively began trying to carve out a strategic territory for themselves in eastern Zaire with the support of locally-based Hutus and members of the Zairean armed forces (FAZ), killing and expelling local Tutsis and other ethnic groups. The picture was complicated by historical rivalries in the area, including widespread resentment of Tutsis resident in South Kivu (known locally as the Banyamulenge), and a long-running dispute over their entitlement to Zairean nationality. The conflict soon spread further south, and in early October the deputy governor of South Kivu ordered the Banyamulenge to leave the country within a week. Although the order was subsequently suspended, it provoked the mobilization of a powerful Tutsi backlash. Tutsi militias, with, according to many reports, covert support from the Tutsi-dominated Rwandan government and its close regional ally, Uganda, made rapid advances against the combined forces of the Hutus and the poorly trained, ill-disciplined FAZ. What had initially appeared to be a regional movement seeking to defend the Tutsi population and to disempower extremist Hutus, soon gathered momentum and emerged as a national rebellion aiming to overthrow the Mobutu regime. Tutsi rebels were joined by dissidents of diverse ethnic origin to form the Alliance des forces démocratiques pour la libération du Congo-Zaïre (AFDL), led by Laurent-Désiré Kabila, a ministerial aide under Lumumba and an active opponent of the Mobutu regime since the 1960s. By early November AFDL forces controlled a substantial area adjoining the border with Rwanda, Burundi and parts of Uganda, including the key towns of Goma and Bukavu. Mobutu's absence, and uncertainties as to the state of his health, contributed to the poor co-ordination of the Zairean government's response to the AFDL, which by the end of November was in control of most of Kivu.

The rebels' success in the east exacerbated anti-Tutsi sentiment in Kinshasa. In November 1996 the HCR–PT demanded the expulsion of all Tutsis from Zairean territory; following attacks on Tutsis and their property, many Tutsi residents of Kinshasa fled across the river to Brazzaville, in the Republic of the Congo. In the same month repeated public demonstrations demanded the resignation of Kengo Wa Dondo (himself, part-Tutsi in origin) for having failed to respond effectively to the insurrection. Mobutu flew back to Kinshasa on 17 December and promptly appointed Gen. Mahele Lieko Bokungu as chief of staff of the joint armed forces. Kengo Wa Dondo remained prime minister, but Mobutu ordered the formation of a crisis government which included some opposition members, although it excluded both main factions of the UDPS and was not approved by the HCR–PT. The continued exclusion of Tshisekedi from the government prompted his supporters to mount a campaign of civil disobedience, and in January 1997 his faction of the UDPS announced its support for the AFDL. In February, following a highly effective general strike in Kinshasa, Mobutu banned all demonstrations and industrial action.

In late January 1997 a counter-offensive by Zairean troops, assisted by foreign mercenaries, failed to make any significant territorial gains. In February the AFDL captured the towns of Shabunda, Kalemie and Kindu; in the same month the Zairean air force began an aerial bombardment of several AFDL-controlled towns. In March, after a brief battle, the AFDL entered the strategically-important northern town of Kinsangani (which had served as the centre of military operations for the government), and in early April Mbuji-Mayi fell to the rebels. Nguza Karl-I-Bond called on his followers (for the most part Shaba secessionists) to support the AFDL. According to international media reports, AFDL troops entering Zaire's 'second city', Lubumbashi, on 9 April were cheered by crowds and greeted as liberators, as government troops withdrew from the city. The Zairean government continued to make allegations that the AFDL offensive was being supported by government troops from Rwanda, Uganda, Burundi and Angola, while the AFDL, in turn, claimed that the Zairean army was being supplemented by white mercenary soldiers and by forces of the insurgent União Nacional para a Independência Total de Angola (UNITA). Several attempts at mediation between the two sides, undertaken by various foreign governments (most notably South Africa) and international organizations, during February-April, failed to halt the escalation of the conflict. With control of all of the country's main productive resources, Kabila was in a commanding position to resist domestic and international calls for compromise.

In March 1997, following the capture of Kisangani, the HCR–PT, although technically inquorate, voted to dismiss Kengo Wa Dondo, who tendered his resignation as prime minister towards the end of the month. He was replaced at the beginning of April by Tshisekedi, who, having offered government posts to members of AFDL (which they refused), announced that he was dissolving the HCR–PT. Parliament, in turn, voted to dismiss Tshisekedi, whose supporters organized a demonstration of support in Kinshasa, only to come under attack from the security forces. On 8 April Mobutu declared a national state of emergency, dismissing the government and ordering the deployment of security forces throughout Kinshasa. Gen. Likulia Bolongo was appointed prime minister at the head of a new 28-member national salvation government, in which the USORAL refused to participate. On 14 and 15 April supporters of the UDPS organized a further two-day general strike in Kinshasa, which was widely observed. An arrest warrant was subsequently issued for Kengo Wa Dondo, who was alleged to have fled to Switzerland with funds from the national treasury.

Following inconclusive peace talks between Mobutu and Kabila, mediated by the South African president, Nelson Mandela, in early May 1997, Mobutu refused to resign and Kabila reiterated his intention to seize the capital by force. A further reorganization of the government was carried out by Mobutu in the same month. A hastily-assembled regional initiative to transfer interim executive power to Monsengwo Pasinya (recently re-elected speaker of the HCR–PT) was rejected by the rebels, and was widely dismissed as a procedural device designed to afford Mobutu a dignified withdrawal from office.

KABILA ASSUMES POWER

On 16 May 1997 Mobutu left Kinshasa (travelling to Togo, and then to Morocco, where he died on 7 September), while many of his supporters and family fled across the border to Brazzaville. On the night of 16 May Mahele Bokungu, the chief of the general staff, was murdered by elements of the presidential guard (reportedly led by Mobutu's son, Kongolo) who suspected him of attempting to negotiate a peaceful transfer of power to the rebels. On 17 May AFDL troops entered Kinshasa (encountering no resistance) and Kabila, speaking from Lubumbashi, declared himself president of the Democratic Republic of the Congo (DRC, the name used between 1964–71), which swiftly gained international recognition. He immediately announced plans to form a provisional government within 72 hours and a constituent assembly within 60 days; presidential and parliamentary elections were to be held in April 1999. On 20 May Kabila arrived in Kinshasa, and on 22 May AFDL forces captured Matadi, giving the AFDL control of most of the country. On 23 May Kabila announced the formation of a government, which, while dominated by members of the AFDL, also included members of the UDPS and of the Front patriotique, and avoided a potentially unpopular preponderance of ethnic Tutsis. No prime minister was appointed, and Tshisekedi was not offered a cabinet post; he refused to recognize the new government, and advocated public protest against the administration, but failed to raise the mass support that he had previously enjoyed. Following several demonstrations, including one in Uvira in which a number of people were reportedly killed by the security forces, on 26 May Kabila issued a decree banning all political parties and public demonstrations. An illegal gathering on 28 May in support of Tshisekedi was dispersed by the army.

On 28 May 1997 Kabila issued a constitutional decree, to remain in force until the adoption of a new constitution. The international community expressed concern that the decree allowed the president to wield near-absolute power, since it accorded him legislative and executive power as well as control over the armed forces and the treasury. Of the previously existing institutions, only the judiciary was not disbanded. On 29 May, at a ceremony attended by the presidents of Uganda, Rwanda, Angola, Burundi and Zambia, Kabila was sworn in as president of the DRC. Despite the concerns of a number of humanitarian organizations regarding the new administration's treatment of refugees, Kabila's assumption of power was widely welcomed by the international community. By 12 June a cabinet of 22 ministers had been appointed. Soon afterwards it was announced that a number of high-ranking officials from the Mobutu period, including the secretary-general of the MPR and the governor of the central bank, had been arrested, while the directors of all parastatal companies had been suspended, pending further investigations. Later in the month the detention overnight of Tshisekedi, following a political address to students, prompted renewed scepticism regarding the Kabila government's commitment to future political pluralism.

In June 1997 the DRC and Rwandan armies were engaged in fighting against a loose alliance comprising soldiers of the former Forces Armées Rwandais (FAR), interahamwe militia and Mai-Mai fighters, in Kivu province. This anti-AFDL alliance particularly targeted the Banyamulenge, thousands of whom fled to Rwanda in August where they were attacked in the Mudende refugee camp later that month. In September, in an attempt to appease the strong anti-Banyamulenge and anti-Tutsi sentiment in Kivu, the government ordered most of the Rwandan army soldiers to return to Rwanda, and replaced the DRC army's Banyamulenge units with those from elsewhere in the country. In November presidential security advisor, Masasu Nindaga, a founder member of the AFDL, was dismissed, and subsequently imprisoned. Clashes between troops loyal to Nindaga and those loyal to Kabila in early December resulted in at least 20 casualties. Nindaga was later sentenced by a military court to 20 years' imprisonment for treason.

A constitutional commission was inaugurated in November 1997, headed by Aniset Kashimura, a minister under Lumumba. The commission was to draw up a draft constitution by March 1998. On 4 January 1998 a cousin of Kabila, Gaëtan Kakudji, was appointed minister of the interior as part of a cabinet reshuffle that effected a general shift in power from Kivu ministers to those from Katanga. On 23 January two UPDS leaders were sentenced by a military tribunal to two years' imprisonment for 'agitating the public', and on 12 February Tshisekedi was once again arrested and this time banished to his home village in Kasaï Oriental until 1 July.

On 3 February 1998, after considerable international pressure, the government announced the closure of the Kapalata military camp near Kisangani, which housed around 3,000 Mai-Mai child soldiers, nearly 300 of whom had recently died of cholera. However, the government rejected international calls for early general elections, with Kabila announcing in mid-February that there would be no elections until 'peace prevailed'. Kabila did, however, announce that a census would be held by August and a referendum on a draft constitution by October.

Clashes between Banyamulenge and other units of the DRC army, and Banyamulenge desertions were reported in Kivu in February 1998, and on 28 February the army chief of staff, James Kabareke (a Rwandan), met various local military leaders on the Rwandan border in an attempt to calm the situation. On 9 March most of the military deserters returned to barracks after being offered an amnesty, but later in the month, reports emerged that a number of them had been interrogated and tortured in Bukavu. Banyamulenge activists complained of a return to conditions experienced during the Mobutu era. Bukavu radio announced on 28 April that a number of Banyamulenge soldiers had been convicted of mutiny and desertion, and that some were to be executed.

The government announced new plans for the protection of human rights on 13 March 1998, following meetings with UN representatives, but, none the less, on the same day seized copies of the annual report of a local human rights group, the Zairean Association for the Defence of Human Rights (AZADHO). The report chronicled a series of abuses allegedly committed by the new government since coming to power, including massacres, pillage and corruption. On 4 April AZADHO was banned by the government for 'indulging in political campaigns rather than objective reports'. In early April fighting again broke out in Kivu, with the army clashing with Mai-Mai rebels and members of Uganda's rebel Allied Democratic Forces (ADF). Kabila visited the region, and accused the UN and international humanitarian agencies of aiding the rebels. On 21 April the UN special rapporteur on human rights in the DRC, Roberto Garreton, informed the UN commission on human rights that abuses were widespread in the DRC; he expressed particular concern at the frequency of death sentences in convictions by military courts, from which there was no right of appeal. Garreton also reported the harassment of opposition political parties, and of non-governmental organizations and the press. The commission subsequently issued a condemnation of the DRC for 'serious violations' of basic freedoms.

Meanwhile, at the end of March 1998 the constitutional commission submitted its draft constitution to Kabila. The document envisaged a five-year presidency, with the president enjoying extensive executive powers. A vice-presidency was to be created, and both English and French were to be official state languages. On 26 May a transitional constituent assembly was established by presidential decree, specifically excluding anyone who held public office during Moutu's presidency. The assembly, holding legislative powers, was to review the draft constitution and prepare it for approval by a national referendum. Kabila has indicated his intention to hold a general election during 1999. In late May 1998 five cabinet ministers were arrested on suspicion of corruption, prompting a major cabinet reshuffle on 1 June. Four new posts were created, including a ministry of human rights. Kabila retained control of the defence ministry.

REBELLION AND REGIONAL INTERVENTION

On 28 July 1998 Kabila issued a decree expelling Rwandan members of the armed forces from the country. In early August a rebellion, reportedly receiving aid from both France and Rwanda, was launched in the east of the DRC. Rebel forces operating as the Rassemblement congolais pour la démocratie (RCD) swiftly captured the eastern border towns of Goma, Bukavu and Uvira. This was denounced by Kabila as a Rwandan invasion of the DRC. (Rwanda denied any involvement in the rebellion at this time.) On 4 August the rebels hijacked a plane from Goma airport and flew to the Kitona military base in the west of the DRC. The rebels swiftly captured the base and the nearby Banana naval installation, and, within a week, had captured the DRC's main port of Matadi and the Inga hydroelectric dam which enabled them to cut off Kinshasa's electricity supply. At least two government ministers, including the minister of foreign affairs, Bizima Karaha, defected to the rebels, and Western embassies advised their nationals to prepare for evacuation; some embassies eventually closed and evacuated their staff. On 19 August at a meeting of ministers of defence of the Southern African Development Community (SADC, which the DRC had joined in September 1997) Zimbabwe and Namibia pledged to assist Kabila. Zimbabwean troops arrived in Kinshasa the following day and secured the international airport. Angola also sent troops from late August which succeeded in recapturing Banana and Kitona, and by the end of August had suppressed rebel activity in the west of the DRC. The RCD, however, increasingly assisted by Rwandan and Ugandan troops, consolidated its control of the eastern DRC, seizing Kisangani, the country's third largest town, apparently without resistance, in late August and went on to capture a series of smaller towns in Kivu throughout September.

Diplomatic initiatives to end the war began on 7–8 September 1998 when the presidents of Zimbabwe, Uganda, Rwanda, Angola, Namibia and the DRC met in Victoria Falls, Zimbabwe, to discuss the conflict, under the chairmanship of the Zambian president, Frederick Chiluba. Although a cease-fire was agreed at the meeting, it was immediately rejected by the RCD which had been denied the opportunity to meet directly with the heads of state, and by Kabila who first demanded the withdrawal of Ugandan and Rwandan troops. The Organization of African Unity (OAU) organized a further round of talks in Addis Ababa, Ethiopia, on 10 September but the RCD was again not invited to attend. On 15 September the annual SADC meeting in Mauritius endorsed the legitimacy of the intervention by Zimbabwe, Namibia and Angola and formally authorized Chiluba to continue his mediation efforts. Two weeks later, at a summit organized by Gabonese president Omar Bongo in Libreville, Gabon, the governments of Gabon, Chad, the Republic of the Congo, the Central African Republic, Equatorial Guinea, Cameroon, Namibia and Angola recognized Kabila as the legitimate head of state of the DRC and condemned the 'external aggression' against him.

In the first major government counter-attack in the eastern DRC, hundreds of Mai Mai fighters and Rwandan Hutu Interahamwe militia attacked Goma on 14 September 1998, but were routed by the rebel troops. Rwanda subsequently accused Kabila of re-arming the extremist Hutu Interahamwe militia (a claim endorsed by the UN commission of enquiry into arms flows in the Great Lakes region) and of supporting their genocidal onslaught on Rwandan Tutsis. Meanwhile Kabila continued his efforts to enlist further support for his government, which resulted in Chad dispatching 2,000 troops to the DRC on 28 September. The RCD claimed that Sudan had also sent 2,000 troops to aid Kabila, but this was denied by the DRC government. The RCD continued its military offensive and on 14 October captured the strategic town of Kindu, which opened the way for the RCD to advance into the DRC's diamond-producing provinces, Kasaï and Katanga. In response, the presidents of Angola, Namibia and Zimbabwe met on 21 October and agreed to increase their military involvement in the war. Although a promised counter-offensive in the eastern DRC did not materialize, Zimbabwe sent additional troops to the DRC shortly after the meeting. At that time further peace initiatives were held in Lusaka, Zambia, although no agreement was formulated. In November a new rebel group emerged called the Mouvement pour la libération du Congo (MLC), led by Jean-Pierre Bemba (the son of a prominent Mobutuist, Bemba Saolona, who joined Kabila's cabinet in 1999). The MLC is based in Equateur and has large numbers of former Zairean soldiers among its ranks. It soon developed increasingly close ties with the Ugandan government while Rwanda remained committed to the RCD.

On 6 November 1998, following talks with South African president Nelson Mandela, Rwandan vice-president Paul Kagame finally confirmed that Rwandan troops were fighting alongside the RCD against Kabila. The admission raised hopes that progress could be made in negotiations to end the war, as did an apparent cease-fire agreement made in Paris, France, during the Francophone summit later that month by the presidents of the DRC, Rwanda and Uganda, and peace talks in late December promoted by Col Muammar al-Qaddafi of Libya, between Kabila and Ugandan president Yoweri Museveni, at which RCD officials were also apparently present. However, it soon became apparent that no real progress had been made, as Kabila continued to insist on the withdrawal of Rwandan and Ugandan troops before he would agree to a cease-fire. The RCD pressed its demands for face-to-face meetings with Kabila, while Rwanda and Uganda insisted that they would only withdraw their troops once their security concerns had been adequately addressed. While diplomatic efforts continued, the RCD extended its control over the eastern DRC, and by the end of 1998 controlled about one-third of the country, from Isiro in the north-east to the Zambian border in the south-east, extending west as far as Bumba on the Congo river and Kindu and Kabalo further south. Since then, neither the rebels nor the government have gained much territory. More significantly, in June the RCD captured the railway junction town of Kamina, which lies on the route to Lubumbashi and advanced to the diamond-mining town of Mbuji–Mayi, but were prevented from seizing it by Zimbabwean troops. In July the MLC captured the strategically significant town of Gbadolite, in Equateur.

As the conflict in the DRC has continued, so has the growth in the numbers of people displaced by it. By mid-2000 it was estimated that more than 300,000 refugees from the DRC were resident in neighbouring countries, while some 1.5m. people were internally displaced. International humanitarian organizations have faced enormous difficulties gaining access to the internally displaced, owing in part to deliberate obstruction by both rebel and government forces. There have been a number of reported massacres on both sides since the civil war began, with an alleged massacre of between 500 and 7,000 people at Makabola in Sud-Kivu in late December 1998 receiving the most international attention. However, while this war has clearly resulted in large numbers of casualties, none of these massacres has been verified and, in the case of Makabola, international investigators failed to find any evidence of mass graves.

In early 1999 Angola intensified its allegations that Zambia was covertly assisting UNITA, weakening Chiluba's mediation initiative, and a consultative meeting held in Lusaka in early January achieved no further progress. A hastily scheduled meeting in Windhoek, Namibia, took place immediately afterwards, with representatives from Rwanda, Uganda, Namibia, Zimbabwe and Angola once more agreeing to a cease-fire in the absence of representatives of both the RCD and DRC government. Although, at Rwanda's insistence, the RCD did not reject the agreement out of hand, it repeated its call for direct negotiations with Kabila before it could commit itself to a cease-fire.

Signs of tension within the RCD became apparent in January 1999 when the movement was restructured against the wishes of some of its prominent members, including the chairman, Ernest Wamba dia Wamba, and some members began to question publicly the alleged dominance of Banyamulenge within the RCD. Wamba dia Wamba's deputy, Arthur Z'Ahidi Ngoma, resigned in mid-February describing the movement as a puppet of Rwanda and Uganda. In mid-May the RCD, in an action supported by Rwanda, but condemned by Uganda, deposed Wamba dia Wamba as its chairman, and replaced him with Emile Ilunga. Wamba dia Wamba denounced this move as illegitimate, and Goma became the headquarters of Ilunga's Rwanda-backed faction. Violence in Kisangani subsequently forced Wamba dia Wamba in October to relocate once more, to Bunia, where he remained under Ugandan army protection. Wamba dia Wamba's faction became known as the RCD-Mouvement de libération (RCD–ML). Despite apparent efforts by Wamba dia Wamba to contain them, ethnic tensions between Hema and Lendu communities in Bunia erupted into violence in late 1999, with fighting continuing in early 2000, resulting in the death of thousands, and the displacement of nearly 200,000.

On 18 April 1999 Museveni and Kabila signed a cease-fire accord in Sirte, Libya, under Libyan mediation, which apparently committed Kabila to direct discussions with Congolese rebels. Representatives of Rwanda and Ilunga's faction were not invited to Sirte, and later announced that they would not be included in the agreement. Rwanda's absence from the Sirte meeting, as well as the division in the RCD, indicated that

the alliance between Rwanda and Uganda in the DRC was disintegrating. On 4 May the presidents of Uganda, Rwanda and Tanzania met in Dodoma, Tanzania, to discuss this breakdown in relations, but the meeting had no discernible impact on subsequent events.

The Lusaka Accord

A peace summit was convened in Lusaka in late June 1999, and culminated in the signing of an accord on 10 July by the presidents of the DRC, Zimbabwe, Angola, Rwanda and Uganda, but by none of the rebel leaderships. The accord provided for an immediate cease-fire, and for combatant forces inside the DRC to establish a Joint Military Commission (JMC), and to disarm identified militia groups, which included the Rwandan Interahamwe, Burundi's Force pour la défense de la démocratie, the Congolese Mai-Mai warriors, and Angola's União Nacional para a Independência Total de Angola (UNITA). The accord also provided a timetable for the withdrawal of foreign forces, the deployment of UN peace-keepers, and the organization of inter-Congolese political negotiations. The JMC was established on 21 July, as was a ministerial committee to which the JMC was to report. Bemba signed the Lusaka accord on 1 August, and on 6 August the UN Security Council authorized the dispatch of 80 UN military observers to Kinshasa and regional capitals as the first stage of the UN's deployment in the DRC; deployment commenced on 13 September. Serious fighting broke out between Rwandan and Ugandan forces in Kisangani in mid-August, which continued for four days and ended with a cease-fire agreement, signed by Museveni and the Rwandan vice-president, Paul Kagame. At the end of the month all 51 founder members of the RCD signed the Lusaka accord following a compromise agreement (which was intended to resolve an acrimonious dispute between the two RCD factions about which grouping had the right to sign).

Kabila named a Mai-Mai commander, Sylvestre Louetcha, as the DRC chief of defence staff in early September 1999. Mai-Mai representatives subsequently asserted that the Mai-Mai were consequently part of the Congolese armed forces and should therefore be removed from the Lusaka list of negative forces. However, no such amendment has been made to the Lusaka accord. Louetcha's appointment was widely interpreted as an attempt by Kabila to benefit from the popularity of the Mai-Mai among many, particularly in South Kivu, as an effective means of combating Rwandan aggression in the region. The JMC, which conducted its first meeting in early October, urged the UN to expedite its decision to dispatch further troops to the DRC. However, later in the month DRC government objections prevented the deployment of some UN observers to positions in the DRC interior. At the end of November the UN Security Council established the UN Organization Mission in the Democratic Republic of the Congo (MONUC).

Internal Political Developments

During 1998 and early 1999 Kabila ordered the arrest of a number of journalists, opposition politicians and prominent civil servants. In October 1998 the minister of finance, Ferdinand Tala Ngai, was arrested for mismanagement of public funds (he was later found guilty of embezzlement) and in November the minister of health, Dr Jean-Baptiste Nsonji, was dismissed and placed under house arrest; in January 1999 the governor of the central bank was arrested and held for five days before being released and allowed to resume his position. On 31 January, following sustained pressure from opposition politicians to lift the ban on political activity, Kabila introduced a new law on political parties which allowed for their registration provided they met a variety of onerous and costly requirements. Virtually all opposition politicians subsequently rejected the initiative as unacceptable. At that time, Kabila announced the formation of village-level Comités du pouvoir populaire (CPP) which were apparently intended to allow the transfer of power from the AFDL to the population as a whole, and in mid-April Kabila proclaimed the dissolution of the AFDL, accusing many of its members of corruption. A cabinet reorganization carried out in March had little political impact as all major government decisions are taken by Kabila. In March Kabila had announced that a national debate would soon be held involving a wide range of DRC political opinion. This was welcomed by Tshisekedi and other opposition politicians until it transpired that the government alone would decide who would be allowed to participate. The RCD was invited to attend, but declined. The national debate was initially scheduled to take place in Rome, Italy, and then in Nairobi, Kenya, but was postponed on both occasions.

On 23 September 1999 Ilunga's faction of the RCD rejected three possible facilitators for the national political dialogue envisaged by the Lusaka accord, representing the OAU, the Rome-based Saint Egidio Community, and the community of francophone states. After a successful meeting between the DRC government and the three rebel groups in Addis Ababa, Ethiopia, over the issue, in mid-December the OAU secretary-general nominated the former Botswanan president, Sir Ketumile Masire, as mediator in the DRC's political dialogue. Masire recommended in January 2000 that 150 representatives from the government, rebels, political opposition and civil society be invited to participate in the negotiations, but rejected the government's suggestion that the discussions be conducted in Kinshasa.

Also in January 2000, religious leaders in the DRC launched 'the national consultation', as a forum in which to prepare for Masire's political dialogue. Kabila supported the initiative, and even suggested it might replace the dialogue. As a result, most opposition politicians boycotted the consultation, which commenced in Kinshasa in late February, as did all three rebel groups. The consultation's final report urged the establishment of a new national assembly, the revision of the Lusaka accord, and the ending of a government ban on political activity. Kabila later rejected this last recommendation, while strongly endorsing the others. In early April the DRC government announced plans for elections to the national assembly by 10 May, which were, however, later abandoned.

In February 2000 Masire made his first visit to Kinshasa, where he was received with hostility by the government. Masire visited the DRC again in March, but was denied permission by the government to travel to rebel-held areas of the DRC. In April Masire proposed that the dialogue begin in July, and suggested Botswana, Ethiopia or Zambia as suitable locations for the discussions. These proposals were, however, rejected by the DRC government on 22 April, which again demanded that the talks take place in Kinshasa. This was immediately rejected by the RCD as unacceptable. During a further visit to Kinshasa in early May Kabila announced that he could no longer wait for the proposed national dialogue, and that a new national assembly would be installed on 1 July. Masire meanwhile visited rebel-held areas of eastern DRC for the first time, and announced that consultations would take place in Benin from early June, involving the DRC government, opposition figures, prominent members of civil society, and the three rebel groups, prior to the commencement of the dialogue on 3 July. However, Kabila notably did not meet Masire, and the DRC government subsequently not only failed to send a delegation to Benin, but confiscated the passports of all the political opposition and civil society delegates, who were due to attend as well. On 11 June the DRC government announced that it no longer had any confidence in Masire and requested that the OAU nominate a replacement.

Reaffirmation of the Lusaka Accord

The UN Security Council commenced a debate about the conflict in the DRC in late January 2000. The presidents of all the countries involved in the conflict participated, and all reaffirmed their commitment to the Lusaka peace accord. Most also urged the rapid deployment of further MONUC forces to prevent the breakdown of the accord. UN secretary-general, Kofi Annan, subsequently recommended to the Security Council that MONUC be increased in size to 500 military observers, supported by some 5,000 combat troops with powers of enforcement, and the possibility of more troops being added if the Lusaka accord was respected by its signatories. This proposal was approved by the Security Council on 24 February, and the mandate of the force was extended to the end of August. Recognising that the 1999 cease-fire agreement had been widely ignored, participants at a meeting of the JMC in early April 2000 agreed to a new cease-fire, which came into effect on 14 April. Fighting subsequently subsided in most areas, although

serious clashes remained commonplace, particularly in Equateur between the MLC and DRC government forces.

At a summit in Algiers, Algeria, on 29 April 2000, which Kabila attended, South Africa and Nigeria affirmed their support for the Lusaka accord, and pledged to provide most of the troops for MONUC. From early May the US ambassador to the UN, Richard Holbrooke, headed a delegation to the DRC and neighbouring countries to assess whether there was sufficient commitment from signatories to the Lusaka accord for MONUC to increase its deployment. Unfortunately for the delegation, fierce fighting erupted once more between Ugandan and Rwandan forces in Kisangani in early May. Despite commitments from both sides to cease hostilities, their troops clashed again a few days later. Kagame and Museveni met in Tanzania in mid-May, and pledged that their troops would withdraw from Kisangani, leaving the town in the hands of an expanded MONUC force. However, further hostilities between Rwandan and Ugandan troops in Kisangani in early June resulted in more than 160 people being killed, and thousands being displaced. Uganda subsequently pledged a unilateral withdrawal from the city, while Rwanda indicated that its troops would remain in position until MONUC forces assumed control. The fighting attracted international condemnation, although a suggestion from Annan that Uganda and Rwanda be subject to sanctions until they withdrew from the DRC was forcibly rejected by both countries.

In late June 2000 Kabila announced the dismissal of three principal ministers for fraudulent practices. In the same month he reiterated that elections would only take place when the Rwandan and Ugandan forces had left the country. However, he had announced in early May that a 300-member transitional parliament would be installed under the programme of democratization. A committee, supervised by the ministry of the interior, selected legislative deputies, from some 5,000 candidates; the nominated deputies, who represented all 11 provinces of the DRC, including the rebel-held areas, were subsequently approved by presidential decree. In early July Kabila endorsed the nomination of the final 60 deputies to the transitional parliament. Later that month he signed a decree providing for the decentralization of the government. Under the new arrangement, which was to take effect following the resolution of the civil conflict, the goverment was to remain based in Kinshasa, while the parliament was to be transferred to Lubumbashi, and the supreme court to Kisangani. On 22 August Kabila inaugurated the new parliament in Lubumbashi, despite criticism from the international community, which accused him of contravening the Lusaka accord. In the same month he finally agreed to the deployment of MONUC troops in government-held territory.

FOREIGN RELATIONS

During the early 1980s, a period of intense superpower rivalry in southern Africa, the Mobutu regime was an important ally of the USA, France and Belgium, receiving large amounts of aid. The ending of superpower conflicts at the end of the 1980s and the increasing prominence being given in aid policies to the issues of democracy and human rights led, however, to a distancing of the relationship between Mobutu and his Western allies. Increasing internal repression and violence drew criticism and condemnation of the Mobutu regime by Belgium, France and the USA, and pressure for Mobutu to relinquish power. They openly blamed Mobutu for the deteriorating internal economy and for political repression, and refused to renew aid to Zaire. In November 1991 a francophone summit due to be held in Kinshasa was relocated in Paris, and France declared that Mobutu would not be welcome. On 22 January 1992 the EC (European Community, now the European Union–EU) announced the suspension of all aid, except humanitarian relief, to Zaire. After the outbreak of rioting in September 1991, when French and Belgian troops intervened to evacuate foreigners and restore order, France, Belgium and the USA became more interventionist, maintaining pressure on Mobutu to reconvene the national conference and to transfer power. The USA insisted that Mobutu must concede power to an interim government and relinquish control over national finances and defence; although it negotiated for Mobutu to remain as titular head of state, owing to concerns that his sudden removal might lead to a rapid breakdown of control over the military apparatus and to anarchy and turmoil.

Zaire's relations with Belgium, France, the USA and the EU improved considerably following the inauguration of Prime Minister Kengo Wa Dondo and his new government in July 1994. Zaire's willingness to co-operate with international initiatives to address the refugee crisis arising from the flight across the Zairean border of more than 2m. Rwandan refugees in 1994–95 resulted in 1996 in the limited resumption of development aid from France and the USA, channelled through non-governmental organizations. By 1996 relations with France had thawed considerably, as Mobutu came to be seen as representative of francophone interests in Africa, interests which had diminished with the establishment of a new anglocentric regime in Rwanda. Most international and regional powers cautiously welcomed the AFDL's victory. France, however, said that it deplored the forcible take-over and called for early elections.

By October 1996, despite reports that large numbers of refugees were beginning to return to Rwanda from Burundi and Tanzania, little progress had been made in repatriating displaced Rwandans from Zaire until the AFDL launched direct attacks on the refugee camps. These attacks led to the rapid return of some 400,000 refugees to Rwanda, reassuring the international aid community that the immediate humanitarian crisis had abated (a number of initiatives for multinational intervention were cancelled at that time), but failed to allay continuing concern as to the whereabouts and welfare of vast numbers of refugees who could not be accounted for. These concerns mounted following reports that the AFDL was increasingly appropriating aid intended for refugees, and of the AFDL's refusal to allow journalists and aid workers into the refugee camps. Following the expiry of an ultimatum, issued to the UN in April 1997 by the AFDL, which demanded the complete repatriation of refugees within 60 days, the AFDL (which by this time was in control of the country) launched its own repatriation programme which was condemned for its brutality by the UN. The government blocked a UN investigative mission until late August, and further obstructed its work until November. In October the humanitarian organization Human Rights Watch released a report containing evidence of mass killings in the eastern DRC, to which the government responded by expelling all humanitarian agencies in the country who worked with refugees. The UN mission eventually began work in December, but was forced to abandon its task a week later. Attempts were made to recommence work in February 1998, but once again the mission had to withdraw and in April the UN secretary-general, Kofi Annan, terminated its activities.

Kabila's government announced a three-year reconstruction and investment programme on 1 August 1997, requiring US $3,000m. in external finance. The programme was poorly received by foreign donors and a conference in Paris on 5 September on development in the DRC failed to generate substantial aid commitments. More encouragingly for the government, a World Bank mission came to Kinshasa in October to begin discussions on rescheduling the DRC's $14,000m. debt. The government presented a revised economic plan to a 'Friends of Congo' conference in Brussels, Belgium, in early December which received a better response than its predecessor. The EU pledged $85m. and Belgium $20m. Shortly afterwards, Kabila visited the People's Republic of China, whose government pledged $150m. A visiting EU delegation in May 1998 specifically ruled out the resumption of long-term development aid to the DRC, primarily because of concerns about the government's human rights record; the USA has expressed similar concerns. The civil war that began in August 1998 stalled virtually all of the previously pledged development assistance; all balance of payments support and debt rescheduling has also been suspended. Emergency humanitarian assistance has been received although this is mostly being directed through international aid agencies.

Since the civil war began, the international community has continued to accord Kabila and his government full diplomatic recognition and international bodies, including the UN Security Council, have repeated their support for the DRC's territorial integrity and their wish for foreign forces to withdraw. However, none of the influential donor nations have taken practical steps to support Kabila or the regional alliance fighting alongside his troops, or indeed to attempt to force Rwanda or Uganda to withdraw. The UN has urged a cease-fire and a peace-keeping force to replace the belligerent troops, but it is clear that no Western countries are prepared to commit troops to this end.

Kabila's reversal early in his presidency of Mobutu's support for Morocco's annexation of Western Sahara was indicative of his desire to place the DRC within the mainstream of OAU members. Kabila has initiated participation by the DRC in a number of regional bodies, and his regime has received recognition by most OAU member countries. Since the rebellion against Kabila broke out in August 1998, the OAU has on a number of occasions denounced 'external aggression' against the DRC and affirmed its support for Kabila, while several of its member states have committed troops to support Kabila's government.

Kabila's principal external support has come from Angola and Zimbabwe, both of which have sent troops to assist in counter-insurgency operations. Both countries have stated that their assistance has been based on the DRC's membership of SADC, although this is clearly not the only, or even the main, reason for their military involvement. Angola is primarily involved as part of its ongoing war against UNITA, but the strong concentration of its troops around Mbuji-Mayi suggests an interest in the DRC's diamond production. Zimbabwe had begun investing heavily in the DRC's mineral wealth before the war broke out and appears to be trying to protect its investments. Indeed, the head of GÉCAMINES, the state mining company, is now a Zimbabwean national. It also seems likely that Zimbabwe, which committed substantial resources to ending Mozambique's civil war, only to see South African businessmen reap the majority of the rewards, is determined to ensure that this does not happen in the DRC. In June 2000, however, the Zimbabwean government announced that it intended to withdraw its combat troops from the DRC.

Other supporters of Kabila are Namibia, Chad, the Republic of the Congo, Cameroon, Equatorial Guinea and Gabon. Only the first two have sent troops, which have played a minor role in the conflict. Namibia's involvement appears to have been in part at Zimbabwe and Angola's insistence. The others seem to have been genuinely alarmed by the precedent that a successful Rwandan and Ugandan-backed rebellion against Kabila would have set for the region. Rwanda and Uganda were instrumental in bringing Kabila to power in 1997 and did so with the hope that he would assure the Banyamulenge of their DRC nationality and assist them in their battles against rebel militia operating from the DRC and in their efforts to extend their economic penetration of the DRC. Kabila carried out all three of these actions during the first year of his presidency, but subsequently allowed matters to lapse and, according to the Rwandan and Ugandan governments, actively encouraged the persecution of the Banyamulenge and sponsored Ugandan and Rwandan rebel militia. This, combined with a growing lack of confidence in Kabila's style of leadership, encouraged Rwanda and Uganda to invade and sponsor new rebel coalitions to overthrow him. There are increasing signs that the two recognize that their bid to depose Kabila may fail, but both seem determined to maintain a military presence in the DRC pending the formulation of satisfactory alternative arrangements to guarantee the security of their interests.

Economy

FRANÇOIS MISSER

MINING AND PETROLEUM

Although the Democratic Republic of the Congo (DRC, formerly Zaire) commands enormous economic potential and is richly endowed with a wide range of resources, the mining sector dominates the economy. In 1990 mining, mineral processing and petroleum extraction accounted for about 17% of gross domestic product (GDP) and around 75% of total export earnings (rising to 92% in 1995, and reaching 81% in 1996 and 1997). In 1995 mining contributed an estimated 4.4% of GDP. The country possesses an abundance of mineral resources, the most important being copper, diamonds, cobalt and zinc; there are also deposits of gold, cassiterite, manganese, cadmium, germanium, silver, wolframite and columbo-tantalite, most of which are exploited only on a small-scale industrial or artisanal basis. Copper, cobalt, zinc and germanium are found mainly in the south-eastern Shaba (formerly Katanga) province, adjoining the Zambian Copperbelt; diamonds are located mainly in Kasaï province, particularly around the towns of Mbuji-Mayi and Tshikapa, although some mining activity is conducted in Bandundu and Province Orientale (formerly Haut-Zaïre) regions. Cassiterite, wolframite, gold and columbo-tantalite are exploited mainly in the Kivu region in the east.

The state-owned mining corporation, the Générale des Carrières et des Mines (GÉCAMINES), was the dominant producer in the 1980s, accounting for more than 90% of copper output, and all production of cobalt, zinc and coal. Production of copper ore remained static in the mid-1980s, consistently totalling around 500,000 metric tons per year, equivalent to about 6% of world output. However, production took a downward trend from 1988 onwards. The international copper market is generally volatile and, as world technology advances, substitute materials, such as aluminium and optical fibres (in telecommunications), are being increasingly used. In addition, other world producers, such as Chile, have established new open-cast, lower-cost mines. Consequently, GÉCAMINES has pursued a policy of vertical integration and increased value added, as opposed to the accelerated production of ore. In the period 1990–93 production was further hampered by strikes, the theft of equipment and concentrate, technical problems and the worsening political situation. These factors led GÉCAMINES to declare, in early May 1991, a partial *force majeure* on its contracts to deliver copper to foreign clients. From total output of 471,500 tons in 1985, production fell steadily to 291,500 tons in 1991, virtually half the average for the first half of the 1980s, and then plunged to just 33,700 tons in 1994. A modest improvement followed in 1995 and 1996, with output rising to 34,000 tons and 42,425 tons, respectively. However, output declined to 38,423 in 1997, to 34,994 tons in 1998, and to 30,067 tons in 1999. Cobalt is mined mainly in association with copper, and world prices for this metal are among the most volatile of all minerals. New equipment, installed by GÉCAMINES in 1995, was expected to boost production of copper and cobalt considerably; GÉCAMINES produced 4,100 tons of cobalt in 1995 and 4,210 tons in 1996. In 1997, despite the company's efforts to recycle scrap metal, production declined to 4,041 tons. In 1998 output further decreased, to 3,944 tons, and to 2,549 tons in 1999. Zinc output has declined sharply in recent years. In 1985 GÉCAMINES produced 64,000 tons, but output then declined steadily to 2,515 tons in 1994, before recovering to 4,510 tons in 1995. However, zinc production in 1996 stood at 3,159 tons and decreased further to 1,686 tons in 1997, and to 1,234 tons in 1998. Intense international pressure to privatize GÉCAMINES prompted the government to attempt to reduce operating costs by merging the three branches of the company in 1995. Subsequent negotiations regarding the privatization of GÉCAMINES foundered, after doubts were raised concerning the integrity of the tendering process.

With the capture of Lubumbashi early in April 1997, Katanga's mining concerns passed into the hands of the Alliance des forces démocratiques pour la libération du Congo-Zaïre (AFDL), led by Laurent-Désiré Kabila, who agreed to honour existing contracts. It was estimated that full rehabilitation of GÉCAMINES would require investment amounting to US $1,000m. A controversial framework agreement was signed in April 1997 between the AFDL and American Mineral Fields International (AMFI), awarding AMFI exclusive rights to conduct feasibility studies for the rehabilitation of the mine and facilities at Kipushi; if these are positive, the DRC's zinc output could rise considerably in the next few years. Prior to its closure in 1993, the mine also produced copper, gold, silver, cadmium, germanium and cobalt. AMFI was also awarded the Kolwezi tailings project, with a maximum annual production of 50,000 metric tons of copper and 6,000 tons of cobalt. In May 1997 the Australian group Broken Hill Pty, together with ISCOR and GENCOR of South Africa and a Swedish- and Canadian-owned company, Lundin, concluded a joint-venture agreement with GÉCAMINES for the exploitation of the Tenké-Fungurumé mine in Katanga. This mine has estimated annual production of 200,000 tons of copper and 6,000 tons of cobalt. A further contract was signed in June, between the Belgian group Forrest International, the US–Finnish OM Group and GÉCAMINES, for the processing of tailings in Lubumbashi, with a projected annual output of 5,000 tons of cobalt, 3,500 tons of copper and 15,000 tons of zinc by mid-1999. However, some confusion arose when the government cancelled AMFI's contract for the Kolwezi tailings project in late 1997; AMFI subsequently alleged that the South African-based Anglo-American Corpn had wrongfully sought to invalidate the AMFI agreement. AMFI initiated court proceedings to this effect although the action was later withdrawn. At that time several international corporations, including Anglo-American, agreed in principle to join a consortium with GÉCAMINES to develop a vast mining project (over 20,000 sq km) in the Kolwezi area. Geologists have estimated that the area has the potential for an annual output of 400,000 tons of copper and 8,000 tons of cobalt; the project has been forecast to cost $1,200m. In early 1998, however, the Congolese government decided to cancel some 15 mining contracts, owing to the failure of foreign enterprises to invest in these projects. In addition, civil conflict, which commenced in early August of that year, acted as a deterrent to foreign investors.

In September 1998 a joint venture agreement was signed between GÉCAMINES and Ridgepoint, a Zimbabwean company. Under this agreement, 80% of the Central Mining Group of GÉCAMINES was handed over to Ridgepoint, which retained the right to market the whole of the joint venture's production. In return, Ridgepoint endeavoured to assist GÉCAMINES to increase substantially the annual production of both copper and cobalt by the end of 1999, to 240,000 metric tons and 6,000 tons, respectively. The government was widely criticized for the agreement as several controversial aspects emerged, resulting in speculation concerning the personal interests of the presidents of the DRC and Zimbabwe in the deal. Late in 1998 a Zimbabwean, Billy Rautenbach, was appointed managing director of GÉCAMINES itself, and announced plans to reduce exploitation costs. In early 1999 the London-based trader MRG Cobalt Sales became the exclusive cobalt marketing agent for GÉCAMINES. A sharp rise in world cobalt prices followed the announcement of the deal. However, the trader withheld these stocks in an attempt to maintain high world prices. As a result, deprived of its cash resources, GÉCAMINES was unable to meet its obligation to its staff and creditors. This provoked strong reactions. In March about 1,000 tons of cobalt, one-quarter of the company's annual output, worth about US $50m., were seized in South Africa and Belgium, by a group of creditors from those countries. As a result, by mid-1999 GÉCAMINES was unable to pay its 25,000 staff; in April GÉCAMINES' labour force in Kinshasa went on strike in protest at the non-payment of their salaries. These problems also deterred foreign mining companies from implementing projects in Katanga. In March 1999 the Canadian Tenke Mining company had declared *force majeure* and closed its offices in the DRC, and ISCOR has abandoned temporarily its plans to rehabilitate the Kamoto mine. Many companies had already withdrawn from the DRC following the cancellation of a number of mining contracts in early 1998. GÉCAMINES' disappointing performance prompted the government in early November 1999 to replace the company's Zimbabwean chairman of the board, Billy Rautenbach. However, in early 2000 the situation continued to deteriorate: cobalt and copper shipments seized in South Africa were auctioned to reimburse the GÉCAMINES' creditors in that country. In March the company's CEO and the DRC government revoked the joint venture between GÉCAMINES and Ridgepoint, the Central Mining Group Corporation, which, according to its management, produced 3,000 tons of cobalt in 1999.

The new chairman of GÉCAMINES signed a contract in early 2000 for a small-scale mining project with a small company, Emak, to be financed by the Belgian corporation, Cobalt Chemical Distribution. In December 1999 the Canadian corporation, Melkior Resources, signed a contract to undertake the mineral development of about 2,800 sq km near Likasi for a period until mid-2002. Melkior also acquired a permit to commence the export of ore and the concentrates for processing from mid-2000.

Meanwhile, Forrest International was discussing with Union Minière plans to develop Rwashi-Etoile deposits, of which reserves were estimated at 1.7m. metric tons of copper and 224,000 tons of cobalt. In October 1999 Union Minière showed a renewed interest in the Congolese copper belt by acquiring, for US $15m., a 20% share in AMFI's interests in Congo Mineral Development (CMD), the joint venture between AMFI and the Anglo-American Corpn for the exploitation of the Kolwezi tailings. Potential production levels of 75,000 tons per annum of copper and up to 12,000 tons per annum of cobalt were estimated. By late 1999 CMD decided to proceed with an experimental plant programme and an environment impact study as part of a larger feasibility study, valued at US $5.5m. In April 2000 the DRC government announced the creation of a Metals Exchange of Lubumbashi to market non-ferrous metals.

Until 1986, when it was overtaken by Australia, Zaire was the world's leading producer of industrial diamonds. Although about 98% of the country's production, from Eastern Kasaï, is of industrial diamonds, gem stones are also found. Official production figures tend to fluctuate and do not give an accurate picture, as there are extensive and elaborate smuggling networks. A report obtained by the Zairean media in early 1993 estimated the value of diamonds smuggled every year at US $300m. The only large-scale producer is the Société Minière de Bakwanga (MIBA), which produced 8.2m. carats in 1987. Output stood at 5.6m. carats in 1995 and 6.5m. carats annually in 1996 and 1997. The remainder of the diamond output is accounted for by artisan diggers (whose share of total output increased from 59% to 69% between 1987–94). Artisan diggers are responsible for the majority of smuggling. Combined with MIBA's output, the total official production for 1996 was 21.9m. carats (compared with 19.7m. carats in 1987), although the real output was higher; total official production for 1997 was 22m. carats. According to estimates from the Bank of Zaire, diamonds became Zaire's principal source of foreign exchange in 1993 ($532m.), ahead of GÉCAMINES products ($225m.) and crude petroleum ($137m.). Diamonds retained this distinction until 1997 (when they accounted for $716m.), again ahead of GÉCAMINES products ($253m.), coffee ($168m.) and crude petroleum ($153m.). De Beers, which marketed all production by MIBA, valued its 1995 output at $400m. In March 1997 the AFDL decided to end this monopoly, allowing American Diamond Buyers, a company associated with AMFI, to open a buying office in Kisangani. Production is now auctioned on a monthly basis, although De Beers remains the principal purchaser. De Beers' local subsidiary, SEDICO (formerly SEDIZA), continues to purchase diamonds from artisan diggers. In 1998, despite the civil conflict, production at MIBA increased by 6.2%, to 6.8m. carats, whereas artisanal output increased by an estimated 23%, to 19.2m. carats. Preliminary estimates for 1999, however, indicated a 22% decline in artisanal production, to some 15m. carats, and a 32% decrease of MIBA's output, to below 5m.

carats. MIBA needed to invest a minimum of $16m. to exploit new kimberlitic deposits which would allow it to increase production to 7.5m. carats by the end of 1999. However, by the end of 1998 MIBA was experiencing difficulties in repaying a $3.2m. loan to the central bank. According to a former financial adviser to President Kabila, these problems were caused, in part, by a requirement that MIBA should contribute to the state budget during 1998 (by a monthly average of $2m.). Between December 1998 and March 1999 MIBA diamond exports decreased from some 550,000 to 200,000 carats per month; the diamond sector as a whole declined in early 1999. On 8 January a presidential decree banned all foreign currency transactions and a further decree stipulated that all diamond dealers were to sell their gems in exchange for Congolese francs (the currency introduced in June 1998—see below). Instead of curbing the fraud, this decision prompted dealers to smuggle a greater proportion of their diamonds out of the DRC, with the result that the value of official production fell from US $35m. in December 1998 to $16m. in February 1999 when the Bourse congolaise des matières précieuses (BCMP, Congolese Precious Materials Exchange), through which all trade in diamonds was to be conducted, commenced operation. The value of artisanal production for the first 10 months of 1999 was $169m., 42.9% lower than that of the corresponding period in 1998.

In January 2000 a ministerial decree allowed traders to pay royalties in US dollars. This resulted in some confusion on the market, since legislation that banned transactions in hard currency was not repealed. Three months later the government decided to prohibit transactions in gold and diamonds at eight specific buildings and zones around the country. Only people with an authorized foreign currency bank account and an office in one of the recognized trade locations were permitted to buy or sell precious minerals.

In March 2000 the trade unions representing MIBA employees criticized the ministry of mines' decision to allocate the company's kimberlite deposits of Tshibwe and its alluvial deposits of Senga-Senga, to SENGAMINES, a Congolese–Zimbabwean joint venture. SENGAMINES is owned by COMIEX, a mainly government-owned company, and by OSLEG, a Zimbabwean corporation. According to the MIBA trade union representative, the government had allocated the company's future reserves to SENGAMINES without any significant compensation. Moreover, such a measure was decided in particularly difficult circumstances for MIBA: during the first quarter of 2000, as a result of periodic power shortages, MIBA had to interrupt frequently the production of its processing units. In addition, spare parts and fuel supplies imported from Zambia and South Africa by MIBA were often intercepted on their way to Eastern Kasai by the Katanga authorities.

Meanwhile, a controversial agreement was signed in June 1999 between the Ugandan-backed wing of the RCD and an offshore company, the First International Bank of Granada. The contract included provisions for the establishment of a private reserve bank and the implementation of a 'sound gold and diamond-backed currency', and the management of the exploitation of resources in rebel-held territories. In turn, the First International Bank committed itself to finance infrastructure projects.

Both the DRC government and the rebels' policies in the mining sector were sharply criticized by the non-armed opposition. In February 2000 its most prominent leader, Etienne Tshisekedi, urged a boycott of all Congolese diamonds, on the grounds that they were used by all sides to finance the civil conflict. Meanwhile, in early October 1999 De Beers had announced its decision to close its buying offices in the country, as part of a larger policy to stop the purchase of 'conflict diamonds'.

Gold output in 1997 was an estimated 394 kg, valued at about US $10.9m., compared with 977 kg, valued at about $17m., in 1996 and 2,200 kg, worth $40m., in 1986. In 1998 output declined sharply to about 100 kg, valued at $1.6m., principally as a result of the occupation of the main gold mines in the east of the country by Ugandan and Rwandan forces from August of that year. Rehabilitation work commenced in 1989 at the main gold mine, the Office des Mines d'Or de Kilo-Moto (OKIMO). In 1990 two foreign companies in the Belgo-Canadian MINDEV consortium were given management contracts for OKIMO, and output was expected to increase steadily during the decade (despite recurrent labour unrest). A new company, the US Barrick Gold Corpn, obtained other exploitation permits from OKIMO in 1996 for 80,000 sq km, of a total of 82,000 sq km. However, by late 1997, the government had reviewed the contract and the area under Barrick Gold's control was reduced to 20,000 sq km. In February 1997 the Ghanaian company, Ashanti Goldfields, entered into discussions with OKIMO about a $25m. mining project. By April 1998, however, a legal dispute had arisen between Ashanti Goldfields and an Australian company, Russel Resources, which both claimed the rights to a 2,000 sq km concession, formerly operated by MINDEV. The private Société Minière du Kivu (SOMINKI) was expected to increase its potential under the new ownership of the Canadian Banro International Capital Inc. (known from May 1996 as Banro Resources Corporation). The reserves of both the former SOMINKI concessions and of the OKIMO concessions have been estimated to exceed 250 tons of gold.The closure of the border with Burundi in May 1996 was expected to limit considerably the persistent problem of large-scale smuggling. In February 1997 Affimet, a Belgian gold dealer and refiner, initiated negotiations with the AFDL to transfer its gold-refining activities from Burundi to Kivu region, whilst the Ugandan company, Caleb International, has expressed an interest in obtaining gold concessions in the region. However, the Fédération des Entreprises du Congo (FEC) protested in March against the continuing smuggling of gold towards Rwanda and Uganda. On 31 July 1998 the government dissolved, by decree, the Société Aurifère du Kivu et Maniema (SAKIMA, formed in 1997 as the successor to SOMINKI, 93%-owned by Banro, 7% by the DRC government) which held 47 concessions totalling 10,271 sq km in the eastern DRC. In August Banro made a request for arbitration to the US-based International Center for the Settlement of Disputes. The company, which protested that the measure was taken without prior warning, claimed $1,000m. against the government. However, the rebels of the Rassemblement congolaise pour la démocratie (RCD), who controlled the area, announced in October 1998 that it had suspended the decree. The RCD has also stated on various occasions that it would not recognize government mining decrees (including the agreement between GÉCAMINES and Ridgepoint), as it opposes the sale of national assets to foreign and private DRC interests. The capture by the RCD of substantial areas of the country has blocked the government's access to the DRC's main gold mines, including both the SAKIMA and OKIMO concessions. Since August 1998, when civil conflict commenced, the DRC government has condemned the illicit trade in diamonds, gold, columbo-tantalite and timber from the rebel territories to Rwanda and Uganda. In April 2000 the UN secretary-general proposed that a team of experts investigate the illegal exploitation of the natural resources of the DRC since the beginning of the civil conflict.

Zaire became a producer of offshore petroleum in 1975, operating from fields on the Atlantic coast and at the mouth of the River Congo. Output averaged around 30,000 barrels per day (b/d) during the second half of the 1980s, with output in 1988 totalling 10.7m. barrels. Output stood at 10m. barrels in 1995, 10.7m. barrels in 1996 and 10.1m. barrels in 1997. The reserves in the Atlantic fields, operated by Zaire Gulf Oil, have declined, but the Belgian–Zairean consortium ZAIREP, operating in the mouth of the River Congo, slightly increased output in 1990. Current campaigns of prospecting, undertaken by both companies, have been hampered by political instability, and only began to benefit the sector in 1996.

In the face of the prolonged economic recession, the country's petroleum output has been broadly equivalent to domestic demand, although the DRC cannot consume its own production as the local refinery is not equipped to treat this exceptionally heavy petroleum. In the longer term, however, unless current onshore exploration near the border with Uganda and Tanzania proves successful, current oil reserves (estimated at around 187m. barrels in 1993) will be exhausted and, in all probability, the DRC will have to continue to import its petroleum requirements. In the third quarter of 1998 the Angolan company, Sonangol, began marketing its refined petroleum products in the DRC, and the South African company, Engen, bought 49% of the shares in ARISTEA, the local subsidiary of the Belgian

company, PETROFINA, which is also a distributor of petroleum products. In January 2000 the Polish corporation announced plans to invest in projects to exploit bitumen reserves in Bas-Congo Province, and to initiate a petroleum offshore exploratory programme. At the same time the US corporation Chevron announced that it would invest US $75m. to develop offshore exploration and production.

AGRICULTURE AND FORESTRY

The DRC's wide range of geography and climate produces an equally wide range of both food and cash crops. The main food crops are cassava, plantains, maize, groundnuts and rice, grown mainly by small-scale subsistence farmers. Cash crops include coffee, palm oil and palm kernels, rubber, cotton, sugar, tea and cocoa, many of which are grown on large plantations. The DRC has the potential to be not only self-sufficient in food but also to be a net exporter. In addition, with the exception of some parts of Kivu and Katanga, it has escaped the droughts which have caused such great damage in other parts of Africa in the last 20 years. The share of agriculture's contribution to GDP remained almost constant throughout the 1980s, standing at 32% in 1981, 33% in 1985 and 32% in 1989. However, the decline of the mining sector (excluding diamonds) contributed to an increase to 45% in the contribution of agriculture to GDP in 1995. In 1996 the agricultural sector employed approximately 66% of the active work-force.

However, the economic condition of agriculture in the DRC has been adversely affected both by the widespread expropriations of privately-owned plantations in the early 1970s and the subsequent decline in output and from poor government funding (only 1% of GDP). The trend has improved since the end of the 1980s, with a strong growth in production of food crops. However, the efficient supply of food to urban population centres is hampered by one of the economy's most damaging structural deficiencies: lack of infrastructure for the transportation of agricultural produce. For example, demand for the staple food, cassava, from the inhabitants of Kinshasa is simply too great to be satisfied by output from the nearby regions of Bas-Congo and Bandundu, and yet the inadequate road network hinders transport of food-stuffs grown in more distant areas. This situation has had serious repercussions in the capital, where it was estimated by the World Bank that child malnutrition had doubled during 1991–94. Estimates of food imports vary widely, ranging from official figures of 157,000 metric tons in 1985 to unofficial estimates of 393,000 tons in that year. There have been indications of an improvement in production of local food crops, but this is difficult to assess accurately as a large proportion are subsistence crops and do not enter the money economy. More recent developments present a mixed outlook. Since the beginning of the 1990s, in most urban centres, an increasing number of inhabitants are growing their own food, either in their own gardens or in public open spaces. In 1995 maize production amounted to 1.2m tons, whereas cassava output, which had increased steadily, totalled 19.3m. tons. In 1995 the European Union (EU) agreed to finance an ECU 90m. programme to support agricultural rehabilitation. The programme is to focus mainly on the renewal of 4,000 km of local roads and 600 km of national roads connecting the rural areas of Northern and Southern Kivu and of Eastern and Western Kasaï with the main cities of these regions in order to provide outlets for the land-locked hinterlands. This programme will particularly benefit Kivu, formerly the principal food-producing area of the DRC, where the economy has been seriously disrupted by massive influxes of refugees from Burundi and Rwanda since 1994, and by local inter-ethnic violence. Nearly three-quarters of the cattle herds there have been destroyed, while any marketable surpluses of beans and potatoes (grown without fertilizers in conditions of extreme shortages) cannot easily be taken to markets in Kisangani and Kinshasa because of unusable roads. The outbreak of civil war in August 1998 considerably aggravated the food security situation in the country. By May 1999 over half the population of Kinshasa was suffering from acute shortages of food. This was caused by a sharp increase in petrol prices, the inability to transport food from the fertile regions of Nord-Kivu which came under rebel control in August, the general climate of unrest which deterred peasants from growing and marketing food and the shortage of foreign currency needed for food imports. The situation deteriorated further during 1999 and 2000, resulting in the reversal of the trade flow of agricultural products. The DRC, which was a net exporter of food staples to the neighbouring Republic of the Congo, commenced the import of Thai rice via Brazzaville. Government attempts to introduce 'magasins du peuple' ('people's stores') to act as price regulators of essential commodities were not successful, since traders were not willing to sell their goods at government prices, which failed to take into account the rapid increase in the rate of inflation (340% in 1999). All this contributed to disrupt further the supply to Kinshasa, and to the other main cities, of food products. The lack of fuel and the deterioration of the road network prompted participants in a conference on the improvement of the food supply to the capital, held in April 2000, to recommend the extensive use of livestock for the transport of commodities. Prospects for 2000 were obscured by a drought in the north and in the north-east of the country during the first quarter of the year.

Export earnings from agriculture, which accounted for approximately 40% of total revenue in 1960, had fallen to only 12.5% by 1994. This decline has been caused in part by the smuggling of coffee (the major agricultural export); it has been estimated that quantities of smuggled coffee are approximately equal to official production figures. In 1994 increased prices for coffee on world markets encouraged growers to intensify their harvesting efforts, and output reached 76,864 metric tons, accounting for 34.9% of total export earnings (compared with just 59,800 tons–10.6%–in 1993). Output retreated to 56,685 tons in 1995, owing to a combination of lower world prices, internal transport difficulties and the lack of foreign exchange needed to purchase fertilizers and pesticides to fight disease, especially in the east of the country. However, while the production of robusta declined by 18% in volume, the arabica output nearly doubled and represented in 1995 about one-quarter of the total production, compared with 14% the previous year. This improvement in arabica output was in part a result of the closure of the Rwandan border through which an estimated 4,000 tons are smuggled annually. In 1995 the Office Zaïrois du Café (OZACAF) drew attention to the continuation of smuggling to Uganda, albeit at a lower level (about 2,000 tons). Production in 1996 fell substantially, with the destruction of numerous plantations in Northern Kivu during the civil war. In 1997, as the result of various factors, including disease, the civil war, and poor seed quality, output fell to 17,299 tons. High taxes on coffee exports also contributed to continued smuggling throughout the year. However, in that year the Office national du Café (ONC), which groups the sector's main producers, launched a US \$3.5m. recovery programme, financed by the International Coffee Organization, the UN Development Programme, and a South African commercial bank. In 1998 output was 21,172 tons, according to the DRC Central Bank, but declined to 18,578 tons in 1999. Prospects for 2000 were unfavourable, since both the principal arabica production areas are in the east of the country, and the main robusta plantations in the region of Equateur. Production of sugar declined from 85,100 tons in 1991 to 75,080 tons in 1992, and has subsequently declined further, reflecting continued civil and industrial unrest. In 1995 output at the Sucrerie de Kiliba totalled only 7,000 tons. Output has continued to decline since then as a result of the occupation of the Kiliba installation by rebels in August 1998. In addition, some 1,000 ha of the Kwilu–Ngongo sugar estate in Bas–Congo were destroyed by flooding in December 1999. In April 2000 strike action suspended production at the Sucrière de Kwilu–Ngongo.

Palm oil production averaged 85,000 tons per year between 1981–86 and was estimated at 95,000 tons in 1988, but only a small percentage is exported. The cost of transporting a ton of palm oil down river from Province Orientale to Matadi is equivalent to that of a Malaysian producer shipping the same quantity of palm oil to the end market in Europe—and thus local producers find they are unable to export at competitive prices. In 1997 palm oil production was 16,781 tons, compared with 18,162 tons in 1996 and 18,076 tons in 1995. In mid-1998 the government hoped to increase production following the conclusion of an agreement with the Malaysian Ideal Palms enterprise for the construction of a palm-oil refinery in the Bandundu region. By the end of 1998 annual production stood

at 16,883 tons, and declined sharply, to some 6,000 tons, in 1999, owing to the conflict prevailing in producing regions such as Equateur and Province Orientale. In the colonial period Zaire had been a sizeable rubber producer. In 1991 it still produced 10,644 tons of rubber but by 1993 production had collapsed to 3,516 tons. Output was less than 3,000 tons in 1995 and rose slightly to 3,333 tons in 1997; in 1998 output stood at 3,216 tons. The lack of investment and maintenance of ageing plantations, and the decrease in world demand, owing to competition from synthetic products, are the main causes for the crisis in the DRC's rubber sector.

During September 1996–May 1997 the agricultural sector was severely disrupted by the ongoing civil war. Traffic on the river Congo was paralysed for several months, and consequently the prices of essential commodities soared in Kinshasa. In Province Orientale, looting prevented much agricultural produce (particularly plantains) from reaching its markets, whilst the movement of hundreds of thousands of refugees from Kivu region towards the interior of the country also affected production. Moreover, according to the FEC, substantial quantities of coffee were once again being smuggled from Kivu into Uganda and Rwanda. Such practices continued in 1999. By April, in order to increase agricultural production, the government decided to requisition and rehabilitate abandoned farms and plantations. Villagers, prisoners and reconstruction brigades were to work on these properties, many of which had belonged to government opponents or to officials of the Mobutu regime. However, widespread looting of these properties followed the announcement of the project. The Congo river basin and Lake Tanganyika offered considerable potential for the development of the fisheries sector. A government report, published in April 2000, estimated the potential catch at 220,000 metric tons of fish (almost twice as much as the country's requirements, estimated at 120,000 tons).

More than 1m. sq km of the DRC's land area is covered by forest (an estimated 6% of the world's woodlands), representing a potential annual production of 6m. cu m. However, only a small proportion of this resource is currently exploited. Canada provided considerable technical assistance for the sector during the 1980s, including the preparation of an exhaustive inventory of forest resources. About 416,500 cu m of logs were felled in 1988, and 107,700 cu m were exported. Following a decline in production, output stood at 163,695 cu m in 1995, rising to 187,000 cu m in 1996 before declining to 128,761 cu m in 1997. In 1998 output increased to 149,160 cu m, but a rebel outbreak in early 1999 in Equateur deprived the companies based in government areas of access to the most significant concessions. As a result, output in 1999 declined by more than 60%, according to Central Bank estimates. Government measures in recent years have been aimed at increasing local value added in the sector, as activity has so far been mainly limited to sawing the wood, with only minimal production of veneer and plywood. A substantial proportion of logging and sawing activity is carried out by SIFORZAL, a subsidiary of the German Danzer Group, with concessions of 2.6m. ha, although in 1996 a Malaysian enterprise was examining the possibility of seeking logging concessions covering 1.5m. ha in Province Orientale and Equateur regions. However, the scarcity of foreign exchange and the lack of alternative means of revenue for the local inhabitants has given rise to fears that excessive logging may be undertaken, devastating the forest environment. In 1996 SIFORZAL expressed concern over the government's failure to allocate taxes imposed on logging towards reafforestation programmes. Further disruption in the forestry sector was caused by the extension of the civil war to the forests of Province Orientale and Equateur and by President Kabila's decision, in January 1999, to impose a state monopoly on the logging sector, officially in order to impose an environmentally-friendly policy. In February the seizure of 40,000 cu m of timber owned by 11 European companies operating in the DRC was ordered, prompting further legal action against the DRC. As a result of this action, in March 6,500 cu m of timber, shipped by the DRC government, was seized in the port of Lisbon, Portugal, at the request of the European companies. At the end of April the companies offered to pay US \$7m. to the treasury in order to be allowed to resume their activities. As a result of an expansion of the rebel control over the forests of Province Orientale and Equateur, in March

2000 SIFORCO (formerly SIFORZAL) decided to transfer its headquarters from the DRC to the Republic of the Congo. The inability to exploit the Equateur resources had prompted the government to launch tenders in Septmeber 1999 for the allocation of 60,000 ha of concessions in Bas–Congo. In May the government indicated that the Bas–Congo forests were over-exploited.

INDUSTRY AND MANUFACTURING

Heavy industrial activity is concentrated in the mining sector and in GÉCAMINES refineries in Katanga province. Prior to the decline in copper production of the late 1980s and early 1990s, the Shituru refinery processed about 225,000 metric tons of copper ore per year and a similar volume was refined 'on toll' in Belgium. In 1990 GÉCAMINES completed a large-scale five-year investment plan to improve copper-mining equipment and related infrastructure. However, GÉCAMINES' copper operation in Katanga suffered severe damage during regional unrest in 1992–93, and rehabilitation costs were estimated at US $1,000m. In addition, according to World Bank estimates at the end of 1994, private investors would be required to absorb debts exceeding $2,000m. The GÉCAMINES recovery programme 1996-2000 includes projects to modernize the Shituru plant, to process tailings at Lubumbashi and Kipushi, and to build a new cobalt processing unit at Kakanda. In the course of 1996 GÉCAMINES signed agreements with a number of foreign companies, concerning in particular the extraction and production of cobalt. A steel mill was set up at Maluku in 1972, during the era of high commodity prices, but it proved to be unprofitable and was closed down in 1986. A refinery at Muanda for the processing of imported light crude petroleum has an installed capacity of 847,000 tons per year but, in 1986, processed less than 90,000 tons. This low level of activity was attributable both to the sharp fall in world oil prices, which meant that it was often cheaper to import refined products, and also to the Zairean government's own liquidity problems, and thus the shortage of funds to pay for crude imports. Extensive studies have been made on the conversion of the refinery to treat the DRC's own rather heavy crude, and external funding for the project is being sought.

The manufacturing sector is dominated by textiles, cement, engineering and agro-industries producing consumer goods. In 1995 manufacturing contributed an estimated 6.5% of GDP (compared with 14% in 1980). Production of most commodities in 1995 was much lower than the 1990 capacity. The sector has been consistently held back on three fronts; firstly, by the lack of foreign exchange to import badly needed spare parts, secondly, by the continuing decline in domestic purchasing power and finally, by chronic electricity cuts. It is estimated that throughout most of the 1980s, manufacturers were operating at just 30% of installed capacity levels. During 1980–90 manufacturing production increased by an annual average of 2.3%. In 1993, however, manufacturing production was estimated to have declined considerably, with production of cement alone thought to have declined by 28% compared with the previous year. A slight recovery was recorded in 1994 and 1995, with the country's three main cement factories increasing sales to 166,000 metric tons and 182,051 tons respectively (compared with 150,000 tons in 1993). Small quantities of cement are exported to the Central African Republic (CAR) and to the Republic of the Congo. In 1995 1.7m. hl of beer were produced in Zaire. A new brewery near Mbuji-Mayi, with an annual production capacity of 96m. litres, came on stream late in that year. Difficulties for the textile industry have been caused by the inadequate roads infrastructure, preventing access to domestic cotton production, and by the smuggling of Chinese-made products; in 1997 the dumping of some 40m. yards of Chinese-made products resulted in the closure of three textile factories in Katanga. By mid-2000 only two textile plants were still operating. In order to protect the domestic textile industry, the government prohibited imports of printed fabrics in April 2000, and signed a framework agreement, which included a commitment to finance the rehabilitation of the equipment.

One of the most important areas of expansion in the sector in the 1990s was informal light industry, especially in the shipyards at Kinshasa and in furniture manufacture. During 1999, however, the restrictions on trading in foreign currency deprived the sector of the finance to import the necessary resources to maintain production. During the first half of 1999 many companies, including the French car manufacture, Peugeot, the cardboard plant Cartoncongo and the Plastica company, ceased operations.

Since the 1991 lootings and riots 1,800 companies from the industrial, financial and trade sectors have ceased operations and more than 100,000 jobs have been lost, according to a trade union report. However, Congolese government officials claimed that the mechanic workshops of the parastatal river transport company ONATRA had significant potential for the establishment of an armament industry. The most recent developments in the sector included the initiation of the production of 'chikwangue' (cassava bread) on an industrial basis in Kinshasa, by a company called Tala-Congo, and the inauguration of a soya-milk plant in February 2000. However, these incidents of progress failed to compensate for the trend of a general 'disindustrialization' of the DRC. In both the mining and manufacturing sectors, unpaid workers tended to sell machinery as scrap metal. Meanwhile, the situation was also extremely critical in the rebel-held areas. In September 1998 the DRC media accused the Ugandan army of the theft of machinery at the Sotexki textile plant in Kisangani, and at the OKIMO gold mines. As a result, the management of Sotexki was forced to close the plant.

ENERGY

The DRC's potential for producing hydroelectric power is rivalled on the African continent only by that of Cameroon. Total potential is considered to be 100,000 MW, while the state electricity board Société Nationale d'Eléctricité, SNEL, estimated installed capacity in 1987 as 2,486 MW. The country's most ambitious infrastructure project to date (which is estimated to account for a substantial proportion of the DRC's foreign indebtedness) is the Inga hydroelectric power project based close to the port of Matadi at the mouth of the River Congo in the west. This comprises two hydroelectric stations, which in 1986 produced 3,100m. kWh, and a 1,725-km high-voltage power line extending almost the entire length of the country from Inga to Kolwezi in the heart of the mining region. Inga produces some of the cheapest power in the world, but the ZOFI industrial free zone set up beside the power stations with the hope of attracting major heavy industry projects (and in particular an aluminium smelter) has proved unsuccessful, so far attracting only a small number of small-scale industrial operations. In early 1990 a project, funded by France and the African Development Bank (ADB), and worth 390m. French francs, was under way to double the capacity of the high-voltage power line over the section from Inga to Kinshasa. The project also included a new transformer post and the reinforcement of the Inga-2 and Lingwala stations. Other components involve a line linking the urban centres of Kolwezi (in Shaba region), Mbuji-Mayi and Kananga as part of an integrated electricity network. Ironically, numerous small towns and villages situated directly along the path of the power line have no access to electricity supplies. However, there are plans for further low-voltage links. The Inga dam supplies some power to the Republic of the Congo. SNEL is also linked to the grid of the Zambian Electricity Supply Corpn (ZESCO) and the South African company ESKOM has carried out joint studies to optimize this connection with those companies and the Zimbabwe Electricity Supply Authority (ZESA). One of ESKOM's strategic objectives is the creation of a southern African grid which could benefit from the energy of the Inga dam. There are supply agreements between the DRC, Zambia and Zimbabwe, and ESKOM provides regular training courses to the technicians and engineers of these three companies. In 1996 ESKOM, SNEL, the Angolan power company ENE and NAMPOWER of Namibia initiated a study to interconnect their national electricity grids to utilize the potential of the Inga dam. In early 1998 ESKOM offered to collaborate with SNEL to improve electricity distribution networks in the DRC. In late 1989 a small hydroelectric power station was inaugurated at Mobayi–Mbongo in Equateur region, on the border with the CAR. In July 1995 discussions were under way between SNEL and the China Machine Building Corpn to increase the capacity of the Mobayi-Mbongo power station (which exports about 2MW to the CAR) and to construct new lines between Businga and the towns of Gemena and Lisala, at an estimated total cost of US $33m. In March 1994 construction began on a 15 MW power plant at Katende on the Lulua river, in Western Kasai province. This project and the construction of the Lubilanji II plant in the neighbouring Eastern Kasaï region are also expected to cost some $33m. A power line was completed early in 1997 that interconnects the power grids of the CAR and SNEL for the provision of supplies from the CAR to Zongo, in the Equateur region of the DRC. The government's three-year stabilization and economic recovery plan (see below) provides for investment of $350m. in the energy sector. The plan aims to increase electricity output, to expand the national grid to rural areas, and to abolish the monopoly of SNEL, allowing private entrepreneurs to enter the market. Since the beginning of the war in August 1998 SNEL has been confronted with worsening problems. President Kabila's decision to offer three months' free electricity to the inhabitants of Kinshasa to reward their response to the rebel attack deprived the company of much-needed cash resources. This was compounded by a loss of 1,500m. Congolese francs in 1998 owing to persistent fraudulent practices and the failure of many customers to honour their bills. In mid-1999 SNEL still required some US $200,000 to replace five pylons destroyed by a storm in February, in order to re-establish power supply to Bandundu. By early May the company also required a $2.5m. loan to rehabilitate two dams in Bas-Congo with a joint capacity of 90 MW. Meanwhile, prospects for the extension of the Lubilanji II hydroelectric dam and for the completion of the Katende plant appeared unlikely by mid-1999. In addition to the occupation of parts of Kasaï Oriental by rebel troops, neither SNEL nor MIBA had the capacity to mobilize the $14m. required to complete the purchase of three new turbines for the Lubilanji plant. This situation prompted MIBA to purchase three 2,000 KV generators in April 1999 to equip a new thermal power plant in Mbuji Mayi at a cost of $2m. In December 1998 a joint venture between SNEL and a group of South African and European operators had been unable to invest $50m. for the construction of several hydroelectric power plants including the Katende project. However, in the second quarter of 1999 SNEL renewed its export contract for the supply of energy to Zimbabwe and Zambia. In June 1999 the DRC and Zimbabwe were discussing, at ministerial level, plans to develop a partnership for the development of the Inga dam. A delegation of the Chinese industrial group Yan Wang visited Mbandaka, in Equateur, in April 1999 in order to assess the possibility of building a hydroelectric dam on the Ruki river.

In 1999,the DRC government requested Italy's financial and technical support to complete the construction of the Inga-3, while the Nigerian government expressed interest in a project to install a high power line between Inga to supply the electricity to Nigeria, through the Republic of the Congo, Gabon and Cameroon. In April 2000 SNEL disclosed new plans, which included a project to construct a 330-KV high power line between Kolwezi in Katanga, and Solwezi in Zambia, to export 1,000 MW to the Southern African countries, the rehabilitation of Inga-1 and Inga-2, and the construction of Inga-3 in two phases (1,700 MW and 3,500 MW) by 2010. The total cost, including the high power lines to Egypt and to Western Africa, was by then estimated at US $11,000m. In January 2000 SNEL and ZESA concluded an agreement for the export of 150 MW to Zimbabwe annually at a cost of $7.2m. However, by March 2000 the total capacity of the DRC had slightly decreased compared with that of the late 1980s, totalling only 2,475 MW, including the Inga-1 power plant (351 MW), Inga-2 (1,426 MW), 493 MW for all the power stations of Katanga and 207 MW for the rest of the country. By this time Kinshasa was suffering from frequent power cuts, as a result of SNEL's inability to meet the growing demand.

WATER

The DRC's huge water reserves have since the late 1980s prompted a number of proposed projects, which, although not implemented due to their huge costs, have, nevertheless, retained the interest of potential investors. In 1988 an Italian company attempted unsuccessfully to establish a project, known as 'Transaqua', to transport water from the Riger Congo to the Sahel region. Twelve years later, in early 2000, the Kinshasa-based Water Trade Corporation and the US-based Sapphire Aqua Corporation announced plans to construct a 2,000-km pipeline from the River Congo, via Port Sudan, to the Middle East and another pipeline of 1,000 km to Southern Africa, via the Okavango Delta. However, by mid-2000 both companies, which had received the required permission from the DRC government to construct and operate the pipelines, were still seeking financing to initiate their project, to be known as the 'Solomon pipelines'.

TRANSPORT AND COMMUNICATIONS

Poor transport and communications infrastructure has proved a major handicap to the DRC's economic development. With a small strip of coastline of just 40 km, the DRC has no deep-water port and depends on the port of Matadi, close to the mouth of the River Congo, for its maritime traffic. By March 2000 the government was attempting to relaunch the activities of the former state-owned Compagnie Maritime Zaïroise (renamed Compagnie Maritime du Congo), and requested that donors provide US $40m. to finance the purchase of two vessels for the resumption of the country's international traffic, which had been suspended in the mid-1990s. In 1989 Matadi handled 273,300 metric tons of mineral exports, compared with 53,000 tons sent via the Tanzanian port of Dar es Salaam and 160,000 tons by the 'southern route' through South Africa. However, in recent years, inadequate maintenance and dredging of the port, coupled with extremely high charges, have contributed to a transfer of activity to the port of Pointe-Noire (Republic of the Congo). The port of Matadi handled 299,464 tons of exports and 812,972 tons of imports in 1995. In 1996 the figures fell to 262,370 tons of exports and 734,412 tons of imports, and in 1997 they were 183,350 tons and 786,024 tons respectively. By early 1999 traffic at the port of Matadi had decreased sharply as a result of the ban on foreign currency transactions. In March only 11 ships entered the port, compared with 27 in December 1998.

Owing to the civil war in Angola, the Benguela railway to the Angolan Atlantic port of Lobito (1,348 km), which offers the shortest rail route to the sea remains closed. Until recently, the country's main transport route was the Voie Nationale, which runs from Matadi to Katanga. It comprises a tortuous circuit of railway from Matadi to Kinshasa, then river transport from Kinshasa to Ilebo, where goods are loaded once more on to the railway. Use of this route has dwindled in recent years owing to poor maintenance, fuel shortages and increased regional insecurity. In 1997 traffic on this line decreased to 338,445 tons from 366,059 tons in 1996, although it increased in 1998 to 374,417 tons. Communications between Kasaï, Katanga and southern Africa, and also in the eastern DRC, improved somewhat as a result of a management contract signed in 1995 between the national railways company (Société nationale des chemins de fer Zaïrois, SNCZ) and a joint Belgian–South African company, Sizarail, for the management of two SNCZ subsidiaries with a total rail network of 4,121 km. In 1996 traffic on the Sizarail network increased to 409,000 tons from 259,000 tons in 1995. However, in May 1997 the incoming administration nationalized Sizarail, and transferred its assets, without compensation, to the national railways company (renamed the Société Nationale des Chemins de Fer du Congo, SNCC). These assets included 14 locomotives and 100 wagons of the South African railway operator Spoornet (a member of the Sizarail consortium); moreover, the SNCC defaulted on debts of some US $22m. owed to Spoornet and of $3.3m. owed to Zambia Railways. In protest, rail traffic via the Zambian border was suspended for several weeks. In 1998 passenger traffic increased to 2.52m. from 2.40m. in 1997. Transport to the north and north-east is possible along the River Congo, and river traffic is probably the single most important means of transport in the country; the national transport office, ONATRA, is responsible for almost 14,000 km of waterways. Passenger and freight services operate between Kinshasa and Kisangani, but the vessels are mainly old and poorly maintained and the journey can take weeks. ONATRA has begun to encounter increasing competition from small private shipowners. Proposals were announced in August 1996 for the privatization of ONATRA, and of the railway line linking Kinshasa with Matadi, on a five-year franchise basis. Since mid-1999, however, traffic on the main waterways, the Congo and the Ubangi rivers, has declined sharply, as a result of the advance of rebel forces along those rivers towards the capital of Equateur, Mbandaka, which, nevertheless, remained under government control in mid-2000. However, in May 2000 the UN Development Programme financed the purchase of 1,000 river boats in order to facilitate the evacuation of staple commodities from Bandundu towards Kinshasa.

The road network is wholly inadequate for a country of the DRC's size: of the estimated 145,000 km of roads, of which some 68,000 km are main roads, only about 2,500 km are surfaced, and most of the road network is in a very poor state of repair. In recent years the situation has become so critical that in Bas-Congo and Province Orientale, local businessmen and churches have contributed to the upkeep of the roads, as the Office des Routes has been unable to cope with this task. A plan to build a road bridge across the River Congo to link Kinshasa with Brazzaville, the capital of the Republic of the Congo, has frequently been raised and the EU has sponsored feasibility studies. The deterioration of the roads was so serious by May 1999, with traffic threatening to be interrupted on four different points on the Kinshasa-Kikwit road, that USAID, Shell RDC, Fina-Congo, Bracongo and Sulfo Industries decided jointly to finance rehabilitation works. At that time, there were also plans to impose a road toll to pay for maintenance work on the Kinshasa-Matadi road, which was also in a poor state of repair. In January 2000 the Office des Routes announced that it had repaired 2,500 km of roads and 14 bridges throughout the country. However, a sharp increase in petrol prices in February contributed to a general standstill of the transport system in the DRC, particularly in the capital, where severe petrol shortages were reported. Domestic air services deteriorated rapidly during the 1980s, as a result of Zaire's economic crisis. Some relief has been provided by a private carrier, Scibe Airlift Cargo, which began operations in 1982. Scibe operates services between the DRC's regional capitals and major towns and by 1985 was carrying more domestic passengers than Air Zaïre. Since the early 1990s Scibe, together with a smaller operator, Shabair, undertook services to Europe and South Africa. In addition, some 40 smaller carriers were providing freight and passenger services in 1995. In late 1996 Zaire Express and Shabair merged to form Zaire Airlines (renamed Congo Airlines in April 1997). In 1997 the new government of the DRC tried to relaunch the activities of the national carrier, renamed Lignes Aériennes du Congo (LAC). However, according to the management, an investment of US $234m. would be necessary to make the LAC fully operational. Safety conditions are poor at the DRC's airports, and accidents have become commonplace. In September 1996 a Belgian construction company, Besix, won a contract to rehabilitate the Kinshasa airport at Ndjili. By mid-May 1999 the Belgian private company CityBird using the rights of the national airline, Lignes Aériennes du Congo (LAC), commenced flights between Kinshasa and Brussels. However, as a result of a legal dispute with the Belgian national carrier, Sabena, CityBird ceased operations a few months later on the Brussels–Kinshasa line. In May 2000 the LAC management announced that the airline was to commence flights to Belgium in June. Meanwhile, Air Tanzania and the LAC signed an agreement to commence flights from Dar es Salaam to Kinshasa and Lubumbashi. The explosion of an arsenal, close to Ndjili airport in April, killed more than 100 persons and destroyed a large part of the airport's installations. As a result, the private carrier Congo Airlines (CAL) lost two Boeing 707 aircraft and a Boeing 727 aircraft. The loss of these aircraft was a disaster for CAL, which had obtained authorization from the DRC government to commence flights to Italy and Angola by the end of 1999. There are several other private airlines, including Katangair and Blue Air Lines. Part of the disaster at Ndjili airport was to be offset, however, by the Canadian government's decision in late April 2000 to finance a US $28m. project to rehabilitate the airport telecommunications and navigation equipment, in order to bring its installations in line with the regulations of the International Civil Aviation Organization. In February 2000 the airstrip of the Mbuji–Mayi airport was extended from 1,900 to 2,300 m, enabling it to become the fifth international airport of the DRC, after Kinshasa and Lubumbashi, then under government control, and the rebel-held cities of Goma and Gbadolite.

Telecommunications facilities within the DRC, operated by the state telecommunications concern, the Office Congolais des Postes et des Télécommunications (OCPT, formerly known as the ONPTZ), are among the worst in Africa and international lines, apart from those to Brussels and Paris, are erratic. In 1980, when Zaire had an estimated 30,000 telephone lines, the ratio to the population was less than one line per 1,000 inhabitants. By 1995 many prominent businessmen and government ministers were using the satellite communications networks provided by two private companies, Telecel and Comcell; these companies have also been developing mobile telecommunications throughout the DRC. In September 1996, it was estimated that the ONPTZ network had shrunk to some 13,000 lines, with the private companies operating an additional 10,000 lines. However, Telecel, the largest private operator, suffered severe losses in 1996–97 during inter-ethnic riots. Government estimates in the mid-1990s indicated that investment of US $200m. would be necessary to rehabilitate the telecommunications infrastructure; SAIT Holland and Inforindus, a Congolese company, subsequently undertook to repair, and temporarily to manage, the network of the OCPT. In early 1998 the US corporation Qualcomm Inc announced plans to invest up to $70m. to establish a wireless local loop system in the DRC. In September 1998 the government seized a 45% stake, owned by Tutsi businessman Miko Kayitare, in Telecel Congo, a subsidiary of the US corporation Telecel International. The government justified its decision (which was denounced as nationalization by the other shareholders) by accusing a number of individuals within Telecel of providing technical assistance to the RDC rebels.

A Global System for Mobile Communications network was established in mid-1999. Its operator, Congolese Wireless Network (CWN), announced plans to increase the number of its clients from 4,000 by the end of 1999 to 100,000 by early 2001. In late 1999 CWN also promised to establish cellular telephone systems in 14 Congolese cities within the next three years. None of the three satellite communications networks, either those of Telecel Congo, Comcell or CWN, were interconnected by the end of 1999. Like Telecel, Comcell has experienced politics-related difficulties with the Kinshasa authorities.

EXTERNAL TRADE

In common with most commodity-producing developing countries, throughout the 1980s Zaire experienced a steady deterioration in its terms of trade, as world market prices for most of its exports failed to keep pace with import price rises. Added to this, the 1980s also brought a massive acceleration in external debt-servicing requirements, making the country's external position even more parlous. Many of the problems now faced by the DRC have their origins in the early 1970s, when commodity prices were relatively high. At that time, following OPEC's first initiative in raising petroleum prices, the international banks found themselves with substantial deposits of 'petro-dollars' and were eager to utilize the funds as loans to developing countries from which they could obtain high rates of interest. With money flowing into the country to support grandiose development projects, such as the Inga hydroelectric station and the steelworks in Maluku, Zaire's import bill rose sharply and a recurrent trade deficit began to accrue, although for several years this was offset to some extent by external borrowing and inflows of foreign aid.

Cushioned by these inflows of funds, the government made little serious effort to regulate the economic situation until the early 1980s. But, as the flow of aid and, in particular, commercial loans began to decrease, the import bill had, perforce, to be cut. Export earnings remained more or less stagnant throughout the 1980s, totalling around US $2,000m. A decline in copper production, however, resulted in export earnings of just $988m. for 1993. By 1995 export earnings had reached $1,453m. and they increased slightly in 1996 to $1,541m., in the wake of increased mineral (except copper) and petroleum output; coffee exports dropped substantially in 1996. In 1997 export earnings in the DRC decreased to $1,389m. as a result of lower world oil prices and of a sharp drop in gold exports. The trend in imports has been similar; the cost of imports totalled around $1,500m. during the 1980s. By 1993 the cost of imports was estimated to have declined to $610m. In 1995 imports increased sharply to $924m. and reached an estimated $1,002m. in 1996. Owing to adverse circumstances created by the civil war, the import bill fell to $807m. in 1997, and to $546.3m. in 1998. Despite a 24.4% decline in export revenue, to $1,051.6m., in 1998, the DRC recorded a trade surplus of $505.3m. in that year.

Until the 1990s, the composition of exports remained fairly constant, with minerals accounting for about 80%, of which GÉCAMINES produced more than half (diamonds between 10% and 15%, according to world prices, crude oil about 10% and gold about 1%). By 1993, however, diamonds accounted for more than half of total exports (53.8%), while all GÉCAMINES products represented only 22.7% of the total, and in 1994 these percentages were 34.9% and 12.2% respectively. Cotton, which was an important source of revenue before independence, is no longer exported, and such output as still exists is used locally. Coffee is the only sizeable agricultural export but its share in export revenue has fluctuated widely in recent years, along with the world coffee market. In 1985 it contributed 9% of export revenue. In the following year it contributed 25%, declining to 9% in 1987 and accounting for only 4.2% of export income in 1990. An increase in world coffee prices in 1994, however, helped to increase the share of coffee in export earnings to almost 40%. An analysis of Zaire's export revenue in 1990 by the World Bank showed copper earning US $1,001m., diamonds $240m., petroleum $227m. and coffee $120m. In 1994 the structure of exports had changed dramatically, with diamonds and coffee exports accounting for $432m. each, ahead of GÉCAMINES products ($151m.) and petroleum ($138m.). In 1997, however, as a result of a lower coffee crop, coffee exports accounted for only 12% of the value of total exports; diamonds represented more than half of total export earnings, and GÉCAMINES products accounted for 18.2%. The DRC's principal imports comprise equipment and spare parts, food and beverages, as well as a substantial amount of luxury goods for resident expatriates and the affluent Congolese business community, and crude oil (when the local refinery is operating) or, more often, petroleum products. In 1998 diamonds remained the DRC's principal export, at $521m., accounting for 49.5% of the total, followed by copper and cobalt ($195.9m. and 18.6%), petroleum ($123.7m. and 11.7%), coffee ($113.3m. and 10.7%) and gold ($1.6m. and 0.15%).

As the former colonial power, Belgium has traditionally been the DRC's main trading partner. Approximately 60% of Zaire's exports went directly to Belgium, but this figure included the substantial amount of blister copper refined in Belgium, most of which was subsequently re-exported. Faltering relations between the two countries since 1988 have intermittently halted the flow of trade and assistance. Between 1991–93 the value of Zairean exports to Belgium decreased from 26,400m. Belgian francs to 14,400m., representing slightly more than 40% of the sale of Zairean goods abroad. Over the same period, the value of imports from Belgium also decreased from 6,500m. to 4,400m. Belgian francs, equivalent to just 20.4% of Zaire's total import bill. In 1994–1996, however, Zaire's exports to Belgium increased again (to 21,700m. Belgian francs in 1994, to 22,110m. francs in 1995 and to 23,250m. francs in 1996), largely as a result of a 72% increase in the value of diamond exports. Belgian exports to Zaire remained modest at 4,600m. Belgian francs in 1994, before rising to 5,880m. francs in 1995 and to 6,520m. francs in 1996. A 'freeze' on foreign aid and export insurance guarantees, imposed by Belgium and many other Western countries, made Zaire increasingly reliant on trade with South Africa. In 1993 South Africa became Zaire's second largest supplier (South African imports amounted to some US $100m.), while Zaire became South Africa's fifth largest African market. By 1997 South Africa's exports to the DRC had nearly doubled, to $192m., while Belgium and Luxembourg accounted for $165m., Nigeria $71m., Hong Kong $48m., and the USA $42m. The USA is an important trading partner. Its percentage share of exports fluctuates, but can reach 30% or more in years when the US administration replenishes strategic stocks such as cobalt. However, the recent reduction in GÉCAMINES' production capacity may oblige the USA to consider other suppliers, such as Zambia. In 1997 South Africa was the DRC's principal source of imports (accounting for 18.6% of the total), followed by Belgium and Luxembourg (16%), Hong Kong (4.7%), and France (4.2%). Belgium and Luxembourg was the DRC's principal market for exports (taking 42.6% of the total), followed by the USA (21.4%),

South Africa (8.4%) and Italy (3.8%). In 1998 South Africa's share of the DRC's imports increased to 25%, followed by Belgium (14.3%), Nigeria (6.8%) and Kenya (4.8%). However, Belgium remained the DRC's principal market for exports in 1998 (taking 51.9% of exports), followed by the USA (13.7%), South Africa (9.4%) and Finland (3.7%).

BALANCE OF PAYMENTS AND EXTERNAL DEBT

During the 1980s the government's extensive deficit spending of the 1970s generated recurrent deficits on the balance-of-payments current account as new sources of external funding evaporated and service payments on debts incurred in earlier years fell due. Faced with this economic deterioration and with no local remedies available, Mobutu became, in 1982, one of the first African leaders to submit his country to an IMF-prescribed austerity programme. In 1983, following IMF and World Bank advice, the Zaire currency was devalued by a massive 77.5%. Subsequent visits by the state commissioner for finance to the 'Paris Club' of official creditors to request reschedulings of the official portion of external debt (accruing to Western governments and Japan) became virtually an annual event, and 'Paris Club' rescheduling agreements were negotiated in each of the years from 1983–86.

Initially, the Zairean government's apparent enthusiasm to fulfil IMF performance targets was favourably received by creditors. By 1986, however, following five years of economic austerity, there were few tangible results. There was little, if any, real growth in the economy and no improvement in the balance of payments. Net outflows of foreign exchange from Zaire now exceeded inflows into the country and the proportion of export earnings devoted to servicing the external debt was more than 25%. Despite a further IMF programme agreed in May 1987, the economy continued to deteriorate. The zaire continued to depreciate; between January and May 1988 it fell by 26% against the US dollar. Disbursement of the IMF funds was also suspended because Fund officials would not accept the projected deficit in the national budget. By June, Mobutu was, once again, threatening to suspend debt repayments. Failure to reach an agreement with the IMF also made impossible a new debt-rescheduling arrangement with the 'Paris Club', the previous agreement having expired in May 1988. The economic stalemate continued into the autumn, but in early November, with inflation almost at an annual rate of 100%, Mobutu announced a further devaluation of the currency and a rise in the retail price of petrol, both measures having been prescribed by the IMF.

In early 1989 the zaire was devalued by a further 8.2% and negotiations were reopened with the IMF. As negotiations continued, the EU postponed the disbursement of an ECU 30m. loan to fund vital imports for manufacturers and the agro-industry sector. The World Bank also delayed a credit of US $75m. for a major transport rehabilitation project. By early May 1989 relations with the IMF had improved distinctly, although a major obstacle remained in the form of growing arrears on earlier IMF credits. At the end of the month there was an unexpected announcement that the government had liquidated these arrears, reportedly by means of a short-term credit of $120m. from a Belgian commercial bank. This opened the way to the release in June of the second tranche of the funding agreed in 1987. Accommodation with the IMF encouraged further loans from other donors and from the 'Paris Club', the World Bank and the EU. IMF performance criteria were met at the end of June and the end of September.

The political and social deterioration from late 1991 brought all negotiations with the IMF to a halt. As a result all rescheduling talks also ceased. No funds were to flow into Zaire for the purpose of structural adjustment or balance-of-payments support until a satisfactory settlement of Zaire's internal crisis had been achieved. In 1992 Zaire suspended virtually all payments on its foreign debt: of total debt service due of US $3,450m., only $79m. was paid. In February 1994 the World Bank closed its office in Kinshasa, and in June 1994 Zaire was suspended from the IMF. Since the civil disturbances of 1991 private investment has virtually ceased, the country having been declared 'a dangerous if not prohibitive risk' for exporters, investors and bankers by all country risk analysis and export credit guarantee insurance organizations of the OECD countries. Various donors, including Belgium, made it clear that suspension from the IMF could only be ended by the installation of a credible government with a feasible economic adjustment programme and plans to exert greater control over the armed forces and increase the efficiency of the central bank. Hopes for a prompt end to the suspension were encouraged by the announcement in July 1994 of the intention of the new prime minister, Kengo Wa Dondo, to regulate treasury disbursements to available resources, and to consider granting autonomous status to the central bank. However, following the visit of an IMF mission to Kinshasa at the end of 1994, the organization concluded that Zaire's draft budget for 1995 did not correspond to its own projections, with expenditure exceeding revenues by some 106,000m. new zaires (approximately $30m.). The control of inflation and the stabilization of the exchange rate were awaited as the concrete signs of recovery upon which donors were prepared to build a support programme. By September 1995, however, there were few signs that Kengo Wa Dondo's government had managed to reduce inflation; indeed, in the space of 12 months the exchange rate against the US dollar had decreased from NZ 1,400=$1 to NZ 7,000=$1. Despite Zaire's inability to fulfil the minimum requirements of the Bretton Woods institutions, its strategic position in Central Africa and Kengo Wa Dondo's apparent efforts to sponsor a transition process and avert a humanitarian crisis prompted the EU to consider the resumption of aid in the autumn of 1995. An ECU 90m. rehabilitation project, aimed at restoring basic infrastructures and at stimulating food production, was subsequently adopted by the EU. A meeting between Kengo Wa Dondo and the IMF managing director took place in mid-1996. However, the outbreak of civil war in September 1996 caused the inflation rate to rise once again, reaching 741% at the end of the year. The need to finance the war effort also prompted the government to cease the repayment of debt arrears to the IMF altogether.

By the end of 1997 total external debt was US $12,330m., of which $8,617m. was long-term debt. Debt service arrears amounted to approximately $9m. in 1997. This situation, combined with the accumulation of arrears to the World Bank and to the IMF, has prevented these institutions from resuming lending to the DRC and from negotiating debt rescheduling. In December 1997, at the 'Friends of Congo' meeting in Brussels, the World Bank sought to mobilize funding through a trust fund for the reconstruction of the DRC's economy, but the response was well below expectations. The lack of co-operation with the UN investigative mission in the eastern DRC (see Recent History) contributed to the lack of donors' enthusiasm; this was further dampened by the government's refusal to endorse the commitments made by the finance minister, Fernand Tala Ngai, to begin monthly payments of $5m. to the IMF from the end of March 1998. Faced with expulsion from the IMF, in June 1998 the government agreed to resume monthly repayments of $1.5m. It is, however, unclear whether these payment arrangements have subsequently been sustained.

On 30 June 1998 a new currency, the Congolese franc (CF), was introduced, equivalent to 100,000 new zaires and to US $1.405. However, as a result of the civil war, by September its value had fallen to CF 3.3 = $1. A presidential decree on 8 January 1999 banned the use of foreign currency for commercial transactions within the DRC and aimed to strengthen the value of the national currency and increase central bank and budget revenues through a tight control of foreign exchange. However, this measure had an adverse effect on the economy. Diamond and gold exporters tended to smuggle a higher proportion of their output rather than trade it for Congolese francs, and, following the ban, foreign suppliers decreased their sales or ceased to supply goods to the DRC (US dollars had accounted for 80% of the value of money in circulation in the DRC). A combination of factors contributed to reduce output. Large parts of the DRC were under rebel control, and therefore unable to supply Kinshasa. At the same time a substantial decrease in the supply of imported spare parts and petrol, caused by the shortage of currency, reduced both production capacity and the ability to transport food from neighbouring regions to the capital. By early 1999 inflation had risen to a monthly rate of 15%. These factors also contributed to a further sharp decline of the Congolese franc which was valued at CF 5.2 = $1 in government-held areas in May 1999 and at CF 3.6 =$1 in rebel-held areas at that time. The new zaire was finally removed from circulation

in June. A devaluation of the Congolese franc, to CF9 = $1, took place in January 2000. However, the difference continued to increase between the official rate and the parallel rate, which was CF 50 = $1 by the end of May 2000. The scarcity of Congolese franc banknotes in the rebel-controlled territories, prompted the rebel groups to maintain the legal currency of the old zaire and the new zaire in these areas. A lucrative practice in which some diplomats, such as the ambassador of Togo to the DRC (who was arrested in March 2000), were involved, according to the Kinshasa authorities, was reported during the first half of 2000; the profiteers bought currency at the lower price of CF 40 = $1 at May 2000 in the rebel-controlled territories, which they would subsequently sell at CF 50 = $1 in Kinshasa. The depreciation of the Congolese franc coincided with a sharp resumption of inflation, which reached 333% in 1999, compared with an estimated 147% in 1998. The main cause for the depreciation was the acute shortage of foreign currency, together with high monetary growth as the government continued to finance its growing budget deficits by printing banknotes.

Total external debt amounted to US $15,172m. by the end of 1998, increasing by $788m. compared with the previous year, owing to the accumulation of arrears. In January 2000 a meeting between President Kabila and an IMF delegation in Libreville prompted expectations regarding an improvement in relations between the DRC government and the Bretton Woods institutions. In February, however, an exploratory mission from the IMF visited Kinshasa without being able to meet President Kabila and concluded that, in addition to the civil conflict, government policies were also responsible for the economic crisis in the DRC. Some amendments to the ban on transactions in foreign currency were nevertheless introduced in March by a presidential decree, which authorized, within some limits, the circulation of foreign currency in 'monetary free zones'.

THE DOMESTIC ECONOMY

During 1968–74 Zaire's real GDP expanded at an average annual rate of 7%, assisted in large part by strong world commodity prices. During the period 1975–80, however, the trend sharply reversed under falling prices for copper, coffee and diamonds, and the impact of Mobutu's 1973 'Zairianization' programme, under which hundreds of industrial, manufacturing and agricultural concerns were expropriated and put under the control of often inexperienced nationals, began to affect GDP performance. During 1980–90 the average annual rate of GDP growth was 1.6%. However, the unrest of 1991–93 resulted in disastrous growth performance, with average annual GDP growth for 1990–96 of –6.6%. Real GDP contracted by only 0.7% in 1995, and was estimated to have risen by 1.3% in 1996. In 1997, however, a contraction of 4.1% was recorded.

The last budget to balance was that for 1989. Estimates for 1993 revealed total revenues of US $300m., accounting for less than half of primary expenditure ($664m.). However, since inflation, and the economy in general, had become seemingly uncontrollable after 1990, the draft budget exercise had become somewhat academic. In November 1993 the government introduced a new currency, the new zaire (each new unit being equivalent to 3m. old zaires), in an attempt at monetary reform. Nevertheless, in the absence of comprehensive adjustment and stabilization programmes, the measure was unable to stem the erosion of the national currency. The unequal allocation of primary expenditure between the executive and the public sector, and between ministries, was singled out as one major reason for the deterioration of the situation. As a result of a lack of budgetary discipline and of a widespread lack of confidence in the new currency, the value of the new zaire collapsed in a matter of months. Between November 1993 and the end of August 1995, the exchange rate against the US dollar decreased from NZ 3 = US $1 to NZ 15,000 = US $1. Annual inflation averaged 79.9% in 1985–90 and 2,477.7% in 1990–96, although by 1996 the inflation rate had fallen to 657%. In 1997 the rate of inflation decreased to just 13.7%. This was a result of the limitation of civil service salary increases, the partial freezing of public enterprises, the decision to cease issuing new banknotes and the effects of the civil war. The decline in demand, which led to a 4.1% contraction in GDP in 1997, has also been cited as a factor. The first post-Mobutu budget, which balanced at $744m., was adopted for 1998. In 1998, however, there was, a resurgence of inflation which had surpassed 70% by November. In December consumer prices increased by 16.2%. The 1999 budget, which was adopted only in May, envisaged a deficit of 859m. Congolese francs (CF) from expenditure of CF 2,958m. and receipts of CF 2,099m. Capital expenditure amounted to 30% of the total, a higher proportion than in previous years. This was intended to provide financing for infrastructure works and for the funding of the activities of the Comités du pouvoir publique (CPP) established in April 1999. Serious difficulties seemed likely in 1999 following a decrease in monthly receipts from an average US $35m. in January–July 1998 to $25m. in August–December 1998. A substantial contraction of GDP was anticipated for 1999 owing to a severe crisis among the DRC's main companies. Both REGIDESCO, the national water company, and SNEL had substantially reduced receipts in 1998 and were, therefore, unable to carry out necessary maintenance and investment expenditure. The occupation by the rebels of large parts of the DRC deprived the economy of the proceeds of the gold, arabica coffee and tea production. In addition, the main diamond producing company, MIBA, underwent serious difficulties, which were made worse by a government requirement that MIBA contribute an average $2m. per month to the state budget, presumably to finance the war effort. The situation deteriorated further in May 1999 when the entire production for that month, some 400,000 carats worth $10m., was seized under the president's orders at Kinshasa airport; by early June company sources were expressing fears of bankruptcy. This uncertainty at MIBA, combined with an increase in fraud and smuggling resulting from the ban on foreign currency transactions, seemed likely to have a damaging effect on the overall performance of the economy in 1999; in previous years diamonds accounted for one-half of total exports. In 1999 GDP contracted by 14.5%, while inflation increased to 333%. Statistics from the Central Bank indicated that production declined in almost all sectors in 1999, particularly in the mining and agricultural sectors. According to the Congolese Federation of Enterprises, in addition to the shortage of hard currency, other factors such as an increasing number of strikes in both the public and the private sector, and the insecurity caused by the war situation, were the principal causes for the decline. In view of the dwindling capacity to collect taxes within this adverse environment, on 1 June 2000 the government launched a campaign to recover forcibly arrears from taxpayers.

ECONOMIC DEVELOPMENT

Unlike the majority of francophone African countries, Zaire never pursued conventional five-year economic development plans. The 'Mobutu Plan' of 1977 was somewhat vague in conception and was never published in full. Although substantial effort and money were expended on the preparation of a Five-Year Plan which was to run from 1986–90, prevailing economic conditions hampered its realization. The Plan was not officially abandoned, but economic policy in the second half of the 1980s was almost entirely devoted to reducing budget deficits and the level of inflation. In November 1989 a paper presented to the legislature stated that expenditure under the plan to date had only been at an implementation rate of 49%, and referred to the 'ambitious and costly five-year plan and the restrictive programme of structural adjustment'. In the wake of serious problems being experienced by GÉCAMINES, the progressive substitution of copper by other materials in world industry (and with Chile having opened one of the world's largest and lowest-cost copper mines in 1990), it became clear that national economic activity in the DRC must become more diversified.

There is vast potential both to rehabilitate and expand the agricultural sector, and to tap the country's huge forestry resources. The DRC's population represents a potentially large consumer base and offers great incentives for developing industry and manufacturing. One of the most immediate obstacles to development remains the lack of infrastructure of all categories—road, rail and river transport and telecommunications. It is to be hoped, also, that the implementation of constitutional and political reform will clear the way for the eradication of endemic financial corruption that has long been an inhibiting factor in the country's economic betterment. However, the context for such fundamental reform is difficult, since the new

administration has not been able to pay wages regularly to its civil servants. Additionally, the dismissal of several ministers accused on corruption charges in May 1998, indicated that such behaviour remained difficult to eradicate. In December 1997 the government asked the international donor community to contribute to a three-year stabilization and economic recovery programme of US $1,682m. Of this total, $946m. was allocated to the rehabilitation of the transport, agriculture and energy sectors, $440m. for political and economic stabilization and $296m. in human capital expenditures, such as health and education. As the result of several factors, including the refusal to resume the payment of arrears owed to the Bretton Woods institutions, a poor human rights record, the cancellation of mining contracts which undermined investors' confidence, and accusations of sponsorship of terrorism against some donors, including Belgium, by mid-June 1998, the new authorities had been unable to secure the levels of external funding with which they planned to finance this programme. Relations with donors deteriorated further owing to the nationalization of gold concessions in Sud-Kivu and the seizure of private shares in Telecel, both of which undermined investor confidence in the DRC. This, combined with a difficult relationship with the IMF, the government's poor human rights record and its refusal to open talks with the RCD rebels, contributed to the failure to secure commitments from Belgium, France and the EU during Kabila's visit to Europe at the end of November 1998. In early 1999, as a result of the reluctance of Western donors, the government decided to pursue an African co-operation strategy with, for example, Zimbabwe and Namibia which had offered revolving credit facilities of $15m. and $25m., respectively, for the purchase of imports. Moreover, in the first quarter of 1999 Kabila urged the government to establish structures for a 'war economy' and an autarchic strategy which would force DRC industries to manufacture their own tyres, tractors and uniforms. In February Kabila announced plans to assemble military equipment in ONATRA workshops. Further initiatives which were unlikely to please donors included the announcement, in early March, that abandoned farms were to be requisitioned and exploited by brigades of prisoners on behalf of the reconstruction ministry and the establishment, in April, of Comités du pouvoir populaire (CPP), reminiscent of the soviets of the former USSR. During the opening ceremony of the CPP congress, President Kabila declared that the CPP were above the administration and were state organs entitled to give instructions to civil servants and to define development strategies. The establishment of the CPP, combined with the fact that opposition parties are not yet fully recognized, seemed unlikely to accommodate Western donors.

The government implicitly admitted that its economic policies had failed in December 1999, when the President decided to suspend both the minister of finance and the minister of planning, on the grounds of 'insubordination'. It was believed that the suspension of both ministers was prompted by their decision to grant permission to Congolese businessmen to use an exchange rate more favourable than the official one. In January 2000, however, both ministers were reinstated without further explanation. Likewise, President Kabila decided in April to replace the managing directors and the chairmen of the board of administrations of eight parastatals, notably SNEL, the Compagnie Maritime du Congo, the Régie de Distribution d'Eau, the OCPT, the ONC, ONATRA, and the Société Nationale d'Assurances. In May the government decided to restructure the Central Bank; however, the 10 highest-ranking directors of the bank and a further 1,000 employees offered their resignation and asked for early retirement, contributing to the general confusion. The DRC's banking sector was, as a whole, experiencing severe difficulties, partly resulting from the decision of Banque Bruxelles Lambert (BBL), which controlled the Union Congolaise de Banques (UCB), to withdraw from the country in 1999. The BBL's action was prompted by the government's refusal to interfere in a dispute between the UCB and some of its former employees who had been dismissed during the Mobutu era, and were claiming $50m. in compensation, exceeding the total capital of the bank. Business sources in Kinshasa expressed fear that this decision might deter even more foreign interests from investing in the country. By 2000 foreign aid had almost come to a halt, with the exception of a US $4.5m. loan from the African Development Bank, allocated in February to finance a capacity building programme in order to improve the management of the DRC's public administration. Beneficiary sectors included the Central Bank, the Office de Gestion de la

Dette and the ministries of transport and education. In March the UN Development Programme announced that it had allocated $47m. to finance several projects in the DRC, but also made apparent that its operational capacity was dependent on an improvement in the economic environment in the country.

Statistical Survey

Sources (unless otherwise stated): Département de l'Economie Nationale, Kinshasa; Institut National de la Statistique, Office Nationale de la Recherche et du Développement, BP 20, Kinshasa; tel. (12) 31401.

Area and Population

AREA, POPULATION AND DENSITY

Area (sq km)	2,344,885*
Population (census result)	
1 July 1984	
Males	14,543,800
Females	15,373,000
Total	29,916,800
Population (provisional UN estimates at mid-year†)	
1996	46,772,000
1997	47,987,000
1998	49,139,000
Density (per sq km) at mid-1998	21.0

* 905,365 sq miles.
† Source: UN *World Population Prospects: The 1998 Revision.* Figures are based on a UN-estimated mid-year population of 37,363,000 in 1990; according to official estimates, however, the population at mid-1990 was 35,562,000.

REGIONS*

	Area (sq km)	Population (31 Dec. 1985)†
Bandundu	295,658	4,644,758
Bas-Zaïre	53,920	2,158,595
Equateur	403,293	3,960,187
Haut-Zaïre	503,239	5,119,750
Kasaï Occidental . . .	156,967	3,465,756
Kasaï Oriental. . . .	168,216	2,859,220
Kivu	256,662	5,232,442
Shaba (formerly Katanga) .	496,965	4,452,618
Kinshasa (city)‡ . . .	9,965	2,778,281
Total	**2,344,885**	**34,671,607**

* In October 1997 a statutory order redesignated the regions as provinces. Kivu was divided into three separate provinces, and several of the other provinces were renamed. There are now 11 provinces: Bandundu, Bas-Congo, Equateur, Kasaï Occidental, Kasaï Oriental, Katanga (formerly Shaba), Kivu-Maniema, Nord-Kivu, Province Orientale (formerly Haut-Zaïre), Sud-Kivu, Kinshasa (city).
† Provisional.   ‡ Including the commune of Maluku.

Source: Département de l'Administration du Territoire.

PRINCIPAL TOWNS (population at census of July 1984)

Kinshasa	2,664,309
Lubumbashi	564,830
Mbuji-Mayi	486,235
Kolwezi	416,122
Kisangani	317,581
Kananga	298,693
Likasi	213,862
Boma	197,617
Bukavu	167,950
Kikwit	149,296
Matadi	138,798
Mbandaka	137,291

Source: UN, *Demographic Yearbook.*

BIRTHS AND DEATHS (UN estimates, annual averages)

	1980–85	1985–90	1990–95
Birth rate (per 1,000) . . .	48.3	47.9	48.2
Death rate (per 1,000) . . .	16.4	15.2	14.7

Expectation of life (UN estimates, years at birth, 1990–95): 51.7 (males 50.0; females 53.5).

Source: UN, *World Population Prospects: The 1998 Revision.*

ECONOMICALLY ACTIVE POPULATION

Mid-1998 (estimates in '000): Agriculture, etc. 13,011; Total labour force 20,279 (Source: FAO, *Production Yearbook*).

Agriculture

PRINCIPAL CROPS ('000 metric tons)

	1996	1997	1998
Rice (paddy)*	430	347	340
Maize*	1,100	1,000	900
Millet*	39	38	36
Sorghum*	50	50	48
Potatoes*	40	40	39
Sweet potatoes*	415	415	410
Cassava (Manioc) . . .	16,800†	16,800*	16,500*
Yams	305*	305	300*
Taro (Coco yam)* . . .	45	45	43
Dry beans*	145	143	140
Dry peas*	70	68	65
Groundnuts (in shell)* . .	585	570	565
Cottonseed*	18	18	17
Palm kernels*	74	72	70
Cabbages*	29	27	25
Tomatoes*	45	43	40
Onions (dry)*	58	56	55
Pumpkins*	44	42	40
Sugar cane*	1,300	1,700	1,700
Oranges*	155	150	145
Grapefruit*	14	12	11
Avocados*	45	43	42
Mangoes*	210	205	200
Pineapples*	145	140	135
Bananas*	405	400	390
Plantains*	2,400	2,300	2,250
Papayas*	213	210	205
Coffee (green)†	59	48	54
Cocoa beans*	7	7	7
Tea (made)*	3	3	3
Tobacco (leaves) . . .	4†	4†	4*
Cotton (lint)*	9	9	9
Natural rubber (dry weight) .	12†	11†	10*

* FAO estimate(s).   † Unofficial figure.

Source: FAO, *Production Yearbook.*

LIVESTOCK ('000 head, year ending September)

	1996	1997	1998
Cattle*	1,150	1,100	1,000
Sheep	1,043†	1,020†	1,020*
Goats	4,172†	4,086†	4,090*
Pigs	1,157	1,183	1,170*

Poultry (FAO estimates, million): 27 in 1996; 25 in 1997; 25 in 1998.

* FAO estimate(s).   † Unofficial figure.

Source: FAO, *Production Yearbook*.

LIVESTOCK PRODUCTS (FAO estimates, '000 metric tons)

	1996	1997	1998
Beef and veal . . .	21	21	21
Mutton and lamb . . .	3	3	3
Goat meat	17	17	17
Pig meat	43	44	44
Poultry meat . . .	24	23	23
Other meat	131	129	129
Cows' milk	8	7	7
Hen eggs	9	8	8

Source: FAO, *Production Yearbook*.

Forestry

ROUNDWOOD REMOVALS ('000 cubic metres, excl. bark)

	1995	1996	1997
Sawlogs, veneer logs and logs for sleepers	300	300	300
Other industrial wood . . .	3,145	3,239	3,324
Fuel wood	45,299	46,568	47,715
Total	48,744	50,107	51,339

Source: FAO, *Yearbook of Forest Products*.

SAWNWOOD PRODUCTION ('000 cubic metres, incl. railway sleepers)

	1995	1996	1997
Total (all broadleaved) . . .	100	100	100

Source: FAO, *Yearbook of Forest Products*.

Fishing

('000 metric tons, live weight)

	1995	1996	1997
Inland waters	154.8	159.0	158.4
Atlantic Ocean	3.9	4.0	3.8
Total catch	158.6	163.0	162.2

Source: FAO, *Yearbook of Fishery Statistics*.

Mining

('000 metric tons, unless otherwise indicated)

	1994	1995	1996
Hard coal*	94	95	95
Copper ore†‡	30.0	30.0	42.2
Cobalt ore†§	0.8	1.6	2.0
Zinc ore†§	0.6	0.8	1.2
Gold ore (kg)*†§ . . .	800	600	1,000
Tin ore†§	1.0	0*	0*
Crude petroleum . . .	1,124	1,146*	1,148*
Diamonds ('000 carats)§ . . .	17,000	17,000	18,000*

* Provisional figures.
† Figures refer to the metal content of ores.
‡ Source: *World Metal Statistics*.
§ Source: US Bureau of Mines.

Source: UN, *Industrial Commodity Statistics Yearbook*.

1997 ('000 metric tons, unless otherwise indicated): Copper 39.7; Cobalt 4.0; Zinc 1.7; Gold (kg) 394; Diamonds ('000 carats) 21.0.

1998 ('000 metric tons, unless otherwise indicated): Copper 35.0; Cobalt 3.9; Zinc 1.2; Gold (kg) 134; Diamonds ('000 carats) 24.5.

Source: Banque Centrale du Congo in *Mining Annual Review 1999*.

Industry

SELECTED PRODUCTS
('000 metric tons, unless otherwise indicated)

	1992	1993	1994
Maize flour	13.0	12.8	10.3
Sugar	81.7	82.3	79.0
Cigarettes ('000 cartons) . .	2,682.1	2,472.5	2,535.0
Beer (million litres) . . .	165.4	148.8	160.7
Soft drinks (million litres) . .	85.3	71.1	75.9
Soaps	38.7	38.6	37.4
Acetylene	39.2	54.3	62.0
Tyres	41.0	26.0	35.6
Cement	208.0	161.7	165.7
Glassware	10.9	12.5	12.9
Diesel and gas oil . . .	52.6	30.7	20.7
Fuel oil	34.3	32.8	9.1
Jet fuel and kerosene . . .	31.4	31.2	1.1
Butane	0.1	10.2	0.2
Premium gasoline . . .	28.3	30.8	8.3
Cotton fabrics ('000 sq metres) .	20,510	15,099	17,804
Printed fabrics ('000 sq metres) .	30,994	28,400	25,900
Footwear ('000 pairs) . . .	934	1,661	1,061
Blankets ('000 units) . .	54	177	94
Metallic furniture ('000 pieces) .	9.0	6.0	7.5
Sheet metal ('000 pieces) . .	144.6	163.4	151.0
Motor cars (units) . . .	131	150	140
Electric energy (million kWh) . .	5,883	5,351	5,006

Source: IMF, *Zaire — Background Information and Statistical Data* (April 1996).

1995 (estimates, '000 metric tons, unless otherwise indicated): Cement 100; Jet fuel 3; Motor gasoline (petrol) 9; Kerosene 10; Gas-diesel (distillate fuel) oils 19; Residual fuel oils 7; Electric energy (million kWh) 5,920.

1996 (estimates, '000 metric tons, unless otherwise indicated): Jet fuel 3; Motor gasoline (petrol) 9; Kerosene 10; Gas-diesel (distillate fuel) oils 18; Residual fuel oils 8; Electric energy (million kWh) 5,408.

Source (for 1995 and 1996): UN, *Industrial Commodity Statistics Yearbook*.

Finance

CURRENCY AND EXCHANGE RATES

Monetary Units
100 new makuta (singular: likuta) = 1 new zaire (NZ).

Sterling and Dollar Equivalents (30 January 1998)
£1 sterling = 196,584 new zaires;
US $1 = 120,000 new zaires;
1,000,000 new zaires = £5.087 = $8.333.

Average Exchange Rate (new zaires per US $)
1993	2.5
1994	1,194.1
1995	7,024

Note: In June 1967 the zaire was introduced, replacing the Congolese franc (CF) at an exchange rate of 1 zaire = CF 1,000. In October 1993 the zaire was replaced by the new zaire (NZ), equivalent to 3m. old zaires. On 30 June 1998 a new Congolese franc (of 100 centimes), equivalent to NZ 100,000, was introduced. For a transitional period, the new zaire and the new franc would both circulate. At 6 July 1998 the official exchange rates were: US $1 = NZ 138,000 or 1.38 new CF (buying) and $1 = NZ 140,000 or 1.40 new CF (selling). In April 1999 the rate was reported to be $1 = 4.505 new CF. The NZ was withdrawn from circulation on 30 June 1999. The official exchange rate was maintained at about 4.5 new CF per US $1 until January 2000, when a new rate of $1 = 9 new CF was introduced. Some of the figures in this Survey are still in terms of old or new zaires.

BUDGET ('000 million new zaires, unless otherwise indicated)

Revenue*	1995	1996	1997
Taxation	1,955	13,787	32,430
Taxes on income, profits, etc. .	700	5,552	10,068
Taxes on payroll and workforce .	27	203	479
Turnover tax . . .	109	1,603	3,931
Excises	286	917	3,475
Import duties . . .	642	4,163	10,534
Export duties . . .	50	453	624
Other tax revenue . .	140	896	3,293
Administrative fees and charges, etc.	48	619	5,781
Other current revenue . .	117	1,282	2,153
Total†	**2,120**	**15,688**	**40,364**

Expenditure	1995	1996	1997
General public services‡ . .	1,646	7,777	26,962
Defence	122	4,482	13,911
Education	27	136	144
Health	25	64	17
Social security and welfare .	n.a.	11	10
Housing and community amenities	1	12	155
Recreational, cultural and religious affairs and services .	19	142	6
Economic affairs and services .	1,194	18,472	37,588
Fuel and energy . .	8	113	321
Agriculture, forestry and fishing	1,183	17,105	287
Mining, manufacturing and construction . . .	1	1,253	36,921
Transport and communications .	2	1	59
Other purposes . . .	255	2,617	80
Interest payments . . .	21	1,009	80
Total†	**3,289**	**33,713**	**78,953**

* Excluding grants received (million new zaires): 1,177,000 in 1995; 17,091,000 in 1996; 32,298,000 in 1997.
† Excluding the operations of the social security system.
‡ Including public order and safety.

Source: IMF, *Government Finance Statistics Yearbook*.

INTERNATIONAL RESERVES (US $ million at 31 December)

	1993	1994	1995
Gold	8.59	10.71	10.83
Foreign exchange . .	46.20	120.69	146.60
Total	**54.79**	**131.40**	**157.43**

1996 (US $ million at 31 December): Foreign exchange 82.50.
1997 (US $ million at 31 December): Gold 15.80.
Source: IMF, *International Financial Statistics*.

MONEY SUPPLY (million new zaires at 31 December)

	1993	1994	1995
Currency outside banks . .	4,693	277,000	1,684,000
Demand deposits at deposit money banks . .	1,618	92,000	187,000
Total money (incl. others) . .	**6,495**	**373,000**	**1,889,000**

Source: IMF, *International Financial Statistics*.

COST OF LIVING
(Consumer Price Index for Kinshasa; base: 1988 = 100)

	1990	1991	1992
Food	785.2	33,900	1,002,187
Rent	771.6	29,658	973,432
Health	1,046.7	50,004	1,881,696
Clothing	488.1	21,019	689,652
Transport and other . . .	930.7	44,134	797,283
All items	**782.4**	**33,867**	**958,367**

All items (base: 1995 = 100): 0.1 in 1993; 15.6 in 1994; 100.0 in 1995; 758.8 in 1996; 2,090.7 in 1997. (Source: IMF, *International Financial Statistics*.)

NATIONAL ACCOUNTS

Expenditure on the Gross Domestic Product
('000 million old zaires at current prices, unless otherwise indicated)

	1993	1994*	1995*†
Government final consumption expenditure . . .	12,462,186	522.2	3,356.1
Private final consumption expenditure . . .	64,305,274	5,417.7	31,924.1
Gross capital formation . .	1,817,933	162.1	982.4
Total domestic expenditure	**78,585,393**	**6,102.0**	**36,262.6**
Exports of goods and services	10,648,434	825.6	5,527.2
Less Imports of goods and services	8,462,269	627.7	5,167.5
GDP in purchasers' values .	**80,771,558**	**6,300.0**	**36,622.3**

* Figures in '000 million new zaires (1 new zaire = 3m. old zaires).
† Estimates.
Source: IMF, *Zaire—Background Information and Statistical Data* (April 1996).

Gross Domestic Product by Economic Activity
('000 million old zaires at current prices, unless otherwise indicated)

	1993	1994*	1995*†
Agriculture, forestry, livestock, hunting, and fishing . .	41,443,328	3,631.2	21,247.6
Mining‡	5,111,950	296.1	1,590.7
Manufacturing . . .	5,523,985	338.6	2,364.8
Construction and public works	797,646	126.2	845.1
Electricity and water . . .	1,793,098	106.8	603.6
Transportation and telecommunications . .	2,833,538	176.0	1,022.6
Trade and commerce . .	17,074,694	1,021.9	6,114.4
Public administration . .	2,743,993	195.4	482.9
Other services . . .	2,796,040	349.5	2,038.1
GDP at factor cost . .	**80,118,272**	**6,241.7**	**36,309.8**
Import duties . . .	653,286	58.3	312.5
GDP at market prices . .	**80,771,558**	**6,300.0**	**36,622.3**

* Figures in '000 million new zaires (1 new zaire = 3m. old zaires).
† Estimates.
‡ Including processing.
Source: IMF, *Zaire—Background Information and Statistical Data* (April 1996).

BALANCE OF PAYMENTS (US $ million)

	1994	1995*	1996†
Exports of goods f.o.b.	1,255	1,632	1,944
Imports of goods f.o.b.	−667	−951	−1,114
Trade balance	589	681	830
Services (net)	−309	−393	−536
Balance on goods and services	280	288	294
Income (net)	−773	−849	−837
Balance on goods, services and income	−493	−561	−543
Current transfers (net)	0	0	−2
Current balance	−493	−561	−545
Capital account (net)	41	51	−11
Financial account (net)	−801	−740	−469
Net errors and omissions	−94	−88	—
Overall balance	−1,347	−1,337	−1,025

*Provisional.   †Estimated.

Source: IMF, *Zaire's Hyperinflation 1990–96* (April 1997).

External Trade

PRINCIPAL COMMODITIES (UN estimates, million old zaires)

Imports c.i.f.	1989	1990	1991
Food and live animals	63,380	121,824	2,172,956
Beverages and tobacco	3,436	6,605	117,812
Crude materials (inedible) except fuels	9,545	18,347	327,252
Mineral fuels, lubricants, etc.	24,436	46,968	837,761
Chemicals	33,217	63,848	1,138,847
Basic manufactures	68,343	131,365	2,343,137
Machinery and transport equipment	102,706	197,414	3,521,243
Miscellaneous manufactured articles	16,418	31,557	562,877
Other commodities and transactions	2,673	5,137	91,628
Total	324,154	623,066	11,113,531

Exports f.o.b.	1989	1990	1991
Food and live animals	93,541	148,201	2,535,635
Beverages and tobacco	5,071	8,035	137,474
Crude materials (inedible) except fuels	14,087	22,319	381,865
Mineral fuels, lubricants, etc.	36,064	57,138	977,599
Chemicals	49,024	77,672	1,328,924
Basic manufactures	100,866	159,807	2,734,207
Machinery and transport equipment	151,581	240,157	4,108,950
Miscellaneous manufactured articles	24,230	38,389	656,814
Other commodities and transactions	3,944	6,249	106,917
Total	478,409	757,967	12,968,384

Source: UN Economic Commission for Africa, *African Statistical Yearbook*.

1994 (US $ million): *Imports c.i.f.*: Mineral fuels 45.4; Total 628.8. *Exports f.o.b.*: Copper 42.8; Cobalt 140.3; Zinc 0.5; Diamonds 293.6; Crude petroleum 123.5; Coffee 158.6; Total 1,271.6. (Source: IMF, *Zaire — Background Information and Statistical Data*, April 1996).

1996 (US $ million): Total imports 921; Total exports 1,629 (Source: *African Economic Digest*).

SELECTED TRADING PARTNERS (US $'000)

Imports c.i.f.	1982	1984*	1985
Belgium-Luxembourg	156,600	116,994	240,918
Brazil	n.a.	87,031	157,716
France	53,400	52,293	118,834
Japan	7,400	20,704	50,147
Netherlands	7,700	31,152	46,107
United Kingdom	29,500	24,339	59,164
USA	60,800	73,600	134,457
Total (incl. others)	475,600	658,741	1,299,282

* Figures for 1983 are not available.

1986 (US $'000): Belgium-Luxembourg 243,929; Brazil 75,238; France 125,981; Japan 47,165; Netherlands 76,275; United Kingdom 49,809; USA 108,143; *Total* (incl. others) 1,331,531.

Exports f.o.b.	1981	1982	1985*
Belgium-Luxembourg	521,300	385,100	165,784
France	25,500	68,100	42,018
Italy	400	200	57,676
Netherlands	2,100	1,500	44,579
Switzerland	71,500	60,500	32,971
United Kingdom	13,700	10,700	21,444
USA	10,900	20,100	228,391
Total (incl. others)	685,200	585,700	796,905

* Figures for 1983 and 1984 are not available.

Source: UN, *International Trade Statistics Yearbook*.

Transport

RAILWAYS (Total traffic, million)

	1988	1989	1990
Passenger-km	465	467	469
Freight (net ton-km)	1,670	1,687	1,655

Source: UN, *Statistical Yearbook*.

ROAD TRAFFIC (motor vehicles in use at 31 December)

	1994	1995*	1996*
Passenger cars	698,672	762,000	787,000
Buses and coaches	51,578	55,000	60,000
Lorries and vans	464,205	495,000	538,000
Total vehicles	1,214,455	1,312,000	1,384,000

* Estimates.

Source: International Road Federation, *World Road Statistics*.

SHIPPING

Merchant Fleet (registered at 31 December)

	1996	1997	1998
Number of vessels	27	27	20
Total displacement ('000 grt)	14.9	14.9	12.9

Source: Lloyd's Register of Shipping, *World Fleet Statistics*.

International Sea-borne Freight Traffic
(estimates, '000 metric tons)

	1988	1989	1990
Goods loaded	2,500	2,440	2,395
Goods unloaded	1,400	1,483	1,453

Source: UN, *Monthly Bulletin of Statistics.*

CIVIL AVIATION (traffic on scheduled services)

	1992	1993	1994
Kilometres flown (million) . .	4	4	6
Passengers carried ('000) . .	116	84	178
Passenger-km (million) . .	295	218	480
Total ton-km (million) . .	56	42	87

Source: UN, *Statistical Yearbook.*

Tourism

	1994	1995	1996
Tourist arrivals ('000) . .	18	35	37
Tourism receipts (US $ million) .	5	5	5

Tourist arrivals: 30,000 in 1997; 53,139 in 1998.

Source: World Tourism Organization, *Yearbook of Tourism Statistics.*

Communications Media

	1995	1996	1997
Radio receivers ('000 in use) . .	14,103	15,970	18,030
Television receivers ('000 in use) .	3,679	5,051	6,478
Telephones ('000 main lines in use)*	36	36	n.a.
Telefax stations (number in use)* .	5,000	5,000	n.a.
Mobile cellular telephones (subscribers)	10,000*	7,200	n.a.
Daily newspapers	9	9	n.a.

Book production (titles published): 64 in 1992.

* Provisional or estimated figure.

Sources: UNESCO, *Statistical Yearbook*; UN Economic Commission for Africa, *African Statistical Yearbook.*

Education

(1994/95)

	Insti-tutions	Teachers	Students		
			Males	Females	Total
Pre-primary* . .	429	768	15,956	17,279	33,235
Primary . .	14,885	121,054	3,218,822	2,198,684	5,417,506
Secondary . .	n.a.	n.a.	943,059	571,264	1,514,323
Higher . .	n.a.	n.a.	n.a.	n.a.	52,501

* Figures refer to 1992/93.

Source: UNESCO, *Statistical Yearbook.*

Directory

Note: Following the proclamation of the Democratic Republic of the Congo in May 1997, it was assumed that the names of public- and private-sector businesses and organizations would be revised to reflect this change in the country's designation. Some entries in this section have been revised in anticipation of this development.

The Constitution

Following the proclamation of the Democratic Republic of the Congo, a 15-point constitutional decree was promulgated on 28 May 1997, which abrogated all previous constitutional dispositions. The decree declared the institutions of the Republic to be the President, the Government and the courts and tribunals; all institutions of the previous regime were suspended, except for the judiciary. All power was to be vested in the Head of State, pending the adoption of a new Constitution. In October 1997 President Kabila appointed a 42-member Constitutional Commission, which was to draft a new constitution by March 1998. The resultant draft Constitution was subsequently referred to a 300-member Constituent Assembly, which was to review the document and submit it to a national referendum. The Assembly was, however, unable to convene, owing to the outbreak of civil war, and the work was undertaken in October by a 12-member Institutional Reform Commission, appointed by Kabila.

EXECUTIVE POWER

The President of the Republic exercises legislative power by decree, following consultation with the Cabinet; he is chief of the executive and of the armed forces and has the authority to issue currency; he has the power to appoint and dismiss members of the Government, ambassadors, provincial governors, senior army officers, senior civil servants and magistrates.

POLITICAL PARTIES

All political parties, with the exception of the Alliance des forces démocratiques pour la libération du Congo-Zaïre (AFDL), were banned by decree on 26 May 1997. In January 1999, however, President Kabila issued a decree legalizing the formation of political parties (see Recent History).

PROVINCIAL GOVERNMENTS

Local government in each province is administered by a provincial governor and deputy governor, who are appointed and dismissed by the President.

The Government

HEAD OF STATE

President: LAURENT-DÉSIRÉ KABILA (assumed power 17 May 1997; inaugurated 29 May 1997).

CABINET
(September 2000)

President and Minister of Defence: LAURENT-DÉSIRÉ KABILA.

Minister of State for Internal Affairs: GAËTAN KAKUDJI.

Minister of State for Foreign Affairs and International Co-operation: ABDOULAYE YERODIA NDOMBASI.

Minister of State for Petroleum Resources: PIERRE-VICTOR MPOYO.

Minister of Justice and Parliamentary Affairs: MWENZE KONGOLO.

Minister of Finance and the Budget: FERDINAND MAWAPANGA MWANAGA.

Minister of Planning and Reconstruction: DENIS KALUME NUMBI.

Minister of the Economy, Commerce and Industry: GRÉGOIRE BAKANDEJA.

Minister of Transport: HENRI MOVASAKANI.

Minister of Housing, Environment and Tourism Development: ANATOLE BISHIKWABO TSHUBAKA.

Minister of Communications: DOMINIQUE SAKOMBI INONGO.

Minister of Post, Telephones and Telecommunications: PROSPER KIBUEY.

Minister of Public Works: YAGI SITOLO.

Minister of Energy: BABI MBAYI.

Minister of Agriculture and Animal Husbandry: ETIENNE KITANGA ESHIMA MUSEBO.

Minister of Human Rights: LÉONARD SHE OKITUNDU.

Minister of National Education: AUGUSTIN RWAKAIKARA KAMARA.

Minister of Youth, Sports and Leisure: DIDIER MUMENGI.
Minister of the Civil Service: CÉLESTIN LWANGI.
Minister of Culture and the Arts: JULIANA LUMUMBA.
Minister of Health: Dr MASHAKO MAMBA.
Minister of Social Affairs: JEANNE EBAMBA BOBOTO.
Minister of Enterprises: NORBERT LIKULIA BOLONGO.
Minister of Labour and Social Security: ANASTASIE MOLEKO MOLIWA.
Minister of Regional Co-operation: ODELIVE META MUTOMBO MUDIAY.

MINISTRIES

All ministries are in Kinshasa.
Office of the President: Hôtel du Conseil Exécutif, ave de Lemera, Kinshasa-Gombe; tel. (12) 30892.
Ministry of Agriculture and Animal Husbandry: Immeuble Sozacom, 3rd floor, blvd du 30 juin, BP 8722 KIN I, Kinshasa-Gombe; tel. (12) 31821.
Ministry of the Civil Service: ave des Ambassadeurs, BP 3, Kinshasa-Gombe; tel. (12) 30209.
Ministry of Culture and the Arts: BP 8541, Kinshasa 1; tel. (12) 31005.
Ministry of Defence: BP 4111, Kinshasa-Gombe; tel. (12) 59375.
Ministry of the Economy, Commerce and Industry: Immeuble Onatra, blvd du 30 juin, BP 8500 KIN I, Kinshasa-Gombe.
Ministry of Energy: Immeuble Snel, 239 ave de la Justice, BP 5137 KIN I, Kinshasa-Gombe; tel. (12) 22570.
Ministry of the Environment, Fisheries and Forests: 15 ave des Cliniques, BP 12348 KIN I, Kinshasa-Gombe; tel. (12) 31252.
Ministry of Finance and the Budget: blvd du 30 juin, BP 12998 KIN I, Kinshasa-Gombe; tel. (12) 31197.
Ministry of Foreign Affairs: place de l'Indépendance, BP 7100, Kinshasa-Gombe; tel. (12) 32450.
Ministry of Health: blvd du 30 juin, BP 3088 KIN I, Kinshasa-Gombe; tel. (12) 31750.
Ministry of Information and the Press: ave du 24 novembre, BP 3171 KIN I, Kinshasa-Kabinda; tel. (12) 23171.
Ministry of Internal Affairs: ave de Lemera, Kinshasa-Gombe; tel. (12) 23171.
Ministry of International Co-operation: ave de Lemera, Enceinte Snel, ave de la Justice, Kinshasa-Gombe; tel. (12) 23171.
Ministry of Justice: 228 ave de Lemera, BP 3137, Kinshasa-Gombe; tel. (12) 32432.
Ministry of Labour and Social Security: blvd du 30 juin, BP 3840, Kinshasa.
Ministry of Mines: Immeuble Snel, 239 ave de la Justice, BP 5137 KIN I, Kinshasa-Gombe; tel. (12) 30336.
Ministry of National Education: Enceinte de l'Institut de la Gombe, BP 3163, Kinshasa-Gombe; tel. (12) 30098.
Ministry of Planning: 4155 ave des Côteaux, BP 9378, Kinshasa-Gombe 1; tel. (12) 31346.
Ministry of Post and Telecommunications: Immeuble Kilou, 4484 ave des Huiles, BP 800 KIN I, Kinshasa-Gombe; tel. (12) 24854.
Ministry of Public Works: Immeuble Travaux Publics, Kinshasa-Gombe.
Ministry of Transport: Immeuble Onatra, blvd du 30 juin, BP 3304, Kinshasa-Gombe; tel. (12) 23660.
Ministry of Youth and Sports: 77 ave de la Justice, BP 8541 KIN I, Kinshasa-Gombe.

President

Laurent-Désiré Kabila declared himself President on 17 May 1997,and was inaugurated on 29 May 1997.

Legislature

The Head of State legislates by decree. In mid-2000 a 300-member transitional Parliament was formed; a selection committee, supervised by the Ministry of Internal Affairs, nominated candidates, who were subsequently approved by the President. Under a further presidential decree, signed in July, the Government was to be decentralized, with the legislature relocating to Lubumbashi. The new Parliament was inaugurated on 22 August in Lubumbashi.

Political Organizations

Comités du pouvoir populaire (CPP): f. 1999 as successor to **Alliance des forces démocratiques pour la libération du Congo–Zaïre** (AFDL, Leader LAURENT-DÉSIRÉ KABILA); committees formed in each village to devolve power to the people; to debate political policy.

Political parties reported to be active in late 1999 included:
Forces novatrices pour l'union et la solidarité (FONUS): Kinshasa; advocates political pluralism; Pres. JOSEPH OLENGHANKOY; Sec.-Gen. JOHN KWET.
Forces politiques du conclave (FPC): Kinshasa; f. 1993; alliance of pro-Mobutu groups, incl the UFERI, led by MPR; Chair. JEAN NGUZA KARL-I-BOND.
Mouvement national du Congo–Lumumba (MNC–Lumumba): Kinshasa; f. 1994; coalition of seven parties, incl. the Parti lumumbiste unifié (PALU), led by ANTOINE GIZENGA; supports the aims of the late Patrice Lumumba; Co-ordinating Cttee PASCAL TABU, MBALO MEKA, OTOKO OKITASOMBO.
Mouvement populaire de la révolution (MPR): f. 1966 by Pres. Mobutu; sole legal political party until Nov. 1990; advocates national unity and opposes tribalism; Leader (vacant); Sec.-Gen. KITHIMA BIN RAMAZANI.
Mouvement pour la libération du Congo (MLC): Equateur; f. 1998; rebel movement; Head JEAN-PIERRE BEMBA.
Parti démocrate et social chrétien (PDSC): 32B ave Tombalbaye, Kinshasa-Gombe; tel. (12) 21211; f. 1990; centrist; Pres. ANDRÉ BO-BOLIKO; Sec. Gen. TUYABA LEWULA.
Rassemblement congolais pour la démocratie (RCD): e-mail congorcd@congorcd.org; internet www.congorcd.org; f. 1998; advocates introduction of a democratic political system; split into two factions in 1999: Ilunga faction: Goma; supported by Rwanda; Pres. Dr EMILE ILUNGA; Wamba dia Wamba faction (Mouvement de libération): Bunia; supported by Uganda; Pres. ERNEST WAMBA DIA WAMBA.
Union des fédéralistes et républicains indépendants (UFERI): Kinshasa; f. 1990; seeks autonomy for province of Katanga; dominant party in the USOR; Pres. JEAN NGUZA KARL-I-BOND; Leader KOUYOUMBA MUCHULI MULEMBE.
Union pour la démocratie et le progrès social (UDPS): Twelfth St, Limete Zone, Kinshasa; e-mail udps@globalserve.net; internet www.udps.org/udps.html; f. 1982; Leader ETIENNE TSHISEKEDI WA MULUMBA; Sec.-Gen. Dr ADRIEN PHONGO KUNDA.
Union pour la République (UPR): Kinshasa; f. 1997 by fmr mems of the MPR; Leader CHARLES NDAYWEL.
Union sacrée de l'opposition radicale (USOR): Kinshasa; f. 1991, comprising c. 130 movements and factions opposed to Pres. Mobutu, in which the UDPS was the dominant party; a radical internal faction, known as the **Union sacrée de l'opposition radicale et ses alliés (USORAL)** (Pres. FRÉDÉRIC KIBASSA MALIBA), emerged in 1994.
Union sacrée rénovée (USR): Kinshasa; f. 1993 by several ministers in fmr Govt of Nat. Salvation; Leader KIRO KIMATE.

Diplomatic Representation

EMBASSIES IN THE DEMOCRATIC REPUBLIC OF THE CONGO

Angola: 4413–4429 blvd du 30 juin, BP 8625, Kinshasa; tel. (12) 32415; Ambassador: MAWETE JOÃO BAPTISTA.
Belgium: Immeuble Le Cinquantenaire, place du 27 octobre, BP 899, Kinshasa; tel. (12) 20110; fax 22120; Ambassador: FRANK DE CONINCK.
Benin: 3990 ave des Cliniques, BP 3265, Kinshasa-Gombe; tel. (12) 33156; Ambassador: ANDRÉ GUY OLOGOUDOU.
Cameroon: 171 blvd du 30 juin, BP 10998, Kinshasa; tel. (12) 34787; Chargé d'affaires a.i.: DOMINIQUE AWONO ESSAMA.
Canada: BP 8341, Kinshasa 1; tel. (88) 41276; Ambassador: VERONA EDELSTEIN.
Central African Republic: 11 ave Pumbu, BP 7769, Kinshasa; tel. (12) 30417; Ambassador: SISSA LE BERNARD.
Chad: 67–69 ave du Cercle, BP 9097, Kinshasa; tel. (12) 22358; Ambassador: MAITINE DJOUMBE.
China, People's Republic: 49 ave du Commerce, BP 9098, Kinshasa; tel. (12) 21207; Ambassador: SUN KUNSHAN.
Congo, Republic: 179 blvd du 30 juin, BP 9516, Kinshasa; tel. (12) 30220; Ambassador: MAURICE OGNAMY.
Côte d'Ivoire: 68 ave de la Justice, BP 9197, Kinshasa; tel. (12) 30440; Ambassador: GILBERT DOH.
Cuba: 4660 ave Cateam, BP 10699, Kinshasa; Ambassador: ENRIQUE MONTERO.
Egypt: 519 ave de l'Ouganda, BP 8838, Kinshasa; tel. (12) 34368; Ambassador: AZIZ ABDEL HAMID HAMZA.

Ethiopia: BP 8435, Kinshasa; tel. (12) 23327; Ambassador: DIEU-DEONNE A. GANGA.

France: 97 ave de la République du Tchad, BP 3093, Kinshasa; tel. (12) 30513; Ambassador: GILDAS LE LIDEC.

Gabon: ave du 24 novembre, BP 9592, Kinshasa; tel. (12) 68325; Ambassador: MICHEL MADOUNGOU.

Germany: 82 ave de Lemera, BP 8400, Kinshasa-Gombe; tel. (12) 33399; fax (satellite) 871-112-0323; Ambassador: HELMUT OHRBRAUN.

Greece: Immeuble de la Communauté Hellénique, 3éme étage, blvd du 30 juin, BP 478, Kinshasa; tel. (88) 44862; fax (12) 21561; e-mail grembkin@ic.cd; Ambassador: PANAYOTIS TH. BAIZOS.

Holy See: 81 ave Goma, BP 3091, Kinshasa; tel. (12) 33128; fax (12) 33346; Apostolic Nuncio: Most Rev. FAUSTINO SAINZ MUÑOZ, Titular Archbishop of Novaliciana.

Iran: 76 blvd du 30 juin, BP 16599, Kinshasa; tel. (12) 31052.

Israel: 12 ave des Aviateurs, BP 8343, Kinshasa; tel. (12) 21955; Ambassador: JAMAR F. GOLAN.

Italy: 8 ave de la Mongala, BP 1000, Kinshasa; tel. (88) 46106; e-mail ambitalykin@raga.net; Ambassador: PIETRO BALLERO.

Japan: Immeuble Citibank, 2e étage, ave Colonel Lukusa, BP 1810, Kinshasa; tel. (88) 45305; fax (satellite) 871-761-21-41-42; e-mail ambj@ic.cd; Ambassador: YASUO TAKANO.

Kenya: 5002 ave de l'Ouganda, BP 9667, Kinshasa; tel. (12) 30117; Ambassador: MWABILI KISAKA.

Korea, Democratic People's Republic: 168 ave de l'Ouganda, BP 16597, Kinshasa; tel. (12) 31566; Ambassador: HAN PON CHUN.

Korea, Republic: 2A ave des Orangers, BP 628, Kinshasa; tel. (88) 20722; Ambassador: CHUN SOON-KYU.

Lebanon: 3 ave de l'Ouganda, Kinshasa; tel. (12) 82469; Chargé d'affaires a.i.: CHEHADE MOUALLEM.

Liberia: 3 ave de l'Okapi, BP 8940, Kinshasa; tel. (12) 82289; Ambassador: JALLA D. LANSANAH.

Mauritania: BP 16397, Kinshasa; tel. (12) 59575; Ambassador: Lt-Col M'BARECK OULD BOUNA MOKHTAR.

Morocco: 4497 ave Lubefu, BP 912, Kinshasa; tel. (12) 34794; Ambassador: ABDELAZIZ BENNIS.

Netherlands: 11 ave Zongo Ntolo, BP 10299, Kinshasa; tel (12) 30733; Ambassador: F. RACKE.

Nigeria: 141 blvd du 30 juin, BP 1700, Kinshasa; tel. (12) 43272; Ambassador: AHMED MOHAMMED KELE.

Portugal: 270 ave des Aviateurs, BP 7775, Kinshasa; tel. (12) 21335; Ambassador: LUÍS DE VASCONCELOS PIMENTEL QUARTIN BASTOS.

Russia: 80 ave de la Justice, BP 1143, Kinshasa 1; tel. (12) 33157; fax (12) 45575; Ambassador: VALERII GAMAIVNE.

South Africa: 17 ave Pumbu, BP 7829, Kinshasa-Gombe; tel. (88) 48287; fax (satellite) 1-212-3723510; Ambassador: (vacant).

Sudan: 83 ave des Treis, BP 7347, Kinshasa; tel. (12) 33200; Ambassador: MUBARAK ADAM HADI.

Sweden: 89 ave de Lemera, BP 11096, Kinshasa; tel. (12) 34084; fax (12) 33683; e-mail ambasuede@ic.cd; Chargé d'affaires a.i.: EVA EMNÉUS.

Togo: 3 ave de la Vallée, BP 10117, Kinshasa; tel. (12) 30666; Ambassador: MAMA GNOFAM.

Tunisia: 67–69 ave du Cercle, BP 1498, Kinshasa; tel. and fax (88) 03901; Chargé d'affaires a.i.: FARHAT BAROUN.

Turkey: 18 ave Pumbu, BP 7817, Kinshasa; tel. (88) 01207; fax (88) 04740; Ambassador: DENIZ UZMEN.

United Kingdom: ave de Lemera, BP 8049, Kinshasa; tel. (88) 46102; fax (satellite) 871-144-7753; e-mail ambrit@ic.cd; Ambassador: DOUGLAS SCRAFTON.

USA: 310 ave des Aviateurs, BP 697, Kinshasa; tel. (12) 21523; fax 21232; Ambassador: WILLIAM L. SWING.

Zambia: 54–58 ave de l'Ecole, BP 1144, Kinshasa; tel. (12) 23038; Ambassador: IAN SIKAZWE.

Judicial System

The Minister of Justice is responsible for the organization and definition of competence of the judiciary; civil, penal and commercial law and civil and penal procedures; the status of persons and property; the system of obligations and questions pertaining to nationality; international private law; status of magistrates; organization of the legal profession, counsels for the defence, notaries and of judicial auxiliaries; supervision of cemeteries, non-profit-making organizations, cults and institutions working in the public interest; the operation of prisons; confiscated property.

There is a Supreme Court in Kinshasa, and there are also nine Courts of Appeal and 36 County Courts. A presidential decree, signed in July 2000, provided for government decentralization, with the Supreme Court relocating to Kisangani.

The Head of State is empowered to appoint and dismiss magistrates.
Supreme Court: cnr ave de la Justice and ave de Lemera, BP 3382, Kinshasa-Gombe; tel. (12) 25104.
 President of the Supreme Court: BIYANGO KETESE.
 Procurator-General of the Republic: MONGULU T'APANGANE.

Religion

Many of the country's inhabitants follow traditional beliefs, which are mostly animistic. A large proportion of the population is Christian, predominantly Roman Catholic, and there are small Muslim, Jewish and Greek Orthodox communities.

CHRISTIANITY
The Roman Catholic Church
The Democratic Republic of the Congo comprises six archdioceses and 41 dioceses. An estimated 51% of the population are Roman Catholics.

Bishops' Conference: Conférence Episcopale de la République Démocratique du Congo, BP 3258, Kinshasa-Gombe; tel. (12) 30082; f. 1981; Pres. Rt Rev. FAUSTIN NGABU, Bishop of Goma.

Archbishop of Bukavu: Most Rev. EMMANUEL KATALIKO, Archevêché, BP 3324, Bukavu; tel. 2707; fax (16) 82060067.

Archbishop of Kananga: Most Rev. GODEFROID MUKENG'A KALOND, Archevêché, BP 70, Kananga; tel. 2477.

Archbishop of Kinshasa: Cardinal FRÉDÉRIC ETSOU-NZABI-BAMUN-GWABI, Archevêché, ave de l'Université, BP 8431, Kinshasa 1; tel. (12) 3723-546.

Archbishop of Kisangani: Most Rev. LAURENT MONSENGWO PASINYA, Archevêché, ave Mpolo 10B, BP 505, Kisangani; tel. (761) 608334; fax (761) 3132898.

Archbishop of Lubumbashi: Most Rev. FLORIBERT SONGASONGA MWITWA, Archevêché, BP 72, Lubumbashi; tel. (2) 34-1442.

Archbishop of Mbandaka-Bikoro: Most Rev. JOSEPH KUMUONDALA MBIMBA, Archevêché, BP 1064, Mbandaka; tel. 2234.

The Anglican Communion
The Church of the Province of the Congo comprises six dioceses.
Archbishop of the Province of the Congo and Bishop of Boga: Most Rev. PATRICE BYANKYA NJOJO, CAC-Boga, POB 21285, Nairobi, Kenya.

Bishop of Bukavu: Rt Rev. FIDÈLE BALUFUGA DIROKPA, CAC-Bukavu, POB 53435, Nairobi, Kenya.

Bishop of Katanga: Rt Rev. ISINGOMA KAHWA, CAZ-Lubumbashi, c/o United Methodist Church, POB 22037, Kitwe, Zambia.

Bishop of Kindu: Rt Rev. ZACHARIA MASIMANGE KATANDA, CAC-Kindu, POB 53435, Nairobi, Kenya; e-mail angkindu@antenna.nl.

Bishop of Kisangani: Rt Rev. SYLVESTRE MUGERA TIBAFA, CAC-Kisangani, BP 861, Kisangani.

Bishop of Nord Kivu: Rt Rev. METHUSELA MUNZENDA MUSUBAHO, CAC-Butembo, POB 21285, Nairobi, Kenya; fax (satellite) 871-166-1121.

Kimbanguist
Eglise de Jésus Christ sur la Terre par le Prophète Simon Kimbangu: BP 7069, Kinshasa; tel. (12) 68944; f. 1921 (officially est. 1959); c. 5m. mems (1985); Spiritual Head HE SALOMON DIALUNGANA KIANGANI; Sec.-Gen. Rev. LUNTADILLA.

Protestant Churches
Eglise du Christ au Congo (ECC): ave de la Justice (face no. 75), BP 4938, Kinshasa-Gombe; f. 1902; a co-ordinating agency for all the Protestant churches, with the exception of the Kimbanguist Church; 62 mem. communities and a provincial org. in each province; c. 10m. mems (1982); Pres. Bishop MARINI BODHO; includes:

Communauté Baptiste du Congo-Ouest: BP 4728, Kinshasa 2; f. 1970; 450 parishes; 170,000 mems (1985); Gen. Sec. Rev. LUSAKWENO-VANGU.

Communauté des Disciples du Christ: BP 178, Mbandaka; tel. 31062; f. 1964; 250 parishes; 650,000 mems (1985); Gen. Sec. Rev. Dr ELONDA EFEFE.

Communauté Episcopale Baptiste en Afrique: 2 ave Jason Sendwe, BP 3866, Lubumbashi 1; tel. (2) 24724; f. 1956; 1,300 episcopal communions and parishes; 150,000 mems (1993); Pres. Bishop KITOBO KABWEKA-LEZA.

Communauté Evangélique: BP 36, Luozi; f. 1961; 50 parishes; 33,750 mems (1985); Pres. Rev. K. LUKOMBO NTONTOLO.

Communauté Lumière: BP 10498, Kinshasa 1; f. 1931; 150 parishes; 220,000 mems (1985); Patriarch KAYUWA TSHIBUMBU WA KAHINGA.

Communauté Mennonite: BP 18, Tshikapa; f. 1960; 40,000 mems (1985); Gen. Sec. Rev. Kabangy Djeke Shapasa.

Communauté Presbytérienne: BP 117, Kananga; f. 1959; 150,000 mems (1985); Gen. Sec. Dr M. L. Tshihamba.

Eglise Missionaire Apostolique: 375 ave Commerciale, BP 15859, Kinshasa 1; tel. (12) 8804569; f. 1986; 5 parishes; 2,500 mems.; Apostle for Africa Lufanga-Ayimou Nanandana.

The Press

DAILIES

L'Analyste: 129 ave du Bas-Congo, BP 91, Kinshasa-Gombe; tel. (12) 80987; Dir and Editor-in-Chief Bongoma Koni Botahe.

Boyoma: 31 blvd Mobutu, BP 982, Kisangani, Dir and Editor Badriyo Rova Rovatu.

Elima: 1 ave de la Révolution, BP 11498, Kinshasa; tel. (12) 77332; f. 1928; evening; Dir and Editor-in-Chief Essolomwa Nkoy ea Linganga.

Mjumbe: BP 2474, Lubumbashi; tel. (2) 25348; f. 1963; Dir and Editor Tshimanga Koya Kakona.

Le Palmarès: Kinshasa; supports Union pour la démocratie et le progrès social; Editor Michel Ladeluya.

Le Phare: BP 15662, Kinshasa 1; tel. (12) 45896; f. 1983; Editor Polydor Muboyayi Mubanga; circ 4,000.

Le Potentiel: Immeuble Ruzizi, 873 ave du Bas-Congo, BP 11338, Kinshasa; tel. (2) 44456; f. 1982; Editor Modeste Mutinga Mutuishayi; circ. 8,000.

La Référence Plus: BP 22520, Kinshasa; tel. (2) 45783; f. 1989; Dir André Ipakala.

Le Soft: Kinshasa; Man. Kinkiey Malumba; Chief Editor Awasi Kharomon.

PERIODICALS

Allo Kinshasa: 3 rue Kayange, BP 20271, Kinshasa-Lemba; monthly; Editor Mbuyu Wa Kabila.

L'Aurore Protestante: Eglise du Christ au Congo, BP 4938, Kinshasa-Gombe; French; religion; monthly; circ. 1,000.

BEA Magazine de la Femme: 2 ave Masimanimba, BP 113380, Kinshasa 1; every 2 weeks; Editor Mutinga Mutwishayi.

Bingwa: ave du 30 juin, zone Lubumbashi no 4334; weekly; sport; Dir and Editor Mateke Wa Mulamba.

Cahiers Economiques et Sociaux: BP 257, Kinshasa XI, (National University of the Congo); sociological, political and economic review; quarterly; Dir Prof. Ndongala Tadi Lewa; circ. 2,000.

Cahiers des Religions Africaines: Faculté de Théologie Catholique de Kinshasa, BP 712, Kinshasa/Limete; tel. (12) 78476; f. 1967; English and French; religion; 2 a year; circ. 1,000.

Le Canard Libre: Kinshasa; f. 1991; Editor Joseph Castro Mulebe.

Circulaire d'Information: Association Nationale des Entreprises du Congo, 10 ave des Aviateurs, BP 7247, Kinshasa 1; tel. (12) 22565; f. 1959; French; legal and statutory texts for the business community; monthly.

La Colombe: 32B ave Tombalbaye, Kinshasa-Gombe; tel. (12) 21211; organ of Parti démocrate et social chrétien; circ. 5,000.

Congo-Afrique: Centre d'Etudes pour l'Action Sociale, 9 ave Père Boka, BP 3375, Kinshasa-Gombe; tel. (12) 34682; f. 1961; economic, social and cultural; monthly; Editors Francis Kikassa Mwanalessa, René Beeckmans; circ. 2,500.

Le Conseiller Comptable: 51 rue du Grand Séminaire, Quartier Nganda, BP 308, Kinshasa; tel. (88) 01216; fax (88) 00075; f 1974; French; public finance and taxation; quarterly; Editor Tomena Foko; circ. 2,000.

Le Courrier du Zaïre: aut. no 04/DIMOPAP 0018/84, 101 Lukolela, Kinshasa; weekly; Editor Nzonzila Ndonzuau.

Cultures au Zaïre et en Afrique: BP 16706, Kinshasa; f. 1973; French and English; quarterly.

Dionga: Immeuble Amassio, 2 rue Dirna, BP 8031, Kinshasa; monthly.

Documentation et Information Protestante (DIP): Eglise du Christ au Congo, BP 4938, Kinshasa-Gombe; tel. and fax (88) 46387; e-mail eccm@ic.cd; French and English; religion.

Documentation et Informations Africaines (DIA): BP 2598, Kinshasa 1; tel. (12) 33197; fax (12) 33196; Roman Catholic news agency reports; 3 a week; Dir Rev. Père Vata Diambanza.

L'Entrepreneur Flash: Association Nationale des Entrepreneurs du Congo, 10 ave des Aviateurs, BP 7247, Kinshasa 1; tel. (12) 22565; f. 1978; business news; monthly; circ. 1,000.

Etudes d'Histoire Africaine: National University of the Congo, BP 1825, Lubumbashi; f. 1970; French and English; history; annually; circ. 1,000.

Horizons 80: Société Congolaise d'Edition et d'Information, BP 9839, Kinshasa; economic affairs; weekly.

Les Kasaï: 161 9e rue, BP 575, Kinshasa/Limete; weekly; Editor Nsenga Ndomba.

Kin-Média: BP 15808, Kinshasa 1; monthly; Editor Ilunga Kasambay.

KYA: 24 ave de l'Equateur, BP 7853, Kinshasa-Gombe; tel. (12) 27502; f. 1984; weekly for Bas-Congo; Editor Sassa Kassa Yi Kiboba.

Libération: Kinshasa; f. 1997; politics; supports the AFDL; weekly; Man. Ngoyi Kabuya Dikateta M'miana.

Mambenga 2000: BP 477, Mbandaka; Editor Bosange Yema Bof.

Le Moniteur de l'Economie (Economic Monitor): Kinshasa; Man. Ed. Félix Nzuzi.

Mwana Shaba: Générale des Carrières et des Mines, BP 450, Lubumbashi; monthly; circ. 25,000.

Ngabu: Société Nationale d'Assurances, Immeuble Sonas Sankuru, blvd du 30 juin, BP 3443, Kinshasa-Gombe; tel. (12) 23051; f. 1973; insurance news; quarterly.

Njanja: Société Nationale des Chemins de Fer Congolais, 115 place de la Gare, BP 297, Lubumbashi; tel. (2) 23430; fax (2) 61321; railways and transportation; annually; circ. 10,000.

NUKTA: 14 chaussée de Kasenga, BP 3805, Lubumbashi; weekly; agriculture; Editor Ngoy Bunduki.

L'Opinion: BP 15394, Kinshasa; weekly; Editor Sable Fwamba Kiependa.

Problèmes Sociaux Zaïrois: Centre d'Exécution de Programmes Sociaux et Economiques, Université de Lubumbashi, 208 ave Kasavubu, BP 1873, Lubumbashi; f. 1946; quarterly; Editor N'Kashama Kadima.

Promoteur Congolais: Centre du Commerce International du Congo, 119 ave Colonel Tshatshi, BP 13, Kinshasa; f. 1979; international trade news; six a year.

Sciences, Techniques, Informations: Centre de Recherches Industrielles en Afrique Centrale (CRIAC), BP 54, Lubumbashi.

Le Sport Africain: 13è niveau Tour adm., Cité de la Voix du Congo, BP 3356, Kinshasa-Gombe; monthly; Pres. Tshimpumpu Wa Tshimpumpu.

Taifa: 536 ave Lubumba, BP 884, Lubumbashi; weekly; Editor Lwambwa Milambu.

Telema: Faculté Canisius, Kimwenza, BP 3724, Kinshasa-Gombe; f. 1974; religious; quarterly; edited by the Central Africa Jesuits; circ. 1,200.

Umoja: 23 Bunkeye Matonge, Kinshasa; weekly; Publr Léon Moukanda Lunyama.

Vision: Kinshasa; 2 a week; independent; Man. Editor Xavier Bonane Yanganzi.

Zaïre Business: Immeuble Amasco, 3968 rue ex-Belgika, BP 9839, Kinshasa; f. 1973; French; weekly.

Zaïre Informatique: Conseil Permanent de l'Informatique au Zaïre, Kinshasa 1; f. 1978; quarterly.

Zaïre Ya Sita: Direction Générale et Administration, 1 rue Luozi Kasavubu, BP 8246, Kinshasa; f. 1968; Lingala; political science; 6 a year.

NEWS AGENCIES

Agence Congolaise de Presse (ACP): 44–48 ave Tombalbaye, BP 1595, Kinshasa 1; tel. (12) 22035; f. 1957; state-controlled; Dir-Gen. Ali Kalonga.

Documentation et Informations Africaines (DIA): BP 2598, Kinshasa 1; tel. (12) 34528; f. 1957; Roman Catholic news agency; Dir Rev. Père Vata Diambanza.

Foreign Bureaux

Agence France-Presse (AFP): Immeuble Wenge 3227, ave Wenge, Zone de la Gombe, BP 726, Kinshasa 1; tel. (12) 27009; Bureau Chief Jean-Pierre Rejette.

Agencia EFE (Spain): BP 2653, Lubumbashi; Correspondent Kanku Sanga.

Agência Lusa de Informação (Portugal): BP 4941, Kinshasa; tel. (12) 24437.

Agenzia Nazionale Stampa Associata (ANSA) (Italy): BP 2790, Kinshasa 15; tel. (12) 30315; Bureau Chief (vacant).

Pan-African News Agency (PANA) (Senegal): BP 1400, Kinshasa; tel. (12) 23290; f. 1983; Bureau Chief Adrien Honoré Mbeyet.

Xinhua (New China) News Agency (People's Republic of China): 293 ave Mfumu Lutunu, BP 8939, Kinshasa; tel. (12) 25647; Correspondent Chen Weibin.

PRESS ASSOCIATIONS

Médias Libres—Médias pour Tous: Kinshasa; org. representing Kinshasa newspapers.

Union de la Presse du Congo: BP 4941, Kinshasa 1; tel. (12) 24437.

Publishers

Aequatoria Centre: BP 276, Mbandaka; f. 1980; anthropology, biography, ethnicity, history, language and linguistics, social sciences; Dir HONORÉ VINCK.

CEEBA Publications: BP 246, Bandundu; f. 1965; humanities, languages, fiction; Man. Dir (Editorial) Dr HERMANN HOCHEGGER.

CELTA (Centre de Linguistique Théorique et Appliquée): BP 4956, Kinshasa-Gombe; tel. (2) 30503; fax (2) 21394; f 1971; language arts and linguistics; Gen. Man. N. KIKO; Dir NTITA NYEMBWE.

Centre de Documentation Agricole: BP 7537, Kinshasa 1; tel. (12) 32498; agriculture, science; Dir PIERTE MBAYAKABUYI; Chief Editor J. MARCELLIN KAPUKUNGESA.

Centre de Recherches Pédagogiques: BP 8815, Kinshasa 1; f. 1959; accounting, education, geography, language, science; Dir P. DETIENNE.

Centre de Vulgarisation Agricole: BP 4008, Kinshasa 2; tel. (12) 71165; fax (12) 21351; agriculture, environment, health; Dir-Gen. KIMPIANGA MAHANIAH.

Centre International de Semiologie: 109 ave Pruniers, BP 1825, Lubumbashi.

Centre Protestant d'Editions et de Diffusion (CEDI): 209 ave Kalémie, BP 11398, Kinshasa 1; tel. (12) 22202; fax (12) 26730; f. 1935; fiction, poetry, biography, religious, juvenile; Christian tracts, works in French, Lingala, Kikongo, etc.; Dir-Gen. HENRY DIRKS.

Commission de l'Education Chrétienne: BP 3258, Kinshasa-Gombe; tel. (12) 30086; education, religion; Man. Dir Abbé MUGADJA LEHANI.

Connaissance et Pratique du Droit Congolais Editions (CDPC): BP 5502, Kinshasa-Gombe; f. 1987; law; Editor DIBUNDA KABUINJI.

Facultés Catholiques de Kinshasa: BP 1534, Kinshasa-Limete; tel. and fax (12) 46965; f. 1957; anthropology, art, economics, history, politics, computer science; five titles in 1994; Dir Mgr LUDIONGO NDOMBASI.

Editions Lokole: BP 5085, Kinshasa 10; state org. for the promotion of literature; Dir BOKEME SHANE MOLOBAY.

Editions Saint Paul: BP 8505, Kinshasa; tel. (12) 77726; fiction, general non-fiction, poetry, religion; Dir Sister FRANKA PERONA.

Les Editions du Trottoir: BP 629, Kinshasa; f. 1989; communications, fiction, literature, drama; Pres. CHARLES DJUNJU-SIMBA.

Librarie les Volcans: 22 ave Pres. Mobutu, BP 400, Goma, Nord-Kivu; f. 1995; social sciences; Man. Dir RUHAMA MUKANDOLI.

Presses Universitaires du Congo (PUC): 290 rue d'Aketi, BP 1682, Kinshasa 1; tel. (12) 30652; f. 1972; scientific publs; Dir Prof. MUMBANZA MWA BAWELE.

Government Publishing House

Imprimerie du Gouvernement Central: BP 3021, Kinshasa-Kalina.

Broadcasting and Communications

TELECOMMUNICATIONS

Comcell: Kinshasa; provides satellite communications network; 4,000 subscribers.

Office Congolais des Postes et des Télécommunications (OCPT): Hôtel des postes, blvd du 30 juin, BP 13798, Kinshasa; tel. (12) 21871; fax (88) 45010; state-owned; 13,000 lines; 40,000 subscribers; Dir-Gen. KAPITAO MAMBWENI.

Telecel-Congo: Kinshasa; provides satellite communications network; largest private operator; 45% nationalized in 1998; 12,000 subscribers.

BROADCASTING

Radio-Télévision Nationale Congolaise (RTNC): BP 3171, Kinshasa-Gombe; tel. (12) 23171; state radio terrestrial and satellite television broadcasts; Dir-Gen. JOSE KAJANGUA.

Radio

Several private radio broadcasters operate in Kinshasa.

Radio Candip: Centre d'Animation et de Diffusion Pedagogique, BP 373, Bunia; state-controlled; under rebel control in late 1998.

La Voix du Congo: Station Nationale, BP 3164, Kinshasa-Gombe; tel. (12) 23175; state-controlled; operated by RTNC; broadcasts in French, Swahili, Lingala, Tshiluba, Kikongo; regional stations at Kisangani, Lubumbashi, Bukavu, Bandundu, Kananga, Mbuji-Mayi, Matadi, Mbandaka and Bunia.

Television

Several private television broadcasters operate in Kinshasa.

Antenne A: Immeuble Forescom, 2e étage, ave du Port 4, POB 2581, Kinshasa 1; tel. (243) 21736; private and commercial station; Dir-Gen. IGAL AVIVI NEIRSON.

Canal Z: ave du Port 6, POB 614, Kinshasa 1; tel. (243) 20239; commercial station; Dir-Gen. FRÉDÉRIC FLASSE.

Tele Kin Malebo (TKM): Kinshasa; private television station; nationalization announced 1997; Dir-Gen. NGONGO LUWOWO.

Télévision Congolais: BP 3171, Kinshasa-Gombe; tel. (12) 23171; govt commercial station; operated by RTNC; broadcasts for 5 hours daily on weekdays and 10 hours daily at weekends.

Finance

(cap. = capital; res = reserves; dep. = deposits; m. = million; brs = branches; amounts in old zaires unless otherwise indicated)

BANKING

A reorganization of the banking sector was expected to follow the introduction as legal tender of a new currency unit, the Congolese franc (CF), which was completed on 30 June 1999.

Central Bank

Banque Centrale du Congo: blvd Colonel Tshatshi au nord, BP 2697, Kinshasa; tel. (12) 20701; f. 1964; cap. and res 50,088.4m. (Dec. 1988); Gov. JEAN-CLAUDE MASANGU MULONGO; 8 brs.

Commercial Banks

African Trade Bank (ATB): ave Lemarinel, BP 3459, Kinshasa-Gombe; tel. (12) 33845; fax (12) 8846991; cap. and res NZ 67,893.3m., total assets NZ 406,946.6m. (Dec. 1996); Pres. ABDALLAH HASSAN WAZNI; Gen. Man. GHAZI ABDALLAH WAZNI.

BANCOR SARL: Immeuble Régidesco-DG, BP 7997, Kinshasa; tel. (12) 20635; fax (satellite) 1-212-3769207; f. 1998.

Banque de Commerce et de Développement (BCD): 87 blvd du 30 juin, Kinshasa; tel. (12) 20106; fax (satellite) 1-703-3902716; e-mail bcd-kin@ic.cd; cap. and res CF 5.2m., total assets CF 29.1m. (Dec. 1998).

Banque Commerciale du Congo SARL (BCDC): blvd du 30 juin, BP 488, Kinshasa; tel. (12) 21693; fax (12) 21770; e-mail bcdc@raga.cd; f. 1909 as Banque du Congo Belge, name changed as above 1997; cap. and res CF 98.6m., total assets CF 240.9m. (Dec. 1998); Pres. NKEMA LILOO; Gen. Man. KASONGO TAIBU; 29 brs.

Banque Congolaise du Commerce Extérieur SARL: blvd du 30 juin, BP 400, Kinshasa 1; tel. (12) 20393; fax (12) 27947; f. 1947, reorg. 1987; state-owned; in liquidation in 1999; cap. and res NZ 19,303.1m., dep. NZ 27,419.9m. (Dec. 1994); Chair. and Gen. Man. GBENDO NDEWA TETE; Dirs MAKUMA NDESEKE, ZIKONDOLO BIWABEKI; 31 brs.

Banque Continentale Africaine (Congo) SCARL: 4 ave de la Justice, BP 7613, Kinshasa-Gombe; tel. (12) 24388; fax (12) 21237; f. 1983; total assets 28,786.5m. (Dec. 1994); Pres. NASIR ABID; Dir-Gen. M. A. DOCHY.

Banque de Crédit Agricole: angle ave Kasa-Vubu et ave M'Polo, BP 8837, Kinshasa-Gombe; tel. (12) 21800; fax (12) 27221; f. 1982 to expand and modernize enterprises in agriculture, livestock and fishing, and generally to improve the quality of rural life; state-owned; in liquidation in 1999; cap. 5m. (Dec. 1991); Pres. MOLOTO MWA LOPANZA.

Banque Internationale de Crédit SCARL (BIC): 191 ave de l'Equateur, BP 1299, Kinshasa 1; tel. (88) 41940; fax (12) 123769600; f. 1994; cap. and res NZ 8,355.4m., total assets NZ 35,077.9m. (Dec. 1995); Pres. PASCAL KINDUELO LUMBU; Man. Dir THARCISSE K. M. MILEMBWE.

Banque Internationale pour l'Afrique au Congo (BIAC): Immeuble Nioki, ave de la Douane, Kinshasa 1; tel. (88) 20612; fax (12) 20120; e-mail biac-rj@raga.net; cap. and res US $1.4m., total assets US $17.4m. (Dec. 1998); Pres. ROBERT JONCHERAY.

Caisse Générale d'Epargne du Congo: 38 ave de la Caisse d'Epargne, BP 8147, Kinshasa-Gombe; tel. (12) 33701; f. 1950; state-owned; Chair. and Man. Dir NSIMBA M'VUEDI; 45 brs.

Citibank NA Congo: Immeuble Citibank Congo, angle aves Col Lukusa et Ngongo Lutete, BP 9999, Kinshasa 1; tel. (12) 20554; fax (12) 21064; f. 1971; cap. and res NZ 199,425.2m., total assets NZ 1,928,804.9m. (Dec. 1996); Pres. ROBERT THORNTON; 1 br.

Fransabank (Congo) SARL: Immeuble Flavica 14/16, ave du Port, BP 9497, Kinshasa 1; tel. (88) 00445376; fax (88) 0046423; f. 1989; cap. and res NZ 7,351.7m., total assets NZ 174,809.7m. (Dec. 1996); Pres. ADNAN WAFIC KASSAR.

Nouvelle Banque de Kinshasa: 1 place du Marché, BP 8033, Kinshasa 1; tel. (12) 26361; fax (12) 20587; f. 1969, nationalized 1975; control transferred to National Union of Congolese Workers in 1989; in liquidation in 1999; cap. NZ 2,000 (1990), res NZ 92,179.4m., dep. NZ 25,396.8m. (Dec. 1994); Pres. MANTOMINA KIALA; 15 brs.

Société Financière de Développement SCARL (SOFIDE): Immeuble SOFIDE, 9–11 angle aves Ngabu et Kisangani, BP 1148, Kinshasa 1; tel. (12) 20676; fax (12) 20788; f. 1970; partly state-owned; provides tech. and financial aid, primarily for agricultural devt; cap. and res NZ 44,610.4m., total assets NZ 519,789.7m. (Dec. 1997); Pres. and Dir-Gen. KIYANGA KI-N'LOMBI; 4 brs.

Stanbic Bank Congo SARL: 12 ave de Mongala, BP 16297, Kinshasa 1; tel. (12) 20028; fax (12) 46216; f. 1973; subsidiary of Standard Bank Investment Corpn (South Africa); cap. and res CF 1.2m., total assets CF 21.3m. (Dec. 1998); Chair. J. N. LEGGETT; Man. Dir NICOLAS CLAVEL; 1 br.

Union de Banques Congolaises (UBC) SARL: angle ave de la Nation et ave des Aviateurs 19, BP 197, Kinshasa 1; tel. (88) 41333; fax (88) 46628; e-mail ubc@ic.cd; f. 1929, renamed as above in 1997; total assets US $ 59.3m. (Dec. 1997); Man. Dir LUC DELVA; 8 brs.

INSURANCE

Société Nationale d'Assurances (SONAS): 3473 blvd du 30 juin, Kinshasa-Gombe; tel. (12) 23051; f. 1966; state-owned; cap. 23m.; 9 brs.

Trade and Industry

At November 1994 the Government's portfolio of state enterprises numbered 116, of which 56 were wholly owned by the Government. The heads of all state-owned enterprises were suspended by decree in June 1997.

DEVELOPMENT ORGANIZATIONS

Caisse de Stabilisation Cotonnière (CSCo): BP 3058, Kinshasa-Gombe; tel. (12) 31206; f. 1978 to replace Office National des Fibres Textiles; acts as an intermediary between the Govt, cotton ginners and textile factories, and co-ordinates international financing of cotton sector.

La Générale des Carrières et des Mines (GÉCAMINES): BP 450, Lubumbashi; tel. (2) 6768105; fax (2) 6768041; f. 1967 to acquire assets of Union Minière du Haut-Katanga; state-owned corpn engaged in mining and marketing of copper, cobalt, zinc and coal; also has interests in agriculture; privatization announced in 1994, subsequently delayed; Exec. Chair. GEORGE FORREST; operates the following enterprise:

GÉCAMINES—Exploitation: mining operations.

Institut National pour l'Etude et la Recherche Agronomiques: BP 1513, Kisangani; f. 1933; agricultural research.

Office National du Café: ave Général Bobozo, BP 8931, Kinshasa 1; tel. (12) 77144; f. 1979; state agency for coffee and also cocoa, tea, quinquina and pyrethrum.

Pêcherie Maritime Congolaise: Kinshasa; DRC's only sea-fishing enterprise.

CHAMBERS OF COMMERCE

Chambre de Commerce, d'Industrie et d'Agriculture du Congo: 10 ave des Aviateurs, BP 7247, Kinshasa 1; tel. (12) 22286.

INDUSTRIAL AND TRADE ASSOCIATIONS

Association Nationale des Entreprises du Congo: 10 ave des Aviateurs, BP 7247, Kinshasa; tel. (12) 24623; f. 1972; represents business interests for both domestic and foreign institutions; Man. Dir EDOUARD LUBOYA DIYOKA; Gen. Sec. ATHANASE MATENDA KYELU.

EMPLOYERS' ASSOCIATION

Fédération des Entreprises du Congo (FEC): Kinshasa; Head JOSE ENDUNDO.

UTILITIES

Electricity

Société Nationale d'Electricité (SNEL): 2831 ave de la Justice, BP 500, Kinshasa; tel. (12) 26893; fax (12) 33735; f. 1970; state-owned; Dir-Gen. PASCAL KUNDA PAKA (acting).

Water

Régie de Distribution d'Eau (REGIDESCO): 65 blvd du 30 juin, BP 12599, Kinshasa; tel. (12) 22792; water supply admin; Dir-Gen. EALE BOMBOLE (acting).

MAJOR COMPANIES

The following are some of the largest companies in terms either of capital investment or employment.

Manufacturing and Trading

BAT Congo SARL: 973 ave Gen. Bobozo, Kingabwa, BP 621, Kinshasa I; tel. (12) 20289; fax (satellite) 871-682-340868; f. 1950; wholly-owned subsidiary of British American Tobacco Co Ltd, London; mfrs of tobacco products; Chair. and Man. Dir B. MAVAMBU ZOYA.

Brasseries, Limonaderies et Malteries du Congo (BRALIMA): 912 ave du Flambeau, BP 7246, Kinshasa; tel. (12) 22141; f. 1923; production of beer, soft drinks and ice; Gen. Man. J. L. HOME.

Compagnie des Margarines, Savons et Cosmétiques au Congo SARL (MARSAVCO CONGO): 1 ave Kalemie, BP 8914, Kinshasa; tel. (12) 24821; f. 1922; subsidiary of Unilever NV; mfrs of detergents, foods and cosmetics; Pres. C. GODDE; 1,100 employees.

Compagnie Sucrière: 1963 ave de Général Bobozo, BP 8816, Kinshasa, and BP 10, Kwilu Ngongo, Bas-Congo; tel. (12) 20476; f. 1925; mfrs of sugar, alcohol, acetylene, oxygen and carbon dioxide; Man. Dir B. MICHEL; Gen. Man. NKAZI BASISULULA; Dir M. LUVIYZ.

Cultures et Elevages du Congo (CELCO) SARL: BP 16796, Kinshasa I; interests in cattle ranches, abattoirs, coffee, cocoa, rubber, oil palm, quinquina plantations and associated processing plants.

IBM World Trade Corporation (Congo): 6 ave du Port, BP 7563, Kinshasa 1; tel. (12) 23358; fax (12) 24029; f. 1954; sale and maintenance of computers and business machines and associated materials; Gen. Man. MUKADI KABUMBU.

Industries Congolaises des Bois (ICB): 23 ave de l'Ouganda, BP 10399, Kinshasa; state forestry and sawmilling enterprise.

Plantations Lever au Congo: 16 ave Colonel Lukusa, BP 8611, Kinshasa I; f. 1911; subsidiary of Unilever NV; plantations of oil palm, rubber, cocoa and tea; Man. Dir A. J. RITCHIE.

NOVATEX: 29B 16ème rue, BP 8456, Kinshasa; principal producer of synthetic fibres.

Société BATA Congolaise: 33 ave Général Bobozo, BP 598, Kinshasa I; tel. (12) 27414; f. 1946; principal shoe mfr in the DRC; Man. Dir JEAN-LOUIS ANTZ; 100 employees.

Société Commerciale et Minière du Congo SA: BP 499, Kinshasa; subsidiary of Lonrho Ltd; engineering, motor trade, insurance, assembly and sale of earth-moving equipment.

Société Congo-Suisse de Produits Chimiques SARL: BP 14096, Kinshasa 1; tel. (12) 24707; sales agent for Ciba-Geigy pharmaceutical products.

Société Générale d'Alimentation (SGA): BP 15898, Kinshasa; state enterprise; import, processing and distribution of foodstuffs; largest chain of distributors in the DRC.

TABAZAIRE: blvd du 30 juin, BP 42, Kinshasa; cigarette mfrs.

Minerals

Fina Recherche Exploitation Pétrolière (FINA REP SPRL): BP 15596, Kinshasa; tel. (12) 20528; fax (12) 20052; exploitation of petroleum; Gen. Man. J. D. NOGUEIRA.

Office des Mines d'Or de Kilo-Moto (OKIMO): BP 219–220, Bunia; state-owned; operates gold mines; Pres. and Sec.-Gen. ISSIKATA TABU.

SHELL RDC: ave du Port 14/16, BP 2799, Kinshasa-Gombe; tel. (12) 21262; f. 1978; marketing of petroleum products; Man. Dir F. J. KOOL; 100 employees.

Société Aurifère du Kivu et Maniema (SAKIMA): f. 1997 as successor to Société Minière du Kivu; 93% owned by Banro Resources Corpn, 7% by DRC government; exploitation of gold; Man. Dir MARIO FLOCCHI.

Société Congo Gulf Oil: blvd du 30 juin, BP 7189, Kinshasa I; tel. (12) 23111; international mining consortium exploiting offshore petroleum at Muanda.

Société Congo—Italienne de Raffinage: BP 1478, Kinshasa I; tel. (12) 22683; fax (12) 25998; f. 1963; petroleum refinery; Pres. LESSEDJINA IKWAME IPU'OZIA; 600 employees.

Société de Développement Industriel et Minière du Congo (SODIMICO): 4219 ave de l'Ouganda, BP 7064, Kinshasa; tel. (12) 32511; subsidiary of GÉCAMINES (see Development Organizations); copper-mining consortium exploiting mines of Musoshi and Kinsenda in Katanga.

Société Minière de Bakwanga (MIBA): BP 377, Mbuji-Mayi, Kasaï Oriental; f. 1961; cap. 27m. zaires; 80% state-owned; industrial diamond mining; CEO TRUDON KATENDE MUTA.

Société Minière du Tenke-Fungurume: Immeuble UCB Centre, 5ème étage, BP 1279, Kinshasa; f. 1970 by international consortium comprising Charter Consolidated of London, Govt of Zaire, Mitsui (Japan), Bureau de Recherches Géologiques et Minières de France,

Léon Tempelsman and Son (USA) and COGEMA (France); copper and cobalt mining; Dir B. L. MORGAN.

Sonangol-Congo: 1513 blvd du 30 juin, BP 7617, Kinshasa 1; tel. (12) 25356; f. 1974; bought by the Sociedade Nacional de Combustíveis de Angola (SONANGOL) in 1998; petroleum refining, processing, stocking and transporting; Dir-Gen. NKOSI PEDRO.

TRADE UNIONS

The Union Nationale des Travailleurs was founded in 1967 as the sole trade union organization. In 1990 the establishment of independent trade unions was legalized, and by early 1991 there were 12 officially recognized trade union organizations.

Union Nationale des Travailleurs du Congo: BP 8814, Kinshasa; f. 1967; comprises 16 unions; Pres. KATALAY MOLELI SANGOL.

Transport

Office National des Transports (ONATRA): BP 98, Kinshasa 1; tel. (12) 24761; fax (12) 24892; operates 12,174 km of waterways, 366 km of railways and road and air transport; administers ports of Kinshasa, Matadi, Boma and Banana; Pres. and Gen. Man. JACQUES MBELOLO BITWEMI.

RAILWAYS

The main line runs from Lubumbashi to Ilebo. International services run to Dar es Salaam (Tanzania) and Lobito (Angola), and also connect with the Zambian, Zimbabwean, Mozambican and South African systems. In 1994 an agreement was concluded with the South African Government for the provision of locomotives, rolling stock and fuel, to help rehabilitate the rail system. In May 1997 the railway system was nationalized.

Kinshasa–Matadi Railway: BP 98, Kinshasa 1; 366 km operated by ONATRA; Pres. JACQUES MBELOLO BITWEMI.

Société Nationale des Chemins de Fer du Congo (SNCC): 115 place de la Gare, BP 297, Lubumbashi; tel. (2) 23430; f. 1974; 4,772 km (including 858 km electrified); administers all internal railway sections as well as river transport and transport on Lakes Tanganyika and Kivu; man. contract concluded with a Belgian-South African corpn, Sizarail, in 1995 for the man. of the Office des Chemins de Fer du Sud (OCS) and the Société des Chemins de Fer de l'Est (SFE) subsidiaries, with rail networks of 2,835 km and 1,286 km respectively; assets of Sizarail nationalized and returned to SNCC control in May 1997; Dir-Gen. R. DIFAND.

ROADS

In 1996 there were approximately 157,000 km of roads, of which some 33,100 km were main roads. In general road conditions are poor, owing to inadequate maintenance. In August 1997 a rehabilitation plan was announced by the Government under which 28,664 km of roads were to be built or repaired. The project was to be partly financed by external sources.

Office des Routes: Direction Générale, ave Ex-Descamp, BP 10899, Kinshasa-Gombe; tel. (12) 32036; construction and maintenance of roads.

INLAND WATERWAYS

The River Congo is navigable for more than 1,600 km. Above the Stanley Falls the Congo becomes the Lualaba, and is navigable along a 965-km stretch from Ubundu to Kindu and Kongolo to Bukama. The River Kasai, a tributary of the River Congo, is navigable by shipping as far as Ilebo, at which the line from Lubumbashi terminates. The total length of inland waterways is 13,700 km.

Régie des voies fluviales: 109 ave Lumpungu, Kinshasa-Gombe, BP 11697, Kinshasa 1; administers river navigation; Gen. Man. NGIAM KIPOY.

Société Congolaise des Chemins de Fer des Grands Lacs: River Lualaba services: Bubundu–Kindu and Kongolo–Malemba N'kula; Lake Tanganyika services: Kamina–Kigoma–Kalundu–Moba–Mpulungu.

SHIPPING

The principal seaports are Matadi, Boma and Banana on the lower Congo. The port of Matadi has more than 1.6 km of quays and can accommodate up to 10 deep-water vessels. Matadi is linked by rail with Kinshasa. The country's merchant fleet numbered 20 vessels and amounted to 12,918 gross registered tons at 31 December 1998.

Compagnie Maritime du Congo SARL: USB Centre, place de la Poste, BP 9496, Kinshasa; tel. (12) 21031; fax (12) 26234; f. 1946; services: North Africa, Europe, North America and Asia to West Africa, East Africa to North Africa; Chair. MAYILUKILA LUSIASIA; Pres. Capt. W. E. BOTENDJU.

CIVIL AVIATION

International airports are located at Ndjili (for Kinshasa), Luano (for Lubumbashi), Bukavu, Goma and Kisangani. There are smaller airports and airstrips dispersed throughout the country.

Blue Airlines: BP 1115, Kinshasa 1; tel. (12) 20455; f. 1991; regional and domestic charter services for passengers and cargo; Man. T. MAYANI.

Compagnie Africaine d'Aviation: Edifice du GAP, blvd du 30 juin, Kinshasa; f. 1992.

Congo Airlines: 1928 ave Kabambare, N'dolo-Kinshasa, BP 12847, Kinshasa; tel. (88) 43947; fax (88) 00235; e-mail cal-fih-dg@ic.cd; f.1994 as Express Cargo, assumed present name in 1997; international, regional and domestic scheduled services for passengers and cargo; Pres. JOSE ENDUNO; CEO STAVROS PAPAIOANNOU.

Eastern Congo Airlines: Bukavu; f. 1997; 60% state-owned, 40% by Belgian interests; Chair. Chief NAKAZIBA CIMANYE.

Filair: BP 14671, Kinshasa; tel. (88) 45702; fax (88) 45702; f. 1987; regional and domestic charter services; Pres. DANY PHILEMOTTE.

Lignes Aériennes du Congo (LAC): 3555-3560 blvd du 30 juin, BP 2111, Kinshasa; tel. (12) 24624; relaunched 1997; national carrier.

Scibe Airlift: BP 614, Kinshasa; tel. (12) 26237; fax (12) 24386; f. 1979; domestic and international passenger and cargo charter services between Kinshasa, Lubumbashi, Bujumbura (Burundi) and Brussels; Pres. BEMBA SAOLONA; Dir-Gen. BEMBA GOMBO.

Zairean Airlines (Congo): 3555–3560 blvd du 30 juin, BP 2111, Kinshasa; tel. (88) 48103; f. 1981; international, regional and domestic services for passengers and cargo; Dir-Gen. Capt. ALFRED SOMMERAUER.

Local charter services are also provided by Trans Service Airlift, Transair Cargo and Wetrafa Airlift.

Tourism

The country offers extensive lake and mountain scenery, although tourism remains largely undeveloped. In 1998 tourist arrivals totalled 53,139, and receipts from tourism amounted to an estimated US $5m. in 1996.

Office National du Tourisme: 2A/2B ave des Orangers, BP 9502, Kinshasa-Gombe; tel. (12) 30070; f. 1959; Man. Dir BOTOLO MAGOZA.

Société Congolaise de l'Hôtellerie: Immeuble Memling, BP 1076, Kinshasa; tel. (12) 23260; Man. N'JOLI BALANGA.

Defence

In August 1999 the troops of President Laurent Kabila were estimated to number 55,000 men, and the navy an estimated 900 men. There were also foreign troops numbering a reported 12,500 men in the country at that time. A civil war began in August 1988 in the east of the country. The strength of the rebel forces was unknown, although at 1 August 1999 they were supported by some 9,000 troops from Uganda and Rwanda. At the end of November 1999 the UN Security Council established the UN Organization Mission in the Democratic Republic of Congo (MONUC). At the end of June 2000 MONUC numbered 258 military observers and 279 civilian personnel, and had a total authorized strength of 5,537 military personnel. The defence budget for 1999 was US $400m.

Defence Expenditure: Estimated at US $308m. in 1997.

Commander-in-Chief: LAURENT-DÉSIRÉ KABILA.

Chief of Staff of the Armed Forces: JOSEPH KABILA.

Education

Primary education, beginning at six years of age and lasting for six years, is officially compulsory. Secondary education, which is not compulsory, begins at 12 years of age and lasts for up to six years, comprising a first cycle of two years and a second of four years. In 1994, according to UNESCO, the total enrolment at primary and secondary schools was equivalent to 52% of the school-age population (males 62%; females 41%); primary enrolment was equivalent to 72% of the school-age population (boys 86%; girls 59%), while the comparable ratio for secondary enrolment was 26% (boys 32%; girls 19%). There are four universities, located at Kinshasa, Kinshasa/Limete, Kisangani and Lubumbashi. According to estimates by UNESCO, the average rate of adult illiteracy in 1995 was 22.7% (males 13.4%; females 32.3%). In the budget for 1997 education received an estimated 144,000m. new zaires (less than 1% of central government expenditure).

Bibliography

Abi-Saab, G. *The United Nations Operations in the Congo 1960–64.* London, Oxford University Press, 1978.

Abdulai, N. *Zaire: Background to the Civil War.* London, ARIB, 1997.

Asch, S. *L'Eglise du Prophète Kimbangu.* Paris, Editions Karthala, 1983.

Bezy, F., Peemans, J. P., and Wantelet, J. M. *Accumulation et sous-développement au Zaïre 1960–1980.* Louvain-la-Neuve, Presses universitaires de Louvain, 1981.

Bontinck, F. *L'évangélisation du Zaïre.* Kinshasa, Saint Paul Afrique, 1980.

Cornevin, R. *Le Zaïre.* Paris, Presses universitaires de France, 1977.

Ekpebu, L. B. *Zaire and the African Revolution.* Ibadan, Ibadan University Press, 1989.

Ekwe-Ekwe, H. *Conflict and Intervention in Africa: Nigeria, Angola and Zaire.* London, Macmillan, 1990.

Gérard-Libois, J. *Katanga Secession,* (trans. by Rebecca Young). Madison and London, University of Wisconsin Press, 1966.

Gourou, P. *La Population du Congo.* Paris, Hachette, 1966.

Hayward, M. F. *Elections in Independent Africa.* Boulder, CO, Westview Press, 1987.

Hochschild, A. *King Leopold's Ghost.* London, Macmillan, 1999.

Huybrechts, A. *Transports et structures de développement au Congo. Etude de progrès économique de 1900 à 1970.* Paris and The Hague, Editions Mouton, 1970.

Jewsiewicki, B. (Ed.). *Etat indépendant du Congo, Congo belge, République démocratique du Congo, République du Zaïre?* Sainte-Foy, Québec, SAFI Press, 1984.

Kamitatu-Massamba, C. *Zaïre, le pouvoir à la portée du peuple.* Paris, Editions de l'Harmattan, 1977.

Kanza, T. *Conflict in the Congo. The Rise and Fall of Lumumba.* Harmondsworth, Penguin, 1972.

Kelly, S. *America's Tyrant: The CIA (Central Intelligence Agency) and Mobutu of Zaire.* Lanham, MD, University of America Press, 1993.

Kronsten, G. *Zaire to the 1990s: Will Retrenchment Work?* London, Economist Intelligence Unit (Economic Prospects Series), 1986.

Leslie, W. J. *Zaire: Continuity and Political Change in an Oppressive State.* Boulder, CO, Westview Press, 1993.

Louis, W. R., and Stengers, J. *E. D. Morel's History of the Congo Reform Association.* Oxford, Clarendon Press, 1968.

Lumumba, P. *Congo My Country.* London, Praeger, 1963.

MacGaffey, J. *The Real Economy of Zaire: An Anthropological Study.* London, James Currey, 1991.

MacGaffey, J., and Mukohya, V. *The Real Economy of Zaire: The Contribution of Smuggling and Other Unofficial Activities to National Wealth.* London, James Currey, 1991.

Marysse, S. *La libération du Congo dans le contexte de la mondialisation.* Antwerp, UFSIA, 1997.

Mbaya, K. (Ed.). *Zaire: What Destiny?* Dakar, CODESRIA, 1993.

Mokoli, M. M. *State Against Development: The Experience of Post-1965 Zaire.* Westport, CT, Greenwood Press, 1992.

Nzongola-Ntalaja, G. *From Zaire to the Democratic Republic of the Congo.* Uppsala, Nordiske Afrikainstitutet, 1999.

Sanqmpam, S. N. *Pseudo-capitalism and the Overpolitical State: Reconciling Politics and Anthropology in Zaire.* Brookfield, VT, Ashgate Press, 1994.

Schatzberg, M. G. *The Dialectics of Oppression in Zaire.* Bloomington, IN, Indiana University Press, 1988.

Shapiro, D., and Tollens, E. *The Agricultural Development of Zaire.* Aldershot, Avebury, 1992.

Vanderlinden, Huybrechts, Mudimbe, Peeters, Van Der Steen and Verhaegen. (Eds). *Du Congo au Zaïre, 1960–1980, essai de bilan.* Brussels, Etudes du CRISP, 1980.

Vanderlinden, J. *La crise congolaise.* Brussels, Complexe, 1985.

Vellut, J.-L., Loriaux, F., and Morimont, F. *Bibliographies historiques du Zaïre à l'époque coloniale (1880–1960).* Louvain-la-Neuve, Tervuren, 1996.

Willame, J. C. *Eléments pour une lecture du contentieux Belgo-Zaïrois.* Les Cahiers du CEDAF, Vol. VI. Brussels, Centre d'etude et de documentation africaines, 1988.

Patrice Lumumba—La crise congolaise revisitée. Paris, Editions Karthala, 1990.

Young, M. C. *Politics in the Congo: Decolonization and Independence.* Princeton, Princeton University Press, 1965.

Young, M. C., and Turner, T. *The Rise and Decline of the Zairean State.* Madison, WI, University of Wisconsin Press, 1985.

For detailed contemporary historical studies, see the annual collection of documents, together with the commentary, published by the Centre de recherche et d'information socio-politique (CRISP), Brussels, starting with *Congo,* 1959.

REPUBLIC OF THE CONGO

Physical and Social Geography

DAVID HILLING

POPULATION

The Congo river forms approximately 1,000 km of the eastern boundary of the Republic of the Congo, the remainder of which is provided by the Oubangui river from just south of the point at which the Equator bisects the country. Across these rivers lies the Democratic Republic of the Congo. To the north, the republic is bounded by the Central African Republic and Cameroon. Gabon lies to the west, and the Cabinda exclave of Angola to the south, adjoining the short Atlantic coastline. Covering an area of 342,000 sq km (132,047 sq miles) the country supported a population of 1,843,421 at the census of 1984. The population was estimated by the UN to have increased to 2,785,000 in mid-1998, giving an average density of only 8.1 inhabitants per sq km. About one-third of the population are dependent on agriculture, mainly of the bush-fallowing type, but this is supplemented where possible by fishing, hunting and gathering. The main ethnic groups are the Vili on the coast, the Kongo (centred on Brazzaville), and the Téké, M'Bochi and Sanga of the plateaux in the centre and north of the country. The principal centres of urban population are the capital, Brazzaville (population estimated at 950,000 in 1997), and the main port of Pointe-Noire (population estimated at 500,000 in the same year).

PHYSICAL FEATURES AND RESOURCES

The exploitation of substantial offshore petroleum deposits represents a major sector of the economy. The immediate coastal zone is sandy in the north, more swampy south of Kouilou, and in the vicinity of Pointe-Indienne yields small amounts of petroleum. A narrow coastal plain does not rise above 100 m,

and the cool coastal waters modify the climate, giving low rainfall and a grassland vegetation. Rising abruptly from the coastal plain are the high-rainfall forested ridges of the Mayombé range, parallel to the coast and achieving a height of 800 m, in which gorges, incised by rivers such as the Kouilou, provide potential hydroelectric power sites. At Hollé, near the Congo-Océan railway and at the western foot of the range, there are considerable phosphate deposits. Mayombé also provides an important export commodity, timber, of which the main commercial species are okoumé, limba and sapele.

Inland, the south-western Niari valley has lower elevation, soils that are good by tropical African standards and a grassland vegetation which facilitates agricultural development. A variety of agricultural products such as groundnuts, maize, vegetables, palm oil, coffee, cocoa, sugar and tobacco, is obtained from large plantations, smaller commercial farms and also peasant holdings. These products provide the support for a more concentrated rural population and the basis for some industrial development.

A further forested mountainous region, the Chaillu massif, is the Congo basin's western watershed, and this gives way north-eastwards to a series of drier plateaux, the Batéké region and, east of the Likoula river, a zone of Congo riverine land. Here are numerous watercourses, with seasonal inundation, and dense forest vegetation, which supports some production of forest products, although the full potential has yet to be realized. The rivers Congo and Oubangui, with tributaries, provide more than 6,500 km of navigable waterway, which are particularly important, owing to the lack of a developed network of roads.

Recent History

PIERRE ENGLEBERT

Revised for this edition by the Editor

The Republic of the Congo became autonomous within the French Community in November 1958, with Abbé Fulbert Youlou as prime minister. Full independence followed on 15 August 1960; in March 1961 Youlou was elected president. Following a period of ethnic tensions and labour unrest, Youlou transferred power in 1963 to a provisional government led by Alphonse Massamba-Débat, who was elected president in December. In 1964 the Mouvement national de la révolution (MNR) was formed, on Marxist-Leninist principles, as the sole political party. In August 1968, Massamba-Débat was deposed by Capt. (later Maj.) Marien Ngouabi in an army coup. A new Marxist-Leninist party, the Parti congolais du travail (PCT), replaced the MNR, and in January 1970 the country was renamed the People's Republic of the Congo.

During the early 1970s ethnic tensions, added to disagreements over political ideology and power struggles within the political élite, contributed to a continuing atmosphere of national instability. In March 1977 Ngouabi was assassinated during an attempted coup by supporters of Massamba-Débat, who was subsequently executed. In April Col (later Brig.-Gen.) Jacques-Joachim Yhombi-Opango, a former chief of staff of the armed forces, was appointed head of state. In February 1979, faced with a collapse in support, Yhombi-Opango surrendered his powers to a provisional committee appointed by the PCT.

In the following month the president of the committee, Col (later Gen.) Denis Sassou-Nguesso, was appointed president of the republic and chairman of the central committee of the PCT.

SASSOU-NGUESSO AND THE PCT

Despite its stated socialist convictions, the Sassou-Nguesso regime adopted an increasingly pro-Western foreign policy and a correspondingly liberal economic policy. However, the main branch of the radical wing of the PCT, known as M-22, remained influential both within the party and the government.

Persistent ethnic rivalries, together with disillusionment with the government's response to the country's worsening economic problems, resulted in an increase in opposition to the Sassou-Nguesso regime during the late 1980s. In July 1987 20 army officers were arrested on suspicion of undermining state security. They were mostly members of the northern Kouyou ethnic group (prominent members of which have included Ngouabi and Yhombi-Opango: Sassou-Nguesso is from a different northern group, the M'Bochi). A commission of enquiry, established by the government, identified the affair as a coup attempt. Although the plot had apparently been instigated by a right-wing army group, it appeared to have some links with M-22. The findings of the enquiry also implicated Yhombi-Opango and his former colleague, Pierre Anga, both of whom were being held under house arrest. Yhombi-Opango, who agreed to appear before the commission of inquiry, was transferred to prison; Anga, however, responded by inciting an armed uprising in his native town of Owando, during which up to 60 people were reported to have been killed. In September government troops suppressed the rebellion with French military assistance. Anga evaded arrest and remained at large until July 1988, when he was killed by Congolese security forces.

At the PCT congress in July 1989 Sassou-Nguesso was re-elected chairman of the party and president of the republic for a further five-year term. In August Alphonse Mouissou Poaty-Souchalaty, elected to the politburo of the ruling party in the previous month, was appointed prime minister, and a new government was announced. At legislative elections, held in September, the single list of 133 candidates was approved by 99.19% of those who used their vote. For the first time the list included candidates who were not members of the PCT. In November Sassou-Nguesso announced a series of extensive reforms, aiming to achieve a liberalization of the economy: state intervention was to be reduced, while private enterprise was to be fostered. In the following month more than 40 prisoners who had been detained without charge since July 1987 were released.

POLITICAL TRANSITION

In February 1990 the government appointed a committee to examine the implications for the Congo of the political changes taking place in Eastern Europe. In July the PCT announced that an extraordinary congress would be convened to formulate legislation enabling the introduction of a multi-party system, and that the PCT's role in mass and social organizations was to be reduced.

In August 1990, on the occasion of the 30th anniversary of the country's independence, Sassou-Nguesso announced the release of several political prisoners, including Yhombi-Opango. In September the Confederation of Congolese Trade Unions (CSC) was refused permission by the government to disaffiliate itself from the PCT. The CSC had also demanded an immediate transition to a plural political system and increased salaries for workers in the public sector. However, in response to a general strike, called in protest by the CSC, the government agreed to permit free elections to the leadership of the trade union organization, and in September the central committee of the PCT decided to allow the immediate registration of new political parties.

In December 1990 Alphonse Poaty-Souchalaty resigned as prime minister over a 'conflict of views' within the PCT on resolving the national crisis. In the same month a hastily convened extraordinary party congress abandoned Marxism-Leninism as its official ideology, and formulated constitutional amendments legalizing a multi-party system. The amendments were subsequently approved by the national people's assembly, and took effect in January 1991. Gen. Goma was appointed prime minister, and shortly afterwards an interim government was installed. From early January the army was instructed to dissociate itself from the PCT, and to remain neutral in its support of democracy.

A national conference on the country's future was convened in February 1991; it was immediately adjourned until mid-March, owing to a dispute over the number and representation of the participant organizations. In a settlement to the dispute opposition movements were allocated seven of 11 seats on the conference's governing body and were represented by 700 of the 1,100 delegates; the Roman Catholic bishop of Owando, Ernest N'Kombo, was elected chairman. The conference voted itself a sovereign body whose decisions were to be binding and not subject to government approval. In April the conference announced that the constitution was to be abrogated and that the national people's assembly and other national and regional institutions were to be dissolved. In June a 153-member legislative higher council of the republic was established under N'Kombo's chairmanship, in order to supervise the implementation of these measures, pending the adoption of a new constitution and the holding of elections. In the same month the prime minister replaced Sassou-Nguesso as head of government, and the country reverted to the name Republic of the Congo. André Milongo, a former World Bank official without formal political

affiliation, succeeded Goma as prime minister. Independent trade unions were also legalized.

In December 1991 the higher council of the republic adopted a draft constitution, which provided for legislative power to be vested in an elected national assembly and senate and for executive power to be held by an elected president. A reshuffle of cabinet posts was announced at the end of December.

Army Discontent

In January 1992, following a reallocation of senior army posts by the prime minister, members of the army, who were reported to be supporters of Sassou-Nguesso, occupied strategic positions in Brazzaville and demanded the reinstatement of military personnel who had allegedly been dismissed because of their ethnic affiliations, the removal of the newly appointed secretary of state for defence and payment of overdue salaries. The government rejected these demands, whereupon the mutinous soldiers demanded Milongo's resignation as prime minister. Armed clashes in Brazzaville at that time between government supporters and mutinous troops resulted in at least five civilian deaths. The crisis was resolved when the secretary of state for defence resigned, and Milongo agreed to reorganize the council of ministers, substantially reducing it in size and appointing a candidate preferred by the army as minister of defence. Milongo assumed personal control of the armed forces.

Electoral Discord

The draft constitution was approved by 96.3% of those who voted at a referendum in March 1992. In May Milongo appointed a new cabinet, whose membership was drawn from each of the country's regions, in order to avoid domination by any one ethnic group. Elections to the new national assembly took place in late June and mid-July. The Union panafricaine pour la démocratie sociale (UPADS) became the majority party, winning 39 of the 125 contested seats, followed by the Mouvement congolais pour la démocratie et le développement intégral (MCDDI), with 29 seats, and the PCT (18 seats). At elections to the senate, held in late July, the UPADS again won a majority (23) of the contested seats (60), followed by the MCDDI, with 13 seats. In August, Pascal Lissouba, the leader of the UPADS and a former prime minister, won 36% and 61% of the votes respectively at two rounds of presidential elections, defeating Bernard Kolelas, the leader of the MCDDI, and President Sassou-Nguesso. Lissouba, whose election campaign had promised the devolution of power from Brazzaville to the regions and the continued implementation of economic reforms, was inaugurated as president at the end of August. At the beginning of September he appointed Maurice-Stéphane Bongho-Nouarra (a member of the UPADS) as prime minister, with a mandate to form a coalition government based on a UPADS–PCT parliamentary alliance. However, shortly after a new cabinet had been named, the PCT terminated the pact, on the grounds that Lissouba had not given it as many ministerial posts as he had promised. The PCT then formed an alliance with the Union pour le renouveau démocratique (URD), a new grouping of seven parties, including the MCDDI. The URD–PCT alliance, which now had a majority of seats in parliament, demanded the right to form a new administration and, at the end of October, won a vote of no confidence in the government. In mid-November Bongho-Nouarra announced the resignation of his government. Soon afterwards President Lissouba, in defiance of demands by the URD–PCT, dissolved the national assembly and announced that new legislative elections would be held in 1993. In response, the URD–PCT coalition commenced a protest campaign of civil disobedience. In early December the chief of staff of the armed forces intervened and, with the barely veiled threat of a military take-over in the background, demanded that the two sides form a transitional government, pending the holding of the fresh parliamentary elections. Claude Antoine Dacosta, a former FAO and World Bank official, was appointed prime minister of the new transitional administration.

INTERNAL CONFRONTATION

At the first round of legislative elections, which took place in early May 1993, the Mouvance présidentielle, comprising the UPADS and its allies, won 62 of the 125 seats in the national assembly, while the URD–PCT coalition secured 49. Protesting that serious electoral irregularities had occurred, the URD–PCT refused to contest the second round of elections in early June (for seats where a clear majority had not been achieved in the first round) and demanded that some of the first-round polls should be repeated. At the second round the Mouvance présidentielle secured an absolute majority (69) of seats in the national assembly. In late June Lissouba appointed a new cabinet, with ex-president Yhombi-Opango as prime minister. During June Bernard Kolelas, the MCDDI leader and chairman of the URD–PCT coalition, nominated a rival cabinet and urged his supporters to force the government to call new elections by means of a campaign of civil disobedience. However, the political crisis soon precipitated violent conflict between armed militias, representing party political and ethnic interests, and the security forces (many of whom were themselves affiliated to the various militias). At the end of June the supreme court ruled that electoral irregularities had occurred at the first round of elections. In mid-July Lissouba declared a state of emergency. In late July the government and the opposition negotiated a truce, and in early August, following mediation by the OAU, France and President Bongo of Gabon, the two sides agreed that the disputed first-round election results should be examined by a committee of impartial international arbitrators and that the second round of elections should be restaged. (The second round already held was consequently annulled by the supreme court). The state of emergency was revoked in mid-August.

Following the repeated second round of legislative elections, which took place at the beginning of October 1993, the Mouvance présidentielle, which secured 65 seats, retained its overall majority in the national assembly. (Therefore the cabinet that had been appointed in June, with Yhombi-Opango as prime minister, remained unchanged.) The URD–PCT, which had amassed 57 seats, agreed to participate in the new assembly. In November, however, confrontations between armed militias, affiliated to political parties, and the security forces erupted once again. During the second half of 1993 activities by militias resulted in serious social and economic disruption and, reportedly, at least 2,000 deaths. A cease-fire was agreed by the Mouvance présidentielle and the opposition at the end of January 1994; nevertheless, fighting continued to erupt sporadically.

In February 1994 the committee of international arbitrators, which had been investigating the conduct of the first round of legislative elections held in May 1993, ruled that the results in eight constituencies were unlawful. In September 1994 six opposition parties, including Sassou-Nguesso's PCT, formed an alliance, the Forces démocratiques unies (FDU), under the chairmanship of Sassou-Nguesso. The alliance, which was affiliated with the URD, included about 15 members of the national assembly, who, it was reported, came mainly from the north of the country, where Sassou-Nguesso enjoyed greatest support.

Coalition Politics

In early December 1994 the government announced its intention to re-form as a coalition administration, including members of the opposition, in the near future. At the end of the month, following the holding of reconciliation talks between the government and the opposition, a co-ordinating body was established to oversee the disarmament of the opposition militias and the restoration of judicial authority. Meanwhile, Lissouba and the two main opposition leaders—Sassou-Nguesso and Kolelas—signed an agreement which sought an end to hostilities between their respective supporters. In early January 1995 it was announced that 2,000 places would be allocated in the national army for former militiamen as soon as their units (reported to number at least 3,000 personnel) were finally disbanded. In mid-January the government resigned and, later in that month, a new coalition council of ministers was appointed, including members of the MCDDI and led by Yhombi-Opango. The FDU, however, refused to participate in the new administration. Some 12 parliamentary deputies defected from the majority UPADS in protest at the lack of representation for south-western Congolese in the newly-appointed council of ministers; they subsequently formed a new party, the Union pour la République, which remained affiliated to the Mouvance présidentielle.

During early 1995 by-elections were contested for seven seats in the national assembly (outstanding since the partially annulled elections of May 1993): five were won by opposition parties and two by the UPADS. In March 1995 the government announced the introduction of measures to restrain state expenditure, including significant reductions in the salaries of government members and a substantial decrease in the number of civil service personnel, in order to secure assistance from the IMF. The Lissouba administration banned all public demonstrations in August, in order to restrict anti-government protest activities by trade unions. In the following month the national assembly approved legislation which severely curtailed the freedom of the press.

In October 1995 the government announced the impending restructuring of the armed forces with the stated aim of achieving a more balanced representation of ethnic and regional interests. In late December political parties from the Mouvance présidentielle and opposition groupings signed a peace pact which required the imminent disarmament of all party militias and the integration into the national security forces of 1,200 former militia members. In February 1996 about 100 soldiers who had previously belonged to militias staged a short-lived mutiny, in order to demand improved pay and conditions; five people were reportedly killed during the unrest. Later in that month the FDU suspended the integration of its militia associates into the national armed forces, claiming that the pact agreed in December 1995 favoured pro-government militias, while under-representing those affiliated to opposition organizations. In March 1996 the government agreed to increase the quota of opposition recruits into the security forces and, consequently, the integration of FDU-affiliated militia members resumed. During 1994–96 some 4,000 militiamen were integrated into the security forces. Nevertheless, activities by armed militia groups continued to be reported. In August 1996, following a local political dispute, some 200 armed militiamen professing allegiance to the FDU (which was subsequently renamed the Forces démocratiques et pátriotiques—FDP), occupied a small town in central Congo for several days.

In late August 1996 Yhombi-Opango resigned as prime minister; he was replaced shortly afterwards by David Charles Ganao, the leader of the Union des forces démocratiques and a former minister of foreign affairs. In early September Ganao appointed an expanded council of ministers, including representatives of the URD. The Ganao administration undertook to continue with the implementation of an economic reform programme which had been agreed with the IMF in June. In early October elections were held for 23 of the 60 seats in the senate. The Mouvance présidentielle retained its majority, winning 12 of the seats, while opposition organizations took 10 seats and one seat was secured by an independent candidate. In January 1997 Sassou-Nguesso returned to the Congo for the first time since 1995, in preparation for the next presidential elections, which were scheduled to take place (concurrently with legislative elections) in July and August.

Factional divisions remained apparent in early 1997, as a number of mutinies and protests erupted, predominantly among newly recruited military personnel affiliated to the Mouvance présidentielle. In February former militiamen blockaded the Congo-Océan railway for several days, and disconnected regional electricity supplies. Their demands, for immediate integration into the regular army at the rank of sergeant and for the dismissal of the commander of their training camp, were subsequently met by Lissouba; the mutineers themselves went unpunished. Opposition politicians accused Lissouba of political and ethnic partiality, when, on several occasions, he was perceived to grant preferential treatment to army members from his native southern Congo, while, during April and May, dismissing several high-ranking northern officers installed under the Sassou-Nguesso administration.

Factional Violence

In a memorandum dated February 1997, 19 opposition parties (including the PCT and the MCDDI) called for the expedited establishment of republican institutions, the free movement of people and goods, and more equitable access to the media and to public funds; in the short term they also requested, as matters of urgency, the establishment of an independent electoral commission, the disarmament of civilians and the deployment of a multinational peace-keeping force, on the basis that the continued existence of armed militias was otherwise likely to lead to a resumption of violence on the scale of that of 1993–94. The government met none of these demands. During May inter-militia unrest did erupt once again, and in early June an attempt by the government to disarm the militia group associated with Sassou-Nguesso's FDP (in preparation for the forthcoming presidential and legislative elections) swiftly developed into a fierce conflict along ethnic and political lines involving militia groups and opposing factions within the regular armed forces. Barricades were erected in Brazzaville, and the city was split effectively into three zones, controlled by supporters of Sassou-Nguesso, Lissouba and Kolelas. The conflict soon became polarized between troops loyal to the Lissouba administration and the rebel forces of Sassou-Nguesso; both sides were allegedly reinforced by mercenaries and by fighters from foreign rebel groups. Despite efforts to mediate—led by Kolelas at a national level and, on behalf of the international community, by President Bongo of Gabon, and Muhammad Sahnoun, the joint UN-OAU special representative to the Great Lakes region—none of the numerous cease-fires signed during mid-1997 led to more than a brief lull in hostilities. An attempt by Lissouba to postpone the impending elections and prolong his presidential mandate beyond the end of August was strongly opposed by Sassou-Nguesso, and both sides were unable to agree on the nature or composition of a proposed government of national unity. In early June French troops assisted in the evacuation of foreign residents from Brazzaville; in mid-June they themselves departed, despite mediators' requests that they remain to protect the civilian population and to attempt to forestall further hostilities.

Fighting between forces loyal to the government and to Sassou-Nguesso intensified in August, spreading to the north. In early September Lissouba appointed a government of national unity, under the premiership of Kolelas, thereby compromising the latter's role as a national mediator and impeding the ongoing negotiations in the Gabonese capital, Libreville. Sassou-Nguesso subsequently refused to accept the offer of five seats for his allies in the council of ministers. In September political organizations loyal to Lissouba formed the Espace républicain pour la défense de la démocratie et l'unité nationale (ERDDUN).

SASSOU-NGUESSO RESUMES POWER

In mid-October 1997 Sassou-Nguesso's forces, assisted by Angolan government troops, won control of Brazzaville and the strategic port of Pointe-Noire. Lissouba was ousted from the presidential palace, and, with Kolelas, fled to Burkina Faso. (They subsequently found refuge in the United Kingdom and the USA.) In late October Sassou-Nguesso was inaugurated as president, having retaken by force the office which he lost at the 1992 presidential election. He appointed a new transitional government in early November. It was reported that some 10,000 people were killed during the civil war and that about 800,000 people were displaced. Brazzaville was ransacked and largely destroyed, while the national infrastructure and institutions were severely disrupted. Upon his accession to power, Sassou-Nguesso decreed that party militias would be disarmed and outlawed as a matter of priority. In late November Lissouba initiated legal proceedings in France in which he accused the petroleum company Elf Congo of complicity in the overthrow of his administration.

In early January 1998 a forum for unity and national reconciliation was convened; the 1,420 delegates at the forum included representatives of most political parties, although ERDDUN refused to participate. The forum approved the immediate commencement of a three-year transition period, pending the organization of presidential and legislative elections in 2001; during the transition period (which could be shortened or prolonged depending upon the prevailing security situation and economic circumstances) a new constitution was to be drafted and submitted to a national referendum. Meanwhile, a 75-member national transitional council was to act as legislative body. The forum also recommended that the leaders of the previous administration should be charged with 'genocide and war crimes'; warrants for the arrest of Lissouba, Kolelas and Yhombi-Opango were issued in November. The national transi-

tional council (which had been elected by delegates at the forum from lists compiled by political and legal commissions and the government) was appointed in mid-January, following the termination of the forum.

Continued Instability

Despite attempts to obtain an enduring peace settlement, clashes continued throughout 1998 in the southern Pool region, a stronghold of the militia loyal to Kolelas (the so-called 'Ninja' militia), causing thousands of refugees to flee the area. In December the violence in the region intensified and spread to the outskirts of Brazzaville, and in late December a full-scale battle for control of Brazzaville broke out between pro-Kolelas forces, allegedly supported by Angolan dissident groups, and Congolese government forces, augmented by Sassou-Nguesso's militia and Angolan government troops. Both sides claimed victory; Kolelas, speaking from the USA, suggested that he might return to take power, while the Congolese authorities denied that there had been a concerted attack on the city, blaming looters and bandits for the eruption of violence. Brazzaville was severely damaged in the fighting, and over 8,000 refugees were reported to have fled into the neighbouring Democratic Republic of the Congo (DRC). Kolelas subsequently denied that his forces had initiated the conflict, describing it as a popular uprising, which had been brutally suppressed by the government and its Angolan allies. In late December government forces, aided by Angolan troops, launched offensives against Kolelas' forces in the south and west of the country.

On 12 January 1999 Sassou-Nguesso appointed a new council of ministers, with the responsibility of restoring security and peace in the south of the country. Itihi Ossetoumba Lekoundzou, the former minister of state for reconstruction and urban development, was appointed minister of defence, a portfolio previously held by Sassou-Nguesso. In mid-January insurgent forces seized the Moukoukoulou hydroelectric dam, while in Brazzaville sporadic fighting continued as government forces sought to assert their control of the southern districts. A French gendarme was killed when an armed group attacked the French embassy, and the French government was reported to be considering evacuating its nationals from the Congo. Fighting was also reported in the south-west of the country, where the militia loyal to ex-president Lissouba was involved in skirmishes with government forces around the strategically important city of Dolisie. In February the military commander of Dolisie was killed in a militia attack on the city's airport, and the battle for control of the city continued throughout February and March.

In late February 1999 the conflict in the area immediately south of Brazzaville intensified, and a further 10,000 people were estimated to have taken refuge in the DRC. By early March, however, the rebel militias had been obliged to withdraw to the Pool region, where clashes continued, and residents began to return to the south of Brazzaville. Many returning refugees later alleged that their properties had been looted by the security forces and by militiamen loyal to Sassou-Nguesso. In early April refugees also began to return to Dolisie, although much of the city's infrastructure had been destroyed in the fighting. In May the army secured the city of Kinkala, capital of the Pool region, and captured the main rebel base in the south-west of the country, while an insurgent attack to the north of Brazzaville was also repulsed. In June and July government forces continued their advances in the south and west of the country; the armed forces also regained control of several railway stations and strategic towns in an attempt to secure the railway line between Brazzaville and Pointe-Noire. In August it was reported that residents of the southern districts of Brazzaville had begun to return to their homes in large numbers, while later in the month the armed forces announced that they had regained control of the railway line between Brazzaville and Pointe-Noire.

Peace Initiatives

The continued success of the armed forces in re-establishing order throughout the country enabled the authorities to pursue a more conciliatory line towards the rebel militias, and in mid-August 1999 Sassou-Nguesso offered to grant an amnesty to militiamen prepared to renounce violence and to surrender their weapons. It was also announced that the government had begun talks with the exiled opposition, although it was announced that the authorities had demanded an end to factional violence as a pre-condition for further discussions. In September it was announced that some 600 militiamen loyal to Kolelas had surrendered to the authorities under the terms of the amnesty proposed by Sassou-Nguesso. In the same month several prominent opposition members, including four former ministers, voluntarily returned to Congo from exile, and in mid-October 12 senior officers, who had been imprisoned for supporting Lissouba, were released at a public ceremony; it was announced that they were to be reintegrated into the armed forces. In October the authorities announced that the armed forces had regained control of all the towns in the Pool region.

In mid-November 1999, following intensive negotiations, the government announced that it had reached agreement with the militias loyal to Lissouba and Kolelas. The agreement, which included provision for a cease-fire and a general amnesty, was, however, described as a 'complete fabrication' by Lissouba and Kolelas themselves. Sassou-Nguesso claimed, however, that the militias had decided themselves to respond to the government's calls for peace, while observers suggested that Lissouba and Kolelas were unaware of the reality of their supporters' military position. In December the national transitional council adopted legislation providing for an amnesty for those militiamen who surrendered their weapons before mid-January 2000. The amnesty, however, excluded the opposition leaders in exile, in particular Lissouba and Kolelas, and the government announced its intention to continue to seek their prosecution for alleged war crimes.

In December 1999 President Bongo of Gabon was designated the official mediator between the government and the militias, and in late December Bongo hosted further discussions in Libreville, Gabon. These discussions led to the signing of a second peace agreement, in the presence of Presidents Bongo and Sassou-Nguesso, by representatives of the armed forces and of the rebel militias. The new agreement provided for further dialogue, for the integration of militiamen into the armed forces and for the opening of a humanitarian 'corridor' to enable displaced persons to return to their homes. Militia leaders continued, however, to demand the withdrawal of Angolan trooops from Congo. None the less, in late December a ceremony of reconciliation was held in Brazzaville between senior government figures and members of the previous Lissouba administration.

By mid-February 2000 it was estimated that some 2,000 former militiamen had surrendered to the authorities, although some sources indicated that up to a further 16,000 militiamen remained at large, principally in the Pool region. The government was forced to acknowledge that it would not be possible to integrate all of the former rebels into the armed forces or the police force, although further job-creation schemes were promised. In the same month the committee in charge of observing the implementation of the peace process announced, at a meeting with President Bongo of Gabon, that the civil war was definitively over. The Congolese government subsequently appealed for funds from the international community in order to begin the process of reconstruction. In the same month it was estimated that around one-half of the estimated 810,000 people displaced by the conflict had returned to their homes.

In May 2000 Kolelas and his nephew, Col Philippe Bikinkita, the minister of the interior in the previous Lissouba administration, were convicted in their absence of operating personal prisons in the southern districts of Brazzaville and of mistreating prisoners and causing their deaths during the 1997 civil war. Both men, at that time in exile in the USA, were sentenced to death and ordered to pay compensation to their victims. Kolelas, who denied the charges, later demanded that an international team investigate the allegations against them. In late May the chairman of the national transitional council, Justin Koumba, announced that in either late 2000 or early 2001 a referendum would be held on the future form of government for the republic, and that presidential, legislative and local government elections would follow. In mid-July, during a visit to Brazzaville, President Bongo of Gabon expressed his satisfaction at the implementation of the peace process, during which

an estimated 3,000 weapons had been surrendered by former militiamen, although he called on the authorities to continue to engage in dialogue with all elements of society in order to establish a permanent settlement.

FOREIGN RELATIONS

Since the 1997 civil war the principal aim of Congolese foreign policy has been to gain international recognition of the legitimacy of the Sassou-Nguesso government, and to ensure the continued support of the Congo's bilateral and multilateral donors. Sassou-Nguesso's exiled political opponents have, however, appealed for international support for their efforts to overthrow the regime.

France, the former colonial power, is the source of more than one-half of total assistance to the Republic of the Congo, the major supplier of imports and the primary business partner in the extraction of petroleum. During the 1997 civil war President Lissouba accused France of favouring the rebel forces of Sassou-Nguesso (who was reported to have allied himself with French petroleum interests) over the elected administration. In April 1998 Lissouba and Kolelas attempted, unsuccessfully, to sue the French petroleum company Elf, claiming that it had provided support for Sassou-Nguesso. In May France decided to normalize relations with the Congo, and to co-operate with the government of Sassou-Nguesso. The Agence française de développement was instructed to co-operate with the Congolese authorities, and began in June to release aid frozen since the 1997 conflict. In July the French government provided further economic assistance, and in September French military instructors were sent to Brazzaville to train the Congolese gendarmerie. Further reconstruction assistance was again promised in January 2000.

In the 1997 conflict Angolan government troops facilitated Sassou-Nguesso's victory by providing tactical support, including the occupation of Pointe-Noire, the Congo's main seaport and focus of the petroleum industry. Angola had accused the Lissouba government of providing assistance both to rebels of the União Nacional para a Independência Total de Angola and to Cabindan separatist guerrillas. In response to international criticism of his role, President dos Santos of Angola announced in early 1998 that the majority of his forces had departed the Congo, and that the role of the remaining troops was merely to help rebuild and train the Congolese army. However, Angolan troops played an important role in the defeat of the rebel attack on Brazzaville in December 1998. In January 1999 the heads of state of Angola, the Congo, and the Democratic Republic of the Congo (DRC) met to agree a common policy on the conflicts in their countries. In December the ministers of the interior of the three countries met in Luanda, Angola and signed a co-operation accord. The accord created a tripartite commission to ensure border security, the free movement of people and goods, the training of personnel, and the provision of assistance to displaced persons. In April 2000 further meetings were held in Kinshasa, DRC, in order to discuss the implementation of the Luanda accord, which was expected to include the formation of joint military patrols. In the same month it was announced that the Angolan and Congolese governments were to investigate the joint exploitation of offshore petroleum resources.

Relations between the Republic of the Congo and the DRC, which had been strained in 1997 after a number of shells fired from Brazzaville exploded in Kinshasa, improved steadily during 1998. In May a bilateral meeting was held to discuss the prevention of the clandestine movement of armed groups across the mutual border, and in August Sassou-Nguesso agreed to extradite rebels to the DRC. A further bilateral meeting was held in September. Relations were, however, damaged later that month when the DRC alleged that the Congo had turned back a DRC navel vessel hoping to enlist some of the thousands of Rwandan Hutus claiming refuge in the Congo into forces loyal to President Kabila. In December 1998 relations were further strained by Congolese claims that rebel militiamen maintained a training camp in the DRC. The DRC strongly denied the report, reiterating its support for Sassou-Nguesso, and later in the month the two countries signed a non-aggression pact and agreed to establish a joint force to guarantee border security. Tension re-emerged in March 1999 when the DRC detained a Congolese passenger boat and accused the Congo of hosting rebel bases, an accusation denied by the Congolese authorities. In April, however, the two countries agreed an accord on the repatriation of refugees, and in May the Congolese government ratified the non-aggression pact agreed in December 1998. In December 1999 Sassou-Nguesso paid a brief visit to President Kabila in order to discuss bilateral

co-operation and the implementation of the tripartite Luanda accord.

The Congo maintains good relations with the Central African Republic and with Gabon, although both countries have expressed unease at the numbers of Congolese refugees entering their territory. China has been an important source of aid since diplomatic relations were established in 1964. Libya is also a significant supporter of the Sassou-Nguesso government.

Economy

EDITH HODGKINSON

Since independence in 1960 economic policy in the Congo has moved from one end of the ideological spectrum to close to the other. For the first decade and a half a systematic policy of state participation in productive enterprise was pursued, although the private sector was initially permitted to continue its activities, especially in mining, forestry and transport. Upon becoming head of state in 1977, Joachim Yhombi-Opango emphasized that the Congo needed a 'mixed' economy and would benefit from the expertise which private investment could provide. Under his successor, Sassou-Nguesso, who ousted him two years later, foreign management consortia were introduced to restructure seriously inefficient nationalized companies, while the petroleum sector was further opened to private foreign investment. In 1989, formally acknowledging the failure of the public sector to stimulate economic growth, the government of Sassou-Nguesso implemented a new policy of economic liberalization, including revised taxation procedures intended to foster private-sector activity. However, full-scale economic restructuring was only undertaken following the devaluation of the CFA franc in January 1994 and it still had some way to go at the beginning of the next decade.

The government of President Lissouba and the IMF agreed in May 1994 on a programme for the privatization of the major public-sector industries (including rail, air and water transport, electricity, the petroleum industry and postal services) and a substantial reduction in the number of civil service personnel. Moreover, in the disposal of public-sector enterprises, whose failure was explicitly recognized, Congolese and foreign investors were to compete on equal terms. On the basis of both intentions stated and actual progress achieved on economic liberalization and budgetary stabilization, the Congo was accorded an enhanced structural adjustment facility (ESAF) by the IMF in 1996. Progress was derailed, however, by the civil war which broke out in 1997, which prompted the Lissouba government to embark on substantial purchases of weaponry and severely disrupted economic activity in Brazzaville, and by the sharp decline in the international price of petroleum, the mainstay of the economy. The new administration of Sassou-Nguesso,which took power in October 1997, inheriting a devastated infrastructure and the urgent need to replenish depleted state coffers following a five-month civil war, immediately confirmed its commitment to privatization. This reaped its reward in July 1998 when the IMF agreed to a special post-conflict recovery credit equivalent to US $10m. which was intended to be followed by another ESAF in 1999. The condition for the support—crucial to obtaining further relief on Congo's very heavy foreign debt burden (see below)—was a comprehensive programme of structural reform, with the privatization of leading parastatal enterprises (including power, water, telecommunications, and the port of Pointe-Noire), the completion of civil service reform, the sale of government shares in the banks and the overhaul of the social security system. The attainment of these objectives was undermined for much of 1999 by the resumption of fighting in the south, and agreeing on a new ESAF took second place to drawing up an emergency post-war assistance programme. In June 2000 the government announced a provisional three-year programme for the rehabilitation and development of the country's social and economic infrastructure. The programme was to be examined in July by a meeting of Congo's external donors, who, it was hoped, would provide

assistance equivalent to about one-third of the cost of the programme.

Partly as a result of Brazzaville's former position as the capital of French Equatorial Africa, and partly because the Congo and Oubangui rivers have long provided the main access to the Central African Republic (CAR) and Chad, services, transport and public administration in particular, have traditionally played an unusually large role in the economy, accounting for close to half of gross domestic product (GDP) in the early 1990s. Until the war in 1997 about 60% of the population—the highest proportion in sub-Saharan Africa—resided in urban areas, principally in Brazzaville. The importance of services has eased, however, as the petroleum sector has developed; in 1995 it accounted for one-third of GDP and in 1997, when it escaped the ravages of the war, 51%. Although over one-half of the country's inhabitants earn their livelihood from agriculture and forestry, this sector accounts for only around one-eighth of GDP. The manufacturing sector makes an even smaller contribution (an estimated 8% in 1996) despite its relatively early development, geared to the markets of the CAR and Chad.

Economic growth has fluctuated widely in the recent past. The mid- and late 1970s saw overall stagnation, and decline in some sectors, as output of petroleum fell and production of potash ceased altogether. However, improved output of petroleum, from 1979 onwards, coincided with increases in international prices for that commodity, which stimulated very high rates of investment by both the public sector and the petroleum companies, and hence strong GDP growth. The collapse of world petroleum prices in 1986 had severe repercussions throughout the economy, initially most acutely felt in major cuts in government spending. GDP initially fell (by 6.8% in 1986) and only slowly recovered over the next few years, with the rise in most years below the rate of population growth. Political turmoil led to a 2.8% fall in GDP in 1993, and the decline deepened in 1994, to 4.8%, because of the impact on domestic demand of the 50% devaluation of the CFA franc in January of that year. The Republic of the Congo benefited less from the devaluation than some other Francophone countries because it did not affect the competitiveness of its major export (petroleum), whose price is denominated in US dollars and determined in the international market. Nevertheless, earnings in local currency terms were boosted, while production geared to the domestic market derived some stimulus from the sharp rise in import costs. Economic performance subsequently improved, with GDP growth rising from 2.6% in 1995 to 6.3% in 1996 as the Nkossa oilfield came on stream. However, the civil war in 1997, which was concentrated on the capital, brought a 2% fall in GDP in that year. The decline was relatively limited because the petroleum industry, based at Pointe-Noire, was largely unaffected by the disorder. The persistent unrest meant that GDP growth was held to an estimated 3%–4% in 1998, but the strong recovery in the petroleum price in the course of 1999 enhanced the GDP growth rate by a further 1%–2%.

AGRICULTURE AND FORESTRY

Since the early 1970s the agricultural sector has suffered from relative neglect, hasty nationalizations, poor management on state farms, and the abandonment of farmwork in favour of salaried employment in the towns. With the exception of palm products, sugar and tobacco, which are grown on modern plantations (particularly in the south-western Niari valley), most agricultural crops are grown by families on small farms. In 1995 an attempt was made to stimulate the agricultural sector with the creation of a joint venture between the Congolese government and the South African Development Co, which employs South African farmers to work 80,000 ha owned by bankrupt parastatals in the Niari valley. Food crop production remains modest, and the country is far from self-sufficient, with the deficit rising through the 1990s. In 1998, according to estimates by the FAO, output of cassava reached 791,000 metric tons and that of sweet potatoes totalled 24,000 tons. Secondary food crops include plantains, yams and maize.

Export crops contribute very little to foreign earnings. Sugar cane and tobacco have traditionally been the most important cash crops, with exports going almost wholly to other countries in the Union douanière et économique de l'Afrique centrale (UDEAC). The state corporation which ran the sugar industry, the Sucrerie du Congo (SUCO), was replaced in 1991 by a joint venture between the government and a French company. Plantations were reorganized and re-equipped, allowing them to satisfy domestic demand. Production of raw sugar increased from an average 30,000 tons in 1989–91 to about 44,000 tons annually in the late 1990s. Tobacco production, which had almost ceased during the 1980s, is also improving, through a development by the French-based Bolloré group, which aims at output of 300 tons a year.

Other export crops include cocoa, coffee and oil palm. Output of both cocoa and coffee is low because colonial era plantations have tended to be neglected. The cocoa crop was generally falling in the 1990s, to around 1,700 tons in 1998, while coffee eased from 1,600 tons in 1994 to 1,300 tons in 1998. Oil palm has fared somewhat better. Palm oil output increased from only 1,093 tons in 1984 to around 16,000 tons annually during the 1990s, as the area under cultivation in state-owned plantations expanded.

Animal husbandry has developed slowly, owing to the prevalence of the tsetse fly and the importance of the forestry sector, which has restricted the availability of pasture. Although numbers of livestock are increasing, the country is not self-sufficient in meat and dairy products. Fishing is not well developed but is carried out commercially on a small scale, especially for tuna. The total fish catch was about 38,100 tons in 1997.

Forestry

Forests cover about 55% of the Congo's total area and are a significant natural resource. Forestry is a major economic activity and timber was the main export until it was superseded by petroleum in the mid-1970s. The principal woods exploited are okoumé, limba and sapele, and there are substantial plantations of eucalyptus in the south-west of the country. Until 1987 the purchase and sale of logs was a monopoly of the state-owned Office Congolaise des Bois, although 95% of production was carried out by the private sector, with foreign companies accounting for a substantial percentage of production. The exploitation by foreign investors of forest resources in the north of the country is being encouraged, while the more accessible but heavily depleted southern forests have been reserved for local interests. The government hopes to stimulate further increases in both production and exports of timber in order to reduce its dependency on exports of petroleum.

Output of timber averaged about 393,000 cu m in the late 1980s, but declined during the early 1990s, to some 167,000 cu m in 1993. The fall in production reflected adverse developments in the export market, notably pressure from environmentalists in western Europe against the use of rainforest timber. Production has increased markedly since the early 1990s, stimulated by the devaluation of the CFA franc in 1994, and in 1998 timber output was 741,100 cu m. Exports have, however, been greatly hindered in recent years by the unrest in the Congo. Companies established in the south-west of the Congo have frequently been obliged to suspend their activities due to military activity, while the frequent suspension of traffic on the Congo-Océan railway has caused congestion and protracted delays in the movement of timber from Brazzaville to Pointe-Noire. As a consequence, since 1997 the majority of timber companies in the north of the country have preferred to export their products by road as far as the port of Douala in Cameroon. Use of this route has,

however, increased both transport costs and delays, as roads are frequently impassable in the rainy season. Environmental concerns remain, although a forestry conservation programme is in place, supported by aid from the World Bank and the UNDP. The government is also attempting to relieve the pressure on virgin forest by requiring forestry companies to replant and by increasing plantation production, in part to serve local demand for fuel wood. The Congolese authorities require timber companies to process at least 60% of their output locally, but this sector is still relatively underdeveloped.

MINING AND ENERGY

Until the 1970s mining was of little significance, with mineral exports accounting for less than 5% of total exports in 1969. By 1984, however, mineral sales provided 90% of export earnings and mining contributed 43% of GDP, reflecting the development of the hydrocarbons sector, which is the only significant mining activity. Although the petroleum sector's contribution to GDP has fluctuated since, reflecting both price and output trends within the sector and the fortunes of the non-petroleum economy, it maintains its overwhelming dominance of export earnings, at around 90% throughout the 1990s.

Onshore deposits were first discovered, at Pointe-Indienne, in 1957. In 1971, when these deposits were almost exhausted, new offshore oilfields were discovered, and their subsequent development has maintained production levels. The Emeraude field went into production in 1972, Loango in 1977, Likouala in 1980, Sendji Marine in 1981, Yanga in 1982, Tchibouela in 1987, Zatchi Marine in 1988 and Nkossa in 1996. Development of the offshore fields has been carried out by Elf Congo and AGIP Recherches Congo, which together account for 98% of the Congo's petroleum production. Annual output increased from 2m.–3m. tons in the late 1970s to an average 9.5m. tons a year in 1993–95. The development of the Nkossa field raised output to 12.3m. tons by 1998, and with AGIP's Kitina field in operation output in 1999 was forecast at 13m. tons. This is likely to be the peak for some time, with production expected to ease down until the middle years of this decade when new fields, at Moho and Bilondo, are due to come on stream. In addition, deposits of natural gas are exploited at Pointe-Indienne.

In line with the continuing programme of privatization, the government's stake in the petroleum industry has been declining. In 1990 the monopoly of the state-owned Société nationale de recherches et d'exploitation pétrolière (HYDRO-CONGO) over the distribution of petroleum products in the Congo was ended. In 1995 the government sold its 25% share in Elf Congo to the French company Elf Aquitaine, which previously held 75% of the share capital, and its 20% share in AGIP Recherches Congo to the majority shareholder, Italy's AGIP. Similarly HYDRO-CONGO's 60% stake in the 1m.-ton capacity petroleum refinery at Pointe-Noire, a joint venture with Elf, was to be taken over by Elf and Shell, as were the state company's distribution activities, under an agreement signed with the Lissouba government in 1997. This agreement was respected by the new Sassou-Nguesso administration, whose initial attempts to buy back the government stake in Elf Congo were rebuffed. A new national petroleum company, the Société nationale des pétroles du Congo (SNPC), was formally created in April 1998 and began operations in early 1999, acting as the repository of the HYDRO-CONGO assets that await privatization as well as the owner of the state's interests in joint ventures.

Lead, zinc, gold and copper are produced in small quantities, and deposits of phosphate and bauxite are known. In 1985 the Congo and Gabon signed an agreement for joint exploitation of the High Ivingo iron ore deposits (estimated at about 1,000m. tons), but the implementation of this scheme will require substantial external funds, together with an improvement in the international market for iron ore. Foreign interest in the non-petroleum mining sector has been increasing in recent years. Magnesium Alloy Corpn of Canada has plans to develop magnesium deposits at Kouilou and a subsidiary of Anglo-American, of South Africa, plans a ferro-silicon smelter.

Production and distribution of electricity have been in the hands of a state-owned corporation, the Société Nationale d'Electricité, since 1967, but this is due to be privatized. Net generating capacity was 118 MW in 1995, of which about three-quarters was accounted for by the hydroelectric stations on the Bouenza and Djoué. The country's enormous hydroelectric potential is underexploited, owing to the low level of domestic consumption and also because the infrastructure is lacking to export output to regional markets.

MANUFACTURING

Manufacturing mainly takes the form of the processing of agricultural and forest products and most of the industry is in Brazzaville, Pointe-Noire and N'Kayi. Many of the larger manufacturing companies were state-owned, but are being transferred to private ownership, or closed down, in accordance with the country's pledges to the IMF.

The industrial development of the 1970s and 1980s had little success. A cement plant was established at Loutété in 1968, reached its peak output in 1971, but subsequently showed a sharp fall in production, despite strong demand from construction programmes, and ceased production in 1987, because of cash-flow problems. The manufacturing sector has been disadvantaged by the high value of the CFA franc, which has undermined its competitiveness, particularly against imports from the neighbouring Democratic Republic of the Congo (formerly Zaire). The 1994 devaluation still left manufacturing at a disadvantage compared with Cameroon. Nevertheless, brewing is a significant industry, and newly-developed eucalyptus plantations have been used to supply a telegraph-pole and charcoal factory. Both also sell to export markets.

TRANSPORT

The Republic of the Congo plays an important role in the trans-equatorial transport system which links Chad, the CAR and parts of Cameroon and Gabon with the Atlantic coast; all of the rail and much of the river portion of the system is located in the Congo. The deep-water port at Pointe-Noire is the terminus of this network, and is central Africa's second most important gateway, after Douala in Cameroon. In 1986 it handled 9.5m. tons of freight, including 5.4m. tons of petroleum, some 552,100 tons of timber (most of this originating in the CAR and floated downstream to the smaller port of Brazzaville, from which it is transported by rail to Pointe-Noire), and about 2.46m. tons of manganese ore from Gabon; transportation of Gabonese manganese ore has now ceased. The river system (in all some 5,000 km is navigable) is also of great significance as a transport artery throughout the country, reaching areas that would otherwise be isolated (particularly in the north).

Some 60%–70% of the traffic on the 515-km Congo-Océan railway (which links Pointe-Noire and Brazzaville, where it connects with transport services on the Congo river) is of an international nature. In the 1970s the saturation of the existing railway capacity and the constraint that this represented on the further development of timber exports prompted a major scheme to increase capacity by two-fifths. Work on realignment was completed in 1985. With the acquisition of new rolling stock, the railway increased its freight handling to 1.4m. tons (excluding manganese) in 1986, compared with 1.15m. tons in 1984. Operations were interrupted by fighting in the area from late 1998 to mid-1999, and substantial rehabilitation work is now needed. Congo-Océan Railways is scheduled for privatization in the near future, as is the administration of the country's rivers and ports. All are currently the responsibility of the Agence Transcongolaise de Communications, which is due to be split into independent units under private management.

Other transport facilities, and especially the road network, are little developed, owing to the great distances and dense equatorial forest. Large areas in the north of the country have no road access, but proposals to build roads there have encountered opposition from environmental groups, as well as funding constraints. Only about 10% of the 12,745 km of roads and tracks are asphalted. In general, poor communications continue to constitute a major obstacle to economic development. There are international airports at Brazzaville and Pointe-Noire, as well as five regional airports and 12 smaller airfields.

FINANCE

The rise in petroleum taxes and royalties from 1978 onwards (at some 110,000m. francs CFA, they constituted 70% of budget revenue in 1981) stimulated a sharp rise in budget development spending at the beginning of the 1980s. This increased 17-fold between 1979–83, and formed the basis of the rapid growth in the economy at the beginning of the 1980s. The fall in petroleum revenues in 1986 threatened almost to double the budget deficit, which had been bloated by rises in the public sector payroll as a result of the oil boom and by the losses incurred by state-owned enterprises. The government turned to the IMF for support and adopted a structural adjustment programme which aimed to restore balance to public finances through cuts in both current and capital spending. The reduction in the former was achieved by means of a wide range of measures, including a 'freeze' on government salaries (the payroll had been increasing steadily during the early 1980s) and the rationalization (including sale to private interests) of several state-owned companies, whose losses had depleted budget resources. However, the deficit continued to rise in both 1987 and 1988, owing to the contraction in the economy. The improvement registered in 1990 with the surge in international petroleum prices after the Iraqi invasion of Kuwait proved short-lived as tax receipts were hit by the political unrest in 1991–92. There was a substantial fall in the deficit in subsequent years, with salary costs held down in both 1994 and 1995, and petroleum revenues in 1996 reflecting the commencement of production at the Nkossa oilfield and amendments in petroleum production-sharing agreements, which increased the government's take from 17.5% to 31%. Under the terms of the enhanced structural adjustment facility (ESAF) agreed by the IMF in 1996, the budget was to record a surplus in 1997, through higher oil revenues, a wider tax base (with the introduction of value-added tax at 18%) and tighter controls on the public sector wage bill, including the dismissal of civil servants with falsified qualifications (an estimated 14% of the total) and early retirement. However, the extra expenditure and slump in revenues generated by the civil war resulted in a very severe imbalance in both 1997 and 1998. The situation was compounded in the latter year; firstly by the sharp fall in the international petroleum price, which halved Congo's budget revenue from petroleum, producing a one-third decline in total receipts, and subsequently by the resumption of fighting late in 1998. The budget forecast for 1999 was therefore of only a limited reduction in the deficit, by around one-eighth to 179,500m. francs CFA (equivalent to around 9% of GDP), with all the fall attributable to cuts on the spending side. In the event oil revenues rebounded because of the recovery in international prices, and on this basis the government planned a 21% rise in spending in 2000, to yield a deficit slightly above the 1999 forecast, of 202,000m. francs CFA.

FOREIGN TRADE AND PAYMENTS

Whereas the Congo's foreign trade was in chronic deficit during the 1960s and 1970s, the expansion of the petroleum sector which began in the late 1970s transformed the situation. In 1978 the Congo recorded a foreign trade deficit of 24,090m. francs CFA, and in 1979 a surplus of 46,150m. With export receipts increasing from only 34,200m. francs CFA in 1978 to 552,600m. in 1984, the surplus reached a peak of 282,600m. francs CFA in that year. The fall in petroleum prices in 1986 more than halved export earnings and, although imports declined as a result of budget austerity, the trade surplus narrowed to only 50,100m. francs CFA. This, in conjunction with higher interest payments on the rapidly-escalating foreign debt, prompted a sharp deterioration in the current account of the balance of payments, from a surplus of US $210m. in 1984 to a deficit of $601m. in 1986. The current account has since remained in deficit, with movements largely reflecting trends on the merchandise account. Therefore a sharp rise in imports in 1996, largely attributable to the purchase of capital equipment for the Nkossa oilfield, raised the current account deficit to a record $1,109m. The imbalance narrowed to around a quarter of this level in 1997 when the trade surplus rebounded from $194m. to $941m., as imports decreased and exports continued to rise, in response to increased shipments of petroleum. The balance deteriorated once more in 1998, in response to trends in petroleum prices, and—for the same reason—was improving in 1999, with a current account deficit of around $500m.

In most years Congo has received relatively low levels of foreign aid because of its oil wealth and poor record on economic management. Net inflows of official development assistance from OECD countries and multilateral agencies were running at around US $120m. annually in the early and mid-1990s, but they surged to $362m. in 1994 (because of additional French aid in the aftermath of the devaluation of the CFA franc) and were again at unusually high levels in 1996 ($430m.) and 1997 ($268m.) as French aid programmes were implemented. With spending disrupted by renewed fighting, net inflows collapsed to only $65m. in 1998. While borrowing (as distinct from grants) from official creditors (multilateral and bilateral) expanded only slowly in the early 1980s, borrowing from private creditors rose sharply, mainly reflecting the expansion in imports, and exceeded that from official sources, to give an external debt of $3,031m. at the end of 1985. This was equivalent to 157% of the country's gross national product (GNP) in that year. The cost of servicing the debt was equivalent to one-quarter of the country's foreign earnings in both 1983 and 1984, and to one-third in 1985—a very substantial burden, which necessitated a rescheduling of the debt. This was accorded after the Congo received IMF approval in 1986 for its structural adjustment programme. Despite further rescheduling, the Congo's debt situation remained dire, and by the end of 1988 the external debt had risen to $4,095m., or 215% of GNP, making the Congo the most heavily indebted African nation (on a per caput basis). The debt-service ratio was 45%, a dangerously high level in

view of the government's practice of borrowing against future petroleum earnings. Backed by the new agreement with the IMF, a new programme of support by external donors, led by France, commenced in 1990, enabling the Congo to pay off some of its debt arrears, notably to the World Bank, which permitted a resumption of lending. Foreign indebtedness fluctuated slightly in the following three years, before reaching a new high of $6,005m. in 1995, equivalent to about three and one-half times the country's GNP (at the new US $: CFA franc parity). The situation has since eased markedly, as the result of a rescheduling of $989m. in liabilities after the currency was devalued and, more significantly, the new round of debt relief extended in 1996, subsequent to IMF approval of an ESAF. Bilateral official creditors granted 'Naples terms' on all liabilities incurred before 1986 (involving write-offs, interest rate reductions and reschedulings equivalent, in all, to a two-thirds reduction in debt). In addition, debts incurred by the Lissouba government to a US petroleum company through the advance payment of oil revenue (a device to which the previous administration had often had recourse) were settled. With some interest arrears met, the country's outstanding debt fell to $5,119m. by the end of 1998. However, it remained extremely high in relative terms, at just over three times total GNP. Moreover, as the war ravaged government finances, arrears on debt service were building up; at the end of 1997 these stood at $1,043m., or $380 per head of the population. In this situation, and given the demands of post-war reconstruction, Congo remains in dire need of additional debt relief.

Statistical Survey

Source (unless otherwise stated): Direction Générale, Centre National de la Statistique et des Etudes Economiques, BP 2031, Brazzaville; tel. and fax 81-59-09.

Area and Population

AREA, POPULATION AND DENSITY

Area (sq km)	342,000*
Population (census results)	
7 February 1974	1,319,790
22 December 1984	1,843,421
Population (UN estimates at mid-year)†	
1996	2,634,000
1997	2,709,000
1998	2,785,000
Density (per sq km) at mid-1998	8.1

* 132,047 sq miles.
† Source: UN, *World Population Prospects: The 1998 Revision.*

REGIONS (estimated population at 1 January 1983)*

Brazzaville	. . 456,383	Kouilou . . .	. 78,738
Pool	. . . 219,329	Lékoumou . .	. 67,568
Pointe-Noire	. . 214,466	Sangha . . .	. 42,106
Bouenza	. . 135,999	Nkayi . . .	. 40,419
Cuvette	. . 127,558	Likouala . .	. 34,302
Niari	. . . 114,229	Loubomo . .	. 33,591
Plateaux	. . 110,379	**Total** . . .	1,675,067

* Figures have not been revised to take account of the 1984 census results.

PRINCIPAL TOWNS (estimated population in 1997)

Brazzaville (capital)	950,000
Pointe-Noire	500,000
Loubomo	83,000

Source: La Zone Franc, *Rapport Annuel.*

BIRTHS AND DEATHS (UN estimates, annual averages)

	1985–90	1990–95	1995–2000
Birth rate (per 1,000) . . .	44.3	44.7	43.6
Death rate (per 1,000) . . .	15.6	16.1	15.8

Source: UN, *Population and Vital Statistics Report.*

Expectation of life (UN estimates, years at birth, 1990-95): 48.9 (males 46.6; females 51.3).
Source: UN, *World Population Prospects: The 1998 Revision.*

EMPLOYMENT ('000 persons at 1984 census)

	Males	Females	Total
Agriculture, etc.	105	186	291
Industry	61	8	69
Services	123	60	183
Total	289	254	543

Mid-1998 (FAO estimates, '000 persons): Agriculture, etc. 483; Total labour force 1,141 (Source: FAO, *Production Yearbook*).

Agriculture

PRINCIPAL CROPS
('000 metric tons)

	1996	1997	1998
Maize†	5	4	2
Sugar cane*	465	480	470
Potatoes*	2	2	2
Sweet potatoes*	25	23	24
Cassava (Manioc)	791†	780	791
Yams*	13	12	13
Other roots and tubers*	36	34	34
Dry beans*	6	6	6
Tomatoes*	10	10	10
Other vegetables (incl. melons)*	37	35	34
Oranges*	4	3	3
Avocados*	26	25	24
Pineapples*	13	13	12
Bananas*	39	38	37
Plantains	76†	76	76*
Palm kernels*	3	3	3
Palm oil*	17	16	15
Groundnuts (in shell)	25*	23	22*
Coffee (green)	1*	1	1*
Cocoa beans	2*	2	2*
Natural rubber*	1	1	1

* FAO estimate(s).   † Unofficial figure(s).

Source: FAO, *Production Yearbook*.

LIVESTOCK ('000 head, year ending September)

	1996*	1997	1998
Cattle	72	75	72
Pigs	46	45	44*
Sheep	114	115	114
Goats	295	286	280*

* FAO estimate(s).

Poultry (FAO estimates, million): 2 in 1996; 2 in 1997; 2 in 1998.

Source: FAO, *Production Yearbook*.

LIVESTOCK PRODUCTS (FAO estimates, '000 metric tons)

	1996	1997	1998
Beef and veal	2	2	2
Pig meat	2	2	2
Poultry meat	6	6	6
Other meat	13	14	15
Cows' milk	1	1	1
Hen eggs	1	1	1

Source: FAO, *Production Yearbook*.

Forestry

ROUNDWOOD REMOVALS ('000 cubic metres, excluding bark)

	1995	1996	1997
Sawlogs, veneer logs and logs for sleepers	636	704	969
Pulpwood	505	120	373
Other industrial wood	334	344	354
Fuel wood	2,358	2,426	2,496
Total	3,833	3,594	4,192

Source: FAO, *Yearbook of Forest Products*.

SAWNWOOD PRODUCTION
('000 cubic metres, including railway sleepers)

	1995	1996	1997
Total (all broadleaved)	62	59	60

Source: FAO, *Yearbook of Forest Products*.

Fishing

('000 metric tons, live weight)

	1995	1996	1997
Freshwater fishes	26.8	25.9	19.0
Boe drum	0.6	0.7*	0.6*
West African croakers*	0.6	0.6	0.6
Sardinellas	11.9	12.1	11.8
Other clupeoids*	1.7	1.7	1.7
Other marine fishes (incl. unspecified)*	3.9	3.9	3.8
Crustaceans	0.3	0.6	0.6*
Total catch	45.8	45.5	38.1

* FAO estimate(s).

Source: FAO, *Yearbook of Fishery Statistics*.

Mining

('000 metric tons, unless otherwise indicated)

	1996	1997	1998
Crude petroleum	10,359	11,586	13,599
Gold (kg)*	5	n.a.	n.a.

* Estimates from the US Bureau of Mines, referring to the metal content of ores.

Sources: UN, *Industrial Commodity Statistics Yearbook*; Banque des Etats de l'Afrique Centrale, *Etudes et Statistiques*.

Industry

SELECTED PRODUCTS ('000 metric tons, unless otherwise indicated)

	1994	1995	1996
Raw sugar*	28	41	42
Veneer sheets ('000 cu metres)*	47	49	50
Jet fuels†	15	16	16
Motor spirit (petrol)†	55	55	56
Kerosene†	50	48	50
Distillate fuel oils†	92	90	92
Residual fuel oils†	268	258	260
Cement	114‡	100‡	n.a.
Electric energy (million kWh)†	431	435	438

1997: Raw sugar ('000 metric tons) 45*; Veneer sheets ('000 cu metres) 50*.
1998: Raw sugar ('000 metric tons) 44*.

* Data from the FAO.
† Provisional figures.
‡ Estimate from the US Bureau of Mines.

Source: mainly UN, *Industrial Commodity Statistics Yearbook*.

Finance

CURRENCY AND EXCHANGE RATES

Monetary Units
100 centimes = 1 franc de la Coopération financière en Afrique centrale (CFA).

Sterling, Dollar and Euro Equivalents (28 April 2000)
£1 sterling = 1,132.20 francs CFA;
US $1 = 722.02 francs CFA;
€1 = 655.96 francs CFA;
10,000 francs CFA = £8.832 = $13.850 = €15.245.

Average Exchange Rate (francs CFA per US $)
1997   583.67
1998   589.95
1999   615.70

Note: The exchange rate of 1 French franc = 50 francs CFA, established in 1948, remained in force until January 1994, when the CFA franc was devalued by 50%, with the exchange rate adjusted to 1 French franc = 100 francs CFA. The relationship to French currency remained in effect with the introduction of the euro on 1 January 1999. From that date, accordingly, a fixed exchange rate of €1 = 655.957 francs CFA has been in operation.

BUDGET ('000 million francs CFA)

Revenue*	1993	1994	1995†
Petroleum revenue	93.9	138.9	131.0
Royalties	44.1	74.4	78.5
Profits tax	0.8	0.2	13.1
Dividends	49.0	64.3	39.4
Tax revenue	83.8	77.8	116.9
Taxes on income and profits .	31.8	34.1	31.4
Excise duty	36.6	30.6	47.8
Domestic petroleum tax . .	0.1	10.3	13.0
Other indirect taxes . .	15.3	2.8	24.7
Other revenue	5.4	3.4	1.5
Total	183.1	220.1	249.4

Expenditure	1993	1994	1995†
Current expenditure . . .	266.4	333.3	315.0
Wages and salaries . .	136.2	130.8	111.1
Local authority subsidies .	7.3	11.1	4.4
Interest payments . . .	56.1	119.0	148.9
Other current expenditure .	66.8	72.3	50.6
Capital expenditure . . .	12.7	27.3	31.6
Sub-total	279.1	360.6	346.6
Less Adjustment for payment arrears	37.9	95.1	71.9
Total (cash basis) . . .	241.2	265.5	274.7

* Excluding grants received ('000 million francs CFA): 0.1 in 1993; 10.4 in 1994; 10.7 in 1995.
† Provisional figures.

Source: IMF, *Republic of Congo — Statistical Annex* (August 1996).

1998 ('000 million francs CFA): Revenue 363.5; Expenditure 432.6.

CENTRAL BANK RESERVES (US $ million at 31 December)

	1997	1998	1999
Gold*	3.24	3.21	2.10
IMF special drawing rights . .	0.01	0.01	0.11
Reserve position in IMF . .	0.72	0.75	0.74
Foreign exchange . . .	59.19	0.08	38.51
Total	63.16	4.05	41.46

* National valuation.

Source: IMF, *International Financial Statistics*.

MONEY SUPPLY ('000 million francs CFA at 31 December)

	1997	1998	1999
Currency outside banks . .	93.26	73.26	102.34
Demand deposits at commercial and development banks . .	68.85	68.39	76.68
Total money (incl. others) . .	166.56	143.98	184.03

Source: IMF, *International Financial Statistics*.

COST OF LIVING
(Consumer Price Index for Africans in Brazzaville; base: 1990 = 100)

	1994	1995	1996
Food (incl. beverages) . . .	139.2	148.6	159.4
All items (incl. others) . . .	141.1	153.8	169.5

Source: ILO, *Yearbook of Labour Statistics*.

All items (base: 1977 = 100): 353.5 in 1996; 433.6 in 1997; 403.7 in 1998 (Source: Banque des Etats de l'Afrique Centrale, *Etudes et Statistiques*).

Expenditure on the Gross Domestic Product

	1996	1997	1998
Government final consumption expenditure	189,100	337,400	199,100
Private final consumption expenditure	582,000	552,900	572,300
Increase in stocks . . .	25,600	4,100	—
Gross fixed capital formation .	337,000	299,000	322,900
Statistical discrepancy . .	−59,100	−500	—
Total domestic expenditure	1,074,600	1,192,900	1,094,300
Exports of goods and services .	829,400	976,000	835,300
Less Imports of goods and services	669,300	834,300	685,900
GDP in purchasers' values	1,234,700	1,334,600	1,243,700

Source: IMF, *International Financial Statistics*.

Gross Domestic Product by Economic Activity

	1993	1994	1995*
Agriculture, hunting, forestry and fishing	85,500	101,300	107,800
Mining and quarrying† . . .			
Manufacturing†	245,400	397,900	410,900
Electricity, gas and water . .	14,900	14,200	14,800
Construction	8,000	16,800	16,100
Trade, restaurants and hotels . .	104,300	113,000	119,000
Transport, storage and communication	71,300	76,900	87,300
Government services . . .	133,800	135,000	130,300
Other services	68,200	80,300	78,700
Sub-total	731,400	935,400	964,900
Import duties	28,700	29,000	39,100
GDP in purchasers' values .	760,100	964,400	1,003,900

* Provisional figures.
† Including petroleum sector (million francs CFA): 184,700 in 1993; 322,400 in 1994; 329,400 (provisional figure) in 1995.

Source: IMF, *Republic of Congo — Statistical Annex* (August 1996).

BALANCE OF PAYMENTS (US $ million)

	1995	1996	1997
Exports of goods f.o.b. . . .	1,167.0	1,554.5	1,744.1
Imports of goods f.o.b. . . .	−650.7	−1,361.0	−802.9
Trade balance	516.3	193.5	941.3
Exports of services . . .	76.3	91.1	55.7
Imports of services . . .	−778.5	−721.1	−565.2
Balance on goods and services	−185.9	−436.5	431.8
Other income received . . .	3.0	11.7	5.1
Other income paid . . .	−459.4	−670.1	−668.9
Balance on goods, services and income	−642.3	−1,094.9	−232.0
Current transfers received . .	30.9	29.9	24.7
Current transfers paid . .	−38.3	−44.0	−44.5
Current balance	−649.7	−1,109.0	−251.9
Investment assets . . .	−10.4	0.4	−3.6
Investment liabilities . .	−69.9	656.8	−170.1
Net errors and omissions . .	120.7	102.1	−122.1
Overall balance	−609.3	−349.7	−547.7

Source: IMF, *International Financial Statistics*.

External Trade

PRINCIPAL COMMODITIES (distribution by SITC, US $ million)

Imports c.i.f.	1993	1994	1995
Food and live animals . .	59.6	87.9	108.6
Meat and meat preparations . .	15.9	23.8	28.2
Fresh, chilled or frozen meat and edible offals .	15.1	21.7	26.8
Meat of bovine animals . .	0.4	11.8	14.8
Poultry (dead) and edible poultry offals (except liver) .	12.4	7.0	8.8
Dairy products and birds' eggs .	10.1	8.7	13.4
Milk and cream . .	7.7	7.2	12.0
Preserved, concentrated or sweetened milk and cream	7.3	6.8	11.4
Fish and fish preparations .	0.2	21.8	16.5
Fresh, chilled or frozen fish .	0.1	10.0	9.3
Frozen fish (excl. fillets) .	0.1	10.0	9.3
Dried, salted or smoked fish	0.1	11.1	6.4
Cereals and cereal preparations .	27.6	23.8	36.8
Semi-milled and milled rice . .	5.1	7.0	12.4
Milled, unbroken rice. .	5.1	6.7	12.4
Flour of wheat or meslin .	18.1	8.2	13.8
Mineral fuels, lubricants, etc.	2.9	5.0	108.7
Petroleum, petroleum products, etc.	2.8	4.9	106.1
Refined petroleum products. .	2.8	3.1	105.5
Gasoline, other light oil .	—	—	38.5
Motor, aviation spirit .	—	—	30.8
Kerosene, incl. jet fuel .	—	—	19.3
Gas oils	—	—	44.5
Animal and vegetable oils, fats and waxes . .	8.3	10.7	1.2
Fixed vegetable oils and fats . .	8.3	10.5	1.2
'Soft' fixed vegetable oils .	0.6	8.5	0.5
Chemicals and related products	54.7	54.8	77.0
Medicinal and pharmaceutical products . . .	39.3	24.6	38.9
Medicaments (incl. veterinary)	38.5	24.0	38.0
Basic manufactures . .	61.6	76.7	69.5
Paper, paperboard and manufactures . . .	8.0	4.8	7.7
Iron and steel . . .	17.8	20.6	15.6
Tubes, pipes and fittings .	14.7	17.7	9.8
'Seamless' tubes and pipes; blanks for tubes and pipes	13.3	15.9	6.5
Iron, steel or aluminium structures and parts . .	0.3	21.7	1.1
Iron or steel structures, etc.. .	0.2	21.6	1.0

Imports c.i.f. — *continued*	1993	1994	1995
Machinery and transport equipment	127.1	112.6	112.6
Machinery specialized for particular industries . .	10.8	17.4	17.3
Civil engineering and contractors' plant and equipment	7.3	12.0	10.0
General industrial machinery, equipment and parts . .	24.9	30.4	32.1
Pumps (except for liquids), compressors, fans, centrifuges, etc.	5.1	9.2	4.4
Electrical machinery, apparatus, etc.	11.8	23.8	19.1
Switchgear, resistors, printed circuits, switchboards, etc. .	5.9	11.4	5.8
Switchgear, switchboards, control panels and parts .	5.9	11.3	5.6
Road vehicles and parts* . .	20.4	20.7	21.2
Passenger motor cars (excl. buses)	8.1	8.4	6.0
Other transport equipment and parts*	47.1	6.5	3.8
Ships, boats and floating structures. . . .	46.9	3.0	0.4
Tugs, special-purpose vessels and floating structures . .	46.7	2.9	0.4
Light-vessels, fire-floats, dredgers, floating cranes, etc..	45.7	—	0.1
Miscellaneous manufactured articles	24.2	36.4	65.2
Professional, scientific and controlling instruments, etc.	8.2	13.3	29.2
Measuring, checking, analysing and controlling instruments, etc.	7.6	11.7	26.4
Total (incl. others) . . .	347.1	395.2	556.0

* Data on parts exclude tyres, engines and electrical parts.

Exports f.o.b.	1993	1994	1995
Crude materials (inedible) except fuels	18.4	124.6	94.2
Cork and wood	17.8	114.6	90.7
Non-coniferous sawlogs and veneer logs	8.7	105.9	80.3
Mineral fuels, lubricants, etc.	911.2	765.3	955.2
Petroleum, petroleum products, etc.	911.2	765.3	955.2
Crude petroleum oils, etc. . .	890.9	746.8	936.3
Total (incl. others) . . .	965.3	917.9	1,089.8

Source: UN, *International Trade Statistics Yearbook*

1996 (million francs CFA): Imports 770,200; Exports 688,100.
1997 (million francs CFA): Imports 522,500; Exports 958,800.
1998 (million francs CFA): Imports 465,000; Exports 747,600.

Source: Banque des Etats de l'Afrique Centrale, *Etudes et Statistiques*.

PRINCIPAL TRADING PARTNERS (US $ million)

Imports c.i.f.	1993	1994	1995
Belgium-Luxembourg . . .	9.7	14.9	19.4
France (incl. Monaco) . . .	114.0	127.5	145.2
Germany	8.4	9.2	15.8
Italy	66.2	17.1	20.8
Japan	11.1	10.2	12.3
Mauritania	—	0.7	5.9
Netherlands	27.5	24.6	30.7
Senegal	1.8	6.0	7.2
United Kingdom	9.0	12.7	16.6
USA	16.1	39.5	44.6
Total (incl. others) . . .	347.1	395.2	555.9

Exports f.o.b.	1993	1994	1995
Angola	10.2	5.1	6.5
Brazil	0.1	14.0	—
Chile	—	15.6	—
France (incl. Monaco)	79.5	56.3	107.3
Germany	2.6	8.1	11.5
Israel	12.8	11.8	—
Italy	226.3	191.8	189.6
Japan	14.4	3.2	3.4
Malta	—	—	31.3
Netherlands	16.6	11.0	130.7
Portugal	1.6	21.9	0.4
Spain	17.3	28.1	0.1
Switzerland-Liechtenstein	12.3	—	—
USA	503.4	386.3	311.1
Total (incl others)	965.3	917.8	1,089.8

Source: UN, *International Trade Statistics Yearbook*.

Transport

RAILWAYS (traffic)

	1993	1994	1995
Passenger-km (million)	312	227	302
Freight ton-km (million)	259	222	266

Source: mainly IMF, *Republic of Congo—Statistical Annex* (August 1996).

ROAD TRAFFIC (estimates, '000 motor vehicles in use at 31 December)

	1994	1995	1996
Passenger cars	33.7	36.3	37.2
Goods vehicles	14.6	15.7	15.5

Source: IRF, *World Road Statistics*.

SHIPPING
Merchant Fleet (registered at 31 December)

	1996	1997	1998
Number of vessels	20	21	20
Total displacement ('000 grt)	6.3	6.7	3.8

Source: Lloyd's Register of Shipping, *World Fleet Statistics*.

Freight Traffic at Pointe-Noire (metric tons)

	1996	1997	1998*
Goods loaded	670,150	708,203	663,480
Goods unloaded	584,376	533,170	486,525

* Figures cover 11 months, excluding December.
Source: Banque des Etats de l'Afrique Centrale, *Etudes et Statistiques*.

Inland Waterways (freight traffic, '000 metric tons)

Port of Brazzaville	1985	1986	1987
Goods loaded	77	77	62
Goods unloaded	407	309	331

CIVIL AVIATION (traffic on scheduled services)*

	1994	1995	1996
Kilometres flown (million)	3	4	4
Passengers carried ('000)	232	267	253
Passenger-km (million)	264	283	279
Total ton-km (million)	40	43	42

* Including an apportionment of the traffic of Air Afrique.
Source: UN, *Statistical Yearbook*.

Tourism

	1996	1997	1998
Foreign tourist arrivals	39,111	25,811	25,082
Tourism receipts (US $ million)	8	3	n.a.

Source: World Tourism Organization, *Yearbook of Tourism Statistics*.

Communications Media

	1994	1995	1996
Radio receivers ('000 in use)	290	300	330
Television receivers ('000 in use)	18	20	30
Telephones ('000 main lines in use)	21	21	21
Mobile cellular telephones (subscribers)	n.a.	n.a.	1,000
Daily newspapers	6	6	6
Non-daily newspapers	n.a.	15	n.a.

1997: Radio receivers ('000 in use) 341; Television receivers ('000 in use) 33.
Sources: UNESCO, *Statistical Yearbook*; UN, *Statistical Yearbook*.

Education

(1996)

	Teachers	Pupils
Pre-primary*	619	4,415
Primary	6,926	489,546
Secondary		
General	5,466	190,409
Vocational	1,746	23,606
Higher†	1,341	16,602

* 1993/94 figures. † 1995 figures.
Source: mainly Ministry of Education, Brazzaville.

Directory

The Constitution

The 1992 Constitution, which provided for legislative power to be exercised by a directly-elected Assemblée nationale and Senate and for executive power to be held by a directly-elected President, was suspended following the assumption of power by Gen. Denis Sassou-Nguesso on 15 October 1997. A Forum for Unity and National Reconciliation was convened in January 1998. Subsequently a 75-member National Transitional Council, elected by delegates at the Forum, was appointed to act as a legislative body pending the organization of national elections in 2001. In November 1998 President Sassou-Nguesso inaugurated a 26-member constitutional committee with responsibility for drafting proposals for a new constitution, to be submitted to a national forum and subsequently to a public referendum.

The Government

HEAD OF STATE

President: Gen. DENIS SASSOU-NGUESSO (assumed power 15 October 1997; inaugurated 25 October 1997).

COUNCIL OF MINISTERS
(July 2000)

Minister at the Presidency responsible for the Cabinet of the Head of State and State Control: GÉRARD BITSINDOU.

Minister at the Presidency responsible for National Defence: ITIHI OSSETOUMBA LEKOUNDZOU.

Minister of State for Agriculture and Livestock: AUGUSTE-CÉLESTIN GONGARAD-NKOUA.

Minister of State for Justice and Keeper of the Seals: JEAN-MARTIN MBEMBA.

Minister of the Economy, Finance and the Budget: MATHIAS DZON.

Minister of Foreign Affairs, Co-operation and Francophone Affairs: RODOLPHE ADADA.

Minister for Transport and Civil Aviation in charge of the Merchant Navy: ISIDORE MVOUBA.

Minister of Territorial and Regional Development: PIERRE MOUSSA.

Minister of Construction, Urban Development, Housing and Land Reform: MARTIN MBERI.

Minister of Equipment and Public Works: Brig. Gen. FLORENT NTSIBA.

Minister of the Interior, Security and Territorial Administration: Brig. Gen. PIERRE OBA.

Minister of Hydrocarbons: JEAN-BAPTISTE TATI LOUTARD.

Minister of Energy and Water Resources: JEAN-MARIE TASSOUA.

Minister of Culture, the Arts and Tourism: MAMBOU AIMÉE GNALI.

Minister of Health, Solidarity and Humanitarian Action: LÉON-ALFRED OPIMBAT.

Minister of Industry, Mines and the Environment: MICHEL MAMPOUYA.

Minister of Forestry and Fishing: HENRI DJOMBO.

Minister of Commerce, Supplies, Small and Medium-sized Enterprises in charge of Handicrafts: PIERRE-DAMIEN BOUSSOUKOU-BOUMBA.

Minister of the Civil Service, Administrative Reforms, and the Promotion of Women: JEANNE DAMBENDZET.

Minister of Communication and Government Spokesman in charge of Relations with the National Assembly: FRANÇOIS IBOVI.

Minister of Primary, Secondary and Tertiary Education in charge of Scientific Research: PIERRE NZILA.

Minister of Technical Education and Vocational Training in charge of Youth Redeployment, Civic Education and Sports: ANDRÉ OKOMBI SALISSA.

Minister of Posts and Telecommunications: JEAN DELLO.

Minister of Labour and Social Security: DAMBERT NDOUANE.

Minister of Industrial Development in charge of the Promotion of the Private Sector: ALPHONSE MBAMA.

MINISTRIES

All Ministries are in Brazzaville.

Office of the President: Palais du Peuple, Brazzaville; internet www.congo-brazza.com/congo.htm.

Ministry of Education: BP 169, Brazzaville; tel. 83-24-60.

Ministry of the Economy, Finance and the Budget: Centre Administratif, Quartier Plateau, BP 2083, Brazzaville; tel. 81-41-43; fax 81-43-45.

Ministry of Foreign Affairs, Co-operation and Francophone Affairs: BP 2070, Brazzaville; tel. 83-20-28.

Ministry of Health, Solidarity and Humanitarian Action: Palais du Peuple, Brazzaville; tel. 81-30-75; fax 81-40-75.

Ministry of Industrial Development and the Promotion of the Private Sector: Centre Administratif, Quartier Plateau, BP 2093, Brazzaville; tel. 81-06-20.

Ministry of Industry, Mines and the Environment: Brazzaville; tel. 83-18-27.

President and Legislature

Gen. Denis Sassou-Nguesso assumed power on 15 October 1997, deposing the elected government of President Pascal Lissouba. Sassou-Nguesso was formally installed as President on 25 October 1997. A Forum for Unity and National Reconciliation was convened in January 1998. Immediately afterwards a 75-member National Transitional Council, elected by delegates at the Forum, was appointed to act as a legislative body pending the organization of national elections in 2001. A new constitution was to be drafted and submitted to a referendum prior to these elections.

Political Organizations

Espace républicain pour la défense de la démocratie et l'unité nationale (ERDDUN); f. 1997; coalition of political organizations opposed to Pres. Sassou-Nguesso; Pres. BERNARD KOLELAS.

Forces démocratiques et patriotiques (FDP): Brazzaville; f. 1994 as an alliance of six political parties; frmly Forces démocratiques unies; Leader Gen. DENIS SASSOU-NGUESSO; Deputy Leader PIERRE NZE.

Convention pour l'alternative démocratique: Leader ALFRED OPIMBA.

Parti congolais du travail (PCT): Brazzaville; f. 1969; sole legal political party 1969–90; Pres. Gen. DENIS SASSOU-NGUESSO; Sec.-Gen. LÉON ZOKONI.

Parti libéral républicain: Leader NICÉPHORE FYLA.

Union nationale pour la démocratie et le progrès (UNDP): f. 1990; Leader PIERRE NZE.

Union patriotique pour la réconstruction nationale: Leader MATHIAS DZON.

Union pour le renouveau nationale: Leader GABRIEL BOKILO.

Front uni des républicains congolais (FURC): e-mail furc@multimedia.com; internet www.multimedia.com/furc; f. 1994; seeks national development on a non-ethnic and non-regional basis; Chair. RAYMOND TIMOTHÉE MACKITA.

Horizon 2000: Brazzaville; f. 1997; coalition of independent republican parties.

Mouvement pour l'unité et la réconstruction: f. 1997 as an alliance of three political parties:

Mouvement pour la démocratie et la solidarité (MDS): Pres. PAUL KAYA.

Rassemblement pour la démocratie et le progrès social (RDPS): Pointe-Noire; f. 1990; Pres. JEAN-PIERRE THYSTÈRE-TCHICAYA; Sec.-Gen. JEAN-FÉLIX DEMBA DELO.

Union pour la République (UR): Brazzaville; f. 1995 by dissident mems of UPADS; Leader BENJAMIN BOUNKOULOU.

Parti du renouvellement et du progrès: Leader HENRI MARCEL DOUMANGUELE.

Parti pour l'unité, le travail et le progrès (PUTP): f. 1995 by fmr mems of the MCDDI; Leader DIDIER SENGHA.

Rassemblement des citoyens (RC): f. 1998 to promote solidarity and tolerance; Leader CLAUDE ALPHONSE SILOU.

Rassemblement pour la démocratie et le développement (RDD): f. 1990; advocates a mixed economy; Chair. SATURNIN OKABE.

Rassemblement démocratique et populaire du Congo: Leader JEAN-MARIE TASSOUA.

Rassemblement pour la démocratie et la République (RDR): f. 1996; Leader Gen. RAYMOND DAMASSE NGOLLO.

Union pour la démocratie congolaise (UDC): f. 1989; advocates economic liberalization; Chair. FÉLIX MAKOSSO.

Union pour la démocratie et la République–Mouinda (UDR–Mouinda): f. 1992; Leader ANDRÉ MILONGO.

Union pour la démocratie et le progrès social (UDPS): f. 1994 by merger of the Union pour le développement et le progrès social and the Parti populaire pour la démocratie sociale et la défense de la République; Leader JEAN-MICHEL BOUKAMBA-YANGOUMA.

Union des forces démocratiques (UFD): Chair. SÉBASTIEN EBAO.

Union panafricaine pour la démocratie sociale (UPADS): Sec.-Gen. MARTIN MBERI.

Union patriotique pour la démocratie et le progrès: Sec.-Gen. CÉLESTIN NKOUA.

Union patriotique des forces Ninjas: f. 1999; political wing of the Ninja militia loyal to fmr prime minister Bernard Kolelas.

Union pour le progrès du peuple congolais: f. 1991; advocates democracy and national unity; Leader ALPHONSE NBIHOULA.

Union pour le progrès social et la démocratie (UPSD): Brazzaville; f. 1991; Pres. ANGE-EDOUARD POUNGUI.

Union pour le renouveau démocratique (URD): f. 1992 as an alliance of seven political parties; Chair. BERNARD KOLELAS; prin. mems:

> **Mouvement congolais pour la démocratie et le développement intégral (MCDDI):** Brazzaville; f. 1990; Sec.-Gen. MICHEL MAMPOUYA.

> **Rassemblement pour la démocratie et le progrès social (RDPS):** see under Mouvement pour l'unité et la réconstruction.

Diplomatic Representation

EMBASSIES IN THE REPUBLIC OF THE CONGO

Following the 1997 conflict and subsequent unrest in Brazzaville, many diplomatic missions have remained closed, or operate with only essential staff.

Algeria: BP 2100, Brazzaville; tel. 83-39-15.

Angola: BP 388, Brazzaville; tel. 81-14-71.

Belgium: BP 225, Brazzaville; tel. 83-29-63; fax 83-71-18.

Cameroon: BP 2136, Brazzaville; tel. 83-34-04.

Central African Republic: BP 10, Brazzaville; tel. 83-40-14.

Chad: BP 386, Brazzaville; tel. 81-22-22.

China, People's Republic: BP 213, Brazzaville; tel. 83-11-20.

Congo, Democratic Republic: 130 ave de l'Indépendance, BP 2450, Brazzaville; tel. 83-29-38.

Cuba: BP 80, Brazzaville; tel. 81-29-80.

Egypt: BP 917, Brazzaville; tel. 83-44-28.

France: rue Alfassa, BP 2089, Brazzaville; tel. 83-14-23; Ambassador: HERVÉ BOLOT.

Gabon: ave Fourneau, BP 2033, Brazzaville; tel. 81-05-90.

Germany: place de la Mairie, BP 2022, Brazzaville; tel. 83-29-90.

Guinea: Brazzaville; tel. 81-24-66.

Holy See: rue Colonel Brisset, BP 1168, Brazzaville; tel. 81-55-80; fax 81-55-81; Apostolic Nuncio: Most Rev. LUIGI PEZZUTO, Titular Archbishop of Turris in Proconsulari.

Italy: 2-3 blvd Lyauté, BP 2484, Brazzaville; tel. 83-25-82.

Korea, Democratic People's Republic: Brazzaville; tel. 83-41-98; Ambassador: HAN BONG CHUN.

Libya: BP 920, Brazzaville.

Nigeria: BP 790, Brazzaville; tel. 83-13-16.

Russia: BP 2132, Brazzaville; tel. 81-19-23; fax 81-50-85; Ambassador: SERGEI NENASHEV.

USA: 70 rue Bayardelle, BP 1015, Brazzaville; tel. 81-14-72; Ambassador: DAVID H. KAEUPER.

Judicial System

The *Acte fondamental* of October 1997 confirmed the independence of the judiciary. The constituent bodies of the judiciary are the Cour suprême (Supreme Court), the Haute cour de la justice (High Court) and the Conseil supérieur de la magistrature (Supreme Council of Magistrates).

Cour suprême: Brazzaville; Pres. GASTON MAMBOUANA.

Religion

At least one-half of the population follow traditional animist beliefs. Most of the remainder are Christians (mainly Roman Catholics).

CHRISTIANITY

The Roman Catholic Church

The Congo comprises one archdiocese and five dioceses. According to Church figures, at 31 December 1998 an estimated 47.8% of the population were adherents.

Bishops' Conference: Conférence Episcopale du Congo, BP 200, Brazzaville; tel. 83-06-29; fax 83-79-08; f. 1992; Pres. Rt Rev. ANATOLE MILANDOU, Bishop of Kinkala.

Archbishop of Brazzaville: Most Rev. BARTHÉLÉMY BATANTU, Archevêché, BP 2301, Brazzaville; tel. 83-17-93; fax 83-17-98.

Protestant Church

Eglise Evangélique du Congo: BP 3205, Bacongo-Brazzaville; tel. 81-43-64; fax 83-77-33; internet services.worldnet.net/adele/Page3.html; f. 1909; autonomous since 1961; 135,811 mems (1993); 105 parishes (1998); Pres. Rev. ALPHONSE MBAMA.

ISLAM

In 1997 an estimated 2% of the population were Muslims. There were 49 mosques in the Congo in 1991.

Comité Islamique du Congo: 77 Makotipoko Moungali, BP 55, Brazzaville; tel. 82-87-45; f. 1988; Leaders HABIBOU SOUMARE, BACHIR GATSONGO, BOUILLA GUIBIDANESI.

The Press

In July 2000 legislation was adopted on the freedom of information and communication. The legislation, which confirmed the abolition of censorship and reduced the penalty for defamation from imprisonment to a fine, specified three types of punishable offence: the encouragement of social tension (including incitement to ethnic conflict), attacks on the authorities (including libels on the head of state or on the judiciary), and libels against private individuals. The terms of the legislation were to be guaranteed by a regulatory body, the Conseil de la liberté de la communication.

DAILIES

Aujourd'hui: Brazzaville; tel. and fax 83-77-44; f. 1991; Man. Dir and Chief Editor FYLLA DI FUA DI SASSA.

L'Eveil de Pointe-Noire: Pointe-Noire.

Journal de Brazzaville: BP 132, Brazzaville.

Mweti: BP 991, Brazzaville; tel. 81-10-87; national news; Dir MATONGO AVELEY; Chief Editor HUBERT MADOUABA; circ. 7,000.

PERIODICALS

Bakento Ya Congo: BP 309, Brazzaville; tel. 83-27-44; quarterly; Dir MARIE LOUISE MAGANGA; Chief Editor CHARLOTTE BOUSSE; circ. 3,000.

Bulletin Mensuel de la Chambre de Commerce de Brazzaville: BP 92, Brazzaville; monthly.

Bulletin de Statistique: Centre Nationale de la Statistique et des Etudes Economiques, BP 2031, Brazzaville; tel. and fax 81-59-09; f. 1977; quarterly; Dir-Gen. DOROTHÉE OUISSIKA.

Le Choc: BP 1314, Brazzaville; weekly; satirical; Chief Editor: JEAN-BAPTISTE BAKOUVOUKA.

Combattant Rouge: Brazzaville; tel. 83-02-53; monthly; Dir SYLVIO GEORGES ONKA; Chief Editor GILLES OMER BOUSSI.

Congo-Magazine: BP 114, Brazzaville; tel. 83-43-81; monthly; Dir GASPARD MPAN; Chief Editor THÉODORE KIAMOSSI; circ. 3,000.

Effort: BP 64, Brazzaville; monthly; general interest.

Le Flambeau: Brazzaville; weekly; independent.

Le Forum: BP 3232, Brazzaville; f. 1992; weekly; Publr MAURICE MASSENGO TIASSE.

Le Gardien: 39 rue Bouenza Talangai, Brazzaville; f. 1993; fortnightly; Publr GILLES ANDAH-LEYET; circ. 2,500.

Jeunesse et Révolution: BP 885, Brazzaville; tel. 83-44-13; weekly; Dir JEAN-ENOCH GOMA-KENGUE; Chief Editor PIERRE MAKITA.

Le Madukutsekele: Brazzaville; f. 1991; weekly; satirical; Editor MATHIEU BAKIMA-BALIELE; circ. 5,000.

La Nouvelle République: Brazzaville; pro-government; weekly.

L'Opinion: Brazzaville; monthly.

Paris-Brazzaville: Brazzaville; weekly; general interest.

Le Pays: f. 1991; weekly; Dir ANTOINE MALONGA.

La Rue Meurt: BP 1258, Brazzaville; f. 1991; satirical weekly magazine; Publr JEAN-PAUL BAFOUIRI; circ. 3,000.

La Semaine Africaine: BP 2080, Brazzaville; tel. 81-03-28; f. 1952; weekly; Roman Catholic; general news and social comment;

circulates widely in francophone equatorial Africa; Dir JEAN-PIERRE GALLET; Chief Editor JOACHIM MBANZA; circ. 7,500.

Le Soleil: f. 1991; weekly; organ of the Rassemblement pour la démocratie et le développement.

Le Stade: BP 114, Brazzaville; tel. 81-47-18; f. 1985; weekly; sports; Dir HUBERT-TRÉSOR MADOUABA-NTOUALANI; Chief Editor LELAS PAUL NZOLANI; circ. 6,500.

Voix de la Classe Ouvrière (Voco): BP 2311, Brazzaville; tel. 83-36-66; six a year; Dir MICHEL JOSEPH MAYOUNGOU; Chief Editor MARIE-JOSEPH TSENGOU; circ. 4,500.

NEWS AGENCIES

Agence d'Information d'Afrique Centrale (ADIAC): Hôtel Méridien, BP 15457, Brazzaville; tel. and fax 81-28-13; e-mail belie@ congonet.cg; internet www.brazzaville-adiac.com; f. 1997; Dirs JEAN-PAUL PIGASSE, BÉLINDA AYESSA; br. in Paris.

Foreign Bureaux

Agence France-Presse (AFP): BP 2144, Brazzaville; tel. 83-46-76.

Associated Press (AP) (USA): BP 2144, Brazzaville.

Inter Press Service (IPS) (Italy): POB 964, Brazzaville; tel. 810565.

Pan-African News Agency (PANA) (Senegal): BP 2144, Brazzaville; tel. 83-11-40; fax 83-70-15.

Reuters (United Kingdom): BP 2144, Brazzaville.

Xinhua (New China) News Agency (People's Republic of China): 40 ave Maréchal Lyauté, BP 373, Brazzaville; tel. 83-44-01.

Publishers

Editions ADIAC: Hôtel Méridien, BP 15457, Brazzaville; tel. and fax 81-28-13; f. 1997; publishes chronicles of current affairs; Dirs JEAN-PAUL PIGASSE, BÉLINDA AYESSA.

Editions 'Héros dans l'Ombre': BP 1678, Brazzaville; tel. 82-23-03; fax 83-50-51; f. 1980; literature, criticism, poetry, essays; President LÉOPOLD PINDY-MAMONSONO.

Imprimerie Centrale d'Afrique (ICA): BP 162, Pointe-Noire; f. 1949; Man. Dir M. SCHNEIDER.

Government Publishing House

Imprimerie Nationale: BP 58, Brazzaville; Man. KIALA MATOUBA.

Broadcasting and Communications

TELECOMMUNICATIONS

Office National des Postes et Télécommunications (ONPT): ave Patrice Lumumba, BP 39, Brazzaville; tel. 81-16-86; operates national telecommunications network; mobile cellular telephone system introduced in 1996; transfer pending to private ownership; Man. Dir BERNARD OKIEMOU.

Celtel Congo: Tour Mayombe 2A, BP 1267, Pointe-Noire; tel. 94-86-02; fax 94-88-75; e-mail celtelcongo@aol.com; Brazzaville; f. 1999; mobile cellular telephone operator and internet access provider; network covers Brazzaville and Pointe-Noire; subsid. of MSI Cellular; Man. Dir ROB GELDERLOOS; 15,000 subscribers (May 2000).

Cyrus International (CYRTEL): Brazzaville; mobile cellular telephone operator; operates as a jt venture between Nexus International (70%), a subsidiary of France Telecom, and the ONPT.

Libertis: Brazzaville; f. 2000; mobile cellular telephone operator.

RADIO AND TELEVISION

Radio Brazzaville: Brazzaville; f. 1999; official station: Man. MONGO SYLM.

Radio Congo Liberté: Brazzaville; f. 1997; operated by supporters of Pres. Sassou-Nguesso.

Radiodiffusion-Télévision Congolaise: BP 2241, Brazzaville; tel. 81-24-73; state-owned; Pres. JEAN-GILBERT FOUTOU; Dir-Gen. GILBERT-DAVID MUTAKALA.

Radio Congo: BP 2241, Brazzaville; tel. 83-03-83; radio programmes in French, Lingala, Kikongo, Subia, English and Portuguese; transmitters at Brazzaville and Pointe-Noire; Dir of Broadcasting THÉOPHILE MIETE LIKIBI.

Télé-Congo: BP 2241, Brazzaville; tel. 81-51-52; began transmission in 1963; operates for 46 hours per week, with most programmes in French but some in Lingala and Kikongo; Dir JEAN-GILBERT FOUTOU.

Radio Rurale: community stations established by the Agence de coopération culturelle et technique (ACCT); transmitters in Sembé, Nkayi, Etoumbi and Mossendjo.

The Republic of the Congo also receives broadcasts from Radio France International and Radio Africa No. 1.

Finance

(cap. = capital; res = reserves; dep. = deposits; m. = million; br. = branch; amounts in francs CFA)

BANKING
Central Bank

Banque des Etats de l'Afrique Centrale (BEAC): BP 126, Brazzaville; tel. 81-10-73; fax 81-10-94; HQ in Yaoundé, Cameroon; f. 1973; bank of issue for mem. states of the Communauté économique et monétaire en Afrique centrale (CEMAC, fmrly Union douanière et économique de l'Afrique centrale); comprising Cameroon, the Central African Repub., Chad, the Repub. of the Congo, Equatorial Guinea and Gabon; cap. and res 209,588.5m., total assets 1,299,052.6m. (Dec. 1998); Gov. JEAN-FÉLIX MAMALEPOT; Dir in Repub. of the Congo PACIFIQUE ISSOIBEKA; br. at Pointe-Noire.

Commercial Banks

Banque Française Intercontinentale "FIBA": angle rue de Reims et rue de Pavic, BP 14579, Brazzaville; tel. 81-40-50; fax 81-50-89; Dir HENRI-JEAN RESCA.

Banque Internationale du Congo (BIDC): ave Amílcar Cabral, BP 33, Brazzaville; tel. 81-07-14; fax 81-16-69; f. 1983; state-owned; privatization pending; total assets 51,980m. (Dec. 1997); Pres. ÉDOUARD EBOUKA BABACKAS; Gen. Man. FRANÇOIS BOUMANDOUKI; 1 br.

Crédit pour l'Agriculture, l'Industrie et le Commerce (CAIC): ave Amílcar Cabral, BP 2889, Brazzaville; tel. 81-09-78; fax 81-09-77; 50% state-owned; Man. Dir DELPHINE MBOUYOU.

Union Congolaise de Banques SARL: ave Amílcar Cabral, BP 147, Brazzaville; tel. 81-58-33; fax 81-47-34; f. 1974; state-owned; transfer pending to private sector; total assets 104,400m. (Dec. 1997); Dir-Gen. GERVAIS BOUITI-VIAUDO; 8 brs.

Co-operative Banking Institution

Mutuelles Congolaises de l'Epargne et de Crédit: BP 13237, Brazzaville; tel. 81-07-57; fax 81-01-68; f. 1994; Dir. JEAN-CLAUDE GARCIA.

Development Bank

Banque de Développement des États de l'Afrique Centrale: Head Office, BP 1177, Brazzaville; tel. 81-17-61; fax 81-18-80; Chair. ZACHARIE PEREVET; Gen. Man. JEAN-MARIE MBIOKA.

Financial Institution

Caisse Congolaise d'Amortissement: ave Foch Beltrando, BP 2090, Brazzaville; tel. 81-57-35; fax 81-52-36; f. 1971; management of state funds; Dir-Gen. ROGER GOSSAKI.

INSURANCE

Assurances et Réassurances du Congo (ARC): ave Amílcar Cabral, BP 977, Brazzaville; tel. 83-01-71; f. 1973; 50% state-owned; to be restructured prior to pending privatization; Dir-Gen. RAYMOND IBATA; brs at Pointe-Noire, Loubomo and Ouesso.

Gras Savoye Congo: BP 139, Brazzaville; tel. 83-43-43; fax 83-43-42; insurance brokers and risk managers; Man. ERIC MANTOT.

Trade and Industry

DEVELOPMENT ORGANIZATIONS

Agence Française de Développement: BP 96, Brazzaville; tel. 81-53-30; fax 81-29-42; French fund for economic co-operation; Dir YVES TERRACOL.

Mission Française de Coopération: BP 2175, Brazzaville; tel. 83-15-03; f. 1959; administers bilateral aid from France; Dir JEAN-BERNARD THIANT.

Office des Cultures Vivrières (OCV): Brazzaville; tel. 82-11-03; f. 1979; state-owned; food-crop development; Dir-Gen. GILBERT PANA.

Société Nationale d'Elevage (SONEL): BP 81, Loutété, Massangui; f. 1964; development of semi-intensive stock-rearing; exploitation of cattle by-products; Man. Dir THÉOPHILE BIKAWA.

CHAMBERS OF COMMERCE

Chambre de Commerce, d'Agriculture et d'Industrie de Brazzaville: BP 92, Brazzaville; tel. 83-21-15; Pres. MAURICE OGNAOY; Sec.-Gen. FRANÇOIS DILOU-YOULOU.

Chambre de Commerce, d'Agriculture et d'Industrie de Loubomo: BP 78, Loubomo.

Chambre de Commerce, d'Industrie et d'Agriculture et des Métiers de Pointe-Noire: 8 ave Charles de Gaulle, BP 665, Pointe-Noire; tel. 94-12-80; fax 94-07-13; f. 1948; Chair. NARCISSE POATY PACKA; Sec.-Gen. JEAN-BAPTISTE SOUMBOU.

INDUSTRIAL AND TRADE ASSOCIATIONS

Office Congolais des Bois (OCB): 2 ave Moe Vangoula, BP 1229, Pointe-Noire; tel. 94-22-38; f. 1974; purchase and marketing of timber products; Man. Dir ALEXANDRE DENGUET-ATTIKI.

Office National de Commercialisation des Produits Agricoles (ONCPA): Brazzaville; tel. 83-24-01; f. 1964; marketing of all agricultural products except sugar; promotion of rural co-operatives; Dir JEAN-PAUL BOCKONDAS.

Office National du Commerce (OFNACOM): Brazzaville; tel. 83-43-99; f. 1964; importer and distributor of general merchandise; monopoly importer of salted and dried fish, cooking salt, rice, tomato purée, buckets, enamelled goods and blankets; Dir-Gen. VALENTIN ENOUSSA NCONGO.

EMPLOYERS' ORGANIZATIONS

Union Nationale des Opérateurs du Congo (UNOC): Brazzaville; employers' assn; operates a professional training centre; Pres. El Hadj DJIBRIL ABDOULAYE BOPAKA.

Union Patronale et Interprofessionnelle du Congo (UNI-CONGO): BP 42, Brazzaville; tel. 81-47-65; fax 81-47-66; f. 1960; employers' asscn; Pres. G. BOUR; Sec.-Gen. J. FUMEY.

UTILITIES

Electricity

Société Nationale d'Electricité (SNEL): 95 ave Paul Doumer, BP 95, Brazzaville; tel. 81-38-58; f. 1967; transfer pending to private ownership; operates hydroelectric plants at Bouenza and Djoué; Dir-Gen. ALPHONSE BOUDONESA.

Water

Société Nationale de Distribution d'Eau (SNDE): rue du Sergent Malamine, BP 229 and 365, Brazzaville; tel. 83-73-26; fax 83-38-91; f. 1967; transfer pending to private-sector ownership; water supply and sewerage; holds monopoly over wells and import of mineral water; Chair. and Man. Dir S. MPINOU.

MAJOR COMPANIES

The following are some of the largest companies in terms of either capital investment or employment. Operations at many of the companies have been suspended or limited since the 1997 civil war and subsequent unrest.

AGIP Recherches Congo: rue Behagle, BP 2047, Brazzaville; tel. 83-11-52; f. 1969; cap. US $7m.; wholly-owned by AGIP (Italy); exploration and exploitation of petroleum resources; Chair. PIETRO CAVANNA; Man. Dir ANTONIO ROSSANI.

BATA SA Congolaise: ave du Général de Gaulle, BP 32, Pointe-Noire; tel. 94-03-26; f. 1965; mfrs of footwear.

Boissons Africaines de Brazzaville (BAB): BP 2193, Brazzaville; tel. 83-20-06; f. 1964; mfrs and markets carbonated drinks and syrups.

Brasseries du Congo: 55 ave du Nouveau Port, BP 105, Brazzaville; tel. 83-85-81; fax 83-25-64; mfrs and markets beer and soft drinks, fruit juices, soda, ice and carbon dioxide; Pres. J. L. HOME; Man. Dir G. J. BOUR; 570 employees.

Les Ciments du Congo (CIMCO): BP 72, Loutété; tel. 92-61-26; f. 1968; name changed as above 1999; 50% owned by Scancem (Norway); Man. Dir OLE KULSETH; 400 employees.

La Congolaise des Bois Impregnés (CBI): BP 820, Pointe-Noire; f. 1986; production of electricity poles from eucalyptus trees.

Elf Congo: BP 761, Pointe-Noire; tel. 94-60-00; also at BP 405, Brazzaville; tel. 83-02-40; f. 1969; cap. US $17.2m.; wholly-owned by Totalfina Elf; exploration and exploitation of petroleum resources; Dir-Gen. LOUIS HEUZÉ.

Eucalyptus du Congo S.A.: BP 1227, Pointe-Noire; tel. 94-04-17; fax 94-40-54; f. 1978; 85% owned by Royal Dutch Shell Group, 15% state owned; production of wood-pulp for export from eucalyptus plantations; Dir GÉRARD PERRIN.

Groupe Cofico SA: BP 13359, Brazzaville; e-mail groupecofico @smartnet.ca; four cos: Congo Finance Corpn, International Import-Export Corpn, Constructions et Gestion Immobilières, Société Agropastorale et d'Aménagement de Boko.

Impressions de Textiles de la République du Congo (IMPRECO): Brazzaville; tel. 81-02-74; fax 83-01-96; f. 1973; 30% state-owned; textile printing.

Minoterie et Aliments de Bétail (MAB): BP 789, Pointe-Noire; tel. 94-19-09; f. 1978; owned by Soufflex, France and Seabord Corp, USA; production of flour and animal feed.

PLACONGO SA: BP 717, Pointe-Noire; tel. 94-02-79; f. 1965 as Société des Placages du Congo; 36% state-owned; rotary peeling of logs.

Régie Nationale des Palmeraies du Congo (RNPC): BP 8, Brazzaville; tel. 83-08-25; f. 1966; state-owned; production of palm oil; Man. Dir RENÉ MACOSSO.

Savonnerie du Congo (SAVCONGO): Brazzaville; tel. 83-10-17; f. 1958; mfrs of soap and domestic cleaning products.

Société Congolaise des Bois (SOCOBOIS): BP 300, Loubomo; tel. 91-02-04; f. 1964; cap. 400m. francs CFA; timber mills.

Société Congolaise Industrielle des Bois (CIB): BP 145, Brazzaville; tel. 83-11-31; fax 83-33-79; logs and timber production

Société Congolaise Industrielle des Bois d'Ouesso: Ouesso; f. 1981; 51% state-owned; forestry production.

Société Congolaise de Pêches Maritimes (COPEMAR): Pointe-Noire; tel. 94-20-32; f. 1981; processing of fish products.

Société d'Economie Mixte de Construction (SEMICO): Brazzaville; f. 1983; 25% state-owned; construction.

Société Forestière Algéro-Congolaise (SFAC): Brazzaville; tel. 83-46-40; f. 1983; timber production and marketing.

Société des Huiles du Congo (HUILCA SA): BP 103, N'Kayi; tel. 92-11-60; f. 1988; 40% state-owned; production of oils and fats, vegetable oil refinery at Brazzaville.

Société Industrielle et Agricole du Tabac Tropical (SIAT): BP 50, Brazzaville; tel. 83-16-15; fax 83-16-72; f. 1945; mfrs of cigarettes; Dir-Gen. BERNARD PUILLET.

Société Industrielle des Bois de Mossendjo (SIBOM): Pointe-Noire; f. 1984; 35% state-owned.

Société Industrielle de Déroulage et de Tranchage (SID-ETRA): BP 1202, Pointe-Noire; tel. 94-20-07; f. 1966; 35% state-owned; forestry, production of sawn wood and veneers; 650 employees.

Société Libanaise de Bois de Placage: Likouala; f. 2000; factory producing logs and plywood from a region of forestry covering 199,000 hectares; 15-year licence granted in 2000.

Société Nationale de Construction (SONACO): Brazzaville, tel. 83-06-54; f. 1979; state-owned; building works; Man. Dir DENIS M'BOMO.

Société Nationale d'Elevage (SONEL): BP 81, Loutété, Massangui; f. 1964; state-owned; development of semi-intensive stockrearing; exploitation of by-products; Man. Dir THÉOPHILE BIKAWA.

Société Nationale d'Exploitation des Bois (SNEB): Pointe-Noire; tel. 94-02-09; f. 1970; state-owned; production of timber; Pres. RIGOBERT NGOULOU; Man. Dir ROBERT ZINGA KANZA.

Société Nationale des Pétroles du Congo (SNPC): Brazzaville; f. 1999 to take over the research and exploration activities of HYDRO–CONGO; cap. 900m. francs CFA.

Société Nationale de Recherches et d'Exploitation Pétrolières (HYDRO-CONGO): Cnr ave Paul Doumer and ave du Camp, BP 2008, Brazzaville; tel. 81-10-13; fax 81-10-25; f. 1973; state-owned; transfer pending to private-sector ownership; production and distribution of petroleum resources; operates petroleum refinery at Pointe-Noire; also mfrs of lubricants; Dir-Gen. Y. A. MONNAELE-NGOLLO.

Société des Silos à Ciment du Congo (SIACIC): Pointe-Noire; Dir Lt-Col FLORENT TSIBA.

Société des Textiles du Congo (SOTEXCO): BP 3222, Brazzaville; tel. 83-33-83; f. 1966; operates cotton-spinning mills, dyeing and weaving plants in Kinsoundi; Man. Dir M. KOMBO-KITOMBO.

Société des Verreries du Congo (SOVERCO): BP 1241, Pointe-Noire; tel. 94-19-19; f. 1977; state-owned; mfrs of glassware; Chair. A. E. NOUMAZALAYE; Man. Dir NGOYOT IBARRA.

TRADE UNIONS

Independent trade unions were legalized in 1991.

Confédération Générale des Travailleurs du Congo (CGTC): Brazzaville; f. 1995; Chair. PAUL DOUNA.

Confédération Nationale des Syndicats Libres (CNASYL): Brazzaville; f. 1994; Sec.-Gen. MICHEL KABOUL MAOUTA.

Confédération Syndicale Congolaise (CSC): BP 2311, Brazzaville; tel. 83-19-23; f. 1964; 80,000 mems.

Confédération Syndicale des Travailleurs Congolais (CSTC): Brazzaville; f. 1993; fed. of 13 trade unions; Chair. DAMAS KIKONI; Sec.-Gen. LOUIS GOUNDOU; 40,000 mems.

Confédération des Syndicats Libres et Autonomes du Congo (COSYLAC): Brazzaville; Pres. RENÉ BLANCHARD SERGE OBA.

Transport

Agence Transcongolaise des Communications (ATC): BP 711, Pointe-Noire; tel. 94-15-32; f. 1969; transfer pending to private-sector ownership; three divisions: Congo-Océan Railways, inland waterways and Brazzaville inland port, and the Atlantic port of Pointe-Noire; Man. Dir Col JEAN-FÉLIX ONGOUYA.

RAILWAYS

There are 515 km of track from Brazzaville to Pointe-Noire. A 286-km section of privately-owned line was used until 1991 to link the manganese mines at Moanda (in Gabon) with the main line to Pointe-Noire. Rail traffic has been severely disrupted since the 1997 civil war. The main line to Pointe-Noire reopened in November 1998 for freight traffic; it has subsequently been affected by unrest. In early 2000 the Government signed two agreements with SNCF of France relating to the repair of the line and associated infrastructure, and to the management of the network.

ATC—Chemin de Fer Congo-Océan (CFCO): BP 651, Pointe-Noire; tel. 94-11-84; fax 94-12-30; f. 1969; entered partnership with Rail Afrique International in June 1998; transfer pending to private ownership; Exec. Vice Pres. ROBERT LAMPARNESSE; Man. Dir Adm. PIERRE GOMBE.

INLAND WATERWAYS

The Congo and Oubangui rivers form two axes of a highly developed inland waterway system. The Congo river and seven tributaries in the Congo basin provide 2,300 km of navigable river, and the Oubangui river, developed in co-operation with the Central African Republic, an additional 2,085 km.

ATC—Direction des Voies Navigables, Ports et Transports Fluviaux: BP 2048, Brazzaville; tel. 83-06-27; waterways authority; Dir MÉDARD OKOUMOU.

Compagnie Congolaise de Transports: Loubomo; f. 1960; Pres. and Dir-Gen. ROBERT BARBIER.

Société Congolaise de Transports (SOCOTRANS): BP 617, Pointe-Noire; tel. 94-23-31; fax 94-45-02; e-mail soco10@calva.com; f. 1977; transport; handling; consignments; Man HENRI BENATOUIL.

Transcap–Congo: BP 1154, Pointe-Noire; tel. 94-01-46; f. 1962; Chair. J. DROUAULT.

SHIPPING

The deep-water Atlantic seaport at Pointe-Noire is the most important port in Central Africa and Brazzaville is one of the principal ports on the Congo river. A major rehabilitation programme began in October 1999, with the aim of establishing Pointe-Noire as a regional centre for container traffic and as a logistics centre for offshore oil exploration. In 1997 708,203 metric tons of goods were loaded at the port of Pointe-Noire, and 533,170 tons were unloaded.

ATC—Direction du Port de Brazzaville: BP 2048, Brazzaville; tel. 83-00-42; port authority; Dir JEAN-PAUL BOCKONDAS.

ATC—Direction du Port de Pointe-Noire: BP 711, Pointe-Noire; tel. 94-00-52; fax 94-20-42; port authority; Dir DOMINIQUE BEMBA.

La Congolaise de Transport Maritime (COTRAM): f. 1984; national shipping co; state-owned.

SAGA Congo: 18 rue du Prophète Lasse Zephirin, BP 674, Pointe Noire; tel. 94-10-16; fax 94-34-04.

ROADS

In 1996 there were an estimated 12,800 km of roads and tracks, including 3,440 km of main roads and 4,150 km of secondary roads. Only about 9.7% of the total network was paved. The principal routes link Brazzaville with Pointe-Noire, in the south, and with Ouesso, in the north. The proposed privatization of national road maintenance services was announced in late 1999.

Régie Nationale des Transports et des Travaux Publics: BP 2073, Brazzaville; tel. 83-35-58; f. 1965; civil engineering, maintenance of roads and public works; Man. Dir HECTOR BIENVENU OUAMBA.

CIVIL AVIATION

There are international airports at Brazzaville (Maya-Maya) and Pointe-Noire (Agostinho Neto). There are also five regional airports, at Dolisie, Nkaye, Owando, Ouesso and Impfondo, as well as 12 smaller airfields. In 1994 the state monopoly on internal flights was terminated, and in 1999 there were 10 airline companies operating in the Congo.

Aéro-Service: ave Charles de Gaulle, BP 1138, Brazzaville; tel. 81-34-88; fax 83-09-47; f. 1967; scheduled and charter services; operates nationally and to regional destinations; Pres. and Dir-Gen. C. GRIESBAUM.

Air Afrique: BP 1126, Pointe-Noire; tel. 94-17-00; see under Côte d'Ivoire; Dir at Pointe-Noire GUY C. CODIJA; Dir at Brazzaville AHMED LAMINE-ALI.

Congo-Aviation: Brazzaville; f. 1994.

Lina Congo (Lignes Nationales Aériennes Congolaises): ave Amílcar Cabral, BP 2203, Brazzaville; tel. 81-30-65; fax 82-80-34; f. 1965; 33% state-owned; operates an extensive internal network; international flights to Gabon and Angola; Man. Dir RAOUL MAIXANT ODZOTO.

Trans Air Congo: ave Amílcar Cabral, BP 2422, Brazzaville; tel. 94-56-43; e-mail TAC10@calva.com; internet www.transaircongo.com; f. 1994; Lebanese-owned private airline operating internal scheduled and international charter flights; Dir BASSAM ELHAGE.

Tourism

The tourism sector has been severely disrupted by political instability and internal unrest. Tourist visitors numbered 25,000 in 1998 (compared with tourist arrivals of 36,072 in 1992). In 1997 earnings from tourism were estimated at US $3m.

Direction Générale du Tourisme et des Loisirs: BP 456, Brazzaville; tel. 83-09-53; f. 1980; Dir-Gen. ANTOINE KOUNKOU-KIBOUILOU.

Defence

In August 1999 the army numbered 8,000, the navy about 800 and the air force 1,200. There were 5,000 men in paramilitary forces. National service is voluntary for men and women, and lasts for two years.

Defence Expenditure: Estimated at 45,000m. francs CFA for 1999.

Supreme Commander of the Armed Forces: Gen. DENIS SASSOU-NGUESSO.

Chief of General Staff of the National People's Army: Gen. JACQUES-YVES NDOULOU.

Education

Education is officially compulsory for 10 years between six and 16 years of age. Primary education begins at the age of six and lasts for six years. Secondary education, from 12 years of age, lasts for seven years, comprising a first cycle of four years and a second of three years. Private education was legalized in 1990. In 1996 there were 489,546 pupils enrolled at primary schools, while 190,409 pupils were receiving general secondary education. In addition, there were 23,606 secondary students attending vocational institutions. In 2000 there were some 20,000 students enrolled in the Marien Ngouabi University in Brazzaville. Some Congolese students also attend further education establishments abroad. In 2000, according to estimates by UNESCO, the average rate of adult illiteracy was 19.3% (males 12.5%, females 25.6%), one of the lowest in Africa. Expenditure on education by the central government was 52,274m. francs CFA in 1995.

Bibliography

Allen, C., Radu, M. S., Somerville, K., et al. *Benin, The Congo, Burkina Faso: Economics, Politics and Society.* New York, Columbia University Press, 1989.

Amin, S., and Coquery-Vidrovitch, C. *Histoire économique du Congo 1880–1968.* Paris, Anthropos, 1969.

Association Rupture-Solidarité. *Congo-Brazzaville: Dérives politiques, catastrophe humanitaire, désirs de paix.* Paris, Editions Karthala, 1999.

Ayessa, B., Pigasse, J. P. *Brazzaville: Chronique 1999.* Brazzaville, Editions ADIAC, 2000.

Balliff, N. *Le Congo.* Paris, Karthala, 1993.

Decalo, S., Thompson, V., and Adloff, R. *Historical Dictionary of the People's Republic of the Congo.* 3rd Edn. Lanham, MD, Scarecrow Press, 1996.

Ekondy, A. *Le Congo-Brazzaville: essai d'analyse et d'explication sociologiques selon la méthode pluraliste.* Berne, Lang, 1983.

Eliou, M. *La formation de la conscience nationale en République populaire du Congo.* Paris, Anthropos, 1977.

Emerging Markets Investment Center. *Congo Investment and Business Guide.* USA, International Business Publications, 1998.

Fegley, R. *The Congo*. Oxford, Clio Press: World Bibliographic Series, 1993.

Gakosso, G-F. *La réalité congolaise*. Paris, La Pensée Universelle, 1983.

Gide, A. *Travels in the Congo*. Ecco Press, 1994.

Lissouba, P. *Conscience du développement et démocratie*. Dakar, 1975.

Congo: Les fruits de la passion partagée. Paris, Odilon, 1997.

MacGaffrey, J., Bazenguissa-Ganga, R. *Congo-Paris: Transnational Traders on the Margins of the Law*. Oxford James Currey Publishers, 2000.

M'Kaloulou, B. *Dynamique paysanne et développement rural au Congo*. Paris, L'Harmattan, 1984.

Ndaki, G. *Crises, mutations et conflits politiques au Congo-Brazzaville*. Paris, L'Harmattan, 1998.

Obenga, B., Makimouna-Ngoualak, J.C. *Congo-Brazzaville: diagnostic et stratégies pour la création de valeur*. Paris, L'Harmattan, 1999.

Obenga, T. *L'Histoire sanglante du Congo-Brazzaville (1959–1997)*. Paris, Présence Africaine, 1998.

Pigasse, J.-P. *Congo: Chronique d'une guerre annoncée*. Brazzaville, Editions ADIAC, 1998.

Rabut, E. *Brazza, commissaire général. Le Congo français (1886–1897)*. Paris, Editions de l'école des hautes études en sciences sociales, 1989.

Rey, P. P. *Colonialisme, néo-colonialisme et transition au capitalisme. Exemple de la Comilog au Congo-Brazzaville*. Paris, 1971.

Sassou-Nguesso, D. *Le Manguier, le fleuve et la souris*. France, Jean-Claude Lattes, 1997.

Soret, M. *Histoire du Congo*. Paris, Berger-Levrault, 1978.

West, R. *Brazza of the Congo*. Newton Abbot, 1973.

CÔTE D'IVOIRE

Physical and Social Geography

R. J. HARRISON CHURCH

The Republic of Côte d'Ivoire is situated on the west coast of Africa, between Ghana to the east and Liberia to the west, with Guinea, Mali and Burkina Faso to the north. Côte d'Ivoire is economically the most important of the states of sub-Saharan francophone Africa. The country has an area of 322,462 sq km (124,503 sq miles), and at the 1988 census the population was 10,815,694, rising to an estimated 14,292,000 in mid-1998 (giving an average population density of 44.3 inhabitants per sq km). There is a diversity of peoples, with the Agni and Baoulé having cultural and other affinities with the Ashanti of Ghana.

From the border with Liberia eastwards to Fresco, the coast has cliffs, rocky promontories and sandy bays. East of Fresco the rest of the coast is a straight sandbar, backed, as in Benin, by lagoons. None of the seaward river exits is navigable, and a canal was opened from the sea into the Ebrié lagoon at Abidjan only in 1950, after half a century's battle with nature.

Although Tertiary sands and clays fringe the northern edge of the lagoons, they give place almost immediately to Archaean and Pre-Cambrian rocks, which underlie the rest of the country. Diamonds are obtained from gravels south of Korhogo, and near Séguéla, while gold is mined at Ity, in the west. The Man mountains and the Guinea highlands on the border with Liberia and Guinea are the only areas of vigorous relief in the country. Substantial deposits of haematite iron ore may be developed near Man for export through the country's second deep-water port of San Pedro. There is considerable commercial potential for large offshore deposits of petroleum and also of natural gas, exploitation of which began in 1995: Côte d'Ivoire aims to become self-sufficient in (and in the medium-term a net exporter of) hydrocarbons. Plans for the development of nickel reserves are proceeding.

Except for the north-western fifth of Côte d'Ivoire, the country has an equatorial climate. This occurs most typically in the south, which receives annual rainfall of 1,250 mm–2,400 mm, with two maxima, and where the relative humidity is high. Much valuable rain forest survives in the south-west, but elsewhere it has been extensively planted with coffee, cocoa, bananas, pineapple, rubber and oil palm. Tropical climatic conditions prevail in the north-west, with a single rainy season of five to seven months, and 1,250 mm–1,500 mm of rain annually. Guinea savannah occurs here, as well as in the centre of the country, and projects southwards around Bouaké.

Recent History

PIERRE ENGLEBERT

Revised for this edition by RICHARD SYNGE

THE HOUPHOUËT-BOIGNY ERA, 1960–93

From independence from French rule in August 1960 until his death in 1993, political life in Côte d'Ivoire was dominated by Dr Félix Houphouët-Boigny. He was the sole candidate for the presidency at every election until 1990, and (despite constitutional provision for the operation of a multi-party system) his Parti démocratique de la Côte d'Ivoire–Rassemblement démocratique africain (PDCI–RDA) was the only legal political party until the same year. During his years in power, President Houphouët-Boigny guided the economic and political evolution of the country without any effective challenge to his rule. Sporadic political unrest was usually without cohesion, and political patronage was successfully used to defuse potential unrest. From the late 1960s efforts were made to 'Ivorianize' public administration and the economy. None the less, France has remained influential in Côte d'Ivoire's political and economic life, and French financial backing, together with membership of the Franc Zone, has been of major influence in Côte d'Ivoire's economic development. A principal guarantee of the security of the state has, moreover, been in the form of a French military base and joint French-Ivorian military exercises.

Houphouët-Boigny supervised wide-ranging economic and political changes in 1980, following a period of economic and social *malaise*. At that time, the question began to arise of an eventual successor to the ageing president. Although Houphouët-Boigny remained reluctant to nominate a vice-president who would automatically succeed him, two likely contenders came to the fore: Philippe Yacé, a former president of the national assembly and secretary-general of the PDCI–RDA, and Henri Konan Bédié, a former ambassador to the USA and minister of finance. The succession issue re-emerged prior to the October 1985 presidential election, with the abolition of the unfilled post of vice-president in a constitutional amendment that allowed only for the president of the legislature to succeed to the presidency on an interim basis. The declared result of the presidential election was a 100% vote for Houphouët-Boigny, although at legislative elections in the following month only 64 of the incumbent deputies were returned. In January 1986 Bédié was re-elected president of the national assembly, and in February Yacé was elected president of the economic and social council, the country's third most senior political office. (He held this post until his death in November 1998.)

By the end of the 1980s Houphouët-Boigny's disinclination to designate a successor, and the absence of any clear indication of his willingness to retire, continued to suppress open political debate, while engendering considerable rivalry among would-be successors. Meanwhile, the president rejected appeals to activate constitutional provisions permitting a multi-party system, on the grounds that political pluralism would impede progress towards national unity.

In early 1990 Côte d'Ivoire experienced unprecedented political upheaval, doubtless influenced by events elsewhere in the region and compounded by the unresolved succession issue and the prospect of economic austerity that was a precondition for assistance by international creditors. Demonstrations involving students and workers centred on the government's austerity policies. Persistent anti-government unrest led to the deployment of troops in Abidjan, and in April, following the death of a student when troops intervened to disperse demonstrators, all educational establishments were closed and the 1989/90 academic year was declared invalid. Aware that to proceed with proposed levies on income entailed too great a political risk

414

and, moreover, would generate only a small proportion of Côte d'Ivoire's revenue requirements, Houphouët-Boigny appointed Alassane Ouattara, the governor of the Banque centrale des états de l'Afrique de l'ouest (the regional central bank), to head a commission whose function would be to formulate adjustment measures both more economically effective and more politically acceptable. In May, furthermore, Houphouët-Boigny agreed to the establishment of a plural political system. At the end of the month a less stringent programme of austerity measures was announced, based on the recommendations of the Ouattara commission.

Under the newly-sanctioned multi-party system opposition groups that had previously operated unofficially now acquired legal status, and numerous new parties were swiftly formed. However, prior to the presidential and legislative elections, due in late 1990, opposition leaders accused the incumbent regime of impeding the reform process, as Houphouët-Boigny refused to accede to demands for a transitional government and for a national conference to discuss Côte d'Ivoire's political future. Security forces intervened at opposition rallies, and in September Houphouët-Boigny accused his opponents of complicity in an alleged plot to assassinate Pope John Paul II at the time of his visit to Côte d'Ivoire. (During his visit the Pope consecrated a basilica in Yamoussoukro, Houphouët-Boigny's birthplace, constructed—officially at Houphouët-Boigny's own expense—at a cost of some 40,000m. francs CFA.)

Côte d'Ivoire's first contested presidential election took place on 28 October 1990, with Houphouët-Boigny challenged by Laurent Gbagbo, the candidate of the Front populaire ivoirien (FPI). The incumbent was elected for a seventh term of office by, according to the official count, 81.7% of those who voted (69.2% of the electorate). The FPI and its allies appealed unsuccessfully to the supreme court to invalidate the election. In November the national assembly approved two constitutional amendments. The first effectively strengthened Bédié's position by providing for the president of the national assembly to assume the functions of the president of the republic, should this office become vacant, until the expiry of the mandate of the previous incumbent. The second allowed for the appointment of a prime minister, a post subsequently awarded to Alassane Ouattara.

Almost 500 candidates, representing some 17 parties, contested the parliamentary elections on 25 November 1990. According to the official results, the PDCI–RDA secured 163 seats in the new legislature, while the FPI won nine (Gbagbo was among the successful FPI candidates). Francis Wodié, the leader of the Parti ivoirien des travailleurs (PIT), was also elected, as were two independent candidates. The incoming national assembly reconfirmed Bédié as its president.

Dissension, Repression and Succession

In May 1991 security forces used violent methods to disperse a students' meeting at the University of Abidjan. Students and academic staff joined demonstrations in protest against the forces' brutality, prompting further intervention by the security forces. The situation deteriorated in June, when members of the Fédération estudiantine et scolaire de Côte d'Ivoire (FESCI) attacked and killed a student who had defied an order to boycott classes. The government ordered that the students' association be disbanded, and deployed security forces on the campus. In July the arrest of 11 students on suspicion of involvement in the death prompted further protests. Tensions eased in August, when the government withdrew troops from the campus and suspended legal proceedings against FESCI activists (although the ban on the students' union remained). However, the political and social climate again deteriorated following the publication, in January 1992, of the findings of a commission of inquiry into the security forces' actions at the university. Although the commission found the chief of the general staff of the armed forces, Gen. Robert Guéï, directly responsible for the acts of violence committed by his troops, Houphouët-Boigny expressed his support for Guéï, and emphasized that neither he nor any of those incriminated by the report would be subject to disciplinary proceedings. Violent demonstrations by FESCI supporters immediately erupted at the university, while opposition parties demanded sanctions against Guéï and called on the government to resign. In February 16 FESCI activists, including the union's

secretary-general, were arrested. A demonstration, organized by the FPI, degenerated into violence, and more than 100 protesters were arrested following clashes with security forces. Among those detained were Gbagbo and René Degny-Segui, the president of the Ligue ivoirienne des droits de l'homme; it was announced that they and other opposition leaders would be prosecuted under the terms of a new presidential ordinance that rendered political leaders responsible for acts of violence committed by their supporters. In late February the FESCI leader was fined and sentenced to three years' imprisonment, convicted of reconstituting a banned organization and of responsibility for acts of vandalism committed by students earlier in the month. In March Gbagbo, Degny-Segui and seven others were each fined and sentenced to two-year prison terms. As the trials continued, opposition deputies began a boycott of the national assembly. In July Houphouët-Boigny (who had recently returned to Côte d'Ivoire after an absence, spent mainly in France, of almost five months) declared an amnesty for all those convicted of political offences since the time of the 1990 disturbances. However, the opposition protested that the amnesty not only prevented detainees from pursuing the right of appeal, but also exempted members of the security forces from charges relating to alleged offences committed during this period.

Houphouët-Boigny left Côte d'Ivoire in May 1993, and subsequently spent six months receiving medical treatment in France and Switzerland. As the president's health failed, controversy was revived concerning the issue of succession. Ouattara and Gbagbo (both of whom were known to have presidential ambitions) were among prominent politicians who denounced the process defined in the constitution, alleging that it effectively endorsed an hereditary presidency—Bédié, like Houphouët-Boigny, was a member of the Baoulé ethnic group from a family of chiefs and cocoa-planters.

President Houphouët-Boigny died in Yamoussoukro on 7 December 1993. Later the same day Henri Konan Bédié made a television broadcast announcing that he was assuming the duties of president of the republic, with immediate effect, in accordance with the constitution. Ouattara initially refused to recognize Bédié's right of succession, but resigned the premiership two days later, after France assumed what was widely regarded as a decisive role in the matter by acknowledging Bédié's legitimacy as president. Daniel Kablan Duncan, hitherto minister-delegate, responsible for the economy, finance and planning, was appointed prime minister. In January 1994 Charles Donwahi was elected president of the national assembly; a prominent member of the PDCI–RDA, he had been vice-president of the legislature since 1991.

THE BÉDIÉ PRESIDENCY

Several months of sporadic labour unrest were brought to an end by Houphouët-Boigny's death, and, largely owing to the two-month period of national mourning, reactions to the 50% devaluation, in January 1994, of the CFA franc were generally more muted in Côte d'Ivoire than in other countries of the region. Despite Bédié's earlier criticism of Ouattara's economic policies, notably the dismantling of the state-owned sector, the new president and prime minister confirmed their commitment to adjustment measures initiated under Ouattara, and accelerated privatization was a major element of financial programmes agreed with international creditors in the mid-1990s. Meanwhile, Bédié conducted an effective purge of Ouattara sympathizers, appointing his own supporters to positions of influence in government agencies, the judiciary and in the state-owned media. Ouattara was, moreover, the subject of virulent attacks in the official daily newspaper, *Fraternité Matin*, which emphasized both his Muslim and Burkinabè origins. Furthermore, the new regime made use of far-reaching legislation governing the press (introduced under Houphouët-Boigny) to prosecute several journalists who were deemed to have been disrespectful to Bédié or to other state officials.

Bédié was elected chairman of the PDCI–RDA in April 1994. His position as head of state was further strengthened by Ouattara's departure for Washington, DC, to take up the post of deputy managing director of the IMF. In June a group of Ouattara loyalists left the PDCI–RDA to form what they termed a moderate, centrist organization, the Rassemblement des républicains (RDR). By the end of the year the new party had supplanted the FPI as the principal parliamentary opposition. Ouattara officially announced his membership of the RDR in early 1995.

The increase in violent crime in Côte d'Ivoire was of particular concern to the Bédié government, and in June 1995 the national assembly approved proposals for legislation permitting the extension of the death penalty (already in existence for murder convictions, although there was no record of its implementation since independence) to cases of robbery with violence. New security operations accompanying the government's anti-crime measures, which frequently targeted non-Ivorian groups, were denounced by Bédié's opponents as indicative of the regime's xenophobic tendencies.

Considerable controversy was caused by the adoption, in December 1994, of a new electoral code, in preparation for the following year's presidential and legislative elections. Opposition parties denounced clauses imposing restrictions on eligibility for public office, in particular requirements that candidates be of direct Ivorian descent and have been continuously resident in Côte d'Ivoire for five years prior to seeking election, both of which were interpreted as being directly aimed at preventing Ouattara from contesting the presidency. The opposition organized several mass demonstrations in Abidjan in mid-1995 to demand the reform of the electoral code and, to reduce government control over the election process, the establishment of an independent electoral commission, as well as the revision of voters' lists. An FPI congress formally adopted Gbagbo as its candidate for the presidency, while the RDR invited Ouattara to stand as its presidential candidate; Ouattara, none the less, announced that he would not attempt to contest the presidency in violation of the law. The PDCI–RDA officially adopted Bédié as the party's presidential candidate. In September, citing the need to ensure the continuation of economic activity, the government imposed a three-month ban on political demonstrations. Opposition groups protested that this was in violation of constitutional recognition of the right to demonstrate, and clashes between demonstrators and security forces persisted.

As the presidential election approached both the FPI and the RDR (whose secretary-general, Djény Kobina, had been expected to replace Ouattara as the party's candidate) stated that they would not be contesting the election as long as the conditions were not 'clear and open'; however, Wodié intended to contest the presidency as the candidate of the PIT. An eruption of violence in Abidjan and in other major towns in early October 1995 was apparently timed to coincide with the opening of an international investment forum in Abidjan. At a meeting between Bédié and representatives of almost 90 political parties, the president reiterated his administration's refusal to submit to opposition demands for the withdrawal of the electoral code, for the postponement of the elections, and for the formation of a transitional government of national unity. No effective progress was made in subsequent meetings between Bédié and opposition parties, and the latter refused to accept a government offer to include opposition representatives on the commission responsible for scrutinizing voters' lists and the results of the elections as sufficient guarantee of the commission's autonomy. Meanwhile, several opposition activists were fined and sentenced to one-year prison terms, convicted of involvement in disturbances.

The 1995 Elections

The presidential election took place, as scheduled, on 22 October 1995, following a week of violent incidents in several towns. The opposition, grouped in a Front républicain (FR), claimed that its call for an 'active boycott' of the poll had been largely successful (despite appeals by Wodié for the opposition vote), while the government claimed that voters had participated both peacefully and in large numbers. Troops were deployed, ostensibly to prevent the disruption of voting by the opposition, although it was reported that polling had proceeded in only one of 60 designated centres in the FPI stronghold of Gagnoa, in the Centre-Ouest region. The official results of the presidential election were announced by the constitutional council five days after the poll. As had been expected, Bédié, with 95.2% of the valid votes cast, secured an overwhelming victory. While most

areas remained generally calm following the election, the apparent persecution of Baoulé around Gagnoa by members of the local majority Bété ethnic group became a cause of considerable concern, as large numbers of Baoulé converged on the town of Gagnoa from surrounding areas. More than 3,500 people, mainly Baoulé, were displaced, and numerous settlements destroyed.

Efforts were intensified to reach an accommodation between the government and opposition prior to the legislative elections, which were scheduled for 26 November 1995. Following a series of discussions, in early November it was announced that the FR had agreed to abandon its threatened boycott of the elections, in return for government concessions regarding the revision of voters' lists; representatives of both the FPI and the RDR were subsequently appointed to the electoral commission. The two principal opposition parties were, however, unable to agree terms for the presentation of a single list of candidates for the national assembly, and submitted separate lists for approval. The opposition suffered a further reverse when the authorities announced that voting in three of Gagnoa's four constituencies, including the constituency that was to have been contested by Gbagbo, was to be postponed, owing to the disruption arising from the recent disturbances; moreover, Kobina's candidacy (in Abidjan's Adjamé constituency) was disallowed, on the grounds that he had been unable to prove direct Ivorian descent. Voting for the legislature was reported to have proceeded generally without incident, and the earliest indications were that the PDCI–RDA had retained a decisive majority. There were clear ethno-geographical trends in the distribution of votes, with a notable loss of support for the PDCI–RDA in the Nord region, in favour of the RDR. The FPI, as expected, secured strong representation in the Centre-Ouest region, while the PDCI–RDA secured overwhelming victories in the Centre, Ouest and Sud-Ouest regions, and had strong support in Abidjan and other major towns. In late December the constitutional council annulled the results of the elections in three constituencies, including the one seat in Gagnoa for which voting had been permitted. The PDCI–RDA thus held 146 seats, the RDR 14, and the FPI nine. (Wodié failed to secure re-election for the PIT.) Donwahi was re-elected president of the national assembly.

In October 1995, shortly before the presidential election, Gen. Gueï was appointed to the government as minister of employment and the civil service. He was replaced in his armed forces command by his former deputy, Cdre Lassana Timité. Duncan reshuffled his government in January 1996. Léon Konan Koffi was transferred from the post of minister of defence to that of minister of state responsible for religious affairs and dialogue with the opposition, while Gueï became minister of sports. At local elections in February the PDCI–RDA won control of 158 communes (of a total of 195); the RDR secured 19 (mainly northern) communes, and the FPI 13 (principally in the west). Electoral turn-out was, however, low.

Undercurrents of Unrest

Reports emerged in the independent press in May 1996 of a coup attempt by disaffected members of the armed forces at the time of the civil unrest that preceded the 1995 presidential election. Gueï's demotion to a relatively minor government post was thus now interpreted as a reaction to unrest in the forces under his command. The minister of defence, Bandama N'Gatta, subsequently referred in a televised statement to 'disloyal' actions within the military in September and October 1995. Later in May 1996 the Ivorian authorities denounced a report by a prominent human rights organization, Amnesty International, in which it was alleged that opposition members in Côte d'Ivoire were, notably since the 1995 election campaign, the target of systematic repression. In the following month *La Voie*, a newspaper closely linked with the FPI (its director, Abou Drahamane Sangaré, also being the party's secretary-general) reported the release, on appeal, of several opposition members who had been detained during pre-election unrest and subsequently convicted in unpublicized trials. The release on bail of further detainees was reported by the same journal in October. *La Voie* also drew attention to the death in custody of several opposition activists who had been arrested in connection with the so-called 'active boycott'.

Meanwhile, the issue of press censorship was again brought to the fore by the imprisonment, in late 1995 and early 1996, of journalists linked to the opposition. Most notably, Sangaré was, together with two other journalists of *La Voie*, sentenced to two years' imprisonment for publishing an article deemed insulting to the head of state. In August 1996 it was announced that these three had refused to submit to preconditions for their release under a presidential amnesty, whereby they would be required to write directly to the head of state seeking a pardon and renouncing any appeal against sentence: in June the court of appeal had confirmed their convictions, and a higher appeal was rejected by the supreme court in November. They were, none the less, pardoned by Bédié in December.

A reorganization of government portfolios in August 1996 appeared to reflect both Bédié's desire to remove from positions of influence figures connected with the insecurity prior to the 1995 elections and his concern to strengthen national security. Among those to leave the government were Guéï, Koffi and Gaston Ouassénan Koné (hitherto minister of security). A new minister of justice and public freedom was appointed, and the secretary-general of the country's new national security council took the rank of minister-delegate to the presidency. In November 1996 the government announced the dismissal or suspension of several members of the armed forces, in accordance with investigations by a military commission into what was now seemingly confirmed as a destabilization plot. In January 1997 Guéï was dismissed from the army: a government communiqué stated that the investigative commission had found that the then armed forces chief had committed 'serious disciplinary offences' in the discharge of his duties. In March it was announced that Bédié had ordered the release from custody of members of the military detained in connection with the events of late 1995.

In October 1996, addressing a congress of the PDCI–RDA, Bédié advocated the opening of government to the parliamentary and non-parliamentary opposition. A commission of inquiry into the 1995 pre-election unrest was inaugurated in December 1996. The RDR and the FPI refused to take up their allotted seats, however, protesting that the opposition had been judged responsible in advance of the inquiry. By-elections for eight parliamentary seats (including those for which voting did not take place or was cancelled in 1995) took place in that month: the FPI won five seats, and the PDCI–RDA three.

After a period of relative calm, there was severe disruption in the higher education sector from late 1996, as students in Abidjan began a protest against the late payment of grants and to demand a modified examinations system. In January 1997 three members of the outlawed FESCI were fined and sentenced to two years' imprisonment, convicted of causing a disturbance outside the ministry of security. Later in the month a student died while fleeing police who disrupted a FESCI meeting, and shortly afterwards, on the eve of a planned boycott of classes, two students were seriously injured in clashes with security forces at the Yopougon campus. The arrest of several leading members of FESCI in February prompted further protests, but tensions were temporarily defused at the end of the month, when Bédié issued a decree pardoning the three students sentenced in January (after they had abandoned their appeal against sentence) and ordering the release of all detained student activists. The establishment was additionally announced of a permanent committee to mediate or arbitrate in future disputes. In April, none the less, disturbances at the University of Bouaké prompted the government to announce the closure of the university and its halls of residence. FESCI began a boycott of classes, and in May the authorities ordered the closure of university residences in Abidjan, owing to persistent disturbances; lectures were to continue, and the resumption of classes at Bouaké was announced at the end of the month. The university year was extended until December, in view of the disruption of recent months, but many students failed to return to classes at the beginning of the new term in September. In October, however, following national consultations on higher education, Bédié revoked the ban on FESCI, and the students' union announced an end to the boycott of classes.

In an interview published by the French journal, *Jeune Afrique,* in mid-1997, Gbagbo stated that, of some 450 opposition activists questioned in connection with election violence in 1995, 70 remained in detention without trial. Most of those detained as a result of the 'active boycott' were released under the terms of a presidential amnesty announced in August 1997; it was reported that 34 people convicted of serious offences (including 13 found guilty of murder) remained in detention in Gagnoa.

Institutional Reforms

Bédié inaugurated the national security council in early August 1997, emphasizing that Côte d'Ivoire's political stability and economic development depended on guaranteed national security and effective measures to combat crime. He also announced that a general audit of the military was to be undertaken, with a view to restructuring, and that the armed forces were to be given additional responsibilities in countering illegal immigration, smuggling and organized crime, as well as in areas such as humanitarian assistance. Opponents of the government denounced the council, which was to be directly responsible to the head of state, as a means of supporting the regime through espionage, intelligence and propaganda.

Charles Donwahi died in early August 1997; he was succeeded as national assembly president by Emile Brou, hitherto the legislature's deputy president.

Wide-ranging constitutional amendments, involving changes to some 40 of the existing document's 76 articles, were approved by a plenary session of the national assembly in late June 1998. The session was boycotted by the RDR, and FPI deputies left the chamber during the debate: the opposition parties objected, in particular, to provisions conferring wider powers on the head of state—specifically a clause allowing the president to delay elections, or the proclamation of election results, on the grounds of 'events, serious troubles or *force majeure*'. The presidential mandate was, furthermore, to be extended to seven years, with no limit on the number of times an incumbent might seek re-election. Conditions of eligibility to seek public office were to be enshrined in the constitution for the first time: most notably, candidates would be required to be Ivorian by birth, of direct Ivorian descent, and to have been continuously resident in Côte d'Ivoire for 10 years. The opposition also denounced arrangements for the composition of a new upper house of the legislature, whereby two-thirds of the members of the new senate were to be indirectly elected and the remainder appointed by the head of state. In early September 1998 Gbagbo and Kobina led a demonstration in Abidjan to denounce the amendments. The government denied foreign radio reports of 15,000 protesters, citing estimates by the security forces of no more than 4,000 participants.

A reorganization of the government in early March 1998 was notable for the appointment of Adama Coulibaly, the deputy secretary-general of the RDR, to the post of minister of transport. Coulibaly's decision to join the government was denounced by the RDR, which emphasized that his appointment had not been sanctioned by the party; Coulibaly was subseqently expelled from the RDR. A further reorganization of the council of ministers in August included the appointment of the PIT leader, Francis Wodié, as minister of higher education and scientific research.

At the end of September 1998 it was reported that Bédié was contemplating granting amnesty to the remainder of those detained in connection with the 1995 'active boycott'. This was expected to apply to 26 detainees, including 13 sentenced to life imprisonment. Bédié subsequently sought contacts with the opposition, with the expressed aim of promoting national reconciliation. In mid-December, it was reported that the PDCI–RDA and the FPI had reached an agreement on democracy and good governance. The authorities agreed to submit a draft amnesty law to the national assembly, together with legislation governing the funding of political parties during elections and the establishment of a national electoral commission. The accord was described by Bédié as a major breakthrough for participatory democracy. Consultations between the government and the RDR, with a view to a similar accord, began in March 1999, but reportedly foundered after only two sessions. The RDR was now led by Henriette Dagba Diabaté, who had assumed the post of party secretary-general following the death, in October 1998, of Djény Kobina. At Kobina's funeral Ouattara, who earlier in the year had announced that he would return to Côte d'Ivoire in mid-1999, upon the expiry of his contract with the IMF, confirmed his intention to contest the presidency at the election due at the end of 2000. The former premier expressed confidence that the rules on eligibility which might prevent his candidacy would have been amended by such time.

There was renewed unrest involving FESCI from April 1999, as students and school pupils boycotted classes in support of demands regarding tuition fees and the disbursement of scholarships and other allowances. Progress apparently made at meetings involving representatives of FESCI and the ministers responsible for secondary and higher education in mid-May was undermined later in the month when five university students and one secondary school pupil were each sentenced to five years' imprisonment for disrupting law and order. At the end of the month, following further demonstrations, the government ordered the closure of all university campuses, asserting that many rooms in halls of residence were, with the collusion of FESCI, being occupied by non-students, and that stockpiles of weapons had been found on campus. FESCI denied these allegations, and strike action proceeded, despite a government ban, in Abidjan and Bouaké from the beginning of June. Meanwhile, it was reported that security forces were seeking actively to apprehend the FESCI leader, Charles Blé Goudé. In late June, following a meeting between Bédié and FESCI, in the presence of the country's religious leaders, the students' strike was suspended pending efforts to secure a lasting settlement of the education crisis. Meanwhile, FESCI continued to demand the release of the detained activists and the reopening of university campuses. Goudé was arrested in late August.

Civil servants joined a 48-hour general strike in early December 1998, and industrial unrest involving various sectors of the public sector continued sporadically throughout the first half of 1999. In mid-June the two main trade union syndicates gave notice of a three-day general strike, after talks with Bédié failed to produce a satisfactory resolution of demands including salary increases and the payment of arrears totalling 3,000m. francs CFA, together with efforts to expedite the processing of pensions and other welfare commitments.

The government was reorganized in mid-August 1999, following the dismissal of ministers responsible for national education, employment and health. The departure of the minister of public health, Maurice Kakou Guikahue, was apparently in connection with the misappropriation, revealed in an audit conducted within the European Union (EU) of EU aid, amounting to some 17,900m. francs CFA, allocated for health care projects. Bédié, who had recently announced renewed efforts to counter corruption in public life, undertook to ensure the repayment of the missing funds.

In August 1999 Alassane Ouattara, who had returned to the country from the USA in July, and who had acquired a certificate confirming his Ivorian identity, was selected as the RDR's presidential candidate. Thereafter the long-simmering confrontation between Bédié and Ouattara quickly escalated, as Bédié continued to insist that he regarded his rival as a Burkinabè citizen and warned that he would suppress any protests on his behalf. When Ouattara's claim to citizenship was subjected to a new inquiry by judicial police, clashes occurred in mid-September between police and supporters of Ouattara in Abidjan. Further demonstrations partly paralysed the city later in the month.

In late October 1999 a court in Dimbokro, Ouattara's birthplace, cancelled his nationality certificate. The news prompted further violent demonstrations in Abidjan, and after some damage to buildings and property was carried out, the authorities ordered the arrest of a number of senior RDR leaders present at the scene. The party's general secretary, Henriette Dagba Diabaté, was among those subsequently found guilty of inciting violence and was sentenced to two years' imprisonment. In early December, while Ouattara was in Paris publicly denouncing the government's actions, a warrant was issued for his arrest.

BRIG.-GEN. GUEÏ ASSUMES POWER

With Bédié's authority and his personal popularity rapidly declining, a mutiny amongst soldiers who converged on Abidjan on 23 December 1999 quickly escalated into a national crisis. The president initially sought to appease the soldiers with the promise of improved pay and conditions; however, the troops subsequently altered their demands to include the reinstatement of Brig.-Gen. Robert Gueï, a popular former army chief of

staff, who had been dismissed by Bédié in October 1995 after his refusal to involve his troops in maintaining order during that year's election campaign. The soldiers, who seized most public buildings, demonstrated their control of the city by firing automatic weapons.

On 24 December 1999 Gueï agreed, after some initial hesitation, to involve himself in the crisis, and having initially described himself as a 'spokesman' for the mutineers, moved quickly to establish a Comité national de salut publique (CNSP) to govern the country. Bédié fled to the French embassy, from where he moved to a French military base. The unexpected coup was apparently widely welcomed within Côte d'Ivoire, where the Bédié regime had been increasingly regarded as authoritarian and corrupt, and Bédié's last hopes of rallying support failed when the commanders of the *gendarmerie* announced their support for the *coup d'état* and deployed their forces in the city on 25 December to prevent looting, which had become widespread. The brief prospect of French military intervention, ostensibly to carry out an evacuation of French nationals, was avoided when Gueï successfully negotiated with the French ambassador Bédié's departure from Libreville, Gabon, on board a French military helicopter. In separate statements of support for the coup, both the RDR and FPI leaders speedily returned to Côte d'Ivoire from their Christmas engagements abroad. France was also quick to accept the coup; the French secretary of state responsible for co-operation, Charles Josselin, stated that his government would establish a dialogue with the new authorities, and noted that France would 'no longer intervene in internal political debates'.

The new authorities rapidly succeeded in restoring order and calm following the events of late December 1999. The CNSP did not at first announce a timetable for a return to civilian rule, but, after having swiftly released the RDR's imprisoned leaders, it was initially interpreted as being solidly behind Ouattara, especially as Intendant-Gen. Lassana Palenfo, a prominent member of the CNSP, had previously held a ministerial portfolio in Ouattara's government. The subsequent formation of an all-party government in January 2000 provoked prolonged disagreements, particularly with the FPI, which, as a result, was eventually better represented than either the RDR or the PDCI—RDA (the latter, in protest at the *coup d'état*, did not officially approve the participation of two of its members in the new government). Several prominent members of the previous government, and a number of senior military officers, continued to be held in detention, despite protests from foreign governments and non-governmental organizations.

In late January 2000 Gueï promised that fresh presidential and legislative elections would be held before 31 October 2000, following a proposed referendum on a new constitution, to be held in July. As the parties, with the exception of the PDCI—RDA, hurriedly confirmed their presidential candidates, the CNSP imposed a temporary ban on political gatherings until after the referendum. Despite the ban, a group of influential PDCI—RDA members began to canvas openly for Gueï himself to stand as the presidential candidate of the former ruling party, although Gueï seemed reluctant to declare his intentions publicly.

The publication of the draft constitution in May 2000 provoked a renewed political crisis, as the articles referring to the eligibility of candidates for the presidency restated the previous position that only candidates with Ivorian nationality and Ivorian parents could stand. In reaction to the protests of the RDR about the clause, which seemed designed to prevent Ouattara's candidacy, Gueï announced a government reshuffle, in which all of the RDR ministers, with the exception of the party's secretary-general, Henriette Dagba Diabaté, were dismissed from their posts. In the reshuffle Gueï also appointed a prime minister, Seydou Diarra. In the same month the authorities in Côte d'Ivoire issued an international warrant for the arrest of former president Bédié, who was living in exile in France, on charges of embezzlement.

In early July 2000 groups of soldiers demanding bonus payments from the transitional government for their part in the December coup mutinied and took to the streets of Abidjan and Bouaké, firing their weapons, and demanding money from residents and businesses. After two days of disturbances, it was announced that the government had reached an agreement with the mutineers, who had returned to barracks. The authorities, who claimed that the protests were in fact an attempt to overthrow the CNSP, subsequently ordered the arrest of 35 soldiers and of four members of the RDR, who were briefly detained on charges of complicity in the troops' actions. A number of soldiers were subsequently sentenced to prison terms for their part in the disturbances.

Despite the earlier unrest and an atmosphere of prevailing tension throughout the country, the referendum on the revised constitution proceeded in relative calm on 23 July 2000, although serious organizational difficulties caused voting to carry on into a second day. It was subsequently announced that 86.5% of voters had expressed their support for the new constitution, which had been supported by all the major parties, and which, among other clauses, granted immunity from prosecution to members of the CNSP and to all those involved in the *coup d'état*. Turn-out in the referendum was estimated at some 56%.

Presidential Elections

In July 2000 a former teacher, Jonas Aka, a citizen of both Côte d'Ivoire and France, who had reportedly intended to stand in the forthcoming presidential election, announced his intention to challenge the new constitution at the United Nations, claiming that the restrictions on the eligibility of presidential candidates violated the right, enshrined in international law, of every citizen to stand for public office. In the same month Ouattara, who asserted that he complied with all the restrictions on eligibility, announced his intention to contest the presidential election, scheduled for 17 September, as the RDR candidate. Former president Bédié also announced that he intended to seek the nomination of the PDCI—RDA, although Gueï was reported to have refused to grant permission for Bédié's return from France.

In early August 2000 Gueï, who had been asked to stand for president by the country's traditional chiefs, surprised observers by also applying to become the candidate of the PDCI—RDA, which was to select its candidate at a conference in mid-August. Gueï's decision to contest the presidency was criticized by France and by the USA as detrimental to the likelihood of the election's being free and fair, although it was believed that Côte d'Ivoire's neighbours were prepared to accept Gueï's candidacy provided that Ouattara was also allowed to stand. In mid-August Gueï announced that the country's four main political parties had agreed in advance to form a coalition government of national unity following the legislative elections. In the same month Gueï announced that he was, contrary to previous reports, to contest the election as an independent. Nineteen other candidates, including Ouattara and Bédié, were also to stand in the election, which was subsequently postponed until 22 October.

In mid-September 2000 members of the armed forces, angered by the late payment of bonuses and by Gueï's decision to stand for president, attacked Gueï's residence, killing two of his bodyguards. Troops loyal to Gueï successfully repelled the mutineers, several of whom were later arrested. The opposition denied any involvement in the attack, which contributed to an atmosphere of extreme tension prior to the presidential election.

FOREIGN RELATIONS AND REGIONAL CONCERNS

Throughout his presidency Houphouët-Boigny was active in regional and international affairs, assisting in the peace process in Angola and, despite strong criticism by the Organization of African Unity (OAU), favouring black African dialogue with the apartheid regime in South Africa. In regional affairs, Côte d'Ivoire under Houphouët-Boigny exerted a strong conservative influence, and tended to favour the maintenance of close links with the West. Relations with France were generally close, and remained cordial following Bédié's accession to the presidency. It was further believed that France had exerted influence over Ouattara not to disrupt the electoral process in Côte d'Ivoire by seeking to contest the presidency in defiance of the law. In 1997 the Bédié administration received assurances from France that France would assist Côte d'Ivoire both in restructuring its armed forces and in establishing a centre for the training of African military personnel for peace-keeping operations. Ivorian troops joined the UN peace-keeping mission in the Central African Republic in April 1998: this was Côte d'Ivoire's first involvement in such an operation.

In 1999 the deterioration in the political situation in Côte d'Ivoire attracted considerable concern among the country's regional and international allies, and in mid-November it was suggested that the Bédié administration's emphasis on the promotion of a sense of nation or 'ivoirité' had helped to provoke outbreaks of violence against Burkinabè migrant workers, who were systematically expelled in November from areas bordering Burkina Faso by indigenous militants. None the less, despite international disapproval of many of the aspects of the Bédié regime, the *coup d'état* in December, which brought Brig.-Gen. Robert Gueï to power, was widely condemned by France, the USA and the OAU, although intervention to restore Bédié was ruled out. In January 2000 the OAU ordered the military regime to announce a schedule for democratic elections or face exclusion from the OAU summit, to be held in July. Gueï subsequently undertook an intensive series of meetings with regional heads of state in order to explain his view of the situation in Côte d'Ivoire and to request their support for the process of transition to democratic rule. Gueï also requested Western governments not to reduce assistance to Côte d'Ivoire. In July, however, reports that the French secretary of state responsible for co-operation, Charles Josselin, had demanded that the Ivorian authorities permit Alassane Ouattara to stand for president, while suggesting that France would disapprove of Gueï's candidacy, provoked violent anti-French demonstrations in Abidjan. Gueï's subsequent announcement that he intended to stand for president was criticized by the international community, and it seemed likely that much international support for Côte d'Ivoire would depend upon the conduct of the presidential and legislative elections scheduled to be held later that year.

Despite considerable evidence to the contrary, Houphouët-Boigny consistently denied that his government was supporting Charles Taylor's National Patriotic Front of Liberia (NPFL), which was instrumental in the overthrow of President Doe in mid-1990 (q.v.). The presence in Côte d'Ivoire of large numbers of refugees from Liberia was increasingly cited by the Ivorian authorities as a cause of the perceived escalation in insecurity in the country, and periodic incursions onto Ivorian territory by members of armed factions in the Liberian conflict provoked considerable disquiet. In mid-1995 Côte d'Ivoire, which had hitherto tended to promote the full integration of refugees into Ivorian society (a process facilitated by the common ethnic origin of communities on both sides of the Côte d'Ivoire–Liberia border), announced the establishment of the first reception centre for Liberian refugees at Guiglo, and stated that further camps would be established. In early 1996 the Ivorian authorities announced that security measures were to be increased in the west (in an effort to prevent further rebel incursions and the infiltration of refugee groups by Liberian fighters, and in July the government proclaimed western Côte d'Ivoire to be a military 'operational zone', extending the powers of the armed forces to act in response to rebel activity. The installation of elected organs of state in Liberia in 1997 facilitated the return of refugees; the office of the UN High Commissioner for Refugees put the number of Liberian refugees in Côte d'Ivoire at 119,900 at the end of 1998, compared with 327,700 at the end of 1996. It was intended that the full repatriation of Liberian refugees should be completed by the end of December 1999.

The reinforcement of security and military operations in western Côte d'Ivoire also followed a period of concern regarding the integrity of the border with Guinea (the demarcation of part of which had long been disputed by the latter). Bilateral relations had been strained in August 1995, after Guinea established a border post in an area assumed to be part of Ivorian territory, claiming the need to prevent incursions into Guinea by Liberian rebels. Despite an announcement in September that the two countries were to co-operate in resolving this and other joint border issues, it was reported in March 1996 that Guinean soldiers had occupied a village in the Sipilou sub-prefecture. Ivorian troops in the region were mobilized in preparation for a military response, although Côte d'Ivoire's minister of defence reaffirmed his government's desire to resolve such border disputes through dialogue.

Economy

EDITH HODGKINSON

For some 20 years following its independence, Côte d'Ivoire was remarkable for its very high rate of economic growth: gross domestic product (GDP) increased, in real terms, at an average annual rate of 11% in 1960–70 and 6%–7% in 1970–80, bringing it into the ranks of middle-income developing countries. During the 1980s, however, the economy entered a period of overall decline, which lasted until the early 1990s. Initially, the economy contracted because of the severe drought of 1982–84 and the weakening in international prices for the country's major export commodities (cocoa and coffee). After a brief return to growth, in 1985 and 1986, as a result of good harvests and higher world prices for most of the country's export commodities, the deterioration in international commodity prices resulted in a decline or stagnation in GDP for seven consecutive years (1987–93). There had been considerable optimism regarding prospects for the Ivorian economy in 1991 with the implementation of a far-reaching programme of structural reform, involving the acceptance by Côte d'Ivoire of an IMF/World Bank programme of fiscal austerity and market liberalization (including the disengagement of the state from both production and service sectors). The 'Plan Ouattara' had ambitious targets: an increase of 5% in GDP by 1995, a doubling in the rate of investment growth, and a reduction by more than one-half in the deficit on the current account of the balance of payments. However, even with financial support from foreign donors and creditors, none of these targets had been achieved by the time Alassane Ouattara relinquished the premiership at the end of 1993. By late 1994, however, a marked recovery was in progress, with GDP growth for the whole year reaching 1.8%, then accelerating to an average of 6.3% per year in 1995–98. The critical factor was the 50% devaluation of the CFA franc in January 1994, which improved the competitiveness, in price terms, of Côte d'Ivoire's timber and non-traditional exports such as fish and rubber at a time when a boom in international prices for coffee was coming to an end. With the programme of structural adjustment well entrenched, the Bédié administration's very positive attitude towards foreign investment, and the major debt relief facilitated by the new Enhanced Structural Adjustment Facility (ESAF) that was accorded by the IMF in February 1998, GDP growth was expected to maintain a robust pace for the remainder of the decade through into the next decade. However, the sharp fall in cocoa and coffee prices in 1999 held GDP growth down to 4.3% in that year, and the expectation was of a further deceleration in the rate of economic growth in 2000, as the military coup in December 1999 was expected to depress inflows of foreign capital, both official and private.

Strong economic growth in the past was a major factor in raising the rate of population growth, to about 3.6% per year, in the late 1980s and early 1990s, one of the highest rates in the world. Expanding employment opportunities attracted immigrants from less prosperous neighbouring countries, particularly Burkina Faso, Guinea and Mali, and immigrants came to constitute almost 40% of the population, providing vital manpower for plantations and urban services. The rate of population growth has slowed recently, however, to an estimated 2% annually, reflecting a decline in the fertility rate and the incidence of AIDS (Côte d'Ivoire is thought to have the highest rate of HIV/AIDS infection in West Africa, at 10% of adults, according to UN estimates in late 1997). The latest UN estimates put the population at 14.6m. in 1998. The rate of urban growth has been rapid (one-half again the overall rate of population growth), with some 44% of the population residing in urban areas in 1995—more than double the proportion in 1960. Abidjan's population was estimated at 3.2m. in 1998, or almost one-quarter of the population. This pressure on Abidjan was a significant factor in the designation of Yamoussoukro as the country's new political capital, although Abidjan remains the principal centre for economic activity.

AGRICULTURE, FORESTRY AND FISHING

Although the Ivorian economy is relatively diversified, it remains dependent on agriculture, which contributes about 30% of GDP and employs some 60%–80% of the economically active population. Agriculture provides about three-quarters of export earnings, and the sector's rapid growth was the basis for the economic expansion of the 1960s and 1970s.

Coffee was formerly the leading cash crop, providing the main source of income for about one-half of Ivorians. However, it has been superseded since the beginning of the 1980s by cocoa, production of which doubled between 1970 and 1979, making Côte d'Ivoire the largest exporter in the world. The country has been the world's largest cocoa producer since 1977/78, when its level of production overtook that of Ghana. Overall output continued to rise, with some fluctuations, reaching a record 1.26m. metric tons in 1995/96 (in the previous four years the crop had averaged 750,000 tons per year). Output was running only slightly below this level, at an average of 1.11m. tons per year, during the following four years. This increase in the cocoa harvest owes much to a major replanting programme implemented by the government in the 1980s, aimed at eliminating ageing cultivation in the traditional cocoa belt, in the south-east, and developing it in the west, where rainfall is abundant. The expansion in cocoa production was also attributable to the transfer to the cultivation of cocoa by many former coffee producers: until 1989 the two crops attracted virtually the same producer price, although the latter was more heavily taxed and is more difficult to grow.

Output of coffee, of which Côte d'Ivoire is among the largest African producers, reached a record level of some 367,000 tons in 1980/81. It has since been in overall decline, and averaged only some 166,000 tons per year in 1991–95, when three-quarters of the country's coffee plants had passed their most productive age. Thus, the surge in international coffee prices in 1993–94 and the leeway provided by the currency devaluation, which allowed increases in the price paid to producers, elicited a relatively modest response in terms of Ivorian output: the crop in 1995/96 was 177,000 tons. By 1996/97 the strength of prices had stimulated a sharp improvement in output, to 323,000 tons. However, production then declined sharply in 1997/98 and 1998/99 (to only 130,000 tons), as a result of both the production cycle and some further switching into cultivation of cocoa because of the narrowing in price differentials (see below). The crop in the latter year was also adversely affected by dry weather. Better climatic conditions were expected to result in a recovery in output, to 269,000 tons, in 1999/2000.

A state marketing agency, the Caisse de stabilisation et de soutien des prix des productions agricoles (Caistab), traditionally purchased all cocoa and coffee production, and during the boom years of 1975–77 this agency bought the crops from producers at prices that were significantly below world market levels, so providing a surplus for investment in other sectors of the economy. However, the subsequent weakening in world prices meant that the government was unable to maintain the real income of producers, and for the four years until 1983/84 and again in 1986/87–1987/88 purchase prices were 'frozen'. After the failure of its attempt to sustain world prices through stockpiling cocoa, the Ivorian government was forced to halve producer prices in the 1989/90 season, to 200 francs CFA per kg for cocoa—their lowest level since 1978—and to 100 francs CFA per kg for coffee. Producer prices for both cocoa and coffee were increased immediately after the January 1994 devaluation, although not to the full extent of the depreciation in the currency's value: the cocoa price was set at 240 francs CFA per kg for the 1993/94 season and 315 francs CFA for 1994/95, while prices for coffee were initially raised to 200 francs CFA per kg and then, with a series of further increases, to 650 francs CFA per kg. The margin between prices for the two subsequently narrowed: the indicative price for cocoa in 1998/99 was 575 francs CFA per kg, and that for coffee 625 francs CFA per kg.

In January 1999 Caistab, which in recent years had operated principally as a consultative body, was privatized, following pressure from the IMF and the World Bank. A new regulatory body, known as New Caistab, was subsequently created, and in August the market for cocoa and coffee was fully opened to competition. However, in November of that year cocoa and coffee farmers undertook a series of protests at the low prices they received for their crops and at what they termed the failure of New Caistab to prepare adequately for the liberalization of the market. The directors of the new body were dismissed in late 1999, and in March 2000 it was announced that New Caistab was to be dissolved and replaced later in the year by a Bureau Ivoirien du Café-Cacao (BICC), which was to be operated by farmers' representatives. Analysts, however, suggested that the low prices, in particular for cocoa, resulted from oversupply and decreased international demand, rather than as a consequence of the liberalization of the market, and it was feared that any attempts by the BICC to inflate artificially the price of coffee or cocoa would prove impossible to sustain in the long term.

With just less than one-half of Côte d'Ivoire's total export earnings provided by sales of cocoa and coffee, both highly vulnerable to international market trends, the government has sought to diversify agricultural production. Since the 1960s Côte d'Ivoire has become a major producer of palm oil, and local processing of palm products has developed. A series of replanting programmes was supported by the World Bank, the European Community (now European Union—EU), France and the United Kingdom. However, the target of becoming the world's leading palm oil producer was abandoned after the sharp fall in world prices in 1987, and only one of the two planned processing mills was constructed. Nevertheless, output of palm oil showed an overall increase in the 1990s, from an average of 236,000 tons per year in 1989–91 to 257,000 tons per year in 1996–98.

Cotton cultivation has done particularly well in recent decades. Production had increased only slowly until the mid-1970s, when the government embarked on a deliberate policy of helping the farmers in the north of the country. In recent years output has averaged about 250,000 tons per year, but a record crop of 337,100 tons was achieved in 1997/98. Côte d'Ivoire thus vies with Burkina Faso and Benin for the position of the Franc Zone's second largest cotton producer (after Mali). Most of the cotton is processed locally in eight ginning complexes, both for export (some 80% of total production) and for the local textile industry.

The rubber industry has also shown growth since the mid-1980s (when output was some 50,000 tons per year), registering an average 71,000 tons per year in 1989–91, but almost 116,000 tons in 1998, as the government pursued plans for Côte d'Ivoire to become Africa's leading rubber producer by the end of the century. The country is also a significant producer of bananas and pineapples, with exports (estimated at 224,000 tons and 160,000 tons, respectively, in 1998) directed principally at the European market.

In recent decades the government has stressed the need to increase output of basic food crops, in which Côte d'Ivoire was not self-sufficient. The country is normally self-sufficient in maize, cassava, yams and plantains, and the government has encouraged the production of rice, large quantities of which are imported. Two of the country's sugar mills have been converted to rice cultivation. By the mid-1980s the rice development programme was proving successful, and output of paddy rice was averaging 1.1m. tons per year in the late 1990s, with a record of 1,287,000 tons in 1997. None the less, output still fails to meet domestic demand, which is rising rapidly as the population moving from rural areas to towns tends to switch its grain preference to rice.

A deficiency in sugar supply and the need to save foreign exchange on sugar imports led the government to initiate a sugar development programme in the 1970s. Two complexes were in operation by 1980, but were producing sugar at twice the cost on the world market. This situation, in conjunction with the need to reduce foreign borrowing, led to the cancellation of six more planned complexes and the reduction of sugar cane plantations, resulting in a decline in sugar production from the 186,000 metric tons recorded in 1982/83 to an average of 127,000 tons per year in the late 1990s.

Forestry has always been a significant source of export earnings, from both logs and sawn timber, and, boosted by enhanced price competitiveness, these displaced both coffee and petroleum products to come second to cocoa in 1994 and 1995, and third (after petroleum) in 1996. Most production is carried out by large integrated firms, many of which are foreign-owned. The area of exploitable timber had fallen to only about 1m. ha in 1987, compared with some 15.6m. ha at independence, because of inadequate reafforestation and the encroachment of agriculture on forest areas. In an attempt to conserve resources, the government therefore restricted commercial production to 3m. cu m per year. With domestic demand rising, the volume available for export declined, with exports falling from 3.1m. cu m (logs) in 1980 to only 29,000 cu m (and 521,000 cu m of sawn timber) in 1992. Export volume has since recovered to a total of 1.3m. cu m in 1994, under the stimulus of much higher earnings in local currency terms. Meanwhile, the World Bank and other external agencies are supporting a reafforestation programme, which includes replanting on 22,000 ha, with a production target of 6.6m. cu m over 35 years. Progress has, however, been disappointing (replanting has recently averaged only 5,000 ha per year), and the government remains committed to a ban on exports of timber once the country's foreign payments position has improved.

Livestock herds are small—in 1998 there were some 1.3m. cattle, 1.3m. sheep and goats and 271,000 pigs—and meat production satisfies only one-third of national demand. Fishing is a significant activity, with industrial fishing accounting for about two-thirds of the annual catch of 65,000–70,000 metric tons. Ivorian participation in this sector is still low, and most traditional fishing is undertaken by non-Ivorians. Domestic production currently meets only about one-third of local demand.

MANUFACTURING AND MINING

The manufacturing sector, which accounted for about 13% of GDP in the early and mid-1990s, is dominated by agro-industrial activities—such as the processing of cocoa, coffee, cotton, oil palm, pineapples and fish. It was stimulated, immediately after independence, by the need to replace goods traditionally imported from Senegal, the manufacturing centre for colonial French West Africa, and it formed one of the most dynamic areas of the economy during this period. Although the main industrial opportunities had been exploited by the mid-1970s, the sector was sustained by the high rate of growth in domestic demand, arising from the rapid increase in the country's population, and it was given a sharp boost by the 1994 devaluation, which greatly enhanced the competitiveness of the local product. Growth in the GDP of the industrial sector (a wider measure, also including mining, construction and utilities) reached 10.3% in 1995 and 8.4% in 1996, and then surged to 13.1% in 1997 as output at the Lion oilfield and Panthère gas field expanded (see below). Meanwhile, since the late 1980s the emphasis of government policy has shifted from import substitution to export promotion, with a higher proportion of local processing—particularly of cocoa and coffee. The agro-industrial sector has also benefited from an influx of foreign investment as the government has disengaged from this sector.

In the past a significant strand in government policy was the attempt to 'Ivorianize' both equity and management. Ivorian-held equity in industrial firms, virtually nil in 1960, had reached almost two-thirds of the total by 1982. However, this was almost entirely held by the government (51.5%), while the private-sector Ivorian share was very small (13.6%). This reflected the development of parastatal organizations during the 1970s as a means of restructuring and diversifying the economy. However, the financial losses being incurred by the parastatal companies became so serious that in 1980 the government reversed its policy regarding these organizations and began to dispose of its interests through outright sale, leasing, or the creation of autonomous co-operatives. An important element of the stabilization programme introduced by Alassane Ouattara in 1990 was an acceleration of the privatization process. Several major companies had been sold off by the end of 1992, including the electricity and water utilities. In all, the government aimed to dispose of 80 of a total of about 140 public companies by the end of 1995. Despite some public disquiet regarding the programme, in particular the extent of French ownership of important sectors of the economy, the Bédié administration stepped up the pace. Among the major disposals that had been realized by the end of 1997 were the state-owned telecommunications company, the palm-oil company and the state sugar company. In 1998 the government's 70% holding in the cotton production and marketing monopoly was sold, while the disposal process for oil refinery was proceeding in 1999, with the sale of the government's 37% stake scheduled for early 2000. A long list of privatizations scheduled for 1999–2000 included companies and agencies in agro-industry, textiles, water, energy, transport (including the domestic airline), communications and banking. However, the whole privatization process was suspended as a result of the military coup in December 1999.

The only significant activity in the mining sector (apart from hydrocarbons) is the extraction of diamonds and gold. Output from the two diamond mines, at Tortiya and Séguéla, is some 15,000 carats annually, but very much larger quantities are produced in illicit operations. Total output was put at 84,300 carats in 1994. The exploitation of deposits of gold-bearing rock at Ity began in 1991, in a joint venture with the Cie française des mines. A second gold mine, at Aniuri, began operations in 1993, in a joint venture between Eden Roc of Canada and the state mining company. Gold output reached a peak of 2,485 kg in 1997, but the fall in its international price caused the Aniuri mine to cease operations in early 1998, reducing production to 1,995 kg in that year. However, there is continuing foreign interest in investing in the sector. Randgold of South Africa bought two concessions in the north-east of the country in 1999. There is considerable potential for nickel mining: in 1996 Falconbridge of Canada signed an agreement with the government to invest US $500m. over five years in the development of reserves at Sipilou and Gounguessou in the north-west, where tests have indicated 54m. tons of nickel ore. In addition, there are substantial iron ore, bauxite and manganese reserves, all largely unworked.

ENERGY

Electricity generating capacity rose very rapidly, from only 41 MW in 1962 to 675 MW in the early 1980s, as the result of the development of hydroelectric plants, which came to account for 90% of all power generated. However, the focus of development switched after the 1982–84 drought severely reduced the contribution of hydroelectric power, and policy is now to develop thermal capacity. Long-discussed plans for a thermal plant at Vridi, utilizing offshore reserves of natural gas, finally came to realization in 1994. A consortium led by United Meridian of the USA has developed the Panthère gas field to supply a 100-MW plant at Vridi, which began to supply the national grid in 1997. With gas output from Panthère more than doubling in 1997, to 139m. cu m, plans were developed to use these resources to expand Côte d'Ivoire's exports of electricity. The target for 2000 was sales of 600m. kWh. The first 144 MW phase of a gas-fired complex at Azito, close to Abidjan, opened in January 1999; the second phase was scheduled for mid-2000 and the third for 2001, bringing total capacity at Azito to 420 MW. Meanwhile, natural gas output is scheduled to double by 2005, with the commencement of production in mid-1999 at the Foxtrot offshore gas field, which is being developed by a US, French and Ivorian consortium.

Côte d'Ivoire has experienced mixed success in the development of its petroleum reserves. Offshore petroleum was discovered in 1975, with reserves at the Bélier field, located 15 km south of Grand Bassam, estimated at 75m. metric tons. A larger discovery was made in the Espoir field (also offshore) in 1980. Output from the two fields reached a peak of 1.1m. tons in 1984, with Espoir accounting for 771,000 tons. Production then declined, and operations at the Espoir field were suspended in 1989, and those at the Bélier field ceased one year later. In addition, offshore exploration for petroleum had virtually ceased by 1984; the Ivorian continental shelf had proved difficult to drill, and its hydrocarbon reserves were found to be dispersed in small pockets. However, a new round of exploration undertaken in the early 1990s proved successful, with a major discovery of offshore petroleum, near Jacqueville and Grand-Lahou, in 1994. A joint venture by United Meridian and the state-owned Société nationale d'opérations pétrolières de la Côte d'Ivoire (PETROCI) began production at the Lion field in April

1995: output reached 894,000 tons in 1996 and 1,027,000 tons in 1997, as nearby offshore blocks were developed. With other foreign companies showing interest in Côte d'Ivoire's offshore reserves, the government is hoping for self-sufficiency in petroleum by the mid-2000s, with the prospect of exports thereafter.

TRANSPORT

The most important transport facility is the deep-water port of Abidjan, rivalled in francophone West Africa only by the iron ore-handling port of Nouadhibou in Mauritania. During the late 1980s and early 1990s Abidjan handled an average of about 10m. tons of freight per year, including shipments to and from Burkina Faso and Mali. This represented a recovery to near the levels recorded in 1980, after several years during which the volume of traffic fell, mainly because of a decline in timber exports and oil imports. By 1998 total freight handled at the port was some 15.2m. tons. Major improvements have been carried out, including the installation of large-scale container-handling facilities, and it is planned to double capacity by 2003. Another port has been developed since 1971 at San Pedro, mainly for timber and cocoa exports; this handled total traffic of more than 1m. tons in 1994.

Côte d'Ivoire has about 68,000 km of classified roads. In all, some 6,000 km of roads are now paved, almost six times the extent in 1970. Repair and extension of the road network has received funding from both multilateral agencies and donor governments (notably France, Germany and Japan). In addition, tolls were introduced on some roads in the mid-1990s, to assist in funding the maintenance of the network. A railway line links Abidjan to Ouagadougou, with 660 km of line in Côte d'Ivoire. The line was managed by a single authority, the Régie du chemin de fer Abidjan–Niger (RAN), but experienced financial and technical difficulties, with both freight and passenger traffic in decline. As a result, RAN was liquidated in 1989, and its Ivorian activities were assumed by the Société ivoirienne des chemins de fer. Management responsibility has since been transferred to SITARAIL, a consortium of French, Belgian, Ivorian and Burkinabè investors. Côte d'Ivoire has international airports at Abidjan, Bouaké and Yamoussoukro, and there are several regional airports.

TOURISM

Tourism developed strongly in the 1970s, with a newly-created ministry stimulating diversification in location (away from the Abidjan area) and in type of visitor (away from business travellers, who previously accounted for almost two-thirds of arrivals). Special tax incentives and government guarantees on loans were offered for hotel construction. The number of tourists increased from some 93,000 in 1974 to 198,900 in 1979, with business visitors accounting for 40% of arrivals. Since then visitor arrivals have fluctuated in the range 200,000–300,000 per year, broadly reflecting trends in world tourism.

PUBLIC FINANCE

Budget spending has risen in parallel with economic growth, with current spending in the past covered from internal sources and investment spending largely financed by foreign borrowing. The deterioration in the economy during the early 1980s, and the associated fall in tax receipts, threatened serious disequilibrium. In response, a series of austerity budgets was adopted, cutting both capital and current expenditure and transforming the budget balance from a record deficit of 361,000m. francs CFA (equivalent to 13% of GDP) in 1982 to a small surplus (83,000m. francs CFA) in 1985. However, the sharp fall in the late 1980s in international prices for Côte d'Ivoire's principal agricultural commodities, and the consequent increase in compensatory transfers to the marketing board, meant that the deficit had risen to 17.1% of GDP by 1989, despite overall reductions in spending. Far more rigorous cuts in expenditure, particularly in agricultural price support, gradually lowered the deficit to 9.9% of GDP in 1992: for the first time in almost a decade the primary budget (i.e. excluding interest payments) recorded a modest surplus. This was enhanced by the reinstatement of export taxes on cocoa and coffee in 1994 (allowed by the impact of currency devaluation), as well as by cuts in the public-sector payroll. The primary budget recorded a surplus, of 217,900m. francs CFA, equivalent to 5.2% of GDP. With the economy in strong recovery in 1995–98, revenue increased sufficiently to allow the government to raise the level of its capital spending while maintaining a surplus on the primary budget (of 210,200m. francs CFA in 1998). The government was thus able to pay off some arrears on its domestic debt. None the less, the budget remained in overall deficit because of the massive burden of interest payments on the foreign debt, representing around one-quarter of total current spending. Under the programme agreed with the IMF for the three-year period 1998–2000, the budget deficit was to be steadily reduced, to only 0.3% of GDP by the end of the period, with the support provided by the debt relief that was accorded after the granting of the ESAF. While the deficit for 1998 was close to the programme target, at 1.8% of GDP as against 1.5%, it widened markedly in 1999, to 2.8% of GDP, largely because of the fall in cocoa revenue. The failure to adhere to programme targets, and the lack of transparency in government finances, prompted the IMF to suspend the ESAF in mid-1999. An IMF mission in February 2000 urged the new government to be more stringent with regard to both expenditure and revenue collection in an attempt to return to the deficit reduction trend.

FOREIGN TRADE AND PAYMENTS

Côte d'Ivoire has had fewer problems with the balance of payments than most comparable African economies. Exports have increased at a faster rate than gross national product (GNP), and they remain the main factor contributing to economic growth.

Côte d'Ivoire's balance of trade has always been in surplus because of the strength of its exports, which have largely been determined by the level of earnings from sales of coffee and cocoa. Thus the recovery in output of both after the drought of the early 1980s brought about a fivefold increase in the surplus in 1984 (to 525,700m. francs CFA), but the sharp fall in international prices for coffee and cocoa after 1986 had halved the surplus by 1988 (to 289,000m. francs CFA). The surplus remained around this level in the years immediately after, with import spending adjusted to reflect trends in receipts from exports. However, the balance improved markedly in 1994, in both US dollar and local currency terms, as the consequence of the devaluation of the CFA franc. This enhanced the profitability of producing exports the prices of which were set in dollars, as well as the price competitiveness of those denominated in local currency. At the same time demand for imports was depressed by their higher cost. The surplus on merchandise trade thus reached US $1,289m. in 1994, compared with $748m. in 1993. Despite pressure on the import bill as a result of the economic recovery, the surplus had risen to just over $1,800m. per year in 1996–98 as earnings from sales of commodities expanded in response to greater supply (boosted by the improvement in producer prices) and still higher international prices.

This improvement in merchandise trade, and the debt relief that followed currency devaluation (see below), virtually eliminated the deficit that had been registered on the current account of the balance of payments in every year since 1986, with a deficit in 1994 of only US $18m. Current payments had deteriorated in the late 1980s because of the narrowing in the trade surplus and the heavy burden of interest payments, owing to earlier, very substantial, foreign borrowing (particularly in the late 1970s), as high prices for cocoa and coffee stimulated ambitious capital investment programmes by the government, and particularly by the state corporations. The annual deficit stabilized

at an average of just over $1,000m. in 1989–93, with some improvement in the final years because of reduced interest payments as the result of debt relief, to register $952m. in 1993. However, the current account reverted to substantial deficit from 1995 onwards, as the increase in the trade surplus was offset by higher outflows on services. Over the period 1995–98 the current-account deficit averaged $341m. per year, equivalent to 3% of GDP, but then widened in 1999 owing to the steep fall in cocoa export earnings in that year, with the ratio to GDP doubling.

Reflecting the difficulties of the 1980s, the external debt has escalated sharply since the beginning of that decade, and at the end of 1993 was more than twice the level of 1980, at US $19,071m. This was equivalent to 211% of GNP in that year, while the cost of debt-servicing had been equivalent to about 35% of the value of exports of goods and services in almost every year since 1981. Both are unmanageable proportions, and by the end of 1993 Côte d'Ivoire's arrears on its long-term debt totalled $3,883m. These arrears had accumulated despite a series of debt reschedulings—of both commercial and official liabilities—facilitated by Côte d'Ivoire's compliance with economic retrenchment programmes agreed with the IMF. The devaluation of the CFA franc in January 1994 threatened to precipitate a crisis, since it doubled the external debt in local currency terms overnight. In common with other Franc Zone countries in Africa, Côte d'Ivoire was the beneficiary of special measures of compensation and relief. The 'Paris Club' of official creditors agreed a new round of debt reschedulings and cancellation, which reduced total debt to $17,395m. by the end of 1994. Côte d'Ivoire also received critically important aid from members of the Organisation for Economic Co-operation and Development and the Organization of the Petroleum Exporting Countries, whose net assistance doubled in 1994, to $1,594m., with most of the increase coming from the International Development Association (the concessionary lending agency of the World Bank), from the IMF and France. As the short-term pressure eased, these net inflows declined over the following two years, to $446m. in 1996. However, Côte d'Ivoire's external position remained very problematic, with arrears on debt obligations reaching $3,504m. by the end of 1996, while its external debt had risen to $19,524m.

The debt relief that was agreed following the IMF's approval of a new ESAF in February 1998 had a considerable positive impact on Côte d'Ivoire's foreign indebtedness. The 'London Club' of commercial creditors agreed to implement a restructuring of US $8,600m. in liabilities that had originally been agreed in November 1996. As a result of the backdating of this arrangement to the end of 1997, the country's foreign debt was reduced by more than $4,000m. from the level at the end of 1996, to $15,609m. The ESAF also facilitated a deal with the 'Paris Club' for debt relief under the World Bank's Heavily Indebted Poor Countries (HIPC) initiative: scheduled to come into effect in March 2001, this represents a saving of $345m. However, with the ESAF suspended and the new uncertainties generated by the military coup of December 1999, the implementation of the HIPC debt relief is likely to be postponed. Meanwhile, the current-account balance remains highly vulnerable to adverse movements in the price and output of cocoa (as 1999's record illustrated). In this situation, a foreign debt that remains close to twice the level of GNP and annual debt service equivalent to around one-quarter of foreign earnings together represent a significant burden.

Statistical Survey

Source (unless otherwise stated): Institut National de la Statistique, BP V55, Abidjan; tel. 20-21-05-38.

Area and Population

AREA, POPULATION AND DENSITY

Area (sq km)	322,462*
Population (census results)	
30 April 1975	6,702,866
1 March 1988	
Males	5,527,343
Females	5,288,351
Total	10,815,694
Population (UN estimates at mid-year)†	
1996	13,816,000
1997	14,064,000
1998	14,292,000
Density (per sq km) at mid-1998	44.3

* 124,503 sq miles.

† Source: UN, *World Population Prospects: The 1998 Revision.*

POPULATION BY ETHNIC GROUP (1988 census)

Ethnic group	Number	%
Akan	3,251,227	30.1
Voltaïque	1,266,235	11.7
Mane Nord	1,236,129	11.4
Krou	1,136,291	10.5
Mane Sud	831,840	7.7
Naturalized Ivorians	51,146	0.5
Others	3,039,035	28.1
Unknown	3,791	0.0
Total	10,815,694	100.0

Source: UN, *Demographic Yearbook.*

POPULATION BY REGION (1988 census)

Region	Population
Centre	815,664
Centre-Est	300,407
Centre-Nord	915,269
Centre-Ouest	1,542,945
Nord	745,816
Nord-Est	514,134
Nord-Ouest	522,247
Ouest	968,267
Sud	3,843,249
Sud-Ouest	647,696
Total	10,815,694

Source: UN, *Demographic Yearbook.*

Note: In January 1997 the Government adopted legislation whereby Côte d'Ivoire's regions were to be renamed. The new regions (with their regional capitals) were to be: Lagoon (Abidjan), Upper Sassandra (Daloa), Savannah (Korhogo), Bandama Valley (Bouaké), Lakes (Yamoussoukro), Middle Comoé (Abengourou), Mountains (Man), Zanzan (Bondoukou), Lower Cavally (San Pedro), Denguélé (Odienné), Marahoué (Bouaflé), Nzi Comoé (Dimbroko), South Comoé (Aboisso), Worodougou (Seguéla), South Bandama (Divo), Agneby (Agboville).

PRINCIPAL TOWNS (population at 1988 census)

Abidjan*	1,929,079	Korhogo	109,445
Bouaké	329,850	Yamoussoukro* . .	106,786
Daloa	121,842		

* The process of transferring the official capital from Abidjan to Yamoussoukro began in 1983.

Source: UN, *Demographic Yearbook.*

BIRTHS AND DEATHS (UN estimates, annual averages)

	1980–85	1985–90	1990–95
Birth rate (per 1,000) . . .	50.1	45.6	38.9
Death rate (per 1,000) . . .	16.0	14.8	14.9

Expectation of life (UN estimates, years at birth, 1990–95): 48.9 (males 47.9; females 50.2).

Source: UN, *World Population Prospects: The 1998 Revision.*

ECONOMICALLY ACTIVE POPULATION

Mid-1998 (estimates in '000): Agriculture, etc. 2,892; Total 5,623 (Source: FAO, *Production Yearbook*).

Agriculture

PRINCIPAL CROPS ('000 metric tons)

	1996	1997	1998
Maize	569	576	547
Millet	60*	65	65*
Sorghum	19†	19	19*
Rice (paddy)	833	1,287	1,223
Sweet potatoes	36*	36	36
Cassava (Manioc) . . .	1,653	1,699	1,700
Yams	2,924	2,986	2,800
Taro (Coco yam) . . .	361	374	355
Pulses*	8	8	8
Tree nuts	33*	27	27*
Sugar cane*	1,320	1,350	1,155
Palm kernels	30	28*	28*
Groundnuts (in shell) . .	147	143	136
Cottonseed	112	142	140*
Coconuts*	205	221	221
Copra*	30	34	34
Tomatoes	130*	137	130
Aubergines (Eggplants)* . .	40	40	40
Chillies and peppers (green)* .	20*	21	21*
Other vegetables* . . .	341	343	343
Oranges	28*	29	29*
Other citrus fruit* . . .	28	28	28
Bananas	219	304	222
Plantains	1,400*	1,441	1,200
Mangoes	6†	9	9*
Pineapples	251	261	227
Other fruit*	13	14	14
Coffee (green)	165	279	332
Cocoa beans	1,254	1,119	1,120
Tobacco (leaves)* . . .	10	10	10
Cotton (lint)	96	114	130
Natural rubber (dry weight) . .	91	108	116

* FAO estimate(s).   † Unofficial figure.

Source: FAO, *Production Yearbook.*

LIVESTOCK ('000 head, year ending September)

	1996	1997	1998*
Cattle	1,286	1,312	1,312
Pigs	290	271	271
Sheep	1,314	1,347	1,347
Goats	1,027	1,053	1,053

Poultry (million): 27 in 1996; 31 in 1997; 31* in 1998.

* FAO estimate(s).

Source: FAO, *Production Yearbook.*

pePan# CÔTE D'IVOIRE

LIVESTOCK PRODUCTS
(FAO estimates unless otherwise indicated, '000 metric tons)

	1996	1997	1998
Beef and veal	40	42	46
Mutton and lamb	5	5	5
Goat meat	4	5	5
Pig meat	14	13	13
Poultry meat	49	50	51
Other meat	28	28	28
Cows' milk	23*	23*	23
Poultry eggs	16*	16	16
Cattle hides	5	6	6
Sheepskins	1	1	1
Goatskins	1	1	1

* Official figure.

Source: FAO, *Production Yearbook*.

Forestry

ROUNDWOOD REMOVALS ('000 cubic metres, excluding bark)

	1995	1996	1997
Sawlogs, veneer logs and logs for sleepers	2,297	2,081	2,054
Other industrial wood	864	884	902
Fuel wood	11,128	11,392	11,624
Total	14,289	14,357	14,580

Source: FAO, *Yearbook of Forest Products*.

SAWNWOOD PRODUCTION
('000 cubic metres, including railway sleepers)

	1995	1996	1997
Coniferous (softwood)	10*	—	—
Broadleaved (hardwood)	696	596	613
Total	706	596	613

* FAO estimate.

Source: FAO, *Yearbook of Forest Products*.

Fishing

('000 metric tons, live weight)

	1995	1996	1997
Freshwater fishes	10.8	11.5	11.5
Bigeye grunt	4.8	4.6*	4.5*
Sardinellas	14.4	13.7*	13.4*
Bonga shad*	10.0	9.5	9.3
Other marine fishes (incl. unspecified)*	29.4	28.0	27.5
Total fish	69.5	67.2	66.2
Crustaceans	0.7	0.7	0.9
Total catch	70.2	67.9	67.2
Inland waters	11.3	12.0	12.0
Atlantic Ocean	58.9	55.9	55.1

* FAO estimate(s).

Source: FAO, *Yearbook of Fishery Statistics*.

Mining

	1996	1997	1998
Gold (kg)	2,054	2,485	1,995
Crude petroleum (barrels)	5,815	5,266	3,806

Source: Banque centrale des états de l'Afrique de l'ouest.

Diamonds ('000 carats): 117.3 in 1992; 98.4 in 1993; 84.3 in 1994.

Industry

SELECTED PRODUCTS ('000 metric tons, unless otherwise indicated)

	1994	1995	1996
Salted, dried or smoked fish*	15.0	0.0	n.a.
Canned fish*	43.6	49.9	n.a.
Palm oil—unrefined*	259	249	n.a.
Raw sugar*	125	119	121
Plywood ('000 cubic metres)	41	58	57
Jet fuel†	61	62	62
Motor gasolene (Petrol)†	425	428	432
Kerosene†	488	490	491
Gas-diesel (Distillate fuel) oils†	685	705	710
Residual fuel oils†	474	477	479
Cement†‡	500	500	n.a.

Cocoa powder (exports, '000 metric tons): 22.1*† in 1988.
Cocoa butter (exports, '000 metric tons): 28.2*† in 1988.
Cotton yarn (pure and mixed, '000 metric tons): 24.7† in 1989.

* Data from FAO.
† Provisional or estimated figure(s).
‡ Data from the US Bureau of Mines.

Source: UN, *Industrial Commodity Statistics Yearbook*.

Electric energy (million kWh): 2,399 in 1996; 2,757 in 1997; 3,984 in 1998 (Source: Banque centrale des états de l'Afrique de l'ouest).

Finance

CURRENCY AND EXCHANGE RATES

Monetary Units
100 centimes = 1 franc de la Communauté financière africaine (CFA).

Sterling, Dollar and Euro Equivalents (28 April 2000)
£1 sterling = 1,132.20 francs CFA;
US $1 = 722.02 francs CFA;
€1 = 655.96 francs CFA;
10,000 francs CFA = £8.832 = $13.850 = €15.245.

Average Exchange Rate (francs CFA per US $)
1997   583.67
1998   589.95
1999   615.70

Note: An exchange rate of 1 French franc = 50 francs CFA, established in 1948, remained in force until January 1994, when the CFA franc was devalued by 50%, with the exchange rate adjusted to 1 French franc = 100 francs CFA. This relationship to French currency remained in effect with the introduction of the euro on 1 January 1999. From that date, accordingly, a fixed exchange rate of €1 = 655.957 francs CFA has been in operation.

BUDGET ('000 million francs CFA)

Revenue*	1996	1997	1998
Tax revenue .	1,040.7	1,112.9	1,142.0
Direct taxes .	252.2	303.5	327.7
Taxes on profits .	126.5	147.2	166.2
Individual income taxes .	77.0	97.8	104.8
Employers' contributions .	19.4	22.4	26.0
Taxes on petroleum products .	100.1	96.9	96.2
Excise taxes .	62.4	61.2	62.8
Value-added tax (VAT) .	28.8	30.5	28.3
Other indirect taxes .	200.1	227.3	240.0
VAT and withholding tax .	136.8	145.6	146.8
Registration and stamp taxes .	24.7	30.6	33.5
Other taxes on imports .	282.5	311.9	320.2
Customs, fiscal and statistical duties	128.6	153.0	162.2
Other import charges .	23.4	20.6	83.3
VAT .	130.5	138.4	170.9
Taxes on exports .	205.7	173.2	158.0
Coffee and cocoa .	196.4	165.9	150.2
Other revenue .	191.2	215.1	246.5
Stabilization fund surplus .	70.1	84.0	131.6
Social security contributions .	74.3	83.1	79.2
Petroleum revenue .	27.8	29.1	17.3
Total .	1,231.9	1,328.0	1,388.5

Expenditure	1996	1997	1998
Wages and salaries .	389.6	408.1	415.2
Social security benefits .	68.8	73.6	76.5
Subsidies and other current transfers .	40.6	54.9	55.9
Other current expenditure .	260.0	285.3	267.6
Investment expenditure .	304.0	372.3	455.9
Interest due on public debt .	322.2	303.2	286.3
Total .	1,385.1	1,497.4	1,557.4

* Excluding grants received ('000 million francs CFA): 40.5 in 1996; 44.1 in 1997; 50.5 in 1998.

Source: IMF, *Côte d'Ivoire: Statistical Appendix* (August 1999).

INTERNATIONAL RESERVES (US $ million at 31 December)

	1997	1998	1999
Gold* .	13.6	13.1	13.1
IMF special drawing rights .	—	0.2	3.4
Reserve position in IMF .	0.2	0.3	0.3
Foreign exchange .	618.1	855.0	628.4
Total .	632.0	868.6	645.2

* Valued at market-related prices.

Source: IMF, *International Financial Statistics*.

MONEY SUPPLY ('000 million francs CFA at 31 December)

	1997	1998	1999
Currency outside banks .	571.8	652.1	615.5
Demand deposits at deposit money banks* .	502.8	562.0	576.7
Checking deposits at post office .	3.6	2.0	3.0
Total money (incl. others) .	1,080.0	1,219.3	1,198.0

* Excluding the deposits of public establishments of an administrative or social nature.

Source: IMF, *International Financial Statistics*.

COST OF LIVING (Consumer Price Index for African households in Abidjan; base: 1995 = 100)

	1997	1998	1999
All items .	106.6	111.6	112.5

Source: IMF, *International Financial Statistics*.

NATIONAL ACCOUNTS
('000 million francs CFA at current prices)
Expenditure on the Gross Domestic Product

	1996	1997	1998*
Government final consumption expenditure	661.6	695.1	690.9
Private final consumption expenditure	3,592.1	3,928.3	4,207.9
Increase in stocks	−25.0	0.0	0.0
Gross fixed capital formation	760.3	957.5	1,181.6
Total domestic expenditure	4,989.0	5,580.8	6,080.5
Exports of goods and services	2,565.0	2,788.4	2,870.6
Less Imports of goods and services	2,142.5	2,384.8	2,458.5
Statistical discrepancy	62.1	—	—
GDP in purchasers' values	5,473.6	5,984.4	6,492.6

* Estimates.

Gross Domestic Product by Economic Activity

	1996	1997	1998*
Agriculture, livestock-rearing, forestry and fishing .	1,512.0	1,587.7	1,688.2
Mining and quarrying .	19.7	19.6	19.5
Manufacturing .	704.9	799.3	906.1
Electricity, gas and water .	249.6	291.2	314.5
Construction and public works .	156.3	199.8	231.6
Transport, storage and communications .	514.4	561.3	623.8
Trade .	929.5	1,030.3	1,128.5
Public administration .	438.3	459.5	462.2
Other services .	693.1	759.2	836.6
Sub-total .	5,217.8	5,708.0	6,211.0
Import duties and taxes .	255.8	276.4	281.6
GDP in purchasers' values	5,473.6	5,984.4	6,492.6

* Estimates.

Source: IMF, *Côte d'Ivoire: Statistical Appendix* (August 1999).

BALANCE OF PAYMENTS (US $ million)

	1996	1997	1998
Exports of goods f.o.b. .	4,532.4	4,636.8	4,482.9
Imports of goods f.o.b. .	−2,673.3	−2,674.5	−2,650.6
Trade balance .	1,859.1	1,962.3	1,832.3
Exports of services .	576.9	574.2	538.8
Imports of services .	−1,471.5	−1,475.3	−1,444.6
Balance on goods and services	964.5	1,061.2	926.4
Other income received .	174.4	180.6	166.4
Other income paid .	−957.7	−965.8	−861.8
Balance on goods, services and income	181.1	275.9	231.0
Current transfers received .	56.6	54.0	49.8
Current transfers paid .	−557.2	−590.6	−587.1
Current balance .	−319.4	−260.8	−306.3
Capital account (net) .	50.8	42.9	35.5
Direct investment abroad .	−0.4	—	—
Direct investment from abroad .	274.4	368.1	426.5
Portfolio investment assets .	−19.5	−16.6	−14.0
Portfolio investment liabilities .	27.1	33.1	37.7
Other investment assets .	−259.1	−300.3	−317.7
Other investment liabilities .	−733.3	−575.7	−655.7
Net errors and omissions .	−35.1	68.2	164.5
Overall balance .	−1,014.6	−641.1	−629.4

Source: IMF, *International Financial Statistics*.

External Trade

PRINCIPAL COMMODITIES ('000 million francs CFA)

Imports c.i.f.	1996	1997	1998
Foodstuffs, beverages and tobacco	256.1	311.3	369.1
Dairy products.	27.8	28.1	32.3
Fish and shellfish (fresh)	75.2	90.5	112.6
Cereals	81.5	104.4	119.0
Rice.	44.7	64.6	81.9
Wheat	25.8	29.7	35.3
Other consumer goods	305.7	346.4	379.9
Pharmaceutical products	61.2	63.3	67.6
Plastic products	60.9	73.1	84.9
Passenger cars.	56.3	59.4	55.0
Raw materials and semi-finished products	556.8	547.3	542.6
Petroleum products	333.1	296.1	262.1
Crude petroleum.	242.5	254.1	195.0
Chemical products	40.9	45.5	45.2
Fertilizers.	22.1	30.9	41.5
Construction materials .	30.4	35.7	36.6
Clinker	25.5	29.9	29.6
Paper and paperboard .	41.8	43.6	48.0
Capital goods	324.8	393.0	472.9
Mechanical	119.0	156.2	160.6
Electrical	55.7	75.7	116.9
Transport equipment	68.1	66.2	80.9
Iron and steel products .	61.6	69.9	94.6
Total (incl. others)	1,443.4	1,598.1	1,746.6

Exports f.o.b.	1996	1997	1998*
Coffee beans	119.8	174.3	176.9
Cocoa beans .	720.3	707.8	735.5
Cotton fibre .	58.7	76.9	67.1
Bananas	44.7	39.9	40.8
Natural rubber	59.6	63.2	48.5
Processed cocoa	95.7	120.0	162.9
Processed coffee .	32.0	33.7	45.3
Sawnwood	141.1	152.3	119.6
Fish products	110.7	126.0	148.6
Crude petroleum.	73.0	98.0	62.2
Petroleum products	251.6	215.8	155.3
Total (incl. others)	2,190.2	2,378.9	2,414.1

* Estimates.

Source: IMF, *Côte d'Ivoire: Statistical Appendix* (August 1999).

PRINCIPAL TRADING PARTNERS (percentage of trade)

Imports	1996	1997	1998
Belgium-Luxembourg	3.0	3.3	3.1
Brazil .	1.1	0.8	1.2
China, People's Repub.	1.8	2.4	2.2
France .	25.1	26.7	28.6
Germany	5.7	4.7	4.6
Italy	4.7	4.3	5.2
Japan .	4.1	4.3	3.4
Netherlands .	3.4	3.7	3.7
Pakistan .	0.1	1.1	0.6
Spain .	2.8	3.2	3.6
Taiwan .	6.6	0.4	0.4
United Kingdom .	2.9	2.9	2.7
USA .	5.9	6.1	5.0

Exports	1996	1997	1998*
Belgium-Luxembourg	2.8	4.2	2.5
Benin	0.9	1.2	1.2
Burkina Faso	2.4	3.0	3.6
Cameroon	0.6	1.2	0.8
France	16.9	17.3	17.1
Germany	5.0	4.8	4.9
Ghana .	2.9	3.7	5.7
Italy	5.7	5.3	5.9
Mali	4.3	4.9	4.8
Netherlands .	16.7	13.2	12.2
Niger .	0.8	1.0	1.1
Senegal .	1.3	1.1	1.1
Spain .	4.0	4.0	3.7
Taiwan .	0.5	0.6	1.3
Togo .	1.6	1.6	1.4
United Kingdom .	2.9	2.6	2.4
USA .	8.2	7.5	9.0

* Estimates.

Source: IMF, *Direction of Trade Statistics,* in IMF, *Côte d'Ivoire: Statistical Appendix* (August 1999).

Transport

RAILWAYS (traffic)

	1991	1992	1993
Passengers ('000)	926	820	744
Passenger-km (million)	199	189	173
Freight ('000 metric tons)	488	484	292
Freight (million net ton-km) .	272	266	168

Source: Société Ivoirienne des Chemins de Fer, Abidjan.

ROAD TRAFFIC (estimates, '000 motor vehicles in use)

	1994	1995	1996
Passenger cars .	255	271	293
Lorries and vans .	140	150	163

Source: IRF, *World Road Statistics.*

SHIPPING
Merchant Fleet (registered at 31 December)

	1996	1997	1998
Number of vessels .	45	43	35
Total displacement ('000 grt) .	12.7	11.4	9.5

Source: Lloyd's Register of Shipping, *World Fleet Statistics.*

International Sea-borne Freight Traffic
(freight traffic at Abidjan, '000 metric tons)

	1993	1994	1995
Goods loaded .	3,882.4	3,702.3	4,172.9
Goods unloaded .	5,936.4	6,183.9	7,227.8

Freight traffic at San Pedro ('000 metric tons, 1994): Goods loaded 883.8; Goods unloaded 184.9.

Source: Banque centrale des états de l'Afrique de l'ouest.

CIVIL AVIATION (traffic on scheduled services)*

	1994	1995	1996
Kilometres flown (million) . .	3	4	5
Passengers carried ('000) . . .	157	175	179
Passenger-km (million) . . .	282	302	307
Total ton-km (million) . . .	40	44	44

* Including an apportionment of the traffic of Air Afrique.

Source: UN, *Statistical Yearbook*.

Tourism

ARRIVALS BY COUNTRY OF RESIDENCE ('000)

	1996	1997	1998
Belgium	4.3	4.2	4.5
Benin	12.5	11.1	14.3
Burkina Faso . . .	11.0	11.9	17.1
Congo, Repub. . . .	6.0	n.a.	7.6
France	66.7	69.0	73.2
Gabon	3.0	n.a.	5.4
Germany	3.2	3.8	3.9
Ghana	5.4	n.a.	6.7
Guinea	8.1	n.a.	12.5
Italy	5.0	14.0	7.6
Mali	10.7	n.a.	15.2
Niger	5.0	n.a.	5.4
Nigeria	7.9	n.a.	14.1
Senegal	13.0	12.1	16.6
Togo	8.7	8.2	10.8
United Kingdom . .	5.1	4.5	5.6
USA	15.3	17.0	18.8
Total (incl. others) . . .	236.9	274.1	301.0

Tourism receipts (US $ million): 75 in 1996; 88 in 1997.

Source: World Tourism Organization: *Yearbook of Tourism Statistics*.

Communications Media

	1994	1995	1996
Radio receivers ('000 in use) . .	1,975	2,100	2,200
Television receivers ('000 in use) .	822	850	870
Telephones ('000 main lines in use)	103	116	130
Mobile cellular telephones			
(subscribers)	—	—	13,549
Daily newspapers			
Number	8	9	12
Average circulation ('000 copies)	190	198	231
Non-daily newspapers			
Number	11	13	15
Average circulation ('000 copies)	205	235	251

1997 ('000 in use): Radio receivers 2,260; Television receivers 900.

Sources: UNESCO, *Statistical Yearbook*; UN, *Statistical Yearbook*.

Education

(1994/95, unless otherwise indicated)

	Institu-tions	Teach-ers	Students		
			Males	Females	Total
Pre-primary . .	281	1,192	13,315	12,323	25,638
Primary . .	7,185	36,058	930,386	679,543	1,609,929
Secondary					
General . .	n.a.	9,505*	313,445	150,365	463,810
Teacher					
training†‡	13	538	n.a.	n.a.	2,821
Vocational‡ .	n.a.	1,424	8,588	2,449	11,037
University level	n.a.	1,657	34,069	9,078	43,147

* Public education only.
† 1993/94 figures.
‡ Data refer only to schools attached to the Ministry of National Education and Basic Training.

1995/96: *Primary:* Institutions 7,401; Students 1,662,265 (males 959,419; females 702,846). *General Secondary:* Students 489,740 (males 327,779; females 161,961).
1996/97: *Pre-primary:* Students 32,141 (males 16,590; females 15,551). *Primary:* Institutions 7,599; Students 1,734,416 (males 993,157; females 741,259). *General Secondary:* Students 534,214 (males 365,201; females 169,013).

Directory

The Constitution

Following the *coup d'état* of 24 December 1999, the Constitution that had been in force, with amendments, since 1960 was suspended. A new Constitution (below) was subsequently prepared by a consultative committee, and was approved by referendum in July 2000.

PREAMBLE

The people of Côte d'Ivoire recognize their diverse ethnic, cultural and religious backgrounds, and desire to build a single, unified and prosperous nation based on constitutional legality and democratic institutions, the rights of the individual, cultural and spiritual values, transparency in public affairs, and the promotion of sub-regional, regional and African unity.

FREEDOMS, RIGHTS AND DUTIES

Articles 1–28: The State guarantees the implementation of the Constitution and guarantees to protect the rights of each citizen. The State guarantees its citizens equal access to health, education, culture, information, professional training, employment and justice. Freedom of thought and expression are guaranteed to all, although the encouragement of social, ethnic and religious discord is not permitted. Freedom of association and demonstration are guar-

anteed. Political parties may act freely within the law, however, parties must not be created solely on a regional, ethnic or religious basis. The rights of free enterprise, the right to a union and the right to strike are guaranteed.

NATIONAL SOVEREIGNTY

Articles 29–33: Côte d'Ivoire is an independent and sovereign republic. The official language is French. Legislation regulates the promotion and development of national languages. The Republic of Côte d'Ivoire is single and indivisible, secular, democratic and social. All its citizens are equal. Sovereignty belongs to the people, and is exercised through referendums and the election of representatives. The right to vote freely and in secret is guaranteed to all citizens over 18 years of age.

HEAD OF STATE

Articles 34–57: The President of the Republic is the Head of State. The President is elected for a five-year mandate (renewable once only) by direct universal suffrage. Candidates must be aged between 40 and 65, and be Ivorian citizens holding no other nationality, and resident in the country, with Ivorian parents. If one candidate does not receive a simple majority of votes cast, a second round of voting takes place between the two most successful candidates. The

President holds executive power, and appoints a Prime Minister to co-ordinate government action. The President appoints the government on the recommendation of the Prime Minister. The President presides over the Council of Ministers, is the head of the civil service and the supreme head of the armed forces. The President may initiate legislation and call referendums. The President may not hold any other office or be a leader of a political party.

NATIONAL ASSEMBLY

Articles 58–83: The national assembly holds legislative power. The national assembly votes on the budget and scrutinizes the accounts of the nation. Deputies are elected for periods of five years by direct universal suffrage. Except in exceptional cases, deputies have legal immunity during the period of their mandate.

INTERNATIONAL AGREEMENTS

Articles 84–87: The President negotiates and ratifies treaties and international agreements. International agreements, which modify internal legislation, must be ratified by further legislation. The Constitution must be amended prior to the ratification of certain agreements if the Constitutional Council deems this necessary.

CONSTITUTIONAL COUNCIL

Articles 88–100: The Constitutional Council rules on the constitutionality of legislation. It also regulates the functioning of government. It is composed of a president, of the former presidents of Côte d'Ivoire and of six councillors named by the President and by the president of the national assembly for mandates of six years. The Council supervises referendums and announces referendum and election results. It also examines the eligibility of candidates to the presidency and the legislature. There is no appeal against the Council's decisions.

JUDICIAL POWER

Articles 101–112: The judiciary is independent, and is composed of the Haute cour de justice, the Cour de cassation, the Conseil d'Etat, the Cour des comptes, and regional tribunals and appeals courts. The Conseil supérieur de la magistrature examines questions relating to judicial independence and nominates and disciplines senior magistrates. The Haute cour de justice judges members of the government in cases relating to the execution of their duties. The Haute cour, which is composed of deputies elected by the national assembly, may only judge the President in cases of high treason.

ECONOMIC AND SOCIAL COUNCIL

Articles 113–114: The Economic and Social Council gives its opinion on proposed legislation or decrees relating to its sphere of competence. The President may consult the council on any economic or social matter.

THE MEDIATOR OF THE REPUBLIC

Articles 115–118: The Mediator is an independent mediating figure, appointed for a non-renewable six-year mandate by the President, in consultation with the president of the national assembly. The Mediator, who may not hold any other office or position, receives immunity from prosecution during the term of office.

OTHER ISSUES

Articles 119–133: Only the President or the national assembly, of whom a two-thirds majority must be in favour, may propose amending the Constitution. Amendments relating to the nature of the presidency or the mechanism whereby the Constitution is amended must be approved by referendum; all other amendments may be enacted with the agreement of the President and of a four-fifths majority of the national assembly. The form and the secular nature of the republic may not be amended. Immunity from prosecution is granted to members of the Comité national de salut public (CNSP) and to all those involved in the change of government of December 1999.

The Government

HEAD OF STATE

President of the Republic and President of the National Committee of Public Salvation (CNSP): Brig.-Gen. ROBERT GUEÏ (assumed power in a *coup d'état* 24 December 1999).

COUNCIL OF MINISTERS
(August 2000)

President of the Republic, President of the CNSP and Minister of Defence: Brig.-Gen. ROBERT GUEÏ.

Prime Minister, responsible for Planning and Development: SEYDOU ELIMANE DIARRA.

Minister of State, responsible for Security: Intendant-Gen. LASSANA PALENFO.

Minister of State, responsible for Transport: Air Commodore ABDOULAYE COULIBALY.

Minister of State, responsible for Youth and Sports: Brig.-Gen. MATHIAS DOUÉ.

Minister of Foreign Relations: CHARLES GOMIS.

Minister of the Interior and Decentralization: Col GRENA MOUASSI.

Minister of Justice and Keeper of the Seals: Me ESSY N'GATTA.

Minister of the Economy and Finance: Prof. MAMADOU COULIBALY.

Minister of Agriculture and Animal Resources: AHMED TIMITE.

Minister of Francophone Affairs and Culture: HENRIETTE DAGBA DIABATÉ.

Minister of Higher Education and Scientific Research: Prof. BAILLY SERI.

Minister of National Education: MICHEL N'GUESSAN AMANI.

Minister of Technical Education and Professional Training: LÉON EMMANUEL MONNET.

Minister of Public Health: JEANINE TAGLIANTE SARACINO.

Minister of Employment and the Civil Service: HUBERT OULAYE.

Minister of Construction and the Environment: Maj. Me HONORÉ ZOHIN.

Minister of the Family and the Promotion of Women: CONSTANCE YAÏ.

Minister of Communication: Naval Lt HENRI SAMA.

Minister of Industry and Tourism: AFFI N'GUESSAN.

Minister of Mining and Energy: MOUSSA TOURE.

Minister of Infrastructure: MICHEL BADIA YORO.

Minister of Trade: Lt-Commdr DJIKALOU SAINT-CYR.

Minister of Social Welfare and National Solidarity: MARTHE BILEY ACHI-BROU.

MINISTRIES

Office of the President: Abidjan.

Office of the Prime Minister: blvd Angoulvant, 01 BP 1533, Abidjan 01; tel. 20-21-11-00; fax 20-21-70-41.

Office of the Minister of State with responsibility for Foreign Affairs: BP V109, Abidjan; tel. 20-22-71-50; fax 20-33-23-08.

Office of the Minister of State with responsibility for the Interior and Decentralization: BP V121, Abidjan; tel. 20-32-23-43.

Office of the Minister of State with responsibility for National Integration: Périmètre de la Présidence, Abidjan; tel. 20-22-04-88; fax 20-32-90-77.

Office of the Minister of State with responsibility for Relations with the Institutions: 04 BP 566, Abidjan 04; tel. 20-22-00-25.

Ministry of Agriculture and Animal Resources: BP V82, Abidjan; tel. 20-21-08-33; fax 20-21-46-18.

Ministry of Culture: Tour E, 22e étape, BP V39, Abidjan; tel. 20-21-40-34; fax 20-21-33-59; e-mail culture.ci@ci.refer.org; internet www.refer.org/ivoir_ct/tur/min.

Ministry of Defence: BP V11, Abidjan; tel. 20-21-26-74; fax 20-22-28-18.

Ministry of Economic Infrastructure: Immeuble POSTEL, 23e étage, BP V6, Abidjan; tel. 20-34-73-15; fax 20-21-30-37.

Ministry of the Economy and Finance: Immeuble SCIAM, 16e étage, ave Marchand, BP V163, Abidjan; tel. 20-21-05-66; fax 20-21-16-90.

Ministry of Employment, the Civil Service and Social Welfare: BP V193, Abidjan; tel. 20-21-42-90; fax 20-22-84-15.

Ministry of Energy: BP V06, Abidjan; tel. 20-34-60-00.

Ministry of the Family and the Promotion of Women: BP V200, Abidjan; tel. 20-21-76-26; fax 20-21-44-61.

Ministry of Foreign Trade Promotion: 04 BP 2302, Abidjan 04; tel. 20-21-37-07; fax 20-21-91-72.

Ministry of Higher Education and Scientific Research: BP V151, Abidjan; tel. 20-21-78-70; fax 20-21-22-25.

Ministry of Housing and Urban Planning: BP V153, Abidjan; tel. 20-21-94-06; fax 20-21-45-61.

Ministry of Industrial Development and Small and Medium-sized Enterprises: Immeuble CCI, 15e étage, BP V65, Abidjan; tel. 20-21-30-88.

Ministry of Information: BP V138, Abidjan; tel. 20-21-11-16; fax 20-22-22-97.

Ministry of Internal Trade Promotion: Immeuble CCIA, 23e étage, BP V142, Abidjan; tel. 20-21-24-35; fax 20-21-23-24.

Ministry of Justice and Human Rights: BP V107, Abidjan; tel. 20-32-08-88; fax 20-33-12-59.

Ministry of Mining and Petroleum Resources: BP V50, Abidjan; tel. 20-21-50-03; fax 20-21-53-20.

Ministry of National Education and Basic Training: BP V120, Abidjan; tel. 20-22-44-17; fax 20-22-69-08; e-mail menfb@ci .refer.org; internet www.refer.org/ivoir_ct/edu/menfb.

Ministry of Public Health: Cité Administrative, Tour C, 16e étage, BP V4, Abidjan; tel. 20-21-08-71; fax 20-21-10-85.

Ministry of Security: BP V241, Abidjan; tel. 20-21-19-50.

Ministry of Technical Education and Professional Training: 20 BP 256, Abidjan 20; tel. 20-21-17-02.

Ministry of Tourism and Handicrafts: Immeuble EECI, place de la République, 01 BP 8538, Abidjan 01; tel. 20-20-65-00; fax 20-22-59-24; e-mail cotedivoire@afri-can.com; internet www.cotedivoire .org.

Ministry of Transport: BP V06, Abidjan; tel. 20-34-60-00.

Ministry of Youth and Sports: BP V136, Abidjan; tel. 20-21-52-51; fax 20-22-48-21.

President and Legislature

Note: Following the *coup d'état* of 24 December 1999, it was announced that new presidential and legislative elections were to take place before 31 October 2000. The following results refer to the last elections conducted under the ousted Bédié regime.

PRESIDENT

Presidential Election, 22 October 1995

Candidate	Votes	% of votes
AIMÉ HENRI KONAN BÉDIÉ	1,640,635	95.25
ROMAIN FRANCIS WODIÉ	65,486	3.80
Abstentions	16,385	0.95
Total	**1,722,506**	**100.00**

ASSEMBLÉE NATIONALE

President: EMILE ATTA AMOAKAN BROU.

General Election, 26 November 1995

Party	Seats
PDCI–RDA	146
RDR	14
FPI	9
Total	**169***

* Voting for three further seats was postponed prior to the election, and the results of voting in three constituencies was annulled by the Constitutional Court in December 1995. By-elections for these and for two other seats took place in December 1996: the FPI won five seats and the PDCI–RDA three.

Advisory Councils

Conseil Constitutionnel: Abidjan; f. 1994; Pres. TIA KONÉ.

Conseil Economique et Social: 04 BP 301, Abidjan 04; tel. 20-21-14-54; Pres. (vacant); Vice-Pres BEDA YAO, GLADYS ANOMA, AUGUSTE DAUBREY, MARTIN KOUAKOU KOUADIO, BERNARD ANO BOA; 120 mems.

Political Organizations

In late 1999 there were some 90 registered political organizations, of which the following were represented in the Assemblée nationale elected in November 1995:

Front populaire ivoirien (FPI): 22 BP 302, Abidjan 22; tel. 21-24-36-76; fax 21-35-35-50; e-mail fpi@africaonline.co.ci; internet www.fpi.ci; f. 1983 in France; social-democratic; Chair. LAURENT KOUDOU GBAGBO; Sec.-Gen. ABOU DRAHAMANE SANGARÉ.

Parti démocratique de la Côte d'Ivoire–Rassemblement démocratique africain (PDCI–RDA): Maison du Parti, Abidjan; f. 1946 as the local section of the Rassemblement démocratique africain; Pres. LAURENT DONA FOLONGO (acting); Sec.-Gen. LAURENT DONA-FOLOGO.

Rassemblement des républicains (RDR): Abidjan; f. 1994, following split from PDCI–RDA; Pres. ALASSANE OUATTARA; Sec.-Gen. HENRIETTE DAGBA DIABATÉ.

Other registered parties include:

The **Congrès démocrate national (CDN):** Nat. Exec. Sec. MOCTAR HAIDARA; the **Front ivoirien du salut (FIS):** Sec.-Gen. N'TAKPE AUCHORET MONNON'GBA; the **Front de redressement national (FRN):** Sec.-Gen. VICTOR ATSEPI; the **Groupement pour la solidarité (GPS):** Pres. ACHI KOMAN; the **Mouvement démocratique et social (MDS):** First Nat. Sec.-Gen. SIAKA TOURÉ; the **Mouvement indépendantistes ivoirien (MII):** Pres. ADOU YAPI; the **Mouvement progressiste de Côte d'Ivoire (MPCI):** Sec.-Gen. AUGUSTIN NANGONE BI DOUA; the **Organisation populaire de la jeunesse (OPJ):** Sec.-Gen. DENIS LATTA; the **Parti africain pour la renaissance ivoirienne (PARI):** Sec.-Gen. DANIEL ANIKPO; the **Parti communiste ivoirien (PCI):** Sec.-Gen. DENIS GUEU DRO; the **Parti fraternel des planteurs, des parents d'élèves et industriels ivoiriens (PFPPEI):** Pres. ERNEST AMESSAN; the **Parti ivoirien pour la démocratie (PID):** Sec.-Gen. FAUSTIN BOTOKO LÉKA; the **Parti ivoirien des travailleurs (PIT):** Sec.-Gen. ANGEL GNONSOA (acting); the **Parti ivoirien de justice et de solidarité (PIJS):** Pres. KEKONGO N'DIEN; the **Parti libéral de Côte d'Ivoire (PLCI):** Sec.-Gen. YADY SOUMAH; the **Parti pour la libération totale de la Côte d'Ivoire (PLTCI):** Sec.-Gen. ELISE ALLOUFOU NIAMIEN; the **Parti pour les libertés et la démocratie (PLD):** Pres. JEAN-PIERRE OUYA; the **Parti national socialiste (PNS):** Pres. RAPHAËL YAPI BEDA; the **Parti ouvrier et paysan de Côte d'Ivoire (POPCI):** Exec. Pres. KOUASSI ADOLPHE BLOKON; the **Parti pour le progrès et la solidarité (PPS):** Sec.-Gen. BAMBA MORIFÉRÉ; the **Parti progressiste ivoirien (PPI):** Pres. SOUMAHORO KASSINDOU; the **Parti pour la protection de l'environnement (PPE):** Sec.-Gen. DIOBA COULIBALY; the **Parti du rassemblement du peuple pour la jeunesse de Côte d'Ivoire (PRJCI):** Sec.-Gen. PHILIPPE ESSIS KHOL; the **Parti pour la reconstruction nationale et la démocratie (PRND):** Pres. MARC JOSEPH BEHED; the **Parti réformiste démocratique ivoirien (PRDI):** Sec.-Gen. RAPHAËL BEUGRÉ KOAMÉ; the **Parti pour la réhabilitation ivoirienne du social et de l'économie (PRISE):** Exec. Pres. GEORGES GRAHOU; the **Parti républicain de Côte d'Ivoire (PRCI):** Sec.-Gen. ROBERT GBAI TAGRO; the **Parti socialiste ivoirien (PSI):** First Nat. Sec. MANDOU-ADJOA KOUAKOU; the **Rassemblement des forces démocratiques (RFD):** Pres. FAKOUROU TOURÉ; the **Rassemblement pour le progrès social (RPS):** Pres. MAMADOU KONÉ; the **Rassemblement pour la République (RPR):** Sec.-Gen. BLAISE BONOUA KODJO; the **Rassemblement des sociaux-démocrates (RSD):** Sec.-Gen. MAHI GUINA; the **Union des libéraux pour la République (ULR):** Pres. CÉLÉSTIN AMON; the **Union nationale des démocrates (UND):** Sec.-Gen. AMADOU KONÉ; the **Union des paysans, des ouvriers et des salariés de Côte d'Ivoire (UPOSCI):** Sec.-Gen. COA KIÉMOKO; the **Union pour le progrès social (UPS):** Sec.-Gen. ALBERT SÉHÉ; and the **Union des sociaux-démocrates (USD):** Sec.-Gen. BERNARD ZADI ZAOUROU.

Diplomatic Representation

EMBASSIES IN CÔTE D'IVOIRE

Algeria: 53 blvd Clozel, Abidjan; tel. 20-32-32-40; Ambassador: MOHAMED SENOUSSI.

Angola: Villa Duplex no 2461, Lot 212, rue des Jardins, Cocody-les-Deux-Plateaux, 16 BP 1734, Abidjan 16; tel. 22-41-38-79; fax 22-41-28-89; Ambassador: SIMEÃO ADÃO MANUEL 'KAFUXY'.

Austria: Immeuble N'Zarama, blvd Lagunaire-Charles de Gaulle, Plateau, 01 BP 1837, Abidjan 01; tel. 20-21-25-00; fax 20-22-19-23; Ambassador: Dr EWALD JÄGER.

Belgium: Immeuble Alliance, ave Terrasson de Fougères, 01 BP 1800, Abidjan 01; tel. 20-21-00-88; Ambassador: PIERRE COLOT.

Benin: blvd André Latrille, Lot 244, Cocody, 09 BP 283, Abidjan 09; tel. 22-41-44-13; fax 22-41-27-89; Ambassador: AUGUSTE C. ALAVO.

Brazil: Immeuble Alpha 2000, rue Gourgas, 01 BP 3820, Abidjan 01; tel. 20-22-23-41; Chargé d'affaires a.i.: FERNANDO JABLONSKI.

Burkina Faso: 2 ave Terrasson de Fougères, 01 BP 908, Abidjan 01; tel. 20-32-13-55; fax 20-32-66-41; Ambassador: LÉANDRE BASSOLE.

Cameroon: Immeuble Général, blvd Botreau Roussel, 01 BP 2886, Abidjan 01; tel. 20-32-33-31; Ambassador: PAUL KAMGA NJIKE.

Canada: Immeuble Trade Centre, ave Nogues, 01 BP 4104, Abidjan 01; tel. 20-32-20-09; fax 20-21-77-28; Ambassador: SUZANNE LAPORTE.

Central African Republic: rue des Combattants, 01 BP 338, Abidjan 01; Ambassador: EMMANUEL BONGOPASSI.

China, People's Republic: 01 BP 3691, Abidjan 01; tel. 22-44-59-00; fax 22-44-67-81; Ambassador: ZHAO BAOZHEN.

Colombia: Tour BIAO, 16e étage, ave Lamblin, 01 BP 3874, Abidjan 01; tel. 20-33-15-15; fax 20-32-47-31; e-mail emcoci@africaonline .co.ci; Chargé d'affaires a.i.: SANTIAGO SALCEDO.

Congo, Democratic Republic: 29 blvd Clozel, 01 BP 3961, Abidjan 01; tel. 20-22-20-80; Ambassador: BAMBI MAVUNGU.

Czech Republic: Immeuble Tropique III, 01 BP 1349, Abidjan 01; tel. 20-21-20-30; fax 20-22-19-06; Chargé d'affaires a.i.: ZDENEK MRKLOVSKY.

Egypt: Immeuble El Nasr, 17e étage, ave du Général de Gaulle, 01 BP 2104, Abidjan 01; tel. 20-22-62-31; fax 20-22-30-53; Ambassador: SAMI YASSA ABDEL SHAHID YASSA.

Ethiopia: Immeuble Nour Al-Hayat, 8e étage, ave Jacques Aka Cocody, 01 BP 3712, Abidjan 01; tel. 20-21-33-65; fax 20-21-37-09; Ambassador: Ato WESSEN BESHAH.

France: rue Lecoeur, quartier du Plateau, 17 BP 175, Abidjan 17; tel. 20-20-04-04; fax 20-22-42-54; Ambassador: FRANCIS LOTT.

Gabon: Cocody Danga Nord, derrière la Direction de la Géologie, 01 BP 3765, Abidjan 01; tel. 22-41-51-54; fax 22-44-75-05; Ambassador: VICTOR MAGNAGNA.

Germany: Immeuble Le Mans, angle blvd Botreau Roussel et ave Nogues, 01 BP 1900, Abidjan 01; tel. 20-21-47-27; fax 20-32-47-29; Ambassador: HANS-ALBRECHT SCHRAEPLER.

Ghana: Résidence de la Corniche, blvd du Général de Gaulle, 01 BP 1871, Abidjan 01; tel. 20-33-11-24; Ambassador: AKUMFI AMEYAW MUNIFIE.

Guinea: Immeuble Crosson Duplessis, 08 BP 2280, Abidjan 08; tel. 20-32-86-00; fax 20-32-82-45; Ambassador: DOMINIQUE KOLY.

Holy See: 08 BP 1347, Abidjan 08 (Apostolic Nunciature); tel. 22-44-38-35; fax 22-44-72-40; e-mail nuntius@comete.ci; Apostolic Nuncio: Most Rev. MARIO ZENARI, Titular Archbishop of Zuglio.

India: Lot 36, impasse Ablaha Pokou, Cocody, Danga Nord, 06 BP 318, Abidjan 06; tel. 22-44-52-31; fax 22-44-01-11; Ambassador: PRADEEP K. GUPTA.

Israel: Immeuble Nour Al-Hayat, ave Chardy, Plateau, 01 BP 1877, Abidjan 01; tel. 20-21-49-53; fax 20-21-87-04; Ambassador: JAACOV REVAH.

Italy: 16 rue de la Canebière, Cocody, 01 BP 1905, Abidjan 01; tel. 22-44-61-70; fax 22-44-35-87; e-mail ambitali@aviso.ci; Ambassador: LUIGI COSTA SANSEVERINO.

Japan: Immeuble Alpha 2000, Tour A, 18e étage, ave Chardy, 01 BP 1329, Abidjan 01; tel. 20-21-28-63; fax 20-21-30-51; Ambassador: MITSUHIRO NAKAMURA.

Lebanon: 01 BP 2227, Abidjan 01; tel. 20-33-28-24; Ambassador: MOHAMED DAHER.

Liberia: Immeuble La Symphonie, ave du Général de Gaulle, 01 BP 2514, Abidjan 01; tel. 20-22-23-59; Chargé d'affaires a.i.: TIAHKWEE JOHNSON.

Mali: Maison du Mali, rue du Commerce, 01 BP 2746, Abidjan 01; tel. 20-32-31-47; Ambassador: LASSANA KEITA.

Mauritania: blvd Latrille, rue de la Paroisse St Jacques, Cocody-les-Deux-Plateaux, 01 BP 2275, Abidjan 01; tel. 22-44-16-43; fax 22-41-05-77; Ambassador: Dr DIAGANA YOUSSOUF.

Morocco: 24 rue de la Canebière, Cocody, 01 BP 146, Abidjan 01; tel. 22-44-58-78; Ambassador: AHMED ASSOULI.

Netherlands: Immeuble Les Harmonies, 2e étage, angle blvd Carde et ave Dr Jamot, Plateau, 01 BP 1086, Abidjan 01; tel. 20-22-77-12; fax 20-21-17-61; Ambassador: PETER VAN LEEUWEN.

Niger: 23 ave Angoulvant, 01 BP 2743, Abidjan 01; tel. 21-35-50-98; Ambassador: MADI KONATÉ.

Nigeria: 35 blvd de la République, 01 BP 1906, Abidjan 01; tel. 20-22-30-82; Ambassador: JONATHAN OLUWOLE COKER.

Norway: Immeuble N'Zarama, blvd du Général de Gaulle, 01 BP 607, Abidjan 01; tel. 20-22-25-34; fax 20-21-91-99; Ambassador: LARS TANGERAAS.

Poland: 04 BP 308, Abidjan 04; tel. 22-44-10-67; fax 22-44-12-35; e-mail polska@globeaccess.net; Chargé d'affaires a.i.: PIOTR MYSLIWIEC.

Russia: Riviera SQ-1 Sud, 01 BP 7646, Abidjan 01; tel. 22-43-09-59; Ambassador: MIKHAIL V. MAIOROV.

Senegal: Résidence Nabil, blvd du Général de Gaulle, 08 BP 2165, Abidjan 08; tel. 20-32-28-76; Ambassador: OUSMANE CAMARA.

South Africa: Villa Marc André, rue Mgr René Kouassi, Cocody Président, 08 BP 1806, Abidjan 08; tel. 22-44-59-63; fax 22-44-74-50; Ambassador: S. NGOMBANE.

Spain: impasse Ablaha Pokou, Cocody, Danga Nord, 08 BP 876, Abidjan 08; tel. 22-44-48-50; fax 22-44-71-22; e-mail embespan@aviso.ci; Ambassador: ALMUDENA MAZARRASA ALVEAR.

Sweden: Immeuble N'Zarama, 4e étage, blvd Lagunaire, 04 BP 992, Abidjan 04; tel. 20-21-24-10; fax 20-21-21-07; e-mail ambsuede@aviso.ci; Ambassador: GÖRAN ANKARBERG.

Switzerland: Immeuble Alpha 2000, rue Gourgas, 01 BP 1914, Abidjan 01; tel. 20-21-17-21; fax 20-21-27-70; Ambassador: PIERRE DE GRAFFENRIED.

Tunisia: Immeuble Pelieu, 6e étage, ave Delafosse, Abidjan 01; tel. 20-22-61-22; Ambassador: MONCEF LARBI.

United Kingdom: Immeuble Les Harmonies, 3e étage, angle blvd Carde et ave Dr Jamot, Plateau, 01 BP 2581, Abidjan 01; tel. 20-22-68-50; fax 20-22-32-21; Ambassador: HAYDON WARREN-GASH.

USA: 5 rue Jesse Owens, 01 BP 1712, Abidjan 01; tel. 20-21-09-79; fax 20-22-32-59; Ambassador: GEORGE MU.

Judicial System

Since 1964 all civil, criminal, commercial and administrative cases have come under the jurisdiction of the Tribunaux de première instance (magistrates' courts), the assize courts and the Court of Appeal, with the Cour de cassation as the highest court of appeal.

Cour de cassation (Supreme Court): rue Gourgas, BP V30, Abidjan; has four chambers: constitutional, judicial, administrative and auditing; Pres. TIA KONÉ.

Courts of Appeal: Abidjan and Bouaké; hear appeals from courts of first instance; Abidjan.

Haute cour de justice (High Court of Justice): composed of Deputies elected from and by the National Assembly; has jurisdiction to impeach the President or other member of the Government.

Courts of First Instance: Abidjan, Pres. ANTOINETTE MARSOUIN; Bouaké: Pres. KABLAN AKA EDOUKOU; Daloa: Pres. WOUNE BLEKA; there are a further 25 courts in the principal centres.

Religion

The Constitution guarantees religious freedom, and this right is generally respected. Religious groups are required to register with the authorities, although no penalties are imposed on a group that fails to register. At the 1988 census it was estimated that about 25.1% of the population were Muslims, 22.8% followed traditional indigenous beliefs, 22.7% were Catholics, 6.6% were Protestants, 1.9% were Harrists, 4.0% practised other religions, while 16.9% had no religious affiliation. It is, however, estimated that the proportion of Muslims is in fact significantly higher, as the majority of unregistered foreign workers are Muslims. Muslims are found in greatest numbers in the north of the country, while Catholics and Protestants are found mostly in the southern, central, and eastern regions. Traditional indigenous beliefs are generally prevalent in rural areas.

ISLAM

Confédération Islamique du Développement de la Côte d'Ivoire: Abidjan.

Conseil National Islamique (CNI): f. 1993; Chair. El Hadj IDRISS KOUDOUSS KONÉ.

Conseil Supérieur Islamique (CSI): f. 1978; Chair. El Hadj MOUSTAPHA DIABY.

Front de la Oumma Islamique: Abidjan.

CHRISTIANITY

The Roman Catholic Church

Côte d'Ivoire comprises four archdioceses and 10 dioceses. At 31 December 1998 Roman Catholics comprised about 12.6% of the total population.

Bishops' Conference: Conférence Episcopale de la Côte d'Ivoire, 01 BP 1287, Abidjan 01; tel. 20-33-22-56; f. 1973; Pres. Most Rev. VITAL KOMENAN YAO, Archbishop of Bouaké.

Archbishop of Abidjan: Most Rev. BERNARD AGRÉ, Archevêché, ave Jean Paul II, 01 BP 1287, Abidjan 01; tel. 20-21-23-08; fax 20-21-40-22.

Archbishop of Bouaké: Most Rev. VITAL KOMENAN YAO, Archevêché, 01 BP 649, Bouaké 01; tel. and fax 63-24-59.

Archbishop of Gagnoa: Most Rev. NOËL KOKORA-TEKRY, Archevêché, BP 527, Gagnoa; tel. 77-25-68; fax 77-20-96.

Archbishop of Korhogo: Most Rev. AUGUSTE NOBOU, Archevêché, BP 12, Korhogo; tel. 86-01-18; fax 86-05-26.

Protestant Churches

Assemblée de Dieu: 04 BP 266, Abidjan 04; tel. 20-37-05-79; fax 20-24-94-65; f. 1960; Pres. GBOAGNON SÉRY APPOLINAIRE.

CB International: BP 109, Korhogo; tel. 86-01-07; fax 86-11-50; f. 1947; fmrly Conservative Baptist Foreign Mission Society; active in evangelism, medical work, translation, literacy and theological education in the northern area and in Abidjan.

Christian and Missionary Alliance: BP 585, Bouaké 01; tel. 63-23-12; fax 63-54-12; f. 1929; 13 mission stations; Dir Rev. DAVID W. ARNOLD.

Eglise du Nazaréen (Church of the Nazarene): 22 BP 623, Abidjan 22; tel. 22-41-07-90; fax 22-41-07-81; e-mail awfcon@ compuserve.com; f. 1988; active in evangelism, ministerial training and medical work; Dir JOHN SEAMAN.

Eglise Protestante Baptiste Oeuvres et Mission: 03 BP 1032, Abidjan 03; tel. 23-45-20-18; fax 23-45-56-41; f. 1975; active in evangelism, teaching and social work; medical centre, 677 places of worship, 285 missionaries and 100,000 mems; Pres. YAYE ROBERT DION.

Eglise Protestante Méthodiste de Côte d'Ivoire: 41 blvd de la République, 01 BP 1282, Abidjan 01; tel. 20-21-17-97; fax 20-22-52-03; c. 650,000 mems; Pres. LAMBERT AKOSSI N'CHO.

Harrist Church: Abidjan; f. 1913 by William Wade Harris; African Protestant denomination; allows polygamous new converts; 100,000 mems, 1,400 preachers, 7,000 apostles.

Mission Evangélique de l'Afrique Occidentale: BP 822, Bouaflé; tel. and fax 68-93-70; e-mail 105344.2207@compuserve.com; f. 1934; 11 mission centres, 59 missionaries; Field Dirs LINDA NAGEL, MARRY SCHOTTE; affiliated church: Alliance des Eglises Evangéliques de Côte d'Ivoire; 254 churches, 65 full-time pastors; Pres. BOAN BI ZRÈ EMMANUEL.

Mission Evangélique Luthérienne en Côte d'Ivoire (MELCI): BP 196, Touba; tel. 70-71-78; f. 1984; active in evangelism and social work; Dir OSCAR NORDBØ.

Union des Eglises Evangéliques du Sud-Ouest de la Côte d'Ivoire and **Mission Biblique:** 08 BP 20, Abidjan 08; f. 1927; c. 250 places of worship.

Other religious groups in Côte d'Ivoire include the Adventist Church, Bossonism (the traditional religious practices of the Akan ethnic group), the Autonomous Church of Celestial Christianity of Oschoffa, the Union of the Evangelical Church of Services and Works of Côte d'Ivoire, the Church of Jesus Christ of the Latter-Day Saints, the Yoruba First Church, the Church of God International Missions, the Church of the Prophet Papa Nouveau, the Pentecostal Church of Côte d'Ivoire, the Messianic Church, the Limoudim of Rabbi Jesus, the Unification Church, Jehovah's Witnesses, and the Inter-denominational Church.

The Press

DAILIES

Actuel: Cocody-les-Deux-Plateaux, 06 BP 2868, Abidjan 06; tel. 22-42-83-27; fax 22-42-63-32; f. 1996; organ of the FPI; Dir MARTIN SOUKOURI BOHOUI.

Douze (Sport): rue Louis Lumière, zone 4C, 10 BP 2462, Abidjan 10; tel. 21-25-54-00; fax 21-35-85-66; f. 1994; Dir RAYES NADY.

Fraternité Matin: blvd du Général de Gaulle, 01 BP 1807, Abidjan 01; tel. 20-37-06-66; e-mail fratmat@africanonline.co.ci; internet www.fratmat.co.ci; f. 1964; official newspaper; Man. Dir MICHEL KOUAMÉ; circ. 80,000.

L'Inter: rue Louis Lumière, Zone 4C, 10 BP 2462, Abidjan 10; tel. 21-25-32-77; fax 21-35-85-66; f. 1998; Dir RAYES NADY.

Ivoir 'Soir: blvd du Général de Gaulle, 01 BP 1807, Abidjan 01; tel. 20-21-95-78; fax 20-37-25-45; internet www.africaonline/co.ci/ AfricaOnline/infos/ivs/ivs.html; f. 1987; organ of the PDCI–RDA; Dir-Gen. EMMANUEL KOUASSI KOKORÉ; circ. 52,000.

Le Jour: 26 ave Chardy, Plateau, 01 BP 2432, Abidjan 01; tel. 20-21-95-78; fax 20-21-95-80; e-mail lejour@africaonline.co.ci; internet www.africaonline.co.ci/infos/lejour.html; f. 1994; Dirs DIEGOU BAILLY, ABDOULAYE SANGARÉ; circ. 16,000.

Le Libéral: Arras III, appt 75, 01 BP 6938, Abidjan 01; tel. 21-25-18-36; f. 1997; organ of the RDR; Dir YORO KONE.

Notre Voie: Cocody-les-Deux-Plateaux, 06 BP 2868, Abidjan 06; tel. 22-42-63-31; fax 22-42-63-32; e-mail gnh@africaonline.co.ci; internet www.africaonline.co.ci/africaonline/infos/notrevoie; f. 1978; organ of the FPI; Dir WANYOU EUGÉNE ALLOU; Editor-in-chief DIABATÉ A. SIDICK.

La Nouvelle République: face Théâtre de la Cité, impasse P. L. Clouzet, Cocody Danga, 09 BP 960, Abidjan 09; tel. 22-41-15-89; fax 22-44-97-10; f. 1994; Dir NOËL YAO.

Le Patriote: rue Marconi prologée, Zone 4C, 22 BP 509, Abidjan 22; tel. 07-83-72-47; fax 20-22-59-26; e-mail lepatriote@globeaccess.net; internet www.lepatriote.ci; Dir PATRICE G. LENONHIN; Editor-in-Chief SINDOU METTE.

Le Populaire–Nouvelle Formule: 19 blvd Angoulvant, résidence Neuilly, Plateau, 01 BP 5496, Abidjan 01; tel. 21-36-34-15; fax 21-36-43-28; Dir RAPHAËL ORE LAKPE.

Soir Info: rue Louis Lumière, zone 4C, 10 BP 2462, Abidjan 10; tel. 21-25-32-77; fax 21-35-85-66; f. 1994; Dir MAURICE FERRO B. BALLY; circ. 10,000–15,000.

La Voie: face Institut Marie-Thérèse Houphouët-Boigny, 17 BP 656, Abidjan 17; tel. 20-37-68-23; fax 20-37-74-76; organ of the FPI; Dir ABOU DRAHAMANE SANGARÉ; Man. MAURICE LURIGNAN.

SELECTED WEEKLIES

Agora: Immeuble Nana Yamoussou, ave 13, rue 38, Treichville, 01 BP 5326, Abidjan 01; tel. 21-25-12-43; f. 1997; Dir FERNAND DÉDÉ.

Argument: 09 BP 3328, Abidjan 09; tel. 20-37-63-96; f. 1998; Dir GUY-BADIETO LIALY.

Le Bélier: Immeuble Citrine, appt 180, Marcory SICOGI, 16 BP 465, Abidjan 16; tel. 21-26-34-06; f. 1993; Dir LAURENT TAPE KOULOU.

Le Changement: Immeuble Ghadar, blvd Giscard d'Estaing, 16 BP 10, Abidjan 16; tel. 21-25-52-52; f. 1991; weekly; Dir BELIWA DAVID GOGBÉ; circ. 10,000.

Citypoche: Immeuble Nour al-Ayat, 18 BP 3136, Abidjan 18; tel. 20-21-91-89; f. 1997; Dir ELIANE STROEHLIN.

Le Démocrate: Maison du Congrès, ave 2, Treichville, 01 BP 1212, Abidjan 01; tel. 21-24-45-88; fax 21-24-25-61; f. 1991; organ of the PDCI–RDA; Dir NOËL YAO.

Mousso: zone 4C, prolongement blvd du 7 décembre, Abidjan; fax 21-35-19-06; f. 1993; Dir MOUSSA SIDIBE.

Notre chance: Immeuble SICOGI, 1er étage, porte escalier E, blvd du Gabon (Marcory), 10 BP 654, Abidjan 10; tel. 21-26-44-28; Dir MICHEL NAHOUA LEPREGNON.

Le Nouvel Horizon: 220 Logements, blvd du Général de Gaulle, Adjamé, 17 BP 656, Abidjan 17; tel. 20-37-68-23; f. 1990; organ of the FPI; Dir ABOU DRAHAMANE SANGARÉ; circ. 15,000.

La Nouvelle Presse: rue des Jardins, Cocody-les-deux-Plateaux, 01 BP 8534, Abidjan 01; tel. 22-41-04-76; fax 22-41-04-15; e-mail jvieyra@africaonline.co.ci; f. 1992; publ. by Centre Africain de Presse et d'Edition; current affairs; Editors JUSTIN VIEYRA, JÉRÔME CARLOS; circ. 10,000.

Le Réveil-Hebdo: face Théatre de la Cité, impasse P. L. Clouzet, Cocody Danga, 09 BP 960, Abidjan 09; tel. 22-44-90-96; fax 22-44-97-10; f. 1993; Dir NOËL YAO.

Sports Magazine: Yopougon-SOGEFIHA, 01 BP 4030, Abidjan 01; tel. 23-45-14-02; f. 1997; Dir JOSEPH ABLE.

Téré: 220 Lgts, blvd du Général de Gaulle, Adjamé Liberté, 20 BP 43, Abidjan 20; tel. and fax 20-37-79-42; organ of the PIT; weekly; Dir ANGÈLE GNONSOA.

La Voie du Compatriote: Adjamé St-Michel; 09 BP 2008, Abidjan 09; tel. 20-37-50-13; f. 1998; Dir SINARI KAL.

La Voix d'Afrique: rue des Jardins, Cocody-les-Deux-Plateaux, 01 BP 8534, Abidjan 01; tel. 22-41-04-76; fax 22-41-04-15; e-mail jvieyra@africaonline.co.ci; publ. by Centre Africain de Presse et d'Edition; monthly; Editor-in-Chief GAOUSSOU KAMISSOKO.

SELECTED PERIODICALS

Côte d'Ivoire Magazine: Présidence de la République, 01 BP 1354, Abidjan 01; tel. 20-22-02-22; f. 1998; quarterly; Dir JEAN-NOËL LOUKO.

La Lettre de l'Afrique de l'Ouest: rue des Jardins, Cocody-les-Deux-Plateaux, 01 BP 8534, Abidjan 01; tel. 22-41-04-76; fax 22-41-04-15; e-mail jvieyra@africaonline.co.ci; f. 1995; publ. by Centre Africain de Presse et d'Edition; six a year; politics, economics, regional integration; Editors JUSTIN VIEYRA, JÉRÔME CARLOS.

La Lettre de la Communication: Cité Administrative, BP V138, Abidjan; tel. 20-21-11-16; Dir PIERRE AYOUN N'DAH.

Maisons et Matériaux: 08 BP 2150, Abidjan 08; tel. 22-42-92-17; monthly; Dir THIAM T. DJENEBOU.

Roots Magazine: 01 BP 1418, Abidjan 01; tel. 22-42-84-74; f. 1998; monthly; Dir DIOMANDÉ DAVID.

RTI-Mag: 08 BP 663, Abidjan 08; tel. 20-33-14-46; fax 20-32-12-06; publ. by Radiodiffusion-Télévision Ivoirienne; listings magazine.

Stades d'Afrique: blvd du Général de Gaulle, 01 BP 1807, Abidjan 01; tel. 20-37-06-66; fax 20-37-25-45; e-mail fratmat@africaonline .co.ci; f. 2000; sports magazine; monthly; Dir-Gen. EMMANUEL KOUASSI KOKORÉ.

Le Succès: 21 BP 3748, Abidjan 21; tel. 20-37-71-64; monthly; Dir AKPLA PLAKATOU.

NEWS AGENCIES

Agence Ivoirienne de Presse (AIP): ave Chardy, 04 BP 312, Abidjan 04; tel. 20-22-71-89; fax 20-21-73-39; e-mail aip@ci.refer.org; internet www.refer.fr/ivoir_ct/med/aip; f. 1961; 12 perm. bureaux; Dir KONÉ SEMGUÉ SAMBA.

Foreign Bureaux

Agence France-Presse (AFP): 18 ave du Docteur Crozet, 01 BP 726, Abidjan 01; tel. 20-21-90-17; fax 20-21-10-36; e-mail afp@ aviso.ci; Dir SERGE ARNOLD.

Associated Press (AP) (USA): 01 BP 5843, Abidjan 01; tel. 22-41-37-49.

Reuters West Africa (United Kingdom): Résidence Les Acacias, 2e étage, appt 203–205, 20 blvd Clozel, 01 BP 2338, Abidjan 01; tel.

20-21-12-22; fax 20-21-30-77; e-mail abidjan.newsroom@reuters .com; West Africa Man. MICHEL CLÉMENT; Bureau Chief NICHOLAS PHYTHIAN.

Xinhua (New China) News Agency (People's Republic of China): Cocody Danga Nord, Lot 46, Abidjan; tel. 22-44-01-24.

PRESS ASSOCIATIONS

Association de la Presse Démocratique Ivoirienne (APDI): Abidjan; f. 1994; tel. 37-06-66; Chair. JEAN-BAPTISTE AKROU.

Union nationale des journalistes de Côte d'Ivoire (UNJCI): Abidjan; Pres. HONORAT DÉ YÉDAGNE.

Publishers

Centre Africain de Presse et d'Edition (CAPE): rue des Jardins, Cocody-les-Deux-Plateaux, 01 BP 8534, Abidjan 01; tel. 22-41-04-76; fax 22-41-04-15; e-mail jvieyra@africaonline.co.ci; Man. JUSTIN VIEYRA.

Centre d'Edition et de Diffusion Africaines (CEDA): square Aristide Briand, 04 BP 541, Abidjan 04; tel. 20-22-22-42; fax 20-32-72-62; f. 1961; general non-fiction; Chair. and Man. Dir VENANCE KACOU.

Centre de Publications Evangéliques: 08 BP 900, Abidjan 08; tel. 22-44-48-05; fax 22-44-58-17; f. 1970; religious; Dir JULES OUOBA.

Nouvelles Editions Ivoiriennes: 01 BP 1818, Abidjan 01; tel. 21-24-07-66; fax 21-24-24-56; e-mail info@mei.co.ci; f. 1972; literature, criticism, essays, drama, religion, art, history; Dir G. LAMBIN.

Université Nationale de Côte d'Ivoire: 01 BP V34, Abidjan 01; tel. 22-44-08-59. f. 1964; academic and general non-fiction and periodicals; Publications Dir GILLES VILASCO.

Government Publishing House

Imprimerie Nationale: BP V87, Abidjan; tel. 20-21-76-11; fax 20-21-68-68.

Broadcasting and Communications

TELECOMMUNICATIONS

Regulatory Authorities

Agence des Télécommunications de Côte d'Ivoire: Immeuble POSTEL 2001, 2e étage, 18 BP 2203, Abidjan 18; tel. 20-34-42-54; fax 20-34-42-58; e-mail atci@africaonline.co.ci; f. 1995; Man. Dir KOUATCHI EBOU.

Conseil des Télécommunications de Côte d'Ivoire: 17 BP 110, Abidjan 17; tel. 20-34-43-04; deals with issues of arbitration.

Service Providers

Côte d'Ivoire-Télécom (CI-Télécom): Immeuble Postel 2000, rue Lecoeur, 17 BP 275, Abidjan 17; tel. 34-34-40-00; fax 34-34-48-28; e-mail info@telecomci.com; internet www.telecomci.com; f. 1991; 51% owned by France Câble Radio; 49% state-owned; Pres. LÉON AKA BONNY; Man. Dir ALAIN PETIT.

Comstar Wireless: Immeuble Alpha 2000, 11e étage, Plateau, Abidjan; tel. 20-22-81-01; fax 20-22-81-05; f. 1996; mobile cellular telephone operator; owned by International Wireless Inc.

Loteny Télécom SA: 12 rue Crossons Duplessis, 01 BP 3685, Abidjan 01; tel. 20-32-32-32; fax 20-32-27-25; e-mail info@telecel.net; internet www.telecel.net; f. 1996; mobile cellular telephone operator; partnership between Telecel International, Access Télécom and Loteny Electronics; Pres. MIKO RWAYITARE.

Société Ivoirienne de Mobiles (SIM): Immeuble Plein Ciel, 5e étage, blvd Valery Giscard d'Estaing, Zone 4C, 11 BP 202, Abidjan 11; tel. 21-23-90-10; fax 21-23-90-11; f. 1996; mobile cellular telephone operator; 70% owned by France Télécom; 70,000 subscribers (June 1999).

BROADCASTING

Radio

Radiodiffusion-Télévision Ivoirienne (RTI): BP V 191, Abidjan 01; tel. 20-21-48-00; e-mail rti@rti.ci; internet www.rti.ci; f. 1962; state-owned; Pres. JOACHIM BONY; Dir-Gen. LEVI NIAMKEY.

La Chaîne Nationale: general FM broadcasts; 280 hrs of programmes weekly; also broadcasts regional news in national languages; 10 studios (eight in Abidjan and two in Bouaké).

Fréquence 2: themed FM broadcasts; entertainment, youth and relaxation; 147 hrs of programming weekly.

Africa Nº 1 Côte d'Ivoire: Abidjan; internet www.africa1.com; FM station; Dir NOËL YAO.

BBC Afrique: Abidjan; broadcasts commenced 1994; FM station operated by British Broadcasting Corpn.

Radio Espoir: 12 BP 27, Abidjan 12; tel. 21-27-60-01; fax 21-27-69-70; f. 1990; broadcasts from Port-Bouët by Roman Catholic Church; Dir Fr GIANFRANCO BRIGNON.

Radio Nostalgie 101.1 FM: Abidjan; internet www.metissacana .sn/nostalgie; f. 1993; subsidiary of Radio Nostalgie (France); music station; Pres. and Man. Dir HAMED BAKAYOKO.

RFI Internationale: Abidjan; operated by Radio France Internationale.

Television

Radiodiffusion-Télévision Ivoirienne (RTI): see above.

La Première Chaîne: 08 BP 883, Abidjan 08; tel. 22-44-90-39; general national and regional broadcasting; French and national languages; Dir KOFFI YOUBOUÉ.

TV 2: 08 BP 883, Abidjan 08; tel. 22-44-90-39; f. 1991; operates in Abidjan and the southern region; local news and current affairs; Dir MAIXENT DEGNEY.

Canal Horizon: Abidjan; e-mail abo.canal@aviso.ci; internet www.canalhorizons.com; broadcasts commenced 1994; subsidiary of Canal Plus (France); 15,000 subscribers (1995).

Côte d'Ivoire also receives international broadcasts from TVS, CNN, MCM Africa and Euronews.

Finance

(cap. = capital; res = reserves; m. = million; br. = branch; amounts in francs CFA)

BANKING

Central Bank

Banque Centrale des Etats de l'Afrique de l'Ouest (BCEAO): angle blvd Botreau Roussel et ave Delafosse, 01 BP 1769, Abidjan 01; tel. 20-21-04-66; fax 20-22-28-52; f. 1962; HQ in Dakar, Senegal; bank of issue for the mem. states of the Union économique et monétaire ouest-africaine (UEMOA, comprising Benin, Burkina Faso, Côte d'Ivoire, Guinea-Bissau, Mali, Niger, Senegal and Togo); cap. and res 806,918m., total assets 4,084,464m. (Dec. 1998); Gov. CHARLES KONAN BANNY; Dir in Côte d'Ivoire LANSINA BAKARY; 5 brs.

Commercial Banks

Bank of Africa–Côte d'Ivoire (BOA–CI): Immeuble ex-BNDA, 11 rue Joseph Anoma, 01 BP 4132, Abidjan 01; tel. 20-33-15-36; fax 20-32-89-93; e-mail c.i.boa@globeaccess.net; 52% owned by Groupe African Financial Holding; cap. and res 4,355m., total assets 31,965m. (Dec. 1998); Chair. PAUL DERREUMAUX; Man. Dir JEAN-PIERRE GALIBERT.

Banque Atlantique–Côte d'Ivoire: Immeuble El Nasir, ave du Général de Gaulle, Plateau, 04 BP 1035, Abidjan 04; tel. 20-21-82-18; fax 20-21-68-52; f. 1978; cap. and res 7,189m., total assets 59,713m. (Dec. 1998); Pres. SERGE GUETTA; Dir-Gen. JACKY VASSEUR.

Banque de l'Habitat de Côte d'Ivoire (BHCI): 22 ave Joseph Anoma, 01 BP 2325, Abidjan 01; tel. 20-22-60-00; fax 20-22-58-18; f. 1993; cap. and res 1,108m., total assets 14,407m. (Dec. 1998); Chair. DAVID AMUAH; Man. Dir LACINA COULIBALY.

Banque Internationale pour le Commerce et l'Industrie de la Côte d'Ivoire SA (BICICI): Tour BICICI, ave Franchet d'Espérey, 01 BP 1298, Abidjan 01; tel. 20-20-16-00; fax 20-20-17-00; f. 1962; 28% owned by Société Financière pour les Pays d'Outre-Mer, 21% by Banque Nationale de Paris, 20% state-owned; cap. and res 29,821m., total assets 345,200m. (Dec. 1998); Chair. and Man. Dir ANGE KOFFY; 39 brs.

Banque Paribas Côte d'Ivoire: Immeuble Alliance, 6e étage, 17 ave Terrasson de Fougères, 17 BP 09, Abidjan 17; tel. 20-21-86-86; fax 20-21-88-23; f. 1984; 85% owned by Banque Paribas (France); cap. and res 2,856m. total assets 26,632m. (Dec. 1998); Chair. FRANÇOIS DAUGE; Man. Dir FRANÇOIS DU PEUTY.

BIAO–Côte d'Ivoire SA (BIAO–CI): 8–10 ave Joseph Anoma, 01 BP 1274, Abidjan 01; tel. 20-20-07-20; fax 20-20-07-00; e-mail biaosq@africaonline.co.ci; internet www.biao.co.ci; f. 1980; 80% owned by Banque Belgolaise; cap. and res 8,301m. total assets 218,298m. (Dec. 1998); Chair. RENÉ AMANY; 32 brs.

Citibank NA: Immeuble Botreau Roussel, 28 ave Delafosse, 01 BP 3698, Abidjan 01; tel. 20-20-90-00; ; fax 20-21-76-85; e-mail citibank@odaci.net; Dir-Gen. MARC H. WIESSING.

Compagnie Bancaire de l'Atlantique Côte d'Ivoire (COBACI): Immeuble Alpha 2000, rue Gourgas, Plateau, 01 BP 522, Abidjan 01; tel. 20-21-28-04; fax 20-21-07-98; e-mail cobaci@africaonline.co.ci; fmrly national branch of Barclays Bank PLC; 99.9% owned by Banque Atlantique–Côte d'Ivoire; cap and res 2,286m., total assets 12,082m. (Dec. 1998); Chair SERGE GUETTA; Man. Dir MICHEL KAHN.

Compagnie Financière de la Côte d'Ivoire (COFINCI): Tour BICICI, 15e étage, ave Franchet d'Espérey, 01 BP 1566, Abidjan 01; tel. 20-21-27-32; fax 20-21-23-46; f. 1974; 72% owned by BICICI; cap. and res 2,337m., total assets 10,183m. (Dec. 1998); Chair. and Man. Dir ANGE KOFFY.

Ecobank–Côte d'Ivoire: Immeuble Alliance, 17 ave Terrasson de Fougères, 01 BP 4107, Abidjan 01; tel. 20-21-10-41; fax 20-21-88-16; e-mail eci@ecobank.com.ci; f. 1989; 93% owned by Ecobank Transnational Inc and subsids (operating under the auspices of the Economic Community of West African States); cap. and res 4,589m., total assets 70,954m. (Dec. 1998); Chair. ABDOULAYE KONÉ; Man. Dir AMIN UDDIN; 1 br.

Société Générale de Banques en Côte d'Ivoire SA (SGBCI): 5–7 ave Joseph Anoma, Plateau, 01 BP 1355, Abidjan 01; tel. 20-20-12-34; fax 20-20-14-92; e-mail ddl.dir@globeaccess.net; f. 1962; 39% owned by Société Générale (France); cap. and res 33,990m., total assets 452,208m. (Dec. 1998); Chair. and Man. Dir TIÉMOKO YADÉ COULIBALY; Man. Dir MICHEL MAIAILLE; 55 brs.

Société Générale de Financement et de Participations en Côte d'Ivoire (SOGEFINANCE): 5–7 ave Joseph Anoma, 01 BP 3904, Abidjan 01; tel. 20-22-55-30; fax 20-32-67-60; f. 1978; 58% owned by SGBCI; cap. and res 1,788m., total assets 6,633m. (Dec. 1998); Chair. and Man. Dir TIÉMOKO YADÉ COULIBALY; Man. Dir ANTOINE YAO CASSAIGNAN.

Société Ivoirienne de Banque (SIB): Immeuble Alpha 2000, 34 blvd de la République, 01 BP 1300, Abidjan 01; tel. 20-20-00-00; fax 20-21-97-41; f. 1962; 51% owned by Crédit Lyonnais (France); 49% state-owned; reduction of state holding to 19% pending; cap. and res 10,955m., total assets 224,308m. (Dec. 1998); Man. Dir JEAN-PIERRE GREYFIE DE BELLECOMBE; 35 brs.

Credit Institutions

Afribail Côte d'Ivoire (Afribail–CI): 01 BP 1274, Abidjan 01; tel. 20-20-07-25; fax 20-20-07-26; 95% owned by (BIAO–CI); cap. and res 623m., total assets 7,375m. (Dec. 1996); Chair. RENÉ AMANY; Man. Dir JACOB AHIWA.

BICI Bail de Côte d'Ivoire: Tour BICICI, 5e étage, ave Franchet d'Espérey, 01 BP 6495, Abidjan 01; tel. 20-22-24-31; fax 20-20-17-00; internet www.bicibail.com; 75% owned by BICICI; cap. and res 1,792m., total assets 13,977m. (Dec. 1997); Pres. ANGE KOFFY; Man. Dir PATRICK MATHIEU.

Compagnie Ivoirienne de Vente à Crédit et Acquisition (CIVECA): angle blvd Roume et ave du Dr Croset, 04 BP 2084, Abidjan 04; tel. 20-22-77-13; fax 20-22-77-35; 87.8% owned by Mutuelle d'Assurance des Taxis Compteur d'Abidjan; cap. and res 826m., total assets 2,343m. (Dec. 1997); Pres. O. YOU TIDJANI; Dir-Gen. DOMINIQUE KONAN KOUAME.

Société Africaine de Crédit Automobilière (SAFCA): Immeuble SAFCA, 1 rue des Carrossiers, Zone 3, 04 BP 27, Abidjan 04; tel. 20-24-91-77; fax 21-35-77-90; e-mail safca@africaonline.co.ci; cap. and res 5,417m., total assets 27,660m. (Dec. 1998); Pres. and Dir-Gen. DIACK DIAWAR.

Société Africaine de Crédit-Bail (SAFBAIL): Immeuble SAFLA, 1 rue des Carrossiers, Zone 3, 04 BP 27, Abidjan 04; tel. 21-24-91-77; fax 21-35-77-90; e-mail safbail@africaonline.co.ci; cap. and res 2,456m., total assets 10,743m. (Dec. 1998); Chair. and Man. Dir DIACK DIAWAR.

SOGEFIBAIL–CI: 26 ave Delafosse, 01 BP 1355, Abidjan 01; tel. 20-32-85-15; fax 20-33-14-93; 35% owned by GENEFITEC, 35% by SOGEFINANCE, 25% by SGBCI; cap. and res 2,145m., total assets 9,515m. (June 1999); Dir PIERRE GABRIEL SIBY.

Financial Institution

Caisse Autonome d'Amortissement: Immeuble SCIAM, ave Marchand, 01 BP 670, Abidjan 01; tel. 20-21-06-11; fax 20-21-35-78; f. 1959; management of state funds; Chair. ABDOULAYE KONÉ; Man. Dir VICTOR KOUAMÉ.

Bankers' Association

Association Professionnelle des Banques et Etablissements Financiers de Côte d'Ivoire (APBEFCI): 01 BP 3810, Abidjan 01; tel. 20-21-20-08; Pres. JEAN-PIERRE MEYER.

STOCK EXCHANGE

Bourse Régionale des Valeurs Mobilières (BRVM): 18 ave Joseph Anoma, 01 BP 3802, Abidjan 01; tel. 20-32-66-85; fax 20-32-66-84; f. 1998 to succeed Bourse des Valeurs d'Abidjan; regional stock exchange serving mem. states of UEMOA; Chair LAMASEH ALEXIS LOOKY; Dir-Gen. KOKOU GOZAN (acting).

BRVM (Antenne Nationale de Côte d'Ivoire): 18 ave Joseph Anoma, 01 BP 1541, Abidjan 01; tel. 20-31-55-50; fax 20-32-47-77; e-mail tbah@brvm.org; Man. TIDIANE AMADOU BAH.

INSURANCE

Abidjanaise d'Assurances: Immeuble Woodin Center, ave Noguès, 01 BP 2909, Abidjan 01; tel. 20-22-46-96; fax 20-22-64-81; e-mail abjassur@africaonline.co.ci.

AFRAM: Immeuble ex-Monopris, 2 ave Noguès, 01 BP 7124, Abidjan 01; tel. 20-32-30-44; fax 20-32-69-72.

AFRICASSUR: blvd Giscard d'Estaing, 01 BP 4092, Abidjan 01; tel. 21-26-05-83.

Assurances Générales de Côte d'Ivoire (AGCI): Immeuble AGCI, ave Noguès, 01 BP 4092, Abidjan 01; tel. 20-32-10-52; fax 20-33-25-79; e-mail agci@africaonline.co.ci; f. 1979; mem. of Groupe NSIA–AGCI since 1996; Chair. and Man. Dir JEAN KACOU DIAGOU.

Assurances Générales de Côte d'Ivoire–Vie (AGCI–Vie): Immeuble AGCI, ave Nogues, 01 BP 4092, Abidjan 01; tel. 20-33-11-31; fax 20-33-25-79; f. 1988; mem. of Groupe NSIA–AGCI since 1996; life; Chair. and Man. Dir JEAN KACOU DIAGOU.

AXA Assurances Côte d'Ivoire: ave Delafosse Prolongée, 01 BP 378, Abidjan 01; tel. 20-21-73-81; fax 20-22-12-43; f. 1981; fmrly l'Union Africaine–IARD; insurance and reinsurance; Chair. JOACHIM RICHMOND; Dir ALEXANDRE AHUI ATTE.

AXA Vie Côte d'Ivoire: 9 ave Houdaille, 01 BP 2016, Abidjan 01; tel. 20-22-25-15; fax 20-22-37-60; f. 1985; fmrly Union Africaine Vie; life assurance and capitalization; Chair. JOACHIM RICHMOND; Dir PATRICE DESGRANGES.

Colina SA: Immeuble Colina, blvd Roume, 01 BP 3832, Abidjan 01; tel. 20-21-65-05; fax 20-22-59-05; f. 1980; e-mail c.dg@colina-sa.com; Chair. MICHEL PHARAON; Dir-Gen. RAYMOND FARHAT.

Mutuelle Centrale d'Assurances: 15 Immeuble Ebrien, 01 BP 1217, Abidjan 01; tel. 20-21-11-24; fax 20-33-18-37.

La Nationale d'Assurances (CNA): Immeuble Symphonie, 30 ave du Général de Gaulle, 01 BP 1333, Abidjan 01; tel. 20-21-49-19; fax 20-22-49-06; e-mail lanationaled'assurance@odaci.net; f. 1972; cap. 400m.; insurance and reinsurance; Chair. SOUNKALO DJIBO; Man. Dir RICHARD COULIBALY.

Nouvelle Société Interafricaine d'Assurances (NSIA): 01 BP 1571, Abidjan 01; tel. 20-22-76-22; fax 20-22-76-20; e-mail nsia@africaonline.co.ci; f. 1995; mem. of Groupe NSIA–AGCI; Chair. and Man. Dir JEAN KACOU DIAGOU.

La Sécurité Ivoirienne: Immeuble La Sécurité Ivoirienne, blvd Roume, Abidjan; tel. 20-21-50-63; fax 20-21-05-67; f. 1971; general; Dir-Gen. JACQUES BARDOUX.

Société Africaine d'Assurances et de Réassurances en République de Côte d'Ivoire (SAFARRIV): Immeuble SAFARRIV, 2 blvd Roume, 01 BP 1741, Abidjan 01; tel. 20-21-91-57; fax 20-21-82-72; e-mail safarriv@globeaccess.net; f. 1975; Pres. TIÉMOKO YADÉ COULIBALY; Man. Dir CHRISTIAN ARRAULT.

Société Ivoirienne d'Assurances Mutuelles–Mutuelle d'Assurances Transports (SIDAM–MAT): Immeuble SIDAM, ave Houdaille, 01 BP 1217, Abidjan 01; tel. 20-21-97-82; fax 20-32-94-39; f. 1970; Chair. ABOU DOUMBIA; Dir-Gen. SOULEYMANE MEITE.

Trade and Industry

GOVERNMENT AGENCIES

Bureau Nationale d'Etudes Techniques et de Développement (BNETD): ancien hôtel 'Le Relais', blvd Hassan II, Cocody, 04 BP 945, Abidjan 04; tel. 22-44-28-05; fax 22-44-56-66; e-mail info@bnetd.sita.net; internet www.bnetd.sita.net; f. 1978 as Direction et Controle des Grands Travaux; management and supervision of major public works projects; Man. Dir ANTOINE ADOU.

Comité de Privatisation: 6 blvd de l'Indénié, 01 BP 1141, Abidjan 01; tel. 20-22-22-31; fax 20-22-22-35: state privatization authority; Pres. JEAN-CLAUDE BROU; Dir NAZAIRE GOUNONGBE.

Compagnie Ivoirienne pour le Développement des Cultures Vivrières (CIDV): 01 BP 2049, Abidjan 01; tel. 20-21-00-79. 1988; production of food crops; Man. Dir BENOÎT N'DRI BROU.

PETROCI Exploration Production SA: Immeuble les Hévéas, 05 BP 2954, Abidjan 01; tel. 20-20-25-00; fax 20-21-68-24; f. 1975; f. 1998 to succeed Société Nationale d'Opérations Pétrolières de la Côte d'Ivoire (PETROCI); transfer to private ownership pending; all aspects of hydrocarbons development; Pres and Man. Dir (vacant).

Société pour le Développement Minier de la Côte d'Ivoire (SODEMI): 31 blvd André Latrille, 01 BP 2816, Abidjan 01; tel. 22-44-29-94; fax 22-44-08-21; f. 1962; geological and mineral research; Pres. NICOLAS KOUANDI ANGBA; Man. Dir JOSEPH N'ZI.

Société de Développement des Plantations Forestières (SODEFOR): blvd François Mitterrand, 01 BP 3770, Abidjan 01; tel. 22-44-46-16; fax 22-44-02-40; f. 1966; establishment and management of tree plantations, management of state forests, marketing of timber products; Pres. Minister of Agriculture and Animal Resources; Man. Dir JEAN-CLAUDE ANEH.

Société pour le Développement des Productions Animales (SODEPRA): Immeuble Les Harmonies, angle blvd Carde et ave Dr Jamot, 01 BP 1249, Abidjan 01; tel. 20-21-13-10; f 1970; rearing of livestock; Man. Dir PAUL LAMIZANA.

DEVELOPMENT AGENCIES

Agence Française de Développement (AFD): 01 BP 1814, Abidjan 01; tel. 22-44-53-05; fmrly Caisse Française de Développement; Dir in Côte d'Ivoire PIERRE MARSET.

Centre pour la Promotion des Investissements en Côte d'Ivoire (CEPICI): BP V152; Abidjan 01; tel. 20-21-40-70; fax 20-21-40-71; investment promotion authority; Dir JEAN-CLAUDE KOUASSI; Gen. Man. M. KOFFIVI.

CHAMBERS OF COMMERCE

Chambre d'Agriculture de la Côte d'Ivoire: 11 ave Lamblin, 01 BP 1291, Abidjan 01; tel. 20-32-92-13; fax 20-32-92-20; Sec.-Gen. GAUTHIER N'ZI.

Chambre de Commerce et d'Industrie de Côte d'Ivoire: 6 ave Joseph Anoma, 01 BP 1399, Abidjan 01; tel. 20-33-16-00; fax 20-32-39-46; f.1992; Pres. SEYDOU ELIMANE DIARRA; Dir-Gen. KONAN KOFFI.

TRADE ASSOCIATIONS

Fédération Ivoirienne des Producteurs du Café et du Cacao (FIPCC): Yamoussoukro; f. 1998; coffee and cocoa growers' assoc.; Chair. CISSÉ LOCINÉ; c. 3,000 mems.

La Nouvelle Caistab: BP V132, Abidjan; tel. 20-20-27-00; fax 20-21-89-94; f. 1964 as Caisse de Stabilisation et de Soutien des Prix des Productions Agricoles (Caistab); fmrly govt agency responsible for controlling price, quality and export of cocoa and coffee; restructured 1995–98 prior to liberalization as autonomous entity in 1999; to be dissolved in 2000 and replaced by Bureau Ivoirien du Café-Cacao; offices in Paris, London and New York; Man. Dir (vacant).

Organisation de Commercialisation de l'Ananas et de la Banane (OCAB): Abidjan; pineapple and banana growers' assoc.

EMPLOYERS' ASSOCIATIONS

Fédération Maritime de la Côte d'Ivoire (FEDERMAR): 04 BP 723, Abidjan 04; tel. 20-21-25-83; Sec.-Gen. VACABA DE MOVALY TOURÉ.

Fédération Nationale des Industries de la Côte d'Ivoire: 01 BP 1340, Abidjan 01; tel. 20-21-71-42; fax 20-21-72-56; f. 1993; Pres. PIERRE MAGNE; Sec.-Gen. DANIEL TEURQUETIL; 280 mems.

Groupement Interprofessionnel de l'Automobile (GIPA): 01 BP 1340, Abidjan 01; tel. 20-21-71-42; fax 20-21-72-56; f. 1953; Pres. BOUAKÉ FOFANA; Sec.-Gen. DANIEL TEURQUETIL; 32 mems.

Syndicat des Commerçants Importateurs, Exportateurs et Distributeurs de la Côte d'Ivoire (SCIMPEX): 01 BP 3792, Abidjan 01; tel. 20-21-54-27; Pres. JACQUES ROSSIGNOL; Sec.-Gen. M. KOFFI.

Syndicat des Entrepreneurs et des Industriels de la Côte d'Ivoire (SEICI): Immeuble Jean Lefèbvre, 14 blvd de Marseille, 01 BP 464, Abidjan 01; tel. 20-21-83-85; f. 1934; Pres. ABDEL AZIZ THIAM.

Syndicat des Exportateurs et Négociants en Bois de Côte d'Ivoire: Immeuble CCIA, 11e étage, 01 BP 1979, Abidjan 01; tel. 20-21-12-39; fax 20-21-26-42; Pres. JEAN-CLAUDE BERNARD.

Syndicat des Producteurs Industriels du Bois (SPIB): Immeuble CCIA, 11e étage, 01 BP 318, Abidjan 01; tel. 20-21-12-39; fax 20-21-26-42; f. 1973; Pres. BRUNO FINOCCHIARO.

Union des Entreprises Agricoles et Forestières: Immeuble CCIA, 11e étage, 01 BP 2300, Abidjan 01; tel. 20-21-12-39; fax 20-21-26-42; f. 1952; Pres. FULGENCE KOFFY.

UTILITIES

Electricity

Compagnie Ivoirienne d'Electricité (CIE): ave Christiani, 01 BP 6932, Abidjan 01; tel. 21-23-33-00; fax 21-24-63-22; f. 1990 to assume electricity distribution network fmrly operated by Energie Electrique de la Côte d'Ivoire; 20% state-owned, 51% controlled by Société Bouygues group (France) and Electricité de France; Pres. MARCEL ZADI KESSY; Dir GÉRARD THEURIAU.

Compagnie Ivoirienne de Production d'Electricité (CIPREL): Tour Sidom, 12e étage, ave Houdaille, 01 BP 4039, Abidjan 01; tel. 20-22-60-97; independent power production.

Gas

Gaz de Côte d'Ivoire (GDCI): 01 BP 1351, Abidjan; tel. 22-44-49-55. 1961; transfer to majority private ownership pending; gas distributor; Man. Dir LAMBERT KONAN.

Water

Société de Distribution d'Eau de la Côte d'Ivoire (SODECI): 1 ave Christiani-Treichville, 01 BP 1843, Abidjan 01; tel. 21-23-30-00; fax 21-24-20-33; f. 1959; production, treatment and distribution of drinking water; 46% owned by SAUR, 51% owned by employees, 3% state-owned; Chair. MARCEL ZADI KESSY; Man. Dir. PIERRE LE TAREAU.

MAJOR COMPANIES

The following are among the largest companies in terms of either capital investment or employment.

Blohorn SA: 01 BP 1751, Abidjan 01; tel. 21-24-90-60; fax 21-25-11-05; f. 1960; cap. 6,040m. francs CFA; 80% owned by Unilever Group; management of industrial complex for processing oil-seeds; production of palm oil and its derivatives, incl. soap, margarine and glycerine; Chair. PIERRE BONNEIL; Vice-Chair. MARTIN RUSHWORTH; 880 employees.

Bois Transformés d'Afrique (BTA): 01 BP 958, Abidjan 01; tel. 20-22-33-04; fax 20-22-74-69; f. 1972; cap. 233.5m. francs CFA; sawmills, plywood factory at Zagné; Dir M. DEKEULENEER.

Carnaud Metalbox SIEM: blvd Giscard d'Estaing, 01 BP 1242, Abidjan 01; tel. 21-35-89-74; fax 21-35-03-94; f. 1954; subsidiary of Carnaud Metalbox (France); cap. 1,889m. francs CFA; mfrs of cans; Chair. PHILIPPE EYMARD; Man. Dir ALAIN ESCAT.

Compagnie des Caoutchoucs du Pakidie (CCP): 01 BP 1191, Abidjan 01; tel. 20-37-15-38; fax 20-37-15-40; f. 1960; cap. 856m. francs CFA; rubber plantations and factory; Chair. FULGENCE KOFFY.

Compagnie Ivoirienne pour le Développement des Textiles (CIDT): route de Béoumi, 01 BP 622, Bouaké 01; tel. 63-30-13; fax 63-41-67; f. 1974; cap. 7,200m. francs CFA; transferred to majority private ownership in 1998; development of cotton production, cotton ginning; Man. Dir SAMBA COULIBALY; 1,713 employees.

Elf Oil Côte d'Ivoire: 01 BP 555, Abidjan 01; tel.20-22-01-33; fax 20-22-87-15; f. 1967; petroleum marketing and distribution; subsidiary of Elf Aquitaine, France; Pres. PIERRE MOERS; Dir-Gen. SERGE BRIQUET.

Ets R. Gonfreville (ERG): route de l'Aéroport, BP 584, Bouaké; tel. 63-32-13; fax 63-46-65; f. 1921; cap. 2,999m. francs CFA; 10.5% state-owned; transfer to private ownership of state holding pending; spinning, weaving, dyeing and printing of cotton textiles; clothing mfrs; Chair. SOUNKALO DJIBO; Man. Dir CLAUDE TRESCOL; 2,452 employees.

Eveready Côte d'Ivoire SA: Zone Industrielle de Vridi, 15 BP 611, Abidjan 15; tel. 21-27-33-84; f. 1969; cap. 894m. francs CFA; wholly-owned subsidiary of Eveready Battery Co (USA); mfrs of batteries; Dir A. CORVEZ.

Filatures, Tissages, Sacs–Côte d'Ivoire SA (FILTISAC): Km 8, route d'Adzopé, 01 BP 3962, Abidjan 01; tel. 20-37-13-02; fax 20-37-09-67; f. 1965; cap. 2,644m. francs CFA; mfrs of polypropylene and jute bags and other packaging; Pres. and Dir-Gen. SIDI MADATALI; 1,700 employees.

Grands Moulins d'Abidjan (GMA): Quai 1, Zone Portuaire, 01 BP 1743, Abidjan 01; tel. 20-21-28-33. 1963; cap. 2,000m. francs CFA; flour milling and production of animal feed; Dir KOUASSI KOUADIO.

Groupe FIBAKO–IVOIREMBAL: 01 BP 306, Abidjan 01; tel. 21-24-04-64; fax 21-24-19-58; f. 1946; fmrly Ficelleries de Bouaké–Société Industrielle Ivoirienne d'Emballage; cap. 950m. francs CFA; spinning, mfrs of sacking and plastic packaging; Man. Dir PHILIPPE GODIN.

Industrie de Transformation des Produits Agricoles (API): Zone Industrielle de Vridi, 15 BP 431, Abidjan 15; tel. 21-35-20-09. 1968; cap. 900m. francs CFA; wholly owned by Cacao Barry Group (France); marketing of cocoa products, processing of cocoa beans; Man. Dir HONORÉ AKPANGNI.

Mobil Oil-Côte d'Ivoire: impasse Paris-Village, 01 BP 1777, Abidjan 01; tel. 20-21-73-20. 1974; cap. 2,000m. francs CFA; distribution of petroleum products; Chair. MICHEL BONNET; Dir J. LABAUNE.

Nandjelait: Zone Industrielle de Vridi, Abidjan 01; f. 1986; cap. 600m. francs CFA; production, packaging and sale of dairy products and by-products; Chair. and Man. Dir ROGER ABINADER.

National Electric-Côte d'Ivoire (NELCI): 16 BP 131, Abidjan 16; f. 1983; cap. 1,000m. francs CFA; assembly of radio and television receivers; Chair. TAMADA TAKASHI.

Nestlé Côte d'Ivoire: rue du Lycée Technique, 01 BP 1840, Abidjan 01; tel. 22-44-44-44; fax 22-44-43-43; f. 1959; cap. 5,518m. francs CFA; subsidiary of Nestlé SA (Switzerland); production of coffee and cocoa products, manufacture and sale of food products; Chair. GEORGES N'DIA KOFFI; Man. Dir FRANÇOIS PRÉVOT.

Omnium Chimique et Cosmétique (COSMIVOIRE): Zone Industrielle de Vridi, 01 BP 3576, Abidjan 01; tel. 21-27-57-32; fax 21-27-28-13; f. 1974; cap. 702m. francs CFA; mfrs of soaps, cosmetics, oils, margarine, butter and alcohol; Pres. ALAIN YACOUBA BAMBARA; Man. Dir YAO KOFFI NOËL.

Palmindustrie: Pointe des Fumeurs, 01 BP V239, Abidjan 01; tel. 21-27-00-70; fax 21-25-47-00; f. 1969; cap. 34,000m. francs CFA; transferred to private ownership in 1996; development of palm, coconut and copra products; Man. Dir BONIFACE BRITO.

Produits Ruraux de Negoce Côte d'Ivoire (PRN CI): rue de Textile, Zone Industrielle de Vridi; 01 BP 3836, Abidjan 01; tel. 21-27-00-60; fax 21-27-00-64; processing, storage and marketing of cocoa and coffee; Man. Dir THOMAS SEGUI.

Société Africaine de Cacao (SACO): rue Pierre et Marie Curie, 01 BP 1045, Abidjan 01; tel. 21-35-44-10. 1956; cap. 1,733m. francs CFA; 65% owned by Cacao Barry Group (France), 35% state-owned; sale of state holding pending; mfrs of cocoa powder, chocolate products, cocoa butter and oil-cake; expansion programme in progress in 1996; Pres. and Man. Dir SEYDOU DIARRA; 670 employees.

Société Africaine de Plantations d'Hévéas (SAPH): 14 blvd Carde, 01 BP 1322, Abidjan 01; tel. 20-21-18-91; fax 20-22-18-67; f. 1956; cap. 10,249m. francs CFA; 38.7% owned by Octide Finance, 30.9% by Société Internationale des Plantations d'Hévéas (France); production of rubber on 17,000 ha of plantations; Pres. and Man. Dir YVES ROLAND.

Société des Caoutchoucs de Grand-Béréby (SOGB): 17 BP 18, Abidjan 17; tel. 20-21-99-47; fax 20-33-25-80; f. 1979; cap. 21,602m. francs CFA; 60% owned by Befin (Belgium), 35% state-owned; rubber plantations and processing; Pres. FULGENCE KOFFI; Gen. Man. MARC MUTSAARS; 4,400 employees.

Société de Conserves de Côte d'Ivoire (SCODI): Quai de Pêche, Zone Industrielle de Vridi, 01 BP 677, Abidjan 01; tel. 21-25-66-74; fax 21-27-05-52; f. 1960; cap. 908m. francs CFA; tuna canning; Chair. PAUL ANTONIETTI; Gen. Man. YVON RIVA.

Société de Construction et d'Exploitation d'Installations Frigorifiques (SOCEF): Port de Pêche, 04 BP 154, Abidjan 04; tel. 21-35-54-42; f. 1962; cap. 900m. francs CFA; mfrs of refrigeration units; Dir GÉRARD CLEMENT.

Société Cotonnière Ivoirienne (COTIVO): BP 244, Agboville; tel. 23-51-70-01; fax 23-51-73-34; f. 1972; cap. 3,600m. francs CFA; textile complex; Pres. MICHEL HEMONNOT; Man. Dir MICHEL DUTRONC.

Société de Galvanisation de Tôles en Côte d'Ivoire (TOLES-IVOIRE): 15 BP 144, Abidjan 15; tel. 21-27-53-38. 1969; cap. 975m. francs CFA; mfrs of galvanized corrugated sheets and other roofing materials; Chair. SIDI MADATALI; Man. Dir PHILIPPE GODIN.

Société de Gestion des Stocks Petroliers de Côte d'Ivoire (GESTOCI): 15 blvd de Vridi, 01 BP 89, Abidjan 01; tel. 21-27-00-50; fax 21-27-17-82; transfer to majority private ownership pending; management of petroleum stocks; Man. Dir KONAN N'GUESSAN.

Société Ivoirienne de Béton Manufacturé (SIBM): 12 rue Thomas Edison, 01 BP 902, Abidjan 01; tel. 21-35-52-71; fax 21-35-82-27; f. 1978; cap. 800m. francs CFA; mem. of Société Africaine de Béton Manufacturé group; mfrs of concrete; Man. Dir DANIEL PAUL.

Société Ivoirienne de Câbles (SICABLE): Zone Industrielle de Vridi, 15 BP 35, Abidjan 15; tel. 21-27-57-35; fax 21-27-12-34; e-mail sicable@globeaccess.net; f. 1975; cap. 740m. francs CFA; 51% owned by Câbles Pirelli; mfrs of electricity cables; Chair. ANDRÉ BOURG; Man. Dir HERVÉ JACOTOT.

Société Ivoirienne de Ciments et Matériaux (SICM-SOCIMAT): blvd du Port, 01 BP 887, Abidjan 01; tel. 21-24-17-34; fax 21-24-27-21; e-mail marfil@cimbelier.ci; f. 1952; cap. 507m. francs CFA; clinker-crushing plant; Chair. JEAN GUILLOT; Man. Dir JOHANN PACHLER.

Société Ivoirienne d'Oxygène et d'Acetylène (SIVOA): 131 blvd de Marseille, 01 BP 1753, Abidjan 01; tel. 21-35-44-71; fax 21-35-80-96; f. 1962; cap. 873m. francs CFA; 20% state-owned, 72% by Air Liquide (France); mfrs of industrial and medical gases; Dir JEAN-PIERRE DESSALLES; 120 employees.

Société Ivoirienne de Raffinage (SIR): route de Vridi, blvd de Petit-Bassam, 01 BP 1269, Abidjan 01; tel. 21-27-01-60; fax 20-21-17-98; f. 1962; cap. 26,000m. francs CFA; 45% owned by PETROCI; transfer to private ownership of state holding pending; operates petroleum refinery at Abidjan; Man. Dir JEAN-PIERRE JANIN; 736 employees.

Société Ivoirienne des Tabacs (SITAB): Zone Industrielle, 01 BP 607, Bouaké 01; tel. 63-35-31. 1971; cap. 4,449m. francs CFA; mfrs of cigarettes; Chair. FRANÇOISE AIDARA; Vice-Chair. and Man. Dir PIERRE MAGNE; 849 employees.

Société Ivoirienne de Trituration de Graines Oléagineuses et de Raffinage d'Huiles Végétales (TRITURAF): 15 BP 324, Abidjan 15; tel. 21-24-90-58; fax 21-24-68-14; f. 1973; cap. 1,300m. francs CFA; 75% owned by Blohorn SA; Chair. PIERRE BONNEIL; Man. Dir GEORGES BROU KOUASSI.

Société de Limonaderies et Brasseries d'Afrique (SOLIBRA): 27 rue du Canal, 01 BP 1304, Abidjan; tel. 21-24-91-33; fax 21-35-97-91; f. 1955; absorbed Société des Brasseries de la Côte d'Ivoire in 1994; cap. 4,100m. francs CFA; mfrs of beer, lemonade and ice at Abidjan, Bouaflé and Yopougon; Chair. PIERRE CASTEL; Man. Dir JACQUES GOCHELY.

Société des Mines d'Ity (SMI): 08 BP 872, Abidjan 08; f. 1989; cap. 600m. francs CFA; 51% owned by Normandy Mining Ltd, 49% by SODEMI; mining of gold reserves (2.0 metric tons per year) at Ity; Pres. ABDOULAYE KONÉ; Man. Dir M. PALANQUE.

Société Multinationale de Bitumes (SMB): blvd de Petit-Bassam, Zone Industrielle de Vridi, 12 BP 622, Abidjan 12; tel. 21-23-70-70; fax 21-27-05-18; f. 1976; cap. 1,218m. francs CFA; 53% owned by SIR; Chair. and Man. Dir MOUSSA TOURÉ; 50 employees.

Société Nationale Ivoirienne de Travaux (SONITRA): route d'Anyama, 01 BP 2609, Abidjan 01; tel. 20-37-13-68. 1963; cap. 2,273m. francs CFA; 55% state-owned; building and construction; Chair. FERNAND KONAN KOUADIO; Man. Dir AMOS SALOMON; 1,393 employees.

Société Nouvelle Abidjanaise de Carton Ondulé (SONACO): Zone Industrielle de Yopougon, 01 BP 1119, Abidjan; tel. 23-46-49-70; fax 23-46-45-06; f. 1964; cap. 1,200m. francs CFA; mfrs of paper goods and corrugated cardboard; Chair. DANIEL FORGET; Man. Dir FÉLIX DADIE; 406 employees.

Société Nouvelle Sifca: rue des Galions, 01 BP 1289, Abidjan 01; tel. 21-24-26-52; fax 21-24-07-90; f. 1964; cap. 2,000m. francs CFA; export of cocoa and coffee, cultivation and processing of rice; Pres. and Man. Dir YVES LAMBELIN; 235 employees.

Société Shell-Côte d'Ivoire: Zone Industrielle de Vridi, 15 BP 378, Abidjan 15; tel. 21-27-00-18; fax 21-27-24-99; f. 1928; cap. 1,800m. francs CFA; 50% holding by PETROCI; transferred to 80% private ownership in 1995; distribution of petroleum products; Pres. and Man. Dir EDOUARD ETTE.

Société de Stockage de Côte d'Ivoire (STOCACI): rue des Thoniers, Zone Portuaire, 01 BP 1798, Abidjan 01; f. 1980; cap. 1,000m. francs CFA; treatment and storage of cocoa and other products; Chair. JEAN ABILE GAL; Vice-Chair. and Man. Dir MADELEINE TCHICAYA.

Société Sucrière de la Côte d'Ivoire (SUCRIVOIRE): 16 ave du Docteur Crozet, 01 BP 2164, Abidjan 01; tel. 20-21-04-79; fax 20-21-07-75; f. 1997, following majority privatization of Société pour le Développement des Cannes à Sucre, l'Industrialisation et la Commercialisation du Sucre (SODESUCRE); 45% state-owned; sugar production; Chair. and Man. Dir JOSEPH KOUAMÉ KRA.

Société de Tubes d'Acier et Aluminium en Côte d'Ivoire (SOTACI): Zone Industrielle de Yopougon, 01 BP 2747, Abidjan 01; tel. 23-45-39-22; fax 23-45-39-25; f. 1978; cap. 1,029m. francs CFA; mfrs of steel and aluminium tubing and pipes; Chair. and Man. Dir MOUSTAPHA KHALIL; Dir JOSÉ HURTADO.

Star Auto: rue Pierre et Marie Curie, 01 BP 4054, Abidjan 01; tel. 21-75-10-00; fax 21-75-10-90; e-mail hdierks@daimlerchrysler.co.ci; f. 1983; cap. 1,619.5m. francs CFA; subsidiary of Daimler-Chrysler AG (Germany); mfrs and distributors of motor vehicles; Chair. E. JONSCHER; Gen. Man. HARM DIERKS.

Union Industrielle Textile de Côte d'Ivoire (UTEXI): Zone Industrielle de Vridi, 15 BP 414, Abidjan 15; tel. 21-27-44-81; fax 21-27-16-16; f. 1972; cap. 3,700m. francs CFA; 12.75% state-owned; spinning and weaving mill at Dimbokro; Chair. JACQUES ROSSIGNOL; Man. Dir NOBOYUKI YOSHIDA.

Union Ivoirienne de Traitement de Cacao (UNICAO): Zone Industrielle de Vridi, 15 BP 406, Abidjan 15; tel. 21-27-14-49; fax 21-27-56-82; e-mail unicao@globeaccess.net; f. 1989; cap. 6,000m. francs CFA; subsidiary of SIFCOM group; processing of cocoa beans; Chair. and Man. Dir YVES LAMBELIN.

UNIWAX: Zone Industrielle de Yopougon, 01 BP 3994, Abidjan 01; tel. 23-46-64-15; fax 23-46-69-42; f. 1967; cap. 1,750m. francs CFA; mfrs of batik fabrics; Chair. JEAN-LOUIS MENUDIER; 757 employees.

Usine de Traitement de Produits Agricoles (UTPA): rue des Thonniers, Zone Portuaire, 01 BP 1798, Abidjan 01; tel. 20-21-16-55; f. 1977; cap. 2,000m. francs CFA; coffee packaging at Abengourou, Kotobi and Daloa; Chair. EMILE ABILE-GAL; Man. Dir ALAIN PERILLAUD.

TRADE UNIONS

Fédération des Syndicats Autonomes de la Côte d'Ivoire (FESACI): Abidjan; Sec. Gen. MARCEL ETTE.

Union Générale des Travailleurs de Côte d'Ivoire (UGTCI): 05 BP 1203, Abidjan 05; tel. 20-21-26-65; f. 1962; Sec.-Gen. HYACINTHE ADIKO NIAMKEY; 100,000 individual mems; 190 affiliated unions.

Transport

RAILWAYS

The 660 km of track in Côte d'Ivoire run from Abidjan to Niangoloko, on the border with Burkina Faso; from there, the railway extends to Kaya, via the Burkinabè capital, Ouagadougou.

SITARAIL–Transport Ferroviaire de Personnel et de Marchandises: Résidence Memanou, blvd Clozel, Plateau, 16 BP 1216, Abidjan 16; tel. 20-21-06-36; fax 20-22-48-47; f. 1995 to operate services on Abidjan–Kaya line; Man. Dir ABDEL AZIZ THIAM.

ROADS

There are about 68,000 km of roads, of which some 6,000 km are paved. Some 68,000m. francs CFA was invested in the road network in 1994–98; projects included the upgrading of 3,000 km of roads and 30,000 km of tracks. Tolls were introduced on some roads in the mid-1990s, to assist in funding the maintenance of the network.

Société des Transports Abidjanais (SOTRA): 01 BP 2009, Abidjan 01; tel. 21-24-90-80; fax 21-25-97-21; f. 1960; 60% state-owned; transfer to majority private ownership pending; urban transport; Man. Dir PASCAL YÉBOUÉ-KOUAMÉ.

SHIPPING

Côte d'Ivoire has two major ports, Abidjan and San Pedro, both of which are industrial and commercial establishments with financial autonomy. Abidjan, which handled some 15.2m. metric tons of goods in 1998, is the largest container and trading port in west Africa. Access to the port is via the 2.7-km Vridi Canal. The port at San Pedro, which handled 1.1m. tons of goods in 1994, remains the main gateway to the south-western region of Côte d'Ivoire.

Port Autonome d'Abidjan (PAA): BP V85, Abidjan; tel. 21-23-80-00; fax 21-23-80-80; e-mail info@paa.ci.org; internet www.paaci.org; f. 1950; public undertaking supervised by the Govt; Man. Dir JEAN-MICHEL MOULOD.

Port Autonome de San Pedro (PASP): BP 339/340, San Pedro; tel. 71-20-80; fax 71-27-85; f. 1971; Man. Dir OGOU ATTEMENE.

AMICI: rue du Havre, Zone Portuaire, 01 BP 4020, Abidjan 01; tel. 21-35-28-50; fax 21-35-28-54.

Compagnie Maritime Africaine–Côte d'Ivoire (COMAF–CI: rond-point du Nouveau Port, 08 BP 867, Abidjan 08; tel. 20-32-40-77; f. 1973; navigation and management of ships; Dir FRANCO BERNARDINI.

Nouvelle SITRAM: rue des Pétroliers, 01 BP 1546, Abidjan 01; tel. 21-36-92-00; fax 21-35-73-93; f. 1967, nationalized in 1976 as Société Ivoirienne de Transport Maritime; returned to private ownership in 1995; services between Europe and west Africa and the USA; Chair. BONIFACE PEGAWAGNABA; Dir Commdt FAKO KONÉ.

SAGA–CI: Immeuble SAGA–CI, rond-point du Nouveau Port, 01 BP 1727, Abidjan 01; tel. 21-23-23-23; fax 21-24-25-06; merchandise handling, transit and storage; Chair. CHARLES BENITAL; Dir DANIEL CHARRIER.

Société Agence Maritime de l'Ouest Africain–Côte d'Ivoire (SAMOA–CI): rue des Gallions, 01 BP 1611, Abidjan 01; tel. 20-21-29-65; f. 1955; shipping agents; Man. Dir CLAUDE PERDRIAUD.

Société Ivoirienne de Navigation Maritime (SIVOMAR): 5 rue Charpentier, zone 2b, Treichville, 01 BP 1395, Abidjan 01; tel. 20-21-73-23; fax 20-32-38-53; f. 1977; shipments to ports in Africa, the Mediterranean and the Far East; Dir SIMPLISSE DE MESSE ZINSOU.

Société Ouest-Africaine d'Entreprises Maritimes en Côte d'Ivoire (SOAEM–CI): 01 BP 1727, Abidjan 01; tel. 20-21-59-69; fax 20-32-24-67; f. 1978; merchandise handling, transit and storage; Chair. JACQUES PELTIER; Dir JACQUES COLOMBANI.

SOCOPAO–Côte d'Ivoire: km 1 blvd de Marseille, 01 BP 1297, Abidjan 01; tel. 21-24-13-14; fax 21-24-21-30; e-mail socopao@africaonline.co.ci; shipping agents; Shipping Dir OLIVIER RANJARD.

CIVIL AVIATION

There are three international airports: Abidjan–Félix Houphouët-Boigny, Bouaké and Yamoussoukro. Work to expand and modernize Abidjan's airport began in mid-1998: the project, costing an estimated 14,000m. francs CFA, was scheduled for completion in late 2000. In addition, there are smaller airports at Bouna, Korhogo, Man, Odienné and San Pedro.

Agence Nationale de l'Aviation Civile: 07 BP 148, Abidjan 07; tel. 21-27-74-24; fax 21-27-63-46; civil aviation authority; Dir JEAN KOUASSI ABONOUAN.

Air Afrique (Société Aérienne Africaine Multinationale): 3 ave Joseph Anoma, 01 BP 3927, Abidjan 01; tel. 20-30-00; fax 20-30-08; internet www.airafrique-airlines.com; f. 1961; 51% owned jtly by the Govts of Benin, Burkina Faso, the Central African Repub., Chad, the Repub. of the Congo, Côte d'Ivoire, Mali, Mauritania, Niger, Senegal and Togo; restructuring in progress; extensive regional flights and services to Europe, North America and the Middle East; Chair. ABDOULAYE SOULE; Chief Exec. PAPE SOW THIAM.

Air Ivoire: place de la République, 01 BP 1027, Abidjan 01; tel. 20-20-66-66; fax 20-33-28-28; internet www.air-ivoire-info.com; f. 1960; state-owned since 1976, transfer to majority private ownership pending; internal flights and services within west Africa; Man. Dir AROUNA DIABAGATÉ.

Tourism

The game reserves, forests, lagoons, coastal resorts, rich ethnic folklore and the lively city of Abidjan are tourist attractions; Côte d'Ivoire also has well-developed facilities for business visitors, including golfing centres. Some 301,000 tourists visited Côte d'Ivoire in 1998; receipts from tourism in 1997 totalled US $88m.

Office Ivoirien du Tourisme et de l'Hôtellerie: Immeuble EECI, place de la République, 01 BP 8538, Abidjan 01; tel. 20-20-65-00; fax 20-20-65-31; e-mail oith@africaonline.co.ci; internet www.tourisme.ci; f. 1992; Dir CAMILLE KOUASSI.

Defence

At 1 August 1999 Côte d'Ivoire's active armed forces comprised an army of 6,800 men, a navy of about 900, an air force of 700, a paramilitary presidential guard of 1,100 and a gendarmerie of 4,400. There was also a 1,500-strong militia, and reserve forces numbered 12,000 men. Military service is by selective conscription and lasts for six months. France supplies equipment and training, and maintains a military presence in Côte d'Ivoire (numbering 570 in August 1999).

Defence Expenditure: Budgeted at 109,000m. francs CFA in 1999.

Inspector-General of the Armed Forces: Rear-Adm. LASSANA TIMITÉ.

Chief of Staff of the Armed Forces: Col-Maj. SOUMAHILA DIABAKITÉ.

Education

At the time of the 1988 census adult illiteracy averaged 65.9% (males 55.6%; females 76.6%); UNESCO estimated the average to be 60.0% in 1995 (males 51.3%; females 69.4%). Education at all levels is available free of charge. Primary education, which is officially compulsory for six years between seven and 13 years of age, begins at the age of six and lasts for six years. Enrolment at primary schools in 1996 was equivalent to 71% of the relevant age-group (82% of boys; 60% of girls). The Ivorian authorities anticipated that the rate of attendance at primary schools would have reached 90% by 2000. Secondary education, from the age of 12, lasts for up to seven years, comprising a first cycle of four years and a second cycle of three years. In 1997 total enrolment at secondary level was equivalent to only 25% of children in the relevant age-group (males 34%; females 16%). The National University at Abidjan has six faculties, and university-level facilities have been constructed in Yamoussoukro. In 1995/96 some 43,000 students were enrolled at university institutions. Total expenditure on education in 1997 was equivalent to 24.9% of total government expenditure (excluding spending on the public debt).

Bibliography

Affou, Y.S. *La relève paysanne en Côte d'Ivoire*. Paris, Editions Karthala, 1990.

Amondji, M. *Félix Houphouët-Boigny et La Côte d'Ivoire*. Paris, Editions Karthala, 1984.

Avenard, J.-M. *Le milieu naturel de la Côte d'Ivoire*. Bondy, France, ORSTOM, 1972.

Azam, J.-P., and Morrisson, C. *The Political Feasibility of Adjustment in Côte d'Ivoire and Morocco*. Paris, OECD, 1994.

Bédié, H. Konan. *Les chemins de ma vie: Entretiens avec Eric Laurent*. Paris, Plon, 1999.

Campbell, W. J., *The Emergent Independent Press in Benin and Côte d'Ivoire: From Voice of the State to Advocate of Democracy*. Westport, Praeger, 1998.

Contamin, B., and Fauré, Y.-A. *La bataille des entreprises publiques en Côte d'Ivoire: L'histoire d'un ajustement interne*. Paris, Editions Karthala, 1990.

Cruise O'Brien, D. B., Dunn, J., and Rathbone, R. (Eds). *Contemporary West African States*. Cambridge, Cambridge University Press, 1989.

Daniels, M. *Côte d'Ivoire*. Santa Barbara, ABC Clio, 1996.

David, P. *Côte d'Ivoire*. Paris, Editions Karthala, 1986.

Diarra, S. *Les faux complots d'Houphouët-Boigny*. Paris, Editions Karthala, 1997.

Domergue-Cloarec. *La Santé en Côte d'Ivoire*. 2 vols. Paris, Académie des Sciences d'Outre-Mer, 1987.

Dozon, J.-P. *La Société bété en Côte d'Ivoire*. Paris, Editions Karthala, 1983.

Dubresson, A. *Villes et industries en Côte d'Ivoire. Pour une géographie de l'accumulation urbaine*. Paris, Editions Karthala, 1989.

Duruflé, G. *L'ajustement structurel en Afrique (Sénégal, Côte d'Ivoire, Madagascar)*. Paris, Editions Karthala, 1987.

Fauré, Y. A., and Médard, J.-F. *Etat et bourgeoisie en Côte d'Ivoire*. Paris, Editions Karthala, 1983.

Gbagbo, L. *Côte d'Ivoire: Pour une alternative démocratique*. Paris, L'Harmattan, 1983.

Gombeaud, J.-L., Moutout, C., and Smith, S. *La Guerre du cacao, histoire secrète d'un embargo*. Paris, Calmann-Lévy, 1990.

Grootaert, C. *Analysing Poverty and Policy Reform: The Experience of Côte d'Ivoire*. Aldershot, Avebury Publishing, 1996.

Harrison Church, R. J. *West Africa*. 8th Edn. London, Longman, 1979.

Lisette, G. *Le Combat du Rassemblement Démocratique Africain*. Paris, Présence Africaine, 1983.

Loucou, J.-N. *Histoire de la Côte d'Ivoire*. Paris, Editions Karthala.

Mehler, A. *Commentaires sur la loi electorale ivoirienne*. Hamburg, 1994.

Mundt, R. *Historical Dictionary of the Ivory Coast*. Metuchen, NJ, Scarecrow Press, 1996.

Rapley, J. *Ivorien Capitalism: African Entrepreneurs in Côte d'Ivoire*. London, Lynne Rienner, 1993.

Rimmer, D. *The Economies of West Africa*. London, Weidenfeld and Nicolson, 1984.

Schneider, H. *Adjustment and Equity in Côte d'Ivoire*. Paris, OECD, 1992.

Siriex, P. H. *Félix Houphouët-Boigny: L'homme de la paix*. Paris, Seghers, 1975.

Touré, A. *La Civilisation quotidienne en Côte d'Ivoire*. Paris, Editions Karthala, 1983.

Vennetie, P. (Ed.). *Atlas de la Côte d'Ivoire*. Paris, Jeune Afrique, 1983.

Verdier, I. (Ed.). *Côte d'Ivoire: 100 Hommes de Pouvoir*. Paris, Indigo Publications, 1996.

Vidal, C. *Sociologie des passions — Côte d'Ivoire, Rwanda*. Paris, Editions Karthala, 1991.

World Bank. *Côte d'Ivoire Living Standards Survey: Design and Implementation*. Washington, DC, International Bank for Reconstruction and Development, 1986.

Zartman, I. W., and Delgado, C. (Eds). *The Political Economy of the Ivory Coast*. New York, Praeger, 1984.

DJIBOUTI

Physical and Social Geography

I. M. LEWIS

The Republic of Djibouti is situated at the southern entrance to the Red Sea. It is bounded on the far north by Eritrea, on the west and south by Ethiopia, and on the south-east by Somalia. Djibouti covers an area of 23,200 sq km (8,958 sq miles), consisting mostly of volcanic rock-strewn desert wastes, with little arable land and spectacular salt lakes and pans. The climate is torrid, with high tropical temperatures and humidity during the monsoon season. The average annual rainfall is less than 125 mm. Only in the upper part of the basaltic range north of the Gulf of Tadjourah, where the altitude exceeds 1,200 m above sea-level, is there continuous annual vegetation.

At 31 December 1990 the population was officially estimated at 519,900, including refugees and other resident non-nationals. According to UN estimates, the population was 623,000 at mid-1998. In 1981 the capital town, Djibouti (whose port and railhead dominate the territory's economy), had a population of about 200,000. The indigenous population is almost evenly divided between the Issa (who are of Somali origin) and the Afar, the former having a slight predominance. Both are Muslim Cushitic-speaking peoples with a traditionally nomadic economy and close cultural affinities, despite frequent local rivalry. The Afar inhabit the northern part of the country, the Issa the southern, and both groups span the artificial frontiers separating the Republic of Djibouti from Ethiopia, Eritrea and Somalia.

Since the development of the port of Djibouti in the early 1900s, the indigenous Issas have been joined by immigrants from the adjoining regions of Somalia. The Afar generally follow more restricted patterns of nomadic movement than the Issa, and a more hierarchical traditional political organization. While they formed a number of small polities, these were linked by the pervasive cleavage running throughout the Afar population between the 'noble' Asaimara (or 'red') clans and the less prestigious Asdoimara (or 'white') clans. There is also a long-established Arab trading community. European expatriates are mainly French, mostly in government employment, commerce and the armed forces.

Recent History

THOMAS OFCANSKY

French interest in the territory that now comprises the Republic of Djibouti dates from the mid-19th century, and was stimulated by subsequent Anglo-French rivalry for control of the entrance to the Red Sea. In 1917 a Franco-Ethiopian railway was completed to carry Ethiopia's trade through Djibouti port.

The territory's indigenous inhabitants, the Afar and the Issa, have strong connections with Ethiopia and Somalia respectively. Until the 1960s, ethnic divisions were not marked; subsequently, however, France's policy of favouring the minority Afar community led to tensions in the territory, then known as French Somaliland (renamed the French Territory of the Afars and the Issas in 1967).

Demands for independence were led by the Issa community, while numbers of Afars, who favoured maintenance of the French connection, were significantly enlarged in the mid-1970s by immigration from Somalia. A unified political movement, the Ligue populaire africaine pour l'indépendance (LPAI), was formed, and, following an overwhelming vote favouring independence at a referendum held in May 1977, the territory became independent on 27 June. Hassan Gouled Aptidon, a senior Issa politician and leader of the LPAI, became the first president of the republic.

Initial intentions to maintain a careful ethnic balance in government were not sustained. In March 1979 Gouled replaced the LPAI with a new political party, the Rassemblement populaire pour le progrès (RPP), whose leadership and policies were to be determined by himself. The two principal Afar-dominated pre-independence parties responded by merging into a clandestine opposition movement, the Front démocratique pour la libération de Djibouti (FDLD).

In June 1981 the first presidential election was held; Gouled, as the sole candidate, received 84% of the popular vote and was thus elected for a further six-year term. The FDLD rejected the election results and, from its base in Addis Ababa, demanded a return to democracy and the release of political prisoners. Soon afterwards, a new opposition party, the Parti populaire djiboutien (PPD), was formed under the leadership of a former premier, Ahmed Dini Ahmed. The leadership was arrested in September and the party banned, but in October, following the adoption of legislation to establish a one-party state, the PPD leaders were released.

ONSET OF OPPOSITION

Until the mid-1980s, there was little overt opposition to the RPP under Gouled's leadership. In January 1986 a bomb was exploded at the RPP headquarters, killing two people. The bombing and the subsequent assassination of a prominent local businessman were followed by intensive security operations, in which more than 1,000 people were arrested. Evidence of open opposition to Gouled attracted wider international attention in May, when Aden Robleh Awalleh, a former cabinet minister, was charged with conducting 'massive propaganda campaigns' against the RPP, and was expelled from the party. Aden Robleh Awalleh fled to Ethiopia, where he announced the formation of a new opposition group, the Mouvement national djiboutien pour l'instauration de la démocratie (MNDID), with the stated aim of restoring a multi-party parliamentary democracy.

At the presidential election held in April 1987 Gouled, the sole candidate, received just over 90% of the votes cast. Concurrently, a single list of candidates for the chamber of deputies was endorsed by 87% of those voting. In November Gouled dissolved the government and appointed a 16-member council of ministers. In February 1988 an attack on the border town of Balho was attributed to the Mouvement populaire de libération, an opposition group based in Ethiopia, and was widely seen as a sign of increasing ethnic tensions.

In April 1989 inter-ethnic hostilities erupted in the capital and the Afar town of Tadjourah. Tension increased in Afar-inhabited areas in May, and in October members of rival clans clashed in the capital. Security forces subsequently arrested several hundred people, some of whom were deported to Gesdir, a remote border region between Djibouti, Ethiopia and Somalia. Sizeable numbers of these deportees were later reported to have been killed by the insurgent Somali National Movement and Issa militiamen.

In January 1990 the FDLD, the MNDID and independent members of the opposition merged to form the Union des mouvements démocratiques (UMD), whose declared aim was to 'unite all the ethnic groups and different political persuasions' and to resolve 'the chaotic situation' existing in the country. In May inter-ethnic strife erupted between the Issa and the Gadabursi communities in the capital. In June units of the Djibouti armed forces raided Tadjourah and arrested Afars who were suspected of involvement in the UMD.

In November 1990 the president reshuffled the council of ministers, introducing one new member and reallocating several portfolios. In so doing, Gouled was believed to have strengthened his position in the ministry of finance, and to have reduced the influence of the former minister of finance and national economy, Mohamed Djama Elabe, who was regarded as a potential presidential successor.

In January 1991 Ali Aref Bourhan, who had led the council of ministers in the period prior to independence, was detained, together with about 100 Afar dissidents, on suspicion of having conspired to assassinate political leaders and senior army officers. Bourhan was subsequently charged with murder, attempted murder and with plotting to destabilize the country. Stricter security measures were applied against disaffection among the Afar community, but the government denied allegations that some Afars who had been arrested had been tortured.

At the fifth RPP congress, held in March 1991, the party resolved that it would remain Djibouti's sole legal political organization. This rejection of political pluralism was widely interpreted as a sign of its increasing insecurity in response to mounting discontent among Djibouti's various clans and clan branches—especially the Afar—at their exclusion from political power.

In April 1991 a former presidential adviser, Mohamed Moussa Kahin, was arrested on suspicion of involvement with the proscribed Mouvement pour l'unité et pour la démocratie (MUD), and in the following month Gouled dismissed two ministers from the government.

CIVIL INSURRECTION

A serious challenge to Gouled's authority appeared in April 1991 with the formation of a new and powerful armed opposition group, the Front pour la restauration de l'unité et de la démocratie (FRUD), which comprised three militant Afar groups, the Front pour la restauration des droits et de la legalité, the Front pour la résistance patriotique djiboutienne and the Action pour la révision de l'ordre à Djibouti. In November the FRUD, with a force of some 3,000 men, launched a full-scale insurrection, and by the end of the month controlled many towns and villages in the north of the country, and was besieging Tadjourah and Obock, which were held by the national army. The government conscripted all men between 18 and 25 years of age, and requested military assistance from France (see below) to repel what it described as external aggression by soldiers loyal to the deposed President Mengistu of Ethiopia. The FRUD denied that it constituted a foreign aggressor (although many of its officers had received training in Ethiopian military camps), claiming that its aim was to achieve political parity for all ethnic groups.

In December 1991 Gouled stated that a national referendum regarding proposed changes in the system of government would be held, but only when the 'external aggressors' had been expelled from the country. At the end of the month, 14 Afar deputies resigned from the RPP (and, therefore, from the chamber of deputies), claiming that its leaders were seeking to protect their privileges rather than the national interest. In January 1992 two ministers resigned, in protest at the government's policy of continuing the war, and subsequently formed the nucleus of a new political movement. In the same month, Gouled appointed a committee to draft a new constitution, intended to provide for a plural political system. Following a meeting in January with senior French officials, the FRUD agreed to open a dialogue with the government, based on an immediate bilateral cease-fire and progress on the promised democratic reforms. The government, however, continued to insist that the FRUD was controlled by foreign interests, describing its military activities as an 'invasion' and responded

to French mediation attempts with complaints that France had failed to honour its defence agreement. By the end of January the government had lost control of most of northern Djibouti, with its garrisons in Tadjourah and Obock kept supplied from the sea.

Attempts by France at achieving a *rapprochement* appeared to be more successful in February 1992, when, following meetings with the FRUD and the Djibouti government it was announced that the FRUD would declare a cease-fire, that France would deploy troops from its Djibouti garrison as a peace-keeping force in the north and that the government would release the FRUD's spokesman in the capital, Abbate Ebo Adou, who had been arrested in late 1991. However, initial hopes that the agreement would facilitate a negotiated settlement were soon disappointed, despite sustained diplomatic efforts by France. In late March 1992 the FRUD announced that it was ending its cease-fire, stating that the deployment of the French peace-keeping forces, which it had initially agreed to, was merely protecting a 'blood-stained dictatorship'. In April Adou was re-arrested, ostensibly for contravening the terms of his release.

Constitutional Manoeuvres

The presidential commission on constitutional reform submitted its report in March 1992 and in April Gouled announced his plans for reform, which, while conceding the principle of political pluralism, proposed few other changes and retained a strong executive presidency. The proposals were rejected as inadequate by the opposition, which demanded the holding of a national constitutional conference, and by the FRUD, although cautiously welcomed by France. The president announced that the reforms would be determined in a national referendum in June, and that legislative elections would follow in July. The mandate of the chamber of deputies, which had been due to expire at the end of May, was later extended for a further five years. The election timetable that the president announced was quickly dismissed as unrealistic, especially since large areas of the country were not under government control. In late June Gouled declared that the referendum would be held in early September, followed by the introduction of a multi-party system in mid-September. Legislative elections would then take place in November.

In July 1992 Gouled granted pardons to a number of opposition figures, including Aden Robleh Awalleh, the exiled leader of the Parti national démocratique (PND), and the leader of the Front des forces démocratiques, Omar Elmi Khaireh. However, in the same month Ali Aref Bourhan and five others (who had been arrested for treason in January 1991) were sentenced to 10 years' imprisonment. Others among the 47 accused received prison sentences of up to six years. The government sustained another defection in August with the announcement that Elaf Orbiss Ali, an Afar, had resigned as minister of labour, in protest against the continuing civil war and deteriorating economic situation, and was joining the Front uni de l'opposition djiboutienne (FUOD), a coalition of opposition parties, including the FRUD.

The draft constitution that the president prepared was approved by referendum on 4 September 1992, with 96.8% voting in favour, according to the ministry of the interior, which claimed a turnout of 75.2% of the 120,000 eligible voters. A proposition to restrict the number of political parties to four was approved by 96.8% of those who voted. However, with two-thirds of the country controlled by the FRUD, which had urged its supporters to boycott the referendum, and no independent observers present, the voting figures were received with some scepticism, notably by France, which refused to endorse the results. The referendum nevertheless facilitated the registration of political parties and the holding of multi-party elections, which, it was announced in October, would take place in December. Applications for registration were at first accepted from only the ruling RPP and the Parti pour le renouveau démocratique (PRD), led by Elabe, which had split from the FUOD in September. Applications from the FRUD and the FUOD were rejected. The application from the PND, which had withdrawn from the FUOD following the pardon and return from exile of Aden Robleh Awalleh, was initially rejected, although it was allowed in October.

Attempts by France to foster negotiations between the government and the FRUD appeared to have achieved success following the announcement in November 1992 that representatives of the two sides were to meet for the first time, under French auspices. However, the meeting was cancelled at short notice by the government, which claimed that the FRUD had failed to honour preconditions, including the release of prisoners of war. In late November France withdrew its troops from northern Djibouti, where they had acted as a buffer between government and rebel forces.

With the opposition largely excluded from the process, the elections held on 18 December 1992, which were monitored by observers from France, the Organization of African Unity (OAU) and the Arab League, provided an easy victory for the RPP, which won all 65 seats in the chamber of deputies and 76.7% of the popular votes. Only the PRD contested the elections (taking one-third of the votes cast in the capital), Awalleh having withdrawn the PND after protesting about irregularities and demanding a postponement of the elections. More than 51% of the electorate abstained from voting, leading to charges from the PND that the chamber was unrepresentative. Renewed fighting was reported in January 1993, with dozens of people said to have been killed in what appeared to be a new government offensive against the FRUD in the Tadjourah area. The army claimed a series of successes during February and March, recapturing FRUD strongholds in the south of the country and severing the rebels' supply routes to the sea. Nevertheless, FRUD achieved a propaganda victory with its first guerrilla attack on the capital in mid-March.

Gouled reshuffled the cabinet in February 1993, preserving a careful ethnic balance, with Issa ministers receiving eight portfolios, and Afar representatives seven, with one portfolio each held by representatives of three other minorities. However, other changes suggested no relaxation of the government's policy, with the transfer of the former minister of the interior, Ahmed Bulaleh Barreh (an opponent of negotiations with the FRUD), to the ministry of defence. The former minister of foreign affairs, Moumin Bahdon Farah, was appointed minister of justice and Islamic affairs, but retained his post as secretary-general of the RPP. Five candidates stood in Djibouti's first contested presidential election, which was held on 7 May: Gouled himself, Elabe (for the PRD), Awalleh (PND) and two independents, Mohamed Moussa Ali 'Tourtour' (actually of the still proscribed MUD, but not representing his party) and Ahmed Ibrahim Abdi. The level of electoral participation was low (at 49.9% of those registered to vote), suggesting an Afar boycott. Official results indicated that Gouled received 60.8% of the votes cast, followed by Elabe (22.0%), Awalleh (12.3%), 'Tourtour' (3.0%) and Abdi (2.0%). The opposition alleged that there had been widespread electoral fraud.

Military and Political Initiatives

Following his re-election as president, Gouled appealed to the FRUD to negotiate with the government. His appeal was rejected, as he proposed that discussions should take place in Djibouti, while the FRUD insisted that it would only meet the government abroad, in the presence of foreign mediators. In mid-1993 the army launched a full-scale offensive on FRUD positions in the centre and north of the country, capturing the FRUD's headquarters on the plateau of Asa Gayla, as well as other towns and areas held by the rebel group. As a result of the hostilities, thousands of the inhabitants of these largely Afar-populated areas fled towards the Ethiopian border. Many rebels retreated into the mountains in the far north of the country. The FRUD continued its struggle, however, launching armed attacks on government forces, including an assault on the army's camp at Tadjourah. Under sustained pressure from the French government, Gouled agreed in December to an exchange of prisoners with the FRUD; later in the month Bourhan and his immediate associates in the alleged coup conspiracy of January 1991 were released.

Relations with France deteriorated in early 1993 as the result of threats by the French government to withhold financial aid, in an attempt to coerce Gouled into negotiations with the FRUD. Counter-insurgency operations were intensified, with the result that, by July, about 80,000 civilians had been displaced by the fighting. In September the Gouled administration was strongly criticized by the international human rights organization Amnesty International for abuses of human rights, inflicted by the army.

The extent of the military reverses inflicted on the FRUD was reflected in the intensification of political activity during late 1993. In October the PRD and the FRUD issued joint proposals for a cease-fire, to be followed by negotiations aimed at forming a transitional 'government of national unity' to supervise the implementation of democratic reforms. These objectives were also defined by two new parties formed in the same month: the Organisation des masses Afars and the Parti centriste et des reformes démocratiques (PCRD). The PCRD, whose leadership comprised former members of the FRUD, announced that it was to seek legal recognition. In December the PRD and the PND launched a co-ordinated campaign to persuade the government to hold new parliamentary elections under the supervision of an independent electoral commission.

In early 1994, again under economic pressure from France, the government agreed to reduce the scale of its military expenditure, although operations against the FRUD continued in February. During March a split developed within the FRUD leadership, several of whose members, led by Ougoureh Kifleh Ahmed, began to seek support within the movement for a negotiated political settlement of the conflict. In May Kifleh Ahmed was expelled from the FRUD executive committee, but re-emerged in the following month, with the claimed support of the majority of FRUD members, as the party's secretary-general. Ali Mohamed Daoud was declared president of the FRUD. The new leaders, who were stated to hold office on a 'provisional' basis, continued to be opposed by several senior FRUD activists, including the party's former president, Ahmed Dini, based in Addis Ababa, who subsequently formed his own faction favouring a continuation of military operations. In late June Kifleh Ahmed and the Djibouti government agreed terms for an immediate cease-fire, and formal negotiations for a peace settlement began in July.

In December 1994 the two sides signed a peace agreement which envisaged the establishment of a coalition government, the implementation of a power-sharing arrangement based on a quota system, and a devolution of power to the regions. In June 1995 Gouled made a significant contribution to the fulfilment of the terms of the agreement by appointing Mohamed Daoud and Kifleh Ahmed to posts in the government. In addition, the agreement offered an amnesty to FRUD insurgents for actions committed before 12 June 1994. In exchange, the FRUD undertook to abandon its military struggle against the Gouled regime and to engage in peaceful political competition. The government also pledged to integrate some FRUD insurgents into the armed forces; indeed, in early 1995, 300 former FRUD insurgents joined the national army. One of the most controversial clauses of the peace agreement concerned a demobilization plan to reduce the size of the army, which had increased from some 2,500 troops before the war to approximately 20,000 at the height of the conflict. The successful implementation of the agreement was hampered further by factionalism within the FRUD. FRUD rebels continued to launch small-scale attacks against government targets during late 1995 and early 1996. Nevertheless, in March 1996 the government granted legal recognition to the FRUD, which became the country's fourth and largest political party. However, at approximately the same time, Ibrahim Chehem Daoud, a former high-ranking official in the FRUD, rejected the reconciliation between the government and the FRUD, and formed a new group, called FRUD-Renaissance.

In August 1997 the anti-government FRUD faction led by Ahmed Dini Ahmed renewed military operations against the Gouled regime. Most of the small-scale attacks occurred in the area around Obock and Tadjourah. FRUD activity was also reported just inside the Ethiopian border. In October the armed forces of Djibouti and Ethiopia launched a joint counter-attack against the FRUD rebels, and in February 1998 the Djiboutian security forces killed 12 members of the armed faction and arrested another 20. In March the rebels launched attacks on the southern towns of Ali Adde, Assamo and Guestir. Meanwhile, Dini unsuccessfully appealed to the Intergovernmental Authority on Development (IGAD) to mediate an end to the conflict. In September the FRUD Dini faction renewed its armed struggle against the Gouled regime by attacking a French water company and a small military post north-west of Obock. Shortly afterwards the rebels assaulted a government convoy in Tadjourah district, resulting in eight fatalities. Another FRUD attack forced government troops to withdraw from the garrison town of Alaili Dadda. In January 1999 the rebels launched attacks on Alaili Dadda and another garrison town, Daddato, near the Eritrean border. According to Dini, the aim of these operations was to force a negotiated settlement to end the 'crisis' affecting Djibouti. It appeared unlikely that the two FRUD factions would be reconciled; in September 1998 Dini's group had distributed leaflets highly critical of the FRUD faction allied to the Gouled regime.

During May–September 1999 landmines planted by FRUD rebels killed more than 20 people and injured some 35 others. In July FRUD insurgents attacked a Djiboutian army garrison in the Medeho region. Neither side released casualty figures, but press reports indicated that the fighting was heavy. In November a clash between FRUD rebels and government troops north of Obock resulted in the death of 15 guerrillas and five Djiboutian army personnel. In February 2000, the FRUD Dini faction concluded another peace agreement with the Djiboutian government. The accord provided for an end to hostilities; the release of prisoners; the rehabilitation of areas affected by the war; the indemnification of war victims; decentralization and autonomy for war-affected areas; the return of military units to positions held prior to the conflict; freedom of movement for persons and goods; the reintegration of FRUD insurgents into their previous positions of employment; and an amnesty for the rebels. In late March the self-exiled Dini returned to Djibouti, whereupon he announced his intention to help implement the peace agreement. In April meetings took place between government and FRUD officials at which the implementation of the agreement signed in February was discussed.

In December 1995 Gouled received medical treatment in France, where he remained in convalescence until March 1996. His prolonged absence from Djibouti prompted a succession crisis within the RPP, between the president's nephew and chief minister, Ismael Omar Gelleh, and his private secretary, Ismael Gedi Hared. In February 1996 a prison riot in the capital (which resulted in two deaths and 29 injuries) provoked a confrontation between the minister of justice and Islamic affairs, Moumin Bahdon Farah (who suggested that the incident had occurred because the cost of maintaining a sizeable army had resulted in poor staffing levels at the prison), and the minister of the interior, Idris Harbi Farah, who attributed the uprising to inadequate prison food supplies. Bahdon Farah's remarks reflected his opposition to Gelleh (whom Harbi Farah supported), who was known to favour a large standing army. In March Bahdon Farah was dismissed from the council of ministers, together with Ahmed Bulaleh Barreh, the minister of defence. Both ministers had openly opposed the December 1994 peace agreement with the FRUD, on the grounds that it strengthened the position of Gelleh and his followers. In April Bahdon Farah established a splinter group of the RPP, the Groupe pour la démocratie de la république (RPP–GDR), which included 13 of the 65 members of the chamber of deputies. The president of the chamber subsequently claimed that the RPP–GDR would remain banned while Bahdon Farah continued to hold his position as secretary-general of the RPP. In May, in an apparent attempt to settle the succession dispute, Gouled expelled Gedi Hared from the RPP's executive committee, together with Bahdon Farah and former ministers Barreh and Ali Mahamade Houmed, all of whom opposed Gelleh. In June Gedi Hared formed a new opposition alliance, the Coordination de l'opposition djiboutienne, embracing the PND, the FUOD and the RPP–GDR. In August Gedi Hared, Bahdon Farah and Barreh were among five people sentenced to six months' imprisonment, and the suspension of their civil rights for five years, for 'insulting the head of state'. The accused reportedly signed a document in May alleging that President Gouled ruled by force and terror. Although the detainees were released from prison in January 1997 (following a presidential pardon), their civil rights were not restored.

In September 1996 an internal dispute arose in the RPP when Gelleh began a discreet campaign against the holding of several positions concurrently, which was aimed at the prime minister

and deputy chairman of the RPP, Barkad Gourad Hamadou. In an apparent attempt to end these internecine disputes, Gouled declared his intention to remain as head of state until the expiry of his term in office in 1999. Moreover, later in September it was announced that a new RPP executive committee had been appointed, and that thenceforth Gouled (as president of the party) would be assisted by three deputies, namely Hamadou, Ahmed Hassan Liban and Gelleh. Mohamed Ali Mohamed, the minister of finance and the economy, was appointed as the RPP's secretary-general. Gouled was re-elected president of the RPP in March 1997. In April the pro-government faction of the FRUD convened its first party congress and announced its intention to participate in the forthcoming legislative elections and to present joint electoral lists with the RPP.

It was reported that in May 1997 more than 200 troops demonstrated in the capital to protest the fact that they had not been paid for more than three months. In addition, there was concern that several hundred demobilized soldiers had received severance payments from the authorities that were considerably lower than anticipated. In September the government commenced the military demobilization programme by announcing that 3,000 troops would leave the armed forces before the end of the year and that another 5,500 would be discharged in 1998. All demobilized soldiers were to receive an indemnity of US $1,000–$2,000, depending on their length of service. In January 1998 it was reported that the European Union (EU) had authorized a contribution of ECU 8.9m. to Djibouti, one-half of which was allocated to the demobilization programme. French financial assistance of an equal amount had been pledged in August 1997. The programme also received support from other international donors.

At the legislative elections, held on 19 December 1997, the RPP-FRUD alliance won all the seats in the chamber of deputies. According to official results, 63.8% of the electorate participated nation-wide, but only 47.8% voted in the capital and 32.9% in Ali-Sabieh. The PND and the PRD presented candidates in some districts and received significant support, but neither succeeded in gaining representation in the chamber. The PRD had suffered a split in May when Abdillahi Hamareiteh was elected as the party's new president (to succeed Elabe, who died in late 1996). A rival faction, led by Kaireh Allaleh Hared, was refused legal recognition. In late December Gouled announced a new council of ministers; minor reshuffles had been effected in April and November.

In February 1999 President Gouled announced his imminent retirement from politics and confirmed that he would not contest the presidential election in April. The RPP then named Gouled's chief minister, Gelleh, as its presidential candidate. According to official results, Gelleh won 74.4% of the votes cast at the presidential election, which was held on 9 April. His only opponent was Moussa Ahmed Idris, who represented an opposition coalition, the Opposition djiboutienne unifiée (ODU), which included the PND, the PRD, and the Dini wing of the FRUD. The rate of voter participation was estimated at 60% of the electorate. Shortly after his election, Gelleh, who had substantial business interests in Ethiopia, described Djibouti and Ethiopia as 'complementary states' and indicated that he was not opposed to the idea of confederation. He pledged to continue the process of political decentralization and to accelerate the reintegration of demobilized soldiers. In mid-May Gelleh reappointed Hamadou as prime minister; a new council of ministers was announced shortly afterwards. In March 2000 the RPP convened its eighth congress, at which its 170-member central committee agreed to the formation of three party commissions (covering discipline, internal co-operation, and press communications) in an attempt to enhance the ruling party's performance. Furthermore, Gelleh was elected to the presidency of the RPP following Gouled's decision to retire from active politics.

Djibouti's record on human rights came under criticism during the late 1990s, with allegations of extrajudicial executions, maltreatment of detainees and the arbitrary arrest of political dissidents. In February 1999 Aref Mohamed Aref (a prominent human rights activist and lawyer) was sentenced to two years in prison for 'attempted fraud and abuse of trust'. His French lawyer was not allowed to plead his case, and Aref claimed that the charges had been made in order to exclude him from the presidential election campaign. Fearing an international campaign for Aref's release, the authorities announced that the government would appoint a commission to examine conditions in Gaboda prison. In May the newly-elected president, Gelleh, ordered the release of Aref and some 40 other prisoners.

In August 1998 the authorities arrested 16 military personnel on suspicion of plotting a coup. In September all but one of the accused, along with Bahdon Farah and Barreh, were given suspended sentences and fined for preparing a 'civil disobedience movement'.

President Gelleh quickly acquired an unfavourable human rights reputation, especially with regard to media and opposition leaders. In August 1999 the authorities arrested Dahar Ahmed Farah, the editor of *Le Renouveau*, and Ali Meidal Wais, the former chief of staff of the army and co-editor of *Le Temps*, both members of the ODU, after they reported FRUD military successes against government troops. In September a court sentenced Farah to one year's imprisonment and jailed Wais for six months. Both publications were also banned for six months. Later that month the police arrested Moussa Ahmed Idriss, the leader of a coalition of factions opposed to Gelleh. After being found guilty of 'rebellion and acts of violence', Idriss received a sentence of four months' imprisonment and a fine; 19 other co-defendants were also given prison sentences. Such activities caused concern among several human rights organizations, and in November the Paris-based International Federation of Human Rights (IFHR) alleged that the Djiboutian authorities were holding some prisoners (particularly those suspected of sympathizing with the FRUD) in inhuman conditions and denying them medical care. Additionally, the IFHR accused government troops of exercising 'ferocious repression' against nomads suspected of belonging to or supporting the FRUD. This pressure undoubtedly contributed to Gelleh's decision in early December to release Moussa Ahmed Idriss and grant clemency to some 250 other prisoners.

In late 1998 French and Djiboutian forces conducted a joint demining operation in Obock, resulting in the destruction of 236 mines and numerous rocket launchers and 82-mm shells. Plans were under way to continue the exercise in other parts of the country. According to the Djiboutian government, both sides in the 1991–94 civil war used anti-personnel mines, especially in the northern part of the country. It was claimed that the Djiboutian army had removed the mines it had planted, but that the FRUD had not. Moreover, in the late 1990s the Dini FRUD faction planted anti-tank mines along the Eritrean border, causing some civilian casualties.

REFUGEES AND EXTERNAL RELATIONS

Djibouti historically has been a refuge for those seeking to escape wars and political persecution. According to the office of the UN High Commissioner for Refugees (UNHCR), at 31 December 1998 there were some 21,600 Somali and 1,900 Ethiopian refugees in Djibouti. It was estimated that there were 3,000 Djiboutian refugees in Ethiopia. In late 1997 an indigenous human rights organization in Djibouti accused Ethiopia of abusing Djiboutian refugees with the apparent intention of persuading them to return to Djibouti. According to UN estimates, Djibouti sheltered some 70,000–100,000 refugees and illegal immigrants from neighbouring countries in early 1998. UNHCR currently provides assistance to 20,400 Somalis and 1,100 Ethiopians resident in Djibouti's three refugees camps. Some 1,500 Ethiopian and Somali refugees are registered with UNHCR in the capital. In March 1998 the Djibouti government requested that UNHCR close its refugee camp in Assamo because of increased activity by FRUD rebels in the area. National and international disputes in the Horn of Africa continue to augment the number of refugees and displaced persons in the region and have led to a decline in trade and services. The resultant destruction of livestock, water resources, and health and education facilities, together with environmental problems such as droughts, floods and epidemics have increased substantially Djibouti's humanitarian aid requirements. In December 1998 some 700 Ethiopian refugees, many of whom had lived in Djibouti since the 1977–78 war between Ethiopia and Somalia, returned to Ethiopia as part of a UNHCR voluntary repatriation programme. Local hostility against refugees surfaced when some Ethiopians claimed that the local police had mistreated them by conducting sporadic raids on their shelters, removing money and other personal effects. The Solidarity Committee for Ethiopian Political Prisoners lodged a complaint with UNHCR and requested that it investigate these and other reports, including religious persecution and rape.

In October 1999 the World Food Programme (WFP) announced that it had launched an operation to provide substantial emergency food relief to some 30,000 Djiboutians. The WFP shipped the food consignment, worth US $198,000, to relieve drought-induced food insecurity in five districts bordering Eritrea and Ethiopia. In late 1999 the UN-Djiboutian drought assessment mission also noted that Djibouti would require food aid unless climatic conditions improved. In January 2000 the WFP indicated that the continued lack of rain had prompted it to launch a $2.7m. emergency relief programme to feed some 100,000 people. The operation was scheduled to continue until June 2000 and was expected to distribute 6,000 metric tons of food. However, by mid-April donors had only pledged about one-half of the required amount.

Because of its geographical position, the maintenance of peaceful relations with both Ethiopia and Somalia has been a vital consideration in Djibouti's foreign policy. The key economic goal of maintaining its share in the rail and sea transport of Ethiopian trade, which was intermittently disrupted by guerrilla action and regional unrest during the late 1970s, was partially realized in 1985 when the governments of Ethiopia and Djibouti agreed to create an independent railway company.

During 1979 Djibouti concluded agreements with both Ethiopia and Somalia for closer co-operation in transport, communications and trade. Regular meetings of frontier boundary commissioners were proposed with Ethiopia in that year, and official visits to Djibouti by high-ranking Ethiopian delegations took place in 1980 and in 1983. In 1985 the two countries concluded a trade and development co-operation agreement, although relations became clouded in the following year when Ethiopia granted asylum to Awalleh and the MNDID.

As a result of Gouled's wish to reconcile the vying factions in the Horn of Africa, Djibouti was instrumental in promoting the creation in 1985 of the six-nation Intergovernmental Authority on Drought and Development (IGADD, now the IGAD), with a permanent secretariat in Djibouti. IGADD's first summit meeting, in January 1986, brought both the Ethiopian and Somali heads of state to Djibouti. In April 1988, following a further meeting of the two leaders in Djibouti, Ethiopia and Somalia agreed to re-establish diplomatic relations, withdraw troops from their common border and exchange prisoners of war.

Relations with Somalia deteriorated following an attack by the Somali National Movement (SNM) on border posts along the Somali-Djibouti border in May 1989. The Somali government had always regarded with suspicion Djibouti's declared neutrality in respect of the Somali-Ethiopian conflict. After the outbreak of armed insurgency in northern Somalia, Somalia accused the Djibouti government of openly supporting the SNM, whose opposition to the Siad Barre regime had many sympathizers among Issa and Isaaq clansmen in Djibouti. In March 1990, when inter-tribal conflict erupted into heavy fighting on the Somali side of the border with Ethiopia, Somalia accused Djibouti of waging armed aggression in its territory. A denial by the Djibouti government did not prevent a further deterioration in relations, and the maritime border between Djibouti and Somalia was closed in October.

In June 1991 Djibouti provided the venue for a preliminary conference of groups from southern Somalia, aimed at forming a transitional Somali government. In October the land borders between Djibouti and Somalia were reopened for the first time since May 1989. Relations between Djibouti and the government of the 'Republic of Somaliland' deteriorated sharply in early 1992 following contacts between the 'Somaliland' authorities and the FRUD. Tensions involving the presence of refugee Issas in the border area were reported in July 1994. In September Djibouti reopened the border post of Loyada, which had been closed for four months because of clashes with armed units from the 'Somaliland'. Relations deteriorated in August 1995, when there were reports of clashes along the border, which, some suggested, had occurred as a result of the involvement of local militia groups in Djibouti in an armed conflict between 'Somaliland' troops and the rebel United Somali Front, which was suspected of receiving clandestine support from Djibouti. In addition, during 1995 Somali pirates reportedly attacked at least 15 vessels in international waters off Djibouti, prompting fears that trade between Djibouti and other countries might be jeopardized. In June 1996, however, Djibouti and 'Somaliland' concluded a 10-point agreement, which included provisions for co-operation on border security and the establishment of trade relations. In September Gouled met Ali Mahdi Mohamed, the leader of the Somali Salvation Alliance, to discuss the possibility of convening a conference in Yemen on Somali reconciliation. A further meeting between Gouled and Ali Mahdi took place in Djibouti in June 1997. In November 1997, following the dispatch of a delegation of officials to 'Somaliland' in September, Djibouti granted the republic official recognition. Shortly afterwards 'Somaliland' established a liaison bureau in Djibouti.

Following the removal of Ethiopia's President Mengistu Haile Mariam, in May 1991, Djibouti established good relations with the successor transitional government in that country. In early 1994 the two nations concluded a co-operation agreement covering a number of subjects, including agriculture, industry, border patrols, use of port facilities, movement of commercial goods and trade subsidies. In August Djibouti and Ethiopia signed a judicial affairs agreement guaranteeing the equality of citizens before one another's courts. The accord also provided for the extradition of criminals. In October Ethiopian President Meles Zenawi made an official visit to Djibouti, his first since he took power in 1991. Meles and Gouled explored ways to improve bilateral relations and reviewed several regional issues and projects being undertaken by the IGADD. Later in the month Djibouti and Ethiopia issued a joint communiqué which pledged both countries to improving economic, transportation, and telecommunications co-operation. Additionally, Gouled and Meles undertook to work for peace and stability throughout the Horn of Africa. In late 1995 Ethiopia announced plans to increase trade with Djibouti, which would be facilitated by the rehabilitation of the Djibouti-Addis Ababa railway. In September 1996 Djibouti and Ethiopia concluded a series of agreements, the most important of which concerned a joint pledge to combat al-Ittihad al-Islam (the Islamic Union Party), a radical group active in western Somalia and eastern Ethiopia. The two countries also promised to increase economic and social co-operation, easing access rules into Djibouti for Ethiopian passenger and freight transport, granting customs exemptions to Ethiopia for imports of salt and fish products from Djibouti, and providing scholarships to Djibouti students studying in Ethiopia. In March 1997 the two countries pledged to fight against smuggling, drugs-trafficking, and other cross-border crimes along their common frontier. During a visit to Addis Ababa in May, President Gouled held discussions with Prime Minister Meles Zenawi on increasing co-operation between IGAD members and on the effect of Djibouti's demobilization programme on Ethiopia's Ogaden region. It was feared that a massive influx of Issa mercenaries from Djibouti could destabilize the region further. In August the two countries pledged to enhance co-operation in matters concerning foreign affairs, trade and industry, education, culture and immigration. In November Djiboutian and Ethiopian officials affirmed their intention to increase bilateral trade. President Gouled, in his capacity as the current chairman of the IGAD, visited Ethiopia and Eritrea in May 1998 to mediate in the border dispute between the two countries; Gouled's efforts proved unsuccessful.

The Eritrean-Ethiopian border dispute, which erupted into open warfare in June 1998, had a significant effect on Djibouti, largely because it allowed Djibouti to prosper as a result of Ethiopia's re-routing of military and non-military imports via Djibouti port. There were allegations, which the Djiboutian government denied, that Ethiopian military forces had been deployed to Djibouti as part of its campaign against Eritrea. Other reports suggested that Ethiopian troops had been deployed to Yoboki, an area some 50 kilometres inside Djibouti, to prevent attacks against Ethiopian truck convoys returning from Djibouti port. In mid-1999 there were unconfirmed reports that two Ethiopian helicopter gunships attacked FRUD rebel camps at Ayri and Dalha. Also in June Djibouti and Ethiopia held their eighth border committee conference in Dire Dawa, during which the two countries agreed to facilitate free cross-border movement of pastoralist people and goods, and to exchange information about border issues. In late 1998 Prime Minister Meles visited Djibouti and held talks with President Gouled and senior government officials on the furthering of existing ties.

Relations with Eritrea, which had been enhanced in late 1997 by the signing of a five-year bilateral agreement, deteriorated in mid-1998 as a result of the dispute between Eritrea and Ethiopia: the Eritrean authorities claimed that Djibouti supported Ethiopia in the conflict. In November, during an OAU mediation committee meeting (on the Eritrea-Ethiopia dispute) in Burkina Faso, attended by the presidents of Burkina Faso, Djibouti, Eritrea, Ethiopia, and Zimbabwe, Eritrean President Issaias Afewerki rejected President Gouled as an impartial negotiator. Djibouti responded by suspending diplomatic relations with Eritrea. In turn, Eritrea demanded that Djibouti withdraw from the OAU mediation committee. In February 1999 Gelleh met an Eritrean delegation in Rome (Italy) to explore ways of restoring relations between the two countries. However, the meeting failed to end the impasse between Eritrea and Djibouti.

In December 1987 President Mitterrand visited Djibouti: the first visit by a French president since 1977. President Gouled made an official visit to France in June 1989, during which he described relations with France as of an 'exceptional quality' and praised the stabilizing influence of the French military presence in Djibouti. However, the French military presence became more controversial following Iraq's invasion of Kuwait in August 1990 and the onset of the 'Gulf crisis'. French troops in Djibouti were reinforced and Djibouti became the operational base for France's participation in the multinational force deployed in Saudi Arabia. By supporting the UN resolutions which were formulated against Iraq, Djibouti jeopardized its future relations with that country, which was emerging as an important supplier of economic and military aid. However, Djibouti's stance during the Gulf War of January–February 1991 strengthened its ties with France, and in February the two countries signed two defence treaties which extended military co-operation. In January 1992, however, there was serious disagreement between France and Djibouti over France's refusal to intervene militarily in the conflict between government forces and the FRUD. Relations remained tense during 1992–93, with France using the threat of withholding its aid, in an attempt to persuade the government to negotiate with the rebels, and showing dissatisfaction with the pace and extent of Gouled's political reforms. A meeting betweeen the two presidents in November 1992 led to the release of French budgetary aid, but France later made clear its irritation at the government's failure to attend a planned meeting with the FRUD. From December Djibouti became the operational centre for French troops participating in multinational (and subsequently UN) operations in Somalia. The facilities of Djibouti airport were also made available for US troop transport. In March 1994 the Franco–Djibouti joint co-operation commission met, for the first time in more than four years, in Djibouti. As a result, the Gouled regime re-established its line of credit with the French government, which had been interrupted because of the war with FRUD insurgents.

France repeatedly sought to end the conflict between the Djibouti government and FRUD insurgents, and in December 1994 a number of influential French parliamentarians expressed the opinion that, if the conflict continued, France should reassess its military commitment to Djibouti. As a result of the peace accord signed on 26 December, relations with France improved. However, tensions remained, primarily concerning French aid to Djibouti. Although in January 1996 the French minister of defence pledged to maintain a military presence in Djibouti, in March he indicated that the French military contingent would probably be reduced by about one-fifth.

During a visit to Djibouti in April 1998 the French minister of defence, Alain Richard, informed Gouled that France planned to reduce its military presence in the country from 3,200 troops to 2,600 by 2000. Richard stressed that France would continue to maintain ground, air and naval forces in Djibouti. It was anticipated that the troop reduction would have a significant negative effect on Djibouti's economy. In October 1998 Gouled made an official visit to France and held discussions with President Jacques Chirac on bilateral relations. In the following month five Djiboutians suspected of involvement in a grenade attack on a cafeteria in Djibouti in 1990 (during which a French child was killed and 15 others were wounded) were sentenced *in absentia* to life imprisonment by a court in France. Three of the accused were held in custody in Djibouti, but it was considered unlikely that they would be handed over to France as Djibouti does not extradite its nationals.

The escalation of hostilities between Eritrea and Ethiopia during 1998–99, and Djibouti's mobilization of troops along its borders with the two countries prompted France to increase its military presence in Djibouti in early 1999. The Franco-Djiboutian defence agreement provided for French assistance in the event of an attack on Djibouti by a foreign country, and, as a precautionary measure, France deployed an anti-aircraft destroyer to the Red Sea and reinforced the Djiboutian air force base where its *Mirage* fighter jets were stationed.

Since becoming president, Gelleh has pursued an aggressive foreign policy, prompted by his belief that a strong Djiboutian presence in the Horn of Africa, the Gulf states and the West will increase the country's prestige and influence. In May 1999 President Gelleh attended a meeting of the Common Market for Eastern and Southern Africa (COMESA) in Kenya. Djibouti had been a founding member of COMESA, but had allowed its membership to lapse because it did not favour making tariff reductions required of all member states. Gelleh reactivated Djibouti's membership largely because of the continuing decline in French aid and the need to make the country more competitive regionally.

In July 1998 a Djiboutian parliamentary delegation visited Sudan to participate in the ninth anniversary of the Bashir regime. The two countries agreed to revitalize IGAD and establish a joint friendship association and a parliamentary forum. In November Gouled visited Libya, Egypt, Morocco, and Yemen.

In August 1998 President Gouled and nine senior officials visited several Far Eastern nations. In Malaysia Gouled signed investment and educational co-operation accords, which, *inter alia*, would afford Djibouti technical aid for the development of the agriculture, power, and transportation sectors. In turn, Malaysian companies were offered investment guarantees in Djibouti. Gouled also visited China, where he held talks with President Jiang Zemin and donated US $10,000 to the Chinese Red Cross Society for its flood relief efforts. In Japan, the Djiboutian delegation received assurances from Prime Minister Keizo Obuchi that Japan would increase its aid programme to Djibouti.

Djibouti's most important regional ally continues to be Ethiopia, and relations between the two countries remain close. In early November 1999 President Gelleh began a four-day visit to Ethiopia, during which he held meetings with President Negasso Gidada, Prime Minister Meles Zenawi and several other Ethiopian ministers. Apart from pledging the full integration of the economies of the two countries, Gelleh and Meles released a joint statement which expressed 'grave concern' about terrorist activities along their common border and laid the groundwork for greater security co-operation. In December 1999 Djibouti and Ethiopia concluded a military co-operation protocol whereby Ethiopia agreed to provide maintenance, spare parts and equipment for the Djiboutian air force.

Djiboutian-Eritrean relations remained tense in 1999. Djibouti accused Eritrea of supporting the FRUD, and allowed its port to be used as a transhipment point for weapons and other military supplies destined for Ethiopia. In July 1999 of that year Gelleh claimed that Eritrea had provided aid for a FRUD attack on the Medeho army camp. In August the pro-government newspaper *La Nation* accused Eritrea of spreading 'regional terrorism'. In October an Eritrean newspaper reported that France had deployed some units stationed in Djibouti to the border with Eritrea, and in November President Gelleh

announced that Djibouti and Eritrea were 'almost in a state of war'. However, in March 2000 the countries announced that they were resuming diplomatic relations, which had been severed in November 1998 following Eritrean accusations that Djibouti was aiding Ethiopia's war effort. The reconciliation had been brokered by Libya. In January 2000 Djibouti and Libya signed an education and scientific co-operation accord. Djibouti also agreed to host a permanent Libyan Educational and Training Mission, which was to facilitate the study of Arabic. Later that month Libya announced that it would support the proposed Somali national reconciliation conference, scheduled to be held in Djibouti in mid-2000. Also in January Djibouti, Sudan and Yemen opened a summit meeting in the Yemeni capital of San'a, at which the three countries discussed security, political, economic and social issues. Sudan and Yemen also expressed support for President Gelleh's plan to host a Somali national reconciliation conference.

In late January 2000 President Gelleh attended a meeting with the Egyptian President, Muhammad Hosni Mubarak, in Cairo, at which the two leaders discussed ways to improve political and economic relations. In addition, they signed a food security agreement, pledged to initiate a commercial air service between the two countries, and made provisions for Djiboutian students to attend the Egyptian International Agriculture Centre and to receive more scholarships to Egyptian universities. Mubarak also expressed support for Gelleh's initiative for a Somali national reconciliation conference in Djibouti.

In May 2000 Gelleh made an official visit to the United Arab Emirates, the main purpose of which was to enlist support for his Somali reconciliation initiative. He also solicited aid for ongoing development initiatives in the housing, health, education and energy sectors.

In late November 1999 Djibouti, Ethiopia, Kenya and Sudan attended the 7th IGAD conference; Eritrea boycotted the meeting owing to tensions with the Gelleh regime. President Gelleh, the organization's current chairman, announced his proposal to hold a Somali national reconciliation conference in Djibouti. This alarmed the leaders of the self-proclaimed 'Republic of Somaliland', which has historically opposed attempts to re-create a unified Somali state, and they expressed their vehement opposition to the plan. The day after the IGAD conference 'Somaliland' closed its border with Djibouti and deployed troops to the Loyada border crossing. The border was, however, reopened the following month. In April 2000 relations deteriorated again after 'Somaliland' refused to allow a Djiboutian delegation to leave their aircraft after landing in Hargeisa. The following day 'Somaliland' once again closed its border with Djibouti. In response, the Djiboutian authorities subsequently closed the Somaliland Liaison Office in Djibouti town, and ordered the 'Somaliland' representative to leave the country. 'Somaliland' officials justified their actions by claiming that Djibouti was encouraging ethnic violence and was responsible for a series of bombings in Hargeisa. Meanwhile, in early 2000 Djibouti levied a 20% increase in the country's taxes on alcohol, qat (a narcotic leaf) and tobacco to help pay for the Somali reconciliation conference. The conference, the 13th such reconciliation meeting to have been convened, opened in Djibouti in May 2000.

In December 1999 Gelleh succeeded in brokering the so-called 'Call of the Homeland' agreement between Sudanese President Omar Hassan Ahmad al-Bashir and Sadiq al-Mahdi, the leader of the opposition Umma Party (UP). The National Democratic Alliance (NDA), a coalition of Sudanese opposition groups which had included the UP (until the latter's suspension of its membership in March 2000), denounced the accord, citing al-Mahdi's failure to secure the alliance's approval prior to the reconciliation.

Economy

THOMAS OFCANSKY

The economy is based on trade through the international port of Djibouti, and its developing service sector, which accounted for an estimated 76.5% of the country's gross domestic product (GDP) in 1998. In addition to the port, there is a railway, which links Djibouti to Addis Ababa in Ethiopia, and a modern airport that can be used by large jet-engined aircraft. The financial sector is growing in importance, aided by the stable and freely convertible Djibouti franc and the absence of exchange controls. A substantial share of the country's receipts derive from the provision of services to the French military garrison (with about 3,400 men in late 1999) and other expatriates.

There is little arable farming in Djibouti, as the land is mainly volcanic desert, one of the least hospitable and most unproductive terrains in Africa, and the country is able to produce only about 3% of its food requirements. More than one-half of the population are pastoral nomads, herding goats, sheep and camels. Agriculture (including hunting, forestry and fishing) provided an estimated 3.6% of GDP in 1998, although some 75.2% of the labour force were employed in this sector in 1991. A 10-year programme to develop fishing was started in 1980, supported by the International Fund for Agricultural Development, and in 1990 the Islamic Development Bank (IDB) agreed to finance the construction of a fish-canning factory with an annual capacity of 1,500 metric tons. In late 1998 Ethiopia Amalgamated and its US partner, Allied International Marketing Corpn, announced plans to establish a joint venture in Djibouti to market agricultural products.

The development of underground water supplies for irrigation is being studied, and deep-water wells have been sunk in an attempt to alleviate the effects of periodic drought. A loan was received in 1987 from the African Development Bank (ADB) to finance a project to supply water to the towns of Djibouti, Ali-Sabieh, Tadjourah and Obock. Relief assistance during periods of periodic drought and flooding has been forthcoming from the European Community (EC, now the European Union—EU), France, Japan, Saudi Arabia and Germany.

Industry is limited to a few small-scale concerns. Regional political uncertainties and high labour costs have discouraged the creation of new industries, despite the existence of a free zone and the major liberalization of investment legislation in 1984, and almost all consumer goods have to be imported. Industry (comprising manufacturing, construction and utilities) provided an estimated 19.9% of GDP in 1998, and engaged 11.0% of the employed labour force in 1991. A power station supplying a mineral-water bottling factory at Tadjourah, the first major industrial project outside the capital, was commissioned in 1981, and a dairy plant (on the outskirts of Djibouti town), a government printing press and an extension to the Boulaos power station were all opened in 1984–85. Plans to privatize the Tadjourah mineral water plant were announced in 1991, but the plant later sustained damage in fighting between government and rebel forces. Djibouti opened its first pharmaceutical factory in 1996, at a cost of US $3m. The company planned to manufacture five generic drugs for the national and regional markets.

Work began in 1986 on a major geothermal exploration project, funded by the World Bank and foreign aid. Although the object of the scheme was to make Djibouti self-sufficient in energy, and possibly able to export gas to neighbouring countries, by the late 1990s Djibouti still relied on imported fuels for 90% of its energy requirements. In 1986 Saudi Arabia granted Djibouti US $21.4m. for the purchase and installation of three electricity generators, with a combined capacity of 15 MW. Total electricity generating capacity rose from 40 MW to 80 MW in 1988, when the second part of the Boulaos power station became operative.

Work on Djibouti's first petroleum refinery at Dorale, began in 1990, with Saudi Arabian private-sector assistance. The US $533m.-refinery was expected to produce 100,000 barrels per day of petrol, kerosene and liquefied gas. The project, which was reported to have been delayed by the conflict between the government and the insurgent Front pour la restauration de l'unité et de la démocratie (FRUD), resumed in 1996. In February 1996 private investors in Djibouti established the Compagnie des Gaz de la Mer Rouge to take over the assets of Air Liquide, a subsidiary of a larger French company. The former, with French technical assistance, sought to manufacture and market industrial gases and to import and export industrial and medical gases.

In December 1997 a US joint venture (comprising Seven Star Minerals and Quest International Resources Corpn) concluded an agreement that granted it exclusive mineral rights to five regions in Djibouti. According to a study by the US Geological Survey in 1992, these areas were likely to contain concentrations of gold, silver, copper, lead and zinc. After Ethiopia halted salt imports from Eritrea in mid-1998, at least six new Djiboutian companies emerged to exploit salt reserves at Lake Assal for the Ethiopian market.

Djibouti's establishment as a free port, in 1981, has helped to arrest a relative decline in total port business, which, affected by competition from rising Arab ports nearby, was virtually stagnant until the completion, in 1985, of a deep-water container terminal, with 'roll-on, roll-off' facilities and a refrigerated warehouse, capable of handling 40,000 metric tons. The rehabilitation of the port's berth facilities, together with dredging and reclamation work, has been proceeding. In 1992 France agreed to lend US $8m. towards continuing modernization of the port facilities, including internal transport and management. As Djibouti has good bunkering and watering facilities and is well placed for transhipment, it was hoped that the addition of these facilities would help the port to regain some of the business that it lost during the closure of the Suez Canal (1967–75), and to increase its competitiveness with the expanding Arab ports. The Gulf crisis of 1990–91 acted as a major stimulus to the port, with total traffic rising to nearly 1.5m. tons in 1990, compared with only 870,000 tons in the previous year. In 1992 Djibouti established a 'flag of convenience' registry, with the aim of attracting international shipowners seeking such facilities. Tax incentives were also offered to shipping companies reinvesting their profits in Djibouti. It was hoped that the port would benefit from an expected increase in Ethiopian traffic, following the independence in 1992 of Eritrea, whose facilities at Assab and Massawa were less developed than those available in Djibouti. In early 1996 Djibouti sought to increase the country's earnings by implementing new tariffs for port services and taxes, including a revised tariff for transit goods and a new fee schedule for exports, imports and transhipments. Activity at Djibouti's port was reported to have declined by 40% in 1995, primarily because business was being diverted to the Eritrean port of Assab and the Somali port of Berbera. However, an administrative reform programme, funded by France and supervised by the port authority of Nantes–Saint-Nazaire, enhanced the port's operations and reputation. The programme aimed to streamline port tariffs, foster closer co-operation between customs and transport officials, and overhaul labour practices. In February 1997 two quays were reopened following a $32m.-renovation, which had been financed by the Japanese government. The French Development Agency subsequently granted loans for the purchase of a tug boat and for the renovation of the port. During 1996 the volume of cargo handled by the port exceeded 1,500m. tons, an increase of 35% compared with the previous year. The increase was attributable primarily to the fact that the US Navy had resumed using Djibouti as a refuelling port. Of the 892 ships that docked at Djibouti port in 1996, just over one-third were container vessels, accounting for one-half of the total gross registered tonnage of 7.8m. tons. The border dispute between Ethiopia and Eritrea in mid-1998 resulted in a substantial increase in activity in Djibouti port after Ethiopia stopped using the ports of Massawa and Assab. In the first three months of the conflict Djibouti port handled almost as much cargo as it did during the whole of 1997. During the first 11 months of 1998 Ethiopian imports via Djibouti port increased by 370%, while exports grew by 113%. Previously, the port was accustomed to handling no more than 10% of Ethiopian transit traffic. In 1998 Ethiopia also leased additional storage capacity in the port area to facilitate the delivery of some 1.6m. tons of cargo a year. To cope with the increased traffic, the government invested considerable sums to upgrade port facilities; more than 1,000 additional workers were hired and the port was opened 24 hours a day. There were problems, however, as local importers experienced delays in the clearing of their shipments because Ethiopian imports received priority, and the lack of space for lorries, containers and storage delayed the processing and onward shipment of imports.

Since the 1980s Djibouti has made considerable advances in developing telecommunications networks. In 1985 a second earth station was inaugurated, linking Djibouti to the telecommunications network of the Arab Satellite Communication Organization, while an undersea telecommunications cable to Saudi Arabia was also installed. In early 1997 the Société de Télécommunications Internationales de Djibouti (STID, a subsidiary of France Cable et Radio) launched a cellular telephone network enabling the country to have internet services. The STID planned to make Djibouti a regional and international transit centre for communications links between Africa and Asia by using submarine optic cables and building a satellite communications station. In December a Japanese telecommunications company, Kokusai Denshiri Denwa Co Ltd, awarded a contract to Elisalat of the United Arab Emirates (UAE) to lay a 5,000-km cable from Mumbai (India) to Djibouti. The proposed cable would pass through Pakistan, the UAE and Oman before linking into European networks.

For many years, the Djibouti government was anxious about its lack of control over the railway linking Djibouti town with Addis Ababa (Ethiopia); 660 km of the line's 781 km pass through the territory of Ethiopia, which employs more than three-quarters of the railway staff. The signing of a new railway agreement with Ethiopia in 1981 brought some improvement, which was further enhanced in 1985, when a joint ministerial meeting between the two countries decided to grant autonomous status to the railway company (the Chemin de Fer Djibouti–Ethiopien, CDE), with the aim of increasing its profitability. A major programme for the replacement of rolling stock and the rehabilitation of track was begun in 1986, with funding from the EU. Further financial assistance from this source was received in 1993. During 1994–95 Djibouti and Ethiopia sought to improve the deteriorating capabilities of the railway, which had been beset by operational problems and had suffered a lack of spare parts and of maintenance. In late 1994 the French Development Agency agreed to extend 55m. French francs in aid for track repair and technical assistance. The World Bank funded short-term technical aid and a programme to improve the railway's spare parts inventory and its telecommunications system. Additionally, the German government, the Kuwait Fund for Arab Economic Development (KFAED) and the IDB have expressed an interest in helping to rehabilitate the railway. In September 1995 the EU pledged US $100m.–$200m., and the French Development Agency agreed to provide 40m. French francs for the rehabilitation project. However, the project was hampered by the persistent theft of railway fittings, and by an incident in mid-1996 when a freight train hit a landmine in Ethiopia, resulting in the death of one passenger. In December 1996 the CDE announced its intention to purchase four new locomotives with a $9.6m. grant from France, significantly reducing the travelling time between Djibouti and Addis Ababa. Meanwhile, interest was reported to have been expressed by the EU, the KFAED, the World Bank, France, Germany and Switzerland in financing a project to replace the CDE's obsolete rail and communications equipment. In February 1997 Djibouti and Ethiopia agreed to grant the CDE autonomous management, thereby opening the way for the participation of private operators in some of the railway's activities. In March Ethiopia revealed that the railway was incurring monthly losses of some $3,000. In April 1998 Djibouti and Ethiopia sought to rectify this situation by announcing plans to cut salaries (which currently account for more than 60% of the CDE's revenue) and eliminate all security checkpoints except for two in Ethiopia and one in

Djibouti. Additionally, the two countries devised an emergency maintenance and repair programme for the CDE's locomotives. France and the EU agreed to contribute $100m. to this scheme, but it was estimated that another $1,500m. would be required for a complete overhaul of the railway. At about the same time, the EU announced that it had hired a consultant on behalf of Djibouti and Ethiopia to prepare a privatization project which would involve selling an operating concession for 20–50 years. The conflict between Eritrea and Ethiopia in 1998–99 substantially increased traffic on the Djibouti–Addis Ababa railway. Total goods carried during 1998 amounted to approximately 200,000 tons, compared with 168,000 tons a year prior to May 1998. The rise in traffic stimulated efforts to rehabilitate existing rolling stock and acquire more locomotives. According to railway officials, the acquisition of additional rolling stock and locomotives could increase carrying capacity to some 400,000 tons a year.

In October 1997 Air Djibouti, which had not been operating for nearly eight years, was ceded to a privately-owned company established by Arab investors. In November 1998 airline officials announced plans to lease an Airbus to reinitiate twice-weekly services to France. Air Djibouti also started services to Uganda and the UAE and planned flights to Saudi Arabia, Ethiopia and Kenya. Plans for a service to Eritrea collapsed after Djibouti suspended diplomatic relations with Eritrea in 1998.

The government's first Development Plan (1982–84) was undertaken to channel foreign aid into a cohesive development strategy. Potential was constrained, however, by the lack of infrastructure, trained labour and natural resources. Nevertheless, a highly successful conference of aid donors was held in Djibouti in 1983, when most of the funds that the country needed for its 1984–89 Development Plan (which envisaged total expenditure of US $570m.) were raised, including more than $100m. from Arab sources. Development projects that had already started included the construction by a Yugoslav contractor of a 114-km 'unity' highway linking Djibouti to Tadjourah. There were also plans for an improved road through Loyada into northern Somalia.

In November 1998 Djibouti's minister of finance presented the 1999–2001 financial plan to parliament, which included plans to enlarge the tax base and improve tax collection; refrain from increasing internal debts while honouring due dates of external debts; and create an export-processing zone and an airport free-zone. He unveiled several short-term projects, including a national road repair scheme and an upgrade to the country's electrical infrastructure. The plan also included provisions for the continuation of the military and police demobilization programme (part-financed by the EU).

Djibouti remains heavily dependent on foreign assistance, which, because of the country's strategic position, is readily forthcoming. The main donors are the EU, France and Saudi Arabia. The Saudi Fund for Development was to provide funds for the renovation of Djibouti's port facilities, and was also to finance housing and educational projects and road construction. Djibouti is a member of the ADB, the IMF, the IDB, the World Bank and its affiliate, the International Finance Corpn, and receives considerable financial support from these organizations.

In 1993, according to estimates by the World Bank, Djibouti's gross national product, measured at average 1991–93 prices, was US $448m., equivalent to $780 per head. In 1997, according to the IMF, Djibouti's GDP, measured at current purchasers' values, was an estimated 89,583m. Djibouti francs. Djibouti's GDP expanded, in real terms, at an average annual rate of 1.2% in 1980–85 and 2.0% in 1985–89, reversing an average annual decline of 2.7% in 1977–79. However, as a result of rapid population increase, GDP per head declined, in real terms, during 1980–86. According to estimates by the IMF, GDP declined, in real terms, in each of the five years 1992–96. Real GDP fell by 2.9% in 1994, by 4.0% in 1995 and by 5.1% in 1996; however, in 1997 GDP increased by an estimated 0.5%. During 1990–98 the population increased by an average of 3.0% per year (according to World Bank estimates), owing partly to the influx of refugees from Ethiopia and Somalia.

Djibouti's total external debt was US $287.8m. at the end of 1998, of which $263.8m. was long-term public debt. Debt-servicing has remained at manageable levels, representing 3.4%

of exports of goods and services in 1997. The annual rate of inflation averaged 5.2% during 1989–96. Consumer prices increased by an estimated 2.0% in 1997.

In 1995 Djibouti recorded a visible trade deficit of US $171.5m., and there was a deficit of $23.0m. on the current account of the balance of payments. According to IMF estimates, in 1998 the principal sources of imports were France (12.5%), Ethiopia (12.0%), Italy (9.2%) and the United Kingdom (6.2%). The principal markets for exports in that year were Somalia (53.0%), Yemen (22.5%) and Ethiopia (5.0%). The principal imports were food and beverages, qat (a narcotic leaf), petroleum products, machinery and electrical appliances, metals and metal products, wood, wood products and furniture and chemical products. Most exports are unclassified.

In September 1990 the government estimated that losses resulting from the crisis in the Gulf would amount (in 1990) to US $218m. This estimate took into account increases in the price of imports (especially petroleum), which were expected to average 15%; increases in transport expenses; and the postponement of investments pledged by Kuwait, Saudi Arabia and Iraq. Losses of state revenues in 1990 were forecast at $23m. There was, however, a doubling of official revenues from Djibouti port, deriving from the war-related traffic. Djibouti's role as a service centre was also enhanced by the Western military intervention in Somalia in 1992.

It was planned to increase substantially public investment in 1990. A total of 10,788m. Djibouti francs was to be invested in projects in the communications, agricultural and fisheries sectors, and in social, environmental and urban improvement schemes. Almost 40% of total expenditure on public projects (about twice the level of 1989) was allocated to projects in the communications sector. It was also proposed to invest 2,058m. Djibouti francs in agriculture and fisheries. Capital expenditure in 1991 was fixed at 13,850m. Djibouti francs, most of which would, again, be directed towards the communications sector; the total budget was projected to balance at 26,000m. Djibouti francs. Internal civil unrest has since had a noticeable impact on investment, with capital spending allocated only 540m. Djibouti francs out of total expenditure of 28,320m. Djibouti francs in the 1993 budget. Capital spending was forecast to account for only 3% of the 1994 budget. Serious flooding in November 1994 caused extensive damage to Djibouti's infrastructure and necessitated emergency relief aid (notably from France) to provide temporary shelters throughout the country, and to assist in the reconstruction of the capital's sewage system.

Djibouti remains reliant on France for budgetary aid. However, despite repeated encouragement from the French government, in early 1995 Djibouti announced that it would not apply to the IMF for assistance with its 1995 budget deficit, estimated at some 225m. French francs. Instead, the Gouled administration hoped to secure new bank loans and financial aid from Arab nations. In addition, Djibouti planned to plead its case before IMF donors at a meeting in Geneva, Switzerland, scheduled for April 1995; however, the conference was subsequently postponed until October 1995. The international financial community responded to Djibouti's budget strategy by insisting that the country, if it hoped to maintain its credit rating with lending banks, would have to honour its loan repayments to the Banque pour le Commerce et l'Industrie–Mer Rouge, a subsidiary of France's Banque Nationale de Paris, although to do so would increase the country's budget deficit. The Djibouti government would also be expected to pay those civil servants with three and four weeks' salary arrears, in order to avoid civil unrest. In pursuit of these goals, the Gouled administration suspended payments to all other creditors and to many of its suppliers. As an incentive to Arab donors, the authorities closed more than 80 establishments serving alcoholic beverages in the capital in order to court the favour of many increasingly Islamist regimes. The failure of this attempt to end reliance on IMF donors to produce any significant gain prompted the Djibouti government to reassess its policy in this area. In April 1995 the council of ministers announced a reduction in budget expenditure of 26.6m. French francs (from 1 July) and launched an initiative to increase public revenues. (Measures which reflected recommendations made by an IMF team which had visited Djibouti earlier in the month.) In July the IMF demanded a budget cut of more than US $37m., and in October insisted on an additional

$11.2m. reduction in civil service salaries. Moreover, in December the IMF informed the Djibouti government that it would have to settle its debts with France before entering a structural adjustment programme, and demanded a comprehensive survey by 31 March 1996 of cross-debts incurred by state-owned companies and the Djibouti government. The IMF stipulated that Djibouti's debt to France (estimated at 2,400m. Djibouti francs) would have to be rescheduled before September 1996. The government's subsequent announcement, in August 1995, of reductions in salaries for government employees and increases in taxes on incomes was fiercely opposed by trade union leaders, who organized a widely-observed one-day general strike in early September. In December the chamber of deputies adopted the 1996 budget, which sought to placate the public as well as the IMF and the World Bank. Plans to increase income tax from 10% to 15% were abandoned, as were taxes of 60% on civil servants' bonuses and indemnities. Consumer taxes on a range of products were reduced, although civil servants' wages were also curtailed.

In April 1996, after months of negotiation, the government and the IMF concluded an agreement for Djibouti's first stand-by credit, equivalent to US $6.7m. Djibouti agreed to implement a range of austerity measures, including the reform of the civil service, a demobilization programme and the restructuring of the country's port, airport, electricity, water, and telecommunications companies. (Under the terms of a $24.2m.-agreement concluded with the World Bank in December 1995, Djibouti was to demobilize 10,000 soldiers and police over a five-year period.) Domestic opposition to the negotiations with the IMF continued, and in early 1996 teachers protested at proposed reforms, resulting in numerous arrests (see Recent History). It was estimated that in 1996 unemployment in Djibouti had reached 58%.

In September 1996 a delegation from the IMF visited Djibouti, and decided to postpone the disbursement of a second tranche of financial aid as it was dissatisfied with Djibouti's progress in undertaking fiscal reforms. In April 1997 Djibouti's minister of finance and the economy led a delegation to the IMF headquarters in Washington, DC, as a result of which the IMF agreed to the disbursal of some US $6.4m. In May the IMF agreed to extend Djibouti's stand-by programme until March 1998, and approved $2.8m. in credits. Meanwhile, in late 1996 the EU pledged ECU 22m. to Djibouti to improve transportation links between Djibouti and Ethiopia, increase available drinking water supplies, and provide additional support for the country's health and education sectors. In January 1997 the International Development Association granted Djibouti credit of $6.5m. to finance technical assistance for the economic reform programme.

Djibouti's agreement with the IMF in April 1996 led to an improvement in the government's relations with France, which had refused to provide concessionary financing to Djibouti until it had reached an understanding with the IMF. Funds were subsequently released by France for a variety of projects in Djibouti, primarily in the sectors of health and education. French aid to Djibouti for 1996 amounted to 162.5m. French francs. In October 1996 France agreed to furnish 53m. French francs in aid to Djibouti (primarily for budgetary assistance and debt relief), and in November it granted Djibouti a structural adjustment subsidy (worth 28m. Franch francs) which was to be disbursed in two tranches. In July 1997 a French financial delegation visited Djibouti and agreed to release the second tranche (10m. French francs) of the structural adjustment grant. Some 3m. French francs was allocated to the health sector, while the remainder was to be used to pay arrears to private-sector suppliers. In addition, Franch agreed to provide 30m. French francs to assist with Djibouti's demobilization programme. (In January 1998 the EU authorized a contribution of ECU 8.9m. to Djibouti, one-half of which was allocated to the programme). In November 1997 French military physicians provided medical assistance to victims of a cholera epidemic in Djibouti, and in December the French government donated 12 tons of medical supplies in an attempt to stem the epidemic, which had infected some 2,500 people and resulted in 50 fatalities. In November 1998 France pledged to provide some 25m. French francs in budgetary support as part of its contribution to Djibouti's economic reform. In January 1999 French officials indicated that France would provide Djibouti with 65m. French francs in financial aid, of which 10m. French francs would be for additional budgetary assistance. The French government also sought to offset the economic impact of the reduction of French troops in Djibouti by authorizing the French army to pay port and airport user fees.

Djibouti's failure to introduce budget reforms prompted an early 1997 meeting with donors who subsequently extended the period for compliance until March 1998. In that month Djibouti adopted a supplementary finance bill to meet IMF demands for a US $9m.-reduction of the budget deficit. The bill envisaged the reduction of public-sector employees' salaries, an increase in taxes on motor fuel and qat and the improvement of debt collection. In June the IMF agreed to extend the current stand-by credit until March 1999 and to augment the amount available under it by about $2.2m.

Despite the sharp rise in Djibouti's port revenues during 1998–99 as a result of the dispute between Eritrea and Ethiopia, several factors continued to plague the Djiboutian economy. For example, in 1999 salaries for civil servants were months in arrears, while the government did little to reduce the number of civil servants or to lower the extensive benefits of state employees. Djibouti also failed to implement tariff reforms that the Arab League's Economic and Social Council appealed for in order to complete the Arab duty-free zone. Such reforms could affect some 15% of Djibouti's imports from Middle Eastern countries.

As mentioned above, the Djiboutian economy received a boost thanks to increased Ethiopian use of its transportation facilities. Activity at Djibouti port during the first half of 1999 rose by 23.3%, compared with figures for the same period in 1998. Freight unloaded increased by 37.9%, but freight loaded decreased by 20%. Over the same six-month period, air freight shipments rose by 24.8%, while passenger air traffic declined by 17.6%. The Djibouti-Addis Ababa railway experienced a 43.1% increase in freight shipments. Despite this growth, a chronic budget deficit (6,058m. Djibouti francs, before allowing for grants received and payment arrears, in the first half of 1999) continued to plague the Djiboutian economy. This was due to declining revenues, which had decreased by 4.5% in comparison with the first half of 1998. Over the same period, government expenditure increased by 33%, while investment expenditure declined by 13.7%.

In October 1999 Djibouti and the IMF agreed to implement a US $26.5m. loan under an Enhanced Structural Adjustment Facility (ESAF) to support the government's three-year economic reform programme (1999–2002). An initial payment of $3.8m. was released immediately. However, disbursement of the balance was conditional on Djibouti's fulfilling its promised programme of economic and financial reform during 1999–2002: this included reforms to tax, revenue administration and budget management; the completion of the army demobilization programme by the end of 2000; the reform of the civil service, thus lowering the wage bill; and the publication of a privatization programme for the six principal state-owned enterprises. According to an economic strategy report released with the ESAF announcement, Djibouti hoped to achieve a 2.3% GDP growth rate in 2000, and during the reform programme, con-

sumer prices were expected to record annual average growth of 2%.

During 1999 French aid to Djibouti remained in a state of flux. In October France closed its external trade promotion office in Djibouti. However, in December the two countries convened a summit to discuss the subject of French aid. The Agence Française de Développement subsequently agreed to a retroactive budgetary assistance grant of US $2.17m. for the 1999 fiscal year. However, according to the IMF, Djibouti still had an estimated $14.3m. fiscal deficit for 1999. Despite the slow but steady reduction in French aid levels, France remained Djibouti's largest bilateral donor. Aside from the aid issue, the presence of the French military garrison in Djibouti continued to be of importance to both countries. In October 1999 the French army chief of staff, Jean Pierre Kelche, visited Djibouti and announced the cessation of further troop withdrawals. Additionally, Kelche indicated that France would deploy new military equipment, such as Leclerc tanks, to Djibouti. At the time of Kelche's visit there were some 3,400 French troops stationed in Djibouti.

In February 2000 Djibouti announced that the shipment of Ethiopian goods through Djibouti port had doubled to an annual total of 4m. metric tons since the outbreak in mid-1998 of the Eritrean-Ethiopian war. Ethiopia's increased use of the port, however, has caused some friction between the two countries. In October 1999 the Ethiopian authorities refused to allow Ethiopian petroleum importers to pay an increase of $1 per ton on petroleum tariffs. During a visit to Ethiopia in November President Gelleh reduced the tariff to $0.5 per ton; however, tensions remained regarding the activities of Djiboutian and Ethiopian import-export and forwarding agents. Despite these problems, increased Ethiopian use of the port convinced Djiboutian officials to launch a $15m. expansion programme, which was expected to triple the handling of the port's yard capacity. The Djiboutian authorities also indicated that Ethiopia owed more than $2m. to Djibouti port for services rendered. In April 2000 the UN started work on a $2.7m. expansion programme, which was to increase the port's handling capacity from 100,000 tons to 147,000 tons per month. In May the Dubai Ports Authority (DPA) signed a 20-year contract to manage Djibouti port. The agreement also empowered the DPA to develop Djibouti's free-trade zone. In an attempt to attract foreign investors, Djibouti issued tax exemptions to several companies, including the Société d'Exploration du Lac, which received permission to import $8.5m. worth of equipment tax free. Other companies that have taken advantage of the concessions include Trans African Transit Service and Djibouti Dry Port, both of which are connected to Djibouti port.

During 1999–2000 Djibouti's inability to settle its debts caused a deterioration in relations with the three international oil companies (Shell, Total Djibouti, and Mobil Oil) that share the Djibouti market (totalling 130,000 metric tons of petroleum imports in 1999). In February 2000 the Banque Nationale de Djibouti announced that the Bank of Africa, which is a subsidiary of AFH Holding of Luxembourg and which has its headquarters in Abidjan, Côte d'Ivoire, had opened a branch in Djibouti.

Statistical Survey

Source (unless otherwise stated): the former Ministère de l'Economie et du Commerce, BP 1846, Djibouti; tel. 351682.

AREA AND POPULATION

Area: 23,200 sq km (8,958 sq miles).

Population: 220,000 (1976 estimate), including Afars 70,000, Issas and other Somalis 80,000, Arabs 12,000, Europeans 15,000, other foreigners 40,000; 519,900 (including refugees and resident foreigners) at 31 December 1990 (official estimate); 623,000 (UN estimate) at mid-1998 (Source: UN, *World Population Prospects: The 1998 Revision*).

Density (mid-1998): 26.9 per sq km.

Principal Towns: Djibouti (capital), population 200,000 (1981); Dikhil; Ali-Sabieh; Tadjourah; Obock.

Births and Deaths (UN estimates, 1990–95): Average annual birth rate 39.0 per 1,000; Average annual death rate 16.2 per 1,000. Source: UN, *World Population Prospects: The 1998 Revision*.

Expectation of Life (UN estimates, years at birth, 1990–95): 48.3 (males 46.7; females 50.0). Source: UN, *World Population Prospects: The 1998 Revision*.

Economically Active Population (estimates, '000 persons, 1991): Agriculture, etc. 212; Industries 31; Services 39; *Total* 282 (males 167, females 115). Source: UN Economic Commission for Africa, *African Statistical Yearbook*.

AGRICULTURE, ETC.

Principal Crops (FAO estimate, '000 metric tons, 1998): Vegetables 22. Source: FAO, *Production Yearbook*.

Livestock (FAO estimates, '000 head, year ending September 1998): Cattle 190; Sheep 470; Goats 507; Asses 8; Camels 62. Source: FAO, *Production Yearbook*.

Livestock Products: (FAO estimates, '000 metric tons, 1998): Beef and veal 3; Mutton and lamb 2; Goat meat 2; Cows' milk 7; Cattle hides 1. Source: FAO, *Production Yearbook*.

Fishing (FAO estimates, metric tons, live weight): Total catch 350 in 1995; 360 in 1996; 340 in 1997. Source: FAO, *Yearbook of Fishery Statistics*.

INDUSTRY

Electric energy (million kWh): 202.5 in 1996; 200.7 in 1997; 133.0 in 1998. Source: IMF, *Djibouti: Statistical Annex* (December 1999).

FINANCE

Currency and Exchange Rates: 100 centimes = 1 Djibouti franc. *Sterling, Dollar and Euro Equivalents* (28 April 2000): £1 sterling = 278.68 Djibouti francs; US $1 = 177.72 Djibouti francs; €1 = 161.46 Djibouti francs; 1,000 Djibouti francs = £3.588 = $5.627 = € 6.194. *Exchange Rate:* Fixed at US $1 = 177.721 Djibouti francs since February 1973.

Budget (provisional, million Djibouti francs, 1998): *Revenue:* Tax revenue 20,258 (Taxes on incomes and profits 4,574, Other direct taxes 4,499, Indirect taxes 10,335; Registration fees, etc. 850); Other revenue (incl. property sales) 2,896; Total 23,154, excl. grants received from abroad (8,079). *Expenditure:* Current expenditure 24,350 (General administration 8,116, Defence 4,013, Mobilization and demobilization 2,083, Education 2,645, Health 1,641, Economic services 931, Transfers 2,534); Capital expenditure 6,077; Sub-total 30,427; Reduction in payment arrears 723; Total 31,150. Source: IMF, *Djibouti: Statistical Annex* (December 1999).

International Reserves (US $ million at 31 December 1999): IMF special drawing rights 0.09; Foreign exchange 69.01; Total 69.10. Source: IMF, *International Financial Statistics*.

Money Supply (million Djibouti francs at 31 December 1998): Currency outside banks 9,099; Demand deposits at commercial banks 20,146; Total money 29,245. Source: IMF, *International Financial Statistics*.

Cost of Living: (Consumer Price Index for expatriates; base: 1989 = 100): All items 137.2 in 1995; 142.9 in 1996; 145.8 (estimate) in 1997. Source: IMF, *Djibouti: Statistical Annex* (August 1998).

Expenditure on the Gross Domestic Product (provisional, million Djibouti francs at current purchasers' values, 1998): Government final consumption expenditure 21,497; Private final consumption expenditure 72,466; Gross capital formation 13,958; *Total domestic expenditure* 107,921; Exports of goods and services 41,449; *Less* Imports of goods and services 58,172; *GDP in purchasers' values* 91,198. Source: IMF, *Djibouti: Statistical Annex* (December 1999).

Gross Domestic Product by Economic Activity (provisional, million Djibouti francs at current factor cost, 1998): Agriculture, hunting, forestry and fishing 2,917; Manufacturing 4,239; Electricity, gas and water 4,850; Construction 6,971; Trade, restaurants and hotels 14,481; Transport, storage and communications 15,824; Finance, insurance, real estate and business services 8,772; Public administration 18,469; Other services 4,340; *GDP at factor cost* 80,863; Indirect taxes *less* subsidies 10,335; *GDP in purchasers' values* 91,198. Source: IMF, *Djibouti: Statistical Annex* (December 1999).

Balance of Payments (US $ million, 1995): Exports of goods f.o.b. 33.5; Imports of goods f.o.b. –205.0; *Trade balance* –171.5; Exports of services 151.4; Imports of services –87.2; *Balance on goods and services* –107.3; Other income received 25.9; Other income paid –8.7; *Balance on goods, services and income* –90.0; Current transfers received 85.4; Current transfers paid –18.4; *Current balance* –23.0; Direct investment from abroad 3.2; Other investment liabilities –5.4; Net errors and omissions 0.7; *Overall balance* –24.5. Source: IMF, *International Financial Statistics*.

EXTERNAL TRADE

Principal Commodities: *Imports c.i.f.* (provisional, million Djibouti francs, 1998): Food and beverages 9,379; Qat 3,049; Petroleum products 2,976; Chemical products 1,114; Clothing and footwear 882; Metals and metal products 1,182; Machinery and electrical appliances 2,613; Vehicles and transport equipment 1,036; Total (incl. others) 24,067. Note: figures refer only to imports for domestic use. Source: IMF, *Djibouti: Statistical Annex* (December 1999). *Exports f.o.b.* (distribution by SITC, US $'000, 1992): Food and live animals 3,292 (Rice 726, Coffee and coffee substitutes 1,773); Crude materials (inedible) except fuels 867; Basic manufactures 771; Machinery and transport equipment 1,260 (Road vehicles and parts 585, Other transport equipment 501); Commodities not classified according to kind 9,481; Total (incl. others) 15,919. Source: UN, *International Trade Statistics Yearbook*.

Principal Trading Partners (US $'000, 1992): *Imports c.i.f.:* Bahrain 3,860; Belgium-Luxembourg 3,455; People's Republic of China 6,724; Denmark 2,543; Ethiopia 17,157; France (incl. Monaco) 58,003; Germany 4,372; India 2,240; Italy 12,064; Japan 14,810; Netherlands 7,771; Saudi Arabia 8,750; Singapore 4,355; Thailand 6,207; United Kingdom 6,955; USA 6,764; Yemen 3,039; Total (incl. others) 219,926. *Exports f.o.b.:* Belgium-Luxembourg 191; Ethiopia 523; France (incl. Monaco) 9,144; Saudi Arabia 1,587; Somalia 664; Thailand 293; Yemen 686; Total (incl. others) 15,919. Source: UN, *International Trade Statistics Yearbook*.

TRANSPORT

Railways (traffic, 1997): Passenger-km ('000) 762; Freight ton-km (million) 232. Source: IMF, *Djibouti: Statistical Annex* (December 1999).

Road Traffic (estimates, motor vehicles in use, 1996): Passenger cars 9,200; Lorries and vans 2,040. Source: International Road Federation, *World Road Statistics*.

Shipping: *Merchant Fleet* (registered at 31 December 1998): 12 vessels (displacement 3,967 grt). Source: Lloyd's Register of Shipping. *Freight Traffic* ('000 metric tons, 1998): Goods loaded and unloaded 808. Source: IMF, *Djibouti: Statistical Annex* (December 1999).

Civil Aviation (1998): Passengers arriving and departing 107,369; Freight loaded and unloaded 7,290 metric tons. Source: IMF, *Djibouti: Statistical Annex* (December 1999).

TOURISM

Tourist Arrivals ('000): 22 in 1994; 21 in 1995; 20 in 1996.

Receipts from Tourism (US $ million): 3 in 1994; 4 in 1995; 4 in 1996. Source: World Tourism Organization, *Yearbook of Tourism Statistics*.

COMMUNICATIONS MEDIA

Newspapers (1995): 1 non-daily (estimated circulation 1,000).

Periodicals (1989): 7 (estimated combined circulation 6,000).

Radio Receivers (1997): 52,000 in use.

Television Receivers (1997): 28,000 in use.

Telephones (1997): 8,257 main lines in use.

Telefax Stations (1996): 142 in use.

Mobile Cellular Telephones (1996): 110 subscribers.

Sources: UNESCO, *Statistical Yearbook*; UN, *Statistical Yearbook*.

EDUCATION

Pre-primary (1996/97): 2 schools; 247 pupils.

Primary (1996/97): 72 schools; 36,896 pupils; 1,096 teachers.

Secondary (1996/97): 13,311 pupils (general 11,367, teacher-training 103, vocational 1,841); 628 teachers (1995/96).

Higher (1996/97): 161 students.

Source: UNESCO, *Statistical Yearbook*.

Directory

The Constitution

In February 1981 the National Assembly approved the first constitutional laws controlling the election and terms of office of the President, who is elected by universal adult suffrage for six years and may serve for no more than two terms. Candidates for the presidency must be presented by a regularly constituted political party and represented by at least 25 members of the Chamber of Deputies. The Chamber, comprising 65 members, is elected for a five-year term.

In October 1984 a new constitutional law was proposed, specifying that, when the office of President falls vacant, the President of the Supreme Court will assume the power of Head of State for a minimum of 20 days and a maximum of 35 days, during which period a new President shall be elected.

Laws approving the establishment of a single-party system were adopted in October 1981. A new Constitution, providing for the establishment of a maximum of four political parties, was approved by national referendum on 4 September 1992 and entered into force on 15 September.

The Government

HEAD OF STATE

President and Commander-in-Chief of the Armed Forces: ISMAEL OMAR GELLEH (inaugurated 7 May 1999).

COUNCIL OF MINISTERS
(August 2000)

Prime Minister: BARKAD GOURAD HAMADOU.

Minister of Justice, Muslim and Penal Affairs, and Human Rights: IBRAHIM IDRISS DJIBRIL.

Minister of the Interior: ABDALLAH ABDILLAHI MIGUIL.

Minister of Defence: OUGOUREH KIFLEH AHMED.

Minister of Foreign Affairs, International Co-operation and Parliamentary Relations: ALI ABDI FARAH.

Minister of Economy, Finance and Privatization: YACIN ELMI BOUH.

Minister of Trade, Industry and Handicrafts: ELMI OBSIEH WA'AYS.

Minister of Agriculture, Livestock and Fishing: ALI MOHAMED DAOUD.

Minister of Communication and Culture, in charge of Post and Telecommunications, and Government Spokesman: RIFKI ABDULKADER BAMAKHRAMA.

Minister of Education: ABDI IBRAHIM ABSIEH.

Minister of Employment and National Solidarity: MOHAMED BARKAT ABDILLAHI.

Minister of Energy and Natural Resources: MOHAMED ALI MOHAMED.

Minister of Equipment and Transportation: OSMAN IDRISS DJAMA.

Minister of Health: MOHAMED DINI FARAH.

Minister of Presidential Affairs, in charge of Investment Promotion: OSMAN AHMED MOUSSA.

Minister of Urban Planning, Housing, the Environment, and National and Regional Development: SOULEIMAN OMAR OUDINE.

Minister of Youth, Sports, Leisure and Tourism: DINI ABDALLAH BILILIS.

Minister-delegate to the Prime Minister in charge of Decentralization: AHMED GUIRREH WABERI.

Minister-delegate to the Prime Minister in charge of Mosque Properties and Muslim Affairs: CHEIK MOGUEH DIRIR.

Minister-delegate to the Prime Minister in charge of the Promotion of Women's, Family and Social Affairs: HAWA AHMED YOUSSOUF.

MINISTRIES

Office of the Prime Minister: BP 2086, Djibouti; tel. 351494; fax 355049.

Ministry of Agriculture, Livestock and Fishing: BP 453, Djibouti; tel. 351297.

Ministry of the Civil Service and Administrative Reform: BP 155, Djibouti; tel. 351464.

Ministry of Defence: BP 42, Djibouti; tel. 352034.

Ministry of the Economy, Finance and Privatization: BP 13, Djibouti; tel. 350297; fax 35601.

Ministry of Education: BP 2102, Djibouti; tel. 350850; internet www.educ.dj.

Ministry of Employment and National Solidarity: Djibouti.

Ministry of Energy and Natural Resources: BP 175, Djibouti; tel. 350340.

Ministry of Foreign Affairs and International Co-operation: BP 1863, Djibouti; tel. 352471.

Ministry of Health: BP 296, Djibouti; tel. 353331; fax 356300.

Ministry of the Interior: BP 33, Djibouti; tel. 350791.

Ministry of Justice, Muslim and Penal Affairs and Human Rights: BP 12, Djibouti; tel. 351506; fax 354012.

Ministry of Labour and Vocational Training: BP 170, Djibouti; tel. 350497.

Ministry of Trade, Industry and Handicrafts: BP 1846, Djibouti; tel. 351682.

Ministry of Transport and Communications: BP 2501, Djibouti; tel. 350971.

Ministry of Urban Planning, Housing, the Environment and National and Regional Development: Djibouti.

Ministry of Youth, Sports, Leisure and Tourism: BP 2506, Djibouti; tel. 355886; fax 356830.

President and Legislature

PRESIDENT

Presidential Election, 9 April 1999

Candidates						Votes	%
ISMAEL OMAR GELLEH (RPP)	.	.	.	.	.	70,993	74.44
MOUSSA AHMED IDRIS (ODU)*	.	.	.	.	.	24,375	25.56
Total	.	.	.	.	.	.	95,368	100.00

* Opposition djiboutienne unifiée, an electoral coalition including the PND, the PRD and the Dini faction of the FRUD.

CHAMBRE DES DÉPUTÉS

Elections for the 65-seat Chamber of Deputies were held on 19 December 1997. The election was contested by the governing Rassemblement populaire pour le progrès (RPP), in alliance with the Front pour la restauration de l'unité et de la démocratie (FRUD), and by the Parti national démocratique (PND) and the Parti du renouveau démocratique (PRD). All 65 seats were won by the RPP-FRUD alliance.

President of the Chamber: SAID IBRAHIM BADOUL.

Political Organizations

Constitutional reforms permitting a maximum of four political parties took effect in September 1992. By late 1999 the following parties were legally recognized:

Front pour la restauration de l'unité et de la démocratie (FRUD): f. 1991 by merger of three militant Afar groups; advocates fair representation in govt for all ethnic groups; commenced armed insurgency in Nov. 1991; split into two factions in March 1994; the dissident group, which negotiated a settlement with the Govt, obtained legal recognition in March 1996 and recognizes the following leaders: Pres. ALI MOHAMED DAOUD; Sec.-Gen. OUGOUREH KIFLEH AHMED; the faction favouring a continuation of mil. operations is led by AHMED DINI AHMED; another dissident group, FRUD–Renaissance (led by IBRAHIM CHEHEM DAOUD), was formed in 1996.

Parti national démocratique (PND): f. 1992; seeks formation of a 'govt of national unity' to supervise implementation of democratic reforms; Chair. ADEN ROBLEH AWALLEH.

Parti du renouveau démocratique (PRD): BP 2198, Djibouti; tel. 356235; fax 351474; f. 1992; seeks to establish democratic parliamentary govt; Pres. ABDILLAHI HAMAREITEH; Sec.-Gen. MAKI HOUMED GABA.

Rassemblement populaire pour le progrès (RPP): Djibouti; f. 1979; sole legal party 1981–92; Pres. ISMAEL OMAR GELLEH; Sec.-Gen. MOHAMED ALI MOHAMED.

The following organizations are banned:

Coordination de l'opposition djiboutienne: f. 1996; alliance of the PND, the FUOD and the RPP–GDR; Leader ISMAEL GEDI HARED.

Front des forces démocratiques (FFD): Leader OMAR ELMI KHAIREH.

Front de libération de la côte des Somalis (FLCS): f. 1963; Issa-supported; has operated from Somalia; Chair. ABDALLAH WABERI KHALIF; Vice-Chair. OMAR OSMAN RABEH.

Front uni de l'opposition djiboutienne (FUOD): f. 1992; based in Ethiopia; united front of internal opposition groups, incl. some fmr mems of the RPP; Leader MAHDI IBRAHIM A. GOD.

Groupe pour la démocratie de la république (RPP–GDR): f. 1996 by a dissident faction of the RPP; Leader MOUMIN BAHDON FARAH.

Mouvement de la jeunesse djiboutienne (MJD): Leader ABDOUL-KARIM ALI AMARKAK.

Mouvement pour l'unité et la démocratie (MUD): advocates political pluralism; Leader MOHAMED MOUSSA ALI ('TOURTOUR').

Organisation des masses Afar (OMA): f. 1993 by mems of the fmr Mouvement populaire de libération; Chair. AHMED MALCO.

Parti centriste et des reformes démocratiques (PCRD): f. 1993 in Addis Ababa, Ethiopia, by a breakaway faction of the FRUD; seeks official registration as an opposition party; Chair. HASSAN ABDALLAH WATTA.

Parti populaire djiboutien (PPD): f. 1981; mainly Afar-supported; Leader MOUSSA AHMED IDRIS.

Union des démocrates djiboutiens (UDD): affiliated to the FUOD; Chair. MAHDI IBRAHIM AHMED.

Union démocratique pour le progrès (UDP): f. 1992; advocates democratic reforms; Leader FARAH WABERI.

Union des mouvements démocratiques (UMD): f. 1990 by merger of two militant external opposition groups; Pres. MOHAMED ADOYTA.

Diplomatic Representation

EMBASSIES IN DJIBOUTI

China, People's Republic: Djibouti; tel. 352246; Ambassador: MENG XIANKE.

Egypt: BP 1989, Djibouti; tel. 351231; Ambassador: IBRAHIM EL-CHOUMI.

Eritrea: BP 1944, Djibouti; tel. 354961; fax 351831; Ambassador: RAMADAN OSMAN MOHAMED (recalled Nov. 1998).

Ethiopia: BP 230, Djibouti; tel. 350718; fax 354803; Ambassador: BERHANU DINKA.

France: 45 blvd du Maréchal Foch, BP 2039, Djibouti; tel. 350963; fax 350272; e-mail ambfrdj@intnet.dj; Ambassador: PATRICK ROUSSEL.

Iraq: BP 1983, Djibouti; tel. 353469; Ambassador: ABDEL AZIZ AL-GAILANI.

Libya: BP 2073, Djibouti; tel. 350202; Ambassador: KAMEL AL-HADI ALMARASH.

Oman: Djibouti; tel. 350852; Ambassador: SAOUD SALEM HASSAN AL-ANSI.

Russia: BP 1913, Djibouti; tel. 352051; fax 355990; Ambassador: MIKHAIL TSVIGOUN.

Saudi Arabia: BP 1921, Djibouti; tel. 351645; fax 352284; Chargé d'affaires a.i.: MOWAFFAK AL-DOLIGANE.

Somalia: BP 549, Djibouti; tel. 353521; Ambassador: MOHAMED SHEK MOHAMED MALINGUR.

Sudan: BP 4259, Djibouti; tel. 356404; fax 356662; Ambassador: ABELWAHAB EL SAWI KHALAFALLA.

USA: Villa Plateau du Serpent, blvd du Maréchal Joffre, BP 185, Djibouti; tel. 353995; fax 353940; e-mail amembadm@bow.intnet.dj; Ambassador: LANGE SCHERMERHORN.

Yemen: BP 194, Djibouti; tel. 352975; Ambassador: MUHAMMAD ABDOUL WASSI HAMID.

Judicial System

The Supreme Court was established in 1979. There is a high court of appeal and a court of first instance in Djibouti; each of the five administrative districts has a 'tribunal coutumier'.

President of the Court of Appeal: KADIDJA ABEBA.

Religion

ISLAM

Almost the entire population are Muslims.

Qadi of Djibouti: MOGUE HASSAN DIRIR, BP 168, Djibouti; tel. 352669.

CHRISTIANITY

The Roman Catholic Church

Djibouti comprises a single diocese, directly responsible to the Holy See. There were an estimated 7,000 adherents in the country at 31 December 1998.

Bishop of Djibouti: Rt Rev. GEORGES PERRON, Evêché, blvd de la République, BP 94, Djibouti; tel. 350140; fax 354831: e-mail evecheat@intnet.dj.

The Anglican Communion

Within the Episcopal Church in Jerusalem and the Middle East, Djibouti lies within the jurisdiction of the Bishop in Egypt.

Other Christian Churches

Eglise Protestante: blvd de la République, BP 416, Djibouti; tel. 351820; fax 350706; e-mail eped@intnet.dj; f. 1957; Pastor FRANCIS MULLER.

Greek Orthodox Church: blvd de la République, Djibouti; tel. 351325; c. 350 adherents; Archimandrite STAVROS GEORGANAS.

The Ethiopian Orthodox Church is also active in Djibouti.

The Press

L'Atout: Palais du peuple, Djibouti; twice a year; publ. by the Centre National de la Promotion Culturelle et Artistique.

Carrefour Africain: BP 393, Djibouti; fax 354916; fortnightly; publ. by the Roman Catholic mission; circ. 500.

La Nation de Djibouti: place du 27 juin, BP 32, Djibouti; tel. 352201; fax 353937; weekly; Dir ISMAEL H. TANI; circ. 4,300.

Le Progrès: Djibouti; weekly; publ. by the RPP; Publr ALI MOHAMED HUMAD.

Le Renouveau: Djibouti; weekly; independent; Editor-in-Chief DAHER AHMED FARAH.

La Republique: Djibouti; weekly; independent; Editor-in-Chief AMIR ADAWEH.

Revue de l'ISERT: BP 486, Djibouti; tel. 352795; twice a year; publ. by the Institut Supérieur d'Etudes et de Recherches Scientifiques et Techniques (ISERT).

Le Temps: Djibouti; opposition newspaper; Owners MOUSSA AHMED IDRIS, ALI MEIDAL WAIS.

NEWS AGENCIES

Agence Djiboutienne d'Information (ADJI): place du 27 juin, BP 32, Djibouti; tel. 355672; fax 353957; internet www.intnet.dj; f. 1978.

Foreign Bureau

Agence France-Presse (AFP): BP 97, Djibouti; tel. 352294; Correspondent KHALID HAIDAR ABDALLAH.

Broadcasting and Communications

TELECOMMUNICATIONS

Djibouti Telecom: Djibouti; f. 2000 to replace Société des Télécommunications Internationales; 100% state-owned; Man. Dir ABDURAHMAN MOHAMED HASSAN.

BROADCASTING

Radio and Television

Radiodiffusion-Télévision de Djibouti (RTD): BP 97, Djibouti; tel. 352294; fax 356502; f. 1957; state-controlled; programmes in French, Afar, Somali and Arabic; 17 hours radio and 5 hours television daily; Dir-Gen. (Radio) ABDI ATTEYEH ABDI; Dir-Gen. (Television) MOHAMED DJAMA ADEN.

Finance

(cap. = capital; res = reserves; dep. = deposits; m. = million; brs = branches; amounts in Djibouti francs)

BANKING

Central Bank

Banque Nationale de Djibouti: BP 2118, Djibouti; tel. 352751; fax 356288; e-mail bndj@intnet.dj; f. 1977; bank of issue; total assets 18,731.6m. (Dec. 1998); Gov. DJAMA MAHAMOUD HAID; Dirs HOUMED ABDOU DAOUD, AHMED OSMAN ALI.

Commercial Banks

Bank of Africa: Djibouti; f. 2000; subsidiary of AFH Holding (Luxembourg); cap. 300m.

Banque Indosuez–Mer Rouge (BIS–MR): 10 place Lagarde, BP 88, Djibouti; tel. 353016; fax 351638; e-mail indomr@intnet.dj; f. 1908; owned by Crédit Agricole Indosuez (France); cap. 1,500m., res 290.3m., dep. 17,811m. (Dec. 1998); Chair. and CEO JEAN-BERNARD ANGLADA.

Banque pour le Commerce et l'Industrie–Mer Rouge (BCI–MR): place Lagarde, BP 2122, Djibouti; tel. 350857; fax 354260; e-mail nespoux@intnet.dj; f. 1954; 51% owned by Banque Nationale de Paris Intercontinentale; cap. 3,000m., res 1,540m., dep. 25,483.3m. (Dec. 1998); Pres. MOHAMED ADEN; Vice-Pres. VINCENT DEROUX; Gen. Man. JOSEPH DETRAUX; 8 brs.

Development Bank

Banque de Développement de Djibouti: angle ave Georges Clemenceau et rue Pierre Curie, BP 520, Djibouti; tel. 353391; fax 355022; f. 1983; 39.2% govt-owned; total assets 3,081m., cap. and res 1,233m. (Dec. 1997); Dir-Gen. ABDOURAHMAN ISMAEL GELLEH.

Banking Association

Association Professionnelle des Banques: c/o Banque pour le Commerce et l'Industrie–Mer Rouge, place Lagarde, BP 2122, Djibouti; tel. 350857; fax 354260; Pres. MOHAMED ADEN.

INSURANCE

Boucher Assurances: AGF–Assurances Générales de France, rue Marchand, BP 200, Djibouti; tel. 353636; fax 353056.

Ethiopian Insurance Corporation: rue de Marseille, BP 2047, Djibouti; tel. 352306.

La Prudence–André Marill: 8 rue Marchand, BP 57, Djibouti; tel. 351150; fax 355623; f.1896.

Trade and Industry

CHAMBER OF COMMERCE

Chambre Internationale de Commerce et d'Industrie: BP 84, Djibouti; tel. 351070; fax 350096; internet www.intnet.dj/public/cicid/index.html; f. 1906; 24 mems, 12 assoc. mems; Pres. SAID ALI COUBECHE; First Vice-Pres. ABDOURAHMAN MAHAMOUD BOREH.

TRADE ASSOCIATION

Office National d'Approvisionnement et de Commercialisation (ONAC): BP 119, Djibouti; tel. 350327; Chair. MOHAMED ABDULKADER.

UTILITIES

Electricity

Electricité de Djibouti (EdD): c/o Ministry of Trade and Industry, BP 1846, Djibouti; tel. 351682; Dir-Gen. DJAMA ALI GELLEH.

Water

Office National des Eaux de Djibouti (ONED): c/o Ministry of Trade and Industry, BP 1846, Djibouti; tel. 351682.

Société des Eaux de Tadjourah: c/o Ministry of Trade and Industry, BP 1846, Djibouti; tel. 351682.

TRADE UNION

Union Générale du Travail: Djibouti; f. 1992 to succeed Union Générale des Travailleurs de Djibouti; confed. of 22 unions; Chair. YUSSUF MOHAMED; Sec.-Gen. ADEN MOHAMED ARDOU.

Transport

RAILWAYS

Chemin de Fer Djibouti–Ethiopien (CDE): BP 2116, Djibouti; tel. 350280; fax 351256; POB 1051, Addis Ababa; tel. 517250; fax 513533; f. 1909, adopted present name in 1981; jtly-owned by Govts of Djibouti and Ethiopia; 781 km of track (121 km in Djibouti) linking Djibouti with Addis Ababa; Pres. SALEH OMAR HILDID; Dir-Gen. ALI ABDALLAH GADID.

ROADS

In 1996 there were an estimated 2,890 km of roads, comprising 1,090 km of main roads and 1,800 km of regional roads; some 12.6% of the roads were paved. Of the remainder, 1,000 km are serviceable throughout the year, the rest only during the dry season. About one-half of the roads are usable only by heavy vehicles. In 1981 the 40-km Grand Bara road was opened, linking the capital with the south. In 1986 the Djibouti–Tadjourah road, the construction of which was financed by Saudi Arabia, was opened, linking the capital with the north. In 1996 the Islamic Development Bank granted Djibouti a loan of US $3.6m. to finance road construction projects.

SHIPPING

Djibouti, which was established as a free port in 1981, handled 720,000 metric tons of freight in 1997.

Port Autonome International de Djibouti: BP 2107, Djibouti; tel. 352331; fax 356187; e-mail port@intnet.dj; internet www.port.dj; Dir ADEN AHMED DOUALE.

Maritime and Transit Service: rue de Marseille, BP 680, Djibouti; tel. 353204; fax 354149.

Principal Shipping Agents

Almis Shipping Line & Transport Co: BP 85, Djibouti; tel. 356996; fax 356998; Man. Dir MOHAMED NOOR.

Cie Générale Maritime: 3 rue Marchand, BP 182, Djibouti; tel. 353825; fax 354778; Gen. Man. HENRI FERRAND.

Cie Maritime et de Manutention de Djibouti: ave des Messageries Maritimes, BP 89, Djibouti; tel. 351028; fax 350466; e-mail comad@intnet.dj; internet www.intnet.dj/comad/index.htm; shipping agents and freight forwarders; Man. Dir ALI A. HETTAM.

Inchcape Shipping Services & Co (Djibouti) SA: 9–11 rue de Genève, BP 81, Djibouti; tel. 353844; fax 353294; e-mail iss@intnet.dj; f. 1942; Dir-Gen. AHMED OSMAN GELLEH.

J. J. Kothari & Co Ltd: rue d'Athens, BP 171, Djibouti; tel. 350219; fax 351778; e-mail kothari@intnet.dj; shipping agents; also ship managers, stevedores, freight forwarders; Dirs S. J. KOTHARI, NALIN KOTHARI.

Mitchell Cotts Djibouti SARL: blvd de la République, BP 85, Djibouti; tel. 351204; fax 355851; Dir FAHMY SAID CASSIM.

Société Maritime L. Savon et Ries: blvd Cheikh Osman, BP 2125, Djibouti; tel. 352351; fax 351103; Gen. Man. J. P. DELARUE.

CIVIL AVIATION

The international airport is at Ambouli, 6 km from Djibouti. There are six other airports providing domestic services.

Air Djibouti (Red Sea Airlines): BP 499, rue Marchand, Djibouti; tel. 356723; fax 356734; f. 1971; fmrly govt-owned, transferred to private ownership in 1997; internal flights and international services to points in Africa, the Middle East and Europe; Chair. SAAD BEN MOUSSA AL-JANAIBI.

Daallo Airlines: BP 2565, Djibouti; tel. 353401; fax 351765; internet www.daallo.com; f. 1992; regional carrier operating services to Somalia, Saudi Arabia and the United Arab Emirates; Man. Dir MOHAMED IBRAHIM YASSIN.

Djibouti Airlines (Puntavia Airline de Djibouti): BP 2240, place Lagarde, Djibouti; tel. 351006; fax 352429; f. 1996; scheduled and charter regional and domestic flights; Man. Dir Mr VABERI.

Tourism

Djibouti offers desert scenery in its interior and watersport facilities on its coast. A casino operates in the capital. There were about 20,000 tourist arrivals in 1996, when receipts from tourism totalled US $4m.

Office National du Tourisme et de l'Artisanat (ONTA): place du 27 juin, BP 1938, Djibouti; tel. 353790; fax 356322; Dir ALI MOHAMED ABDALLAH.

Defence

Arrangements for military co-operation exist between Djibouti and France, and in August 1999 there were about 2,600 French military personnel stationed in Djibouti. The total armed forces of Djibouti itself, in which all services form part of the army, numbered some 9,600 (including 200 naval and 200 air force personnel). There were also paramilitary forces numbering 1,200 gendarmes, as well as a 3,000-strong national security force. Conscription of all men between 18 and 25 years of age was introduced in 1992.

Defence Expenditure: Budgeted at 3,900m. Djibouti francs in 1999.

Commander-in-Chief of the Armed Forces: Pres. ISMAEL OMAR GELLEH.

Chief of Staff of the Army: Gen. FATHI AHMED HUSSEIN.

Education

The government has overall responsibility for education. Primary education generally begins at six years of age and lasts for six years. Secondary education, usually starting at the age of 12, lasts for seven years, comprising a first cycle of four years and a second of three years. In 1996 the total enrolment at primary and secondary schools was equivalent to 26% of the school-age population (31% of boys; 22% of girls), while primary enrolment was equivalent to 39% of pupils in the relevant age-group (44% of boys; 33% of girls) and secondary enrolment was equivalent to 14% of pupils in the relevant age-group (17% of boys; 12% of girls). Provisional budgetary current expenditure on education in 1998 was 2,645m. Djibouti francs, equivalent to 8.7% of total government expenditure. In 1996/97

there were 36,896 primary school pupils and 13,311 pupils receiving general secondary and vocational education (including teacher training). As Djibouti has no university, students seeking further education study abroad, mainly to France. In 1995, according to UNESCO estimates, the rate of illiteracy among the population aged 15 years and over was 53.7% (males 39.6%; females 67.2%).

Bibliography

Coubba, A. *Djibouti: Une nation en otage*. Paris, L'Harmattan, 1993.

Koburger, C. W. *Naval Strategy East of Suez: the Role of Djibouti*. New York, Praeger, 1992.

Laudouze, A. *Djibouti, Nation carrefour*. Paris, Editions Karthala, 1982.

Oberle, P., and Hugot, P. *Histoire de Djibouti: des origines à la république*. Paris, Editions Présence Africaine, 1985.

Schrader, P. J. *Djibouti*. Oxford, Clio Press, 1991.

'Ethnic Politics in Djibouti: From the "Eye of the Hurricane" to "Boiling Cauldron", in *African Affairs*, Vol. 92, No. 367 (April 1993), pp 203–221.

Tholomier, R. *Djibouti: Pawn of the Horn of Africa*. Metuchen, NJ, Scarecrow Press, 1981.

Thompson, V., and Adloff, R. *Djibouti and the Horn of Africa*. London, Oxford University Press, 1968.

Tramport, J. *Djibouti Hier: de 1887 à 1939*. Paris, Hatier, 1990.

Weiss, E. *Djibouti: Évasion*. Paris, Editions du Fer à Marquer, 1990.

Woodward, P. *The Horn of Africa: State Politics and International Relations*. London, Tauris, 1996.

EQUATORIAL GUINEA

Physical and Social Geography

RENÉ PÉLISSIER

The Republic of Equatorial Guinea occupies an area of 28,051 sq km (10,831 sq miles). Geographically, the main components of the republic are the islands of Bioko (formerly known as Fernando Póo), covering 2,017 sq km, and Annobón (also known as Pagalu), 17 sq km; and, on the African mainland, bordered to the north by Cameroon, to the south and east by Gabon and westwards by the Gulf of Guinea, lies the province of Río Muni (also formerly known as Mbini), 26,017 sq km, including three coastal islets, Corisco (15 sq km), and the Great and Little Elobeys (2.5 sq km).

Bioko is a parallelogram-shaped island, 72 km by 35 km, formed from three extinct volcanoes. To the north lies the Pico de Basilé (rising to 3,007 m above sea-level), with an easy access. In the centre of the island are the Moka heights, while, further south, the Gran Caldera forms the remotest and least developed part of the island. The coast is steep to the south. Malabo is the only natural harbour. Crop fertility is high, owing to the combination of volcanic soils and plentiful rainfall. At the southern extremity of the Guinean archipelago lies the remote island of Annobón, south of the island of São Tomé.

Mainland Río Muni is a jungle enclave, from which a coastal plain rises steeply toward the Gabonese frontier. Its main orographic complexes are the spurs of the Monts de Cristal of Gabon. The highest peaks are Piedra de Nzas, Monte Mitra and Monte Chime, all rising to 1,200 m. The main river is the Mbini (formerly known as the Río Benito), non-navigable except for a 20-km stretch, which bisects the mainland province. On the Cameroon border is the Río Campo; its tributary, the Kye, is the de facto eastern border with Gabon. The coast is a long beach, with low cliffs towards Cogo. There is no natural harbour.

The country has an equatorial climate with heavy rainfall, especially in Bioko. The average temperature of Malabo is 25°C and the average rainfall is in excess of 2,000 mm. Humidity is high throughout the island, except on the Moka heights. Río Muni has less debilitating climatic conditions.

According to the July 1983 census, which recorded a total population of 300,000, there were 240,804 inhabitants in Río Muni, 57,190 on Bioko and 2,006 on Annobón. The population was estimated by the UN to be 431,000 at mid-1998. The main city is Malabo (with 15,253 inhabitants at the 1983 census), the capital of Bioko and of the republic, as well as the main economic, educational and religious centre. The other town of note is Luba. Bubi villages are scattered in the eastern and western parts of the island. On the mainland the only urban centre is the port of Bata, which had a population of 24,100 in 1983. Other ports are Mbini and Cogo. Inland, Mikomeseng, Nkumekie, Ebebiyín and Evinayong are small market and administrative centres. The country is divided into seven administrative provinces: Bioko Norte, Bioko Sur and Annobón for the two main islands; Centro-Sur, Kié-Ntem, Litoral and Wele-Nzas for the mainland and its adjacent islets.

The ethnic composition of Equatorial Guinea is unusually complex for so small a political unit. The Fang are the dominant group in Río Muni, where they are believed to comprise 80%–90% of the population. North of the Mbini river are the Ntumu Fang, and to the south of it the Okak Fang. Coastal tribes—notably the Kombe, Balengue and Bujeba—have been pushed towards the sea by Fang pressure. Both Fang and coastal peoples are of Bantu origin. Since independence in 1968, many inhabitants of Río Muni have emigrated to Bioko, where they have come to dominate the civil and military services. The Bubi, who are the original inhabitants of Bioko, may now number about 5,000. The Fernandino, of whom there are a few thousand, are the descendants of former slaves liberated by the British, mingled with long-settled immigrants from coastal west Africa. The working population of Annobón are mainly seafarers and fishermen.

The official languages are Spanish and, since February 1998, French. In Río Muni the Fang language is spoken, as well as those of coastal tribes. Bubi is the indigenous language on Bioko, although Fang is also widely used in Malabo, and Ibo is spoken by the resident Nigerian population.

Recent History

MARISÉ CASTRO

The Republic of Equatorial Guinea, comprising the region of Río Muni, on the African mainland, and the islands of Bioko, Annobón, Corisco and the Elobeys, was granted independence on 12 October 1968, after 190 years of Spanish colonial rule. Francisco Macías Nguema, a mainland Fang from the Esangui clan, took office as president of the new republic, following multi-party elections in which he had received the support of a moderate coalition grouping.

In office, Macías Nguema moved swiftly to suppress opposition, and to assert his absolute power through a 'reign of terror'. The brutal nature of the regime led to the flight of as many as one-third of the total population, including nearly all of the skilled and educated elements of Equato-Guinean society. Macías Nguema obtained much of his economic and military aid from Eastern bloc countries; relations with Spain deteriorated, and serious disputes arose regionally with Gabon and Nigeria. The country's economy, centred on cocoa plantations on Bioko and relying on imported African labour, was devastated by the excesses of Macías Nguema's regime.

OBIANG NGUEMA'S PRESIDENCY

In August 1979 Lt-Col (now Gen.) Teodoro Obiang Nguema Mbasogo, the commander of the national guard and a nephew of the president, deposed Macías, who fled from the capital, was captured and executed in September. Obiang Nguema announced the restoration of the rule of law, but banned all political parties and ruled through a supreme military council (SMC), which continued to be dominated by the Esangui clan. However, sustained pressure from exiled opposition groups, together with the government's need to secure foreign economic assistance, compelled Obiang Nguema to grant political concessions. In December 1981 the first civilians were appointed to the SMC, and in August 1982 a new constitution was approved by 95% of voters in a referendum. Provisions for the protection of human rights and for a limited form of popular representation were incorporated in the constitution, and Obiang Nguema was appointed to a seven-year term as president. At elections held in August 1983 all candidates were nominated by the president, to serve for a term of five years in a unicameral legislature with virtually no independent legislative powers.

During the 1980s there were a number of reports of attempted *coups d'état*. One in 1986, was promoted by the minister of defence, Lt-Col Fructuoso Mba Onaña Nchama, an uncle of the president. Obiang Nguema created a 'governmental party', the Partido Democrático de Guinea Ecuatorial (PDGE), while still resisting demands for multi-party democracy. The higher ranks of the civil service and armed forces remained firmly in the hands of the president's Esangui clan, and elections continued to be overtly manipulated by the government. At legislative elections held in July 1988, all of the PDGE candidates were returned, receiving 99.2% of the votes cast. Numerous arrests followed an alleged fourth unsuccessful coup attempt in August.

The first presidential election since 1968 took place in June 1989, with Obiang Nguema, the sole candidate, receiving 99% of the votes cast. The election was not conducted by secret ballot. An amnesty for political detainees was proclaimed in August. However, the international human rights organization, Amnesty International, has since reiterated long-standing accusations against the government of detaining and mistreating its political opponents. The Roman Catholic church, which claims the allegiance of the majority of the population, has also been active in criticizing the regime's human rights abuses.

Opposition Pressures

Under growing internal and international pressure, Obiang Nguema eventually conceded the principle of political plurality in July 1991. A new constitution containing such provisions was approved by referendum in mid-November; however, the few human rights safeguards contained in the 1982 constitution were removed. In early January 1992 a number of new laws were promulgated, which included legislation on political parties and on freedom of assembly and demonstration. This was followed, in mid-January, by the formation of a new transitional government and the implementation of a general amnesty which included all political exiles. However, these reform measures failed to meet the opposition's expectations. Provisions of the new constitution exempted Obiang Nguema from any judicial procedures arising from his presidential tenure, while Equato-Guinean citizens who also held foreign passports and persons not continuously resident in Equatorial Guinea for 10 years were barred from standing as election candidates. This measure thus effectively excluded virtually all exiled political opponents from participation in national political life. In addition, the legislation on political parties required each organization to submit a deposit of 30m. francs CFA as a condition of registration, and prohibited the use of funds from abroad for this purpose. The president indicated that legislative and presidential elections would not be held until the current mandates of the legislature and of the president had expired, in 1993 and 1996 respectively. The transitional government included only PDGE members, although the party's 'liberal' wing was represented, notably by the new foreign minister, Benjamín Mba Ekua. The first two opposition parties, the Unión Popular (UP) and Partido Liberal, were legalized in June 1992, and in September an alliance of opposition organizations, the Plataforma de Oposición Conjunta (POC), was created.

During January 1992 the UN published a report that criticized the human rights record of the Equato-Guinean authorities and some of the provisions incorporated in the new constitution. Throughout 1992 the security forces continued to arrest members of opposition parties. In early November two Spanish businessmen were charged with plotting against the government; they were found guilty in late November, sentenced to 12 years' imprisonment, and simultaneously pardoned. In December about 100 anti-government protesters were arrested in Malabo; however, they were released soon afterwards.

In January 1993, following the promulgation of an electoral law, further arrests of opposition members took place. In the following month the UN published another report alleging a serious disregard for human rights by the Obiang Nguema regime, and appointed a 'Special Rapporteur for Equatorial Guinea'. During February and March the government and several opposition organizations negotiated a national pact, which stipulated conditions for the conduct of the forthcoming legislative elections; these included the freedom to organize political activity and equal access by all parties to the media. However, the government was soon accused of violating the pact. In May five opposition members were arrested while attending a political meeting, and in August further arrests took place of political opponents accused of attempting to overthrow the government; one detainee died, reportedly as a result of torture. During August violent clashes occurred on the island of Annobón between anti-government demonstrators and security forces. Accusations by the Equato-Guinean authorities that Spain had incited the unrest were strenuously denied by the Spanish government.

Multi-party legislative elections took place in November 1993. They were, however, boycotted by most of the parties in the POC alliance, in protest at Obiang Nguema's refusal to review contentious clauses of the electoral law or to permit international observers to inspect the electoral register. Although OAU representatives attended as observers, the UN declined a request by the Equato-Guinean authorities to monitor the elections, asserting that correct procedures were evidently not being implemented. Following a turn-out variously estimated at between 30%-50% of the electorate, the PDGE won 68 of the 80 seats in the house of representatives; of the six opposition parties which presented candidates, the Convención Social-democrática Popular won six seats, the Unión Democrática y Social de Guinea Ecuatorial secured five seats and the Convención Liberal Democrática obtained one seat. Prior to the elections, opposition politicians were reported to have been harassed by the security forces and during the polling irregularities in procedures were allegedly widespread. In early December the government announced that henceforth all party political gatherings would be subject to prior official authorization. In mid-December Silvestre Siale Bileka, prime minister in the interim government, became prime minister of the new administration. His council of ministers included no opposition representatives.

In June 1994, in response to pressure from international aid donors, the government agreed to modify the controversial electoral law and to conduct a preliminary electoral census prior to the holding of local elections. In September, however, the authorities began to compile a full population census, instead of preparing for the local elections, which had been scheduled for November. The census was boycotted by opposition parties, and there were numerous arrests in ensuing clashes with the security forces. The local elections were postponed. During late November and early December the Convergencia para la Democracia Social (CPDS) held the first congress of an opposition political party to take place within Equatorial Guinea.

In early 1995 the constitution and electoral law were amended to reduce from 10 to five years the minimum time required for candidates to have been resident in Equatorial Guinea. In April several leaders of the opposition Partido del Progreso de Guinea Ecuatorial (PPGE), including its president, Severo Moto Nsa, were sentenced to terms of imprisonment, having been convicted of treason by a military court. (Moto Nsa received a sentence of 28 years.) These proceedings were widely condemned by the international community, and in August, following representations by President Chirac of France on behalf of Moto Nsa, Obiang Nguema unexpectedly pardoned all the convicted PPGE members.

Local elections (which had been postponed in 1994—see above) eventually took place in September 1995. Contested by 14 parties, they were the first truly representative multi-party elections to take place since independence. The electoral roll had been drafted with assistance from the UN, and the elections were monitored by a team of 27 international observers; observers representing the government and opposition parties were also present at polling stations. The six member parties of the POC presented a united front, offering a single candidate in each constituency. Although no major problems were reported during the election campaigns, the ruling PDGE was accused of electoral fraud and harassment once polling was under way. The initial results indicated that opposition parties had won an overwhelming victory; however, the official results credited the ruling party with a majority of the votes cast in two-thirds of local administrations. Judicial appeals by the opposition against the outcome, supported by the team of international observers, were rejected.

At a presidential election held in February 1996 Obiang Nguema was returned to office for a third term, securing more than 90% of the votes cast. The election was boycotted by influential opposition parties, in protest at alleged electoral irregularities and official intimidation, and because their preferred candidate, Armancio Gabriel Nze, was not permitted to run for the POC. The electoral roll drawn up by the UN in 1995 was discarded in favour of an allegedly fraudulent list produced by the government, and the conduct of the elections was severely criticized by foreign observers. In March 1996 Obiang Nguema appointed a new prime minister, Angel Serafin Seriche Dougan (hitherto a vice-minister); a new, enlarged council of ministers was announced in the following month.

In early 1996 disagreements within the POC led to the withdrawal of two parties from the alliance. The government attempted to capitalize on the disunity by issuing a decree in March that effected the organization's immediate dissolution. In August Obiang Nguema issued a decree promoting himself to the rank of general. In November a military court found 11 army officers guilty of conspiring to overthrow the government; all were sentenced to terms of imprisonment.

In February 1997 Obiang Nguema conceded that human rights violations (particularly in Río Muni) were damaging his government's international reputation. Measures that were apparently being taken by the government to prevent official torture and to punish those responsible were dismissed by human rights organizations and opposition politicians as an empty gesture designed to appease potential foreign donors; acts of violence and intimidation allegedly carried out by members of the security forces continued to be reported.

In April 1997 a new national pact was signed by representatives of the government and of 13 opposition parties, following two months of negotiations; however, the CPDS, a leading opposition party instrumental in the establishment of the POC, was excluded from the talks. In May 1997 Moto Nsa was arrested by the Angolan authorities, having been discovered on board a boat carrying a consignment of arms, which were reportedly intended for use in a planned *coup d'état* in Equatorial Guinea. Moto Nsa was released in June and subsequently sought refuge in Spain. Meanwhile, the PPGE was banned. The party subsequently split, with one faction demanding Moto Nsa's expulsion from the party; other party members defected to the ruling PDGE. In August Moto Nsa and 11 others were convicted *in absentia* of treason; Moto Nsa was sentenced to 101 years' imprisonment. During July and August 1997 a large number of people belonging to the PPGE and the (not yet legalized) Fuerza Demócrata Republicana (FDR) were arrested. In September a national economic conference on priority investment areas for Equatorial Guinea's soaring petroleum revenues (see Economy) was held in Bata. Delegates included representatives of opposition parties.

In January 1998 the government resigned. Shortly afterward Seriche Dougan was re-appointed as prime minister and a new, enlarged council of ministers was formed. A notable appointment was that of Teodoro Obiang, the president's eldest son, as minister of forestry and environment. In the following month a new electoral law was passed, which banned political coalitions; this was expected to disadvantage the opposition at the next legislative elections.

In late January 1998 armed protestors launched three successive attacks against mainly military targets on Bioko, killing four soldiers and three civilians. The attacks were alleged to have been perpetrated by members of the secessionist Movimiento para la Autodeterminación de la Isla de Bioko (MAIB), which was founded in 1993 to represent the island's indigenous Bubi population, who, following independence, had become outnumbered and marginalized by the dominant Fang. A wave of repressive measures, orchestrated by the government against the Bubi and the local resident Nigerian community, ensued; hundreds of people were arrested and many severely tortured. A maximum security alert was declared throughout the country. In late May 1998 some 116 detainees, including two Nigerians and four Spaniards, were tried by a military court in connection with the January attacks, on charges including terrorism and

treason. Fifteen of the defendants were found guilty of the most serious charges and sentenced to death; in response to international pressure, however, the death sentences were commuted to terms of life imprisonment in September. More than 70 were found guilty of lesser offences and sentenced to terms of imprisonment varying from six to 27 years. In July Martin Puye, a prominent MAIB leader who had been sentenced to 27 years in prison following the May trial, died in detention, arousing widespread international condemnation of the conditions of imprisonment in Equatorial Guinea.

The country's second multi-party legislative elections (which had been postponed in November 1998) were finally held in early March 1999 amid numerous allegations concerning electoral fraud and the harassment of opposition candidates and election workers, many of whom were expelled from the voting stations that they were monitoring. During the electoral campaign several members of opposition parties were arrested, including election candidates. Roman Catholic priests on Río Muni, who were suspected of sympathizing with the opposition, were recalled to Bata and forbidden to leave the city for the duration of the elections. In many districts of the mainland voters were required to cast their votes publicly. The elections were contested by 13 parties (excluding the PPGE, which had been banned in 1997—see above), and there was an estimated turn-out of some 99% of the electorate. The ruling PDGE claimed to have obtained more than 90% of the votes cast, increasing its representation from 68 to 75 of the 80 parliamentary seats. Two opposition parties, the UP and the CPDS, gained four seats and one seat respectively, but refused to participate in the new administration. Together with five other opposition parties they rejected the results and demanded the annulment of the elections on the grounds that the electoral law had been violated. The Malabo court of appeal dismissed their petition, accusing the opposition of dishonesty; the case was subsequently taken to the Supreme Tribunal. Following the election Seriche Dougan was reappointed to the premiership; a new cabinet was announced in late July. The new government instituted measures to purge corruption. During the first three months in office, the new administration dismissed hundreds of civil servants, including a number of high-ranking officials. This was followed in January 2000 by the dismissal of judicial officials, including the president of the supreme court and the president of the constitutional court. Silvestre Siale Bileka, a former prime minister, was appointed president of the supreme court.

In late March 2000 the government announced that municipal elections would be held on 28 May. The electoral campaign began on 13 May; however, the CPDS, the UP and the Alianza Democrática Progresista (ADP) announced they would not participate in the elections. Consequently, the PDGE obtained 95.7% of the votes cast and won power in all 30 municipal councils. There was an estimated turn-out of 91% of the electorate. The opposition dismissed the elections as invalid.

During the UN Human Rights Commission in late March 2000, the new Special Representative for Equatorial Guinea, severely criticized the Equatorial Guinean authorities of systematic and serious human rights violations. It was further stated that, despite some minor advances, there was not real democracy in the country and accused the government of refusing to authorize the formation of human rights non-governmental organizations (NGO).

Early in 1999 unregistered opposition parties in exile in Spain formed the Coordinadora de la Oposición Conjunta (CODE), which grouped Moto Nsa's faction of the PPGE, the MAIB, FDR, Foro-Democracia Guinea Ecuatorial, Unión Democrática Independiente and Unión para la Reconciliación y el Progreso. Following the March legislative elections, CODE announced the creation of a Civil-Military Front and a government in exile, which aimed to overthrow President Obiang and promote democratic change. On at least two occasions in March and April opposition leaders were prevented from travelling abroad.

Equato-Guinean exiles have reacted cautiously to Obiang Nguema's efforts to encourage their return. His regime's authoritarian ethos, together with reports of persistent human rights abuses, corruption and economic stagnation, have tended to discourage the great majority of emigrés. During the Macías period, the most influential exiled opposition party had been the Alianza Nacional para la Restauración Democrática de

Guinea Ecuatorial (ANRD). Based in Geneva, Switzerland, it achieved a semi-representative, if unofficial, standing with UN bodies. Following Obiang Nguema's accession to power, however, ANRD's influence declined, and the exiled opposition split into numerous small and shifting groups, many of which were based in Spain. The PPGE, founded in 1983, emerged as a particularly influential opposition party during the late 1980s. Moto Nsa, the PPGE's leader during 1983–97, was appointed secretary-general of the Junta Coordinadora de las Fuerzas de Oposición Democrática, which was formed in Zaragoza, Spain, in 1983, as a co-ordinating body for exiled opposition groups. Political liberalization in Gabon led during 1990 to the emergence of Libreville as a new centre of activity for the Equato-Guinean opposition in exile. The most significant of these groups was the Unión para la Democracia y el Desarollo Social (UDDS), founded in September 1990 and led by Antonio Sibacha Bueicheku. A coalition of parties dominated by the UDDS was formed in Libreville, in April 1991, under the title of Coordinación Democrática de los Partidos de Oposición de Guinea Ecuatorial. Following the government's amnesty for political exiles in January 1992 and the enactment of legislation in that month legalizing a multi-party political system, the opposition began to prepare for the legislative elections due to take place in 1993 (see above). The POC was dissolved in March 1996. In early 1999 opposition parties exiled in Spain formed the CODE (see above).

Foreign Relations

Equatorial Guinea's relations with Spain, the former colonial power (which has traditionally provided substantial economic aid), have been consistently strained by reports of internal corruption, the misuse of aid funds and abuses of human rights. In December 1993 the Spanish consul in Bata was expelled 'for interference in the country's internal affairs', following an alleged meeting between the consul and members of opposition parties. The Spanish government recalled its ambassador and reduced aid to the country by 50%, excluding humanitarian assistance, from the beginning of January 1994. The ban was extended to all forms of aid at the end of the month. The European Union (EU) has also withdrawn financial assistance and the United Nations Development Programme has suspended a number of projects. In April 1994 negotiations commenced between the Equato-Guinean and Spanish governments, with a view to resuming full Spanish financial assistance. In June aid donors met representatives of the Obiang Nguema administration and opposition parties; it was agreed that assistance would be resumed gradually, on condition that improvements were made in both the human rights situation and the democratization process. Relations with Spain improved considerably in 1996, with the installation of a new Spanish government; in 1997 negotiations recommenced between the two countries concerning the resumption of economic co-operation and aid. Opposition politicians expressed dismay at the *rapprochement,* which they believed would reduce international pressures on the Obiang Nguema government to install a truly democratic political system in Equatorial Guinea. However, bilateral relations became strained once again during the second half of 1997, when Spain granted refugee status to the Equato-Guinean dissident Moto Nsa (see above), and deteriorated further in 1998. The Obiang Nguema regime has continued to accuse Spain of interfering in Equatorial Guinea's domestic affairs and of attempting to destabilize the country by providing funds to opposition organizations, and of attempting to re-colonize the country. Spanish citizens were frequently subjected to detention and expulsion. The Spanish government was still prepared to negotiate further assistance, but continued to insist that future aid would be dependent upon progress towards democratization. Spanish assistance to Equatorial Guinea resumed after the two governments signed, in October 1999, a new three-year co-operation pact, which was not conditional on improvements in the government's observance of human rights and democratization.

In the early 1980s Obiang Nguema attempted to move the country away from Spanish influence and into France's economic sphere. In December 1983 Equatorial Guinea became a member of the Union douanière et économique de l'Afrique centrale (which was replaced by the Communauté économique et monétaire en Afrique centrale—CEMAC—in 1999), and in August 1984 it joined the Banque des états de l'Afrique centrale (BEAC). Full entry to the Franc Zone followed in January 1985, when the CFA franc replaced the epkwele as the national currency. The increasing level of French economic influence was reflected in the president's regular attendance at Franco-African summit meetings, and in an extended curriculum of French-language classes in Equato-Guinean schools. In February 1998 French became Equatorial Guinea's second official language. Obiang Nguema has also sought to establish amicable relations with countries outside Europe, particularly China and the Democratic People's Republic of Korea. In September 1996 an agreement on economic co-operation was signed with China. In July 1998, during a visit to Iran by the Equato-Guinean minister of foreign affairs and co-operation, it was agreed that the two countries would establish full diplomatic relations, and several co-operation arrangements were signed in the areas of agriculture, health and technology. Co-operation has also been promoted with Latin American countries, notably Mexico and Cuba. During Obiang Nguema's visit to Cuba in November 1999, a co-operation agreement between the two countries was signed in the areas of health, education and agriculture. Later in January 2000, another agreement was signed under which Equato-Guinean radio and television technicians were to be trained in Cuba. The first group of about 80 students, arrived in Cuba in February, followed in March by the arrival in Equatorial Guinea of about 150 Cuban medical personnel. Military aid from Morocco, which replaced that from Cuba after 1979, remained crucial to the maintenance of his regime until 1994, when most Moroccan troops were withdrawn from Equatorial Guinea, apart from a small number of guards overseeing the president's security. Some military aid has also been received from the USA. During the late 1990s Obiang Nguema sought to improve Equatorial Guinea's relations with the EU. In October 1997 he visited Brussels with a view to negotiating the resumption of EU assistance; in January 1998, however, the EU announced that it would not resume co-operation with Equatorial Guinea until notable progress had been achieved in improving human rights. The Obiang Nguema government responded in July by threatening to withdraw Equatorial Guinea from the Lomé Convention.

Regionally, Equatorial Guinea's relations with Nigeria deteriorated when, in 1988, Nigeria threatened to invade Bioko to eject South African personnel, who were alleged to be installing a satellite-tracking station and extending Malabo airport, in preparation for a military assault on the Niger delta oilfields. The affair was eventually resolved in 1990 by reciprocal state visits by the two heads of state. In mid-1994, following a visit to Nigeria by Obiang Nguema, the two countries agreed to co-operate in the establishment of an international commission to demarcate maritime borders in the Gulf of Guinea. Cameroon and São Tomé and Príncipe were also expected to become members. These negotiations between Equatorial Guinea and Nigeria were complicated by the presence of substantial reserves of petroleum in the disputed offshore areas. Since 1996 the two countries have held regular meetings to discuss, primarily, the issue of the maritime borders. Relations with Gabon have come under strain, as the result of unresolved frontier disputes, revived by petroleum exploration activity in southern Mbini. In May 1993 Equatorial Guinea and South Africa established diplomatic relations, and in January 1994 diplomatic relations with Israel were resumed. Relations with South Africa continued to improve, and in 1999 several South African companies became involved in various economic and social projects in Equatorial Guinea. As part of a programme of cost-saving measures, the US government closed its diplomatic mission in Malabo in 1996. In March 2000 the Spanish charter of the aid organization Médecins sans frontières suspended work in Equatorial Guinea in protest against the corruption and alleged manipulation of humanitarian aid by the government.

Economy

MARISÉ CASTRO

Revised for this edition by the Editor

The economy of Equatorial Guinea was traditionally based on agriculture and forestry, the principal products being timber, cocoa, coffee, palm oil, bananas and cassava. During the 1990s, however, the petroleum sector became increasingly important, leading to unprecedented levels of economic growth. In 1996, according to estimates by the World Bank, Equatorial Guinea's gross national product (GNP), measured at average 1994–96 prices, was US $217m., equivalent to $530 per head. Equatorial Guinea's GNP totalled $444m. in 1997, equivalent to $1,050 per head and during the same period, it was estimated, GNP per head increased, in real terms, at an average annual rate of 12.1%. In 1990–97 the population increased by an annual average of 2.5%. According to estimates by the World Bank, Equatorial Guinea's gross domestic product (GDP) increased, in real terms, by an annual average of 22.9% in 1992–98. Real GDP advanced by 29.1% in 1996, by 71.2% in 1997 and by an estimated 22% in 1998. The recent exceptional growth in GDP derives from vastly increased petroleum production and the commencement in 1992 of petroleum exports, which has very significantly improved Equatorial Guinea's economic prospects.

AGRICULTURE, FORESTRY AND FISHING

Agriculture, including hunting, forestry and fishing, contributed an estimated 21.8% of GDP in 1998 (compared with 51.6% of GDP in 1995) and employed an estimated 71.2% of the active population in the same year. Timber from the mainland province of Río Muni accounted for 25.8% of export revenue in 1996. There are some 1.3m. ha of timber estimated to be suitable for lumbering operations, of which only 597,000 ha had been conceded to timber production in 1993. However, timber output was stimulated by the devaluation of the national currency, the CFA franc, in January 1994, and concessions were granted for more than 1m. ha of land in 1995. This massive growth in the forestry sector has called into question its sustainability. The environmental impact on easily accessible areas close to the coast or to navigable waterways has already been devastating. It is estimated that during 1900–95 Equatorial Guinea lost 0.7% of its forest annually. According to the IMF, at the current rate of extraction, available resources would be exhausted by the year 2012. The principal exploited species of wood are *okoumé* and *akoga*. In 1967, the year before independence, production by Spanish concessionaires reached nearly 340,000 metric tons. Output subsequently declined sharply, and amounted to a mere 1,000 tons in 1978. Production and exports recovered quickly after the overthrow of Macías Nguema in 1979, although annual production remained considerably below the level of 300,000 cu m until 1992, when it soared to 613,000 cu m; in 1993 and 1994 output rose further, to 638,000 cu m and 714,000 cu m respectively, and annual production was estimated at 811,000 cu m in both 1995 and 1996. Exports totalled 216,559 cu m in 1994 and an estimated 281,000 cu m in 1995. The government's wish to increase the proportion of processed to unprocessed exports has largely failed to materialize, despite the construction in 1982, with Italian aid, of a sawmill with an annual capacity of 20,000 cu m. Exploitation rights to sizeable areas of forest were granted by Obiang Nguema to foreign (mainly French and Spanish) concessionaires. Following many years of stagnation, the sector grew rapidly throughout the mid-1990s (see above). By the end of 1995 there were 38 timber concessions, as compared with 15 at the end of 1993. This was attributable not only to the devaluation of 1994, but also to an increased demand for *okoumé* and reportedly to the failure to enforce cultivation guidelines, which has allowed concessionaires to fell trees officially set aside for conservation. In 1990 the government had adopted a forestry action plan, which aimed to revitalize timber production and emphasized the necessity of implementing reafforestation measures.

Cocoa, which provided 2.9% of export earnings in 1996, is the main crop of Bioko, where its cultivation accounts for about 90% of the country's total output. Production of cocoa fell sharply from about 38,000 tons annually before independence to less than 7,000 tons by the early 1980s; output has subsequently stagnated, totalling an estimated 4,000 tons in 1997 (or 2%–3% of the world market). Prior to independence an area in excess of 41,000 ha was under cocoa cultivation, underpinned by high guaranteed prices on the Spanish domestic market. More than 800 plantations belonged to Africans, but most of the land and production was controlled by Europeans. Nationalized under Macías Nguema, the cocoa plantations were intially offered back to their former owners after the coup of 1979. However, many plantations remained unclaimed and others were subsequently re-confiscated; most are now owned by members of the presidential entourage, and are managed by two Spanish companies. They are worked on a share-cropping basis by local small farmers. Only about one-third of the land that was cultivated before independence is now exploited, and most of the trees are old and poorly tended. In March 2000 the government threatened to expropriate some of the smallholdings around Malabo, which it had granted to small farmers to develop agricultural production, on the grounds that output had not increased, and that in some instances plots had remained uncultivated for several years. A five-year cocoa rehabilitation project for 7,550 ha, initiated in 1985 by the World Bank and supported by a variety of donors, achieved little success. In 1991 the World Bank initiated a 10-year rehabilitation scheme, under which strictly commercial criteria were to be applied, to preclude any accusations of uneconomic subsidies. Under the programme, it was hoped that yields would be increased through replanting and the control of plant pests and diseases. The programme also provided for a gradual expansion in the areas under cultivation, with the promotion of diversification into other crops in areas of marginal cocoa production. The cocoa rehabilitation scheme was part of a wider agricultural project, which attracted a pledge of US $18m. from the World Bank and lesser sums from other donors.

Coffee is the third most important export commodity, but it lags far behind timber and cocoa. The Spanish administration encouraged smallholder cultivation in Río Muni for the Spanish market during the 1940s. In 1968, the year of independence, exports stood at just under 8,500 metric tons, part of which represented coffee from Gabon and Cameroon (smuggled over the frontier to benefit from higher Spanish prices). By 1979–80, exports had dwindled to just over 100 tons. Production gradually recovered and was estimated at 7,000 tons in 1996. However, it is believed that about two-thirds of the harvest is smuggled into Gabon to benefit from that country's higher producer prices. In 1988 it was estimated that there were nearly 20,000 ha planted with coffee, divided among some 25,000 households. The quality is poor and the yields are extremely low.

Cassava, cocoyam, sweet potatoes, plantain, bananas, rice, maize, palm oil and eggs are all produced for the domestic market. There are eventual prospects of substantial food exports to Gabon, which is persistently short of foodstuffs and which already imports plantain from Río Muni. The government is promoting the production of spices (vanilla, pepper and coriander) for export.

Livestock raising almost disappeared from the country during the Macías Nguema period. In 1986 the African Development Bank (ADB) provided a loan of US $12.6m. to revive cattle-rearing on the high pastures of Moka, in Bioko, to a level comparable to that prevailing prior to independence, when the island was self-sufficient in beef and dairy products. The cattle herd was estimated at 5,000 head in 1997, and a slaughterhouse was in operation. In Río Muni the emphasis was on poultry raising, again with ADB support, and by the end of the 1980s Río Muni was again well supplied with chickens and eggs.

At independence, some 5,000 people worked in the fishing industry, and those of Annobón (Pagalu) were renowned as skilled fishermen. Tuna from Annobón waters and shellfish from Bioko were processed locally and exported. Under Macías Nguema, the fishing industry collapsed, and the former USSR was granted a fishing monopoly. This was terminated in 1980, and replaced by agreements with Spain in 1980, with Nigeria in 1982 (renewed in 1991), and with the European Community (EC, now the European Union—EU) in 1983 (renewed in 1986 and 1989). In 1989 the EC paid 6m. European Currency Units (ECU) for an agreed monthly tonnage catch by European fishing vessels, mainly Spanish and French. The agreement expired in 1992, and was renewed in 1994. The EU has also financed research and training schemes to improve Equatorial Guinea's own artisanal fishing operations. The overall catch rose from around 1,000 tons in 1981–82 to an estimated 3,700 tons in 1994, of which a negligible proportion came from artisanal fisherman. Shellfish constituted nearly one-half of the total catch. In 1996 the overall catch totalled 2,306 tons. By 1999 it had risen to between 6,000–8,000 tons annually. A tuna-processing factory at the port of Luba on Bioko, which was financed by Spanish aid, was due to begin production in the early 1990s; it was hoped that the plant would stimulate local involvement in the fishing industry.

INDUSTRY, MINING, POWER AND COMMUNICATIONS

In 1984 the offshore Alba gas and condensate field was discovered by Spain's Repsol on behalf of Empresa Guineano-Española de Petróleos (Gepsa), a joint venture between the government and Repsol. However, Gepsa was dissolved in 1990, and the concession was taken over, on a production-sharing basis, by a consortium of US independent operators, led by Walter International. Production began in late 1991, at a rate of 1,200 barrels per day (b/d), and was shipped to a storage complex near Malabo. The first consignment of condensates left Bioko in early 1992. Output rose to 6,700 b/d, in 1995, and was expected to increase further during the late 1990s. Walter International carried out further successful exploration work in neighbouring blocs near Bioko, and between April 1992 and March 1993 it was reported that the company had exported some 1.2m. barrels of high-grade petroleum valued at US $23m. In 1999 Equatorial Guinea exported 36m. barrels valued at $400m. In 1995 the Northern Michigan Electric Co (NOMECO) took over the operation of the Alba wells. Petroleum production has greatly increased since October 1995, when Mobil Oil Corpn's Zafiro field came on stream; Mobil, which has invested $130m. in the country, began to produce 40,000 b/d from Zafiro in August 1996, which had doubled to 80,000 b/d by late 1997. Mobil's production reached 100,000 b/d by 1999 and with the coming into production of the new field, Jade, in March 2000, production was expected to rise to 145,000 b/d. In February 1998 Mobil announced that it would invest a further $1,200m. to expand and develop the sector. Test drilling is now under way in the Topacio prospect, also controlled by Mobil, in which United Meridien International Corpn (UMIC) has a 25% stake. The Topacio prospect could potentially yield a further 40,000 b/d. UMIC is the majority shareholder and operator for blocs A, C and D, to the north of Bioko, where test drilling commenced in late 1996. The French company Elf Aquitaine has been exploring offshore concessions near Río Muni, and in 1996 was planning to set up several Equato-Guinean–Gabonese joint ventures in order to circumvent a territorial dispute between Equatorial Guinea and Gabon regarding offshore fields in the vicinity of the islands of Corisco and the Great and Little Elobeys. In addition, the US company Triton, in partnership with the South African oil and gas exploration group Energy Africa, have started exploration of the Ceiba oilfield on the coast opposite Mbini, in the Río Muni Basin. Production was expected to begin early in 2001, at a rate of 50,000 b/d. An increasing number of oil companies have been showing an interest in Equatorial Guinea. The contribution of the petroleum sector to GDP was 17.9% in 1995, rising to an estimated 41.9% in 1996. In the latter year the sector provided 67.7% of export earnings. The Equato-Guinean petroleum fields also contain considerable

reserves of natural gas, most of which, however, is currently flared. In February 1988 the US companies CMS Energy (NOMECO's parent company) and Samedan Oil signed a deal with the Equato-Guinean government to construct a petrochemical plant near Malabo, at a cost of $300m. Consequently, flaring was to cease and the natural gas was expected to become a marketable commodity. A US $400m. methanol plant was scheduled to be completed during 2000; it is designated to process most of the natural gas now being flared. The condensate output of the Alba fields has been forecast to rise substantially, eventually generating as much as $300,000 per day. Equatorial Guinea also has reserves of gold, iron ore, manganese, tantalum and uranium, but these have yet to be exploited.

On Bioko the existing electricity distribution system supplies only the towns of Malabo and Riaba. In 1987 funding was finalized for the construction of a 3.6-MW hydroelectric power station on the Riaba river (Bioko), at a total cost of US $32.1m., and the project was officially opened in 1989. There have been commissioning problems with the power station, and disputes over electricity tariffs with a French company, Saur-Afrique, which manages the distribution of electricity on the island. During the dry season the Malabo diesel plant supplements output from Riaba. A further 3.6-MW power station, constructed with aid from the People's Republic of China, at Bikomo, near Bata, supplies 90% of Río Muni's energy requirements. In February 2000 a new thermal power station to supply Malabo, which had been under construction for two years, at a cost of US $13.5m., came on stream.

Before independence, there was a diversified and flourishing light industrial sector, centred in Malabo; this infrastructure was effectively ruined by Macías Nguema and has yet to be fully restored. The manufacturing sector contributed only 0.7% of GDP in 1996. Two sawmills in Bata currently account for most of the country's industrial activity; the town also has a small cement works and a bleach factory. Food-processing and soap production are carried out on a small scale. Cocoa fermenting and drying is the only manufacturing industry on Bioko.

Since independence the entire Equato-Guinean road network has fallen into disrepair. During the early 1990s Spain allocated much of its economic aid towards the repair of roads on Bioko, in order to allow the cocoa plantations in the Luba and Riaba areas to re-enter production. A group of international donors are providing assistance for the upgrading of road access from the town of Mbini in Río Muni to Cogo on the Gabonese frontier, much of which is currently impassable in the rainy season; it is hoped that this will stimulate exports of foodstuffs to Gabon. 'Food for work' programmes are also being introduced, in order to maintain the network of feeder roads. There are no railways.

The harbour which handles by far the largest volume of exports is Bata, in Río Muni; the port is used by the timber companies, and handled nearly 125,990 metric tons of exports in 1990. The Italian government provided some US $5m. for the rehabilitation of the port in 1987, on condition that the facility be operated by a joint Italo-Equato-Guinean company. The initial aim was to increase the handling capacity of Bata to 500,000 tons per year, and eventually to 1m. tons. There have, however, been long delays in implementing this project. Malabo has an excellent natural harbour (formed by a sunken volcanic crater), which has been rehabilitated by a French company. There are regular shipping services to Europe, but maritime communications between Malabo, Bata and Annobón are erratic, and there is little maritime traffic with neighbouring mainland states.

There is an international airport at Malabo (Santa Isabel airport). A larger international airport at Bata, constructed with Italian aid, was completed in 1995. France has provided funds to upgrade facilities at Santa Isabel airport. Attempts to form a national airline have been bedevilled by mismanagement and alleged corruption. Aerolíneas Guinea Ecuatorial, founded in 1982, had collapsed by 1985. Its successor, the Compañía Ecuato-Guineana de Aviación, was established in 1986 as a partnership between the government and Air Inter-Gabon. After incurring heavy losses, the company went into liquidation in 1990, but has continued to operate limited regional and domestic services, and provides a weekly service to Madrid. Scheduled international services are provided by IBERIA, between Malabo and Madrid, Cameroon Airlines (Cam-Air), between Malabo and Douala, and Air Afrique, operating services to Cotonou (Benin) and Abidjan (Côte d'Ivoire). New Air Afrique services to Nigeria, France and Portugal were planned in the late 1990s. Swissair is also developing international services from Malabo.

AID, FINANCE AND DEVELOPMENT

Traditionally, the economy relied to a great extent on good relations with Spain, which supplied aid totalling 17,000m. pesetas during the period 1979–86. In addition to aid of 2,000m. Spanish pesetas in 1989, Spain also cancelled repayment of one-third of Equatorial Guinea's debt of 5,000m. pesetas, with the remaining two-thirds to be repaid over 14 years, with eight years' grace. In February 1990 Spain signed an agreement to provide a further US $100m. of aid, to be disbursed over four years, covering education, health, administrative reform and economic infrastructure. The Spanish government stated that this involved expenditure amounting to 11 times as much per caput as for any of the other hispanophone countries receiving Spanish assistance. In 1991 Spain waived a further one-third of the country's debt.

During the early 1990s Spanish assistance to Equatorial Guinea totalled about 350m. pesetas annually. However, in January 1994 Spain suspended one-half of its aid following a diplomatic contretemps. A tentative agreement for the gradual resumption of full assistance was made in mid-1994, and further negotiations took place in the late 1990s. In 1998 Spanish aid totalled just over 1.5m. pesetas, of which just over two-thirds were allocated to health and education. France is the second main provider of aid; French assistance rose sharply after Equatorial Guinea joined the various French-sponsored regional economic associations for Central Africa in 1983–85.

In January 1985 Equatorial Guinea entered the Franc Zone. The Banco de Guinea Ecuatorial (the former central bank and bank of issue) ceased operation, and the epkwele, which had been linked to the Spanish peseta, was replaced by the franc CFA at a rate of 4 bipkwele = 1 franc CFA. It was hoped that Equatorial Guinea's entry into the Franc Zone would bring the country out of isolation by encouraging foreign trade and investment. In July 1985 the 'Paris Club' of Western creditor governments granted a rescheduling, over 10 years, of 246m. French francs of debt, with a five-year period of grace. According to the IMF, during 1991–95 total scheduled external debt-servicing amounted to an annual average of 89% of GDP; however, total cash payments on the external debt (including payments on arrears) averaged some 14% of domestic revenue over the same period. According to the World Bank, Equatorial Guinea's total external debt reached US $306.1m. at the end of 1998.

Loans and grants have come from a variety of other Western and Middle Eastern sources, as well as from China and Nigeria, but none on the scale of those provided by Spain and France. An international aid conference, held in Geneva in April 1982, aimed to provide US $140m. for development projects. In November 1988 a second international aid conference pledged a total of $63m. in support of Equatorial Guinea's medium-term investment programme (1989–91). In December 1988 the IMF granted a structural adjustment facility (SAF) of SDR 11.7m. (Equatorial Guinea had received its first IMF stand-by credit, totalling SDR 9.2m., in July 1985.) However, in February 1990 the IMF refused to make any further payments, and shortly afterwards a World Bank mission announced that it was not prepared to make any recommendation for the implementation of a structural adjustment programme. Both multilateral agencies declared themselves particularly dissatisfied with the government's failure to eradicate the budgetary deficit, which stood, according to estimates by the Banque des Etats de l'Afrique

Centrale (BEAC, the Franc Zone's regional central bank), at 2,512m. francs CFA in 1989. In 1990, when the budget deficit fell to an estimated 585m. francs CFA, the government adopted measures to reduce the deficit further which included liberalizing import prices, stimulating private investment and raising the tariffs charged by public utilities. By 1994 the budget, according to an optimistic estimate by the BEAC, showed a surplus of 1,169m. francs CFA; the surplus was estimated to have narrowed to 142m. francs CFA in 1995. However, figures from the IMF present a very different picture: in 1994 the overall budget deficit (including grants) stood at 3,950m. francs CFA on a commitment basis, and at 2,090m. francs CFA on a cash basis, and in 1995 the deficit was estimated at 4,595m. francs CFA on a commitment basis and at 9,689m. francs CFA on a cash basis (following substantial arrears payments brought about by the devaluation of the CFA franc). The multilateral agencies also expressed concern at the continuing deficit on the current account of the balance of payments, which stood at $24.66m. in 1991, although this was offset, to some extent, by inflows of foreign aid.

The commencement in 1992 of petroleum exports was expected to generate a significant improvement in both the balance of payments and budgetary deficits during the 1990s. On the basis of the then promising economic outlook, the IMF agreed to unblock the disbursement of SAF funds in December 1991. The government introduced an economic programme for 1994–96, supported by an SDR 12.9m. three-year enhanced structural adjustment facility (ESAF) from the IMF, which aimed to accelerate the diversification of the economy and the reform of the public sector, and to restructure the financial sector. Under the programme it was expected that the real rate of economic growth could be increased while containing inflation at 35% and reducing the current account deficit. However, while petroleum exports initially had a significant effect on the deficit on the current account of the balance of payments, which decreased, according to the IMF, from US $45.5m. in 1991 to only $0.6m. in 1994, the sector had little direct impact on the budgetary deficit (which totalled 8,318m. francs CFA in 1996 and an estimated 3,754m. francs CFA in 1998). By 1996 the current account deficit had soared to $344m. Potential revenue from the profitable petrolem and timber sectors has been undermined by the inefficient taxation system. In addition, it has been alleged that members of the Equato-Guinean regime have profited personally from national oil revenues. While non-tax revenue from the petroleum sector did increase during 1992–95, it amounted on average only to some 10% of export earnings, which is low by regional standards.

The devaluation of the CFA franc had a limited positive impact on Equatorial Guinea's economic prospects, although it was found necessary to impose price restraints on bread, medicines and petroleum to protect vulnerable sections of the population from economic hardship brought about by the reduction in their consumer purchasing power. Products for export were rendered more competitive on the international market and inflationary pressures were initially successfully contained, with consumer prices increasing, according to estimates from the IMF, by only 11.4% in 1995. (Prices rose by an annual average of 31.5% in the year to July 1996.) Prices increased by an annual average of 3.0% in 1997, and by 7.8% in 1998. However, recent improvements in the trade balance are in part the result of a decreased purchasing power brought about by reductions in foreign aid; the re-establishment of good relations with the international donor community remains a priority, particularly in view of the reliance of the export base on timber and petroleum, and the finite nature of the reserves of these commodities. Having regard to the frequent allegations of corruption in Equato-Guinean public life, greater public accountability in the use of government funds is also much to be desired.

Statistical Survey

Source (unless otherwise stated): Dirección Técnica de Estadística, Secretaría de Estado para el
Plan de Desarrollo Económico, Malabo.

AREA AND POPULATION

Area: 28,051 sq km (10,831 sq miles): Río Muni 26,017 sq km, Bioko 2,017 sq km, Annobón 17 sq km.

Population: 246,941 (Río Muni 200,106, Bioko 44,820, Annobón 2,015) at December 1965 census; 300,000 (Río Muni 240,804, Bioko 57,190, Annobón 2,006), comprising 144,268 males and 155,732 females, at census of 4–17 July 1983. (Source: Ministerio de Asuntos Exteriores, Madrid); 431,000 (UN estimate) at mid-1998.

Provinces (population, census of July 1983): Kié-Ntem 70,202, Litoral 66,370, Centro-Sur 52,393, Wele-Nzas 51,839, Bioko Norte 46,221, Bioko Sur 10,969, Annobón 2,006.

Principal Towns (population at 1983 census): Malabo (capital) 15,253, Bata 24,100.

Births and Deaths (UN estimates, annual averages): Birth rate 43.5 per 1,000 in 1990–95; Death rate 18.0 per 1,000 in 1990–95. Source: UN, *World Population Prospects: The 1998 Revision.*

Expectation of Life (UN estimates, years at birth, 1990–95): 48.0 (males 46.4; females 49.6) (Source: UN, *Demographic Yearbook.*)

Economically Active Population (persons aged 6 years and over, 1983 census): Agriculture, hunting, forestry and fishing 59,390; Mining and quarrying 126; Manufacturing 1,490; Electricity, gas and water 224; Construction 1,929; Trade, restaurants and hotels 3,059; Transport, storage and communications 1,752; Financing, insurance, real estate and business services 409; Community, social and personal services 8,377; Activities not adequately defined 984; Total employed 77,740 (males 47,893, females 29,847); Unemployed 24,825 (males 18,040, females 6,785); Total labour force 102,565 (males 65,933, females 36,632). Note: Figures are based on un-adjusted census data, indicating a total population of 261,779. The adjusted total is 300,000. Source: International Labour Office, *Yearbook of Labour Statistics.*

AGRICULTURE, ETC.

Principal Crops (FAO estimates, '000 metric tons, 1998): Sweet potatoes 35; Cassava 49; Coconuts 8; Palm kernels 3; Bananas and plantains 15; Cocoa beans (unofficial estimate) 5; Green coffee 6. Source: FAO, *Production Yearbook.*

Livestock (FAO estimates, '000 head, year ending September 1998): Cattle 5; Pigs 5; Sheep 36; Goats 8. Source: FAO, *Production Yearbook.*

Forestry (1997): Roundwood removals ('000 cu m): Fuel wood 447 (assumed to be unchanged since 1983); Sawlogs, veneer logs and logs for sleepers 364; Total 811. Source: FAO, *Yearbook of Forest Products.*

Fishing (FAO estimates, metric tons, live weight): Total catch 2,306 in 1995; 5,040 in 1996; 6,090 in 1997. Source: FAO, *Yearbook of Fishery Statistics.*

MINING

Crude Petroleum ('000 metric tons): 821.7 in 1996; 2,754.6 in 1997; 4,036.7 (provisional) in 1998. Source: IMF, *Equatorial Guinea: Recent Economic Developments* (October 1999).

INDUSTRY

Palm Oil (FAO estimates, '000 metric tons): 5.0 in 1996; 5.0 in 1997; 5.0 in 1998. Source: FAO, *Production Yearbook.*

Veneer Sheets ('000 cubic metres): 9 in 1995; 9 (FAO estimate) in 1996; 9 (FAO estimate) in 1997. Source: FAO, *Yearbook of Forest Products.*

Electric Energy (million kWh): 19 in 1993; 19 in 1994; 20 in 1995. Source: UN, *Industrial Commodity Statistics Yearbook.*

FINANCE

Currency and Exchange Rates: 100 centimes = 1 franc de la Coopération financière en Afrique centrale (CFA). *Sterling, Dollar and Euro Equivalents* (28 April 2000): £1 sterling = 1,132.20 francs CFA; US $1 = 722.02 francs CFA; €1 = 655.96 francs CFA; 10,000 francs CFA = £8.832 = $13.850. = €15.245. *Average Exchange Rate* (francs CFA per US dollar): 583.67 in 1997; 589.95 in 1998; 615.70 in 1999. *Note:* An exchange rate of 1 French franc = 50 francs CFA, established in 1948, remained in force until January 1994, when the CFA franc was devalued by 50%, with the exchange rate adjusted to 1 French franc = 100 francs CFA. This relationship to French currency remained in effect with the introduction of the euro on

1 January 1999. From that date, accordingly, a fixed exchange rate of €1 = 655.957 francs CFA has been in operation.

Budget (estimates, million francs CFA, 1998): *Revenue:* Petroleum sector 53,489; Taxation 14,608 (Taxes on income and profits 2,253; Taxes on domestic goods and services 6,501; Taxes on international trade 5,064; Other taxes 786); Other revenue 7,080; Total revenue 75,177, excl. grants from abroad (1,797). *Expenditure:* Current expenditure 33,788 (Wages and salaries 9,129; Other goods and services 12,917; Subsidies and transfers 7,284; Interest payments 4,458); Capital expenditure 29,410; Unclassified expenditure 17,530; Total expenditure 80,728. Source: IMF, *Equatorial Guinea: Recent Economic Developments* (October 1999).

International Reserves (US $ million at 31 December 1998): IMF special drawing rights 0.01; Foreign exchange 0.79; Total 0.80. Source: IMF, *International Financial Statistics.*

Money Supply ('000 million francs CFA at 31 December 1999): Currency outside deposit money banks 12.06; Demand deposits at deposit money banks 16.39; Total money 28.45. Source: IMF, *International Financial Statistics.*

Cost of Living (Consumer price index; base: January 1990 = 100): 161.1 in 1996; 166.0 in 1997; 179.0 (estimate) in 1998. Source: IMF, *Equatorial Guinea: Recent Economic Developments* (October 1999).

Expenditure on the Gross Domestic Product ('000 million francs CFA at current prices, 1997): Government final consumption expenditure 32.0; Private final consumption expenditure 133.2; Gross capital formation 190.8; *Total domestic expenditure 356.0;* Exports of goods and services 292.9; *Less* Imports of goods and services 358.4; *GDP in purchasers' values* 290.5. Source: IMF, *Equatorial Guinea: Recent Economic Developments* (October 1999).

Gross Domestic Product by Economic Activity (million francs CFA at current prices, 1997): Agriculture, hunting, forestry and fishing 67,268; Petroleum sector 187,429; Manufacturing 962; Electricity, gas and water 3,121; Construction 5,768; Trade, restaurants and hotels 8,819; Transport and communications 1,920; Finance, insurance, real estate and business services 1,967; Government services 8,235; Other services 2,823; *Sub-total* 288,312; Import duties 2,205; *GDP in purchasers' values* 290,517. Source: IMF, *Equatorial Guinea: Recent Economic Developments* (October 1999).

Balance of Payments (US $ million, 1996): Exports of goods f.o.b. 175.31; Imports of goods f.o.b. –292.04; *Trade balance* –116.73; Exports of services 4.88; Imports of services –184.58; *Balance on goods and services* –296.43; Other income received 0.16; Other income paid –45.18; *Balance on goods, services and income* –341.44; Current transfers received 4.03; Current transfers paid –6.62; *Current balance* –344.04; Direct investment from abroad 376.18; Other investment liabilities –62.43; Net errors and omissions 24.82; *Overall balance* –5.46. Source: IMF, *International Financial Statistics.*

EXTERNAL TRADE

Principal Commodities (distribution by SITC, US $ '000, 1990): *Imports c.i.f.:* Food and live animals 4,340; Beverages and tobacco 3,198, (Alcoholic beverages 2,393); Crude materials (inedible) except fuels 2,589 (Crude fertilizers and crude minerals 2,102); Petroleum and petroleum products 4,738; Chemicals and related products 2,378; Basic manufactures 3,931; Machinery and transport equipment 35,880 (Road vehicles and parts 3,764, Ships, boats and floating structures 24,715); Miscellaneous manufactured articles 2,725; Total (incl. others) 61,601. *Exports f.o.b.:* Food and live animals 6,742 (Cocoa 6,372); Beverages and tobacco 3,217 (Tobacco and tobacco manufactures 2,321); Crude materials (inedible) except fuels 20,017 (Sawlogs and veneer logs 12,839, Textile fibres and waste 7,078); Machinery and transport equipment 24,574 (Ships, boats and floating structures 23,852); Total (incl. others) 61,705. Source: UN, *International Trade Statistics Yearbook.*

1997 (US $ '000): Imports c.i.f. 352,800; Exports f.o.b. 498,444. Source: IMF, *Equatorial Guinea: Recent Economic Developments* (October 1999).

Principal Trading Partners (US $ '000, 1991): *Imports c.i.f.:* Cameroon 29,141; France 5,915; Italy 3,001; Liberia 22,032; Spain 11,640; USA 33,366; Total (incl. others) 113,545. *Exports f.o.b.:* Cameroon 47,212; Gabon 2,389; Netherlands 2,103; Nigeria 8,955; São Tomé and Príncipe 1,952; Spain 11,645; Total (incl. others) 86,151. Source: UN, *International Trade Statistics Yearbook.*

TRANSPORT

Road Traffic (estimates, motor vehicles in use at 31 December 1996): Passenger cars 1,520; Lorries and vans 540; Total 2,040. Source: IRF, *World Road Statistics*.

Shipping: *Merchant Fleet* (at 31 December 1998): Vessels 87; Total displacement 58,506 grt. Source: Lloyd's Register of Shipping, *World Fleet Statistics*. International Sea-borne Freight Traffic ('000 metric tons, 1990): Goods loaded 110; Goods unloaded 64. Source: UN, *Monthly Bulletin of Statistics*.

Civil Aviation (traffic on scheduled services, 1996): Passengers carried ('000) 15; Passenger-km (million) 7. Source: UN, *Statistical Yearbook*.

COMMUNICATIONS MEDIA

1996: 175,000 radio receivers in use; 4,000 television receivers in use; 4,000 main telephone lines in use; 100 telefax stations in use; 61 mobile cellular telephone subscribers; 1 daily newspaper (estimated circulation 2,000); Book production 17 titles (1988). Sources: UNESCO, *Statistical Yearbook*; UN, *Statistical Yearbook*.

EDUCATION

Primary (1993/94): Schools 781; Teachers 1,381; Pupils 75,751.
Secondary and Further (1993/94): Teachers 588; Pupils 16,616.
Higher (1990/91): Teachers 58; Pupils 578.
Source: UNESCO, *Statistical Yearbook*.

Directory

The Constitution

The present Constitution was approved by a national referendum on 16 November 1991 and amended in January 1995. It provided for the introduction of a plural political system and for the establishment of an 80-member legislative House of Representatives. The term of office of the President is seven years, renewable on an indefinite number of occasions. The President is immune from prosecution for offences committed before, during or after his tenure of the post. The House of Representatives serves for a term of five years. Both the President and the House of Representatives are directly elected by universal adult suffrage. The President appoints a Council of Ministers, headed by a Prime Minister, from among the members of the House of Representatives.

The Government

HEAD OF STATE

President and Supreme Commander of the Armed Forces: Gen. (TEODORO) OBIANG NGUEMA MBASOGO (assumed office 25 August 1979; elected President 25 June 1989; re-elected 25 February 1996).

COUNCIL OF MINISTERS
(July 2000)

Prime Minister and Head of Government: ANGEL SERAFIN SERICHE DOUGAN.

First Deputy Prime Minister: MIGUEL OYONO NDONG MIFUMU.

Second Deputy Prime Minister and Minister for the Interior and Local Corporations: DEMETRIO ELO NDONG NSEFUMU.

Minister of State at the President's Office: ALEJANDRO EVUNU OWONO ASANGONO.

Minister of State for Parliamentary Relations and Judicial Affairs, Government Spokesman: ANTONIO FERNANDO NVE NGU.

Minister of State for Communications and Transport: MARCELINO OYONO NTUTUMU.

Minister of State for Labour and Social Security: RICARDO MANGUE OBAMA NFUBE.

Minister of State for Agriculture, Forestry, Fisheries and the Environment: TEODORO NGUEMA OBIANG MANGUE.

Minister of State for Information, Tourism and Culture: LUCAS NGUEMA ESONO.

Minister of Foreign Affairs and International Co-operation: SANTIAGO NSOBEYA EFUMAN.

Minister of Justice and Worship: RUBÉN MAYA NSUE.

Minister of the Economy and Finance: MIGUEL ABIA BITEO.

Minister of Education, Science and Francophone Affairs: SANTIAGO NGUA NFUMU EYANG.

Minister of Industry, Commerce and Small and Medium-sized Enterprises: CONSTANTINO EKONG NSUE.

Minister of Mines and Energy: CRISTÓBAL MAÑANA ELA.

Minister of Social Affairs and Women's Development: TERESA EFUA ASANGONO.

Minister of Public Works, Housing and Urban Affairs: FLORENTINO NKOGO NDONG.

Minister of Planning and Economic Development: FORTUNATO OFA MBO.

Minister of Health and Social Welfare: JUAN ANTONIO NTUTUMU.

Minister of Youth and Sports: VIDAL CHONI BEKOBA.

Minister of the Civil Service and Administrative Reforms: FERNANDO MABALE MBA NNOMO.

MINISTRIES

All ministries are in Malabo.

Ministry of Agriculture, Forestry, Fisheries and the Environment: Apdo 504, Malabo.

Ministry of the Economy and Finance: Malabo; tel. (9) 31-05; fax (9) 32-05.

Ministry of Foreign Affairs and International Co-operation: Malabo; tel. (9) 32-20.

Ministry of Mines and Energy: Calle 12 de Octobre s/n, Malabo; tel. (9) 35-67; fax (9) 33-53.

Legislature

CÁMARA DE REPRESENTANTES DEL PUEBLO
(House of Representatives)

Speaker: SALOMON NGUEMA OWONO.

General Election, 7 March 1999

Party		Seats
Partido Democrático de Guinea Ecuatorial (PDGE)	.	75
Unión Popular (UP)	.	4
Convergencia para la Democracia Social (CPDS)	. .	1
Total	. . . .	**80**

Political Organizations

Acción Popular (AP): Pres. MIGUEL ESONO.

Alianza Democrática Progresista (ADP): Pres. VICTORINO BOLEKIA.

Alianza Nacional para la Restauración Democrática de Guinea Ecuatorial (ANRD): 95 Ruperto Chapi, 28100 Madrid, Spain; tel. (1) 623-88-64; f. 1974; Sec.-Gen. LUIS ONDO AYANG.

Convención Liberal Democrática (CLD): Pres. ALFONSO NSUE MIFUMU.

Convención Socialdemocrática Popular (CSDP): Leader SECUNDINO OYONO.

Convergencia para la Democracia Social (CPDS): Pres. SANTIAGO OBAMA; Sec.-Gen. PLÁCIDO MICÓ ABOGO.

Coordinación Democrática de los Partidos de Oposición de Guinea Ecuatorial: based in Libreville, Gabon; f. 1991; coalition of the following groups:

Frente Democrático para la Reforma: Sec.-Gen. BIYONGO BI-TUNG.

Movimiento Nacional para la Nueva Liberación de Guinea Ecuatorial.

Partido Republicano.

Partido de Reunificación (PR).

Unión para la Democracia y el Desarrollo Social (UDDS): f. 1990; Sec.-Gen. ANTONIO SIBACHA BUEICHEKU.

Coordinadora de la Oposición Conjunta (CODE): based in Spain; f. 1999; Leader JOAQUÍN ELEMA BORENGUE; includes:

Foro-Democracia Guinea Ecuatorial (FDGE).

Fuerza Demócrata Republicana (FDR): f. 1995; Chair. FELIPE ONDO OBIANG.

Movimiento para la Autodeterminación de la Isla de Bioko (MAIB): f. 1993 by Bubi interests seeking independence of Bioko; Spokesman JOAQUÍN MAHO.

Partido del Progreso de Guinea Ecuatorial (PPGE): f. 1983; Christian Democrat; faction led by SEVERO MOTO NSA (another faction operates outside CODE).

Unión Democrática Independiente (UDI): Leader DANIEL OYONO.

Unión Popular (UP): f. 1992; socialist; Leader ANDRÉS MOISÉS MBA ADA.

Unión para la Reconciliación y el Progreso (URP).

Partido de la Convergencia Social Demócrata (PCSD): Pres. BUENAVENTURA MOSUY.

Partido Democrático de Guinea Ecuatorial (PDGE): Malabo; f. 1987; sole legal party 1987–92; Chair. Gen. (TEODORO) OBIANG NGUEMA MBASOGO.

Partido Social Demócrata (PSD): Pres. BENJAMÍN BALINGA.

Partido Socialista (PS): Sec.-Gen. TOMÁS MACHEBA.

Unión Democrática Nacional (UDEMA): Pres. JOSÉ MECHEBA.

Unión Democrática y Social de Guinea Ecuatorial (UDS): Pres. CARMELO MODÚ AKUNE.

Diplomatic Representation

EMBASSIES IN EQUATORIAL GUINEA

Cameroon: 37 Calle Rey Boncoro, Apdo 292, Malabo; tel. and fax (9) 22-63; Ambassador: JOHN NCHOTU AKUM.

China, People's Republic: Malabo; Ambassador: XU SHAOHAI.

France: Carretera del Aeropuerto, Apdo 326, Malabo; tel. (9) 20-05; Ambassador: GÉRARD BRUNET DE COURSSOU.

Gabon: Apdo 648, Douala, Malabo; tel. (9) 420; Ambassador: JEAN-BAPTISTE MBATCHI.

Korea, Democratic People's Republic: Malabo; Ambassador: PAK MYONG HAK.

Nigeria: 4 Paseo de los Cocoteros, Apdo 78, Malabo; tel. (9) 23-86; Chargé d'affaires: EDWARD NWADA.

Russia: Malabo; Ambassador: LEV ALEKSANDROVICH VAKHRAMEYEV.

Spain: Parque de las Avenidas de Africa, Malabo; tel. (9) 20-20; fax (9) 26-11; Ambassador: JACOBO GONZÁLEZ-ARNAO.

Judicial System

The structure of Judicial Administration was established in 1981. The Supreme Tribunal in Malabo, consisting of a President of the Supreme Tribunal, the Presidents of the three chambers (civil, criminal and administrative), and two magistrats from each chamber, is the highest court of appeal. There are Territorial High Courts in Malabo and Bata, which also sit as courts of appeal. Courts of first instance sit in Malabo and Bata, and may be convened in the other provincial capitals. Local courts may be convened when necessary.

President of the Supreme Tribunal: SILVESTRE SIALE BILEKA.

Religion

An estimated 90% of the population are adherents of the Roman Catholic Church. Traditional forms of worship are also followed.

CHRISTIANITY

The Roman Catholic Church

Equatorial Guinea comprises one archdiocese and two dioceses. There were an estimated 370,304 adherents in the country at 31 December 1998.

Bishops' Conference: Arzobispado, Apdo 106, Malabo; tel. (9) 24-16; f. 1984; Pres. Rt Rev. ANACLETO SIMA NGUA, Bishop of Bata.

Archbishop of Malabo: Most Rev. ILDEFONSO OBAMA OBONO, Arzobispado, Apdo 106, Malabo; tel. (9) 29-09; fax (9) 21-76.

Protestant Church

Iglesia Reformada Evangélica de Guinea Ecuatorial (Evangelical Reformed Church of Equatorial Guinea): Apdo 195, Malabo; f. 1960; c. 8,000 mems; Sec.-Gen. Rev. JAIME SIPOTO.

The Press

El Patio: Apdo 180, Malabo; tel. (9) 27-20; fax (9) 27-22; Spanish; cultural review; 6 a year; publ. by Centro Cultural Hispano-Guineano; Editor GABRIELA GÓMEZ-PIMPOLLO.

El Sol: 24 Calle Camerún, Apdo 944, Malabo; f. 1994; Spanish; weekly; Chief Editor FERMÍN-NVO MBOMIO AVOMO; circ. 3,500.

Hoja Parroquial: Malabo; weekly.

La Gaceta: Malabo; f. 1996; bi-weekly.

La Verdad: Malabo; opposition monthly; publ. by the Convergencia para la Democracia Social; Editor PLÁCIDO MIKÓ ABOGO.

Voz del Pueblo: Malabo; publ. by the Partido Democrático de Guinea Ecuatorial.

FOREIGN NEWS BUREAU

Agencia EFE (Spain): 50 Calle del Presidente Nasser, Malabo; tel. (9) 31-65; Bureau Chief DONATO NDONGO-BIDYOGO.

Publisher

Centro Cultural Hispano-Guineano: Apdo 180, Malabo; tel. (9) 27-20; fax (9) 27-22.

Broadcasting and Communications

RADIO

Radio Africa and Radio East Africa: Apdo 851, Malabo; e-mail pabcomain@aol.com; commercial station; owned by Pan American Broadcasting; music and religious programmes in English.

Radio Malabo: Malabo; Spanish and French programmes.

Radio Nacional de Guinea Ecuatorial: Apdo 749, Barrio Comandachina, Bata; tel. (8) 25-92; fax (8) 20-93; and Apdo 195, 90 ave 30 de Agostó, Malabo; tel. (9) 22-60; fax (9) 20-97; govt-controlled; commercial station; programmes in Spanish, French and vernacular languages; Dir (Bata) SEBASTIÁN ELÓ ASEKO; Dir (Malabo) JUAN EYENE OPKUA NGUEMA.

TELEVISION

Televisión Nacional: Malabo; broadcasts in Spanish and French; Dir ANTONIO NKULU OYE.

Finance

(cap. = capital; p.u. = paid up; res = reserves; m. = million; br. = branch; amounts in francs CFA)

BANKING

Central Bank

Banque des Etats de l'Afrique Centrale (BEAC): Apdo 510, Malabo; tel. (9) 20–10; fax (9) 20–06; HQ in Yaoundé, Cameroon; f. 1973; bank of issue for mem. states of the Communauté économique et monétaire de l'Afrique centrale (CEMAC, fmrly Union douanière et économique de l'Afrique centrale), comprising Cameroon, the Central African Repub., Chad, the Repub. of the Congo, Equatorial Guinea and Gabon; cap. and res 210,014m., total assets 1,303,226m. (June 1999); Gov. JEAN-FÉLIX MAMALEPOT; Dir in Equatorial Guinea BALTHAZAR EDJO'O ENGONGA.

Commercial Banks

Caisse Commune d'Epargne et d'Investissement Guinea Ecuatorial (CCEI-GE): Pres. Nasser St, POB 428, Malabo; tel. (9) 31-21; fax (9) 33-11; f. 1995; dep. 4,725m. (Dec. 1998); Man. Dir JOSEPH TINDJOU.

Société Générale des Banques GE (SGBGE): 6 Calle de Argelia, Apdo 686, Malabo; tel. (9) 93-37; fax (9) 33-66; f. 1986, present name adopted 1998; 60% owned by Société Générale SA (France), 33% state-owned; dep. 10,330m. (Dec. 1998); Pres. CASTRO NVONO AKELE; Gen. Man. CHARLES SANLAVILLE; brs in Bata and Malabo.

Development Banks

Banco de Fomento y Desarrollo (BFD): Malabo; f. 1998; 30% state-owned; cap. 50m.

Banque de Développement des Etats de l'Afrique Centrale (see Franc Zone, p. 127).

Financial Institution

Caja Autónoma de Amortización de la Deuda Pública: Ministry of the Economy and Finance, Malabo; tel. (9) 31-05; fax (9) 32-05; management of state funds; Dir-Gen. BALTASAR ESONO-EWORO NFONO.

Trade and Industry

GOVERNMENT AGENCIES

Cámaras Oficiales Agrícolas de Guinea: Bioko and Bata; purchase of cocoa and coffee from indigenous planters, who are partially grouped in co-operatives.

Empresa General de Industria y Comercio (EGISCA): Malabo; f. 1986; parastatal body jtly operated with the French Société pour l'Organisation, l'Aménagement et le Développement des Industries Alimentaires et Agricoles (SOMDIA); import-export agency.

Oficina para la Cooperación con Guinea Ecuatorial (OCGE): Malabo; f. 1981; administers bilateral aid from Spain.

DEVELOPMENT ORGANIZATION

Sociedad Anónima de Desarrollo del Comercio (SOADECO–Guinée): Malabo; f. 1986; parastatal body jtly operated with the French Société pour l'Organisation, l'Aménagement et le Développement des Industries Alimentaires et Agricoles (SOMDIA); development of commerce.

CHAMBER OF COMMERCE

Cámara de Comercio, Agrícola y Forestal de Malabo: Apdo 51, Malabo; tel. (9) 151.

INDUSTRIAL AND TRADE ASSOCIATIONS

INPROCAO: Malabo; production, marketing and distribution of cocoa.

Total Ecuatoguineana de Gestion (GE–Total): Malabo; f. 1984; 50% state-owned, 50% by CFP-Total (France); petroleum marketing and distribution; Chair. of Bd of Dirs Minister of Public Works, Housing and Urban Affairs.

UTILITIES
Electricity
ENERGE: Malabo; state-owned electricity board.

TRADE UNIONS

A law permitting the establishment of trade unions was introduced in 1992.

Transport

RAILWAYS

There are no railways in Equatorial Guinea.

ROADS

In 1996 there were an estimated 2,880 km of roads and tracks.

Bioko: a semi-circular tarred road serves the northern part of the island from Malabo down to Batete in the west and from Malabo to Bacake Grande in the east, with a feeder road from Luba to Moka and Bahía de la Concepción.

Río Muni: a tarred road links Bata with the town of Mbini (Río Benito) in the west; another road, partly tarred, links Bata with the frontier post of Ebebiyín in the east and then continues into Gabon; other earth roads join Acurenam, Mongomo and Anisok.

SHIPPING

The main ports are Bata (general cargo and most of the country's export timber), Malabo (general), Luba (bananas, timber), Mbini and Cogo (timber).

CIVIL AVIATION

There are two international airports, at Malabo (Santa Isabel Airport) and Bata (the latter was completed with Italian aid in 1995). The national carrier, EGA–Ecuato Guineana de Aviación (which has been in liquidation since 1990), continues to provide limited regional and domestic services, as well as a weekly service to Madrid. Scheduled services between Malabo and Madrid are operated by IBERIA, Líneas Aéreas de España, and Swissair is also developing an international service from Malabo. Cameroon Airlines (CAM-AIR) carries passengers between Malabo and Douala (Cameroon). Air Afrique operates a cargo service linking Equatorial Guinea with West African destinations.

EGA–Ecuato Guineana de Aviación: Apdo 665, Malabo; tel. (9) 23-25; fax (9) 33-13; regional and domestic passenger and cargo services.

Tourism

Tourism remains undeveloped. Future interest in this sector would be likely to focus on the unspoilt beaches of Río Muni and Bioko's scenic mountain terrain.

Defence

In August 1999 there were 1,100 men in the army, 120 in the navy and 100 in the air force. There was also a paramilitary force, referred to both as 'Antorchas' and 'Ninjas', which was trained by French military personnel. Military service is voluntary. Spain and Morocco have provided military advisers and training since 1979. Military aid has also been received from the USA.

Defence Expenditure: Estimated at 4,000m. francs CFA in 1999.

Supreme Commander of the Armed Forces: Gen. (TEODORO) OBIANG NGUEMA MBASOGO.

Education

Education is officially compulsory and free for five years between the ages of six and 11 years. Primary education starts at six years of age and normally lasts for five years. Secondary education, beginning at the age of 12, spans a seven-year period, comprising a first cycle of four years and a second cycle of three years. In 1982 the total enrolment at primary and secondary schools was equivalent to 81% of the school-age population. In 1993/94 primary education in nine grades was provided for 75,751 pupils in 781 schools with 1,381 teachers. More advanced education for 16,616 pupils was provided in that year, with 588 teachers. In 1990 there were 578 students in higher education, the majority enrolled at distance-learning institutions.

Since 1979, assistance in the development of the educational system has been provided by Spain. Two higher education centres, at Bata and Malabo, are administered by the Spanish Universidad Nacional de Educación a Distancia. The French government also provides considerable financial assistance. In 1995, according to UNESCO estimates, the average rate of adult illiteracy was 21.5% (males 16.9%; females 32.8%). In 1993 budgetary expenditure on education by the central government amounted to 734m. francs CFA (1.8% of total public expenditure).

Bibliography

Agencia Española de Cooperación Internacional. *Segundo plano marco de cooperación entre el Reino de España y la República de Guinea Ecuatorial.* Madrid, AECI, 1990.

Castro A., Mariano, and de la Calle Muñoz, M. L. *Geografía de Guinea Ecuatorial.* Madrid, Programa de Colaboración Educativa con Guinea Ecuatorial, 1985.

Castroviejo Bolívar, Javier, Juste Balleste, Javier, and Castelo Alvarez, Ramón. *Investigación y conservación de la naturaleza en Guinea Ecuatorial.* Madrid, Oficina de Cooperación con Guinea Ecuatorial, 1986.

Cohen, R. (Ed.). *African Islands and Enclaves.* London, Sage Publications, 1983.

Cronjé, S. *Equatorial Guinea: The Forgotten Dictatorship.* London, 1976.

Economist Intelligence Unit. *Gabon, Equatorial Guinea, Country Profile.* London, annual.

Eman, A. *Equatorial Guinea during the Macías Nguema régime.* Washington DC, 1983.

Fegley, R. *Equatorial Guinea: An African tragedy.* New York, Peter Lang, 1989.

González-Echegaray, C. *Estudios Guineos: Filología.* Madrid, IDEA, 1964.

Estudios Guineos: Etnología. Madrid, IDEA, 1964.

Jakobeit, C. 'Äquatorialguinea' in Hanisch, R. and Jakobeit, C. (Eds). *Der Kakaoweltmarkt,* Vol. 2. Hamburg, Deutsches Übersee-institut, 1991.

Klitgaard, R. *Tropical Gangsters.* London, I. B. Tauris, 1990.

Liniger-Goumaz, M. *Guinea Ecuatorial: Bibliografía General.* 5 vols. Bern and Geneva, 1976–85.

Equatorial Guinea: An African Historical Dictionary. Metuchen, NJ, Scarecrow Press, 2000.

De la Guinée équatoriale nguemiste. Eléments pour le dossier de l'afro-fascisme. Geneva, Editions du Temps, 1983.

Statistics of Nguemist Equatorial Guinea. Geneva, Editions du Temps, 1986.

Small is not always Beautiful: The Story of Equatorial Guinea. London, Hurst, 1988.

Martín de Molino, A. *Los Bubis, ritos y creencias.* Malabo, Centro Cultural Hispano-Guineano, 1989.

Miranda Díaz, M. *España en el continente africano.* Madrid, IDEA, 1963.

Ndongo Bidyogo, D. *Historia y Tragedia de Guinea Ecuatorial.* Madrid, Cambio, 1977.

Nguema-Obam, P. *Aspects de la religion fang.* Paris, Editions Karthala, 1984.

Pélissier, R. *Los Territorios Españoles de Africa.* Madrid, 1964.

Africana. Bibliographies sur l'Afrique luso-hispanophone (1800–1980). Orgeval, Editions Pélissier, 1981.

Sundiata, I. K. *Equatorial Guinea.* Boulder, CO, Westview Press, 1990.

de Unzueta y Yuste, A. *Islas del Golfo de Guinea (Elobeyes, Corisco, Annobón, Príncipe y Santo Tomé).* Madrid, Institito de Estudios Políticos, 1945.

Historia geográfica de Fernando Póo. Madrid, IDEA, 1947.

ERITREA

Physical and Social Geography

MILES SMITH-MORRIS

The State of Eritrea, which formally acceded to independence on 24 May 1993, covers an area of 121,144 sq km (46,774 sq miles). Its territory includes the Dahlak islands, a low-lying coralline archipelago offshore from Massawa. Eritrea, which has a coastline on the Red Sea extending for almost 1,000 km, is bounded to the north-west by Sudan, to the south and west by Ethiopia, and to the south-east by Djibouti. The terrain comprises the northern end of the Ethiopian plateau (rising to more than 2,000 m above sea-level), where most cultivation takes place, and a low-lying semi-desert coastal strip, much of which supports only pastoralism. Lowland areas have less than 500 mm of rainfall per year, compared with 1,000 mm in the highlands. Average annual temperatures range from 17°C in the highlands to 30°C in Massawa. The Danakil depression in the south-east descends to more than 130 m below sea-level and experiences some of the highest temperatures recorded on earth, frequently exceeding 50°C. Much of the coniferous forest that formerly covered the slopes of the highlands has been destroyed by settlement and cultivation; soil erosion is a severe problem.

The extent of Eritrea's natural resources awaits fuller exploration and evaluation. Copper ores and gold were mined from the Eritrean plateau in prehistoric times and there has been some extraction of iron ore. The Dallol depression, south of Massawa, is known to have valuable potash deposits. Some exploration for petroleum has taken place in Red Sea coastal areas; oil seepages and offshore natural gas discoveries have been reported.

The population of Eritrea was enumerated at just over 2.7m. in the Ethiopian census of 1984, but the war for independence resulted in large-scale population movements. Some 500,000 refugees fled to neighbouring Sudan and a significant, but unquantified, number of Eritreans has remained in Ethiopia. At mid-1991, according to official Ethiopian sources, the population of the Eritrean territory was estimated at 3,435,500. A total of 1.2m. people registered to vote in the April 1993 referendum, 860,000 of them within Eritrea, leading to estimates of a domestic population of about 2m. At mid-1998, according to UN estimates, Eritrea's population totalled 3,577,000. The population is fairly evenly divided between Tigrinya-speaking Christians, the traditional inhabitants of the highlands, and the Muslim communities of the western lowlands, northern highlands and east coast.

Recent History

ALAN RAKE

Modern Eritrea dates from the establishment of an Italian colony at the end of the 19th century. From a small concession gained near Assab in 1869, the Italians extended their control to Massawa in 1885 and to most of Eritrea by 1889. In the same year the Ethiopian emperor, Menelik, and the Italian government signed the Treaty of Uccialli, which effectively recognized Italian control over Eritrea (and from which Italy derived its subsequent claim to a protectorate over Ethiopia). The period of Italian rule (1889–1941) and the subsequent years under British military administration (1941–52) created a society, economy and polity more advanced than in the semi-feudal Ethiopian empire. Following the Second World War, Ethiopia, which historically regarded Eritrea as an integral part of its territory, intensified its claims to sovereignty. The strategic interests of the USA and its influence in the newly-founded UN resulted in a compromise, in the form of a federation between Eritrea and Ethiopia. No federal institutions were established, and Eritrean autonomy was systematically stifled. In 1962 Eritrea was reconstituted as a province of Ethiopia.

THE LIBERATION STRUGGLE

The dissolution of the federation brought forth a more militant Eritrean nationalism, whose political roots had been established during the process of consultation for the disposal of the Italian colony in the latter part of the period of British rule. The Eritrean Liberation Movement, founded in 1958, was succeeded by the Eritrean Liberation Front (ELF), which began an armed struggle in 1961. Organizational and ideological differences erupted into violence within the ELF in the mid-1960s, as the result of demands for reform from the increasing numbers of educated guerrilla fighters, particularly those from the Christian highlands and the Muslim eastern lowland towns. A reformist group separated from the ELF and formed the Popular Liberation Forces (renamed the Eritrean People's Liberation Front, EPLF, in 1977). A major consequence of the split was the civil war of 1972–74. Some reformists remained within the ELF, although most of these eventually left in two stages, the first group breaking away in 1977–78 and the second (the Sagem group joining the EPLF) in 1985, following a second civil war. These desertions destroyed the ELF as a coherent military organization, although a number of disaffected factions remained loyal to it and suspicious of the EPLF. The most influential groups remaining outside the EPLF have been those associated with Ahmed Nasser, leader of the ELF–Revolutionary Council (ELF–RC), and an Islamic movement which emerged during the 1980s among refugees in Sudan. The EPLF leadership consolidated a highly centralized and disciplined political and military organization, in contrast to the more loosely organized and factionalized ELF.

The 1974 revolution in Ethiopia and its violent aftermath brought thousands of new recruits into the resistance groups. Even greater numbers of recruits joined the EPLF after the Mengistu regime launched its 'red terror' campaign in Asmara, and following its capture of smaller cities such as Keren and Decamhare in 1977. The retreat from the cities and liberated highland areas in 1978 brought with it thousands of young peasants, both male and female. From 1978 the EPLF consolidated the defence of its base area in the north. Through the 1980s the EPLF pushed back the Ethiopian forces on all fronts, capturing large quantities of heavy artillery and tanks, and transforming itself from a guerrilla force into a regular army. Ethiopian defeats gave the EPLF control of the north, the west (formerly the ELF's heartland) and, finally, the east coast with the capture of Massawa port in 1990. The EPLF broke through the Decamhare front in May 1991 and entered Asmara, the capital. The retreating Ethiopian forces left the city largely undamaged. The discipline of the Eritrean People's Liberation Army (EPLA) and the extensive network of secret cells in the capital helped to ensure a smooth transition from liberation movement to government.

Concurrent with the liberation of Asmara in 1991 was the London Conference under the chairmanship of the US assistant secretary of state for Africa. Representatives of the EPLF attended in a delegation separate from the Ethiopian People's Revolutionary Democratic Front, now in control of Ethiopia and sympathetic to Eritrean nationalist aspirations. Both the USA and the Ethiopian delegation accepted the EPLF as the provisional government, and the latter agreed to hold a referendum on independence in 1993. Ethiopian assent to this process played an important role in the international legitimation of Eritrea's path to independence. In advance of the referendum, the EPLF formed a government and established ministries, most of whose key personnel were drawn from the EPLF. Although the international and regional political context was favourable for the transition to independence, the international economic context, prolonged warfare, drought and the legacy of neglect and destruction left by the Ethiopian forces placed the new government in straitened circumstances; 80% of the population were still dependent on food aid and urban economic activity had virtually ceased. Over and above these domestic problems was the task of attracting back and reintegrating around 750,000 refugees. Of these, some 500,000 were in Sudan, 90% of whom would require extensive financial assistance to return. An additional legacy of war was the scale of fatalities, which were estimated at 60,000–75,000.

In the absence of any significant sources of domestic revenue for reconstruction, the task of rebuilding fell largely on the 75,000-strong EPLA, the members of which received a small stipend for their work. Administrative and technical cadres took government positions, skilled fighter-workers were used to reconstruct manufacturing industry and many ordinary fighters were drafted to undertake the arduous work of road and other infrastructural repair. Finance for reconstruction came largely from contributions by Eritreans abroad and from assistance by foreign governments and non-governmental organizations. Without full legal sovereignty, access to loans and assistance from international financial institutions was limited, but in 1993 this formal constraint was removed. In April a UN-supervised referendum took place in an atmosphere of national celebration. Of the 1,102,410 Eritreans who voted, 99.8% endorsed national independence. The anniversary of the liberation of Asmara, 24 May, was proclaimed Independence Day, and on 28 May the State of Eritrea formally attained international recognition.

INDEPENDENCE AND TRANSITIONAL GOVERNMENT

Following Eritrea's accession to independence, a four-year transitional period was declared, during which preparations were to proceed for establishing a constitutional and pluralist political system. At the apex of the transitional government were three state institutions: the consultative council (the executive authority formed from the ministers, provincial governors and heads of government commissions); the national assembly (the legislative authority formed from the central committee of the EPLF, together with 30 members from the provincial assemblies and 30 members appointed by the central committee); and the judiciary. One of the national assembly's first acts was the election of a head of state. To little surprise, Issaias Afewerki, the secretary-general of the EPLF, was elected, by a margin of 99 votes to five.

Internal Politics

President Afewerki appointed a new consultative council in June 1993, comprising 14 ministers (all members of the EPLF politburo) and 10 regional governors. Ramadan Muhammad Nur was removed from the politically sensitive post of governor of Danakil province (where he had successfully contained Afar nationalism) and was appointed minister of local government. Another prominent EPLF member, Petros Solomon, was allocated the defence portfolio. The third congress of the EPLF was convened at Nakfa, in Sahel province, in February 1994. There the EPLF effected the formal transformation from a military front to a national movement for peace and democracy (the People's Front for Democracy and Justice, PFDJ), hoping to embrace all Eritreans (except those accused of collaboration during the liberation struggle). The party congress also confirmed its support for a plural political system which was to be

included in the final draft of a new constitution, which (together with legislation to regulate the formation of political parties) was to be submitted for approval by a national referendum. Afewerki was elected chairman of an 18-member executive committee (while remaining head of state, and leader of the PFDJ). A 75-member PFDJ central committee was elected (an additional 75 members were to be elected by PFDJ regional committees).

In March 1994 the national assembly adopted a series of resolutions whereby the former executive body, the consultative council, was formally superseded by a state council. Other measures adopted by resolutions of the assembly included the creation of a 50-member constitutional commission, and the establishment of a committee charged with the reorganization of the country's administrative divisions. It was decided that the national assembly would henceforth comprise 75 members of the PFDJ central committee, and 75 directly elected members. However, no mechanism was announced for their election. All but eight of the 50-member constitutional commission were government appointees, and there was no provision for any opposition participation in the interim system. Later in the month Afewerki carried out a ministerial reshuffle, which was widely interpreted as an attempt to formalize a separation of the functions of the government and the PFDJ executive. Ramadan Muhammad Nur left the government, together with Amin Muhammad Sa'id, the minister of information and culture, following his nomination as secretary-general of the PFDJ. One of the first actions of the new state council was to draft legislation governing investment, which aimed to achieve a significant liberalization of trade.

International conferences on the draft constitution were held in the capital in July 1994 and in January 1995. The symposia were presided over by Dr Berekhet Habteselassie, the chairman of the draft constitutional commission. Many foreign constitutional experts were invited to attend and discuss the draft document, and there was extensive popular consultation, with more than 1,000 meetings throughout the country, attended by some 500,000 Eritreans. However, no opposition parties or opponents of the regime were invited to contribute. A third stage of consultation began in October 1995, when former soldiers of the EPLF armed forces were invited to discuss the draft law.

In April 1995 the minister of defence, Mesfin Hagos, was replaced by Sebhat Ephrem, previously the minister of health. Reports suggested that Hagos had been demoted because his popularity with the armed forces posed a threat to Afewerki, with whom he had recently contested a number of sensitive issues. In May Afewerki announced that the 30,000-strong civil service was to be reduced by one-third. All ministries (with the exceptions of interior and defence) would be subject to the rationalization programme, and 6,500 civil servants who had not been combatant members of the EPLF were made redundant immediately. In the same month the national assembly approved a law reducing the previous 10 administrative regions to six, each with regional, sub-regional and village administrations. In November the assembly approved new names for the regions, unrelated to the ethnic groups which inhabit them, and finalized details of their exact boundaries and sub-divisions.

The Eritrean Orthodox Church was a notable casualty of the Ethiopian occupation of the country at the time of the liberation war. Several monasteries were occupied by Ethiopian soldiers and many of the religious instructors and their students were killed. Much church land was confiscated and was never returned by the Ethiopian government. The current Eritrean government, in an attempt to raise revenue, sought to sell the land back to the church at arbitrary prices. These events provoked considerable dissatisfaction within the church, and a movement promoting secession from the Ethiopian church gained widespread support. In June 1994 Eritrea sent five abbots from Eritrean monasteries to the headquarters of the Coptic church in Cairo, where they were inducted as bishops by Shenouda III, the Coptic Orthodox pontiff. In September the first bishops of the Eritrean Orthodox Church were consecrated at a ceremony conducted in Cairo. These consecrations signified the formal separation of the Eritrean Orthodox Church from the Ethiopian Orthodox Church as an independent body. In May 1998 Archbishop Philippos was installed as the first Eritrean patriarch by Shenouda III in Asmara.

Since the establishment of the EPLF government, an effective ban on other political groups had been in effect. The ELF opposition claimed that many political prisoners remained incarcerated in a number of provincial towns. In April 1994 26 members of the ELF–RC faction were detained in Ethiopia; other ELF–RC members were reported to have been forcibly repatriated to Eritrea. Meanwhile, the country's Jehovah's Witnesses encountered alleged discrimination as a result of their refusal to recognize the state of Eritrea. Jehovah's Witnesses had elected not to fight in the war of secession, vote in the 1993 referendum, or fulfil military service obligations. Consequently they were denied Eritrean citizenship and some were reported to have been evicted from state-owned housing.

Major demobilization of freedom fighters began following the 1993 referendum, and in May 1994 compulsory military service was introduced to compensate for the contraction of the armed forces. All Eritreans between 18 and 40 years of age (with certain exceptions) were obliged to undertake six months' military training and 12 months' service; about 250,000 young men were due to be trained in the following five years. Some observers suggested that government strategy was to reduce the power of troublesome veteran freedom fighters, while introducing a malleable younger element into the armed forces. High-ranking officers were also reorganized, with the aim of removing political agitators and those who were not members of the PFDJ from the armed forces. In July disillusioned war veterans took hostage the director of the rehabilitation centre at Mai Habar and demanded to meet the president to discuss the meagre rehabilitation benefits. Moreover, in December fighting erupted when government officials attempted to take by force hundreds of Eritreans (recently deported to Massawa from Saudi Arabia) to the military training camp at Sawa in order to undertake national service. In July 1995 further clashes were reported between government troops and groups of young men refusing to report for national service. By mid-1995 the membership of the armed forces had been reduced from 95,000 to 55,000, and plans were in place for a further cut of 20,000 men. The USA reportedly pledged funds and training for Eritrea's military after Afewerki's visit to the USA in January 1995. By mid-1995 there were 30 US military advisers present in Keren. In April 1996 ranks were introduced into the armed forces for the first time. Several senior officers were promoted to the rank of general, including the minister of defence, Sebhat Ephrem.

December 1996 was marked by a number of assassinations, including the former commanding officer of the ELF, Abubekar Al-Hussein, and a recently-promoted colonel. Meanwhile, numerous people were wounded in a bomb attack in Habero. A former military commander of the radical religious opposition group, the Eritrean Islamic Jihad (EIJ), was also killed in December. The government blamed most of these incidents on the EIJ, although some analysts suggested that they were perpetrated by pro-government elements involved in internal disputes. Others linked the killings to an anti-corruption investigation which started in December. During the investigation PFDJ members responsible for the party's Red Sea Trading Corpn were found guilty (by a closed tribunal) of involvement in a smuggling operation with customs officials and sentenced to lengthy terms of imprisonment.

In early 1997 a constituent assembly was established to discuss and ratify the draft constitution. The constituent assembly comprised 527 members, of whom 150 were from the national assembly, and the remainder were selected from representatives of Eritreans residing abroad or elected by regional assemblies (adhering to a 30% quota for women). On 23 May the constituent assembly unanimously adopted the constitution, instituting a presidential regime, with a president elected for a maximum of two five-year terms. According to the constitution, the president, as head of state, was empowered to appoint, with the approval of the national assembly, the ministers, the commissioners, the auditor-general, the president of the central bank and judges of the supreme court. The president's mandate could be revoked should two-thirds of the members of the national assembly so demand. 'Conditional' political pluralism was authorized. Following the adoption of the constitution, the constituent assembly was disbanded, having empowered a transitional national assembly (comprising the 75 members of the PFDJ, 60 members of the constituent assembly

and 15 representatives of Eritreans residing abroad) to act as the legislative body until the holding of national elections. Meanwhile, in February 1997 President Afewerki carried out a discreet but extensive cabinet reshuffle. Plans to hold legislative elections during 1993 were postponed indefinitely following the outbreak of hostilities with Ethiopia (see below).

Opposition to the Eritrean government continued in the late 1990s, primarily from disaffected nationals residing abroad. In November 1997 reports emerged of the existence of a clandestine radio station, 'The Voice of Free Eritrea', apparently broadcasting from Sudan, both in Arabic and in English. It claimed to represent the Eritrean National Alliance, a group of Eritrean opposition organizations formed in Khartoum in late 1996.

Regional Concerns

Eritrea gradually increased its international contacts during 1993. Diplomatic ties were established with Sudan, Ethiopia, Israel, Australia and Pakistan, and several international organizations, shortly after independence. In July Eritrea and Ethiopia signed an agreement for the joint use of the ports of Assab and Massawa, while in August it was reported that 90,000 Ethiopian prisoners of war had been released by the Eritrean government. In September the first meeting of the Ethiopian-Eritrean joint ministerial commission was held in Asmara, during which agreement was reached on measures to allow the free movement of nationals between each country, and on cooperation regarding foreign affairs and economic policy. However, cordial relations with several Arab states deteriorated following the publication and dissemination of articles critical of the Afewerki administration by the militant EIJ based in Sudan.

Relations between the transitional government and Sudan, which had supported the EPLF during the war, deteriorated in December 1993, following an incursion by members of the EIJ from Sudan. In a clash with Eritrean forces, all the members of the group, and an Eritrean commander, were killed. In response to the incident, President Afewerki stressed the links between the EIJ and the Sudanese National Islamic Front, led by Dr Hassan at-Turabi, implying that the latter had prior knowledge of the incursion. However, following a swift denial by the Sudanese government that it would ever interfere in the affairs of neighbouring states, Afewerki reaffirmed his support for the Sudanese authorities and his commitment to improving bilateral relations.

In August 1994 Eritrea and Sudan signed an agreement concerning borders, security and the repatriation of refugees, and in November the office of the UN High Commissioner for Refugees (UNHCR) initiated a repatriation programme for Eritrean refugees currently in Sudan. Some 500,000 Eritreans had taken refuge in Sudan in the early 1990s as a result of separatist conflicts, although by 1995 an estimated 125,000 had returned spontaneously, particularly following Eritrea's accession to independence. Owing to delays in the implementation of the UNHCR programme, an estimated 342,300 Eritrean refugees remained in Sudan in late 1998. It was estimated that, as a result of the conflict between Ethiopia and Eritrea in 2000 (see below), a further 90,000 Eritreans had sought refuge in Sudan during May–June. In July, however, following the cessation of hostilities, the UNHCR began operations to repatriate tens of thousands of Eritrean refugees.

Relations between Eritrea and Sudan deteriorated in late 1994, when the Eritrean authorities accused Sudan of training 400 terrorists. Sudan accused Eritrea of training some 3,000 Sudanese rebels in camps within Eritrea. In December Eritrea severed diplomatic relations with Sudan. Further destabilization followed in early 1995 after attacks and infiltration in Barka Province by commandos of the military wing of the EIJ. The insurgents deployed land-mines on border roads, and a number of schools, dispensaries and buses were destroyed. The Eritrean authorities subsequently identified six alleged terrorist training camps on the Sudanese side of the border, and also claimed that large numbers of Eritrean refugees in Sudan had been arrested by Sudanese security forces. Sudan responded by proposing Eritrea's suspension from the Intergovernmental Authority on Drought and Development (IGADD, now the Intergovernmental Authority on Development–IGAD), which had been attempting to mediate in Sudan's civil war. The Sudanese government strongly criticized Eritrea for hosting a series of conferences in Asmara for Sudan's opposition grouping, the National Democratic Alliance (NDA), in December 1994, June 1995 and January 1996. The Sudanese minister of foreign affairs complained that Eritrea was deliberately encouraging military activity against Sudan. In February 1996 the Eritrean government granted Sudanese opposition leaders permission to use Sudan's embassy in Asmara as their headquarters; limited radio transmissions to Sudan were also allowed. Several attacks on government vehicles in Eritrea in April were claimed by the EIJ.

Relations with Sudan remained hostile throughout 1996. In July the Eritrean authorities denied reports in the Sudanese media that its troops had attacked Sudanese forces across the border. The Sudanese government was becoming increasingly convinced that Eritrea, Ethiopia, Uganda and Kenya formed part of a US-backed anti-Sudanese alliance. This was of considerable concern to Eritrean Muslims who constituted approximately one-half of the country's population.

In January 1997 the NDA launched an attack from Eritrea on Sudanese forces in the border region, resulting in numerous casualties. Sudan, however, blamed the incident on Eritrea's armed forces. Meanwhile, Eritrea claimed that the EIJ was training more than 4,000 Eritrean Muslims in Sudan to launch attacks against the Eritrean authorities from Sudanese bases in Eritrea. In June Eritrea's minister of foreign affairs, Haile Woldetensae, announced that in May the security forces had thwarted a plot by the Sudanese government to assassinate Afewerki. This prompted further clashes between Eritrean and Sudanese forces on the frontier during July; Eritrean recruits were sent to reinforce units of the NDA based in the border area. In August there were reports that Sudanese military aircraft had repeatedly crossed into Eritrean airspace, dropping bombs around Karora. In February 1998 the Sudanese government closed the border with Eritrea to prevent infiltration by anti-government forces into Sudan. The Eritrean authorities denied reports of infiltration and clashes along the border.

Sudan took advantage of the ongoing war between Ethiopia and Eritrea (see below) by resolving its differences with Ethiopia further and discomfiting Eritrea. In March 1999 the Alliance of Eritrean National Forces (AENF) was launched in Khartoum, by 10 Eritrean opposition organizations. It was led by Abdallah Idriss, the chairman of an ELF faction, who had consistently opposed the Afewerki government from exile. The AENF declared that it would establish a government in exile and commence negotiations over the border dispute with Ethiopia. But the AENF, composed of conflicting religious and ethnic factions, was accused of largely being a creation of Sudan and Ethiopia. By mid-year Sudan indicated its willingness to improve its relations with Eritrea too. In May President Afewerki and his Sudanese counterpart signed a reconciliation agreement in Qatar, which, *inter alia*, would restore diplomatic relations. In June Sudan accused Eritrea of violating the agreement by allowing a Sudanese opposition group to hold a rally in Asmara. However, following President Afewerki's decision to order Sudanese anti-government activists occupying the Sudanese embassy building to vacate the premises and cease political activities, relations between the two countries quickly improved. In January 2000 Eritrea handed back the Sudanese embassy building to the Sudanese authorities and the embassies in Asmara and Khartoum were subsequently reopened. Furthermore, Eritrea's minister of foreign affairs pledged that no military or hostile acts would be launched from Eritea into Sudan and concurrently oversaw the reopening of the common border. Just days later the Sudanese president, Lt-Gen. Omar Hassan Ahmad al-Bashir, made an unplanned visit to Asmara, where he met President Afewerki.

In November 1995 Eritrea's minister of foreign affairs, Petros Solomon, held talks with President Gouled in Djibouti. As a result, both countries pledged to enhance bilateral co-operation. Allegations made in a Yemeni newspaper in December that Eritrean troops had made an incursion into north-east Djibouti were vehemently denied by Eritrea. In April 1996 Gouled reportedly rejected a map (produced in Italy in 1935) submitted by Solomon, which apparently indicated that a 20-km strip of land currently claimed by Djibouti was, in fact, Eritrean territory. Concurrently, reports emerged of the attempted occupation of a border post in Djibouti (within the disputed territory) by Eritrean troops. Relations between the two countries subse-

quently improved; however, in November 1998 Djibouti suspended diplomatic relations with Eritrea, following allegations by the Eritrean authorities that it was supporting Ethiopia in the Eritrea–Ethiopia border conflict. In March 2000 Djibouti announced that it had resumed diplomatic relations with Eritrea.

In early May 1994, following a three-day official visit to France (the first such visit undertaken to a Western nation since independence), President Afewerki announced that substantial financial commitments had been secured from the French government for the rehabilitation of the airport and the water-supply system in Asmara.

In November 1996 a Chinese military delegation visited Asmara, indicating China's support for Eritrea's policy in the region. In December 1997 the US department of defense financed two projects associated with Massawa port, justifying the expenditure by arguing that future military manoeuvres in the area around the Red Sea would involve US forces. There were also reports that the USA was considering transferring its military base from Saudi Arabia to Eritrea. A US airbase had existed at Kagnew some 30 years earlier. In February 1998 Eritrea established diplomatic relations with Libya, following a visit to that country by President Afewerki. The Eritrean embassy in the Libyan capital, Tripoli, was duly opened in July 1999, and Libya played an important mediatory role between Djibouti and Eritrea prior to those countries' re-establishing diplomatic relations in March 2000.

Dispute over Hanish Islands

In November 1995 there were reports that Eritrean troops had attempted to land on the Red Sea island of Greater Hanish, one of three islands (the others being Lesser Hanish and Zuqar) claimed by both Eritrea and Yemen. The invasion attempt had reportedly been prompted by Yemen's announced intention to develop Greater Hanish as a tourist resort, and its subsequent refusal to comply with an Eritrean demand that the island be evacuated. The disputed islands had been used by Eritrea (with apparent Yemeni approval) during its struggle for independence from Ethiopia. Yemen subsequently resumed its claims to the islands, because of both their strategic importance (located close to a principal shipping lane) and the possibility of discovering lucrative petroleum reserves in their surrounding waters. Negotiations in Eritrea and Yemen failed to defuse the crisis, and in mid-December fighting erupted between the two sides, resulting in the deaths of six Eritrean and three Yemeni soldiers. Two days later Eritrea and Yemen agreed to a cease-fire, but fighting resumed on the following day, and Eritrean forces succeeded in occupying Greater Hanish. The cease-fire was adhered to thenceforth, and some 180 captured Yemeni soldiers were released at the end of the month. The Ethiopian and Egyptian governments attempted, unsuccessfully, to broker an agreement, and in January 1996 France assumed the mediatory role. In May representatives of Eritrea and Yemen signed an arbitration accord in Paris, France, whereby the two sides agreed to submit the dispute to an international tribunal. France subsequently undertook to observe and supervise military movements in the area around the disputed islands. In August, despite the accord, Eritrean troops occupied Lesser Hanish; however, later in the month Eritrea withdrew its soldiers after mediation by France and a UN Security Council edict to evacuate the island forthwith. In October Eritrea and Yemen confirmed that they would submit the dispute to an international tribunal. A five judge arbitration court was established in the United Kingdom and started work in April 1997. In October 1998 the tribunal ruled that the Hanish islands belonged to Yemen and had been illegally occupied by Eritrea. Both countries accepted the ruling, and shortly afterwards they agreed to establish a joint committee to strengthen bilateral co-operation. Some observers suggested that Eritrea did not contest the ruling because it had to concentrate on the far more serious conflict that had developed with Ethiopia. In March Eritrea and Yemen had exchanged ambassadors. In December 1999 the Hanish arbitration tribunal announced that Eritrean fishermen would still be permitted to engage in artisanal fishing around the Hanish islands.

Conflict with Ethiopia

Relations with Ethiopia deteriorated in late 1997 as disagreements arose following Eritrea's introduction of a new currency, the nakfa (see Economy). In late December there was a military confrontation around an Eritrean army post on the frontier in northern Dankalia, an area where Ethiopian rebels were reported to be operating. Several thousand Eritreans who had settled in western Tigrai were told to leave the region or adopt Ethiopian nationality. In May 1998 fighting erupted between Eritrean and Ethiopian troops in the border region after both countries accused the other of having invaded their territory. As many as 100 people were killed around the towns of Badme and Sheraro. Although the two countries had established a joint committee in 1993 to examine the border issue, the conflict erupted before any progress had been made. President Afewerki claimed that Ethiopia had been building up troop strength, continuously establishing new border posts and harassing Eritreans living in the area. Both sides subsequently reinforced their troops on the border, digging trenches and building defences.

President Gouled of Djibouti and Susan Rice, the US assistant secretary of state for Africa, attempted, unsuccessfully, to defuse the conflict. Other mediation efforts were made by Libya, Kenya and the Organization of African Unity (OAU), but the main initiative was devised by the USA and Rwanda. They drafted a peace plan which depended on both sides withdrawing from the land occupied since hostilities began in May 1998. Ethiopia broadly accepted the plan but Eritrea refused to withdraw its troops and the initiative collapsed. Both sides reinforced their troops during June and fighting broke out at Zelambessa, near Adigrat, and at Biru on the road to Assab. Regular artillery bombardments and aerial bombing raids were carried out, resulting in numerous Eritrean and Ethiopian casualties. Flights between the two countries were cancelled and Ethiopia boycotted the ports of Assab and Massawa, rerouting trade through Djibouti port. In mid-June Eritrea and Ethiopia accepted a US proposal for an aerial cease-fire, but a UN Security Council resolution passed later that month, demanding the immediate cessation of hostilities, was not adhered to. Meanwhile, there were mutual recriminations concerning the alleged widespread arrest of Eritreans in Ethiopia and of Ethiopians residing in Eritrea.

During the uneasy lull which followed the initial battles in May 1998, both sides raced to increase their military capabilities. Despite an appeal by the UN for an arms embargo, Russia supplied Eritrea with five MiG-29 fighters, four Mi-17 helicopters, one MiG-29 UB training aircraft and 200 Igla transportable surface-to-air missiles; it also provided Ethiopia with Sukhoi-27 fighter aircraft, Mi-24 helicopter gunships and Mi-8 cargo helicopters. Eritrea was reported to have spent US $90m. in 1998 on Russian armaments, plus $150m. on weapons from other East European countries including Bulgaria, Poland and Romania. Ethiopia's arms purchases were reported to be at least twice as much. By the end of 1999 it was estimated that Ethiopia's army numbered 320,000 (including 100,000 untrained volunteers) and that of Eritrea totalled 270,000 (including 80,000 national servicemen).

By mid-1998 the OAU had become the most important mediator in the conflict. Anthony Lake, a former US national security adviser, also made a series of visits to both countries, but made little progress. Eritrea insisted on bilateral demilitarization and technical demarcation of the borders, while Ethiopia demanded Eritrean withdrawal form the disputed area before negotiation. However, the two sides agreed not to resume fighting until the OAU mediation was completed.

In December 1998 the OAU proposed a peace plan that included an immediate cease-fire, no further aerial bombardments, demarcation and demilitarization of the border area, and the deployment of an international peace-keeping force. All these points were accepted by both parties, but Eritrea refused to withdraw from the disputed Badme area, arguing that it was Eritrean land, populated by ethnic Eritreans, and that there was no reason to withdraw while negotiations continued.

The war of words over the peace proposals ended in early February 1999 when Ethiopia claimed that Eritrea had bombed the town of Adigrat, contravening the aerial embargo. The newly equipped Ethiopian army launched a series of attacks on Eritrean positions at Badme, Zelambessa and Bure, on the road to the port of Assab. The scale of the conflict was without parallel in Africa. Hundreds of thousands of troops were involved in the fighting; both sides were exceptionally well-armed with modern weapons. Infantry advanced under the cover of tanks in the teeth of heavy artillery across minefields and deep entrenchments. Independent observers estimated that up to 30,000 men were killed. Foreign correspondents taken to the central front at Tsorona counted 300 Ethiopian bodies in one small area where Ethiopian footsoldiers had advanced behind tanks.

Ethiopia's 'Operation Sunset' was a Pyrrhic victory, but its troops advanced several miles into Eritrean territory, occupying 120 miles in the Badme area. Eritrea claimed to have destroyed 25 Ethiopian tanks before their troops made an orderly withdrawal. Ethiopia may have exaggerated its victory, but Eritrea hastily agreed to accept the OAU peace plan in full, including the withdrawal from the disputed territories. As Eritrea accepted the OAU proposals, Ethiopia continued its advance, repeatedly resorting to aerial and artillery bombardments. In March 1999, as Ethiopian troops attempted to push forward, Eritrea claimed to have destroyed a further 57 tanks.

In April 1999 the fighting diminished significantly, with both sides saying they were prepared to implement the OAU peace plan but accusing the other of violating its conditions. In May Ethiopia carried out aerial bombardments along the front line, striking fuel depots and the port of Massawa. Ethiopia mounted another major three-day battle at the end of May on the Mereb-Setit front, roughly in the centre of the heavily mined front line. The outcome was inconclusive, with thousands of casualties on both sides. In June 1999 fighting once again broke out between the two countries along the common border. Eritrea failed in its attempt to recapture Badme and sustained heavy losses in the process. Despite the claims of both sides that they were prepared to accept and implement the OAU peace proposals, fighting continued.

The war was a major issue at the OAU heads of state summit held in Algiers in July 1999 where, following mediatory talks, both sides confirmed their commitment to the OAU's framework agreement. President Afewerki announced that Eritrean troops would be withdrawn from all territory captured from Ethiopia since 6 May 1998. Under the terms of the agreement Ethiopia was also required to withdraw from all Eritrean territory captured since 6 February 1999, which, in effect, would see both sides return to their pre-war positions. The UN subsequently announced that it would demarcate the border using colonial maps originally drawn up by Italy. Afewerki accepted these technical agreements in August and stated that the prospects for peace were better than at any time over the preceding 18 months. However, Eritrea subsequently accused Ethiopia of attempting to stall proceedings after Ethiopia requested clarification of the technical arrangements to end the conflict. In September Ethiopia informed the OAU that it had rejected the peace agreement, owing to inconsistencies contained therein. The national radio stations of Eritrea and Ethiopia both accused their counterparts of using the dispute as a pretext to rearm, and arms and military material continued to arrive in both countries in large quantities; it was reported in late 1999 that both countries were spending at least US $1m. per day on the war.

There were reports of numerous clashes between Eritrean and Ethiopian troops throughout late 1999 and early 2000. Furthermore, both countries continued to promote and assist opposition groups hostile to their foe. Ethiopia encouraged the AENF to operate from its territory, while Eritrea, in turn, supplied arms to anti-Ethiopian groups, including the Oromo Liberation Front (OLF) and the Ogaden National Liberation Front (ONLF). In late February 2000 Lake and Ahmed Ouyahia, the prime minister of Algeria and the OAU's special envoy, began their visits to Asmara and Addis Ababa with the aim of persuading the two countries to accept the OAU's peace proposals. Despite the fact that no agreement was reached, the OAU claimed that significant progress had been made. In March the Eritrean government agreed to allow the port of Assab to be used for the transport of huge quantities of food aid destined for Ethiopia. Once again severe drought in the Horn of Africa meant that millions of Ethiopians were threatened with starvation. Despite the ongoing war between the two countries, President Afewerki agreed to requests from the USA to establish a food corridor from the coastal port to Ethiopia; however, reports published in the Ethiopian press suggested that this offer had been rejected by the Ethiopian government. In late April 2000 delegations from Ethiopia and Eritrea agreed to attend OAU-sponsored talks in Algiers, although neither side would agree to meet face to face. Instead, Algerian diplomats acted as mediators between the two sides. The talks collapsed after six days with the Ethiopians blaming the Eritreans for the lack of progress and vice versa.

In mid-May 2000, just days after the UN special envoy Richard Holbrooke had visited the two countries and warned that a resumption of hostilities and the outbreak of a new round of fighting was very close, Ethiopia launched an offensive on the Mereb-Setit front near the disputed towns of Badme and Zelambessa and succeeded in repulsing the Eritrean forces. The UN Security Council immediately adopted a resolution, which provided for the imposition of sanctions and an embargo on the sale of all military supplies to the two warring countries if hostilities did not cease within three days. Meanwhile, it was reported that eight Eritrean divisions had been destroyed, and Eritrea claimed to have killed some 25,000 Ethiopian troops in the first few days of fighting. Hostilities continued despite growing fears of a mounting humanitarian crisis. It was estimated that between 500,000 and 1m. Eritreans had fled as the conflict spread into Eritrea, with many seeking refuge in Sudan. The crisis was exacerbated by the ongoing drought and shortage of food, with about 850,000 Eritreans and an estimated 8m. Ethiopians in need of emergency assistance. The UN Security Council subsequently voted unanimously to impose a 12-month arms embargo on the two countries in an attempt to prevent any further intensification of hostilities; however, hours after this announcement Ethiopia declared that it had captured the key strategic town of Barentu, in south-west Eritrea, and had taken full control of the western front. As Ethiopian forces continued to drive deeper into Eritrean territory and Ethiopian military aircraft carried out bombing raids on strategic positions in Eritrea, foreign diplomats and other expatriates were urged to leave the country. Ethiopia launched a massive new offensive, which led to the capture of Zelambessa, and on 25 May the Eritrean government announced that it would withdraw troops from the disputed areas, although Afewerki refused to acknow-

ledge defeat and stated that this was a 'gesture of goodwill' designed to revive the peace talks. He claimed that the decision to withdraw troops from the area was a response to the plea by the OAU that the two countries redeploy their troops and de-escalate the conflict. Nevertheless, fighting continued in several areas, despite announcements emanating from the Ethiopian government that it had no designs on Eritrean territory.

Ethiopian forces continued to capture Eritrean towns over the following days, although both sides had by this stage agreed to attend peace talks under the auspices of the OAU, which began on 29 May 2000 in Algiers. This, however, did not prevent Ethiopian aircraft from bombing the military airfield in Asmara in late May, which the Eritrean government claimed made 'a mockery' of the peace talks and prompted it to appeal for urgent international intervention. On 31 May the prime minister of Ethiopia, Meles Zenawi, announced that the war with Eritrea was over and that his troops had withdrawn from most of the territory that they had captured from Eritrea. Nevertheless, fighting continued to take place whilst discussions were ongoing in Algiers, with each side accusing the other of resuming hostilities. Eritrea accused Ethiopia of launching a huge attack on the Red Sea port of Assab; however, this claim was denied by the Ethiopian authorities. As fighting continued into mid-June, following extensive negotiations, both sides expressed their readiness, in principle, to accept the OAU's cease-fire agreement. On 18 June the ministers of foreign affairs from the two countries signed a peace agreement, which provided for an immediate cease-fire and the deployment of a UN peace-keeping force in a 24-km buffer zone inside Eritrea until the disputed 966-km border had been demarcated. In early July delegations from both Eritrea and Ethiopia attended a meeting in Washington, DC, USA, at which experts from the two countries and from international organizations discussed outstanding technical issues, including the demarcation of the border and compensation for damages incurred during the conflict, in the course of which it was estimated that some 100,000 people had been killed and more than 1m. people had been displaced. In mid-September the UN Security Council approved the deployment of a 4,200-strong UN Mission in Ethiopia and Eritrea (UNMEE) peace-keeping force on the Eritrean side of the common border. UNMEE was given an initial mandate of six months and was charged with monitoring and ensuring that both Eritrea and Ethiopia comply with their agreement on the cessation of hostilities, including the redeployment of their respective forces to agreed positions.

Economy

ALAN RAKE

Revised for this edition by DAVID STYAN

Statistics on Eritrea's economy improved markedly in the late 1990s. The IMF estimated Eritrea's GDP at factor cost in 1999 at 5,321m. nakfa. With a substantial proportion of Eritreans living outside the country, many in Europe and the Gulf states, remittances play a key role in the economy. Domestic and IMF figures indicated an inflow of private remittances of almost US $200m. in 1999. With net factor payments estimated at one-half of this sum, and indirect taxes of 508m. nakfa, total GNP at current market prices in 1999 was estimated at 6,817m. nakfa. The same figures suggest that real GDP growth averaged 3.5% during both 1998 and 1999. However, the previously weak statistical base and the substantial economic dislocation, due to the Ethio-Eritrean war in the two years to May 2000, mean these figures should be treated with caution. In particular, the sharp increases in military expenditure, coupled with enforced mobilization of diaspora communities, have further heightened the role of remittances. The long-term consequences of the rupture of trade ties with Ethiopia, hitherto Eritrea's principal trading partner, in mid-1998 further confuse the economic outlook. Assuming the June 2000 peace settlement holds, substantial additional funds will be required both for reconstruction

and for immedite humanitarian assistance, as at least 30% of the population has been displaced by fighting.

AGRICULTURE

By far the most important sector of the economy is agriculture, which, despite a reduction in food production of roughly 40% over the period 1980–90, still sustains 90% of the population. In 1999 agricultural production (including forestry and fishing) accounted for an estimated 16.0% of GDP. The sector employs an estimated 75% of the working population. Most sedentary agriculture is practised in the highlands, where rainfall is sufficient to cultivate the main crops: teff (an indigenous grain), sorghum, millet, barley and wheat. In 1992, which was described as a satisfactory year in agricultural terms, some 315,000 ha of land were cultivated, and the harvest was good enough to satisfy an estimated 54% of Eritrea's food requirements. The grain harvest increased from some 70,000 metric tons in 1991 to 250,000–300,000 tons in 1992, but 1993 was a disastrous year, following the almost complete failure of the rains and persistent problems caused by crop pests. There was a substantial cereal deficit, and much of the country required the distribution of emergency food aid. In June 1993 the World Food Programme announced the launch of a six-month emergency food operation (including several food-for-work projects) to assist more than 500,000 Eritreans suffering serious food shortages. The 1994 harvest was considerably better than in the previous few years, owing to high levels of rainfall and an extensive government programme of rehabilitation of communications and irrigation systems. Nevertheless, agricultural production remains erratic. After an improved harvest in 1994/95, agricultural output was poor in the three following years. In 1998/99 there was a bumper grain harvest of 468,000 tons. As in much of the Horn of Africa, grain production was slashed by poor rains in 1999, leaving more than 50% of Eritrea's population critically dependent upon food assistance at the height of the war with Ethiopia in May 2000. With more than 1m. people displaced, and planting impossible in some of the most fertile areas, total food aid imports of 380,000 tons will be required during 2000/01. In 1996 a small enterprise was established in Eritrea to export cut flowers and fruit, initially to the Netherlands, Germany and Israel. The number of livestock in Eritrea (severely depleted during the war) has increased since 1992, primarily as a result of improved animal husbandry and access to veterinary services, and has led to the export of live animals.

Land reform legislation was promulgated in 1994, whereby the government was to maintain ownership of all land, but farmers would be allowed a life-time lease on currently held land. In addition, every Eritrean citizen would automatically qualify for the right to use a specific plot throughout their life. The government initiated agricultural resettlement projects for demobilized soldiers and introduced a special credit scheme for ex-combatants to facilitate the establishment of new farms and co-operatives. In January 1995 two loans for agricultural development were granted: US $12.7m. from the International Fund for Agricultural Development (IFAD) and $5.3m. from the joint IFAD-Belgium Survival Fund Programme. In February 1996 Japan pledged aid worth $3m. to assist in the development of the agricultural sector. In late 1997 the African Development Bank (ADB) awarded Eritrea a loan of $13.9m. to finance a livestock-breeding project; an additional $16m. was allocated to the fisheries sector.

As a result of serious environmental degradation (caused directly and indirectly by the war of independence), water scarcity and unreliable rainfall, projects have been undertaken to build water reservoirs and small dams. In an attempt to prevent soil erosion, more than 40,000 km of badly eroded hillsides have been terraced and 22m. new trees planted. In 1994 the European Development Fund (EDF) committed ECU 3.6m. (US $4m.) for the construction of five small-scale irrigation dams. In 1997 the ADB granted a loan worth $11.6m. to finance an irrigated horticulture development project, repayable over a 50-year period, which included 10 years' grace.

Fisheries are a potential growth area for the Eritrean economy. Fishing of sardines, anchovies, tuna, shark and mackerel is practised in the waters of the Red Sea. An FAO-sponsored conference was held in Massawa in March 1993 to discuss measures to develop Eritrea's marine fishery resources. UN fishery experts have estimated that Eritrea has the potential to achieve annual yields of around 70,000 metric tons. Although fishing activity is on a very small scale, the total catch has increased considerably in recent years, amounting to 3,212 tons in 1996. The total catch declined to 978 tons in 1997, increasing to 1,786 tons in 1998. In the past, government price controls and a poor transport infrastructure discouraged the development of a domestic market, with the result that much of the catch was smuggled abroad. In 1994 the China State Construction and Engineering Co was awarded a 3.7m. birr contract to build a new fishing centre at the port of Massawa. The contract was part of a US $5.4m.-scheme funded by the UN Development Programme (UNDP), to develop fishery projects for Eritrea. By early 1996 fishing fleets from Saudi Arabia, the United Kingdom, Greece, the Netherlands and Israel were licensed to operate in the area, and were exporting sardines, tuna, shrimps and lobsters. The companies have been building cold storage and processing facilities in Massawa.

INDUSTRY

Eritrea's industrial base traditionally centred on the production of glass, cement, footwear and canned goods. Although some of the 42 public-sector factories—producing textiles, footwear, beverages and other light industrial goods—were operating in 1991, they were doing so at only one-third of capacity. By 1995 production had increased considerably, mostly as a result of substantial government aid. The government calculated that the cost of industrial recovery would be US $20m. for the private sector and $66m. for the state sector. In 1999 industrial production (comprising mining, manufacturing, construction and utilities) accounted for an estimated 27.3% of GDP.

The manufacturing sector provided an estimated 9.8% of GDP in 1999. All public enterprises in the sector are currently scheduled for divestment or liquidation, following the initiation of a programme of privatization in 1995. Since independence several small manufacturing companies have been established, including a contact lens factory that exports to countries in Europe, Africa and Asia. Until mid-1997 imported petroleum was processed at the Assab refinery, whose entire output of petroleum products was delivered to Ethiopia. Eritrea purchases its own petroleum requirements from Ethiopia under a quota arrangement; however, trade between the two countries was disrupted by the outbreak of hostilities in May 1998.

MINING AND POWER

Eritrea's mineral resources are believed to be of significant potential value, although in 1999 mining and quarrying accounted for less than 0.1% of GDP. Of particular importance, in view of Eritrea's acute energy shortage, is the possibility of large reserves of petroleum and natural gas beneath the Red Sea. In early 1993 the government made petroleum exploration regulations more stringent, and British Petroleum, which had signed a contract for petroleum exploration with the former Ethiopian regime, had its exploration rights invalidated. A US petroleum company, Amoco, and the International Petroleum Corpn of Canada were the only two remaining companies with concessions. The latter had operating rights in the 31,000 sq km Danakil block along the Eritrean coast, where there are believed to be good prospects for petroleum and gas discoveries. In November 1993 a new code of practice regulating the petroleum sector was promulgated, allowing companies a 25-year licence, renewal periods of 10 years and fiscal advantages. Several prominent international petroleum companies expressed an interest in exploration and distribution. A local company, Prima, backed by expatriate Eritrean shareholders and Shell-Eritrea, was expected to handle internal distribution. In October 1995 the government signed an agreement with Anadarko Petroleum Corpn of the USA for a seven-year prospecting contract, worth US $28.5m. Anadarko began its seismic studies for petroleum in the Zula block (containing the Dahlak islands) in November 1996. In September 1997 Anadarko signed a second production-sharing agreement to explore the Edd block, extending more than 6.7m. acres south of its Zula permit and stretching almost as far as the Hanish islands. Anadarko undertook to spend a further $23m. on prospecting and announced that it would begin drilling in both blocks in 1998. The company sold AGIP of Italy a 30% shareholding in the Zula block before serious drilling began in May 1998. The Eritrean authorities were in discussion with various US companies in early 1998 in an attempt to attract investors to two offshore blocks that had been operated by major petroleum companies in the 1980s. However, Anadarko's first three deep drills were dry. The last drill was sunk in the Edd block in early 1999. By then the company was reported to be in short supply of capital in a discouraging market. The war with Ethiopia showed no sign of ending and the international price of petroleum remained weak. The company began reducing operations by removing most of its operational staff in May, although nominal representation was maintained in Asmara.

The ageing and inefficient refinery at Assab was closed in late 1997; the government announced that it would import refined petroleum for the immediate future.

Gold-bearing seams exist in many of the igneous rocks forming the highlands of Eritrea. There are at least 15 gold-mines and a large number of prospects close to Asmara, and the potential for new discoveries in the area is considered good. There are two regions of widespread gold mineralization in the western lowlands, at Tokombia and Barentu. Other mineral resources include potash, zinc, magnesium, copper, iron ore and marble. In April 1995 a new mining law was promulgated, which declared all mineral resources to be state assets, but recognized an extensive role for private investors in their exploitation. Investor companies would enjoy a concessionary tax regime, pay royalties of 2%–5% and encounter no restriction on repatriating profits. The government retained the right to acquire a 10% share in any mining undertaking. In December applications to explore for gold and base metals were received from numerous foreign companies. Particular interest was expressed in the old Eritrean mines that had been exploited until the early 1940s. In March 1996 Canada's Reese Mining Co signed two agreements with Eritrea for the exploration of gold and copper reserves. In the following month the government signed exploration agreements with Western Mining of Australia and Ghana's Ashanti Goldfields. In late 1996 Golden Star Resources of Canada, and its subsidiary, Pan African Resources, began drilling for diamonds in the Adi Rassi area. During 1997 several Italian companies began prospecting for the much prized Eritrean marble at Embamadre, Shiraro-Dichima and Wor-Heewere quarries. It was anticipated that the companies would seek to establish joint ventures with Eritrean partners.

Eritrea's economic performance is hampered by its lack of capacity to produce energy. Total production of electricity in 1998 was 186m. kWh, 74% of which was in the capital, Asmara. Electricity is provided to only some 10% of the population, the remainder relying on fuelwood and animal products. Attempts are being made to harness the plentiful and clear sunlight for solar energy. By mid-1994, 37 schools and three hospitals had been purpose-built to operate on solar power. With an increase in the use of solar power, it was hoped that the demand for wood for fuel (from the rapidly diminishing forests, already severely denuded by the liberation war) would decline. In September 1994 the Kuwait Fund for Arab Economic Development allocated US $158m. for a project to upgrade the production and distribution of electricity in Eritrea. In March 1996 the government announced plans to construct a barrage, at a cost of $45m., at Toker, some 50 km from Asmara. The barrage was expected to increase water reserves for Asmara, although no immediate plans were announced for its use in generating electricity. In mid-1997 Korean contractors were scheduled to commence work on the construction of a $114m. power station (Hirgigo) at Massawa. The station was to have an initial output of 80 MW produced by four 20 MW diesel generators, and was to be financed primarily by Arab and Italian donors. Meanwhile, in late 1996, work commenced on the construction of a 2,000-metric ton gas depot at Massawa (funded by public and private capital) to provide additional storage facilities. A total of $200m. was to be invested in power generation by 2000. The Italian government guaranteed the financing of $75m. for three electricity power transmission lines linking Massawa power station with Asmara and the other major towns in the north. Kuwait pledged $16.5m. for the expansion of Beleza power station located to the north of Asmara.

RECOVERY AND REHABILITATION PROGRAMME

In March 1993 the International Development Association (IDA), part of the World Bank, approved a credit of SDR 18.1m. (US $25m.) to support Eritrea's two-year Recovery and Rehabilitation Programme (involving total investment of $147m.), which was to be funded by a series of loans on concessionary terms. The second largest contributor was Italy, which pledged $24.3m. Contributions were also promised by a number of other European countries, the European Union (EU) and the UNDP. The main components of the programme were: agricultural and industrial input, equipment for infrastructural development, mechanical, electrical and telecommunications spare parts, construction materials for social utilities and cottage industries, and support for administration and economic planning. In 1994 the 'Paris Club' of official creditors granted Eritrea a long-term loan of $250m. to fund rehabilitation and development programmes.

FOREIGN TRADE AND PAYMENTS

According to preliminary IMF data, in 1999 Eritrea had a trade deficit of US $481m., with exports earning only $26m. Revenue from exports of services totalled $74m. and inward private transfers (remittances from workers abroad) were $243m. The positive balance on Eritrea's capital account stood at $136m., including loans of $84m. and foreign direct investment inflows totalling $36m. This, coupled with official transfers and short-term capital inflows, left a preliminary overall balance of $8m., the first such surplus for five years. However, again this data should be treated with caution, with the actual level of remittances and loans contracted during the war inevitably remaining the subject of considerable uncertainty. In 1998 the principal sources of non-petroleum imports were Italy (accounting for 17.4% of the total), the United Arab Emirates (16.2%), Saudi Arabia (14.6%), and Germany (5.6%). Exports in that year were mostly to Sudan (27.3%), Ethiopia (26.6%), Japan (13.2%) and Italy (5.3%). The principal exports to these countries were crude materials, food and live animals, and basic manufactures. The main non-petroleum imports were machinery and transport equipment (38.5% of the total), basic manufactures, and food and live animals.

IMF preliminary figures suggested that Eritrea's overall budget deficit in 1999 totalled 2,929m. nakfa. With 376.4m. nakfa offset by external grants, the total deficit fell to 2,552m. nakfa, representing 37.4% of GNP. In 1997 the total budget deficit had decreased to 331m. nakfa, some 10% of GNP, the onset of war thus triggering a sharp deterioration. According to ministry of finance figures, Eritrea's total external debt stood at $464m. in January 2000, 29% of which was owed to the World Bank's IDA; loans worth $84m. were disbursed during 1999. Bank of Eritrea price data, based on the Asmara price index, suggest that urban inflation averaged 16.6% in the year to December 1998. However, prices stabilized during the first half of 1999 as the effects of the improved 1998 harvests reduced grain prices. The poor 1999 main harvests, coupled with shortages due to war, underpin forecasts of inflation of at least 15%–20% during 2000.

In May 1993 Eritrea was admitted to the group of African, Caribbean and Pacific (ACP) countries party to the Lomé Convention. In September an IMF delegation visited Asmara and held talks with the government regarding Eritrea's application to join the Fund, and in July 1994 Eritrea became the 179th member of the IMF, with an initial quota of SDR 11.5m. Eritrea sought to show the international donor community its commitment to implementing a liberal trade and exchange regime and developing an export-orientated domestic economy. As early as January 1992 Eritrea and Ethiopia signed an agreement whereby the port of Assab became a free port for Ethiopia, and which provided for tax-free trade between the two countries, using the Ethiopian birr as currency. In October 1994 Eritrea and Ethiopia signed a further agreement to allow the free movement of goods between the two countries without payment of customs dues. A tariff agreement providing for a free-trade zone and the basis for future economic union between the two countries was announced by the Ethiopian government in May 1995.

In late 1996 Afewerki and a trade delegation visited Italy, the United Kingdom and the USA in an attempt to promote investment in Eritrea. In mid-1996 28 US companies operating in Eritrea had established an American Business Council to protect their interests and to assist local Eritrean businesses involved in promoting or selling US merchandise.

CONSTRUCTION, TRANSPORT AND TOURISM

In 1993 the government adopted a two-year Recovery and Rehabilitation Programme, which supported infrastructure and construction projects. Public enterprises, particularly cement, metalworks and limestone factories, underwent rehabilitation, while emphasis was also placed on the rebuilding of government offices, commercial and residential buildings and the reconstruction of roads and infrastructure. In 1995 a Republic of Korea company started work on Eritrea's biggest housing scheme; it was anticipated that the US $70m.-project would provide accommodation for some 1,300 families in the outskirts of Asmara.

Construction work on a new airport in Massawa began in April 1996. In 1993 the government announced plans for the rehabilitation of the Asmara–Massawa railway line, which had been severely damaged during the war. The government initially sought estimates for the repair work from foreign companies, but in 1995 decided that the rehabilitation should be undertaken locally. In early 1997 the line was formally inaugurated.

Significant progress has been made in rehabilitating the port of Massawa, which was heavily bombed by Ethiopia during the liberation struggle. The port was obstructed by shipwrecked vessels, and much of the city was reduced to rubble. By late 1994 the harbour had been cleared by the US navy, and port activity has since accelerated. In 1991 104 small ships visited the port; however, in 1998 some 463 vessels docked at the port. The government announced a long-term project to build a container terminal at the port, as well as a liquefied petroleum gas terminal. Finance for both projects was to be sought from foreign investors. In mid-1996 Italy and the IDA pledged loans of US $21m. and $18m., respectively, to fund the repair and refurbishment of the port, including the construction of the container terminal, the extension of quays and the development of customs facilities. It was anticipated that finance would also be sought to improve facilities at Assab port (which then handled the majority of Ethiopia's external trade). In December 1997 the US Department of Defense provided finance totalling $700,000 for two projects associated with Massawa port: the construction of an area to accommodate commercial aircraft and an annexe to the town's hospital. In late 1997 the World Bank approved an IDA loan of $30m. for the improvement of Massawa and Assab ports. A framework for the commercial management of the ports was also approved. In Massawa priority was given to the dredging of the harbour and the extension of the docks; in Assab the main objective was to accelerate the transfer of cargo through the purchase of cargo-handling equipment. Both ports were virtually closed to Ethiopian trade with the outbreak of hostilities between the two countries in May 1998. As a result of the conflict, activity at Assab port declined markedly: some 322 vessels docked at the port in 1998, compared with 628 in the previous year.

The construction and repair of roads and bridges remained a priority. In September 1997 Japan pledged US $10m. in aid for the purchase of road construction machinery.

Tourism in Eritrea remains undeveloped and has been further damaged by two years of war (1998–2000). Nevertheless, new construction activity in Massawa has resulted in the rehabilitation of three hotels with a combined capacity of 160 beds, and the government remains optimistic that the number of tourist arrivals will gradually increase. In 1995 a US company had expressed interest in building a US $200m.-casino and hotel complex (and desalination plant) on the Dahlak islands. However, the development of visitor facilities on these islands, which have considerable potential for eco-tourism, has been impeded by the demarcation dispute between Eritrea and Yemen. In late 1996 it was announced that an Italian company had won a contract to build Eritrea's first five-star hotel. It was estimated that the 200-room hotel would cost $17.5m. to construct. The divestment of state-owned hotels remained integral to the government's privatization programme. Despite the intensification of the war with Ethiopia after May 1998, many infrastructure projects continued. In May a Republic of Korea company, Kingnam, agreed to establish a cement factory at a cost of $50m. The IDA announced it would provide finance to build hospitals in Barentu and Mendefera, and a blood bank in Asmara. The Saudi Development Fund loaned $20m. of the construction of the Mendefera–Barentu road. The fighting of May–June 2000 severely damaged infrastructure, notably roads along the border regions and the towns of Barentu and Tesseney, which were occupied by Ethiopian troops.

ECONOMIC POLICY AND AID

In August 1994 the national assembly approved a long-awaited programme of economic reforms governing investment, land tenure, monetary and fiscal policy and trade. The programme represented a major change from a wartime command economy to a liberal market economy, designed for peace. Private investment was to be liberalized, and government involvement reduced to a regulatory capacity (with the exception of the provision of assistance for depressed regions). Private and foreign investors were to be treated equally, and remission of capital and profits was to be unrestricted, but employment for Eritrean nationals would be prioritized. The 43 state enterprises were scheduled for privatization, and 11 state-owned hotels were also expected to be sold. Nearly 45,000 houses, nationalized during the Ethiopian occupation, were to be returned to their owners. It was announced that small export-orientated businesses would qualify for competitive exchange rates and loans under the Recovery and Rehabilitation Programme (see above). The privatization programme began to make serious progress in the second half of 1997. International investors purchased the Eritrea Shoe factory, the Gash Cigarette factory and the Red Sea Soap factory, but little foreign interest was expressed in the Asmara Brewery. Some criticism was levelled at the revised land tenure law, as the government had declared itself to be the owner of all land, with Eritreans and foreign investors receiving usufructuary rights for farming, development and housing. In October 1994 a new tariff regime was adopted; it was hoped that this measure would curb inflation but encourage trade and investment. Capital goods and raw materials were subject to minimal tariffs of less than 3%, whereas tariffs on some luxury goods were fixed as high as 50%.

Following independence, the government allocated considerable expenditure to financing the demobilization and reintegration of ex-combatants. During 1993–96 the demobilization programme was estimated to have cost 300m. birr. The government has remained committed to restructuring the public administration and reforming taxation policy in order to reduce the widening budget deficit. The government's commitment to restructuring public administration and reforming tax policy in order to reduce budget deficits was derailed by the war with Ethiopia. The war also heightened the reluctance of key foreign donors to commit significant sums to capital projects.

Pledges of financial aid from international organizations became more frequent in 1994. The EU promised US $4.1m., under the Lomé agreement, for diverse projects such as the demobilization of the army and the provision of health equipment, veterinary services and pharmaceutical supplies. A further ECU 20m. was allocated in November for the upgrading of the Asmara–Massawa road, for drilling wells and for establishing schools and health centres. In addition, the European Investment Bank pledged $10m. to upgrade telecommunication networks in Massawa and Keren. In late 1996 it was announced that Norway was to provide an additional $7m. in aid to improve the telecommunications service. (In November 1997 Daewoo of the Republic of Korea signed an agreement with Eritrea to upgrade the telecommunications system by 2000.)

Eritrea's first donor conference was convened by the World Bank in France in December 1994. Donors pledged US $250m. in international aid for 1995. The World Bank promised $25m., the ADB $50m., Kuwait $20m., and Saudi Arabia $50m. The EU, which had already pledged $200m. since 1992, offered a further $30m. for 1995. However, an economic memorandum, prepared by the World Bank, expressed concern regarding the Eritrean government's ability to provide counterpart funds to discharge the substantial range of international commitments. It also stressed the acute shortage of skilled manpower in key sectors, and the absence of essential statistics, necessary for effective economic planning. In late 1995 the IDA announced that it would fund community-based micro-projects in the areas of health and irrigation, to the value of $25m., as well as a $20m.-project aimed at rehabilitating and expanding capacity in Eritrea's ports. The IDA allocated a further $18.3m. to the health sector in late 1997, and in January 1998 it approved credit worth $60m. to support recruitment and training programmes in an attempt to resolve Eritrea's manpower crisis. In early 1997 the Arab Bank for Economic Development in Africa granted Eritrea $10m. to finance improvements to the drinking water network. In April the World Bank approved a $6.3m. credit to finance feasibility and engineering studies in the construction and transport sectors. However, in September 1999 the World Bank announced that it was to halt all new funding for Eritrea until the conflict with Ethiopia had been brought to a peaceful conclusion.

During late 1996 the government imposed severe restrictions on non-governmental organizations (NGO) operating in Eritrea.

Thenceforth NGO would be permitted to operate only in the education and health sectors, and expatriate personnel would be required to pay income tax at 38%. Many NGO expressed concern that the restrictions would prevent them from continuing their work in Eritrea. In early 1998 several key western NGO withdrew from the country. During 1999 the Eritrean government invited back selected NGO in an attempt to alleviate the humanitarian consequences of the fighting with Ethiopia. Further NGO and US emergency assistance was expected following the signing of a cease-fire with Ethiopia in June 2000.

ECONOMIC ASPECTS OF WAR

In July 1997 a decree was promulgated, announcing the creation of the nakfa as the national currency (Eritrea had retained the Ethiopian birr as its monetary unit since independence), initially at par with the birr. The nakfa became legal tender in November; however, its introduction led to conflict with Ethiopia. In the period prior to the change of currency Eritrea manipulated the exchange rate, offering 10%–15% more birr to the US dollar, angering Ethiopia, and encouraging smuggling; it also led to speculation that the nakfa would not maintain parity with the birr. The Ethiopian authorities responded by announcing that all trade and service transactions between the two countries would have to be conducted using 'hard' currency. Cross-border commerce subsequently virtually halted as Eritrean traders encountered difficulties with the letter-of-credit trading system and the lengthy customs checks. In November both countries announced that they would use foreign currency to settle trade accounts between themselves. By the beginning of 1998 the new nakfa coins and notes had been introduced in Eritrea and the Ethiopian birr had been withdrawn from circulation. The dispute over the nakfa was one of the contributing factors that led to the outbreak of hostilities between the two countries in May 1998.

Economic Impact of the War

Eritrea introduced conscription and sent an estimated 270,000 men to the war, using the lull after the initial hostilities in May 1998 to rearm. It purchased light arms, artillery, military equipment and tanks from Bulgaria, Romania, other Eastern European countries and Italy. Belgian police seized 91 containers of military equipment destined for the Gedam Construction Co of Asmara. Eritrea bought five new MiG-29s from Russia, and when these proved difficult to operate a further six, older MiG-21s were purchased from Moldova. Both sides spent several hundred million dollars on weapons from suppliers and international arms dealers who insisted on cash in advance. While the FAO reported that Eritrea had the world's second-lowest calorie intake in the world, the country was estimated to be spending at least US $1m. a day on the war. The Ethiopian government claimed that Eritrea had seized 134,000 metric tons of food stranded at the port of Assab at the beginning of the war.

The government had to cope with hundreds of thousands of displaced persons and tens of thousands of Eritreans expelled from Ethiopia. In addition, trade with Ethiopia, which previously accounted for two-thirds of Eritrean exports, virtually ceased. Activity at the port of Assab declined sharply as most of Eritrea's war material was routed through Massawa.

President Afewerki toured the world trying to raise funds which would indirectly help the war effort. In January 1999 he was in Belgium, arranging EDF finance for transport, water and food security projects. In February he attempted, unsuccessfully, to join the Arab League, which he considered as a potential source of finance. He made overtures to Col Qaddafi in Libya, and resolved Eritrea's differences with Yemen, however, few Arab countries were prepared to reward his endeavours with financial assistance.

In mid-2000 it was still too early to assess the full economic impact of Eritrea's effective defeat following the Ethiopian offensives of May. Many of the estimated 260,000 Eritreans uprooted in earlier fighting were displaced for a second time. An estimated additional 500,000 people fled the fighting in central and western Eritrea, with 75,000 entering Sudan in late May. The need to feed, clothe and shelter these displaced people, coupled with acute food shortages caused by the failure of the main 1999 harvests, placed severe financial strains on the government and expatriate Eritreans who have partially funded the war and relief effort. Total government expenditure increased by 48% in 1998, and by a further 21%, to 4,629m. nakfa, in 1999, the equivalent of 68% of GNP. Even if the cease-fire holds, levels of defence expenditure are likely to remain at their 1999 levels—official Eritrean data suggest budgeted expenditure of around US $15m. per month.

Statistical Survey

Source (unless otherwise stated): Ministry of Trade and Industry, POB 1844, Asmara; tel. (1) 118386; fax (1) 120586.

Area and Population

AREA, POPULATION AND DENSITY*

Area (sq km)	121,144†
Population (census results)	
9 May 1984	
Males	1,374,452
Females	1,373,852
Total	2,748,304
Population (UN estimate at mid-year)	
1998	3,577,000
Density (per sq km) at mid-1998	29.5

* Including the Assab district.
† 46,774 sq miles.

PRINCIPAL TOWN (estimated population at mid-1990)

Asmara (capital) 358,100
Source: UN, *Demographic Yearbook.*

BIRTHS AND DEATHS (UN estimates, averages per year)

	1980–85	1985–90	1990–95
Birth rate (per 1,000) . . .	45.2	44.7	43.1
Death rate (per 1,000) . .	20.0	17.0	15.5

Expectation of life (UN estimates, years at birth, 1990–95): 49.6 (males 48.0; females 51.4).

Source: UN, *World Population Prospects: The 1998 Revision.*

Agriculture

PRINCIPAL CROPS ('000 metric tons)

	1996*	1997*	1998
Wheat	10	12	23
Barley	25	20	57
Maize	5	11	29
Millet	25	19	52
Sorghum	54	59	27
Potatoes	40	40	25
Other roots and tubers	70	70	n.a.
Pulses	33	33	33
Groundnuts (in shell)	2	2	2
Sesame seed	6	6	5
Linseed	1	1	1
Vegetables	30	30	46
Fruits and berries	5	5	21

* FAO estimates (Source: FAO, *Production Yearbook*).

LIVESTOCK ('000 head, year ending September)

	1996*†	1997*†	1998
Cattle	1,320	1,320	1,386
Sheep	1,530	1,530	1,607
Goats	1,400	1,400	1,470
Camels	69	69	72

Poultry*† (million): 4 in 1996; 4 in 1997; 4 in 1998.

* Source: FAO, *Production Yearbook*.
† FAO estimates.

LIVESTOCK PRODUCTS (FAO estimates, '000 metric tons)

	1996	1997	1998
Beef and veal	10	10	10
Mutton and lamb	5	5	5
Goat meat	5	5	5
Poultry meat	6	6	6
Cows' milk	31	31	31
Goats' milk	7	7	7
Sheep's milk	4	4	4
Hen eggs	6	6	6
Wool: greasy	1	1	1
Cattle hides	2	2	2
Sheepskins	1	1	1
Goatskins	1	1	1

Source: FAO, *Production Yearbook*.

Fishing

(metric tons, live weight)

	1996	1997	1998
Groupers	140	36	23
Snappers	222	12	36
Grunts and sweetlips	366	12	42
Emperors	753	15	25
Barracudas	185	14	45
Jacks and crevalles	815	9	123
Narrow-barred Spanish mackerel	181	172	181
Total catch (incl. others)	3,212	978	1,786

Finance

CURRENCY AND EXCHANGE RATES

Monetary Units

100 cents = 1 nakfa.

Sterling, Dollar and Euro Equivalents (28 April 2000)

£1 sterling = 14.90 nakfa;
US $1 = 9.50 nakfa;
€1 = 8.63 nakfa;
1,000 nakfa = £67.13 = $105.26 = €115.86.

Note: Following its secession from Ethiopia in May 1993, Eritrea retained the Ethiopian currency, the birr. An exchange rate of US $1 = 5.000 birr was introduced in October 1992 and remained in force until April 1994, when it was adjusted to $1 = 5.130 birr. Further adjustments were made subsequently. In addition to the official exchange rate, the Bank of Eritrea applied a marginal auction rate (determined at fortnightly auctions of foreign exchange, conducted by the National Bank of Ethiopia) to aid-funded imports and to most transactions in services. A more depreciated preferential rate applied to remittances of foreign exchange by Eritreans abroad, to proceeds from exports and to most payments for imports. On 1 April 1997 Eritrea unified the official and preferential exchange rates at $1 = 7.20 birr (which had been the preferential rate since January 1996). In November 1997 the Government introduced a separate national currency, the nakfa, replacing (and initially at par with) the Ethiopian birr. The exchange rate in relation to the US dollar was initially set at the prevailing unified rate, but from 1 May 1998 a mechanism to provide a market-related exchange rate was established.

BUDGET (million birr/nakfa)

Revenue*	1995	1996	1997†
Tax revenue	715.6	830.4	959.4
Direct taxes	339.7	380.0	447.9
Taxes on personal income	74.2	113.6	117.2
Taxes on business profits	185.0	230.7	292.9
Rehabilitation tax	73.2	23.3	18.1
Domestic sales tax (incl. stamp duties)	151.0	180.7	212.8
Import duties and taxes	224.9	269.7	298.7
Port fees and charges	233.5	281.9	444.3
Other current revenue	396.1	277.6	619.1
Capital revenue	0.0	0.0	20.0
Total	1,345.2	1,389.9	2,042.8

Expenditure	1995	1996	1997†
Current expenditure	2,131.3	1,883.3	1,445.5
General services	1,090.3	1,233.1	886.0
Internal affairs	110.7	74.7	56.6
Regional administration	48.6	40.6	55.5
Foreign affairs	71.5	77.1	84.5
Defence‡	770.5	968.1	634.2
Economic services	235.1	186.4	140.8
Agriculture and natural resources	30.1	15.4	32.8
Mining and energy	17.8	93.1	190.7
Construction and urban development	88.5	61.8	9.7
Transport and communications	97.6	85.4	85.0
Social services	226.9	188.0	279.5
Education and training	97.6	70.7	139.3
Health	75.3	56.0	81.1
Demobilization of ex-combatants	41.8	14.0	0.0
Capital expenditure	548.7	838.2	1,143.3
General services	54.4	163.9	99.6
Economic development	410.4	471.4	709.7
Agriculture and natural resources	272.5	256.1	180.6
Trade, industry and tourism	25.1	35.0	83.1
Construction, transport and communications	93.8	73.6	242.1
Social development	83.9	202.9	334.0
Education	15.5	49.3	99.3
Health	35.5	87.7	55.0
Total	2,680.0	2,721.5	2,588.8

* Excluding grants received (million birr/nakfa): 491.0 in 1995 (current 170.6, capital 320.4); 508.6 in 1996 (current 194.6, capital 314.0); 290.5 (provisional) in 1997 (current 32.7, capital 257.8).
† Provisional figures.
‡ Including some demobilization costs.

Source: IMF, *Eritrea: Selected Issues* (September 1998).

MONEY SUPPLY (million birr/nakfa at 31 December)

	1995	1996	1997
Demand deposits at banks . .	1,295.8	1,670.9	1,616.6

Source: IMF, *Eritrea: Selected Issues* (September 1998).

COST OF LIVING*
(price index for Asmara at December; base: January 1992 = 100)

	1995	1996	1997
All items	141.3	146.1	161.5

* The index has been constructed using estimated weights for various categories of commodity prices, compiled by the Ministry of Trade and Industry.

Source: IMF, *Eritrea: Selected Issues* (September 1998).

NATIONAL ACCOUNTS (million birr/nakfa at current prices)
Gross Domestic Product by Economic Activity

	1995	1996	1997*
Agriculture, forestry and fishing .	390.9	371.8	390.3
Mining and quarrying . . .	2.1	3.6	4.5
Manufacturing†	501.9	571.4	656.0
Electricity and water . . .	52.5	56.2	65.1
Construction	235.6	412.3	515.4
Wholesale and retail trade . .	921.9	1,050.2	1,134.1
Transport and communications .	453.4	475.3	488.9
Financial services . . .	57.8	68.1	85.7
Dwellings and domestic services .	79.0	95.6	103.7
Public administration and services	758.8	648.3	706.8
Other services	43.0	50.5	50.8
GDP at factor cost . . .	3,496.9	3,803.3	4,201.4
Indirect taxes, *less* subsidies .	375.9	450.4	511.5
GDP in purchasers' values .	3,872.8	4,253.7	4,712.9

* Provisional figures.
† Including handicrafts and small-scale industry.

Source: IMF, *Eritrea: Selected Issues* (September 1998).

BALANCE OF PAYMENTS (US $ million)

	1995	1996	1997
Exports of goods f.o.b. . . .	80.6	95.3	53.1
Imports of goods c.i.f. . . .	−403.8	−513.7	−489.5
Trade balance	−323.2	−418.5	−436.4
Exports of services . . .	90.8	104.8	148.3
Imports of services . . .	−43.7	−53.7	−93.4
Balance on goods and services	−276.1	−367.3	−381.5
Other income (net) . . .	7.6	−7.3	−3.4
Balance on goods, services and income	−268.5	−374.6	−384.9
Private unrequited transfers (net) .	215.3	243.9	348.4
Official unrequited transfers (net) .	71.0	79.9	41.4
Current balance . . .	17.8	−50.8	4.9
Direct investment (net) . .	n.a.	36.7	38.3
Official long-term capital (net) .	8.2	7.4	28.4
Short-term capital (net) . . } Net errors and omissions . . }	−92.3	−68.5	−183.1
Overall balance . . .	−66.3	−75.2	−111.5

Source: IMF, *Eritrea: Selected Issues* (September 1998).

External Trade

PRINCIPAL COMMODITIES (million birr/nakfa)

Imports c.i.f. (excl. petroleum)	1996*	1997*	1998
Food and live animals . . .	542.9	599.9	460.0
Beverages and tobacco . .	23.5	22.4	20.2
Crude materials (inedible) except fuels	116.5	67.7	43.7
Animal and vegetable oils, fats and waxes	55.0	57.6	71.3
Chemicals and related products .	209.7	182.8	152.5
Basic manufactures . . .	733.8	678.5	642.5
Machinery and transport equipment	1,091.1	1,158.2	1,039.6
Miscellaneous manufactured articles	250.8	242.7	231.1
Total (incl. others) . . .	3,062.8	3,062.0	2,702.2

Exports f.o.b.	1996*	1997*	1998
Food and live animals . . .	92.4	81.3	58.3
Beverages and tobacco . .	26.2	8.9	0.3
Crude materials (inedible) except fuels	123.0	129.5	89.1
Chemicals and related products .	13.4	8.2	4.1
Basic manufactures . . .	88.3	64.3	26.1
Machinery and transport equipment	27.7	10.8	4.7
Miscellaneous manufactured articles	146.6	70.9	13.8
Total (incl. others) . . .	520.4	375.3	196.5

* Source: IMF, *Eritrea: Selected Issues* (September 1998).

PRINCIPAL TRADING PARTNERS (million birr/nakfa)

Imports c.i.f. (excl. petroleum)	1996*	1997	1998
Belgium	84.1	26.8	47.3
Djibouti	78.6	79.0	58.1
Ethiopia	261.8	274.6	25.0
Germany	217.0	168.2	152.6
Italy	429.1	420.1	469.8
Japan	111.2	125.5	107.1
Korea, Repub. . . .	126.0	99.7	118.3
Netherlands	49.4	51.2	60.1
Saudi Arabia . . .	465.6	480.6	393.9
Sudan	97.9	20.3	22.0
Sweden	19.3	22.9	19.0
United Arab Emirates . .	365.9	402.0	436.5
United Kingdom . . .	68.5	142.1	128.9
USA	83.1	96.4	114.5
Total (incl. others) . . .	3,062.9	3,062.2	2,702.2

Exports f.o.b.	1996*	1997*	1998
Ethiopia	342.4	238.1	52.2
Italy	22.3	18.3	10.4
Japan	0.0	0.0	26.0
Saudi Arabia . . .	20.0	7.3	2.3
Sudan	51.5	62.3	53.7
USA	39.9	3.2	4.1
Total (incl. others) . . .	520.4	375.3	196.5

* Source: IMF, *Eritrea: Selected Issues* (September 1998).

Transport

ROAD TRAFFIC (motor vehicles in use)

	1996	1997	1998
Number of registered vehicles . .	27,013	31,276	35,942

SHIPPING
Merchant Fleet (registered at 31 December)

	1996	1997	1998
Number of vessels . . .	4	6	7
Displacement (grt) . . .	830	6,777	7,335

Source: Lloyd's Register of Shipping, *World Fleet Statistics*.

CIVIL AVIATION

	1996	1997	1998
Passengers ('000) . . .	168.1	173.8	105.2

Tourism

ARRIVALS BY NATIONALITY

	1996	1997	1998
Ethiopia.	248,814	275,534	117,087
Total (incl. others) . . .	416,596	409,544	187,647

Tourism receipts (US $ million): 69 in 1996.
Source: World Tourism Organization, *Yearbook of Tourism Statistics*.

Communications Media

	1995	1996	1997
Radio receivers ('000 in use) . .	310	330	345
Television receivers ('000 in use) .	1	1	1
Telephones ('000 main lines in use)	17	19	21
Telefax stations (number in use) .	777	1,101	n.a.

Book production (1993): 106 titles (including 23 pamphlets) and 420,000 copies (including 60,000 pamphlets). Figures for books, excluding pamphlets, refer only to school textbooks (64 titles; 323,000 copies) and government publications (19 titles; 37,000 copies).
Telephones ('000 main lines in use): 24 in 1998.
Sources: mainly UNESCO, *Statistical Yearbook*; UN, *Statistical Yearbook*.

Education

(1996/97)

	Institutions	Teachers	Pupils
Pre-primary	61	207	7,443
Primary	549	5,476	240,737
Secondary:			
General	n.a.	1,959	88,054
Teacher-training . . .	n.a.	33	359
Vocational	n.a.	79	674
University and equivalent level* .	n.a.	198	3,096

* Figures refer to 1997/98.

Source: UNESCO, *Statistical Yearbook*.

Directory

The Constitution

On 23 May 1997 the Constituent Assembly unanimously adopted the Eritrean Constitution. A presidential regime was instituted, with the President to be elected for a maximum of two five-year terms. The President, as Head of State, has extensive powers and appoints, with the approval of the National Assembly (the Legislature), the ministers, the commissioners, the Auditor-General, the president of the central bank and the judges of the Supreme Court. The President's mandate can be revoked if two-thirds of the members of the National Assembly so demand. 'Conditional' political pluralism is authorized. Pending the election of a new National Assembly, legislative power was to be held by a Transitional National Assembly, comprising the 75 members of the PFDJ Central Committee, 60 members of the former Constituent Assembly and 15 representatives of Eritreans residing abroad.

The Government

HEAD OF STATE

President: ISSAIAS AFEWERKI (assumed power May 1991; elected President by National Assembly 8 June 1993).

CABINET
(August 2000)

President: ISSAIAS AFEWERKI.
Minister of Defence: Gen. SEBHAT EPHREM.
Minister of Justice: FAWZIA HASHIM.
Minister of Foreign Affairs: HAILE WOLDETENSAE.
Minister of Information: BARAKI GEBRESELASSIE.
Minister of Finance: GEBRESELASSIE YOSIEF.
Minister of Trade and Industry: ALI SAYYID ABDULLAH.
Minister of Agriculture: AREFAINE BERHE.
Minister of Local Government: MAHMOUD AHMED SHERIFO.
Minister of Labour and Human Welfare: ASKALU MENKERIOS.
Minister of Fisheries: PETROS SOLOMON.

Minister of Construction: ABRAHA ASFAHA.
Minister of Energy and Mines: TESFAI GEBRESELASSIE.
Minister of Education: OSMAN SALIH MUHAMMAD.
Minister of Health: Dr SALIH MEKKI.
Minister of Transport and Communications: SALEH KEKIA.
Minister of Tourism: AHMED HAJI ALI.
Minister of Land, Water and the Environment: TESFAI GHIRMAZION.

MINISTRIES AND COMMISSIONS

Office of the President: POB 257, Asmara; tel. (1) 119701; fax (1) 125123.
Ministry of Agriculture: POB 1048, Asmara; tel. (1) 181499; fax (1) 181415.
Ministry of Construction: POB 841, Asmara; tel. (1) 119077; fax (1) 120661.
Ministry of Defence: POB 629, Asmara; tel. (1) 115493; fax (1) 124920.
Ministry of Education: POB 5610, Asmara; tel. (1) 113044; fax (1) 113866.
Ministry of Energy and Mines: POB 5285, Asmara; tel. (1) 116872; fax (1) 127652.
Ministry of Finance: POB 896, Asmara; tel. (1) 118131; fax (1) 127947.
Ministry of Fisheries: POB 923, Asmara; tel. (1) 114271; fax (1) 112185.
Ministry of Foreign Affairs: POB 190, Asmara; tel. (1) 127838; fax (1) 123788; e-mail tesfai@wg.eol.
Ministry of Health: POB 212, Asmara; tel. (1) 117549; fax (1) 112899.
Ministry of Information: POB 242, Asmara; tel. (1) 117111; fax (1) 124647.
Ministry of Justice: POB 241, Asmara; tel. (1) 127739; fax (1) 126422.
Ministry of Labour and Human Welfare: POB 5252, Asmara; tel. (1) 181846; fax (1) 181649; e-mail mlhw@eol.com.er.

Ministry of Land, Water and the Environment: POB 976, Asmara; tel (1) 118021; fax (1) 123285.

Ministry of Local Government: POB 225, Asmara; tel. (1) 127734.

Ministry of Tourism: POB 1010, Asmara; tel. (1) 126997; fax (1) 126949; e-mail ona@eol.com.ar.

Ministry of Trade and Industry: POB 1844, Asmara; tel. (1) 118386; fax (1) 110586.

Ministry of Transport and Communications: POB 6465, Asmara; tel. (1) 114307; fax (1) 127048; e-mail motc_rez@eol.com.er.

Eritrean Relief and Refugee Commission: POB 1098, Asmara; tel. (1) 182222; fax (1) 182970; e-mail john@errec.er.punchdown.org.

Land and Housing Commission: POB 348, Asmara; tel. (1) 117400.

Provincial Administrators

There are six administrative regions in Eritrea, each with regional, sub-regional and village administrations.

Anseba Province: ALAMIN SHEIKH SALIH.

Debub Province: MESFIN HAGOS.

Debubawi Keyih Bahri Province: ABDELLA ADEM.

Gash-Barka Province: MUSTAFA NUR HUSSEIN.

Maakel Province: WELDENKIEL ABRAHA.

Semenawi Keyih Bahri Province: IBRAHIM IDRIS TOTIL.

Legislature

NATIONAL ASSEMBLY

In accordance with transitional arrangements formulated in Decree No. 37 of May 1993, the National Assembly consists of the Central Committee of the People's Front for Democracy and Justice (PFDJ) and 60 other members: 30 from the Provincial Assemblies and an additional 30 members, including a minimum of 10 women, to be nominated by the PFDJ Central Committee. The legislative body 'outlines the internal and external policies of the government, regulates their implementation, approves the budget and elects a president for the country'. The National Assembly is to hold regular sessions every six months under the chairmanship of the President. In his role as Head of the Government and Commander-in-Chief of the Army, the President nominates individuals to head the various government departments. These nominations are ratified by the legislative body. In March 1994 the National Assembly voted to alter its composition: it would henceforth comprise the 75 members of the Central Committee of the PFDJ and 75 directly elected members. In May 1997, following the adoption of the Constitution, the Constituent Assembly empowered a Transitional National Assembly (comprising the 75 members of the PFDJ, 60 members of the former Constituent Assembly and 15 representatives of Eritreans residing abroad) to act as the legislature until elections were held for a new National Assembly.

Chairman of the Transitional National Assembly: ISSAIAS AFEWERKI.

Political Organizations

At independence in May 1993, many of the rival political organizations to the Eritrean People's Liberation Front (now the People's Front for Democracy and Justice) declared their support for the transitional Government.

Democratic Movement for the Liberation of Eritrea: opposition group; Leader HAMID TURKY.

Eritrean Islamic Jihad (EIJ): radical opposition group; in Aug. 1993 split into a mil. wing and a political wing, led by Sheikh MOHAMED ARAFA.

Eritrean Liberation Front (ELF): f. 1958; commenced armed struggle against Ethiopia in 1961; subsequently split into numerous factions (see below); mainly Muslim support; opposes the PFDJ; principal factions:

> **Eritrean Liberation Front–Central Command (ELF–CC):** f. 1982; Chair. ABDALLAH IDRISS.

> **Eritrean Liberation Front–National Council (ELF–NC):** Leader HASSAN ALI ASSAD.

> **Eritrean Liberation Front–Revolutionary Council (ELF–RC):** Leader IBRAHIM MOHAMED ALI.

People's Front for Democracy and Justice (PFDJ): POB 1081, Asmara; tel. (1) 121399; fax (1) 120848; f. 1970 as the Eritrean Popular Liberation Forces, following a split in the Eritrean Liberation Front; renamed the Eritrean People's Liberation Front in 1977; adopted present name in Feb. 1994; Christian and Muslim support;

in May 1991 took control of Eritrea and formed provisional Govt; formed transitional Govt in May 1993; Chair. ISSAIAS AFEWERKI; Sec.-Gen. ALAMIN MOHAMED SAID.

Red Sea Afar Democratic Organization: Afar opposition group; Sec.-Gen. Ato AMIN AHMMAD.

Diplomatic Representation

EMBASSIES IN ERITREA

China, People's Republic: 16 Ogaden St, POB 204, Asmara; tel. (1) 185271; fax (1) 185275; Ambassador: SHI YONGJIU.

Denmark: Ras Dashan St 11, POB 6300, Asmara; tel. (1) 124346; fax (1) 124343; e-mail dkemb@eol.com.er; Chargé d'affaires a.i.: PETER TRUELSEN.

Djibouti: POB 5589, Asmara; tel. (1) 354961; fax (1) 351831; Ambassador: AHMAD ISSA.

Egypt: POB 5577, Asmara; tel. (1) 123603; fax (1) 123294; Ambassador: Dr RIFAT AL-ANSARI.

Ethiopia: Franklin D. Roosevelt St, Asmara; tel. (1) 116365; fax (1) 116144; Ambassador: AWALOM WOLDU (recalled May 1998).

France: POB 209, Asmara; tel. (1) 126599; fax (1) 121036; e-mail af@gemel.com.er; Ambassador: LOUIS LE VERT.

Germany: 24 Ogaden Ave, POB 5589, Asmara; tel. (1) 182670; fax (1) 182900; Ambassador: ELMAR TIMPE.

Israel: POB 5600, Asmara; tel. (1) 185626; fax (1) 185550; e-mail isremb@eol.com.er; Ambassador: RAPHAEL WALDEN.

Italy: POB 220, Asmara; tel. (1) 120160; fax (1) 121115; e-mail iea@eol.com.er; Ambassador: ANTONIO BANDINI.

Libya: Asmara.

Russia: POB 5667, Asmara; tel. (1) 127172; fax (1) 182033; Ambassador: ALEKSANDR OBLOV.

Saudi Arabia: POB 5599, Asmara; tel. (1) 120171; fax (1) 121027; Ambassador: ABDUL R. IBRAHIM AT-TOELMI.

Sudan: Asmara.

USA: 34 Zera Yacob St, POB 211, Asmara; tel. (1) 120004; fax (1) 127584; Ambassador: WILLIAM D. CLARKE.

Yemen: POB 5566, Asmara; tel. (1) 114434; fax (1) 117921; Ambassador: Dr AKRAM ABD AL-MARIK AL-QABRI.

Judicial System

The judicial system operates on the basis of transitional laws which incorporate pre-independence laws of the Eritrean People's Liberation Front, revised Ethiopian laws, customary laws and post-independence enacted laws. The independence of the judiciary in the discharge of its functions is unequivocally stated in Decree No. 37, which defines the powers and duties of the Government. It is subject only to the law and to no other authority. At present, the court structure is composed of first instance sub-zonal courts, appellate and first instance zonal courts, appellate and first instance high courts and a panel of high court judges, presided over by the president of the high court, as a court of last resort. With the implementation of the 1997 ratified Constitution, a supreme court will be established, whose judges will be appointed by the President of the State, subject to confirmation by the National Assembly.

High Court: POB 241, Asmara; tel. (1) 115210.

Religion

Eritrea is almost equally divided between Muslims and Christians. Most Christians are adherents of the Orthodox Church, although there are Protestant and Roman Catholic communities. A small number of the population follow traditional beliefs.

CHRISTIANITY

The Eritrean Orthodox Church

In September 1993 the separation of the Eritrean Orthodox Church from the Ethiopian Orthodox Church was agreed by the respective church leaderships. The Eritrean Orthodox Church announced that it was to create a diocese of each of the country's then 10 provinces. The first five bishops of the Eritrean Orthodox Church were consecrated in Cairo in September 1994. In May 1998 Eritrea's first Patriarch (Abune) was consecrated in Asmara.

Patriarch (Abune): Archbishop PHILIPPOS.

The Roman Catholic Church

At 31 December 1998 there were an estimated 133,192 adherents in the country.

Bishop of Asmara: Rt Rev. ZEKARIAS YOHANNES, 19 Gonder St, POB 244, Asmara; tel. (1) 120206; fax (1) 126519.

Bishop of Barentu: Rt Rev. LUCA MILESI, POB 9, Barentu; tel. (1) 120631; fax (1) 122322.

Bishop of Keren: Rt Rev. TESFAMARIAM BEDHO, POB 460, Keren; tel. (1) 401907; fax (1) 401604; e-mail cek@gemel.com.er.

The Anglican Communion

Within the Episcopal Church in Jerusalem and the Middle East, Eritrea lies within the jurisdiction of the Bishop in Egypt.

Leader: ASFAHA MAHARY.

ISLAM

Eritrea's main Muslim communities are concentrated in the western lowlands, the northern highlands and the eastern coastal region.

Leader: Sheikh AL-AMIN OSMAN AL-AMIN.

The Press

Chamber News: POB 856, Asmara; tel. (1) 120045; fax (1) 120138; monthly; Tigrinya, Arabic and English; publ. by Asmara Chamber of Commerce.

Eritrea Profile: POB 247, Asmara; f. 1994; weekly; English; publ. by the Ministry of Information and Culture.

Hadas Eritra (New Eritrea): Asmara; f. 1991; three times a week; in English, Tigrinya and Arabic; govt publ.; Editor YITBAREK ZEROM; circ. 25,000.

Newsletter: POB 856, Asmara; tel. (1) 120045; fax (1) 120138; e-mail encc@aol.com.er; monthly; Tigrinya, Arabic and English; publ. by Eritrean National Chamber of Commerce; Editor MUHAMMED-SFAF HAMMED.

Trade and Development Bulletin: POB 856, Asmara; tel. (1) 121388; fax (1) 120138; monthly; Tigrinya, Arabic and English; publ. by Asmara Chamber of Commerce; Editor TAAME FOTO.

Broadcasting and Communications

Ministry of Transport and Communications (Communications Department): POB 4918, Asmara; tel. (1) 115847; fax (1) 126966; e-mail motc_rez@eol.com.er; Dir-Gen. ESTIFANOS AFEWERKI.

TELECOMMUNICATIONS

Telecommunications Services of Eritrea: 11 Semaetat St, POB 234, Asmara; tel. (1) 117547; fax (1) 120938; f. 1991; Gen. Man. GOITOM OGBAZGHI.

BROADCASTING
Radio

Voice of the Broad Masses of Eritrea (Dimseehafash): POB 242, Asmara; tel. (1) 117111; fax (1) 124847; govt-controlled; programmes in Arabic, Tigrinya, Tigre, Amharic, Afar and Kunama; Dir-Gen. MAHMUD CHIRUM.

Television

ERI-TV: Asmara; f. 1992; govt station providing educational, tech. and information service; broadcasting began in 1993 in Arabic and Tigrinya; transmissions limited to Asmara and surrounding areas.

Finance

(cap. = capital; dep. = deposits; m. = million; brs = branches; amounts in Ethiopian birr)

In November 1997 Eritrea adopted the nakfa as its unit of currency, replacing the Ethiopian birr, which had been Eritrea's monetary unit since independence.

BANKING
Central Bank

Bank of Eritrea: POB 849, 21 Awet St, Asmara; tel. (1) 123036; fax (1) 123162; e-mail tekieb@boe.gov.er; f. 1993; bank of issue; Gov. TEKIE BEYENE.

Other Banks

Commercial Bank of Eritrea: POB 219, Asmara; tel. (1) 121844; fax (1) 124887; f. 1991; dep. 5,100m. (Dec. 1996); Gen. Man. YAMANE TESFAI; 15 brs.

Eritrean Development and Investment Bank: POB 1266, Asmara; tel. (1) 123787; f. 1996; cap. 45m.; provides medium- to long-term credit; 13 brs.

Housing and Commerce Bank of Eritrea: POB 235, Asmara; tel. (1) 120350; fax (1) 120401; e-mail hcbe@gemel.com.er; f. 1994; cap. 33m., total assets 1,008m. (Dec. 1998); finances residential and commercial construction projects and commercial loans; CEO Dr ARAIA TSEGGAI; 7 brs.

INSURANCE

National Insurance Corporation of Eritrea: Asmara Bldg, POB 881, Asmara; tel. (1) 123000; fax (1) 123240; e-mail nice@eol.com.er; Gen. Man. ZERU WOLDEMICHAEL.

Trade and Industry
CHAMBER OF COMMERCE

Eritrean National Chamber of Commerce: POB 856, Asmara; tel. (1) 121388; fax (1) 120138; e-mail encc@aol.com.er.

TRADE ASSOCIATION

Red Sea Trading Corporation: 29/31 Ras Alula St, POB 332, Asmara; tel. (1) 127846; fax (1) 124353; f. 1983; import and export services; operated by the PFDJ; Gen. Man. KUBROM DAFLA.

UTILITIES
Electricity

Eritrean Electricity Authority (EEA): Asmara.

Water

Dept of Water Resources: Asmara; tel. (1) 119636; fax (1) 124625.

Transport

Eritrea's transport infrastructure was severely damaged during the three decades of war prior to independence. International creditors have since provided loans for the repair and reconstruction of the road network and for the improvement of port facilities.

RAILWAYS

The 306-km railway connection between Agordat, Asmara and the port of Massawa was severely damaged during the war of independence and ceased operation in 1975. In 1999 an 81-km section of the Asmara–Massawa line (between Massawa and Embatkala) became operational; the 36-km railway connection between Embatkala and Asmara was under rehabilitation.

Eritrean Railway: POB 6081, Asmara; tel. (1) 123365; fax (1) 201785; Co-ordinator, Railways Rehabilitation Project AMANUEL GEBRESELLASIE.

ROADS

In 1997 there were approximately 3,900 km of roads in Eritrea, of which some 900 km were paved. Roads that are paved require considerable repair, as do many of the bridges across seasonal water courses destroyed in the war. Road construction between Asmara and the port of Massawa was given particular priority in the Recovery and Rehabilitation Programme.

SHIPPING

Eritrea has two major seaports: Massawa, which sustained heavy war damage in 1990, and Assab, which has principally served Addis Ababa, in Ethiopia. Under an accord signed between the Ethiopian and Eritrean Governments in 1993, the two countries agreed to share the facilities of both ports. Since independence, activity in Massawa has increased substantially; however, activity at Assab declined following the outbreak of hostilities with Ethiopia in May 1998. In 1998 a total of 463 vessels docked at Massawa, handling 1.2m. metric tons of goods; 322 vessels docked at Assab, which handled 1.0m. tons of goods.

Dept of Maritime Transport: POB 679, Asmara; tel. (1) 121317; fax (1) 121316; e-mail motc_rez@eol.com.er; Dir-Gen. IBRAHIM SAÏD IDRIS.

Port and Maritime Transport Authority: POB 851, Asmara; tel. (1) 111399; fax (1) 113647; Dir WELDE MIKAEL ABRAHAM.

Eritrean Shipping Lines: 80 Semaetat Ave, POB 1110, Asmara; tel. (1) 120359; fax (1) 120331; f. 1992; provides shipping services in Red Sea and Persian (Arabian) Gulf areas and owns and operates four cargo ships; Gen. Man. TEWELDE KELATI.

CIVIL AVIATION

The international airport is at Asmara.

Civil Aviation Department: POB 252, Asmara; tel. (1) 124335; fax (1) 124334; e-mail motc_rez@eol.com.er; handles freight and

ERITREA

passenger traffic for eight scheduled carriers which use Asmara airport; Dir-Gen. PAULOS KAHSAY.

Eritrean Airlines: POB 222, Asmara; tel. (1) 181822; fax (1) 181255; Man. Dir ABRAHA GHIRMAZION.

Tourism

The Ministry of Tourism is overseeing the development of this sector, although its advance since independence has been inhibited by the country's war-damaged transport infrastructure, and by subsequent conflicts with Ethiopia and other regional tensions. Eritrea possesses many areas of scenic and scientific interest, including the Dahlak Islands (a coralline archipelago rich in marine life), off shore from Massawa, and the massive escarpment rising up from the coastal plain and supporting a unique ecosystem. In 1998 tourist arrivals in Eritrea totalled 187,647, compared with 409,544 in 1997; in 1996 tourism receipts amounted to US $69m.

Eritrean Tourism Service Corporation: Asmara; operates govt-owned hotels.

Defence

In August 1999 Eritrea's active armed forces were estimated to number as many as 200,000 (of whom up to 150,000 were conscripts), including an army of about 180,000 and a navy of 1,100. In addition, there were some 120,000 reserves. National service is compulsory for all Eritreans between 18 and 40 years of age (with certain exceptions), for an 18-month period, including six months of military training. The defence budget for 1999 was estimated at US $236m. In September 2000 the UN Security Council approved the establishment of the UN Mission in Ethiopia and Eritrea (comprising 4,200 peace-keeping troops), which was to be deployed on the Eritrean side of the two countries' common border.

Education

Education is provided free of charge in government schools and at the University of Asmara. There are also some fee-paying private schools. Education is officially compulsory for children between seven and 13 years of age. Primary education begins at the age of seven and lasts for five years. Secondary education, beginning at 12 years of age, lasts for as much as six years, comprising a first cycle of two years and a second of four years. In 1996 the total enrolment at primary and secondary schools was equivalent to 37% of the school-age population (41% of boys; 33% of girls). In that year primary enrolment included 31% of children in the relevant age-group (males 32%; females 29%), while the comparable ratio for secondary enrolment was only 16% (males 17%; females 15%). Government expenditure on education and training in 1997 was estimated at 238.6m. nakfa (9.2% of total spending). By mid-1994 Eritrea had about 600 schools, almost three times as many as in 1991. In 1997 there were 3,096 students enrolled at the University of Asmara or at equivalent-level institutions. The overall rate of adult illiteracy in Eritrea in the mid-1990s was estimated to be 80%; among demobilized women fighters the rate was believed to be as high as 95%.

Bibliography

Abbay, A. *Identity Jilted or Re-imagining Identity? The Divergent Paths of the Eritrean and Tigrayan Nationalist Struggles.* Lawrenceville, NJ, Red Sea Press, 1998.

Cliffe, L., and Davidson, B. (Eds) *The Long Struggle of Eritrea for Independence and Constructive Peace.* Nottingham, Spokesman, 1988.

Connell, D. *Against All Odds: A Chronicle of the Eritrean Revolution.* Trenton, NJ, Red Sea Press, 1993.

Constitutional Commission of Eritrea. *Constitutional Proposals for Public Debate.* Asmara, Adulis Printing Press, 1995.

Doornbos, M., Cliffe, L., and Markakis, J. (Eds) *Beyond Conflict in the Horn: The Prospects of Peace and Development in Ethiopia, Somalia, Eritrea and Sudan.* Lawrenceville, NJ, Red Sea Press, 1992.

Doornbos, M., and Tesfai, A. (Eds). *Post-conflict Eritrea: Prospects for Reconstruction and Development.* Lawrenceville, NJ, Red Sea Press, 1999.

Duffield, M., and Prendergast, J. *Without Troops and Tanks: Humanitarian Intervention in Ethiopia and Eritrea.* Lawrenceville, NJ, Red Sea Press, 1995.

Ellingson, L. *The Emergence of Eritrea, 1958–1992.* London, James Currey Publishers, 1993.

Erlich, H. *The Struggle over Eritrea 1962–78.* Stanford, CA, Hoover Institution, 1983.

Fegley, R. *Eritrea.* Oxford, Clio Press, 1995.

Firebrace, J., and Holland, S. *Never Kneel Down.* Trenton, NJ, Red Sea Press, 1985.

Fukui, K., and Markakis, J. (Eds). *Ethnicity and Conflict in the Horn of Africa.* London, James Currey, 1994.

Gebregergis, T. *Eritrea: An Account of an Eritrean Political Exile on his Visit to Liberated Eritrea: December 1991–March 1992.* Amsterdam, Liberation Books, 1993.

Gebre-Medhin, J. *Peasants and Nationalism in Eritrea.* Trenton, NJ, Red Sea Press, 1989.

Ghebre-Ab, H. (Ed.). *Ethiopia and Eritrea: A Documentary Study.* Trenton, NJ, Red Sea Press, 1993.

Gorke, I., Klingebiel, S., et al. *Promoting the Reintegration of Former Female and Male Combatants in Eritrea.* Berlin, German Development Institute, 1995.

Iyob, R. *The Eritrean Struggle for Independence: Domination, Resistance, Nationalism 1941–93.* Cambridge, Cambridge University Press, 1995.

Kibreab, G. *Ready and Willing . . . But Still Waiting: Eritrean Refugees in Sudan and the Dilemmas of Return.* Uppsala, Life and Peace Institute, 1996.

Killion, T. *Historical Dictionary of Eritrea.* Lanham, MD, Scarecrow Press, 1998.

Legum, C., and Lee, B. *Conflict in the Horn of Africa.* London, Rex Collings, 1977.

Lewis, I. M. (Ed.). *Nationalism in the Horn of Africa.* London, Ithaca Press, 1983.

Machida, R. *Eritrea: The Struggle for Independence.* Trenton, NJ, Red Sea Press, 1987.

Markakis, J. *National and Class Conflict in the Horn of Africa.* Cambridge, Cambridge University Press (African Studies Series No. 55), 1988.

Medhanie, T. *Eritrea: The Dynamics of a National Question.* Amsterdam, B. R. Grunner, 1986.

Eritrea and Neighbours in the 'New World Order': Geopolitics, Democracy and 'Islamic Fundamentalism'. Munster, LIT, 1994.

Mesghenna, Y. *Italian Colonialism: A Case Study of Eritrea 1869–1934.* Lund, University of Lund, 1989.

Negash, T. *Italian Colonialism in Eritrea, 1882–1941: Policies, Praxis and Impact.* Uppsala, Almqvist and Wiksell International, 1987.

No Medicine for the Bite of a White Snake: Notes on Nationalism and Resistance in Eritrea 1890–1940. Uppsala, University Press, 1987.

Eritrea and Ethiopia: The Federal Experience. New Brunswick, NJ, Transaction Publishers, 1997.

Negash, T., and Tronvoll, K. *Brothers at War.* Oxford, James Currey Publishers, 2000.

Papstein, R. *Eritrea: A Tourist Guide.* Lawrenceville, NJ, Red Sea Press, 1995.

Pateman, R. *Eritrea: Even the Stones are Burning.* Trenton, NJ, Red Sea Press, 1990.

Eritrea: Revolution at Dusk. Trenton, NJ, Red Sea Press, 1991.

Pool, D. *From Guerillas to Government.* Oxford, James Currey Publishers, 2000.

Prouty, C., and Rosenfeld, E. *Historical Dictionary of Ethiopia and Eritrea.* 2nd Edn. Lanham, MD, and London, Scarecrow Press, 1994.

Sherman, R. *Eritrea: The Unfinished Revolution.* New York, Praeger, 1980.

Tekle, A. (Ed.). *Eritrea and Ethiopia: From Conflict to Co-operation.* Lawrenceville, NJ, Red Sea Press, 1994.

Tesfagiorgis, G. H. (Ed.). *Emergent Eritrea: Challenges of Economic Development.* Lawrenceville, NJ, Red Sea Press, 1993.

Trevaskis, G. K. *Eritrea: A Colony in Transition.* London, Oxford University Press, 1960.

United Nations. *The United Nations and the Independence of Eritrea.* New York, United Nations Department of Public Information, 1996.

Weini, M. *A Small Village in the Highlands of Eritrea: a Study of the People, their Livelihood and Land Tenure during the Times of Turbulence.* Lawrenceville, NJ, Red Sea Press, 1998.

With, P. *Politics and Liberation: the Eritrean Struggle, 1961–1986.* Aarhus, Denmark, University of Aarhus, 1987.

Wolde-Yesus, A. *Eritrea: Root Causes of War and Refugees.* Baghdad, Sinbad, 1992.

Yohannes, O. *Eritrea, a Pawn in World Politics.* University Press of Florida, 1991.

ETHIOPIA

Physical and Social Geography

G. C. LAST

The Federal Democratic Republic of Ethiopia is a land-locked country in the Horn of Africa, covering an area of 1,133,380 sq km (437,600 sq miles). Ethiopia's western neighbour is Sudan; to the south it has a common border with Kenya; and to the east and south-east lie the Republic of Djibouti and the Somali Democratic Republic. To the north and north-east lies the State of Eritrea.

PHYSICAL FEATURES

Elevations range from around 100 m below sea-level in the Dallol Depression (Kobar Sink), on the north-eastern border with Eritrea, to a number of mountain peaks in excess of 4,000 m above sea-level, which dominate the plateaux and of which the highest is Ras Dashen, rising to 4,620 m.

The southern half of Ethiopia is bisected by the rift valley, ranging between 40–60 km in width and containing a number of lakes. In the latitude of Addis Ababa, the western wall of the rift turns north and runs parallel to the west coast of Arabia, leaving a wide plain between the escarpment and the Red Sea coast of Eritrea. The eastern wall of the rift turns to the east in the latitude of Addis Ababa, forming an escarpment looking north over the Afar plains. The escarpments are nearly always abrupt, and are broken at only one point near Addis Ababa where the Awash river descends from the rim of the plateau.

The plateaux to the west of the rift system dip gently towards the west and are drained by right bank tributaries of the Nile system, which have carved deep and spectacular gorges. The plateaux to the north of Lake Tana are drained by the Tekeze and Angareb rivers, headwaters of the Atbara. The central plateaux are drained by the Abbai (Blue Nile) river and its tributaries. The Abbai rises in Lake Tana and is known as the Blue Nile in Sudan. Much of the flood water in the Blue Nile system comes from the left-bank tributaries, which rise in the high rainfall region of south-west Ethiopia. This southern region is also drained by the Akobo, Gilo and Baro rivers which form the headwaters of the Sobat river. The only river of significance to the west of the rift valley which is not part of the Nile system is the Omo, which drains southwards into Lake Turkana and is known in its upper course as the Gibie. The lower trough of the Omo has, in recent years, been the site of interesting archaeological discoveries of early human occupation, pre-dating the early remains at Olduvai in Tanzania. The rift valley itself contains a number of closed river basins, including the largest, the Awash, which flows north from the rift valley proper into the Afar plain and terminates in Lake Abe. It is in the middle and lower Awash regions of the rift valley that even earlier remains of man have been discovered, in the locality of Hadow, below the escarpment to the east of Dessie. The highlands to the east of the rift are drained south-eastwards by the headstreams of the Webi-Shebelli and Juba river systems.

The location of Ethiopia across a series of major fault lines and its association with earth movements, particularly in the Afar plains, which are related to the continuing drift of the African continent away from the Asian blocks, makes it highly susceptible to minor earth tremors.

CLIMATE, VEGETATION AND NATURAL RESOURCES

Ethiopia lies within the tropics but the wide range of altitude produces considerable variations in temperature conditions which are reflected in the traditional zones of the *dega* (the temperate plateaux), the *kolla* (hot lowlands) and the intermediate frost-free zone of the *woina dega*. The boundaries between these three zones lie at approximately 2,400 m and 1,700 m above sea-level. Average annual temperature in the *dega* is about 16°C, in the *woina dega* about 22°C and in the *kolla* at least 26°C. A main rainy season covers most of the country during June–August, when moist equatorial air is drawn in from the south and west.

Ethiopia is extremely vulnerable to drought conditions, particularly in the low-lying pastoral areas, and along the eastern escarpment where there is a widespread dependence upon the spring rains (*belg*). The development of cultivation in areas of marginal rainfall has accentuated this problem.

Despite the significant variations in local climates and in the distribution of rainfall, Ethiopia's climatic conditions can be described generally in terms of well-watered highlands and uplands, mostly receiving at least 1,000 mm of rain a year with the exception of the Tigraian plateau, and dry lowlands, generally having less than 500 mm of rain, with the significant exception of the Baro and Akobo river plains in the south-west, which lie in the path of summer rain-bearing winds.

The natural vegetation of the plateaux and highlands above 1,800 m is coniferous forest (notably *zigba* and *tid*), but these forests have now largely disappeared, existing only in the more inaccessible regions of the country. In the south-west higher rainfall with lower elevations and higher temperatures has produced extensive broad-leafed rain forests with a variety of species including abundant *karraro*. Previously densely forested areas in the former Illubabor and Kaffa Administrative Regions of the south-west have now, with the extension of all-weather road systems, been subject to extensive commercial exploitation and the activities of a growing population of traditional cultivators, with devastating impact on the natural vegetation.

Above the tree line on the plateaux are wide expanses of mountain grassland. The highlands are the site of settled agriculture in which some 4m. farmers produce a variety of grain crops. The growth of population and the depletion of resources in forest cover and soil has led to the practice of farming in areas which are very marginal and unreliable in rainfall, notably along the eastern escarpment. This has exacerbated the drought and famine conditions that have developed since 1973 and have been repeated with growing severity in 1984, 1990, 1999 and 2000. In particular, the most important traditional grain crop, teff, used in the highlands for the production of the staple food, injera, has been most seriously affected. This has had a notable impact, as these populations do not adapt easily to replacement crops (and relief supplies) of maize and rice.

In the lowlands, dependent on rainfall conditions, there is a range of dry-zone vegetation. Extensive natural range-lands, particularly in the Borena and Ogaden plains in the south, are an important resource in Ethiopia and currently support some 30m. head of cattle.

Drought conditions, which began in 1972–73, in association with abnormal conditions affecting the whole Sahel region of Africa, have completely disrupted the pastoral economy in many areas, resulting in a high mortality rate both of humans and livestock and severely depleting vegetation cover.

To add to Ethiopia's problems is the frequent invasion by the so-called 'desert' locust. There are breeding grounds of this insect in the drier regions of the country, but much of the damage is done by large swarms of adults, which can contain more than 25m. locusts, each eating its own weight in vegetation daily, and which originate in the semi-desert areas of Sudan, Saudi Arabia, Somalia and Kenya.

Although the exploitation of gold and copper ores on the Eritrean plateau dates from prehistoric times, relatively little is known of the potential mineral resources of Ethiopia; by the mid-1990s only about one-quarter of the country had been geologically mapped. Probably the area with the highest mineral potential lies in the west and south-west (in the Wollega, Illubabor and Kaffa regions). There are alluvial gold workings in the Adola area of the Sidamo region, and platinum deposits near Yubdo in the Wollega region. Potentially valuable deposits of potash have been located in the Dallol Depression; their exploitation awaits the development of other infrastructure and effective joint operations between Ethiopia and Eritrea.

Exploration for petroleum was carried out for some years in the Ogaden region without success. More recently, attention has been diverted to the southern borders of Ethiopia. In the Bale region between the rivers Web and Webi-Shebelli, it has been reported that petroleum reserves have been identified. The geothermal power potential of extensive sources in the Afar plain region is being evaluated.

Ethiopia commands excellent potential for the generation of hydroelectric power. A number of plants are in operation along the course of the Awash river, while numerous sites have been identified along the Blue Nile river basin, at which power production could be coupled with irrigation schemes.

POPULATION

According to a census that was conducted in May 1984 (which was estimated to have reached 85% of the population), the total population (excluding Eritrea, but including an estimate for areas not covered by the census) was 39,868,501 (males 20,062,453, females 19,806,048). The average annual population growth rate for Ethiopia in 1985–94 was 2.9%. The large percentage of the population aged 19 years or less, together with the early age of marriage in Ethiopia, contributed to the rapidly increasing population growth rate during the 1980s.

However, the annual population growth rate during 1990–96 declined to 2.2%.

According to a census conducted in October 1994, the total population was 49,218,178 (males 24,564,929, females 24,653,249). The population of the capital had increased to 2,084,588, while a further eight towns each had more than 105,000 inhabitants. The growth rates in these larger urban settlements are high. At mid-1999 the country's population was officially estimated to be 61,672,000, with overall density of population of 54.4 inhabitants per sq km. However, this average conceals a very wide variation among the regions, as might be expected from the multiplicity of natural environments.

The distribution of population generally reflects the pattern of relief. The highlands, having a plentiful rainfall, are the home of settled agriculture and contain nearly all of the major settlements. Land more than 2,000 m above sea-level was, in the past, free of the malarial mosquito, a factor contributing to the non-occupation of lowlands that are suitable for farming. However, recent evidence shows that this traditional limit is being breached as average temperatures rise and the mosquito adapts to higher elevations. It would not be unreasonable to assume that 10% of the population live below 1,000 m, 20% at 1,000 m–1,800 m and 70% above the 1,800 m contour line. The distribution of population has been affected by recurrent droughts, which have forced many people to leave their traditional areas in search of emergency aid; and by the erstwhile government's policy of resettling famine victims from the former Tigrai and Wollo Administrative Regions in newly-established villages in the lowlands of the south-west; additionally, the civil war, which intensified in 1989–91, caused the displacement of large numbers of the population.

The implementation of new administrative regions ('States'), which are based on ethnic distributions, has resulted in movement of minority groups, and the continued massive recruitment of young men for the war with Eritrea is likely to have long-term implications for population growth and distribution.

Recent History

PATRICK GILKES

THE ETHIOPIAN EMPIRE

Ethiopia's history as an organized and independent polity dates from about 100 BC with a kingdom at Axum in the northern regional state (*killil*) of Tigrai. The Axumite empire, as it later became, covered the northern part of the present state of Ethiopia and included part of Eritrea down to the coast around Massawa and Zula. It was converted to Christianity in the fourth century AD. In the fourth and sixth centuries, it extended across the Red Sea, but its core lay in the northern Ethiopian highlands. When Axum collapsed in the eighth century, power shifted south to Lasta, and later to Shoa. In the 16th century, 50 years of conflict with the Muslim sultanate of Adal exhausted both; they fell an easy prey to the Oromos, a pastoral people who expanded from the south.

By the late 18th century, although powerless emperors and the Ethiopian Orthodox (Coptic) Church provided an element of continuity, real power was in the hands of provincial nobles from the highlands, Tigraian, Oromo and Amhara, who fought for control of the throne. In the 1880s Yohannes IV from Tigrai region successfully fended off Egyptians, Italians and Dervishes; his successor, Menelik of Shoa, reunited and expanded the empire to the east, south and west of Shoa, taking over largely Oromo-inhabited areas rich in coffee, gold, ivory and slaves. Menelik's successes coincided with the arrival of the European colonial powers. He defeated the Italians at the battle of Adua in 1896, but under the subsequent treaty Italy retained control of Eritrea.

Menelik (who died in 1913) presided over the first stages of Ethiopia's modernization; Haile Selassie (emperor during 1930–74) turned Ethiopia into a centralized autocracy. The process was interrupted by the Italian invasion and conquest of 1935–41, but after Ethiopia's liberation, a by-product of Italy's involvement in the Second World War, Haile Selassie continued a largely successful policy of centralization, playing off the United Kingdom, which came close to occupying Ethiopia after 1941 (it only withdrew from the Ogaden in 1948 and the Reserved Haud area in 1954), against the USA. In 1952, after protracted discussions, Eritrea, a UN-mandated territory after the war, was federated with Ethiopia. Haile Selassie immediately began dismantling its institutions, including the press, trade unions, political parties and the elected parliament, all anathema to his own highly centralized structure of control. In 1962 Eritrea became a province of Ethiopia, igniting the Eritrean struggle for independence. Orginally led by the Eritrean Liberation Front (ELF) which drew most of its support from Muslim pastoralists in lowland areas, by the early 1970s it was joined by the Eritrean People's Liberation Front (EPLF), which was more representative of the Tigraian Christian highland agriculturalists.

Haile Selassie supplied the trappings of a more modern state, including, in 1955, a constitution with an elected, though powerless, parliament. He made no real effort to effect necessary changes in land policy, or adjust the hierarchies of administrative power. Ethiopia remained essentially feudal, with small Amhara-dominated modern sectors in the bureaucracy and in industry. These provided the impetus for opposition among non-Amhara nationalities, in Tigrai region in 1943, among Oromos and Somalis in Bale in 1963–70, and after 1961 in Eritrea. Haile Selassie himself preferred to concentrate on international affairs. Addis Ababa became the headquarters of the Organization of African Unity (OAU), and the UN Economic Commission for Africa. His main ally was the USA: Ethiopia, the main recipient of US aid in Africa in the 1950s and 1960s, provided the USA with a major communications base at Kagnew, in Eritrea.

Long-term weaknesses of the regime included a growing agrarian crisis, inequitable distribution of land, and lack of development. More immediately, the costs of the revolt in Eritrea after 1961, drought and famine in Wollo in 1972–74 (in which 200,000 people died), and, by 1973, Haile Selassie's own near-senility and his failure to designate an heir, fuelled the grievances of the military, students (with no employment prospects), and workers. A series of army mutinies, started in January 1974, were paralleled by civilian strikes. Attempts at reform by a new prime minister made little progress, and from June a co-ordinating committee of the armed forces began to arrest leading officials. Haile Selassie was deposed in September, with hardly a murmur of dissent. The monarchy was formally abolished in March 1975.

MILITARY RULE

The imperial regime was replaced by the Provisional Military Administrative Council (PMAC), or Dergue, a group of 109 soldiers up to the rank of major. A popular soldier, Lt-Gen. Aman Andom, from Eritrea, was drafted in as head of state, but disagreements over how to deal with the Eritrean revolt led to his death only two months later. At the same time, 57 former high-ranking military and civilian officials were summarily executed, including two former prime ministers and 17 generals.

Under the influence of left-wing intellectuals returning from abroad, the PMAC began to see itself as the vanguard of an Ethiopian revolution. In December 1974 Ethiopia was declared a socialist state, and a programme of revolutionary reforms called *Ethiopia Tikdem* ('Ethiopia First'), was initiated. Over the next few months more than 100 companies were nationalized or partly taken over by the state; trade unions were restructured; rural and urban land was nationalized in March and July 1995 respectively; thousands of students were dispatched to the countryside on a national campaign for development; more than 30,000 local, electively-led peasant associations were created with responsibility for tax collection, judicial affairs and administration; and similar associations, *kebeles*, were established in towns, with pyramids of higher-level organizations, district, regional and national.

In April 1976 the theory of the revolution was outlined in the 'national democratic revolution programme', essentially the work of a Marxist-Leninist group, the All-Ethiopia Socialist Movement (MEISON) which wanted a Soviet-style communist party, but was prepared to accept the need for temporary military rule. Its rival, the Ethiopian People's Revolutionary Party (EPRP), another and more popular Marxist-Leninist grouping, argued for the immediate creation of a civilian government, and also supported the Eritrean struggle. Their disputes, over ideology and control of the new institutions, intensified into urban terrorism, and spilt over into the Dergue. In December 1976 pro-EPRP Dergue members appeared to have won the arguments; in February 1977 the first vice-chairman of the Dergue, Lt-Col Mengistu Haile Mariam, seized power with MEISON support. The head of state, Gen. Teferi Banti, and five other leading members of the Dergue were executed. Mengistu became head of state and chairman of the PMAC. He subsequently launched, originally on behalf of his ally MEISON, the 'red terror' campaign, aimed at eliminating the EPRP. Tens of thousands were killed or tortured, particularly in urban areas. MEISON did not benefit. In mid-1977 Mengistu turned against it too, and by late 1978 both organizations had been virtually eliminated.

The ideological and power struggles were intensified by a deteriorating military situation in Eritrea, where the guerrillas had captured all but five towns, and in the south and south-east where Somalia attempted to take advantage of the weakness of the central administration and the army. In July 1977 Somalia, claiming the Somali-inhabited area of the Ogaden, invaded to support the Western Somali Liberation Front (WSLF) guerrillas which it had been arming and training. Within five months Somali forces had overrun most of the south and south-east, and the town of Harar was under attack. However, the overstretched Somali army ran out of supplies, just as Ethiopia, with Cuban help in training a 300,000-strong militia force in just six months, received a massive influx of Soviet weapons, including hundreds of tanks, and fighter aircraft. (By 1991 the USSR had provided Ethiopia with some US $8,000m. of military equipment.) So-

malia, previously a close ally of the USSR, expelled its Soviet military advisers and severed relations with Cuba; Ethiopia, in turn, suspended relations with the USA. In early 1978, with its new weaponry and the help of 16,000 Cuban troops, the Ethiopian army drove out the Somali army. It then moved to Eritrea. Within a few months it had retaken most of the towns, forcing the ELF to revert to guerrilla operations, and pushing the EPLF into the far north around the remote town of Nakfa. There the Ethiopian forces lost their momentum, and over several years accumulated serious losses in a series of unsuccessful attacks including the 'Red Star' offensive, personally commanded by Mengistu. Meanwhile, continuing religious, ethnic and ideological differences among the Eritrean movements erupted into civil war in 1981; the EPLF, in alliance with the Tigrai People's Liberation Front (TPLF) from neighbouring Tigrai region, forced the ELF into Sudan in 1982, where they were disarmed and later fragmented.

After the military successes of 1978, Mengistu turned his attention to organizing a political party. Disputes among existing small Marxist-Leninist political organizations led him to opt for a party of individuals. The Commission for Organizing the Party of the Working People of Ethiopia was established in 1979; loyalty rather than ideology became the prime criterion for membership. Various revolutionary women's, youth, peasant and trade union associations were founded, and the Workers' Party of Ethiopia was formally inaugurated in September 1984. It failed to attract either support or loyalty from the general population, being seen as a vehicle for the regime's control.

NATIONALITIES ISSUES AND THE OVERTHROW OF MENGISTU

The PMAC was no more successful with its major problem, the issue of nationalities. The rhetoric of the revolution raised expectations among various nationalities, particularly Oromos, Somalis, Afars and Tigraians. (The EPLF insisted Eritrea was a colonial issue not a nationalist one, partly to avoid problems with its nine nationalities.) The government had one partial success with the Afars when a 'progressive' Afar National Liberation Movement (ANLM) appeared, prepared to accept the PMAC's version of regional autonomy. ANLM members were appointed local administrators, but the speed of progress towards autonomy satisfied no one. No advance was made in autonomy for Somalis or Oromos. Somalia, despite its defeat in 1978, continued its support for the WSLF and the Somali Abo Liberation Front (which operated in Bale and Sidamo regions) until the mid-1980s when both movements, suffering from internal splits, collapsed. Relations between the two governments finally improved in 1988 as threats from their opponents grew. By the early 1980s, the Oromo Liberation Front (OLF), advocating self-determination for the Oromo people and the use of Oromo culture and language, was gaining support from peasants critical of government efforts to establish co-operatives; originally, the Dergue's greatest support had been among Oromo peasantry who had benefited from the land reforms of 1975. The OLF remained militarily small, but was able to operate along the Sudan border of western Wollega where it had some EPLF support, and in an area south-west of Harar. Most serious for the government was the success of the TPLF. Established in 1975, this received arms and training from the EPLF. In 1977–78 it drove out other opponents, notably the Ethiopian Democratic Union, an exile-based group which included former aristocracy, and the left-wing EPRP, which had taken up armed struggle. Gaining considerable support from the effects of the 'red terror' campaign, and its calls for Tigraian self-determination, the TPLF moved steadily left, setting up the Marxist–Leninist League of Tigrai in 1983. Like the Eritreans and Oromos, it was able to use the Sudan border, moving 200,000 people into Sudan during the famine of 1984–85. Throughout the 1980s Ethiopia–Sudan relations were poor, with each country supporting the other's dissidents. Relations between the TPLF and the EPLF were strained for several years in the 1980s, but after 1988, when they were once more co-operating, the TPLF was rapidly able to take over the whole of Tigrai region.

The regime's response to the growth of the nationality movements was, originally, only military. A political response was attempted following the disastrous famine of 1984–85, which had eradicated any gains made by state farms, and a heavily criticized and ill-organized resettlement programme, abandoned after two years, which had moved some 600,000 people into the south and west; how many died is unknown. The new constitution of 1987 provided for an 835-seat elected legislature, the national shengo, and for the creation of several autonomous regions based on ethnicity: Tigrai for the Tigraian people; Dire Dawa for Issa Somalis; the Ogaden region for other Somalis; and Assab for Afars in both Eritrea and Ethiopia. These allowed for elected assemblies with control over health, education, development, finance and taxation. In 1990, following an attempted coup the previous year, Mengistu made further concessions. Ethiopian socialism was abandoned; opposition groups were invited to participate in a unity party; free market principles replaced economic planning; and peasants were allowed to bequeath land to their children. The peasantry were quick to abandon the highly unpopular enforced villagization policy, and the area of land under cultivation increased significantly.

However, Mengistu's overtures failed to satisfy either the EPLF or the TPLF; both were determined to oust him, regarding this as a prerequisite for achievement of their aims. Mengistu's military situation deteriorated steadily after 1988 following a major defeat at Af Abet in Eritrea; Massawa was captured by the EPLF in February 1990, severing supply lines for the army in Eritrea. Disillusionment grew steadily within the army, which was previously prepared to accept Mengistu because of his determination to keep Eritrea and his commitment to a united Ethiopia; his apparent refusal to accept any political solution was finally seen as a liability. The economy was collapsing as fast as the military and political situation. The price of coffee, Ethiopia's sole foreign exchange earner, was falling, and supplies of cheap Soviet petroleum ceased in mid-1989. The revolution in Eastern Europe precipitated a complete collapse of Ethiopia's overseas alliances, and the loss of critically necessary arms supplies. Mengistu tried to replace his Soviet allies with Israel, promising to allow the Ethiopian Jews (Falashas) to leave (13,000 had been flown from Sudan to Israel in a secret airlift in 1984); for a few months Israel provided cluster bombs and anti-guerrilla training, but, under strong US pressure, this support was stopped. However, in May 1991 as the regime collapsed, with government consent the Israelis took control of Addis Ababa airport for 36 hours to evacuate a further 14,000 of the remaining Falasha population.

Once in control of Tigrai region in 1989, the TPLF established a united front, the Ethiopian People's Revolutionary Democratic Front (EPRDF), with the Ethiopian People's Democratic Movement, a largely Amhara organization that the TPLF had created as a surrogate group to fight outside Tigrai region, and subsequently renamed the Amhara National Democratic Movement. As the EPRDF advanced further south it created other organizations: the Oromo People's Democratic Organization (OPDO), after the OLF refused to join the EPRDF, and a short-lived officers' movement (EDORM). The TPLF remained the major element in the front, but its own original demands for self-determination were replaced by its commitment to the removal of Mengistu and the establishment of a democratic government in Addis Ababa.

In January 1991 the EPRDF produced a new political programme which did not mention Marxism and was moderate and democratic enough to be acceptable to the USA. As the guerrillas closed in on Addis Ababa, Mengistu's armies ceased to fight. On May 21 Mengistu fled to Zimbabwe where he was granted political asylum. The USA presided over peace talks in London, in an attempt to provide an orderly transfer of power from the government. The government delegation did not even have time to surrender before the USA, fearing a collapse of law and order in Addis Ababa, invited the EPRDF to enter Addis Ababa. On 28 May the EPRDF entered the city and subsequently established an interim government, a move criticized by the OLF as premature. The EPLF attended the conference but as an observer only, to mark Eritrea's *de facto* independence; it subsequently established a provisional government in Eritrea pending the holding of a referendum in April 1993, when 99.8% of voters demonstrated overwhelming support for independence. *De jure* independence came in May 1993. Relations with Ethiopia were formalized by a series of agreements covering defence, security, trade and the economy, and on the use of Assab, given

status as a free port because of its particular importance to Ethiopia, land-locked by the independence of Eritrea.

THE EPRDF AND ETHNIC POLITICS

In July 1991 the EPRDF convened a national conference attended by representatives of some 20 political organizations to discuss Ethiopia's political future and establish a transitional government. The EPRDF prepared the agenda, drafted a national charter providing for an 87-seat council of representatives to govern during a two-year transition period, created some of the political groups which attended, and organized seat allocations. The EPRDF chairman, Meles Zenawi, was elected head of state; the vice-chairman of the EPRDF, Tamirat Layne, became prime minister. Some 32 political organizations were subsequently represented on the council, with the EPRDF's component parts occupying 32 of the 87 seats. The next largest group on the council was the OLF with 12 seats. The Oromos were allocated a total of 27 seats but they were divided between five different organizations. The portfolios of the council of ministers were similarly distributed with 17 ministers from seven different organizations being appointed.

From the outset, the EPRDF made it clear it would support Eritrean independence, and emphasized self-determination for Ethiopia's nationalities within a federal system as the answer to the political problem of a multi-ethnic state. The EPRDF originally established 12 self-governing regions with two chartered cities. After changes including the merger of four regions in the south west, the new constitution of 1994 created the regional states (*killil*) of Tigrai, Afar, Amhara, Oromia, Benishangul-Gumuz, Southern Peoples, Gambela, and Harar, together with Addis Ababa and the administrative area of Dire Dawa. The basis of the new states is ethnicity and language, although equally they reflect political power. Tigrai region, the home of the TPLF, lost a large area of desert, and gained the rich farming lands of Setit Humera along the Sudanese border. The Oromo region brought together most of four former regions, while nationalities that were widely spread, like the Amhara and the Gurage, and those who sought a centralized state, were not favoured by the new system.

The first stage of implementation of the new policies was the organization of local administrative elections, conducted in 1992, followed by regional nationality elections. By mid-1993 the elected regional assemblies were functioning to a greater or lesser extent. Regions were expected, in theory at least, to raise their own funding after 1993, but this has proved difficult. The bulk of revenue still comes from central government sources. In 1994 there was a significant decline in agricultural production, and the threat of large-scale famine was only averted with substantial imports. Agricultural production subsequently improved, but government claims to have achieved food self-sufficiency in 1996–97 appeared premature. There were significant food shortages in 1999 and 2000, largely owing to poor rains, with more than 8m. people needing food aid by early 2000. The war with Eritrea (see below) also had a serious effect on transport and production. Distribution of resources remained a subject of controversy.

Numerous political parties emerged, mostly ethnically based. More than 100 parties had appeared by early 1993, although the May 1995 elections were contested by only 49. As Tigrains constitute no more than 7% of the population, the EPRDF created surrogate parties or 'democratic organizations' with which it could form alliances and which it intended should eventually join the EPRDF, although only one has formally done so since the EPRDF's takeover—the Southern Ethiopian People's Democratic Union, established in 1992. This approach has complicated the political process. The existence of the EPRDF's OPDO was a major reason for the breakdown in relations with the OLF, despite the OLF's position in government. In the months preceding the 1992 elections, there were numerous clashes as the two organizations manoeuvred for position in the Oromo regions. Both also sought to remove other nationalities from their areas. Just before the elections, the OLF and several other groups pulled out, and the OLF also withdrew from the government. Its criticisms of the election were supported by international observers who reported harassment, intimidation, failures to deliver registration and voting cards or to organize election committees. The EPRDF and its supporting parties did extremely well in almost every region, and even in Addis Ababa it surprisingly won all but three of the regional seats. Elections were briefly postponed in Afar and Somali regions, where EPRDF support was less well organized. After its withdrawal from government, the OLF attempted to revive guerrilla activity. Most of its fighters were quickly apprehended but small groups continued to operate; western diplomatic efforts to reconcile the OLF and the EPRDF made little progress, and an OLF congress in April 1998 took a stronger line towards the idea of an independent Oromo state. In 1999, with Eritrean support, the OLF infiltrated several hundred Eritrean-trained fighters through Somalia into southern Ethiopia. Operating along Ethiopia's southern border, they caused considerable disruption as well as tension between Ethiopia and Kenya, although they were largely rounded up by Ethiopian security forces by the end of the year. Subsequently, the OLF claimed responsibility for several bomb explosions on the Addis Ababa–Djibouti railway.

Elections for a constituent assembly in June 1994 demonstrated that the EPRDF had become a disciplined, tightly organized and highly centralized front using government resources to great effect. The main opposition groups boycotted the election. In December the constituent assembly ratified the draft constitution (including controversial articles on the right to self-determination and secession, and state ownership of land) with little change from the approved draft, although recognition of *Shari'a* law for Muslims was included, following a major demonstration in Addis Ababa.

The final stage in the creation of the Federal Democratic Republic of Ethiopia came in May 1995 with elections to the federal parliamentary assembly (the council of people's representatives) and to the regional state councils, which elect representatives to the upper house (the council of the federation). Executive power lies with a prime minister, chosen by the majority party in the federal assembly. The EPRDF and its allies won an overwhelming victory, and Meles Zenawi, as chairman of the EPRDF, and of the TPLF which is still the dominant element in the EPRDF, became prime minister in August 1995; Dr Negasso Gidada of the OPDO was elected president. In Tigrai region the TPLF took all seats for both the federal and state assemblies; EPRDF parties were equally successful in Amhara and Oromia regions. Despite Addis Ababa's reputation as a centre for opposition, the EPRDF won all 92 local assembly seats; independents took only two of the city's 23 federal assembly seats. In Afar and Somali regions, after postponements, pro-EPRDF parties won narrow victories; in neither case did this stop guerrilla activities by opposition parties seeking greater autonomy or secession. Overall the election results were seriously undermined by the decision of most opposition parties to boycott, claiming insufficient access to media, extensive arrest and harassment of their officials and closure of party offices. International observers generally agreed with the criticisms; there was a consensus that the elections were neither free nor fair.

EPRDF control of the political process and of the political debate left the opposition in disarray. The Coalition of Alternative Forces for Peace and Democracy in Ethiopia (CAFPDE), which brings together some 30 groups, was established in 1993, following a conference in Paris, France. An attempt to hold a second conference in Addis Ababa in December was disrupted by the arrest of seven leading participants on arrival, prompting strong international criticism. Under the chairmanship of Dr Beyene Petros, who also heads the opposition Southern Ethiopian People's Democratic Coalition (SEPDC), CAFPDE includes ethnic and non-ethnic parties and professional bodies, and, in theory, some exile-based organizations. It finally achieved official registration in July 1996, and has been a major critic of EPRDF policies on land, rents and leases, the economy and human rights. However, EPRDF pressure and its control of the media, coupled with CAFPDE's own divisions, have limited its impact; when the SEPDC took part in district elections in 1997 it failed to win any seats. Another opposition party targeted by the EPRDF was the All-Amhara Peoples Organization (AAPO), whose chairman, Prof. Asrat Woldeyes, was accused of inciting violence, and jailed for a total of five years after a series of trials; numerous other AAPO officials have been detained, though seldom tried. Prof. Asrat was re-

leased from his fourth trial on grounds of ill-health in December 1998 after strong international pressure; he died in the USA in May 1999. Twenty-three others accused with him were given sentences of between three and 20 years, despite detailed allegations of torture. The AAPO has always rejected such allegations. In 1999 the AAPO split, with a significant number of members joining a new Ethiopian Democratic Party. The AAPO was also affected by leadership problems, which were only resolved six weeks before the May 2000 election.

As expected, the EPRDF won an overwhelming victory at the legislative elections held on 14 May 2000, although opposition parties were allowed to win some seats in the federal house of people's representatives (with the minister of defence losing his seat to an AAPO candidate), and slightly more in the regional assembly elections. According to the National Electoral Board (NEB), the EPRDF coalition won seats in 348 of the 505 constituencies where voting took place and where the results were allowed to stand. The seven main Ethiopian-based opposition parties subsequently claimed numerous irregularities had occurred, including physical abuse, intimidation of monitors and vote-rigging. In the months before the election, the opposition complained that candidates had been refused registration and endorsement, and supporters had often been harassed and arrested; local administrators had been partial and the state media had failed to provide promised services. Most opposition complaints, although largely substantiated by independent sources, were rejected by the NEB. However, four weeks after the election the NEB did announce new elections in 16 constituencies of the Southern Nations, Nationalities and Peoples State after complaints by the SEPDC. In early September voting took place in the Somali regional state (voting had earlier been postponed, owing to severe drought in the region). The counting of votes was disrupted, owing to a power failure; however, initial reports indicated that the Somali People's Democratic Party was on course to win the majority of the 23 seats available.

Armed opposition has appeared in several regions, including the Afar and Benishangul-Gumuz, as well as from the externally based OLF and the Ogaden National Liberation Front (ONLF), a Somali region party which split in 1995 allowing the pro-government Ethiopian Somali Democratic League (ESDL) to win elections in 1995 and 2000, although relations between the EPRDF and the regional government have remained uneasy. The OLF and the ONLF, which signed a military co-operation agreement in July 1996, demand greater autonomy and firmer commitments to possible independence. They claim the EPRDF has no intention of allowing secession, deliberately making the process lengthy and difficult—secession would require a two-thirds' majority in the regional legislature, a majority vote in a federally organized referendum, and an agreed transfer of power over a three-year period. Another Somali organization, the Islamic Union Party (al-Ittihad al-Islam), is fighting for an Islamic state. Al-Ittihad claimed responsibility for bomb explosions in hotels in Addis Ababa and Dire Dawa in early 1996, and for the attempted assassination in July of the minister of transport, a Somali and the chairman of the ESDL, although not for explosions in Harar in February 1997, and in Addis Ababa and Dire Dawa in April. The EPRDF responded from 1996 with a series of cross-border attacks into Somalia, aiming to disrupt al-Ittihad and its allies, occupying several towns and villages for much of 1997, and supplying arms to movements opposed to al-Ittihad in Somalia. These operations intensified in 1999 when Eritrea attempted to distract Ethiopia's attention from the war along the Ethio-Eritrean border by supplying the OLF and various Somali factions opposed to Ethiopia.

In 1996 the extent of corruption began to cause concern. In October the deputy prime minister and minister of defence, Tamirat Layne, was dismissed and detained. He was finally sentenced to 18 years' imprisonment in February 2000. Hundreds of officials in different *killils* have been removed since 1996, following extensive self-awareness (*gimgema*) sessions, or EPRDF-organized peace, democracy and development conferences. Few, however, have appeared in court, leading to opposition claims that the dismissals had been political rather than ethical.

The EPRDF also encountered opposition in other areas as it tried to ensure control of all professional bodies. Its regional linguistic education policy was opposed by the Ethiopian Teachers Association (ETA) which claimed it threatened the status of Amharic as a national language. Numerous members of the ETA were dismissed or detained. Its chairman, Dr Taye Wolde-Semayat, was arrested on his return from Europe in May 1996, and given a 15-year prison sentence in July 1999; he is regarded as a prisoner of conscience by the international human rights organization Amnesty International. Another leading ETA member was shot and killed by police in May 1997. The Confederation of Ethiopian Labour Unions opposed the EPRDF's privatization policies and the IMF stabilization programme. Three of its leaders fled the country in April 1999. There was trouble, too, in the Ethiopian Orthodox Church, with opposition to the patriarch, Abune Paulos, a Tigraian appointed in 1992 after his predecessor, an appointee of the previous government, was retired on grounds of ill health. In January 1997 a monk was shot and killed in church while apparently trying to assassinate the Patriarch. Accusations of maladministration, nepotism, misappropriation of funds and heresy, underline continuing dissension within the church.

The EPRDF's decision to continue state ownership of land, although coupled with security of usage, was widely resented. In the Amhara region complaints over land redivision appeared in 1997; peasants from Gojjam protested in Addis Ababa, and were supported by university students. Further demonstrations in 1997 followed sharp and unpopular rent rises in Addis Ababa. Other policies were more popular. By the end of 1994 more than 30,000 (mostly Tigraian) fighters had been demobilized, and recruitment was later widened to provide for a more national and professional army, under US prompting.

Human rights has emerged as a contentious issue, with international and local human rights organizations making serious criticisms. The EPRDF has used its 1992 press law to arrest or detain dozens of editors, owners and journalists, largely, it appeared, on the basis of criticism or questioning of government policy. Ethiopia has subsequently detained more journalists than any other country in Africa; around 200 at various times and 27 others have fled the country. Although the independent Ethiopian Free Journalists' Association, established in 1993, finally obtained official recognition in March 2000, there were still eight journalists in prison in June 2000, with a further 31 on bail. A series of Ethiopian Human Rights Council reports since 1992 has detailed alleged extrajudicial killings, disappearances and numerous cases of arbitrary arrest and imprisonment. The majority of the 20,000 Oromos detained in 1992 on suspicion of guerrilla activity were released by late 1994, and detention camps closed; nearly 300 were brought to trial in 1995. However, there have been a number of reports that hundreds of executions and disappearances have taken place in Oromo areas from 1993 onwards. In October 1997 three alleged OLF members were shot down by police in the street; in December 31 Oromos were charged in connection with several bomb attacks in April, including seven members of the Human Rights League, set up a year earlier. Amnesty International has condemned detentions without trial, disappearances and the use of torture, which by 1998 appeared to be frequent. The long delays over the trials of the senior officials of the former regime also raised comment, although few disagreed with the special prosecutor's intention to charge them with crimes against humanity. In February 1994 Ethiopia requested the extradition of the former leader, Col Mengistu, but the Zimbabwe government consistently refused. The trial of 69 former senior officials (23 *in absentia*, including Mengistu) on charges of crimes against humanity and war crimes began in December 1994, although proceedings have been adjourned on numerous occasions. In 1999 the Special Prosecutor suggested that the trial might last another 10 years unless the justices speeded up the process. In November 1999 South Africa refused a request from the Ethiopian government to extradite Mengistu, after it emerged that he was receiving medical treatment in that country. Meanwhile, in February 1997 the special prosecutor's office announced that it was going to put another 5,198 people on trial on charges of genocide and war crimes, nearly 3,000 of them *in absentia*. These trials are moving more quickly and some verdicts have already been delivered. The government held a conference in May 1998 to discuss establishing a human rights commission and the post of ombudsman; neither Amnesty International nor Human Rights

Watch, both of which produced critical reports in 1998, were invited.

EXTERNAL AFFAIRS

Internationally, the EPRDF continued to maintain good relations with the USA and with European powers. The 'Paris Club' of official creditors and international agencies have provided generous amounts of loans and grants, although the IMF, concerned about delays in liberalizing trade, interest and exchange rates, suspended a structural adjustment facility in October 1997 for a year. More recently it has been worried by the effects of the war with Eritrea and the diversion of resources this has involved. The USA regards Ethiopia as crucial to stability in the Horn of Africa and in containing Sudan and 'radical' Islam. Relations with Sudan deteriorated sharply in 1995, following the apparent Sudanese complicity in the attempted assassination of President Mubarak of Egypt in Addis Ababa in June. Ethiopia, together with Uganda and Eritrea, backed Sudanese opposition forces, providing arms, training and, in 1996, artillery support. Although during 1996 and early 1997 Sudan protested at alleged border incursions by Ethiopian troops, relations have steadily improved since 1998, following Ethiopia's conflict with Eritrea. In March 2000 10 agreements to improve cross-border security between Ethiopia and Sudan were signed.

Ethiopia has adopted an assertive regional role, heading OAU efforts to foster a peace settlement in Somalia; it hosted reconciliation conferences in Addis Ababa in 1993 and at Sodere in January 1997, where 26 Somali factions agreed on a process to establish a transitional government. Ethiopia ascribes its failure in part to Egypt's subsequent Cairo conference of Somali factions. In turn, Egypt considers Ethiopian plans to construct dams on the Blue Nile as a serious threat to its water supplies. However, in November 1999 Ethiopia, Egypt and Sudan all signed an agreement for strategic co-operation on the Nile. Ethiopia has supported efforts to give the Djibouti-based Intergovernmental Authority on Development (IGAD), which includes Djibouti, Eritrea, Ethiopia, Kenya, Sudan and Uganda, a more active political and security role regionally, including mediation in the conflicts in Somalia and Sudan. The Ethiopian–Eritrean war, however, as well as the poor relations between Eritrea and both Sudan and Djibouti, has meant that IGAD's effectiveness has been severely limited. In 1994 Ethiopia provided a battalion of troops for UN peace-keeping operations in Rwanda, and in 1996 offered troops for OAU operations in Burundi; it supports US proposals for an African peace-keeping force. Meles was OAU chairman in 1995–96. Ethiopia has established close relations with Israel and formed closer links with Saudi Arabia. Furthermore, Ethiopia signed a security agreement with Yemen in October 1999. Relations with Djibouti were consolidated when Djibouti replaced Assab as Ethiopia's main outlet to the sea, and with the election of Ethiopian-born Ismail Omar Gelleh as Djibouti's new president in May 1999.

Conflict with Eritrea

Political and economic policies since May 1998 have been dominated by the war with Eritrea. Relations had been cordial until 1997, with Eritrean independence generally, if sometimes reluctantly, accepted in Ethiopia. There were, none the less, tensions: Ethiopians resented the costs of using their former port of Assab, and unreciprocated Eritrean access to residence and employment rights in Ethiopia; Eritrea was offended by Ethiopia's reaction to its new currency, the nakfa, introduced in 1997, by Ethiopia's subsequent insistence on using 'hard' currencies in all transactions, and by its unilateral improvement in relations with Sudan. Eritrea's desire to formalize its boundaries after 1993 led it into a series of disputes with Sudan, Yemen (over the Hanish Islands in the Red Sea) and Djibouti; in 1998 it was the turn of Ethiopia. Despite the close links between Prime Minister Meles and President Issaias Afewerki of Eritrea, in May 1998 a minor border dispute escalated after several Eritrean troops were killed. Eritrea dispatched substantial reinforcements, and took over three areas previously under Ethiopian administration but claimed by Eritrea. Casualties rapidly escalated as Ethiopian aircraft attacked Asmara airport and Eritrean aircraft bombed Adigrat and Mekele. In June negotiations between the two countries, under the auspices of the Italian government and US President Bill Clinton, resulted in an aerial cease-fire. Other efforts at mediation made little progress, although the level of fighting diminished as both sides, accusing the other of responsibility for the conflict, built up substantial forces along their common border, mobilizing armies of more than 300,000 and buying hundreds of millions of dollars-worth of weapons from Russia, Eastern Europe and China.

Both sides also embarked on extensive propaganda campaigns. In June 1998 Ethiopia began a process of expelling Eritreans, and by early 2000 more than 65,000 had been deported to Eritrea. The move was strongly criticized by Amnesty International. Ethiopia also accused Eritrea, less convincingly, of forcibly expelling thousands of its nationals. Both countries, which began the registration of each other's nationals in 1999–2000, claimed that their citizens had been seriously mistreated. Hundreds of thousands of people in the border areas were displaced by the fighting.

The uneasy military calm along the border was broken in February 1999 when an Ethiopian offensive retook Badme, prompting several months of fighting, during which hundreds of people were killed. Each side accused the other of breaking the aerial cease-fire and escalating the conflict. An Ethiopian attack on Tsorona near the Eritrean-occupied town of Zelambessa was soundly defeated in March, as were two Eritrean attempts to recapture Badme in March and June, all resulting in heavy casualties. There were signs in 1999 that the conflict might spread elsewhere in the Horn of Africa. Eritrea provided arms and assistance to Ethiopian opposition groups, including the OLF and the ONLF, through Somalia, and encouraged Djiboutian opposition forces to attack the Ethiopian-Djibouti railway, threatening Ethiopia's link to the sea. Ethiopia responded by assisting the Eritrean opposition Alliance of Eritrean National Forces, which was established in Sudan in March 1999.

Mediation efforts made slow progress. In June 1998 the OAU established a mediation committee in an attempt to end the dispute, and in July an OAU delegation visited the two countries. The committee presented its report to the Ethiopian and Eritrean ministers of foreign affairs at a meeting in Ouagadougou, Burkina Faso, in August. The OAU proposals, which were based on original suggestions made by the USA and Rwanda, were rejected by Eritrea, necessitating the convening of a special meeting of the mediation committee in Ouagadougou in November. Prime Minister Meles and President Afewerki attended different sessions of the meeting, at which the heads of state of Burkina Faso, Djibouti and Zimbabwe were also present. Ethiopia welcomed the committee's proposals, which stressed the need to demilitarize and demarcate the disputed region, but Eritrea rejected the plans and accused Djibouti of favouring Ethiopia in the conflict. Other international mediation attempts continued in late 1998 (including that of Anthony Lake, a former US national security adviser), but failed to resolve the dispute.

Ethiopia continued to insist on Eritrea's withdrawal from all Ethiopian territory; however, Eritrea repeatedly rejected this demand, thus continuing to inhibit progress. The deadlock continued into May 1999 as Eritrea steadfastly refused to withdraw from the territory that it occupied, and, despite the UN Security Council's repeated insistence on an immediate cessation of fighting, Ethiopian military aircraft bombed the Eritrean port of Massawa.

In mid-July 1999 the Algerian president, Abdelaziz Bouteflika, attempted to mediate between Ethiopia and Eritrea at the OAU summit meeting in Algiers. The deadlock appeared to have been broken when the two warring countries confirmed their commitment to the OAU peace proposals, under which both sides would withdraw from all territory captured since the outbreak of the conflict, thus effectively returning both sides to their pre-war frontiers. However, the situation was complicated by Eritrean demands for war reparations and Ethiopian requests for clarification of the technical arrangements regarding the withdrawal of troops from the disputed territory. In August Eritrea formally accepted the latest OAU peace plan;

however, in the following month Ethiopia announced that it had rejected the proposals because, in its opinion, the technical arrangements were inconsistent with the other elements (the framework agreement and the modalities) of the peace propositions and did not guarantee a return to the *status quo ante*. Both sides remained distrustful of each other and were reported to be re-arming on a large scale. In October Eritrea claimed Zelambessa as its sovereign territory, and, while both sides publicly insisted that they were intent on finding a peaceful solution to the conflict, their mutual reluctance to make concessions meant that the situation remained deadlocked.

There were reports of numerous clashes between Ethiopian and Eritrean troops throughout late 1999 and early 2000; however, in late April 2000 delegations from Ethiopia and Eritrea agreed to attend OAU-sponsored talks in Algiers, although neither side would agree to meet face to face. Instead Algerian diplomats acted as messengers between the two sides. The talks collapsed after six days with the Ethiopians blaming the Eritreans for the lack of progress and vice versa.

In mid-May 2000, just days after the UN special envoy Richard Holbrooke had visited Ethiopia and Eritrea and warned that a resumption of hostilities and the outbreak of a new round of fighting was very close, Ethiopia launched an offensive on the Mereb-Setit front near the disputed towns of Badme and Zelambessa and succeeded in repelling the Eritrean forces. The UN Security Council immediately adopted a resolution, which provided for the imposition of sanctions and an embargo on the sale of all military supplies to the two warring countries if hostilities did not cease within three days. Nevertheless, the fighting continued despite growing fears of a mounting humanitarian crisis; it was estimated that 8m. Ethiopians were in need of emergency assistance. The UN Security Council subsequently voted unanimously to impose a 12-month arms embargo on the two countries in an attempt to prevent any further intensification of hostilities; however, hours after this announcement Ethiopia declared that it had captured the key strategic town of Barentu in south-west Eritrea and had taken full control of the western front. Ethiopia launched a massive new offensive, which led to the capture of Zelambessa, and on 25 May the Eritrean government announced that it would withdraw troops from the disputed areas. However, fighting persisted in several areas, despite this declaration.

Ethiopian forces continued to capture Eritrean towns over the following days, although both sides had by this stage agreed to attend peace talks under the auspices of the OAU, which began on 29 May 2000 in Algiers. Despite this, Ethiopian aircraft bombed the military airfied in Asmara in late May, which prompted the Eritrean government to appeal for urgent international intervention. On 31 May Prime Minister Meles announced that the war with Eritrea was over and that his troops had withdrawn from most of the territory that they had captured from Eritrea. Nevertheless, fighting continued to take place whilst discussions were ongoing in Algiers, with each side accusing the other of restarting hostilities.

On 18 June 2000 both sides signed revised OAU peace proposals in Algiers. These were more favourable to Ethiopia than the earlier peace framework, allowing for a return to the pre-May 1998 border positions (without prejudice to any final settlement), for a security zone 25 km inside the Eritrean frontier and the insertion of a UN peace-keeping force, and for the future demarcation of the border according to colonial treaties and international law. The problems of demarcation and of compensation seemed likely to delay any final settlement for a long time.

In mid-September 2000 the UN Security Council approved the deployment of a 4,200-strong UN Mission in Ethiopia and Eritrea (UNMEE) peace-keeping force on the Eritrean side of the common border. UNMEE was given an initial mandate of six months and was charged with monitoring and ensuring that both Eritrea and Ethiopia comply with their agreement on the cessation of hostilities, including the redeployment of their respective forces to agreed positions.

Economy

DAVID STYAN

With some 60m. people, Ethiopia has Africa's third-largest population, after Nigeria and Egypt. It has the ninth-largest land area on the continent, and has abundant agricultural, mineral and hydrological resources. Despite this, most Ethiopians face acute rural impoverishment, their livelihoods critically dependent upon unstable, rain-fed agriculture. Ethiopians live some of the hardest, shortest lives in the world, with the lowest per caput consumption levels, and the highest incidence of malnutrition and infant mortality. Although around 30m. Ethiopians are under 16 years of age, poverty and mininal infrastructure means access to health and education services is chronically low. The lowest road-density in Africa exacerbates the isolation and vulnerability of many rural communities, particularly in years of drought. Estimated annual per caput incomes of US $110 are one-quarter the average for sub-Saharan Africa.

Economic reforms since 1991 have brought significant improvements in both economic policy and performance, but they have so far failed to produce sustained economic growth and poverty reduction. Reforms remain overshadowed by the legacy of decades of stagnation and daunting structural weaknesses. In 1998–2000 economic prospects were further undermined by an internecine war with Eritrea.

ECONOMIC STRUCTURES

Ethiopians' individual livelihoods and aggregate economic well-being depend almost entirely upon agriculture. National accounts, the accuracy of which, as with most official Ethiopian data, should be treated with considerable caution, suggest that more than 50% of gross domestic product (GDP) stems from agriculture. With the lowest level of urbanization in Africa, 85% of the population remains dependent directly or indirectly upon the land. Coffee alone accounts for more than two-thirds of export earnings, with hides, skins and the stimulant *qat* the other significant earners. Industry represents only 12% of national income, while services, including the state bureaucracy and the defence forces, account for one-third of formal economic activity. Ethiopia has a diverse agricultural profile, with cropping patterns and livelihoods differing widely both between and within highland communities. Coffee and root crops are grown in the fertile central and southern areas, while the semi-arid eastern and southern lowlands are characterized largely by pastoral economies, notably of Somalis and Afars. Ethiopia contains the largest total livestock herds in Africa.

Despite such significant internal economic and geographical disparities, poverty is endemic throughout the country. The fragmentary aggregate national and international data available suggests that Ethiopia has some of the weakest development indicators in the world. In 1997 life expectancy at birth was 49 years. Only one-third of children of primary school age attend school, and in 1995 enrolment rates in secondary and higher education were equivalent to 11% and 0.7% of children in the relevant age-group respectively. In that year, according to UNESCO estimates, only 33.2% of the adult population were literate. Young children suffer the brunt of poverty; infant mortality is around 11%, while a further 1.8% of children do not survive beyond their fifth birthday. Lack of health care and poor sanitation account for the largest number of deaths. In the light of these statistics, it is little surprise that Ethiopia lies 169th out of the 174 countries listed in the UN Development Programme's human development index. Ethiopia's population is increasing at around 3% per annum: at current rates of growth the population is expected to reach 100m. by 2015.

Although Ethiopians are now formally administered within nine, ostensibly equal, regional states, economically the administrative units are exceedingly uneven. The vast majority of economic production is in just four states: the capital Addis Ababa (denominated region 14), Amhara (region 3), Oromia (region 4) and the heterogeneous southern nationalities' region.

These four contain almost 90% of the country's population and account for two-thirds of regional expenditure. National economic integration is hampered by poor internal transport. The road network is largely a legacy of the brief Italian occupation of the 1930s. Low density of roads, and their centralization on the hub of Addis Ababa, impedes intra-regional agricultural trade as well as famine relief. Since 1995 road building has been a government priority, accounting for around 20% of capital expenditure.

The largest single unexploited resource is rivers. The chronic instability of agricultural production could be partially alleviated by increased irrigation. At present only an estimated 4% of cultivatable land is even partially irrigated. Much of this is along the southern Awash valley. Similarly, Ethiopia's hydro-electric potential is largely untapped. Both the Awash and Blue Nile river basins could produce abundant electricity. The Blue Nile, which snakes through the central highlands from Lake Tana, supplies 80% of total Nile waters to Sudan and Egypt.

With the partial exception of gold, Ethiopia's mineral resources also remain mostly unexploited, representing less than 1% of GDP in the late 1990s. The country has considerable proven reserves of gold, coal, potassium, tantalum and iron ore. In the mid-1990s a series of foreign mining companies bought concessions to explore for gold in the country's three main goldfields. In 1997 the government sold the largest operating mine, Lega Dembi, to the Ethio-Saudi Alamoudi group. Minerals used in construction, such as limestone and marble, are produced, the latter also being exported. In addition, since 1995 there has been limited exploration for semi-precious gemstones.

ECONOMIC STAGNATION AND REFORM

Given these structural constraints, sustained economic improvement is difficult, even with policies conducive to growth. However, between the revolution in 1974 and the late 1980s, economic policy was largely unfavourable to growth, state ownership of the means of production and distribution constraining agricultural development. The government's emphasis on state farms, large-scale rural resettlement and collectivization schemes undermined agricultural production, while civil war in the provinces of Eritrea and Tigrai, recurrent drought and environmental decay reinforced economic stagnation.

Initial land reforms resulted in limited increases in productivity, but these were often undermined by insecure tenures and disincentives to production. Social indicators did improve, notably in health and literacy, though rarely to the levels claimed. Despite nationalization and state control of banks, inbred fiscal and monetary conservatism helped check inflation. However, the nationalization of industry, centralized control of distribution and considerable investment in state farms and prestige industrial projects failed to produce sustained industrial growth. Peasants' quotas, lack of agricultural incentives, poor access to credit and fertilizers and tight political control via hierarchical peasants' associations were all inimical to rural investment and entrepreneurship. Poor agrarian production was further stunted by the famine of 1984–85. Modest economic recovery came with subsequent harvests, and from 1988 there was a loosening of economic controls. Such liberalization was too little too late. Successive military defeats in the north from 1989 weakened central government and further disrupted the highland economy.

REFORMS SINCE 1991

Economic dislocation owing to war, culminating in the overthrow of the government in 1991, saw the collapse of tax collection and export earnings, while poor harvests further stunted growth in 1991–93. In addition to managing the economic consequences of the rapid demobilization of some 300,000 troops, the new government had to disentangle the assets, liabilities, infrastructure and personnel of the Ethiopian and nascent Eritrean states. The Eritrean economy was, *de facto*, managed entirely independently from May 1991. Until late 1997 it continued to use the Ethiopian birr in what was in effect a currency union, buttressed by a series of bilateral agreements guaranteeing free movement of people and goods between the two countries. This arrangement ruptured in 1998 with the outbreak of hostilities (see below).

Upon taking power, the Ethiopian People's Revolutionary Democratic Front (EPRDF) rapidly jettisoned its *dirigiste* Marxist dogma, and immediateley embarked on market reform and structural adjustment. Despite limited experience and personnel, the government has retained tight control of the content and timing of the reform programme. Relations with donors and allies have occasionally been frosty; in 1997–98 a dispute with the IMF over the pace of financial-sector reform sparked a nine-month break in relations. However, the authorities won praise from donors for resolute 'ownership' of reform, and by 1998 had become one of the World Bank's favoured clients in sub-Saharan Africa.

The government has implemented extensive economic reforms in four broad areas: the dismantling of direct controls and deregulation of both domestic and foreign trade; the overhaul of government taxation and expenditure, implemented in tandem with the restructuring of the civil service along federal lines; financial liberalization, including the devaluation of the birr and the fostering of private banking and insurance markets; and privatization.

In rural areas market reforms have produced largely positive results, with increased output, prices and revenues for peasants. In towns, the benefits of liberalization have been less clear: wholesale and retail trade is now almost exclusively in private hands, but significant barriers to investment, including poor infrastructure, state bureaucracy and convoluted systems of urban land-leases, remain. The government has formulated extensive sectoral investment programmes, notably for transport, health and education, to be implemented at federal and state level. However, these are critically dependent upon external donor funding, and also require improvements in capital budget and project implementation, particularly by smaller regional administrations.

The EPRDF has eschewed comprehensive planning, but it does have a loose, medium-term economic framework for federal and regional economic development. This 'agricultural development-led industrialization' strategy aims to promote medium-scale industries based on agricultural processing in the larger regional capitals. It envisages the integration of such agro-processing plants with programmes to improve productivity in small-holder agriculture as well as larger-scale commercial farms. Despite deregulation and the ability of regional governments to grant licences for commercial farming, large-scale commercial agriculture remains beset with problems of infrastructure, land tenure and licensing.

Although several hundred small state-owned retail outlets were quickly sold, the privatization of larger companies has been piecemeal, slow and far from transparent. In April 1999 the government announced plans to dispose of interests in 120 of the remaining 163 state-owned companies over the next three years. Despite financial liberalization, banking and insurance remain dominated by the state. A similar situation prevails in terms of attempts to encourage foreign direct investment. Ethiopia's investment code has been liberalized three times since 1992, most recently in early 1998.

RECENT DEVELOPMENTS

Since 1991 government economic policy has been characterized by continuity, caution and slow but steady reform. Despite the shift from 'transitional' to federal government in 1995, and a progressive restructuring and devolution of regional and local government since 1992, there have been few changes to the broad orientation of economic policy as laid out in 1991–93. This coherence and consistency is largely due to the continuity of personnel. Notwithstanding what is often perceived as an obsession with secrecy and national autonomy, disagreements with key donors have surfaced only over the sequencing and timing of reforms, notably in the financial sector. The gradual pace of reform, and the secondary role accorded to foreign donors' advice, have contributed to economic stability.

According to IMF figures, gross domestic product (GDP) increased by an average of 4% per year during 1992–95 and by an average of 5% per year during 1996–99. With inflation and annual population growth of around 3%, this represented only marginal per caput improvements. Yet such aggregate data mask erratic fluctuations, due primarily to variations in rain-fed agriculture. Preliminary data suggest that real income per head fell significantly in the two fiscal years from July 1998–July 2000. Negative growth of −0.5% in 1997/98 reflected unseasonable rains. Although main crop harvests improved in 1998, the impact of war and crop failures in 1999 severely undermined the ambitious 7.8% annual growth rate target and associated stringent fiscal targets set in the government's 1998–2001 policy framework paper issued with the IMF in September 1998.

Annual inflation averaged 2.3% during 1993–97, despite significant devaluation of the birr and extensive market deregulation. Official measurements of inflation are driven primarily by fluctuations in grain prices, in turn determined by harvest and supply conditions. Thus in years of good harvests prices fall; deflation of 6.4% was recorded in 1996/97. Poor main-crop harvests in late 1998 led to price rises, although these were dampened by the release of food security reserves and by food imports. Improved harvests in 1998 reduced inflation, and while subsequent shortages fuelled steep food price rises, provisional official figures suggested that annual inflation during 1998–99 was around 4%, in line with government targets. Since 1997 there have been improvements in the quality of consumer price data, which is now collected nationally. An inflation target of 4% per annum to 2001 was set in mid-1998.

Central and regional government expenditure in 1997/98 was budgeted at 11,460m. birr (US $1,650m.), representing 25% of GDP. Expenditure had risen by an average of 5% in nominal terms over the previous four years, the increase largely favouring health and education expenditure. The structures of the Ethiopian state's expenditure and revenues have been reformed in conjunction with the eleboration of a federal state with nine regional states. The country's two significant urban, commercial centres, Addis Ababa and Dire Dawa, are administered separately. The formulae delineating tax-raising and expenditure prerogatives of central and regional governments remain somewhat convoluted, prompting accusations of poor transparency and accountability of regional authorities. The two small western regions bordering Sudan, and the mainly pastoral Afar and Somali regional administrations have all experienced corruption and frequent changes in personnel. However, despite evidence of increasing dishonesty in recent years, large-scale graft and corruption remains much lower in Ethiopia than in other sub-Saharan states.

EXTERNAL TRADE

External tariffs have been simplified and reduced extensively since 1992. However, at least 60% of Ethiopia's export earnings depend upon coffee, and thus are hostage to exceedingly volatile international prices. Falling coffee prices, coupled with significant planned increases of imports under successive adjustment and investment programmes, mean that both Ethiopia's overall trade position and terms of trade weakened in the mid-1990s. A current-account deficit of around US $500,000 was registered in 1997/98, representing almost 8% of GDP. Around one-half of this deficit was met by official donor transfers. Hides and skins are Ethiopia's other main export, earning $49.6m. in 1998. Qat is also exported, largely to Somalia. Ethiopia runs a small surplus of invisible earnings, largely owing to the performance of Ethiopian Airlines and Ethiopian Shipping Lines Corpn, the latter having prospered, in spite of the lack of a home port.

The Ethiopian birr has been devalued progressively since 1992, moving from US $1 = 2.07 birr to $1 = just over 8 birr in April 2000. Since mid-1993 the rate of the birr has been determined by auctions supervised by the national bank. In 1998 these became essentially wholesale auctions, supplying foreign exchange to an increasingly liberalized retail banking sector. The cautious pace of reform was successful, achieving a phased devaluation with minimal inflation and a steady narrowing of parallel market premium.

PROBLEMS AND PROSPECTS

Acute, perennial food shortages remain the most immediate and protracted economic problem confronting the majority of Ethiopians. Since 1991 the government, via its Disaster Prevention and Preparedness Commission (DPPC), and donors have made significant improvements to the country's famine early-warnings systems. An emergency food security reserve has been established and food relief storage and distribution networks have been improved. Nevertheless, most rural communities remain highly vulnerable, owing to acute poverty and the vagaries of weather and pests. In times of shortage, aid efforts are hampered by the rural isolation of many highlanders. Most settlements are inaccessible by road, particularly during the long rainy season (June–September) when need is often greatest. In both 1994/95 and 1999 harvest failures left an estimated 4.5m. people in need of food assistance. Erratic regional harvests in 1999 created additional severe shortages in both highland and pastoral areas. In January 2000 the DPPC appealed for 900,000 metric tons of food aid to assist an estimated 8m. people. In 1998 and 1999 Afar and Somali pastoralists also encountered severe hardship as a result of prolonged drought and the collapse of livestock prices. The latter was triggered by Saudi Arabia's ban on livestock imports from the Horn of Africa. The ban was lifted in May 1999.

In the longer term, without significant improvements in agricultural productivity the Ethiopian economy will be unable to generate the agricultural surplus necessary both to fund economic diversification and support the inevitable acceleration of urbanization. Only via sustained improvements in rural productivity, primarily via irrigation and increased fertilizer application, can living standards be improved. Currently less than 5% of cultivable land is even partially irrigated. Moreover Ethiopia has the lowest rates of fertilizer application in Africa. Although the government is now heavily promoting its use, many peasants resist, not least because of high cost, unreliable returns and fears of exacerbating the acute soil erosion experienced in the highlands. There is also minimal use of pesticides, further contributing to low and inconsistent yields.

A second weakness is Ethiopia's dependence upon a single export crop, coffee. For almost four decades coffee has routinely accounted for two-thirds of Ethiopia's foreign exchange earnings. Fluctuations in international coffee prices greatly accentuate the inherent instability of the Ethiopian economy. In 1998/99 the US $368m. earned from coffee represented a 17.4% reduction on the previous year, despite record export volumes of 137,000 metric tons, 133,000 tons, worth $445.7m., having been sold in 1997/98. Ethiopia is unique among African coffee producers in consuming much of the crop at home; an estimated 300,000 tons of coffee is produced annually. Since 1996 limited steps have been taken to improve the quality of Ethiopian coffee exports. Washing and processing facilities have been advanced, and the production of premium brands has been promoted. Most coffee is produced by smallholders. Since 1991 the marketing and export of coffee has increasingly been in private hands. Attempts to diversify exports away from coffee have so far shown few results. Flowers, fruit and vegetables for export are produced, but the quality of finishing, packaging and marketing lags behind that of neighbouring competitors such as Kenya.

Ethiopia's economy is, and will remain for the foreseeable future, highly dependent on external donor funding. With a projected total trade deficit of around 15% of GDP in the period 1998–2001, once services and private transfers are taken into account, an overall current-account deficit of around 8.5% of GDP is forecast. This leaves an external financing requirement of some US $8,600m. over the three-year period. Some $5m. of this is expected to be concessional debt relief, the bulk of this sum representing the cancellation of rouble debts to the former USSR accumulated prior to 1991. In early 1999 Ethiopia hoped to join the IMF/World Bank initiative for heavily-indebted poor countries. The World Bank conducted a preliminary assessment of Ethiopia in 1999, although finalization of the proposed financial assistance package of $636m. was postponed owing to the hostilities between Ethiopia and Eritrea. Other key donors effectively suspended new project-lending in mid-1999. However, by 1998 actual disbursement was already lagging significantly behind pledges, largely owing to constraints in implementation capacity, which have been further restricted by the war effort. In September 2000 the World Bank announced that it was to resume financial assistance to Ethiopia, which had been suspended for more than two years.

Transparency and accountability in economic policy-making remains problematic. Despite extensive liberalization, many markets remain far from competitive. The piecemeal privatization process and the allocation of urban land-leases in particular have attracted accusations of favouritism and regional bias in policy-making. An Ethio-Saudi entrepreneur, Mohamed Hussein Alamoudi, has established extensive interests in real-estate, hotels, beverages, banking, insurance, agriculture and mining. A second group of conglomerates are owned and managed by members or affiliates of the ruling party, particularly in the media and distribution sectors, prompting allegations that public contracts are awarded on the basis of party ties or ethnic favouritism. Critics of the government claim that the economic influence and political connections of such consortia have squeezed smaller, genuinely independent entrepreneurs out of crucial markets, undermining private investor confidence. Such issues are not helped by the constrained nature of public debate of economic issues. Although the situation has improved since 1991, there is little press debate or general public understanding of economic policy-making.

THE ECONOMIC IMPACT OF WAR WITH ERITREA

The initial, short-term, aggregate economic impact of the 1998–2000 conflict with Eritrea was surprisingly limited. Disruption to agricultural production was restricted largely to Tigrai, where 385,000 people were reportedly displaced. Disturbance to land-locked Ethiopia's foreign trade was also less than initially forecast. The decision to suspend use of the Eritrean ports of Assab and Massawa and to channel all foreign trade via Djibouti was taken unilaterally by Ethiopia. The flexibility of Djibouti's port facilities and the efficiency of road haulage from Djibouti to Addis Ababa and the highlands ensured a continuous flow of goods to and from Ethiopia. Currency and trade questions played a key role in the genesis of the conflict. The debilitating fiscal impact of a festering stalemate appeared to have fuelled Ethiopia's efforts decisively to reconfigure the military balance via the offensives of May–June 2000. However, even if the June 2000 peace settlement holds, the maintenance of the current high levels of defence spending is inevitable for the foreseeable future. In September 1999 a World Bank study estimated the total annual costs of the war at around 3,000m. birr; subsequent arms purchases and the cost of the battles in mid-2000 will have further swollen expenditure in the fiscal year to July 2000. The war has inevitably dented the reporting and transparency of economic and fiscal data. During the war senior government officials stated that the cost of conflict had been met largely by deferring capital expenditure, implying severe cuts in sectoral investment programmes, and sharp reductions in health and education expenditure. The optimistic targets for both investment, originally scheduled to rise to 22% of GDP per annum by 2001, and the government's overall fiscal stance now appear untenable. The elaborate timetable and targets for further reform—notably in the financial sector—outlined in the September 1998 policy framework paper, were rendered obsolete by the financial pressures of war and higher military expenditure. Further depreciation of the birr is also likely, owing in large part to declining international coffee prices.

Finally, war further erodes domestic and international confidence in the economy. The expulsion of more than 50,000 largely urban Ethiopian citizens with family ties to Eritrea has undermined both the government's legal commitment to property rights and general investor confidence. The apparently arbitrary criteria and rationale behind the expulsions exacerbates economic uncertainty. Up to 300,000 other citizens with family ties to Eritrea could also face expulsion. Many, like those already expelled, are entrepreneurs and are seeking to leave the country, usually to industrialized states, not Eritrea.

The immediate crisis of the war with Eritrea adds to the deeper pressures of rapid population growth and slow agrarian change. Political uncertainty, low economic growth and investment undermine already limited opportunities for employment and education, and inevitably fuel migration. Ethiopians have long migrated, usually temporarily, to the countries of the Arabian Peninsula. Over the past 15 years or so middle-class and urban youth have fled to the USA and the northern countries of the European Union. Given the poverty at home, such external migration is likely to intensify, heightening the role that remittances from abroad will play in Ethiopia's economy.

Statistical Survey

Source (unless otherwise stated): Central Statistical Authority, POB 1143, Addis Ababa; tel. (1) 553010; fax (1) 550334.

Note: Unless otherwise indicated, figures in this Survey refer to the territory of Ethiopia after the secession of Eritrea in May 1993.

Area and Population

AREA, POPULATION AND DENSITY

Area (sq km)	1,133,380*
Population (census results)	
9 May 1984†	39,868,501
11 October 1994	
Males	26,910,698
Females	26,566,567
Total	53,477,265
Population (official estimates at mid-year)	
1997	58,117,000
1998	59,880,000
1999	61,672,000
Density (per sq km) at mid-1999	54.4

* 437,600 sq miles.
† Including an estimate for areas not covered by the census.

ADMINISTRATIVE DIVISIONS (estimated population at mid-1999)

	Population ('000)		
	Males	Females	Total
Regional States			
1 Tigrai	1,767	1,826	3,593
2 Afar	667	521	1,188
3 Amhara	7,938	7,912	15,850
4 Oromia	10,833	10,861	21,694
5 Somali	1,952	1,650	3,602
6 Benishangul/Gumuz . .	264	259	523
7 Southern Nations, Nationalities and Peoples	6,029	6,103	12,132
8 Gambela	105	101	206
9 Harari	78	76	154
Chartered Cities			
1 Dire Dawa	154	152	306
2 Addis Ababa	1,169	1,255	2,424
Total	30,956	30,716	61,672

PRINCIPAL TOWNS (census results of October 1994)

Addis Ababa (capital)	2,084,588
Dire Dawa	164,851
Nazret.	127,842
Harar	122,932
Mekele	119,779
Jimma.	119,717
Dessie	117,268
Bahir Dar	115,531
Debrezit	105,963

Source: UN, *Demographic Yearbook*.

BIRTHS AND DEATHS (UN estimates, annual averages)

	1980–85	1985–90	1990–95
Birth rate (per 1,000). . . .	48.0	49.0	46.5
Death rate (per 1,000) . . .	22.1	20.0	19.2

Expectation of life (UN estimates, years at birth, 1990–95): 45.2 (males 43.9; females 46.7).

Source: UN, *World Population Prospects: The 1998 Revision*.

ECONOMICALLY ACTIVE POPULATION (official estimates, ISIC Major Divisions, persons aged 10 years and over, mid-1995)*

	Males	Females	Total
Agriculture, hunting, forestry and fishing	12,681,037	8,924,280	21,605,317
Mining and quarrying . .	12,114	4,426	16,540
Manufacturing	224,106	160,889	384,995
Electricity, gas and water. .	14,799	2,267	17,066
Construction.	55,906	5,326	61,232
Trade, restaurants and hotels. .	335,353	600,584	935,937
Transport, storage and communications	87,975	15,179	103,154
Financing, insurance, real estate and business services . .	14,513	4,938	19,451
Community, social and personal services	777,907	474,317	1,252,224
Total labour force . . .	14,203,710	10,192,206	24,395,916

* The figures exclude persons seeking work for the first time, totalling 210,184 (males 100,790; females 109,394), but include other unemployed persons.

Source: ILO, *Yearbook of Labour Statistics*.

Mid-1998 (estimates in '000): Agriculture, etc. 21,788; Total labour force 26,175 (Source: FAO, *Production Yearbook*).

Agriculture

PRINCIPAL CROPS ('000 metric tons)

	1996	1997	1998
Wheat	1,162	1,093	1,143
Barley	1,125	1,062	1,095
Maize	3,164	2,987	2,344
Oats	84	67	56
Millet (Dagusa)	244	296	260
Sorghum	1,808	2,040	1,083
Other cereals	1,792	1,928	1,216
Potatoes*	360	360	365
Sweet potatoes*	159	159	160
Yams*	265	265	266
Other roots and tubers* . .	1,270	1,270	1,275
Dry beans*	400	400	410
Dry peas*	160	160	165
Dry broad beans* . . .	284	284	285
Chick-peas*	127	127	128
Lentils*	36	36	37
Other pulses*	131	131	133
Sugar cane*	1,600	1,600	1,650
Soybeans*	23	23	24
Groundnuts (in shell)* . .	56	56	57
Castor beans*	15	15	15
Rapeseed*	82	82	83
Sesame seed*	33	33	34
Linseed*	32	32	33
Safflower seed*	35	35	36
Cottonseed†	30	30	30
Cotton (lint)†	15	15	15
Vegetables and melons* . .	590	589	596
Bananas*	80	80	81
Other fruit (excl. melons)* . .	149	149	150
Tree nuts*	68	68	69
Coffee (green)†	230	228	204
Tobacco (leaves)	4†	4†	4*
Fibre crops (excl. cotton)*. .	17	17	18

* FAO estimate(s).   † Unofficial figure(s).

Source: FAO, *Production Yearbook*.

LIVESTOCK (FAO estimates, '000 head, year ending September)

	1996	1997	1998
Cattle	29,900	29,900	29,900
Sheep	21,800	21,850	21,850
Goats	16,800	16,850	16,850
Asses	5,200	5,200	5,200
Horses	2,750	2,750	2,750
Mules	630	630	630
Camels	1,020	1,030	1,030
Pigs	22	23	23

Poultry (FAO estimates, million): 55 in 1996; 55 in 1997; 55 in 1998.

Source: FAO, *Production Yearbook.*

LIVESTOCK PRODUCTS (FAO estimates, '000 metric tons)

	1996	1997	1998
Beef and veal	236	236	236
Mutton and lamb	80	80	80
Goat meat	63	63	63
Pig meat	1	1	1
Poultry meat	73	73	73
Other meat	134	134	134
Cows' milk	740	740	740
Goats' milk	93	93	93
Sheep's milk	55	55	55
Butter	10	10	10
Cheese	3	3	3
Hen eggs	74	74	74
Honey	31	31	31
Wool:			
greasy	12	12	12
clean	6	6	6
Cattle hides	47	47	47
Sheepskins	14	14	14
Goatskins	13	13	13

Source: FAO, *Production Yearbook.*

Forestry

ROUNDWOOD REMOVALS ('000 cubic metres, excl. bark)

	1995	1996	1997
Sawlogs, veneer logs and logs for sleepers	16	92	60
Pulpwood	23	7	7
Other industrial wood	2,266	2,340	2,416
Fuel wood	46,727	48,251	49,827
Total	49,032	50,690	52,310

Source: FAO, *Yearbook of Forest Products.*

SAWNWOOD PRODUCTION
('000 cubic metres, incl. railway sleepers)

	1995	1996	1997
Total	33	33	33

Source: FAO, *Yearbook of Forest Products.*

Fishing

('000 metric tons, live weight)

	1995	1996	1997
Total catch (freshwater fishes)	6.3	8.8	10.4

Source: FAO, *Yearbook of Fishery Statistics.*

Mining

('000 metric tons, unless otherwise indicated)

	1993	1994	1995
Gold (kilograms)	3,404	2,370*†	4,500*†
Salt (unrefined)†	53	5	5
Limestone ('000 cu metres)†	100	261	n.a.
Kaolin†	1*	0*	n.a.
Gypsum†	3	31	54
Clay†	1	0	n.a.
Marble ('000 sq metres)†	n.a.	n.a.	184

Gold (kilograms): 5,000*† in 1996.

* Provisional figure.

† Data from US Bureau of Mines.

Source: UN, *Industrial Commodity Statistics Yearbook.*

Industry

SELECTED PRODUCTS
('000 metric tons, unless otherwise indicated; year ending 7 July)

	1992/93*	1993/94	1994/95
Edible oils	4.0	4.2	5.6
Wheat flour	62.3	74.7	116.0
Flour of other cereals	0.3	2.3	1.6
Macaroni and pasta	5.7	11.2	19.1
Raw sugar	136.7	123.3	129.3
Wine ('000 hectolitres)	68.9	57.3	70.9
Beer ('000 hectolitres)	522.3	634.4	723.5
Mineral waters ('000 hectolitres)	159.3	199.3	298.4
Soft drinks ('000 hectolitres)	553.8	546.2	710.5
Cigarettes (million)	1,932.0	1,468.4	1,582.8
Cotton yarn (metric tons)	3,448	5,669	4,934
Woven cotton fabrics ('000 sq metres)	36,423	60,591	50,016
Nylon fabrics ('000 sq metres)	3,840	3,752	4,910
Leather footwear ('000 pairs)	928.8	1,999.2	1,159.4
Canvas and rubber footwear ('000 pairs)	2,030.9	1,609.4	2,196.3
Plastic footwear ('000 pairs)	123.5	62.3	395.7
Paper	—	—	7.1
Soap	17.3	15.0	15.2
Tyres ('000)	99.8	171.3	167.5
Clay building bricks ('000)	19.8	19.5	19.3
Quicklime	3.7	2.7	4.9
Cement	377.1	464.4	609.3

* Including Eritrea.

Electricity (estimates, million k Wh): 1,399 in 1993; 1,302 in 1994; 1,328 in 1995; 1,316 in 1996 (Source: UN, *Industrial Commodity Statistics Yearbook*).

1996 ('000 metric tons; data from FAO): Wheat flour 185; Raw sugar 182 (Source: UN, *Industrial Commodity Statistics Yearbook*).

Finance

CURRENCY AND EXCHANGE RATES
Monetary Units
100 cents = 1 birr.

Sterling, Dollar and Euro Equivalents (28 April 2000)
£1 sterling = 12.841 birr;
US $1 = 8.189 birr;
€1 = 7.440 birr;
1,000 birr = £77.87 = $122.12 = €134.41.

Average Exchange Rate (birr per US $)
1997	6.7093
1998	7.1159
1999	7.9423

GENERAL BUDGET (million birr, year ending 7 July)

Revenue*	1995/96	1996/97†	1997/98†
Taxation	4,723.3	5,358.2	5,261.1
Taxes on income and profits .	1,848.8	1,745.3	1,849.5
Personal income . . .	337.4	366.3	429.3
Business profits . . .	1,222.3	1,264.7	1,088.6
Domestic indirect taxes. .	1,155.6	1,289.9	1,180.6
Sales/excise taxes . .	955.3	1,067.9	942.2
Alcohol and tobacco .	359.2	397.9	356.1
Import duties	1,694.4	2,025.1	2,037.2
Customs duties . . .	889.1	1,066.9	1,012.4
Excise taxes	805.3	958.2	1,024.8
Export duties	119.5	138.5	181.2
Other revenue	2,242.9	2,519.3	3,139.1
Government investment income	822.4	1,118.5	1,400.4
Reimbursements and property sales	177.4	116.4	92.2
Proceeds from privatization .	—	347.0	312.5
Total	**6,966.2**	**7,877.5**	**8,400.2**

* Excluding grants received from abroad (million birr): 1,096.8 in 1995/96; 1,504.0† in 1996/97; 1,273.3† in 1997/98.
† Estimate(s).

Expenditure	1995/96	1996/97*	1997/98*
Current expenditure . . .	5,582.2	5,717.4	7,094.9
General services . . .	1,949.5	1,860.2	287.5
Organs of state . . .	343.1	239.2	287.5
Judiciary	66.6	220.2	258.9
Defence	771.9	334.7	2,083.5
Public order and security .	347.4	185.2	216.4
Economic services . . .	620.5	661.0	659.9
Agriculture and natural resources	378.6	408.0	486.5
Social services	1,422.0	1,488.4	1,723.1
Education	941.0	1,025.7	1,126.8
Health	328.1	331.5	400.4
Pension payments . . .	290.6	303.4	308.7
Interest and charges . .	922.5	918.7	835.6
External assistance (grants)†	142.7	256.5	160.0
Capital expenditure . . .	3,562.6	4,299.8	4,265.1
Economic development . .	2,618.8	3,000.4	2,451.1
Agriculture and settlement .	357.7	277.2	370.2
Water and natural resources .	422.2	513.2	464.0
Mining and energy . .	384.4	796.0	429.0
Industry.	358.3	288.1	93.2
Road construction . .	670.6	742.1	898.5
Transport and communications	218.0	385.5	194.7
Financial agencies . .	207.1	n.a.	n.a.
Social development. . .	712.0	843.5	1,013.4
Education	441.9	421.9	436.8
Public health . . .	153.9	251.8	276.9
Urban development and housing	116.2	169.8	299.7
General services and compensation . . .	231.8	355.9	305.6
External assistance (grants)† .	n.a.	100.0	495.0
Equity contribution . . .	1,049.2	—	100.0
Total	**10,194.0**	**10,017.2**	**11,460.1**

* Estimates.
† Imputed value of goods and services provided mainly in kind.
Source: National Bank of Ethiopia.

NATIONAL BANK RESERVES (US $ million, at 31 December)

	1997	1998	1999
Gold*	0.4	0.4	0.3
IMF special drawing rights .	0.1	0.1	0.1
Reserve position in IMF . .	9.5	10.0	9.7
Foreign exchange . . .	491.4	501.0	448.7
Total	**501.5**	**511.5**	**458.8**

* National valuation.
Source: IMF, *International Financial Statistics*.

MONEY SUPPLY (million birr, at 31 December)

	1997	1998	1999
Currency outside banks . . .	4,964	3,978	4,507
Demand deposits at commercial banks	5,123	5,326	6,018
Total money	**10,087**	**9,304**	**10,524**

Source: IMF, *International Financial Statistics*.

COST OF LIVING (General Index of Retail Prices for Addis Ababa, excluding rent; base: 1990 = 100)

	1993	1994	1995
Food	160.4	176.7	198.6
Fuel, light and soap* . . .	133.1	134.1	142.4
Clothing.	189.9	170.3	175.8
All items (incl. others) . .	**155.3**	**167.1**	**183.9**

* Including certain kitchen utensils.
Source: ILO, *Yearbook of Labour Statistics*.
All items: 174.6 in 1996; 168.1 in 1997 (Source: IMF, *International Financial Statistics*).
1998 (including rent; base: 1997 = 100): Food 101.8; All items 100.9 (Source: UN, *Monthly Bulletin of Statistics*).

NATIONAL ACCOUNTS
(million birr at current prices; year ending 7 July)
Expenditure on the Gross Domestic Product

	1995/96	1996/97	1997/98
Government final consumption expenditure	4,158	4,526	6,251
Private final consumption expenditure	31,291	32,831	35,472
Gross capital formation . . .	7,246	7,049	7,927
Total domestic expenditure .	**42,695**	**44,406**	**49,650**
Exports of goods and services . .	4,962	6,731	7,251
Less Imports of goods and services	9,719	9,672	11,866
GDP in purchasers' values .	**37,938**	**41,465**	**45,035**

Source: IMF, *International Financial Statistics*.

Gross Domestic Product by Economic Activity
(at constant 1980/81 factor cost)

	1995/96	1996/97	1997/98
Agriculture, hunting, forestry and fishing	7,206.2	7,453.9	6,687.0
Mining and quarrying . . .	55.4	62.6	68.9
Manufacturing	881.0	932.8	986.9
Electricity, gas and water. . .	203.2	215.1	223.1
Construction.	349.3	379.6	412.1
Trade, hotels and restaurants. .	1,115.5	1,208.9	1,263.3
Transport, storage and communications . . .	799.2	853.2	907.8
Finance, insurance and real estate	879.7	954.5	999.2
Public administration and defence	1,391.5	1,483.4	1,848.3
Education	298.0	311.1	327.0
Health	154.0	160.1	175.9
Domestic and other services . .	654.1	694.7	731.5
Total	**13,987.1**	**14,709.9**	**14,631.0**

Source: IMF, *Ethiopia: Recent Economic Developments* (September 1999).

BALANCE OF PAYMENTS (US $ million)

	1996	1997	1998
Exports of goods f.o.b.	417.5	588.3	568.3
Imports of goods f.o.b.	−1,002.2	−1,018.7	−1,042.2
Trade balance	**−584.7**	**−430.5**	**−473.9**
Exports of services	377.2	390.7	431.3
Imports of services	−349.8	−396.2	−418.5
Balance on goods and services	**−557.0**	**−436.0**	**−461.1**
Other income received	51.3	37.2	47.8
Other income paid	−76.1	−67.0	−59.6
Balance on goods, services and income	**−582.0**	**−465.8**	**−472.9**
Current transfers received	679.0	450.4	627.9
Current transfers paid	−7.5	−7.6	−21.0
Current balance	**89.4**	**−23.0**	**134.0**
Investment assets	−306.8	318.5	45.1
Investment liabilities	−192.8	−77.3	−68.6
Net errors and omissions	−56.6	−646.7	−493.5
Overall balance	**−466.7**	**−428.6**	**−383.1**

Source: IMF, *International Financial Statistics*.

External Trade

PRINCIPAL COMMODITIES (distribution by SITC, US $ '000)

Imports c.i.f.	1994	1995	1996
Food and live animals	150,811	123,677	26,783
Cereals and cereal preparations	121,279	84,432	19,287
Mineral fuels, lubricants, etc.	n.a.	124,378	119,455
Crude petroleum oils, etc.	80,274	67,197	47,285
Refined petroleum products	65,795	57,000	71,822
Chemicals and related products	n.a.	n.a.	n.a.
Medicinal and pharmaceutical products	32,622	29,561	26,634
Medicaments	n.a.	27,499	22,282
Manufactured fertilizers	8,821	60,967	66,171
Basic manufactures	n.a.	n.a.	n.a.
Rubber manufactures	33,962	36,033	51,258
Textile yarn, fabrics, etc.	31,688	47,121	52,761
Iron and steel	n.a.	58,530	80,544
Universals, plates and sheets	n.a.	45,714	55,910
Machinery and transport equipment	n.a.	n.a.	n.a.
Electrical machinery, apparatus, etc.*	n.a.	53,255	69,459
Road vehicles and parts†	146,467	198,335	194,946
Passenger motor cars (excl. buses)	n.a.	43,304	57,066
Motor vehicles for goods transport, etc.	n.a.	102,023	94,397
Parts and accessories for cars, buses, lorries, etc.†	n.a.	23,373	22,097
Total (incl. others)	918,589	1,121,297	1,117,884

* Excluding telecommunications and sound equipment.

† Excluding tyres, engines and electrical parts.

Exports f.o.b.	1994	1995	1996
Food and live animals	n.a.	n.a.	n.a.
Vegetables and fruit	2,561	16,111	3,495
Coffee, tea, cocoa and spices	n.a.	270,829	278,485
Coffee and coffee substitutes	218,430	270,707	278,485
Crude materials (inedible) except fuels	n.a.	n.a.	n.a.
Raw hides, skins and furskins	48,315	56,450	71,078
Raw hides and skins (excl. furs)	48,315	56,450	71,078
Cattle hides	n.a.	8,809	4,559
Sheep skins	n.a.	24,301	50,114
Mineral fuels, lubricants, etc.	17,409	11,842	13,701
Petroleum, petroleum products, etc.	17,409	11,842	13,701
Total (incl. others)	334,894	414,483	417,411

Exports f.o.b. (US $ '000, 1997): Vegetables and fruit 23,576; Coffee, tea, cocoa and spices 382,703 (Coffee and coffee substitutes 382,314); Raw hides, skins and furskins 60,590 (Raw hides and skins, excl. furs 60,590); Total (incl. others) 557,376.

Exports f.o.b. (US $ '000, 1998): Vegetables and fruit 39,958; Coffee, tea, cocoa and spices 420,313 (Coffee and coffee substitutes 419,763); Raw hides, skins and furskins 49,572 (Raw hides and skins, excl. furs 49,572); Total (incl. others) 593,393.

Source: National Bank of Ethiopia.

PRINCIPAL TRADING PARTNERS (million birr)

Imports c.i.f.	1995	1996	1997*
Belgium-Luxembourg	217.4	160.2	114.4
China, People's Repub.	163.4	207.5	366.1
Denmark	66.3	83.4	n.a.
Djibouti	174.3	186.5	40.0
France	183.7	130.2	149.5
Germany	539.6	504.9	749.5
India	177.2	243.8	430.6
Italy	863.8	863.9	726.7
Japan	588.5	565.9	796.8
Kenya	214.9	211.3	154.9
Korea, Repub.	155.6	200.6	358.5
Netherlands	194.1	342.2	344.9
Saudi Arabia	828.4	724.7	735.2
Sweden	198.7	188.6	n.a.
Turkey	36.6	83.7	121.3
United Kingdom	417.5	321.6	454.7
USA	910.4	374.5	358.5
Total (incl. others)	7,041.7	7,103.1	7,615.1

* Preliminary estimates.

Exports f.o.b.	1996	1997	1998*
Belgium-Luxembourg	54.7	142.5	176.2
Djibouti	230.9	298.9	147.0
France	94.2	127.5	144.0
Germany	827.1	811.9	984.4
Israel	8.8	18.9	56.1
Italy	206.7	307.8	270.3
Japan	333.6	441.0	479.5
Netherlands	35.9	57.5	73.8
Saudi Arabia	296.3	337.1	392.5
Switzerland	21.9	62.6	22.8
United Kingdom	86.6	115.0	98.1
USA	169.9	448.0	271.2
Total (incl. others)	2,783.1	3,941.3	3,966.0

* Preliminary estimates.

Source: IMF, *Ethiopia: Recent Economic Developments* (September 1999).

Transport

RAILWAYS (traffic, year ending 7 July)*

	1996/97	1997/98	1998/99
Addis Ababa–Djibouti:			
Passenger-km (million) . . .	157	167	150
Freight (million net ton-km) .	106	90	116

* Including traffic on the section of the Djibouti–Addis Ababa line which runs through the Republic of Djibouti. Data pertaining to freight include service traffic.

Source: Ministry of Transport and Communications, Addis Ababa.

ROAD TRAFFIC (motor vehicles in use, year ending 7 July)

	1996/97	1997/98	1998/99
Cars	42,318	48,307	48,534
Buses and coaches . . .	22,460	21,959	24,199
Lorries and vans . . .	24,367	26,000	26,007
Motorcycles and mopeds . .	1,151	1,172	1,353
Road tractors . . .	5,888	5,445	5,367
Total	96,184	102,883	105,460

Source: Ministry of Transport and Communications, Addis Ababa.

SHIPPING

Merchant Fleet (registered at 7 July)

	1997	1998	1999
Number of vessels . . .	11	11	12
Displacement (grt) . . .	86,592	81,508	82,503

Source: Ethiopian Shipping Lines Corporation.

International Sea-borne Shipping (freight traffic, '000 metric tons, year ending 7 July)

	1996/97	1997/98	1998/99
Goods loaded	242	201	313
Goods unloaded	777	1,155	947

Source: Ministry of Transport and Communications, Addis Ababa.

CIVIL AVIATION (traffic on scheduled services, year ending 7 July)

	1996/97	1997/98	1998/99
Kilometres flown (million) .	28	n.a.	n.a.
Passengers carried ('000) . .	808	807	779
Passenger-km (million) . .	1,915	1,944	1,999
Total ton-km (million) . .	129	149	115

Source: Ministry of Transport and Communications, Addis Ababa.

Tourism

TOURIST ARRIVALS BY COUNTRY OF ORIGIN

	1996	1997	1998
Canada	3,811	4,703	3,421
Djibouti	4,247	6,197	4,698
France	4,029	4,818	3,837
Germany	5,554	6,081	5,151
India	2,069	2,066	2,067
Italy	7,621	7,458	6,922
Japan	2,830	2,868	2,383
Kenya	5,336	6,769	4,821
Netherlands	2,504	2,983	2,455
Russia	3,702	2,869	3,460
Saudi Arabia	4,246	5,277	3,620
Sudan	3,485	2,408	3,516
Switzerland	3,159	3,443	2,950
United Kingdom	6,424	6,769	5,949
USA	8,819	9,762	8,002
Yemen	3,920	4,475	3,148
Total (incl. others)*	108,885	114,732	116,686

* Including Ethiopian nationals residing abroad.

Receipts from tourism (US $ million): 28 in 1996; 36 in 1997.

Source: World Tourism Organization, *Yearbook of Tourism Statistics*.

Communications Media

	1994	1995	1996
Telephones ('000 main lines in use)*	138	142	149
Telefax stations (number in use)* .	1,057	1,445	1,624
Radio receivers ('000 in use) .	10,550	10,900	11,300
Television receivers ('000 in use) .	230	250	300
Daily newspapers:			
Number	4	4	4
Average circulation ('000 copies)	81†	92†	86

* Year ending 30 June.
† Estimate.

Book production: 240 titles (including 93 pamphlets) in 1991.

Non-daily newspapers: 17 in 1995 (average combined circulation 159,000).

1997 ('000 in use): Television receivers 11,750; Radio receivers 320.

Source: mainly UNESCO, *Statistical Yearbook*.

Education

(1998/99)

	Institutions	Teachers	Students
Pre-primary	793	2,487	90,321
Primary	11,051	112,405	5,702,223
Secondary:			
General	386	13,078	521,728
Teacher-training . . .	12	273	5,378
Vocational . . .	16	548	3,374
University level . . .	4	1,674	40,936
Other higher	8	554	16,104

Source: Ministry of Education, Addis Ababa.

Directory

The Constitution

In July 1991 a national conference elected a transitional Government and approved a charter under the provisions of which the Government was to operate until the holding of democratic elections. The charter provided guarantees for freedom of association and expression, and for self-determination for Ethiopia's different ethnic constituencies. The transitional Government was to be responsible for drafting a new constitution to replace that introduced in 1987. A Constituent Assembly, dominated by representatives of the EPRDF, was elected in June 1994. It ratified the draft Constitution (already approved by the transitional Council of Representatives) in December. The Constitution of the Federal Democratic Republic of Ethiopia provides for the establishment of a federal government and the division of the country into nine states, one chartered city (Addis Ababa) and one Administrative Council (Dire Dawa). It also provides for regional autonomy, including the right of secession. Simultaneous elections of deputies to the federal and state parliaments were conducted on 7 May 1995. The new Constitution came into effect on 22 August 1995.

The Government

HEAD OF STATE

President: Dr NEGASSO GIDADA (took office 22 August 1995).

COUNCIL OF MINISTERS
(August 2000)

Prime Minister: MELES ZENAWI.

Deputy Prime Minister and Head of Economic Affairs: Dr KASSA YLALA.

Deputy Prime Minister and Minister of Defence: TEFERA WALWA.

Minister of Foreign Affairs: SEYOUM MESFIN.

Minister of Health: Dr ADEM IBRAHIM.

Minister of Energy and Mines: EZEDIN ALI.

Minister of Economic Development and Co-operation: GIRMA BIRU.

Minister of Information and Culture: WOLDE MIKAEL CHAMO.

Minister of Education: GENET ZEWDE.

Minister of Agriculture: Dr MENGISTU HULUKA (acting).

Minister of Commerce and Industry: KASAHUN AYELE.

Minister of Finance: SUFYAN AHMED.

Minister of Justice: WEREDE WOLDU WOLDE.

Minister of Works and Urban Development: HAILE SELASSIE ASEGIDE.

Minister of Labour: HASAN ABDELA.

Minister of Water Resources: SHIFERAW JARSO.

Minister and Head of the Revenue Collectors Board: DESTA AMARE.

Minister of Transport and Communications: MOHAMOUD DIRIR GHEDDI (acting).

MINISTRIES AND COMMISSIONS

Office of the Prime Minister: POB 1013, Addis Ababa; tel. (1) 552044.

Ministry of Agriculture: POB 62347, Addis Ababa; tel. (1) 152816; fax (1) 512984.

Ministry of Commerce and Industry: POB 704, Addis Ababa; tel. (1) 518025; fax (1) 515411.

Ministry of Defence: POB 125, Addis Ababa; tel. (1) 445555.

Ministry of Economic Development and Co-operation: POB 2559, Addis Ababa; tel. (1) 552800.

Ministry of Education: POB 1367, Addis Ababa; tel. (1) 553133.

Ministry of Energy and Mines: POB 486, Addis Ababa; tel. (1) 518250; fax (1) 517874.

Ministry of Finance: POB 1905, Addis Ababa; tel. (1) 552400; fax (1) 551355.

Ministry of Foreign Affairs: POB 393, Addis Ababa; tel. (1) 447345; fax (1) 514300.

Ministry of Health: POB 1234, Addis Ababa; tel. (1) 518031; fax 519366.

Ministry of Information and Culture: POB 1020, Addis Ababa; tel. (1) 517020.

Ministry of Justice: POB 1370, Addis Ababa; tel. (1) 517390.

Ministry of Labour: POB 2056, Addis Ababa; tel. (1) 517080.

Ministry of Transport and Communications: POB 1238, Addis Ababa; tel. (1) 516166; fax (1) 515665.

Ministry of Water Resources: POB 5744, Addis Ababa, tel. (1) 611111; fax (1) 610885.

Ministry of Works and Urban Development: POB 3386, Addis Ababa; tel. (1) 150000.

Regional Governments

Ethiopia comprises nine regional governments, one chartered city (Addis Ababa) and one Administrative Council (Dire Dawa), which are vested with authority for self-administration. The executive bodies are respectively headed by Presidents (regional states) and Chairmen (Addis Ababa and Dire Dawa).

PRESIDENTS

Tigrai: GEBRU ASRAT.
Afar: ESMAEL ALISERO.
Amhara: ADDISO LEGGESE.
Oromia: KUMA DEMEKSA.
Somali: MUHAMMED MUALIN ALI.
Benishangul/Gumuz: YAREGAL AYSHESHIM.
Southern Nations, Nationalities and Peoples: ABATE KISHO.
Gambela: OKALO GNIGELO.
Harari: GEZALI MUHAMMED.

CHAIRMEN

Dire Dawa: SOLOMON HAILU.
Addis Ababa: ALI ABDO.

Legislature

FEDERAL PARLIAMENTARY ASSEMBLY

The legislature comprises an upper house, the House of the Federation (Yefedereshn Mekir Bet), with 108 seats (members are selected by state assemblies and are drawn one each from 22 minority nationalities and one from each professional sector of the remaining nationalities, and serve for a period of five years), and a lower house of 548 directly-elected members, the House of People's Representatives (Yehizbtewekayoch Mekir Bet), who are also elected for a five-year term.

Speaker of the House of the Federation: ALMAZ MEKO.

Yehizbtewekayoch Mekir Bet
(House of People's Representatives)

Speaker: DAWIT YOHANES.

General Election, 14 May 2000

Party	Seats
Oromo People's Democratic Organization (OPDO)	177
Amhara National Democratic Movement (ANDM)	134
Tigrai People's Liberation Front (TPLF)	38
Walayta, Gamo, Gofa Dawro Konta People's Democratic Organization (WGGPDO)	27
Ethiopian People's Revolutionary Democratic Front (EPRDF)	19
Sidama People's Democratic Organization (SPDO)	18
Gurage Nationalities Democratic Movement (GNDM)	15
Kafa Shaka People's Democratic Organization (KSPDO)	10
Afar National Democratic Party (ANDP)	8
Gedeyo People's Revolutionary Democratic Front (GPRDF)	7
South Omo People's Democratic Movement (SOPDM)	7
Benishangul Gumuz People's Democratic Unity Front (BGPDUF)	6
Bench Madji People's Democratic Organization (BMPDO)	5
Kembata, Alabaa and Tembaro (KAT)	4
Gambela People's Democratic Front (GPDF)	3
South Ethiopia People's Democratic Front (SEPDF)	3
Ethiopian Democratic Unity Party (EDUP)	2
Hadiya National Democratic Organization (HNDO)	2
Southern Ethiopian People's Democratic Union (SEPDU)	2
All Amhara People's Organization (AAPO)	1
Argoba People's Democratic Movement (APDM)	1
Burgi People's Democratic Union (BPDU)	1
Hadiya National Democratic Organization (HNDO)	1
Kore Nationality Democratic Organization (KNDO)	1
Oromo Liberation Unity Front (OLUF)	1
Oromo National Congress (ONC)	1
Oyda Nationality Democratic Organization (ONDO)	1
Silte People's Democratic Unity Party (SPDUP)	1
Yem People's Democratic Unity Party (YPDUP)	1
Independents	8
Total*	**505**

* Owing to irregularities and violence at a number of polling stations, voting was scheduled to be reheld in 16 constituencies. Furthermore, voting was postponed in the Somali regional state because of severe drought affecting the area.

Political Organizations

Afar People's Democratic Organization (APDO): fmrly Afar Liberation Front (ALF); based in fmr Hararge and Wollo Admin. Regions; Leader ISMAIL ALI SIRRO.

Coalition of Alternative Forces for Peace and Democracy in Ethiopia (CAFPDE): f. 1993 as a broadly-based coalition of groups opposing the EPRDF; split into two factions in Dec. 1999, led by former Vice-Chairman KIFLE TIGNEH ABATE and by Dr BEYENE PETROS.

Coalition of Ethiopian Democratic Forces (COEDF): f. 1991 in the USA by the Ethiopian People's Revolutionary Party–EPRP (the dominant member), together with a faction of the Ethiopian Democratic Union (EDU) and the Ethiopian Socialist Movement (MEISON); opposes the EPRDF; Chair. MERSHA YOSEPH.

Coalition of Ethiopian Opposition Political Organizations (CEOPO): f. 1998 in France as a coalition of groups opposing the EPRDF; Chair. NEGEDE GOBEZIE; Chair. (Ethiopia) KIFLEH TIGNEH ABATE.

Ethiopian Democratic Unity Party (EDUP): Addis Ababa; f. 1984 as Workers' Party of Ethiopia; adopted present name in 1990, when its Marxist-Leninist ideology was relaxed and membership opened to non-Marxist and opposition groups; sole legal political party until May 1991; Sec.-Gen. Lt-Gen. TESFAYE GEBRE KIDAN.

Ethiopian National Congress (ENC): USA-based organization aims to form a unified opposition among anti-Govt parties; Chair. GEBEYEHU IJUGU.

Ethiopian National Democratic Party (ENDP): f. 1994 by merger of five pro-Govt orgs with mems in the Council of Representatives; comprises: the Ethiopian Democratic Organization, the Ethiopian Democratic Organization Coalition (EDC), the Gurage People's Democratic Front (GPDF), the Kembata People's Congress (KPC), and the Wolaita People's Democratic Front (WPDF); Chair. FEKADU GEDAMU.

Ethiopian People's Revolutionary Democratic Front (EPRDF): Addis Ababa; f. 1989 by the TPLF as an alliance of insurgent groups seeking regional autonomy and engaged in armed struggle against the EDUP Govt; Leader MELES ZENAWI; in May 1991, with other orgs, formed transitional Govt; alliance comprises:

Amhara National Democratic Movement (ANDM): based in Tigrai; represents interests of the Amhara people; fmrly the Ethiopian People's Democratic Movement (EPDM); adopted present name in 1994; Sec.-Gen. TEFERA WALWA.

Oromo People's Democratic Organization (OPDO): f. 1990 by the TPLF to promote its cause in Oromo areas; based among the Oromo people in the Shoa region; Dep. Sec.-Gen. KUMA DEMEKSA.

Tigrai People's Liberation Front (TPLF): f. 1975; the dominant org. within the EPRDF; Leader MELES ZENAWI.

Gambela People's Democratic Front (GPDF): pro-Govt group based in the Gambela region; Chair. AKILO NIGILIO.

Oromo Liberation Front (OLF): seeks self-determination for the Oromo people; participated in the Ethiopian transitional Govt until June 1992; Chair. DAOUD IBSA GUDINA; Vice-Chair. ABDULFATTAH A. MOUSSA BIYYO.

Somali Abo Liberation Front (SALF): operates in fmr Bale Admin. Region; has received Somali military assistance; Sec.-Gen. MASURAD SHU'ABI IBRAHIM.

Somali Democratic Party: f. 1998 by merger of Ogaden National Liberation Front (ONLF) and the Ethiopian Somali Democratic League (ESDL—an alliance comprising the Somali Democratic Union Party, the Issa and Gurgura Liberation Front, the Gurgura Independence Front, the Eastern Gabooye Democratic Organization, the Eastern Ethiopian Somali League, the Horyal Democratic Front, the Social Alliance Democratic Organization, the Somali Abo Democratic Union, the Shekhash People's Democratic Movement, the Ethiopian Somalis' Democratic Movement and the Per Barreh Party); Chair. MOHAMOUD DIRIR GHEDDI; Sec.-Gen. SULTAN IBRAHIM.

Southern Ethiopian People's Democratic Coalition (SEPDC): opposition alliance; Chair. Dr BEYENE PETROS.

Southern Ethiopian People's Democratic Union (SEPDU): f. 1992 as an alliance of 10 ethnically-based political groups from the south of the country; was represented in the transitional Council of Representatives, although five of the participating groups were expelled from the Council in April 1993.

Western Somali Liberation Front (WSLF): POB 978, Mogadishu, Somalia; f. 1975; aims to unite the Ogaden region with Somalia; maintains guerrilla forces of c. 3,000 men; has received support from regular Somali forces; Sec.-Gen. ISSA SHAYKH ABDI NASIR ADAN.

A coalition of the following Oromo organizations was formed in 1991:

Oromo Abo Liberation Front (OALF): Chair. MOHAMMED SIRAGE.

Oromo People's Democratic Organization (OPDO): see above.

United Oromo Liberation Front: f. 1995 by merger of United Oromo People's Liberation Front and Islamic Front for the Liberation of Oromia; Chair. AHMAD MUHAMMAD SARO.

Other ethnic organizations seeking self-determination for their respective groups include: the **Abugda Ethiopian Democratic Congress**; the **Afar Revolutionary Democratic Unity Front (ARDUF):** Pres. MUHYADIN MAFTAH KEDIR; the **All-Amhara People's Organization (AAPO):** Leader KEGNAZMATCH NEGUEA TIBEB; the **Burji People's Democratic Organization**; the **Daworo People's Democratic Movement**; the **Gedeo People's Democratic Organization (GPDO):** Leader ALESA MENGESHA; the **Hadia People's Democratic Organization**; the **Harer National League**; the Somali-based **Islamic Union Party (al-Ittihad al-Islam)**, seeking self-determination for the Ogaden; the **Jarso Democratic Movement**; the **Kaffa People's Democratic Union (KPDU)**; the **Kefa People's Democratic Movement**; the **Sidama Liberation Movement**; and the **Yem Nationality Movement**.

Other organizations in opposition to the Ethiopian Government include: the **Democratic Unity Party (DUP):** Chair. AHMAD ABD AL-KARIM; the **Ethiopian Medhin Democratic Party:** Leader Col GOSHU WOLDE; the **Ethiopian National Democratic Organization**; the **Ethiopian People's Democratic Unity Organization (EPDUO):** Leader TADESE TILAHUN; the **Ethiopian People's Revolutionary Party (EPRP)**; the **Gambela People's Democratic Congress (GPDC):** Leader UPAMA UBOYA; the monarchist **Moa Ambessa Party** and the **National Democratic Union**.

Other political organizations include the **Ethiopian Democratic Action Group:** Chair. EPHREM ZEMIKAEL; and **Forum 84**.

Diplomatic Representation

EMBASSIES IN ETHIOPIA

Algeria: POB 5740, Addis Ababa; tel. (1) 652300; fax (1) 650187; Ambassador: DELMI BOUDJEMAÂ.

Angola: POB 2962, Addis Ababa; tel. (1) 510085; fax (1) 514922; e-mail angola.embassy@telecom.net.et; Ambassador: TOKO D. SERÃO.

Austria: POB 1219, Addis Ababa; tel. (1) 712144; fax (1) 712140; Ambassador: THOMAS MICHAEL BAIER.

Belgium: POB 1239, Addis Ababa; tel. (1) 611813; fax (1) 613646; e-mail embel.et@telecom.net.et; Ambassador: LEOPOLD CARREWYN.

Bulgaria: POB 987, Addis Ababa; tel. (1) 610032; fax (1) 613373; Chargé d'affaires a.i.: MIROSLAV KOMAROV.

Burkina Faso: POB 19685, Addis Ababa; tel. (1) 615863; fax (1) 612094; e-mail ambfet@telecom.net.et; Ambassador: LÉANDRE BASSOLET.

Burundi: POB 3641, Addis Ababa; tel. (1) 651300; Ambassador: ANTOINE NAMOBWA.

Cameroon: Bole Rd, POB 1026, Addis Ababa; fax (1) 518116; Ambassador: JEAN-HILAIRE MBÉA MBÉA.

Canada: Old Airport Area, Higher 23, Kebele 12, House No. 122, POB 1130, Addis Ababa; tel. (1) 713022; fax (1) 713033; Ambassador: JOHN R. SCHRAM.

Chad: Addis Ababa; fax (1) 612050; Ambassador: MAHAMAT ABDELKERIM.

China, People's Republic: POB 5643, Addis Ababa; Ambassador: JIANG ZHENGYUN.

Congo, Democratic Republic: Makanisa Rd, POB 2723, Addis Ababa; tel. (1) 204385; Ambassador: (vacant).

Congo, Republic: POB 5571, Addis Ababa; tel. (1) 154331; Ambassador: VICTOR NIMI.

Côte d'Ivoire: POB 3668, Addis Ababa; tel. (1) 711213; Ambassador: PIERRE YÉRÉ.

Cuba: Jimma Road Ave, POB 5623, Addis Ababa; tel. (1) 202010; Ambassador: MARIANO M. L. BETANCOURT.

Czech Republic: POB 3108, Addis Ababa; tel. (1) 516132; fax (1) 513471; Ambassador: ZDENĚK POLÁČEK.

Djibouti: POB 1022, Addis Ababa; tel. (1) 613200; fax (1) 612786; Ambassador: DILEITA MOHAMED DILEITA.

Egypt: POB 1611, Addis Ababa; tel. (1) 113077; Ambassador: MUHAMMAD ASIM IBRAHIM.

Equatorial Guinea: POB 246, Addis Ababa; Ambassador: SALVADOR ELA NSENG ABEGUE.

Eritrea: POB 2571, Addis Ababa; tel. (1) 514302; fax (1) 514911; Ambassador: GRMAY ASMEROM (recalled February 1999).

Finland: Tedla Desta Bldg, Bole Rd, POB 1017, Addis Ababa; tel. (1) 513900; Chargé d'affaires a.i.: LAURI KANGAS.

France: Kabana, POB 1464, Addis Ababa; tel. (1) 550066; fax (1) 551441; Ambassador: JACQUES DEWATRE.

Gabon: POB 1256, Addis Ababa; tel. (1) 611090; fax (1) 613700; Ambassador: EMMANUEL MENDOUME-NZE.

Germany: Kabana, POB 660, Addis Ababa; tel. (1) 550433; fax (1) 551311; Ambassador: HERBERT HONSOWITZ.

Ghana: POB 3173, Addis Ababa; tel. (1) 711402; fax (1) 712511; Ambassador: BENJAMIN G. GODWYLL.

Greece: off Debre Zeit Rd, POB 1168, Addis Ababa; tel. (1) 654911; fax (1) 654883; internet www.telecom.net.et/~greekemb; Ambassador: VASSILIOS N. VASSALOS.

Guinea: POB 1190, Addis Ababa; tel. (1) 651308; fax (1) 512826; Ambassador: MAMADI DIAWARA.

Holy See: POB 588, Addis Ababa (Apostolic Nunciature); tel. (1) 712100; fax (1) 711499; e-mail vatican.embassy@telecom.net.et; Apostolic Nuncio: Most Rev. SILVANO M. TOMASI, Titular Archbishop of Asolo.

Hungary: Abattoirs Rd, POB 1213, Addis Ababa; tel. (1) 651850; Ambassador: Dr SÁNDOR ROBEL.

India: Kabana, POB 528, Addis Ababa; tel. (1) 552100; fax (1) 552521; Ambassador: KADAKATH PATHROSE ERNEST.

Indonesia: Mekanisa Rd, POB 1004, Addis Ababa; tel. (1) 712014; fax (1) 710877; Ambassador: ROCHSJAD DAHLAN.

Iran: POB 70488, Addis Ababa; tel. (1) 200794; fax (1) 711915; email csiri@telecom.net.et; internet www.telecom.net.et/~iranet/; Ambassador: SEYED HOSSEIN RAJABI.

Ireland: POB 9585, Addis Ababa; tel. (1) 710835; fax (1) 710852; e-mail ireland.emb@telecom.net.et; Chargé d'affaires a.i.: PAULINE CONWAY.

Israel: POB 1266, Addis Ababa; tel (1) 610999; fax (1) 612456; Ambassador: AVI A. GRANOT.

Italy: Villa Italia, POB 1105, Addis Ababa; tel. (1) 553042; fax (1) 550218; e-mail italembadd@telecom.net.et; Ambassador: MARCELLO RICOVERI.

Jamaica: National House, Africa Ave, POB 5633, Addis Ababa; tel. (1) 613656; Ambassador: OWEN A. SINGH.

Japan: Sunshine Bldg, Bole Rd, POB 5650, Addis Ababa; tel. (1) 511088; fax (1) 511350; Ambassador: TAKEHISA NOGAMI.

Kenya: Fikre Mariam Rd, POB 3301, Addis Ababa; tel. (1) 610303; Ambassador: GEORGE AGOI.

Korea, Democratic People's Republic: POB 2378, Addis Ababa; Ambassador: MUN SONG MO.

Korea, Republic: Jimma Rd, Old Airport Area, POB 2047, Addis Ababa; tel. (1) 444490; Ambassador: DEUK PO KIM.

Kuwait: Higher 20, Kebele 17, House No. 128, Bole Rd, Addis Ababa; tel. (1) 615411; fax (1) 612621; Ambassador: MUHAMMAD AL-AWADHI.

Lesotho: POB 7483, Addis Ababa; tel. (1) 614368; fax (1) 612837; Ambassador: J. T. METSING.

Liberia: POB 3116, Addis Ababa; tel. (1) 513655; Ambassador: MARCUS M. KOFA.

Libya: POB 5728, Addis Ababa; Chargé d'affaires a.i.: OMAR ELHADI SHENSHEN.

Madagascar: Addis Ababa; Ambassador: CHRISTIAN RÉMI RICHARD.

Malawi: POB 2316, Addis Ababa; tel. (1) 615866; fax (1) 615436; e-mail malemb@telecom.net.et; Ambassador: Mrs S. A. KALINDE.

Mali: Addis Ababa; Ambassador: S. Y. SIDIBE.

Mexico: Tsige Mariam Bldg 292/21, 4th Floor, Churchill Rd, POB 2962, Addis Ababa; tel. (1) 443456; Ambassador: CARLOS FERRER.

Morocco: POB 60033, Addis Ababa; tel. (1) 531700; fax (1) 511828; e-mail morocco.emb@telecom.net.et; Chargé d'affaires a.i.: AZZEDINE HADDAOUI.

Mozambique: POB 5671, Addis Ababa; Ambassador: ALEXANDRE ZANDAMELA.

Namibia: Higher 17, Kebele 19, House No. 002, POB 1443, Addis Ababa; tel. (1) 611966; fax (1) 612677; e-mail embassy@telecom .net.et; Ambassador: EDDIE S. AMKNOGO.

Netherlands: POB 1241, Addis Ababa; tel. (1) 711100; fax (1) 711577; e-mail netherlands.emb@telecom.net.et; internet www .telecom.net.et/~nethemb/body.htm; Ambassador: PIETER J. T. MARRES.

Niger: Debrezenit Rd, Higher 18, Kebele 41, House No. 057, POB 5791, Addis Ababa; tel. (1) 651175; Ambassador: ASSANE IGODOE.

Nigeria: POB 1019, Addis Ababa; tel. (1) 550644; Ambassador: BROWNSON N. DEDE.

Norway: POB 8383, Addis Ababa; tel. (1) 710799; fax (1) 711255; Ambassador: S. OSKARSSON.

Poland: Bole Rd, POB 1123, Addis Ababa; tel. (1) 610197; Ambassador: TADEUSZ WUJEK.

Romania: 17 Woreda, Kebele 19, 10 Bole Rd, POB 2478, Addis Ababa; tel. (1) 610156; fax (1) 611191; Chargé d'affaires a.i.: VASILE BONDARET.

Russia: POB 1500, Addis Ababa; tel. (1) 552061; fax (1) 613795; Ambassador: VLADIMIR A. VOLKOV.

Rwanda: Africa House, Higher 17, Kebele 20, POB 5618, Addis Ababa; tel. (1) 610300; fax (1) 610411; Ambassador: Dr NGOGA PASCAL.

Saudi Arabia: Old Airport Area, POB 1104, Addis Ababa; tel. (1) 448010; Ambassador: SAOUD A. M. AL-YAHAYA.

Senegal: Africa Ave, POB 2581, Addis Ababa; tel. (1) 611376; Ambassador: PAPA LOUIS FALL.

Sierra Leone: POB 5619, Addis Ababa; tel. (1) 710033; Ambassador: IBRAHIM M. BABA KAMARA.

Somalia: Addis Ababa; Ambassador: ABRAHIM HAJI NUR.

South Africa: POB 1091, Addis Ababa; tel. (1) 713034; fax (1) 711330; Ambassador: W. NHLAPO.

Spain: Entoto St, POB 2312, Addis Ababa; tel. (1) 550222; fax (1) 551131; Ambassador: AURORA BERNÁLDEZ.

Sudan: Kirkos, Kebele, POB 1110, Addis Ababa; tel (1) 515241; fax (1) 517030; Ambassador: OSMAN AS-SAYED.

Sweden: Ras Ababa Aregaye Ave, POB 1029, Addis Ababa; tel. (1) 511255; fax (1) 515830; Ambassador: JOHAN HOLMBERG.

Switzerland: Jimma Rd, Old Airport Area, POB 1106, Addis Ababa; tel. (1) 711107; fax (1) 712177; Ambassador: PAOLO BROGINI.

Tanzania: POB 1077, Addis Ababa; tel. (1) 441064; Ambassador: CHARLES BEHSTEVAN.

Toso: Addis Ababa; Ambassador: KATI OHARA KORGA.

Tunisia: Wereda 17, Kebele 19, Bole Rd, POB 100069, Addis Ababa; tel. (1) 612063; fax (1) 614568; e-mail embassy.tunisia@telecom .net.et; Ambassador: HAMID ZAOUCHE.

Turkey: POB 1506, Addis Ababa; tel. (1) 613161; fax (1) 611688; e-mail turk.emb@telecom.net.et; Ambassador: MURAT BILHAN.

United Kingdom: POB 858, Addis Ababa; tel. (1) 612354; fax (1) 610588; e-mail b.emb4@telecom.net.et; Ambassador: (vacant).

USA: Entoto St, POB 1014, Addis Ababa; tel. (1) 550666; fax (1) 551328; e-mail usembassy@telecom.net.et; internet www.telecom .net.et/~usemb-et/; Ambassador: TIBOR P. NAGY, Jr.

Venezuela: Debre Zeit Rd, POB 5584, Addis Ababa; tel. (1) 654790; Chargé d'affaires a.i.: ALFREDO HERNÁNDEZ-ROVATI.

Viet Nam: POB 1288, Addis Ababa; Ambassador: NGUYEN DUY KINH.

Yemen: POB 664, Addis Ababa; Ambassador: MANSUR ABD AL-JALIL ABD AL-RAB.

Yugoslavia: POB 1341; Addis Ababa; tel. (1) 517804; Ambassador: IGOR JOVOVIĆ.

Zambia: POB 1909; Addis Ababa; tel. (1) 711302; Ambassador: SIMATTA AKAPELWA.

Zimbabwe: POB 5624, Addis Ababa; tel. (1) 183872; Ambassador: T. A. G. MAKOMBE.

Judicial System

Special People's Courts were established in 1981 to replace the former military tribunals. Judicial tribunals are elected by members of the urban dwellers' and peasant associations. In 1987 the Supreme Court ceased to be administered by the Government and became an independent body. In October 1993, however, the transitional Council of Representatives approved draft amendments empowering the Ministry of Justice to assume the functions of prosecutor; the office of prosecutor was to operate as a division under the Ministry.

The Supreme Court: Addis Ababa; tel. (1) 448425; comprises civil, criminal and military sections; its jurisdiction extends to the supervision of all judicial proceedings throughout the country; the Supreme Court is also empowered to review cases upon which final rulings have been made by the courts (including the Supreme Court) where judicial errors have occurred; Pres. ASEFA LIBEN.

The High Court: Addis Ababa; hears appeals from the Provincial and sub-Provincial Courts; has original jurisdiction.

Awraja Courts: Regional courts composed of three judges, criminal and civil.

Warada Courts: Sub-regional; one judge sits alone with very limited jurisdiction, criminal only.

Religion

About 45% of the population are Muslims and about 40% belong to the Ethiopian Orthodox (Tewahido) Church. There are also significant Evangelical Protestant and Roman Catholic communities. The Pentecostal Church and the Society of International Missionaries carry out mission work in Ethiopia. There are also Hindu and Sikh religious institutions. Virtually all of Ethiopia's small Jewish population had been evacuated by the Israeli Government by mid-1999. It has been estimated that 5%–15% of the population follow animist rites and beliefs.

CHRISTIANITY
Ethiopian Orthodox (Tewahido) Church
The Ethiopian Orthodox (Tewahido) Church is one of the five oriental orthodox churches. It was founded in AD 328, and in 1989 had

more than 22m. members, 20,000 parishes and 290,000 clergy. The Supreme Body is the Holy Synod and the National Council, under the chairmanship of the Patriarch (Abune). The Church comprises 25 archdioceses and dioceses (including those in Jerusalem, Sudan, Djibouti and the Western Hemisphere). There are 32 Archbishops and Bishops. The Church administers 1,139 schools and 12 relief and rehabilitation centres throughout Ethiopia.

Patriarchate Head Office: POB 1283, Addis Ababa; tel. (1) 116507; Patriarch (Abune) Archbishop PAULOS; Gen. Sec. L. M. DEMTSE GEBRE MEDHIN.

The Roman Catholic Church

At 31 December 1998 Ethiopia contained an estimated 68,357 adherents of the Alexandrian-Ethiopian Rite and 378,113 adherents of the Latin Rite.

Bishops' Conference: Ethiopian and Eritrean Episcopal Conference, POB 21322, Addis Ababa; tel. (1) 550300; fax (1) 553113; f. 1966; Pres. Most Rev. BERHANE-YESUS DEMEREW SOURAPHIEL, Archbishop of Addis Ababa.

Alexandrian-Ethiopian Rite

Adherents are served by one archdiocese (Addis Ababa) and one diocese (Adigrat).

Archbishop of Addis Ababa: Most Rev. BERHANE-YESUS DEMEREW SOURAPHIEL, Catholic Archbishop's House, POB 21903, Addis Ababa; tel. (1) 111667; fax (1) 553113.

Latin Rite

Aherents are served by the five Apostolic Vicariates of Awasa, Harar, Meki, Nekemte and Soddo-Hosanna, and by the Apostolic Prefecture of Jimma-Bonga.

Other Christian Churches

The Anglican Communion: Within the Episcopal Church in Jerusalem and the Middle East, the Bishop in Egypt has jurisdiction over seven African countries, including Ethiopia.

Armenian Orthodox Church: Deacon VARTKES NALBANDIAN, St George's Armenian Church, POB 116, Addis Ababa; f. 1923.

Ethiopian Evangelical Church (Mekane Yesus): Pres. Rev. YADESA DABA, POB 2087, Addis Ababa; tel. (1) 531919; fax (1) 534148; e-mail eecmy.co@telecom.net.et; f. 1959; affiliated to Lutheran World Fed., All Africa Conf. of Churches and World Council of Churches; c. 3.2m. mems (1999).

Greek Orthodox Church: Metropolitan of Axum Most Rev. PETROS GIAKOUMELOS, POB 571, Addis Ababa.

Seventh-day Adventist Church: Pres. TINSAE TOLESSA, POB 145, Addis Ababa; tel. (1) 511319; e-mail sdaeum@telecom.net.et; f. 1907; 130,000 mems.

ISLAM

Leader: Haji MOHAMMED AHMAD.

JUDAISM

A phased emigration to Israel of about 27,000 Falashas (Ethiopian Jews) took place during 1984–91. An estimated further 4,000 Falashas were assisted to emigrate to Israel in mid-1999, leaving only a small number remaining in the country.

The Press

DAILIES

Addis Zemen: POB 30145, Addis Ababa; f. 1941; Amharic; publ. by the Ministry of Information and Culture; Editor-in-Chief (vacant); circ. 40,000.

The Daily Monitor: POB 22588, Addis Ababa; tel (1) 611880; fax (1) 518409; f. 1993; English; Editor-in-Chief LULLIT MICKAEL; circ. 6,000.

Eletawi Addis (Addis Daily): Addis Ababa; f. 2000; Amharic; Editors-in-Chief SOLOMON ABATE, DEREJE DESTA.

Ethiopian Herald: POB 30701, Addis Ababa; tel. (1) 119050; f. 1943; English; publ. by the Ministry of Information and Culture; Editor-in-Chief KIFLOM HADGOI; circ. 37,000.

PERIODICALS

Abyotawit Ethiopia: POB 2549, Addis Ababa; fortnightly; Amharic.

Addis Tribune: Tambek International, POB 2395, Addis Ababa; tel. (1) 615228; fax (1) 615227; e-mail tambek@telecom.net.et; internet www.addistribune.ethiopiaonline.com; f. 1993; weekly; English; Editor-in-Chief (vacant); circ. 6,000.

Addis Zimit: POB 2395, Addis Ababa; tel. (1) 118613; fax (1) 552110; f. 1993; weekly; Amharic; Editor-in-Chief (vacant); circ. 8,000.

Al-Alem: POB 30232, Addis Ababa; tel. (1) 158046; fax (1) 516819; f. 1941; weekly; Arabic; publ. by the Ministry of Information; Editor-in-Chief TELSOM AHMED; circ. 2,500.

Berisa: POB 30232, Addis Ababa; f. 1976; weekly; Oromogna; publ. by the Ministry of Information; Editor BULO SIBA; circ. 3,500.

Beza: Addis Ababa; weekly; Editor-in-Chief YARED KEMFE.

Birhan Family Magazine: Addis Ababa; monthly; women's magazine.

Birritu: National Bank of Ethiopia, POB 5550, Addis Ababa; tel. (1) 517430; fax (1) 514588; e-mail nbe.excd@telecom.net.et; f. 1968; six a year; Amharic and English; business, insurance and financial news; circ. 6,000; Editor-in-Chief SEMENEH ADGE.

Ethiopis Review: Editor-in-Chief TESFERA ASMARE.

Mabruk: Addis Ababa; weekly; Editor-in-Chief TESAHALENNE MENGESHA.

Maebel: Addis Ababa; weekly; Amharic; Editor-in-Chief ABERA WOGI.

Meskerem: Addis Ababa; quarterly; theoretical politics; circ. 100,000.

Negarit Gazzetta: POB 1031, Addis Ababa; irregularly; Amharic and English; official gazette.

Nigdina Limat: POB 2458, Addis Ababa; tel. (1) 513882; fax (1) 511479; monthly; Amharic; publ. by the Ethiopian Chamber of Commerce; circ. 6,000.

Press Digest: POB 12719, Addis Ababa; tel. (1) 511301; fax (1) 513523; e-mail phoenix.universal@telecom.net.et; f. 1993; weekly.

Tequami: Addis Ababa; weekly; Editor-in-Chief SAMSON SEYUM.

Tinsae (Resurrection): Addis Ababa; tel. (1) 116507; Amharic and English; publ. by the Ethiopian Orthodox Church.

Tobia Magazine: POB 22373, Addis Ababa; tel. (1) 114359; e-mail akpac@telecom.net.et; monthly; Amharic; Gen. Man. WOLE GURMU; circ. 30,000.

Tobia Newspaper: POB 22373, Addis Ababa; tel. (1) 114359; e-mail akpac@telecom.net.et; weekly; Amharic; Gen. Man. WOLE GURMU; circ. 25,000.

Wetaderna Alamaw: POB 1901, Addis Ababa; fortnightly; Amharic.

Yezareitu Ethiopia (Ethiopia Today): POB 30232, Addis Ababa; weekly; Amharic and English; publ. by the Ministry of Information and Culture; Editor-in-Chief IMIRU WORKU; circ. 30,000.

NEWS AGENCIES

Ethiopian News Agency (ENA): Patriot St, POB 530, Addis Ababa; tel. (1) 550011; fax (1) 551609; e-mail ena@telecom.net.et; Chief AMARE AREGAWI.

Foreign Bureaux

Agence France-Presse (AFP): POB 3537, Addis Ababa; tel. (1) 511006; Chief SABA SEYOUM.

Agenzia Nazionale Stampa Associata (ANSA) (Italy): POB 1001, Addis Ababa; tel. (1) 111007; Chief BRAHAME GHEBREZGHI-ABIHER.

Associated Press (AP): Addis Ababa; tel. (1) 161726; Correspondent ABEBE ANDUALAM.

Deutsche Presse-Agentur (dpa) (Germany): Addis Ababa; tel. (1) 510687; Correspondent GHION HAGOS.

Informatsionnoye Telegrafnoye Agentstvo Rossii—Telegrafnoye Agentstvo Suverennykh Stran (ITAR—TASS) (Russia): Addis Ababa; tel. (1) 181255; Bureau Chief GENNADII G. GABRIELYAN.

Prensa Latina (Cuba): Gen. Makonnen Bldg, 5th Floor, nr Ghion Hotel, opp. National Stadium, Addis Ababa; tel. (1) 519899; Chief HUGO RIUS BLEIN.

Reuters (UK): Addis Ababa; tel. (1) 156505; Correspondent TSEGAYE TADESSE.

Rossiiskoye Informatsionnoye Agentstvo—Novosti (RIA—Novosti) (Russia): POB 239, Addis Ababa; Chief VITALII POLIKARPOV.

Xinhua (New China) News Agency (People's Republic of China): POB 2497, Addis Ababa; tel. (1) 515676; fax (1) 514742; Correspondent CHEN CAILIN.

PRESS ASSOCIATION

Ethiopian Journalists' Association: POB 5911, Addis Ababa; tel. (1) 128198; Chair. IMERU WORKU (acting).

Publishers

Addis Ababa University Press: POB 1176, Addis Ababa; tel. (1) 119148; fax (1) 550655; f. 1968; educational and reference works in English; Editor MESSELECH HABTE.

Ethiopia Book Centre: POB 1024, Addis Ababa; tel. (1) 116844; f. 1977; privately-owned; publr, importer, wholesaler and retailer of educational books.

Kuraz Publishing Agency: POB 30933, Addis Ababa; tel. (1) 551688; state-owned.

Government Publishing House

Government Printing Press: POB 1241, Addis Ababa.

Broadcasting and Communications

TELECOMMUNICATIONS

Ethiopian Telecommunications Corpn (ETC): POB 1047, Addis Ababa; tel. (1) 510500; fax (1) 515777; etc-hq@telecom.net.et; internet www.telecom.net.et; Man. Dir ASMARE ABATE.

BROADCASTING

Radio

Radio Ethiopia: POB 1020, Addis Ababa; tel. (1) 121011; f. 1941; Amharic, English, French, Arabic, Afar, Oromifa, Tigre, Tigrinya and Somali; Gen. Man. KASA MILOKO.

Radio Torch: Addis Ababa; f. 1994; Amharic; autonomous station; Gen. Man. SEIFU TURE GETACHEW.

Radio Voice of One Free Ethiopia: Amharic; broadcasts twice a week; opposes current Govts of Ethiopia and Eritrea.

Voice of the Revolution of Tigrai: POB 450, Mekele; tel. (4) 400600; fax (4) 405485; f. 1985; Tigrinya and Afargna; broadcasts 57 hours per week; supports Tigrai People's Liberation Front.

Television

Ethiopian Television: POB 5544, Addis Ababa; tel. (1) 516977; fax (1) 512685; f. 1964; semi-autonomous station; accepts commercial advertising; programmes transmitted from Addis Ababa to 26 regional stations; Dir-Gen. WOLE GURMU.

Finance

(cap. = capital; p.u. = paid up; res = reserves; dep. = deposits; m. = million; brs = branches; amounts in birr)

BANKING

Central Bank

National Bank of Ethiopia: POB 5550, Addis Ababa; tel. (1) 517430; fax (1) 514588; e-mail nbe@telecom.net.et; f. 1964; bank of issue; cap. and res 1,117.5m., dep. 6,022.8m. (May 1999); Gov. TEKLEWOLD ATNAFU; Vice-Gov. ALEMSEGED ASSEFA; 4 brs.

Other Banks

Awash International Bank: POB 12638, Addis Ababa; tel. (1) 612919; fax (1) 614477; e-mail awash.bank@telecom.net.et; f. 1994; cap. and res 66.6m., dep. 455.4m. (December 1999); Gen. Man. LEIKUN BERHANU; 18 brs.

Bank of Abyssinia: POB 12947, Addis Ababa; tel. (1) 514130; fax (1) 511575; e-mail abyssinia@telecom.net.et; f. 1905 (closed 1935 and reopened 1996); commercial banking services; cap. and res 28.0m., dep. 255.4m. (March 1999); CEO TEKALIGN GEDAMU; 7 brs.

Commercial Bank of Ethiopia: Unity Sq., POB 255, Addis Ababa; tel. (1) 511271; fax (1) 533858; f. 1943, reorg. 1996; state-owned; cap. and res 1,076.6m., dep. 14,263.8m. (March 1999); Pres. TILAHUN ABBAY; 168 brs.

Construction and Business Bank: Higher 21, Kebele 04, POB 3480, Addis Ababa; tel. (1) 512300; fax (1) 515103; e-mail cbb@telecom.net.et; f. 1975 as Housing and Savings Bank; provides credit for construction projects and a range of commercial banking services; state-owned; cap. p.u. 68.7m., total assets 1,045.3m. (March 1999); Gen. Man. ADMASSU TECHANE; 20 brs.

Dashen Bank: POB 12752, Addis Ababa; tel. (1) 650286; fax (1) 653037; e-mail dashenbank@telecom.net.et; cap. and res 48.9m., dep. 489.4m. (June 1999); CEO LULSEGED TEFERI; 16 brs.

Development Bank of Ethiopia: POB 1900, Addis Ababa; tel. (1) 511188; fax (1) 511606; provides devt finance for industry and agriculture, technical advice and assistance in project evaluation; state-owned; cap. and res 385.2m., dep. 727.7m. (March 1999); Gen. Man. MOGES CHEMERE; 32 brs.

United Bank: POB 19963, Addis Ababa; tel. (1) 655222; fax (1) 655243; f. 1998; commercial banking services; cap. and res 24.8m., dep. 37.1m. (June 1999); Gen. Man. KEBEDE TEMESGEN; 5 brs.

Wegagen Bank: POB 1018, Addis Ababa; tel. (1) 655015; fax (1) 653330; e-mail wegagen@telecom.net.et; f. 1997; commercial

banking services; cap. and res 43.0m.; dep. 218.4m. (March 1999); CEO BRUTAYIT DAWIT ABDI; 13 brs.

INSURANCE

Africa Insurance Co: POB 12941, Addis Ababa; tel. (1) 517861; fax (1) 510376; Gen. Man. ALEM TESFATSION.

Awash Insurance Co: POB 12637, Addis Ababa; tel. (1) 614420; fax (1) 614419; Gen. Man. TSEGAYE KEMAS.

Ethiopian Insurance Corpn: POB 2545, Addis Ababa; tel. (1) 512400; fax (1) 517499; e-mail eic.md@telecom.net.et; internet www.telecom.net.et/~eic; f. 1976; Man. Dir HABTAMU HAILE MARIAM.

Global Insurance SC: POB 180112, Addis Abba; tel. (1) 158498; fax (1) 710808; f. 1997; Gen. Man. YESUF IBRAHIM.

Lion Insurance SC: POB 661, Addis Ababa; tel. (1) 513305; fax (1) 710091; f. 1998; Gen. Man. TESFAYE NATNAEL.

National Insurance Co of Ethiopia: POB 12645, Addis Ababa; tel. (1) 116417; fax (1) 650660; Man. Dir HABTEMARIAM SHUMGIZAW.

Nile Insurance Co: POB 12836, Addis Ababa; tel. (1) 150580; fax (1) 514592; f. 1995; Gen. Man. MAHTSENTU FELEKE.

Nyala Insurance SC: POB 12753, Addis Ababa; tel. (1) 340532; fax (1) 349474; e-mail nisco@telecom.net.et; Man. Dir NAHU-SENAYE ARAYA.

United Insurance Co: POB 1156, Addis Ababa; tel. (1) 515656; fax (1) 513258; e-mail united.insurance@telecom.net.et; Gen. Man. EYESSUS W. ZAFU.

Trade and Industry

CHAMBERS OF COMMERCE

Ethiopian Chamber of Commerce: Mexico Sq., POB 517, Addis Ababa; tel. (1) 518240; fax (1) 517699; f. 1947; city chambers in Addis Ababa, Asella, Awasa, Bahir Dar, Dire Dawa, Nazret, Jimma, Gondar, Dessie, Mekele and Shashemene; Pres. ASCHALEW HAILE; Sec.-Gen. ADANE GUDINA.

Addis Ababa Chamber of Commerce: POB 2458, Addis Ababa; tel. (1) 513882; fax (1) 511479; e-mail AAchamber1@telecom.net.et; internet www.addischamber.com.

INDUSTRIAL AND TRADE ASSOCIATIONS

Ethiopian Beverages Corporation: POB 1285, Addis Ababa; tel. (1) 186185; Gen. Man. MENNA TEWAHEDE.

Ethiopian Cement Corporation: POB 5782, Addis Ababa; tel. (1) 552222; fax (1) 551572; Gen. Man. REDI GEMAL.

Ethiopian Chemical Corporation: POB 5747, Addis Ababa; tel. (1) 184305; Gen. Man. ASNAKE SAHLU.

Ethiopian Coffee Export Enterprise: POB 2591, Addis Ababa; tel. (1) 515330; fax (1) 510762; f. 1977; Gen. Man. DERGA GURMESSA.

Ethiopian Food Corporation: POB 2345, Addis Ababa; tel. (1) 518522; fax (1) 513173; f. 1975; produces and distributes food items including edible oil, ghee substitute, pasta, bread, maize, wheat flour etc.; Gen. Man. BEKELE HAILE.

Ethiopian Fruit and Vegetable Marketing Enterprise: POB 2374, Addis Ababa; tel. (1) 519192; fax (1) 516483; f. 1980; sole wholesale domestic distributor and exporter of fresh and processed fruit and vegetables, and floricultural products; Gen. Man. KAKNU PEWONDE.

Ethiopian Grain Trade Enterprise: POB 3321, Addis Ababa; tel. (1) 653166; fax (1) 652792; e-mail egte@telecom.net.et; Gen. Man. GIRMA BEKELE.

Ethiopian Handicrafts and Small-Scale Industries Development Agency: Addis Ababa; tel. (1) 157366; f. 1977.

Ethiopian Import and Export Corporation (ETIMEX): Addis Ababa; tel. (1) 511112; fax (1) 515411; f. 1975; state trading corpn under the supervision of the Ministry of Commerce and Industry; import of building materials, foodstuffs, stationery and office equipment, textiles, clothing, chemicals, general merchandise, capital goods; Gen. Man. ASCHENAKI G. HIWOT.

Ethiopian Livestock and Meat Corporation: Addis Ababa; tel. (1) 159341; fax (1) 513520; f. 1984; state trading corpn responsible for the devt and export of livestock and livestock products; Gen. Man. GELANA KEJELA.

Ethiopian National Metal Works Corporation: Addis Ababa; fax (1) 510714; Gen. Man. ALULA BERHANE.

Ethiopian Oil Seeds and Pulses Export Corporation: POB 5719, Addis Ababa; tel. (1) 550597; fax (1) 553299; f. 1975; Gen. Man. ABDOURUHMAN MOHAMMED.

Ethiopia Peasants' Association (EPA): f. 1978 to promote improved agricultural techniques, home industries, education, public health and self-reliance; comprises 30,000 peasant asscns with c. 7m. mems; Chair. (vacant).

Ethiopian Petroleum Enterprise: POB 3375, Addis Ababa; fax (1) 512938; e-mail ethpetroleum@telecom.net.et; f. 1976; Gen. Man. YIGZAW MEKONNEN.

Ethiopian Pharmaceuticals and Medical Supplies Corporation (EPHARMECOR): POB 21904, Addis Ababa; tel. (1) 134577; fax (1) 752555; f. 1976; manufacture, import, export and distribution of pharmaceuticals, chemicals, dressings, surgical and dental instruments, hospital and laboratory supplies; Gen. Man. GIRMA BEPASSO.

Ethiopian Sugar Corporation: POB 133, Addis Ababa; tel. (1) 519700; fax (1) 513488; Gen. Man. ABATE LEMENGH.

National Leather and Shoe Corporation: POB 2516, Addis Ababa; tel. (1) 514075; fax (1) 513525; f. 1975; produces and sells semi-processed hides and skins, finished leather, leather goods and footwear; Gen. Man. GIRMA W. AREGAI.

National Textiles Corporation: POB 2446, Addis Ababa; tel. (1) 157316; fax (1) 511955; f. 1975; production of yarn, fabrics, knitwear, blankets, bags, etc.; Gen. Man. FIKRE HUGIANE.

Natural Gums Processing and Marketing Enterprise: POB 62322, Addis Ababa; tel. (1) 159930; fax (1) 518110; f. 1976; Gen. Man. AREGA HABTEWOLD.

UTILITIES
Electricity

Ethiopian Electric Power Corporation (EEPCO): De Gaulle Sq., POB 1233, Addis Ababa; tel. (1) 111443; fax (1) 551324; Chair. HAILE SELASSIE ASEGIDE; Gen. Man. TESFA ALEM GEBRE IYESUS.

Water

Addis Ababa Water Sewerage Authority: Addis Ababa.

Water Resources Development Authority: POB 1045, Addis Ababa; tel. (1) 612999; fax (1) 611245; Gen. Man. GETACHEW GIZAW.

TRADE UNIONS

Ethiopian Trade Union (ETU): POB 3653, Addis Ababa; tel. (1) 514366; f. 1975; comprises nine industrial unions and 22 regional unions with a total membership of 320,000 (1987); Chair. (vacant).

Transport
RAILWAYS

Djibouti-Ethiopian Railway (Chemin de Fer Djibouti-Ethiopien–CDE): POB 1051, Addis Ababa; tel. (1) 517250; fax (1) 513533; f. 1909, adopted present name in 1981; jtly-owned by Govts of Ethiopia and Djibouti; 781 km of track (681 km in Ethiopia), linking Addis Ababa with Djibouti; Pres. SALEH OMAR HILDID; Dir-Gen. ALI ABDALLAH GADID.

ROADS

In 1998 the total road network comprised an estimated 26,053 km of primary, secondary and feeder roads, of which 3,656 km were paved, the remainder being gravel roads. In addition, there are some 30,000 km of unclassified tracks and trails. A highway links Addis Ababa with Nairobi in Kenya, forming part of the Trans-East Africa Highway. In early 1998 the World Bank granted Ethiopia a loan of US $309.2m. to help finance the first five-year phase of an ambitious 10-year government programme to rebuild and upgrade rural and urban roads.

Comet Transport Enterprise: POB 2402, Addis Ababa; tel. (1) 151864; fax (1) 514254; f. 1994; Gen. Man. FELEKE YIMER.

Ethiopian Freight Transport Corporation: Addis Ababa; restructured into five autonomous enterprises in 1994.

Ethiopian Road Transport Authority: POB 2504, Addis Ababa; tel. (1) 510244; fax (1) 510715; enforcement of road transport regulations, registering of vehicles and issuing of driving licences; Gen. Man. KASAHUN H. MARIAM.

Ethiopian Roads Authority: POB 1770, Addis Ababa; tel. (1) 517170; fax (1) 514866; f. 1951; construction and maintenance of roads, bridges and airports; Gen. Man. TESFA MICHAEL NAHUSENAI.

Public Transport Corporation: POB 5780, Addis Ababa; tel. (1) 153117; fax (1) 510720; f. 1977; urban bus services in Addis Ababa and Jimma, and services between towns; restructured into three autonomous enterprises in 1994 and scheduled for privatization; Man. Dir AHMED NURU.

SHIPPING

The formerly Ethiopian-controlled ports of Massawa and Assab now lie within the boundaries of the State of Eritrea (q.v.). Although an agreement exists between the two Governments allowing Ethiopian access to the two ports, which can handle more than 1m. metric tons of merchandise annually, in mid-1998 Ethiopia ceased using the ports, owing to the outbreak of hostilities. Ethiopia's maritime

trade currently passes through Djibouti (in the Republic of Djibouti), and also through the Kenyan port of Mombasa. At 7 July 1999 Ethiopia's registered merchant fleet numbered 12 vessels, with a total displacement of 82,503 grt.

Ethiopian Shipping Lines Corporation: POB 2572, Addis Ababa; tel. (1) 518280; fax (1) 519525; e-mail esl@telecom.net.et; f. 1964; serves Red Sea, Europe, Mediterranean, Gulf and Far East with its own fleet and chartered vessels; Chair. G. TSADKAN GEBRE TENSAY; Gen. Man. AMBACHEW ABRAHA.

Marine Transport Authority: Maritime Dept, POB 1861, Addis Ababa; tel. (1) 158227; fax (1) 515665; f. 1993; regulates maritime transport services; Chair. TESHOME WOLDEGIORGIS.

Maritime and Transit Services Enterprise: POB 1186, Addis Ababa; tel. (1) 510666; fax (1) 514097; f. 1979; handles cargoes for import and export; operates shipping agency service; Chair. DESTA AMARE; Gen. Man. AHMED YASSIN.

CIVIL AVIATION

Ethiopia has two international airports (at Addis Ababa and Dire Dawa) and around 40 airfields. Bole International Airport in the capital handles 95% of international air traffic and 85% of domestic flights. A programme to modernize the airport, at an estimated cost of 819m. birr (US $130m.), was to be undertaken during 1997–2001. Several domestic airports are currently under construction and are due to be completed in 2000.

Civil Aviation Authority: POB 978, Addis Ababa; tel. (1) 610277; fax (1) 612533; e-mail civilaviation@telecom.net.et; constructs and maintains airports; provides air navigational facilities; Dir-Gen. MESHESHA BELAYNEH.

Ethiopian Airlines: Bole International Airport, POB 1755, Addis Ababa; tel. (1) 612222; fax (1) 611474; e-mail eal@telecom.net.et; internet www.flyethiopian.com; f. 1945; operates regular domestic services and flights to 47 international destinations in Africa, Europe, Middle East, Asia and the USA; CEO BISRAT NIGATU.

Tourism

Ethiopia's tourist attractions include the early Christian monuments and churches, the ancient capitals of Gondar and Axum, the Blue Nile Falls and the National Parks of the Semien and Bale Mountains. Tourist arrivals in 1996 totalled 108,885 and provided US $28m. in foreign exchange. In 1998 116,686 tourists visited Ethiopia.

Ethiopian Tourism Commission: POB 2183, Addis Ababa; tel. (1) 517470; fax (1) 513899; e-mail tour-com@telecom.net.et; f. 1964; formulates national tourism policy, publicizes tourist attractions and regulates standards of tourist facilities; Commr YOUSUF ABDULLAHI SUKKAR.

Defence

Following the fall of Mengistu's government and the defeat of his army in May 1991, troops of the Eritrean People's Liberation Front (EPLF) and the Ethiopian People's Revolutionary Democratic Front (EPRDF) were deployed in Eritrea and in Ethiopia respectively. In June 1993 EPRDF forces were estimated at about 100,000. In October 1993 it was announced that preparations were under way to create a 'multi-ethnic defence force'. Extensive demobilization of former members of the Tigrai People's Liberation Front has since taken place. In September 1996 the Government sold its naval assets. Owing to hostilities with Eritrea in 1998–2000, there was a large increase in the size of the armed forces and in defence expenditure during this period. In August 1999 Ethiopia's armed forces numbered an estimated 325,000 in active service.

Defence Expenditure: Budgeted at 3,500m. birr in 1999.

Education

Education in Ethiopia is available free of charge, and, after a rapid growth in numbers of schools, it became compulsory between the ages of seven and 13 years. Since 1976 most primary and secondary schools have been controlled by local peasant associations and urban dwellers' associations. Primary education begins at seven years of age and lasts for eight years. Secondary education, beginning at 15 years of age, lasts for a further four years, comprising two cycles of two years, the second of which provides preparatory education for entry to the tertiary level. In 1996 total enrolment at primary schools was equivalent to 43% of children in the appropriate age-group (55% of boys; 30% of girls); enrolment at secondary schools was equivalent to 12% (14% of boys; 10% of girls) of children in the relevant age-group. The 1997/98 budget allocated an estimated 13.6% (1,563.6m. birr) of total expenditure to education. A major literacy campaign was launched in 1979. By 1990 more than 23m. people had been enrolled for tuition programmes, and the rate of adult illiteracy had reportedly been reduced to 23% (compared with 96% in 1970). The campaign subsequently lost momentum, however,

and in 1995, according to UNESCO estimates, the rate of adult illiteracy had risen to 66.8% (males 60.1%; females 73.5%). There are 12 institutions of higher education in Ethiopia, with a total of 57,040 enrolled students in 1998/99. There is a considerable shortage of qualified teachers, which is particularly acute in secondary schools, which rely heavily on expatriate staff.

Bibliography

Abbink, J. *Ethiopian Society and History: A Bibliography of Ethiopian Studies 1957–1990*. Leiden, African Studies Centre, 1990.

Abegaz, B. (Ed.). *Essays on Ethiopian Economic Development*. Aldershot, Avebury, 1994.

Abir, M. *Ethiopia and the Red Sea: The Rise and Decline of the Solomonic Dynasty and Muslim–European Rivalry in the Region*. London, Frank Cass, 1980.

Abraham, K. *Ethiopia: from Bullets to the Ballot Box: The Bumpy Road to Democracy and the Political Economy of Transition*. Lawrenceville, NJ, Red Sea Press, 1994.

Africa Watch. *Evil Days: 30 Years of War and Famine in Ethiopia*. New York, Human Rights Watch, 1991.

Agyeman-Duah, B. *The United States and Ethiopia: Military Assistance and the Quest for Security 1953–1993*. Lanham, MD, University Press of America, 1994.

Bekele, S. (Ed.). *An Economic History of Ethiopia. Vol.* I: *The Imperial Era, 1941–1974*. Dakar, CODESRIA, 1995.

Clapham, C. *Transformation and Continuity in Revolutionary Ethiopia*. Cambridge, Cambridge University Press, 1988.

Del Boca, A. *The Ethiopian War 1935–1941*. Chicago, University of Chicago Press, 1969.

Doornbos, M., Cliffe, L., Ahmed, A.G.M., and Markakis, J. (Eds). *Beyond Conflict in the Horn: The Prospects of Peace and Development in Ethiopia, Somalia, Eritrea and Sudan*. Lawrenceville, NJ, Red Sea Press, 1992.

Dugan, J., and Lafore, L. *Days of Emperor and Clown, The Italo-Ethiopian War 1935–1936*. New York, Doubleday, 1973.

Erlich, H. *Ethiopia and the Middle East*. Boulder, CO, and London, Lynne Rienner Publishers, 1994.

Fukui, K., and Markakis, J. (Eds). *Ethnicity and Conflict in the Horn of Africa*. London, James Currey, 1994.

Ghebre-Ab, H. (Ed.). *Ethiopia and Eritrea: A Documentary Study*. Trenton, NJ, Red Sea Press, 1993.

Gilkes, P. *The Dying Lion: Feudalism and Modernization in Ethiopia*. London, Julian Friedmann, 1974.

Griffin, K. (Ed.). *The Economy of Ethiopia*. New York, St Martin's Press, 1992.

Gurdon, C. (Ed.). *The Horn of Africa*. London, University College London Press, 1994.

Haile Selassie I. *The Autobiography of Emperor Haile Selassie I. 'My Life and Ethiopia's Progress.'* Oxford, Oxford University Press, 1976.

Haile-Selassie, T. *The Ethiopian Revolution, 1974–1991: From a Monarchical Autocracy to a Military Oligarchy*. London, Kegan Paul International, 1997.

Hammond, J. *Fire from the Ashes: A Chronicle of the Revolution in Tigray, Ethiopia, 1975–1991*. Lawrenceville, NJ, Red Sea Press, 1999.

Hansson, G. *The Ethiopian Economy 1974–94: Ethiopia, Tikdem and After*. London, Routledge, 1995.

Harbeson, J. W. *The Ethiopian Transformation*. Boulder, CO, Westview Press, 1988.

Hassen, M. *The Oromo of Ethiopia: A History 1570–1860*. Lawrenceville, NJ, Red Sea Press, 1994.

Henze, P. *Layers of Time: A History of Ethiopia*, London, Hurst, 2000.

Iyob, R. *The Eritrean Struggle for Independence: Domination, Resistance, Nationalism 1941–93*. Cambridge, Cambridge University Press, 1995.

Jalata, A, *Oromia and Ethiopia: State Formation and Ethnonational Conflict, 1868–1992*. Boulder, CO, Lynne Rienner Publishers, 1993.

Jansson, K., Harris, M., and Penrose, A. *The Ethiopain Famine*. London, Zed Books, 1987.

Katsuyoski, F., and Markakis, J. (Eds). *Ethnicity and Conflict in the Horn of Africa*. London, James Currey, 1994.

Kebbede, G. *The State and Development in Ethiopia*. Atlantic Highlands, NJ, Humanities Press, 1992.

Keller, E. J. *Revolutionary Ethiopia: From Empire to People's Republic*. Bloomington, Indiana University Press, 1989.

Last, G. C. 'Introductory Notes on the Geography of Ethiopia', in *Ethiopia Observer*, Vol. VI, No. 2, 1962.

Levine, D. *Greater Ethiopia: The Evolution of a Multicultural Society*. Chicago, University of Chicago Press, 1974.

Lockot, H. W. *The Mission: The Life, Reign and Character of Haile Selassie I*. London, Hurst, 1992.

Marcus, H. G. *Ethiopia, Great Britain and the United States, 1941–1974*. Berkeley, University of California Press, 1983.

A History of Ethiopia. Berkeley, University of California Press, 1994.

Haile Selassie I: The Formative Years 1892–1936. Berkeley, University of California Press, 1987.

Markakis, J. *National and Class Conflict in the Horn of Africa*. Cambridge, Cambridge University Press (African Studies Series, No. 55), 1988.

Negash, T. *Rethinking Education in Ethiopia*. New Brunswick NJ, Transaction Publishers, 1996.

Eritrea and Ethiopia: The Federal Experience. Uppsala, Nordiska Africainstitutet, 1997.

Ofcansky, T. P., and Berry, L. (Eds). *Ethiopia: A Country Study*. Washington, DC, USGPO, 1991.

Olmstead, J. *Woman between Two Worlds: Portrait of an Ethiopian Rural Leader*. Champaign, IL, University of Illinois Press, 1997.

Ottaway, M. *Soviet and American Influence in the Horn of Africa*. New York, Praeger, 1982.

(Ed.). *The Political Economy of Ethiopia*. New York, Praeger, 1990.

Pankhurst, A. *Resettlement and Famine in Ethiopia: The Villagers' Experience*. Manchester, Manchester University Press, 1992.

Pankhurst, R. *Economic History of Ethiopia, 1880–1935*. Addis Ababa, 1968.

History of Ethiopian Towns: From Middle Ages to Early Nineteenth Century. Stuttgart, Steiner Verlag, 1982.

History of Ethiopian Towns: From Mid Nineteenth Century to 1935. Stuttgart, Steiner Verlag, 1985.

The Ethiopians. Oxford, Blackwell, 1999.

Parker, B. *Ethiopia: Breaking New Ground*. Oxford, Oxfam Publishing, 1995.

Patman, R. G. *The Soviet Union in The Horn of Africa*. Cambridge, Cambridge University Press, 1990.

Pausewang, S., et al. (Eds). *Ethiopia: Rural Development Options*. London, Zed Books, 1990.

Phillipson, D. W. *Ancient Ethiopia*. London, British Museum Press, 1998.

Pickett, J. *Economic Development in Ethiopia: Agriculture, the Market and the State*. Paris, OECD, 1991.

Prouty, C., *Empress Taytu and Menilek II: Ethiopia 1883–1910*. London, Ravens Educational and Development Services, 1986.

Prouty, C., and Rosenfeld, E. *Historical Dictionary of Ethiopia and Eritrea*. 2nd Edn. Lanham, MD, and London, Scarecrow Press, 1994.

Relief Society of Tigray. *Tigray: The Struggle for Development*. Makelle, REST, 1993.

Sbacchi, A. *Ethiopia under Mussolini: Fascism and the Colonial Experience*. London, Zed Press, 1985.

Sellassie, H. B. *Conflict and Intervention in the Horn of Africa*. New York and London, Monthly Review Press, 1980.

Tadesse, K. *The Generation: A History of the Ethiopian People's Revolutionary Party*. Lawrenceville, NJ, Red Sea Press, 1993.

Tareke, G. *Ethiopia: Power and Protest*. New York, Cambridge University Press, 1991.

Tiruneh, A. *The Ethiopian Revolution 1974–87*. Cambridge, Cambridge University Press, 1993.

Ullendorff, E. *The Ethiopians: An Introduction to Country and People*. Oxford, Oxford University Press, 1973.

Wubner, M., and Abate, Y. *Ethiopia: Transition and Development in the Horn of Africa*. Boulder, CO, Westview Press, 1988.

Zegeye, A., and Pausewang, S. (Eds). *Ethiopia in Change: Peasantry, Nationalism and Democracy*. London, British Academic Press, 1994.

Zewde, B. *A History of Modern Ethiopia 1855–1974*. London, James Currey, 1991.

GABON

Physical and Social Geography

DAVID HILLING

Lying along the Equator, on the west coast of Africa, the Gabonese Republic covers an area of 267,667 sq km (103,347 sq miles) and comprises the entire drainage basin of the westward-flowing Ogooué river, together with the basins of several smaller coastal rivers such as the Nyanga and Como.

The low-lying coastal zone is narrow in the north and south but broader in the estuary regions of the Ogooué and Gabon. South of the Ogooué numerous lagoons, such as the N'Dogo, M'Goze, and M'Komi, back the coast, and the whole area is floored with Cretaceous sedimentary rocks, which at shallow depth yield oil. The main producing oil fields are in a narrow zone stretching southwards from Port-Gentil, both on- and off-shore. The interior consists of Pre-Cambrian rocks, eroded into a series of plateau surfaces at heights of 450–600 m and dissected by the river system into a number of distinct blocks, such as the Crystal mountains, the Moabi uplands and the Chaillu massif. This area is one of Africa's most mineralized zones, with the large-scale exploitation of manganese and uranium contributing significantly to Gabon's economy. There are also deposits of high-grade iron ore, gold and diamonds.

Gabon has an equatorial climate, with uniformly high temperatures, high relative humidities and mean annual rainfalls of 1,500–3,000 mm. About 85% of the country's area is covered with rain forest, one of the highest national proportions in the world, and wood from the okoumé tree provided the basis for the country's economy until superseded by minerals in the 1960s. Grassland vegetation is restricted to the coastal sand zone south of Port-Gentil and parts of the valleys of the Nyanga, upper N'Gounié and upper Ogooué.

Agricultural development in the potentially rich forest zone has been limited by the small size of the country's population. At the July 1993 census the population was enumerated at 1,014,976, and in mid-1998, according to UN estimates, totalled 1,188,000, giving an average density of only 4.4 inhabitants per sq km. As the population is small in relation to national income, Gabon has the highest level of income per head in mainland sub-Saharan Africa, although many of the country's enterprises depend on labour imported from neighbouring countries. The three main urban concentrations may now account for more than one-half of the population; in 1988 Libreville, the capital, had more than 352,000 inhabitants, Port-Gentil, the centre of the petroleum industry, 164,000, and Franceville/Moanda, the mining centres, 75,000. The major rural concentrations are found in Woleu N'Tem, where coffee and cocoa are the main cash crops, and around Lambaréné, where palm oil and coffee are important. The country's principal ethnic groups are the Fang (30%) and the Eshira (25%). The resident French population is estimated at 20,000.

Recent History

PIERRE ENGLEBERT

Revised for this edition by the Editor

ONE-PARTY GOVERNMENT

Formerly part of French West Africa, Gabon was granted internal autonomy in 1958 and became fully independent on 17 August 1960. Léon M'Ba, the new republic's president, established Gabon as a one-party state. Following his death in November 1967 M'Ba was succeeded by his vice-president, Albert-Bernard (later Omar) Bongo, who organized a new ruling party, the Parti démocratique gabonais (PDG). Gabon enjoyed relative political stability during the 1970s and experienced rapid growth under a liberal economic system which attracted foreign capital investment; in 1975 Gabon, a significant regional producer of petroleum, joined the Organization of the Petroleum Exporting Countries (OPEC). Social and political strains, deriving from the rapid growth of the economy in the mid-1970s and its subsequent decline, began to emerge in the early 1980s, led by the Mouvement de redressement national (MORENA), a moderate opposition group. MORENA accused Bongo of corruption and personal extravagance and demanded the restoration of a plural political system. Bongo, however, maintained his commitment to a single-party framework, within which he undertook to allow democratic debate. MORENA formed a government-in-exile in Paris and nominated a candidate to challenge Bongo in the presidential election of November 1986, but was prevented from organizing a campaign. Bongo was duly re-elected for a further seven-year term, with 99.97% of the vote.

Following a deterioration in the economy, compulsory reductions in salaries for public-sector employees in October 1988 provoked strike action. Bongo's subsequent announcement that economic reforms and austerity measures would, henceforth, be pursued only to the extent that they did not undermine social and political stability, had a detrimental effect on the country's negotiations with its external creditors.

MORENA, which had been preoccupied with internal divisions since 1987, resumed its campaign against the government in early 1989. In May, however, the movement's chairman, Fr Paul M'Ba Abessole, visited Gabon and, after a meeting with Bongo, announced that he and many of his supporters would return to the country in the near future. M'Ba Abessole subsequently declared his support for Bongo's regime and in early 1990, following his removal from the leadership of MORENA, formed a new organization, MORENA des bûcherons (renamed Rassemblement national des bûcherons in 1991 to avoid confusion with the rival MORENA–originels).

A number of arrests took place in October 1989, following an alleged conspiracy to overthrow the government. It was claimed that the detainees, who included senior members of the security forces and prominent public officials, had acted in concert with a Paris-based opposition group, the Union du peuple gabonais (UPG). Further arrests followed in November, after the alleged discovery of a second plot against the government.

CONSTITUTIONAL TRANSITION

A series of strikes and demonstrations by students and workers in early 1990 reflected increasing public discontent with economic conditions. In late February a 'special commission for democracy', established in January by the PDG central committee, submitted a report, which contained an explicit condemnation of the one-party system. On the following day, Bongo announced that immediate and fundamental political reforms would be introduced. However, his replacement of the PDG with the Rassemblement social-démocrate gabonais (RSDG), which was intended to attract a diverse ideological following, did little to allay popular discontent.

In March 1990 Bongo announced that legislative elections, scheduled for April, were to be postponed for six months to allow time for the constitution to be amended. It was also proposed that a multi-party system be introduced, under the supervision of the RSDG, at the end of a five-year transitional period. However, a national conference of some 2,000 delegates, which was convened in late March to formulate a programme for the transfer to a plural democracy, rejected Bongo's proposals and voted instead for the immediate creation of a multi-party system and the formation of an interim government, to hold office only until the October legislative elections. Bongo acceded to the conference's decisions, and in April Casimir Oye Mba, the governor of the Banque des états de l'Afrique centrale, was appointed prime minister in a transitional administration, which included several opposition members.

In May 1990 PDG and legislative approval was given to constitutional amendments to facilitate the transition to a multi-party system. The existing presidential mandate (effective until January 1994) was to be respected; thereafter, elections to the presidency would be contested by more than one candidate and the tenure of office would be reduced to five years, renewable only once. At the same time, Bongo resigned as secretary-general of the PDG (claiming that a party political role was now incompatible with his position as head of state), and the post was assumed by Jean Adiahénot. These far-reaching changes, however, were overshadowed by the repercussions of the death, in suspicious circumstances, of Joseph Rendjambe, the secretary-general of an opposition movement, the Parti gabonais du progrès (PGP). Demonstrators, who alleged Bongo's complicity in the death, attacked property belonging to the president and his associates. A country-wide curfew was imposed as unrest spread. French troops were dispatched to Gabon to protect the interests of the 20,000 resident French nationals, and several hundred Europeans were evacuated. The strength of the Gabonese economy was for a time jeopardized by the severe disruption of the petroleum sector resulting from the disorders. A state of emergency was imposed in Port-Gentil and its environs, and at least two deaths were reported after Gabonese security forces intervened to restore order. In early June 1990 it was announced that the French military reinforcements were to be withdrawn. The national curfew was lifted in early July, although the state of emergency remained in force in the area surrounding Port-Gentil.

Legislative Elections

Legislative elections were scheduled for 16 and 23 September 1990; however, only political parties which had registered during the national conference in March were allowed to present candidates. The first round of the elections, on 16 September, was disrupted by violent protests by voters, who claimed that electoral fraud was being practised in favour of the PDG. Following allegations by opposition parties of widespread electoral irregularities, results in 32 constituencies were declared invalid, although the election of 58 candidates (of whom 36 were members of the PDG) was confirmed. The transitional government subsequently conceded that malpractices had occurred, and the second round of the elections was postponed until 21 and 28 October. A commission representing both the PDG and opposition parties was established to supervise polling. At the elections in October, the PDG won an overall majority, with 62 seats, while opposition candidates secured 55 seats.

The formation of a government of national unity was announced on 27 November 1990; Oye Mba, the prime minister of the former interim government, was appointed as prime minister. Sixteen portfolios were allocated to members of the PDG, with the remaining eight distributed among members of five opposition parties. Three other opposition movements refused Bongo's offer of inclusion in the government. A new draft constitution, which was promulgated on 22 December, endorsed reforms included in the transitional constitution introduced in May. Further measures included the proposed establishment of an upper house, to be known as the senate, which

was to control the balance and regulation of power. This proposal, however, was strongly opposed by the opposition parties. A constitutional council was also to replace the administrative chamber of the supreme court and a national communications council was to be formed to ensure the impartial treatment of information by the state media.

The final composition of the national assembly was determined in March 1991, when elections took place in five constituencies where the results had been annulled, owing to alleged irregularities. Following the completion of the elections, the PDG secured 66 seats, while the PGP obtained 19, the Rassemblement national des bûcherons (RNB, formerly MORENA des bûcherons) 17, MORENA–originels seven, the Association pour le socialisme au Gabon (APSG) six, the Union socialiste gabonais (USG) three, and two smaller parties one seat each.

Opposition Realignments and Social Unrest

In May 1991 six opposition parties formed an alliance, known as the Coordination de l'opposition démocratique (COD). The COD announced its withdrawal from the national assembly, and demanded the full and immediate implementation of the new constitution, the appointment of a new prime minister, the submission of constitutional proposals for consideration by the national assembly, and access to the state-controlled media. Following a general strike, which was organized by the COD, Bongo dissolved the council of ministers, affirmed his intention fully to implement the new constitution, and announced that, in accordance with the constitution, a constitutional court and a national communications council had been created. In a further attempt to appease public discontent, Bongo pardoned more than 200 political prisoners. However, opposition parties within the COD refused to participate in the new government, of which Oye Mba was appointed prime minister. Later in June, opposition deputies terminated their boycott of the national assembly and resumed parliamentary duties. On 22 June a new coalition government was formed which retained 14 members of the previous council of ministers and included representatives of MORENA–originels, the USG and the APSG.

In February 1992 three political associations, MORENA–originels, the Parti socialiste gabonais (PSG) and the USG, formed an alliance, known as the Forum africain pour la reconstruction (FAR). Later in February the government announced that a multi-party presidential election would take place in December 1993, two months before the expiry of Bongo's term of office.

Widespread strikes and demonstrations continued during 1992 and 1993; in February, following protests by students demanding additional scholarship grants, the university was closed, and a ban on public demonstrations and gatherings was imposed. Later in February the COD organized a one-day general strike in Port-Gentil (which was only partially observed), followed by a one-day 'dead city' campaign in Port-Gentil and Libreville. In late February the government reopened the university, and lifted the ban on political gatherings and demonstrations. In March, however, a protester was killed, during a demonstration by teachers in support of improvements in salary and working conditions. The COD subsequently instigated a further one-day 'dead city' campaign in Libreville. In early April, in an attempt to regain public support, the PDG organized a pro-government rally in the capital.

In July 1992 the national assembly adopted a new electoral code (which had been submitted by the government), despite protests by the FAR that the government had failed to comply with the demands presented by the COD in October 1991. Later in July 1992 a motion of censure against the government, proposed by opposition deputies in the national assembly in response to the postponement of local government elections, was defeated. The cabinet was reshuffled in August, and in December three members of the PDG, including a former minister, were expelled from the party, after establishing a faction, known as the Cercle des libéraux réformateurs (CLR).

In April 1993 there were widespread protests and demonstrations in central and southern Gabon at the poor quality of living conditions resulting from the lack of social infrastructure, particularly road facilities and reliable water supplies in rural areas. In the same month Jules Bourdès-Ogouliguendé (who had left the PDG in January) resigned as president of the national assembly, prior to standing as a candidate in the forthcoming presidential election. Pierre-Claver Maganga Moussavou, the leader of the PSD, and Alexandre Sambat, a former ambassador to the USA, subsequently declared their candidacies. In July Bongo reshuffled the council of ministers, following the resignation of the minister with responsibility for labour and employment, Simon Oyono Aba'a, who had been nominated as the presidential candidate of MORENA–originels. In October Bongo formally announced that he was to contest the presidential election; by the end of that month 16 candidates had emerged (of which three subsequently withdrew in favour of Bongo), including M'Ba Abessole, the leader of the PGP, Pierre-Louis Agondjo-Okawé, and a former prime minister, Léon Mébiame.

In early November 1993 five political groups (the PDG, the USG, the APSG, the CLR and the Parti de l'unité du peuple gabonais) agreed to support Bongo's candidacy in the presidential election, while eight opposition candidates established an informal alliance, known as the Convention des forces du changement (CFC). Later that month a number of demonstrations were staged by members of the CFC, in protest at alleged irregularities in the electoral register. Following public disorders in early December, the government agreed to a partial revision of electoral lists, but rejected opposition demands for a postponement of the election.

Presidential Election and Political Retrenchment

At the presidential election, which took place on 5 December 1993, Bongo was re-elected with 51.18% of votes cast, while M'Ba Abessole secured 26.51% of the votes; some 86% of the registered electorate participated. The official announcement of the results provoked rioting by opposition supporters, in which several foreign nationals were attacked (apparently as a result of dissatisfaction with international observers, who declared that the elections had been properly conducted). Security forces intervened, and a national curfew and state of alert (which included a ban on demonstrations) were subsequently imposed. M'Ba Abessole, however, rejected the election results, and established a 'high council of the republic' (HCR), which included the majority of the presidential candidates, as part of a parallel government. Despite generally favourable reports by international observers on the conduct of the elections, the opposition appealed to the constitutional court to annul the results, on the grounds that the government had perpetrated electoral malpractice. In mid-December Bongo strongly denounced the establishment of the HCR, and invited the unsuccessful presidential candidates to take part in a government of national consensus. As a result of the administrative confusion, local government elections, which were due to take place in late December, were postponed until March 1994.

In early January 1994 the Bongo administration was accused by the USA of human rights violations, after three opposition leaders, including two presidential candidates, were prevented from leaving the country. Later that month the constitutional court endorsed the election results, and on 22 January Bongo was inaugurated as president. M'Ba Abessole subsequently redesignated the HCR as the 'high council for resistance', and urged his supporters to refuse to pay taxes and to boycott the local government elections (which were again postponed, to August). In mid-February the national curfew and the state of alert, in force since the previous December, were lifted, only to be reimposed later that month, after a general strike, in support of demands for an increase in salaries to compensate for a devaluation of the CFA franc in January, degenerated into violence. Security forces destroyed the transmitters of Radio Liberté, a radio station owned by the RNB (which had supported the strike), and attacked M'Ba Abessole's private residence, leading to further clashes with protesters. Strike action was suspended after four days, following negotiations between the government and trade unions; nine people had been killed during that period, according to official figures (although the opposition claimed that a total of 38 had died). At the end of February the minister of state control, in charge of parastatal affairs, left the government and the PDG, citing his disagreement with the increasingly authoritarian stance adopted by Bongo.

In March 1994 Oye Mba submitted his resignation and dissolved the council of ministers; later that month he was re-appointed as prime minister and, following the opposition's rejection of his offer to participate in a government of national unity, a 38-member administration was formed. The size of the new government, in view of the deterioration in the economy, attracted widespread criticism. In the same month the national assembly approved a constitutional amendment providing for the establishment of a senate (which the opposition resisted) and repealing legislation that prohibited unsuccessful presidential candidates from participating in the government within a period of 18 months.

In June 1994 opposition parties agreed to a further postponement of the local government elections, to early 1995. In August opposition parties announced that they were prepared to participate in a coalition government, on condition that it was installed on a transitional basis pending new legislative elections. In September negotiations between the government and opposition took place in Paris, under the auspices of the Organization of African Unity (OAU), in order to resolve remaining differences concerning the results of the presidential election and the proposed formation of a government of national unity. In mid-September the RNB, which took part in the discussions, indicated that it would refuse to join a coalition government.

Coalition Problems

At the end of September 1994 an agreement was reached, as a result of the Paris meetings, whereby a transitional coalition government was to be installed, with local government elections scheduled to take place after a period of one year, followed by legislative elections six months later; the electoral code was to be revised and an independent electoral commission established, in an effort to ensure that the elections be conducted fairly. In early October Oye Mba resigned from office and dissolved the council of ministers. Shortly afterwards Bongo appointed Dr Paulin Obame-Nguema, a member of the PDG who had served in former administrations, as prime minister. Obame-Nguema subsequently formed a 27-member council of ministers, which included six opposition members. The composition of the new government was, however, immediately criticized by the opposition, on the grounds that it was entitled to one-third of ministerial portfolios in proportion to the number of opposition deputies in the national assembly; the HCR announced that the opposition would boycott the new administration, which, it claimed, was in violation of the Paris accord. Four opposition members consequently refused to accept the portfolios allocated to them, although two of these finally agreed to join the government. (The portfolios that remained vacant were later assigned to a further two opposition members.) Following the inauguration of the council of ministers in early November, a motion expressing confidence in the new prime minister was adopted by 99 of 118 votes cast in the national assembly. In the same month associates of Bongo established an informal grouping, known as the Mouvement des amis de Bongo.

In January 1995 controversy emerged over the extent of the authority vested in the national assembly, after members of the HCR refused to participate in the drafting of the new electoral code until the Paris agreement was ratified. The constitutional court subsequently ruled that the national assembly was not empowered, under the terms of the constitution, to ratify the agreement. In early February, however, opposition deputies ended a boycott of the national assembly, following a further ruling by the constitutional court that the national assembly was entitled to act as a parliamentary body, pending the installation of a senate after the legislative elections in 1996, but that the constitutional provisions adopted under the terms of the Paris agreement would require endorsement by referendum. Following a pronouncement by the authorities that all illegal immigrants remaining in Gabon by mid-February would be arrested, some 55,000 foreign nationals left the country by the stipulated date. In April Bongo announced that a referendum to endorse the constitutional amendments would take place on 25 June. In the same month, in accordance with the Paris accord, the cabinet approved legislation providing for the release of prisoners detained on charges involving state security. Later in April Gabon withdrew its ambassador from Paris, in protest at reports in the French media containing allegations about the president's private life, and a number of anti-French demonstrations in support of Bongo took place in Libreville. (The national communications council had rejected government efforts to ban two pro-opposition newspapers, which had published French press reports considered to be critical of Bongo.) At the national referendum (which had been postponed until 24 July), the constitutional amendments were approved by 96.48% of votes cast, with 63.45% of the electorate participating. In September 1995, following dissent within the UPG, Sébastien Mamboundou Mouyama, the minister of social affairs and national solidarity, was elected party chairman, replacing Pierre Mamboundou. However, the latter subsequently regained the leadership of the UPG. (Mamboundou Mouyama formed a new political party, the Mouvement alternatif, in August 1996.)

Local and Legislative Elections

During early 1996 opposition parties criticized the government for delaying the implementation of the electoral timetable contained in the Paris accord. At the beginning of May, following a meeting attended by all the officially recognized political parties, Bongo agreed to establish a national electoral commission to formulate a timetable for local, legislative and senatorial elections, in consultation with all the official parties. It was also decided that access to state-controlled media and election funding should be equitably divided. Obame-Nguema's government resigned at the beginning of June, in accordance with the Paris agreement. Bongo, however, rejected the resignation on the grounds that the government should, before leaving office, organize the elections and finalize pending agreements with the International Monetary Fund (IMF) and the World Bank. At the beginning of October the national electoral commission adopted a timetable for legislative elections: the first round was to take place on 17 November, with a second round scheduled for 1 December. HCR representatives denounced the timetable, withdrew their participation from the commission and demanded the postponement of the local and legislative elections. In mid-October Pierre-Claver Maganga Moussavou, the leader of the PSD, was compelled to resign from the government, following his condemnation of the electoral timetable. The chairman of the HCR claimed that the 'dismissal' was a violation of the Paris accord. Later that month a minor reshuffle of the council of ministers was effected. Meanwhile, the government announced the suspension of salary payments for teachers, who had been on strike since 1 October in protest against the government's suspension of their housing allowances. The teachers' unions subsequently announced their intention to seek legal redress.

Organizational problems disrupted the local elections, which were held on 20 October 1996, having been postponed twice previously; according to reports, only 15% of the electorate participated. The PDG gained control of the majority of the municipalities, although the PGP secured victory in Port-Gentil, while the RNB was successful in the north of the country. Elections in Fougamou (where voting had not taken place) and Libreville (where the results had been invalidated) were eventually rescheduled for 24 November, although the RNB demanded the validation of the original results. On 24 November the RNB secured 62 of the 98 seats available in Libreville; M'Ba Abessole was subsequently elected mayor.

Legislative elections were rescheduled on several occasions, owing to the delay in the release of the local election results and the failure to revise electoral registers in time. The first round of the elections took place on 15 December 1996, without major incidents. Later that month it was reported that the PDG had obtained 47 of the 55 seats that were decided in the first round of voting. The opposition disputed the results, and there were demands for protest marches and a boycott of the second round of voting. The PDG secured a substantial majority of the remaining seats in the second round, which was held on 29 December, winning 84 seats, while the RNB obtained seven, the PGP six and independent candidates four, with the remaining 14 seats shared by the CLR, the UPG, the USG and others. Polling was unable to proceed for the five remaining seats, and results in a number of other constituencies were later annulled, owing to irregularities. (Following by-elections held in August 1997, during which five people were reportedly killed in violent incidents in north-east Gabon, the PDG held 88 seats, the PGP

nine and the RNB five.) Guy Ndzouba Ndama was elected president of the new national assembly. Following the legislative elections, the prime minister and his council of ministers resigned on 24 January 1997, in accordance with the terms of the constitution. Obame-Nguema was reappointed prime minister on 27 January, and a new council of ministers, dominated by members of the PDG, was announced on the following day. The PGP had refused to participate in the new government.

Elections to the new senate took place on 26 January and 9 February 1997, with senators to be elected by members of municipal councils and departmental assemblies. The PDG won 53 of the senate's 91 seats, while the RNB secured 20 seats, the PGP four, the Alliance démocratique et républicaine (ADERE) three, the CLR one, and the RDP one, with independent candidates obtaining nine seats. The results for a number of seats were annulled, however, and in subsequent by-elections, held later that year, the PDG increased its representation to 58 seats, while the RNB held 20 seats and the PGP four.

Institutional Changes and Electoral Discord

On 18 April 1997, at a congress of deputies and senators, constitutional amendments which extended the presidential term to seven years, provided for the creation of the post of vice-president and formally designated the senate as an upper chamber of a bicameral legislature, were adopted, despite the protests of opposition leaders who objected to the creation of a vice-presidency and demanded that a referendum be held. The vice-president was to deputize for the president when required, but was not to have any power of succession. In late May 1997 Didjob Divungui-di-N'Dingue, a senior member of the ADERE and a candidate in the 1993 presidential election, was appointed to the new position. Although officially part of the HCR, the ADERE had signed a number of local electoral agreements with other parties, including the PDG, prior to the legislative elections.

In April 1998 the government announced the establishment of a national democracy council, a consultative body whose members were to include the prime minister, the presidents of the senate and the national assembly, and the leaders of all political parties with parliamentary representation. Meanwhile, opposition parties had been highly critical of a nation-wide 'republican tour' made by Bongo during early 1998, claiming that it was tantamount to electioneering prior to the presidential election, due to be held later that year. Divisions within the leadership of the RNB led to a split in the party in July, following the expulsion of its secretary-general, Pierre-André Kombila, who was subsequently elected to lead a dissident group within the party.

In September 1998 opposition parties withdrew their members from the national electoral commission in protest at alleged irregularities in the voter registration process for the forthcoming presidential election. In mid-October President Bongo confirmed that he was to seek re-election; his candidature was formally accepted later that month, together with those of Kombila, M'Ba Abessole and Alain Egouang Nze for the RNB, Pierre Mamboundou for the HCR, Maganga Moussavou for the PSD, and two independents.

At the presidential election, which was held on 6 December 1998, Bongo was re-elected by 66.55% of votes cast, while Mamboundou received 16.54% of the votes and M'Ba Abessole secured 13.41%. The reported rate of participation was 53.8%. Opposition parties rejected the results, again alleging electoral malpractice, amid confusion over the size of the newly-registered electorate (after official statements gave contradictory figures) and doubts regarding the neutrality of French observers to the election. A proposal by Bongo for discussions was rejected by the main parties, which demanded the fulfilment of a number of preconditions prior to talks, including the annulment of the election. None the less, Bongo was inaugurated as president on 21 January 1999, and a new 42-member council of ministers, headed by Jean-François Ntoutoume Emane, was subsequently appointed. A minor reshuffle took place in February. In early 1999 student demonstrations and strike action by civil servants severely disrupted health and education services; further industrial action by university teachers occurred in April and June 2000. In December 1999 it was announced that Bongo had reduced the Council of Ministers in size from 42 to 31 members.

In August 2000 four opposition parties, including the RNB, formed a coalition, the Front des Parties du Changement, in preparation for legislative and local elections scheduled to be held in 2001.

EXTERNAL CONCERNS

President Bongo has pursued a policy of close co-operation with France in the fields of economic and foreign affairs. In October 1992 Bongo represented the then French president, François Mitterrand, at a Franco-African summit meeting which took place in Libreville. On a visit to Gabon in July 1996, the French president, Jacques Chirac, urged the industrialized countries to continue to give economic aid to the African nations. Relations became strained in March 1997, however, when allegations that Bongo had been a beneficiary in an international fraud emerged, during a French judicial investigation into the affairs of the petroleum company Elf-Aquitaine. The chairman of Elf-Gabon, André Tarallo, was temporarily detained, and bank accounts in Switzerland and the British Virgin Islands, said to contain Gabonese government funds, were blocked. In response, Bongo cancelled a visit to France and reportedly threatened to impose economic sanctions on French petroleum interests in Gabon. He insisted that the Elf enquiry was a matter for the French judiciary and was not the concern of Gabon. Tarallo, who had been replaced as chairman of Elf-Gabon, came under further investigation in November 1997. In October 1999 a further judicial investigation into the affairs of Elf-Aquitaine, carried out by Swiss authorities, revealed that Tarallo had used bank accounts in that country secretly to transfer large sums of money to several African heads of state, among them Bongo. Bongo denied personally receiving direct payments from Elf and maintained that such 'bonus' payments were made only to the Gabonese government. However, a report released in November, following a separate investigation by the US Congress into money 'laundering' and corruption among political figures, alleged that the US banking group Citibank had assisted Bongo in transferring 'political gifts', including some US $50m. contributed to his 1993 election campaign fund, which had been paid into 'offshore' accounts by Elf.

Bongo has often acted as an intermediary in regional disputes, chairing the OAU *ad hoc* committee seeking to resolve the border dispute between Chad and Libya, and encouraging dialogue between Angola and the USA. In 1997 he intervened in civil conflicts in Zaire (now the Democratic Republic of the Congo, DRC), the Central African Republic and the Republic of the Congo. In July of that year the government expressed concern at the large numbers of refugees arriving in Gabon and subsequently announced plans for repatriation. In July 1999 the government appealed for international assistance following a further influx of refugees fleeing renewed fighting in the DRC. At the Gulf of Guinea summit held in Libreville in November the seven countries represented agreed to form the Commission du golfe de guinée (CGG), a consultation framework designed to promote co-operation and development among the member countries as well as to take measures towards the prevention and resolution of conflicts between them. In the same month Gabon established diplomatic relations with Libya.

In January 2000 African leaders and representatives of the IMF met in Libreville to discuss the alleviation of poverty in Africa. Later in the same month, under the framework of Renforcement des capacités africaines de maintien de la paix (RECAMP) (a French initiative designed to enhance the abilities of African countries to intervene in conflicts on their own continent), a military exercise involving personnel from eight countries from the Central African region took place in Lambaréné, Gabon. Known as 'Gabon 2000', the exercise was orientated towards conflict resolution and was supported with technical assistance from eight industrialized nations, including France, Belgium, the United Kingdom and the USA.

In February 1996 the northern part of Gabon was quarantined in response to an outbreak of Ebola haemorrhagic fever, in which at least 13 people died, according to the World Health Organization (WHO). In April it was reported that the World Bank and the World Wide Fund for Nature were seeking to identify areas of equatorial forest for conservation, amid fears that increasing exploitation by logging companies would imperil the survival of indigenous plant and animal species. It was also feared that opening up the forest could lead to another outbreak of the Ebola virus, which is believed to reside in small, forest-dwelling animals. In October a second outbreak claimed 14 lives in the north-east of the country, and by January 1997 a further 40 deaths had been reported.

Economy

EDITH HODGKINSON

The combination of a small population, estimated at 1.19m. in mid-1998, and plentiful petroleum resources has given Gabon one of the highest incomes per head in sub-Saharan Africa. In 1993—the year before the devaluation of the CFA franc—its gross national product (GNP) per head was equivalent to US $4,050; even after devaluation, the figure by 1998 was a comfortable $4,170. It therefore ranks as an upper-middle-income country. However, reflecting the dominance of the petroleum sector, and hence the vulnerability to trends in world prices for this commodity, the rate of economic growth has fluctuated widely in recent decades. While growth in gross domestic product (GDP) averaged 9.5% per year in 1965–80, after the collapse in petroleum prices in 1986 the average declined to 0.8% in 1985–90. The 1990s saw an improvement, because of the development of the Rabi-Kounga oilfield, to an average of 3.2% per year in 1990–97. In 1998, however, the economy contracted by around 4%, owing to the combination of steeply falling petroleum prices and a downturn in Asian demand for timber, while 1999 saw only a modest recovery, with GDP estimated to have risen by under 2%.

The earlier period of rapid growth contained the petroleum boom of the mid-1970s, when the surge in domestic production, prompted by higher world prices, generated government investment spending and borrowing which left the country with a heavy debt burden and increased its vulnerability to adverse trends in the international economy—petroleum prices, interest rates and the value of the US dollar. Consequently, since the mid-1980s, the government has had to undertake a series of economic adjustment programmes, designed to reduce the external current-account deficit while promoting the development of non-petroleum activities. Private enterprise was encouraged, and a policy of retrenchment in the public sector initiated, including the rationalization of public-sector enterprises. Progress has been very limited in all these areas, and the non-petroleum economy remained very weak; the disbursement of IMF funds was suspended on occasion, due to lack of compliance with performance criteria. Following the devaluation of the CFA franc by 50% in relation to the French franc in January 1994, the government adopted a programme for economic recovery, supported, as in the past, by IMF funding, in the form of a stand-by credit, and with similar objectives. However, shortcomings in implementation and the Fund's dissatisfaction with public financial transparency delayed the award of an extended Fund facility (EFF) until November 1995. The targets of the 1995–98 programme, supported by this funding, included an improvement in the rate of return on petroleum resources; a thorough reform of the tax revenue system; a reduction in current budget spending (including retrenchment in the payroll); higher implementation of the budget's capital expenditure programme; and privatization of public-sector enterprises. The objectives of this programme were broadly, if not completely, achieved by the end of 1998. A number of major privatizations had been realized (the power utility) or agreed (the railway company), while others were in preparation, with restructuring under way for telecommunications services and the national airline. Some significant tax reforms had been introduced, including the extension of value-added tax to forestry companies, the removal of some tax privileges accorded to specific sectors and an investment code consistent with the recommendations of the IMF. Tight monetary and fiscal policies have offset the strong inflationary impact of the currency's devaluation to reduce the rate from an average 36% in 1994 to 0.7% in 1996, 4% in 1997 and 2.1% in 1998—well below the 5% target set in the programme agreed with the IMF. The downturn in the economy in 1998, however, brought with it a sharp rise in Gabon's debt arrears, which made the negotiation of a new agreement with the IMF in 1999, the price for any prospect of debt relief, a priority. Consequently the government continued with its privatization programme by completing the transfer of the railway company to private ownership. However, other planned divestments were still unrealized in early 2000, essentially because of vested interests, at high political levels, in their retention by the state. The IMF also wanted more far-reaching economic reform than the government envisaged, inluding larger reductions in government spending with a greater contraction in the size of the civil services. Thus, the expectation was that an enhanced structural adjustment facility (ESAF) would not be agreed before the end of 2000.

AGRICULTURE

Owing to the density of the tropical rain forest, only a small proportion of land area is suitable for agricultural activity, and only 2% is estimated to be under cultivation. With nearly 50% of the population living in towns and a poor road infrastructure, the contribution to GDP of the agriculture, forestry and fishing sector is very modest, at around 7–8% in the 1990s. The country lacks self-sufficiency in staple crops, and over one-half of food requirements have to be imported. Until the late 1980s the focus of public investment was industry and infrastructure, notably the Transgabonais railway, and the sector's growth lagged far behind the expansion of the overall economy. Agricultural GDP was rising by an average of only about 1% per year in the 1980s, and then declined by around 2% per year in the 1990s. This situation both generated, and was exacerbated by, a steady drift of population to the towns.

The principal cash crops are palm oil, sugar cane and rubber. Of these, palm oil is the most important, although export potential is limited, owing to intense competition from producers in the Far East. A parastatal organization, the Société de développement de l'agriculture au Gabon (AGROGABON), manages plantations covering 7,500 ha, which produced around 3,000 metric tons per year in the late 1990s. Production of refined sugar increased from negligible levels to 21,000 tons in 1989, with the development of a large-scale complex at France-ville designed to produce 30,000 tons annually. It has since decreased to around 16,000 tons per year, covering the domestic requirement but leaving little surplus for export. In the 1980s the government decided to promote the development of rubber as an export crop, and four plantations have been developed by the state-owned Société de développement de l'hévéaculture (HEVEGAB). Two of these, at Mitzic, began exporting in 1992; production in 1997 reached 10,098 tons. Cocoa and coffee were once relatively significant cash crops, with a small amount available for export, but outputs of both have been falling since the 1980s, with annual cocoa crops down from 1,500–2,000 tons to some 800 tons in recent years. Coffee output has declined to only 120 tons in 1997, from around 1,000 tons per year at the beginning of the decade.

Animal husbandry was, for many decades, hindered by the prevalence of the tsetse fly, but 1980 saw the importation of the first tsetse-resistant cattle. Livestock numbers have risen, with 39,000 head of cattle estimated in 1998 (compared with an average of 31,000 in 1989–91), 208,000 pigs (169,000) and 259,000 sheep and goats (241,000). The Société gabonaise de développement d'élevage (an offshoot of AGROGABON) manages three cattle ranches, covering 14,000 ha. Poultry farming is mainly on a smallholder basis. The fishing catch falls well below total demand (some 45,000 metric tons); the domestic industrial catch was only 11,000 tons in 1997. Resources are still not fully exploited, but under a three-year fisheries agreement signed with the EU in 1998, EU trawlers are allowed to fish up

to 9,000 tons a year, in return for aid funds and a levy on the catch.

FORESTRY

Tropical forests cover some 85% of Gabon's total land area. Until the commencement of mineral exploitation in the early 1960s, the economy was dependent upon the timber industry. Okoumé and ozigo are the most important timbers, accounting for 75% of Gabon's timber exports. Gabon's forests contain an estimated 100 other species of commercially exploitable hard and soft woods. Gabon currently ranks as Africa's fourth largest producer of tropical wood, and the world's largest exporter of okoumé wood. About 50 companies are active in the forestry sector, which is dominated by a small number of European enterprises. Gabonese enterprises are involved in small-scale timber production.

Output of timber has fluctuated since independence, mainly in response to international demand and to movements in the value of the US dollar in relation to the CFA franc, which affect the sector's competitiveness as regards suppliers in south-east Asia. Output averaged some 1.6m. cu m a year in 1990–92 and exports 1.4m. cu m, but then increased steadily because of production controls in some Asian countries and the unsettled political climate in several of Gabon's African competitors. Devaluation in 1994 gave a significant additional boost by doubling earnings in terms of local currency (they reached 195,000m. francs CFA in 1994 from 90,000m. francs CFA in 1993). Production increased to 2.67m. cu m by 1997, when exports of okoumé reached 1.85m. cu m and total timber export earnings were US $416m. The fall in demand from Asian countries, as their economies contracted in the wake of the region's financial and currency crisis in 1997, resulted in a one-third fall in both export volumes and earnings in 1998, to 1.84m. cu m and $282m. respectively. Exports were stagnant in 1999, but were expected to increase in 2000 as the recovery in Asian economies gathered pace. The total amount of timber cut is thought to be much higher than the official production figures, and there is concern that continuing expansion in the sector may prove unsustainable with the present low level of reforestation. The government has imposed ceilings on production (which tend to be exceeded), but a more effective constraint on the ability to meet foreign demand is the inadequacy of the transport infrastructure.

The state-owned Société nationale des bois du Gabon (SNBG) retains its monopoly in the marketing and export of okoumé, but only to 'traditional' markets (Europe, Africa, and the Americas), with sales of other woods liberalized as part of the restructuring of this much-criticized parastatal. Gabon, like most African timber producers, exports the vast majority of its wood in the form of raw logs. One of the government's aims is to raise the share of locally processed wood from its present level of about 10% to 50%. However, this will be difficult to achieve because the infrastructure for exporting logs is already well-established and the trade very lucrative.

MINING

The source of Gabon's economic growth since the 1970s has been the exploitation of the country's mineral wealth, principally petroleum and, to a lesser extent, manganese and uranium. In 1997 petroleum and petroleum products accounted for an estimated 77% of total export earnings, while the contribution of manganese was 5% and that of uranium just under 1%. Previously a member of OPEC, Gabon withdrew from the organization in 1996, after production from the Rabi-Kounga field had raised national output well above the quota set by OPEC—a ceiling that Gabon was not prepared to impose on its industry.

The petroleum industry remains by far the dominant sector of the economy, even as its contribution fluctuates from year to year with trends in world prices and the value of the US dollar. Thus its share of GDP, totalling 40.4% in 1980, fell to a low of 16.5% in 1986, and, following the Gulf crisis and the development of Rabi-Kounga, increased to an estimated 43.5% in 1997.

Exploitation began in 1956, but significant growth only commenced after 1967, with the coming into production of the Gamba-Ivinga deposits and the exploitation of the offshore Anguille deposit. Production was largely offshore until January 1989, when the massive Rabi-Kounga onshore deposit entered production. Output rapidly exceeded projections, reaching

135,000 barrels per day (b/d) by early 1990. National output reached 13.5m. metric tons in 1990, compared with 7.9m. tons in 1988 and 10.2m. tons in 1989; exports were 12.5. tons in 1990, up from 8.6m. tons in the preceding year. Volumes of both output and exports increased in every year to 1997, when they reached a peak of 19.4m. tons (370,000 b/d). Gabon ranks as sub-Saharan Africa's third largest petroleum producer. Rabi-Kounga, which accounts for about one-half of total petroleum exports, remains the country's principal oilfield, but its output has begun to decline. With only small new fields developed, national output fell to 18.8m. tons in 1998 and reached an estimated 17.6m. tons in 1999. This decline is likely to continue as exploration activity has been diminishing for some years, while Gabon has suffered from the greater attraction of exploration in Angola and the Republic of the Congo (which explains Elf-Aquitaine's reduced involvement in recent years—see below) and the international shortage of deep-water drilling rigs. Its eighth licensing round, in 1997–98, which opened up 100,000 sq km of virgin acreage offshore (equivalent to the entire area already under licence) met a poor response, with acceptable bids for only three of the 12 blocks on offer. The remaining deep-water areas were due to be reoffered, together with a few onshore areas earlier relinquished, in the ninth licensing round in mid-2000, with the likelihood of better fiscal terms.

The main producer was previously Elf-Gabon (a 25/75 joint venture between the government and Elf-Aquitaine) but it was overtaken in 1993 by Shell-Gabon, which operates the Rabi-Kounga field in association with Elf-Gabon and Amerada-Hess. In 1997 there were 25 producing fields, with a number of other foreign companies participating, including AGIP (which had replaced Elf as the largest holder of exploration acreage), Total, Conoco, Occidental, Marathon, Amoco, OMV, Santa Fe and Repsol. An important new producer appeared in 1995, when a South African company, Energy Africa, acquired a 40% interest in three satellite fields of Rabi-Kounga and smaller interests in a number of offshore fields.

The bulk of production is exported as crude (the country's refining capacity is some 800,000 metric tons), with the USA, France, Argentina and Brazil as the major markets. Export earnings have mirrored output and price trends, with an increase in most years since 1986, when US $758m. was recorded, to $2,346m. in 1997. Reflecting the fall in world prices in 1998, earnings in that year declined to $1,518m. Yielding income to the government in the form of royalties, taxes on company profits, exploration permits, and dividends and returns from the 15 fields in which it has equity, petroleum provided around 60% of budget revenue in 1997.

Since 1962, manganese ore has been mined at Moanda, near Franceville, by the Cie minière de l'Ogooué (COMILOG). Gabon has estimated reserves of 45m. metric tons, representing around one-quarter of known world reserves. Virtually all production is exported (almost wholly in ore form) through the port of Owendo, the opening of which in 1988 stimulated volumes, which reached an all-time peak of 2.4m. tons in the following year. Previously most export ore was transported through the neighbouring Congo to the port of Pointe-Noire. Despite a slight decline in shipments in 1990, to 2.2m. tons, in that year Gabon overtook South Africa as the world's principal exporter of manganese ore. In 1993 the South African group, Gencor, acquired a 15% holding in COMILOG from US Steel; other shareholders are Eramet of France, which took a 47% equity in 1995, the Société nationale d'investissement and private Gabonese interests. Production had been tending to decrease in 1991–93 but recovered to 2.04m. tons in 1997, a level it has broadly maintained since.

The exploitation of uranium began in 1958. Deposits were mined at Mounana and the ore concentrated before export by the Cie des mines d'uranium de Franceville (COMUF), a consortium largely controlled by French interests but with a 26% share held by the Gabonese government. Gabonese uranium was marketed through the French Atomic Energy Commission. Production averaged some 500–600 metric tons a year in the 1990s, down from its 1988 peak of 930 tons, or around one-half of the industry's capacity. This reflected the decline in world demand, and hence prices, as nuclear power programmes were cut back. The situation worsened after China entered the market as a supplier. In response to the fall in prices and the prospect

of continuing oversupply, COMUF first reduced its work-force (by two-thirds in 1995) and then, with reserves approaching exhaustion, ceased production in March 1999.

One of the largest iron-ore deposits in the world, some 850m. tons, at Belinga in the north-east of Gabon, remains unexploited because the government has been unable to secure the funds necessary for a 237-km spur to the Transgabonais railway, to transport the ore. Alluvial deposits of gold are exploited on a small scale, with output estimated at some 80 kg per year. Stimulated by the decline in costs after the 1994 devaluation and changes in the mining code introduced in 1997, foreign companies are showing strong interest both in gold mining and in the exploitation of deposits of niobium and phosphates. Cluff Mining of Australia was carrying out detailed studies in early 2000 on the Mabounié niobium deposit, with plans to produce 4,000 metric tons per year. Lead, zinc and baryte deposits are known to exist. Marble is quarried at Doussé-Oussou.

MANUFACTURING AND POWER

Gabon's manufacturing sector is relatively small, accounting for an estimated 5.8% of GDP in 1997. A substantial part of this contribution is represented by oil refining and timber processing. Other manufacturing industries include the processing of agricultural products, cement, soap, paint, industrial gas, cigarettes and textiles. Gabon has sought to develop large-scale natural-resource-based industries, but since its own domestic market is very small, these can for the most part be viable only in the context of the Communauté économique et monétaire en Afrique centrale (CEMAC), the successor to the Union douanière et économique de l'Afrique centrale, of which Gabon is one of the six member countries. Gabon imports substantial quantities of manufactured products from other CEMAC countries, but exports little to its CEMAC partners other than refined petroleum. In addition to competition from suppliers in CEMAC, which increased as the movement of goods was liberalized, Gabon's manufacturing industries face a challenge from smuggled goods.

Electricity is produced and distributed by the Société d'énergie et d'eau du Gabon (SEEG), a parastatal whose management was taken over by a consortium of French and Canadian interests in 1993 and which was then privatized in 1997, with 51% going to a consortium led by France's Cie générale des eaux and the balance sold to the Gabonese public. This was the first major privatization under the programme agreed with the IMF in 1996. Generation is both hydroelectric and thermal (gas-fired), with slightly over one-half of total capacity (310 MW net in 1997) hydroelectric. There is considerable potential for expansion in this sector.

TRANSPORT

Despite substantial investment in the Transgabonais railway and foreign backing for road development in the 1990s, the surface transportation system is inadequate. Until 1979 there were no railways except for the cableway link between the Congo border and the Moanda manganese mine, and the main rivers are navigable only for the last 80–160 km of their course to the Atlantic Ocean. The road network is poorly developed and much of it is unusable during the rainy seasons. In 1996 there were an estimated 7,670 km of roads, of which only some 8.2% was asphalted. The government's aim was to surface some 1,400 km of the road network by 2000, with a target of 3,580 km in the long term.

The Transgabonais railway scheme is among the most prestigious achievements of the Bongo presidency, opening up hitherto inaccessible areas and those more accessible from the Republic of Congo, such as the mineral-rich Franceville area. The 679-km railway required total investment of 800,000m.–900,000m. francs CFA between 1974 and 1986, which is not likely to be paid off, and external donors have been highly critical of the expenditure involved. It proved difficult to find financial backing for even the first 340-km section of the rail line, linking Owendo and Booué; work was completed in 1983. Work on the 357-km second section of the Transgabonais, from Booué to Franceville, was completed in 1986. Plans for a third section of 237 km, from Booué to Belinga, intended to enable exploitation of the large iron-ore deposits in the north-east of the country, were suspended, owing to lack of finance, and available resources reallocated to the completion of the Booué–Franceville stretch. By 1989 the line linking Libreville and Franceville was fully operational. The inauguration, in late 1988, of the minerals-handling terminal at Owendo resulted in an increase in revenue for the operator of the railway, the Office du chemin de fer transgabonais (OCTRA). In 1996 the Transgabonais earned revenue of 21,757m. francs CFA, of which 57% came from the transport of logs, 8% from manganese and 13% from passengers. OCTRA was one of the major state assets due to be sold under the programme agreed with the IMF for 1995–98. In late 1998 Le Transgabonais, a consortium headed by the state-owned timber concern, SNBG, took over the rail line on a 20-year operating concession.

The main port for petroleum exports is Port-Gentil, which also handles logs (floated down the Ogooué river) as does Owendo, the principal mineral port. A third deep-water port operates at Mayumba.

Air transport plays an extremely important role in the economy, particularly because the dense forest, which covers much of the country, makes other modes of transport impracticable. Libreville's Léon M'Ba international airport was modernized and expanded in the late 1980s, bringing capacity to 1.5m. passengers by 1990. As well as five domestic airports (Libreville, Port-Gentil, Franceville, Lambaréné and Moanda), there are several small airfields owned mainly by large companies working in the region. In 1977, following its withdrawal from Air Afrique, Gabon established its own international air carrier, Air Gabon, in which the state has an 80% interest. After drastic restructuring measures and against domestic opposition, the company was due to be sold by 2000.

FINANCE

In the first period of petroleum exploitation the government budget was sustained by rapidly increasing income, but the investment requirements of the Transgabonais were largely met by borrowing at non-concessionary rates in the late 1970s, resulting in a serious deterioration in the fiscal position, which pushed the budget into deficit by 1983. The situation was gravely exacerbated by the collapse in petroleum prices in 1986, which reduced government revenue from petroleum by one-quarter. In that year the deficit peaked at 186,700m. francs CFA (equivalent to 11.7% of GDP). Despite the completion of the Transgabonais and the surge in petroleum revenue in 1990 and 1991, the budget remained in deficit (on a commitment basis) because of two sets of pressure on current expenditure—debt service and the very high salary bill. The gap was, however, narrowed in 1993–94, and in 1995 a small surplus, of 79,700m. francs CFA (3.2% of GDP), was registered. This was the result of a combination of factors: petroleum production was continuing to rise steadily while the January 1994 devaluation had doubled petroleum operators' incomes in local currency terms; the growth in the salary bill was at last controlled; and the burden of debt service was eased by the major rescheduling of the bilateral debt (see below). The budget surplus was maintained at around the 1995 level in 1996, with the fall in interest payments offsetting the stagnation in petroleum revenues, but then surged to an estimated 179,300m. francs CFA in 1997, as revenue was boosted by much higher petroleum receipts. The sharp fall in petroleum prices led to a return to deficit in 1998, of 60,000m. francs CFA. The budget for 1999 forecast a substantial increase in the deficit, to 625,256m. francs CFA. However, this figure was based on pessimistic assumptions on petroleum production and prices, and also included the clearance of all the arrears to domestic and foreign creditors that had accumulated in 1998. The government's aim was to persuade domestic interests to accept decreases in budget spending and to convince the IMF that external debt obligations were unmanageable, thus making debt rescheduling essential. The latter had not been achieved by the end of 1999, so the proposed budget for 2000 forecast another large increase in the deficit, to 1,360,500m. francs CFA; yet again, petroleum production and price forecasts were set at low levels, and the settlement of debt arrears at high, for essentially political reasons.

FOREIGN TRADE AND PAYMENTS

Gabon has sustained a considerable surplus on its foreign trade, even through periods of quite marked fluctuation in petroleum

prices, because the import demand of its small population has remained relatively modest. Exports are normally three times the value of imports, and even though the latter has been augmented by major investment spending, a large proportion of this investment has served to generate rapidly increased earnings, from petroleum, timber and manganese. Even in the crisis year of 1986, when spending on the Transgabonais was still high and export earnings were halved, the value of imports was still 10% lower than that of exports, at 339,100m. francs CFA against 372,000m. francs CFA. Subsequently this favourable gap widened markedly, to average a surplus of 316,000m. francs CFA per year in 1987–93. It then surged to an average 940,000m. francs CFA per year in 1994–96, with the devaluation windfall in petroleum earnings more than matching the increase in expenditure on imports by an economy with very limited capacity for import substitution. Although less spectacular in US dollar terms, from US $1,481m. in 1993 to an annual average of $1,835m. in 1994–97, the improvement was substantial. After falling by more than one-half in 1998, to $805m., owing to lower petroleum and timber receipts, the surplus increased to an estimated $1,214m. in 1999.

Whereas previously the current account had been in modest surplus in most years, the surplus on foreign trade has been exceeded by the deficit on the invisibles side of the account (services and transfers) in nearly every year since 1985. This deficit is the result of high outflows on interest payments on the foreign debt and on remittances of profits and dividends by the petroleum industry. The current-account balance is very sensitive to movements in the petroleum price. Thus the current-account deficit increased dramatically from US $163m. in 1985 to $1,058m. in 1986, when petroleum prices collapsed, while the surge in petroleum prices after the Iraqi invasion of Kuwait in 1990 produced a surplus of $168m. in 1990. Devaluation generated a surplus on the current account of $320m. in 1994, as spending on imported goods and services was depressed, and the increase in petroleum earnings in 1996, as Rabi-Kounga's output reached its peak, boosted the current-account surplus to $326m. in that year. The surplus was eliminated in 1998, when the fall in petroleum and timber earnings produced a current-account deficit of $781m. Although the subsequent improvement in petroleum prices narrowed the deficit, it was estimated to have returned to around the $300m. level in 1999 and 2000 because of lower petroleum export volumes.

The overall deficit on the balance of payments has been augmented by outflows on the capital account, as the heavy foreign borrowing which characterized the late 1970s and early 1980s came to an end while the debt-repayment burden has been high. 'Exceptional financing' (the postponement of due debt-service payments) has made the most significant contribution in most recent years to covering the payments gap, as Gabon has built up arrears on its foreign debt. That debt reached a peak of US $4,223m. at the end of 1991, equivalent to 87% of GNP; of this $539m. represented arrears. The situation became worse in 1992–93, by the end of which period arrears had increased to $1,100m., or 28% of the country's total foreign debt of $3,861m. Yet its high GDP per head, and its poor record of compliance with commitments to the IMF, meant that Gabon was not a priority candidate for debt relief. The currency devaluation of January 1994 changed the environment. Against the background of the stand-by agreement with the IMF, both the 'Paris Club' of official bilateral creditors and the 'London Club' of commercial creditors agreed to debt rescheduling. Maturities on the official debt falling due in the period April 1994–March 1995, and all arrears, were rescheduled over 15 years, with a two-year period of grace. The 'London Club' restructured all commercial debt contracted before 1986. The debt situation was alleviated further by France's cancellation in 1994 of 50% of the loans contracted through the Caisse française de développement (CFD) and the cancellation of some $78m. in obligations in July 1996. As a result, the external debt declined slightly from a new high of $4,360m. at the end of 1995 to $4,285m. by the end of 1997. The sharp deterioration in the current payments balance in 1998 led to an accumulation of arrears on the foreign debt, totalling $164m., which resulted in the total external debt increasing to $4,425m. by the end of that year.

Despite Gabon's high income levels and the foreign investment its petroleum sector attracts, inflows of foreign aid, while relatively modest, have been significant in underpinning both the budget and the balance of payments. In the period 1991–93 net disbursements of official development assistance averaged US $105m. per year, with 85% coming from France, much of it representing support for the overvalued CFA franc. The devaluation of 1994, and the associated external support, brought a sudden surge in inflows, to a net $182m. in that year (of which $150m. came from France) and an average of $135m. per year in 1995–96. Net inflows of aid fell back sharply in 1997 and 1998, to an average of $41.7m. a year, as Gabon's short-term needs eased. But the economy's downturn in 1998 high-lighted the fragility of the country's balance of payments situation, and for most of 1999 foreign exchange reserves were between $1m. and $2m.—or less than one day's import cover. That fragility will continue while the country remains dependent on the export of a very limited range of raw materials and the infrastructural and funding constraints on their growth and the economy's diversification. Solution of these problems is becoming more urgent in that, in the absence of major new petroleum discoveries on the scale of Rabi-Kounga, Gabon's petroleum production—which currently generates almost one-half of GDP—is forecast to lose 50% of its 1996 level by 2003.

Statistical Survey

Source (unless otherwise stated): Direction Générale de l'Economie, Ministère de la Planification, de l'Economie et de l'Administration Territoriale, Libreville.

Area and Population

AREA, POPULATION AND DENSITY

Area (sq km)	267,667*
Population (census results)	
8 October 1960–May 1961	448,564
31 July 1993	
Males	501,784
Females	513,192
Total	1,014,976
Population (official estimate at mid-year)†	
1998	1,188,000
Density (per sq km) at mid-1998	4.4

* 103,347 sq miles.
† Source: UN, *Population and Vital Statistics Report.*

REGIONS (1993 census, provisional)

Region	Area (sq km)	Population*	Density (per sq km)	Chief town
Estuaire . . .	20,740	462,086	22.3	Libreville
Haut-Ogooué . .	36,547	102,387	2.8	Franceville
Moyen-Ogooué .	18,535	41,827	2.3	Lambaréné
N'Gounié . .	37,750	77,871	2.1	Mouila
Nyanga . .	21,285	39,826	1.9	Tchibanga
Ogooué-Ivindo .	46,075	48,847	1.1	Makokou
Ogooué-Lolo .	25,380	42,783	2.1	Koula-Moutou
Ogooué-Maritime .	22,890	98,299	4.3	Port-Gentil
Woleu-N'Tem .	38,465	97,739	2.5	Oyem
Total . . .	**267,667**	**1,011,665**	**3.8**	

* Excluding 45 persons in unspecified regions.
Source: UN, *Demographic Yearbook.*

PRINCIPAL TOWNS (population in 1988)

Libreville (capital) .	352,000	Franceville . . .	75,000
Port-Gentil . .	164,000		

BIRTHS AND DEATHS (UN estimates, annual averages)

	1980–85	1985–90	1990–95
Birth rate (per 1,000) . .	33.1	35.7	36.6
Death rate (per 1,000) . .	18.1	17.0	16.1

Expectation of life (UN estimates, years at birth, 1990–95): 52.3 (males 50.8; females 54.0).
Source: UN, *World Population Prospects: The 1998 Revision.*

ECONOMICALLY ACTIVE POPULATION
(estimates, '000 persons, 1991)

	Males	Females	Total
Agriculture, etc.	187	151	338
Industry	62	9	71
Services	69	26	95
Total labour force . . .	**318**	**186**	**504**

Source: UN Economic Commission for Africa, *African Statistical Yearbook.*
Mid-1998 (estimates, '000 persons): Agriculture, etc. 216; Total 535.
Source: FAO, *Production Yearbook.*

Agriculture

PRINCIPAL CROPS ('000 metric tons)

	1996	1997	1998
Maize*	30	31	31
Cassava (Manioc)*	210	215	215
Yams*	140	140	140
Taro (Coco yam)* . . .	57	58	58
Vegetables*	33	34	34
Bananas*	10	11	11
Plantains*	260	260	260
Cocoa beans†	1	1	1
Groundnuts (in shell)* . . .	16	17	17
Sugar cane*	173	175	173

* FAO estimates.   † Unofficial figures.
Source: FAO, *Production Yearbook.*

LIVESTOCK (FAO estimates, '000 head, year ending September)

	1996	1997	1998
Cattle	39	39	39
Pigs.	208	208	208
Sheep	173	173	173
Goats	86	86	86

Poultry (FAO estimates, million): 3 in 1996; 3 in 1997; 3 in 1998.
Source: FAO, *Production Yearbook.*

LIVESTOCK PRODUCTS

1998 (FAO estimates, '000 metric tons): Meat 28; Hen eggs 2.
Source: FAO, *Production Yearbook.*

Forestry

ROUNDWOOD REMOVALS ('000 cubic metres)

	1995	1996	1997
Sawlogs, veneer logs and logs for sleepers	1,990	1,990	1,990
Fuel wood	2,356	2,424	2,493
Total	4,346	4,414	4,483

Source: FAO, *Yearbook of Forest Products*.

SAWNWOOD PRODUCTION
('000 cubic metres, incl. railway sleepers)

	1995	1996	1997
Total	170	170	170

Source: FAO, *Yearbook of Forest Products*.

Fishing

('000 metric tons, live weight)

	1995	1996	1997
Tilapias	2.6*	3.6	4.2
Torpedo-shaped catfishes	2.0*	2.1	2.1
Other freshwater fishes*	3.0	4.2	3.6
Sea catfishes	0.4	2.8	2.7
Grunts, sweetlips, etc.	0.9	0.8	0.9
Bobo croaker	1.0	0.9	0.8
West African croakers	2.1	4.0	3.1
Barracudas	0.4	1.1	0.9
Lesser African threadfin	1.9	3.8	3.2
Sardinellas	1.2	1.9	0.9
Bonga shad	11.8	13.0	14.7
Other marine fishes (incl. unspecified)	11.3	5.6	5.7
Total fish	39.4	43.9	42.6
Southern pink shrimp	0.9	1.0	1.4
Other crustaceans and molluscs	0.2	0.5	0.7
Total catch	40.4	45.3	44.7

* FAO estimate(s).

Source: FAO, *Yearbook of Fishery Statistics*.

Mining

('000 metric tons, unless otherwise indicated)

	1994	1995	1996
Crude petroleum	17,214	18,246	19,250
Natural gas (petajoules)	30	32	32*
Uranium ore (metric tons)†	736	740*	n.a.
Manganese ore*†‡	663	893	923
Gold (kilograms)*†‡	72	70	70

* Provisional or estimated figure(s).
† Figures refer to the metal content of ores.
‡ Data from the US Bureau of Mines.
Source: UN, *Industrial Commodity Statistics Yearbook*.

Industry

PETROLEUM PRODUCTS ('000 metric tons)

	1994	1995	1996*
Liquefied petroleum gas*	8	8	9
Motor spirit (petrol)	33	33	35
Kerosene*	85	88	90
Jet fuel*	70	70	72
Distillate fuel oils	260	274	258
Residual fuel oils*	278	280	145
Bitumen (asphalt)	4	4	4

* Provisional or estimated figures.
Source: UN, *Industrial Commodity Statistics Yearbook*.

SELECTED OTHER PRODUCTS
('000 metric tons, unless otherwise indicated)

	1994	1995	1996
Palm oil (crude)*	3	3	n.a.
Flour*	31	27	26
Cement†	126	130	n.a.
Electric energy (million kWh)‡	933	940	953

* Data from the FAO.
† Data from the US Bureau of Mines.
‡ Estimated production.
Beer ('000 hectolitres): 819 in 1990; 814 in 1991; 785 in 1992.
Soft drinks ('000 hectolitres): 413 in 1990; 439 in 1991; 410 in 1992.
Source: UN, *Industrial Commodity Statistics Yearbook*.
Plywood (FAO estimates, '000 cu metres): 25 in 1995; 25 in 1996; 25 in 1997 (Source: FAO, *Yearbook of Forest Products*).
Veneer sheets (FAO estimates, '000 cu metres): 2 in 1995; 5 in 1996; 10 in 1997 (Source: FAO, *Yearbook of Forest Products*).

Finance

CURRENCY AND EXCHANGE RATES
Monetary Units
100 centimes = 1 franc de la Coopération financière en Afrique centrale (CFA).

Sterling, Dollar and Euro Equivalents (28 April 2000)
£1 sterling = 1,132.20 francs CFA;
US $1 = 722.02 francs CFA;
€1 = 655.96 francs CFA;
10,000 francs CFA = £8.832 = $13.850 = €15.245.

Average Exchange Rate (francs CFA per US $)
1997   583.67
1998   589.95
1999   615.70

Note: An exchange rate of 1 French franc = 50 francs CFA, established in 1948, remained in force until January 1994, when the CFA franc was devalued by 50%, with the exchange rate adjusted to 1 French franc = 100 francs CFA. This relationship to French currency remained in effect with the introduction of the euro on 1 January 1999. From that date, accordingly, a fixed exchange rate of €1 = 655.957 francs CFA has been in operation.

BUDGET ('000 million francs CFA)

Revenue	1995	1996*	1997†
Petroleum revenue	469.2	562.1	562.6
Profits tax	265.5	341.8	330.0
Royalties	155.8	182.7	192.2
Production-sharing and assets	18.0	22.6	25.4
Dividends	30.0	15.0	15.0
Non-petroleum revenue	288.2	306.0	352.0
Tax revenue	277.7	293.9	346.2
Direct taxes	76.8	80.2	100.3
Company taxes	42.7	45.0	61.2
Individual taxes	34.1	35.2	39.0
Indirect taxes	61.7	43.0	64.0
Turnover taxes	51.6	29.4	56.0
Taxes on goods and services	10.1	13.6	8.0
Taxes on refined petroleum products	4.3	n.a.	n.a.
Taxes on international trade and transactions	128.7	147.8	175.9
Import duties	110.7	125.2	148.5
Export duties	18.0	22.6	27.4
Other revenue	21.0	35.0	11.9
Total	757.4	868.1	914.7

Expenditure	1995	1996*	1997†
Current expenditure	514.9	522.2	540.7
Wages and salaries	178.1	184.8	189.3
Other goods and services	112.9	142.6	150.2
Transfers and subsidies	23.0	21.6	23.3
Interest payments	201.0	173.1	177.9
Capital expenditure	136.0	154.3	215.4
Sub-total	650.9	676.5	756.1
Adjustment for payment arrears	53.6	125.1	170.0
Total (cash basis)	704.5	801.6	926.1

* Preliminary figures.
† Estimates.

Source: IMF, *Gabon: Statistical Annex* (February 1999).

INTERNATIONAL RESERVES (US $ million at 31 December)

	1997	1998	1999
Gold*	3.74	3.69	n.a.
IMF special drawing rights	—	0.01	0.01
Reserve position in IMF	0.09	0.09	0.15
Foreign exchange	282.51	15.30	17.79
Total	286.34	19.09	n.a.

* Valued at market-related prices.

Source: IMF, *International Financial Statistics*.

MONEY SUPPLY ('000 million francs CFA at 31 December)

	1997	1998	1999
Currency outside banks	121.03	124.72	105.26
Demand deposits at commercial and development banks	174.41	156.99	161.85
Total money (incl. others)	298.25	283.12	268.61

Source: IMF, *International Financial Statistics*.

COST OF LIVING
(Retail Price Index for African families in Libreville; base: 1995 = 100)

	1996	1997
All items	100.7	104.7

Source: IMF, *International Financial Statistics*.

NATIONAL ACCOUNTS ('000 million francs CFA at current prices)
Expenditure on the Gross Domestic Product

	1995	1996*	1997†
Government final consumption expenditure	291.0	327.4	339.5
Private final consumption expenditure	1,064.9	1,174.7	1,217.7
Increase in stocks	24.5	—	—
Gross fixed capital formation	561.3	676.4	794.9
Total domestic expenditure	1,941.7	2,178.5	2,352.1
Exports of goods and services	1,455.5	1,780.2	1,923.0
Less Imports of goods and services	922.1	1,067.9	1,261.5
GDP in purchasers' values	2,475.2	2,890.8	3,013.7

* Preliminary figures.
† Estimates.

Source: IMF, *Gabon: Statistical Annex* (February 1999).

Gross Domestic Product by Economic Activity

	1995	1996*	1997†
Agriculture, livestock, hunting and fishing	123.7	130.8	138.8
Forestry	75.1	71.0	85.7
Petroleum exploitation and research	951.3	1,226.7	1,247.5
Other mining	51.7	54.2	58.6
Manufacturing	146.4	162.2	167.1
Electricity and water	35.4	38.8	36.4
Construction and public works	92.8	102.4	116.3
Trade	246.4	287.1	245.8
Transport	129.5	135.3	143.4
Financial services	11.9	11.8	13.0
Government services	235.1	245.5	267.1
Other services	265.2	300.1	345.4
GDP at factor cost	2,364.4	2,765.8	2,865.1
Import duties	110.7	125.0	148.5
GDP in purchasers' values	2,475.2	2,890.8	3,013.7

* Preliminary figures.
† Estimates.

Source: IMF, *Gabon: Statistical Annex* (February 1999).

BALANCE OF PAYMENTS (US $ million)

	1993	1994	1995
Exports of goods f.o.b.	2,326.2	2,365.3	2,642.9
Imports of goods f.o.b.	−845.1	−776.7	−898.5
Trade balance	1,481.1	1,588.6	1,744.4
Exports of services	311.1	219.6	272.9
Imports of services	−1,022.7	−826.7	−949.4
Balance on goods and services	769.5	981.4	1,067.8
Other income received	32.1	11.9	13.4
Other income paid	−658.3	−509.9	−783.5
Balance on goods, services and income	143.4	483.4	297.7
Current transfers received	48.0	18.7	4.4
Current transfers paid	−240.5	−184.8	−202.3
Current balance	−49.1	317.4	99.8
Direct investment abroad	−2.5	—	n.a.
Direct investment from abroad	−113.7	−99.6	−113.4
Other investment assets	−7.8	−258.6	−5.4
Other investment liabilities	−265.2	−386.7	−293.9
Net errors and omissions	−13.6	254.6	−108.2
Overall balance	−451.9	−173.0	−421.2

Source: IMF, *International Financial Statistics*.

External Trade

PRINCIPAL COMMODITIES

Imports c.i.f. (US $ million)*	1993	1994	1996
Food and live animals . .	131.5	105.8	145.7
Meat and meat preparations .	34.8	32.0	37.8
Fresh, chilled or frozen meat	31.5	28.9	32.8
Fresh or frozen bovine meat	16.7	13.1	10.1
Dairy products and birds' eggs .	16.1	10.7	15.5
Fish and fish preparations .	15.4	8.7	13.6
Cereals and cereal preparations	35.5	32.3	48.4
Beverages and tobacco .	17.7	15.5	23.1
Mineral fuels, lubricants, etc. .	14.5	17.1	31.6
Petroleum, petroleum products,			
etc.	14.3	16.9	28.3
Refined petroleum products	14.2	16.8	27.4
Chemicals and related			
products . . .	83.6	70.1	93.0
Medicinal and pharmaceutical			
products . . .	30.7	18.4	33.4
Medicaments (incl. veterinary)	28.3	16.7	30.7
Basic manufactures . .	123.8	112.1	150.2
Paper, paperboard and			
manufactures . . .	19.4	14.1	16.8
Iron and steel	30.9	27.3	37.3
Tubes, pipes and fittings .	23.7	19.7	24.3
Machinery and transport			
equipment . .	316.4	314.3	351.9
Power-generating machinery and			
equipment . .	26.9	25.9	26.3
Machinery specialized for			
particular industries . .	21.0	46.4	36.9
Civil engineering and			
contractors' plant and			
equipment	12.1	30.9	23.2
General industrial machinery,			
equipment and parts .	67.0	82.2	105.9
Pumps for liquids, etc. . .	10.7	14.1	10.0
Other pumps, centrifuges, etc.	14.6	18.5	35.8
Office machines and automatic			
data-processing equipment .	15.2	12.3	19.7
Telecommunications and sound			
equipment . . .	19.0	16.6	22.8
Other electrical machinery,			
apparatus, etc. . . .	40.0	29.8	42.8
Switchgear, etc., and parts .	15.3	9.1	11.9
Road vehicles and parts . .	68.7	57.6	84.2
Passenger motor cars (excl.			
buses)	30.8	18.6	29.4
Motor vehicles for goods			
transport, etc. . .	18.8	14.1	23.3
Goods vehicles (lorries and			
trucks)	17.7	13.2	19.8
Other transport equipment .	57.8	42.8	12.3
Ships, boats and floating			
structures . . .	50.8	37.9	4.1
Miscellaneous manufactured			
articles	77.9	62.3	89.1
Professional, scientific and			
controlling instruments, etc.	21.3	16.9	29.8
Measuring and controlling			
instruments . .	15.3	14.3	24.2
Total (incl. others) . .	774.9	707.5	898.1

* Figures for 1995 are not available.

Source: UN, *International Trade Statistics Yearbook*.

Exports ('000 million francs CFA)	1995	1996*	1997†
Petroleum and petroleum products	1,055.4	1,335.1	1,369.6
Manganese	66.4	77.6	88.9
Timber	172.6	196.0	257.7
Uranium	15.5	13.2	11.7
Total (incl. others) . .	1,319.2	1,631.6	1,776.3

* Preliminary figures.
† Estimates.

Source: IMF, *Gabon: Statistical Annex* (February 1999).

PRINCIPAL TRADING PARTNERS (US $ million)

Imports c.i.f.*	1993	1994	1996
Belgium-Luxembourg . .	22.5	24.5	37.1
Cameroon . . .	6.3	12.0	12.1
Côte d'Ivoire . . .	6.3	7.6	13.7
France (incl. Monaco) . .	370.4	281.4	384.8
Germany . . .	27.8	39.7	41.1
Italy	24.3	29.6	31.3
Japan	n.a.	n.a.	53.8
Morocco . . .	10.1	4.5	6.6
Netherlands . . .	36.0	35.1	40.8
Panama	—	11.3	
SACU†	3.5	4.5	9.3
Spain	11.2	11.4	21.0
Thailand . . .	4.3	3.3	15.3
United Kingdom . . .	29.4	45.1	42.8
USA	71.0	83.5	93.4
Total (incl. others) . .	774.9	707.5	898.1

Exports f.o.b.*	1993	1994	1996
Canada	52.3	—	—
Chile	81.6	22.6	17.5
China, People's Repub. . .	29.4	54.5	136.2
France (incl. Monaco) . .	505.6	361.6	239.8
Gibraltar . . .	17.2	42.0	n.a.
Israel	9.9	19.8	34.5
Japan	n.a.	n.a.	66.1
Korea, Repub. . . .	16.1	35.4	24.2
Morocco . . .	14.5	76.2	16.8
Netherlands . . .	2.9	89.0	30.7
Netherlands Antilles . .	n.a.	n.a.	121.4
Portugal . . .	1.9	91.2	6.3
Singapore . . .	17.1	40.6	2.0
Spain	32.9	92.5	36.8
Switzerland-Liechtenstein .	10.8	9.8	34.7
United Kingdom . . .	93.1	61.8	7.3
USA	1,388.2	1,192.9	2,015.3
Total (incl. others) . .	2,637.0	2,391.0	3,145.6

* Figures for 1995 are not available.
† Southern African Customs Union, comprising Botswana, Lesotho, Namibia, South Africa and Swaziland.

Source: UN, *International Trade Statistics Yearbook*.

Transport

RAILWAYS (traffic)

	1995	1996*	1997†
Passengers carried ('000) . .	175.8	191.9	195.5
Freight carried ('000 metric tons)	3,012.9	2,973.0	2,959.0

* Preliminary figures.
† Estimates.

Source: IMF, *Gabon: Statistical Annex* (February 1999).

ROAD TRAFFIC (estimates, motor vehicles in use)

	1994	1995	1996
Passenger cars . . .	22,310	24,000	24,750
Lorries and vans . . .	14,850	15,840	16,490

Source: IRF, *World Road Statistics*.

INTERNATIONAL SEA-BORNE SHIPPING
(freight traffic, '000 metric tons)

	1988	1989	1990
Goods loaded	8,890	10,739	12,828
Goods unloaded . . .	610	213	212

Source: UN, *Monthly Bulletin of Statistics*.

GABON

CIVIL AVIATION (traffic on scheduled services)

	1994	1995	1996
Kilometres flown (million)	6	7	7
Passengers carried ('000)	481	508	431
Passenger-kilometres (million)	719	623	728
Total ton-kilometres (million)	96	89	100

Source: UN, *Statistical Yearbook*.

Tourism

	1995	1996	1997
Tourist arrivals	127,332	141,170	167,197
Tourism receipts (US $ million)	7	7	n.a.

Sources: Centre Gabonais de Promotion Touristique (GABONTOUR) and World Tourism Organization, *Yearbook of Tourism Statistics*.

Communications Media

	1994	1995	1996
Radio receivers ('000 in use)	189	195	201
Television receivers ('000 in use)	49	51	60
Telephones ('000 main lines in use)	31	32	35
Telefax stations (number in use)	n.a.	360	503
Mobile cellular telephones (subscribers)	2,581	4,000	6,800
Daily newspapers:			
Number	1	2	2
Average circulation ('000 copies)	20	30	33

1997 ('000 in use): Radio receivers 208; Television receivers 63.

Sources: UNESCO, *Statistical Yearbook*; UN, *Statistical Yearbook*.

Education

(1996)

	Institu-tions	Teachers	Males	Females	Total
Pre-primary*	9	37	465	485	950
Primary	1,147	4,944	126,208	124,398	250,606
Secondary:					
General	88	1,107	31,318	28,863	60,181
Technical	5	181	5,521	1,033	6,554
Vocational	6	52	291	189	480
University level*	2	299	2,148	852	3,000
Other higher	n.a.	257†	1,033‡	315‡	1,348‡

* 1991/92 figures. † 1983/84 figure. ‡ 1986/87 figure.

Sources: Ministère de l'Education Nationale; UNESCO, *Statistical Yearbook*.

Directory

The Constitution

The Constitution of the Gabonese Republic was adopted on 14 March 1991. The main provisions are summarized below:

PREAMBLE

Upholds the rights of the individual, liberty of conscience and of the person, religious freedom and freedom of education. Sovereignty is vested in the people, who exercise it through their representatives or by means of referenda. There is direct, universal and secret suffrage.

HEAD OF STATE*

The President is elected by direct universal suffrage for a five-year term, renewable only once. The President is Head of State and of the Armed Forces. The President may, after consultation with his ministers and leaders of the National Assembly, order a referendum to be held. The President appoints the Prime Minister, who is Head of Government and who is accountable to the President. The President is the guarantor of national independence and territorial sovereignty.

EXECUTIVE POWER

Executive power is vested in the President and the Council of Ministers, who are appointed by the Prime Minister, in consultation with the President.

LEGISLATIVE POWER

The National Assembly is elected by direct universal suffrage for a five-year term. It may be dissolved or prorogued for up to 18 months by the President, after consultation with the Council of Ministers and President of the Assembly. The President may return a bill to the Assembly for a second reading, when it must be passed by a majority of two-thirds of the members. If the President dissolves the Assembly, elections must take place within 40 days.

The Constitution also provides for the establishment of an upper chamber (the Senate), to control the balance and regulation of power.

POLITICAL ORGANIZATIONS

Article 2 of the Constitution states that 'Political parties and associations contribute to the expression of universal suffrage. They are formed and exercise their activities freely, within the limits delineated by the laws and regulations. They must respect the principles of democracy, national sovereignty, public order and national unity'.

JUDICIAL POWER

The President guarantees the independence of the Judiciary and presides over the Conseil Supérieur de la Magistrature. Supreme judicial power is vested in the Supreme Court.

* A constitutional amendment, adopted by the legislature on 18 April 1997, extended the presidential term to seven years and provided for the creation of the post of Vice-President.

The Government

HEAD OF STATE

President: El Hadj OMAR (ALBERT-BERNARD) BONGO (took office 2 December 1967, elected 25 February 1973, re-elected December 1979, November 1986, December 1993 and December 1998).

Vice-President: DIDJOB DIVUNGUI-DI-N'DINGUE.

COUNCIL OF MINISTERS
(August 2000)

Prime Minister and Head of Government: JEAN-FRANÇOIS NTOU-TOUME EMANE.

Vice-Prime Minister, Minister of National Solidarity and Social Welfare: EMMANUEL ONDO-METHOGO.

Minister of State for Equipment and Construction: ZACHARIE MYBOTO.

Minister of State for Planning, Development and Territorial Administration: CASIMIR OYÉ MBA.

Minister of State for Foreign Affairs, Co-operation and Francophone Affairs: JEAN PING.

Minister of State for Communications, Posts and Information Technology: JEAN-RÉMY PENDY-BOUYIKI.

Minister of State for Labour, Employment and Professional Training: PAULETTE MISSAMBO.

Minister of State for the Interior, Security and Decentralization: ANTOINE MBOUMBOU MIYAKOU.

Minister of State for Housing, Urbanization and Cadastral Services: JACQUES ADIAHÉNOT.

Minister of Mining, Energy and Water Resources: PAUL TOUNGUI.

Minister of Justice, Guardian of the Seals: PASCAL DÉSIRÉ MISSONGO.

Minister of Water, Forestry, Fishing, Reafforestation and the Environment: RICHARD ONOUVIET.

Minister of Transport and Merchant Navy: Gen. IDRISS NGARI.

Minister of Trade, Tourism, Industrial Development and Crafts: ALFRED MABICKA.

Minister of National Education and Government Spokesperson: ANDRÉ MBA OBAME.

Minister of National Defence: ALI BONGO.

Minister of Economic Affairs, Finance, the Budget and Privatization: ÉMILE DOUMBA.

Minister of Higher Education, Research and Technology: ANDRÉ-DIEUDONNÉ BERRE.

Minister of Public Health and Population: FAUSTIN BOUKOUBI.

Minister of Agriculture, Livestock and Rural Development: FABIEN OWONO ESSONO.

Minister of Culture, the Arts, Popular Education, Youth and Sports: DANIEL ONA-ONDO.

Minister of Small- and Medium-sized Enterprises: PAUL BIYOGHE-MBA.

Minister of Family Affairs and Women: ANGELIQUE NGOMA.

There were also eight Ministers Delegate.

MINISTRIES

Office of the Prime Minister: BP 546, Libreville; tel. 77-89-81.

Ministry of Agriculture, Livestock and Rural Development: BP 551, Libreville; tel. 72-09-60.

Ministry of the Civil Service, Administrative Reform and Modernization of the State: BP 496, Libreville; tel. 76-38-86.

Ministry of Communications, Posts and Information Technology: Libreville.

Ministry of Culture, the Arts and Popular Education: BP 2280, Libreville; tel. 76-61-83.

Ministry of Economic Affairs, Finance, the Budget and Privatization: BP 165, Libreville; tel. 76-12-10; fax 76-59-74.

Ministry of Equipment and Construction: BP 49, Libreville; tel. 76-38-56; fax 74-80-92.

Ministry of Family Affairs and Women: BP 5684, Libreville; tel. 77-50-32.

Ministry of Foreign Affairs, Co-operation and Francophone Affairs: BP 2245, Libreville; tel. 73-94-65.

Ministry of Higher Education and Research Technology: BP 2217, Libreville; tel. 72-41-08.

Ministry of Housing, Urbanization and Cadastral Services: BP 512, Libreville; tel. 77-31-02.

Ministry of Human Rights and Relations with Constitutional Institutions: Libreville.

Ministry of the Interior, Security and Decentralization: BP 2110, Libreville; tel. 72-00-75.

Ministry of Justice: BP 547, Libreville; tel. 74-66-28; fax 72-33-84.

Ministry of Labour, Employment and Professional Training: BP 4577, Libreville; tel. 74-32-18.

Ministry of Mining and Energy: BP 576, Libreville; tel. 77-22-39.

Ministry of National Defence: BP 13493, Libreville; tel. 77-86-94.

Ministry of National Education: BP 6, Libreville; tel. 76-13-01; fax 74-14-48.

Ministry of National Solidarity and Social Welfare: Libreville.

Ministry of Planning, Development and Territorial Administration: Libreville.

Ministry of Public Health and Population: BP 50, Libreville; tel. 76-36-11.

Ministry of Small- and Medium-sized Enterprises and Crafts: BP 3096, Libreville; tel. 74-59-21.

Ministry of Social Welfare: Libreville.

Ministry of Tourism and the Environment: BP 178, Libreville; tel. 76-34-62.

Ministry of Trade and Industrial Development: Libreville.

Ministry of Transport and Marine Resources: BP 803, Libreville; tel. 74-71-96; fax 77-33-31.

Ministry of Water, Forestry, Fishing and Reafforestation: BP 3974, Libreville; tel. 76-01-09; fax 76-61-83.

Ministry of Youth and Sports: BP 2150, Libreville; tel. 74-00-19; fax 74-65-89.

President and Legislature

PRESIDENT

Presidential Election, 6 December 1998

Candidate	% of votes
El Hadj Omar (Albert-Bernard) Bongo	66.55
Pierre Mamboundou	16.54
Fr Paul M'Ba Abessole	13.41
Pierre-André Kombila	1.54
Pierre-Claver Maganga Moussavou	0.99
Others	0.97
Total	100.00

ASSEMBLÉE NATIONALE

President: GUY NDZOUBA NDAMA.

Secretary-General: PIERRE NGUEMA-MVE.

General Election, 15 and 29 December 1996

Party	Seats
Parti démocratique gabonais (PDG)	84
Rassemblement national des bûcherons (RNB)	7
Parti gabonais du progrès (PGP)	6
Independents	4
Cercle des libéraux réformateurs (CLR)	3
Union du peuple gabonais (UPG)	2
Union socialiste gabonais (USG)	2
Others	7
Total	115*

* Voting was unable to proceed normally in five constituencies, and results in a number of other constituencies were later annulled. Following subsequent by-elections, the PDG held 89 seats, the PGP nine and the RNB six.

SÉNAT

President: GEORGES RAWIRI.

Secretary-General: FÉLIX OWANSANGO DEACKEU.

Election, 26 January and 9 February 1997*

Party	Seats
Parti démocratique gabonais (PDG)	53
Rassemblement national des bûcherons (RNB)	20
Independents	9
Parti gabonais du progrès (PGP)	4
Alliance démocratique et républicaine (ADERE)	3
Cercle des libéraux réformateurs (CLR)	1
Rassemblement pour la démocratie et le progrès (RDP)	1
Total	91

* Following the annulment of a number of results, the PDG gained a further five seats at by-elections held later in 1997.

Political Organizations

Alliance démocratique et républicaine (ADERE): Pres. MBOUMBOU NGOMA; Sec.-Gen. DIDJOB DIVUNGUI-DI-N'DINGUE.

Association pour le socialisme au Gabon (APSG): Pres. V. MAPANGOU MOUCANI MOUETSA.

Cercle des libéraux réformateurs (CLR): f. 1993 by breakaway faction of the PDG; Leader JEAN-BONIFACE ASSELE.

Cercle pour le renouveau et le progrès (CRP).

Congrès pour la démocratie et la justice: Pres. JULES BOURDES OGOULIGUENDE.

Convention des forces du changement: f. 1993 as an informal alliance of eight opposition presidential candidates.

Coordination de l'opposition démocratique (COD): f. 1991 as an alliance of eight principal opposition parties; Chair. SÉBASTIEN MAMBOUNDOU MOUYAMA.

Forum africain pour la reconstruction (FAR): f. 1992; a factional alliance within the COD; Leader Prof. LÉON MBOU-YEMBI; comprises three political parties:

Mouvement de redressement national (MORENA-originels): f. 1981 in Paris, France; Leader (vacant).

Parti socialiste gabonais (PSG): f. 1991; Leader Prof. LÉON MBOYEBI.

Union socialiste gabonais (USG): Leader Dr SERGE MBA BEKALE.

Front national (FN): f. 1991; Leader MARTIN EFAYONG.

Gabon Avenir: f. 1999; Leader SYLVESTRE OYOUOMI.

Mouvement alternatif: f. 1996; Leader SÉBASTIEN MAMBOUNDOU MOUYAMA.

Mouvement pour la démocratie, le développement et la reconciliation nationale (Modern): Libreville; f. 1996; Leader GASTON MOZOGO OVONO.

Parti démocratique gabonais (PDG): BP 268, Libreville; tel. 70-31-21; fax 70-31-46; f. 1968; sole legal party 1968–90; Leader OMAR BONGO; Sec.-Gen. SIMPLICE GUEDET MANZELA.

Parti gabonais du centre indépendant (PGCI): Leader JEAN-PIERRE LEMBOUMBA LEPANDOU.

Parti gabonais du progrès (PGP): f. 1990; Pres. PIERRE-LOUIS AGONDJO-OKAWÉ; Sec.-Gen. ANSELME NZOGHE.

Parti des libéraux démocrates (PLD): Leader MARC SATURNIN NAN NGUEMA.

Parti social-démocrate (PSD): f. 1991; Leader PIERRE-CLAVER MAGANGA MOUSSAVOU.

Parti de l'unité du peuple gabonais (PUP): Libreville; f. 1991; Leader LOUIS GASTON MAYILA.

Rassemblement des démocrates (RD): f. 1993.

Rassemblement pour la démocratie et le progrès (RDP): Pres. PIERRE EMBONI.

Rassemblement des Gaullois: Libreville; f. 1994, registered 1998; 5,000 mems; Pres. MAX ANICET KOUMBA-MBADINGA.

Rassemblement national des bûcherons (RNB): f. 1990 as MORENA des bûcherons; Leader Fr PAUL M'BA ABESSOLE; Sec.-Gen. Prof. VINCENT MOULENGUI BOUKOSSO.

Union pour la démocratie et le développement Mayumba (UDD).

Union démocratique et sociale (UDS): f. 1996; Leader HERVÉ ASSAMANET.

Union nationale pour la démocratie et le développement (UNDD): f. 1993; supports President Bongo.

Union du peuple gabonais (UPG): f. 1989 in Paris, France; Leader PIERRE MAMBOUNDOU.

Diplomatic Representation

EMBASSIES IN GABON

Algeria: BP 4008, Libreville; tel. 73-23-18; fax 73-14-03; e-mail ambalgabon@tiggabon.com; Ambassador: ABDELHAMID CHEBCHOUB.

Angola: BP 4884, Libreville; tel. 73-04-26; fax 73-76-24; Ambassador: BERNARDO DOMBELE M'BALA.

Argentina: BP 4065, Libreville; tel. 74-05-49; Ambassador: HUGO HURTUBEI.

Belgium: BP 4079, Libreville; tel. 73-29-92; Ambassador: VICTOR WEI.

Bénin: BP 3851, Akebe, Libreville; tel. 73-76-82; fax 73-77-75; Ambassador: TIMOTHÉE ADANLIN.

Brazil: BP 3899, Libreville; tel. 76-05-35; fax 74-03-43; e-mail emblibreville@inet.ga; Ambassador: SERGIO SEABRA DE NORONAHA.

Cameroon: BP 14001, Libreville; tel. 73-28-00; Ambassador: JEAN KOE NTONGA.

Canada: BP 4037, Libreville; tel. 74-34-64; fax 74-34-66; e-mail lbrve@dfait-maeci.gc.ca; Ambassador: ROBERT NOBLE.

Central African Republic: Libreville; tel. 72-12-28; Ambassador: FRANÇOIS DIALLO.

China, People's Republic: BP 3914, Libreville; tel. 74-32-07; Ambassador: GUO TIANMIN.

Congo, Democratic Republic: BP 2257, Libreville; tel. 74-32-53; Ambassador: KABANGI KAUMBU BULA.

Congo, Republic: BP 269, Libreville; tel. 73-29-06; Ambassador: PIERRE OBOU.

Côte d'Ivoire: BP 3861, Libreville; tel. 73-82-68; Ambassador: GÉORGES GOHO BAH.

Egypt: BP 4240, Libreville; tel. 73-25-38; fax 73-25-19; Ambassador: SIHAM SALEM RAHMY MOKHTAR.

Equatorial Guinea: BP 1462, Libreville; tel. 75-10-56; Ambassador: CRISANTOS NDONGO ABA MESSIAN.

France: blvd de l'Indépendance, BP 2125, Libreville; tel. 76-20-31; fax 74-48-78; e-mail ambafran@inet.ga; Ambassador: PHILIPPE SELZ.

Germany: blvd de l'Indépendance, BP 299, Libreville; tel. 76-01-88; fax 72-40-12; e-mail amb-allegmagne@inet.ga; Ambassador: ADALBERT RITTMÜLLER.

Guinea: BP 4046, Libreville; tel. 73-85-09; Ambassador: MOHAMED SAMPIL.

Holy See: blvd Monseigneur Bessieux, BP 1322, Libreville (Apostolic Nunciature); tel. 74-45-41; Apostolic Nuncio: Most Rev. MARIO ROBERTO CASSARI, Titular Archbishop of Tronto.

Iran: BP 2158, Libreville; tel. 73-05-33; Ambassador: AHMAD SOBHAM.

Italy: Immeuble Personnaz et Gardin, rue de la Mairie, BP 2251, Libreville; tel. 74-28-92; fax 74-80-35; e-mail ambiasciata-italia@internetgabon.com; Ambassador: LUDOVICO TASSONI ESTENSE DE CASTELVECCHIO.

Japan: BP 3341, Libreville; tel. 73-22-97; fax 73-60-60; Ambassador: ASAHI HIDEKI.

Korea, Republic: BP 2620, Libreville; tel. 73-40-00; fax 73-00-79; Ambassador: OH SANG-SHIK.

Lebanon: BP 3341, Libreville; tel. 73-96-45; Ambassador: CHARAMY HABIB AYOUB.

Mauritania: BP 3917, Libreville; tel. 74-31-65; Ambassador: El Hadj THIAM.

Morocco: BP 3983, Libreville; tel. 77-41-51; fax 77-41-50; Ambassador: MOHAMED GHALI TAZI.

Nigeria: BP 1191, Libreville; tel. 73-22-03; Ambassador: IGNATIUS HEKAIRE AJURU.

Philippines: BP 1198, Libreville; tel. 72-34-80; Chargé d'affaires a.i.: ARCADIO HERRERA.

Russia: BP 3963, Libreville; tel. 72-48-68; fax 72-48-70; Ambassador: USEVOLD SOUKHOV.

São Tomé and Príncipe: BP 489, Libreville; tel. 72-09-94; Ambassador: URBINO JOSÉ GONHALVES BOTELÇO.

Senegal: BP 3856, Libreville; tel. 77-42-67; Ambassador: OUMAR WELE.

South Africa: Immeuble les Arcades, 142 rue des Chavannes, BP 4063, Libreville; tel. 77-45-30; fax 77-45-36; Ambassador: MONGEHI SAMUEL MONAISA.

Spain: Immeuble Diamant, blvd de l'Indépendance, BP 2105, Libreville; tel. 72-12-64; fax 74-88-73; Ambassador: DOMINGO DE SILOS MANSO GARCÍA.

Togo: BP 14160, Libreville; tel. 73-29-04; Ambassador: AHLONKO KOFFI AQUEREBURU.

Tunisia: BP 3844, Libreville; tel. 73-28-41; Ambassador: EZZEDINE KERKENI.

USA: blvd de la Mer, BP 4000, Libreville; tel. 76-20-03; Ambassador: JAMES V. LEDESMA.

Venezuela: BP 3859, Libreville; tel. 73-31-18; fax 73-30-67; Ambassador: VÍCTOR CROQUER-VEGA.

Yugoslavia: Libreville; tel. 73-30-05; Ambassador: ČEDOMIR STRBAC.

Judicial System

Supreme Court: BP 1043, Libreville; tel. 72-17-00; three chambers: judicial, administrative and accounts; Pres. BENJAMIN PAMBOU-KOMBILA.

Constitutional Court: Libreville; tel. 72-57-17; fax 72-55-96; Pres. MARIE MADELEINE MBORANTSUO.

Courts of Appeal: Libreville and Franceville.

Court of State Security: Libreville; 13 mems; Pres. FLORENTIN ANGO.

Conseil Supérieur de la Magistrature: Libreville; Pres. El Hadj OMAR BONGO; Vice-Pres. Pres. of the Supreme Court (ex officio).

There are also Tribunaux de Première Instance (County Courts) at Libreville, Franceville, Port-Gentil, Lambaréné, Mouila, Oyem, Koula-Moutou, Makokou and Tchibanga.

Religion

About 60% of Gabon's population are Christians, mainly adherents of the Roman Catholic Church. About 40% are animists, and fewer than 1% are Muslims.

CHRISTIANITY
The Roman Catholic Church

Gabon comprises one archdiocese and three dioceses. At 31 December 1998 the estimated number of adherents in the country was equivalent to 50.4% of the total population.

Bishops' Conference: Conférence Episcopale du Gabon, BP 2146, Libreville; tel. 72-20-73; f. 1989; Pres. Most Rev. BASILE MVÉ ENGONE, Archbishop of Libreville.

Archbishop of Libreville: Most Rev. BASILE MVÉ ENGONE, Archevêché, Sainte-Marie, BP 2146, Libreville; tel. 72-20-73.

Protestant Churches

Christian and Missionary Alliance: active in the south of the country; 16,000 mems.

Eglise Evangélique du Gabon: BP 10080, Libreville; tel. 72-41-92; f. 1842; independent since 1961; 120,000 mems; Pres. Pastor SAMUEL NANG ESSONO; Sec. Rev. EMILE NTETOME.

The Evangelical Church of South Gabon and the Evangelical Pentecostal Church are also active in Gabon.

The Press

Afric'Sports: BP 3950, Libreville; tel. 76-24-74; monthly; sport; CEO SERGE ALFRED MPOUHO; Man. YVON PATRICE AUBIAN; circ. 5,000.

Le Bûcheron: BP 6424, Libreville; tel. 72-50-20; f. 1990; weekly; official publ. of the Rassemblement national des bûcherons; Editor DÉSIRÉ ÉNAME.

Bulletin Evangélique d'Information et de Presse: BP 80, Libreville; monthly; religious.

Bulletin Mensuel de la Chambre de Commerce, d'Agriculture, d'Industrie et des Mines: BP 2234, Libreville; tel. 72-20-64; fax 74-64-77; monthly.

Bulletin Mensuel de Statistique de la République Gabonaise: BP 179, Libreville; monthly; publ. by Direction Générale de l'Economie.

La Cigale Enchantée: Libreville; bi-monthly; satirical.

L'Economiste Gabonais: BP 3906, Libreville; quarterly; publ. by the Centre gabonais du commerce extérieur.

Gabon d'Aujourd'hui: BP 750, Libreville; weekly; publ. of the Ministry of Culture, the Arts and Popular Education.

Gabon Libre: BP 6439, Libreville; tel. 72-42-22; weekly; Dir DZIME EKANG; Editor RENÉ NZOVI.

Gabon-Matin: BP 168, Libreville; daily; publ. by Agence Gabonaise de Presse; Man. HILARION VENDANY; circ. 18,000.

La Griffe: BP 4928, Libreville; tel. 74-73-45; f. 1990; weekly; independent; satirical; Editor-in-Chief RAPHAEL NTOUTOUME NKOGHE; Editor NDJOUMBA MOUSSOCK.

Journal Officiel de la République Gabonaise: BP 563, Libreville; f. 1959; fortnightly; Man. EMMANUEL OBAMÉ.

Ngondo: BP 168, Libreville; monthly; publ. by Agence Gabonaise de Presse.

Le Progressiste: blvd Léon-M'Ba, BP 7000, Libreville; tel. 74-54-01; f. 1990; Dir BENOÎT MOUITY NZAMBA; Editor JACQUES MOURENDE-TSIOBA.

La Relance: Libreville; tel. 70-31-66; weekly; publ. of the Parti démocratique gabonais; Pres. JACQUES ADIAHÉNOT; Dir RENÉ NDEMEZO'O OBIANG.

Le Reveil: BP 20386, Libreville; tel. and fax 73-17-21; weekly; Man. ALBERT YANGARI; Editor RENÉ NZOVI; circ. 8,000.

La Voix du Peuple: BP 4049, Libreville; tel. 76-20-45; f. 1991; Publisher Parti de l'unité du peuple gabonais; weekly, Editor-in-Chief JEAN KOUMBA; Editor MAURIC-BLAISE NDZADIENGA MAYILA; circ. 4,000.

Sept Jours: BP 213, Libreville; weekly.

L'Union: Sonapresse, BP 3849, Libreville; tel. 73-58-61; fax 73-58-62; f. 1974; 75% state-owned; daily; official govt publ.; Man. Dir ALBERT YANGARI; Editor NGOYO MOUSSAVOU; circ. 20,000.

NEWS AGENCIES

Agence Gabonaise de Presse (AGP): BP 168, Libreville.

Association Professionnelle de la Presse Ecrite Gabonais (APPEG): BP 3849, Libreville; e-mail wmestre@gabon-presse.org.

BERP International: BP 8483, Libreville; tel. and fax 77-58-81; e-mail BERP8483@hotmail.com; Dir ANTOINE LAWSON.

Foreign Bureau

Agence France-Presse (AFP): Immeuble Sogapal, Les Filaos, BP 788, Libreville; tel. 76-14-36; fax 72-45-31; e-mail afp-libreville@tiggabon.com; Dir JEAN-PIERRE REJETE.

Publishers

Gabonaise d'Imprimerie (GABIMP): BP 154, Libreville; tel. 70-22-55; fax 70-31-85; f. 1973; Dir BÉATRICE CAILLOT.

Multipress Gabon: blvd Léon-M'Ba, BP 3875, Libreville; tel. 73-22-33; f. 1973; Chair. PAUL BORY.

Société Imprimerie de l'Ogooué (SIMO): BP 342, Port-Gentil; f. 1977; Man. Dir URBAIN NICOUE.

Société Nationale de Presse et d'Edition (SONAPRESSE): BP 3849, Libreville; tel. 73-21-84; f. 1975; Pres. and Man. Dir JOSEPH RENDJAMBE.

Broadcasting and Communications

TELECOMMUNICATIONS

Office des Postes et des Télécommunications (OPT): BP 20 000, Libreville; tel. 78-70-05; fax 78-67-70; scheduled for privatization during 1999; Dir-Gen. THOMAS SOUAH.

Société des Télécommunications Internationales Gabonaises (TIG): BP 2261, Libreville; tel. 78-77-56; fax 74-19-09; f. 1971; cap. 3,000m. francs CFA; 61% state-owned; planning and devt of international telecommunications systems; Man. Dir A. N'GOUMA MWYUMALA.

BROADCASTING
Radio

The national network, 'La Voix de la Rénovation', and a provincial network broadcast for 24 hours each day in French and local languages.

Africa No. 1: BP 1, Libreville; tel. 76-00-01; fax 74-21-33; e-mail africa1@inet.ga; internet www.africa1.com; f. 1980; 35% state-controlled; international commercial radio station; daily programmes in French and English; Pres. LOUIS BARTHÉLEMY MAPANGOU; Mans MICHEL KOUMBANGOYE, FRANÇOIS MOREAU.

Radiodiffusion-Télévision Gabonaise (RTG): BP 150, Libreville; tel. 73-20-25; f. 1959; state-controlled; Dir-Gen. JOHN JOSEPH MBOUROU; Dir of Radio GILLES TERENCE NZOGHE.

Radio Fréquence 3: f. 1996.

Radio Génération Nouvelle: f. 1996; Dir JEAN-BONIFACE ASSELE.

Radio Mandarine: f. 1995.

Radio Soleil: f. 1995; affiliated to Rassemblement national des bûcherons.

Radio Unité: f. 1996.

Television

Radiodiffusion-Télévision Gabonaise (RTG): BP 150, Libreville; tel. 73-21-52; fax 73-21-53; f. 1959; state-controlled; Dir-Gen. JOHN JOSEPH MBOUROU; Dir of Television JULES CÉSAR LEKOGHO.

Télé-Africa: Libreville; tel. 76-20-33; private channel; daily broadcasts in French.

Télédiffusion du Gabon: f. 1995.

Finance

(cap. = capital; res = reserves; dep. = deposits; m. = million; brs = branches; amounts in francs CFA)

BANKING
Central Bank

Banque des Etats de l'Afrique Centrale (BEAC): BP 112, Libreville; tel. 76-13-52; fax 74-45-63; HQ in Yaoundé, Cameroon; f. 1973; bank of issue for mem. states of the Communauté économique et monétaire de l'Afrique centrale (CEMAC, fmrly Union douanière et économique de l'Afrique centrale), comprising Cameroon, the Central African Repub., Chad, the Repub. of the Congo, Equatorial Guinea and Gabon; cap. and res 210,014m., total assets 1,303,226m. (June 1999); Gov. JEAN-FÉLIX MAMALEPOT; Dir in Gabon PHILIBERT ANDZEMBE; 3 brs in Gabon.

Commercial Banks

Banque Gabonaise et Française Internationale (BGFI): BP 2253, Libreville; tel. 76-23-26; fax 74-08-94; e-mail bgfi@internetgabon.com; internet www.bgfi.com; f. 1972; 33.4% state-owned; cap. and res 23,706.5m., dep. 65,499.7m. (Dec. 1999); Chair. PATRICE OTHA; Dir-Gen. HENRI-CLAUDE OYIMA; 3 brs.

Banque Internationale pour le Commerce et l'Industrie du Gabon, SA (BICIG): ave du Colonel Parant, BP 2241, Libreville; tel. 76-26-13; fax 74-64-10; e-mail bicigdoi@inet.ga; f. 1973; 27.7% state-owned; cap. and res 50,403m., total assets 256,000m. (Dec.

1998); Pres. Etienne Guy Mouvagha Tchioba; Man. Dir Emile Doumba; 9 brs.

Banque Internationale pour le Gabon: Immeuble Concorde, blvd de l'Indépendance, BP 106, Libreville; tel. 76-26-26; fax 76-20-53.

Banque Populaire du Gabon 'La Populaire': blvd d'Indépendance, BP 6663, Libreville; tel. 72-86-88; fax 72-86-91; e-mail bapo10@calva.com; f. 1996; cap. 700m., total assets 4,950m. (Dec. 1998); Pres. Jean-Marc Ekoh Ngyema; Dir-Gen. Samson Ngomo.

Crédit Foncier du Gabon: blvd de l'Indépendance, BP 3905, Libreville; tel. 72-47-45; fax 76-08-70; 90% state-owned; under enforced administration since June 1996; Interim Admin. Fabien Ovono-Ngoua.

Union Gabonaise de Banque, SA (UGB): ave du Colonel Parant, BP 315, Libreville; tel. 77-70-00; fax 76-46-16; f. 1962; 25% state-owned; cap. 5,000m., dep. 101,339m., total assets 122,356m. (Dec. 1998); Chair. Marcel Doupamby-Matoka; Pres. Pierre-Parfait Gondjout; Man. Dir Jean-Claude Dubois; 6 brs.

Development Banks

Banque Gabonaise de Développement (BGD): rue Alfred Marche, BP 5, Libreville; tel. 76-24-29; fax 74-26-99; e-mail bdg@internetgabon.com; f. 1960; 69% state-owned; cap. and res 26,859.3m. (Dec. 1998); Pres. Michel Anchouey; Chair. Victor Afene; Dir-Gen. Richard Onouviet.

Banque Gabonaise et Française Internationale Participations: BP 2253, Libreville; tel. 76-23-26; fax 74-08-94; e-mail bgfi@internetgabon.com; internet www.bgfi.com; f. 1997; cap. 1,500m. (Dec. 1999); Dir-Gen. Henri-Claude Oyima.

Banque Nationale de Crédit Rural (BNCR): ave Bouet, BP 1120, Libreville; tel. 72-47-42; fax 74-05-07; f. 1986; 74% state-owned; cap. 1,350m., total assets 6,885m. (Dec. 1998); Pres. Gérard Meyo M'Emane; Man. Dir Georges Issembe.

Société Nationale d'Investissement du Gabon (SONADIG): BP 479, Libreville; tel. 72-09-22; fax 74-81-70; f. 1968; state-owned; cap. 500m.; Pres. Antoine Oyieye; Dir-Gen. Massala Tsamba.

Financial Institution

Caisse Autonome d'Amortissement du Gabon: BP 912, Libreville; tel. 74-41-43; management of state funds; Dir-Gen. Maurice Eyamba Tsimat.

INSURANCE

Agence Gabonaise d'Assurance et de Réassurance (AGAR): BP 1699, Libreville; tel. 74-02-22; fax 76-59-25; f. 1987; Man. Dir Louis Gaston Mayila.

Assurances Générales Gabonaises (AGG): ave du Colonel Parant, BP 2148, Libreville; tel. 76-09-73; fax 76-57-41; f. 1974; Dir-Gen. Alain Weller.

Assureurs Conseils Franco-Africains du Gabon (ACFRA-GABON): BP 1116, Libreville; tel. 72-32-83; Chair. Frédéric Marron; Dir M. Garnier.

Assureurs Conseils Gabonais-Faugère et Jutheau & Cie: Immeuble Shell-Gabon, rue de la Mairie, BP 2138, Libreville; tel. 72-04-36; fax 76-04-39; represents foreign insurance cos; Dir Gérard Milan.

Groupement Gabonais d'Assurances et de Réassurances (GGAR): Immeuble les Horizons, blvd Triomphal Omar Bongo, BP 3949, Libreville; tel. 74-28-72; f. 1985; Chair. Rassaguiza Akerey; Dir-Gen. Denise Ombagho.

Mutuelle Gabonaise d'Assurances: ave du Colonel Parant, BP 2225, Libreville; tel. 72-13-91; fax 76-47-49; Sec.-Gen. M. Yeno-Olingot.

Omnium Gabonais d'Assurances et de Réassurances (OGAR): 546 blvd Triomphal Omar Bongo, BP 201, Libreville; tel. 76-15-96; fax 76-58-16; f. 1976; 10% state-owned; general; Pres. Marcel Doupamby-Matoka; Man. Dir Edouard Valentin.

Société Nationale Gabonaise d'Assurances et de Réassurances (SONAGAR): ave du Colonel Parant, BP 3082, Libreville; tel. 76-28-97; f. 1974; owned by l'Union des Assurances de Paris (France); Dir-Gen. Jean-Louis Messan.

SOGERCO-Gabon: BP 2102, Libreville; tel. 76-09-34; f. 1975; general; Dir M. Rabeau.

L'Union des Assurances du Gabon (UAG): ave du Colonel Parant, BP 2141, Libreville; tel. 74-34-34; fax 74-14-53; f. 1976; Chair. Albert Alewina Chaviot; Dir Ekomie Afene.

Trade and Industry

GOVERNMENT AGENCY

Conseil Economique et Social de la République Gabonaise: BP 1075, Libreville; tel. 73-19-46; fax 73-19-44; comprises representatives from salaried workers, employers and Govt; commissions on economic, financial and social affairs and forestry and agriculture; Pres. Louis Gaston Mayila.

DEVELOPMENT ORGANIZATIONS

Agence Française de Développement: BP 64, Libreville; tel. 74-33-74; fax 74-51-25; fmrly Caisse Française de Développement; Dir Antoine Baux.

Agence Nationale de Promotion de la Petite et Moyenne Entreprise (PROMO-GABON): BP 3939, Libreville; tel. 74-31-16; f. 1964; state-controlled; promotes and assists small and medium-sized industries; Pres. Simon Boulamatari; Man. Dir Jean-Fidèle Otando.

Centre Gabonais de Commerce Extérieur (CGCE): BP 3906, Libreville; tel. 76-11-67; promotes foreign trade and investment in Gabon; Man. Dir Michel Leslie Teale.

Commerce et Développement (CODEV): BP 2142, Libreville; tel. 76-06-73; f. 1976; 95% state-owned, proposed transfer to private ownership announced 1986; import and distribution of capital goods and food products; Chair. and Man. Dir Jérôme Ngoua-Bekale.

Mission Française de Coopération: BP 2105, Libreville; tel. 76-10-56; fax 74-55-33; administers bilateral aid from France; Dir Jean-Claude Quirin.

Office Gabonais d'Amélioration et de Production de Viande (OGAPROV): BP 245, Moanda; tel. 66-12-67; f. 1971; development of private cattle farming; manages ranch at Lekedi-Sud; Pres. Paul Kounda Kiki; Dir-Gen. Vincent Eyi-Ngui.

Palmiers et Hévéas du Gabon (PALMEVEAS): BP 75, Libreville; f. 1956; state-owned; palm-oil production.

Société de Développement de l'Agriculture au Gabon (AGRO-GABON): BP 2248, Libreville; tel. 76-40-82; fax 76-44-72; f. 1976; 92% state-owned; Man. Dir André Paul-Apandina.

Société de Développement de l'Hévéaculture (HEVEGAB): BP 316, Libreville; tel. 72-08-29; fax 72-08-30; f. 1981; 99.9% state-owned; development of rubber plantations in the Mitzic, Bitam and Kango regions; Chair. François Owono-Nguema; Man. Dir Raymond Ndong-Sima.

Société Gabonaise de Recherches et d'Exploitations Minières (SOGAREM): blvd de Nice, Libreville; state-owned; research and development of gold mining; Chair. Arsène Bounguenza; Man. Dir Serge Gassita.

Société Gabonaise de Recherches Pétrolières (GABOREP): BP 564, Libreville; tel. 75-06-40; fax 75-06-47; exploration and exploitation of hydrocarbons; Chair. Hubert Perrodo; Man. Dir P. F. Leca.

Société Nationale de Développement des Cultures Industrielles (SONADECI): Libreville; tel. 76-33-97; f. 1978; state-owned; agricultural development; Chair. Paul Kounda Kiki; Man. Dir Georges Bekalé.

CHAMBER OF COMMERCE

Chambre de Commerce, d'Agriculture, d'Industrie et des Mines du Gabon: BP 2234, Libreville; tel. 72-20-64; fax 74-64-77; f. 1935; regional offices at Port-Gentil and Franceville; Pres. Joachim Boussamba-Mapaga; Sec.-Gen. Dominique Mandza.

EMPLOYERS' ORGANIZATIONS

Confédération Patronale Gabonaise: BP 410, Libreville; tel. 76-02-43; fax 74-86-52; f. 1959; represents industrial, mining, petroleum, public works, forestry, banking, insurance, commercial and shipping interests; Pres. J. C. Baloche; Sec.-Gen. Eric Messerschmitt.

Conseil National du Patronat Gabonais (CNPG): Libreville; Pres. Rahandi Chambrier; Sec.-Gen. Thomas Franck Eya'a.

Syndicat des Entreprises Minières du Gabon (SYNDIMINES): BP 260, Libreville; Pres. André Berre; Sec.-Gen. Serge Gregoire.

Syndicat des Importateurs Exportateurs du Gabon (SIMPEX): Libreville; Pres. Albert Jean; Sec.-Gen. R. Tyberghein.

Syndicat des Producteurs et Industriels du Bois du Gabon: BP 84, Libreville; tel. 72-26-11; fax 77-44-43; Pres. Heiric Cheneau.

Syndicat Professionnel des Usines de Sciages et Placages du Gabon: Port-Gentil; f. 1956; Pres. Pierre Berry.

Union des Représentations Automobiles et Industrielles (URAI): BP 1743, Libreville; Pres. M. Martinent; Sec. R. Tyberghein.

Union Nationale du Patronat Syndical des Transports Urbains, Routiers et Fluviaux du Gabon (UNAPASYFTU-ROGA): BP 1025, Libreville; f. 1977; Pres. Laurent Bellal Bibang-Bi-Edzo; Sec.-Gen. Martin Kombila-Mombo.

UTILITIES

Société d'Energie et d'Eau du Gabon (SEEG): BP 2082, Libreville; tel. 72-19-11; fax 76-11-34; f. 1950; 51% owned by Compagnie

Générale des Eaux (France) and Electricity Supply Board International (Ireland); controls 35 electricity generation and distribution centres and 32 water production and distribution centres; Chair. of Bd FRANÇOIS OMBANDA.

MAJOR COMPANIES

The following are some of the largest private and state-owned companies in terms of either capital investment or employment.

L'Auxiliaire du Bâtiment J.-F. Aveyra (ABA): BP 14382, Libreville; tel. 70-44-80; f. 1977; cap. 1,000m. francs CFA; production of construction materials, plastics; Chair. JEAN-FRANÇOIS AVEYRA; Man. Dir G. DUTILH.

Compagnie Forestière du Gabon (CFG): BP 521, Port-Gentil; tel. 55-20-45; fax 55-36-43; f. 1945; cap. 6,785m. francs CFA; 63% state-owned; production of okoumé plywood and veneered quality plywoods; Chair. MICHEL ESSONGHÉ; 1,975 employees.

Compagnie des Mines d'Uranium de Franceville (COMUF): BP 260, Libreville; tel. 76-43-10; fax 76-43-41; f. 1958; cap. 5,050m. francs CFA; 25% state-owned; uranium mining at Mounana (due to cease production in May 1999); Man. Dir EGIDE BOUNDONO-SIMANGOYE; 150 employees.

Compagnie Minière de l'Ogooué (COMILOG): BP 27-28, Moanda; tel. 66-10-00; fax 66-11-57; f. 1953; cap. 32,812.5m. francs CFA; 30% state-owned; manganese mining at Moanda; Pres. CLAUDE VILLAIN; Man. Dir MARCEL ABEKE; 1,400 employees.

Elf-Gabon: BP 525, Port-Gentil; tel. 55-60-00; fax 55-18-08; f. 1934; cap. 76,500m. francs CFA; 25% state-owned, 57% owned by Elf-Aquitaine group; prospecting for and mining of petroleum; Chair. JEAN-FRANÇOIS GAVALDA; Man. Dir MARC COSSÉ; 643 employees.

Gabo-Ren: Port-Gentil; f. 1975; cap. 1,600m. francs CFA; 33% state-owned, 32% owned by Elf-Gabon, 35% owned by N'Ren Corpn; mfrs of artificial ammonia and urea.

Leroy-Gabon: BP 69, Libreville; tel. 72-14-14; fax 76-15-94; f. 1976; cap. 2,080m. francs CFA; forestry; Chair. and Man. Dir JEAN LEPRINCE.

Mobil Oil Gabon: Zone Industrielle Sud Owendo, BP 145, Libreville; tel. 70-05-48; fax 70-05-87; e-mail mobil@komo.tiggabon.com; f. 1974; cap. 547m. francs CFA; storage and distribution of petroleum products; Chair. ARNAUD BLOVIN.

PIZO Shell SA: Libreville; tel. 74-01-01; fax 76-02-44; f. 1987; cap. 1,875m. francs CFA; subsidiary of Shell Group; Man. Dir JEAN-BAPTISTE BIKULOU.

Rougier Océan Gabon SA (ROG): BP 130, Libreville; tel. 74-31-50; fax 74-31-48; cap. 1,200m. francs CFA; forestry and mfr of plywood; Chair. MAURICE ROUGIER; Dir HERVÉ BOZEC.

Shell Gabon: BP 146, Port-Gentil; tel. 55-26-62; fax 55-80-50; f. 1960; cap. 15,000m. francs CFA; owned 75% by Royal Dutch-Shell group, 25% state-owned; exploration and production of hydrocarbons; Chair. and Man. Dir PAUL ROWLANDS.

Société Bernabé Gabon: BP 2084, Libreville; tel. 74-34-32; fax 76-05-21; cap. 1,000m. francs CFA; metallurgical products, construction materials, hardware; Man. Dir J. P. BERGER; Finance Dir J. LE GAL.

Société des Brasseries du Gabon (SOBRAGA): 20 blvd Léon M'Ba, BP 487, Libreville; tel. 73-23-66; fax 70-09-21; f. 1966; cap. 1,558m. francs CFA; mfrs of beer and soft drinks; Chair. and Man. Dir PIERRE CASTEL; Dir M. PALU.

Société des Ciments du Gabon: BP 477, Libreville; tel. 70-20-25; fax 70-27-05; f. 1976; cap. 12,505m. francs CFA; 91.44% state-owned, 8.55% owned by Elf-Gabon; clinker crushing works at N'Toum, Owendo (Libreville) and Franceville; Chair. LÉONARD ANDJEMBE; Dir-Gen. EMMANUEL NZE BEKALE.

Société d'Exploitation des Produits Oléagineux du Gabon (SEPOGA): BP 1491, Libreville; tel. 76-01-92; fax 74-15-67; f. 1977; cap. 732m. francs CFA; 25% state-owned, 14% owned by Shell Gabon; production and marketing of vegetable oils; Chair. PAUL KOUNDA-KIKI; Man. Dir EDMUND SCHEFFLER.

Société Gabonaise des Ferro-Alliages (SOGAFERRO): BP 2728, Moanda; f. 1974; cap. 1,000m. francs CFA; 10% state-owned; manganese processing; Chair. Dr HERVÉ MOUTSINGA; Man. Dir GILLES DE SEAUVE.

Société Gabonaise de Raffinage (SOGARA): BP 530, Port-Gentil; tel. 55-36-52; fax 56-34-73; f. 1965; cap. 1,200m. francs CFA; 25% state-owned; refines locally-produced crude petroleum; Chair. RENÉ RADEMBINO CONIQUET; Man. Dir JEAN FIDÈLE OTANDO; 455 employees.

Société Gabonaise des Textiles (SOGATEX): f. 1987; 36.5% state-owned; mfrs of garments.

Société de la Haute Mondah (SHM): BP 69, Libreville; tel. 72-22-29; f. 1939; cap. 888m. francs CFA; forestry, plywood and sawmilling; Man. Dir M. DEJOIE.

Société Industrielle d'Agriculture et d'Elevage de Boumango (SIAEB): BP 68, Franceville; tel. 67-72-88; f. 1977; cap. 1,740m.

francs CFA; 35% state-owned; maize, soya, rice and poultry production; Man. Dir JEAN-JACQUES DUBOIS.

Société Industrielle Textile du Gabon (SOTEGA): Libreville; tel. 72-19-29; f. 1968; cap. 260m. francs CFA; 15% state-owned; textile printing; Chair. RAPHAËL EBOBOCA; Man. Dir M. MARESCAUX.

Société Italo-Gabonaise des Marbres (SIGAMA): BP 3893, Libreville; tel. 72-25-83; f. 1974; cap. 542m. francs CFA; operates a marble quarry and factory at Doussé Oussou; Man. Dir FRANCO MARCHIO.

Société Meunière et Avicole du Gabon (SMAG): BP 609, Libreville; tel. 70-18-76; fax 70-28-12; f. 1968; cap. 1,341m. francs CFA; partly state-owned; production of eggs, cattle-food, flour, bread; Chair. J. LOUIS VILGRAIN; Man. Dir X. THOMAS.

Société des Mines de Fer de Mekambo (SOMIFER): Libreville; tel. 73-28-58; f. 1960; cap. 900m. francs CFA; 49% state-owned; mineral prospecting and mining; Chair. ADAMA DIALLO; Dir JEAN AUDIBERT.

Société de Mise en Valeur du Bois (SOMIVAB): BP 3893, Libreville; tel. 78-18-27; cap. 1,550m. francs CFA; forestry, sawmill, mfrs of sleepers for Transgabon railway; Chair. HERVÉ MOUTSINGA; Man. Dir FRANCO MARCHIO.

Société Nationale des Bois du Gabon (SNBG): BP 67, Libreville; tel. 76-47-94; fax 76-02-11; f. 1944; cap. 4,000m. francs CFA; 51% state-owned; has a monopoly of marketing all okoumé production; Chair. EGIOE BONDONO-SIMAGOYE; 230 employees.

Société National Immobilière (SNI): BP 515, Libreville; tel. 76-05-81; fax 74-76-00; e-mail snigabon@internetgabon.com; f. 1976; cap. 1,250m. francs CFA; 77% state-owned; housing management and development; CEO ANTOINE N'GOUA.

Société Pizo de Formulation de Lubrifiants (PIZOLUB): BP 699, Port-Gentil; tel. 55-28-40; fax 55-03-82; f. 1978; cap. 500m. francs CFA; 25% state-owned; mfrs of lubricating materials; Chair. MARCEL SANDOUNGOUT; Dir-Gen. PIERRE RIPOLL.

Société Sucrière du Haut-Ogoooué (SOSUHO): BP 1180, Libreville; tel. 72-00-51; fax 73-91-83; f. 1974; cap. 500m. francs CFA; 54% state-owned; sugar production and agro-industrial complex at Ouélé; Chair. A. H. AKENDENGUE; Dir-Gen. JEAN ZEPHIRIN ENGANDGI.

TRADE UNIONS

Confédération Gabonaise des Syndicats Libres (CGSL): BP 8067, Libreville; tel. 77-37-82; fax 74-45-25; f. 1991; Sec.-Gen. FRANCIS MAYOMBO; 16,000 mems.

Confédération Syndicale Gabonaise (COSYGA): BP 14017, Libreville; f. 1969 by the Govt, as a specialized organ of the PDG, to organize and educate workers, to contribute to social peace and economic development, and to protect the rights of trade unions; Gen. Sec. MARTIN ALLINI.

Transport

RAILWAYS

The construction of the Transgabonais railway, which comprises a section running from Owendo (the port of Libreville) to Booué (340 km) and a second section from Booué to Franceville (357 km), was completed in 1986. By 1989 regular services were operating between Libreville and Franceville. Some 2m. metric tons of freight and 200,000 passengers were carried on the network in 1996. In 1998 the railways were transferred to private management.

Office du Chemin de Fer Transgabonais (OCTRA): BP 2198, Libreville; tel. 70-24-78; fax 70-20-38; f. 1972; management transferred to the private sector in late 1998; Dir-Gen. CÉLESTIN NDOLIA-NHAUD.

ROADS

In 1996 there were an estimated 7,670 km of roads, including 30 km of motorways, 3,780 km of main roads and 2,420 km of secondary roads; about 8.2% of the road network was paved.

INLAND WATERWAYS

The principal river is the Ogooué, navigable from Port-Gentil to Ndjolé (310 km) and serving the towns of Lambaréné, Ndjolé and Sindara.

Compagnie de Navigation Intérieure (CNI): BP 3982, Libreville; tel. 72-39-28; fax 74-04-11; f. 1978; state-owned; responsible for inland waterway transport; agencies at Port-Gentil, Mayumba and Lambaréné; Chair. JEAN-PIERRE MENGWANG ME NGYEMA; Dir-Gen. JEAN LOUIS POUNAH-NDJIMBI.

SHIPPING

The principal deep-water ports are Port-Gentil, which handles mainly petroleum exports, and Owendo, 15 km from Libreville, which services mainly barge traffic. The main ports for timber are at Owendo, Mayumba and Nyanga, and there is a fishing port at Libreville. The construction of a deep-water port at Mayumba is planned. A new terminal for the export of minerals, at Owendo, was opened in 1988. In 1998 the merchant shipping fleet had a total displacement of 26,532 grt. In 1997 the Islamic Development Bank granted a loan of 11,000m. francs CFA for the rehabilitation of Gabon's ports.

Compagnie de Manutention et de Chalandage d'Owendo (COMACO): BP 2131, Libreville; tel. 70-26-35; f. 1974; Pres. GEORGES RAWIRI; Dir in Libreville M. RAYMOND.

Office des Ports et Rades du Gabon (OPRAG): BP 1051, Libreville; tel. 70-00-48; fax 70-37-35; f. 1974; state-owned; national port authority; Pres. ALI BONGO; Dir-Gen. MARTIN LOURY.

SAGA Gabon: BP 518, Port-Gentil; tel. 55-54-00; fax 55-21-71; Chair. G. COGNON; Man. Dir J. C. SIMON.

Société Nationale d'Acconage et de Transit (SNAT): BP 3897, Libreville; tel. 70-04-04; fax 70-13-11; f. 1976; 51% state-owned; freight transport; Dir-Gen. GUSTAVE BONGO.

Société Nationale de Transports Maritimes (SONATRAM): BP 3841, Libreville; tel. 74-06-32; fax 74-59-67; f. 1976; relaunched 1995; 51% state-owned; river and ocean cargo transport; Man. Dir RAPHAEL MOARA WALLA.

Société du Port Minéralier d'Owendo: f. 1987; majority holding by Cie Minière de l'Ogooué; management of a terminal for minerals at Owendo.

SOCOPAO–Gabon: BP 4, Libreville; tel. 70-21-40; fax 70-02-76; f. 1983; freight transport and storage; Dir DANIEL BECQUERELLE.

CIVIL AVIATION

There are international airports at Libreville, Port-Gentil and Franceville, 65 other public and 50 private airfields linked mostly with the forestry and petroleum industries.

Air Affaires Gabon: BP 3962, Libreville; tel. 73-25-13; fax 73-49-98; f. 1975; domestic passenger chartered and scheduled flights; Chair. RAYMOND BELLANGER; Dir-Gen. DIEUDONNÉ MFOUBOU MOUDHOUMA.

Air Service Gabon (ASG): BP 2232, Libreville; tel. 73-24-08; fax 73-60-69; f. 1965; charter flights; Chair. JEAN-LUC CHEVRIER; Gen. Man. FRANÇOIS LASCOMBES.

Compagnie Nationale Air Gabon: BP 2206, Libreville; tel. 73-00-27; fax 73-01-11; f. 1951 as Cie Aérienne Gabonaise; began operating international services in 1977, following Gabon's withdrawal from Air Afrique (see under Côte d'Ivoire); 80% state-owned; internal and international cargo and passenger services; Chair. MARTIN BONGO; Dir-Gen. RENÉ MORVAN.

Société de Gestion de l'Aéroport de Libreville (ADL): BP 363, Libreville; tel. 73-62-44; fax 73-61-28; e-mail adl@inet.ga; f. 1988; 26.5% state-owned; management of airport at Libreville; Pres. CHANTAL LIDJI BADINGA; Dir-Gen. PIERRE ANDRÉ COLLET.

Tourism

Tourist arrivals were estimated at 167,197 in 1997, and receipts from tourism totalled US $7m. in 1996. The tourism sector is being extensively developed, with new hotels and associated projects and the promotion of national parks. In 1996 there were 74 hotels, with a total of 4,000 rooms.

Centre Gabonais de Promotion Touristique (GABONTOUR): BP 2085, Libreville; tel. 72-85-04; fax 72-85-03; e-mail gabontour@internetgabon.com; internet www.internetgabon.com; f. 1988; Dir-Gen. JOSEPH ADJEMBIMANDE.

Office National Gabonais du Tourisme: BP 161, Libreville; tel. 72-21-82.

Defence

In August 1999 the army consisted of 3,200 men, the air force of 1,000 men, and the navy of an estimated 500 men. Paramilitary forces numbered 4,800 (including a gendarmerie of 2,000). Military service is voluntary. France maintains a detachment of 700 troops in Gabon.

Defence Expenditure: Budgeted at an estimated 77,000m. francs CFA for 1999.

Commander-in-Chief of the Armed Forces: Gen. AUGUSTIN ANGUILEY.

Education

Education is officially compulsory for 10 years between six and 16 years of age: in 1993 89% of children in the relevant age-group attended primary and secondary schools (90% of boys; 88% of girls). Primary and secondary education is provided by the state and mission schools. Primary education begins at the age of six and lasts for six years. Secondary education, beginning at 12 years of age, lasts for up to seven years, comprising a first cycle of four years and a second of three years. The Université Omar Bongo, at Libreville, had 2,741 students in 1986. The Université des Sciences et des Techniques de Masuku, at Franceville, was opened in 1986, with an enrolment of 550 students. Many students go to France for university and technical training. In 1995, according to estimates by UNESCO, adult illiteracy averaged 36.7% (males 26.3%; females 46.6%). The 1994 budget allocated 78,850m. francs CFA (19% of total administrative spending) to expenditure on education.

Bibliography

Aicardi de Saint-Paul, M. *Le Gabon du roi Denis à Omar Bongo.* Paris, Editions Albatros, 1987 (trans. by Palmer, A. F., and Palmer, T. as *Gabon: The Development of a Nation*). New York and London, Routledge, 1989.

Ambourouë-Avaro, J. *Un peuple gabonais à l'aube de la colonisation.* Paris, Editions Karthala, 1983.

Barnes, J. F. *Gabon: Beyond the Colonial Legacy.* Boulder, CO, Westview Press, 1992.

Bongo, O. *El Hadj Omar Bongo par lui-même.* Libreville, Multipress Gabon, 1988.

Bory, P. *The New Gabon.* Monaco, 1978.

Bouquerel, J. *Le Gabon.* Paris, Presses universitaires de France, 1970.

Deschamps, H. *Traditions orales et archives du Gabon.* Paris, Berger-Levrault, 1962.

Economist Intelligence Unit. *Gabon, Equatorial Guinea, Country Profile.* London, annual.

Fernandez, J. W. *Bwiti.* Princeton, NJ, Princeton University Press, 1982.

Gardinier, D. E. *Historical Dictionary of Gabon.* Lanham, MD, Scarecrow Press, 1994.

Gaulme, F. *Le Pays de Cama Gabon.* Paris, Editions Karthala, 1983.

Le Gabon et son ombre. Paris, Editions Karthala, 1988.

McKay, J. 'West Central Africa', in Mansell Prothero, R. (Ed.), *A Geography of Africa*, London, 1969.

Péan, P. *Affaires africaines.* Paris, Fayard, 1983.

Raponda-Walker, A. *Notes d'histoire du Gabon.* Montpellier, Imprimerie Charité, 1960.

Vennetier, P. 'Problems of Port Development in Gabon and Congo', in Hoyle, B. S., and Hilling, D. (Eds), *Seaports and Development in Tropical Africa.* London, 1970.

Les Plans de Développement des Pays d'Afrique Noire. 4th Edn. Paris, Ediafric, 1977.

L'Economie Gabonaise. Ediafric, Paris, 1977.

Yates, D. *The Rentier State in Africa: Oil Dependency and Neocolonialism in the Republic of Gabon.* Trenton, NJ, Africa World Press, 1996.

THE GAMBIA

Physical and Social Geography

R. J. HARRISON CHURCH

The Republic of The Gambia occupies an area of 11,295 sq km (4,361 sq miles). Apart from a very short coastline, The Gambia is a semi-enclave in Senegal, with which it shares some physical and social phenomena, but differs in history, colonial experience and certain economic affiliations. Its population (enumerated at 1,025,867 in April 1993, according to provisional census results) is, however, one of the fastest-growing of mainland Africa: the government reported a rate of population growth of 4.2% in 1996. According to UN estimates, the population numbered 1,229,000 in mid-1998, producing a density of 108.8 inhabitants per sq km.

The Gambia essentially comprises the valley of the navigable Gambia river. Around the estuary (3 km wide at its narrowest point) and the lower river, the state is 50 km wide, and extends eastward either side of the navigable river for 470 km. In most places the country is only 24 km wide with but one or two villages within it on either bank, away from mangrove or marsh. The former extends about 150 km upstream, the limit of the tide in the rainy season, although in the dry season and in drought years the tide penetrates further upstream. Annual rainfall averages 1,150 mm. Coastal erosion has been increasing since 1980, and it is estimated that between 4 m–5 m of coastal land was lost during the period 1990–94.

Small ocean-going vessels can reach Kaur, 190 km upstream, throughout the year; Georgetown, 283 km upstream, is accessible to some small craft. River vessels regularly call at Fatoto, 464 km upstream, the last of 33 wharf towns served by schooners or river boats. Unfortunately, this fine waterway is underutilized because it is separated from most of its natural hinterland by the nearby frontier with Senegal.

Some mangrove on the landward sides has been removed for swamp rice cultivation. Behind are seasonally flooded marshes with freshwater grasses, and then on the upper slopes of Tertiary sandstone there is woodland with fallow bush and areas cultivated mainly with groundnuts and millet.

The Gambia has no commercially exploitable mineral resources, although deposits of petroleum have been identified.

The principal ethnic groups are the Mandinka, Fula, Wollof, Jola, Serahule, Manjago and Bambara. There is also a small but influential Creole (Aku) community. Each ethnic group has its own vernacular language, although the official language is English.

Recent History

JOHN A. WISEMAN

Revised for this edition by the Editor.

Following the establishment of a coastal trading settlement at Bathurst (now Banjul) in 1816, the extension of British control over the territory now comprising the Republic of The Gambia was completed by the close of the 19th century. Political life during the colonial period developed slowly, but following the extension of the franchise to all adults after 1960 two political parties came to the fore: the United Party (UP), which attracted support from urban coastal interests, and the rurally based Protectorate People's Party (PPP, subsequently the People's Progressive Party), led by Dr (later Sir) Dawda Jawara, a country veterinary officer. The PPP emerged as the dominant party in pre-independence elections in 1962, and subsequently attracted the support of the coastal political élite. On 18 February 1965 The Gambia became an independent state, within the Commonwealth, with Jawara as prime minister.

JAWARA AND THE PPP, 1965–94

From independence in 1965 until the military *coup d'état* of July 1994, political life and government control were firmly concentrated in the hands of Jawara and the PPP. Jawara remained the central figure in Gambian politics, becoming president when the country opted for republican status in 1970. The UP went into decline after independence, and in 1975 was eclipsed by a new opposition party, the National Convention Party (NCP), whose leader Sherif Dibba, had formerly been a leading figure in the PPP. The late 1970s also saw the formation of a number of small Marxist-inspired groups, among them the Gambia Socialist Revolutionary Party (GSRP) and the Movement for Justice in Africa–The Gambia (MOJA–G), and of a number of clandestine 'underground' groups.

In July 1981, while Jawara was out of the country, dissident members of the paramilitary field force (the country had no army at this time) allied with some of the small radical groupings to attempt a *coup d'état*. Jawara secured from Senegal the support of troops to help suppress the insurgency, and, following a week of fierce fighting in and around Banjul, the rebellion was crushed. At least 1,000 people (and possibly double that number) were killed in the conflict: many of these casualties resulted from the release and arming of convicts from prison in Banjul, who conducted a campaign of looting and murder. As the Jawara government was returned to power some 1,000 people were detained, although many were soon released without being brought to trial. Among those charged was Sherif Dibba, who was subsequently acquitted and released.

There were two important ramifications of the coup attempt. The first was the establishment of a confederation with Senegal in February 1982. The Senegambian confederation was always more favoured by Senegal authorities than it was by the Gambians, and for most of the decade the pattern of relationships was one of the former's trying to establish ever greater unity while the smaller partner perceived the need to preserve its independent sovereignty: fears of Senegalese domination have long been a feature of Gambian political consciousness. The confederal partners' differences of approach produced numerous disagreements and tensions, and in September 1989 the Senegambian confederation was formally dissolved.

The second development arising from the coup attempt was the establishment of a Gambian army. Initially the army was raised as part of a confederal army, which tended to be dominated in terms of finance and leadership by Senegal, but the subsequent dissolution of the confederation left the Gambian national army (GNA) as an independent force. Even before the 1994 coup there were several indications of disaffection within the GNA. In June 1991 Gambian soldiers who had served in Liberia, as members of the ECOMOG force of the Economic Community of West African States (ECOWAS), staged a protest in Banjul over the late payment of allowances and general conditions of service. In February 1992 senior officers managed to contain a similar protest within the confines of the army barracks.

Following the 1981 coup attempt, the PPP retained its dominance in Gambian party politics. At elections held in May 1982 Jawara was re-elected president, with 72% of the votes, overwhelmingly defeating Dibba (who conducted his campaign from detention). Once again the PPP emerged with a clear majority in parliament, winning 27 seats, compared with three obtained by the NCP and five by independent candidates. Two new political parties appeared during 1986: the Gambia People's Party (GPP), under the leadership of Assan Musa Camara, who (like Dibba in the 1970s) had previously been a leading figure in the PPP, and the People's Democratic Organization for Independence and Socialism (PDOIS), led by Halifa Sallah and Sam Sarr—both of whom had been detained briefly in 1981. With a distinctive socialist approach, the PDOIS offered a clear ideological choice to the electorate (in reality, the other major parties differed little in terms of political doctrine). However, at the May 1987 elections neither of the new parties took a single parliamentary seat. The NCP increased its representation in parliament to five elective seats, but all of the remainder were won by the PPP. In the presidential election Jawara took 59% of the votes, defeating Dibba (27%) and Camara (14%). Prior to the April 1992 elections Jawara announced that he wished to retire from politics, but was said to have been persuaded by his party colleagues to seek re-election once more. He proceeded to secure 58% of the popular vote. Dibba (who won 22% of the votes), Camara and two others also contested the presidency. Although the 1992 elections (the last before the imposition of military rule) marked an upturn in support for opposition parties—in the parliamentary elections the NCP won six seats, the GPP two, and independent candidates three—the results did not deviate significantly from the pattern set in all previous post-independence elections, and Jawara and the PPP (whose parliamentary representation had been reduced to 25 members) retained comfortable majorities.

Jawara reshuffled his cabinet following the 1992 elections. One of the more unexpected aspects of this reorganization was the promotion to the vice-presidency of Saihou Sabally, regarded by many as tainted by allegations of corruption, in place of the widely respected Bakary Dabo (who now took the finance portfolio). Sabally's appointment fuelled increasingly outspoken allegations of corruption and mismanagement in public life. In late 1993 leading Christian and Islamic clerics in Banjul publicly accused the government of corruption, embezzlement and lack of financial accountability, which they claimed were causing hardship for the majority of the population and benefiting only a few élite. In January 1994 Jawara announced the establishment of an independent public complaints commission, with the aim of combating corruption in public life. However, while public dissatisfaction with the PPP regime certainly appeared to be increasing in late 1993 and early 1994, there was little indication of the dramatic political change that was shortly to occur.

MILITARY GOVERNMENT

On 22 July 1994 Jawara and his government were overthrown by a military *coup d'état*. Although the coup appears to have had little or no advance planning, it took place without bloodshed and met with very little resistance. Soldiers from the GNA seized key installations, including the airport and national radio headquarters, and marched on government buildings in Banjul. Jawara and some of his government colleagues (including vice-president Sabally), boarded a US naval vessel that was anchored off the coast in preparation for scheduled training exercises involving US marines and the GNA. Jawara appealed unsuccessfully for the rebels to return to barracks, and for the US marines to put down the coup, and he and his entourage were disembarked in Senegal. (Jawara subsequently took up residence in the United Kingdom.) In The Gambia, meanwhile, senior members of the army and the police, together with those

members of the government who had not escaped, were arrested and placed in detention. That evening radio broadcasts were made announcing that government was now in the hands of an armed forces provisional ruling council (AFPRC), led by Lt (later Col) Yahya Jammeh. The other members of the council were Lts Sana Sabally, Sadibou Hydara, Edward Singhateh and Yankuba Touray (all of whom were susequently promoted to the rank of captain). While they were of diverse ethnic background, the common feature of this group was their extreme youth: none was more than 30 years of age at the time of the coup. The AFPRC announced the suspension of the constitution, a ban on all political parties and political activity, the temporary closure of the country's borders and a dusk-to-dawn curfew, and gave warning that they would 'mercilessly crush' any opposition to the take-over. Jammeh's early speeches, justifying the coup by portraying the Jawara regime as corrupt, inefficient and not truly democratic, while promising 'a new era of freedom, progress, democracy and accountability', resembled many postcoup speeches in other African states. The absence of any mention of specific changes to be sought in the country's political or economic system probably reflected the rather precipitate manner in which the coup had occurred. Although not articulated by the new regime, grievances specific to the army—such as the late or non-payment of salaries to soldiers involved in ECOMOG operations in Liberia, poor standards of food and accommodation for troops, and the lack of prospects for promotion caused by the deployment in senior positions in the GNA of officers seconded in accordance with a bilateral defence accord with Nigeria—could also be regarded as motives for the coup. Jammeh announced the formation of a provisional cabinet, comprising both soldiers and civilians. Almost immediately, however, two military members of the cabinet were dismissed and arrested. The frequency of cabinet changes has been a continuous feature of the Jammeh regime. In order to increase the technical competence of the cabinet, Jammeh appointed two ex-PPP ministers: Bakary Dabo resumed the finance portfolio, and Fafa M'bai (a minister of justice in the early 1980s, who had led an anti-corruption campaign but subsequently himself been implicated in allegations of financial impropriety and forced to resign) as minister of justice and attorney-general, but both appointments proved relatively brief. Dabo was dismissed in October 1994 and fled the country in the following month (see below), while M'bai was removed from office in March 1995 and subsequently arrested and charged with corruption.

International reaction to the military take-over, especially from major aid donors such as the USA, the European Union (EU), the United Kingdom and Japan, was generally unfavourable, and, when attempts to persuade the AFPRC to restore the elected regime failed, efforts were concentrated on a fairly rapid return to democratic rule. Arab donor states such as Saudi Arabia and Kuwait agreed, none the less, to continue funding aid projects; relations with Libya improved significantly, and the restoration of full diplomatic relations (severed in 1980) in November 1994 was accompanied by Libyan aid. Diplomatic links were established with Taiwan in July 1995, whereupon the People's Republic of China (which had maintained aid to The Gambia following the coup) suspended relations.

In September 1994 the AFPRC established several commissions of inquiry to examine allegations of corruption and maladministration in the public sector under Jawara. Commissions examining the assets of public officers, the working of government departments and public corporations, as well as the issue of land allocation, were set up under the guidance of senior legal practitioners, recruited from Sierra Leone and Ghana as well as locally. Many prominent political figures and civil servants from the Jawara period, together with large numbers of business executives (many of whom had strong political connections), were summoned before the commissions to answer for their past actions; cases involving individuals who had fled the country since the coup were examined in their absence. Even allowing for the fact that the commissions were designed, in part, to discredit the previous regime, they were seen to act according to due legal process and without direct interference from the military AFPRC, and they undoubtedly uncovered significant and genuine evidence of widespread, systematic corruption, as well as high levels of bureaucratic confusion and chaos. The commissions continued to operate in 1995–98.

The AFPRC survived an attempted counter-coup from within the military in November 1994 in which the coup leader and several other officers were killed. Allegations of summary executions following the defeat of the coup attempt were denied by the authorities. Several senior PPP figures were arrested but later released. Bakary Dabo fled to Senegal amid unsubstantiated government assertions that he had been involved in the plot. A significant repercussion of this coup attempt was that the British government issued a warning to travellers that The Gambia was unsafe, causing most major tour companies in the United Kingdom to suspend operations in The Gambia. This had devastating consequences for the tourist industry (see Economy).

An even more serious attempt at a coup took place in January 1995, when two of the most senior AFPRC members, vice-chairman Sana Sabally and the minister of the interior, Sadibou Hydara, reportedly attempted to assassinate Jammeh and seize power. The attempt was defeated, and Sabally and Hydara were imprisoned. Hydara died in prison in June. Edward Singhateh was promoted to the post of AFPRC vice-chairman, while Capt. Lamin Bajo and Capt. Ebou Jallow were appointed to the council as minister of the interior and AFPRC spokesman, respectively. Official reports of events surrounding the attempted *putsch* were contradicted by persistent rumours in The Gambia (by their nature impossible to substantiate) that Jammeh had fabricated allegations of a coup in order to eliminate those whom he regarded as potential rivals. With their detention, an open campaign of vilification of Sabally and Hydara was undertaken by the remaining members of the AFPRC. In December Sabally was sentenced by court martial to nine years' imprisonment for plotting to overthrow Jammeh.

Unity within the reorganized AFPRC was short-lived. In October 1995 Ebou Jallow fled the country amid accusations that he had embezzled government funds amounting to US $3m. and was conspiring with members of the banned PPP. Jallow denied the theft, and accused Jammeh's regime of tyranny and corruption—producing documentary evidence purportedly relating to the latter, although in January 1998 a Swiss court ordered Jallow to return US $3m. held in a private bank account there. In December two further senior military figures (not AFPRC members) fled the country: these were Capt. Pa Sanneh, head of the Gambian contingent of ECOMOG, and Maj. David Coker, third-in-command of the GNA.

The frequency of arrests of politicians and journalists (and for foreign—mainly Liberian and Sierra Leonean—journalists, deportations), as well as allegations of the harassment of civilians by the military, fuelled accusations of authoritarianism on the part of the Jammeh regime. There was considerable national outrage in June 1995, when the body was discovered of Ousman Koro Ceesay, since March the finance minister (and an 'honorary member' of the AFPRC): although the authorities attributed his death to a motor accident, rumours circulated of more suspicious circumstances. Ceesay was replaced in the government by Bala Garba Jahumpa, a former minister of finance. In that month the AFPRC established a new police organization, the national intelligence agency (NIA), which was given wide powers of surveillance and arrest, and in August the restoration of the death penalty (abolished in 1993) was attributed to an increase in the incidence of murder. A government decree issued in November 1995 accorded the minister of the interior (an AFPRC member) unlimited powers of arrest and detention without charge: the decree appeared to have been frequently used against suspected opponents of the regime, and there were increasingly frequent allegations of the torture of political detainees.

Constitutional Debate

Of paramount importance following the seizure of power by the military was the issue of a return to democratic civilian rule, to which the AFPRC consistently expressed its commitment. Much public debate focused on the timetable for, and manner of, such a restoration. In October the AFPRC announced what it termed its programme of rectification and transition to democratic constitutional rule, which provided for the restitution of elected civilian organs of state in 1998—four years from the seizure of power. This timetable was widely criticized both within The Gambia and abroad. Gambian trade unions, professional associations, former opposition politicians and journalists united to condemn the length of the proposed transitional period. Internationally, the intended duration of military rule was denounced by the United Kingdom, the USA, the European Union (EU) and the Commonwealth, as well as by human rights groups and many others. Apparently in response to such generally adverse reactions, Jammeh announced at the end of November 1994 the establishment of a national consultative committee (NCC) to examine the question of the transition, and indicated that he was willing to reconsider the timetable. The NCC consisted of 23 members appointed by the AFPRC: its chairman was Dr Lenrie Peters, a widely respected writer and physician, and it included representatives of trade unions, religious groups, women's organizations, professional associations and leading traditional chiefs. Following nation-wide consultations and meetings with representatives of The Gambia's aid donors, in January 1995 the NCC recommended to the AFPRC that the transition period be reduced to two years from the time of the coup, a timetable which had majority support within the country and was more likely to be acceptable to external creditors. Jammeh subsequently agreed to accept the revised programme, but rejected a further NCC suggestion that an interim civilian government be established while he remained as head of state. The reduction in the proposed duration of military rule was generally welcomed in The Gambia and abroad; however, prominent creditors, including the EU and the USA, continued to withhold assistance, stating that they wished to see a shorter period of transition to civilian government.

After some delay, attributed to financial problems, the AFPRC established a constitutional review commission (CRC) in April 1995, under the chairmanship of a Ghanaian lawyer, Justice Gilbert Mensah Quaye. The CRC began a series of public hearings, at which all citizens were invited to make proposals regarding constitutional change. One of the most contentious issues to emerge at the public hearings, and one much discussed in the Gambian press, was the question of what should be the minimum age for presidential candidates. Underlying this debate was the widespread belief that Jammeh was himself planning to contest the presidency in 1996, although Jammeh consistently refused to confirm or deny this. Those suggesting a minimum age of 40 were interpreted as seeking to preclude Jammeh's candidature. There was at this time increasing criticism that Jammeh's tours of the country resembled an election campaign, while civilian politicians were still forbidden by military decree to organize political meetings of any sort. Jammeh's cause was, moreover, now supported by the July 22 Movement: although ostensibly a non-governmental development organization, the movement appeared to be functioning politically.

The CRC submitted its draft document to the AFPRC in November 1995, although none of its findings was made public until March 1996—prompting suspicion in some quarters that in the intervening period the AFPRC had been able to accept, amend, or reject the commission's recommendations without public consultation. In April it was announced that the elections were to be postponed, on the grounds that there was insufficient time to complete preparations, and in May voting was set for September (presidential) and December (legislative); the ban on political parties was to remain in place until after the constitutional referendum, which was to take place in August. Many aspects of the constitution and the new electoral arrangements provoked concern among opponents of the AFPRC, who stated that the transition process had now been manipulated to promote Jammeh's election to the presidency and give political advantage to his supporters. The stipulation that presidential candidates must be aged between 30 and 65 years ensured Jammeh's eligibility for office, while preventing many veteran politicians from participating; there was to be no restriction on the number of times a president might seek re-election. The revised demarcation of constituency boundaries, it was alleged, would unduly favour the incumbent regime, and significant financial obstacles to political organizations seeking elected public office had been presented by raising both the deposit required from candidates and the proportion of the vote necessary to secure the deposit's return. Meanwhile, human rights organizations were critical of effective provision in the proposed constitution for the revocation of political freedoms in the event of a state of public emergency.

In January 1996 Jawara was charged *in absentia* with embezzlement, following investigations into the alleged diversion of proceeds (estimated at more than US $11m.) from the sale of petroleum donated by Nigeria; similarly charged was a Sierra Leonean business executive, now resident in Panama. Moreover, the possible involvement in the affair of a former vice-president of Sierra Leone, Abdulai Conteh, who had been resident in The Gambia since 1993, was also reported to have been investigated during anti-corruption proceedings: Conteh was briefly detained in mid-October 1995 and subsequently ordered to leave the country. During March–April 1996 the confiscation was ordered of the assets in The Gambia of Jawara and 11 former government members. In July the minister of health and social welfare was arrested and charged with the misappropriation of state funds.

The referendum on the constitution took place (one day later than scheduled) on 8 August 1996. The rate of participation was high (more than 85%), and more than 70.4% of voters were reported to have endorsed the new document. A presidential decree was issued on 14 August reauthorizing party political activity. Shortly afterwards, however, it was announced that the PPP, the NCP and the GPP were to be prohibited from contesting the forthcoming elections, as were all holders of executive office in the 30 years prior to the 1994 military takeover; thus, the only pre-coup parties authorized to contest the elections were the PDOIS and the People's Democratic Party. The effective ban on participation in the restoration of elected institutions of all those associated with political life prior to July 1994 provoked strong criticism from the Commonwealth, whose Ministerial Action Group on the Harare Declaration (CMAG) had hitherto made a significant contribution to the transition process. At the same time it was announced that, following consultations between the military authorities and the independent electoral commission (which had expressed concern that political organizations would have insufficient time to campaign for the elections), the presidential poll was to be postponed by two weeks, to 26 September 1996.

ELECTIONS AND BEYOND

As the ban on all political organizations remained in force until only weeks before the presidential election, the formation of parties was a fairly rushed affair. As had been widely anticipated, the July 22 Movement transformed itself into an official political grouping to support Jammeh's campaign for the presidency, styling itself the Alliance for Patriotic Reorientation and Construction (APRC). The PDOIS nominated Sidia Jatta as its presidential candidate. Some of the elements associated with the pre-1994 parliamentary parties formed the United Democratic Party (UDP) under the leadership of a prominent human rights lawyer, Ousainou Darboe, who became the party's candidate. Hamat Bah was to contest the presidency as the candidate of the 'personalist' National Reconciliation Party (NRP). In early September 1996 Jammeh and his AFPRC colleagues formally retired from the GNA: Jammeh was to contest the presidency as a civilian, as required by the constitution.

The short presidential campaign was widely condemned by opponents of the Jammeh regime as having been neither free nor fair, while international observers, including CMAG, expressed doubts as to the credibility of the election. The state-owned media, including the recently established television service, promoted Jammeh while offering minimal coverage of the other candidates' campaigns. Moreover, the APRC enjoyed privileged access to government finance and resources. There were reports of violence and intimidation, often involving military personnel, directed especially at the UDP. As polling proceeded, on 26 September 1996, Ousainou Darboe sought refuge in the Senegalese embassy in Banjul, having received threats to his life; he remained there until the end of the month. The official results of voting, issued on 27 September, gave Jammeh 55.77% of the votes. Darboe polled 35.84%, Bah 5.52% and Jatta 2.87%. A further set of 'leaked' results later indicated a victory for Darboe, but these had limited credibility. The dissolution of the AFPRC was also announced on 27 September: pending the legislative elections, the cabinet was to be the sole provisional governing body. Jammeh was inaugurated as president on 18 October. In early November an unconditional amnesty was proclaimed for more than 40 political detainees, among them former government ministers detained since July 1994.

Following considerable debate among the opposition parties as to whether to participate in the legislative elections, now scheduled (after a further postponement) for 2 January 1997, all decided to present candidates. Only the APRC had the organization and finance to field candidates in all 45 constituencies (in five of these they were unopposed); the UDP was to contest 34 seats, the PDOIS 17, and the NRP five. The APRC again made full use of state resources and media, but violence and intimidation were generally acknowledged as having occurred at a much reduced level. Some opposition activists, including one UDP candidate, were, none the less, detained for all or part of the campaign period. Voting took place as scheduled, and the Gambian authorities, opposition groups and most international observers expressed broad satisfaction at the conduct of the poll. The official results of the elections gave the APRC 28 seats (plus the five unopposed) in the new national assembly, with 52% of the votes cast. The UDP won seven seats, with 34% of the votes, the PDOIS one seat, with 8%, and the NRP two seats, with 2%; two independent candidates also secured seats. Jammeh's presidency thus had the backing of a significant legislative majority. As head of state, Jammeh was empowered by the constitution to nominate four additional members of parliament, from whom the speaker (and deputy speaker) would be chosen. The opening session of the national assembly, held on 16 January, accordingly elected Mustapha Wadda, previously secretary-general of the APRC and secretary at the presidency, as speaker. This session denoted the full entry into force of the constitution and thus the inauguration of the second republic.

In early February 1997 most remaining long-term political detainees, including army and police personnel, were released. Later in the month, none the less, there were new arrests: among those detained were Lt Landing Sanneh, the commander of the state guard, and Maj. Pa Modou Ann, the commander of the newly-established Gambia national guards. In March Isatou Njie-Saidy, secretary of state for health, social welfare and women's affairs, was appointed vice-president, the first woman to hold this position. However, most of the powers and duties hitherto associated with the vice-presidency were transferred to the secretary of state for the office of the president, a post now held by Edward Singhateh (who, at 27, remained too young to hold the office of vice-president).

In the national assembly a high proportion of the debate in the legislature's first months was taken up with procedural disputes, as opposition members accused Jammeh of failing to abide by the constitution. Furthermore, opposition representatives complained that their use of the national assembly as a platform for criticism of the government was restricted by the actions of the legislature's speaker (appointed by Jammeh) in frequently blocking parliamentary questions and operations. Thus, attempts by the opposition to instigate investigations into what they alleged were serious instances of corruption within government repeatedly failed.

In April 1997 the trial began (in camera) of five alleged mercenaries suspected of involvement in the November 1996 attack on the Farafenni barracks. The accused apparently confirmed press reports at the time of the attack that they had formed part of a 40-strong commando group, trained in Libya and led by Kukoi Samba Sanyang, which had fought for Charles Taylor's National Patriotic Front of Liberia during the early 1990s. Four of the accused (three Gambians and one Senegalese national) were subsequently sentenced to death—the fifth defendant had died in detention in May 1997. In early October, however, the supreme court ruled that the convictions, on charges of treason, were not sustainable, and ordered that the four be retried on conspiracy charges. Meanwhile, the arrest of a further mercenary had been reported in mid-April; some 13 other suspects remained at large.

In July 1997 an attack, attributed to former GNA troops, on a military installation at Kartong, near the Senegalese border, resulted in the death of at least one soldier; weapons were stolen during the raid. In late October 1998 three former members of the armed forces were sentenced to death for their part in the raid.

In July 1997 CMAG reiterated its previous concerns regarding the lack of a 'fully inclusive' political system in The Gambia, urging the immediate removal of the ban on political activities by certain parties and individuals; the group also sought demonstration of the Jammeh administration's expressed commitment to the observance of human rights and the rule of law, and appealed to the government to investigate allegations of the harassment of members of the opposition. In September, none the less, CMAG reported signs of progress in the democratization process. However, the tax on the registration of independent radio stations was more than doubled in January 1998, prompting opposition protests of censorship. In the following month the main independent station, Citizen FM, was ordered to cease broadcasts, shortly after its director and a station journalist were arrested. (The station had recently broadcast information regarding the NIA, although the closure was attributed by the authorities to the station's failure to pay taxes.) The director of Citizen FM, Baboucar Gaye, subsequently launched a legal appeal against the closure of the station and the *New Citizen* newspaper. Gaye's appeal was finally heard in late May 2000, after a series of lengthy postponements, which had prompted accusations that the government was employing delaying tactics. In July of that year the high court reversed the original judgment and ordered the authorities to return the apparatus of Citizen FM to Gaye. The state of the independent media again gave cause for concern in May 1999, when the *Daily Observer*, the only remaining newspaper which openly criticized the government, was bought from its Liberian owner by Amadou Samba, a Gambian businessman closely associated with Jammeh. Despite Samba's assurances that he would not interfere in editorial matters, the news editor, Demba Jawo, and other journalists associated with criticisms of government policy were subsequently removed from their posts. In July *The Independent*, a privately-owned newspaper, which had been recently launched, was ordered to suspend publication because of alleged irregularities in its registration. Critics of the government, however, suggested that the suspension had been provoked by an article written by a member of the UDP, which accused the Jammeh regime of widespread corruption.

Opposition activists continued to allege harassment by the government throughout 1998 and early 1999. In May 1998 nine people were arrested in a raid on the mosque at Brikama, among those detained was a prominent critic of Jammeh, Lamine Wa Juwara. A member of the UDP, Juwara had initiated a lawsuit seeking compensation for alleged wrongful imprisonment during the transition period. The UDP leader, Ousainou Darboe, was also briefly imprisoned shortly afterwards. In July a seminar on government structures, attended by several international organizations, was interrupted by members of the APRC's militant 'Action Group' who forcibly removed Juwara. The government blamed Juwara for fomenting unrest, but promised to investigate the incident; meanwhile, critics claimed that the activities of the 'Action Group' had official support. In the same month Juwara's claim for damages, arising from his 20-month detention following the 1994 coup, was rejected by the supreme court on the grounds that the constitution contained a clause granting immunity to the former AFPRC in connection with the transition period.

In January 1999 Jammeh unexpectedly announced a major cabinet reshuffle, dismissing four ministers. At the same time the managing director of the National Water and Electricity Co was dismissed. No official explanation was given for the changes, although it was rumoured that a recent audit had revealed financial mismanagement in some government departments.

In late May 1999 the leader of the youth wing of the UDP, Momodou Shyngle Nyassi, was abducted by the security forces and reportedly subjected to ill-treatment. He was released without charge after nearly a month, following the intervention of the Gambian high court and diplomatic pressure from the EU. Nyassi later declared his intention to take legal action against his abductors, who he alleged included members of the July 22 Movement (a branch of the APRC). In June, in response to international criticism of his government's treatment of the independent press and of the opposition, Jammeh spoke out against western donor countries, which he accused of using aid as a conduit for the imposition of western standards of democracy and human rights on countries with different cultural values.

In September 1999 international attention was again focused on Jammeh's attitude to the press, when a reporter and editor were arrested after the publication of an article in *The Observer* alleging that a Senegalese helicopter had flown over Jammeh's home village and exchanged gunfire with presidential guards. In December staff from *The Independent* newspaper were arrested and charged with libel following the publication of an article suggesting that Jammeh had divorced his wife and remarried. The government was further embarrassed in October by the flight to Senegal of the APRC secretary-general, Phokay Makalo, who had allegedly embezzled party funds, while in January 2000 an APRC deputy was detained on suspicion of drugs-trafficking. In late December 1999 Jammeh dismissed the secretary of state for agriculture, and in early 2000 a further minor cabinet reshuffle was carried out.

In December 1999 Jammeh called an extraordinary congress of the APRC in order to discuss the culture of embezzlement described in a report into official corruption by the auditor-general. Jammeh's announcement at the end of the congress that corrupt officials would be pursued through the courts irrespective of their political affiliation was welcomed by the opposition, although critics of the government noted that Jammeh had promised to rid The Gambia of corruption when he assumed power in 1994. Jammeh subsequently dismissed the Gambian ambassadors to France and Belgium, whose embassies had been criticized by the report. Further allegations of government corruption emerged in early January 2000 after the disclosure, during legal proceedings in the United Kingdom, that significant sums generated by the sale of petroleum had been paid into an anonymous Swiss bank account. The crude petroleum had been granted to The Gambia for trading purposes by the Nigerian government between August 1996 and June 1998, reportedly in recognition of Jammeh's opposition in 1995 to the imposition of sanctions by the Commonwealth against Nigeria. The UDP leader, Ousainou Darboe, subsequently alleged that Jammeh had illegally diverted more than US $1.9m. of the proceeds of the sale of the petroleum. Jammeh vigorously denied any involvement in the matter, and the government offered no further comment. Journalists continued, however, to attempt to uncover the beneficiaries of the Swiss bank account, while in May 2000 opposition deputies demanded that the national assembly create a commission of inquiry to investigate the allegations; the motion was, however, blocked by APRC deputies, who requested more time to allow them to study documents obtained by the UDP relating to Jammeh's alleged involvement in the matter.

On 15 January 2000 the security forces announced that they had forestalled an attempted military coup. It was reported that, during efforts to arrest the conspirators, Lt Almamo Manneh of the state guard had been killed, and the commander of the state guard, Lt Landing Sanneh, who was the officer in charge of security at the presidential palace, had been wounded. Another member of the state guard was killed on the following day while attempting to evade arrest. The secretary of state for the interior, Ousman Badjie, strenuously denied rumours that the authorities had invented the plot as a pretext to purge the state guard and as a means of diverting press attention from the petroleum scandal. Lt Sanneh's wife continued, however, to deny that her husband had been involved in a coup attempt, while opponents of the government demanded to see evidence of the existence of the plot. None the less, the government refused to release further details on the grounds that they might prejudice any future criminal proceedings.

In March 2000 the secretary of state for justice was replaced; no reason was given for the dismissal. In the same month it was announced that municipal and rural elections were to be held in November, while presidential elections were to be held in October 2001. Five political parties announced their intention of contesting the 118 seats for municipal and regional councillors in what were to be the first local elections to be held since 1992. In late March 2000 Col (retd) Sam Sillah was appointed president of the UDP. Sillah was expected to contest the presidential elections, scheduled for late 2001.

In mid-April 2000 student demonstrations took place in Banjul, Brikama and Serrekunda to protest at the authorities' handling of the death of a student, who had been found dead in March in reportedly suspicious circumstances in a firemen's barracks. The demonstrations subsequently degenerated into serious disturbances, during which houses were looted and police and fire stations burned down. Following the intervention of the security forces, 14 people were killed and 30 were injured in Banjul and Brikama. The authorities initially denied that the security forces had fired on the crowd, suggesting that the demonstrators had included foreigners and armed bandits. However, autopsies later confirmed that the security forces had in fact used live ammunition against the demonstrators. Schools remained closed following the disturbances, and a heavy police presence was reported on the streets of Banjul, while foreign tourists were warned to remain inside their hotels. President Jammeh, who decreed a week of national mourning to commemorate the victims of the violence, later established an eight-member commission of inquiry in order to investigate the disturbances. However, in May its chairman, chief justice Felix Lartey, was obliged to appeal publicly for witnesses, owing to the widespread public cynicism regarding the independence of the commission. Later in the month Jammeh assured the UN secretary-general, Kofi Annan, who was visiting The Gambia, that those responsible for the deaths would be brought to justice, and he called for co-operation with the commission of inquiry's investigations.

In May 2000 the secretary of state for territorial administration and religious affairs, Capt. (retd) Lamin Bajo, was dismissed from his post. In mid-June it was announced that the UDP leader, Ousainou Darboe, had been arrested by police and accused, along with 80 of his supporters, of murdering an APRC activist. In the same month four men, including Lt Lalo Jaiteh, Jammeh's former aide-de-camp, were arrested on suspicion of planning a *coup d'état*. In August the detainees were committed for trial on charges of treason.

In July 2000 Jammeh reportedly threatened, in the course of a speech to an APRC youth rally, to bury those who threatened the stability of The Gambia six feet deep. His comment was seized upon by the press and by the opposition as a veiled threat to anyone seeking to challenge his regime. Fatoumata Jahumpa, the president's director of press and public relations subsequently criticized the press for ignoring the statements on policy made by Jammeh in his speech in favour of provoking controversy. Jahumpa also accused human rights activists, who she claimed had been spreading rumours of illegal detentions and executions, of being opposition activists seeking to denigrate the government. Later in the month two journalists were briefly detained by police following the publication of an article in *The*

Independent alleging that a number of prisoners had been detained for several years without charge.

In early August 2000 the administrative secretary of the APRC suggested that it would not be possible to hold local government elections in late November as scheduled, since the national assembly had yet to approve the local government act, which was intended to regulate voter registration and electoral boundaries. In the same month the premises of the independent radio station, Radio 1 FM, were attacked by arsonists; it was widely believed that the attack was connected to the station's popular Sunday Newshour programme, which had recently featured a critical interview with Fatoumata Jahumpa.

FOREIGN RELATIONS

The Gambia maintains generally good relations with most countries in the region. Despite the presence in Senegal of prominent opponents of his regime, Jammeh has sought to improve relations with that country, and in January 1996 the two countries signed an agreement aimed at increasing bilateral trade and at minimizing cross-border smuggling. A further agreement, concluded in April 1997, was designed to facilitate the trans-border movement of goods destined for re-export. In June the two countries agreed to take joint measures to combat insecurity, illegal immigration, arms-trafficking and drugs-smuggling. In January 1998 the Senegalese government welcomed an offer by Jammeh to mediate in the conflict in the southern province of Casamance (see Recent History of Senegal): the separatist MFDC is chiefly composed of the Diola ethnic group, of which Jammeh is a member. In June 1999 Jammeh hosted a meeting of the various rebel factions in Banjul, the purpose of which was to facilitate agreement amongst them prior to negotiations with the Senegalese government. In late June 1998 Jammeh also offered to mediate in the conflict between the government and rebel forces in Guinea-Bissau; the rebel leader, Gen. Ansumane Mane, was a Diola of Gambian extraction, and many refugees from Sierra Leone had taken refuge in The Gambia. In January 1999 The Gambia agreed to provide troops for an ECOMOG peace-keeping mission in Guinea-Bissau. After the defeat of goverment forces in Guinea-Bissau in May 1999, the Gambian authorities secured in June the safe passage of former President Vieira to The Gambia on medical grounds, from where he departed for Portugal. In late June the interim president of Guinea-Bissau, Malam Bacai Sanha, visited Jammeh to thank him for his intervention; both presidents expressed their desire to co-operate to attain a lasting peace in the region, and a joint communiqué to that effect was signed in April 2000. The Gambia also maintains particularly cordial relations with Nigeria, Libya and Taiwan.

Economy

JOHN A. WISEMAN

Revised for this edition by the Editor.

Apart from the development of a significant tourist industry, the principal features of the Gambian economy have altered relatively little in the post-independence period. The country has remained poor, underdeveloped, and dependent. The often stated goal of transforming the country into the 'Singapore of Africa' would appear to have no foundation in reality. With a small population of little more than 1m. (1,229,000, according to UN estimates, at mid-1998), high levels of illiteracy, no significant mineral resources, a poorly-developed infrastructure and an erratic, arid climate, the prospects for dramatic economic development are slight. Official statistics on the economy have not been noted for their reliability, partly due to administrative weakness and partly due to a significant (and inherently unmeasurable) informal sector. More positively, there has been a moderate improvement in health and education provision, access to safe drinking water has widened, and life expectancy has increased while infant mortality has declined. Most importantly, the country has, despite widespread poverty, avoided the

famine and food insecurity experienced in many other African states.

AGRICULTURE AND FISHING

More than 70% of the Gambian population are directly dependent on agriculture for their livelihood, making this sector overwhelmingly the largest employer of labour, accounting for an estimated 73% of the labour force in 1998. For the most part, agricultural production is still organized through small-scale peasant units in which kinship predominates: over 90% of agricultural production is derived from this type of farming. Traditional patterns of shifting cultivation are widely used, and the bulk of production is for subsistence purposes. Large-scale plantation agriculture, whether privately-operated or state-run, is minimal. Women play a key role in the agricultural labour force, especially in the cultivation of subsistence crops. Attempts by the Jawara administration to increase capital investment in agriculture, such as by the establishment of the Agricultural

Development Bank in 1981, largely failed as a result of corruption and mismanagement. Large loans were made to powerful élites who then defaulted on repayments, causing the bank's collapse. Foreign non-governmental organizations (NGOs) have become the main source of investment capital for small-scale peasant farmers. The most crucial factor affecting agricultural production is the level of rainfall. Since the mid-1960s the country has experienced recurrent drought, of varying severity, which has adversely affected production levels and led to significant environmental degradation, especially the damage caused by the penetration of saline river water.

The predominant cash crop in The Gambia is groundnuts, first introduced from America in the 18th century. About one-half of cultivated land is devoted to groundnuts—although this proportion has been declining slowly since the early 1970s. While the country produces less than 1% of the world's exported groundnuts, the national significance of the crop is immense. Some 20% of groundnut production is for domestic consumption by growers, the rest being cultivated for export, particularly in a processed form (groundnut-processing constitutes the major industrial activity). The cultivation of groundnuts is almost entirely undertaken by men, who therefore have major control over cash income in rural areas. The government-controlled Gambia Produce Marketing Board (GPMB) had a monopoly over the purchase and export marketing of groundnuts from 1973 until 1990, when this was removed to allow competition from the private sector. In common with other crops, fluctuations in rainfall levels have a major effect on production levels from year to year. Additionally, the relative levels of official prices paid to producers in The Gambia and in neighbouring Senegal are a major determinant in groundnut sales. In years when producer prices are high in Senegal much of the Gambian crop is smuggled across the border into Senegal: estimates suggest, for example, that in 1986/87 some 50%–70% of Gambian groundnuts were sold in Senegal. Official statistics on groundnut production tend to be somewhat misleading. Even allowing for problems of measurements, the 1996/97 groundnut crop was reported to be the worst in living memory. Recorded production of 16,000 metric tons was less than half that of 1995/96 and only about one-tenth of annual crops during the boom years of the 1970s. The dramatic decline was officially attributed to a number of factors, including poor seed varieties, low rainfall, shortage of fertilizers, bureaucratic inefficiency and labour shortages caused by migration to urban areas. Production recovered, however, in late 1990s.

For subsistence purposes, rice is a more important crop than groundnuts. Most of the crop is consumed by producers and their families, although some is sold locally; the country remains a net importer of rice. Traditionally rice has been grown (almost entirely by women) in the swamplands along the edge of the Gambia river, but since independence there have been several projects intended to expand pump-irrigated rice production, the majority of which were supported by foreign technical assistance. While increased rice production would provide the best route to the goal of self-sufficiency in basic foodstuffs, the rate of population growth continues to exceed increases in output. Other important subsistence crops include millet, sorghum and cassava. In recent years there has been some expansion of fruit cultivation (bananas, mangoes, papayas and oranges) and horticulture. Produced mainly for subsistence purposes and local sales, these also provide about 5% of export earnings, with the export of fruit and vegetables accounting for an estimated 6.6% of export earnings in 1999. Livestock-rearing makes a contribution to subsistence in many parts of the country. Cattle, especially the more disease-resistant N'Dama strain, are an important source of meat, milk and hides. Most peasant farmers raise small numbers of goats, sheep and chickens. Fishing, largely using traditional methods, is an important source of local food, while the export of fish and fish products accounted for an estimated 12.6% of total exports in 1999.

The 1999 budget speech revealed further problems for Gambian agriculture when it was announced that the previous year had seen a 25% decline in output in the agricultural sector, which included a 48% decline in fisheries. In 1998 there were also serious problems with government purchasing arrangements for the groundnut crop with the result that many farmers sold their produce in Senegal. In January 1999 the government took over the assets of the privately-owned Gambia Groundnut Corpn (GGC) and therefore also became involved in the marketing of groundnuts. The IMF strongly criticized the take over, and stressed the importance of a rapid resolution to the government's dispute with the GGC in order to ensure the successful marketing of the 1999/2000 crop and the restoration of investor confidence in the groundnut sector.

TOURISM

The post-independence development of the tourist industry represents the most important and successful attempt at economic diversification and expansion in The Gambia. Prior to the 1994 *coup d'état* tourism had risen to become the country's largest source of foreign exchange. The industry began in 1965, but it was not until 1972 that its development was seriously undertaken by the government with the creation of 'tourism development areas'. Tourists initially came mainly from Sweden, but these were rapidly overtaken in numbers by British visitors, who came to constitute between one-third and one-half of tourist arrivals. Despite some diversification, the vast majority of tourists are still from western Europe. Tourism in The Gambia is mostly in the form of 'packages' organized by major western European (especially British) tour operators, whose decisions on whether or not to expand the promotion of tourism to The Gambia have a very major impact on the development of the industry. The independent, 'non-package' tourist sector has remained very small. Largely for climatic reasons the main tourist season runs from October to April, during which time The Gambia has the considerable advantage of warm, dry conditions. Apart from rainfall in May–September, climatic disadvantages in this period include extreme heat and humidity, rendering The Gambia much less attractive to tourists. Attempts to promote off-season tourism have been generally ineffective, and most employees in the sector are thus laid off during these months. The rainy season marks the most active period in farming, but evidence suggests that very few workers in tourism actually return to farming during the tourist low-season. Despite its significant attractions for ornithologists and for those with an interest in African life and culture, The Gambia is mainly perceived by visitors as a 'beach' destination. Hotel development, to international standards, has therefore taken place mainly in the coastal areas and especially in the strip running from Bakau to Kotu Point. Attempts to attract tourists up-river for at least part of their stay have met with little success, apart from short day-trips organized by the hotels and tour companies. In a good year The Gambia might expect to receive up to 100,000 tourists, but actual numbers are sensitive to a number of factors, including economic conditions in western Europe and, of late, political uncertainty in The Gambia itself. According to the IMF, about one-third of the formal-sector workforce was employed in the tourist sector in 1992/93; elsewhere, it has been estimated that some 10% of the population are totally dependent on earnings from the industry. A considerable amount of tourist-related employment lies in the informal sector, which is not amenable to statistical measurement. Although there are official, government-recognized tourist guides, there are very many more unofficial guides who make their living by providing a variety of services for tourists. Woodcarvers, silversmiths, potters, tailors, weavers and—especially—taxi drivers receive considerable income from the tourist trade.

Inevitably, the tourist industry is extremely vulnerable to political developments. Tourist arrivals declined following the failed 1981 coup attempt, but the rapid return to political normality meant that this was a temporary downturn. The aftermath of the 1994 *coup d'état* posed more serious problems. European tour operators had emphasized the image of the democratic stability of the country for many years, but this image was negated by the military's seizure of power. Following the November 1994 attempted coup, the British government advised travellers that The Gambia was an 'unsafe' destination, and as a consequence most of the major British tour operators withdrew from the country; the Swedish and Danish governments offered similar warnings. Although the official advice was changed by March 1995, tourist numbers for 1994/95, at some 43,000, were less than one-half of the level in 1993/94, causing the closure of many hotels and mass unemployment in the tourist sector. For the 1995/96 season some of the main foreign tour companies chose to recommence operations in The Gambia, but others decided to maintain the suspension until the political situation became clearer. The 1995/96 season (with about 72,000 tourists) was thus better than the previous one, although arrivals remained well below pre-coup levels. To compensate for the decline in arrivals from western Europe, the government inaugurated an annual 'Roots Festival' in May 1996, designed to attract African-American visitors; the success of this venture, in terms of numbers, was relatively slight, although the festival has subsequently been much more successful. During 1996/97 there was for the first time some success in attracting significant numbers of German tourists. A new airport terminal building was opened in October 1997, as the volume of tourists began to return to pre-coup levels. The success in restoring tourist numbers to pre-coup levels was, however, thrown into uncertainty by the decision of the government in April 1999 to institute a ban on all-inclusive package holidays from the start of the next tourist season. The move, which was designed to encourage more participation by local entrepreneurs in the tourist industry, was opposed by several tour operators whose involvement is crucial to the industry.

FINANCE, AID AND TRADE

At independence the Gambian pound replaced the colonial West African Currency Board pound, at parity with sterling. This parity was maintained up to the inauguration of the Central Bank of The Gambia in March 1971. In July of that year the dalasi (divided into 100 bututs) was adopted as the new national currency, with an exchange rate of D5 = £1. With minor adjustments this rate was retained until, as part of the economic recovery programme (ERP—see below), the fixed exchange was abandoned and replaced by a floating rate. In recent years a rate of D15–D20 = £1 has prevailed, and there has been very little difference between official and informal rates (unlike in many sub-Saharan African countries, the latter is only slightly higher than the former).

The Gambia has since independence been heavily dependent on external funding from a variety of bilateral and multilateral sources. Development assistance has frequently exceeded more than one-half of gross national product. Until the 1994 coup the major foreign donors were the European Union (EU), the USA, the United Kingdom, Canada, the Nordic countries, Japan, Saudi Arabia and the People's Republic of China. Opposition by most of the donor community to the imposition of military rule resulted in significant reductions in disbursements of development aid. The EU, for example, halved financial assistance (from US $20m. to $10m.), and announced that it had no plans to renew its aid programme until elected civilian government had been restored. Most government-to-government bilateral aid programmes were either scaled down or abandoned. In an attempt to compensate for these losses, the Jammeh regime has tried to foster new sources of foreign assistance. Taiwan, notably, agreed to lend some $35m. following the restoration of diplomatic relations (severed in 1974) in July 1995; assistance was also forthcoming for the Gambian army. (The restoration of links with Taiwan led to a corresponding severance of ties with, and thus a loss of co-operation by, the People's Republic of China.) Taiwan announced an increase in its development funding in January 1997. By 1998 Taiwan had become the country's biggest unilateral aid donor. (It was widely believed that The Gambia's accession to a non-permanent seat on the UN Security Council influenced this increase in Taiwanese assistance.) The Gambia was also reported to have received significant financial assistance from Libya upon the restoration of diplomatic relations in November 1994 (after an interval of almost 15 years), and co-operation accords have, additionally, been signed with Cuba and with Iran. In 1999 Morocco announced extensive aid programmes for The Gambia; The Gambia had supported Morocco in the dispute over Western Sahara at the United Nations Security Council, while in March President Jammeh had married a Moroccan woman. The country has continued to receive considerable amounts of aid from a wide variety of (mostly Western) charitable NGOs; such aid is mainly targeted at projects designed to help the rural poor. More than 100 NGOs were operating in The Gambia in the mid-1990s. A further source of external finance is the remittances of Gambians working abroad, mainly in western Europe and the USA, to their families in The Gambia.

About one-third of The Gambia's gross domestic product (GDP) is derived from re-exports: goods imported into The Gambia under low import tariffs are then re-exported (not always in a legal manner) to other countries of the region, principally to Senegal but often as far afield as Guinea, Guinea-Bissau and Mali. Some aspects of this trade are politically sensitive, and have periodically led to border problems with Senegal (see below). By the late 1990s political instability in Guinea-Bissau and in the Casamance region of Senegal was causing disruption in the re-export trade and was blamed, in the 1999 budget speech, for a 12% shortfall in tax revenue arising from decreases in import revenues associated with this trade.

ECONOMIC RESTRUCTURING

Having performed relatively strongly in the 10 years after independence, the Gambian economy then entered a decline which by the mid-1980s had reached crisis proportions. The balance of payments was in increasing deficit, leading to an accumulation of external payments' arrears and increased external borrowing. Government expenditure continued to expand, unsupported by a parallel expansion of state revenue. Increased government intervention in the economy through loan-guarantee schemes, extended parastatal activity, subsidized interest rates and exchange and price controls had the effect of distorting the economy, and by 1984 The Gambia was unable to meet its obligations to the IMF, causing the latter to consider a ban on further drawings by the country. In response to this crisis the Jawara administration adopted its ERP in August 1985: drawn up in consultation with, and with support from, the IMF and the World Bank, this represented a significant attempt to restructure the Gambian economy. In common with other similar, IMF-inspired economic adjustment programmes undertaken elsewhere in Africa, the primary goals of the ERP were to restructure the economy by means of a reduction of unprofitable state involvement and a liberalization of economic mechanisms. One of the first measures of the ERP was the floating, in January 1986, of the dalasi by means of the creation of an inter-bank market for foreign exchange, resulting in the devaluation of the national currency. There was a 120% depreciation in the first six months, with further falls in subsequent years until a *de facto* stabilization was achieved by the early 1990s. This policy resulted in the rechannelling of significant amounts of foreign exchange from the informal sector into the official sector. The ERP also entailed considerable retrenchment in the civil service, with the loss of about 20% of jobs in the government sector. Meanwhile, producer prices for groundnuts were increased, and these two measures in combination went some way towards correcting the urban bias in the Gambian economy. The central bank first raised, then decontrolled, interest rates. Parastatal organizations were either privatized or subjected to strict financial discipline through performance contracts. For a time at least efforts were made to combat customs fraud, which led to an increase of one-third in revenue from such duties. The positive medium-term effects of the ERP included fiscal stabilization, significant reductions in inflation and higher rates of GDP growth. The programme for sustained development (PSD), inaugurated in 1990, was essentially a continuation of the economic policies of the ERP. The GPMB and the Gambia Utilities Corpn were privatized under the PSD in 1993.

Although, as noted above, the Gambian economy was damaged by reductions in foreign aid and the temporary collapse of the tourist industry following the military take-over, the Jammeh regime has not pursued any significant reversals of macroeconomic policy, and has consistently pledged its commitment to 'free-market capitalism'. Following a decline of 4.0% in 1994/95, GDP was estimated to have increased by 3.1% in 1995/96—largely reflecting the partial recovery in tourist numbers—and by 2.1% in 1996/97. Currency exchange rates remained relatively stable following the *coup d'état*, with only minor depreciations against the US dollar and the pound sterling.

For 1996/97, additional government revenues were to be derived notably by raising the retail price of petrol and by increasing fees for issuing passports. A 6% increase in public-sector pay was announced, offsetting a projected 5% rate of inflation. GDP growth of 2% was forecast for the year. A budget for the six months to the end of 1997 was presented in June of that year (thereafter, the financial year was to coincide with the calendar year).

Presenting the budget for 1998, the government stated that reserve levels, inflation and other monetary aggregates had remained broadly within target during 1998. Growth of 8.9% in 1997 and of an estimated 2.8% in 1998 in the agricultural sector contrasted with a decline of 11.1% in 1999, while the services sector continued to expand (by an estimated 5.8% in 1998), largely reflecting strong performances in the tourism and telecommunications industries. Export revenue increased in both 1998 and 1999, to some D290m. in 1999, although the cost of imports over the same period also increased, to some D2,207m. in 1999.

Despite the apparent stabilization of the economy in the post-coup period, there has been criticism in some quarters of the new regime's enthusiasm for ambitious infrastructural and other 'prestige' projects. Most of these projects have been financed by international loans. The extent of these loans was revealed in the January 1999 budget speech when it was admitted that the country's international debt had tripled since 1995; a state of affairs which may prove problematic in terms of The Gambia's long-term economic prospects. The government's long-term aim, outlined in its *Vision 2020* document published in September 1996, setting targets for all sectors of the economy, for education, health care, welfare, the environment and public administration, is to achieve the status of a middle-income economy within 25 years. The Jammeh administration hoped, moreover, that the return to government by elected civilian institutions, from early 1997, would prompt a return to the full support by the international economic community that will be essential to the achievement of strong and sustained growth. Crucial support for the Gambian economy came from the IMF, which in mid-1998 approved funding under its Enhanced Structural Adjustment Facility (ESAF) for the three-year period 1998–2000. The programme aimed to achieve real GDP growth averaging some 4.5% annually, and to restrict average inflation to 3% per year. Excluding grants, the fiscal deficit was to be reduced to the equivalent of 4.0% of GDP in 1998 and to 1.9% by the end of the period covered by the ESAF, from the equivalent of 7.8% of GDP in 1997, while the deficit on the current account of the balance of payments (before official transfers) was to be maintained at about 10% of GDP. A fundamental aim of the programme was to be encourage further private-sector development: to this end, the government had undertaken in the 1998 budget to sign binding agreements with several parastatals, notably the port authority, public transport corporation, social security and housing fund and the telecommunications and utilities operators, to reduce the role of the state on condition of the attainment of certain performance criteria. The government's decision to take over the struggling Gambia Groundnut Corporation was therefore criticized by the IMF, during the second annual ESAF review, which took place

in November 1999, as injurious to the ESAF programme's stated aim of increasing the role of the private sector and of enhancing investor confidence in The Gambia. The IMF, none the less, later announced that it was to make the second annual loan under the programme available as scheduled, although it called on the government to consolidate previous progress made in economic reform and to strengthen the fiscal position, in order to free resources for increased social and investment expenditure, during the remaining two years of the programme.

In July 2000 it was announced that preliminary indicators suggested that The Gambia might be eligible for further international assistance under the terms of the IMF-sponsored Heavily Indebted Poor Countries Initiative (HIPC Initiative). It was therefore hoped that, following further scrutiny, The Gambia would qualify for further reduction in its external debt repayments.

RELATIONS WITH SENEGAL

The formal dissolution, in September 1989, of the Senegambia confederation (see Recent History), and subsequent allegations regarding Senegal's economic 'harassment' of The Gambia, raised serious questions regarding future economic relations between the two countries. During 1990 the Senegalese authorities eased restrictions on cross-border traffic, and the conclusion, in January 1991, of a new co-operation treaty confirmed several existing bilateral agreements governing such areas as defence and security, transport and telecommunications, health, trade, fishing, agriculture and energy. None the less, Senegal's closure, in September 1993, of the border between the two countries prompted protests by The Gambia that its overland trading links had been blocked.

Economic relations with Senegal did not improve following the imposition of military rule in The Gambia. Although Jammeh announced that the Senegalese restrictions on cross-border trade were to be revoked following a visit to Senegal in September 1994, this failed to materialize. In retaliation, in April 1995 the Gambian authorities raised the tolls on the Yellitenda–Bambatenda ferry (Senegal's main link with its southern province of Casamance) by 1,000% for Senegalese vehicles, forcing these to use the much longer Tambacounda route; the increase was, however, abandoned in June. In January 1996 the Senegalese and Gambian governments agreed to end restrictions on cross-border trade between the two countries, subject to the implementation of measures designed to prevent smuggling. A further agreement, concluded in April 1997, was to facilitate trans-border movement of goods destined for re-export. In late 1997 and early 1998 an escalation in the conflict in the Casamance region of southern Senegal (q.v.) prompted large numbers of refugees to cross into The Gambia; Jammeh has subsequently mediated in the conflict (see Recent History). Both countries have maintained their membership of the sub-regional Gambia River Basin Development Organization, to which Guinea and Guinea-Bissau also belong. This organization is principally concerned with promoting development by means of regional co-operation and the joint exploitation of shared natural resources.

Statistical Survey

Source (unless otherwise stated): Department of Information, 14 Daniel Goddard St, Banjul; tel. 225060; fax 227230.

Area and Population

AREA, POPULATION AND DENSITY

Area (sq km)	11,295*
Population (census results)	
15 April 1983	
Total	687,817
15 April 1993	
Males	514,530
Females	511,337
Total	1,025,867
Population (UN estimates at mid-year)†	
1996	1,150,000
1997	1,189,000
1998	1,229,000
Density (per sq km) at mid-1998	108.8

* 4,361 sq miles.
† Source: UN, *World Population Prospects: The 1998 Revision.*

ETHNIC GROUPS

1993 census (percentages): Mandinka 39.60; Fula 18.83; Wollof 14.61; Jola 10.66; Serahule 8.92; Serere 2.77; Manjago 1.85; Bambara 0.84; Creole/Aku 0.69; Others 1.23.

PRINCIPAL TOWNS (population at 1993 census)

Banjul (capital) . .	42,326	Lamin . . .	10,668
Brikama . .	41,761	Gunjur . . .	9,983
Bakau . . .	28,882	Basse . . .	9,265
Farafenni . .	20,956	Soma . . .	7,988
Serrekunda . .	18,901	Bansang . .	5,743
Sukuta . . .	16,667		

BIRTHS AND DEATHS (UN estimates, annual averages)

	1985–90	1990–95	1995–2000
Birth rate (per 1,000) . .	46.3	43.3	40.6
Death rate (per 1,000) . .	21.2	19.2	17.4

Expectation of life (UN estimates, years at birth, 1990–95): 45.0 (males 43.4; females 46.6).

Sources: UN, *World Population Prospects: The 1998 Revision*; UN, *Population and Vital Statistics Report.*

ECONOMICALLY ACTIVE POPULATION*
(persons aged 10 years and over, 1993 census)

	Males	Females	Total
Agriculture, hunting and forestry	82,886	92,806	175,692
Fishing	5,610	450	6,060
Mining and quarrying . .	354	44	398
Manufacturing	18,729	2,953	21,682
Electricity, gas and water supply	1,774	84	1,858
Construction	9,530	149	9,679
Wholesale and retail trade; repair of motor vehicles, motorcycles and personal and household goods	33,281	15,460	48,741
Hotels and restaurants . .	3,814	2,173	5,987
Transport, storage and communications	13,421	782	14,203
Financial intermediation . .	1,843	572	2,415
Other community, social and personal service activities .	25,647	15,607	41,254
Activities not adequately defined	10,421	6,991	17,412
Total	207,310	138,071	345,381

* Figures exclude persons seeking work for the first time.
Mid-1998 (estimates in '000): Agriculture, etc. 500; Total 682 (Source: FAO, *Production Yearbook*).

Agriculture

PRINCIPAL CROPS ('000 metric tons)

	1996	1997	1998*
Millet	61	66	66
Sorghum	14	13	13
Rice (paddy)	20	17	17
Maize	10	8	8
Cassava (Manioc) . . .	6*	6*	6
Pulses	4*	4*	4
Palm kernels . . .	2*	2*	2
Groundnuts (in shell) . .	46	78	78
Vegetables	8*	8*	8
Fruits	4*	4*	4
Cottonseed	3*	1*	1

* FAO estimate(s).
Source: FAO, *Production Yearbook.*

LIVESTOCK ('000 head, year ending September)

	1996	1997	1998*
Cattle	323	346	346
Goats	224	250	250
Sheep	159	182	182
Pigs	14	14	14
Asses	35*	35*	35
Horses	19*	19*	19

Poultry (million)*: 1 in 1996; 1 in 1997; 1 in 1998.
* FAO estimate(s).
Source: FAO, *Production Yearbook.*

LIVESTOCK PRODUCTS (FAO estimates, '000 metric tons)

	1996	1997	1998
Beef and veal	3	3	3
Goat meat	1	1	1
Mutton and lamb . . .	1	1	1
Poultry meat	1	2	2
Other meat	1	1	1
Cows' milk	7	7	7
Poultry eggs	1	1	1

Source: FAO, *Production Yearbook.*

Forestry

ROUNDWOOD REMOVALS
('000 cubic metres, excluding bark)

	1995	1996	1997
Sawlogs, veneer logs and logs for sleepers	106	106	106
Other industrial wood . .	7	7	7
Fuel wood	1,108	1,114	1,126
Total	1,221	1,227	1,239

Source: FAO, *Yearbook of Forest Products.*

Fishing

('000 metric tons, live weight)

	1995	1996	1997
Tilapias	1.1	1.2	1.1
Other freshwater fishes	1.5	1.5	1.5
Tonguefishes	0.9	0.5	0.3
Sea catfishes	0.8	0.2	1.2
Croakers and drums	1.4	1.3	1.0
Bonga shad	13.9	22.6	21.5
Other marine fishes (incl. unspecified)	2.8	3.5	5.4
Total fish	22.4	30.8	32.0
Southern pink shrimp	0.4	0.3	—
Other crustaceans and molluscs	0.5	0.5	0.3
Total catch	23.3	31.6	32.3
Inland waters	2.5	2.5	2.5
Atlantic Ocean	20.8	29.1	29.8

Source: FAO, *Yearbook of Fishery Statistics*.

Industry

SELECTED PRODUCTS

	1993	1994	1995
Salted, dried or smoked fish ('000 metric tons)*	0.9	1.1	0.9
Palm oil—unrefined ('000 metric tons)*	3	3	3
Electric energy (million kWh)†	73	73	74

* Data from the FAO.   † Provisional or estimated figures.

Source: UN, *Industrial Commodity Statistics Yearbook*.

Palm oil—unrefined (FAO estimates, '000 metric tons): 3 in 1996; 3 in 1997; 3 in 1998. Source: FAO, *Production Yearbook*.

Finance

CURRENCY AND EXCHANGE RATES

Monetary Units
    100 butut = 1 dalasi (D).

Sterling, Dollar and Euro Equivalents (28 April 2000)
    £1 sterling = 19.264 dalasi;
    US $1 = 12.285 dalasi;
    €1 = 11.161 dalasi;
    1,000 dalasi = £51.91 = $81.40 = €89.60.

Average Exchange Rate (dalasi per US $)
    1997   10.200
    1998   10.643
    1999   11.395

BUDGET (million dalasi, year ending 30 June)

Revenue*	1996/97‡	1997	1998
Tax revenue	670.7	714.8	751.2
Direct taxes	153.4	168.6	185.1
Taxes on personal incomes	71.7	72.3	76.4
Taxes on corporate profits	74.4	81.8	93.7
Indirect taxes	517.3	546.2	566.1
Domestic taxes on goods and services	237.4	71.5	65.3
Domestic sales tax	219.9	57.1	63.0
Taxes on international trade	280.0	474.7	500.8
Customs duties	279.8	119.7	145.1
Sales tax on imports	—	146.4	149.9
Petroleum taxes	—	208.5	205.8
Duty	—	178.6	177.3
Sales tax	—	29.9	28.5
Other current revenue	77.7	84.8	80.4
Government services and charges	36.9	40.1	35.1
Interest, dividends and property	29.8	23.0	38.6
Central Bank profit	—	17.4	4.0
Total	748.4	799.6	831.6

Expenditure†	1996/97‡	1997	1998
Current expenditure	726.5	794.6	799.7
Expenditure on goods and services	551.9	470.9	447.4
Personal emoluments, allowances and pensions	250.5	269.3	282.9
Other charges	301.4	201.6	164.5
Goods and services	—	201.6	164.5
Interest payments	174.6	214.7	236.9
Internal	117.4	155.2	180.4
External	57.2	59.5	56.5
Subsidies and current transfers	—	109.0	115.4
Development expenditure	249.3	349.9§	259.9§
Total	975.8	1,144.5	1,059.6

* Excluding grants received (million dalasi): 29.9 in 1996/97; 53.0 in 1997; 88.5 in 1998.
† Excluding lending minus repayments (million dalasi): −20.9 in 1997; −31.2 in 1998.
‡ Year ending 30 June.
§ Including foreign-financed extrabudgetary expenditure (million dalasi): 150.4 in 1996/97; 60.6 in 1997.

Source: Department of State for Finance and Economic Affairs, Banjul.

INTERNATIONAL RESERVES (US $ million at 31 December)

	1997	1998	1999
IMF special drawing rights	0.11	0.42	0.67
Reserve position in IMF	2.00	2.09	2.04
Foreign exchange	93.92	103.85	108.54
Total	96.04	106.36	111.25

Source: IMF, *International Financial Statistics*.

MONEY SUPPLY (million dalasi at 31 December)

	1997	1998	1999
Currency outside banks	360.51	347.55	379.72
Demand deposits at commercial banks	268.90	279.02	336.32
Total money	629.41	626.57	716.04

Source: IMF, *International Financial Statistics*.

COST OF LIVING
(Consumer Price Index for Banjul and Kombo St Mary's; base: 1974 = 100)

	1997	1998	1999
Food	1,511.8	1,565.8	1,628.8
Fuel and light	2,145.8	1,854.9	2,076.0
Clothing*	937.5	981.8	999.9
Rent	1,409.6	1,431.3	1,428.6
All items (incl. others) . . .	1,441.5	1,457.3	1,512.9

* Including household linen.

NATIONAL ACCOUNTS
(million dalasi at current prices, estimates)
Expenditure on the Gross Domestic Product

	1996/97*	1997	1998
Government final consumption expenditure	690.3	735.1	743.2
Private final consumption expenditure	3,070.1	3,120.6	3,352.5
Increase in stocks . . . }	771.5	715.1	812.9
Gross fixed capital formation . }			
Total domestic expenditure .	4,531.9	4,570.8	4,908.7
Exports of goods and services .	1,844.7	1,883.5	2,262.2
Less Imports of goods and services	2,375.0	2,303.1	2,746.5
GDP in purchasers' values .	4,001.6	4,151.2	4,424.3
GDP at constant 1976/77 prices	609.1	639.2	669.3

* Year ending 30 June.

Gross Domestic Product by Economic Activity

	1996/97*	1997	1998
Agriculture, hunting, forestry and fishing	946.4	983.6	1,056.2
Manufacturing	217.4	223.3	225.7
Electricity and water . . .	56.1	66.5	72.1
Construction	200.1	216.2	229.8
Trade, restaurants and hotels .	619.4	671.3	741.5
Transport and communications .	604.1	565.8	600.7
Business services and housing .	274.2	276.0	299.6
Government services . . .	368.2	383.9	407.1
Other services† . . .	184.0	218.9	225.4
GDP at factor cost . .	3,469.9	3,605.5	3,858.3
Indirect taxes, *Less* Subsidies .	531.7	545.7	566.0
GDP in purchasers' values .	4,001.6	4,151.2	4,424.3

* Year ending 30 June.
† Including banking and insurance, net of imputed bank service charges.
Source: IMF, *The Gambia: Selected Issues* (August 1999).

BALANCE OF PAYMENTS (US $ million, year ending 30 June).

	1995	1996	1997
Exports of goods f.o.b. . .	122.96	118.75	119.61
Imports of goods f.o.b. . .	−162.53	−217.10	−207.09
Trade balance . . .	−39.57	−98.35	−87.48
Exports of services . . .	53.71	101.21	109.35
Imports of services . . .	−69.25	−77.03	−74.67
Balance on goods and services.	−55.11	−74.17	−52.81
Other income received . .	4.37	6.01	3.73
Other income paid . . .	−9.58	−9.28	−11.30
Balance on goods, services and income	−60.32	−77.44	−60.38
Current transfers received .	55.81	35.10	45.04
Current transfers paid . .	−3.68	−5.35	−8.22
Current balance . . .	−8.19	−47.70	−23.56
Capital account (net) . . .	—	8.52	5.74
Direct investment from abroad .	7.78	10.80	11.98
Other investment assets . .	−3.66	5.62	10.28
Investment liabilities . .	20.65	42.18	17.19
Net errors and omissions . .	−15.63	−4.94	−14.22
Overall balance . . .	0.95	14.47	7.40

Source: IMF, *International Financial Statistics.*

External Trade

PRINCIPAL COMMODITIES (million dalasi)

Imports c.i.f.	1997	1998	1999
Food and live animals . . .	570.9	956.6	726.3
Beverages and tobacco . . .	48.9	74.4	83.1
Raw materials	28.9	26.6	36.5
Mineral fuels, lubricants, etc. . .	124.4	142.8	121.3
Animal and vegetable oils . .	62.8	98.7	66.8
Chemicals	170.0	131.2	116.1
Manufactured goods classified by material	160.0	241.1	253.9
Machinery and transport equipment	373.7	502.7	456.4
Miscellaneous manufactured articles	201.7	207.5	273.1
Total (incl. others)	1,773.8	2,426.4	2,206.9

Exports f.o.b.*	1997	1998	1999
Groundnuts and groundnut products	49.2	139.9	197.6
Fish and fish products . . .	44.2	33.6	36.6
Fruit and vegetables	11.5	25.9	19.2
Cotton products	9.6	6.7	2.4
Total (incl. others)	139.4	229.4	289.8

* Excluding re-exports (million dalasi) 11.0 in 1997; 50.2 in 1998; 23.2 in 1999.

PRINCIPAL TRADING PARTNERS (million dalasi)

Imports c.i.f.	1997	1998	1999
Belgium	86.8	163.1	126.8
China, People's Repub. . . .	68.9	140.5	140.8
Côte d'Ivoire	104.3	145.2	89.8
France (incl. Monaco) . .	167.3	220.6	148.3
Germany	148.0	179.6	305.3
Hong Kong	50.5	82.8	96.7
Italy	47.9	30.6	31.8
Japan	55.3	77.2	71.5
Netherlands	84.5	163.8	105.3
Senegal	42.8	38.1	50.0
Spain	67.8	87.1	38.1
Thailand	6.2	125.6	27.3
United Kingdom	261.2	338.5	235.1
USA	171.2	168.9	109.2
Total (incl. others) . . .	1,773.8	2,426.4	2,206.9

Exports f.o.b.	1997	1998	1999
Belgium	7.3	16.8	24.2
China, People's Repub. . . .	2.6	6.9	1.4
France (incl. Monaco) . . .	27.5	153.9	2.3
Germany	3.5	20.6	10.1
Hong Kong	2.6	1.4	0.8
Japan	3.2	5.3	2.1
Netherlands	7.4	9.0	3.3
Senegal	5.3	7.3	5.9
Spain	29.2	8.9	7.7
United Kingdom	22.0	34.8	15.7
USA	6.5	1.4	3.0
Total (incl. others) . . .	150.4	279.6	313.0

Transport

ROAD TRAFFIC (estimates, motor vehicles in use)

	1995	1996	1997
Passenger cars	6,972	6,925	7,267
Lorries and vans	3,778	4,045	4,147

SHIPPING

Merchant Fleet (registered at 31 December)

	1996	1997	1998
Number of vessels	6	7	8
Total displacement (grt)	1,490	1,600	1,884

Source: Lloyd's Register of Shipping, *World Fleet Statistics*.

International Sea-borne Freight Traffic ('000 metric tons)

	1996	1997	1998
Goods loaded	55.9	38.1	47.0
Goods unloaded	482.7	503.7	493.2

CIVIL AVIATION (traffic on scheduled services)

	1992	1993	1994
Kilometres flown (million)	1	1	1
Passengers carried ('000)	19	19	19
Passenger-km (million)	50	50	50
Total ton-km (million)	5	5	5

Source: UN, *Statistical Yearbook*.

Tourism

FOREIGN VISITORS BY COUNTRY OF ORIGIN*

	1996	1997	1998
Belgium	6,366	3,795	3,703
Denmark	2,445	2,237	2,836
Germany	4,692	18,460	22,189
Netherlands	13,207	10,365	10,762
Sweden	6,317	5,478	5,574
United Kingdom	37,295	38,378	37,437
Total (incl. others)	76,814	84,758	91,106

* Air charter tourist arrivals.

1998/99 (Air charter tourist arrivals, year ending 30 June): 119,983.

Receipts from tourism (million dalasi): 162.4 in 1994/95; 307.5 in 1995/96; 308.4 in 1996/97.

Source: National Tourist Office, Banjul.

Communications Media

	1994	1995	1996
Radio receivers ('000 in use)	176	182	189
Television receivers ('000 in use)	4	4	4
Daily newspapers			
Number	2	1	1
Average circulation ('000 copies)	2*	1	2
Books published†			
Titles	21	n.a.	14
Copies ('000)	20	n.a.	10

* Estimate.   † Including pamphlets: 5 titles, 9,000 copies in 1994.

Telephones: ('000 main lines in use, excluding public call offices, year ending 31 March): 18 in 1994/95; 19 in 1995/96; 21 in 1996/97.
Telefax stations (number in use, year ending 31 March): 700 in 1994/95; 1,030 in 1995/96; 1,096 in 1996/97.
Mobile cellular telephones (subscribers, year ending 31 March): 812 in 1994/95; 1,442 in 1995/96; 3,096 in 1996/97.
Non-daily newspapers (1996): 4; Average circulation (estimate) 6,000 copies.

Sources: UNESCO, *Statistical Yearbook*; UN, *Statistical Yearbook*.

Education

(1998/99, unless otherwise indicated)

		Students		
	Teachers	Males	Females	Total
Pre-primary	408*	15,205	13,618	28,823
Primary	4,578	81,360	69,043	150,403
Junior Secondary	1,338	20,142	14,018	34,160
Senior Secondary	598	8,102	4,507	12,609
Tertiary*	155	1,018	573	1,591

* 1994/95 figure(s).

Source: Department of State for Education, Banjul.

Directory

The Constitution

Following the *coup d'état* of July 1994, the 1970 Constitution was suspended and the presidency and legislature, as defined therein, dissolved. A Constitutional Review Commission was inaugurated in April 1995; the amended document was approved in a national referendum on 8 August. The new Constitution of the Second Republic of The Gambia entered into full effect on 16 January 1997.

Decrees issued during the transition period (1994–96) are deemed to have been approved by the National Assembly and remain in force so long as they do not contravene the provisions of the Constitution of the Second Republic.

The Constitution provides for the separation of the powers of the executive, legislative and judicial organs of state. The Head of State is the President of the Republic, who is directly elected by universal adult suffrage. No restriction is placed on the number of times a President may seek re-election. Legislative authority is vested in the National Assembly, comprising 45 members elected by direct universal suffrage and four members nominated by the President of the Republic. The Speaker and Deputy Speaker of the Assembly are elected, by the members of the legislature, from among the President's nominees. The Constitution upholds the principle of executive accountability to parliament. Thus, the Head of State appoints government members, but these are responsible both to the President and to the National Assembly. Ministers of cabinet rank take the title of Secretary of State. Committees of the Assembly have powers to inquire into the activities of ministers and of government departments, and into all matters of public importance.

In judicial affairs, the final court of appeal is the Supreme Court. Provision is made for a special criminal court to hear and determine all cases relating to the theft and misappropriation of public funds.

The Constitution provides for an Independent Electoral Commission, an Independent National Audit Office, an Office of the Ombudsman, a Lands Commission and a Public Service Commission, all of which are intended to ensure transparency, accountability and probity in public affairs.

The Constitution guarantees the rights of women, of children and of the disabled. Tribalism and other forms of sectarianism in politics are forbidden. Political activity may be suspended in the event of a state of national insecurity.

The Government

HEAD OF STATE

President: Col (retd) Dr Alhaji YAHYA A. J. J. JAMMEH (proclaimed Head of State 26 July 1994; elected President 26 September 1996).

Vice-President: ISATOU NJIE-SAIDY.

THE CABINET
(August 2000)

President: Col (retd) Dr Alhaji YAHYA A. J. J. JAMMEH.

Vice-President and Secretary of State for Women's Affairs: ISATOU NJIE-SAIDY.

Secretary of State for Presidential Affairs, responsible for the National Assembly, the Civil Service, Fisheries and Natural Resources: Capt. (retd) EDWARD SINGHATEH.

Secretary of State for Youth and Sports: Capt. (retd) YANKUBA TOURAY.

Secretary of State for the Interior and Religious Affairs: OUSMAN BADJIE.

Secretary of State for Trade, Industry and Employment: MUSA SILLAH.

Secretary of State for Foreign Affairs: MOMADOU LAMINE SEDAT JOBE.

Secretary of State for Education: THERESE NDONG-JATTA.

Secretary of State for Tourism and Culture: SUSAN WAFFA-OGOO.

Secretary of State for Agriculture: HASSAN SALLAH.

Secretary of State for Works, Communications and Information: SARJO JALLOW.

Secretary of State for Finance and Economic Affairs: FAMARA JATTA.

Secretary of State for Local Government: MOMODOU NAI CEESAY.

Secretary of State for Justice and Attorney-General: PAP CHEYASSIN SECKA.

Secretary of State for Health and Social Welfare: ABDOULIE M. SALLAH.

Secretary-General: JULIA JOINER.

MINISTRIES

Office of the President: State House, Banjul; tel. 227881; fax 227034.

Office of the Vice-President and Department of State for Defence: State House, Banjul; tel. 227822; fax 227034.

Department of State for Agriculture and Natural Resources: The Quadrangle, Banjul; tel. 228291; fax 223578.

Department of State for Education: Bedford Place Bldg, POB 989, Banjul; tel. 227236; fax 224180.

Department of State for Finance and Economic Affairs: The Quadrangle, Banjul; tel. 228291; fax 227954.

Department of State for Foreign Affairs: 4 Col Muammar Ghadaffi Ave, Banjul; tel. 225654; fax 223578.

Department of State for Health, Social Welfare and Women's Affairs: The Quadrangle, Banjul; tel. 227881; fax 228505.

Department of State for the Interior and Religious Affairs: 71 Dobson St, Banjul; tel. 228511; fax 223063.

Department of State for Justice: Col Muammar Ghadaffi Ave, Banjul; tel. 228181; fax 225352.

Department of State for Local Government: The Quadrangle, Banjul; tel. 228291.

Department of State for Tourism and Culture: New Administrative Bldg, The Quadrangle, Banjul; tel. 228496; fax 227753.

Department of State for Trade, Industry and Employment: Independence Drive, Banjul; tel. 228229.

Department of State for Works, Communication and Information: MID Rd, Kanifing, Banjul; tel. 227449; fax 226655.

Department of State for Youth and Sports: The Quadrangle, Banjul; tel. 227449; fax 225066.

President and Legislature

PRESIDENT

Presidential Election, 26 September 1996

Candidate	Votes	% of votes
YAHYA A. J. J. JAMMEH	220,011	55.77
OUSAINOU DARBOE	141,387	35.84
HAMAT N. K. BAH	21,759	5.52
SIDIA JATTA	11,337	2.87
Total	**394,494**	**100.00**

NATIONAL ASSEMBLY

Speaker: MUSTAPHA WADDA.

General Election, 2 January 1997

Party	Seats
Alliance for Patriotic Reorientation and Construction	33*
United Democratic Party	7
National Reconciliation Party	2
People's Democratic Organization for Independence and Socialism	1
Independents	2
Total	**45†**

* Including five seats taken in constituencies in which the party was unopposed.

† The President of the Republic is empowered by the Constitution to nominate four additional members of parliament.

Political Organizations

Alliance for Patriotic Reorientation and Construction (APRC): GAMSTAR Bldg, Banjul; f. 1996; Chair. President YAHYA A. J. J. JAMMEH.

National Reconciliation Party (NRP): Banjul; f. 1996; Leader HAMAT N. K. BAH.

People's Democratic Organization for Independence and Socialism (PDOIS): Banjul; f. 1986; radical socialist; Leaders HALIFA SALLAH, SAM SARR, SIDIA JATTA.

People's Democratic Party: Bojang Kunda, Brikama, Kombo Central, Western Division; e-mail bikiling@qanet.gm; f. 1991; Pres. Dr LAMINE BOJANG.

United Democratic Party (UDP): Banjul; f. 1996; Pres. Col (retd) SAM SILLAH; Leader OUSAINOU DARBOE.

Note: The **Gambia People's Party**, of ASSAN MUSA CAMARA, the **National Convention Party**, of SHERIF MUSTAPHA DIBBA, and the **People's Progressive Party**, of fmr Pres. Sir DAWDA KAIRABA JAWARA, were banned from contesting the 1996 presidential election and the 1997 legislative elections.

Diplomatic Representation

EMBASSIES AND HIGH COMMISSIONS IN THE GAMBIA

China (Taiwan): 26 Radio Gambia St, Kanifing South, POB 916, Banjul; tel. 374041; fax 374055; Ambassador CHEN-HSIUNG LEE.

Liberia: Garba-Jahumpa Rd, Bakau Newtown, POB 2982, Banjul; tel. 496775; fax 496775; Chargé d'affaires a.i.: ERIC R. TOGBA.

Libya: Fajara, Banjul; tel. 493434; Chargé d'affaires a.i.: ABDUSSALAM ABUZAID.

Nigeria: Garba Jahumpa Rd, Bakau Newtown, POB 630, Banjul; tel. 495803; fax 496456; High Commissioner: AYUBA JACOB NGBAKO.

Senegal: Kairaba Ave, POB 385, Banjul; tel. 373752; fax 373750; Ambassador: Gen. MOMODOU DIOP.

Sierra Leone: 67 Daniel Goddard St, POB 448, Banjul; tel. 228206; fax 229814; High Commissioner: IBRAHIM MORIKEH FOFANA.

United Kingdom: 48 Atlantic Rd, Fajara, POB 507, Banjul; tel. 495133; fax 496134; e-mail bhcbanjul@gamtel.gm; High Commissioner: JOHN PERROTT.

USA: The White House, Kairaba Ave, Fajara, PMB 19, Banjul; tel. 392856; fax 392475; internet www.usembassy-gambia.com; Ambassador: GEORGE WILLIFORD BOYCE HALEY.

Judicial System

The judicial system of The Gambia is based on English Common Law and legislative enactments of the Republic's Parliament which include an Islamic Law Recognition Ordinance whereby an Islamic Court exercises jurisdiction in certain cases between, or exclusively affecting, Muslims.

The Constitution of the Second Republic guarantees the independence of the judiciary. The Supreme Court is defined as the final court of appeal. Provision is made for a special criminal court to hear and determine all cases relating to theft and misappropriation of public funds.

Supreme Court of The Gambia: Law Courts, Independence Drive, Banjul; tel. 227383; fax 228380; consists of the Chief Justice and four other judges.

Chief Justice: FELIX LARTEY.

The Banjul Magistrates Court (f. 1997), the **Kanifing Magistrates Court** and the **Divisional Courts** are courts of summary jurisdiction presided over by a magistrate or in his absence by two or more lay justices of the peace. There are resident magistrates in all divisions. The magistrates have limited civil and criminal jurisdiction, and appeal from these courts lies with the Supreme Court.

Islamic Courts have jurisdiction in matters between, or exclusively affecting, Muslim Gambians and relating to civil status, marriage, succession, donations, testaments and guardianship. The Courts administer Islamic (Shari'a) Law. A cadi, or a cadi and two assessors, preside over and constitute an Islamic Court. Assessors of the Islamic Courts are Justices of the Peace of Islamic faith.

District Tribunals have appellate jurisdiction in cases involving customs and traditions. Each court consists of three district tribunal members, one of whom is selected as president, and other court members from the area over which it has jurisdiction.

Attorney-General: PAP CHEYASSIN SECKA.

Solicitor-General: RAYMOND SOCK.

Religion

About 85% of the population are Muslims. The remainder are mainly Christians, and there are a few animists, mostly of the Jola and Karoninka ethnic groups.

ISLAM

Banjul Central Mosque: Box Bar Road, Banjul; tel. 228094; Imam Ratib Alhaji ABDOULIE M. JOBE; Dep. Imam Ratib Alhaji TAFSIR GAYE.

Imam Ratib of Banjul: Alhaji ABDOULIE M. JOBE, King Fahd Bun Abdul Aziz Mosque, 39 Lancaster St, POB 562, Banjul; tel. 228094.

Supreme Islamic Council: Banjul; Chair. Alhaji BANDING DRAMMEH.

CHRISTIANITY

The Gambia Christian Council: POB 27, Banjul; tel. and fax 392092. 1966; seven mems (churches and other Christian bodies); Chair. Rev. TITUS K. A. PRATT (Gen. Supt of the Methodist Church of The Gambia); Sec.-Gen. HANNAH ACY PETERS.

The Anglican Communion

The diocese of The Gambia, which includes Senegal and Cape Verde, forms part of the Church of the Province of West Africa. The Archbishop of the Province is the Bishop of Koforidua, Ghana. There are about 1,500 adherents in The Gambia.

Bishop of The Gambia: Rt Rev. SOLOMON TILEWA JOHNSON, Bishopscourt, POB 51, Banjul; tel. 227405; fax 373803; e-mail 106617.1404@compuserve.com.

The Roman Catholic Church

The Gambia comprises a single diocese (Banjul), directly responsible to the Holy See. At 31 December 1998 there were an estimated 33,000 adherents of the Roman Catholic Church in the country. The diocese administers a development organization (Caritas, The Gambia), and runs 63 schools and training centres. The Bishop of Banjul is a member of the Inter-territorial Catholic Bishops' Conference of The Gambia and Sierra Leone (based in Freetown, Sierra Leone).

Bishop of Banjul: Rt Rev. MICHAEL J. CLEARY, Bishop's House, POB 165, Banjul; tel. 393437; fax 390998.

Protestant Churches

Abiding Word Ministries: POB 207, Serrekunda; tel. 394035; fax 394035; e-mail ncwc.awm@commit.gm; Senior Pastor Rev. FRANCIS FORBES.

Methodist Church: POB 288, Banjul; f. 1821; tel. 227425; Chair. and Gen. Supt Rev. TITUS K. A. PRATT.

The Press

All independent publications are required to register annually with the Government and to pay a registration fee.

The Daily Observer: POB 131, Banjul; tel. 496608; fax 496878; internet www.qanet.gm/Observer; f. 1992; daily; independent; Man. Dir SARRIANG CEESAY.

Foroyaa (Freedom): Bundunka Kunda, POB 2306, Serrekunda; tel. 393177; fax 393177; e-mail foroyaa@commit.gm; weekly; publ. by the PDOIS; Editors HALIFA SALLAH, SAM SARR, SIDIA JATTA.

The Gambia Daily: Dept of Information, 14 Daniel Goddard St, Banjul; tel. 225060; fax 227230; e-mail gamna@gamtel.ga; f. 1994; govt organ; Dir of Information EBRUMA COLE; circ. 500.

The Gambia Onward: Banjul; 3 a week; Editor RUDOLPH ALLEN.

The Gambian: 60 Lancaster St, Banjul; 3 a week; Editor NGAING THOMAS.

The Gambian Times: 21 OAU Blvd, POB 698, Banjul; tel. 445; f. 1981; fortnightly; publ. by the PPP; Editor MOMODOU GAYE.

The Independent: next to A-Z Supermarket, Kairaba Ave, Banjul; f. 1999; 2 a week; independent; internet www.qanet.gm/Independent; Editor-in-Chief BABA GALLEH JALLOW; Man. Editor YORRO JALLOW.

The Nation: People's Press, 3 Boxbar Rd, POB 334, Banjul; fortnightly; Editor W. DIXON-COLLEY; circ. 1,000.

New Citizen: 40 Sait Matty Rd, POB 1021, Bakau, Banjul; independent; suspended publication in February 1999; Dir BABOUCAR GAYE.

The Point: 2 Garba Jahumpa Rd, Fajara, Banjul; tel. 497441; fax 497442; internet www.qanet.gm/point; f. 1991; 2 a week; Man. Editor DEYDA HYDARA; circ. 4,000.

The Spectator: Banjul; tel. 226072; e-mail thespectatormagazine@yahoo.com; f. 1999; independent; weekly magazine.

The Toiler: 31 OAU Blvd, POB 698, Banjul; Editor PA MODOU FALL.

The Worker: 6 Albion Place, POB 508, Banjul; publ. by the Gambia Labour Union; Editor M. M. CEESAY.

NEWS AGENCIES

Gambia News Agency (GAMNA): Dept of Information, 14 Daniel Goddard St, Banjul; tel. 225060; fax 227230; e-mail gamna@gamtel.ga; Dir EBRIMA COLE.

Spice News Services: 62 Mosque Rd, Latrikunda German, Serrekunda; c/o POB 630, Banjul; e-mail ahes_ttsmart_spi@hotmail.com.

PRESS ASSOCIATION

Gambia Press Union: 10 Atlantic Rd, Fajara, POB 1440, Banjul; tel. 497945; fax 497946; e-mail gpu@qanet.gm; affiliated to West African Journalists' Association; Pres. DEMBA A. JAWO.

Publisher

Government Printer: MacCarthy Sq., Banjul; tel. 227399.

Broadcasting and Communications

TELECOMMUNICATIONS

Gambia Telecommunications Co Ltd (GAMTEL): Gamtel House, 3 Nelson Mandela St, POB 387, Banjul; tel. 229999; fax 227214; e-mail gen-info@gamtel.gm; internet www.gamtel.gm; f. 1984; state-owned; Man. Dir BAKARY K. NJIE.

BROADCASTING

Radio

Citizen FM: Banjul; independent commercial broadcaster; broadcasts suspended following government intervention in February 1999; Propr BABOUCAR GAYE; News Editor EBRIMA SILLAH.

Farafenni Community Radio: Farafenni; tel. 735527.

FM B Community Radio Station: Brikama; tel. 483000; FM broadcaster.

Gambia Radio and Television Services: Serrekunda Exchange Complex, Kairaba Ave, Serrekunda; tel. 374223; fax 374242; e-mail tombongs@hotmail.com; internet www.qanet.com; f. 1962; non-commercial broadcaster funded by Gambia Telecommunications Company; radio broadcasts in English, Mandinka, Wolof, Fula, Jola, Serer and Serahuli; Dir TOMBONG SAIDY.

Radio 1 FM: 44 Kairaba Ave, POB 2700, Serrekunda, Fajara; tel. 394900; fax 396071; e-mail george.radio1@qanet.gm; f. 1990; private station broadcasting FM music programmes to the Greater Banjul area; Dir GEORGE CHRISTENSEN.

Radio Gambia: Mile 7, Banjul; tel. 495101; fax 495932.

Radio Syd: POB 279/280, Banjul; tel. and fax 226490; f. 1970; medium-wave commercial station broadcasting mainly music; programmes in English, French, Spanish, Wolof, Mandinka, Fula, Jola and Serahuli; also tourist information in Swedish; Dir CONSTANCE WADNER ENHÖRNING; Man. BENNY HOLGERSON.

Sud FM: ECOWAS Ave, POB 94, Banjul; tel. 222359; fax 222394.

West Coast Radio: Manjai Kunda, POB 2687, Serrekunda; tel. 460911; fax 461193; e-mail wcr@delphi.com; FM broadcaster.

The Gambia also receives broadcasts from Radio Democracy for Africa (f. 1998); a division of the Voice of America.

Television

Gambia Radio and Television Services: (see Radio); television broadcasts commenced 1996.

Finance

(cap. = capital; res = reserves; dep. = deposits; m. = million;
brs = branches; amounts in dalasi)

BANKING
Central Bank

Central Bank of The Gambia: 1–2 Ecowas Ave, Banjul; tel.
228103; fax 226969; e-mail centralbank.gambia@qanet.gm; f. 1971;
bank of issue; monetary authority; cap. and res 4.0m., dep. 993.6m.
(1998); Gov. Momodou Clarke Bajo; Gen. Man. Valdemar R. Jensen.

Other Banks

Arab-Gambian Islamic Bank: 7 Ecowas Ave, POB 1415, Banjul;
tel. 223773; fax 223770; e-mail agib@qanet.gm; f. 1996, operations
commenced 1997; 30.1% owned by Islamic Development Bank; cap.
6.1m., total assets 46.2m. (Dec. 1998); Chair. Dr Omar Zuhair Hafiz;
Man. Dir Mamour Malick Jagne.

Continent Bank Ltd: 61 Ecowas Ave, POB 142, Banjul; tel. 222000;
fax 229711; e-mail continent.bank@gamtel.gm; internet www
.gambianews.com/continentbank; f. 1990; cap. 4m., dep. 65m. (Nov.
1999); Chair. Karim Bayzid; Gen. Man. Murad Bayzid; 2 brs.

First International Bank Ltd: 6 OAU Blvd, POB 1997, Banjul;
tel. 202000; fax 202000; e-mail fib@gamtel.gm; f. 1999; 52.5% owned
by Slok Nigeria Ltd; cap. 10m.; Chair. Dr Babacar Ndiaye; Man. Dir
Alhaji T. S. Alieun Njie.

**International Bank for Commerce and Industry (Gambia)
Ltd:** 11a Liberation Ave, POB 211, Banjul; tel. 218144; fax 229312;
f. 1997; owned by Banque Mauritanienne pour le Commerce et
l'Industrie; cap. and res 18.8m., dep. 182.4m. (Dec. 1998); Chair.
Sidi Mohamed Abbass; Man. Dir Baba Ouldah; 2 brs.

Standard Chartered Bank Gambia Ltd: 8 Ecowas Ave, POB
259, Banjul; tel. 228681; fax 227714; f. 1978; 75% owned by Standard
Chartered Holdings BV, Amsterdam; cap. and res 80.6m., dep.
523.5m. (Dec. 1998); Chair. Dr Peter John N'Dow; Chief Exec. S.
Tsikirayi; 4 brs.

Trust Bank Ltd (TBL): 3–4 Ecowas Ave, POB 1018, Banjul; tel.
225778; fax 225781; e-mail trust@gamtel.gm; f. 1992; fmrly Meridien
BIAO Bank Gambia Ltd, name changed 1997; 30% owned by Data
Bank, 20% by Social Security and Housing Finance Corpn, 10% by
Boule & Co Ltd; cap. and res 16.0m., total assets 212.8m. (Dec.
1998); Chair. Ken Ofori Atta; Man. Dir Pa Macoumba Njie (acting);
2 brs.

INSURANCE

There were seven insurance companies and four insurance brokers
operating in The Gambia at the end of 1998.

Capital Insurance Co Ltd: 22 Anglesea St, POB 485, Banjul; tel.
228544; fax 229219; f. 1986; Man. Dir Joseph C. Fye.

The Gambia National Insurance Co Ltd: 19 Kairaba Ave, Fajara,
POB 750, Banjul; tel. 395726; fax 395716; e-mail info@gnic.gm;
internet www.gnic.gm; f. 1974; privately-owned; Chair. Bai Matarr
Drammeh; 3 brs.

GAMSTAR Insurance Co Ltd: July 22 Sq., POB 1276, Banjul;
tel. 226021; fax 229755; Man. Dir Bai Ndogo Faal.

Greater Alliance Insurance Co: 10 Nelson Mandela St, POB 930,
Banjul; tel. 227839; fax 226687; f. 1989; Man. Dir Abor Forster.

Senegambia Insurance Co Ltd: 7 Nelson Mandela St, POB 880,
Banjul; tel. 228866; fax 226820; f. 1984; Man. Dir Alhaji Babou A. M.
Ceesay; Gen. Man. Pa Alassan Jagne.

Insurance Association

Insurance Association of The Gambia (IAG): Banjul.

Trade and Industry
GOVERNMENT AGENCIES

Indigenous Business Advisory Services: Serrekunda; tel.
496098.

National Environmental Agency (NEA): 5 Fitzgerald St, Banjul;
tel. 228056; fax 229701.

National Investment Promotion Authority (NIPA): Independence Drive, Banjul; tel. 228332; fax 229220; f. 1994 to replace the
National Investment Bd; CEO S. M. Mboge.

National Trading Corpn of The Gambia Ltd (NTC): 1–3 Liberation Avenue, POB 61, Banjul; tel. 228323; fax 227790; f. 1973;
transfer pending to private-sector ownership; Man. Dir. Charbel N.
Elhajj; 15 brs.

CHAMBER OF COMMERCE

Gambia Chamber of Commerce and Industry: NTC Complex,
Ecowas Ave, POB 333, Banjul; tel. 227042; fax 229671; e-mail

gcci@delphi.com; f. 1961; Pres. Bai Ndongo Fall; Chief Exec. Kebba
T. N'Jai.

UTILITIES

National Water and Electricity Company (NAWEC): 10th St
East, POB 609, Fajara; tel. 496430; fax 496971; e-mail info@
nawec.com; internet www.nawec.com; f. 1996, in 1999 control was
transferred to the Bassau Development Corporation, Côte d'Ivoire,
under a 15-year contract; Man. Dir. Alagie Conteh.

CO-OPERATIVES

Federation of Agricultural Co-operatives: Banjul.

The Gambia Co-operative Union (GCU): POB 505, Banjul; tel.
374788; fax 392582; f. 1959; co-operative for groundnut producers;
Gen. Man. Lamin Willy Jammeh; 110,000 mems.

MAJOR COMPANIES

Banjul Breweries Ltd: Kanifing Industrial Estate, Kombo St Mary
Division, Banjul; tel. 392566; fax 392266; e-mail banbrew@
gamtel.gm; internet www.julbrew.gm; f. 1975; owned by Brauhaase
(Germany); Gen. Man. A. F. Huberts; 160 employees.

BIMEX Co Ltd: POB 2588, Serrekunda; tel. 372395; fax 390601;
e-mail bimex.banjul@commit.gm; building materials.

Boule & Co Ltd: 3/4 Liberation Ave, NTC Complex, POB 602,
Banjul; tel. 227746; fax 227790; f. 1976; e-mail boule@gamtel.gm;
internet www.gambianet.com/boule; general merchants; Chair. and
Man. Dir Charbel N. Elhajj.

CFAO (Gambia): 14 Wellington St, POB 297, Banjul; tel. 227473;
fax 227472; f. 1887; general merchants; Chair. R. P. Couerbe; Man.
G. Durand; 100 employees.

K. Chellaram & Sons (Gambia) Ltd: POB 275, Banjul; tel.
392912; fax 392910; e-mail chellbanjul@gamtel.gm; f. 1958; importers and general merchants; Man. Dir Nitin Chellaram; 35
employees.

EDLA Gambia Ltd: Kotu West, POB 2932, Serrekunda; tel.
460396; fax 460396; e-mail 113775,312@compuserve.com; secondhand building materials, tractors, trucks, household equipment.

Elof Trading Co Ltd: 40 Kanifing Industrial Estate, POB 95,
Banjul; tel. 394522; fax 390599; f. 1991; general merchants; Dirs
Kamal Melki, Nawal Melki; also **The Milky Way:** f. 1983.

Fass Upper Saloum Enterprises: 80 Garba Juhumpa Rd, POB
1328, Banjul; tel. 497878; electrical supplies and building materials.

The Gambia Groundnut Corpn (GGC): Banjul; subject to a take-
over by the government in 1999; Gen. Man. Richard Kettlewell.

Gambia Oilseeds Processing and Marketing Co Ltd: Marina
Foreshore, Banjul; tel. 227572; fax 228037; assumed 'core' assets of
The Gambia Produce Marketing Board in 1993.

Gamsen Construction: 50 Garba Jahumpa Rd, Bakau, POB 2844,
Serrekunda; tel. 497448; fax 497449; construction and civil engineering; jtly owned by ALFRON and ATEPA Technologies, Senegal.

Gamworks Agency: 19 Kairaba Ave, POB 2640, Serrekunda; tel.
375340; fax 375344.

General Suppliers and Construction Services: Kairaba Ave,
POB 316, Banjul; tel. 461795; fax 461795; construction services
and suppliers.

International Pelican Seafood Ltd: Banjul; f. 1997; seafood processing.

Lenrie Holdings: Banjul; import-export agency; Chair. Lenrie
Peters.

S. Madi (Gambia) Ltd: 10c Nelson Mandela St, POB 255/256,
Banjul; tel. 227372; fax 226192; e-mail s-madi@qanet.gm; general
merchants, agents for Lloyd's of London; Man. Dir Jane H. Clement.

Maurel and Prom: 22 Ecowas Ave, Banjul; fax 228942; general
merchants; Man. J. Eschenlohr.

New Gambia Industrialists: 3 Essa Joof Rd, POB 954, Banjul; tel.
373185; fax 373185; civil, mechanical and electrical design; building
contractors.

Nyambai Sawmill: 10 Moukhtara St, POB 447, Banjul; tel. 392512;
fax 393085; e-mail moukhtara.gambia@commit.gm; timber and
woodwork.

Shell Marketing (Gambia) Ltd: Dobston St, POB 263, Banjul;
tel. 228028; fax 227992; marketing and sale of petroleum products;
Gen. Man. Adama Faal.

SIFAM Co Ltd: 18 Sayerr Jobe Ave, Serrekunda; tel 375954; spare
parts and building materials.

Sosseh & Sons Engineering Co Ltd: 34 Liberation Ave, POB
701, Banjul; marine and production engineering.

TAF Holding Co Ltd: Cemetery Rd, Kanifing Industrial Estate,
POB 121, Banjul; tel. 392333; fax 390033; e-mail taf@commit.gm.

TAF Building Materials: Mamadi Manjang Highway, POB 121, Banjul; tel. 392333; fax 390033; e-mail taf@commit.gm.

TAF Construction Ltd: Cemetery Rd, Kanifing Industrial Estate, POB 121, Banjul; tel. 392333; fax 390033; e-mail taf@commit.gm; building contractors.

Zingli Manufacturing Co Ltd: Kanifing Industrial Estate, POB 2402, Serrekunda; tel. 392282; mfrs of corrugated iron and wire.

TRADE UNIONS

Association of Gambia Sailors: c/o 31 OAU Blvd, POB 698, Banjul; tel. 223080; fax 227214.

Dock Workers' Union: Albert Market, POB 852, Banjul; tel. 229448; fax 225049.

Gambia Labour Union: 6 Albion Place, POB 508, Banjul; tel. 641; f. 1935; Pres. B. B. KEBBEH; Gen. Sec. MOHAMED CEESAY; 25,000 mems.

Gambia Workers' Confederation: 12 Clarkson St, POB 979, Banjul; f. 1958 as The Gambia Workers' Union, present name adopted in 1985; Sec.-Gen. PA MODOU FALL.

The Gambia National Trades Union Council (GNTUC): Trade Union House, 31 OAU Blvd, POB 698, Banjul; Sec.-Gen. IBRIMA GARBA CHAM (acting).

Transport

Gambia Public Transport Corporation: Factory St, Kanifing Industrial Estate, POB 801, Kanifing; tel. 392230; fax 392454; f. 1975; operates road transport and ferry services; Chair. SALIFU KUJABI; Man. Dir BAKARY HOUMA.

RAILWAYS

There are no railways in The Gambia.

ROADS

In 1996 there were an estimated 2,700 km of roads in The Gambia, of which 850 km were main roads, and 520 km were secondary roads. In that year only about 35% of the road network was paved. Some roads are impassable in the rainy season. The expansion and upgrading of the road network is planned, as part of the Jammeh administration's programme to improve The Gambia's transport infrastructure. Among intended schemes is the construction of a motorway along the coast, with the aid of a loan of US $8.5m. from Kuwait. In early 1999 Taiwan agreed to provide $6m. for road construction programmes, and in early 2000 work began on the construction of a dual carriageway between Serrekunda-Mandina-Ba, supported by funds from the Islamic Development Fund.

Gambia Public Transport Corpn (GPTC): Banjul; tel. 392230; fax 392454; provides bus services; state-owned.

SHIPPING

The River Gambia is well suited to navigation. A weekly river service is maintained between Banjul and Basse, 390 km above Banjul, and a ferry connects Banjul with Barra. Small ocean-going vessels can reach Kaur, 190 km above Banjul, throughout the year. Facilities at the port of Banjul were modernized and expanded during the mid-1990s, with the aim of enhancing The Gambia's potential as a transit point for regional trade. In 1999 three advanced storage warehouses were commissioned with total storage space of 8,550 sq m.

Gambia Ports Authority: Liberation Ave; POB 617, Banjul; tel. 227266; fax 227268; e-mail gamport@gamtel.gm; internet www.gamport.gm; Man. Dir IBRAHIMA JANGANA.

The Gambia River Transport Co Ltd: 61 Liberation Ave, Banjul; tel. 227664; river transport of groundnuts and general cargo; Man. Dir. LAMIN JUWARA; 200 employees.

The Gambia Shipping Agencies Ltd: Liberation Ave, Banjul; tel. 227518; fax 227929; shipping agents and forwarders; Man. NILS LANGGAARD SORENSEN; 30 employees.

Interstate Shipping Co (Gambia) Ltd: POB 437, Banjul; tel. 227644; fax 229347; transport and storage.

CIVIL AVIATION

Banjul International Airport, at Yundum, 27 km from the capital, handled some 275,000 passengers and 3,000 metric tons of cargo in 1992. Construction of a new terminal, at a cost of some US $10m., was completed in late 1996. Facilities at Yundum have been upgraded by the US National Aeronautics and Space Administration (NASA), to enable the airport to serve as an emergency landing site for space shuttle vehicles.

Gambia Civil Aviation Authority: Banjul National Airport, Yundum; tel. 472831; fax 472190.

Gambia International Airlines: Banjul International Airport, PMB, Banjul; tel. 472753; fax 472750; e-mail gia-gambia@delphi.com; f. 1996; state-owned; sole handling agent at Banjul, sales agent; Man. Dir VICTOR J. CARVALHO.

Tourism

Tourists are attracted by The Gambia's beaches and also by its abundant birdlife. A major expansion of tourism facilities was carried out in the early 1990s. Although there was a dramatic decline in tourist arrivals in the mid-1990s (owing to the political instability), the tourism sector recovered well; an estimated 90,810 visitors arrived during the 1997/98 season, and 119,983 in 1998/99. An annual 'Roots Festival' was inaugurated in 1996, with the aim of attracting African-American visitors to The Gambia.

National Tourist Office: Dept of State for Tourism and Culture, New Administrative Bldg, The Quadrangle, Banjul; tel. 229563; fax 224019; Dir of Tourism M. B. O. CHAM.

The Gambia Hotels' Association: c/o The Bungalow Beach Hotel, POB 2637, Serrekunda; tel. 465288; fax 466180; Chair. ARDY SARGE.

Defence

In August 1999 the Gambian National Army comprised 800 men, including a marine unit of about 70 men and a presidential guard. Military service has been mainly voluntary; however, the Constitution of the Second Republic, which entered into full effect in January 1997, makes provision for conscription.

Defence Expenditure: Estimated at D180m. in 1999.

Chief of Staff of the Army: Col BABUCAR JATTA.

Education

Primary education, beginning at seven years of age, is free but not compulsory and lasts for six years. Secondary education, from 13 years of age, comprises a first cycle of five years and a second, two-year cycle. In 1998/99 total primary enrolment was equivalent to 72% of children in the relevant age-group, while it was also estimated that a further 10% attended Koranic schools (Madrassas). In the same year secondary enrolment was equivalent to 78% of the appropriate age-group, compared with an enrolment ratio of 35% in 1991/92. According to UNESCO estimates, adult illiteracy in 1995 averaged 69.1% (males 62.2%, females 75.6%). The Jammeh administration has, since 1994, embarked on an ambitious project to improve educational facilities and levels of attendance and attainment. A particular aim, expressed in the government's Revised Education Policy for 1998–2005, has been to improve access to schools for pupils in rural areas. Post-secondary education is available in teacher training, agriculture, health and technical subjects. Some 1,591 students were enrolled at tertiary establishments in 1994/95. The establishment of a university remains a priority, and a cost and financing study was carried out in 1998. In the government budget for 1998 education was allocated an estimated D152.9m., equivalent to almost 22% of recurrent budgetary spending.

Bibliography

Amnesty International. *The Gambia: Democratic Reforms Without Human Rights*. London, 1997.

Bridges, R. C. (Ed.). *Senegambia*. Aberdeen University African Studies Group, 1974.

Cooke, D., and Hughes, A. 'The Politics of Economic Recovery: The Gambia's Experience of Structural Adjustment, 1985—94', in *The Journal of Commonwealth and Comparative Politics,* Vol. 35, No. 1, London, Frank Cass, 1997.

Dieke, P. U. C. 'Tourism in The Gambia: Some Issues in Development Policy', in *World Development,* Vol. 21, No. 2, Oxford, Pergamon Press, 1993.

Gailey, H. A. *A History of The Gambia*. London, Routledge and Kegan Paul, 1964.

    Historical Dictionary of The Gambia. 2nd Edn. Metuchen, NJ, Scarecrow Press, 1987.

Gamble, D. P. *A General Bibliography of The Gambia*. Boston, G. K. Hall and Co, 1979.

    The Gambia, World Bibliographical Series, Vol. 91. Oxford, Clio Press, 1988.

Gray, J. M. *A History of the Gambia*. New York, Barnes and Noble, and London, Cass, 1966.

Harrison Church, R. J. *West Africa*. 8th Edn. London, Longman, 1979.

Hughes, A. 'From Colonialism to Confederation: the Gambian Experience of Independence 1965–1982', in Cohen, R. (Ed.), *African Islands and Enclaves*. London, Sage Publications, 1983.

    'The Senegambian Confederation', in *Contemporary Review,* February 1984.

    (Ed.). *The Gambia: Studies in Society and Politics*. University of Birmingham Centre of West African Studies, 1991.

    'The Collapse of the Senegambian Confederation', in *The Journal of Commonwealth and Comparative Politics,* Vol. 30, No. 2, London, Frank Cass, 1992.

Hughes, A., and Gailey, A. *Historical Dictionary of The Gambia*. Metuchen, NJ, Scarecrow Press, 2000.

Hughes, A., and Perfect, D. *Political History of The Gambia, 1816–1922*. London, C. Hurst & Co, 1996.

Jarrett, H. R. *A Geography of Sierra Leone and Gambia*. Harlow, Longman, 1981.

McPherson, M. F., and Radelet, S. C. (Eds). *Economic Recovery in The Gambia: Insights for Adjustment in Sub-Saharan Africa*. Cambridge, MA, Harvard Institute for International Development, 1995.

People's Progressive Party Special Editorial Commission. *The Voice of the People, the Story of the PPP, 1959–1989*. Banjul, The Gambia Communications Agency and Barou-Ueli Enterprises, 1992.

Radelet, S. 'Reform without Revolt: The Political Economy of Economic Reform in The Gambia', in *World Development,* Oxford, Pergamon Press, Vol. 28, No. 8, 1992.

Rice, B. *Enter Gambia: The Birth of an Improbable Nation*. London, Angus and Robertson, 1968.

Robson, P. *Integration, Development and Equity: Economic Integration in West Africa*. London, Allen and Unwin, 1983.

Sallah, T. M. 'Economics and Politics in The Gambia', in *The Journal of Modern African Studies,* Vol. 28, No. 4, 1990.

Sweeney, P. (Ed.). *The Gambia and Senegal*. London, APA, 1996.

Tomkinson, M. *Gambia*. London, Michael Tomkinson Publishing, 1999.

Wiseman, J. A. *Democracy in Black Africa: Survival and Revival*. New York, Paragon House, 1990.

    'Military Rule in The Gambia: An Interim Assessment', in *Third World Quarterly,* Vol. 17, No. 5, London, 1996.

    'The Gambia: From Coup to Elections', in *Journal of Democracy,* Vol. 9, no. 2, Washington, DC, 1998.

Wiseman, J. A., and Vidler, E. 'The July 1994 Coup d'Etat in The Gambia: The End of an Era', in *The Round Table,* No. 333, Abingdon, Carfax, 1995.

Wright, D. R. *The Early History of Niumi*. Ohio University Center for International Studies, 1977.

Yeebo, Z. *State of Fear in Paradise: The Coup in The Gambia and the Prospect for Democracy*. London, African Research and Information Bureau, 1995.

GHANA

Physical and Social Geography

E. A. BOATENG

PHYSICAL FEATURES

Structurally and geologically, the Republic of Ghana exhibits many of the characteristics of sub-Saharan Africa, with its ancient rocks and extensive plateau surfaces marked by prolonged sub-aerial erosion. About half of the surface area is composed of Pre-Cambrian metamorphic and igneous rocks, most of the remainder consisting of a platform of Palaeozoic sediments believed to be resting on the older rocks. These sediments occupy a substantial area in the north-central part of the country and form the Voltaic basin. Surrounding this basin on all sides, except along the east, is a highly dissected peneplain of Pre-Cambrian rocks at an average of 150–300 m above sea-level but containing several distinct ranges of up to 600 m. Along the eastern edge of the Voltaic basin and extending right down to the sea near Accra is a narrow zone of highly folded Pre-Cambrian rocks forming the Akwapim-Togo ranges. These ranges rise to 300–900 m above sea-level, and contain the highest points in Ghana. Continuing northwards across Togo and Benin, they form one of west Africa's major relief features, the Togo-Atakora range.

The south-east corner of the country, below the Akwapim-Togo ranges, is occupied by the Accra-Ho-Keta plains, which are underlain by the oldest of the Pre-Cambrian series (known as the Dahomeyan) and contain extensive areas of gneiss, of which the basic varieties weather to form heavy but agriculturally useful soils. Extensive areas of young rocks, formed between the Tertiary and Recent ages, are found only in the broad delta of the Volta in the eastern part of the Accra plains, and in the extreme south-west corner of the country along the Axim coast; while in the intervening littoral zone patches of Devonian sediments combine with the rocks of the Pre-Cambrian peneplain to produce a coastline of sandy bays and rocky promontories.

Most of the country's considerable mineral wealth, consisting mainly of gold, diamonds, manganese and bauxite, is associated with the older Pre-Cambrian rocks, although there are indications that petroleum may be available in commercial quantities in some of the younger sedimentaries.

The drainage is dominated by the Volta system, which occupies the Voltaic basin and includes the vast artificial lake of 8,502 sq km formed behind the hydroelectric dam at Akosombo. A second dam is sited at Kpong, 8 km downstream from Akosombo. Most of the other rivers in Ghana, such as the Pra, Birim, Densu, Ayensu and Ankobra, flow between the southern Voltaic or Kwahu plateau and the sea. Most are of considerable local importance as sources of drinking water, but are hardly employed for irrigation purposes.

CLIMATE AND VEGETATION

Climatic conditions are determined by the interaction of two principal airstreams: the hot, dry, tropical, continental air mass or harmattan from the north-east, and the moist, relatively cool, maritime air mass or monsoon from the south-west across the Atlantic. In the southern part of the country, where the highest average annual rainfall (of 1,270–2,100 mm) occurs, there are two rainy seasons (April–July and September–November), while in the north, with annual averages of 1,100–1,270 mm, rainfall

occurs in only a single season between April and September, followed by a long dry season dominated by the harmattan. There is much greater uniformity as regards mean temperatures, which average 26°–29°C. These temperatures, coupled with the equally high relative humidities, which fall significantly only during the harmattan, tend to produce oppressive conditions, relieved only by the relative drop in temperature at night, especially in the north, and the local incidence of land and sea breezes near the coast.

Vegetation in Ghana is determined mainly by climate and soil conditions. The area of heavy annual rainfall broken by one or two relatively short dry seasons, to be found in the south-west portion of the country and along the Akwapim-Togo ranges, is covered with evergreen forest in the wetter portions and semi-deciduous forest in the drier portions, while the area of rather lower rainfall, occurring in a single peak in the northern two-thirds of the country and the anomalously dry area around Accra, are covered with savannah and scrub. Prolonged farming activities and timber exploitation have reduced the original closed forest vegetation of some 82,000 sq km to about 24,000 sq km, while in the savannah areas prolonged cultivation and bush burning have also caused serious degradation of the vegetation.

POPULATION

Ghana covers an area of 238,537 sq km (92,100 sq miles). The March 1984 census recorded a population of 12,296,081, giving an approximate density of 51.5 inhabitants per sq km. In mid-1998, according to UN estimates, the population had increased to 19,162,000, with a density of 80.3 inhabitants per sq km. The high rate of population growth, together with the influx of large numbers—mostly youth from the rural areas into the urban centres—coupled with a virtually stagnant economy and the lack of adequate employment openings, has created serious social and political problems. In view of these demographic trends, the government has initiated a campaign of family planning and population control, and aims to improve living standards through increased economic development. The highest densities occur in the urban and cocoa-farming areas in the southern part of the country, and also in the extreme north-eastern corner, where intensive compound farming is practised.

There are no less than 75 spoken languages and dialects, each more or less associated with a distinct ethnic group. The largest of these groups are the Akan, Mossi, Ewe and the Ga-Adangme, which, according to 1991 estimates, formed respectively 52.4%, 15.8%, 11.9% and 7.8% of the population. Any divisive tendencies which might have arisen from this situation have been absent, largely as a result of governmental policies; however, a distinction can be made between the southern peoples, who have come most directly and longest under the recent influence of European life and the Christian religion, and the northern peoples, whose traditional modes of life and religion have undergone relatively little change, owing mainly to their remoteness from the coast. One of the most potent unifying forces has been the adoption of English as the official language, although it is augmented by eight major national languages.

Recent History

T. C. McCASKIE

Revised for this edition by RICHARD SYNGE

Following the Second World War, a sustained political campaign to secure independence for the Gold Coast from British colonial rule led to the emergence in 1949 of the Convention People's Party. Its leader, Dr Kwame Nkrumah, became prime minister of an indigenous ministerial government popularly elected in 1951. Subsequent progress towards full independence followed a UN-supervised plebiscite in May 1956, when the British-administered section of Togoland, a UN Trust Territory, voted to join the Gold Coast in an independent state. On 6 March 1957 the new state of Ghana was granted independence within the Commonwealth, becoming the first British dependency in sub-Saharan Africa to attain independence under majority rule. Ghana became a republic on 1 July 1960, with Nkrumah as executive president.

Under Nkrumah's leadership, Ghana established close relations with the USSR and its allies, while remaining economically dependent on Western countries. Within Ghana, political dissent was suppressed and opponents of Nkrumah were liable to imprisonment without trial. Following widespread discontent at the country's worsening economic problems, and at widespread political corruption, Nkrumah was deposed by a military coup in February 1966, led by Gen. Joseph Ankrah. In October 1969 power was returned to an elected civilian government led by Dr Kofi Busia, a prominent opposition activist from the Nkrumah period. Busia proved unable to resolve Ghana's economic problems, and in January 1972 the armed forces again took power, under the leadership of Lt-Col (later Gen.) Ignatius Kutu Acheampong. A modest improvement in Ghana's economic situation was achieved by the military junta, which announced in 1977 (despite strong public opposition to the plans, and indications of dissent within the armed forces) that it intended to relinquish power to a new government following a general election, to take place in June 1979. These arrangements, however, were forestalled in July 1978 by Lt-Gen. (later Gen.) Frederick Akuffo, the chief of the defence staff, who assumed power in a bloodless *coup d'état*.

THE RAWLINGS COUPS

Tensions within the army became evident in May 1979 when a group of junior military officers led by Flt-Lt Jerry Rawlings staged an unsuccessful coup attempt. Following a brief period in detention, Rawlings and his associates successfully seized power, amid great popular acclaim. In June an Armed Forces Revolutionary Council (AFRC) was formed by Rawlings, and Acheampong, Akuffo and other senior officers were swiftly tried, convicted of corruption, and executed.

The AFRC indicated that its assumption of power was temporary, and the general election took place in June 1979, as scheduled. The People's National Party (PNP), led by Dr Hilla Limann, emerged with the largest number of parliamentary seats and formed a coalition government with support from the smaller United National Convention. Dr Limann took office as president in September. However, dissatisfaction with measures taken by the government to improve the economy provoked renewed discontent within the armed forces. On 31 December 1981 Rawlings seized power for the second time, assuming the chairmanship of a Provisional National Defence Council (PNDC). On this occasion, Rawlings expressed no intention of restoring power to civilian politicians; instead, the PNDC adopted measures to 'democratize' political decision-making and to decentralize power. City and district councils were replaced by People's Defence Committees (PDC), in an attempt to create mass participation at local level, and to encourage public awareness and vigilance.

The 'democratization' of the army led to the creation of factions, and to the increasing division of military personnel along ethnic lines. Unsuccessful attempts to overthrow Rawlings were reported in November 1992, and again in early 1993. Although Rawlings and the PNDC remained under challenge from exiled opponents, based mainly in the United Kingdom and in neighbouring Togo, there was some improvement in economic conditions during 1984. During 1985, however, the PNDC detected a further attempt from within the army to overthrow the regime; five conspirators, allegedly linked to dissidents in Togo, were executed in May.

INTERNAL CONCERNS

The PNDC became increasingly preoccupied with domestic security in 1986 and 1987. In March 1986 a number of people were tried for involvement in a conspiracy to overthrow the government by dissident Ghanaians; several executions were subsequently carried out. In June 1987 the PNDC announced further arrests in connection with an alleged conspiracy to overthrow the government. Seven further arrests took place in November; on this occasion the detainees included former officials of the PNDC.

Various administrative reforms were introduced by the PNDC from late 1984 to 1988. In December 1984 the PDC were redesignated committees for the defence of the revolution (CDR). In December 1986 Rawlings announced that the PNDC was to seek a national mandate through district assembly elections, scheduled for mid-1987. In July 1987, however, these elections were postponed until the final quarter of 1988, and it was announced that the ban on political parties was to remain in force.

Elections to district assemblies were held in three stages, between December 1988 and February 1989. The PNDC reserved one-third of seats for its own nominees, and retained the power to scrutinize and disqualify individual candidates, although it was envisaged that the elected district assemblies would move towards regional representation, and ultimately form a national body which would supersede the PNDC.

However, the envisaged adoption of democratic reforms continued to be overshadowed by grave economic problems. In 1988 the universities were closed for four months, following renewed student unrest. In December of that year the PNDC discontinued free secondary and university education, and in the following month inaugurated a student loan scheme, provoking considerable student discontent. In addition, the PNDC's attempts to implement economic reforms were impeded by widespread mismanagement and corruption in the commercial sector. In 1989 further controls were imposed on the media; in March of that year newspaper and magazine licences became subject to review under new legislation.

In September 1989 an attempted coup took place, led by Maj. Courage Quashigah, a former commander of the military police and a close associate of Rawlings. Quainoo was subsequently dismissed as commander of the armed forces, although he remained a member of the PNDC. (Rawlings himself assumed control of the armed forces until June 1990, when Mensa-Wood was appointed to that post.) Quashigah and four other members of the security forces were charged with conspiring to assassinate Rawlings. In January 1990 five further arrests were made in connection with the coup attempt. In August the human rights organization Amnesty International criticized the continued detention of Quashigah and six other members of the security forces.

CONSTITUTIONAL TRANSITION

In 1990 there were increasing demands for an end to the ban on political activities and associations, and for the abolition of a number of laws, particularly those concerning the detention of suspects. In July of that year, in response to pressure from Western donors to increase democracy in return for a continuation in aid, the PNDC announced that a national commission for democracy (NCD), under the chairmanship of Justice Annah, a member of the PNDC, would organize a series of regional debates, which would review the decentralization process, and consider Ghana's political and economic future. In August, however, a newly-formed political association, the Movement for Freedom and Justice (MFJ), criticized the NCD, claiming that it was too closely associated with the PNDC. In addition, the MFJ demanded the abolition of a number of laws, the release of political prisoners, the end of press censorship, and the immediate restoration of democratic government. The PNDC, however, advocated a 'national consensus', rather than a return to the discredited political system. In September the MFJ accused the PNDC of intimidation, after security forces suppressed its inaugural meeting.

On 30 December 1990 Rawlings announced that a constitution was to be introduced by the end of 1991. The NCD was to present a report on the democratic process with reference to the series of regional debates. The PNDC was to consider the recommendations, and then convene a consultative body to determine constitutional reform. However, the MFJ and other opponents of the PNDC criticized the absence of a timetable for political reform and the lack of information on the composition of the proposed consultative body.

In late March 1991 the NCD presented its report, which recommended the election of an executive president for a fixed term, the establishment of a national assembly, and the creation of the post of prime minister. Rawlings announced that the PNDC would consider the report and submit recommendations to the proposed national consultative body, which was to be established in May, and to start work in July. On 10 May, contrary to previous expectations, the PNDC endorsed the restoration of a plural political system, and accepted the NCD's recommendations. It was emphasized, however, that the formation of political associations remained prohibited. The MFJ immediately challenged the veracity of the PNDC's announcement, and the state-controlled press accused the MFJ of planning subversive action. In late May a 260-member consultative assembly was established, which was to review recommendations by a government-appointed committee of constitutional experts. A new constitution was subsequently to be submitted for endorsement by a national referendum.

In June 1991 the PNDC announced an amnesty for political exiles, excepting those implicated in acts of subversion against the government. In early August a newly-formed alliance of opposition movements, human rights organizations and trade unions, including the MFJ and the socialist New Democratic Movement (NDM), known as the Co-ordinating Committee of Democratic Forces of Ghana (CCDFG), demanded that a constitutional conference be convened to determine a schedule for the transition to democracy, and that legislation prohibiting political activities be immediately repealed. Later in August the committee submitted a series of recommendations for constitutional reform, which included the establishment of a legislature, a council of state and a national security council. It was proposed that a president, who would also be c-in-c of the armed forces, would be elected by universal suffrage for a four-year term of office. However, the subsequent review of the draft constitution by the consultative assembly was impeded by opposition demands for a boycott, on the grounds that the number of government representatives in the assembly was too high. Two organizations, representing students and the legal profession, refused to attend. In the same month Rawlings announced that presidential and legislative elections would take place in late 1992.

In December 1991 Amnesty International reiterated claims that a number of prisoners in Ghana were detained for political dissension. In the same month the government announced the establishment of an interim national electoral commission (INEC), which was to assume functions formerly allocated to the NCD: the demarcation of electoral regions, and the supervision of public elections and referenda. In January 1992 the government extended the allocated period for the review of the draft constitution, originally scheduled for completion by the end of 1991, to the end of March 1992, provoking widespread speculation that Rawlings planned to delay the democratic process. In February, however, preparations for the forthcoming multi-party elections commenced; the PNDC subsequently carried out a government reshuffle. In March Rawlings announced

a programme for constitutional transition, which was to be completed in January 1993. The new constitution was to be submitted for endorsement by national referendum on 28 April 1992. Legislation permitting the formation of political associations was to be introduced on 18 May, despite opposition demands that a multi-party system be adopted prior to the referendum. A presidential election was to take place on 3 November, and was to be followed by legislative elections on 8 December. Later in March the government granted an amnesty to 17 prisoners, who had been convicted of subversion, including Quashigah.

At the end of March 1992 the consultative assembly endorsed the majority of the constitutional recommendations, which were subsequently presented for approval by the PNDC. However, the proposed creation of the post of prime minister was rejected by the assembly; executive power was to be vested solely in the president, who would appoint a vice-president. In addition, the draft constitution included a provision that members of the government be exempt from prosecution for acts committed during the PNDC's rule; opposition groups subsequently condemned the legislation, on the grounds that it contravened human rights. At the national referendum held on 28 April, however, the adoption of the draft constitution was approved by 92% of votes cast, with 43.7% of the electorate voting.

In May 1992 the government introduced legislation which ended the ban on the formation of political associations imposed in 1981; political parties were required to apply to the INEC for legal recognition. Under the terms of the legislation, however, 21 former political organizations remained proscribed, while emergent parties were not permitted to use the names or slogans of these organizations. Moreover, the permitted amounts of individual financial contributions to parties were restricted. Later in May Komla A. Gbedemah, a former member of the Nkrumah government, and 28 other prominent opposition figures, unsuccessfully applied to the high court to disallow the legislation, which, it was claimed, was biased in favour of the PNDC. At the end of May the government announced that the legislation had been amended to allow the INEC to impose a new limit for individual financial contributions.

In June 1992 a number of political organizations emerged, many of which were established by supporters of former politicians; six opposition groups subsequently obtained legal status. In the same month a coalition of pro-government organizations, the National Democratic Congress (NDC), was formed to contest the elections on behalf of the PNDC. However, an existing alliance of supporters of Rawlings, known as the Eagle Club, refused to join the NDC, and formed the Eagle Party of Ghana, subsequently known as the EGLE (Every Ghanaian Living Everywhere) Party. In July Rawlings denied that he was associated with the Eagle Club, and rejected an offer by the EGLE Party to represent it in the presidential election. In August the government promulgated legislation regulating the conducting of the forthcoming elections, which included a stipulation that, if no presidential candidate received more than 50% of votes cast, a second ballot between the two candidates with the highest number of votes would take place within 21 days.

In September 1992, in accordance with the new constitution, Rawlings retired from the armed forces (although he retained the title of c-in-c of the armed forces in his capacity as head of state), and was subsequently chosen as the presidential candidate of the NDC. (The NDC later formed an electoral coalition with the EGLE Party and the National Convention Party, NCP.) A member of the NCP, Kow Nkensen Arkaah, became Rawlings' vice-presidential candidate. Four other political groups nominated presidential candidates: the People's Heritage Party (PHP); the National Independence Party (NIP); the People's National Convention (PNC, which nominated ex-president Limann); and the New Patriotic Party (NPP). Although the establishment of a united opposition to Rawlings was discussed, the parties failed to achieve agreement, owing, in part, to the apparent conviction of the NPP (which was recognized as the strongest of the movements) that its presidential candidate, Prof. A. A. Boahen, could defeat Rawlings.

Electoral Discord

In preparation for the November 1992 presidential election, and for the subsequent legislative elections, the INEC divided Ghana into 200 constituencies. Despite controversy over the accuracy of the high number of registered voters, the PNDC, acting through the INEC, refused to carry out a revision of the electoral register. However, the INEC did arrange for the forthcoming election to be monitored by Commonwealth observers. During the pre-election period, Rawlings enacted a number of popular measures, which included substantial wage increases for civil servants and other public sector workers, and, in October, the introduction of legislation that restricted (but did not abolish) the PNDC's powers of detention without trial. However, these measures were widely viewed as electoral bribes, and their popular impact was limited. Later in October the high court dismissed an application by the MFJ for an injunction to prevent Rawlings from contesting the presidential election, on the grounds that he was not a Ghanaian national (his father was Scottish), and that he remained accountable for charges in connection with the May 1979 and December 1981 coups. Prior to the election, widespread outbreaks of sporadic violence between NPP and NDC supporters were reported.

Less than 48.3% of the registered electorate voted in the presidential election, which took place, as scheduled, on 3 November 1992. Rawlings secured 58.3% of the vote, while Boahen obtained 30.4%, Limann 6.7%, the NIP candidate, Kwabena Darko, 2.8%, and the PHP candidate, Lt-Gen. (retd) E. A. Erskine, 1.7% of votes cast. Rawlings, with more than 50% of the vote, was declared the winner. The Commonwealth observers subsequently declared that the conducting of the election had been both free and fair. However, the opposition parties, led by the NPP, claimed that widespread electoral irregularities had taken place. A curfew was imposed in Kumasi (Ashanti), following incidents of violence, and rioting by opposition supporters, in which an NDC ward chairman was killed; in addition, a series of explosive devices were detonated in Accra and Tema. The government subsequently rescheduled the legislative elections for 22 December. Later in November a prominent member of the PHP was detained, together with other opposition supporters, on the grounds of complicity in the bombings.

In early December 1992 Boahen announced that the opposition had direct evidence of electoral fraud perpetrated by the government. The opposition parties declared, however, that they would not legally challenge the result of the presidential election, but that they would boycott the forthcoming legislative elections. Accordingly, these elections (which had been postponed until 29 December) were contested only by the NDC and its allies, the EGLE Party and the NCP. On this basis, the NDC obtained 189 of the 200 seats in the parliament, while the NCP secured eight seats, the EGLE Party one seat, and independent candidates two seats. On 7 January 1993 Rawlings was sworn in as president of the Fourth Republic, the PNDC was dissolved and the new parliament was inaugurated.

THE FOURTH REPUBLIC

In early January 1993 a number of the severe economic austerity measures, introduced under the 1993 budget, resulted in an immediate increase in transport and supply costs, and food prices. The NPP, the PNC, the NIP and the PHP subsequently formed an alliance, known as the Inter-Party Co-ordinating Committee (ICC), which strongly criticized the budget (widely believed to have been formulated under the terms of the World Bank and the IMF), and announced that it was to act as an official opposition to the government, despite its lack of representation in the parliament. In March Rawlings submitted nominations for members of the cabinet and other ministers for approval by the parliament. In the same month the two main perpetrators of the bombings in November 1992 were fined and sentenced to 10 years' imprisonment. In early April the NPP published a book, entitled *The Stolen Verdict,* which provided detailed evidence of alleged malpractice by the NDC and the INEC in the presidential election. On 14 April elections were held for the 10 regional seats in the council of state, and in May a 17-member cabinet (which included a number of members of the former PNDC administration) was sworn in. International approval of the series of election results was apparently indicated by subsequent pledges of economic assistance for Ghana. However, the member parties of the ICC continued to dispute the results of the presidential election. In August the NPP (which had apparently been adversely affected by discrimination

in the allocation of government contracts) announced that it was prepared to recognize the legitimacy of the election results, thereby undermining the solidarity of the ICC. In November, in accordance with the constitution, a 20-member national security council, chaired by Arkaah, was established. In December the PHP, the NIP and a faction of the PNC (all of which represented supporters of ex-president Nkrumah) merged to form the People's Convention Party (PCP).

Ethnic Tensions and Security Concerns

In February 1994 long-standing hostility between the Konkomba ethnic group, which originated in former Togoland, and the land-owning Nanumba escalated, following demands by the Konkomba for traditional status that would entitle them to own land; some 500 people were killed in ethnic clashes in the Northern Region. The government subsequently dispatched troops to the Northern Region to restore order and imposed a state of emergency in seven districts for a period of three months; however, skirmishes between a number of ethnic factions continued, and it was reported that some 6,000 Konkomba had fled to Togo.

In March 1994 Rawlings carried out a minor reshuffle of the government. Later that month district assembly elections took place (except in the seven districts where the state of emergency remained in force); although the elections were contested on a non-party basis, it was reported that candidates who were unofficially supported by the NPP had secured the majority of seats in a number of the district assemblies. Negotiations between representatives of the various ethnic groups involved in the conflict in the Northern Region began in April, under government sponsorship. In the same month it was reported that the authorities had discovered a conspiracy to overthrow the government, which apparently involved threats to kill Quashigah (the instigator of the September 1989 coup attempt) and the editors of two private newspapers; the opposition, however, questioned the veracity of these claims. In May 1994 the NPP announced that it was to withdraw from reconciliation discussions between the government and the opposition, owing to lack of progress. In the same month a cabinet reshuffle took place, and the state of emergency in force in the Northern Region (where a total of 1,000 people had been killed, and a further 150,000 displaced) was extended for one month. In early June, however, the seven ethnic factions involved in the fighting signed a peace agreement that provided for the imposition of an immediate cease-fire and renounced violence as a means of settling disputes over land-ownership. The government subsequently announced that troops were to be permanently stationed in the Northern Region in order to pre-empt further conflict, and appointed a negotiating team, which was to attempt to resolve the inter-ethnic differences. The state of emergency was extended for a further month in June, and again in July. In early August, however, the government announced that order had been restored in the region, and ended the state of emergency.

In September 1994 five civilians, who had allegedly conspired to overthrow the government, were charged with treason. In October two men were arrested for allegedly attempting to transport armaments illicitly to the Northern Region; an increase in tension in the region was reflected by further arrests, in connection with violent incidents in which several people had been killed. Following a joint rally of the NPP, the PNC and the PCP in November, the parties announced that they would present a single candidate to contest the presidential election in 1996. Meanwhile, rumours emerged of ill-feeling between Rawlings and Vice-President Arkaah, reflecting increasing division between the NDC and NCP. In January 1995 Arkaah discounted speculation that Rawlings was responsible for allegations, which had appeared in an independent newspaper, of an illicit relationship between Arkaah and a minor, and attributed blame to subversive elements. In the same month, however, the government denied a reported statement by Arkaah that he had refused a request by Rawlings for his resignation.

In March 1995 the government imposed a curfew in the Northern Region in response to renewed ethnic violence, in which about 100 were killed. In April a joint committee, comprising prominent members of the Konkomba and Nanumba ethnic groups, was established in an effort to resolve the conflict. Meanwhile, the imposition, in February, of value-added tax

(VAT) under that year's budget prompted widespread protests, while civil servants threatened to initiate strike action if the government failed to increase salaries following the ensuing rise in consumer prices; a series of demonstrations, which was organized by a grouping of opposition leaders, Alliance for Change, culminated in May, when five people were killed in clashes between government supporters and protesters. Later that month the national executive committee of the NCP decided to withdraw the party from the government coalition, claiming that the NDC had dominated the alliance. However, Arkaah (a member of the NCP) subsequently announced that he was to retain the office of vice-president on the grounds that his mandate had not expired. In June the authorities agreed to suspend VAT, and reinstated the sales tax that had previously been in force. In July the long-serving minister of finance, Kwesi Botchwey, resigned, apparently as a result of disagreement with the government's economic policies; a minor reorganization of the council of ministers ensued. At a by-election in the same month, the vacant seat was secured by a joint candidate of the PNC, NPP, NCP and PCP. In October the chairman of the NCP resigned, following dissent within the party. In November a commission of human rights and administrative justice (CHRAJ) commenced investigations into allegations of corruption on the part of government ministers and civil servants.

In January 1996 an alleged incident in which Rawlings assaulted Arkaah during a meeting of the council of ministers prompted further speculation of discord between the president and vice-president; opposition parties subsequently demanded that Rawlings resign. Proposals by the government for widely-ranging constitutional amendments came before parliament in the same month, provoking intense hostility from opposition parties and from many traditional chiefs. The draft legislation contained proposals for changes regarding a number of issues: the composition of the public services; the chairmanship and future nature of the prison service, the armed forces council and the police council; the participation of chiefs in politics; and dual citizenship. Rawlings reshuffled the council of ministers in March.

Elected Government

In April 1996 presidential and parliamentary elections were scheduled for 10 December, although this was later changed to 7 December to meet constitutional requirements. Nominations of candidates were to take place in September. In May Kwame Pianim, prospective presidential candidate for the NPP, was disqualified from the elections on the grounds of his conviction for treason in 1982. In the same month it was announced that the Popular Party for Democracy and Development (PPDD), a group formed in 1992 by supporters of Nkrumah, was to merge with the PCP. The PPDD also announced its support for unity with the NPP. In June Thomas Appiah resigned for personal reasons as chairman of the NCP and vice-chairman of the PCP. In July the NCP announced that it had removed Kow Nkensen Arkaah as its leader, following his selection as presidential candidate by the PCP. In August the NPP and PCP announced their formation of an electoral coalition, to be known as the Great Alliance; it was subsequently announced that John Kufuor, of the NPP, was to be the Great Alliance's presidential candidate, with Arkaah, of the PCP, as the candidate for the vice-presidency. The NCP stated that it would support the NDC in the forthcoming elections, while the PNC announced its intention to contest the elections alone; Edward Mahama was subsequently selected as the PNC's presidential candidate. In September Rawlings was nominated as the NDC's presidential candidate. By 18 September, the official deadline for the nomination of candidates, only the Progressive Alliance (the NDC, the EGLE party and the Democratic People's Party–DPP), the Great Alliance and the PNC had succeeded in having their nomination papers accepted. In early October the NCP, which, according to the national electoral commission, had not presented the appropriate papers, declared its intention to take legal action against the commission to force it to accept the nomination of the party's candidates. In mid-October the electoral commission denied accusations that it had shown bias against the NCP. The selection of common candidates provoked a lengthy dispute between the NPP and the PCP, with the parties contradicting each other regarding previous agreements on the distribution

of seats. In late October at least 20 people were wounded in clashes between NDC and NPP militant supporters in Tamale (in the north) and Kibi (in the north-east). In November a network of domestic election observers, comprising 25 groups (including religious councils, the TUC, and civil servants' and journalists' associations), was created to oversee the December elections. The resignation of the minister of the interior in October was followed, in November, by the resignations of the minister of trade and industry and the presidential aide on cocoa affairs, following corruption allegations against them published in an interim report by the CHRAJ. Reports of a number of violent incidents prior to the elections included a fatal attack on an NDC activist near Kumasi, allegedly carried out by NPP supporters, which prompted a temporary ban on all political activity in the area.

The presidential and parliamentary elections took place, as scheduled, on 7 December 1996. Rawlings was re-elected as president by 57.2% of votes cast, while Kufuor secured 39.8% of the votes. In the parliamentary poll the NDC's representation was reduced to 133 seats, while the NPP won 60 seats, the PCP five and the PNC one seat. Voting was postponed in the constituency of Afigya Sekyere East, in Ashanti, because of a legal dispute concerning the eligibility of candidates. (The seat was subsequently won by the NPP in a by-election held in June 1997.) Despite opposition claims of malpractice, international observers declared that the elections had been conducted fairly, and a high electoral turnout of 76.8% was reported. Following the announcement of the election results, about 15 people were injured in clashes between NDC and opposition supporters in Bimbila, south-east of Tamale. Later in December Kofi Annan, a Ghanaian, was elected to serve a five-year term as secretary-general of the UN. At the end of that month the PCP announced that its electoral alliance with the NPP had broken down. On 7 January 1997 Rawlings was sworn in as president.

The lengthy process of appointing a new council of ministers resulted in a protracted dispute between the NDC and the opposition, prompting a series of parliamentary boycotts by the NPP, which insisted that all ministerial appointees be approved by the parliamentary appointments committee prior to assuming their duties. In late February 1997 opposition parties filed a writ in the supreme court preventing Kwame Peprah, the reappointed minister of finance, from presenting the budget. Owing to the NDC's parliamentary majority, however, procedures were approved to allow those ministers who had been retained from the previous government to avoid the vetting process. The majority of ministerial appointments were made during March and April, although a number of posts were not filled until June. In early June the supreme court ruled that all presidential nominees for ministerial positions had to be approved by parliament, even if they had served in the previous government. Following the ruling, the NPP left the chamber on several occasions when ministers attempted to address parliament. The government subsequently announced that ministers who had participated in the previous administration were prepared to undergo vetting procedures.

Following increasing accusations of government corruption, President Rawlings dismissed a minister of state in February 1998, after a committee of inquiry discovered lapses of propriety regarding a sea defence project for which the minister was responsible. In August the NCP and the PCP merged to form a new movement, the Convention Party (CP). In October the NPP again nominated Kufuor as its presidential candidate, to contest the election scheduled to take place in the year 2000. (Under the terms of the constitution, Rawlings was prohibited from seeking re-election to a third term in office, and had announced that the incumbent vice-president, Prof. John Evans Atta Mills, was to contest the election on behalf of the NDC.) In November 1998 Rawlings reorganized the government. At an NDC congress, which took place in December, the party constitution was amended to create the position for Rawlings of 'life chairman' of the party. In March 1999 a Ghanaian officer, Capt. James Owoo, who had allegedly been involved in attempts to remove the PNDC government in the 1980s, was arrested by ECOMOG forces in Sierra Leone (see below), and was transported to Accra. It was subsequently announced that Owoo had been charged with conspiring to overthrow the Rawlings government in 1998. Following dissatisfaction within the NDC at the changes carried out at the party congress, in June 1999 a disaffected group of party members formed a new political group, the National Reform Party (NRP).

Joint opposition demonstrations, organized by the NRP, NPP, PNC and CP in protest at alleged economic mismanagement, corruption and hardship, were staged in Accra on 25 November 1999. The ruling PNDC responded with a national rally in the impoverished Nima district of the capital, at which Rawlings accused the opposition of conducting a persistent campaign of misinformation and distortion. Opinion polls published at the time indicated that the NDC had 36% of voter support, against 24% for its nearest rival, the NPP.

In February 2000 Atta Mills formally announced his candidature for the NDC presidential nomination in the election due to be held later that year. In April the electoral register was reviewed in preparation for the election and the president ordered an amnesty for about 1,000 prisoners, including two former army officers convicted of subversion more than 10 years previously. Atta Mills was officially nominated as the NDC presidential candidate at the end of that month. By mid-2000 a number of opposition parties, including the CP, NRP, NPP and PNC, had also presented candidates to contest the presidential election, which was scheduled to take place on 8 December.

FOREIGN POLICY UNDER THE RAWLINGS GOVERNMENTS

In 1984 the PNDC established close links with the government of Capt. Thomas Sankara in the neighbouring state of Burkina Faso. Sankara, who seized power in August 1983, based the working structure of his 'revolution' on that of the PNDC. During 1984 Ghana also revived its involvement with the foreign policy structures of the African community, and in September of that year was elected to the chairmanship of the OAU liberation committee. In August 1986 the governments of Ghana and Burkina Faso agreed to establish a high-level political commission which would be responsible for preparing a 10-year time-table for the political union of the two countries. Agreements were also made to harmonize their currencies and their energy, transport, trade and educational systems, and in September and October a joint military exercise was held. Following a military coup in Burkina Faso in October 1987, relations between the two countries were temporarily strained, but subsequently improved, after meetings between Rawlings and Sankara's successor, Capt. Blaise Compaoré. In March 1998 Ghana and Burkina Faso agreed to establish a standing commission to manage water bodies common between the two countries. Tensions had previously arisen over Burkinabè plans to build hydroelectric dams on a major tributary of the Volta river.

In July 1985 relations between Ghana and the USA became strained when a distant relative of Rawlings, Michael Agbotui Soussoudis, was arrested by the US authorities and charged with espionage. He was subsequently convicted, and sentenced to 20 years' imprisonment. Shortly afterwards, four members of the diplomatic missions in Accra and Washington were expelled by the respective governments. In December, however, following secret negotiations between the PNDC and the Reagan administration, Boussoudis was exchanged for a number of identified CIA agents in Ghana. In the same month Joseph H. Mensah, the leader of the exiled Ghana Democratic Movement, was arrested in the USA, with two other Ghanaians, and put on trial for attempting to purchase military equipment for shipment to dissidents in Ghana. (However, charges against Mensah were invalidated by legal technicalities.) Tension between the two countries increased in March 1986, when it was discovered that a Panamanian-registered freighter en route from Buenos Aires, Argentina, to Rio de Janeiro was transporting arms and ammunition, while its 18-member crew comprised a number of known mercenaries and US veterans of the Viet Nam war. The PNDC claimed that the vessel had been destined for subversive operations against Ghana, and had been financed by a Ghanaian dissident with alleged links with the CIA. During their trial in Brazil, eight members of the crew admitted that the charges were substantially true and that the dissident, named as Godfrey Osei, had purchased the weaponry in Argentina by posing as an agent of the Ghanaian government. The eight men were sentenced to terms of imprisonment, but three of them subsequently escaped to the USA, with, according

to the Ghanaian government, the assistance of the CIA. A visit to Ghana in March 1998 by US President Clinton signified the improved relations between the two countries during the 1990s.

Relations with Togo deteriorated sharply in May 1986, following the arrest in Ghana of eight people on charges of subversion: they had allegedly been operating from a base in Togo. In June seven of the defendants were executed. In September an attempted coup in Togo was blamed, in turn, by the Togolese government on infiltrators from Ghana. The frontiers were closed, and in the following month the PNDC accused the Togolese authorities of maltreating the Ghanaians who had been detained in connection with the coup attempt. Although the borders were reopened in February 1987, relations between the two states remained strained.

Between December 1988 and January 1989 more than 130 Ghanaians were deported from Togo, where they were alleged to be residing illegally. In October 1991 the governments of Ghana and Togo signed an agreement on the free movement of goods and persons between the two countries. In October 1992, however, Ghana denied claims by the Togo government that it was implicated in subversive activity by Togolese dissidents based in Ghana. (By late 1992 more than 100,000 Togolese had taken refuge in Ghana, following the deterioration in the political situation in Togo.) In January 1993 Ghana announced that its armed forces were to be mobilized, in reaction to concern at the increasing civil unrest in Togo. In March the government of Togo accused Ghana of supporting an armed attack on the military camp at Lomé, where the Togolese president, Gen. Gnassingbe Eyadéma, resided. In January 1994 relations with Togo again became strained, following a further attack on Eyadéma's residence, which was claimed by the Togolese authorities to have been staged by armed dissidents based in Ghana. The Ghanaian chargé d'affaires in Togo was subsequently arrested, while Togolese forces killed 12 Ghanaians and bombarded a customs post at Aflao and several villages near the border between the two countries. Ghana, however, denied the accusations of involvement in the coup attempt, and threatened to retaliate against further acts of aggression. In May allegations by the Togolese government that Ghana had been responsible (owing to lack of border security) for bomb attacks in Togo resulted in further tension between the two nations. Later that year, however, relations between the two countries improved, and in November full diplomatic links were formally restored, with the appointment of a Ghanaian ambassador in Togo. In the following month Togo's border with Ghana, which had been closed in January 1994, was reopened. After discussions between Eyadéma and Rawlings in July 1995, an agreement was reached, providing for the reconstitution of the Ghana-Togo joint commission for economic, social and technical co-operation and the Ghana-Togo border demarcation commission. In August the Togolese governmment denied involvement in the assassination of a political opponent who had taken refuge in Ghana. In February 1996 both parliaments established friendship groups to examine ways of easing tensions. By the end of 1996 some 48,000 Togolese refugees were estimated to have received payment for voluntary repatriation. Eyadéma and Rawlings met again in Accra in May 1998, amid an easing of relations between the two countries. In August 1999, following Togolese incursions into Ghanaian territory and airspace, delegations from the two countries met in Ghana's Volta Region for discussions regarding the border situation. In September the Ghanaian government proposed that the Ghana–Togo border demarcation commission resume operations.

In November 1993 attacks in Ghana on Ivorian footballers and their supporters prompted violent reprisals against the Ghanaian community in Côte d'Ivoire, leading to 25 deaths. More than 10,400 Ghanaians resident in Côte d'Ivoire were subsequently repatriated, while Ghana formally protested to the Ivorian authorities. However, relations with Côte d'Ivoire improved, following the establishment of a joint commission to investigate the violence in December.

Ghana has participated in the Monitoring Group (ECOMOG) of the Economic Community of West African States (ECOWAS), which was dispatched to Liberia in August 1990 following the outbreak of conflict between government and rebel forces in that country (see chapter on Liberia). In mid-1994 some 1,000 Ghanaian troops remained in Liberia. In August of that year

Rawlings, who replaced the Beninois president as chairman of the conference of heads of state and government of ECOWAS, indicated that Ghana was to consider the withdrawal of troops from Liberia. However, it subsequently appeared that the Ghanaian contingent would remain in ECOMOG until peace was achieved, while Rawlings mediated continuing negotiations between the warring Liberian factions. In May 1996 an ECOWAS meeting, to discuss the situation in Liberia, took place at Rawlings' insistence, following intense fighting in Monrovia, Liberia. Ghana granted temporary asylum to some 2,000 Liberian war refugees, but insisted that no more could be accepted in the future. Financial assistance was received from the government of Canada for the care of the Liberian refugees. In July anxiety was expressed by Rawlings and by the government of Mali that the continuance of conflict in Liberia could impede the economic aims of ECOWAS. By mid-1997, however, some 17,000 Liberian refugees had arrived in Ghana. In late July the Nigerian head of state, Gen. Sani Abacha, succeeded Rawlings as chairman of ECOWAS. In June 1997 the Ghanaian government announced the establishment of a task force to monitor the situation in Sierra Leone, following the staging of a military coup in the previous month (see chapter on Sierra Leone). By late 1998 most of the ECOMOG forces in Liberia had been redeployed in Sierra Leone, owing to continuing unrest in that country; at mid-2000 military and civilian police personnel from Ghana were participating in the expanded UN Mission in Sierra Leone (UNAMSIL).

Economy

LINDA VAN BUREN

The Ghanaian economy is based primarily on the country's lucrative gold and cocoa sectors, although some success has been achieved towards diversification. Cocoa production was established in the country, mainly as an African smallholder crop, in the latter part of the 19th century. In the late 1950s, at the time of its political independence, Ghana was the world's leading exporter of cocoa, and this crop continued to account for 45%–70% of commodity exports in most years from the early 1970s until the 1990s, when increased mineral revenues led to a decline in cocoa's share of exports, to some 37% in 1997. The country has been known as a source of gold for many centuries; large-scale extraction commenced in the 1880s, and the sector underwent a major revival in the 1990s, which subsequently proved to be sustainable, despite a weakness in the international price of gold. Exports of timber from Ghana's forests also began in the 1880s.

At independence in 1957, Ghana possessed one of the strongest economies in Africa. However, the economy declined sharply in the following 25 years. During that period, real per caput income fell, and the government tax base was diminished by falling incomes and production and by an increase in smuggling. The resulting large deficits led to rising inflation and a burgeoning external debt burden. It also resulted in lower expenditure on, and a general neglect of, the country's infrastructure, as well as its education and health services.

By the time the second Rawlings government came to power in 1981, per caput income had diminished by one-third since 1966, and inflation was running at 142%. The new government took steps to reduce corruption and restore the basis of economic production and growth through two Economic Recovery Programmes (ERPs), developed in close collaboration with the World Bank and the IMF. ERP I, introduced in 1983, was the stabilization phase of the economy's recovery, while ERP II, covering the period 1987–90, was the structural adjustment and development stage of that recovery. Most of the subsequent policy initiatives of the government were designed under the two ERPs.

With the introduction in 1992 of its new multiparty constitution, followed by elections at the end of the year, Ghana suffered a brief period of economic uncertainty, compounded by difficulties in fiscal management and reduced earnings from cocoa and gold. Government expenditure briefly exceeded stipulated levels, after pay increases were awarded to civil servants, resulting in a suspension of programmed assistance from a number of donor agencies. In the aftermath of the elections, Rawlings's new constitutional government (little changed from its predecessor) was forced to adopt unpopular measures in its 1993 budget, and imposed sharp increases in the price of fuel, which prompted protests from trade unions and from the political parties that had boycotted the parliamentary elections.

Under the 1992 Rawlings government, the emphasis of economic policy shifted more fully towards the stimulation of the private sector as an essential part of its declared strategy of accelerated growth and the alleviation of poverty. In 1993 the government announced the liberalization of the investment code and radical revisions to tax and price-control laws. The sale of part of the government's stake in Ashanti Goldfields Co on the London and Accra stock exchanges in April 1994 represented a new stage in the opening up of the economy to foreign portfolio investment, a move which proved timely for investors from South Africa. Government holdings in a number of other companies were also sold. The government, however, continued to acknowledge the need to alleviate poverty and raise standards of living for most Ghanaians, and opted to maintain expenditure on education and basic health.

The international community has continued to support Ghana's reform efforts. Donors in June 1993 pledged US $2,100m. for 1993 and 1994 to meet Ghana's anticipated balance-of-payments difficulties. The IMF in mid-1995 approved a three-year, $258m. enhanced structural-adjustment facility (ESAF) and then in March 1998 extended the ESAF period by a further year, to June 1999, together with a $110m. loan under the facility. In May 1999 the IMF approved a new three-year ESAF of $209.4m. in support of Ghana's economic reform programme for 1999–2001. After an IMF review of Ghana's economic situation, the Fund released a further $30m.-tranche of this ESAF in November 1999.

POLICY OBJECTIVES OF THE ERP

Exchange rate and trade policy reforms were given priority in the recovery programmes, resulting in a progressive nominal devaluation of the official cedi rate between early 1983 and early 1986. A weekly foreign-exchange auction for specified transactions, but excluding cocoa exports, was introduced in September 1986. This two-tier structure was unified in February 1987, thereby ending discrimination against cocoa exports and an unrealistically low cedi exchange rate for certain specified imports, particularly petroleum. The long-established quantitative restrictions on imports, which were still in force in 1986 because of continued currency overvaluation, were lifted from almost all raw materials, spare parts and capital goods, and were replaced by a fairly uniform rate of customs tariff on most imports. Two further main reforms in exchange and trade arrangements followed. The first of these was the release of foreign exchange for importers of consumer goods by allowing their participation in the auction. The second was the licensing of a number of foreign-exchange bureaux, which were empowered to buy and sell foreign exchange independently. Policies adopted in 1992 included the abolition of the weekly foreign auction, with the aim of making exchange-rate determination a function of a freely operating interbank market. The cedi steadily depreciated in value, however, averaging C649.06 = US $1 in 1993, C956.71 = $1 in 1994, C1,200.43 = $1 in 1995, C1,637.23 = $1 in 1996, C2,050.17 = $1 in 1997, and C2,314 = $1 in 1998. By May 1999 the rate was C2,417 = $1, indicating that the rate of depreciation had slowed substantially; the cedi depreciated by only 3% in January–September 1998. Further upheaval followed, however, and in less than two years the cedi had depreciated by 49% and stood at C4,774 = $1 as of 30 May 2000. Indeed, in only the first five months of 2000 the cedi lost 26% of its value against the US dollar. The IMF formula for dealing with the adverse effects on the Ghanaian economy of external trade weaknesses continued to be the maintenance of 'adequate' international reserves; moreover, the preferred method of restraining inflation continued to be to raise already-high interest rates and to restrict government expenditure. Meanwhile, the Ghanaian government stressed the need to protect the poorest people from the weakness of the cedi and from the resultant high prices of many items on the domestic market.

In the area of public finance, the ERP aimed to raise the revenue base of the government, which had declined sharply by the early 1980s. The programme placed emphasis on a series of policies to simplify and rationalize sales and customs taxes, to improve tax administration, and to manage petroleum and other administered prices more efficiently to reduce the subsidy burden. In the case of direct taxes, a main objective was to amend tax brackets and exemptions in order to reduce the degree of progressiveness, which was seen as a main incentive for non-compliance. In the case of indirect taxes, the main objective was to integrate the *ad hoc* excise taxes on a wide range of goods into a reformed sales tax. In 1995 the government introduced value-added tax (VAT) at a rate of 17.5%, but public reaction against the move, in the form of political protests and riots, was so strong that the tax was withdrawn. In February 1997 the minister of finance announced that new VAT legislation was to be brought before parliament, with the intention of re-introducing the tax from 1 January 1998. The VAT law was finally passed in February 1998, and VAT came into force in December 1998 at a rate of 10%. The ERP also sought to rationalize the import tariff as the central instrument of trade protection. Finally, and as a by-product of exchange-rate policies, the major devaluations of the currency significantly boosted, in cedi terms, tax revenues on cocoa earnings.

In the area of budgetary expenditure, successive IMF programmes sought to monitor and limit government expenditure while changing the structure of that expenditure; the civil-service and parastatal payrolls were progressively reduced. Major changes were introduced in price and subsidy policies. ERP I introduced a series of rises in cocoa producer prices to encourage higher production levels. A 1987 World Bank credit introduced a scheme to relate Ghanaian producer prices to world prices on a formula basis. Price controls were relaxed on some 700 items, effectively terminating the implicit social contract on wages and prices which had operated through the 1970s and the early 1980s. The result was that many items became more readily available, but often at a price too high for many consumers. Subsidies on a number of items, such as fertilizers and pesticides, were at first reduced and in many cases later removed.

The 1983 ERP also provided for changes to the policy of state ownership. At an early stage a consultant study recommended that 80 of 235 state enterprises be converted into joint ventures with the private sector, be completely divested, or in a few cases be liquidated. Progress was initially slow, but some 52 enterprises had been divested by mid-1993, of which 33 were sold to foreign investors, and by 1996, more than 180 had been disposed of. In addition, some parastatal companies previously considered to be 'strategic', such as Ghana Airways and the Posts and Telecommunications Corpn (now Ghana Telecommunication Co), were designated for transfer to the private sector. Government shares in mining and banking were transferred to the private sector in 1994 and 1995. In early 1996 the government indicated that it intended to accelerate the privatization process; the World Bank extended a US $26.45m. credit towards Ghana's $36.25m. privatization scheme, which was due for completion in December 2001. About 20 state-owned enterprises were offered for sale in 1998. The International Finance Corpn (IFC), the private-sector organ of the World Bank, became very active in Ghana during the late 1980s and the 1990s, adding no fewer than 25 Ghanaian companies to its portfolio during that period. Assistance was sometimes in the form of an equity participation, but was more often as a loan, varying in size from $120,000 for a corrugated-carton manufacturer in 1991 to $6.58m. for an open-pit gold-mining operation in 1988.

The 1989 ESAF supported the unification, in mid-1990, of the auction and foreign bureau exchange rates, further privatization measures, a further relaxation of trade restrictions, and the liberalization of fuel prices. Ghana's first stock exchange, based in Accra, began functioning in late 1990 with three stockbroking firms. By May 2000 the stock exchange had 22 stockbrokers and 21 listed companies in manufacturing, mining, banking and insurance.

Ghana's economic programme for 1995–97 aimed to increase real growth in gross domestic product (GDP) to 5.5%, to reduce inflation to 5% (subsequently revised to 15%), to reduce the external current-account deficit to 2.7% of GDP, and to achieve a budgetary surplus of 1.3% of GDP by 1997. At the end of the period, assessments indicated that real GDP growth was 5.1% in 1997, inflation was running at 20%, and the current-account deficit had fallen from 8.3% of GDP in 1996 to 6.4% in 1997. The out-turn budgetary surplus, however, exceeded the target comfortably, as 3.4% of GDP. New targets were set for 1998, including real GDP growth of 5.6%, real GDP per caput growth of 2.5%, inflation of not more than 11% by the end of 1998 (and of not more than 5.5% by the end of 1999), a current-account deficit equivalent to not more than 7.3% of GDP and the maintenance of gross international reserves sufficient to cover 2.7 months of imports. The budgetary surplus was forecast at 4% of GDP in 1998. Only some of these targets were achieved; out-turn figures for 1998 indicated that real GDP growth, at 4.7%, failed to meet the target; that real GDP per caput grew only by 1.8%; and that inflation increased dramatically in March and April, owing to drought, before declining to an official annual rate of 15.7% in December 1998, still far higher than the targeted rate. However, the current-account deficit, at 6% of GDP, was successfully restrained, and the gross international reserves were, according to the IMF, consistently higher than the amount targeted. Real GDP growth in 1999 was only about 4.4%, failing to meet the target of 5.5% for that year. GDP growth for 2000 was targeted at 5.0%.

ECONOMIC PERFORMANCE UNDER THE ERP

By the end of 1982 Ghana's economy was severely flawed. Against this general background, economic performance since 1983 can be considered very successful, although further progress is necessary to achieve broad-based growth at all levels of the economy.

Real GDP increased at an average rate of 3% per annum in 1980–90 and 4.4% in 1990–99. The deficit on the current account of the balance of payments, which had increased to US $603m., was reduced by more than one-half in 1998, to $261m. In 1999, particularly in the second half of the year, Ghana's balance of payments came under heavy pressure during a period of weak demand for the country's exports. Whereas an overall balance-of-payments surplus of $59.9m. had been projected, an actual deficit of $93m. for that year was recorded. The government's efforts to reduce inflation were only partially successful, even before the 1995 VAT fiasco. Although the rate of inflation was effectively controlled in 1990 and 1991, it increased sharply following the political transition of 1992 and on an end-of-period basis amounted to 27.7% in 1993, 34.2% in 1994, 70.8% in 1995, 32.7% in 1996, 20.8% in 1997 and officially 15.7% in 1998. The rate of inflation decelerated to 9.4% at May 1999, the lowest level since March 1992. However, inflation subsequently increased dramatically. The end-of-period inflation rate was targeted at 12% for 2000 and at 8% for 2000–02. The main reason for the doubling of inflation in 1995 was the introduction of VAT, but food shortages in the first quarter of the year also contributed. The lack of a sufficiently developed financial sector rendered the imposition of high interest rates largely ineffective in curbing inflation in the face of intense currency speculation.

Private investment was deterred in the early 1990s by perceptions both of financial instability and of political obstacles placed in the way of businesses owned by known opponents of the government, while anticipated flows of foreign and Ghanaian private capital were not realized. New investment was concentrated in relatively few areas, principally in gold mining and, to a lesser extent, in tourism. Much of the economy is based on short-term trading activity, and it was the services sector that exhibited the strongest growth during the recovery period. In 1999 the highest level of growth (5%, compared with 6% in 1998) was recorded by the services sector, while the industrial sector expanded by 4.9% and agriculture by 3.9%. Agriculture continued to make the largest contribution to GDP, at 36.5%, followed by the services sector, with 29.2%, and industry, with 25.2%.

As the economy recovered, imports increased sharply, from US $499.7m. in 1983 to $2,128m. in 1997, and to an estimated $2,896m. in 1998, on a free-on-board (f.o.b.) basis. Official estimates indicated that total f.o.b. imports amounted to $2,792m., representing a 3.6% reduction compared with 1998. Exports (f.o.b.) amounted to an estimated $2,031m. in 1999, a decline compared with 1998, as the terms of trade suffered for both of Ghana's principal exports, cocoa and gold. In volume terms, exports of both these commodities increased, but lower prices resulted in a decrease in receipts. Substantial inflows of external concessionary assistance maintained the overall balance of payments in surplus in most years of the 1990s, at $53.2m. in 1993, $172.1m. in 1994 and $256.5m. in 1995, although the $83.1m. surplus forecast for 1996 became a $14m. overall deficit, before recovering to a surplus of $25m., followed by an estimated surplus of $99m. in 1998. Although surpluses of $77m. (later revised to $59.9m.) in 1999, $34m. in 2000 and $88m. in 2001 were projected, a rapid decline in the terms of trade in the second half of 1999 prompted a $93m. shortfall on the overall balance for that year; the balance for 2000 was targeted to neither increase nor decline.

POPULATION

According to the results of the March 1984 census, Ghana's population had increased by 43% since 1970, to reach 12.3m. The heaviest concentrations were in the regions of Ashanti (2.1m.), Eastern (1.7m.), Greater Accra (1.4m.), and Volta (1.2m.). The least populous regions were Upper East and Upper West. About 50% of the population were under 15 years of age, and 40% lived in or around the principal metropolitan areas. Ghana's population became increasingly urbanized, with an estimated 5.5% rise in the average annual growth rate of the urban population in 1980–85, compared with an average annual growth rate of 3.4% for the whole country over the same period. During 1990–96, according to World Bank estimates, the population increased by an average of 2.7% per year. In August 1996 the minister of finance announced that a population census would be carried out in 1998, at a cost of C2,000m.; however, the census was subsequently rescheduled to take place in 2000.

At the 1984 census the Ghanaian labour force was about 5.6m., of whom 41% worked in agriculture and 23% were engaged in service industries. Despite opposition from trade unions, the recognition of chronic over-employment in the public sector resulted in attempts to reduce the public-sector workforce, while raising the wages of remaining employees, by redeployment of labour to the agricultural sector. By 1998 54.7% of the labour force worked in the agricultural sector, while only 7.7% were employed in the service sector, largely as a result of the government's efforts to reduce public-sector employees. In order to help those affected by its economic retrenchment policies, the government launched the Programme of Action to Mitigate the Social Costs of Adjustment (PAMSCAD) in 1988 and obtained pledges of US $140m. from donors to finance it. The first part of the PAMSCAD comprised a series of schemes to generate employment for those (about 45,000) affected by the job losses in the public sector during 1988–90. The second part aimed to strengthen community social programmes, including self-help groups. The final part was intended to provide the most vulnerable groups in society with basic needs, such as water and sanitation, health care, nutrition and housing. In 1995 redundant staff of the Ghana Cocoa Board (COCOBOD, see below) were to be retrained under a C890m. national programme, funded by the European Union (EU) and the government. In the following year a C4,000m. Entrepreneurial Scheme, partly funded by the African Development Bank (ADB), was introduced by the government to encourage former civil servants to find employment in the agricultural sector. A further round of public-sector wage and price revisions was implemented in January 1997.

AGRICULTURE

In 1999 the agricultural sector (including forestry and fishing) accounted for 36.5% of GDP and employed more than one-half of the working population. Cocoa is traditionally Ghana's most important cash crop, occupying more than one-half of all the country's cultivated land. Output declined steadily during the 1970s, owing to a lack of financial incentives for farmers, an overvalued cedi, unreliable payment procedures, low producer prices, ageing and diseased trees, shortages of fertilizers and vital pesticides, and poor transport and distribution services. The decline continued into the 1980s, exacerbated by drought, bush fires and smuggling (this activity, mainly into Côte d'Ivoire, Togo and Burkina Faso, led to losses of about 50,000 metric tons of cocoa per year).

In October 1983 the government launched a US $130m. campaign under ERP I to revitalize the cocoa sector. The Cocoa Marketing Board (CMB) was reorganized to implement the campaign more efficiently. Cash incentives were offered to farmers to replant crops, and producer prices were increased by 67% in cedi terms, though in terms of real purchasing power the price rise had little effect. Essential inputs, such as insecticides, building materials and sprayers, were made available, and improvements were made to transport and distribution services. Financial assistance was provided by the World Bank. Attention was also focused on estate rehabilitation and disease control in the major growing areas in the Ashanti and Western Regions (although the areas worst affected by disease were the Eastern and Central Regions). Progress was slow, owing to shortages of labour, resistance by farmers to the uprooting of old trees in order to prevent the spread of disease to new pods, and continued doubts about the adequacy of price incentives. Although more than 3m. hybrid cocoa pods were distributed to private farmers for planting in mid-1985, many farmers chose to plant food crops rather than cocoa, because they preferred to be provided with essential commodities rather than receive payment in cedis. Later in 1985 the CMB was reorganized as COCOBOD, and in July 1986 a new agreement, proposed by the World Bank, fixed the level of producer prices. In Ghana 320,000 ha of cocoa farming land were designated as special zones for rehabilitation and spraying to prevent black pod disease. Under ERP II, the government aimed to increase cocoa production to more than 350,000 metric tons per year. However, this target initially proved to be over-optimistic, and output remained below 300,000 metric tons per year, totalling only 243,000 tons in 1991/92, 240,000 tons in 1993 and 270,000 tons in 1994. Subsidies on fertilizers were abolished, and high rates of interest discouraged farmers from seeking credit from the commercial banks. In late 1997, however, global cocoa prices reached a nine-year high, at £1,186 per metric ton, enabling the government to act swiftly to make good on its promise of sharing out this good fortune with the farmers. In June 1997 the government raised the producer price of cocoa from C1.2m. per metric ton to C1.8m., an increase of 50%. Following this measure, the farmer received 54% of the estimated f.o.b. price received from the sale of cocoa by the government to overseas purchasers, and it was announced that this proportion was to rise to 60% by the year 2000; in October 1998 the proportion increased to 56%. By the late 1990s cocoa output was on target, at 325,000 tons in 1995/96, 330,000 tons in 1996/97, 370,000 tons in 1997/98, 409,360 tons in 1998/99, and an estimated 407,000 tons in 1999/2000. New cocoa-output targets of 500,000 tons by the year 2004/05 and 700,000 tons by 2009/10 were set. The volume of exports of cocoa beans increased by 3% in 1999, to 336,043 tons; but at the same time the value of cocoa exports declined sharply, by 12%, to $541m. The government in 1998 restated its intention to resist pressure from the IMF and the World Bank to liberalize the external marketing of cocoa, which was still carried out exclusively by the government. In July 1993 COCOBOD was deprived of its monopoly over the internal marketing of cocoa, and three trading companies were licensed to purchase cocoa direct from farmers; by 1999 18 companies had been licensed to buy cocoa from the producers. Cocoa achieved the highest growth level of any agricultural subsector, at 11.1% in 1995. In 1996 export earnings from cocoa reached $508.6m., exceeding the $425.3m. target by almost 20%. In 1997 the government proposed that the Produce Buying Co was to be floated on the Ghana Stock Exchange; this measure was implemented in February 2000.

Ghana also achieved some diversity in cash-crop production during the 1990s. Output of edible oil crops in 1999 amounted to 920,000 metric tons of oil-palm fruit, 310,300 tons of coconuts, 212,490 tons of groundnuts in shells and 55,000 tons of karite nuts (sheanuts). On a small scale, both for local consumption and for export, Ghanaian farmers have begun to grow such crops as cashew nuts, brazil nuts, oranges, lemons, limes, apples, melons, papayas, mangoes, avocados, tomatoes, cucumbers, onions, green beans, aubergines, chillies, okra, peppercorns, ginger and raspberries. In 1996 export promotion villages were established to produce a number of high-value export crops.

Food production is based principally on the farming of cassava, yams, cocoyams (taro), plantains and maize. After severe fluctuations of output in the 1970s and the early 1980s, staple food production had increased to 6.8m. metric tons by 1988. Despite severe floods, a crop surplus was reported in 1989. Ethnic conflict in the north of the country (a principal agricultural region) in 1994 adversely affected the sector; nevertheless, maize production increased to 1.0m. tons in 1995, according to the FAO, compared with 574,000 tons in 1985. In 1999 Ghana produced 7.8m. tons of cassava (an increase of 8.6%, compared with 7.2m. tons in 1998), 3.2m. tons of yams (an increase of 23.4%, compared with 2.6m. tons in 1998), 2.05m. tons of plantains, and 1.7m. tons of cocoyams; all these crops had larger harvests in 1999 than in 1998. The maize harvest of 1.0m. tons was about the same level as in 1998, but the 1999 sorghum crop, at 302,020 tons, had declined by 22%, compared with 387,400 tons in 1998, and the millet harvest declined from 172,000 tons in 1998 to 159,750 tons in 1999. Only paddy rice experienced an upturn, from 193,600 tons in 1998 to 209,750 tons in 1999. Still, while external factors had a severe negative impact on the overall inflation rate during 1999, food prices achieved greater stability, declining from an annual inflation rate of 21.8% for the period ending December 1998 to just 3.8% in May, and remained, according to government estimates, in single digits for the remainder of 1999.

To maintain the continuity of food supplies throughout the year, the government established a national food security and buffer stock system. A price-support structure, to combat fluctuating producer prices, was introduced in 1985, and other reforms included selling state farms back to the private sector. The ministry of agriculture also set up a national resource allocation committee, which aimed to rationalize the distribution of inputs and equipment. The ministry drew up a pilot scheme for intensive food-crop production in the Accra plains, on previously unused land.

In 1987 the government introduced a four-year agricultural programme, which included proposals to privatize certain services provided by the secretariat for agriculture and to reorganize its planning and research unit. In 1991 the government implemented a Medium Term Agricultural Development Programme (1991–2000), which aimed to achieve complete self-sufficiency in food by the year 2000. The programme included proposals to diversify staple crops and improve livestock production; farmers were to receive subsidized loans from local banks to purchase high-yield seed and fertilizers. In 1997 the government announced that the outgrower scheme in the cultivation of oil palms and other cash crops had been so successful that it was to be used as the basis for similar schemes in other food and cash crops, particularly cereals and tubers. The yield of yams was to be improved by the use of better cultivation techniques.

Cattle farming is restricted to the Northern Region and the Accra plains. Production of meat is insufficient to meet local annual demand of about 200,000 metric tons. Imports of livestock from adjacent countries have been considerable, though declining in recent years, owing to shortages of foreign exchange. To revitalize the livestock sector, the government undertook to rehabilitate and restock the six cattle stations at Pong-Tamale, Ejura, Babile, Kintampo, Amrahia and Nungua. An outbreak of African swine fever occurred in 1999 in parts of the Central and Greater Accra regions, but was successfully contained in February 2000. The government paid C1,050m. in compensation to pig farmers whose stock had to be slaughtered to control the disease. Domestic fisheries (marine and Volta Lake) supply only about one-half of the country's total annual demand of 600,000 tons. The total catch in 1995 was 344,460 tons. The fisheries sector increased by 1.8% in 1998, and by 1.0% in 1999.

Ghana has extensive forests, mostly in the south-west, and developed a substantial timber export industry during the 1960s. The establishment of a Timber Marketing Board (TMB), with powers to fix minimum contract prices, marked the begin-

ning of a decline in this sector, and in 1985 the TMB was replaced by the Forest Products Inspection Bureau and the Timber Export Development Board. Efforts are proceeding to promote timber exports, which are projected eventually to reach 700,000 cu m per year. However, exports declined from 614,000 cu m in 1994 to 364,768 cu m in 1996. The government has undertaken to phase out exports of raw logs and to encourage local processing of timber products, following the introduction in late 1993 of duty incentives for imports of sawmilling and other equipment. Forest replanting, which was being carried out at an annual rate of 11,000 ha in the early 1970s, had declined to 4,000 ha per year by the late 1980s. Ghana, however, possesses enough timber to meet its foreseeable domestic and export requirements until the year 2030. In 1989 a forest management programme was initiated, financed by US $30.6m. from the IDA. The World Bank also made $39.4m. available for forest protection. In 1996 the government decided to prohibit mineral exploration in areas classified as forest reserve; however, in late 1997 the ministry of lands and forests issued new guidelines, under which companies submitting an Environmental Management Plan and paying for forest rehabilitation would be permitted to carry out mining exploration within rainforest reserves. Export earnings from timber increased to $165.4m. in 1994 (compared with $88m. in 1989), becoming Ghana's third most important export, before falling back to $146.9m. in 1996, 31% short of the $212.4m. target. Timber exports amounted to $174m. in 1999. The forestry sector accounted for an estimated 3.7% of GDP and for 9.4% of total export earnings in 1996. In 1995 more than 800,000 teak trees were planted on a 250-ha site at Somanya, in the Eastern Region by a joint Ghanaian-Dutch company which planned to bring a further 450 ha under teak during 1996 and to cover some 10,000 ha with teak in the Ashanti Region by the year 2000. A wood industry training centre at Ejisu, near Kumasi, was opened in 1998. The government provided funding in 1999 to the Forest Research Institute to enable it to develop seedlings for distribution to tree farmers. Most of Ghana's timber was still exported in the form of sawlogs, and the government was promoting industries that would add value to Ghana's timber before export; more than 95% of all roundwood removals in Ghana were for locally consumed fuelwood.

MANUFACTURING

Apart from traditional industries such as food processing, Ghana has a number of long-established large and medium-sized enterprises, including a petroleum refinery and plants producing textiles, vehicles, cement, paper, chemicals and footwear, and some export-based industries, such as cocoa-processing and wood-processing plants.

The manufacturing industries have traditionally been underused, high-cost and strongly dependent on imported equipment and materials. Expansion has been deterred by low levels of investment, by transport congestion and by persistent shortages of imported materials and spares. Moreover, the consistent overvaluation of the cedi and the irregularity of supply have increased the attractiveness of imports relative to home-produced goods.

Manufacturing output stagnated in the 1970s and then declined sharply in the early 1980s, and the sector's contribution to Ghana's total GDP fell from 22% in 1973 to under 5% before the commencement of ERP I in 1983. There was an increase to 8% in 1986, and to nearly 10% of GDP in 1990. This recovery was assisted by freer access to imports, following the liberalization measures implemented under the adjustment programme. Almost all industries continued to be affected by shortages of raw materials, spare parts and other imported machinery, irregular electricity supplies, and inflation. These factors, together with poor planning, lack of co-ordination, and duplication, especially in the soap, textile and beverage industries, reduced average capacity utilization to as low as 20% in 1985. However, manufacturing output recovered somewhat in 1986, as more capital equipment was purchased by producers, using the new foreign-exchange auctions. In 1988 the rate of capacity utilization reached 62%. Manufacturing GDP increased by an average of 3.6% per year in 1985–95, by 4.0% in 1998, and by 4.8% in 1999. The contribution of the industrial sector to total GDP increased from less than 12% in 1983 to an estimated

25.2% in 1999. Industrial GDP increased at an average annual rate of 5.4% in 1985–95, 3.2% in 1998 (the decline being mainly a result of electricity shortages), and 4.9% in 1999.

Among the largest capital-intensive industries in Ghana is an aluminium smelter at Tema, operated by the Volta Aluminium Co (VALCO), which is owned by the multinational Kaiser Aluminum and Chemical Corpn (90%) and the Reynolds Metals Co (10%). Although the Tema plant has a potential output capacity of 200,000 metric tons of primary aluminium per year, production was running at less than 50,000 tons annually in the mid-1980s, owing to lower world demand and reduced energy supplies from the drought-stricken Akosombo hydroelectricity plant. Although production at Tema recovered to 152,000 tons in 1997, output of only 56,000 tons was estimated for 1998, owing to electricity shortages. Other developments in the manufacturing sector during the 1980s included the reopening of a glass factory at Aboso, with a capacity of 25,000 tons per year; a US $36m. project to increase palm oil production, including the opening of a new $15m. palm oil mill in 1987, with a capacity of 25,000 tons per year; a new cement factory using local raw materials; the rehabilitation of Ghana Sugar Estates to produce alcohol; Chinese funding for three rice mills; and the construction of a citronella distillation plant at Bonso. Privatization of the manufacturing sector accelerated in 1993, and the Divestiture Implementation Committee undertook to sell the government's shares in a number of enterprises, including the Tema food complex, the Ghana Industrial Holding Co's pharmaceutical subsidiary, the Bonsa Tyre Co (including its rubber estate) and cocoa processing factories in Tema and Takoradi. The divestiture programme was expanded in 1994 and 1995 to include some important state-owned enterprises. In 1996 a number of enterprises, including Coca-Cola Ltd, experienced higher production, employment and export levels following privatization. Coca-Cola announced in May 1999 that it was to invest $10m. in its bottling and production industry in Ghana.

Evidence of increasing foreign investor confidence is apparent in the repurchase by multinationals, such as Unilever and Guinness, of shares in their Ghanaian operations that had been held by government. In an attempt to encourage new investments by US corporations, the government repealed some restrictive legislation, and in early 1993 prepared new investment legislation for presentation to parliament. This enactment sharply reduced the minimum capital requirements for new foreign investment and reserved very few activities exclusively for Ghanaians. Dividends, profits and the original investment capital could be repatriated freely in convertible currency, and tax incentives and benefits were improved. In 1995 the government introduced the free zone act, established the Ghana Free Zones Board and invited companies to invest in export-processing activities in Ghana. The board's role was strictly regulatory, and companies were allowed 100% ownership of free-zone enterprises. Investors were granted total exemption from duties on imported raw materials, exemption from withholding tax on dividends, and from income tax in the first 10 years (with an income tax rate of not more than 8% in the second 10 years). In addition, companies were allowed to sell up to 30% of their output into the Ghanaian market. By 1997 over 60 companies had applied for free-zone licences. By February 2000 the government acknowledged that measures were required to prevent 'leakages' from the zone into the domestic market.

MINING

Mining production increased by 3.0% in 1999, compared with a rise of 6.1% in 1998. The fall in growth was due largely to the weakness of the international price of gold. The volume of Ghana's gold exports increased by 9% in 1999, but the value rose by only 3% as the international gold price continued to stagnate. Gold is Ghana's principal mineral export and has accounted for an increasing proportion of total export earnings in recent years, replacing cocoa as the leading export commodity in 1992. Ghana produced 2.5m. oz of gold in 1999, compared with 2.3m. oz in 1998 (ranking as the tenth-largest gold producer in the world). The principal mine is situated at Obuasi and is the ninth largest in the world. It is operated by the Ashanti Goldfields Co, which is part owned by Lonrho PLC of the United

Kingdom. The potential of Ashanti Goldfields was demonstrated by the successful flotation of 26% of its shares on the London and Accra stock exchanges in April 1994. With the shares selling at more than $20 per unit, the government received more than $300m. and the company more than $50m. The government retained a 31% share in the company. In August 1995 Ashanti placed 3m. new shares without the participation of the government, whose share declined from 31% to 28.8%, or of Lonrho, whose shareholdings fell to 41.4%. In 1996, amid speculation regarding a possible takeover by South Africa's Anglo American Corpn, Ashanti acquired the UK's Cluff Resources, International Gold Resources of Toronto and GLAMCO, and concluded a merger with Australia's Golden Shamrock Mines. The company also became listed on the New York and Toronto stock exchanges. The government reduced its shareholding to 19%, with Lonrho owning 34%.

In 1992 substantial new investment was under way in the gold mining sector, with Ashanti Goldfields (which accounted for two-thirds of Ghana's official production in 1996) implementing a number of measures to expand its output. The company has initiated a programme, at an estimated cost of US $250m., to increase production capacity from underground sources to 600,000 oz per year, established a new open-pit sulphide operation, and developed a new surface operation, with an estimated output of 38,000 oz per year. Output at the main Obuasi mine reached 940,000 oz in 1995 and exceeded 1m. oz in 1996, before declining to 850,000 oz in 1998. Nevertheless, pre-tax profits at Ashanti Goldfields declined by 46% in 1996, to $60.1m., owing to increased operating costs at Obuasi. Corrective action, proposed in 1997, included the renegotiation of large supply contracts, the rationalization of the labour force and the elimination of high-cost contractors. Meanwhile, the global price for gold plunged to a 20-year low of $325 per oz in July 1997, and then deteriorated even further, to $276.8 per oz in May 1999. Miners initiated strike action in support of demands for salary increases in May 1999. The other major investments in gold were largely from private sources, while the activities of the government-owned State Gold Mining Corpn (SGMC) continued to be hindered by technical difficulties. Following the political changes in South Africa, investors from that country bought Tarkwa Goldfields from the SGMC in the mid-1990s, and almost immediately the inflow of new investment became evident as new facilities were constructed, virtually transforming the Tarkwa site (where gold reserves are measured at 13m. oz). In 1997 plans to develop the northern reef at Tarkwa were strongly opposed by villagers who were dissatisfied with the resettlement terms that they had been offered. As of June 1997, 123 local and 74 foreign mine operators were active in Ghana.

Following exploration and development by private investors from 1985, several medium-scale gold producers, mainly using open-pit methods, commenced production in 1991/92. These included Teberebie Goldfields, Billiton Bogusu, Ghana Australian Goldfields, Goldenrae Mining Co (which ceased operations in 1993) and Bonte. Some received financial support and equity contributions from development finance companies, particularly the IFC and European bilateral institutions. Gold mining investment in the period 1987–91 totalled some US $600m. The highest-producing companies after Ashanti in 1993–95 were Teberebie Goldfields, controlled by Pioneer Group of the USA (235,470 oz in 1995), Ghana Australian Goldfields at Iduapriem (124,279 oz in 1995) and Billiton Bogusu, owned by Gencor of South Africa (107,677 oz in 1995). In 1992 the government announced its intention to draft, in consultation and discussion with mining companies, legislation to regulate the conduct of the companies, following a report on the impact of gold mining on the environment.

Diamonds, which are mainly industrial stones, are mined both by Ghana Consolidated Diamonds (formerly Consolidated Africa Selection Trust) at Akwatia and by local diggers. Total recorded production dwindled from 3.2m. carats in 1960 to 442,000 carats in 1987, and to only 300,000 carats in 1988. Diamond output recovered as a result of efforts to regularize small-scale mining after 1990, and reached about 500,000 carats in 1992, advancing to 739,967 carats in 1994 but then falling back to 631,337 carats in 1995.

Ghana entered petroleum production in 1978, when a US company began extracting petroleum from the continental shelf near Saltpond. Reserves at Saltpond were estimated at 7m. barrels, but average output during the early 1980s was only 1,250 barrels per day (b/d). In 1986 another US company ceased operations at Saltpond, owing to a decline in profits. In 1983 the government established the Ghana National Petroleum Corpn (GNPC) to develop offshore areas under production-sharing contracts. In 1984 foreign oil companies were invited to bid for exploration and production licences in 70% of its offshore blocks. Exploration and production rights were set out under the 1984 Petroleum Law, which allowed the government to take an initial 10% share in any venture, with the option of buying 50% of production and holding a 50% royalty on output. As of 1993, however, following some exploratory drilling, no commercial quantities of petroleum had been identified, although various gas projects for power generation were in the process of being developed. In June 1997, Santa Fe, a US company, announced a production-sharing contract with the ministry of mines and energy and the GNPC which entitled Santa Fe to carry out exploratory oil and gas activities in the 10,500 sq km Keta Block, located at the delta of the Volta. Some 80% of the concession is offshore. Ghana's proven reserves of petroleum were estimated at about 16m. barrels in December 1995. In that year the decision was taken to re-appraise a natural gas deposit at Cape Three Points, discovered initially in 1974, and in 1997 the GNPC signed agreements with two foreign consortia for offshore exploration and production in the area. In September 1995 Ghana joined Nigeria, Togo and Benin in signing an agreement to proceed with the construction of a US $270m. West African gas pipeline from Nigeria to the three recipient countries. The country's sole refinery, the 45,000 b/d Tema oil refinery (TOR), was operated by the Ghanaian-Italian Petroleum Co and was owned by GNPC. A new unit was to be built at the refinery to convert excess residual fuel into petrol and liquefied petroleum gas (LPG). Plans for a partial privatization of the TOR by the end of 1999 were announced, with 30% to be sold to a 'strategic investor' with management control and 25% to be floated on the stock exchange; however, parliament in November 1998 objected to the sale of the TOR, as well as the Ghana Oil Co (GOC), on the grounds that these were 'strategic assets'. This prompted the IMF in January 1999 to urge the government to continue its privatization plans as scheduled. Nigeria is the principal supplier of crude petroleum to Ghana; other suppliers include Iran, Libya and Algeria. The GNPC disposed of some of its non-petroleum assets in March 1998, and paid off its debt to the Bank of Ghana in April of that year.

Ghana possesses substantial reserves of bauxite, although only a small proportion, at Awaso in the Western Region, is currently mined. Exploitation of these deposits is carried out by the Ghana Bauxite Co (GBC), in which the government holds a 55% interest. Bauxite output, which is all exported, fell from more than 300,000 metric tons per year during the 1950s to less than 30,000 tons by the mid-1980s, owing to the rapid deterioration of the railway line linking Awaso with port facilities at Takoradi. Following the virtual closure of the line in 1984, the GBC temporarily ceased operations, although output recovered to 170,000 tons in 1985, as repairs to the rail link progressed. Production had increased further to 426,100 tons by 1994 and reached 513,000 tons in 1995, before falling to an estimated 413,200 tons in 1996. Plans to utilize the large bauxite deposits at Kibi for the VALCO aluminium smelter at Tema failed to materialize because of funding difficulties and opposition from Kaiser Aluminum, which currently imports bauxite from Jamaica for use at the Tema plant.

Manganese ore is mined at Nsuta, in the Western Region, by Ghana National Manganese Corpn. Despite obsolete equipment and limited transport facilities at Takoradi Port and the main railway, ore production of 230,000–260,000 metric tons annually was achieved in the second half of the 1980s, increasing to 319,000 tons in 1991, but declining to 269,700 tons in 1994 and 100,000 tons in 1995, before increasing dramatically to an estimated 447,900 tons in 1996. Albeit that production recently has averaged at about one-half of the output levels in the 1960s, Ghana ranks as the world's eighth largest producer of manganese.

In 1986 the government introduced a new mineral code, whereby new mining projects were required to be self-financing in foreign exchange and were granted external account status. The new code made Ghana highly attractive to foreign investors, but almost all of their interest has been focused on gold, with remaining finance being directed to the diamond industry. In February 2000 the government confirmed plans to intensify aerial geophysical surveys and seismic monitoring activities, and to upgrade old geological maps, in order to identify the country's mineral reserves more efficiently.

ELECTRICITY

Until the opening of the Akosombo hydroelectricity plant on the Volta Lake in 1966, electricity production came solely from diesel generators that were operated by the Electricity Corpn of Ghana (ECG) or by the mines. In 1986 the Akosombo plant, with an installed generating capacity of 912 MW, and later the 160-MW Kpong plant, together provided virtually all of Ghana's electricity needs, and allowed electricity to be exported to Togo and Benin—when rain was sufficient. Drought in the early 1980s and again in 1998 caused the plants to operate far below capacity, leading to power interruptions. In the early 1980s the Volta River Authority (VRA), which operates electricity supply from the Volta Lake, was forced to restrict output, owing to a reduction of water levels after two years of drought. Sporadic interruptions in the electricity supply ensued, and major commercial consumers, such as the Volta Aluminium Co (VALCO, which takes, on average, more than 60% of the power supply from Akosombo), were forced to reduce production levels. An improvement in rainfall from 1984 allowed a return to full output. A project to extend the electricity supply to the Northern, Upper West and Upper East Regions from Brong Ahafo, in order to curtail reliance on diesel generators in the north, was financed by bilateral and multilateral credits. In May 1994, however, following poor rainfall, the VRA was again obliged to restrict output, with VALCO agreeing to a reduction of 22% in its energy allocation. Drought again led to power rationing in February–June 1998, with the government seeking emergency sources of electricity from abroad and many domestic enterprises, including VALCO, operating at markedly reduced capacity. Aware that power shortages severely restrict industrial output and result in substantial levels of lost revenue, the government in 1999 announced that it was to establish a transitional power system development plan to prevent the recurrence of power cuts following drought. During 1999 480 communities were brought within the national grid. The government in 1999 also supported the West African Gas Pipeline Project; this US $821m.-multinational scheme was to be financed with both public- and private-sector funds, and was due for completion by July 2002.

The expansion of the Kpong hydroelectricity plant and the linking of the power systems of Ghana and Côte d'Ivoire are expected to facilitate a growth in electricity exports. However, plans to build a 450-MW hydroelectricity plant at Bui, on the Black Volta, to provide electricity for export and to supply northern Ghana, were delayed by funding difficulties. The construction of the country's first gas-fired power generation plant (at a projected cost of US $400m.) at Aboadze, near Takoradi, was completed in December 1997 and added 200 MW to the national grid, until an explosion in March 1998 put one of the two 100-MW turbines out of action. CMS Energy Corpn of the USA announced in February 1999 that it was to build, own and operate a $60m. 110-MW electricity-generating unit at the site of the VRA's Takoradi thermal power plant near Aboadze, with completion expected in mid-2000. Initially CMS was to hold 90% of the equity, with the VRA owning the other 10%, although as part of the agreement the VRA was to have an option to increase its share later to up to 50%. The VRA was to be the main customer for the scheme's electricity output, under a long-term contract. The facility constituted the first stage of a 330-MW expansion of the existing Takoradi plant. Takoradi, due to commence commercial operations in late 1999, initially using light crude oil as fuel, was to be converted to natural gas, sourced from Nigeria and Côte d'Ivoire. The installation was intended to be the 'anchor customer' for the proposed West African gas pipeline from Nigeria. The construction of a nuclear reactor at Kwabenya, near Accra, which commenced in 1964 (but was suspended during 1966–74) was completed in January 1995. Western Power Co's 125-MW power barge facility, with Japanese funding, was to be completed by the end of 1999. An ECG scheme to restore 80 MW of generating capacity and to improve the distribution at the Tema Industrial Estate was due for completion by the end of 2000. Eleven more district capitals were connected to the national electricity grid in 1995, and the last 25 district capitals were subsequently to be connected, using $165m. of donor funding. By 1996 the ECG owed the VRA more than C50,000m., and the debt was increasing by some C1,500m. per month. In February 1997 the government announced that it was to convert the ECG into a limited-liability company. Under pressure from the World Bank, a new Public Utilities Regulatory Commission introduced a 90% increase in water and electricity tariffs in February 1998 and a further 100% rise in September, with the aim of eliminating all arrears of the power utilities by the end of 1999.

PUBLIC FINANCE

Since 1983 fiscal policies have been designed to reduce the imbalances in government finances and to foster economic growth. Capital spending, and the proportion of both revenue and expenditure to GDP, have increased significantly. From 1987 increasing emphasis has been laid on improving economic incentives and tax administration, with the result that, in 1992, corporate tax rates were considerably lower than before the reform process. Receipts from import duties expanded during 1987–90, increasing from 16% to 25% of total revenue. Another important source of revenue has been petroleum taxes. Export duties declined as a percentage of total revenue from 35% in 1983 to 5% in 1993, but increased to 14% in 1996. The generally declining contribution of receipts from the cocoa tax to total revenue reflected substantial real increases in producer prices paid to farmers, and greater efficiency in the collection of other taxes, notably income taxes. In 1998 Ghana collected C2,728,468m. in total revenue; although this amount was 3.7% below the C2,834,000m. projected, it was still 25.4% higher than the revenue received in 1997 (a significant accomplishment given that corporate income tax yielded 16% less revenue than forecast in 1998 because electricity shortages had reduced both production and taxable profits). In 1999 Ghana collected C3,089,100m. in total revenue; although this figure was 13.2% higher than that of 1998, it was, nevertheless, 6% lower than the projected figure of C3,294,000m., largely owing to cocoa export duties, non-tax revenue, project grants and loans having all failed to meet their targets. Total expenditure in 1999 amounted to C5,845,500m., 3.6% less than the projected figure of C6,063,700m. The 2000/2001 balanced budget, announced in February 2000, projected total expenditure and revenue at C8,633,100m.

Government expenditure was realigned in the 1980s, with the aim of increasing both civil service wages and capital expenditure on infrastructure, agriculture, education and health. The rationalization of the civil service involved the redeployment of some 50,000 civil servants in the period 1987–90. Nevertheless, the public-sector wage bill grew from C297,000m. in 1994 to C431,000m. in 1995, to C613,000m. in 1996, and to C1,516,300m. in 1999, with C1,722,000m. projected for 2000. Defence expenditure has remained low, representing 7.5% of total expenditure in 1985, according to official statistics, and declining to 4% of proposed total expenditure by 1999.

Ghana's heavy use of IMF facilities has contributed significantly to the country's foreign debt. Total external debt stood at US $5,306m. at 31 December 1999, compared with $6,077.6m. at 31 December 1998. During 1999 debt repayments exceeded new obligations, resulting in a $771.6m. reduction in total debt stock. Most of the country's other borrowings are long-term and at concessionary rates, but the debt-servicing burden remains substantial; the ratio of debt service to exports of goods and services was 35.7% in 1996, declining to 31.6% in 1997 and to 28.1% in 1998, with 24.5% projected in 1999, 24.7% in 2000 and 18.7% in 2001. The cost of servicing Ghana's foreign debt amounted to US $32.3m. in 1997 and to $27.4m. in 1998. The cost of servicing the government's domestic debt was more than twice as high as that of servicing its overseas debts, at an outturn of C861,369m. in 1998, compared with C645,000m. in 1997. The government blamed this sharp increase in domestic

borrowing on the need to absorb excess liquidity and to help reduce inflation. Yet during the same year the government increased the money supply by 34%, adding C452,000m., to bring the total to C1,785,000m. The 1998 budget pledged to keep money-supply growth to a maximum of 20%, and the 2000 budget aimed to restrain it to below 16%. The government has, nevertheless, given priority to its debt-servicing obligations, resulting in an improvement in the country's credit rating; Ghana had no external payments' arrears in 1996, 1997 or 1998 (end of period assessment by the IMF). Private banks have proved increasingly willing to extend short-term credit to Ghana for a variety of financial operations, including US $40m. to COCOBOD for the purchase of the cocoa crop for the 1993/94 season, followed by $150m. for 1994/95, $225m. in 1995/96, $225m. in 1996/97 and $275m. in 1997/98. In support of Ghana's continuing adherence to its reform programme—not least in making a second effort to introduce VAT—the World Bank in June 1998 announced a single-tranche, one-off US $50m. 'equivalent credit' to Ghana and acknowledged achievements such as raising the primary domestic surplus to 3.3% of GDP in 1997 and bringing inflation down from 60% in 1995 to 20% in 1997. The 1999 target was a primary domestic surplus of 3.8% of GDP. Although the second attempt did result in the introduction of VAT, the level of compliance with this unpopular measure was less than the government would have hoped. The 2000 budget promised improved collection of VAT by registered traders, better monitoring and surveillance and a narrowing of the scope of exemptions from the tax.

DOMESTIC COMMERCE AND FINANCE

A small number of large and long-established foreign companies continue to be important in the import trade, though they have now largely withdrawn from retail transactions, except for department stores in the major towns and for certain 'technical' goods. Since 1962 the publicly-owned Ghana National Trading Corpn (GNTC), created by purchase of A. G. Leventis and Co, has existed alongside the expatriate companies. At the retail level, independent Ghanaian and other African traders compete with the GNTC and with Lebanese and a few Indian businesses. The complex and highly fragmented trade in locally produced foodstuffs is almost wholly in African ownership.

Between 1968–83 many aspects of trade in Ghana were reserved for Ghanaian ownership, but by the mid-1980s foreign investment was again encouraged. In 1986 the government introduced a new investment code, offering a range of fiscal and trade incentives and inducements. The priority sectors, designated for special treatment under the new code, were agriculture, import substitution industries, construction and tourism. The government continues to stress the importance of private investment and has reduced public-sector investment in the development of basic key industries. Public-sector investment accounted for only 28% of total proposed investment under ERP I. Shares were floated on the Ghana Stock Exchange in such groups as Paterson Zochonis Ghana Ltd, UTC Estates, CFAO (Ghana) Ltd and Unilever Ghana Ltd.

The banking sector has expanded and undergone substantial reform since the mid-1980s. In 1999 there were nine commercial banks as well as three development banks, four merchant banks and a number of rural banks. The Bank of Ghana has strengthened its supervisory role and in June 1992 assumed control of the assets of the Ghana Co-operative Bank. Home Finance Co Ltd, Standard Chartered Bank Ghana Ltd and the Social Security Bank were listed on the stock exchange in 1996.

TRANSPORT

The country's two major ports are both artificial: Takoradi, built in the 1920s, and Tema, which was opened in 1961 to replace the Accra roadstead, and which became an industrial centre. The rehabilitation of the two ports, at an estimated cost of US $100m., was completed in 1990. An additional programme to rehabilitate Takoradi commenced in mid-1995. Facilities are to be upgraded further in a $365m. project, which also aims to give greater operational autonomy to both ports. The Ghana Ports and Harbours Authority undertook the dredging of the ports in 1996. The Ghana merchant shipping fleet had a total displacement of 225,000 gross registered tons in 1982, but its size was subsequently reduced, as the national Black Star Line disposed of some of its ships, owing to recurrent labour disputes and an increasing debt burden. Total displacement stood at 115,465 grt in 1998.

There are 1,300 km of railway, forming a triangle between Takoradi, Kumasi and Accra-Tema. Exports traditionally accounted for the greater part of railway freight tonnage, but cocoa and timber were diverted to the roads as rail facilities deteriorated, and the railways have required a regular government subsidy since 1976. In 1988 the IDA and the ADB provided a credit of US $42m. towards a project to rehabilitate the Western Line railway from Kumasi to Takoradi. Equipment worth $12.8m. was also provided by the IDA to help to repair faulty track. In 1996 the government committed US $150m. towards further upgrading the Western Line to link the mining areas with Takoradi port. In 1995 Ghana Railway Corpn took delivery of three new locomotives and 60 goods wagons, funded by Germany's Kreditanstalt für Wiederaufbau (KFW) and Japan's Overseas Economic Co-operation Fund (OECF).

In 1996 there were an estimated 37,800 km of classified roads, of which 24.1% were paved. The road system is good by tropical African standards, but its maintenance was a constant problem from the early 1960s. Vehicle spare parts were also scarce, and the internal distributive system deteriorated physically. In 1991 the government initiated a major five-year programme of road development and rehabilitation, at an estimated cost of US $142.3m. Work commenced in 1996 on eight new roads with a combined length of 466 km and a combined cost of C326,500m. The overwhelming focus of construction in the transport sector in the late 1990s was on roads, with work being completed on four new roads in 1996. In addition, 87 km of roads were gravelled in that year and a further 213 km were resurfaced, including two roads in the Obuasi area. Government spending on road construction in 1999 was expected to total C603,500m., with C832,700m. projected in 2000 and C863,900m. in 2001. However, the minister of finance announced during his 1999 budget speech that 'in an effort to demonstrate the feasibility of private-sector financing of toll roads' and 'for the purposes of improving cost recovery', tolls were to be introduced on 'newly-reconstructed or -rehabilitated' roads and bridges. Existing roads designated for toll status included Tema–Akosombo, Yamoransa–Takoradi, Yamoransa–Anwiankwanta, Accra–Yamoransa, Accra–Kumasi, Kumasi–Dunkwa, Tema–Aflao and Kumasi–Kintampo. The creation of the Volta Lake, stretching some 400 km inland from the Akosombo dam, opened up new possibilities for internal transportation, but lake transport is still relatively modest. The budget for 2000 allocated funding for 11 road projects and the construction of 28 bridges. Two of the road projects involved port access. The road linking Ashaiman and Tema, and the 1.8-km Africana Road linking the business centre of Takoradi to the port, were both to be rehabilitated. In the late 1980s the Federal Republic of Germany financed a project to construct new ports on the lake, and to establish a new cargo and passenger service. There is an international airport at Kotoka, near Accra, and other airports at Kumasi, Sunyani, Takoradi, Tamale and Wa serve inland traffic. The national airline is Ghana Airways.

FOREIGN TRADE AND AID

Ghana has traditionally been an exporter of primary products, mainly gold, cocoa and timber, and an importer of capital goods, foodstuffs and mineral fuels. In 1993 the ministry of trade and industry established a special unit to promote non-traditional exports. By 1998 revenue from non-traditional exports had increased to US $180m. (compared with $70m. in 1993), and the sector had significant potential for the future.

Ghana's visible trade balance was in deficit throughout the 1990s, increasing steadily to an estimated shortfall of US $383.8m. in 1998, with $382.3m. projected for 1999. Substantial deficits on invisible trade (services and transfers), accentuated by high payments to service the external debt, resulted in increasing deficits on the current account since 1981. Current-account shortfalls reached $528.3m. in 1996 and $729.9m. in 1997, but declined sharply, to $12m. in 1998, increasing again to $616m. (excluding official transfers) in 1999. The outlook for 2000 was a current account deficit of $684m. (excluding official transfers), equivalent to 10.7% of GDP.

In the 1990s the Western industrialized nations comprised Ghana's major trading partners, although useful links were maintained with countries of the former Eastern bloc, with which Ghana developed trade relations in the early 1980s (in 1984 the USSR accounted for one-quarter of Ghanaian exports). In 1995 the principal export destinations were the United Kingdom (representing 14.7% of the total), Germany (12%), the USA (11.5%) and France (7.8%). The major sources of imports in 1989 were Nigeria (22.3%), which provided most of Ghana's petroleum imports, the United Kingdom (16.7%), the USA (10%) and Germany (8%). In 1997 Ghana's main trading partners were the United Kingdom, Germany, the USA and Nigeria.

Although the level of donor pledges has risen dramatically since 1980, disbursement of funds has often been slow. In 1999 efforts by the Ghanaian government to meet IMF and World Bank requirements continued to be impeded by popular resistance to reform measures, including the introduction of VAT, increased electricity tariffs and road tolls. In the international arena the World Bank and the IMF continued to urge restraint in foreign and domestic borrowing, greater openness in the accounting of state-owned enterprises such as the ECG, the liberalization of the external marketing of cocoa, and the privatization of the Produce Buying Co, the Tema oil refinery and the Ghana Oil Co. Nevertheless, after many years of instigating reforms which initially seemed to produce no real results, the Ghanaian government can now demonstrate tangible achievements in export diversification, in incoming foreign investment, in the availability of a far wider range of consumer goods in the domestic marketplace, and even in some economic resilience in view of unfavourable external trade factors.

Statistical Survey

Source (except where otherwise stated): Central Bureau of Statistics, POB 1098, Accra; tel. (21) 66512.

Area and Population

AREA, POPULATION AND DENSITY

Area (sq km) .	238,537*
Population (census results)	
1 March 1970 .	8,559,313
11 March 1984	
Males .	6,063,848
Females .	6,232,233
Total .	12,296,081
Population (UN estimates at mid-year)†	
1996 .	18,154,000
1997 .	18,656,000
1998 .	19,162,000
Density (per sq km) at mid-1998 .	80.3

* 92,100 sq miles.
† Source: UN, *World Population Prospects: The 1998 Revision.*

POPULATION BY REGION (1984 census)

Western .	1,157,807
Central .	1,142,335
Greater Accra .	1,431,099
Eastern .	1,680,890
Volta .	1,211,907
Ashanti .	2,090,100
Brong-Ahafo .	1,206,608
Northern .	1,164,583
Upper East .	772,744
Upper West .	438,008
Total .	12,296,081

Principal ethnic groups (1991 estimates, percentage of total population): Akan 52.4, Mossi 15.8, Ewe 11.9, Ga-Adangme 7.8, Guan 11.9, Gurma 3.3%, Yoruba 1.3%.

PRINCIPAL TOWNS (population at 1984 census)

Accra (capital).	867,459	Takoradi .	61,484
Kumasi .	376,249	Cape Coast .	57,224
Tamale .	135,952	Sekondi .	31,916
Tema .	131,528		

BIRTHS AND DEATHS (UN estimates, annual averages)

	1980–85	1985–90	1990–95
Birth rate (per 1,000) .	45.0	43.1	40.1
Death rate (per 1,000) .	13.1	11.9	10.6

Expectation of life (UN estimates, years at birth, 1990–95): 58.0 (males 56.3; females 59.7).

Source: UN, *World Population Prospects: The 1998 Revision.*

ECONOMICALLY ACTIVE POPULATION (1984 census)

	Males	Females	Total
Agriculture, hunting, forestry and fishing	1,750,024	1,560,943	3,310,967
Mining and quarrying .	24,906	1,922	26,828
Manufacturing .	198,430	389,988	588,418
Electricity, gas and water .	14,033	1,404	15,437
Construction .	60,692	3,994	64,686
Trade, restaurants and hotels .	111,540	680,607	792,147
Transport, storage and communications .	117,806	5,000	122,806
Financing, insurance, real estate and business services .	19,933	7,542	27,475
Community, social and personal services .	339,665	134,051	473,716
Total employed .	2,637,029	2,785,451	5,422,480
Unemployed .	87,452	70,172	157,624
Total labour force .	2,724,481	2,855,623	5,580,104

Source: ILO, *Yearbook of Labour Statistics.*

Mid-1998 (estimates in '000): Agriculture, etc. 5,212; Total 9,086 (Source: FAO, *Production Yearbook*).

Agriculture

PRINCIPAL CROPS ('000 metric tons)

	1996	1997	1998
Maize .	1,008	996	1,015
Millet .	193	114	162
Sorghum .	353	333	355
Rice (paddy) .	216	197	281
Sugar cane* .	110	110	110
Cassava (Manioc) .	7,111	7,000	7,172
Yams .	2,275	2,408	2,703
Taro (Coco yam) .	1,552	1,530	1,577
Onions* .	25	25	25
Tomatoes* .	160	160	160
Green chillies and peppers* .	70	70	70
Eggplants (Aubergines)* .	6	6	6
Pulses* .	15	16	16
Oranges* .	50	50	50
Lemons and limes* .	30	30	30
Mangoes* .	4	4	4
Bananas* .	4	4	4
Plantains .	1,823	1,878	1,878*
Pineapples* .	35	35	35
Palm kernels .	35†	35*	35*
Groundnuts (in shell) .	133	135*	135*
Coconuts* .	240	240	240
Copra* .	10	10	10
Coffee (green) .	6	6*	6*
Cocoa beans .	403	400†	380†
Tobacco (leaves) .	1†	2*	2*

* FAO estimate(s). † Unofficial figure.
Source: FAO, *Production Yearbook.*

LIVESTOCK ('000 head, year ending September)

	1996	1997	1998
Horses* .	2	2	2
Asses* .	13	13	13
Cattle .	1,248	1,150*	1,150*
Pigs .	318	395*	395*
Sheep .	2,207	2,100*	2,100*
Goats .	2,340	2,200*	2,200*

Poultry (million): 13 in 1996; 13* in 1997; 13* in 1998.

* FAO estimate(s).
Source: FAO, *Production Yearbook.*

LIVESTOCK PRODUCTS (FAO estimates, '000 metric tons)

	1996	1997	1998
Beef and veal	21	20	20
Mutton and lamb	6	6	7
Goat meat	5	6	6
Pig meat	8	9	9
Poultry meat	12	12	13
Other meat	91	91	89
Cows' milk	28	27	27
Hen eggs	14	14	14
Cattle hides	3	3	2

Source: FAO, *Production Yearbook*.

Forestry

ROUNDWOOD REMOVALS ('000 cubic metres, excl. bark)

	1995	1996	1997
Sawlogs, veneer logs and logs for sleepers	1,194	1,166	1,166
Other industrial wood	89	89	89
Fuel wood	25,190	25,190	25,190
Total	26,473	26,445	26,445

Source: FAO, *Yearbook of Forest Products*.

SAWNWOOD PRODUCTION ('000 cubic metres, incl. railway sleepers)

	1995	1996	1997
Coniferous (softwood)*	54	54	54
Broadleaved (hardwood)	558	550	550*
Total	612	604	604

* FAO estimate(s).

Source: FAO, *Yearbook of Forest Products*.

Fishing

('000 metric tons, live weight)

	1995	1996	1997
Freshwater fishes	60.0	73.6	70.0
Bigeye grunt	14.8	13.6	19.8
Jack and horse mackerels	9.5	10.9	17.5
Round sardinella	67.8	118.4	49.4
Madeiran sardinella	13.2	13.6	14.2
Other sardinellas	14.1	20.1	36.0
Bonga shad	1.1	1.2	9.8
European anchovy	65.5	98.3	82.7
Skipjack tuna	18.6	21.4	28.5
Yellowfin tuna	9.3	11.4	18.4
Chub mackerel	12.5	15.6	19.9
Other marine fishes (incl. unspecified)	61.3	73.4	74.5
Crustaceans and molluscs	5.6	5.1	5.8
Total catch	353.3	476.6	446.5
Inland waters	60.0	73.6	70.0
Atlantic Ocean	293.3	403.0	376.5

Source: FAO, *Yearbook of Fishery Statistics*.

Mining

('000 metric tons, unless otherwise indicated)

	1995	1996*	1997*
Gold ('000 kilograms)†	51.3	48.3	53.5
Diamonds ('000 carats)	622.7	714.3	585.5
Manganese ore‡	100.0	266.8	333.4
Bauxite	513.0	383.4	500.7

* Estimates.
† Figures refer to the metal content of ores.
‡ Figures refer to gross weight. The estimated manganese content was 101,000 metric tons in 1996.

Source: IMF, *Ghana: Selected Issues* (January 1999).

Industry

SELECTED PRODUCTS ('000 metric tons, unless otherwise indicated)

	1994	1995	1996
Groundnut oil*	25	21	17
Coconut oil*	6	6	6
Palm oil*	100	100	105
Palm kernel oil*	9	9	9
Motor spirit (petrol)*	215	218	218
Kerosene*	125	127	128
Diesel and gas oil*	214	215	215
Cement	1,350†	1,400†	1,575
Aluminium (unwrought)‡§	140.7	135.4	137.0
Electric energy (million kWh)*	6,155	6,159	6,036

* Provisional or estimated figures.
† Data from US Bureau of Mines.
‡ Primary metal only.
§ Data from *World Metal Statistics* (London).

1997 and 1998 (estimates, '000 metric tons): Groundnut oil 18, Coconut oil 6, Palm oil 100, Palm kernel oil 10.

Sources: FAO, *Quarterly Bulletin of Statistics*; UN, *Industrial Commodity Statistics Yearbook*.

Finance

CURRENCY AND EXCHANGE RATES
Monetary Units
100 pesewas = 1 new cedi.

Sterling, Dollar and Euro Equivalents (28 April 2000)
£1 sterling = 6,817.8 cedis;
US $1 = 4,347.8 cedis;
€1 = 3,950.0 cedis;
10,000 cedis = £1.467 = $2.300 = €2.532.

Average Exchange Rate (cedis per US $)
1997 2,050.17
1998 2,314.15
1999 2,647.32

GENERAL BUDGET ('000 million new cedis)

Revenue*	1995	1996	1997
Tax revenue	1,138.5	1,710.6	2,070.0
Taxes on income, profits and			
capital gains . . .	275.0	433.3	606.4
Individual . . .	80.8	131.1	225.1
Corporate . . .	157.2	242.3	293.1
Other unallocated taxes on			
income . . .	37.0	59.9	88.3
Domestic taxes on goods			
and services . .	503.7	732.4	833.4
General sales, turnover or			
value-added tax . .	210.1	329.6	407.4
Excises (excl. petroleum) . .	69.6	112.6	111.6
Petroleum revenue . .	224.0	290.2	314.3
Taxes on international trade			
and transactions . .	359.9	544.9	630.2
Import duties . . .	202.6	267.2	364.3
Export duties . . .	157.2	277.7	265.9
Non-tax revenue	446.1	287.0	376.7
Total	1,584.6	1,997.5	2,446.7

Expenditure†	1993	1994‡	1995‡
General public services . .	83.9	145.4	93.6
Defence	39.5	30.9	34.5
Public order and safety . .	30.8	23.9	42.9
Education	179.2	207.6	258.7
Health	56.6	58.6	73.6
Social security and welfare .	57.8	112.3	138.8
Housing and community amenities	12.4	16.8	48.7
Other community and			
social services . . .	10.1	20.6	—
Economic services . . .	129.7	137.3	199.3
Agriculture, forestry and fishing	28.4	26.8	18.5
Mining, manufacturing and			
construction . . .	11.0	18.5	24.6
Utilities	7.0	12.8	21.5
Transport and communications .	79.5	75.5	116.7
Other economic services .	3.8	3.7	18.0
Other purposes . . .	162.7	338.9	342.7
Interest payments . . .	134.8	230.1	328.8
Sub-total	762.7	1,092.3	1,232.8
Special efficiency payments§ . .	50.8	64.0	51.4
Total	813.5	1,156.3	1,284.2
Current	694.3	n.a.	n.a.
Capital	135.3	n.a.	n.a.
Adjustment for payment arrears‖	−16.0	n.a.	n.a.

* Excluding grants received ('000 million new cedis): 280.1 in 1995; 291.1 in 1996; 262.2 in 1997. Also excluded are the proceeds from the divestiture of state-owned enterprises ('000 million new cedis): 106.2 in 1995; 143.5 in 1996; 105.7 in 1997.
† Excluding lending minus repayments ('000 million new cedis): 8.0 in 1993; 8.3 in 1994; 15.8 in 1995. Also excluded is capital expenditure resulting from foreign financing ('000 million new cedis): 286.9 in 1993; 456.0 in 1994; 564.8 in 1995.
‡ Excluding unallocable expenditure.
§ Including provision for redeployment, retraining and relocation of public-sector employees.
‖ Minus sign indicates an increase in arrears.
Source: IMF, *Ghana: Selected Issues* (January 1999).

INTERNATIONAL RESERVES (US $ million at 31 December)

	1997	1998	1999
Gold*	n.a.	78.8	78.9
IMF special drawing rights . .	3.4	59.7	18.2
Reserve position in IMF . .	23.4	24.5	56.5
Foreign exchange . . .	n.a.	292.8	379.1
Total	n.a.	455.8	532.7

* National valuation.
Source: IMF, *International Financial Statistics*.

MONEY SUPPLY ('000 million new cedis at 31 December)

	1997	1998	1999
Currency outside banks . .	981.82	1,083.63	1,186.14
Deposits of non-financial public			
enterprises . . .	6.32	3.17	2.76
Demand deposits at deposit money			
banks	776.54	982.53	939.25
Total money (incl. others) . .	1,767.26	2,073.12	2,129.41

Source: IMF, *International Financial Statistics*.

COST OF LIVING (Consumer Price Index; base: 1995 = 100)

	1997	1998	1999
All items	187.4	214.8	241.5

Source: IMF, *International Financial Statistics*.

NATIONAL ACCOUNTS ('000 million new cedis at current prices)

National Income and Product

	1995	1996	1997
GDP in purchasers'			
values	7,418.0	10,633.1	14,113.4
Net factor income from abroad .	−155.1	−220.0	273.9
Gross national product .	7,262.9	10,413.1	13,839.5
Less Consumption of fixed capital	359.8	560.5	996.7
National income in market			
prices	6,903.1	9,852.6	12,842.8

Source: IMF, *International Financial Statistics*.

Expenditure on the Gross Domestic Product

	1995	1996	1997
Government final consumption			
expenditure . . .	921.7	1,345.0	1,743.8
Private final consumption			
expenditure	6,108.1	8,800.3	11,267.0
Increase in stocks . . .	5.4	6.2	127.3
Gross fixed capital			
formation	1,028.1	1,464.2	3,338.2
Total domestic expenditure .	8,063.3	11,615.7	16,476.3
Exports of goods and			
services	1,898.9	2,537.6	2,794.6
Less Imports of goods and services	2,544.2	3,520.1	5,157.5
GDP in purchasers' values .	7,418.0	10,633.1	14,113.4
GDP at constant 1990 prices .	2,530.3	2,661.1	2,796.7

Source: IMF, *International Financial Statistics*.

Gross Domestic Product by Economic Activity

	1995	1996	1997
Agriculture and livestock . .	2,351.0	3,440.0	3,848.7
Forestry and logging . . .	211.0	297.0	477.2
Fishing	444.0	680.0	724.2
Mining and quarrying . . .	371.0	536.0	719.8
Manufacturing	723.0	979.0	1,277.5
Electricity, water and gas . .	206.0	302.0	425.7
Construction	582.0	856.0	1,199.6
Transport, storage and communications . . .	303.0	423.0	580.4
Wholesale and retail trade . .	465.0	654.0	917.0
Finance, real estate and business services . . .	302.6	430.0	586.6
Public administration, defence and other government services	825.0	1,124.0	1,377.0
Other community, social and personal services . . .	185.0	249.0	341.6
Private non-profit services . .	72.0	97.0	133.2
GDP at factor cost . .	7,040.6	10,067.0	12,608.5
Indirect taxes, *less* subsidies .	712.0	1,272.0	1,504.9
GDP in purchasers' values .	7,752.6	11,339.0	14,113.4

Source: IMF, *Ghana: Selected Issues* (January 1999).

BALANCE OF PAYMENTS (US $ million)

	1996	1997	1998
Exports of goods f.o.b. . .	1,570.1	1,489.9	1,813.2
Imports of goods f.o.b. . .	−1,937.0	−2,128.2	−2,346.0
Trade balance . . .	−366.9	−638.3	−532.8
Exports of services . .	156.8	164.9	175.9
Imports of services . .	−456.4	−505.0	−540.5
Balance on goods and services	−666.5	−978.4	−897.4
Other income received . .	23.5	26.7	26.7
Other income paid . .	−163.4	−158.1	−163.0
Balance on goods, services and income	−806.4	−1,109.8	−1,033.7
Current transfers received .	497.9	576.5	701.0
Current transfers paid . .	−16.2	−16.4	−17.1
Current balance . . .	−324.7	−549.7	−349.8
Capital account (net) . .	−1.0	−1.0	−1.0
Direct investment from abroad .	120.0	82.6	55.8
Other investment assets . .	−179.4	33.1	87.9
Other investment liabilities .	344.5	378.1	215.3
Net errors and omissions . .	1.8	34.5	117.5
Overall balance . . .	−38.8	−22.4	125.7

Source: IMF, *International Financial Statistics*.

External Trade

PRINCIPAL COMMODITIES (US $ million)

Imports	1996	1997	1998
Food and live animals . .	267.4	361.1	536.2
Rice	53.8	46.5	106.0
Mineral fuels, lubricants, etc. .	55.4	341.8	159.5
Crude petroleum . .	21.5	139.1	97.1
Petroleum products . .	30.6	200.7	52.0
Chemicals	100.7	110.6	100.7
Machinery and transport equipment . . .	876.7	1,270.8	1,293.0
Passenger cars (incl. buses)	127.7	114.5	154.9
Lorries and trucks . .	134.7	224.0	229.8
Miscellaneous manufactured articles . .	105.9	116.1	40.3
Total (incl. others) . .	2,839.7	3,033.6	3,329.8

Exports	1996	1997	1998
Cocoa beans	494.7	384.8	541.6
Cocoa products . . .	73.2	92.7	78.2
Timber and timber products .	147.8	170.5	171.0
Gold	681.6	545.1	679.4
Electricity	58.2	67.6	40.9
Total (incl. others) . . .	1,698.0	1,753.7	1,811.6

Source: Ministry of Trade and Industry, Accra.

PRINCIPAL TRADING PARTNERS (US $ million)

Imports	1996	1997	1998
Belgium	68.1	87.7	136.7
China, People's Repub. . .	96.7	76.0	105.8
France	123.6	118.5	129.2
Germany	341.6	237.6	277.4
India	72.2	61.7	77.5
Italy	108.6	130.3	152.7
Japan	176.0	167.0	159.9
Korea, Republic . . .	59.8	68.3	110.2
Netherlands . . .	108.9	146.6	153.2
Nigeria	262.5	163.6	44.9
South Africa . . .	48.1	70.5	90.6
Spain	82.1	77.4	102.2
United Kingdom . . .	453.1	472.8	383.8
USA	360.7	395.2	390.0
Total (incl. others) . .	2,839.7	3,033.6	3,329.8

Exports	1996	1997	1998
Belgium . . .	32.3	35.3	65.4
France . . .	60.5	80.5	77.8
Germany . . .	142.6	117.8	93.8
Italy	44.8	49.7	57.0
Japan . . .	58.4	75.1	55.3
Netherlands . .	165.3	211.8	202.4
South Africa . .	6.1	3.2	41.3
Spain . . .	31.3	31.9	31.9
Switzerland . .	486.3	437.1	418.0
Togo	19.0	14.9	60.0
United Kingdom . .	369.5	284.4	364.5
USA	49.2	33.8	69.2
Total (incl. others) . .	1,639.8	1,586.1	1,770.6

Source: Ministry of Trade and Industry, Accra.

Transport

RAILWAYS (traffic)

	1996
Passengers carried ('000)	2,100
Freight carried ('000 metric tons)	857
Passenger-km (million)	208
Net ton-km (million)	152.8

Source: *Railway Directory*.

ROAD TRAFFIC ('000 motor vehicles in use at 31 December)

	1994	1995*	1996*
Passenger cars . . .	90.0	90.0	90.0
Lorries and vans . . .	44.7	45.0	45.0

* Estimates.

Source: International Road Federation, *World Road Statistics*.

SHIPPING

Merchant Fleet (registered at 31 December)

	1996	1997	1998
Number of vessels . . .	195	206	205
Total displacement ('000 grt) .	134.7	129.7	115.5

Source: Lloyd's Register of Shipping.

International Sea-borne Freight Traffic (estimates, '000 metric tons)

	1991	1992	1993
Goods loaded	2,083	2,279	2,424
Goods unloaded . . .	2,866	2,876	2,904

Source: UN Economic Commission for Africa, *African Statistical Yearbook*.

CIVIL AVIATION (traffic on scheduled services)

	1994	1995	1996
Kilometres flown (million) . .	5	5	6
Passengers carried ('000) . .	182	186	197
Passenger-km (million) . .	478	611	655
Total ton-km (million) . .	72	86	91

Source: UN, *Statistical Yearbook*.

Tourism

ARRIVALS BY NATIONALITY

	1995	1996	1997
Côte d'Ivoire	13,750	14,657	15,646
France	10,334	11,016	11,759
Germany	13,799	14,709	15,702
Liberia	7,500	7,995	8,534
Netherlands	6,924	7,380	7,878
Nigeria	39,254	41,842	44,667
Togo	8,560	9,124	9,739
United Kingdom . . .	24,762	26,395	28,177
USA	18,864	20,108	21,465
Total (incl. others)* . . .	286,000	304,860	325,434

* Includes Ghanaian nationals resident abroad: 77,850 in 1995; 82,984 in 1996; 88,585 in 1997.

Source: World Tourism Organization, *Yearbook of Tourism Statistics*.

Receipts from tourism (US $ million): 233 in 1995; 248 in 1996; 266 in 1997 (Source: mainly UN, *Statistical Yearbook*).

Communications Media

	1994	1995	1996
Radio receivers ('000 in use) . .	3,880	4,000	4,250
Television receivers ('000 in use) .	1,500	1,600	1,650
Telephones ('000 main lines in use)	50	63	78
Telefax stations (number in use)* .	4,500	5,000	5,000
Mobile cellular telephones (subscribers)	3,336	6,200	12,766
Daily newspapers			
Number	4	4	4
Average circulation ('000 copies)	310*	310*	250

* Provisional or estimated figure(s).

1997 ('000 in use): 4,400 radio receivers, 1,730 television receivers.

Sources: UNESCO, *Statistical Yearbook*; UN, *Statistical Yearbook*.

Education

(1989/90, unless otherwise indicated)

	Institutions	Teachers	Students
Pre-primary	4,735	15,152	323,406
Primary (public only)[1] . .	12,134	71,863	2,154,646
Secondary			
General (public only) . .	n.a.	39,903[2]	841,722[3]
Teacher training . .	38[4]	1,001	15,723
Vocational (public only) . .	20[5]	1,247	22,578[3]
University	5[6]	700[7]	10,700[6]

[1] 1994/95 figures.
[2] 1990/91 figure.
[3] 1991/92 figure.
[4] 1988 figure.
[5] 1988/89 figure.
[6] 1992 figure.
[7] Excluding the University of Ghana.

Source: mainly UNESCO, *Statistical Yearbook*.

1992: *Primary* 10,623 institutions, 1,800,000 students (estimate); *Junior secondary* 5,136 institutions, 569,000 students (estimate); *Senior secondary* 404 institutions, 147,000 students (estimate); *Higher* 52,000 students.

Source: African Development Bank.

Directory

The Constitution

Under the terms of the Constitution of the Fourth Republic, which was approved by national referendum on 28 April 1992, Ghana has a multi-party political system. Executive power is vested in the President, who is Head of State and Commander-in-Chief of the Armed Forces. The President is elected by universal adult suffrage for a term of four years, and appoints a Vice-President. The duration of the President's tenure of office is limited to two four-year terms.

It is also stipulated that, in the event that no presidential candidate receives more than 50% of votes cast, a new election between the two candidates with the highest number of votes is to take place within 21 days. Legislative power is vested in a 200-member unicameral Parliament, which is elected by direct adult suffrage for a four-year term. The Council of Ministers is appointed by the President, subject to approval by the Parliament. The Constitution also provides for a 25-member Council of State, principally comprising presidential nominees and regional representatives, and a 20-

member National Security Council (chaired by the Vice-President), both of which act as advisory bodies to the President.

The Government

HEAD OF STATE

President and Commander-in-Chief of the Armed Forces: Flt-Lt (retd) JERRY JOHN RAWLINGS (assumed power as Chairman of Provisional National Defence Council 31 December 1981; elected President 3 November 1992; re-elected 7 December 1996).

Vice-President: Prof. JOHN EVANS ATTA MILLS.

COUNCIL OF MINISTERS
(August 2000)

Minister of Defence: Lt-Col ENOCH K. T. DONKOH.

Minister of National Security: KOFI TOTOBI-QUAKYI.

Minister of Finance: RICHARD KWAME PEPRAH.

Minister of Parliamentary Affairs: Dr KWABENA ADJEI.

Minister of Foreign Affairs: JAMES VICTOR GBEHO.

Attorney-General and Minister of Justice: Dr OBED ASAMOAH.

Minister of Local Government: CECILIA JOHNSON.

Minister of Education: EKWOW SPIO-GARBRAH.

Minister of the Interior: NII OKAIDJA ADAMAFIO.

Minister of Food and Agriculture: J. H. OWUSU-ACHEAMPONG.

Minister of Health: Dr KWAME DANSO-BUAFO.

Minister of Roads and Transport: EDWARD SALIA.

Minister of Tourism: MIKE GIZO.

Minister of Trade and Industry: DAN ABODAKPI.

Minister of Youth and Sports: ENOCH T. MENSAH.

Minister of Lands and Forestry: Dr CHRISTINA AMOAKO-NUAMA.

Minister of Works and Housing: ISAAC ADJEI-MENSAH.

Minister of Communications: JOHN MAHAMA.

Minister of Employment and Social Welfare: Alhaji MOHAMMED MUMUNI.

Minister of the Environment, Science and Technology: CLETUS APUL AVOKA.

Minister of Mines and Energy: Dr JOHN EBU.

Minister of State for Planning and Regional Economic Co-operation and Integration: KWAMENA AHWOI.

Minister of State at the Presidency responsible for Chieftancy Affairs and State Protocol: D. O. AGYEKUM.

Presidential Staffer: JOHN E. AFFUL.

REGIONAL MINISTERS
(August 2000)

Ashanti: KOJO YANKAH.

Brong Ahafo: DAVID OSEI-WUSU.

Central: JACOB ARTHUR.

Eastern: PATIENCE AIDOW.

Greater Accra: JOSHUA ALABI.

Northern: Alhaji SEIDU IDDI.

Upper East: DONALD ADABRE.

Upper West: Alhaji AMIDU SULEMANA.

Volta: Lt-Col CHARLES K. AGBENAZA.

Western: ESTHER LILY NKANSAH.

MINISTRIES

Office of the President: POB 1627, Osu, Accra.

Ministry of Communications: POB M41, Accra; tel. (21) 228011; fax (21) 229786.

Ministry of Defence: Burma Camp, Accra; tel. (21) 777611; fax (21) 773951.

Ministry of Education: POB M45, Accra; tel. (21) 665421; fax (21) 664067.

Ministry of Employment and Social Welfare: POB M84, Accra; tel. (21) 665421; fax (21) 667251.

Ministry of the Environment, Science and Technology: POB M232, Accra; tel. (21) 662626; fax (21) 666828; e-mail barnes@africaonline.com.gh.

Ministry of Finance: POB M40, Accra; tel. (21) 665441; fax (21) 667069; internet www.finance.gov.gh.

Ministry of Food and Agriculture: POB M37, Accra; tel. (21) 665421; fax (21) 663250; e-mail mofa@africaonline.com.gh.

Ministry of Foreign Affairs: POB M53, Accra; tel. (21) 664951; fax (21) 665363.

Ministry of Health: POB M44, Accra; tel. (21) 665421; fax (21) 663810.

Ministry of the Interior: POB M42, Accra; tel. (21) 665421; fax (21) 667450.

Ministry of Justice: POB M60, Accra.

Ministry of Lands and Forestry: POB M212, Accra; tel. (21) 665421; fax (21) 666801.

Ministry of Local Government: POB M50, Accra; tel. (21) 665421; fax (21) 661015.

Ministry of Mines and Energy: POB M212, Accra; tel. (21) 667151; fax (21) 668262.

Ministry of National Security: Accra.

Ministry of Parliamentary Affairs: Parliament House, Accra; tel. (21) 664716.

Ministry of Roads and Transport: POB M38, Accra; tel. (21) 665421; fax (21) 668340.

Ministry of Tourism: POB 4386, Accra; tel. (21) 666701; fax (21) 666182.

Ministry of Trade and Industry: POB M85, Accra; tel. (21) 665421; fax (21) 664115; e-mail gatewayl@ghana.com.

Ministry of Works and Housing: POB M43, Accra; tel. (21) 665421; fax (21) 663268.

Ministry of Youth and Sports: POB 1272, Accra; tel. (21) 665421; fax (21) 663927.

President and Legislature

PRESIDENT

Presidential Election, 7 December 1996

Candidates	% of votes
Flt-Lt (retd) JERRY RAWLINGS (NDC).	57.2
JOHN KUFUOR (Great Alliance*)	39.8
EDWARD MAHAMA (PNC) .	3.0
Total .	**100**

* An electoral coalition comprising the New Patriotic Party (NPP) and the People's Convention Party (PCP).

PARLIAMENT

Speaker: Justice DANIEL F. ANNAN.

Legislative Election, 7 December 1996

	Seats
National Democratic Congress (NDC) .	133
New Patriotic Party (NPP)	60
People's Convention Party (PCP)*.	5
People's National Convention (PNC)	1
Total† .	**200**

* Merged with the non-parliamentary National Convention Party to form the Convention Party in August 1998.
† Voting in one constituency was postponed. At a by-election in June 1997 the seat was won by the NPP.

COUNCIL OF STATE

Chairman: Alhaji MUMUNI BAWUMIA.

Political Organizations

Convention Party (CP): Accra; f. 1998 by merger of the National Convention Party (f. 1992) and the People's Convention Party (f. 1993); Nkrumahist.

Democratic People's Party (DPP): Accra; f. 1992; Chair. T. N. WARD-BREW.

EGLE (Every Ghanaian Living Everywhere) Party: Accra; pro-Govt alliance; Co-Chair. OWORAKU AMOFA, Capt. NII OKAI.

Ghana Democratic Republican Party (GDRP): Accra; f. 1992; Leader Dr KOFI AMOAH.

Great Consolidated People's Party (GCPP): Leader DAN LARTEY; Chair. E. B. MENSAH.

National Democratic Congress (NDC): Tamale; f. 1992; pro-Govt alliance; Leader Flt-Lt (retd) JERRY JOHN RAWLINGS; Chair. Alhaji ISSIFU ALI; Sec.-Gen. Alhaji HUUDU YAHAYA.

National Reform Party (NRP): Accra; f. June 1999 by a break-away group of the National Democratic Congress; Nat. Chair. PETER KPORDUGBE (acting); Nat. Sec. KYERETWIE OPOKU (acting).

New Patriotic Party (NPP): Private Mail Bag, Accra-North; tel. (21) 227951; fax (21) 224418; e-mail npp@africaonline.com.gh; f. 1992 by supporters of the fmr Prime Minister, Dr Kofi Busia, and Dr J. B. Danquah; Chair SAMUEL ARTHUR ODOI-SYKES; Sec.-Gen. DANIEL BOTWE.

People's National Convention (PNC): Accra; f. 1992 by supporters of the fmr Pres., Dr Kwame Nkrumah; Chair. EDWARD MAHAMA; Pres. JOHN EDWIN.

United Ghana Movement (UGM): Accra.

Diplomatic Representation

EMBASSIES AND HIGH COMMISSIONS IN GHANA

Algeria: 22 Josif Broz Tito Ave, POB 2747, Accra; tel. (21) 776719; fax (21) 776828; e-mail amb.dz.acc@n.c.s.com.gh; Ambassador: HASSANE RABEHI.

Benin: 19 Volta St, Second Close, Airport Residential Area, POB 7871, Accra; tel. (21) 774860; fax (21) 774889; Ambassador: SÊDJORO THÉOPHILE HOUESSINON.

Brazil: 24 Sir Arku Korsah Rd, Roman Ridge Ambassadorial Area, POB CT 3859, Accra; tel. (21) 774921; fax (21) 778566; e-mail brasemb@ighmail.com; Ambassador: PAULO AMÉRICO V. WOLOWSKI.

Bulgaria: 3 Kakramadu Rd, East Cantonments, POB 3193, Accra; tel. (21) 772404; fax (21) 774231; e-mail bulembgh@ghana.com; Chargé d'affaires: GEORGE MITEV.

Burkina Faso: 772/3, Asylum Down, off Farrar Ave, POB 651, Accra; tel. (21) 221988; Ambassador: EMILE GOUBA.

Canada: No. 46, Independence Ave, POB 1639, Accra; tel. (21) 228555; fax (21) 773792; High Commissioner: (vacant).

China, People's Republic: No. 7, Agostinho Neto Rd, Airport Residential Area, POB 3356, Accra; tel. (21) 774527; Ambassador: LI ZUPEI.

Côte d'Ivoire: F710/2 18th Lane, off Cantonments Rd, POB 3445, Christiansborg, Accra; tel. (21) 774611; fax (21) 773516; Ambassador: AMON TANOE EMMANUEL.

Cuba: 20 Amilcar Cabral Rd, Airport Residential Area, POB 9163 Airport, Accra; tel. (21) 775868; Ambassador: JUAN CARRETERO.

Czech Republic: C260/5, Kanda High Rd No. 2, POB 5226, Accra-North; tel. (21) 223540; fax (21) 225337; e-mail accraczemb@ighmail.com; Ambassador: JINDŘICH JUNEK.

Denmark: 67 Dr Isert Rd, 8th Ave Extension, North Ridge, POB C596, Accra; tel. (21) 226972; fax (21) 228061; e-mail accamb@accamab.um.dk; Ambassador: OLE BLICHER-OLSEN.

Egypt: 27 Fetreke St, Roman Ridge Ambassadorial Estate, POB 2508, Accra; tel. (21) 776925; fax (21) 776795; Ambassador: MOHAMED EL-ZAYAT.

Ethiopia: 6 Adiembra Rd, East Cantonments, POB 1646, Accra; tel. (21) 775928; fax (21) 776807; Ambassador: Dr KUWANG TUTILAM.

France: 12th Rd, off Liberation Ave, POB 187, Accra; tel. (21) 774480; fax (21) 778321; Ambassador: DIDIER FERRAND.

Germany: Valdemosa Lodge, Ridge Rd No. 6, North Ridge, POB 1757, Accra; tel. (21) 221311; fax (21) 221347; Ambassador: CHRISTIAN NAKONZ.

Guinea: 11 Osu Badu St, Dzorwulu, POB 5497, Accra-North; tel. (21) 777921; fax (21) 760961; Ambassador: DORE DIALE DRUS.

Holy See: 8 Drake Ave, Airport Residential Area, POB 9675, Accra; tel. (21) 777759; fax (21) 774019; Apostolic Nuncio: Most Rev. ANDRÉ DUPUY, Titular Archbishop of Selsea (Selsey).

Hungary: 14 West Cantonments, off Switchback Rd, POB 3072, Accra; tel. (21) 777234; Chargé d'affaires a.i.: IMRE SOSOVICSKA.

India: 9 Ridge Rd, Roman Ridge, POB 3040, Accra; tel. (21) 775601; fax (21) 772176; High Commissioner: DILJIT SINGH PANNUN.

Iran: 12 Sir Arku Korsah St, Roman Ridge, POB 12673, Accra North; tel. (21) 777043; Ambassador: KIUMARS FOTUHI-QIYAM.

Italy: Jawaharlal Nehru Rd, POB 140, Accra; tel. (21) 775621; fax (21) 777056; e-mail ambital@ghana.com; Ambassador: MARIO FUGAZZOLA.

Japan: 5th Ave Extension, West Cantonments, POB 1637, Accra; tel. (21) 765066; fax (21) 762553; Ambassador: SHOSUKE ITO.

Korea, Democratic People's Republic: 139 Nortei Ababio Loop, Ambassadorial Estate, POB 13874, Accra; tel. (21) 777825; Ambassador: RI JAE SONG.

Korea, Republic: 3 Abokobi Rd, East Cantonments, POB 13700, Accra North; tel. (21) 776157; Ambassador: HWANG PU-HONG.

Lebanon: F864/1 off Cantonments Rd, OSU, POB 562, Accra; tel. (21) 776727; fax (21) 764290; e-mail lebanon@ighmail.com; Ambassador: CHARBEL AOUN.

Liberia: 10 West Cantonments, off Jawaharlal Nehru Rd, POB 895, Accra; tel. (21) 775641; Ambassador: ELWOOD GREAVES.

Libya: 14 Sixth St, Airport Residential Area, POB 9665, Accra; tel. (21) 774820; Secretary of People's Bureau: Dr FATIMA MAGAME.

Mali: Agostino Neto Rd, Airport Residential Area, POB 1121, Accra; tel. (21) 666423; Ambassador: MUPHTAH AG HAIRY.

Netherlands: 89 Liberation Rd, Thomas Sankara Circle, POB 3248, Accra; tel. (21) 773644; fax (21) 773655; Ambassador: HELN C. R. M. PRINCEN.

Niger: E104/3 Independence Ave, POB 2685, Accra; tel. (21) 224962; Ambassador: OUMAROU YOUSSOUFOU.

Nigeria: Josif Broz Tito Ave, POB 1548, Accra; tel. (21) 776158; High Commissioner: T. A. OLU-OTUNLA.

Pakistan: 11 Ring Rd East, Danquah Circle, POB 1114, Accra; tel. (21) 776059; High Commissioner: Dr ABDUL KABIR.

Poland: 2 Akosombo St, Airport Residential Area, POB 2552, Accra; tel. (21) 775972; fax (21) 776108; Chargé d'affaires a.i.: KAZIMIERZ MAURER.

Romania: North Labone, Ward F, Block 6, House 262, POB 3735, Accra; tel. (21) 774076; Chargé d'affaires a.i.: GHEORGHE V. ILIE.

Russia: 856/1, 13th Lane, Ring Rd East, Osu, POB 1634, Accra; tel. (21) 775611; fax (21) 772699; e-mail russia@ghana.com; Ambassador: PAVEL D. PAVLOV.

Saudi Arabia: 10 Noi Fetreke St, Roman Ridge, Airport Residential Area, POB 670, Accra; tel. (21) 774311; Chargé d'affaires a.i.: ANWAR ABDUL FATTAH ABDRABBUH.

South Africa: 10 Klottey Crescent, Labone North, POB 298, Accra; tel. (21) 762380; fax (21) 762381; e-mail sahcgh@africaonline.com.gh; High Commissioner: JOSIAH MOTSEPE.

Spain: Drake Ave Extension, Airport Residential Area, POB 1218, Accra; tel. (21) 774004; fax (21) 776217; Ambassador: FERNANDO CORRAL.

Switzerland: 9 Water Rd S.I., North Ridge Area, POB 359, Accra; tel. (21) 228125; fax (21) 223583; Ambassador: PETER SCHWEIZER.

Togo: Togo House, near Cantonments Circle, POB C120, Accra; tel. (21) 777950; fax (21) 777961; Ambassador: ASSIONGBOR FOLIVI.

United Kingdom: Osu Link, off Gamel Abdul Nasser Ave, POB 296, Accra; tel. (21) 221665; fax (21) 7010655; e-mail high.commission@accra.mail.fco.gov.uk; High Commissioner: IAN W. MACKLEY.

USA: Ring Road East, POB 194, Accra; tel. (21) 775347; fax (21) 776008; internet www.usia.gov/posts/ghana; Ambassador: KATHRYN DEE ROBINSON.

Yugoslavia: 47 Senchi St, Airport Residential Area, POB 1629, Accra; tel. (21) 775761; Ambassador: LAZAR COVIĆ.

Judicial System

The civil law in force in Ghana is based on the Common Law, doctrines of equity and general statutes which were in force in England in 1874, as modified by subsequent Ordinances. Ghanaian customary law is, however, the basis of most personal, domestic and contractual relationships. Criminal Law is based on the Criminal Procedure Code, 1960, derived from English Criminal Law, and since amended. The Superior Court of Judicature comprises a Supreme Court, a Court of Appeal, a High Court and a Regional Tribunal; Inferior Courts include Circuit Courts, Circuit Tribunals, Community Tribunals and such other Courts as may be designated by law.

Supreme Court: Consists of the Chief Justice and not fewer than nine other Justices. It is the final court of appeal in Ghana and has jurisdiction in matters relating to the enforcement or interpretation of the Constitution.

 Chief Justice: ISAAC KOBINA ABBAN.

Court of Appeal: Consists of the Chief Justice and not fewer than five Judges of the Court of Appeal. It has jurisdiction to hear and determine appeals from any judgment, decree or order of the High Court.

High Court: Comprises the Chief Justice and not fewer than 12 Justices of the High Court. It exercises original jurisdiction in all matters, civil and criminal, other than those for offences involving treason. Trial by jury is practised in criminal cases in Ghana and the Criminal Procedure Code, 1960, provides that all trials on indictment shall be by a jury or with the aid of Assessors.

Circuit Courts: Exercise original jurisdiction in civil matters where the amount involved does not exceed C100,000. They also have jurisdiction with regard to the guardianship and custody of infants, and original jurisdiction in all criminal cases, except offences where the maximum punishment is death or the offence of treason. They have appellate jurisdiction from decisions of any District Court situated within their respective circuits.

District Courts: To each magisterial district is assigned at least one District Magistrate who has original jurisdiction to try civil suits in which the amount involved does not exceed C50,000. District Magistrates also have jurisdiction to deal with all criminal cases, except first-degree felonies, and commit cases of a more serious nature to either the Circuit Court or the High Court. A Grade I District Court can impose a fine not exceeding C1,000 and sentences of imprisonment of up to two years and a Grade II District Court may impose a fine not exceeding C500 and a sentence of imprisonment of up to 12 months. A District Court has no appellate jurisdiction, except in rent matters under the Rent Act.

Juvenile Courts: Jurisdiction in cases involving persons under 17 years of age, except where the juvenile is charged jointly with an adult. The Courts comprise a Chairman, who must be either the District Magistrate or a lawyer, and not fewer than two other members appointed by the Chief Justice in consultation with the Judicial Council. The Juvenile Courts can make orders as to the protection and supervision of a neglected child and can negotiate with parents to secure the good behaviour of a child.

National Public Tribunal: Considers appeals from the Regional Public Tribunals. Its decisions are final and are not subject to any further appeal. The Tribunal consists of at least three members and not more than five, one of whom acts as Chairman.

Regional Public Tribunals: Hears criminal cases relating to prices, rent or exchange control, theft, fraud, forgery, corruption or any offence which may be referred to them by the Provisional National Defence Council.

Special Military Tribunal: Hears criminal cases involving members of the armed forces. It consists of between five and seven members.

Religion

At the 1960 census the distribution of religious groups was: Christians 42.8%, traditional religions 38.2%, Muslims 12.0%, unclassified 7.0%.

CHRISTIANITY

Christian Council of Ghana: POB 919, Accra; tel. (21) 776725; f. 1929; advisory body comprising 14 Protestant churches; Chair. (vacant); Gen. Sec. Rev. DAVID A. DARTEY.

The Anglican Communion

Anglicans in Ghana are adherents of the Church of the Province of West Africa, comprising 12 dioceses, of which seven are in Ghana.

Archbishop of the Province of West Africa and Bishop of Koforidua: Most Rev. ROBERT OKINE, POB 980, Koforidua; tel. (81) 2329.

Bishop of Accra: Rt Rev. JUSTICE OFEI AKROFI, Bishopscourt, POB 8, Accra; tel. (21) 669125.

Bishop of Cape Coast: Rt Rev. KOBINA QUASHIE, Bishopscourt, POB A233, Cape Coast; tel. (42) 2637.

Bishop of Kumasi: Rt Rev. DANIEL YINKAH SARFO, Bishop's Office, POB 144, Kumasi; tel. and fax (51) 24117.

Bishop of Sekondi: (vacant), POB 85, Sekondi; tel. (21) 6048; fax (21) 669125.

Bishop of Sunyani: Rt Rev. THOMAS AMPAH BRIENT, Bishop's House, POB 23, Sunyani; fax (61) 7023; e-mail deegyab@ighmail.com.

Bishop of Tamale: Rt Rev. EMMANUEL ARONGO, POB 110, Tamale; tel. (71) 2018; fax (71) 22849.

The Roman Catholic Church

Ghana comprises three archdioceses and 15 dioceses. At 31 December 1998 there were 2,172,490 adherents in the country, equivalent to 9.7% of the total population.

Ghana Bishops' Conference: National Catholic Secretariat, POB 9712, Airport, Accra; tel. (21) 500491; fax (21) 500493; f. 1960; Pres. Most Rev. PETER K. APPIAH-TURKSON, Archbishop of Cape Coast.

Archbishop of Accra: Most Rev. DOMINIC KODWO ANDOH, Chancery Office, POB 247, Accra; tel. (21) 222728; fax (21) 231619.

Archbishop of Cape Coast: Most Rev. PETER KODWO APPIAH-TURKSON, Archbishop's House, POB 112, Cape Coast; tel. (42) 33471; fax (42) 33473.

Archbishop of Tamale: Most Rev. GREGORY EBO KPIEBAYA, Gumbehini Rd, POB 163, Tamale; tel. (71) 22425; fax (71) 22425.

Other Christian Churches

African Methodist Episcopal Zion Church: Sekondi; Pres. Rev. Dr ZORMELO.

Christian Methodist Episcopal Church: POB 3906, Accra; Pres. Rev. YENN BATA.

Evangelical-Lutheran Church of Ghana: POB 197, Kaneshie; tel. (21) 223487; fax (21) 223353; Pres. Rt Rev. Dr PAUL KOFI FYNN; 21,700 mems.

Evangelical-Presbyterian Church: POB 18, Ho; tel. (91) 755; f. 1847; Moderator Rt Rev. D. A. KORANTENG; 295,000 mems.

Ghana Baptist Convention: POB 1979, Kumasi; tel. (51) 5215; f. 1963; Pres. Rev. FRED DEEGBE; Sec. Rev. FRANK ADAMS.

Mennonite Church: POB 5485, Accra; fax (21) 220589; f. 1957; Moderator Rev. Dr TEI-KWABLA; Sec. ISAAC K. QUARTEY; 4,800 mems.

Methodist Church of Ghana: Liberia Rd, POB 403, Accra; tel. (21) 228120; fax (21) 227008; Pres. Rt Rev. Dr SAMUEL ASANTE ANTWI; Sec. Rev. MACLEAN AGYIRI KUMI; 341,000 mems.

Presbyterian Church of Ghana: POB 1800, Accra; tel. (21) 662511; fax (21) 665594; f. 1828; Moderator Rt Rev. ANTHONY ANTWI BEEKO; Sec. Rev. Dr D. N. A. KPOBI; 422,500 mems.

Seventh-day Adventists: POB 1016, Accra; tel. (21) 223720; fax (21) 227024; e-mail waumsda1@ghana.com; 1943; Pres. P. O. MENSAH; Sec. SETH A. LARMIE.

The African Methodist Episcopal Church, the F'Eden Church and the Society of Friends (Quakers) are also active in Ghana.

ISLAM

There is a substantial Muslim population in the Northern Region. The majority are Malikees.

Chief Imam: CHEICK USMAN NUBUSHARABUTU.

The Press

DAILY NEWSPAPERS

Daily Graphic: Graphic Rd, POB 742, Accra; tel. (21) 228911; fax (21) 669886; e-mail graphic@ghana.com; internet www.graphic.com.gh; f. 1950; state-owned; Editor ELVIS ARYEH; circ. 100,000.

The Ghanaian Times: New Times Corpn, Ring Rd West, POB 2638, Accra; tel. (21) 228282; fax (21) 229398; e-mail newtimes@ghana.com; internet www.gtimes.com.gh; f. 1958; state-owned; Editor CHRISTIAN AGGREY; circ. 45,000.

PERIODICALS

Weekly

Bombshell: Crossfire Publications, POB 376, Sakumono, Accra; tel. (21) 234750; fax (21) 233172; Editor BEN ASAMOAH.

Business and Financial Times: POB 2157, Accra; tel. and fax (21) 223334; e-mail bft@africaonline.com.gh; internet www.bftgh.com; f. 1989; Man. Editor JOHN HANSON; Editor WALLY ODOOM; circ. 20,000.

Catholic Standard: Accra.

Champion: POB 6828, Accra-North; tel. (21) 229079; Man. Dir MARK D. N. ADDY; Editor FRANK CAXTON WILLIAMS; circ. 300,000.

Christian Chronicle: Accra; English; Editor GEORGE NAYKENE.

The Democrat: Democrat Publications, POB 13605, Accra; tel. (21) 76804; Editor L. K. NYAHO.

Echo: POB 5288, Accra; f. 1968; Sun.; Man. Editor M. K. FRIMPONG; circ. 40,000.

Entertaining Eye: Kad Publications, POB 125, Darkuman-Accra; Editor NANA KWAKYE YIADOM; circ. 40,000.

Evening Digest: News Media Ltd, POB 7082, Accra; tel. (21) 221071; Editor P. K. ANANTITETTEH.

Experience: POB 5084, Accra-North; Editor ALFRED YAW POKU; circ. 50,000.

Free Press: Tommy Thompson Books Ltd, POB 6492, Accra; tel. (21) 225994; independent; English; Editor EBEN QUARCOO.

Ghana Life: Ghana Life Publications, POB 11337, Accra; tel. (21) 229835; Editor NIKKI BOA-AMPONSEM.

Ghana Palaver: Palaver Publications, POB 15744, Accra-North; tel. (21) 232495; Editor BRUCE QUANSAH.

Ghanaian Chronicle: General Portfolio Ltd, Private Mail Bag, Accra-North; tel. (21) 227789; fax (21) 775895; e-mail chronicle@africaonline.com.gh; internet www.ghanaian-chronicle.com; Editor EBO QUANSAH; circ. 60,000.

Ghanaian Dawn: Dawn Publications, POB 721, Mamprobi, Accra; Editor MABEL LINDSAY.

The Ghanaian Voice: Newstop Publications, POB 514, Mamprobi, Accra; Editor DAN K. ANSAH; circ. 100,000.

The Gossip: Gossip Publications, POB 5355, Accra-North; Editor C. A. ACHEAMPONG.

Graphic Showbiz: Graphic Rd, POB 742, Accra; tel. (21) 228911; fax (21) 669886; e-mail graphic@ncs.com.gh; state-owned.

Graphic Sports: Graphic Rd, POB 742, Accra; tel. (21) 228911; state-owned; Editor JOE AGGREY; circ. 60,000.

The Guide: Western Publications Ltd, POB 8253, Accra-North; tel. (21) 232760; Editor KWEKU BAAKO Jnr.

High Street Journal: POB 7974, Accra-North; tel. (12) 239835; fax (12) 239837; e-mail hsaccra@ghana.com; Editor SHEIKH ABUTIATE.

The Independent: Clear Type Press Bldg Complex, off Graphic Rd, POB 4031, Accra; tel. and fax (12) 661091; f. 1989; Editor RICHMOND KEELSON.

The Mirror: Graphic Rd, POB 742, Accra; tel. (21) 228911; fax (21) 669886; f. 1953; state-owned; Sat.; Editor E. N. V. PROVENCAL; circ. 90,000.

The New Ghanaian: Tudu Publishing House, POB 751, Tamale; tel. (71) 22579; Editor RAZAK EL-ALAWA.

New Nation: POB 6828, Accra-North; Editor S. N. SASRAKU; circ. 300,000.

Private Eye: Kad Life Books Channels, POB 125, Accra; tel. (21) 230684; Editor AWUKU AGYEMANG-DUAH.

Public Agenda: P. A. Communications, POB 5564, Accra-North; tel. (21) 238821; fax (21) 231687; e-mail isodec@ncs.com.gh; f. 1994; Editor YAO GRAHAM; circ. 12,000.

Sporting News: POB 5481, Accra-North; f. 1967; Man. Editor J. OPPONG-AGYARE.

The Standard: Standard Newspapers & Magazines Ltd, POB 765, Accra; tel. (21) 220165; Editor ISAAC FRITZ ANDOH; circ. 10,000.

Statesman: Kinesic Communications, POB 846, Accra; tel. and fax (21) 233242; official publ. of the New Patriotic Party; Editor HARUNNA ATTAH.

Voice: Accra.

The Weekend: Newstop Publications, POB 514, Mamprobi, Accra; tel. and fax (21) 226943; Editor EMMANUEL YARTEY; circ. 40,000.

Weekly Events: Clear Type Image Ltd, 29 Olympic Street (Enterprise House), Kokomlemle, POB 7634, Accra-North; tel. (21) 223085; Editor JORIS JORDAN DODOO.

Weekly Insight: Militant Publications Ltd, POB K272, Accra New Town, Accra; tel. (21) 660148; f. 1993; independent; English; Editor KWESI PRATT Jnr.

Weekly Spectator: New Times Corpn, Ring Road West, POB 2638, Accra; tel. (21) 228282; fax (21) 229398; state-owned; f. 1963; Sun.; Editor WILLIE DONKOR; circ. 165,000.

Other

Africa Flamingo: Airport Emporium Ltd, POB 9194, Accra; monthly; Editor FELIX AMANFU; circ. 50,000.

African Observer: POB 1171, Kaneshie, Accra; tel. (012) 231459; bi-monthly; Editor STEVE MALLORY.

African Woman: Ring Rd West, POB 1496, Accra; monthly.

AGI Newsletter: c/o Asscn of Ghana Industries, POB 8624, Accra-North; tel. (21) 777283; e-mail agi@ighmail.com; f. 1974; quarterly; Editor (vacant); circ. 1,500.

Akwansosem: Ghana Information Services, POB 745, Accra; tel. (21) 228011; quarterly; in Akuapim Twi, Asanti Twi and Fante; Editor KATHLEEN OFOSU-APPIAH.

Armed Forces News: General Headquarters, Directorate of Public Relations, Burma Camp, Accra; tel. (21) 776111; f. 1966; quarterly; Editor ADOTEY ANKRAH-HOFFMAN; circ. 4,000.

Boxing and Football Illustrated: POB 8392, Accra; f. 1976; monthly; Editor NANA O. AMPOMAH; circ. 10,000.

Business and Financial Concord: Sammy Tech Consult Enterprise, POB 5677, Accra-North; tel. (21) 232446; fortnightly; Editor KWABENA RICHARDSON.

Chit Chat: POB 7043, Accra; monthly; Editor ROSEMOND ADU.

Christian Messenger: Presbyterian Book Depot Bldg, POB 3075, Accra; tel. and fax (21) 662415; f. 1883; English; also **The Presbyterian** (in Twi and Ga); quarterly; Editor G. B. K. OWUSU; circ. 40,000.

Drum: POB 1197, Accra; monthly; general interest.

Ghana Journal of Science: Ghana Science Asscn, POB 7, Legon; monthly; Editor Dr A. K. AHAFIA.

Ghana Official News Bulletin: Information Services Dept, POB 745, Accra; English; political, economic, investment and cultural affairs.

Ideal Woman (Obaa Sima): POB 5737, Accra; tel. (21) 221399; f. 1971; fortnightly; Editor KATE ABBAM.

Insight and Opinion: POB 5446, Accra; quarterly; Editorial Sec. W. B. OHENE.

Legon Observer: POB 11, Legon; fax (21) 774338; f. 1966; publ. by Legon Society on National Affairs; fortnightly; Chair. J. A. DADSON; Editor EBOW DANIEL.

Police News: Police HQ, Accra; monthly; Editor S. S. APPIAH; circ. 20,000.

The Post: Ghana Information Services, POB 745, Accra; tel. (21) 228011; f. 1980; monthly; current affairs and analysis; circ. 25,000.

Radio and TV Times: Ghana Broadcasting Corpn, Broadcasting House, POB 1633, Accra; tel. (21) 221161; f. 1960; quarterly; Editor SAM THOMPSON; circ. 5,000.

The Scope: POB 8162, Tema; monthly; Editor EMMANUEL DOE ZIORKLUI; circ. 10,000.

Students World: POB M18, Accra; tel. (21) 774248; fax (21) 778715; e-mail aframpub@ighmail.com; f. 1974; monthly; educational; Man. Editor ERIC OFEI; circ. 10,000.

The Teacher: Ghana National Asscn of Teachers, POB 209, Accra; tel. (21) 221515; fax (21) 226286; f. 1931; quarterly; circ. 30,000.

Truth and Life: Gift Publications, POB 11337, Accra-North; monthly; Editor Pastor KOBENA CHARM.

The Watchman: Watchman Gospel Ministry, POB GP 4521, Accra; tel. (21) 502011; fax (21)507428; e-mail sonlife@africaonline.com.gh; fortnightly; Pres. and CEO DIVINE P. KUMAH; Chair. Dr E. K. OPUNI.

NEWS AGENCIES

Ghana News Agency: POB 2118, Accra; tel. (21) 665136; fax 669841; e-mail ghnews@ncs.com.gh; f. 1957; Gen. Man. SAM B. QUAICOE; 10 regional offices and 110 district offices.

Foreign Bureaux

Associated Press (AP) (USA): Accra; Bureau Chief P. K. COBBINAH-ESSEM.

Xinhua (New China) News Agency (People's Republic of China): 2 Seventh St, Airport Residential Area, POB 3897, Accra; tel. (21) 772042.

Deutsche Presse-Agentur (Germany) and **Reuters** (UK) are also represented.

Publishers

Advent Press: POB 0102, Osu, Accra; tel. (21) 777861; f. 1937; Gen. Man. EMMANUEL C. TETTEH.

Adwinsa Publications (Ghana) Ltd: Advance Press Bldg, 3rd Floor, School Rd, POB 92, Legoh Accra; tel. (21) 221654; f. 1977; general, educational; Man. Dir KWABENA AMPONSAH.

Afram Publications: 9 Ring Rd East, POB M18, Accra; tel. (21) 774248; fax (21) 778715; e-mail aframpub@ighmail.com; f. 1974; textbooks and general; Man. Dir ERIC OFEI.

Africa Christian Press: POB 30, Achimota; tel. (21) 244147; fax (21) 220271; f. 1964; religious, fiction, theology, children's; Gen. Man. RICHARD A. B. CRABBE.

Allgoodbooks Ltd: POB AN10416, Accra-North; tel. (21) 665629; fax (21) 302993; e-mail allgoodbooks@hotmail.com; f. 1968; children's; Man. MARY ASIRIFI.

Asempa Publishers: POB GP919, Accra; tel. (21) 233084; fax (21) 235140; e-mail asempa@ncs.com.gh; f. 1970; religion, social issues, African music, fiction, children's; Gen. Man. Rev. EMMANUEL B. BORTEY.

Baafour and Co: POB K189, Accra New Town; f. 1978; general; Man. B. KESE-AMANKWAA.

Benibengor Book Agency: POB 40, Aboso; fiction, biography, children's and paperbacks; Man. Dir J. BENIBENGOR BLAY.

Black Mask Ltd: 17 Watson Ave, Adabraka, Accra; tel. (21) 234577; f. 1979; textbooks, plays, novels, handicrafts; Man. Dir YAW OWUSU ASANTE.

Editorial and Publishing Services: POB 5743, Accra; general, reference; Man. Dir M. DANQUAH.

Educational Press and Manufacturers Ltd: POB 9184, Airport-Accra; tel. (21) 220395; f. 1975; textbooks, children's; Man. G. K. KODUA.

Encyclopaedia Africana Project: POB 2797, Accra; tel. (21) 776939; f. 1962; reference; Dir J. O. VANDERPUYE.

Frank Publishing Ltd: POB MB414, Accra; tel. (21) 240711; f. 1976; secondary school textbooks; Man. Dir FRANCIS K. DZOKOTO.

Ghana Publishing Corpn: PMB Tema; tel. (221) 2921; f. 1965; textbooks and general fiction and non-fiction; Man. Dir F. K. NYARKO.

Ghana Universities Press: POB GP4219, Accra; tel. (21) 500300; fax (21) 501930; f. 1962; scholarly and academic; Dir K. M. GANU.

Golden Wings Publications: 26 Mantse Kwao St, POB 1337, Accra; educational and children's; Man. Editor GREGORY ANKRAH.

Miracle Bookhouse: POB 7487, Accra-North; tel. (21) 226684; f. 1977; general; Man. J. APPIAH-BERKO.

Moxon Paperbacks: POB M160, Accra; tel. (21) 761175; fax (21) 777971; f. 1967; travel and guide books, fiction and poetry, Africana, telephone directory; Man. Dir JAMES MOXON.

Sam-Woode Ltd: A.979/15 Dansoman High Street, POB 12719, Accra-North; tel. (21) 305287; fax (021) 310482; internet www .samwoode@africaonline.com.gh; educational and children's; Chair. KWESI SAM-WOODE.

Sedco Publishing Ltd: Sedco House, 5 Tabon St, North Ridge, POB 2051, Accra; tel. (21) 221332; fax (21) 220107; e-mail sedco@ africaonline.com.gh; f. 1975; educational; Man. Dir COURAGE K. SEGBAWU.

Sheffield Publishing Co: Accra; tel. (21) 667480; fax (21) 665960; f. 1970; religion, politics, economics, science, fiction; Publr RONALD MENSAH.

Unimax Publishers Ltd: 42 Ring Rd South Industrial Area, POB 10722, Accra-North; tel. (21) 227443; fax (21) 225215; e-mail unimax@africaonline.com.gh; atlases, educational and children's; Dir EDWARD ADDO.

Waterville Publishing House: POB 195, Accra; tel. (21) 663124; f. 1963; general fiction and non-fiction, textbooks, paperbacks, Africana; Man. Dir H. W. O. OKAI.

Woeli Publishing Services: POB NT601, Accra New Town; tel. and fax (21) 229294; f. 1984; children's, fiction, academic; Dir W. A. DEKUTSEY.

PUBLISHERS' ASSOCIATIONS

Ghana Book Development Council: POB M430, Accra; tel. (21) 229178; f. 1975; govt-financed agency; promotes and co-ordinates writing, production and distribution of books; Exec. Dir D. A. NIMAKO.

Ghana Book Publishers' Association: c/o Africa Christian Press, POB 430, Achimota; Sec. E. B. BORTEY.

Private Newspaper Publishers' Association of Ghana (PRINPAG): POB 125, Darkuman, Accra; Gen. Sec. K. AGYEMANG DUAH.

Broadcasting and Communications

TELECOMMUNICATIONS

Ghana Telecommunication Co Ltd: Posts and Telecommunications Bldg, Accra-North; tel. (21) 221001; fax (21) 667979; f. 1995; 30% transferred to private ownership in 1997; Dir-Gen. JOSEPH AGGREY-MENSAH; Man. Dir ADNAN ROFIEE.

BROADCASTING

There are internal radio broadcasts in English, Akan, Dagbani, Ewe, Ga, Hausa and Nzema, and an external service in English and French. There are three transmitting stations, with a number of relay stations. There is a total of eight main colour television transmitters. The Ghana Broadcasting Corporation operates two national networks, Radio 1 and Radio 2, which broadcast from Accra. There is also an FM station in Accra (known as Radio GAR), a regional FM station at Bolgatanga and a community FM station at Apam, as well as an external service which broadcasts in English and French.

Ghana Broadcasting Corporation: Broadcasting House, POB 1633, Accra; tel. (21) 221161; fax (21) 221153; e-mail gtv@ncs.com.gh; f. 1935; Dir-Gen. Dr KOFI FRIMPONG; Dir of TV Prof. MARK DUODU; Dir of Radio CRIS TACKIE.

Finance

(cap. = capital; res = reserves; dep. = deposits; m. = million; brs = branches; amounts in cedis)

BANKING

The commercial banking sector comprised nine commercial banks, four development banks and four merchant banks in 1998. There were also 130 rural banks and several non-banking financial institutions.

Central Bank

Bank of Ghana: High Street, Thorpe Rd, POB 2674, Accra; tel. (21) 666902; fax (21) 662996; e-mail secretary@bog.gov.gh; f. 1957; bank of issue; cap. and res 200,504m., dep. 696,921m. (Dec. 1997); Chair. and Gov. KWABENA DUFFOUR.

Commercial and Development Banks

Agricultural Development Bank: Cedi House, Liberia Rd, POB 4191, Accra; tel. (21) 662758; fax (21) 662846; e-mail adb@ africaonline.com.gh; internet www.ghanaclassifieds.com/adb/; f. 1965; 79% state-owned; credit facilities for farmers and commercial

banking; cap. and res 77,658.4m., dep. 119,463.0m. (Dec. 1997); Chair. NATHAN QUAO; Man. Dir PERCIVAL A. KURANCHIE; 34 brs.

Bank for Housing and Construction (BHC): Okofoh House, 24 Kwame Nkrumah Ave, POB M1, Adabraka, Accra; tel. (21) 220033; fax (21) 229631; e-mail bhc@ghana.com; f. 1973; 50% state-owned; cap. 1,000m. (Dec. 1995); Chair. K. TWUM BOAFO; Man. Dir L. A. ADJAIDOO.

Ghana Commercial Bank Ltd: POB 134, Accra; tel. (21) 664914; fax (21) 662168; e-mail gcbmail@ncs.com.gh; f. 1953; 59.1% state-owned; cap. and res 101,613m., dep. 555,607m. (Dec. 1997); Chair. JOHN SEY; Man. Dir WILLIAM PANFORD BRAY (acting); 145 brs.

Ghana Co-operative Bank Ltd: Kwame Nkrumah Ave, POB 5292, Accra-North; tel. (21) 663131; fax (21) 662359; f. 1970; 81% state-owned; cap. 2,913.7m. (Dec. 1994); Chair. W. E. INKUMSAH (acting); Man. Dir S. A. DONKOR; 21 brs.

Leasafric Ghana Ltd: 7 Main St, Tesano, POB C2430, Accra; tel. (21) 240140; fax (21) 228375; e-mail leasafric@africaonline.com.gh; cap. 893m. (Dec. 1996); Chair. JOHN KOBINA RISHCARDSON; Man. Dir SETH K. DEI.

National Investment Bank Ltd (NIB): 37 Kwame Nkrumah Ave, POB 3726, Accra; tel. (21) 669301; fax (21) 240030; f. 1963; 86.5% state-owned; provides long-term investment capital, jt venture promotion, consortium finance man. and commercial banking services; cap. 3,259.7m., dep. 58,867.5m. (Dec. 1997); Chair. NICHOLAS AKPEBU; Man. Dir MAHMOUD HANTOUR; 11 brs.

National Trust Holding Co Ltd: Martco House, Okai Mensah Link, off Kwame Nkrumah Ave, POB 9563 KIA, Airport, Accra; tel. (21) 238492; fax (21) 229975; e-mail nthc@ghana.com; internet www.nthcghana.com; f. 1976 to finance Ghanaian acquisitions of indigenous cos; also assists in their development and expansion, and provides financial advisory services; cap. 500m. (1999); Chair. JACOB BRUCE YIRERONG; Acting Man. Dir PAUL EFFAH OTENG.

Prudential Bank Ltd: Kingsway Stores Bldg, 34 Kwame Nkrumah Ave, POB 9820, Accra; tel. (21) 226322; fax (21) 226803; f. Aug. 1996; Chair. and Man. Dir JOHN SACKAH ADDO.

Social Security Bank Ltd (SSB): POB 13119, Accra; tel. (21) 221726; fax (21) 220713; e-mail ssb@ghana.com; internet www.ssb.com.gh; f. 1976; cap. 6,734.5m., dep. 277,309.1m. (Dec. 1996); Chair. FRANCIS E. Y. ATTIPOE; Man. Dir PRYCE K. THOMPSON.

Trust Bank Ghana Ltd: 68 Kwame Nkrumah Ave, POB 1862, Accra; tel. (21) 240049; fax (21) 240056; e-mail trust@gh.com; f. 1996; cap. and res 15,347.2m., dep. 60,078.9m. (Dec. 1997); Chair. ALEX AWUKU; Man. Dir JEAN-MARIE MARQUEBREUCQ; 6 brs.

Merchant Banks

CAL Merchant Bank Ltd: 45 Independence Ave, POB 14596, Accra; tel. (21) 221056; fax (21) 231913; e-mail calbank@calbankgh .com; internet www.africaonline.com.gh/cal/; f. 1990 as Continental Acceptances Ltd; cap. and res 17,816.1m., dep. 45,795.2m. (Dec. 1998); Chair. LOUIS CASELY-HAYFORD; Man. Dir JUDE KOFI BUCKNOR.

Ecobank Ghana Ltd (EBG): 19 Seventh Ave, Ridge West, Accra; tel. (21) 229532; fax (21) 667127; e-mail ecobank@ghana.com; internet www.ghanaclassifieds.com/ecobank; f. 1989; 93.7% owned by Ecobank Transnational Inc (operating under the auspices of the Economic Community of West African States); cap. and res 33,861.4m., dep. 215,878.3m. (Dec. 1997); Chair. EDWARD PATRICK LARBI GYAMPOH; Man. Dir JEAN N. AKA.

First Atlantic Merchant Bank Ltd: Atlantic Place, 1 Seventh Ave, Ridge West, POB C1620, Cantonments, Accra; tel. (21) 231433; fax (21) 231399; e-mail fambl@ghana.com; f. 1995; cap. and res 4,563.9m., dep. 35,307.6m. (Dec. 1998); Chair. SAM JONAH; Man. Dir JUDE ARTHUR.

Merchant Bank (Ghana) Ltd: Merban House, 44 Kwame Nkrumah Ave, POB 401, Accra; tel. (21) 666331; fax (21) 667305; e-mail merban-services@ighmail.com; internet www.ghana classifieds.com/merchantbank; f. 1972; cap. and res 17,497.0m., dep. 166,828.0m. (Dec. 1998); Chair. Dr JOHN RICHARDSON; Man. Dir CHRIS N. NARTEY; 4 brs.

Foreign Banks

Barclays Bank of Ghana Ltd (UK): High St, POB 2949, Accra; tel. (21) 664901; fax (21) 667420; e-mail barclays@africaonline.com.gh; f. 1917; 10% state-owned; cap. and res 58,628m., dep. 485,302m. (Dec. 1998); Chair. NANA WEREKO AMPEM; Man. Dir K. QUANSAH; 25 brs.

Standard Chartered Bank Ghana Ltd (UK): 3rd Floor, Accra, High St Building, POB 768, Accra; tel. (21) 664591; fax (21) 667751; e-mail dzaney@scb.ghana.nhs.compuserve.com; f. 1896; cap. and res 87,861.0m., dep. 715,188.0m. (Dec. 1998); Chair. DAVID ANDOH; CEO VISHNU MOHAN; 28 brs.

STOCK EXCHANGE

Ghana Stock Exchange (GSE): Cedi House, 5th Floor, Liberia Rd, POB 1849, Accra; tel. (21) 669908; fax (21) 669913; e-mail stockex@ncs.com.gh; internet www.gse.com.gh; 52 mems; Man. Dir YEBOAH AMOAH.

INSURANCE

Ghana Union Assurance Co Ltd: POB 1322, Accra; tel. (21) 664421; fax (21) 664988; f. 1973; Man. Dir KWADWO DUKU.

The Great African Insurance Co Ltd: POB 12349, Accra North; tel. (21) 227459; fax (21) 228905; f. 1980; Man. Dir KWASI AKOTO.

The State Insurance Corporation of Ghana: POB 2363, Accra; tel. (21) 666961; fax (21) 662205; f. 1962; state-owned; all classes of insurance; Man. Dir B. K. QUASHIE.

Social Security and National Insurance Trust: Pension House, POB M149, Accra; tel. (21) 667742; fax (21) 662226; f. 1972; covers over 650,000 contributors; Dir-Gen. HENRY G. DEI.

Vanguard Assurance Co Ltd: Insurance Hall, Derby House, Derby Ave, POB 1868, Accra; tel. (21) 666485; fax (21) 668610; f. 1974; general accident, marine, motor and life insurance; Man. Dir NANA AWUAH-DARKO AMPEM; 7 brs.

Several foreign insurance companies operate in Ghana.

Trade and Industry

GOVERNMENT AGENCIES

Divestiture Implementation Committee: F35/5 Ring Road East, North Labone; POB CT102, Cantonments, Accra; tel. (21) 772049; fax (21) 773126; e-mail dicgh@ncs.com.gh; f. 1988; Exec. Sec. EMMANUEL AGBODO.

Food Production Corporation: POB 1853, Accra; f. 1971; state corpn providing employment for youth in large-scale farming enterprises; controls 76,900 ha of land (16,200 ha under cultivation); operates 87 food farms on a co-operative and self-supporting basis, and rears poultry and livestock.

Ghana Export Promotion Council (GEPC): Republic House, Tudu, POB M146, Accra; tel. (21) 228813; fax (21) 668263; e-mail gepc@ighmail.com; f. 1974; Exec. Sec. TAWIA AKYEA.

Ghana Food Distribution Corporation: POB 4245, Accra; tel. (21) 228428; f. 1971; buys, stores, preserves, distributes and retails foodstuffs through 10 regional centres; Man. Dir E. H. K. AMANKWA.

Ghana Free Zones Board: POB M626, Accra; tel. (21) 780532; fax (21) 670536; e-mail gfzb@ighmail.com; internet www.africaonline .com.gfzb; f. 1996; approves establishment of cos in export processing zones; Exec. Sec. GEORGE ABOAGYE.

Ghana Industrial Holding Corporation (GIHOC): POB 2784, Accra; tel. (21) 664998; f. 1967; controls and manages 26 state enterprises, including steel, paper, bricks, paint, pharmaceuticals, electronics, metals, canneries, distilleries and boat-building factories; also has three subsidiary cos and four jt ventures; Chair. J. E. K. MOSES; Man. Dir J. K. WILLIAMS.

Ghana Investment Promotion Centre: Central Ministerial Area, POB M193, Accra; tel. (21) 665125; fax (21) 663801; e-mail gipc@ ghana.com; internet www.gipc.org.gh; f. 1981; negotiates new investments, approves projects, registers foreign capital and decides extent of govt participation; Chair. P. V. OBENG.

Ghana National Trading Corporation (GNTC): POB 67, Accra; tel. (21) 664871; f. 1961; organizes exports and imports of selected commodities; over 500 retail outlets in 12 admin. dists.

Ghana Standards Board: c/o POB M245, Accra; tel. (21) 500065; fax (21) 500092; f. 1967; establishes and promulgates standards; promotes standardization, industrial efficiency and development and industrial welfare, health and safety; operates certification mark scheme; 403 mems; Dir Rev. Dr E. K. MARFO.

National Board for Small-scale Industries: Ministry of Trade and Industry, POB M85, Accra; f. 1985; promotes small and medium-scale industrial and commercial enterprises by providing credit, advisory services and training.

State Farms Corporation: Accra; undertakes agricultural projects in all regions but Upper Region; Man. Dir E. N. A. THOMPSON (acting).

State Housing Construction Co: POB 2753, Accra; f. 1982 by merger; oversees govt housing programme.

CHAMBER OF COMMERCE

Ghana National Chamber of Commerce: POB 2325, Accra; tel. (21) 662427; fax (21) 662210; e-mail gncc@ncs.com.gh; f. 1961; promotes and protects industry and commerce, organizes trade fairs; 2,500 individual mems and 8 mem. chambers; Pres. ATO AMPIAH; Exec. Dir SAL D. AMEGAVIE.

INDUSTRIAL AND TRADE ASSOCIATIONS

Best Fibres Development Board: POB 1992, Kumasi; f. 1970; promotes the commercial cultivation of best fibres and their processing, handling and grading.

Ghana Cocoa Board (COCOBOD): POB 933, Accra; tel. (21) 221212; fax (21) 667104; e-mail cocobod@africaonline.comigh; f. 1985; monopoly purchaser of cocoa until 1993; responsible for purchase, grading and export of cocoa, coffee and shea nuts; also encourages production and scientific research aimed at improving quality and yield of these crops; controls all exports of cocoa; CEO JOHN NEWMAN.

Grains and Legumes Development Board: POB 4000, Kumasi; tel. (51) 4231; f. 1970; state-controlled; promotes and develops production of cereals and leguminous vegetables.

Minerals Commission: 9 Switch Rd, Residential Area, Cantonments, POB M248, Accra; tel. (21) 772783; fax (21) 773324; e-mail mincom@ncs.com.gh; f. 1984; supervises, promotes and co-ordinates the minerals industry; CEO KOFI ANSAH.

Timber Export Development Board: POB 515, Takoradi; tel. (31) 22921; fax (31) 23339; e-mail timbod@ghana.com; f. 1985; promotes the sale and export of timber; CEO SAMUEL KWESI APPIAH.

EMPLOYERS' ORGANIZATION

Ghana Employers' Association: 122 Kojo Thompson Rd, POB 2616, Accra; tel. (21) 228455; fax (21) 228405; f. 1959; 400 mems; Pres. ISHMAEL E. YAMSON; Vice-Pres. ATO AMPIAH.

Affiliated Bodies

Association of Ghana Industries: Trade Fair Centre, POB 8624, Accra-North; tel. and fax (21) 779793; e-mail agi@ghana.com; internet www.agi-org.gh; f. 1957; Pres. Prince KOFI KLUDJESON; Exec. Dir ANDREW E. QUAYSON.

Ghana Booksellers' Association: POB 10367, Accra-North; tel. (21) 773002; fax (21) 773242; Pres. SAMPSON BRAKO; Gen. Sec. FRED J. REIMMER.

Ghana Chamber of Mines: 2nd Floor, Diamond House, POB 991, Accra; tel. (21) 665355; fax (21) 662926; f. 1928; Pres. PETER BRADFORD; Exec. Dir SAM POKU.

Ghana Electrical Contractors' Association: POB 1858, Accra.

Ghana National Association of Teachers: POB 209, Accra; tel. (21) 221515; fax (21) 226286; f. 1931; Pres. G. N. NAASO; Gen. Sec. PAUL OSEI-MENSAH.

Ghana National Contractors' Association: c/o J. T. Osei and Co, POB M11, Accra.

Ghana Timber Association (GTA): POB 246, Takoradi; f. 1952; promotes, protects and develops timber industry; Chair. TETTEH NANOR.

UTILITIES

Electricity

Electricity Corporation of Ghana (ECG): Electro-Volta House, POB 521, Accra; tel. (21) 664941; fax (21) 666262; e-mail ecgho@gh.com; Man. Dir MUSA B. ADAM.

Ghana Atomic Energy Commission: POB 80, Legon/Accra; tel. (21) 400310; fax (21) 400807; e-mail secgaec@ncs.com.gh; f. 1963; promotes, develops and utilizes nuclear techniques; construction of a research reactor at Kwabenya, near Accra, which was begun in 1964, was completed in 1995; Chair. Prof. KWAME SARPONG.

Volta River Authority: POB MB77, Accra; tel. (21) 664941; fax (21) 662610; e-mail orgsrv@accra.rva.com; internet www.vramis .ncs.com.gh; f. 1965; controls the generation and distribution of electricity; Chair. and CEO E. A. K. KALITSI.

Water

Ghana Water and Sewerage Corporation: POB M194, Accra; tel. (21) 666781; f. 1966 to provide, distribute and conserve water supplies for public, domestic and industrial use, and to establish, operate and control sewerage systems; Man. Dir T. B. F. ACQUAH.

MAJOR COMPANIES

The following are among the largest companies in terms of either capital investment or of employment.

Ashanti Goldfields Co Ltd: Gold House, Patrice Lumumba Rd, Roman Ridge, POB 2665, Accra; tel. (21) 722190; fax (21) 775947; e-mail ernestab@aqcnet.com; internet www.ashanti.com.gh; f. 1897, reorg. 1994; gold mining; leases mining and timber concessions from the Govt, which holds a 19% interest; 34% is held by Lonrho PLC and 47% by private investors; Chair. MICHAEL BECKETT (acting); CEO SRINIVASAN VENKATAKRISHNAN; 9,500 employees.

Cocoa Processing Co Ltd: PMB, Tema; tel. (22) 202926; fax (22) 206657; e-mail cocoapro@africaonline.com.gh; f. 1981; controlled by COCOBOD; mfrs of cocoa products; Man. Dir PAUL AWUA.

Elf Oil Ghana Ltd: 95 Kojo Thompson Rd, POB 553, Accra; tel. (21) 221445; fax (21) 221453; f. 1965 as BP Ghana Ltd; changed name 1992; shares held by Elf Oil Africa Ltd, National Investment

Bank, National Trust Holding Co Ltd, Elf Employees' Credit Union; marketing and distribution of petroleum products, fuelling marine vessels at Tema and Takoradi, and aircraft at Kotoka International Airport, Accra; Man. Dir Marc Bellocq-Dessus; 122 employees.

Ghana Bauxite Co Ltd: POB 1, Awaso; 20% state-owned; fmrly British Aluminium Co Ltd; mining of bauxite at Awaso with loading facilities at Takoradi; Man. Dir T. Cregg.

Ghana Breweries Ltd: POB 114, Achimota, Accra; tel. (21) 402988; fax (21) 400673; f. 1988 by the merger of the Achimota Brewery Co Ltd and the Kumasi Brewery Ltd; Chair. Ishmael E. Yamson; Man. Dir Martin Eson-Benjamin.

Ghana Consolidated Diamond Co Ltd: POB M108, Accra; tel. (21) 664577; fax (21) 664635; f. 1986; grades, values and processes diamonds, buys all locally won, produced or processed diamonds; engages in purchasing, grading, valuing, export and sale of local diamonds; Chair. Kofi Agyeman; Man. Dir Joseph Ansafo-Mensah.

Ghana National Manganese Corporation: POB M183, Ministry PO, Accra; tel. (21) 666607; fax (21) 666562; f. 1975 following nationalization of mine at Nsuta; Chair. Nana Akuamoah Boateng Ababio (acting); Man. Dir Col (retd) E. T. Oklah.

Ghana National Petroleum Corporation: Private Mail Bag, Tema; tel. (22) 206020; fax (22) 205449; e-mail gapc@ncs.com.gh; internet www.gupc.com.gh; f. 1983; exploration, development, production and disposal of petroleum; CEO Tsatsu Tsikata.

State Construction Corporation: Ring Rd West, Industrial Area, Accra; state corpn with a labour force of 7,000; Man. Dir David Boateng.

State Fishing Corporation: POB 211, Tema; tel. (221) 6177; fax (221) 2336177; f. 1961; govt-sponsored deep-sea fishing, distribution and marketing (incl. exporting) org; transfer to private-sector ownership proposed in 1991; owns 5 deep-sea fishing trawlers; CEO Dr Isaac C. N. Morrison.

State Gold Mining Corporation: POB 109, Tarkwa; Accra Office, POB 3634; tel. (21) 775376; f. 1961; manages 4 gold mines; CEO F. Awua-Kyerematen.

Tema Oil Refinery (TOR) Ltd: POB 599, Tema; tel. (21) 302881; fax (22) 302884; f. 1963; sole oil refinery in Ghana; state-controlled since 1977; Man. Dirs W. S. Parker, A. S. K. Aidoo, L. Prempeh; 360 employees.

Total Ghana Ltd: 3 Yiyiwa St, Abelenkpe, Accra; tel. (21) 772309; fax (21) 764951; e-mail totalgha@ghana.com; f. 1960; subsidiary of Total Paris; distribution of petroleum products, incl. liquefied petroleum gas; Man. Dir Jean-Jacques Cestari.

Unilever Ghana Ltd: POB 64, Kwame Nkrumah Ave, Accra; tel. (21) 664985; fax (21) 664808; f. 1955 as United Africa Co of Ghana Ltd; comprises 6 divisions and assoc. cos; subsidiary of Unilever plc, United Kingdom; agricultural, industrial, specialized merchandising, distributive and service enterprises; Chair. Ishmael Yamson; 1,200 employees.

Volta Aluminium Co Ltd (VALCO): POB 625, Tema; tel. (21) 231004; fax (21) 231423; owned by Kaiser Aluminium and Chemical Corpn (90%) and the Reynolds Metal Co (10%); operates an aluminium smelter at Tema (annual capacity 200,000 metric tons); Chair. Jim Chapman; Man. Dir Ron Helton.

West African Mills Co Ltd: Effia Junction Industrial Estate, POB 257 and 218, Takoradi; tel. (31) 22511; fax (31) 23394; f. 1992; formerly Cocoa Processing Co; produces high-grade cocoa products for export; Man. Dir Jelle Kuiper; 350 employees.

CO-OPERATIVES

In 1998 there were 11,154 registered co-operative societies, grouped into four sectors: industrial, financial, agricultural and service.

Department of Co-operatives: POB M150, Accra; tel. (21) 666212; fax (21) 772789; f. 1944; govt-supervised body, responsible for registration, auditing and supervision of co-operative socs; Registrar R. Buachie-Aphram.

Ghana Co-operatives Council Ltd: POB 4034, Accra; tel. (21) 232195; f. 1951; co-ordinates activities of all co-operative socs; comprises five active nat. asscns and two central organizations; Sec.-Gen. Thomas Andoh.

The five national associations and two central organizations include the Ghana Co-operative Marketing Asscn Ltd, the Ghana Co-operative Credit Unions Asscn Ltd, the Ghana Co-operative Distillers and Retailers Asscn Ltd, and the Ghana Co-operative Poultry Farmers Asscn Ltd.

TRADE UNIONS

Ghana Trades Union Congress (GTUC): Hall of Trade Unions, POB 701, Accra; tel. (21) 662568; fax (21) 667161; f. 1945; 17 affiliated unions; all activities of the GTUC were suspended in 1982; Chair. Interim Man. Cttee E. K. Aboagye; Sec.-Gen. Christian Appiah-Agyei.

Transport

RAILWAYS

Ghana has a railway network of 1,300 km, which connects Accra, Kumasi and Takoradi.

Ghana Railway Corporation: POB 251, Takoradi; tel. (31) 22181; fax (31) 23797; f. 1977; responsible for the operation and maintenance of all railways; Man. Dir M. K. Arthur.

ROADS

In 1996 Ghana had an estimated total road network of 37,800 km, including 30 km of motorways, 5,230 km of main roads, and 9,620 km of secondary roads; some 24.1% of the road network was paved. A five-year Road Sector Expenditure Programme, costing US $259m., commenced in 1995.

Ghana Highway Authority: POB 1641, Accra; tel. (21) 666591; fax (21) 665571; f. 1974 to plan, develop, administer and maintain trunk roads and related facilities; CEO B. L. T. Sakibu.

State Transport Corporation: Ring Rd West, POB 7384, Accra; tel. (21) 221912; f. 1965; Man. Dir Lt-Col Akyea-Mensah.

SHIPPING

The two main ports are Tema (near Accra) and Takoradi, both of which are linked with Kumasi by rail. A project to upgrade facilities at both ports, at a cost of US $365m., was to commence in 1998. In 1996 some 6.7m. metric tons of goods were handled at the two ports.

Ghana Ports and Harbour Authority: POB 150, Tema; tel. (22) 202631; fax (22) 202812; e-mail ghpa@ghana.com; holding co for the ports of Tema and Takoradi; Dir Gen. K. T. Dovlo.

Alpha (West Africa) Line Ltd: POB 451, Tema; operates regular cargo services to west Africa, the UK, the USA, the Far East and northern Europe; shipping agents; Man. Dir Ahmed Edgar Collingwood Williams.

Black Star Line Ltd: 4th Lane, Kuku Hill Osu, POB 248, Accra; tel. (21) 2888; fax (21) 2889; f. 1957; state-owned; transfer to private sector pending in 1997; operates passenger and cargo services to Europe, the UK, Canada, the USA, the Mediterranean and West Africa; shipping agents; Chair. Magnus Addico; Man. Dir Capt. V. N. Attuquayefio.

Bunktrad Shipping and Trading Ltd: 4th Floor, Trust Towers, POB 14801, Accra; tel. (21) 238401; fax (21) 236121; e-mail bunktrad @africaonline.com.gh; charters tankers.

Holland West-Afrika Lijn NV: POB 269, Accra; POB 216, Tema; and POB 18, Takoradi; cargo services to and from North America and the Far East; shipping agents.

Liner Agencies and Trading (Ghana) Ltd: POB 214, Tema; tel. (22) 202187; fax (22) 202189; international freight services; shipping agents; Dir J. Ossei-Yaw.

Remco Shipping Lines Ltd: POB 3898, Accra; tel. (21) 224609.

Scanship (Ghana) Ltd: CFAO Bldg, High St, POB 1705, Accra; tel. (21) 664314; shipping agents.

Association

Ghana Shippers' Council: Enterprise House, 5th Floor, opp. Barclay's Bank, High St, POB 1321, Accra; tel. (21) 666915; fax (21) 668768; e-mail shippers@ncs.com.gh; f. 1974; represents interests of c. 3,000 registered Ghanaian shippers; also provides cargo-handling and allied services; CEO M. T. Addico.

CIVIL AVIATION

The main international airport is at Kotoka (Accra). There are also airports at Takoradi, Kumasi, Sunyani, Tamale and Wa. The construction of a dedicated freight terminal at Kotoka Airport was completed in 1994.

Ghana Civil Aviation Authority: Kotoka International Airport, Accra; tel. (21) 776171; fax (21) 773293; e-mail centre-gcaa@ighmail.com; internet www.gcaa.com.gh.

Gemini Airlines Ltd: America House, POB 7328, Accra-North; tel. (21) 665785; f. 1974; operates weekly cargo flight between Accra and London; Dir V. Owusu; Gen. Man. P. F. Okine.

Ghana Airways Ltd.: Plot 9, Ghana Airways Avenue, Ghana Airways House, POB 1636, Accra; tel. (21) 773321; fax (21) 773316; e-mail ghanaairways@ighmail.com; internet www.ghanaairways.com;

f. 1958; state-owned; transfer to private sector pending in 1999; operates regional services and international routes to West African, Asian and European destinations, and to the USA and South Africa; Chair. of Bd VICTORIA ADDY; CEO EMMANUEL L. QUARTEY.

Tourism

Ghana's attractions include fine beaches, game reserves, traditional festivals, and old trading forts and castles. In 1996 a 15-year Integrated National Tourism Development Plan was initiated, under which annual tourist arrivals were targeted to exceed 1m. by 2020. In 1997 325,434 tourists visited Ghana, with revenue from tourism totalling US \$266m.

Ghana Tourist Board: POB 3106, Accra; tel. (21) 685441; fax (21) 662375; e-mail gtb@africaonline.com.gh; f. 1968; Exec. Dir DOREEN OWUSU-FIANKO (acting).

Ghana Association of Tourist and Travel Agencies: Ramia House, Kojo Thompson Rd, POB 7140, Accra; tel. (21) 228933; Pres. JOSEPH K. ANKUMAH; Sec. JOHNNIE MOREAUX.

Ghana Tourist Development Co Ltd: POB 8710, Accra; tel. (21) 776109; fax (21) 772093; f. 1974; develops tourist infrastructure, incl. hotels, restaurants and casinos; operates duty-free shops; Man. Dir ALFRED KOMLADZEI.

Defence

In August 1999 Ghana's total armed forces numbered 7,000 (army 5,000, navy 1,000 and air force 1,000). The headquarters of the Defence Commission of the OAU is in Accra. In March 2000 the government restructured the armed forces; the army was subse-quently organized into north and south commands, and the navy into western and eastern commands.

Defence Expenditure: Estimated at C310,000m. in 1998.

Commander-in-Chief of the Armed Forces: Flt-Lt (retd) JERRY RAWLINGS.

Chief of Defence Staff: Lt-Gen. B. K. AKAFIA.

Commander of the Navy: Rear-Adm. OSEI OWUSO-ANSAH.

Commander of the Air Force: Air Vice-Marshal J. A. BRUCE.

Commander of the Army: Maj.-Gen. J. H. SMITH.

Education

Education is officially compulsory for eight years, between the ages of six and 14 years. Primary education begins at the age of six and lasts for six years. Secondary education begins at the age of 12 and lasts for a further seven years, comprising a first cycle of four years and a second cycle of three years. Following four years of junior secondary education, pupils are examined to determine admission to senior secondary school courses, or to technical and vocational courses. In 1994 primary enrolment was equivalent to 79% of children in the relevant age-group (boys 84%; girls 74%), while the comparable ratio for secondary enrolment in 1991 was 36% (boys 44%; girls 28%). It was estimated that 52,000 students were enrolled in higher education in 1992, with about 10,700 students attending the country's five universities. Tertiary institutions also included 38 teacher-training colleges, seven diploma-awarding colleges, 21 technical colleges and six polytechnics. Expenditure on education by the central government in 1995 was C255,792m. (15.1% of total spending); expenditure on education rose to 19.9% of total government spending in 1996. According to UNESCO estimates, the average rate of adult illiteracy in 1995 was 36.1% (males 25.3%; females 46.6%).

Bibliography

Adjei, M. *Death and Pain: Rawlings Ghana, The Inside Story.* London, Black Line Publishing Ltd, 1994.

Afrifa, A. A. *Ghana Coup d'Etat.* London, Frank Cass, 1967.

Agbodeka, F. *An Economc History of Ghana from the Earliest Times.* Accra, Ghana Universities Press, 1993.

Allman, J. M. *The Quills of the Porcupine: Asante Nationalism in an Emergent Ghana.* Madison, University of Wisconsin Press, 1993.

Anin, T. E. *Essays on the Political Economy of Ghana.* London, Selwyn, 1991.

Armah, K. *Nkrumah's Legacy.* London, Rex Collings, 1974.

Aryeetey, E. *The Formal Financial Sector in Ghana after the Reforms.* London, Overseas Development Institute, 1996.

Austin, D. *Politics in Ghana 1946–60.* Oxford University Press, 1964.

Awoonor, K. N. *Ghana: A Political History from Pre-European to Modern Times.* Accra, Ghana, Woeli Publishing Services, 1990.

Babatope, E. *The Ghana Revolution from Nkrumah to Jerry Rawlings.* Enugu, Fourth Dimension Publishers, 1984.

Baynham, S. *The Military and Politics in Nkrumah's Ghana.* Boulder, CO, Westview Press, 1988.

Boateng, E. A. *A Geography of Ghana.* 2nd Edn. Cambridge University Press, 1970.

Brown, C. K. (Ed.). *Rural Development in Ghana.* Accra, Ghana University Press, 1986.

Brydon, L., and Legge, K. *Adjusting Society: The World Bank, the International Monetary Fund and Ghana.* London, Tauris, 1996.

Busia, K. A. *Africa in Search of Democracy.* London, Routledge and Kegan Paul, 1967.

Chazan, N. *An Anatomy of Ghanaian Politics: Managing Political Recession 1969–1982.* Boulder, CO, Westview Press, 1983.

Cruise O'Brien, D. B., Dunn, J., and Rathbone, R. (Eds). *West African States.* Cambridge, Cambridge University Press, 1989.

Davidson, B. *Black Star. A View of the Life and Times of Kwame Nkrumah.* London, Panaf Books, 1974.

Dickson, K. B. *A Historical Geography of Ghana.* Cambridge University Press, 1969.

Donkor, K. *Structural Adjustment and Mass Poverty in Ghana.* Aldershot, Ashgate, 1997.

Dumor, E. K. *Ghana, OAU and Southern Africa: An African Response to Apartheid (1957–1972).* Oxford, ABC; Ghana University Press, 1991.

Edgerton, R. B. *The Fall of the Ashante Empire.* New York and London, Free Press, 1995.

Foster, P., and Zolberg, A. R. (Eds). *Ghana and the Ivory Coast: Perspectives and Modernization.* University of Chicago Press, 1972.

Frimpong, J. H. *The Vampire State in Africa: The Political Economy of Decline in Ghana.* London, James Currey, 1991.

Goodall, H. B. *Beloved Imperialist.* Durham, Pentland Press, 1998.

Graham, R. *The Aluminium Industry and the Third World: Multinational Corporations and Underdevelopment.* London, Zed Press, 1982.

Greenhalgh, P. *West African Diamonds: An Economic History 1919–83.* Manchester University Press, 1985.

Gyimah-Boardi, E. (Ed.). *Ghana under PNDC Rule.* Dakar, CODESRIA, 1993.

Hansen, E. *Ghana under Rawlings: Early Years.* Oxford, ABC; Malthouse Press, 1991.

Hansen, E., and Ninwin, K. A. (Eds). *State Development and Politics in Ghana.* Dakar, CODESRIA, 1990.

Hayward, M. F. *Elections in Independent Africa.* Boulder, CO, Westview Press, 1987.

Herbst, J. *The Politics of Reform in Ghana, 1982–1991.* Berkeley, University of California Press, 1993.

Huq, M. M. *The Economy of Ghana: The First 25 Years since Independence.* London, Macmillan, 1988.

Jeffries, R. *Class, Power and Ideology in Ghana.* Cambridge University Press, 1978.

Jones, T. *Ghana's First Republic.* London, Methuen, 1976.

Kay, G. (Ed.). *The Political Economy of Colonialism in Ghana: A Collection of Documents and Statistics 1900–60.* Cambridge University Press, 1972.

Killick, A. *Development Economics in Action: A Study of Economic Policies in Ghana.* London, Heinemann, 1978.

Kimble, D. *Political History of Ghana.* London, Oxford University Press, 1963.

Milne, J. *Kwame Nkrumah — A Biography.* London, PANAF Books, 2000.

Ninwin, K. A., et al. *Ghana's Political Transition, 1990–1993.* Accra, Freedom Publishers, 1996.

Ninwin, K. A., and Drah, F. K. (Eds). *The Search for Democracy in Ghana: A Case Study in Political Instability in Africa.* Accra, Asempa Publishers, 1987.

Ghana's Transition to Constitutional Rule. Accra, Ghana University Press; Oxford, ABC, 1991.

Political Parties and Democracy in Ghana's Fourth Republic. Accra, Woeli Publishing Services, 1993.

Obeng-Fosu, P. *Industrial Relations in Ghana: The Law and Practice.* Oxford, ABC; Ghana University Press, 1991.

Ofori, S. *Regional Policy and Regional Planning in Ghana.* Brookfield, VT, Ashgate Publishing, 1997.

Okeke, B. E. *4 June: A Revolution Betrayed.* Enugu, Ikenga Publishers, 1982.

Oquaye, M. *Politics in Ghana 1972–1979.* Accra, Tornado Publications, 1980.

Owusu-Ansah, D., and McFarland, M. D. *Historical Dictionary of Ghana.* 2nd Edn. Lanham, MD, Scarecrow Press, 1995.

Pinkney, R. *Ghana under Military Rule 1966–1969.* London, Methuen, 1972.

Quay, R. *Underdevelopment and Health Care in Africa: The Ghanaian Experience.* Lewiston, Edwin Mellen Press, 1996.

Rimmer, D. *The Economies of West Africa.* London, Weidenfeld and Nicolson, 1984.

Staying Poor: Ghana's Political Economy, 1950–1990. Oxford, Pergamon, 1992.

Roe, Alan, Schneider, H., and Pyatt, G. *Adjustment and Equity in Ghana.* Paris, OECD, 1992.

Sarpong, P. *Ghana in Retrospect.* Oxford, ABC; Ghana Publishing Corporation, 1991.

Sarris, A., and Shams, H. *Ghana under Structural Adjustment: The Impact on Agriculture and the Rural Poor.* New York University Press, 1991. (IFAD Studies in Rural Poverty).

Shillington, K. *Ghana and the Rawlings Factor.* London, Macmillan, 1992.

Ward, W. E. F. *A History of Ghana.* London, Allen and Unwin, 1958.

Yeebo, Z. *Ghana: The Struggle for Popular Power—Rawlings: Saviour or Demagogue?* Accra, New Beacon Books, 1992.

GUINEA

Physical and Social Geography

R. J. HARRISON CHURCH

The Republic of Guinea covers an area of 245,857 sq km (94,926 sq miles), containing exceptionally varied landscapes, peoples and economic conditions. The census of 31 December 1996 recorded a population of 7,164,823 (giving an average density of 29.1 inhabitants per sq km). The population is concentrated in the plateau area of central Guinea: about one-quarter of the population is estimated to be living in Conakry and its environs.

Guinea's coast is part of the extremely wet south-western sector of west Africa, which has a monsoonal climate. Thus Conakry, the capital, has five to six months with almost no rain, while 4,300 mm fall in the remaining months. The coastline has shallow drowned rivers and estuaries with much mangrove growing on alluvium eroded from the nearby Fouta Djallon mountains. Much of the mangrove has been removed, and the land bunded for rice cultivation. Only at two places, Cape Verga and Conakry, do ancient hard rocks reach the sea. At the latter they have facilitated the development of the port, while the weathering of these rocks has produced exploitable deposits of bauxite on the offshore Los Islands.

Behind the swamps a gravelly coastal plain, some 65 km wide, is backed by the steep, often sheer, edges of the Fouta Djallon, which occupies the west-centre of Guinea. Much is over 900 m high, and consists of level Primary sandstones (possibly of Devonian age) which cover Pre-Cambrian rocks to a depth of 750 m. The level plateaux, with many bare lateritic surfaces, are the realm of Fulani herders. Rivers are deeply incised in the sandstone. These more fertile valleys were earlier cultivated with food crops by slaves of the Fulani, and then with bananas, coffee, citrus fruits and pineapples on plantations under the French. Falls and gorges of the incised rivers have great hydro-electric potential. This is significant in view of huge deposits of high-grade bauxite located at Fria and Boké. The climate is still monsoonal but, although the total rainfall is lower—about 1,800 mm annually—it is more evenly distributed than on the coasts as the rainy season is longer. In such a mountainous area there are sharp variations in climatic conditions over a short distance, and from year to year.

On the Liberian border the Guinea highlands rise to 1,752 m at Mt Nimba, where substantial deposits of haematite iron ore are eventually to be developed. These rounded mountains contrast greatly with the level plateaux and deep narrow valleys of the Fouta Djallon. Rainfall is heavier than in the latter, but is again more evenly distributed, so that only two or three months are without significant rain. Coffee, kola and other crops are grown in the forest of this remote area. Diamonds are mined north of Macenta and west of Beyla, and gold at Siguiri and Léro.

Recent History

PIERRE ENGLEBERT

Revised for this edition by the Editor

THE SEKOU TOURÉ PERIOD

On 2 October 1958, having rejected membership of a proposed community of self-governing French overseas territories, French Guinea became the independent Republic of Guinea. Ahmed Sekou Touré, the secretary-general of the Parti démocratique de Guinée–Rassemblement démocratique africain (PDG–RDA), which had led the campaign for independence, became the republic's first president, and the PDG–RDA the sole political party. Punitive economic reprisals were taken by the departing French authorities, and French aid and investment were suspended. Sekou Touré's government initially obtained assistance from the USSR and withdrew from the Franc Zone in 1960, but after 1961 the USA became a more significant source of aid.

Radical socialist policies were applied to Guinea's internal economy. In 1975 all private trading was forbidden, and financial transactions were supervised by the government's 'economic police', who were themselves widely suspected of extortion and smuggling. Resentment against their activities culminated in August 1977 in widespread demonstrations and rioting, as a so-called 'women's revolt' in Conakry quickly extended to other towns. In response, Sekou Touré disbanded the 'economic police' and permitted the resumption (from July 1979) of small-scale private trading. In 1978 it was decided to merge the PDG–RDA and the state, and in January 1979 the country was renamed the People's Revolutionary Republic of Guinea.

Diplomatic relations with France (which had effectively ceased in 1965) were resumed in 1976, and in the following year the two countries reached an agreement on economic co-operation, including an undertaking by the French government to curb the activities of Guinean dissidents in Paris. In 1978 Sekou Touré declared a policy of 'co-operation with capitalist as well as socialist states'. The government sought also to improve relations with Côte d'Ivoire and Senegal, and increased its participation in regional organizations.

CONTÉ AND THE CMRN

Sekou Touré died suddenly in March 1984. Before a successor could be chosen, the army staged a *coup d'état* in April, and a Comité militaire de redressement national (CMRN) seized power. Its principal leaders, Col (later Gen.) Lansana Conté and Col Diarra Traoré, who became president and prime minister respectively, had both held senior positions for some years. A semi-civilian government was appointed, and efforts were furthered to improve regional relations and links with potential sources of economic aid (most notably France). In May the country resumed the designation of Republic of Guinea. The PDG–RDA and organs of Sekou Touré's 'party state' were dismantled under this second republic, which was initially greeted with great enthusiasm. State surveillance and control were ended, and many political detainees were freed. In the first months of his presidency Conté adopted an open style of government, inviting constructive advice and criticism from all sectors of society.

Undercurrents of Opposition

In December 1984 Conté abolished the office of prime minister, demoting Traoré to a lesser cabinet post. In July 1985, while Conté was attending a regional summit meeting in Togo, Traoré attempted a *coup d'état,* supported mainly by members of the police force. Troops loyal to Conté swiftly regained control, and the president returned, to public acclaim, two days later. Traoré and many of his family were arrested, and the armed forces conducted a purge of his suspected sympathizers; in all, more than 200 arrests were made. Among those executed in the immediate aftermath of the coup attempt were Traoré and a half-brother of Sekou Touré. About 60 other military officers were later sentenced to death following secret trials. (Sekou Touré's widow and son were released following an amnesty for 67 political prisoners in January 1988.)

The coup attempt effectively strengthened Conté's position, allowing him to pursue the extensive economic reforms demanded by the World Bank and the IMF as a prerequisite for the disbursement of new funds. The syli was devalued and replaced in January 1986 by a revived Guinean franc. Civil service reform entailed numerous redundancies; many state-owned enterprises were dissolved or offered for sale, and the banking system was overhauled. In December 1985 Conté reorganized the council of ministers, introducing a majority of civilians for the first time since he took power and creating resident 'regional' ministries. Opposition to the reform programme was revealed in late 1987 by unrest within the armed forces and the civil service, while high levels of inflation provoked public demonstrations in Conakry in January 1988. Two high-ranking government members were subsequently transferred to regional ministries.

Meanwhile, a process of limited democratization was proceeding. In October 1988, commemorating the 30th anniversary of the country's independence, Conté declared an amnesty for 39 political prisoners, including some of those implicated in the 1985 coup attempt. At the same time he announced the establishment of a committee to draft a new constitution, which would be submitted for approval in a national referendum. In October 1989 Conté revealed plans whereby a Comité transitoire de redressement national (CTRN) would succeed the CMRN and oversee a five-year transitional period prior to the establishment of a two-party political system under an elected president and legislature. In February 1990 an amnesty was announced for all remaining political detainees and exiled dissidents.

As elsewhere in the region, discontent with economic austerity tended most frequently to manifest itself in the education sector. A teachers' strike in early 1990, in protest at inadequate pay and conditions, led to the replacement of the minister of education. Tensions resurfaced in November, when four students were killed during clashes with security forces.

Conté appealed in November 1990 for the return to Guinea of political exiles. However, three members of an illegal opposition movement, the Rassemblement populaire guinéen (RPG), were imprisoned later in the month. Rejecting widespread demands for an accelerated programme of political reform, the government proceeded with its plan for a gradual transition to a two-party political system. The draft constitution (*loi fondamentale*) was submitted to a national referendum in December, and was declared to have been approved by 98.7% of those who voted (some 97.4% of the registered electorate). The period of transition to civilian rule thus began, and in February 1991 the 36-member CTRN was inaugurated, under the chairmanship of Conté. Military officers continued to hold the most sensitive posts in a new government, implying that the president intended to ensure the continued loyalty of the armed forces.

In May 1991, as academic staff again took strike action, the government announced a doubling of civil servants' salaries, together with increases in some social allowances and a halving of the salaries of members of the council of ministers and of the CTRN. However, the trade unions deemed these concessions to be insufficient, and a widely-observed general strike effectively paralysed the capital. In the same month the leader of the RPG, Alpha Condé, returned to Guinea after a long period of exile in France and Senegal. Security forces dispersed a meeting of his supporters, and the government subsequently imposed a ban on unauthorized meetings and demonstrations. In June one person was killed when security forces opened fire on a gathering of demonstrators outside the police headquarters in Conakry, to where Condé had been summoned in connection with the seizure of allegedly subversive materials. Some 60 arrests were reported, while Condé sought refuge in the Senegalese embassy, where he remained for several weeks before being granted political asylum in Senegal.

Contrary to the earlier scheme for political change, in October 1991 Conté announced that the registration of an unlimited number of political parties would come into effect on 3 April 1992 (the eighth anniversary of the coup that had brought him to power), and that legislative elections would take place before the end of 1992 in the context of a full multi-party political system. In late 1991 the Conté administration denied allegations made by Amnesty International of the persecution, imprisonment and torture of political opponents.

CONTÉ AND THE THIRD REPUBLIC

The constitution of the third republic was promulgated on 23 December 1991. In January 1992 Conté ceded the presidency of the CTRN (whose membership was reduced to 15), in accordance with constitutional provision for the separation of the powers of the executive and legislature. In the following month most military officers and all *Guinéens de l'extérieur* (former dissidents who had returned from exile after the 1984 coup) were removed from the government: it later became apparent that some of these long-serving ministers had left public office in order to establish a pro-Conté political party, the Parti de l'unité et le progrès (PUP).

The RPG was among the first parties to be legalized in April 1992, and Alpha Condé returned to Guinea in June. Other than the RPG, the most prominent challengers to the PUP were the Parti pour le renouveau et le progrès (PRP), led by a well-known journalist, Siradiou Diallo, and the Union pour la nouvelle République (UNR), led by Mamadou Bâ. However, the generally fragmented nature of the opposition undermined attempts to persuade the government to convene a national political conference. The opposition alleged that the PUP was benefiting from state funds, and that the government was coercing civil servants into joining the party; there was also evidence that the government was favouring development projects in areas of potential PUP support. Clashes between pro- and anti-Conté activists (seemingly fuelled by ethnic rivalries) occurred frequently from mid-1992, and in October the government again banned all unauthorized public gatherings. In that month Conté was reported to have escaped an assassination attempt when gunmen opened fire on the vehicle in which he was travelling.

In December 1992 the government announced the indefinite postponement of the legislative elections, which had been scheduled for the end of the month, citing technical and financial difficulties. It was later indicated that the elections would be organized in late 1993, and that (contrary to the preference of most opposition parties) they would be preceded by the presidential election. The principal opposition parties failed in their attempts to form an electoral alliance, with the aim of preventing a divided opposition vote from benefiting Conté and the PUP. Thus, there were eight candidates for the presidential election, which was scheduled for 5 December 1993. Conté's main challengers were Condé, Diallo and Bâ. In September the government banned all political gatherings and marches, following violent incidents in Conakry when police opened fire on demonstrators, as a result of which, according to official figures, some 18 people were killed (unofficial reports claimed as many as 63 deaths). In October, at an unprecedented meeting between Conté and representatives of 43 political organizations, it was agreed to establish an independent electoral commission. However, controversy immediately arose regarding its composition and also the government's decision to place it under the jurisdiction of the powerful ministry of the interior and security. Opposition candidates demanded that the presidential election be postponed, citing technical and procedural irregularities and delays. Objections were also voiced that the PUP was able to hold electoral rallies, while the opposition remained subject to the ban imposed in September. In late November the government announced a two-week postponement of the presidential poll, admitting that technical preparations for voting were incomplete.

At least four deaths resulted from outbreaks of violence in Conakry and in the interior prior to the presidential election. A further six people were reported to have been killed as voting proceeded on 19 December 1993. Despite confused reports of opposition appeals for a boycott of the poll (and the absence of voters' lists in some polling centres), the rate of participation was, officially, 78.5% of the registered electorate. The official results were confirmed by the supreme court in early January 1994: Conté was elected at the first round of voting, having secured an absolute majority (51.70%) of the votes cast. Condé, his nearest rival, took 19.55% of the votes; however, the supreme court's invalidation (having found evidence of malpractice) of the results of voting in the Kankan and Siguiri prefectures, in both of which Condé had won more than 90% of the votes, fuelled opposition claims that the poll had been manipulated in favour of Conté.

Conté (who had, as required by the constitution, resigned from the armed forces in order to contest the presidency) was inaugurated as president on 29 January 1994. His stated priorities were to strengthen national security and unity and to promote economic growth.

In May 1994 Bâ, asserting his lack of confidence in the Guinean opposition movement, expressed the UNR's willingness to recognize Conté as the country's legitimately elected head of state. Relations between the government and opposition otherwise remained generally poor, and the RPG in particular protested that its activists were being harassed by members of the armed forces. The brief detention, in June, of eight senior armed forces officers, including the deputy chief of staff of the air force, prompted rumours of a coup plot; the government confirmed that certain members of the armed forces had participated in a 'political' meeting, in contravention of their terms of service, but denied the existence of any conspiracy. In September the authorities refuted RPG assertions that attempts had been made to assassinate Condé. The ban on political gatherings was ended in November, but the government emphasized that rallies should not be confused with street demonstrations. The announcement, shortly afterwards, that there would be no facilities abroad to allow expatriate Guineans to vote in the forthcoming legislative elections (following violent disturbances at polling stations outside Guinea at the 1993 presidential election) provoked criticism by opposition parties and by members of the electoral commission, who stated that the disenfranchisement of Guineans abroad was in contravention of both the constitution and the electoral code. The UNR condemned the decision, and withdrew its support for Conté. In February 1995 it was announced that the president was to readopt his military rank.

In December 1994 the government announced new measures aimed at combating organized crime and other serious offences. As well as the creation of a special police unit to counter banditry, the enforcement of the death penalty was envisaged, together with stricter policies governing immigration and asylum for refugees: the Conté administration has frequently attributed the increase in insecurity to the presence of large numbers of refugees (see Foreign and Regional Affairs, below) in Guinea. In January 1996 international human rights organizations expressed concern at the rejection by the supreme court of appeals against six death sentences.

In March 1995 it was announced that elections to the new national assembly would take place on 11 June. Parties of the so-called 'radical' opposition (principally the RPG, the PRP and the UNR) frequently alleged harassment of their activists by the security forces, claiming that efforts were being made to prevent campaigning in areas where support for the opposition was likely to be strong. They also denounced the PUP's use of portraits of Conté on campaign posters and literature, since the head of state was constitutionally required to distance himself from party politics. A total of 846 candidates, from 21 parties, contested the national assembly's 114 seats. As preliminary results indicated that the PUP had won an overwhelming majority in the legislature, the radical opposition protested that voting had been conducted fraudulently, stating that they would take no further part in the electoral process and that they would boycott the national assembly. According to the official results, the PUP won 71 seats—having taken 30 of the country's 38 single-member constituencies, together with 41 of the 76 seats allocated by proportional representation. Eight other parties won representation, principal among them the RPG, which took 19 seats, the PRP and the UNR, both of which won nine seats. Some 63% of the electorate were reported to have voted. The results were confirmed by the supreme court in July, whereupon the new legislature formally superseded the CTRN. At local elections in late June the PUP won control of 20 of the country's

36 municipalities, while the RPG, the PRP and the UNR, which had presented a co-ordinated campaign, took 10.

In July 1995 the three radical opposition parties joined forces with nine other organizations in a new opposition front, the Coordination de l'opposition démocratique (Codem), which indicated its willingness to enter into a dialogue with the authorities. At a subsequent meeting with a representative of Codem, the minister of the interior, Alsény René Gomez, rejected purported evidence of electoral fraud as not affecting the overall credibility of the results. The inaugural session of the national assembly, on 30 August, was attended by representatives of all the elected parties. Boubacar Biro Diallo, of the PUP, was elected as the new parliament's speaker; the PUP and its allies also took control of all other prominent posts in the legislature, despite previous indications that some would be allocated to the opposition.

Military Unrest

In early February 1996 Conté was reportedly seized as he attempted to flee the presidential palace during a mutiny by disaffected elements of the military. He was released after making concessions including a doubling of salaries and immunity from prosecution for those involved in the uprising. (He had already agreed to the demand that the minister of defence, Col Abdourahmane Diallo, be dismissed, assuming responsibility for defence himself.) About 50 people (some of them civilians) were killed and 100 injured as rebels clashed with forces loyal to the Conté regime. In all, as many as 2,000 soldiers, including members of the presidential guard, were believed to have joined the rebellion. Despite Conté's undertaking that there would be no punitive action, several officers—apparently among them some of those detained in June 1994—were arrested shortly afterwards, and both Conté and Gomez stated that any legal proceedings would be a matter for the judiciary. That there had been a coup attempt was only admitted by Conté almost three weeks after the mutiny. Members of Codem subsequently withdrew from a parliamentary commission that had been established to investigate the circumstances surrounding the rebellion, apparently in protest at Conté's allusions to opposition links with anti-government elements within the military.

Among the initial recommendations of the parliamentary commission was a complete depoliticization of the military, accompanied by the demilitarization of political life; the need to restore discipline within the armed forces was emphasized. In late March 1996 it was announced that eight members of the military (four of them senior officers) had been charged with undermining state security in connection with the coup attempt. A reinforcement of security measures followed the assassination of the commander (a close associate of Conté) of the Alpha Yaya military barracks, where the February rebellion had begun, apparently in reprisal against the charges. Calm was quickly restored, and Conté left his barracks for the first time since early February to meet President Alpha Oumar Konaré of Mali, who arrived in Conakry to discuss terms for the release into Guinean custody of one of the alleged perpetrators of the coup attempt, who had taken refuge in the Malian embassy. In early April it was reported in Guinea that the Malian authorities had handed over the officer, having received assurances that his rights would be respected; however, Mali subsequently recalled its ambassador from Conakry, protesting that Guinean forces had stormed the embassy to make the arrest. By June some 42 members of the armed forces had reportedly been charged in connection with the coup plot. An international warrant was also issued for the arrest of Commdr Joseph Gbago Zoumanigui, suspected of being a main conspirator, who was rumoured to have fled the country. Meanwhile, 10 people, some of them civilians, were said to have been detained in connection with the assassination of the army commander in the previous month.

The replacement, in April 1996, of two close associates of Conté, the armed forces chief of staff and the governor of Conakry (also a military officer), was regarded as an indication of the president's commitment to a restructuring of both the civilian and military administration. An armed forces conference was convened in June to consider the reorganization of the military, at which there was consensus regarding several of the parliamentary commission's recommendations for reform. In

July Conté announced (for the first time under the third republic) the appointment of a prime minister. The premiership was assigned to a non-partisan economist, Sydia Touré. A comprehensive reorganization of the government included the departure of Gomez and the division of the ministry of the interior into two separate departments (one responsible for territorial administration and decentralization, the other for security), and the appointment of a new minister of justice; Conté retained the defence portfolio. Touré stated that his government's priorities were to be economic recovery and the combating of institutionalized corruption, with the aim of securing renewed assistance from the international donor community, and of attracting increased foreign investment; the new prime minister, who assumed personal responsibility for the economy, finance and planning, announced immediate measures to reduce public expenditure by one-third—although the salary increases for the military conceded by Conté in February were to be honoured. The installation of Touré's technocrat-led government was generally well received, although controversy arose in some quarters, most notably within the PUP, after it emerged that Touré (who held dual Guinean-Ivorian citizenship, and had formerly been an aide to Alassane Ouattara—Côte d'Ivoire's prime minister in 1990–93) had been appointed premier in accordance with an Ivorian-brokered arrangement. Touré responded to criticism that there was no constitutional provision for the post of prime minister by stating that his appointment was in accordance with the article of the constitution empowering the president of the republic to appoint ministers and to delegate part of his functions.

The removal from office of Gomez was welcomed by opposition groups. However, one of his last actions as minister of the interior, authorizing the establishment of a foundation dedicated to the philosophy of Sekou Touré, was particularly criticized by the Union des forces démocratiques de Guinée, which was active in representing the interests of victims of the Sekou Touré regime. The party had also condemned the rehabilitation of Sekou Touré and recent legislation granting full privileges to members of the former president's family as trivializing the crimes of the 'party state'.

In November 1996 the RPG's headquarters in Conakry was ransacked and damaged by fire, apparently following clashes between supporters of Condé and a group of students. Four prominent members of the RPG were subsequently arrested, and in the following month Codem announced its intention to establish a militia, with the aim of resisting further detentions of opposition activists. The minister of territorial administration and decentralization responded that no political party had the right to establish an armed force, and emphasized that the law would be applied vigorously against those seeking to foster what he termed a spiral of violence in Guinea. The four RPG officials were sentenced to two years' imprisonment in June, having been convicted of violence and causing injury to others.

In February 1997 (following the conclusion of a new financing arrangement with the IMF) Touré relinquished control of the economy portfolio to his two ministers-delegate, Ousmane Kaba and Ibrahima Kassory Fofana, who now became, respectively, minister of planning and co-operation and minister of the economy and finance. The issue of the premiership remained controversial, and in May, in response to parliamentary appeals for the establishment of a post of constitutional prime minister, the government stated that for the constitution to vest powers directly in an office of prime minister would result in political instability and confusion.

Meanwhile, in August 1996 40 of those detained in connection with the February mutiny were released from custody; charges remained against three suspects (including Zoumanigui). The announcement, in June 1997, that a state security court was to be established to deal with matters of exceptional jurisdiction, and that its first task would be to try the alleged leaders of the previous year's mutiny, provoked outrage among opposition parties and prompted strong protests by the national lawyers' association. Particular concerns were that there was no constitutional provision for such a court, that its members were to be personally appointed by Conté (the tribunal's president was to be Commdr Sama Pannival Bangoura, the head of the Alpha Yaya barracks), and that the trial of the alleged mutineers would be held in camera. The opposition again warned of the

potential consequences should Conté renege on his pledge that there would be no reprisals for those involved in the rebellion. Rumours circulated with increasing frequency that Guinean dissidents, among them the fugitive Zoumanigui, were conspiring with rebels and mercenary groups in Sierra Leone and Liberia to overthrow Conté. Opposition parties asserted that the Conté regime itself was the source of the rumours.

Political Tensions

It was announced in September 1997 that an independent national electoral commission would not be constituted to supervise the forthcoming presidential election (due in December 1998), and that the minister of territorial administration and decentralization was to be responsible for the revision of the voters' register. The ministers of security and of planning and co-operation left the government in October 1997, as part of a reorganization of portfolios in which a new minister of the interior and decentralization, Zaïnoul Abidine Sanoussi, was appointed. The former minister of territorial administration and decentralization, Dorank Assifat Diassény, was transferred to the higher education and scientific research portfolio, but was subsequently appointed minister of national defence (thereby becoming the first civilian to hold this position since the 1984 *coup d'état*).

In a report presented in October 1997 the Association guinéenne des droits de l'homme accused the Guinean security forces of daily atrocities, alleging the systematic ill-treatment of detainees. The association expressed particular concern at the continued detention of civilians related to the suspects in the 1996 mutiny, and at the detention without trial, in solitary confinement, of Liberian and Sierra Leonean nationals. The detention of three Belgian nationals, arrested with a Guinean associate in early 1997, was similarly condemned. In November 1997 it was revealed that 53 soldiers, detained since the mutiny, had in a joint letter to the national assembly alleged that they had been tortured following their arrest and complained of their conditions of confinement. The authors of the letter appealed, in the absence of an amnesty law, for the legislature to exert pressure on the judiciary to ensure a fair trial. In December Agence France-Presse reported that the same soldiers had alleged that many senior military officers remained in their posts despite their complicity in the mutiny. Among the officers identified by the detainees were the present and former chiefs of staff of the armed forces, as well as Sama Pannival Bangoura and his predecessor at the Alpha Yaya barracks.

A total of 96 defendants were brought before the state security court in mid-February 1998, to answer charges related to the attempted coup two years earlier; hearings were immediately adjourned, after defence lawyers complained that they had had no access to their clients for the past four months. Reportedly among the defendants was the former minister of defence dismissed by Conté on the second day of the mutiny. Hearings resumed in March; however, defence lawyers reportedly refused to represent their clients, on the grounds that their rights were being infringed by the state security court. Proceedings were again adjourned, and the court did not reconvene until mid-September. At the end of the month 38 of the accused received custodial sentences ranging from seven months to 15 years, some with hard labour (Zoumanigui was convicted *in absentia*); 51 defendants were acquitted.

Political tensions increased when, in late March 1998, Bâ and two other UNR deputies were arrested, following violent incidents in which nine people were killed in Kaporo, a suburb of Conakry which was a stronghold of the UNR. The government alleged that Islamist extremists were implicated in the violence; however, other observers described the incidents as confrontations along ethnic lines between residents of the district whose homes were threatened with demolition and contingents of the security forces. Following the arrest, in early April, of two RPG deputies who had attended a political rally in eastern Guinea, Codem organized an opposition boycott of the opening session of the national assembly. Both deputies were released after three days. In early May the legislature approved a motion urging the release of the arrested deputies. Bâ was released in early June, following a trial verdict which was described as 'lenient'. In early September the two other UNR deputies resumed their seats in the legislature, having been released from custody. The two stated that they had been well treated while in detention, but deplored the conditions in which other prisoners were being held. In October opposition activists who had been imprisoned in June in connection with the violent clashes in Kaporo were released under a presidential pardon. In late October the national assembly speaker was suspended from the PUP, after he denounced what he termed 'atrocious and inhuman torture' of detainees, notably those held in connection with the 1996 mutiny; a further statement by Diallo in the following month expressed regret at the ruling party's 'insolent contempt for the law'.

Codem was 'critial of the government's preparations for the forthcoming presidential election, notably proposals for the establishment of a new body, the Haut conseil aux affaires électorales (HCE), to act in conjunction with the ministry of the interior and decentralization in preparing and supervising the poll. The 68-member HCE was to be composed of representatives of the presidential majority, together with opposition delegates, ministerial representatives and members of the civic society. A ban on public demonstrations was imposed by the HCE in early November 1998. The opposition again asserted that the PUP was abusing the state apparatus in support of Conté's re-election campaign. Conté was challenged by four candidates: Mamadou Boye Bâ, representing the Union pour le progrès et le renouveau (formed in September by a merger of the UNR and the PRP), Alpha Condé (who had been resident abroad since early 1997, owing to fears for his personal safety) for the RPG, Jean-Marie Doré for the Union pour le progrès de Guinée, and Charles-Pascal Tolno (a former education minister who had been dismissed from the government in 1993) for the Parti du peuple de Guinée. Voting proceeded, according to schedule, on 14 December 1998, despite several violent incidents during the election campaign, including, in late November, the lynching of a local government official in Farannah. Further violence followed the arrest, two days after the poll, of Condé, who was accused of seeking to leave the country illegally (Guinea's borders had been sealed prior to the election) and of seeking to recruit troops to destabilize the country. By the end of the month at least 12 people were reported to have been killed as a result of violence in Conakry, Kankan, Siguiri and Baro. Condé was formally charged in late December with having recruited mercenaries with the aim of overthrowing the Conté regime. Some 100 other opposition activists remained in detention, among them Marcel Cros, the leader of the Parti démocratique africain de Guinée, who was accused of the illegal possession of firearms. Meanwhile, the opposition withdrew its representatives from the HCE, denouncing the conduct of the election as fraudulent. The official results, issued by the HCE on 17 December and confirmed by the supreme court two weeks later, confirmed a decisive victory for Conté, with 56.1% of the valid votes cast. Bâ took 24.6% and Condé 16.6%. The electoral turn-out was 71.4% of the registered electorate.

At his inauguration, on 30 January 1999, President Conté announced that his forthcoming term of office would witness a period of economic growth and social progress for all sectors of society. He further emphasized that his government would ensure the defence of individual freedoms and security, and gave an undertaking that all abuses, including those committed by the security forces, would be severely punished. In early March, following several weeks of speculation, Lamine Sidimé, the chief justice of the supreme court, was appointed prime minister. Sidimé, a *guinéen de l'extérieur* originating from Haut Guinée, had no party political affiliation. Fofana was reappointed as minister of the economy and finance. (It had been rumoured that Fofana, widely credited with Guinea's recent economic successes, would himself be awarded the premiership.) Assifat, redesignated minister at the presidency, retained the national defence portfolio, while Sanoussi was appointed minister at the presidency, in charge of foreign affairs. Former chief of staff Col Oumar Sanko was among those removed from post as a result of an effective purge of the military high command in mid-March: 18 officers were dismissed, accused of high treason, and a further 13 retired early, on the grounds of what were termed serious faults arising from the 1996 mutiny.

Impending local government elections were postponed in early June 1999. In mid-June Codem denounced government proposals to extend the mandate of the president of the republic

from five years to seven. However, the chairman of the constitutional committee of the national assembly gave assurances that this, if adopted, would take effect from the presidential election in 2003, and would not be applied retroactively.

Throughout the first half of 1999 opposition groups and human rights organizations urged the release from detention of Alpha Condé and other activists arrested at the time of the presidential election. In February Condé's defence lawyers withdrew from the case, citing serious violations of the rule of law and exercise of legal practice on the part of the authorities; in particular, defence counsel complained of being denied free access to Condé (who was reportedly held in solitary confinement), of the 'politicization' of the case, and of the authorities' refusal to allow a French defence lawyer to enter the country. The RPG leader's lawyers resumed their defence in April, stating that the authorities had taken their concerns into account. In mid-July it was announced that Condé's trial would begin in early September; however, a decreee published in mid-August declaring that the RPG leader would be tried by the State Security Court provoked further controversy. Moreover, it was reported that foreign lawyers would not be permitted to represent Condé. In the event, Condé's trial did not proceed as scheduled, while his lawyers protested that neither the defence nor the prosecution had received any documentation relating to the trial. Trials of other opposition activists were pursued in the mean time. In mid-March 13 RPG officials were sentenced to four months' imprisonment, convicted of disturbing public order; they were released at Conté's behest. A further 15 activists were sentenced *in absentia* to five years' detention. The trial began in mid-July 1999 of 20 mainly-RPG activists, arrested following the murder of the local official in Farannah in late 1998; some 50 people were charged in connection with this incident, but most had since absconded.

It was reported in June 1999 that the authorities had agreed to release some 10,000m. FG in order to pay soldiers who were threatening a rebellion against the regime. Rumours of disaffection in some quarters of the military continued to circulate, frequently linked to the insecurity in the region of Guinea's borders with Sierra Leone and Liberia. In late September the authorities launched a campaign to register all foreigners resident in the capital, while violence during student demonstrations in mid-October was blamed by the government on 'external elements'. In November the Codem claimed that many of its activists had been arrested and subjected to ill-treatment in an attempt by the authorities to gather evidence prior to the trial of Alpha Condé, while in early December the government banned a protest march planned by the Codem in order to complain at the continued detention of Condé. In the same month a senior journalist at *L'Indépendant Plus* was briefly detained by the police, following the newspaper's publication of allegations relating to official corruption. Also in December health workers undertook industrial action in order to press for the opening of negotiations regarding their working conditions.

In January 2000 a major government reshuffle was announced, and several senior ministers were dismissed. The reorganization was widely believed to have been occasioned by the release of disappointing economic figures for 1999. In February members of the national assembly, including members of the PUP, called on the president to release Alpha Condé. The deputies noted that Condé possessed parliamentary immunity from prosecution, and suggested that his release would encourage democracy in Guinea.

In mid-April 2000, some 16 months after the initial arrests, the trial began of Condé and his 47 co-defendants on charges that included plotting to kill President Conté, hiring mercenaries and threatening state security. However, after the judge rejected the defence's calls for the trial to be abandoned and for the defendants to be released, lawyers for the defence withdrew from the case, claiming that they would be unable properly to defend their clients. In the resultant atmosphere of confusion, the trial was again temporarily postponed. The defendants subsequently alleged that they had been tortured while in detention, while the general secretary of the ruling PUP attacked the foreign press, who had criticized the conduct of the trial, accusing them of being manipulated by 'a coalition of the Socialist International and freemasonry'. When the case reopened in early May, Condé and his co-defendants rejected a defence team appointed by the court, and the trial was again postponed. At the reopening of the trial in late May Condé refused to speak, while all the defendants denied the charges against them; a further adjournment was subsequently granted in order to allow the defence to prepare their case. When proceedings reopened in mid-August the prosecution called for a sentence of life imprisonment for Condé, and in mid-September Condé was sentenced to five years' imprisonment, while six other defendants also received prison terms.

On 25 June 2000 local elections were held to elect some 660 council members in 38 constituencies. Eight parties presented candidates at the elections, and observers reported that, with the exception of a few clashes between members of the opposition and of the PUP in central Conakry, voting had taken place in an atmosphere of calm. Observers noted, however, that there had been little enthusiasm for the elections in those districts in the interior of the country where the government had invalidated the opposition's list of candidates. The elections were, however, followed by a series of clashes between members of the security forces and UPR members, who claimed that the delayed announcement of the election results resulted from the determination of the authorities to falsify the results in favour of the PUP. It was reported that at least five people had been killed and many more injured during demonstrations. It was subsequently announced that the PUP and its allies had won control of 33 of the 38 constituencies, while the opposition had gained control of the remainder. In the same month Conté carried out a further ministerial reshuffle; no reason was given for the changes.

EXTERNAL AFFAIRS

Of particular concern to the Guinean authorities during the 1990s was the internal instability of neighbouring Liberia, Sierra Leone and Guinea-Bissau. These conflicts in Guinea's neighbouring states have, in particular, led to an enormous influx of refugees, who in the late 1990s were estimated to number some 5%–10% of the total population of Guinea.

In August 1990 Guinean armed forces were stationed along the border with Liberia, following a series of incursions by deserters from the Liberian army. Guinean army units also participated in the ECOMOG cease-fire monitoring group of the Economic Community of West African States (ECOWAS) that was dispatched to Liberia in that month, and in April 1991 it was announced that a Guinean contingent was to be deployed in Sierra Leone to assist that country in repelling violations of its territory by the National Patriotic Front of Liberia (NPFL), led by Charles Taylor. Following the *coup d'état* in Sierra Leone in April 1992, ex-president Momoh of that country took asylum in Guinea, although the Conté government expressed its wish to establish 'normal' relations with the new regime led by Capt. Valentine Strasser, and announced that Guinean forces would remain in Sierra Leone.

In October 1992 the Guinea government confirmed for the first time that it was providing training facilities for Liberian forces; however, assurances were given that those receiving military instruction were not, as had been widely rumoured, members of the anti-Taylor United Liberation Movement of Liberia for Democracy (ULIMO), but that they were to constitute the first Liberian government forces following the eventual restoration of peace. In March 1993 the NPFL protested to the UN that ULIMO had launched an armed attack on NPFL-held territory from Guinea, and threatened reprisals should further offensives occur. Although Guinea continued to deny support for ULIMO, it was admitted that, contrary to earlier indications, Liberian forces trained in Guinea (at the request of the Liberian interim government) had already returned to Liberia. Efforts were undertaken from early 1994 to reinforce security along Guinea's borders, following recent incursions by both ULIMO and NPFL fighters.

A resurgence of violence in Liberia in September 1994, following a coup attempt in that country, caused as many as 50,000 refugees to cross into Guinea. Moreover, an intensification of hostilities involving government and rebel forces in Sierra Leone, in January 1995, resulted in a further influx of refugees. In July the government issued a statement reaffirming Guinea's determination to ensure the defence of its territory and security of its population, and indicating that attacks by Liberian fac-

tions against border areas would not be tolerated. In December, following the conclusion earlier in the year of a new peace accord for Liberia, it was reported that arrangements were being finalized for the repatriation of Liberian refugees from Guinea. Several thousand refugees were also reported to have crossed into Liberia, following the reopening of a border point that had been blocked by the NPFL since 1994.

Like his predecessor, Strasser took refuge in Guinea after he was deposed in January 1996. None the less, close co-operation was developed with the new regime, and President Ahmed Tejan Kabbah made several visits to Guinea both before and after his election to the presidency in March of that year. Kabbah in turn fled to Guinea in May 1997, and established a government-in-exile, following the seizure of power in Sierra Leone by forces led by Maj. Johnny Paul Koroma. Military reinforcements were deployed to protect Guinea's border, and 1,500 Guinean troops were dispatched in support of the Nigerian-led ECOMOG force in Sierra Leone. Guinea joined other members of the international community in condemning the subversion of constitutional order in Sierra Leone; following an *ad hoc* conference of ECOWAS ministers of foreign affairs, which was convened in Conakry in June, Guinea became a member of the 'committee of four' (with Côte d'Ivoire, Ghana and Nigeria) charged with ensuring the implementation of decisions and recommendations pertaining to the situation in Sierra Leone. A conference communiqué appealed for international assistance for Guinea and other countries of the sub-region affected by the influx of refugees as a result of the coup. The total number of refugees in Guinea was estimated at 435,300 at the end of 1997; however, the operation leading to the return of Kabbah from Conakry to Sierra Leone in March 1998 to resume the presidency again led to an influx of thousands of refugees from Sierra Leone, while fighting in April in eastern Sierra Leone between ECOMOG forces and soldiers supporting Koroma caused a further influx of refugees and the closure of parts of the border.

In June 1999 it was reported that the Guinean army was conducting an offensive in the border region with Sierra Leone, with the aim of curbing the activities of the Sierra Leone People's Army, a guerrilla group held responsible for a series of raids in southern Guinea to procure food and livestock. (In April it had been reported that a refugee camp at Mollah had been sacked by local residents following an attack, blamed on rebels harboured at the camp, in which two people had been killed.) Meanwhile, the Liberian government delivered a formal note of protest to the Guinean authorities in April, in response to what it termed an invasion from Guinea of the border town of Voinjama, in Lofa County, by a group of rebels (later stated to be members of ULIMO) who had briefly held hostage aid workers and foreign diplomats before being repelled by the Liberian armed forces. The Guinean government denied the accusations, reiterating that Guinea had never been, and would never be, used as a base for destabilization of another country, and emphasizing its commitment to the pursuit of peace in the sub-region. It was reported that the raid on Voinjama had caused more than 1,300 Liberian refugees to cross into south-east Guinea.

In August 1999 the Liberian government again claimed that an invasion force had entered northern Liberia from Guinea. The Liberian government declared a state of emergency, and the border between the two countries was closed with immediate effect. Guinea again denied any involvement, and urged international observers to visit the border areas to verify that incursions were not originating in Guinea. Later in the month ECOWAS ministers of foreign affairs agreed to establish a commission in an effort to resolve the chronic border instability in the region. However, in the following month it was alleged that 28 people had been killed in attacks by Liberian troops on Guinean villages; Liberia subsequently denied the allegations. None the less, at an extraordinary summit meeting of eight ECOWAS leaders held in mid-September Presidents Conté and Taylor made pledges of friendship and non-aggression. The summit condemned the attacks, without apportioning blame, and recommended that the functions of the Mano River Union (see p. 152) be reactivated, and that its members (Guinea, Liberia and

Sierra Leone) should establish a joint security commission and exchange information relating to border security. The summit also requested international assistance for the large number of refugees displaced as a result of the attacks.

Liberia reopened its border with Guinea in February 2000, and in April the ministers of security of Guinea, Liberia and Sierra Leone agreed to create a joint technical committee of experts on security issues within the Mano River Union, and to allow reciprocal inspections of border areas. Military officials from the three countries also met in May in order to consider strategies for peace and security in the region. However, in July the Liberian government reported renewed fighting in the Lofa region, following an attack by rebel groups allegedly operating from Guinea. The Liberian government, which dispatched reinforcements to the area, accused the Guinean authorities of complicity in the attack, and threatened to attack the rebel groups in their Guinean bases. Guinea denied any involvement in the attacks, and accused the Liberian government of deliberate misinformation. In late August President Taylor expressed his government's continued commitment to work towards a peaceful settlement within the framework of the Mano River Union, while reaffirming his determination to defend Liberian territory from attack.

In general, the Conté administration maintains good relations with the French government, which is Guinea's primary source of financial and technical assistance. However, the progress of the trial of the opposition leader Alpha Condé remained a source of concern to the French authorities, and during his visit to Guinea in July 1999 President Jacques Chirac of France sought assurances from the government that the trial would be 'transparent'. A meeting of the joint commission for Franco-Guinean co-operation took place in Conakry in November 1999. However, in mid-2000 a meeting of francophone parliamentarians called on Guinea's donor countries to suspend assistance in protest at the conduct of the Condé trial. Guinea, a member of the Organization of the Islamic Conference, has also forged links with other Islamic states, notably signing several co-operation agreements with Iran in the mid-1990s. Guinea has also received significant material assistance from Libya and from the People's Republic of China.

Economy

EDITH HODGKINSON

Revised for this edition by the Editor

With substantial mineral deposits and excellent agricultural potential, Guinea could be one of the richest countries in west Africa. Yet the economic record since independence has been disappointing overall. The country's gross domestic product (GDP) expanded, in real terms, at an average rate of 3.0% per year in 1970–80, reflecting the rapid development of the bauxite sector during that decade, but declined by an average of 1.4% per year in 1980–85. The causes of Guinea's relatively poor performance during this period were largely political. First, there was the abrupt severance of the country's links with France in 1958, which was followed by the withdrawal of French officials and the discontinuation of aid, as well as the loss of the leading traditional market for Guinea's exports. Second, the newly independent Guinea immediately sought to set up a socialist economy, with direct state control of production and consumption in virtually every sector—an objective demanding managerial input that Guinea lacked, and which resulted in great inefficiency and waste. Mining, the one economic sector where state control was diluted, developed as an enclave, with admittedly major benefits for Guinea's export earnings but little linkage and feedback into the rest of the economy, which remained essentially based on agriculture and which suffered from Sekou Touré's system of highly centralized management. The economy consequently became even more dualistic, with the development of a large informal sector in response to the near monopoly of the state over formal economic activity. In an attempt to remove at least the domestic constraints on growth, the Conté regime has introduced a series of policy reforms, agreed with the IMF and the World Bank. These include the transfer to private interests, or elimination, of the parastatal organizations, the liberalization of foreign trade and the abolition of price controls, together with monetary and banking reforms and a reduction in the number of civil service personnel. The recovery programme has received substantial international support, in the form of debt relief and new funds from bilateral and multilateral sources. Such reforms have enjoyed considerable success, and real GDP growth in 1990–98 averaged 4.2% per year, with some acceleration since 1993. GDP growth was 4.3% in 1998, with an increase of 5% forecast for 1999. None the less, GDP per head, at some US $555 in 1997, has remained relatively low. A more telling indication of living standards is provided by two demographic statistics: life expectancy at birth was only 46.5 years in 1997 (the average for sub-Saharan Africa was 48.9 years), and one-fifth of all live-born children die before the age of five.

POPULATION AND EMPLOYMENT

Population growth has been relatively slow, owing to the high level of emigration during the Sekou Touré regime. Therefore, while the population was stated to be 4.5m. (excluding adjustment for underenumeration) at the 1983 census, a further 2m. Guineans (some of whom returned following the 1984 coup) were estimated to be living abroad. The census conducted in December 1996 enumerated a population of 7,164,823, including some 640,000 refugees. The urban population numbered 2.1m.

The active labour force in the early 1990s was estimated at about 3m. The majority are employed in the rural sector, although the share has eased from 78% of the total at the 1983 census to about two-thirds in the mid-1990s, with an increasing proportion now engaged in industrial and service activities. A little more than one-half of salaried employees are concentrated in the public sector, which has rendered more difficult the Conté government's aim of reducing the number of civil service personnel by 50%. By early 1995 the number of employees in the public sector had been reduced to about 48,000, compared with some 90,000 in 1986. However, the real contraction is less significant, as some of the losses resulted from the transfer to private ownership of state-owned interests. Thus, 8,000 employees of the state mining companies were removed from the public payroll in 1990. The diminution in job opportunities in the public sector, previously guaranteed to all university graduates, has caused a rapid increase in urban unemployment and fuelled student unrest.

AGRICULTURE, FORESTRY AND FISHING

Despite the rapid development and potential of the mining sector, agriculture remains an important economic activity in terms of value of output (an estimated 22% of GDP in 1998) and the most significant in terms of employment (see above). Under the Sekou Touré regime agricultural production was depressed by the low official prices paid to producers, government controls on marketing, and the production tax on crops and livestock, which led to large-scale smuggling of produce by peasant farmers. The collective agricultural units, which occupied a dominant role in agriculture, and the Pouvoirs révolutionnaires locaux, which controlled the transport and marketing of agricultural production, were highly inefficient. The government of Lansana Conté immediately abolished collectives, raised producer prices and ended the production tax. Improvements to the infrastructure (notably to the road network) and the easier availability of farm credits began to stimulate an increase in production by small-scale farmers.

Production of foods has thus been recovering in recent years, to about 20% more than the average in 1979–81. In 1998 output of paddy rice (cultivated mainly in the Forest Guinea area) was 764,000 metric tons, while production of cassava was 812,000 tons, sweet potatoes 135,000 tons and maize 89,000 tons. The rise in output has, in the long term, failed to keep pace with population growth, so that Guinea—a net exporter of food in the past—now imports large quantities, representing about double the value of its agricultural exports. The staple crops are supplemented by the substantial livestock herd (raised by traditional methods), estimated by FAO in 1998 at 2.3m. cattle, 669,000 sheep and 820,000 goats.

The major commercial crops are bananas, coffee, pineapples, oil palm, groundnuts and citrus fruit. The banana plantations, which suffered in the late 1950s from disease and, with independence, from the withdrawal of European planters and the closing of the protected French market, have shown a good recovery, with output averaging about 150,000 metric tons per year in the late 1990s. Officially recorded coffee output fluctuated widely in the Sekou Touré era—in some years net imports were recorded—because of smuggling to neighbouring countries, where higher prices were obtainable. Before independence Guinea exported about 20,000 tons of coffee annually. Higher prices paid to producers in the late 1980s prompted more output to be sold on the official domestic market: production rose strongly, from 6,900 tons in 1985/86 to in excess of 20,000 tons per year in the late 1990s. Similarly pineapple production, having fallen from 25,000 tons per year in the late 1960s to about one-half of this level in 1970, had increased to about 67,000 tons per year by the late 1990s. An export trade in fruit and vegetables for the European market has been developed, as quality-control and transportation links have improved. Because of the overvaluation of the currency until 1985, exports of bananas, coffee, oil palm and other crops were subsidized out of the proceeds of import taxes. This practice ceased under the Conté regime, and production of cash crops is being stimulated by the more realistic exchange rate. In 1986 a nine-year project was launched to plant 13,000 ha with rubber and oil palm in Forest Guinea, with the aim of re-establishing, in a modified form, the plantation agriculture that was characteristic of the colonial period, and of attracting foreign investment to this sector. Meanwhile, a cotton development scheme, aided by France, was inaugurated in 1985, aiming to produce a total of 43,000–50,000 tons from plantations in Haute Guinée (where it is the largest single development project) and Moyenne Guinée. However, progress has been disappointing, with output of seed cotton reaching its highest level at only 19,670 tons in 1992/93 before decreasing again owing to unfavourable weather and a reduction in the area planted as farmers transferred to other economic activities, notably gold mining. Output was estimated at 14,000 tons in 1998. The government is attempting to keep the programme in operation by means of increasing producer prices, reducing supply costs and subsidizing agricultural equipment.

There is considerable potential for timber production, with forests covering more than two-thirds of the land area. Timber resources are currently used mainly for fuel, with production of roundwood (by small-scale producers) totalling 5.4m. cu m in 1997. An integrated forestry industry is planned.

The fishing sector remains relatively undeveloped. Only a small proportion of the total catch from Guinean waters—103,000 metric tons in 1997—has been accounted for by indigenous fleets, the rest having been taken by factory ships and industrial trawlers. Since 1983 the Guinean government has concluded a series of fishing accords with the European Community (EC, now European Union—EU). It has since been agreed to award foreign licences exclusively to EU fleets, in an effort to preserve the viability of fish stocks on the continental shelf. Inadequate local infrastructure has been a constraint on the development of this sector, but improvements are now being made. The African Development Bank is helping to finance the establishment of onshore facilities and the supply of equipment for small-scale fishermen. In addition, the rehabilitation of the port of Conakry includes the installation of deep-freeze equipment to serve the fishing industry.

MINING AND POWER

Guinea's most dynamic sector and most important source of foreign exchange, providing more than 90% of recorded export revenues for much of the 1980s and around 80% in the 1990s, is mining. It has been contributing around one-fifth of GDP each year since the end of the 1980s. In 1995 the government introduced revisions to the mining code created in 1984, which were intended to encourage foreign investment and to redefine the state's new non-participatory role in the mining sector. The government also announced the foundation of the Centre de Promotion et de Développement Miniers (CPDM), which was to act as the advisory and regulatory body for the mining sector. Foreign investment was further encouraged by the completion in 1998 of a comprehensive evaluation of Guinea's mineral resources by the German Federal Institute for Geosciences and Natural Resources. In the late 1990s some 128 exploration licences were issued, and it was hoped that increased production in subsequent years would, to a large extent, offset the effects of depressed world commodity prices. Currently bauxite, diamonds and gold are commercially exploited, but it is also hoped that deposits of iron-ore and nickel may prove viable. The further development of the sector is, however, dependent on improvements in infrastructure and power supply.

Bauxite and Alumina

The country possesses 30% of the world's known bauxite reserves, with a very high-grade ore. Guinea ranks second only to Australia in terms of ore production, and is the world's largest exporter of bauxite. Since the mid-1980s, however, bauxite revenues have been affected by a weakening in world demand for aluminium and the considerable surplus in world production capacity. Annual output has been running at around the 12m.–17m. metric tons level since the early 1980s, reaching a recent high of 18.39m. tons in 1996. Current expansion and rehabilitation programmes at the country's mines are projected to increase annual output to 20m. tons, and it is hoped that a restructuring of the sector, through the reduction in the state interest to 15% of equity, will enhance both investment and efficiency.

The exploitation of bauxite reserves at Fria, by the Cie internationale pour la production de l'alumine Fria (an international consortium that included Pechiney), began in the 1930s. Processing into alumina began in 1960, at what remains the country's only smelter. Following independence, the government took a 49% share in the company, which was renamed Friguia. The smelter's output eased from a peak of 692,000 metric tons (recorded in 1980, and close to the plant's total capacity of 700,000 tons annually) to some 640,000 tons in 1999. In October 1998 the international consortium ceded its 51% stake in Friguia to the Guinean government. The government subsequently formed in late 1999 a controlling company, the Alumina Company of Guinea Ltd (ACG-GUINEA), and concluded a management and technical assistance agreement with the Reynolds Metal Company of the USA, by which it was hoped to achieve significant improvements in production efficiency.

The country's principal bauxite mine is at Boké-Sangaredi, in the north-west, which was commissioned in 1973 by the Cie des bauxites de Guinée, a joint venture between the government and the Halco group (an international consortium of Canadian, US, French, German and Australian aluminium companies). The government holds 49% of the capital and receives 65% of the mine's net profits. The scheme involved investment of US $400m., including infrastructural development—142 km of railway and a port at Kamsar. Output increased from around 900,000 metric tons per year to the complex's full capacity (at that time) of 10m. tons in 1981, eased subsequently, and then rose to 13.6m. tons in 1999.

A similar agreement to that signed with Halco was concluded in 1969 by Guinea and the USSR for the working of bauxite deposits at Debélé, near Kindia. Production by the Office des bauxites de Kindia began in 1974 and averaged about 3m. tons per year, as against design capacity of 5m. tons, in the late 1980s. Following the dissolution of the USSR, the company suffered severe financial difficulties, and output has fluctuated around the 1m.–2m. metric tons level since the company was reorganized as the Société des bauxites de Kindia in 1992: production was 1.3m. tons in 1999. A majority stake is now held by a Ukrainian company. The Société des bauxites de Dabola-Tougué, established as a joint venture with Iran, plans to develop reserves at Dabola and Tougué and eventually to operate an alumina-processing plant. Production from the mine has yet to start. Initial output is planned at 3.5m. tons a year, reaching 10m. tons eventually. However, exports will depend on an upgrading of the rail link to Conakry. A joint Russian-Ukrainian scheme to extract bauxite from deposits at Dian-Dian, for processing in those two countries, was announced in 1996, but funding has yet to be obtained.

Diamonds

Production of diamonds rose in the late 1960s, to reach 80,000 carats per year in the early 1970s: the official figure did not include substantial illicit production, and mining was suspended in the late 1970s to prevent smuggling and theft. In 1980 the government allowed the resumption of diamond mining by private companies, and AREDOR–Guinée was founded in 1981 with Australian, Swiss, British and—for the first time in Guinea—International Finance Corpn participation. The government had a 50% holding and was to take 65% of net profits. AREDOR–Guinée began production in 1984, and output reached a peak of 204,000 carats in 1986. However, mining was suspended in 1994. AREDOR has since been restructured under new ownership. In 1992 the government revoked the ban (imposed in 1985) on small-scale prospecting in order to stimulate investment by foreign companies. Of a recorded 379,639 carats exported in 1997, 342,187 were from artisanal producers.

Gold

Gold is mined both industrially and by individuals (the latter smuggle much of their output abroad). A joint venture with Belgian interests, the Société Aurifère de Guinée (SAG), was established in 1985 to develop gold mining in the Siguiri and Mandiana districts. Alluvial production began in 1988, and reached 2,000 kg in the following year; however extraction ceased in 1992, owing to financial and technical difficulties and conflicts with artisanal miners. Golden Shamrock of Australia took a 70% interest in the project, which was in turn taken over by Ghana's Ashanti Goldfields in 1996; production by SAG (renamed Société Ashanti Goldfields de Guinée) resumed in early 1998, with output in its first year estimated at 160,000 oz. The Société minière de Dinguiraye (a joint venture with Norwegian, Australian and French interests) began production at the Léro site in 1995; output in 1998 was in the region of 52,000 oz. The Norwegian-based Kenor is currently developing an extension of the mine east of the Karta river. Several other foreign enterprises are also actively prospecting for gold.

Iron-Ore

Working of the iron-ore deposits on the Kaloum peninsula (near Conakry) was begun in 1953 by an Anglo-French group, and provided a stable output of about 700,000 metric tons per year in 1960–69, when operations were abandoned. An ambitious project for the exploitation of the far superior deposits at Mt Nimba, which has proven reserves of 600 tons of ore, has been discussed for many years. The original proposals failed to attract sufficient capital, since commitments by potential customers for the ore were far below the planned level of output (an eventual 15m. tons per year). A scaled-down version of the project was to be undertaken by Nimba International Mining Co (Nimco), a joint venture of the governments of Guinea and Liberia (each with a stake of 20%) and the Euronimba consortium of international mining interests. This US $500m. scheme envisaged transport via an 18-km rail spur for processing in Liberia, with export through that country's port of Buchanan. The conflict in Liberia during the early and mid-1990s prevented any progress on the proposal, but with peace formally restored in the second half of 1997 the project again became feasible. The immediate issue to be settled is the export route to be used, as the rail line to Buchanan was damaged during the civil war. A new company to succeed Nimco was being formed in 1999 by the government of Guinea and Euronimba. It is now planned to extract some 20m. tons of ore annually, to be transported through Guinean territory to the coast for shipment.

Energy

Installed electricity generation capacity is currently estimated at 245 MW, of which one-half is privately operated, notably by mining companies. Supplies of energy outside the mining and industrial sector are vastly inadequate, with less than one-tenth of the population receiving electricity from the national grid; even Conakry is subject to frequent and prolonged power-cuts during dry periods. In June 2000 it was admitted that only one of Guinea's nine power stations was operational, as seven had been destroyed during the political crisis of 1996, while one had broken down. None the less, the country has a very large, as yet unexploited, hydroelectric potential, estimated at some 6,000 MW. Several ambitious projects for the development of hydro-electric facilities on the Konkouré river finally came to fruition—in a much reduced form—in 1999, with the commissioning of a 75-MW plant at Garafiri. This, together with a planned station at Kaléta, 100 km downstream (scheduled for completion in 2002), was to increase total generating capacity by 155 MW. As part of the economic reform programme, the national power corporation has been restructured, to allow the participation of Canadian and French companies. It is envisaged that the electricity network be extended to cover the whole country by 2004.

MANUFACTURING

The principal aim of Guinea's small manufacturing sector, which accounts for only 4%–5% of GDP, has been import-substitution, but the experience of the state-run projects that were established under Sekou Touré was disappointing. Lack of foreign exchange for raw materials, of skilled workers and of technical expertise, combined with poor management and low domestic purchasing power, meant that most of the plants were operating substantially below capacity. The sector has been rationalized under the Conté administration, with the former state-run textile and fruit-processing companies closed and no new factories established. Manufacturing is now largely limited to food, drinks and cigarettes, and basic inputs such as cement, metal manufacturers and fuel products, all geared to the domestic market. As part of the programme of stimulating the private sector, the investment code has been liberalized to give equal treatment to foreign capital and individuals, while the government has disengaged from participation in a total of 300 companies since 1987. However, the privatization programme has attracted criticism on two counts: that the government did not put an adequate value on the assets divested, and that the capacity of the new owners to undertake the necessary rehabilitation was not assured.

TRANSPORT INFRASTRUCTURE

The inadequacy of Guinea's transport infrastructure has been cited by the World Bank as the 'single most severe impediment to output recovery'. None the less, some major improvements have been made since the mid-1980s. The road network is being almost entirely reconstructed, to restore links between Conakry and the country's interior, while road tracks have been built to open up rural areas. The network comprised an estimated 30,500 km of roads (of which some 5,030 were paved) in 1996. The rail network is better developed, but is entirely geared to serving the bauxite sector: a 135-km heavy-gauge railway links the Boké bauxite deposits with the deep-water port at Kamsar, which handles around 9m. tons per year and is thus the country's major export outlet in tonnage terms. The 662-km public rail line from Conakry to Kankan is in very poor condition, but is now being renovated, with French aid. The port of Conakry, which handled 3.9m. tons of foreign trade in 1999, has been extended and modernized as part of a programme that envisages the construction of naval-repair and deep-water port facilities. A petroleum terminal is also planned for Conakry. The international airport at Conakry handled some 290,000 passengers in 1997; there are several smaller airfields in the interior.

FINANCE

Government revenue remains heavily reliant on income from the mining sector, but this contribution declined sharply from a peak of 60% in 1987 to about 25% in the late 1990s. Although mining revenue rose strongly in the mid- and late 1970s, reflecting the growth of the bauxite sector, current expenditure exceeded revenue, owing to the government's policy of providing jobs in the public sector to all graduates, combined with the rising losses of the state enterprises and the growing burden of servicing the foreign debt. Thus, by 1981 the deficit of the public sector was equivalent to around one-fifth of GDP, with parastatal enterprises alone accounting for some three-quarters of the deficit.

As part of Guinea's programme for economic stabilization, inaugurated in 1986 with support from the IMF, consumer subsidies were reduced or eliminated, while the activities of state enterprises were curtailed and employment in the civil service was to be reduced by more than one-half. This severe fiscal austerity proved difficult to implement, and the government was obliged to rescind some of the price increases resulting from the devaluation of the currency in 1986, while the reduction in civil service personnel was finally achieved only in 1995. None the less, the budget balance improved as the government succeeded in raising its revenue from non-mining activities 10-fold in 1987–95, through changes in the tax system and improvements in collection. This was particularly significant, as mining revenue fell in every year from 1990 to 1994. Expenditure, meanwhile, has benefited from the liquidation or sale of the state's industrial and commercial enterprises. The current budget has thus been in surplus in every year since 1989: a surplus equivalent to 2.7% of GDP was recorded in 1998. The overall budget (i.e. taking into account both grants and capital expenditure) remains in deficit, but as a proportion of GDP this has declined in almost every year, from 6.6% in 1988 to 2.8% in 1996, although there was some regression, to 4.2%, in 1997. (Excluding grants, the deficit has fallen from 8.4% of GDP in 1989 to 6.0% in 1997.) However, this still represents an addition to already high debt stocks, which in turn increases the burden of interest payments on the current budget. The multilateral institutions, the support of which is essential to secure the external funding needed to make up the budgetary shortfall, have maintained their pressure for rigid spending control. The fiscal targets for 1996 came under pressure when the military insurrection early in the year extracted a promise from President Conté of substantial pay increases for the army, prompting the IMF to suspend the enhanced structural adjustment facility (ESAF). However, the new government under prime minister Sydia Touré, subsequently introduced measures to restrain spending and improve tax collection (including the introduction of a value-added tax), which kept the result for the year close to target. The IMF thus accorded a new ESAF in early 1997; under the programme that this supported, the overall budget deficit (before grants) was to narrow to 5.7% of GDP in 1999 and 2000.

Guinea's budgetary resources were, however, weakened in 1999 both by the depression in world mineral prices, which resulted in a sharp decline in revenue from sales of bauxite and alumina, and by continued regional instability, which required Guinea to commit substantial financial resources towards supplying peace-keeping forces, strengthening border security and providing for large numbers of refugees. Meanwhile, the IMF expressed concern at weaknesses, particularly in fiscal revenue collection, and the annual funding under the ESAF originally agreed in early 1997 was delayed until the end of 1999, when support under the Poverty Reduction and Growth Facility (the successor to the ESAF) was granted in three yearly instalments. Fiscal reform and the elimination of administrative inefficiency and corruption were to remain priorities for 2000–01, together with efforts to encourage increased private investment. It was also intended that reform to the system of customs and tariffs would contribute to an estimated rise in revenue from 10.4% of GDP in 1999 to 11.5% of GDP in 2000.

An important element of the economic liberalization initiated in the final years of the Sekou Touré regime and pursued with vigour by the Conté administration was the reform of the banking sector, ending the state monopoly by allowing the establishment of private commercial banks and then closing down the six state-controlled institutions. This is gradually drawing in funds that previously flowed to the parallel economy. In a further significant disengagement from the banking sector, the government plans to privatize the Banque internationale pour le commerce et l'industrie de la Guinée (BICI–GUI), in which it holds a 51% stake (foreign interests hold 40%); BICI–GUI accounts for 45% of the country's banking resources and for about one-third of credits to the private sector.

FOREIGN TRADE AND PAYMENTS

With the development of bauxite resources from the early 1970s, the country's external trade position greatly improved. The sharp rise in bauxite exports resulted in strong growth in export earnings after 1975, and sales of bauxite and alumina contributed more than 90% of recorded earnings in the early 1980s. Export earnings were subsequently bolstered by contributions from sales of diamonds and gold, which accounted for 15% of the total in 1990. The sustained growth in exports throughout this period allowed a similarly strong rise in spending on imports, in large part reflecting capital investment in the mining sector. However, as earnings from bauxite and alumina declined from 1991 onwards, and spending on imports was relatively little changed, the trade account moved into deficit, reaching a peak of US $170m. in 1994. The value of illicit exports to neighbouring countries (consisting largely of agricultural products) was, in the past, estimated at some $100m. per year, with the proceeds being used mainly to finance illicit imports. It was hoped that the devaluation of the currency and increases in agricultural producer prices would attract more trade into legal channels. By the mid-1990s these measures seemed to be having some effect, and, with bauxite and alumina earnings recovering from their trough of 1994, the trade account had moved back into surplus by 1996; the surplus was maintained at an estimated $137.4m. in 1998. Nevertheless, the current account has remained in deficit because of high outflows on services (including interest payments and profit remittances), although the shortfall declined from an average annual total of more than $200m. in 1994–96 to $118.5m. in 1998.

A significant positive item on the current account has for decades past been inflows of official aid. The country's *rapprochement* with France and adherence to the Lomé Conventions (the aid and trade agreements with the EC), in conjunction with the change of political regime in 1984, resulted in a rapid increase in the flow of official development assistance (both grants and loans) from non-Eastern bloc countries and agencies. This averaged US $359m. (net) per year in 1988–96, and totalled $382m. in 1997. While France remains by far the most significant bilateral source of aid funds, the World Bank (through its concessionary lending agency, the International Development Association) and the European Commission are the largest multilateral lenders, providing a net $380m. and $267m., respectively, in 1992–96.

The deficit on the current account has been financed by inflows of investment in the mining sector and by borrowing, both private and governmental. Guinea's foreign debt rose very sharply, from US $137m. in 1960 to $1,387m. at the end of 1981—equivalent to 86% of the country's gross national product (GNP) in that year—a level that was broadly maintained in the following four years. Although the burden of servicing the debt was alleviated by concessionary interest rates on most of the borrowing and by the buoyancy of Guinean exports, it remained at a high level throughout this period, fluctuating within the range of 14%–24% of exports of goods and services, and obligations were not discharged in full. Arrears on both repayment and interest had apparently reached $300m. at the time of the 1984 coup. In early 1986, following final agreement between the IMF and the Conté administration on the terms of the economic stabilization programme (which included a 93% devaluation of the currency), the country's Western creditors agreed to a rescheduling of debt, covering arrears and debt-service due up to early 1987. However, with the external debt and debt-service continuing to rise, the 'Paris Club' of official creditors rescheduled debt in every year from 1990 to 1992. With a rising share of concessionary loans, this meant that, while total foreign debt remained close to 100% of GNP (at $3,110m. at the end of 1994, it was equivalent to 94% in that year), the debt-service ratio was kept at a manageable 11%–14% in 1992–94. Another round of rescheduling, in January 1995, was under the highly concessionary 'Naples terms', and included the cancellation of one-half of debt-servicing liabilities due in 1994 and 1995 to France, Germany, Norway and the USA. While the ratio almost doubled in 1995, to 25%, because of a surge in repayments to reduce arrears, the latter kept down the increase in the total debt, with an end-year figure of $3,242m., while 1996 saw a stabilization, with total debt stocks at $3,240m. (equivalent to 87.5% of GNP). The award of the new ESAF in 1997 generated another round of 'Paris Club' restructuring, again under 'Naples terms', and Guinea was also permitted to convert up to 20% of its outstanding debt (i.e. double the usual limit) into local-currency equity in the form of investment in development projects. Total debt at the end of that year was $3,520m. (95.3% of GNP), while the cost of debt-servicing was equivalent to 21.5% of the value of exports of goods and services. Total debt at the end of 1998 fell slightly, to $3,546m., and the cost of debt-servicing in that year was equivalent to 19.5% of revenue from exports of goods and services.

Debt relief and continued inflows of new funds are essential to the Guinean economy, since the country's export base remains narrow, over-dependent on one commodity (bauxite) and thus highly vulnerable to fluctuations in international prices for that commodity. It is therefore of great significance that in late 1999 the IMF and the World Bank approved the principles of eligibility of Guinea for the heavily indebted poor countries initiative, which, it is hoped, will allow Guinea to benefit from highly reduced terms of debt repayment. The current account of Guinea's balance of payments is expected to continue in deficit for some time, as the country's dependence on imports—particularly of food and petroleum—will still be high. Meanwhile, budgetary support from external sources is vital to the success of the sometimes unpalatable economic adjustment process, by enabling the Conté administration to respond to domestic pressure for an improvement in living standards.

Statistical Survey

Source (unless otherwise stated): Service de la Statistique Générale, Conakry; tel. 44-21-48.

Area and Population

AREA, POPULATION AND DENSITY

Area (sq km) .	245,857*
Population (census results)	
4–17 February 1983	4,533,240†
31 December 1996‡	
Males	3,496,150
Females	3,668,673
Total	7,164,823
Density (per sq km) at census of 1996	29.1

* 94,926 sq miles.
† Excluding adjustment for underenumeration.
‡ Provisional figure, including refugees from Liberia and Sierra Leone (estimated at 640,000).

PRINCIPAL TOWNS (population at 1996 census)

Conakry (capital)	1,091,483	Kankan	261,341
Kindia	287,607	Labé	249,515
N'Zérékoré	282,772		

BIRTHS AND DEATHS (UN estimates, annual averages)

	1980–85	1985–90	1990–95
Birth rate (per 1,000)	51.3	47.3	44.1
Death rate (per 1,000)	23.8	22.0	19.4

Expectation of life (UN estimates, years at birth, 1990–95): 44.5 (males 44.0; females 45.0).

Source: UN, *World Population Prospects: The 1998 Revision.*

ECONOMICALLY ACTIVE POPULATION
(persons aged 10 years and over, census of 1983, provisional)

	Males	Females	Total
Agriculture, hunting, forestry and fishing	856,971	566,644	1,423,615
Mining and quarrying	7,351	4,890	12,241
Manufacturing	6,758	4,493	11,251
Electricity, gas and water	1,601	1,604	3,205
Construction	5,475	3,640	9,115
Trade, restaurants and hotels	22,408	14,901	37,309
Transport, storage and communications	17,714	11,782	29,496
Finance, insurance, real estate and business services	2,136	1,420	3,556
Community, social and personal services	82,640	54,960	137,600
Activities not adequately defined*	101,450	54,229	155,679
Total labour force	1,104,504	718,563	1,823,067

* Includes 18,244 unemployed persons (not previously employed), whose distribution by sex is not available.

Source: ILO, *Yearbook of Labour Statistics.*

Mid-1998 (estimates in '000): Agriculture, etc. 3,091; Total labour force 3,655 (Source: FAO, *Production Yearbook*).

Agriculture

PRINCIPAL CROPS ('000 metric tons)

	1996	1997	1998
Maize	82	85	89
Millet	8	8*	8*
Sorghum	6	5*	5*
Rice (paddy)	673	716	764
Other cereals	110	118*	117*
Sweet potatoes	132*	135*	135
Cassava (Manioc)	667	732	812
Yams	90*	95*	89
Taro (Coco yam)	24	27	29
Pulses*	60	60	60
Coconuts*	18	18	18
Cottonseed	5	9*	14*
Cotton (lint)	6	10	16
Vegetables	476*	476*	476
Sugar cane*	220	220	220
Citrus fruits*	205	215	215
Bananas	150*	150*	150
Plantains	435*	430*	429
Mangoes	76	75*	85
Pineapples	65*	67*	72
Other fruits*	44	46	45
Palm kernels	52	52*	52*
Groundnuts (in shell)	145	158	174
Coffee (green)	23	20*	21
Cocoa beans	5†	6†	6*
Tobacco (leaves)*	2	2	2

* FAO estimate(s).   † Unofficial figure.

Source: FAO, *Production Yearbook*.

LIVESTOCK ('000 head, year ending September)

	1996	1997	1998
Cattle	2,246	2,291	2,337
Sheep	631	650	669
Goats	758	788	820
Pigs	48	51	53
Horses*	3	3	3
Asses*	2	2	2

* FAO estimates.

Poultry (million): 7 in 1996; 8 in 1997; 9 in 1998.

Source: FAO, *Production Yearbook*.

LIVESTOCK PRODUCTS (FAO estimates, '000 metric tons)

	1996	1997	1998
Beef and veal	15	15	15
Poultry meat	2	3	3
Mutton and lamb	1	2	2
Goat meat	3	3	3
Other meat	6	4	5
Cows' milk	50	55	59
Goats' milk	5	5	5
Sheep's milk	2	2	2
Poultry eggs	8	8	8
Cattle hides	2	2	3

Source: FAO, *Production Yearbook*.

Forestry

ROUNDWOOD REMOVALS ('000 cubic metres, excl. bark)

	1995	1996	1997
Sawlogs, veneer logs and logs for sleepers	170	170	170
Other industrial wood	512	524	531
Fuel wood	4,541	4,642	4,700
Total	5,223	5,336	5,401

Source: FAO, *Yearbook of Forest Products*.

SAWNWOOD PRODUCTION ('000 cubic metres, incl. railway sleepers)

	1995	1996	1997
Total (all broadleaved)	85	85*	85*

* FAO estimate.

Source: FAO, *Yearbook of Forest Products*.

Fishing

('000 metric tons, live weight)

	1995	1996	1997
Freshwater fishes	3.1	2.8	3.6
Tonguefishes	2.5	2.1	4.3
Sea catfishes	4.8	4.4	4.0
Bobo croaker	4.4	3.8	6.7
West African croakers	5.7	4.4	6.9
Porgies and seabreams	5.4	4.8	5.1
Mullets	1.8	1.9	1.3
Carangids	3.0	8.1	6.5
Sardinellas	4.5	5.3	4.6
Bonga shad	23.6	26.1	29.6
Chub mackerel	0.3	1.3	2.2
Other marine fishes (incl. unspecified)	11.2	10.1	19.3
Total fish	70.2	75.1	94.0
Panaeus shrimps	1.0	1.0	1.6
Cuttlefish and bobtail squids	6.4	5.7	6.5
Other crustaceans and molluscs	0.7	0.5	0.5
Total catch	78.4	82.3	102.6

Source: FAO, *Yearbook of Fishery Statistics*.

Mining

	1990	1991	1992
Bauxite ('000 metric tons)	15,341	14,862	13,625
Diamonds ('000 carats)*	127	97	95

Bauxite ('000 metric tons): 13,761 in 1994; 17,733† in 1995; 18,393† in 1996.

* Data from the US Bureau of Mines.
† Source: *World Metal Statistics* (London).

Source: UN, *Industrial Commodity Statistics Yearbook*.

Gold (mineral content of ore, metric tons): 7.0 in 1996; 7.1 in 1997; 13.1 in 1998 (Source: Gold Fields Mineral Services Ltd, *Gold Survey 1999*).

Industry

SELECTED PRODUCTS ('000 metric tons, unless otherwise indicated)

	1994	1995	1996
Salted, dried or smoked fish*	11.0	11.0	n.a.
Raw sugar*	19	19	19
Alumina (calcined equivalent)†	640	566	600
Electric energy (million kWh)‡	532	537	n.a.

* Data from FAO.
† Data from the US Bureau of Mines.
‡ Provisional or estimated figures.

Source: UN, *Industrial Commodity Statistics Yearbook*.

Palm oil (unrefined): 50 in 1994; 50 (estimate) in 1995; 55 in 1996; 55 (estimate) in 1997; 50 in 1998 (Source: FAO, *Production Yearbook*).

Finance

CURRENCY AND EXCHANGE RATES

Monetary Units
100 centimes = 1 franc guinéen (FG or Guinean franc).

Sterling, Dollar and Euro Equivalents (31 January 2000)
£1 sterling = 2,974.0 Guinean francs;
US $1 = 1,831.6 Guinean francs;
€1 = 1,793.4 Guinean francs;
10,000 Guinean francs = £3.362 = $5.460 = €5.576.

Average Exchange Rate (Guinean francs per US $)
1996   1,004.0
1997   1,095.3
1998   1,236.8

BUDGET ('000 million Guinean francs)

Revenue*	1996	1997	1998
Mining-sector revenue . . .	106.8	123.0	126.4
Special tax on mining products .	101.5	116.1	116.7
Other revenue	291.8	353.0	370.4
Tax revenue	266.0	320.5	337.5
Taxes on income and profits .	43.5	46.0	48.1
Personal	26.0	26.1	26.1
Corporate	8.9	9.5	9.5
Taxes on domestic production and trade	166.2	200.6	217.4
Value-added tax (VAT)† .	58.0	108.8	96.4
Excise surcharge . . .	11.1	9.0	8.5
Petroleum excise tax . .	66.7	63.9	66.3
Taxes on international trade .	56.3	74.0	71.9
Import duties . . .	49.6	71.1	67.8
Total	398.6	475.9	496.7

Expenditure‡	1996	1997	1998
Current expenditure . . .	350.7	377.4	388.1
Wages and salaries . .	173.4	171.7	181.2
Other goods and services .	75.0	83.9	89.8
Subsidies and transfers .	50.3	54.3	53.0
Interest payments . .	52.1	67.4	64.1
Public investment programme .	288.6	341.5	250.4
Domestically financed . .	48.7	39.7	41.4
Externally financed . .	239.9	301.7	209.0
Restructing of banking system .	–	6.0	13.6
Sub-total	639.4	724.9	652.1
Adjustment for payments arrears§	–9.1	56.6	66.9
Total (cash basis) . . .	630.3	781.5	719.0

* Excluding grants received ('000 million Guinean francs): 122.5 in 1996; 127.8 in 1997; 127.8 in 1998.
† VAT, introduced in August 1996, replaced the turnover tax. Includes VAT (turnover tax before 1996) on imports.
‡ Excluding lending minus repayments ('000 million Guinean francs): 1.5 in 1997; 3.9 in 1998.
§ Minus sign indicates an increase in arrears.

Source: IMF, *Guinea: Statistical Appendix* (February 2000).

INTERNATIONAL RESERVES (US $ million at 31 December)

	1995	1996	1997
IMF special drawing rights . .	7.45	0.77	2.66
Reserve position in IMF . .	0.10	0.11	0.10
Foreign exchange . . .	79.21	86.46	118.88
Total	86.76	87.34	121.63

Source: IMF, *International Financial Statistics*.

1998: IMF special drawing rights 1.43; Reserve position in IMF 0.11.
1999: IMF special drawing rights 1.29; Reserve position in IMF 0.10.

MONEY SUPPLY (million Guinean francs at 31 December)

	1995	1996	1997
Currency outside banks . .	167,144	154,420	191,635
Demand deposits at commercial banks	104,060	112,590	130,430
Total (incl. others) . . .	274,125	273,465	331,666

Source: IMF, *International Financial Statistics*.

COST OF LIVING
(Consumer Price Index; base: 1991 = 100)

	1996	1997	1998
Food	141.2	140.7	154.7
Fuel and light	120.0	123.3	124.9
Clothing	117.0	124.0	123.0
Housing	124.3	126.0	129.5
All items (incl. others) . .	134.2	136.8	143.8

Source: IMF, *Guinea: Statistical Appendix* (February 2000).

NATIONAL ACCOUNTS

Expenditure on the Gross Domestic Product
('000 million Guinean francs at current prices)

	1996	1997	1998
Government final consumption expenditure	325.5	345.0	337.4
Private final consumption expenditure	3,135.9	3,282.0	3,625.0
Increase in stocks . . .	65.0	57.0	59.0
Gross fixed capital formation . .	607.7	674.1	738.6
Total domestic expenditure .	4,134.1	4,358.1	4,760.0
Exports of goods and services .	739.8	844.1	1,010.8
Less Imports of goods and services	898.7	936.5	1,093.0
GDP in purchasers' values . .	3,975.1	4,265.8	4,677.7
GDP at constant 1994 prices .	3,663.2	3,840.5	4,012.5

Gross Domestic Product by Economic Activity
('000 million Guinean francs at constant 1994 prices)

	1996	1997	1998
Agriculture, hunting, forestry and fishing	746.2	784.3	824.8
Mining and quarrying . . .	588.9	608.4	630.3
Manufacturing	140.0	146.3	153.9
Electricity, gas and water . .	18.1	19.2	20.8
Construction	309.1	328.3	350.6
Trade	1,013.9	1,065.6	1,116.8
Transport	216.2	226.6	243.6
Administration	187.7	175.9	166.1
Other services	321.5	336.9	356.1
GDP at factor cost . . .	3,541.6	3,691.4	3,863.0
Indirect taxes	121.6	149.1	149.6
GDP in purchasers' values . .	3,663.2	3,840.5	4,012.5

Source: IMF, *Guinea: Statistical Appendix* (February 2000).

BALANCE OF PAYMENTS (US $ million)

	1996	1997	1998
Exports of goods f.o.b. . . .	636.5	630.1	692.9
Imports of goods f.o.b. . . .	−525.3	−512.5	−572.0
Trade balance	111.2	117.6	120.9
Exports of services . . .	124.1	110.7	110.8
Imports of services . . .	−422.2	−321.6	−390.3
Balance on goods and services .	−186.8	−93.3	−158.6
Other income received . .	12.8	7.7	9.0
Other income paid . . .	−105.7	−121.3	−90.0
Balance on goods, services and income	−279.8	−206.9	−239.6
Current transfers received . .	137.8	131.4	145.4
Current transfers paid . .	−35.3	−15.6	−24.3
Current balance . . .	−177.3	−91.1	−118.5
Direct investment abroad .	−0.5	—	—
Direct investment from abroad	23.8	17.3	17.8
Portfolio investment assets .	—	—	−82.7
Other investment assets . .	−19.8	−99.1	−14.7
Other investment liabilities .	44.0	−7.5	146.6
Net errors and omissions . .	69.9	49.8	−64.5
Overall balance . . .	−59.9	−130.6	−116.0

Source: IMF, *International Financial Statistics*.

External Trade

PRINCIPAL COMMODITIES (US $ million)

Imports c.i.f.	1996	1997	1998*
Vegetable products . . .	72.1	80.4	54.2
Prepared foodstuffs; beverages and tobacco .	52.5	58.1	76.9
Mineral products	92.0	83.8	85.8
Products of the chemical or allied industries, plastics and rubber	64.8	67.2	61.9
Textiles and textile articles . .	28.6	27.2	23.4
Base metals and articles thereof	42.5	44.1	43.7
Machinery and mechanical appliances . .	111.5	112.9	126.8
Vehicles, vessels and other transport equipment . .	55.5	33.9	40.4
Total (incl. others) . . .	583.7	572.5	571.8

Exports f.o.b.	1996	1997	1998*
Bauxite	309.0	322.6	324.3
Alumina	103.0	94.5	100.2
Diamonds	42.2	56.8	51.2
Gold	82.2	79.8	125.3
Coffee	13.5	31.6	23.3
Fish	27.5	35.8	38.5
Total (incl. others) . . .	612.7	660.0	709.2

* Estimates.

Source: IMF, *Guinea: Statistical Appendix* (February 2000).

PRINCIPAL TRADING PARTNERS (percentage of trade)*

Imports f.o.b.	1996	1997	1998
Austria	0.3	0.2	1.8
Belgium-Luxembourg . .	8.1	9.2	7.9
Canada	1.2	0.5	1.4
China, People's Repub. . .	2.1	3.8	5.6
Côte d'Ivoire . . .	14.0	6.3	6.6
France (incl. Monaco) . .	16.2	25.0	24.8
Germany	1.6	2.1	2.5
Hong Kong	2.1	1.9	4.0
India	3.6	1.1	1.0
Italy	3.2	3.9	4.1
Japan	4.4	4.2	3.0
Netherlands	2.9	2.8	3.9
Nigeria	1.5	0.6	0.5
Senegal	1.4	1.4	1.8
Singapore	0.5	1.0	1.1
South Africa . . .	0.1	2.6	2.3
Spain	2.2	2.9	3.3
Switzerland	0.3	0.4	1.3
United Kingdom . . .	1.8	4.1	2.7
USA	6.6	8.3	9.8

Exports f.o.b.	1996	1997	1998
Belgium-Luxembourg . . .	4.3	6.7	13.7
Cameroon . . .	3.0	3.8	3.8
Canada	7.7	3.1	2.2
Côte d'Ivoire . . .	—	—	1.0
France (incl. Monaco) . .	8.5	12.8	6.9
Germany	4.1	3.6	3.5
Ireland	10.4	11.1	12.2
Italy	5.3	3.3	1.9
Netherlands	0.4	0.1	1.3
Norway	2.4	2.5	0.7
Spain	10.9	17.5	12.4
Switzerland	1.3	0.6	—
Ukraine	—	—	6.7
United Kingdom . . .	3.0	4.1	0.4
USA	33.2	23.1	16.4

Source: IMF, *Guinea: Statistical Appendix* (February 2000).

Transport

RAILWAYS (estimated traffic)

	1991	1992	1993
Freight ton-km (million) . . .	660	680	710

Source: UN Economic Commission for Africa, *African Statistical Yearbook*.

ROAD TRAFFIC (estimates, motor vehicles in use)

	1994	1995	1996
Passenger cars	13,160	13,720	14,100
Lorries and vans	18,000	19,400	21,000

Source: IRF, *World Road Statistics*.

SHIPPING
Merchant Fleet (registered at 31 December)

	1996	1997	1998
Number of vessels . . .	25	30	30
Total displacement ('000 grt) . .	6.7	9.0	11.2

Source: Lloyd's Register of Shipping, *World Fleet Statistics*.

International Sea-borne Freight Traffic (Port of Conakry, '000 metric tons)

	1998	1999
Goods loaded	2,194	2,089
Goods unloaded	1,680	1,851

Source: Poste d'Expansion Economique, Conakry.

GUINEA

CIVIL AVIATION (traffic on scheduled services)

			1994	1995	1996
Kilometres flown (million)	.	.	1	1	1
Passengers carried ('000)	.	.	30	30	31
Passenger-km (million)	.	.	27	48	50
Total ton-km (million)	.	.	4	5	5

Source: UN, *Statistical Yearbook*.

Tourism

FOREIGN VISITOR ARRIVALS

							1997	1998
Belgium	.	.	.	.	.	.	1,026	1,386
France	.	.	.	.	.	.	3,009	4,550
Germany	.	.	.	.	.	.	788	846
Italy	.	.	.	.	.	.	1,469	1,850
Lebanon	.	.	.	.	.	.	495	1,765
United Kingdom	.	.	.	.	.	.	974	1,080
Total (incl. others)	.	.	.	.	.	.	17,000	23,000

Receipts from tourism (US $ million): 6 in 1996; 5 in 1997.

Source: World Tourism Organization, *Yearbook of Tourism Statistics*.

Communications Media

	1994	1995	1996
Radio receivers ('000 in use) . . .	310	325	350
Television receivers ('000 in use) . .	50	65	75
Telephones ('000 main lines in use) .	9	11	n.a.
Telefax stations (number in use) . .	n.a.	n.a.	1,000
Mobile cellular telephones (subscribers)	812	950	950
Non-daily newspapers:			
Number	n.a.	n.a.	1
Average circulation ('000 copies) .	n.a.	n.a.	20

1997 ('000 in use): Radio receivers 357; Television receivers 85.

Sources: UNESCO, *Statistical Yearbook*; UN, *Statistical Yearbook*.

Education

(1997/98, unless otherwise indicated)

	Institu-tions	Teachers	Students		
			Males	Females	Total
Pre-primary .	202*	594	n.a.	n.a.	30,857
Primary .	3,723	13,883	425,644	249,088	674,732
Secondary:					
General . .	n.a.	5,099	114,212	39,449	153,661
Teacher training†	n.a.	194†	288‡	271‡	559‡
Vocational .	n.a.	1,114§	3,009‡	1,637‡	4,646‡
Tertiary* . .	n.a.	307	780	1,098	1,878

* 1996/97 figure(s). † 1993/94 figure. ‡ 1995/96 figure. § 1992/93 figure.

Source: UNESCO, *Statistical Yearbook*.

Directory

The Constitution

The Constitution (*Loi fondamentale*) of the Third Republic of Guinea was adopted in a national referendum on 23 December 1990 and promulgated on 23 December 1991. An 'organic law' of 3 April 1992, providing for the immediate establishment of an unlimited number of political parties, countermanded the Constitution's provision for the eventual establishment of a two-party political system. There was to be a five-year period of transition, overseen by a Comité transitoire de redressement national (CTRN), to civilian rule, at the end of which executive and legislative authority would be vested in organs of state elected by universal adult suffrage in the context of a multi-party political system. The CTRN was dissolved following the legislative elections of June 1995.

The Constitution defines the clear separation of the powers of the executive, the legislature and the judiciary. The President of the Republic, who is Head of State, must be elected by an absolute majority of the votes cast, and a second round of voting is held should no candidate obtain such a majority at a first round. The duration of the presidential mandate is five years, and elections are by universal adult suffrage. Any candidate for the presidency must be aged between 40 and 70 years, must not be a serving member of the armed forces, and must be proposed by a political party. The President is Head of Government, and is empowered to appoint ministers and to delegate certain functions. The legislature is the 114-member Assemblée nationale. One-third of the assembly's members are elected as representatives of single-member constituencies, the remainder being appointed from national lists, according to a system of proportional representation. The legislature is elected, by universal suffrage, with a five year mandate

The Government

HEAD OF STATE

President: Gen. LANSANA CONTÉ (took office 4 April 1984; elected 19 December 1993; re-elected 14 December 1998).

COUNCIL OF MINISTERS
(August 2000)

President of the Republic and President of the Council of Ministers: Gen. LANSANA CONTÉ.

Prime Minister: LAMINE SIDIMÉ.

Minister at the Presidency, in charge of Foreign Affairs: HADJA MAWA BANGOURA CAMARA.

Minister at the Presidency, in charge of National Defence: DORANK ASSIFAT DIASSÉNY.

Minister of Security: SÉKOU KOUREISSY CONDÉ.

Minister of Justice, Keeper of the Seals: ABOU CAMARA.

Minister of Territorial Administration and Decentralization: MOUSSA SOLANO.

Minister of the Economy and Finance: CHEICK AHMADOU CAMARA.

Minister of Planning and Co-operation: El Hadj THIERNO MAMADOU CELLOU DIALLO.

Minister of Trade, Industry and Small and Medium-sized Enterprises: MARIAMA DÉO BALDE.

Minister of Mines, Geology and the Environment: IBRAHIMA SOUMAH.

Minister of Agriculture and Livestock: JEAN PAUL SARR.

Minister of Fishing and Aquaculture: MANSA MOUSSA SIDIBÉ.

Minister of Water and Energy: NIANKOYE FASSOU SAGNO.

Minister of Public Works and Transport: CELLOU DALEIN DIALLO.
Minister of Town Planning and Housing: Dr ALPHA OUSMANE DIALLO.
Minister of Communications: MAMADY CONDÉ.
Minister of Pre-university and Civil Education: GERMAIN DOUALAMOU.
Minister of Technical Education and Professional Training: FODÉ SYLLA.
Minister of Higher Education and Scientific Research: EUGÈNE CAMARA.
Minister of Public Health: Dr MAMADOU SALIOU DIALLO.
Minister of Youth, Sports and Culture: ABDEL KADER SANGARÉ.
Minister of Tourism, Hotels and Handicrafts: SYLLA KOUMBA DIAKITÉ.
Minister of Employment and the Civil Service: LAMINE KAMARA.
Minister of Social Affairs, Women's Promotion and Children's Affairs: MARIAMA ARIBOT.
Minister Secretary-General of the Presidency: El Hadj FODÉ BANGOURA.
Secretary-General of the Government: El Hadj OUSMANE SANOKO.

MINISTRIES

Office of the Prime Minister: Cité des Natíons, Conakry; tel. 41-52-83.
Ministry of Administrative Reform and Labour: blvd du Commerce, Conakry; tel. 44-29-01.
Ministry of Animal Husbandry and Fishing: Cité du Port, Conakry; tel. 41-12-58.
Ministry of Communications and Culture: Boulbinet, BP 617, Conakry; tel. 41-50-01; fax 41-47-97.
Ministry of the Economy and Finance: blvd du Commerce, Conakry; tel. 45-17-95.
Ministry of Education and Scientific Research: blvd du Commerce, Conakry; tel. 41-19-01.
Ministry of Foreign Affairs: blvd du Commerce, Conakry; tel. 41-33-42.
Ministry of Forestry: Cité du Port, Conakry; tel. 44-12-18.
Ministry of Higher Education and Scientific Research: face à la Cathédrale Sainte-Marie, Conakry; tel. 41-19-01.
Ministry of Justice: face Immeuble 'La Paternelle', Conakry; tel. 45-29-06.
Ministry of Local Government and Decentralization: Conakry; tel. 44-11-06.
Ministry of Mines, Geology and the Environment: BP 295, Conakry; tel. 45-45-26; fax 41-49-13.
Ministry of National Defence: Camp Samory Touré, Conakry; tel. 41-42-44.
Ministry of Planning and Co-operation: Conakry; tel. 41-40-12.
Ministry of Private Sector Promotion, Industry and Trade: blvd du Commerce, Conakry; tel. 44-49-20.
Ministry of Public Health: blvd du Commerce, Conakry; tel. 41-20-32.
Ministry of Social Affairs, Women's Promotion and Children's Affairs: Corniche-Ouest, face au Terminal Conteneurs du Port de Conakry, Conakry; tel. 41-20-15; fax 41-46-60.
Ministry of Technical and Professional Training: face aux Jardins du 2 Octobre, Conakry; tel. 41-44-84.
Ministry of Territorial Administration and Decentralization: près de la Gendarmerie Nationale; Conakry; tel. 41-44-15.
Ministry of Town Planning and Housing: blvd du Commerce, Conakry; tel. 41-32-00.
Ministry of Youth and Sports: ave du Port, Conakry; tel. 44-19-19; fax 41-19-26.

President and Legislature

PRESIDENT
Election, 14 December 1998

Candidate	% of votes
LANSANA CONTÉ (PRP)	56.11
MAMADOU BOYE BÂ (UPR)	24.62
ALPHA CONDÉ (RPG)	16.58
JEAN-MARIE DORÉ (UPG)	1.72
CHARLES-PASCAL TOLNO (PPG)	0.95
Total	100.00

ASSEMBLÉE NATIONALE
Speaker: El Hadj BOUBACAR BIRO DIALLO.
General election, 11 June 1995

Party	Seats
PUP	71
RPG	19
PRP*	9
UNR*	9
UPG	2
Djama	1
PDG—AST	1
PDG—RDA	1
UNP	1
Total	114

* The Parti pour le renouveau et le progrès (PRP) and the Union pour la nouvelle République (UNR) merged in September 1998 to form the Union pour le progrès et le renouveau (UPR).

Advisory Council

Conseil Economique et Social: Immeuble FAWAZ, Corniche Sud, Coléaah, Commune de Matam, BP 2947, Conakry; tel. 45-31-23; fax 45-31-24; f. 1997; 45 mems; Pres. MICHEL KAMANO; Sec.-Gen. MAMADOU BOBO CAMARA.

Political Organizations

There were 46 officially registered parties in mid-2000, of which the following were the most important.
Parti démocratique de Guinée—Ahmed Sekou Touré (PDG—AST): f. 1994, following split from PDG—RDA.
Parti démocratique de Guinée—Rassemblement démocratique africain (PDG—RDA): f. 1946, revived 1992; Leader El Hadj ISMAËL MOHAMED GASSIM GUSHEIN.
Parti Djama: Leader MOHAMED MANSOUR KABA.
Parti du peuple de Guinée (PPG): Leader CHARLES-PASCAL TOLNO.
Parti de l'unité et du progrès (PUP): supports Pres. Conté; Sec.-Gen. ABOUBACAR SOMPAORÉ.
Rassemblement populaire guinéen (RPG): Leaders ALPHA CONDÉ, AHMED TIDIANE CISSÉ.
Union des forces républicaines (UFR): Conakry; f. 1992; social-liberal party; Pres. SIDIYA TOURÉ; Sec.-Gen. BAKARY ZOUMANIGUI.
Union pour le progrès de Guinée (UPG): Sec.-Gen. JEAN-MARIE DORÉ.
Union pour le progrès et le renouveau (UPR): f. 1998 by merger of the Parti pour le renouveau et le progrès and the Union pour la nouvelle République; Pres. SIRADIOU DIALLO.
Union nationale pour le progrès (UNP): Leader PAUL LOUIS FABER.
Note: The **Coordination de l'opposition démocratique (Codem)** was established in July 1995, under the leadership of MAMADOU BOYE BÂ, as an alliance of 12 opposition groups. Leading mems include the UPR and the RPG.

Diplomatic Representation

EMBASSIES IN GUINEA
Algeria: Commune de Kaloum, face Etat Major de la Gendarmerie Nationale, BP 1004, Conakry; tel. 44-15-03; fax 41-15-08.
Canada: Corniche Sud, BP 99, Commune de Matam, Conakry; tel. 46-23-95; fax 41-42-36; Ambassador: DENIS BRIAND.
China, People's Republic: Quartier Donka, Cité Ministérielle, Commune de Dixinn, BP 714, Conakry; tel. 41-48-35; Ambassador: XU MENGSHUI.
Congo, Democratic Republic: Quartier Almamya, ave de la Gare, Commune du Kaloum, BP 880, Conakry; tel. 45-15-01.
Cuba: Corniche-Nord, Coronthie, Commune du Kaloum, BP 71, Conakry; tel. 44-42-68; fax 41-50-76; Ambassador: LUIS DELGADO PÉREZ.
Egypt: Corniche-Sud, près des Abattoirs, Commune de Matam, BP 389, Conakry; tel. 41-23-94.
France: Immeuble Chavanel, blvd du Commerce, BP 570, Conakry; tel. 41-16-05; fax 41-27-08; Ambassador: CHRISTOPHE PHILIBERT.
Germany: 2e blvd, Commune de Kaloum, BP 540, Conakry; tel. 41-15-06; fax 45-22-17; e-mail diplogerma@eti-bull.net; Ambassador: PIUS FISCHER.

Ghana: Immeuble Ex-Urbaine et la Seine, BP 732, Conakry; tel. 44-15-10; Ambassador: Air Vice-Marshal J. E. A. KOTEI.

Guinea-Bissau: Quartier Bellevue, Commune de Dixinn, BP 298, Conakry.

Iran: Commune de Dixinn, BP 310, Conakry; tel. 41-15-98; Ambassador: JAVAD ROWSHAN ZAMIR QOROQI.

Italy: BP 84, Village Camayenne, Conakry; tel. 46-23-32.

Japan: Lanseboundji, Corniche Sud, Commune de Matam, BP 895, Conakry; tel. 41-36-07; fax 41-25-75; Ambassador: KEIICHI KITABAN.

Korea, Democratic People's Republic: BP 723, Conakry; Ambassador: PAK CHANG SUK.

Liberia: Cité Ministérielle, Donka, Commune de Dixinn, BP 18, Conakry; tel. 42-26-71; Ambassador: TARGAN WANTEE.

Libya: Commune de Kaloum, BP 1183, Conakry; tel. 41-41-72.

Mali: La Minière, Commune de Dixinn, BP 299, Conakry; tel. 41-15-39.

Morocco: Cité des Nations, Villa 12, Commune du Kaloum, BP 193, Conakry, tel. 41-36-86; fax 41-38-16.

Nigeria: Corniche Sud, Quartier de Matam, BP 54, Conakry; tel. 41-43-75; Ambassador: PETER N. OYEDELE.

Russia: BP 329, Conakry; tel. 46-37-25; fax 41-27-77; Ambassador: IGOR I. STOUDENNIKOV.

Saudi Arabia: Près de l'hôtel Camayenne, Commune de Dixinn, BP 611, Conakry; tel. 41-24-86.

Senegal: BP 842, Conakry; tel. and fax 44-44-13; Ambassador: MAKHILY GASSAMA.

Sierra Leone: Quartier Bellevue, face aux cases présidentielles, Commune de Dixinn, BP 625, Conakry; tel. 44-50-08; Ambassador: Commdr MOHAMED DIABY.

Togo: ave de la République, Immeuble Kaloum, Commune du Kaloum, BP 3633, Conakry; tel. 41-47-72.

Ukraine: Cité des Nations, Commune du Kaloum, BP 2067, Conakry; tel. 41-47-93; fax 41-47-08.

USA: rue KA 038, Commune du Kaloum, BP 603, Conakry; tel. 41-15-20; fax 41-15-22; e-mail amemconakry.adm@eti-bull.net; internet www.eti-bull.net/usembassy; Ambassador: JOYCE E. LEADER.

Yugoslavia: près du Cinéma la Coléah, Commune de Matam, BP 1154, Conakry; tel. 46-42-65; Ambassador: DANILO MILIĆ.

Judicial System

The Constitution of the Third Republic embodies the principle of the independence of the judiciary, and delineates the competences of each component of the judicial system, including the Higher Magistrates' Council, the Supreme Court, the High Court of Justice and the Magistrature. A restructuring of the judicial system is being undertaken, with international financial and technical support, as part of the programme of structural adjustment.

President of the Supreme Court: LAMINE SIDIMÉ.

Director of Public Prosecutions: ANTOINE IBRAHIM DIALLO.

Note: A State Security Court was established in June 1997, with exceptional jurisdiction to try, 'in times of peace and war', crimes against the internal and external security of the State. Members of the court are appointed by the President of the Republic. There is no constitutional provision for the existence of such a tribunal.

President of the State Security Court: Commdr SAMA PANNIVAL BANGOURA.

Religion

It is estimated that 95% of the population are Muslims and 1.5% Christians.

ISLAM

National Islamic League (NIL): Conakry; f. 1988; Sec.-Gen. El Hadj AHMED TIDIANE TRAORÉ.

CHRISTIANITY

The Anglican Communion

Anglicans in Guinea are adherents of the Church of the Province of West Africa, comprising 12 dioceses. The diocese of Guinea and Guinea-Bissau (as the diocese of Guinea) was established in 1985 as the first French-speaking diocese in the Province. The Archbishop of the Province is the Bishop of Koforidua, Ghana.

Bishop of Guinea and Guinea-Bissau: (vacant), Cathédrale Toussaint, BP 1187, Conakry; tel. 45-13-23.

The Roman Catholic Church

Guinea comprises one archdiocese and two dioceses. At 31 December 1998 Roman Catholics in Guinea comprised about 2.0% of the total population.

Bishops' Conference: Conférence Episcopale de la Guinée, BP 1006 bis, Conakry; tel. and fax 41-32-70; Pres. Most Rev. ROBERT SARAH, Archbishop of Conakry.

Archbishop of Conakry: Most Rev. ROBERT SARAH, Archevêché, BP 2016, Conakry; tel. and fax 41-32-70.

The Press

Regulatory Authority

Conseil National de la Communication (CNC): Conakry; f. 1991; regulates the operations of the press, and of radio and television; regulates political access to the media; nine mems; two meetings each week; Pres. EMILE TOMPAPA.

Newspaper and Periodicals

L'Evénement de Guinée: BP 796, Conakry; tel. 44-33-91; monthly; independent; f. 1993; Dir BOUBACAR SANKARELA DIALLO.

Fonike: BP 341, Conakry; sport and general; Dir IBRAHIMA KALIL DIARE.

Horoya (Liberty): Coléah, BP 191, Conakry; tel. 41-34-75; fax 45-10-16; e-mail horoya@leland-gn.org; govt daily; Dir OUSMANE CAMARA.

L'Indépendant: route du Palais du Peuple, BP 2427, Conakry; tel. 41-57-62; fax 41-43-19; e-mail indepdt@mirinet.net.gn; internet www.mirinet.net.gn/indepdt; weekly; also L'Indépendant Extra; Publr ABOUBACAR SYLLA; Editor-in-Chief ABDOULAYE TOP SYLLA.

Journal Officiel de Guinée: BP 156, Conakry; fortnightly; organ of the Govt.

La Lance: route du Palais du Peuple, BP 2427, Conakry; tel. and fax 41-23-85; e-mail lalance@mirinet.net.gn; internet www.mirinet.net.gn/lynx/lce; weekly; general information; Dir SOULEYMANE DIALLO.

Le Lynx: Immeuble Baldé Zaïre Sandervalia, BP 4968, Conakry; tel. 41-23-85; fax 41-23-85; e-mail le-lynx@mirinet.net.gn; internet www.mirinet.net.gn/lynx; f. 1992; weekly; satirical; Editor SOULEYMAN E. DIALLO.

L'Observateur: Conakry; independent; Dir SEKOU KONE.

L'Oeil: Conakry; independent; weekly; Dir of Publishing ISMAËL BANGOURA.

Le Scribe: 124 rue MO-268, BP 1305, Conakry; tel. 22-75-87; e-mail lescribe@mirinet.net.gn; internet www.mirinet.net.gn/lescribe; f. 1997; evangelical Christian magazine; Dir JOSEPH SOURO CAMARA; Editor-in-Chief PIERRE CAMARA.

3-P Plus (Parole-Plume-Papier); 7e ave Bis Almamyah, BP 5122, Conakry; tel. 45-22-32; fax 45-29-31; e-mail 3p-plus@mirinet.net.gn; internet www.mirinet.net.gn/3p_plus; journal of arts and letters; 6 a year; Dir MOHAMED SALIFOU KEÏTA.

NEWS AGENCY

Agence Guinéenne de Presse: BP 1535, Conakry; tel. 46-54-14; f. 1960; Man. Dir MOHAMED CONDÉ.

PRESS ASSOCIATION

Association Guinéenne des Editeurs de la Presse Indépendante (AGEPI): Conakry; f. 1991; an asscn of independent newspaper publ; Chair. BOUBACAR SANKARELA DIALLO.

Publishers

Editions du Ministère de l'Education Nationale: Direction nationale de la recherche scientifique, BP 561, Conakry; tel. 44-19-50; f. 1959; general and educational; Dir Prof. KANTÉ KABINÉ.

Editions SKK: Conakry; Propr SIDIKI KUBÉLÉ KEITA.

Broadcasting and Communications

TELECOMMUNICATIONS

Regulatory Bodies

Direction Nationale des Postes et Télécommunications: Conakry; tel. 41-40-97; fax 44-20-12; f. 1997; regulates transport, postal and telecommunications services; Dir. KOLY CAMARA.

Comité National de Coordination des Télécommunications (CNCT): BP 5000, Conakry; tel. 41-40-79; fax 41-20-28; Exec. Sec. SEKOU BANGOURA.

Service Providers

Société des Télécommunications de Guinée (SOTELGUI): 4e Blvd, BP 2066, Conakry; tel. 41-12-12; f. 1993; privatized 1995; internet www.leland-gn.org; 60% owned by Telkom Malaysia; 40% state-owned; also provides mobile cellular services; Man. JEAN-BAPTISTE KANTARA.

Spacetel Guinée SA: Conakry; f. 1994; mobile cellular telephone operator; operates with a range of 50km around Conakry; 5,000 subscribers (1998).

Télécel-Guinea SA: Conakry; tel. 41-33-44; f. 1994; mobile cellular telephone operator; 60% owned by Télécel International; 40% owned by Guinean investors; operates with a range of 50km around Conakry; 900 subscribers (1997).

Wireless International: Conakry; mobile cellular telephone operator; operating licence pending.

BROADCASTING
Regulatory Authority

Conseil National de la Communication (CNC): see above.

Radio

Radiodiffusion-Télévision Guinéenne (RTG): BP 391, Conakry; tel. 44-22-05; broadcasts in French, English, Créole-English, Portuguese, Arabic and local languages; Dir-Gen. JUSTIN MOREL.

The establishment of a network of rural radio stations is in progress.

Television

Radiodiffusion-Télévision Guinéenne (RTG): (see Radio); transmissions in French and local languages.

Finance

(cap. = capital; res = reserves; m. = million; brs = branches; amounts in Guinean francs)

BANKING
Central Bank

Banque Centrale de la République de Guinée (BCRG): 12 blvd du Commerce, BP 692, Conakry; tel. 41-26-51; fax 41-48-98; f. 1960; bank of issue; Gov. IBRAHIMA CHÉRIF BAH; Dep. Gov. FODÉ SOUMAH.

Commercial Banks

Banque Internationale pour le Commerce et l'Industrie de la Guinée (BICI—GUI): ave de la République, BP 1484, Conakry; tel. 41-45-15; fax 41-39-62; f. 1985; 51% state-owned; cap. and res 15,830m., total assets 197,815m. (Dec. 1998); transfer to private ownership pending; Pres. IBRAHIMA SOUMAH; Man. Dir JEAN-PIERRE BAJON-ARNAL; 11 brs.

Banque Populaire Maroco-Guinéenne (BPMG): Immeuble SCIM, ave de la République, BP 4400, Conakry 1; tel. 41-23-60; fax 41-32-61; f. 1991; 35% owned by Crédit Populaire du Maroc (Morocco), 20% state-owned, cap. and res 708m., total assets 28,345m. (Dec. 1996); Dir AMRANI SIDI MOHAMED; 3 brs.

Ecobank Guinée: BP 5687, Conakry; tel. 45-58-77; fax 45-42-41; e-mail ecobank@mirinet-net.com; activities commenced 1999; wholly owned by Ecobank Transnational Inc. (operating under the auspices of the Economic Community of West African States); Man. Dir KUMLAN ADJARHO OWEH.

First American Bank of Guinea: Blvd du Commerce, angle 9ème Ave, BP 4540, Conakry; tel. 41-34-32; fax 41-35-29; f. 1994; jt-owned by Mitan Capital Ltd, Grand Cayman and El Hadj Haidara Abdourahmane Chérif, Mali.

International Commercial Bank: 4e ave Boulbinet, K.A. 020, Bât. 346, BP 3547, Conakry; tel. 41-25-89; fax 41-25-92.

Société Générale de Banques en Guinée: ave de la République, BP 1514, Conakry 1; tel. 41-17-46; fax 41-25-65; f. 1985; 34% owned by Société Générale (France); cap. and res 7,892m., total assets 101,555m. (Dec. 1998); Pres. ROGER SERVONNET; Man. Dir JEAN-CLAUDE ROBERT.

Union Internationale de Banque en Guinée (UIBG): 6e ave, angle 5e blvd, BP 324, Conakry; tel. 41-43-09; fax 41-42-77; f. 1987; 68% owned by Crédit Lyonnais Global Banking (France); cap. and res 2,224m., total assets 36,726m. (Dec. 1998); Pres. ALPHA AMADOU DIALLO; Man. Dir CHARLES ROSSNER.

Islamic Bank

Banque Islamique de Guinée: Immeuble Nafaya, ave de la République, BP 1247, Conakry; tel. 41-50-86; fax 41-50-71; e-mail bigconakry@eti-bull.net; f. 1983; 68.5% owned by Dar al-Maal al-Islami (DMI Trust); cap. and res 1,514m., total assets 21,046m. (Dec. 1998); Pres. ADERRAOUF BENESSAIAH; Man. Dir ABDELMAJID BENJELLOUN.

INSURANCE

Société Guinéenne d'Assurance Mutuelle (SOGAM): Conakry; tel. 41-50-57; fax 41-25-57.

Société Nouvelle d'Assurance de Guinée (SONAG): BP 3363, Conakry; tel. 41 49 77; fax 41-43-03.

Union Guinéenne d'Assurances et de Réassurances (UGAR): Place des Martyrs, BP 179, Conakry; tel. 41-48-41; fax 41-17-11; f. 1989; 40% owned by AXA (France), 35% state-owned; cap. 2,000m.; Man. Dir RAPHAËL Y. TOURÉ.

Trade and Industry
GOVERNMENT AGENCIES

Centre de Promotion et de Développement Minier (CPDM): BP 295, Conakry; tel. 41-15-44; fax 41-49-13; e-mail cpdm@mirinet.net.gn; f. 1995; promotes investment and co-ordinates devt strategy in mining sector; Dir MORCIRÉ SYLLA.

Entreprise Nationale Import-Export (IMPORTEX): BP 152, Conakry; tel. 44-28-13; state-owned import and export agency; Dir MAMADOU BOBO DIENG.

Office de Promotion des Investissements Privés (OPIP): BP 2024, Conakry; tel. 41-49-85; fax 41-39-90; internet www.mirinet.net.gn/opip; f. 1992; promotes private investment; Dir BEN YALLA SYLLA.

DEVELOPMENT ORGANIZATIONS

Agence Française de Développement (AFD): 5e ave, Conakry; tel. 41-25-69; fax 41-28-74; e-mail 3621/debroisee@afd.fr; fmrly Caisse Française de Développement; Dir in Guinea EMMANUEL DEBROISE.

Mission Française de Coopération: Conakry; administers bilateral aid; Dir in Guinea ANDRÉ BAILLEUL.

CHAMBERS OF COMMERCE

Chambre d'Agriculture de Guinée: Conakry; tel. 42-28-81.

Chambre de Commerce, d'Industrie et d'Artisanat de Guinée: BP 545, Conakry; tel. 46-42-16; fax 41-42-17; f. 1985; Pres. OUSMANE BALDE; Sec.-Gen. MOHAMED SAID FOFANA; 70 mems.

Chambre Economique de Guinée: BP 609, Conakry.

TRADE AND EMPLOYERS' ASSOCIATIONS

Association des Commercants de Guinée: BP 2468, Conakry; tel. 41-30-37; fax 45-31-66; Sec.-Gen. OUMAR CAMARA.

Association des Femmes Entrepreneurs de Guinee (AFEG): BP 790, Conakry; fax 41-32-06.

Conseil National du Patronat Guinéen: c/o Hann & Cie, BP 431, Conakry; tel. 41-36-51; fax 44-37-12; Pres. MAMADOU SYLLA.

Fédération Patronale de l'Agriculture et de l'Elévage (FEPAE): BP 5684, Conakry; tel. 22-95-56; fax 41-54-36; Pres. MAMDOU SYLLA; Sec.-Gen. MAMADY CAMARA.

Groupement des Importateurs Guinéens (GIG): BP 970, Conakry; tel. 42-18-18; fax 42-19-19; Pres. FERNAND BANGOURA.

UTILITIES
Electricity

Barrage Hydroélectrique de Garafiri: BP 1770, Conakry; tel. 41-50-91.

Entreprise Nationale d'Electricité de Guinée (ENELGUI): BP 322, Conakry; tel. 41-42-43; fax 41-17-51; production of electricity; Man. Dir BOKARY SYLLA.

Société Guinéenne d'Electricité (SOGEL): Conakry; f. 1994; majority ownership held jtly by Hydro-Québec (Canada), Electricité de France and SAUR (France), 33% owned by ENELGUI; production, transport and distribution of electricity.

Water

Service National d'Aménagement des Points d'Eau (SNAPE): BP 2064, Conakry; tel. 41-18-93; fax 41-50-58.

Société d'Exploitation des Eaux de Guinée (SEG): BP 446, Conakry; tel. 41-43-67; fax 41-43-69.

Société Nationale des Eaux de Guinée (SONEG): BP 825, Conakry; tel. and fax 41-43-81; f. 1988; national water co.

MAJOR COMPANIES

The following are among the largest companies in terms either of capital investment or employment.

Alumina Company of Guinea Ltd (ACG-GUINEA): BP 1762, Conakry; f. 1999 to replace Friguia (f. 1957); 100% govt-owned;

mining of bauxite and production of alumina; technical and management agreement with Reynolds Metal Co. (USA).

AREDOR-Guinée: BP 1218, Conakry; tel. 44-31-12. 1981 (as Association pour la recherche et l'exploitation de diamants et de l'or); operations suspended 1994, restructured 1996; cap. US $8m.; 85% owned by First City Mining Ltd; diamond mining and gold; 1,200 employees.

BONAGUI: Z.I. Matoto, BP 3009, Conakry; tel. 41-18-92; fax 41-24-91; f. 1986; cap. 2,607m. FG; privately owned; soft-drinks bottling factory. Man. ERIC BOULANGER; 147 employees.

Ciments de Guinée: Route de Kindia, Km 30, BP 3621, Conakry 2; tel. 41-45-12; fax 41-45-13; one cement plant (Sinfonia) with annual production capacity of 300,000 metric tons; owned by Holderbank (Switzerland), Man. Dir PATRICK VANDERESSE.

Compagnie des Bauxites de Guinée: BP 523, Conakry; tel. 41-12-13; fax 41-28-14; f. 1964; cap. US $2m.; 49% state-owned, 51% owned by Halco (Mining) Inc (a consortium of interests from USA, Canada, France, Germany and Australia); bauxite mining at Boké; Pres. JOHN L. PERVOLA; Vice-Pres. G. COKER; 2,796 employees.

Compagnie des Eaux Minérales de Guinée: Conakry; f. 1987; owned by Cie générale des eaux (France); mineral water bottling plant.

FFA Ernst & Young: BP 1762, Conakry; tel. 41-28-31; fax 44-59-77; e-mail ffaeygui@leland-gn.org; f. 1987; Dir CHRISTIAN MION.

Mobil Oil (Guinea): autoroute Fidel Castro, Commune de Matam, BP 305, Conakry; tel. 46-52-74; fax 78-93-78; petroleum and gas exploration and distribution; owned by ExxonMobil Corpn (USA); Gen. Man. AYITE AMOUZOU KODJO.

Nimba International Mining Co (Nimco): BP 837, Conakry; tel. 41-30-68; fax 41-50-04; f. 1990; undergoing restructuring in 1999; cap. US $120m.; development of high-grade iron deposit at Mt Nimba.

Office de Développement de la Pêche artisanale et de l'Aquaculture en Guinée (ODEPAG): 6 ave de la République, BP 1581; Conakry; tel. 44-19-48; development of fisheries and fish-processing.

Shell de Guinée: BP 312, Conakry; tel. 46-37-37; fax 46-49-12; e-mail corporate@csgcky.simis.com; distribution of petroleum products; owned by Royal Dutch Shell; Dir-Gen. CHRISTOPHE BOULANGER

Société d'Aquaculture de Koba (SAKOBA): BP 4834, Conakry; tel. 44-24-75; fax 41-46-43; f. 1991; 49% state-owned, 51% owned by private Guinean and French interests; prawn-farming venture with a planned annual capacity of 1,300 metric tons of frozen shrimps for export by 1997; 700 employees; Mans SEPIA International (France).

Société Ashanti Goldfields de Guinée (SAG): BP 1006, Conakry; tel. 41-58-09; fax 41-15-45; e-mail danso@leland-gn.org; f. 1985 as Société Aurifère de Guinée, name changed 1997; cap. US $20m.; 70% owned by Ashanti Goldfields Co Ltd (Ghana); gold prospecting and exploitation at Koron.

Société des Bauxites de Dabola-Tougué (SBDT): BP 2859, Conakry; tel. and fax 41-47-21; f. 1992; owned jtly by Govts of Guinea and Iran; bauxite mining at Dabola and Tougué; Dir-Gen. A. SAADATI.

Société des Bauxites de Kindia (SBK): BP 613, Conakry; tel. 41-38-28; fax 41-38-29; f 1969, as Office des Bauxites de Kindia (a jt-venture with the USSR), production began 1974; named changed 1992; owned by Nikolaev (Ukraine); bauxite mining at Debélé; Man. Dir IBRAHIMA BAH; 1,700 employees.

Société Guinéenne des Hydrocarbures (SGH): BP 892, Conakry; tel. 46-12-56; f. 1980; 50% state-owned; research into and exploitation of offshore petroleum reserves.

Société Guinénne de Lubrifs et d'Emballages (SOGUILUBE): BP 709, Conakry; tel. 44-25-33; fax 44-49-92; blends lubricants; owned by Royal Dutch Shell.

Société Guinéenne de Pêche (SOGUIPECHE): Conakry; f. 1987; 51% state-owned, 49% owned by Jego-Query (France); fishing and processing of fish products.

Société Guinéo-Arabe d'Alumine: BP 554, Conakry; f. 1975 by Guinean govt and six Arab govts; to open and develop production of aluminium at Ayekoe; estimated production 1m. tons annually.

Société Libyo-Guinéenne pour le Développement Agricole et Agro-industriel (SALGUIDIA): BP 622, Conakry; 44-31-34; fax 41-13-09; cap. 15m. FG; f. 1997; fmrly Société Industrielle des Fruits Africains; fruit growing (pineapples, grapefruit, oranges and mangoes); fruit canning and juice extracting; marketing.

Société Minière de Dinguiraye: BP 2162, Conakry; tel. 46-36-81; fax 46-35-73; e-mail smd.gui@eti-bull.net; 85% owned by Delta Gold Mining—owned by Kenor ASA (Norway); exploitation of gold deposits at Karta Mine, nr Léro and devt of other areas of Dinguiraye concession; Man. Dir PETER CONNERY.

Société Minière et de Participation Guinée-Alusuisse: Conakry; f. 1971; owned by Guinean govt and Alusuisse (Switzer-land); to establish bauxite mine and aluminium smelter at Tougué; estimated production of bauxite 8m. metric tons annually.

Société de Pêche de Kamsar (SOPEKAM): Kamsar Free Zone; f. 1984; 40% state-owned, 40% Universal Marine & Shark Products (USA); fishing and processing of fish products; fleet of 18 fishing vessels.

TGH Plus SA: BP 1562, Conakry; tel. 46-40-01; fax 46-49-12; f. 1993; natural gas distribution; private co; Chair. BAH ALIMOU YALI; Man. Dir DIALLO SAIKOU OUMAR.

Total Guinée: BP 306, Conakry; tel. 41-50-35; fax 45-49-17; f. 1988 as Société Guinnéenne des Carburants; storage of petroleum products.

TRADE UNION

Confédération des travailleurs de Guinée (CTG): BP 237, Conakry; f. 1984; Sec.-Gen. Dr MOHAMED SAMBA KÉBÉ.

Transport

RAILWAYS

There are 662 km of 1-m gauge track from Conakry to Kankan in the east of the country, crossing the Niger at Kouroussa. The line is to be upgraded over two years: the contract for the first phase was awarded to a Slovak company in early 1997. Three lines for the transport of bauxite link Sangaredi with the port of Kamsar in the west, via Boké, and Conakry with Kindia and Fria, a total of 383 km. In late 1996 the Government of Iran announced its intention to construct a railway linking the Dabola-Tougué bauxite deposits with Conakry: the preliminary contract was secured by Slovak State Railways. Plans exist for the eventual use of a line linking the Nimba iron-ore deposits with the port of Buchanan in Liberia.

Office National des Chemins de Fer de Guinée (ONCFG): BP 589, Conakry; tel. 44-46-13; fax 41-35-77; f. 1905; Man. Dir MOREL MARGUERITE CAMARA.

    Chemin de Fer de Boké: BP 523, Boké; operations commenced 1973.

    Chemin de Fer Conakry–Fria: BP 334, Conakry; operations commenced 1960; Gen. Man. A. CAMARA.

    Chemin de Fer de la Société des Bauxites de Kindia: BP 613, Conakry; tel. 41-38-28; operations commenced 1974; Gen. Man. K. KEITA.

ROADS

In 1996 there were an estimated 30,500 km of roads, including 4,300 km of main roads and 7,960 km of secondary roads; about 5,030 km of the road network were paved. An 895-km cross-country road links Conakry to Bamako, in Mali, and the main highway connecting Dakar (Senegal) to Abidjan (Côte d'Ivoire) also crosses Guinea. The road linking Conakry to Freetown (Sierra Leone) forms part of the Trans West African Highway, extending from Morocco to Nigeria.

La Guinéenne-Marocaine des Transports (GUIMAT): Conakry; f. 1989; owned jtly by Govt of Guinea and Hakkam (Morocco); operates national and regional transport services.

Société Générale des Transports de Guinée (SOGETRAG): Conakry; f. 1984; 63% state-owned; bus operator.

SHIPPING

Conakry and Kamsar are the international seaports. Conakry handled 3.9m. metric tons of foreign trade in 1999, while in 1994 some 12m. tons of bauxite were transported to Kamsar for shipment.

GETMA SA: 60 blvd du Commerce, BP 1648, Conakry; tel. 41-42-78; fax 41-42-73; e-mail getma-gui@eti-bull.net; marine transportation.

Port Autonome de Conakry: BP 715, Conakry; tel. 44-27-37.

Société Navale Guinéenne (SNG): BP 522, Conakry; tel. 44-29-55; fax 41-39-70; f. 1968; state-owned; shipping agents; Dir-Gen. NOUNKÉ KEITA.

SOAEM; blvd du Commerce, BP 3177, Conakry; tel. 41-25-90; fax 41-20-25.

SOTRAMAR: Kamsar; f. 1971; exports bauxite from mines at Boké through port of Kamsar.

CIVIL AVIATION

There is an international airport at Conakry-Gbessia, and smaller airfields at Labé, Kankan and Faranah. Facilities at Conakry have been upgraded, at a cost of US $42.6m.; the airport handled some 290,000 passengers in 1997.

Air Dabia: 7e Ave, Almamya, Conakry; tel. 45-39-05; fax 45-35-27; private; two weekly flights to Banjul, The Gambia.

Guinée Air Service: Aéroport Conakry-Gbessia; tel. 41-27-61.

Guinée Inter Air: Aéroport Conakry-Gbessia; tel. 41-37-08.

Nouvelle Air Guinée: 6 ave de la République, BP 12, Conakry; tel. 44-46-02; f. 1960; transfer pending to one-third private ownership; regional and internal services; Dir-Gen. El Hadj NFA MOUSSA DIANE.

Société de Gestion et d'Exploitation de l'Aéroport de Conakry (SOGEAC): Conakry; f. 1987; manages Conakry-Gbessia international airport; 51% state-owned.

Tourism

Some 23,000 tourists visited Guinea in 1998; receipts from tourism in 1997 totalled US $5m. Under a major tourism development project announced in 1995, 186 tourist sites were to be renovated, and access to them improved, and it was planned to increase the number of hotel beds from less than 800 to 25,000 by 1999.

Office Nationale du Tourisme: Immeuble al-Iman, 6e ave de la République, BP 1275, Conakry; tel. 45-51-63; fax 45-51-64; e-mail ontour@leland-gn.org; internet www.mirinet.net.gn/ont; f. 1997; Dir-Gen. IBRAHIM A. DIALLO.

Defence

In August 1999 Guinea's active armed forces numbered 9,700, comprising an army of 8,500, a navy of 400 and an air force of 800.

Paramilitary forces comprised a republican guard of 1,600 and a 1,000-strong gendarmerie, as well as a reserve 'people's militia' of 7,000. Military service is compulsory (conscripts were estimated at some 7,500 in 1998) and lasts for two years.

Defence Expenditure: Budgeted at 75,000m. FG in 1999.

Chief of Staff of Armed Forces: Col KERFALA CAMARA.

Education

Education is provided free of charge at every level in state institutions. Primary education, which begins at seven years of age and lasts for six years, is officially compulsory. In 1997, however, enrolment at primary schools was equivalent to only 54% of children in the relevant age-group (males 68%; females 41%). Secondary education, from the age of 13, lasts for seven years, comprising a first cycle (collège) of four years and a second (lycée) of three years. Enrolment at secondary schools in 1997 was equivalent to only 14% of children in the appropriate age-group (males 20%; females 7%). There are universities at Conakry and Kankan, and other tertiary institutions at Maneah, Boké and Faranah. In 1993, according to the national literary service, the average rate of adult illiteracy was 72% (males 61%; females 83%). UNESCO estimates put average illiteracy at 64.1% in 1995 (males 50.0%; females 78.0%). Budget estimates for 1997 allocated 67,400m. FG to education (equivalent to 9.2% of total budgetary expenditure).

Bibliography

Adamolekun, L. *Sekou Touré's Guinea*. London, Methuen, 1976.

Ameillon, B. *La Guinée, bilan d'une indépendance*. Paris, Maspero, 1964.

Arulpragasam, J., and Sahn, D. E. *Economic Transition in Guinea: Implications for Growth and Poverty*. New York, New York University Press, 1997.

Binns, M. *Guinea*. Oxford, Clio Press, 1996.

Canale, J. S. *La République de Guinée*. Paris, Editions Sociales, 1970.

Dhada, M. *Warriors at Work: How Guinea was Set Free*. Niwot, University Press of Colorado, 1994.

Diallo, A. *Le mort de Diallo Telli*. Paris, Editions Karthala, 1983.

Dicko, A. A. *Journal d'une défaite: autour du référendum du 28 septembre 1958 en Afrique noire*. Paris, L'Harmattan, 1992.

Europe Outremer. *La Guinée d'aujourd'hui*. Paris, 1979.

Hair, P. E. H., Jones, A., and Law, R. *Barbot on Guinea*. London, the Hakluyt Society, 1992.

Kake, I. B. *Sekou Touré, le héros et le tyran*. Paris, Jeune Afrique Livres, 1987.

Keita, S. K. *Ahmed Sekou Touré, l'homme et son combat anticolonial (1922–58)*. Conakry, Editions SKK, 1998.

Lewin, A. *La Guinée*. Paris, Presses Universitaires de France, 1984.

O'Toole, T. E. *Historical Dictionary of Guinea*. Metuchen, NJ, Scarecrow Press, 1988.

Rimmer, D. *The Economies of West Africa*. London, Weidenfeld and Nicolson, 1984.

Rivière, C. *Guinea: The Mobilization of a People* (trans. by Thompson, V., and Adloff, R.). Ithaca, NY, Cornell University Press, 1977.

Soriba Camara, S. *La Guinée sans la France*. Paris, Presse de la Fondation nationale des sciences politiques, 1977.

Touré, S. *L'expérience guinéenne et l'unité africaine*. Paris, Présence africaine, 1959.

L'action politique du parti démocratique en Guinée. Conakry, 1962.

GUINEA-BISSAU

Physical and Social Geography

RENÉ PÉLISSIER

The Republic of Guinea-Bissau is bounded on the north by Senegal and on the east and south by the Republic of Guinea. Its territory includes a number of coastal islets, together with the offshore Bissagos or Bijagós archipelago, which comprises 18 main islands. The capital is Bissau.

The country covers an area of 36,125 sq km (13,948 sq miles), including some low-lying ground which is periodically submerged at high tide. Except for some higher terrain (rising to about 300 m above sea-level), close to the border with Guinea, the relief consists of a coastal plain deeply indented by *rias*, which facilitate internal communications, and a transition plateau, forming the *planalto* de Bafatá in the centre, and the *planalto* de Gabú, which abuts on the Fouta Djallon.

The country's main physical features are its meandering rivers and wide estuaries, where it is difficult to distinguish mud, mangrove and water from solid land. The principal rivers are the Cacheu, also known as Farim on part of its course, the Mansôa, the Geba and Corubal complex, the Rio Grande and, close to the Guinean southern border, the Cacine. Ocean-going vessels of shallow draught can reach most of the main population centres, and there is access by flat-bottomed vessels to nearly all significant outposts except in the north-eastern sector.

The climate is tropical, hot and wet with two seasons. The rainy season lasts from mid-May to November and the dry season from December to April. April and May are the hottest months, with temperatures ranging from 20°C to 38°C, and December and January are the coldest, with temperatures ranging from 15°C to 33°C. Rainfall is abundant (1,000–2,000 mm per year in the north), and excessive on the coast. The interior is savannah or light savannah woodland, while coastal reaches are covered with mangrove swamps, rain forest and tangled forest.

The first official census since independence, conducted in April 1979, recorded a population of 753,313. At the census of December 1991 the National Census and Statistics Institute enumerated the population at 983,367. According to UN estimates, the total was 1,161,000 at mid-1998. The main population centre is Bissau, which had 197,610 inhabitants at the 1991 census. Bafatá, Bolama, Farim, Cantchungo, Mansôa, Gabú, Catió and Bissorã are the other important towns. Prior to the war of independence, the main indigenous groups were the Balante (about 32% of the population), the Fulani or Fula (22%), the Mandyako (14.5%), the Malinké or Mandingo (13%), and the Pepel (7%). The non-Africans were mainly Portuguese civil servants and traders, and Syrian and Lebanese traders. Although Portuguese is the official language, a Guinean *crioulo* is the lingua franca. In 1990–95, according to UN estimates, the average life expectancy at birth was 41.8 years for men and 45.2 years for women.

Recent History

LUISA HANDEM PIETTE

Revised for this edition by the Editor

The campaign for independence in Portuguese Guinea (now the Republic of Guinea-Bissau) began in the 1950s with the formation of the Partido Africano da Independência da Guiné e Cabo Verde (PAIGC), under the leadership of Amílcar Cabral. Armed resistance began in the early 1960s, and by 1972 the PAIGC was in control of two-thirds of the country. In January 1973 Cabral was assassinated by PAIGC dissidents. The subsequent escalation of hostilities prompted the deployment of some 40,000 Portuguese troops. Guinea-Bissau unilaterally declared its independence from Portugal on 24 September 1973 under the presidency of Luis Cabral, the brother of Amílcar Cabral. The heavy losses sustained by the Portuguese in 1973–74 have been cited as a contributory factor in the military *coup d'état* in Portugal in April 1974. In August Portugal withdrew its forces from Guinea-Bissau and on 10 September it recognized the country's independence. Guinea-Bissau became a single party state governed by the PAIGC. The party introduced measures to lay the foundations for a socialist state. However, the government adopted a non-aligned stance in its foreign relations, receiving military aid from the Eastern bloc and economic assistance from Western countries and Arab states. Friendly relations with Portugal were renewed.

By 1980, however, Guinea-Bissau's economic condition had deteriorated, owing partly to drought, but also to the policies of Cabral. Agricultural output had fallen below pre-independence levels, the state-controlled retail network had proved inadequate, and the country's meagre economic resources were being deployed in projects of questionable utility.

Until 1980, the PAIGC supervised both Cape Verde and Guinea-Bissau, the two constitutions remaining separate, but with a view to eventual unification. These arrangements were abruptly terminated by Cape Verde in November 1980, when Cabral was overthrown by the prime minster, João Bernardo Vieira, and a military-dominated revolutionary council took control of government.

VIEIRA AND THE PAIGC, 1980–99

The period following the 1980 coup was one of considerable political ferment, with major shifts in the leadership, although President Vieira remained the dominant force. The unrest was attended by further economic decline, which prompted Vieira to bring some former opponents of the regime into the government, and to recruit Portuguese-trained civil servants into the bureaucracy.

In May 1982 Vieira postponed forthcoming elections and assumed the portfolios of defence and security in a cabinet reshuffle. Vítor Saúde Maria, vice-chairman of the ruling council of the revolution and former minister of foreign affairs, was appointed prime minister. A struggle ensued for primacy between Vieira and Saúde Maria. The issue was eventually decided in Vieira's favour, and in March 1984 Saúde Maria sought asylum in the Portuguese embassy, and several of his political associates were expelled from the PAIGC.

A new constitution was introduced in May 1984, following elections to a new legislative assembly. A government reshuffle ensued, which reduced the number of ministers and brought into office a number of younger and better-trained officials. The overall effect of these changes was to consolidate the position of Vieira as head of state, chief of government, c-in-c of the armed forces and head of the PAIGC, and to assemble a government in which the emphasis was placed on economic competence.

In November 1985 the first vice-president, Col Paulo Correia, and several senior army officers were arrested for allegedly attempting to lead a coup. In July 1986 six people, accused of involvement in the alleged conspiracy, were reported to have died in prison. Later in the same month, 12 of those arrested were condemned to death, and 41 were sentenced to hard labour. Correia and five others were executed, but the remaining six had their death sentences commuted, following international appeals for clemency. In order to discourage the creation of personal power-bases, Vieira replaced a number of multi-functional ministries with smaller administrative portfolios. In December 1988 four of those imprisoned following the 1985 attempted coup were released under an amnesty. All the remaining prisoners had been released by January 1990.

Economic liberalization was accelerated in the late 1980s. In August 1986 the government abolished trading restrictions and allowed private traders to import and export goods. At the fourth PAIGC congress, held in November, Vieira introduced further proposals to reduce state controls over trade and the economy, and to increase foreign investment. These moves were supported by the congress, which re-elected him as secretary-general of the PAIGC for a further four years. In 1987 the government and the World Bank agreed on a structural adjustment programme which included further liberalization measures for the economy. These were accompanied by a restructuring of the state investment programme and a reduction in levels of public-sector employment, and were followed by a 41% devaluation of the Guinea peso. Although Vieira promised that the domestic effects of the latter would be offset by government subsidies on essential commodities, political tension increased, amid rumours that about 20 army officers had been arrested for plotting against the president.

In early 1989 it was announced that the PAIGC had set up a six-member constitutional revision commission. Regional elections were held in early June, at which all candidates were nominated by the PAIGC. The electoral commission reported a 95.8% turnout of eligible voters, although this figure was disputed by other sources. The 473 councillors convened in mid-June to elect the national assembly, which in turn elected the council of state. Vieira was confirmed as president for a second five-year term. In January 1990 Vieira announced the formation of two commissions to review, respectively, the programme and statutes of the PAIGC and the laws on land ownership, in preparation for the fifth PAIGC congress, due to be held in November. The government was reshuffled in March.

Constitutional Transition

In April 1990, from its base in Lisbon, an emigré opposition group, the Resistência da Guiné-Bissau–Movimento Bafatá (RGB–MB), proposed political negotiations with the PAIGC, with the implied threat that civil war might ensue should its demands for reform not be met. Shortly afterwards, in the wake of mounting international pressure for political democratization, Vieira gave approval in principle to the introduction of a multi-party political system. It was stated that the necessary constitutional amendments would be implemented in late 1990, following a special congress of the PAIGC, and that the next presidential election, due in 1994, could be contested by two or more candidates. In June 1990 another external opposition movement, the Frente da Luta para a Libertação da Guiné (FLING), demanded an immediate conference of all political parties. In August Vieira informed a meeting of the PAIGC central committee that members of the national assembly would in future be elected by universal adult suffrage. A national conference on the transition to democracy was held in October, attended by 350 representatives of the government, the ruling party and private organizations. The conference voted in favour of the holding of a national referendum on the nature of political reforms to be introduced. There was also support for the establishment of a transitional government to oversee the democratization process, and for the abolition of the PAIGC's political monopoly.

Rumours of an attempted coup were widespread in November and December 1990, although these were consistently denied by the government. Vieira returned early from a visit to Taiwan at the beginning of November, cancelling a planned trip to Japan; some observers linked his return to the flight to Portugal of Saúde Maria, the former prime minister, and the former armed forces minister, Umaru Djalo, where they obtained political asylum.

At an extraordinary conference of the PAIGC, which opened in January 1991, Vieira confirmed that the transition to a multi-party system would be completed by 1993, when a presidential election would be held. During the transitional period, the armed forces would become independent of the PAIGC, and the party would cease to be the country's dominant social and political force.

Constitutional amendments, formally terminating single-party rule, were approved unanimously by the national assembly in May 1991. The reforms terminated the PAIGC's role as the leading political force and Vieira indicated that legislative elections would be held before 1993. The new arrangements also severed the link between the party and the armed forces, and guaranteed the operation of a free-market economy. To prevent the formation of regionally-based or separatist organizations, it was stipulated that new parties seeking registration must obtain at least 100 signatures from each of the nine provinces, with a total of 2,000 signatures required for registration; these regulations were revised in August, when the numbers of signatures required were halved to 50 and 1,000 respectively. A number of opposition parties were created following the introduction of the legislation. The Frente Democrática Social (FDS), set up clandestinely in 1990 and led by Rafael Barbosa, split into two factions in mid-1991: the Frente Democrática (FD), led by Aristides Menezes, and the Partido Unido Social Democrático (PUSD), led by Saúde Maria. In November the FD became the first party to be legalized by the supreme court, formally ending 17 years of one-party politics.

The PAIGC met in December 1991 to discuss its strategy for the first democratic elections. As part of this process, Vieira extensively reshuffled the cabinet in late December. The post of prime minister, which had been abolished in May 1984, was revived with the appointment of Carlos Correia to the position. Other cabinet changes included the appointment of Samba Lamine Mane as minister of defence and of João Cruz Pinto as minister of justice. In addition Vieira relinquished the post of minister of the interior to Abubacar Baldè. Filinto de Barros was appointed minister of finance. The reshuffle included the removal of Col Camara, the first vice-president, who had been accused of involvement in smuggling of arms to separatist guerrillas in Senegal's southern Casamance region.

Three further opposition parties were registered in December 1991 and January 1992: the Resistência da Guiné-Bissau–Movimento Bah-Fatah (RGB–MB) (the party changed its name prior to legalization, from Resistência da Guiné-Bissau–Movimento Bafatá, owing to a constitutional ban on parties with names connoting regional or tribal affiliation), led by Domingos Fernandes Gomes, the FDS, and the PUSD. Three other parties had yet to achieve recognition and another was formed in January, following a further split in the FDS: the Partido para a Renovação Social (PRS), led by former FDS vice-chairman Koumba Yala. In late January, four opposition parties: the RGB–MB, FDS, PUSD and the Partido da Convergência Democrática (PCD), led by Vítor Mandinga, agreed to set up a 'democratic forum' for consultations. They demanded that the government dissolve the political police and cease using state facilities for political purposes. They also called for a revision of press law, free access to media, the creation of an electoral commission and the declaration of election dates in consultation with all the opposition parties.

An opposition demonstration, the first to be permitted by the government, was held in Bissau in March 1992, attended by an estimated 30,000 people. Following a meeting in the same month of the PAIGC national council, it was announced that presidential and legislative elections would take place in November and December, respectively. The meeting also elected Manuel Saturnino da Costa as the new permanent secretary to the party's central committee, replacing Vasco Cabral, who had held the post since 1987. Following a second application for official recognition, the FLING was legalized in May. In that month a dissident group known as the 'Group of 121' broke away from the PAIGC to form a new party, the Partido de Renovação e Desenvolvimento (PRD), led by João da Costa, a former minister of health under Luis Cabral. The PRD called for the establishment of a transitional government pending democratic elections and for the dissolution of the political police. In mid-May the leader of the RGB–MB, Domingo Fernandes, returned from a six year exile in Portugal. Following his return Fernandes and the leaders of the FD, PCD, FDS and the PUSD met Vieira to discuss the political reform programme. As a result of the talks it was decided that commissions would be set up to oversee and facilitate the organization of the forthcoming elections.

In July 1992 the leader and founder of the FLING, François Kankoila Mendy, returned to Guinea-Bissau after 40 years in exile. In the following month, in response to opposition demands for the establishment of a national conference to oversee the transition to multi-party democracy, Vieira inaugurated the Comissão Multipartidária de Transição (Multi-party Transition Commission), charged with drafting legislation in preparation for democratic elections. All officially recognized parties were to be represented on the commission, although it was boycotted by the recently recognized Partido Democrático do Progresso (PDP), led by Amine Michel Saad, which alleged that the commission's work would be biased in favour of the PAIGC. Several other political parties were given legal status during the second half of 1992; these included the PRD, the Movimento para a Unidade e a Democracia (MUDE), led by former education minister Filinto Vaz Martins, and the PRS.

In October 1992 Vieira again reshuffled the council of ministers, dismissing eight ministers who had served in the cabinet since the country's independence in 1974. Other changes included the establishment of a new ministry of territorial administration, replacing the three resident ministries for the provinces.

In November 1992 the government announced that the presidential and legislative elections, scheduled for that month, were to be postponed until March 1993. The delay arose from a disagreement concerning the sequence in which the two sets of elections should be held; contrary to government proposals, the opposition parties insisted that the legislative elections take place prior to the presidential elections.

Legislation preparing for the transition to a pluralist democracy was approved by the national assembly in February 1993, and in the following month a four-member commission was appointed to supervise the forthcoming elections. However, reports in mid-March of a coup attempt against the Vieira government threatened to disrupt the progress of democratic transition. Initial reports indicated that Maj. Robalo de Pina, commander of the Forças de Intervenção Rápida (an élite guard of some 30 soldiers responsible for protecting the president), had been assassinated in what appeared to be an army mutiny, provoked by disaffection at poor standards of pay and living conditions. About 50 people were arrested in connection with the mutiny, including the leader of the PRD, João da Costa. Opposition politicians, however, alleged that the incident had been contrived by the government in an effort to discredit its political opponents and to maintain its hold on power. It was announced that the suspects would be brought to trial in August. Da Costa and nine other members of the PRD in detention were released in June, but banned from political activity. In April public-sector unions organized a three-day general strike in support of demands for wage increases and payment of arrears. In May, following a further split in the FDS, a new political party, the Partido da Convenção Nacional (PCN), was formed, although it was not granted official registration. In July Vieira announced that simultaneous presidential and legislative multi-party elections would be held on 27 March 1994. In August da Costa was rearrested for allegedly violating the conditions of his parole, prompting renewed accusations by opposition politicians that the government's actions were politically motivated. Following a threatened boycott of the national electoral commission by the opposition, da Costa was released.

In January 1994, when João da Costa came to trial, several of his co-defendants retracted statements implicating him in the coup attempt, and it was claimed that accusations against

him had been fabricated by the director-general of state security, Col João Monteiro, who had presided over the military commission of inquiry which had investigated the coup attempt. In early February da Costa was acquitted.

Multi-Party Elections

One week before the designated election date, set for 27 March 1994, Vieira announced a further postponement of the elections owing to financial and technical difficulties, including delays in the electoral registration process and inadequacies in the functioning of the regional electoral commissions. Voter registration for the postponed elections was conducted between 11–23 April. On 11 May it was announced that the elections would be held on 3 July, with a 21-day period of electoral campaigning to begin on 11 June. In early May six opposition parties, the FD, FDS, MUDE, PDP, PRD and the Liga para a Proteção da Ecologia (LIPE), formed an electoral coalition, the União para a Mudança (UM). Later in May a further five opposition parties, the FLING, PRS, PUSD, RGB–MB and the Foro Cívico da Guiné (FCG), announced the establishment of an informal alliance under which each party reserved the right to present its own candidates in the elections.

The elections took place on schedule on 3 July 1994, although voting was extended for two days owing to logistical problems. Eight candidates contested the presidency, while 1,136 candidates contested the 100 legislative seats. The PAIGC secured a clear majority in the national people's assembly, winning 62 seats, but the results of the presidential election were inconclusive, with Vieira winning 46.3% of the votes, while his nearest rival, Koumba Yalla of the PRS, secured 21.9% of the votes. As no candidate had obtained an absolute majority, a second round presidential election between the two leading candidates was conducted on 7 August. Despite receiving the combined support of all the opposition parties, Yalla was narrowly defeated, securing 48.0% of the votes to Vieira's 52.0%. Yalla subsequently contested the results of the election, accusing the PAIGC of electoral fraud and claiming that the state security police had sought to intimidate opposition supporters. Yalla's claims were, however, rejected and on 20 August he accepted the results of the election, but announced that the PRS would not participate in the new government. International observers later declared the elections to have been free and fair. Vieira was inaugurated as president on 29 September 1994 and, following considerable delays owing to divisions within the PAIGC, eventually appointed Manuel Saturnino da Costa as prime minister in late October. The council of ministers was appointed in November comprising solely members of the PAIGC.

Post-Election Politics

In April 1995 the FD, FDS, MUDE, PDP and the PRD reconsolidated themselves within the UM coalition and elected João da Costa as president and Amine Michel Saad as its secretary-general. The LIPE, which had two representatives in the legislature and was a member of the original UM coalition, did not join the new organization, which obtained legal status in November. In August registration was granted to a new party, the Partido Social Democrático, which was formed by dissidents from the RGB–MB.

In May 1996 the national people's assembly rejected a motion of censure, proposed by the RGB–MB, against the government. The vote followed sustained demands by opposition parties for the government's resignation on grounds of incompetence and its inability to resolve the socio-economic problems of the country. In early November government plans to join the Union économique et monétaire ouest-africaine (UEMOA) were rejected by the national people's assembly. A report by the parliamentary economic and financial commission recommended a transition period of two years before joining the francophone regional organization. However, in late November, on receiving a plea from Vieira, the legislature approved a constitutional amendment authorizing the government to seek membership of the UEMOA, which it duly attained in March 1997. Guinea-Bissau subsequently entered the Franc Zone on 17 April, the national currency was replaced by the franc CFA, and the Banque centrale des états de l'Afrique de l'ouest (BCEAO) assumed the central banking functions of the Banco Central da Guiné-Bissau.

In May 1997, in the light of what Vieira described as a serious political crisis, da Costa was dismissed. Carlos Correia was subsequently appointed prime minister and took office in the following month, when a new 14-member cabinet was inaugurated.

In August 1997 the country's principal trade union, the União Nacional dos Trabalhadores da Guiné (UNTG) organized a four-day general strike in support of demands for public-sector salaries to be increased in line with those of other countries belonging to the Franc Zone. The union claimed that entry into the Franc Zone had exacerbated inflation and that the government had failed to adopt measures to compensate for the impact of membership on living standards. The government subsequently agreed to increase public-sector salaries by 50%, with effect from January 1998.

On 11 October 1997 Correia was dismissed, bringing to an end an institutional crisis that began with his inauguration as prime minister in June. The legislative process had been obstructed by opposition deputies who claimed that, by omitting to consult those parties represented in the legislature on Correia's appointment, Vieira had acted unconstitutionally. In August the matter was referred to the supreme court, which ruled, in early October, that Vieira had indeed contravened the constitution. Following consultations with party leaders, Vieira reappointed Correia on 13 October, with the full support of the main opposition parties.

In January 1998 some 10 separatists from the Senegalese region of Casamance were killed, and a further 40 arrested, following clashes with the armed forces in two towns on the northern border of Guinea-Bissau. The armed forces had recently deployed reinforcements along the border with Casamance to prevent the separatists from entering the country. In late January, following the seizure in Guinea-Bissau of a cache of weapons, a number of officers of the armed forces were arrested on charges of supplying arms to the Casamance separatists. In early February the minister of defence announced the dismissal of the chief of staff of the armed forces, Brig. Ansumane Manè, on the grounds of dereliction of duty, in view of the fact that the weapons impounded in the previous month had been taken from a military depot of the Guinea-Bissau armed forces.

In March 1998, following protest by opposition parties at delays in the organization of legislative elections, an independent national elections commission was established. The elections were due to be held in July. In April a new political party, the União Nacional para a Democracia e o Progresso (UNDP), led by former minister of the interior Abubacar Baldè, was established. In that month Ansumane Manè publicly accused the minister of defence and a group of officers of the armed forces of involvement in arms-trafficking to the Casamance separatists, a practice which he maintained was long-established and continued with the acquiescence of Vieira.

At the sixth PAIGC congress, held May 1998, Vieira was re-elected president of the party, while Paulo Medina was elected to the newly-created post of permanent secretary; the post of secretary-general was abolished.

Army Rebellion

In June 1998 rebel troops, led by Ansumane Manè, seized control of the Bra military barracks in the capital, as well as other strategic locations in the city, including the international airport. Manè subsequently formed a 'military junta for the consolidation of democracy, peace and justice' and demanded the resignation of Vieira and his administration and the conduct of free and democratic elections in July. With the support of 1,300 Senegalese and 400 Guinean soldiers, troops loyal to the government attempted unsuccessfully to regain control of rebel-held areas of the city, and heavy fighting ensued. In the following days more than 3,000 foreign nationals were evacuated from the capital by ship to Senegal. An estimated further 200,000 residents of Bissau fled the city, prompting fears of a humanitarian disaster, with the hostilities preventing aid organizations from distributing emergency food and medical supplies to the refugees. Fighting continued into July, with many members of the Guinea-Bissau armed forces reportedly defecting to the side of the rebels. On 26 July, following mediation by a delegation from the lusophone commonwealth body, the Comunidade dos

Países de Língua Portuguesa (CPLP, see below), the government and the rebels agreed to implement a truce. On 25 August representatives of the government and the rebels met, under the auspices of the CPLP and ECOWAS, on Sal island, Cape Verde, where agreement was reached to transform the existing truce into a cease-fire. The accord provided for the reopening of the international airport and for the deployment of international forces to maintain and supervise the cease-fire.

In September 1998 talks between the government and the rebels resumed in Abidjan, Côte d'Ivoire. However, the rebels' demand that all Senegalese and Guinean forces be withdrawn from the country as a precondition to a definitive peace agreement was rejected by the government. The rebels, in turn, rejected a proposal for the establishment by Senegal of a buffer zone within Guinea-Bissau territory along the border with Casamance. In October the rebels agreed to a government proposal for the creation of a demilitarized zone separating the opposing forces in the capital. However, before the proposal could be formally endorsed, the cease-fire collapsed as fighting erupted in the capital and several other towns. On 20 October the government imposed a nation-wide curfew, and on the following day Vieira declared a unilateral cease-fire. By that time almost all of the government troops had defected to the rebel forces, which were believed to control about 99% of the country. On 23 October Brig. Manè agreed to observe a 48-hour truce to allow Vieira time to clarify his proposals for a negotiated peace settlement, and agreement was subsequently reached for direct talks to be held in Banjul, The Gambia. At the talks, which took place on 29 October, the rebels confirmed that they would not seek Vieira's resignation. Further talks, held under the aegis of ECOWAS, in Abuja, Nigeria, resulted in the signing of a peace accord on 1 November. Under the terms of the accord, the two sides reaffirmed the cease-fire of 25 August, and resolved that the withdrawal of Senegalese and Guinean troops from Guinea-Bissau be conducted simultaneously with the deployment of an ECOMOG (ECOWAS Cease-fire Monitoring Group) interposition force, which would guarantee security on the border with Senegal. It was also agreed that a government of national unity would be established, to include representatives of the rebel junta, and that presidential and legislative elections would be held no later than March 1999. In early November 1998 agreement was reached on the composition of a joint executive commission to implement the peace accord. In late November the commission approved the structure of the new government, which was to comprise 10 ministers and seven secretaries of state. On 3 December Francisco José Fadul was appointed prime minister, and later that month Vieira and Manè reached agreement on the allocation of portfolios to the two sides. The first contingent of 100 ECOMOG troops arrived in late December.

In January 1999 Fadul announced that presidential and legislative elections would not take place in March as envisaged in the Abuja accord, and would not be conducted until the end of the year. Also in January agreement was reached between the government, the rebel military junta and ECOWAS on the strength of the ECOMOG interposition force, which was to comprise some 710 troops. Agreement was also reached on a timetable for the withdrawal of Senegalese and Guinean troops from the country. However, at the end of January hostilities resumed in the capital resulting in numerous fatalities and the displacement of some 250,000 residents. On 9 February talks between the government and the rebels produced agreement on a cease-fire and provided for the immediate withdrawal of Senegalese and Guinean troops. At a meeting held in Lomé, Togo, on 17 February Vieira and Manè pledged never again to resort to armed conflict. On 20 February the new government of national unity was announced. The disarmament of rebel troops and those loyal to the president, as provided for under the Abuja accord, began in early March. The withdrawal of Senegalese and Guinean troops was completed that month following an extension of the deadline, from 28 February to 16 March, owing to logistical problems. In April a report was released by the national assembly exonerating Manè of charges of trafficking arms to the Casamance rebels. Although the report, which had been due for release in June 1998 when hostilities began, called for the reinstatement of Manè as chief of staff of the armed forces, it revealed that Vieira's presidential guard had been heavily implicated in the arms trafficking.

TRANSITIONAL GOVERNMENT

In early May 1999 Vieira announced that legislative and presidential elections would take place on 28 December. However, on 7 May, to widespread condemnation by the international community, Vieira was overthrown by the rebel military junta. Fighting had erupted in Bissau on the previous day when rebel troops seized stockpiles of weapons that had been held at Bissau airport since the disarmament of the rival forces in March. The rebels, who claimed that their actions had been prompted by Vieira's refusal to allow his presidential guard to be disarmed, surrounded the presidential palace and forced its surrender. Vieira subsequently took refuge at the Portuguese embassy, where on 10 May he signed an unconditional surrender. The president of the national assembly, Malam Bacai Sanha, was appointed acting president of the republic pending a presidential election. The government of national unity, including the ministers appointed by Vieira, remained in office. At a meeting of the ruling bodies of the PAIGC that month, Manuel Saturnino da Costa was appointed to replace Vieira as party president, while Flavio Proença was appointed permanent secretary. At a tripartite meeting conducted in late May by representatives of the government, the military junta and the political parties, agreement was reached that Vieira should stand trial for his involvement in arms-trafficking to the Casamance separatists and for political and economic crimes relating to his terms in office. Vieira subsequently agreed to stand trial, but only after receiving medical treatment abroad, after which, he pledged, he would return to Guinea-Bissau. At a meeting of ECOWAS foreign ministers held in Togo that month Vieira's overthrow was condemned and demands were made for him to be permitted to leave Guinea-Bissau. It was also decided that ECOMOG forces would be withdrawn from the country; the last ECOMOG troops left in early June. That month Vieira was permitted to leave Guinea-Bissau to seek medical treatment in France. Sanha cited humanitarian reasons for allowing Vieira's departure, but stressed that he would return to stand trial. In the same month Sanha asserted that presidential and legislative elections would take place by 28 November. In July constitutional amendments were introduced limiting the tenure of presidential office to two terms and abolishing the death penalty. It was also stipulated that the country's principal offices of state could only be held by Guinea-Bissau nationals born of Guinea-Bissau parents. In September an extraordinary congress of the PAIGC voted to expel Vieira from the party. Also expelled were the former prime minister Carlos Correia and five ministers from his administration, while the incumbent minister of defence and freedom fighters, Francisco Benante, was appointed president of the party. In October a mass grave was discovered containing the bodies of 22 people thought to have been executed during the Vieira regime. An earlier such discovery, of 14 bodies, had been made in the previous month. Later in October the attorney-general, Amine Michel Saad, announced that he had sufficient evidence to prosecute Vieira for crimes against humanity and expressed his intention to seek Vieira's extradition from Portugal.

THE YALA PRESIDENCY

Presidential and legislative elections were conducted on 28 November 1999, with voting extended for a further day owing to logistical problems. As no candidate received the necessary 50% of the votes to win the presidential election outright, the leading candidates, Koumba Yala of the PRS and Malam Bacai Sanha of the PAIGC, were to contest a second round of voting in January 2000. Of the 102 seats in the legislature (enlarged from 100) the PRS secured 38 seats, the RGB—MB 28, the PAIGC 24, the Aliança Democrática four, the UM three, the Partido Social Democrático (PSD) three, and the FDS and the UNDP each obtained one seat. In that month former president Luis Cabral returned from Portugal to Guinea-Bissau for the first time since he was exiled following his removal from power by Vieira in a military coup in 1980.

In December 1999 thousands of soldiers, who had fought in support of the military junta to oust Vieira, conducted a protest in the capital to demand the payment of salary arrears and war allowances. The soldiers returned to barracks following promises of payment by the government. In November the World Bank had announced that it was to finance a three-year, US \$425m.-plan to demobilize and reintegrate the thousands of former civilians who had taken up arms in the recent conflict.

At the second round of the presidential election, which was conducted on 16 January 2000, Yala secured victory with 72% of the votes cast. Yala assumed power on 17 February and installed a new council of ministers, which included members of several former opposition parties, later that month. Caetano N'Tchama of the PRS was appointed prime minister. The election was subsequently judged by international observers to have been 'free and fair'. In April Fernando Correia was appointed minister of defence to replace Lt-Col Veríssimo Correia Seabra. In May it was reported that tensions were increasing between Yala and certain elements in the army, who viewed the head of the military junta, Gen. Ansumane Manè, as the rightful leader of the country, on the grounds that it was he who had ousted Vieira from power. The refusal of Lamine Sagna, the commander of the national navy, to resign, following his dismissal by Yala (Sagna had allegedly received bribes in return for the release of a Korean fishing boat that had entered Guinea-Bissau's waters illegally) further exacerbated the tensions. However, Sagna subsequently agreed to stand down following an agreement by Yala to co-operate and communicate further with the military. Also in that month a new political party, the Aliança Socialista da Guiné-Bissau (ASG), was formed, under the leadership of the former chairman of the national human rights commission, Fernando Gomes.

FOREIGN AFFAIRS

In its foreign relations, Guinea-Bissau is motivated primarily by the need to solicit aid, and secondly by a sense of vulnerability to the economic interests of its larger and more prosperous francophone neighbours, Senegal and Guinea. As a result, the country has actively promoted co-operation with Portugal, even to the point of proposing an 'escudo zone' (an idea in which other lusophone African countries have shown no interest). Relations with Portugal deteriorated in October 1987, after patrol boats detained six Portuguese vessels for alleged illegal fishing in Guinea-Bissau's territorial waters. Portugal retaliated by suspending non-medical aid, but reversed this decision in early November, after the vessels were released. Shortly afterwards, the head of security at the embassy of Guinea-Bissau in Lisbon sought political asylum, alleging that the diplomatic mission was preparing to organize the assassinations of prominent members of the exiled RGB–MB, which had its headquarters in Lisbon. These allegations were vigorously denied by the government of Guinea-Bissau. During a brief visit to Lisbon in October 1988,Vieira raised the question of the RGB–MB's activities with President Soares of Portugal. As a sign of further commitment to *rapprochement* between the two countries, the Portuguese prime minister, Cavaco Silva, visited Guinea-Bissau in March 1989, when both governments promised increased bilateral co-operation, and agreed to continue to promote relations between African lusophone states. President Soares' visit to Guinea-Bissau in November 1989 included discussions on the issue of extending dual nationality to Guinea-Bissau citizens resident in Portugal. In January 1990 a co-operation agreement between Portugal and Guinea-Bissau allowed a credit facility in conversions of the Guinea peso to the Portuguese escudo at an agreed rate. Links with Portugal were strengthened further by visits during 1990 by Cavaco Silva and by the Portuguese ministers for foreign affairs and the environment. In July 1996 Vieira paid an official visit to Portugal, during which agreement was reached on improved bilateral relations, particularly in the area of defence. In the same month Guinea-Bissau was among the five lusophone African nations which, together with Brazil and Portugal, formally established the Comunidade dos Países de Língua Portuguesa (CPLP), a lusophone commonwealth intended to benefit each member state by means of joint co-operation on technical, cultural and social matters. Diplomatic relations were established with Taiwan in May 1990. In October 1995 da Costa headed a ministerial delegation on a six-day official visit to Taiwan, with the aim of strengthening ties between the two nations. In November 1995 Guinea-Bissau became a non-permanent member of the UN Security Council, for a period of two years. In May 1996 Guinea-Bissau and Morocco signed a co-operation agreement establishing the foundations for improved economic, technical, cultural and scientific co-operation.

Relations with neighbouring countries have been improving in recent years and those between Guinea-Bissau and Cape Verde, which had deteriorated following the coup in 1980, have gradually become closer. The two countries signed a bilateral co-operation agreement in February 1988 and agreed to liquidate certain joint shipping interests which predated the 1980 coup. A boundary dispute with the Republic of Guinea was resolved in Guinea-Bissau's favour by the International Court of Justice (ICJ) in February 1985. In August 1989 a similar dispute arose between Guinea-Bissau and Senegal over the demarcation of maritime borders, which had been based on a 1960 agreement between the former colonial powers, France and Portugal. Guinea-Bissau brought proceedings against Senegal in the ICJ after rejecting an international tribunal's ruling in favour of Senegal. Guinea-Bissau requested direct negotiations with Senegal and invited President Mubarak of Egypt (as president of the OAU) and President Soares of Portugal to act as mediators. In April 1990 Guinea-Bissau accused Senegal of repeated territorial violations, following the seizure of a Soviet vessel operating in Guinea-Bissau territorial waters and several infringements of Guinea-Bissau's air-space. In early May Guinea-Bissau and Senegal appeared close to military conflict after a reconnaissance platoon of the Senegalese army entered Guinea-Bissau territory. However, the detachment was withdrawn, and military confrontation was avoided. Following a meeting between Vieira and President Diouf of Senegal in late May, the two heads of state affirmed their commitment to seeking a peaceful solution to the dispute. A meeting of the two countries' joint commission in July failed to make any significant progress towards determining an agreed maritime boundary. The meeting, the first for nine years, did result in an agreement to establish a commission to monitor security on the common land border (a response to claims by Senegal that Guinea-Bissau had supported separatists in Senegal's Casamance region). Action by the Senegalese armed forces against the separatists led to the flight of several hundred refugees to Guinea-Bissau in late 1990. The Bissau government has been involved in negotiations between the Senegal government and the Casamance separatists which led to the signing in Bissau of a cease-fire agreement in May 1991. However, violence again erupted in Casamance in the second half of 1991.

In November 1991 the ICJ ruled that the agreement concluded between France and Portugal in 1960 regarding the demarcation of maritime borders between Guinea-Bissau and Senegal remained valid. In October 1993 the presidents of Guinea-Bissau and Senegal signed an agreement providing for the joint management and exploitation of the countries' maritime zones (see Economy). The agreement, which was for a renewable 20-year period, was expected to put a definitive end to the countries' dispute over the demarcation of their common maritime borders.

In December 1995 the legislature authorized the ratification of the October 1993 accord. In November 1995 the ICJ announced that Guinea-Bissau had abandoned all proceedings regarding the border dispute with Senegal.

Relations with Senegal have, however, continued to be strained by separatist violence in the Casamance region. In December 1992, following an attack by separatists that resulted in the deaths of two Senegalese soldiers, Senegalese aircraft bombarded border villages in Guinea-Bissau, killing two people and injuring three. Vieira protested to the Senegalese authorities and denied Senegalese claims that the government was providing support for the rebels. The Senegalese government apologized and offered assurances that there would be no repetition of the incident. In March 1993, in an apparent attempt to convince Senegal that it did not support the rebels, the government handed over Abbé Augustin Diamacouné Senghor, one of the exiled leaders of the Casamance separatists, to the Senegalese authorities. In late 1994 the number of Senegalese refugees in Guinea-Bissau was estimated to total 13,600. In February 1995 the Senegalese air force bombarded the village of Ponta Rosa in Guinea-Bissau, close to the border with Senegal. Despite an acknowledgement by the Senegalese authorities that the bombing had occurred as the result of an error, the Senegalese military conducted a similar attack later in the same month, when the border village of Ingorezinho came under artillery fire. In March, in an attempt to forge a rapprochement between the two countries, President Diouf visited Guinea-Bissau to provide a personal apology for the two recent incidents and to offer the commitment that Senegal would respect Guinea-Bissau's sovereignty. In September, following a meeting at Gabú, in Guinea-Bissau, between representatives of both governments, agreement was reached to strengthen co-operation and establish regular dialogue concerning security on the countries' joint border. However, a further attack by the Senegalese air force in October, which resulted in injuries to several Guinea-Bissau nationals, prompted the legislature to establish a commission of inquiry to investigate such border incidents. In November Manuel Saturnino da Costa paid a three-day visit to Senegal, aimed at strengthening co-operation between the two countries. In June 1996 a meeting held at Kolda, in Senegal, between ministerial delegations from Guinea-Bissau and Senegal resulted in renewed commitments to improved collaboration on security.

In April 2000 there were renewed reports of a number of incidents on the border between Senegal and Guinea-Bissau. Five people were alleged to have been killed as a result of bombardments in the border region of Casamance; however, the Senegalese government denied accusations that its troops had entered Guinea-Bissau, and in May requested assistance from Guinea-Bissau to resolve the Casamance conflict. Also in that month, calls by the Senegalese president, Abdoulaye Wade, for the presence of UN military observers along the border between the two countries, were rejected by Yala. However, in July Yala agreed to provide assistance to Senegal, in the hope of finding a rapid solution to the separatist conflict in that country.

Economy

MILES SMITH-MORRIS

Revised for this edition by the Editor

INTRODUCTION

According to the World Bank, in terms of average income, Guinea-Bissau is the sixteenth poorest country in the world. In 1998, according to World Bank estimates, Guinea-Bissau's gross national product (GNP), measured at average 1996–98 prices, was US $184m., equivalent to only $160 per head. During 1990–98, it was estimated, GNP per head decreased, in real terms, at an average rate of 1.3% per year. Over the same period the population increased at an average annual rate of 2.5%. Guinea-Bissau's gross domestic product (GDP) increased, in real terms, at an average annual rate of 1.1% in 1990–98. Real GDP rose by an estimated 4.8% in 1997, but declined by an estimated 27.7% in 1998.

Following independence in 1974, the government established a centrally-planned economy, and an ambitious investment programme, financed mainly by foreign borrowing, was initiated, with emphasis on the industrial sector. However, the economy, which had been adversely affected by the campaign for independence, continued to deteriorate, partly as a result of the government's policies, and by the late 1970s Guinea-Bissau had an underdeveloped agricultural sector, a growing external debt, dwindling exports and escalating inflation.

In the 1980s the government initiated a policy of economic liberalization, in an attempt to reverse the decline in the economy. In 1983 measures were initiated to liberalize the trading sector, to increase producer prices and to encourage private enterprise. Although the measures of adjustment succeeded in increasing agricultural production and exports in 1984, the momentum behind the reforms slowed in 1985–86. By the end of 1986, export earnings had fallen, and the production of many goods had been halted, as the depletion of the country's reserves of foreign exchange made it difficult to import fuel or spare parts. In response to the deteriorating economic situation, the government adopted a structural adjustment programme (SAP) for 1987–90 (see below), which aimed to strengthen the role of the private sector by removing controls over prices and marketing, and by reforming the public sector. In 1990 the government began the reform of the country's public enterprises and initiated the first phase of its programme of privatization. By mid-1995 the process of removing subsidies from public enterprises, which began in 1991, had been virtually completed.

AGRICULTURE AND FISHING

Agriculture is the principal economic activity. The agricultural sector (including forestry and fishing) engaged an estimated 83.3% of the working population and accounted for an estimated 62.4% of GDP in 1998. Agriculture in Guinea-Bissau is entirely an African activity, since there are no European settlers. The main cash crops are cashew nuts (which accounted for an estimated 83.9% of total merchandise exports in 1998) and cotton. In addition, rice, roots and tubers, maize, millet, sorghum and groundnuts are produced. Livestock and timber production are also important. The fishing industry is developing rapidly; earnings from fishing exports and the sale of fishing licences now represent the country's second largest source of export revenue. Among food crops, rice is the staple food of the population. The southern region of Tombali accounts for about 70% of the country's rice production. Production of swamp rice and upland rice amounted to about 70,000 metric tons per annum in the pre-war period, and some rice was exported in years of good harvests. The FAO estimate for the production of paddy rice in 1998 was 125,000 tons. The government is promoting a project aimed at achieving an annual harvest of 30,000 tons of rice from new fields. The droughts of 1977, 1979–80 and 1983 drastically reduced rice production, and in 1986/87 the overall food deficit reached an estimated 17,000 tons. By 1989 it had risen to 165,700 tons, owing to locust depredation and late and insufficient rain for the 1988/89 crop. Agricultural output was maintained in 1990, despite another year of inadequate rains. Cereal output in 1991 declined by 58.2%, compared with the previous year, from 250,400 tons in 1990 to 104,704 tons in 1991, but had recovered to 183,000 tons by 1998. Maize, beans, cassava, sorghum and sweet potatoes play an important part at the village level. Rice imports increased sharply in recent years, accounting for some 40% of domestic rice consumption in the late 1990s, and thus depressing the market for domestic produce.

Traditional exports are groundnuts (18,000 metric tons produced in 1998, according to FAO estimates), grown in the interior as an extension of the Senegalese cultivation, oil-palm products in the islands and on the coast, and coconuts. In 1977 groundnut exports of 16,335 tons, accounted for 60% of total export earnings. However, in 1992 only about 400 tons, worth US $200,000, were exported, and by 1993, according to the IMF, exports of groundnuts had ceased altogether. Exports of palm kernels amounted to 10,600 tons, worth $1.3m., in 1983, but by 1994 had declined to 800 tons, worth about $100,000. Cashew nuts are a relatively recent crop, with an expanding production, estimated at 6,000 tons in 1987, rising to 46,500 tons in 1994. In that year export earnings from cashew nuts totalled $31m., or 93.4% of total export revenue. Cashew nut exports declined to $18.6m. in 1996, when it accounted for 86.1% of total export revenue, before recovering to an estimated $50.8m. in 1997 (94.2%). However, it was estimated that exports of cashew nuts had fallen again, to $22.4m., in 1998. Most of Guinea-Bissau's cashew nuts are purchased by India.

In the government's development plans, priority has been given to agriculture, with the aim of achieving self-sufficiency in food. A sugar refinery (with an annual capacity of 10,000 metric tons), capable of satisfying domestic needs, is being built at Gambiel and will be supplied from new irrigated plantations covering an area of 6,000 ha. An agro-industrial complex at Cumeré is capable of processing 50,000 tons of rice and 70,000 tons of groundnuts annually. It is estimated that these schemes, together with the projected construction of a thermoelectric power station, will require an investment of US $200m., mainly from external sources. The government has nationalized most of the land but does grant private concessions to work the land and has maintained the rights of those tilling their fields. The regime also confiscated the property of former pro-Portuguese Guineans and introduced state control over foreign trade and domestic retail trade through 'people's shops', whose inefficiency and corruption led to serious shortages of consumer goods and contributed to the downfall of the Cabral regime in 1980. In 1983/84 the government partially privatized the state-controlled trading companies, and raised producer prices by about 70%, in an attempt to accelerate agricultural output. Despite the introduction of these measures, Guinea-Bissau continued to operate a 'war economy', superimposed upon a rudimentary peasant economy where most products are bought and sold by the state. Since 1987, however, plans have been accelerated for the removal of price controls on most agricultural products, except essential goods, and for the liberalization of internal marketing systems. In 1992 the government disbanded the people's militia, a paramilitary corps charged with monitoring the economic sector inside the country. The approval of long-awaited legislation on land reform, which would allow the allocation of land for private ownership and provide a delimitation of communal land, was still pending in mid-1999.

The fishing industry has expanded rapidly since the late 1970s, and it has been estimated that the potential annual catch in Guinea-Bissau's waters could total nearly 250,000 metric tons, although by 1995 less than 10% of this level was actually being realized and revenue from fish exports had declined to less than 1% of total export revenue (US $200,000). Fishing exports recovered to an estimated $700,000 in 1997.

Revenue from fishing licences reached 9,100m. francs CFA in 1997, an increase of some 100% on 1995. If illegal fishing could be effectively prevented, fishing could become Guinea-Bissau's main source of revenue. In 1994 it was estimated that annual losses from illegal fishing by foreign vessels in Guinea-Bissau's waters amounted to $25m. Industrial fishing is conducted principally by foreign vessels operating under licence. In 1980 Guinea-Bissau entered into an agreement with the European Community (EC, now the European Union—EU), under the terms of which EC vessels were allowed to fish in Guinea-Bissau's waters in return for aid. The arrangement has since been renewed and updated on seven occasions. The latest of these was in June 1997, when a new four-year fishing agreement was signed with the EU, allowing European vessels to catch 12,600 tons of fish per year in Guinea-Bissau's waters in return for annual compensation of ECU 9m. In 1990 the African Development Bank (ADB) agreed to lend $15m. for a project to develop fishing for export at Cacine, in the south. In 1993 an agreement was signed with Senegal providing for the joint management of the countries' maritime zones, with fishing resources to be divided according to the determination of a joint management agency, formally established in 1995 (see also below). In 1989 there were 1,200 artisanal fishing vessels, of which some 20% were motorized, providing a total catch of 10,000 tons per year. According to estimates by the ministry of fishing, in 1996 the number of artisanal vessels had increased to some 2,500, of which 25% were motorized, providing a total catch of 52,000 tons per year. In 1998 a fisheries research institute was under construction, with assistance from Taiwan, at a cost of $3m.

Cattle-breeding is a very important activity among Balante and Muslim tribes of the interior. In 1998 there were 510,000 head of cattle, 335,000 pigs, 305,000 goats and 275,000 sheep, according to FAO estimates. Meat consumption is significant, and some hides and skins are exported. Tree-felling was temporarily halted while a full assessment of resources was made, but exports resumed in 1986, reaching US $1m., and production totalled 583,000 cu m in 1997, according to FAO estimates. Earnings from the export of rough and processed timber totalled $1.5m in 1995, declining to an estimated $600,000 in 1997. In the 1988–91 Development Plan, forestry was allocated a high priority by the government, and a reafforestation programme was to be implemented.

INDUSTRY, MINING AND TRANSPORT

There is little industrial activity other than food-processing, brewing and wood- and cotton-processing. Industry (including mining, manufacturing, construction and power) employed 4.1% of the economically active population in 1994 and provided an estimated 12.7% of GDP in 1998. According to the World Bank, industrial GDP decreased, in real terms, at an average annual rate of 1.4% in 1990–98. A car assembly plant, with a capacity of 500 vehicles per year, was reopened in 1986, following the government's encouragement of the private sector. An agreement between Guinea-Bissau, Portugal and the USA was signed in 1987 for the establishment of an experimental credit fund to encourage private enterprise. In July 1989 an agreement was signed with Portugal, under which a Portuguese company was to reopen a plastics factory which had ceased production in 1984. Manufacturing contributed 7% of GDP in 1997. Energy is derived principally from thermal and hydroelectric power. In 1998 domestic electricity production totalled 40.1m. kWh. In that year imports of petroleum and petroleum products comprised an estimated 9.8% of the value of total imports. In 1987 work began on the construction of an 8,000-kW diesel-electric power station, funded by the USSR; its completion, together with the rehabilitation of the Bissau thermal power station and purchase of a new 3.5 MW generating unit, formed part of a project aimed at increasing total generating capacity to 15.4 MW. In 1992 the European Investment Bank (EIB) agreed to provide ECU 7.5m. towards financing the project.

The mining sector has still to be developed, and prospecting for bauxite, petroleum and phosphates is in progress. A large deposit of 200m. metric tons of bauxite was reported in the Boé area in 1972, but exploitation has not yet become economic. In 1981 a French exploration team announced the discovery of 200m. tons of phosphates in Cacheu and Oio. In 1987 the government negotiated for financial backing to exploit phosphate deposits in the northern region. Petroleum exploration has resumed; an offshore zone, contested with Guinea until 1985, may contain significant deposits. A second maritime zone, on the border with Senegal, was also the subject of a jurisdictional dispute until October 1993, when an agreement was signed with Senegal providing for the joint management of the countries' maritime zones. The agreement, which was to operate for an initial 20-year period, provided for an 85%–15% division of petroleum resources between Senegal and Guinea-Bissau respectively. Guinea-Bissau formally ratified the agreement in December 1995. In 1984 the government reached agreement with a group of foreign petroleum companies concerning prospecting in an offshore concession covering 4,500 sq km, and in 1985 licences for exploration of some 40 offshore blocks were offered on favourable terms, following the relaxation of Guinea-Bissau's hydrocarbons law. A US petroleum company, Pecten, began exploratory drilling in its offshore permits in 1990. In July of that year the government announced that a new exploration programme was to begin in 1991; a joint commission had been formed with Guinea to facilitate exploration in the two countries' maritime border area. In 1996 a Canadian petroleum company, Petrobank, agreed terms for a joint venture with the state petroleum company of Guinea-Bissau to explore an offshore block covering some 280,000 ha. Petrobank's initial investment was to total US $1m.

For strategic reasons, an impressive network of 3,500 km of roads (540 km tarred) was built from Bissau to the north and north-east in 1972. The road system is poor, however, especially during the rainy season. In early 1989 grants totalling US $31.3m. were provided by the ADB, the Arab Bank for Economic Development in Africa and the EC for road improvements. The road from São Domingos to M'Pack in Senegal, built with aid from the EC and Italy, opened in 1990. In 1996, according to International Road Federation estimates, there were some 4,400 km of roads, of which 453 km were paved. Water transport could be much developed, as 85% of the population live within 20 km of a navigable waterway. In 1984 work began on a project, expected to cost $47.4m., to enlarge Bissau harbour and to rehabilitate four river ports. The construction of a new river port at N'Pungda began in 1986, to improve rice distribution to the northern region. There are also plans to expand the international airport at Bissau. In 1991 Guinea-Bissau and Portugal signed an air transport agreement, under which the Portuguese national airline, TAP, would provide equipment and technicians to help Air Bissau to improve internal services, as well as increasing the frequency of Lisbon-Bissau flights from two to three per week.

EXTERNAL TRADE, FINANCE AND DEVELOPMENT

Serious external trade imbalances persist. Exports rose from US $7.5m. in 1986 to $15.3m. in 1987, as a result of the devaluation of the peso in May, and to $15.9m. in 1988. The value of exports continued to rise, to $17.5m. in 1989, $21.5m. in 1990 and $23m. in 1991, in spite of the devaluation of the Guinea peso, which in 1991, when the exchange rate averaged 3,659 pesos = $1, was worth less than one-half of its value of two years earlier. According to IMF figures, the value of exports totalled only $6.5m. in 1992, but increased to $16m. in 1993, and to $33.2m. in 1994 before declining to $23.9m. in 1995 and to $21.6m. in 1996, then increasing again to $48.5m. in 1997 but falling to an estimated $26.7m. in 1998. Devaluation of the peso continued, with the average exchange rate reaching 6,934 pesos = $1 in 1992, 10,082 pesos = $1 in 1993, 12,892 pesos = $1 in 1994, 18,073 pesos = $1 in 1995 and 26,373 pesos = $1 in 1996. Meanwhile, the demand for manufactured goods, machinery, fuel and food has ensured a high level of imports, averaging $60m. per year in the 1980s. However, foreign exchange controls and the closure of some state enterprises caused a large fall in imports of industrial raw materials. Imports totalled $51.2m. in 1986, falling to $48.8m. in 1987 and rising again in 1988 to about $57m., according to IMF figures. Imports continued to rise reaching $78m. in 1989 and $93m. in 1990 before falling slightly to $78m. in 1991. According to IMF figures, the value of imports totalled $83.5m. in 1992, but declined to $53.8m. in 1993, and to $52.4m. in 1994, reflecting tightened fiscal and monetary policies, rising slightly to $59.3m. in 1995, to $68.9m. in 1996 and to $88.6m. in 1997. Imports were estimated at

$63.1m. in 1998. In that year the principal source of imports was the Netherlands (38.8%); other major suppliers were Portugal, the People's Repubic of China, Japan and Spain. In that year India, a major importer of cashew nuts, was the principal market for exports (85.9%); other significant purchasers were Portugal, France and Spain. The principal exports in 1998 were cashew nuts, cotton, shrimp and logs. The principal imports in that year were food and live animals, petroleum and petroleum products, electrical equipment and machinery, and transport equipment.

In 1993 the budgetary deficit was equivalent to 13.1% of GDP and stood at 310,134m. Guinea pesos, falling to 244,172m. pesos in 1994 and to 66,600m. pesos in 1995. In 1996 the budgetary deficit stood at 14,400m. francs CFA (equivalent to 10.2% of GDP), increasing to 24,580m. francs CFA in 1997, but decreasing to an estimated 19,700m. francs CFA (including grants from abroad and net lending) in 1998 (equivalent to 16.4% of GDP). Grants from abroad continue to be the major source of revenue, accounting for 45.5% of the total for 1998. The deficit on the current account of the balance of payments reached US $79.04m. in 1991, increasing to $104.18m. in 1992, before decreasing to $65.48m. in 1993, and to $50.63m. in 1994. The deficit increased to $50.65m. in 1995 and to $60.43m. in 1996, but decreased to $30.28m. in 1997. In 1990–98 the average annual rate of inflation was 41.5%. Consumer prices increased by an average of 15.2% in 1994, by 45.4% in 1995, by 50.7% in 1996, by 49.1% in 1997, by 6.5% in 1998, but fell by 0.7% in 1999. The shortfalls in the economy are offset by inflows of foreign aid, which averaged more than $60m. per year in 1981–85, increasing from $72.2m. in 1986 to $106.3m. in 1987. The increase was due principally to a rise in multilateral assistance, especially from the World Bank, the African Development Fund (ADF) and the EC. In recent years, the Netherlands and the Scandinavian countries have been important aid-donors. Guinea-Bissau has attended various Franco-African summit conferences and has been a signatory to successive Lomé Conventions.

An extensive re-organization of Guinea-Bissau's banking system has been under way since 1989, involving the replacement of Banco Nacional da Guiné-Bissau by three institutions: a central bank, a commercial bank (Banco Internacional da Guiné-Bissau, which began operations in March 1990), and a national credit bank, established in September 1990, to channel investment. A fourth financial institution, responsible for managing aid receipts, was subsequently created with assistance from the EC, the US Agency for International Development, Sweden and Portugal. In 1991 the government authorized the establishment of privately-operated foreign exchange bureaux.

In November 1987 Guinea-Bissau applied to join the Franc Zone, but withdrew its application in January 1990 following the formulation of an exchange rate agreement with Portugal linking the Guinea peso rate to that of the Portuguese escudo. This accord was considered to form the initial stage in the creation of an 'escudo zone'. However, in August 1993 Guinea-Bissau renewed its application to join the Franc Zone. Guinea-Bissau joined the Union économique et monétaire ouest-africaine in March 1997 and was admitted to the Franc Zone on 17 April. The Guinea peso and the franc CFA co-existed for a period of three months to allow for the gradual replacement, at foreign exchange offices, of the national currency at a rate of 1 franc CFA = 65 Guinea pesos. With the entry of Guinea-Bissau into the Franc Zone, the Banco Central da Guiné-Bissau ceased to operate as the country's central bank and its functions were assumed by the Banque centrale des états de l'Afrique de l'ouest (BCEAO), which has its headquarters in Dakar, Senegal.

President Vieira's government aimed to downgrade many of the prestigious projects that had been initiated by Cabral's administration, and to emphasize rural development. In order to achieve a coherent policy, a Development Plan for 1983–86 was prepared in 1982. In December 1983 the peso was devalued by 50%, with the new official exchange rate set at 88 pesos = SDR 1, as part of a programme of economic stabilization, which aimed to liberalize trade and to increase activity in the private sector. In 1986 trading restrictions were lifted, allowing private traders to import and export goods, although the two state-owned enterprises retained their monopolies in rice, petroleum products and various other commodities.

After consultations with the World Bank, the IMF and other external donors, Guinea-Bissau initiated an SAP covering the period 1987–90. The programme was to be wholly financed by external aid totalling US $46.4m. The SAP included proposals to liberalize the economy and to reform public administration and enterprises. It aimed to achieve a real GDP growth rate of at least 3.5% per year, a lower annual inflation rate (of about 8%) and a reduction in the current account and budgetary deficits. In May 1987 the peso was devalued by about 60%, with the official rate set at 650 pesos = US $1, and new taxes and higher tariffs were introduced. Civil servants' salaries were substantially increased in the late 1980s. In 1988 a reduction of government subsidies on petroleum products increased their average price by 40%.

The Development Plan (1989–92) aimed to consolidate the progress made under the SAP in the reduction of the state's role in the economy, and the growth of private investment. Emphasis was on social development. The agricultural and fishing sectors were to be given priority as a means of achieving self-sufficiency and reducing the balance-of-payments deficit. By the end of 1989, Guinea-Bissau's total external debt was estimated at US $458m., of which $427m. was public and publicly-guaranteed long-term debt. Overall debt-servicing charges for that year totalled $11.6m., or 43% of exports. In October 1989, the 'Paris Club' of Western official creditors, including Belgium, France, Sweden and Switzerland, agreed to reschedule $21m. of principal and interest due from end-October 1989 to December 1990. In September 1989 Belgium agreed to reschedule $2.5m. of Guinea-Bissau's debt. Portugal announced in October 1990 that it would convert Guinea-Bissau's debt of $14.5m. into a Guinea peso fund to be used to support development projects. At the end of the year Portugal released a $6m. credit to the government as part of the financial agreement concluded in January (see above). In January 1989, following the removal of subsidies, fuel prices rose a further 40%, and this was quickly followed by a 33% increase in the price of bread. Further fuel price increases followed in the early 1990s, linked to the depreciation of the Guinea peso against the US dollar and in response to the rise in world petroleum prices that accompanied the Gulf crisis.

In January 1989 the government announced the adoption of a US $104.6m.-investment programme, to be funded entirely by external donors, which was to supplement development projects already proceeding under the SAP. In an attempt to stimulate foreign trade, restrict 'black market' activity and restrain inflation, customs duties and general taxes on imported goods were reduced in April. In the following month international donor countries pledged allocations of $120m., of which 40% was to assist in financing the balance-of-payments deficit, and the remainder to meet general financing requirements. In accordance with these agreements, the World Bank approved a $23.4m. loan to support the second stage of the SAP, introduced in 1987. Under the second stage of the SAP, the government undertook to extend the aims of its economic liberalization programme, with particular emphasis on the privatization of state-owned enterprises.

In June 1990 President Vieira initiated new measures to attract domestic and foreign private investment. It was stated that most of the 50 public enterprises were to be restructured and made more efficient although some strategic sectors, such as telecommunications, electricity and infrastructure, were expected to remain under state control. A decree on privatization was adopted in March 1991, defining areas of state intervention in the economy and outlining the rules for transferring state holdings in public enterprises to the private sector. Nine enterprises were listed for initial privatization, including the 'people's shops', the national brewery and the fishing enterprise, SEMAPESCA. Of these, seven were sold for a total of US $6m. The second phase of privatizations began in early 1994. The government's failure to meet some of the targets of the adjustment programme led, however, to a suspension of international financing when the IMF declined to renew its structural adjustment facility. Among funding suspended as a result was the third tranche of the World Bank's structural adjustment loan, totalling $6.5m.; negotiations on a resumption of World Bank funding began in July 1992 and, in July 1993, it was announced that credits were finally to be resumed. However, in the following month, the World Bank reversed its decision, owing to the government's delay in making repayments on its external debt. In January 1995 the IMF approved a series of loans totalling $13.6m. under an enhanced structural adjustment facility in support of the government's economic reform programme. The loans were to be disbursed over a three-year period. In 1992 the International Development Association announced a loan of $7.2m. to help finance an economic management project. The project, which aimed to improve the government's management and monitoring of economic policy, was to cost a total of $8m. Among the measures involved in the project were a modernizing of the budget process and reform of the tax structure. In 1993 the government initiated a $63m.-public investment programme. The programme, which concentrated predominantly on public works, was to be funded by $32.5m. in aid and $29.5m. in loans contracted by the government, which was itself to provide the remaining $1m. By the end of 1998 total external debt had risen to $964.4m., of which $873.1m. was long-term public debt. In that year the cost of debt servicing was equivalent to 25.6% of the total value of exports of goods and services. Efforts to renegotiate the country's external debt were being made with the assistance of the UN Development Programme. In March 1998 the IMF announced its approval of the government's execution of its structural adjustment programme for 1995–98, thus improving Guinea-Bissau's eligibility for debt relief under the Heavily Indebted Poor Countries initiative.

In February 1998 the government announced a further stage in its privatization programme; some 20 public and parastatal companies in the sectors of telecommunications, tourism, fishing and port and airport management were to be divested, in an effort to restructure and stabilize the economy.

As part of the enhanced structural adjustment facility (ESAF) agreed in 1995, the IMF provided US $6.5m. in support of the government's programme for 1997/98. The programme aimed to achieve annual GDP growth of 5%. However, the economy received a serious reverse following the military uprising of June 1998. Several months of intense fighting in the capital resulted in the extensive destruction of public buildings, causing serious disruption to government and services, and of private business premises. In addition, as many as 400,000 people were displaced by the conflict, imposing a serious burden on the country's underdeveloped infrastructure and necessitating appeals for high levels of humanitarian aid. Following the overthrow of President Vieira in May 1999, the prime minister, Francisco José Fadul, urged the international community to continue with economic aid, in particular with the $200m. funding awarded earlier that month at a Geneva round table meeting on Guinea-Bissau that had been organized by the UN and Guinea-Bissau's development partners. In June the country's banking system, which had been suspended for more than a year during the hostilities, resumed operations. In July the EU granted Guinea-Bissau emergency aid worth 580m. escudos to assist those affected by the armed conflict. That month Bissau airport reopened to commercial traffic for the first time since the outbreak of hostilities. In September the IMF awarded $3m. in emergency aid in support of the government's reconstruction and economic recovery programme. The programme, which, it was estimated, would cost some $138m., focused on the reconstruction of housing and basic infrastructure, the demobilization of former combatants and the strengthening of private-sector operations. Supported by a strong recovery in agricultural production and an increase in cashew exports, as well as by private and public investment in reconstruction, GDP was expected to increase by 8.7% in 1999, while devaluation of 2.1% was envisaged. In January 2000 the IMF approved a $2m.-loan in emergency assistance, which, it was hoped, would assist the government's economic recovery programme. The funds were expected to be used to accelerate demobilization, decrease military spending and improve health and education facilities, which had been damaged during the 1998–99 conflict. In April 2000 the ADB agreed to provide $500m. in funding for the improvement of Guinea-Bissau's health system.

Statistical Survey

Area and Population

AREA, POPULATION AND DENSITY

Area (sq km) .	36,125*
Population (census results)	
16–30 April 1979	753,313
1 December 1991	
Males	476,210
Females .	507,157
Total	983,367
Population (UN estimates at mid-year)†	
1996	1,111,000
1997	1,136,000
1998	1,161,000
Density (per sq km) at mid-1998	32.1

* 13,948 sq miles.

† Source: UN, *World Population Prospects: The 1998 Revision.*

POPULATION BY REGION (1991 census)

Bafatá .	143,377
Biombo .	60,420
Bissau .	197,610
Bolama/Bijagos .	26,691
Cacheu .	146,980
Gabú .	134,971
Oio .	156,084
Quinara .	44,793
Tombali .	72,441
Total .	983,367

PRINCIPAL TOWNS (population at 1979 census)

Bissau (capital) . .	109,214	Catió . . .	5,170
Bafatá . . .	13,429	Cantchungo† . .	4,965
Gabú* . . .	7,803	Farim . . .	4,468
Mansôa . . .	5,390		

* Formerly Nova Lamego.   † Formerly Teixeira Pinto.

BIRTHS AND DEATHS (UN estimates, annual averages)

	1980–85	1985–90	1990–95
Birth rate (per 1,000). . .	44.7	43.9	43.3
Death rate (per 1,000) . .	25.1	23.1	21.4

Expectation of life (UN estimates, years at birth, 1990–95): 43.5 (males 41.8; females 45.2).

Source: UN, *World Population Prospects: The 1998 Revision.*

ECONOMICALLY ACTIVE POPULATION
('000 persons at mid-1994)

	Males	Females	Total
Agriculture, etc. . . .	195	175	370
Industry. . . .	15	5	20
Services	80	14	94
Total	290	194	484

Source: UN Economic Commission for Africa, *African Statistical Yearbook.*

Mid-1998 (estimates in '000): Agriculture, etc. 450; Total 540 (Source: FAO, *Production Yearbook*).

Agriculture

PRINCIPAL CROPS ('000 metric tons)

	1996	1997	1998
Rice (paddy)	120	125*	125*
Maize	9	9†	9*
Millet	21	29†	29*
Sorghum	22	19*	19*
Roots and tubers* . . .	77	77	77
Groundnuts (in shell) . . .	17	18*	18*
Cottonseed	2	2*	2*
Coconuts*	43	44	44
Copra*	8	8	8
Palm kernels*	8	8	8
Vegetables and melons* . .	24	25	25
Plantains*	35	36	36
Other fruits*	36	36	36
Sugar cane*	6	6	6
Cashew nuts*	38	38	38
Cotton (lint)*	1	1	1

* FAO estimate(s).   † Unofficial figure.

Source: FAO, *Production Yearbook*.

LIVESTOCK (FAO estimates, '000 head, year ending September)

	1996	1997	1998
Cattle	500	510	510
Pigs	330	335	335
Sheep	270	275	275
Goats	295	305	305

Source: FAO, *Production Yearbook*.

LIVESTOCK PRODUCTS (FAO estimates, '000 metric tons)

	1996	1997	1998
Beef and veal	4	4	4
Pig meat	10	10	10
Cows' milk	13	13	13
Goats' milk	3	3	3

Source: FAO, *Production Yearbook*.

Forestry

ROUNDWOOD REMOVALS
('000 cubic metres, excluding bark)

	1995	1996	1997
Sawlogs, veneer logs and logs for sleepers* .	40	40	40
Other industrial wood . .	117	119	121
Fuel wood†	422	422	422
Total	579	581	583

* Assumed to be unchanged since 1971.
† Assumed to be unchanged since 1979.

Source: FAO, *Yearbook of Forest Products*.

SAWNWOOD PRODUCTION
('000 cubic metres, including railway sleepers)

	1995	1996	1997
Total*	16	16	16

* Assumed to be unchanged since 1971.

Source: FAO, *Yearbook of Forest Products*.

Fishing

('000 metric tons, live weight)

	1995	1996*	1997*
Inland waters	0.3*	0.3	0.3
Atlantic Ocean . . .	6.1*	6.8	7.0
Total catch	6.3	7.0	7.3

* FAO estimate(s).

Source: FAO, *Yearbook of Fishery Statistics*.

Industry

SELECTED PRODUCTS

	1996	1997	1998
Vegetable oils (million litres) . .	4.3	4.1	n.a.
Electric energy (million kWh) . .	47.6	48.2	40.1

Source: IMF, *Guinea-Bissau: Statistical Annex* (October 1999).

Finance

CURRENCY AND EXCHANGE RATES

Monetary Units
100 centimes = 1 franc de la Communauté financière africaine (CFA).

Sterling, Dollar and Euro Equivalents (28 April 2000)
£1 sterling = 1,132.20 francs CFA;
US $1 = 722.02 francs CFA;
€1 = 655.96 francs CFA;
10,000 francs CFA = £8.832 = $13.850 = €15.245.

Average Exchange Rate (francs CFA per US $)
1997   583.67
1998   589.95
1999   615.70

Note: An exchange rate of 1 French franc = 50 francs CFA, established in 1948, remained in force until January 1994, when the CFA franc was devalued by 50%, with the exchange rate adjusted to 1 French franc = 100 francs CFA. This relationship to French currency remained in effect with the introduction of the euro on 1 January 1999. From that date, accordingly, a fixed exchange rate of €1 = 655.957 francs CFA has been in operation. Following Guinea-Bissau's admission in March 1997 to the Union économique et monétaire ouest-africaine, the country entered the Franc Zone on 17 April. As a result, the Guinea peso was replaced by the CFA franc, although the peso remained legal tender until 31 July. The new currency was introduced at an exchange rate of 1 franc CFA = 65 Guinea pesos. At 31 March 1997 the exchange rate in relation to US currency was $1 = 36,793.3 Guinea pesos. The average exchange rate (Guinea pesos per US $) was: 18,073 in 1995; 26,373 in 1996. Some of the figures in this survey are still in terms of Guinea pesos.

BUDGET (million francs CFA)

Revenue*	1997	1998
Tax revenue	12,456.5	4,514.8
Income taxes	1,992.8	857.7
Business profits	1,290.1	460.9
Individuals	624.6	381.7
Consumption taxes	2,400.1	461.2
On imports	2,363.8	432.6
General sales tax . . .	—	588.5
Taxes on international trade and transactions	7,290.5	2,265.6
Import duties	2,583.8	1,356.8
Export duties	2,466.3	214.3
Port service charges . .	2,240.5	694.5
Other taxes	759.1	256.5
Non-tax revenue	11,515.5	2,079.1
Entrepreneurial and property income	584.2	110.4
Fees and duties	9,189.8	899.9
Fishing licences . . .	8,994.9	763.9
Total	23,972.0	6,593.9

Expenditure†

	1997	1998
Current expenditure	17,069.9	22,683.2
Wages and salaries.	4,873.6	5,663.7
Goods and services	6,134.1	5,563.5
Transfers	4,441.6	3,294.1
Scheduled external interest payments . .	1,620.5	8,161.9
Capital expenditure	27,882.6	7,499.8
Total	**44,952.4**	**30,183.1**

* Excluding grants received ('000 million francs CFA): 20.0 in 1997; 3.9 in 1998.
† Excluding net lending ('000 million francs CFA): 20.6 in 1997; −0.1 in 1998.

Source: IMF, *Guinea-Bissau: Statistical Annex* (October 1999).

CENTRAL BANK RESERVES (US $ million at 31 December)

	1997	1998	1999
IMF special drawing rights . .	0.06	0.03	0.08
Foreign exchange . . .	33.65	35.73	35.21
Total	**33.70**	**35.76**	**35.28**

Source: IMF, *International Financial Statistics.*

MONEY SUPPLY (million francs CFA at 31 December)

	1997	1998	1999
Currency outside banks . . .	20,137	17,642	24,186
Demand deposits at deposit money banks	16,431	14,476	14,476
Total money (incl. others) . .	**36,625**	**32,194**	**39,420**

Source: IMF, *International Financial Statistics.*

COST OF LIVING (Consumer Price Index; base: 1995 = 100)

	1997	1998	1999
Food, beverages and tobacco . .	224.7	239.4	237.7

Source: IMF, *International Financial Statistics.*

NATIONAL ACCOUNTS (million francs CFA at current prices)
Expenditure on the Gross Domestic Product

	1995	1996	1997
Government final consumption expenditure	10,033	10,891	18,118
Private final consumption expenditure	117,485	132,206	141,323
Increase in stocks	154	5,624	27
Gross fixed capital formation .	22,373	21,248	21,278
Total domestic expenditure	**150,045**	**169,969**	**180,746**
Exports of goods and services . .	16,051	17,304	38,370
Less Imports of goods and services	42,122	47,932	60,154
GDP in purchasers' values .	**123,974**	**139,340**	**158,961**

Source: IMF, *International Financial Statistics.*

Gross Domestic Product by Economic Activity
(estimates)

	1997	1998
Agriculture, hunting, forestry and fishing . .	84,094	78,831
Mining and quarrying		
Manufacturing	17,250	11,134
Electricity, gas and water		
Construction	6,307	4,071
Trade, restaurants and hotels . . .	36,601	23,624
Transport, storage and communications . .	3,614	2,333
Finance, insurance, real estate, etc. . . .		
Community, social and personal services (excl. government)	1,389	897
Government services	4,751	3,067
GDP at factor cost	**154,006**	**119,956**
Indirect taxes	2,744	1,357
GDP at market prices	**156,750**	**121,313**

Source: IMF, *Guinea-Bissau: Statistical Annex* (October 1999).

BALANCE OF PAYMENTS (US $ million)

	1995	1996	1997
Exports of goods f.o.b. . . .	23.90	21.61	48.86
Imports of goods f.o.b. . . .	−59.34	−56.80	−62.49
Trade balance . . .	**−35.44**	**−35.19**	**−13.63**
Exports of services . . .	5.69	6.96	8.00
Imports of services . . .	−29.91	−29.25	−26.15
Balance on goods and services	**−59.66**	**−57.48**	**−31.78**
Other income paid	−21.09	−18.65	−14.30
Balance on goods, services and income	**−80.75**	**−76.13**	**−46.08**
Current transfers received . .	31.42	15.70	15.80
Current transfers paid . . .	−1.32	—	—
Current balance . . .	**−50.65**	**−60.43**	**−30.28**
Capital account (net) . . .	49.20	40.70	32.20
Other investment assets . .	—	—	−5.80
Other investment liabilities . .	−28.25	−12.30	7.83
Net errors and omissions . .	−11.26	−11.44	−15.87
Overall balance . . .	**−40.96**	**−43.46**	**−11.92**

Source: IMF, *International Financial Statistics.*

External Trade

PRINCIPAL COMMODITIES (US $ million)

Imports c.i.f.	1996	1997	1998*
Food and live animals . .	25.1	31.1	17.1
Rice	13.9	22.2	10.2
Sugar	1.4	0.7	0.5
Oil	2.2	2.1	0.6
Dairy products . . .	2.0	2.5	2.7
Beverages and tobacco . .	4.0	6.7	1.5
Other consumer goods . .	4.6	8.5	1.7
Durable consumer goods .	1.6	3.0	0.5
Non-durable consumer goods .	2.2	4.1	0.6
Petroleum and petroleum products	9.3	9.5	6.2
Diesel fuel and gasoline . .	6.5	6.6	6.0
Construction materials . .	7.7	8.5	1.2
Transport equipment . .	9.4	12.5	4.1
Passenger vehicles . .	2.5	3.3	1.6
Freight vehicles . .	5.8	7.8	2.0
Electrical equipment and machinery . . .	6.5	8.5	4.5
Total (incl. others) . . .	**68.9**	**88.6**	**63.1**

* Provisional figures.

Exports f.o.b.			1996	1997	1998*
Cotton .	.	.	1.3	0.1	1.5
Cashew nuts.	.	.	18.6	45.6	22.4
Fish.	.	.	0.7	0.5	0.5
Shrimp	.	.	0.6	0.4	0.5
Wood products	.	.	0.8	1.2	0.5
Logs .	.	.	0.5	0.4	0.3
Total (incl. others)	.	.	21.6	48.5	26.7

* Provisional figures.

Source: IMF, *Guinea-Bissau: Statistical Annex* (October 1999).

PRINCIPAL TRADING PARTNERS

Imports (million pesos)								1984
France	.	.	.	.	.	.	.	232.7
Germany, Fed. Repub.	.	.	.	.	.	.	213.7
Italy	.	.	.	.	.	.	.	110.4
Netherlands .	.	.	.	.	.	.	215.6
Portugal .	.	.	.	.	.	.	924.0
Senegal	.	.	.	.	.	.	.	362.0
Sweden .	.	.	.	.	.	.	70.2
USSR	.	.	.	.	.	.	.	462.7
USA .	.	.	.	.	.	.	.	192.4
Total (incl. others)	.	.	.	.	.	.	3,230.7

Source: Ministry of Planning, Bissau.

Exports (US $ '000)							1981
China, People's Repub.	.	.	.	.	.	.	1,496
France	.	.	.	.	.	.	1,376
Portugal .	.	.	.	.	.	.	2,890
Senegal	.	.	.	.	.	.	1,122
Spain	.	.	.	.	.	.	4,058
Sweden .	.	.	.	.	.	.	1,627
Switzerland .	.	.	.	.	.	.	1,617
United Kingdom .	.	.	.	.	.	1,211
Total (incl. others)	.	.	.	.	.	.	15,730

Source: UN, *International Trade Statistics Yearbook*.

Transport

ROAD TRAFFIC (motor vehicles in use, estimates)

			1994	1995	1996
Passenger cars	.	.	5,940	6,300	7,120
Commercial vehicles .	.	.	4,650	4,900	5,640

Source: International Road Federation, *World Road Statistics*.

SHIPPING
Merchant Fleet (registered at 31 December)

			1996	1997	1998
Number of vessels	.	.	21	21	23
Total displacement (grt) .	.	.	5,891	5,617	6,079

Source: Lloyd's Register of Shipping, *World Fleet Statistics*.

International Sea-Borne Freight Traffic
(UN estimates, '000 metric tons)

				1991	1992	1993
Goods loaded	.	.	.	40	45	46
Goods unloaded .	.	.	.	272	277	283

Source: UN Economic Commission for Africa, *African Statistical Yearbook*.

CIVIL AVIATION (traffic on scheduled services)

			1994	1995	1996
Kilometres flown (million)	.	.	1	1	1
Passengers carried ('000) .	.	.	21	21	21
Passenger-km (million)	.	.	10	10	10
Total ton-km (million)	.	.	1	1	1

Source: UN, *Statistical Yearbook*.

Communications Media

	1994	1995	1996
Radio receivers ('000 in use) .	.	42	45	47
Telephones ('000 main lines in use)	9	9	8
Telefax stations (number in use) .	480	500	500
Daily newspapers:			
Number .	.	.	.	1	1	1
Average circulation ('000 copies)	6	6	6

1997: Radio receivers 49,000 in use.

Sources: UNESCO, *Statistical Yearbook*; UN, *Statistical Yearbook*.

Education

(1988)

	Insti-tutions	Teachers	Students Males	Students Females	Students Total
Pre-primary .	.	5	43	384	370	754
Primary .	.	632*	3,065*	50,744	28,291	79,035
Secondary:						
General .	.	n.a.	617†	3,588	1,917	5,505
Teacher training.	.	n.a.	33	137	39	176
Vocational .	.	n.a.	74	593	56	649
Tertiary .	.	n.a.	n.a.	380	24	404

* 1987 figures.   † 1986 figure.

Primary (1994/95): 100,369 students (63,415 males; 36,954 females).

Source: UNESCO, *Statistical Yearbook*.

Directory

The Constitution

A new Constitution for the Republic of Guinea-Bissau was approved by the National People's Assembly on 16 May 1984 and amended in May 1991, November 1996 and July 1999 (see below). The main provisions of the 1984 Constitution were:

Guinea-Bissau is an anti-colonialist and anti-imperialist Republic and a State of revolutionary national democracy, based on the people's participation in undertaking, controlling and directing public activities. The Partido Africano da Independência da Guiné e Cabo Verde (PAIGC) shall be the leading political force in society and in the State. The PAIGC shall define the general bases for policy in all fields.

The economy of Guinea-Bissau shall be organized on the principles of state direction and planning. The State shall control the country's foreign trade.

The representative bodies in the country are the National People's Assembly and the regional councils. Other state bodies draw their powers from these. The members of the regional councils shall be directly elected. Members of the councils must be more than 18 years of age. The National People's Assembly shall have 150 members, who are to be elected by the regional councils from among their own members. All members of the National People's Assembly must be over 21 years of age.

The National People's Assembly shall elect a 15-member Council of State, to which its powers are delegated between sessions of the Assembly. The Assembly also elects the President of the Council of State, who is also automatically Head of the Government and Commander-in-Chief of the Armed Forces. The Council of State will later elect two Vice-Presidents and a Secretary. The President and Vice-Presidents of the Council of State form part of the Government, as do Ministers, Secretaries of State and the Governor of the National Bank.

The Constitution can be revised at any time by the National People's Assembly on the initiative of the deputies themselves, or of the Council of State or the Government.

Note: Constitutional amendments providing for the operation of a multi-party political system were approved unanimously by the National People's Assembly in May 1991. The amendments stipulated that new parties seeking registration must obtain a minimum of 2,000 signatures, with at least 100 signatures from each of the nine provinces. (These provisions were adjusted in August to 1,000 and 50 signatures, respectively.) In addition, the amendments provided for the National People's Assembly (reduced to 100 members) to be elected by universal adult suffrage, for the termination of official links between the PAIGC and the armed forces, and for the operation of a free-market economy. Multi-party elections took place in July 1994.

In November 1996 the legislature approved a constitutional amendment providing for Guinea-Bissau to seek membership of the Union économique et monétaire ouest-africaine and of the Franc Zone.

In July 1999 constitutional amendments were introduced limiting the tenure of presidential office to two terms and abolishing the death penalty. It was also stipulated that the country's principal offices of state could only be held by Guinea-Bissau nationals born of Guinea-Bissau parents.

The Government

HEAD OF STATE

President of the Republic and Commander-in-Chief of the Armed Forces: KOUMBA YALA (assumed power 17 February 2000).

COUNCIL OF MINISTERS
(August 2000)

Prime Minister: CAETANO N'TCHAMA.

Deputy Prime Minister and Minister of Economic and Social Reconstruction: FAUSTINO FADUT IMBALI.

Minister of Defence and Freedom Fighters: FERNANDO CORREIA.

Minister of Internal Administration: ANTÓNIO ARTUR SANHA.

Minister of Foreign Affairs and International Co-operation: YAIA DJALLO.

Minister of Finance: PURNA BIA.

Minister of the Economy: HELDER VAZ LOPES.

Minister of Justice: ANTONIETA ROSA GOMES.

Minister of Education, Science and Technology: JOÃO JOSÉ SILVA MONTEIRO.

Minister of Health: ANTÓNIO BAMBA.

Minister of War Veterans: IANCUBA INDJAI.

Minister of Social Infrastructure: CARLITO BARAI.

Minister of Agriculture and Forestry: ALAMARA NIASSE.

Minister of Natural Resources and the Environment: FRANSICO JOSÉ FERNANDO JUNIOR.

Minister of Administration and Labour: DAUDA SOW.

There are, in addition, nine Junior Ministers.

MINISTRIES
All of the ministries are located in Bissau.

Office of the Prime Minister: Avda Unidade Africana, CP 137, Bissau; tel. 211308; fax 201671.

Ministry of Agriculture, Forestry and Fisheries: Avda Amílcar Cabral, CP 102, Bissau; tel. 202251; fax 201157.

Ministry of Defence and Freedom Fighters: Amura, Bissau; tel. 213297.

Ministry of Economy and Finance: CP 67, Avda 3 de Agosto, Bissau; tel. 215193; fax 214586.

Ministry of Education, Science and Technology: Rua Areolino Cruz, Bissau; tel. 202244.

Ministry of Foreign Affairs and International Co-operation: Rua General Omar Torrijo, Bissau; tel. 202752; fax 202378.

Ministry of Health: CP 50, Bissau; tel. 201107; fax 201701.

Ministry of Internal Administration: Avda Unidade Africana, Bissau; tel. 201527.

Ministry of Justice: Avda Amílcar Cabral, CP 17, Bissau; tel. 202187.

Ministry of Social Infrastructure: CP 14, Bissau; tel. 202466; fax 201137.

President and Legislature

PRESIDENT
Presidential Election, First Ballot, 28 November 1999

Candidate	% of Votes
KOUMBA YALA (PRS)	38.8
MALAM BACAI SANHA (PAIGC)	23.4
FAUSTINO IMBALI (PUSD/RGB—MB)	8.2
FERNANDO GOMES (Independent)	7.0
JOÃO TATIS SÁ (Independent)	6.5
ABUBACAR BALDÈ (UNDP)	5.4
Total (incl. others)	100.0

Second Ballot, 16 January 2000

Candidate	% of Votes
KOUMBA YALA (PRS)	72.0
MALAM BACAI SANHA (PAIGC)	28.0
Total	100.0

NATIONAL PEOPLE'S ASSEMBLY
General Election, 28 November 1999

	Seats
Partido para a Renovação Social (PRS)	38
Resistência da Guiné-Bissau—Movimento Bah-Fatah (RGB–MB)	28
Partido Africano da Independência da Guiné e Cabo Verde (PAIGC)	24
Aliança Democrática (AD)	4
União para a Mudança (UM)	3
Partido Social Democrático (PSD)	3
Frente Democrática Social (FSD)	1
União Nacional para a Democracia e o Progresso (UNDP)	1
Total (incl. others)	102

Political Organizations

Aliança Democrática (AD): c/o National People's Assembly, Bissau.

Aliança Socialista da Guiné-Bissau (ASG): Bissau; f. 2000; Leader FERNANDO GOMES.

Foro Cívico da Guiné (FCG): Bissau; Leader ANTONIETA ROSA GOMES.

Frente Democrática Social (FDS): c/o National People's Assembly, Bissau; f. 1991; legalized in Dec. 1991; Leader RAFAEL BARBOSA.

Frente da Luta para a Libertação da Guiné (FLING): Bissau; f. 1962 as an external opposition movement; legally registered in May 1992; Leader FRANÇOIS KANKOILA MENDY.

Liga Guineense de Protecção Ecológica (LIPE): Bairro Missirá 102, CP 1290, Bissau; tel. and fax 252309; f. 1991; ecology party; Pres. Alhaje BUBACAR DJALÓ.

Partido Africano da Independência da Guiné e Cabo Verde (PAIGC): CP 106, Bissau; f. 1956; fmrly the ruling party in both Guinea-Bissau and Cape Verde; although Cape Verde withdrew from the PAIGC following the coup in Guinea-Bissau in Nov. 1980, Guinea-Bissau has retained the party name and initials; Pres. FRANCISCO BENANTE; Perm. Sec. FLAVIO PROENÇA.

Partido da Convergência Democrática (PCD): Bissau; Leader VÍTOR MANDINGA.

Partido para a Renovação Social (PRS): c/o National People's Assembly, Bissau; f. 1992 by four mems of the Frente Democrática Social; officially registered in Oct. 1992; Leader (vacant).

Partido Social Democrático (PSD): c/o National People's Assembly, Bissau; f. 1995 by breakaway faction of RGB–MB; Leader JOAQUIM BALDÉ; Sec.-Gen. GASPAR FERNANDES.

Partido Unido Social Democrático (PUSD): Bissau; f. 1991; officially registered in Jan. 1992; Leader (vacant).

Resistência da Guiné-Bissau–Movimento Bah-Fatah (RGB–MB): c/o National People's Assembly, Bissau; f. 1986 in Lisbon, Portugal, as Resistência da Guiné-Bissau–Movimento Bafatá; adopted present name prior to official registration in Dec. 1991; maintains offices in Paris (France), Dakar (Senegal) and Praia (Cape Verde); Chair. HELDER VAZ LOPES.

União para a Mudança (UM): c/o National People's Assembly, Bissau; f. 1994 as coalition to contest presidential and legislative elections, re-formed April 1995; comprises following parties:

> **Frente Democrática (FD):** Bissau; f. 1991; officially registered in Nov. 1991; Pres. CANJURA INJAI; Sec.-Gen. MARCELINO BATISTA.

> **Movimento para a Unidade e a Democracia (MUDE):** Bissau; officially registered in Aug. 1992; Leader FILINTO VAZ MARTINS.

> **Partido Democrático do Progresso (PDP):** Bissau; f. 1991; officially registered in Aug. 1992; Pres. of Nat. Council AMINE MICHEL SAAD.

> **Partido de Renovação e Desenvolvimento (PRD):** Bissau; f. 1992 as the 'Group of 121' by PAIGC dissidents; officially registered in Oct. 1992; Leaders MANUEL RAMBOUT BARCELOS, AGNELO REGALA.

União Nacional para a Democracia e o Progresso (UNDP): c/o National People's Assembly, Bissau; f. 1998; Leader ABUBACAR BALDÉ.

Diplomatic Representation

EMBASSIES IN GUINEA-BISSAU

Brazil: Rua São Tomé, Bissau; tel. 201327; fax 201317; Ambassador: LUIZ FERNANDO NAZARETH.

China (Taiwan): Avda Amílcar Cabral 35, CP 66, Bissau; tel. 201501; fax 201466.

Cuba: Rua Joaquim N'Com 1, Bissau; tel. 213579; Ambassador: DIOSDADO FERNÁNDEZ GONZÁLEZ.

Egypt: Avda Omar Torrijos, Rua 15, CP 72, Bissau; tel. 213642; Ambassador: MOHAMED REDA FARAHAT.

France: Avda 14 de Novembro, Bairro de Penha, Bissau; tel. 201610; fax 253142; Ambassador: FRANÇOIS CHAPPELLET.

Guinea: Rua 14, no. 9, CP 396, Bissau; tel. 212681; Ambassador: MOHAMED LAMINÉ FODÉ.

Libya: Rua 16, CP 362, Bissau; tel. 212006; Representative: DOKALI ALI MUSTAFA.

Portugal: Rua Cidade de Lisboa 6, Apdo 276, Bissau; tel. 201261; fax 201269; Ambassador: FRANCISCO HENRIQUES DA SILVA.

Russia: Avda 14 de Novembro, Bissau; tel. 251036; fax 251050; Ambassador: VIKTOR M. ZELENOV.

Senegal: Avda Omar Torrijos 43A, Bissau; tel. 211561; Ambassador: MAMADOU NIANG.

USA: CP 297, 1067 Bissau; tel. 252273; fax 252282; Ambassador: PEGGY BLACKFORD.

Judicial System

Judges of the Supreme Court are appointed by the Conselho Superior da Magistratura.

President of the Supreme Court: MAMADU SALIU DJALO PIRES.

Religion

According to the 1991 census, 45.9% of the population are Muslims, 39.7% are animists and 14.4% are Christians, mainly Roman Catholics.

CHRISTIANITY

The Roman Catholic Church

Guinea-Bissau comprises a single diocese, directly responsible to the Holy See. The Bishop participates in the Episcopal Conference of Senegal, Mauritania, Cape Verde and Guinea-Bissau, currently based in Senegal. At 31 December 1998 there were an estimated 135,252 adherents in the country.

Bishop of Bissau: JOSÉ CÂMNATE NA BISSIGN, CP 20, Avda 14 de Novembro, 1001 Bissau; tel. 251057; fax 251058.

The Anglican Communion

Anglicans in Guinea-Bissau are adherents of the Church of the Province of West Africa, comprising 12 dioceses.

Bishop of Guinea and Guinea-Bissau: (vacant), BP 1187, Conakry, Guinea.

The Press

Baguerra: Bissau; owned by the Partido da Convergência Democrática.

Banobero: Bissau; weekly; Dir FERNANDO JORGE PEREIRA.

Correio-Bissau: Bissau; weekly; f. 1992; Editor-in-Chief JOÃO DE BARROS; circ. 9,000.

Journal Nô Pintcha: Bissau; daily; Dir Sra CABRAL; circ. 6,000.

NEWS AGENCY

Agência Noticiosa da Guinea (ANG): CP 248, Bissau; tel. 212151.

Broadcasting and Communications

TELECOMMUNICATIONS

Guiné-Telecom: Bissau; 49% state-owned.

RADIO AND TELEVISION

An experimental television service began transmissions in 1989. Regional radio stations were to be established at Bafatá, Cantchungo and Catió in 1990. In 1990 Radio Freedom, which broadcast on behalf of the PAIGC during Portuguese rule and had ceased operations in 1974, resumed transmissions.

Radiodifusão Nacional da República da Guiné-Bissau: CP 191, Bissau; govt-owned; broadcasts in Portuguese on short-wave, MW and FM; Dir FRANCISCO BARRETO.

Rádio Bombolom: f. 1996; independent; Dir AGNELO REGALA.

Rádio Pidjiguiti: f. 1995; independent.

Finance

(cap. = capital; res = reserves; m. = million; brs = branches; amounts in francs CFA unless otherwise indicated)

BANKING

Central Bank

Banque Centrale des Etats de l'Afrique de l'Ouest (BCEAO): Avda Amílcar Cabral, CP 38, Bissau; tel. 215548; fax 201305; HQ in Dakar, Senegal; f. 1955; bank of issue for the mem states of the Union économique et monétaire ouest-africaine (UEMOA, comprising Benin, Burkina Faso, Côte d'Ivoire, Guinea-Bissau, Mali, Niger, Senegal and Togo); cap. and res 806,918m., total assets 4,084,464m.; (Dec. 1998); Gov. CHARLES KONAN BANNY; Dir in Guinea-Bissau LUÍS CÂNDIDO LOPES RIBEIRO.

Other Banks

Banco Internacional da Guiné-Bissau: Avda Amílcar Cabral, CP 74, 1064 Bissau; tel. 201256; fax 201033; e-mail bigb@sol .gtelecom.gw; f. 1989; cap. 3,260m. Guinea pesos (Dec. 1993); 26% state-owned, 25% by Guinea-Bissau enterprises and private interests, 49% by Crédito Predial Português (Portugal); Chair. FIL-INTO E. BARROS; Gen. Man. JOSÉ ANTÓNIO TAVARES DA CRUZ.

Banco Totta e Açores (Portugal): Rua 19 de Setembro 15, CP 618, Bissau; tel. 214794; fax 201591; Gen. Man. CARLOS MADEIRA.

Caixa de Crédito da Guiné: Bissau; govt savings and loan institution.

Caixa Económica Postal: Avda Amílcar Cabral, Bissau; tel. 212999; postal savings institution.

STOCK EXCHANGE

In 1998 a regional stock exchange, the Bourse Régionale des Valeurs Mobilières, was established in Abidjan, Côte d'Ivoire, to serve the member states of the UEMOA.

INSURANCE

In 1979 it was announced that a single state-owned insurer was to replace the Portuguese company Ultramarina.

Trade and Industry

The Government has actively pursued a policy of small-scale industrialization to compensate for the almost total lack of manufacturing capacity. Following independence, it adopted a comprehensive programme of state control, and in 1976 acquired 80% of the capital of a Portuguese company, **Ultramarina**, a large firm specializing in a wide range of trading activities, including ship-repairing and agricultural processing. The Government also held a major interest in the **CICER** brewery (until its privatization in 1996) and created a joint-venture company with the Portuguese concern **SACOR** to sell petroleum products. Since 1975 three fishing companies have been formed with foreign participation: **GUIALP** (with Algeria), **Estrela do Mar** (with the former USSR) and **SEMAPESCA** (with France), all of which were awaiting divestment in 1998. In December 1976 **SOCOTRAM**, an enterprise for the sale and processing of timber, was inaugurated. It operates a factory in Bissau for the production of wooden tiles and co-ordinates sawmills and carpentry shops throughout the country. In 1998 SOCOTRAM was in the process of being divested through separate sales of its regional operational divisions. The restructuring of several further public enterprises was proceeding in the late 1990s, as part of the Government's programme to attract private investment.

Empresa Nacional de Pesquisas e Exploração Petrolíferas e Mineiras (PETROMINAS): Rua Eduardo Mondlane 58, Bissau; tel. 212279; state-owned; regulates all prospecting for hydrocarbons and other minerals; Dir-Gen. ANTÓNIO CARDOSO.

CHAMBER OF COMMERCE

Associação Comercial, Industrial e Agrícola da Guiné-Bissau: Bissau; f. 1987; Pres. CANJURA INJAI.

UTILITIES

Electricity and Water

EAGB: Bissau; operated under contract by private management co.

TRADE UNION

União Nacional dos Trabalhadores da Guiné (UNTG): 13 Avda Ovai di Vievra, CP 98, Bissau; tel. 212094; Pres. DEFEJADO LIMA DA COSTA; Sec.-Gen. MÁRIO MENDES CORREA.

Legislation permitting the formation of other trade unions was approved by the National People's Assembly in 1991.

Transport

RAILWAYS

There are no railways in Guinea-Bissau. In March 1998 Guinea-Bissau and Portugal signed an agreement providing for the construction of a railway linking Guinea-Bissau with Guinea.

ROADS

In 1996, according to International Road Federation estimates, there were about 4,400 km of roads, of which 453 km were paved. A major road rehabilitation scheme is proceeding, and an international road, linking Guinea-Bissau with The Gambia and Senegal, is planned. In 1989 the Islamic Development Bank granted more than US $2m. towards the construction of a 111-km road linking north and south and a 206-km road between Guinea-Bissau and Guinea.

SHIPPING

Under a major port modernization project, the main port at Bissau was to be renovated and expanded, and four river ports were to be upgraded to enable barges to load and unload at low tide. The total cost of the project was estimated at US $47.4m., and finance was provided by the World Bank and Arab funds. In 1986 work began on a new river port at N'Pungda, which was to be partly funded by the Netherlands.

CIVIL AVIATION

There is an international airport at Bissau, which there are plans to expand, and 10 smaller airports serving the interior.

Transportes Aéreos da Guiné-Bissau (TAGB): Aeroporto Osvaldo Vieira, CP 111, Bissau; tel. 201277; fax 251536; f. 1977; domestic services and flights to France, Portugal, the Canary Islands (Spain), Guinea and Senegal; Dir Capt. EDUARDO PINTO LOPES .

Air Bissau: CP 111, Bissau; tel. 251063; fax 251008.

Tourism

Centro de Informação e Turismo: CP 294, Bissau; state tourism and information service.

Defence

In August 1999 the armed forces totalled 9,250 men: army 6,800, navy 350, air force 100, and the paramilitary gendarmerie 2,000.

Defence Expenditure: Budgeted at US $10m. in 1999.

Commander-in-Chief of the Armed Forces: Gen. ANSUMANE MANÉ.

Education

Education is officially compulsory only for the period of primary schooling, which begins at seven years of age and lasts for six years. Secondary education, beginning at the age of 13, lasts for up to five years (a first cycle of three years and a second of two years). In 1988 the total enrolment at primary and secondary schools was equivalent to 38% of the school-age population (males 49%; females 27%). In 1994 enrolment at primary schools of children in the relevant age-group was equivalent to 62% (males 79%; females 45%). In 1988 enrolment at secondary schools was equivalent to 7% (males 9%; females 4%). Expenditure on education by the central government in 1989 was 5,051m. pesos (2.7% of total spending). In 1997 the IDA approved a credit of US $14.3m. for a project to expand and upgrade the education system. Mass literacy campaigns have been introduced: according to UNESCO estimates, however, the average rate of adult illiteracy in 1995 was still very high at 68.5% (males 52.5%; females 83.7%). In 1991 plans were announced for the establishment of the country's first university.

Bibliography

Andreini, J.-C., and Lambert, M.-L. *La Guinée-Bissau.* Paris, 1978.

Cabral, A. *Unity and Struggle* (collected writings) (trans. by M. Wolfers). London, Heinemann Educational, 1979.

Cabral, L. *Crónica da Libertação.* Lisbon, O Jornal, 1984.

Cann, J. P. *Counter-insurgency in Africa: The Portuguese Way of War 1961–1974.* Westport, CT, Greenwood Press, 1997.

Chabal, P. *Amílcar Cabral—Revolutionary Leadership and People's War.* Cambridge, Cambridge University Press, 1983.

Chaliand, G. *Lutte armée en Afrique.* Paris, Maspero, 1967. As *Armed Struggle in Africa.* New York and London, Monthly Review Press, 1969.

Davidson, B. *The Liberation of Guiné.* Harmondsworth, Penguin Books, 1969.

No Fist is Big Enough to Hide the Sky: The Liberation of Guinea-Bissau and Cape Verde. 2nd Edn. London, Zed Press, 1984.

Fisas Armengol, V. *Amílcar Cabral y la Independencia de Guinea-Bissau.* Barcelona, Nova Terra, 1974.

Galli, R., and Jones, D. *Guinea-Bissau: Politics, Economics and Society.* New York and London, Pinter Publishers, 1987.

Henry, C. *Les Iles où dansent les enfants défunts: age, sexe et pouvoir chez les Bijagós de Guinée-Bissau.* Paris, CNRS, 1994.

Lobban, R. A. *Historical Dictionary of the Republics of Guinea-Bissau and Cape Verde.* Folkestone, Kent, Bailey Bros and Swinfen, 1981.

Lobban, R. A., and Mendy, P. K. *Historical Dictionary of Guinea-Bissau.* 2nd Edn. Lanham, MD, Scarecrow Press, 1997.

Lopes, C. *Guinea-Bissau: From Liberation Struggle to Independent Statehood.* Boulder, CO, Westview Press, 1987.

Mettas, J. *La Guinée portugaise au vingtième siècle.* Paris, Académie des Sciences d'Outre-mer, 1984.

Monteiro, A. I. *O programa de Ajustamento Estrutural na Guiné-Bissau.* INEP, Bissau, 1996.

da Mota Teixeira, A. *Guiné Portuguesa.* 2 vols. Lisbon, 1964.

Núñez, B. *Dictionary of Portuguese-African Civilization.* Vol. I. London, Hans Zell, 1995.

Paulini, T. *Guinea-Bissau, Nachkoloniale Entwicklung eines Agrarstaates.* Göttingen, 1984.

Pereira, L. T., and Moita, L. *Guiné-Bissau: Três Anos de Independência.* Lisbon, CIDAC, 1976.

Proença, C. S. *Os efeitos da política de estabilização e ajustamento estrutural no bem-estar das famílias urbanas: o caso de Bissau 1986–93.* ISEG, Lisbon, 1998.

Rimmer, D. *The Economies of West Africa.* London, Weidenfeld and Nicolson, 1984.

Rudebeck, L. *Guinea-Bissau.* Uppsala, 1974.

Problèmes de pouvoir populaire et de développement. Uppsala, Scandinavian Institute of African Studies, Research Report 63.

World Bank. *Guinea-Bissau: A Prescription for Comprehensive Adjustment.* Washington DC, 1988.

KENYA

Physical and Social Geography

W. T. W. MORGAN

PHYSICAL FEATURES

The total area of the Republic of Kenya is 580,367 sq km (224,081 sq miles) or 569,137 sq km (219,745 sq miles) excluding inland waters (mostly Lake Turkana and part of Lake Victoria). Kenya is bisected by the Equator and extends from approximately 4°N to 4°S and 34°E to 41°E.

The physical basis of the country is composed of extensive erosional plains, cut across ancient crystalline rocks of Pre-Cambrian age. These are very gently warped—giving an imperceptible rise from sea level towards the highlands of the interior which have their base at about 1,500 m above sea-level. The highlands are dominated by isolated extinct volcanoes, including Mt Kenya (5,200 m) and Mt Elgon (4,321 m), while outpourings of Tertiary lavas have created plateaux at 2,500–3,000 m. The Great Rift Valley bisects the country from north to south and is at its most spectacular in the highlands, where it is some 65 km across and bounded by escarpments 600–900 m high. The trough is dotted with lakes and volcanoes which are inactive but generally associated with steam vents and hot springs. Westwards the plains incline beneath the waters of Lake Victoria, and eastwards they have been down-warped beneath a sediment-filled basin, which may hold deposits of petroleum.

CLIMATE AND NATURAL RESOURCES

Although Kenya lies on the Equator, its range of altitude results in temperate conditions in the highlands above 1,500 m, with temperatures which become limiting to cultivation at about 2,750 m, while Mt Kenya supports small glaciers. Average temperatures may be roughly calculated by taking a sea-level mean of 26°C and deducting 1.7°C for each 300 m of altitude. For most of the country, however, rainfall is more critical than temperature. Only 15% of the area of Kenya can be expected to receive a reliable rainfall adequate for cultivation (750 mm in four years out of five). Rainfall is greatest at the coast and in the west of the country, near Lake Victoria and in the highlands, but the extensive plains below 1,200 m are arid or semi-arid. In the region of Lake Victoria and in the highlands west of the Rift Valley, rain falls in one long rainy season. East of the Rift Valley there are two distinct seasons: the long rains (March–May) and the short rains (September–October).

The high rainfall areas tend to be intensively cultivated on a small-scale semi-subsistence basis with varying amounts of cash cropping. Food crops are in great variety, but most important and widespread are maize, sorghum, cassava and bananas. The principal cash crops, which provide the majority of exports, are tea, coffee (*arabica*), pyrethrum and sisal. The first three are particularly suited to the highlands and their introduction was associated with the large-scale farming on the alienated lands of the former 'White Highlands'. Horticultural produce (in particular cut flowers) is an increasingly significant export. The dairy industry is important both for domestic consumption and for export. The herds of cattle, goats, sheep and camels of the dry plains support a low density of mainly subsistence farmers. Fisheries are of local importance around Lake Victoria and are of great potential at Lake Turkana.

Soda ash is mined at Lake Magadi in the Rift Valley. Deposits of fluorspar, rubies, gold, salt, vermiculite, iron ore and limestone are also exploited. However, mineral resources make a negligible contribution to Kenya's economy.

POPULATION AND CULTURE

A total population of 15,327,061, excluding estimated under-enumeration of 5%, was recorded at the census of August 1979. The provisional results of the August 1989 census (also believed to be underenumerated) indicated a total population of 21,443,636. At mid-1997 the population was officially estimated at 33,144,000. The resultant overall density of 57.1 inhabitants per sq km is extremely unevenly distributed, with approximately three-quarters of the population contained in only 10% of the area; densities approach 400 per sq km on the small proportion of the land that is cultivable. About 15% of the population reside in urban areas, principally in Nairobi (population provisionally estimated to be 1,346,000 at the 1989 census) and Mombasa (465,000 at the 1989 census, provisional results). The towns also contain the majority of the non-African minorities of some 89,185 Asians, 34,560 Europeans and 41,595 Arabs (1989 census, provisional results).

Kenya has been a point of convergence of major population movements in the past, and, on a linguistic and cultural basis, the people have been divided into Bantu, Nilotic, Nilo-Hamitic (Paranilotic) and Cushitic groups. Persian and Arab influence at the coast is reflected in the Islamic culture. Kiswahili is the official language, although English, Kikuyu and Luo are widely understood.

Recent History

ALAN RAKE

With revisions by the Editor

COLONIAL RULE TO THE KENYATTA ERA

Kenya, formerly known as British East Africa, was declared a British protectorate in 1895, primarily to secure a route to Uganda. Subsequent white settlement met with significant African armed resistance by 1914, and by the early 1920s some African political activity had begun to be organized. In 1944 the Kenya African Union (KAU), an African nationalist organization, was formed, demanding African access to white-owned land. Leadership of the movement, which drew its main support from the Kikuyu, passed in 1947 to Jomo Kenyatta, himself a Kikuyu. During 1952–56 a campaign of terrorism was conducted by the Mau Mau, a predominantly Kikuyu secret society. A state of emergency was declared by the British authorities, Kenyatta was detained and a ban on all political activity remained in force until 1955. During this period, two Luo political activists, Tom Mboya and Oginga Odinga, came to prominence. Following the removal of the state of emergency in January 1960, a transitional constitution was introduced, legalizing political parties and according Africans a large majority in the legislative council. The KAU was reorganized as the Kenya African National Union (KANU), and Mboya and Odinga were elected to the party's leadership. Following his release in August 1961, Kenyatta assumed the presidency of KANU, which won a decisive victory at the general election of May 1963. Kenyatta became prime minister in June, and independence followed on 12 December. The country was declared a republic (with Kenyatta as president) exactly one year later.

By 1965 KANU had become divided into a 'conservative' wing, led by Mboya, and a 'radical' group, led by Odinga, who left KANU to form the Kenya People's Union (KPU), which accused the government of furthering the interests of a small privileged class. Kenyatta moved swiftly to curtail the activities of the KPU, introducing legislation giving the government powers of censorship and the right to hold suspects in detention without trial. Following the assassination of Mboya in July 1969, the KPU was banned and Odinga was placed in detention, where he remained for 15 months. At a general election in December only KANU members were offered as candidates.

During the early 1970s President Kenyatta became increasingly reclusive and autocratic, although he was elected, unopposed, for a third five-year term in September 1974. At a general election in October (in which, once again, KANU members were the sole candidates), more than one-half of the members of the previous assembly were defeated. Kenyatta died in August 1978.

THE MOI PRESIDENCY

With the support of Charles Njonjo, the attorney-general and an influential associate of the elderly Kenyatta, the presidency passed to Daniel arap Moi, the vice-president, in October 1978. A programme to reform Kenya's corrupt bureaucracy was initiated, and in December all political detainees were released. President Moi, a Kalenjin, emphasized regional representation in the new style of government. In 1980 Moi succeeded in bringing Odinga and his substantial (predominantly Luo) following back into KANU. Nevertheless, Odinga continued to oppose the use of military facilities in Kenya by the USA, and to denounce the government's economic management. A 'detribalization' campaign was introduced in mid-1980, whereby virtually every Kenyan organization title which had a tribal implication was renamed.

During 1981 disagreements between the president's two close associates, Njonjo and Mwai Kibaki, the vice-president, became unbridgeable; intense factional disputes also developed between their respective supporters. Kibaki eventually won the power struggle, gaining Njonjo's home affairs portfolio at a cabinet reshuffle in February 1982. Meanwhile, Moi appeared to be growing increasingly intolerant of criticism. In May 1982 Odinga and another former MP were expelled from KANU for advocating the formation of a new political party, and in the following month Kenya constitutionally became a one-party state.

Onset of Opposition

In August 1982 a section of the Kenya air force attempted to overthrow the government. The revolt, in which there was a considerable degree of Luo involvement, was swiftly crushed by the army. An estimated 3,000 arrests followed, and the air force was disbanded. Nairobi university, which had also been a focus of support for the rebellion, was temporarily closed. Odinga was placed under house arrest (from which he was freed in October 1983), and the Luo information minister, Peter Aringo, was dismissed. By March 1983, when the government had sufficiently recovered from the political paralysis that followed the revolt, death sentences passed on the perpetrators were suspended and most of the remaining detainees were released. Conciliatory moves, aimed at some of the sources of political unrest, included a new code of conduct for politicians in office, and an investigation of the civil service.

The country's mood of political uncertainty during the early part of 1983 was compounded by suggestions, promoted by Moi, that certain unspecified foreign powers were grooming an unnamed Kenyan politician to take over as president. The name of Charles Njonjo, the minister for constitutional affairs, was eventually mentioned in the national assembly in connection with the allegation, prompting Njonjo's suspension from the cabinet and from KANU. Following an inconclusive official inquiry, Njonjo withdrew from public life. A further inquiry also resulted in a purge of Njonjo's political supporters.

In September 1983, a year earlier than constitutionally required, general elections took place, in which Moi was returned unopposed for a second presidential term. Only 48% of the electorate participated in the poll, which was followed by wide-ranging changes in the cabinet. A minor government reshuffle took place in January 1985. Moi's political strategy during that year was dominated by a recruitment drive to revitalize the membership of KANU.

The 'Mwakenya Conspiracy'

In March 1986 it was revealed that several Kenyans had been detained under security provisions, and that others were to face charges of publishing seditious documents: during the ensuing 12 months, a 'conspiracy' known as Mwakenya (a Swahili acronym for the 'Union of Nationalists to Liberate Kenya') became the focal point of Kenyan politics. Although Moi alleged that Mwakenya comprised the same 'tribalistic élite' that had fostered the 1982 coup attempt, it became apparent that the movement embraced a wide spectrum of opposition to the Moi presidency.

In August 1986 the annual KANU party conference approved a 'queue-voting' system to replace the secret ballot in the preliminary stage of a general election. The new procedure, whereby voters were to queue publicly in support of the candidate of their choice, was opposed by church leaders on the grounds that it would discourage voting by church ministers, civil servants and others whose political impartiality was necessary for their work. In December the national assembly adopted constitutional amendments which increased the power of the president by transferring control of the civil service to the president's office, and reduced the independence of the judiciary by giving the head of state the power to dismiss the attorney-general and the auditor-general without endorsement by a legal tribunal. No votes were cast in opposition to the amendments, but two MPs who had openly questioned the virtue of the changes were briefly detained in January 1987. By early 1987, more than 100 people had been detained in connection with Mwakenya, some of them receiving lengthy terms of imprisonment, and the political climate had become reminiscent of the months preceding the 1982 coup attempt. In April 1987 Odinga, still the most prestigious opponent of the government, made an unprecedented public declaration of opposition to Moi's political management; the government, opting for caution, took no action against Odinga, who repeated his criticism of the Moi regime in July and August. The administration did, however, make allegations of involvement with Mwakenya against several influential church leaders.

Although the government may have over-reacted in its anxieties about Mwakenya, the movement none the less represented genuine undercurrents of discontent. Its followers comprised a broad spectrum of opposition elements, including Kikuyu peasants, urban intellectuals (often, but not exclusively, Luo), and elements of the established political network. Most threatening for the government was the fact that Mwakenya was apparently confined to no particular region.

Political Retrenchment

From early 1987 international criticism of Moi's government intensified, as further allegations emerged of human rights abuses in Kenya. The government's response to this criticism reflected, for the most part, its continuing hostility both to external pressure and internal opposition. In April, however, Moi ordered the dismissal of members of the police force found to be guilty of corruption, criminal activity or brutality. Two months later the minister of foreign affairs was replaced, reportedly on the grounds that he was failing effectively to defend Kenya's record on human rights. In July Amnesty International published a report which accused the Kenyan authorities of seeking to silence political opposition by detention without trial and by torture.

In October and November 1987 serious rioting broke out among Muslims in Mombasa, following a government ban on an Islamic public meeting. The government's fear of destabilization by foreign powers was reflected in the detention, in November, of seven student leaders, one of whom was imprisoned for allegedly spying on behalf of Libya. These arrests led to mass student demonstrations during December; clashes between students and riot police resulted, to the dismay of the government, in the brief detention and alleged mistreatment of four Western journalists. Nairobi university was temporarily closed, and its student organization banned.

In early 1988 the government made some minor concessions to international criticism of its conduct towards its opponents. In January the minister of state for security was demoted following a controversy over the brief detention of two US human rights activists who were allegedly in possession of 'subversive' documents, and in February the president ordered the release of nine political detainees, several of whom later claimed that they had been tortured while in custody.

A general election to the national assembly, held in March 1988, provided only limited indication of Moi's popularity. Prior to the parliamentary polling, the president was returned unopposed for a third term of office. The open-air 'queue-voting' technique of candidate selection, conducted in February, produced a KANU-approved list to contest 123 of the 188 elective seats (65 candidates, including the president, were returned unopposed). Potential candidates who were unpopular with the Moi administration (such as Odinga) were excluded from seeking election, and seats were largely contested on local and personality issues rather than on national policies. In an extensive government reshuffle following the election, Mwai Kibaki was demoted from the vice-presidency to the post of minister of health (it was widely believed that the president was disquieted by Kibaki's popularity among the Kikuyu), and replaced by Josephat Karanja, a relatively obscure politician with no popular following.

The independence of the judiciary from the executive was effectively removed in July 1988, when the national assembly assented to constitutional amendments which allowed the president to dismiss judges at will, and which increased the period of detention, from 24 hours to 14 days, of people suspected of capital offences. These measures led to an intensification of criticism of the government's record on human rights, especially from church leaders and lawyers. Moi subsequently accused foreigners of acting in concert with Kenyan church leaders against the government. Moi indicated that he was considering the arrests of 'roaming' foreigners and the curtailment of freedom of worship.

Elections to the leadership of KANU were held in September 1988; Moi was confirmed as president of the party, and Kibaki was replaced by Karanja as party vice-president. Allegations of malpractice in the KANU elections were made by Kibaki, among others, and in December Kenneth Matiba, the minister of transport and communications, resigned and was expelled from KANU after criticizing the conduct of the party elections.

Karanja's period of influence was short-lived: in February 1989 he became the subject of a campaign of vilification by fellow MPs, which culminated, in April, in a unanimous parliamentary vote expressing 'no confidence' in him. He was widely accused of attempting to establish himself as a rival to President Moi and of pursuing tribal interests. In addition, he encountered allegations from some quarters of conspiring with the Ugandan government to destabilize Kenya. In May Karanja, who had denied the charges against him, resigned from the posts of Kenyan vice-president and vice-president of KANU. Moi appointed Prof. George Saitoti, the minister of finance, as the country's new vice-president and announced a major cabinet reshuffle. Shortly afterwards, Karanja resigned from the national assembly, and in June he was expelled from KANU.

In June 1989 Moi, who was clearly sensitive to continuing international criticism of his human rights record, released all political prisoners who were being detained without trial, and offered an amnesty to dissidents living in exile. While this action was applauded by Amnesty International, that organization repeated allegations that many convicted Kenyan political prisoners had received unfair trials. In November part of Nairobi university was closed, owing to student unrest.

In February 1990, the minister of foreign affairs and international co-operation, Dr Robert Ouko, died in suspicious circumstances. Accusations that the Moi administration was implicated in Ouko's death led to anti-government riots in Nairobi and the western town of Kisumu. Moi responded by banning all demonstrations from the beginning of March, and requested an investigation by British police into Dr Ouko's death (the results of this were presented to the Kenyan authorities in

September, and in October Moi ordered a judicial inquiry into the affair). In April the minister of information and broadcasting, Waruru Kanja, was dismissed, following allegations on his part that Ouko's death was politically motivated. Pressure on the government to terminate KANU's political monopoly increased in May with the formation of a broad alliance of intellectuals, lawyers and church leaders (under the leadership of the former cabinet minister, Kenneth Matiba) which sought to legalize political opposition. In July Moi ordered the arrests of several of the alliance's leaders, including Matiba and Raila Odinga, the son of the former vice-president. Serious rioting ensued in Nairobi and its environs, and sporadic unrest was reported in the hinterland of the Kikuyu-dominated Central province; more than 20 people were killed in the disturbances, and more than 1,000 rioters were reportedly arrested. The KANU leadership responded to international criticism by denouncing the advocates of multi-party political reform as 'tribalists' in the pay of 'foreign masters', seeking to undermine national unity. Moi accused the US government of interfering in the country's internal politics after one of the dissident leaders was granted refuge in the US embassy in Nairobi. In August a prominent Anglican bishop, who had publicly criticized the government, died in a car crash, following threats to his life from members of the cabinet; the most senior of these, Peter Okondo, the minister of labour, subsequently resigned his post. The government ordered a public inquest into the bishop's death. In November Amnesty International reported that several hundreds of people detained at the time of the July riots remained in custody, and accused the Kenyan authorities of torturing some prisoners. During late 1990 seven people were arrested and charged with treason.

In December 1990, having considered the findings of a political review committee that had recently tested public opinion, KANU abolished the system of 'queue-voting' approved by the party in 1986, and resolved to cease expulsions of party members. In January 1991 KANU agreed to readmit to the party a number of people who had previously been expelled. Oginga Odinga founded the National Democratic Party (NDP) in the following month, and was subsequently harrassed by the Kenyan authorities: he was arrested briefly in May, shortly before the court of appeal rejected his application to register the (subsequently disbanded) NDP as a political party.

In March 1991 a prominent human rights lawyer and magazine editor was arrested and charged with sedition, having accused the president of promoting the interests of his native Kalenjin tribe, and having published the manifesto of the banned NDP. The charge was withdrawn in May, following widespread exposure of the case in the international media. In that month Moi reiterated his offer of an amnesty for dissident Kenyans in exile abroad. Soon afterwards the government announced the release from imprisonment of Kenneth Matiba, who was reportedly suffering from ill health. In June several religious leaders and lawyers formed a body, known as the Justice and Peace Convention, which aimed to promote freedom of political expression. In the following month four of those arrested during the unrest of July 1990 were found guilty of sedition and each sentenced to seven years' imprisonment. During July 1991 a human rights organization, Africa Watch, published allegations that the government was permitting the torture of detainees and exerting undue influence on the judiciary. In August six opposition leaders, including Oginga Odinga, formed a new political movement, the Forum for the Restoration of Democracy (FORD); the government immediately outlawed the grouping, but it continued to operate.

In September 1991 the judicial inquiry into the death of Dr Ouko was presented with evidence that he had been murdered. In November Moi dismissed Nicholas Biwott from the post of minister of industry, in response to widespread suspicion that the latter was implicated in the alleged assassination. Shortly afterwards Moi ordered the dissolution of the judicial inquiry. A suspect was eventually charged with the murder, but was acquitted in July 1994.

In November 1991 several members of FORD were arrested prior to a planned pro-democracy rally in Nairobi; protestors at the rally (which took place despite a government ban) were dispersed by the security forces. The Kenyan authorities were condemned internationally for suppressing the demonstration, and most of the opposition activists who had been detained were subsequently released. During that month bilateral and multilateral creditors suspended aid to Kenya for 1992, pending the acceleration of both economic and political reforms; the donors emphasized, in particular, the desirability of an improvement in Kenya's human rights record.

Political Pluralism and Ethnic Tensions

In early December 1991 a special conference of KANU delegates, chaired by Moi, acceded to the domestic and international pressure for reform, and resolved to permit the introduction of a multi-party political system. Soon afterwards the constitution was accordingly amended. Several new political parties were registered from the beginning of 1992.

In mid-December 1991 Moi dismissed the minister of manpower development and employment, Peter Aringo, who had publicly criticized the government; Aringo subsequently resigned as chairman of KANU. Later in that month Mwai Kibaki, the minister of health and former vice-president, resigned from the government, in protest against alleged electoral malpractice by KANU and against the unsatisfactory outcome of the judicial inquiry into the death of Dr Ouko. Kibaki immediately founded the Democratic Party (DP). Five other ministers and deputy ministers resigned their posts in December 1991 and January 1992.

During the first half of 1992 as many as 2,000 people were reportedly killed and some 20,000 made homeless as a result of tribal clashes in western Kenya. Opposition leaders accused the Moi administration of covertly inciting the violence as a means of discrediting the progress towards a multi-party political system, while the government countered that the exacerbation of existing ethnic tensions was an inevitable result of the new political freedoms. In March the government banned all political rallies, purportedly in a bid to suppress the unrest, and restrictions were placed on the activities of the press. A two-day general strike, organized by FORD to demand the release of political prisoners and the removal of the ban on political rallies, was held in April: the government acceded to the latter demand shortly afterwards.

In mid-May 1992 some 34 members of the opposition were arrested, following the publication in the national media of unsubstantiated allegations that elements within the government were plotting to assassinate opponents of the Moi regime. Later in that month the security forces violently suppressed a pro-Islamic demonstration in Mombasa. In June, during the period of voter-registration for the forthcoming presidential and legislative elections (see below), opposition parties protested that administrative and legal obstacles were effectively disenfranchising some sectors of the electorate. In June KANU published draft legislation stipulating that a successful presidential candidate must receive at least one-quarter of all votes cast in at least five of the country's eight provinces: this measure was intended to encourage political participation along national rather than ethnic lines.

From mid-1992 FORD was weakened by mounting internal divisions; in August the organization split into two opposing factions, and in October these were registered as separate political parties, FORD–Asili and FORD–Kenya, respectively led by Kenneth Matiba and Oginga Odinga.

Presidential and parliamentary elections were held concurrently in late December 1992. At the presidential election Moi was re-elected, winning 36.35% of the votes, ahead of Kenneth Matiba (26.00%), Mwai Kibaki (19.45%) and Oginga Odinga (17.48%). Of the 188 elective seats in the national assembly, KANU won 100 (including 16 uncontested), FORD–Asili and FORD–Kenya secured 31 each, the DP took 23, and the remainder were divided between the Kenya Social Congress, the Kenya National Congress and an independent candidate. (In November 1994 one FORD–Kenya representative and the independent member were found guilty of electoral malpractice and retrospectively disqualified from the elections.) Some 15 former cabinet ministers lost their seats. Votes were cast predominantly in accordance with ethnic affiliations, with the two largest tribes, the Kikuyu and Luo, overwhelmingly rejecting KANU. The leaders of FORD–Asili, FORD–Kenya and the DP initially launched a campaign to have the results declared invalid, alleging that gross electoral irregularities had taken

place. In January 1993, however, a Commonwealth monitoring group concluded that the outcome of the elections reflected 'the will of the people', despite accusing the government of corruption, intimidation and incompetence.

In early January 1993 Moi was sworn in for a fourth five-year term as president. An extensive reshuffle of cabinet posts followed in mid-January. In February the government impounded copies of three opposition publications which allegedly contained seditious material, and in April four opposition members were arrested and charged with participating in an illegal demonstration. During April the World Bank agreed to release foreign aid which had been suspended since November 1991. At the beginning of May 1993 a general strike was called by the Central Organization of Trade Unions (COTU) to demand wage increases and the dismissal of Prof. Saitoti as vice-president and minister of planning and national development. The former demand was partially met; however, COTU's secretary-general was arrested and charged with inciting industrial unrest.

In May 1993 Sheikh Khalid Balala, a leader of the banned radical-fundamentalist Islamic Party of Kenya (IPK), threatened to declare a 'jihad' against the government and called for the assassination of cabinet ministers; Balala was subsequently arrested on charges of sedition. In an attempt to counter support for the IPK, KANU sponsored a rival Muslim party, the United Muslims of Africa, whose stated objective was to end 'the domination and oppression of indigenous African tribes by rich Arabs'. Behind the ethnic rivalry, however, lay a serious economic conflict centred on local feelings about the purchase of high-value land in tourist coastal areas by 'outsiders'—namely Asians, whites and certain government ministers.

Tribal clashes which occurred during 1993, described by church organizations as the most serious since independence, were most acute in the Rift Valley and on the borders between land occupied by the Masai, Kikuyu and Kalenjin tribes. Hundreds of Kikuyu families were driven from their farms, which were then allegedly occupied mainly by Kalenjins. Foreign observers who toured the Rift Valley in mid-1993 accused the government of failing to contain the fighting and of pursuing a policy of 'ethnic cleansing'. President Moi sealed off part of the region in September, ostensibly to prevent further hostilities, although the opposition claimed that his real aim was to suppress criticism of the government. Following significant escalation of the violence in October, Moi accused his opponents of fomenting a civil war and increased the powers of the security forces. Five prominent Kikuyu who were arrested in connection with raids on police stations during October included the human rights activist Koigi wa Wamwere, who had been released earlier in the year following his arrest on charges of treason. In November the international human rights organization Africa Watch reiterated allegations that the ethnic violence had been deliberately exploited by Moi and his associates in order to undermine the move towards political pluralism. The organization estimated that 1,500 people had been killed and 300,000 displaced since the clashes began.

In January 1994 Oginga Odinga died; he was succeeded as the chairman of FORD–Kenya by Michael Kijana Wamalwa, hitherto the party's vice-chairman. At the time of Odinga's death, the rift between FORD–Kenya and FORD–Asili had widened considerably. During January Dr Richard Leakey, director of the Kenya Wildlife Service (KWS) and a third-generation white Kenyan, resigned after coming under attack from a number of government ministers. Although Leakey was respected internationally for his efforts at ending the poaching of elephants and for obtaining substantial financial support for the protection of Kenya's game reserves (a vital element in the country's tourism industry), it was alleged that he was doing little to protect the farmers on and around the reserves whose crops were being ravaged by the wildlife.

In April 1994, following further outbreaks of violence in part of the Rift Valley between the Kikuyu and the Kalenjin, Moi reimposed a security zone and curfew on the area. Roman Catholic bishops and opposition leaders repeated the long-standing allegations that the government was fully responsible for fomenting the unrest. Allegations of serious fraud involving the misappropriation of government funds abounded during 1994, incriminating opposition activists as well as government supporters. This apparent widespread corruption, together with the continuing adoption of tactics of repression by the government and the ineffectual state of the divided and poorly-organized opposition, led to major popular discontent and social alienation; the rates of crime and urban violence increased significantly and ethnic unrest continued to simmer. Meanwhile, university staff and employees of the public health sector organized strike action to protest at the government's refusal to recognize their respective trade unions and to grant improved conditions of employment.

In June 1994 the main opposition groups, excluding FORD–Asili, formed a loose coalition, the United National Democratic Front (UNDA), in an attempt to gain a tactical advantage at future elections; however, UNDA was subsequently divided by disagreements. Disunity was also becoming apparent within individual opposition parties, with vying factions evident within both FORD–Kenya and FORD–Asili. The IPK suffered a set-back when, in December, the government withdrew the right to Kenyan citizenship from its leading spokesman, Sheikh Balala (also a citizen of Yemen); Balala, who was abroad at the time, was also banned from re-entering Kenya. (He was eventually permitted to return to Kenya in July 1997, in order to resolve the issue of his citizenship.) In May 1995 several opposition activists, including Gitobu Imanyara, a former secretary-general of FORD–Kenya, and Paul Muite, an influential human rights lawyer and also a former FORD–Kenya supporter, formed a new political grouping, Safina (the Swahili term for 'Noah's Ark'). The new party, whose primary stated aims were to combat corruption and human rights abuses and to introduce an electoral system of proportional representation, was chaired by Mutari Kigano, also a human rights lawyer. The former KWS director, Dr Leakey, was appointed as Safina's secretary-general, thereby attracting beneficial international attention to the enterprise. Moi, apparently regarding the party, and, in particular, Dr Leakey as a significant threat, launched a series of bitter personal attacks against the white Kenyan, accusing him of harbouring 'colonialist' ambitions. Safina's application for official registration was rejected. The party strongly rebuffed accusations by the government that it was illegally funded from abroad.

During the mid-1990s Kenya's apparently deteriorating human rights situation came under intense domestic and international scrutiny. In April 1995 the country's Roman Catholic bishops published a pastoral letter in which they once again strongly condemned the government, accusing it of betraying the nation by eroding the independence of the judiciary and by condoning police brutality and endemic corruption. In mid-1995 leading human rights organizations expressed particular concern over physical assaults on Safina officials (including Dr Leakey) by members of KANU's youth wing, as well as the government's refusal officially to register Safina, and the lengthy trial of the human rights activist Koigi wa Wamwere, who had been charged in 1993 in connection with a raid on a police station (see above). Wamwere was eventually found guilty in October 1995 of attempted robbery and sentenced to a term of imprisonment; Amnesty International and opposition members of the national assembly alleged that the prosecution's evidence had been fabricated. In November the Kenyan authorities revealed that 810 prisoners had died in custody since the beginning of 1995. In December Amnesty International reported that the security forces were systematically torturing criminal suspects and opposition activists. In response to its critics (and in order to ensure continuing inflows of foreign assistance), the Moi administration provisionally withdrew controversial draft legislation in January 1996 that would have severely restricted the freedom of the press and, in July, inaugurated a human rights committee to investigate alleged humanitarian abuses by the Kenyan authorities. During July, however, Moi announced, and subsequently reiterated, that constitutional reforms (strongly advocated by foreign donors) would not be considered prior to the next legislative and presidential elections, which were scheduled to take place in late 1997.

The rising rates of crime and urban violence continued to arouse concern. During the latter part of 1995 several foreign diplomatic missions and personnel were attacked by armed robbers; a British high commission official who was shot in his car subsequently died of his injuries. In December the Kenyan

authorities, under pressure to allay the fears of the resident foreign communities and to protect the national tourism industry, organized a rounding-up of illegal aliens, who were alleged to be largely responsible for the crime wave.

Despite the prospect of national elections in 1997, during much of the mid-1990s the opposition remained deeply fractured and disorganized. Although the main opposition organizations (excluding FORD–Asili) formed a new alliance in November 1995, with Leakey as its chief co-ordinator, widening divisions in and between the parties ensured that the co-operation was ineffectual and short-lived. By the end of 1995 some 11 national assembly delegates who had been elected in December 1992 as representatives of opposition groupings had reportedly defected to the ruling KANU; several subsequent defections occurred during 1996–97. FORD–Asili and FORD–Kenya were paralysed by leadership struggles in early 1996; Martin Shikuku claimed to have unseated Matiba as chairman of the former, while in the latter Raila Odinga nominated a rival party executive to that led by Kijana Wamalwa. A FORD–Kenya party congress, held in April to settle Odinga's challenge, ended in disorder. Meanwhile, Safina remained effectively powerless, owing to the government's refusal to grant it registered status. In December Odinga was reportedly expelled from FORD–Kenya; Odinga (who claimed to have resigned from the party) subsequently announced that he was joining the National Development Party (NDP), of which he was appointed leader in May 1997. Rivalries also began to emerge within KANU itself, apparently motivated by the desire to gain political advantage in anticipation of Moi's demise or retirement, given his age and that the constitution permitted him to stand for only one further term as president.

At a public rally in September 1996 Moi pardoned two self-confessed guerrillas, who were said to have admitted to belonging to a clandestine group that had plotted to assassinate the president and other prominent Kenyans; they were also claimed to have revealed a plot to free Wamwere from detention. However, it was widely considered that the allegations had been fabricated in an attempt to discredit the opposition. In December Wamwere was released on bail in order to seek medical treatment abroad; his conviction was eventually quashed in November 1997. In January 1997 Amnesty International published a report that accused the government of failing to halt the widespread torture of detainees. In the same month the re-appointment to the cabinet of Biwott (a principal suspect in the inquiry into the death of Robert Ouko in 1990) provoked considerable disquiet. In February 1997 Kenya became a signatory to the UN Convention Against Torture and Other Cruel, Inhuman and Degrading Treatment or Punishment. Shortly afterwards the death of a prominent student activist in suspicious circumstances let to nation-wide anti-government demonstrations on campuses.

Concerns continued to be voiced in the mid-1990s over levels of corruption in Kenyan society. In May 1996 the opposition-dominated public accounts committee accused a number of senior members of the government of withholding information vital to its investigation into the collapse of several Kenyan banks, a matter believed to be connected with losses of an estimated US $430m. in public funds on allegedly fraudulent claims for export tax rebates. In June 1997 proceedings were abandoned in the high court against a prominent businessman implicated in the affair (which became known as the 'Goldenberg' scandal); although the attorney-general announced that a retrial would take place, international donors accused the government of doing little to recover the lost revenue or to bring those responsible to justice. (Plans for a retrial were under way in mid-1999.)

At the beginning of August 1997 the IMF suspended loan disbursements to Kenya, pending the implementation of decisive action to eliminate official corruption and to improve the system of revenue collection; the Moi administration subsequently announced the inauguration of an anti-corruption authority.

It was widely believed by opposition politicians that, short of considerable constitutional reform, Moi and KANU would inevitably win the presidential and parliamentary elections scheduled for 1997. In particular, it was alleged that constituency boundaries had been gerrymandered and should be altered, and that, while Moi would be extremely likely to gain the highest number of votes in a first presidential ballot, given a second round of voting requiring an overall majority of votes, a single opposition candidate might emerge victorious. Moi, however, having promised a constitutional review, repeatedly refused to contemplate its initiation until after the 1997 elections. In April 1997 the national convention assembly (along with its executive council, the NCEC) was established at a conference in Limuru as an inclusive forum involving representatives of non-governmental organizations, religious groups and opposition parties (notably excluding supporters of Matiba and Odinga). In early May the NCEC attempted to hold a rally in Nairobi, but security forces prevented supporters from entering the venue and violent confrontations ensued. At the end of the month, shortly after Matiba announced that he was resigning as a member of parliament on the grounds that he did not recognize the government's authority, security forces intervened to disperse a rally organized by Matiba and Odinga. Demands for constitutional reform intensified in mid-June, when opposition parliamentarians rendered the budget speech inaudible and security forces clashed with demonstrators on the streets of Nairobi. The budget was subsequently approved, despite opposition claims that it could not be properly debated as nobody had been able to hear its contents.

In early July 1997, on the anniversary of the pro-democracy demonstrations of 1990, illegal rallies were held across Kenya in support of constitutional reform. International outrage was expressed at the conduct of the security forces, who, as well as using excessive force to disperse demonstrators, attacked worshippers in the Anglican cathedral in Nairobi and were widely reported to have committed unprovoked acts of violence against passers-by. The disturbances continued for several days, and a number of people were killed. In mid-July 1997 Moi met opposition and religious leaders to discuss constitutional reform, and announced that the opposition was free to hold registered public meetings, in anticipation of new, more lenient legislation. In what was widely viewed as an attempt to regain control of the reform process, KANU's executive council recommended the establishment of a constitutional review commission. Despite misgivings, the NCEC agreed to enter into dialogue with the Moi administration; in late August, however, the government withdrew from the talks, following serious outbreaks of criminal violence in and around Mombasa. While the government blamed the NCEC for orchestrating the attacks, the NCEC in turn alleged that the government was inciting inter-ethnic conflict with the aim of depriving opposition supporters from the predominantly Luo region of the opportunity to vote in the forthcoming elections, by forcing them to flee their homes. Although the dialogue between the NCEC and the Moi administration had broken down, representatives of both KANU and opposition parties succeeded in persuading parliament that the introduction of some constitutional reforms would be necessary in order to avert further bloodshed. Consequently in early September 1997 the national assembly approved legislation that amended the constitution with the stated aim of ensuring free and fair democratic elections: detention without trial was ended, greater freedom granted to hold political rallies without prior authorization, opposition members were appointed to the electoral commission organizing the impending elections, rules governing the registration of political parties were eased, and more equitable access to the state-owned media was permitted. By October some 22 political parties had been registered, although Safina remained barred from official recognition. Both Moi and KANU benefited from the freer registration procedure, as the creation of new political organizations rendered the opposition ever more fractured and ineffectual. Despite the new legislation enabling the opposition to organize more public rallies, several meetings were broken up, with considerable violence, by the security forces during September and October. In mid-October Moi ordered the police to stop disrupting peaceful opposition rallies.

Elections and Internal Concerns

The presidential and legislative elections, which took place concurrently on 29 December 1997, were undermined by poor organization, logistical difficulties and violence, as well as by allegations of electoral fraud. Moi was declared the winner of the presidential poll, which was contested by 15 candidates, obtaining 40.64% of the valid votes cast. He won easily in the

coastal region, north-east, Rift Valley and Western province, but received only one-third of the votes in the Eastern province. Mwai Kibaki, the DP leader and former vice-president, came second, winning 31.49% of the votes cast. At the legislative election KANU secured 107 of the 210 elected seats in the enlarged national assembly, with the DP taking 39 seats, the NDP 21, FORD–Kenya 17 and the Social Democratic Party 15. Safina (which had eventually obtained registration in November and had consequently conducted only a short campaign) took five seats. KANU (having received government patronage and with better organization and finances than its opponents) won 2.4m. votes, compared with 3.2m. for the combined opposition. It was the only major party which drew support from all ethnic groups, although voting was, as in 1992, predominantly conducted in accordance with ethnic allegiances. Despite KANU's success, several cabinet ministers and assistant ministers were not re-elected to the national assembly. Moi was inaugurated for a fifth (and final) term as president in January 1998. Shortly afterwards he appointed a new cabinet. Significantly, he did not reappoint Prof. Saitoti (who had held the post since 1989) to the vice-presidency, leaving the position vacant, evidently in order not to give any indication of his preferred successor. There were no Kikuyu or Luo ministers. The cabinet was reorganized in February. Following the elections, Kibaki petitioned the high court to declare Moi's re-election invalid. A group of independent Kenyan observers had, none the less, pronounced the electoral process 'satisfactory'.

In early 1998 inter-ethnic violence erupted once again in the volatile Rift Valley: the disturbances were blamed by the government on bitterness in the Kikuyu and Luo communities at the outcome of the elections, and by the Kikuyu and Luo on persecution by the security forces and by the smaller tribal groups which had voted for Moi and KANU. During January and February about 100 fatalities were reported to have ensued from clashes between the Kikuyu and Kalenjin in the Laikipia area; in all more than 300,000 people were believed to have been displaced. The violence appeared to closely resemble the inter-ethnic conflict of 1992, with well-organized armed Kalenjin raiders forcing Kikuyu to flee their homes. The police reportedly failed to intervene effectively. Government troops reportedly embarked upon a programme of disarmament in the Rift Valley in early May. In July the authorities organized a judicial inquiry into the causes of both the 1992 and 1998 tribal disturbances.

During early 1998 Raila Odinga, who had robustly contested the presidential election, unexpectedly adopted a policy of *rapprochement* with Moi: he was frequently seen at the president's side at public functions, and the two men appeared to have formed an unofficial alliance of the NDP and KANU, creating considerable disquiet in both organizations. Moi also won the co-operation of FORD–Kenya, assuring KANU of a comfortable majority in parliament. A consultative forum on the constitutional review process was inaugurated in April, with the aim of organizing the long-anticipated constitutional review commission.

In early August 1998 a car bomb exploded at the US embassy in central Nairobi (concurrently with a similar attack on the US mission to Dar es Salaam, Tanzania). Some 254 people were killed in Nairobi and more than 5,000 suffered injuries. The attacks were believed to have been co-ordinated by international Islamic fundamentalist terrorists, led by a Saudi Arabian dissident, Osama bin Laden, and, in mid-August, the USA retaliated by launching air strikes against targets associated with bin Laden in Afghanistan and Sudan. In the aftermath of the bomb attacks, Kenyan investigators and US federal agents made extensive nation-wide enquiries, concentrating their search for the perpetrators particularly on the Muslim community in Mombasa and the surrounding coastal region. In October the US government approved the provision of a US $38m. humanitarian aid programme for Kenyan victims of the embassy bomb. During that month evidence emerged that young Kenyan Muslims had been systematically recruited for military training by international Islamic guerrilla groups. Meanwhile, the government banned five local Islamic aid organizations, provoking deep resentment among Kenyan Muslims. Nation-wide protest demonstrations were held in October; these, however, did not attract a high level of support and revealed significant rifts between moderate and extremist Islamists. Subsequently the government permitted two of the organizations to resume operations. In early February 1999 the high court refused to permit the extradition to the USA of a Palestinian resident of Mombasa, who was accused of planting the Nairobi bomb.

In mid-February 1999 Turkish agents in Nairobi captured Abdullah Ocalan, the leader of the Kurdistan Workers' Party, which is engaged in an armed struggle against the Turkish government; Ocalan was returned to Turkey, where he was subsequently tried and, in late June, sentenced to death. He had reportedly entered Kenya clandestinely at the beginning of February, and had been sheltered at the Greek embassy. The precise role of the Moi administration in Ocalan's arrest remained unclear. Subsequently several Kenyan diplomatic missions in Europe were occupied by Kurdish protesters. Shortly after the capture of Ocalan, Moi dismissed two leading members of the police force and a senior immigration official who had been implicated in the affair.

Moi reorganized the cabinet in February 1999. Most significantly Simon Nyachae, the minister of finance, hitherto regarded as a potential presidential successor, exchanged portfolios with the minister of industrial development, Yekokanda Francis Masakhalia; this effectively represented a demotion for Nyachae, who had played a leading role in efforts to combat corruption and financial mismanagement in the public sector. The removal of Nyachae from the treasury was unpopular with the IMF. Nyachae, claiming to have been victimized by powerful senior figures allegedly involved in corrupt activities, immediately resigned from his new post. Following Nyachae's departure from the cabinet, Micah Cheserem, governor of the central bank of Kenya, became the most prominent national campaigner against senior-level corruption. Masakhalia was a close associate of Nicholas Biwott, the former minister of industry who had been implicated in the suspicious death of Dr Robert Ouko in 1990. (Biwott had been reinstated in the cabinet in 1997, and was widely believed to have become Moi's closest adviser.) In early April 1999 Prof. Saitoti was reappointed to the position of vice-president (vacant since January 1998). A minor reshuffle of the cabinet took place later in April 1999. Saitoti, however, was rumoured to be implicated in the 'Goldenberg' financial scandal that had been uncovered in 1996 (see above). At the end of June 1999 the national assembly defeated a motion of 'no confidence' in Saitoti's vice-presidency, which had been proposed by an NDP deputy on the basis of Saitoti's alleged connections with the affair. Dr Leakey, evidently disappointed by the failure of the opposition to present a united and effective alternative to KANU, announced his intention to retire from politics in October 1998; during the previous month he had been reappointed as director the KWS. In late July 1999, however, Leakey (who appeared to have formed a vastly improved relationship with Moi) was nominated head of the civil service and secretary to the cabinet, responsible for combating the corruption that was allegedly widespread in the public services. Masakhalia, having failed to make a significant impact as minister of finance, was replaced in mid-August by Chrysanthus Okemo, previously the minister of energy.

During early 1999 controversy arose over the composition of the proposed constitutional review commission. Many non-governmental organizations applied for representation on the commission, and most were approved by the attorney-general. Problems emerged, however, over the relative influence that KANU, opposition groupings and civil bodies would command, with KANU being accused by the opposition of seeking an unjustified level of representation on the commission. In late May Moi stated that the constitutional review process should, instead, be conducted by parliament, proposing that the national assembly should appoint a legal team to draft reforms. The NCEC, concerned that the ruling party would then use its parliamentary majority to sabotage the reform process, strongly opposed this. In early June the NCEC organized a protest march in Nairobi, which was broken up by the security forces. The establishment of the commission was suspended throughout the second half of 1999. In December the national assembly voted in favour of appointing a parliamentary select commission to review the situation.

Moi's eldest son, Jonathan Kipkemboi Torotich, a prominent Kenyan businessman, announced in September 1998 that he intended to enter politics on the eventual retirement of his father. In March 1999 Moi confirmed that he would relinquish power following the expiry of his current term of office in 2002.

In September 1999 Moi carried out an extensive reshuffle of the cabinet, reducing the number of government ministers from 27 to 15. The rationalization, in which a considerable number of ministries were merged, was the work of Dr Leakey in his new capacity as head of the civil service. He said that reductions would also have to be made in the numbers of civil servants. The opposition claimed that the rationalization was more a matter of show than of substance. Not one senior minister lost his position in the cabinet. International donors also expressed their disappointment at the seemingly inadequate and limited efforts to tackle corruption. The chief justice, Zaccheus Chesoni, died in September and was replaced by Bernard Chunga, formerly the director of public prosecutions.

In December 1999 a political rally organized by Kenya's main opposition parties in Nairobi ended in violence and was dispersed by the police; one person was killed and several were injured. KANU supporters were believed to have provoked the unrest. The rally had been called to press for a popular constitutional review process. This was supported by the churches, which had become increasingly involved in pursuing their own version of constitutional reform during 1999. A group called Ufungamano announced that it would hold its own constitutional review process as an alternative to the official KANU-supported select commission working through parliament. Ufungamano said that it would canvas public opinion directly and produce its own recommendations. Another protest group, entitled the Stakeholders' Support Group (SSG), declared that it would campaign against the resumption of IMF aid (originally discontinued in 1997) until the government had carried out sufficient reforms. The SSG wanted the IMF to list the necessary reforms and declare whether they had been carried out before resuming aid to Kenya.

An IMF team visited Kenya in mid-February 2000 and expressed its satisfaction at the reforms initiated since Leakey's appointment; the latter's efforts, however, to investigate and eliminate corruption at the highest level were thwarted by senior KANU politicians who were still diverting development funds and exploiting vulnerable commodity boards. Kenya's anti-corruption authority, which had been established in 1997 at the Fund's insistence, had still not prosecuted a single case by the end of March 2000. Consequently, the IMF team left Kenya without approving the expected credits or balance-of-payments support. Other donors refused to disburse aid unless the IMF gave the lead. On his return to Kenya from a summit meeting in the USA in February, Moi was given the news that the latest round of talks with the IMF had failed. The president declared that he would personally take charge of all future negotiations with the IMF.

Raila Odinga of the NDP, who was now a government loyalist, was chosen to head the parliamentary select commission charged with reviewing constitutional reform. The opposition boycotted the commission's inaugural meeting in January 2000. An alternative meeting was called by the churches in the same month; the churches, however, wishing to keep their movement out of politics, refused to share the platform with the mainly Kikuyu opposition leaders. As Odinga's commission started to hold hearings around the country, he won some support in Luo areas, but encountered difficulties in holding hearings in Kikuyu territory. The debate seemed to be dividing along ethnic lines as some 50 Kikuyu KANU parliamentary members came out in support of a measure of constitutional reform. Odinga completed his review in the first four months of 2000, and on 27 April introduced the Kenya Constitutional Amendment Report, which had been drafted by his commission, to parliament. Odinga's NDP and KANU supported the amendment, while the main opposition parties, including the DP and the FORD groupings, boycotted the debate. This meant that a sizeable parliamentary majority approved the amendment. Its effect was to remove the constitutional process from public discussion and entrust it to 15 commissioners, appointed by the President, with parliamentary advice. Politically the move was seen as a victory for the alliance between KANU (representing the Kalenjin and minority tribes) and the Luos of the NDP. The Kikuyus were almost entirely excluded from the process. It was reported that the commission favoured constitutional changes involving the introduction of a ceremonial presidency (a position that was expected to be taken by Moi), a vice-presidency (a powerless post to be given to an opposition leader) and a prime minister (a post targeted by Odinga). These proposals were still opposed by the Kikuyu and the Ufungamao coalition, but, having been defeated in parliament, they were restricted to extra-parliamentary opposition.

Although Moi was not due to step down from the presidency until December 2002 (when he would be 80 years old), the succession struggle among high-ranking members of KANU started in earnest in 2000. The ostracized leader Simon Nyachae, who had been dismissed as minister of finance in February 1999, announced his intention to stand for the presidency. Other prominent figures within KANU said that they would challenge Prof. Saitoti for the vice-presidency. The leaders of all the main opposition parties also began manoeuvering tactically to put themselves in a strong position to contest the posts.

In February 2000 ethnic clashes broke out in Laikipia and Isolio in central Kenya between pro-government pastoralist tribes and established Kikuyu farmers. The opposition press claimed that the riots had been deliberately provoked by the government against its Kikuyu opponents. Most of the Laikipia farmers supported the opposition DP.

EXTERNAL RELATIONS

Uniquely in Africa, President Kenyatta left the conduct of foreign relations to his ministers of foreign affairs and never travelled outside the country. On his accession to power, however, President Moi resumed presidential direction of foreign affairs. Throughout the years of Kenyatta's presidency, Kenya remained unconvinced of the benefits of close integration with its neighbours through the East African Common Services Organization and its successor, the East African Community (EAC). During the early 1970s major political and economic tensions developed between the EAC member states, and by July 1977 the Community had ceased to function. Throughout the period of Idi Amin's regime in Uganda, Kenya maintained an official stance of strict neutrality towards that country, although relations with Tanzania gradually deteriorated to a level of outright hostility by the time of Kenyatta's death in 1978. The collapse in April 1979 of the Amin regime raised hopes of better relations generally in east Africa, but Kenya was deeply suspicious of Tanzania's military role in Uganda. A meeting in January 1980 between President Moi and Presidents Nyerere of Tanzania and Binaisa of Uganda failed to allay these anxieties. The accession of Dr Milton Obote to the presidency of Uganda in December 1980, however, was followed by a sustained improvement in Kenya's relations with both Uganda and Tanzania. In November 1983 the three countries reached agreement on the distribution of the assets and liabilities of the EAC. Shortly afterwards, the border between Kenya and Tanzania (closed in 1977) was reopened, and in December the two countries agreed to establish full diplomatic relations. In 1986 agreement was reached on a trade treaty and on the establishment of a joint co-operation commission.

When the National Resistance Army (NRA) seized power in Uganda in January 1986, Moi offered full co-operation to the new Ugandan president, Yoweri Museveni. However, relations became less cordial as Moi became increasingly distrustful of the radical nature of the new regime in Kampala. Additionally, the Kenyan authorities became anxious that continued unrest in Uganda could provide a source of arms for opposition supporters in Kenya. Tension grew during 1986 over alleged Kenyan interference in freight deliveries to Uganda that were routed through Mombasa, and, in early 1987, this was intensified following the death in Kenyan police custody of a Ugandan national. In May Uganda protested at Kenya's alleged closure of the land frontier. The tension eased somewhat in June, when it became apparent that the movement of traffic between the two countries was possible.

The *détente*, however, proved to be short-lived. In September 1987 Uganda claimed that Kenya was harbouring anti-Museveni rebels, and stationed troops at its border with Kenya. These claims were denied, and Moi warned that any infiltration by Ugandan troops in Kenya would encounter fierce retaliation. The influx of some 2,000 Ugandan refugees into Kenya strained relations further. In December Ugandan troops were alleged to

have entered Kenya illegally in pursuit of rebels, and for several days the Ugandan and Kenyan armed forces exchanged fire across the border, which was temporarily closed to traffic. The Kenyan government expelled the Ugandan high commissioner and a number of other Ugandan citizens. Later in December, Presidents Moi and Museveni agreed to withdraw troops from either side of the border and to allow the resumption of normal traffic. In January 1988 the two countries signed a joint communiqué which provided for mutual co-operation in resolving problems relating to the flow of traffic across the common border. This *rapprochement* was disrupted in July, when the Ugandan government accused Kenya of complicity in smuggling weapons to a rebel group in northern Uganda, and security was tightened along the Kenya–Uganda border to prevent alleged incursions by Ugandan troops. In October Uganda complained that Kenya had been intermittently obstructing the movement of Ugandan traffic across the border. In March 1989 the Ugandan government strongly denied Kenyan allegations that Ugandan troops had been involved in an attack by Ugandan cattle-rustlers on Kenyan security forces earlier in that month, and that a Ugandan military aircraft had been responsible for the bombing of a town in north-western Kenya shortly afterwards. In August 1990 Moi visited Museveni, indicating a renewed *détente* between Kenya and Uganda. In November 1991 the presidents of Kenya, Uganda and Tanzania met in Nairobi, and declared their commitment to developing mutual co-operation. In November 1994 the three leaders met at Arusha, Tanzania, and established a permanent tripartite commission for co-operation, with a view to reviving the defunct EAC; progress was hindered, however, by a renewed deterioration in relations between Kenya and Uganda. During early 1995 the Moi administration protested strongly to the UN, following the granting of refugee status in Uganda to Brig. John Odongo (also known as Stephen Amoke), leader of the February Eighteen Popular Resistance Army, a previously unknown outlawed Kenyan guerrilla movement. The Moi administration lent no credence to subsequent claims by the Ugandan government to have deported Odongo to a third country (reported to be Ghana). Following the intervention of the newly-elected President Benjamin Mkapa of Tanzania, Moi and Museveni were publicly reconciled in January 1996, and undertook to co-operate over the planned relaunch of the EAC. In March Moi, Museveni and Mkapa, meeting in Nairobi, formally inaugurated the Secretariat of the Permanent Tripartite Commission for East African Co-operation. A treaty for the re-establishment of the EAC (providing for the promotion of free trade among the member states, with the eventual introduction of a single currency, for the development of infrastructure, tourism and agriculture within the Community, and for the establishment of a regional legislative assembly and court) was ratified by the heads of state of Kenya, Tanzania and Uganda in June 2000.

In December 1980 and May 1981 Lt-Col Mengistu Haile Mariam of Ethiopia made state visits to Kenya; the two countries subsequently signed a treaty of friendship and co-operation, and a mutual defence pact. Relations with the government of Meles Zenawi in Ethiopia came under strain in 1997, following an increased incidence of cross-border cattle-rustling, including an attack in March 1997 in which 16 members of the Kenyan security forces were killed. A number of communiqués were subsequently signed by representatives of the two countries, agreeing to tighten border security, to take measures to prevent arms and drugs-smuggling and to enhance trade. Somalia has traditionally laid claim to part of north-eastern Kenya, where there is a large ethnic Somali population. In mid-1981, however, President Moi held talks with the Somali president, Siad Barre, at which the latter renounced these territorial claims. In July 1984, during a state visit to Somalia by the Kenyan leader, Presidents Moi and Siad Barre pledged to increase bilateral co-operation between their respective countries. In early 1989, however, friction developed between the Kenyan government and ethnic Somalis from both north-eastern Kenya and Somalia, when Somali poachers were alleged to be largely responsible for the depletion of Kenyan elephant numbers; it was reported that several thousand ethnic Somalis had been ordered to evacuate areas near the game parks. In April 1991, following the overthrow and flight of President Siad Barre in January of that year, the new Somali government accused the Moi regime of providing assistance to Barre and his supporters, who had taken refuge in Kenya. During the early 1990s the Kenyan government mediated between the rival factions in the Somali civil war. In May 1992 the Kenyan authorities negotiated permanent asylum for Barre in Nigeria. Relations between Kenya and Libya deteriorated in April 1987, when five Libyan diplomats were expelled for alleged subversive activities. In the following month a Kenyan newspaper published an unsubstantiated report that Libya was training dissidents from Kenya to overthrow the government. In December the government closed the Libyan diplomatic mission in Nairobi. Diplomatic relations between Kenya and Libya were eventually restored in July 1998. Relations between Kenya and Sudan deteriorated in June 1988, as they exchanged mutual accusations of aiding rebel factions. In early 1989 Sudan rekindled a long-standing dispute with Kenya over the sovereignty of territory on the Kenyan side of the Kenya–Sudan border, known as the 'Elemi triangle', which is believed to contain substantial deposits of petroleum. In October 1997 negotiations commenced in Nairobi between representatives of the Sudanese government and the Sudan People's Liberation Army, under the chairmanship of the Kenyan minister of foreign affairs. In November 1998 some 189 people (mainly Somalis) were found to have been massacred in north-eastern Kenya; Ethiopian guerrillas belonging to the Oromo Liberation Front (OLF) were widely believed to be responsible. In January 1999 the Kenyan government protested to the Ethiopian authorities, following an incursion into Kenya by Ethiopian security forces, who were reported to be in pursuit of OLF rebels. In May Kenya deployed additional troops at the two countries' common frontier, following a series of landmine explosions in the region, which had resulted in several fatalities. Ethiopian troops allegedly made a further incursion into Kenyan territory in early July.

In October 1995, despite strong condemnation from foreign governments, the Kenyan authorities refused to permit the UN international criminal tribunal for Rwanda, at Arusha in Tanzania, which was investigating war crimes committed in 1994, access to alleged Rwandan perpetrators of genocide who were now in Kenya. In June 1996 Kenya closed the Rwandan embassy in Nairobi in protest at the Rwandan government's refusal to waive diplomatic immunity for an embassy official who was suspected of plotting a murder in Kenya; the diplomat was deported. In September 1996, however, the first arrest in Kenya was made of a Rwandan Hutu suspected of involvement in genocide. Kenya strongly denied accusations, in November, of supplying arms to Rwandan Hutu rebels operating from within Zaire. Following the *coup d'état* in Burundi in July 1996, Kenya, along with other countries of the region, imposed full economic sanctions on the administration of Maj. Pierre Buyoya; these sanctions were subsequently relaxed, and were eventually withdrawn in January 1999. In November and December 1996 regional summit meetings were held in Nairobi to discuss the crisis in the Great Lakes region. Relations between the Kenyan and Rwandan governments improved during 1997, when further Rwandan Hutus were arrested by the Kenyan security forces to stand trial on charages of genocide at the UN tribunal.

At 31 December 1995, according to a report from UNHCR, Kenya was sheltering an estimated 239,500 refugees, including about 200,000 from Somalia. The Moi government, which claims that the refugees place an intolerable burden on the country's resources, has repeatedly requested the UN to repatriate the total refugee population. By mid-1998 an estimated 155,000 Somalis had been repatriated from Kenya, with assistance from UNHCR. However, continuing instability in Somalia during the late 1990s resulted in further influxes of refugees to Kenya. Kenya's total refugee population stood at 238,200 at the end of 1998.

In north-eastern Kenya the endemic problem of unrest erupted again in mid-1999 as regional problems spread across Kenya's borders. Somali militia overwhelmed the Ammuma border post in June and seized arms, a number of Kenyan army trucks and other military equipment. In July the Kenyan navy

was, for the first time, placed on alert and ordered to guard the maritime borders and intercept any hostile craft from Somalia. On land, the Kenyan government reported frequent penetration of its borders, an influx of outlaws and a strong increase of incidents of smuggling. In August Moi retaliated by ordering the immediate closure of the Somali border; the border remained closed until April 2000. In December 1999 armed militiamen dressed in Somali army uniforms crossed the border with Kenya and attacked a police post. Violent clashes along the border between Kenya and Somali recurred in February 2000. Fierce fighting between the Awlyahan and Muhammad Zuberi clans in Doble, Somalia, resulted in more than 30 deaths. When unrest spread across the Kenyan frontier, Kenya's north-eastern provincial commissioner sealed the border with heavily-armed security personnel. The following week Merille bandits from Ethiopia attacked Turkana homesteads north of Marsabit. Security forces killed 35 raiders. In May more than 70 people were reported to have been killed in a major clash between Somalis and Boran tribesmen.

President Moi has made a number of overseas visits and has taken an active interest in continental affairs. In 1989 he offered his services as mediator between vying forces in Ethiopia and Mozambique, and in 1991 he took the chairmanship in peace talks between warring Somali factions. An important development in foreign affairs under Moi has been Kenya's support of US military commitments in the Indian Ocean. In 1980 Kenya permitted the USA to use port and air base facilities in Kenya, in return for increased US military assistance.

The Moi administration has consistently received international criticism of its record on human rights. Following the violent disruption by Kenyan security forces of a meeting in Kenya between a US congressman and a Kenyan church leader in January 1987, the USA temporarily suspended aid allocations to Kenya. In August the US administration suspended military aid of US $5m., in protest at the Kenyan government's arrest of opposition figures during the previous month; the funds were eventually released in February 1991. In October 1990 Kenya severed diplomatic relations with Norway, following protests by the Norwegian government about the arrest on treason charges during that month of a Kenyan dissident who had previously been in exile in Norway; Norway subsequently suspended aid allocations to Kenya. Diplomatic relations were restored in February 1994, although Norway declined to resume assistance. In mid-November 1991, following international protests at arrests by the Kenyan security forces of opposition leaders who had organized a pro-democracy rally, the Kenyan government accused US, German and Swedish diplomats of assisting Kenyan dissidents (allegations which were vigorously denied). In response, Germany withdrew its ambassador for 'consultations'. Later in November, following the decision by donor nations and organizations to withhold aid to Kenya, the USA announced that it was suspending assistance worth $28m. In July 1995 the United Kingdom withheld financial aid to Kenya, pending an improvement in the Moi administration's human rights policies and economic management. Despite these setbacks, strategic considerations have ensured the contribution of the informal military alliance between Kenya and the USA. Following the devastating bomb attack on the US embassy in Nairobi in August 1998 (see above), US federal agents were dispatched to Kenya on an investigative mission.

By the late 1990s the view was widely held that Moi's prestige as a senior African statesman had been undermined both by his government's human rights record at home, and, abroad, by the demise of many of his political allies and the emergence of younger, more radical African leaders who viewed his style of government as unacceptable. Nevertheless, under the Moi administration Kenya has enjoyed relatively good regional relations. During the late 1990s Kenya worked consistently within the Intergovernmental Authority on Development (IGAD, see p. 134) to enhance regional co-operation. In May 1999 Moi was elected chairman of the Common Market for Eastern and Southern Africa (COMESA, see p. 117).

Economy

LINDA VAN BUREN

INTRODUCTION

In the 21st century agriculture remains the main occupation and source of income of the majority of Kenyans, not only sustaining most of the rural population through subsistence crops or jobs on large agricultural estates, but also making a major contribution to gross domestic product (GDP), export earnings and government revenue. But in the nearly four decades since independence in 1963, Kenya has seen the rise of a substantial middle class encompassing all ethnic groups in the country. This middle class, engaged primarily in the services and manufacturing sectors, accounts for both the production and the consumption that are necessary to sustain these sectors, which are substantially more important to this economy than would normally be expected in a country of Kenya's income level. Before independence, the disproportionate development of manufacturing, processing and service industries was bound up with the early presence in Kenya of a substantial number of non-African settlers, whose high incomes generated demand. Since independence, the demand necessary to sustain these sectors has come primarily from the growing African middle class, as well as from the presence of large numbers of non-Kenyans, both as residents (expatriate staff of non-governmental organizations and multinational companies) and as visitors (tourists and business travellers).

The population of Kenya at the census of 24 August 1989 (believed to be underenumerated) was 21,443,636. On the eve of the census of 24 August 1999 the total population was officially estimated at 28.7m. Much of Kenya's population is concentrated in the central highlands, the coastal strip and the lake area. According to official estimates, only about one-quarter of the population lived in urban areas in 1999; the three largest cities were Nairobi (with 1.4m. inhabitants), Mombasa (with about 1m.) and Kisumu (with about 400,000). The average rate of population increase was 3.4% per annum in 1980–90, but fell to 2.6% per annum in 1990–96, according to World Bank estimates, and to 2.4% in 1998–99. In 1985 the country's average annual birth rate, at 5.4%, was the highest in the world; by 1995, however, the rate stood at 3.5%, one of the lowest in sub-Saharan Africa. The rate of infant mortality was 57 per 1,000 live births in 1996, compared with 102 per 1,000 in 1970.

At independence in 1963, formal sector agriculture in Kenya was export orientated and was based upon large-scale commercial agriculture of the settled 'White Highlands' and on European- and Asian-owned plantations. Much of the government's agricultural effort in the early years of independence was devoted to a land reform programme designed to transfer land from the European settlers and to resettle Africans upon it. Later, the government turned its attention to the Kenyanization of commerce, which at that time was dominated by non-African and frequently non-citizen businesses.

Kenya's record in the first 15 years or so after independence placed it, in terms of the growth of output, among the most successful of African developing countries. From independence until 1980, the economy progressed at a cumulative annual rate of growth of 6.8% in real terms, with growth in the industrial sector reaching 9.7% per year during the 1970s. This expansion was financed by a substantial inflow of capital as well as by domestic sources.

Throughout the 1980s, the economy was characterized by a boom-and-bust pattern, depending on the global prices of coffee and tea and the presence or absence of drought in food-growing areas. Then, in 1992, Kenya experienced negative GDP growth of 0.8%, owing to a combination of political and ethnic instability, the suspension of bilateral balance of payments assistance and other exogenous factors. The introduction of a new round of economic reforms in 1993, together with greater political stability and the resumption of aid, heralded a return to positive GDP growth: a rate of 0.4% was recorded in 1993, improving to 2.7% in 1994 and 4.8% in 1995, before slowing to 4.6% in 1996, 2.3% in 1997, 1.8% in 1998 and an estimated 1.3% in 1999. The annual inflation rate rose steadily during the early 1990s, to 15.8% per annum in 1990, 19.8% in 1991, 29.5% in 1992 and 45.8% in 1993. During the first three months of 1993 the annual rate of inflation soared to 60% (and, at times, to more than 100%, according to unofficial sources), owing to the effects of the suspension of international donor aid and the deregulation of prices in 1992 (see below). By the end of 1993 the inflation rate had been contained, and the annual rate for 1994 was 29.0%. Consumer prices rose by just 1.6% in 1995, but soared to 9.1% in 1996 and 11.2% in 1997, before falling back to 6.6% in 1998 and, further, to 3.5% in 1999. These improvements were achieved by limiting the growth of the money supply to 10% per annum. GDP at current prices rose from US $9,071m. in 1997 to $9,961m. in 1998 and to an estimated $10,443m. in 1999, according to Central Bank of Kenya figures. Meanwhile, real per caput GDP declined from $283 in 1997, to $282 in 1998 and to $279 in 1999.

AGRICULTURE

Agriculture continues to dominate Kenya's economy. Although the agricultural sector's direct contribution to GDP has declined slightly in recent years, it remains significant, accounting, with forestry and fishing, for 24.6% of GDP in 1998. The sector's indirect contribution to GDP is also very important: the World Bank estimates that agriculture-based subsectors of the manufacturing and services sectors provide about 30% of GDP annually. The principal cash crops, tea and coffee, ranked second and third respectively, behind tourism, as sources of foreign exchange in 1992–95. About 70% of the working population made their living on the land in 1999, compared with 80% in 1980. More than one-half of total agricultural output is subsistence production. The sector grew by just 1.1% in the year to February 2000; virtually all of that growth was accounted for by coffee, while output of tea, sugar cane and sisal declined. The disappointing agricultural performance was blamed on adverse weather as well as on the high cost of credit compared with real returns.

Agricultural output is greatly dependent upon the weather, since only about 20% of Kenya's irrigation potential has been harnessed. The huge Bura scheme on the Tana river was designed to grow mainly cotton, while the government-managed schemes at Mwea and Ahero grow primarily rice. A National Water Master Plan estimates Kenya's total irrigation potential at 352,400 ha. Of this, only about 75,000 ha has been developed, and almost all of that area is irrigated from surface water. The plan has two main targets: 140 small-scale irrigation schemes of some 7,000 ha, each costing about US $7m., at a unit cost of $1,000 per ha; and 160 larger-scale schemes at a cost of $5,730 per ha, of which 18 have been shortlisted for further study. A target set in 1989 of bringing 1,000 ha into irrigation annually has not been met; only about 200–300 ha have been brought into irrigation per year, owing in part to economic reforms which abolished government grants and replaced them with loans that farmers have to repay.

In the early 1960s, as a result of land reform and increased coffee production on African farms, the share of small farms in marketed output grew rapidly; by 1976 this share had reached about one-half. There are around 1.7m. smallholders in the monetary sector and 3,200 large farms, ranches and plantations. There is an acute shortage of arable land, and only 7% of the country is classified as first-class land. The majority of smallholders have plots of less than 2 ha, and successive subdivision of plots among farmers' heirs impels large numbers of people to travel to towns in search of employment.

Kenya's leading export crop is tea, followed by coffee (almost all of it high-grade arabica) and horticultural produce. High-quality tea has been a rapidly expanding crop since the early 1970s, and overtook coffee as the top agricultural export earner in 1989. In 1998 tea earned two and one-half times as much export revenue as coffee. Tea output declined, however, by 6.6%

in the year to February 2000, to 254,548 metric tons, compared with 272,452 tons in the year to February 1999. At the same time, the average tea price decreased from US $2,000 per ton to $1,800. These two factors together forced earnings from tea exports down by 10.7% from $479.0m. in the 11 months to January 1999 to $427.9m. in the 11 months to January 2000. In 1998 Kenya ranked as the world's second largest exporter of tea, behind Sri Lanka, and ahead of China and India. In the 1990s Kenya replaced India as the United Kingdom's principal tea supplier, providing about 40% of British tea imports. Pakistan was also an important customer. The share of tea in Kenya's export earnings rose from 13.7% in 1982 to more than 28% in 1984, when production of tea reached a then record 203,590 tons. Drought in all growing areas and the disruption to farming caused by ethnic clashes in western regions restricted output to 188,000 tons in 1992. However, record tea crops followed in subsequent years, of 211,170 tons in 1993, 245,030 tons in 1995 and 294,165 tons in 1998. The total area planted with tea rose from 87,473 ha in 1989 to 117,000 ha in 1996, of which almost 80,000 ha were controlled by about 196,000 smallholders, accounting for some 65% of total output.

The share of small farms in the total area under tea expanded rapidly under the high-density settlement schemes of the Kenya Tea Development Authority (KTDA), which established 45 tea factories in 14 districts and distinguished itself as one of the most successful parastatals in Africa. In July 1992 the government announced the forthcoming transfer of tea factories to the private sector, and in 1998 details of the privatization were made public. Each tea factory was to become an independent company, while the KTDA was to convert to a management company, to be known as the Kenya Tea Development Agency. Of the remaining assets of the old KTDA, a 50% share was to be retained by the new KTDA, 25% was to be divided evenly among the 45 tea factory companies, and the remaining 25% was to be distributed among the companies in accordance with the proportion of management fees that they had paid to the old KTDA between 1983 and 1998. An unregistered entity, entitled the Kenya Union of Small-Scale Tea Owners (KUSSTO), was subsequently created as an alternative to the KTDA and called for wide-ranging reforms of the tea sector. The country's large tea estates, grouped in the Kenya Tea Growers' Association, cover about 31,017 ha. In the late 1990s smallholders' yields (at 1,810 kg per ha) were still lower than those of the large plantations (2,929 kg per ha), but were increasing as smallholders' bushes reached maturity.

The rise of the tea sector coincided with a decline in coffee production. Until October 1992 the Coffee Board of Kenya (CBK) controlled coffee production and handled much of its marketing. Since then, however, the marketing of coffee has been liberalized and the role of the CBK has nominally been confined to licensing, regulation and research. In addition, coffee auctions are now conducted in US dollars. Small-holders accounted for 117,677 ha of the total 156,304 ha planted with coffee in 1986, when they produced about 60% of the crop. Until the abandonment of coffee quotas by the International Coffee Organization (ICO) in July 1989, Kenya's production consistently exceeded its quota allocations, with the result that buyers were sought on the open market, mainly in the Middle East. Although Kenya's premium arabica coffee has long commanded a high price, the instability of the coffee market (in April 1992 world coffee prices were, in nominal terms, at a 22-year 'low', and overall 1992 prices were only one-third of their 1980 level) acted as a disincentive to Kenyan producers, many of whom decided to abandon coffee-growing in favour of more profitable crops. In 1989 a coffee development scheme, aimed at raising productivity and improving farmers' access to credit, was initiated with the support of the Commonwealth Development Corpn and the World Bank. The seven-year, US $107m. scheme also provided for the construction of 65 processing factories and the rehabilitation of a further 275 such installations. With the deregulation of coffee marketing in 1992, official production figures declined even further, to 85,300 metric tons in that year and to 75,100 tons in 1993. Output recovered to 79,000 tons in 1994, to 95,400 tons in 1995, and, according to the ICO, to 103,192 tons in 1996. The subsequent rapid decline in output was blamed by the government on 'structural constraints in marketing and inefficient supplies of farm inputs': production fell to 86,642 tons in 1997 and to just 57,000 tons in 1998. Output recovered by one-third in 1999, reaching 70,963 tons in the year to February 2000. The volume gain was offset, however, by a 39% drop in the average price fetched, which fell from an average of $3,452.80 per ton during the year to February 1999 to just $2,091.80 per ton in the year to February 2000. In 1999 and 2000 coffee growers experienced delays in payments, and some of them resorted to selling their coffee in local 'unofficial' markets. A proportion of Kenya's coffee crop made its way across the border into Uganda. In February 1995 Kenya, together with four other African coffee producers, agreed to participate in coffee price guarantee contract arrangements sponsored by the Eastern and Southern Africa Trade and Development Bank under the auspices of the Common Market for Eastern and Southern Africa (COMESA). This plan sought to promote producer price guarantees in place of stock retention schemes. The contract guarantee arrangements were to indemnify producers against prices falling below an agreed contract price. None the less, during 1994–99 global coffee prices declined by some 40%, with no sign of an imminent recovery. In March 1997 the Coffee Millers' Forum (subsequently renamed the Coffee Millers' Association) was founded to advocate further liberalization of the coffee marketing sector, which remained dominated by the still-powerful CBK. Although the CBK was instructed to issue marketing licences to all suitable applicants, a deposit of Ks. 1,000m. was required as security, which, it was argued, few applicants could afford.

The Kenya Sugar Authority was established in 1971 to develop the growing and processing of sugar cane. In 1980 there was a surplus of 150,000 metric tons of sugar for export after domestic demand of 275,000 tons had been met. By 1990, domestic consumption (which may have included an undetermined amount of demand for sugar intended for illegal export to neighbouring countries) had increased to 537,999 tons, against production of 431,836 tons. In order to meet part of the shortfall, some 64,050 tons of sugar were imported. Output declined to 303,292 tons in 1994, when 174,048 tons of sugar were imported. Domestic production had recovered to 401,610 tons by 1997, but the sector continued to suffer structural problems. Cheap imported sugar meant that Kenyan producers were unable to sell their output at a profit, and large stockpiles accumulated, assessed at 35,000 tons (with a value of Ks. 1,300m.) in August 1998. In that month the government reacted by raising the duty on imported sugar from 20% to 40%. In 1998 it was estimated that Kenya produced 410,000 tons of sugar, consumed 457,000 tons, imported 73,000 tons, and legally exported 26,000 tons. The sugar-cane harvest rose from 4.9m. tons in 1998 to 5.2m. tons in 1999. The government challenged the country's sugar producers in that year, pledging that it would ban imports of sugar into Kenya if they, in turn, would terminate illegal exports to neighbouring countries. Cane is sold to the sugar companies by smallholders and co-operatives. Of the seven sugar companies, the first to be privatized were Miwani (in late 1993, with the government retaining a 49% interest), and west Kenya. The largest company by far is Mumias, whose privatization has been the subject of lengthy debate. At first it was proposed that, through a public issue on the Nairobi Stock Exchange, the government was to reduce its share in Mumias from 70% to 30%, with 25% to go to the cane growers and factory workers. However, the government subsequently opted for a 'rights' issue, allowing existing shareholders, including Tate & Lyle of the United Kingdom, first call on the share offering. Both Mumias and Chemelil were brought to the point of sale, but, in February 1999, the government announced that the sale completions would be postponed, owing to prospects for 'low price realization'.

Production of cotton increased steadily in the 1970; however, output of lint subsequently slumped from 62,179 bales (each of 480 lb or 218 kg) in 1978/79 to 18,306 bales in 1995. Although production had recovered to 30,000 bales by 1997/98, Kenya still imported about 40,000 bales in that year. Nevertheless, potential output of lint is estimated at more than 220,000 bales. The reasons for the poor performance include low prices, an erratic payments system, inefficient marketing, and drought. Output of seed cotton declined from 15,200 metric tons in 1998 to about 15,000 tons in 1999, while cotton seed production fell from 10,100 tons in 1998 to about 10,000 tons in 1999, and cotton lint output decreased from 5,000 tons to 4,900 tons. The

Cotton Board of Kenya was radically reorganized during the early 1990s, and the transfer to private-sector ownership of the country's 15 cotton ginneries commenced in 1995.

Kenya became self-sufficient in tobacco in 1983, with production at about 6,600 metric tons. Production of tobacco rose by 24% in 1987, and included 5,212 tons of flue-cured, 126 tons of burley and 1,658 tons of fire-cured tobacco. The 1999 tobacco crop was estimated at 10,000 tons.

Kenya is the world's third largest producer of sisal. However, output of sisal, which reached a peak of 86,526 metric tons in 1974, had dwindled to only 26,000 tons in 1999. Revenue from the crop averaged an estimated US $11m. per annum in the early 1990s. The number of large estates fell from about 60 in 1954 to 19 in the mid-1990s. Global sisal prices reached a 12-year low in 1992, but recovered during 1993–96, benefiting Kenyan producers. Kenya exports only sisal fibre, having no processing industry. Small amounts of abaca (Manila hemp) are also produced: output was about 40 tons in 1999.

Kenya supplies 65%–70% of the world market for pyrethrum. In the early 1990s there were about 30,000 ha under pyrethrum, its output being mainly linked to co-operatives. The Pyrethrum Board of Kenya allocates quotas and attempts to improve production and its quality. In the late 1980s production ranged from 7,500 tons to about 10,000 tons annually. By the early 1990s, however, the increasing use of biological insecticides (particularly in the USA, the mainstay of Kenyan pyrethrum exports), had led to declining levels of demand for this commodity. Nevertheless, growing environmental concern in developed countries over the use of synthetic pesticides contributed to a modest upturn in demand for Kenya's output in the late 1990s. Kenya produced about 7,000 tons of dried pyrethrum flowers in 1999.

Kenya's high elevation favours the cultivation of a variety of fruits and vegetables, and in 1995 horticultural produce became Kenya's fourth most important source of foreign exchange, after tourism, tea and coffee. Fresh flowers, fruit and vegetables are air-freighted to Europe and the Middle East. In the late 1990s about 2,000 metric tons per week of air-freight space was available for this produce on northbound flights via Jomo Kenyatta International Airport. Production increased from 1.5m. kg in 1968 to 548m. kg in 1993, while earnings from horticultural exports rose from US $76m. in 1980 to an estimated $157m. in 1991. Output of fresh vegetables alone reached 688m. kg in 1998, declining to 662m. kg in 1999, with produce ranging from lettuce to cucumbers, tomatoes, onions, garlic, leeks, carrots, cabbages, green beans, broad beans, peas, pimentos and peppercorns. According to the Kenya Flower Council, Kenya accounts for 60% of African cut flower exports, in terms of value, and is the world's fourth-largest exporter of cut flowers. In 1997 Kenyan growers exported 35,000 metric tons of cut flowers to Europe, equivalent to 5m. stems per day. Two large companies account for most of the production, which is concentrated mainly on large-scale farms in the Naivasha region of Central province. The vegetables and fruit, other than pineapples, are grown mainly by smallholders. Kenya began exporting fresh pineapples in 1988, and in 1999 output totalled 290,000 tons of fresh pineapples (down from 300,000 tons in 1998), 90,291 tons of canned pineapples and 36,116 tons of pineapple juice. In that year the citrus sector produced 27,000 tons of oranges, 15,000 tons of grapefruits and smaller amounts of lemons, limes, pomelos and tangerines. The United Kingdom imports 44% of the vegetables and fruit. In 1997 a 10% 'suspended duty' was imposed on imports of certain fruits, in order to protect local growers.

Kenya's principal food crop is maize. Output levels depend heavily on weather conditions and tend to follow a boom or bust cycle. After the drought-affected crop of 2.1m. metric tons in 1993, production totalled 3.1m. tons in 1994 and 2.8m. tons in 1995, in which year some 1.4m. ha were planted with maize, yielding 1,964 kg per ha. Drought substantially reduced the 1996/97 maize crop, necessitating the importation of famine-relief maize, and also affected the 1997/98 maize crop (only 2.07m. tons were produced in the latter year). Improved weather conditions boosted the 1998 maize crop to 2.45m. tons. An infestation of army worms, however, contributed to a 14% decline in maize output, to 2.1m. tons, in 1999. In 1998–2000 18 districts, primarily in the north of the country, were affected by drought. Aid agencies distributed 75,000 tons of food valued at US $43m. in three northern districts in February–June 2000. The loss-making National Cereals and Produce Board (NCPB) was to be restructured under an agreement that Kenya signed with the World Bank in 1986 for a US $71.5m. agricultural adjustment programme, and with additional aid from the EC (European Community, now the European Union–EU). The government liberalized grain marketing in 1993 to allow more private-sector involvement, although it reserved for itself the power to 'make selected targeted interventions where market forces may not be effective'. The NCPB purchased about 1.4m. 90-kg bags of maize worth Ks. 2,000m. from Kenyan farmers during the 1999/2000 growing season. Part of these reserves were distributed in 2000 to several thousand people in Wajir and other drought-stricken areas, primarily in the north of the country.

Kenya has a high consumer demand for wheat, but normally provides less than 50% of its requirements. A major wheat expansion programme increased the area under wheat from 95,000 ha in 1993 to 155,000 ha in 1994. Yields, which were 2,025 kg per ha in 1979–81, had fallen to 1,259 kg per ha by 1992, but recovered to an estimated 2,129 kg per ha in 1995. Output increased from 150,000 metric tons in 1993 to about 277,000 tons in 1994, reaching a record 330,000 tons in 1995, before falling back to 315,000 tons in 1998 and further declining to 135,000 tons in 1999. In 1990 production costs for wheat were reported to have a foreign exchange component of about 80%, compared with 50% for maize production. In 1996, it was estimated, it cost a farmer Ks. 700 to produce one kg of wheat, whereas he received a producer price of Ks. 1,200 and the global price was equivalent to Ks. 1,069. In 1997, however, following the implementation of new liberalization measures, the farmer's costs increased to Ks. 1,500 per kg of wheat, while the producer price amounted to Ks. 1,100 and the global price was Ks. 900. In both years the producer price exceeded the global price and therefore contained a state-funded subsidy, which displeased the IMF and other lenders.

Livestock and dairy production are important both for domestic consumption and for export. The country had an estimated 14.1m. cattle in 1998. Some 1.8m. head of cattle were slaughtered in 1995, producing 240,000 metric tons of beef. The national dairy herd numbered an estimated 4.4m. in 1995 and produced an estimated 2.4m. tons of milk in 1998. A substantial proportion of dairy cattle are in small herds of up to 10 animals. Kenya has traditionally exported butter, cheese and skimmed milk powder, and maintains strategic stocks of these products. An outbreak of rinderpest in January 1997 had been brought under control by October of that year. An epidemic of Rift Valley fever, which strikes both livestock and humans, occurred between October 1997 and March 1998, but by March 1999 the World Health Organization estimated the risk as 'minimal or negligible.' The country had an estimated 108,000 pigs, 5.7m. sheep and 7.5m. goats in 1998. In 1995 some 4.51 head of sheep and goats were slaughtered, producing 51,000 tons of mutton, lamb and goat meat. In 2000 drought once again emphasized the growing pressure on Kenya's grazing lands, resulting in incidents of agrarian unrest.

INDUSTRY

Kenya is the most industrially developed country in east Africa, with a relatively good infrastructure, extensive transport facilities and considerable private-sector activity. Nevertheless, the manufacturing sector contributed only 13.3% of GDP in 1998. The annual increase in the output of the sector averaged 10.5% in 1965–80, but had retreated to 3.7% by 1991. Growth in manufacturing output recovered to 4.9% in 1992, partly owing to the effects of the liberalization of foreign exchange controls in that year (see below). By the late 1990s, however, growth had virtually stagnated, at 1.7% in 1998 and 0.9% in 1999. The government blamed the low growth figures on inefficiency arising from the dilapidation of the infrastructure, from the dumping of cheap imports and insufficient supply of electric power (see below). The manufacturing sector employs fewer than 200,000 people. It suffered from stringent import controls during the late 1970s and the 1980s, with 60%–70% of its inputs having to be imported, and was also hindered during that period by delays in the issuing of import licences and by controls on ex-factory prices. In addition the steady devaluation of the shilling in the 1980s and 1990s increased the costs of those manufacturers heavily dependent on imported inputs. Manufacturing is, in practice, based on import-substitution, although the government is now putting great emphasis on developing export-orientated industries. In 1990 imports of goods intended for the manufacture of exports were exempted from import duty and value added tax. Kenyan manufacturers hoped to find new markets among the member countries of COMESA (formerly the PTA). Major industries include petroleum refining (using imported crude petroleum), the processing of agricultural products, vehicle assembly, the exploitation of soda-ash reserves, the production of chemicals, publishing and printing and the manufacture of textiles and clothing, cement, electrical equipment, tyres, batteries, paper, ceramics, machinery, metal products, rubber, leather goods and wood and cork products. Petroleum refining provided about 9% of export earnings in 1993. About one-half of the investment in the industrial sector is foreign-owned, and, of this, the United Kingdom owns about one-half. The USA is the second most important foreign investor.

The massive Panafrican Paper Mills' plant at Webuye commenced production in 1975. A major expansion raised annual production capacity from 66,000 metric tons to 90,000 tons. The government owns 40% of the company's shares. A partly Swedish-owned company, Tetra Pak Converters, began production of laminated milk cartons in 1983.

The textile industry performed relatively well following independence, and diversification was encouraged in the clothing and leather industries. By 1993 some 65 textile factories were operating in the country, of which about 40 were engaged in manufacturing under bond for export. The expansion in the sector was mostly induced by Kenya's unrestricted access to the US market, which encouraged manufacturers in Asian countries to use Kenya as a conduit for their goods and thus to bypass US-imposed quotas. However, in 1994 the US authorities imposed a quota on Kenyan textile imports, quantities of which had increased suspiciously. The industry swiftly collapsed: by the late 1990s only a few factories remained in operation, and those at a much reduced rate of production. In 1998 it was estimated that 10,000 Kenyans had lost jobs in the textiles sector as a consequence of the quota. There are three vehicle assembly plants: Associated Vehicle Assemblers (AVA), General Motors Kenya and Leyland Kenya. They produce trucks, commercial vehicles, pickups, minibuses, four-wheel drive vehicles and passenger cars from kits supplied from abroad. General Motors Kenya in Nairobi started assembly of a passenger car, the Uhuru, in 1985 and by 1999 was assembling Chevrolet and Opel passenger cars. Bedford vehicles and several types of Isuzu models including 62-seater Isuzu buses; the company sells both to the Kenyan market and to Uganda, Tanzania, Rwanda and Burundi. AVA in Mombasa assembles five models of Toyota vehicles. A small proportion of Kenyan-assembled vehicles are also exported to Sudan and Malawi. Domestic sales of locally-produced vehicles reached 13,600 in 1987, an increase of more than 30% from 1986. About 30% of components are produced locally and this proportion is to be increased. The government has announced plans to reduce its 35% interest in Leyland Kenya and its 51% interest in the other two assembly firms. Tyres are manufactured by Firestone East Africa. The parent company, the US-based Firestone Corpn, reduced its share in the enterprise from 80% to 18% in 1985. An expansion programme for 1989–92, with a projected cost of Ks. 450m., sought to increase production capacity from 500,000 tyres per year to 700,000 tyres per year. Steel processing, for the construction industry and for re-export, is a growing industry; 14 steel mills were operational in May 1997, with a further three scheduled to open by the end of the year. Controversy arose in 1996 over revelations that a bullet factory was being built at Eldoret by the Belgian corporation Fabrique Nationale de Herstal. Construction briefly ceased after fears were raised that the ammunition might be used in conflicts in volatile countries in the region, but resumed in March 1997 after Kenya, at the Belgian government's insistence, pledged not to export output to neighbouring states. Cement, produced by the Bamburi Portland Cement Co and East African Portland Cement, was one of the most successful industries during the 1980s and by the late 1990s the country was producing about 1.5m. tons of cement

per annum. During the 1990s, however, this industry suffered the effects of irregular supplies of imported inputs, an increasingly competitive export market and the fall in the value of the US dollar (the currency in which cement earnings are denominated). Bamburi was building a new 1m. ton-per-annum clinker grinding plant in Nairobi in 1999. The Blue Circle/La Farge group increased its investment in East African Portland Cement by US $5m. in 1998. The domestic use of cement declined by 15.9% in the year to February 1999, from 1.14m. metric tons to 960,729 tons. There are three glassware factories, two owned by the Madhvani Group, and one by Kenya Breweries Ltd. There is a sheet glass factory at Mombasa. Charcoal is produced from coffee husks by Kenya Planters' Co-operative Union at Nairobi and is exported to the Middle East, as well as being used locally to replace some of the wood charcoal. A machine-tool manufacturing plant is being set up at Nairobi, in a joint venture with an Indian firm, and will include a training centre. Kenya Breweries Ltd, part of the East African Breweries Group, has four brewing plants, and it exports a small percentage of its beer. In June 1997 a Ks. 1,500m. bottling line was commissioned at the company's Nairobi premises. In April of that year South African Breweries announced that it was to invest in a brewery at Thika, scheduled to become operational in 1998 at a production capacity of 800,000 hl.

The Mombasa petroleum refinery, which is 50%-owned by the state, with the remaining 50% held by a group of international oil companies (BP, Caltex, Exxon and Shell), entered production in 1963. It is capable of handling 4.2m. metric tons of crude petroleum annually, although only 2.1m. tons were handled in 1987. Refined petroleum products were, until recently, Kenya's largest source of foreign exchange, but the refinery needs modernizing; its shareholders have announced investments to carry out the work. Plans to extend the Mombasa-to-Nairobi oil pipeline as far as the Ugandan border were pledged financing of US $120m. in 1990. The petroleum sector was deregulated in 1994.

In 2000 the Investment Promotion Centre (IPC) identified several subsectors of manufacturing in which incoming private-sector foreign investment would be especially welcome. They included paper products (especially coated white lined chipboard and newsprint), textile equipment and inputs such as dyes, metallurgy, electrical equipment, electronics, pharmaceuticals, gelatin capsules, ink for ballpoint pens, PVC granules made from ethyl alcohol, ceramics and sheet glass.

MINERALS

Mining activity in Kenya is as yet limited, but prospecting is continuing. Soda ash, Kenya's principal mineral export, is extracted at Lake Magadi, in the Rift Valley; output is estimated at 350,000 metric tons per year. In 1997 a Canadian company, Tiomin Resources, announced the discovery of mineral sands at Kwale, 105 km south of Mombasa, containing reserves of 200m. tons of titanium- and zirconium-bearing sands. These discoveries followed earlier discoveries at Kwale of rutile, zircon and ilmenite. Tiomin Resources announced the results of a positive feasibility study by an Australian firm and a South African company in May 2000. The study found that the Kwale titanium-bearing sands presented 'robust economics', with a projected lifespan of at least 14 years and an expected capital payback period of not more than 3.5 years. The project was expected to produce 300,000 tons of ilmenite, 75,000 tons of rutile and 37,000 tons of premium zircon annually during its first six years of operation. The company expected to have won all the necessary permits from the Kenyan government, to have signed long-term sales contracts and to have secured project financing for the US $137m.-scheme by the end of December 2000. Kenya's other principal mineral products are gold, salt, vermiculite and limestone. A fluorspar ore deposit in the Kerio valley in Rift Valley province has been mined since 1975: it produced 80,630 tons in 1992, and has a total capacity of 102,000 tons. The extraction of extensive deposits of rubies began in 1974; gems of up to 30 kg have been reported. Deposits of tsavorite, a grossularite garnet discovered at Tsavo in the 1970s have received high valuations. In the 1990s a new tsavorite source was discovered at Lokirima, in the north-west. Other minerals identified in Kenya include apatite, graphite, kaolin, kyanite, rubies, topazes and green tourmalines. Searches for chromite, nickel, fluorspar and vermiculite in Central province, and for chromite, nickel and copper in the Kerio valley are being undertaken. Prospecting for petroleum and gas has continued intermittently on and off shore, but so far without significant results. Under an Oil Exploration Act, introduced in 1984, exploitation by foreign oil companies would be on a production-sharing basis. Exploration concessions have been taken by Amoco, Compagnie Française des Pétroles (CFP–Total), Marathon Oil Co, Mobil, Fina (of Belgium) and Petro-Canada, operating either independently or in consortia. In 1988 CFP–Total discovered traces of gas and oil in a test well drilled in Isiolo district, in the northwest. It was the 20th well to be drilled in Kenya since exploration began in the 1950s; the others, mostly in coastal areas, had all been dry. Several concessions came due for renewal in 1988, and Total's discovery, and the discovery of a deposit in Turkana district, revived the oil companies' flagging interest, although the commercial value of these finds is not yet known. In 1989 a four-year exploration agreement was awarded to a consortium comprising Total, Amoco, Marathon and Texaco; this related to an area covering 32 sq km of the Wajir and Mandera districts in the north-east of the country. New agreements were entered into in 1990 with Amoco and Shell Exploration.

POWER

Electricity, apart from small local stations, is supplied inland by hydroelectric plants in the Tana river basin and by the geothermal station at Olkaria, and at the coast by an oil-fired plant. This is supplemented by a bulk supply of 30 MW from Owen Falls in Uganda under a 50-year agreement signed in 1958. However, the revival of Uganda's economy in the 1990s led to increased demand for electricity there; an agreement was reached in 1997 that Kenya would pay a higher rate for electricity imported from Uganda. Hydroelectric plants supply about 75% of total generating capacity. There are five major stations on the Tana river: Gitaru (40 MW), Kiambere (144 MW), Kamburu (40 MW), Kindaruma, (40 MW) and Masinga (40 MW). Kiambere was commissioned in 1988, increasing Kenya's total generating capacity to 715 MW. Another station, with a capacity of 105 MW, operates at Turkwel Gorge in Turkana district. The Olkaria geothermal scheme in the Rift Valley, 90 km from Nairobi, began production in 1981 and now has three 15-MW generators in operation, with plans for a further two 64-MW units, to become operational in 2000 and 2001 respectively. In 1997 it was announced that the Japanese government was funding a hydropower project at Sondu-Miriu with a generating capacity of 60-MW. The drought of 1996–97 necessitated seven months of power rationing, and the urgent need for expansion in the sector became apparent. However, the tendering of contracts to Iberafrica of Spain, to supply a 44-MW diesel-fuelled unit for the Nairobi South power plant, and to Sabah Shipyard of Indonesia, to provide a 43-MW barge-mounted unit at Kipevu, near Mombasa, lacked transparency, according to the IMF: together with the government's failure to rationalize the energy sector, this was presented as a reason for the suspension of IMF aid in August 1997 (see below). In mid-1999 construction of Kipevu II was reportedly at an advanced stage, and power-purchase agreements had already been signed. Two further 'fast-track' units, to be situated at Kakuru and Eldoret, were being planned in mid-1999. In 1997 the Kenya Power Co was established, to deal exclusively with the generation of electricity; the Kenya Power and Lighting Co continued to be responsible for electricity transmission and distribution. In July 1997 the World Bank approved a US $125m. loan towards Kenya's continuing $1,000m. energy sector investment project. A rural electrification programme was under way in 1999. Drought reduced the amount of water in the system in the late 1990s, and in May 2000 Kenya Power & Lighting Co (KPLC) introduced a severe rationing of power, in which domestic customers suffered a 12-hour blackout every day, and industrial consumers endured a 12-hour blackout every night. Lack of electricity was expected to reduce manufacturing output significantly, leading to job suspensions, smaller company profits (if not losses), a negative GDP growth rate for 2000 and substantially reduced government revenues as taxable company profits shrank. The following unrest compelled KPLC to bring in additional capacity, and within days it had arranged for delivery of two 55-MW diesel-powered generators for Lanet

and Eldoret. It also sought to increase the 30 MW of power it had been importing from Uganda to 50 MW, following the completion of that country's $230m.-Kiyira hydroelectric power station near Jinja.

COMMUNICATIONS

Kenya's extensive transport system includes road, rail, air, and coastal and inland waterways. Full container-handling facilities were built at Mombasa, the chief port, to deal with the volume of containers, which expanded from 50,000 20-ft (6-m) equivalent units (TEU) in 1982 to nearly 103,000 TEU in 1985. The modern container-handling terminal was opened in 1983, and the country's first inland clearance depot for containers, at Embakasi on the outskirts of Nairobi, began operating in 1984, followed by other inland container ports at Kisumu and Eldoret. In 1993 it was announced that Mombasa's Kilindini port was to be expanded by 1,200 ha. Mombasa provides access to the sea for Uganda, Burundi, Rwanda and the eastern part of the Democratic Republic of the Congo. In April 1998 the World Bank's International Finance Corpn (IFC) pledged US $10m. to the private-sector Kenyan company Grain Bulk Handlers Ltd towards the building of the first modern bulk handling and storage terminal for unloading grain and fertilizer at Mombasa port. The $32m. facility's rated capacity was the unloading of 10,000 metric tons per day, and it was expected to handle about one-half of the east African region's food imports in its first year. Although faced with competition from Dar es Salaam, in Tanzania, which was undergoing modernization, Mombasa handled 7,991,822 tons in 1992, compared with 7,143,876 tons in 1991. In 1995 a study by Canadian consultants found that, although Mombasa still handled more than twice as much cargo as Dar es Salaam, volume at the Tanzanian port was growing by 10% per annum compared to 2% annual growth at Kenya's main port. Transit cargo passing through the port to neighbouring states (including northern Tanzania) increased sharply from 527,418 tons in 1991 to 1,209,977 tons in 1992. The government acknowledged in 1997 that the diversion into the Kenyan market of goods nominally in transit had become a serious problem, and promised measures to tighten controls on transit cargo. For this reason, the transport of fuel by road to Ethiopia, Sudan and Somalia was banned, and it was required that all fuel products from the Mombasa refinery to those countries be shipped by sea. By December 1997 an increase in berthing delays was reported, with 25,000-ton vessels typically having to wait four days for a berth and as long as 12 days to unload. The completion in 1999 of the new bulk handling terminal was expected to help reduce waiting times. The Kenya Ports Authority (KPA), undergoing restructuring during the late 1990s in preparation for privatization, introduced a $70 surcharge per container and prepared to reduce its work-force. By 2000 the KPA was still waiting for the government to proceed with its privatization, and also to act on upgrading its container-handling equipment. The KPA had increased the number of container crane moves from five to 10 per hour and hoped to boost it even further, to 15 moves per hour; in order to achieve this target, however, the KPA would need to replace some of its out-of-date equipment. In the longer term, the KPA is seeking private-sector investors to build, operate and transfer (BOT) two additional container terminals.

Kenya Airways has operated its own international services since the break-up of East African Airways. In April 1989 the airline inaugurated a freighter service to Europe: fresh flowers and vegetables were the main outward cargo. In 1992 Kenya Airways underwent a major reorganization in preparation for privatization, which took place in 1996 when KLM Royal Dutch Airlines paid US $24m. for a 26% stake. African Express Airkenya, a private passenger airline, began operating regular services between Kenya and Europe in 1986. Construction of the country's third international airport, at Eldoret in central Kenya (President Moi's home town) was completed in 1996, at an estimated cost of $49m. Critics, including international donors, considered the facility to be an unnecessary waste of resources. Meanwhile, Jomo Kenyatta International and Moi International Airports were modernized during the mid-1990s. It was reported in June 2000 that Kenya Airways planned to update its fleet with the purchase of 10 new Boeing aircraft at a cost of $1,000m. over the period 2001–2005.

A 590-km road between Kitale and Juba, in Southern Sudan, provides an all-weather road link between the two countries. Rebuilding of 175 km of Kenyan roads, with financing by the EU and Germany, began in 1990 as part of the 'northern corridor' scheme to improve access for land-locked countries to Mombasa port. In early 1990 Japan promised to provide almost US \$200m. in concessionary finance to help develop road infrastructure and airports. In February 1996 the World Bank approved a \$165m. loan to finance the urgent rehabilitation of the important Nairobi–Mombasa road link. Construction of the Ks. 349.3m. trans-Mara highway commenced in 1996. A \$155m. programme to rehabilitate urban road surfaces, with financial assistance from the World Bank, was to commence in 1997. A senior government official estimated in May 2000 that only about 57% of Kenya's road system was in 'usable condition' and that to bring the entire network up to standard would cost \$631m. In January 1999 the IFC approved a \$1m. loan to the Kenyan private-sector company Multiple Hauliers (EA) Ltd, which is the largest cross-border road transporter in the region and the largest transporter of fuel to Uganda. The funds were to go towards the purchase of 16 new prime movers with tanker trailers, costing \$2.8m.

The railway in Kenya runs from the coast at Mombasa, through Nairobi, to western Kenya, and on to points in Tanzania and Uganda. A three-year project to improve Kenya Railways Corpn's operations, at an expected cost of US \$45.5m., was carried out in 1987–89, and was aimed, in particular, at making the railways more competitive in the freight market. In 1995/96 Kenya Railways Corpn made a loss, and in 1997 the government proposed that locomotives and rolling stock be leased out to private operators. In February 1999 the government acknowledged the need to accelerate the privatization of Kenya Railways Corpn.

Under a major telecommunications development project, funded by the World Bank and started in 1983, international subscriber dialling was introduced in 1984. Kenya had 240,000 telephones in use in 1995 (compared with 106,000 in 1984). In February 1997 the government announced plans to install 2.7m. new telephone lines, of which 300,000 were to be in rural areas; this would increase the number of telephone lines per 1,000 inhabitants from nine in 1995 to around 60. A US company was contracted to supply wireless local loop systems to Kenya. In August 1992 a Ks. 2,380m. radio transmitter, in the Ngong hills near Nairobi, was inaugurated, reportedly bringing 95% of the population within range of radio transmissions. There is an earth satellite station at Longonot. During 1999 Kenya Posts and Telecommunications Corpn was to be divided, pending privatization, into three entities: Telkom Kenya, the Postal Corpn of Kenya and the Communications Commission of Kenya (a regulatory body).

TOURISM

Kenya's tourism sector has exhibited steady and strong growth in most years since independence, and by the 1990s the sector had become the country's largest source of foreign exchange. The number of tourist arrivals rose from 894,300 in 1998 to 969,300 in 1999, while revenue from tourism increased from Ks. 17,500m. in 1998 to Ks. 21,400m. in 1999. However, preliminary assessments for 2000 indicated that tourism, like most other sectors of the Kenyan economy, was not performing well. Mombasa and the coastal hotels were exempted from the electricity rationing in May 2000 (see above) in order to protect the tourism industry. In late 1998 a tourism endowment fund was established with assistance from the EU, and increased government funding was allocated under the 1998/99 budget for improved tourism promotion. To encourage the local financing of projects to develop tourism facilities, qualifying projects were allowed a zero value-added tax rating. Germany and the United Kingdom provide the largest number of tourists.

BALANCE OF PAYMENTS AND DEBT

Kenya typically has a substantial deficit in visible trade with countries outside Africa. Its terms of trade have fluctuated quite widely since the mid-1970s, but, overall, there has been a general decline. The visible trade deficit was less than Ks. 600m. in 1977, but had climbed to Ks. 25,000m. by 1990 and to Ks. 159,000m. by 1995. Exports, on a free-on-board (f.o.b.) basis,

declined by 12.8%, from US \$2,012m. in 1998 to \$17,755m. in 1999, while imports, on a cost, insurance and freight (c.i.f.) basis, also fell by 12.7%, from \$3,337m. to \$2,912m. Therefore, the ratio of imports to exports remained virtually the same in 1999, with export revenue covering about 60% of import costs, but, owing to the lower levels, the trade deficit narrowed by 12.7%, from \$1,325m. in 1998 to \$1,157m. in 1999. The services account, boosted by tourism, consistently showed a surplus in the late 1990s; the largest surplus was in 1999 at \$895m., compensating for more than three-quarters of the visible shortfall. The current account of the balance of payments has shown a deficit in most years; the smallest current-account shortfall of the late 1990s was \$84m. in 1996, while the largest was \$463m. in 1998. An improvement was achieved in 1999, when the deficit narrowed by 43%, to \$262m. The overall balance of payments has fluctuated in recent years; a \$139m. deficit in 1995 was followed by a \$438m. surplus in 1996, but the balance was negative again in 1997, at \$29m. An overall surplus of \$57m. in 1998 dwindled to a \$6m. surplus in 1999. Kenya's reserves of foreign exchange stood at \$80m. at the end of 1992, compared with \$460m. in 1985, having been deliberately depleted in order to relieve pressure on the balance of payments. By the end of 1993 reserves had recovered to \$437m., and at the end of 1994 they stood at \$588m., subsequently increasing to \$853m. at the end of 1995, to \$925m. by July 1997 and to \$1,140m. at 31 December 1999, sufficient to cover 3.1 months' worth of imports. Import cover had lengthened to 3.4 months by 31 March 2000. Following pressure from IMF and the World Bank Kenya has liberalized the sale of foreign exchange. It is estimated that overseas holdings by Kenyan residents amount to at least \$4,000m.

Kenya's total external debt, which had reached US \$6,893m. at the end of 1996, declined to \$5,600m. at the end of June 1998 and to \$5,360m. at March 2000. This was compounded by a domestic debt of Ks. 163,400m., equivalent to \$22,000m., also at the end of March 2000. Total debt service for July 1999–March 2000 amounted to \$486.2m., and in January 2000 the debt-service ratio as a percentage of exports of goods and services was 18.9%.

FOREIGN TRADE AND AID

In an attempt to reduce dependence on fluctuating world prices for its main agricultural commodities, the government has made efforts to stimulate non-traditional exports including horticultural produce, canned pineapple products, handicrafts, clothing, leather, cement, soda ash and fluorspar. The stimulation of exports of manufactured goods, including textiles, paper and vehicles, has also been a priority. Manufacturing was hampered by restrictions on imports of raw materials, parts and machinery until 1992, when these restrictions began to be removed gradually. In 1993 manufactured products accounted for 29% of Kenya's total exports. After crude oil and petroleum products, the largest import bill in that year was for industrial machinery and transport equipment. Consumer goods accounted for only about 15% of the total.

The United Kingdom is traditionally the most important non-African trading partner, accounting for 9% of Kenyan exports and 10% of its imports in 1998. The main source of imports is the United Arab Emirates, Kenya's main supplier of crude oil. Other suppliers of imports in 1998 were the USA, Japan, Germany, Italy, France and the Netherlands. Regional trade is important to Kenya, which has consistently had a favourable trade balance with its neighbours, to which it exports petroleum products, food and basic manufactures in particular. After the re-opening of the Kenya/Tanzania border (closed from 1977–83) trade with Tanzania was limited by that country's lack of foreign exchange. However, exports to Tanzania advanced during the 1990s and, according to the IMF, accounted for some 13% of Kenya's total exports in 1995. Official trade with Uganda was depressed from the 1970s. By 1995, however, Uganda was Kenya's largest export market, accounting for 15.7% of total exports, according to IMF figures. A significant amount of goods are smuggled into Uganda from Kenya. The revival of the East African Community (EAC) should stimulate trade between Kenya, Tanzania and Uganda. A treaty for the re-establishment of the EAC providing for the promotion of free trade between the member states (envisaging the eventual introduction of a single currency), and for the development of infrastructure, tourism and agriculture within the Community, was finally ratified by the Kenyan, Tanzanian and Ugandan heads of state in June 2000.

Aid

Since independence, Kenya has received substantial amounts of development aid. The World Bank-sponsored Consultative Group of aid donors to Kenya meets regularly, usually every two years, to pledge financing for the country's development strategy. The sources of aid have diversified considerably in recent years. The share provided by the United Kingdom has fallen, while multilateral agencies, particularly the World Bank and the European Development Fund, have increased their share. In 1989 the Federal Republic of Germany, Kenya's principal bilateral creditor at that time, announced that it would cancel the total debt of US $435m. in return for increased Kenyan investment in projects aimed at protecting the environment. Japan also increased its aid to Kenya, becoming the largest bilateral donor. Kenya received the approval of the IMF for its management of the economy during the late 1980s, particularly for having reduced the rate of increase in money supply. However, the budgetary deficit remained a problem, as did the losses incurred by the country's parastatal bodies. In April 1989 the government reached agreement with the IMF and the World Bank on the release of funds to support an economic programme for 1989–91. Relations with the international donor community were strained towards the end of 1989, when the government proposed building a 60-storey media complex at a cost of $200m., with 'offshore' commercial financing. At a special January 1990 meeting, donors expressed concern that the new loans would raise the debt-service ratio and would slow productive investment. The USA agreed to cancel Kenya's debt on condition that the government agreed to abandon its plans for the media complex, which it subsequently did. In November 1991, however, the 'Paris Club' of Western official creditors declared a moratorium on aid to Kenya, pending the implementation of economic and political reforms. Following the holding of multi-party elections in December 1992 (see Recent History), lending resumed in April 1993. Total development aid from all sources amounted to $894m. in 1993, and in December the IMF agreed to a one-year enhanced structural adjustment facility (ESAF) arrangement totalling $61.97m., of which one-half was disbursed immediately. At a 'Paris Club' meeting in January 1994 donors pledged a total of $850m. for 1994; a further $800m. was pledged in December 1994, but much of this remained undisbursed, following 'informal talks' between the government and donors in Paris in July 1995, at which strong reservations were expressed about the Moi regime's economic management and human rights record. In September 1995 the IMF withheld a $216m. ESAF, pending decisive action by the Kenyan authorities to eradicate allegedly endemic corruption. At a meeting in Paris in March 1996 donors announced a $730m. aid package for Kenya; however, as a substantial proportion of the assistance pledged for 1994 had not yet been disbursed, doubts were expressed as to whether the 1996 assistance represented wholly new funds. The IMF agreed to release the $216m. ESAF in April 1996; however, the second tranche of $37m., scheduled for release in November, was postponed, owing to concerns over the slow progress of privatization and reform, particularly in the power sector. In July 1997, following the collapse of court proceedings in a corruption scandal (see Recent History), the IMF once again delayed disbursement. In August the IMF suspended disbursement of the second and third tranches of the ESAF, shortly after the government's dismissal of a customs official who was taking measures to prevent corruption in revenue collection. Kenya resumed discussions with creditors in February 1998 and reached agreement with the 'Paris Club' for a rescheduling of $70m. of debt, of which $31.6m. was interest accrued from January 1992. Repayments were to be over a 10-year period, with three years' grace, and were to be at a fixed interest rate of 3.5% for the first four and a half years and then at a rate of 0.8% above the London Inter-Bank Offered Rate (Libor) for the remaining years. In exchange, creditors agreed to waive two-thirds of the interest. In addition, 60% of the remainder was to be capitalized, according to a treasury source.

In December 1999 the IMF, from which no new lending had been forthcoming for some months, concluded that 'Kenya's economic performance weakened over the last decade because of the failure to sustain prudent macroeconomic policies, the slow pace of structural reform, and the persistence of governance problems'. Indicating that lending rates had risen above 20% in real terms, the Fund also observed that the costs of conducting business in Kenya were high, 'because of corruption, a deteriorating infrastructure and an inefficient parastatal sector'. Among the inefficient parastatals, utilities and transport services were singled out for particular criticism. All of these factors, the IMF concluded, had adversely affected investor and donor confidence.

PUBLIC FINANCE

The budgets of the 1980s carried increasingly worrying levels of deficit; that for 1986-87, at Ks. 8,080m., was equivalent to 7% of GDP, while the 1987/88 budgetary deficit was equivalent to 6.7% of GDP. During the early and mid-1990s the budgetary deficit fluctuated, exceeding the 1992/93 (5.3%) and IMF ceiling of 5% of GDP in 1990/91 (at 5.6% of GDP), 1993/94 (more than 7%), while falling well within the target in 1991/92 (1.4%) and in 1994/95 (2%). In 1995/96 expenditure of Ks. 153,220m. and revenue amounting to Ks. 145,500m. created a budgetary deficit of Ks. 7,712m., equivalent to less than 1% of GDP. The fiscal year 1996/97 saw a significant overspend, incurred by imports of famine-relief maize, high levels of domestic debt-servicing, salary increases and the registration of voters for the forthcoming elections. In order to pay for these additional expenses, a Supplementary Appropriation Bill was passed by the national assembly, releasing some Ks. 5,750m. Even so, the budgetary deficit amounted to less than 2% of GDP. The 2000/01 budget speech, presented in mid-June 2000, confirmed that revenue collected during 1999/2000 had fallen some Ks. 2,000m. short of the forecast. One of the reasons was that the industrial sector, which had been hit by severe power rationing limiting companies' electricity supply to 32 hours per week, had produced less and had, therefore, created less taxable income. Another reason, however, was that existing revenue-collection methods were inefficient. The decision was taken, therefore, to concentrate revenue collection in the hands of a sole agency, the Kenya Revenue Authority.

DEVELOPMENT PLANNING

Development policy in Kenya emphasizes the role of private enterprise in industry and commerce, and foreign investment is actively encouraged. Direct participation by the state in productive enterprises is limited, and in recent years the government has been withdrawing from unprofitable joint ventures. In 1991 the government announced that all remaining unproductive, 'non-strategic' state-owned companies were to be transferred to private-sector ownership; details of the impending privatization of some 207 such companies had been released by mid-1993. By June 1997 148 of these companies had been either privatized or dissolved. However, concerns were raised in 1997 over the slow pace of the privatization process which had been scheduled for completion by the end of the year; this could in part be attributed to the poor performance of some parastatals, but there were also suspicions that the government was unwilling to divest itself of some lucrative assets. The IMF welcomed the government's announcement in 1999 that it was to sell off its remaining shares in the Kenya Commercial Bank Ltd (KCB) and to divest itself of 49% of Telkom Kenya Ltd, as well as to privatize other parastatals. The Fund was critical, however, of the government's 'unanticipated outlays', which were equivalent to 0.9% of GDP, to bail out the state-owned National Bank of Kenya (NBK). A government task force reported in April 1999 that the NBK's stock of domestic arrears was 'much higher than originally thought' and revealed 'weaknesses in expenditure control and circumvention of relevant financial regulations'. The Fund agreed, however, to Kenya's plan to help the NBK to 'satisfy the minimum capital adequacy ratios' first and to privatize it only after this ratio had been strengthened and after the sale of the KCB had been completed.

Kenya's first Development Plan, revised in 1966, covered the period 1964–70. Important objectives of the plan included the Kenyanization of the economy, until then largely in expatriate hands. Subsequent five-year plans stressed rural development and were aimed at achieving a better incomes balance between urban and rural areas. In 1986 the government published details of a programme for economic reform (Sessional Paper No. 1), which aimed to increase productivity, provide incentives and stimulate investment in the private sector, develop and diversify agricultural and industrial exports and to create jobs in rural areas.

A sixth Development Plan, covering the period 1989–93, aimed primarily to increase earnings of foreign exchange and to generate employment through the expansion of the industrial sector. The plan also aimed to reduce the rate of population growth, by promoting family planning; statistics demonstrate that significant progress was made towards this aim. In 1990 import duty and value added tax were withdrawn from goods intended for the manufacture of exports, in order to stimulate industrial expansion. During the first half of 1992, however, following the imposition by foreign donors in November 1991 of a moratorium on aid (see above), the government implemented a sweeping programme of economic reforms: these included the liberalization of imports, exports and exchange control, the streamlining of government ministries, price deregulation and a reduction in the bureaucracy surrounding incoming foreign investment. Although the reform measures were briefly suspended in March 1993, having been denounced by President Moi as 'dictatorial and suicidal', they were reintroduced in May, following the announcement by the World Bank in April that it would resume aid allocations to Kenya. In a speech delivered for him in early May 1994, President Moi vowed to continue with the policy of economic liberalization already under way. The Kenyan currency was devalued by 32% between July 1991 and June 1992, by 37% in February 1993, and by 23% in April 1993. According to an assessment made by the IMF in May 1994 Kenya has made 'important headway' in tightening monetary conditions. The Kenya shilling, the IMF pointed out, had 'appreciated' from over Ks. 80=US $1 to about Ks. 60=US $1 during the previous 12 months. In May 1994 the government announced the liberalization of foreign exchange controls which would allow commercial banks to undertake foreign exchange transactions without reference to the Central Bank. The new measures, which took immediate effect, meant that the Kenyan shilling became fully convertible against other world currencies. The shilling at first exhibited marked stability when exposed to market forces: immediately after flotation, in May 1994, its value stood at Ks. 56.48=US $1, and in 1995 it had strengthened to an annual average rate of Ks. 51.43=US $1. However, the value of the Kenyan currency declined from Ks. 53.90 = US $1 in June 1997 to Ks. 64.02 = US $1 in October of that year. The currency suffered again as the economic crisis deepened in mid-2000. As urban Kenyans endured power rationing, rural Kenyans in some parts of the country faced ever-worsening drought conditions, leading to malnutrition, hunger and even starvation. In June President Moi issued an appeal to overseas donors for Ks. 11,500m. worth of food aid. Amid all these factors, the shilling depreciated by a full 2% in a single month, from a monthly average of Ks. 76.00 = US $1 in May 2000 to a monthly average of Ks. 77.55 = US $1 in June of that year.

The eighth Development Plan (1997–2001) differed from previous plans in that it aimed primarily to foster an enabling environment for the private sector, rather than emphasizing the state's role in raising and sustaining growth. The targeted average annual growth rate for the economy was 5.9%, entailing annual investment equivalent to more than 25% of GDP. Stated methods included the curbing of corruption and the enhancement of revenue collection, the rationalization of the tax system, reform in the civil service and in public enterprises and further market liberalization. However, the plan was jeopardized by the suspension of IMF assistance in August 1997. It also failed to meet its GDP growth targets.

REGIONAL ARRANGEMENTS AND PROBLEMS

In 1967 Kenya, Tanzania and Uganda founded the East African Community (EAC), which comprised a customs union and a range of public services, including the East African Development Bank, operated on a collectively-managed basis. During the early 1970s, however, major economic and political tensions developed between the EAC's member countries. By July 1977 the railways had effectively become national enterprises, East African Airways had broken up and Kenya had launched its own Kenya Airways, Tanzania had closed its border with Kenya, and official trade between the two countries was suspended: for all practical purposes, the EAC had ceased to exist. The East African Development Bank, however, continued to function.

Negotiations concerning the distribution of the EAC's assets and liabilities among the former member states continued intermittently for six years, under the chairmanship of a World Bank-appointed mediator. Agreement was eventually reached in 1983, and a new era of improved relations between the three countries seemed possible. Kenya was allocated a 42.5% share of the assets, whose value was put at $898m., while Tanzania received 32.5% and Uganda 25%. In addition, Uganda was to be paid compensation of US $191m. by the other two partners, because their shares of the assets were calculated as greater than the equity shares which they held in the former community corporations. Kenya started to pay this compensation by transferring some of its railway rolling stock to Uganda. An immediate result of the settlement was the re-opening of the Kenya/Tanzania border, which provided some limited opportunities for Kenyan exporters. The two countries' airlines resumed inter-state flights in 1984 and there have been agreements on overland transport, the cross-border transport of tourists, an expanded air service and co-operation in shipping and port services. In November 1994 the leaders of Kenya, Tanzania and Uganda established a permanent tripartite commission for East African co-operation, and in March 1996 the commission's secretariat was formally inaugurated. A treaty for the re-establishment of the EAC, providing for the promotion of free trade between the member states, the development of the region's infrastructure and economy, and the creation of a regional legislative assembly and court, was approved by Kenya and Uganda in November 1999 and was finally ratified by Tanzania in June 2000 (see above).

PROBLEMS AND PROSPECTS

Kenya's high rate of population growth has imposed major strains upon the economy, in terms of public expenditure, as well as threatening social stability. However, government initiatives to encourage family planning have had significant success in reducing the rate in recent years. The average fertility rate fell from 7.8 children per adult female in 1980 to 4.6 in 1995, and the population growth rate declined from an average of 3.4% per year in 1980–90 to 2.6% in 1990–96. Another major constraint to growth has been the balance-of-payments problem. External factors contributing to the sharp slowdown included deteriorating terms of trade, with rising prices for petroleum and other imports and generally low world prices for Kenya's commodities. Internal factors included: lack of incentives to agricultural producers in some sectors; shortages of imported inputs for manufacturers; high government spending; an overvalued currency; low wages, which have declined in real terms, and consequent poor productivity; and too much stress on industries relying heavily on expensive imported materials and equipment.

Pressure from the IMF, the World Bank and bilateral donors helped to persuade the government to take a firm grip on the economy and on public spending by late 1982. In that year President Moi stressed the government's commitment to encouraging the private sector and foreign investment, both public and private. Following the collapse of a number of financial institutions, owing to the malpractice and mismanagement of their directors, the government formed a committee in 1996 to investigate the scandal and to restore public confidence in Kenya's financial system. A further wave of bank collapses led the government to take action again in 1994 to strengthen the sector. However, two more banks collapsed in mid-1996, apparently as a result of bad debts linked to major cases of corruption. The IFC supported two Kenyan banks with loans, providing, in June 1998, US $10m. to the Development Bank of Kenya (one of the few long-established private-sector lending institutions in Africa), and, in January 1999, $30m. to the Kenya Commercial Bank (KCB), thereby signalling the World Bank's approval of the privatization of the oldest and largest financial institution in the country (see above). The KCB was to lend the proceeds of the loan to small and medium-sized export-orientated enterprises in the agricultural, manufacturing and tourism sectors.

During the 1990s progress was made towards solving some of Kenya's economic problems. Liberalization made imported inputs more freely available and eased currency distortions, and government expenditure was more restrained. In addition, productivity levels improved, with gross output per employee increasing by 135% in 1980–92, and the privatization of unprofitable state-owned companies taking place. However, there remained many serious flaws in the economy's basic structure, and pressure on land and the lack of alternative employment for the growing numbers of landless people represented serious long-term difficulties. The sweeping programme of economic reforms implemented by the government in 1992 attempted to address these problems, although the positive effects of the reforms were slow to permeate through the economy. By early 1993 measures to liberalize agricultural marketing had prod-

uced mixed results, but the introduction of foreign-exchange retention accounts had clearly facilitated the importation of raw materials by manufacturers. The effects on the economy of widespread corruption became increasingly manifest during the late 1990s and contributed in no small measure to the economic crisis of 2000. The government only began to take decisive action against those responsible, however, following the suspension of IMF loans in August 1997. Meanwhile, civic unrest in mid-1997 and the resumption of inter-ethnic conflict in the Rift Valley in early 1998 threatened both the tourism industry and foreign investment. Hopes were high in Nairobi in mid-2000 that the long-standing impasse with the IMF was about to come to an end. Investor confidence was unlikely to be restored unless a new IMF agreement could be finalized, but it remained to be seen whether an improvement would quickly ensue even after such an arrangement were put into place.

Statistical Survey

Source (unless otherwise stated): Central Bureau of Statistics, POB 30256, Nairobi; tel (2) 338111; fax (2) 330426.

Area and Population

AREA, POPULATION AND DENSITY

Area (sq km)	580,367*
Population (census results)†	
24 August 1979	15,327,061
24 August 1989	
Males	10,628,368
Females	10,815,268
Total	21,443,636
Population (official estimates at mid-year)	
1995	30,522,000
1996	31,806,000
1997	33,144,000
Density (per sq km) at mid-1997	57.1

* 224,081 sq miles. Total includes 11,230 sq km (4,336 sq miles) of inland water.
† Excluding adjustment for underenumeration.

PRINCIPAL ETHNIC GROUPS (census of August 1989)

African	21,163,076	European . .	34,560
Arab . . .	41,595	Other* . .	115,220
Asian . .	89,185	**Total** . .	21,443,636

* Includes persons who did not state 'tribe' or 'race'.

PRINCIPAL TOWNS (estimated population at census of August 1989)

Nairobi (capital) .	1,346,000	Meru . .	78,100
Mombasa . .	465,000	Thika . .	57,100
Kisumu* . .	185,100	Kitale . .	53,000
Nakuru . .	162,800	Kisii . .	44,000
Eldoret* . .	104,900	Kericho . .	40,000
Nyeri* . .	88,600	Malindi* . .	35,200

* Boundaries extended between 1979 and 1989.

BIRTHS AND DEATHS (UN estimates, annual averages)

	1980-85	1985-90	1990-95
Birth rate (per 1,000) . . .	48.7	45.5	37.5
Death rate (per 1,000) . . .	13.2	11.6	10.6

Expectation of life (UN estimates, years at birth, 1990–95): 56.8 (males 55.3; females 58.4).

Source: UN, *World Population Prospects: The 1998 Revision.*

ECONOMICALLY ACTIVE POPULATION
(estimates, '000 persons, 1991)

	Males	Females	Total
Agriculture, etc. . . .	4,587	3,270	7,857
Industry	657	159	816
Services	972	615	1,587
Total	6,216	4,044	10,260

Source: UN Economic Commission for Africa, *African Statistical Yearbook.*

Mid-1998 (estimates in '000): Agriculture, etc. 11,310; Total labour force 14,826 (Source: FAO, *Production Yearbook*).

Agriculture

PRINCIPAL CROPS ('000 metric tons)

	1996	1997	1998
Wheat	320*	252	250†
Rice (paddy)	60†	55	55†
Barley	60†	57	65†
Maize	2,160*	2,214	2,450*
Millet†	49	55	55
Sorghum†	120	130	130
Potatoes	270†	377	380†
Sweet potatoes† . . .	730	720	730
Cassava (Manioc)† . . .	880	900	910
Pulses†	250	240	250
Cottonseed*	8	15	10
Cotton lint*	4	8	5
Coconuts	60†	72	72†
Vegetables (incl. melons) . .	656†	666	668†
Sugar cane†	4,650	4,450	4,900
Oranges†	27	27	28
Grapefruits†	16	16	17
Pineapples†	300	290	300
Bananas†	225	225	230
Plantains†	380	380	390
Cashew nuts	6	9	9†
Coffee (green)	97	87	57*
Tea (made)	257	221	294*
Tobacco (leaves) . . .	10*	10*	10†
Sisal	28	28	29†

* Unofficial figure(s).   † FAO estimate(s).

Source: FAO, *Production Yearbook.*

LIVESTOCK ('000 head, year ending September)

	1996	1997	1998
Cattle	13,838*	13,414	14,116*
Sheep†	5,600	5,600	5,700
Goats†	7,500	7,400	7,500
Pigs†	106	105	108
Camels†	820	820	825

Poultry (FAO estimates, million): 27† in 1996; 29 in 1997; 29† in 1998.

* Unofficial figure.   † FAO estimate(s).

Source: FAO, *Production Yearbook*.

LIVESTOCK PRODUCTS ('000 metric tons)

	1996	1997	1998
Beef and veal	280*	270	280*
Mutton and lamb* . . .	23	22	23
Goats' meat*	30	29	30
Pig meat*	5	5	5
Poultry meat* . . .	52	55	55
Other meat	31*	32	31*
Cows' milk	2,280*	2,300	2,375*
Sheep's milk*	25	25	25
Goats' milk*	94	93	94
Butter and ghee . . .	2†	2*	2*
Poultry eggs* . . .	45	48	49
Honey	24*	25	25*
Wool:			
greasy*	2	2	2
clean*	1	1	1
Cattle hides*	44	43	44
Goatskins*	9	9	9

* FAO estimate(s).   † Unofficial figure.

Source: FAO, mainly *Production Yearbook*.

Forestry

ROUNDWOOD REMOVALS
('000 cubic metres, excluding bark)

	1995	1996	1997
Sawlogs, veneer logs and logs for sleepers*	460	460	460
Pulpwood*	357	357	357
Other industrial wood . . .	1,067	1,093	1,116
Fuel wood	38,204	39,118	39,981
Total	40,088	41,028	41,914

* Annual output is assumed to be unchanged since 1989.

Source: FAO, *Yearbook of Forest Products*.

SAWNWOOD PRODUCTION
('000 cubic metres, including railway sleepers)

	1995	1996	1997
Total*	185	185	185

* Annual output is assumed to be unchanged since 1989.

Source: FAO, *Yearbook of Forest Products*.

Fishing

('000 metric tons, live weight)

	1995	1996	1997
Silver cyprinid	56.8	49.7	40.3
Nile tilapia	11.8	10.3	14.0
Other tilapias	7.6	7.6	19.3
Mouthbrooding cichlids . .	4.8	3.9	2.5
Nile perch	102.5	97.1	73.6
Other fishes (incl. unspecified) .	7.8	10.0	9.7
Other aquatic animals . . .	1.3	1.4	1.7
Total catch	192.7	180.1	161.0
Inland waters	187.2	174.2	154.9
Indian Ocean	5.5	5.9	6.1

Source: FAO, *Yearbook of Fishery Statistics*.

Mining

('000 metric tons)

	1993	1994	1995
Soda ash	216	224	124
Fluorspar	78.7*	89.2	80.2
Salt*†	75	75	74
Limestone flux	31	31	31

* Data from the US Bureau of Mines.   † Estimates.

Source: UN, *Industrial Commodity Statistics Yearbook*.

Industry

SELECTED PRODUCTS ('000 metric tons, unless otherwise indicated)

	1993	1994	1995
Wheat flour	143	191	237
Raw sugar	375	303	384
Beer ('000 hectolitres) . .	3,589	3,250	3,474
Cigarettes (million) . . .	7,267	7,319	7,932
Cement	1,417	1,470	1,566
Jet fuels	298	295	262
Motor spirit (petrol) . . .	329	329	305
Kerosene	128	126	112
Gas-diesel (distillate fuel) oils .	529	539	476
Residual fuel oil	664	630	527
Electric energy (million kWh) .	3,396	3,538	3,747

Source: UN, *Industrial Commodity Statistics Yearbook*.

Electric energy (million kWh): 3,744 in 1996; 4,368 in 1997 (Source: UN, *Monthly Bulletin of Statistics*).

Finance

CURRENCY AND EXCHANGE RATES

Monetary Units

100 cents = 1 Kenya shilling (Ks.);

Ks. 20 = 1 Kenya pound (K£).

Sterling, Dollar and Euro Equivalents (28 April 2000)

£1 sterling = Ks. 117.38;

US $1 = Ks. 74.86;

€1 = Ks. 68.01;

Ks. 1,000 = £8.519 sterling = $13.359 = €14.704.

Average Exchange Rate (Ks. per US $)

1997	58.732
1998	60.367
1999	70.326

Note: The foregoing information refers to the Central Bank's mid-point exchange rate. However, with the introduction of a foreign exchange bearer certificate (FEBC) scheme in October 1991, a dual exchange rate system is in effect. In May 1994 foreign exchange transactions were liberalized and the Kenya shilling became fully convertible against other currencies.

BUDGET (Ks. million, year ending 30 June)

Revenue*	1993/94	1994/95	1995/96
Tax revenue	91,537	108,516	123,008
Taxes on income and profits .	36,570	43,287	48,054
Taxes on goods and services .	40,276	44,918	52,203
Value-added tax . . .	29,049	24,298	28,404
Excise duties . . .	11,227	19,332	22,612
Taxes on international trade .	14,691	18,598	21,176
Import duties . . .	14,691	18,598	21,176
Non-tax revenue . . .	11,286	16,615	22,494
Property income . . .	1,604	3,802	8,401
Administrative fees and charges	2,408	4,471	3,786
Total	102,823	125,131	145,502

Expenditure†	1993/94	1994/95	1995/96
General administration . .	18,486	18,003	33,621
Defence	5,320	7,367	9,039
Social services . . .	32,260	44,195	39,387
Education	22,575	30,717	29,501
Health	7,076	9,595	8,872
Housing, community amenities and social welfare . .	2,609	3,883	1,014
Economic services . . .	26,514	32,857	29,643
General administration. .	2,729	2,637	2,929
Agriculture, forestry and fishing	12,031	10,069	9,454
Mining, manufacturing and construction. . . .	2,137	4,858	1,572
Electricity, water, gas and steam	2,153	4,191	2,745
Roads	3,536	6,242	7,571
Other transport and communications . . .	2,473	3,336	4,386
Other economic services .	1,455	1,524	986
Interest on public debt . .	46,652	31,823	37,245
Unallocated	1,718	1,428	3,619
Sub-total	130,950	135,672	152,554
Adjustment to cash basis . .	933	−658	659
Total	131,883	135,014	153,213

* Excluding grants received (Ks. million): 4,025 in 1993/94; 5,508 in 1994/95; 5,815 in 1995/96.

† Including lending minus repayments (Ks. million): 2,516 in 1993/94; 1,592 in 1994/95; 2,840 in 1995/96.

1996/97 (Ks. million, year ending 30 June): Tax revenue 129,230, Non-tax revenue 20,019, Total revenue (excl. grants 5,783) 149,249; Total expenditure 168,403.

Source: IMF, *Kenya: Selected Issues and Statistical Appendix* (August 1998).

INTERNATIONAL RESERVES (US $ million at 31 December)

	1997	1998	1999
Gold*	23.1	—	—
IMF special drawing rights . .	0.7	0.6	2.4
Reserve position in IMF . .	16.7	17.5	17.1
Foreign exchange . . .	770.6	765.0	772.2
Total	811.1	783.1	791.7

* National valuation of gold reserves (80,000 troy oz in 1997).

Source: IMF, *International Financial Statistics*.

MONEY SUPPLY (Ks. million at 31 December)

	1997	1998	1999
Currency outside banks . . .	36,178	38,713	42,963
Demand deposits at commercial banks.	46,258	47,273	56,849
Total money (incl. others) .	91,037	94,092	109,506

Source: IMF, *International Financial Statistics*.

COST OF LIVING (Consumer Price Index for low-income group in Nairobi; annual averages; base: 1990 = 100)

	1995	1996	1997
Food, beverages and tobacco . .	309.8	335.2	387.7
Fuel and light	223.6	249.0	265.7
Rent	297.0	318.7	357.0
All items (incl. others) . . .	297.1	318.7	357.0

1998: Food, beverages and tobacco 401.6; All items 377.8 (Source: UN, *Monthly Bulletin of Statistics*).

NATIONAL ACCOUNTS (Ks. million at current prices)

Expenditure on the Gross Domestic Product

	1997	1998	1999
Government final consumption expenditure . . .	100,770	112,365	125,276
Private final consumption expenditure . . .	450,664	520,404	537,483
Increase in stocks . . .	5,400	6,210	6,798
Gross fixed capital formation .	109,870	113,087	117,793
Total domestic expenditure	666,704	752,066	787,350
Exports of goods and services .	174,835	172,087	188,390
Less Imports of goods and services	220,596	225,915	238,511
GDP in purchasers' values*	627,436*	698,958*	737,230
GDP at constant 1982 prices .	115,469	116,444	n.a.

* Including adjustment.

Source: IMF, *International Financial Statistics*.

Gross Domestic Product by Economic Activity (at factor cost)

	1994	1995	1996*
Agriculture, hunting, forestry and fishing	112,646	122,602	130,471
Mining and quarrying . . .	714	724	741
Manufacturing	36,155	38,911	45,645
Electricity, gas and water . .	4,481	5,097	5,515
Construction.	16,954	18,340	20,012
Trade, restaurants and hotels. .	48,016	64,760	82,895
Transport, storage and communication . . .	25,259	30,313	34,277
Finance, insurance, real estate and business services . .	61,794	68,873	79,055
Other services	32,045	34,497	36,869
Total	338,065	384,116	435,479

* Estimates.

Source: IMF, *Kenya: Selected Issues and Statistical Appendix* (August 1998).

BALANCE OF PAYMENTS (US $ million)

	1996	1997	1998
Exports of goods f.o.b. . . .	2,083.3	2,062.6	2,013.1
Imports of goods f.o.b. . . .	−2,598.2	−2,948.4	−3,028.7
Trade balance	−514.8	−885.9	−1,015.6
Exports of services . . .	936.2	914.3	837.6
Imports of services . . .	−854.0	−823.1	−665.9
Balance on goods and services	−432.6	−794.7	−843.9
Other income received . .	21.4	23.0	41.2
Other income paid . . .	−242.2	−254.9	−214.7
Balance on goods, services and income	−653.4	−1,026.6	−1,017.3
Current transfers received . .	585.4	649.3	654.4
Current transfers paid . .	−5.4	—	—
Current balance . . .	−73.5	−377.3	−363.0
Capital account	−0.4	—	—
Direct investment abroad. . .	0.5	−2.1	—
Direct investment from abroad .	12.7	19.7	11.4
Portfolio investment liabilities .	7.5	34.2	1.3
Other investment assets . .	628.2	549.3	678.4
Other investment liabilities . .	−59.9	−238.3	−129.0
Net errors and omissions . . .	−128.2	134.8	−125.5
Overall balance	387.0	120.2	73.7

Source: IMF, *International Financial Statistics.*

External Trade

PRINCIPAL COMMODITIES (distribution by SITC, US $ million)

Imports c.i.f.	1994	1995	1996
Food and live animals . . .	317.0	121.9	185.0
Cereals and cereal preparations .	180.5	69.0	122.5
Wheat and meslin (unmilled) .	52.8	45.1	103.6
Crude materials (inedible) except fuels . . .	55.3	65.5	59.6
Mineral fuels, lubricants, etc .	269.2	414.1	452.1
Petroleum and petroleum products	264.5	402.2	444.2
Animal and vegetable oils and fats	95.8	150.5	136.2
Chemicals and related products	370.8	428.6	465.2
Medicinal and pharmaceutical products	68.7	84.7	84.7
Fertilizers (manufactured) . .	79.9	44.4	83.0
Plastic materials, etc . . .	79.6	108.9	111.8
Basic manufactures . . .	312.7	477.9	435.8
Paper, paperboard and manufactures . . .	28.8	53.1	65.4
Iron and steel	126.9	202.4	159.8
Machinery and transport equipment . . .	593.7	942.9	864.5
Machinery specialized for particular industries . .	80.6	157.4	144.5
General industrial machinery, equipment and parts . .	95.7	153.5	137.1
Telecommunications and sound equipment . . .	44.5	43.0	35.7
Other electrical machinery, apparatus, etc. . .	53.6	92.9	80.5
Road vehicles and parts . .	214.0	351.7	305.8
Passenger motor cars (excl. buses)	83.3	133.0	97.1
Motor vehicles for goods transport and special purposes	73.3	125.8	125.5
Miscellaneous manufactured articles	116.0	202.0	139.3
Total (incl. others) . . .	2,142.5	2,818.0	2,749.6

Exports f.o.b.	1994	1995	1996
Food and live animals . . .	828.3	933.8	1,042.7
Fish and fish preparations . .	38.6	35.3	57.6
Cereals and cereal preparations	11.0	71.1	69.2
Vegetables and fruit . . .	109.8	130.9	156.9
Sugar, sugar preparations and honey	10.8	22.4	42.8
Coffee (green and roasted) . .	258.8	291.6	287.6
Tea	375.6	362.4	397.1
Beverages and tobacco. . .	56.7	47.5	47.6
Crude materials (inedible) except fuels . .	164.6	180.3	189.1
Cut flowers and flower buds . .	53.4	64.9	72.2
Mineral fuels, lubricants, etc .	66.9	112.3	139.6
Petroleum and petroleum products	66.6	111.8	139.1
Chemicals and related products	109.3	119.4	126.6
Soap, cleansing and polishing preparations . . .	33.0	39.8	45.0
Basic manufactures . . .	255.2	280.5	290.5
Cement	40.8	34.4	44.6
Iron and steel	76.5	95.5	92.3
Miscellaneous manufactured articles	94.1	84.0	101.8
Total (incl. others) . . .	1,618.7	1,826.1	1,992.2

Source: UN, *International Trade Statistics Yearbook.*

PRINCIPAL TRADING PARTNERS (US $ million)

Imports c.i.f.	1995	1996	1997
Australia	8.9	24.5	35.4
Belgium-Luxembourg . . .	151.4	90.0	62.2
China	59.8	46.1	63.9
France (incl. Monaco) . .	143.7	137.4	122.3
Germany	191.6	166.7	218.8
India	154.1	161.1	141.2
Indonesia	70.6	107.6	108.6
Italy	141.5	90.9	79.7
Japan	289.5	205.3	246.9
Netherlands	83.7	78.6	81.8
Saudi Arabia	99.6	138.7	175.7
Singapore	30.4	38.6	30.9
SACU*	209.8	209.4	374.8
Switzerland–Liechtenstein . .	32.2	44.7	42.4
United Arab Emirates . .	225.5	223.7	326.9
United Kingdom	349.0	358.9	370.6
USA	114.8	147.0	242.6
Total (incl. others) . . .	2,817.9	2,749.6	3,278.4

Exports f.o.b.†‡	1995	1996	1997
Belgium-Luxembourg . . .	43.4	39.0	32.7
Congo, Democratic Republic . .	41.0	33.4	42.3
Egypt	58.0	75.1	52.4
Ethiopia	53.3	40.1	n.a.
France (incl. Monaco) . .	46.4	39.3	44.0
Germany	155.2	154.2	131.0
Italy	31.8	35.9	38.6
Netherlands	86.1	111.6	97.5
Pakistan	110.6	91.5	88.5
Rwanda	34.2	35.2	64.7
Somalia	31.6	40.3	34.2
Sudan	21.5	23.5	33.8
Sweden	29.4	20.8	31.0
Tanzania	216.1	238.7	281.8
Uganda	277.1	306.0	311.5
United Kingdom	197.6	215.6	237.7
USA	49.6	55.5	58.2
Total (incl. others) . . .	1,826.0	1,992.2	2,061.9

* Southern African Customs Union, comprising Botswana, Lesotho, Namibia, South Africa and Swaziland.

† Excluding exports of gold.

‡ Country data exclude exports of bunkers and ship stores (included in total).

Source: UN, *International Trade Statistics Yearbook.*

Transport

RAILWAYS (traffic)

	1990	1991	1992*
Passengers carried ('000) .	3,109	2,635	2,563
Passenger-km (million) . .	677	658	557
Freight carried ('000 metric tons) .	3,317	3,581	2,821
Freight ton-km (million) . .	1,865	1,627	1,755

* Provisional.

1994: Passenger-km (million) 408; Freight ton-km (million) 874 (Source: UN, *Statistical Yearbook*).

ROAD TRAFFIC (estimates, motor vehicles in use at 31 December)

	1994	1995	1996
Motor cars . . .	265,000	271,000	278,000
Buses and coaches . .	17,460	18,240	19,200
Goods vehicles (incl. vans) . .	54,450	58,000	62,000
Road tractors . . .	27,440	28,000	28,420
Motor cycles and mopeds . .	29,400	30,690	32,000

Source: International Road Federation, *World Road Statistics*.

SHIPPING
Merchant Fleet (registered at 31 December)

	1996	1997	1998
Number of vessels . . .	38	38	39
Total displacement ('000 grt) .	19.8	20.6	20.9

Source: Lloyd's Register of Shipping, *World Fleet Statistics*.

International Sea-borne Freight Traffic
(estimates, '000 metric tons)

	1990	1991	1992*
Goods loaded	2,297	1,791	2,083
Goods unloaded	5,192	5,310	5,810

* Provisional.

CIVIL AVIATION (traffic on scheduled services)

	1994	1995	1996
Kilometres flown (million) .	16	16	17
Passengers carried ('000) . .	754	740	779
Passenger-km (million) . .	1,737	1,757	1,838
Total ton-km (million) . .	215	211	214

Source: UN, *Statistical Yearbook*.

Tourism

FOREIGN TOURIST ARRIVALS
(number of visitors by country of origin)

	1996	1997	1998
France	40,400	48,139	41,764
Germany	107,900	157,516	136,658
Italy	44,900	53,704	48,592
Sweden	n.a.	34,618	32,034
Switzerland . . .	24,600	39,357	34,145
Tanzania . . .	84,200	112,535	108,310
Uganda	57,200	70,281	60,974
United Kingdom . .	106,000	153,082	132,811
USA	48,900	65,658	61,944
Total (incl. others) . . .	1,003,000*	1,000,559	894,300
Tourism receipts (US $ million)	474	n.a.	n.a.

* Departures.

Source: World Trade Organization, *Yearbook of Tourism Statistics*.

1999: Foreign tourist arrivals 969,300.

Tourism receipts (Ks. million): 17,500 in 1998; 21,400 in 1999.

Communications Media

	1994	1995	1996
Radio receivers ('000 in use) . .	2,400	2,600	3,000
Television receivers ('000 in use) .	295	500	700
Telephones ('000 main lines in use)*	229	240	261
Telefax stations (number in use)*†	3,500	3,800	3,800
Mobile cellular telephones (subscribers)* . . .	1,990	2,279	2,804
Book production (titles)‡ . .	300	n.a.	n.a.
Daily newspapers:			
Titles	n.a.	5	4
Average circulation ('000 copies)	358	450†	263

* Year ending 30 June.
† Estimated figure(s).
‡ Excluding pamphlets.
1997: 3,070,000 radio receivers in use; 730,000 television receivers in use.
Sources: UNESCO, *Statistical Yearbook*; UN, *Statistical Yearbook*.

Education

(1995, unless otherwise indicated)

	Institutions	Teachers	Pupils
Primary	15,906*	181,975	5,544,998
Secondary:			
General secondary . . .	2,878	41,484	632,388
Technical† . . .	36	1,147	11,700
Teacher-training . . .	26	808‡	18,992§
Universities‖	4	4,392	35,421

* 1994 figure. † 1988 figures. ‡ 1985 figure.
§ 1992 figure. ‖ 1990 figures.
Sources: Ministry of Education, Nairobi; UNESCO, *Statistical Yearbook*.

Directory

The Constitution

The Constitution was introduced at independence on 12 December 1963. Subsequent amendments, including the adoption of republican status on 12 December 1964, were consolidated in 1969. A further amendment in December 1991 permitted the establishment of a multi-party system. In September 1997 the National Assembly approved legislation which amended the Constitution with a view to ensuring free and fair democratic elections. All political parties were granted equal access to the media, and detention without trial was prohibited. In addition, the opposition was to participate in selecting the 12 nominated members of the National Assembly and 10 of the 12 members of the supervisory Electoral Commission. An amendment to the Constitution, approved by the National Assembly in November 1999, reduced the level of presidential control over the legislative process. The Constitution can be amended by the affirmative vote on Second and Third Reading of 65% of the membership of the National Assembly (excluding the Speaker and Attorney-General).

The central legislative authority is the unicameral National Assembly, in which there are 210 directly elected Representatives, 12 nominated members and two ex-officio members, the Attorney-General and the Speaker. The maximum term of the National Assembly is five years from its first meeting (except in wartime). It can be dissolved by the President at any time, and the National Assembly may force its own dissolution by a vote of 'no confidence', whereupon Presidential and Assembly elections have to be held within 90 days.

Executive power is vested in the President, Vice-President and Cabinet. Both the Vice-President and the Cabinet are appointed by the President, who must be a member of the Assembly and at least 35 years of age. Election of the President, for a five-year term, is by direct popular vote; the winning candidate at a presidential election must receive no less than 25% of the votes in at least five of Kenya's eight provinces. If a President dies, or a vacancy otherwise occurs during a President's period of office, the Vice-President becomes interim President for up to 90 days while a successor is elected.

The Government

HEAD OF STATE

President: DANIEL ARAP MOI (took office 14 October 1978; elected August 1983, commenced further term of office February 1988, re-elected December 1992 and 29 December 1997).

CABINET
(August 2000)

Vice-President: Prof. GEORGE SAITOTI.

Minister of Home Affairs, Heritage and Sport: NOAH KATANA NGALA.

Minister of Finance: CHRYSANTHUS BARNABAS OKEMO.

Minister of Planning: GIDEON M. NDAMBUKI.

Minister of Foreign Affairs and International Co-operation: Dr BONAYA GODANA.

Minister of Education: STEPHEN KALONZO MUSYOKA.

Minister of Science and Technology: HENRY KIPRONO KOSGEY.

Minister of Vocational Training: ISAAC RUTO.

Minister of Labour: JOSEPH NGUTU.

Minister of Transport and Communications: W. MUSALIA MUDAVADI.

Minister of Energy: Dr YEKOKANDA FRANCIS OMOTO MASAKHALIA.

Minister of Water Development: KIP'NGENO ARAP NG'ENY.

Minister of the Environment: FRANCIS M. NYENZE.

Minister of Mineral Exploration: JACKSON KALWEO.

Minister of Agriculture: CHRIS MOGERE OBURE.

Minister of Rural Development: HUSSEIN MAALIM MOHAMED.

Minister of Tourism, Trade and Industry: KIPYATOR NICHOLAS KIPRONO BIWOTT.

Minister of Public Works and Housing: WILLIAM CHERUIYOT MOROGO.

Minister of Public Health: Prof. SAM ONGERI.

Minister of Medical Services: Dr AMUKOWA F. ANANGWE.

Minister of Local Government: JOHN JOSEPH KAMOTHO.

Minister of Lands and Settlement: JOSEPH NYAGAH.

MINISTRIES

Office of the President: Harambee House, Harambee Ave, POB 30510, Nairobi; tel. (2) 227411.

Office of the Vice-President and Ministry of Home Affairs, Heritage, Culture and Sport: Jogoo House 'A', Taifa Rd, POB 30520, Nairobi; tel. (2) 228411.

Ministry of Agriculture, Livestock Development and Rural Development: Kilimo House, Cathedral Rd, POB 30028, Nairobi; tel. (2) 718870; fax (2) 720586.

Ministry of Education, Science and Technology: Jogoo House 'B', Harambee Ave, POB 30040, Nairobi; tel. (2) 334411; e-mail elimul@africaonline.co.ke.

Ministry of Energy: Nyayo House, Kenyatta Ave, POB 30582, Nairobi; tel. (2) 333551.

Ministry of the Environment and Natural Resources: Maji House, Ngong Rd, POB 49720, Nairobi; tel. (2) 716103.

Ministry of Finance and Planning: Treasury Bldg, Harambee Ave, POB 30007, Nairobi; tel. (2) 338111; fax (2) 330426; e-mail mof@form-net.com.

Ministry of Foreign Affairs and International Co-operation: Treasury Bldg, Harambee Ave, POB 30551, Nairobi; tel. (2) 334433.

Ministry of Health: Medical HQ, Afya House, Cathedral Rd, POB 30016, Nairobi; tel. (2) 717077; fax (2) 725902.

Ministry of Human Resource Development: Nairobi.

Ministry of Information, Transport and Communications: Telecom House, Ngong Rd, POB 52692, Nairobi; tel. (2) 729200; fax (2) 726362.

Ministry of Labour and Human Resource Development: Social Security House, Bishop Rd, POB 40326, Nairobi; tel. (2) 729800.

Ministry of Lands and Settlement: Ardhi House, Ngong Rd, POB 30450, Nairobi; tel. (2) 718050.

Ministry of Local Government: Jogoo House 'A', Taifa Rd, POB 30004, Nairobi; tel. (2) 217475; e-mail mlog@form-net.com.

Ministry of Roads and Public Works: Ministry of Works Bldg, Ngong Rd, POB 30260, Nairobi; tel. (2) 717008; fax (2) 720044; e-mail ps@roadsnet.go.ke.

Ministry of Tourism, Trade and Industry: Utalii House, 5th Floor, off Uhuru Highway, POB 30027, Nairobi; tel. (2) 331030.

President and Legislature

PRESIDENT
Election, 29 December 1997

Candidates	Votes	%
DANIEL ARAP MOI	2,445,801	40.64
MWAI KIBAKI	1,895,527	31.49
RAILA AMOLO ODINGA	665,725	11.06
MICHAEL CHRISTOPHER KIJANA WAMALWA	505,542	8.40
CHARITY KALUKI NGILU	469,807	7.81
MARTIN J. SHIKUKU	36,302	0.60
Total	6,018,704	100.00

NATIONAL ASSEMBLY

Speaker: FRANCIS XAVIER OLE KAPARO.

General Election, 29 December 1997

Party	Seats
KANU	107
DP	39
NDP	21
FORD—Kenya	17
SDP	15
Safina	5
FORD—People	3
KSC	1
FORD—Asili	1
SPK	1
Total	210*

* In addition to the 210 directly elected seats, 12 are held by nominees. The Attorney-General and the Speaker are, *ex officio*, members of the National Assembly.

Political Organizations

Democratic Party (DP): Nairobi; f. 1991; Pres. MWAI KIBAKI; rival faction led by NGENGI MUIGAI.

Forum for the Restoration of Democracy—Asili (FORD—Asili): POB 48647, Nairobi; f. 1992; Chair. MARTIN J. SHIKUKU.

Forum for the Restoration of Democracy—Kenya (FORD—Kenya): Nairobi; f. 1992; predominantly Luo support; Chair. MICHAEL CHRISTOPHER KIJANA WAMALWA.

Forum for the Restoration of Democracy for the People (FORD—People): Nairobi; f. 1997 by fmr mems of FORD—Asili; Chair. KENNETH STANLEY NJINDO MATIBA; Sec.-Gen. KIMANI WA NYOIKE.

Kenya African National Union (KANU): POB 72394, Nairobi; f. 1960; sole legal party 1982–91; Pres. DANIEL ARAP MOI; Chair. WILSON NDOLO AYAH; Sec.-Gen. JOHN JOSEPH KAMOTHO.

Kenya National Congress (KNC): f. 1992; Chair. KATANA MKANGI.

Kenya National Democratic Alliance Party (KENDA): f. 1991; Chair. MUKARU NG'ANG'A.

Kenya Social Congress (KSC): f. 1992; Chair. GEORGE MOSETI ANYONA; Sec.-Gen. ONESMUS MBALI.

Labour Party Democracy: Chair. MOHAMED IBRAHIM NOOR.

Liberal Party: Chair. WANGARI MAATHAI.

National Development Party (NDP): f. 1994; Chair. RAILA ODINGA; Sec.-Gen. Dr CHARLES MARANGA.

Party of Independent Candidates of Kenya (PICK): Leader: JOHN HARUN MWAU.

Patriotic Pastoralist Alliance of Kenya: f. 1997; represents the interests of northern Kenyan pastoralist communities; Leaders KHALIF ABDULLAHI, IBRAHIM WOCHE, JACKSON LAISAGOR.

People's Alliance for Change in Kenya (PACK): Nairobi; f. 1999; aims to unite diverse ethnic groups; Sec.-Gen. OLANG SANA.

People's Union of Justice and New Order: Kisumu; Islamic support; Leader WILSON OWILI.

Safina ('Noah's Ark'): Nairobi; f. 1995; aims to combat corruption and human rights abuses and to introduce proportional representation; Chair. FARAH MA'ALIM; Sec.-Gen. MWANDAWIRO MGHANGA.

Social Democratic Party (SDP): Nairobi; f. 1992; Chair. CHARITY KULUKI NGILU; Sec.-Gen. APOLLO NJONJO.

United Democratic Movement: Nairobi; Chair. FRED OKIKI AMAYO; Sec.-Gen. MAURICE KAMAU RUBIA.

United Patriotic Party of Kenya: Chair. MUNYUA WAIYAKI.

The following organizations are banned:

February Eighteen Resistance Army: believed to operate from Uganda; Leader Brig. JOHN ODONGO (also known as STEPHEN AMOKE).

Islamic Party of Kenya (IPK): Mombasa; f. 1992; Islamic fundamentalist; Chair. SHEIKH KHALIFA MUHAMMAD (acting); Sec.-Gen. ABDULRAHMAN WANDATI.

Diplomatic Representation

EMBASSIES AND HIGH COMMISSIONS IN KENYA

Algeria: Comcraft House, 4th Floor, Haile Selassie Ave, POB 53902, Nairobi; tel. (2) 213864; fax (2) 337286; e-mail algerianembassy@form-net.com.

Argentina: Posta Sacco, 6th Floor, University Way, POB 30283, Nairobi; tel. (2) 335242; fax (2) 217693; e-mail argentina@form-net.com; Ambassador: JOSÉ MARÍA CANTILO.

Australia: ICIPE House, River Side Drive, off Chiromo Rd, POB 39341, Nairobi; tel. (2) 445034; fax (2) 444617; High Commissioner: PHILIP GREEN.

Austria: City House, 2nd Floor, Wabera St, POB 30560, Nairobi; tel. and fax (2) 331792; e-mail austria@africaonline.co.ke; Ambassador: FRANZ HÖRLBERGER.

Bangladesh: Lenana Rd, POB 41645, Nairobi; tel. (2) 583354; fax (2) 562817; High Commissioner: Dr M. AFSARUL QADER.

Belgium: Muthaiga, Limuru Rd, POB 30461, Nairobi; tel. (2) 741564; fax (2) 442701; e-mail belgianembke@form-net.com; Ambassador: LEO WILLEMS.

Brazil: Jeevan Bharati Bldg, 4th Floor, Harambee Ave, POB 30754, Nairobi; tel. (2) 332649; fax (2) 336245; Ambassador: MÁRIO AGUSTO SANTOS.

Burundi: Development House, 14th Floor, Moi Ave, POB 44439, Nairobi; tel. (2) 575113; fax (2) 219005; Ambassador: GERMAIN NKESHIMANA.

Canada: Comcraft House, 6th Floor, Haile Selassie Ave, POB 30481, Nairobi; tel. (2) 214804; fax (2) 226987; High Commissioner: GERRY CAMPBELL.

Chile: International House, 5th Floor, Mama Ngina St, POB 45554, Nairobi; tel. (2) 331320; fax (2) 215648; e-mail echileke@form-net.com; Ambassador: Dr VICENTE SÁNCHEZ.

China, People's Republic: Woodlands Rd, Hurlingham, POB 47039, Nairobi; tel. (2) 722559; fax (2) 746402; Ambassador: AN YONGYU.

Colombia: International House, 8th Floor, POB 48494, Nairobi; tel. (2) 246770; fax (2) 246771; e-mail embcol@form-net.com; Ambassador: Dr GERMÁN GARCÍA-DURÁN.

Congo, Democratic Republic: Electricity House, Harambee Ave, POB 48106, Nairobi; tel. (2) 229771; fax (2) 334539; Ambassador: (vacant).

Cyprus: Eagle House, 5th Floor, Kimathi St, POB 30739, Nairobi; tel. (2) 220881; fax (2) 331232; High Commissioner: PAVLOS HADJI-TOFIS.

Czech Republic: Embassy House, Harambee Ave, POB 48785; tel. (2) 210494; fax (2) 223447; e-mail nairobi@embassy.mzv.cz; Chargé d'affaires: ZDENĚK DOBIÁŠ.

Denmark: HFCK Bldg, 11th Floor, Kenyatta Ave, POB 40412, Nairobi; tel. (2) 331088; fax (2) 331492; e-mail dkembnbo@africaonline.co.ke; Ambassador: KLAUS DAHLGAARD.

Djibouti: Comcraft House, 2nd Floor, Haile Selassie Ave, POB 59528, Nairobi; tel. (2) 339640; Ambassador: SALEH HAJI FARAH.

Egypt: Harambee Plaza, 7th Floor, Haile Selassie Ave, POB 30285, Nairobi; tel. (2) 570360; fax (2) 570383; Ambassador: MOHAMMED ASIM IBRAHIM.

Eritrea: New Rehema House, Raphta Rd, POB 38651, Nairobi; tel. (2) 443163; fax (2) 443165; Ambassador: GIRMAY GEBREMARIAM.

Ethiopia: State House Ave, POB 45198, Nairobi; tel. (2) 723027; fax (2) 723401; e-mail ethembnb@africaonline.co.ke; Ambassador: TOSHOME TOGA.

Finland: International House, 2nd Floor, Mama Ngina St, POB 30379, Nairobi; tel. (2) 334777; fax (2) 335986; e-mail finland@form-net.com; Ambassador: LAURI KANGAS.

France: Barclays Plaza, 9th Floor, Loita St, POB 41784, Nairobi; tel. (2) 339783; fax (2) 339421; e-mail ienkenya@form-net.com; Ambassador: JACQUES DEPAIGNE.

Germany: Williamson House, 8th Floor, 4th Ngong Ave, POB 30180, Nairobi; tel. (2) 712527; fax (2) 714886; e-mail ger-emb@form-net.com; Ambassador: MICHAEL GERDTS.

Greece: Nation Centre, 13th Floor, Kimathi St, POB 30543, Nairobi; tel. (2) 228465; fax (2) 216044; Ambassador: (vacant).

Holy See: Apostolic Nunciature, Manyani Rd West, Waiyaki Way, POB 14326, Nairobi; tel. (2) 442975; fax (2) 446789; e-mail nunciokenya@form-net.com; Apostolic Nuncio: Most Rev. GIOVANNI TONUCCI, Titular Archbishop of Torcello.

Hungary: Ole Odume Rd, POB 61146, Nairobi; tel. (2) 560060; fax (2) 560114; e-mail huembnai@africaonline.co.ke; Ambassador: ANDRÁS TÓTH.

India: Jeevan Bharati Bldg, 2nd Floor, Harambee Ave, POB 30074, Nairobi; tel. (2) 225104; fax (2) 334167; e-mail hcindia@form-net.com; High Commissioner: T. P. SREENIVASAN.

Indonesia: Utalii House, 3rd Floor, Uhuru Highway, POB 48868, Nairobi; tel. (2) 215874; fax (2) 340721; Ambassador: DALINDRA AMAN.

Iran: Dennis Pritt Rd, POB 49170, Nairobi; tel. (2) 720343; fax (2) 339936; Ambassador: HAMID MOAYYER.

Iraq: Loresho Ridge, POB 49213, Nairobi; tel. (2) 580262; fax (2) 582880; Chargé d'affaires a.i.: SABAH-TALAT-KADRAT.

Israel: Bishop's Rd, POB 30354, Nairobi; tel. (2) 722182; fax (2) 715966; Ambassador: MENASHE ZIPORI.

Italy: International House, 9th Floor, Mama Ngina St, POB 30107, Nairobi; tel. (2) 337356; fax (2) 337056; e-mail afra@form-net.com; Ambassador: Dr ALBERTO BALBONI.

Japan: ICEA Bldg, 15th Floor, Kenyatta Ave, POB 60202, Nairobi; tel. and fax (2) 332955; Ambassador: MORIHISA AOKI.

Korea, Republic: Anniversary Towers, 15th Floor, University Way, POB 30455, Nairobi; tel. (2) 333581; fax (2) 332839; e-mail koremb@form-net.com; Ambassador: KWON JONG RAK.

Kuwait: Muthaiga Rd, POB 42353, Nairobi; tel. (2) 761614; fax (2) 762837; e-mail kuwaitembassy@form-net.com; Chargé d'affaires a.i.: JABER SALEM HUSSAIN EBRAHEEM.

Lesotho: International House, 4th Floor, Mama Ngina St, POB 44096, Nairobi; tel. (2) 224876; fax (2) 337493; High Commissioner: (vacant).

Malawi: Waiyaki Way (between Mvuli and Church Rds), POB 30453, Nairobi; tel. (2) 440569; fax 440568; High Commissioner: M. V. L. PHIRI (acting).

Mexico: Kibagare Way, off Loresho Ridge, POB 14145, Nairobi; tel. (2) 582850; fax (2) 581500; e-mail embmexke@form-net.com; Ambassador: ARTURO GONZÁLEZ.

Morocco: Diamond Trust House, 3rd Floor, Moi Ave, POB 61093, Nairobi; tel. (2) 222361; fax (2) 222364; e-mail embassymorocco@form-net.com; Chargé d'affaires a.i.: DRISS KASSIMI.

Mozambique: Bruce House, 3rd Floor, Standard St, POB 66923, Nairobi; tel. (2) 221979; fax (2) 222446; High Commissioner: PAULO ELIAS CIGARRO.

Netherlands: Uchumi House, 6th Floor, Nkrumah Ave, POB 41537, Nairobi; tel. (2) 227111; fax (2) 339155; e-mail holland@form-net.com; Ambassador: RUUD J. TREFFERS.

Nigeria: Lenana Rd, Hurlingham, POB 30516, Nairobi; tel. (2) 564116; fax (2) 564117; High Commissioner: CLARKSON N. UMELO.

Norway: Rehani House, 8th Floor, Kenyatta Ave, POB 46363, Nairobi; tel. (2) 337121; fax (2) 216009; Chargé d'affaires a.i.: OVE DANBOLDT.

Pakistan: St Michel Rd, Westlands Ave, POB 30045, Nairobi; tel. (2) 443911; fax (2) 446507; High Commissioner: (vacant).

Poland: Kabarnet Rd, Woodley, POB 30086, Nairobi; tel. (2) 566288; fax (2) 727701; e-mail polambnairobi@form-net.com; Ambassador: ADAM T. KOWALEWSKI.

Portugal: Reinsurance Plaza, 10th Floor, Aga Khan Walk, POB 34020, Nairobi; tel. (2) 338990; fax (2) 214711; Ambassador: JOSÉ LAMEIRAS.

Romania: POB 48412, Nairobi; tel. (2) 743209; fax (2) 741696; e-mail roembken@africaonline.co.ke; Ambassador: Prof. NICOLAE COMAN.

Russia: Lenana Rd, POB 30049, Nairobi; tel. (2) 722462; fax (2) 721888; Ambassador: BORIS SEPTOV.

Rwanda: International House, 12th Floor, Mama Ngina St, POB 48579, Nairobi; tel. (2) 560178; fax (2) 561932.

Saudi Arabia: Muthaiga Rd, POB 58297, Nairobi; tel. (2) 762781; fax (2) 760939; Chargé d'affaires: IBRAHIM AMMAR.

Slovakia: Milimani Rd, POB 30204, Nairobi; tel. (2) 721896; fax (2) 721898.

Somalia: POB 30769, Nairobi; tel. (2) 580165; fax (2) 581683.

South Africa: Lonhro House, 14th Floor, Standard St, POB 42441, Nairobi; tel. (2) 215616; fax (2) 223687; High Commissioner: GRIFFITHS M. MEMELA.

Spain: Bruce House, 5th Floor, Standard St, POB 45503, Nairobi; tel. (2) 335711; fax (2) 332858; Ambassador: FERMÍN PIETRO-CASTRO ROUMIER.

Sri Lanka: Rose Ave, off Lenana Rd, POB 48145, Nairobi; tel. (2) 227577; fax (2) 225391; e-mail slhckeny@user.africaonline.co.ke; internet www.lk/dipmissionf.html; High Commissioner: J. D. A. WIJEWARDENA.

Sudan: Minet-ICDC Bldg, 7th Floor, Mamlaka Rd, POB 48784, Nairobi; tel. (2) 720853; fax (2) 721015; Ambassador: OMER EL-SHEIKH.

Swaziland: Transnational Plaza, 3rd Floor, Mama Ngina St, POB 41887, Nairobi; tel. (2) 339231; fax (2) 330540; High Commissioner: Prince MBILINI DLAMINI.

Sweden: International House, 10th Floor, Mama Ngina St, POB 30600, Nairobi; tel. (2) 229042; fax (2) 218908; Ambassador: LARS-GÖRAN ENGFELDT.

Switzerland: International House, 7th Floor, Mama Ngina St, POB 30752, Nairobi; tel. (2) 228735; fax (2) 217388; e-mail sdckenya@form-net.com; Ambassador: Dr ARMIN KAMER.

Tanzania: Continental House, Uhuru Highway, POB 47790, Nairobi; tel. (2) 721742; fax (2) 218269; High Commissioner: MIRISHO SAM HAGGAI SARAKIKYA.

Thailand: Ambassador House, Rose Ave, POB 58349, Nairobi; tel. (2) 715800; fax (2) 715801; e-mail thainbi@form-net.com; Ambassador: PONGSAK DISYATAT.

Turkey: Gigiri Rd, off Limuru Rd, POB 30785, Nairobi; tel. (2) 520404; fax (2) 521237; Ambassador: MANZU BUYUKDAVRAS.

Uganda: Uganda House, 5th Floor, Kenyatta Ave, POB 60853, Nairobi; tel. (2) 330801; fax (2) 330970; High Commissioner: J. TOMUSANGE.

United Kingdom: Upper Hill Rd, POB 30465, Nairobi; tel. (2) 714699; fax (2) 719486; e-mail bhcinfo@iconnect.co.ke; internet www.britain.or.ke; High Commissioner: Sir JEFFREY JAMES.

USA: Mombasa Rd, POB 30137, Nairobi; tel. (2) 334141; fax (2) 340838; Ambassador: JOHNNIE CARSON.

Venezuela: Ngong/Kabarnet Rd, POB 34477, Nairobi; tel. (2) 574646; fax (2) 337487; e-mail embavene@africaonline.co.ke; Chargé d'affaires a.i.: NOEL D. QUINTERO.

Yemen: cnr Ngong and Kabarnet Rds, POB 44642, Nairobi; tel. (2) 564379; fax (2) 564394; Ambassador: AHMAD MAYSARI.

Yugoslavia: State House Ave, Nairobi; tel. (2) 720670.

Zambia: Nyerere Rd, POB 48741, Nairobi; tel. (2) 724850; fax (2) 718494; High Commissioner: ENESS CHISHALA CHIYENGE.

Zimbabwe: Minet-ICDC Bldg, 6th Floor, Mamlaka Rd, POB 30806, Nairobi; tel. (2) 721071; fax (2) 726503; High Commissioner: LUCAS PANDE TAVAYA.

Judicial System

The Kenya Court of Appeal: POB 30187, Nairobi; the final court of appeal for Kenya in civil and criminal process; sits at Nairobi, Mombasa, Kisumu, Nakuru and Nyeri.

    Chief Justice: BERNARD CHUNGA.

    Justices of Appeal: MATHEW MULI, J. M. GACHUHI, J. R. O. MASIME, J. E. GICHERU, R. O. KWACH, EFFIE OWUOR.

The High Court of Kenya: Harambee Ave, POB 30041, Nairobi; tel. (2) 221221; e-mail hck-lib@nbnet.co.ke; has unlimited criminal and civil jurisdiction at first instance, and sits as a court of appeal from subordinate courts in both criminal and civil cases. The High Court is also a court of admiralty. There are two resident puisne judges at Mombasa and at Nakuru, and one resident puisne judge at Eldoret, Kakamega, Kisumu, Nyeri, Kisii and Meru.

Resident Magistrates' Courts: have country-wide jurisdiction, with powers of punishment by imprisonment up to five years or by fine up to K£500. If presided over by a chief magistrate or senior resident magistrate the court is empowered to pass any sentence authorized by law. For certain offences, a resident magistrate may pass minimum sentences authorized by law.

District Magistrates' Courts: of first, second and third class; have jurisdiction within districts and powers of punishment by imprisonment for up to five years, or by fines of up to K£500.

Kadhi's Courts: have jurisdiction within districts, to determine questions of Islamic law.

Religion

Most of the population hold traditional African beliefs, although there are significant numbers of African Christians. The Arab inhabitants are Muslims, and the Indian population is partly Muslim and partly Hindu. The Europeans and Goans are predominantly Christian. Muslims are found mainly along the coastline; however, the Islamic faith has also established itself among Africans around Nairobi and among some ethnic groups in the northern districts. East Africa is also an important centre for the Bahá'í faith.

CHRISTIANITY

National Council of Churches of Kenya: Church House, Moi Ave, POB 45009, Nairobi; tel. (2) 242278; fax (2) 224463; f. 1943 as Christian Council of Kenya; 35 full mems and eight assoc. mems; Chair. Rev. JOSEPH WAITHONGA; Sec.-Gen. Rev. MUTAVA MUSYIMI.

The Anglican Communion

Anglicans are adherents of the Church of the Province of Kenya, which was established in 1970. It comprises 28 dioceses, and has about 2.5m. members.

Archbishop of Kenya and Bishop of Nairobi: Most Rev. Dr DAVID M. GITARI, POB 40502, Nairobi; tel. (2) 714755; fax (2) 718442; e-mail ackenya@insightkenya.com.

Greek Orthodox Church

Archbishop of East Africa: NICADEMUS of IRINOUPOULIS, Nairobi; jurisdiction covers Kenya, Tanzania and Uganda.

The Roman Catholic Church

Kenya comprises four archdioceses and 17 dioceses. At 31 December 1998 there were an estimated 7.0m. adherents in the country.

Kenya Episcopal Conference: Kenya Catholic Secretariat, POB 13475, Nairobi; tel. (2) 443133; fax (2) 442910; e-mail csk@users.africaonline.co.ke; f. 1976; Pres. Rt Rev. JOHN NJUE, Bishop of Embu.

Archbishop of Kisumu: Most Rev. ZACCHAEUS OKOTH, POB 1728, Kisumu; tel. (35) 43950; fax (35) 42415.

Archbishop of Mombasa: Most Rev. JOHN NJENGA, Catholic Secretariat, Nyerere Ave, POB 83131, Mombasa; tel. (11) 471320; fax (11) 473166; e-mail msadio@africaonline.co.ke.

Archbishop of Nairobi: Most Rev. RAPHAEL NDINGI MWANA'A NZEKI, Archbishop's House, POB 14231, Nairobi; tel. (2) 441919; fax 447027; e-mail arch-nbo@africaonline.co.ke.

Archbishop of Nyeri: Most Rev. NICODEMUS KIRIMA, POB 288, Nyeri; tel. (34) 30446.

Other Christian Churches

Africa Inland Church in Kenya: Pres. Rev. Dr TITUS GITHUMBI.

African Christian Church and Schools: POB 1365, Thika; tel. (151) 47; f. 1948; Moderator Rt Rev. JOHN NJUNGUNA; Gen. Sec. Rev. SAMUEL MWANGI; 50,000 mems.

Directory

African Church of the Holy Spirit: POB 183, Kakamega; f. 1927; Exec. Sec. Rev. Pres. Rev. Dr Byrum Makokha; 20,000 mems.

African Israel Nineveh Church: Nineveh HQ, POB 701, Kisumu; f. 1942; High Priest Rt Rev. John Kivuli, II; Gen. Sec. Rev. John arap Tonui; 350,000 mems.

Baptist Convention of Kenya: POB 14907, Nairobi; Pres. Rev. Eliud Mungai.

Church of God in East Africa: Pres. Rev. Dr Bairam Makokha.

Evangelical Fellowship of Kenya: Co-ordinator Rt Rev. Arthur Gitonga; Sec.-Gen. Dr Washington Ng'eng'i.

Evangelical Lutheran Church in Kenya: POB 874, Kisii; tel. (381) 20237; Bishop Rev. Francis Onderi Nyamwaro; 55,000 mems.

Methodist Church in Kenya: POB 47633, Nairobi; tel. (2) 724841; f. 1862 (autonomous since 1967); Presiding Bishop Rev. Dr Zablon Nthamburi; 610,000 mems (1996).

Presbyterian Church of East Africa: POB 48268, Nairobi; tel. (2) 504417; fax (2) 504442; Moderator Rt Rev. Dr Jesse Kamau; Sec.-Gen. Rev. Dr Samuel Mwaniki.

Other denominations active in Kenya include the Africa Gospel Church, the African Brotherhood Church, the African Independent Pentecostal Church, the African Interior Church, the Episcopal Church of Kenya, the Free Pentecostal Fellowship of Kenya, the Full Gospel Churches of Kenya, the Lutheran Church in Kenya, the National Independent Church of Africa, the Pentecostal Assemblies of God, the Pentecostal Evangelistic Fellowship of God and the Reformed Church of East Africa.

BAHÁ'Í FAITH

National Spiritual Assembly: POB 47562, Nairobi; tel. (2) 725447; mems resident in 9,654 localities.

ISLAM

Supreme Council of Kenyan Muslims (SUPKEM): Nat. Chair. Prof. Abd al-Ghafur al-Busaidy; Sec.-Gen. Mohammed Khalif.

Chief Kadhi: Nassor Nahdi.

The Press

PRINCIPAL DAILIES

Daily Nation: POB 49010, Nairobi; tel. and fax (2) 337710; e-mail nation@insightkenya.com; internet www.nationaudio.com; f. 1960; English; owned by Nation Media Group; Editor-in-Chief Wangethi Mwangi; Man. Editor Joseph Odindo; circ. 170,000.

East African Standard: POB 30080, Nairobi; tel. (2) 540280; fax (2) 553939; e-mail online@eastandard.net; internet www.eastandard.net; f. 1902; Group Man. Editor Waruru Wachiro; circ. 60,000.

Kenya Leo: POB 30958, Nairobi; tel. (2) 332390; f. 1983; Kiswahili; KANU party newspaper; Group Editor-in-Chief Amboka Andere; circ. 6,000.

Kenya Times: POB 30958, Nairobi; tel. (2) 332390; f. 1983; English; KANU party newspaper; Group Editor-in-Chief Amboka Andere; circ. 10,000.

The People: POB 48647, Nairobi; tel. (2) 449269; fax (2) 446640; e-mail info@people.co.ke; f. 1993; Editor-in-Chief George Mbugguss; circ. 40,000.

Taifa Leo: POB 49010, Nairobi; tel. (2) 337691; Kiswahili; f. 1960; daily and weekly edns; owned by Nation Media Group; Editor Robert Mwangi; circ. 57,000.

Kenya has a thriving vernacular press, but titles are often short-lived. Newspapers in African languages include:

Kihooto (The Truth): Kikuyu; satirical.

Mwaria Ma (Honest Speaker): Karatina, Nyeri; f. 1997; Publr Canon Jamlick M. Miano.

Mwihoko (Hope): POB 734, Muranga; f. 1997; Roman Catholic.

Nam Dar: Luo.

Otit Mach (Firefly): Luo.

SELECTED PERIODICALS
Weeklies and Fortnightlies

The Business Chronicle: POB 53328, Nairobi; tel. (2) 544283; fax (2) 532736; f. 1994; weekly; Man. Editor Musyoka Kyendo.

Coastweek: Oriental Bldg, 2nd Floor, Nkrumah Rd, POB 87270, Mombasa; tel. (11) 313767; fax (11) 225003; e-mail coastwk@africaonline.co.ke; internet www.coastweek.com; f. 1978; English; weekly; Editor Adrian Grimwood; circ. 40,000.

The East African: POB 49010 Nairobi; tel. (2) 337710; fax (2) 213946; e-mail nation@insightkenya.com; internet www

.nationaudio.com/news/eastafrican/current; f. 1994; weekly; English; owned by Nation Media Group; Editor-in-Chief Wangethi Mwangi; Man. Editor Mbatau wa Ngai.

The Herald: POB 30958, Nairobi; tel. (2) 332390; English; sponsored by KANU; Editor Job Mutungi; circ. 8,000.

Kenrail: POB 30121, Nairobi; tel. (2) 221211; fax (2) 340049; English and Kiswahili; publ. by Kenya Railways Corpn; Editor J. N. Luseno; circ. 20,000.

Kenya Gazette: POB 30746, Nairobi; tel. (2) 334075; f. 1898; official notices; weekly; circ. 8,000.

Post on Sunday: Nairobi; weekly; independent; Editor-in-Chief Tony Gachoka.

The Standard on Sunday: POB 30080, Nairobi; tel. (2) 540280; fax (2) 553939; English; Man. Editor Fred Mutiso; circ. 90,000.

Sunday Nation: POB 49010, Nairobi; f. 1960; English; owned by Nation Media Group; Man. Editor Bernard Nderitu; circ. 170,000.

Sunday Times: POB 30958, Nairobi; tel. (2) 337798; Group Editor Amboka Andere.

Taifa Jumapili: POB 49010, Nairobi; f. 1987; Kiswahili; owned by Nation Media Group; Editor Robert K. Mwangi; circ. 56,000.

Taifa Weekly: POB 49010, Nairobi; tel. (2) 337691; f. 1960; Kiswahili; Editor Robert K. Mwangi; circ. 68,000.

Trans Nzoia Post; POB 34, Kitale; weekly.

The Weekly Review: POB 42271, Nairobi; tel. (2) 251473; fax (2) 222555; f. 1975; English; Man. Dir Jaindi Kisero; circ. 16,000.

What's On: Rehema House, Nairobi; tel. (2) 27651; Editor Nancy Kairo; circ. 10,000.

Monthlies

Africa Law Review: Tumaini House, 4th Floor, Nkrumah Ave, POB 53234, Nairobi; tel. (2) 330480; fax (2) 230173; e-mail alr@africalaw.org; f. 1987; English; Editor-in-Chief Gitobu Imanyara.

East African Medical Journal: POB 41632, Nairobi; tel. (2) 712010; fax (2) 724617; e-mail eamj@healthnet.or.ke; English; f. 1923; Editor-in-Chief Prof. William Lore; circ. 4,500.

East African Report on Trade and Industry: POB 30339, Nairobi; journal of Kenya Asscn of Mfrs; Editor Gordon Boy; circ. 3,000.

Executive: POB 47186, Nairobi; tel. (2) 555811; fax (2) 557815; e-mail sstms@africaonline.co.ke; f. 1980; business; Editor Tom Maliti; circ. 25,000.

Kenya Export News: POB 30339, Nairobi; tel. (2) 340010; fax (2) 218845; English; publ. for Kenya External Trade Authority, Ministry of Tourism, Trade and Industry; Editor Prof. Samuel Njoroge; circ. 5,000.

Kenya Farmer (Journal of the Agricultural Society of Kenya): c/o English Press, POB 30127, Nairobi; tel. (2) 20377; f. 1954; English and Kiswahili; Editor Robert Irungu; circ. 20,000.

Kenya Yetu: POB 8053, Nairobi; tel. (2) 250083; fax (2) 340659; f. 1965; Kiswahili; publ. by Ministry of Information, Transport and Communications; Editor M. Ndavi; circ. 10,000.

Nairobi Handbook: POB 30127, Accra Rd, Nairobi; Editor Mrs R. Ouma; circ. 20,000.

News from Kenya: POB 8053, Nairobi; tel. (2) 253083; fax (2) 340659; publ. by Ministry of Information, Transport and Communications.

PC World (East Africa): Gilgil House, Monrovia St, Nairobi; tel. (2) 246808; fax (2) 215643; f. 1996; Editor Andrew Karanja.

Presence: POB 10988, Nairobi; tel. (2) 561103; fax (2) 560420; f. 1984; economics, law, women's issues, fiction.

Sparkle: POB 47186, Nairobi; tel. (2) 555811; fax (2) 557815; f. 1990; children's; Editor Anna Ndila.

Today in Africa: POB 60, Kijabe; tel. (154) 64210; English; Man. Editor Mwaura Njoroge; circ. 13,000.

Other Periodicals

African Ecclesial Review: POB 4002, Eldoret; tel. (321) 61218; fax (321) 62570; e-mail gabapubs@net2000ke.com; f. 1969; scripture, religion and development; 6 a year; Editor Agatha Radoli; circ. 2,500.

Afya: POB 30125, Nairobi; tel. (2) 501301; fax (2) 506112; e-mail amrefkco@africaonline.co.ke; journal for medical and health workers; quarterly.

Busara: Nairobi; literary; 2 a year; Editor Kimani Gecau; circ. 3,000.

East African Agricultural and Forestry Journal: POB 30148, Nairobi; f. 1935; English; quarterly; Editor J. O. Mugah; circ. 1,000.

Eastern African Economic Review: POB 30022, Nairobi; f. 1954; 2 a year; Editor J. K. Maitha.

Economic Review of Agriculture: POB 30028, Nairobi; tel. (2) 728370; f. 1968; publ. by Ministry of Agriculture, Livestock Development and Rural Development; quarterly; Editor Okiya Okoiti.

Education in Eastern Africa: Nairobi; f. 1970; 2 a year; Editor JOHN C. B. BIGALA; circ. 2,000.

Finance: Nairobi; monthly; Editor-in-Chief NJEHU GATABAKI.

Inside Kenya Today: POB 8053, Nairobi; tel. (2) 340010; fax (2) 340659; English; publ. by Ministry of Information, Transport and Communications; quarterly; Editor M. NDAVI; circ. 10,000.

Kenya Education Journal: Nairobi; f. 1958; English; 3 a year; Editor W. G. BOWMAN; circ. 5,500.

Kenya Statistical Digest: POB 30007, Nairobi; tel. (2) 338111; fax (2) 330426; publ. by Ministry of Finance and Planning; quarterly.

Target: POB 72839, Nairobi; f. 1964; English; 6 a year; religious; Editor FRANCIS MWANIKI; circ. 17,000.

NEWS AGENCIES

Kenya News Agency (KNA): Information House, POB 8053, Nairobi; tel. (2) 223201; f. 1963; Dir S. MUSANDU.

Foreign Bureaux

Agence France-Presse (AFP): International Life House, Mama Ngina St, POB 30671, Nairobi; tel. (2) 230613; fax (2) 230649; e-mail afpkenya@net2000ke.com; Bureau Chief DIDIER LAPEYRONIE.

Agenzia Nazionale Stampa Associata (ANSA) (Italy): Agip House, POB 20444, Nairobi; tel. (2) 711338; fax (2) 229383; Rep. ADOLFO D'AMICO.

Associated Press (AP) (USA): Chester House, Koinange St, POB 47590, Nairobi; tel. (2) 250168; fax (2) 221449; e-mail naiburo@ap.org; Bureau Chief SUSAN LINNÉE.

Deutsche Presse-Agentur (dpa) (Germany): Chester House, 1st Floor, Koinange St, POB 48546, Nairobi; tel. (2) 330274; fax (2) 221902; e-mail lapkya@form-net.com; Bureau Chief Dr HUBERT KAHL.

Informatsionnoye Telegrafnoye Agentstvo Rossii—Telegrafnoye Agentstvo Suverennykh Stran (ITAR—TASS) (Russia): Likoni Lane, POB 49602, Nairobi; tel. and fax (2) 721978; e-mail itartass@swiftkenya.com; Correspondent ANDREI K. POLYAKOV.

Inter Press Service (IPS) (Italy): Press Centre, Chester House, Koinange St, POB 54386, Nairobi; tel. (2) 335418; Correspondent HORACE AWORI.

Kyodo Tsushin (Japan): Koinange St, POB 58281, Nairobi; tel. (2) 243250; fax (2) 230448; e-mail kyodonew@africaonline.co.ke; Bureau Chief OHNO KEIICHIRO.

Newslink Africa (UK): POB 3325, Nairobi; tel. (2) 241339; Correspondent PAMPHIL KWEYUH.

Reuters (UK): Finance House, 12th Floor, Loita St, POB 34043, Nairobi; tel. (2) 330261; fax (2) 338860; e-mail nairobi.newsroom@reuters.com; Bureau Chief DAVID FOX.

United Press International (UPI) (USA): POB 76282, Nairobi; tel. (2) 337349; fax (2) 213625; Correspondent JOE KHAMISI.

Xinhua (New China) News Agency (People's Republic of China): Ngong Rd at Rose Ave, POB 30728, Nairobi; tel. and fax (2) 711685; Pres. and Editor-in-Chief Prof. FLAMINGO Q. M. CHEN.

Publishers

Academy Science Publishers: POB 14798, Nairobi; tel. (2) 8844015; fax (2) 884406; e-mail aas@arcc.permanet.org; f. 1989; part of the African Academy of Sciences.

Amecea Gaba Publications: Amecea Pastoral Institute, POB 4002, Eldoret; tel. (321) 61218; fax (321) 62570; e-mail gabapubs@net2000ke.com; f. 1989; anthropology, religious; Dir Sister AGATHA RADOLI.

Camerapix Publishers International: POB 45048, Nairobi; tel. (2) 448923; fax (2) 448926; e-mail info@camerapix.com; internet www.camerapix.com; f. 1960; travel, topography, natural history; Dirs SALIM AMIN, RUKHSANA HAQ.

East African Educational Publishers Ltd: cnr Mpaka Rd and Woodvale Grove, Westlands, POB 45314, Nairobi; tel. (2) 444700; fax (2) 448753; e-mail eaep@africaonline.co.ke; f. 1965; academic, educational, creative writing; some books in Kenyan languages; Man. Dir HENRY CHAKAVA.

Evangel: Lumumba Drive, Roysambu, POB 28963, Nairobi; tel. (2) 802033; fax (2) 860840; e-mail evanglit@maf.org; f. 1952; religious; Man. Dir D. TRASK.

Foundation Books: POB 73435, Nairobi; tel. (2) 765485; f. 1974; biography, poetry; Man. Dir F. O. OKWANYA.

Kenway Publications Ltd: POB 45314, Nairobi; tel. (2) 444700; fax (2) 448753; e-mail eaep@africaonline.co.ke; f. 1981. general, regional interests; Chair. HENRY CHAKAVA.

Kenya Literature Bureau: Bellevue Area, off Mombasa Rd, POB 30022, Nairobi; tel. (2) 506142; fax (2) 505903; f. 1977; parastatal body under Ministry of Education, Science and Technology; literary,

educational, cultural and scientific books and journals; Man. Dir S. C. LANG'AT.

Jomo Kenyatta Foundation: POB 30533, Nairobi; tel. (2) 557222; fax (2) 531966; e-mail publish@jomokenyattaf.com; f. 1966; primary, secondary, university textbooks; Man. Dir IDRIS M. FARAH.

Longman Kenya Ltd: Funzi Road, Industrial Area, POB 18033, Nairobi; tel. (2) 5413457; fax (2) 540037; f. 1965; textbooks and educational materials; Gen. Man. JANET NJOROGE.

Macmillan Kenya (Publishers) Ltd: POB 30797, Nairobi; tel. (2) 220012; fax (2) 212179; e-mail dmuita@macken.co.ke; f. 1970; atlases, children's educational, guide books, literature; Man. Dir DAVID MUITA.

Newspread International: POB 46854, Nairobi; tel. (2) 331402; fax (2) 607252; f. 1971; reference, economic development; Exec. Editor KUL BHUSHAN.

Oxford University Press (Eastern Africa): Waiyaki Way, ABC Place, POB 72532, Nairobi; tel. (2) 440555; fax (2) 443972; f. 1954; children's, educational and general; Regional Man. ABDULLAH ISMAILY.

Paulines Publications-Africa: POB 49026, Nairobi; tel. (2) 447202; fax (2) 442097; e-mail paulines@iconnect.co.ke; f. 1985; children's, educational; religious; Dir Sister TERESA MARCAZZAN.

Transafrica Press: Kenwood House, Kimathi St, POB 48239, Nairobi; tel. (2) 331762; f. 1976; general, educational and children's; CEO JOHN NOTTINGHAM.

Government Publishing House

Government Printing Press: POB 30128, Nairobi.

PUBLISHERS' ORGANIZATION

Kenya Publishers' Association: POB 18650, Nairobi; tel. (2) 223262; fax (2) 339875; f. 1971; Chair. GACHECHE WARUINGI.

Broadcasting and Communications

TELECOMMUNICATIONS

Kencel Communications Ltd: Nairobi; operates mobile telephone network.

Telkom Kenya Ltd: Teleposta Towers, Kenyatta Ave, POB 30301, Nairobi; tel. (2) 251071; e-mail mdtelkomaeafix.net; f. 1999; operates, jtly with Vodafone Airtouch (UK), cellular telephone co Safaricom Ltd; Man. Dir AUGUSTINE CHESEREM.

Regulatory Authority

Communications Commission of Kenya (CCK): Kijabe St, Longonot Place, POB 14448, Nairobi; tel. (2) 240165; fax (2) 252547; e-mail cckaeafix.net; internet www.cck.go.ke; f. 1999; Dir-Gen. and CEO SAMUEL K. CHEPKONG'A.

BROADCASTING

Radio

Kenya Broadcasting Corporation (KBC): Broadcasting House, Harry Thuku Rd, POB 30456, Nairobi; tel. (2) 334567; fax (2) 220675; internet www.africaonline.co.ke/africaonline/netradio.html; f. 1989; state corpn responsible for radio and television services; Chair. Dr JULIUS KIANO; Man. Dir SIMEON ANABWANI.

> **Radio:** National service (Kiswahili); General service (English); Vernacular services (Borana, Burji, Hindustani, Kalenjin, Kikamba, Kikuyu, Kimasai, Kimeru, Kisii, Kuria, Luo, Luhya, Rendile, Somali, Suba, Teso and Turkana).

Capital FM: Lonrho House, Standard St, POB 74933, Nairobi; tel. (2) 210020; fax (2) 332349; e-mail lynxahl@users.africaonline.co.ke; commercial station broadcasting to Nairobi and environs.

Igra Broadcast Network: Westlands Estate, Nairobi; Muslim station broadcasting to Nairobi and environs.

Nation 96.4 FM: Nairobi; commercial station owned by Nation Media Group.

Television

Kenya Broadcasting Corporation (KBC): (see Radio).

> **Television:** KBC–TV, financed by licence fees and commercial advertisements; services in Kiswahili and English; operates on four channels for c. 50 hours per week. KBC–II: private subscription service.

Kenya Television Network (KTN–TV): POB 56985, Nairobi; tel. (2) 227122; fax (2) 214467; internet www.kenyaweb.com/ktn; commercial station; Chair. MWAKIO SIO.

Nation TV: POB 49010, Nairobi; f. 1999; commercial station; owned by Nation Media Group; Man. Dir SAM COMPTON.

Finance

(cap. = capital; res = reserves; dep. = deposits; m. = million;
brs = branches; amounts in Kenya shillings)

BANKING
Central Bank

Central Bank of Kenya (Banki Kuu Ya Kenya): Haile Selassie Ave, POB 60000, Nairobi; tel. (2) 226431; fax (2) 340192; e-mail cbk@africaonline.co.ke; internet www.centralbank.go.ke; f. 1966; bank of issue; cap. and res 1,672m., dep. 65,048m. (June 1996); Gov. MICAH KIPRONO CHESEREM; Dep. Gov. Dr T. N. KIBUA.

Commercial Banks

African Banking Corporation Ltd: ABC-Bank House, Koinange St, POB 46452, Nairobi; tel. (2) 223922; fax (2) 222437; e-mail abcbank@form-net.com; f. 1995; cap. and res 280m., dep. 2,264m. (Dec. 1998); Exec. Chair. ASHRAF SAVANI; Gen. Man. GHULAM HUSSAIN SHEIKH; 7 brs.

Akiba Bank Ltd: Fedha Towers, 2nd Floor, Muindi Mbingu St, POB 49584, Nairobi; tel. (2) 331709; fax (2) 225694; e-mail akiba @form-net.com; internet www.kenyaweb.com/eabsgroup; cap. 400m. (Dec.1998); Exec. Chair. L. J. PANDIT.

Barclays Bank of Kenya Ltd: Barclays Plaza, Loita St, POB 30120, Nairobi; tel. (2) 332230; fax (2) 213915; f. 1978; cap. and res 8,169m., dep. 60,954m. (Dec. 1998); Chair. SAMUEL O. J. AMBUNDO; Man. Dir GARETH GEORGE; 87 brs.

Biashara Bank of Kenya Ltd: Jethalal Chambers, Biashara St, POB 30831, Nairobi; tel. (2) 221064; fax 221679; e-mail business@biasharabank.com; f. 1984; cap. and res 227.9m., dep. 1,602.1m. (Dec. 1997); Chair. S. B. P. SHAH; CEO N. D. CHUDASAMA.

CFC Bank Ltd: CFC Centre, Chiromo Rd, POB 72833, Nairobi; tel. (2) 340091; fax (2) 223032; cap. 500m. (Dec. 1998); Chair. P. K. JANI; Man. Dir N. MAJMUDAR.

Chase Bank (Kenya) Ltd: Prudential Assurance Bldg, Wabera St, POB 28987, Nairobi; tel. (2) 244035; fax (2) 246334; e-mail chasebank@form-net.com; cap. 404m. (Dec. 1998); Chair. BIPIN YORA; Man. Dir ZAFRULLAH KHAN.

Commercial Bank of Africa Ltd: Commercial Bank Bldg, cnr Wabera and Standard Sts, POB 30437, Nairobi; tel. (2) 228881; fax (2) 335827; internet www.cba.co.ke; f. 1962; owned by Kenyan shareholders; cap. and res 1,489m., dep. 9,953m. (Dec. 1999); Chair. M. H. DA GAMA-ROSE; Man. Dir I. O. AWUONDO; 11 brs.

Consolidated Bank of Kenya Ltd: Koinange St, POB 51133, Nairobi; tel. (2) 340920; fax (2) 340213; f. 1989; state-owned; cap. and res 1,326m. (Dec. 1998); Chair. ANDREW LIGALE; Man. Dir E. K. MATHIU.

Delphis Bank Ltd: Finance House, Koinauge St, POB 44080, Nairobi; tel. (2) 228461; fax (2) 219469; e-mail delphiskenya@iconnect.co.ke.; internet www.delphisbank.com.; f. 1991; cap. and res. 465m., dep. 3,650m. (Dec. 1998); Chair. J. K. CHANDE; Man. Dir N. R. C. PANICKER.

Development Bank of Kenya Ltd: Finance House, Loita St, POB 30483, Nairobi; tel. (2) 340401; fax (2) 338426; e-mail dbk@africaonline.co.ke; f. 1963 as Development Finance Co of Kenya, current name adopted 1996; owned by Industrial and Commercial Devt Corpn, govt agencies of Germany and the Netherlands, the Commonwealth Development Corpn and the International Finance Corpn, Washington; cap. and res 1,180m., dep. 747m. (Dec. 1998); Chair. Prof. HAROUN NGENY KIPKEMBOI MENGECH; Gen. Man. JOHN VIJEDI BOSSE.

Equatorial Commerce Bank Ltd: POB 52467, Nairobi; tel. (2) 331122; fax (2) 331606; e-mail ecb@iconnect.co.ke; cap. 306m. (Dec. 1998); Chair. S. M. C. THOMSON; Man. Dir T. N. KHWAJA.

Kenya Commercial Bank Ltd: Kencom House, Moi Ave, POB 48400, Nairobi; tel. (2) 339441; fax (2) 338006; e-mail kcbhq@form.net.com; f. 1970; 35% state-owned; cap. and res 10,144m., dep. 60,768m. (Dec. 1998); Exec. Chair. PETER C. J. O. NYAKIAMO; Gen. Man. E.C.A. SAINA; 180 brs and sub-brs.

Middle East Bank Kenya Ltd: Exchange Bldg, Kenyatta Ave, POB 47387, Nairobi; tel. (2) 335170; fax (2) 336182; e-mail mebkenya@nbnet.co.ke; f. 1981; 75% owned by Kenyan shareholders; cap. and res 635m., dep. 3,156m. (Dec. 1999); Chair. A. A. K. ESMAIL; Man. Dir S. S. DINAMANI; 2 brs.

National Bank of Kenya Ltd (Banki ya Taifa La Kenya Ltd): National Bank Bldg, Harambee Ave, POB 72866, Nairobi; tel. (2) 226471; fax (2) 330784; e-mail fimaga@nbnet.co.ke; f. 1968; 64.5% state-owned; cap. 1,000m., dep. 19,288m. (Dec. 1998); Exec. Chair. JOHN P. N. SIMBA; Man. Dir REUBEN MARAMBII; 25 brs.

Stanbic Bank Kenya Ltd: Stanbic Bank Bldg, Kenyatta Ave, POB 30550, Nairobi; tel. (2) 335888; fax (2) 330227; e-mail stanbic@africaonline.co.ke; f. 1992; 82% owned by Standard Bank Investment Corpn Ltd (Botswana), 11% state-owned; cap. and res 994m., dep. 5,852m. (Dec. 1998); Chair. J. B. WANJUI; Man. Dir P. J. W. LEWIS-JONES; 2 brs.

Standard Chartered Bank Kenya Ltd: Standard House, Moi Ave, POB 30003, Nairobi; tel. (2) 330200; fax (2) 330506; f. 1987; owned by Standard Chartered Holdings (Africa) BV (Netherlands); cap. 824m. (Dec. 1998), dep. 26,262m. (Dec. 1997); Chair. HARRINGTON AWORI; CEO L. S. GIBSON; 43 brs.

Trans-National Bank Ltd: Trans-National Plaza, 2nd Floor, Mama Ngina St, POB 34353, Nairobi; tel. (2) 339201; fax (2) 339227; e-mail tnbl@form-net.com; f. 1985; cap. and res 711m., dep. 1,008m. (Dec. 1997); Chair. MWAKAI SIO; Man. Dir PATRICK NOBLE; 5 brs.

Trust Bank Ltd: Trustforte Bldg, Moi Ave, POB 46342, Nairobi; tel. (2) 226413; fax (2) 334995; e-mail in@chiefmngr hotrustbnk.com.ke; f. 1988; placed under statutory management Sept. 1998; cap. 500m. (Dec. 1997); 21 brs.

Victoria Commercial Bank Ltd: Victor House, Kimathi St, POB 41114, Nairobi; tel. (2) 228732; fax (2) 220548; f. 1987 as Victoria Finance Co Ltd, name changed 1996; cap. and res 370.7m., dep. 3,513.8m. (Dec. 1997); Chair. SILVANO KOLA; Gen. Man. YOGESH KANJI PATTNI.

Merchant Banks

Barclays Merchant Finance Ltd: Barclays Plaza, Loita St, POB 46661, Nairobi; tel. (2) 331324; fax (2) 331396; Man. Dir GARETH A. GEORGE.

Diamond Trust Bank of Kenya Ltd: Nation Centre, 8th Floor, Kimathi St, POB 61711, Nairobi; tel. (2) 210988; fax (2) 336836; f. 1945; cap. 318m. (Dec. 1998); Chair. J. B. GALBRAITH; Man. Dir M. P. MANJI.

Kenya Commercial Finance Co Ltd: Kenyan House, 6th Floor, Moi Ave, POB 21984, Nairobi; tel. (2) 339074; fax (2) 215881; e-mail kcfc@net2000ke.com; f. 1971; cap. 300m., dep. 4,042m. (1998); Chair. PETER C. J. O. NYAKIAMO; Chief Man. M. S. FAZAL.

Kenya National Capital Corporation Ltd: POB 73469, Nairobi; tel. (2) 336077; fax (2) 338217; f. 1977; 60% owned by National Bank of Kenya, 40% by Kenya National Assurance Co; cap. 80m., dep. 1,024m. (1996); Chair. R. GITAU; Gen. Man. C. M. KIBUNJA.

National Industrial Credit Bank Ltd (NIC): NIC House, Masaba Rd, POB 44599, Nairobi; tel. (2) 718200; fax (2) 718232; e-mail nic@iconnect.co.ke; cap. 330m. (Dec. 1998); Chair. N. M. MUGWANDIA; Man. Dir M. N. DAVIDSON.

Standard Chartered Financial Services Ltd: International House, 1st Floor, Mama Ngina St, POB 40310, Nairobi; tel. (2) 336333; fax (2) 334934; owned by Standard Chartered Bank Kenya; cap. and res 161.7m., dep. 1,700m. (Dec. 1992); Chair. A. CLEARY; Man. Dir W. VON ISENBURG.

Foreign Banks

ABN AMRO Bank NV (Netherlands): Nyerere Rd, POB 30262, Nairobi; tel. (2) 710455; fax (2) 713391; e-mail abnamro@africaonline.co.ke; internet www.abnamro.com; Gen. Man. ADRIAN VAN DER POL; 2 brs.

Bank of Baroda (India): Bank of Baroda Bldg, cnr Mondlane St and Tom Mboya St, POB 30033, Nairobi; tel. (2) 228405; fax (2) 333089; Exec. Chair. C. K. DAIYA; 6 brs.

Bank of India: Kenyatta Ave, POB 30246, Nairobi; tel. (2) 221414; fax (2) 229462; CEO PUNDARIK SANYAL.

Citibank NA (USA): Citibank House, Upperhill Rd, POB 30711, Nairobi; tel. (2) 711221; fax (2) 714811; Gen. Man. PETER H. HARRIS.

Crédit Agricole Indosuez (France): Reinsurance Plaza, Taifa Rd, POB 69562, Nairobi; tel. (2) 215859; fax (2) 214166; Regional Man. BENOÎT DESTOPPELAIRE.

First American Bank of Kenya Ltd (USA): ICEA Bldg, 6th/7th Floors, Kenyatta Ave, POB 30691, Nairobi; tel. (2) 215936; fax (2) 333868; e-mail fabk@africaonline.co.ke; f. 1987; cap. and res 750m., dep. 4,454m. (Dec. 1998); Chair. N. N. MERALI; Man. Dir MANLIO BLASETTI; 2 brs.

Habib Bank AG Zurich (Switzerland): National House, Koinange St, POB 30584, Nairobi; tel. (2) 334984; fax (2) 218699; Gen. Man. IQBAL ALLAWALA.

MashreqBank PSC (UAE): ICEA Bldg, Kenyatta Ave, POB 11129, Nairobi; tel. (2) 330562; fax (2) 330792; e-mail m6cbd@gsm.net.com; Gen. Man. SYED AKHTAR IMAN.

Co-operative Bank

Co-operative Bank of Kenya Ltd: Co-operative House, Haile Selassie Ave, POB 48231, Nairobi; tel. (2) 228453; fax (2) 240690; e-mail coopbankpr@form-net.com; f. 1968; cap. and res 2,323.4m., dep. 14,900m. (Dec. 1998); Chair. HOSEA KIPLAGAT; Man. Dir ERASTUS K. MUREITHI; 28 brs.

Development Banks

East African Development Bank: Bruce House, 4th Floor, Standard St, POB 47685, Nairobi; tel. (2) 340642; fax (2) 216651; Man. D. HOROHO.

Industrial Development Bank Ltd (IDB): National Bank Bldg, 18th Floor, Harambee Ave, POB 44036, Nairobi; tel. (2) 337079; fax (2) 334594; e-mail idbkenya@swiftkenya.com; f. 1973; 49% state-owned; cap. and res 721m. (Dec. 1998); Chair. R. K. CHESHIRE; Man. Dir L. A. MASAVIRU.

STOCK EXCHANGE

Nairobi Stock Exchange (NSE): Nation Centre, 1st Floor, Kimathi St, POB 43633, Nairobi; tel. (2) 230692; fax (2) 224200; e-mail nse@arcc.or.ke; f. 1954; 58 mems (July 1997); Chair. JIMNAH M. MBARU; CEO KIBBY KARRITHI.

INSURANCE

American Life Insurance Co: POB 30364, Nairobi; tel. (2) 711242; fax (2) 723146; f. 1964; general; Man. Dir ERWIN BREWSTER.

Apollo Insurance Co Ltd: POB 30389, Nairobi; tel. (2) 223562; fax (2) 339260; e-mail insurance@apollo.co.ke; f. 1977; life and general; CEO ASHOK K. M. SHAH.

Blue Shield Insurance Co Ltd: POB 49610; Nairobi; tel. (2) 219592; fax (2) 337808; f. 1983; life and general.

Cannon Assurance (Kenya) Ltd: Haile Selassie Ave, POB 30216, Nairobi; tel. (2) 335478; fax (2) 331235; e-mail info@cannon.co.ke; internet www.cannon.co.ke; f. 1964; life and general; Man. Dir I. J. TALWAR.

Fidelity Shield Insurance Ltd: POB 47435, Nairobi; tel. (2) 430635; fax (2) 445699.

Heritage AII Insurance Co Ltd: CFC Centre, Chiromo Rd, POB 30390, Nairobi; tel. (2) 749118; fax (2) 748910; e-mail info@heriaii .com; f. 1976; general; Man. Dir J. H. D. MILNE.

Insurance Co of East Africa Ltd (ICEA): ICEA Bldg, Kenyatta Ave, POB 46143, Nairobi; tel. (2) 221652; fax (2) 338089; e-mail hof@icea.co.ke; internet www.icea.co.ke; life and general; Man. Dir J. K. NDUNGU.

Jubilee Insurance Co Ltd: POB 30376, Nairobi; tel. (2) 340343; fax (2) 216882; f. 1937; life and general; Chair. ABDUL JAFFER.

Kenindia Assurance Co Ltd: Kenindia House, Loita St, POB 44372, Nairobi; tel. (2) 333100; fax (2) 218380; e-mail kenindia@users .africaonline.co.ke; f. 1978; life and general; Exec. Dir R. S. BEDI.

Kenya Reinsurance Corporation Ltd (KenyaRe): Reinsurance Plaza, Taifa Rd, POB 30271, Nairobi; tel. (2) 240188; fax (2) 339161; e-mail kenyare@africaonline.co.ke; f. 1970; Man. Dir PETER KENNETH.

Lion of Kenya Insurance Co Ltd: POB 30190, Nairobi; tel. (2) 710400; fax (2) 711177; e-mail lionnbi@form-net.com; f. 1978; general; CEO J. P. M. NDEGWA.

Mercantile Life and General Assurance Co Ltd: POB 20860, Nairobi; tel. (2) 218244; fax (2) 215528; e-mail mercantile@ form-net.com; Gen. Man. SUPRIYO SEN.

Monarch Insurance Co Ltd: Chester House, 2nd Floor, Koinange St, POB 44003, Nairobi; tel. (2) 330042; fax (2) 340691; e-mail monarch@form-net.com; f. 1975; general; Exec. Dir R. A. VADGAMA.

Pan Africa Insurance Co Ltd: POB 30065, Nairobi; tel. (2) 252168; fax (2) 217675; e-mail insure@pan-africa.com; f. 1946; life and general; Man. Dir WILLIAM OLOTCH.

Phoenix of East Africa Assurance Co Ltd: Ambank House, University Way, POB 30129, Nairobi; tel. (2) 338784; fax (2) 211848; general; Man. Dir D. K. SHARMA.

Prudential Assurance Co of Kenya Ltd: Yaya Centre, Argwings Kodhek Rd, POB 76190, Nairobi; tel. (2) 567374; fax (2) 567433; f. 1979; general; Man. Dir JOSEPH MURAGE.

PTA Reinsurance Co (ZEP-RE): Anniversary Towers, University Way, POB 42769, Nairobi; tel. (2) 212792; fax (2) 224102; e-mail zep-re@africaonline.co.ke; internet www.zep.re.com; f. 1992; Man. Dir S. M. LUBASI.

Royal Insurance Co of East Africa Ltd: Mama Ngina St, POB 40001, Nairobi; tel. (2) 717888; fax (2) 712620; f. 1979; general; CEO S. K. KAMAU.

Standard Assurance (Kenya) Ltd: POB 42996, Nairobi; tel. (2) 224721; fax (2) 224862; Man. Dir WILSON K. KAPKOTI.

UAP Provincial Insurance Co of East Africa Ltd: Old Mutual Bldg, Kimathi St, POB 43013, Nairobi; tel. (2) 330173; fax (2) 340483; f. 1980; general; CEO E. C. BATES.

United Insurance Co Ltd: POB 30961, Nairobi; tel. (2) 227345; fax (2) 215609; Man. Dir G. KARRUIKI.

Trade and Industry

GOVERNMENT AGENCIES

Export Processing Zones Authority: POB 50563, Nairobi; tel.

(2) 712800; fax (2) 713704; e-mail epzahq@africaonline.co.ke; established by the Govt to promote investment in Export Processing Zones; CEO SILAS ITA.

Export Promotion Council: POB 40247, Nairobi; tel. (2) 228534; fax (2) 218013; f. 1992; promotes exports; CEO PETER MUTHOKA

Investment Promotion Centre: National Bank Bldg, 8th Floor, Harambee Ave, POB 55704, Nairobi; tel. (2) 221401; fax (2) 336663; f. 1982; promotes and facilitates local and foreign investment; Exec. Chair. Dr JOSEPH N. K. ARAP NGOK.

Kenya National Trading Corporation Ltd: Yarrow Rd, off Nanyuki Rd, POB 30587, Nairobi; tel. (2) 543121; fax (2) 532800; f. 1965; promotes national control of trade in both locally produced and imported items; exports coffee and sugar; CEO S. W. O. OGESSA.

Settlement Fund Trustees: POB 30449, Nairobi; administers a land purchase programme involving over 1.2m. ha for resettlement of African farmers.

DEVELOPMENT ORGANIZATIONS

Agricultural Development Corporation: POB 47101, Nairobi; tel. (2) 338530; fax (2) 336524; f. 1965 to promote agricultural development and reconstruction; CEO Dr WALTER KILELE.

Agricultural Finance Corporation: POB 30367, Nairobi; tel. (2) 333733; a statutory organization providing agricultural loans; Gen. Man. G. K. TOROITICH.

Development Finance Company of Kenya Ltd: Finance House, Loita St, POB 30483, Nairobi; tel. (2) 340401; fax (2) 338426; e-mail dbk@africaonline.co.ke; f. 1963; private co with govt participation; Chair. H. N. K. ARAP MENGECH; Gen. Man. J. V. BOSSE.

Horticultural Crops Development Authority: POB 42601, Nairobi; tel. (2) 337381; fax (2) 228386; f. 1968; invests in production, dehydration, processing and freezing of fruit and vegetables; exports of fresh fruit and vegetables; Chair. KASANGA MULWA; Man. Dir M. A. S. MULANDI.

Housing Finance Co of Kenya Ltd: Rehani House, Kenyatta Ave, POB 30088; Nairobi; tel. (2) 333910; fax (2) 334670; e-mail hfck@hfck.co.ke; f. 1965; Chair. TITUS T. NAIKUNI; Man. Dir WALTER MUKURIA.

Industrial and Commercial Development Corporation: Uchumi House, Aga Khan Walk, POB 45519, Nairobi; tel. (2) 229213; fax (2) 333880; e-mail icdcexe@africaonline.co.ke; f. 1954; govt-financed; assists industrial and commercial development; Chair. JOHN NGUTHU MUTIO; Exec. Dir K. ETICH ARAP BETT.

Kenya Fishing Industries Ltd: Nairobi; Man. Dir ABDALLA MBWANA.

Kenya Industrial Estates Ltd: Nairobi Industrial Estate, Likoni Rd, POB 78029, Nairobi; tel. (2) 530551; fax (2) 534625; f. 1967 to finance and develop small-scale industries.

Kenya Industrial Research and Development Institute: POB 30650, Nairobi; tel. (2) 557762; f. 1942, reorg. 1979; restructured 1995; research and development in industrial and allied technologies including engineering, commodity technologies, mining and power resources; Dir Dr H. L. KAANE.

Kenya Tea Development Authority: POB 30213, Nairobi; tel. (2) 21441; f. 1964 to develop tea growing, manufacturing and marketing among African smallholders; in 1994/95 it supervised an area of 76,968 ha, cultivated by 289,270 registered growers; operates 45 factories; privatization pending; Chair. STEPHEN M. IMANYARA; Man. Dir EUSTACE G. KARANJA.

CHAMBER OF COMMERCE

Kenya National Chamber of Commerce and Industry: Ufanisi House, Haile Selassie Ave, POB 47024, Nairobi; tel. (2) 334413; fax (2) 340664; f. 1965; 53 brs; Nat. Chair. G. KASSIM OWANGO; CEO REM O. OGANA.

INDUSTRIAL AND TRADE ASSOCIATIONS

Central Province Marketing Board: POB 189, Nyeri.

Coffee Board of Kenya: POB 30566, Nairobi; tel. (2) 332896; fax (2) 330546; f. 1947; Chair. JOHN NGARI ZACHARIAH; Gen. Man. AGGREY MURUNGA.

East African Tea Trade Association: Tea Trade Centre, Nyerere Ave, POB 85174, Mombasa; tel. (11) 315687; fax (11) 225823; e-mail eatta@africaonline.co.ke; f. 1957; organizes Mombasa weekly tea auctions; Exec. Sec. LUCY MICHENI; 200 mems.

Fresh Produce Exporters' Association of Kenya: Nairobi; Chair. JAMES MATHENGE.

Kenya Association of Manufacturers: POB 30225, Nairobi; tel. (2) 746005; fax (2) 746028; e-mail kam@users.africaonline.co.ke; Chair. MANU CHANDARIA; Exec. Sec. LUCY MICHENI; 200 mems.

Kenya Dairy Board: POB 30406, Nairobi.

Kenya Flower Council: POB 24856, Nairobi; tel. and fax (2) 883041; e-mail kfc@africaonline.co.ke; internet www .kenyaflowers.co.ke; regulates production of cut flowers; Exec. Dir MICHAEL MORLAND.

Kenya Meat Corporation: POB 30414, Nairobi; tel. (2) 340750; f. 1953; purchasing, processing and marketing of beef livestock; Chair. H. P. BARCLAY.

Kenya Planters' Co-operative Union Ltd: Nairobi; coffee cultivation and processing; Chair. J. M. MACHARIA; Gen. Man. MATHEW S. NASIBU.

Kenya Sisal Board: Mutual Bldg, Kimathi St, POB 41179, Nairobi; tel. (2) 223457; f. 1946; CEO J. H. WAIRAGU; Man. Dir KENNETH MUKUMA.

Kenya Sugar Authority: NSSF Complex, 9th Floor, Bishops Rd, POB 51500, Nairobi; tel. (2) 710600; fax (2) 723903; e-mail ksa@ users.africaonline.co.ke; Chair. LUKE R. OBOK; CEO F. M. CHAHONYO.

Mild Coffee Trade Association of Eastern Africa (MCTA): Nairobi; F. J. MWANGI.

National Cereals and Produce Board: POB 30586, Nairobi; tel. (2) 536028; fax (2) 542024; e-mail cereals@africaonline .co.ke; f. 1995; grain marketing and handling, provides drying, weighing, storage and fumigation services to farmers and traders, stores and manages strategic national food reserves, distributes famine relief; Chair. JAMES MUTUA; Man. Dir Maj. W. K. KOITABA.

Pyrethrum Board of Kenya: POB 420, Nakuru; tel. (37) 211567; fax (37) 45274; f. 1935; 14 mems; Chair. J. J. ARIKA; CEO J. C. KIPTOON.

Tea Board of Kenya: POB 20064, Nairobi; tel. (2) 572421; fax (2) 562120; f. 1950; regulates tea industry on all matters of policy, licenses tea planting and processing, combats pests and diseases, controls the export of tea, finances research on tea, promotes Kenyan tea internationally; 17 mems; Chair. JOHNSTONE O. MORONGE; CEO STEPHEN NKANATA.

EMPLOYERS' ORGANIZATIONS

Federation of Kenya Employers: Waajiri House, Argwings Kodhek Rd, POB 48311, Nairobi; tel. (2) 721929; fax (2) 721990; Chair. J. P. N. SIMBA; Exec. Dir TOM DIJU OWUOR; the following are affiliates:

Association of Local Government Employers: POB 52, Muranga; Chair. S. K. ITONGU.

Distributive and Allied Industries Employers' Association: POB 30587, Nairobi; Chair. P. J. MWAURA.

Engineering and Allied Industries Employers' Association: POB 48311, Nairobi; tel. (2) 721929; Chair. D. M. NJOROGE.

Kenya Association of Building and Civil Engineering Contractors: Nairobi; Chair. G. S. HIRANI.

Kenya Association of Hotelkeepers and Caterers: POB 46406, Nairobi; tel. (2) 726642; fax (2) 714401; f. 1944; Chair. P. MURIUKI.

Kenya Bankers' (Employers') Association: Nairobi; tel. (2) 330200; Chair. J. A. M. DOCHERTY.

Kenya Sugar Employers' Union: Kisumu; Chair. L. OKECH.

Kenya Tea Growers' Association: POB 320, Kericho; tel. (2) 21010; fax (2) 32172; Chair. M. K. A. SANG.

Kenya Vehicle Manufacturers' Association: POB 1436, Thika; Chair. C. PETERSON.

Motor Trade and Allied Industries Employers' Association: POB 48311, Nairobi; tel. (2) 721929; fax (2) 721990; Exec. Sec. G. N. KONDITI.

Sisal Growers' and Employers' Association: POB 47523, Nairobi; tel. (2) 720170; fax (2) 721990; Chair. A. G. COMBOS.

Timber Industries Employers' Association: POB 18070, Nairobi; Chair. H. S. BAMBRAH.

UTILITIES
Electricity

The Kenya Power and Lighting Co (KPLC): Stima Plaza, Kolobot Rd, POB 30099, Nairobi; tel. (2) 243366; fax (2) 337351; e-mail isd@form-net.com; state-owned; co-ordinates electricity transmission and distribution; Man. Dir SAMUEL GICHURU.

Kenya Electricity Generating Co Ltd (KenGen): Stima Plaza, Phase 3, Kolobot Rd, Parklands, POB 47936, Nairobi; tel. (2) 248833; fax (2) 248848; e-mail kengen@africaonline.co.ke; f. 1997 as Kenya Power Co, present name adopted 1998; generates 90% of Kenya's energy requirements; Man. Dir EDWIN WASUNNA.

MAJOR COMPANIES

The following are among the largest companies in terms either of capital investment or employment.

BAT (Kenya) Ltd: Likoni Rd, Industrial Area, POB 30000, Nairobi; tel. (2) 533555; fax (2) 531717; f. 1956; subsidiary of British American Tobacco Co Ltd, UK; mfrs of tobacco products; Exec. Dir E. MWANIKI.

Bata Shoe Co (Kenya) Ltd: POB 23, Limuru; tel. (154) 71620; fax (154) 71145; e-mail bata@net2000ke.com; f. 1943; mfrs of footwear; Man. Dir A. FERNANDEZ.

A. Baumann and Co Ltd: Nairobi Baumann House, Haile Selassie Ave, POB 40538, Nairobi; tel. (2) 536490; fax (2) 536411; e-mail baumann@net2000ke.com; f. 1926; active in Kenya and Uganda; exporters and importers of electrical, engineering and agricultural products, and mfrs of carbon brushes and soft alloys; has business in Kenya; also holds substantial investments in numerous local cos and industries; Chair. N. NGANGA; Man. Dir P. O'CONNOR.

Consolidated Holdings Ltd: POB 11854, Nairobi; fax (2) 553939; f. 1919; cap. K£2,140,410; holding co with interests in Kenya in newspaper publication and the distribution of foreign newspapers and magazines; Chair. M. W. HARLEY; Man. Dir R. S. HOLT.

East Africa Industries: Commercial St, Industrial Area, POB 30062, Nairobi; tel. (2) 542000; fax (2) 543912; f. 1942; mfrs of toothpaste, body lotions, soaps, detergents, edible oils; Chair. HEINZ ARNOLD; CEO J. B. WANJUI.

East African Portland Cement Co Ltd: Longonot Place, Kijabe St, POB 40101, Nairobi; tel. (2) 226551; fax (2) 211936; f. 1932; cement mfrs; Chair. A. LULU; Man. Dir J. G. MAINA.

Firestone East Africa (1969) Ltd: POB 30429, Nairobi; tel. (2) 559922; fax (2) 544241; f. 1969; tyre and tube mfrs; Chair. N. N. MERALI; Man. Dir A. DIBAGGIO.

General Motors Kenya Ltd: cnr Enterprise and Mombasa Rds, Industrial Area, POB 30527, Nairobi; tel. (2) 556588; fax (2) 544178; f. 1975; motor vehicle assembly; Man. Dir CHRIS PETERSON.

Kenya Breweries Ltd: Thika Rd, POB 30161, Nairobi; tel. (2) 802701; fax (2) 802054; f. 1920; mfrs of lager beers and malted barley; Chair. J. G. KIEREINI; Man. Dir M. J. KARANJA.

Kenya Co-operative Creameries Ltd: Creamery House, Dakar Rd, POB 30131, Nairobi; tel. (2) 532535; fax (2) 544879; f. 1925; processes and markets the bulk of dairy produce; Man. Dir J. P. L. NYABERI.

Kenya Vehicle Manufacturers Ltd: POB 1436, Thika; tel. (151) 21711; fax (151) 21689; e-mail kvm@arcc.co.ke; motor vehicle mfrs; Man. Dir D. PERCIVAL.

Magadi Soda Co Ltd: POB 1, Magadi; tel. (303) 33000; fax (303) 32088; f. 1926; processors of salt and soda ash for export; Man. Dir T. T. NAIKUNI.

Panafrican Paper Mills (East Africa) Ltd: Kenindia House, Loita St, POB 30221, Nairobi; tel. (2) 335489; fax (2) 215692; f. 1970; mfrs of paper, paperboard and pulp; CEO N. K. MOHATTA.

TRADE UNIONS

Central Organization of Trade Unions (Kenya) (COTU): Solidarity Bldg, Digo Rd, POB 13000, Nairobi; tel. (2) 761375; fax (2) 762695; f. 1965 as the sole trade union fed.; Chair. PETER G. MUTHEE; Sec.-Gen. JOSEPH J. MUGALLA; the following unions are affiliates:

Amalgamated Union of Kenya Metalworkers: POB 73651, Nairobi; tel. (2) 211060; Gen. Sec. F. E. OMIDO.

Bakers', Confectionary Manufacturing and Allied Workers' Union: POB 57751, Nairobi; tel. (2) 229920.

Dockworkers' Union: POB 98207, Mombasa; tel. (11) 491427; f. 1954; Gen. Sec. J. KHAMIS.

Kenya Airline Pilots' Association: POB 57505, Nairobi; tel. (2) 716986.

Kenya Building, Construction, Civil Engineering and Allied Trades Workers' Union: POB 49628, Nairobi; tel. (2) 336414; Gen. Sec. JOHN MURUGU.

Kenya Chemical and Allied Workers' Union: POB 73820, Nairobi; tel. (2) 338815. Gen. Sec. WERE DIBI OGUTO.

Kenya Electrical Trades Allied Workers' Union: POB 47060, Nairobi; tel. (2) 334655.

Kenya Engineering Workers' Union: POB 73987, Nairobi; tel. (2) 333745; Gen. Sec. JUSTUS MULEI.

Kenya Game Hunting and Safari Workers' Union: Nairobi; tel. (2) 25049; Gen. Sec. J. M. NDOLO.

Kenya Jockey and Betting Workers' Union: POB 55094, Nairobi; tel. (2) 332120.

Kenya Local Government Workers' Union: POB 55827, Nairobi; tel. (2) 217213; Gen. Sec. WASIKE NDOMBI.

Kenya National Union of Fishermen: POB 83322, Nairobi; tel. (2) 227899.

Kenya Petroleum Oil Workers' Union: POB 48125, Nairobi; tel. (2) 338756; Gen. Sec. JACOB OCHINO.

Kenya Plantation and Agricultural Workers' Union: POB 1161, Nakuru; tel. (37) 212310; Gen. Sec. STANLEY MUIRURI KARANJA.

Kenya Quarry and Mine Workers' Union: POB 332120, Nairobi; f. 1961; Gen. Sec. WAFULA WA MUSAMIA.

Kenya Railway Workers' Union: Rahu House, Mfangano St, POB 72029, Nairobi; tel. (2) 213091; f. 1952; Nat. Chair. FRANCIS O'LORE; Sec.-Gen. PETER GITONGA MUTHEE.

Kenya Scientific Research, International Technical and Allied Institutions Workers' Union: Ngumba House, Tom Mboya St, POB 55094, Nairobi; tel. (2) 215713; Sec.-Gen. FRANCIS D. KIRUBI.

Kenya Shipping, Clearing and Warehouse Workers' Union: POB 84067, Mombasa; tel. (11) 312000.

Kenya Shoe and Leather Workers' Union: POB 49629, Nairobi; tel. (2) 533827; Gen. Sec. JAMES AWICH.

Kenya Union of Commercial, Food and Allied Workers: POB 46818, Nairobi; tel. (2) 212545.

Kenya Union of Domestic, Hotel, Educational Institutions, Hospitals and Allied Workers: POB 41763, Nairobi; tel. (2) 336838.

Kenyan Union of Entertainment and Music Industry Employees: Nairobi; tel. (2) 333745.

Kenya Union of Journalists: POB 47035, Nairobi; tel. (2) 3376691; Gen. Sec. GEORGE ODIKO.

Kenya Union of Printing, Publishing, Paper Manufacturers and Allied Workers: POB 72358, Nairobi; tel. (2) 331387; Gen. Sec. JOHN BOSCO.

Kenya Union of Sugar Plantation Workers: POB 36, Kisumu; tel. (35) 22221; Gen. Sec. ONYANGO MIDIKA.

National Seamen's Union of Kenya: Mombasa; tel. (11) 312106; Gen. Sec. I. S. ABDALLAH MWARUA.

Tailors' and Textile Workers' Union: POB 72076, Nairobi; tel. (2) 338836.

Transport and Allied Workers' Union: POB 45171, Nairobi; tel. (2) 545317; Gen. Sec. JULIAS MALII.

Union of Posts and Telecommunications Employees: POB 48155, Nairobi; tel. (2) 27314.

Independent Unions

Kenya Medical Practitioners' and Dentists' Union: not officially registered; Nat. Chair. GIBBON ATEKA.

Kenya National Union of Teachers: POB 30407, Nairobi; f. 1957; Sec.-Gen. AMBROSE ADEYA ADONGO.

Universities Academic Staff Union: Nairobi; not officially registered; Interim Chair. Dr KORWA ADAR.

Transport

RAILWAYS

In 1999 there were some 2,700 km of track open for traffic.

Kenya Railways Corporation: POB 30121, Nairobi; tel. (2) 221211; fax (2) 224156; f. 1977; Man. Dir A. HARIZ.

ROADS

At the end of 1996 there were an estimated 63,800 km of classified roads, of which 6,360 km were main roads and 19,600 km were secondary roads. Only an estimated 13.9% of road surfaces were paved. An all-weather road links Nairobi to Addis Ababa, in Ethiopia, and there is a 590-km road link between Kitale (Kenya) and Juba (Sudan). The rehabilitation of the important internal road link between Nairobi and Mombasa (funded by a US $165m. loan from the World Bank) was undertaken during the late 1990s.

Abamba Public Road Services: POB 40322, Nairobi; tel. (2) 556062; fax (2) 559884; operates bus services from Nairobi to all major towns in Kenya and to Kampala in Uganda.

East African Road Services Ltd: Nairobi; tel. (2) 764622; f. 1947; operates bus services from Nairobi to all major towns in Kenya; Chair. S. H. NATHOO.

Nyayo Bus Service Corp.: POB 47174, Nairobi; tel. (2) 803588; f. 1986; operates bus services within and between major towns in Kenya.

Speedways Trans-Africa Freighters: POB 75755, Nairobi; tel. (2) 544267; private road haulier; CEO HASSAN KANYARE.

SHIPPING

The major international seaport of Mombasa has 16 deep-water berths, with a total length of 3,044 m, and facilities for the offloading of bulk carriers, tankers and container vessels. Mombasa port handled more than 8.5m. metric tons of cargo in 1998. An inland container depot with a potential full capacity of 120,000 20-ft (6-m) equivalent units was opened in Nairobi in 1984. Two further inland depots were scheduled to begin operating in the mid-1990s at Eldoret and Kisumu.

Kenya Ports Authority: POB 95009, Mombasa; tel. (11) 312211; fax (11) 311867; f. 1978; sole operator of coastal port facilities, and operates three inland container depots; Man. Dir L. MWANGOLA.

Kenya Cargo Handling Services Ltd: POB 95187, Mombasa; tel. (11) 25955; division of Kenya Ports Authority; Man. Dir JOSHUA KEGODE.

Inchcape Shipping Services Kenya Ltd: POB 90194, Mombasa; tel. (11) 314245; fax (11) 314224: Man. Dir DAVID MACKAY.

Kenya Shipping Agency Ltd: POB 84831, Mombasa; tel. (11) 220501; fax (11) 314494; e-mail ksamba@africaonline.co.ke; f. 1967; 60% govt-owned, 40% owned by Southern Shield Group; dry cargo, container, bulk carrier and tanker agents; Chair. RAY KESTER; Man. Dir JONATHAN MTURI.

Lykes Lines: POB 30182, Nairobi; tel. (2) 332320; fax (2) 723861; services to USA ports.

Mackenzie Maritime Ltd: Maritime Centre, Archbishop Makarios Close, POB 90120, Mombasa; tel. (11) 221273; fax (11) 316260; e-mail mml@africaonline.co.ke; shipping agents; Man. Dir M. M. BROWN.

Marship Ltd: Jubilee Bldg, Moi Ave, POB 80443, Mombasa; tel. (11) 314705; fax (11) 316654; f. 1986; shipbrokers, ship management and chartering agents; Man. Dir MICHELE ESPOSITO.

Mitchell Cotts Kenya Ltd: Cotts House, Wabera St, POB 30182, Nairobi; tel. (2) 221273; fax (2) 214228.

Motaku Shipping Agencies Ltd: Tangana Rd, POB 80419, Mombasa; tel. (11) 314770; fax (11) 311816; e-mail motaku@formnet.com.

PIL (Kenya) Ltd: POB 43050, Mombasa; tel. (11) 225361; fax (11) 312296.

Shipmarc Ltd: POB 99543, Mombasa; tel. (11) 229241; fax (11) 315673; e-mail shipmarc@form-net.com.

Southern Line Ltd: POB 90102, Mombasa; tel. (11) 20507; operating dry cargo and tanker vessels between East African ports, Red Sea ports, the Persian (Arabian) Gulf and Indian Ocean islands.

Spanfreight Shipping Ltd: Cannon Towers, Moi Ave, POB 99760, Mombasa; tel. (11) 315623; fax (11) 312092; e-mail a23ke464@gncomtext.com; Exec. Dir DILIPKUMAR AMRITLAL SHAH.

Star East Africa Co: POB 86725, Mombasa; tel. (11) 314060; fax (11) 312818; shipping agents and brokers; Man. Dir YEUDA FISHER.

CIVIL AVIATION

Jomo Kenyatta International Airport (JKIA), in south-eastern Nairobi, Moi International Airport, at Mombasa, and Eldoret International Airport (which opened in 1997) all service international flights. Wilson Airport, in south-western Nairobi, and airports at Malindi and Kisumu handle internal flights. Kenya has about 150 smaller airfields. The rehabilitation and expansion of JKIA and Moi International Airport was undertaken during the late 1990s. A new cargo handling facility, The Nairobi Cargo Centre, opened at JKIA in June 1999, increasing the airport's capacity for storing horticultural exports.

Kenya Airports Authority: Jomo Kenyatta International Airport, POB 19001, Nairobi; tel. (2) 822950; fax (2) 822078; f. 1991; state-owned; responsible for the provision, management and operation of all airports and private airstrips; Man. Dir JANET WANGERA.

African Airlines International: POB 74772, Nairobi; tel. (2) 824333; fax (2) 823999; placed under receivership mid-1999; CEO Capt. MUSA BULHAN.

Airkenya Aviation: Wilson Airport, POB 30357, Nairobi; tel. (2) 605730; fax (2) 500845; e-mail info@airkenya.com; internet www.airkenya.com; f. 1985; operates internal scheduled and charter passenger services; Man. Dir JOHN BUCKLEY.

Blue Bird Aviation Ltd: Wilson Airport, Langata Rd, POB 52382, Nairobi; tel. (2) 506004; fax (2) 602337; e-mail bbal@form-net.com.

Eagle Aviation (African Eagle): POB 93926, Mombasa; tel. (11) 434502; fax (11) 434249; e-mail eaglemsa@africaonline.co.ke; f. 1986; scheduled regional and domestic passenger and cargo services; Chair. RAJA TANUJ; CEO Capt. KIRAN PATEL.

East African Safari Air: Mombasa; operates charter service.

Kenya Airways Ltd: Jomo Kenyatta International Airport, POB 19002, Nairobi; tel. (2) 823000; fax (2) 823757; e-mail gmurira @kenya-airways.com; internet www.kenyaairways.co.uk; f. 1977; in private-sector ownership since 1996; passenger services to Africa, Asia, Europe and Middle East; freight services to Europe; internal services from Nairobi to Kisumu, Mombasa and Malindi; also operates a freight subsidiary; Chair. ISAAC OMOLO OKERO; CEO RICHARD NYAGA.

CIVIL AVIATION AUTHORITY

Kenya Directorate of Civil Aviation: Jomo Kenyatta International Airport, POB 30163, Nairobi; tel. (2) 822950; f. 1948; under Kenya govt control since 1977; responsible for the conduct of civil aviation; advises the Govt on civil aviation policy; Dir J. P. AYUGA.

Tourism

Kenya's main attractions for visitors are its wildlife, with 25 National Parks and 23 game reserves, the Indian Ocean coast and an equable year-round climate. A decline in the number of tourist arrivals from the mid-1990s was attributed both to competition from other countries of the region, and to perceptions of high rates of crime and shortcomings in security within Kenya. There were an estimated 969,300 visitors in 1999. Earnings from the sector totalled Ks. 21,400m. in that year.

Kenya Tourism Board: Nairobi; internet www.kenyatourism.com; f. 1996; promotes Kenya as a tourist destination, monitors the standard of tourist facilities; Chair. UHURU KENYATTA.

Kenya Tourist Development Corporation: Utalii House, 11th Floor, Uhuru Highway, POB 42013, Nairobi; tel. (2) 330820; fax (2) 227815; e-mail info@ktdc.co.uk; internet www.ktdc.co.uk; f. 1965; Chair. PAUL KITOLOLO; Man. Dir JOHN A. M. MALITI.

Defence

In August 1999 Kenya's armed forces numbered 24,200, comprising an army of 20,500, an air force of 2,500 and a navy of 1,200. Military service is voluntary. The paramilitary police general service unit was 5,000 strong in 1999. Military assistance is received from the United Kingdom, and from the USA, whose Rapid Deployment Force uses port and onshore facilities in Kenya. In June 1998 Kenyan, Tanzanian, Ugandan and US troops launched a joint military training initiative, which was regarded as a significant landmark in efforts to revive regional co-operation during the late 1990s.

Defence Expenditure: Budgeted at Ks. 16,000m. for 1999/2000.
Commander-in-Chief of the Armed Forces: DANIEL ARAP MOI.
Chief of Armed Forces General Staff: Gen. DAUDI TONJE.

Education

The government provides, or assists in the provision of, schooling. Primary education, which is compulsory, is provided free of charge. The education system involves eight years of primary education (beginning at six years of age), four years at secondary school and four years of university education. The language of instruction from the secondary stage onwards is English. The total enrolment at primary schools increased from about 900,000 in 1963 to 5,545,000 in 1995, taught by some 181,975 teachers. The number of pupils in secondary schools increased from 31,923 in 1963 to 632,388 in 1995, taught by some 41,484 teachers. Primary enrolment in 1995 was equivalent to 85% of children in the relevant age-group. In the same year, however, secondary enrolment was equivalent to only 24% of the appropriate age-group (males 26%; females 22%). A survey conducted in 1994 revealed that some 30% of pupils leaving primary schools were without access to secondary education. According to estimates by UNESCO, the adult literacy rate in 1995 was 77.3% (males 85.6%; females 69.1%). Enrolment on the government adult literacy programme stood at 111,997 in 1995. There are four state universities, with total enrolment of 35,421 students in 1990, and three chartered private universities. The education sector was allocated Ks. 33,554m. in the budget for 1996/97 (representing 16.7% of total budgeted expenditure by the central government).

Bibliography

arap Moi, D. T. *Kenya African Nationalism: Nyayo Philosophy and Principles.* London, Macmillan, 1986.

Azam, J.-P., and Daubrée, C. *Bypassing the State: Economic Growth in Kenya, 1964–1990.* Pans, OECD, 1997.

Bailey, J. *Kenya: The National Epic.* Nairobi, East African Education Publishers, 1993 (Pictorial history).

Bates, R. H. *Beyond the Miracle of the Market: The Political Economy of Agrarian Development in Kenya.* Cambridge, Cambridge University Press, 1992.

Bennett, G. *Kenya, A Political History: The Colonial Period.* London, Oxford University Press, 1963.

Berman, B., and Lonsdale, J. *Unhappy Valley: Clan, Class and State in Colonial Kenya.* London, James Currey, 1988.

Bourmand, D. *Histoire politique du Kenya.* Paris, Editions Karthala, 1988.

Central Bank of Kenya. *Kenya: Land of Opportunity.* Nairobi, Central Bank of Kenya, 1991.

Clough, M. S. *Mau Mau Memoirs: History, Memory and Politics.* Boulder, CO, Lynne Reinner, 1998.

Cohen, D. W., and Odhiambo, E. S. A. *Burying SM: The Politics of Knowledge and the Sociology of Power in Africa.* London, James Currey, 1992.

Coughlin, P., and Gerrishon, K. I. (Eds). *Kenya's Industrialization Dilemma.* Nairobi, Kenyan Heinemann, 1991. [Contains industrial studies carried out under the Industrial Research Project].

Eshiwani, G. S. *Education in Kenya since Independence.* Nairobi, East African Educational Publishers, 1993.

Fogken, D., and Tellegen, W. *Tied to the Land: Living Conditions of Labourers on Large Farms in Trans-Nzoia District, Kenya.* Leiden, African Studies Centre, 1995.

Govt of Kenya. *Economic Reforms for 1996–1998: The Policy Framework Paper.* Nairobi, Govt Printing Press, 1996.

Haugerud, A. *The Culture of Politics in Modern Kenya.* Cambridge, Cambridge University Press, 1995.

Hayward, M. F. *Elections in Independent Africa.* Boulder, CO, Westview Press, 1987.

Himbara, D. *Kenyan Capitalists, the State and Development.* Boulder, CO, Lynne Rienner Publishers, 1993.

Hoorweg, J., Fogken, D., and Klaver, W. *Seasons and Nutrition at the Kenya Coast.* Brookfield, VT, Ashgate Publishing, 1996.

Kanogo, T. *Squatters and the Roots of Mau Mau, 1905–63.* London, James Currey, 1987.

Kenyatta, J. *Facing Mount Kenya.* London, Heinemann, 1979.

Killick, T. (Ed.). *Papers on the Economy of Kenya: Performance, Problems and Politics.* London, Heinemann Educational, 1983.

King, K. *Jua Kali Kenya: Change and Development in an Informal Economy, 1970–1995.* Athens, OH, Ohio University Press, 1996.

Kitching, G. N. *Class and Economic Change in Kenya: The Making of an African Bourgeoisie 1905–1970.* Yale University Press, 1980.

Leys, C. *Underdevelopment in Kenya: The Political Economy of Neo-Colonialism.* London, Heinemann Educational, 1975.

Little, P. D. *The Elusive Granary: Herder, Farmer and State in Northern Kenya.* Cambridge, Cambridge University Press, 1992.

Malobe, W. O. *Mau Mau and Kenya: An Analysis of a Peasant Revolt.* Bloomington, Indiana University Press, 1993.

Mboya, T. *The Challenge of Nationhood.* London, André Deutsch, 1970.

Miller, N., and Yeager, R. *Kenya: The Quest for Prosperity.* Boulder, CO, Westview Press, 1994.

Morton, A. *Moi: The Making of an African Statesman.* London, Michael O'Mara Books, 1998.

Mungeam, G. H. *British Rule in Kenya, 1898–1912.* London, Clarendon Press, 1966.

Mwau, G., and Handa, J. *Rational Economic Decisions and the Current Account in Kenya.* Aldershot, Avebury, 1995.

Ndegwa, P. *Development and Employment in Kenya: A Strategy for the Transformation of the Economy; Report of the Presidential Committee on Employment.* Southwell, Leishman and Taussig, 1991.

Nowrojee, B. *Divide and Rule: State-Sponsored Ethnic Violence in Kenya.* Washington, DC, Human Rights Watch and Africa Watch, 1993.

Ochieng, W. R., and Maxon, R. M. *An Economic History of Kenya.* Nairobi, East African Educational Publishers, 1992.

Ogot, B. A. (Ed.). *Politics and Nationalism in Colonial Kenya.* Nairobi, East African Publishing House, 1972.

Ogot, B. A., and Ochieng, W. R. (Eds). *Decolonization and Independence in Kenya, 1940–1993.* London, James Currey, 1995.

Ojany, F. F., and Ogendo, R. B. *Kenya: A Study in Physical and Human Geography.* London, Longman, 1973.

Otiende, J. E., Wamahiu, S. P., and Karugu, A. M. *Education and Development in Kenya: An Historical Perspective*. Nairobi, Oxford University Press, 1992.

Ouma, S. J. *Development in Kenya through Co-operatives*. Revised Edn. Nairobi, Shirikon, 1989.

Pearson, S., et al. *Agricultural Policy in Kenya*. Ithaca, NY, Cornell University Press, 1995.

Presley, C. A. *Kikuyu Women and Social Change in Kenya*. Boulder, CO, Westview Press, 1992.

Somjee, S. *Material Culture of Kenya*. Nairobi, East African Educational Publications, 1993.

Swainson, N. *The Development of Corporate Capitalism in Kenya, 1918–1977*. London, Heinemann, 1980.

Thomas-Slayter, B., and Rocheleau, D. *Gender, Environment and Development in Kenya: A Grassroots Perspective*. Boulder, CO, Lynne Rienner, 1995.

Throup, D. W. *Economic and Social Origins of Mau Mau, 1945–53*. London, James Currey, 1987.

Trench, C. C. *Men Who Ruled Kenya: The Kenya Administration 1892–1963*. London, Radcliffe Press, 1993.

wa Wamwere, K. *The People's Representative and the Tyrants: or, Kenya, Independence without Freedom*. Nairobi, New Concept Typesetters, 1993.

Widner, J. A. *The Rise of a Party State in Kenya: From 'Harambee' to 'Nyayo'*. Berkeley, University of California Press, 1992.

Willis, J. *Mombasa, the Swahili and the Making of the Mijikenda*. New York, Oxford University Press, 1993.

World Bank. *Kenya: Re-investing in Stabilization and Growth through Public Sector Adjustment*. Washington, DC, World Bank, 1992. (World Bank Country Study).

LESOTHO

Physical and Social Geography

A. MacGREGOR HUTCHESON

PHYSICAL FEATURES

The Kingdom of Lesotho, a small, land-locked country of 30,355 sq km (11,720 sq miles), is enclosed on all sides by South Africa. It is situated at the highest part of the Drakensberg escarpment on the eastern rim of the South African plateau. About two-thirds of Lesotho is very mountainous. Elevations in the eastern half of the country are generally more than 2,440 m above sea-level, and in the north-east and along the eastern border they exceed 3,350 m. This is a region of very rugged relief, bleak climate and heavy annual rainfall (averaging 1,905 mm), where the headstreams of the Orange river have incised deep valleys. Westwards the land descends through a foothill zone of rolling country, at an altitude of 1,830–2,135 m, to Lesotho's main lowland area. This strip of land along the western border, part of the high veld, averages 40 km in width and lies at an altitude of about 1,525 m. Annual rainfall averages in this region are 650–750 mm, and climatic conditions are generally more pleasant. However, frost may occur throughout the country in winter, and hail is a summer hazard in all regions. The light, sandy soils which have developed on the Karoo sedimentaries of the western lowland compare unfavourably with the fertile black soils of the Stormberg basalt in the uplands. The temperate grasslands of the west also tend to be less fertile than the montane grasslands of the east.

POPULATION AND NATURAL RESOURCES

The population at mid-1992 was estimated to be 1,932,879, (including 126,647 absentee workers in South Africa). In mid-1998, according to UN estimates, the population numbered 2,062,000, giving an average density of 67.9 inhabitants per sq km. The noticeable physical contrasts between east and west of Lesotho are reflected in the distribution and density of the population. While large parts of the mountainous east (except for valleys) are sparsely populated, most of the fertile western strip, which carries some 70% of the population, has densities in excess of 200 inhabitants per sq km (the national average in 1989 was 56.0 per sq km). Such population pressure, further aggravated by steady population growth, has resulted in (i) the permanent settlement being pushed to higher levels (in places to 2,440 m) formerly used for summer grazing, and on to steep slopes, thus adding to the already serious national problem of soil erosion; (ii) an acute shortage of cultivable land and increased soil exhaustion, particularly in the west; (iii) land holdings which are too small to maintain the rural population; and (iv) the country's inability, in its current stage of development, to support all its population, thus necessitating the migration of large numbers of workers to seek paid employment in South Africa. It was estimated in 1995 that some 25% of the adult male labour force were employed in South Africa, mainly in the mines. The number of Basotho employed in South Africa declined somewhat in the late 1990s, however, reaching about 18% of the male labour force in 1999. Lesotho's economy depends heavily on their remitted earnings, and a migratory labour system on this scale has grave social, economic and political implications for the country.

Lesotho's long-term development prospects largely rely upon the achievement of optimum use of its soil and water resources. Less than 13% of the country is cultivable and, since virtually all of this is already cultivated, only more productive use of the land can make Lesotho self-sufficient in food (20% of domestic needs are currently imported from South Africa). The high relief produces natural grasslands, well suited for a viable livestock industry, but this has been hindered through inadequate pasture management, excessive numbers of low-quality animals and disease. Lesotho and South Africa are jointly implementing the Highlands Water Project (see Economy), which will provide employment for thousands of Basotho and greatly improve Lesotho's infrastructure. Reserves of diamonds have been identified in the mountainous north-east, and there are small surface workings at Lemphane, Liquobong and Kao. Uranium deposits have been located near Teyateyaneng in the north-west, but their exploitation must await a sustained improvement in world prices. The search for other minerals is continuing.

Recent History

RICHARD BROWN

Revised for this edition by CHRISTOPHER SAUNDERS

Lesotho, formerly known as Basutoland, became a British protectorate in 1868, at the request of the Basotho people's chief, who feared Boer expansionism. Basutoland was annexed to Cape Colony (now part of South Africa) in 1871 but became a separate British colony in 1884, and was administered as one of the high commission territories in southern Africa (the others being the protectorates of Bechuanaland, now Botswana, and Swaziland).

Modern party politics began in 1952 with the founding of the Basutoland Congress Party (BCP, renamed the Basotho Congress Party in 1966) by Dr Ntsu Mokhehle. The BCP decisively won elections to the legislative council, held in 1960. Basutoland's first general election, held on the basis of universal adult suffrage, took place in April 1965. The majority of seats in the new legislative assembly were won by the Basutoland National Party (BNP, renamed the Basotho National Party at independence), a conservative group which had the support of the South African government. Following the election, Moshoeshoe II, the paramount chief, was recognized as king. The

BNP's leader, Chief Leabua Jonathan, became prime minister. Basutoland became independent, as the Kingdom of Lesotho, on 4 October 1966.

JONATHAN AND THE BNP, 1966–86

In January 1967 executive power was transferred from the king to the prime minister. A general election was held in January 1970, when the opposition BCP appeared to have won a majority of seats in the national assembly. Chief Jonathan declared a state of emergency, suspended the constitution and arrested Mokhehle and other leaders of the BCP. The election was annulled, and the country effectively passed under the prime minister's control. Moshoeshoe went briefly into exile, but returned in December after agreeing to take no part in politics. The BCP split into an 'internal' faction, whose members were willing to accept the political status quo, and an 'external' faction, whose members demanded a return to normal political life: the latter group was led by Mokhehle who, following a coup attempt in 1974, fled the country.

Despite Lesotho's economic dependence on South Africa and the government's official policy during the 1970s of 'dialogue' with its neighbour, Jonathan repeatedly criticized the South African government's policy of apartheid, and declared his support for the prohibited African National Congress of South Africa (ANC). During the late 1970s Jonathan accused the South African government of supporting the Lesotho Liberation Army (LLA), the military wing of the 'external' faction of the BCP, which was conducting a campaign of violence: this was denied by South Africa. The cancellation by Chief Jonathan of elections promised to take place in 1985 increased the hostility of the LLA, which launched a number of attacks on BNP targets late in that year.

Lesotho's reluctance to sign a joint non-aggression pact was a persistent cause of friction during this period. In 1984 South Africa threatened to impound consignments of armaments destined for Lesotho, and to impose economic sanctions. On 1 January 1986 South Africa blockaded its border with Lesotho, impeding access to vital supplies of food and fuel. Five leading Lesotho politicians opposed to the government were arrested on their return from talks in Pretoria, South Africa, and there were reports of fighting between factions of the armed forces.

MILITARY RULE, 1986–93

On 15 January 1986 troops of the Lesotho paramilitary force, led by Maj.-Gen. Justin Lekhanya, surrounded government buildings. Five days later Lekhanya (who had recently returned from 'security consultations' in South Africa), together with Maj.-Gen. S. K. Molapo, the commander of the security forces, and S. R. Matela, the chief of police, deposed the Jonathan government.

The new regime established a military council, headed by Lekhanya and including five other senior officers of the paramilitary force (which was subsequently replaced by the Royal Lesotho Defence Force–RLDF). In late January 1986 a council of ministers was sworn in, comprising three officers and 17 civilians, predominantly civil servants and professional men, and including one former member of Jonathan's cabinet. The national assembly was dissolved, and all executive and legislative powers were vested in the king, acting on the advice of the military council. One week after the coup, about 60 members of the ANC were deported from Lesotho, and on the same day the South African blockade was lifted.

The main opposition groups initially welcomed the military take-over. The exception was Mokhehle's wing of the BCP, which demanded the immediate restoration of the 1966 constitution, the integration of the LLA into Lesotho's armed forces and the holding of free elections within six months. All formal political activity was suspended by the military council in March 1986. Chief Jonathan died in April 1987.

In September 1986 the council of ministers was reorganized (giving increased responsibility to Lekhanya), and the military council held discussions with the leaders of the five main opposition parties. The suspension of political activity continued, however, and opposition to the military council was discouraged. In April 1988 the five main opposition parties appealed to the Organization of African Unity (OAU), the Commonwealth and the South African government to restore civilian rule. In the following month Mokhehle, after 14 years of exile, was allowed to return to Lesotho for peace talks, together with other members of the BCP. The government agreed to guarantee the personal security of those returning, on certain conditions, the most important of these being that members of the LLA were to be prohibited from joining the RLDF. It was widely believed that the South African government had played a part in promoting this reconciliation. In 1989 the LLA was reported to have been disbanded, and by 1990 the two factions of the BCP had apparently reunited under the leadership of Mokhehle.

In mid-1989 some elements within the government were reported to have sought the removal of Lekhanya from the chairmanship of both the military council and the council of ministers, following reports in the international media that implicated him in the fatal shooting of a civilian at Maseru in December 1988: it was claimed that Lekhanya had falsely attributed responsibility for the incident to a subordinate. In September 1989, at an inquest into the death (which was reportedly instigated at the request of members of the military

council), Lekhanya admitted the truth of the allegations; nevertheless, a verdict of justifiable homicide was returned.

In early 1990 conflict developed between Lekhanya and King Moshoeshoe. In February Lekhanya dismissed three members of the military council and one member of the council of ministers, reportedly owing to their alleged involvement in a coup plot. Following the king's refusal to approve the changes to the military council, Lekhanya suspended his executive and legislative powers. Lekhanya promised that a return to civilian government would take place in 1992, and, to reassure business interests, a programme for privatizing state enterprises was announced. In March 1990 the military council assumed the executive and legislative powers which were previously vested in the king, and Moshoeshoe (who remained head of state) went into exile, in England. Later in March one of the dismissed members of the military council, Lt-Col Sekhobe Letsie, was charged with the murder in 1986 of two former government ministers (who had been regarded as leading opponents of Lekhanya) and their wives. In June a national constituent assembly was inaugurated to draft a new constitution acceptable to the majority of Basotho; its members included Lekhanya, together with members of the council of ministers, traditional chiefs, local councillors, businessmen and representatives of banned political parties.

In October 1990 Lekhanya invited King Moshoeshoe to return from exile. However, the king announced that his return would be conditional upon the lifting of military rule and the formation, by representatives of all political parties, of an interim government, pending the restoration of the 1966 constitution and the holding of an internationally supervised general election. On 6 November 1990 Lekhanya promulgated an order deposing the king with immediate effect. Lesotho's 22 principal chiefs elected Moshoeshoe's eldest son, Prince Bereng Seeisa, as the new king, and on 12 November he succeeded to the throne, as King Letsie III, having undertaken not to involve himself in the political life of the country.

On 30 April 1991 Lekhanya was removed as chairman of the military council in a coup led by Col (later Maj.-Gen.) Elias Phitsoane Ramaema, a member of the military council. Col Ramaema succeeded Lekhanya as chairman of that body, which was immediately reorganized, along with the council of ministers; Ramaema's announcement that there would be no changes in government policy indicated that the coup resulted from a conflict of personalities rather than from a divergence of political aims. In May Ramaema announced the repeal of the law that had banned party political activity in 1986. However, a tense atmosphere prevailed following the coup.

In June 1991 20 officers were dismissed from the RLDF, following an unsuccessful attempt to overthrow Ramaema and to reinstate Lekhanya; the latter was placed under house arrest during August-September, owing to allegations that a further counter-coup was being plotted. By July the national constituent assembly had drafted a new constitution. In September the council of ministers was restructured.

In June 1992 it was announced that elections would take place in late November. The council of ministers was reshuffled in late June. Following talks in England with Ramaema, under the auspices of the secretary-general of the Commonwealth, former King Moshoeshoe returned to Lesotho in July. In August two members of the military council were dismissed, following allegations against them of corruption.

MOKHEHLE IN GOVERNMENT

The transition from military rule to democratic government, which had been scheduled to take place in November 1992, was postponed at short notice; the general election eventually took place on 27 March 1993. The BCP swept to power, winning all 65 seats in the new national assembly. Mokhehle, the leader of the BCP, was sworn in as prime minister on 2 April, and, on the same day, King Letsie swore allegiance to the new constitution (which took effect following the election). Although independent local and international observers pronounced the general election to be broadly free and fair, the BNP, which had the support of members of the former military regime, alleged widespread irregularities and refused to accept the results; the BNP also subsequently declined the BCP government's offer of two seats in the newly established senate.

Army Unrest

In late 1993 serious discontent emerged within the armed forces. A mutiny in November by about 50 junior officers in the RLDF, was apparently precipitated by a proposal to place the military under the command of a senior member of the LLA—as part of government efforts to integrate LLA activists (many of whom were still in South Africa) with the RLDF. Skirmishes followed near Maseru in January 1994, involving rebellious troops and forces loyal to the government. Although the rebels' leaders maintained that their actions were linked to demands for increased pay, it was widely believed that the mutiny reflected broader political differences within the military. Mediation efforts involving representatives of Botswana, South Africa, Zimbabwe, the Commonwealth, the OAU and the UN failed to prevent a day of more serious fighting (between about 600 rebels and a 150-strong loyalist contingent) before a truce took effect. At the beginning of February the rival factions surrendered their weapons and returned to barracks, in accordance with a Commonwealth-mediated peace accord. In all, at least five soldiers and three civilians were reported to have been killed in the conflict.

There was renewed army unrest in April 1994, when the deputy prime minister, Selometsi Baholo (who also held the finance portfolio), was shot dead during an abduction attempt by disaffected troops, who also briefly detained four other ministers. In May police officers demanding increased pay and allowances briefly took hostage the minister of information and broadcasting and acting finance minister, Mpho Malie. Agreement was subsequently reached on increased allowances, and the government announced the formation of an independent commission to review the salary structures of civil servants. Meanwhile, the minister responsible for natural resources, Monyane Moleleki, fled to South Africa and subsequently resigned from the government. A commission to investigate the armed forces unrest of January and April began work in July.

'Royal Coup'

In July 1994 Mokhehle appointed a commission of inquiry into the circumstances surrounding the dethronement of former King Moshoeshoe II in 1990. In the following month, however, King Letsie petitioned the high court to abolish the commission on the grounds of bias on the part of its members. On 17 August Letsie made a radio broadcast announcing that he had dissolved parliament, dismissed the Mokhehle government and suspended sections of the constitution, citing 'popular dissatisfaction' with the BCP administration. A provisional government was to be established, pending a general election, which was to be organized by an independent commission. Following the king's broadcast, several thousand people gathered outside the royal palace in Maseru to demonstrate their support for the deposed government. However, army and police support for Letsie's 'royal coup' was evident, and clashes between demonstrators and the security forces resulted in four deaths (a further death was reported in disturbances two days later). A night-time curfew was imposed on the day of the broadcast. A prominent human rights lawyer, Hae Phoofolo, was appointed chairman of the transitional council of ministers, and the secretary-general of the BNP, Evaristus Retselisitsoe Sekhonyana, was appointed minister of foreign affairs. Phoofolo identified as a priority for his administration the amendment of the constitution to facilitate the restoration of Moshoeshoe. In the mean time, King Letsie was to act as executive and legislative head of state. A two-day general strike, co-ordinated by the BCP and the Lesotho Council of Non-governmental Organizations, in support of the ousted government effectively paralysed economic activity in Maseru in late August.

The suspension of constitutional government was widely condemned outside Lesotho. The presidents of Botswana, South Africa and Zimbabwe led diplomatic efforts to restore the elected government, supported by the OAU and the Commonwealth. Several countries threatened economic sanctions against Lesotho, and the USA withdrew financial assistance. King Letsie and Mokhehle attended negotiations in Pretoria in late August 1994, at which Letsie was urged to reinstate all elected institutions. In September King Letsie and Mokhehle signed an agreement, guaranteed by Botswana, South Africa and Zimbabwe, providing for the restoration of Moshoeshoe as reigning

monarch, and for the immediate restitution of the elected organs of government; the commission of inquiry into Moshoeshoe's dethronement was to be abandoned; persons involved in the 'royal coup' were to be immune from prosecution; the political neutrality of the armed forces and public service was to be guaranteed, and consultations were to be undertaken with the expressed aim of broadening the democratic process.

In October 1994 Sekhonyana was ordered to pay a heavy fine (or serve two years' imprisonment) after being convicted of sedition and the incitement to violence earlier in the year of army and police troops against former LLA members.

In the following month legislation providing for the reinstatement of Moshoeshoe was presented to the national assembly; the bill was unanimously approved on 2 December, and was subsequently endorsed by the senate. Accordingly, on 25 January 1995 Moshoeshoe II, who undertook not to intervene in politics, was restored to the throne, following the voluntary abdication of Letsie III, who took the title of crown prince.

Internal Discord

The director and another senior officer of the national security service (NSS) were held hostage by junior officers (who were demanding improved terms and conditions of service) for three weeks in March 1995, and were released only after intervention by the Commonwealth secretary-general. The BNP, meanwhile, alleged that the government was forming a private security force with the participation of former members of the Azanian People's Liberation Army (APLA), the military wing of the Pan-Africanist Congress of South Africa.

In April 1995 government representatives and military officials from Lesotho, Botswana, South Africa and Zimbabwe met in Maseru to discuss progress in the restoration of constitutional order in Lesotho. The conference examined the recommendations of the commission of inquiry into the army mutiny of 1994; these included a streamlining of existing forces, a clearer definition of their functions, and improved training. In May 1995 two people were shot dead in Maseru during rioting which had erupted while police were maintaining an indefinite 'go slow', as part of their continuing salary campaign. In June the BCP complained of persistent harassment of its members by the NSS. In previous weeks several members of the national assembly were reported to have been abducted and interrogated; at least one was questioned in connection with the discovery of arms caches allegedly linked to the APLA. Apparently in an attempt to deter further indiscipline, the government announced 15% salary increases for all sectors of the armed and security forces, thus bringing their pay into line with remuneration for other public-sector employees.

Renewed concerns that the Mokhehle administration was not honouring its expressed commitment to trade union rights resulted in a huge demonstration in August 1995 in Maseru to protest against proposed legislation that would prevent public servants from joining trade unions. The protesters demanded, moreover, that Mokhehle abandon plans to reduce earlier salary increases that were now said to have been granted in error. A six-day 'national forum' was convened in September to examine the exercise of democracy in Lesotho and the country's stability and development since 1993. In the same month, however, Amnesty International urged the Mokhehle government to act to eliminate abuses of human rights by the security forces.

King Moshoeshoe was killed in a motor accident in January 1996. The crown prince was formally elected by the college of chiefs to succeed his father, and returned to the throne, resuming the title King Letsie III, in February. Like his father in January 1995, Letsie undertook not to involve the monarchy in any aspect of political life.

Following a five-month trial, in early February 1996 three former senior public officials were sentenced to a total of 120 year's imprisonment, having been convicted by the high court of the theft of more than M2m. in state funds from the Central Bank of Lesotho. In late February premises of the national radio service were seized by a small group that broadcast an apparently groundless statement that the government had been overthrown. The alleged perpetrators of the 'false coup', reported as being, Makara Sekautu, the president of the opposition United Party, two former members of the Lesotho Defence Force (LDF, as the RLDF had been redesignated) and a former member of the NSS, were charged in March with high treason; in March 1997 three of the accused, including Sekautu, were given prison sentences.

Political Realignments

Five government ministers were removed from office in May 1996, among them the minister of justice and human rights, law and constitutional affairs, Molapo Qhobela. The dismissed ministers were unofficially said to have been linked to efforts to bring about the annulment of elections that had taken place in March to the national executive committee (NEC) of the BCP (Qhobela, notably, had been replaced as the party's deputy leader by Bethuel Pakalitha Mosisili, the deputy prime minister). Further government changes followed the resignation, in mid-May, of the ministers of finance and economic planning and of trade and industry. In November, none the less, the results were invalidated by the high court, and the previous committee (elected in 1995) was empowered to organize a new internal party election. Divisions within the BCP were exacerbated in January 1997, when Moleleki, who had returned to the government in November 1996 as minister of information and broadcasting, intimated in an official statement that an attempt was under way to destabilize the government. Although Moleleki did not name the suspected conspirators in this statement, Qhobela, reinstated as deputy leader of the BCP, asserted that the minister had, in fact, directly accused him and other senior members of the party during an interview with the external service of the British Broadcasting Corpn. The conflicting claims apparently led to unsubstantiated rumours of an imminent coup attempt. A new NEC, elected later in January, was dominated by Qhobela and his supporters, but in mid-February these elections were in turn invalidated by the high court. The court ordered that Qhobela's 1995 committee organize yet another election, to be held at the end of February 1997, at the BCP annual conference. However, there was considerable confusion as the prime minister and other party members opposed to the 1995 committee were expelled from the conference. In early March, moreover, Qhobela's NEC announced that it had dismissed Mokhehle as BCP leader in accordance with a decision of the conference, prompting uproar in the national assembly. A government statement insisting that Mokhehle remained leader of the BCP failed to dispel divisions within the party.

There was further confusion in February 1997, when eight police officers, who were resisting arrest for alleged involvement in the fatal shooting of three officers in October 1995, seized control of the police headquarters in Maseru, with the support of a small group of colleagues; the rebel officers claimed to have dismissed senior officers and appointed their own police commissioner. A strike by supporters of the mutineers within the force resulted in the closure of police stations. After government efforts failed to persuade the rebels to surrender, the LDF was mobilized and swiftly regained control of the police headquarters. More than 100 police officers (some of whom had taken refuge in the royal palace) were arrested, and 10 alleged leaders of the rebellion were subsequently remanded in custody on charges of sedition and contravention of internal security legislation. However, two of the instigators of the mutiny (including one of the officers indicted for murder) evaded arrest and fled to South Africa to seek political asylum, which they were reported to have been granted the following month. Meanwhile, suggestions that 14 South Africans arrested in Maseru while the rebellion was in progress belonged to an élite police unit dispatched from South Africa to restore order in Lesotho were denied by the authorities in both countries. The arrests coincided with a claim by Qhobela that mercenaries had been brought into Lesotho to assassinate members of the BCP.

In mid-March 1997 Mokhehle announced his intention to retire from politics prior to the 1998 elections, citing ill health and old age. In the following month the high court ruled that Mokhehle was to remain interim leader of the BCP, and that elections for his successor were to be held before the end of July. Also in April the national assembly approved legislation for a reduction in the age of eligibility to vote (from 21 to 18 years), and for the establishment of a three-member independent electoral commission. The creation of such a body had been a recommendation of the 1995 'national forum'.

In early June violent clashes between supporters of the opposing groups in the ruling party led to two deaths in the southeast. As a result of the intense rivalry within the party, and despite his earlier statement suggesting his imminent retirement, Mokhehle resigned from the BCP and formed a new political party, the Lesotho Congress for Democracy (LCD), to which he transferred executive power. Opposition leaders denounced the move as a political coup, declaring that Mokhehle should have resigned from his position as prime minister, sought a dissolution of the national assembly and held new elections. However, some 38 members of the national assembly joined the LCD, while the BCP staged a parliamentary walk-out in protest at the formation of the new ruling party. The LCD denied that Mokhehle had contravened the constitution, as he was supported by a majority in the national assembly. Meanwhile, a demonstration in support of demands for the prime minister's resignation was widely attended. Later that month Mokhehle announced that the NEC that had been elected by the BCP in March 1996 was to perform the executive duties of the LCD. In early July 1997 opposition parties organized a protest march to the royal palace, in defiance of a government ban, to demand the resignation of Mokhehle and the appointment of an interim government. Qhobela was elected leader of the BCP at the party's annual conference in late July.

Following the designation, by the speaker of the national assembly, of the BCP as the official opposition party in late August 1997, several BCP deputies who objected to the ruling, including 18 who had failed to stand during the speaker's entrance procession, were suspended from the national assembly. Meanwhile, journalists had been attempting forcibly to enter the chamber, after the speaker had prohibited the public and the media from attending parliamentary sessions. In mid-October members of the senate (most of whom apparently refused to recognize the legitimacy of Mokhehle's government) voted to suspend discussion of proposed legislation, pending the king's response to appeals for the dissolution of the national assembly. At the annual conference of the LCD, held in late January 1998, Mokhehle resigned as leader, and was made honorary life president of the party. (He died in January 1999.) In February 1998 Mosisili was elected to replace him as party leader. Later that month the national assembly was dissolved in preparation for legislative elections.

The coronation of King Letsie III took place on 31 October 1997, at a ceremony in Maseru attended by some 15,000 citizens, as well as several regional leaders.

ELECTIONS AND INTERNAL UNREST

Elections to an expanded national assembly took place on 23 May 1998. The LCD secured 78 of the 80 seats, while the BNP won one seat. Voting in the remaining constituency was postponed, owing to the death of a candidate. Prior to the election, opposition parties had unsuccessfully submitted an application to the high court for a postponement, on the grounds that the electoral commission had not allowed sufficient time for parties to examine the electoral roll. Despite the pronouncement of regional and international observers that the election had been fair, it was reported that several hundred people demonstrated in Maseru, protesting against the results and accusing both the LCD and the electoral commission of irregularities. Mosisili was later elected prime minister by the national assembly, and a new cabinet was appointed at the beginning of June. At the end of that month more than 200 defeated opposition candidates filed petitions in the high court calling for the annulment of the election results and a re-examination of the ballot papers. In July, after the court granted the complainants access to the relevant documentation, and evidence of irregularities began to emerge, anti-government protests broke out in the capital. In early August crowds besieged the royal palace and demanded that the king exercise his power to annul the elections and appoint a government of national unity. Letsie, however, declined to act.

SADC Intervention

As protests escalated in Maseru, the Southern African Development Community (SADC) intervened, under South African leadership. A commission was appointed under Pius Langa, the deputy president of South Africa's constitutional court, to investigate the allegations of electoral fraud. However, publication of the completed report was delayed; when it was eventually released it stated that, while voting irregularities had occurred, they were insufficient to invalidate the results of the election.

Meanwhile, influential elements within the LDF had openly declared their support for the opposition, and junior officers forced a number of senior commanders to flee into South Africa. Prime Minister Mosisili, fearing a possible collapse of law and order and an imminent military coup, sought assistance from other SADC countries. South African troops arrived in late September 1998, followed by a military contingent from Botswana. 'Operation Boleas', as the intervention was named, caused outrage in Lesotho, and on their entry into Maseru, the South African contingent met considerably fiercer resistance from the LDF than it had expected. Within a few days at least 68 soldiers on both sides were killed, a number of them at the hydroelectric dam deep in the mountains in the interior of the country, where an army camp came under attack. Extensive looting took place of shops and businesses in Maseru, which the SADC soldiers did little to prevent. The possibility of political motivation behind the looting, as a means of protest against the South African 'invasion', was suspected, although its rapid spread to other towns resulted in serious damage to the economy, as well as the flight of thousands of people into the countryside and to South Africa. With the gradual restoration of calm and with South African mediation an Interim Political Authority (IPA), representing the various parties, was formed to prepare the way for new general elections, to be held within 18 months. The remaining South African and Botswanan troops were withdrawn in May 1999, although a small number of advisers remained behind until May 2000 to continue training the LDF.

The IPA

The multi-party IPA, which was inaugurated in December 1998, rapidly became embroiled in controversy over electoral arrangements for the proposed elections. The government wished the existent voting system to remain, but the BNP (under the leadership of Lekhanya following Sekhonyana's death in November 1998) demanded a system of full proportional representation, on the South African model. Following protracted negotiations, the issue was eventually referred to arbitration. In October 1999 a tribunal appointed to resolve the divisions proposed a system combining both simple majority voting (for 80 seats) and proportional representation (for 50 new seats), which was accepted by the IPA. An agreement to this effect was signed by the government and the IPA in December. However, when the draft legislation on the new electoral system was introduced into parliament in February 2000, the LCD-dominated national assembly rejected it, prompting the IPA to accuse the government of reneging on its undertaking to abide by the tribunal's decision and the December accord. The LCD subsequently proposed to the legislature that the country should retain the existing simple majority system, which had led to the 1998 violence, and which the opposition had rejected. The LCD-sponsored legislation was endorsed by the national assembly, but rejected by the senate, on the grounds that it differed from the electoral model approved by the IPA. Several weeks of political stalemate ensued, and, as the end of the 18-month period during which fresh elections were to have been held approached, in May 2000, a sense of crisis developed. Opposition parties urged the IPA to demand the dissolution of parliament and the replacement of the LCD government with one of national unity. Intense diplomatic efforts were made by the SADC, Scandinavian diplomats and the Commonwealth to broker an agreement between Lesotho's political parties. The opposition accepted that a postponement of the elections was now inevitable, but blamed the LCD and the national assembly for stalling the process. Following mediation, the opposition parties agreed to the LCD remaining in office, in return for assurances that the electoral system would be changed as soon as possible.

In mid-May 2000 the IPA and the government adopted a provisional electoral timetable; Mosisili announced that a general election would be held between March and May 2001, on the grounds that there was insufficient time to prepare for a poll in 2000. The IPA was to remain in existence until the

results of the election were announced. In July 2000 the election date was provisionally set for 26 May 2001, although legislation pertaining to a new voting system had still to be finalized and approved by parliament. Political leaders remained divided over the proposed expansion of the national assembly and the number of seats to be decided by simple majority voting and by proportional representation.

RELATIONS WITH SOUTH AFRICA

Crucial to Lesotho's external affairs has been its relationship with South Africa, to whose support the Jonathan regime owed some of its initial success. In 1970 Lesotho and Malawi were the only countries to abstain on an OAU resolution calling on Western powers not to supply arms to South Africa. Perhaps as a result of his dwindling support among the Basotho population, who were disaffected by his pro-South African policies, Jonathan made a number of increasingly sharp criticisms of the South African government from 1972, and in November 1974 revived Lesotho's claim to 'conquered territory' in South Africa's Orange Free State (OFS, now the Free State Province). A vigorous anti-South African stance at the UN and OAU in the first half of 1975 increased tensions between the two countries. Lesotho's refusal to recognize South Africa's proclamation of an 'independent' Transkei in October 1976 led the Transkeian authorities to demand visas from visiting Lesotho nationals. In December Lesotho protested to the UN about this action. In February 1978 the Transkei authorities imposed stringent border controls, which virtually halted all cross-border traffic, cutting off Basotho migrant workers from mines in South Africa. Jonathan added to South African ire when he attended the non-aligned conference in Havana, Cuba, in September 1979 and again attacked apartheid. The first meeting of the leaders of Lesotho and South Africa since 1967 took place in August 1980 and produced a preliminary agreement on the Highlands Water Project (HWP, see Economy), an advantageous scheme for Lesotho to supply water to South Africa.

During 1982–83 relations with South Africa deteriorated sharply, following allegations of South African armed raids against ANC sympathizers in Lesotho. In April 1983 Jonathan announced that Lesotho was effectively in a state of war with South Africa. South Africa responded in the following month by applying strict border controls on its main frontier with Lesotho, resulting in food shortages. The border controls were eased in June, after a meeting between both countries in which they agreed to curb cross-border guerrilla infiltration, but were reimposed in July. Further talks with South Africa followed, and, soon afterwards, Lesotho declared that it had received an ultimatum from the republic, either to expel (or repatriate) some 3,000 refugees or to face the economic consequences. In September two groups of refugees left the country.

Relations with South Africa remained at a low ebb for most of 1984. In March Chief Jonathan alleged that the South African government had encouraged dissident exiles to form a new opposition party, the Basotho Democratic Alliance (BDA), as part of a conspiracy to overthrow the government. In April the party was officially registered, and its chairman reportedly confirmed that South Africa had promised to provide financial support to the BDA for the forthcoming election campaign. Relations between the two countries were further marred during 1984 by South African attempts to coerce Lesotho into signing a joint non-aggression pact, similar to the Nkomati Accord, agreed in March 1984 with Mozambique. Lesotho's continued refusal to sign such a pact led South Africa to impound consignments of armaments destined for Lesotho, and to threaten further economic sanctions in August, including the suspension of the HWP. However, after talks between the two countries in the following month, and an announcement by Lesotho that the ANC had agreed to withdraw completely from its territory, relations improved slightly in October, when South Africa released the arms that it had impounded and resumed talks on the HWP. Tension was renewed during 1985, as, with unrest spreading in South Africa, Jonathan refused South African requests to expel ANC refugees and to discuss a mutual security pact with South Africa. In December there was a raid on Maseru, ostensibly carried out by the LLA, for which Jonathan publicly blamed South Africa, and again refused to hand over refugees or to discuss a security treaty. On 1 January 1986 South Africa imposed strict controls at border crossing-points (see above), claiming the need to exclude 'terrorists'.

Following the military coup of January 1986 (in which South Africa denied having any role), the new government proved to be more amenable to South Africa's policy on regional security. It was agreed that neither country would allow its territory to be used for attacks on the other; South African refugees began to be flown out, and South Africa withdrew its special border checks on 25 January. By August more than 200 South African refugees, believed to be ANC members, were reported to have been expelled from Lesotho (although the Lesotho government did not permit their extradition directly to South Africa). Additionally, the new government agreed to create a joint security committee and to proceed with the HWP. In March Lekhanya travelled to Pretoria and met President Botha of South Africa. The two leaders reiterated the principles of mutual respect and non-interference. In October the treaty for the HWP was signed by Lesotho and South Africa. In April 1987 the two countries signed an agreement to establish a joint trade mission. Lesotho

and South Africa concluded 'friendly and successful' negotiations on issues relating to their common border in March 1988. Lesotho and South Africa agreed to establish diplomatic relations, at ambassadorial level, in May 1992.

In December 1992 South Africa alleged that terrorist attacks on South African targets were being launched from Lesotho. In April 1993, however, the new Lesotho government declared its intention to co-operate closely with South Africa, and, following the election of an ANC-dominated government in 1994, relations became cordial. On an official visit to Lesotho in July 1995, President Mandela stressed the importance of good relations between the two countries, and their mutual interest in the success of the HWP. Friction continued, however, over the persistent problem of cross-border cattle thefts and the still unresolved claim by Lesotho to 'conquered territory' in the former OFS. Following the SADC intervention of September 1998 (see above), which provoked a mixed reaction among Basotho, South African influence on the affairs of Lesotho increased further, as a large number of South Africans attempted to help bring stability to the kingdom.

Economy

LINDA VAN BUREN

As the kingdom of Lesotho is completely surrounded by South Africa geographically, its economic and political fortunes are inextricably linked to those of its much larger neighbour. Both prior to and since independence in 1966, Lesotho has relied heavily on remittances from Basotho citizens working in South Africa, primarily in the gold mines. In the late 1990s, however, the economic fragility of this arrangement became sharply apparent following the fall in the world price of gold to below US $300 per oz in December 1997. Gold-mining companies hastened to reduce their costs and their work-forces during 1998, as the gold price continued to decline. Thousands of miners lost their jobs, and priority for employment was given to South African citizens. Unemployed Basotho—estimated to number 70,000—returned to the kingdom, where few jobs were available, while the government lost the significant revenues generated by these workers' remittances. Whereas these remittances were equivalent to about two-thirds of gross national product (GNP) in 1990, they had fallen to one-third by 1997. This high proportion reflects a continuing lack of opportunities in the domestic formal sector, despite government attempts to develop manufacturing and services, and severe pressure on agricultural land. About 86% of the resident population live in rural areas, and about 18% of the male labour force were employed as migrant workers in South Africa in 1999, compared with an estimated 45% in 1987 and an estimated 25% in 1995. In January 2000 68,400 Basotho worked in South African mines, a decline of 15% from the 80,400 employed in January 1999. Migrant workers' remittances also declined by about 15% in 1999, to M1,200m.

The population of Lesotho was estimated at 2.1m. in mid-1999. During 1990–98, it was estimated, the population increased at an average annual rate of 2.5%. The pressure on productive land is reflected in the wide disparity of population density. In the lowlands of the west, where virtually all arable land and 70% of the population are concentrated, the population density reaches 200 inhabitants per sq km, compared with a national average density of an estimated 67.9 per sq km. at mid-1998. Only 11% of Lesotho's land is arable. The resulting problems of land shortage, soil erosion and falling productivity have been compounded by recurrent drought.

Lesotho's economic performance has also been adversely affected by the problems of the intimately linked South African economy—particularly in terms of the depreciation in the value of the South African rand, which is at par with the Lesotho currency unit, the loti (plural: maloti). Unusually, Lesotho's GNP has traditionally been more than twice as large as its gross domestic product (GDP) because of the importance of remittances from Basotho migrants. In years when the world gold price is low, Lesotho's GNP grows much more slowly than

its GDP. Lesotho's GDP increased, in real terms, by an average of 7.2% per year in 1990–98. In 1998 real GDP declined by 3.6%, although a return to positive growth was achieved in 1999, when an increase of 2.5% was recorded, according to World Bank estimates. In June 2000 the world gold price was still low, at US $285.9 per oz. Some 50,000 redundancies were declared in South African gold mines in 1997 alone, and for the jobs that remained, South African nationals received preference over foreign workers.

The country's internal tensions (see Recent History) influenced the 1999/2000 budget, in which total expenditure was forecast to rise by 2.9% over the 1998/99 level. Total revenue and grants were expected to rise by 8.6%, assisted by a 14% increase in receipts from the customs revenue pool of the Southern African Customs Union (SACU, see below). The budget deficit for 1999/2000 was forecast at M333m., equivalent to 5.4% of GNP.

AGRICULTURE

Although only about 11% of the total land area of 30,355 sq km can support arable cultivation, a further 66% is suitable for pasture, and subsistence agriculture is the primary occupation for the great majority of Basotho (86% of the internal labour force in 1998. It accounts for about one-fifth of export earnings. The sector's contribution to GDP fluctuates with changes in yields caused by soil erosion, the prevalence of poor agricultural practices, and the impact of drought on several occasions during the 1990s, including 1998. Agriculture accounted for 47% of GDP in 1970 and for 17.3% in 1998/99. Apart from increases in the use of fertilizers and tractors since 1970, the sector remains largely unmodernized. Most crops continue to be produced using traditional methods, by peasant farmers who have little security of tenure under existing laws.

Maize is the staple crop, accounting for 60% of the total planted area, followed by sorghum with 30%. Lesotho produced 124,549 metric tons of maize in 1999, 5% more than in 1998; the 1999 sorghum crop of 33,340 tons represented an increase of 46% over the 1998 harvest. Summer wheat is so far the only crop to have been exported in significant quantities, with most exports sold to South Africa. Food imports have been required in recent years, as drought recurs frequently. In December 1996 and January 1997, the long rains were too plentiful, causing some waterlogging and reducing yields. Small quantities of barley and oats are also grown. Other crops include beans, peas, melons and vegetables. The considerable potential of the livestock sector has been little exploited, although cattle exports have traditionally accounted for about one-third of agricultural exports, with wool and mohair providing a further 30% each.

In 1998 the national herd was estimated at 580,000 cattle, 1.1m. sheep and 730,000 goats, having suffered severe depletion during the early 1980s as a result of the drought. The Livestock Products Marketing Service was established in 1973 as a state monopoly for marketing and improving production. One of its major projects, construction of an export-orientated abattoir in Maseru, was completed in 1983. This facility, and associated fattening pens, aimed initially to satisfy domestic demand, and eventually to extend into exports to regional and European Community (EC, now European Union–EU) markets. Milk production is also being promoted. Allegations were raised in South Africa's national assembly in September 1999 that Lesotho residents were moving large nubers of domestic animals from South Africa across the border into Lesotho.

The government is implementing a programme for food security, based on the development of small-scale irrigated agricultural schemes and the general improvement of rural water supplies. About 30 sq km were under irrigation in 1993. The Lesotho Agricultural Development Bank (LADB) was established in 1980 as the sole source of farmers' credit, and was to play an important part in the self-sufficiency programme; however, it was declared bankrupt and closed in 1998, and was in the process of being liquidated in 2000.

MANUFACTURING, MINING AND TOURISM

Confronted by the chronic problems of agriculture, and by the need to create jobs for a rapidly expanding resident population, Lesotho has promoted development in other sectors, with varying degrees of success. Its main assets are proximity and duty-free access to the South African market, and abundant labour. Lesotho enjoys one of the lowest average rates of adult illiteracy in Africa (18.6% in 1995, according to UNESCO estimates), and emigrant Basotho workers command an excellent reputation in South Africa. The World Bank's International Development Association approved a US $21m. credit in April 1999 in support of the first phase, running from June 1999 to December 2002, of a 12-year education-sector development programme designed to enhance the level of skills of the Lesotho labour force. Until the mid-1990s, South Africa actively discouraged the development of competing industries in Lesotho.

The Lesotho National Development Corpn (LNDC), founded in 1967, and the Basotho Enterprises Development Corpn (BEDCO), which provides finance to local entrepreneurs, have been the main bodies stimulating manufacturing development, promoting a wide variety of small industries, including tyre retreading, tapestry weaving, shoemaking, food processing, electric lamp assembly, diamond cutting and polishing, and the production of clothing (particularly denim jeans), candles, beverages, ceramics, explosives, furniture, fertilizers, television sets and jewellery. Lesotho Wool & Mohair seeks to add value locally by manufacturing garments from the country's wool and mohair before export. Inducements to foreign companies have included generous allowances and tax 'holidays', duty-free access to the EU and SACU markets, the provision of industrial infrastructure and the construction of industrial estates in Maseru and Maputsoe, with further estates planned elsewhere in the country. During the late 1980s, when the international community imposed economic sanctions against South Africa, the government intensified its efforts to encourage the involvement of South African firms in Lesotho. In 1996 the government again announced incentives for South African companies relocating to Lesotho. Industrial developments during the 1980s which were supported by the LNDC included a project designed to double the capacity of the Basotho Fruit and Vegetable Cannery at Mazenod, the establishment of a tyre company, a concern manufacturing parachutes for sporting and military purposes, a brewery and soft drinks plant in Maseru, and two new steel plants and a wire products factory near the capital. By 1989 the LNDC was promoting 51 companies which employed more than 10,000 workers. In 1991 a Chinese company opened a television assembly plant. For its part, BEDCO has had some success in encouraging small-scale enterprises, with strong financial support from Canada. Up to 3,000 new jobs are estimated to have been created during 1975–95. As a result of these efforts, the GDP of the industrial sector increased at an average annual rate of 7.1% in 1980–90, and by 9.2% per year in 1990–98, but declined by 12.4% in 1998/99. Manufacturing's

contribution to GDP increased from about 6% in 1986 to an estimated 17.0% in 1998/99. The political unrest of September 1998 (see Recent History) caused some US $70m. worth of damage in Maseru alone, resulted in the loss of an estimated 4,000 jobs and severely dented investor confidence in Lesotho; according to some estimates, South African companies sustained M2,000m. in losses caused by the crisis. The LNDC launched a major initiative in 1999 to attract foreign investors back to the kingdom, with concessions which included a 15% corporate tax rate for manufacturing companies, accelerated depreciation allowances for plants and machinery, exemption from withholding and secondary taxes on dividends, and reduced water and electricity charges. One project supported by the LNDC and Lesotho Bank is Pioneer Plastics (Pty) Ltd, a US $455,000-project to manufacture polyethylene film bags in Lesotho, which has the potential of gaining an immediate 28% share of the market, rising to 40% in four years' time. The World Bank's private-sector institution, the International Finance Corpn (IFC), is also active in Lesotho, seeking to develop small and medium-sized enterprises, to diversify and deepen financial markets, to revive the extractive industries, to put existing industrial assets to more productive use, and to develop the country's physical infrastructure. The IFC has invested in two companies in the kingdom: Lesotho Quality Aggregate Industries (Pty) Ltd and Upper Qeme Holdings (Pty) Ltd.

Tourism has seen significant development since independence. In the 1990s the sector became both a major source of employment and the second largest source of invisible earnings, after workers' remittances. Tourist arrivals (including same-day visitors), principally from South Africa, reached 323,868 in 1997 before declining to 289,819 in 1998.

Diamond mining was limited to small artisanal diggings, exploited by primitive methods, until 1977, when a small modern mine at Letseng-la Terai, developed and administered by De Beers Consolidated Mines of South Africa, entered production. Most of the diamonds were of industrial quality, although a few unusually large gemstones were also reportedly found. Recovery rates, at only 2.8 carats per 100 metric tons, proved to be the lowest of any mine in the De Beers group, and operations ceased in 1982. In the late 1990s, however, the government was exploring the feasibility of reopening the Letseng-la Terai mine. Co-operatives using labour-intensive methods still recover a small quantity of low-grade diamonds.

POWER

Lesotho's major exploitable natural resource is running water. After much uncertainty over economic and technical feasibility, the governments of Lesotho and South Africa signed a treaty in October 1986 to create the Highlands Water Project (HWP). The agreement for this huge and controversial scheme was reconfirmed in the mid-1990s, after the change of government in South Africa. Parastatal bodies in each country were assigned responsibility for the implementation of the project; in the kingdom the parastatal was the Lesotho Highlands Development Authority (LHDA). A massive undertaking for any country (particularly for one as small as Lesotho), with costs originally estimated at US $3,770m., the HWP proposed the diversion of water from Lesotho's rivers for export to South Africa, with self-sufficiency in hydro-generated electricity as the major by-product. The prospective throughput of water was projected at 77 cu m per second by the time the scheme is completed in the year 2017, although at the end of the $2,500m. Phase 1A, in 1998, the rate was to be about 18 cu m per second. The HWP was expected to have a generating capacity of 200 MW by the year 2003, of which Phase 1A accounted for 72 MW for Lesotho. About 75% of the cost of Phase 1A was raised in southern Africa (including some 57% from banks), with diversified external sources providing the balance, including $110m. from the World Bank in 1989. The commercial segment of the debt was to be met from royalty payments received on water sales to South Africa. Construction of Phase 1A began in 1989 and was completed nine years later. Phase 1B, the total cost of which was projected to be $1,100m., was also to be funded largely from South African capital and money markets and from the water users themselves ($825m. in all, also equivalent to 75%). Other sources of finance for Phase 1B include the European Investment Bank with $110m., foreign export-credit-backed commercial loans with \$60m., the Development Bank of Southern Africa with \$45m., and the Lesotho government with \$25m. The World Bank's share of the funding, at \$45m., is only 4% of the total. Excavation began in 1991, and Phase 1A, which included the Katse dam, was sufficiently complete in 1997 for water delivery to begin. However, in mid-1997, as the first delivery of water to South Africa and the first M110m. annual royalty payment to Lesotho were about to be made, rumours became widespread that the troubled scheme was far too ambitious and was about to be downsized. The World Bank had observed that the scheme had been under poor management, and there were even suggestions that it might not fund the remaining four phases. After several months of deliberation, the World Bank did finally announce in June 1998 that it would lend \$45m. in support of Phase 1B, which would involve the construction of the 145 m-high Mohale dam on the Senqunyane river, a 15 m weir on the Matsoku river, and water tunnels from both these sites to deliver 11.8 cu m. of water per second to Katse dam, there linking up with the facilities that were built in Phase 1A, which transfer the water to South Africa. Phase 1A had been beset by dismissals, strikes and opposition from environmental, trade-union and other groups. In September 1996, during a labour dispute which led to the dismissal of more than 2,000 workers, at least five workers were shot dead and some 30 others were injured in clashes between the security forces and former employees. The contractors eventually agreed to take back 1,700 workers. A further problem was that many of the 1,750 families who had been displaced by the first stage of Phase I had received little or none of the compensation they had been promised. The World Bank acknowledged that the scheme's 'social targets' had not been achieved, suggesting a reluctance to proceed with the displacement of upwards of 8,000 more families to allow the construction of a further five dams. Nevertheless, the continuation of Phase 1B was expected to contribute 6.5% of Lesotho's GDP in 1998, fuel a full 65% of projected GDP growth in that year, and create the 'equivalent of' 40,000 full-time jobs. Nevertheless, the Lesotho government had to meet M61.1m. in debt-service payments in that year in respect of the project. In November 1999 the Lesotho government announced that a number of foreign companies (from countries such as Canada, France, Italy, South Africa and the United Kingdom) had offered bribes in order to win HWP construction contracts. The World Bank pledged financial support for an investigation into bribery and corruption in connection with the scheme, and in December a civil court found the former chief executive of the LHDA guilty of having accepted about US \$2m. in bribes from the contractors. In May 2000 construction of Phase 1B's Mohale tunnel was reported to be behind schedule, owing to 'inefficiency of organization and management on the site'.

The water treaty negotiated with South Africa covered the legal framework of the project and the pricing and volume of water to be sold. One of the most contentious aspects of the treaty was the control of water delivery. There were strong fears, both in Lesotho and among its neighbours, that unless Maseru controlled the supplies, the country would be even more dependent on South Africa, because the republic could delay the transfer of water payments as a form of leverage. The treaty addresses part of the problem, with South Africa due to pay monthly royalties in cash, regardless of water delivered, plus a unit cost component based on each cu ft of water delivered.

TRANSPORT AND COMMUNICATIONS

Owing to its mountainous terrain, much of Lesotho was, until recently, virtually inaccessible except by horse or light aircraft. However, a substantial network of nearly 5,000 km of tracks, passable by four-wheel-drive vehicles, has now been built up, largely by 'food for work' road builders in the mountain areas, and by 1996 some 887 km of tarred roads had been constructed. The road between Leribe, in the north, and Tsoaing, beyond Maseru, has been bitumenized. In 1983 the first section of the southern perimeter road from Tsoloane to Mohale's Hoek was completed with aid from the Arab Bank for Economic Development in Africa, and in 1984 the EC agreed to finance the next stage, to the Mekaling river. Finance from the EC was also made available in 1984 for the third stage, from Mekaling to Quthing. Other projects to build or rehabilitate roads included the construction of a new road linking Mohale's Hoek to Quthing

and also of 300 km of new roads under the HWP, which commenced in 1987. In 1996 the World Bank's IDA granted US \$40m. towards the government's rolling five-year road programme. In 1990 a bilateral agreement was reached with South Africa for the joint construction of a bridge over the Caledon river, for the transportation of equipment to the HWP. Lesotho's economic development has relied heavily on South African road and rail outlets, a dependence which was graphically illustrated in 1983–86, when the South African government instituted road blocks and checks, as a form of economic sanctions, which had severely debilitating effects on the Lesotho economy. A greater degree of independence in international communications was reached after the Maseru international airport became operational in mid-1986. In 1998 Lesotho had three airports with paved runways and 25 with unpaved runways. Lesotho has 2.6 km of railway line, which is operated as part of South Africa's railway system.

EMPLOYMENT, WAGES AND MIGRANT LABOUR

Lesotho's dependence on South Africa is also reflected in the extent of migrant labour. Of the estimated total labour force of 689,000 in 1996, more than one-quarter worked in South Africa, 87,421 of them as miners. This exodus is caused by land shortage, by the depressed state of agriculture, by the lack of employment opportunities and by low wages in the formal sectors. Unemployment was officially estimated at 40% in 1999, and well over one-half of the population are thought to be either unemployed or underemployed. Only the finite labour demands of the construction phases of the HWP have prevented it from reaching an even higher level.

The Lesotho economy's dependence on receipts from services and transfers, in the form of migrants' remittances, has traditionally been reflected in the fact that the country's GNP is generally more than double GDP. (In most other African states the net outflow of remittances means that GDP is greater than GNP.) Net private capital flows amounted to US \$14m. in 1994, or 7.3% of GNP. Apart from their obvious role in financing the large trade gap, the remittances were central to the income of up to 60% of families and were also used by the government to finance development. The Lesotho Deferred Payment Scheme was set up in 1974, at the instigation of the Lesotho government, and, as it was compulsory, it was widely criticized by labour-relations groups. It also served as an impetus to encourage Basotho to conceal their employment from the authorities in the hope of retaining more of their wage. Under the scheme, the South African employer of a Lesotho national was required to deposit 60% of his wage into a special account at Lesotho Bank every month; this proportion was reduced to 30% in 1990. Although the employee was permitted to make two withdrawals during the contract period, of up to a total of 50% of the accumulated balance, the remainder was, of course, available to the Lesotho government. The National Union of Miners has long called for the abolition of the scheme, and a commission established in South Africa to investigate migrant labour in that country recommended that the scheme be phased out over a period of five years. In any case, South Africa's policy (announced in late 1995) of granting permanent residency rights to migrant workers could deprive Lesotho of this important source of income. It was decided that migrant workers who had voted in the 1994 South African election, and who were in South Africa before 30 June 1996, would be eligible for 'permanent status'. By March 1996 some 37,000 applications had been approved, although it was not specified how many of these were from Lesotho nationals.

The decline in the number of migrant workers since 1990 holds potentially serious implications for Lesotho's economy. In 1985 the government invited the International Labour Office to assess alternative employment prospects. The resulting report emphasized the creation of small-scale enterprises, employing up to 50 people each, as the main area of potential job development, although such a policy would require far more active investment efforts from government. In 1996 the government announced incentives for South African manufacturing companies, particularly those in labour-intensive industries, relocating to Lesotho. However, once South Africa entered the post-sanctions era, interest in Lesotho as a gateway into that lucrative market rapidly dwindled.

SACU AND THE MONETARY AGREEMENTS

Together with Botswana, Namibia, South Africa and Swaziland, Lesotho is a member of the Southern African Customs Union (SACU), which dates formally from 1910, when the Union (now the Republic) of South Africa was established. The 1969 SACU agreement provided for payments to Botswana, Lesotho and Swaziland (the BLS countries) to be made on the basis of their share of goods imported by SACU countries, multiplied by an 'enhancement' factor of 1.42 as a form of compensation for the BLS countries' loss of freedom to conduct a completely independent economic policy, and for the costs that this restriction involved in trade diversion and loss of investment. SACU revenue was paid two years in arrears and earned no interest, but even so, for Lesotho it formed up to 70% of government recurrent revenues in some years. Lesotho resisted attempts by South Africa to renegotiate the terms governing SACU. However, pressure on SACU grew after the Mandela government came to power in South Africa. The longer-term role of SACU in southern Africa's changed environment was unclear, in view of South Africa's negotiations with Europe over a free-trade agreement with the EU, which was finalized in February 1999, and also the Southern African Development Community's plan to establish a 14-nation free-trade area by the year 2005, which would include all the members of SACU. A commodity which illustrates the dilemma well is beef. The European beef protocol permitted qualifying African developing countries (the four small SACU members are developing countries, but South Africa is not) to sell beef to the EU at a price well above the going market rate. The EU then sold some of the excess beef it acquired in this manner to South Africa at a much-reduced price, an arrangement not bearing much resemblance to 'free trade'. The advent of an EU-South African free-trade agreement could cause the four smaller members of SACU to lose income they had received in statutory shared SACU customs duties ranging between US $1,900m. and $3,500m. per year, according to unofficial estimates. Although allocated the smallest share of this sum, of the four countries, Lesotho is the most dependent on that source of revenue.

In December 1974 the governments of Lesotho, Swaziland and South Africa concluded the Rand Monetary Agreement (RMA). Under this agreement, Lesotho received interest on rand currency circulating in Lesotho, at a rate of two-thirds of the current yield to redemption of the most recent issues of long-dated South African government stock offered the previous year. In January 1980, however, Lesotho followed Botswana and Swaziland in their moves towards monetary independence by introducing its own currency, the loti, replacing the South African rand at par. This measure was designed to give Lesotho greater control over factors influencing its development and over cash outflows by Basotho visiting South Africa. In July 1986 the RMA was superseded by a new agreement, establishing the Tripartite Monetary Area (TMA, now the Common Monetary Area–CMA) comprising Lesotho, Swaziland and South Africa (and later including Namibia, which became independent in 1990). Under the CMA arrangements, Lesotho may determine the exchange rate of its own currency, but to date the loti has remained at par with the rand.

EXTERNAL TRADE AND PAYMENTS

Until the 1980s, Lesotho was largely able to ignore its balance of payments; owing to its membership of the South African-dominated RMA, situations which in other countries would have shown up as a balance-of-payments problem would, in Lesotho, have appeared as a general credit shortage. In fact, this happened only rarely until the 1980s, as Lesotho's chronic trade deficit, resulting from a limited export base and large requirements of food imports, was more than offset by current transfers, migrant remittances and surpluses on the capital account of the balance of payments. As a result of a sharp decline in export earnings from 1980, combined with a reduction in aid receipts and an increase in imports, deficits on the current account of the balance of payments were incurred. Towards the end of the 1980s, as donors became concerned about the government's management of the economy, aid disbursements began to be withheld from time to time. In 1988 an IMF programme of reforms was implemented. In 1989 the current account of the balance of payments registered a surplus of US $10.4m., fol-

lowed by surpluses of $65m. in 1990, $83.1m. in 1991, $37.6m. in 1992, $29.3m. in 1993 and $108.1m. in 1994. However, these surpluses were created by the large ratio of migrants' remittances to the size of the internal economy of Lesotho. In 1994 imports of goods and services, at $874.4m., far exceeded exports of goods and services, at $181.3m., leaving a deficit of $693.2m. Recognizing the need to redress this balance, the IMF approved an $11m. stand-by credit in September 1995 in support of Lesotho's economic programme for 1995/96, which set targets of GNP growth of at least 7.4%, inflation of not more than 7.8%, a budget surplus of 2% of GNP based on total budgetary revenue equivalent to 29% of GNP, the maintenance of enough foreign reserves to cover 5.8 months of imports and a current-account deficit (exclusive of private transfers) of not more than 1.6% of GNP. The current-account target was not met, however, as the outturn showed a current-account deficit equivalent to 2.0% of GNP. In September 1996 the IMF approved a $10m. stand-by credit—the only one it granted to any African country in 1996/97—for Lesotho's economic programme whose targets for 1996/97 were real GNP growth of 10.2%, inflation of not more than 10.0%, a budget surplus of 1.3% of GNP based on recurrent expenditure of not more than 10.3% of GNP and a current-account deficit of not more than 1.8% of GNP. Lower workers' remittances, together with reduced SACU customs revenue, made it difficult to sustain such targets in 1997/98. The current-account deficit was equivalent to 29.7% of GDP in 1998 and to 23.5% of GDP in 1999. Per-capita GNP was equivalent to US $570 in 1998 and to only $530 in 1999; per-capita GDP was less than $300 per annum. The political instability of 1998 (see Recent History) led to a decline in real GDP of 3.6% in that year, but a recovery was achieved in 1999, when GDP growth was again positive, at 2.5%. Internal unrest also caused inflation to soar; the rate of inflation had been lowered to just 3.7% before the crisis, but the ensuing destruction and looting significantly reduced the supply of many goods in the market, thereby increasing prices and boosting inflation to 18.9% in 1999.

South Africa is Lesotho's main trading partner. In 1998 SACU countries were the main source of Lesotho's imports, supplying 89.7%, and were the destination for 65.4% of its exports, while most of the rest went to North America. The principal imports in 1997 were maize, other foodstuffs, building materials, clothing, vehicles, machinery, medicines and petroleum products. The principal exports in 1998 were clothing, footwear, foodstuffs and wool. Lesotho is associated with the EU under the provisions of the Lomé Convention, according duty-free access to EU markets for all exports except those covered by the EU's Common Agricultural Policy, which will benefit only from a small preference. The short-term effect on Lesotho's exports has been small.

PUBLIC FINANCE

In 1995 the Mokhehle government unveiled its plans for a five-year privatization programme. A government privatization unit was set up to decide the future of 31 public enterprises, including the BEDCO (see above), the Drug Service Organization, the Lesotho Electricity Corpn, the Lesotho Water and Sewerage Authority, Radio Lesotho, the Lesotho Housing and Development Corpn, the Lesotho National Abattoir and Feedlot Complex, the Lesotho Handknits Project, Air Lesotho, Lesotho Flour Mills, Lesotho Pharmaceutical Corpn, the Lesotho Telecommunications Corpn and tourism installations such as a car-hire firm and the Marakabei Lodge at Ha Marakabei on the Senqunyane river. Critics of the privatization programme, led by trade-union organizations, argued that selling off these enterprises would only make Lesotho more dependent on South Africa. They maintained that Lesotho Flour Mills in particular should not be privatized for reasons of food security.

Between 1980 and 1986 Lesotho's receipts of net development assistance fell by over 40% in real terms. Lesotho's disbursed public debt more than doubled during 1980–84 to $134m., or 24.3% of GNP, and then rose to $462.6m. at the end of 1992, resulting in a debt-service ratio of 5.2%, as a percentage of exports of goods and services, equivalent to 43.4% of GNP. By the end of 1996 total external public debt had risen to $627.9m., equivalent to 52.5% of that year's GNP. Total external debt stood at $692.1m. at the end of 1998, equivalent to 64.7% of GNP. In that year the cost of debt-servicing was equivalent to 8.4% of revenue from exports of goods and services. Debt-service obligations were equivalent to 5.4% of GNP in 1998/99 and to a projected 8.1% in 1999/2000.

Lesotho continues to face formidable economic challenges. The acute shortage of fertile land, the problem of soil erosion, and the backward state of agriculture make it highly unlikely that this sector can absorb the increase in population that is now resulting from returning migrants. Much will depend on the attitudes of the government in South Africa, on the benefits to be derived from the HWP, and on the government's ability to find alternative sources of revenue to the Lesotho Deferred Payment Scheme of emigrant workers' remittances and SACU receipts.

Statistical Survey

Source (unless otherwise stated): Bureau of Statistics, POB 455, Maseru 100; tel. 323852.

Area and Population

AREA, POPULATION AND DENSITY

Area (sq km)	30,355*
Population (census results)†	
12 April 1976	
Males	458,260
Females	605,928
Total	1,064,188
12 April 1986 (provisional)	1,447,000
Population (UN estimates at mid-year)‡	
1996	1,970,000
1997	2,016,000
1998	2,062,000
Density (per sq km) at mid-1998	67.9

* 11,720 sq miles.
† Excluding absentee workers in South Africa, numbering 152,627 (males 129,088; females 23,539) in 1976.
‡ Source: UN, *World Population Prospects: The 1998 Revision.* Figures include absentee workers in South Africa.

1992 (official estimates): Population 1,932,879, including 126,647 absentee workers in South Africa.

DISTRICTS (*de jure* population at 1986 census, provisional)*

District	Population
Berea	194,600
Butha-Buthe	100,600
Leribe	257,900
Mafeteng	195,600
Maseru	311,200
Mohale's Hoek	164,400
Mokhotlong	74,700
Qacha's Nek	64,000
Quthing	110,400
Thaba-Tseka	104,100
Total	1,577,500

* Including absentee workers in South Africa.

Note: Each district has the same name as its chief town.

Capital: Maseru, population 45,000 in 1976.

BIRTHS AND DEATHS (UN estimates, annual averages)

	1980–85	1985–90	1990–95
Birth rate (per 1,000) . . .	38.9	37.6	36.4
Death rate (per 1,000) . . .	13.8	12.4	11.3

Expectation of life (UN estimates, years at birth, 1990–95): 58.3 (males 57.0; females 59.7).

Source: UN, *World Population Prospects: The 1998 Revision.*

ECONOMICALLY ACTIVE POPULATION

Mid-1998 (estimates in '000): Agriculture, etc. 331; Total 862 (Source: FAO, *Production Yearbook*).

In 1999 about 18% of the total adult male labour force were in employment in South Africa.

Agriculture

PRINCIPAL CROPS ('000 metric tons)

	1996	1997	1998
Wheat	30	34	14*
Maize	188	142	94†
Sorghum	36	29	20*
Roots and tubers* . . .	70	75	80
Pulses	10	18	11*
Vegetables*	23	22	18
Fruit*	16	15	13

* FAO estimate(s). † Unofficial figure.

Source: FAO, *Production Yearbook.*

LIVESTOCK (FAO estimates, '000 head, year ending September)

	1996	1997	1998
Cattle	585	590	580
Sheep	1,150	1,200	1,100
Goats	750	760	730
Pigs	70	75	65
Horses	114	115	114
Asses	150	155	150
Mules	1	1	1

Poultry (million): 2 in 1996; 2 in 1997; 2 in 1998.

Source: FAO, *Production Yearbook.*

LIVESTOCK PRODUCTS (FAO estimates, '000 metric tons)

	1996	1997	1998
Cows' milk	26	27	26
Beef and veal . . .	14	14	14
Mutton and lamb . . .	4	4	4
Goat meat	2	2	2
Pig meat	4	4	3
Poultry meat . . .	2	2	2
Other meat	3	3	3
Hen eggs	1	1	1
Wool:			
greasy	3	4	4
clean	2	2	2

Source: FAO, *Production Yearbook.*

Forestry

ROUNDWOOD REMOVALS
('000 cubic metres, excluding bark)

	1995	1996	1997
Total (all fuel wood) . . .	719	728	737

Source: FAO, *Yearbook of Forest Products.*

Fishing

(FAO estimates, metric tons, live weight)

	1995	1996	1997
Common carp	16	16	18
North African catfish . . .	2	2	2
Other freshwater fishes . .	8	10	10
Total catch	26	28	30

Source: FAO, *Yearbook of Fishery Statistics.*

Finance

CURRENCY AND EXCHANGE RATES
Monetary Units
100 lisente (singular: sente) = 1 loti (plural: maloti).

Sterling, Dollar and Euro Equivalents (28 April 2000)
£1 sterling = 10.6921 maloti;
US $1 = 6.8185 maloti;
€1 = 6.1946 maloti;
1,000 maloti = £93.53 = $146.66 = €161.43.

Average Exchange Rate (maloti per US $)
1997   4.60796
1998   5.52828
1999   6.10948

Note: The loti is fixed at par with the South African rand.

BUDGET (million maloti, year ending 31 March)

Revenue*	1996/97	1997/98	1998/99†
Tax revenue	1,553.8	1,794.9	1,715.8
Taxes on net income and profits	299.0	340.1	363.3
Company tax . . .	52.6	69.7	70.2
Individual income tax . .	204.6	221.7	248.9
Taxes on goods and services .	241.6	273.3	307.8
Sales tax	193.9	223.5	252.0
Petrol levy	46.0	47.4	53.8
Taxes on international trade and			
transactions. . . .	1,006.0	1,172.7	1,033.4
Customs duties . . .	1,006.0	1,172.7	1,033.4
Non-tax revenue	480.8	452.1	515.6
Administative fees, charges and			
non-industrial sales . .	82.0	106.9	66.4
Total	2,034.6	2,247.0	2,231.4

Expenditure‡	1996/97	1997/98	1998/99†
General public services . .	488.2	673.4	929.1
Public order, safety and defence	220.2	326.9	407.8
Health, social security and welfare	204.4	190.4	249.5
Education and community services	472.6	524.2	639.4
Economic services . . .	791.9	895.1	751.6
Agriculture and rural			
development. . . .	223.4	233.5	180.9
Commerce, tourism and industry	20.7	29.3	63.3
Water, energy and mining . .	281.7	222.9	185.1
Roads	172.5	365.7	300.3
Other transport and			
communications . . .	93.6	43.7	22.1
Unallocable and other purposes	94.4	58.3	260.4
Total	2,051.5	2,341.4	2,830.1
Current	1,177.8	1,473.1	2,158.9
Capital‡	873.7	868.3	671.2

* Excluding grants received (million maloti): 203.4 in 1996/97; 178.7 in
1997/98; 142.8 (provisional) in 1998/99.
† Provisional figures. Revised totals for 1998/99 (in million maloti) are:
Revenue 2,171.6, excluding grants received (120.0); Expenditure 2,438.4
(Current 1,942.7, Capital 495.7), excluding net lending (0.0).
‡ Including lending minus repayments (million maloti): 11.0 in 1996/97.
Source: mainly IMF, *Lesotho: Recent Economic Developments and Selected
Issues* (August 1999).

INTERNATIONAL RESERVES (US $ million at 31 December)

	1997	1998	1999
IMF special drawing rights . .	1.20	1.22	1.17
Reserve position in IMF . . .	4.75	4.98	4.85
Foreign exchange . . .	565.78	568.89	493.54
Total	571.74	575.08	499.56

Source: IMF, *International Financial Statistics.*

MONEY SUPPLY (million maloti at 31 December)

	1997	1998	1999
Currency outside banks . .	89.92	134.50	122.66
Demand deposits at commercial			
banks	672.46	836.92	821.27
Total money	762.39	971.41	943.93

Source: IMF, *International Financial Statistics.*

COST OF LIVING (Consumer Price Index; base: 1990 = 100)

	1994	1995	1996
All items	168.9	184.5	201.7

1999 (base: 1995 = 100): All items 135.2.
Source: IMF, *International Financial Statistics.*

NATIONAL ACCOUNTS
(million maloti at current prices, year ending 31 March)
Expenditure on the Gross Domestic Product

	1996/97	1997/98*	1998/99*
Government final consumption			
expenditure	817.4	1,383.1	1,544.1
Private final consumption			
expenditure	4,347.6	4,469.4	5,006.8
Increase in stocks . . . }			
Gross fixed capital formation . }	2,406.3	2,700.5	1,755.2
Total domestic expenditure†	7,571.2	8,553.0	8,306.1
Exports of goods and services .	1,392.8	1,318.0	1,458.9
Less Imports of goods and services	4,737.9	5,125.1	4,923.9
GDP in purchasers' values .	4,226.2	4,745.9	4,841.2
GDP at constant 1995 prices	3,806.4	3,963.9	3,749.2

* Estimates.
† Including adjustment.

Gross Domestic Product by Economic Activity*

	1996/97	1997/98	1998/99
Agriculture, forestry and fishing .	671.0	702.5	752.9
Mining and quarrying . .	3.1	3.7	3.9
Manufacturing . . .	609.7	693.9	741.4
Electricity, gas and water. .	171.6	316.6	324.7
Construction. . . .	699.0	726.4	588.7
Trade, restaurants, and hotels .	395.8	437.7	400.4
Transport and communications .	144.2	160.0	163.0
Finance, insurance, real estate			
and business services . .	369.5	400.8	423.7
Government services . . .	710.2	819.1	904.5
Other services . . .	44.9	50.0	54.8
Sub-total	3,819.1	4,310.7	4,358.1
Less Imputed bank service charge	92.7	93.5	95.7
GDP at factor cost . .	3,726.4	4,217.2	4,262.4
Indirect taxes, *less* subsidies . .	499.8	528.7	578.8
GDP in purchasers' values . .	4,226.2	4,745.9	4,841.2

* Estimates for fiscal years, based on sectoral data for calendar years
compiled by the Lesotho Bureau of Statistics.
† Provisional data.
Source: IMF, *Lesotho: Recent Economic Developments and Selected Issues*
(August 1999).

BALANCE OF PAYMENTS (US $ million)

	1996	1997	1998
Exports of goods f.o.b.	186.9	196.1	193.4
Imports of goods f.o.b.	−998.6	−1,024.4	−866.0
Trade balance	**−811.8**	**−828.3**	**−672.5**
Exports of services	42.6	86.9	53.6
Imports of services	−55.9	−67.6	−52.2
Balance on goods and services	**−825.1**	**−809.0**	**−671.2**
Other income received	453.0	447.4	357.7
Other income paid	−119.5	−110.0	−123.6
Balance on goods, services and income	**−491.6**	**−471.6**	**−437.1**
Current transfers received	190.2	202.9	158.0
Current transfers paid	−1.1	−0.5	−1.2
Current balance	**−302.5**	**−269.2**	**−280.2**
Capital account (net)	45.5	44.5	22.9
Direct investment from abroad	287.5	268.1	264.8
Other investment assets	−7.0	−5.0	−1.7
Other investment liabilities	70.1	60.5	53.0
Net errors and omissions	23.3	42.1	56.8
Overall balance	**116.9**	**141.0**	**115.6**

Source: IMF, *International Financial Statistics.*

External Trade

PRINCIPAL COMMODITIES

Imports c.i.f. ('000 maloti)	1979	1980	1981
Food and live animals	68,559	76,918	82,902
Beverages and tobacco	13,725	16,233	21,761
Clothing	31,652	34,452	36,733
Machinery and transport equipment	44,084	58,397	74,647
Petroleum products	22,848	31,633	37,766
Chemicals	16,372	18,853	28,229
Footwear	10,556	12,423	14,338
Total (incl. others)	**303,612**	**360,757**	**439,375**

Total imports (million maloti): 497.8 in 1982; 539.7 in 1983; 634.5 in 1984; 751.0 in 1985; 803.3 in 1986; 954.8 in 1987; 1,327.5 in 1988; 1,552 in 1989; 1,738 in 1990; 2,242 in 1991; 2,564 in 1992; 2,839 in 1993; 3,000 in 1994; 3,576 in 1995; 4,303 in 1996; 4,722 in 1997; 4,699 in 1998 (Source: IMF, *International Financial Statistics*).

Exports (million maloti)	1996	1997	1998
Foodstuffs, etc.	33.8	43.8	41.2
Livestock materials	32.9	29.2	24.4
Wool	22.7	23.5	21.0
Chemicals and petroleum	24.7	16.6	9.0
Road vehicles	18.5	32.7	16.1
Furniture and parts	10.8	11.3	3.1
Clothing, etc.	368.8	403.4	472.2
Footwear	153.1	177.4	253.6
Total (incl. others)	**812.1**	**903.8**	**998.5**

Source: IMF, *Lesotho: Recent Economic Developments and Selected Issues* (August 1999).

PRINCIPAL TRADING PARTNERS (million maloti)

Imports*	1996	1997	1998
Africa	4,462.3	4,704.4	4,436.1
SACU†	4,417.7	4,687.1	4,408.0
Asia	254.0	394.8	309.2
Hong Kong	8.2	22.6	19.2
Japan	24.6	24.7	21.0
Taiwan	154.5	192.1	183.5
European Union	55.4	87.5	40.5
North America	23.7	52.5	84.2
USA	14.2	18.6	34.7
Total (incl. others)	**4,815.6**	**5,253.5**	**4,915.7**

Exports	1996	1997	1998
Africa	569.6	581.4	654.9
SACU†	562.6	580.0	652.9
European Union	43.6	11.7	7.4
North America	198.5	308.4	333.1
Total (incl. others)	**812.1**	**902.5**	**998.7**

* Valuation exclusive of import duties. Figures also exclude donated food.
† Southern African Customs Union, of which Lesotho is a member; also including Botswana, Namibia, South Africa and Swaziland.

Source: IMF, *Lesotho: Recent Economic Developments and Selected Issues* (August 1999).

Transport

ROAD TRAFFIC (estimates, motor vehicles in use at 31 December)

	1994	1995	1996
Passenger cars	9,900	11,160	12,610
Lorries and vans	20,790	22,310	25,000

Source: IRF, *World Road Statistics.*

CIVIL AVIATION (traffic on scheduled services)

	1994	1995	1996
Kilometres flown (million)	1	1	1
Passengers carried ('000)	27	25	17
Passenger-km (million)	9	8	6
Total ton-km (million)	1	1	1

Source: UN, *Statistical Yearbook.*

Tourism

	1996	1997	1998
Tourist arrivals*	311,802	323,868	289,819
Tourism receipts (US $ million)	19	20	n.a.

* Figures refer to arrivals at frontiers from visitors abroad and include same-day visitors.

Source: World Tourism Organization, *Yearbook of Tourism Statistics.*

Communications Media

	1994	1995	1996
Radio receivers ('000 in use)	n.a.	n.a.	100
Television receivers ('000 in use)	n.a.	n.a.	50
Daily newspapers:			
Number	2	2	2
Average circulation ('000 copies)	14	14	15
Non-daily newspapers:			
Number	n.a.	n.a.	7
Average circulation ('000 copies)	n.a.	n.a.	74

Telephones ('000 main lines in use, year ending 31 March): 15 in 1993/94; 16* in 1994/95; 18 in 1995/96.

Telefax stations (number in use, year ending 31 March): 480 in 1994/95; 569 in 1995/96; 600 in 1996/97.

Mobile cellular telephones (subscribers): 1,262 in 1996/97.

* Estimate.

1997: Radio receivers ('000 in use) 104; Television receivers ('000 in use) 54.

Sources: UNESCO, *Statistical Yearbook;* UN *Statistical Yearbook.*

Education

(1996/97)

	Institutions	Teachers	Students Males	Females	Total
Primary	1,249	7,898	178,481	196,147	374,628
Secondary:					
General	n.a.	2,817	27,742	39,712	67,454
Technical and vocational	n.a.	61	241	437	678
University-level	n.a.	373	1,171	1,743	2,914
Other tertiary*	n.a.	201	934	766	1,700

* Including teacher-training.

Source UNESCO, *Statistical Yearbook.*

Directory

The Constitution

The Constitution of the Kingdom of Lesotho, which took effect at independence in October 1966, was suspended in January 1970. A new Constitution was promulgated following the March 1993 general election. Its main provisions are summarized below:

Lesotho is an hereditary monarchy. The King, who is Head of State, has no executive or legislative powers. Executive authority is vested in the Cabinet, which is headed by the Prime Minister, while legislative power is exercised by the 80-member* National Assembly, which is elected, at intervals of no more than five years, by universal adult suffrage in the context of a multi-party political system. There is also a Senate, comprising 22 traditional chiefs and 11 nominated members. The Prime Minister is the official head of the armed forces.

* With effect from the May 1998 general election, the National Assembly was expanded from 65 members to 80 members; a further expansion, to 130 members, was agreed by the Interim Political Authority in December 1999 (see Recent History).

The Government

HEAD OF STATE

HM King LETSIE III (acceded to the throne 7 February 1996).

CABINET
(August 2000)

Prime Minister and Minister of Defence and Public Service: BETHUEL PAKALITHA MOSISILI.

Deputy Prime Minister and Minister of Finance and Development Planning: KELEBONE ALBERT MAOPE.

Minister of Agriculture, Cooperatives and Land Reclamation: VOVA BULANE.

Minister of Foreign Affairs: MOTSOAHAE THOMAS THABANE.

Minister of Education: ARCHIBALD LESAO LEHOHLA.

Minister of Justice, Human Rights, Law, Constitutional Affairs and Rehabilitation: SHAKANE MOKHEHLE.

Minister of Employment and Labour: NOT'SI VICTOR MOLOPO.

Minister of Local Government and Home Affairs: MOPSHATLA MABITLE.

Minister of the Environment, Gender and Youth Affairs: MATHABISO LEPONO.

Minister of Industry, Trade and Marketing: MPHO MELI MALIE.

Minister of Health and Social Welfare: TEFO MABOTE.

Minister of Tourism, Sports and Culture: MLALELE MOTAUNG.

Minister of Communication (Broadcasting, Posts and Telecommunications): NYANE MPHAFI.

Minister in the Prime Minister's Office: SEPHIRI ENOCH MOTANYANE.

Minister of Natural Resources: MONYANE MOLELEKI.

Minister of Works and Transport: MOFELEHETSI SALOMONE MOERANE.

MINISTRIES

Office of the Prime Minister: POB 527, Maseru 100; tel. 311030; fax 310102.

Ministry of Agriculture, Cooperatives and Land Reclamation: POB 24, Maseru 100; tel. 323561; fax 310349.

Ministry of Communication (Broadcasting, Posts and Telecommunications): POB 36, Maseru 100; tel. 323561; fax 310003.

Ministry of Defence and Public Service: Private Bag A166, Maseru 100; tel. 316570; fax 310319.

Ministry of Education: POB 47, Maseru 100; tel. 313045; fax 310206.

Ministry of Employment and Labour: Private Bag A116, Maseru 100; tel. 322565; fax 310374.

Ministry of the Environment, Gender and Youth Affairs: Maseru.

Ministry of Finance and Development Planning: POB 395, Maseru 100; tel. 311100; fax 310157.

Ministry of Foreign Affairs: POB 1378, Maseru 100; tel. 311150; fax 310178.

Ministry of Health and Social Welfare: POB 514, Maseru 100; tel. 314404; fax 310467.

Ministry of Industry, Trade and Marketing: POB 747, Maseru 100; tel. 317454; fax 310326.

Ministry of Justice, Human Rights, Law and Constitutional Affairs: POB 402, Maseru 100; tel. 322683; fax 310365.

Ministry of Local Government Home Affairs: POB 174, Maseru 100; tel. 323771; fax 310319.

Ministry of Natural Resources: POB 426, Maseru 100; tel. 323163; fax 310520.

Ministry of Tourism, Sports and Culture: POB 52, Maseru 100; tel. 313034; fax 310194.

Ministry of Works and Transport: POB 20, Maseru 100; tel. 311362; fax 310125.

Legislature

PARLIAMENT

National Assembly

Speaker: NTLHOI MOTSAMAI.

General Election, 23 May 1998

Party	% of votes	Seats
Lesotho Congress for Democracy . . .	60.72	78
Basotho National Party	24.47	1
Others	14.81	–
Total	100.00	79*

* Voting for one seat was postponed, owing to the death of a candidate.

Senate

Speaker: Chief SEMPE LEJAHA.

The Senate is an advisory chamber comprising 22 traditional chiefs and 11 members appointed by the monarch.

Political Organizations

Basotho Congress Party (BCP): POB 111, Maseru; f. 1952; Leader TSELISO MAKHAKHE.

Basotho Democratic Alliance (BDA): Maseru; f. 1984; Pres. S. C. NKOJANE.

Basotho National Party (BNP): POB 124, Maseru 100; f. 1958; Leader JUSTIN METSING LEKHANYA; Sec.-Gen. MAJARA MOLAPO; 280,000 mems.

Khokanyana-Phiri Democratic Alliance: Maseru; f. 1999; alliance of opposition parties, incl.:

Christian Democratic Party: Maseru.

Communist Party of Lesotho (CPL): Maseru; f. 1962 (banned 1970–91); supported mainly by migrant workers employed in South Africa; Sec.-Gen. MOKHAFISI KENA.

Kopanang Basotho Party (KBP): Maseru; f. 1992; campaigns for women's rights; Leader LIMAKATSO NTAKATSANE.

National Independence Party (NIP): Maseru; f. 1984; Pres. ANTHONY C. MANYELI.

Popular Front for Democracy (PFD): Maseru; f. 1991; Leader LEKHETHO RAKUANE.

Progressive National Party (PNP): Maseru; f. 1995 following split in the BNP; Leader Chief PEETE NKOEBE PEETE.

Social Democratic Party: Maseru; Leader MASITISE SELESO.

Lesotho Congress for Democracy (LCD); Maseru; f. 1997 as a result of divisions within the BCP; Chair. PHEBE MOTEBANG; Leader BETHUEL PAKALITHA MOSISILI; Dep. Leader KELEBONE ALBERT MAOPE; 200,000 mems.

Lesotho Labour Party (LLP): Maseru; f. 1991; Leader PATRICK SALIE.

Marematlou Freedom Party (MFP): POB 0443, Maseru 105; tel. 315804; f. 1962; Leader VINCENT MOEKETSE MALEBO; Dep. Leader THABO LEANYA: 300,000 mems.

Sefate Democratic Union (SDU): Maseru; Leader BOFIHLA NKUEBE.

United Democratic Party (UDP): POB 776, Maseru 100; f. 1967; Chair. BEN L. SHEA: Leader CHARLES D. MOFELI; Sec.-Gen. MOLOMO NKUEBE; 26,000 mems.

United Party (UP): Maseru; Pres. MAKARA SEKAUTU (imprisoned for high treason March 1997).

Diplomatic Representation

EMBASSIES AND HIGH COMMISSIONS IN LESOTHO

China, People's Republic: POB 380, Maseru 100; tel. 316521; fax 310489; Ambassador: CHEN LAIYUAN.

Denmark: Site 11, Industrial Area, POB 1259, Maseru 100; tel. 323630; fax 310138; Ambassador: ALF JÖNSSON.

Korea, Democratic People's Republic: Maseru; Ambassador: AN KYONG HYON.

South Africa: Lesotho Bank Tower, 10th Floor, Kingsway, Private Bag A266, Maseru 100; tel. 315758; fax 310128; e-mail sahcis@lesoff.co.za; High Commissioner: M. JAPHET NDLOVU.

United Kingdom: Linare Rd, POB MS521, Maseru 100; tel. 313961; fax 310120; e-mail hcmaseru@bhc.org.ls; internet www.lesoff.co.za/bhcmaseru; High Commissioner: KAYE W. OLIVER.

USA: 254 Kingsway, POB 333, Maseru 100; tel. 312666; fax 310116; e-mail amles@lesoff.co.za; internet www.usembassy.org.ls; Ambassador: KATHERINE H. PETERSON.

Judicial System

HIGH COURT

The High Court is a superior court of record, and in addition to any other jurisdiction conferred by statute it is vested with unlimited original jurisdiction to determine any civil or criminal matter. It also has appellate jurisdiction to hear appeals and reviews from the subordinate courts. Appeals may be made to the Court of Appeal.

Chief Justice: JOSEPH LEBONA KHEOLA.

Judges: M. L. LEHOHLA, W. C. M. MAQUTU, B. K. MOLAI, T. E. MONAPATHI, K. GUNI, G. MOFOLO, M. RAMOLIBELI.

COURT OF APPEAL

President: ISMAIL MAHOMED.

Judges: T. BROWDE, G. P. KOTZE, R. N. LEON, J. N. STEYN.

SUBORDINATE COURTS

Each of the 10 districts possesses subordinate courts, presided over by magistrates.

JUDICIAL COMMISSIONERS' COURTS

These courts hear civil and criminal appeals from central and local courts. Further appeal may be made to the high court and finally to the court of appeal.

CENTRAL AND LOCAL COURTS

There are 71 such courts, of which 58 are local courts and 13 are central courts which also serve as courts of appeal from the local courts. They have limited civil and criminal jurisdiction.

Religion

About 90% of the population profess Christianity.

CHRISTIANITY

African Federal Church Council: POB 70, Peka 340; f.1927; co-ordinating org. for 48 African independent churches; Co-ordinator Rev. S. MOHONO.

Christian Council of Lesotho: Maseru 100; tel. 323639; fax 310310; f. 1973; six mem. and four assoc. mem. churches; Chair. Rev. LEBOHANG KHEEKHE; Sec. R. M. TAOLE.

The Anglican Communion

Anglicans in Lesotho are adherents of the Church of the Province of Southern Africa. The Metropolitan of the Province is the Archbishop of Cape Town, South Africa. Lesotho forms a single diocese, with an estimated 100,000 members.

Bishop of Lesotho: Rt Rev. JOSEPH MAHAPU TSUBELLA, Bishop's House, POB 87, Maseru 100; tel. 311974; fax 310161; e-mail jandjgay@lesoff.com.

The Roman Catholic Church

Lesotho comprises one archdiocese and three dioceses. At 31 December 1998 there were some 894,299 adherents of the Roman Catholic Church.

Lesotho Catholic Bishops' Conference: Catholic Secretariat, POB 200, Maseru 100; tel. 312525; fax 310294; f. 1972; Pres. Most Rev BERNARD MOHLALISI, Archbishop of Maseru.

Archbishop of Maseru: Most Rev. BERNARD MOHLALISI, Archbishop's House, 19 Orpen Rd, POB 267, Maseru 100; tel. 312565; fax 310425; e-mail archmase@adelfang.co.za.

Other Christian Churches

African Methodist Episcopal Church: POB 223, Maseru 100; tel. 322616; f. 1903; 11,295 mems.

Dutch Reformed Church in Africa: POB 454, Maseru 100; tel. 314669; f. 1957; 7,396 mems (1991).

Lesotho Evangelical Church: POB 260, Maseru 100; tel. 323942; f. 1833; independent since 1964; Moderator Rev. G. L. SIBOLLA; Exec. Sec. Rev. A. M. THEBE; 211,000 mems (1990).

Methodist Church of Southern Africa: POB 81, Maseru 100; tel. 322412; f. 1927; Supt Rev. D. SENKHANE; c. 10,000 mems and adherents (1989).

Other denominations active in Lesotho include the Apostolic Faith Mission, the Assemblies of God, the Full Gospel Church of God and the Seventh-day Adventists. There are also numerous African independent churches.

BAHÁ'Í FAITH

National Spiritual Assembly: POB 508, Maseru 100; tel. 312346; fax 310092; mems resident in 431 localities.

The Press

Lentsoe la Basotho: POB 353, Maseru 100; tel. 323561; fax 310003; e-mail lbmin@lesoff.co.za; f. 1974; weekly; Sesotho; publ. by Ministry of Information and Broadcasting; Editor KAHLISO LEBENYA; circ. 3,000.

Leselinyana la Lesotho (Light of Lesotho): POB 7, Morija 190; tel. 360244; fax 360005; f. 1866; fortnightly; Sesotho, with occasional articles in English; publ. by Lesotho Evangelical Church; Editor A. B. THOALANE; circ. 10,000.

Lesotho Today: POB 36, Maseru 100; tel. 323586; fax 310003; weekly; English; publ. by Ministry of Information and Broadcasting; Editor T. TSEPANE; circ. 7,000.

Lesotho Weekly: POB 353, Maseru 100; weekly.

Makatolle: POB 111, Maseru 100; tel. 850990; f. 1963; weekly; Sesotho; Editor M. RAMANGOEI; circ. 2,000.

The Mirror: POB 903, Maseru 100; tel. 315602; fax 310216; f. 1986; weekly; English; Editor NAT MOLOMO; circ. 4,000.

MoAfrika: POB 7234, Maseru 100; tel. 325034; f. 1990; weekly; Sesotho; Editor-in-Chief CANDI RAMAINOANE; circ. 5,000.

Moeletsi oa Basotho: Mazenod Institute, POB 18, Mazenod 160; tel. 350465; fax 350010; f. 1933; weekly; Roman Catholic; Sesotho; Editor Fr G. TLABA; circ. 20,000.

Mopheme (the Survivor): POB 14184, Maseru; tel. and fax 311670; e-mail mopheme@lesoff.co.za; weekly; English; Editor LAWRENCE KEKETSO; circ. 2,500.

Public Eye: POB 14129, Maseru; tel. 3201414; fax 310614; e-mail voicened@lesoff.co.za; twice a week; English; Editor BETHUEL THA; circ. 5,000.

The Sun: POB 1013, Maseru; weekly; English; Editor M. RANOUKU; circ. 6,500.

Thebe ea Khotso: POB 15303, Maseru; Sesotho; Editor MOHAPI MOTBA; circ. 7,000.

Shoeshoe: POB 36, Maseru 100; tel. 323561; fax 310003; quarterly; women's interest; publ. by Ministry of Information and Broadcasting.

Southern Star: POB 7590, Maseru; tel. 312269; fax 310167; e-mail baffoe@iafrika.co.za; weekly; English; Editor JOE MOKEFI; circ. 1,500.

NEWS AGENCIES

Lesotho News Agency (LENA): POB 36, Maseru 100; tel. 315317; fax 310003; f. 1986; Dir LEBOHANG LEJAKANE; Editor KHOELI PHOLOSI.

Foreign Bureau

Inter Press Service (IPS) (Italy): c/o Lesotho News Agency, POB 36, Maseru 100; Correspondent LEBOHANG LEJAKANE.

Publishers

Longman Lesotho (Pty) Ltd: POB 1174, Maseru 100; tel. 317340; fax 310118; Man. Dir SEYMOUR R. KIKINE.

Macmillan Boleswa Publishers Lesotho (Pty) Ltd: POB 7545, Maseru 100; tel. 317340; fax 310047.

Mazenod Institute: POB 39, Mazenod 160; tel. 350224. 1933; Roman Catholic; Man. Fr B. MOHLALISI.

Morija Sesuto Book Depot: POB 4, Morija 190; tel. and fax 360204; f. 1862; owned by the Lesotho Evangelical Church; religious, educational and Sesotho language and literature.

St Michael's Mission: The Social Centre, POB 25, Roma; tel. 316234; f. 1968; religious and educational; Man. Dir Fr M. FERRANGE.

Government Publishing House

Government Printer: POB 527, Maseru; tel. 313023.

Broadcasting and Communications

TELECOMMUNICATIONS

Lesotho Telecommunications Corporation: POB 1037, Maseru 100; tel. 211000; fax 310014; transfer pending to private sector; Man. Dir P. C. RAFEKILA.

VCL Communications: Development House, Kingsway Rd, POB 7387, Maseru 100; tel. 212000; fax 311079; f. 1996; jt venture between Lesotho Telecommunications Corpn and Vodacom (Pty) Ltd; operates mobile cellular telephone network.

BROADCASTING

Lesotho National Broadcasting Service: POB 552, Maseru 100; tel. 323561; fax 310003; programmes in Sesotho and English; radio transmissions began in 1964 and television transmissions in 1988; Dir MOLAHLEHI LETLOTLO; Dir of Programming MAMONYANE MATSABA.

Finance

(cap. = capital; res = reserves; dep. = deposits; m. = million; brs = branches; amounts in maloti)

BANKING
Central Bank

Central Bank of Lesotho: cnr Airport and Moshoeshoe Rds, POB 1184, Maseru 100; tel. 314281; fax 310051; e-mail cbl@pixie.co.za; internet www.centralbank.org.ls; f. 1980; bank of issue; cap. and res 670.3m., dep. 2,568.1m. (Dec. 1998); Gov. and Chair. S. M. SWARAY.

Commercial Banks

Lesotho Bank: Central Services, Lesotho Bank Centre, Kingsway, POB 1053, Maseru 100; tel. 315737; fax 314333; f. 1972; transferred to majority private ownership in Aug. 1999; 70% owned by Standard Bank Lesotho Ltd; commercial bank, also carries out development banking functions; cap. and res 114m. (1998); Chair. Dr 'MUSI MOKETE; Gen. Man. NKOPANE MONYANE; 15 brs.

Nedbank Lesotho: Standard Bank Bldg, 1st Floor, Kingsway, POB 1001, Maseru 100; tel. 312696; fax 310025; frmrly Standard Chartered Bank Lesotho Ltd; owned by Nedcor Bank Ltd (South Africa); cap. 8.3m., total assets 197.4m. (Dec. 1995); Man. Dir DAVE WATTS; 3 brs and 7 agencies.

Standard Bank Lesotho Ltd: Bank Bldg, 1st Floor, Kingsway, POB 115, Maseru 100; tel. 312423; fax 310068; e-mail stanbicles@abg.sbic.co.za; f. 1957 as Barclays Bank DCO; frmrly Stanbic Bank Lesotho Ltd, present name since 1997; owned by Standard Bank Investment Corpn Ltd; cap. and res 43m., dep. 299m. (1998); Chair. ROBERT E. NORVAL; Man. Dir M. WOOLER; 6 brs.

Development Bank

Lesotho Building Finance Corporation (LBFC): Private Bag A59, Maseru 100; tel. 313514; fax 310348; state-owned; Man. Dir N. MONYANE; 3 brs.

INSURANCE

Alliance Insurance Co Ltd: POB 1118, Maseru West 105; tel. 312357; fax 310313; Man. Dir JACK BECKER.

Lesotho National Insurance Co (Pty) Ltd: Private Bag A65, Lesotho Insurance House, Kingsway, Maseru 100; tel. 313031; fax 310007; e-mail inig@lesoff.co.za; f. 1977; Chair. Dr M. SENAOANA; CEO M. MOLELEKOA.

Metropolitan Life Ltd: POB 645, Maseru; tel. 323970; fax 317126; Regional Man. E. L. TSHABALALA.

Minet Kingsway Lesotho (Pty) Ltd: POB 993, Maseru 100; tel. 313540; fax 310033; f. 1969; Chair. R. A. DAVISON; Man. Dir A. T. WHITEHORN.

Thebe Hosken Insurance Brokers (Pty) Ltd: Options Bldg, 1st Floor, Pioneer Rd, Private Bag A244, Maseru 100; tel. 313018; fax 310513; Chair. C. J. SOUNES; Man. Dir G. M. WILSON.

Trade and Industry
GOVERNMENT AGENCIES

Privatization Unit: c/o Ministry of Finance and Development Planning, Private Bag A249, Maseru 100; tel. 317902; fax 317551; Dir MOTHUSI MASHOLOGU.

Trade Promotion Unit: c/o Ministry of Trade and Industry, POB 747, Maseru 100; tel. 322138; fax 310121.

DEVELOPMENT ORGANIZATIONS

Lesotho Highlands Development Authority: POB 7332, Maseru 100; tel. 311280; fax 310060; internet www.lesoff.co.za/lhda; f. 1986 to supervise the Highlands Water Project, being undertaken jtly with South Africa; Chair. H. M. MHLANGA; CEO MAKASE MARUMO.

Lesotho National Development Corporation (LNDC): Development House, 1st Floor, Kingsway Rd, Private Bag A96, Maseru 100; tel. 312012; fax 310038; e-mail lndc@pixie.co.za; internet www.lndc.org.ls; f. 1967; 90% state-owned; cap. M40m.; interests include candle, carpet, tyre-retreading, explosives, fertilizer, clothing, jewellery and furniture factories, potteries, two diamond prospecting operations, an abattoir, a diamond-cutting and polishing works, a housing co, a brewery and an international hotel with a gambling casino; Chair. Minister of Industry, Trade and Marketing; CEO SOPHIE MOHAPI.

Basotho Enterprises Development Corporation (BEDCO): POB 1216, Maseru 100; tel. 312094; fax 310455; e-mail bedco@lesoff.co.za; f. 1980; promotes and assists in the establishment and development of small-scale Basotho-owned enterprises; CEO P. MOKHESI.

Lesotho Co-operatives Handicrafts: Maseru; f. 1978; marketing and distribution of handicrafts; Gen. Man. KHOTSO MATLA.

CHAMBER OF COMMERCE

Lesotho Chamber of Commerce and Industry: POB 79, Maseru 100; tel. 323482; fax 310414.

INDUSTRIAL AND TRADE ASSOCIATIONS

Livestock Marketing Corporation: POB 800, Maseru 100; tel. 322444. 1973; sole org. for marketing livestock and livestock products; liaises closely with marketing boards in South Africa; projects include an abattoir, tannery, poultry and wool and mohair scouring plants; Gen. Man. S. R. MATLANYANE.

Produce Marketing Corporation: Maseru. 1974; Gen. Man. M. PHOOFOLO.

EMPLOYERS' ORGANIZATION

Association of Lesotho Employers: POB 1509, Maseru 100; tel. 315736. 1961; represents mems in industrial relations and on govt bodies, and advises the Govt on employers' concerns; Pres. BRIAN MCCARTHY; Exec. Dir T. MAKEKA.

UTILITIES

Lesotho Electricity Corporation: POB 423, Maseru 100; tel. 312236; fax 310093; f. 1969; Chair. B. T. PEKECHE; Man. Dir M. S. SHALE.

Water and Sewerage Authority: POB 426, Maseru; tel. 312449; fax 310006.

MAJOR COMPANIES

Berea Steel Industries Co: POB 809, Maseru 100; tel. 326344; fax 322825; production of steel.

Forrest Construction Pty Ltd: POB 856, Maseru; tel. 312931; fax 312932; e-mail forrest@adelfang.co.za; f. 1972; civil engineering and construction; Man. Dir J. M. FORREST.

Kingsway Construction: Private Bag A53, Maseru 100; tel. 313161; fax 310137; e-mail kingsway@lesoff.co.za; f. 1986; Chair. T. HENDRY.

Lesotho Brewing Co Pty Ltd: POB 746, Maseru; tel. 311111; fax 310020; e-mail lbcsabi@icon.co.za; f. 1981; beer and non-alcoholic beverages; Chair. S. MOHAPI; Man. Dir E. MARRIOTT.

Lesotho Flour Mills: Private Bag A62, Maseru 100; tel. 313498; fax 310037; e-mail lesflour@lesoff.co.za; f. 1979; flour milling; Man. Dir J. H. VAN DER MOLEN.

Lesotho Milling Co Pty Ltd: POB 39, Maputsoe; tel. 430622; fax 430010; maize, groats and meal; Man. Dir J. B. GAGCKE.

Lesotho Pharmaceutical Corporation: POB 256, Mafeteng 900; tel. 700326; fax 700002; pharmaceutical products; Man. Dir M. P. POSHOLI.

Lesotho Sandstone Co Pty Ltd (LESACO): Private Bag A241, Maseru 100; tel. 322443; fax 310081; e-mail rifa@lesoff.co.za; mining and quarrying; Man. Dir R. FACTA; Chair. L. G. FACTA.

Lesotho Textiles Pty: POB 7432, Maseru 100; tel. 314647; fax 310004; clothing mfrs; Chair. and Man. Dir R. E. STOCKDALE.

TRADE UNIONS

Construction and Allied Workers Union of Lesotho (CAWULE): Maseru.

Lesotho General Workers' Union: POB 322, Maseru 100; f. 1954; Chair. J. M. RAMAROTHOLE; Sec. T. MOTLOHI.

Lesotho Transport and Telecommunication Workers' Union: Maseru 100; f. 1959; Pres. M. BERENG; Sec. P. MOTRAMAI.

Lesotho University Teachers' and Researchers' Union (LUTARU): Maseru.

National Union of Construction and Allied Workers: Maseru; f. 1967; Pres. L. PUTSOANE; Sec. T. TLALE.

National Union of Printing, Bookbinding and Allied Workers: PO Mazenod 160; f. 1963; Pres. G. MOTEBANG; Gen. Sec. CLEMENT RATSIU.

Union of Shop Distributive and Allied Workers: Maseru 100; f. 1966; Pres. P. BERENG; Sec. J. MOLAPO.

Transport

RAILWAYS

Lesotho is linked with the South African railway system by a short line (2.6 km in length) from Maseru to Marseilles, on the Bloemfontein/Natal main line.

ROADS

In 1996 Lesotho's road network totalled 4,955 km, of which 884 km were main roads and 1,255 km were secondary roads. About 17.9% of roads were paved. In 1996 the International Development Association granted US $40m. towards the Government's rolling five-year road programme. From 1996/67 an extra-budgetary Road Fund was to finance road maintenance. In March 2000 a major road network was opened, linking Maseru with the Mohale Dam.

CIVIL AVIATION

King Moshoeshoe I International Airport is at Thota-Moli, some 20 km from Maseru. There are 40 smaller airfields in Lesotho. International services between Maseru and Johannesburg are operated by South African Airlink.

Lesotho Airways Corpn: POB 861, Maseru 100; tel. 324507; fax 310617; domestic and international passenger services; privatized 1999; Man. Dir MICHAEL SCHRIENER.

Tourism

Spectacular mountain scenery is the principal tourist attraction. In 1998 there were 289,819 tourist arrivals (including same-day visitors). Receipts from tourism in 1997 totalled about US $20m.

Lesotho Tourist Board (Boto Ea Tsa Boeti Lesotho): POB 1378, Maseru 100; tel. 313760; fax 310108; f. 1983; Man. Dir MANDISA MASHOLOGU.

Defence

Military service is voluntary. The Lesotho Defence Force (formerly the Royal Lesotho Defence Force) comprised 2,000 men in August 1999.

Defence Expenditure: Budgeted at M177.5m. for 1998/99.

Commander of the Lesotho Defence Force: Maj.-Gen. MAKHULA MOSAKENG.

Education

All primary education is available free of charge, and is provided mainly by the three main Christian missions (Lesotho Evangelical, Roman Catholic and Anglican), under the direction of the Ministry of Education and Training, Sports, Culture and Youth Affairs. Lesotho has one of the highest levels of literacy among African countries: according to the population census of 1986, the average rate of adult illiteracy was 30% for males and 11% for females. According to estimates by UNESCO, the rate in 1995 averaged 18.6% (males 29.9%; females 8.1%). Education at primary schools is officially compulsory for seven years between six and 13 years of age. Secondary education, beginning at the age of 13, lasts for up to five years, comprising a first cycle of three years and a second of two years. Of children in the relevant age-group in 1996, 63% (males 58%; females 68%) were enrolled at primary schools, while only 17% (males 12%; females 22%) were enrolled at secondary schools. The National University of Lesotho had some 1,800 students in the mid-1990s. Of projected expenditure by the central government in the 1998/99 financial year, M639.4m. (22.6%) was allocated to education and community services.

Bibliography

Ambrose, D. *Maseru: An Illustrated History*. Morija, Morija Museum and Archives, 1993.

Ambrose, D. P., and Perry, J. W. B. *Atlas for Lesotho*. Cape Town, Longman Southern Africa, 1974.

Bardill, J. E., and Cobbe, J. *Lesotho: Dilemmas of Dependence in Southern Africa*. Boulder, CO, Westview Press, 1985.

Lesotho: Profiles. Boulder, CO, Westview Press, 1985.

Burman, S. *Chiefdom, Politics and Alien Law: Basutoland under Cape Rule, 1871–1884*. London, Macmillan in association with St Antony's College, Oxford, 1981.

Cervenka, Z., et al. *Botswana, Lesotho, Swaziland*. Bonn, Deutsche Afrika-Gesellschaft, 1974.

Duncan, T., et al. *Support Against Apartheid: An Evaluation of 28 Years of Development Assistance to Lesotho: Final Report*. Stockholm, Swedish International Development Authority, 1994.

Eldredge, E. A. *A South African Kingdom: The Pursuit of Security in Nineteenth-Century Lesotho*. Cambridge, Cambridge University Press, 1993.

Ferguson, J. (Ed.). *The Anti-Politics Machine: Development, Depoliticization and Bureaucratic State Power in Lesotho*. Cambridge, Cambridge University Press; Cape Town, David Philip, 1990.

Franklin, A. S. *Land Law in Lesotho: The Politics of the 1979 Land Act*. Aldershot, Avebury; Brookfield, VT, Ashgate Publishing, 1995.

Gary, J., et al (Ed.). *Lesotho's Long Journey: Hard Choices at the Crossroads: A Comprehensive Overview of Lesotho's Historical, Social, Economic and Political Development With a View to the Future*. Maseru, Sechaba Consultants, 1995. (Commissioned and funded by Irish Aid).

Gary, J., and Hall, D. *Poverty in Lesotho*. Maseru, Sechaba Consultants, 1994.

Gill, S. J. *A Short History of Lesotho, From the Late Stone Age Until the 1993 Elections*. Morija, Morija Museum and Archives, 1993.

Haliburton, G. *Historical Dictionary of Lesotho*. Metuchen, NJ, Scarecrow Press, 1977.

Konczacki, Z. A., et al. *Studies in the Economic History of Southern Africa*. Vol. II. London, Cass, 1991.

Kowet, D. K. *Land, Labour Migration and Politics in Southern Africa: Botswana, Lesotho and Swaziland*. New York, Africana Publishing, 1979.

Lundahl, M., and Petersson, L. *The Dependent Economy: Lesotho and the Southern Africa Customs Union*. Boulder, CO, Westview Press, 1991.

Machobane, L. B. B. J. *Government and Change in Lesotho, 1800–1966: A Study of Political Institutions*. Maseru, Macmillan Lesotho, 1990.

Mapetla, E. R. M., and Rembe, S.W. *Decentralisation and Development in Lesotho*. Roma, National University of Lesotho, 1989.

Maqutu, W. C. M. *Contemporary Constitutional History of Lesotho*. Mazenod, Mazenod Institute, 1990.

Milazi, D. *The Politics and Economics of Labour Migration in Southern Africa. What are the Key Issues?* Maseru, Lesotho Printing and Publishing Co, 1984.

Mochebelele, M.T., et al. *Agricultural Marketing in Lesotho*. Ottawa, International Development Research Centre, 1992.

Murray, C. *Families Divided: The Impact of Migrant Labour in Lesotho*. Cambridge, Cambridge University Press; Johannesburg, Ravan Press, 1981.

Orpen, J. M. *History of the Basutos of South Africa*. Mazenod, Mazenod Institute, 1988.

Rule, S. *Elections in Lesotho: May 1998*. Johannesburg, Electoral Institute of South Africa, 1998.

Rwelamira, M. *Refugees in a Chess Game: Reflections on Botswana, Lesotho and Swaziland Refugee Policies*. Trenton, NJ, Red Sea Press, 1990.

Southall, R., and Petlane, T. (Eds). *Democratisation and Demilitarisation in Lesotho: The General Election of 1993 and its Aftermath*. Pretoria, Africa Institution of South Africa, 1996.

Van der Wiel, A. C. A. *Migratory Wage Labour: Its Role in the Economy of Lesotho*. Maseru, Mazenod Book Centre, 1977.

Van Rensburg, P. *Another Development for Lesotho: Alternative Development Strategies for the Mountain Kingdom*. Gaborone, Foundation for Education with Production, 1989.

Winai-Strom, G. *Development and Dependence in Lesotho, the Enclave of South Africa*. Uppsala, Scandinavian Institute of African Studies, 1979.

Migration and Development: Dependence on South Africa: A Study of Lesotho. Revised Edn. Uppsala, Scandinavian Institute of African Studies; Trenton, NJ, Red Sea Press, 1986.

Witzsch, G. *Lesotho Environment and Environmental Law*. Roma, National University of Lesotho, 1992.

LIBERIA

Physical and Social Geography

CHRISTOPHER CLAPHAM

The Republic of Liberia was founded in 1847 by freed black slaves from the USA who were resettled from 1821 onwards along the western Guinea coast between Cape Mount (11° 20' W) and Cape Palmas (7° 40' W). Liberia extends from 4° 20' N to 8° 30' N with a maximum breadth of 280 km between Buchanan and Nimba. The country occupies an area of 97,754 sq km (37,743 sq miles) between Sierra Leone to the west, the Republic of Guinea to the north, and Côte d'Ivoire to the east.

PHYSICAL FEATURES AND POPULATION

An even coastline of 570 km, characterized by powerful surf, rocky cliffs and lagoons, makes access from the Atlantic Ocean difficult, except at the modern ports. The flat coastal plain, which is 15–55 km wide, consists of forest and savannah. The interior hills and mountain ranges, with altitudes of 180–360 m, form part of an extended peneplain, covered by evergreen (in the south) or semi-deciduous (in the north) rain forests. The northern highlands contain Liberia's greatest elevations, which include the Nimba mountains, reaching 1,752 m above sea-level, and the Wologisi range, reaching 1,381 m. The descent from the higher to the lower belts of the highlands is characterized by rapids and waterfalls.

Liberia has two rainy seasons near Harper, in the south, and one rainy season (from May to October) in the rest of the country. From Monrovia, on the coast in north-west Liberia, with an average of 4,650 mm per year, rainfall decreases towards the south-east and the hinterland, reaching 2,240 mm per year at Ganta. Average temperatures are more extreme in the interior than at the coast. Monrovia has an annual average of 26°C, with absolute limits at 33°C and 14°C respectively. At Tappita temperatures may rise to 44°C in March and fall to 9°C during cool harmattan nights in December or January. Mean water temperature on the coast is 27°C.

The drainage system consists of 15 principal river basins, of which those of the Cavalla river, with an area of 30,225 sq km (including 13,730 sq km in Liberia), and of the St Paul river, with an area of 21,910 sq km (11,325 sq km in Liberia), are the largest. The water flow varies considerably and may reach over 100,000 cubic feet per second (cfs) at the Mt Coffee gauge of the St Paul river in August or decrease to 2,000 cfs during the dry season in March.

The first Liberian census enumerated a population of 1,016,443 in April 1962. According to the second census, in February 1974, an increase of 47.9%, to 1,503,368, had taken place, indicating an average annual growth rate of 3.36%, one of the highest in Africa. A third census, held in February 1984, enumerated a total population of 2,101,628. According to UN estimates, the resident population had increased to 2,439,966 in 1997, and to 2,826,143 in early 1999, following the return of Liberian refugees to the country. There were some 90,000 refugees from Sierra Leone resident in Liberia in October 1999.

The 1984 census officially recognized 16 principal ethnic groups in the Liberian population, comprising 96% of the population. The remaining population consisted of non-Liberian Africans (2%) and 'non-ethnic' Liberians (principally descendants of the original settlers—2%). The main ethnic groups were the Kpelle (numbering 408,176 in 1984), living in Bong County and other central areas of the country, and the Bassa (291,106), in the Buchanan region. Other prominent ethnic groups were the Krahn (79,352), living mainly in Grand Gedeh County, the Mandingo (107,186), a predominantly Muslim group widely distributed throughout the country, and the Gio and Mano of Nimba County (164,823 and 149,277 respectively).

The demographic pattern of Liberia is characterized by a number of features typical of developing countries: a high birth rate (estimated at 46.4 per 1,000 in 1996), a high proportion of children under 15 years of age (estimated at 45.1% of the total population in 1996) and a low expectation of life at birth (estimated at 49 years in 1996). The average population density is low (28.9 inhabitants per sq km in 1999), but urbanization has been rapid, resulting in an estimated 45.6% of the population living in urban areas in 1996. The population of Monrovia, including Congotown, increased from 80,992 in 1962 to 208,629 in 1978, and to 421,058 in 1984; influxes of people displaced by the fighting may have taken the population above 1.3m. during the 1989–96 war.

The war caused massive displacements of population: at many times during the conflict one-third of the population were living as refugees and a further one-third were internally displaced. The repatriation of refugees commenced in 1997 but was still far from complete in June 2000. About 240,000 refugees returned to Liberia during 1998, leaving some 310,000 in neighbouring countries at the end of the year. It was thought that about three-quarters of the internally displaced had returned home by May 1999. About another 100,000 refugees repatriated during 1999, leaving about 200,000 who were unable or who had refused to repatriate; of the latter, between one-half and three-quarters were reported to be of the Mandingo and Krahn ethnic groups, or former residents of Lofa County. The Office of the UN High Commissioner for Refugees (UNHCR) declared Lofa County not safe for repatriation in June 2000, owing to continuing insecurity (see below). Excess mortality due to the conflict is estimated at 150,000 or 200,000 by various sources; this, and wartime reductions in fertility, substantially slowed the natural growth of population during the 1990s.

Recent History

QUENTIN OUTRAM

Based on an earlier article by GILL TUDOR

Liberia was founded by liberated black slaves from the USA, resettled along the western Guinea coast under the auspices of US philanthropic organizations. However, these settlements were not formally placed under US sovereignty. Liberia became an independent republic on 26 July 1847. Control was extended inland from the 1890s, although the peoples of the interior were not fully subdued until the 1920s. In the mid-1920s socio-economic conditions began to undergo considerable change when the US-owned Firestone Plantations Co began operations in Liberia, establishing massive rubber estates, and becoming the country's principal private-sector employer.

Until 1980 Liberian politics was dominated by descendants of the original settlers, known as Americo-Liberians; their True Whig Party (TWP) maintained uninterrupted rule for almost a century. William Tolbert, who became president in 1971, took the country into the Mano River Union, which provided for increased economic co-operation with Sierra Leone, and the Economic Community of West African States (ECOWAS). During the late 1970s, however, Liberia was adversely affected by declining world demand for its principal exports, iron ore and rubber. The resultant decline in living standards prompted the formation of a radical opposition group, the Progressive Alliance of Liberia, which in December 1979, under the leadership of Gabriel Baccus Matthews, organized itself as the Progressive People's Party (PPP). Popular support for the PPP increased rapidly.

THE DOE REGIME

In April 1980 Tolbert was assassinated in a military coup, led by Master Sgt (later Gen.) Samuel Doe. A People's Redemption Council (PRC) was formed, comprising military personnel together with representatives of the TWP, the PPP and the radical Movement for Justice in Africa (MOJA). The constitution was suspended, political parties were proscribed, and several leading officials of the previous administration were publicly executed. During 1981–82 Doe increasingly asserted control over the PRC, removing those with a different ideological outlook. In August 1981 five members of the PRC were executed for seditious conspiracy. By late 1982 numerous other ministers, including Matthews were removed from the government and several heads of public companies were dismissed, following allegations of malpractice. In October 1983 the army commander, Brig.-Gen. Thomas Quiwonkpa (who had been accused of plotting against the government), was dismissed from the PRC, and fled the country.

In July 1984, following its endorsement by national referendum, a new constitution was approved. The PRC was replaced by an interim national assembly, under Doe's chairmanship, and the ban on political organizations was lifted, in anticipation of presidential and legislative elections, scheduled for January 1985, after which the new constitution would come into force.

In August 1984 Doe formed the National Democratic Party of Liberia (NDPL) and announced that he was to contest the presidential elections. Other newly-established parties included the Liberian People's Party (LPP), the successor to MOJA; the United People's Party (UPP), a reconstituted PPP; the Unity Party (UP); the Liberian Action Party (LAP); and the Liberian Unification Party (LUP). However, the registration of political parties was impeded by considerable legal difficulties (including a prohibitive financial qualification). Opposition leaders were briefly detained, following an attempt to assassinate Doe in April 1985. Only three parties besides the NDPL—the LAP, the LUP and the UP—were eventually registered in time for the elections, which finally took place in October. There were allegations of electoral fraud, and the chairman of the government-appointed electoral commission conceded that extensive irregularities had occurred. It was later announced that Doe had been elected to the presidency, with 50.9% of the votes cast. (Many independent observers, however, believed the leader of the LAP, Jackson Doe, to have been the actual winner.) At concurrent elections to the bicameral national assembly, the NDPL secured 22 of the 26 seats in the senate and 51 of the 64 seats in the house of representatives. The LAP rejected the results, and refused to take up the seats awarded to them.

In November 1985 an attempted military coup, led by Brig.-Gen. Quiwonkpa, was suppressed by troops loyal to the government. Quiwonkpa and a number of his supporters were killed, and subsequent fighting between rebels and government forces resulted in at least 600 deaths. Opposition leaders were detained, and meetings of students and others likely to be critical of the government were banned.

The formal installation of a civilian government under the new constitution in January 1986 failed to achieve internal stability and international acceptance. Although Doe appealed for national reconciliation, only a few members of the opposition

parties agreed to accept posts in his government. In March the LAP, LUP and UP formed an alliance, known as the Liberia Grand Coalition. In March 1988 Gabriel Kpolleh, the leader of the LUP, was arrested on charges of conspiring to overthrow the government; in October he and nine others were sentenced to 10 years' imprisonment. In July 1988 Doe announced that a former PRC vice-chairman, Nicholas Podier, had been killed while allegedly preparing to organize a coup from bases in Côte d'Ivoire. Liberia's relations with neighbouring countries became strained during Doe's leadership, although links were established with Nigeria.

CIVIL CONFLICT AND ECOMOG INTERVENTION

In late December 1989 an armed insurrection by rebel forces began in the north-eastern border region of Nimba County. The rebels claimed to represent a previously unknown opposition movement, the National Patriotic Front of Liberia (NPFL), led by Charles Taylor, a former government official who was being sought for trial on charges of corruption. In early 1990 several hundred deaths ensued in the course of fighting between the Liberian army (the Armed Forces of Liberia, AFL) and the rebels, which swiftly developed into a conflict between Doe's ethnic group, the Krahn, and the local Gio and Mano tribes. Both the Krahn-dominated army and the rebel forces were responsible for numerous atrocities against civilians; a large proportion of the local population took refuge in neighbouring Côte d'Ivoire and Guinea. By April the NPFL had overcome government resistance in Nimba County, and in May it extended its control to the remainder of the country, apart from the capital, Monrovia. The NPFL military offensive on Monrovia began in early July, and Taylor repeatedly demanded Doe's resignation as a precondition for a cease-fire. Taylor's authority as self-proclaimed head of a national patriotic reconstruction assembly (NPRA) was, however, challenged by a breakaway faction, known as the Independent National Patriotic Front of Liberia (INPFL), led by Prince Yormie Johnson, whose troops, estimated to number less than 500, rapidly gained control of parts of central Monrovia. Repeated efforts by ECOWAS to negotiate a cease-fire proved unsuccessful, and in late August it dispatched a sea-borne force, comprising some 4,000 troops, provided by Ghana, Nigeria, Sierra Leone, The Gambia and Guinea, to enforce peace in the region. Doe and Johnson agreed to accept the ECOWAS monitoring group (ECOMOG), but its initial occupation of the port area of Monrovia (which had been under Johnson's control), encountered armed opposition by Taylor's forces.

On 30 August 1990 ECOWAS convened a national conference in the Gambian capital, Banjul, although the NPFL refused to attend. Exiled representatives of Liberia's principal political parties, churches and other groups elected Dr Amos Sawyer, the leader of the LPP, as president of an interim government of national unity (IGNU). In late August it was reported that the AFL, which supported Doe, and Johnson's INPFL, had formed an alliance against the NPFL. In September, however, discussions between the AFL and INPFL, held under ECOMOG supervision, led to armed clashes, during which Doe was captured and subsequently killed by the INPFL.

In October 1990 ECOMOG launched an armed offensive, with the aim of establishing a neutral zone in Monrovia to separate the three warring factions, and subsequently gained control of central Monrovia. Thus, Liberia became effectively divided between two administrations: Monrovia was placed under the jurisdiction of the IGNU, which was maintained in power by ECOMOG, while most of the remainder of the country was controlled by the NPFL. Taylor continued to assert his claim to the presidency, and, later that month, established a rival administration, the NPRA, based at Gbarnga, in Bong County (in central Liberia). On 22 November Sawyer was formally installed as interim president in Monrovia. An initial cease-fire was signed at Bamako, Mali, in late November.

Following further negotiations, under the auspices of ECOWAS, a peace agreement was signed in Yamoussoukro, Côte d'Ivoire, in October 1991, whereby all Liberian warring factions were to be encamped and disarmed, and national elections were to be conducted under ECOWAS supervision. Although the cease-fire was maintained, efforts to re-establish a national government failed, largely as a result of Taylor's refusal to disarm NPFL forces and to submit to the authority of ECOMOG, which he believed to be prejudiced in favour of Sawyer. Taylor also cited the increasing threat presented by a new opposition group, the United Liberation Movement of Liberia for Democracy (ULIMO), as a reason not to disarm. ULIMO, led by Raleigh Seekie, was formed in Sierra Leone in June 1991 by former supporters of Doe and immediately declared its opposition to the NPFL. Its forces entered northwestern Liberia in September 1991, and from November clashes with the NPFL occurred in the Mano River Bridge area in the south-west of the country.

ULIMO denounced the Yamoussoukro accord, and progress towards a settlement was also inhibited by the rival sources of external support for ECOMOG and the NPFL. ECOMOG, while formally representing all members of ECOWAS, largely comprised forces of its anglophone members, dominated by Nigeria (although Guinea also supported ECOMOG, and Senegalese troops participated in the force from September 1991 until early 1993). The NPFL received supplies and consignments of armaments through neighbouring Côte d'Ivoire from Burkina Faso, although support from both countries was periodically restrained as a result of diplomatic pressure.

The INPFL initially co-operated with the IGNU, and participated in a 28-member interim national assembly, established in January 1991. In August, however, the INPFL withdrew from the interim government, and its role in the conflict declined; the movement was dissolved in September 1992.

In early 1992 there appeared to be some prospect of a permanent settlement. Roads linking Monrovia and territory under the control of the NPFL were opened, and in April ECOMOG began to deploy troops in NPFL-controlled areas, with the aim of disarming all factions and creating conditions that would allow elections to take place. In May, however, following the execution of six Senegalese soldiers by NPFL forces, ECOMOG withdrew its troops to Monrovia. In late July ECOWAS announced that it would impose economic sanctions on the NPFL if Taylor did not fully comply with the conditions of the Yamoussoukro agreement within 30 days. In August ULIMO attacked the NPFL from Sierra Leone, with considerable success, gaining control of large areas of Lofa and Cape Mount Counties in western Liberia.

In mid-October 1992 the NPFL launched a major offensive against ECOMOG positions in the outskirts of Monrovia, and captured a number of strategic areas, effectively besieging the capital and resulting in the temporary closure of Spriggs Payne airport, the city's principal link with the international community. The NPFL recruited boys, some as young as eight, and executed large numbers of civilians who refused to join its forces.

ECOMOG abandoned its previous peace-keeping stance for a directly combatant role; Nigerian aircraft under ECOMOG command bombed NPFL positions. In late November 1992 the UN security council imposed a mandatory arms embargo on all factions in the conflict (excluding ECOMOG), and authorized the UN secretary-general to send a special envoy to Liberia. The former president of Zimbabwe, Canaan Banana, was appointed as OAU representative. In early January 1993, following a new offensive, ECOMOG forces regained control of the outskirts of Monrovia, and advanced along the coast, capturing the airport at Robertsfield (which was severely damaged and closed to civilian traffic) later that month, the Firestone rubber plantation at Harbel in mid-February, and the principal port of Buchanan in early April.

In early 1993 ULIMO intensified its attacks in western Liberia, gaining control of Cape Mount and Bomi Counties and the greater part of Lofa County. In March ULIMO accepted an invitation to join the IGNU, although its relations with the government and ECOMOG remained uneasy, and in early April ECOMOG disarmed ULIMO forces in Monrovia, in the interests of public safety. (ULIMO had split into two factions, of which one, led by Raleigh Seekie and subsequently by Maj.-Gen. Roosevelt Johnson, principally comprised Krahn and operated from Sierra Leone. The other faction, led by Alhaji G. V. Kromah, was predominantly Islamic and Mandingo, and operated from Guinea.) In June more than 600 refugees were killed by faction members at the Harbel rubber plantation. The IGNU accused the NPFL of perpetrating the massacre. In September 1993, however, a UN investigation concluded that AFL troops were

responsible; a number of AFL units were withdrawn to Monrovia and disarmed.

In July 1993 a peace conference, attended by all factions involved in the hostilities, was convened under the auspices of the UN and ECOWAS in Geneva, Switzerland. After several days of negotiations, the IGNU, the NPFL and ULIMO agreed to a cease-fire (which was to be monitored by UN observers and a reconstituted peace-keeping force), and to the formation of a transitional government. The peace accord was formally signed on 25 July at an ECOWAS summit meeting, held in Cotonou, Benin. The agreement provided for the IGNU to be replaced by a Liberian national transitional government (LNTG), headed by a five-member council of state (which was to include representatives of the factions), pending presidential and legislative elections. In response to demands by Taylor, the dominance of the Nigerian contingent in ECOMOG was to be considerably reduced; the new peace-keeping force was to be supplemented with additional troops from other West African states.

At the end of July 1993 the cease-fire took effect. In early August, however, ECOMOG claimed that the NPFL had violated the peace agreement by repeatedly entering territory under the control of the peace-keeping force. In mid-August the IGNU and the factions reached agreement on the membership of the council of state. However, its inauguration (originally scheduled for 24 August) was to be postponed, pending the disarmament of all warring factions. Subsequent delays in the deployment of UN observers and additional peace-keeping troops resulted in a protracted impasse: Taylor refused to permit the disarmament of NPFL forces prior to the arrival of the additional troops (owing to his scepticism regarding ECOMOG's neutrality) while the IGNU continued to insist that the installation of the transitional authorities take place in conjunction with the disarmament process.

In September 1993 the UN security council approved the establishment of the UN Observer Mission in Liberia (UNOMIL), which was to co-operate with ECOMOG and the OAU in supervising the transitional process. Meanwhile, it was feared that renewed hostilities in several areas of the country would jeopardize the peace accord. A further armed faction, known as the Liberia Peace Council (LPC), comprising members of the Krahn ethnic group, together with a number of disaffected AFL troops, emerged in September 1993, and subsequently entered into conflict with the NPFL in south-eastern Liberia. A large number of civilians fled to Buchanan from Rivercess and Grand Bassa Counties, in response to fighting in the region. The LPC, which was led by Dr George Boley (a prominent member of ULIMO), claimed to be a non-partisan movement established in response to what it claimed to be continued atrocities perpetrated by the NPFL. In December fighting between ULIMO and a newly-formed movement, the Lofa Defence Force (LDF), was also reported in Lofa County, apparently in retaliation against alleged acts of violence committed by ULIMO forces in the region.

In late December 1993 the contingents of additional ECOMOG troops from Tanzania and Uganda began to arrive. At the end of February 1994 the council of state elected David Kpormakpor, a representative of the IGNU, as its chairman. In early March units belonging to UNOMIL and the expanded ECOMOG force were deployed, and the disarmament of all factions commenced. On 7 March the council of state was inaugurated; it was envisaged that the presidential and legislative elections (which were originally scheduled for February) would take place in September. However, the disarmament process was subsequently impeded by an increase in inter-factional fighting; in addition to continuing hostilities involving the LPC and the NPFL, more than 200 people were killed in clashes between members of the two ULIMO factions, particularly in the region of Tubmanburg, north of Monrovia (where the organization was based). The hostilities were prompted by Krahn resentment at the predominance of the Mandingo among ULIMO representatives in the transitional institutions; the factions became entirely divided into two separate militias: ULIMO–K (led by Kromah, a Mandingo) and ULIMO–J (led by Johnson, a Krahn). In May, following continued disputes over its composition, a 19-member cabinet was installed, comprising seven members of the NPFL (which held the disputed portfolios of justice and foreign affairs), seven of ULIMO and five of the IGNU.

In early September 1994 a meeting of the NPFL, the AFL and ULIMO–K was convened, under the aegis of the Ghanaian president, Jerry Rawlings, at Akosombo, Ghana. On 12 September Taylor, Kromah and the AFL chief of staff, Lt-Gen. Hezekiah Bowen, signed a peace accord. This provided for an immediate cessation of hostilities and the establishment later that month of a reconstituted council of state, in which four of the members were to be nominated by the three warring factions, while the remaining member was to be selected by a national conference of prominent civilians; presidential and general elections were rescheduled for October 1995, and the new government was to be installed in January 1996. However, the proposed installation of a predominantly military council of state prompted widespread criticism.

Meanwhile, following clashes between dissident members of the NPFL and troops loyal to Taylor near Gbarnga, the minister of labour, Thomas Woewiyu, claimed that he had replaced Taylor as leader of the NPFL. In mid-September 1994 disaffected members of the AFL, led by a former officer who had served in the Doe administration, Gen. Charles Julu, seized the presidential residence in Monrovia, but were subsequently overpowered by ECOMOG forces. The NPFL dissidents, apparently in alliance with elements of the AFL, ULIMO, the LPC and the LDF, took control of Gbarnga in September 1994; forces loyal to Taylor retreated to the town of Palala, to the east of Gbarnga, while Taylor was said to have taken refuge in Côte d'Ivoire.

In early October 1994 the council of state removed Bowen from the post of AFL chief of staff, on the grounds that he had failed to respond effectively to Julu's coup attempt in September; Bowen, however, refused to relinquish office. In the same month ECOMOG announced a reduction in its peace-keeping forces deployed in Liberia, citing a lack of financial resources and the failure of the international community to assist in the peace process; the UN security council extended the mandate of UNOMIL, but also announced a reduction in personnel (which then numbered 368), in view of the lack of progress achieved. In early November 1994 Ghana reiterated its warning that it would withdraw from ECOMOG if the warring factions failed to reach a peace settlement, while the Nigerian government withdrew military equipment from the peace-keeping force. Later that month a conference, attended by Bowen, Taylor, Woewiyu, Boley and the leader of the LDF, François Massaquoi, together with representatives of the LNTG and a group of civilian politicians, known as the Liberian National Conference (LNC), was convened in the Ghanaian capital, Accra, to discuss preparations for the installation of a reconstituted council of state, in accordance with the Akosombo agreement. However, a subsequent decision, endorsed by ECOWAS, that the AFL nominate a representative in conjunction with the 'Coalition Forces' (an informal alliance comprising the NPFL dissidents, the LPC, the LDF and elements of ULIMO–K) resulted in contention, with both Bowen and Boley claiming a seat in the proposed council of state. Negotiations were adjourned at the end of November, after the participants failed to agree on the composition of the new transitional administration.

In early December 1994 the NPFL regained control of much of the territory, including Gbarnga, that the NPFL dissidents had captured in September. On 22 December, after the peace conference was reconvened in Accra, the participants reached agreement on a cease-fire, which was to enter into force later that month. Additional accords reaffirmed the terms of the Akosombo agreement, including provisions for the establishment of demilitarized zones throughout Liberia and for the installation of a reconstituted council of state; new institutions were to be installed on 1 January 1996, following multi-party elections. Later in December 1994 the Nigerian government reduced its ECOMOG contingent to 6,000 from about 10,000, in accordance with its stated aim gradually to withdraw from Liberia. The cease-fire, which entered into force on 28 December, was widely observed, despite reports of skirmishes between supporters of ULIMO–J, the AFL and the NPFL around Monrovia.

Negotiations on the membership of the council of state, impeded by Taylor's persistent demands that he be granted the chairmanship, continued until early February 1995 when a compromise arrangement was negotiated, whereby Chief Tamba

Tailor, the traditional ruler who had been nominated by ULIMO and the NPFL, would assume the office of chairman, while Charles Taylor and Kromah would become joint vice-chairmen. In the same month reports of renewed hostilities between the NPFL and the LPC in south-eastern Liberia prompted concern that any agreement reached by the armed factions would be undermined. In early March the Tanzania government announced that its ECOMOG contingent (which numbered 800) was to be withdrawn from Liberia by the end of that month.

In April 1995 about 62 civilians were massacred by unidentified armed groups in the town of Yosi, near Buchanan, after hostilities between the NPFL and the LPC resumed in the region; renewed fighting in other parts of Liberia was also reported. At the end of April the withdrawal of the Tanzanian contingent of ECOMOG commenced. In May an ECOWAS summit meeting was convened in Abuja, Nigeria, to discuss the Liberian conflict; however, Charles Taylor failed to attend the meeting, and a number of issues regarding the composition of the council of state remained unresolved. It was subsequently announced that the installation of the council of state was to be postponed until the constituent factions demonstrated commitment to the observance of the cease-fire and to the disarmament process.

In June 1995 clashes took place at the border with Côte d'Ivoire, apparently between LPC and NPFL forces. In July the Guinean government attributed border incursions, in which several people were killed, to NPFL forces. At the end of that month peace negotiations resumed in Monrovia, which, however, Charles Taylor again failed to attend, continuing to demand the position of first vice-president in the new council of state, despite the recommendations of the summit meeting in May that the five members representing the warring factions be granted equal status as joint vice-chairmen. Meanwhile, the UN special representative in Liberia indicated that UNOMIL's mandate (which had progressively been renewed) would be allowed to expire in mid-September unless sufficient progress was achieved in the peace process.

TRANSITIONAL COUNCIL OF STATE

On 19 August 1995, following a further ECOWAS summit meeting (convened at Abuja, Nigeria), the warring factions signed a peace accord providing for the installation of a reconstituted council of state, which was to remain in power for a period of one year, pending elections: an academic with no factional affiliations, Prof. Wilton Sankawulo, was to assume the office of chairman, while the other seats were to be allocated respectively to Charles Taylor, Kromah, Boley, the representative of the LNC, Oscar Quiah and Tamba Tailor. Later that month a cease-fire entered into force, in accordance with the terms of the peace agreement. The new transitional council of state was formally installed on 1 September; at the inauguration ceremony the UN special representative announced that the elections were to take place on 20 August 1996. A new transitional council of ministers, comprising members of the seven factions that had signed the peace agreement, was subsequently formed. Later in September the UN Security Council extended UNOMIL's mandate until the end of January 1996. Reports emerged, however, that clashes between the ULIMO factions had resumed in Lofa County, while the armed factions had failed to commence disarmament in compliance with the peace accord. At the end of September about 65 civilians were killed by NPFL forces in Nimba County.

In October 1995, at an emergency meeting of ECOWAS, the governments of Nigeria, Ghana, Côte d'Ivoire, Burkina Faso and Togo pledged to contribute additional forces to ECOMOG (which then numbered 7,269), to ensure the effective implementation of the peace process. In mid-December the deployment of ECOMOG forces commenced, in accordance with the Abuja peace agreement. Following continued clashes between the ULIMO factions, however, ULIMO–J attacked ECOMOG troops in the region of Tubmanburg. ECOMOG was obliged to suspend deployment of its forces, and launched a counter-offensive in an attempt to restore order. Hostilities continued in early 1996, with large numbers of civilians killed or displaced. At the end of January unidentified forces attacked members of UNOMIL in the region of Tubmanburg. In March the council of state announced the removal of Johnson (who had hitherto held the rural development portfolio) from the cabinet. A number of ULIMO–J forces remained loyal to Johnson, however, and clashes erupted between the two factions. Johnson's troops allegedly killed a supporter of the new leadership, and the council of state subsequently ordered that he be arrested on charges of murder. Johnson, however, refused to surrender to the authorities and became effectively besieged in his private residence in central Monrovia.

In early April 1996 forces representing the new government, led by Charles Taylor and supported by ULIMO–K, launched an offensive against Johnson and his supporters. Members of the LPC and AFL (which were predominantly Krahn) supported Johnson's forces, while the NPFL and ULIMO–K opposed them. Fighting rapidly intensified in central Monrovia, resulting in the displacement of large numbers of civilians, who fled the capital or took refuge in embassy compounds. ECOMOG (which had refrained from military intervention) deployed its forces in the region of Monrovia, with the aim of negotiating between the warring factions; following a lull in the fighting, however, a number of Johnson's supporters staged attacks in the residential area of Mamba Point (where embassies and offices of humanitarian organizations were situated) and seized a number of civilians, including 40 Lebanese nationals and 25 Nigerian members of ECOMOG, as hostages. The US government began to evacuate US citizens and other foreign nationals from the US embassy (where some 20,000 civilians had taken shelter). Johnson's supporters, together with their hostages and several thousand civilians, took refuge in former army barracks, known as the Barclay Training Centre, in Monrovia, where they were surrounded by NPFL and ULIMO–K forces. President Rawlings of Ghana (in his capacity as chairman of ECOWAS) urged Johnson to surrender in exchange for pledges of safe conduct, and appealed to the council of state to suspend military action against him. Following negotiations, with mediation by ECOMOG, the warring factions agreed to a cease-fire; Johnson was to surrender to ECOMOG, pending further negotiations, while the hostages held by his supporters were to be released. Johnson's forces subsequently released 27 Lebanese hostages.

The cease-fire agreement proved unsuccessful, however, and NPFL and ULIMO–K forces launched renewed attacks against the Barclay Training Centre. Further discussions took place between an ECOMOG delegation and Johnson's supporters, who demanded guarantees of protection for members of the Krahn ethnic group as a precondition for surrender. The evacuation of foreign nationals continued, while the US government dispatched warships to the region, with the stated aim of ensuring the protection of US diplomatic staff in Monrovia. Later in April 1996 a further cease-fire agreement was reached under the aegis of the US government, the UN and ECOWAS; under the terms of the accord, ECOMOG troops were subsequently deployed throughout Monrovia, while the majority of the remaining hostages, including the foreign nationals, were released by Johnson's supporters.

In early May 1996 an emergency summit meeting was abandoned, after the heads of state of the majority of member countries failed to attend. Meanwhile, during the absence of Johnson (who had left the country under US protection, to attend the planned summit meeting), the NPFL launched a further attack against the Barclay Training Centre. The resumption of intense fighting prompted further large numbers of civilians to flee to Monrovia Free Port in an attempt to leave the country, attracting international concern. A Nigerian freighter transporting some 4,000 Liberians was refused entry by other West African coastal nations until, following considerable international pressure, the Ghanaian government agreed to accept the refugees. At the end of May the UN Security Council renewed the mandate of UNOMIL for a further three months, but warned the armed factions that international support would be withdrawn if fighting continued; UNOMIL was henceforth to comprise only the five military and 20 civilian personnel remaining in the country following the evacuation of a further 93 observers in April. In early June Johnson's supporters agreed to disarm and to leave the Barclay Training Centre, while an ECOWAS arbitration mission commenced discussions with the faction leaders in an effort to restore the peace process. ECOMOG troops gained control of the Barclay Training Centre, although a number of Johnson's supporters subsequently

refused to leave Monrovia, in contravention of the agreement. Meanwhile, clashes resumed between ULIMO–K and ULIMO–J forces in Grand Cape Mount County.

In August 1996, at an ECOWAS conference in Abuja, the principal faction leaders (apart from Johnson, who remained abroad) signed a further peace agreement. A reconstituted council of state was to be installed by the end of that month, with a former Liberian senator, Ruth Perry, replacing Sankawulo as chairman; Taylor and Boley were to remain members of the new administration. Under a revised timetable, elections were to take place at the end of May 1997, and power was to be transferred to an elected government by mid-June, while the armed factions were to be dissolved by the end of January of that year. In order to implement the new timetable, ECOMOG (which then numbered 8,500) was to be reinforced. Faction leaders who failed to comply with the new agreement would be subject to sanctions, including travel restrictions, the 'freezing' of business assets and exclusion from the elections, while the establishment of a war crimes tribunal was recommended. The mandate of UNOMIL was extended for a further three months to the end of November, and the mission was to be expanded to 34 personnel; the announcement was accompanied by further warnings that the international community would withdraw its representatives from the country if the armed factions failed to demonstrate their commitment to the peace process. In early September Perry was inaugurated as chairman of the council of state.

The implementation of the peace process gained impetus, following the new Abuja accord. Taylor, Boley and Kromah ordered their followers to withdraw from territory under their control, and by late August the removal of some roadblocks had commenced. The cease-fire was generally observed, although skirmishes were reported in various areas, notably between the NPFL and the LPC in south-eastern Liberia and between the two ULIMO factions in the west. Under the terms of the peace agreement, Johnson was reinstated to a reorganized cabinet at the end of September 1996, becoming minister of transport. The reopening of roads allowed humanitarian organizations to resume operations in regions that had previously been inaccessible, and reports of severe famine in Tubmanburg, in western Liberia, attracted international attention; however, activity by faction members continued to prevent free movement in much of the country. The delivery of UN relief supplies to Sinje, in Grand Cape Mount County, inadvertently caused a massacre, with members of one of the two ULIMO factions killing a number of civilians in a raid to steal the food supplies. In early October ECOMOG demanded that ULIMO–J remove its roadblocks from the main highways in western Liberia. ECOMOG troops subsequently encountered no armed resistance when they took control of the region; by the end of the month they had also gained control of the southern port of Greenville. In early November it was announced that ECOMOG was to be reinforced by about 2,300 personnel from several West African states, including Nigeria, Ghana and Mali; Niger and Burkina Faso had pledged contingents for the first time, while Côte d'Ivoire was to dispatch medical personnel. UNOMIL's mandate was extended until the end of March 1997.

On 31 October 1996 the peace process suffered another serious threat, with an apparent assassination attempt against Charles Taylor by unidentified assailants when he arrived at the offices of the council of state. Taylor was unharmed but at least three of his aides were killed. Taylor accused Boley and Johnson of instigating the attack, although they both denied involvement. ECOMOG arrested about 20 people, mainly members of the LPC. Taylor refused to attend subsequent meetings of the council of state, on security grounds, but the incident remained largely inconclusive and did not prove an impediment to the peace process.

The process of disarmament officially recommenced in late November 1996, with ECOMOG deploying troops throughout much of the country, and establishing demilitarized zones to separate the warring factions. Progress was very slow, however; by the end of December the UN reported that about 6,000 of an estimated total of 60,000 rebel forces had been disarmed at the 11 official demobilization points. In January 1997 the national disarmament and demobilization commission revised the estimated number of combatants, to a total of only 23,416. ECOMOG agreed that the estimate of 60,000 (based on claims by faction leaders) was exaggerated and announced that a more realistic number would be 30,000–35,000. Shortly before the end of January (the stipulated date for the completion of disarmament under the terms of the Abuja accord), the number of combatants demobilizing suddenly increased; by the end of that month ECOMOG announced that about 23,000 had been disarmed. The deadline was extended by a further week to allow the process to be completed, and ECOMOG declared that 91% of forces had been disarmed at the end of that period, although final figures were inconsistent. The faction leaders all declared that their movements had been officially dissolved in accordance with the Abuja agreement, and Taylor and Kromah announced the reconstruction of their military organizations into the civilian National Patriotic Party (NPP) and All Liberia Coalition Party respectively.

THE 1997 ELECTIONS

In mid-February 1997 ECOWAS confirmed that voting by proportional representation would take place on 30 May to elect a president and a bicameral parliament, comprising a 64-seat house of representatives and a 26-seat senate. At the end of February, Taylor, Kromah and Boley resigned from the council of state in order to contest the presidential election; they were replaced by nominees from their respective organizations. The office of the UN high commissioner for refugees (UNHCR) drafted a programme for a mass repatriation of refugees, which was to commence in May and continue for 18 months, at a cost of US $60m. The mandate of UNOMIL was again extended, to the end of June.

During a nationwide search for illicit armaments in March and April 1997, ECOMOG discovered two large arms caches at Kromah's residences in Monrovia and Voinjama, as well as two major caches in the NPFL stronghold of Nimba County and smaller quantities of armaments at the residences of Taylor and Boley. Kromah was placed under house arrest and threatened with prosecution and exclusion from the elections but was subsequently released without charge, after issuing a public apology. ECOMOG was progressively reinforced during the first half of 1997, and by May had reached a total strength of about 13,000.

Several political parties which had become inactive during the civil conflict re-emerged and a number of civilian candidates presented their candidacy for the presidency, including the former ministers, Gabriel Baccus Matthews and Togba-Nah Tipoteh. An attempt in late March 1997 by an alliance of seven of the long-standing parties (the LPP, UPP, LAP, TWP, NDPL, LUP and UP) to agree on a single presidential candidate failed when some of the parties rejected a poll which had been won by Cletus Wotorson of the LAP. The selection of a new seven-member independent electoral commission was impeded by disagreements, with Taylor contesting the appointment of the chairman. The body was finally inaugurated in early April, but the delay affected the electoral timetable. By early May it was evident that preparations for the poll were not adequately advanced, and all the parties, apart from Taylor's NPP, demanded a postponement. ECOWAS acted decisively in the dispute, announcing later that month that the first round of voting would be rescheduled for 19 July, with a second round taking place on 2 August if no presidential candidate won more than 50% of votes cast. A total of 13 candidates were to contest the presidential election, including Ellen Johnson-Sirleaf, a political exile from the Doe regime and hitherto a director of the UN development programme. Taylor was generally viewed as the most popular candidate, with a well-organized campaign, financed by profits accrued from unofficial exports and supported by his private radio station (the only one broadcasting nationwide), Kiss FM. Johnson-Sirleaf, who contested the election on behalf of the UP, quickly emerged as his closest rival. A 10-day voter registration census commenced in late June, but was extended by a few days in some areas, owing to adverse weather conditions.

The electoral campaign was conducted peacefully, apart from a few clashes between rival supporters and allegations of a further conspiracy to assassinate Taylor. Voting, which took place on 19 July 1997, was also without serious incident, apart from some logistical difficulties. More than 500 international observers, who monitored the electoral process, declared that no serious irregularities had occurred (although both Johnson-Sirleaf and Kromah complained of malpractice). According to the final results, Taylor secured an outright victory, with 75.3% of the votes cast, while Johnson-Sirleaf obtained 9.6% of the votes; in the legislative elections the NPP won 49 seats in the house of representatives and 21 seats in the senate. Taylor was duly inaugurated as president on 2 August. ECOWAS ended the economic sanctions that had been imposed against Liberia, although the UN armaments embargo remained in force. UNOMIL was dissolved, following the expiry of its final mandate at the end of September 1997, with a small UN peace-building support office remaining in Monrovia. (In 1999 the mandate of the UN office was extended to December 2000.)

TAYLOR IN OFFICE

Taylor made his inaugural speech on 2 August 1997. It emphasized national reconciliation, national unity, human rights and economic restructuring. The new legislature, convened in the same month, subsequently confirmed the 1985 constitution. Although, like the original 1847 constitution, this was based on the constitution of the USA with a division of powers between the executive, legislature and judiciary, in practice, the presidency was pre-eminent. The state was highly centralized: the 13 counties had no independent revenue-raising powers and were governed by county superintendents directly appointed by the president and subject to dismissal by him. Three county superintendents were dismissed by Taylor in early 2000, apparently for voicing opposition to presidential policy. In response to complaints from members of the Grebo ethnic group in Grand Gedeh County who alleged that they had been marginalized by Krahn in the north of the county, the house of representatives approved legislation providing for the establishment of a new county, River Gee, to be created from lower Grand Gedeh. The senate approved the proposal in March 2000.

The legislature has been inactive under Taylor's administration. Many meetings of the house of representatives had to be abandoned as inquorate in 1999. Most new legislation was introduced by the executive; examination of proposed legislation and the government budget often appeared lax. The judiciary remained weakened by inadequate funding and shortages of qualified personnel; in some rural areas the court system was effectively in abeyance during 1999 and a reversion to traditional forms of justice administration was reported in some localities. The judiciary remained subject to political, social and financial pressures limiting its independence. In October 1999 the acting president of the Liberia National Bar Association complained that court decisions were enforced selectively by the executive. However, in January 2000 the courts succeeded in convicting Henric Cassel, a brother-in-law of Taylor, on charges of murder.

In June 2000 the vice-president, Enoch Dogolea, died in Côte d'Ivoire, where he had been taken for medical treatment after becoming ill; he was replaced in late July by a former ambassador, Moses Blah. In early August the government established a commission to investigate the circumstances of Dogolea's death, following rumours that he had been murdered.

Political Parties

Shortly after his election in 1997 Taylor appointed a number of opposition politicians to the government, allegedly as a gesture of reconciliation. Roosevelt Johnson was appointed as minister for rural development. Alhaji Kromah became the chairman of the national commission on reconciliation. Cletus Wotorson, the leader of the LAP, became a presidential advisor in 1997 and defended the executive's legislation on mining and natural resources in 2000. In January 1998 Raleigh Seekie, the founder of ULIMO, was appointed as auditor-general and Larmin Kawai, a prominent member of the LPP, was appointed as minister of transport. Critics interpreted the appointment of opposition figures to the government as an attempt to incorporate and stifle the opposition. Political opposition may have been intimidated by the murder in November 1997 of Samuel Dokie and members of his family subsequent to an order for their arrest issued by the head of the special security service. Dokie was a former ally of Taylor's during the war, but had joined the group of NPFL dissidents, led by Thomas Woewiyu in 1994. In March

1999 the president of the senate, Charles Brumskine, who was considered to be a moderate figure in the NPP, fled the country expressing fears for his personal security. A new political party, the New Democratic Alternative for Liberia Movement, or 'New Deal', was formed in June 1999, and held its first national congress at the end of the year; its offices were ransacked by about 20 members of the security forces in March 2000. Otherwise, party political activity has been limited and this has prompted comment even from within the executive and the ruling party. In April 1998 Taylor urged the opposition to gain more credibility, and in January 1999 Blamo Nelson, Taylor's chief of cabinet, complained that the opposition parties had no strength. At the first UPP convention since the elections in December 1999, Gabriel Baccus Matthews resigned from the chairmanship of the party after 13 years. His successor, Wesley Johnson, pledged to co-operate with the government. The strongest political opposition to Taylor's policies has come from within the NPP itself; in February 2000 delegates to the NPP convention complained that high-level corruption was responsible for the country's lack of progress. In the same month complaints emerged from a number of quarters that Taylor was replacing qualified government personnel with NPP supporters. Taylor subsequently denied that Liberia was becoming a one-party state.

In April 1999 it was announced that nationwide municipal and chieftaincy elections were to be postponed indefinitely owing to lack of funds; nevertheless, in mid-May some such elections were conducted in Margibi, Nimba and Grand Bassa Counties, together with by-elections for the senate and house of representatives. It was reported that voter registration for the elections was low, partly as a result of poor levels of education. In the meantime, the elective positions were held by presidential nominees.

The Press

Despite the constitution, numerous incidents of harassment of journalists and editors by members of the government, the judiciary and the security forces have been reported since Taylor assumed office. Attempts were made to close down Radio Veritas, which was operated by the Catholic Archdiocese, in December 1997, and the independent Star Radio was shut down for several weeks in January 1998. In October of that year Star Radio's short-wave service was suspended on government orders, effectively confining its broadcasts to the Greater Monrovia area. In March 2000 Radio Veritas and Star Radio were forcibly closed down by the government; Radio Veritas was allowed to resume broadcasts later that month. Broadcasts of Star Radio remained suspended at mid-2000, despite an official protest by the US government.

Staff of local human rights organizations and churches have also been subject to harassment and arbitrary arrest. In 1998 Koffi Woods, the director of the Catholic Justice and Peace Commission, left the country for several weeks, citing concern for his personal security. In December 1999 James Torh, the head of a children's rights group, was arrested and charged with sedition, apparently after implying that Liberia was governed by criminals in an address at a Monrovia high school. The arrest attracted international condemnation. In February 2000 a Catholic priest, Father Boniface Tye, was arrested and charged with seditious libel, after having allegedly referred to Taylor as a former rebel and his administration as a rebel government.

ECOMOG and Army Restructuring

Relations between Taylor and ECOMOG remained poor until the redeployment of most of ECOMOG's forces to Sierra Leone in late 1998. Two issues caused continual disputes: Taylor's refusal to allow ECOMOG to restructure the AFL in accordance with the Abuja-I and II Accords, and strong suspicions of Taylor's continuing support for the RUF in Sierra Leone. Taylor early expressed his view that the restructuring of the armed forces was a matter for the elected government, while ECOMOG's field commander, Gen. Victor Malu, voiced concern that the government would not construct a neutral and ethnically-balanced army. ECOMOG's concerns were reiterated by Roosevelt Johnson, who claimed that Taylor was recruiting his own supporters for the armed forces. In November 1997 ECOMOG threatened to withdraw from Liberia over the issue; Taylor, for

his part, demanded that ECOWAS replace Malu. A compromise was reached early in 1998 under which ECOMOG remained in Liberia and was to assist in the training of security forces, but Taylor continued with his insistence that the restructuring of the AFL and other security forces be carried out by the government. Malu was replaced by Gen. Timothy Shelpidi. In December 1998 a commission, headed by Taylor's chief of cabinet, recommended that the AFL should be reduced in size from its then strength of 15,000 to 6,000. Taylor's plans for restructuring the AFL finally emerged in February 2000. They were largely concerned with management issues but observers expected that Krahn representation in the military would be reduced. Implementation of the programme commenced in May 2000. Tension over Taylor's role in Sierra Leone also increased soon after the 1997 elections when Taylor insisted that his own security forces, rather than ECOMOG troops, be deployed at the border with Sierra Leone. Shelpidi later stated that NPFL combatants had been deployed at the border area, as members of the armed forces had been transferred to Sierra Leone to assist the Revolutionary United Front (RUF), in exchange for diamonds. However, the issue did not become prominent until after the upsurge in RUF attacks in Sierra Leone after October 1998, by which time most of the ECOMOG forces in Liberia had been redeployed to Sierra Leone (see below).

By late 1998 only about 2,000 Nigerian and Ghanaian troops belonging to the ECOMOG contingent remained in Monrovia, and in January 1999 it was announced that most of these remaining troops were to be relocated to Sierra Leone. A small number of ECOMOG troops remained in the country in mid-1999 to supervise a programme for the destruction of armaments surrendered by the armed factions. In late July Taylor presided at the public burning of weapons in Monrovia; it was intended that this ceremony should symbolize the end of hostilities. Following the completion of the armaments destruction process in October 1999, the remaining ECOMOG troops left, thus bringing a final end to the ECOMOG presence in Liberia.

Following the ending of the civil conflict, inadequate measures to demobilize and reintegrate large numbers of former combatants has precipitated unrest. In May 1998 two uprisings took place at the AFL's Barclay Training Centre, apparently as a result of discontent about arrangements for demobilization and retirement; at least two people were killed. Former combatants demonstrated outside the UN Peace Building Office in Monrovia in July 1999, demanding resettlement benefits from the international community. Soon afterwards about 100 armed former combatants ransacked the house of Commany Wesseh, the director of the Centre for Democratic Empowerment, alleging that his comments on a radio broadcast would obstruct international aid to them. The UN resident representative in Liberia announced an emergency aid package for some 20,000 registered former combatants in late 1999. In December 1999 it was reported that some 5,000 former combatants had found employment in the security forces, but that 10,000, including many amputees, had still not been resettled. In February 2000 armed former combatants attacked the offices of Freedom Gold in Sinoe County, alleging that it was mining a gold deposit that they had discovered. In March 2000 former combatants staged another demonstration in Monrovia to demand the removal of the leadership of their organization, whom they accused of misappropriating funds; the organization's offices were seized and an interim leadership installed.

National Security

Taylor reappointed his cousin, Joe Tate, as police director in 1997. Tate had been accused by the US government of directing and participating in the looting of Monrovia during the 1996 fighting and was subsequently removed from his post at the insistence of the international community. The US government cancelled its programme of aid to the Liberian security forces in protest at Tate's reappointment and in April 1998 demanded his removal. Tate was killed in an air crash in August 1999; his successor, Paul Mulbah, has, according to the US Department of State, made greater efforts to curb abuses of human rights by the security forces during his tenure of the police directorship.

Security agencies have proliferated under Taylor's administration, and had increased to eight by the end of 1999. A National Bureau of Investigation (NBI) was established in that year, despite some opposition from the legislature. In addition, almost every large organization, including government ministries, parastatals and private businesses, and some prominent individuals, now employ private security forces. Reports of harassment by 'security forces', often unidentified, have been frequent and continuous during Taylor's administration. In October 1999 three officers belonging to one of the security agencies were placed under investigation, following allegations of torture made by a Ghanaian national. In the same month the Grand Bassa county superintendent reported persistent complaints of torture and illegal detention by security forces in the county. In December the local chairman of the NPP in Grand Gedeh County reported that harassment and looting by security forces had prompted some residents to abandon their farms and others to flee towns; there were similar reports from Lower Lofa.

In August 1997 Taylor accused Kromah of reassembling elements of ULIMO–K across the border, with the ultimate aim of destabilizing the government in Monrovia. Kromah denied the accusations and, in a gesture demonstrating an apparent acceptance of his denials, he was appointed to head the country's national reconciliation commission in December. Further tensions erupted in Monrovia in March 1998 when Roosevelt Johnson accused Taylor's security agents of arresting and assaulting his bodyguards and claimed that his own life was under threat. Government officials met Johnson to ease tension, but he was subsequently removed from the cabinet, and appointed ambassador to India. Johnson subsequently refused to accept the post and left Liberia, supposedly for medical treatment. Also in March 1998, Kromah, who, like Johnson, had expressed fears for his own safety, was removed from his position as head of the reconciliation commission and was replaced by a prominent member of the NPP. Kromah, too, left the country. In August 1998 Johnson's unexpected return to Liberia precipitated major disturbances. In September security forces attempted to capture Johnson and staged an offensive against his residence and base. Unofficial reports indicated that about 300 people (mainly Krahn) had been killed in the ensuing fighting and in summary executions carried out by Taylor's forces. The Liberian government stated that about 53 people had been killed. After clashes with Taylor's forces, Johnson and about 23 of his supporters succeeded in taking refuge in the US embassy compound. Taylor's men pursued him into the compound and two US security guards were injured in the ensuing fracas. The government demanded that US embassy officials surrender Johnson to the Liberian authorities. After discussions between the US embassy and the Liberian government, however, Johnson was allowed to leave the country for Sierra Leone. In October 32 civilians (several, including Johnson and Kromah, *in absentia*) were charged with treason; of these, 19 were arrested and their trial began in November. Nine AFL officers, all Krahn, were also arrested, and were accused of collaborating to overthrow the government and were charged with sedition. In early December the government abandoned proceedings against five of the civilians on trial for treason who had turned state witness. In April 1999 13 of the civilian defendants, all of them Krahn, were each sentenced to 10 years' imprisonment. Appeals for clemency addressed to the president by elders in Grand Gedeh County in December met with no response. The sedition trial continued until February 2000; four of the nine soldiers were then convicted and were each sentenced to 10 years' imprisonment with hard labour.

There were two serious security incidents in 1999. In April an unidentified force of about 20 armed militia attacked the town of Voinjama, in Lofa County. Members of a UN assessment mission, including a European diplomat, who were in the region at the time were briefly taken hostage. AFL troops rapidly regained control of the town. Taylor blamed the Guinean government for the attack and made a formal protest; Guinea denied, however, that the attack had been staged from Guinean territory and any other involvement. The incident prompted some 6,000 Liberians in the area to flee to Guinea.

The second incident, which took place in August 1999, was much more serious. An initially unidentified group, later named as the Joint Forces for the Liberation of Liberia (JFLL), captured five towns in Foya and Kolahun districts of Lofa. Taylor announced the attack and ordered the imposition of a state of emergency in upper Lofa County in early August. The JFLL seized about 50 international aid staff, including six expatriates and about 50 of their dependants. Government forces largely regained control of the area later that month, and all of the hostages were freed by mid-August, although sporadic fighting continued into October. There was speculation that the JFLL comprised former members of ULIMO–K, although Taylor reported that Alhaji Kromah had dissociated himself from the attack. Taylor once again accused Guinea of providing shelter to Liberian dissidents and closed the Liberia-Guinea border. (Guinea once again denied the charge.) The fighting prompted the exodus of some 25,000 civilians. In addition, about 10,000 Sierra Leonean refugees in the area fled south and were eventually relocated to the Sinje refugee camp in Grand Cape Mount County.

In September 2000 it was reported that more than 13,000 civilians had been displaced in Lofa County, following protracted fighting (which had commenced in July) between government forces and unidentified rebels; Liberia again accused the Guinean government of supporting the dissidents. Early in September Taylor suspended from office the minister of defence, Daniel Chea, after it emerged that the efforts of government troops to suppress rebel activity had been impeded by severe food shortages and logistical difficulties.

Domestic Unrest

Ethnic tensions have clearly subsided since the early years of the civil conflict. Nevertheless, Krahn and the predominantly Muslim Mandingo have continued to encounter substantial hostility. Some 18,000 Krahn fled to Côte d'Ivoire following the attack in September 1998 on Roosevelt Johnson's base in Monrovia, alleging that they had been targeted by security forces. Tensions rose in Lofa, Bong and Nimba Counties as Mandingo refugees returning at the end of the war discovered their residences to be occupied by squatters. Conflicts over traditional shrines between the Mandingo and Lorma ethnic groups erupted in Lofa County in December 1998. In February 1999 Mandingoes in Nimba County complained that they were being harassed by local residents and that they were being prevented from mining. In September an allegedly ethnically-motivated massacre in which up to 25 Mandingo were killed occurred at Nikibozou in Lofa County. A number of peace initiatives by local groups and the Inter-Faith Mediation Committee during 1998 and 1999 attempted to secure a reconciliation between the groups concerned throughout these conflicts. In February 2000 a previously unknown Jihad Movement urged Muslims to resign from government posts in protest at mosque burnings in Lofa. A few days later, police ransacked the home of the leader of the movement, Lartin Konneh, and Konneh himself disappeared. A warrant was subsequently issued for his arrest on charges of treason.

The other principal cause of domestic unrest during Taylor's administration has been the Liberian school system; the main issue has been the non-payment of salaries due to teachers. Teachers have threatened strike action, boycotted their classes, withheld examination results and demonstrated, sometimes with the active support of their students, in an attempt to force the payment of salary arrears and over other grievances. A strike by teachers in the Monrovia consolidated school system in December 1999 was only ended after presidential intervention. Strike action by teachers in Nimba County precipitated a riot in early 2000. In January 2000 the authorities at the University of Liberia announced its closure until September, owing to lack of funding. Taylor warned the students, many of whom are former combatants, against violence. A few days later he announced that the Oriental Timber Company (see Economy, below) had agreed to spend US $2m. on renovating the campus and to donate one-half of its profits to the University; Libya also agreed to assist the University financially. The unrest subsequently subsided.

INTERNATIONAL RELATIONS

Taylor remained critical of ECOWAS policy towards Sierra Leone in the first months of his administration. In October 1997 Taylor criticized ECOMOG's use of military force in its efforts to reinstate the elected Sierra Leonean president, Ahmad Tejan Kabbah. Liberia announced that ECOMOG would no longer be permitted to launch aerial attacks from Liberian territory against the junta in Freetown. The junta included members of the RUF, which Taylor's NPFL had covertly supported from the early 1990s (see chapter on Sierra Leone). ECOMOG ousted the junta, following a major offensive in February 1998, and shortly afterwards accused Liberia of training remnants of the former regime's forces for a counter-attack; the Liberian government denied the charge. Since the reinstatement of President Kabbah in March 1998, Liberia's relations with Sierra Leone and its rebels have, on the surface, conformed with ECOWAS policy, but the international community has made increasingly strong accusations that Taylor has continued to support the RUF covertly. In July 1998 Liberia attended a mini-summit, under Nigerian auspices, of ECOWAS, Sierra Leone and the UN secretary-general in Abuja; Taylor welcomed the deployment of ECOMOG observers along the Liberia-Sierra Leone border, and agreed with Sierra Leone to seek ways of controlling the activities of former combatants. In late December 1998 Liberia closed its border with Sierra Leone in response to the escalation in civil conflict caused by the RUF offensive against the Sierra Leonean capital, Freetown. Taylor pledged his support to Kabbah but the ECOMOG commander, Gen. Shelpidi, by this time based in Sierra Leone, accused Liberia of contravening the UN arms embargo on Sierra Leone, by supplying armaments to the RUF, in exchange for diamonds. The governments of the USA, the United Kingdom and Ghana made similar statements and accusations in January 1999. In February Sierra Leone accused Liberia of allowing RUF training camps on its territory, and in March ECOMOG charged Taylor with permitting armaments from Burkina Faso to reach the Sierra Leonean rebels via Liberian territory. Taylor denied the accusations, admitting only that some Liberian nationals might be operating as mercenaries in Sierra Leone (a response which Shelpidi rejected). Taylor signed the July 1999 Lomé Agreement, under which Foday Sankoh, the RUF leader, joined the government of Sierra Leone as vice-president and chairman of the commission for the management of strategic resources. Taylor hosted meetings, described as 'reconciliatory', between Sankoh and Johnny Paul Koroma, the head of the Sierra Leone Armed Forces Ruling Council, in late September. A mini-summit between Taylor, President Kabbah of Sierra Leone, and the Guinean President, Lansana Conté, was hosted by President Obasanjo of Nigeria under ECOWAS auspices in the same month. Taylor, Kabbah and Conté agreed to establish a joint border team and exchange information on political dissidents in the context of a reactivated Mano River Union. In response to a Liberian statement made in October that dissidents were training in southern Sierra Leone, Kabbah promised to conduct a 'census' of Liberians in the area. The main road route across the Liberia–Sierra Leone border was reopened in the same month after a 10-month closure. Measures to establish a joint Mano River Union security committee to supervise a joint security patrol of Liberia's borders with Sierra Leone and Guinea were reported to be underway in February 2000. Meanwhile, in December 1999 it was reported that Sam Bockarie, the RUF field commander, was refusing to disarm and was no longer taking orders from Sankoh; Taylor offered to mediate the dispute and it was agreed that Bockarie would stay in Liberia until the disarmament process was completed.

The collapse of the Lomé Agreement brought about by the RUF attacks on peace-keepers of the UN Mission in Sierra Leone (UNAMSIL) in late April and early May 2000 once again raised questions over Taylor's role in the Sierra Leone conflict (see chapter on Sierra Leone). The UN secretary-general appealed for action to halt reported rebel movements into Sierra Leone from Guinea and Liberia. Press reports suggested that Taylor was training RUF fighters under the control of Bockarie. Simultaneously, ECOWAS mandated Taylor to ensure that the RUF complied with the Lomé Agreement and Taylor assisted in negotiating the release of UNAMSIL hostages held by the RUF. Liberia alleged that Liberian dissidents were fighting, together with pro-government forces in Sierra Leone and were a danger to Liberia's security, and denounced the decision to place the captured Sankoh on trial as 'stupidity'. In June the British government once more referred to links between the

RUF and 'supporters in Liberia' and called for a UN boycott of uncertificated diamonds from Sierra Leone. In early July the UN Security Council adopted a resolution prohibiting the international sale of diamonds originating with the RUF, and demanding that the Liberian government (which continued to act as a transit point for many RUF diamonds) comply with the ban. In August four journalists (including two British nationals), who had been preparing a television documentary on the Liberian government, were arrested in Monrovia on charges of espionage. Later that month, however, they were released without being charged, following international criticism of their detention.

Taylor's concern over persistent reports of activity by Liberian dissidents in Guinea, possibly including former members of ULIMO–K, continued to adversely affect Liberia's relations with its northern neighbour. In February 1999 Taylor reiterated claims that the Guinean government was providing support to Liberian dissidents, and Taylor submitted a formal protest to the Guinean government after the attack on Voinjama in April. Guinea denied that the offensive had been staged from its territory. During the attack on Lofa by the JFLL in August the charges of Guinean involvement were repeated and again denied. The Liberian border with Guinea was closed. In September Guinea accused Liberia of invading border villages in Guinea. The ECOWAS mini-summit between Taylor, Conté and Kabbah of Sierra Leone, held in an attempt to resolve these issues, has been mentioned above. Liberia accepted that no regular Guinean armed forces had been involved in attacks on Liberian territory. Liberia reopened its side of the Guinea–Liberian border in February 2000, but the Guinean authorities kept their side closed.

The December 1999 coup in Côte d'Ivoire has had little impact on relations between Liberia and Côte d'Ivoire. Shortly after his inauguration in 1997, Taylor reaffirmed diplomatic recognition for Taiwan, which had, according to some reports, contributed funds to Taylor's electoral campaign and which publicly pledged large amounts of financial assistance for Liberia. The People's Republic of China subsequently severed links with Monrovia and closed the Liberian consulate in Hong Kong. After Taylor's return from another visit to Taiwan in February 2000 there was speculation that relations between Taiwan and Liberia were less cordial, especially in view of Liberia's continuing non-voting status at the UN due to its unpaid debts to the organization. Taylor's relations with Libya, which dated back to 1987, were reaffirmed by Taylor's visit to the country in October 1997, when the Libyan leader, Col Muammar al-Qaddafi, welcomed Taylor's 'revolutionary' role in Africa. Taylor made a further visit in September 1999. Libya has responded by funding substantial aid projects in Liberia, and in May 2000 Libya also dispatched helicopters and medical personnel to assist in the evacuation of wounded UNAMSIL peace-keepers from Sierra Leone.

Taylor's links with Libya have impeded Liberian relations with the USA. However, the incursion of Liberian security forces pursuing Roosevelt Johnson into the US embassy compound in August 1998 had the greatest adverse impact. The US government temporarily closed the embassy, and deployed a naval vessel near the Liberian coast. The US chargé d'affaires demanded that the Liberian authorities initiate an investigation into the incident and formally apologize. In November this apology was finally made, and it was subsequently announced that an investigation would be conducted into the incident in co-operation with the UN. US relations with Liberia were subsequently declared to be gradually improving by local US diplomats.

Taylor's administration bears many similarities to those of Tubman and Tolbert. There is the same outward show of a commitment to the rule of law and to democratic norms and practices, symbolized by the Liberian constitution and the close connection to the USA which it represents. Behind this lies the reality of a powerful presidency, an ineffective opposition, a vocal but weak civil society, and a sustained record of human rights abuses. Liberia's recent international relations are markedly different from those of the Tubman and Tolbert eras, however. While Tubman and Tolbert, with the assistance of the

USA, successfully insulated Liberia from the political instability affecting neighbouring countries during the decolonization period and after, in recent years Liberia has been a major source

of instability in the region. In fact, a lasting peace in the region seems inconceivable without substantial changes in the Liberian polity.

Economy

QUENTIN OUTRAM

The Liberian economy has, historically, presented a strong contrast between a traditional, low-productivity, subsistence agriculture sector, in which poverty was endemic, and a modern, monetized, largely foreign-owned export-orientated sector. The modern sector provided revenues to the state and allowed its leaders and functionaries to enjoy relatively high standards of living. Although the export sector has nineteenth-century origins, its real beginning can be dated to the start of production at the Firestone rubber plantation in 1926. Iron ore exports commenced in the 1950s, and from the 1960s iron ore was Liberia's most valuable export. In the late 1970s and 1980s crises in the world economy caused economic stagnation and political upheaval for Liberia.

During 1984–86, according to UN estimates, Liberia's gross domestic product (GDP) declined, in real terms, at an average annual rate of 1.6%. In 1987–89 GDP increased by an average of 2.8% per year. The subsequent civil conflict devastated the economy during the 1990s. Agricultural activity was abandoned as civilians fled regions of conflict; infrastructure and major capital assets were looted and destroyed. According to recent IMF estimates, in 1990 real GDP collapsed to 35% of the level in 1987. In early 1992 some economic activity resumed in the territory controlled by the rebel forces of the National Patriotic Front of Liberia (NPFL), led by Charles Taylor. Nevertheless, the decline in agricultural output, the collapse of the iron ore industry and the cessation of most private and public services resulted in continuing falls in real GDP. IMF estimates indicated that in 1994 real GDP may have fallen to as low as 10% of the level in 1987, and continued at that level in 1995 and 1996. Some economic recovery followed presidential and legislative elections in 1997, but continuing instability impeded fundamental changes to the Liberian economy. Agricultural activity continued to provide a subsistence living for the majority of the population. Exports of primary commodities to the international market have once again become of the greatest importance in the modern sector, but, following the civil conflict, while rubber remained significant, the sector was increasingly dominated by logging, diamonds and gold.

AGRICULTURE

Agriculture (including forestry and fishing) accounted for more than 70% of the labour force in the 1980s, and contributed 36.7% of the country's GDP in 1989. The main cash crop was rubber; small quantities of coffee and cocoa were also produced. The principal food crops were, and continue to be, rice and cassava (manioc), and these crops, together with palm oil and some fish or meat, form the basis of the national diet. The civil conflict particularly affected rural areas, prompting much of the population employed in the sector to take refuge in neighbouring states, or in the capital, Monrovia. Consequently, agricultural production fell dramatically during the conflict, to less than one-half of the level of 1989 (according to the FAO). Production of cereals (almost exclusively rice) was particularly adversely affected, collapsing to less than one-fifth of the 1989 level by 1994.

Paddy rice production averaged more than 290,000 metric tons per year in the late 1980s; there were also substantial imports of rice, averaging 96,000 tons annually during the same period, largely to satisfy urban markets. Following the outbreak of war, production of paddy rice was estimated to have declined to as low as 50,000 tons in 1994, and much of the population became dependent on emergency relief grain. The UN World Food Programme (WFP), which was responsible for most of the food aid to Liberia during this period, provided well over 100,000 tons of food annually to Liberia throughout the war. Distribution

of relief outside the ECOMOG 'safe haven' around Monrovia was frequently interrupted by the activities of the armed factions and there were intermittent reports of starvation among civilians. Food shortages were also reported in Monrovia, especially during major refugee influxes and during the 1996 fighting in the capital. Nevertheless, the relative calm in rural areas brought about by the Abuja I peace accord allowed rice production to increase to some 95,000 tons in 1996 (equivalent to about 30% of pre-war output). With the end of the fighting, and the return of refugees and displaced civilians, rice production recovered to about 170,000 tons in 1997, to 210,000 tons in 1998, and to a projected 255,000 tons in 1999 (equivalent to 70% and 85% of pre-war output, respectively). Production in 1999 was adversely affected by insecurity in Lofa County, where fighting broke out during the growing season, and was limited by poor road conditions in the south-east of the country. Nevertheless, the large numbers of refugees and displaced civilians in Liberia, Sierra Leone, Guinea, Côte d'Ivoire and Ghana continued to be dependent on food aid and almost 70,000 tons of food aid was provided to this region by the WFP in 1998 and 1999. In 2000 the WFP appealed for some 55,000 tons for the same purposes. Food aid to Liberia from the USA continued throughout 1999, both in the form of contributions to WFP programmes, and in the form of contributions to Food for Work, Food for Education and other programmes designed to assist post-war rehabilitation.

Production of cassava increased rapidly in the late 1980s, from 280,000 metric tons in 1985 to 446,000 tons in 1989. Since cassava requires less consistent attention than rice and the tubers can be left in the ground for some time after they are ready for harvest, production of cassava was not as badly disrupted by the civil conflict. During the conflict production declined to a low of 175,000 tons in 1995, according to FAO estimates. Recovery from the war is now regarded by the FAO as practically complete, as far as cassava is concerned, with production running at an estimated 313,000 tons in 1999. Rice and cassava production have benefited from the distribution of seeds and tools by UN agencies and non-governmental organizations. After these distributions were first co-ordinated in 1995, the number of beneficiaries increased from 64,000 in 1995 to 134,000 in 1998, before declining to 75,000 in 1999, as needs diminished.

The pre-war rubber sector was divided about equally in terms of land area between a domestically-owned sector, comprising both smallholders and commercially-operated plantations, and a small number of large foreign-owned concessions. Employment in rubber production was about 15,000 in the concession sector and perhaps 28,000 in the domestically-owned sector, and accounted for about 15% of total employment in the economy. Crude rubber and latex, together, were Liberia's second-largest export earner in the 1980s, generating US $110m. in 1988 (28% of total export earnings). The concessions produced about 70% of total annual production, which stood at around 100,000 metric tons in the late 1980s. The largest of the concessions, Firestone, had long been Liberia's largest private-sector employer, with about 7,000 employees at its 53,000-ha Harbel plantation east of Monrovia before the war. Firestone sold its Liberian interests to the Japanese tyre company Bridgestone in 1988, and the company is now known as Bridgestone/Firestone; Firestone Polymers continues to be responsible for local management of the plantation. There are now two other foreign-owned plantations, owned respectively by the Liberian Agricultural Co (LAC) and Kumpulan Guthrie. Prominent among the domestically-owned plantations are the Salala Rubber Corporation, formerly owned by a Dutch-German company, employing at least 500 workers in late 1997, and the Cavalla Rubber Corporation plantation in Maryland County, formerly owned by Firestone, employing more than 1,200 in late 1998.

Production at the Firestone plantation was suspended in 1990, as its employees fled. Following an agreement with the alternative administration of Charles Taylor, Firestone resumed operations in February 1992, but was severely disrupted little more than one year later by the capture of Harbel and Buchanan from the NPFL by ECOMOG (see Recent History). Over-tapping by illegal producers and the cutting down of trees for firewood and charcoal damaged up to one-half of the plantation during the war. The plantation was reactivated in mid-1997, with a labour force of 2,000, rising to 3,000 by March 1998, and to 4,000 by March 2000. It achieved output equal to 40% of capacity in February 1998 and 65% by September 1999, and was expected to process about 25,000–30,000 metric tons of dry-weight latex in 1999. Production was adversely affected by a labour strike, however, commencing in June 1998, in support of demands for a 37% pay increase, followed by another in September over allegedly unfair labour practices. The capacity of the Firestone Agricultural Workers' Union to pursue its demands was weakened by leadership disputes during 1999 and 2000.

The LAC plantation comprises 10,500 ha east of Buchanan, in Grand Bassa County, and employed 3,000 people before the war. In April 1990 the plantation was occupied by the NPFL, who looted vehicles, slaughtered the livestock raised by the company to help feed its labour force, and demanded fuel, food and other supplies. Expatriate staff returned to resume operations in the following month, and by August it was operating at about 50% capacity. At one time owned by the US rubber company Uniroyal, 75% of the plantation's share capital has been purchased by a Luxembourg-registered affiliate of Société Financière des Caoutchoucs Luxembourg (SOCFINAL). SOCFINAL planned to rehabilitate the plantation with a US $7m.-programme to reconstruct the factory, workers' camps, roads and bridges and to extend the plantation by 2,500 ha. It sought a $3.5m.-loan from the International Finance Corporation, the World Bank's private-sector lending affiliate, in support of the project. Rehabilitation began in February 2000 with the employment of 26 workers, increasing to 275 shortly afterwards. The Kumpulan Guthrie plantation is 8,000 ha north of Monrovia, in Bomi County. ULIMO–J fighters organized illegal tapping on the plantation, sometimes using forced labour. Its new Malaysian owners announced plans to rehabilitate the plantation in early 1998.

The civil conflict resulted in severe disruption of production in the rubber sector as a whole. According to data produced by the International Rubber Study Group, output fell to 10,000 metric tons in 1994. Post-war recovery was initially fairly rapid, with output estimated at 49,000 tons in 1997, but growth has since slowed in view of local production difficulties and the 1998 Asian economic crisis. The Asian crisis precipitated a fall in buying prices in Liberia of nearly 50%. Quality controls imposed in November 1998 by Firestone, which acted as a buyer and processor for the smallholder sector, as well as a direct producer, also contributed to the difficulties faced by smallholders. The minister of finance, Elie Saleeby, admitted in January 1999 that market conditions might prevent the full rehabilitation of Liberia's rubber sector. Investment in the sector was undermined by the collapse into receivership in early 2000 of the natural rubber traders Lewis & Peat, which had made long-term investments in the Liberian rubber industry. USAID announced in November 1999 a US $3.5m. programme to aid the Liberian rubber sector, which was to be implemented in collaboration with Firestone. A promise of assistance from Libya to establish a rubber-processing plant in Liberia was announced in May 2000.

Another important plantation product is palm nuts, from which, according to FAO estimates, some 42,000 metric tons of palm oil were produced in 1999. In addition to some 1,620 ha of smaller plantations (mainly in the Kakata area), there is a large estate at New Cess, near Buchanan in Grand Bassa County, with some 2,940 ha under cultivation; before the civil conflict the estate was operated by the Liberia Industrial Corpn (LIBINC). Another large estate, of some 1,860 ha at Wangakor, near Robertsport in Grand Cape Mount County, belonging to the Liberian-owned West African Agricultural Corporation

(WAAC), started production in 1972. In south-eastern Liberia the Liberian Palm Products Corporation (LPPC), a subsidiary of the Liberian Produce Marketing Company (LPMC), has been developing two larger programmes at Buto, near Juarzon in Sinoe County (3,040 ha), and at Dube in Grand Gedeh County (4,050 ha), with technical assistance from SODEPALM of Côte d'Ivoire.

Coffee production is centred in northern Liberia, between Voinjama and Kolahun, where mainly *Coffea robusta* is cultivated. Prior to the outbreak of the civil conflict, production was fairly stable, totalling 8,000–10,000 metric tons per year, of which about one-half was consumed locally. The total declined to an average of 3,000 tons per year during the war, according to FAO estimates, and there has been little sign of any substantial recovery, not least because of the continuing insecurity in the area. Cocoa was introduced into Maryland County from Equatorial Guinea, but an attempt to develop a cocoa plantation near Ganta in Nimba County ended in failure. Production during the civil conflict declined to negligible levels and has not recovered.

Problems have also occurred at the Liberia Sugar Corporation plantation at Barrake in Maryland County. By 1980 an area of 600 ha had been cultivated with sugar cane, but the original Taiwanese management withdrew after Liberia recognized the People's Republic of China. In January 1983 Chinese advisers arrived to assist in the management and rehabilitation of the plantation. By 1987, however, the plantation was in need of further rehabilitation, and Cuba agreed to provide the necessary assistance. An average annual production of 220,000 metric tons was recorded in 1989–91.

FAO estimates indicated that there were some 210,000 sheep, 220,000 goats, 120,000 pigs and 36,000 head of cattle in Liberia in 1999. In the same year, the FAO estimated that the country produced some 18,000 metric tons of meat, of which about one-third was game meat (still a significant source of protein in rural areas).

NATURAL RESOURCES

Fish production increased from 1,180 metric tons in 1960 to 18,731 tons in 1987, of which marine fish comprised three-quarters. Sea fishing was adversely affected by the war, inland fishing less so. The 1997 catch totalled only 8,580 tons, according to FAO estimates, divided almost equally between the marine and freshwater catches.

Liberia has substantial forest and mineral resources. Historically, the Liberian state has regulated the country's forest and mineral resources under separate arrangements administered by separate authorities. During the period of the war economy, however, these differences disappeared as the factions sought to exploit whatever resources were under their control, and in 1999–2000 the Taylor administration introduced important new legislation affecting the exploitation of all of Liberia's natural resources. In the pre-war period forestry development was the responsibility of the Forestry Development Authority (FDA), whereas mineral resources were the responsibility of the ministry of lands and mines. Academic studies of the mining sector conducted in the 1960s and 1970s queried the developmental efficacy of the state's management of the sector, and in 1987 a USAID study also questioned the capacity of the government to manage and conserve its forest resources. Taylor's new administration initially focused its attention on the mineral sector. In June 1997 the transitional government signed an extensive mineral exploration agreement with South Africa's Amalia Gold Mining and Exploration Ltd, which was endorsed by Taylor's government after the elections later that year. All of Liberia's unallocated mineral rights were assigned to a new body, the Liberia Resources Corporation (LIBERESCO), of which 60% was owned by the government and 40% by a subsidiary of Amalia, Holistic Resources. These plans were thrown into confusion in March 1998, however, when Amalia suspended its shares on the Johannesburg stock exchange amidst accusations of malpractice and was shortly afterwards placed under liquidation by one of its creditors. In June the Liberian government announced that it had cancelled its agreement with Amalia.

During the first two years of Taylor's administration there were few developments affecting the forestry sector. In 1999–2000, however, a number of changes were announced, some with the aim of appeasing the international community and resulting in the disbursement of aid, and some which have had the effect of delivering much of Liberia's natural resources into the personal control of the presidency. Taylor inaugurated the National Environmental Commission of Liberia in 1999, with funding partly provided by the UN Development Programme (UNDP) and a remit of environmental protection, nature conservation and the sustainable management of Liberia's natural resources. The Commission has yet to have a discernible impact on the logging industry. The Liberian legislature ratified the UN convention on biological diversity in late 1999 in the hope that this would prompt the disbursement of aid from the UN Global Environment Facility. In October Taylor announced a review of forestry regulation and asserted government ownership of the Liberian forest. In December licences to log 2m. acres (8,000 sq km) held by Liberian-owned companies were cancelled.

Legislation for the enactment of a new forestry law, a new minerals and mining law and a strategic commodities law was introduced in early 2000. Taylor publicized requirements in the new laws for companies to attend to the health, educational and environmental concerns of the concession areas in which they operated, and requirements to process natural resources into semi-finished or finished products. The national forestry law, in the form adopted by the house of representatives in March, granted the National Investment Commission authority to review all concession agreements. The strategic commodities law, adopted by the house of representatives in February, designated a number of natural resources as 'strategic' commodities and granted the presidency sole powers to negotiate, conclude and sign all contracts concerning them. Gold, diamonds, iron ore and logs were to be included under the 'strategic' designation.

FORESTRY

Liberia possesses substantial forest reserves; forest covers 4.5m. ha (or 46.8% of the total land area of Liberia), with wooded land accounting for another 2.0m. ha (or 20.7% of land area). There is one protected area of rain forest, designated as such in 1983, the 1,300 sq km Sapo National Park, in Sinoe County; an extension of the park, to 2,000 sq km, was under discussion in late 1999. A new nature reserve around Lake Piso, in Grand Cape Mount County, was declared in 1999. Historically, smallholder agriculture has been responsible for 95% of all deforestation, and the use of trees for domestic fuel, directly in rural areas and in the form of charcoal in urban areas, has dwarfed the activities of commercial timber producers. Nevertheless, by the late 1980s virtually all significant national forest land was under concessionary arrangements with commercial logging companies. The mass population displacements during the civil war inhibited deforestation from agricultural activities and the insecurity of the time inhibited large-scale logging operations. Despite a probable increase in charcoal production owing to the collapse of electricity supplies, the FAO estimates that during 1990–95 only 134,000 ha of total forest cover were lost.

Timber production increased markedly from the 1960s. Production of sawlogs and veneer logs reached more than 1m. cu m in 1988, with other industrial roundwood contributing 154,000 cu m in the same year. Although a large sawmill and a plywood mill near Greenville commenced production in the mid-1970s, output of sawnwood and other timber products was less than expected for most of the 1980s. Output of sawnwood showed an increase, to 411,000 cu m, in 1988, but production of wood-based panels remained limited, with 5,000 cu m of veneer sheets produced in 1988 and 3,000 cu m of plywood. More than 90% by value of Liberia's timber exports continued to be in the form of roundwood. Exports of roundwood reached 681,000 cu m in 1988, with a value of US $88m. Despite the bombing of Buchanan and Greenville ports by ECOMOG in 1993, and despite the withdrawal of many logging companies as the security situation deteriorated, the decline in the production of roundwood is believed to have been only limited before 1995. According to FAO estimates, output of sawlogs and veneer logs continued at more than 750,000 cu m annually in 1990–94, but declined to 29,000 cu m in 1995. Many of the 48 timber companies present in Liberia before the war re-established their operations in NPFL territory after the end of the first period of conflict and exported through Buchanan and other ports under Taylor's control, paying taxes to Taylor's 'Greater Liberia' regime. Log-

ging companies came to similar arrangements with other factions as factional territories shifted during subsequent conflict. However, the sawmill and plywood mills near Greenville were destroyed during the war and production of veneer sheets and plywood was suspended in 1992.

Post-war recovery in the forestry sector was initially slow. Production of sawlogs and veneer logs increased to 75,000 cu m in 1997 and to 157,000 cu m in 1998. In 2000 the activities of the Oriental Timber Company (OTC) attracted widespread attention, both domestically and abroad. The OTC was invited to carry out extraction and other activities in a large concession covering some 1.0m.–1.6m. ha in Grand Bassa, Rivercess and Sinoe Counties. The OTC upgraded the 108-mile dirt road connecting Buchanan and Greenville in late 1999 and early 2000. Complaints from Grand Bassa that the company had destroyed houses and cash crops along the Buchanan–Greenville road without compensation emerged in November 1999. The OTC has also taken over the management of Buchanan port. Extraction rates have been estimated to be running at an annual rate of 800,000–1,100,000 cu m; the latter figure approaches the maximum annual pre-war output of the entire Liberian logging industry. The OTC is reported to be clear felling, a practice inconsistent with sustainable forestry management and allegedly in violation of FDA regulations. Armed guards working for the OTC have allegedly opened fire indiscriminately and prevented access to the concession area by FDA officials. Accusations of tax evasion by the OTC have also been reported. The OTC's operations, however, enjoy the clear support of President Taylor: public officials were warned against harassing the company at the launch of the OTC's Buchanan–Greenville road project. Criticism of the OTC's operations by the Grand Bassa County superintendent resulted in his dismissal in December 1999. (Although he was reinstated a few days later in response to local protests, he was dismissed again in February 2000.)

MINING

Since the opening of Liberia's first iron ore mine in 1951, mining, first of iron ore, and more recently of gold and diamonds, has superseded Liberia's traditional dependence on rubber. Other mineral resources discovered or believed likely to exist in Liberia include nickel, cobalt, barite, kyenite, bauxite, platinum, colombo-tantalite, manganese, chromium, uranium, lead, graphite, rutile, ilmenite, zircon, silica sand and ceramic clay. These resources have not been exploited. Iron ore mining was the principal extraction industry prior to the civil conflict. The value of iron ore exports exceeded that of rubber exports in 1961, and Liberia soon became one of the world's main exporters of iron ore. In the 1980s, however, the reduction in international demand for iron ore severely depressed production and export earnings: production was just over 8.0m. metric tons (iron content) in 1988, yielding US $220m. in export earnings (equivalent to 55% of total export revenue). Four main deposits have been exploited to date: at Bomi Hills (by the Liberian Mining Company) from 1951, the Mano River deposit (by the National Iron Ore Company) from 1961, The Mount Nimba South deposit, just south of the Guinean border (by the Liberian-American Minerals Company—LAMCO) from 1963, and at Bong mines north of Kakata (by the Bong Mining Company—BMC) from 1965. These were the highest grade of the 11 principal deposits known to exist. The Mount Nimba project involved a $300m.-investment to construct the plant and infrastructure, including a 274-km railway from the mine at Yekepa to the coast, a pelletizing plant and a new port at Buchanan. Production at Bomi Hills and Mano River ended in 1977 and 1985 respectively, owing to the exhaustion of the high- and medium-grade ores at those sites. LAMCO ceased production in July 1989, after the extraction of 230m. tons of iron ore, and in view of a contracting world market for ore. LAMCO's assets were transferred to a government-owned holding company, the Liberian Mining Company (LIMINCO), in September 1989. LIMINCO reached agreement with the British-based African Mining Consortium to manage operations at Yekepa. The resumption of mining was suspended at the start of the civil conflict in December 1989, but continued in 1990 at the end of the first war until early 1993. However, the deposit on the Liberian side of the Guinea border is now largely exhausted and operations are not expected to be resumed. Remaining stockpiles of iron ore at Buchanan were sold in 1999. The BMC mine at Bong Mines also suspended operations early in the civil conflict, in June 1990, and the site, near some of the most heavily contested territory of the war, was devastated by fighting and looting. After the civil conflict ended, the cost of rehabilitating the facilities was found to be greater than the value of the remaining reserves; the mine is now permanently closed and the BMC has been dissolved. Wartime production of the industry declined from 2.5m. tons (iron content) in 1990 to 1.1m. tons in 1992. No further production has taken place and the Liberian iron ore industry is now defunct. Liberia may, however, gain some benefit from the exploitation of Guinea's iron ore deposits just over the border from Yekepa. Economic exploitation of this deposit required the use of a refurbished Yekepa–Buchanan railway. The Taiwanese China Steel Corporation undertook an assessment of LIMINCO's infrastructure in December 1998. In February 2000 it was announced that a London-based mining group, Billiton, was leading negotiations to establish a 20m. tons per-year mining operation in the area.

Alluvial gold has been exploited since the 1940s in an area near Zwedru (Tchien) in Grand Gedeh County and exploration for primary (lode) gold in the 1970s quickly focused on this area. The primary gold reserves of this area have been estimated at 2m. metric tons, with a gold content of 2g per ton. Further exploration and exploitation have been focused on alluvial gold. Reserves are distributed throughout the country, but the most significant occurrences are in western Liberia between the Lofa and Mano Rivers, in Bong and Nimba Counties along the St John River and Ya Creek, and in the south-east of the country. Liberia's total reserves of gold are estimated at 3m. oz. Production was small-scale with some 6,000–14,000 diggings for gold and diamonds believed to exist before the war. The prevalence of illicit production, before, during and since the civil conflict, renders output estimates highly uncertain, but, according to official figures, annual gold production increased from 359 kg in 1982 to 677 kg in 1988. Production continued throughout the war, organized by the ULIMO–J, ULIMO–K, NPFL and LPC factions, both in alliance with foreign companies and directly with labour supplied by factions and, in the south-east, forced labour. The proceeds are believed to have financed arms purchases and to have augmented the personal fortunes of the factional leaders. The US Geological Survey (USGS), formerly the US Bureau of Mines, estimated Liberian wartime production at 500–800 kg annually; with the return of peace, production was estimated to have declined to 500 kg in 1997 and 1998. Official Liberian government figures estimated production at 670 kg in 1999.

Diamond deposits were first discovered in the lower Lofa river area in 1957, and continued westwards to the border with Sierra Leone at the Mano River. These deposits consisted of both alluvial deposits, and kimberlites and kimberlite dykes, and yielded both industrial and gem diamonds. Alluvial diamond occurrences have also been located in the Cavalia and Ya Creek drainage systems in Nimba County, in Grand Bassa and Montserrado Counties, and there have been reports of discoveries near Greenville. Reserves are estimated at about 10m. carats. Official data on production and exports were believed to be distorted by illicit production and smuggling. However, the officially-recorded value of diamond exports reached a pre-war record of US $49.4m. in 1973, when 812,000 carats were exported. By the mid-1980s officially-recorded exports had declined to about 200,000 carats annually, and continued at low levels until the outbreak of the war in 1989: according to the USGS, 263,000 carats of industrial diamonds and 67,000 carats of gem diamonds were produced in 1988. As with gold, the warring factions became heavily involved in diamond production. Conflicts between the NPFL, ULIMO–J and ULIMO–K forces in western Liberia from 1993 onwards were motivated, in whole or part, and greatly exacerbated by the desire to obtain control over diamond workings. The USGS estimates annual production in 1994–96, at about 40,000–60,000 carats of gem diamonds and 60,000–90,000 carats of industrial diamonds. The annual value of diamond exports during the war, estimated from Belgian data on diamond imports en route to Antwerp, was reckoned to be $300m.–$500m. These included diamonds originating from elsewhere in Africa. Owing to the high margins charged by dealers, the Liberian value of diamond exports

during the war period may have been as low as $30m.–$50m. per year.

Much of the mining for gold and diamonds in Liberia continues to be illicit, with the government admitting its inability to control an estimated 6,000 miners operating illegally in the country, compared to some 400 who are officially registered. The USGS estimated production in 1997 and 1998 at about 60,000 carats (gem) and 90,000 carats (industrial). The involvement of mining companies in this sector has produced varied results. Mano River Resources, which has been active in Liberia since 1995 and has shares listed on the London and Vancouver stock exchanges, has acquired rights to more than 8,000 sq km in the gold fields of western Liberia; exploration at King George-Larjor, in Grand Cape Mount County, continued in 1999 with promising results. A diamond exploration programme on its Bea Mountain and Kpo Range licences began in early 2000. Freedom Gold acquired a three-year exploration licence covering more than 200,000 acres in Sinoe County and commenced operations in the area in late 1999. Other exploration projects have proved less successful. President Mines of Canada obtained three-year exploration licences covering more than 500 sq km in the diamond fields of the Lofa and Mano river valleys in August 1997, but claimed in August 1998 that the licences had been transferred to the chief executive of its Liberian operating subsidiary without its knowledge. Its operations appeared to have been suspended in 2000. The Greater Diamond Mining Company acquired mining licences in the Mano River area, in Lofa County, and in Cocopa, Nimba County, in 1997 or 1998. Greater Diamond is a subsidiary of Greater Ministries International of the USA; the latter company's investment schemes were banned by financial regulators in a number of states in the USA between 1995 and 1999. Greater Diamond's operations in Liberia are now reported to be inactive.

In October 1999 Global Witness, an investigative human rights and environment organization, launched a campaign to prevent the funding of civil war in Africa by diamond sales. Research by Partnership Africa Canada, published in January 2000, demonstrated that Belgian imports of diamonds from Liberia far exceeded the Liberian diamond mining capacity and reported the widespread view that diamonds were being smuggled out of Sierra Leone via Liberia. It urged that an international embargo be imposed on Liberian diamond sales by the UN Security Council. In June 2000, after the collapse of the Lomé Agreement in Sierra Leone, the British government also demanded a UN boycott on uncertificated diamonds from Sierra Leone.

INDUSTRY

Companies such as Firestone and LAMCO assisted in the development of Liberia's technical and social infrastructure by constructing roads, ports, airfields, schools and hospitals. Their contribution to the development of manufacturing industry was, nevertheless, limited, as few secondary industries based on iron ore, or rubber, were established. Government policy for the development of manufacturing industry was designed to promote import substitution through tax and customs incentives until the early 1970s, when emphasis was placed on the establishment of industries to add value to Liberia's production of primary commodities. This emphasis was maintained by the Doe regime and has continued under Taylor's administration. In 1975 the government established a free-trade zone next to the Monrovia 'free port'. None of Liberia's policies with regard to the industrial sector have had much success, however. The restricted significance of the manufacturing sector to the Liberian economy was indicated by its contribution of a mere 7.3% to the country's GDP in 1989, and by the size of its workforce, which represented only about 6% of the total labour force in 1990. Before the civil conflict the manufacturing sector had few companies of any size, and many firms were owned and operated by only one person. Enterprises were concentrated in food and drink manufacture, building materials, and the clothing and furniture trades. Large-scale industry included a 125,000-ton capacity cement factory, owned by the Liberian Cement Corporation (CEMENCO), which commenced operations in 1968, and a 15,000 barrel/day oil refinery, which was initially largely owned by US oil interests but was acquired by the Doe regime's Liberia Petroleum Refining Corporation (LPRC) in the early

1980s. A steel-rolling mill, using scrap metal from naval vessels, was constructed by Hong Kong shipping interests and commenced operations in 1988. Other large-scale plants included the rubber factories at the concession sites and the beverage industry, represented by a Coca-Cola and other bottling plants and by a brewery. The largest Liberian-owned manufacturing company was the Mesurado Group, which manufactured detergents, soap, industrial gases and animal foods. Its assets were confiscated by the Doe regime, and it subsequently collapsed.

Many manufacturing enterprises were seriously affected by the depressed state of the economy in the 1980s and increased interference and harassment by government and military personnel. Manufacturing industry, which is principally located in and around Monrovia, was badly affected by the initial assault on the capital in 1990, by 'Operation Octopus' in 1992, and again by the renewed outbreak of war in Monrovia in mid-1996. The petroleum refinery had to reduce its output in 1982, owing to the effects of inadequate maintenance, and at the end of that year ceased refining operations entirely as shortages of foreign exchange prevented its purchase of crude petroleum. Since that time Liberia has again been dependent on imports of refined petroleum products. The LPRC enjoyed a monopoly over the import of petroleum products and this function survived the collapse of its refining operations. In January 1991 the cost of rehabilitating the LPRC's facilities after war damage was projected at US $7m., but in 2000 there were no plans to undertake this project. The LPRC's import monopoly has attracted the attention of the IMF and the government is under pressure to liberalize the market in petroleum products. The reconstruction and development of the manufacturing sector since the civil conflict has been limited. The Coca-Cola bottling plant and the CEMENCO installation have resumed operations, although work at the latter has been hindered by power supply failures. A plastics installation was established in the industrial free zone in January 1999.

Prior to the outbreak of the civil conflict, the main impediments to industrialization were the limited size of the domestic market, corrupt governance, an ill-educated workforce and the poor domestic transport, communications and financial infrastructures. Attempts to enlarge the market through regional economic integration, which have been conducted under the auspices of ECOWAS since the latter's formation in 1975, have proved almost entirely unsuccessful. The outcome of renewed attempts by ECOWAS in 1999 and 2000 to promote regional integration through investment in transport links and progress towards monetary union has yet to be seen.

TRANSPORT, POWER AND TELECOMMUNICATIONS AND UTILITIES

Liberia's road network is inadequate and mostly in very poor repair. In 1996 the road network totalled an estimated 10,600 km, of which about 657 km were paved. A main road between Monrovia and Freetown, Sierra Leone, which was completed in 1988, reduced the distance between the two capitals from 1,014 to 544 km. Another major road links Monrovia to Ganta in Nimba County. Road connections between Monrovia and the south-east of the country are very poor and coastal shipping remains a significant mode of transport on this route. The principal roads in Liberia were closed for most of the civil conflict and free movement was prevented by roadblocks installed by the various armed factions. Most of the principal roads were reopened during the 1995–96 disarmament process, but remain in poor repair with some rural areas continuing to be inaccessible by road during the rainy season. Some feeder roads have been rehabilitated by local residents in conjunction with non-governmental organizations. In December 1998 logging company representatives agreed to rehabilitate roads and bridges after a meeting with Taylor, and logging companies have become a significant, although sometimes unwilling, source of rural infrastructural development in the areas in which they operate. Ambitious plans to construct two new highways were announced in late 1999; the first was planned to connect coastal towns from Robertsport in the west to Harper in the south-east, while the second was planned to extend from the south-east, through the interior, to Mendekoma in the far north-west. Road transport between Liberia and Sierra Leone was suspended following the closure of the border in December 1998, and government checkpoints were installed on roads leading to the border. The border with Sierra Leone was reopened in October 1999. The border with Guinea was closed in August 1999, and had not been reopened at mid-2000.

The railways from Monrovia to Mano River via Bomi Hills (145 track-km), from Monrovia to the Bong Mine (78 track-km) and from Buchanan to Yekepa (267 track-km) were constructed for the transport of iron ore. The latter railway was also utilized for the transport of logs and rubber and for the Guinea transit trade. A passenger service operated on the Buchanan–Yekepa route prior to the civil conflict. The closure of Liberia's iron ore industry has resulted in the cessation of all traffic on these lines.

In December 1998 the Liberian-registered merchant fleet, according to Lloyd's Register of Shipping, comprised 1,717 vessels, with a total displacement of 60.5m. gross registered tons (grt). None of this fleet is owned by Liberian nationals. Although it remained the second largest national fleet in the world in terms of tonnage, and recorded a marginal increase of registered tonnage in 1999, the long-term decline from a 1982 peak of 81.5m. grt reflected the fall in the number of oil tankers, competition from other 'open registry' states, and growing international opposition to 'open registry' shipping. The management of the Liberian registry was, from its inception in 1949, conducted by the International Trust Company (ITC), an associate company of International Registries Incorporated (IRI) of New York. Since the registry is, for all intents and purposes, managed from the USA, it was little affected by the civil conflict. In 1998 Liberia instituted court proceedings against the IRI, alleging that it had diverted business from the Liberian registry. An out of court settlement was reached in May 1999, under which the management of the registry was transferred to a new company, also based in the USA, the Liberia International Ship and Corporate Registry (LISCR) from January 2000; it was expected that about 80% of ITC staff would be transferred to the LISCR.

Liberia's principal ports are Monrovia Free Port, Buchanan, Greenville and Harper. The 1992 offensive on Monrovia resulted in the suspension of most shipping activity. It subsequently resumed, but activities at all the ports remained dependent on developments in the fighting. In 1993 ECOMOG imposed a 19-km coastal exclusion zone, and in April–May 1996 Monrovia Free Port was again closed to commercial shipping owing to the renewed conflict in the capital. The Danish shipping company Maersk resumed direct services to Monrovia in late 1996, followed by the British-based OT Africa Lines (OTAL). Port traffic increased markedly after the elections in 1997, and ECOMOG ended the coastal exclusion zone in September of that year. Taiwan pledged US $1m. of aid to rehabilitate Monrovia Free Port in July 1998. In mid-2000, however, OTAL reported that the quay was partially collapsed, and that dredging equipment at the port was inadequate. The port at Buchanan has been rehabilitated by the Oriental Timber Company. Greenville and Harper are shallow-water ports used mainly for the export of logs.

Liberia's principal airports before the civil war were Robertsfield International Airport (RIA), at Harbel, 56 km east of Monrovia, and the smaller James Spriggs Payne Airport, at Monrovia. International air traffic reached a total of 52,954 passengers arriving and 55,541 departing in 1985, compared with 24,724 arrivals and 28,281 departures in 1970. Between 1970 and 1985 the quantities of air cargo loaded and unloaded increased from 242 to 1,247 metric tons, and from 1,142 to 1,624 tons respectively. In 1990 the civil conflict in Monrovia resulted in severe damage to the RIA, which remained closed to civilian traffic during the remainder of the conflict. A number of airlines maintained international services from James Spriggs Payne Airport, with occasional suspensions owing to fighting in Monrovia. The airport was damaged, but was reopened in June 1996. The RIA was reopened to civilian airlines in December 1997. In May 1999 Taiwan donated US $4.5m. of equipment to enable RIA to meet international safety standards. Air Afrique resumed services to RIA in January 2000, and in February Ghana Airways announced that it would resume direct flights to the USA in August 2000.

Estimated electricity production increased from 328.8m. kWh in 1972 to 904m. kWh in 1985, with production by the government-owned Liberian Electricity Corporation (LEC) accounting for just under one-half of the total. The LEC operated two systems, the Monrovia Grid, serving Montserrado and parts of the adjacent four counties, and the Rural Electrification Network, serving the remainder of the country through isolated diesel generators. The dependence of the Monrovia Grid on hydroelectric power from the Mt Coffee plant resulted in shortages of electricity during the dry season. Total electricity production declined to 565m. kWh in 1990, and to 450m. kWh in 1991. In December 1990 the Mt Coffee dam was reported to have been completely destroyed, and mains electricity supplies have been erratic or non-existent during and since the end of the civil conflict; businesses and other organizations are dependent on privately-owned generators. The Liberian government signed a memorandum of understanding in 1998 with Consolidated Associates Engineering Development (CAED), a US energy supply company, under which CAED was to lease the LEC's facilities and supply electricity throughout Liberia. The LEC condemned the agreement in April 1999, and cast doubt on the ability of CAED to raise the necessary finance for the LEC's reconstruction. In 1999 Taylor appointed a special task force to oversee the restoration of street lighting in Monrovia by 2000. In the event, LEC managed to restore some lighting only temporarily. In February 2000 Taylor announced that funds did not exist to restore the city's electricity and that, in any case, his priority was road-building. Citizens requiring electricity were advised to purchase generators.

The central water supply and sewage disposal system in Monrovia was damaged during the 1992 offensive on the capital. A severe shortage of safe water continued in Monrovia, alleviated by a European Union-operated distribution system using water tankers. Outbreaks of disease linked to unsafe water supplies remained a major problem in rural areas. Little progress has been made on the restoration of water supplies in Monrovia. In 1999 piped water was available two days a week to Bushrod Island, the industrial area near Monrovia, but elsewhere in Monrovia people continued to rely on EU distribution or on hand-pumping water from wells. In April 2000 a severe water shortage was caused in parts of Monrovia when diesel pumps broke down. Repairs carried out by the EU finally relieved the shortage in May. Almost all of the installations of the Liberian Telecommunications Corporation (LTC) were damaged during the war and rehabilitation of the network has been slow, hindered by substantial levels of telephone fraud and poor revenue collection. Total capacity was estimated at 6,000 fixed and 10,000 mobile lines in 1998. In 1999 the LTC acquired a wireless local loop system, with a capacity of 2,250 lines. Plans to privatize the LTC by selling a 60% stake to a US corporation, Spectronics International, were impeded by a dispute between Spectronics and the Liberian government in late 1999. In the mean time, the telephone system continues to be unreliable and operates only in parts of Monrovia; most telecommunications are conducted by radio. The most recent estimate in Liberia of 0.2 telephone lines per 100 inhabitants is one of the lowest in Africa. Two internet service providers commenced operations in 1998, but both were closed down in 1999; Liberia is now the only country in Africa without local internet access.

MONEY AND BANKING

From 1940 until August 1998 the Liberian dollar was nominally maintained at par with the US dollar; since 1998 the US–Liberian dollar exchange rate has been market-determined. US banknotes were and remain legal tender in Liberia, and US notes circulate alongside Liberian currency. Following the military coup in 1980, the value of US dollar notes in circulation declined from $10.5m. in 1980 to $4.2m. in 1984, while Liberian coins in circulation rose from $11.6m. to $31.3m. over the same period, and to $46.6m. by the end of 1985. Doe issued a $5 coin from 1981, and a $5 banknote, now known as the 'JJ Roberts' from 1989. Rapid inflation in local currency terms resulted in a substantial premium for US notes. In early 1992 the interim administration introduced new banknotes, known as 'Liberty' dollars, in an attempt to demonetize currency held by the NPFL administration, the National Patriotic Reconstruction Assembly (NPRA), and a fluctuating exchange rate emerged between new

and old notes, depending on developments in the conflict. The resulting threefold currency system (US dollars, JJ Roberts and Liberty dollars) continued until 2000. During the war the Liberty dollar circulated in the Monrovia area; possession of the Liberty dollar in factional territory was dangerous and the US and JJ Roberts dollars predominated in these areas. The Liberty dollar was the weakest of the three currencies on the Monrovia parallel money market. After the 1997 elections Liberty dollars traded at 40–45 to the US dollar, the JJ Roberts at 20–22. In February 1998 the government announced its intention to maintain a 1:2 exchange rate between the JJ Roberts and the Liberty dollars. The Liberty dollar is the *de facto* local unit of account so that values expressed in 'Liberian dollars' refer to the Liberty dollar; this includes the usually quoted US-Liberian dollar exchange rates. During 1998 the Liberty traded at an average of L$ 41 to the US dollar, in 1999 at an average of L$ 42. Plans to withdraw both the JJ Roberts and Liberty dollars and issue a new banknote to replace them were announced in February 1998, but implementation of this reform was delayed until March 2000.

Before the civil war the banking system comprised 14 commercial banks and the National Bank of Liberia (NBL). The banking system was in substantial difficulties before the war with the inter-bank clearing system close to collapse. During the war the majority of the commercial banks were closed and the NBL was rendered largely inoperative. In November 1999 a new central bank, the Central Bank of Liberia (CBL), was established. At this point five commercial banks were in operation: two were branches of foreign banks, two were locally-incorporated subsidiaries and one was a locally-owned subsidiary. The CBL has introduced measures to supervise the commercial banking sector and restore the inter-bank clearing system. However, the commercial banking system remains hindered by substantial difficulties, resulting from an uncertain legal environment and the wartime collapse of the Liberian economy. Some 85% of commercial bank loans were non-operative at the end of 1998.

In April 2000 Liberia signed an accord with five other ECOWAS states outside the CFA zone (Gambia, Ghana, Guinea, Nigeria and Sierra Leone) to establish a monetary union of the six countries in 2004. The plan is dependent on the attainment of economic targets in each country, including: an inflation rate of no more than 9% in 2000 and 5% by 2003; foreign-exchange reserves sufficient to cover three months' imports by the end of 2000 and six months' imports by 2003; central bank financing of government budget deficits of more than 10% of revenue by the end of 2000; and deficits limited to no more than 5% of GDP by 2000 and 4% by 2002. The plan is also clearly dependent on the attainment of peace and stability throughout the six states.

PUBLIC FINANCE AND AID

A substantial rate of growth in government revenue between 1945 and 1981 failed to keep pace with increased levels of government expenditure, which, especially with the decline in the growth rate of revenue during the recession of the late 1970s, resulted in heavy budgetary deficits. Following the 1980 coup, the Doe government inherited an external public debt of US $400m. and a budgetary deficit of $56m. Increased domestic expectations after the coup of April 1980, together with a decline in foreign business confidence and the weakness of the international iron ore market, placed further strains on the economy. In addition, private-sector liquidity fell sharply, as both local and foreign investors moved their convertible assets abroad. The increasing fiscal crisis contributed to the collapse of the Doe government in 1980. In 1991–93 the national budget related only to the small part of the national territory controlled by the Interim Government of National Unity (IGNU), while the NPRA in the interior imposed levies on the local population and on companies exporting through the port of Buchanan and through Côte d'Ivoire. IGNU expenditure was principally financed by funds from the maritime registry. Government finances were disrupted by the wholesale looting in April–May 1996, and the National Bank of Liberia remained closed for several months. Following the installation of a new government in August 1997, it was announced that national reserves amounted to only $17,000, while public-sector salary arrears totalled $2.5m., and there was a central bank deficit of L $118m. The new minister of finance committed the IGNU to fiscal discipline and accountability. In October the legislature adopted a balanced interim budget of L $536.4m., which was to remain in force until the end of the year. The 1998 budget was projected at L $1,660m. (US $41m.), of which 80% was allocated to defence, with most of the remainder allocated to education, health and agriculture. Revenue was to be derived from business and sales taxes, import and export duties and revenue from the maritime registry. In May 1998 the government announced that it had paid all arrears in salaries. Nevertheless, demonstrations and other actions to force the payment of wage and salary arrears continued to affect various public-sector organizations into 2000. The 1999 budget proposed a 55% increase in expenditure, to L $2,600m. (US $64m.), and a substantial reduction in the share allocated to defence. The budget proposals were accompanied by an announcement that the finance ministry would henceforth be the sole revenue collecting agency, eliminating the independent revenue collections by the ministries of land, and mines, among other authorities. Following an IMF recommendation, a review of government payrolls to eliminate 'ghost' workers was also announced. Judging by subsequent labour disputes, this policy has been pursued with some seriousness. Taylor's 2000 budget was an interim one, covering only January–June 2000, due to a change in the fiscal year. Expenditure was targeted at an annual rate of a little over L $4,000m. (US $100m.), with 33% allocated to roads, 15% to health, 15% to education, 14% to 'millennium projects' (development) and 12% to agriculture. As in 1999, the interim 2000 budgeted expenditure was to be funded entirely by tax revenue and income from the maritime registry. Although Taylor promised that there would be no extra budgetary expenditure since his 1999 budget, the IMF discovered US $13.4m. of extra-budgetary expenditures in a half-yearly review of the 1999 budget, and it was evident that expenditure made by logging and other companies on infrastructure construction at the behest of the government failed to appear in the government budget. The government budgets have offered no indication as to the size of, or the uses made of, the government's income from the logging and minerals sectors.

The willingness of the USA to increase its aid, from some US $10m. in 1979 to $64m. in 1985, undoubtedly encouraged the Doe government to maintain Liberia's traditional alignment with Western countries. However, US aid was sharply reduced, to $43m., in 1986. In February 1987 a US federal agency reported that $12m. of aid had been diverted to unauthorized use, with a further $16.5m. unaccounted for. The release of further US aid was subsequently made conditional upon Liberian acceptance of 17 US-appointed operational experts to supervise revenue collection and government expenditure. The experts arrived in Liberia in late 1987 but left after only one year of a projected two-year stay, owing to their failure to control unauthorized presidential allocations and the revenues of public corporations. In 1988 US aid was further reduced, to $31m. From 1990, however, the USA provided emergency assistance to counteract the effects of the civil conflict. Total US government assistance over the 1990–96 civil war period amounted to more than $450m. Total net official development assistance (ODA) from the Organization for Economic Community and Development development assistance committee countries, and multilateral organizations over the same period exceeded $900m., almost all of which was humanitarian aid. Liberia's net ODA receipts declined to $75m. in 1997 and to $73m. in 1998, compared with $171m. in 1996, as peace reduced the necessity for humanitarian aid. The USA has been Liberia's largest donor in the post-war period, followed by the European Union (EU) and UN agencies.

In April 1998 donors, including the EU, the USA and the UN, pledged grants of US $220m. to finance the first year of a $438m.-national reconstruction programme, which had been presented by the Liberian government. Despite this, Taylor accused the international community of rejecting the Liberian government, and attributed the conceded failure of the first year of his administration to the lack of international aid. Most international assistance has been devoted to refugee resettlement, health, food security and post-conflict reconstruction. Aid

has continued to be provided to UN field agencies in Liberia, to non-governmental organizations and directly to communities; little has been channelled through government ministries. Western diplomats and officials have indicated that this would continue until the government demonstrated an ability to manage aid funds efficiently and without corruption, control the security forces and attend to human rights abuses.

THE MACRO-ECONOMY AND INTERNATIONAL DEBT

The rapid expansion of the Liberian economy in the 1950s and 1960s was largely generated by exports of rubber, iron ore and timber and infrastructural projects financed by foreign aid. After the first major decline in international prices in 1974 rubber and iron ore exports stagnated. It is from this period that Liberia's macro-economic problems stem. Public-sector deficits increased from negligible levels in 1975 to 15% of GDP in 1979; external debt nearly quadrupled. Export volumes broadly declined throughout the 1980s and stagnating or declining export unit values exacerbated the effects on the economy. The Doe regime borrowed massively, almost entirely from abroad and mainly at commercial rates, and used the funds obtained to finance unproductive public investments and maintain domestic consumption. As early as 1982 Liberia's external public debt had increased to US $726m., equivalent to 75% of GDP. By 1988 external public debt had risen to $1,800m., equivalent to 164% of GDP, and debt-service payments due would have taken 40% of export earnings.

Not surprisingly, Liberia's relations with the IMF deteriorated badly in the 1980s. Liberia received successive standby credits from the IMF: for SDR 55.0m. in September 1982, for a further SDR 55m. in September 1983, and for SDR 42.8m. in December 1984; the last of these was suspended within one week, owing to repayment arrears on a previous loan. Successive debt-rescheduling schedules were agreed in December 1981, December 1983 and December 1984. In January 1986 Liberia was declared ineligible for further drawings on the IMF, and in February 1988 the IMF closed its mission in Monrovia, claiming that the governmment had not seriously attempted to reform the economy. The World Bank suspended disbursements in December 1986. In March 1990 the IMF declared Liberia a 'non-co-operating' country, and threatened expulsion from the Fund, owing to the government's failure to pay outstanding arrears; Liberia owed an estimated US $396m. to the IMF and $65m. to the African Development Bank (ADB).

The conflict resulted in the suspension of debt-service payments and the arrears accumulated at an accelerating rate. IMF estimates suggest that real GDP declined by more than 25% in 1989, by over 50% in 1990 and continued to fall rapidly until 1995 (when real GDP stood at less than 10% of the level achieved in 1987). These estimates may well exaggerate the collapse of the Liberian economy, and are difficult to reconcile with the substantial exports from Liberia recorded by importing countries throughout the 1990s, but the devastation brought to the Liberian economy by the civil conflict is undeniable. In August 1994 the transitional government resumed negotiations with the IMF after paying arrears of only L $1m.; however, the continuing conflict and political confusion prevented further discussions. By 1997 accumulated arrears had increased Liberia's external public debt to a figure now estimated by the IMF to be US $2,447m. This is an exceptionally high figure, equivalent to about $800 per head of the 1999 de jure population of perhaps 3m., and the IMF accepted that Liberia's external debt burden was unsustainable. Nevertheless, there is no immediate prospect of Liberia benefiting from the World Bank's highly indebted poor countries initiative.

Relations between the international financial institutions and Liberia registered some improvement after the 1997 elections. A joint IMF, World Bank and African Development Bank assessment mission visited Liberia in September of that year. Although Liberia's appeal for a 75% debt cancellation and a rescheduling of the remainder met with no response, the IMF decided in March 1998 to refrain from initiating moves to suspend Liberia's voting rights in view of its recent efforts to co-operate with the IMF, in particular Liberia's regular monthly token payments of arrears to the Fund. Further joint IMF, World Bank and donor assessment visits in 1999 and 2000 registered some satisfaction with the improving security situation and the macro-economy. IMF staff estimated that the economy expanded by more than 100% in 1997 and by nearly 30% in 1998, and projected growth rates of more than 20% in 1999 and 2000. Officially recorded exports have increased, and are projected to grow at similar rates. Even so, GDP in 1999 was estimated to stand at only about one-third of 1987 levels. The US-Liberian dollar exchange rate has remained stable and consumer price inflation has been negligible. The government has planned on the basis of balanced budgets. However, the IMF, World Bank and donors voiced continuing concerns over budgetary transparency, contract award practices, the regulation of rice imports, the monopoly position of the Liberian Petroleum Refining Company and, more fundamentally, governance, the rule of law and human rights abuses.

ECONOMIC PROSPECTS

The post-war period has seen a rapid recovery of the subsistence agriculture sector, as refugees and displaced civilians returned to their farms. There has been a rapid increase in the exploitation of Liberia's timber, diamond and gold resources but this has been managed with scant regard for sustainability. The recovery of the health and education sectors has been heavily dependent on humanitarian aid. Reconstruction and development of the country's economic infrastructure has been slow or non-existent. The international aid and investment required for the rehabilitation and development of Liberia's public sector was likely to be conditional on government attempts to combat corruption, control the security forces, and attend to human rights abuses.

Statistical Survey

Sources (unless otherwise stated): the former Ministry of Planning and Economic Affairs, POB 9016, Broad Street, Monrovia.

Area and Population

AREA, POPULATION AND DENSITY

Area (sq km)	97,754*
Population (census results)	
1 February 1974	1,503,368
1 February 1984 (provisional)	
Males	1,063,127
Females	1,038,501
Total	2,101,628
Population (official estimates at mid-year)†	
1995	2,759,714
1996	2,819,540
1997	2,879,366
Density (per sq km) at mid-1997	29.5

* 37,743 sq miles.

† Figures are based on a mid-1985 estimate of 2,161,454, with an assumed increase of 59,826 per year thereafter. According to UN estimates, the mid-year population of Liberia increased from 2,193,000 in 1985 to 2,579,000 in 1990, but declined to 2,090,000 in 1995, before rising to 2,402,000 in 1997 and 2,666,000 in 1998 (Source: UN, *World Population Prospects: The 1998 Revision*).

ADMINISTRATIVE DIVISIONS (population at 1984 census)

Counties:		Nimba . . .	313,050
Bomi . . .	66,420	Rivercess . . .	37,849
Bong . . .	255,813	Sinoe . . .	64,147
Grand Bassa . .	159,648	Territories:	
Grand Cape Mount .	79,322	Gibi . . .	66,802
Grand Gedeh . .	102,810	Kru Coast . .	35,267
Lofa . . .	247,641	Marshall . .	31,190
Maryland . .	85,267	Sasstown . .	11,524
Montserrado . .	544,878	**Total** . .	2,101,628

Note: The counties of Grand Kru and Margibi were subsequently established. In June 1998 the creation of a further county, River Gee, was approved by the House of Representatives.

PRINCIPAL TOWN

Monrovia (capital), population 421,058 at 1984 census.

BIRTHS AND DEATHS (UN estimates, annual averages)

	1980–85	1985–90	1990–95
Birth rate (per 1,000) . . .	47.0	46.7	41.7
Death rate (per 1,000) . . .	15.9	14.4	23.6

Expectation of life (UN estimates, years at birth, 1990–95): 38.8 (males 37.5; females 40.1).

Source: UN, *World Population Prospects: The 1998 Revision*.

ECONOMICALLY ACTIVE POPULATION

	1978	1979	1980
Agriculture, forestry, hunting and fishing	355,467	366,834	392,926
Mining	25,374	26,184	28,047
Manufacturing . . .	6,427	6,631	7,102
Construction . . .	4,701	4,852	5,198
Electricity, gas and water .	245	246	263
Commerce	18,668	19,266	20,636
Transport and communications .	7,314	7,549	8,086
Services	49,567	51,154	54,783
Others	28,555	29,477	31,571
Total	496,318	512,193	548,615

Mid-1998 (estimates in '000): Agriculture, etc. 747; Total 1,089 (Source: FAO, *Production Yearbook*).

Agriculture

PRINCIPAL CROPS ('000 metric tons)

	1996	1997	1998
Rice (paddy)*	94	168	210
Sweet potatoes†	17	17	17
Cassava (Manioc)* . . .	213	283	313
Yams†	20	20	20
Taro (Coco yam)† . . .	20	20	20
Coconuts†	7	7	7
Palm kernels†	10	11	11
Vegetables and melons† . .	76	76	76
Sugar cane†	245	250	250
Oranges†	7	7	7
Pineapples†	7	7	7
Bananas†	85	90	90
Plantains†	33	35	35
Natural rubber (dry weight)* . .	25	28†	28†

* Unofficial figures.   † FAO estimate(s).

Source: FAO, *Production Yearbook*.

LIVESTOCK (FAO estimates, '000 head, year ending September)

	1996	1997	1998
Cattle	36	36	36
Pigs	120	120	120
Sheep	210	210	210
Goats	220	220	220

Poultry (FAO estimates, million): 4 in 1996; 4 in 1997; 4 in 1998.

Source: FAO, *Production Yearbook*.

LIVESTOCK PRODUCTS (FAO estimates, metric tons)

	1996	1997	1998
Pig meat	4,000	4,000	4,000
Poultry meat	5,000	6,000	6,000
Other meat	9,000	8,000	8,000
Cows' milk	1,000	1,000	1,000
Hen eggs	4,000	4,000	4,000

Source; FAO, *Production Yearbook*.

Forestry

ROUNDWOOD REMOVALS ('000 cubic metres, excluding bark)

	1995	1996	1997
Sawlogs, veneer logs and logs for sleepers	100	29	75
Other industrial wood	130	138	152
Fuel wood	4,506	4,608	4,794
Total	4,736	4,775	5,021

Source: FAO, *Yearbook of Forest Products*.

SAWNWOOD PRODUCTION
('000 cubic metres, including railway sleepers)

	1995	1996	1997
Total	90	90	90

Source: FAO, *Yearbook of Forest Products*.

Fishing

('000 metric tons, live weight)

	1995	1996	1997
Inland waters	4.0	4.0	4.0
Atlantic Ocean	5.2	3.2	4.6
Total catch	9.2	7.2	8.6

Source: FAO, *Yearbook of Fishery Statistics*.

Mining

	1990	1991	1992
Iron ore ('000 metric tons)*	2,490	804	1,142
Industrial diamonds ('000 carats)	60	60	90
Gem diamonds ('000 carats)†	40	40	60
Gold (kilograms)*†	600	600	700

* Figures refer to the metal content of ores.
† Data from the US Bureau of Mines.

Gold (metal content, kilograms): 500 in 1994; 500 in 1995; 700 (estimate) in 1996 (data from the US Bureau of Mines).

Source: UN, *Industrial Commodity Statistics Yearbook*.

Industry

SELECTED PRODUCTS
('000 metric tons, unless otherwise indicated)

	1991	1992	1993
Palm oil*	25	25	30
Cigarettes (million)†	22	22	n.a.
Cement‡	2	8	8
Electric energy (million kWh)	450	460	480

* FAO estimates.
† Data from the US Department of Agriculture.
‡ Provisional or estimated figures.

Electric energy (million kWh): 480 in 1994; 486 in 1995.

Source: UN, *Industrial Commodity Statistics Yearbook*.

Palm oil (FAO estimates, '000 metric tons): 39 in 1996; 42 in 1997; 42 in 1998. (Source: FAO, *Production Yearbook*).

Finance

CURRENCY AND EXCHANGE RATES

Monetary Units
100 cents = 1 Liberian dollar (L $).

Sterling, Dollar and Euro Equivalents (28 April 2000)
£1 sterling = L $1.5681;
US $1 = L $1.0000;
€1 = 90.85 cents;
L $100 = £63.77 = US $100.00 = €110.07.

Exchange Rate
Since 1940 the Liberian dollar has been officially at par with the US dollar.

BUDGET (public sector accounts, L $ million, year ending 30 June)

Revenue*	1985/86	1986/87	1988†
Tax revenue	172.7	172.4	203.8
Taxes on income and profits	71.7	61.5	72.1
Taxes on property	1.1	2.3	2.6
Taxes on domestic transactions	44.9	57.7	53.3
Taxes on foreign trade	51.6	48.6	73.6
Other taxes	3.4	2.3	2.2
Other current revenue	7.7	8.0	8.9
Capital revenue	0.3	0.2	0.1
Total	180.7	180.6	212.8

Expenditure‡	1985/86	1986/87	1988†
General public services . .	51.3	51.3	67.8
Defence	21.0	23.5	26.5
Education	38.8	42.8	31.3
Health	15.6	18.7	14.5
Social security and welfare . .	2.3	2.5	2.9
Housing and community amenities	2.7	2.6	2.1
Recreational, cultural and religious affairs and services .	7.2	6.4	4.2
Economic affairs and services .	94.4	72.8	79.8
Fuel and energy . . .	7.3	4.5	17.4
Agriculture, forestry, fishing and hunting	21.0	23.6	14.1
Mining, manufacturing and construction	13.1	6.4	2.1
Transport and communications .	19.8	18.2	15.0
Other purposes . . .	40.6	42.9	54.3
Total	273.9	263.5	283.4
Current§	205.3	226.1	244.7
Capital	68.6	37.4	38.7

* Excluding grants received from abroad (L \$ million): 25.0 (current 17.0, capital 8.0) in 1985/86; 18.0 (current 12.2, capital 5.8) in 1986/87.
† Beginning in 1988, the fiscal year was changed to coincide with the calendar year.
‡ Excluding net lending (L \$ million): 22.7 in 1985/86; 19.0 in 1986/87; 21.3 in 1988.
§ Including interest payments (L \$ million): 40.6 in 1985/86; 42.9 in 1986/87; 41.2 in 1988.

Source: IMF, *Government Finance Statistics Yearbook*.

INTERNATIONAL RESERVES (US \$ million at 31 December)

	1997	1998	1999
Reserve position in IMF . .	0.04	0.04	0.04
Foreign exchange . . .	0.38	0.58	0.39
Total	0.42	0.62	0.43

Source: IMF, *International Financial Statistics*.

MONEY SUPPLY (L \$ million at 31 December)

	1997	1998	1999
Currency outside banks* . .	576.6	565.5	556.9
Demand deposits at commercial banks	110.0	1,005.5	1,247.9
Total money . . .	686.8	1,571.0	1,804.8

* Figures refer only to amounts of Liberian coin in circulation. US notes and coin also circulate, but the amount of these in private holdings is unknown. The amount of Liberian coin in circulation is small in comparison to US currency.

Source: IMF, *International Financial Statistics*.

COST OF LIVING
(Consumer Price Index for Monrovia; base: 1980 = 100)

	1986	1987	1988
Food	107.8	108.0	128.8
Fuel and light	127.2	127.4	128.1
Clothing	124.9	144.8	157.5
Rent	103.8	104.1	105.1
All items (incl. others) . . .	123.2	129.4	141.8

1989: Food 141.2 (average for January–October); All items 150.2.
1990 (January–June): Food 160.7; All items 162.4.
Source: ILO, *Yearbook of Labour Statistics*.

NATIONAL ACCOUNTS (L \$ million at current prices)
Expenditure on the Gross Domestic Product

	1987	1988	1989
Government final consumption expenditure	143.9	136.3	141.6
Private final consumption expenditure	713.9	733.3	656.8
Increase in stocks* . . .	7.0	3.5	4.0
Gross fixed capital formation .	120.4	115.3	96.8
Statistical discrepancy . .	22.9	39.1	48.2
Total domestic expenditure .	1,008.1	1,027.5	947.4
Exports of goods and services . .	438.2	452.3	521.4
Less Imports of goods and services	356.8	321.5	275.2
GDP in purchasers' values .	1,089.5	1,158.3	1,193.6
GDP at constant 1981 prices .	1,015.0	1,043.7	1,072.8

* Figures refer only to stocks of iron ore and rubber.

Gross Domestic Product by Economic Activity

	1987	1988	1989
Agriculture, hunting, forestry and fishing	381.8	412.0	410.7
Mining and quarrying . . .	105.0	115.0	122.3
Manufacturing	73.1	80.4	81.6
Electricity, gas and water . .	19.0	18.8	19.0
Construction	32.7	28.8	26.3
Trade, restaurants and hotels .	60.1	64.2	63.3
Transport, storage and communications . . .	75.3	79.1	79.1
Finance, insurance, real estate and business services . .	119.2	136.1	141.8
Government services . . .	108.5	109.7	139.4
Other community, social and personal services . . .	34.4	35.5	35.5
Sub-total	1,009.1	1,079.6	1,119.0
Less Imputed bank service charge .	18.3	27.1	36.5
GDP at factor cost . . .	990.8	1,052.5	1,082.5
Indirect taxes, *less* subsidies .	99.0	105.8	111.3
GDP in purchasers' values .	1,089.5	1,158.3	1,193.6

Source: UN, *National Accounts Statistics*.

BALANCE OF PAYMENTS (US \$ million)

	1985	1986	1987
Exports of goods f.o.b. . . .	430.4	407.9	374.9
Imports of goods f.o.b. . . .	−263.8	−258.8	−311.7
Trade balance . . .	166.6	149.1	63.2
Exports of services . . .	34.6	56.9	52.5
Imports of services . . .	−80.2	−80.5	−74.2
Balance on goods and services .	121.0	125.5	41.5
Other income received . . .	3.7	2.1	5.2
Other income paid . . .	−131.8	−183.3	−188.3
Balance on goods, services and income	−7.1	−55.7	−141.6
Current transfers received . .	130.0	97.9	50.0
Current transfers paid . . .	−67.6	−59.9	−53.5
Current balance . . .	55.3	−17.7	−145.1
Direct investment from abroad .	−16.2	−16.5	38.5
Portfolio investment assets . .	4.4	5.6	—
Other investment assets . .	−9.3	−7.1	4.3
Other investment liabilities . .	−128.9	−199.1	−228.1
Net errors and omissions . .	−108.7	−73.4	30.3
Overall balance	−203.4	−294.0	−300.1

Source: IMF, *International Financial Statistics*.

External Trade

PRINCIPAL COMMODITIES (US $ million)

Imports c.i.f.	1986	1987	1988
Food and live animals	53.6	58.7	47.3
Rice	12.1	17.7	27.9
Mineral fuels, lubricants, etc.	52.9	69.8	55.3
Refined petroleum products	52.5	67.1	n.a.
Motor spirit and other light fuels	12.1	14.2	n.a.
Chemicals and related products	26.3	22.1	15.3
Basic manufactures	36.0	55.3	48.0
Machinery and transport equipment	59.1	73.5	82.3
Miscellaneous manufactured articles	18.1	14.2	15.4
Total (incl. others)	259.0	307.6	272.3

Exports f.o.b.	1986	1987	1988
Coffee and substitutes	16.3	9.0	5.6
Cocoa	9.0	5.9	6.3
Natural rubber and gums	70.9	89.4	110.2
Wood in the rough or roughly squared	33.1	35.5	32.0
Iron ore and concentrates	248.4	218.0	219.7
Diamonds	6.6	11.0	8.8
Total (incl. others)	408.4	382.2	396.3

Source: UN, *International Trade Statistics Yearbook*.

1989 (L $ million): Total exports f.o.b. 461.16 (iron ore 235.05, rubber 119.93, logs 91.98). Source: National Bank of Liberia, *Quarterly Statistical Bulletin*.

PRINCIPAL TRADING PARTNERS (US $ million)*

Imports c.i.f.	1986	1987	1988
Belgium-Luxembourg	8.5	11.2	15.0
China, People's Repub.	7.1	14.7	4.8
Denmark	10.6	7.6	5.9
France (incl. Monaco)	6.5	6.4	4.7
Germany, Fed. Repub.	32.7	52.3	39.5
Italy	2.5	2.2	7.3
Japan	20.1	15.0	12.0
Netherlands	20.6	26.8	14.4
Spain	2.5	6.6	3.1
Sweden	2.4	0.6	4.6
United Kingdom	24.2	18.4	12.7
USA	42.5	58.0	57.7
Total (incl. others)	259.0	307.6	272.3

Exports f.o.b.	1986	1987	1988
Belgium-Luxembourg	29.2	23.2	28.2
France (incl. Monaco)	33.1	33.2	33.2
Germany, Fed. Repub.	114.5	109.2	108.1
Italy	70.3	63.4	63.2
Japan	4.9	1.0	4.8
Netherlands	14.4	11.5	10.5
Spain	16.4	17.8	13.4
United Kingdom	7.2	8.8	6.3
USA	93.2	73.9	74.6
Total (incl. others)	408.4	382.2	396.3

* Imports by country of origin; exports by country of last consignment.
Source: UN, *International Trade Statistics Yearbook*.

Transport

RAILWAYS (estimated traffic)

	1991	1992	1993
Passenger-km (million)	406	417	421
Freight ton-km (million)	200	200	200

Source: UN Economic Commission for Africa, *African Statistical Yearbook*.

ROAD TRAFFIC (estimates, vehicles in use at 31 December)

	1994	1995	1996
Passenger cars	13,720	10,340	9,400
Goods vehicles	26,000	28,420	32,000

Source: International Road Federation, *World Road Statistics*.

SHIPPING

Merchant Fleet (registered at 31 December)

	1996	1997	1998
Number of vessels	1,684	1,697	1,717
Displacement ('000 gross registered tons)	59,988.9	60,058.4	60,492.1

Source: Lloyd's Register of Shipping.

International Sea-borne Freight Traffic (estimates, '000 metric tons)

	1991	1992	1993
Goods loaded	16,706	17,338	21,653
Goods unloaded	1,570	1,597	1,608

Source: UN Economic Commission for Africa, *African Statistical Yearbook*.

CIVIL AVIATION (traffic on scheduled services)

	1990	1991	1992
Passengers carried ('000)	32	32	32
Passenger-km (million)	7	7	7
Total ton-km (million)	1	1	1

Source: UN, *Statistical Yearbook*.

Communications Media

	1994	1995	1996
Radio receivers ('000 in use)	670	675	715
Television receivers ('000 in use)	55	56	60
Telephones ('000 main lines in use)	5	5	n.a.
Daily newspapers Number	8	8	6
Average circulation ('000 copies, estimates)	35	35	35

1997: Radio receivers ('000 in use) 790; Television receivers ('000 in use) 70.
Sources: UNESCO, *Statistical Yearbook*; UN, *Statistical Yearbook*.

Education

	1983	1984	1985
Schools	1,284	1,830	1,691
Teachers	7,202	9,817	9,856
Students	245,673	275,243	260,560

1986: Students 250,322.
Source: Ministry of Education, Monrovia.
Primary school pupils (1986): 80,048.
University (1987): 444 teachers; 4,855 students (males 3,698; females 1,157).
Other higher (1987): 28 teachers; 240 students (males 220; females 20).
Source: UNESCO, *Statistical Yearbook*.

Directory

The Constitution

The Constitution, promulgated on 6 January 1986 (and amended in July 1988), provides for the division of state authority into three independent branches: the executive, the legislature and the judiciary. Executive powers are vested in the President, who is Head of State, Head of Government and Commander-in-Chief of the Liberian armed forces, and who is elected by universal adult suffrage for a six-year term (renewable only once). Legislative power is vested in the bicameral National Assembly, comprising the 26-member Senate and the 64-member House of Representatives. Members of the House of Representatives are directly elected for a term of six years, while two Senators are elected from each of Liberia's counties* for a term of nine years. The President appoints a Cabinet, subject to the approval of the Senate. The Constitution provides for a multi-party system of government, and incorporates powers to prevent the declaration of a one-party state, the dissolution of the legislature or the suspension of the judiciary. The Constitution may be amended by a two-thirds majority of both houses of the National Assembly.

* There were 13 counties at the time of the 1997 senatorial elections. The establishment of a 14th county was approved by the House of Representatives in June 1998.

The Government

HEAD OF STATE

President: CHARLES GHANKAY TAYLOR (took office 2 August 1997).
Vice-President: MOSES BLAH.

CABINET
(August 2000)

Minister of Agriculture: Dr ROLAND C. MASSAQUOI.
Minister of Commerce and Industry: AMELIA WARD.
Minister of Defence: DANIEL CHEA.
Minister of Education: Dr EVELYN WHITE-KANDAKAI.
Minister of Finance: NATHANIEL BARNES.
Minister of Foreign Affairs: MONIE CAPTAN.
Minister of Health and Social Welfare: Dr PETER COLEMAN.
Minister of Information, Culture and Tourism: JOE WOR-LORBAH-MULBAH.
Minister of Internal Affairs: MAXWELL POE.
Minister of Justice: EDDINGTON VARMAH.
Minister of Labour: CHRISTIAN NEUFVILLE.
Minister of Lands, Mines and Energy: JENKINS DUNBAR.
Minister of National Security: PHILIP KAMAH.
Minister of Planning and Economic Affairs: LAMI KAWAH.
Minister of Posts and Telecommunications: CHARLES BRIGHT.
Minister of Public Works: EMMET TAYLOR.
Minister of Rural Development: Lt-Gen. (retd) HEZEKIAH BOWEN.
Minister of Transport: BRAHIMA KABAH.
Minister of Youth and Sports: FRANÇOIS MASSAQUOI.
Minister of State of Presidential Affairs: JONATHAN TAYLOR.
Minister of State of Planning and Economic Affairs: WISSEH MCCLAIN.
Minister of State without Portfolio: AUGUSTINE ZAYZAY.

MINISTRIES

Office of the President: Executive Mansion, POB 10-9001, Capitol Hill, 1000 Monrovia 10; e-mail emansion@liberia.net.
Ministry of Agriculture: Tubman Blvd, POB 10-9010, 1000 Monrovia 10.
Ministry of Commerce and Industry: Ashmun St, POB 10-9014, 1000 Monrovia 10.
Ministry of Defence: Benson St, POB 10-9007, 1000 Monrovia 10.
Ministry of Education: E. G. N. King Plaza, Broad St, POB 10-1545, 1000 Monrovia 10; tel. and fax 226216.
Ministry of Finance: Broad St, POB 10-9013, 1000 Monrovia 10; tel. 227235.
Ministry of Foreign Affairs: Mamba Point, POB 10-1002, 1000 Monrovia 10; tel. 227616.

Ministry of Health and Social Welfare: Sinkor, POB 10-9004, 1000 Monrovia 10.
Ministry of Information, Culture and Tourism: Capitol Hill, POB 10-9021, 1000 Monrovia 10; tel.and fax 226269.
Ministry of Internal Affairs: cnr Warren and Benson Sts, POB 10-9008, 1000 Monrovia 10.
Ministry of Justice: Ashmun St, POB 10-9006, 1000 Monrovia 10.
Ministry of Labour: Mechlin St, POB 10-9040, 1000 Monrovia 10.
Ministry of Lands, Mines and Energy: Capitol Hill, POB 10-9024, 1000 Monrovia 10.
Ministry of National Security: 1000 Monrovia 10.
Ministry of Planning and Economic Affairs: Broad St, POB 10-9016, 1000 Monrovia 10.
Ministry of Posts and Telecommunications: Carey St, 1000 Monrovia 10.
Ministry of Presidential Affairs: Executive Mansion, Capitol Hill, 1000 Monrovia 10.
Ministry of Public Works: Lynch St, POB 10-9011, 1000 Monrovia 10.
Ministry of Rural Development: POB 10-9030, 1000 Monrovia 10.
Ministry of Transport: 1000 Monrovia 10.
Ministry of Youth and Sports: New Port St, POB 10-9040, 1000 Monrovia 10.

President and Legislature

PRESIDENT

Presidential Election, 19 July 1997

	Votes	% of votes
CHARLES TAYLOR (NPP)	468,443	75.33
ELLEN JOHNSON-SIRLEAF (UP)	59,557	9.58
Alhaji G. V. KROMAH (ALCOP)	25,059	4.03
CLETUS WOTORSON (Alliance of Political Parties)	15,969	2.57
GABRIEL BACCUS MATTHEWS (UPP)	15,604	2.51
Dr TOGBA-NAH TIPOTEH (LPP)	10,010	1.61
Dr GEORGE BOLEY (NDPL)	7,843	1.26
Dr HENRY MONIBA (LINU)	6,708	1.08
FIYAH GBOLIE (PDPL)	3,497	0.56
MARTIN SHERIF (NRP)	2,965	0.48
CHEA CHEAPOO (PPP)	2,142	0.34
Dr HENRY FAHNBULLEH (RAP)	2,067	0.33
Dr GEORGE T. WASHINGTON (FDP)	2,016	0.32
Total	621,880	100.00

LEGISLATURE

Senate

Elections to the 26-member Senate took place on 19 July 1997, with each county electing two Senators. The National Patriotic Party secured 21 seats, the Unity Party three seats, and the All Liberian Coalition Party two seats.

House of Representatives

Speaker: NYUDUEH MORKONMANA.

General Election, 19 July 1997

Party	Seats
National Patriotic Party	49
Unity Party	7
All Liberian Coalition Party	3
Alliance of Political Parties*	2
United People's Party	2
Liberian People's Party	1
Total	64

* Coalition of the Liberian Action Party and the Liberian Unification Party.

Political Organizations

At the end of January 1997 the armed factions in Liberia officially ceased to exist as military organizations; a number of them were reconstituted as political parties, while long-standing political organizations re-emerged. Elections in July of that year were contested by 13 political associations.

All Liberian Coalition Party (ALCOP): f. 1997 from elements of the fmr armed faction, the United Liberation Movement of Liberia for Democracy; Leader Alhaji G. V. KROMAH.

Free Democratic Party (FDP): Leader Dr GEORGE T. WASHINGTON.

Liberian Action Party (LAP): f. 1984; Leader CLETUS WOTORSON.

Liberian National Union (LINU): Leader HENRY MONIBA.

Liberian People's Party (LPP): f. 1984 by fmr members of the Movement for Justice in Africa; Leader TOGBA-NAH TIPOTEH.

Liberian Unification Party (LUP): f. 1984; Leader LAVELI SUPU-WOOD.

National Democratic Party of Liberia (NDPL): f. 1997 from the fmr armed faction, the Liberia Peace Council; Leader Dr GEORGE E. SAIGBE BOLEY.

National Patriotic Party (NPP): f. 1997 from the fmr armed faction, the National Patriotic Front of Liberia; won the majority of seats in legislative elections in July; Leader CHARLES GHANKAY TAYLOR; Sec.-Gen. CHRISTIAN HERBERT.

National Reformation Party (NRP): Leader MARTIN SHERIF.

People's Democratic Party of Liberia (PDPL): Leader FIYAH GBOLIE.

People's Progressive Party (PPP): Leader CHEA CHEAPOO.

Reformation Alliance Party (RAP): Leader HENRY BOIMAH FAHN-BULLEH.

United People's Party (UPP): f. 1984 by fmr mems of the Progressive People's Party, which led opposition prior to April 1980 coup; Leader GABRIEL BACCUS MATTHEWS.

Unity Party (UP): f. 1984; Leader ELLEN JOHNSON-SIRLEAF.

Diplomatic Representation

EMBASSIES IN LIBERIA

Algeria: Capitol By-Pass, POB 2032, Monrovia; tel. 224311; Chargé d'affaires a.i.: MUHAMMAD AZZEDINE AZZOUZ.

Cameroon: 18th St and Payne Ave, Sinkor, POB 414, Monrovia; tel. 261374; Ambassador: VICTOR E. NDIBA.

Congo, Democratic Republic: Spriggs Payne Airport, Sinkor, POB 1038, Monrovia; tel. 261326; Ambassador: (vacant).

Côte d'Ivoire: Tubman Blvd, Sinkor, POB 126, Monrovia; tel. 261123; Ambassador: CLÉMENT KAUL MELEDJE.

Cuba: 17 Kennedy Ave, Congotown, POB 3579, Monrovia; tel. 262600; Ambassador: M. GAUNEANO CARDOSO TOLEDO.

Egypt: POB 462, Monrovia; tel. 226226; fax 226122; Ambassador: FAROUK GHONEIM.

Germany: Oldest Congotown, POB 34, Monrovia; tel. 261460; Ambassador: Dr JÜRGEN GEHL.

Ghana: cnr 11th St and Gardiner Ave, Sinkor, POB 471, Monrovia; tel. 261477; Ambassador: G. R. NIPAH.

Israel: Gardiner Ave, between 11th and 12th Sts, Sinkor, Monrovia; tel. 262861; Ambassador: MOSHE ITAN.

Italy: Mamba Point, POB 255, Monrovia; tel. 224580; Ambassador: Dr. ENRIC'ANGIOLO FERRONI-CARLI.

Korea, Republic: 10th St and Payne Ave, Sinkor, POB 2769, Monrovia; tel. 261532; Ambassador: KIM YONG-JIP.

Lebanon: 12th St, Monrovia; tel. 262537; Chargé d'affaires: GABRIEL GEARA.

Libya: Monrovia; Ambassador: MUHAMMAD UMAR AT-TABI.

Morocco: Tubman Blvd, Congotown, Monrovia; tel. 262767; Chargé d'affaires a.i.: Dr MOULAY ABBES AL-KADIRI.

Nigeria: Congo Town, POB 366, Monrovia; tel. 227345; fax 226135; Ambassador: JOSHUA IROHA.

Poland: cnr 10th St and Gardiner Ave, Sinkor, POB 860, Monrovia; tel. 261113; Chargé d'affaires a.i.: ZBIGNIEW REJMAN.

Romania: 81 Sekou Touré Ave, Sinkor, POB 2598, Monrovia; tel. 261508; Chargé d'affaires a.i.: SILVESTRA ZUGRAV.

Russia: Payne Ave, Sinkor, POB 2010, Monrovia; tel. 261304; Ambassador: VASILII S. BEBKO.

Senegal: Monrovia; Ambassador: MOCTAR TRAORÉ.

Sierra Leone: Tubman Blvd, POB 575, Monrovia; tel. 261301; Ambassador: WILFRED KANU.

Spain: Capitol Hill, POB 275, Monrovia; tel. 221299; Ambassador: MANUEL DE LUNA.

Sweden: POB 335, Monrovia; tel. 261646; Chargé d'affaires a.i.: OVE SVENSSON.

Switzerland: Old Congo Rd, POB 283, Monrovia; tel. 261065; Chargé d'affaires a.i.: CHARLES HALLER.

USA: 111 United Nations Drive, Mamba Point, POB 10-0098, Monrovia; tel. 222991; Ambassador: BISMARCK MYRICK.

Judicial System

In February 1982 the People's Supreme Tribunal (which had been established following the April 1980 coup) was renamed the People's Supreme Court, and its chairman and members became the Chief Justice and Associate Justices of the People's Supreme Court. The judicial system also comprised People's Circuit and Magistrate Courts. The five-member Supreme Court (composed of representatives of the interim Government and of the NPFL) was established in January 1992 to adjudicate in electoral disputes.

Chief Justice of the Supreme Court of Liberia: GLORIA M. MUSU-SCOTT.

Religion

Liberia is officially a Christian state, although complete religious freedom is guaranteed. Christianity and Islam are the two main religions. There are numerous religious sects, and many Liberians hold traditional beliefs.

CHRISTIANITY

Liberian Council of Churches: 16 St, Sinkor, POB 10-2191, 1000 Monrovia; tel. 226630; fax 226132; f. 1982; 11 mems, two assoc. mems, one fraternal mem.; Pres. Rt Rev. Dr W. NAH DIXON; Gen. Sec. Rev. STEVEN W. MUIN.

The Anglican Communion

The diocese of Liberia forms part of the Church of the Province of West Africa, incorporating the local Protestant Episcopal Church. Anglicanism was established in Liberia in 1836, and the diocese of Liberia was admitted into full membership of the Province in 1982. In 1985 the Church had 125 congregations, 39 clergy, 26 schools and about 20,000 adherents in the country. The Metropolitan of the Province is the Bishop of Koforidua, Ghana.

Bishop of Liberia: Rt Rev. EDWARD NEUFVILLE, POB 10-0277, 1000 Monrovia 10; tel. 224760; fax 227519.

The Roman Catholic Church

Liberia comprises the archdiocese of Monrovia and the dioceses of Cape Palmas and Gbarnga. At 31 December 1998 there were an estimated 114,240 adherents in the country, equivalent to 4.8% of the total population. The Bishops participate in the Interterritorial Catholic Bishops' Conference of the Gambia, Liberia and Sierra Leone (based in Freetown, Sierra Leone).

Archbishop of Monrovia: Most Rev. MICHAEL KPAKALA FRANCIS, Catholic Mission, POB 2078, Monrovia; tel. 227245; fax 226175.

Other Christian Churches

Assemblies of God in Liberia: POB 1297, Monrovia; f. 1908; 14,578 adherents, 287 churches; Gen. Supt JIMMIE K. DUGBE, Sr.

Lutheran Church in Liberia: POB 1046, Monrovia; tel. 226633; fax 226262; e-mail lwfliberia@compuserve.com; 35,600 adherents; Pres. Bishop SUMOWARD E. HARRIS.

Providence Baptist Church: cnr Broad and Center Sts, Monrovia; f. 1821; 2,500 adherents, 300 congregations, 6 ministers, 8 schools; Pastor Rev. A. MOMOLUE DIGGS; associated with:

> **The Liberia Baptist Missionary and Educational Convention, Inc:** POB 390, Monrovia; tel. 222661; f. 1880; Pres. Rev. J. K. LEVEE MOULTON; Nat. Vice-Pres. Rev. J. GBANA HALL; Gen. Sec. CHARLES W. BLAKE.

United Methodist Church in Liberia: cnr 12th St and Tubman Blvd, POB 1010, 1000 Monrovia 10; tel. 223343; f. 1833; c. 70,000 adherents, 487 congregations, 450 ministers, 300 lay pastors, 38 schools; Resident Bishop Rev. ARTHUR F. KULAH; Sec. Rev. JULIUS SARWOLO NELSON.

Other active denominations include the National Baptist Mission, the Pentecostal Church, the Presbyterian Church in Liberia, the Prayer Band and the Church of the Lord Aladura.

ISLAM

The total community numbers about 670,000.

National Muslim Council of Liberia: Monrovia; Leader Shaykh KAFUMBA KONNAH.

The Press

NEWSPAPERS

Daily Observer: 11 Broad St, POB 1858, 1000 Monrovia 10; tel. 223545; f. 1981; independent; 5 a week; Editor-in-Chief STANTON B. PEABODY; circ. 30,000.

Herald: Monrovia; f. 1987; Catholic weekly; Editor RUFUS DARPOH.

The Inquirer: Monrovia; Man. Editor GABRIEL WILLIAMS.

New Times: Monrovia; Man. Editor RUFUS DARPOH; Editor JEFF MUTADA.

Sunday Express: Mamba Point, POB 3029, Monrovia; weekly; Editor JOHN F. SCOTLAND; circ. 5,000.

Sunday People: POB 3366, Monrovia; 2 a week; Editor D. G. PYNE-DRAPER.

PERIODICALS

Concord Times: Monrovia; English; independent; weekly; Man. Editor LYNDON PONNIE; circ. 3,000.

Daily Listener: POB 35, Monrovia; monthly; Man. CHARLES C. DENNIS; circ. 3,500.

The Eye: POB 4692, Monrovia; daily; Editor H. B. KINBAH.

Journal of Commerce, Industry & Transportation: POB 9041, Monrovia; tel. 222141.

The Kpelle Messenger: Kpelle Literacy Center, Lutheran Church, POB 1046, Monrovia; Kpelle-English; monthly; Editor Rev. JOHN J. MANAWU.

Liberian Star: POB 691, Monrovia; f. 1954; monthly; Editor HENRY B. COLE; circ. 3,500.

Palm: Johnson and Carey Sts, POB 1110, Monrovia; 6 a year; Editor JAMES C. DENNIS.

The People Magazine: Bank of Liberia Bldg, Suite 214, Carey and Warren Sts, POB 3501, Monrovia; tel. 222743; f. 1985; monthly; Editor and Publr CHARLES A. SNETTER.

Plain Talk: POB 2108, Monrovia; daily; Editor-in-Chief N. MACAULAY PAYKUE.

X-Ray Magazine: c/o Liss Inc, POB 4196, Monrovia; tel. 221674; f. 1985; monthly; health; Man. Editor NMAH BROPLEH.

PRESS ORGANIZATION

Press Union of Liberia: Monrovia; f. 1985; Pres. SUAH DEDDEH.

NEWS AGENCIES

Liberian News Agency (LINA): POB 9021, Capitol Hill, Monrovia; tel. 222229; Dir-Gen. ERNEST KIAZOLY (acting).

Foreign Bureaux

Agence France-Presse (AFP): Monrovia; Rep. JAMES DORBOR.

United Press International (UPI) (USA): Monrovia; Correspondent T. K. SANNAH.

Xinhua (New China) News Agency (People's Republic of China): Adams St, Old Rd, Congotown, POB 3001, Monrovia; tel. 262821; Correspondent SUN BAOYU.

Reuters (UK) is also represented in Liberia.

Publisher

Government Publishing House

Government Printer: Government Printing Office, POB 9002, Monrovia; tel. 221029.

Broadcasting and Communications

TELECOMMUNICATIONS

Liberia Telecommunications Corporation: Monrovia; CEO CHARLES ROBERTS.

Monrovia Communications Corporation (MONCOM): Monrovia; tel. 4057001; fax 4052002.

BROADCASTING

Radio

ELBC—The Voice of Peace, Harmony and Reconciliation: Liberian Broadcasting System, POB 594, Monrovia; tel. 224984; f. 1960; programmes in English, French and Liberian vernaculars; Asst Dir-Gen. (Radio) NOAH A. BORDOLO.

Kiss FM: Owned by Pres. Charles Ghankay Taylor; country-wide broadcasts.

LAMCO Broadcasting Station (ELNR): LAMCO Information and Broadcasting Service, Nimba; Liberian news, music, cultural, political and educational programmes in English; carries national news and all programmes of ELBC; also local news in English and African languages (Mano, Gio, Bassa, Vai, Lorma, Kru, Krahn, Grebo and Kpelle); also relays BBC World Service and African Service news broadcasts; Dir T. NELSON WILLIAMS.

Liberia Rural Communications Network: POB 10-02176, 1000 Monrovia 10; tel. 271368; f. 1981; govt-operated; rural development and entertainment programmes; Dir J. RUFUS KAINE (acting).

Radio ELWA (Eternal Love Winning Africa): POB 192, Monrovia; tel. 271669; f. 1954; operated by SIM International (formerly Sudan Interior Mission); religious broadcasts in English; Broadcasting Dir LEE J. SONIUS.

Radio Liberia (Liberia Communications Network): Totota; short-wave service operated by the National Patriotic Party.

Radio Liberty: FM radio station; associated with former faction leader, Dr George Boley.

Radio Monrovia: Monrovia; independent FM radio station.

Star Radio: Sekou Toure Ave, Mamba Point, Monrovia; tel. 226820; fax 227360; e-mail star@liberia.net; independent news and information station; f. July 1997 by Fondation Hirondelle, Switzerland, with funds from the US Agency for International Development; broadcasts in English, French and 14 African languages; Dir GEORGE BENNETT.

Voice of America: Monrovia; funded by the US Govt; broadcasts in English, French, Swahili, Hausa and Portuguese.

Television

ELTV: Liberian Broadcasting System, POB 594, Monrovia; tel. 224984f. 1964; commercial station, partly govt-supported.

Finance

(cap. = capital; res = reserves; dep. = deposits; m. = million; br. = branch; amounts in Liberian dollars)

BANKING

Most banking operations in Liberia were suspended in 1990, as a result of the disruption caused by the civil conflict. A number of commercial banks subsequently resumed operations.

Central Bank

National Bank of Liberia: Broad St, POB 2048, Monrovia; tel. 222497; f. 1974; bank of issue; cap. and res 17.1m., dep. 70.7m. (1986); Gov. ELI SALEEBY.

Other Banks

Agricultural and Co-operative Development Bank: Carey and Warren Sts, POB 10-3585, Monrovia; tel. 224385; fax 221500; f. 1977; 65% govt-owned; cap. 6.6m. (Dec. 1989), res. 6.7m., dep. 30.6m. (Dec. 1987); Pres. and CEO JEROME M. HODGE; Gen. Man. ETHEL DAVIS; 6 brs.

Citibank (Liberia): Ashmun St, POB 280, Monrovia; tel. 224991; f. 1935; cap. 0.5m.; Gen. Man. THIERRY BUNGINER; 1 br.

Eurobank Liberia Ltd: Broad and Warren Sts, POB 2021, 1000 Monrovia; tel. 224873; fax 225921; cap. 1m. (Dec. 1992); Chair. GEORGES PHILIPPE; Pres. DONALD S. REYNOLDS.

First Commercial and Investment Bank: cnr Ashmun and Mechlin Sts, POB 1442, Monrovia; tel. 222498; fax 222351; cap. 3.6m. (Dec. 1991); Chair. and Pres. EDWIN J. COOPER.

International Trust Co of Liberia: 80 Broad St, POB 10-292, Monrovia; tel. 226279; fax 226159; f. 1948; cap. 2m. (1989), dep. 96.4m. (Dec. 1996); Pres. A. N. STEWART; Gen. Man. Gen. THOMAS JEFFREY; 1 br.

Liberia Finance and Trust Corporation: Broad St, POB 3155, Monrovia; tel. 221020; cap. 0.8m. (Dec. 1984); Chair. G. ALVIN JONES; Pres. C. T. O. KING, III.

Liberian Bank for Development and Investment (LBDI): Ashmun and Randall Sts, POB 547, Monrovia; tel. 227140; fax 226359; f. 1961; cap. 5.2m. (March 1991), dep. 34.1m. (Dec. 1993); Chair. ELIE E. SALEEBY; Gen. Man. FRANCIS A. DENNIS.

Liberian Trading and Development Bank Ltd (TRADEVCO): 57 Ashmun St, POB 10-293, Monrovia; tel. 221800; fax 225035; f. 1955; wholly-owned subsidiary of Mediobanca SpA (Italy); cap. and res 3.2m., dep. 64.7m. (June 1995); Chair. and Pres. GIORGIO PICOTTI.

National Housing Bank: Water St, POB 10-0818, Monrovia; tel. 221402; Pres. CHARLES SIRLEAF.

Banking Association

Liberia Bankers' Association: POB 292, Monrovia; mems include commercial and development banks; Pres. LEN MAESTRE.

INSURANCE

American International Underwriters, Inc: Carter Bldg, 39 Broad St, POB 180, Monrovia; tel. 224921; general; Gen. Man. S. B. MENSAH.

American Life Insurance Co: Carter Bldg, 39 Broad St, POB 60, Monrovia; f. 1969; life and general; Vice-Pres. ALLEN BROWN.

Insurance Co of Africa: 80 Broad St, POB 292, Monrovia; f. 1969; life and general; Pres. GIZAW H. MARIAM.

Lone Star Insurances Inc: 51 Broad St, POB 1142, Monrovia; tel. 222257; property and casualty.

Minet James Liberia Inc: POB 541, Monrovia; Man. Dir EDWARD MILNE.

National Insurance Corporation of Liberia (NICOL): LBDI Bldg Complex, POB 1528, Sinkor, Monrovia; tel. 262429; f. 1984; state-owned; sole insurer for govt and parastatal bodies; also provides insurance for the Liberian-registered merchant shipping fleet; Man. Dir MIATTA EDITH SHERMAN.

Royal Exchange Assurance: Ashmun and Randall Sts, POB 666, Monrovia; all types of insurance; Man. RONALD WOODS.

United Security Insurance Agencies Inc: Randall St, POB 2071, Monrovia; life, personal accident and medical; Dir EPHRAIM O. OKORO.

Trade and Industry

GOVERNMENT AGENCIES

Budget Bureau: Capitol Hill, POB 1518, Monrovia; Dir EMMANUEL GARDNER.

General Services Agency (GSA): Sinkor, Monrovia; Dir PAUL MULBAH.

DEVELOPMENT ORGANIZATIONS

Forestry Development Authority: POB 3010, 1000 Monrovia; tel. 224940; fax 226000; responsible for forest management and conservation; Man. Dir ROBERT TAYLOR.

Liberia Industrial Free Zone Authority: Bushrod Island, POB 9047, Monrovia; f. 1975; 98 mems; Man. Dir GBAI M. GBALA.

National Investment Commission (NIC): Former Executive Mansion Bldg, POB 9043, Monrovia; tel. 225163; f. 1979; autonomous body negotiating investment incentives agreements on behalf of Govt; promotes agro-based and industrial development; Chief CYRIL ALLEN.

CHAMBER OF COMMERCE

Liberia Chamber of Commerce: POB 92, Monrovia; tel. 223738; f. 1951; Pres. DAVID A. B. JALLAH; Sec.-Gen. LUESETTE S. HOWELL.

INDUSTRIAL AND TRADE ASSOCIATIONS

Liberian Produce Marketing Corporation: POB 662, Monrovia; tel. 222447; f. 1961; govt-owned; exports Liberian produce, provides industrial facilities for processing of agricultural products and participates in agricultural development programmes; Man. Dir TIJANI GARBA.

Liberian Resources Corporation (LIBRESCO): controls Liberia's mineral resources; 60% govt-owned; 40% owned by South African co, Amalia Gold.

Mesurado Industrial Complex: POB 142, Monrovia; Liberian-owned cos; products include detergents, soap, industrial gases; Pres. P. BONNER JALLAH.

EMPLOYERS' ASSOCIATION

National Enterprises Corporation: POB 518, Monrovia; tel. 261370; importer, wholesaler and distributor of foodstuffs, and wire and metal products for local industries; Pres. EMMANUEL SHAW, Sr.

UTILITIES

Electricity

Liberia Electricity Corporation: Waterside, POB 165, Monrovia; Man. Dir IAN YAPP.

MAJOR COMPANIES

The following are among the largest companies in terms either of capital investment or employment. In 1990 the majority of industrial companies were forced to suspend activity, owing to the disruption caused by the civil war. Commercial activity normalized following a peace agreement, which was reached in August 1996.

Bong Mining Co Ltd: POB 538, Monrovia; tel. 225222; fax 225770; f. 1958; iron ore mining, upgrading of crude ore and transportation of concentrate and pellets to Monrovia Free Port for shipment abroad; capacity: 4.5m. tons of concentrate and 3m. tons of pellets

annually; Pres. HANSJOERG RIETZSCH; Gen. Man. HANS-GEORG SCHNEIDER; 2,200 employees.

Bridgestone Firestone Co: POB 140, Harbel; f. 1926 by Firestone Rubber Co (USA); acquired by Japanese co, Bridgestone, in 1988, although Firestone retained control of local management; operations severely disrupted during 1990–92 and 1993–97; Man. Dir CLYDE TABOR; c. 3,000 employees.

Liberia Cement Corporation (CEMENCO): POB 150, Monrovia; tel. 222650; fax 226219; mfrs of Portland cement; Gen. Man. H. WALLWITZ.

The Liberia Co: POB 45, Broad St, Monrovia; f. 1947; shipping agents Delta Steamship Lines; owns COCOPA rubber plantations; Pres. J. T. TRIPPE (New York); Vice-Pres. J. M. LIJNKAMP (Monrovia); 850 employees.

Liberian International American Corporation (LIAC): mining of iron ore.

Liberian Iron and Steel Corporation (LISCO): POB 876, Monrovia; f. 1967; mining of iron ore.

Liberian Mining Co (LIMINCO): Monrovia; govt-owned; mining of iron ore; assumed control of LAMCO JV Operating Co in 1989; operations suspended in 1993.

Liberia Petroleum Refining Corporation (LPRC): POB 90, Monrovia; tel. 222600; sole producer of domestically produced fuels, with designed capacity of 15,000 b/d; products include diesel fuel, fuel oils, liquid petroleum gas; supplies domestic market and has limited export facilities for surplus products; Man. Dir P. DAVIS.

Mesurado Industrial Complex: POB 142, Monrovia; Liberian-owned cos; products include detergents, soap, industrial gases, windows and animal feeds; Pres. P. BONNER JALLAH.

National Iron Ore Co Ltd: POB 548, Monrovia; f. 1958; 85% govt-owned co mining iron ore at Mano river; Gen. Man. S. K. DATTA RAY.

Shell Liberia Ltd: Bushrod Island, POB 360, Monrovia; f. 1920; inc in Canada; distributors of petroleum products; Man. M. Y. KUENYEDZI; 15 employees.

Texaco Exploration Belize Inc: ULRC Bldg, Randall St and United Nations, Monrovia; oil and gas exploration; Pres. C. R. BLACK.

United States Trading Co: POB 140, Monrovia; f. 1949; distribution of Firestone products; Ford USA and UK vehicle sales and service, wholesalers and retailers of foodstuffs and beverages.

TRADE UNIONS

Congress of Industrial Organizations: 29 Ashmun St, POB 415, Monrovia; Pres. Gen. J. T. PRATT; Sec.-Gen. AMOS N. GRAY; 5 affiliated unions.

Labor Congress of Liberia: 71 Gurley St, Monrovia; Sec.-Gen. P. C. T. SONPON; 8 affiliated unions.

Liberian Federation of Labor Unions: J. B. McGill Labor Center, Gardnersville Freeway, POB 415, Monrovia; f. 1980 by merger; Sec.-Gen. AMOS GRAY; 10,000 mems (1983).

Transport

RAILWAYS

Railway operations were suspended in 1990, owing to the civil conflict. Large sections of the 480-km rail network were subsequently dismantled.

Bong Mining Co Ltd: POB 538, Monrovia; tel. 225222; fax 225770; f. 1965; Gen. Man. HANS-GEORG SCHNEIDER.

Liberian Mining Co: Monrovia; tel. 221190; govt-owned; assumed control of LAMCO JV Operating Co in 1989.

National Iron Ore Co Ltd: POB 548, Monrovia; f. 1951; Gen. Man. S. K. DATTA RAY.

ROADS

In 1996 the road network in Liberia totalled an estimated 10,600 km, of which about 657 km were paved. The main trunk road is the Monrovia–Sanniquellie motor road, extending north-east from the capital to the border with Guinea, near Ganta, and eastward through the hinterland to the border with Côte d'Ivoire. Trunk roads run through Tapita, in Nimba County, to Grand Gedeh County and from Monrovia to Buchanan. A bridge over the Mano river connects with the Sierra Leone road network, while a main road links Monrovia and Freetown (Sierra Leone). The use of the road network was subject to considerable disruption from 1990, as a result of the armed conflict in Liberia. Following a peace agreement in August 1996, most of the principal roads were reopened to commercial traffic in early 1997.

SHIPPING

In December 1998 Liberia's open-registry fleet (1,717 vessels), the second largest in the world (after Panama) in terms of gross tonnage, had a total displacement of 60.5m. grt. Commercial port activity in Liberia was frequently suspended from 1990, as a result of the armed conflict, but resumed in late 1996.

Bureau of Maritime Affairs: POB 10-9042, 1000 Monrovia 10; fax 226069.

Liberia National Shipping Line (LNSL): Monrovia; f. 1987; jt venture by the Liberian Govt and private German interests; routes to Europe, incl. the UK and Scandinavia.

National Port Authority: POB 1849, Monrovia; tel. 221454; f. 1967; administers Monrovia Free Port and the ports of Buchanan, Greenville and Harper; Man. Dir ELSIE DOGSIE BADIO.

CIVIL AVIATION

Liberia's principal airports are Roberts Field International Airport, at Harbel, 56 km east of Monrovia, and James Spriggs Payne Airport, at Monrovia. There are more than 100 other airfields and airstrips. As a result of the armed conflict in Liberia, normal air services were suspended in 1990. James Spriggs Payne Airport was reopened in mid-1996. Roberts Field International Airport was re-opened at the end of 1997; it was announced that US $50m. was required for its rehabilitation.

ADC Liberia Inc: Monrovia; f. 1993; services to the United Kingdom, the USA and destinations in West Africa.

Air Liberia: POB 2076, Monrovia; f. 1974 by merger; state-owned; scheduled passenger and cargo services; Man. Dir JAMES K. KOFA.

Defence

The total strength of the Armed Forces of Liberia (AFL) in mid-1998 was an estimated 14,000. It was envisaged that the AFL was to be reorganized to comprise an army of about 3,400, a navy of 1,100 and an air force of 500. In late 1999 the remaining troops belonging to the ECOWAS Cease-Fire Monitoring Group (ECOMOG) were redeployed to Sierra Leone, owing to the increased rebel activity in that country.

Defence Expenditure: Estimated at US $45m. in 1998.

Chief of Staff of the Armed Forces of Liberia: Lt-Gen. PAUL JOHNSON.

Education

Primary and secondary education are available free of charge, except for an annual registration fee of about L $10. Education is officially compulsory for 10 years, between six and 16 years of age. Primary education begins at seven years of age and lasts for six years. Secondary education, beginning at 13 years of age, lasts for a further six years, divided into two cycles of three years each. In 1986 the total enrolment at primary schools was equivalent to only 35% of children in the relevant age-group; in 1984 the comparable ratio for secondary schools was 17%. In late 1995 total enrolment of school-age children was estimated at only 25%. A total of 5,056 students were enrolled at the University of Monrovia in 1994. Other higher education institutes include the Cuttington University College (controlled by the Protestant Episcopal Church), a college of technology and a computer science institute. In 1986 enrolment in tertiary education was equivalent to 2.5% of the relevant age group (males 3.7%, females 1.2%). UNESCO estimated that 54.8% of the adult population (males 38.4%; females 71.6%) remained illiterate in 1995. Following elections in July 1997, the new government was to rehabilitate large numbers of children who had been recruited to fight for the armed factions during the period of civil conflict. The government announced that about 15% of projected expenditure in the interim 2000 budget (covering only January–June 2000) was being allocated to education.

Bibliography

Alao, A. *The Burden of Collective Goodwill: The International Involvement in the Liberian Civil War.* Aldershot, Ashgate, 1998.

Clapham, C. *Liberia and Sierra Leone: An Essay in Comparative Politics.* Cambridge University Press, 1976.

Corder, S. H. *Liberia under Military Rule.* Monrovia, 1980.

Cruise O'Brien, D. B., Dunn, J., and Rathbone, R. (Eds). *Contemporary West African States.* Cambridge, Cambridge University Press, 1989.

Dolo, E. *Democracy versus Dictatorship: The Quest for Freedom and Justice in Africa's Oldest Republic, Liberia.* Lanham, MD, University Press of America, 1996.

Dunn, D. E. *The Foreign Policy of Liberia During the Tubman Era 1944–71.* Hutchinson Benham, 1979.

Dunn, D. E., and Holsoe, S. E. *Historical Dictionary of Liberia.* Metuchen, NJ, Scarecrow Press, 1986.

Dunn, D. E., and Tarr, S. B. *Liberia: A National Polity in Transition.* Metuchen, NJ, Scarecrow Press, 1988.

Ellis, S. *The Mask of Anarchy: The Destruction of Liberia and the Religious Dimension of an African Civil War.* London, C. Hurst & Co., 1999.

Fahnbulleh, H. B., Jr. *The Diplomacy of Prejudice: Liberia in International Politics 1945–1970.* Vantage Press, 1986.

Gifford, P. *Christianity and Politics in Doe's Liberia.* New York, Cambridge University Press, 1993.

Givens, W. *Liberia: The Road to Democracy under the Leadership of Samuel Kanyon Doe.* London, Kensal Press, 1986.

Horton A. P. *Liberia's Underdevelopment.* Lanham, MD, University Press of America, 1994.

Huberich, C. H. *The Political and Legislative History of Liberia.* 2 vols. New York, 1947.

Keih, G. K. Jr. *Dependency and the Foreign Policy of a Small Power.* Lewiston, NY, Edwin Mellen Press, 1992.

Liebenow, J. G. *Liberia: The Quest for Democracy.* Bloomington, Indiana University Press, 1987.

Magyar, K. P., and Gontel-Morgan (Eds). *Peace-keeping in Africa: ECOMOG in Liberia.* Basingstoke, Macmillan, 1998.

Rimmer, D. *The Economies of West Africa.* London, Weidenfeld and Nicolson, 1984.

Sawyer, A. *The Emergence of Autocracy in Liberia: Tragedy and Challenge.* San Francisco, ICS Press, 1992.

Schulze, W. *A New Geography of Liberia.* London, Longman, 1973.

Sisay, H. B. *Big Powers and Small Nations.* Lanham, MD, University Press of America, 1985.

US Library of Congress. *Liberia during the Tolbert Era: A Guide.* Washington, DC, 1984.

Vogt, M. A. (Ed.). *Liberian Crisis and ECOMOG: A Bold Attempt at Regional Peace-keeping.* Lagos, Gabumo Publishing Co, 1992.

Wonkeryor, E. L. *Liberia's Military Dictatorship: A 'Fiasco' Revolution.* Chicago, Smugglers' Press, 1985.

MADAGASCAR

Physical and Social Geography

VIRGINIA THOMPSON

PHYSICAL FEATURES

The Democratic Republic of Madagascar comprises the island of Madagascar, the fourth largest island in the world, and several much smaller offshore islands. Madagascar lies 390 km from the east African mainland across the Mozambique channel. It extends 1,600 km from north to south and is up to 570 km wide. The whole territory covers an area of 587,041 sq km (226,658 sq miles). Geologically, the main island is basically composed of crystalline rock, which forms the central highlands that rise abruptly from the narrow eastern coastal strip and descend gradually to the wide plains of the west coast.

Topographically, Madagascar can be divided into six fairly distinct regions. Antsiranana province, in the north, is virtually isolated by the island's highest peak, Mt Tsaratanana, rising to 2,800 m above sea level. Tropical crops can be grown in its fertile valleys, and the natural harbour of Antsiranana is an important naval base. Another rich agricultural region lies in the north-west, where a series of valleys converge on the port of Mahajanga. To the south-west along the coastal plains lies a well-watered region where there are large animal herds and crops of rice, cotton, tobacco, and manioc. The southernmost province, Toliary (Tuléar), contains most of Madagascar's known mineral deposits, as well as extensive cattle herds, despite the almost total lack of rainfall. In contrast, the hot and humid climate of the east coast favours the cultivation of the island's most valuable tropical crops—coffee, vanilla, cloves, and sugar cane. Although this coast lacks sheltered anchorages, it is the site of Madagascar's most important commercial port, Toamasina. Behind its coral beaches a continuous chain of lagoons, some of which are connected by the Pangalanes Canal, provides a partially navigable internal waterway. The island's mountainous hinterland is a densely populated region of extensive rice culture and stock raising. Despite its relative inaccessibility, this region is Madagascar's administrative and cultural centre, the focal point being the capital city of Antananarivo.

Climatic conditions vary from tropical conditions on the east and north-west coasts to the hotness and dryness of the west coast, the extreme aridity of the south and the temperate zone in the central highlands. Forests have survived only in some areas of abundant rainfall, and elsewhere the land has been eroded by over-grazing and slash-and-burn farming methods. Most of the island is savannah-steppe, and much of the interior is covered with laterite. Except in the drought-ridden south, rivers are numerous and flow generally westward, but many are interspersed by rapids and waterfalls, and few are navigable except for short distances.

POPULATION AND CULTURE

Geography and history account for the diversity and distribution of the population, which was enumerated at 12,092,157 at the census of August 1993. The island's 18 principal ethnic groups are the descendants of successive waves of immigrants from such diverse areas as south-east Asia, continental Africa and Arab countries. The dominant ethnic groups, the Merina (estimated at 1,993,000 in 1974) and the Betsileo (920,600), who inhabit the most densely populated central provinces of Antananarivo and Fianarantsoa, are of Asian-Pacific origin. In the peripheral areas live the tribes collectively known as côtiers, of whom the most numerous are the Betsimisaraka (1,134,000) on the east coast, the Tsimihety (558,100) in the north, and the Antandroy (412,500) in the south. Population density ranges from 30 inhabitants per sq km on the central plateaux to 2 per sq km along much of the west coast. At the 1993 census the average density was 20.6 inhabitants per sq km. Although continuous migrations, improved means of communication and a marked cultural unity have, to some extent, broken down geographical and tribal barriers, traditional ethnic antagonisms—notably between the Merina and the côtiers—remain close to the surface.

Increasing at an average annual rate of 2.8% during 1980–96, the Malagasy are fast exceeding the island's capacity to feed and employ them. Estimates from the 1974–75 census indicated that more than half the population was under 20 years of age, that the large foreign element was rapidly declining, and that the urban component was steadily growing. French nationals, who numbered some 50,000 before 1972, dwindled to fewer than 15,000 by 1986. In 1981 there were some 5,000 Indians holding French nationality and an equal number of creoles. The Comorans, who were formerly the second largest non-indigenous population group and were concentrated in the Mahajanga area (60,000 in 1976), have become an almost negligible element there, owing to the repatriation of about 16,000 after the clashes between them and the Malagasy in December 1976. Also inhabiting the west coast are the 10,000 or so Indian nationals, who are also unpopular with the Malagasys because of their social clannishness and their wealth, acquired through control of the textile and jewellery trades and of urban real estate. Administratively, the Asians are organized into congrégations, each headed by a representative chosen by them but appointed by and responsible to the government. A Chinese community, numbering about 10,000, is dispersed throughout the east-coast region, where they are principally employed as grocers, small-scale bankers, and traders in agricultural produce.

More than 82% of the Malagasy still live in rural areas, but the towns are attracting an increasing percentage of the fast-growing youthful population, thus aggravating urban socio-economic problems. Antananarivo, the capital, is by far the largest city (estimated population: 662,585 in 1985) and continues to expand, as do all the six provincial capitals.

Recent History
MERVYN BROWN

Madagascar was annexed by France in 1896. The imposition of colonial rule did not, however, resolve the basic ethnic conflict between the dominant Merina tribe, based on the central plateau, and the coastal peoples (*côtiers*), The introduction in 1946 of elected deputies from Madagascar to the French parliament brought two opposing parties to the fore: the Mouvement démocratique pour la rénovation malgache, a predominantly Merina group favouring immediate independence, and the Parti des déshérités de Madagascar (PADESM), a *côtier* party opposed to rapid constitutional change. Following violent ethnic and partisan confrontations during 1947, in which about 80,000 people were killed, the French authorities suspended all political activity.

INDEPENDENCE

New constitutional arrangements introduced by France in 1956 opened the way to a resumption of political activity. The predominantly *côtier*-supported Parti social démocrate (PSD), formed from progressive elements of PADESM, and led by a schoolteacher, Philibert Tsiranana, emerged as the principal party. In October 1958 Madagascar became a self-governing republic within the French Community. In 1959 Tsiranana was elected president. Full independence as the Malagasy Republic followed on 26 June 1960.

Following Tsiranana's accession to power, the PSD, which practised a moderate, pragmatic socialism, was joined by nearly all of its early rivals. The only significant opposition was the left-wing Parti du congrès de l'indépendance de Madagascar (AKFM), led by Richard Andriamanjato, a Merina Protestant pastor and mayor of Antananarivo. The rivalry between the two parties reflected the continuing antagonisms between Merina and *côtiers*. Tsiranana's policies were generally favourable to French interests.

Following a period of economic decline in the late 1960s, a serious agrarian uprising, accompanied by student unrest, broke out in 1971. Following the suppression of the disorder, a new radical opposition group, the Mouvement national pour l'indépendance de Madagascar (MONIMA), led by Monja Jaona and based in the agricultural south-west of the island, where the uprising had begun, became a significant opposition movement, also attracting urban and student support. As the sole candidate in the presidential election of January 1972, Tsiranana was re-elected with 99.9% of the votes cast, but this result bore little relation to the true state of political opinion. In May, following a resurgence of violent protest, Tsiranana relinquished power to Gen. Gabriel Ramanantsoa, the Merina chief of staff of Madagascar's armed forces.

MILITARY GOVERNMENT

Ramanantsoa moved swiftly to restore public order. A referendum conducted in October 1972 obtained the endorsement of 96% of the voters for Ramanantsoa to govern for a transitional period of five years, while a new constitutional structure was established.

The promotion of Malagasy as the official language and the 'Malagasization' of education was welcomed by student and nationalist opinion, but revived fears among *côtiers* of Merina domination. Nationalists and radicals, including the extreme left-wing Mouvement pour le pouvoir prolétarien (MFM), led by Manandafy Rakotonirina, supported the major changes in foreign policy: the establishment of diplomatic relations with the People's Republic of China, the Soviet bloc countries and Arab nations; the withdrawal from the Franc Zone and the Organisation commune africaine et mauricienne (OCAM); and, in particular, the renegotiation of the co-operation agreements with France, which resulted in the evacuation of French air and naval bases.

However, Ramanantsoa's authority was undermined by the country's worsening trade and financial position, disunity in the armed forces and the government, and continuing discord between *côtiers* and Merina. Contention arose in the cabinet where a radical faction, led by Col Richard Ratsimandrava demanded administrative and political reform, based on a revival of the traditional communities, known as *fokonolona*.

On 31 December 1974 the mobile police, a mainly *côtier* force, staged an attempted coup in protest at Merina domination of the armed forces. A prolonged crisis ensued. In February 1975 Ramanantsoa transferred power to Col Richard Ratsimandrava, who was, however, assassinated six days later. Gen. Gilles Andriamahazo immediately assumed power. Martial law and press censorship were imposed, and political parties suspended. In June 1975 Andriamahazo was succeeded as head of state by Lt-Commdr Didier Ratsiraka, a *côtier* and a former minister of foreign affairs. Ratsiraka established a supreme revolutionary council (CSR), originally entirely military, to supervise a government that principally comprised civilians. The financial sector, shipping, the petroleum refinery and mineral resources were nationalized, as was the leading French-owned trading company, the Société Marseillaise. Ratsiraka declared his intention to carry out administrative and agrarian reforms based on the *fokonolona*, reorganize the armed forces as an 'army of development' and pursue a non-aligned foreign policy. At a referendum held in December, Ratsiraka's proposals were endorsed by 94.66% of voters. Ratsiraka was elected to a seven-year term as president, the country was renamed the Democratic Republic of Madagascar, and the 'Second Republic' was proclaimed.

THE SECOND REPUBLIC

Having reorganized the CSR with a predominantly civilian base, in March 1975 Ratsiraka formed the Avant-garde de la révolution malgache (AREMA) as the nucleus of the Front national pour la défense de la révolution socialiste malgache (FNDR), the only political organization permitted by the constitution. Several existing parties subsequently joined the FNDR, including the MONIMA, the MFM and the Elan populaire pour l'unité nationale (known as the Vonjy), which comprised left-wing elements of the former PSD. Local government elections, which took place in 1977, led to divisions within the FNDR. MONIMA withdrew from the FNDR, and was subsequently banned. Strains within AREMA also became apparent within the national assembly, where a number of disparate right-wing and left-wing factions had emerged. In August the membership of the CSR was extended to include leaders of the former political parties, and a larger number of *côtiers*, in an effort to achieve political equilibrium.

The incidence of severe drought during 1978–80 provoked sporadic outbreaks of violence in rural areas. Monja Jaona, who had called for a general strike and was subsequently detained, was released in early 1981; MONIMA subsequently rejoined the FNDR, and Jaona was appointed to the CSR. Ratsiraka, meanwhile, attempted to establish himself in the international community as a spokesman for the developing countries and as the leading advocate of the demilitarization of the Indian Ocean. His 'non-aligned' foreign policy manifested itself chiefly in hostility to what he perceived as 'Western imperialism', in conjunction with close relations with the USSR and other Eastern bloc countries.

Although opposed by Monja Jaona at a presidential election held in November, Ratsiraka was re-elected by 80% of the vote, while Jaona won only 20% of the votes cast. Jaona denounced the result as fraudulent, and called for a general strike in support of demands for a new poll. Following rioting in December, Jaona was arrested and expelled from the CSR. In August 1983 elections to the 137-member national assembly took place. AREMA secured 117 seats in the legislature.

Social Unrest

Urban violence increased dramatically in the 1970s and early 1980s, with groups of unemployed citizens harassing and extorting money from people in the capital, especially those opposed to the government. To counter their activities, students and other youths, mainly of bourgeois families, organized vigilante societies which practised the oriental martial art of kung-fu. Clashes between the two groups resulted in a ban on the practice of kung-fu in September 1984, which provoked further rioting from kung-fu adherents and resulted in 50 deaths during further disturbances in December. A reorganization of the council of ministers, carried out in February 1985, was intended to confirm the regime's socialist direction in the face of 'deviationist' tendencies and increased liberalism in the economic sector. In August security forces attacked the headquarters of the kung-fu societies, which the government accused of planning a coup attempt; some 50 people were killed and over 200 arrested. (At the trial of 245 kung-fu adherents in March 1988, the majority of the defendants were acquitted.)

In the rural south of Madagascar there were further disorders in 1986–87, following severe famine in the region. In November 1986 violent demonstrations, resulting in a number of deaths, occurred at Toamasina, the principal Malagasy port, in protest at food shortages and the introduction of measures to rationalize the port. Violence erupted again in early 1987, when Indian and Pakistani traders in southern towns were attacked, and their property burnt and looted. The Asian community had long been unpopular with the Malagasys, who resented its control of the retail sector and relative prosperity. In June 56 people who had taken part in the riots were imprisoned.

In 1987 opposition within the FNDR to Ratsiraka appeared to be increasing. The MSM and the Vonjy, joined later by the Parti socialiste monima (VSM), began to co-operate openly with MONIMA in opposing government policies and, from May 1987, in demands for the resignation of the government and the holding of new elections. The MSM, the Vonjy and MONIMA also decided to contest the presidential elections, which were due to take place in 1989. Ratsiraka subsequently announced that legislative and local government elections, scheduled for 1988, would be postponed respectively until May and September 1989. In February 1988 the prime minister, Gen. Désiré Rakotoarijaona, resigned, ostensibly on grounds of ill-health, and was succeeded by the minister of public works, Lt-Col Victor Ramahatra. In January 1989 the constitution was amended to allow Ratsiraka to bring forward the presidential election from November to March. In February the MFM, the Vonjy and the VSM announced the formation of an opposition alliance, the Alliance démocratique de Madagascar (ADM), but retained separate presidential candidates. In the same month restrictions on the freedom of the press were relaxed, and the abolition of press censorship was announced.

At the presidential election, which took place in March 1989, Ratsiraka was elected to a third term of office, receiving 62% of the total votes cast (compared with 80% at the previous election). Manandafy Rakotonirina, the candidate of the MFM (which had now moved from the extreme left to a market-orientated liberalism), obtained 20% of the votes, while the Vonjy candidate, Dr Jérôme Marojama Razanabahiny, secured 15% and Monja Jaona of MONIMA only 3%. Later in March a new political movement, the AKFM/Fanavaozana, was formed by Richard Andriamanjato, in response to the refusal of the AKFM to support his presidential candidature. Allegations by the ADM of electoral fraud led to subsequent rioting. The membership of the cabinet remained unchanged following Ratsiraka's inauguration, but six members of the CSR, including Rakotonirina and Andriamanjato, were dismissed for opposing his re-election. At the end of April the ADM declared its intention to boycott the forthcoming legislative elections, but this threat was withdrawn when Ratsiraka promised to allow representatives of the opposition parties to observe polling procedures. At the legislative elections in May, AREMA increased its previously substantial parliamentary majority by a further three seats, winning 120 of the 137 parliamentary seats. The MFM, which obtained seven seats, rejected the results, alleging fraud. The Vonjy secured four seats, the AKFM/Fanavaozana three seats, the original AKFM two seats and MONIMA only one. The abstention rate was high, averaging 25% of registered voters and reaching almost 35% in some urban constituencies.

Political Reform

Despite AREMA's electoral success, widespread discontent with the government continued among the intellectual and urban classes. In August 1989 Ratsiraka reorganized both the CSR and the government, removing members of doubtful loyalty and replacing them with strong supporters. The fragile opposition alliance was divided by the reappointment of Monja Jaona to the CSR, together with the vice-president of the Vonjy and some minor opposition figures, while several economic and technical specialists were appointed to the government. Shortly before the government reshuffle, Ratsiraka convened a meeting of the FNDR (the first to be held since 1982), at which the constituent parties were invited to submit proposals for the future of the FNDR and a possible revision of the 1975 constitution. He also consulted privately with leaders of the churches and other opinion groups. However, demands by the FFKM for the abolition of the FNDR's monopoly on political activity, as well as the elimination of socialist references in the constitution, received wide support.

In the first round of local government elections (to the *fokontany*) in September 1989, AREMA again gained the majority of votes, except in Antananarivo, but the average abstention rate was 30%. AREMA's electoral strength and a divided opposition enabled Ratsiraka to limit constitutional changes. The amendments adopted by parliament in December abolished the requirement for political parties to be members of the FNDR, thus effectively dissolving the FNDR itself. However, the privileged status of socialism in the constitution was retained. Nevertheless, provisions were made for a multi-party system, backed by economic liberalism imposed by the International Monetary Fund (IMF) and the new freedom of the press, which opposition newspapers were using increasingly to criticize the government. In the early months of 1990 a number of new parties were formed. Two former PSD ministers established a centre-right party, the Mouvement des démocrates chrétiens malgaches (MDCM), while the Vonjy was seriously weakened by the departure of André Resampa and nine other leading members to relaunch the PSD, with Resampa as secretary-general.

In March 1990 the government formally assented to the resumption of multi-party politics. Numerous organizations subsequently emerged, some of them small left-wing parties supporting the president which joined with AREMA, the old AKFM and elements of the Vonjy and MONIMA, to form a new coalition, the Mouvement militant pour le socialisme malagasy (MMSM). Other new parties, notably the Union nationale pour le développement et la démocratie (UNDD), led by a medical professor, Albert Zafy, joined the MFM, AKFM/Fanavaozana and the newly-formed MDC and PSD in opposition to the government. The MFM now changed its name to Mouvement pour le progrès de Madagascar, while retaining the same Malagasy initials, MFM.

On 13 May 1990 a group of armed rebels seized control of the radio station at Antananarivo and broadcast an announcement that Ratsiraka's regime had been overthrown. A crowd gathered outside the station to demonstrate its support. Six people were killed and 50 injured in the subsequent suppression of the revolt by security forces. Of the 11 rebels arrested and brought to trial in December, several were acquitted and the others received short prison sentences.

Meanwhile, the withdrawal of Soviet support following the collapse of communism in the USSR compelled Ratsiraka to look to the Western countries, particularly France, for economic aid. These improved relations were demonstrated by a state visit by President Mitterrand in June 1990, during which it was announced that Madagascar's US $750m. debt to France had been cancelled and that France would be permitted to resume use of the facilities at the naval base at Antsiranana.

In mid-1990 the FFKM invited all political associations to attend conferences, which were to take place in August and December, to discuss a programme of reform. However, Ratsiraka criticized the FFKM's intervention, and parties belonging to the MMSM refused to participate in the discussions. At the conference, held in December, 16 opposition factions, together with trade unions and other groups, established an informal alliance, under the name Forces vives (FV), to co-ordinate proposals for constitutional reform. The leading figures of FV were Zafy (UNDD), Rakotonirina (MFM) and Andriamanjato (AKFM/

Fanavaozana). In the same month the national people's assembly adopted legislation that abolished press censorship, ended the state monopoly of radio and television and permitted the establishment of private broadcasting stations in partnership with the government. In January 1991 Ratsiraka announced that further constitutional amendments would be adopted by the assembly at its next meeting in May. It was later indicated that the main change would be the replacement of the supreme revolutionary council by an elected senate.

Confrontation and General Strike

At the session of the national people's assembly in May 1991, FV supporters forced their way into the chamber to submit their alliance's proposals for amending the constitution; these included the elimination of references to socialism, a reduction in the powers of the president and a limit on the number of terms he could serve. However, the only amendments considered were those presented by the government, which, although numerous, did not meet the FV's basic demands. In early June the FV leadership demanded that a constitutional conference be convened. When the government failed to respond, the FV called a general strike from 10 June, and began a series of peaceful demonstrations, in support of demands for the resignation of the president and the appointment of a new 'provisional government', which would include opposition leaders. The army and police did not intervene in the demonstrations, and similar gatherings took place in the provincial capitals.

The strike was widely supported in the civil service, banks, major firms and transport and, together with the daily demonstrations, resulted in the suspension of economic activity in the capital. In July 1991 various negotiations between the FV and the MMSM, with the mediation of the FFKM or the French embassy, failed, owing to the FV's insistence on the resignation of the president. Ratsiraka refused to resign, on the grounds that he had been democratically elected. In response, the FV maintained that the 1989 elections were not democratic (since only political parties adhering to the FNDR were allowed to operate), and denounced abuses of human rights and widespread corruption in the government and in the president's family. In mid-July the FV appointed its own 'provisional government', with a retired general, Jean Rakotoharison, as president and Zafy as prime minister. 'Ministers' of the 'provisional government' then began to occupy various ministry buildings, with the assistance of civil servants observing the strike. Later in July Ratsiraka announced a state of emergency, reimposed censorship, and prohibited mass meetings. This had little effect, however, as the army and police took no action to enforce it. In the next few days Zafy and three other FV 'ministers' were abducted and held in various army camps. There were also murders of several FV leaders in Toamasina and Antsiranana.

On 28 July 1991 Ratsiraka dissolved his government and pledged to organize a referendum on a new constitution by the end of the year. At a demonstration on the folllowing day, however, the FV insisted on the president's resignation, the lifting of the state of emergency and the release of their 'ministers'. (They were released unharmed on the following day.) On 8 August Ratsiraka nominated a new prime minister, Guy Razanamasy, hitherto the mayor of Antananarivo, who invited the FV to join the government. The offer was rejected, and on 10 August the FV organized a large but peaceful protest march on the president's residence to demand his resignation. The president's bodyguard fired into the crowd, killing 100 and wounding many more. On the same day a further 20 people were killed in the suppression of a similar demonstration in Mahajanga. The French government subsequently suspended military aid and advised Ratsiraka to resign, offering him asylum in France. The Roman Catholic archbishop of Antananarivo joined those calling for the president's resignation, and the FFKM announced that it was abandoning its role as mediator and would henceforth support the FV. Later that month Ratsiraka declared Madagascar to be a federation of six states, under his presidency, and claimed to command the support of five provinces, where AREMA held the majority of seats in regional councils. On 26 August Razanamasy formed a government, which contained some defectors from the FV, including Resampa. The state of emergency was modified, but Razanamasy warned that civil servants would be dismissed unless they

returned to work by 4 September. On that day, however, the FV, which had denounced the new government as 'puppets' of Ratsiraka, organized a massive demonstration, which halted all economic activity in Antananarivo.

During September and October 1991 the FV continued to organize frequent demonstrations and maintain the general strike at an effective level, ensuring the closure of all ports except for Toamasina. Ratsiraka was sustained by support from the provinces and was able to exploit divisions within the opposition, notably between Rakotonirina's MFM, which favoured a constitutional settlement, and the majority of radicals led by Zafy. Meanwhile, the army and the aid donors increased their pressure on all parties to reach a settlement including a consensus government.

Interim Settlement

Following an ultimatum from the army, an interim agreement was signed on 31 October 1991 by Razanamasy and representatives of the FV, MMSM and FFKM, providing for the suspension of the constitution and the creation of a transitional government, which was to remain in office for a maximum period of 18 months, pending the adoption of a new constitution and the holding of elections. Under the agreement, Ratsiraka remained as president with the ceremonial duties of head of state and titular head of the armed forces, but relinquished all executive powers. A 31-member Haute autorité de l'état (HAE), under Zafy, and a 130-member advisory Conseil de redressement économique et social (CRES), headed jointly by Andriamanjato and Rakotonirina, replaced the CSR and the national people's assembly, while Razanamasy's government was to be expanded to include members of the FV.

In February 1992 the interim authorities suspended the elected bodies (nearly all controlled by AREMA and supporting Ratsiraka) at the various levels of local government and replaced them with special delegations. In the same month proposals for a new constitution and electoral code were compiled at a series of regional forums, and delegates were elected to attend a national forum, which was convened in Antananarivo in late March. After attacks against the conference hall and an attempt to assassinate Zafy, the forum was moved to a military camp. At the end of March security forces fired at supporters of Ratsiraka, led by Monja Jaona, who had marched on the camp; eight people, including a former minister, were killed.

Ratsiraka reasserted his intention to stand for re-election, and called for a federalist draft constitution to be submitted to a referendum as an alternative to the unitary draft being considered by the forum. After much debate, a clause was included in the electoral code excluding the candidature of anyone who had been elected president twice under the second republic. The constitution adopted by the forum, subject to approval by the transitional authorities and at a national referendum, was of a parliamentary type, with a constitutional president, a senate and a national assembly elected by proportional representation, and executive power vested in a prime minister elected by the assembly. The referendum on the constitution was scheduled for 21 June 1992, and was to be followed by presidential elections in August and legislative elections in October. However, continuing lack of agreement within the government and the HAE regarding the exclusion of Ratsiraka from the presidential elections and the extent of the future president's powers delayed the publication of the draft constitution and therefore caused the referendum to be postponed. Despite attempts by federalist supporters of Ratsiraka to disrupt the referendum, the new constitution was approved on 19 August by 73% of votes cast.

The federalists subsequently intensified pressure for Ratsiraka's right to stand for re-election. After a number of violent incidents involving federalists, including the temporary seizure of the airport at Antsiranana and the bombing of the railway track linking Toamasina and the capital, the transitional authorities agreed to allow Ratsiraka to contest the election. A further seven candidates, including Zafy and Rakotonirina, were also to participate in the elections. In the first round of the presidential election, which was conducted peacefully under international supervision on 25 November 1992, Zafy secured 45% of votes cast, while Ratsiraka obtained 29% and Rakotonirina 10% of the vote. The second round, which was contested by the two leading candidates, took place on 10 February 1993. Most of the other candidates transferred their support to Zafy, who obtained a substantial majority of 67% of the vote, against 33% for Ratsiraka. Zafy was formally invested as president in late March, amid violent clashes between security forces and federalists in northern Madagascar. However, the transitional authorities continued to function, pending the formation of a new government after the legislative elections (which were rescheduled for 16 June). In accordance with a constitutional stipulation, Zafy resigned as president of the UNDD in May.

In early June 1993 two people were killed and a further 40, including Monja Jaona, arrested, after security forces attacked federalists who had seized the prefecture building in Toliary. On 16 June the elections to the national assembly (which had been reduced from 184 to 138 seats) were contested under a system of proportional representation by 121 political parties and some 4,000 candidates. Several elements of the FV coalition presented separate lists of candidates; however, the remaining parties in the alliance, known as the Cartel HVR, proved the most successful group, securing 45 seats; Rakotonirina's MFM obtained 16 seats, while a new pro-Ratsiraka movement, FAMIMA, won only 11 seats. Intensive inter-party negotiations prior to the first meeting of the assembly resulted in some shifting in party support for the various candidates contesting the post of prime minister. In the election on 9 August, Rakotonirina obtained 32 votes and Roger Ralison (the candidate of the Cartel) 45 votes. The winner, with 55 votes, was Francisque Ravony, who was the favoured candidate both of Zafy and the business community. Ravony, a respected lawyer and a son-in-law of former president Tsiranana, had served as deputy prime minister in the transitional government. The leader of the AKFM/Fanavaozana, Richard Andriamanjato, was elected speaker of the national assembly.

THE THIRD REPUBLIC

At the end of August 1993 Ravony formed a new council of ministers, which was endorsed by 72% of deputies in the national assembly, together with his programme, which emphasized economic recovery based on free-market policies, and measures to eradicate corruption. The latter resulted in the arrest in September of 12 senior civil servants, who were accused of misappropriating World Bank credits equivalent to US $10m. Effective action regarding economic recovery subsequently proved difficult, however, owing, in part, to the fragmented nature of the national assembly, which comprised some 25 separate parties; these became grouped into two informal coalitions of equal size (and a small number of independent deputies), known respectively as the HVR group (which included supporters of Zafy and Andriamanjato) and G6. However, neither was specifically a government or opposition organization, and ministers were appointed from both alliances and also from the independent members. Despite the immediate necessity for substantial assistance from the World Bank and IMF to sustain the economy, a number of deputies opposed the acceptance of structural adjustment measures, required by the World Bank and IMF as a precondition to the approval of financial credit, owing to the additional widespread hardship that would ensue. A strike by civil servants in January 1994 opposed IMF demands for substantial retrenchment in the civil service and a 'freeze' of public sector salaries. In early 1994 a number of severe cyclones further damaged the economy, and weakened the government's ability to resist the demands of the World Bank and IMF. In May agreement was reached with the World Bank and IMF on a framework agreement for 1995–96, including further structural adjustment reforms. In June, however, the reform programme was rejected by a majority in the national assembly.

Ravony's position was undermined by public opposition from Zafy and Andriamanjato, who rejected the IMF and World Bank demands as an affront to national sovereignty and favoured financial arrangements with private enterprises (known as 'parallel financing'). In July 1994 31 deputies belonging to the G6 coalition proposed a motion of censure against Ravony for failing to conclude an agreement with the Bretton Woods institutions, which was, however, defeated with the assistance of the HVR group. In August Ravony reorganized the council of ministers to reflect the HVR's support; the president of the

LEADER/Fanilo party, Herizo Razafimahaleo, subsequently resigned, after his portfolio was divided.

Andriamanjato, with the support of Zafy and the governor of the central bank, continued to pursue 'parallel financing' arrangements, notably one with Prince Constantin of Liechtenstein, whose company established a subsidiary, Flamco Madagascar. In October 1994 Flamco's directors, who included two of Andriamanjato's sons, were accused of misappropriating funds advanced by the government and other irregularities. The continuing decline of the economy and the inflationary effects of the flotation of the currency and an increase in fuel prices in May prompted demands from the main G6 parties for the resignation of the president, the prime minister and the speaker, while the HVR group urged the resignation of the prime minister and the minister of finance.

In January 1995, at the insistence of the Bretton Woods institutions, Ravony dismissed the governor of the central bank. In a balancing move to appease the HVR group, the minister of finance also resigned, with Ravony assuming the portfolio himself. The government subsequently pledged to undertake further austerity measures, while the IMF and World Bank approved the doubling of the minimum wage and additional expenditure on health and education to counteract the effect of the structural adjustment reforms.

In March 1995 two leaders of a minor opposition group were arrested, after announcing the establishment of a 'parallel government', while members of the HVR group staged a demonstration urging the resignation of the prime minister. In June members of the G6 group staged a demonstration urging the impeachment of Zafy, on the grounds that he had exceeded his constitutional powers and supported Andriamanjato's demands for 'parallel financing'. At the same time Ravony strengthened his parliamentary position by recruiting additional deputies to his (hitherto single-member) party, Committee for the Support of Democracy and Development in Madagascar (CSDDM). The CSDDM then joined the G6, which became the G7, constituting a clear majority in the assembly. In July Zafy publicly criticized Ravony, and, at his instigation, the HVR group in the national assembly proposed a motion of censure against the prime minister, which was, however, rejected by a large majority.

Zafy subsequently announced that he could not co-operate with Ravony and called a referendum for 17 September 1995 to endorse a constitutional amendment, whereby the president, rather than the national assembly, would select the prime minister. Ravony, who had reorganized the cabinet to reflect changes in the composition of his support in the national assembly, announced that he would resign when the result of the referendum was formally announced in October. He also declined to campaign against the referendum, and many of his supporters decided to express their disapproval by abstaining from voting. In the referendum, notable for a high degree of abstention, the constitutional amendment was approved by 63.5% of the valid votes.

Ravony and his government duly resigned and President Zafy appointed the leader of his own party, the UNDD, Emmanuel Rakotovahiny, as prime minister. The new government contained no members of the G7 majority group and was heavily weighted in favour of the UNDD at the expense of other groups from the former HVF. Six parties formerly supporting the president immediately demanded a change of government and a new prime minister, and accused Zafy of seeking to create a UNDD one-party state.

The government, with very little support in the assembly, was further weakened by public disagreement between the prime minister and the finance minister over the 1996 budget, and could make no progress in negotiations with the IMF and the World Bank. In February 1996 a new radical extra-parliamentary group, SFFF (led by prominent figures from the Ratsiraka regime), held demonstrations in support of demands for the departure of the president, a provisional government of national recovery and yet another new constitution. Public discontent was expressed by strikes of university students and railway workers and an unprecedented strike by officials of the finance ministry, joined by customs officials at the ports, calling for the resignation of their minister who, it was later revealed, had been convicted of corruption in 1982. Under increasing pressure to change the government, Zafy offered a reshuffle but insisted on retaining Rakotovahiny as prime minister. In April most of the parties which previously supported Zafy joined in a new group, the Rassemblement pour la Troisième République (RP3R), to oppose him. At the same time, the FFKM returned to the public stage to appeal for a new government, an agreement with the IMF and World Bank and the elimination of corruption in the government. The managing director of the IMF, Michel Camdessus, made it clear during a visit to Madagascar that the IMF could negotiate only with a cohesive government united in favour of agreements with the Bretton Woods institutions.

When Zafy failed to carry out even the government reshuffle that he had promised, the G7 and RP3R joined on 16 May 1996 in a motion of censure against the government, which, requiring a two-thirds' majority, was carried by 109 votes to 15. Rakotovahiny resigned and Zafy appointed a non-political prime minister, Norbert Ratsirahonana, hitherto the president of the constitutional high court and a leading member of the Protestant Reformed Church. Ratsirahonana's programme, emphasizing economic reform in the context of agreements with the IMF and World Bank and action on poverty, corruption and crime, won general approval. He proposed a government including a number of members of the G7 majority group and only one UNDD member. However, Zafy vetoed all but one G7 minister and insisted on the retention of five UNDD members and other ministers from the previous government. Most G7 and RP3R deputies therefore walked out when Ratsirahonana presented his government and programme to the assembly on 10 June. However, in July Ratsirahonana obtained a vote of confidence by linking it with legislation necessary for the agreements with the IMF and World Bank. There were further strikes, by transport drivers protesting against an increase in the fuel tax, and by civil servants protesting against the politicization of civil service appointments.

On 26 July 1996 the assembly voted the impeachment of the president, for various violations of the constitution, by 99 votes to 34. After giving Zafy a month to contest the charges, the constitutional high court endorsed the impeachment and removed him from office; on the same day Zafy resigned. The court appointed the prime minister, Ratsirahonana, to act as interim president pending the outcome of a new presidential election, to be held within two months. He formed a new government, excluding those ministers whom Zafy had forced him to accept. Despite the impeachment, Zafy immediately declared himself a candidate for the presidential election, and was joined by ex-president Ratsiraka, acting president Ratsirahonana and 12 other candidates, including most of the leaders of the main political parties.

The Return of Ratsiraka

In the first round of the presidential election on 3 November 1996, marked by a high abstention rate, Ratsiraka came first with 37% of the valid votes, followed by Zafy with 23%. In the run-off on 29 December Ratsiraka won narrowly with 51% of the valid votes to Zafy's 49%, but, with abstentions and spoilt votes comprising 52% of the electorate, less than 25% of the electorate voted for the winning candidate. In February 1997 Ratsiraka appointed as prime minister Pascal Rakotomavo, who formed a government consisting largely of technocrats.

During the election campaign Ratsirahonana had successfully completed negotiations with the IMF, leading in due course to a resumption of international aid and debt-relief arrangements. Ratsiraka's first act was to visit Washington and New York (USA), Paris (France) and Brussels (Belgium) to reassure the donor community of his intention to adhere to the reform programme approved by the IMF. He announced his intention to fulfil an electoral promise to submit to a national referendum two alternative new constitutions. The legislative elections due in August 1997 were postponed for 10 months so that they could be held under whatever new constitutional arrangements emerged from the referendum; the national assembly's mandate was subsequently extended, with the approval of the constitutional high court. The opposition, led by Zafy, condemned the delay (which was officially to allow time for the distribution of newly compulsory identity cards for voters), and declared it to be a violation of the constitution.

The government decided that the referendum would concern amendments to the existing constitution rather than two alternative new constitutions. These revisions were so extensive that they amounted to an almost totally new constitution reverting to a presidential regime, greatly increasing the president's powers at the expense of the legislature and weakening the independence of the judiciary. They also provided for a considerable degree of decentralization of government to the provinces. The national assembly, in which the opposition had a majority, attempted to disrupt the referendum process by motions of censure of the government and, on 4 February 1998, impeachment of the president. Although both motions were carried, they failed to achieve the two-thirds' majority needed for them to be effective. Most opposition parties decided not to campaign actively for a 'No' vote in the referendum. Despite this, the amendments were only narrowly adopted on 15 March, by 51% of the valid votes cast by 66% of the electorate. The amended constitution provided that President Ratsiraka could complete his term of office and could be re-elected twice rather than only once.

Elections to an enlarged 150-member national assembly took place on 17 May 1998 under a new electoral law, which favoured the larger parties: the previous system of proportional representation using party lists was replaced by 82 single-member constituencies and a form of proportional representation for 34 two-member constituencies. Ratsiraka's party, AREMA, although receiving only 25% of the votes, won 63 of the 150 seats. The 19 seats won by its government coalition partners, LEADER/Fanilo and AKFM/Fanavaozana, assured the government of a majority in the assembly. Independent candidates received 27% of the votes and 32 seats. The parties of Andriamanjato (AKFM/Fanavaozana) and Rakotonirina (MFM) won only three seats each, and neither party leader was re-elected. On 23 July Ratsiraka appointed as prime minister Tantely Andrianarivo, who formed a coalition government dominated by AREMA but including members of other parties and some independents. The former deputy prime minister, Herizo Razafimahaleo, who had hoped to be prime minister, resigned while leaving his party LEADER/Fanilo in the government.

Subsequently the government was strengthened by the support of the Rassemblement pour le socialisme et la démocratie (RPSD) and 24 independent deputies. However, disillusionment with the goverment's economic performance, notably the long delay in obtaining the release of additional structural adjustment funds from the World Bank and the IMF, led to a loss of support. The opposition divided into two groups: the radicals, including Zafy's Asa, fahamarinana, fampandrosoana, arinda (AFFA) and Rakotonirina's MFM, who called for the overthrow of the government and a new constitution; and the moderates, led by Ratsirahonana's Ny asa vita no ifampitsara (AVI), who engaged in more constructive opposition.

Local government elections, originally scheduled for October 1993, were repeatedly postponed, owing to disagreement over proposals to restructure and decentralize government by the creation of more local authorities. In response to pressure from the World Bank and IMF to reduce administrative expenditure, the government proposed a two-tiered structure of 28 regions (replacing six provinces) and 1,278 communes. Elections to the communes were held in November 1995, but those to the regions, scheduled for August 1996, were postponed because of the crisis over the impeachment of the president. Subsequently the amended constitution of 1998 reverted to three tiers of local government (provinces, regions and communes). Elections to the communes took place on 14 November 1999. AREMA was confirmed as the largest party, although, with 41% of the vote, it was some way short of an overall majority. Popular disillusionment with politicians resulted in massive rejection of candidates from political parties in favour of independent candidates. Most notably, Marc Ravelomanana, the head of the country's largest agro-industrial processor, was elected mayor of Antananarivo. Following AREMA's poor performance in the elections, Pierrot Rajaonarivelo, the deputy prime minister, resigned as secretary-general of the party. Elections to the regional and provincial councils were postponed to unspecified dates in 2000. Meanwhile, the establishment of the Senate, as provided for in the 1992 constitution, continued to be delayed by failure to decide on the method of election of senators and was still pending in mid-2000.

In complete reversal of Ratsiraka's foreign policies, in the early 1990s Ravony's government established relations with Israel, South Africa, the Republic of Korea and (for trade and economic purposes only) Taiwan. These arrangements were not altered after Ratsiraka's return as president in 1997. The minister of foreign affairs, Herizo Razafimahaleo, made the promotion of the economy the main focus of foreign policy and moved to strengthen relations with South Africa, the newly industrialized countries of South-East Asia and the Far East. France remained the principal trading partner and supplier of bilateral aid. Political relations with France became even closer

after the settlement, in October 1998, of the long-standing dispute over compensation for nationalized French assets. Disagreement remained over the sovereignty of the Iles Glorieuses and three other uninhabited islets in the Mozambique Channel, which are claimed by France, but in February 2000 it was agreed that the islands would be co-administered by France, Madagascar and Mauritius, without prejudice to the question of sovereignty. In 1999 relations with the People's Republic of China were somewhat strained by popular resentment at a large influx of Chinese small traders undercutting Malagasy shopkeepers.

Economy
GILL TUDOR
Revised for this edition by the Editor

In 1998, according to estimates by the World Bank, Madagascar's gross national product (GNP), measured at average 1996–98 prices, was US $3,741m., equivalent to $260 per head. On the basis of GNP per head, Madagascar was among the world's 28 poorest countries in that year. In 1990–98, it was estimated, GNP per head declined, in real terms, by an annual average of 1.2%, while the population increased by an annual average of 3.2%. Madagascar's GDP increased, in real terms, by an average of 1.3% annually in 1990–98; the economy registered real GDP growth of 2.1% in 1996, 3.7% in 1997 and 3.9% in 1998. In the mid-1980s it was estimated that 65% of the population were in the subsistence sector. However, the urban population represented more than 23% of this total in 1990.

THE RURAL SECTOR

The rural economy accounts for 80% of Madagascar's export revenues and supplies most of the raw materials needed for industry. The agricultural sector (including forestry and fishing) accounted for an estimated 30.2% of GDP, and engaged an estimated 75.5% of the country's labour force in 1998. The production of both food and export crops, except cotton, either stagnated or declined after President Ratsiraka first took power in 1975, mainly as a result of the imposition of doctrinaire socialist principles and natural disasters. The island's agricultural sector also suffered from adverse climatic conditions, a lack of insecticides, spare parts and fertilizers, and the poor maintenance of rural roads. The imposition of co-operative societies and state farms on a reluctant peasantry also contributed to the agricultural sector's poor performance. Agricultural GDP increased at an average annual rate of 1.5% in 1990–98, according to the World Bank; the IMF estimated growth of 1.5% in 1998. The introduction of higher producer prices during the 1980s aimed to increase output of food crops, in particular, and eventually to achieve self-sufficiency in food. However, in view of the problems of quotas, low world prices and international competition, a major policy objective is to improve the quality of export crops, while limiting the expansion in output. The diversification of both food and export crops is also a priority. The forestry sector has been badly neglected, and 84% of domestic fuel needs are supplied by wood and charcoal. In 1995, according to UN estimates, about 26% of the land area was covered by forests. A US $66m. aid arrangement was agreed at a donors' meeting in Paris in February 1990 to support the first stage of a long-term environmental action plan. In August 1989 a 'debt-for-nature' exchange, the first for Africa, was arranged: the USA donated $1m. to the Worldwide Fund For Nature (WWF) to apply towards the acquisition, costing $2.1m., of government commercial debts at a 55% discount from a consortium of international banks, and to use the money for environmental projects. The experiment proved successful, and further debt-conversion agreements, involving international organizations, were subsequently negotiated. By late 1995 WWF was reported to have redeemed about $5m. of Malagasy debt, for $2.3m.

Paddy rice is the main crop grown by 70% of the population, whose basic food is rice (the average annual per caput consump-

tion is about 135 kg, the highest of any country in the world), and it occupies about 1.18m. ha, or approximately one-half the area under cultivation. Output of paddy remained constant at an average annual level of about 2m. metric tons for some years but the cyclones of January 1982 caused flooding which damaged the paddy crop and necessitated imports of about 356,000 tons of rice, at great cost, during that year. In early 1984 a further four cyclones destroyed some 40,000 ha of rice fields, and in March 1986 a cyclone destroyed rice fields and damaged Toamasina, the major port. A further cyclone in January 1990 destroyed rice fields and coffee plantations, especially in the south-east. The area planted to rice was subsequently reduced, while output of potatoes and maize was increased. In 1986 the government abolished virtually all controls on the rice trade, except for a minimum purchasing price of 90 Malagasy francs per kg and the maintenance of buffer stocks by the state. The estimated harvest in 1986 was 2.1m. tons, and in 1987 2.2m. tons. Imports of about 162,000 tons were necessary in both years but these were reduced to 75,000 tons in 1989, and to 50,000 tons in 1990 (with production reaching an estimated 2.4m. tons in that year). Severe drought in 1991–92 necessitated some 60,000 tons of imports. Rice production totalled an estimated 2.3m. tons in 1991, but increased to 2.5m. tons in 1992, and to 2.6m. tons in 1993. It fell back to 2.4m. tons in 1994 as a result of cyclone damage, leading to imports of 179,000 tons in that year, but rebounded to 2.5m. tons in 1995, when imports totalled 71,911 tons. Fresh cyclone damage in January 1996 in the major rice-growing area of Ambatondrazaka was estimated to have destroyed as much as 5% of that year's crop. However, rice imports declined to 34,684 tons in 1996, with production remaining constant at 2.5m. tons, before increasing to 2.6m. tons in 1997. The country suffered extensive crop damage again in early 1997, when cyclones struck both the south-east and the north-east. Heavy rains, brought by the cyclones, led to an increase in the number of locusts, which destroyed rice fields and maize plantations in the south and covered 4–5m. ha by June 1998. Rice production declined to 2.2m. tons in 1998, which constituted only some 60% of domestic consumption. In that year rice imports totalled 89,287 tons. Paddy rice production increased by 7.8% in 1999, despite very low yields. Further cyclones between February and April 2000 caused the loss of 150,000 tons of rice paddy. There is a need for improved husbandry and for the introduction of higher-yielding varieties, as well as an improved distribution system. Other important staple crops are maize, cassava, bananas and sweet potatoes.

Madagascar's main cash crops are coffee, vanilla and cloves. The most important is coffee (97% of it robusta, although arabica production is encouraged), which, in the 1980s, accounted for about 24% of total export earnings and engaged 25% of the working population. Output in the 1980s was generally about 80,000–84,000 metric tons per year, almost double the export quota allocated by the International Coffee Organization (ICO). Madagascar thus had considerable quantities for disposal on the non-quota market. Domestic consumption has risen steadily in recent years, to about 15,000 tons per year. There was a dramatic decline in world coffee prices after the ICO agreement collapsed in July 1989, leading to a loss in export revenue of over US $20m. that year; coffee export earnings came to $76.8m. Despite a recovery in prices, export earnings from coffee declined further in 1990, to $38.8m., owing partly to cyclone damage and lower crop quality. Coffee earnings stagnated until 1994, when a surge in world prices raised Madagascar's coffee exports to $79m., equivalent to 24% of total exports. Prices declined between 1994 and 1998, when coffee exports accounted for 17.2% of the value of total exports. In 1999 coffee production totalled 28,000 tons and export earnings from coffee were $29.5m. In 2000 a programme to relaunch the sector was in progress, headed by the National Coffee Marketing Committee and financed by the European Union (EU). It was envisaged that coffee production would not exceed 25,000 tons in 2000.

Madagascar is the world's largest producer of natural vanilla, accounting for more than half the world's output. Vanilla accounted for 4.3% of Madagascar's total export revenue in 1997, and only 3.0% in 1998. The USA and France are the main purchasers. Output has fluctuated widely, between 600 metric tons and 1,800 tons a year. Owing to competition from cheap synthetic substitutes, the value of Madagascar's high-quality natural vanilla is determined by its scarcity, and the government has therefore followed a policy of limiting exports. The country has operated a quota and price cartel system with Réunion and the Comoros, although by late 1994 this was starting to crumble; a huge build-up of stocks led the government to destroy vanilla amounting to more than the total volume of annual world consumption. Madagascar exported only 543 tons in 1993, but exports more than doubled to 1,182 tons in 1994 (yielding earnings of 182,641m. Malagasy francs), before falling back to 602 tons in 1995, and to 640 tons in 1996. Export earnings continued to decline thereafter, reaching 38,718m. Malagasy francs in 1998. However, earnings from vanilla production increased dramatically, by 61%, in 1999, when they totalled US $25.5m. Cyclone damage in the north-east of the country resulted in the loss of a considerable percentage of the crop in 2000. However, exporters estimated that production would still reach between 800 and 950 tons in that year. Reform of the vanilla sector has been a key prerequisite for further funding from the Bretton Woods institutions (see below), and in 1994 the government implemented a number of changes, including abolition of the guaranteed producer price. Free-market prices for farmers have since plunged, discouraging production. In May 1997, however, the government's decision to abolish export tax (levied at 25%) was welcomed. The government also replaced the state vanilla marketing board by a supervisory parastatal, the Madagascar Vanilla Institute (IVAMA), which had been due to be transferred in late 1996 to private-sector control. In early 1997, however, it was reported that the government had decided to abolish IVAMA, in response to pressure from the World Bank.

Production of cloves in the early 1980s was at a level of 10,000–12,000 metric tons per year and accounted for about a quarter of export earnings, but in 1983 the main buyer, Indonesia, suspended purchases and Madagascar was left with large quantities of unsold stocks. New markets were found in Sri Lanka and the Far East, and exports recovered by 1985 to 11,600 tons. In 1987 there was a collapse in world prices, following the emergence of Indonesia as a clove exporter, while liberalization of marketing in Madagascar led to an excess of cloves on the market, depressing prices further. Production subsequently rose as farmers responded to liberalization. Official figures show a leap in output from 12,500 tons in 1993 to 23,000 tons in 1994. Exports totalled 17,128 tons in 1995, but declined considerably to 7,268 tons in 1996, with revenue falling by more than 50% in the latter year, to 22,814m. Malagasy francs. By 1998 export revenue from cloves had fallen further, to 14,804m. Malagasy francs, as production and prices declined, owing to continued competition from Indonesia.

Lychees and small quantities of pepper and ylang-ylang (an essence used in the perfume industry) are also exported. Production of seed cotton declined steadily, from 42,900 metric tons in 1984/85 to 27,000 tons in 1987/88. However, 41,000 tons were harvested in 1988/89 and exports resumed, after a period of several years. Production fell back to between 20,000 tons and 27,000 tons a year in the early to mid-1990s. Sisal is a minor export crop, adversely affected for a number of years by synthetic

substitutes. World prices have improved, but drought in the south in 1988 caused the closure of three major sisal estates. Annual production is between 10,000-20,000 tons. There are five sugar factories, of which four have been rehabilitated with French aid, increasing their output from 80,000 tons a year to an average of some 120,000 tons in the late 1980s. The fifth factory, near Morondava on the west coast, was built with Chinese assistance and began operating in 1987, with an annual capacity of 22,000 tons. All factories are managed by the state-owned Société Siramamy Malagasy. Nevertheless, the sugar estates have suffered from under-investment and several have been threatened with closure because of debts. Production of sugar cane has averaged about 2m. tons a year in the 1990s. Imports of sugar are necessary to meet domestic requirements; in 1992 11,092 tons were imported from Mauritius and Réunion. Groundnuts, pineapples, coconuts, butterbeans and tobacco are also grown.

Sea fishing by coastal fishermen is being industrialized, with assistance from Japan and France. Shrimp fishing has expanded considerably, and has now become an important source of export revenue; the catch of shrimps and prawns reached 9,900 metric tons in 1995, yielding export revenue of 200,695m. Malagasy francs. The main markets are France and Japan. Small quantities of lobster are also exported. A temporary ban on imports of animal products from Madagascar, which was imposed in August 1997 on the grounds of poor hygiene, was particularly damaging to the shellfish industry; export revenue from shrimps and prawns declined to 41,423m. Malagasy francs in that year. The sector recovered to some extent in 1998, when revenue totalled 81,732m. Malagasy francs, after eight of the 50 companies affected by the ban were allowed to resume exports to EU countries in November 1997. The embargo on fish products was fully lifted in mid-1999. Export earnings from fish products increased by 6% in 1999. In 1998 the total catch amounted to 116,400 tons. Fish farming is a rapidly growing industry, with some 50,000 ha of suitable territory in swamps along the west coast. Vessels from EU countries, Japan and Russia fish by agreement for tuna and prawns in Madagascar's exclusive maritime zone, extending to 370 km (200 nautical miles) off the coast. A US $18m. tuna-canning complex has been established as a joint venture with a French company at Antsiranana, financed predominantly by France and the European Investment Bank (EIB). The EIB, the International Finance Corpn (IFC) and France are providing funds for Pêcheries de Nossy Bé to replace three trawlers and to modernize the shrimp-processing plant at Hellville in the north-west. In late 1997 the Caisse Française de Développement (now Agence Française de Développement) awarded a subsidy of 2.5m. French francs as part of a larger French subsidy of 12.3m. French francs to help Madagascar to improve its levels of hygiene in the fisheries export sector.

Madagascar has about 10.3m. head of cattle; however, cattle are generally regarded as an indication of wealth rather than as sources of income, and the development of a commercial beef sector is difficult. Nevertheless, there is some ranching and 145,000 metric tons of beef and veal were produced commercially in 1998, according to FAO estimates. Some beef is exported, but volumes have declined in recent years, to about 800 tons a year, despite an EU quota of 11,000 tons. There is an urgent need to revive veterinary sevices, improve marketing and rehabilitate abattoirs, partly to meet EU import standards. Live animals and some canned corned beef are exported to African countries, the Gulf states and Indian Ocean islands. There are scarcely any dairy cattle and the three milk processing plants use imported milk powder. There were some 1.7m. pigs in 1998, according to FAO estimates, but pigmeat is a luxury item and only about 54,000 tons were produced commercially in that year. Subsequently some 70% of the country's pig herds have been destroyed by disease. According to the FAO, there were some 1.3m. goats in 1998. Poultry are raised on a small-scale, non-commercial basis.

INDUSTRY

Industry accounted for an estimated 13.5% of Madagascar's GDP in 1998 and employed about 2.2% of the labour force in 1993. The island's major industrial centres, other than mines, are located in the High Plateaux or near Toamasina port. Food processing accounts for about one-half of all industrial value added. Textiles, brewing, paper and soap are also important sectors. There are cement plants at Mahajanga and Toamasina. However, in the late 1980s average annual production of cement was only about 40,000 metric tons, necessitating imports of about 250,000 tons per year; by 1993 production had declined to 36,397 tons and in 1994 it plunged to only 8,524 tons before recovering in subsequent years to reach 44,102 tons in 1997. A fertilizer plant at Toamasina, which began operations in 1985, produces 90,000 tons per year of urea- and ammonia-based fertilizers. Other industries include the manufacture of wood products and furniture, tobacco, agricultural machinery and the processing of agricultural products. Industrial GDP increased at an average annual rate of 1.5% in 1990–98, according to the World Bank; growth was estimated at 2.0% in 1996.

In June 1986 the government introduced a new investment code, which provided incentives for domestic and foreign private investment in activities outside the public sector, particularly in manufacturing for the export market. All military and strategic industries, including those in the energy sector, dockyards and ship repair yards, remained in the control of the Office militaire national pour les industries stratégiques (OMNIS), renamed the Office des mines nationales et des industries stratégiques under President Zafy (see Recent History). The country's fifth investment code, which took effect in January 1990, introduced incentives to attract foreign private investors, in particular. This enactment was strongly opposed by many politicians and also by local business people. Rules regarding foreign exchange and the number of expatriate employees have been relaxed and private investors are granted tax incentives. In the case of small and medium-sized enterprises, profits are exempt from corporation tax for the first five years, after which there is tax relief for a further five years. A number of export processing zones (EPZ) have been established, and have attracted foreign investors' interest, particularly from South-East Asia, Mauritius and France. A preliminary agreement has been signed with a consortium of Hong Kong interests, involving projected investment totalling US $650m. over 15 years. In 1996 125 manufacturing businesses were operating in the EPZ, employing a total of 36,700 workers. Labour is cheaper and corporation tax lower in the Malagasy EPZ than in those in Mauritius, but there are much higher risks for companies producing for export. A new investment code was approved in mid-1996 to simplify procedures for potential investors.

In March 1990 the International Development Association (IDA) approved a credit of US $48m. to finance the government's project to develop private enterprises. The funds were to be directed towards private businesses, or allocated to the development of training and extension services, to the restructuring of the chamber of commerce and to the establishment of an investment promotion agency. In mid-1994 the IFC approved an equity investment amounting to about $1.1m. in the Madagascar Capital Development Fund (an investment fund established by a French bank), which was to assist export-orientated companies.

MINING

Madagascar has sizeable deposits of a wide range of minerals, but in many cases they are in remote areas, making commercial exploitation difficult and expensive. However, chromite, graphite and mica are all exported, as are small quantities of semi-precious stones, such as topaz, garnet and amethyst. Chromite output (chromium ores and concentrates) before 1976 was approximately 200,000 metric tons per year, although in the early 1980s production had declined to very low levels. In 1993 output increased to 144,311 tons, compared with 64,200 tons in 1988, but declined to 75,000 tons in 1994 (despite a maximum annual capacity of 160,000 tons) before recovering to 140,000 tons by 1997. The main deposits of chromium ore are at Andriamena, but it is also mined at Befandriana Nord. Graphite output was also very low in the early 1980s; after increasing to 18,500 tons in 1990, production again declined, to 14,659 tons in 1994; output stood at only 11,295 tons in 1996, but recovered to some 14,000 tons in 1997. Production of mica reached 1,800 tons in 1986, but declined thereafter, amounting to only 317 tons in 1996; it recovered to some 500 tons in 1997. The government is inviting private mining companies to exploit the country's gold deposits, which were nationalized in 1975.

Official production has been only a few kilograms a year, but it has been estimated that 2–3 tons annually is mined unofficially by small prospectors. In 1994 the government established an agency to purchase the output of these prospectors. A proposed major project to revive the mining of ilmenite (titanium ore), which ceased in 1977, has aroused considerable controversy on environmental grounds; the deposits, whose exploitation could earn an estimated US $550m. over a 30-year period, are located in an area of primeval rain forest and sand-dunes in the south-east of the island. The project, which received government support in 1997, pending the completion of further studies, would also necessitate the construction of a new port. However, operations were not expected to commence before 2000. Other potential mineral projects include the eventual exploitation of an estimated 100m. tons of bauxite at Manantenina in the south-east of the country, and of coal deposits, also estimated at 100m. tons. In 1998 a feasibility and environmental assessment of nickel and cobalt deposits in central Madagascar was initiated. The discovery of sapphires in early 1997 in the north of the island prompted the arrival of thousands of unofficial miners, whose activities were causing serious damage to the Ankarana nature reserve. A further discovery in southern Madagascar in 1998 aroused the interest of foreign investors, and sapphires worth some $100m. were reported to have been mined by early 1999. In March the government ordered the suspension of sapphire mining, pending the results of studies into the effects of exploitation on the environment; however, unauthorized mining continued on a wide scale. In early 2000 a new mining code came into force, setting out the legal and environmental framework for the sector. Further legislation being drafted with regard to mining projects envisaged investment of more than $200m.

ENERGY

Madagascar's prospects for reducing fuel imports have been improved by the development of hydroelectric power and by a reduction in the cost of imported crude petroleum (which absorbed 7.1% of the country's total export earnings in 1998). The Andekaleka hydroelectric scheme, which began operations in 1982, supplies Antananarivo and Antsirabe areas, as well as the Andriamena chromite mine. A second stage to extend this grid to Toamasina is planned, but finance has yet to be secured. There are seven hydroelectric stations, which provided an estimated 78.3% of electricity production in 1998 while the remainder came from thermal installations. Fuel wood and charcoal is estimated to provide 84% of the country's total energy needs. Petroleum products account for 11% of energy consumption and the remaining 5% is provided by electricity. Many mines and factories have their own small diesel- or steam-powered generators. In April 1994 the government announced plans for the construction of a solar-energy electricity power plant, at a projected cost of US $3,400m. In April 1996 the IDA financed a $46m. project comprising various energy programmes including the promotion of energy efficiency and the rehabilitation and development of equipment, facilities and feasibility studies.

In 1980 the government announced that deposits of petroleum had been located and that the Petroleum Code would be revised. In the following decade several foreign companies signed concession agreements with the government to prospect in a number of areas, particularly in the Morandava basin, in western Madagascar. In 1990 BHP Australia signed an agreement to explore the Mahajanga area in the north west. As a result of the war in the Persian Gulf in late 1990 and early 1991, interest among Western petroleum companies in locating deposits of petroleum outside the Gulf region increased and, in Madagascar, Shell began drilling at three onshore sites in mid-1991. In 1993, however, it completed its exploratory programme and in 1994 announced that it was terminating its activities. So far, only non-commercial deposits of oil and gas have been found, although contracts for further exploration were granted in 1997 and 1999. Studies are continuing on deposits of heavy petroleum at Tsimororo.

For some years the USSR provided about two-thirds of Madagascar's imports of petroleum, some on a concessionary financing basis. However, in 1988 the USSR suspended deliveries of petroleum to Madagascar, owing to unpaid bills totalling some

US $240m. Madagascar was subsequently obliged to buy Iranian crude petroleum at market prices. Petroleum is also supplied by Libya and Gabon. The Toamasina refinery has the capacity to produce about 747,000 tons annually, but only an estimated 150,300 tons of petroleum products were exported in 1998. The World Bank has been urging the privatization of the refinery. In late 1995, also under World Bank pressure, the government relinquished the state monopoly on retail sales of petroleum products. The privatization of Solitany Malagasy (SOLIMA), the state petroleum company, was still pending in mid-2000 owing principally to disagreement over petroleum prices; potential buyers wanted to increase petroleum prices, which had already almost trebled during 1999, while the government considered this to be politically unacceptable and instead offered to pay subsidies direct to the petroleum companies.

TRANSPORT

Madagascar's mountainous topography has hindered the development of adequate communications and the infrastructure is also prone to cyclone damage. Even major routes may be impassable in bad weather. In 1996 there were 49,837 km of classified roads, of which 8,528 km were main roads and 17,310 km were secondary roads; some 11.6% of the road network was paved. In 1987 there were 39,500 km of unclassified roads, used only in favourable weather. In 1988 a programme to rehabilitate 4,781 km of roads (of which 1,500 km tarred) by 1993 was initiated. The US $144m. project was to be financed by the IDA, the EC (European Community, now the European Union—EU), Switzerland and Norway. In June 1989 the European Development Fund (EDF) granted $10m. for road rehabilitation in the north and west of the country and in 1992 the Arab Bank for Economic Development in Africa lent a further US $7m. to improve roads in tourist areas. In late 1997 the IDA granted US$35m. in credit for a four-year programme for the rehabilitation of urban roads and other infrastructure.

In 1999 there were 883 km of railway. Three lines in the north of the country primarily served the capital, while the fourth (in the south) linked Fianarantsoa to the east coast. In 1986 the World Bank agreed to lend US $12m. to finance the rehabilitation of the northern railway network, and the 40-km extension of one line. A 72-km extension to a line on the northern system was opened in 1986. In 1994 'Cyclone Geralda' damaged the line from Antananarivo to Toamasina so extensively that the World Bank recommended its replacement by a road link. Plans were mooted in 1997 to privatize the railway network; however, the age and poor condition of the network were likely to discourage potential buyers.

Domestic air services are important to Madagascar, on account of its size, difficult terrain and poor quality of road and rail networks. There are 211 airfields, two-thirds of which are privately owned. The main international airport is at Antananarivo. In 1996 the government invited bids for a rehabilitation project including nine of Madagascar's airports. The national airline, Air Madagascar, is 90% owned by the government. Under the government's new liberalization measures, Air Madagascar lost its monopoly on domestic services in 1995, although few competitors have emerged. On international routes, Air Madagascar effectively operates a duopoly with Air France. The French charter airline, Air Outre-Mer (AOM), began flights to Antananarivo in 1995, but was banned from landing in Madagascar soon afterwoods. The South African company, Inter Air, began charter flights to Madagascar in 1995 and was joined by a French company, Corsair, in late 1996. The privatization of Air Madagascar continued to be delayed owing to outstanding debts. In April 2000 it was announced that divestment had been postponed again and would not take place that year.

Toamasina and Mahajanga, the principal seaports, suffer from lack of storage space and equipment. Toamasina port handles about 70% of Madagascar's foreign trade and was in the process of being enlarged and modernized, until 80% of the port was destroyed by a cyclone in March 1986. (It suffered further serious damage from 'Cyclone Geralda' in 1994.) In January 1987 the IDA agreed to provide a US $16m. credit for a $34.8m. project to rehabilitate 10 ports. France, Germany and the UK are also financing the project. Toamasina is independently managed but the other ports are operated by the Malagasy

Ports Authority. Coastal shipping is conducted mainly by private companies. The country's 18 ports handled a total of 1,434,349 tons of freight in 1993 (819,093 tons inward and 615,256 tons outward). In 1984 the government initiated a development project to restore more than 200 km of the Pangalanes canal, which runs for 600 km near the east coast from Toamasina to Farafangana. In early 1990 432 km of the canal between Toamasina and Mananjary were navigable.

TOURISM

In 1989 the government introduced a tourism investment programme, which aimed to achieve 100,000 tourist arrivals by 1995. The government planned to exploit specialist markets represented by the growing number of visitors who are attracted by Madagascar's unusual varieties of wildlife. A number of state-owned hotels were transferred to private-sector ownership, and a French adviser was appointed to prepare a new tourism plan. The French group Savana and its parent company, Pullman–International Hotels, were to implement the tourism project at a total cost of US $234m., of which $30m. was provided by the government, mainly for infrastructural costs. An hotel group, partly owned by Mauritian interests, began the construction of a 200-room luxury hotel in the capital. There were 4,208 hotel rooms and 52,923 tourist arrivals in 1990, when tourist receipts amounted to $37m.; in 1991, however, the number of tourist arrivals declined by 34%, to 34,891, in reaction to the country's internal unrest. Tourist arrivals numbered 74,619 in 1995, considerably less than the original target number, with revenue from tourism amounting to $63m. Tourist arrivals increased in 1996 to an estimated 82,681, with tourist receipts at $64.7m. Tourist arrivals increased further, to 100,762, in 1997 when receipts totalled $73m. In 1998 tourist arrivals numbered 121,207. In 1999 receipts totalled $87m., making tourism the country's second most important source of foreign currency earnings.

EXTERNAL TRADE AND BALANCE OF PAYMENTS

During the period 1977 to 1987 Madagascar's unfavourable trade balance steadily worsened. Despite a brief rise in the value of exports in 1980, imports increased even faster than before, owing to the official policy of industrialization and over-riding emphasis on investment.

As the balance-of-payments problems became increasingly severe, the government was obliged to yield to pressure from the IMF, the World Bank and Western aid donors and creditors to liberalize trade and to adjust the Malagasy franc exchange rate. The reforms succeeded in reducing the external current account deficit from 14.6% of GDP in 1980 to 8.7% in 1986, when it was US $136m. The deficit declined from $149m. in 1988, to $84m. in 1989, as a result of improved export earnings in that year. Following a sharp increase in imports, the deficit on the current account rose to $265m. in 1990; it subsequently recovered slightly, amounting to $198m. in 1992, but increased again to reach $291m. in 1996. The government has aimed to reduce import restrictions and to introduce comprehensive tariff reforms. In February 1988 simplified import procedures were introduced, and the government also announced the removal of export duties from all goods except those, such as coffee, handled by state marketing boards. The trade deficit was converted to a surplus of $1m. in 1989; in 1990, however, a deficit of $249m. was recorded. In 1998 the trade deficit stood at $154m., and there was a deficit of $301m. on the current account of the balance of payments. The principal exports in 1998 were textiles, coffee, shrimps and prawns, and petroleum products. The principal imports in that year included chemical products, transport equipment, minerals (chiefly crude petroleum), base metals and machinery.

The principal source of imports in 1998 was France (24.0%); other major suppliers were Germany, Iran, the Southern African Customs Union (SACU) countries and Japan. France was also the principal market for exports (accounting for 39.3% of exports in that year); other important purchasers were Mauritius, the USA, Germany and Réunion. A national office opened in Paris (France) in January 1998 to promote tourism and artisanal work, and to facilitate potential investment in Madagascar.

ECONOMIC POLICY, PLANNING AND AID

Ratsiraka's initial 'strategy for development', embodied in a Plan covering three stages over the period 1978–2000, proved unsuccessful after only two years, principally as a result of the government's failure to take into consideration Madagascar's inadequate supply of the raw materials which were needed to operate some of the projected (or even existing) factories, the growing rice deficit, and the lack of spare parts and consumer-goods inducements. By mid-1980 the external debt had risen to US $680m.; Ratsiraka appealed successfully to the IMF for an $85m. loan, and later requested that France cancel Madagascar's debt. By 1981 many of Madagascar's traditional suppliers refused to grant credit to its government.

In return for a further stand-by loan of about US $80m. in May 1982, the IMF required the government to devalue the Malagasy franc by 15%; to channel state investments into the agricultural sector, to increase payments to farmers for paddy rice and cotton; and to restrict any increase in the minimum wage to 4.5%. Fulfilment of these and other drastic demands was immediately visible in the 1983 budget allocations, and was also reflected by a revision of national policies under which the state would either retain its monopoly or hold a majority share in certain vital sectors such as mining and hydrocarbons, but in most other areas would allow private entrepreneurs to invest in, and initiate, new projects. Although there was an improvement in the supply of provisions to urban consumers, as a result of the increase in payments to farmers and the liberalization of the rice trade in 1983–84, there was a noticeable rise in the cost of living, while successive devaluations of the Malagasy franc, together with the failure to make any appreciable increase in the wages of non-agricultural workers, placed the cost of basic necessities beyond the means of the average Malagasy. Even with the overall improvements in Madagascar's economic condition, the declining level of production, especially in export crops, caused an increasing dependence on costly imports (particularly fuel and rice) and on foreign aid.

In April 1985 the IMF approved a stand-by arrangement of SDR 29.5m. to support Madagascar's economic and financial programme during 1985–86. At a World Bank-sponsored Consultative Group meeting in April 1986, donors made commitments of about US $600m. for 1986–87. In May the IMF agreed to grant Madagascar two facilities, totalling SDR 32.7m., to offset the effects of the cyclone in March and the shortfalls in export earnings during the previous year. A devaluation of the Malagasy franc in August (see below), and further liberalization of trade and distribution, encouraged the IMF to provide a three-year stand-by arrangement of SDR 30m. in September. In October the 'Paris Club' of official creditors agreed to reschedule SDR 73.8m. of debts for 1986 and SDR 99.2m. for 1987.

In June 1986 a new investment code was introduced, providing incentives for domestic and foreign investment, particularly in manufacturing for the export market. Also in 1986 the government abolished most state controls on the internal rice trade. In 1987 further measures were introduced to encourage exports by allowing exporters to fix prices directly with foreign purchasers, and imposing a duty, equal to 10% of the import licence, on importers. The Malagasy franc was devalued by 20% in August 1986. There were several subsequent adjustments, and in June 1987 the currency was devalued by a further 41%. The government's reform measures resulted in the approval of a US $100m. structural adjustment loan arrangement from the World Bank and several bilateral donors. In August 1987 the IMF agreed to provide a new stand-by facility of SDR 42.2m. over three years, which included a structural adjustment facility (SAF). In the same month the 'London Club' of commercial creditors agreed to reschedule $59.4m. of debt.

At a meeting in Paris in January 1988, the World Bank-sponsored Consultative Group agreed to provide Madagascar with US $700m. in quick-disbursing aid, conditional upon the rescheduling of debts due to the 'Paris Club' later in the year. The donors strongly commended the Malagasy government's structural adjustment programme. The budget deficit had been reduced to the equivalent of 4% of GDP in 1986 (compared with 18.4% in 1980), and price controls had been lifted from most products and fixed profit margins had been virtually abolished by the end of 1987. In early 1988 the government stated its commitment to rationalize the public sector by closing loss-making nationalized enterprises and selling off many others. At the end of 1988 the IMF approved a 10-month stand-by facility of SDR 13.3m. to replace a credit of SDR 30m. which had expired in March 1988, without being fully drawn. Conditions of the new arrangement included further trade liberalization, stricter controls on government spending, the return of state banks to private-sector ownership, the opening up of financial markets to foreign competition, and improved credit access for producers. This was in addition to the three-year SAF due to expire in August 1990. The IDA released $125m. in July 1988 to support the government's plan to reform the public sector, and made available a credit of $22m. for social programmes.

The new IMF agreement opened the way for further pledges from donors attending a meeting in October 1988 of the 'Paris Club', which agreed to reschedule US $212m. of debt and to cancel $37m. of principal. The Federal Republic of Germany cancelled $116m. of debt in 1988, and in 1989 France decided to write off one-third of the debt owed to it, or about $471.4m. Debt-servicing costs were reduced from $271m. in 1987 to $221m. in 1988. The latest debt relief measures decreased further costs, but in 1988 debt servicing still represented 53.7% of export earnings. In May 1989 the IMF gave approval for a three-year enhanced structural adjustment facility (ESAF), to replace the 10-month stand-by agreement. The credit of SDR 76.9m. was to give support to the programme covering the period 1989–1991 which aims to promote growth of per caput income in real terms and to stabilize the financial sector. As part of the liberalization programme the government removed all price subsidies in March 1989.

Total external debt was estimated at US $3,449m. at the end of 1989, although this represented a decline in US dollar terms compared with 1987, as a result of the devaluation in June of that year. Despite the 'Paris Club' rescheduling of debt-service arrangements in 1988, debt-service payments still represented 33.1% of the value of exports of goods and services in 1991; this ratio had declined to 9.6% by 1994, but this was largely because much of the debt service due went unpaid, leading to a steep build-up in arrears. External debt at the end of 1998 totalled $4,394m., of which $4,107m. was long-term public debt; the cost of debt-servicing in that year was estimated to be equivalent to 14.7% of the value of exports of goods and services. Madagascar received a net total of $289m. in official development assistance from members of the OECD's development assistance committee in 1994, of which $273m. was in grant form. The main bilateral donors were France and Japan, while the World Bank's IDA and the EU were the principal multilateral donors. In 1988 the rate of inflation (which had declined to an average of 9.9% in 1984) increased to an average of 27%, owing to the abolition of price controls and the devaluation of the currency, which resulted in higher prices for imported goods. The rate fell back to an average of just over 11% per year in 1990–93, but consumer prices escalated again in 1994 and 1995 (by 39% and 49.1% respectively) as a result of further devaluation, less disciplined monetary policy and the effects of the boom in world coffee prices. The rate of inflation slowed to 19.8% in 1996 and to 4.5% in 1997 before increasing to 6.2% in 1998, giving an average of 18.0% per year in 1990–98. The rate of inflation increased to 14% in 1999, owing mainly to a steep rise in petroleum prices and a decline in the value of the currency.

Liberalization of the banking sector has attracted foreign private banks to Madagascar. Société Générale became the main shareholder in 1998 with the purchase of 70% of Banky Fampandrosoana ny Varotra (BFV). Banque Nationale de Paris owns 37.5% of Banque Malgache de l'Océan Indien (BMOI), which was officially opened in January 1990. Belgian and German banks also own a percentage of BMOI, as do about 300 Malagasy shareholders. Privatization of the remaining state bank, Bankin'ny Tantsaha Mpamokatra (BTM), was completed in late 1999 with Bank of Africa purchasing 60% of the shares; the bank was subsequently renamed BTM–BOA.

In 1991 a public investment programme (1991–93), financed by the World Bank, IMF and other international donors, was initiated. The programme, which cost an estimated US $1,000m., again emphasized the liberalization of trade and the financial sector, the encouragement of foreign and domestic investment, a reduction in the role of parastatal bodies, and increased producer prices. Following a prolonged general strike in the second half of 1991, however, the programme was deferred, pending the fulfilment of certain conditions, which included the transfer of a number of parastatal organizations to the private sector and a reduction in public expenditure.

The general strike in 1991 severely affected the financial sector: despite a substantial decline in capital expenditure, the ensuing fall in tax revenue, in conjunction with increased expenditure on personnel, prompted a rise in the budgetary deficit in 1991, to 272,400m. Malagasy francs (equivalent to 5.5% of GDP). Reserves of foreign exchange, which totalled US $223.7m. at the end of 1988 (excluding gold), declined to $89m. Economic conditions failed to improve in 1992, owing to the continued lack of political stability. In 1993 the new government initiated negotiations with the Bretton Woods institutions to obtain funding for a further economic reform programme. Following a report by a joint mission by the World Bank and IMF in early 1994, however, the organizations insisted that a number of economic reforms be implemented as a precondition to the disbursement of funds to support a new structural adjustment programme. Severe cyclones in early 1994 resulted in a further deterioration in economic conditions, increasing the necessity for substantial external assistance, while the French government indicated that continuing aid for reforms was conditional on an agreement between Madagascar and the Bretton Woods institutions. In May the government accepted the conditions imposed by the World Bank and IMF, notably the 'floating' of the Malagasy franc (which resulted in an immediate devaluation), the removal of price controls, further 'privatization' (93 state-owned enterprises had been either liquidated or transferred to the private sector in 1988–92), and measures to reduce budgetary expenditure, including substantial retrenchment in the civil service. A 'framework agreement', signed by the government and the Bretton Woods institutions in June, provided for the introduction of further reforms (including the removal of price controls and measures to reduce budgetary expenditure), prior to the adoption of a structural adjustment programme later that year. However, parliamentary opposition to the implementation of the economic austerity measures impeded subsequent progress (see Recent History). In October, in compliance with demands by the IMF and World Bank, the prime minister undertook to suspend arrangements with private enterprises whereby the government obtained financial assistance independently from the Bretton Woods institutions, and the dismissal, in early 1995, of the governor of the central bank fulfilled a further precondition to the resumption of credit from the World Bank and IMF. In February the government accepted a number of economic reforms (similar to those agreed in June 1994), including the imposition of a new tax on petroleum products and restrictions on loans by the central bank to private enterprises; subject to the successful implementation of these measures, the IMF was to reschedule Madagascar's external debt arrears and resume financial disbursements later in 1995. In September of that year, however, a World Bank mission reported delays in the implementation of a number of prescribed economic reforms.

Political paralysis in early 1996, including a bitter feud between the prime minister, Emmanuel Rakotovahiny, and the finance minister, Jean-Claude Raherimanjato, continued to stall reforms deemed necessary for agreement on new structural adjustment financing. The managing director of the IMF, Michel Camdessus, visited Antananarivo at the end of April and subsequently said that no new deal with the Fund would be possible without a cabinet reshuffle. The appointment of Norbert Ratsirahonana as prime minister in May 1996, followed by a government vote of confidence in reforms regarded as conditions for further IMF support, raised hopes of a breakthrough. IMF

officials arrived in Madagascar in August for more talks; they agreed the government's economic policy framework document (1996–99) setting out the measures needed to satisfy the aid donors. The document was primarily concerned with controlling inflation, promoting growth and investment, and improving the working of the foreign exchange market. Specific provisions included the ending of monopolies (public or private), a major improvement in tax collection and a concentration of government expenditure on education, security and road improvement. In November 1996 the IMF approved a three-year loan (equivalent to US $118m.) in support of the economic reform programme for 1996–99. Following his re-election in December 1996, President Ratsiraka affirmed his commitment to the implementation of the structural adjustment programme. Subsequent negotiations with the 'Paris Club' of official creditors resulted in the restructuring of Madagascar's debt, with an agreement to reduce its value by 67%. In March 1997 the World Bank approved a structural adjustment loan of $70m., and further aid was forthcoming from the EU and the African Development Bank.

Economic indicators in 1997–98 were favourable, with real GDP growth exceeding population growth and a reduction in the rate of inflation, but slow progress with structural reforms (particularly privatization) and a deterioration in fiscal performance prompted the IMF to delay the disbursement of a second structural adjustment credit. Privatization policies had made little progress for various reasons. Opposition to the process within both the government and parastatal organizations was substantial, while political uncertainty persisted surrounding proposed changes to the constitution and legislative elections in 1998 (see Recent History). The privatization proposals also reinforced demands by French petroleum companies for compensation for the nationalization of their assets under the first Ratsiraka government. The involvement of trade unions in the arrangement of compensation agreements for employees and a strike by civil servants in early 1998 also complicated what little progress was attempted. However, by late 1998 the payment of compensation to most of the nationalized petroleum interests, including the French companies, had cleared the way for the privatization of SOLIMA. Additionally, by May 1999, terms of settlement had been agreed on the question of compensation for all French businesses nationalized in 1970s.

In late 1998 the government announced measures to widen the tax base and improve customs and tax administration, including the removal of exemptions and an extension in the application of value-added tax. Meanwhile, following the sale of the state-owned Banky Fampandrosoana ny Varotra in December, the government pledged to complete the first phase of its privatization progamme (involving 46 companies, of which 37 had still to be sold or liquidated) by June 2000. The World Bank's decision to grant structural adjustment credits worth US $116.4m. in May 1999 was followed in July by the IMF's approval of a second annual loan, of some $36m., under an extension of the enhanced structural adjustment facility that was approved in November 1997. However, progress in the government's privatization programme stalled, and in mid-2000 several major enterprises, including Air Madagascar, Télécom Malagasy and SOLIMA, remained under state control, thus delaying the release of World Bank and IMF funding. Proceeds from the privatization programme totalled only $7.2m. in 1999, compared with the figure of $83m. forecast for that year. However, tax receipts improved in 1999 to meet the IMF target of 11.3% of GNP. It was also envisaged that tax collection would improve by 25% in 2000. Investment was equivalent to only 12.3% of GNP in 1999, the low level being due largely to investors' reluctance to commit finance pending the resolution of the government's problems with the Bretton Woods institutions.

Statistical Survey

Source (unless otherwise stated): Banque des Données de l'Etat, BP 485, Antananarivo; tel. 21613.

Area and Population

AREA, POPULATION AND DENSITY

Area (sq km)	587,041*
Population (census results)	
1974–75†	7,603,790
1–19 August 1993	
Males	5,991,171
Females	6,100,986
Total	12,092,157
Population (official estimates at mid-year)‡	
1996	13,494,000
1997	13,872,000
1998	14,260,000
Density (per sq km) at mid-1998	24.3

* 226,658 sq miles.

† The census took place in three stages: in provincial capitals on 1 December 1974; in Antananarivo and remaining urban areas on 17 February 1975; and in rural areas on 1 June 1975.

‡ Source: IMF. *Madagascar: Statistical Annex* (March 1999).

PRINCIPAL ETHNIC GROUPS (estimated population, 1974)

Merina (Hova) .	1,993,000	Sakalava . .	470,156*
Betsimisaraka .	1,134,000	Antandroy . .	412,500
Betsileo . .	920,600	Antaisaka . .	406,468*
Tsimihety . .	558,100		

* 1972 figure.

PRINCIPAL TOWNS (population at 1974–75 census)

Antananarivo		Mahajanga	
(capital) . .	406,366	(Majunga) . .	65,864
Antsirabé . .	78,941	Toliary	
Toamasina		(Tuléar) . .	45,676
(Tamatave) .	77,395	Antsiranana	
Fianarantsoa .	68,054	(Diégo-Suarez) .	40,443

The population of Antananarivo was estimated to be 662,585 in 1985.

BIRTHS AND DEATHS (UN estimates, annual averages)

	1980–85	1985–90	1990–95
Birth rate (per 1,000) . . .	46.5	46.2	45.9
Death rate (per 1,000) . .	15.5	14.8	12.6

Expectation of life (UN estimates, years at birth, 1990–95): 55.5 (males 54.0; females 57.0).

Source: UN, *World Population Prospects: The 1998 Revision.*

ECONOMICALLY ACTIVE POPULATION ('000 persons)

	1991	1992	1993
Agriculture	4,926	5,057	5,100
Manufacturing and mining . .	82	84	86
Construction	44	45	46
Trade, banking and insurance .	141	145	149
Transport and telecommunications	40	41	42
Administration	180	193	208
Other activities*	240	246	243
Total labour force . . .	5,653	5,811	5,874

* Including artisans and domestic servants.

Source: IMF, *Madagascar: Statistical Annex* (March 1999).

1993 census (persons aged 10 years and over): Total labour force 5,299,563 (males 3,181,509; females 2,118,054) (Source: ILO, *Yearbook of Labour Statistics*).

Mid-1998 (estimates in '000): Agriculture, forestry and fishing 5,492; Total labour force 7,310 (Source: FAO, *Production Yearbook*).

Agriculture

PRINCIPAL CROPS ('000 metric tons)

	1996	1997	1998
Maize	180	178	152
Rice (paddy)	2,500	2,558	2,447
Sugar cane	2,150	2,160	2,180
Potatoes . . .	280	280	280
Sweet potatoes . .	500	510	510
Cassava (Manioc) . .	2,353	2,418	2,404
Taro (Coco yam)† .	150	160	155
Dry beans . . .	68	70	72
Vegetables and melons† .	349	354	357
Oranges† . . .	83	83	84
Bananas† . . .	250	260	265
Avocados† . . .	22	23	24
Mangoes† . . .	202	204	205
Pineapples† . . .	50	51	52
Other fruits† . .	221	223	225
Groundnuts (in shell) . .	36	36	34
Cottonseed . . .	16	16*	23
Cotton (lint)* . . .	11	11	15
Coconuts† . . .	83	84	84
Copra† . . .	10	10	10
Coffee (green) . .	68	55	60
Cocoa beans . .	4	4	4†
Tobacco (leaves) . .	4	4	4†
Sisal	17	18	19†

* Unofficial figure(s). † FAO estimate(s).

Source: FAO, *Production Yearbook.*

LIVESTOCK ('000 head, year ending September)

	1996	1997	1998†
Cattle	10,320	10,331	10,335
Pigs	1,629	1,662	1,670
Sheep	756	760†	765
Goats	1,329	1,330†	1,340

Chickens (million): 16* in 1996; 17† in 1997; 17† in 1998.

Ducks (million): 3* in 1996; 3† in 1997; 3† in 1998.

Turkeys (million): 2* in 1996; 2† in 1997; 2† in 1998.

* Unofficial figure. † FAO estimate(s).

Source: FAO, *Production Yearbook.*

LIVESTOCK PRODUCTS (FAO estimates, '000 metric tons)

	1996	1997	1998
Cows' milk . . .	484	485	486
Beef and veal . .	145	145	145
Pig meat . . .	53	54	54
Poultry meat . .	50	52	53
Hen eggs . . .	13	13	13
Honey	4	4	4
Cattle hides . . .	20	20	20

Source: FAO, *Production Yearbook.*

Forestry

ROUNDWOOD REMOVALS
('000 cubic metres, excluding bark)

	1995	1996	1997
Sawlogs, veneer logs and logs for sleepers	95	42	34
Other industrial wood*	339	339	339
Fuel wood	9,092	9,372	9,688
Total	9,526	9,753	10,061

* Annual output assumed to be unchanged since 1977.

Source: FAO, *Yearbook of Forest Products.*

SAWNWOOD PRODUCTION
(FAO estimates, '000 cubic metres, including railway sleepers)

	1995	1996	1997
Coniferous (softwood)	20	20	20
Broadleaved (hardwood)	64	64	64
Total	84	84	84

Source: FAO, *Yearbook of Forest Products.*

Fishing

('000 metric tons, live weight)

	1995	1996	1997
Inland waters:			
Freshwater fishes	30.0	30.0	30.0
Indian Ocean:			
Marine fishes	71.5	70.0	71.6
Marine crabs	1.3	1.0	1.0
Tropical spiny lobsters	0.4	0.4	0.4
Shrimps and prawns	9.9	10.5	10.8
Molluscs	0.7	0.9	0.9
Other aquatic animals	1.8	1.8	1.8
Total catch	115.7	114.5	116.4

Source: FAO, *Yearbook of Fishery Statistics.*

Mining

(metric tons)

	1995	1996	1997
Chromite*	105,747	139,272	140,000
Salt	70,560	41,750	46,702
Graphite (natural)	16,119	11,295	14,000
Mica	432	317	500

* Figures refer to gross weight. The estimated chromium content is 27%.

Source: IMF, *Madagascar: Statistical Annex* (March 1999).

Industry

SELECTED PRODUCTS (metric tons, unless otherwise indicated)

	1995	1996	1997
Raw sugar	90,052	87,608	82,343
Beer ('000 hectolitres)	318.8	347.8	457.9
Cigarettes	1,969	3,371	3,159
Woven cotton fabrics (million metres)	24.3	11.1	11.6
Leather footwear ('000 pairs)	132	158	162
Plastic footwear ('000 pairs)	547	409	339
Paints	1,855	2,350	2,397
Soap	16,654	16,500	15,071
Motor spirit—petrol ('000 cu metres)	64.9	70.6	96.6
Kerosene ('000 cu metres)	48.8	54.4	72.1
Gas-diesel (distillate fuel) oil ('000 cu metres)	111.1	93.7	125.3
Residual fuel oils ('000 cu metres)	204.5	159.5	211.5
Cement	38,000	38,349	44,102
Electric energy (million kWh)*	552.0	563.2	616.3

* Production by the state-owned utility only, excluding electricity generated by industries for their own use.

Source: IMF, *Madagascar: Statistical Annex* (March 1999).

Finance

CURRENCY AND EXCHANGE RATES

Monetary Units
100 centimes = 1 franc malgache (franc MG—Malagasy franc).

Sterling, Dollar and Euro Equivalents (28 April 2000)
£1 sterling = 11,338.6 francs MG;
US $1 = 7,230.8 francs MG;
€1 = 6,569.2 francs MG;
100,000 francs MG = £8.819 = $13.830 = €15.223.

Average Exchange Rate (Malagasy francs per US $)
1997 5,090.9
1998 5,441.4
1999 6,283.8

GENERAL BUDGET ('000 million francs MG)

Revenue*	1994	1995	1996
Tax revenue	702.2	1,120.8	1,374.2
Taxes on income, profits and capital gains	150.7	167.8	258.2
Corporate	68.5	83.2	163.6
Individual	40.6	58.6	59.0
Domestic taxes on goods and services	201.4	298.5	341.7
General sales, turnover or value-added tax	177.5	242.3	166.8
Excises	5.9	0.8	74.4
Taxes on international trade and transactions	335.6	633.8	750.3
Import duties	320.0	589.8	731.6
Export duties	15.6	43.9	18.7
Other current revenue	55.0	28.0	30.4
Entrepreneurial and property income	18.2	10.6	0.6
Capital revenue	4.8	0.8	2.6
Total	762.0	1,149.6	1,407.2

Expenditure†	1994	1995	1996
General public services	181.9	174.6	493.1
Defence	84.6	118.6 {	151.2
Public order and safety			59.2
Education	187.0	264.6	255.5
Health	83.3	136.6	191.3
Social security and welfare	32.9	61.6	26.0
Housing and community amenities	49.4	67.0	n.a.
Recreational, cultural and religious affairs and services	1.0	13.1	6.7
Economic affairs and services	432.8	658.9	n.a.
Agriculture, forestry, fishing and hunting	109.1	143.1	285.7
Mining and mineral resources, manufacturing and construction	58.4	71.1	n.a.
Transportation and communication	105.6	121.1	36.1
Other purposes	681.4	849.2	862.8
Interest payments	491.8	687.9	759.2
Sub-total	**1,734.3**	**2,344.2**	**2,799.1**
Current	1,165.5	1,535.4	1,696.4
Capital	568.8	808.8	1,102.7
Adjustment for payment arrears‡	−75.0	−619.4	−564.1
Total	**1,359.3**	**1,724.8**	**2,235.0**

* Excluding grants received ('000 million francs MG): 274.0 in 1994; 392.1 in 1995; 683.4 in 1996.
† Excluding lending minus repayments ('000 million francs MG): 44.3 in 1994; 29.7 in 1995; 73.1 in 1996.
‡ Minus sign indicates an increase in arrears.

Source: IMF, *Government Finance Statistics Yearbook*.

INTERNATIONAL RESERVES (US $ million at 31 December)

	1997	1998	1999
IMF special drawing rights	0.1	—	0.1
Foreign exchange	281.5	171.3	227.0
Total	**281.6**	**171.4**	**227.2**

Source: IMF, *International Financial Statistics*.

MONEY SUPPLY ('000 million francs MG at 31 December)

	1996	1997	1998
Currency outside banks	829.4	1,020.3	1,169.9
Demand deposits at deposit money banks	1,338.3	1,643.7	1,783.1
Total money	**2,167.7**	**2,663.9**	**2,953.2**

Source: IMF, *International Financial Statistics*.

COST OF LIVING (Consumer Price Index for Madagascans in Antananarivo; base: 1990 = 100)

	1996	1997	1998
Food	346.0	360.1	381.7
All items*	339.3	354.6	376.6

* Excluding rent.
Source: UN, *Monthly Bulletin of Statistics*.

NATIONAL ACCOUNTS ('000 million francs MG at current prices)
Expenditure on the Gross Domestic Product

	1997	1998	1999
Government final consumption expenditure	1,378.1	1,524.9	1,841.9
Private final consumption expenditure	16,081.7	18,026.1	20,104.7
Increase in stocks } Gross fixed capital formation	2,156.9	2,558.3	3,127.4
Total domestic expenditure	**19,616.7**	**22,109.3**	**25,074.0**
Exports of goods and services	3,937.3	4,358.8	5,710.9
Less Imports of goods and services	5,476.8	6,078.7	7,716.3
GDP in purchasers' values	**18,077.8**	**20,389.4**	**23,068.7**
GDP at constant 1984 prices	**2,045.7**	**2,126.2**	**2,222.6**

Source: IMF, *International Financial Statistics*.

Gross Domestic Product by Economic Activity

	1989	1990	1991
Agriculture, hunting, forestry and fishing	1,181.7	1,334.3	1,488.4
Mining and quarrying	16.1	14.9	14.8
Manufacturing	471.6	492.6	530.6
Electricity, gas and water	42.7	78.7	87.0
Construction	48.7	61.7	52.6
Trade, restaurants and hotels	351.6	426.2	498.0
Transport, storage and communications	623.9	721.6	747.9
Finance, insurance, real estate and business services	58.7	64.6	70.0
Public administration and defence	190.9	240.7	284.4
Other services	658.7	756.9	791.9
GDP at factor cost	**3,644.6**	**4,192.0**	**4,565.5**
Indirect taxes, *less* subsidies	360.7	409.6	340.9
GDP in purchasers' values	**4,005.3**	**4,601.6**	**4,906.4**

Source: UN Economic Commission for Africa, *African Statistical Yearbook*.

BALANCE OF PAYMENTS (US $ million)

	1996	1997	1998
Exports of goods f.o.b.	509	516	538
Imports of goods f.o.b.	−629	−694	−693
Trade balance	**−120**	**−178**	**−154**
Exports of services	293	272	291
Imports of services	−373	−386	−436
Balance on goods and services	**−200**	**−292**	**−299**
Other income received	6	20	25
Other income paid	−169	−115	−103
Balance on goods, services and income	**−363**	**−387**	**−377**
Current transfers received	94	156	109
Current transfers paid	−23	−35	−33
Current balance	**−291**	**−266**	**−301**
Capital account (net)	5	115	103
Direct investment from abroad	10	14	17
Other investment assets	37	135	−68
Other investment liabilities	86	−39	−25
Net errors and omissions	59	25	−25
Overall balance	**−94**	**−16**	**−299**

Source: IMF, *International Financial Statistics*.

External Trade

PRINCIPAL COMMODITIES (million francs MG)

Imports c.i.f.	1996	1997	1998
Animal products	41,489	31,054	23,060
Vegetable products	123,160	179,366	209,037
Wheat and meslin	58,202	17,408	84,893
Rice	34,684	85,063	89,287
Animal or vegetable fats, oils and waxes	65,520	127,199	73,645
Food oils	40,623	98,020	55,712
Prepared foodstuffs	37,167	85,129	114,500
Mineral products	295,782	109,032	306,716
Crude petroleum	178,453	47,156	195,014
Chemical products	305,971	420,279	411,362
Pharmaceutical products	61,669	115,176	95,348
Plastic materials	56,947	86,868	93,555
Rubber manufactures	67,439	63,080	62,056
Rubber tyres	49,576	44,322	41,029
Paper, paperboard, etc.	79,716	94,341	117,323
Base metals and articles thereof	162,796	196,607	266,712
Iron and steel	75,202	89,955	145,903
Machinery and mechanical appliances (non-electric)	210,186	227,423	254,895
Electrical machinery and appliances	193,262	202,450	228,883
Radio and television equipment	104,791	96,258	112,291
Transport equipment	214,846	316,391	313,012
Passenger cars and buses	73,180	115,774	140,689
Lorries	80,749	101,922	106,639
Total (incl. others)	2,056,108	2,392,164	2,748,989

Exports f.o.b.	1996	1997	1998
Animal products	233,919	87,679	123,654
Shrimps and prawns	178,627	41,423	81,732
Vegetable products	471,104	437,564	436,199
Coffee (green)	232,242	168,397	218,922
Vanilla	47,988	49,196	38,718
Cloves	22,814	62,764	49,969
Litchis	25,052	16,996	14,804
Prepared foodstuffs	30,730	15,066	9,966
Mineral products	227,557	134,424	143,858
Graphite	33,061	35,716	36,382
Chromium ores	151,610	45,712	49,540
Petroleum products	39,414	40,851	53,772
Chemical products	24,920	30,894	35,039
Wood, cork and articles thereof	25,277	38,860	57,245
Textiles and textile articles	117,400	286,922	268,083
Cotton fabrics	43,612	89,865	179,416
Total (incl. others)	1,215,702	1,139,067	1,273,767

Source: Ministère du commerce et de la consommation.

PRINCIPAL TRADING PARTNERS (million francs MG)

Imports	1996	1997	1998
Belgium-Luxembourg	35,539	44,147	39,960
China, People's Repub.	94,410	128,287	131,531
France	638,339	388,689	660,021
Germany	12,193	126,282	198,242
India	35,339	51,062	59,742
Iran	187,198	50,785	197,992
Italy	40,578	71,606	61,028
Japan	118,265	176,887	163,037
Malaysia	33,632	29,531	32,108
Netherlands	23,261	34,932	30,771
Pakistan	2,432	58,965	49,452
Romania	17,440	4,684	40,500
Singapore	47,497	36,435	19,328
SACU*	169,140	161,028	165,787
United Kingdom	47,459	67,491	69,161
USA	102,889	130,160	108,151
Total (incl. others)	2,056,108	2,392,164	2,748,989

* Southern African Customs Union, comprising Botswana, Lesotho, Namibia, South Africa and Swaziland.

Exports	1996	1997	1998
Belgium-Luxembourg	53,179	44,329	597
France	385,865	388,689	500,841
Germany	77,513	69,015	57,557
Italy	53,896	42,261	46,858
Japan	192,659	36,885	24,773
Mauritius	47,691	55,592	87,180
Netherlands	19,333	14,651	8,059
Portugal	16,570	3,360	16,055
Réunion	69,184	63,194	48,550
Singapore	19,124	43,134	34,907
Spain	27,563	32,963	18,674
United Kingdom	36,956	45,414	35,933
USA	50,797	53,571	76,589
Total (incl. others)	1,215,702	1,139,067	1,273,767

Source: Ministère du commerce et de la consommation.

Transport

RAILWAYS (traffic)

	1996	1997	1998
Passengers carried ('000)	321	359	293
Passenger-km (millions)	38	37	35
Freight carried ('000 metric tons)	242	227	213
Ton-km (millions)	82	81	71

Source: Réseau National des Chemins de Fer Malagasy.

ROAD TRAFFIC (vehicles in use)

	1994	1995	1996*
Passenger cars	54,821	58,097	60,480
Buses and coaches	3,797	4,332	4,850
Lorries and vans	35,931	37,232	37,972
Road tractors	488	560	619

* Estimates.

Source: IRF, *World Road Statistics*.

SHIPPING

Merchant Fleet (registered at 31 December)

	1996	1997	1998
Number of vessels	99	101	101
Displacement ('000 gross registered tons)	39.3	40.1	41.7

Source: Lloyd's Register of Shipping, *World Fleet Statistics*.

International Sea-borne Freight Traffic ('000 metric tons)

	1987	1988	1989
Goods loaded:			
Mahajanga	17	18	29.4
Toamasina	252	350	360.6
Other ports	79	100	137.4
Total	348	468	527.4
Goods unloaded:			
Mahajanga	37	32	30.8
Toamasina	748	778	708.9
Other ports	48	53	52.0
Total	833	863	791.7

1990 ('000 metric tons): Goods loaded 540; Goods unloaded 984 (Source: UN, *Monthly Bulletin of Statistics*).

CIVIL AVIATION (traffic on scheduled services)

	1993	1994	1995
Kilometres flown (million) . .	7	7	8
Passengers carried ('000) . . .	419	451	497
Passenger-km (million) . .	499	567	631
Total ton-km (million) . . .	72	74	89

Source: UN, *Statistical Yearbook*.

Tourism

TOURIST ARRIVALS BY NATIONALITY

	1996	1997	1998
Canada and USA	5,462	2,015	2,424
Comoros.	1,675	n.a.	n.a.
France	28,459	51,389	61,815
Germany	14,738	4,030	4,850
Italy	6,969	6,046	7,273
Mauritius	1,429	1,814	3,394
Réunion	4,577	4,030	12,121
Switzerland	5,870	3,023	4,847
United Kingdom	3,970	n.a.	3,636
Total (incl. others) . . .	82,681	100,762	121,207

Tourism receipts (US $ million): 65 in 1996; 73 in 1997.

Source: World Tourism Organization, *Yearbook of Tourism Statistics*.

Communications Media

	1994	1995	1996
Radio receivers ('000 in use) . .	2,740	2,850	2,950
Television receivers ('000 in use) .	280	295	305
Telephones ('000 main lines in use)	34	33	n.a.
Book production*:			
Titles	114	131	119
Copies ('000)	287	292	296
Daily newspapers:			
Number	7	6	5
Circulation ('000 copies) . .	60	59	66
Non-daily newspapers:			
Number	31	31	n.a.
Circulation ('000 copies) . .	90	90	n.a.
Other periodicals:			
Number	55	n.a.	n.a.
Circulation ('000 copies) . .	108†	n.a.	n.a.

* Including pamphlets (42 titles and 106,000 copies in 1994).

† Estimate.

1997: ('000 in use) Radio receivers 3,050; Television receivers 325.

Sources: UNESCO, *Statistical Yearbook*; UN, *Statistical Yearbook*.

Education

(1995/96, unless otherwise indicated)

	Insti-tutions	Teach-ers	Pupils Males	Females	Total
Pre-primary* . .	n.a.	n.a.	28,657	29,186	57,843
Primary . . .	13,325	44,145	836,506	801,681	1,638,187
Secondary:					
General . . .	n.a.	16,795	150,542	151,493	302,035
Teacher training† .	n.a.	58	199	142	341
Vocational‡ .	n.a.	1,092	5,708	2,430	8,138
University level§ .	n.a.	921	9,976	8,482	18,458

* 1994/95 figures.
† 1993/94 figures.
‡ Public education only.
§ 1996/97 figures.

Source: UNESCO, *Statistical Yearbook*.

Directory

The Constitution

The Constitution of the Third Republic of Madagascar was endorsed by national referendum on 19 August 1992, but was substantially altered by amendments that were endorsed in a national referendum on 15 March 1998. The amended Constitution enshrines a 'federal-style' state, composed of six autonomous provinces—each with a governor and up to 12 general commissioners (holding executive power) and a provincial council (holding legislative power). It provides for a government delegate to each province, who is charged with supervising the division of functions between the state and the province. The bicameral legislature consists of the National Assembly (the lower house), which is elected by universal adult suffrage, under a mixed system of single-seat constituencies and a form of proportional representation, for a five-year term of office. The Constitution also provides for a Senate (the upper house), of which one-third of the members are to be presidential nominees and two-thirds are to be elected in equal numbers by each of the autonomous provinces. The constitutional Head of State is the President. If no candidate obtains an overall majority in the presidential election, a second round of voting is to take place a maximum of 30 days after the publication of the results of the first ballot. Any one candidate can be elected for a maximum of three five-year terms. The powers of the President were greatly increased by constitutional amendments of March 1998: he has the power to determine general

state policy in the Council of Ministers, to call referendums on all matters of national importance and to dissolve the National Assembly not less than one year after a general election. Executive power is vested in a Prime Minister, who is appointed by the President. The President appoints the Council of Ministers, on the recommendation of the Prime Minister.

The Government

HEAD OF STATE

President: Adm. (retd) DIDIER RATSIRAKA (took office 9 February 1997).

COUNCIL OF MINISTERS
(August 2000)

Prime Minister and Minister of Finance and the Economy: TANTELY RENÉ GABRIO ANDRIANARIVO.

Deputy Prime Minister in charge of the Budget and the Development of the Autonomous Provinces: PIERROT JOCELYN RAJAONARIVELO.

Minister of Water and Forests: RIJA RAJOHNSON.

Minister of Higher Education: JOSEPH SYDSON.

Minister of the Development of the Private Sector and Privatization: CONSTANT HORACE.

Minister of the Population, the Status of Women and Children: NOELINE JAOTODY.

Minister of Energy and Mines: CHARLES RASOZA.

Minister of Tourism: BLANDIN RAZAFIMANJATO.

Minister of Secondary and Primary Education: NIVOSON JACQUIT SIMON.

Minister of Technical Education and Professional Training: BONIFACE LEVELO.

Minister of Youth and Sports: Capt. NDRIANASOLO.

Minister of Foreign Affairs: LILA RATSIFANDRIAMANANA.

Minister of Information, Culture and Communications: FREDO BETSIMIFIRA.

Minister of Health: HENRIETTE RAHANTALALAO.

Minister of Scientific Research: SOLAY GEORGES RAKOTONIRAINY.

Minister of Justice: ANACLET IMBIKY.

Minister of Public Works: Col. JEAN ÉMILE TSARANAZY.

Minister of Town Planning: HERIVELONA RAMANANTSOA.

Minister of Posts and Telecommunications: NY HASINA ANDRIAMANJATO.

Minister of Transport and Meteorology: CHARLES ANGELO MARC RASOLONAY.

Minister of the Civil Service: ALICE RAZAFINAKANGA.

Minister of Agriculture: MARCEL THÉOPHILE RAVELOARIJAONA.

Minister of Fishing and Fish Stocks: HOUSSENE ABDALLAH.

Minister of Industrialization and Craftsmanship: MAMY RATOVOMALALA.

Minister of the Environment: ALPHONSE.

Minister of Animal Husbandry: RAKOTONDRASOA.

Minister of Commerce and Consumer Affairs: ALPHONSE RANDRIANAMBININA.

Minister of the Armed Forces: Gen. MARCEL RANJEVA.

Minister of the Interior: Brig. JEAN JACQUES RASOLONDRAIBE.

State Secretary at the Ministry of the Interior in charge of Public Security: BEN MAROUF AZALY.

State Secretary at the Ministry of the Armed Forces in charge of the Gendarmerie: Gen. JEAN PAUL BORY.

MINISTRIES

Office of the Prime Minister: BP 248, Mahazoarivo, 101 Antananarivo; tel. (20) 2225258; fax (20) 2235258.

Ministry of Agriculture: BP 301, Anosy, 101 Antananarivo; tel. (20) 2224710; fax (20) 2226561.

Ministry of Animal Husbandry: BP 484, Antsahavola, Antananarivo; tel. (20) 2224026; fax (20) 2266896.

Ministry of the Armed Forces: BP 08, Ampahibe, 101 Antananarivo; tel. (20) 2222211; fax (20) 2235420.

Ministry of the Budget and the Development of the Autonomous Provinces: BP 61, Antaninarenina, Antananarivo; tel. (20) 2230173; fax (20) 2264680.

Ministry of the Civil Service: BP 270, Cité des 67 Hectares, Tsaralalana, 101 Antananarivo; tel. (20) 2221541; fax (20) 2233856.

Ministry of Commerce and Consumer Affairs: BP 454, Ambohidahy, Antananarivo; tel. (20) 2227292; fax (20) 2231280.

Ministry of the Development of the Private Sector and Privatization: BP 674, Antaninarenina, 101 Antananarivo; tel. (20) 2220284; fax (20) 2228508.

Ministry of Energy and Mining: BP 527, Antaninarenina, Antananarivo; tel. (20) 2225515; fax (20) 2232554.

Ministry of the Environment: Ampandrianomby, 101 Antananarivo; tel. (20) 2240908.

Ministry of Finance and the Economy: BP 61, Antaninarenina, 101 Antananarivo; tel. (20) 2230173; fax (20) 2234530.

Ministry of Fishing and Fish Stocks: BP 1699, Ampandrianomby, 101 Antananarivo; tel. (20) 2240650; fax (20) 2241655.

Ministry of Foreign Affairs: BP 448, Anosy, 101 Antananarivo; tel. (20) 2221198; fax (20) 2234484.

Ministry of Health: Ambohidahy, 101 Antananarivo; tel. (20) 2223697.

Ministry of Higher Education: BP 4163, Tsimbazaza, 101 Antananarivo; tel. (20) 2227185; fax (20) 2223897.

Ministry of Industrialization and Craftsmanship: BP 527, Antaninarenina, 101 Antananarivo; tel. (20) 2225515; fax (20) 2227790; e-mail celenv@sinergic.mg.

Ministry of Information, Culture and Communications: BP 305, 101 Antananarivo; tel. (20) 2227092; fax (20) 2229448.

Ministry of the Interior: BP 2310, Anosy, 101 Antananarivo; tel. (20) 2223084; fax (20) 2235579.

Ministry of Justice: BP 231, Faravohitra, 101 Antananarivo; tel. (20) 2224030; fax (20) 2262376.

Ministry of the Population, Women's Affairs and Children: Ambohijatovo, 101 Antananarivo; tel. (20) 2223075; fax (20) 2227394.

Ministry of Posts and Telecommunications: BP 163, Antaninarenina, 101 Antananarivo; tel. (20) 2223267; fax (20) 2235894.

Ministry of Public Works: BP 295, Anosy, 101 Antananarivo; tel. (20) 2223215; fax (20) 2234946.

Ministry of Scientific Research: 21 rue Fernand Kasanga, BP 6224, Andoharano-Tsimbazaza, 101 Antananarivo; tel. (20) 2233288; fax (20) 2224075; e-mail cidst@bow.dts.mg.

Ministry of Secondary and Basic Education: BP 267, Anosy, 101 Antananarivo; tel. (20) 2221325; fax (20) 2224765.

Ministry of Technical Education and Professional Training: Complexe scolaire, Ampefiloha, BP 793, 101 Antananarivo; tel. (20) 2226014; fax (20) 2225176.

Ministry of Tourism: BP 610, Tsimbazaza, 101 Antananarivo; tel. (20) 2226298; fax (20) 2226719.

Ministry of Town Planning: BP 3378, Anosy, 101 Antananarivo; tel. (20) 2235617; fax (20) 2235613.

Ministry of Transport and Meteorology: BP 4139, Anosy, 101 Antananarivo; tel. (20) 2224604; fax (20) 2224001.

Ministry of Water and Forests: BP 243, Antsahavola, Antananarivo; tel. (20) 2264588; fax (20) 2266896.

Ministry of Youth and Sports: Ambohijatovo, Place Goulette, 101 Antananarivo; tel. (20) 2267604; fax (20) 2263174.

President and Legislature

PRESIDENT

Presidential Election, First Ballot, 3 November 1996

Candidate	% of votes
Adm. (retd) DIDIER RATSIRAKA	36.6
Prof. ALBERT ZAFY	23.4
HERIZO RAZAFIMAHALEO	15.1
NORBERT RATSIRAHONANA	10.1
Pastor RICHARD ANDRIAMANJATO	4.9
Others	9.9
Total	100.0

Second Ballot, 29 December 1996

Candidate	% of votes
Adm. (retd) DIDIER RATSIRAKA	50.71
Prof. ALBERT ZAFY	49.29
Total	100.00

LEGISLATURE

The Constitution provides for a bicameral legislature, comprising a Senate and a National Assembly. However, no Senate had been established by early 2000.

National Assembly

President: Prof. ANGE ANDRIANARISOA.

General Election, 17 May 1998

Party	Seats
AREMA	63
LEADER/Fanilo	16
AVI	14
RPSD	11
AFFA	6
AKFM/Fanavaozana	3
MFM	3
Fihaonana	1
GRAD/Iloafo	1
Independents	32
Total	150

Political Organizations

Following the restoration of multi-party politics in March 1990, more than 120 political associations emerged, of which nine secured representation in the National Assembly in 1998. The following were among the more influential political organizations in early 2000:

AKFM/Fanavaozana (AKFM/Renouveau): f. 1989 by fmr mems of the Marxist Parti du congrès de l'indépendance de Madagascar (AKFM); liberal orientation; Leader Pastor RICHARD ANDRIAMANJATO.

Asa, fahamarinana, fampandrosoana, arinda (AFFA—Action, Truth, Development and Harmony): f. 1998; opposition party; Leader Prof. ALBERT ZAFY.

Association pour la renaissance de Madagascar (Andry sy riana enti-manavotra an'i Madigasikara—AREMA): f. 1975 as Avant-garde de la révolution malgache; adopted present name 1997; party of Pres. DIDIER RATSIRAKA; Sec.-Gen. (vacant).

Committee for the support of democracy and development in Madagascar (CSDDM): f. 1993; Leader FRANCISQUE RAVONY.

Fihaonana: f. 1990; Leader GUY RAZANAMASY.

Groupe de réflexion et d'action pour le développement de Madagascar (GRAD/Iloafo): f. 1992 by its Leader TOVONANAHARY RABETSITONTA.

LEADER/Fanilo: f. 1993 as a party of 'non-politicians'; supports Pres. Ratsiraka; Leader HERIZO RAZAFIMAHALEO.

MASTERS: f. 1997 by ALAIN RAMAROSON following his dismissal as Pres. of political dept of the Hery Velona Rasalama (HVR, now disbanded); Leader ALAIN RAMAROSON.

Mouvement pour le progrès de Madagascar (Mpitolona ho amin'ny fandrosoan'ny Madagasikara—MFM): 101 Antananarivo; f. 1972 as Mouvement pour le pouvoir prolétarien (MFM), adopted present name in 1990; advocates liberal and market-orientated policies; Leader MANANDAFY RAKOTONIRINA; Sec.-Gen. GERMAIN RAKOTONIRAINY.

Ny asa vita no ifampitsara (AVI)—('People are judged by the work they do'): f. 1997 to promote human rights, hard work and development; Leader NORBERT RATSIRAHONANA.

Parti sociale démocrate (PSD): f. 1957; party of fmr Pres. Tsiranana; ruling party 1958–72; relaunched 1990; Leader Mme RUFFINE TSIRANANA.

Rassemblement pour le socialisme et la démocratie (RPSD): f. 1993 by fmr mems of PSD; Leader EVARISTE MARSON; Sec.-Gen. JEAN EUGÈNE VONINAHITSY.

Vonjy iray tsy mivaky (VITM—Elan populaire pour l'unité nationale): f. 1973; centrist; supports Pres. Ratsiraka; Leader Dr JÉRÔME MAROJAMA RAZANABAHINY.

Diplomatic Representation

EMBASSIES IN MADAGASCAR

China, People's Republic: Ancien Hôtel Panorama, BP 1658, 101 Antananarivo; Ambassador: MA ZHIXUE.

Egypt: 47 ave Lénine, BP 4082, Ankadifotsy, 101 Antananarivo; tel. (20) 2225233; fax (20) 2227959; Ambassador: ALY ELKARAKSY.

France: 3 rue Jean Jaurès, BP 204, 101 Antananarivo; tel. (20) 2239898; fax 2239927; e-mail ambatana@dts.mg; Ambassador: STANISLAS LEFEBVRE DE LABOULAYE.

Germany: 101 rue du Pasteur Rabeony Hans, BP 516, Ambodirotra, 101 Antananarivo; tel. (20) 2223802; fax (20) 2226627; Ambassador: KLAUS D. SOMMER.

Holy See: Amboniloha Ivandry, BP 650, 101 Antananarivo; tel. (20) 2242376; fax (20) 2242384; e-mail noncapmg@dts.mg; Apostolic Nuncio: Most Rev. BRUNO MUSARO, Titular Archbishop of Abari.

India: 4 làlana Emile Rajaonson, Tsaralalana, BP 1787, 101 Antananarivo; tel. (20) 2223334; fax (20) 2233790; Ambassador: Dr PRABHAKAR JHA.

Indonesia: 26–28 rue Patrice Lumumba, BP 3969, 101 Antananarivo; tel. (20) 2224915; fax (20) 2232857; Chargé d'affaires a.i.: SLAMET SUYATA SASTRAMIHARDZA.

Iran: route Circulaire, Lot II L43 ter, 101 Antananarivo; tel. (20) 2228639; fax (20) 2222298; Ambassador: ALI AMOUI.

Italy: 22 rue Pasteur Rabary, BP 16, Ankadivato, 101 Antananarivo; tel. (20) 2221217; fax (20) 2223814; e-mail ambanta@simicro.mg; Ambassador: ROSARIO GUIDO NICOSIA.

Japan: 8 rue du Dr Villette, BP 3863, Isoraka, 101 Antananarivo; tel. (20) 2226102; fax (20) 2221769; Ambassador: TOSHIO WATANABE.

Korea, Democratic People's Republic: Ambohibao, 101 Antananarivo; tel. (20) 2244442; Ambassador: RI HYONG YON.

Libya: Lot IIB, 37A route Circulaire Ampandrana-Ouest, 101 Antananarivo; tel. (20) 2221892; Chargé d'affaires: MANSUR MILAD AL-KADUSHI.

Mauritius: Anjaharay, route Circulaire, BP 6040, Ambanidia 101, Antananarivo; tel. (20) 2221864; fax (20) 2221939; Ambassador: GHISLAINE HENRY.

Russia: BP 4006, Ivandry-Ambohijatovo, 101 Antananarivo; tel. (20) 2242827; fax (20) 2242642; Ambassador: YOURI N. MERZLIAKOV.

Switzerland: BP 118, 101 Antananarivo; tel. (20) 2262997; fax (20) 2228940; Chargé d'affaires: ROSMARIE SCHELLING.

United Kingdom: Lot II I164 ter, Alarobia, Amboniloha, BP 167, 101 Antananarivo; tel. (20) 2249378; fax (20) 2249381; e-mail ukembant@simicro.mg; Ambassador: CHARLES F. MOCHAN.

USA: 14–16 rue Rainitovo, Antsahavola, BP 620, 101 Antananarivo; tel. (20) 2221257; fax (20) 2234539; Ambassador: SHIRLEY ELIZABETH BARNES (designate).

Judicial System

CONSTITUTIONAL HIGH COURT

Haute Cour Constitutionnelle: 101 Antananarivo; interprets the Constitution and rules on constitutional issues; nine mems; Pres. VICTOR BOTO.

HIGH COURT OF JUSTICE

Haute Cour de Justice: 101 Antananarivo; nine mems.

SUPREME COURT

Cour Suprême: Palais de Justice, Anosy, 101 Antananarivo; Pres. ALICE RAJAONAH (acting); Attorney-General COLOMBE RAMANANTSOA (acting); Chamber Pres. YOLANDE RAMANGASOAVINA, FRANÇOIS RAMANANDRAIBE.

COURT OF APPEAL

Cour d'Appel: Palais de Justice, Anosy, 101 Antananarivo; Pres. AIMÉE RAKOTONIRINA; Pres of Chamber CHARLES RABETOKOTANY, PÉTRONILLE ANDRIAMIHAJA, BAKOLALAO RANAIVOHARIVONY, BERTHOLIER RAVELONTSALAMA, LUCIEN RABARIJHON, NELLY RAKOTOBE, ARLETTE RAMAROSON, CLÉMENTINE RAVANDISON, GISÈLE RABOTOVAO, JEAN-JACQUES RAJAONA.

OTHER COURTS

Tribunaux de Première Instance: at Antananarivo, Toamasina, Antsiranana, Mahajanga, Fianarantsoa, Toliary, Antsirabé, Ambatondrazaka, Antalaha, Farafangana, Maintirano; for civil, commercial and social matters, and for registration.

Cours Criminelles Ordinaires: tries crimes of common law; attached to the Cour d'Appel in Antananarivo but may sit in any other large town. There are also 31 Cours Criminelles Spéciales dealing with cases concerning cattle.

Tribunaux Spéciaux Economiques: at Antananarivo, Toamasina, Mahajanga, Fianarantsoa, Antsiranana and Toliary; tries crimes specifically relating to economic matters.

Tribunaux Criminels Spéciaux: judges cases of banditry and looting; 31 courts.

Religion

It is estimated that more than 50% of the population follow traditional animist beliefs, some 43% are Christians (about one-half of whom are Roman Catholics) and the remainder are Muslims.

CHRISTIANITY

Fiombonan'ny Fiangonana Kristiana eto Madagasikara (FFKM)/Conseil Chrétien des Eglises de Madagascar/Christian Council of Churches in Madagascar: Vohipiraisama, Ambohijatovo-Atsimo, BP 798, 101 Antananarivo; tel. (20) 2229052; f. 1980; four mems and one assoc. mem.; Pres. Pastor EDMOND RAZAFIMAHALEO; Gen. Sec. Rev. LALA ANDRIAMIHARISOA.

Fiombonan'ny Fiangonana Protestanta eto Madagasikara (FFPM)/Fédération des Eglises Protestantes à Madagascar/Federation of the Protestant Churches in Madagascar: VK 3 Vohipiraisana, Ambohijatovo-Atsimo, BP 4226, 101 Antananarivo; tel. (20) 2220144; f. 1958; two mem churches; Pres. Pastor EDMOND RAZAFIMAHEFA; Gen. Sec. Rev. Dr ROGER ANDRIATSIRATAHINA.

The Anglican Communion

Anglicans are adherents of the Church of the Province of the Indian Ocean, comprising six dioceses (four in Madagascar, one in Mauritius and one in Seychelles). The Archbishop of the Province is the Bishop of Antananarivo. The Church has about 160,000 adherents in Madagascar, including the membership of the Eklesia Episkopaly Malagasy (Malagasy Episcopal Church), founded in 1874.

Bishop of Antananarivo (also Archbishop of the Province of the Indian Ocean): Most Rev. RÉMI JOSEPH RABENIRINA, Evêché Anglican, Lot VK57, Ambohimanoro, 101 Antananarivo; tel. (20) 2220827; fax (20) 2261331; e-mail eemdants@dts.mg.

Bishop of Antsiranana: Rt Rev. KEITH BENZIES, Evêché Anglican, BP 278, 201 Antsiranana; tel. (20) 8222650; e-mail eemdants@dts.mg.

Bishop of Mahajanga: Rt Rev. JEAN-CLAUDE ANDRIANJAFIMANANA, BP 169, 401 Mahajanga; e-mail eemdmaha@dts.mg.

Bishop of Toamasina: Rt Rev. DONALD WESTWOOD SMITH, Evêché Anglican, rue de la Fraternité, BP 531, 501 Toamasina; tel. (20) 5332163.

The Roman Catholic Church

Madagascar comprises three archdioceses and 15 dioceses. At 31 December 1998 the number of adherents in the country represented about 23.6% of the total population.

Bishops' Conference: Conférence Episcopale de Madagascar, 102 bis ave Maréchal Joffre, Antanimena, BP 667, 101 Antananarivo; tel. (20) 2220478; fax (20) 2224854; f. 1969; Pres. Cardinal ARMAND RAZAFINDRATANDRA, Archbishop of Antananarivo.

Archbishop of Antananarivo: Cardinal ARMAND RAZAFINDRATANDRA, Archevêché, Andohalo, BP 5159, 101 Antananarivo; tel. (20) 2220726, fax (20) 2224854.

Archbishop of Antsiranana: Most Rev. MICHEL MALO, Archevêché, BP 415, 201 Antsiranana; tel. (20) 8221605.

Archbishop of Fianarantsoa: Most Rev. PHILIBERT RANDRIAMBOLOLONA, Archevêché, place Mgr Givelet, BP 1440, Ambozontany, 301 Fianarantsoa; tel. (20) 7550672; fax (20) 7524854.

Other Christian Churches

Fiangonan' i Jesoa Kristy eto Madagasikara/Eglise de Jésus-Christ à Madagascar: Lot 11 B18, Tohatohabato Ranavalona 1, Trano 'Ifanomezantsoa', BP 623, 101 Antananarivo; tel. (20) 2226845; fax (20) 2226372; e-mail fjkm@dts.mg; f. 1968; Pres. Rev. EDMOND RAZAFIMAHEFA; Gen. Sec. Rev. LALA RASENDRAHASINA; 2m. mems.

Fiangonana Loterana Malagasy (Malagasy Lutheran Church): BP 1741, 101 Antananarivo; tel. (20) 2222347; Pres. Rev. RABENOROLAHY; 600,000 mems.

The Press

In December 1990 the National People's Assembly adopted legislation guaranteeing the freedom of the press and the right of newspapers to be established without prior authorization.

PRINCIPAL DAILIES

Bulletin de l'Agence Nationale d'Information 'Taratra' (ANTA): 3 rue du R. P. Callet, Behoririka, BP 386, 101 Antananarivo; tel. (20) 2221171; f. 1977; French; Man. Dir JEANNOT FENO.

L'Express de Madagascar: BP 3893, 101 Antananarivo; tel. (20) 2221934; fax (20) 2262894; f. 1995; French and Malagasy; Editor SYLVAIN RANDRIANAHINORO; circ. 10,000.

Imongo Vaovao: 11K 4 bis Andravoahangy, BP 7014, 101 Antananarivo; tel. (20) 2221053; f. 1955; Malagasy; Dir CLÉMENT RAMAMONJISOA; circ. 10,000.

Madagascar Tribune: Immeuble SME, rue Ravoninahitriniarivo, BP 659, Ankorondrano, 101 Antananarivo; tel. (20) 2222635; fax (20) 2234753; f. 1988; independent; French and Malagasy; Editor RAHAGA RAMAHOLIMIHASO; circ. 12,000.

Maresaka: 12 làlana Ratsimba John, Isotry, 101 Antananarivo; tel. (20) 2223568; f. 1953; independent; Malagasy; Editor M. RALAIARIJAONA; circ. 5,000.

Midi Madagasikara: làlana Ravoninahitriniarivo, BP 1414, Ankorondrano, 101 Antananarivo; tel. (20) 2269779; fax (20) 2227351; e-mail midi@dts.mg; internet www.dts.mg/midi/; f. 1983; French and Malagasy; Dir MAMY RAKOTOARIVELO; circ. 25,500.

PRINCIPAL PERIODICALS

Afaka: 101 Antananarivo; Malagasy and French; Dir MAX RATSIMANDISA; circ. 5,000.

Basy Vava: Lot III E 96, Mahamasina Atsimo, 101 Antananarivo; tel. (20) 2220448; f. 1959; Malagasy; Dir GABRIEL RAMANANJATO; circ. 3,000.

Bulletin de la Société du Corps Médical Malgache: Imprimerie Volamahitsy, 101 Antananarivo; Malagasy; monthly; Dir Dr RAKOTOMALALA.

Dans les Media, Demain: Immeuble Jeune Afrique, 58 rue Tsiombikibo, BP 1734, Ambatovinaky, 101 Antananarivo; tel. (20)

2227788; fax (20) 2230629; f. 1986; independent; weekly; Dir HONORÉ RAZAFINTSALAMA; circ. 2,500.

Feon'ny Mpiasa: Lot M8, Isotry, 101 Antananarivo; trade union affairs; Malagasy; monthly; Dir M. RAZAKANAIVO; circ. 2,000.

Fiaraha-Miasa: BP 1216, 101 Antananarivo; Malagasy; weekly; Dir SOLO NORBERT ANDRIAMORASATA; circ. 5,000.

Gazetinao: Lot IPA 37, BP 1758, Anosimasina, 101 Antananarivo; tel. (20) 2261979; French and Malagasy; monthly; Dir ETIENNE M. RAKOTOMAHANINA; circ. 3,000.

La Gazette d'Antsirabé: 110 Antsirabé; f. 1989; Dir VOLOLOHARIMANANA RAZAFIMANDIMBY; circ. 7,000.

Gazety Medikaly: 101 Antananarivo; tel. (20) 2227898; f. 1965; medical; monthly; Dir PAUL RATSIMISETA; circ. 2,000.

Isika Mianakavy: Ambatomena, 301 Fianarantsoa; f. 1958; Roman Catholic; Malagasy; monthly; Dir J. RANAIVOMANANA; circ. 21,000.

Journal Officiel de la République de Madagascar: BP 248, 101 Antananarivo; tel. (20) 2265010; fax 2225319; f. 1883; official announcements; Malagasy and French; weekly; Dir HONORÉE ELIANNE RALALAHARISON.

Journal Scientifique de Madagascar: BP 3855, Antananarivo; f. 1985; Dir Prof. MANAMBELONA; circ. 3,000.

Jureco: Immeuble SOMAGI, 120 rue Rainandriamampandry, 101 Antananarivo; tel. (20) 2220237; fax (20) 2234238; e-mail somagi@bow.dts.mg; internet www.dts.mg/jureco; law and economics; monthly; Dir MBOARA ANDRIANARIMANANA.

Lakroan'i Madagasikara: Maison Jean XXIII, Mahamasina Sud, 101 Antananarivo; tel. (20) 2221158; f. 1927; Roman Catholic; French and Malagasy; weekly; Dir LOUIS RASOLO; circ. 25,000.

Mada—Économie: 15 rue Ratsimilaho, BP 3464, 101 Antananarivo; tel. (20) 2225634; f. 1977; reports events in south-east Africa; monthly; Editor RICHARD-CLAUDE RATOVONARIVO; circ. 5,000.

Mpanolotsaina: BP 623, 101 Antananarivo; tel. (20) 2226845; fax (20) 2226372; e-mail fjkm@dts.mg; religious, educational; Malagasy; quarterly; Dir RAYMOND RAJOELISOL.

Ny Mpamangy-FLM: 9 rue Grandidier Isoraka, BP 538, Antsahamanitra, 101 Antananarivo; tel. (20) 2232446; f. 1882; monthly; Dir Pastor JEAN RABENANDRASANA; circ. 3,000.

Ny Sakaizan'ny Tanora: BP 538, Antsahaminitra, 101 Antananarivo; tel. (20) 2232446; f. 1878; monthly; Editor-in-Chief DANIEL PROSPER ANDRIAMANJAKA; circ. 5,000.

PME Madagascar: rue Hugues Rabesahala, BP 953, Antsakaviro, 101 Antananarivo; tel. (20) 2222536; fax (20) 2234534; f. 1989; French; monthly; economic review; Dir ROMAIN ANDRIANARISOA; circ. 3,500.

Recherche et Culture: BP 907, 101 Antananarivo; tel. (20) 2226600; f. 1985; publ. by French dept of the University of Antananarivo; 2 a year; Dir GINETTE RAMAROSON; circ. 1,000.

Revue Ita: BP 681, 101 Antananarivo; tel. (20) 2230507; f. 1985; controlled by the Ministry of Population; monthly; Dir FILS RAMALANJAONA; circ. 1,000.

Revue de l'Océan Indien: Communication et Médias Océan Indien, rue H. Rabesahala, BP 46, Antsakaviro, 101 Antananarivo; tel. (20) 2222536; fax (20) 2234534; f. 1980; quarterly; Man. Dir GEORGES RANAIVOSOA; Sec.-Gen. HERY M. A. RANAIVOSOA; circ. 5,000.

Sahy: Lot VD 42, Ambanidia, 101 Antananarivo; tel. (20) 2222715; f. 1957; political; Malagasy; weekly; Editor ALINE RAKOTO; circ. 9,000.

Sosialisma Mpiasa: BP 1128, 101 Antananarivo; tel. (20) 2221989; f. 1979; trade union affairs; Malagasy; monthly; Dir PAUL RABEMANANJARA; circ. 5,000.

Valeurs—L'Hebdomadaire de Madagascar: Antananarivo; f. 1995; weekly; Dir RIJA RASENDRATSIROFO.

Vaovao: BP 271, 101 Antananarivo; tel. (20) 2221193; f. 1985; French and Malagasy; weekly; Dir MARC RAKOTONOELY; circ. 5,000.

NEWS AGENCIES

Agence Nationale d'Information 'TARATRA' (ANTA): 7 rue Jean Ralaimongo, Ambohiday, BP 386, 101 Antananarivo; tel. and fax (20) 2236047; e-mail anta@blanbir.mg; f. 1977; Man. Dir JOÉ ANACLET RAKOTOARISON.

Foreign Bureaux

Associated Press (AP) (USA): BP 73, 101 Antananarivo; tel. (20) 2380971; e-mail madapp@bow.dts.mg; Correspondent CHRISTIAN CHADEFAUX.

Korean Central News Agency (KCNA) (Democratic People's Republic of Korea): BP 4276, 101 Antananarivo; tel. (20) 2244795; Dir KIM YEUNG KYEUN.

Xinhua (New China) News Agency (People's Republic of China): BP 1656, 101 Antananarivo; tel. (20) 2229927; Chief of Bureau WU HAIYUN.

Reuters (UK) is also represented in Madagascar.

Publishers

Edisiona Salohy: BP 4226, 101 Antananarivo; Dir MIRANA VOLO-LOARISOA RANDRIANARISON.

Editions Ambozontany: BP 40, 301 Fianarantsoa; tel. (20) 7550603; f. 1962; religious and school textbooks; Dir R. F. GIAMBRONE.

Foibe Filankevitry Ny Mpampianatra (FOFIPA): BP 202, 101 Antananarivo; tel. (20) 2227500; f. 1971; textbooks; Dir Frère RAZAF-INDRAKOTO.

Madagascar Print and Press Co (MADPRINT): rue Rabesahala, Antsakaviro, BP 953, 101 Antananarivo; tel. (20) 2222536; fax (20) 2234534; f. 1969; literary, technical and historical; Dir GEORGES RANAIVOSOA.

Maison d'Edition Protestante Antso: 19 rue Venance Manifatra, Imarivolanitra, 101 Antananarivo; tel. (20) 2220886; f. 1962; religious, school, social, political and general; Dir HANS ANDRIAMAMPI-ANINA.

Imprimerie Nouvelle: PK 2, Andranomahery, route de Majunga, BP 4330, 101 Antananarivo; tel. (20) 2223330; fax (20) 2269225; Dir EUGÈNE RAHARIFIDY.

Nouvelle Société de Presse et d'Edition (NSPE): Immeuble Jeune Afrique, 58 rue Tsiombikibo, BP 1734, Ambatorinaky, 101 Antananarivo; tel. (20) 2227788; fax (20) 2230629.

Office du Livre Malgache: Lot 111 H29, Andrefan' Ambohijana-hary, BP 617, 101 Antananarivo; tel. (20) 2224449; f. 1970; children's and general; Sec.-Gen. JULIETTE RATSIMANDRAVA.

Société de Presse et d'Edition de Madagascar: Antananarivo; non-fiction, reference, science, university textbooks; Man. Dir RAJAO-FERA ANDRIAMBELO.

Société Malgache d'Edition (SME): BP 659, Ankorondrano, 101 Antananarivo; tel. (20) 2222635; fax (20) 2222254; f. 1943; general fiction, university and secondary textbooks; Man. Dir RAHAGA RAMAH-OLIMIHASO.

Société Nouvelle de l'Imprimerie Centrale (SNIC): làlana Ravoninahitriniarivo, BP 1414, 101 Antananarivo; tel. (20) 2221118; f. 1959; science, school textbooks; Man. Dir MARTHE ANDRIAMBELO.

Imprimerie Takariva: 4 rue Radley, BP 1029, Antanimena, 101 Antananarivo; tel. (20) 2222128; f. 1933; fiction, languages, school textbooks; Man. Dir PAUL RAPATSALAHY.

Trano Printy Fiangonana Loterana Malagasy (TPFLM): BP 538, 9 ave Général Gabriel Ramanantsoa, 101 Antananarivo; tel. (20) 2223340; fax (20) 2262643; e-mail impluth@dts.mg; f. 1877; religious, educational and fiction; Man. RAYMOND RANDRIANATOANDRO.

Government Publishing House

Imprimerie Nationale: BP 38, 101 Antananarivo; tel. (20) 2223675; all official publs; Dir JEAN DENIS RANDRIANIRINA.

Broadcasting and Communications

TELECOMMUNICATIONS

Mobile cellular telephone networks are operated by Antaris, Sacel and Télécel.

Office Malgasy d'Etudes et de Régulation des Télécommunications (OMERT): f. 1997; Gen. Man. GILBERT ANDRIANIRINA RAJOANASY.

Société Anonyme Télécom Malgasy (TELMA): BP 763, Antananarivo 101; tel. (20) 2242705; fax (20) 2242654; 66% state-owned, 34% owned by France Cable et Radio; Chair. MAMIHARILALA RASOLO-JAONA; Dir-Gen. BRUNO ANTRIATAVISON.

BROADCASTING

Radio

Radio Nationale Malagasy: BP 442, 101 Antananarivo; tel. (20) 2232715; fax (20) 2232715; e-mail radmad@dts.mg; state-controlled; broadcasts in French, Malagasy and English; Dir FÉLIX MALAZARIVO.

Le Messager Radio Evangélique: BP 1374, 101 Antananarivo; tel. (20) 2234495; broadcasts in French, English and Malagasy; Dir JOCELYN RANJARISON.

Radio Antsiva: Lot VA, 21 Ambohitantely, 101 Antananarivo; tel. (20) 2234330; broadcasts in French, English and Malagasy; Dir JEAN VICTOR RALIARISON.

Radio Feon'ny Vahoaka (RFV): 103 Immeuble Ramaroson, 8e étage, 101 Antananarivo; tel. (20) 2233820; broadcasts in French and Malagasy; Dir ALAIN RAMAROSON.

Radio Korail: BP 6325, 101 Antananarivo; tel. and fax (20) 2224494; f. 1993; broadcasts in French and Malagasy; Dir ALAIN RAJAONA.

Radio Lazan'iarivo (RLI): Lot V A49, Andafiavaratra, 101 Antananarivo; tel. (20) 2229016; broadcasts in French, English and Malagasy; Dir IRÈNE RAVALISON.

Radio Tsioka Vao (RTV): BP 315, Tana; tel. (20) 2221749; f. 1992; broadcasts in French, English and Malagasy; Dir DETKOU DEDONNAIS.

Television

Télévision Nasionaly Malagasy: BP 1202, 101 Antananarivo; tel. (20) 2222381; state-controlled; broadcasts in French and Malagasy; Dir-Gen. RAZAFIMAHEFA HERINIRINA LALA.

Finance

(cap. = capital; res = reserves; dep. = deposits; m. = million; brs = branches; amounts in Malagasy francs)

BANKING

Central Bank

Banque Centrale de Madagascar: ave de la Révolution Socialiste Malgache, BP 550, 101 Antananarivo; tel. (20) 2221751; fax (20) 2227596; f. 1973; bank of issue; cap. and res 8,574.2m., dep. 2,123,021.7m. (Dec. 1998); Gov. GASTON RAVELOJAONA; Dir-Gen. FERDINAND VELOMITA.

Other Banks

Banky Fampandrosoana ny Varotra (BFV): 14 làlana Jeneraly Rabehevitra, BP 196, 101 Antananarivo; tel. (20) 2220691; fax (20) 2234554; f. 1977 by merger; 70% owned by Société Générale (France), 30% state-owned; cap. and res 15,681.1m., dep. 569,046.3m. (1995); Chair. HENRI GUDIN DU PAVILLON; 28 brs.

Banque Malgache de l'Océan Indien (BMOI) (Indian Ocean Malagasy Bank): place Philibert Tsiranana, BP 25 Bis, Antaninar-enina, Antananarivo 101; tel. (20) 2234609; fax (20) 2234610; e-mail bmoi.st@simicro.mg; inernet www.bmoi.mg; f. 1990; 37.5% owned by Banque Nationale de Paris; cap. and res 118,800m., total assets 916,504m. (Dec. 1998); Pres. GASTON RAMENASON; Dir-Gen. ROBERT DURBEC; 8 brs.

Banque de Solidarité Malgache (BSM): Antananarivo; f. 2000; cap 24,000m.

BFV—Société Générale: BP 440, Antananarivo 101; tel. (20) 2220043; fax (20) 2234535; f. 1999; 70% owned by Société Générale (France) and 30% state-owned; Pres. HENRI GUDIN DU PAVILLON.

BNI—Crédit Lyonnais Madagascar: 74 rue du 26 Juin 1960, BP 174, 101 Antananarivo; tel. (20) 2223951; fax (20) 2233749; e-mail info@bni.mg; 33% state-owned; f. 1976; cap. and res 165,800m., total assets 1,310,000m. (Dec. 1998); Dir-Gen. DANIEL BOURGERY; 22 brs.

BTM—BOA: 2 place de l'Indépendance, BP 183, 101 Antananarivo; tel. (20) 2239100; fax (20) 2221398; e-mail btmdi@dts.mg; internet www.takelaka.dts.mg/btmdi; f. 1976 as Bankin'ny Tantsaha Mpa-mokatra (BTM), name changed as above 1999; 60% owned by Bank of Africa, 15% state-owned; specializes in rural development; cap. and res –185,783m., total assets 676,642m. (Dec. 1998); Pres. PAUL DERREUMAUX; Dir-Gen. BERNARD HAIZET; 60 brs.

Union Commercial Bank (UCB): 77 rue Solombavambahoaka Frantsay, Antsahavola, BP 197, 101 Antananarivo; tel. (20) 2227262; fax (20) 2228740; e-mail ucb.int@dts.mg; f. 1992; 70% owned by Mauritius Commercial Bank Ltd; cap. and res 10,997m., dep. 92,631m. (Dec. 1996); Pres. RAYMOND HEIN; Gen. Man. PAUL GIBLIN; 2 brs.

INSURANCE

ARO (Assurances Réassurances Omnibranches): Antsahavola, BP 42, 101 Antananarivo; tel. (20) 2220154; fax (20) 2234464; Pres. DÉSIRÉ RAJOBSON; Dir-Gen. HENRI RAJERISON.

Assurance France-Madagascar: 7 rue Rainitovo, BP 710, 101 Antananarivo; tel. (20) 2223024; fax (20) 2223024; f. 1951; Dir SAMUELSON RAOILY.

Compagnie Malgache d'Assurances et de Réassurances: Immeuble 'Ny Havana', Zone des 67 Ha, BP 3881, 101 Antananarivo; tel. (20) 2226760; fax (20) 2224303; f. 1968; cap. 16,050m. (1996); Dir-Gen. ROLAND RASAMOELY.

Mutuelle d'Assurances Malgasy (MAMA): Lot 1F, 12 bis, rue Rainibetsimisaraka, Ambalavao-Isotry, BP 185, 101 Antananarivo; tel. (20) 2222508; Pres. FRÉDÉRIC RABARISON.

Ny Havana: BP 3881, Antananarivo 101; tel. (20) 2226760; fax (20) 2224303; Dir-Gen. ROLAND RASAMOELY.

Société Malgache d'Assurances, Faugère, Jutheau et Cie: 13 rue Patrice Lumumba, BP 673, 101 Antananarivo; f. 1952; tel. (20) 2223162; Dir ANDRIANJAKA RAVELONAHIANA.

Trade and Industry

DEVELOPMENT ORGANIZATIONS

Office des mines nationales et des industries stratégiques (OMNIS): 21 làlana Razanakombana, BP 1 bis, 101 Antananarivo; tel. (20) 2224439; fax (20) 2222985; e-mail omnis@online.mg; f. 1976; promotes the exploration and exploitation of mining resources, in particular oil resources; Dir-Gen. ACKRAM MOHAJY ANDRIAMANDAMINY.

Société d'Etude et de Réalisation pour le Développement Industriel (SERDI): 78 bis, ave Lénine Ankaditapaka, BP 3180, 101 Antananarivo; tel. (20) 2221335; fax (20) 2229669; f. 1966; 85% state-owned; to be privatized in 1998; Dir-Gen. RAOILISON RAJAONARY.

CHAMBER OF COMMERCE

Fédération des Chambres de Commerce, d'Industrie et d'Agriculture de Madagascar: 20 rue Paul Dussac, BP 166, 101 Antananarivo; tel. (20) 2221567; 12 mem. chambers; Pres. JEAN RAMAROMISA; Chair. HENRI RAZANATSEHENO; Sec.-Gen. HUBERT RATSIANDAVANA.

TRADE ASSOCIATION

Société d'Intérêt National des Produits Agricoles (SINPA): BP 754, rue Fernand-Kasanga, Tsimbazaza, Antananarivo; tel. (20) 2220558; fax (20) 2220665; f. 1973; monopoly purchaser and distributor of agricultural produce; Chair. GUALBERT RAZANAJATOVO; Gen. Man. JEAN CLOVIS RALIJESY.

EMPLOYERS' ORGANIZATIONS

Groupement des Entreprises de Madagascar (GEM): Kianja MDRM sy Tia Tanindrazana, BP 1338, 101 Antananarivo; f. 1973; eight nat. syndicates and four regional syndicates comprising 444 cos and 44 directly affiliated cos; Pres. GASTON RAMENASON: Sec.-Gen. ZINAH RASAMUEL RAVALOSON.

Syndicat des Importateurs et Exportateurs de Madagascar: 2 rue Georges Mandel, BP 188, 101 Antananarivo; Pres. M. FONTANA.

Syndicat Indépendant des Exportateurs de Vanille de Madagascar: Antalaha; 18 mems; Pres. MICHEL GERMAIN MING.

Syndicat des Industries de Madagascar: Immeuble Kobana Soanierana; BP 1695, 101 Antananarivo; tel. (20) 2223608; fax (20) 2233043; f. 1958; Chair. PATRICK RAJAONARY.

Syndicat des Planteurs de Café: 37 làlana Razafimahandry, BP 173, 101 Antananarivo.

Syndicat Professionnel des Agents Généraux d'Assurances: Antananarivo; f. 1949; Pres. SOLO RATSIMBAZAFY; Sec. IHANTA RANDRIAMANDRANTO.

UTILITIES

Electricity and Water

Jiro sy Rano Malagasy (JIRAMA): BP 200, 149 rue Rainandriamampandry, Faravohitra, Antananarivo; tel. (20) 2220031; fax (20) 2233806; f. 1975; state-owned; scheduled for transfer to private sector in 2001; controls production and distribution of electricity and water; Chair. GÉRARD ANDRIAMILEROVASON; Dir RATSIMISETA ANDRIANTSIFERANA.

MAJOR COMPANIES

The following are some of the largest in terms either of capital investment or employment.

Brasseries STAR Madagascar: BP 3806, Antananarivo; tel. (20) 2227711; fax (20) 2234682; f. 1953; cap. 10,090.9m. FMG; mfrs of beer and carbonated drinks. Pres. H. FRAISE; Gen. Man. YVAN COUDERC.

Compagnie des Ciments Malgaches: BP 302, Mahajanga; cap. 625m. FMG; cement works; Pres. JULES PLAQUET; Dir J. SCHNEEBERGER.

Compagnie Salinière de Madagascar: rue Béniowsky, BP 29, 201 Antsiranana; tel. (20) 8221373; fax (20) 8229394; e-mail csm@simicro.mg; f. 1895; cap. 1,312m. FMG; exploitation of salt marshes; Pres. GÉRARD MUTRICY; Dir-Gen. JEAN-YVES MORVAN; 200 employees (1999).

Coralma: Immeuble ARO Antsahavola, BP 1083, 101 Antananarivo; tel. (20) 2225189; fax (20) 2228037; e-mail coralmad@dts.mg; f. 1989; production and distribution of tobacco; Administrator ERIC DAHLSTRÖM.

La Cotonnière d'Antsirabé (COTONA): route d'Ambositra, BP 45, Antsirabé; tel. (20) 4449422; fax (20) 4449222; e-mail saga@cotona.com; f. 1952; 39.3% state-owned; cap. 46,528m. FMG; spinning, weaving, printing and dyeing of textiles; Dirs-Gen. SALIM ISMAIL, AZIZ HASSAM ISMAIL; 2,372 employees (1995).

Ets Gallois: BP 159, Antananarivo; cap. 220m. FMG; production of graphite and sisal; Pres. and Dir-Gen. HENRY GALLOIS.

Kraomita Malagasy (KRAOMA): BP 936, Ampefihola, Antananarivo; tel. (20) 2224304; fax (20) 2224654; e-mail kraoma@dts.mg; internet tabelaka.dts.mg\kraoma; f. 1966 as Cie Minière d'Andriamena (COMINA); cap. 1,540m. FMG; 100% state-owned; chrome mining and concentration; Dir-Gen. CHRISTIAN RANAIVO; 450 employees (2000).

Laboratoires Pharmaceutiques Malgaches (FARMAD): BP 828, Antananarivo 101; tel. (20) 2246622; fax (20) 2244775; pharmaceutical mfrs.

Nouveaux Ateliers de Construction Métallique: 352 route Circulaire, BP 1073, Antananarivo 101; tel. (20) 2223136; fax (20) 2233744; e-mail alubat@simicro.mg; internet www.lk-oi.com/alubat; mfrs of cutlery, tools, implements and metal parts; Dir-Gen. JACQUES KWAN HUA; 55 employees (1999).

Omnium Industriel de Madagascar: BP 207, Antananarivo; tel. (20) 2222373; fax (20) 2228064; f. 1929; cap. 1,300m. FMG; mfrs of shoes and luggage; operates a tannery; Pres. and Dir-Gen. H. J. BARDAY; 1,000 employees (1999).

Papeteries de Madagascar (PAPMAD): BP 1756, Ambohimanambola, 101 Antananarivo; tel. (20) 2220635; fax (20) 2224394; f. 1963; cap. 1,308m. FMG; paper-making; Pres. and Dir-Gen. P. RAJAONARY; 800 employees (1999).

Société Agricole du Domaine de Pechpeyrou: BP 71, Tolagnaro; f. 1947; cap. 192m. FMG; sisal growing.

Société Américaine, Grecque et Malgache 'Industrie de la Viande': Antananarivo; cap. 300m. FMG; abattoir, meat-canning, mfrs of meat products; Pres. and Dir-Gen. G. S. REPAS; Dir T. C. BACOPOLOUS.

Société Commerciale Laitière (SOCOLAIT): BP 4126; Antananarivo; tel. (20) 2222282; fax (20) 2222279; cap. 2,800m. FMG; dairy products; Pres. SOCOTALY KARMALY.

Société des Cigarettes Melia de Madagascar: route d'Ambositra 110, BP 128, Antsirabé; tel. (20) 2248241; f. 1956; cap. 881m. FMG; mfrs of cigarettes; Pres. and Dir-Gen. PHILIPPE DE VESINNE LARUE; Dir GUY RAVELOMANANTSOA.

Société d'Etudes de Constructions et Réparations Navales (SECREN): rue Lavigerie, BP 135, 201 Antsiranana; tel. (20) 8229321; fax (20) 8229326; e-mail secren@dts.mg; 37.5% state-owned; f. 1975; transfer to the private sector pending; cap. 2,600m. FMG; ship-building and repairs; Dir-Gen. JEAN ROBERT GARA; Gen. Man. CHRISTOPHE J. NOSY HARINONY; 1,150 employees (1999).

Société de Fabrication de l'Océan Indien: Tanjombato, BP 132, Antananarivo 101; tel. (20) 2246776; plastics.

Société de Filature et de Tissage de Madagascar (FITIM): BP 127, Mahajanga; tel. (20) 6222127; fax (20) 6229345; f. 1930; cap. 1,444m. FMG; spinning and weaving of jute; Pres. C. A. WILLIAM RAVONINJATOVO; Dir-Gen. HATIM HASSANALY; 240 employees.

Société Malgache de Collecte et de Distribution: BP 188, 101 Antananarivo; tel. (20) 2224871; fax (20) 2225024; f. 1972; Chair. HENRI RASAMOELINA; Gen. Man. NORBERT RAZANAKOTO.

Société Malgache de Cosmetiques et de Parfumerie: Tanjombato, BP 852, Antananarivo 101; tel. (20) 2246408; fax (20) 2247079; e-mail somalco@simicro.mg; perfumery, cosmetics and toothpaste; Pres. GOULSENBANOU BARDAY; Dir-Gen. NIGAR BARDAY; 56 employees (1999).

Société Malgache d'Exploitations Minières (SOMEM): BP 266, Antananarivo; f. 1926; cap. 130m. FMG; mining of graphite and mica; Pres. JEAN SCHNEIDER; Dir-Gen. LUCIEN DUMAS.

Société Malgache de Pêcherie (SOMAPECHE): BP 324, Mahanga; 33% state-owned; cap. 200m. FMG; sea fishing; Pres. J. RABEMANANJARA; Dir-Gen. J. BRUNOT; 1,200 employees (1996).

Société Malgache de Raffinage: BP 433, Toamasina; tel. (20) 5332773; fax (20) 5333705; f. 1964; cap. 2.5m. FMG; state-owned; refinery for petroleum imported from the Middle East, principally Iran; Dir-Gen. JACQUES GLANTENET.

Société Siramamy Malagasy (SIRAMA): BP 1633, Antananarivo; tel. (20) 2225235; fax (20) 2227231; e-mail sirama@dts.mg; f. 1949; state-owned; transfer to the private sector announced in 1997; cap. 2,500m. FMG; sugar refinery at St Louis; Chair. GEORGES SOLOFOSON; Pres. GABRIEL DAHER; Dir-Gen. MOHAMED RACHIDY; 14,359 employees (1999).

Société Textile de Majunga (SOTEMA): BP 375, Mahajanga; tel. (20) 6227568; fax (20) 6234533; f. 1967; cap. 3,510m. FMG; spinning, weaving, printing and finishing textiles, finished garments; Pres. LÉON RAJAOBELINA; 2,800 employees.

Société Verrerie Malagasy (SOVEMA): BP 84, Toamasina; f. 1970; 31.2% state-owned; cap. 235.6m. FMG; bottles and glass articles; Pres. and Dir-Gen. A. SIBILLE.

Solitany Malagasy (SOLIMA): 2 ave Grandidier, BP 140, Antananarivo; tel. (20) 2220633; fax (20) 2235328; e-mail solimacm@dts.mg; f. 1976; transfer to the private sector pending; cap. 2,505m. FMG; imports, transports and refines crude petroleum; produces and exports petroleum products; Chair. ALBERT ANDRIANTSOA RASOMANAMA; Man. Dir LOUIS CHRISTIAN NTSAY; 1,646 employees (1995).

TRADE UNIONS

Cartel National des Organisations Syndicales de Madagascar (CARNOSYAMA): BP 1035, 101 Antananarivo.

Confédération des Travailleurs Malgaches (Fivomdronamben'ny Mpiasa Malagasy—FMM): Lot IVM 133 A Antetezanafovoany I, BP 846, 101 Antananarivo; tel. (20) 2224565; f. 1957; Sec.-Gen. JEANNOT RAMANARIVO; 30,000 mems.

Fédération des Syndicats des Travailleurs de Madagascar (Firaisan'ny Sendika eran'i Madagaskara—FISEMA): Lot III, rue Pasteur Isotry, 101 Antananarivo; f. 1956; Pres. DESIRÉ RALAMBOTAHINA; Sec.-Gen. M. RAZAKANAIVO; 8 affiliated unions representing 60,000 mems.

Fédération des Travailleurs Malagasy Révolutionnaires (FISEMARE): Lot IV N 77, Ankadifots, BP 1128, Antananarivo-Befelatanana; tel. (20) 2221989; f. 1985; Pres. PAUL RABEMANANJARA.

Sendika Kristianina Malagasy—SEKRIMA (Christian Confederation of Malagasy Trade Unions): Soarano, route de Mahajanga, BP 1035, 101 Antananarivo; tel. (20) 2223174; f. 1937; Pres. MARIE RAKOTOANOSY; Gen. Sec. RAYMOND RAKOTOARISAONA; 158 affiliated unions representing 40,000 mems.

Sendika Revolisakionera Malagasy (SEREMA): 101 Antananarivo.

Union des Syndicats Autonomes de Madagascar (USAM): Ampasadratsarahoby, Lot 11 H67, Faravohitra, BP 1038, 101 Antananarivo; Pres. NORBERT RAKOTOMANANA; Sec.-Gen. VICTOR RAHAGA; 46 affiliated unions representing 30,000 mems.

Transport

RAILWAYS

In 1999 there were 883 km of railway, all 1-m gauge track. The northern system, which comprised 720 km of track, links the east coast with Antsirabé, in the interior, via Moramanga and Antananarivo, with a branch line from Moramanga to Lake Alaotra. The southern system, which comprised 163 km of track, links the east coast with Fianarantsoa.

Réseau National des Chemins de Fer Malgasy: 1 ave de l'Indépendance, BP 259, Soarano, 101 Antananarivo; tel. (20) 2220521; fax (20) 2222288; f. 1909; transfer to private sector pending; Administrator DANIEL RAZAFINDRABE.

ROADS

In 1996 there were 49,837 km of classified roads, of which 8,528 km were main roads and 17,310 km were secondary roads; about 11.6% of the road network was paved. In 1987 there were 39,500 km of unclassified roads, used only in favourable weather.

INLAND WATERWAYS

The Pangalanes Canal runs for 600 km near the east coast from Toamasina to Farafangana. In 1984 the Government initiated a project to rehabilitate more than 200 km of the canal by 1988, at a cost of 18.5m. Malagasy francs. In early 1990 432 km of the canal between Toamasina and Mananjary were navigable.

SHIPPING

There are 18 ports, the largest being at Toamasina, which handles about 70% of total traffic, and Mahajanga. In 1987 Madagascar received foreign loans totalling US $34.8m., including a credit of $16m. from the World Bank, to finance a project to rehabilitate 10 ports.

Compagnie Générale Maritime (CGM): BP 69, 501 Toamasina; tel. (20) 5332312; fax (20) 5331037; f. 1976 by merger; Dir-Gen. GILLES-LOUIS TROIANO.

Compagnie Malgache de Navigation (CMN): rue Toto Radona, BP 1621, 101 Antananarivo; tel. (20) 2225516; f. 1960; coasters; 13,784 grt; 97.5% state-owned; to be privatized in 1999; Pres. ELINAH BAKOLY RAJAONSON; Dir-Gen. ARISTIDE EMMANUEL.

Navale et Commerciale Havraise Peninsulaire (NCHP): rue Rabearivelo Antsahavola, BP 1021, 101 Antananarivo; tel. (20) 2222502; Rep. JEAN PIERRE NOCKIN.

Société Nationale Malgache des Transports Maritimes (SMTM): 6 rue Indira Gandhi, BP 4077, 101 Antananarivo; tel. (20) 2227342; fax (20) 2233327; f. 1963; 59% state-owned; to be privatized in 1999; services to Europe; Chair. ALEXIS RAZAFINDRATSIRA; Dir-Gen. ANDRIONORO RAMANANTSOA.

CIVIL AVIATION

The international airport is at Antananarivo, while the airports at Mahajanga, Toamasina and Nossi-Bé can also accommodate large jet aircraft. There are 211 airfields, two-thirds of which are privately owned. In 1996 the Government invited tenders for a rehabilitation project, which was to include nine of the major airports. Later that year the Government authorized private French airlines to operate scheduled and charter flights between Madagascar and Western Europe.

Société Nationale Malgache des Transports Aériens (Air Madagascar): 31 ave de l'Indépendance, BP 437, 101 Antananarivo; tel. (20) 2222222; fax (20) 2225728; e-mail airmaddu@dts.mg; internet www.air-mad.com; f. 1962; 89.58% state-owned; transfer to the private sector pending; extensive internal routes connecting all the principal towns; external services to France, Germany, Italy, Singapore, the Comoros, Kenya, Mauritius, Réunion, Seychelles and South Africa; Chair. and Man. Dir NIRINA ANDRIAMANERASOA.

Direction de l'Aviation Civile: BP 921, Anosy, 101 Antananarivo; tel. (20) 2227715; fax (20) 2230444; Pres. NIRINA ANDRIAMANERASOA; Dir-Gen. ROLLAND BESOA RAZAFIMAHARO.

Transports et Travaux Aériens de Madagascar: Immeuble Fiaro, Ampefiloha, BP 876, 101 Antananarivo; tel. (20) 2227036; fax (20) 2230540; e-mail tamdg@dts.mg; internet www.madagascar-contacts.com/tam; f. 1959; Pres. ANDRIAMALAGASY RABEARIVELO; Dir-Gen. JEAN LOUIS RAJAONARIVELO.

Tourism

Madagascar's attractions include unspoiled scenery, many unusual varieties of flora and fauna, and the rich cultural diversity of Malagasy life. The tourism sector is undergoing expansion; the Government has declared a target of 230,000 tourist arrivals annually by 2000. In 1998 a total of 121,207 tourists visited Madagascar. Revenue from tourism in 1997 was estimated at US $73m. The number of hotel rooms increased from some 3,040 in 1991 to an estimated 8,090 in 1998.

Direction du Tourisme de Madagascar: Ministry of Tourism, Tsimbazaza, BP 610, 101 Antananarivo; tel. (20) 2226298; fax (20) 2226710.

La Maison du Tourisme de Madagascar: place de l'Indépendance, BP 3224, 101 Antananarivo; tel. (20) 2235178; fax (20) 2269522; e-mail mtm@simicro.mg; internet www.tourisme.madagascar.com; Exec. Dir IRÈNE ANDRÉAS RANDRIANJAFISOLO.

Defence

In August 1999 total armed forces numbered 21,000 men: army 20,000, navy 500 and air force 500. There is a paramilitary gendarmerie of 7,500.

Defence Expenditure: Budgeted at an estimated 273,000m. Malagasy francs in 1999.

Chief of Armed Forces General Staff: Gen. ISMAIL MONIBOU.

Education

Education is officially compulsory between six and 13 years of age. Madagascar has both public and private schools, although legislation that was enacted in 1978 envisaged the progressive elimination of private education. Primary education generally begins at the age of six and lasts for five years. Secondary education, beginning at 11 years of age, lasts for a further seven years, comprising a first cycle of four years and a second of three years. In 1995 primary enrolment was equivalent to 92% of children in the relevant age-group (males 92%; females 91%). In that year secondary enrolment was equivalent to 16% of children in the relevant age-group (males 16%; females 16%). Enrolment in tertiary education in 1993 was equivalent to 3.9% of the relevant age-group (males 4.4%; females 3.4%). In 1999 the OPEC Fund granted a loan worth US $10m. to support a government programme to improve literary standards and to increase access to education. According to UNESCO estimates, 54.3% of the adult population (males 40.2%; females 68.0%) remained illiterate in 1995. The budget for 1996 allocated 255,500m. Malagasy francs (9.1% of total expenditure) to education.

Bibliography

Allen, P. M. *Madagascar: Conflicts of Authority in the Great Island.* Boulder, CO, Westview Press, 1995.

Archer, R. *Madagascar depuis 1972, la marche d'une révolution.* Paris, Editions l'Harmattan, 1976.

Bastian, G. *Madagascar, étude géographique et économique.* Nathan, 1967.

Bradt, H., and Brown, M. *Madagascar.* Oxford, Clio Press, 1993.

Brown, Sir M. *Madagascar Rediscovered.* London, Damien Tunnacliffe, 1978.

A History of Madagascar. London, Damien Tunnacliffe, 1995.

Cadoux, C. *La République malgache.* Paris, Berger-Levrault, 1970.

Chaigneau, P. *Rivalités politiques et Socialisme à Madagascar.* Paris, Centre des Hautes Etudes sur l'Afrique et l'Asie Modernes, 1985.

Covell, M. *Madagascar. Politics, Economics and Society.* London, Frances Pinter, 1987.

Historical Dictionary of Madagascar. Lanham, MD, Scarecrow Press, 1995.

Deleris, F. *Ratsiraka: Socialisme et Misère à Madagascar.* Paris, L'Harmattan, 1986.

Deschamps, H. *Histoire de Madagascar.* 4th Edn. Paris, Berger-Levrault, 1972.

Dodwell, C. *Madagascar Travels.* London, Hodder and Stoughton, 1995.

Drysdale, H. *Dancing with the Dead: A Journey through Zanzibar and Madagascar.* London, Hamish Hamilton, 1991.

Duruflé, G. *L'Ajustement structurel en Afrique (Sénégal, Côte d'Ivoire, Madagascar).* Paris, Editions Karthala, 1987.

Feeley-Harnick, G. *A Green Estate: Restoring Independence in Madagascar.* Washington, DC, Smithsonian Institution Press, 1991.

de Gaudusson, J. *L'Administration malgache.* Paris, Berger-Levrault, 1976.

Heseltine, N. *Madagascar.* London, Pall Mall, 1971.

Hugon, P. *Economie et enseignement à Madagascar.* Paris, Institut International de Planification de l'Education, 1976.

Litalien, R. *Madagascar 1956–1960, Etape vers la décolonisation.* Paris, Ecole Pratique des Hautes Etudes, 1975.

Massiot, M. *L'organisation politique, administrative, financière et judiciaire de la République malgache.* Antananarivo, Librairie de Madagascar, 1970.

Mutibwa, P. *The Malagasy and the Europeans: Madagascar's Foreign Relations 1861–95.* London, Longman, 1974.

Pascal, R. *La République malgache: Pacifique indépendance.* Paris, Berger-Levrault, 1965.

Pryor, F. L. *Malawi and Madagascar: The Political Economy of Poverty, Equity and Growth.* New York, Oxford University Press, 1991.

Rabemananjara, J. *Nationalisme et problèmes malgaches.* Paris, 1958.

Rabenoro, C. *Les relations extérieures de Madagascar, de 1960 à 1972.* Paris, Editions l'Harmattan, 1986.

Raison-Jourde, F. *Les souverains de Madagascar.* Paris, Editions Karthala, 1983.

Rajémis-Raolison, R. *Dictionnaire historique et géographique de Madagascar.* Fianarantsoa, Librairie Ambozontany, 1966.

Rajoelina, P. *Quarante années de la vie politique de Madagascar, 1947–1987.* Paris, L'Harmattan, 1988.

Rajoelina, P., and Ramelet, A. *Madagascar, la grande île.* Paris, L'Harmattan, 1989.

Ralaimihoatra, E. *Histoire de Madagascar.* 2 vols. Antananarivo, Société Malgache d'Editions, 1966–67.

Ramahatra, O. *Madagascar: Une économie en phase d'ajustement.* Paris, Editions l'Harmattan, 1989.

Schuurman, D., and Ravelojoana, N. *Madagascar.* London, New Holland, 1997.

Sharp, L. A. *The Possessed and the Dispossessed.* Berkeley, University of California Press, 1993.

Spacensky, A. *Madagascar: Cinquante ans de vie politique (de Ralaimongo à Tsiranana).* Paris, Nouvelles Editions Latines, 1970.

Thompson, V., and Adloff, R. *The Malagasy Republic.* Stanford, CA, Stanford University Press, 1965.

Tronchon, J. *L'insurrection malgache de 1947.* Paris, Editions Karthala, 1986.

Vérin, P. *Madagascar.* Paris, Editions Karthala, 1990.

Vindard, G. R., and Battistini, R. *Bio-geography and Ecology of Madagascar.* The Hague, 1972.

Wilson, J. *Lemurs of the Lost World.* 2nd Edn. London, Impact Books, 1995.

MALAWI

Physical and Social Geography

A. MacGREGOR HUTCHESON

The land-locked Republic of Malawi extends some 840 km from north to south, varying in width from 80 to 160 km. It has a total area of 118,484 sq km (45,747 sq miles), including 24,208 sq km (9,347 sq miles) of inland water, and is aligned along the southern continuation of the east African rift valley system. There are land borders with Tanzania to the north, with Zambia to the west, and with Mozambique to the south and east. Frontiers with Mozambique and Tanzania continue to the east, along the shores of Lake Malawi.

Malawi occupies a plateau of varying height, bordering the deep rift valley trench which averages 80 km in width. The northern two-thirds of the rift valley floor are almost entirely occupied by Lake Malawi, which is 568 km in length and varies in width from 16 km to 80 km. The lake covers an area of 23,310 sq km, and has a mean surface of 472 m above sea-level. The southern third of the rift valley is traversed by the River Shire, draining Lake Malawi, via the shallow Lake Malombe, to the River Zambezi. The plateau surfaces on either side of the rift valley lie mainly at 760–1,370 m, but very much higher elevations are attained; above the highlands west of Lake Malawi are the Nyika and Viphya plateaux and the Dedza mountains and Kirk Range, which rise to between 1,524 and 2,440 m in places. South of Lake Malawi are the Shire highlands and the Zomba and Mulanje mountain ranges; the Zomba plateau rises to 2,100 m, and Mt Mulanje, the highest mountain in central Africa, to 3,050 m above sea-level.

The great variations in altitude and latitudinal extent are responsible for a wide range of climatic, soil and vegetational conditions within Malawi. There are three climatic seasons. During the cool season, from May to August, there is very little cloud, and mean temperatures in the plateau areas are 15.5°C–18°C, and in the rift valley 20°C–24.5°C. The coldest month is July, when the maximum temperature is 22.2°C and the minimum 11.7°C. In September and October, before the rains, a short hot season occurs when humidity increases: mean temperatures range from 27°C–30°C in the rift valley, and from 22°C–24.5°C on the plateaux at this time. During October/November temperatures exceeding 37°C may be registered in the low-lying areas. The rainy season lasts from November to April, and over 90% of the total annual rainfall occurs during this period. Most of Malawi receives an annual rainfall of 760–1,015 mm, but some areas in the higher plateaux experience over 1,525 mm.

Malawi possesses some of the most fertile soils in south-central Africa. Of particular importance are those in the lake-shore plains, the Lake Chilwa-Palombe plain and the upper and lower Shire valley. Good plateau soils occur in the Lilongwe-Kasungu high plains and in the tea-producing areas of Thyolo, Mulanje and Nkhata Bay districts. Although just over half the land area of Malawi is considered suitable for cultivation, rather less than 50% of this area is cultivated at present; this is an indication of the agricultural potential yet to be realized. The lakes and rivers have been exploited for their considerable hydroelectric and irrigation potential.

Malawi is one of the more densely populated countries of Africa, with 7,988,507 inhabitants (an average density of 67.4 per sq km) at the 1987 census. There were an estimated 10,441,000 inhabitants at mid-1997, giving a population density of 88.1 per sq km. According to UN projections, Malawi's population will increase to 11.4m. by the middle of the year 2000. However, population patterns are expected to be affected by the high rate of incidence of AIDS, which is particularly prevalent in urban areas. Labour has been a Malawian resource for many years, and thousands of migratory workers seek employment in neighbouring countries, particularly in South Africa.

As a result of physical, historical and economic factors, Malawi's population is very unevenly distributed. The Southern Region, the most developed of the three regions, contains more than half the population, while the Northern Region has only about 12%. New investment in the Northern and Central Regions and the movement of the capital from Zomba to a new site at Lilongwe in the early 1970s have made some progress towards redressing these regional imbalances.

Recent History

RICHARD BROWN

Revised for this edition by the Editor

In 1891 the British government declared a protectorate over the area that came to be known as Nyasaland. An agricultural economy was established by white settlers. Agrarian grievances of the African population led in 1944 to the formation of the Nyasaland African Congress (NAC), which unsuccessfully opposed a federation of Nyasaland in 1953 with the territories of Northern and Southern Rhodesia as the Federation of Rhodesia and Nyasaland (FRN). In 1958 Dr Hastings Kamuzu Banda, a physician who had retained close links with the NAC despite being resident abroad for nearly 40 years, returned to assume the leadership of the NAC. A period of civil disorder followed, during which the NAC was banned and Dr Banda was imprisoned. During his detention, Banda organized the new Malawi Congress Party (MCP). The British government, faced with the choice of maintaining control by armed force, or preparing the territory for independence, released Banda in 1960.

Elections held in August 1961 gave the MCP a decisive victory. Full self-government followed in January 1963; Banda became prime minister in February, and the FRN was dissolved in December. On 6 July 1964 Nyasaland became the independent state of Malawi.

THE BANDA REGIME

On 6 July 1966 Malawi officially became a republic and a one-party state, with Banda as president: he was voted president-for-life in 1971. No political opposition was tolerated, and the various exiled opposition groups, of which the most prominent were the Socialist League of Malawi and the Malawi Freedom Movement proved ineffectual. The treatment of political detainees by the Banda regime attracted repeated criticism by Amnesty International and other international human rights organizations, while within the MCP no political figure was permitted to emerge as an obvious successor to the ageing president. In 1983 rivalry was reported to have developed between Dick Matenje, the secretary-general of the MCP and a minister without portfolio, and John Tembo, the governor of the Reserve Bank of Malawi, concerning the eventual succession to the presidency. Matenje and three other senior politicians died in May, apparently in a road accident, but exiled opposition members claimed that they had been murdered while trying to leave the country (see below).

In March 1992 the government was exposed to unprecedented criticism from the influential Roman Catholic church in Malawi, with the publication by its bishops of an open letter criticizing the state's alleged abuses of human rights. Pressure on the government intensified later in that month, when about 80 Malawian political exiles gathered in Lusaka, Zambia, to devise a strategy to precipitate political reforms. In April Chakufwa Chihana, a prominent trade union leader who had demanded multi-party elections, returned to Malawi from exile and was immediately arrested. The Banda regime was seriously threatened from within the country in May, when industrial unrest in the southern city of Blantyre escalated into violent anti-government riots; these spread to Lilongwe, and reportedly resulted in at least 40 deaths. Shortly afterwards international donors suspended all non-humanitarian aid to Malawi, pending an improvement in the government's observance of human rights. In June several hundred people were arrested and charged with circulating seditious material.

Elections to an enlarged legislature took place in June 1992, at which 675 MCP candidates contested 141 elective seats in the national assembly: 45 candidates were returned unopposed, five seats remained vacant, owing to the disqualification of some candidates, and 62 former members of the national assembly lost their seats. Opposition groups challenged the government's claim of a turnout of about 80% of the electorate. Chihana was released from detention in July, but was rearrested and subsequently imprisoned for sedition.

In September 1992 a group of opposition politicians formed the Alliance for Democracy (AFORD), a pressure group operating within Malawi under the chairmanship of Chihana, which aimed to campaign for democratic political reform. Another opposition organization, the United Democratic Front (UDF), was formed in the same month. In October Banda reluctantly conceded to demands for a national referendum by secret ballot on the introduction of multi-party democracy. In January 1993 more than 100,000 anti-government demonstrators attended a rally in Blantyre. During that month LESOMA and another party, the Malawi Democratic Union, merged to form the United Front for Multi-party Democracy, based in Zambia. In March MAFREMO dissolved itself and its membership joined AFORD.

TRANSITION TO DEMOCRACY

The referendum on the introduction of democratic reform took place in mid-June 1993. Although the government had disrupted the activities of opposition groups prior to the referendum, the latter secured a decisive victory, with 63.2% of voters supporting the reintroduction of multi-party politics. A turn-out of 67% of the electorate was recorded. The opposition received especially strong support in the north and south of the country, while voters in the central region mainly remained loyal to the MCP. Following the referendum, Banda rejected opposition demands for the immediate installation of a government of national unity. He agreed, however, to establish a national executive council, to oversee the transition to a multi-party system, and a national consultative council to draft a new constitution. Both councils were to comprise members of the government and the opposition. Banda announced a general amnesty for thousands of political exiles, and stated that a general election would be held, on a multi-party basis, within a year. (Chihana had been released from prison a few days before the referendum, having served six months of his sentence.) In late June the constitution was amended to allow the registration of political parties other than the MCP: by mid-August five organizations, including AFORD and the UDF, had been accorded legal status. A UN-sponsored forum on the transition to democracy was held in Malawi in July; it was agreed that the UN would continue to play a supporting role in the country during the transitional period.

In September 1993 Banda carried out an extensive cabinet reshuffle, including the appointment of Hetherwick Ntaba as minister of external affairs, a post held by Banda himself since 1964. In October 1993 Banda became seriously ill and underwent neurological surgery in South Africa. Having rejected opposition demands for the election of an apolitical interim head of state, in mid-October the office of the president announced the formation of a three-member presidential council, which was to assume executive power in Banda's absence. As required by the constitution, the council was placed under the chairmanship of the new secretary-general of the MCP, Gwanda Chakuamba. (Chakuamba, a former government minister, had been sentenced to 22 years' imprisonment in 1981, after having been convicted of sedition; he was released in July 1993.) The two other members were also senior MCP officials, John Tembo and Robson Chirwa, the minister of transport and communications. In early November the presidential council reshuffled the cabinet, as a result of which Banda was without ministerial responsibilities for the first time since 1964. In mid-November 1993 the national assembly passed the constitutional amendment bill, which included the repeal of the institution of life presidency, the reduction of the qualifying age for a presidential candidate from 40 to 35 years, the repeal of the requirement that election candidates be members of the MCP, the repeal of the right of the president to nominate members of the legislature exclusively from the MCP, and the lowering of the minimum voting age from 21 to 18 years. The national assembly also amended the public security act, repealing all provisions permitting detention without trial.

Having made a rapid and unexpected recovery, Banda resumed full presidential powers on 7 December 1993 and the presidential council was dissolved. Shortly afterwards, in response to increasing pressure from the opposition, the government amended the constitution to provide for the appointment of an acting president in the event of the incumbent being incapacitated. In February 1994 the MCP announced that Banda was to be the party's presidential candidate in the forthcoming general election, which was scheduled to take place on 17 May; Chakuamba was selected as the MCP's candidate for the vice-presidency. In the same month the national assembly approved an increase in the number of elected legislative members in the approaching general election from 141 to 177.

Meanwhile, the MCP announced in September 1993 that the Malawi Young Pioneers (MYP), a widely-feared paramilitary section of the ruling party, were to be gradually disarmed. In December, following the murder of three soldiers by MYP members, members of the regular army undertook a peremptory campaign to close MYP offices and camps. In the ensuing violence, which was believed to have been exacerbated by long-standing tensions between the army and the MYP, 32 people were reported to have been killed. Following his recovery from surgery, Banda appointed a minister of defence (having previously himself retained the defence portfolio) to oversee the MYP disarmament process and investigate army grievances. By early January 1994 it was reported that the disarmament of the MYP had been satisfactorily completed; it was also reported, however, that several thousand MYP members had crossed the border into Mozambique to take refuge in rebel bases. In late January the governments of Malawi and Mozambique agreed to a programme for the repatriation of the MYP forces from Mozambican territory; however, in May (three months after the MYP was officially disbanded) it was reported that at least 2,000 armed MYP members remained in Mozambique. In June 1996 it was further reported that former MYP members had formed a terrorist group, known as the Movement for the Restoration of Democracy in Malawi (MRDM), in Mozambique.

On 16 May 1994 a provisional constitution was adopted by the national assembly. The new document provided for the appointment of a constitutional committee and of a human rights commission, and abolished the system of 'traditional' courts. Banda's domination of the country finally ended with the multi-party elections held on the following day. In the four-candidate presidential contest, Bakili Muluzi, leader of the UDF, obtained 47.3% of the votes; Banda himself won 33.6%, and Chakufwa Chihana (of AFORD) 18.6%. The UDF won 84 of the 177 parliamentary seats, the MCP 55 seats and AFORD 36 seats. (The results of voting in two constituencies were invalidated.) In the absence of strong ideological differences between the parties, regional and ethnic allegiances predominated: AFORD won all 33 of the Northern Region's seats; the MCP was strongly supported in the Central Region; and the UDF won most of the seats in the Southern Region. The expected UDF–AFORD coalition did not materialize, however, and one month after the elections AFORD agreed instead to work with the MCP, thus compelling the UDF to form a government without a parliamentary majority.

THE MULUZI GOVERNMENT

President Muluzi and his vice-president, Justin Malewezi, were inaugurated later in May 1994. The principal aims of the new administration were defined as being to alleviate poverty and ensure food security, and to combat corruption and the mismanagement of resources. The closure was announced of three prisons where abuses of human rights were known to have taken place; an amnesty was granted to the country's remaining political prisoners, and all death sentences were commuted to terms of life imprisonment. The new government was dominated by the UDF, but also included members of the Malawi National Democratic Party and the United Front for Multi-party Democracy. Attempts to recruit members of AFORD into a coalition administration initially failed, owing to disagreements regarding the allocation of senior portfolios, and in June AFORD and the MCP signed what was termed a 'memorandum of understanding' whereby they would function as an opposition front. The Muluzi government was thus deprived of a majority in the national assembly, which was inaugurated at the end of June. In August it was announced that Banda, while remaining honorary life president of the MCP, was to retire from active involvement in politics. Chakuamba, as vice-president of the MCP, effectively succeeded to the party leadership.

Government changes in September 1994 included the appointment of Chihana to the post of second vice-president and minister of irrigation and water development: AFORD members were also allocated responsibility for agriculture, transport, research and the environment. None the less, the AFORD–MCP 'memorandum of understanding' remained in force until January 1995, when AFORD, acknowledging that the new government had made significant progress in the restoration of political stability and the establishment of democracy, announced an end to its co-operation with the MCP. The creation of the post of second vice-president necessitated a constitutional amendment, and provoked severe criticism from the MCP. Moreover, the national constitutional conference, which met in February to consider refinements to the document prior to its official promulgation, recommended that the post be abolished. In late March, however, the national assembly (in the absence of MCP deputies, who boycotted the vote) approved the retention of the second vice-presidency; the assembly also approved the establishment—although not before May 1999—of a second chamber of parliament, the senate, as well as a constitutional clause requiring that senior state officials declare all personal assets within two months of assuming their post. A further reorganization of the cabinet took place in August 1995.

In June 1994 Muluzi announced the establishment of an independent commission of inquiry to investigate the deaths of Matenje and his associates in May 1983. In January 1995, in accordance with the findings of the commission, Banda was placed under house arrest; Tembo and two former police officers were arrested and detained, and the four were charged with murder and conspiracy to murder. A former inspector-general of the police, who was alleged, *inter alia*, to have destroyed evidence relating to the deaths, was charged later in the month. Cecilia Kadzamira, Tembo's niece and the former president's 'official hostess', was charged in early April with conspiracy to murder. The trial opened in late April, but was immediately adjourned, owing to Banda's absence from court (his defence counsel asserted that he was too ill to stand trial), and to the failure of the state prosecution to submit, as required, certain evidence to the defence. Banda failed to appear at a resumed hearing in May, and was stated by medical consultants to be unable to attend the trial. Banda remained under house arrest, while proceedings against Tembo, Kadzamira and other defendants resumed in July. In September Tembo and the two former police officers were granted bail, and most restrictions on

Banda's movements were ended. The case against Kadzamira was abandoned in mid-December, owing to lack of evidence, and later in the month Banda, Tembo and the other defendants were acquitted of conspiracy to murder and to defeat justice. The director of public prosecutions subsequently appealed against the verdict, complaining that the presiding judge had effectively instructed the jury to acquit the defendants. In January 1996 an MCP-owned newspaper printed a statement by Banda in which he admitted that he might unknowingly have been responsible for brutalities perpetrated under his regime, and apologized to Malawians for 'pain and suffering' inflicted during his presidency. In July 1995 Tembo and four other members of the Banda regime were charged with conspiring to murder the Roman Catholic bishops who had published criticisms of the former administration in 1992.

In July 1995 lawyers acting for Banda demanded that Muluzi explain the apparent payment of a substantial sum to a witness in the trial of Banda and his associates. Meanwhile, there were further allegations that the Muluzi administration had been involved in questionable financial transactions. It emerged in mid-1995 that the president had authorized the payment of some K6.2m. from the state poverty alleviation account to UDF members of parliament (to enable the payment of loans to their constituents); there was also evidence of the involvement of government ministers in the smuggling of maize to neighbouring countries. Moreover, few ministers had complied with the constitutional requirement regarding the declaration of assets. An investigation of Banda's financial interests was initiated in September. Muluzi announced in February 1996 that an independent anti-corruption bureau was to be established to investigate allegations of corruption.

The cabinet was reorganized in July 1995. Later in that month the UDF and AFORD signed a formal co-operation agreement. Many government offices were closed for a week in August, as civil servants undertook industrial action in support of their demands for increases in salary. The government declared the strike illegal, but withdrew threatened sanctions after the industrial action was cancelled; negotiations regarding pay increases ensued. In October the president and vice-president of the Malawi Democratic Party (MDP) were acquitted on charges of intimidating the head of state: in July MDP leaders had demanded Muluzi's resignation, stating that the population had lost confidence in his administration.

In December 1995 Chihana warned that AFORD might withdraw from the coalition government, alleging that the UDF was using public funds to secure political influence, and complaining of a lack of openness in the Muluzi administration. Chihana resigned from the government in May 1996, expressing his intention to devote himself more fully to the work of his party. The post of second vice-president remained vacant following a reorganization of the cabinet shortly afterwards. In late May Bitwell Kawonga, another AFORD minister, resigned. In June AFORD withdrew from its coalition with the UDF (which meant the loss of a parliamentary working majority for the government) and declared that AFORD ministers still in the cabinet should resign; Dr Mponda Mkandawire, the minister of natural resources, subsequently stepped down and the party appointed a new 'shadow cabinet', which included Kawonga and Mkandawire. Five members were dismissed from AFORD's national executive, having refused to relinquish their ministerial posts. A reorganization of the cabinet in July included the appointment of a further AFORD member. Meanwhile, AFORD and the MCP insisted that AFORD ministers who had disobeyed instructions to resign should be regarded as members of the UDF, as they were effectively maintaining that party's parliamentary majority. The rejection of this demand resulted in a parliamentary boycott by both opposition parties. In September a UDF member of the national assembly (a former government minister) resigned from the party, and a further eight members were reportedly threatening to resign, in response to Muluzi's controversial appointment of a new UDF regional governor for the south. In December the AFORD ministers remaining in the cabinet asserted that they were independent and had not joined the UDF. In March 1997 AFORD stated that the party would continue its boycott until the ministers resigned both their government posts and parliamentary seats. Meanwhile, the high court dismissed a case, brought by the opposition parties, that the previous sitting of parliament be declared illegal and unconstitutional. In April the MCP ended its parliamentary boycott, following a meeting between Muluzi and Chakuamba, at which Muluzi had allegedly promised to amend the constitution to prevent parliamentary delegates from changing their political affiliation without standing for re-election. Minor government changes were made in May.

Tembo and Kadzamira were again arrested in September 1996, and were charged, along with several others, with conspiracy to murder and attempted murder. Although they had been arrested in connection with the recent shooting of a Lebanese trader, the charges were reported to relate to a plot to kill three government ministers in 1995. In January 1997 it was announced that Banda was to be charged with embezzling state funds for the establishment of a private school; however, in May he was discharged as medically unfit to attend court. In July the supreme court dismissed an appeal against the acquittal, in December 1995, of Banda and Tembo on murder charges, shortly after Muluzi reportedly requested that all criminal cases against Banda be discontinued. In the same month Banda announced his intention to resign as president of the MCP. In November 1997 Banda died in South Africa, where he had been undergoing emergency medical treatment. He was accorded a state funeral, with full military honours, which was attended by some 100,000 Malawians.

Strike action by civil servants during April–May 1997 caused considerable disruption, notably to health services and air traffic. A government-appointed commission had recently recommended salary increases of as much as 300% for public-sector employees; however, the government insisted that immediately to grant increases of this order would necessitate unacceptable measures of retrenchment in other areas of public expenditure. In early May, following a number of arrests, it was reported that the majority of personnel had returned to work.

In July 1997 the cabinet was reorganized, and a number of ministries were merged or abolished, as part of the government's reform of the civil service; former members of AFORD remained in the cabinet. A national economic council was established to assume the responsibilities of the former ministry of economic planning and development. In September Muluzi demanded that the MCP apologize for atrocities committed by the Banda regime, in the light of new evidence that Matenje and his associates had indeed been murdered in May 1983. In December 1997 AFORD decided against a merger with the MCP, instead favouring an alliance. Muluzi completed the restructuring of his government in March 1998, further reducing the number of ministries.

Preparations for forthcoming presidential and legislative elections dominated domestic politics in 1998 and early 1999. In June 1998 the national assembly approved legislation that provided for the replacement of the current multiple-ballot electoral system with the use of a single ballot, and for a reinforcement of the authority and independence of the electoral commission. In November legislation was adopted to allow presidential and parliamentary elections to run concurrently (as Muluzi's term was due to end several weeks earlier than that of the national assembly), and the elections were subsequently scheduled for 18 May 1999. An electoral alliance between the MCP and AFORD, which was officially announced in February 1999, created serious divisions within the MCP, when the party's leader and presidential candidate, Gwandaguluwe Chakuamba, chose Chakufwa Chihana, the leader of AFORD, as the candidate for the vice-presidency, in preference to John Tembo. Thousands of Tembo's supporters were reported to have mounted protests to demand Chakuamba's resignation. The Chakuamba-Chihana alliance also provoked a wider dispute with the UDF and the electoral commission, which claimed that the arrangement was unconstitutional, but in April the high court dismissed their petition. Also in April Muluzi inaugurated the human rights commission, which had been a provision of the 1995 constitution. Meanwhile, the elections were postponed until 25 May, owing to delays in the registration of voters. In February the national assembly adopted a report by the electoral commission which had caused considerable controversy by recommending the creation of a further 72 parliamentary seats, including an additional 42 in the Southern Region, a UDF

stronghold. In response to widespread opposition to the proposals, however, only 16 of the 72 seats were approved.

After a further postponement, the presidential and legislative elections were held on 15 June 1999. The turn-out was high, with some 93.8% of registered voters reported to have participated. Muluzi was re-elected to the presidency, securing 51.37% of the votes cast, while Chakuamba obtained 43.30% and Kamulepo Kalua of the MDP 1.43%. Two other candidates contested the election, but each received less than 1% of the vote. At the elections to the expanded national assembly, some 658 candidates and 11 parties contested the 193 seats. The ruling UDF won 93 seats, while the MCP secured 66 seats, AFORD 29 seats and independent candidates four seats. (Voting in the remaining constituency was later postponed until October, owing to the death of a candidate.) Traditional regional loyalties were strongly in evidence, with AFORD winning some 85% of the seats in the Northern Region, the MCP securing 75% of the Central Region's seats and the UDF obtaining 86% of the seats available in the Southern Region. The opposition disputed the results and violent clashes ensued in the northern districts. Despite declarations from international observers that the elections were largely free and fair, the MCP–AFORD alliance filed two petitions with the high court, challenging Muluzi's victory and the results in 16 districts. The opposition alleged irregularities in the voter registration process and claimed that Muluzi's win was unconstitutional, as he had failed to gain the support of 50% of all registered voters. None the less, Muluzi was inaugurated later that month and a new cabinet was appointed. In July the high court ordered the electoral commission to allow opposition lawyers access to voting materials from the disputed districts, but the commission subsequently appealed against the order. In August the UDP regained a parliamentary majority when the four independent deputies decided to ally themselves with the UDF, of which they had all previously been members.

In September 1999 two members of the electoral commission were suspended for allegedly sympathizing with the opposition and in December a report published by the electoral commissions forum of the Southern African Development Community (SADC) emphasized the failings of the Malawian electoral commission and recommended that in future it consist solely of members with no party political affiliation. Also in December a re-count of votes cast in the presidential election in June began and later that same month lawyers representing the MCP-AFORD alliance claimed to have discovered evidence of electoral fraud carried out to the benefit of the UDF. Meanwhile, in October by-elections were held in three constituencies with UDF candidates winning all of the three available seats, thus increasing the number of deputies supporting the UDF to 100. In early March 2000 Muluzi effected a cabinet reshuffle, prompted, it was speculated, by allegations of high-level corruption. Notable changes included the appointment of Mathews Chikoanda, hitherto governor of the central bank, as minister of finance and economic planning to replace Cassim Chilumpha, who was given responsibility for the ministry of education, sports and culture. Chilumpha had recently come under investigation by the anti-corruption bureau, following media reports questioning the legality of circumstances surrounding the awarding of a pre-shipment contract. In May the high court dismissed the opposition's case disputing Muluzi's victory in June 1999 and declared his election to the presidency lawful. It was subsequently reported that the opposition had appealed to the supreme court to overturn the high court's ruling.

Ongoing divisions within the leadership of the MCP prompted the defection of two of the party's deputies to the UDF in May 2000 and escalated thereafter. In June Tembo, the vice-president of the MCP, was designated as the new leader of the opposition in the national assembly, after deputies voted to suspend Chakuamba, the incumbent, from the chamber for a period of one year, on the grounds that he had persistently boycotted legislative proceedings. In early August the two factions of the MCP held separate conventions in Blantyre and Lilongwe, which elected Chakuamba and Tembo, respectively, as presidents of the party. The high court annulled the results of both leadership elections pending a full hearing on the legitimacy of the two conventions. Local government elections were to be held in November 2000.

REGIONAL RELATIONS

Banda's establishment of diplomatic relations with South Africa in 1967 alienated him for a time from most other African leaders, as did his promotion of friendly relations with Portugal under the pre-1974 right-wing regime. Following independence, Malawi's relations with its neighbours, Tanzania and Zambia, were strained by disputes over territorial boundaries: during the late 1960s Malawi claimed that its natural boundaries included the whole of the northern half of Lake Malawi, and extended at least 160 km north of Tanzania's Songwo river, as well as east and west into Mozambique and Zambia. Full diplomatic relations with Zambia were established in 1971, but it was not until 1985 that diplomatic relations were established with Tanzania. However, Malawi did become a member of the Southern African Development Co-ordination Conference in 1980, and in 1993 was a founder member of its successor organization, the SADC. Following talks in April 1994, the presidents of Tanzania and Malawi agreed that social and economic relations between the two countries should be improved, and that the joint commission on co-operation (which had last met in 1983) should be re-established. An agreement formalizing cross-border trade was signed in August 1996.

The Banda regime gave support neither to the Frente de Libertação de Moçambique (Frelimo) nor to the Patriotic Front (PF), during their respective independence struggles in Mozambique and Zimbabwe, and in 1982 the Mozambique government alleged that its opponents, members of the Resistência Nacional Moçambicana (Renamo), were operating from bases in Malawi. In October 1984 Malawi and Mozambique signed a general co-operation agreement, establishing a joint commission to regulate their relations. In July 1986, however, the chief of staff of Mozambique's armed forces alleged that Malawi was actively assisting the guerrillas of Renamo. Despite Banda's denial of these allegations, President Machel of Mozambique warned that, if Malawi continued to assist Renamo, he would close the border between the two countries, thereby denying Malawi its most direct access to the sea. In October 1986 President Machel was killed in an aeroplane crash in South Africa. The South African government claimed that documents which had been discovered in the crash wreckage revealed a plot by Mozambique and Zimbabwe to overthrow the Malawi government. Angry protests from the Malawi government to Mozambique and Zimbabwe were met by denials of the accusations. In December Malawi and Mozambique signed a further agreement on defence and security matters, which was believed to include co-operation in eliminating Renamo operations. In April 1987 it was confirmed that Malawi troops had been stationed in Mozambique to protect the strategic railway line linking Malawi to the Mozambican port of Nacala.

In July 1988 relations between the two countries were consolidated when President Chissano of Mozambique made a state visit to Malawi, during which he stated that he did not believe Malawi to be supporting Renamo. In December Malawi, Mozambique and the UN High Commissioner for Refugees (UNHCR) signed an agreement to promote the voluntary repatriation of an estimated 650,000 Mozambican refugees who had fled into Malawi over the previous two years, as a result of the continuing unrest in Mozambique, and who were placing a considerable burden on the country's resources; the number of refugees continued to rise, however, reaching about 1m. by mid-1992. Following the signing of a general peace agreement for Mozambique in October 1992, all Malawian troops had been withdrawn from Mozambique by June 1993. However, in mid-1994 an estimated 600,000 Mozambican refugees still remained in Malawi. By early 1996 the majority of the refugees had been repatriated in an operation organized by UNHCR. In March 1995 President Chissano visited Malawi, and the two countries agreed to review their joint defence and security arrangements to reflect problems such as drugs-trafficking and arms-smuggling. Following a meeting of the joint defence and security commission in mid-1996, a subcommittee to regulate border issues, and joint committees on security and police matters at national, regional, district and local levels, were to be established. At the commission's eighth session, in early 1998, the Malawian government expressed concern over uncertainty regarding the whereabouts of remaining MYP members. (In September 1997 10 Malawians had been detained in Mozambique on suspicion of destabilizing border areas.) In June 1998 the government of Malawi issued a statement in response to allegations that the MCP had been involved in the death of Samora Machel, then president of Mozambique, in October 1986. The government undertook to co-operate fully with any investigation into the plane crash in which Machel had died.

Malawi's relations with Zimbabwe improved during the 1980s, despite the Banda regime's hostility to the PF prior to Zimbabwe's independence, and absence from the independence celebrations in 1980. Diplomatic relations were subsequently established, and in 1986 a joint permanent commission was formed. In April 1990 Banda was a guest of honour at celebrations for Zimbabwe's 10th anniversary of independence.

The Muluzi government has undertaken a more active role in foreign affairs, offering troops for the UN peace-keeping operation in Rwanda and undertaking joint military exercises with US troops within Malawi. During 1995, as chairman of the Common Market for Eastern and Southern Africa (COMESA), Muluzi acted as mediator in a long-standing frontier dispute between Sudan and Uganda.

Economy

LINDA VAN BUREN

In the post-Banda era Malawi rapidly managed to rescue the economy from its downward spiral of the early 1990s and to obtain the confidence of donors in its recovery strategy. However, that much still remained to be done was evident in October 1999, when Malawi presented its adjustment strategy, and again in May 2000, when donors assessed its progress. In 1998 Malawi's GNP per caput ranked among the lowest in the world, at US $210, according to the World Bank. The rate of inflation, which had been more than 18% for over a decade, soared to 75% at the end of 1995, and was officially estimated at 57% in March 1999 and at some 35% in March 2000. The budget deficit in the mid-1990s grew far beyond any lender's acceptable level, in relation to GDP. The country's economic advancement is restrained by problems of subsistence agriculture, low educational levels, a shortage of skilled personnel, a lack of mineral resources, overdependence on one principal export crop, inadequate infrastructure and import-dependent industries, which have been compounded by the limitations of a landlocked position and a small domestic market.

ECONOMIC BACKGROUND

During the 1970s Malawi benefited from a sharp rise in investment, supported by favourable government policies and an influx of foreign aid and capital. The concurrent expansion of commercial output led to a doubling of production of export crops, and also placed Malawi among the few countries of sub-Saharan Africa where food production kept pace with population growth. In the social services sector extensive donor-supported programmes sought to improve the provision of education, health services, water supply and sanitation. Rapid growth in the domestic economy was, however, paralleled by a poor performance of the economy externally.

Malawi was beset by drought during 1979–81, and GDP growth, in real terms, declined to an average rate of 2.5% per year during the period 1980–90. In 1981 the government, supported by the IMF and the World Bank, initiated a reform programme. The economy responded rapidly, helped by the return of favourable rains in 1982 and a resurgence of agricultural output. A further reform programme, launched in 1986, reduced subsidies and reorganized some major parastatal bodies, but GDP growth fell to 2.8% in that year, compared with the target of 4.2%. Economic performance in 1992 was adversely affected by severe drought, an unprecedented level of industrial unrest and the decision by international donors in May of that year to link all future non-humanitarian aid to the Banda government's progress in upholding human rights. According to government figures, GDP declined, in real terms, by 7.3% in 1992, while (following two devaluations of the national currency) the annual rate of inflation averaged 23.2%, compared with 8.2% in 1991. More than one-half of the population experienced food shortages in that year. Favourable weather conditions in 1992–93 retrieved the situation, and official figures estimated real GDP growth at 9.7% in 1993. The new Muluzi government inherited an unstable fiscal and monetary situation in 1994. In addition, serious drought returned in 1993/94, and real GDP decreased by 10.2% in 1994. The decline in GDP was reversed in 1995 when growth of 9.0% was recorded. Ambitious recovery targets were set for the late 1990s; however, in October 1999, the government conceded that most of its economic aims had not been achieved. Real GDP increased by an officially estimated 4.5% in 1999, as against a target of 5%, and inflation reached 57% in March 1999 before being reduced to about 30% in the first half of 2000.

AGRICULTURE

Agriculture is the most important sector of the economy, and, with forestry and fishing, it accounted for 35.3% of GDP (at constant 1994 prices) in 1998. Agricultural GDP grew at an average annual rate of 8.9% in 1990–98 and, according to the central bank, by an estimated 3.7% in 1998. An estimated 83.6% of the working population were engaged in agriculture in 1998. The vast majority of these people work in the smallholder sector, which accounts for nearly 80% of the cultivated area and of agricultural output, which is mostly on a subsistence basis. The principal cash crops are tobacco (which accounted for an estimated 64.4% of total export earnings in 1996), tea and sugar cane. Maize is the principal food crop, and is grown almost entirely by smallholders; output increased by 40% from 1.77m. metric tons in 1998 to 2.48m. tons in 1999. The sorghum harvest increased from 17,000 tons in 1994 to 55,000 tons in 1996 and, after declining to 41,473 tons in 1998, it rose by 45% to an estimated 60,000 tons in 1999. Maize has been exported in some years and imported in others, depending on weather conditions; the import of some 87,000 metric tons of maize was required in 1998. Potatoes, pulses, plantains and cassavas are also important food crops. Malawi produced about 31,000 metric tons of groundnuts in shells in 1994 and 1995 and 40,000 tons in 1996, before harvesting a record crop of 108,298 tons in 1998, followed by a similar amount in 1999. From this was obtained an output of 9,750 tons of groundnut oil in 1998. The sunflower-seed crop of about 6,000 tons in 1998 yielded 1,320 tons of sunflower-seed oil, and the 1999 harvest was an estimated 7,000 tons of seeds. The output of green coffee beans declined from 3,900 tons in 1998 to 3,600 tons in 1999. The leading export crop, tobacco, was grown on an estimated 130,000 ha in 1995, but on only about 105,000 ha in 1999. Output of tobacco leaves declined from 158,113 tons in 1997 to 124,550 tons in 1998 and to 112,800 tons in 1999, with a 33% fall in burley production alone in 1999. On average, Malawi's tobacco growers achieved a yield of 1,074 kg per ha in 1999, compared with 2,102 kg per ha in neighbouring Zimbabwe. The crop is sold at auction from April to October. International prices have declined in recent years, however, owing mainly to smaller demand from the big tobacco companies, and the effects have permeated the whole Malawian economy.

Malawi's principal agricultural exports are tobacco, tea, sugar, coffee and large, hand-shelled, confectionery-grade groundnuts. Cassava, rice, medium-staple cotton and sunflower seed are also exported. Smallholder crops are marketed for export by the Agricultural Development and Marketing Corpn (ADMARC) and, since the mid-1990s, by private traders. Since the implementation, after 1981, of more favourable pricing arrangements, together with the introduction of new hybrid varieties, efforts have been made to diversify the range of commercial smallholder crops, to improve the productivity of

food and export crops and to raise rural incomes. A growing horticultural sector is expanding into a variety of export crops, from the more traditional cabbages, tomatoes and onions to such items as chestnuts, nutmeg, fennel and vanilla. Malawi also produced 2,000 tons of tung nuts in 1999, the oil from which is used in paints and varnishes as a drying agent, and to provide a water-resistant finish. In September 1997 the Malawi Export Promotion Council proposed that the best alternative export crop to tobacco was paprika, which until then was being produced only on a small scale by two companies. Assistance was obtained from several donors, led by the International Development Association (IDA). The IDA has also helped to finance, in association with the International Fund for Agricultural Development (IFAD), a scheme instigated in 1988 to improve the availability of credit to small-scale farmers. This scheme formed part of government plans to double the coverage of seasonal credit to about 30% of smallholders by 1995. Efforts to expand commercial production of crops, especially for export, and to raise rural incomes took two forms—the expansion of commercial smallholding schemes and the National Rural Development Programme (NRDP). The 20-year NRDP, introduced in 1977, centred on eight principal agricultural development regions, covering one-fifth of the country; by 1985 more than 80% of Malawi's smallholders were involved in the programme. The scheme was aimed at increasing crop yields by encouraging simple improvements in farming techniques, with greater use of fertilizers, pest control and irrigation. The programme was intended to stimulate farmers with very small plots (40% of all smallholders) to achieve self-sufficiency in food production, and to enable larger smallholders to produce a surplus for market. However, growth in smallholder output lost momentum during the late 1980s, amounting to only 2.6% in 1988, compared with growth of 7% in the estate sector; the NRDP was consequently suspended in that year. In 1998 the government introduced a new smallholder initiative, the Starter Pack Scheme, in which about 3m. smallholder farmers were to receive a pack containing 10 kg of improved-yield maize, sorghum and legume seeds and 10 kg of fertilizers. The scheme sought to increase smallholder maize production by 15,000 tons. The liberalization of agricultural marketing and production arrangements undertaken by the Muluzi government in the mid-1990s contributed, together with favourable weather conditions, to substantial increases in smallholder production, estimated by the IMF to amount to 34% in 1995 and 40% in 1996. Nevertheless, in 1998 fertilizer prices rose by an average 56% for the three most commonly used types, owing to the sharp depreciation of the kwacha.

Livestock improvements have made the country self-sufficient in meat and liquid milk. The national herd comprised 1.4m. sheep and goats, 800,000 cattle and 240,000 pigs in 1998. Traditionally, almost all livestock has been kept by smallholders, but in the 1990s the government began encouraging beef production as a diversification away from tobacco for the large estates, as global demand for tobacco continued to decline. In June 2000 an outbreak of foot-and-mouth disease occurred in the northern district of Mzimba, placing 35,000 head of cattle at risk. Fish provides about 70% of animal protein consumption, and the fishing sector is thought to employ about 220,000 people, but the annual catch decreased during 1990–95 by 9.3% per annum, to 53,700 metric tons in 1995, compared with a peak of 74,100 tons in 1990. The annual catch totalled 63,600 tons in 1996, but declined to 56,300 tons in 1997. Much of the commercial fishing activity centres on Nkhotakota, on the western shore of Lake Malawi. The lake has more than 500 species of fish, including several species of tilapia, such as *chambo* (known as *kambuli* when young) and *makumba*; the tilapia catch in 1997 was 4,494 tons. Fish stocks in some of Malawi's lakes have been almost obliterated by overfishing (as drought reduces crops and impels more people to fish in order to survive), by declining water levels and by pollution. The good maize crop of 1999 was expected to relieve some of this pressure on lake stocks. In May 2000 the Danish International Development Agency pledged US $1.4m. to reclaim Lake Chilwa, which covers an area of 10,426 sq km and is home to 10 species of fish. The lake had been suffering from agro-chemical pollution and also from the proliferation of non-native fast-growing aquatic plants, such as water hyacinth and mesquite, which block out the sunlight on which many native species depend for survival. In July 2000 it was reported that overfishing had resulted in a complete cessation of fish exports in 1999.

Timber and pulpwood plantations have been developed since the early 1970s, with the area under state plantations totalling 20,800 ha in 1985. In addition, 54,000 ha of pine and eucalyptus were planted on the Viphya plateau, in the north, to supply a pulp and paper project. The project focused on development of part of the Viphya plantation, and the construction of processing facilities. The scheme aimed eventually to provide employment for several thousand people, not only in forestry but also in infrastructural development, which includes the construction of a port on the lake at Chintheche and a new town. The total area under forests in 1990 was 35,000 sq km. Acacia, conifers and baobab trees grow in the highlands. Malawi holds the responsibility for the South African Development Community (SADC) Forestry Sector Co-ordinating Unit and has the highest rate of deforestation of all the SADC states, at 1.6% per annum.

Major Exports

Malawi is the second-largest producer of tobacco in Africa, after Zimbabwe. The crop sustains some 6,500 estates and provides a cash income for about 66,000 tenant smallholders. It is by far the most important export, accounting for an estimated 64.4% of total export earnings in 1996, a less than optimal year, as the quality of the crop was reduced, owing to excessive rainfall. Malawi is the only significant African producer of burley, which is the most important of the six types of tobacco cultivated in Malawi. Output of this variety achieved record levels in several consecutive years after 1991, the first year in which its cultivation on smallholdings was permitted (the production of burley had previously been confined to estates), and quotas for burley production on smallholdings were eliminated. The importance of burley increased greatly in the early 1980s, when strong world demand encouraged a major expansion in output. Output of flue-cured tobacco, which traditionally has been grown only on estates, and of the four types of tobacco traditionally cultivated by smallholders (dark-fire-cured, southern-dark-fired, sun/air-cured and oriental) is declining. The average price fetched for Malawi flue-cured in 1998 was US $1.35 per kg, down from $1.66 in 1997; in comparison, Zimbabwe's 1998 flue-cured crop earned on average $2.06 per kg, down from $2.46 in 1997. However, when the 1999 auction season opened in April, Malawi leaf fetched an average of $2.20 per kg in the first week, raising hopes that the dismal performance of 1998 might not be repeated after all. Forecasts at June 1999 were that the sector would record a $16m. deficit, as against an $80m. loss in 1998. The government is trying to improve smallholder production and output of flue-cured tobacco through instructional and training programmes aimed at improving yields, but low international demand in the late 1990s placed heavy downward pressure on prices. In May 1998 one auction floor in northern Malawi was closed when farmers objected to prices of less than 100 US cents per kg, and even at the Lilongwe and Blantyre auction floors, prices fell by 50% for flue-cured and by 30% for burley in 1998. When the 2000 auction season opened in April, prices failed to rise above US $2.00 per kg (at one point declining to 10 cents per kg), and growers suspended sales. Malawi's tobacco industry was left to consider its mixed prospects; global demand remained sluggish, but the tense political situation in Zimbabwe in 2000 was placing downward pressure on supply.

Malawi is, after Kenya, Africa's second-largest producer and exporter of tea. In 1995 Malawi had about 20,000 ha planted with tea: 88% of the land under cultivation was controlled by large estates, and the remainder was worked by 5,200 smallholders. Output of tea rose from 34,500 tons in 1995 to 46,102 tons in 1998; the 1999 harvest was estimated at some 43,000 tons. In 1994 Malawi accounted for almost 14% of all African tea exports. Tea provided about 12% of Malawi's total export earnings in 1998. The United Kingdom is by far the most important foreign purchaser. The tea sector was confronted in 1997 by the imposition of an 8% levy on all tea exports (reduced to 4% in the 1997/98 budget), together with a significant fall in world demand for the Indochinese variety of tea predominant in Malawi. Efforts by the government to persuade the country's tea growers to transfer to a more popular hybrid met with strong resistance, despite the establishment by the EU of a US $8m. fund, intended to provide an income for growers until newly planted bushes became productive.

Much of Malawi's sugar production, amounting to some 129,000 metric tons per year, is consumed locally. The principal foreign customer is the EU, followed by the USA. The Sugar Co of Malawi (Sucoma) owns two sugar factories in Chikwawa District, Southern Region, and in Nkhotakota, Central Region. In 1997 Lonrho of the United Kingdom, which had owned a majority share of Sucoma, sold its holding to Illovo Sugar Corpn of South Africa, and in November of that year Sucoma carried out a share flotation on the Malawi Stock Exchange. Despite allegations of smuggling and corruption in the sugar-distribution sector, the price of Sucoma's shares rose by 64% in kwacha terms in the first six months of trading. The Dwangwa sugar project, covering some 5,250 ha of the Central Region, commenced operations in 1979. In 1996 export earnings from sugar provided 7.8% of total export receipts. Lonrho announced a sugar expansion project to meet increasing local demand in 1992, and production of raw sugar increased considerably in 1994, to 185,000 metric tons, following the completion of the expansion programme at Nchalo. Malawi produced 1.75m. tons of sugar cane in 1998.

Malawi's output of seed cotton rose from 36,381 tons in 1998 to an estimated 38,000 tons in 1999, yielding 25,400 tons of cottonseed and 9,900 tons of cotton lint in that year. ADMARC agreed to buy the 1999/2000 crop at a price of 8–10 US cents per kg of lint, but farmers, whose costs had increased significantly, were not satisfied with this offer, and in May 2000 some threatened to burn their lint in protest against the low prices.

INDUSTRY

Development of Malawi's extremely limited industrial base was accorded high priority at independence, and subsequent rapid expansion increased manufacturing output by an average of 11% per year in the 1970s. During the early 1980s growth slowed to less than 3% per year, owing to a combination of factors, including the impact of drought on domestic demand and the scarcity of foreign exchange for imports (the sector is heavily dependent on imports). Manufacturing entered a recession after 1985, but by 1988 the sector recovered slightly, benefiting from the effects of the trade and industrial policy adjustment programme, and from the associated influx of donor funds. Output subsequently contracted, partly as a result of the aid ban. Industry (including manufacturing, construction and power) contributed 16.7% of GDP (at constant 1994 prices) in 1998.

Government encouragement of private enterprise led initially to the attraction of foreign private direct investment and management expertise, especially in collaboration with the government-owned Malawi Development Corpn (MDC), established in 1964. In common with other major parastatal bodies, however, the MDC became subject to major reorganization and management restructuring in 1985. Small-scale industrial development has been promoted by the Small Enterprise Development Organization of Malawi (SEDOM). The single largest industrial sector concern during the period when Dr Banda held power was the Press Corpn. Nominally a private company but indirectly controlled by Banda, Press had interests throughout the modern sector of the economy. Often in joint-venture arrangements with foreign companies, these interests included tobacco and sugar estates, cattle ranching, ethanol production, civil engineering, transport, retail and wholesale trade, property development, and banking and insurance. The proposed flotation of Press Corpn shares on the stock exchange (see below) continued to be delayed, however, owing mainly to a dispute over ownership between the government and the Malawi Congress Party. In 1997 it was announced that the Malawi Iron and Steel Corpn and Plastic Products Corpn were to be privatized. In June 1999 the management of all parastatal enterprises was undergoing reorganization. The government targeted 30 enterprises for privatization, of which nine had been privatized by October 1999 and a further five had been 'brought to the point of sale'. Some of the more significant divestitures planned included assets held by the MDC and ADMARC, as well as the remaining government shares in the Commercial Bank of Malawi.

Malawi has provided an attractive range of incentives for potential investors, including low-cost estate sites, tariff protection, exclusive licensing where justified, generous investment allowances and unrestricted repatriation of capital, profits and dividends. However, the rate of new investment has been inhibited by the small size of the local market and the limited possibilities for exports. Although new investment has not created as many new jobs as the government had hoped, owing to the capital-intensive nature of some operations, employment in industry more than doubled between 1980 and 1992. In November 1999 Malawi's textile industry was dealt a severe blow when South Africa banned the import of some Malawian textiles and imposed a prohibitively high duty on others. South Africa accused Malawi of being a conduit through which cheap Asian-manufactured textiles were flooding the region's markets, a charge which Malawi denied. After the ban, six of the 14 Malawian textile-exporting companies closed down, with the reported loss of 3,000 jobs. In July 2000, following several months of bilateral discussions, it was reported that Malawian textile exports to South Africa would resume before the end of the year.

Mining

Deposits of a number of minerals, including bauxite, asbestos, coal, phosphates, gemstones, uranium, vermiculite, granite, glass sands, graphite and several types of construction stone, have been discovered, but only a few industrial minerals have so far been exploited to any extent, notably limestone by the Portland Cement Co (Malawi). During the 1980s the company rehabilitated its clinker and cement works and expanded its quarry at Changalame, with the aim of producing a small surplus of limestone for export. Cement output stood at approximately 120,000 metric tons in 1996. There has been some exploitation of Malawi's coal reserves; production at the Kaziwiziwi mine near Livingstonia, in northern Malawi, was terminated in 1984, after less than a year's operation, because it was deemed to be uneconomic. The state-owned Mining Investment and Development Corpn (MIDCOR) later reopened the mine. After Kaziwiziwi reached depletion, coal production transferred in 1992 to the Mchenga mine, which was estimated to contain some 2.3m. metric tons of bituminous coal, with a further 20m. tons in the vicinity. Production averaged 7,500 tons per month in 1998, for use in domestic and regional industries. In June 1999 the government announced that a private-sector buyer was to be sought for the whole of its 100% holding in Mchenga Coal Mines Ltd, which at full capacity could produce 8,000 tons per month, supplying a regional demand of about 12,500 tons per month. Further coal deposits, of poorer quality, lie at Ngana and Mwabvi. In 1989 large high-quality phosphate reserves were discovered, which could potentially be utilized for local fertilizer production. Local fertilizer production would be of great benefit to farmers and would help reduce the import bill, but development of the deposits would require a substantial capital investment. Clays suitable for use in the production of ceramics have also been identified.

Reserves of vermiculite exist at Fereme, and in 1997 a feasibility study was carried out on the prospects for the export of this mineral to Zimbabwe. Semi-precious stones are mined, mostly on an artisanal basis; in 1997 Minex, a joint venture between MIDCOR and a South African company, was involved in the rehabilitation of facilities at Chimwadzulu for the extraction of corundum, including some sapphires and rubies. In 1997 the Geological Survey Department reported that deposits of gold had been found at Mwanza and on the outskirts of Lilongwe and that there were indications of diamond reserves at Livingstonia. An international mining forum was to take place in Malawi in August 2000, following a survey that led to the discovery of deposits of diamonds, other gemstones, gold, marble and granite.

Cost factors have prevented the exploitation of Malawi's most important mineral discovery so far, the bauxite reserves in the Mulanje area, which have been assessed at almost 29m. metric tons of ore, containing an average of 43.9% alumina. Their development would involve heavy transport costs, owing to the remote location of the area, supplemented by further transport costs to the coast, making their exploitation uneconomic in present world market conditions. The feasibility of the project could improve if development of Malawi's hydroelectric capacity were to result in sufficient low-cost power to meet the substan-

tial requirements of alumina smelting. Indeed, a major restraint on the sector's expansion is that current levels of electricity generation are insufficient for most heavy industrial mining.

Power

The Electricity Supply Commission of Malawi (ESCOM) operates both thermal and hydroelectric power stations in its grid; the latter supply 85% of the central grid's generating capacity of 190 MW. Three plants on the Middle Shire river account for 76% of hydroelectric capacity: Tedzani (40 MW); Nkula A (24 MW), which was completed in 1985; and Nkula B (80 MW). Outside the grid, ESCOM operates four small diesel sets in remote areas in the north, and in 1998 there were 30 MW of privately-owned capacity, of which about 50% was operated by the sugar estates. Although the central grid is currently operating at below capacity (with sales of 800m. kWh in 1995), ESCOM has invested in new capacity, in an attempt to satisfy projected future demand, as well as reinforcing the existing grid. In April 2000 ESCOM announced the completion of a seven-year hydroelectric power scheme, at a cost of K5,900m., which was expected to result in an increase in generating capacity of 128 MW by 2003. Lack of foreign exchange for spare parts resulted in interruptions to the electricity supply in the mid-1990s. Even with the expansion of electricity output, the majority of Malawi's energy requirements are supplied by fuel wood, which has accounted for some 90% of energy needs (compared with 3% for hydropower, 4% for petroleum products and 1% for coal) in recent years. The Muluzi government has, however, announced that it intends to reduce dependence on this source. In November 1998 electricity tariffs were increased by 35% in a bid to place ESCOM on a firmer financial footing in preparation for its privatization. A further increase of 15% was imposed in July 1999. Petroleum and diesel fuel constitute Malawi's principal imports; in 1995 petroleum products comprised 10.7% of the value of total imports; in 1996 fuel imports totalled approximately 220m. litres. In 1982 a factory to produce ethyl alcohol (ethanol) from molasses went into production, and in its first five years of operation it produced 6.8m. litres of ethanol annually, for 20% blending with petrol, equivalent to 10% of Malawi's petrol needs. Full design capacity of 8.5m. litres per year was reached in 1988. The government intended to increase ethanol production to 20m. litres per year in the 1990s, subject to its commercial value. Just over 16,000 tons of coal were imported in 1988 (compared with 70,000 tons in 1982). Serious shortfalls in the supply of petroleum products occurred in the mid-1990s, prompting research (funded by the World Bank) which was to produce contingency plans, and to evaluate a minimum level below which rationing of petroleum products should automatically take effect. The retail prices of petroleum prices were increased by 55%–80% in October 1998, as part of the ongoing structural-reform programme.

Transport and Tourism

Malawi Railways developed an internal rail network covering 789 km, extending to Mehinji on the Zambian border. It also operated 465 km of the 830-km single-line rail link from Salima, on the central lake shore, to Mozambique's Indian Ocean port of Beira. Another rail link provided access to the port of Nacala, north of Beira. The loss-making railway underwent restructuring in preparation for its privatization, and was offered for sale in July 1998. Seven international companies entered bids, including South Africa's Spoornet, but the winning bid came from CFM/SDCN, a consortium owned by Mozambique's Empresa Nacional dos Portos e Caminhos de Ferro de Moçambique (CFM) and the USA's Railroad Development Corpn., and also including Portugal's Tertir and South Africa's Rennies. In December 1999 Malawi Railways was transferred to its new owners, who pledged to invest US $26m. into the Malawian railway system. The railway was subsequently renamed the Central East African Railway Co. At the time of transfer, only about 10% of the rolling stock was operational, but by June 2000 the consortium reported that it had returned nearly 90% to active service.

Moves to provide Malawi with a cheaper alternative outlet to the sea began in 1983/84, when the United Kingdom upgraded the 65-km unpaved road linking Karonga, near the northern end of Lake Malawi, to Mbeya, in southern Tanzania, so providing

Malawi with access to the Tanzania–Zambia railway as far as the port of Dar es Salaam. A new 'northern corridor' scheme completed in 1992 at a cost of US $110m. involved a 750-km section of the Tazara railway line between Dar es Salaam and Mbeya, a 250-km road link from Mbeya to Chilumba port at the northern end of Lake Malawi, and a 400-km journey along the lake to Chipoka port, to link with the southern transport network.

Malawi was also to benefit from the US $600m. 'Beira corridor' scheme, supported by a group of international donors under the guidance of the SADC. Work on the Beira railway line began in 1985. At the same time rehabilitation of Malawi's rail link to Nacala was being undertaken. In October 1989, after a cease-fire was agreed along the line in Mozambique, the Nacala link was reopened. Traffic resumed slowly, owing to the disrepair of the line and to the uncertain security situation.

Malawi's road network, totalling 15,137 km (21.2% tarred) in 1997, is being steadily upgraded, in particular the lake-shore Kamuzu Highway, which provides the main land link between the remote Northern Region and the Central and Southern Regions. Feeder and crop-extraction roads are also being extended. Road transport grew steadily during the period when Malawi's rail outlets were closed. The World Bank's IDA announced a credit of US $30m. in June 1999 towards the maintenance and rehabilitation of Malawi's roads, in a bid to reform road-sector financing and to address a backlog of road-maintenance projects. Japan extended a grant of $12m. in the same month for the construction of a bridge over the Shire river in the south, to improve access to the Nacala corridor.

Malawi has one main international airport at Lilongwe, three domestic airports and the former main international airport at Blantyre, which still serves some regional airlines. Lilongwe is regularly served by a number of international and regional airlines, as well as by the national carrier Air Malawi. In 2000 the decision as to whether to privatize part or all of Air Malawi was still awaited. Airline officials expressed a preference for seeking a 'strategic partner' rather than offering the entire company for sale. Plans were announced to divide the carrier, in July 2000, into three separate entities; Air Malawi Cargo was to concentrate on cargo services, Airport Handling on all ground duties and Air Malawi on commercial passenger services.

The government is currently aiming to expand the tourism sector, which has grown substantially since Malawi began to develop its considerable tourist potential in the mid-1970s. The sector was, however, adversely affected in the 1980s by recession in South Africa, which accounts for the majority of visitors to Malawi, but recovered in the early 1990s. Tourism receipts in 1997 totalled US $7m. The number of visitors reached 205,248 in that year, but declined to 176,573 in 1998. Political instability in Zimbabwe in 2000 was expected to deter many tourists from visiting any part of the region. In March 1997 shares in Blantyre Hotels were floated on the Malawi Stock Exchange. In 1999 the government was actively seeking foreign-investment partners in such tourism projects as hotels and lodges around Lake Malawi and in game-viewing areas, time-share developments, hotels and restaurants in the main cities and in lakeside resorts, cruise boats on Lake Malawi and casinos.

EXTERNAL TRADE AND PAYMENTS

Malawi's prospects for sustained development depend upon the achievement of improved export performance, especially in the industrial sector. The primary producer's dependence on international commodity trade is heightened in Malawi's case by a lack, so far, of exportable minerals. Agricultural products still account for about 90% of domestic export receipts, with tobacco providing more than two-thirds of total foreign exchange earnings at a time when global demand for the controversial crop is weakening. Exports of manufactured goods, mainly clothing, footwear and cattle cake, increased during the 1980s, but still provided only 6% of all export earnings in 1996. Even this low level was expected to decline after South Africa severely restricted imports of Malawian textile products in late 1999. However, according to the IMF, non-traditional exports increased by more than 150% per annum during 1995–96 in terms of volume, albeit from a restricted base. The principal imports in the 1990s were diesel fuel and petroleum (by far the largest

item, accounting for 11% of all imports in 1996), machinery and transport equipment, piece goods, and medical and pharmaceutical goods. In 1997 merchandise imports c.i.f. of US $783m. exceeded merchandise exports f.o.b. of $567m., leaving a visible trade deficit of $216m. It is estimated that imports c.i.f. in 1998 amounted to $717m., exceeding exports f.o.b. of $509m. by $208m. In 1996 the Eastern and Southern Africa Trade and Development Bank announced the funding of a structured pre-shipment financing facility of $50m. to support the growth of exports from Malawi.

Malawi's major trading partners have not changed over the years, although the volume of trade with the United Kingdom has declined. In 1996 the main export destinations were the USA, South Africa, Germany and Japan, while the principal suppliers of Malawi's imports were South Africa and Zimbabwe.

Malawi has sustained a deficit on the current account of its balance of payments in every year since 1966, with a particularly sharp deterioration in 1979 and 1980, when the shortfall increased from an average of 8% of GDP to 23.5%. However, following the introduction of the economic stabilization programme in 1981, some recovery was noted. The current-account deficit stood at US $162m. in 1995, down from $450m. in 1994. The IMF assessed Malawi's current-account deficit (including official transfers) at 9.3% of GDP in 1997, at an estimated 8.9% of GDP in 1998 and at a projected 8.8% of GDP in 1999. The Muluzi government's recovery programme aimed to achieve an overall balance-of-payments surplus of US $81m. for 1998, a target which was not only met but was exceeded, with a surplus of $91m. recorded for that year. The overall balance was expected to fall to a surplus of $65m. for 1999. Against a target of gross international reserves sufficient to cover 3.5 months' worth of imports, gross reserves covering 4.5 months' worth were attained.

PUBLIC FINANCE AND BANKING

With the introduction of the first economic adjustment programme in 1981, the overall budget deficit began to improve, and by 1985/86 it had fallen to 6.6% of GDP. However, this was largely attributable to a sharp decrease in development expenditure, which declined by an annual average of 2% in real terms. Owing to a rise in the costs of debt-servicing and transport, and to an increase in losses by parastatal enterprises, recurrent expenditure expanded, in real terms, by 10% per year, resulting in a deficit that had to be financed by domestic and foreign borrowing. The budget deficit rose to 9.1% of GDP in 1992/93. The 1994/95 budget, presented in March 1994, was widely seen as an attempt to influence the elections, with its emphasis on social expenditure and the reduction in the number of income-tax payers. The government's pre-election spending contributed to a deficit of about K500m. in May 1994, 2.5 times the figure agreed with the IMF. A supplementary budget in October 1994 helped to stabilize, if briefly, the downward-floating kwacha, but did not prevent inflation from reaching 37% by the end of the year. The regular budget of March 1995 attempted to reduce the deficit by controlling expenditure, enhancing revenue collection and stimulating agricultural exports, which were favoured by the low kwacha. Even so, the deficit soared, and the World Bank credits the Muluzi government that came to power in 1995 with reducing the budgetary deficit by a full 20 percentage points of GDP over the following two years. In the financial year ending 31 March 1997 the overall budget deficit was K1,086m. (equivalent to 3.1% of GDP). The deficit for 1999, however, was expected to widen to 12.9% of GDP excluding grants, or 5.8% including grants. In October 1999 the government announced that it aimed to reduce the overall fiscal deficit excluding grants to 11.5% of GDP and to limit the domestic primary deficit to 2% of GDP.

The network of banking services includes a central bank, three commercial banks, a savings bank and a development bank. The First Merchant Bank of Kenya commenced banking operations in Malawi in July 1995. Foreign exchange bureaux were also licensed. In 1999 the Muluzi government rescued the failing Malawi Savings Bank (MSB) with funds equivalent to 0.5% of GDP and announced that financial and administrative links between the postal system and the MSB, which had contributed to the latter's financial problems, had largely been severed. The Malawi Stock Exchange was established in March 1995 under guidance from a Zimbabwean company, although once launched it was managed by Malawians. By 1999 six companies were listed.

The Reserve Bank of Malawi began issuing its own notes in 1965, the basic currency unit then being the Malawi pound, which stood at par with sterling. In February 1971 a decimal currency was introduced, with the kwacha, divided into 100 tambala, as the unit of exchange. The exchange rate of the kwacha was originally linked to that of sterling, but an active exchange-rate policy was introduced in 1974. From 1984 the kwacha exchange rate was related to a 'basket' of the currencies of Malawi's seven principal trading partners. As part of the Reserve Bank's management of the exchange rate, the kwacha was subject to regular trade-related devaluations between 1982 and 1994. In February 1994, when the exchange rate was K2.50 = US \$1, the kwacha was 'floated', with the result that it depreciated by 25% in three months, relative to the US dollar. Its decline continued, and by June 1997 the rate was K15.34 = US \$1; a year later, in June 1998, the rate had plunged to K26.50 = US \$1, with devastating effects on domestic prices for all imported items, not least fertilizers and other agricultural inputs. This depreciation contributed to an inflation level of more than 75% in 1994; by March 1997 the annual rate of inflation had been reduced, to 6.7%, according to official figures, or to about 20%, according to other financial sources. As revenue for Malawi's principal export, tobacco, plummeted ever further, in dollar terms, the kwacha's value also declined steeply, reaching K43.99 = US \$1 in June 1999. The kwacha remained stable at about this level for 10 months, but in April 2000, affected by the problems on Malawi's tobacco auction floors (see above), it lost 17% of its value in six weeks.

FOREIGN AID AND GOVERNMENT DEBT

Malawi began to undertake significant commercial borrowing in the mid-1970s, initially to finance development programmes. International organizations replaced bilateral donors as the main source of foreign funding, granting 78.8% of foreign aid given in 1994, with the IDA as the leading multilateral creditor. As a proportion of outstanding debt, commercial borrowing increased from less than 2% in 1976 to more than 24% in 1980. After 1979 non-concessionary borrowing rose sharply, as the government resorted to the banks to help to finance the budget deficit. This led to a substantial increase in total public debt-service payments. 'Paris Club' debt reschedulings in 1982 and 1983 substantially reduced payment obligations, but by 1984 the effects of this relief were coming to an end, and in 1984/85 service payments increased sharply. In 1986/87 they were equivalent to 41% of total export earnings. World Bank figures for 1994 indicate that the Muluzi government inherited a total external debt of \$2,025m., equivalent to 163.2% of Malawi's GNP in that year, compared to US \$830m. in 1980. By the end of 1998 total debt had grown, albeit considerably more slowly, to \$2,444m. In Banda's last year of power foreign reserves had dwindled to \$48m., enough to cover less than three weeks' worth of imports; by January 1997 international reserves had been replenished and stood at \$218m., sufficient to cover about 3.6 months' worth of imports. In January 1999 total disbursed and outstanding foreign debt amounted to \$2,374m., and the IMF expected this figure to rise to \$2,680m. by January 2000 and to \$2,798m. in January 2001. Foreign reserves stood at \$235m. in December 1998, enough to cover 3.5 months' worth of imports; by October 1999 reserves were able to cover 4.5 months' worth of imports.

The United Kingdom was Malawi's major aid donor in the years after independence, and has remained an important source of funding. Similarly, South Africa has been a significant source of donor aid, particularly in providing finance for the

purpose-built capital Lilongwe, where construction of government buildings began in 1968. Other major donors are the EU (currently the main donor overall), France, Canada, the USA, Germany, Denmark, Japan, the African Development Bank, the IDA and the World Bank. In May 1990 the World Bank consultative group on Malawi approved \$508m. in support of the economic recovery programme for 1990/91, but in May 1992 it suspended all non-humanitarian aid, linking future assistance to an improvement in Malawi's human-rights record. Following the multi-party elections in 1994 (see Recent History), Germany, the USA and the United Kingdom all indicated that they would provide increased future levels of aid. The eighth consultative group meeting for Malawi, held in May 1997, agreed enough firm pledges to cover all of Malawi's estimated US \$319m. external financing needs in that year. In December 1998 the consultative group held its meeting in Malawi for the first time and pledged to meet in full Malawi's estimated \$1,250m. financing needs for 1998–2000. At a three-day meeting in Lilongwe in May 2000, 24 international donors pledged balance-of-payments support but also expressed concern over the continuing high rate of inflation and some relapses in the government's commitment to economic reform. One US source reportedly observed that Malawi's budget was 'overburdened by unauthorized and wasteful spending and the inability of parastatals to service their debts'.

In November 1994 the World Bank approved a US \$40m. supplementary financing arrangement under the Entrepreneurship Development and Drought Recovery Credit. Following an unsuccessful adjustment programme, supported by an eight-month IMF stand-by arrangement, the government adopted a comprehensive economic reform programme in 1995. With assistance from the IMF and other donors, it was aimed at achieving GDP growth of 9.9% in 1995 and of 7% annually during 1996–98, at containing the external current-account deficit and at bringing about significant reductions in both the rate of inflation and the budget deficit. A wide-ranging programme of economic liberalization was to include the privatization of many state concerns and the ending of most agricultural monopolies and subsidies, and measures were instituted to promote foreign investment in all sectors. In June 1998 the government announced that it was to remove 21 institutions from the public budget by the end of the year, including organizations involved in mining development, pulpwood production, sports, university education, industrial research and technological development. Public expenditure was to be restricted through the implementation of a cash budget system, the restructuring of parastatal companies and reductions in the public payroll, while government revenue would be enhanced by fiscal reforms, including improved efficiency in the collection of import duties, the planned introduction of a value-added tax and the establishment of an independent National Revenue Authority. A civil service census was conducted in October 1995, and some 20,000 employees were discharged, while restraints were placed on further public recruitment. Donors have expressed some satisfaction at the progress of the Muluzi government's reforms, and the IMF released further loans under its ESAF arrangement in December 1996 and December 1998, worth some \$22m. and \$27m., respectively. However, the economic and infrastructural problems that the Muluzi government inherited in 1994, combined with the agricultural sector's vulnerability to climatic conditions and the country's continuing reliance on tobacco as its main source of foreign exchange, render heavy dependence on foreign aid a continuing necessity. To ensure that this foreign aid continues to be forthcoming, the government will be required to introduce more unpopular measures, such as the retrenchment of at least 1,300 government employees, and will have to reduce the rate of inflation by 10%, lower the fiscal deficit to the equivalent of 1.4% of GDP by 2001, and maintain stricter control over the money supply, which, even by government assessments, grew by 29% in 1999.

Statistical Survey

Sources (unless otherwise indicated): Ministry of Information and Tourism, POB 494, Blantyre; Reserve Bank of Malawi, POB 30063, Capital City, Lilongwe 3; tel. 780600; fax 782752.

Area and Population

AREA, POPULATION AND DENSITY

Area (sq km)	118,484*
Population (census results)	
20 September 1977	5,547,460
1–21 September 1987	
Males	3,867,136
Females	4,121,371
Total	7,988,507
Population (official estimates at mid-year)	
1995	9,788,000
1996	10,114,000
1997	10,441,000
Density (per sq km) at mid-1997	88.1

* 45,747 sq miles. The area includes 24,208 sq km (9,347 sq miles) of inland water.

Ethnic groups (1977 census): Africans 5,532,298; Europeans 6,377; Asians 5,682; others 3,103.

REGIONS (provisional figures at mid-1994)

Region	Area (sq km)*	Estimated population	Density (per sq km)	Regional capital
Southern . . .	31,753	4,980,500	156.9	Blantyre
Central . . .	35,592	3,907,000	109.8	Lilongwe
Northern . . .	26,931	1,145,100	42.5	Mzuzu
Total . . .	94,276	10,032,600	106.4	

* Excluding inland waters, totalling 24,208 sq km.

PRINCIPAL TOWNS (estimated population at mid-1994)

Blantyre . . .	446,800	Mzuzu.	62,700
Lilongwe (capital) .	395,500*	Zomba.	62,700

* Including Limbe.

BIRTHS AND DEATHS (UN estimates, annual averages)

	1980–85	1985–90	1990–95
Birth rate (per 1,000). . . .	53.5	51.9	50.2
Death rate (per 1,000) . . .	21.6	20.7	22.1

Expectation of life (UN estimates, years at birth, 1990–95): 42.0 (males 41.5; females 42.5).

Source: UN, *World Population Prospects: The 1998 Revision.*

ECONOMICALLY ACTIVE POPULATION*
(persons aged 10 to 64 years, 1987 census)

	Males	Females	Total
Agriculture, hunting, forestry and fishing	1,293,606	1,674,327	2,967,933
Mining and quarrying . . .	6,977	187	7,164
Manufacturing	79,293	18,483	97,776
Electricity, gas and water. .	8,306	527	8,833
Construction.	45,006	1,869	46,875
Trade, restaurants and hotels.	75,491	18,954	94,445
Transport, storage and communications	23,323	1,540	24,863
Financing, insurance, real estate and business services . .	4,418	1,172	5,590
Community, social and personal services	113,763	33,276	147,039
Activities not adequately defined .	9,120	2,765	11,885
Total employed	1,659,303	1,753,100	3,412,403
Unemployed	36,549	8,801	45,350
Total labour force	1,695,852	1,761,901	3,457,753

* Excluding armed forces.

Mid-1998 (estimates in '000): Agriculture, etc. 4,138; Total 4,944 (Source: FAO, *Production Yearbook*).

Agriculture

PRINCIPAL CROPS ('000 metric tons)

	1996	1997	1998
Rice (paddy).	73	66	67
Maize	1,793	1,226	1,725
Millet	20	16	19*
Sorghum	55	40	48*
Potatoes*	380	380	385
Cassava (Manioc)*	190	200	200
Dry beans	85*	89	90*
Chick-peas*	39	39	40
Lentils*	1	1	1
Other pulses*	151	151	153
Groundnuts (in shell) . . .	40	69	108
Sunflower seed	18	5	6*
Cottonseed†	55	30	29
Cotton (lint)†	22	12	11
Cabbages*	30	25	26
Tomatoes*	35	30	32
Onions (dry)	25*	15	18*
Other vegetables.	175*	171	172*
Mangoes	34*	30*	32
Bananas*	91	90	90
Plantains*	200	200	202
Citrus fruits*	2	2	2
Other fruit*	184	179	182
Sugar cane	1,860	1,750*	1,750*
Coffee (green)	4†	5†	5*
Tea (made)	37	44*	46
Tobacco (leaves)	142	158	125

* FAO estimate(s).   † Unofficial figure(s).

Source: FAO, *Production Yearbook.*

LIVESTOCK ('000 head, year ending September)

	1996	1997*	1998*
Cattle	700	750	800
Pigs	220	230	240
Sheep	110	110	120
Goats	1,257	1,260	1,270

Poultry (million, year ending September): 14 in 1996; 14* in 1997; 15* in 1998.

* FAO estimate(s).

Source: FAO, *Production Yearbook*.

LIVESTOCK PRODUCTS (FAO estimates, '000 metric tons)

	1996	1997	1998
Beef and veal	16	18	20
Goat meat	5	5	5
Pig meat	11	12	13
Poultry meat	14	14	15
Cows' milk	32	34	36
Hen eggs	18	18	19

Source: FAO, *Production Yearbook*.

Forestry

ROUNDWOOD REMOVALS ('000 cubic metres, excluding bark)

	1995	1996	1997
Sawlogs, veneer logs and logs for sleepers	130	130	130
Other industrial wood	355	361	370
Fuel wood	8,635	8,787	9,007
Total	9,120	9,278	9,507

Source: FAO, *Yearbook of Forest Products*.

SAWNWOOD PRODUCTION
(FAO estimates, '000 cubic metres, including railway sleepers)

	1995	1996	1997
Coniferous (softwood)	30	30	30
Broadleaved (hardwood)	15	15	15
Total	45	45	45

Source: FAO, *Yearbook of Forest Products*.

Fishing

('000 metric tons, live weight)

	1995	1996	1997
Carps, barbels, etc.	0.5	0.5	0.5
Tilapias	3.9	5.1	4.5
Torpedo-shaped catfishes	n.a.	4.6	n.a.
Other freshwater fishes	49.3	53.4	51.3
Total catch	53.7	63.6	56.3

Source: FAO, *Yearbook of Fishery Statistics*.

Mining

('000 metric tons, unless otherwise indicated)

	1996	1997	1998
Coal	69.9	63.2	54.2
Limestone	175.6	258.0	171.9
Lime	3.2	1.9	2.6
Gemstones (kilograms)	848.6	351.2	933.6
Aggregate (cubic metres)	58,700	162,538	182,616

Source: *Mining Annual Review 1999*.

Industry

SELECTED PRODUCTS ('000 metric tons, unless otherwise indicated)

	1992	1993	1994
Raw sugar	200	114	185
Beer ('000 hectolitres)	774	763	811
Cigarettes (million)	1,000	1,020	1,127
Blankets ('000)	1,300	894	895
Cement	108	117	122
Electric energy (million kWh)*	792	795	801

1995: Raw sugar 222,000 metric tons; Cement 120,000 metric tons; Electric energy 803 million kWh*.
1996: Raw sugar 218,000 metric tons.

* Provisional or estimated figure(s).

Source: UN, *Industrial Commodity Statistics Yearbook*.

Finance

CURRENCY AND EXCHANGE RATES

Monetary Units
100 tambala = 1 Malawi kwacha (K).

Sterling, Dollar and Euro Equivalents (28 April 2000)
£1 sterling = 76.299 kwacha;
US $1 = 48.657 kwacha;
€1 = 44.205 kwacha;
1,000 Malawi kwacha = £13.11 = $20.55 = €22.62.

Average Exchange Rate (kwacha per US $)
1997   16.4442
1998   31.0727
1999   44.0881

BUDGET (K million, year ending 30 June)

Revenue*	1997/98†	1998/99‡	1999/2000§
Tax revenue‖	7,928.3	9,800.1	12,139.2
Taxes on income and profits	3,467.7	4,500.0	5,762.0
Companies	1,420.2	1,811.0	2,472.0
Individuals	2,047.6	2,689.0	3,290.0
Taxes on goods and services	2,671.1	3,685.0	5,161.1
Surtax	2,236.7	3,053.8	4,662.0
Excise duties	407.7	599.7	465.0
Taxes on international trade	1,976.4	1,871.5	1,684.0
Import duties	1,708.0	1,833.5	1,648.0
Non-tax revenue	533.3	2,157.1	1,209.6
Treasury Fund receipts	262.0	370.5	372.5
Departmental receipts	136.4	668.9	689.1
Sale of maize	40.0	1,053.0	—
Total	8,461.6	11,957.2	13,348.8

Expenditure	1997/98†	1998/99‡	1999/2000§
General public services . . .	2,420.1	4,536.5	5,599.0
Defence	461.4	456.9	637.8
Public order and safety . . .	501.1	585.9	843.2
Education	2,442.7	2,154.4	3,583.9
Health	992.3	1,945.6	2,668.1
Social security and welfare .	1,280.0	837.9	1,649.4
Housing and community amenities	437.1	996.3	1,356.6
Recreational, cultural and other social services	163.7	102.6	346.0
Economic affairs and services . .	1,678.2	1,931.4	4,646.8
Agriculture and natural resources	776.0	963.3	2,524.2
Transport and communications .	643.0	616.5	1,508.3
Unallocable expenditure . . .	2,836.4	3,705.2	1,711.4
Total	**13,213.0**	**17,252.7**	**23,042.2**
Current¶	11,404.9	12,770.3	14,505.7
Capital	1,808.1	4,482.4	8,536.5

* Excluding grants received (K million): 2,092.4 (provisional) in 1997/98; 4,251.0 (revised estimate) in 1998/99; 7,900.0 (forecast) in 1999/2000.
† Figures are provisional and refer to the 15 months beginning 1 April 1997.
‡ Revised estimates.
§ Forecasts.
‖ After deduction of tax refunds (K million): 218.6 (provisional) in 1997/98; 285.0 (revised estimate) in 1998/99; 510.0 (forecast) in 1999/2000.
¶ Including interest on debt (K million): 2,080.8 (provisional) in 1997/98; 2,286.9 (revised estimate) in 1998/99; 1,659.0 (forecast) in 1999/2000.
Source: Ministry of Finance.

INTERNATIONAL RESERVES (US $ million at 31 December)

	1997	1998	1999
Gold*	0.54	0.55	0.54
IMF special drawing rights . .	0.09	6.82	0.39
Reserve position in IMF . .	3.00	3.15	3.07
Foreign exchange	159.15	259.77	247.15
Total	**162.78**	**270.28**	**251.15**

* National valuation.
Source: IMF, *International Financial Statistics.*

MONEY SUPPLY (K million at 31 December)

	1997	1998	1999
Currency outside banks . .	1,375.33	1,999.39	2,992.02
Demand deposits at commercial banks	1,824.45	2,771.19	3,641.75
Total money (incl. others) .	**3,200.64**	**4,999.24**	**6,651.15**

Source: IMF, *International Financial Statistics.*

COST OF LIVING (National Consumer Price Index; base: 1995 = 100)

	1997	1998	1999
All items	150.2	194.9	282.4

Source: IMF, *International Financial Statistics.*

NATIONAL ACCOUNTS

Expenditure on the Gross Domestic Product
(K million at current prices)

	1996	1997	1998
Government final consumption expenditure	4,634.2	5,241.5	7,426.2
Private final consumption expenditure	31,175.9	35,934.8	44,456.5
Increase in stocks	900.0	1,000.0	1,288.6
Gross fixed capital formation . .	3,404.5	4,079.7	5,973.3
Total domestic expenditure .	**39,687.4***	**46,254.0***	**59,144.6**
Exports of goods and services . .	7,743.8	9,619.3	15,468.0
Less Imports of goods and services	11,895.6	14,314.5	22,207.7
GDP in purchasers' values . .	**35,535.6**	**41,558.8**	**52,404.9**
GDP at constant 1978 prices .	**1,136.8**	**1,209.5**	**1,285.6**

* Including adjustment.
Source: IMF, *International Financial Statistics.*

Gross Domestic Product by Economic Activity
(K million at constant 1994 prices)

	1996	1997	1998
Agriculture, forestry and fishing .	4,279.7	4,419.8	4,582.8
Mining and quarrying . . .	100.2	106.7	111.9
Manufacturing	1,661.5	1,672.8	1,659.1
Electricity and water	151.8	160.7	170.5
Construction	218.1	222.3	232.6
Distribution	2,645.1	2,971.2	3,125.9
Transport and communications .	492.8	530.0	529.6
Finance, insurance and business services	852.1	917.9	908.4
Ownership of dwellings . .	171.5	176.4	181.5
Private social services . . .	236.5	260.1	262.0
Government services . . .	1,167.6	1,200.5	1,220.9
Sub-total	**11,976.9**	**12,638.4**	**12,985.2**
Less Imputed bank service charges	312.3	392.0	333.1
GDP at factor cost . . .	**11,664.6**	**12,246.4**	**12,652.1**

BALANCE OF PAYMENTS (US $ million)

	1992	1993	1994
Exports of goods f.o.b. . .	399.9	317.5	362.6
Imports of goods f.o.b. . .	−415.0	−340.2	−639.0
Trade balance	**−15.0**	**−22.8**	**−276.4**
Exports of services . . .	28.5	30.0	22.2
Imports of services . . .	−338.8	−260.1	−233.7
Balance on goods and services	**−325.4**	**−252.9**	**−488.0**
Other income received . .	6.3	2.2	1.9
Other income paid . . .	−83.4	−70.9	−87.8
Balance on goods, services and income	**−402.5**	**−321.6**	**−573.9**
Current transfers received . .	155.2	167.9	139.7
Current transfers paid . .	−37.7	−11.9	−15.4
Current balance . . .	**−284.9**	**−165.6**	**−449.6**
Investment assets . . .	11.9	−11.8	—
Investment liabilities . . .	81.7	200.6	122.0
Net errors and omissions . .	144.8	0.7	292.6
Overall balance . . .	**−46.5**	**24.0**	**−35.1**

Source: IMF, *International Financial Statistics.*

External Trade

PRINCIPAL COMMODITIES (distribution by SITC, US $ million)

Imports c.i.f.	1994	1995
Food and live animals	75.9	52.9
Cereals and cereal preparations	57.6	42.1
Maize (unmilled)	37.8	25.8
Mineral fuels, lubricants, etc.	41.2	55.8
Petroleum, petroleum products, etc.	39.7	53.3
Refined petroleum products	37.5	51.1
Animal and vegetable oils, fats and waxes	11.0	15.3
Fixed vegetable oils and fats	9.7	14.7
Chemicals and related products	81.6	112.6
Medicinal and pharmaceutical products	11.3	39.7
Medicaments	8.0	36.7
Manufactured fertilizers	26.7	37.7
Nitrogenous fertilizers (mineral or chemical)	17.7	21.6
Urea	7.2	10.5
Artificial resins, plastic materials, etc.	13.5	12.2
Products of polymerization, etc.	11.7	11.1
Basic manufactures	112.4	90.8
Rubber manufactures	15.0	8.3
Rubber tyres, tubes, etc.	11.6	5.4
Paper, paperboard, etc.	18.6	15.9
Paper and paperboard (not cut to size or shape)	13.3	12.9
Textile yarn, fabrics, etc.	24.8	25.6
Iron and steel	19.5	15.1
Universals, plates and sheets	11.1	6.1
Machinery and transport equipment	175.3	138.0
Machinery specialized for particular industries	36.0	21.4
General industrial machinery, equipment and parts	18.8	14.1
Telecommunications and sound equipment	15.6	4.5
Other electrical machinery, apparatus, etc.	17.3	15.9
Road vehicles and parts*	66.3	64.9
Passenger motor cars (excl. buses)	15.3	14.7
Motor vehicles for goods transport, etc.	26.1	30.1
Goods vehicles (lorries and trucks)	22.9	29.1
Miscellaneous manufactured articles	31.6	27.2
Total (incl. others)	539.3	500.5

* Excluding tyres, engines and electrical parts.

Exports f.o.b.	1994	1995
Food and live animals	79.9	79.6
Vegetables and fruit	4.9	10.9
Sugar, sugar preparation and honey	24.8	19.7
Sugar and honey	24.8	19.7
Raw beet and cane sugars	17.6	16.2
Coffee, tea, cocoa and spices	45.3	44.2
Coffee and coffee substitutes	14.8	15.5
Coffee (incl. husks and skins) and substitutes containing coffee	14.8	15.5
Unroasted coffee, husks and skins	14.8	15.5
Tea and maté	30.0	26.6
Tea	30.0	26.6
Beverages and tobacco	198.7	300.0
Tobacco and tobacco manufactures	198.2	295.7
Unmanufactured tobacco; tobacco refuse	196.7	293.8
Unstripped tobacco	67.9	70.8
Stripped or partly stripped tobacco	128.9	223.1
Crude materials (inedible) except fuels	10.5	11.3
Basic manufactures	20.0	17.0
Textile yarn, fabrics, etc.	15.1	11.1
Woven cotton fabrics (excl. narrow or special fabrics)	12.0	7.1
Unbleached fabrics (not mercerized)	10.8	6.5
Machinery and transport equipment	13.3	8.6
Miscellaneous manufactured articles	12.6	15.0
Clothing and accessories (excl. footwear)	11.2	13.4
Total (incl. others)	337.1	433.4

Source: UN, *International Trade Statistics Yearbook*.

1996 (K million): Total imports c.i.f. 9,544.9; Total exports f.o.b. 7,214.1.
1997 (K million): Total imports c.i.f. 12,847.7; Total exports f.o.b. 8,827.4.
1998 (K million): Total imports c.i.f. 19,792.9; Total exports f.o.b. 16,410.

Sources (for 1996–98): Malawi Government, *Economic Report*, and IMF, *International Financial Statistics*.

PRINCIPAL TRADING PARTNERS (US $ million)*

Imports c.i.f.	1994	1995
Austria	11.0	8.0
China, People's Repub.	17.6	15.8
France (incl. Monaco)	12.7	8.4
Germany	21.7	46.6
India	21.7	15.9
Italy	9.2	5.0
Japan	35.1	24.9
Korea, Repub.	6.9	5.6
Malaysia	4.0	6.8
Mozambique	4.4	15.1
SACU†	174.1	159.8
United Kingdom	82.2	78.9
USA	18.4	13.1
Zambia	13.4	6.1
Zimbabwe	55.0	39.9
Total (incl. others)	539.3	500.4

Exports f.o.b.							1994	1995
Australia	.	.	.	.	.	.	4.2	5.6
Austria	.	.	.	.	.	.	3.4	3.6
Belgium-Luxembourg	.	.	.	.		8.2	6.5
China, People's Repub.	.	.	.	.		4.1	1.5
Czech Republic.	.	.	.	.	.	1.9	4.7
France (incl. Monaco)	.	.	.	.		10.4	43.3
Germany	.	.	.	.	.	.	51.7	58.9
Hungary	.	.	.	.	.	.	4.8	6.4
India	.	.	.	.	.	.	—	4.7
Japan	.	.	.	.	.	.	27.5	21.8
Mozambique	.	.	.	.	.		7.6	9.9
Netherlands	.	.	.	.	.		26.0	39.4
New Zealand	.	.	.	.	.		3.4	2.5
SACU†	.	.	.	.	.	.	45.5	44.8
Spain	.	.	.	.	.	.	4.3	12.6
Switzerland-Liechtenstein	.	.	.		15.9	17.5
Tanzania	.	.	.	.	.		2.2	6.5
United Kingdom	.	.	.	.		41.2	30.0
USA	.	.	.	.	.	.	32.6	57.0
Zambia	.	.	.	.	.	.	4.1	5.1
Zimbabwe	.	.	.	.	.		8.0	7.1
Total (incl. others)	.	.	.	.		337.1	433.3

* Imports by country of production; exports by country of last consignment.
† Southern African Customs Union, comprising Botswana, Lesotho, Namibia, South Africa and Swaziland.
Source: UN, *International Trade Statistics Yearbook*.

Transport

RAILWAYS (traffic)

	1996	1997	1998
Passengers carried ('000) . .	339,000	452,000	349,000
Freight ('000 metric tons). .	132,000	167,000	197,000

Source: Ministry of Finance and Economic Planning, *Economic Report 1999*.

ROAD TRAFFIC (estimates, motor vehicles in use at 31 December)

	1994	1995	1996
Passenger cars . . .	23,520	25,480	27,000
Lorries and vans . . .	26,000	29,000	29,700

Source: International Road Federation, *World Road Statistics*.

SHIPPING
Inland waterways (lake transport)

	1996	1997	1998
Freight ('000 metric tons). .	13,000	10,000	14,000
Passengers carried ('000) . .	191,000	133,000	115,000

Source: Ministry of Finance and Economic Planning, *Economic Report 1999*.

CIVIL AVIATION (traffic on scheduled services)

	1994	1995	1996
Kilometres flown (million) . .	3	3	3
Passengers carried ('000) . .	142	149	153
Passenger-kilometres (million) .	289	110	115
Total ton-kilometres (million) . .	28	14	14

Source: UN, *Statistical Yearbook*.

Tourism

FOREIGN TOURIST ARRIVALS BY COUNTRY OF RESIDENCE

	1996	1997	1998
East Africa*	28,644	30,363	26,112
Mozambique	27,004	28,624	24,617
North America	5,645	5,984	5,146
South Africa†	21,526	22,818	19,623
United Kingdom and Ireland . .	14,261	15,117	13,001
Zambia	49,292	52,250	44,935
Zimbabwe.	26,262	27,838	23,941
Total (incl. other)	193,628	205,248	176,573

* Includes Kenya, Uganda and Tanzania.
† Includes South Africa, Botswana, Lesotho and Swaziland.
Tourism receipts (US $ million): 9 in 1995; 5 in 1996; 7 in 1997.
Source: World Tourism Organization, *Yearbook of Tourism Statistics*.

Communications Media

	1994	1995	1996
Radio receivers ('000 in use) . .	2,450	2,480	2,525
Telephones ('000 main lines in use)	33	34	35
Telefax stations (number in use) .	924	1,086	1,192
Mobile cellular telephones (subscribers) . . .	n.a.	382	3,700
Book production*:			
Titles	243	182	117†
Copies ('000)	n.a.	n.a.	9,174†
Daily newspapers:			
Titles	1	1‡	5
Average circulation ('000 copies)	25	25‡	n.a.
Non-daily newspapers:			
Titles	n.a.	n.a.	4
Average circulation ('000 copies)	n.a.	n.a.	120‡

* Including pamphlets (106 in 1994).
† School textbooks (first editions only).
‡ Estimate.
1997 ('000 in use): Radio receivers 2,600.
Sources: UNESCO, *Statistical Yearbook*; UN, *Statistical Yearbook*.

Education

(1995/96)

	Insti-tutions	Teachers	Students		
			Males	Females	Total
Primary . . .	3,706	49,138	1,528,564	1,358,543	2,887,107
Secondary:					
General . . .	n.a.	2,948	90,003	49,383	139,386
Teacher training .	n.a.	145*	996	475	1,471
Vocational . .	n.a.	79	n.a.	n.a.	1,054
Higher:					
Universities . .	6†	329	2,917	955	3,872
Other higher . .	n.a.	202*	959	730	1,689

* Estimate.
† 1994/95 figure.
Source: UNESCO, *Statistical Yearbook*.

Directory

The Constitution

A new Constitution, replacing the (amended) 1966 Constitution, was approved by the National Assembly on 16 May 1994, and took provisional effect for one year from 18 May. During this time the Constitution was to be subject to review, and the final document was promulgated on 18 May 1995. The main provisions (with subsequent amendments) are summarized below:

THE PRESIDENT

The President is both Head of State and Head of Government. The President is elected for five years, by universal adult suffrage, in the context of a multi-party political system. The Constitution provides for up to two Vice-Presidents.

PARLIAMENT

Parliament comprises the President, the Vice-President(s) and the National Assembly. The National Assembly has 193 elective seats, elections being by universal adult suffrage, in the context of a multi-party system. Cabinet ministers who are not elected members of parliament also sit in the National Assembly. The Speaker is appointed from among the ordinary members of the Assembly. The parliamentary term is normally five years. The President has power to prorogue or dissolve Parliament.

In 1995 the National Assembly approved proposals for the establishment of a second chamber, the Senate, to be implemented in 1999.

EXECUTIVE POWER

Executive power is exercised by the President, who appoints members of the Cabinet.

The Government

HEAD OF STATE

President: Dr (ELSON) BAKILI MULUZI (took office 21 May 1994; re-elected 15 June 1999).
Vice-President: JUSTIN MALEWEZI.

CABINET
(August 2000)

President and Head of Government: Dr BAKILI MULUZI.

Vice-President and Minister responsible for Privatization: JUSTIN MALEWEZI.

Minister of Agriculture and Irrigation Development: LEONARD MANGULAMA.

Minister of Natural Resources and Environmental Affairs: HARRY THOMSON.

Minister of Foreign Affairs and International Co-operation: LILIAN PATEL.

Attorney-General and Minister of Justice: PETER FACHI.

Minister of Finance and Economic Planning: MATHEWS CHIKAONDA.

Minister of Home Affairs and Internal Security: MANGEZA MALOZA.

Minister of State for Presidential Affairs: KEN LIPENGA.

Minister of Tourism, National Parks and Wildlife: GEORGE MTAFU.

Minister of Sports and Culture: MOSES DOSSI.

Minister of Commerce and Industry: SAMUEL KALIYOMA PHUMISA.

Minister of Health and Population: ALEKE BANDA.

Minister of State in the President's Office, responsible for People with Disabilities: GEORGE CLAVER.

Minister of Transport and Public Works: BROWN MPINGANJIRA.

Minister of Lands, Housing, Physical Planning and Surveys: THENGO MALOYA.

Minister of State in the President's Office, responsible for Districts and Local Government Administration: PATRICK MBEWE.

Minister of Education, Science and Technology: CASSIM CHILUMPHA.

Minister of State in the President's Office, responsible for Statutory Corporations: BOB KHAMISA.

Minister of Water Development: YUSUF MWAWA.
Minister of Defence: RODWELL MUNYENYEMBE.
Minister of Information: CLEMENT STAMBULI.
Minister of Women, Youth and Community Services: MARY BANDA.
Minister of Labour and Vocational Training: PETER CHUPA.
Minister without Portfolio: ULADI MUSSA.

There are also nine Deputy Ministers.

MINISTRIES

Office of the President and Cabinet: Private Bag 301, Capital City, Lilongwe 3; tel. 782655; fax 783654.

Ministry of Agriculture and Irrigation Development: POB 30144, Capital City, Lilongwe 3; tel. 784299; fax 784656.

Ministry of Commerce and Industry: POB 30366, Capital City, Lilongwe 3; tel. and fax 780680.

Ministry of Defence: Private Bag 43, Lilongwe 3; tel. 782200; fax 781282.

Ministry of District and Local Government Administration: POB 30312, Lilongwe 3; tel. 784500; fax 782130.

Ministry of Education, Science and Technology: Private Bag 328, Capital City, Lilongwe 3; tel. 784800; fax 782873.

Ministry of Finance and Economic Planning: POB 30049, Capital City, Lilongwe 3; tel. 782199; fax 781679.

Ministry of Foreign Affairs and International Co-operation: POB 30315, Capital City, Lilongwe 3; tel. 782211; fax 782434.

Ministry of Health and Population: POB 30377, Capital City, Lilongwe 3; tel. 783044; fax 783109.

Ministry of Home Affairs and Internal Security: Private Bag 331, Lilongwe 3; tel. 780177; fax 784067.

Ministry of Information: Private Bag 310, Lilongwe 3; tel. 783233; fax 784568.

Ministry of Justice: Private Bag 333, Capital City, Lilongwe 3; tel. 782411; fax 782176.

Ministry of Labour and Vocational Training: Private Bag 344, Capital City, Lilongwe 3; tel. 783277; fax 783805; e-mail labour@eo.wn.apc.org.

Ministry of Lands, Housing, Physical Planning and Surveys: Private Bag 311, Lilongwe 3; tel. 784766; fax 781389.

Ministry of Natural Resources and Environmental Affairs: Private Bag 350, Lilongwe 3; tel. 782600; fax 780260.

Ministry of Sports and Culture: Lilongwe.

Ministry of Statutory Corporations: POB 30061, Lilongwe 3; tel. 784266; fax 784110.

Ministry of Tourism, National Parks and Wildlife: Private Bag 326, Lilongwe 3; tel. 743969; fax 780650.

Ministry of Transport and Public Works: Private Bag 322, Capital City, Lilongwe 3; tel. 80344; fax 784678.

Ministry of Water Development: Tikwere House, Private Bag 350, Capital City, Lilongwe 3; tel. 782600; fax 780260.

Ministry of Women, Youth and Community Services: Private Bag 330, Capital City, Lilongwe 3; tel. 780411; fax 780826.

President and Legislature

PRESIDENT

Presidential Election, 15 June 1999

Candidate	Votes	% of votes
BAKILI MULUZI (UDF) . . .	2,442,685	51.37
GWANDAGULUWE CHAKUAMBA (MCP–AFORD) . . .	2,106,790	44.30
KAMULEPO KALUA (MDP) . .	67,856	1.43
Rev. DANIEL NKHUMBWE (CNU) .	24,347	0.51
BINGU WA MUTHARIKA (UP) . .	22,073	0.46
Invalid votes	91,671	1.93
Total	**4,755,422**	**100.00**

NATIONAL ASSEMBLY

Speaker: SAMUEL LEMMOTH MPASU.

General Election, 15 June 1999

Party	Seats
UDF	93
MCP	66
AFORD	29
Independents	4
Total*	192

* Voting in the remaining constituency was postponed, owing to the death of a candidate. The seat was won by a candidate of the UDF at a by-election in October (see Recent History).

Political Organizations

Alliance for Democracy (AFORD): Private Bag 28, Lilongwe; f. 1992; in March 1993 absorbed membership of fmr Malawi Freedom Movement; Pres. CHAKUFWA CHIHANA; First Vice-Pres. JOHN MHANGO; Second Vice-Pres. UNISON MWANGISA; Sec.-Gen. ZHIOBAT SHIWANGO.

Congress for National Unity (CNU).

Congress for the Second Republic (CSR): Leader KANYAMA CHIUME.

Forum Party (FP): f. 1997; Leader KALONGA STAMBULI.

Malawi Congress Party (MCP): Private Bag 388, Lilongwe 3; tel. 730388; f. 1959; sole legal party 1966–93; leadership under dispute in early August 2000.

Malawi Democratic Party (MDP): Pres. KAMULEPO KALUA.

Malawi Democratic Union (MDU): Pres. JAMES TABUNA DISENTIKUBA.

Mass Movement for the Young Generation (MM): Lilongwe; f. 1998; Interim Pres. CHAIMA BANDA.

Movement for the Restoration of Democracy in Malawi: f. 1996; terrorist group based in Mozambique consisting of fmr Malawi Young Pioneers.

National Unity Party (NUP).

People's Democratic Party (PDP).

Social Democratic Party (SDP): Pres. ISON KAKOME.

United Democratic Front (UDF): POB 5446, Limbe; f. 1992; Pres. BAKILI MULUZI; Vice-Pres. JUSTIN MALEWEZI; Sec.-Gen. SAMUEL LEMMOTH MPASU.

United Front for Multi-party Democracy (UFMD): f. 1992 by three exiled political groups: the Socialist League of Malawi, the Malawi Freedom Party and the Malawi Democratic Union; Pres. EDMOND JIKA.

United Party (UP): f. 1997; Interim Chair. BINGU WA MUTHARIKA.

Diplomatic Representation

EMBASSIES AND HIGH COMMISSIONS IN MALAWI

China (Taiwan): Area 40, Plot No. 9, POB 30221, Capital City, Lilongwe 3; tel. 783611; fax 784812; Ambassador: CHEN HSI-TSAN.

Denmark: Area 14/40, Private Bag 396, Lilongwe 3; tel. 784825; fax 784961; e-mail denmal@malawi.net; Ambassador: BO JENSEN.

Egypt: POB 30451, Lilongwe 3; tel. 730300; fax 730865; Ambassador: ESSAM ABDEL RAHMAN IBRAHIM.

Germany: POB 30046, Lilongwe 3; tel. 782555; fax 780250; Ambassador: Dr JÜRGEN HELLNER.

Korea, Republic: POB 30583, Lilongwe 3; Ambassador: SON MYONG-SON.

Mozambique: POB 30579, Lilongwe 3; tel. 784100; fax 781342; High Commissioner: DANIEL MBANZE.

South Africa: British High Commission Bldg, Capital Hill, POB 30043, Lilongwe 3; tel. 783722; fax 782571; High Commissioner: LLEWELLYN CREWE-BROWN.

United Kingdom: British High Commission Bldg, Capital Hill, POB 30042, Lilongwe 3; tel. 782400; fax 782657; e-mail britcom@malawi.net; High Commissioner: GEORGE FINLAYSON.

USA: Area 40, Plot 18, POB 30016, Lilongwe 3; tel. 783166; fax 740474; Ambassador: ROGER MEECE.

Zambia: POB 30138, Lilongwe 3; tel. 782635; fax 784349; High Commissioner: Col (retd) LAWRENCE M. H. HAAMAUNDU.

Zimbabwe: POB 30187, Lilongwe 3; tel. 784988; fax 782382; e-mail zimhighcomllw@malawi.net; High Commissioner: E.T. MANYIKA.

Judicial System

The courts administering justice are the Supreme Court of Appeal, High Court and Magistrates' Courts.

The High Court, which has unlimited jurisdiction in civil and criminal matters, consists of the Chief Justice and five puisne judges. Traditional Courts were abolished under the 1994 Constitution. Appeals from the High Court are heard by the Supreme Court of Appeal in Blantyre.

High Court of Malawi: POB 30244, Chichiri, Blantyre 3; tel. 670255; fax 670213; Registrar W. W. QOTO.

Chief Justice: RICHARD A. BANDA.

Justices of Appeal: L. A. UNYOLO, H. M. MTEGHA, J. B. KALAILE, D. G. TAMBALA, A. S. E. MSOSA.

High Court Judges: M. P. MKANDAWIRE, I. J. MTAMBO, D. F. MWAUNGULU, A. K. C. NYIRENDA, D. S. L. KUMANGE, G. M. CHIMASULA PHIRI, E. B. Z. KUMITSONYO, CHIUDZA BANDA, L. B. T. NDOVIE, W. M. HANJA HANJA, E. B. TWEA, R. R. MZIKAMANDO, J. M. ANSAH, R. R. CHINANGWA.

Religion

About 75% of the population profess Christianity. The Asian community includes Muslims and Hindus, and there is a small number of African Muslims. Traditional beliefs are followed by about 10% of the population.

CHRISTIANITY

Malawi Council of Churches: POB 30068, Capital City, Lilongwe 3; tel. 783499; fax 783106; f. 1939; 19 mems and 12 associates; Chair. Rt Rev. JAMES TENGATENGA; Gen. Sec. Rev. Dr A.C. MUSOPOLE.

The Anglican Communion

Anglicans are adherents of the Church of the Province of Central Africa, covering Botswana, Malawi, Zambia and Zimbabwe. The Church comprises 12 dioceses, including three in Malawi. The Archbishop of the Province is the Bishop of Botswana. There are about 80,000 adherents in Malawi.

Bishop of Lake Malawi: Rt Rev. PETER NATHANIEL NYANJA, POB 30349, Capital City, Lilongwe 3; fax 731966.

Bishop of North Malawi: Rt Rev. JACKSON BIGGERS, POB 120, Mzuzu; e-mail biggers@malawi.net.

Bishop of Southern Malawi: Rt Rev. JAMES TENGATENGA, Private Bag 1, Chilema, Zomba; tel. 539203; fax 539207; e-mail angsoma@malawi.net.

Protestant Churches

Church of Central Africa (Presbyterian): comprises three synods in Malawi (Blantyre, Livingstonia and Nkhoma); Blantyre Synod: POB 413, Blantyre; tel. and fax 633942; Co-ordinator Rev. J. J. MPHATSE; more than 1m. adherents in Malawi.

Evangelical Association of Malawi: Lilongwe; tel. and fax 730373; e-mail evangelicalassmw@malawi.net; Chair. Rev. MVULA J. MVULA; Gen. Sec. FRANCIS MKANDAWIRE.

The Indigenous Baptist Convention of Malawi: POB 51083, Limbe; tel. 643224; Chair. Rev. S. L. MALABWANYA; Gen. Sec. Rev. M. T. KACHASO GAMA.

The Lutheran Church of Central Africa: POB 748, Blantyre; tel. 630821; fax 630821; f. 1963; evangelical and medical work; Co-ordinator J. M. JANOSEK; 35,000 mems. in Malawi.

Seventh-day Adventists: POB 951, Blantyre; tel. 620264; fax 620528; e-mail 1016631763@malawi.net; Pres. B. E. MALOPA; Exec. Sec. R. R. MZUMARA.

The African Methodist Episcopal Church, the Churches of Christ, the Free Methodist Church, the Pentecostal Assemblies of God and the United Evangelical Church in Malawi are also active.

The Roman Catholic Church

Malawi comprises one archdiocese and six dioceses. At 31 December 1998 some 18.0% of the total population were adherents of the Roman Catholic Church.

Episcopal Conference of Malawi: Catholic Secretariat of Malawi, Chimutu Rd, POB 30384, Capital City, Lilongwe 3; tel. 782079; fax 782019; e-mail ecm@malawi.net; f. 1969; Pres. Rt Rev. FELIX EUGENIO MKHORI, Bishop of Chikwawa.

Archbishop of Blantyre: Most Rev. JAMES CHIONA, Archbishop's House, POB 385, Blantyre; tel. 633905; fax 636107.

BAHÁ'Í FAITH

National Spiritual Assembly: POB 5849, Limbe; tel. and fax 640996; f. 1970; mems resident in over 1,500 localities.

The Press

ABA Today: POB 5861, Limbe; f. 1982; monthly; publ. by African Businessmen's Association of Malawi.

Boma Lathu: POB 494, Blantyre; tel. 620266; fax 620039; f. 1973; monthly; Chichewa; publ. by the Ministry of Information; circ. 100,000.

Business and Development News: POB 829, Development House, Victoria Avenue, Blantyre; f. 1973; monthly.

The Daily Times: Private Bag 39, Ginnery Corner, Blantyre; tel. 671566; fax 671233; e-mail dailytimes@mailexcite; f. 1895; Mon.–Fri.; English; Editor-in-Chief MIKE KAMWENDO; circ. 22,000.

Kuunika: PO Nkhoma, Lilongwe; f. 1909; monthly; Chichewa; Presbyterian; Editor Rev. M. C. NKHALAMBAYAUSI; circ. 6,000.

Malawi Life: Private Bag 39, Ginnery Corner, Blantyre; tel. 671566; f. 1991; monthly magazine; English.

Malawi Government Gazette: Government Printer, POB 37, Zomba; tel. 523155; f. 1894; weekly.

Malawi News: Private Bag 39, Ginnery Corner, Blantyre; tel. 671566; fax 671114; f. 1959; weekly; English, Chichewa; Editor HORACE SOMANJE; circ. 30,000.

The Mirror: POB 30721, Blantyre; tel. 675043; f. 1994; weekly; English; Editor-in-Chief GEORGE TUKHUWA; circ. 10,000.

Moni: POB 5592, Limbe; tel. 651139; fax 651171; f. 1964; monthly; Chichewa and English; circ. 40,000.

The Monitor: POB 2521, Blantyre; tel. 673901; f. 1993; daily; English; Publisher CLEMENT STANBULI; circ. 7,000.

Moyo: Health Education Unit, POB 30377, Lilongwe 3; bi-monthly; English; publ. by Ministry of Health; Editor-in-Chief W. G. BOMBA.

Nation: POB 30408, Chichiri, Blantyre; f. 1993; weekly; English; independent; Editor ALFRED NTONGA; circ. 10,000.

Odini: POB 133, Lilongwe; tel. 721388; fax 721141; f. 1950; fortnightly; Chichewa and English; Roman Catholic; Dir P. I. AKOMENJI; circ. 12,000.

This is Malawi: POB 494, Blantyre; tel. 620266; fax 620807; e-mail alivuza@malawi.net; internet www.maform.malawi.net; f. 1964; monthly; English and Chichewa edns; publ. by the Dept of Information; Editor ANTHONY LIVUZA; circ. 5,000.

The Weekly Chronicle: POB 40521, Lilongwe; f. 1993; weekly; English, independent; Editor WILLIE ZINGANI; circ. 5,000.

NEWS AGENCIES

Malawi News Agency (MANA): Mzuza; tel. 636122; f. 1966.

Foreign Bureau

Newslink Africa (UK): POB 2688, Blantyre; Correspondent HOBBS GAMA.

Publishers

Christian Literature Association in Malawi: POB 503, Blantyre; tel. 620839; f. 1968; general and religious publs in Chichewa and English; Gen. Man. J. T. MATENJE.

Likuni Press and Publishing House: POB 133, Lilongwe; tel. 721388; fax 721141; f. 1949; publs in English and Chichewa; Gen. Man. (vacant).

Mzuzu Publishing Co: POB 225, Nkhata Bay; tel. 352353; f. 1977; Exec. Chair. M. W. KANYAMA CHIUME.

Popular Publications: POB 5592, Limbe; tel. 651833; fax 651171; e-mail mpp@malawi.net; f. 1961; general and religious; Gen. Man. VALES MACHILA.

Government Publishing House

Government Printer: POB 37, Zomba; tel. 523155.

Broadcasting and Communications

TELECOMMUNICATIONS

Malawi Telecoms Ltd: Glyn Jones Rd, POB 537, Blantyre; tel. 620977; fax 620188; f. 2000 following division of Malawi Posts and Telecommunications Corpn into two separate entities.

Mobile Systems International (MSI): f. 1998; operates the Celtel mobile cellular telephone network; Man. Dir DAVID BAMFORD.

Telekom Networks Malawi (TNM): tel. 641088; fax 644683; e-mail abakar@malawi.net; operates mobile cellular telephone network; CEO ABU BAKAR ABDUL RAHMAN.

BROADCASTING
Radio

Malawi Broadcasting Corporation: POB 30133, Chichiri, Blantyre 3; tel. 671222; fax 671257; e-mail dgmbc@malawi.net; f. 1964; statutory body; semi-commercial, partly state-financed; two channels; programmes in English, Chichewa, Chitumbuka, Lomwe and Yao; Chair. Maj. Gen. B. NAMWAL; Dir Gen. WILSON PANKUKU (acting); Dir of News and Current Affairs MOLLAND NKHATA.

Television

Television Malawi: f. 1999; broadcasts 55 hours per week, of which 10 hours are produced locally; relays programmes from France, Germany, South Africa and the United Kingdom; Co-ordinator BENSON TEMBO.

Finance

(cap. = capital; res = reserves; dep. = deposits; m. = million; brs = branches; amounts in kwacha)

BANKING
Central Bank

Reserve Bank of Malawi: POB 30063, Capital City, Lilongwe 3; tel. 780600; fax 782752; e-mail gov@malawi.net; f. 1965; bank of issue; cap. and res 610.7m., dep. 1,921.8m. (Dec. 1997); Gov. ELIYAS BWANALI; Gen. Mans. G. G. LENGU, I. C. BONONGWE, B. J. A. KHORIYO; br. in Blantyre.

Commercial Banks

Commercial Bank of Malawi Ltd: POB 1111, Blantyre; tel. 620144; fax 620360; e-mail combank@malawi.net; internet www.combank-MW.Malawi.net; f. 1970; 22% state-owned; cap. and res 462.9m., dep. 3,992.6m. (Dec. 1998); Chair. TIMON SAM MANGWAZU; CEO VICTOR MBEWE; 13 brs.

Finance Bank of Malawi: Finance House, Victoria Ave, POB 421, Blantyre; tel. 624799; fax 622957; e-mail makhan@malawi.net; cap. and res 23.4m, total assets 257.1m. (June 1998); Chair. Dr R. L. MAHTANI; Man. Dir N.A. QURESHI (acting).

National Bank of Malawi: Victoria Ave, POB 945, Blantyre; tel. 620622; fax 620606; e-mail natbank@malawi.net; internet www.natbank.malawi.net; f. 1971; cap. and res 1,295.1m., dep. 5,749.0m. (Dec. 1999); Chair. F. A. JUMBE; CEO T. J. O. BARNES; 13 brs; agencies throughout Malawi.

Development Bank

Investment and Development Bank of Malawi Ltd (INDEBANK): Indebank House, Kaushong Rd, Top Mandala, POB 358, Blantyre; tel. 620055; fax 623353; e-mail indebank@malawi.net; f. 1972; cap. and res 73.5m., total assets 236.9m. (Dec. 1997); provides loans to statutory corpns and to private enterprises in the agricultural, industrial, tourism, transport and commercial sectors; Chair. CHRISTOPHER BARROW; Gen. Man. M. J. M. PHIRI.

Merchant Banks

First Merchant Bank Ltd: Delamere House, Ground Floor, Victoria Ave, POB 122, Blantyre; tel. 624889; fax 621987; e-mail fmbhq@malawi.net; cap. and res 54.5m., total assets 533.0m. (Dec. 1998); Chair RASIKBHAI C. KANTARIA; Gen. Man. K. N. CHATURVEDI.

Leasing and Finance Co of Malawi Ltd: Indebank House, 1st Floor, Top Mandala, POB 1963, Blantyre; tel. 620233; fax 620275; e-mail lfc@malawi.net; f. 1986; cap. 8.0m., dep. 265.8m. (Aug. 1999); Chair. AGNES VALERA; Gen. Man. J. N. WHITEHEAD.

National Finance Co Ltd: Plantation House, POB 821, Blantyre; tel. 623670; fax 620549; e-mail natfin@malawi.net; f. 1958; cap. 15.0m., total assets 166.4m. (Dec. 1999); Chair. T. J. O. BARNES; Gen. Man. M. T. BAMFORD.

Savings Bank

Malawi Savings Bank: Umboyo House, Victoria Ave, POB 521, Blantyre; tel. 625111; fax 621929; e-mail msb@msb.mw.net; state-owned; total assets 551.1m. (1998); Chair. RASPICIOUS DZANJALIMODZI; Gen. Man. IAN BONONGWE.

STOCK EXCHANGE

Malawi Stock Exchange: Able House, Ground Floor, cnr Hannover Ave and Chilembwe Rd, POB 2598, Blantyre; tel. 821783; fax 624353; f. 1995; Chair. C. MPANDE; CEO THOM MPINGANJIRA.

INSURANCE

National Insurance Co Ltd: NICO House, POB 501, Blantyre; tel. 622699; fax 622364; e-mail nico@nico.malawi.net; f. 1971; transferred to private sector in 1998; cap. and res 104.7m. (Sept.

1997); offices at Blantyre, Lilongwe, Mzuzu and Zomba; agencies country-wide; CEO and Man. Dir. FELIX L. MLUSU.

Old Mutual Malawi: POB 393, Blantyre; tel. 620677; fax 622649; e-mail oldmutual@malawi.net; f. 1845; Gen. Man. MARIUS WALTERS.

Royal Insurance Co Ltd: POB 442, Blantyre; tel. 624044; fax 623862; Gen. Man. COLIN BOYS.

United General Insurance Co Ltd: POB 383, Blantyre; tel. 621577; fax 621980; e-mail ugi@malawi.net; Gen. Man. I. KUMWENDA.

Trade and Industry

GOVERNMENT AGENCIES

Malawi Export Promotion Council: Delamere House, POB 1299, Blantyre; tel. 620499; fax 635429; f. 1974; Gen. Man. G. I. L. MANG-OCHI.

Malawi Investment Promotion Agency (MIPA): Private Bag 302, Capital City, Lilongwe 3; tel. 780800; fax 781781; e-mail mipa@eo.wn.apc.org; f. 1993; promotes and facilitates local and foreign investment; CEO WATIPASO MKANDAWIRE.

Privatization Commission: POB 937, Blantyre; tel. 623655; fax 621248; f. 1996 to oversee privatization programme.

DEVELOPMENT ORGANIZATIONS

Agricultural Development and Marketing Corporation (ADMARC): POB 5052, Limbe; tel. 640500; fax 640486; f. 1971; govt agency; markets agricultural crops produced by smallholder farmers; exports confectionery-grade groundnut kernels, maize, cassava and sunflower seed; primary marketing of tobacco, wheat and beans, peas and other seeds; co-operates with commercial cos in the cultivation and processing of agricultural produce; Chair. J. STEVENS; Gen. Man. FRIDAY JUMBE.

Malawi Development Corporation (MDC): MDC House, Glyn Jones Rd, POB 566, Blantyre; tel. 620100; fax 620584; e-mail mdcgm@malawi.net; internet www.mdc.malawi.net; f. 1964; state-owned; provides finance and management advice to commerce and industry; 23 subsidiary and assoc. cos; Chair. Dr JERRY A. A. JANA; Gen. Man. ELVAS B. KADZAKO.

Small Enterprise Development Organization of Malawi (SEDOM): POB 525, Blantyre; tel. 622555; fax 622781; f. 1982; tech. and management advice to indigenous small-scale businesses.

CHAMBER OF COMMERCE

Malawi Chamber of Commerce and Industry: Chichiri Trade Fair Grounds, POB 258, Blantyre; tel. 671988; fax 671147; e-mail mcci@eo.wn.apc.org; f. 1892; 400 mems; Chair. MARK KATSONGO PHIRI.

INDUSTRIAL AND TRADE ASSOCIATIONS

Smallholder Coffee Authority: POB 20133, Luwinga, Mzuzu 2; tel. 332899; fax 332902; e-mail mzuzucoffee@malawi.net; producers of arabica coffee.

Smallholder Sugar Authority: Blantyre.

Smallholder Tea Authority: POB 80, Thyolo.

Tea Association of Malawi Ltd: POB 930, Blantyre; tel. 671355; fax 671427; f. 1936; 20 mems; Man. Dir G. D. BANDA.

Tobacco Association of Malawi: POB 31360, Lilongwe 3; tel. 783099; fax 783493; e-mail tama@eo.wn.apc.org; f. 1929; 60,000 mems; Pres. ALBERT W. KAMULAGA.

Tobacco Exporters' Association of Malawi: Private Bag 403, Kanengo, Lilongwe 4; tel. 710663; fax 710668; f. 1930; 10 mems; Chair. CHARLES A. M. GRAHAM; Exec. Sec. H. M. MBALE.

EMPLOYERS' ORGANIZATIONS

Employers' Consultative Association of Malawi (ECAM): POB 2134, Blantyre; tel. 671337; f. 1963; 500 mems; Chair. D. KAMBAUWA; Exec. Dir W. L. DAMBULENI.

Master Builders', Civil Engineering Contractors' and Allied Trades' Association: POB 311, Blantyre; tel. 622966; f. 1955; 70 mems (1994); Chair. B. CLOW.

Master Printers' Association of Malawi: POB 2460, Blantyre; f. 1962; 21 mems; Chair. PAUL FREDERICK.

National Automotive Franchise Holders' Association of Malawi: POB 311, Blantyre; tel. 624754; fax 622966; f. 1954; 42 mems (1989); Chair. D. H. DRAUDE.

UTILITY
Electricity

Electricity Supply Commission of Malawi (ESCOM): ESCOM House, Haile Selassie Rd, POB 2047, Blantyre; tel. 622000; fax 622008; f. 1966; controls electricity distribution; Chair. LUKE JUMBE; CEO REYNOLD DUNCAN.

MAJOR COMPANIES

The following are among the largest companies in terms of capital investment or employment.

Auction Holdings Ltd: POB 40035, Kanengo, Lilongwe; tel. 765377; fax 765384; e-mail ahll@malawi.net; f. 1962; cap. K121.9m. (1998); tobacco and tobacco products; Chair. F. A. JUMBE; Gen. Man. G. C. MSONTHI.

BATA Shoe Company (Malawi) Ltd: POB 936, Blantyre; tel. 670511; mfrs of shoes; Man. Dir H. STROHMAYER.

BAT (Malawi) Ltd: POB 428, Blantyre; tel. 670033; fax 670808; f. 1942; mfrs of cigarettes; Chair. and Man. Dir SAISUL ISLAM.

Blantyre Netting Co: POB 30575, Blantyre; tel. 671227; fax 672597; polypropylene woven sacks, ropes, bristles, strapping tapes, nylon twines, nets; Man. Dir H. ANADKAT.

Brown and Clapperton: POB 1582, Blantyre; tel. 670011; fax 677821; f. 1929; mfrs of engineering, metal and electrical products; CEO ROBIN WRIXON.

Carlsberg Malawi Brewery Ltd: POB 1050, Heavy Industrial Area, Blantyre; tel. 670133; fax 671903; mfrs of beer; CEO C. L. MPHANDE.

Chemical Manufacturers Ltd: POB 30242, Chichiri, Blantyre 3; tel. 671536; fax 671915; f. 1981; mfrs and distributers of industrial chemical products; Man. Dir ATHOL ESTMENT.

Chillington Agrimal (Malawi) Ltd: POB 143, Blantyre; tel. 670933; fax 670651; mfrs of agricultural hand tools, hoes and implements; Gen. Man. C. J. PEVERELLE.

CTM (Malawi) Ltd: POB 5350, Limbe; mfrs of textiles; Man. Dir CHRISTOPHER GEORGE GEASLEY.

David Whitehead and Sons (Malawi) Ltd: POB 30070, Chichiri, Blantyre; tel. 670644; fax 671639; cap. and res K98m. (1998); mfrs of textile fabrics and yarns; CEO N. A. WILLIAMSON; Chair. J. MALANGE.

Grain and Milling Co Ltd: POB 5847, Limbe; tel. 645055; fax 643342; grain millers; Man. Dir C. C. BAILIE.

Import and Export Co of Malawi Ltd: POB 1106, Blantyre; tel. 670999; fax 671160; e-mail i&e@malawi.net; f. 1984; wholesale, retail and packaging; Chair. E. KAZEMBE; Man. Dir M. D. KONSON.

International Timbers Ltd: POB 5050, Limbe; tel. 640399; fax 640959; e-mail itl-itml@malawi.net; f. 1907; cap. K6.6m.; foresters and sawmillers of home-grown eucalyptus timber; mfrs of tobacco packing material, structural laminated timber, woodblock flooring, pallets and wooden packaging material, commercial plywood, block-board, tea chests and flush panel doors; Chair. D. VAN LELYVELD; Man. Dir EDWARD J. GOREHAM.

Lever Brothers (Malawi) Ltd: POB 5151, Tsiranana Rd, Limbe; tel. 641100; fax 645720; f. 1963; mfrs of soaps, detergents, cooking oils, foods, beverages and chemicals; CEO ROBERT CLARKE.

Lonrho (Malawi) Ltd: POB 5498, Churchill Rd, Limbe; tel. 640000; fax 640427; f. 1963; cap. K5m.; total issued cap. of Lonrho group cos in Malawi: c. K70m.; Chair. G. A. JAFFU; operates the following subsidiaries:

> **The Central Africa Co Ltd:** Tobacco and special crops.
>
> **Chibuku Products Ltd:** Brewing.
>
> **Farming and Engineering Services Ltd:** Agricultural equipment.
>
> **Lonrho Motors (Malawi) Ltd:** POB 918, Blantyre; tel. 644677; fax 645904; e-mail lonmotors@malawi.net; motor trading.
>
> **Lonrho Properties Ltd:** POB 5498, Limbe; tel. 640000; fax 640427; construction and property management; Gen. Man. T. O. D. KANYUKA.

Toyota Malawi Ltd: POB 430, Blantyre; tel. 641332; fax 645369; e-mail toyotamalawi@malawi.net; f. 1964; cap. K122m. (1998); motor trading; Man. Dir J. J. CONNELL.

Malawi Distilleries Ltd: POB 924, MacLeod Rd, Heavy Industrial Site, Blantyre; tel. 670722; fax 670813; e-mail maldist@malawi.net; f. 1967; cap. K83m.; sole producer of potable spirits for local consumption and export; Man. Dir. J. A. CALVIN.

Malawi Iron and Steel Corporation: POB 143, Blantyre; tel. 674307; fax 670651; foundry operators.

Mandala Ltd: POB 49, Blantyre; tel. 621011; fax 623107; e-mail mandalace@malawi.net; f. 1908; cap. K22.6m. (1998); conglomerate involved in agriculture, insurance and motor trade industries; CEO R. M. SHARP.

National Oil Industries Ltd: POB 143; Macleod Rd, Blantyre; tel. 670155; mfrs of cooking oils, cotton-seed cake and millers of rice; Gen. Man. F. A. JUMBE.

Packaging Industries (Malawi) Ltd: POB 30533, Chichiri, Blantyre 3; tel. 670533; fax 671283; e-mail pim@malawi.net; f. 1969; cap. K13m. (1998); mfrs of cardboard boxes, paper sacks and liquid packaging containers; Chair. N. CUMMING; Man. Dir S. A. ITAYE.

PEW Ltd: POB 30038, Chichiri, Blantyre 3; tel. 671155; fax 671437; e-mail pew@malawi.net; fmrly Plumbing and Engineering Works; f. 1968; cap. US $282.5m. (1997); mfrs of coachworks, bus bodies, road and farm trailers, truck bodies, tankers and GRP products; Chair. A. D. C. CHILEMBWE; Gen. Man. JOHN H. MSOLOMBA.

Plastic Products Ltd: POB 907, Blantyre; tel. 670455; fax 670664; e-mail ppl@malawi.net; mfrs of polythene bags; Gen. Man. ROBERT KAPYEPYE.

The Portland Cement Co (1974) Ltd: POB 523, Heavy Industrial Area, Blantyre; tel. 671933; fax 671026; e-mail portland@malawi .net; f. 1974; cap. K14.5m. (Dec. 1997); mfrs and distributors of cement; projected annual capacity: 140,000 metric tons; Chair. J. BRAITHWAITE; CEO ROGER MORTON.

Press Corpn Ltd: POB 30238, Lilongwe; tel. 784411; fax 780523; e-mail presscorporation@malawi.net; f. 1983; cap. and res K2,294m. (1998); holding co operating through 19 subsidiaries and four associate cos in distribution, banking, insurance, manufacturing and processing; Chair. Dr J. A. JANA; CEO R. A. PITCHFORD.

Press and Shine Clothing Ltd: Private Bag 362, Lilongwe 3; tel. 781700; fax 784239; mfrs of bedlinen and garments; Exec. Man. M. KINDINGER.

Press Steel Industries Ltd: POB 30116, Lilongwe 3; tel. 765088; fax 765848; metal rollers.

PROMAT Ltd: POB 30041, Lilongwe 3; tel. 765388; fax 730653; e-mail promat@eo.wn.apc.org; mfrs of polyvinylchloride (PVC)-U pipes, high-density polyethylene pipes, PVC hosepipes.

Raiply Malawi Ltd: Private Bag 1, Chikangawa, Mzimba; tel. 333944; fax 333642; mfrs of plywood, blockboard and timber.

Southern Bottlers Ltd: POB 406, Blantyre; tel. 670022; fax 670689; cap. K100m. (1998); mfrs of soft drinks; Chair. C. BARROW; Man. Dir CHADWICK MPHANDE.

Sugar Corpn of Malawi Ltd: Private Bag 580, Limbe; tel. 643988; fax 640135; e-mail illovo@malawi.net; f. 1965; cap. K488.9m. (1999); sugar production and processing; Chair. F. A. JUMBE; Man. Dir B. M. STEWARDSON.

Universal Industries Ltd: POB 507, Blantyre; tel. 670055; fax 677408; e-mail unibisco@malawi.net; mfrs of confectionery; Chair. and Man. Dir D. K. AMIN.

TRADE UNIONS

Trades Union Congress of Malawi (TUCM): POB 5094, Limbe; f. 1964; 6,500 mems; Chair. KEN WILLIAM MHANGO; Gen. Sec. EATON V. LAITA; the following are among the principal affiliated unions:

Building Construction, Civil Engineering and Allied Workers' Union: Limbe; tel. 650598; f. 1961; 6,000 mems; Chair. W. I. SOKO; Gen. Sec. G. SITIMA.

Railway Workers' Union of Malawi: POB 5393, Limbe; tel. 640844; f. 1954; 3,000 mems; Pres. THOMAS CHISAKANIZA; Gen. Sec. MACDONALD LUWANJA.

Other unions affiliated to the TUCM are the Commercial and Allied Workers' Union, the Civil Servants' Trade Union, the Hotels, Food and Catering Workers' Union, the Local Government Employees' Union, the Plantation and Agricultural Workers' Union, the Teachers' Union of Malawi, the Textile, Garment, Guards and Leather Workers' Union, the Transport and General Workers' Union and the Sugar Plantation and Allied Workers' Union. The TUCM and its affiliated unions had a total membership of 450,000 in 1995.

Transport

RAILWAYS

The Central East African Railways Co (fmrly Malawi Railways) operates between Nsanje (near the southern border with Mozambique) and Mchinji (near the border with Zambia) via Blantyre, Salima and Lilongwe, and between Nkaya and Nayuchi on the eastern border with Mozambique, covering a total of 797 km. The Central East African Railways Co and Mozambique State Railways connect Malawi with the Mozambican ports of Beira and Nacala. These links, which traditionally form Malawi's principal trade routes, were effectively closed during 1983–85, owing to insurgent activity in Mozambique. The rehabilitation of the rail link to Nacala was completed in October 1989. There is a rail/lake interchange station at Chipoka on Lake Malawi, from where vessels operate services to other lake ports in Malawi.

Central East African Railways Co Ltd: POB 5144, Limbe; tel. 640844; fax 643262; f. 1994 as Malawi Railways Ltd; sold to a consortium owned by Mozambique's Empresa Nacional dos Portos e Caminhos de Ferro de Moçambique and the USA's Railroad Corpn

in mid-1999 and subsequently renamed as above; CEO ROBERT MORTENSEN; Gen. Man. BRADLEY KNAPP.

ROADS

In 1997 Malawi had a total road network of some 15,137 km, of which some 3,203 km were paved. In addition, unclassified community roads total an estimated 10,000 km. All main roads, and most secondary roads, are all-weather roads. Major routes link Lilongwe and Blantyre with Harare (Zimbabwe) Lusaka (Zambia) and Mbeya and Dar es Salaam (Tanzania). A 480-km highway along the western shore of Lake Malawi links the remote Northern Region with the Central and Southern Regions. A project to create a new trade route, or 'Northern Corridor', through Tanzania, involving road construction and improvements in Malawi, was completed in 1992.

Road Transport Operators' Association: Makata Industrial Site, POB 30740, Chichiri, Blantyre 3; tel. 670422; fax 671423; f. 1956; 254 mems (1995); Chair. E. MUHOMED.

CIVIL AVIATION

Lilongwe (formerly Kamuzu) International Airport was opened in 1982. There is another main airport, at Blantyre, which serves a number of regional airlines, and three domestic airports.

Air Malawi Ltd: 4 Robins Rd, POB 84, Blantyre; tel. 620811; fax 620042; e-mail it@airmalawi.malawi.net; internet www .africaonline.co.ke/airmalawi; f. 1967; restructuring in preparation for privatization began in 1999; scheduled domestic and regional services, scheduled services to the United Kingdom suspended in June 1999; Chair. B. G. BOWLER; CEO Capt. A. WISDOM B. MCHUNGULA.

Tourism

Fine scenery, beaches on Lake Malawi, big game and an excellent climate form the basis of the country's tourist potential. The number of foreign visitor arrivals declined from 205,248 in 1997 to 176,573 in 1998; receipts from tourism totalled US $7m. in 1997. The Ministry of Tourism, National Parks and Wildlife aims to attract 500,000 visitors annually by 2000.

Department of Tourism: POB 402, Blantyre; tel. 620300; fax 620947; f. 1969; responsible for tourist policy; inspects and licenses tourist facilities, sponsors training of hotel staff and publs tourist literature; Director of Tourism Services F. MASIMBE.

Tourism Development and Investment Co (TDIC): Blantyre; f. 1988 by Malawi Development Corpn to operate hotels and tours; Chief Exec. FRANCIS MBILIZI.

Defence

Malawi's defence forces in August 1999 comprised a land army of 5,000, a marine force of 220 and an air force of 80; all form part of the army. There was also a paramilitary police force of 1,000. In late 1997 the army received training in peace-keeping operations from US soldiers.

Defence Expenditure: Budgeted at K637.8m. in 1999/2000.

Commander-in-Chief of the Armed Forces: Lt-Gen. JOSEPH CHIMBAYO.

Education

Primary education, which is officially compulsory, begins at six years of age and lasts for up to eight years. Secondary education, which begins at 14 years of age, lasts for four years, comprising two cycles of two years. In 1995 the total enrolment at primary and secondary schools was equivalent to 100% of the school-age population (males 106%; females 94%). In that year primary school enrolment was equivalent to 134% of children in the relevant age-group (males 140%; females 127%), but the comparable ratio for secondary enrolment was 17% (males 21%; females 12%). A programme to expand education at all levels has been undertaken; however, the introduction of free primary education in September 1994 was reported to have resulted in severe overcrowding in schools; primary school enrolment in 1992 had been equivalent to only 52% of the relevant age-group. In January 1996 the International Development Association granted US $22.5m. for the training of 20,000 new teachers, appointed in response to the influx. In mid-1997 additional funding was provided by the African Development Bank for the construction of primary and secondary schools, and in April 1998 the World Bank approved a loan of K1,200m. to improve access to secondary education. The University of Malawi had 3,601 students in 1994/95. Some students attend institutions in the United Kingdom and the USA. According to provisional figures, current expenditure on education in the 1997/98 budget was K2,111.6m. (equivalent to 20.4% of total current expenditure. In 1987, according to census results, the average rate of adult illiteracy was 51.5% (males 34.7%; females 66.5%). A five-year adult literacy programme was launched in 1986, and in 1987 two teacher-training colleges were opened. However, in 1995, according to UNESCO estimates, the average rate of adult illiteracy was 44.0% (males 28.3%; females 58.7%).

Bibliography

Bafael, B. R. *A Short History of Malawi*. Limbe, Popular Publishers, 1980.

Baker, C. *Seeds of Trouble: Government Policy and Land Rights in Nyasaland, 1946–1964*. London, British Academic Press, 1993.

Catholic Institute for International Relations. *Malawi: Moment of Truth*. London, CIIR, 1993.

Crosby, C. A. *Historical Dictionary of Malawi*. 2nd Edn. Metuchen, NJ, Scarecrow Press, 1993.

Cullen, T. *Malawi: A Turning Point*. Edinburgh, Pentland Press, 1994.

Economist Intelligence Unit. *Country Report: Zimbabwe, Malawi*. No. 2, 1986, London, EIU, 1986.

Harrigan, J. *From Dictatorship to Democracy*. Aldershot, Ashgate Publishing Ltd, 2000.

Jere, N., and Mkandawire, D. S. *An Outline of Our Government*. Blantyre, Christian Literature Association of Malawi, 1982.

Kibble, S. *Dependency and Choice: Malawi's Links with South Africa*. Leeds, African Studies Unit, University of Leeds, 1988.

Lienau, C. *Malawi*. Darmstadt, Wissenschaftliche Buchgesellschaft, 1981.

Lwanda, J. L. C. *Kamuzu Banda of Malawi: A Study in Promise, Power and Paralysis: Malawi under Dr Banda, 1961 to 1993*. Glasgow, Dudu Nsomba Publishers, 1993.

   Promises, Power Politics and Poverty: Democratic Transition in Malawi, 1961–1996. Glasgow, Dudu Ngemba Publishers, 1996.

Macdonald, R. J. (Ed.). *From Nyasaland to Malawi: Studies in Colonial History*. Nairobi, East African Publishing House, 1976.

Martin, C. G. C. *Maps and Surveys of Malawi: A History of Cartography and the Land Survey Profession*. Cape Town, Balkema, 1980.

Meinhardt, H. *Die Rolle des Parlaments in Autoritaeren Malawi*. Hamburg, Institut für Afrika-Kunde, 1993.

Mhone, G. C. Z. (Ed.). *Malawi at the Crossroads: The Post-Colonial Political Economy*. Harare, SAPES Books, 1992.

Milazi, D. *The Politics and Economics of Labour Migration in Southern Africa: What are the Key Issues?* Maseru, Lesotho Publishing Co, 1986.

Mtewa, M. *Malawi: Democratic Theory and Public Policy*. Cambridge, MA, Schenkmann, 1984.

Mwhakasunguru, A. K. *The Rural Economy of Malawi: A Critical Analysis*. Bergen, CMI, 1986.

Nzunda, M. S., and Ross, K. R. (Eds). *Church, Law and Political Transition in Malawi 1992–1994*. Gweru, Mambo, 1995.

Pachai, B. *The Early History of Malawi*. London, Longman, 1972.

   Malawi: The History of a Nation. New York, Longman, 1973.

   Land and Politics in Malawi 1875–1975. Kingston, Ontario, Limestone Press, 1978.

Phiri, D. D. *From Nguni to Ngoni*. Limbe, Popular Publishers, 1982.

Spring, A. *Agricultural Development and Gender Issues in Malawi*. Lanham, MD, University Press of America, 1995.

Vaughan, M. *The Story of an African Famine: Gender and Famine in Twentieth-Century Malawi*. Cambridge, Cambridge University Press, 1987.

Wells, A. J. *An Introduction to the History of Central Africa: Zambia, Malawi and Zimbabwe*. Oxford, Oxford University Press, 1985.

White, L. *Magomero: Portrait of an African Village*. Cambridge, Cambridge University Press, 1987.

Williams, T. D. *Malawi: The Politics of Despair*. Ithaca, NY, Cornell University Press, 1978.

World Bank. *Malawi: Human Resources and Poverty: Profile and Priorities for Action*. Washington, DC, World Bank, 1996.

Young, A., and Young, D. *A Geography of Malawi*. 2nd Edn. London, Evans, 1987.

MALI

Physical and Social Geography

R. J. HARRISON CHURCH

With an area of 1.24m. sq km (478,841 sq miles), the Republic of Mali is only slightly smaller than Niger, west Africa's largest state. Like Niger and Burkina Faso, Mali is land-locked. Bordering on seven countries, it extends about 1,600 km from north to south, and roughly the same distance from east to west, with a narrowing at the centre. The population was 7,696,348 at the census of April 1987, and was estimated by the United Nations at 10,694,000 in mid-1998 (giving an average density of 8.6 inhabitants per sq km).

The ancient Basement Complex rocks of Africa have been uplifted in the mountainous Adrar des Iforas of the north-east, whose dry valleys bear witness to formerly wetter conditions. Otherwise the Pre-Cambrian rocks are often covered by Primary sandstones, which have bold erosion escarpments at, for example, Bamako and east of Bandiagara. At the base of the latter live the Dogon people, made famous by Marcel Griaule's study. Where the River Niger crosses a sandstone outcrop below Bamako, rapids obstruct river navigation, giving an upper navigable reach above Bamako, and another one below it from Koulikoro to Ansongo, near the border with Niger.

Loose sands cover most of the rest of the country and, as in Senegal and Niger, are a relic of drier climatic conditions. They are very extensive on the long border with Mauritania and Algeria.

Across the heart of the country flows the River Niger, a vital waterway and source of fish. As the seasonal floods retreat, they leave pasture for thousands of livestock desperate for food and water after a dry season of at least eight months. The retreating floods also leave damp areas for man, equally desperate for cultivable land in an arid environment. Flood water is sometimes retained for swamp rice cultivation, and has been made available for irrigation, particularly in the 'dead' south-western section of the inland Niger delta.

The delta is the remnant of an inland lake, in which the upper River Niger once terminated. In a more rainy era this overflowed to join the then mighty Tilemsi river, once the drainage focus of the now arid Adrar des Iforas. The middle and lower courses of the Tilemsi now comprise the Niger below Bourem, at the eastern end of the consquential elbow turn of the Niger. The eastern part of the delta, which was formed in the earlier lake, is intersected by 'live' flood-water branches of the river, while the relic channels of the very slightly higher western part of the delta are never occupied naturally by flood water and so are 'dead'. However, these are used in part for irrigation water retained by the Sansanding barrage, which has raised the level of the Niger by an average of 4.3 m.

Mali is mainly dry throughout, with a rainy season of four to five months and a total rainfall of 1,120 mm at Bamako, and of only seven weeks and an average fall of 236 mm at Gao. North of this there is no rain-fed cultivation, but only semi-desert or true desert, which occupies nearly one-half of Mali. The exploitation of gold reserves, most of which are located near the borders with Senegal and Guinea, is becoming an increasingly important activity. Modest quantities of diamonds are mined near the border with Senegal.

Distances to the nearest foreign port from most places in Mali are at least 1,300 km, and, not surprisingly, there is much seasonal and permanent emigration.

Recent History

PIERRE ENGLEBERT

Revised for this edition by the Editor

The former French colony of Soudan merged with Senegal in April 1959 to form the Federation of Mali, which became independent on 20 June 1960. Senegal seceded two months later, and the Republic of Mali was proclaimed on 22 September. President Modibo Keita declared the country a one-party state, under his Union soudanaise–Rassemblement démocratique africain (US–RDA). Keita's Marxist regime severed links with France and developed close relations with the Eastern bloc. In November 1968 Keita was deposed in an army coup d'état, and a Comité militaire pour la libération nationale was formed, with Lt (later Gen.) Moussa Traoré as president.

THE TRAORÉ PERIOD

The new regime promised a return to civilian rule when Mali's economic problems (now exacerbated by drought in the Sahel region) had been overcome. Relations with France improved, and French budgetary aid ensued, while internal political debate was overshadowed by the ravages of the 1968–74 drought. In 1976 a new ruling party, the Union démocratique du peuple malien (UDPM), was established, and presidential and legislative elections followed in 1979. Traoré, as sole candidate for the presidency, received 99% of the votes cast, while a single list of UDPM candidates was elected to the legislature. From 1981 the Traoré regime undertook a programme of economic reform, which was pursued despite the return of severe droughts in 1983–84. Following his unopposed re-election to the presidency in 1985, Traoré vigorously pursued measures to suppress public corruption: in December 1987 nine people were sentenced to death, convicted of embezzling public funds; four others received death sentences in 1989.

At elections to the national assembly in June 1988, provision was made for up to three UDPM-nominated candidates to contest each of the 82 seats. In September Traoré ordered the closure of the detention facilities at the Taoudenni salt mines, in northern Mali, and reduced the sentences of (or released) its 78 prisoners, among them several of those implicated in a 1978 coup attempt.

Doubtless influenced by political events elsewhere in the region, in March 1990 Traoré initiated a nation-wide series of conferences to consider the exercise of democracy within and by the ruling party. Although many political activists, especially in Bamako, spoke in favour of reform, Traoré stated that diverse political opinions must be expressed within the framework of the UDPM. Mali's first cohesive opposition movements began to emerge in the second half of the year: among the most prominent were the Comité national d'initiative démocratique

(CNID) and the Alliance pour la démocratie au Mali (ADEMA), which organized mass pro-democracy demonstrations in December. In January 1991 Traoré again relinquished the defence portfolio—this time to Brig.-Gen. Mamadou Coulibaly, the air force chief of staff. Gen. Sékou Ly, minister of the interior and basic development, issued warnings to the opposition groups that their political activities must cease. Rallies were organized to denounce the restrictions, and protests intensified following the arrest of the leader of an unofficial students' organization. Two demonstrators were killed when security forces intervened to suppress violent protests in Bamako led by students, school pupils and lawyers. Schools and colleges throughout Mali were closed by the authorities for several weeks, as unrest spread, and armoured vehicles were deployed in the capital.

ARMY INTERVENTION AND POLITICAL REFORM

Violent pro-democracy demonstrations in March 1991 were harshly repressed by the security forces: official figures later revealed that 106 people were killed, and 708 injured, during three days of unrest. Traoré promised political reforms, but refused to accede to demands for his resignation. On 26 March it was announced that Traoré had been arrested. A military Conseil de réconciliation nationale (CRN), led by Lt-Col (later Lt-Gen.) Amadou Toumani Touré, assumed power, and the constitution, government, legislature and the UDPM were dissolved. Following negotiations with ADEMA, the CNID and other reformist political groups, the CRN was swiftly succeeded by a 25-member Comité de transition pour le salut du peuple (CTSP), chaired by Touré, whose function was to be to oversee a transition to a democratic, civilian political system. It was announced that municipal, legislative and presidential elections would be organized by the end of the year, and that the armed forces would withdraw from political life in early 1992. In April 1991 Soumana Sacko, working in the Central African Republic as a UN development official, and briefly minister of finance and trade in 1987, accepted an invitation to return to Mali to head a transitional, civilian-dominated government.

The CTSP, while affirming its commitment to the policies of economic adjustment that had been adopted by the Traoré administration, sought to remove from positions of influence all those considered to have been implicated in the corrupt practices of the previous regime. Efforts were initiated to recover funds allegedly embezzled by Traoré and his associates, rumoured to total some US $2,000m. (roughly equivalent to the country's foreign debt), which were said to have been deposited in bank accounts overseas. Sékou Ly, Mamadou Coulibaly and Ousmane Coulibaly, the chief of staff of the army, were among the senior officials arrested in connection with the brutal repression of the unrest prior to Traoré's overthrow, while other prominent figures were accused of 'economic crimes'. The council of ministers and the CTSP were reorganized following the discovery, in July 1991, of a coup plot, allegedly involving several members of the new regime.

An amnesty was proclaimed for most political prisoners detained under Traoré, and provision was made for the registration of political parties. The CNID was legalized as the Congrès national d'initiative démocratique (led by a prominent lawyer, Mountaga Tall), while ADEMA (chaired by Alpha Oumar Konaré, an historian, archaeologist and founder of an influential cultural co-operative, who had briefly been a government minister in the late 1970s) adopted the additional title of Parti panafricain pour la liberté, la solidarité et la justice. Modibo Keita was posthumously rehabilitated in May 1991, and his US–RDA was revived.

A national conference was convened in Bamako in late July 1991, and during its two-week session some 1,800 delegates prepared a draft constitution for what was to be designated the third republic of Mali, together with an electoral code and a charter governing political parties. Later in August seven government ministers and about one-half of the members of the CTSP were replaced, following reports implicating them in the repression prior to the coup. In November it was announced that the period of transition to civilian rule was to be extended until 26 March 1992. (The delay was attributed principally to the CTSP's desire first to secure an agreement with Tuareg groups in the north—see below.) The constitutional referendum, originally scheduled for 1 December 1991, thus took place on

12 January 1992, when the document was approved by 99.8% of those who voted (only about 43% of the electorate). Municipal elections followed one week later, contested by 23 of the country's 48 authorized parties. ADEMA enjoyed the greatest success, winning 214 of the 751 local seats, while the US–RDA took 130 seats and the CNID 96. The rate of abstention by voters was, however, almost 70%. Legislative elections eventually took place on 23 February and 8 March, amid allegations that the electoral system was unduly favourable to ADEMA. Of the 21 parties that submitted candidates, 10 secured seats in the 129-member national assembly: ADEMA won 76 seats (with 48.4% of the votes cast), the CNID nine (with 5.5%) and the US–RDA eight (with 17.6%). Overall, only about one-fifth of the electorate voted.

Nine candidates contested the first round of the presidential election, on 12 April 1992 (the date for the transition to civilian rule having again been postponed). The largest share of the votes (some 45%) was won by Konaré. A second round of voting, contested by the ADEMA leader and his nearest rival, Tiéoulé Mamadou Konaté of the US–RDA, followed two weeks later, at which Konaré won 69% of the votes cast. Again, participation by voters was little more than 20%.

THE KONARÉ PRESIDENCY

Alpha Oumar Konaré was sworn in as president of the third republic on 8 June 1992. Younoussi Touré, formerly the director in Mali of the Banque centrale des états de l'Afrique de l'ouest, was designated prime minister. While most strategic posts in Touré's government were allocated to members of ADEMA, the US–RDA and the Parti pour la démocratie et le progrès (PDP) were also represented. In July Aly Nouhoun Diallo, ADEMA's political secretary, was elected president of the national assembly; opposition deputies boycotted the vote, in protest against their perceived lack of political influence in a system excessively dominated by ADEMA.

In February 1993 ex-president Traoré, Sékou Ly, Mamadou Coulibaly and Ousmane Coulibaly were sentenced to death, after having been convicted of 'premeditated murder, battery and voluntary manslaughter' at the time of the March 1991 disturbances; 29 other defendants were acquitted. Appeals against the death sentences were rejected by the supreme court in May. However, no execution was known to have been carried out since 1980, and in early 1996 Konaré asserted that no death penalty would be exacted during his presidency. Charges relating to 'economic crimes' remained against Traoré, his wife and other members of the discredited regime.

Younoussi Touré resigned the premiership in April 1993, following several weeks of student protests against the government's austerity measures, and was replaced by Abdoulaye Sekou Sow. The new prime minister, who was not affiliated to any political party, appointed a council of ministers dominated by ADEMA and its supporters, but which also included opposition representatives: most notably, three ministries were allocated to the CNID. Members of ADEMA, the CNID and the US–RDA soon expressed dissatisfaction at their exclusion from the decision-making process, which they believed to be excessively dominated by Konaré and the council of ministers, and a reorganization of the government in November was prompted by the resignation of ADEMA's vice-president, Mohamed Lamine Traoré, from his ministerial post. Sow's 'streamlined' council of ministers included a new minister responsible for finance (a controversial programme of austerity measures, announced in September, had failed to prevent the suspension of assistance by the IMF and the World Bank). ADEMA remained the majority party in the government, which also included representatives of the CNID, the PDP and the Rassemblement pour la démocratie et le progrès (RDP). The US–RDA withdrew from the coalition shortly afterwards. In December it was revealed that a plot to assassinate Konaré, Sow and Aly Nouhoun Diallo, orchestrated by Traoré's former aide-de-camp (who had been detained since July, accused of the misappropriation of state funds), had been thwarted.

Political and social tensions were exacerbated by the 50% devaluation, in January 1994, of the CFA franc. Sow, who had been experiencing increasing difficulty in securing support for his policies from ADEMA, resigned in February, and was replaced as prime minister by Ibrahim Boubacar Keita—since

November 1993 the minister of foreign affairs, Malians abroad and African integration, who was said to be both a member of ADEMA's radical tendency and a close associate of Konaré. The CNID and the RDP withdrew from the government coalition, protesting that they had not been consulted about the changes; a new, ADEMA-dominated government was appointed, from which the PDP in turn withdrew (although its representative in the council of ministers resigned from the party, in order to retain his portfolio).

Sow's resignation failed to avert renewed unrest in the education sector, as students and school pupils protested against the currency's depreciation and demanded compensatory grant increases. Violent demonstrations in Bamako in February 1994 prompted the closure of schools and colleges, and the detention in March of the students' union leader provoked further violent disturbances. A day of 'inaction', organized by opposition groups in late March, was deemed by the authorities to have been poorly supported, although the opposition claimed that much of the economic life of the capital had been disrupted. Salaries in the state sector were increased by 10% with effect from April, and by a further 5% in October. In November cadets who had been dismissed from the gendarmerie following strike action prompted by the delayed payment of arrears seized weapons and erected barricades in Bamako: one person was killed, and about 300 cadets were arrested.

In September 1994, the election of Keita to the presidency of ADEMA precipitated the resignation of prominent party members, including Mohamed Lamine Traoré and the secretary-general, Mouhamedou Dicko. Disaffected members of ADEMA formed the Mouvement pour l'indépendance, la renaissance et l'intégration africaines (MIRIA) in December. In January 1995 an application for legalization by a revived UDPM was rejected by the supreme court (an earlier application had been disallowed in 1993). However, the Mouvement patriotique pour le renouveau (MPR), established by several of those who had sought to revive the UDPM, was granted official status later in the month. A 'breakaway' movement from the CNID was registered in September as the Parti pour la renaissance nationale (PARENA); ADEMA and PARENA established a political alliance in February 1996, and its chairman and secretary-general were appointed to the government in July. In October it was announced that a prominent member of the MPR and former minister under Traoré, Mady Diallo, had been arrested, together with several armed forces officers, following the discovery of a plot to assassinate Konaré, Keita and other government ministers. Diallo was later released, but was again detained in early April 1997. The trial of Diallo and six members of the military began in early March 1998.

A new electoral code was approved by the national assembly in early January 1997. An earlier version, adopted in September 1996, had been denounced by the opposition parties as being unduly favourable to ADEMA's interests, and certain clauses had subsequently been deemed inadmissible by the constitutional court. (Opposition deputies, who had boycotted the vote on the first revision, participated in the parliamentary debate but did not vote on the amended code.) Under the new code the composition of the Commission électorale nationale indépendante (CENI), the body responsible for overseeing the forthcoming presidential, legislative and municipal elections, was to comprise 14 representatives of political parties (seven for the majority party and seven for the opposition parties combined), together with eight representatives of the government and eight non-political members. The national assembly also approved an increase in the number of parliamentary seats from 129 to 147.

Dates for the forthcoming elections were revised, after the CENI announced that it would be unable to organize the parliamentary elections according to the original schedule, owing to legal, technical and financial difficulties. The first round of the legislative election (which had been due to take place on 9 March) thus took place on 13 April 1997, despite opposition demands for a further postponement. More than 1,500 candidates, mainly representing 36 of the country's 63 political parties, sought election to the enlarged national assembly. There was considerable confusion at polling stations, with a shortage of electoral materials compounded by anomalies and omissions in voting lists. As early results showed a clear victory for

ADEMA (which was the only party to have won any seats outright), the main opposition parties condemned the results as fraudulent, and announced their intention to withdraw from the second round. Some 20 people (among them an opposition candidate for the presidency) were reported to have been injured as security forces intervened to disperse an opposition demonstration in Bamako, organized to protest against the conduct of the elections and to demand the resignation of the government and the disbandment of the CENI. Konaré, the government and the chairman of the electoral commission all admitted that there had been organizational difficulties at the first round, but stated that the poll had been honestly conducted and appealed to the opposition to participate in the second round. (Independent national and international monitors, for their part, recognized that the conduct of the poll had been flawed but not fraudulent.) However, the opposition parties confirmed that they would boycott the second round, and also withdrew their candidates from the presidential and municipal elections. In late April the constitutional court annulled the first round of voting; while welcoming the cancellation, the opposition none the less expressed its dissatisfaction that the results had been invalidated on the grounds of irregularities, rather than fraud.

The first round of the presidential election was subsequently postponed, by one week, until 11 May 1997. Konaré emphasized that he had no wish to be the sole candidate. In early May Mamadou Maribatrou Diaby, the leader of the Parti pour l'unité, la démocratie et le progrès, announced that he was prepared to contest the presidency. However, the so-called 'radical' opposition collective adhered to its demands for the cancellation of the ongoing electoral process, for the complete revision of the voters' register, and, in the mean time, for the resignation of the government and the appointment of a transitional administration. The constitutional court rejected a petition filed by the opposition seeking the cancellation of the presidential poll, and voting proceeded on 11 May, generally in an atmosphere of calm. The results of voting, published by the CENI five days after the poll, confirmed an overwhelming victory for the incumbent Konaré, with 84.4% of the votes, while Diaby took 3.6%. These results included votes cast for the eight radical opposition candidates, whose names were required to be posted at polling centres since they had not given formal notification of their withdrawal from the contest; the final results, as issued by the constitutional court on 24 May, excluded the votes for boycotting candidates, and thus allocated 95.9% of the valid votes cast to Konaré and 4.1% to Diaby. Claiming success for its campaign for a boycott of the election, the radical opposition stated that the low rate of participation by voters, 28.4% of the registered electorate, effectively invalidated Konaré's victory. (The turn-out was, none the less, higher than that recorded at the 1992 election.) International observers, meanwhile, expressed satisfaction at the fair conduct of the poll.

Political tensions escalated following the presidential election, as the radical opposition, refusing to recognize the legitimacy of Konaré's second mandate, resisted the president's attempts at reconciliation. At the end of May 1997 the municipal elections were postponed indefinitely. On 8 June, the day of Konaré's investiture, there were violent disturbances in Bamako, and Mountaga Tall, Almany Sylla (the RDP chairman and leader of the opposition collective) and Sogal Maïga (the MPR secretary-general) were among five opposition leaders arrested and charged with 'non-recognition of the results of the presidential election' and with opposition to state authority, as well as with arson and incitement to violence. They were released on bail in mid-June, shortly after the first round of the legislative elections, due on 6 July, had been postponed by two weeks. Meanwhile, several opposition activists were sentenced to three months' imprisonment for their part in recent disturbances. While some opposition parties announced their intention to present candidates for the national assembly, 18 opposition parties, whose collective embraced the broadest political spectrum—linking the late president Keita's US-RDA with the MPR (the effective successor to Moussa Traoré's UDPM) and the CNID (which had, together with ADEMA, led the opposition to Traoré's one-party state)—reiterated their refusal to re-enter the electoral process unless their demands were met in full.

Two people were reported to have been killed in violence in San on the eve of legislative voting, and there were violent disturbances in Bamako and elsewhere, as a result of which, according to opposition claims, some 40 people were injured and 50 arrests were made. Voting took place on 20 July 1997: a total of 17 parties (including five 'moderate' opposition parties), as well as small number of independent candidates, contested seats in the national assembly. As at the presidential election, the radical opposition claimed that its appeal to the electorate to boycott the poll had been successful, and that the low rate of participation by voters (about 12% of the registered electorate in Bamako, and 22% elsewhere) would render the assembly illegitimate. The official results confirmed the large majority of ADEMA. A second round of voting was held for eight seats on 3 August. The final results allocated 130 seats to ADEMA (including one seat won in alliance with the Convention patriotique pour le progrès), eight to PARENA, four to the Convention démocratique et sociale (CDS), three to the Union pour la démocratie et le développement (UDD) and two to the PDP. Both rounds of legislative voting were stated by international monitors to have been conducted fairly.

Konaré undertook a series of consultations with representatives of the political majority and opposition, and there were indications that he was prepared to concede the allocation of public funds to opposition parties, acknowledging that ADEMA was disproportionately advantaged by the prevailing system. However, the ruling party strongly disapproved of the president's relatively conciliatory approach towards the radical opposition; meanwhile, neither Konaré nor ADEMA was willing to compromise on the key element of the opposition's demands, the issue of the legitimacy of the recently-elected institutions, asserting that the validity of the presidential and legislative polls had been confirmed both by the constitutional court and by independent monitors.

Meanwhile, the political climate deteriorated further with the lynching of a police-officer at an opposition rally in Bamako following the second round of legislative voting. Several opposition leaders, among them Tall, Sylla and the MIRIA leader, Mohamed Lamine Traoré, were subsequently arrested, and 10 activists were charged with violence, assault and battery and were transferred to detention centres outside the capital. All 10 were acquitted of inciting violence and complicity to murder in April 1998. In early September 1997, none the less, Konaré held a meeting with some 20 opposition leaders, including representatives of the radical opposition, at which he proposed the formation of a broadly-based coalition government. A new government was appointed in mid-September, again with Keita as prime minister: the new administration included a small number of representatives of the moderate opposition parties (such as the UDD and the PDP), alongside ADEMA and its allies. It was emphasized that this was not a transitional administration, and close associates of the president held the finance, foreign affairs and territorial administration and security portfolios. In late October a presidential pardon was granted to all political activists charged during the election period and its aftermath (including the opposition leaders arrested in August). At the end of the month, however, the opposition parties repeated their warning that they would not participate in the municipal elections unless the voters' register had been updated.

In late 1997 the Malian government denied allegations made in a report by the human rights organization, Amnesty International, of complicity in the torture of detainees. The report cited in particular cases of the ill-treatment of political activists during the recent election period. In early December the government adopted measures regarding the decentralization of prison administration; a decree ordering the closure of the prison at Kidal (like Taoudenni, a symbol of torture and repression under previous regimes) was stated as exemplifying the government's commitment to promoting human rights. Shortly afterwards Konaré formally commuted some 21 death sentences—most notably including those imposed on ex-president Traoré and his associates.

In the meantime, although several parties had withdrawn from the radical opposition collective, little progress was made towards full political reconciliation. In early 1998 the radical opposition announced that it would not attend a planned national forum (a regular feature of political life under the third republic), and in mid-February 13 parties confirmed their intention to boycott the forthcoming municipal elections: the radical opposition stated that the voters' register remained unreliable, and denounced the government for planning the elections in the absence of a wider political settlement. The opposition warned that rallies and demonstrations would resume, while indicating willingness to negotiate with Konaré. The local elections, scheduled for 19 April, were subsequently cancelled, and in mid-April the radical opposition announced that it was prepared to accept a mediation initiative by former US president Jimmy Carter. (Since his withdrawal from Malian political life the leader of the 1991 coup, Amadou Toumani Touré, had become involved in the crisis-management work of the US-based Carter Center.) During a recent visit to Mali Carter had proposed that all parties recognize the legitimacy of Konaré's presidential mandate, and recommended the dissolution and recomposition of the CENI, what was termed a 'consensual' revision of voters' lists, and the holding of communal elections before the end of June. While accepting the principle of mediation, the radical collective warned of an imminent campaign of nation-wide civil disobedience. During May, however, the opposition's strength was undermined by a split in the US–RDA, as 29 members of the party's political bureau announced their recognition of Konaré's election; the party chairman, Mamadou Bamou Touré, suspended these members, prompting the dissidents to question the legitimacy of his leadership. In the same month, furthermore, a meeting took place between Keita, in his capacity as leader of ADEMA, and Sogal Maïga of the MPR, with the expressed aim of defusing the political climate. At the meeting, Keita was reported as having responded positively to a request by the MPR that outstanding legal proceedings against former members of the Traoré regime be expedited.

Municipal voting began in mid-1998, as elections took place in 19 communes on 21 June. Violence was reported in Bamako prior to the poll, and MIRIA accused ADEMA militants of setting fire to the opposition party's headquarters; several opposition activists were arrested in the CNID stronghold of Segou for allegedly attempting to sabotage voting. The remaining radical opposition parties boycotted the elections, at which ADEMA won control of 16 councils. Voting in the majority of communes (a total of 682) was scheduled to take place in November, but was subsequently postponed until April 1999 to allow for the resolution of administrative problems and, in addition, for negotiations on participation by all political tendencies.

In mid-October 1998 the trial for 'economic crimes' began in Bamako of ex-president Traoré, his wife Mariam, her brother, Abraham Douah Cissoko (the former head of customs), together with a former minister of finance under the Traoré regime, Tiena Coulibaly, and the former representative in France of the Banque de développement du Mali, Moussa Koné. All five were accused of embezzlement of public funds and illegal enrichment while in office. In January 1999 Traoré, his wife and brother-in-law were sentenced to death, having been convicted of 'economic crimes' to the value of some US $350,000; the original claims had cited embezzled funds amounting to $4m. Coulibaly and Koné were acquitted. However, in September Konaré, as expected, commuted the death sentences to terms of life imprisonment. In 2000 ex-president Traoré travelled to the Algerian capital, Algiers, for medical treatment, returning to imprisonment in Mali later in the year.

Only four of the 19 radical opposition parties took part in the national forum on Mali's political and institutional problems, held in Bamako in late January 1999. On the eve of the forum Bamou Touré (whose faction of the US–RDA was to boycott the talks) indicated his willingness to recognize the legitimacy of Konaré's presidency, in return for opposition participation in government and the holding of early legislative elections. On the third day of the forum some 20 people were reported to have been injured when police intervened to disperse a meeting of MPR activists, which was to have been followed by a protest march to the forum. In February it was reported that the Parti progressiste soudanais (PPS), which had attended the forum, had been expelled from the radical collective. In March the PPS announced that they were to contest the forthcoming municipal elections. A number of other members of the radical opposition subsequently announced that they would also take part.

On 2 May 1999 about 30 parties took part in the first tranche of the municipal elections. Many radical opposition parties refused, however, to participate. It was reported that of the 7,124 seats available in 492 communes in the regions of Kayes, Koulikoro, Sikasso and Ségou, the ADEMA had won 4,193, the PARENA 857 and the UDD 425. The CDS, the US–RDA, the Bloc pour la démocratie et l'intégration africaine (BDIA), and the Parti malienne pour le développement et le renouveau each obtained more than 100 seats. On 6 June municipal elections for 190 communes in the regions of Gao, Kidal, Mopti, and Tombouctou took place. According to provisional results, ADEMA obtained 1,739 of the 2,823 available seats, while the US–RDA won 213, PARENA 110 and the UDD 108. The remaining seats were divided between various parties and independents. On 21 June elections were held in a further 19 communes. ADEMA won 16 of the 19 mayoralties at stake and 282 of the councillors' seats. PARENA also performed strongly, while in the north 11 seats were won by an independent list composed of members of the BDIA and dissident members of ADEMA. Elections for the remaining 682 communes remained to be held.

On 19 July 1999 the Union nationale des travailleurs du Mali (UNTM), Mali's main trade union federation, called for a 48-hour general strike across the country. The strike followed the breakdown of negotiations with the government, through which the UNTM had hoped to secure improvements in prospects for state employees, a reduction in the cost of basic commodities, and an end to recent electricity shortages. The UNTM further accused the government of having broken its promise, made in 1998, to review public sector salaries. The strike, which was reportedly widely observed, subsequently spread from the public to the private sector. In mid-August the UNTM and the government agreed a 7% increase in the salaries of public-sector employees and workers in state-owned companies. None the less, in late September health-sector employees undertook industrial action in support of their claims for improved working conditions. The strike lasted until mid-October, when a compromise was reached with the government.

In September 1999 President Konaré launched what he termed a 'clean hands' campaign with the dismissal of a number of senior public officials, including some directors of state-owned companies, suspected of corrupt practices. Konaré later announced the creation of a commission to examine the extent of corruption and fraud among state officials and to review all reports received on the issue since 1992. Konaré emphasized that he expected that legal proceedings would be undertaken against any official criticized in the committee's report. In November 1999 the former director of the state postal service, Lansina Togda, was arrested on suspicion of having trafficked in stamps. In January 2000 the commission's report detailed widespread irregularities in the management of state-owned companies and a lack of transparency in local government. The independent press subsequently demanded the prosecution of offenders and the confiscation of illegally-acquired wealth.

In mid-February 2000 Ibrahim Boubacar Keita submitted his government's resignation. Observers suggested that Keita had decided to concentrate on his role as the leader of ADEMA, in the hope of promoting his candidature in the next presidential election, scheduled for 2002; Konaré was barred under the constitution from seeking a further term in office. An extensively reorganized council of ministers was subsequently appointed, with Mandé Sidibé as prime minister. In July a significant proportion of the ADEMA party called for an extraordinary congress, which would undermine Keita's prospects of securing the party's candidacy to succeed Konaré as president; however, the numbers calling for such action did not amount to the required two-thirds of the party's branches, or a majority of the executive committee. Meanwhile, opposition parties attempted to adopt a united approach for the 2002 election campaign through a grouping known as the Collectif de l'opposition malienne, although several parties, including MIRIA, preferred to maintain an independent approach. There was also some support, both within the country and from Malians living in Senegal and Niger, for Amadou Toumani Touré, the leader of the 1991 coup and subsequent transitional regime, to stand as a candidate in the presidential elections.

ETHNIC TENSIONS

Ethnic violence emerged in the north in mid-1990, as large numbers of light-skinned Tuaregs, who had migrated to Algeria and Libya during periods of drought, began to return to Mali and Niger (q.v.). In July of that year the Traoré government, which claimed that Tuareg rebels were attempting to establish a secessionist state, imposed a state of emergency in the Gao and Tombouctou regions, and the armed forces began a repressive campaign against the nomads. In September the Malian government announced that a new administrative region was to be established in the north-eastern Kidal area. In January 1991 representatives of the Traoré government and of two Tuareg groups, the Mouvement populaire de l'Azaouad (MPA) and the Front islamique-arabe de l'Azaouad (FIAA), meeting in Tamanrasset, Algeria, signed a peace accord: there was to be an immediate cease-fire, and the state of emergency was revoked. Tuareg military prisoners were released in March. Following the overthrow of the Traoré regime, the transitional administration affirmed its commitment to the Tamanrasset accord, and representatives of the Tuaregs were included in the CTSP. However, unrest continued in the north, and in June Amnesty International reported incidences of the harsh repression of Tuaregs by the armed forces. Thousands of Tuaregs, Moors and Bella (the descendants of the Tuaregs' black slaves, some of whom remained with the nomads), had fled to neighbouring countries to escape retaliatory attacks by the armed forces and the sedentary black population, while there had been many casualties in the Malian armed forces.

During the second half of 1991 the MPA was reported to have lost the support of more militant members, and a further group, the Front populaire de libération de l'Azaouad (FPLA), emerged to claim responsibility for several attacks. In December a 'special conference on the north' was convened in Mopti. With Algerian mediation, representatives of the transitional government and of four Tuareg groups—the MPA, the FIAA, the FPLA and the Armée révolutionnaire de libération de l'Azaouad (ARLA)—agreed in principle to a peace settlement. Negotiations resumed in the Algerian capital in January 1992, at which the Malian authorities and the MPA, the FIAA and the ARLA (now negotiating together as the Mouvements et fronts unifiés de l'Azaouad—MFUA) formally agreed to implement the Mopti accord; the FPLA was reported not to have attended the Algiers sessions. A truce entered into force in February, and further talks in Algiers culminated, in March, in the drafting of a 'national pact', which was signed in Bamako by the Malian authorities and the MFUA on 11 April. In addition to the provisions of the Mopti accord, the pact envisaged special administrative structures for the country's three northern regions, the incorporation of Tuareg fighters into the Malian armed forces, the demilitarization of the north and the instigation of efforts more fully to integrate Tuaregs in the economic and political fields.

Sporadic attacks, particularly against members of the northern majority Songhai, continued. None the less, the implementation of the 'national pact' was pursued: joint patrols were established, and Konaré visited the north in November 1992 to inaugurate the new administrative structures. In February 1993 the Malian government and the MFUA signed a preliminary accord facilitating the integration of Tuaregs into the national army. In May the FPLA's secretary-general, Rhissa Ag Sidi Mohamed, declared the rebellion at an end and returned to Mali (from his base in Burkina Faso), urging FPLA fighters to participate in the pact. During the second half of 1993, however, Tuareg leaders expressed concern that difficulties in repatriating refugees and in the implementation of the 'national pact' were the cause of renewed attacks in the north. In February 1994 the assassination of the MPA's military leader (a principal architect of the peace process, who had joined the Malian army under the 'national pact') was allegedly perpetrated by the ARLA, and clashes between the MPA and the ARLA continued for several weeks before the two groups were reconciled.

In May 1994, at a meeting in Algiers, agreement was reached by the Malian government and the MFUA regarding the integration of 1,500 former rebels into the regular army and of a further 4,860 Tuaregs into civilian sectors; the MFUA agreed to dismantle its military bases in the north, while the government reaffirmed its commitment to the pursuit of development projects. The agreement was, however, undermined by an intensification of violence in this area, and tensions between the 'integrated' Tuareg fighters and regular members of the Malian armed forces periodically escalated into violence. Meanwhile, a Songhai-dominated resistance movement, the Mouvement patriotique malien Ghanda Koy ('Masters of the Land'), emerged and there were rumours of official complicity in its actions against the Tuaregs. Meeting in Tamanrasset in June, the Malian authorities and the MFUA agreed on the need for the reinforcement of the army presence in areas affected by the violence, and for the more effective integration of Tuareg fighters.

In August 1994 agreement was reached by Mali, Algeria, representatives of the UN High Commissioner for Refugees (UNHCR) and the International Fund for Agricultural Development regarding the voluntary repatriation from Algeria of Malian refugees. The accord, whereby the Malian authorities undertook to respect the fundamental rights of the Tuaregs, and which guaranteed international protection for Tuareg refugees, was welcomed by the Tuaregs: the MFUA pledged the reconciliation of the Tuareg movements and reiterated its commitment to the 'national pact'; however, the talks were not attended by representatives of the 'dissident' Tuaregs of the FIAA (whose commitment to the peace process had been increasingly called into question), and unrest continued. In September Amnesty International expressed concern at the deaths of increasing numbers of civilians as a result of the conflict, denouncing what it termed a cycle of violence as a result of which attacks by armed Tuareg and Moorish groups were followed by retaliatory attacks by the Malian armed forces on light-skinned civilians. Hostilities intensified, and in October, following an attack (for which the FIAA claimed responsibility) on Gao and retaliatory action, as a result of which, according to official figures, 66 people were killed, both the government and the MFUA appealed for an end to the violence.

The government subsequently appeared to adopt a less conciliatory approach towards the Tuareg rebels, and in the weeks following the Gao attack the army announced the capture of several rebel bases. In January 1995 representatives of the FPLA and Ghanda Koy, meeting in Bourem, issued a joint statement urging an end to hostilities in the north. Shortly afterwards the FIAA leader, Zahabi Ould Sidi Mohamed, asserted that his organization was willing to co-operate with the government and with other Tuareg groups in the restoration of peace. Discussions involving Tuareg groups, Ghanda Koy and representatives of local communities took place in subsequent weeks, and in April an agreement was signed providing for co-operation in resolving hitherto contentious issues. Ministerial delegations, including representatives of the organs of state, the MFUA and Ghanda Koy, toured the north, as well as refugee areas in Algeria, Burkina and Mauritania, with the aim of promoting reconciliation and awareness of the peace programme. Konaré also visited those countries, and made direct appeals to refugees to return to participate in the process of reconstruction. In June the FIAA announced an end to its armed struggle.

As part of the programme of 'normalization' in the north, initiatives were undertaken in mid-1995 to restore civilian local government to areas affected by the conflict, as well as education and health-care facilities and basic utilities. In July representatives of the government and of Mali's creditors met at Tombouctou, where they agreed development strategies for the northern regions; the MFUA and Ghanda Koy issued a joint statement in support of the decisions taken at the conference.

By February 1996 some 3,000 MFUA fighters and Ghanda Koy militiamen had registered and surrendered their weapons at designated centres in the north, under an encampment programme initiated in November 1995 in preparation for the eventual integration of former rebels into the regular army or civilian structures. The MFUA and Ghanda Koy subsequently jointly affirmed their adherence to Mali's constitution, national unity and territorial integrity, and advocated the full implementation of the 'national pact' and associated accords. They further proclaimed the 'irreversible dissolution' of their respective movements.

In September 1997 the graduation of MFUA and Ghanda Koy contingents in the gendarmerie was reported as marking the accomplishment of the integration of all Malian fighters within the regular armed and security forces. In the following month the former FPLA leader, Rhissa Ag Sidi Mohamed, who had not previously been regarded as a party to the peace process, returned to Mali and expressed his willingness to join efforts to consolidate peace and promote the development of the north. None the less, following a tour of the region in November 1997, the ministers of justice and of the armed forces and veterans expressed concern that the continued proliferation of weapons, as well as the inadequacy of military and administrative structures in the area, could result in renewed unrest.

From 1995 significant numbers of refugees were reported to be returning voluntarily to Mali. Such returns were accompanied by repatriations of smaller numbers under UNHCR supervision from Algeria and Mauritania. The process of repatriating some 42,000 Malian refugees from Mauritania was completed, and the last camp there closed, in July 1997. The remaining refugee camps in Burkina (where, in all, 160,000 Malians were reported to have sought shelter at some time during the conflict) were closed in December 1997. In November 1996, meanwhile, Mali, Niger and UNHCR signed an agreement for the repatriation of 25,000 Malian Tuaregs from Niger. In June 1998 the last groups of refugees returned from Algeria. Observers have, however, expressed concern at the continuing insecurity in northern Mali and the prevalence of armed attacks and robberies.

In mid-July 1999 clashes were reported in Gao and Kidal between members of the Arab and Kounta communities. The conflict had been provoked by disagreements between the two communities following the municipal elections in the town of Tarkint. Despite mediation efforts, 10 people were reportedly killed in the violence, and security forces were deployed in the area to prevent further disturbances. Meanwhile, ethnic violence was also reported in the Kayes region, where eight people were killed in a dispute between Soninké farmers and Fulani (Peul) herders over access to water and pasture. Numerous such disputes between the two ethnic groups had been reported in the area since early 1999, and at the end of July the Malian authorities brokered a peace agreement, which was signed by representatives of both communities and by the president of the assemblée nationale. The peace agreement envisaged a programme of disarmament and a conference to investigate the causes of, and possible solutions to, the recent disturbances in the region. In August the Malian security forces constructed an additional 15 guard posts in the north of the country (near the border with Senegal and Mauritania) in the hope of curbing the increase in ethnic and political violence and in cross-border banditry. In October, however, clashes over the division of territory and control again led to an outbreak between the two sides, in which up to 40 people were estimated to have been killed.

EXTERNAL RELATIONS

In recent years the presence in neighbouring countries of large numbers of refugees from the conflict in northern Mali, and the attendant issue of border security, has dominated Mali's regional relations. From 1995, following the programme of 'normalization' in the north, significant numbers of refugees began to return voluntarily to Mali, and the process of repatriation was completed by mid-1998. The north of the country remains, however, vulnerable to continuing insecurity and, particularly, to cross-border banditry. In May 1998 the ministers of the interior of Mali, Senegal and Mauritania met to strengthen co-operation and border controls, and in December Mali and Senegal decided to reinforce border security. Following a visit by Konaré to Algiers in February 1999 Mali and Algeria also agreed to revive their joint border committee to promote development and stability in the region. In March 1999 Konaré visited Mauritania to discuss border security, however, in June a dispute over watering rights escalated into an armed conflict between neighbouring Malian and Mauritanian communities, in which 13 people were killed. The two governments responded to the disturbances by increasing border patrols, and by sending a joint delegation to the villages involved. In August, at a meeting in Dakar, Senegal, the Malian, Mauritanian and Senegalese ministers of the interior agreed to establish an operational unit drawn from the police forces of the three countries in order to ensure security in the area of their joint border. Mali also maintains particularly good relations with Côte d'Ivoire and with Libya. Mali was a founder member, with Libya, of the Community of the Sahel-Saharan States (see p. 151), established in Tripoli in 1997.

The government of France granted financial support for the recovery efforts that were necessary after March 1991, and promised continued aid for Mali's programme of economic adjustment. French financial assistance was also forthcoming for the implementation of the 'national pact' between the Malian government and Tuareg movements. None the less, the Konaré regime has sought to develop what it considers a more equal relationship with its former colonial ruler. From mid-1996, moreover, a series of much-publicized expulsions from France of illegal immigrants, among them many Malians, was generally criticized in Mali, with the process of repatriation by chartered aircraft being condemned by the Konaré administration as a violation of basic dignity. The issue of immigration was a principal focus of discussions during a visit by the French prime minister, Lionel Jospin, in December 1997 (the first visit by a French premier to independent Mali). Konaré appealed for humanity in French policy towards immigrants, while Jospin gave assurances that the mass expulsions by chartered aircraft would cease. Regarding Mali's domestic tensions, Jospin appealed to the opposition movement not to boycott the democratic process. The French prime minister also undertook to relieve Mali's bilateral debt. Further progress on immigration was achieved in September 1998 with the establishment of a Franco-Malian joint committee on immigration, intended to promote co-operation on the repatriation of migrants and their reintegration into Malian society. In August 1999, however, the French ambassador to Mali was summoned to the ministry of foreign affairs and Malians abroad in order to explain the allegedly violent repatriation of a Malian citizen from France.

During his first term in office President Konaré regarded the development of a wider international role for Mali as a priority in foreign policy. Mali has, notably, contributed actively to UN peace-keeping forces, and has been prominent in efforts to establish an African military crisis-response force. In late 1996 and early 1997, moreover, Amadou Toumani Touré led a regional mediation effort to resolve the crisis in the Central African Republic (CAR), and in February 1997 a Malian military contingent was dispatched to the CAR as part of a regional surveillance mission. Malian troops remained in the CAR, until February 2000, as part of the UN peace-keeping mission which succeeded the regional force in April 1998. In February of that year Mali, together with Mauritania and Senegal, was among the principal participants in military exercises conducted in eastern Senegal.

In February 1999 488 Malian troops joined the peace-keeping forces of the Economic Community of West African States (see ECOMOG, p. 128) in Sierra Leone. In response to domestic criticism of this intervention, the Malian authorities emphasized that the troops would take on a purely peace-keeping role and would not be involved in any hostilities between Sierra Leone's ECOMOG-supported government forces and rebels. In May, however, several members of the Malian contingent were reported to have been killed, and many more taken hostage, by rebel forces in fighting around the town of Port Loko. News of the casualties provoked widespread indignation in Bamako, and demands for the withdrawal of Malian troops. In early August 150 soldiers withdrew from Sierra Leone, and further withdrawals were expected to follow. The Malian authorities announced that a small number of troops would remain in Sierra Leone to assist with the disarmament programme in that country. It was reported that during the six-month mission seven Malian soldiers had been killed and 10 seriously injured, while one was missing.

Economy

EDITH HODGKINSON

Revised for this edition by the Editor

Mali, the second largest country in francophone west Africa, is sparsely populated (with a density of 8.6 inhabitants per sq km at mid-1998) and land-locked, and most parts are desert or semi-desert, with the economically viable area confined to the Sahelian-Sudanese regions irrigated by the River Niger, which comprise about one-fifth of the total land area. The rate of economic growth in recent decades has been affected by drought, changes in the terms of international trade, as well as political instability. There have thus been wide fluctuations in trends in real gross domestic product (GDP) from year to year. Overall GDP increased at an average rate of 4.9% per year in the 1970s and by 2.8% in the 1980s; growth in 1990–97 averaged 3.3%. Progress was particularly erratic in the early 1990s: GDP declined by 0.9% in 1991, as political upheaval and difficulties in the agricultural sector depressed the economy. There was renewed growth, of 8.3%, in 1992, with the reflation of the economy assisted by strong expansion in cotton output. GDP fell by 2.5% in 1993, largely owing to the economic paralysis that preceded the devaluation of the CFA franc, and to pressure from the IMF for fiscal restraint. The stimulus to the agricultural sector that resulted from the 50% devaluation of the currency in January 1994 coincided with a marked increase in world commodity prices in that year. Growth of 2.3% in 1994 progressed to 6.4% in 1995, as the agricultural sector prospered, investment in infrastructure stimulated the services sector, and fiscal pressures began to ease. The recovery continued in 1996 and 1997, with growth rates estimated at 4.0% and 6.7% respectively. GDP growth in 1998 was estimated at 4.6%. With the prospect of further expansion in exports of cotton (which have recently accounted for about one-half of total export earnings) and gold (as new capacity comes into production), Mali's immediate prospects for economic growth were good. None the less,

Mali remains among the world's poorest countries, with gross national product (GNP) per head equivalent to only some US $250 in 1998—ranking it just behind that of Nigeria but behind other west African countries such as Ghana, Guinea or Senegal—and it remains both highly vulnerable to external shocks and highly dependent on external funds. Mali's external debt remains at a high level, despite the rescheduling of commitments on highly concessionary terms by official creditors in 1996.

Under the supervision of the World Bank and the IMF, Mali has, since 1998, been implementing adjustment policies that have concentrated on macroeconomic stabilization; fiscal consolidation and tax reform; the liberalization of price and trade policies; regulatory reform; and the reform of public enterprises and the agricultural sector. In early 1999 the IMF concluded that, overall, Mali had achieved important progress in its programme of reform, although the economic situation remained fragile and the agenda of outstanding reforms substantial. In addition to the return to GDP growth since 1994, inflation had been contained at about 4% and Mali had retained the competitive advantage resulting from the devaluation of the CFA franc in 1994. The external current account deficit (excluding official transfers) was estimated to have declined from 9.25% of GDP in 1997 to 8.75% in 1998. Monetary policy was assessed as prudent and the overall deficit of the central government (excluding grants) had been reduced from nearly 8% of GDP in 1997 to 7.5% in 1998. A more efficient and more rigorously enforced tax regime had led to a rise in the tax revenue/GDP ratio to more than 13.5% in 1998, compared with 12.5% in 1996. Total government expenditure and net lending had been reduced by 0.75% to 22.75% of GDP in 1998. Meanwhile, expenditure on health and education had risen to 34% of the government's current expenditure, or 3.6% of GDP, in 1998.

In recognition of the progress achieved in recent years Mali became eligible, in September 1998, for further concessionary relief on its external debt. This became available from 31 December 1999 under the Bretton Woods institutions' Highly Indebted Poor Countries (HIPC) initiative.

Mali's population, which was 7,696,348 at the census of April 1987, is (according to official figures) increasing at a rate of about 2.6% per year (relatively low because of emigration). The UN mid-year estimate for 1998 was 10.7m. About 5% of the population are nomadic, and 27% urban, with the only significant agglomerations at the capital, Bamako, and the regional capitals. Persistent drought throughout the Sahelian region during the 1970s and early 1980s drew a significant part of the nomadic population to the settled areas, with the result that parts of the Gao and Tombouctou (Timbuktu) regions are now deserted. The conflict between government and Tuareg forces in the first half of the 1990s reinforced this trend, with many thousands seeking refuge in neighbouring countries, although the restoration of peace has resulted in the return of large numbers of refugees.

In the absence, until the 1990s, of strong economic growth or structural change, employment patterns have changed little since independence. Subsistence agriculture remains the dominant economic activity. There is still significant seasonal migration (during the agricultural off-season) to Côte d'Ivoire and Senegal, and some 3m. Malians are thought to work abroad, with France also an important host country. Wage employment is very low, and is concentrated in the state sector and in formal-sector businesses in Bamako.

AGRICULTURE

As noted above, agriculture, in particular subsistence agriculture, dominates Mali's economy. In 1998 the sector engaged more than 80% of the total labour force, but contributed only an estimated 45% of the country's GDP. The reduction of the disparity between these figures depends on the successful completion of irrigation programmes—based on the Niger and Senegal rivers—in order to obviate the effects of the periodic droughts that affect the country. In recent decades these have combined with institutional failings and low producer prices to hinder agricultural development.

Agricultural exports account for about 75% of Mali's total exports, but further development is constrained by the inadequacy of the country's transport infrastructure for the movement of perishable goods over long distances. Pending the improvement of that infrastructure, the government has begun to promote the development of small-scale agro-industry in order to increase the proportion of processed goods among agricultural exports.

Millet and sorghum—two basic food crops—are essentially produced at subsistence level. Output of cereals was badly affected by the droughts of the early 1970s and early 1980s: production of millet, sorghum and maize, which had been 1.3m. metric tons in 1976/77, declined to less than one-half of this level in 1984/85, while that of rice, at 103,400 tons in that year, continued to be substantially below earlier levels. The cereals deficit consequently reached 481,000 tons in 1985, about one-half of which was covered by food aid. Since then there has been a recovery, largely the consequence of the return of adequate rainfall in the late 1980s, and exportable surpluses were recorded in both 1989/90 and in 1994/95. In the latter year output of millet, sorghum and maize together reached a record 1,966,300 tons. In 1996/97 production of millet, sorghum and maize declined to an estimated 1,568,600 tons. Cereal imports remained necessary in most years: there was a surplus of 65,000 tons in 1997/98, but a deficit of 54,000 tons was forecast for the 1998/99 season.

Production of rice, meanwhile, has generally increased steadily since the mid-1990s. In 1994/95 output totalled an unprecedented 469,100 tons, and in 1996/97 production rose by more than 30%, compared with 1995/96, to an estimated 614,000 tons. In 1997/98 record production of 663,200 tons was achieved. An important factor in the improvement in rice production has been the reform of the parastatal Office du Niger. This agency was originally established by the French colonial authorities to irrigate the Niger delta, mainly for the cultivation of cotton. For many years the agency operated at a substantial financial loss,

with about one-third of its irrigated area remaining uncultivated. In 1986 a rehabilitation programme was initiated which aimed to rationalize the organization's management and to increase the total cultivable area to more than 100,000 ha, of which 46,730 ha were to be planted with rice. The restructuring of the Office was largely completed by 1994. In 1988 a programme was inaugurated to improve the irrigation network for the cultivation of rice both on the Office du Niger land and in the inland delta of the Niger in the Ségou region. Yields of rice remained low until the mid-1990s (largely owing to poor levels of rainfall), although yields exceeded 5 tons/ha in 1996. In the late 1990s the Office du Niger began to delegate responsibility for the irrigation of a further estimated 1m. ha of land to private rice growers. There is considerable potential, once self-sufficiency has been achieved, for the export of rice to regional markets.

By far the most important cash crop is cotton, and this dominates the agricultural sector. About 99% of the crop is exported and cotton accounts for 50%–60% of Mali's total exports. Mali is easily the leading producer in the Franc Zone and ranks second only to Egypt on the African continent. Production is in the southern region, by means of village co-operatives co-ordinated by the parastatal Cie Malienne pour le développement des textiles (CMDT), in which the Cie française pour le développement des fibres textiles has a 40% interest. After suffering from the droughts of the 1970s and early 1980s output of seed cotton increased substantially, to reach 367,000 tons (320,000 tons marketed) in 1992/93. It then eased back somewhat, to average some 270,000 tons per year in 1993/94 and 1994/95, before the 47% rise in the producer price following the 1994 devaluation of the CFA franc, in conjunction with strong international prices, and the connected expansion of the area cultivated, boosted marketed output to 405,940 tons in 1995/96. A further sharp expansion was recorded in 1996/97, to as much as 500,000 tons, aided by increased growth in the west of the country. Production rose to 522,000 tons in 1997/98, but fell to 485,621 tons in 1998/99. In a reaction to lower world prices for cotton, some producers planted cereal crops rather than cotton seed, and production was expected to fall significantly in 1999/2000, probably to less than 400,000 tons.

Groundnut production, which had reached a high point of 205,000 tons in 1975/76, declined sharply in the early 1980s, but recovered over the following decade, attaining a new record of 213,000 tons in 1994/95. However, many growers switched to cotton production in the following season, resulting in a decline in the groundnut harvest in 1995/96, to 155,541 tons. Groundnut production totalled 134,000 tons in 1996/97, and an estimated 138,000 tons in 1997/98. Production is mainly for domestic consumption.

Livestock-raising accounts for about one-half of the agricultural sector's contribution to GDP, and is the principal economic activity in the north. After cotton, livestock has represented Mali's second highest recorded export (although gold now vies for this position), and large numbers of live animals are smuggled across the country's borders. Livestock numbers fell during the droughts of the 1970s and early 1980s (the last is thought to have caused the deaths of 40%–80% of the national herd). None the less, at 5.7m. cattle and 14.5m. sheep and goats in 1998, Mali's herd remains by far the largest in francophone west Africa. The drought also tended to move livestock-rearing from the north to the south, where it is geared towards export to Côte d'Ivoire and Ghana. This trade has received a strong stimulus from the currency's devaluation.

Fishing on the Niger produces an annual catch of about 65,000 tons, although this was more than doubled in 1995, and very substantially exceeded again in 1996 and 1997. The sector remains very vulnerable to drought, to the effects of large-scale dam building on the upper reaches of the river, and to pollution from urban centres.

MINING AND POWER

Deposits of bauxite, copper, iron ore, manganese and uranium have been located but not yet exploited, largely because of the country's land-locked position and lack of infrastructure. Marble is mined at Bafoulabé, and phosphate rock at Gao, but by far the most important mineral currently being exploited is gold. With one exception, all of Mali's gold-mines are open-cast.

Consequently production costs are extremely low and this factor has allowed the foreign operators detailed below to withstand the 25% decline in the world price of gold that occurred in 1996–98. The government has also begun to implement a programme for the development of the gold sector elaborated by the World Bank; a comprehensive topographical survey of potential gold reserves is also envisaged. In August 1999 a new mining code was adopted by the Malian government, which it was hoped would increase foreign investment in the sector. The code limits the government to a 20% stake in mining companies, and provides an improved legal framework for investment. Taxation of the sector was, however, to be increased, and new taxes were imposed on the sale, transfer and renewal of mining licences, while new requirements were also introduced in the areas of employment conditions, environmental protection, and worker safety.

After considerable delay, production at the Kalana gold-mine began in 1985, supported by credits from the USSR. Planned capacity was 2,000 kg per year, but official output averaged only 400 kg per year in 1985–90. Exploitation of the reserves was suspended in 1992, amid rumours that much of the production had bypassed official channels under the Traoré regime. Syama, in the south—the first post-Traoré mining venture—was established by a consortium led by BHP-Utah (which took 65% of the shares). Although gold production reached 6,200 kg in 1995, BHP sold its interest to Randgold of South Africa in mid-1996, citing operational difficulties and Syama's incompatibility with BHP's global corporate strategy. Randgold has since increased its stake to 75%. Mali's largest gold-mining project, Sadiola Hill, is a joint venture between the Canadian operator Iamgold and South Africa's De Beers offshoot, Anglo American. The deposit was expected to produce 10,000 kg annually from 1997 (the first year of commercial output) to 2005, with some of the lowest operating costs in the world despite the lack of mining infrastructure in the Kayes region. Actual output from Sadiola exceeded 12,000 kg in 1997, while Syama produced 4,100 kg. Total gold exports reached 18,500 kg in 1997, from 6,580 kg in 1996, largely reflecting the entry into production of Sadiola. Modernization at Syama, meanwhile, was expected to increase output to between 6,000 kg–7,000 kg. Production from Randgold's Loulo deposit began in late 1999, while a new company, in which the Malian government was to have a 20% share, was to be formed to exploit the Kodieran deposit. Kalana was acquired in 1996 by a consortium including Ghana's Ashanti Goldfields, although industry sentiment is divided as to whether this was a worthwhile purchase. Following the discovery of the Morila field in the south, with a potential total production of 150 tons of gold over a 12-year period, Rangold sold 50% of its share in the project to AngloGold in a joint venture, in July 2000; production was to start in October and a subsidiary of AngloGold was to operate the site. Other Australian, South African, Japanese and (especially) Canadian companies are active in exploration. A joint venture between Canada's Mink Minerals and Ashton Pty of Australia is investigating kimberlite pipes in the Kéniéba area of the south-west, in the hope of locating exploitable deposits of diamonds.

Mali suffers from a serious shortage of energy. In many areas there is no supply of electricity, and in others quantities are insufficient to meet, for example, the requirements of agriculture and the mining sector. Some 80% of the 335m. kWh of electricity generated in 1996 were hydroelectric in origin, provided by the Selingué facility on the Sankarani river. The proportion is scheduled to rise as a second dam is constructed on the river, at Koruba, and as the Manantali project on the Senegal river begins production. The operation of the last (constructed at a cost of some US $600m.) is to be supervised by the Organisation pour la mise en valeur du fleuve Sénégal, in which both Mauritania and Senegal also participate. Mali is to receive 52% of the annual output of the hydroelectric plant (projected at 200 MW). Construction of the dam was completed in 1988, but the installation of generating equipment was delayed by disagreements over supply routes, as well as the deterioration in relations between Mauritania and Senegal in 1989–90, so that the dam was not formally inaugurated until 1992. After further problems with funding and cross-border arrangements, Manantali is now expected to come into full operation in 2001, when Mali's network is to be linked to the Ivorian national grid, via a line from the north of Côte d'Ivoire to the Syama gold-mine and thence to Selingué. In July 2000 Belgium provided an interest-free loan of 2,600m. francs CFA for the construction of two high-voltage power stations in Bamako. In the mean time, much of the country's energy demand is met by fuel wood and charcoal, which has resulted in considerable deforestation. Mali currently imports all of the petroleum it requires, but the exploration of indigenous reserves is under way.

MANUFACTURING

Manufacturing activity, largely directed to meet local demand, is concentrated in Bamako, mainly taking the form of agricultural processing and the manufacture of consumer goods. Manufacturing contributed some 6% of GDP in 1998. The incomplete statistics available suggest general stagnation in industry throughout the 1970s and much of the 1980s, with several agricultural processing plants (particularly oilseed-crushing mills) operating well below capacity owing to a lack of supply. Smuggling of cheaper goods from Nigeria (while the CFA franc remained overvalued) and competition from the more developed manufacturing companies in Côte d'Ivoire also depressed the sector. During the mid-1980s more than 75% of industrial turnover was accounted for by state companies, which operated nine of the 12 major food sector plants—a legacy of the Keita era. The 40 parastatal bodies generally proved to be inefficient and unprofitable. Following the failure of successive governments to improve its performance, the sector has been substantially reorganized, under pressure from the IMF and other foreign creditors.

TRANSPORT

The first years of the 1960s saw very substantial investment (one-fifth of total planned investment spending) in road-building, after the dissolution of the short-lived federation with Senegal in 1960 and Mali's withdrawal from the Franc Zone in 1962, disrupted traditional trading outlets. However, road communications remain poor: of some 15,000 km of classified roads, only about one-third are all-weather roads. Mali's main access to the sea is via the Bamako–Abidjan (Côte d'Ivoire) road. Construction of a road linking Bamako with Dakar (Senegal), also a port city, is being financed by the European Development Fund and is due to be completed by 2003. The 575-km all-weather road between Sévaré and Gao, which was opened in 1987, forms part of the Trans-Sahara Highway connecting Algeria with Nigeria. A major donor-funded programme for the modernization of the transport infrastructure, in progress since the mid-1990s, aims to restore 3,000 km of roads (including the vital link between Mabako and Sévaré) and also part of the very dilapidated 1,286-km rail link from Bamako to Dakar. The state-owned Régie des chemins de fer du Mali is seeking private capital. The Bamako–Dakar rail link is a particularly important one, as it is by this route that some 500,000 tons of Mali's freight is transported annually. It is hoped that the rehabilitation of the rail link will allow an increase in the volume of goods thus transported to some 750,000 tons annually. Owing to the inadequacy of the road and rail facilities, the country's inland waterways are of great importance to the transport infrastructure. The River Niger is used for bulk transport during the rainy season, while traffic on the Senegal is expected to improve as a result of the completion of the Manantali hydro project, which should stabilize the water level and facilitate uninterrupted access to the sea.

FINANCE

Mali adopted a very ambitious capital spending programme at independence, and state companies were established to operate the main sectors of the economy (including foreign trade, transport and mineral exploration). In the event, the bureaucratic superstructure became highly developed—administrative spending rose by an average 11%–12% per year in 1959–68, while the economy grew by a small fraction of this rate. Most state enterprises were operating at a loss. The simultaneous, and related, deterioration in the balance-of-payments situation led Mali in 1967 to seek to rejoin the Franc Zone and the Union monétaire ouest-africaine (UMOA), from which it had withdrawn in 1962. The conditions of the agreement providing for such a reintegration included a reduction in the activities of state enterprises and a 'freeze' on wages, to reduce the budget deficit. These measures undoubtedly contributed to the downfall of the Keita regime in 1968. (The final stage in the return to financial integration with other francophone countries of the region came in 1984, when Mali rejoined UMOA and readopted the CFA franc as its currency.) The recovery programme to cover the period 1970–73, drawn up with French advice, provided for a reduction in infrastructure and social investment, the dismantling of co-operatives, the abandonment of mineral exploration, and the winding up of some state industries. The budget deficit in fact continued, and French subsidies were substantially in excess of the agreed upper limit, as any serious reduction in spending would have alienated the large and influential bureaucracy.

Beginning in 1981, the Traoré government, under pressure from the IMF, the World Bank and bilateral donors, undertook a programme of economic reform. Adjustment measures included the ending of state monopolies, the restructuring or transfer to private ownership of parastatal organizations, the liberalization of the marketing of agricultural products and the easing of price controls. One objective of these measures, which included the unpopular cessation of guaranteed jobs within the civil service for graduates, was to curtail budgetary expenditure. However, the budget deficit remained at a high level, with revenues depressed by the weak foreign trade performance (in 1985) and the sharp decline in world cotton prices (in 1986). The deficit was reduced in 1987, as Mali failed to fulfil its debt-servicing obligations, but increased again in 1988 and 1989, as some debt arrears were paid off in order to secure the resumption of IMF funding: the shortfall thus reached a record 62,100m. francs CFA (after grants) in 1989 (equivalent to 9.5% of GDP). The budget deficit was then brought down to less than one-half of this level by 1991, through a combination of higher tax revenue in conjunction with a decline in current expenditure (as employment in the civil service was rationalized and the functions of the state agricultural produce boards were scaled down). Compliance with the adjustment programme agreed with the IMF and the World Bank was essential if Mali was to secure the external funds, mostly in the form of grants, needed for the budget. In 1991, for example, grants constituted one-third of total budgetary revenue. However, the unpopularity of the austerity programme, particularly as it affected employment among graduates, contributed to the downfall of President Traoré in March 1991. The new administration recognized none the less that there was no feasible alternative to complete acceptance of IMF-prescribed policies, and the deficit was held at a level similar to the 1990–91 average in 1992 and 1993 essentially by means of cuts in expenditure. However, there was little improvement in the tax regime, and overall fiscal performance was therefore deemed inadequate by the IMF and the World Bank, which suspended all assistance to Mali in October 1993.

Negotiations with the Bretton Woods institutions resumed following the 50% devaluation, in January 1994, of the CFA franc. The World Bank and the IMF agreed, respectively, to provide 157,000m. and 50,000m. francs CFA in budgetary support for 1994–96, thereby allowing the government to establish a special fund to assist those social groups most severely affected by the devaluation, to increase public-sector salaries and to raise the official minimum wage. Reflecting the increase in spending obligations, the 1994 budget recorded a much higher deficit, at 73,100m. francs CFA (after grants). Allowing for currency depreciation, this represented a real increase of about one-sixth. If external grants are excluded, the deficit was 141,200m. francs CFA, equivalent to 13.7% of GDP. In 1995 this ratio declined to 10.5% (129,000m. francs CFA), as a moderate increase in spending was more than offset by an improvement in tax receipts. After grants, the deficit was 50,700m. francs CFA, equivalent to 4.1% of GDP. The programme agreed with the IMF in early 1996, to secure its continued financial support under the Enhanced Structural Adjustment Facility (ESAF) for the following three years, provided for further progress along these lines, with the fiscal deficit (excluding foreign grants) targeted to narrow gradually to 7.7% of GDP by 1998. Towards the end of 1997 an IMF mid-term review declared itself satisfied with budgetary performance (with a fiscal deficit of 107,800m.

francs CFA, or 11.3% of GDP) in 1996. In 1997, according to the IMF, Mali's fiscal deficit (on a commitment basis) amounted to 115,500m. francs CFA, or 31,300m. francs CFA after grants. Excluding grants, this was equivalent to 7.9% of GDP in that year. In 1998 the Fund estimated that Mali's fiscal deficit (on a commitment basis) totalled 199,600m. francs CFA, or 45,200m. francs CFA after grants. Excluding grants, this was equivalent to 7.5% of GDP. These figures exemplify Mali's continuing reliance on foreign grants to compensate for budgetary shortfalls. The government consolidated the improvement in its fiscal position in 1998 by implementing further domestic tax reforms, including the introduction of a single-rate value-added tax at 18%, and the expansion of the tax base in order to compensate for possible losses of revenue following the introduction of a common external tariff within UMOA on 1 January 2000.

FOREIGN TRADE AND PAYMENTS

In recent decades Mali's trade balance has been in chronic deficit, although there has been an overall improvement since the early 1970s, when exports typically represented only one-half of the value of imports. However, Mali's trade deficit remained high, as the two rounds of increases in international petroleum prices (in 1973–74 and 1979–80) and the impact of drought on cereals production necessitated increased spending on imports. By 1985 the trade deficit (a record US $152m.) was equivalent to 86.5% of the value of merchandise exports. Significantly lower deficits, averaging some $96m., were recorded annually in 1986–91, as rising sales of gold and an increase in the volume of cotton exports helped to offset weaknesses in international prices for these commodities while imports showed only modest growth. The balance deteriorated once again in 1992, to a deficit of $149m., as exports declined and imports rose, although the situation was somewhat better in 1993 (when the deficit was $105m.). Devaluation had a beneficial impact on the trade balance, lowering the deficit to $102m. in 1994. According to the Franc Zone secretariat of the Banque de France, the trade deficit remained in the region of $100m. in both 1995 and 1996. Export earnings have been boosted by the sharp increase in cotton production (in response to much higher local prices), by higher demand from Côte d'Ivoire for Malian livestock, and by enhanced gold production. Import spending, meanwhile, has been contained as a result of higher prices, tight management of demand and improved domestic food supply. In 1997 Mali recorded a visible trade surplus of $9.7m. owing, largely, to the tripling of gold exports in that year.

There are two important offsets to Mali's customary trade deficit, namely aid inflows and emigrants' remittances. The latter averaged about US $85m. annually in 1992–95, according to Franc Zone secretariat figures. Aid inflows are substantially higher, averaging some $450m. per year in 1991–95 and totalling $505m. in 1996—equivalent to about one-fifth of GNP and representing more than 70% of gross domestic investment. France, in particular, has maintained a high level of support for the structural adjustment programme, in the form of budgetary grants as well as loans and debt relief. Despite considerable development assistance, Mali's current-account deficit has remained substantial, totalling $273.2m. in 1996 and $178.4m. in 1997. According to the IMF, Mali's current account deficit (inclusive of official transfers) was an estimated 2.9% of GDP in 1997 and, according to the World Bank, 7.1% in 1998. None the less, exceptional financing from the World Bank and the IMF has contributed to an increase in foreign-exchange reserves from the equivalent of less than two months' import cover in the late 1980s to an estimated six months' in 1997.

Because of the high grant element in the development assistance that Mali receives, its debt-servicing payments had, until the mid-1980s, remained low—8.3% of total foreign earnings in 1983. However, the drought of 1983–85 necessitated a rapid increase in external borrowing, from US $879m. at the end of 1982 (equivalent to less than 75% of GNP) to $1,468m. by the end of 1985 (120% of GNP in that year). Despite the cancellation of significant amounts of bilateral debt during this period, and the increasingly concessionary nature of inflows, the burden of servicing the debt rose substantially, owing to the decline in international prices for cotton. In the absence, after 1986, of a formal agreement with the IMF, there were no formal debt-relief concessions. Thus, as the external debt continued to accumulate (reaching $2,040m. by the end of 1988), so did arrears on the servicing of the debt. In October 1988, however, following agreement with the IMF on a programme of economic adjustment, Mali became the first debtor country to benefit from a system of exceptional debt relief that had been agreed in principle at that year's summit meeting of industrialized nations, held in Toronto, Canada, which made provision for preferential relief for countries with persistent debt-servicing difficulties. In addition, Mali was one of the world's 35 poorest countries whose official debt to France was cancelled at the beginning of 1990 (when Mali's debt of $240m. to that country was written off). None the less, the external debt, which had risen again, to $2,595m. by the end of 1991, continued to represent a substantial burden on this poor economy. The debt-service ratio in that year was reduced to a tolerable level—7.9%, from 11.9% in 1990—only because of the non-payment of some obligations. Thus there remained a continuing need for both debt relief and new funding, and the 'Paris Club' of Western official creditors agreed in November 1992 to a further round of rescheduling, on enhanced 'Toronto terms'. However, with debt at the end of 1993 equivalent to 110% of GNP, at $2,902m., Mali was a prime candidate for the special measures of debt relief that followed the devaluation of the CFA franc in January 1994 (which had doubled the external debt in local currency terms). Major bilateral aid sources, led by France, thus cancelled a proportion of debt and rescheduled repayments. Cancellations meant that the foreign debt increased only modestly in 1994, to $2,694m., but this was, owing to devaluation, equivalent to 149% of GNP, while the debt-service ratio increased to 18.0%. The rise in the latter reflected the resumption of payment of debt-servicing obligations in full, and Mali has continued to meet its payments' requirements since. With Mali's economic performance continuing to be to the satisfaction of the IMF and the World Bank, and the securing of another three-year access to the ESAF in April 1996, further debt relief was granted by the country's external creditors in May of that year, under the highly concessionary 'Naples terms', whereby two-thirds of eligible debt was cancelled. The strict guidelines for the 'Naples terms',

however, meant that relatively little debt fell into this category, and the net benefit to Mali is estimated to have been only $50m. Total external debt stood at US $3,020m. at the end of 1996, while the debt-service ratio was equivalent to 17.9% of exports of goods and services.

In 1998 Mali qualified as eligible for the HIPC initiative of the World Bank and the IMF. In September the Bretton Woods institutions granted the country debt relief of $250m., of which the World Bank was to contribute $95m. and the IMF $18m. Other multilateral and bilateral creditors were to provide the remainder. According to the World Bank, Mali's total external debt amounted to $2,880m. in September 1998. The annual cost of servicing the debt was equivalent to 12.6% of the value of exports of goods and services in 1998. Mali may in future also benefit from substantial relief on debts to the former USSR (estimated by Malian sources at some $600m.), as Russia's entry to the 'Paris Club' is conditional upon a more realistic valuation of past debts. In the medium term, however, the country will remain highly dependent on inflows of aid to underpin the budget and to compensate the funding shortfall on the current account.

TOURISM

In 2002 Mali will host the African Nations Cup football tournament and, in preparation for this event, the government has begun to implement a social development programme—'Mali 2002'—which will also benefit the country's nascent tourist industry. Up to 90,000 tourists visit Mali each year, but the development of the industry is handicapped by the country's inadequate transport infrastructure and by a shortage of hotels. Under the 'Mali 2002' programme, which will cost an estimated 2,500m. French francs, the construction of two new international airports and the renovation of two existing ones is envisaged. Other projects include the construction and refurbishment of hotels to accommodate the teams participating in the tournament, and the improvement of telecommunications infrastructure. It is planned, for instance, to double the number of hotel beds available in Tombouctou, Mali's principal tourist destination.

Statistical Survey

Source (unless otherwise stated): Direction de la Statistique et de l'Informatique, Ministère des Finances, BP 234, Koulouba, Bamako; tel. 22-56-87; fax 22-88-53.

Area and Population

AREA, POPULATION AND DENSITY

Area (sq km)	1,240,192*
Population (census results)†	
16 December 1976	6,394,918
1–30 April 1987	
Males	3,760,711
Females	3,935,637
Total	7,696,348
Population (UN estimates at mid-year)‡	
1996	10,186,000
1997	10,436,000
1998	10,694,000
Density (per sq km) at mid-1998	8.6

*478,841 sq miles.
† Figures refer to the *de jure* population.
‡ Source: UN, *World Population Prospects: The 1998 Revision.*

PRINCIPAL ETHNIC GROUPS (estimates, 1963)

Bambara . . .	1,000,000	Malinke . . .	200,000
Fulani . . .	450,000	Tuareg . . .	240,000
Marka . . .	280,000	Sénoufo . . .	375,000
Songhai . . .	230,000	Dogon . . .	130,000

ADMINISTRATIVE DIVISIONS (*de jure* population at 1987 census)

District					
Bamako . . .	658,275				
Regions*					
Ségou . . .	1,339,631		Kayes . . .		1,067,007
Sikasso . . .	1,310,810		Tombouctou . .		459,318
Mopti . . .	1,282,617		Gao		380,722
Koulikoro . .	1,197,968				

* An eighth region, Kidal, was established in May 1991.

PRINCIPAL TOWNS (population at 1976 census)

Bamako (capital) .	404,000	Sikasso . . .		47,000
Ségou	65,000	Kayes		45,000
Mopti	54,000			

1995 (estimates): Bamako 800,000; Ségou 88,000; Mopti 75,000; Sikasso 74,000; Gao 55,000 (Source: Secrétariat du Comité Monétaire de la Zone Franc, *La Zone Franc—Rapport Annuel 1997*).

1996: Bamako (mid-year estimate) 809,552 (Source: UN, *Demographic Yearbook*).

BIRTHS AND DEATHS (UN estimates, annual averages)

	1980–85	1985–90	1990–95
Birth rate (per 1,000) . . .	50.8	50.8	49.8
Death rate (per 1,000) . . .	22.3	19.1	17.8

Expectation of life (UN estimates, years at birth, 1990–95): 50.9 (males 50.0; females 52.6).

Source: UN, *World Population Prospects: The 1998 Revision.*

ECONOMICALLY ACTIVE POPULATION

Mid-1998 (estimates in '000): Agriculture, etc. 4,321; Total 5,266.

Source: FAO, *Production Yearbook.*

Agriculture

PRINCIPAL CROPS ('000 metric tons)

	1996	1997	1998*
Millet	765	739	739
Sorghum	710	540	540
Rice (paddy)	463	614	614
Maize	248	290	290
Other cereals	17	19	19
Sugar cane	293	285	285
Sweet potatoes . . .	16	16*	16
Yams*	15	11	11
Tomatoes	23	21*	21
Onions (dry)	47	45*	45
Other vegetables . . .	252	252*	252
Mangoes	51	51*	51
Pulses	82	57	57
Groundnuts (in shell) . .	157	134	134
Cottonseed	211	240	270
Cotton (lint)	169	190	215

* FAO estimate(s).

Source: FAO, *Production Yearbook.*

LIVESTOCK ('000 head, year ending September)

	1996	1997	1998*
Cattle	5,708	5,725*	5,725
Sheep	5,703	5,950*	5,950
Goats	8,135	8,550*	8,550
Pigs	64	65	65
Horses	123	135*	135
Asses	638	650*	650
Camels	327	365*	365

Poultry (million): 23 in 1996; 24* in 1997; 24* in 1998.

* FAO estimate(s).

Source: FAO, *Production Yearbook.*

LIVESTOCK PRODUCTS (FAO estimates, '000 metric tons)

	1996	1997	1998
Cows' milk	140	140	140
Sheep's milk	85	89	89
Goats' milk	167	168	168
Beef and veal . . .	86	86	90
Mutton and lamb . . .	19	21	21
Goat meat	31	32	33
Poultry meat	26	26	28
Other meat	26	27	27
Poultry eggs	12	12	12
Cattle hides	13	13	14
Sheepskins	4	5	5
Goatskins	4	5	5

Source: FAO, *Production Yearbook.*

Forestry

ROUNDWOOD REMOVALS ('000 cubic metres, excluding bark)

	1995	1996	1997
Sawlogs, veneer logs and logs for sleepers	4	4	4
Other industrial wood . .	403	416	429
Fuel wood	6,124	6,316	6,511
Total	**6,531**	**6,736**	**6,944**

Source: FAO, *Yearbook of Forest Products.*

SAWNWOOD PRODUCTION ('000 cubic metres, incl. railway sleepers)

	1995	1996	1997
Total (all broadleaved) . . .	13	13	13

Source: FAO, *Yearbook of Forest Products.*

Fishing

('000 metric tons, live weight)

	1995	1996	1997
Total catch (freshwater fishes) .	132.9	111.9	99.6

Source: FAO, *Yearbook of Fishery Statistics.*

Mining

	1996	1997	1998
Gold (kilograms)	7,340	16,725	22,826

Source: Banque centrale des états de l'Afrique de l'ouest.

Salt ('000 metric tons, provisional or estimated figures): 5 in 1995; 6 in 1996 (Source: US Bureau of Mines in UN, *Industrial Commodity Statistics Yearbook*).

Industry

SELECTED PRODUCTS ('000 metric tons, unless otherwise indicated)

	1994	1995	1996
Salted, dried or smoked fish . .	12.1	12.0	12.1
Raw sugar	27	25	25
Cement	14	13	21
Electric energy (million kWh) .	276	312	336

Source: mainly UN, *Industrial Commodity Statistics Yearbook.*

1997: Raw sugar ('000 metric tons) 26; Electric energy (million kWh) 385.4.

1998: Raw sugar (FAO estimate, '000 metric tons) 26; Electric energy (million kWh) 414.4.

Sources: FAO, *Production Yearbook*; Banque centrale des états de l'Afrique de l'ouest.

Finance

CURRENCY AND EXCHANGE RATES

Monetary Units

100 centimes = 1 franc de la Communauté financière africaine (CFA).

Sterling, Dollar and Euro Equivalents (28 April 2000)

£1 sterling = 1,132.20 francs CFA;
US $1 = 722.02 francs CFA;
€1 = 655.96 francs CFA;
10,000 francs CFA = £8.832 = $13.850 = €15.245.

Average Exchange Rate (francs CFA per US $)

1997   583.67
1998   589.95
1999   615.70

Note: An exchange rate of 1 French franc = 50 francs CFA, established in 1948, remained in force until January 1994, when the CFA franc was devalued by 50%, with the exchange rate adjusted to 1 French franc = 100 francs CFA. This relationship to French currency remained in effect with the introduction of the euro on 1 January 1999. From that date, accordingly, a fixed exchange rate of €1 = 655.957 francs CFA has been in operation.

BUDGET ('000 million francs CFA)*

Revenue†	1996	1997	1998‡
Budgetary revenue	185.0	207.9	227.7
Tax revenue	172.8	196.3	216.8
Taxes on net income and profits	34.5	37.8	35.8
Payroll tax	3.7	3.9	4.2
Property taxes	6.4	4.9	4.6
Domestic taxes on goods and services	25.4	26.5	29.9
Value-added tax	22.8	23.0	23.7
Taxes on international trade	94.5	112.6	122.8
Value-added tax on imports	31.6	34.2	34.6
Petroleum import duties	24.6	29.2	36.8
Other tax revenue	8.4	10.6	19.5
Stamp duties	5.3	5.3	5.0
Payment of tax arrears	2.0	1.9	9.2
Other current revenue	12.2	11.6	10.9
Special funds and annexed budgets	20.9	21.8	17.9
Social security fund	19.1	20.1	16.3
Total	205.9	229.7	245.6

Expenditure§	1996	1997	1998‡
Budgetary expenditure	303.9	328.6	351.4
Current expenditure	137.1	167.7	168.8
Personnel	50.6	56.8	59.2
Supplies	20.1	25.2	25.1
Scholarships	4.3	4.3	4.3
Interest payments (scheduled)	14.5	13.8	15.3
Capital expenditure	161.7	156.4	179.1
Externally financed	137.3	124.5	140.1
Public enterprise sector adjustment programme	2.5	2.1	2.0
Voluntary departure programme	0.0	0.6	0.1
National Pact	2.7	1.8	1.4
Special funds and annexed budgets	20.7	21.8	17.9
Social security fund	18.9	20.1	16.3
Sub-total	324.6	350.4	369.3
Adjustment for payments arrears	18.0	7.0	10.0
Adjustment to cash basis	1.0	1.4	0.0
Total	343.6	358.8	379.3

* Figures represent a consolidation of the central government budget, special funds and annexed budgets.
† Excluding grants received ('000 million francs CFA): 96.5 in 1996; 84.2 in 1997; 74.4 in 1998.
‡ Estimates.
§ Excluding net lending ('000 million francs CFA): −10.6 in 1996; −5.2 in 1997; −4.0 in 1998.

Source: IMF, *Mali: Selected Issues and Statistical Appendix* (April 1999).

INTERNATIONAL RESERVES (US $ million at 31 December)

	1997	1998	1999
Gold*	5.8	5.5	5.6
IMF special drawing rights	0.1	0.1	0.6
Reserve position in IMF	11.8	12.4	12.1
Foreign exchange	403.0	390.4	337.0
Total	420.7	408.4	355.3

* Valued at market-related prices.

Source: IMF, *International Financial Statistics.*

MONEY SUPPLY ('000 million francs CFA at 31 December)

	1997	1998	1999
Currency outside banks	129.5	135.3	123.4
Demand deposits	126.2	131.8	142.3
Total money (incl. others)	256.0	267.6	266.0

Source: IMF, *International Financial Statistics.*

COST OF LIVING (Consumer Price Index; base: 1995 = 100)

	1997	1998	1999
All items	106.4	110.7	109.4

Source: IMF, *International Financial Statistics.*

NATIONAL ACCOUNTS
('000 million francs CFA at current prices)

Expenditure on the Gross Domestic Product

	1996	1997	1998
Government final consumption expenditure	210.6	216.8	228.9
Private final consumption expenditure	1,059.6	1,065.4	1,104.3
Increase in stocks	−42	−30	12
Gross fixed capital formation	316.4	345.2	372.2
Total domestic expenditure*	1,497.6	1,572.1	1,717.7
Exports of goods and services	267.6	349.2	385.2
Less Imports of goods and services	472.7	489.4	552.6
GDP in purchasers' values	1,292.5	1,431.9	1,550.3

* Including adjustment.

Source: IMF, *International Financial Statistics.*

Gross Domestic Product by Economic Activity

	1996	1997	1998*
Agriculture, livestock-rearing, forestry and fishing	589.1	574.1	640.7
Mining	27.7	67.3	92.6
Manufacturing			
Electricity and water	100.9	112.7	117.1
Construction and public works	71.2	80.6	86.2
Transport and telecommunications	70.8	81.4	88.0
Trade	205.3	219.9	227.6
Other marketable services	60.5	62.9	65.4
Public administration	102.7	104.8	110.3
GDP at factor cost	1,228.2	1,303.7	1,427.9
Import duties	94.5	112.6	122.4
GDP in purchasers' values	1,322.7	1,416.3	1,550.3

* Preliminary figures.

Source: Banque centrale des états de l'Afrique de l'ouest.

BALANCE OF PAYMENTS (US $ million)

	1995	1996	1997
Exports of goods f.o.b.	441.8	433.5	561.6
Imports of goods f.o.b.	−556.8	−551.5	−551.9
Trade balance	**−115.0**	**−118.0**	**9.7**
Exports of services	87.6	87.6	82.1
Imports of services	−434.5	−382.8	−345.6
Balance on goods and services	**−461.9**	**−413.2**	**−253.8**
Other income received	8.3	10.9	10.6
Other income paid	−48.9	−67.1	−61.7
Balance on goods, services and income	**−502.6**	**−469.3**	**−304.8**
Current transfers received	266.8	246.1	170.0
Current transfers paid	−48.0	−50.0	−43.5
Current balance	**−283.8**	**−273.2**	**−178.4**
Capital account (net)	126.2	136.4	108.6
Direct investment from abroad	111.4	84.1	39.4
Other investment assets	−52.3	4.1	−12.4
Other investment liabilities	59.6	86.4	25.7
Net errors and omissions	−13.0	−8.8	7.9
Overall balance	**−52.0**	**29.0**	**−9.2**

Source: IMF, *International Financial Statistics*.

External Trade

PRINCIPAL COMMODITIES ('000 million francs CFA)

Imports c.i.f.	1995	1996	1997*
Foodstuffs	55.4	58.0	63.5
Cereals	10.9	12.8	12.2
Sugar	16.8	17.2	17.6
Milk	11.9	9.9	12.2
Machines and vehicles	123.0	115.4	129.1
Petroleum products	42.4	52.2	61.1
Construction materials	39.6	39.8	47.1
Chemical products	35.2	36.8	39.2
Textiles and leather	21.7	23.3	25.7
Total (incl. others)	**374.8**	**395.1**	**438.2**

Exports f.o.b.	1995	1996	1997*
Cotton	129.2	135.0	161.2
Cotton fibre	126.9	132.6	158.7
Livestock	40.0	30.0	30.7
Gold	35.6	39.8	117.2
Total (incl. others)	**220.5**	**221.8**	**327.7**

* Estimates.

Source: IMF, *Mali: Selected Issues and Statistical Appendix* (April 1999).

PRINCIPAL TRADING PARTNERS (US $ million)*

Imports	1995	1996	1997
Belgium-Luxembourg	33.81	33.89	n.a.
China, People's Repub.	27.61	16.75	15.28
Côte d'Ivoire	166.21	202.51	222.76
France (incl. Monaco)	191.52	218.82	199.45
Germany	17.00	26.82	21.70
Spain	12.42	15.48	17.50
United Kingdom	41.71	41.71	43.30
Total (incl. others)	**987.94**	**1,106.64**	**1,125.65**

Exports	1995	1996	1997
Belgium-Luxembourg	17.76	12.39	n.a.
China, People's Repub.	33.04	12.37	24.98
Côte d'Ivoire	2.90	4.23	4.65
France (incl. Monaco)	6.91	4.94	7.03
Germany	3.73	2.87	3.77
Spain	7.76	7.82	7.20
Total (incl. others)	**236.77**	**281.70**	**262.89**

* Data are compiled on the basis of reporting by Mali's trading partners.

Source: IMF, *Mali: Selected Issues and Statistical Appendix* (April 1999).

Transport

RAILWAYS (traffic)

	1993	1994	1995
Passenger-km (million)	845.9	794.8	929.6
Freight ton-km (million)	460.9	453.2	501.5

Source: Banque centrale des états de l'Afrique de l'ouest.

ROAD TRAFFIC (estimates, motor vehicles in use)

	1994	1995	1996
Passenger cars	24,250	24,750	26,190
Lorries and vans	16,000	17,100	18,240

Source: IRF, *World Road Statistics*.

CIVIL AVIATION (traffic on scheduled services)*

	1994	1995	1996
Kilometres flown (million)	2	3	3
Passengers carried ('000)	69	74	75
Passenger-km (million)	215	223	225
Total ton-km (million)	34	36	37

* Including an apportionment of the traffic of Air Afrique.

Source: UN, *Statistical Yearbook*.

Communications Media

	1994	1995	1996
Radio receivers ('000 in use)	465	500	550
Television receivers ('000 in use)	14	20	40
Telephones ('000 main lines in use)	15	17	21
Mobile cellular telephones (subscribers)	n.a.	n.a.	1,187
Daily newspapers:			
Number	2	2	3
Estimated average circulation ('000 copies)	10	11	12

Book production (first editions, excluding pamphlets): 14 titles (28,000 copies) in 1995.

1997: Radio receivers 570,000 in use; Television receivers 45,000 in use.

Sources: UNESCO, *Statistical Yearbook*; UN, *Statistical Yearbook*.

Tourism

	1995	1996	1997
Tourist arrivals ('000) . .	42	98	75
Tourist receipts (US $ million) .	25	29	26

Source: World Tourism Organization, *Yearbook of Tourism Statistics*.

Education

(1997/98, unless otherwise indicated)

	Institutions	Teachers	Students		
			Males	Females	Total
Pre-primary . . .	197	675	11,910	11,638	23,548
Primary* . . .	2,511	10,853	512,345	350,530	862,875
Secondary:					
General . .	n.a.	4,549†	111,162	55,260	166,372
Teacher-training .	n.a.	77‡	1,052	494	1,596
Vocational . .	n.a.	526‡	13,485	6,706	20,191
University level . .	n.a.	796‡	11,085	2,762	13,847

* Data exclude recognized Medersas (Islamic schools).
† 1994/95 figure.
‡ 1996/97 figure.

Source: UNESCO, *Statistical Yearbook*.

Directory

The Constitution

The Constitution of the Third Republic of Mali was approved in a national referendum on 12 January 1992. The document upholds the principles of national sovereignty and the rule of law in a secular, multi-party state, and provides for the separation of the powers of the executive, legislative and judicial organs of state.

Executive power is vested in the President of the Republic, who is Head of State and is elected for five years by universal adult suffrage. The President appoints the Prime Minister, who, in turn, appoints other members of the Council of Ministers.

Legislative authority is exercised by the unicameral Assemblée nationale, which is elected for five years by universal adult suffrage.

The Constitution guarantees the independence of the judiciary. Final jurisdiction in constitutional matters is vested in a Constitutional Court.

The rights, freedoms and obligations of Malian citizens are enshrined in the Constitution. Freedom of the press and of association are guaranteed.

Note: A constitutional bill was adopted by the Assemblée nationale in January 1997, providing for an increase, with effect from that year's legislative elections, in the number of deputies from 129 to 147.

The Government

HEAD OF STATE

President: ALPHA OUMAR KONARÉ (took office 8 June 1992; re-elected 11 May 1997).

COUNCIL OF MINISTERS
(August 2000)

Prime Minister, Minister of Integration: MANDÉ SIDIBÉ.

Minister of Rural Development: AHMED EL MADANI DIALLO.

Minister of Facilities, National Development, the Environment and Town Planning: SOUMAILA CISSÉ.

Minister of Foreign Affairs and Malians Abroad: MODIBO SIDIBÉ.

Minister of the Armed Forces and Former Combattants: SOUMEYLOU BOUBÈYE MAÏGA.

Minister of Social Development, Solidarity and the Elderly: FATOUMATA N'DIAYE DIAKITÉ.

Minister of Education: MOUSTAPHA DICKO.

Minister of Security and Civil Protection: Gen. TIÉCOURA DOUMBIA.

Minister of Youth and Sports: ADAMA KONÉ.

Minister of Communications: ASCOFARÉ OULÉMATOU TAMBOURA.

Minister for the Promotion of Children and the Family: DIARRA AFOUSSATOU THIÉRO.

Minister of Industry, Trade and Transport: TOURÉ ALIMATA TRAORÉ.

Minister of Territorial Administration and Local Collectives: OUSMANE SY.

Minister of Justice, Keeper of the Seals: ABOULAYE OGOTEMBELY POUDIOUGOU.

Minister of Health: TRAORÉ FATOUMATA NAFO.

Minister of the Economy and Finance: BAKARI KONÉ.

Minister of Handicrafts and Tourism: ZAKYATOU OUALETT HALATINE.

Minister of State-Administered Estates and Housing Affairs: BOUARÉ FILY SISSOKO.

Minister of Mining, Energy and Water Resources: ABOUBACARY COULIBALY.

Minister of Employment and Vocational Training: MAKAN MOUSSA SISSOKO.

Minister of Culture: PASCAL BABA COULIBALY.

MINISTRIES

Office of the President: BP 1463, Koulouba, Bamako; tel. 23-00-29; fax 23-00-26.

Office of the Prime Minister, Ministry of Integration: quartier du Fleuve, BP 790, Bamako; tel. 22-55-34; fax 22-85-83.

Ministry of the Armed Forces and Former Combattants: route de Koulouba, BP 2083, Bamako; tel. 22-50-21; fax 23-23-18.

Ministry of Culture and Communications: quartier du Fleuve, BP 116, Bamako; tel. 22-26-47; fax 22-83-19.

Ministry of the Economy and Finance: BP 234, Koulouba, Bamako; tel. 22-57-26; fax 22-88-53.

Ministry of Education: BP 71, Bamako; tel. 22-24-50; fax 22-21-26.

Ministry of Employment and Vocational Training: route de Koulouba, Bamako; tel. 22-34-31; fax 22-34-31.

Ministry of Foreign Affairs and Malians Abroad: Koulouba, Bamako; tel. 22-21-50; fax 22-52-26.

Ministry of Handicrafts and Tourism: quartier du Fleuve, BP 1759, Bamako; tel. 22-80-58; fax 23-02-67; internet www.undp.org/fomli.

Ministry of Health: BP 232, Koulouba, Bamako; tel. 22-53-02; fax 23-02-03.

Ministry of Industry, Trade and Transport: quartier du Fleuve, BP 234, Koulouba, Bamako; tel. 22-56-87; fax 22-88-53.

Ministry of Justice: quartier du Fleuve, BP 97, Bamako; tel. 22-26-51; fax 23-00-63.

Ministry of Mining, Energy and Water Resources: BP 238, Bamako; tel. 22-35-47.

Ministry for the Promotion of Women, Children and the Family: Torokorobougou, BP 2688, Bamako; tel. 28-74-42; fax 28-75-04; e-mail mpfef@fib.com.

Ministry of Rural Development: BP 1676, Bamako; tel. and fax 23-19-39.

Ministry of Territorial Administration and Local Collectives: face Direction de la RCFM, BP 78, Bamako; tel. 22-42-12.

Ministry of Youth and Sports: route de Koulouba, BP 91, Bamako; tel. 22-31-53; fax 23-10-87.

President and Legislature

PRESIDENT

Presidential Election, 11 May 1997

Candidate	Votes	% of votes
ALPHA OUMAR KONARÉ	1,056,819	95.90
MAMADOU MARIBATROU DIABY . . .	45,160	4.10
Total	**1,101,979**	**100.00**

ASSEMBLÉE NATIONALE

President: ALY NOUHOUN DIALLO.
General Election, 20 July and 3 August 1997

Party	Seats
ADEMA	130*
PARENA	8
CDS	4
UDD	3
PDP	2
Total	**147**

* Including one seat won in alliance with the COPP.

Advisory Councils

Conseil Economique et Social: Bamako; f. 1987; Chair. MOUSSA BALLA COULIBALY.

Cour Constitutionnelle: BP 213, Bamako; tel. 22-56-32; fax 23-42-41; f. 1994; Pres. ABDOULAYE DICKO; Sec.-Gen. BOUBACAR TAHOUATI.

Political Organizations

In early 2000, when there were some 70 functioning political groups, the most active parties included:

Alliance pour la démocratie au Mali—Parti pan africain pour la liberté, la solidarité et la justice (ADEMA): BP 1791, Bamako; tel. 22-03-68; f. 1990 as Alliance pour la démocratie au Mali; Chair. IBRAHIM BOUBACAR KEITA; Sec.-Gen. BOKRI TRETA.

Bloc pour la démocratie et l'intégration africaine—Faso Jigi (BDIA—Faso Jigi): BP 2833, Bamako; tel. 77-17-09; fax 20-82-93; f. 1993; liberal and democratic; Vice Pres. YOUSSOUF TRAORÉ.

Congrès national d'initiative démocratique (CNID): BP 2572, Bamako; tel. 21-42-75; fax 22-83-21; f. 1990; Chair. Me MOUNTAGA TALL; Sec.-Gen. N'DIAYE BA.

Convention démocratique et sociale (CDS): Bamako; f. 1996; Chair. MAMADOU BAKARY SANGARÉ.

Convention patriotique pour le progrès (COPP): Bamako; f. 1997; Leader MAMADOU GACKOU.

Convention pour la république et la démocratie (CRD): Bamako; f. 1999; centrist opposition alliance; Pres. MAMADOU GACKO.
  Convention du parti populaire: Bamako.
  Parti pour la démocratie et le renouveau: Bamako.
  Union pour la démocratie et le développement (UDD): Bamako; f. 1991 by supporters of ex-President Traoré; merged with Parti socialiste pour le progrès et le développement in Aug. 1999; Leader MOUSSA BALLA COULIBALY.

Mouvement pour l'indépendance, la renaissance et l'intégration africaines (MIRIA): Bamako; e-mail lemiria@iquebec.com; internet www.iquebec.com/miria; f. 1994 following split in ADEMA; Leaders MOHAMED LAMINE TRAORÉ, MOUHAMEDOU DICKO.

Mouvement patriotique pour le renouveau (MPR): Bamako; f. 1995; linked to fmr UDPM; Pres. Dr CHOGUEL MAÏGA.

Parti africain pour la renaissance nationale (PARENA): Bamako; f. 1995, following split in CNID; supports Pres. Konaré; Chair. YORO DIAKITÉ; Sec.-Gen. TIÉBILÉ DRAMÉ.

Parti pour la démocratie et le progrès (PDP): BP 1823, Bamako; tel. and fax 22-64-52; f. 1991; Leader: Me IDRISSA TRAORÉ.

Parti malien pour le développement et le renouveau (PMDR): Bamako.

Parti progressiste soudanais (PPS): Bamako; Sec.-Gen. OUMAR DICKO.

Parti pour l'unité, la démocratie et le progrès (PUDP): Bamako; Chair. MAMADOU MARIBATROU DIABY.

Rassemblement pour la démocratie et le progrès (RDP): BP 2110, Bamako; tel. 22-30-92; fax 22-67-95; f. 1990; Chair. ALMAMY SYLLA.

Rassemblement pour la démocratie et le travail (RDT): Bamako; Leader ALI GNANGADO.

Rassemblement nationale pour la démocratie (RND): Bamako; f. 1997 by 'moderate' breakaway group from RDP; Chair. ABDOULAYE GAFA KAPO.

Union des forces démocratiques pour le progrès (UFDP): Bamako; f. 1991; Sec.-Gen. Col. YOUSSOUF TRAORÉ.

Union soudanaise—Rassemblement démocratique africain (US—RDA): BP E 1413, Bamako; tel. and fax 21-45-22; f. 1946; sole party 1960–68, banned 1968–1991; 'moderate' faction split from party in 1998; Leader MAMADOU BAMA TOURÉ.

Diplomatic Representation

EMBASSIES IN MALI

Algeria: route de l'aéroport, Daoudabougou; tel. 22-51-76; fax 22-93-74; Ambassador: AHMED FERHAT ZERHOUNI.

Burkina Faso: rue 244, BP 9022, quartier de l'Hippodrome, Bamako; tel. 22-31-71; fax 22-92-66; e-mail ambafaso@datatech.toolnet.org; Ambassador: SOPHIE SOW.

Canada: route de Koulikoro, BP 198, quartier de l'Hippodrome, Bamako; tel. 21-22-36; fax 21-43-62; Ambassador: YVES BOULANGER.

China, People's Republic: route de Koulikoro, quartier de l'Hippodrome, BP 112, Bamako; tel. 21-35-97; fax 22-35-97; Ambassador: LI YONGQIAN.

Côte d'Ivoire: place Patrice Lumumba, BP E 3644, Bamako; tel. 22-03-89; fax 22-13-76.

Egypt: ave de l'OUA, BP 44, Badalabougou-est; tel. 22-35-65; fax 22-08-91; Ambassador: ABDELSALAM YEHIA EL-TAWIL.

France: square Patrice Lumumba, BP 17, Bamako; tel. 22-29-51; fax 22-31-36; Ambassador: CHRISTIAN CONNAN.

Germany: rue de l'OUA, Badalabougou-Est, Lotissement A6, BP 100, Bamako; tel. 22-32-99; fax 22-96-50; Ambassador: KARL PRINZ.

Guinea: Immeuble Saybou Maïga, quartier du Fleuve, BP 118, Bamako; tel. 22-29-75; fax 23-08-97.

Iran: quartier de l'Hippodrome, BP 2136, Bamako; tel. 21-35-93; fax 21-07-31; Ambassador: MOJTABA SHAFII.

Iraq: BP 2512, Badalabougou-est; tel. 22-38-60; fax 22-24-16; Chargé d'affaires a.i.: JASSIM N. MSAWIL.

Libya: Immeuble Nimaga, Ngolonina, BP 1670, Bamako; tel. 22-25-18; fax 22-66-97; Chargé d'affaires a.i.: ABDEL MANSUR.

Korea, Republic: face autocars sise Sotelma, BP 76, Sogoniko; tel. 22-51-83; fax 22-51-83.

Mauritania: route de Koulikoro, quartier de l'Hippodrome, BP 135, Bamako; tel. 22-48-15; fax 22-49-08; Ambassador: BILAL OULD WERZEG.

Morocco: ave de L'OUA, BP 2013, Bamako; tel. 22-21-23; fax 22-77-87; Ambassador: LARBI ROUDIÉS.

Netherlands: angle rue 437 et route de Koulikoro, BP 2220, quartier de l'Hippodrome, Bamako; tel. 21-95-82; fax 21-36-17.

Nigeria: BP 57, Badalabougou; tel. 22-57-71; fax 22-52-84; Chargé d'affaires: M. O. KUFORIJI.

Russia: BP 300, Niaréla, Bamako; tel. 22-55-92; fax 22-99-26; Ambassador: PAVEL PETROVSKII.

Saudi Arabia: route de l'aéroport, Sogoniko; tel; 22-25-28; fax 22-50-74; Chargé d'affaires: MUHAMMAD RAJAMIRI.

Senegal: ave Nelson Mandela, quartier de l'Hippodrome, BP 42, Bamako; tel. 21-82-74; fax 21-17-80; Ambassador: MAMADOU LAITY NDIAYE.

USA: angle rue Rochester NY et rue Mohamed V, BP 34, Bamako; tel. 22-36-78; fax 22-37-12; internet http//www.usa.org.ml; Ambassador: MICHAEL E. RANNEBERGER.

Judicial System

The 1992 Constitution guarantees the independence of the judiciary.

Supreme Court: BP 7, Bamako; tel. 22-24-06; f. 1969; judicial section comprises two civil chambers, one commercial chamber, one social chamber and one criminal chamber; in addition, there are administrative and financial regulatory sections; Pres. LOUIS BASTIDE; Sec.-Gen. HENRIETTE BOUNSLY.

President of the Bar: Me MAGATTÉ SÈYE.

There is a Court of Appeal, two Tribunaux de première instance (Magistrates' Courts) and also courts for labour disputes.

Religion

It is estimated that about 80% of the population are Muslims, while 18% follow traditional animist beliefs and some 2% are Christians.

ISLAM

Association Malienne pour l'Unité et le Progrès de l'Islam (AMUPI): Bamako; state-endorsed Islamic governing body.

Chief Mosque: place de la République, Bagadadji, Bamako.

CHRISTIANITY

The Roman Catholic Church

Mali comprises one archdiocese and five dioceses. At 31 December 1997 there were an estimated 115,123 Roman Catholics, comprising about 0.9% of the total population.

Bishops' Conference: Conférence Episcopale du Mali, Archevêché, BP 298, Bamako; tel. 22-54-99; fax 22-52-14; f. 1973; Pres. Rt Rev. JEAN-GABRIEL DIARRA, Bishop of San.

Archbishop of Bamako: JEAN ZERBO, Archevêché, BP 298, Bamako; tel. 22-54-99; fax 22-52-14.

Other Christian Churches

There are several Protestant mission centres, mainly administered by US societies.

The Press

The 1992 Constitution guarantees the freedom of the press. In 1997 there were 8 daily newspapers, 18 weekly or twice-weekly publications and 6 monthly or twice-monthly publications.

DAILY NEWSPAPERS

Les Echos: Hamdallaye, ave Cheick Zayed, porte no 2694, BP 2043, Bamako; tel. 29-62-89; fax 26-76-39; e-mail jamana@malinet.ml; f. 1989; publ. by Jamana cultural co-operative; circ. 30,000; Dir Gen. HAMIDOU KONATÉ; Editor-in-Chief ABOUBACAR SALIPH DIARRA.

L'Essor—La Voix du Peuple: square Patrice Lumumba, BP 141, Bamako; tel. 22-36-83; fax 23-43-13; e-mail amap@djata.malinet.ml; f. 1949; pro-Government newspaper; Editor SOULEYMANE DRABO; circ. 3,500.

Info Matin: rue 56/350, Bamako Coura, BP E 4020, Bamako; tel. 23-82-09; fax 23-82-27; e-mail redaction@info-matin.com; Dir SAMBI TOURÉ.

Le Républicain: Niornirambougou, BP 1484, Bamako; tel. 23-00-32; fax 23-00-34; f. 1992; independent; Dir TIÉBILÉ DRAMÉ; Editor EBRAHIM TRAORÉ.

PERIODICALS

26 Mars: Bamako; f. 1998; weekly; independent; Editor BOUBACAR SANGHARE.

L'Afro-Arabe Revue: rue Mohamed V, BP 2044, Bamako; quarterly; Editor MOHAMED BEN BABA AHMED; circ. 1,000.

L'Aurore: rue 438 P 298, BP 3150, Bamako; tel. 22-69-22; fax 22-69-22; f. 1990; fortnightly; independent; Dir KARAMOKO N'DIAYE.

Barakela: Bamako; monthly; publ. by the Union nationale des travailleurs du Mali.

Le Carcan: Immeuble Babou Yarra, porte 58, BP E 1688, Bamako; tel. 23-40-28; Dir ABDOUL KARIM DRAMÉ.

Carrefour: Immeuble S.K. Hamadallaye, BP E 1985, Bamako; tel. 22-49-01; Dir MAHAMANE IMRANE COULIBALY.

Cauris: rue 464, porte 278, Badialan 1, BP 3041, Bamako; tel. 22-59-99; Dir KARAMAKO N'DIAYE.

Citoyen: Bamako; f. 1992; fortnightly; independent.

Le Courrier: rue 42, Hamdallaye Marché, Bamako; tel. 22-69-22; Dir SADOU A. YATTARA.

La Cravache: rue 127, porte 460, Bamako; tel. and fax 22-15-73; Dir EMMANUEL B. DAOU.

Danbe: Bamako; f. 1990; organ of the CNID.

L'Indépendant: Immeuble Sossoh, 2ème étage, BP E 1040, Bamako; tel. and fax 23-27-27; Dir SAOUTI HAÏDARA.

L'Inspecteur: Immeuble Alpha Gamby, bloc 6, BP 2725, Bamako; tel. 23-21-32; Dir ALY DIARRA.

Jamana—Revue Culturelle Malienne: BP 2043, Bamako; BP E 1040f. 1983; e-mail jamana@malinet.ml; quarterly; organ of Jamana cultural co-operative.

Journal Officiel de la République du Mali: BP 1463, Bamako; official gazette.

Kabaaru: Mopti; monthly; Fulbé language; rural interest; Editor BADAMA DOUCOURÉ; circ. 5,000.

Kabako: rue 228, porte 474, quartier de l'Hippodrome, BP 9005, Bamako; tel. 23-29-12; Dir MACORO CAMARA.

Kibaru: BP 1463, Bamako; monthly; Bambara and three other languages; rural interest; Editor AMADOU GAGNY KANTÉ; circ. 5,000.

Le Malien: rue 497, porte 277, Badialan III, BP E 1558, Bamako; tel. 23-57-29; weekly; Dir C. F. KEITA.

Mali Muso (Women of Mali): Bamako; quarterly; publ. by the Union des femmes du Mali; circ. 5,000.

Nouvel Horizon: rue 433, porte 94, Niaréla, BP 942, Bamako; tel. 77-30-46; weekly; independent; Dir CHOUAIDOU TRAORÉ; Editor SEMBI TOURÉ.

L'Observateur: Galérie Djigué, rue du 18 juin, BP E 1002, Bamako; tel. and fax 23-06-89; Dir BELCO TAMBOURA.

La Roue: Quinzambougou, BP 2043, Bamako; pre-independence journal, revived 1990; independent.

Le Scorpion: rue 42, Hamdallaye Marché, BP 1258, Bamako; tel. 22-98-35; fax 22-69-22; Dir MAHAMANE HAMÈYE CISSÉ.

Le Soir de Bamako: rue 433, porte 94, Niaréla, BP E 2578, Bamako; tel. 23-85-78; Dir CHOUAIDOU TRAORÉ.

Le Soudanais: rue 261, porte 100, Lafia secteur II, BP E 535, Bamako; tel. 22-21-79; Dir. KISSIMA GAKOU.

Sud-Info: rue 127, porte 460, Bamako; tel. 22-15-73; independent; Dir CHEICK OUMAR KONARÉ.

Sunjata: BP 141, Bamako; monthly; social, economic and political affairs; Editor SOUMEYLOU MAÏGA; circ. 3,000.

Le Tambour: rue 497, porte 295, Badialan III, BP E 289, Bamako; tel. and fax 22-75-68; Dir YÉRO DIALLO.

Le Temps: rue Samba Ibrahim Diawara, porte 848, BP 5032, Bamako; tel. and fax 23-02.29; Dir FAKOROBA COULIBALY.

La Voix de l'Opposition: Bamako; f. 1997 by collective of 'radical' opposition parties; weekly.

Yiriwa: BP 2043, Bamako; f. 1990; independent.

Le Zénith: Immeuble Tidiany Sylla, BP E 3881, Bamako; tel. 77-22-68; Dir IBRAHIM DIALLO.

NEWS AGENCIES

Agence Malienne de Presse et Publicité (AMAPP): Ministry of Culture and Communications, quartier du Fleuve, BP 116, Bamako; tel. 22-26-47; fax 22-83-19; f. 1977; Dir GAOUSSOU DARBO.

Foreign Bureaux

Agence France-Presse (AFP): BP 778, Bamako; tel. 22-07-77.

Rossiiskoye Informatsionnoye Agentstvo—Vesti (RIA—Vesti (Russia): BP 193, Bamako; tel. 22-45-25.

IPS (Italy), Reuters (UK) and Xinhua (New China) News Agency (People's Republic of China) are also represented in Mali.

PRESS ASSOCIATIONS

Association des Editeurs de la Presse Privée (ASSEP): BP 1258, Bamako; tel. 22-98-45; Pres. SADOU ABDOULAYE YATTARA.

Association des Femmes de la Presse Privée: Porte 474, rue 428, BP E 731, Bamako; tel. 21-29-12; Pres. FANTA DIALLO.

Association des Journalistes Professionels des Médias Privés du Mali (AJPM): BP E 2456, Bamako; tel. 22-19-15; fax 23-54-78; Pres. MOMADOU FOFANA.

Association des Professionnelles Africaines de la Communication (APAC MALI): Porte 474, rue 428, BP E 731, Bamako; tel. 21-29-12; Pres. MACORO CAMARA DIABY.

Maison de la Presse: BP E 2456, Bamako; tel. 22-19-15; fax 23-54-78; e-mail Maison-Presse@cefib.com; internet www.cefib.com/presse/introduction.htm; independent media association.

Réseau des Journalistes Economiques du Mali (RJEM): BP E 3717, Bamako; tel. 77-16-67; Co-ordinator HAWOYE TOURÉ.

Union Nationale des Journalistes Maliens (UNAJOM): BP 141, Bamako; tel. 22-36-83; fax 23-43-13; e-mail amap@djata.malinet.ml; Pres. OUSMANE MAÏGA.

Publishers

EDIM SA: ave Kassé Keïta, BP 21, Bamako; tel. 22-40-41; f. 1972 as Editions Imprimeries du Mali, reorg. 1987; general fiction and non-fiction, textbooks; Chair. and Man. Dir IBRAHIMA BERTHE.

Editions Donniya: Cité du Niger, BP 1273, Bamako; tel. 21-46-46; fax 21-90-31; e-mail donniya@malinet.ml; internet www.cefib.com/impcolor/donniya.htm; f. 1996; general fiction, history, reference and children's books.

Broadcasting and Communications

TELECOMMUNICATIONS

Société des Télécommunications du Mali (SOTELMA): route de Koulikoro, BP 740, Bamako; tel. 21-52-80; fax 21-30-22; e-mail khalima@sotelma.ml; internet www.sotelma.net; f. 1989; state-owned; 49% privatization pending; Pres. and Man. Dir SAMBA SOW.

BROADCASTING

Radio

Office de Radiodiffusion-Télévision Malienne (ORTM): BP 171, Bamako; tel. 21-20-19; fax 21-42-05; e-mail ortm@spider.toolnet .org; f. 1957; state-owned; radio programmes in French, Bambara, Peulh, Sarakolé, Tamachek, Sonrai, Moorish, Wolof, English; Man. Dir SIDIKI KONATE.

Chaîne 2: Bamako; f. 1993; radio broadcasts to Bamako.

In the late 1990s there were some 56 authorized private radio stations and an estimated 16 unauthorized stations, including:

Fréquence 3: Bamako; f. 1992; commercial.

Radio Bamakan: Marché de Médine, BP E100, Bamako; tel. 21-27-60; fax 22-53-66; e-mail diallom@ifrance.com; f. 1991; community station; 104 hours of FM broadcasts weekly; Man. MODIBO DIALLO.

Radio Binkan: Bangui; FM broadcasts to Bangui.

Radio Guintan: Bangui; FM broadcasts to Bangui.

Radio Jamana: Nioro; tel. 52-18-57.

Radio Kayira: Bamako; f. 1992; supports the CNID.

Radio Klédu: Bamako; f. 1992; commercial; Propr MAMADOU COULIBALY.

Radio Liberté: Nouveau Marché de Médine, BP 5015, Bamako; tel. 22-05-81; f. 1991; commercial station broadcasting 24 hours daily.

Radio Balanzan: Ségou.

Radio Patriote: Bangui; FM broadcasts to Bangui.

Radio Rurale: Kayes; tel. 52-14-76; community stations established by the Agence de coopération culturelle et technique (ACTT); transmitters in Niono, Kadiolo, Bandiagara and Kidal.

Sahel FM: Immeuble Hamet Niang, Grand Marché, BP 394, Kayes; tel. 52-21-87; f. 1995, broadcasts began 1997; Man. Dir MOUCTAR THIAM.

Radio Tabalé: BP 697, Bamako; tel. and fax 22-78-70; f. 1992; independent public-service station broadcasting 57 hours weekly; Dir TIÉMOKO KONÉ.

Radio France International, the Voix de l'Islam, and the Gabonese-based Africa No. 1 began FM broadcasts in Mali in 1993; broadcasts by Voice of America and the World Service of the British Broadcasting Corpn are also transmitted via private radio stations.

Television

Office de Radiodiffusion-Télévision Malienne (ORTM): (see Radio); Dir of Television CHEICK HAMALLA TOURÉ.

Multicanal SA: Quinzambougou, BP E 1506, Bamako; tel. 21-49-64; e-mail sandrine@multi-canal.com; internet www.multi-canal.com; private subscription broadcaster; relays international broadcasts; Pres. ISMAÏLA SIDIBÉ.

TV Klédu: 600 ave Modibo Keïta, BP E 1172, Bamako; tel. 23-90-00; fax 23-70-50; e-mail info@tvkledu.com; internet www.cefib.com/tvkledu; private cable TV operator; relays international broadcasts.

Finance

(cap. = capital; res = reserves; m. = million; brs = branches; amounts in francs CFA)

BANKING

Central Bank

Banque Centrale des Etats de l'Afrique de l'Ouest (BCEAO): square Lumumba, BP 206, Bamako; tel. 22-37-56; fax 22-47-86; f. 1962; HQ in Dakar, Senegal; bank of issue for the mem. states of Union économique et monétaire ouest-africaine (UEMOA, comprising Benin, Burkina Faso, Côte d'Ivoire, Guinea-Bissau, Mali, Niger, Senegal and Togo); cap. and res 806,918m., total assets 4,084,464m. (Dec. 1998); Gov. CHARLES KONAN BANNY; Dir in Mali IDRISSA TRAORÉ; br. at Mopti.

Commercial Banks

Bank of Africa—Mali (BOA): 418 ave de la Marne, Bozola, BP 2249, Bamako; tel. 21-85-88; fax 21-46-53; e-mail boamali@datatech .toolnet.org; internet www.pelsys.com/boa; f. 1982; cap. and res 3,026m., total assets 50,158m. (Dec. 1998); Chair. BOUREIMA SYLLA; Man. Dir RENÉ PHILIPPE BACH; 5 brs.

Banque Commerciale du Sahel SA (BCS–SA): rue 127 x 122, Boyola, BP 2372, Bamako; tel. 21-01-95; fax 21-05-35; f. 1982; fmrly Banque Arabe Libyo-Malienne pour le Commerce Extérieur et le Développement; 50% owned by Libyan-Arab Foreign Bank, 49.5% state-owned; cap. and res 2,096m., total assets 15,243m. (Dec. 1998); Dir-Gen. MOHAMED SAAD EL ATRACH.

Banque de l'Habitat du Mali (BHM): ave Kassé Keïta, BP 2614, Bamako; tel. 22-91-90; fax 22-93-50; f. 1996; fmrly Société des Chèques Postaux et de la Caisse d'Epargne; 50% owned by Institut National de Prévoyance Social; 20% state-owned; cap. 1,350m.; Dir-Gen. MAMADOU SAMBA DIARRA.

Banque International pour le Commerce et l'Industrie au Mali SA (BICIM): Immeuble Nimagala, blvd du Peuple, BP B72, Bamako; tel. 23-33-70; fax 23-33-73; e-mail bicim-sa@cefib.com; f. 1999; 50% owned by SFOM Interafrica, 20% by Banque National de Paris, 15% by Banque Mauritanienne pour le Commerce International; Pres. LUC VIDAL; Sec. Gen. JEAN-PAUL GONÇON

Banque Internationale pour le Mali (BIM—SA): Immeuble de Bolibana, blvd de l'Indépendance, BP 15, Bamako; tel. 22-51-11; fax 22-45-66; e-mail bim@malinet.ml; internet www.malinet.ml/pratique/bim/index.html; f. 1981; fmrly BIAO—Mali, present name since 1995; 61.5% state-owned; cap. and res 3,184m., total assets 65,500m. (Dec. 1996); Chair. MAHAMAR OUMAR MAÏGA; Man. Dir ASSANA SY; 4 brs.

Banque Malienne de Crédit et de Dépôts SA (BMCD): ave Modibo Keïta, BP 45, Bamako; tel. 22-53-36; fax 22-79-50; e-mail bmcd@malinet.ml; internet www.bmcd-mali.com; f. 1961; previously state-owned; 49.98% acquired by a consortium of the Banque de Développement du Mali and the Banque Marocaine du Commerce Extérieur SA in 2000; initial cap. 100,000m. francs CFA; Dir-Gen. SALIF NAMBALA KEÏTA (acting).

Ecobank Mali: place de la Nation, quartier du Fleuve, BP 1272, Bamako; tel. 23-33-00; fax 23-33-05; e-mail ecobank@cefib.mali; f. 1998; 50% owned by Ecobank Transnational Inc., 30% by Ecobank Bénin, 20% by Ecobank Togo; cap. and res 1,452m., total assets 4,453m. (Dec. 1998); Pres. SEYDOU DJIN SYLLA; Man. Dir BENOÎT ZANNOU.

Development Banks

Banque de Développement du Mali SA (BDM): ave Modibo Keïta, BP 94, Bamako; tel. 22-20-50; fax 22-50-85; f. 1968; 20% state-owned, 20% owned by BCEAO, 20% by Banque ouest-africaine de développement; cap. and res 4,884m., total assets 101,714m. (Dec. 1996); Chair. Minister of Finance and Trade; Man. Dir ABDOULAYE DAFFÉ; 11 brs.

Banque Nationale de Développement Agricole—Mali (BNDA—Mali): Immeuble Caisse Autonome d'Amortissement, quartier du Fleuve, BP 2424, Bamako; tel. 22-64-64; fax 22-29-61; f. 1981; 41.8% state-owned; cap. and res. 19,116m., total assets 53,558m. (Dec. 1998); Chair. and Man. Dir BAKARY TRAORÉ; 21 brs.

Financial Institutions

Direction Générale de la Dette Publique: Immeuble Caisse Autonome d'Amortissement, quartier du Fleuve, BP 1617, Bamako; tel. 22-29-35; fax 22-07-93; management of the public debt; Dir NAMALA KONÉ.

Société Malienne de Financement (SOMAFI): BP 3643, Bamako; tel. 22-18-66; fax 22-18-69; e-mail somafi@malinet.ml; f. 1997; cap. and res 327m., total assets 720m. (Dec. 1998); Man. Dir ERIC LECLÈRE.

STOCK EXCHANGE

Bourse Régionale des Valeurs Mobilières (BRVM): Chambre de Commerce et de l'Industrie du Mali, place de la Liberté, BP E 1398, Bamako; tel. 23-23-54; fax 23-23-59; f. 1998; national branch of BRVM (regional stock exchange based in Abidjan, Côte d'Ivoire, serving the mem. states of UEMOA); Man. AMADOU DJÉRI BOCOUM.

INSURANCE

Les Assurances Générales de France (AGF): ave du Fleure, BP 190, Bamako; tel. 22-58-18.

Assurance Colina SA: Immeuble SOMIEX, BP 953, Bamako; tel. 224792; fax 226713; f. 1990; cap. 600m.; Dir-Gen. MAMADOU CISSÉ.

Caisse Nationale d'Assurance et de Réassurance (CNAR): Immeuble CNAR, square Patrice Lumumba, BP 568, Bamako; tel. 22-31-17; fax 22-23-29; f. 1969; state-owned; cap. 50m.; Dir-Gen. F. KEÏTA; 10 brs.

Compagnie d'Assurance Privée—La Soutra: BP 52, Bamako; tel. 22-36-81; fax 22-55-23; f. 1979; cap. 150m.; Chair. AMADOU NIONO.

Compagnie d'Assurance et de Réassurance de Mali: BP 1822, Bamako; tel. 22-60-29.

Compagnie d'Assurance Sabu Nyuman: Bamako Coura 135–136, BP 1822, Bamako; tel. 226029; fax 225750; f. 1984; cap. 250m.; Dir-Gen. MOMADOU SANOGO.

Lafía Assurances: ave de la Nation, BP 1542, Bamako; tel. 223551; fax 225224; f. 1983; cap. 50m.; Dir-Gen. ABDOULAYE TOURÉ.

Trade and Industry

GOVERNMENT AGENCIES

Centre d'Etudes et de Promotion Industrielle (CEPI): BP 1980, Bamako; tel. 22-22-79; fax 22-80-85.

Compagnie Malienne pour le Développement des Textiles (CMDT): BP 487, Bamako; tel. 22-24-62; fax 22-81-41; f. 1975; cap. 1,500m. francs CFA; 60% state-owned, 40% owned by Cie Française pour le Développement des Fibres Textiles; cotton cultivation, ginning and marketing; Chair. and Man. Dir DRISSA KEITA.

Direction Nationale des Affaires Économiques (DNAE): rue de Sotuba, BP 210, Bamako; tel. 22-23-14; fax 22-02-256; involved in economic and social affairs.

Direction Nationale des Travaux Publics (DNTP): ave de la Liberté, BP 1758, Bamako; tel. and fax 22-29-02; administers public works.

Office du Niger: BP 106, Ségou; tel. 32-02-92; fax 32-01-43; f. 1932; taken over from the French authorities in 1958; restructured in mid-1990s; cap. 7,139m. francs CFA; principally involved in cultivation of food crops; Pres. and Man. Dir NANCOMA KEÏTA.

Office des Produits Agricoles du Mali (OPAM): BP 132, Bamako; tel. 22-37-55; fax 22-04-06; f. 1965; cap. 5,800m. francs CFA; state-owned; manages National (Cereals) Security Stock, administers food aid, responsible for sales of cereals and distribution to deficit areas; Man. Dir ABDOULAYE KOITA.

Société Nationale de Recherches et d'Exploitation des Ressources Minières du Mali (SONAREM): BP 2, Kati; tel. 27-20-42; state-owned; Man. Dir MAKAN KAYENTAO.

DEVELOPMENT ORGANIZATIONS

Agence Française de Développement (AFD): BP 32, Bamako; tel. 22-28-42; fmrly Caisse Française de Développement; Dir GÉRARD PINCE; Head of Mission H. KAHANE.

Office de Développement Intégré du Mali-Ouest (ODIMO): square Patrice Lumumba, Bamako; tel. 22-57-59; f. 1991 to succeed Office de Développement Intégré des Productions Arachidières et Céréalières; development of diversified forms of agricultural production; Man. Dir ZANA SANOGO.

Service de Coopération et d'Action Culturelle: Square Patrice Lumumba, BP 84, Bamako; tel. 21-83-38; fax 21-83-39; e-mail scac@cefib.com; administers bilateral aid from France; Dir MICHEL COLIN DE VERDIÈRE.

CHAMBER OF COMMERCE

Chambre de Commerce et d'Industrie du Mali: place de la Liberté, BP 46, Bamako; tel. 22-50-36; fax 22-21-20; f. 1906; Pres. DRAHAMANE HAMIDOU TOURÉ; Sec.-Gen. DABA TRAORÉ.

EMPLOYERS' ASSOCIATIONS

Association Malienne des Exportateurs de Légumes (AMELEF): BP 1996, Bamako; f. 1984; Pres. BADARA FAGANDA TRAORÉ; Sec.-Gen. BIRAMA TRAORÉ.

Association Malienne des Exportateurs de Ressources Animales (AMERA): Centre Malien de Commerce Extérieur, BP 1996, Bamako; tel. 22-56-83; f. 1985; Pres. AMBARKÉ YERMANGORE; Admin. Sec. ALI HACKO.

UTILITIES

Electricity

Energie du Mali (EDM): square Patrice Lumumba, BP 69, Bamako; tel. 22-30-20; fax 22-84-30; e-mail sekou.edm@cefib.com; f. 1961, restructuring in progress from 1994; state-owned, managed by consortium of Franco-Canadian interests; 60% privatization pending; planning, construction and operation of all power-sector facilities; cap. 7,880m.; Dir-Gen. FREDERIC BAUDIN; 1,350 employees.

Enertech GSA: marché de Lafiabougou, BP 1949, Bamako; tel. 22-37-63; fax 22-51-36; f. 1994; cap. 20m.; solar energy producer; Dir MOCTAR DIAKITE.

Société de Gestion de l'Energie de Manantali (SOGEM): Immeuble 790 Hippodrome, rue 235 x 236, BP E 4015, Bamako; f. to generate and distribute electricity from the Manantali HEP project, under the auspices of the Organisation pour la mise en valeur du fleuve Sénégal.

Gas

Maligaz: route de Sotuba, BP 5, Bamako; tel. 22-23-94; gas distribution.

MAJOR COMPANIES

The following are among the major private and state-owned companies in terms of capital investment or employment.

Abattoir Frigorifique de Bamako: Zone Industrielle, BP 356, Bamako; tel. 22-24-67; fax 22-99-03; f. 1965; cap. 339m. francs CFA; state-owned; transfer to 80% private ownership, as Société des Abattoirs Frigorifiques de Bamako, announced in 1996; Man. Dir El Hadj YOUSSOUF CAMARA.

Béton Mali: BP 2410, Bamako; cap. 350m. francs CFA; mfrs and distributors of construction materials; Chair. and Man. Dir MAMADOU DIATIGUI DIARRA.

Compagnie Malienne de Développement Textile (CMDT): BP 487, Bozda; tel. 22-24-62; fax 22-81-41; f. 1974; cap. 1,000m. francs CFA; production of cotton fibre; Dir PRISSA KEITA; 6,808 employees.

Compagnie Malienne des Textiles (COMATEX): route de Markala, BP 52, Ségou; tel. 32-01-83; fax 32-01-29; f. 1968; cap. 4,250m. francs CFA; production of unbleached fibre and textiles; Pres. M. KEITA; 2,027 employees.

Elf Oil Mali: BP 13, Bamako; tel. 22-29-71; fax 22-80-27.

Ets Peyrissac–Mali: ave de la République, BP 168, Bamako; tel. 22-20-62; f. 1963; cap. 300m. francs CFA; distributors of motor vehicles; Dir FRANÇOIS GRULOIS.

Grands Moulins du Mali (GMM): BP 324, Koulikoro; tel. 22-36-64; fax 22-58-74; f. 1982; cap. 600m. francs CFA; mfrs of flour and animal feed; Chair. and Man. Dir GÉRARD ACHCAR; 89 employees.

Huilerie Cotonnière du Mali (HUICOMA): c/o CMDT, BP 2434, Bamako; tel. 22-68-91; fax 22-68-84; f. 1979; cap. 1,500m. francs CFA; 50% owned by CMDT, 40% state-owned; processing of oilseeds; Dir of Operations ABEL KEITA.

Industrie Textile du Mali (ITEMA): Zone Industrielle, BP 299, Bamako; tel. 22-46-47; f. 1972; producer of textiles; cap. 1,500m. francs CFA; 799 employees.

Mobil Oil Mali: quartier TSF, Zone Industrielle, BP 145, Bamako; tel. 22-25-97; fax 22-68-82; f. 1974; cap. 321m. francs CFA; distribution of petroleum products; Dir-Gen. JEAN-PIERRE LEYNAUD.

Pharmacie Populaire du Mali (PPM): ave Houssa Travele, BP 277, Bamako; tel. 22-46-25; fax 22-90-34; f. 1960; cap. 400m. francs CFA; majority state-owned; import and marketing of medicines and pharmaceutical products; Man. Dir Dr ABDOULAYE DIALLO.

Shell Mali SA: BP 199, Bamako; tel. 21-24-52; fax 21-76-15; f. 1963; Gen. Man. IBRA DIENG.

Société des Brasseries du Mali (BRAMALI): BP 442, Bamako; f. 1981; cap. 500m. francs CFA; mfrs of beer and soft drinks; Chair. and Man. Dir SEYDOU DJIM SYLLA.

Société d'Equipement du Mali (SEMA): Face Ecole Cathédrale, BP 163, Bamako; tel. 22-50-71; fax 23-06-47; f. 1961; construction and public works; cap. 140m. francs CFA; Dir MAMADOU DIAKITE; 51 employees.

Société d'Exploitation des Mines d'Or de Sadiola SA (SEMOS): Bamako; f. 1994; 38% owned by Anglo American Corpn (South Africa), 38% by Iamgold (Canada); devt of gold deposits at Sadiola Hill.

Société Industrielle de Karité (SIKAMALI): Bamako; f. 1980; cap. 938m. francs CFA; processors of shea-nuts (karité nuts); Dir DRISSA SANGARÉ.

Société Karamoko Traoré et Frères (SOKATRAF): BP 88, Mopti; f. 1975; cap. 318m. francs CFA; import/export; Chair. and Man. Dir DRAMANE TRAORÉ.

Société Malienne d'Etudes et de Construction de Matériel Agricole (SMECMA): BP 1707, Bamako; tel. 22-40-71; f. 1974; cap. 251.4m. francs CFA; mfrs of agricultural equipment; Chair. AHMED AG HAMANI; Man. Dir BOUBACAR NANTÉGUÉ MALLE.

Société Malienne de Piles Electriques (SOMAPIL): route de Sotuba, Zone Industrielle, BP 1546, Bamako; tel. 22-46-87; fax 22-29-80; f. 1975; cap. 500m. francs CFA; mfrs of batteries; Chair. KOUMAN DOUMBIA; Man. Dir GÉRARD HELIX.

Société Malienne de Produits Chimiques (SMPC): BP 1560, Bamako; f. 1987; cap. 250m. francs CFA; sale of part of state holding (c. 20%) authorized in 1996; mfrs and distributors of insecticides; Chair. and Man. Dir ISSA KONDA.

Société Malienne de Profilage et de Transformation des Métaux (TOLMALI): quartier TSF, Zone Industrielle, Bamako; tel. 22-33-35; fax 22-53-77; f. 1978; cap. 250m. francs CFA; mfrs of iron and steel construction materials and aluminium utensils.

Société Malienne de Sacherie (SOMASAC): BP 74, Bamako; tel. 22-49-41; f. 1971; cap. 462.5m. francs CFA; production of sacking from dah and kenaf fibre and manufacture of sacks; Chair. DOSSOLO TRAORÉ; Man. Dir ERNEST RICHARD.

Société des Mines de Loulo (SOMILO): Loulo; fax 22-81-87; f. 1987; cap. 2,133m. francs CFA; 51% owned by Randgold Resources

(Jersey); exploration and development of gold deposits at Loulo; Chair. MAMADOU TOURÉ; Man. Dir ROBERT KRUH.

Société Minière de Syama (SOMISY): Syama; tel. 22-28-06; f. 1990; cap. 9,000m. francs CFA; 75% owned by Randgold Resources (Jersey), 20% state-owned; exploitation of gold reserves at Syama; Gen. Man. GERHARD VAN JAARSVELD; 221 employees.

Société Nationale des Tabacs et Allumettes du Mali (SON-ATAM): route de Sotuba, Zone Industrielle, BP 59, Bamako; tel. 22-49-65; fax 22-23-72; f. 1968; cap. 2,177m. francs CFA; state-owned; transfer to private ownership pending; production of cigarettes and matches; Chair. MOUSSA BABA DIARRA; Man. Dir BOUBACAR DEMBÉLÉ; 820 employees.

Tannerie de l'Afrique de l'Ouest: Bamako; f. 1994; jt venture by private Malian interests and Curtidos Corderroura (Spain); processing of skins and hides; 150 employees.

Total Texaco Mali: BP 26, Badala; tel. 22-58-22; fax 22-59-98; f. 1976; cap. 393m. francs CFA; distribution of gas, petroleum and insecticides; 45 employees.

Usine Malienne de Produits Pharmaceutiques (UMPP): zone Industrielle, BP 2286, Bamako; tel. 22-51-61; fax 22-51-69; e-mail umpp1@datatech.toolnet.org; f. 1983; cap. 2,551m. francs CFA; producer of pharmaceutical products; 209 employees.

TRADE UNION FEDERATION

Union nationale des travailleurs du Mali (UNTM): Bourse du Travail, blvd de l'Indépendance, BP 169, Bamako; tel. 22-20-31; f. 1963; Sec.-Gen. SIAKA DIAKITÉ.

There are, in addition, several non-affiliated trade unions.

Transport

RAILWAYS

Mali's only railway runs from Koulikoro, via Bamako, to the Senegal border (642 track-km). The line continues to Dakar, a total distance of 1,286 km. The track is in very poor condition, and is frequently closed during the rainy season. In 1995 the Governments of Mali and Senegal agreed to establish, with a view to privatization, a joint company to operate the Bamako–Dakar line. Some 501,500 tons of freight were handled on the Malian railway in 1995. Plans exist for the construction of a new rail line linking Bamako with Kouroussa and Kankan, in Guinea.

Régie du Chemin de Fer du Mali (RCFM): rue Baba Diarra, BP 260, Bamako; tel. 22-59-68; fax 22-83-88; f. 1960; privatization pending; Pres. DIAKARIDIA SIDIBÉ.

ROADS

The Malian road network in 1996 comprised an estimated 15,100 km, of which about 5,820 km were main roads and 5,710 km were secondary roads. About 1,830 km of the network were paved. A bituminized road between Bamako and Abidjan (Côte d'Ivoire) provides Mali's main economic link to the coast; construction of a road linking Bamako and Dakar (Senegal) is to be financed by the European Development Fund. The African Development Bank also awarded a US $31.66m. loan to fund the Kankan–Kouremale–Bamako road between Mali and Guinea. A road across the Sahara to link Mali with Algeria is also planned.

Compagnie Malienne de Transports Routiers (CMTR): BP 208, Bamako; tel. 22-33-64; f. 1970; state-owned; Man. Dir MAMADOU TOURÉ.

INLAND WATERWAYS

The River Niger is navigable in parts of its course through Mali (1,693 km) during the rainy season from July to late December. The River Senegal was, until the early 1990s, navigable from Kayes to Saint-Louis (Senegal) only between August and November, but its navigability was expected to improve following the inauguration, in 1992, of the Manantali dam, and the completion of works to deepen the river-bed.

Compagnie Malienne de Navigation (CMN): BP 10, Koulikoro; tel. 26-20-94; fax 26-20-09; f. 1968; state-owned; river transport and shipbuilding; Pres. and Man. Dir YACOUBA DIALLO.

Société Navale Malienne (SONAM): rue Achkhabad Niaréla, BP 10, Bamako; tel. 22-60-52; fax 22-60-66; f. 1981; transferred to private ownership in 1986; Chair. ALIOUNE KEÏTA.

Société Ouest-Africaine d'Entreprise Maritime (SOAEM): rue Mohamed V, BP 2428, Bamako; tel. 22-58-32; fax 22-40-24; maritime transport co.

CIVIL AVIATION

The principal airport is at Bamako-Senou. The other major airports are at Bourem, Gao, Goundam, Kayes, Kita, Mopti, Nioro, Ségou, Tessalit and Tombouctou. There are about 40 small airfields. Mali's airports are being modernized with external financial assistance.

Direction Nationale de l'Aéronautique Civile: Bamako; tel. 22-55-24.

Air Affaires Mali: BP E 3759, Badalabougou, Bamako; tel. 22-61-36.

Air Afrique: square Patrice Lumumba, BP 2651, Bamako; tel. 22-76-86; fax 22-61-36; see under Côte d'Ivoire; Dir in Mali B. DJIBO.

Mali Tombouctou Air Service (MALITAS): BP 27, Bamako; tel. 22-57-19; f. 1988 to succeed Air Mali; partial sale of state holding (20%) authorized in 1996; domestic services; Chair. AMADOU OUSMANE SIMAGA.

Société des Transports Aériens (STA): BP 1809, Bamako; f. 1984; privately-owned; local services; Man. Dir MELHEM ELIE SABBAGUE.

Tourism

Mali's rich cultural heritage is promoted as a tourist attraction. In 1999 the Government launched a three-year cultural and tourism development programme centred on Tombouctou, Gao and Kidal. About 75,000 tourists visited Mali in 1997, when receipts from tourism totalled US $26m. A total of 90,000 tourists were estimated to have visited Mali during the 1999–2000 tourist season, generating revenue of about $90m.

Office Malien du Tourisme et de l'Hôtellerie (OMATHO): porte 71, rue Mohamed V, BP 191, Bamako; tel. 22-56-73; fax 22-55-41; e-mail tombouctou2000@tourisme.gov.ml; internet www.tourisme.gov.ml; f. 1995; Dir AGUIBOU GUISSÉ.

Defence

In August 1999 the active Malian army numbered some 7,350 men: land army 6,900, naval force about 50 (with three patrol boats on the River Niger), air force 400. Paramilitary forces comprised a gendarmerie (1,800 men), republican guard (2,000), militia (3,000) and national police (1,000). Military service is by selective conscription and lasts for two years.

Defence Expenditure: Estimated at 29,000m. francs CFA in 1999.

Chief of Staff of the Armed Forces: Col TOUMANI CISSOKO.

Chief of Staff of the Army: Col PANGASSY SANGARE.

Education

Education is provided free of charge and is officially compulsory for nine years between seven and 16 years of age. Primary education begins at the age of seven and lasts for six years. Secondary education, from 13 years of age, lasts for a further six years, generally comprising two cycles of three years each. The rate of school-enrolment in Mali is among the lowest in the world: in 1997 total enrolment at primary and secondary schools excluding Medersas (Islamic schools) was equivalent to only 32% of children in the relevant age-group (males 39%; females 25%). Primary enrolment in 1997 was equivalent to 49% of the appropriate age-group (males 58%; females 40%), while secondary enrolment was equivalent to only 13% (males 17%; females 8%). Tertiary education facilities include the national university, developed in the mid-1990s. Hitherto, many students have received higher education abroad, mainly in France and Senegal. In 1988, according to official figures, illiteracy among persons aged six years and over averaged 81.2% (males 73.6%; females 88.6%). UNESCO estimated the average rate of adult illiteracy in 1995 at 67.7% (males 60.0%; females 74.9%). The draft budget for 2000 allocated around 25,000m. francs CFA to education.

Bibliography

Bastian, D. E., Myers, R. A., Stamm, A. L. *Mali*. Oxford, ABC-Clio, 1994.

de Benoist, J.-R. *Eglise et pouvoir colonial au Soudan français*. Paris, Editions Karthala, 1987.

Bingen, R. J., Staatz, J. M., Robinson, D. (Eds). *Democracy and Development in Mali*. Michigan, The Michigan State University Press, 2000.

Cissé, Y. T., and Kamissoko, W. *La grande geste du Mali, des origines à la fondation de l'empire*. Paris, Editions Karthala, 1988.

Cola Cissé, M., et al. *Le Mali: Le Paysan et L'Etat*. Paris, L'Harmattan, 1981.

Daum, C. *Les Maliens en France. Les associations d'émigrés de la région de Kayes*. Paris, Editions Karthala, 1998.

Davies, S. *Adaptable Livelihoods: Coping with Food Insecurity in the Malian Sahel*. New York, St. Martin's Press, 1996.

Decraene, P. *Le Mali*. Paris, Presses universitaires de France, 1980.

Diakite, Y. *La Fédération du Mali: sa création et les causes de son éclatement*. Bamako, Ecole Normale Supérieure de Bamako, 1985.

Diarrah, Cheikh O. *Le Mali de Modibo Keita*. Paris, L'Harmattan, 1986.

Diop, M. *Histoire des classes sociales dans l'Afrique de l'Ouest. Tome 1: Le Mali*. Paris, L'Harmattan.

Foltz, W. J. *From French West Africa to Mali Federation*. Yale University Press, 1965.

Gaudio, A. *Le Mali*. Paris, Editions Karthala, 1988.

Gibbal, J. M. *Genii of the River Niger*. Chicago, University of Chicago Press, 1994.

Harrison Church, R. J. *West Africa*. 8th Edn. London, Longman, 1979.

Imperato, P. J. *Historical Dictionary of Mali*. Metuchen, NJ, Scarecrow Press, 1987.

Mali: A Search for Direction. Boulder, CO, Westview Press, 1989.

Jenkins, M. *To Timbuktu: A Journey down the Niger*. New York, William Morrow & Co Inc, 1997.

Maharaux, A. *L'Industrie au Mali*. Paris, L'Harmattan, 1986.

Maiga, Abdoul B. C. *La politique africaine du Mali de 1960 à 1980*. Bamako, Ecole Normale Supérieure de Bamako, 1983.

Mariko, K. *Les Touaregs Ouelleminden*. Paris, Editions Karthala, 1984.

Poulton, R.-E., and ag Youssouf, I. *A Peace of Timbuktu*. Geneva, UNIDR, 1998.

Raimbault, M., and Sanogo, K. (Eds). *Recherches archaéologiques au Mali*. Paris, Editions Karthala, 1991.

Rimmer, D. *The Economies of West Africa*. London, Weidenfeld and Nicolson, 1984.

Snyder, F. G. *One-Party Government in Mali: Transition towards Control*. New Haven and London, Yale University Press, 1965.

Stamm, A., et al. *Mali (Bibliography)*. Oxford, Clio Press, 1998.

Sy, M. S. *Recherches sur l'exercice du pouvoir politique en Afrique noire (Côte d'Ivoire, Guinée, Mali)*. Paris, 1965.

MAURITANIA

Physical and Social Geography

DAVID HILLING

Covering an area of 1,030,700 sq km (397,950 sq miles), the Islamic Republic of Mauritania forms a geographical link between the Arab Maghreb and Black West Africa. Moors, heterogeneous groups of Arab/Berber stock, form about two-thirds of the population, which totalled 1,864,236 at the April 1988 census. According to UN estimates, the population totalled 2,529,000 at mid-1998 (giving an average population density of 2.5 persons per sq km).

The Moors are divided on social and descent criteria, rather than skin colour, into a dominant group, the Bidan or 'white' Moors, and a group, probably of servile origin, known as the Harratin or 'black' Moors. All were traditionally nomadic pastoralists. The country's black African inhabitants traditionally form about one-third of the total population, the principal groups being the Fulani (20%) and the Wolof (12%). They are mainly sedentary cultivators and are concentrated in a relatively narrow zone in the south of the country.

During the drought of the 1970s and early 1980s, there was mass migration to the towns, and the urban population increased from 18% of the total in 1972 to as much as 35% in 1984. The population of Nouakchott was 134,986 at the time of the 1977 census, but this was estimated to have risen to 667,300 by 1998. The populations of towns such as Nouadhibou (22,365 in 1977) and Kaédi (20,356) were estimated to have increased to 88,313 and 40,633, respectively, by 1996. There has been a general exodus from rural areas and an associated growth of informal peri-urban encampments. In 1963 about 83% of the population was nomadic, and 17% sedentary, but by 1988 only 12% remained nomadic, while 88% were settled, mainly in the larger towns.

Two-thirds of the country may be classed as 'Saharan', with rainfall absent or negligible in most years and always less than 100 mm. In parts vegetation is inadequate to graze even the camel, which is the main support of the nomadic peoples of the northern and central area. Traditionally this harsh area has produced some salt, and dates and millet are cultivated at oases such as Atar. Southwards, in the 'Sahelian' zone, the rainfall increases to about 600 mm per year; in good years vegetation will support sheep, goats and cattle, and adequate crops of millet and sorghum can be grown. There is evidence that the 250 mm precipitation line has moved 200 km further south since the early 1960s, as Saharan conditions encroach on Sahelian areas. In 1983 rainfall over the whole country reached an average of only 27% of that for the period 1941–70, and was only 13% in the pasturelands of the Hodh Oriental region. Average annual rainfall in the early 1990s was reported to be only 100 mm. The Senegal river has been at record low levels, and riverine cultivation in the seasonally inundated *chemama* lands has been greatly reduced. Larger areas of more systematic irrigation could be made possible by dams which have been constructed for the control of the river.

Geologically, Mauritania is a part of the vast western Saharan 'shield' of crystalline rocks, but these are overlain in parts with sedimentary rocks, and some 40% of the country has a superficial cover of unconsolidated sand. Relief has a general north-east/south-west trend, and a series of westward-facing scarps separate monotonous plateaux, which only in western Adrar rise above 500 m. Locally these plateaux have been eroded, so that only isolated peaks remain, the larger of these being known as *kedia* and the smaller as *guelb*. These are often minerally enriched; however, reserves of high-grade iron ore in the *djbel le-hadid* ('iron mountains') of the Kédia d'Idjil were nearing exhaustion in the late 1980s, and production ceased in 1992. Mining at a neighbouring *guelb*, El Rhein (some 40 km to the north), began in 1984, while the exploitation of the important M'Haoudat deposit (55 km to the north of Zouérate) began in 1994. Gypsum is currently mined on a small scale, and reserves of gold, phosphates, sulphur and rock salt have been identified.

In 1991 Arabic was declared to be the official language. The principal vernacular languages, Poular, Wolof and Solinke were, with Arabic, recognized as 'national languages'. French is still widely used, particularly in the commercial sector.

Recent History

PIERRE ENGLEBERT

Revised for this edition by the Editor

OULD DADDAH AND THE PPM

Mauritania achieved independence from France on 28 November 1960. Moktar Ould Daddah, whose Parti du regroupement mauritanien (PRM) had won all the seats in the previous year's general election, became head of state. All parties subsequently merged with the PRM to form the Parti du peuple mauritanien (PPM), and Mauritania was declared a one-party state in 1964. A highly centralized and tightly controlled political system was imposed on a diverse political spectrum. Some elements among the Moorish population favoured union with Morocco, and, although each government included a small minority of black Mauritanians, the southern population feared Arab domination.

In the early 1970s the Ould Daddah government undertook a series of measures to assert Mauritania's political, cultural and economic independence. Economic and cultural agreements signed with France at independence were renegotiated, and Mauritania announced its intention to withdraw from the Franc Zone and introduce its own currency, the ouguiya. In 1974 the foreign-owned iron-ore mines, which provided 80% of national exports, were nationalized. The period of reform culminated in the adoption, in 1975, of a charter for an Islamic, national, central and socialist democracy.

For the next four years Mauritanian political life was dominated by the question of the Spanish-controlled territory of the Western Sahara, sovereignty of which was claimed by both Morocco and Mauritania. In November 1975, despite a ruling made in the previous month by the International Court of Justice that the territory's people were entitled to self-determination, Spain, Morocco and Mauritania concluded the Madrid Agreement, whereby Spain agreed to cede the territory in February 1976 for division between its northern and southern neighbours. However, the occupation of the territory by Mauritania and Morocco met with fierce resistance from guerrillas of the Frente Popular para la Liberación de Saguia el-Hamra y Río de Oro, known as the Frente Polisario (Polisario Front), which had, with Algerian support, proclaimed a 'Sahrawi Arab Democratic Republic' (SADR). With the assistance of Moroccan troops, Mauritania occupied Tiris el Gharbia, the province it had been allocated under the Madrid Agreement, but resistance by Polisario forces continued. Guerrilla attacks were mounted both in the new province and inside Mauritania's 1960 frontiers (most notably on the economically vital railway linking the iron-ore deposits near Zouérate with the port of Nouadhibou).

Despite a rapid expansion of its army, Mauritania became increasingly dependent on support from Moroccan troops and on financial assistance from France and conservative Arab states. Within Mauritania the war was popular only with the pro-Moroccan tendency: large sections of the Moorish population had ties of kinship with the Sahrawi insurgents and felt no commitment to the conflict. Mauritania was unable to defend itself militarily, and its economy was in ruins.

SALEK AND HAIDALLA

In July 1978 Ould Daddah was overthrown and detained in a bloodless military coup. Power was assumed by a military committee for national recovery (CMRN), headed by the chief of staff, Lt-Col (later Col) Moustapha Ould Mohamed Salek, which suspended the constitution and dissolved the national assembly and PPM. Two days after the coup Polisario announced a cease-fire with Mauritania; this was accepted by the new government but proved difficult to maintain with Moroccan troops still on Mauritanian territory. With an outbreak of racial tensions between blacks and Moors in early 1979 adding to political instability, Salek assumed absolute power in March, replacing the CMRN with a military committee for national salvation (CMSN). In May Lt-Col Mohamed Khouna Ould Haidalla was appointed prime minister, and in the following month Salek resigned and was succeeded as president by Lt-Col Mohamed Mahmoud Ould Ahmed Louly. In July Polisario announced an end to the cease-fire; later in the month the Organization of African Unity (OAU) appealed for a referendum to be held in Western Sahara. These events provided the impetus for Mauritania's withdrawal from the war: Haidalla declared that Mauritania had no territorial claims in Western Sahara, a decision that was formalized in the Algiers Agreement, signed with Polisario in August. King Hassan of Morocco then announced that his country had taken over Tiris el Gharbia 'in response to local wishes'.

Haidalla displaced Louly as president in January 1980, and dismissed several members of the CMSN. Some of those dismissed were to form the nucleus of exiled opposition movements, including the Paris-based Alliance pour une Mauritanie démocratique, led by Ould Daddah, who was released from prison in 1979. Following growing tensions within the CMSN, Haidalla formed a civilian government in December 1980, and published a draft constitution with provision for a multi-party system. In April 1981, however, the army chief of staff, Lt-Col (later Col) Maawiya Ould Sid'Ahmed Taya, became prime minister of a new military government, and the draft constitution was abandoned.

Mauritania, which had recognized the legitimacy of Polisario but not that of the SADR, found it increasingly difficult to maintain neutrality in the Western Sahara conflict, especially after October 1981, when Morocco bombed Sahrawi bases in northern Mauritania and threatened reprisals against Mauritania itself. In 1982 Mauritania supported the admission of SADR to the OAU, although it was not until February 1984 that Mauritania itself formally recognized the SADR.

THE TAYA PRESIDENCY

Popular discontent with Haidalla's rule led to a bloodless *coup d'état* in December 1984, led by Col Taya. The new government introduced major economic reforms, which attracted support from foreign donors, and sought a political *rapprochement* with supporters of Ould Daddah by appointing three members of the ex-president's government to ministerial posts. Ould Daddah was himself officially pardoned and invited to return home, but chose to remain in exile.

Ethnic Unrest

The second half of the 1980s witnessed growing unrest among the black Mauritanian population—resentful at what they perceived as the increasing Arabicization of the country by the Moorish community. The distribution of a document entitled the *Oppressed Black African Manifesto* in April 1986 provoked the arrest, in September, on charges of 'undermining national unity', of a number of prominent black Mauritanians. Civil disturbances involving the black community led to further arrests. The government responded by stressing the Islamic, rather than Arab, character of Mauritanian culture and by accelerating the introduction of *Shari'a* (Islamic) law. At municipal council elections in December 1986, provision was made for up to four lists of candidates in each municipality, although formal political organizations remained illegal. The Taya regime pledged to continue the process of democratization, with the eventual introduction of direct legislative and presidential elections.

Racial tensions were again highlighted by the arrest, in October 1987, of 51 members of the black Toucouleur ethnic group, following the discovery of a coup plot. Three military officers were sentenced to death, and 41 others were imprisoned. In early 1988 it was claimed that more than 500 black personnel had been dismissed from the army, gendarmerie and national guard, as a result of disturbances that had followed the executions of the three convicted officers.

In mid-1988 it was reported that some 600 people, including members of the armed forces, were arrested, as part of a short-lived purge of light-skinned Bidan supporters of the pro-Iraqi Baathist movement (which had hitherto been influential in the CMSN, and was also known to be sympathetic to Moroccan interests). In September 13 opponents of the government, all alleged to have Baathist links, were convicted of undermining state security and of recruiting military personnel on behalf of an unnamed country. This estrangement of the pro-Moroccan faction was viewed in some quarters as a shift in the government's position to that which had been advocated by Haidalla (who was released from detention in December), and raised questions concerning Mauritania's professed neutrality in the Western Sahara question.

Friction with Senegal

The persistence of ethnic divisions within Mauritania was exemplified by the country's three-year border dispute with Senegal. The deaths, in April 1989, of two Senegalese, following a disagreement over grazing rights with Mauritanian livestock-breeders, provoked a crisis that was exacerbated by long-standing ethnic and economic rivalries. In the aftermath of the border incident Mauritanian nationals residing in Senegal were attacked, and their businesses ransacked (the retail trade in Senegal had hitherto been dominated by some 300,000 mainly light-skinned Mauritanians resident in that country). Senegalese nationals in Mauritania (an estimated 30,000, many of whom were employed in the manufacturing sector), together with black Mauritanians, suffered similar attacks, and it was believed that by early May several hundred people, mainly Senegalese, had been killed. Operations to repatriate nationals of both countries commenced, with international assistance. It was alleged that Mauritania exploited the crisis to expel members of its black indigenous population to Senegal. In addition, many black Mauritanians fled, or were expelled to Mali. In July the human rights organization Amnesty International expressed concern that violations of human rights were taking place in Mauritania, and in November it recommended that the Taya government conduct an inquiry into allegations of the torture and murder of black Mauritanians.

Despite international mediation attempts, and both countries' expressed commitment to the principle of a negotiated settlement to the dispute, Senegal's insistence on the inviolability of the border, as defined at the time of French colonial rule, and Mauritania's demand that its traders returning from Senegal receive compensation from the government of that country, remained the greatest impediments to a solution. The two countries suspended diplomatic relations in August 1989. There were further outbreaks of violence at the end of the year, when black Mauritanians sheltering in Senegal crossed the frontier (with, the Taya government asserted, the complicity of the

Senegalese armed forces) with the intention of reclaiming their property. OAU mediation efforts in early 1990 were thwarted by military engagements in the border region, resulting in several deaths. Subsequent initiatives were equally unsuccessful, and in July telephone connections between the two countries were severed. (All transport links between Mauritania and Senegal had been suspended during 1989.)

Hopes of a *rapprochement* were further undermined in late 1990, when the Mauritanian authorities accused Senegal of complicity in an alleged attempt to overthrow Taya. In December several sources reported the arrests of large numbers of black Halpulaars in Mauritania. The government confirmed that many arrests (of both military personnel and civilians) had been made in connection with a foiled coup conspiracy, but denied suggestions that detainees had been tortured. The Senegalese government denied any involvement in the alleged plot, and bilateral relations further deteriorated. In early 1991 incidents were reported in which Mauritanian naval vessels had opened fire on Senegalese fishing boats, apparently in Senegal's territorial waters; in March several deaths allegedly resulted from a confrontation on Senegalese territory, following an incursion by Senegalese troops into Mauritania.

In March 1991 60 of those who had been detained following the alleged coup plot were released. Further clemency measures were announced shortly thereafter, as a result of which the government stated that almost all the country's political prisoners had been freed; however, other sources maintained that several hundred of those who had been arrested in late 1990 remained in detention.

Constitutional Reform

In April 1991 Taya announced that proposals for a new constitution, which would permit the introduction of a multi-party political system, were to be submitted for approval in a national referendum. The announcement coincided with an upsurge in overt political opposition. In May and June demonstrations were held in Nouakchott by women demanding to know the fate of their relatives who had 'disappeared' following the alleged coup plot in November 1990; also in June there were anti-government protests in Nouadhibou. Tracts and open letters, condemning the Taya government and demanding that a national conference be convened to deliberate the country's political future, began to circulate. The draft constitution was submitted to a national referendum on 12 July 1991. According to official results, 97.9% of those who voted (85.3% of the registered electorate) endorsed the proposals. However, opposition movements claimed that the turn-out had been as low as 8% of registered voters. The new constitution accorded extensive powers to the president of the republic, who was to be elected, by universal suffrage, for a period of six years, with no limitation placed on further terms of office. Provision was made for a bicameral legislature (comprising a national assembly, to be elected by universal suffrage every five years, and a senate, to be appointed by municipal leaders with a six-year mandate), as well as for a constitutional council, an economic and social council and a supreme Islamic council. The CMSN would remain in power pending the inauguration of the new organs of state. Arabic was designated as the sole official language.

Following the adoption of the constitution, legislation permitting registration of political parties took effect. Among the first parties to be accorded official status was the pro-government Democratic and Social Republican Party (DSRP), which was criticized by the opposition for its privileged access to the state apparatus; also influential in the first months of political pluralism were the Mauritanian Party for Renewal (which included ex-president Haidalla among its members) and the Union of Democratic Forces (UDF).

A general amnesty for all those accused or convicted of undermining state security was announced in July 1991, prompting the Dakar-based opposition group, the Forces de libération africaine de Mauritanie (FLAM), which had maintained a sporadic campaign of attacks on official targets, to suspend its military operations. However, the limitations of the democratization process became evident in August, when a further women's demonstration was violently dispersed by the security forces. In that month Amnesty International published a list of 339 people (mostly Halpulaars), who were alleged to

have died in detention, primarily as a result of torture, since the disclosure of the November 1990 coup plot.

Four candidates, including Taya, Ahmed Ould Daddah (the half-brother of the country's first president), who, while not at the time affiliated to any party, was supported by the UDF, and former CMRN chairman Salek, participated in the presidential election, which took place on 17 January 1992. According to official results, Taya obtained 62.7% of the poll (51.7% of the registered electorate voted); his nearest rival, Ahmed Ould Daddah, received 32.8% of the votes cast. The defeated candidates denounced Taya's victory as fraudulent, and appealed unsuccessfully to the supreme court to declare the election invalid. (Independent observers stated that some 'administrative' errors had undoubtedly occurred, but otherwise agreed that the election had been fairly conducted.) Unrest following the election led to at least two deaths and more than 160 arrests; the government subsequently imposed a temporary dusk-to-dawn curfew in Nouakchott and Nouadhibou. By early February all those who had been detained in the post-election violence had been released. Shortly before the presidential election FLAM had announced that it was to resume military operations.

'Democratized' Government

By late February 1992 six opposition parties that had initially intended to contest elections to the national assembly had withdrawn their candidates, claiming that the electoral process favoured the DSRP. At the elections, which took place on 6 and 13 March, the DSRP won 67 of the chamber's 79 seats, with all but two of the remaining seats being secured by independent candidates. The rate of participation by voters was reportedly low. It was stated that each of the country's ethnic groups was represented in the assembly. Other than the DSRP, only one party presented candidates for the senate (elections to which followed on 3 and 10 April). The DSRP emerged with a majority in the upper house, with 36 senators; 17 independent candidates were elected, the remaining three seats being reserved for representatives of Mauritanians resident abroad.

At his inauguration, on 18 April 1992, President Taya designated Sidi Mohamed Ould Boubacar, hitherto the minister of finance, as prime minister. The only military officer in the new government was Col Ahmed Ould Minnih, as minister of defence. Included in the new government were three black ministers and one opposition representative. Ould Boubacar, a French-trained technocrat, was known to have extensive experience of financial management and had previously been involved in the country's negotiations with the IMF. However, his relative lack of experience in other areas of government suggested that Taya intended to retain a dominant role in the political process. The new government announced plans to restructure the judicial system and to reform the civil service. The two legislative chambers were inaugurated later in April. The national assembly elected Cheikh Sid'Ahmed Ould Baba, a Harratin (black Moors who had formerly been slaves) as its president, and Dieng Boubou Farba, a Toucouleur, became president of the senate. Ahmed Ould Daddah and his supporters formally joined the principal opposition to Taya's administration, the UDF (which was renamed the UDF–New Era), in June.

The devaluation of the ouguiya, in October 1992, precipitated violent protests in the capital, as traders immediately imposed sharp increases in the prices of basic household commodities. The government gave assurances that measures would be taken to offset the adverse social consequences of the currency's depreciation, and compensatory salary increases were introduced in all sectors in January 1993.

Although the government placed particular emphasis on the multi-ethnic character of its administration, tensions remained. In May 1993 parliament approved legislation pardoning all those (specifically including members of the army and security forces) convicted of crimes committed in connection with 'armed operations and acts of violence and terrorism' in the three years preceding Taya's inauguration as elected president. Security forces forcibly dispersed a demonstration in Nouakchott organized by opponents of the measure, who protested that the period covered by the amnesty had been one of severe repression by the armed forces of black dissidents.

Mauritania's first multi-party municipal elections took place in January and February 1994, at which the DSRP won control of 172 of the country's 208 administrative districts. The UDF–New Era won control of 17 districts, the remainder being taken by independent candidates. Opposition groups, including the UDF–New Era, protested that the elections had been fraudulently conducted, to the benefit of the DSRP. (Prior to the elections several people, reported to be activists of both the DSRP and opposition parties, had been arrested in connection with alleged electoral malpractice, while several parties, anticipating fraud, boycotted the polls.) The DSRP's control of the political process was confirmed at elections to renew one-third of the senate's membership in April and May.

Shortly before the first round of municipal voting the president of the unauthorized Mauritanian Human Rights Association (MHRA), Cheikh Sadibou Camara (who was also a member of the prominent opposition party, the Union for Democracy and Progress, UDP) was detained for several days, reportedly on charges of incitement to agitation. Camara had apparently reported to a visiting delegation of international human rights organizations that children of Harratin had been abducted and sold into slavery. (Mauritanian law regards any reference to slavery, which was formally abolished in 1980, as injurious to national unity.) International human rights monitors protested that the government's assertion that Camara belonged to an unauthorized organization was invalid, since the MHRA had on several occasions applied for and been denied legal status, despite constitutional guarantees of the right of free association. Earlier in January 1994 Mauritania's first independent trade union confederation was legalized, following a protracted dispute between its leaders and the authorities.

Internal Tensions

Meanwhile, there was renewed concern regarding Mauritania's observance of civil rights. In September 1994 seven independent journals suspended publication, in protest at alleged increased censorship measures. None the less, the authorities continued to enforce strict press controls, suspending journals deemed critical of the Taya administration.

From the final months of 1993 there was increasing evidence of the government's desire to counter activities by Islamist organizations. More than 90 alleged members of illicit Islamist organizations were arrested in September 1994, among them a former government minister, 10 religious leaders and several foreign nationals. In the following month an amnesty was granted to the detainees after several of their number had made broadcast 'confessions' regarding their membership of extremist groups. Among those who admitted to belonging to an Islamist movement in Mauritania (Hasim) were prominent members of the UDF–New Era. The Taya government, which accused foreign Islamist groups of promoting extremism in Mauritania, subsequently prohibited the delivery of political speeches in places of worship and outlawed several Islamist organizations.

An increase of some 25% in the price of bread in January 1995 (following the imposition of value-added tax on food products and industrial supplies) led to riots in Nouakchott. Several prominent opposition figures, including Ahmed Ould Daddah and the UDP leader, Hamdi Ould Mouknass, were temporarily placed under house arrest, accused of organizing the disturbances. The government subsequently adopted measures aimed at controlling the prices of essential consumer goods.

Government changes in February 1995 included the appointment of new ministers of finance and of defence. In March the Movement of Independent Democrats, which until 1994 had been a member of the UDF–New Era, announced that it was to join the DSRP. Internal tensions within the UDF–New Era threatened to undermine the influence of the party, as dissident groups complained of excessive centralization around Ahmed Ould Daddah's leadership. In July several UDF–New Era members were reported to have defected to the UDP. In mid-1995, none the less, six opposition parties, including the UDF–New Era and the UDP, announced they had agreed a series of joint demands regarding future elections: these included the compilation of an accurate voters' register, the formulation of what they termed a 'consensual' electoral code, and guarantees of judicial independence and impartiality on the part of the administration.

In October 1995 the Taya administration declared the Iraqi ambassador *persona non grata*, and demanded his departure

from Mauritania. The expulsion coincided with reports of a foiled coup in Mauritania, allegedly sponsored by the Iraqi government, which, it was claimed, had funded 'secret organizations' in Mauritania with the intention of securing confidential information concerning the country's strategic installations. A series of arrests ensued, primarily within the ranks of alleged pro-Iraqi Baathist activists. Among those arrested were several journalists, two parliamentarians (one from the DSRP, the other from the UDP), the secretary-general of the national assembly, officers in the armed forces and a police commissioner. In December 52 defendants stood trial on charges of forming an illegal organization: eight of the accused were sentenced to one year's imprisonment, 11 received short suspended sentences, and 33 were acquitted. In January 1996 all 52 were discharged on appeal.

Also in January 1996 Taya appointed Cheikh el Avia Ould Mohamed Khouna (hitherto minister of fisheries and marine economy) to replace Boubacar as prime minister. (Boubacar was subsequently elected secretary-general of the DSRP.) A new council of ministers was formed, comprising most members of the previous administration and incorporating six new members. Additional changes in February and March included the appointment of Lemrabott Sidi Mahmoud Ould Cheikh Ahmed (hitherto minister of national education) as minister of foreign affairs and co-operation—replacing Mohamed Salem Ould Lekhel, who had been credited with the 'normalization' of relations with Israel and the improvement of relations with Gulf states after the 1990–91 crisis in the region of the Persian (Arabian) Gulf. Meanwhile, it was announced that the general election (originally scheduled to be held in early 1997) would be brought forward to October 1996, thus enabling the incoming national assembly to vote on the budget for 1997 at the new session. In March the UDP announced its intention to boycott elections to renew one-third of the senate (scheduled to be held in April), in protest at the government's failure to address the opposition's electoral demands. The results of the elections confirmed the dominance in the senate of the DSRP, which won 17 of the 18 seats contested; the remaining seat was taken by an independent candidate. Despite their initial reluctance, by mid-1996 most political parties, including the UDF–New Era, had agreed to participate in the forthcoming legislative elections. Meanwhile, in June the UDP expelled four of its senior members for their alleged involvement in a defamation campaign against the party, after it had been proposed that the UDP secretary-general be dismissed.

At the legislative elections, held on 11 and 18 October 1996, the DSRP reaffirmed its authority, winning 71 of the 79 seats in the national assembly. The Rally for Democracy and National Unity, closely allied with the administration, also secured a seat. Action for Change (AC) was the only opposition party to win a seat in the assembly, the remainder being secured by independent candidates. Several opposition parties disputed the validity of the results, and denounced censorship measures imposed in the period preceding the elections. Moreover, the UDP, which had participated in the first round of the elections, withdrew from the second round in protest at what it alleged were unfair electoral procedures. Later in October, following the formal resignation of the government, the prime minister named a new council of ministers.

In January 1997 several opposition leaders, including Messaoud Ould Boulkheir, the AC chairman, and Mohamed Hassaoud Ould Ismael, the secretary-general of the People's Progressive Party (PPP), were arrested on charges of maintaining 'suspicious relations' with Libya. Boulkheir and several others were released at the end of the month, and Ismael was freed in February, although five others (all PPP members) were sentenced to short terms of imprisonment for conspiring to break the law. In April four of the five convicted were acquitted by the court of appeal.

In February 1997 five prominent opposition parties, including the AC and the UDF–New Era, announced the formation of a coalition Opposition Parties' Front. In April the coalition staged a demonstration in the capital to protest at price increases, corruption, and restrictions placed on political parties and trade unions. Ahmed Ould Daddah subsequently announced that the coalition would boycott the forthcoming presidential election.

At the presidential election, held on 12 December 1997, Taya was returned to office with 90.9% of the valid votes cast; his nearest rival, Mohamed Lemine Ch'bih Ould Cheikh Melainine (who had resigned from the DSRP in 1996), obtained 7.0% of the vote. Three others contested the election, including Kane Amadou Mokhtar, Mauritania's first black presidential candidate. Opposition parties, which had unsuccessfully demanded the establishment of an independent electoral commission, alleged that there had been widespread electoral fraud and claimed that the official rate of voter participation (some 73.8% of the registered electorate) was unrealistically high. Taya subsequently appointed Mohamed Lemine Ould Guig, a university academic, as prime minister, and a new council of ministers, which included three women, was installed. There were further government changes in January, February and March 1998.

In January 1998 Mauritanian lawyers undertook a strike in protest at the arrest, earlier in the month, of several human rights activists (including Cheikh Sadibou Camara of the MHRA and Brahim Ould Ebetti, a lawyer) who had participated in a French television programme on the subject of the persistence of slavery in Mauritania. In the following month the security forces arrested eight people and injured 20 others prior to an AC-organized demonstration in the capital to denounce slavery in the country and to demand the activists' release. Several politicians and trade unionists were dispatched to the interior and placed under house arrest. Although five activists were fined and sentenced to 13 months' imprisonment, in March they received a presidential pardon.

Elections to renew 18 of the Senate's 56 seats took place in April 1998. All but one of the seats contested were won by members of the DSRP; an independent candidate secured the remaining seat. The council of ministers was reorganized in July and October, and in November, following the appointment of Cheikh el Avia Ould Mohamed Khouna (hitherto minister of foreign affairs and co-operation, and formerly premier) as prime minister.

In March 1998 serious internal divisions in the UDF–New Era caused a split in the party, with two rival factions (led by Ahmed Ould Daddah and Moustapha Ould Bedreddine, respectively) claiming leadership of the UDF. Ahmed Ould Daddah and two other members of his UDF faction were placed under house arrest in December after they demanded that a public inquiry be held into allegations that the government had agreed to allow Israeli nuclear waste to be stored underground in Mauritanian territory. The detainees were released in January 1999, following demonstrations in Nouadhibou and Nouakchott to protest at their arrest. In March they were acquitted of charges of threatening public order by a Mauritanian court.

Meanwhile, in January 1999 the DSRP claimed victory in most of the 208 districts contested at municipal elections. The polls in Nouakchott and two other municipalities were annulled (and contested again in February) owing to charges of electoral fraud. The DSRP won all the seats contested at the rescheduled elections in Nouakchott, although only 16% of the registered electorate participated in the poll. The principal opposition parties boycotted both rounds of elections.

Partial elections to the Senate took place on 7 and 14 April 2000. The majority of seats were secured by the DSRP, although the UDP and the National Union for Democracy and Development each won one seat, and three seats were gained by independent candidates. Later that month Daddah was again detained two days prior to a meeting of the UDF—NE at which he was expected to address the acquisition of wealth by associates of President Taya. His call for the meeting to take place was officially considered a public incitement to violence against the Taya regime. Two members of the UDF were also arrested and several people were injured following protest against Daddah's arrest. He was released later that month. In mid-September President Taya effected a cabinet reshuffle and appointed Fatimetou Mint Mohamed Saleck to the newly-created post of secretary of state in charge of the development and promotion of information technology.

External Issues

Renewed diplomatic initiatives resulted in a meeting, held in July 1991 in Guinea-Bissau, of the foreign ministers of Mauritania and Senegal, at which it was agreed in principle to reopen the Mauritania–Senegal border and to resume diplomatic relations. (However, the issues of the demarcation of the border and the fate of Mauritanian refugees in Senegal were not discussed.) Bilateral contacts continued during the second half of the year, and in November Presidents Taya and Diouf met while attending the francophone summit meeting in France. Full diplomatic links were restored in April 1992, and the process of reopening the border began in May. However, major issues remained unresolved. In June representatives of the refugees published an open letter in which they appealed for international assistance for repatriation efforts, together with the return of property confiscated by the Mauritanian authorities and payment compensation for the 'humiliation' suffered as a result of their earlier expulsion. Moreover, Mauritanian refugees in Senegal insisted that, as long as their national identity (_mauritanité_) was not recognized by the Taya government, they would not return to Mauritania. Further tensions were reported in September 1993, when the Mauritanian authorities announced that Senegalese nationals would henceforth be required to fulfil certain criteria, including currency-exchange requirements, before being allowed to remain in (or enter) Mauritania. Although concern was expressed that such conditions might be used to prevent the return of black Mauritanians who had fled to Senegal in 1989, in late 1994 the governments of Mauritania and Senegal agreed measures to facilitate the free movement of goods and people between the two countries, and in early 1995 it was reported that diplomatic initiatives with a view to the repatriation of black Mauritanians from Senegal were in progress. A census conducted by the office of the UN High Commissioner for Refugees (UNHCR) in mid-1995 indicated that there were some 66,000 Mauritanian refugees in Senegal.

In January 1996 several hundred Mauritanian refugees staged demonstrations in northern Senegal, protesting at the Mauritanian government's proposed repatriation programme, and insisting that their earlier demands be met and that the repatriation process be organized by UNHCR in co-operation with the two governments. By late 1997 the number of Mauritanian refugees in Senegal had declined to 56,200. In September 1998 it was reported that the Senegalese authorities were no longer issuing the remaining refugees with travel documents.

Relations with Mali were also dominated at this time by the issue of refugees, which was the subject of senior-level bilateral negotiations. The problem of Mauritanian refugees in Mali was compounded by the presence in Mauritania of light-skinned Malian Tuaregs and Moors and also Bella (for further details, see Recent History of Mali), who, the Malian authorities asserted, were launching raids on Malian territory from bases in Mauritania. Following reports that Malian troops had, in turn, crossed into Mauritania in pursuit of rebels, the two countries agreed in early 1993 to begin work on a precise demarcation of their joint border, which was concluded in September 1993. In April 1994 Mauritania, Mali and UNHCR representatives signed an agreement for the eventual voluntary repatriation of Malian refugees from Mauritania. The Tuareg refugee camp in Mauritania closed in mid-1997, following the repatriation of some 42,000 Malians. According to UNHCR, there were some 11,100 Mauritanian refugees in Mali at the end of 1998.

Meanwhile, in April 1994 Mauritania, Mali and Senegal agreed to strengthen military co-operation, with the aim of improving joint border security. In January 1995 the governments of the three countries undertook to co-operate in resolving joint border issues and in combating extremism, arms-smuggling and drugs-trafficking. In mid-1996, at the conclusion of a meeting in Nouakchott of ministers responsible for the interior, the three established joint security measures on their common borders. In July 1997 the respective countries' chiefs of general staff held a meeting in Mali to discuss measures to combat banditry in the region. In May 1998 the three countries' ministers responsible for the interior held a meeting in Nouakchott in an attempt to strengthen relations and consider ways of ensuring the security and stability of nationals living in the common border area. In the previous month there had been reports of cattle thefts and attacks on locals in eastern Senegal, allegedly by Mauritanian refugees residing in the area. In August 1999 ministers responsible for security from Mauritania,

Mali and Senegal met in Dakar to discuss measures to address the increase in violent incidents on their common borders. An agreement was subsequently signed, which provided for the establishment of a special operational unit drawn from the police forces of the three countries to combat border crime.

In early June 2000 relations between Mauritania and Senegal deteriorated after Mauritania accused the new Senegalese administration of relaunching an irrigation project, which involved the use of joint waters from the River Senegal. The dispute escalated when the Mauritanian authorities requested that all of its citizens living in Senegal return home and issued the estimated 100,000 Senegalese nationals living in Mauritania with a 15-day deadline by which to leave the country. Tension was further heightened when the Mauritanian minister of communication and relations with parliament accused the Senegalese government of 'approaching and offering means of propaganda' to groups hostile to the Mauritanian government. In mid-June, following mediation by King Muhammad VI of Morocco and the presidents of The Gambia and Mali, the Mauritanian minister of the interior announced that the decision to expel Senegalese citizens had been withdrawn and that Mauritanians living in Senegal could remain there, provided they felt safe. President Wade of Senegal visited Mauritania later that month and announced that the irrigation project had been abandoned. Nevertheles, it was estimated that some 25,000 Senegalese had left Mauritania and that more than one-half of the 11,000 officially-registered Mauritanians living in Senegal had returned to their home country.

Although France has remained an important source of aid and technical assistance, the Taya regime has sought increasingly to enhance links with the other countries of the Maghreb and with the wider Arab world. In February 1989 Mauritania became a founder member, with Algeria, Libya, Morocco and Tunisia, of a new regional economic organization, the Union of the Arab Maghreb (UMA). The member states subsequently formulated 15 regional co-operation conventions. In February 1993, however, it was announced that, given the differing economic orientations of each signatory, no convention had actually been implemented, and the organization's activities were to be 'frozen'. None the less, meetings of UMA leaders continued to be convened annually. Taya made an official visit to Algeria in 1995, which culminated in a reaffirmation of both countries' commitment to consolidating bilateral relations and to combating 'all manifestations of terrorism'. Relations were strengthened further when Algeria's prime minister and president visited Mauritania in April and July 1996, respectively.

Mauritania has generally enjoyed cordial relations with Iraq (exemplified by the prominent role of the Baathist movement in Mauritanian public life). In April and May 1990 the government denied persistent rumours that it was allowing Iraq to test long-range missiles on Mauritanian territory. Following Iraq's invasion of Kuwait, in August of that year, Mauritania condemned the deployment of troops in the region of the Persian (Arabian) Gulf by those countries that opposed the Iraqi action. Individual Mauritanians volunteered to support Iraq's armed forces, and demonstrations in protest against what was regarded as a US-led offensive took place in Nouakchott. Mauritanian support for Iraq during the 1990–91 crisis resulted in the loss of financial assistance from other countries of the Gulf region. During 1993, however, Mauritania sought to improve its relations with Kuwait and its allies, and there was a perceived loss of influence for Iraqi sympathizers. In April 1994 Kuwait's first deputy prime minister and minister of foreign affairs visited Mauritania, and the two countries issued a joint communiqué in which the Taya government emphasized its recognition of Kuwait's borders, as defined by the UN in 1993.

Mauritania's relations with France improved significantly in the early 1990s, following the introduction of political reforms. Taya made an official visit to France in December 1993, during which he held discussions, described as 'fruitful' with President François Mitterrand and the prime minister, Edouard Balladur. Bilateral relations were consolidated in September 1997 and in February 1998 as a result of reciprocal official visits made by President Jacques Chirac of France and Taya, respectively. However, relations deteriorated abruptly in 1999, following the arrest by the French authorities in July of Ali Ould Dah, a captain in the Mauritanian army, who was attending a training course in France. Dah was charged with torturing, in 1991, fellow Mauritanian soldiers suspected of participating in the unsuccessful attempt to overthrow the Taya administration in 1990. The charges were brought at the request of human rights organizations under the 1984 International Convention against Torture and Other Cruel, Inhuman or Degrading Treatment or Punishment, to which France is a signatory. The Mauritanian government responded by suspending military co-operation with France (expelling French military advisers from Mauritania and recalling army officers receiving training in French institutions) and introducing visas for French nationals visiting Mauritania. In late September a court in Montpellier, France, ordered Dah's release from custody, although he was required to remain in France until the end of legal proceedings. By April 2000, however, Dah had illicitly returned to Mauritania. In July two French nationals, including the first secretary to the French ambassador to Mauritania, were expelled from Mauritania. They had been accused of partaking in anti-Mauritanian activities and of spying in connection with the Dah case.

In February 1998 some 3,500 troops from several west African countries, primarily Mauritania, Mali and Senegal, participated in military exercises in Senegal's border area as part of a French-sponsored initiative to train African forces to conduct regional peace-keeping operations under the auspices of the UN and the OAU.

In November 1995, during a European-Mediterranean conference in Barcelona, Spain, Mauritania signed an agreement to recognize and establish relations with Israel. The Libyan government denounced the *rapprochement*, closed its embassy in Mauritania and severed all economic assistance to the country. The Mauritanian government responded by closing the Libyan cultural centre in Nouakchott. Diplomatic relations between the two countries were, however, restored in March 1997.

In October 1998 Mauritania's minister of foreign affairs and co-operation visited Israel and held talks with the prime minister, Binyamin Netanyahu. The visit was strongly criticized by the Arab League, which argued that it contravened the League's resolutions on the suspension of the normalization of relations with Israel. Shortly afterwards the Taya administration denied reports in Western media that it had agreed to store Israeli nuclear waste in Mauritania. In October 1999 Mauritania established full diplomatic relations with Israel—the first Arab country to do so (with the exception of Egypt and Jordan under their respective peace treaties with Israel). The announcement provoked widespread criticism from other Arab nations, particularly from Iraq, with which Mauritania severed diplomatic relations in November (following allegations that Iraq was planning acts of subversion in Mauritania), as well as from opposition groups within Mauritania.

In December 1999 the Prime Minister announced Mauritania's withdrawal from the Economic Community of West African States (ECOWAS), owing to decisions adopted by the organizations at its summit earlier in the month, including the integration of the armed forces of member states and the removal of internal border controls and tariffs.

Economy

EDITH HODGKINSON

Revised for this edition by the Editor

Mauritania has few natural resources other than minerals, and its economy was almost entirely traditional and rural, based on livestock and agriculture, until the rapid development of the mining industry, in the 1960s and 1970s, enormously increased export earnings and government revenues. The country's gross domestic product (GDP) rose, in real terms, at an average rate of 8% per year during the 1960s. The growth rate fluctuated in the 1970s as a result of drought, trends in demand for iron ore, and disturbances in output, owing to the activities of the Polisario Front (see Recent History).

During the early 1980s the economy contracted (by an annual average of 1.0% in 1981–84) in the wake of a world recession in demand for iron ore and the burden of servicing a high level of foreign debt, much of it arising from ill-considered investments made during the more prosperous years of the mid-1970s. Persistent drought was also a factor. The sole offsetting element was the dynamic growth of the fishing sector. The further expansion of this sector, together with the recovery in agricultural production when the drought ended, resulted in a recovery in GDP growth in 1985–88, to an average of 3.2% annually (slightly below the target of real GDP growth of 4% per year that had been envisaged in the programme for economic and financial recovery for that period). The rate of growth accelerated to 5.5% in 1989; however, decline in revenue from the fishing sector, together with disruption caused by the dispute with Senegal and the withdrawal of funding from Middle Eastern sources—as a consequence of Mauritania's support for Iraq at the time of the crisis in the region of the Persian (Arabian) Gulf—resulted in a decline, of 1.8%, in GDP in 1990. The following year saw growth of 2.6%, despite lower output in both the fishing and mining sectors. There was modest growth, estimated at 1.7%, in 1992, while a growth rate of 5.5% in 1993 was attributed to successes achieved under the government's programme of economic adjustment. GDP growth has since remained solid, averaging 4.7% per year during 1994–96. According to the IMF, GDP increased by 3.2% in both 1997 aand 1998, and by 4.3% in 1999. In 1998, according to estimates by the World Bank, Mauritania's gross national product (GNP) was US $1,033m., equivalent to $410 per head. This level of GNP per head places Mauritania in the category of low-income developing countries (in earlier years, Mauritania had been classified as a lower middle-income developing country). According to the World Bank, Mauritania's per caput GNP ranks it below neighbouring countries like Senegal and almost equal to Haiti.

Mauritania has undergone a series of economic reform programmes sponsored by the World Bank and the IMF since the early 1980s. The Taya regime formulated a one-year economic recovery programme, in agreement with the IMF, when it came to power at the end of 1984. This was incorporated in the 1985–88 programme, which aimed to reduce budget and balance-of-payments deficits by means of more stringent criteria for selecting public investment projects. Emphasis was given to immediately productive schemes in fishing and agriculture, and to the rehabilitation of existing capacity and infrastructure in mining and transport. The achievements of the programme were to be consolidated under the terms of the 1989–91 economic support and revival programme, aided by an enhanced structural adjustment facility from the IMF (that was awarded in May 1989). The programme aimed to achieve real average GDP growth of 3.5% per year during 1989–91 by fostering private enterprise while restructuring and rehabilitating the banking system. However, economic growth averaged only 2.1% over the period, below the estimated annual population growth rate of 2.6%. Nevertheless, the broad terms of the programme, and its GDP growth targets, were maintained for the subsequent IMF-supported reforms in 1992–95, while real annual growth targets were revised to 4.4% for the 1995–97 programme.

In the late 1990s donors sought a greater commitment from the government to creating a wider role for the private sector in the economy. The private sector was reported to have contributed more than 60% of GDP in 1996, and its share in total investment was growing (15.5% in 1997, compared with 10% in 1996). However, donors claimed that government investment practice continued to consolidate the position of the country's economic oligarchy at the expense of the diffusion of wealth and the creation of domestic markets. Complementary foreign investment remained very low. Nevertheless, since 1990 the government had ceded control in 19 of some 41 parastatal companies and, in the agreement concluded with the World Bank in late 1998 (see below), it undertook to privatize posts and telecommunications, public utilities and Air Mauritanie.

In May 1999 Mauritania concluded a further agreement with the World Bank and the IMF as part of its ongoing programme of economic reform. Under the terms of the agreement, Mauritania expected to receive some US $450m. in support from the Bank and the Fund. In July 1999 the IMF approved a three-year loan worth $56.53m. to support the government's 1999–2002 economic programme. The programme aimed to achieve real GDP growth of 5.0% and to lower the inflation rate to 2.5% by 2002. (Projections for the year 2000 envisaged real GDP growth of 4.4% and an inflation rate of 3.5%.)

The total population of Mauritania was 1,864,236 at the census of April 1988, implying an average population growth of about 2.6% per year during the preceding decade. UN estimates for mid-1998 indicate a population of 2.53m., although some uncertainty has been caused by population movements arising from the dispute with Senegal. Mauritania's average population density (2.5 per sq km) is the lowest in West Africa. The severe drought of the early 1970s, with its destruction of livestock, and the growth of the modern sector caused a significant diminution in numbers of those living a nomadic or semi-nomadic way of life. In 1965 these were estimated to total 83% of the population, but by 1988 the proportion had declined to 12%. A trend towards settlement in urban areas has been apparent, with an average annual growth rate of the urban population of 6.8% between 1980–95. About 53% of the population was urban in 1996, compared with 14% in 1970; of these, more than 80% live in the capital, Nouakchott. More than 50% of Mauritania's population is affected by poverty and in 2000 the Mauritanian government began to formulate a Poverty Reduction Strategy Paper which aimed to address the problem of wide-scale poverty in the country.

AGRICULTURE

As mining has developed, the contribution of agriculture and livestock-rearing to GDP has declined—from about 44% in 1960 to 24.7% in 1997 (although 53.4% of the economically active population were employed in the sector in 1998). Less than 1% of the land receives sufficient rainfall to sustain crop cultivation, which is largely confined to the riverine area in the extreme south.

The serious drought of the early 1970s destroyed a large part of the livestock herds (cattle numbered 2m. in 1970), while the harvest of millet and sorghum fell to below its normal level. The return of drought in subsequent years resulted in a further decline in production and livestock numbers, and the grain crop was estimated at 35,000 metric tons in 1979/80. In 1980/81 and 1981/82 there was a good recovery in output of cereals, but the severe drought of 1982–84 caused production to decline sharply, to only one-tenth of domestic requirements in 1983/84. Improved rainfall brought a very strong recovery in subsequent years, while the introduction of paddy rice cultivation proved highly successful, contributing to a total cereal crop of 183,600 tons in 1989/90. However, inadequate rains reduced the crop out-turn to an average of just over 100,000 tons in the following three years. As a result of considerable investment in irrigation and extension services by the government and foreign donors, the area planted with cereals increased dramatically in 1993/94 and 1994/95, by nearly 30% and 90% respectively, which, combined with good rains, produced a bumper harvest of 200,400 tons in 1994/95. Improvements in irrigation have led to a continued rise in rice production, from 25,000 tons in the 1992/93 season to 67,000 tons in 1996/97 (despite a very poor overall cereal crop in the latter year). In late 1998 the FAO forecast that Mauritania's total production of cereals would amount to about 202,600 tons in the 1998/99 crop year, an increase of 39.1% compared with 1997/98. The estimated total included 88,800 tons of sorghum, 6,300 tons of millet, 10,000 tons of maize and 51,900 tons of rice. The improvement in production was attributed to the use of new varieties of rice and to a good distribution of rains.

Even in non-drought years cereal imports are needed to satisfy domestic demand (which has increased as a result of urbanization). In the drought years 1982–84 commercial grain imports were as high as 300,000 metric tons, supplemented by more than 100,000 tons of food aid. However, by 1994 the import requirement had fallen to 81,000 tons, supplemented by 25,000 tons of food aid. Herding (which is the main occupation of the rural population, and whose contribution to GDP is more than three times that of crop cultivation) was even more adversely affected by the droughts: in 1984 cattle numbers had fallen to about 1m., and sheep and goats to 5.7m. They subsequently recovered to near pre-drought levels, but then fell again in the early 1990s; in 1998, according to the FAO, the number of cattle had recovered to an estimated 1.3m., while sheep and goats were estimated to number 10.3m.

The military regime committed itself to a comprehensive rural development programme, concentrating on rebuilding livestock herds and providing reliable water supplies. The 1985–88 economic and financial recovery programme gave priority to the rural sector, which was allocated 35% of total investment, compared with only 10% in the previous (1981–85) plan. The major project in the 1980s was the Gorgol valley irrigation scheme, representing investment of US $100m., with the World Bank, the European Community (EC, now European Union—EU), Saudi Arabia, Libya and France providing more than 85% of the funds. The scheme has provided irrigation for 3,600 ha of rice, sugar, wheat and maize since the inauguration of the dam in 1985. Two similar projects are in progress: one at Boghé, on the Senegal river, and the other based on a number of small dams in the centre and west of the country. In total, the three schemes are projected to bring some 30,000 ha into cultivation. The construction of dams at Djama, in Senegal (completed in 1985), and at Manantali in Mali (completed in 1988), under the auspices of the Organization for the Development of the Senegal River (OMVS), was expected to provide a further 16,000 ha of irrigated land, but its contribution so far has been limited by technical and political problems.

An Oasis Development Project, financed by the International Fund for Agricultural Development, was under way in 1994–95. The project, estimated to cost US $17.2m., aimed to improve incomes and living conditions of 9,500 poor and rural families in 120 oases and 20 villages in five of the country's regions through the development of water resources and conveyance systems. In 1996 Mauritania won funding of some $76.5m. from various donors for a major five-year irrigation project along the Senegal river. In late 1999 the World Bank granted funding worth $102m. to support irrigated agricultural projects in Mauritania.

FISHING

The fishing sector is an important component both of local food supplies and of exports, and employed about 25,000 people in 1998. The Société mauritanienne de commercialisation de poissons, SA, the marketing organization responsible for all exports of frozen fish, is currently in the process of being privatized. The potential annual harvest in Mauritanian waters was once estimated at as much as 600,000 metric tons, but declining catches and concern about over-exploitation of fish stocks have led to a less optimistic reassessment. The potential of the sector has never been fully realized, not least because much of Mauritania's coastal territory is uninhabitable.

The rapid extension of foreign participation in the industry during the 1970s, which exceeded the growth of the fish-processing sector at Nouadhibou, obliged the government to reformulate its fishing policy in 1980. Thus, it abrogated existing agreements permitting foreign-based vessels to fish Mauritanian waters, and required foreign companies or governments to form joint ventures with Mauritanian interests, with the latter holding a majority of the equity capital. After 1983 all catches made in Mauritanian waters had to be landed in the country for processing and export, and from mid-1984 until the monopoly was ended in 1992 all sales had to be directed through the state fishing company. Agreements have been reached with fishing companies from the EU, Japan, Russia, Ukraine, the Republic of Korea and the People's Republic of China, among others.

After protracted negotiations, a fishing agreement with the EC was signed in 1987. Covering a three-year period, the agreement granted fishing rights to vessels of EC countries in return for US $23.7m. in compensation, but excluded some categories of fish and vessels. The subsequent three-year accord, concluded in 1990, maintained broadly the same terms, but made provision for the protection of fish stocks and for monetary compensation of $64m. A further arrangement with the EC was negotiated in 1993, and in 1996 a five-year accord was signed with the EU. The new accord increased substantially Mauritania's annual compensation entitlement (including licence fees), from around $10.7m. in the previous three-year treaty, to $75.4m. The annual catch quota was raised from 76,050 metric tons to 183,392 tons. For the first time EU vessels were allowed to trawl the deep-water (pelagic) species which were previously exploited by Mauritanian joint-venture companies (many of which had become inoperative). As part of the accord, the EU agreed to increase local employment in the industry from around 400 workers to 1,000 and to observe an annual two-month rest period (September and October) to protect species during their peak reproductive season.

The former requirement that foreign enterprises land and process their catch in Mauritania boosted fish exports and earnings, which in 1983 reached 312,100 metric tons (from only 14,600 in 1979) and UM 8,773m., respectively, causing fish to become, for the first time, a more important source of export earnings than iron ore—a position that was maintained in 1984, despite a recovery in sales of iron ore in that year, and in 1985. In 1986 the value of exports of fish reached a record UM 20,330m. and their volume a record 388,400 tons. In that year the fishing sector (including processing) accounted for about one-tenth of GDP, and the 1985–88 recovery programme allocated almost 9% of total new project investment (UM 3,520m.) to further fisheries development, with around one-half destined for a ship-repair yard in Nouadhibou, which became operational in late 1989. However, the volume and value of catches declined in the late 1980s, as some international fleets moved their operations elsewhere and because of the depletion of stocks earlier in the decade. By 1991 the sector's contribution to GDP had declined to 6%, with fish exports (of 205,000 tons) valued at UM 18,926m. Earnings improved by almost 45% in 1993, when exports of fish and fish products accounted for some 56% of the value of total exports, and the contribution of fishing to GDP recovered to 7%. Export volumes declined by 38% in 1994, however, to a total of 196,100 tons, reducing the contribution of the fishing sector to 5% of GDP. (In terms of foreign exchange earnings, the decline was partly offset by higher prices.) This provoked the government to rethink its fishing policy and in late 1995 it imposed a one-month suspension of all fishing operations, in an attempt to allow marine stocks (particularly octopus and squid) to recover. It also revised its system of allocating fishing licences, replaced deep-sea export licences with access fees and introduced production-sharing agreements. In spite of the temporary fishing ban, fish exports recovered sharply, totalling 287,000 tons in 1995 and 366,000 tons in 1996. In 1997 exports declined to 220,000 tons, according to official estimates. Nevertheless, the value of exports of fresh and frozen fish in that year (US $200m.), supplemented by some $60m. in licence fees payable by the EU, accounted for about 13% of GNP. Over-fishing remains a concern, however, especially as the government has no effective means of enforcing the ban imposed on fishing in September and October. The economic consequences of the 1997 decline in exports were further compounded by a fall in international prices for some species, particualry cephalopods, owing in part to a fall in Asian demand. The sector's future is also compromised by the poor state of the Mauritanian fleet, only 60% of which is now considered operational.

Substantial external assistance has been made available for the reform of the fishing sector. As part of the revised national policy, the government's surveillance capabilities have been strengthened and the Centre for Oceanographic and Fisheries Research regularly compiles and publishes information of permissible catch levels. Many aid-funded projects have targeted artisanal fishing, for which the government adopted a new strategy in 1997. In that year fish exports provided some 50% of total foreign income, compared with about 66% in 1996. The government hopes to arrest this decline by concluding a more favourable agreement with the EU that will permit joint ventures and stipulate that catches in Mauritanian waters should be landed for processing in the country. In the absence of such improved terms, the government may extend the offshore exclusion zone from 9 km to 19 km and reduce the number of licences granted. According to some observers, the government has been prepared to accept successive devaluations of the ouguiya (the most recent, of 11%, took place in July 1998) since the weakening of the currency acts as a direct subsidy to the fishing and mining sectors.

MINING AND POWER

While the vast majority of the population still depends on agriculture and livestock for its livelihood, the country's economic growth prospects were transformed during the 1960s by the discovery and exploitation of reserves of iron ore and copper, which made Mauritania one of West Africa's wealthiest countries in terms of per caput income. In the late 1990s iron ore still accounted for about 11% of Mauritania's GNP and for about 40% of the country's exports. The Guelbs region has workable reserves of iron ore estimated at 5,000m.–6,000m. metric tons. These are being developed by the former Société anonyme des mines de fer de Mauritanie (MIFERMA), established in 1959 by the French government. Mauritania nationalized these holdings in 1974, and they became part of the state mining corporation, the Société nationale industrielle et minière (SNIM). During 1960–72 about 70,800m. francs CFA was invested in the development of the Kédia d'Idjil mines, including the construction of a 670-km railway and a mineral port. Production of ore, which began in 1963, reached 11.7m. tons (gross weight) in 1974, but by 1978 had fallen to 7.3m. tons, owing in part to attacks on the supply line by guerrillas of the Polisario Front. Following the cease-fire of 1978, production began to recover. However, the mines' fortunes were subsequently eclipsed by a fall in foreign demand, caused by economic recession. By the late 1980s the Kédia d'Idjil mines were nearing exhaustion, and production ceased in 1992. Meanwhile, SNIM began exploitation of the lower-grade (36%, compared with a metal content of as much as 60% at Kédia d'Idjil) iron ore deposits at El Rhein, some 40 km north of the Kédia d'Idjil mines. Production under the first stage of the project began in 1984, increasing total national output to 11.5m. tons in 1990. However, production declined to 10.3m. tons in 1991 and to only 8.3m. tons in 1992, as technical problems at El Rhein meant that the deposit yielded little more than 2m. tons per year, far less than the 'break-even' level of 3m. tons annually. The second stage of the project, a new mine at Oum Arwagen, was thus allowed to lapse. The company's main interest has now been transferred to the deposits at M'Haoudat, near Zouérate (estimated to contain recoverable reserves of 100m. tons), which revealed potential for annual production of about 5.6m. tons of high-grade (60%–65%) ore. Financing for the project, estimated to total US $172m., was supplied by the African Development Bank (ADB), the European Investment Bank, France and SNIM. Work on the scheme began in December 1991, and the mine was inaugurated in April 1994. As part of the project the mineral port at Point-Central, 10 km south of Nouadhibou, has been modernized and expanded, with a new plant to mix different concentrate types. With the entry into production of the M'Haoudat scheme, the government hoped to sustain overall output averaging 12m. tons of ore annually, over at least 25 years. Total production reached 11.3m. tons in

1995, 11.4m. tons in 1996 and 11.7m. tons in 1997, while exports rose from 8.0m. tons in 1992 to 11.7m. tons in 1997. In April 1997 SNIM began construction of its $200m. iron pelletization project, which will increase domestic value-added by reducing impurities in the iron-bearing ore, and provide an estimated 5,000 additional jobs in Nouadhibou. The government hoped to raise output to 15.5m. tons of ore per year. In 1997 SNIM invested $43m. in iron-ore mining, and a further $72m. in 1998, especially in pelletization projects.

In 1967 the Société minière de Mauritanie (SOMIMA), of which the government took full control in 1975, was formed to exploit the copper reserves at Akjoujt, then estimated at 32m. metric tons. Production began in 1970, with 3,000 tons of copper concentrate. Output rose to a peak of 28,982 tons in 1973, but ceased altogether in 1978, owing to the low grades of the deposit. A new company, the Société arabe des mines de l'Inchiri (SAMIN), was formed in 1981 by the government and Arab interests in order to reopen the mine, with projected annual production of 105,000 tons, exploiting more extensive reserves than earlier estimated, at a cost of US $100m. Projected annual output was subsequently lowered to 65,000 tons, and investment reduced to $40m. In early 1991 SOMIMA established a joint-venture company, Mines d'or d'Akjoujt (MORAK), with Australian interests and the International Finance Corpn, to extract gold from Akjoujt. Operations began in April 1992 and ended in early 1996, when the deposit was depleted, but the partners in MORAK were expected to start a new venture to mine an estimated 25m. tons of deeper copper reserves at the site. In the late 1990s a new company, Guelb Moghrein Mines d'Akjoujt (GEMAK), was established to construct a new mine in order to resume the exploitation of copper and gold deposits in Akjoujt. Construction of the mine commenced in mid-1998 and was scheduled to be completed in late 1999. It is estimated that the new mine will produce some 802,000 oz of gold, 366,000 tons of copper and 2,100 tons of cobalt over a 13-year period. The cost of the project has been estimated at $181m. General Gold Resources, an Australian exploration company, was reported to have contributed funding of A $6.1m. in order to obtain a 50%-share in the GEMAK copper/gold project. The state-owned SAMIN holds the remaining 50%-share.

In June 1995 the government granted General Gold Resources exclusive rights to explore and exploit minerals in the south of the country. In November 1996 General Gold Resources applied for a new mining permit covering a region close to the northern border with Western Sahara. In June 1995 France awarded a substantial grant for gold prospecting in the Inchiri region. In July 1998 it was reported that exploration permits (mainly for gold and diamonds) recently granted included one in Amsaga province to a joint venture between SNIM and the Office Mauritanien de Recherches Géologiques (OMRG); one in Tasiast province to General Gold Resources; and one in Inchiri province to a joint venture between OMRG, the French Bureau de Recherches Géologiques and General Gold Resources. The grant of a permit to explore for diamonds in Tiris province was reported to be pending for SNIM, while others had already been granted for Tasiast province, Bir Moghrein and Guelb Richat. In March 1999 it was reported that geologists had discovered diamond deposits in northern Mauritania. By late 1999 two companies had reported progress with their diamond exploration projects, and in March 2000 the Mauritanian government granted the US company Brick Capital Corporation a licence to prospect for diamonds in the Tiris Zemmour province.

Mauritania's total gypsum reserves are estimated at 4,000m. metric tons, among the largest in the world. Production rose substantially with the reopening in 1984 of the N'Drahamcha quarry, north of Nouakchott, by the Société arabe des industries métallurgiques mauritano-koweïtienne (SAMIA). Owing to technical and transport problems, total output declined from a peak of 19,400 tons in 1987 to less than 3,000 tons a year, both in 1991 and 1992.

As part of the reduction in the government's role in the economy, SNIM was opened to private participation in 1978, and Arab governments and institutions now hold 29% of the renamed concern. SNIM is involved in prospecting for tungsten (wolfram), iron, petroleum, phosphates and uranium (the latter, in the north of the country, was temporarily interrupted by the guerrilla war). Phosphate reserves estimated at more than

135m. metric tons have been located at Bofal, near the Senegal river. In October 1998 SAMIA was granted a permit to begin exploiting these reserves in co-operation with foreign partners. Phosphate mining was to be carried out in two phases. In the first phase, which was scheduled to be completed in 1999, SAMIA aimed to produce sufficient phosphates to meet domestic fertilizer requirements and provide an exportable surplus. In the second phase phosphoric acid would be produced for export. In October 1999 highly valuable blue granite deposits were discovered in the north of the country.

Exploratory drilling for petroleum began at the offshore Autruche field in 1989. A consortium led by an Australian company, Hardman Resources, is currently seeking financial partners to develop the Shafr el Khanjar field, where potential reserves are estimated at 290m.–850m. barrels. In April 2000 President Taya announced that the drilling of exploitation vents would commence in February 2001.

Reflecting the needs of mineral development, electricity generation has expanded rapidly since the late 1960s, from 38.4m. kWh in 1967 to 176.4m. kWh in 1996. About one-half of the electricity is now generated by hydroelectric installations built on the Senegal river under the OMVS scheme (see above). SNIM generates electrical power for its production centres from two diesel-powered plants at Zouérate, and from the Point-Central plant in Nouadhibou. A power line that will enable Mauritania to utilize electricity generated at the Manantali installation (which was opened in 1992) is to be constructed; Mauritania would receive 15% of the target of generation of 800m. kWh.

A butane gas depot, with a capacity of 2,500 cu m, was inaugurated in mid-1995 at Kiffa, in southern Mauritania. Consumption of butane gas in the country was reported to have increased from 5,000 metric tons in 1988 to 13,000 tons in 1994. The EU is currently subsidizing the distribution of bottles and burners in the hope of encouraging 55% of households to convert to gas for cooking by 2000.

MANUFACTURING

There is, as yet, no significant industrial development outside the mining sector and the fish-processing industry. Initially, development had concentrated on import substitution. However, as income from iron mining rose during the early 1970s, the government promoted the development of large-scale, capital-intensive manufacturing projects, in which it participated directly. These included the petroleum refinery at Nouadhibou, which entered production in 1978, with an annual capacity of 1m. metric tons. In the event, this wholly government-financed project was closed by the new regime. After reopening in 1982 (with Algerian assistance), the refinery closed again after only six months. However, an agreement on rehabilitation was reached with Algeria in 1985, and operations resumed in mid-1987. More than three-quarters of its total annual output of 1.5m. tons are exported. A sugar refinery was completed in 1977, but it was closed after less than one year's operation because its dependence on imported sugar made it uneconomic. The plant was reactivated in 1982, with assistance from Algeria, as a sugar-packaging operation, but finally closed in 1990. The government also planned to establish plants to produce 500,000 tons of steel and 30,000 tons of copper by 1979/80. SAMIA (see above) was formed in 1974, with Kuwaiti participation, to build the plants, and operations at the steel mill, which has product capacity of 36,000 tons and uses both scrap and imported billets, began in 1981. The mill failed to reach capacity production, and closed in 1984, but reopened in 1987 as a joint venture with Jordanian and Kuwaiti participation. In total, however, these projects proved to be unprofitable and a major burden on state finances. Although government enterprises remain of major importance, the Taya administration is no longer placing emphasis on large-scale capital-intensive projects, but is, instead, encouraging development by the private sector and the establishment of small- and medium-scale operations, aimed at low-level import substitution. Long-term tax concessions are offered for private investors, especially for those aiming to create local employment, increase exports or establish projects outside the two main cities. Meanwhile, the development of fish-processing units at Nouadhibou, as a result of the government's fisheries policy, made this sub-sector into the single most important manufacturing activity, accounting for as much as 4% of annual

GDP. However, several plants have since closed, mainly because of high utility costs, a lack of skilled labour and inadequate port facilities. In April 1996 poor hygiene standards prompted the EU to impose a three-month ban on imports of fish landed in Mauritania. In 1997 the manufacturing sector contributed 10.9% of GDP.

A major strand in current policy is the rationalization of the public sector. In mid-1990 the World Bank, in co-operation with Arab donors, Spain and the Federal Republic of Germany, agreed to provide US $40m. in support of a programme to reduce, or eliminate, state monopolies, to transfer some state enterprises to private ownership, and to restructure some strategic enterprises (such as SNIM, the fish-export monopoly and the power utility). It was envisaged that one-half of Mauritania's 80 parastatal organizations would have been thus 'privatized' or liquidated by mid-1991. Although this target was not attained, there has been solid progress. The reform of the banking system, under the 1989–91 programme, had already entailed the streamlining of government banking institutions. Five textile and fishing companies were liquidated, the petroleum-products sector was fully liberalized, and the monopolies in fish-marketing, insurance and tea-importing have been ended. By mid-1996 only seven companies remained wholly under state ownership, with a further 50 majority- or part-owned by the government.

TRANSPORT INFRASTRUCTURE

Transport and communication in Mauritania is difficult, with sparse coverage and a lack of maintenance, although infrastructure related to mineral development is of a high standard. The iron ore port of Point-Central, 10 km to the south of Nouadhibou, can accommodate 150,000-ton bulk carriers (a 670-km railway line links the port with the iron-ore deposits at Zouérate and has been extended by 40 km to the El Rhein deposit and by 30 km to M'Haoudat), while Nouakchott's capacity was expanded to 950,000 tons with the completion, in 1986, of a 500,000-ton deep-water facility, financed and constructed by the People's Republic of China. This development reduced the country's dependence on transportation through Senegal, and the excess capacity that the port currently represents could be used for gypsum and copper exports, and for traffic to Mali. Outside the mineral shipment network, communications are at present still poor: in 1996 there were some 7,600 km of roads and tracks, of which less than 1,800 km were tarred. The 1,100-km Trans-Mauritania highway, linking Nouakchott with the south-eastern part of the country, was completed in 1985. Its construction was aided by foreign, principally Arab, funds. In late 1994 the European Development Fund granted ECU 7.4m. to help finance the country's second road programme. In 1996 the ADB granted a US $12.8m. loan towards upgrading the road between Akjoujt and Atar. The work is part of the $26m. 'route transmaghrébine', designed to improve access to the north-eastern part of the country and eventually to improve transport links between Mauritania and its north-eastern neighbours. The Senegal river is navigable for 210 km throughout the year (navigability should eventually be extended, with the completion of the Manantali dam), and there are three major river ports, at Rosso, Kaédi and Gouraye. There are international airports at Nouakchott and Nouadhibou and 13 small regional airports. In mid-1998 Air Mauritanie stood on the verge of bankruptcy, and in order to avert this the airline's fleet was reduced to a single aircraft. Under the terms of an agreement concluded with the World Bank in late 1998 (see below), the government undertook to privatize the airline and planned, by the end of 1999, to have sold all but 15% of its 68%-holding to the private sector. In June 2000 the Mauritanian government announced that it had sold the majority of its holding in Air Mauritanie and retained only an 11% stake.

FINANCE

Mauritania's budget situation was transformed by mineral development. The MIFERMA contract allowed the temporary liquidation of the chronic budget deficit and commitment of funds to capital development. Spending increased as a result of the guerrilla war and the administrative costs associated with the annexed territory of Western Sahara (abandoned in 1979). Consequently, ordinary expenditure rose by 11% in 1977 and was predicted to rise by 18% in 1978. The cease-fire allowed a much slower rise in current spending in 1978 (only 7%) and a projected fall of 9% in 1980, to UM 9,948m. However, the budget continued in deficit, reaching UM 5,423m. on current spending and UM 8,095m. on total spending in 1979. In return for IMF stand-by credits, successive Mauritanian governments have since 1980 attempted to restrain the level of budgetary spending and to raise current revenue. The overall deficit fell sharply, to around UM 1,800m. per year in both 1982 and 1983, but rose to an estimated UM 4,000m. in 1984, owing to the rising cost of servicing the foreign debt and to the impact of the drought. The 1985–88 recovery programme aimed to balance the current budget in 1986 and to generate a surplus by 1988. In its first year, however, the overall deficit reached an unprecedented UM 9,341m., as debt arrears were discharged. None the less, the current budget did achieve the intended balance, and the overall deficit eased to about UM 900m. in 1986, before widening to UM 2,000m. in 1987. The deficit increased again in the following two years, to reach UM 6,300m. in 1989. Improvements in revenue from taxes, in conjunction with strict controls on expenditure, reduced the deficit to an average of UM 3,930m. per year in 1990–92 (equivalent to 4.4% of GDP). The deficit widened sharply in 1993 to UM 8,860m. (equivalent to almost 8% of GDP), largely reflecting the costs of restructuring the banking sector and of servicing the external debt (see below), together with increased social costs. A slight fall in debt-service payments and better revenue collection reduced the deficit to UM 3,190m. in 1994 (2.5% of GDP). On 1 January 1995 the government imposed value-added tax of 5% on food products and of 14% on industrial supplies in an attempt to raise current revenue. The tax proved unpopular and riots erupted in Nouakchott when the price of bread increased by some 25%. However, the government was able to achieve a fiscal surplus of UM 1,580m. (1.1% of GDP) in 1995. The government subsequently announced the introduction of measures to check monopoly and speculation and the expansion of the remit of SONIMEX, the state's essential goods distribution company, to encompass all essentials including rice, milk, vegetable oil and bread. In line with the 1995–97 reform programme, the government has continued to restrain current expenditure while broadening the tax base by reducing exemptions granted to externally financed government projects, and strengthening collection procedures, particularly for imports. The budget surplus increased in 1996 to UM 11,260m. (an estimated 7.5% of GDP). Although the government projected an increase in expenditure, particularly towards the social sectors, during the 1997–99 programme, the fiscal balance remained in surplus. According to the IMF, there was a surplus of 4.2% of GDP in 1997. The government decided not to incorporate all fishing revenue in the budget: of the UM 11,000m. annual receipts, only UM 4,000m. was included in the current budget; the remainder was to be placed in accounts abroad, reflecting concerns both about the economy's growing dependence on a single depletable resource and the short-term capacity of the economy to absorb productively the large influx of resources. In 1998 the government forecast a balanced budget of UM 48,620m., an increase of some 8% compared with 1997. It was reported that the operating budget would be increased by 12% in order to finance a population census and owing to higher spending on health and education. In 1999 Mauritania's budget was forecast to balance at UM 53,358m. It was reported that 32.7% of investment expenditure in that year was to be targeted at infrastructural development. Other aims of the 1999 budget were the diversification of agricultural production, the preservation of fishing resources and the further development of the mining sector. In 2000 the government forecast Mauritania's budget to balance at UM 58,000m. and projected that some UM 3,000m. would be used to attempt to alleviate poverty. The government also pledged to reduce taxes in order to improve private investments and to facilitate the creation of new jobs.

FOREIGN TRADE AND PAYMENTS

Foreign trade has been transformed by the development, firstly, of the mineral sector and, secondly, of fishing. The value of Mauritania's exports increased from 3,200m. francs CFA (mainly cattle)—equivalent to UM 650m.—in 1959 to UM 8,013m. in 1976, of which 6,919m. came from iron ore. Despite the heavy import requirements of mining development, imports

rose less rapidly—from 7,000m. francs CFA (UM 1,400m.) in 1959 to UM 8,072m. in 1976. International reserves, which were only US $3m. at the end of 1970, reached $143m. in early 1975. However, the trade account deteriorated in subsequent years, recording a deficit of UM 5,137m. in 1979, on exports of UM 6,733m. (of which iron ore accounted for some 90%). The major reasons were a weakening in the demand for iron ore, and increased spending on imports of petroleum. Tighter control on the growth in imports of capital equipment and consumer goods, the recovery in iron-ore prices and the sevenfold increase in earnings from fish exports resulted in a narrowing in the trade gap in subsequent years, to only UM 294m. in 1981. After a sharp rise in the deficit in 1982, as a result of the decline in earnings from iron ore and the increase in petroleum imports with the opening of the refinery, foreign trade moved into surplus in 1983. Import spending was curbed by the government's austerity programme and by a decrease in the import of petroleum products, while export revenue benefited from the near-doubling in earnings from fish. The trade surplus almost doubled in 1984, and again in 1985, as export totals were enlarged by the rise in iron ore shipments and imports eased further, with an increase in food aid (reducing the need for commercial purchases) and the completion of the first stage of investment at the *guelbs* mine project. The devaluation of the ouguiya in 1985 reinforced these trends, and higher earnings from sales of iron ore and the further devaluation of the ouguiya in relation to the US dollar effectively doubled ouguiya-denominated export receipts during 1984–89. The balance of trade remained positive until 1992 when a sharp fall in earnings from iron ore (resulting from both lower volumes and international prices) and a large increase in capital imports caused a substantial regression into deficit, of some $55m. Following a small surplus in 1993, a continuing decline in the volume of imports, combined with a sharp rise in exports in the latter year, produced a trade surplus of $184m. in 1995. Official estimates indicated a reduced trade surplus, of $96m., in 1996, owing to a substantial increase in imports. (It must be borne in mind that significant cross-border trade is not recorded in these statistics.) Such fluctuations in the trade balance were largely responsible for changes in the deficit (before official transfers) on the current account of the balance of payments, although this remained substantial throughout the late 1980s and into the 1990s. Net of official transfers, the current-account deficit averaged $146m. per year in 1986–88. The current account continued in deficit, averaging $80m. per year in the period 1990–94. In 1995 and 1996, however, the current account registered modest surpluses of $22m., owing mainly to large trade surpluses. Despite the substantial decline in fisheries exports during 1997, the current account surplus was expected to narrow as the government continued to contain the demand for imports. According to the IMF, in 1998 there was a deficit of $11m. on the current account. However, in 1999 a surplus of $41m. was recorded, largely owing to an excellent agricultural season and a recovery in the fisheries sector.

The substantial trade surpluses that occurred every year during 1965–74 enabled Mauritania to service its extensive foreign borrowing, while reaching a payments surplus in 1971–74. This allowed Mauritania to leave the West African Monetary Union in 1973 and establish its own currency, the ouguiya, not linked to the franc. In the less favourable payments situation in subsequent years, Mauritania's reserves were sustained by continuing capital borrowing. The country's external public debt reached US $632.2m. (disbursed) at the end of 1976, and its service payments in that year reached 33% of total foreign earnings, compared with only 3.8% in 1974. The foreign debt declined in the following years, reaching $590m. at the end of 1979, but the burden of repayment and interest remained at the same level because of the country's substantial borrowing of commercial funds. Despite a rescheduling of debt obtained by the regime that came to power in 1978, indebtedness continued to rise, totalling $1,342m. at the end of 1984, which was almost double the level of GNP in that year. In addition, arrears of more than $100m., not agreed with lenders, had accrued by the end of 1984, and the debt burden was forecast to rise again in subsequent years. Against the background of the economic stabilization programme agreed with the IMF, the Taya government secured reschedulings of its debt to official creditors in

1985, 1986 and 1987, on the latter occasion obtaining a 15-year rescheduling (including five years' grace) on repayment. Moreover, Mauritania continued to receive substantial aid, of which more than one-half was in grant form, from non-communist countries and multilateral agencies: such funding averaged $242m. per year in 1985–88. However, the debt rose inexorably, to $2,054m. at the end of 1987 (equivalent to 247% of annual GNP), and arrears on interest payments had doubled by 1988, to $52m. The debt-service ratio neared 25% of foreign earnings during most of this period. Mauritania was one of the African countries classified by the World Bank as 'debt-distressed' (i.e., without rescheduling, its debt-service ratio would exceed more than 30% of external earnings in 1988–90) and was thus eligible for the system of exceptional debt-relief that was agreed in principle at the summit meeting of industrialized nations, held in Toronto, Canada, in June 1988. Accordingly, in June 1989 the 'Paris Club' of Western official creditors agreed to reschedule $52m. of the country's external debt. Some bilateral donors agreed to relief: in both 1988 and 1989 the Federal Republic of Germany cancelled official trade obligations, and in mid-1990 France cancelled official loans, totalling $60m., contracted before the end of 1988. In all, debts totalling $180m. were cancelled in 1989. While the foreign debt continued to rise, to $2,233m. by the end of 1991, debt-rescheduling agreements meant that the debt-service ratio was reduced to 20.4% of the value of exports of goods and services in that year—although this continued to represent a considerable burden on the Mauritanian economy. Moreover, interest arrears continued to accumulate, totalling $121m. by the end of 1992 (although the total debt fell slightly, to $2,134m.). Mauritania's failure to pay off debt arrears or to achieve the fiscal targets agreed with the IMF for 1989–91 meant that no further debt relief was accorded until early 1993, when, following the IMF's agreement to extend an enhanced structural adjustment facility for the period to September 1995, the 'Paris Club' agreed to cancel one-half of the interest due on non-concessional debt and to reschedule the remainder over 23 years, with payment due to begin only after 10 years. This round of debt relief represented savings for Mauritania amounting to more than $200m. and was followed by debt-restructuring packages of $91m. and $67m. in subsequent years. Nevertheless, although arrears were reduced, the total

debt continued to rise to $2,320m. at the end of 1995. The debt-service ratio increased to 30.1% of the value of exported goods and services in 1993, and was 21.5% in 1995. In early 1995 the IMF approved a $63m. loan, extending an enhanced structural adjustment facility to support the government's financial and economic reform programme for 1995–97. Towards the end of 1996 almost the entire stock of foreign privately-contracted commercial debt (of $92m.) was retired through a discounted buy-back operation funded by the World Bank and other donors. By the end of 1998 total external debt stood at $2,589m. (of which 85.5% was long-term public debt), while the cost of debt-servicing was equivalent to 27.7% of the value of exports of goods and services.

In late 1998 Mauritania concluded a three-year (1999–2001) agreement with the World Bank that will allow it, in 2001, to reschedule some US $130m. of its external debt under the heavily-indebted poor countries (HIPC) initiative of the World Bank and the IMF. In return, Mauritania undertook to privatize the posts and telecommunications sectors, public utilities (water and electricity) and the national air carrier, Air Mauritanie. A second phase of the agreement, to be implemented in its final year, relates to Mauritania's monetary policies and the control of the exchange market. The agreement was to be complemented by measures to protect fish stocks and reform the country's tax regime. On the successful implementation of the agreement, Mauritania will become eligible for large-scale balance-of-payments support from the IMF, the ADB and the EU. In February 2000 Mauritania became one of the first countries to receive assistance under the joint IMF/World Bank HIPC initiative, which would amount to a reduction of Mauritania's debt by $622m. in net present value terms, representing savings of an estimated 40% of annual debt-service obligations. Additionally, the 'Paris Club' of donor countries agreed in March to cancel $80m.-worth of Mauritania's external debt, representing 90% of the debt-service charges owed to the 'Paris Club' donors.

The support of foreign donors remains essential to stimulate the key sectors of the economy. Planned investment in 1998–2001 of UM 124,000m. in infrastructure, rural development and industry will depend on grants and loans for up to 90% of the required funds. Given this level of dependency, it would not be possible for the government to continue its reform programme without some rescheduling of its external debt.

Statistical Survey

Figures exclude Mauritania's section of Western Sahara, annexed in 1976 and relinquished in 1979.

Source (unless otherwise stated): Office National de la Statistique, BP 240, Nouakchott; tel. 25-28-80; fax 25-51-70; internet www.ons.mr.

Area and Population

AREA, POPULATION AND DENSITY

Area (sq km)	1,030,700*
Population (census results)†	
1 January 1977.	1,338,830
5–20 April 1988	
Males	923,175
Females	941,061
Total	1,864,236
Population (UN estimates at mid-year)	
1996	2,394,000
1997	2,461,000
1998	2,529,000
Density (per sq km) at mid-1998	2.5

* 397,950 sq miles.

† Figures include estimates for Mauritania's nomad population (444,020 in 1977; 224,095 in 1988).

REGIONS

Region	Chief town	Area ('000 sq km)	Population (1988 census)*
Hodh el Chargui . . .	Néma	183	212,203
Hodh el Gharbi . .	Aïoun el Atrous	53	159,296
Assaba	Kiffa	37	167,123
Gorgol	Kaédi	14	184,359
Brakna	Aleg	33	192,157
Trarza	Rosso	68	202,596
Adrar	Atar	215	61,043
Dakhlet-Nouadhibou .	Nouadhibou	22	63,030
Tagant	Tidjikja	95	64,908
Guidimaka . . .	Sélibaby	10	116,436
Tiris Zemmour . .	F'Derik	253	33,147
Inchiri	Akjoujt	47	14,613
Nouakchott . . .	Nouakchott	1	393,325
Total		1,030	1,864,236

* Source: UN, *Demographic Yearbook*.

PRINCIPAL TOWNS (population at census of January 1977)

Nouakchott (capital) . . 134,986	Zouérate 17,947
Nouadhibou	Atar 16,394
(Port-Etienne) . . 22,365	Rosso 15,888
Kaédi 20,356	

1996 (estimates): Nouakchott 608,228; Nouadhibou 88,313; Kaédi 40,633.

BIRTHS AND DEATHS (UN estimates, annual averages)

	1980–85	1985–90	1990–95
Birth rate (per 1,000) . .	42.3	43.6	42.6
Death rate (per 1,000) . .	18.5	16.2	14.7

Expectation of life (UN estimates, years at birth, 1990–95): 51.4 (males 49.9; females 53.1).

Source: UN, *World Population Prospects: The 1998 Revision.*

ECONOMICALLY ACTIVE POPULATION
(estimates, '000 persons, 1994)

	Males	Females	Total
Agriculture, etc.	332	98	430
Industry	69	11	80
Services	155	22	177
Total	556	131	687

Source: UN Economic Commission for Africa, *African Statistical Yearbook.*

Mid-1998 (estimates in '000): Agriculture, etc. 605; Total labour force 1,134 (Source: FAO, *Production Yearbook*).

Agriculture

PRINCIPAL CROPS ('000 metric tons)

	1996	1997	1998
Rice (paddy)	64*	67	81
Maize	14	6	12
Millet	8	3	1
Sorghum	145	46	57
Potatoes.	1†	1	1†
Sweet potatoes . . .	2†	2	2†
Yams	3†	3	3†
Pulses	33	34	34
Vegetables	10	8	11
Dates	20*	36*	12
Watermelons	1*	1	1†
Groundnuts (in shell). . .	2	2	2†

* Unofficial figure.   † FAO estimate(s).

Source: FAO, *Production Yearbook.*

LIVESTOCK ('000 head, year ending September)

	1996	1997	1998
Cattle	1,312	1,312*	1,312*
Goats	4,133	4,133	4,133*
Sheep	6,199	6,199	6,200*
Asses*	155	155	155
Horses	19†	20*	20*
Camels	1,127	1,182	1,183

Poultry (million): 4* in 1996; 4 in 1997; 4* in 1998.

* FAO estimate(s).   † Unofficial figure.

Source: FAO, *Production Yearbook.*

LIVESTOCK PRODUCTS ('000 metric tons)

	1996	1997	1998
Beef and veal	10	10	10*
Mutton and lamb* . . .	15	15	15
Goat meat*	10	10	10
Poultry meat*	4	4	4
Other meat	19	19	19*
Cows' milk*	107	108	91
Sheep's milk*	84	84	84
Goats' milk*	90	90	92
Poultry eggs*	5	5	5
Cattle hides*	2	1	1
Sheepskins*	2	2	2
Goatskins*	1	1	1

* FAO estimate(s).

Source: FAO, *Production Yearbook.*

Forestry

ROUNDWOOD REMOVALS
('000 cubic metres, excluding bark)

	1995	1996	1997
Sawlogs, veneer logs and logs for sleepers	1	1	1
Other industrial wood . .	5	5	5
Fuel wood	8	9	9
Total	14	15	15

Source: FAO, *Yearbook of Forest Products.*

Fishing

(FAO estimates, '000 metric tons, live weight)

	1995	1996	1997
Freshwater fishes . . .	5.5	6.0	6.0
Flatfishes	2.2	2.2	2.2
Groupers and seabasses . .	7.5	7.4	7.3
Meagre	6.3	6.2	6.1
Porgies, seabreams, etc. . .	7.4	7.3	7.2
Sardinellas	3.2	3.1	3.1
Other marine fishes (incl. unspecified)	24.7	26.5	26.0
Total fish	56.8	58.7	57.9
Marine crustaceans . . .	0.5	0.5	0.5
Cuttlefishes and bobtail squids .	5.1	4.3	3.7
Octopuses	25.4	21.5	18.3
Other cephalopods . . .	2.2	1.9	1.6
Total catch	90.0	87.0	82.0

Source: FAO, *Yearbook of Fishery Statistics.*

Mining

('000 metric tons)

	1996	1997	1998*
Iron ore: gross weight . .	11,400	11,700	11,400
metal content . .	7,000*	7,000*	7,000

* Estimate(s).

Source: US Geological Survey.

Industry

SELECTED PRODUCTS ('000 metric tons, unless otherwise indicated)

	1992	1993	1994
Frozen and chilled fish* . .	8.3	8.3	8.3
Salted, dried and smoked fish* .	0.9	1.7	1.7
Electric energy (million kWh). .	137.1	147.7	155.9

Electric energy (million kWh): 168.0 in 1995; 185.7 in 1996; 199.4 in 1997.

* Data from FAO.

Source: mainly UN, *Industrial Commodity Statistics Yearbook*.

Finance

CURRENCY AND EXCHANGE RATES

Monetary Units
5 khoums = 1 ouguiya (UM).

Sterling, Dollar and Euro Equivalents (28 April 2000)
£1 sterling = 373.21 ouguiyas;
US $1 = 238.00 ouguiyas;
€1 = 216.22 ouguiyas;
1,000 ouguiyas = £2.679 = $4.202 = €4.625.

Average Exchange Rate (ouguiyas per US $)
1997   151.853
1998   188.476
1999   209.514

BUDGET ('000 million ouguiyas)

Revenue*	1995	1996	1997
Budgetary revenue . . .	32.8	44.5	44.6
Tax revenue	23.6	26.3	26.0
Taxes on income and profits .	8.2	7.4	8.3
Taxes on goods and services .	7.5	10.9	11.8
Value-added tax . .	4.5	4.8	5.0
Turnover taxes . .	0.3	3.2	3.6
Tax on petroleum products .	1.5	1.5	1.8
Other excises . . .	1.0	1.2	1.1
Taxes on international trade .	7.5	7.4	5.4
Import taxes . . .	4.7	5.6	5.4
Export tax on fish . .	2.7	1.7	0.0
Other current revenue . .	8.0	17.4	17.8
Fishing royalties and penalties	3.5	14.0	14.4
Revenue from public enterprises . . .	0.5	0.4	0.6
Capital revenue . . .	1.2	0.9	0.8
Special accounts . . .	0.4	0.2	0.3
Total	**33.2**	**44.7**	**44.8**

Expenditure	1995	1996	1997
Current expenditure . . .	24.6	26.2	27.7
Wages and salaries. . .	7.0	7.4	8.0
Goods and services. . .	6.9	7.3	8.2
Transfers and subsidies .	2.3	2.4	2.5
Military expenditure . .	3.6	3.7	3.7
Interest on public debt . .	4.5	4.9	4.9
Other (incl. unclassified) .	0.3	0.4	0.3
Capital expenditure and net lending	9.5	10.2	9.7
Fixed capital formation. .	7.0	8.3	8.5
Restructuring and net lending .	2.5	1.9	1.2
Total†	**34.4**	**36.7**	**37.9**

* Excluding grants received.
† Including adjustments.

Source: IMF, *Mauritania: Recent Economic Developments* (April 1999).

INTERNATIONAL RESERVES (US $ million at 31 December)

	1997	1998	1999
Gold*	3.3	3.3	3.3
IMF special drawing rights . .	0.4	—	—
Foreign exchange . . .	200.4	202.8	224.3
Total	**204.1**	**206.2**	**227.6**

* Valued at market-related prices.

Source: IMF, *International Financial Statistics*.

MONEY SUPPLY (million ouguiyas at 31 December)

	1997	1998	1999
Currency outside banks . . .	5,854	5,801	5,963
Demand deposits at deposit money banks	11,629	17,321	13,697
Total money (incl. others) . .	**17,579**	**23,358**	**19,675**

Source: IMF, *International Financial Statistics*.

COST OF LIVING (Consumer Price Index for Mauritanian households in Nouakchott; base: 1985 = 100)

	1996	1997	1998
Food	222.2	231.6	251.9
Clothing.	179.2	195.4	216.1
Housing	222.0	230.5	241.7
All items (incl. others) . . .	**209.3**	**218.8**	**236.3**

NATIONAL ACCOUNTS

Expenditure on the Gross Domestic Product
('000 million ouguiyas at current prices)

	1995	1996	1997
Government final consumption expenditure	19.6	20.9	22.3
Private final consumption expenditure*	109.0	117.4	130.1
Increase in stocks . . }	22.2	28.8	29.1
Gross fixed capital formation . }			
Total domestic expenditure .	**150.7**	**167.2**	**181.6**
Exports of goods and services .	70.0	70.9	66.1
Less Imports of goods and services	82.2	87.9	81.0
GDP in purchasers' values . .	**138.6**	**150.1**	**166.7**
GDP at constant 1985 prices .	**71.6**	**74.9**	**78.6**

* Including public enterprises. Figures are obtained as a residual.

Source: IMF, *Mauritania: Recent Economic Developments* (April 1999).

Gross Domestic Product by Economic Activity
(million ouguiyas at current prices)

	1995	1996	1997
Agriculture, hunting, forestry and fishing	31,134	33,232	37,117
Mining and quarrying . .	13,441	13,440	16,075
Manufacturing . . .	14,160	16,117	16,447
Electricity, gas and water . }	11,471	12,766	14,344
Construction. . . . }			
Trade, restaurants and hotels. .	20,064	22,287	25,511
Transport, storage and communications . . .	9,239	10,282	12,627
Public administration . .	14,743	15,684	16,852
Other services . . .	9,235	10,210	11,270
GDP at factor cost . . .	**123,488**	**134,018**	**150,242**
Indirect taxes, *less* subsidies .	15,131	16,124	16,688
GDP in purchasers' values .	**138,619**	**150,142**	**166,930**

Source: IMF, *Mauritania: Recent Economic Developments* (April 1999).

BALANCE OF PAYMENTS (US $ million)

	1996	1997	1998
Exports of goods f.o.b.	480.0	423.6	358.6
Imports of goods f.o.b.	−346.1	−316.5	−318.7
Trade balance	133.9	107.2	40.0
Exports of services	31.6	34.9	34.0
Imports of services	−231.3	−200.0	−152.5
Balance on goods and services	−65.8	−57.9	−78.6
Other income received	0.9	1.4	2.5
Other income paid	−45.9	−40.3	−34.0
Balance on goods, services and income	−110.8	−96.8	−110.2
Current transfers received	217.5	157.9	198.3
Current transfers paid	−15.5	−13.3	−10.8
Current balance	91.3	47.8	77.2
Direct investment from abroad	—	—	0.1
Portfolio investment liabilities	−0.4	—	−0.4
Other investment assets	236.0	191.1	190.1
Other investment liabilities	−321.6	−208.4	−215.7
Net errors and omissions	−1.0	−3.0	−8.1
Overall balance	4.2	27.6	43.2

Source: IMF, *International Financial Statistics*.

External Trade

PRINCIPAL COMMODITIES (million ouguiyas)

Imports c.i.f.	1994	1995	1996
Dairy products	2,030	1,927	1,784
Tea	325	326	600
Rice	1,214	1,346	2,648
Sugar	2,346	3,118	3,203
Cement	1,082	1,200	1,698
Hydrocarbons	1,367	6,873	10,589
Total (incl. others)	44,694	64,144	63,485

Exports f.o.b.	1994	1995	1996
Iron ore	21,025	25,401	28,200
Fish, crustaceans and molluscs	24,853	34,639	37,981
Total (incl. others)	50,710	64,815	67,431

PRINCIPAL TRADING PARTNERS (million ouguiyas)

Imports c.i.f.	1992	1993	1994
Algeria	2,330	3,698	2,578
Belgium	1,755	1,713	2,091
Canada	n.a.	1,269	n.a.
China, People's Repub.	1,816	1,470	n.a.
France	12,430	18,074	14,665
Germany	2,291	4,749	2,906
Italy	n.a.	n.a.	1,410
Japan	1,051	2,189	1,629
Netherlands	863	2,573	891
Spain	3,010	3,122	2,980
Thailand	1,208	n.a.	1,047
USA	1,810	5,940	4,291
Total (incl. others)	35,362	53,749	44,694

Exports f.o.b.	1992	1993	1994
Belgium	3,023	2,759	3,388
Côte d'Ivoire	1,666	2,283	1,712
France	2,988	5,972	7,141
Germany	n.a.	n.a.	1,441
Italy	4,365	7,001	7,094
Japan	9,981	11,192	14,511
Nigeria	802	1,497	n.a.
Spain	3,768	5,572	5,225
Switzerland	n.a.	1,932	2,643
USSR (former)	2,737	3,320	1,362
United Kingdom	1,606	2,358	1,603
USA	905	n.a.	n.a.
Total (incl. others)	37,019	51,109	50,710

1995 (million ouguiyas): *Imports c.i.f.*: France 19,017; Spain 4,494; Total imports (incl. others) 64,144; *Exports f.o.b.*: Japan 14,577; Italy 9,891; Total exports (incl. others) 64,815.
1996 (million ouguiyas): *Imports c.i.f.*: France 18,730; Spain 4,393; Total imports (incl. others) 63,485; *Exports f.o.b.*: Japan 15,495; Italy 12,053; Total exports (incl. others) 67,431.

Transport

RAILWAYS

1984: Passengers carried 19,353; Passenger-km 7m.; Freight carried 9.1m. metric tons; Freight ton-km 6,142m.

Freight ton-km (million): 6,365 in 1985; 6,411 in 1986; 6,473 in 1987; 6,535 in 1988; 6,610 in 1989; 6,690 in 1990; 6,720 in 1991; 6,810 in 1992; 6,890 in 1993 (figures for 1988–93 are estimates) (Source: UN Economic Commission for Africa, *African Statistical Yearbook*).

ROAD TRAFFIC (estimates, '000 motor vehicles in use)

	1994	1995	1996
Passenger cars	16.8	17.5	18.8
Commercial vehicles	9.0	9.3	10.5

Source: IRF, *World Road Statistics*.

SHIPPING
Merchant Fleet (registered at 31 December)

	1996	1997	1998
Number of vessels	131	135	140
Total displacement (grt)	42,679	42,998	47,959

Source: Lloyd's Register of Shipping, *World Fleet Statistics*.

International Sea-borne Freight Traffic (estimates, '000 metric tons)

	1991	1992	1993
Goods loaded	10,100	10,300	10,400
Goods unloaded	690	715	724

Source: UN Economic Commission for Africa, *African Statistical Yearbook*.

CIVIL AVIATION (traffic on scheduled services)*

	1994	1995	1996
Kilometres flown (million)	3	4	4
Passengers carried ('000)	216	228	235
Passenger-km (million)	289	301	306
Total ton-km (million)	41	44	44

* Including an apportionment of the traffic of Air Afrique.

Source: UN, *Statistical Yearbook*.

Tourism

Tourist arrivals (estimates, '000): 12 in 1984; 13 in 1985; 13 in 1986.

Receipts from tourism (US $ million): 7 in 1984; 5 in 1985; 8 in 1986; 14 in 1987; 12 in 1988; 13 in 1989; 15 in 1990; 15 in 1991; 15 in 1992; 15 in 1993.

Sources: UN Economic Commission for Africa, *African Statistical Yearbook;* UN, *Statistical Yearbook.*

Communications Media

	1995	1996	1997
Radio receivers ('000 in use) . . .	340	350	360
Television receivers ('000 in use) .	55	59	62
Telephones ('000 main lines in use) .	9	10	n.a.
Daily newspapers			
Number	1	2	n.a.
Average circulation ('000 copies) .	1*	1*	n.a.

* Estimate.

Telefax stations (number in use): 302 in 1995; 4,030 in 1996.

Sources: UNESCO, *Statistical Yearbook;* UN, *Statistical Yearbook.*

Education

(1995/96, unless otherwise indicated)

	Institu-tions	Teach-ers	Students		
			Males	Females	Total
Pre-primary* . . .	36	108	n.a.	n.a.	800
Primary	1,854†	n.a.	135,533	132,683	289,945
Secondary					
General	n.a.	1,865	32,608	16,613	49,221
Teacher training . .	2‡	43	803	327	1,130
Vocational . .	3‡	159	999§	415§	1,414§
University level. . }	4 {	214	6,708	1,463	8,171
Other higher . . }	{	56	302	23	325

* 1992/93 figures.
† 1994/95 figure.
‡ 1991/92 figure.
§ Excluding health-related programmes.

1996/97: Primary: 2,392 schools; 6,225 teachers; 312,671 pupils (165,843 boys; 146,828 girls).
1997/98: Primary: 330,199 students; Secondary: 56,120 students; Tertiary: 9,256 students.

Source: mainly UNESCO, *Statistical Yearbook.*

Directory

While no longer an official language under the terms of the 1991 Constitution (see below), French is still widely used in Mauritania, especially in the commercial sector. Many organizations are therefore listed under their French names, by which they are generally known.

The Constitution

The Constitution of the Arab and African Islamic Republic of Mauritania was approved in a national referendum on 12 July 1991.

The Constitution provides for the establishment of a multi-party political system. The President of the Republic is elected, by universal adult suffrage (the minimum age for voters being 18 years), for a period of six years: no limitations regarding the renewal of the presidential mandate are stipulated. Legislative power is vested in a National Assembly (elected by universal suffrage for a period of five years) and in a Senate (elected by municipal leaders with a six-year mandate—part of its membership being elected every two years). The President of the Republic is empowered to appoint a head of government. Provision is also made for the establishment of a Constitutional Council and a Supreme Islamic Council (both of which were inaugurated in 1992), as well as an Economic and Social Council.

The Constitution states that the official language is Arabic, and that the national languages are Arabic, Poular, Wolof and Solinke.

The Government

HEAD OF STATE

President: Col MAAWIYA OULD SID'AHMED TAYA (took office 12 December 1984; elected President 17 January 1992; re-elected 12 December 1997).

COUNCIL OF MINISTERS
(September 2000)

Prime Minister: CHEIKH EL AVIA OULD MOHAMED KHOUNA.

Minister Counsellor to the Presidency: AHMED OULD SIDI BABA.

Minister of Foreign Affairs and Co-operation: AHMED OULD SID'AHMED.

Minister of Defence: KABA OULD ELEWA.

Minister of Justice: LEMRABOTT SIDI MOHAMED OULD CHEIKH AHMED.

Minister of the Interior, Posts and Telecommunications: DAH OULD ABDELJELIL.

Minister of Finance: KAMARA ALY GUELADIO.

Minister of Fisheries and Marine Economy: MOHAMED EL MOCTAR OULD ZAMEL.

Minister of Economic and Development Affairs: MOHAMED OULD NANNI.

Minister of Trade, Handicrafts and Tourism: DIOP ABDOUL HAMET.

Minister of National Education: SID'EL MOCTAR OULD NAGI.

Minister of Industry and Mines: ISHAGH OULD RAJEL.

Minister of Equipment and Transport: BA AMADOU RACINE.

Minister of Culture and Islamic Affairs: ISSELMOU OULD SIDI MOUSTAPHA.

Minister of the Civil Service, Labour, Youth and Sports: BABA OULD SIDI.

Minister of Water and Energy: CHEIKH AHMED OULD EZZAHAF.

Minister of Rural Development and the Environment: AHMEDY OULD HAMADY.

Minister of Health and Social Affairs: MOHAMED SALEM OULD MERZOUG.

Minister of Communication and Relations with Parliament: RACHID OULD SALEH.

Minister, Secretary-General of the Presidency: SIDI MOHAMED OULD BOUBACAR.

Minister, Secretary-General of the Government: BA SILEYE.

President of the Court of Audit: MOHAMED LEMINE OULD GUIG.

Secretary of State, in charge of Civil Status: KHADIJETOU MINT BOUBOU.

Secretary of State for Literacy and Basic Education: DEDDOUD OULD ABDELLAHI.

Secretary of State, in charge of Women's Issues: MINTATA MINT HEDEID.

Secretary of State, in charge of Union of the Arab Maghreb Affairs: CHEYAKH OULD ELY.

Secretary of State, in charge of the Development and Promotion of Information Technology: FATIMETOU MINT MOHAMED SALECK.

MINISTRIES

Office of the President: Présidence de la République, BP 184, Nouakchott; tel. 25-23-17.

Ministry of the Civil Service, Labour, Youth and Sports: Nouakchott.

Ministry of Culture and Islamic Affairs: BP 223, Nouakchott; tel. 25-11-30.

Ministry of Defence: BP 184, Nouakchott; tel. 25-20-20.

Ministry of Economic and Development Affairs: BP 238, Nouakchott; tel. 25-16-12; fax 25-51-10.

Ministry of Equipment and Transport: BP 237, Nouakchott; tel. 25-33-37.

Ministry of Finance: BP 181, Nouakchott; tel. 25-20-20.

Ministry of Fisheries and Marine Economy: BP 137, Nouakchott; tel. 25-24-76; fax 25-31-46.

Ministry of Foreign Affairs and Co-operation: BP 230, Nouakchott; tel. 25-26-82; fax 25-28-60.

Ministry of Health and Social Affairs: BP 177, Nouakchott; tel. 25-20-52; fax 25-22-68.

Ministry of Industry and Mines: BP 387, Nouakchott; tel. 25-33-37; fax 25-35-82.

Ministry of the Interior, Posts and Telecommunications: BP 195, Nouakchott; tel. 25-20-20.

Ministry of Justice: BP 350, Nouakchott; tel. 25-10-83.

Ministry of National Education: BP 387, Nouakchott; tel. 25-12-37; fax 25-12-22.

Ministry of Rural Development and the Environment: BP 366, Nouakchott; tel. 25-15-00; fax 25-74-75.

Ministry of Trade, Handicrafts and Tourism: BP 182, Nouakchott; tel. 25-35-72; fax 25-76-71.

Ministry of Water and Energy: Nouakchott; tel. 25-26-88; fax 25-26-99.

Office of the Secretary-General of the Government: BP 184, Nouakchott.

President and Legislature

PRESIDENT

Election, 12 December 1997

	Votes	% of total
MAAWIYA OULD SID'AHMED TAYA . . .	801,190	90.94
MOHAMED LEMINE CH'BIH OULD CHEIKH MELAININE	61,869	7.02
MOULAYE EL HASSAN OULD JEYID . . .	8,165	0.93
MOHAMED MAHMOUD OULD MAH . . .	6,443	0.73
KANE AMADOU MOKHTAR	3,342	0.38
Total	**881,009**	**100.00**

In addition, there were 19,191 blank or invalid votes.

SENATE

President: DIENG BOUBOU FARBA.

Elections to the 56-member Senate took place on 3 and 10 April 1992. It was reported that 36 candidates of the Democratic and Social Republican Party (DSRP) were elected; 17 seats were won by independent candidates, and a further three senators were to represent the interests of Mauritanians resident abroad. Part of the Senate is subject to re-election every two years: accordingly, elections for 17 senators took place on 15 and 22 April 1994, while elections for the three representatives of Mauritanians abroad were conducted by the Senate on 14 May. The DSRP retained its majority in the upper house following these elections and those held on 12 and 19 April 1996 for 18 senatorial seats. At elections to 18 of the Senate's seats on 17 April 1998 one seat was secured by an independent candidate and the remainder were taken by members of the DSRP. Partial elections to the Senate took place on 7 and 14 April 2000; the Union for Democracy and Progress and the National Union for Democracy and Development each secured one seat, three seats were won by independent candidates and the remaining 13 were taken by the DSRP.

NATIONAL ASSEMBLY

President: Commdt (retd) CHEIKH SID'AHMED OULD BABA.

General Election, 11 and 18 October 1996

	Seats
Democratic and Social Republican Party	71
Action for Change	1
Rally for Democracy and National Unity	1
Independent	6
Total	**79**

Advisory Councils

Constitutional Council: f. 1992; includes six mems, three nominated by the Head of State and three designated by the Presidents of the Senate and National Assembly; Pres. DIDI OULD BOUNAAMA; Sec.-Gen. MOHAMED OULD M'REIZIG.

Supreme Islamic Council (al-Majlis al-Islamiya al-A'la'): f. 1992; Chair. MOHAMED MOKTAR OULD M'BALAH.

There is provision in the 1991 Constitution for the establishment of an Economic and Social Council.

Political Organizations

There are currently about 21 officially registered parties, among which the most influential are:

Action for Change (AC): f. 1995 to represent the interests of Harratin (black moors who had formerly been slaves); Leader MESSAOUD OULD BOULKHEIR; Sec.-Gen. IBRAHIM ASSAR.

Alliance for Justice and Democracy: f. 2000; breakaway group from AC; Leaders ALPHA DIALLO, ABDOULAYE KEBE.

Democratic Centre Party (DCP): Leader MOULAYE MOHAMED.

Democratic and Social Republican Party (DSRP): tel. 25-58-55; internet www.prds.mr; f. 1991; absorbed Movement of Independent Democrats in 1995; Leader Col MAAWIYA OULD SID'AHMED TAYA; Sec.-Gen. MOHAMED YEHDIH OULD MOCTAR EL HASSAN.

Mauritanian Party for Renewal (MPR): f. 1991; Leader MOULAYE EL HASSAN OULD JEYID.

National Union for Democracy and Development (NUDD): f. 1997; Leader TIDJANE KOITA.

People's Progressive Party (PPP): f. 1991; Leader TALEB OULD JIDDOU; Sec.-Gen. MOHAMED HASSAOUD OULD ISMAEL.

Popular Front: f. 1998; social-liberal; Leader MOHAMED LEMINE CH'BIH OULD CHEIKH MELAININE.

Rally for Democracy and National Unity (RDNU): f. 1991; Chair. AHMED OULD SIDI BABA.

Socialist and Democratic People's Union (SDPU): f. 1991; Leader MOHAMED MAHMOUD OULD MAH.

Union for Democracy and Progress (UDP): f. 1993; Pres. EL ARABY OULD KERKOUB; Sec.-Gen. SIDI OULD AHMED DEYA.

Union of Democratic Forces (UDF): BP 5290, Nouakchott; tel. 25-66-96; fax 25-65-70; e-mail mailbox@ufd-en.org; internet www.ufd-en.org; f. 1991; restructured as the UDF—New Era (following internal divisions) in 1994; divided into two factions in 1998, one led by AHMED OULD DADDAH and the other by MOUSTAPHA OULD BEDREDDINE.

United Social Democratic Party (USDP): f. 1995; Leader MOHAMED LEMIND OULD MOHAMED BABOU.

Unauthorized but influential is the Islamic **Ummah Party** (the Constitution prohibits the operation of religious political organizations), founded in 1991 and led by Imam SIDI YAHYA. The clandestine **Forces de libération africaine de Mauritanie (FLAM)** was formed in 1983 to represent black Africans in Mauritania.

Diplomatic Representation

EMBASSIES IN MAURITANIA

Algeria: BP 625, Nouakchott; tel. 25-40-07; Ambassador: ABDELKRIM BEN HOCINE.

China, People's Republic: BP 196, Nouakchott; Ambassador: ZHANE JUNQI.

Congo, Democratic Republic: BP 487, Nouakchott; tel. 25-28-36; e-mail ambardc.rim@caramail.com; Chargé d'affaires a.i. TSHIBASU MFUAD.

Egypt: BP 176, Nouakchott; Ambassador: MOHAMED WAGI EL JIBALY.

France: BP 231, rue Ahmed Ould M'Hamed, Nouakchott; tel. 25-17-40; Ambassador: JEAN-PAUL TAIX.

Gabon: BP 38, Nouakchott; tel. 25-29-19; Ambassador: JACQUES BONAVENTURE ESSONGHE.

Germany: BP 372, Nouakchott; tel. 25-17-29; fax 25-17-22; Ambassador: Dr STEPHAN KRIER.

Iraq: Nouakchott; tel. 25-20-55; fax 25-49-61; Chargé d'affaires a.i.: KADHM ABD AL-HAMID ERHADHY.

Israel: Tevragh-Zenia Ilot-A-516, Nouakchott; tel.25-46-10; fax 25-46-12; e-mail nouakchott@israel.org; Ambassador: FREDDY EYTAN.

Korea, Republic: BP 324, Nouakchott; tel. 25-37-86; fax 25-44-43; Chargé d'affaires a.i.: WON CHOL-KIM.

Morocco: BP 621, Nouakchott; tel. 25-14-11; Ambassador: ABDERRAHMANE BEN OMAR.

Nigeria: BP 367, Nouakchott; BALLA MOHAMED SANI.

Qatar: BP 609, Nouakchott; tel. 25-23-99; fax 25-68-87; Ambassador: SHAMLAN MARZOUK ASH-SHAMLAN.

Russia: BP 251, Nouakchott; tel. 25-19-73; fax 25-57-96; Ambassador: VALERII SUKHIN.

Saudi Arabia: BP 498, Nouakchott; tel. 25-26-33; Ambassador: MOHAMED AL FADH EL ISSA.

Senegal: BP 611, Nouakchott; Ambassador: (vacant).

Spain: BP 232, Nouakchott; tel. 25-20-80; fax 25-40-88; Ambassador: ENRIQUE RUIZ MOLERO.

Tunisia: BP 681, Nouakchott; tel. 25-28-71; Ambassador: ABDEL WEHAB JEMAL.

USA: BP 222, Nouakchott; tel. 25-26-60; fax 25-25-89; Ambassador: TIMBERLAKE FOSTER.

Judicial System

The Code of Law was promulgated in 1961 and subsequently modified to integrate modern law with Islamic institutions and practices. The main courts comprise three courts of appeal, 10 regional tribunals, two labour tribunals and 53 departmental civil courts. A revenue court has jurisdiction in financial matters.

Shari'a (Islamic) law was introduced in February 1980. A special Islamic court was established in March of that year, presided over by a magistrate of Islamic law, assisted by two counsellors and two *ulemas* (Muslim jurists and interpreters of the Koran).

Supreme Court: Palais de Justice, Nouakchott; tel. 25-21-63; f. 1961; intended to ensure the independence of the judiciary; the court is competent in juridical, administrative and electoral matters; Pres. MAHFODH OULD LEMRABOTT.

Court of Audit (Cour des Comptes): Nouakchott; audits all govt institutions; Pres. MOHAMED LEMINE OULD GUIG.

Religion

ISLAM

Islam is the official religion, and the population are almost entirely Muslims of the Malekite rite. The major religious groups are the Tijaniya and the Qadiriya. Chinguetti, in the region of Adrar, is the seventh Holy Place in Islam.

CHRISTIANITY

Roman Catholic Church

Mauritania comprises the single diocese of Nouakchott, directly responsible to the Holy See. The Bishop participates in the Bishops' Conference of Senegal, Mauritania, Cape Verde and Guinea-Bissau, based in Dakar, Senegal. At 31 December 1998 there were an estimated 4,500 adherents, mainly non-nationals, in the country.

Bishop of Nouakchott: Rt Rev. MARTIN ALBERT HAPPE, Evêché, BP 5377, Nouakchott; tel. 25-04-27; fax 25-37-51.

The Press

Ach-Chaab: BP 371-618, Nouakchott; tel. 25-29-40; daily; Arabic; also publ. in French (**Horizons**); publ. by Agence Mauritanienne de l'Information; Dir-Gen. MOHAMED EL-HAFED OULD MAHAM.

Le Calame: BP 1059, Nouakchott; weekly; French and Arabic; independent; Pblr HABIB OULD MAHFOUD; circ. 2,000.

L'Essor: BP 5310, Nouakchott; tel. 29-19-83; fax 25.04.07; e-mail lessor@caramail.com; monthly; economics; Dir SIDI EL-MOCTAR CHEÏGUER.

Eveil-Hebdo: BP 587, Nouakchott; f. 1991; weekly; independent; Pblr MAMADOU SY; circ. 2,000.

Journal Officiel: Ministry of Justice, BP 350, Nouakchott; fortnightly.

Nouakchott-Info: BP 1905, Nouakchott; tel. 25-02-71; fax 25-54-84; e-mail nouakinfo@toptechnology.mr; Dir CHEIKHNA OULD NENNI.

In addition, there are a number of Arabic-language newspapers, mostly published on a weekly-basis.

NEWS AGENCIES

Agence Mauritanienne de l'Information (AMI): BP 371, Nouakchott; tel. 25-29-40; fax 25-45-87; e-mail ami@mauritania.mr; internet www.mauritania.mr/amil; fmrly Agence Mauritanienne de Presse; state-controlled; Dir MOHAMED OULD HAMADY.

Foreign Bureaux

Xinhua (New China) News Agency (People's Republic of China): Nouakchott; Correspondent WANG TIANRUI.

Agence France-Presse and Reuters (UK) are also represented in Mauritania.

Publishers

Imprimerie Commerciale et Administrative de Mauritanie: BP 164, Nouakchott; textbooks, educational.

Imprimerie Nationale: BP 618, Nouakchott; tel. 25-44-38; fax 25-44-37; f. 1978; state-owned; Pres. RACHID OULD SALEH.

Government Publishing House

Société Nationale d'Impression: BP 618, Nouakchott; Pres. MOUSTAPHA SALECK OULD AHMED BRIHIM.

Broadcasting and Communications

TELECOMMUNICATIONS

Société Mauritanienne des Télécommunications (MAURITEL): BP 7000, Nouakchott; tel. 25-23-40; fax 25-17-00; e-mail webmaster@mauritel.mr; internet www.opt.mr; Dir Col. AHMEDOUL OULD MOHAMED EL KORY.

BROADCASTING

Radio

Radio de Mauritanie (RM): ave Nasser, BP 200, Nouakchott; tel. and fax 25-21-64; e-mail rm@mauritania.mr; f. 1958; state-controlled; five transmitters; radio broadcasts in Arabic, French, Sarakolé, Toucouleur and Wolof; Dir SID BRAHIM OULD HAMDINOU.

Television

Télévision de Mauritanie (TVM): BP 5522, Nouakchott; tel. 25-40-67; fax 25-40-69; Dir YESLEM OULD EBNOU ABDEN.

Finance

(cap. = capital; res = reserves; dep. = deposits; m. = million; brs = branches; amounts in ouguiyas)

BANKING

Central Bank

Banque Centrale de Mauritanie (BCM): ave de l'Indépendance, BP 623, Nouakchott; tel. 25-22-06; fax 25-27-59; f. 1973; bank of issue; cap. 200m.; Gov. MAHFODH OULD MOHAMED ALI; 4 brs.

Commercial Banks

Banque al-Baraka Mauritanienne Islamique (BAMIS): ave du Roi Fayçal, BP 650, Nouakchott; tel. 25-14-24; fax 25-16-21; f. 1985; 50% owned by al-Baraka Group (Saudi Arabia); cap. 3,700m. (Feb. 1998); Chair. CHERIF OULD ABDALLAHI; Man. Dir ABDALLAHI OULD MOKHTAR.

Banque pour le Commerce International (BCI): BP 5050, Nouakchott; tel. 29-28-76; fax 29-28-77; e-mail bci@opt.mr; Pres. and Dir-Gen. ISSELMOU OULD DIDI TAJEDINE.

Banque de l'Habitat de Mauritanie (BHM): BP 5559, Nouakchott; tel. 25-34-90; fax 25-34-95; cap. 1,425.0m., total assets 2,437.2m. (Dec. 1997); Pres. AHAMED SALEM OULD BOUNA MOKHTAR; Dir-Gen. MOUSSA FALL.

Banque Mauritanienne pour le Commerce International (BMCI): Immeuble BMCI, ave Nasser, Tevragh Zeina, BP 622, Nouakchott; tel. 25-28-26; fax 25-20-45; f. 1974; privately-owned; cap. and res 2,764.3m., total assets 16,297.4m. (Dec. 1998); Pres. MOULAYE O. HACEN ABASS; Dir-Gen. TIDIANI BEN AL-HOUSSEIN; 4 brs.

Banque Nationale de Mauritanie (BNM): ave Nasser, BP 614, Nouakchott; tel. 25-26-02; fax 25-33-97; e-mail BNM10@opt.mr; f. 1988; privately-owned; cap. and res 1,428.6m., dep. 9,031.2m. (Dec. 1997); Pres. ISMAIL OULD ABEIDNA; Man. Dir MOHAMED O. A. O. NOUEIGUED.

Chinguitty Bank: ave Nasser, Tevragh Zeina, BP 626, Nouakchott; tel. 25-21-73; fax 25-33-82; f. 1972; 50% state-owned, 50% owned by Libyan Arab Foreign Bank; cap. and res 2,186.6m., total assets 6,797.7m. (Dec. 1998); Pres. HASSEN OULD SALEH; Gen. Man. DAW AMAR ABDALLA; br. at Nouadhibou.

Générale de Banque de Mauritanie pour l'Investissement et le Commerce (GBM): ave de l'Indépendance, BP 5558, Nouakchott; tel. 25-36-36; fax 25-46-47; f. 1996; privately-owned; Pres. and Gen. Man. MOHAMED OULD BOUAMATOU.

INSURANCE

Assurances Générales de Mauritanie: BP 2141, avenue Charles de Gaulle TZA Ilot A 667, Nouakchott; tel. 29-29-00; fax 29-29-11; Man. MOULAYE ELY BOUAMATOU.

Cie Nationale d'Assurance et de Réassurance (NASR): 12 ave Gamal-Abdel-Nasser, BP 163, Nouakchott; tel. 25-26-50; fax 25-18-18; f. 1994; state-owned; Pres. ABDELLAHI OULD MOCTAR; Dir-Gen. ABDERRAHMANE OULD BOUBOU.

Société Anonyme d'Assurances de Mauritanie (SAAR): BP 2841, Nouakchott; tel. 25-30-56.

TAAMIN: BP 5164, Nouakchott; tel. 29-40-02; fax 29-40-02; e-mail taamin@toptechnology.mr; Dir-Gen. MOULAYE EL HACEL OULD MOCTAR-HACEN.

Trade and Industry

DEVELOPMENT ORGANIZATIONS

Agence Française de Développement (AFD): quartier des Ambassades, BP 211, Nouakchott; tel. 25-23-09; Dir MARC JAUDOIN.

Mission Française de Coopération: BP 203, Nouakchott; tel. 25-21-21; administers bilateral aid from France; Dir MAURICE DADOUCHE.

Société Arabe Mauritano-Libyenne de Développement Agricole (SAMALIDA): BP 658, Nouakchott; tel. 25-37-15; f. 1980; cap. UM 350m.; 51% state-owned, 49% owned by Govt of Libya; Dir-Gen. O. TURKI.

Société Nationale pour le Développement Rural (SONADER): BP 321, Nouakchott; tel. 25-40-56; fax 25-32-86; e-mail sonader@toptechnology.mr; internet www.sonader.mr; Dir-Gen. SIDI MOHAMED OULD MEINE.

CHAMBER OF COMMERCE

Chambre de Commerce, d'Agriculture, d'Elevage, d'Industrie et des Mines de Mauritanie: BP 215, Nouakchott; tel. 25-22-14; f. 1954; Chair. KANE YAYA.

INDUSTRIAL AND TRADE ASSOCIATIONS

NAFTEC, SA: BP 679, Nouakchott; tel. 25-26-51; fax 25-25-42; f. 1980; cap. UM 120m.; govt is a minority shareholder; import and distribution of petroleum products; fmrly Société Mauritanienne de Commercialisation des Produits Pétroliers; Dir-Gen. BRAHIM NOUH.

Société Mauritanienne de Commercialisation de Poissons, SA (SMCP): Avenida Media, BP 259, Nouadhibou; tel. 24-53-90; fax 24-55-66; f. 1984; cap. UM 500m.; govt is a minority shareholder; until 1992 monopoly exporter of demersal fish and crustaceans; Pres. MOHAMED SALEM OULD LEKHAL; Dir-Gen. BOIJEL OULD HEMEID.

Société Nationale d'Importation et d'Exportation (SONIMEX): BP 290, Nouakchott; tel. 25-14-72; f. 1966; cap. UM 914m.; 74% state-owned; import of foodstuffs and textiles, distribution of essential consumer goods, export of gum-arabic; Pres. MOHAMED KHATTRY OULD SEGANE; Dir-Gen. BABAHA OULD AHMED YOURA.

EMPLOYERS' ORGANIZATION

Confédération Générale des Employeurs de Mauritanie (CGEM): BP 383, Nouakchott; tel. 25-19-90; fax 25-91-08; e-mail germe@opt.mr; f. 1974; professional asscn for all employers active in Mauritania; Pres. SIDI MOHAMED ABASS; Sec.-Gen. CHEIKH OULD MOHAMED HACEN.

UTILITIES

Electricity and Water

Société Nationale d'Eau et d'Electricité (SONELEC): ave de l'Indépendance, BP 355, Nouakchott; tel. 25-23-08; fax 25-39-95; f. 1968; cap. UM 400m.; state-owned; production and distribution of electricity and water; Dir-Gen. Col SIDI OULD RIHA.

Gas

Société Mauritanienne des Gaz (SOMAGAZ): POB 5089, Nouakchott; tel. 25-18-71; fax 25-31-74; Dir-Gen. BAZEIDINE OULD NE.

MAJOR COMPANIES

The following are some of the largest companies in terms of either capital investment or employment:

Cie Mauritano-Coréenne de Pêche (COMACOP): BP 527, Nouakchott; tel. 25-37-47; f. 1977; cap. UM 230m.; fishing and freezer complex; Chair. and Man. Dir ABDOU OULD AL HACHEME.

Guelb Moghrein Mines d'Akjoujt (GEMAK): BP 9, Akjoujt; tel. 25-64-23; fax 26-63-20; f. 1991 as Mines d'Or d'Akjoujt (MORAK); cap. US $30m.; 50% owned by SAMIN, 50% by General Gold Resources (Australia); exploitation of gold, copper and other ores at Akjoujt; Dep. Gen. Man. MOCTAR OULD MOHAMED EL HACEN.

NAFTAL, SA: BP 73, Nouadhibou; tel. 74-52-40; f. 1981 as Société Mauritanienne des Industries de Raffinage (SOMIR); cap. UM 4,600m.; operates a petroleum refinery and negotiates overseas transactions; Chair. ABDELMADJID KAZI TANI; Man. Dir MOHAMED OTHMANI.

Société Algéro-Mauritanienne des Pêches (ALMAP): BP 321, Nouadhibou; tel. 74-51-48; f. 1974; cap. UM 180m.; 51% state-owned, 49% owned by Govt of Algeria; fishing, processing of fishery products; Dir BRAHIM OULD BOIDAHA; 500 employees.

Société Arabe du Fer et de l'Acier (SAFA): BP 114, Nouadhibou; tel. 24-56-03; f. 1984; cap. UM 450m.; 33% owned by SNIM; steel rolling mill; Chair. MOHAMED SALECK OULD HEYINE; Man. Dir AHMEDOU OULD JIDDOU.

Société Arabe des Industries Métallurgiques (SAMIA): BP 1248, Nouakchott; tel. 25-44-55; fax 29-05-85; f. 1974; cap. UM 762m.; 50% owned by SNIM, 50% by Kuwait Real Estate Investment Consortium; extraction of gypsum and production of plaster of Paris; Man. Dir MOHAMED SALEM OULD CHEIKH.

Société Arabe Libyenne-Mauritanienne des Ressources Maritimes (SALIMAUREM): BP 75, Nouadhibou; tel. 74-52-41; f. 1978; cap. UM 2,300m.; 50% state-owned, 50% owned by Libyan-Arab Finance Co; fishing and fish processing; freezer factory; Chair. AHMED OULD GHNAHALLA; Dir-Gen. SALA MOHAMED ARIBI.

Société Arabe des Mines de l'Inchiri (SAMIN): BP 9, Akjoujt; tel. 76-71-04; f. 1981; cap. UM 3,276m.; 37.5% state-owned, 62.5% owned by Arab interests; Chair. TAHER TABET; Man. Dir SIDI MALEK.

Société de Construction et de Gestion Immobilière de Mauritanie (SOCOGIM): BP 28, Nouakchott; tel. 25-17-75; f. 1974; cap. UM 583m.; 89% state-owned; Chair. ABDALLAH OULD MOHAMEDEN; Man. Dir AHMED OULD MOHAMED KHAIROU.

Société Mauritanienne d'Allumettes (SOMAURAL): BP 44, Nouakchott; tel. 25-24-81; fax 25-49-33; f. 1971; matches; Chair. ABDALLAHI OULD NOUEIGUED.

Société Nationale Industrielle et Minière (SNIM): BP 42, Nouadhibou; tel. 24-51-74; fax 24-53-96; f. 1972; cap. UM 9,059.5m.; 80% state-owned; balance held by Islamic Development Bank and private Kuwait and Jordan interests; exploitation, processing and marketing of minerals; Chair. CHEIKH SID'EL MOKTAR OULD CHEIKH ABDALLAHI; Man. Dir MOHAMED SALECK OULD HEYINE; 4,400 employees.

TRADE UNIONS

Confédération Générale des Travailleurs de Mauritanie: Nouakchott; f. 1992; obtained official recognition in 1994.

Confédération Libre des Travailleurs de Mauritanie: Nouakchott; f. 1995; Sec.-Gen. SAMORI OULD BEYI.

Union des Travailleurs de Mauritanie (UTM): Bourse du Travail, BP 630, Nouakchott; f. 1961; Sec.-Gen. MOHAMED BRAHIM (acting); 45,000 mems.

Transport

RAILWAYS

A 670-km railway connects the iron-ore deposits at Zouérate with Nouadhibou; a 40-km extension services the reserves at El Rhein, and a 30-km extension those at M'Haoudat. Motive power is diesel-electric. The Société Nationale Industrielle et Minière (SNIM) operates one of the longest (2.4 km) and heaviest (22,000 metric tons) trains in the world.

SNIM—Direction du Chemin de Fer et du Port: BP 42, Nouadhibou; tel. 74-51-74; fax 74-53-96; e-mail m.khalifa.beyah@snim.com; f. 1963; Gen. Man. MOHAMED SALECK OULD HEYINE; Dir KHALIFA OULD BEYAH.

ROADS

In 1996 there were about 7,660 km of roads and tracks, of which main roads comprised some 2,800 km, and 11.3% of the road network was paved. The 1,100-km TransMauritania highway, completed in 1985, links Nouakchott with Néma in the east of the country. Plans exist for the construction of a 7,400-km highway, linking Nouakchott with the Libyan port of Tubruq (Tobruk). In August 1999 the Islamic Development Bank granted Mauritania a loan worth US $9.4m. to help finance the rebuilding of the Chouk-Kiffa road.

Société Mauritanienne des Transports (SOMATRA): Nouakchott; tel. 25-29-53; f. 1975; Pres. CHEIKH MALAININE ROBERT; Dir-Gen. MAMADOU SOULEYMANE KANE.

INLAND WATERWAYS

The River Senegal is navigable in the wet season by small coastal vessels as far as Kayes (Mali) and by river vessels as far as Kaédi; in the dry season as far as Rosso and Boghé, respectively. The major river ports are at Rosso, Kaédi and Gouraye.

SHIPPING

The principal port, at Point-Central, 10 km south of Nouadhibou, is almost wholly occupied with mineral exports. There is a commercial and fishing port at Nouadhibou. The deep-water Port de l'Amitié at Nouakchott, built and maintained with assistance from the People's Republic of China, was opened in 1986. The port, which has a total capacity of 1m. metric tons annually, handled 776,608 tons in 1997 (compared with 479,791 tons in 1990); the port cleared 429 vessels in 1997 (compared with 244 in 1990). In 1998 Mauritania's merchant fleet consisted of 140 vessels and had a total displacement of 47,959 grt.

Port Autonome de Nouakchott: BP 267/5103, El Mina, Nouakchott; tel. 25-14-53; fax 25-16-15; f. 1986; deep-water port; Dir-Gen. MOHAMED MAHMOUD OULD DEH.

Port Autonome de Nouadhibou: BP 236, Nouadhibou; tel. 74-51-34; f. 1973; state-owned; Pres. HABIB ELY; Dir-Gen. HAMADA OULD DERWICH.

Shipping Companies

Cie Mauritanienne de Navigation Maritime (COMAUNAM): 119 ave Gamal-Abdel-Nasser, BP 799, Nouakchott; tel. 25-36-34; fax 25-25-04; f. 1973; 51% state-owned, 49% owned by govt of Algeria; nat. shipping co; forwarding agent, stevedoring; Chair. MOHAND TIGHILT; Dir-Gen. KAMIL ABDELKADER.

Société d'Acconage et de Manutention en Mauritanie (SAMMA): BP 258, Nouadhibou; tel. 74-52-63; fax 74-52-37; f. 1960; freight and handling, shipping agent, forwarding agent, stevedoring; Dir-Gen. DIDI O. BIHA; Dept Chief SADEGH O. BABA.

Société Générale de Consignation et d'Entreprises Maritimes (SO GE CO): BP 351, Nouakchott; tel. 25-22-02; fax 25-39-03; f. 1973; shipping agent, forwarding, stevedoring; Man. Dir SID'-AHMED ABEIDNA.

Société Mauritanienne pour la Pêche et la Navigation (SMPN): BP 40254, Nouakchott; tel. 25-36-38; fax 25-37-87; e-mail smpn@toptechnology.mr; Dir-Gen. ABDALLAHI OULD ISMAIL.

VOTRA: BP 454, Nouakchott; tel. 25-24-10; fax 25-31-41; Dir-Gen. ABDERRAHMANE OULD CHOUAÏB.

CIVIL AVIATION

There are international airports at Nouakchott and Nouadhibou, an airport at Néma, and 23 smaller airstrips. Facilities at Nouakchott were expanded considerably in the late 1980s and early 1990s.

Air Afrique: BP 51, Nouakchott; tel. 25-25-45; fax 25-49-44; see under Côte d'Ivoire.

Air Mauritanie (Société d'Economie Mixte Air Mauritanie): BP 41, Nouakchott; tel. 25-22-11; fax 25-64-70; f. 1974; 60% state-owned, 20% owned by Air Afrique; domestic and regional passenger and cargo services; Dir-Gen. SIDI ZEIN.

Tourism

Mauritania's principal tourist attractions are its historical sites, several of which have been listed by UNESCO under its World Heritage Programme, and its game reserves and national parks. Some 13,000 tourists visited Mauritania in 1986. Receipts from tourism in 1993 totalled an estimated US $15m.

Direction du Tourisme: BP 246, Nouakchott; tel. 25-35-72; f. 1988; Dir KANE ISMAILA.

SOMASERT: BP 42, Nouadhibou; tel. 74-90-42; fax 74-90-43; subsidiary of SNIM responsible for promoting tourism, managing hotels and organizing tours; Dir-Gen. ABDERRAHMANE OULD DOUA.

Defence

In August 1999 the total armed forces numbered an estimated 15,650 men: army 15,000, navy about 500, air force 150. Full-time membership of paramilitary forces totalled about 5,000. Military service is by authorized conscription, and lasts for two years.

Defence Expenditure: Budgeted at UM 5,400m. in 1999.

Chief of Staff of the Armed Forces: Col MOULAYE OULD BOULKHREIS.

Chief of Staff of the National Gendarmerie: Lt-Col NE OULD ABDEL MALEK.

Education

Primary education, which is officially compulsory, begins at six years of age and lasts for six years. In 1996 total enrolment at primary schools was equivalent to 79% of children in the relevant age-group (84% of boys; 75% of girls). Secondary education begins at 12 years of age and lasts for six years, comprising two cycles of three years each. The total enrolment at secondary schools in 1995 was equivalent to only 16% of children in the appropriate age-group (21% of boys; 11% of girls). At the time of the 1988 census the average rate of adult illiteracy was 64.9% (males 53.9%; females 75.4%). According to UNESCO estimates, adult illiteracy averaged 62.5% (males 51.3%; females 73.7%) in 1995. A plan to make Arabic the compulsory first language in all schools (which had been postponed in 1979, following protests from the French-speaking south) was reintroduced in April 1988. In 1997/98 a total of 9,256 students were enrolled at Mauritania's four higher education institutions (including the University of Nouakchott, opened in 1983). Expenditure on education in 1995 was equivalent to 16.2% of total government expenditure in that year. In April 1995 the World Bank approved a US $35m. loan to improve the country's educational system.

Bibliography

Bader, C., and Lefort, F. *Mauritanie, la vie réconciliée.* Paris, Fayard, 1990.

Balta, P., and Rulleau, C. *Le Grand Maghreb, des indépendances à l'an 2000.* Paris, Editions La Découverte, 1990.

Belvaude, C. *La Mauritanie.* Paris, Editions Karthala, 1989.

Calderini, S., Cortese, D., and Webb, J. L. A. *Mauritania.* Oxford, ABC Clio, 1992.

Clausen, U. *Demokratisierung in Mauritanien: Einfuehrung und Dokumente.* Hamburg, Deutsches Orient-Institut, 1993.

de Chassey, C. *Mauritania 1900–1975.* Paris, Harmattan, 1984.

Garnier, C., and Ermont, P. *Désert fertile: un nouvel état, la Mauritanie.* Paris, Hachette, 1960.

Gerteiny, A. G. *Mauritania.* London, Pall Mall; New York, Praeger, 1967.

Hudson, S. *Travels in Mauritania.* London, Virgin Books, 1990.

Human Rights Watch, Africa. *Mauritania's Campaign of Terror: State-Sponsored Repression of Black Africans.* New York, 1994.

Ould-May, M. *Global Restructuring and Peripheral States: The Carrot and the Stick in Mauritania.* Lanham, MD, Littlefield Adams, 1996.

Pazzanika, A. G. *Historical Dictionary of Mauritania.* Lanham, MD, Scarecrow Press, 1996.

Rimmer, D. *The Economies of West Africa.* London, Weidenfeld and Nicolson, 1984.

Toupet, C., and Pitte, J.-R. *La Mauritanie.* Paris, PUF, 1977.

Westebbe, R. M. *The Economy of Mauritania.* New York and London, Praeger, 1971.

Wolff, W. J., van der Land, J., Nienhuis, P. H., and de Wilde, P. A. W. J. (Eds). *Ecological Studies in the Coastal Waters of Mauritania.* London, Kluwer Academic Publishers, 1993.

MAURITIUS

Physical and Social Geography

The Republic of Mauritius, comprising the islands of Mauritius and Rodrigues, together with the Agalega Islands and the Cargados Carajos Shoals, lies in the Indian Ocean 800 km east of Madagascar. The island of Mauritius covers 1,865 sq km (720 sq miles) in area. It is a volcanic island, consisting of a plain rising from the north-east to the highest point on the island, Piton de la Rivière Noire (827 m above sea-level) in the south-west, interspersed by abrupt volcanic peaks and gorges, and is almost completely surrounded by a coral reef. Including Rodrigues and its other islands, the republic occupies a land area of 2,040 sq km (788 sq miles).

The climate is sub-tropical maritime, but with two distinct seasons; additionally, the warm dry coastal areas contrast with the cool rainy interior. Mauritius and Rodrigues are vulnerable to cyclones, particularly between September and May.

Rodrigues, a volcanic island of 104 sq km (40 sq miles) surrounded by a coral reef, lies 585 km east of the island of Mauritius. Its population was enumerated at 34,204 in the 1990 census, and was estimated to number 35,332 in December 1998. Mauritius has two dependencies (together covering 71 sq km with 167 inhabitants at the 1990 census, and an estimated population of 170 in December 1998): Agalega, two islands 935 km north of Mauritius; and the Cargados Carajos Shoals (or St Brandon Islands), 22 islets without permanent inhabitants but used as a fishing station, 370 km north-north-east of Mauritius.

Mauritius claims sovereignty over Tromelin, a small island without permanent inhabitants, 556 km to the north-west. This claim is disputed by Madagascar and France. Mauritius also seeks the return of Diego Garcia, a coral atoll in the Chagos Archipelago, about 1,900 km to the north-east. The archipelago was formerly administered by Mauritius but in 1965 became part (and in 1976 all) of the British Indian Ocean Territory (see p. 229).

The population of Mauritius was enumerated at 1,058,942 at the July 1990 census, and was officially estimated at 1,174,400 in mid-1999, giving a density of 596.4 inhabitants per sq km. During 1985–95 the population increased at an average annual rate of only 1.0%, owing, in part, to higher emigration and a decline in the birth rate. Almost 42% of the population reside in the urban area extending from Port Louis (the capital and business centre) on the north-west coast, to Curepipe in the island's centre. The population is of mixed origin, including people of European, African, Indian and Chinese descent. English is the official language, and Creole (Kreol), derived from French, the lingua franca. The most widely spoken languages at the 1990 census were Creole (35.9%) and Bhojpuri (32.5%).

Recent History

Revised by the Editor

The islands of Mauritius and Rodrigues passed from French into British control in 1810. Subsequent settlement came mainly from east Africa and India, and the European population has remained predominantly francophone.

The Indian community in Mauritius took little part in politics until 1947, when the franchise was extended to adults over the age of 21 years who could establish simple literacy in any language. This expansion of the electorate deprived the Franco-Mauritian and Creole communities of their political dominance, and the Mauritius Labour Party (MLP), led by Dr (later Sir) Seewoosagur Ramgoolam, consolidated the new political role of the Indian community. The Parti Mauricien Social Démocrate (PMSD) emerged to represent traditional Franco-Mauritian and Creole interests, under the leadership of Gaëtan (later Sir Gaëtan) Duval. With impetus from Ramgoolam's MLP, Mauritius proceeded to independence, within the Commonwealth, on 12 March 1968, with Ramgoolam as prime minister of a coalition government which was subsequently extended to include the PMSD.

In November 1965 the United Kingdom transferred the Chagos Archipelago (including the atoll of Diego Garcia), a Mauritian dependency about 2,000 km (1,250 miles) north-east of the main island, to the newly-created British Indian Ocean Territory (see p. 229). Mauritius has subsequently campaigned for the return of the islands, which have been developed as a major US military base.

From 1970, the strongest opposition to the Ramgoolam coalition came from a newly-formed left-wing group, the Mouvement Militant Mauricien (MMM), led by Paul Bérenger. The MMM attracted considerable public support during a period of labour unrest, and at the general election held in December 1976 the MMM emerged as the largest single party in the legislative assembly, although with insufficient seats to form a government. Ramgoolam, however, was able to form a new coalition with the PMSD, which, despite resurgences of public disorder, retained power for its full legislative term.

THE JUGNAUTH COALITIONS, 1982–95

At elections to the legislative assembly in June 1982, an alliance of the MMM and Parti Socialiste Mauricien (PSM) won all 60 elective seats on the main island. Anerood (later Sir Anerood) Jugnauth became prime minister and appointed Bérenger as minister of finance. In March 1983, however, following discord within the cabinet over Bérenger's stringent economic policies and his attempts to make Creole (Kreol) the official language (despite the Indian descent of the majority of the population), Bérenger and his supporters resigned. Jugnauth formed a new government, and in early April formed a new party, the Mouvement Socialiste Militant, which, in May, amalgamated with the PSM and was renamed the Mouvement Socialiste Mauricien (MSM). However, the new government lacked a majority in the legislative assembly, and Jugnauth was obliged to dissolve the assembly in June. At a general election in August, an alliance comprising the MSM, the MLP and the PMSD, obtained a decisive majority. Jugnauth remained as prime minister, with Duval as deputy prime minister.

In December 1983 draft legislation that would allow Mauritius to become a republic failed to gain sufficient support in the legislative assembly, owing, in part, to disagreements over the extent of the powers to be granted to the president of the proposed republic. In the same month Sir Seewoosagur Ramgoolam was appointed governor-general. Satcam (later Sir Satcam) Boolell subsequently became leader of the MLP, but was dismissed from the cabinet in February 1984. In response, the MLP withdrew from the coalition; however, a number of MLP deputies continued to support the government. During 1985 the Jugnauth government began to incur public dissatisfaction, which was increased by the introduction in April of legislation banning material that was judged to be damaging to the administration. Serious public disquiet arose in December, when four members of the legislative assembly were arrested in the Netherlands on charges of drug smuggling. In January 1986, following Jugnauth's refusal to comment on allegations that other deputies were involved in the affair, four cabinet ministers resigned. A new government formed by Jugnauth retained the political balance of the previous administration. In March five MSM deputies, including three who had resigned as ministers in January, withdrew their support from the coalition.

In June 1986, in response to pressure from within the MSM, Jugnauth appointed a commission of inquiry to investigate the drugs scandal. In the following month, however, three ministers resigned, citing lack of confidence in Jugnauth's leadership. The government retaliated by expelling 11 MSM dissidents from the party. In November, following a report by the commission of inquiry into the drugs affair, four MSM deputies resigned from the legislative assembly, thus reducing the MSM/PMSD coalition's strength in the legislature to only 30 of the 62 elective seats. In the subsequent political realignment, the MMM regained the support of several deputies who had previously left the coalition. In January 1987 Jugnauth announced that a general election would take place later that year.

In March 1987 the commission of inquiry issued a further report alleging that six deputies of the MSM/PMSD alliance had been involved in drug-trafficking. In the same month further allegations associated Sir Gaëtan Duval, a deputy prime minister, with the affair. However, Duval's subsequent offer of resignation was rejected by Jugnauth. In May Diwakar Bundhun, the minister of industry, was dismissed, after openly criticizing Jugnauth. Having lost majority support in the legislative assembly, Jugnauth announced that a general election was to take place in August.

At the general election held on 30 August 1987 an electoral alliance comprising the MSM, the PMSD and the MLP won 39 of the 60 elective seats on the main island, although it received only 49.8% of total votes cast. The MMM, which campaigned with two smaller parties in an opposition alliance, won 21 seats, obtaining 48.1% of votes cast. Dr Paramhansa (Prem) Nababsingh subsequently became the leader of the MMM and of the opposition in the assembly, replacing Bérenger, who had failed to secure a seat. In September Jugnauth appointed a new council of ministers. Later that month the new government announced plans to make Mauritius a republic within the Commonwealth.

In August 1988, following a disagreement over employment policies, Sir Gaëtan Duval, the leader of the PMSD, left the government, together with his brother, Hervé Duval, the minister of industry. The opposition demanded Jugnauth's resignation in February 1989, following his expression of support for a former high commissioner to the United Kingdom, who had been arrested on drug-smuggling charges. Two attempts on Jugnauth's life (in November 1988 and March 1989) were attributed by him to criminals involved in drug-trafficking. In June Sir Gaëtan Duval was temporarily detained on suspicion of involvement in a political assassination in 1971.

In July 1990 the MMM and MSM agreed to form an alliance to contest the next general election, and to proceed with constitutional measures, which would allow Mauritius to become a republic. Under the proposed new constitution, Bérenger would assume the presidency, while Jugnauth would remain as executive prime minister, with Nababsingh as deputy prime minister. However, the draft amendments, which were submitted to the legislative assembly in mid-August, were opposed by members of the MLP (in alliance with the PMSD), and Jugnauth failed to secure the necessary parliamentary majority. He subsequently dismissed Boolell, as well as two ministers belonging to the MSM, who had refused to support the proposed amendments. A further three ministers representing the MLP also resigned, leaving only one MLP member in the government. Boolell subsequently relinquished the leadership of the MLP to Dr Navinchandra Ramgoolam (the son of Sir Seewoosagur Ramgoolam, who died in December 1985). In September 1990 Jugnauth announced the formation of a new coalition government, in which the six vacant ministerial posts were awarded to the MMM, while Nababsingh became one of the three deputy prime ministers.

In August 1991 Jugnauth dissolved the legislative assembly; the ensuing general election took place on 15 September. An alliance of the MSM, the MMM and the Mouvement des Travaillistes Démocrates (MTD) won 57 of the 62 elective seats, while the alliance of the MLP and the PMSD secured only three seats. Members of the Organisation du Peuple Rodriguais (OPR) were returned to the remaining two seats. However, members of the opposition, including Dr Ramgoolam and Sir Gaëtan Duval, alleged electoral malpractice, and refused to attend the inaugural session of the legislative assembly. Jugnauth subsequently formed a new government, to which nine representatives of the MMM (including Bérenger, who became minister of external affairs) and one representative of the MTD were appointed. Later in September Sir Gaëtan Duval resigned from the legislative assembly. In the following month the MLP/PMSD alliance refused to participate in municipal elections, in which the MSM/MMM/MTD alliance won 125 of the 126 contested seats.

In October 1991 Jugnauth announced that, subject to the approval of constitutional amendments by a majority of 75% of members of the legislative assembly, Mauritius would become a republic within the Commonwealth on 12 March 1992. However, Duval asserted that the creation of a republic would permit Jugnauth to assume absolute power, and demanded that the proposed amendments be submitted to a national referendum. In December 1991 the constitutional changes were approved by 59 of the 66 deputies in the legislative assembly. (The seven members of the MLP/PMSD alliance in the assembly refused to vote, on the grounds that the amendments provided for an increase in executive power, to the detriment of the legislature.) Under the terms of the revised constitution, the governor-general, Sir Veerasamy Ringadoo, who had been nominated by Jugnauth, was to assume the presidency for an interim period, pending the election of a president and vice-president, for a five-year term, by a simple majority of the legislative assembly (which would be renamed the national assembly). However, the MLP/PMSD alliance criticized these provisions, and demanded that the president be elected by universal suffrage. The constitution vested executive power in the prime minister, who would be appointed by the president, and would be the parliamentary member best able to command a majority in the national assembly. On 12 March 1992 Ringadoo officially became interim president, replacing the British monarch, Queen Elizabeth II, as head of state. Later that month the government announced that Cassam Uteem, the minister of industry and industrial technology and a member of the MMM, was to be nominated to the presidency after a period of three months. (Under the terms of the alliance between the MSM and the MMM, members of the MMM were to be appointed to the presidency and vice-presidency, while Jugnauth was to remain as prime minister.) Uteem was duly elected president by the national assembly in June, with Sir Rabindrah Ghurburrun as vice-president.

In October 1992 Ramgoolam announced that he was to return to the United Kingdom to complete legal studies, despite a constitutional stipulation suspending the mandate of a parliamentary member who was absent from sessions of the national assembly for a period of more than three months. Plans by Ramgoolam to return to Mauritius in time to comply with this condition were thwarted by the curtailment of a parliamentary session in December and the convening of a further session, in January 1993, without prior notice. In June, however, an attempt by the government to unseat Ramgoolam was rejected by the supreme court, which criticized the 'unreasonable' timing of the parliamentary session in January.

Following a number of disagreements between the MMM and MSM, the government coalition was further weakened in August 1993, when candidates of the PMSD secured the three vacant seats in a municipal by-election (in a constituency where the MMM traditionally attracted most support). Later in August, following an unexpected success by the PMSD in municipal elections in a constituency that traditionally favoured the MMM, a meeting between Bérenger and Ramgoolam prompted speculation that an alliance between the MMM and MLP was contemplated. Shortly afterwards, Jugnauth dismissed Bérenger from the council of ministers, on the grounds that he had repeatedly criticized government policy.

The removal of Bérenger precipitated a serious crisis within the MMM, whose political bureau decided that the other nine members of the party who held ministerial portfolios should remain in the coalition government. Led by Nababsingh, the deputy prime minister, and the minister of industry and industrial technology, Jean-Claude de l'Estrac, supporters of the pro-coalition faction announced in October 1993 that Bérenger had been suspended as secretary-general of the MMM. Bérenger and his supporters responded by expelling 11 MMM officials from the party, and subsequently obtaining a legal ban on Nababsingh and de l'Estrac from using the party name. The split in the MMM led in November to a government reshuffle, in which the remaining two MMM ministers supporting Bérenger were replaced by members of the party's pro-coalition faction.

In April 1994 the MLP and the MMM announced that they had agreed terms for an alliance to contest the next general elections. Under its provisions, Ramgoolam was to be prime minister and Bérenger deputy prime minister, with cabinet portfolios allocated on the basis of 12 ministries to the MLP and nine to the MMM. In the same month, three MPs from the MSM withdrew their support from the government.

Nababsingh and the dissident faction of the MMM, having lost Bérenger's legal challenge for the use of the party name, formed a new party, the Renouveau Militant Mauricien (RMM), which formally commenced political activity in June 1994. In the same month, Jugnauth declared that the government would remain in office to the conclusion of its mandate in September 1996. In August 1994 a number of cabinet posts were reallocated.

In November 1994, during the course of a parliamentary debate on electoral issues, Bérenger and de l'Estrac accepted a mutual challenge to resign their seats in the national assembly and to contest by-elections. In the following month the MSM indicated that it would not oppose RMM candidates in the two polls. In January 1995, however, Jugnauth unsuccessfully sought to undermine the MLP/MMM alliance by offering electoral support to the MLP. The by-elections, held in February, were both won by MLP/MMM candidates, and Bérenger was returned to the national assembly. Following these results, Jugnauth opened political negotiations with the PMSD, whose leader, Luc Xavier Duval (the son of Sir Gaëtan Duval), agreed to enter the coalition as minister of industry and industrial technology and minister of tourism. The cabinet post of attorney-general and minister of justice, previously held by Jugnauth, was also allocated to the PMSD, and Sir Gaëtan Duval accepted an appointment as economic adviser to the prime minister. As a result, however, of widespread opposition within the PMSD to participation in the coalition, Luc Xavier Duval left the government in October, and Sir Gaëtan Duval subsequently resumed the leadership of the party. The minister for Rodrigues, representing the OPR, also resigned from the cabinet.

MLP/MMM COALITION

In November 1995 the government was defeated in a parliamentary vote, requiring a two-thirds' majority to introduce a constitutional requirement for instruction in oriental languages to be provided in primary schools. Jugnauth dissolved the national assembly, and at the subsequent general election in December the MLP/MMM alliance won a decisive victory: of the 62 elected seats, the MLP secured 35 seats, the MMM obtained 25 seats and the OPR two seats. Under constitutional arrangements providing representation for unsuccessful candidates attracting the largest number of votes, Sir Gaëtan Duval re-entered the national assembly, together with two members of the Mouvement Rodriguais and a representative of Hizbullah, an Islamic fundamentalist group. Ramgoolam became prime minister of the new MLP/MMM coalition, with Bérenger as deputy prime minister with responsibility for foreign and regional relations. The more equitable distribution of the country's recent prosperity was identified as a primary aim of the new government. Sir Gaëtan Duval died in May 1996 and was succeeded in the national assembly and as leader of the PMSD by his brother, Hervé Duval, although Luc Xavier Duval continued to command a significant personal following within the party.

Evidence of strains within the MLP/MMM coalition began to emerge in June 1996, when austerity proposals, put forward by Rundheersing Bheenick, the minister of finance, in the 1995/96 budget, aroused considerable opposition from the MMM. Bheenick subsequently resigned, and the finance portfolio was

taken over by Ramgoolam until November, when an extensive reallocation of ministerial responsibilities was carried out.

THE MLP IN POWER

More serious divisions within the coalition government emerged in late 1996, when differences were reported between Ramgoolam and Bérenger over the allocation of ministerial responsibilities, and the perception by the MMM of delays in the implementation of social and economic reforms. In January 1997 rumours had begun to circulate of a possible political alliance between the MMM and the MSM, and in March it was reported that Ramgoolam intended to seek support from certain members of the PMSD should the MMM decide to withdraw from the government. Bérenger's criticism of the coalition's performance intensified in the following months, and culminated in late June in his dismissal from the government and the consequent withdrawal of the MMM from the coalition. Following unsuccessful efforts by Ramgoolam to draw the PMSD into a new administration, an MLP cabinet was formed by Ramgoolam, who additionally asumed Bérenger's former responsibilities for foreign affairs. Bheenick returned to the government as minister of economic development and regional co-operation. Ahmed Rashid Beebeejaun, minister of land transport, shipping and public safety in the former coalition, left the MMM and retained his former portfolio as an independent. Ramgoolam emphasized his determination to remain in office for the full legislative term to December 2000. In late June 1997 the national assembly re-elected Cassam Uteem to a second five-year term as president. A prominent supporter of the MLP, Angidi Verriah Chettiar, was elected vice-president.

Following the dissolution of the MLP/MMM alliance, Bérenger sought to assume the leadership of a consolidated political opposition to the government. In August 1997 two small parties, the Mouvement Militant Socialiste Mauricien (MMSM) and the Rassemblement pour la Réforme (RPR), agreed to support Bérenger in this aim. The alliance was extended to include a breakaway faction of the PMSD, known as the 'Vrais Bleus', under the leadership of Hervé Duval, who had been replaced as party leader by his nephew, Charles Gaëtan Xavier-Luc Duval, an opponent of co-operation with the MMM. In April 1998 the MMM, the MMSM, the RPR and the 'Vrais Bleus' formed an electoral coalition, the Alliance Nationale, to contest a by-election for a vacant seat in the national assembly. The seat, which was retained by the MLP, had also been sought by Jugnauth on behalf of the MSM, which remained unrepresented in the national assembly. Jugnauth subsequently opened negotiations with Bérenger for an MSM/MMM electoral alliance, and in December both parties agreed terms for a joint list of candidates. Ramgoolam, following a government reshuffle in October, announced proposals in the following month for an all-party review of the republic's electoral system, with a view to considering the adoption of proportional representation. In mid-1999 the MLP announced that it would endorse the candidature of Xavier-Luc Duval at a legislative by-election due to take place in September.

In February 1999 Mauritius experienced three days of serious rioting, following the death in police custody of a popular Creole musician. The public disorders, during which many banks and businesses were forced to close and damage estimated at £20m. was caused, were widely interpreted as an indication of the resentment felt by many in the Creole community, which has remained at the margin of the island's recent economic prosperity. Lesser disorders took place on Rodrigues, whose population is predominantly Creole, in early May. Meanwhile, civil unrest continued in the capital, Port Louis, culminating in an arson attack on a well-known casino in the Chinese quarter in May. Sources close to the National Intelligence Unit claimed that a group of Islamic fundamentalists could have been responsible for the attack; the gaming house was only a few metres from the capital's largest mosque. Bérenger claimed that the police had failed to protect civilians during the riots, and there was a widespread belief that the police and government were unable to maintain law and order properly. In December the government enacted legislation granting it wide powers to suppress public disorder.

In February 1999 Jugnauth assumed the leadership of the informal MSM/MMM alliance. An agreement creating a federation of the two parties stipulated that Jugnauth would serve as prime minister in any future government formed by the alliance. Bérenger was appointed deputy leader of the alliance, and was to be deputy prime minister in the event of the alliance winning the legislative elections (due to be held in late 2000). However, the appointment of Jugnauth's son Pravind as deputy leader of the MSM later that year caused divisions within the alliance. Members of the MMM claimed that Jugnauth was attempting to establish a political dynasty and feared that, in the event of an electoral victory, Pravind would be in line for the post of prime minister—assuming Sir Anerood retired from politics or was otherwise unavailable. By July 2000 it was believed that the MMM was taking preparatory steps towards re-forming an alliance with the MLP.

A reorganization of the council of ministers was carried out in October 1999, following the victory of Xavier-Luc Duval in a by-election the preceding month. Duval was appointed minister of industry, commerce, corporate affairs and financial services (regarded as the third most important post in the government hierarchy); Clarel Malherbe, whose government post Duval took, was left with a portfolio including domestic transport and marine and port development. The inclusion of financial services in Duval's portfolio effectively removed some power from the minister of finance, Moorthy Sunassee. In September 2000 the government announced several popular measures in a bid to influence public opinion in its favour ahead of the elections. The measures included the cancellation of a debt of 6m. rupees contracted by cattle breeders in 1987, the granting of permission to taxi owners to purchase duty-free cars every four years instead of every five years, and an extension of the National Development Housing Company repayment period from 15 to 25 years. The council of ministers also decided to offer free public transport to students and the elderly, and to allocate six plots of land to squatters. In addition, it extended the tenure of land lease from 20 to 99 years, at a cost of 100 rupees annually instead of the current 1,500 rupees.

A general election was held on 11 September 2000. There was a high rate of participation, with 81% of the 790,000 registered electors casting their ballots. The result was a significant victory for the opposition MSM/MMM alliance, which had remained united despite apparent signs of division earlier in the year. The alliance won a total of 54 of the 62 directly elective seats in the national assembly, with the remaining seats (up to a maximum of eight) to be filled by candidates appointed by the independent electoral commission, under the 'best loser' system. Sir Anerood Jugnauth became prime minister again, while Paul Bérenger was appointed deputy prime minister and minister of finance. The new council of ministers was named a week later and was sworn in on 20 September.

Economy*
DONALD L. SPARKS
Revised for this edition by the Editor

Mauritius* is a relatively small island (less than 800 sq miles, with a population of 1.2m.). Unlike most other members of the Organization of African Unity (OAU), Mauritius is classified by the World Bank as an 'upper middle income' economy. Unlike most other countries in the sub-Saharan region, Mauritius has achieved good rates of economic growth during the past two decades. Mauritius' gross domestic product (GDP) increased, in real terms, at an average annual rate of 5.0% in 1990–97. Real GDP increased, according to official estimates, by 5.1% in the year to June 1996, by 5.6% in 1996/97 and by 5.6% in 1997/98. Mauritius was traditionally dependent on sugar production, and economic growth was therefore vulnerable to adverse climatic conditions and changes in international prices for sugar. However, the dominance of sugar in the economy has been eclipsed by the steadily expanding manufactured exports and financial services sectors and by tourism; the contribution of revenue from sugar to GDP declined from 13% in 1979 to less than 6% in 1997, when it accounted for about 23% of total export earnings. In 1998, according to estimates by the World Bank, Mauritius' gross national product (GNP), measured at average 1996–98 prices, was US $4,329m., equivalent to $3,730 per head. During 1985–95, according to an earlier World Bank estimate, GNP per head increased, in real terms, by 5.4% per year, while the population rose at an average annual rate of 1%. The inflation rate averaged 6.8% in 1997, 6.8% in 1998 and 6.9% in 1999. It was estimated that about 6.4% of the labour force were unemployed in 1999.

SUGAR

Until recently, with the increasing importance of tourism and light industry (including textiles), agriculture formed the backbone of Mauritius' economy, and sugar dominated the sector. Sugar cane is grown on a total of 72,750 ha (accounting for more than three-quarters of the island's arable land). There are 17 large estates, covering 48,000 ha, all but one privately owned and each with a factory for processing the estate sugar and the cane grown by planters in the surrounding areas. The other land under sugar cane, producing over 40% of the total crop, is owned by 452 'big' planters and 35,000 'small' planters. Plans for the rationalization of the sugar sector, announced in 1996, were expected to reduce the number of sugar mills from seven to four by 2000, in order to increase efficiency and improve unit costs. Many of the 'small' sugar planters, who are mostly Indo-Mauritian and who cultivate about one-quarter of the total land under cane, have grouped themselves into co-operatives to facilitate the consignment of cane to the factories on the estates. Some 33,100 workers (6.8% of the labour force in 1998) are employed in the sugar industry, and represent about one-half of the agricultural labour force. A bulk sugar terminal, opened in 1980 with an annual capacity of 350,000 metric tons, is the third largest in the world. The Mauritius Sugar Syndicate markets all manufactured sugar, while the main estates are grouped into the Mauritius Sugar Producers' Association. Cyclones, however, periodically cause severe damage to the crop. This problem beset the industry in 1992 and 1994 and again in 1995, when sugar production was about 540,000 tons. Output recovered to almost 588,500 tons in 1996, partly as a result of better weather conditions, and also through an increase in the area under sugar cultivation (see below). Output in 1997 was 620,600 tons and production in 1998 rose to 628,528 tons.

In 1975 Mauritius acceded to the sugar protocol of the first Lomé Convention, which was signed in that year by the European Community (EC, now the European Union–EU) and 46 developing countries. Under this protocol and its successors, Mauritius receives a basic annual quota of 500,000 metric tons of raw cane sugar, and is the principal exporter of sugar to the EU, which comprises the main market for Mauritian sugar. Other important customers are the USA, Canada and New Zealand. Local consumption is about 37,000 tons per year. Mauritius has benefited from the EC quota arrangement in that, for these exports, the guaranteed price has been much higher than the 'spot' price on the world market. However, since 1982 the EC price has remained almost static, despite annual rounds of protracted and often acrimonious negotiations. In 1989 the price was reduced by 2%. Sugar import quotas, operated since 1982 by the USA, have been extremely detrimental to Mauritius. The disappointing sugar crop in 1995 (see above) fell short of the 585,000 tons required to meet the EU threshold

* Although Rodrigues is an integral part of the Republic of Mauritius, most economic data refer to the island of Mauritius only. The figures in this section therefore refer only to the main island, unless otherwise stated.

quota level, and posed the risk that Mauritius could lose its preferential treatment under the EU Sugar Protocol. To meet its full quota allocations (inclusive of an additional EU sugar quota of 85,000 tons annually under the special preferential sugar agreement), Mauritius requires an annual output of approximately 625,000 tons. In an effort to stimulate production, the government transferred about 1,000 ha from tea to sugar cultivation during 1995–96. In 1996 Mauritian sugar exports under the EU quota totalled 538,800 tons.

Apart from poor weather in some years, problems affecting the industry in recent years have included low world prices, ageing machinery in the factories, and the high level of the sugar export levy, which was introduced in 1980. In 1984 the government established the Mauritius Sugar Authority to co-ordinate and monitor a Sugar Action Plan (SAP) covering the period 1985–90, and one of its main features was the easing of the levy. Five factories were to be closed during that period, and the area planted with sugar was to be reduced by 1% per year, to encourage the growing of more food crops. Under the SAP, the island was divided into five sugar regions, each supervised by a public company in which small planters were encouraged to buy shares. The SAP also covered the modernization of sugar factories and the development of power stations fired by bagasse (the fibrous remnants of sugar cane after milling).

Progress was made during the 1990s in improving yields through the introduction of irrigation and new strains of sugar cane. The large-scale Northern Plains irrigation scheme was targeted to increase yields per acre from 25 metric tons of cane to 42 tons. Molasses and rum are important sugar by-products, and are also exported by Mauritius. A five-year agricultural development plan, launched in 1989–90, aimed to increase the significance of the agricultural sector. About one-half of the programme's new funds (Rs 7,300m.) was to be allocated to the sugar industry, with much of it specifically going to bagasse energy production. In 1992 the government initiated a new agricultural plan, and in the following year introduced legislation that provided additional agricultural incentives, and reduced the sugar export duty rate.

Poor weather once again affected sugar production on the island in 1999. Rainfall during the months of November and December 1998 had been only 33% and 7% of the normal average respectively, and in January 1999 the rainfall was again only 7% of the normal average, making it the driest January for 50 years. As a result of the drought, sugar production fell by more than 40%, to 373,300 metric tons, compared with 628,528 tons in 1998. Revenue from sugar production for 1999/2000 was estimated at Rs 5,100m. (equivalent to US $204m.), much lower than the Rs 9,200m. ($368m.) recorded during the previous year. This had a considerable effect on economic growth during 1999/2000, which was estimated at 3% instead of the 5% initially forecast by the government.

Sugar output was expected to be low again in 2000, with the government predicting a shortfall of an estimated 103,000 metric tons on its quota. However, this would be a marked improvement over the substantially reduced 1999 crop. Revenue for the 2000 crop was forecast at Rs 7,300m. (US $289m.), higher than that of 1999, but still Rs 2,000m. less than that of 1998. This represented a reduction of 27% in earnings for the industry. Prospects for the sugar industry in mid-2000 were mixed; while the government projected a decrease in sugar production, about 400 ha of land was simultaneously being converted from sugar cultivation to other purposes. However, the government also gave its approval for the construction of a refinery, which was expected to process 100,000 tons of Brazilian sugar per year for export to the EU.

AGRICULTURE AND FISHING

Agriculture's contribution to GDP was estimated to have fallen to 5.7% in 1999 (compared with 20% in 1970). Agricultural activity currently faces a number of difficulties unrelated to adverse weather conditions. Labour costs have been rising sharply, as have the prices of agricultural inputs and land. Producer prices have not kept pace with these factors, and the government has not allocated sufficient resources to agricultural extension and other services. In 1999 agricultural employment, according to government figures, represented 11.5% of the active labour force, compared with 15.1% in 1990.

Tea production, once a significant component of the island's economy, has been adversely affected since the late 1980s by rising production costs and the low level of prices on world markets. Export revenue from this source fell by 67%, between 1985–88, when the volume of tea exported declined from 7,000 tons to 5,400 tons annually. Exports of tea in 1995 were 2,900 tons, declining to 1,390 tons in 1996, to 435 tons in 1997, 194 tons in 1998 and to just 47 tons in 1999. In 1998 tea output totalled only 1,500 tons. Most tea-growing is carried out by about 1,500 smallholders, grouped into co-operatives. The supervision of the sector is carried out by the Mauritius Tea Factories Co (TeaFac), owned jointly by several state bodies and by tea producer co-operatives. TeaFac currently operates four factories, which account for about 75% of tea exports, and is responsible for export sales. The tea industry receives support from state subsidies.

Tobacco is the other main cash crop, after sugar and tea. Production has been expanded to the point where locally manufactured cigarettes are composed entirely of local tobacco apart from certain luxury grades. Output, which was 422 metric tons in 1970, was subsequently expanded to about 1,000 tons per year. Practically all tobacco is grown and processed by British-American Tobacco (BAT–Mauritius). Output during the late 1990s averaged about 700 tons per year.

Subsistence farming is conducted on a small scale, although the cultivation of food crops is becoming more widespread in view of the need to diversify the economy and reduce food imports. Food accounted for an estimated 11.8% of the total cost of imports in 1999. The expansion of vegetable cultivation and experiments in intercropping with sugar have resulted in self-sufficiency in potatoes and nearly all other vegetables. Other crops now being experimentally intercropped with sugar are maize, rice, vanilla and groundnuts. A tree-planting programme began in 1982, with the aim of providing one-half of the country's timber needs by the mid-1990s.

Mauritius produces only 10% of its total beef requirements, and about 20% of its total consumption of dairy products, the remainder having to be imported mainly from New Zealand, Australia and South Africa. Mauritius is, however, self-sufficient in pork, eggs and poultry. A National Dairy Board was established in 1985, and several projects were initiated, including a cattle improvement scheme and a study on the potential of deer farming. Most cattle fodder has to be imported, in particular maize from South Africa, at considerable cost. Studies have been conducted on the possible production of high-protein feeding-stuffs, as by-products of sugar cane.

The fishing industry is being regenerated, with assistance from Japan and Australia in particular, and commercial fishing is gradually expanding. Vessels from Japan, Taiwan and the Republic of Korea fish in offshore waters and tranship between 15,000 and 16,000 metric tons of fish, mostly tuna, every year. Since the mid-1970s, there has been a noticeable increase in illegal fishing by foreign companies in Mauritian waters. A joint-venture tuna-canning factory, owned 49% by Japanese interests, was set up in 1972 and exports to EU countries. A second tuna-canning plant, with an initial capacity of 10,000 tons per year, was opened in 1988. A new fishing port at Trou Fanfaron, built with Japanese grant aid, was opened in 1985, with a handling capacity of about 6,000 tons of fish per year. The experimental farming of prawns has been a success, and there are hopes for export potential in this field.

INDUSTRY

Until the 1970s, the industrial sector was effectively limited to the import substitution of basic consumer products, such as food, beverages, tobacco, footwear, clothing, metal products, paints and board for furniture, made from bagasse.

However, in view of the limited domestic market, the high level of unemployment and the emphasis on reducing dependence on the sugar sector, the government adopted a policy of export promotion by developing the Export Processing Zone (EPZ), concentrating on labour-intensive processing of imported goods for the export market. Within the EPZ, the government offers both local and foreign investors attractive incentives, including tax 'holidays', exemption from import duties on most raw materials and capital goods, free repatriation of capital, profits and dividends, low-price electricity, etc. About 60% of invested capital is locally-held, a further 25% is owned by Hong Kong entrepreneurs, and the remainder is supplied mainly by Pakistani, Indian, French, German and British interests. By September 1988 there were 586 enterprises in the EPZ, employing about 90,700 workers. However, the growth of employment subsequently slowed, and in 1993, when there were 554 enterprises (down from 556 in 1992), EPZ employment declined to 83,500, its lowest level since 1987. The decline both in new enterprises and employment continued in 1994 and into 1995, when a total of 494 businesses were employing 82,220 workers. New investment also declined, to Rs 800m. in 1994, a fall of 11% on the 1993 total.

The fastest-growing EPZ sectors have been textiles and clothing, which now account for about 80% of total EPZ exports, more than 68% of EPZ enterprises, and 91% of EPZ labour. Mauritius is among the world's largest exporters of new woollen goods. Other rapidly growing sectors include electronics components and diamond processing, and emphasis has been put on the development of precision engineering (electronics, watch and instrument making, etc.) and skilled crafts (diamond cutting and polishing, furniture, quality goods, etc.). Other products include toys, razor blades, nails, industrial chemicals, detergents, rattan furniture, plastic goods, tyres and assembly of recording cassettes. During the 1990s the government encouraged diversification in EPZ activities, with particular emphasis on the textile sector.

In 1986 exports from the EPZ replaced sugar as Mauritius' main source of export revenue. The import content, however, represents about 70%–75% of EPZ export earnings, and the high cost of imported materials and components has been reflected in net foreign exchange revenue. EPZ exports rose by 6.7% to Rs 16,533m. in 1994, when these exports accounted for 67.4% of the value of all of Mauritius' exports. Increased productivity in the clothing and textile sectors led to a rise of 10.5% in EPZ exports in 1995, to Rs 18,267m. EPZ exports advanced by 15% to Rs 21,001m. in 1996, by 9.8% to Rs 23,049m. in 1997, by an estimated 13.1% to Rs 26,075m. in 1998, and by 11% to Rs 28,952m. in 1999. The EU is the principal market for these exports, accounting for about 70% of the total. According to the World Bank, however, shortcomings in training and lack of modernization restrict the zone's productivity.

As a result of increasing labour costs, many firms in the EPZ are using more capital-intensive technologies; this will affect employment in the next few years. The demand for skilled personnel in various business sectors, including marketing, management, accounting and computing, has also exceeded the number of suitable candidates, and the government began to address this problem in 1999 by expediting the grant of labour permits to non-nationals possessing relevant professional qualifications. Emphasis on the potential of the textiles sector has prompted the creation of a Rs 200m. fund to modernize textile equipment, and a centre of textile technology has also been established by the University of Mauritius. Following changes in the GATT and the subsequent implementation of the world-wide Multi-fibre Arrangement under the World Trading Organization (WTO), Mauritius' EPZ is faced by considerable challenges, particularly in relation to increased international competition in its principal export sectors. Additionally, exports by lower-cost producers in China, India and East Africa could eventually imperil Mauritius' EPZ's comparative advantage.

Mauritius has a large, and growing, informal sector. Women comprise almost one-third of the economically active population, although they represent up to 65% of the work-force in the EPZ. Unemployment, however, has been rising since 1991 and was estimated at about 6.4% of the labour force in 1999. In that year agriculture employed 57,300 workers (representing 11.5% of the work-force), manufacturing 148,300 (29.8%) and government 62,600 (12.6%). The total work-force, including the informal sector, was 496,900 in 1999.

TOURISM

Mauritius is an attractive destination for European visitors, and tourism is now the third most important source of foreign exchange, after sugar and textiles. Arrivals of foreign tourists increased from 27,650 in 1970 to an estimated 578,100 in 1999. In that year the greatest number of visitors were from France (30.3%), Réunion (14.5%), the United Kingdom (10.2%), South Africa (8.1%) and Germany (7.8%). In 1999 revenue from this source was estimated at Rs 13,670m. (US $542.8m.). To safeguard the natural amenities of the island, the government is implementing measures to curtail and, where possible, reverse environmental damage which has been caused by the uncontrolled expansion of tourism in the recent past. In an effort to harmonize environmental considerations with higher rates of hotel room occupancy, the government has, since 1990, largely ceased issuing permits to build new hotels. Although small private hotels are exempt from the ban, their room occupancy rates have remained at around 50%, and government measures have been promised to assist this sector. The overall room occupancy rate for 1999 was 71%. Tourism provided employment, directly and indirectly, for almost 83,000 people in 1999. This sector, however, also contributes to the rise in costly imports, especially foodstuffs.

COMMUNICATIONS

There are approximately 1,905 km of classified roads, of which 31 km are motorways, 902 km are are other main roads and 582 km are secondary roads. The road network is good, considering the mountainous terrain, and about 93% of the roads are paved. A motorway connects Port Louis with the Plaisance international airport. There are a number of road projects planned or under way, including a new road from Pamplemousse to Grande Baie, and the reconstruction of the Nouvelle France–Mahébourg road. Port Louis, the major commercial port, underwent modernization and expansion during the 1990s, with loan finance from the World Bank.

The international airport at Plaisance is served by 15 airlines. In 1999 the airport handled about 41,000 metric tons of freight and more than 1m. passengers. Plans for its expansion, proceeding in the late 1990s and expected to cost about Rs 800m., reflect a 50% increase in the number of international arrivals since the late 1980s. Proposals for the construction of a second airport, at Plaine-les-Roches, in the north of the island, were under consideration in mid-1999. Air Mauritius, which is 51% government-owned, generates about one-half of total passenger traffic.

POWER AND WATER

Mauritius relies on imports for most of its energy needs. However, owing to the normally abundant rainfall and precipitous water courses, about 25% of electricity is generated from hydro sources. Most of the supply, however, is provided by diesel-powered thermal stations. The sugar estates generate electricity from bagasse. The 30-MW Champagne hydroelectric scheme started operating in late 1984. A 20-MW gas-powered generating plant in the north, built with French aid, came on stream in 1988. Energy demand is increasing at about 12% per year. It is estimated that Mauritius could produce up to 350m. kWh of electricity per year by using bagasse as a fuel, compared with current annual production of about 34m. kWh. There is a 21.7-MW bagasse-fuelled station attached to the Flacq United Estates sugar factory, and a French-financed bagasse pelletization pilot plant, Bagapel, operates at the nearby Deep River–Beau Champ sugar estate. The object is to establish bagasse as a year-round fuel; currently it is available only in the harvesting season. Two 15-MW bagasse-fired power stations are planned. Studies on wave power and wind power are also being carried out. Water supply and distribution are well developed, with only 0.75% of the population without piped provision. Subterranean reserves are tapped to supply industry, the principal consumer. Imports of petroleum products comprised an estimated 6.1% of the value of merchandise imports in 1999.

BALANCE OF PAYMENTS, FINANCE AND AID

Following the favourable movement in world sugar prices in the mid-1970s, Mauritius was able to close its trade gap for the first time in 1974. The trade balance returned to deficit between 1975 and 1986, and in 1987 a sharp rise in imports led to a deficit of Rs 1,000m. In 1990 and 1991 trade deficits of Rs 5,700m. and Rs 5,300m. respectively were recorded, increasing to Rs 5,800m. in 1992. The visible trade deficits have been caused by increases in EPZ imports for manufacturing inputs, and in imported fuel costs, disappointing sugar harvests and the fixed price for sugar exports to the EC. In 1993 the trade deficit totalled Rs 6,800m., and in 1994 the shortfall advanced to Rs 9,800m. As a result of the decline in exports from the EPZ, export volume rose by only 5%, to Rs 24,700m., in 1994. Imports, however, advanced by 13.7% to a record Rs 34,500m. Exports rose by an estimated 10% in 1995, reflecting growth in both the EPZ and non-EPZ export sectors. In that year agricultural production increased and sugar exports rose in value by about 8%. Mauritius' intake of imports remained virtually static in 1995, compared with an increase of 13.4% in 1994. This deceleration in import growth was, however, in large part attributable to the cessation of substantial purchases of aircraft and ships, which had previously affected import totals. In 1995 Mauritius recorded a visible trade deficit of US $240.5m. In 1996 the visible trade deficit rose to $294.6m., advancing to $436m. in 1997, before decreasing to $266.1m. in 1998.

The principal domestic exports are clothing and textiles, sugar and molasses, and the principal imports are textile yarn and fabrics, petroleum products and food. In 1999 the principal source of imports was France (14.9%); other major suppliers were South Africa (10.7%), India (8.8%) and the United Kingdom (4.8%). The principal market for exports (taking 33.5% of exports in that year) was the United Kingdom; other significant purchasers were France (18.4%), the USA (17.9%) and Germany (4.4%). The importance of South Africa in Mauritius' trade with Southern Africa is expected to increase significantly as the recently-created Common Market for Eastern and Southern Africa (COMESA) becomes fully operational. Mauritius has also been actively promoting economic initiatives to advance the trading interests of countries on the Indian Ocean rim, and in 1998 joined the government of Mozambique in establishing a 100,000-ha special economic zone on the Mozambique mainland. Proposals to establish a second such zone were announced in November. Mauritius maintains an active commitment to the Indian Ocean Commission (IOC), the Indian Ocean Rim Association for Regional Co-operation (IOR–ARC) and the South African Development Community (SADC).

The overall balance of payments remained in surplus from 1985/86 until 1990, when a deficit of US $119.3m. on the current account of the balance of payments was recorded. This declined to $18.2m. in 1991 and to only $100,000 in 1992. In 1993 the deficit on the current account of the balance of payments rose to $92m., advancing to $232.1m. in 1994, but declining to $21.9m. in 1995. In 1996 there was surplus of $34m. on the current account of the balance of payments, but in 1997 a deficit of $88.9m. was recorded. A small surplus, of $3.3m., was recorded in 1998, but the recovery did not last, and a deficit of $52.3m. was recorded in 1999. Mauritius' external debt totalled $2,482m. at the end of 1998, of which $1,152m. was long-term public debt; in that year the cost of debt-servicing was equivalent to 11.3% of the value of exports of goods and services. Mauritius has an excellent international credit rating.

Mauritius' economic advances of the mid-1980s, precipitated by the growth of the EPZ sector, enabled the government to introduce far-reaching measures to encourage economic expansion. The 1986/87 budget maintained taxes at their existing level, extended welfare benefits (particularly to workers in the EPZ sector) and reduced customs duties on many items. The budget for 1987/88 included proposals to liberalize banking regulations and to provide tax incentives, in order to stimulate international trading interest in the newly established stock exchange and to develop offshore banking activities (see below). To lessen a forecast budgetary shortfall in 1989/90, the government introduced increased excise taxes, although subsidies were maintained on food staples such as rice and flour. Proposals were announced to introduce a harmonized system of customs tariffs and to develop re-export and transhipment activities by establishing a duty-free processing zone for bulk imports. In 1990/91 there was an estimated budgetary deficit of Rs 877m. (equivalent to 1.9% of GDP), which the government financed by increased borrowing on the domestic market. In 1991/92 however, the budgetary deficit declined to Rs 67.2m., and in 1992/93 there was a modest budgeting surplus of Rs 221.4m. A return to deficit spending followed in 1993/94, with a budgetary shortfall of Rs 195.4m. Successive deficits (excluding figures for grants and lending), of Rs 1,105.8m. and Rs 2,795m. were

recorded for 1994/95 and 1995/96 respectively. The budgetary deficit for 1996/97 was estimated at Rs 1,984m., while the deficit for 1997/98 decreased to Rs 1,119m. Additional finance was to be obtained from the privatization of state enterprises, and the imposition of a value-added tax (VAT) from September 1998 to replace the previous sales tax. The budget for 1999/2000, announced in July 1999, envisaged a deficit of US $142m., representing 3.2% of GDP. Its provisions included measures to stimulate foreign investment in the island and reductions in customs duties on products imported from member countries of COMESA. The 2000/2001 budget was boosted by revenue of Rs 3,000m. raised from the sale of 40% of the government's shares in Mauritius Telecom, and by VAT revenues, which were Rs 800m. higher than forecast. However, there was concern at the high level of public spending (almost Rs 31,000m.), and the sum required to service the national debt, which was projected to rise by Rs 4,000m. in 2000/2001 to reach a record Rs 10,400m. Despite the exceptional amounts of revenue available, the budgetary deficit fell only marginally, to 2.9% of GDP, compared with 3.2% in the previous year.

In 1981 the government obtained a structural adjustment loan (SAL) of US $15m. from the World Bank, to finance the three-year economic programme introduced in 1979. Later in 1981 a second one-year stand-by credit of about $30m. was approved by the IMF, but was suspended in May 1982, as a result of the government's failure to meet IMF conditions. Agreement was reached with the IMF in 1983 for a further facility of SDR 49.8m., and the World Bank subsequently approved a new SAL of $45m. Meanwhile, Mauritius' other main aid donors showed their confidence in the government's austerity programme when, in June 1983, at a meeting of the World Bank-sponsored consultative group, they pledged some $53m. in balance-of-payments support. In early 1984 disagreement arose between Mauritius and the IMF over the release of the remaining half of the stand-by facility. Disbursement of the remainder of the World Bank's second SAL was also delayed until 1985, when the sugar restructuring plan was finally introduced. Sectoral loans of about $25m. for the sugar sector and $25m. for the industrial sector were agreed with the World Bank, following lengthy negotiations during late 1985 and throughout 1986. Agreement was reached with the IMF for an SDR 49m. stand-by facility, over 18 months, and SDR 7.5m. in compensatory financing for the shortfall in export earnings. Owing to the delay in negotiating the new arrangement, the government turned to European money markets for balance-of-payments support to enable the country to meet its immediate external debt-servicing obligations. In 1984 the government signed a $40m. Euroloan agreement with a consortium of banks. When the IMF arrangement expired in 1986, the government decided to defer negotiations on a new facility, owing to the country's strong economic performance. At a special donors' meeting organized by the World Bank, held in Paris in 1989, $90m. was made available to finance a five-year environment protection programme, which laid emphasis on improvements to water and sewage treatment.

A new three-year Development Plan was introduced in 1993, with the aim of further modernizing and diversifying of the economy. The plan envisaged an increased pace of privatization of public enterprises, and provided for the creation of new incentives and institutions to assist the private sector.

As part of a long-term strategy to establish Mauritius as an international financial centre, controls on the movement of foreign exchange were relaxed in 1986. From July 1988 commercial banks were allowed to settle all import payments without having to refer to the central bank. In 1989 the government also announced further measures to liberalize foreign exchange controls. An offshore banking facility was established in that year, under legislation adopted in 1988. By 1997 a total of seven offshore banks were in operation. The government also implemented a series of incentives to encourage companies to incorporate locally and to offer a minimum of 25% of their shares on the stock exchange, which opened in Port Louis in 1989. Investors in these companies were to be exempt from tax on 35% of all dividend payments, and annual profits of up to Rs 100,000 from the sale of these securities were also to be exempt. Mauritius has strengthened trade and investment relations with South Africa since the early 1990s. China and Mauritius signed a technical co-operation and economic agreement in 1990, which provided Mauritius with an interest-free loan of US \$5.3m. for infrastructure projects. The Mauritius financial services sector has actively sought to attract capital from Hong Kong, following that territory's reversion to Chinese sovereignty in 1997. In addition, the island has become a significant provider of offshore banking and investment services for a number of south Asian countries (particularly India), as well as for countries in the SADC and IOR–ARC groupings.

ECONOMIC PROSPECTS

Despite its relatively favourable economic performance in recent years. Mauritius faces a number of problems and uncertainties. Prominent among these is the rate of population growth, which projects a population of more than 1.5m. people by the year 2010, exclusive of the numbers of *émigré* Mauritians, estimated at about 50,000, who are expected to return to the island following retirement. This demographic trend is expected to pose the economy with considerable challenges.

The EPZ sector, which has led the island's industrial expansion in recent years, was expected to show growth of less than 8% annually in the late 1990s. As the base of export diversification is unlikely to be widened in the short term, a sharper decline in this sector can be expected. The government is proceeding with proposals to diversify the EPZ's industrial base and to improve vocational, technical and professional training for the industrial sector. Inflation, which has so far been held within manageable levels, reached 6.9% in 1999. The expansion of tourism, an economic mainstay of recent years, is challenged by the prospect of overcrowding and environmental damage.

Mauritius' infrastructure is beginning to show need of heavy investment in projects such as roads, telecommunications and public utilities. A World Bank report, published in 1989, stressed the need for economic diversification to minimize the country's vulnerability to fluctuations in the international economy. Mauritius is faced by increased competition in the international textile market, and any future alteration in its privileged access to the EU markets would necessitate the industry's becoming more competitive, with the use of newer, costly technology. Foreign direct investment into Mauritius increased during the 1980s, owing primarily to the expansion in the EPZ. By 1991, however, this investment fell sharply, following a slackening in EPZ growth. This decreased investment led in turn to a further decline in the EPZ, which continued in the mid-1990s. The new coalition government, which came to power in late 1995 under Dr Navinchandra Ramgoolam, remained committed to a free market economy, while recognizing the need to raise the living standards of the less prosperous strata of Mauritian society. In 1996 the government reintroduced the cycle of five-year plans into national development strategies, with emphasis on education, housing and health.

The drought in 1999 had a hugely negative impact on sugar export revenues, resulting in a trade deficit 50% larger than that recorded for the previous year. The loss of sugar production equated to about 3.2% of GDP; this, in turn, had an adverse effect on the rate of economic growth (sugar exports account for about 9% of total GDP). A more long-term cause for concern was the gradual decline of foreign direct investment (FDI) during the 1990s. The main reason for this decline has been that Mauritius is no longer competitive with regard to its labour costs, which average about US \$1.41 per hour—much higher than those in some competing countries, e.g. Indonesia at 24 cents and Madagascar at 41 cents. Increasing costs and logistical problems also reduce the country's competitiveness.

However, Mauritius is undergoing an economic transformation and is becoming increasingly less dependent on its traditional sources of income. After the success of the Mauritius Freeport, plans were announced to build the Riche Terre Freeport Business Park (RTFB). The RTFB will be based around an integrated framework to promote business, industry, trade and services in a 350 ha location to the north of Port Louis. The park will contain various zones for business, community services, hotel and recreational facilities, light manufacturing, logistics, telecommunications and a specialized training centre. The Mauritius Offshore Business Activities Authority (MOBAA) is keen to promote the country as a centre for international business. A flexible regulatory framework based on international 'best practice principles' and strict rules to prevent money laundering have attracted more than 10,000 companies to Mauritius, establishing the country as an important international business centre in the Indian Ocean region. Wide membership of various regional trade organizations, exchange controls and free repatriation of profits without withholding taxes have meant that Mauritius has rapidly become the major offshore financial centre for that region, accounting for nearly 40% of foreign direct investment into India through a variety of different funds. Given the general diversification and stability of its economy, Mauritius can reasonably expect to achieve its government's target of GDP growth of between 5.5% and 6.5% annually by the start of the 21st century.

Statistical Survey

Source (unless otherwise stated): Central Statistical Office, LIC Centre, President John F. Kennedy St, Port Louis; tel. 212-2316; fax 211-4150; e-mail cso@intnet.mu; internet www.ncb.intnet.mu/cso.htm.

Area and Population

AREA, POPULATION AND DENSITY

Area (sq km)	2,040*
Population (census results)	
2 July 1983†	1,002,178
1 July 1990‡	
Males	529,089§
Females	529,686§
Total	1,058,942
Population (official estimates at mid-year)§	
1997	1,147,706
1998	1,159,729
1999	1,174,400
Density (per sq km) at mid-1999§	596.4

* 788 sq miles.
† Including an adjustment of 1,746 for underenumeration.
‡ Including an adjustment of 2,115 for underenumeration.
§ Islands of Mauritius and Rodrigues only (area 1,969 sq km).

ISLANDS

	Area (sq km)	Population	
		2 July 1983 Census*	1 July 1990 Census†
Mauritius . .	1,865	968,609‡	1,024,571‡
Rodrigues . .	104	33,082	34,204
Other islands . .	71	487	167

* Figures relate to the *de facto* population.
† Figures relate to the *de jure* population.
‡ Including adjustment for underenumeration.

ETHNIC GROUPS

Island of Mauritius, mid-1982: 664,480 Indo-Mauritians (507,985 Hindus, 156,495 Muslims), 264,537 general population (incl. Creole and Franco-Mauritian communities), 20,669 Chinese.

LANGUAGE GROUPS (census of 1 July 1990)*

Arabic	1,686
Bhojpuri	343,832
Chinese	17,652
Creole	379,288
English	888
French	22,367
Hindi	38,181
Marathi	17,732
Tamil	47,953
Telegu	21,033
Urdu	45,311
Other languages	120,737
Total	**1,056,660**

* Figures refer to the languages of cultural origin of the population of the islands of Mauritius and Rodrigues only. The data exclude an adjustment for underenumeration. The adjusted total was 1,058,775.

PRINCIPAL TOWNS (estimated population at mid-1998)

Port Louis (capital)	147,131		Curepipe	79,614
Beau Bassin/Rose Hill	100,616		Quatre Bornes	76,798
Vacoas/Phoenix	98,464			

BIRTHS, MARRIAGES AND DEATHS*

	Registered live births		Registered marriages		Registered deaths	
	Number	Rate (per 1,000)	Number	Rate (per 1,000)	Number	Rate (per 1,000)
1992	22,902	21.1	11,408	10.5	7,023	6.5
1993	22,329	20.3	11,576	10.5	7,433	6.8
1994	21,795	19.6	11,414	10.3	7,402	6.7
1995	20,549	18.3	10,624	9.5	7,465	6.7
1996	20,763	18.3	10,700	9.4	7,670	6.8
1997	20,012	17.4	10,887	9.5	7,988	7.0
1998	19,434	16.8	10,898	9.4	7,839	6.8
1999	20,313	17.3	11,291	9.6	7,943	6.8

* Figures refer to the islands of Mauritius and Rodrigues only. The data are tabulated by year of registration, rather than by year of occurrence.

Expectation of life (years at birth, 1994–96): Males 66.6; Females 74.3 (Source: UN, *Demographic Yearbook*).

EMPLOYMENT (persons aged 12 years and over)

	1997	1998	1999*
Agriculture, hunting, forestry and fishing	59,300	58,000	57,300
Mining and quarrying	1,400	1,400 ⎫	148,300
Manufacturing	136,700	143,300 ⎭	
Electricity, gas and water	3,300	3,300	3,200
Construction	36,800	36,600	37,900
Trade, restaurants and hotels	75,300	79,900	82,700
Transport, storage and communications	29,900	30,500	30,900
Financing, insurance, real estate and business services	16,000	17,000	17,900
Community, social and personal services	114,300	115,000 ⎫	118,700
Activities not adequately defined	2,500	2,600 ⎭	
Total employed	**475,500**	**487,600**	**496,900**
Males	322,300	328,100	332,500
Females	153,200	159,500	164,400

Unemployed ('000 persons): 29 in 1997; 29.4 in 1998; 33.3* in 1999.

* Provisional figure(s).

Agriculture

PRINCIPAL CROPS ('000 metric tons)

	1996	1997	1998
Potatoes	11	18	18*
Pulses*	2	2	2
Coconuts	1	1	1
Cabbages	8	6	6*
Tomatoes	11	12	12*
Pumpkins, squash and gourds	16	15*	16*
Cucumbers and gherkins	6	6*	7*
Aubergines (Eggplants)	2	3*	3*
Onions (dry)	6	5	5*
Carrots	3	3	3*
Sugar cane	5,260	5,797	5,800*
Pineapples	3	2	2*
Bananas	9	9	9*
Tobacco (leaves)	1	1	1
Groundnuts (in shell)	1	1	1

* FAO estimate(s).

Source: FAO, *Production Yearbook*.

Tea (made) ('000 metric tons): 2.5 in 1996; 1.8 in 1997; 1.5 in 1998 (Source: International Tea Committee).

LIVESTOCK (FAO estimates, '000 head, year ending September)

	1996	1997	1998
Cattle	37	37	37
Pigs	18	18	18
Sheep	7	7	7
Goats	92	93	93

Poultry (FAO estimates, million): 3 in 1996; 3 in 1997; 3 in 1998.

Source: FAO, *Production Yearbook*.

LIVESTOCK PRODUCTS ('000 metric tons)

	1996	1997	1998
Beef and veal	2	2*	2*
Poultry meat*	20	21	21
Cows' milk*	25	25	25
Hen eggs*	5	5	5

* FAO estimate(s).

Source: FAO, *Production Yearbook*.

Forestry

ROUNDWOOD REMOVALS ('000 cubic metres, excluding bark)

	1995	1996	1997
Sawlogs, veneer logs and logs for sleepers	4	6	6
Other industrial wood	2	3	3
Fuel wood	6	7	7
Total	**12**	**15**	**15**

SAWNWOOD PRODUCTION
('000 cubic metres, including railway sleepers)

	1995	1996	1997
Total	2	3	3

Source: FAO, *Yearbook of Forest Products*.

Fishing

('000 metric tons, live weight)

	1995	1996	1997
Emperors (Scavengers) . .	6.2	5.1	5.0
Skipjack tuna	3.8	1.9	2.9
Yellowfin tuna	1.7	0.7	0.9
Other fishes (incl. unspecified) .	4.8	4.3	4.5
Crustaceans and molluscs .	0.4	0.4	0.3
Total catch	16.9	12.4	13.7

Source: FAO, *Yearbook of Fishery Statistics.*

Industry

SELECTED PRODUCTS (metric tons, unless otherwise indicated)

	1997	1998	1999
Raw sugar	620,588	628,528	373,300
Molasses	165,802	168,500	132,000
Rum (hectolitres) . .	95,537	93,437	n.a.
Beer and stout (hectolitres) .	339,529	366,400	362,800
Electric energy (million kWh) .	1,193	1,396	1,559

Finance

CURRENCY AND EXCHANGE RATES

Monetary Units
100 cents = 1 Mauritian rupee.

Sterling, Dollar and Euro Equivalents (28 April 2000)
£1 sterling = 40.28 rupees;
US $1 = 25.69 rupees;
€1 = 23.34 rupees;
1,000 Mauritian rupees = £24.83 = $38.93 = €42.85.

Average Exchange Rate (Mauritian rupees per US $)
1997   21.057
1998   23.993
1999   25.186

BUDGET (million rupees, year ending 30 June)*

Revenue†	1995/96	1996/97	1997/98‡
Taxation	11,488	14,001	15,686
Taxes on income, profits and			
capital gains . . .	1,973	2,287	2,409
Individual taxes . .	991	1,220	1,238
Corporate taxes . . .	982	1,067	1,171
Taxes on property . . .	895	976	1,101
Taxes on financial transactions	658	786	919
Domestic taxes on goods and			
services	3,710	5,157	6,007
General sales, turnover or			
value-added taxes . .	1,357	2,442	2,725
Excises	1,162	1,276	1,530
Alcoholic beverages .	628	645	682
Taxes on specific services .	848	1,062	1,325
Taxes on international trade and			
transactions . . .	4,899	5,570	6,157
Import duties . . .	4,889	5,570	6,157
Other current revenue . .	1,124	2,410	2,598
Entrepreneurial and property			
income	646	1,954	2,073
Administrative fees and			
charges, non-industrial and			
incidental sales . . .	287	318	369
Total	12,612	16,411	18,284

Expenditure§	1995/96	1996/97	1997/98‡
General public services . .	1,800	2,032	2,260
Defence	242	224	189
Public order and safety . .	1,569	1,697	1,666
Education	2,724	3,378	3,507
Health and sanitation . .	1,431	1,567	1,768
Social security and welfare .	2,984	3,787	4,237
Housing and community amenities	921	1,208	1,251
Recreational, cultural and			
religious affairs and services .	302	328	334
Economic affairs and services .	2,391	2,560	2,591
Agriculture, forestry, fishing and			
hunting	977	902	1,052
Transport and communications .	621	596	366
Other purposes . . .	2,963	3,569	4,170
Public debt interest . .	2,332	2,875	3,503
Transfers to local government .	631	694	666
Total	17,327	20,350	21,973
Current	14,586	17,208	19,316
Capital	2,741	3,142	2,657

* Figures exclude the operations of the National Pensions Fund and 22
  extra-budgetary units of the central Government. The accounts of local
  government councils are also excluded.
† Excluding grants received from abroad (million rupees): 220 in 1995/96;
  63 in 1996/97; 216 in 1997/98.
‡ Provisional.
§ Excluding lending minus repayments (million rupees): 840 in 1995/96;
  2,286 in 1996/97; 152 in 1997/98.

Source: IMF, *Mauritius: Selected Issues and Statistical Appendix*
(October 1999).

INTERNATIONAL RESERVES (US $ million at 31 December)

	1997	1998	1999
Gold*	6.1	11.9	12.3
IMF special drawing rights .	30.3	32.2	22.1
Reserve position in IMF . .	9.9	10.4	19.9
Foreign exchange . . .	653.0	516.5	689.1
Total	699.3	571.0	743.4

* Valued at market-related prices.
Source: IMF, *International Financial Statistics.*

MONEY SUPPLY (million rupees at 31 December)

	1997	1998	1999
Currency outside banks . .	5,410.4	5,832.9	6,126.7
Demand deposits at deposit money			
banks	5,194.5	5,730.2	5,844.8
Total money (incl. others) . .	10,611.0	11,590.0	12,001.8

Source: IMF, *International Financial Statistics.*

COST OF LIVING
(Consumer Price Index; base: July 1996–June 1997 = 100)

	1997	1998	1999
Food and non-alcoholic beverages .	101.9	110.1	117.1
Alcoholic beverages and tobacco .	106.4	122.1	144.0
Clothing and footwear . .	100.5	105.2	112.0
Fuel and electricity . . .	100.7	100.3	100.5
Housing and household operations	101.3	105.1	110.2
All items (incl. others) . . .	102.5	109.5	117.1

NATIONAL ACCOUNTS (million rupees in current prices)

Components of the Gross National Product

	1995	1996*	1997*
Compensation of employees . .	28,360	31,100	33,719
Operating surplus . . . }	32,334	36,907	41,235
Consumption of fixed capital . }			
Gross domestic product (GDP) at factor cost . . .	60,694	68,007	74,954
Indirect taxes	8,688	9,700	11,650
Less Subsidies	300	408	650
GDP in purchasers' values .	69,082	77,299	85,954
Factor income received from abroad	908 }	−789	−325
Less Factor income paid abroad .	1,240 }		
Gross national product (GNP) at market prices . . .	68,750	76,510	85,629

* Figures are provisional. Revised totals (in million rupees) are: GDP in purchasers' values 77,310 in 1996, 86,428 in 1997; GNP at market prices 76,521 in 1996, 86,054 in 1997.

Expenditure on the Gross Domestic Product

	1997	1998	1999
Government final consumption expenditure . . .	10,428	11,413	12,555
Private final consumption expenditure . . .	54,865	62,104	69,527
Increase in stocks . . .	1,888	1,958	46
Gross fixed capital formation . .	23,430	23,075	30,100
Total domestic expenditure .	90,611	98,550	112,228
Exports of goods and services .	54,357	65,711	68,235
Less Imports of goods and services	58,540	66,543	74,084
GDP in purchasers' values .	86,428	97,718	106,379
GDP at constant 1992 prices .	63,840	67,523	69,836

Source: IMF, *International Financial Statistics*.

Gross Domestic Product by Economic Activity (at factor cost)

	1997	1998*	1999†
Agriculture, forestry, hunting and fishing	6,687	7,428	5,375
Mining and quarrying . .	120	127	135
Manufacturing . . .	18,250	20,996	22,837
Electricity, gas and water . .	1,758	1,419	1,450
Construction	4,564	5,030	5,600
Trade, restaurants and hotels .	13,163	14,594	16,373
Transport, storage and communications . . .	8,617	10,325	11,405
Financing, insurance, real estate and business services . .	12,163	14,279	16,409
Government services . . .	7,829	8,800	9,800
Other services . . .	4,386	5,079	5,744
Sub-total	77,537	88,077	95,128
Less Imputed bank service charges	2,675	3,264	3,899
Total	74,862	84,813	91,229

* Revised figures.
† Provisional figures.

BALANCE OF PAYMENTS (US $ million)

	1997	1998	1999
Exports of goods f.o.b. . .	1,600.1	1,669.3	1,589.3
Imports of goods f.o.b. . .	−2,036.1	−1,933.3	−2,136.5
Trade balance	−436.0	−264.0	−547.2
Exports of services . . .	893.7	916.9	1,070.3
Imports of services . . .	−656.3	−718.0	−660.7
Balance on goods and services.	−198.6	−65.0	−137.7
Other income received . . .	47.0	47.8	34.9
Other income paid . . .	−64.6	−74.4	−53.4
Balance on goods, services and income . . .	−216.3	−91.7	−156.2
Current transfers received . .	206.4	186.8	196.6
Current transfers paid . .	−79.0	−91.8	−92.7
Current balance . . .	−88.9	3.3	−52.3
Capital account (net) . . .	−0.5	−0.8	−0.5
Direct investment abroad . .	−3.2	−13.7	−6.4
Direct investment from abroad .	55.3	12.2	49.4
Portfolio investment assets . .	−96.8	43.6	38.4
Portfolio investment liabilities .	30.6	−28.7	−15.3
Other investment assets . .	−115.7	−66.7	−9.9
Other investment liabilities . .	111.2	27.3	4.8
Net errors and omissions . .	73.4	−41.9	181.6
Overall balance	−34.6	−65.4	189.7

Source: IMF, *International Financial Statistics*.

External Trade

PRINCIPAL COMMODITIES (million rupees)

Imports c.i.f.	1997	1998	1999
Food and live animals . . .	6,091	6,826	6,744
Dairy products and birds' eggs .	964	733	629
Fish and fish preparations .	867	1,113	793
Crude materials (inedible) except fuels	1,567	1,931	1,667
Mineral fuels, lubricants, etc. . .	3,471	3,145	4,046
Refined petroleum products .	3,021	2,636	3,507
Chemicals	3,340	3,890	3,883
Basic manufactures . . .	14,947	17,251	17,069
Textile yarn, fabrics, etc .	9,103	7,216	7,225
Textile yarn and thread . .	n.a.	4,063	4,412
Textile fabrics . . .	n.a.	3,153	2,813
Iron and steel . . .	1,077	1,286	1,122
Machinery and transport equipment	11,702	11,369	17,850
Machinery specialized for particular industries . .	1,682	1,895	2,488
General industrial machinery, equipment and parts .	1,076	1,823	1,796
Electrical machinery, apparatus, etc. (excl. telecommunications and sound equipment)	1,263	1,407	1,898
Road motor vehicles . .	2,139	2,764	4,100
Aircraft, marine vessels and parts	n.a.	741	3,176
Miscellaneous manufactured articles	3,804	4,233	4,830
Total (incl. others) . . .	46,093	49,742	57,337

Exports f.o.b. (EPZ)*	1997	1998	1999
Fish and fish preparations . .	894	939	952
Clothing	18,142	21,121	22,947
Other textiles . . .	1,309	1,062	1,769
Pearls and precious stones . .	476	446	625
Watches and clocks . . .	409	508	585
Total (incl. others) . . .	23,049	26,075	28,952

MAURITIUS

Exports f.o.b. (non-EPZ)†	1997	1998	1999
Sugar (raw)	7,495	8,907	8,009
Clothing	n.a.	1,030	207
Total (incl. others)	8,839	11,687	8,938

* Exports from the Export Processing Zone (EPZ) only.

† Figures refer to domestic exports, excluding exports from the Export Processing Zone (EPZ). Also excluded are re-exports, totalling (in million rupees): 1,130 in 1997; 1,567 in 1998; 1,478 in 1999.

PRINCIPAL TRADING PARTNERS (million rupees)*

Imports c.i.f.	1997	1998	1999
Australia	1,547	1,694	1,836
Belgium	773	778	1,187
China, People's Repub.	2,006	2,601	3,235
France	7,623	5,527	8,520
Germany	2,164	2,056	2,147
Hong Kong	1,987	2,499	2,130
India	4,521	4,617	4,745
Indonesia	533	1,054	840
Italy	1,333	1,823	2,001
Japan	1,966	2,530	3,412
Korea, Repub.	478	1,091	873
Madagascar	642	747	595
Malaysia	1,060	1,419	1,914
Pakistan	618	725	711
Saudi Arabia	470	1,033	1,273
Singapore	1,020	1,112	1,063
South Africa	5,650	5,172	6,150
Switzerland	853	948	932
Taiwan	1,258	1,222	1,184
United Kingdom	2,574	2,584	2,592
USA	1,367	1,635	2,400
Total (incl. others)	46,093	49,742	57,337

Exports f.o.b.	1997	1998	1999
Belgium	675	782	952
France	5,990	6,995	7,234
Germany	1,860	2,219	1,731
Italy	1,272	1,407	1,249
Madagascar	1,193	1,629	1,815
Netherlands	744	900	922
Portugal	760	989	472
Réunion	477	549	571
Spain	818	935	999
Switzerland	463	525	556
United Kingdom	11,356	13,203	13,156
USA	4,687	6,505	7,006
Total (incl. others)	32,863	39,282	39,248

* Imports by country of origin; exports by country of destination.

Source: Mauritius Export Development and Investment Authority.

Transport

ROAD TRAFFIC (vehicles in use)

	1997	1998	1999
Private vehicles			
Cars	68,691	46,300	48,000
Motorcycles and mopeds	104,798	109,100	110,900
Commercial vehicles			
Buses	2,359	2,367	2,300
Taxis	4,721	4,761	4,900
Goods vehicles	24,342	24,200	26,900
Government vehicles	4,971	5,049	n.a.

SHIPPING

Merchant Fleet (registered at 31 December)

	1996	1997	1998
Number of vessels	50	55	51
Total displacement ('000 grt)	243.6	274.5	206.0

Source: Lloyd's Register of Shipping, *World Fleet Statistics*.

Sea-borne Freight Traffic ('000 metric tons)

	1997	1998	1999
Goods unloaded	2,902	3,129	3,355
Goods loaded*	950	1,033	1,198

* Excluding ships' bunkers.

CIVIL AVIATION (traffic)

	1997	1998	1999
Aircraft landings	7,049	7,320	7,612
Freight unloaded (metric tons)	17,443	17,500	20,300
Freight loaded (metric tons)	20,762	19,600	20,700

Tourism

FOREIGN TOURIST ARRIVALS

Country of Residence	1997	1998	1999
France	145,173	162,775	175,400
Germany	43,993	43,826	45,200
India	13,220	12,629	n.a.
Italy	35,255	36,614	36,700
Madagascar	10,143	9,213	n.a.
Réunion	82,628	83,966	83,700
South Africa	51,249	49,676	46,600
Switzerland	16,105	16,178	n.a.
United Kingdom	46,022	52,299	58,700
Total (incl. others)	536,125	558,195	578,100

Tourism earnings (million rupees): 10,070 in 1997; 11,890 in 1998; 13,670 in 1999.

Communications Media

	1994	1995	1996
Radio receivers ('000 in use) . .	405	410	415
Television receivers ('000 in use) .	245	248	252
Telephones ('000 main lines in use)	129	148	184
Telefax stations (number in use) .	18,000	20,000	25,000
Mobile cellular telephones			
(subscribers)	5,706	11,735	23,000
Book production*			
Titles	84	64	80
Copies ('000)	100	116	163
Daily newspapers			
Number	6	5	6
Average circulation ('000 copies)	75	80	85
Non-daily newspapers			
Number	28	25	29
Average circulation ('000 copies)	n.a.	70†	n.a.

1997: Radio receivers ('000 in use) 420; Television receivers ('000 in use) 258; Telephones ('000 main lines in use) 223; Mobile cellular telephones (subscribers) 44,000.

* Including pamphlets (21 titles and 19,000 copies in 1994).
† Estimate.

Sources: partly UNESCO, *Statistical Yearbook*; UN, *Statistical Yearbook*.

Education

(1998/99)

	Institutions	Students
Primary	287	133,489
General secondary	135	95,187
University	1	3,667*
Institute of Education	1	3,092†
Lycée Polytechnique	1	584†

Teachers: Primary 5,200 in 1996/97; General secondary 4,710 in 1996/97; Higher 474 in 1995/96.

* 1996/97 academic year.
† 1997/98 academic year.

Directory

The Constitution

The Mauritius Independence Order, which established a self-governing state, came into force on 12 March 1968, and was subsequently amended. Constitutional amendments providing for the adoption of republican status were approved by the Legislative Assembly (henceforth known as the National Assembly) on 10 December 1991, and came into effect on 12 March 1992. The main provisions of the revised Constitution are listed below:

HEAD OF STATE

The Head of State is the President of the Republic, who is elected by a simple majority of the National Assembly for a five-year term of office. The President appoints the Prime Minister (in whom executive power is vested) and, on the latter's recommendation, other ministers.

COUNCIL OF MINISTERS

The Council of Ministers, which is headed by the Prime Minister, is appointed by the President and is responsible to the National Assembly.

THE NATIONAL ASSEMBLY

The National Assembly, which has a term of five years, comprises the Speaker, 62 members elected by universal adult suffrage, a maximum of eight additional members and the Attorney-General (if not an elected member). The island of Mauritius is divided into 20 three-member constituencies for legislative elections. Rodrigues returns two members to the National Assembly. The official language of the National Assembly is English, but any member may address the Speaker in French.

The Government

HEAD OF STATE

President: CASSAM UTEEM (took office 30 June 1992; re-elected 28 June 1997).
Vice-President: ANGIDI VERRIAH CHETTIAR.

COUNCIL OF MINISTERS
(September 2000)

Prime Minister, Minister of Defence and Home Affairs, and Minister of External Communications: Sir ANEROOD JUGNAUTH.
Deputy Prime Minister and Minister of Finance: PAUL BÉRENGER.
Minister of Industry, Commerce and International Trade: JAYA KRISHNA CUTTAREE.
Minister of Agriculture, Food Technology and Natural Resources: PRAVIND KUMAR JUGNAUTH.

Minister of Social Security, National Solidarity and Senior Citizens' Welfare and Reform Institutions: SAMIOULLAH LAUTHAN.
Minister of Local Government, Rodrigues and Rural and Urban Development: GEORGES PIERRE LESJONGARD.
Minister of Public Utilities: ALAN GANOO.
Minister of Tourism: NANDCOOMAR BODHA.
Minister of Environment: RAJESH ANAND BHAGWAN.
Minister of Public Infrastructure and Inland Transport: ANIL KUMAR BACHOO.
Minister of Civil Service Affairs and Administrative Reforms: AHMAD SULLIMAN JEEWAH.
Minister of Labour and Industrial Relations: SHOWKUTALLY SOODHUN.
Minister of Women's Rights, Child Development and Family Welfare: MARIA ARIANNE NAVARRE-MARIE.
Minister of Foreign Affairs and Regional Co-operation: ANIL KUMARSINGH GAYAN.
Minister of Education and Scientific Research: LOUIS STEVEN OBEEGADOO.
Minister of Health and Quality of Life: ASHOCK KUMAR JUGNAUTH.
Minister of Arts and Culture: MOTEE RAMDASS.
Minister of Fisheries: LOUIS SYLVIO MICHEL.
Minister of Economic Development, Financial Services and Corporate Affairs: KHUSHHAL CHAND KHUSHIRAM.
Minister of Co-operatives: PREMDUT KOONJOO.
Minister of Housing and Lands: MOOKHESSWUR CHOONEE.
Minister of Information Technology and Communications: DEELCHAND JEEHA.
Attorney-General and Minister of Justice and Human Rights: EMMANUEL JEAN LEUNG SHING.
Minister of Training, Skills Development and Productivity: SANGEET FOWDAR.

MINISTRIES

President's Office: State House, Port Louis; tel. 454-3021; fax 464-5370; e-mail statepas@intnet.mu; internet ncb.intnet.mu/presiden.htm.

Prime Minister's Office: Government Centre, Port Louis; tel. 202-9010; fax 208-8619; internet ncb.intnet.mu/pmo.htm.

Ministry of Agriculture, Food Technology and Natural Resources: Renganaden Seeneevassan Bldg, 9th Floor, Port Louis; tel. 212-0814; fax 212-4427; internet neb.intnet.mu/moa.

Ministry of Arts and Culture: Renganaden Seeneevassen Bldg, 7th Floor, cnr Pope Hennessy and Maillard Sts, Port Louis; tel. 212-9993; fax 212-9366; e-mail culture@intnet.mu; internet ncb.intnet.mu/mac.

Ministry of Civil Service Affairs and Administrative Reform: Government Centre, Port Louis; tel. 201-1035; fax 212-9528; e-mail civser@bow.intnet.mu; internet ncb.intnet.mu/mcsa.htm.

Ministry of Economic Development, Productivity and Regional Development: Emmanuel Anquetil Bldg, 9th Floor, Sir Seewoosagur Ramgoolam St, Port Louis; tel. 201-2533; fax 212-4124; e-mail medrc@intnet.mu; internet ncb.intnet.mu/medrc.htm.

Ministry of Education and Scientific Research: IVTB House, Pont Fer, Phoenix; tel. 698-0464; fax 698-2550; e-mail meduhrd@bow.intnet.mu; internet ncb.intnet.mu/meduhrd.htm.

Ministry of Employment, Manpower Resources and Technical Training: NPF Bldg, 6th Floor, cnr Jules Koenig and Maillard Sts, Port Louis; tel. 242-1462.

Ministry of Energy and Water Resources: Government Centre, Port Louis; tel. 201-1087; fax 208-6497.

Ministry of External Communications: Air Mauritius Bldg, 5th Floor, Port Louis; tel. 210-3537; fax 211-7708; internet ncb.intnet.mu/ecoi.htm.

Ministry of Finance: Government Centre, Port Louis; tel. 201-2557; fax 208-9823; e-mail mof@bow.intnet.mu; internet ncb.intnet.mu/mof.htm.

Ministry of Fisheries and Co-operatives: Life Insurance Corpn of India Bldg, President John F. Kennedy St, Port Louis; tel. 211-2470; internet ncb.intnet.mu/fishco.

Ministry of Foreign Affairs and International Trade: Level 5, New Government Centre, Port Louis; tel. 201-1416; fax 208-8087; e-mail facrem@bow.intnet.mu; internet ncb.intnet.mu/mfa.htm.

Ministry of Health and Quality of Life: Emmanuel Anquetil Bldg, Sir Seewoosagur Ramgoolam St, Port Louis; tel. 201-1911; fax 208-0375; e-mail mohql@intnet.mu; internet ncb.intnet.mu/moh.

Ministry of Housing and Lands: Moorgate House, Port Louis; tel. 212-6022; fax 212-7482; internet ncb.intnet.mu/housing.

Ministry of Industrial Relations: Ming Court, cnr Eugène Laurent and GMD Atchia Sts, Port Louis; tel. 212-3049; fax 212-3070.

Ministry of Industry, Commerce, Corporate Affairs and Financial Services: Air Mauritius Centre, 7th Floor, John F. Kennedy St, Port Louis; tel. 201-7100; fax 212-8201; e-mail minic@intnet.mu; internet ncb.intnet.mu/mic.htm.

Ministry of Justice: Jules Koenig St, Port Louis; tel. 208-5321.

Ministry of Local Government, Outer Islands Development and Small and Medium Enterprises and Handicraft: Emmanuel Anquetil Bldg, cnr Sir Seewoosagur Ramgoolam and Jules Koenig Sts, Port Louis; tel. 201-1215; e-mail minlogov@intnet.mu; internet ncb.intnet.mu/mlge.

Ministry of Local Government and Environment (Environment Division): Ken Lee Tower, Barracks St, Port Louis; tel. 212-8332; fax 212-9407; e-mail enviro@bow.internet.mu.

Ministry of Public Infrastructure: Moorgate House, 4th Floor, Sir W. Newton St, Port Louis; tel. 208-3063; fax 208-7149; internet ncb.intnet.mu/mpi.

Ministry of Public Utilities: Medcor Bldg, 10th Floor, John F. Kennedy St, Port Louis; tel. 210-3994; fax 208-6497; e-mail minpuuti@intnet.mu; internet ncb.intnet.mu/mpu.htm.

Ministry for Rodrigues: Fon Sing Bldg, 5th Floor, Edith Cavell St, Port Louis; tel. 208-8472; fax 212-6329; e-mail minrodr@bow.intnet.mu; internet ncb.intnet.mu/rdgs.

Ministry of Social Security, National Solidarity and Senior Citizens' Welfare: Renganaden Seeneevassen Bldg, Jules Koenig St, Port Louis; tel. 212-9813; fax 212-8190 e-mail mssns@intnet.mu; internet ncb.intnet.mu/ssns.htm.

Ministry of Telecommunications and Information Technology: Level 9, Air Mauritius Centre, John F. Kennedy St, Port Louis; tel. 210-0201; fax 212-1673; e-mail mintelit@intnet.mu; internet ncb.intnet.mu/mtit.htm.

Ministry of Tourism and Leisure: Air Mauritius Centre, Level 12, John Kennedy St, Port Louis; tel. 210-1329; fax 208-6776; e-mail mot@intnet.mu; internet ncb.intnet.mu/mot.

Ministry of Trade and Shipping: Government Centre, Port Louis; tel. 201-1067; fax 212-6368.

Ministry of Women, Family Welfare and Child Development: C.S.K. Bldg, cnr Remy Ollier and Emmanuel Anquetil Sts, Port Louis; tel. 240-1377; fax 240-7717; e-mail mwfwcd@bow.intnet.mu; internet ncb.intnet.mu/mwfw.htm.

Ministry of Youth and Sports: Emmanuel Anquetil Bldg, Sir Seewoosagur Ramgoolam St, Port Louis; tel. 201-1242; fax 212-6506; internet ncb.intnet.mu/sports.

Legislature

NATIONAL ASSEMBLY

Speaker: RAMESH JEEWOOLALL.

General Election, 11 September 2000

Party	Seats*
Mouvement Socialiste Mauricien (MSM)/Mouvement Militant Mauricien (MMM)	54
Mauritius Labour Party (MLP)/Parti Mauricien Social Démocrate (PMSD)	6
Organisation du Peuple Rodriguais (OPR)	2

* Additional members were to be appointed from the unsuccessful candidates who attracted the largest number of votes.

Political Organizations

Comité d'Action Musulman (CAM): POB 882, Port Louis; f. 1958; Muslim support; Pres. YOUSSUF MOHAMMED.

Hizbullah: Port Louis; Islamist.

Mauritius Labour Party (MLP): 7 Guy Rozemont Sq., Port Louis; tel. 212-6691; e-mail labour@intnet.mu; internet www.labour.intnet.mu; f. 1936; Leader Dr NAVINCHANDRA RAMGOOLAM; Chair. JEAN-FRANÇOIS CHAUMIÈRE; Sec.-Gen. SARAT DUTT LALLAH.

Mouvement Militant Mauricien (MMM): 21 Poudrière St, Port Louis; tel. 212-6553; fax 208-9939; internet mmm.intnet.mu; f. 1969; socialist; Chair. AHMAD JEEWAH; Leader PAUL BÉRENGER; Sec.-Gen. IVAN COLLENDAVELLOO.

Mouvement Rodriguais: Port Mathurin, Rodrigues; tel. 831-1876 (Port Mathurin); tel. and fax 686-8859 (Port Louis); f. 1992; represents the interests of Rodrigues; Leader JOSEPH (NICHOLAS) VON-MALLY.

Mouvement Socialiste Militant (MSM): Sun Trust Bldg, 31 Edith Cavell St, Port Louis; tel. 212-8787; fax 208-9517; f. 1983 by fmr mems of the MMM; dominant party in subsequent coalition govts until Dec. 1995; Leader Sir ANEROOD JUGNAUTH; Chair. JOE LESJON-GARD; Sec.-Gen. VISHWANATH SAJADAH.

Organisation du Peuple Rodriguais (OPR): Port Mathurin, Rodrigues; represents the interests of Rodrigues; Leader LOUIS SERGE CLAIR.

Parti Mauricien Social Démocrate (PMSD): Melville, Grand Gaube; also known as the Parti Mauricien Xavier-Luc Duval (PMXD); centre-right; Leader CHARLES GAËTAN XAVIER-LUC DUVAL; Sec.-Gen. JACQUES PANGLOSE.

Minor parties include the **Mouvement Militant Socialiste Mauricien** (Leader MADUN DULLOO) the **Rassemblement pour la Réforme** (Leader SHEILA BAPPOO), the **Renouveau Militant Mauricien** (Leader Dr PARAMHANSA (PREM) NABABSINGH), the **'Vrais Bleus'** (Leader HERVÉ DUVAL), the **Parti Socialiste Ouvrier** (Gen. Sec. DIDIER EDMOND), the **Rassemblement pour l'Organisation des Créoles, Lalit** and the **Mouvement Republicain**.

Diplomatic Representation

EMBASSIES AND HIGH COMMISSIONS IN MAURITIUS

Australia: Rogers House, President John F. Kennedy St, Port Louis; tel. 208-1700; fax 208-8878; e-mail austhc@intnet.mu; High Commissioner: CHRIS MARCHANT.

China, People's Republic: Royal Rd, Belle Rose, Rose Hill; tel. 454-9111; fax 464-6012; Ambassador: XIA SHOUAN.

Egypt: King George V Ave, Floreal, Port Louis; tel. 696-5012; fax 686-5575. Ambassador: SAMIRA EKDAWI.

France: 14 St George's St, Port Louis; tel. 208-3755; fax 208-8145; Ambassador: RENÉ FORCEVILLE.

India: Life Insurance Corpn of India Bldg, 6th Floor, President John F. Kennedy St, POB 162, Port Louis; tel. 208-3775; fax 208-6859; High Commissioner: L. R. NARAYAN.

Madagascar: Guiot St, Pasceau, Floreal, Port Louis; tel. 686-5015; fax 686-7040; Ambassador: BERTRAND RAZAFINTSALAMA.

Pakistan: Anglo-Mauritius House, Intendance St, Port Louis; tel. 212-6547; fax 212-6548; High Commissioner: IKRAM KARIM FAZLI.

Russia: Queen Mary Ave, POB 10, Floreal; tel. 696-1545; fax 696-5027; e-mail rusemb.mu@intnet.mu; Ambassador: V. M. NESTERUSHKIN.

South Africa: BAI Bldg, 4th Floor, 25 Pope Hennessy St, POB 908, Port Louis; tel. 212-6925; fax 212-6936; High Commissioner: MBULELO RAKWENA.

United Kingdom: Les Cascades Bldg, Edith Cavell St, POB 1063, Port Louis; tel. 211-1361; fax 211-1369; e-mail bhc@intnet.mu; High Commissioner: DAVID SNOXELL.

USA: Rogers House, President John F. Kennedy St, Port Louis; tel. 208-9764; fax 208-9534; Ambassador: HAROLD W. GEISEL.

Judicial System

The laws of Mauritius are derived both from the French Code Napoléon and from English Law. The Judicial Department consists of the Supreme Court, presided over by the Chief Justice and eight other Judges who are also Judges of the Court of Criminal Appeal and the Court of Civil Appeal. These courts hear appeals from the Intermediate Court, the Industrial Court and 10 District Courts. The Industrial Court has special jurisdiction to protect the constitutional rights of the citizen. There is a right of appeal in certain cases from the Supreme Court to the Judicial Committee of the Privy Council in the United Kingdom.

Chief Justice: ARIANGA PILLAY.

Senior Puisne Judge: B. SIK YUEN.

Puisne Judges: V. BOOLELL, K. P. MATADEEN, Mrs R. N. NARAYEN, E. BALANCY, P. LAM SHANG LEEN.

Religion

Hindus are estimated to comprise more than 50% of the population, with Christians accounting for some 30% and Muslims 17%. There is also a small Buddhist community.

CHRISTIANITY
The Anglican Communion

Anglicans in Mauritius are within the Church of the Province of the Indian Ocean, comprising six dioceses (four in Madagascar, one in Mauritius and one in Seychelles). The Archbishop of the Province is the Bishop of Antananarivo, Madagascar. In 1983 the Church had 5,438 members in Mauritius.

Bishop of Mauritius: Rt Rev. REX DONAT, Bishop's House, Phoenix; tel. 686-5158; fax 697-1096; e-mail diocese_mauritius@ecunet.org.

Presbyterian Church of Mauritius

Minister: Pasteur ANDRÉ DE RÉLAND, 11 Poudrière St, Port Louis; tel. 208-2386; f. 1814.

The Roman Catholic Church

Mauritius comprises a single diocese, directly responsible to the Holy See. At 31 December 1999 there were an estimated 310,000 adherents in the country, representing about 24% of the total population.

Bishop of Port Louis: Rt Rev. MAURICE PIAT, Evêché, 13 Mgr Gonin St, Port Louis; tel. 208-3068; fax 208-6607; e-mail eveche@intnet.mu.

BAHÁ'Í FAITH

National Spiritual Assembly: POB 538, Port Louis; tel. 212-2179; mems resident in 190 localities.

ISLAM

Mauritius Islamic Mission: Noor-e-Islam Mosque, Port Louis; Imam S. M. BEEHARRY.

The Press

DAILIES

China Times: 24 Emmanuel Anquetil St, POB 325, Port Louis; tel. 240-3067; f. 1953; Chinese; Editor-in-Chief LONG SIONG AH KENG; circ. 3,000.

Chinese Daily News: 32 Rémy Ollier St, POB 316, Port Louis; tel. 240-0472; f. 1932; Chinese; Editor-in-Chief WONG YUEN MOY; circ. 5,000.

L'Express: 3 Brown Sequard St, POB 247, Port Louis; tel. 212-4365; fax 208-8174; e-mail sentinelle@bow.intnet.mu; internet www.lexpress-net.com; f. 1963; English and French; Editor-in-Chief JEAN-CLAUDE DE L' ESTRAC; circ. 35,000.

Maurice Soir: Port Louis; f. 1996; Editor SYDNEY SELVON; circ. 2,000.

Le Mauricien: 8 St George St, POB 7, Port Louis; tel. 208-3251; fax 208-7059; f. 1907; English and French; Editor-in-Chief GILBERT AHNEE; circ. 35,000.

L'Observateur: Port Louis; f. 1997; French.

Le Quotidien: 12 Dr Seetulsingh St, Port Louis; tel. 211-4800; fax 211-7479; e-mail quotidie@bow.intnet.mu; f. 1996; English and French; Dirs JACQUES DAVID, PATRICK MICHEL; circ. 30,000.

Le Socialiste: Manilall Bldg, 3rd Floor, Brabant St, Port Louis; tel. 208-8003; English and French; Editor-in-Chief Dr MONAF KHEDARUN; circ. 1,000.

The Sun: 31 Edith Cavell St, Port Louis; tel. 212-4820; fax 208-9517; English and French; Editor-in-Chief SUBASH GOBIN; circ. 4,000.

The Tribune: Port Louis; f. 1999; Publr HARISH CHUNDUNSING.

WEEKLIES AND FORTNIGHTLIES

5-Plus Dimanche: Résidence des Palmiers, 198 Royal Rd, Beau Bassin; tel. 454-3353; fax 454-3420; f. 1994; English and French; Editor-in-Chief FINLAY SALESSE; circ. 30,000.

5-Plus Magazine: Résidence des Palmiers, 198 Royal Rd, Beau Bassin; tel. 454-3353; fax 454-3420; f. 1990; English and French; Editor-in-Chief PIERRE BENOÎT; circ. 10,000.

Business Magazine: TN Tower, 1st Floor, 13 St George St, Port Louis; tel. 211-1925; fax 211-1926; f. 1993; English and French; Editor-in-Chief LYNDSAY RIVIÈRE; circ. 6,000.

Le Croissant: cnr Velore and Noor Essan Mosque Sts, Port Louis; tel. 240-7105; English and French; Editor-in-Chief RAYMOND RICHARD NAUVEL; circ. 25,000.

Le Dimanche: 5 Jemmapes St, Port Louis; tel. 212-1177; f. 1961; English and French; Editor RAYMOND RICHARD NAUVEL; circ. 25,000.

La Gazette des Iles: Port Louis; historical journal.

L'Hebdo-Militant: Port Louis.

Impact News: 6 Grandcourt, Port Louis; tel. 240-8567; English and French; Editor-in-Chief CADER SAIB.

Lalit de Klas: 153B Royal Rd, G.R.N.W., Port Louis; tel. 208-2132; English, French and Creole; Editor ASHOK SUBRON.

Le Lotus: 73 Prince of Wales St, Rose Hill; tel. 208-4068; English and French; Editor-in-Chief MOGANADEN PILLAY.

Le Mag: Industrial Zone, Tombeay Bay; tel. 247-1005; fax 247-1061; f. 1993; English and French; Editor (vacant); circ. 8,000.

Mauritius Times: 23 Bourbon St, POB 202, Port Louis; tel. and fax 212-1313; f. 1954; e-mail mtimes@intnet.mu; English and French; Editor-in-Chief BICKRAMSINGH RAMLALLAH; circ. 15,000.

Le Militant Magazine: 7 Lord Kitchener St, Port Louis; tel. 212-6050; fax 208-2291; f. 1989; English and French; Editor-in-Chief MITRADEV PEERTHUM; circ. 2,000.

Mirror: 39 Emmanuel Anquetil St, Port Louis; tel. 240-3298; Chinese; Editor-in-Chief NG KEE SIONG; circ. 4,000.

News on Sunday: Port Louis; f. 1996; Editor SYDNEY SELVON.

Le Nouveau Militant: 21 Poudrière St, Port Louis; tel. 212-6553; fax 208-2291; f. 1979; publ. by the Mouvement Militant Mauricien; English and French; Editor-in-Chief J. RAUMIAH.

Le Rodriguais: Saint Gabriel, Rodrigues; tel. 831-1613; fax 831-1484; f. 1989; Creole, English and French; Editor JACQUES EDOUARD; circ. 2,000.

Star: 14 Orléans St, Port Louis; tel. 212-2736; English and French; Editor-in-Chief Dr HASSAM RUHOMALLY.

Style: Port Louis; women's interest; weekly.

Sunday: 31 Edith Cavell St, Port Louis; tel. 208-9516; fax 208-7059; f. 1966; English and French; Editor-in-Chief SUBASH GOBIN.

La Vie Catholique: 28 Nicolay Rd, Port Louis; tel. 242-0975; fax 242-3114; f. 1930; English and French; Editor-in-Chief MONIQUE DINAN; circ. 15,000.

Week-End: 8 St George St, Port Louis; tel. 208-3252; fax 208-7059; f. 1966; French and English; Editor-in-Chief GÉRARD CATEAU; circ. 80,000.

Week-End Scope: 8 St George St, Port Louis; tel. 208-3251; fax 208-7059; English and French; Editor-in-Chief AHMAD SALARBUX.

OTHER SELECTED PERIODICALS

CCI–INFO: 3 Royal St, Port Louis; tel. 208-3301; fax 208-0076; e-mail mcci@intnet.mu; internet www.mcci.org; English and French; f. 1995; publ. of the Mauritius Chamber of Commerce and Industry.

Ciné Star Magazine: 64 Sir Seewoosagur Ramgoolam St, Port Louis; tel. 240-1447; English and French; Editor-in-Chief ABDOOL RAWOOF SOOBRATTY.

Education News: Edith Cavell St, Port Louis; tel. 212-1303; English and French; monthly; Editor-in-Chief GIAN AUBEELUCK.

Le Message de L'Ahmadiyyat: c/o Ahmadiyya Muslim Asscn, POB 6, Rose Hill; tel. 464-1747; fax 454-2223; e-mail jamaatmu@bow.intnet.mu; French; monthly; Editor-in-Chief ZAFRULLAH DOMUN; circ. 3,000.

Le Progrès Islamique: 51 Solferino St, Rose Hill; f. 1948; English and French; monthly; Editor N. SOOKIA.

PROSI: Plantation House, Port Louis; tel. 212-3302; fax 212-8710; f. 1969; sugar industry journal; monthly; Dir JACQUES DINAN; circ. 2,750.

La Voix d'Islam: Parisot Rd, Mesnil, Phoenix; f. 1951; English and French; monthly.

NEWS AGENCY
Foreign Bureau

Newslink Africa (UK): Port Louis; Correspondent NASEEM ACKBARALLY.

Publishers

Bukié Banané: 8 Edwin Ythier St, Rose Hill; tel. 454-2327; f. 1979; Creole literature, poetry and drama; Man. Dir DEV VIRAHSAWMY.

Business Publications Ltd: TN Tower, 1st Floor, St George St, Port Louis; tel. 211-1925; fax 211-1926; f. 1993; English and French; Dir LYNDSAY RIVIÈRE.

Editions du Dattier: 82 Goyavier Ave, Quatre Bornes; tel. 466-4854; fax 446-3105; e-mail dattier@intnet.mu; English and French; Dir JEAN-PHILIPPE LAGESSE.

Editions de l'Océan Indien Ltée: Stanley, Rose Hill; tel. 464-6761; fax 464-3445; f. 1977; textbooks, literature; English and French; Gen. Man. (vacant).

Editions Le Printemps: 4 Club Rd, Vacoas; tel. 696-1017; fax 686-7302; e-mail elp@bow.intnet.mu; Man. Dir A. I. SULLIMAN.

Broadcasting and Communications

TELECOMMUNICATIONS

Mauritius Telecommunications Authority (MTA): Port Louis; f. 1999; regulatory authority; Chair. RAJESKUMAR UNNUTH.

Mauritius Telecom: Telecom Tower, Edith Cavell St, Port Louis; tel. 203-7000; fax 208-1070; e-mail mtelcom@intnet.mu; f. 1992; govt-controlled; proposals for transfer of a 40% interest to the private sector were proceeding in early 2000; provides all telecommunications services; Chair. MILAN MEETARBHAN; Exec. Dir MEGH PILAY.

BROADCASTING

In 1997 the Supreme Court invalidated the broadcasting monopoly held by the Mauritius Broadcasting Corporation.

Radio

Mauritius Broadcasting Corporation: Broadcasting House, Louis Pasteur St, Forest Side; tel. 675-5001; fax 676-7332; f. 1964; independent corpn operating the two national radio services and two television channels; Chair. DENIS RIVET; Dir-Gen. BIJAYE MADHOU.

Television

Mauritius Broadcasting Corporation: (see Radio, above).

Finance

(cap. = capital; res = reserves;
dep. = deposits; m. = million; brs = branches; amounts in Mauritian
rupees, unless otherwise stated)

BANKING

Central Bank

Bank of Mauritius: Sir William Newton St, POB 29, Port Louis; tel. 208-4164; fax 211-1355; e-mail bomrd@bow.intnet.mu; internet www.bom.intnet.mu; f. 1967; bank of issue; cap. and res 10m., dep. 3,004.1m. (June 1998); Gov. RAMESHUAR BASANT ROI; Man. Dir BABOO RAJENDRANATHSING GUJADHUR.

Principal Commercial Banks

Bank of Baroda: Sir William Newton St, POB 553, Port Louis; tel. 208-1504; fax 208-3892; e-mail bobgen@intnet.mu; cap. and res. 19.9m., dep. 396m. (March 1998); Pres. R. A. ALMEIDA; 6 brs.

Banque Nationale de Paris Intercontinentale: 1 Sir William Newton St, POB 494, Port Louis; tel. 208-4147; fax 208-8143; e-mail bnpidom@intnet.mu; internet www.maurirent.com/bnpi; Pres. MICHEL PÉBEREAU; Man. Dir MICHEL GRILLO; 2 brs.

Barclays Bank PLC, Mauritius: Sir William Newton St, POB 165, Port Louis; tel. 208-2685; fax 208-2720; Dir JACQUES DE NAVACELLE; 21 brs.

Delphis Bank Ltd: 16 Sir William Newton St, POB 485, Port Louis; tel. 208-5061; fax 208-5388; e-mail info@delphis-mauritius.com; internet www.delphis-mauritius.com/delphis; f. 1991; cap. and res 246.3m., dep. 3,330m. (Dec. 1998); Man. Dir VIJAY KUMAR RAMPHUL.

Hongkong and Shanghai Banking Corporation Ltd: place d'Armes, POB 50, Port Louis; tel. 208-1801; fax 208-8449; internet www.hongkongbank.com; CEO PAUL LEECH.

Indian Ocean International Bank Ltd: 34 Sir William Newton St, POB 863, Port Louis; tel. 208-0121; fax 208-0127; f. 1978; cap. and res 201.5m., dep. 854.2m. (June 1998); Chair. and Man. Dir S. M. CUNDEN; 8 brs.

Mauritius Commercial Bank Ltd: MCB Centre, 9–15 Sir William Newton St, Port Louis; tel. 208-5000; fax 208-7054; e-mail mcb.pub-rel@intnet.mu; internet www.mcbgroup.com; f. 1838; cap. and

res 2,173m., dep. 44,282m. (June 1998); Pres. ADOLPHE VALLET; Gen. Man. PIERRE GUY NOËL; 40 brs.

South East Asian Bank Ltd: Max City Bldg, 2nd Floor, cnr Rémy Ollier and Louis Pasteur Sts, Port Louis; tel. 216-8826; fax 241-7379; e-mail seab@intnet.mu; f. 1989; cap. and res 105.9m., dep. 750.4m. (Dec. 1998); CEO VINCENT LEE; 5 brs.

State Bank of Mauritius Ltd: State Bank Tower, 1 Queen Elizabeth II Ave, Port Louis; tel. 202-1111; fax 202-1234; e-mail sbm@sbm.intnet.mu; internet www.sbm.online.com; f. 1973; cap. and res 2,914m., dep. 20,288m. (June 1999); Chair. SEETANAH LUTCHMEENARAIDOO; CEO MUNI KRISHNA T. REDDY; 52 brs.

Development Bank

Development Bank of Mauritius Ltd: La Chaussée St, POB 157, Port Louis; tel. 208-0241; fax 208-8498; e-mail dbmltd@bow.intnet.mu; internet www.mauritius-island.com./dbm; f. 1964; 65% govt-owned; cap. and res 1,278.2m., dep. 3,022.8m. (June 1998); Chair. K. SACCARAM; Man. Dir RANAPARTAB TACOURI.

Principal 'Offshore' Banks

Banque Internationale des Mascareignes: Le Caudan Waterfront, 4th Floor, Barkly Wharf, Port Louis; tel. 212-4978; fax 212-4983; e-mail bim@bow.intnet.mu; f. 1991; jt venture of Caisse d'Epargne Provence Alpes Corse de France, Crédit Lyonnais de France and Mauritius Commercial Bank Ltd; cap. US $6m. (1999); Chair. MICHEL VALIDIRE; Gen. Man. HIMMAT KALSIA.

SBI International (Mauritius) Ltd: SICOM Bldg, 10th Floor, Sir Célicourt Antelme St, POB 376, Port Louis; tel. 212-2054; fax 212-2050; e-mail sbilmaur@intnet.mu; f. 1989; subsidiary of the State Bank of India; cap. and res US $14.4m., dep. US $120.7m. (Dec. 1998); Chair. M. BAGUANI; Man. Dir M. MADHUKAR.

Bank of Baroda, Banque Nationale de Paris Intercontinentale, Barclays Bank PLC, African Asian Bank, PT Bank International Indonesia, Investec Bank (Mauritius) and HSBC Bank PLC also operate 'offshore' banking units.

STOCK EXCHANGE

Stock Exchange Commission: SICOM Bldg, Sir Célicourt Antelme St, Port Louis; tel. 208-8735; fax 208-8676; f. 1993; supervisory authority; Chair. DHIREN DABEE (acting); CEO Ms SHARDA DINDOYAL.

Stock Exchange of Mauritius: Cascades Bldg, 2nd Floor, Edith Cavell St, Port Louis; tel. 212-9541; fax 208-8409; e-mail stockex@bow.intnet.mu; internet lynx.intnet.mu/sem; f. 1989; 11 mems; Chair. SYDNEY BATHFIELD; CEO SUNIL BENIMADHU.

INSURANCE

Albatross Insurance Co Ltd: 22 St George St, POB 116, Port Louis; tel. 207-9007; fax 208-4800; e-mail albatros@bow.intnet.mu; f. 1975; Chair. DEREK TAYLOR; Man. Dir JEAN DE LA HOGUE.

Anglo-Mauritius Assurance Society Ltd: Swan Group Centre, 10 Intendance St, POB 837, Port Louis; tel. 211-2312; fax 208-8956; e-mail anglomtius@intnet.mu; f. 1951; Chair. J. M. ANTOINE HAREL; CEO JEAN DE FONDAUMIÈRE.

British American Insurance Co (Mauritius) Ltd: BAI Bldg, 25 Pope Hennessy St, POB 331, Port Louis; tel. 208-3637; fax 208-3713; e-mail bai@bow.intnet.mu; f. 1920; Chair. DAWOOD RAWAT; Man. Dir ALAIN C. Y. CHEONG.

Indian Ocean General Assurance Ltd: 35 Corderie St, POB 865, Port Louis; tel. 212-4125; fax 212-5850; f. 1971; Chair. SAM M. CUNDEN; Man. Dir D. A. CUNDEN.

Island Insurance Co Ltd: Labourdonnais Court, 5th Floor, cnr Labourdonnais and St Georges Sts, Port Louis; tel. 212-4860; fax 208-8762; e-mail consult@intnet.mu; Chair. CARRIM A. CURRIMJEE; Man. Dir OLIVIER LAGESSE.

Jubilee Insurance (Mauritius) Ltd: PCL Bldg, 4th Floor, 43 Sir William Newton St, POB 301, Port Louis; tel. 210-3678; fax 212-7970; e-mail jubilee@intnet.mu; f. 1998; Chair. and CEO ABDUL M. JAFFER.

Lamco International Insurance Ltd: 12 Barracks St, Port Louis; tel. 212-0233; fax 208-0630; e-mail lamco@intnet.mu; f. 1978; Chair. A. B. ATCHIA; Gen. Man. A. S. KARKHANIS.

Life Insurance Corporation of India: LIC Centre, President John F. Kennedy St, Port Louis; tel. 212-5316; fax 208-6392; Chief Man. Mr ATIMBAH.

Mauritian Eagle Insurance Co Ltd: 10 Dr Ferrière St, POB 854, Port Louis; tel. 208-1485; fax 208-8608; f. 1973; Chair. CHRISTIAN DALAIS; Exec. Dir GUY LEROUX.

Mauritius Union Assurance Co Ltd: 4 L'Homme St, POB 233, Port Louis; tel. 208-4185; fax 212-2962; e-mail mua@bow.intnet.mu; f. 1948; Chair. Sir MAURICE LATOUR-ADRIEN; Gen. Man. JOHN NOËL LAM CHUN.

The New India Assurance Co Ltd: Bank of Baroda Bldg, 3rd Floor, 15 Sir William Newton St, POB 398, Port Louis; tel. 208-1442; fax 208-2160; e-mail niassurance@intnet.mu; Chief Man. P. K. KATHURIA.

La Préservatrice Foncière: 6 Dumas St, Port Louis; tel. 212-1352; fax 208-3604; Dirs MAURICE MARTIN, FRANÇOIS MARTIN.

La Prudence Mauricienne Assurances Ltée: Le Caudan Waterfront, 2nd Floor, Barkly Wharf, POB 882, Port Louis; tel. 208-8935; fax 208-8936; e-mail prudence@intnet.mu; Chair. ROBERT DE FROBERVILLE; Man. Dir FÉLIX MAUREL.

Rainbow Insurance Co Ltd: 23 Edith Cavell St, POB 389, Port Louis; tel. 212-5767; fax 208-8750; f. 1976; Chair. B. GOKULSING; Man. Dir PREVIN RENBURG.

Seagull Insurance Ltd: Blendax House, 3rd Floor, Dumas St, POB 1058, Port Louis; tel. 212-0867; fax 208-2417; Chair. Y. V. LAI FAT FUR; Man. Dir O. GUNGABISSOON.

State Insurance Co of Mauritius Ltd (SICOM): SICOM Bldg, Sir Célicourt Antelme St, Port Louis; tel. 208-5406; fax 208-7662; e-mail mail@sicom.intnet.mu; f. 1975; Chair. RAMESH SUNT; Man. Dir Mrs K. BHOOJEDHUR-OBEEGADOO.

Stella Insurance Co Ltd: 17 Sir Seewoosagur Ramgoolam St, POB 852, Port Louis; tel. 208-0056; fax 208-1639; e-mail stellain@intnet.mu; internet www.stellain.com; f. 1977; Chair. and Man. Dir R. KRESHAN JHOBOO.

Sun Insurance Co Ltd: 2 St George St, Port Louis; tel. 208-0769; fax 208-2052; f. 1981; Chair. Sir KAILASH RAMDANEE; Man. Dir A. MUSBALLY.

Swan Insurance Co Ltd: Swan Group Centre, 10 Intendance St, POB 364, Port Louis; tel. 211-2001; fax 208-6898; e-mail swan@bow .intnet.mu; f. 1955; Chair. J. M. ANTOINE HAREL; CEO JEAN DE FONDAU-MIÈRE.

L. and H. Vigier de Latour Ltd: Les Jamalacs Bldg, Old Council St, Port Louis; tel. 212-2034; fax 212-6056; Chair. and Man. Dir L. J. D. HENRI VIGIER DE LATOUR.

Trade and Industry

GOVERNMENT AGENCIES

Agricultural Marketing Board (AMB): Dr G. Leclézio Ave, Moka; tel. 433-1980; fax 433-4837; e-mail agbd@intnet.mu; markets certain locally produced food crops; also collects and distributes milk and provides cold store facilities.

Mauritius Meat Authority: Abattoir Rd, Roche Bois, POB 612, Port Louis; tel. 242-5884; fax 242-4695; e-mail msa@bow.intnet.mu; licensing authority; controls and regulates sale of meat and meat products; also purchases and imports livestock and markets meat products.

Mauritius Sugar Authority: Ken Lee Bldg, 2nd Floor, Edith Cavell St, Port Louis; tel. 208-7466; fax 208-7470; Exec. Dir G. RAJPATI.

Mauritius Tea Board: Wooton St, Curepipe Rd, Curepipe; tel. 675-3497; responsible for the tea industry; also promotes diversification into other crops.

DEVELOPMENT ORGANIZATIONS

Mauritius Export Development and Investment Authority (MEDIA): BAI Bldg, 2nd Floor, 25 Pope Hennessy St, POB 1184, Port Louis; tel. 208-7750; fax 208-5965; f. 1985 to promote exports of goods and services and to encourage export-orientated investment; Chair. RAJKAMAL TAPOSEEA; CEO CHAND BHADAIN.

Mauritius Freeport Authority: Deramann Tower, 3rd Floor, 30 Sir William Newton St, Port Louis; tel. 212-9627; fax 212-9626; e-mail freeport@bow.intnet.mu; internet www.mauritius.freeport .com; f.1990; Chair. Prof. EDOUARD LIM FAT; Dir-Gen. GÉRARD SANSPEUR.

Mauritius Offshore Business Activities Authority (MOBAA): Barkly Wharf, 5th Floor, le Caudan Waterfront, Old Pavilion St, Port Louis; tel. 210-7000; fax 212-9459; e-mail mobaa@intnet.mu; internet www.mobaa.net; f.1992; regulates and supervises 'offshore' commercial activities; Dir SATYADEV DEONARAIN BIKOO.

State Investment Corporation Ltd (SIC): Fon Sing Bldg, 2nd Floor, 12 Edith Cavell St, Port Louis; tel. 212-2978; fax 208-8948; provides support for new investment and transfer of technology, in agriculture, industry and tourism; CEO RAJIV BEEHARRY.

CHAMBERS OF COMMERCE

Chinese Chamber of Commerce: 35 Dr Joseph Rivière St, Port Louis; tel. 208-0946; fax 242-1193; Pres. JEAN KOK SHUN.

Mauritius Chamber of Commerce and Industry: 3 Royal St, Port Louis; tel. 208-3301; fax 208-0076; e-mail mcci@ intnet.mu; internet www.mcci.org; f. 1850; 416 mems; Pres. DEREK TAYLOR; Sec.-Gen. JEAN-CLAUDE MONTOCCHIO (until May 2000).

INDUSTRIAL ASSOCIATION

Mauritius Sugar Producers' Association: Plantation House, Duke of Edinburgh Ave, Port Louis; tel. 212-0295; fax 212-5727; e-mail mspa@intnet.mu; Chair. ARNAUD DALAIS; Dir P. DE L'. D' ARIFAT.

EMPLOYERS' ORGANIZATION

Mauritius Employers' Federation: Cerné House, 1st Floor, Chaussée St, Port Louis; tel. 212-1599; fax 212-6725; e-mail mef@ intnet.mu; f. 1962; Pres. FRANÇOIS WOO; Dir Dr AZAD JEETUN.

UTILITIES
Electricity

Central Electricity Board: Teste de Buch St, Curepipe; tel. 675-5010; fax 675-7958; f. 1952; state-operated; Chair. SUBASH JEEPAUL Dir-Gen. EDDY ASTRUC.

Water

Central Water Authority: St Paul-Phoenix; tel. 686-5071; fax 686-6264; e-mail cwa@bow.intnet.mu; state-operated.

MAJOR COMPANIES

Compagnie Sucrière de St Antoine Ltée: Cerné House, La Chaussée, Port Louis; tel. 283-9545; fax 283-9551; mfrs of sugar products.

International Distillers (Mauritius) Ltd: POB 661, Plaine Lauzun; tel. 212-6896; fax 208-6076; e-mail idmltd@intnet.mu; mfrs, importers and distributors of wines and spirits.

Les Moulins de la Concorde Ltée: Cargo Peninsula, Quay D, Port Louis; tel. 240-8180; fax 240-8171; millers; Chair. ARMAND MAUDAVE.

Mauritius Chemical and Fertilizer Industry Ltd: Chaussée Tromelin, POB 344, Port Louis; tel. 242-5077; fax 240-9969; e-mail mcfi@bow.intnet.mu; mfrs of agricultural chemicals and fertilizers; Chair. J. M. ANTOINE HAREL.

Prince's Tuna (Mauritius) Ltd: Caudan, POB 131, Port Louis; tel. 212-3746; fax 212-5876; e-mail mlan@intnet.mu; processors of tuna fish; Chair. J. MUTCH.

TRADE UNIONS
Federations

Federation of Civil Service Unions (FCSU): Jade Court, Rm 308, 3rd Floor, Jummah Mosque St, Port Louis; tel. 216-1977; fax 216-1475; f. 1975; 65 affiliated unions with 22,000 mems (1997); Pres. RASHID IMRITH; Sec. SOONDRESS SAWMYANDER.

General Workers' Federation: 19B Poudrière St, Port Louis; tel. 212-3338; Pres. BEEDIANAND JHURRY; Sec.-Gen. FAROOK AUCHOYBUR.

Mauritius Federation of Trade Unions: Arc Bldg, 3rd Floor, cnr Sir William Newton and Sir Seewoosagur Ramgoolam Sts, Port Louis; tel. 208-9426; f. 1958; four affiliated unions; Pres. FAROOK HOSSENBUX; Sec.-Gen. R. MAREEMOOTOO.

Mauritius Labour Congress: 8 Louis Victor de la Faye St, Port Louis; tel. 212-4343; fax 208-8945; f. 1963; 55 affiliated unions with 70,000 mems (1992); Pres. NURDEO LUCHMUN ROY; Gen. Sec. JUGDISH LOLLBEEHARRY.

Principal Unions

Government Servants' Association: 107A Royal Rd, Beau Bassin; tel. 464-4242; f. 1945; Pres. A. H. MALLECK-AMODE; Sec.-Gen. S. P. TORUL; 14,000 mems (1984).

Government Teachers' Union: 3 Mgr Gonin St, POB 1111, Port Louis; tel. 208-0047; fax 208-4943; f. 1945; Pres. JUGDISH LOLLBEE-HARRY; Sec. SHEIKH NASHIR RAMJAN; 4,358 mems (1998).

Nursing Association: Royal Rd, Beau Bassin; tel. 464-5850; f. 1955; Pres. CASSAM KUREEMAN; Sec.-Gen. FRANCIS SUPPARAYEN; 2,040 mems (1980).

Organization of Artisans' Unity: 42 Sir William Newton St, Port Louis; tel. 212-4557; f. 1973; Pres. AUGUSTE FOLLET; Sec. ROY RAMCHURN; 2,874 mems (1994).

Plantation Workers' Union: 8 Louis Victor de la Faye St, Port Louis; tel. 212-1735; f. 1955; Pres. C. BHAGIRUTTY; Sec. N. L. ROY; 13,726 mems (1990).

Port Louis Harbour and Docks Workers' Union: 19B Poudrière St, Port Louis; tel. 208-2276; Pres. M. VEERABADREN; Sec.-Gen. GERARD BERTRAND; 2,198 mems (1980).

Sugar Industry Staff Employees' Association: 1 Rémy Ollier St, Port Louis; tel. 212-1947; f. 1947; Chair. T. BELLEROSE; Sec.-Gen. G. CHUNG KWAN FANG; 1,450 mems (1997).

Textile, Clothes and Other Manufactures Workers' Union: Thomy d'Arifat St, Curepipe; tel. 676-5280; Pres. PADMATEE TEELUCK; Sec.-Gen. DÉSIRÉ GUILDAREE.

Union of Bus Industry Workers: 19B Poudrière St, Port Louis; tel. 212-3338; Pres. BABOOA; Sec.-Gen. F. AUCHOYBUR; 1,783 mems (1980).

Union of Employees of the Ministry of Agriculture and other Ministries: Royal Rd, Curepipe; tel. 686-1847; f. 1989; 2,131 mems (1988); Sec. P. JAGARNATH.

Union of Labourers of the Sugar and Tea Industry: Royal Rd, Curepipe; f. 1969; Sec. P. RAMCHURN; 2,150 mems (1980).

Transport

RAILWAYS

There are no operational railways in Mauritius.

ROADS

In 1997 there were 1,905 km of classified roads, of which 31km were motorways, 902km were other main roads, and 582 km were secondary roads. About 93% of the road network is paved. An urban highway links the motorways approaching Port Louis. A motorway connects Port Louis with Plaisance airport.

SHIPPING

Mauritius is served by numerous foreign shipping lines. In 1990 Port Louis was established as a free port to expedite the development of Mauritius as an entrepôt centre. In 1995 the World Bank approved a loan of US $30.5m. for a programme to develop the port. At 31 December 1998 Mauritius had a merchant fleet of 51 vessels, with a combined displacement of 206,039 grt.

Mauritius Ports Authority: Port Administration Bldg, POB 379, Mer Rouge, Port Louis; tel. 240-0415; fax 240-0856; e-mail mpaisd@bow.intnet.mu; f. 1976; Chair. GILBERT PHILIPPE; Dir-Gen. Capt. JEAN WONG CHUNG TOI.

Ireland Blyth Ltd: 1 Queen St, POB 58, Port Louis; tel. 208-2811; fax 208-1014; Chair. P. A. DALAIS; CEO and Man. Dir G. C. DALAIS; 3 vessels.

Islands Services Ltd: Rogers House, 5 President John Kennedy St, POB 60, Port Louis; tel. 208-6801; fax 208-5045; services to Indian Ocean islands; Chair. Sir RENÉ MAINGARD; Exec. Dir Capt. RENÉ SANSON.

Mauritius Shipping Corporation Ltd: St James Court, Suite 417/418, St Denis St, Port Louis; tel. 210-6120; fax 210-5176; e-mail mauriship@intnet.mu; f. 1985; Pres. Y. ABDULLATIFF; Man. Dir SUREN RAMPHUL.

Rogers & Co Ltd: 5 President John F. Kennedy St, POB 60, Port Louis; tel. 208-6801; fax 208-5045; e-mail rogers@rogers.intnet.mu; internet www.rogersgroup.net; Chair. Sir J. EMILE SÉRIES; CEO TIMOTHY TAYLOR; 3 vessels.

Société Mauricienne de Navigation Ltée: 1 rue de la Reine, POB 53, Port Louis; tel. 208-3241; fax 208-8931; e-mail iblsh@bow.intnet.mu; Man. Dir Capt. FRANÇOIS DE GERSIGNY.

CIVIL AVIATION

Sir Seewoosagur Ramgoolam international airport is at Plaisance, 4 km from Mahébourg. Work on the construction of additional runway and air traffic control facilities, at an estimated cost of Rs 800m., was proceeding in 1999. Proposals are being considered for the construction of a second airport, at Plaine-les-Roches, in the north of the island.

Air Mauritius: Air Mauritius Centre, President John F. Kennedy St, POB 441, Port Louis; tel. 207-7070; fax 208-8331; e-mail mkcare@airmauritius.intnet.mu; internet www.airmauritius.com; f. 1967; 51% state-owned; services to 28 destinations in Europe, Asia, Australia and Africa; Chair. and Man. Dir N. MALLAM-HASHAM.

Tourism

Tourists are attracted to Mauritius by its scenery and beaches, the pleasant climate and the blend of cultures. Accommodation capacity totalled 14,995 beds in 1998. The number of visitors increased from 300,670 in 1990 to 578,100 in 1999, when the greatest numbers of visitors were from France (30.3%), Réunion (14.5%), the United Kingdom (10.2%), South Africa (8.1%) and Germany (7.8%). Revenue from tourism in 1999 was estimated at Rs 13,670m.

Mauritius Tourism Promotion Authority: Air Mauritius Centre, 11th Floor, President John F. Kennedy St, Port Louis; tel. 210-1545; fax 212-5142; e-mail mtpa@intnet.mu; internet www.mauritius.net; Chair. ARMAND MAUDAVE; Dir Dr KARL A. MOOTOOSAMY.

Defence

The country has no standing defence forces, although there is a special 1,000-strong police mobile unit to ensure internal security and a coastguard numbering 500.

Defence Expenditure: Budgeted at Rs 400m. in 1999/2000.

Education

In 1995, according to UNESCO estimates, the average rate of adult illiteracy was 17.8% (males 13.6%; females 21.8%), one of the lowest rates in sub-Saharan Africa. Education is officially compulsory for seven years between the ages of five and 12. Primary education begins at five years of age and lasts for six years. Secondary education, beginning at the age of 11, lasts for up to seven years, comprising a first cycle of three years and a second of four years. Primary and secondary education are available free of charge. In 1996 enrolment at primary schools included 98% of both males and females in the relevant age-group. In the same year the number of children attending secondary schools was equivalent to 64% of the appropriate age-group (males 63%; females 66%). The government exercises indirect control of the large private sector in secondary education. The University of Mauritius, founded in 1965, had 3,667 students in 1997/98; in addition, many students receive further education abroad. Of total proposed expenditure by the central government (excluding transfers to local government) in 1999/2000, Rs 4,056.5m. (equivalent to 13.4% of total government spending) was budgeted for education, arts and culture.

OTHER ISLANDS

Rodrigues

The island of Rodrigues covers an area of 104 sq km. Its population, which was ennumerated at 34,204 at the 1990 census, was officially estimated to number 35,332 in December 1998. Formerly also known as Diego Ruys, Rodrigues is located 585 km east of the island of Mauritius, and is administered by a resident commissioner. Rodrigues is currently represented in the national assembly by four members. Fishing and farming are the principal activities, while the main exports are cattle, salt fish, sheep, goats, pigs and onions. The island is linked to Mauritius by thrice-weekly air and monthly boat services.

The Lesser Dependencies

The Lesser Dependencies (area 71 sq km, population enumerated at 167 at the 1990 census and estimated at 170 in December 1998) are the Agalega Islands, two islands about 935 km north of Mauritius, and the Cargados Carajos Shoals (St Brandon Islands), 22 islets without permanent inhabitants, lying 370 km north-north-east. Mauritius also claims sovereignty over Tromelin Island, 556 km to the north-west. This claim is disputed by Madagascar, and also by France, which maintains an airstrip and weather station on the island.

Bibliography

Addison, J., and Hazareesingh, K. *A New History of Mauritius.* Oxford, ABC; Rose Hill, Editions de l'Océan Indien,1991.

Alladin, I. *Economic Miracle in the Indian Ocean: Can Mauritius Show the Way?* Port Louis, Editions de l'Océan Indien, 1993.

Baker, P. *Kreol: A Description of Mauritian Creole.* London, Hurst, 1972.

Benedict, B. *Indians in a Plural Society: A Report on Mauritius.* London, HMSO, 1961.

   Mauritius, A Plural Society. London, 1965.

Bissoonoyal, B. *A Concise History of Mauritius.* Bombay, Bharatiya Vidya, 1963.

Bowman, L. W. *Mauritius: Democracy and Development in the Indian Ocean.* Boulder, CO, Westview Press, 1991.

Cohen, R. *African Islands and Enclaves.* London, Sage Publications, 1983.

Dukhira, C. D. *Mauritius and Local Government Management.* Oxford, ABC; Port Louis, Editions de l'Océan Indien; Bombay, LSG Press, 1992.

Favoreu, L. *L'île Maurice.* Paris, Berger-Levrault, 1970.

Ingrams, W. H. *A Short History of Mauritius.* London, Macmillan, 1931.

International Monetary Fund. *Mauritius: Recent Economic Developments and Selected Issues.* Washington, DC, 1997.

Jones, P., and Andrews, B. *A Taste of Mauritius.* London, Macmillan, 1982.

Lehembre, B. *L'île Maurice.* Paris, Editions Karthala, 1984.

Mahadeo, T. *Mauritian Cultural Heritage.* Port Louis, Editions de l'Océan Indien, 1995.

Mathur, H. *Parliament in Mauritius.* Oxford, ABC; Rose Hill, Editions de l'Océan Indien, 1991.

Ramgoolam, Sir S. *Our Struggle: 20th Century Mauritius.* New Delhi, Vision Books, 1982.

Selvon, S. *Historical Dictionary of Mauritius.* 2nd Edn. Metuchen, NJ, Scarecrow Press, 1991.

Simmons, A. S. *Modern Mauritius: The Politics of Decolonization.* Bloomington, IN, Indiana University Press, 1982.

Titmuss, R. M., and Abel-Smith, B. *Social Policies and Population Growth in Mauritius.* Sessional Paper No. 6 of 1960, London, Methuen, reprinted by Frank Cass, 1968.

Toussaint, A. *Port Louis, deux siècles d'histoire (1735–1935).* Port Louis, 1946.

   Bibliography of Mauritius 1501–1954. Port Louis, 1956.

   Histoire des îles Mascareignes. Paris, Berger-Levrault, 1972.

World Bank. *Mauritius: Economic Memorandum: Recent Developments and Prospects.* Washington, DC, 1983.

   Mauritius: Managing Success. Washington DC, 1989.

   Mauritius: Expanding Horizons. Washington, DC, 1992.

Wright, C. *Mauritius.* Newton Abbot, David and Charles, 1974.

MOZAMBIQUE

Physical and Social Geography

RENÉ PÉLISSIER

The Republic of Mozambique covers a total area of 799,380 sq km (308,641 sq miles). This includes 13,000 sq km of inland water, mainly comprising Lake Niassa, the Mozambican section of Lake Malawi. Mozambique is bounded to the north by Tanzania, to the west by Malawi, Zambia and Zimbabwe, and to the south by South Africa and Swaziland.

With some exceptions towards the Zambia, Malawi and Zimbabwe borders, it is generally a low-lying plateau of moderate height, descending through a sub-plateau zone to the Indian Ocean. The main reliefs are Monte Binga (2,436 m above sea-level), the highest point of Mozambique, on the Zimbabwe border in Manica province, Monte Namúli (2,419 m) in the Zambézia province, the Serra Zuira (2,227 m) in the Manica province, and several massifs which are a continuation into northern Mozambique of the Shire highlands of Malawi. The coastal lowland is narrower in the north but widens considerably towards the south, so that terrain less than 1,000 m high comprises about 45% of the total Mozambican area. The shore-line is 2,470 km long and generally sandy and bordered by lagoons, shoals and strings of coastal islets in the north.

Mozambique is divided by at least 25 main rivers, all of which flow to the Indian Ocean. The largest and most historically significant is the Zambezi, whose 820-km Mozambican section is navigable for 460 km. Flowing from eastern Angola, the Zambezi provides access to the interior of Africa from the eastern coast.

Two main seasons, wet and dry, divide the climatic year. The wet season has monthly averages of 26.7°–29.4°C, with cooler temperatures in the interior uplands. The dry season has June and July temperatures of 18.3°–20.0°C at Maputo. Mozambique is vulnerable to drought and attendant famine, which severely affected much of the country during the 1980s, particularly during the period 1982–84 and again during 1986–87. In late 1992 it was estimated that 3.2m. people were threatened with food shortages as a result of drought.

The census taken by the Portuguese authorities in December 1970 recorded a total population of 8,168,933, and the population increased to 11,673,725, excluding underenumeration (estimated at 3.8%), by the census of 1 August 1980. At the census of 1 August 1997 the population stood at 16,099,246, and at mid-2000 it was estimated at 17,242,240. The population density was 21.6 per sq km at mid-2000. Mozambique's population increased by an annual average of 2.6% during 1990–98.

North of the Zambezi, the main ethnic groupings among the African population, which belongs to the cultural division of Central Bantu, are the Makua-Lomwe groups, who form the principal ethno-linguistic subdivision of Mozambique and are believed to comprise about 40% of the population. South of the Zambezi, the main group is the Thonga, who feature prominently as Mozambican mine labourers in South Africa. North of the Thonga area lies the Shona group, numbering more than 1m. Southern ethnic groups have tended to enjoy greater educational opportunities than those of other regions. The government has sought to balance the ethnic composition of its leadership, but the executive is still largely of southern and central origin.

Mozambique is divided into 11 administrative provinces, one of which comprises the capital, Maputo, a modern seaport whose population was 989,386 at 1 August 1997. The second seaport of the country is Beira. Other towns of importance include Nampula, on the railway line to Niassa province and Malawi, and Matola.

Recent History

JOÃO GOMES CRAVINHO

Revised for this edition by MAREK GARZTECKI

The territory now comprising the Republic of Mozambique came under Portuguese control in the 19th century and became a Portuguese 'overseas province' in 1951. Nationalist groups began to form in the early 1960s, eventually uniting in the Frente de Libertação de Moçambique (Frelimo), under the leadership of Eduardo Mondlane, in 1962. In 1964 Frelimo launched a military campaign for independence against the colonial regime, that subsequently developed into a serious conflict, engaging thousands of Portuguese troops by the early 1970s. Following the assassination of Mondlane in 1969, Samora Machel was elected leader. After the military coup in Portugal in April 1974, the Portuguese authorities agreed to hand over power to a transitional Frelimo-dominated government, and full independence followed on 25 June 1975, when the People's Republic of Mozambique was declared, with Machel as its president.

The new Frelimo government implemented a centrally planned economy and one-party state, and in 1977 Frelimo declared itself to be a 'Marxist-Leninist vanguard party.' Despite impressive advances in the fields of public health, social welfare and education, Frelimo's policy of *socialização do campo* (socialization of the countryside) succeeded in antagonizing most of the country's peasantry (which accounted for 80% of the population); collective agriculture was promoted, traditional beliefs and ceremonies were prohibited, *regulos* (tribal kings) were stripped of their powers and church-run social projects were closed.

CIVIL WAR

In its foreign policy Frelimo embraced international activism during the late 1970s, implementing sanctions against the white regime in Rhodesia, by cutting off its main transport route via the Mozambican port of Beira. It also allowed Robert Mugabe's Zimbabwe African National Union (ZANU) forces to set up bases on its territory and mount cross-border raids. The Rhodesian authorities responded by arming and providing support to the dissident Movimento Nacional de Resistência de Moçambique (MNR).

By 1991, following the emergence of an independent Zimbabwe, South Africa became the MNR's main supporter. Under South African tutelage the MNR, now renamed Resistência Nacional Moçambicana (Renamo), rapidly expanded from some 500 to a force of an estimated 8,000 guerrillas. Renamo concentrated its attacks on the symbols of Frelimo achievements, such as schools, health centres, social projects and transport infrastructure, and acquired a reputation for brutality, including mass murders of civilians as well as mutilations. Furthermore, the government and Renamo became involved in super-power rivalry, serving as proxies for the Soviet Union and the west respectively. Mozambique's problems were further aggravated by catastrophic droughts.

POLITICAL LIBERALIZATION

In October 1986 President Machel was killed when the aircraft in which he was travelling crashed (see below). He was succeeded as president by Joaquim Chissano, the former minister of foreign affairs. Fundamental changes in Frelimo's political and economic philosophy began to emerge in 1987, when an economic recovery programme, the Programa de Reabilitação Econômica (PRE), was launched; it included wide-ranging policy reforms designed to move the country away from socialist central planning towards a free-market economy (see Economy). In 1989 the party renounced its Marxist-Leninist orientation, embracing social democracy and opening its membership to all. In January 1990 draft proposals for a new constitution were published, providing for the direct election of the president and people's assembly by universal suffrage. Renamo was invited to contest the elections, provided that it abandoned violence and acknowledged the legitimacy of the state. The draft constitution, which was submitted to public debate during 1990, provided for the separation of Frelimo and the state, the independence of the judiciary and the right to strike.

These political developments represented attempts to create a framework for a diplomatic solution to the civil war, by reducing the disparity between the aims of the government and those of Renamo. The process of political change was further advanced in August 1990, when Frelimo announced that multi-party legislative elections were to take place in 1991, and that the country's name was to be changed from the People's Republic of Mozambique to the Republic of Mozambique.

The new constitution was formally approved by the people's assembly at the beginning of November 1990 and took effect at the end of the month. Provisions outlawing censorship and enshrining freedom of expression had been added to the earlier draft after representations by local journalists; the constitution also abolished the death penalty. The new constitution was welcomed by Western aid donors but rejected by Renamo as the product of an unrepresentative, unelected body.

The renamed assembly of the republic met for the first time in December 1990. One of its first acts was to pass legislation allowing the formation of new political parties, which took effect in February 1991. In March President Chissano announced that general elections would be held in 1992. A number of political parties announced their intention to apply for legal status under the new legislation. Prominent among these were the Partido Liberal e Democrático de Moçambique (Palmo), which described itself as 'anti-socialist' and whose manifesto expressed views critical of white, mixed race and Asian Mozambicans; the União Nacional Moçambicana (Unamo), described as 'social democratic' and composed of disaffected guerrillas who had left Renamo, and the Movimento Nacionalista Moçambicana–Partido Moçambicano da Social Democracia (Monamo–PMSD), based in Portugal. A fourth party, the Congresso Independente de Moçambique (Coinmo), founded in Kenya in 1985, was led by Vítor Marcos Saene, son of an exiled Frelimo dissident.

Evidence of opposition to the change-over to multi-party democracy emerged in late June 1991 when a conspiracy against the government was discovered, leading to the arrests of a number of serving and retired army officers, as well as civilians. In August, the minister of the interior, Col Manuel José António, was questioned in connection with the alleged coup conspiracy, although the case against him was dropped in February 1992, on the grounds that he had been instrumental in bringing the coup attempt to the attention of the authorities, and he returned to his duties in April. Mabote was acquitted of all charges by the supreme court in September, and 13 others were released under a general amnesty in October.

Frelimo held its sixth congress in August 1991, re-electing Chissano as party chairman and electing its central committee by secret ballot for the first time. Feliciano Gundana, the minister of the presidency, was appointed to the new post of party secretary-general. New legislation on trade union activity was passed by parliament in December, allowing workers to form trade unions of their choice, to join and resign from unions at will and establishing unions as self-regulating and autonomous organizations, free from outside interference.

New political parties continued to organize during late 1991 and early 1992 in preparation for the forthcoming elections, with several of the newly-registered parties, including Renamo, holding conventions, one of the conditions for registration. The formal end to one-party politics came in March with the official registration of Unamo as the first legal opposition party. Earlier, a long-standing opponent of Frelimo, Domingos Arouca, in exile in Portugal since 1975, returned to launch the local organization of his Frente Unido de Moçambique (Fumo), formed in exile in 1976. Arouca declared his intention to form a 'third force', between Frelimo and Renamo on the political spectrum, and invited the co-operation of other opposition parties. In late June 1992 the leader of Palmo, Martins Bilal, announced that eight parties, including Palmo, had agreed to work together to present a 'third force' in opposition to Frelimo and Renamo.

The government published a draft electoral law in March 1993 proposing the establishment of a 21-member national electoral commission, chaired by a member of the supreme court, to organize and supervise the elections. A multi-party conference, convened in late April to discuss the law, collapsed when 12 opposition parties announced that they would boycott the conference until their demands for accommodation and logistical support were met. Following the collapse of the discussions, the 12 opposition parties called for the establishment of a transitional coalition administration pending the elections. The demand was rejected by the government. The conference met again in late July, after the opposition parties agreed to end their boycott in return for promises of state funding in 1994, but was again disrupted by the withdrawal of Renamo, which alleged that the draft electoral law contravened the peace agreement, which had been signed in October 1992 (see below).

MOZAMBIQUE–SOUTH AFRICA SECURITY ISSUES

The high economic cost of the conflict with Renamo prompted Mozambique to enter into discussions with the South African government in late 1983. Negotiations in early 1984 culminated in the Nkomati Accord, a non-aggression treaty, in which both sides bound themselves not to give material aid to opposition movements in each other's countries, and to establish a joint security commission. Effectively, this meant that Mozambique would prevent the African National Congress of South Africa (ANC) from conducting military operations from its territory, while South Africa would cease to support Renamo. The government immediately restricted the organization's presence to a diplomatic mission in Maputo. For its part, however, the South African government effectively ignored the accord. The disruption resulting from continuing Renamo operations in Mozambique was considerable, and by August 1984 Renamo forces were active in all 10 of Mozambique's provinces, with the capital coming increasingly under threat. The South African government, however, denied any involvement in the continuing Renamo activity.

The escalating internal conflict led the Frelimo government to warn South Africa in August 1984 that both the accord and associated plans for economic co-operation were under threat unless Renamo activity was halted. South Africa responded by convening a number of separate but parallel talks with Renamo and Frelimo government representatives during August and September, which culminated, in early October, in the so-called 'Pretoria Declaration' in which a cease-fire was agreed in principle between the Frelimo government and the rebels, and a tripartite commission, comprising Frelimo, Renamo and South African representatives, was established to implement the truce. In November, however, Renamo withdrew from the peace negotiations, citing the Frelimo government's continued refusal to recognize its legitimacy. The rebel movement also announced the launching of a major country-wide offensive. In December the South African government denied Mozambican claims that it was continuing to support Renamo, and made further, unsuccessful attempts in early 1985 to persuade Renamo to negotiate with the Frelimo government.

Meanwhile, the joint security commission, established between South Africa and Mozambique under the provisions of the Nkomati accord, continued to meet to review the situation, but Renamo activity in Mozambique continued. In March 1985 the two countries reiterated their continued commitment to the accord, and South Africa announced that a restricted air space, partly aimed at preventing support from reaching Renamo guerrillas from South African territory, would be established in the border area with Mozambique. This was followed in April by an announcement that a joint operational centre dealing with security and other matters relating to the Nkomati Accord, would be established on the border between Mozambique and South Africa. However, in the same month, Renamo guerrilla activity effectively severed rail links between the two countries.

The worsening security situation precipitated a meeting in June 1985 in Harare, Zimbabwe, between President Machel, Robert Mugabe (the prime minister of Zimbabwe) and President Nyerere of Tanzania, at which it was agreed that Tanzania and Zimbabwe would support Mozambique, and, in particular, that Zimbabwe would augment its military presence in Mozambique. This arrangement resulted in the capture, in August, of the largest Renamo base, the so-called 'Casa Banana' in Sofala province, and of other major rebel bases in the area. Not only were large quantities of weapons captured, but also incriminating documentation concerning South African support for Renamo since the signing of the Nkomati Accord. Some of these documents were published, compelling the South African government to confirm the allegations, although claiming that its continued contacts with Renamo were designed to promote peace negotiations between the guerrillas and the Frelimo government. In mid-October Mozambique unilaterally suspended the joint security commission.

In early 1986 the Mozambique government's military situation deteriorated sharply. This was most graphically illustrated by the recapture in February of the 'Casa Banana' base by Renamo forces, who encountered no serious opposition from fleeing government troops. This military reverse dismayed the Zimbabweans, who had been instrumental in capturing the base; it was eventually recaptured by them in April.

The second half of 1986 was dominated both by a deterioration in the military situation and by the sudden death of President Samora Machel: in October a Soviet civilian aircraft carrying the president, on his return from a meeting in Zambia of leaders of the 'front-line' states, crashed just inside South African territory, killing the president, together with two of his aides and the minister of transport, Luís Santos. Controversy has continued to surround the causes of the crash, especially over the strong possibility of South African involvement. Following the disaster, Mozambican demonstrators attacked the South African trade mission in Maputo, in protest against South Africa's suspected involvement in the incident.

In October the South African government banned the recruitment of Mozambican miners, and was to repatriate some 60,000 Mozambicans already employed in South African mines, in retaliation for an alleged increase in activity by ANC guerrillas in the Mozambique border region. (In January 1987 this decision was relaxed in respect of about 30,000 of the Mozambican mineworkers.) In January 1987 a joint report, compiled by Mozambican, Soviet and South African experts, was presented to an international board of inquiry, established to investigate the crash. The board concluded that pilot error, and not sabotage, had caused the accident, although some observers suggested that the examination of the course of events was not sufficiently thorough. (In May 1998 it was announced that South Africa's Truth and Reconciliation Committee was to examine evidence relating to the crash.)

Following the death of Machel in October 1986, Mozambique applied intense pressure on Malawi, including threats of military action, to induce its neighbour to cease accommodating Renamo, and in December a joint security agreement was signed between the two states. In April 1987 Chissano confirmed the presence of some 300 Malawian troops guarding part of the railway line from the Malawi frontier to Nacala, in northern Mozambique. Malawi's willingness to co-operate with Mozambique was endangered in November 1987, when it was reported that Mozambique government forces had shot down a Malawian civilian aircraft (which they claimed to have violated Mozambican airspace), killing 10 people. The Mozambique government expressed its regret, and a joint investigation by the two countries into the incident led to

the drafting of new regulations on air safety. By mid-1988 the number of Malawian troops in Mozambique had increased to 600, and in July, during a state visit to Malawi, Chissano praised the country for its support of his government. In December 1988 Mozambique, Malawi, and the United Nations High Commissioner for Refugees (UNHCR) signed an agreement to promote the voluntary repatriation of Mozambican refugees in Malawi.

The Mozambican army was so ill-equipped and malnourished that it was often unable to hold even well-defended positions. However, government troops became more successful at repulsing rebel attacks during 1987, although Renamo continued to cause widespread disruption. In February Zimbabwean and Mozambican troops recaptured five towns in northern Mozambique which Renamo had seized in late 1986. This signified a general shift in the balance of power, with Renamo increasing its operations in the south, while government troops registered important successes in the north and along the coastline. In March 1987 the government carried out a major reorganization of the armed forces, which included the establishment of highly-trained commandos and the arrival of reinforcements from Zimbabwe and Tanzania. The apparent cessation of covert aid by Malawi to Renamo may also have been significant.

An open raid in late May 1987 by South African security forces on alleged ANC bases in metropolitan Maputo effectively signalled the demise of the Nkomati Accord. Renewed accusations of South African support for Renamo were made in July, when the rebels were allegedly responsible for the massacre of 424 civilians in the southern Mozambican town of Homoine. South Africa denied any involvement in the incident, however, and offered to investigate its circumstances jointly with Mozambique. International opinion was further outraged by successive attacks attributed to Renamo, including the ambush, in October, of a convoy travelling from Maputo on the main north–south road, in which more than 270 people were killed. The rebels were also reported to have conducted a series of cross-border raids into Zambia and, especially, Zimbabwe; between June and December some 80 Zimbabwean civilians were allegedly killed by Renamo guerrillas.

In December 1987 President Chissano announced a 'law of pardon', offering to release on parole or shorten the sentences of repentant convicted prisoners; he also offered amnesty for members of Renamo willing to surrender their weapons. By December 1988 it was claimed by the Mozambican authorities that more than 3,000 rebels had defected to its side; these included two prominent members of the European branch of Renamo, both of whom accused South Africa of continuing complicity in the affairs of the organization. The amnesty was initially to have expired in December 1988, but was extended for a further 12 months. Meanwhile, government troops made important advances against Renamo.

The defection of some Renamo members appeared to have been prompted by bitter divisions within the organization. The main disagreement was between the proponents and opponents, such as Afonso Dhlakama (the leader of Renamo), of a peaceful resolution of the armed conflict by means of negotiation with the Frelimo government and by a reduction of links with South Africa.

In late 1987 and early 1988 the governments of Mozambique and South Africa held discussions aimed at reviving the Nkomati Accord. A bomb attack in Maputo in April 1988, in which an exiled South African anti-apartheid activist was severely injured, threatened to undermine the progress made in negotiations. However, a series of discussions between Mozambique, South Africa and Portugal led to an agreement by these countries, signed in November 1987, to restore the Cahora Bassa dam in Mozambique (see Economy). In September 1988 President Chissano met the South African president, P. W. Botha, in Mozambique, as a result of which Mozambique and South Africa established a joint commission for co-operation and development, and South Africa agreed to provide non-lethal military aid for the protection of the Cahora Bassa power lines. In addition, South Africa agreed to give assistance for improvements to Maputo harbour and to the road and rail links between Mozambique and South Africa, and in November restrictions on the recruitment of Mozambican mineworkers in South Africa were withdrawn. In February 1989 South Africa proposed a peace initiative for Mozambique, whereby the USA was to mediate a settlement between the Mozambican government and Renamo; however, the two parties in the conflict rejected this offer. In the following month a senior US government official claimed that supplies were still reaching Renamo from South Africa. Nevertheless, during a visit to Mozambique in July by the then leader of the South African National Party, F. W. de Klerk, Chissano accepted that the South African government no longer supported the rebel organization.

PEACE INITIATIVES

In June 1989 the government launched a peace initiative containing 12 principles, which demanded the cessation of acts of terrorism, guaranteed the right of political participation to all 'individuals' who renounced violence, recognized the principle that no group should impose its will on another by force and demanded that all parties should respect the legitimacy of the state and of the constitution. In mid-1989 Presidents Moi of Kenya and Mugabe of Zimbabwe agreed to mediate between Renamo and the Mozambique government, and in August officials from the Mozambique Christian Council met representatives from Renamo in Nairobi to discuss the 12 principles. However, Renamo rejected the plan, demanding its recognition as a political entity, the introduction of multi-party elections and the withdrawal of Zimbabwean troops from Mozambique. Nevertheless, there was indirect contact between Renamo and the government during late 1989. In mid-November Presidents Moi and Mugabe invited both parties to hold direct negotiations. Although the government subsequently agreed to this offer in principle, it continued to deny formal recognition to Renamo. The role of Presidents Mugabe and Moi as mediators came to an end after Renamo refused to attend a meeting between the protagonists that had been arranged to take place in Malawi in June 1990.

However, in July 1990 the first direct talks between the two sides were held in Rome, Italy, and further talks were held in August. A third round of talks, due to start in September, was postponed after Renamo alleged that the government had begun a new military offensive. The two sides met again in Rome in November when Renamo presented a list of demands as conditions for a cease-fire, including the withdrawal of all foreign troops from the country and the abandonment of the new constitution. Three weeks of talks culminated in the signing on 1 December of a partial cease-fire agreement. This provided for the withdrawal of Zimbabwean forces to within 3 km of the Beira and Limpopo transport 'corridors'. In exchange, Renamo agreed to cease hostilities and refrain from attacking the 'corridors'. The cease-fire was to be monitored by a joint verification commission (JVC) comprising representatives from 10 countries. The withdrawal of Zimbabwean troops to the 'corridors' was completed by the end of December but a number of violations of the cease-fire, mostly attributed to Renamo, were reported in January 1991.

A brief round of the peace talks was held in mid-December 1990, but proved inconclusive; the fifth round, in late January and early February 1991, collapsed after Renamo rejected a JVC report accusing it of breaching the cease-fire provisions. Later in February, Renamo announced that it would resume attacks. However, in March Renamo was reported to be ready to resume negotiations and declared a unilateral cease-fire over the Easter period. Attacks by Renamo during the early months of 1991 included the first, for more than a year, on the transport 'corridor' from Nacala port in northern Mozambique to Malawi. This had not been covered by the partial cease-fire agreement because of the lack of rebel activity in the area at the time.

Following a meeting between Renamo and members of the JVC in mid-April 1991 to discuss alleged violations of the cease-fire, direct talks resumed in Rome, Italy, on 6 May. The talks, which ended on 10 June, were reported to have agreed on a timetable for the discussion of outstanding issues, including setting a date for the cessation of hostilities and for the calling of general elections.

The seventh round of peace talks began in Rome in August 1991 and was suspended on 9 August, to give Renamo time to consider proposals made by the mediators which would allow it to begin political activities in Mozambique as soon as a cease-fire had been agreed, but requiring it to recognize the existing constitution. Renamo was, however, reported to have made a

new demand: that the UN should take control of the administration during the period between a cease-fire and the elections. This demand was abandoned at the next round of talks, in October, which ended with clear signs of progress, including the signing by the two sides of a protocol said to represent a recognition by Renamo of the government's legitimacy and its agreement to begin operating as an opposition political party. In return, the government was reported to have undertaken not to enact legislation before the elections on any of the issues under discussion at the talks. The establishment of a commission to oversee the eventual cease-fire was also agreed. In the following month, it was agreed that Renamo would function as a political party immediately after a cease-fire.

Relations with Malawi deteriorated sharply at the end of December 1991, when Mozambique protested about Malawi's sudden closure of the border crossing at Milange, one of the major entry points to Mozambique. The closure, that halted international relief consignments to Zambézia province, was thought to be linked to political conflicts within Malawi. The border crossing was eventually re-opened in January 1992.

The role of Mugabe as a mediator resumed following talks with Chissano in December 1991. In mid-January 1992, Mugabe and President Banda of Malawi held direct discussions with Renamo leader Afonso Dhlakama, in Malawi, in an effort to expedite the peace talks, although it was reported that one of Renamo's main demands—the withdrawal of the 7,000 Zimbabwean troops from Mozambique—was not discussed. The ninth round of peace talks began in Rome on 21 January but remained deadlocked for several weeks because of demands by Renamo that the government commit itself to a revision of the constitution. In mid-March, however, a third protocol was signed, establishing the principles for the country's future electoral system. The protocol provided for a system of proportional representation for the legislature, with legislative and presidential elections to take place simultaneously within one year of the signing of a cease-fire. A national electoral commission was to be set up to oversee the elections, with one-third of its members appointed by Renamo. The protocol also guaranteed freedom of the press and media as well as of association, expression and movement.

Rebel activity within Mozambique, with attacks on the fringes of major cities, including Maputo, Beira and Chimoio, continued during March 1992. Convoys carrying relief supplies were also attacked and in April the Red Cross sought guarantees from Renamo that it would not attack relief shipments. Following appeals by Chissano and the Italian minister of foreign affairs for other countries, including the USA, Portugal, France and Britain, to participate in the peace talks as observers, US assistant secretary of state Herman Cohen met Dhlakama in Malawi in late April. At the meeting he was understood to have persuaded the rebel leader to concentrate on discussing proposals for a cease-fire, rather than political issues, at the next round of talks. There was speculation that the increasingly severe drought in Mozambique (see below) was having an impact on Renamo's forces, and increasing the chances for a peaceful settlement. However, when, after a series of delays, the peace talks re-opened in Rome in mid-June, Renamo's negotiators immediately departed from the agreed agenda to revive the constitutional issue, resulting in a further deadlock. After meetings in July with the presidents of South Africa and Zimbabwe, Chissano announced that he was prepared to meet Dhlakama. In early August, following three days of discussions in Rome, Chissano and Dhlakama signed a joint declaration committing the two sides to a total cease-fire by 1 October 1992, as part of a general peace agreement which would provide for presidential and legislative elections within one year. Dhlakama rejected Chissano's offer of an immediate armistice, on the grounds that the mechanisms necessary to guarantee such a truce had first to be implemented. The two leaders did agree, however, to guarantee the political rights and freedoms and personal security of all Mozambican citizens and political parties, and to accept the role of the international community, particularly the UN, in monitoring and guaranteeing the peace agreement.

In mid-September 1992 Chissano and Dhlakama met in Gaborone, Botswana, to attempt to resolve the military and security issues which had remained deadlocked since the first substantive talks on the subjects in early July. At the talks

Chissano offered to establish an independent commission to monitor and guarantee the impartiality of the Serviço de Informação e Segurança do Estado (SISE, State Information and Security Service), a body which Renamo claimed to be merely a successor to the disbanded political police. It was also agreed that the joint national defence force would number 30,000 troops. As the talks continued, aid agencies warned that up to 3.2m. people in Mozambique were threatened with food shortages due to the drought. In mid-September Renamo agreed to open two transport corridors to allow food aid to reach some of those in need in areas under its control in central Mozambique, although it insisted that most areas could be supplied by air.

The Acordo Geral de Paz

Following a brief delay a peace agreement, known as the Acordo Geral de Paz (AGP), was eventually signed on 4 October 1992. It provided that a general cease-fire was to come into force immediately after ratification of the treaty by the assembly of the republic. Both the Renamo and the government forces were to withdraw to assembly points within seven days of ratification. A new 30,000-strong national defence force, the Forças Armadas de Defesa de Moçambique (FADM), would then be created, drawing on equal numbers from each side, with the remaining troops surrendering their weapons to a UN peace-keeping force within six months. A cease-fire commission, incorporating representatives from the government, Renamo and the UN, would be established to assume responsibility for supervising the implementation of the truce regulations. In overall political control of the peace process would be the Comissão de Supervisão e Controle (CSC, Supervision and Control Commission), comprising representatives of the government, Renamo and the UN, with responsibilities including the supervision of the cease-fire commission and other commissions charged with establishing the joint armed forces and reintegrating demobilized soldiers into society, as well as verifying the withdrawal of foreign troops from Mozambique. In addition, Chissano was to appoint a national commission with the task of supervising the SISE. Presidential and legislative elections were to take place, under UN supervision, one year after the signing of the general peace agreement, provided that it had been fully implemented and the demobilization process completed.

The AGP was duly ratified by the assembly of the republic, and came into force on 15 October 1992. However, in the week that followed, the government accused Renamo of systematically violating the accord. The rebels had reportedly occupied four strategically-positioned towns in central and northern Mozambique. Dhlakama subsequently claimed that Renamo's actions had been defensive manoeuvres, and, in turn, accused government forces of violating the accord by advancing into Renamo territory. However, there was speculation as to the extent to which the Renamo leader was able to control his forces. The UN Security Council, meanwhile, agreed to appoint a special representative for Mozambique, former Italian parliamentarian and UN development programme official Aldo Ajello, and dispatch 25 military observers, the first of whom arrived in Maputo on 15 October.

In mid-December the UN Security Council approved a plan for the establishment of the UN Operation in Mozambique (ONUMOZ), providing for the deployment of some 7,500 troops, police and civilian observers to oversee the process of demobilization and formation of the new national armed forces, and to supervise the forthcoming elections.

ONUMOZ Intervention

The commander of the UN military force, Maj.-Gen. Lélio Gonçalves Rodrigues da Silva, assumed his post in February 1993. There were continued delays in the deployment of the peace-keeping force, with the UN experiencing difficulty in persuading member nations to commit troops. Renamo, in turn, refused to begin demobilizing its forces until the UN force was in place. The location of the 49 assembly points was not agreed until late February. Renamo withdrew from the CSC and the cease-fire commission in mid-March, protesting that its officials had not been provided with necessary accommodation, transport and food. In early April Dhlakama announced that his forces would begin to report to assembly points only when Renamo received US $15m. to support its political activities. The first UN troops

became operational in the Beira corridor on 1 April, and in mid-April the Zimbabwean troops guarding the Beira and Limpopo corridors finally withdrew, six months behind schedule. On 14 April the UN Security Council expressed serious concern at the delays, calling for the timetable for implementation of the peace treaty to be finalized.

Renamo, however, continued to use its demands for finance to delay the demobilization process, claiming, in late May, that it needed US $100m. from the international community to transform itself into a political party. In early June a meeting in Maputo of the CSC announced a formal postponement of the election date to October 1994 (one year behind the original schedule), and called for immediate action on establishing assembly points and commencing the formation of the new national armed forces. The CSC meeting was followed by a meeting of aid donors which revealed growing impatience among the international community with the repeated delays in implementing the peace agreement and with Renamo's escalating demands for funds. The meeting produced additional promises of support for the peace process, bringing the total pledged by donors to US $520m., including support for the repatriation of 1.5m. refugees from neighbouring countries, the resettlement of 4m.–5m. displaced people and the reintegration of some 80,000 former combatants into civilian life, as well as for emergency relief and reconstruction. The UN also agreed to establish a trust fund of $10m. to finance Renamo's transformation into a political party, with use of the funds requiring approval by both Renamo and the UN. A second trust fund, accessible to all political parties, was to be established once the national electoral commission had been formed, following the eventual approval of a new electoral law.

In July 1993 Renamo announced new conditions to the advancement of the peace process, initially insisting on the recognition of its own administration, to operate parallel to that of the government. This demand was later revised, with Renamo seeking appointments to five of the country's 11 provincial governorships. However, in early September, following direct talks between Chissano and Dhlakama an agreement was signed, whereby Renamo was to appoint three advisers to each of the incumbent provincial governors to advise on all issues relating to the reintegration of areas under Renamo control into a single state administration. It was also agreed that the UN be requested to provide a police corps to supervise the activities of the national police and ensure neutrality in areas under Renamo control. In late October 1993 the CSC approved a new timetable covering all aspects of the peace process, including the elections in October 1994.

In early November 1993 the UN Security Council adopted a resolution renewing the mandate of ONUMOZ for a further six months. In addition, it responded to the joint request by the government and Renamo for a UN police corps by authorizing the deployment of 128 police observers. In mid-November consensus was finally reached on the text of the electoral law, which was duly promulgated on 29 December.

At a meeting of the CSC in mid-November 1993 an agreement was signed providing for the confinement of troops to begin on 30 November. The process was to have concluded by the end of December. However, by that date less than 15% of the total number of troops for confinement had entered assembly points. In January 1994 the UN expressed concern at the slow pace at which government troops were assembling. In mid-January 540 military instructors (comprising government and Renamo troops who had been trained by British instructors in Zimbabwe) arrived in Mozambique to begin training the FADM. However, owing to logistical and financial problems, formal training was repeatedly postponed and eventually only a fraction of the originally planned numbers was trained.

The national electoral commission was inaugurated in early February 1994. It included 10 members from the government, seven from Renamo, three from the other opposition parties and an independent chairman. On 23 February the UN Security Council announced that, in response to demands made by Dhlakama for a reinforcement of the UN police corps monitoring the confinement areas, it would be increasing their number from 128 to 1,144. By the end of February only 50% of troops had entered assembly points and none had officially been demobilized. In early March, in an effort to expedite the confinement process, the government announced its decision to begin the unilateral demobilization of its troops. Renamo responded by beginning the demobilization of its troops on 18 March. In early April Lt-Gen. Lagos Lidimo, the nominee of the government, and former Renamo guerrilla commander Lt-Gen. Mateus Ngonhamo were inaugurated as the high command of the FADM.

On 11 April 1994 Chissano issued a decree establishing the date of the general election as 27–28 October. On 5 May the UN Security Council adopted a resolution renewing the mandate of ONUMOZ for the final period, ending on 15 November, subject to review in July and September. Voter registration for the elections began on 1 June and was due to continue until 15 August, with the total potential electorate estimated at some 7.89m. people.

The confinement and demobilization processes continued to make slow progress and consequently the deadline for troop confinement was extended, beyond the beginning of the electoral process, to 8 July 1994, with demobilization to be completed by 15 August. On that date, according to figures issued by ONUMOZ, a total of 64,277 government troops had registered at confinement points, of which 48,237 had been demobilized. The total number of Renamo troops registered was 22,790, of which 14,925 had been demobilized, thus making it impossible for Renamo to supply its quota of 15,000 troops to the FADM. At that point only 7,375 troops from both sides had enlisted in the FADM (4,134 government troops; 3,241 Renamo troops). The deadline for registration at confinement points was subsequently extended to 31 August, after which date it was to continue at three centres in the north, centre and south of the country. On 16 August, in accordance with the provisions of the AGP, the government Forças Armadas de Moçambique were formally dissolved and its functions transferred to the FADM, which was duly inaugurated as the country's official armed forces on the same day. During July and August a series of mutinies and demonstrations occurred involving troops from both sides stationed in confinement areas. The soldiers were protesting at poor conditions and the slow pace of demobilization. In August Renamo formally registered as a political party. In the same month the Partido Nacional Democrático, the Partido Nacional de Moçambique and Palmo formed an electoral coalition, the União Democrático (UD).

Presidential and legislative elections were held on 27–28 October 1994. Only hours before the beginning of the poll Renamo withdrew, claiming that conditions were not conducive to free and fair elections. Following intense international pressure, Renamo abandoned its boycott in the early hours of 28 October, necessitating the extension of the voting by a day.

The official election results were issued by the national electoral commission on 19 November 1994. In the presidential election Chissano secured an outright majority (53.30%) of the votes, thus avoiding the need for a second round of voting. His closest rival was Dhlakama, who received 33.73% of the votes. In the legislative election Frelimo also secured an overall majority, winning 129 of the 250 seats, while Renamo obtained 112 and the UD the remaining nine seats. Renamo received considerable support in central and northern Mozambique, and won a majority of the votes in five of the country's 11 provinces (including the most economically important in the country). The level of participation by the electorate was considerable, with some 80% of the total registered voters exercising their right to vote. Dhlakama subsequently accepted the results of the elections, although he maintained that there had been irregularities. The UN recognized the occurrence of irregularities, but asserted that these were insufficient to have affected the overall credibility of the poll, which it declared to have been free and fair. (This view was endorsed by international observers at the elections, who numbered some 2,300.) In mid-November the UN Security Council adopted a resolution extending the mandate of ONUMOZ until the inauguration of the new government: the withdrawal of ONUMOZ troops and police was to be completed by 31 January 1995. In December 1994 the cease-fire commission issued its final report, according to which ONUMOZ had registered a combined total of 91,691 government and Renamo troops during the confinement process, of whom 11,579 had enlisted in the FADM (compared with the 30,000 envisaged in the general peace accord). In practice, demobilization had

continued until 15 September, with special cases still being processed the day before the elections.

THE RETURN OF REFUGEES

In January 1993 the office of the United Nations High Commissioner for Refugees (UNHCR) estimated that there were 1.7m. Mozambican refugees in neighbouring countries. In June 1993 UNHCR began its official voluntary repatriation programme with the return of a small group from an estimated total of 140,000 refugees in Zimbabwe. In August Mozambique, UNHCR and Swaziland signed a tripartite agreement providing for the return of 24,000 refugees from Swaziland, and in mid-October the first contingent arrived in Mozambique (the programme was completed in June 1994). The first 300 of an estimated 25,000 refugees in Zambia also returned in October. In the same month a tripartite agreement was signed with South Africa, providing for the voluntary repatriation of some 350,000 Mozambican refugees. However, in January 1994 it was reported that South Africa had expressed its intention to begin expelling refugees from April. In February UNHCR reported that some 600,000 refugees had returned from neighbouring countries in 1993, although the majority had done so spontaneously. By January 1994 only 20,167 refugees were reported to have returned through UNHCR repatriation schemes. The complete repatriation programme was expected to last a total of three years and to cost US $203m. In March 1995 UNHCR reportedly announced that it would cease repatriating Mozambican refugees from South Africa at the end of that month because the process had become too expensive. According to a report by the International Organization of Migration, issued in November 1994, there were still 684,000 'internally displaced' people in Mozambique at that time. However, an estimated 3m. had been successfully resettled since the signing of the AGP. In May 1995 UNHCR reported that a total of 1.7m. refugees had returned to Mozambique from six southern African countries (although only 363,000 had done so through its voluntary repatriation programme), and that only Malawi was, at the time, still in the process of repatriating an estimated total of 39,000 remaining refugees. Expenditure on the repatriation process then totalled some US $152m. In November the process was reported to have been completed, some seven months ahead of schedule.

POST-ELECTION POLITICS

Chissano was inaugurated as president on 9 December 1994, and the new government was sworn in on 23 December. All the portfolios were assigned to members of Frelimo. Demands by Renamo that it be assigned the governorships of the five provinces where it won a majority of the votes in the legislative elections were rejected by Chissano: three new provincial governors appointed in January 1995 were all members of Frelimo. At the first session of the new legislature, the assembléia da república, which began on 8 December 1994, a dispute concerning the voting procedure employed to elect the assembly's chairman resulted in the withdrawal of the Renamo and UD deputies, who had unsuccessfully demanded a secret ballot; both parties had abandoned the legislative boycott by the end of December, although not before the conclusion of the first session.

In March 1995 the minister of national defence announced that, once legislation had been enacted allowing for the reintroduction of compulsory military service, a further 4,500 troops would be drafted into the FADM in that year. The total strength of the FADM would be defined by government policy, and the figure of 30,000 envisaged in the general peace accord would not necessarily be observed. During that and subsequent months there were several incidents of insurrection involving members of the FADM who were demanding salary increases and improved conditions. By the end of March all ONUMOZ troops and police had withdrawn from Mozambique, two months later than originally envisaged, and only a small unit of ONUMOZ officials remained in the country. (Legislation providing for the reintroduction of compulsory military service was approved by the assembléia da república in November 1997.)

At the second national conference of opposition parties, held in May in Inhambane province, an extra-parliamentary forum was established through which parties without representation in the legislature intended to convey their concerns to the executive and legislative bodies. In October there was an outbreak of rioting in Maputo when hundreds of demonstrators looted shops and blockaded roads in protest at the acute increase in the price of basic commodities. In November Mozambique was admitted as a full member of the Commonwealth (see p. 118), in which it had held observer status since 1987.

During 1995 the activities, principally in the border province of Manica, of a Zimbabwean dissident group, known as 'Chimwenje', came under increasing scrutiny. The group, which was alleged to have associations with Renamo, was believed to be preparing for military incursions into neighbouring Zimbabwe, where it sought the overthrow of President Mugabe. In early 1996, following a series of armed confrontations between 'Chimwenje' and the Mozambican security forces, the Chissano government announced its intention to expel the dissidents from Mozambique. In June, following a series of armed attacks on both sides of the Mozambique-Zimbabwe border believed to have been perpetrated by 'Chimwenje', bilateral discussions held between the governments of Mozambique and Zimbabwe resulted in an agreement to combine and intensify efforts to combat the activities of the dissidents. The group was eventually suppressed in late 1996, through joint military action by both countries.

In February 1996 the government proposed that municipal elections, which the Constitution stipulated must be conducted no later than October 1996, be held in 1997. Delays in the election process had resulted from a dispute between the government and the parliamentary opposition regarding the scope of the elections: the opposition demanded simultaneous local elections throughout Mozambique, while the government sought to hold elections only in those areas that had attained municipal status. This would have excluded almost 60% of the population, as the process of establishing functioning nation-wide municipal administration was exected to be completed only by 2003. In October 1996 parliament approved a constitutional amendment differentiating between municipalities (including 23 cities and 116 other district capitals) and administrative posts (numbering 394). Each of these units would have its own elected council and mayor. In June 1997 the government announced that the municipal elections would be conducted, in 23 cities and 10 towns, on 27 December 1997. However, it was widely assumed that the logistics of the electoral process would require that the elections be delayed for several months. Also in June Renamo and 10 other opposition parties established a co-ordinating council of the opposition, with a view to presenting a concerted political alternative to the ruling party at the forthcoming municipal elections.

In May 1996 the government signed an agreement with South Africa under the terms of which some 200,000 ha of farmland in northern Mozambique were to be leased to South African farmers. The agreement, which was estimated to be worth some US $800m. to Mozambique, was criticized by opposition parties and abroad. However, in 1997, the South African Chamber for Agricultural Development (SACADA), that was to provide the initial capital for the joint venture, jointly with the Mozambique government, failed to remit its share, and by mid-1999 Mozambique was seeking to remove it from the project. Also in that year, the granting of 236,000 ha in area south of Maputo, including a wildlife reserve, to an American entrepreneur, for the creation of a luxury resort, caused serious controversy.

Debate continued during 1997 and the first half of 1998 concerning the revision of the law on land tenure. Existing legislation placed all land in the hands of the state. Various levels of state authority had the capacity to offer land concessions, giving rise to multiple claims for the same area of land. Moreover, the law did not adequately address matters relating to disputes over land use, particularly when one claim resulted from an official concession and another from customary but unwritten law. Donors strongly urged the introduction of new land legislation and made their approval of the US $200m. Proagri programme for the support of agriculture (see Economy) conditional upon certain guarantees for peasant land-tenure rights. In October 1998 donors pledged $46m. for the first phase of the programme.

In May 1997 a wave of anti-government demonstrations began in the central city of Beira, spreading gradually to Quelimane, Nampula, Chimoio and Inhambane. The initial demonstration was organized by Renamo in order to protest at the exclusion of a number of towns from the municipal elections. Clashes between the demonstrators and police resulted in some 25 arrests, including those of two local Renamo leaders. Subsequently, demonstrations took place to demand the release of those arrested. With the escalation of the demonstrations, the protests broadened to express opposition to police brutality, the high cost of living, and the disparities in development between southern Mozambique and the rest of the country.

In late May 1997 Frelimo held its seventh party congress, the first such congress since the introduction of the multi-party system. Chissano was re-elected unopposed as the leader of the party.

In August 1997 the government announced that, owing to delays in the disbursement by international donors of funding for the voter registration process, the municipal elections would not be conducted until 1998: the elections were subsequently scheduled for 29 May. In January Renamo claimed that the registration process, which had taken place in November 1997, had been fraudulent, and threatened to boycott the forthcoming elections unless a further registration of voters was conducted. The national electoral commission conceded that certain material errors had occurred in the registration process but claimed that these affected only a minor percentage of the electorate and that efforts to correct the register would ensure that it remained valid. In March 1998 the government announced that the elections had been further postponed and would take place on 30 June. In April Renamo and 15 other opposition parties officially announced their withdrawal from the elections, and Renamo subsequently began a vigorous campaign to dissuade the electorate from voting. In the event, very few opposition parties contested the elections of 30 June, and Frelimo's main opposition came from independent candidates. Frelimo secured all the mayoral posts and took control of all the municipal authorities contested. However, the voter turnout was just 14.6%, greatly reducing the legitimacy of the newly-elected representatives and prompting Renamo to demand the annulment of the elections.

In October 1998 the government published draft constitutional amendments that envisaged substantial changes to the country's political system, including a reduction in presidential powers and concomitant increase in those of the prime minister as well as separating the jurisdictions of central government and local administration. If approved, the amendments would confer the status of head of government on the prime minister, transferring this from the president—who would remain head of state. The president would no longer be able to appoint the prime minister without first consulting parliament, and would dismiss and appoint ministers only on the proposal of the prime minister. In addition, a council of state would be formed as a consultative body to advise the president. The underlying aim of the proposed changes was to make provision for a situation in which a president and government could be drawn from different parties. The constitutional debate, which was due to take place at an extraordinary sitting of the legislature beginning on 20 July, was, however, postponed indefinitely earlier in that month. In October 1998 the government presented draft electoral legislation governing the conduct of presidential and legislative elections scheduled for 1999.

By the end of February 1999 only 45,000 of the total of some 150,000 people of the age-group required to register for conscription had done so. In May thousands of workers conducted a demonstration at the annual May Day parade in the capital in support of demands for wage increases and an end to the large number of redundancies resulting from the privatization of public companies.

Under the constitution, the five-year term of the president and the national assembly was to end in November 1999. However, political disputes and administrative delays made it increasingly unlikely that elections would be held in that year, posing serious constitutional problems. One of the principal causes of the delay was Renamo's insistence on the need to re-register the entire electorate. The electoral process was further delayed by the late appointment of the national elections commission at the end of March. In late May the government announced that voter registration would take place between 20 July and 17 September—thus allowing for elections to take place in late November. However, Renamo protested that a longer period, of 75 days, would be necessary in order to ensure that the majority of the population, resident in the countryside, be able to register in time. That month Renamo announced that it was to conduct its first peacetime congress in late July in Chimoio, at which it would discuss a revision of its programme and party statutes. However, the congress was later postponed indefinitely. In June Frelimo announced that Chissano would stand as its presidential candidate. In the following month 11 opposition parties, led by Renamo, signed an agreement to contest the forthcoming elections as a coalition, styled Renamo–União Eleitoral (Renamo–UE), presenting a single list of legislative candidates with Dhlakama as its presidential candidate.

1999 ELECTIONS AND PROBLEMS OF 2000

Presidential and legislative elections took place on 3–5 December 1999. In the presidential contest Chissano defeated Dhlakama (his sole challenger), taking 52.29% of the valid votes cast. Frelimo secured an outright majority in the legislative elections, winning 133 of the 250 seats in the assembléia da república; Renamo-UE obtained the remaining seats. Renamo rejected the outcome, claiming that the vote had been fraudulent, and appealed to the Supreme Court (which was exercising the functions of the Constitutional Council, that was yet to be established). However, international monitors declared the elections to have been free and fair. In January 2000, following the Supreme Court rejection of the appeal by Renamo against the results of the elections, Dhlakama publicly accused the Supreme Court judges of being manipulated by Frelimo. Later that month it was reported that, in contravention of legislation requiring political parties to be based in the capital, Renamo had moved its headquarters to Beira, leaving only a small delegation in Maputo. On 15 January Chissano was sworn in for a further five-year presidential term, and subsequently effected a substantial reshuffle of the council of ministers. However, Dhlakama refused to attend the investiture, and Renamo continued to dispute the legitimacy of the newly-elected government. In February Dhlakama issued an ultimatum to the government, giving it 10 days in which to conduct a recount of the votes or agree to new elections, failing which, he announced, Renamo would unilaterally declare the establishment of a parallel government in the central and northern regions of the country. However, the deadline of a similar ultimatum, issued in January, had passed without incident.

In February 2000 Mozambique suffered massive flooding in southern and central areas, following the heaviest rainfall recorded in the country for some 50 years. The unseasonal heavy rains in December and January triggered a severe swelling of the Limpopo and other rivers that drain through southern Mozambique. Moreover, the effects of Cyclone Eline, which struck the country in mid-February, further compounded the widespread devastation caused to the country's social and eco-

nomic infrastructure. It was thought that the poor management of upstream dams in South Africa and Zimbabwe may have contributed to the flooding, following the sudden release of floodwaters from the weakened and overflowing reservoirs. The resulting catastrophe left an estimated 2m. people seriously affected by the flooding, of whom some 1m. were in need of assistance and 500,000 were reported to have been displaced. The number of confirmed deaths was put at 640; some 127,000 ha of crops (10% of the country's cultivated land) were destroyed, and many livestock, including over 20,000 head of cattle, lost. Large sections of the country's transport infrastructure were destroyed, and many villages were washed away; refugees were also affected by the rapid spread of diseases such as malaria, cholera and dysentery. In March the Paris Club of bilateral creditor countries agreed to defer Mozambique's debt repayments for a period of 12 months. In early May the Mozambique government requested $450m. in aid at a conference of international donors, held in Rome, Italy, to help finance the reconstruction of the country; the donor countries subsequently pledged $452.9m. The World Bank later estimated the cost of losses at between $270m. and $430m. By late May it was announced that 70% of the displaced flood victims had been resettled.

In May 2000 thousands of workers took part in a May day march, where they demanded the establishment of labour tribunals, which had been announced by the government in 1992, but were not yet in existence; workers also demanded an increase in the minimum wage and the return of price controls. Also in that month an attack on a police station in the northern province of Nampula, in which five people were killed, was believed to have been carried out by members of Renamo. Comments made earlier that month by Dhlakama, in which he had threatened to regroup demobilized Renamo soldiers and seize control of the country, were condemned by the prime minister, Pascoal Mocumbi. The Renamo political delegate for Nampula province was subsequently arrested. In the following month it was revealed that negotiations were taking place between Chissano and Renamo. However, it was also announced by Renamo that the party had suspended its demands for new elections, as funding would not be available following the flooding earlier that year. In early July a senior member of Renamo, Raul Domingos, was suspended from the party, pending an investigation into the negotiations in June between Domingos and the minister for transport and communications, Tomás Salomão, during which Domingos was alleged to have demanded an estimated $500,000 to assist in personal loan repayments, up to $1m. per month for Renamo, and a $10,000 per month salary for Dhlakama. Also in that month, Renamo announced that it was to boycott the election of the new National Elections Commission (CNE), scheduled to take place on 26 July, in which Renamo was entitled to hold seven seats, on the grounds that it did not recognize the government's authority.

Economy

JOÃO GOMES CRAVINHO

Revised for this edition by Marek Garztecki

INTRODUCTION

Mozambique's post-independence economy has suffered the damaging effects of a guerrilla war, drought, floods, famine, the displacement of population, and a severe scarcity of skilled workers and foreign exchange. These difficulties are compounded by a large visible trade deficit, with export earnings covering only about 15-30% of import costs, and high levels of debt repayments, although substantial debt relief has reduced servicing to a more sustainable level in recent years. As a result, Mozambique is heavily reliant on foreign credits. Following the signing of the Nkomati Accord with South Africa in March 1984, the US government announced that its ban on direct bilateral aid to Mozambique had been lifted. In the same year Mozambique acceded to the third Lomé Convention, thus becoming

eligible for assistance from the European Community (EC, now the European Union–EU), and became a member of the IMF and the World Bank.

In 1998, according to estimates by the World Bank, Mozambique's gross national product (GNP), measured at average 1996–98 prices, was US $3,478m., equivalent to only about $210 per head. Between 1990–98, it was estimated, GNP per head increased, in real terms, at an average rate of 3.5% per year. Over the same period the population increased by an average of 2.6% per year. Signs of economic recovery began to emerge at the end of the 1980s with real growth in gross domestic product (GDP) averaging 5.4% in 1987–89. Economic growth declined during 1990–92, owing to drought, the effects of the war on production and reduced foreign support; GDP growth averaged only 0.8% during this period, according to the World Bank. With an end to the drought and prospects for sustained peace, GDP increased by 19.3% in 1993, by 5.0% in 1994, by 1.5% in 1995, by 6.4% in 1996, by 8.0% in 1997, by 12% in 1998, and by an estimated 10.0% in 1999. Between 1994–98 the Mozambican economy was one of the fastest growing in the world, with GDP growth averaging 8.3%. The annual average rate of inflation was 53.7% in 1985–96. With the impact of economic reforms, the rate of inflation fell from 160% in 1987 to 35.2% in 1991, before increasing to 45.2% in 1992 and to 76.2% in 1993, owing to an acute devaluation of the currency. The inflation rate for 1994 was 70%, declining to 54.4% in 1995, and fell sharply to 16.3% in 1996. Under the government's economic programme for 1996-98 it was intended to reduce inflation to 10% by the end of 1998, but by the end of 1997 inflation had already fallen to 5.8%. According to the central bank, in 1998 Mozambique recorded negative inflation of 1.3%, before recording inflation of 4.8% in 1999, just below the government target rate of 5.5%. In the first quarter of 2000 the monthly rate of inflation increased to 12.0%, reflecting the economic disruption caused by the floods. There was a marked appreciation of the metical against the currencies of its major trading partners, in particular the South African rand, during 1999. However, it was expected that a reversal of this trend would be encouraged by the central bank, following concerns that the strength of the metical negatively impacted on the country's export performance.

In January 1987 the government initiated an economic recovery programme (Programa de Reabilitação Econômica—PRE) for 1987–90, which was supported by the IMF, and which aimed to increase economic efficiency and to reduce internal and external deficits, by a 'liberalization' of the economy (see below).

Meanwhile, the implementation of the PRE began with two substantial devaluations of the metical, from US $1 = 40 meticais to US $1 = 200 meticais in January 1987, and to US $1 = 400 meticais in June 1987. Subsequent devaluations, by 12.5% in January 1988, 22.4% in July 1988, 6.9% in October 1988, and through subsequent monthly adjustments brought the official exchange rate to US $1 = 12,100 meticais by August 1999. Other major components of the PRE included fiscal measures, with a planned reduction of the budget deficit from 50% of expenditure in 1986 to 25% in 1987, an increase in income taxes, and a reduction in government wage costs and government subsidies, and monetary measures, including the maintenance of stringent control on the rate of credit growth and the increased linkage of wages to productivity. Other measures under the programme included a deregulation of some prices previously controlled by the government, the stimulation of the private sector in industry and agriculture, the focusing of resources on activities of import-substitution or those yielding a high level of value added, the stimulation of exports, and a review of procedures for the allocation of foreign exchange. Price rises were duly introduced in 1988, during the second phase of the PRE, when basic commodity prices were increased. In urban centres the price of maize rose by nearly 300%, that of rice by nearly 600%, and that of sugar by 400%. In an effort to offset the impact of these rises, the government announced an increase in minimum wages. However, enterprises were expected to limit overall increases in wage costs to 45%. The prices of petroleum, electricity and meat were increased in early 1989. In February 1990 further increases in food prices were announced.

In June 1990 the IMF approved an enhanced structural adjustment facility (ESAF) of SDR 85.40m. to support a further programme of economic reforms (1990–92), which aimed to increase the role of the private sector, to promote foreign investment and to improve access to imports and supplies of industrial inputs. The programme was intended to raise the annual growth rate of GDP to 6.0%, and to limit the current account deficit on the balance of payments to 30% of GDP (compared to an estimated 74.4% in 1989). In June 1994 the IMF announced a further loan of SDR 29.4m. under the ESAF to support economic reforms in 1994/5. A meeting of the consultative group of aid donors in Paris in December 1990 resulted in pledges of nearly US $1,200m. for 1991: $400m. for debt relief (including the writing off of $19m. of debt), and $761m. in food and project aid. A number of reforms linked to the PRE were introduced in late 1990 and early 1991, including the establishment of a

secondary foreign exchange market and the introduction of new incentives for foreign investors. Pledges totalling $1,125m. (48% in grant form) were made at the December 1991 consultative group meeting, although 80% of this consisted of debt relief, rather than new finance. In March 1992 the government unveiled a three-year plan for sharp cuts in public expenditure. The plan, prepared in consultation with the IMF, provided for reductions in investment in agriculture, mining and manufacturing, accompanied by a programme of privatizations in these areas, with the emphasis shifting to rehabilitation of infrastructure. Plans to sell off a number of major state-owned enterprises were announced in early 1992. By mid-1993 some 180 state enterprises had been transferred to private ownership, 80% of which were sold to Mozambican investors. A new investment code was approved by the legislature in 1993, providing identical fiscal and customs benefits to both local and foreign investors. By the end of 1995 some 1,000 state-owned enterprises had been privatized. By the end of 1999 over 80% of the formerly state-owned enterprises had been privatized, in what was considered to be one of the world's most successful privatization programmes.

During 1993 the government introduced a national reconstruction plan to account for post-war reconstruction needs. A World Bank report, prepared for the December 1993 consultative group meeting of donors in Paris, estimated that Mozambique would require external funding totalling US $1,494m. in 1994, including $405m. in debt relief. The same document estimated that the cost of the peace process (including demobilization, demining, assistance for returning refugees and displaced people and the conduct of elections) would reach $400m. A further consultative group meeting was held in March 1995 in Paris at which pledges were made for $784m. of the estimated total of $1,105m. needed for 1995. Three of the major donors—the USA, Britain and Germany—stipulated that their funding was conditional on continued democratization and good governance in Mozambique. In June 1995 the minister of planning and finance revealed that delays in the disbursement of funds pledged by donor countries were forcing the state to borrow more heavily than anticipated from banks. As a result restrictions on credit for business were tightened considerably in order to maintain total credit within the limits imposed by the IMF. A meeting of the consultative group of aid donors in Paris in April 1996 resulted in pledges of $567.5m., excluding debt relief, while the government agreed to continue and intensify its programme of privatization and liberalization of the economy. In June 1996 the IMF approved a three-year loan of $110m., under its ESAF, to support the government's economic reform programme for 1996–98. The objectives of the programme included a reduction in the annual inflation rate to 10% by 1998, and average annual GDP growth, excluding energy production, of 5% for the three-year period.

At the May 1997 consultative group meeting of donors in Paris, Mozambique received praise for its success in the implementation of economic reforms, as reflected in its positive economic indicators for 1996. Consequently, the government's funding requirements for 1997 were met with little discussion; pledges amounted to US $641.5m., with an additional $193.5m. for debt reduction. In June 1997 the IMF approved a $35m. loan for Mozambique. The prospect of reducing Mozambique's debt burden improved following the decision by the 'Paris Club' of official creditors to admit Russia as a member. Since Mozambique owed substantial debts to Russia (which inherited them from the Soviet Union), this cleared the way for Mozambique to benefit from the IMF and World Bank's Heavily Indebted Poor Countries (HIPC) debt-reduction initiative. A programme under HIPC terms was approved in April 1998.

In September 1998 a meeting of the World Bank Consultative Group agreed to meet in full the government's external financing requirements for 1999 of US $490m. (excluding debt relief). A further $150m. was pledged by the Bretton Woods institutions in October 1998 to finance economic rehabilitation programmes in 1999. Following discussions with the IMF in early 1999, a set of macroeconomic targets were set for that year, including real GDP growth of 9% and average annual inflation of 5.5%. The IMF also revised Mozambique's GDP figure for 1998 giving a new official total of $3,900m., equivalent to $240 per caput (the UN had earlier estimated per capita GDP at $143 for 1998).

In June 1999 the IMF announced that Mozambique was to receive US $3,700m. in debt relief under the HIPC initiative, reducing the country's external debt by almost two-thirds. As a result Mozambique's external debt-service obligations were to fall to an annual average of $73m. in 1999-2005, compared with an average of $169m. that would have been due in the absence of the HIPC relief. In April 2000 the IMF agreed to grant Mozambique a further $600m. in debt relief under the enhanced terms of the HIPC initiative. The value of the country's debt-stock was reduced to $1,700m. and, according to the minister of planning and finance, Luísa Diogo, the cost of annual debt servicing would be reduced from $104m. in 1999 to an estimated $23m.–$24m. in the following years. Furthermore, following massive flooding in the southern and central regions of the country in February 2000 (see Recent History), in mid-March the 'Paris Club' of official creditors agreed to defer all payments due on the country's external debt, valued at $73m., for a period of one year (it had originally been hoped that the debt would be cancelled altogether). However, a number of conditions were attached to the debt relief package, including the maintenance of a stable economic environment and the implementation of the poverty reduction strategy in the areas of social development and public-sector reform. Also in that month the IMF authorized the release of $50m. under the Poverty Reduction and Growth Facility (PRGF). In June, following a meeting of the World Bank Consultative Group, international aid donors pledged an estimated $530m. for 2000 and $560m. for 2001 to Mozambique, and praised the country's recent economic reforms.

AGRICULTURE

In periods of stability, 80%–90% of the total working population have been engaged in agriculture, and about 80% of exports in the late 1960s were of agricultural origin. Although only 5% of arable lands are cultivated, agriculture accounted for 32.3% of Mozambique's GDP in 1997. The major cash crops are cotton (accounting for 8.9% of export earnings in 1998), cashew nuts (7.6%), sugar (3.4%) and copra (2.0%). Maize, bananas, rice, tea, sisal and coconuts are also grown, and the main subsistence crop is cassava. Large-scale modern agriculture before independence was mainly under Portuguese control. About 3,000 farms and plantations were known to exist, employing more than 130,000 people on more than 1.6m. ha, while African plots covered some 2.8m. ha. Since independence, agricultural production has been adversely affected by several factors: the internal conflict which prevented nearly 3m. Mozambicans from farming the land; the scarcity of skilled labour, following the post-independence exodus by the Portuguese; low crop yields from some state farms; the collapse of rural transport and marketing systems, owing to general insecurity and disorganization; drought, flooding, cyclones and insect pests which have combined to destroy food crops in large areas of the country (notably in the south and the Zambézia region). Agricultural GDP increased by an estimated annual average of 1.6% during 1980–90. During 1990–98 agricultural production increased by an estimated average of 4.8% per year. Agricultural production increased by 8.0% in 1998.

During 1996 and 1997 a major programme for the promotion of Mozambican agriculture, entitled Proagri, was drawn up. The five-year programme, which aimed to increase state capacity and co-ordination in all areas of agricultural production, began in 1999 with the support of all major donors, at a total cost of some US $200m.; in October 1998 donors pledged $46m. for the first phase of the programme. Following the wave of land seizures in Zimbabwe in the late 1990s, discussions were under way in 1998/99 concerning the possible resettlement of 150 white Zimbabwean farmers in the sparsely populated central province of Manica. However, in 2000 the possible number of Zimbabwean farmers seeking resettlement increased dramatically. Up to $27m. was expected to be invested by the farmers, creating an estimated 40,000 jobs.

The development of the cultivation of cashew nuts is a relatively recent occurrence. Production of cashew nuts was 204,000 metric tons in 1974. Output decreased by 44% between 1973 and 1976 and continued to decline until 1984, owing to inefficient marketing practices by state enterprises, lack of transportation and the effects of drought. In an attempt to increase production levels, the government doubled producer prices for the crop.

Output of cashews was estimated at 50,000 tons in 1988/89 but fell to 22,000 tons in 1989/90 due to poor weather conditions and security problems. The expansion in production resulted largely from a French-financed rehabilitation programme. Production recovered to 31,000 tons in 1990/91 and to 54,000 tons in 1991/92, before falling to 24,000 in 1992/93 due to a shortage of rainfall. In 1993 the African Development Bank (ADB) granted US $20m. for a five-year programme to rehabilitate the industry. In the two subsequent seasons marketed cashew production was stable at around 35,000 tons per year, but in 1995/96 a 15-year record high was reached with 60,000 tons. However, production declined to 43,000 tons in 1996/97, but increased to 49,000 tons in 1997/98 and to 51,000 tons in 1998/99. Output was expected to decline in 2000 as a result of the floods (see Recent History), with parts of the country traditionally accounting for up to 32% of cashew production severely affected. In June 1998 the cashew secretariat, which had been created to encourage the cultivation of cashew trees, was abolished. The secretariat had been intended to organize a massive programme to replace ageing and diseased stock; US $47.6m. was made available from the mid-1980s for planting 1.5m. trees per year. However, industry sources suggest that much of this money was misappropriated. In 1998 the Nacala Cashew Centre harvested 2.5 tons of cashew nuts from a new species of tree, the dwarf cashew. In late 1991 the government authorized the export of cashews in unprocessed form, mainly to India for the first time since 1976, because of the inability of processing plants to cope with increased output. Following demands by the World Bank that the industry be privatized, in 1994 and 1995 the government sold the processing factories to six Mozambican trading companies for $9.1m. This attracted significant local investment and resulted in the expansion of the workforce from 6,700 to 9,000. A request by the World Bank that restrictions on the export of unprocessed cashews should not be reintroduced was vociferously opposed by producers and by the government. However, a compromise was subsequently reached whereby the government agreed to impose an export tax of 20% for unprocessed cashew nuts during 1995-96, which would then gradually be phased out by 2000. However, by mid-1997 the debate concerning the liberalization of unprocessed cashew exports had resumed as several Mozambican processing plants reduced staff numbers as a result of the increasing proportion of unprocessed exports. By February 1999 all but three of the country's 14 principal cashew processing plants had closed owing to the lack of raw materials. Furthermore, marketed production decreased by 9,000 tons between 1998/99 and 1999/2000, although climatic conditions and the poor condition of the plantations, neglected during the civil war, were also contributing factors. Facing a growing demand for an outright ban on the export of unprocessed cashews, the Mozambique government passed a bill, in September 1999, increasing the existing 14% tax to between 18% and 22%, with an exact level to be established each year, depending on the existing conditions.

Cotton has traditionally been the main cash crop of northern Mozambique, with more than 500,000 African growers in the Cabo Delgado, Niassa, Nampula and Zambézia provinces. Production of seed (unginned) cotton was 144,000 metric tons in 1973, but by 1984 had fallen to less than 20,000 tons, and in 1985 marketed production reached only 5,700 tons. A programme for rehabilitating the cotton sector is under way, with help from foreign companies. Nearly all cotton is cultivated by peasant producers working in concession areas where large companies have sole right of purchase. Total production was 50,000 tons in 1996, when exports earned $20m. Production increased to 70,000 tons in 1997, and reached 90,000 tons in 1998, the highest level since independence.

Sugar was produced by large cane-growing companies, such as the Sena Sugar Estates Ltd, on a tributary of the Zambezi, the Companhia Colonial do Buzi, south of Beira, and the Sociedade Agrícola do Incomati, north of Maputo. This formerly monopolistic system produced 227,823 metric tons of sugar in 1975, but export earnings fell from 575m. escudos in 1975 to 260m. escudos in 1977. All the companies were nationalized and entrusted to Cuban experts, who sought unsuccessfully to restore pre-independence levels of production. Climatic conditions, combined with production difficulties, reduced raw sugar production to 126,000 tons in 1982, and to a record 'low' of 17,000 tons in

1986. However, output increased to about 55,000 tons in 1987. Sugar production has increased dramatically since the peace agreement. In 1994 some 234,000 tons were produced, increasing to 313,000 tons in 1995 and 320,000 tons in 1996 before declining to 279,000 tons in 1997, but increasing to 369,000 tons in 1998. Production of refined sugar reached 38,240 tons in 1998, an increase of nearly 50% on 1997 when production totalled 25,229 tons, increasing to 50,700 tons in 1999. As part of government plans to rehabilitate the industry, the African Development Fund provided $55m. for the rehabilitation of the Mafambisse sugar complex in Sofala province. In June 1998 it was announced that agreement had been reached between the Mozambican government and a consortium of private Mauritian companies to rehabilitate the Luabo and Marromeu sugar refineries belonging to the defunct Sena Sugar Estates Ltd. The new company, Société Marromeu, will have a share capital of $27m. and aims to invest around $70m., with a view to beginning sugar production in 2001; it was hoped that production would reach 40,000 tons in that year, increasing to 120,000 tons per year. In June 1999 the Maragra sugar company, near Maputo (which had been purchased in 1996 by Illovo Sugar Ltd of South Africa) reopened, producing 6,200 tons. However, in February 2000 the mill, as well as its adjoining plantation, were affected by the floods (see Recent History), destroying some $30m. of the $50m. investment. Consequently, estimated production of 12,000 tons per year was not expected to be achieved before 2002.

In 1986 Mozambique ranked eighth, after Kenya, Malawi, Tanzania, Zimbabwe, Rwanda, South Africa and Mauritius, among African producers of tea. The Zambézia hills and mountains, close to the Malawi border, are the main producing area. The country produced 18,795 metric tons of made tea in 1973 but output fell to 13,143 tons in 1975. It rose to 22,190 tons in 1981 but declined again, to an estimated 1,500 tons in 1988. The destruction by Renamo, in February 1987, of equipment at five tea-processing factories, which had been rehabilitated at a cost of about US $30m., led to a further decline in output. An increase in production in 1990 and 1991 was reversed by drought and in 1997 production stood at only 2,000 tons. Production was estimated at 1,600 tons in 1999. The principal markets for Mozambican tea are the United Kingdom and the USA, and exports earned 1,212m. meticais in 1981, when shipments totalled 18,000 tons. Following the sharp fall in production since 1981, the value of tea exports declined, to 51m. meticais in 1986, according to government figures. Exports of tea reached a peak of $800,000 in 1991 and have since declined considerably.

Copra is produced mainly on immense coconut plantations on the coastal belt of the Zambézia and Nampula provinces. It is also a popular crop among Africans who use the oil and other copra products in daily life. In 1972 copra exports totalled 43,938 metric tons. Production levels have fluctuated in recent years, reaching an estimated 60,000 tons in 1980, but declining to 5,200 tons in 1989, due largely to a fall in prices. Since then output has increased significantly, reaching an estimated 76,000 tons in 1998. Exports of copra earned US $5.0m. in 1998. As in Angola, sisal was introduced by German planters. It is a typical plantation crop, concentrated principally on about 20 estates west of Nacala and Pemba; annual production has been consistent during the 1990s at around 24,000 tons.

For many years after independence the normal maize crop was far below the level needed to meet domestic requirements. However, with the advent of peace and successive years of favourable climatic conditions in 1994–96, the shortfall in this staple crop continued to be diminished. In 1997/98 there was a surplus of 51,850 tons of maize; there were also surpluses of sorghum and millet (18,250 tons) and cassava (100,000 tons) despite the loss of some 60,000 ha of crops owing to drought and flooding. A problem remains, nevertheless, in that surpluses from the north and centre of the country reach the areas in deficit in the south (particularly the large urban markets around Maputo) at greatly inflated prices due to high transport costs, making it cheaper to import maize from South Africa and to export surpluses from the north and centre of the country to Tanzania and Malawi. Rehabilitation of the commercial networks that link the areas with surplus maize to neighbouring countries and to the ports of Nacala and Beira is needed to eliminate this problem in the medium term. According to the FAO, the harvest totalled 947,000 tons in 1996, increasing to

1.04m. tons in 1997, to 1.12m. tons in 1998 and was estimated at 1.19m. tons in 1999. The principal maize-producing areas in the north were largely unaffected by the floods in February 2000. About 120,000 tons of rice were produced in the irrigated lowlands in 1974, falling to an estimated 66,000 tons in 1993. However, by 1998 production had risen to 191,000 tons. In the late 1990s significant efforts were made to rehabilitate the vast rice fields between Massingir and Chokwe, in the Limpopo valley; however, these were almost entirely destroyed by the floods in early 2000. Total cereal production stood at 1.5m. tons in 1997 and 1.7m. tons in 1998. Oil seeds, such as sesame and sunflower seeds and, above all, groundnuts (estimated at 126,000 tons in 1997 and 143,000 tons in 1998), allow for some exports to Portugal. Processing of vegetable oils produces more than 25,000 tons annually. Bananas (production estimated at 87,000 tons in 1998) and citrus fruits (42,000 tons produced in 1998) are exported, as well as potatoes (production estimated at 75,000 tons in 1998), tobacco and kenaf (a jute-like fibre).

Livestock is still of secondary importance, owing partly to the prevalence of the tsetse fly over about two-thirds of the country. Most of the cattle are raised south of the Save river, particularly in the Gaza province which has about 500,000 head. In 1998 estimated figures were: 1.30m. cattle; 123,000 sheep; 388,000 goats and 176,000 pigs. During colonial times the Limpopo *colonato* and the area surrounding Maputo had European cattle ranches to provide the capital with meat and dairy products. Mozambique now has to import fresh and prepared meat.

In the early years after independence the government sought to establish communal agriculture at the village level. From 1976 onwards, more than 1,500 communal villages were formed, and agricultural co-operatives and state farms established, in an effort to 'socialize' the rural sector. Between 1975 and 1985 the state sector accounted for 40%–50% of marketed production, while the co-operative sector averaged only 1%. However, several state farms proved to be uneconomic, and since 1983 the government has given increased priority to improving production from small farms in the family sector. From 1984 onwards, several state farms were divided into individual peasant holdings. Further reforms have taken place as part of the 1987–90 PRE: subsidies have been reduced, and the prices of some agricultural products have been deregulated. Private producers and traders were encouraged with higher producer prices. In October 1987 a fund for agricultural and rural development was established by the Banco Popular de Desenvolvimento, with the aim of assisting peasant farmers and co-operatives to improve their output. However, various difficulties have rendered this programme almost inoperational and rural credit remains inaccessible for the vast majority of peasant producers.

During 1981–84 a severe drought prevailed in eight out of the 10 provinces and 4m. people were seriously affected. Further problems were caused by floods and cyclones in 1984, and in both 1983 and 1984 there was a steady deterioration in the overall situation in the agricultural sector. In 1983 an estimated 1m. tons of cassava, equivalent to about one-third of the total annual crop, were lost because of drought. In the six southern provinces, agricultural production had declined by about 70%–80%, and some 550,000 tons of cereals were required to offset crop losses in 1983/84. In 1984 it was estimated that 600,000–900,000 tons of maize imports would be required for 1984/85, and the total cereal import requirement for that period (including commercial imports) was estimated at 620,000 tons. Mozambique received considerable international assistance during the drought. However, distribution of food supplies was persistently hampered by security and transport problems, owing to Renamo guerrilla activity. Because of the ravaged state of agriculture, FAO experts believed that a long-term modernization programme of agricultural methods was needed to reduce the national food production deficit.

In 1986 a combination of drought conditions and the escalation of rebel activity in the latter part of the year resulted in a famine: some 4m. people were threatened with starvation. In 1987 the UN launched an appeal for US $247m. in humanitarian aid to ease the problem; it was estimated that 800,000 tons of food aid would be required in 1987/88. Following a meeting of UN member-states held in March 1987, international donors increased their pledges of aid: of increased shipments of cereals pledged, the USA was to send 194,000 tons, and the EC 105,000 tons, in 1987. The outlook was equally bleak in the following year. Agricultural production was further hampered by the inadequate level of rainfall over much of the country in late 1987, and by floods in early 1988. Locusts were reported to have destroyed 80% of the cereal crop in Inhambane province in 1988. In March of that year the UN launched an appeal, on behalf of the government, for $380m. in emergency aid; it was estimated that 710,000 tons of cereals were needed for 1988/89. In 1989 the government appealed, through the UN, for $383m. in emergency funding for 1989/90. It was estimated that 916,000 tons of food aid were required to meet the needs of some 7.7m. people who were facing severe food shortages. The government requested a further $136m. in emergency aid for 1990/91. The food supply situation continued to deteriorate during 1990. In December the World Bank warned that half the population faced starvation or serious deprivation. In April 1991 the overall food deficit was put at 1.1m. tons.

With much of southern Africa suffering from severe drought, the food supply situation in Mozambique deteriorated further in 1992, with that year's harvests expected to yield only 30% of normal levels. Total cereal production was estimated at 236,000 tons, compared to 724,000 tons in 1990, the last year of normal rainfall. Almost complete harvest failure was reported from the south and centre of the country. A report prepared by the government and UN agencies to support an appeal for international assistance in May put the number of people threatened with famine at 3.15m., with a further 6m. in need of additional food supplies. The report estimated Mozambique's total food aid needs for the next 12 months at more than 1.3m. tons valued at US $270.7m.; the government appealed for total emergency assistance of $457.5m. to cover food aid and logistical needs. The first deaths from starvation were reported in late May. Conditions among Mozambican refugees in Malawi were also reported to be deteriorating as their numbers continued to grow, reaching 985,000 by June, with the number increasing by 8,000 a month. With the return of normal rains and the establishment of a cease-fire, the food supply improved in 1993, although the UN estimated that 1m. people, excluding refugees, would still require direct food aid in 1993/94. By the end of 1993, however, with hostilities at an end, there were indications that Mozambique was recovering its capacity to support itself. Although noting that it would be premature to declare an end to the emergency, a report prepared with UN assistance put the country's emergency needs for 1994/95 at $211m., less than half the figure for 1993/94, with an estimated 119,340 tons of food aid needed for 500,000–800,000 people. These predictions proved to be correct despite a setback in March 1994 when a cyclone hit the fertile northern province of Nampula. The damage caused by the February 2000 floods was concentrated primarily in the four southern provinces, accounting for some 7% of the country's total agricultural production. Although there was a surplus in the cereals produced by the most fertile, northern provinces, the breakdown of the transportation system prevented the supplies from being sent to the south, where they were most needed. Consequently, in July 2000, the price for maize in Nampula fell below the cost level, while Gaza and Maputo had to rely on imports.

Forestry has developed chiefly along the Beira railway and in the wetter Zambézia province. Some eucalyptus plantations have been established in the south of the country to produce wood for paper, but the long-term ecological effects of these plantations are a matter of concern. Most of the exports are sawn timber, construction timber, etc., with a ready market in South Africa. In 1990 a South African company formed a joint venture with the Banco Popular de Desenvolvimento to produce timber products in Beira. It was hoped that a US $86.5m. investment by a South African company, Mondi Forests, would help regenerate the sector. The forestry sector is affected by widespread corruption, with numerous small companies felling hardwood trees indiscriminately, particularly in the central provinces of Zambézia, Manica and Sofala. Much of the wood is then exported illegally at greatly reduced prices. During the late 1990s the volume of production averaged 18.5m. cu m.; it was also the country's fourth most valuable export, worth $13.8m. in 1997.

Fishing is a relatively recent development along Mozambique's extensive coastline. Shrimp exports totalled $70.3m. in 1996 before increasing to $90.2m. in 1997. Fish catches, including shrimps, totalled 26,900 tons in 1995, 34,900 tons in 1996 and 39,600 tons in 1997. Although Mozambique is still not self-sufficient in fish, domestic catches cover about 34% of consumption at present, compared with 6% in 1979. The potential annual catch is estimated at 500,000 tons of fish and 14,000 tons of shrimps. In July 1998 the EU ended a ban on imports of fresh fish from Mozambique that had been imposed in December 1997 in response to concerns that the fish might transmit cholera. Although the ban excluded deep-frozen prawns, it cost the country an estimated $400,000 in lost export earnings. In May 1998 Spain announced that it would finance a small-scale fishing complex in Cabo Delgado, at a cost of $500,000. In May 1999 Japan announced that it was to provide funding of $3.4m. for the upgrading of Maputo's fishing port. Construction was to begin in late 1999 and was to include renovation of the quay and the installation of new cold storage facilities.

MINERALS

Mozambique has considerable mineral resources, although exploitation has been limited by internal unrest. The value of mineral exports was US $1.1m. in 1987, $2.4m. in 1988 and $1m. in 1989. Mining contributed 0.3% of GDP in 1998. There are confirmed coal reserves of some 10,000m. tons, but so far output has remained relatively low. The Moatize coal mine, near Tete has an annual production capacity of 600,000 tons, although output was only 84,500 tons in 1989 (compared with 574,800 tons in 1975), owing to a lack of facilities for transporting the coal to Beira port, and to rebel attacks against the railway to Beira. Exports of coal from Moatize declined from pre-independence levels of some 100,000 tons per year to only 19,000 tons in 1990, and to 400 tons in 1993 owing to flooding in the Moatize mines. However, there are plans to revive the industry, with a new coal-handling terminal at Beira increasing annual capacity from 400,000 tons to 1.2m. tons. Renovation work on the railway to the port, having been repeatedly delayed as a result of the security situation, resumed in July 1990. The EC was providing funding of $72m. for the project. The government signed bilateral agreements which envisaged an increase in annual coal production levels to about 3m. tons by 1995, although the plan was later postponed for several years. The rehabilitation project envisaged foreign investment in mining projects of more than $600m., and in railway and port infrastructural work of almost $500m. The loans were to be repaid in coal. However, the Moatize–Beira railway line still awaited rehabilitation in mid-2000.

Mozambique has significant reserves of tantalite, but only small quantities are exported. There are deposits of ilmenite in the area north of the mouth of the Zambezi river. In 1989 the Irish-based Kenmare Resources Co joined the government in a joint venture to exploit graphite deposits at Ancuabe, in Cabo Delgado province. Mining commenced in 1994, and was expected to produce about 5,000 tons annually, at 98% carbon. A US $150m. titanium-mining joint venture in Nampula province between Kenmare Resources Co and Broken Hill Proprietary (BHP) of Australia was suspended, following the withdrawal of BHP from the project in mid-1999. In 1999 the largest reserve of titanium in the world (estimated at 100m. tons) was discovered in the district of Chibuto, in the province of Gaza. Commercial exploitation of the reserve was expected to begin in 2001. Investigations have also been proceeding along the coast to confirm deposits of ilmenite, zircon and titano-magnetite, and smaller reserves of rutile and monazite. Preliminary assessments estimated the heavy mineral content at 2.2m.–5m. tons, depending upon the method of extraction, with possible revenues of $44m. per year. A mineral sands mining project in Chibuto district, 160 km north of Maputo, was being developed in 1998 by a South African company, Southern Mining Corporation. The mining of iron ore began in the mid-1950s and production of ore averaged about 6m. tons (60%–65% iron) annually in the early 1970s. Production was disrupted by the civil war and ceased altogether between 1975 and 1984. At present, output is stockpiled and the resumption of exports of iron ore depends upon the eventual rehabilitation of the rail link between the mines at Cassinga and the coast. A major deposit of 360m. tons estimated reserves exists near Namapa in Nampula province. Plans for two major iron-ore reduction plants were being studied by prospective investors in mid-2000. Bauxite is mined in the Manica area; in the early 1990s several thousand tons annually were exported direct by licence to Zimbabwe. Further deposits near Tete were reported to be awaiting the completion of the Cahora Bassa power complex to be processed in Vila Fontes on the Zambezi. New deposits of manganese, graphite, fluorite, platinum, nickel, radioactive minerals (e.g. uranium), asbestos, iron, diamonds and natural gas (of which there are confirmed reserves of about 60,000m. cu m) have been found. An Israeli company is mining emeralds and garnets in Zambézia province.

In October 1987 Lonrho, a multinational conglomerate, signed a 25-year agreement for rights in five blocks on a seam in Manica province to prospect for gold; in 1990 the company announced the formation of a joint venture with the Mineral Resources Ministry, Aluviões de Manica, with plans to produce 20 kilos of gold per month from alluvial deposits in the Revuè and Chua river basins. Reserves in the province are estimated at 50 metric tons. In 1996 total official extraction of gold was just 50.3 kg. In June 1993 Italy agreed to provide US $19m. to rehabilitate the Montepuez marble quarry in Cabo Delgado province and to build a processing factory in Pemba. Annual production from the quarry was projected at 8,100 cubic metres, with Portugal and South Africa identified as potential export markets.

Mozambique imports all its petroleum supplies. Following a US $700,000 study in 1998, the National Iranian Oil Co and Petronoc of Malaysia indicated their interest in constructing a refinery in Beira, to produce 100,000 barrels per day. The refinery would take two years to complete and would cost $1,200m. Petroleum prospecting has been carried out by US, French, German and South African companies, both offshore near the Rovuma river basin and Beira and on the mainland, but so far only gas has been found. Petroleum prospecting resumed in late 1994, following a three-year hiatus, with initial exploration focusing on the Rovuma basin and the southern coast. In May 1998 an agreement was signed with Norway, providing $4.5m. for the development of the Mozambican petroleum sector. In May 2000 the French company TotalFina-Elf commenced a technical evaluation of a new, deep-water concession, 300 km east of Beira. In recent years a critical shortage of foreign exchange has drastically reduced Mozambique's imports of crude petroleum, and severe shortages of fuel have ensued. The government has aimed to encourage foreign investment in the minerals sector. The state energy company Empresa Nacional de Hidrocarbonetos de Moçambique (ENH) was to commence the sale of a new round of energy exploration licences to foreign companies in late 2000. Extraction of gas from the Pande field in southern Inhambane province was to begin with the assistance of a US $30m. loan from the World Bank agreed in April 1994. The field's reserves are estimated at 55,000m. cu metres. Sales of the gas to South Africa, which was expected to be the principal consumer, were to begin in 1998, following the construction of a 900-km pipeline. The project was subsequently delayed following dispute between the US-based energy conglomerate Enron, involved in the project, and the Mozambique government, over the extent of Enron's rights in the South African market where it was unable to challenge successfully the monopoly of SASOL Ltd (South Africa). In 1997 Enron abandoned its plans to sell gas directly to South Africa. In May 1998 the government signed a production-sharing agreement with an international consortium, led by SASOL Ltd and ARCO (USA), under the terms of which the consortium was to invest at least $30m. over a seven-year period in gas exploration in the Temane region of Inhambane province. In November the consortium revealed that it could produce between 23m. and 50m. cu ft of gas per day for the next 50 years. Sales of the gas domestically and in South Africa (and potentially in Zimbabwe) were to amount to some $200m. per year.

POWER

Electricity production, totalling 658m. kWh in 1975, increased to 4,940m. kWh in 1977, of which 4,490m. was hydroelectric. Total production reached 14,000m. kWh in 1980, but by 1996 had dwindled to 560m. kWh. The main component of the Mozambican power-generating industry is the Cahora Bassa dam, built and operated by the Portuguese authorities. By 1982 Cahora

Bassa had a generating capacity of 2,075 MW. The supply of power to South Africa commenced in mid-1977, and by 1983 South Africa was receiving about 98% of Cahora Bassa's output. In March–April 1984 tripartite talks between Mozambique, Portugal and South Africa resulted in an agreement whereby Mozambique was to receive a share of the revenues, which had previously been paid exclusively to Portugal. Under the new agreement, Mozambique acquired an 18% stake in the company managing the dam, Hidroelétrica de Cahora Bassa (HCB). However, frequent sabotage of power lines by Renamo subsequently halted supplies from the dam to the South African grid. By March 1987 Cahora Bassa was reported to be operating at only 0.5% of its potential capacity. However, Mozambique, Portugal and South Africa signed an agreement in June 1988 to restore operations at the dam. Under the agreement, 1,400 km of power lines (of which 900 km traversed areas under Renamo control) were to undergo rehabilitation and an armed force was to be established to protect the lines, following the completion of the repair work. However, rehabilitation was continually delayed as a result of the security situation. A programme to rehabilitate the lines, at an estimated cost of US $130m., began in July 1995, with funding from South Africa ($50m.), Portugal ($25m.) and the remainder from the EU, the European Investment Bank and the Caisse Française de Développement. However, a dispute concerning the price that South Africa should pay for electricity from Cahora Bassa delayed the resumption of exports, which were scheduled to begin in 1997. Transmission commenced in mid-1998 but was suspended in September, for a period of six months, when South Africa reneged on an agreement to increase payments. Supplies resumed in March 1999 at the original tariff pending international arbitration. The first arbitration hearings were scheduled to begin in late April 2000. An agreement for Zimbabwe, which faces power shortages, to buy electricity from Cahora Bassa was signed in April 1992. The project involved the construction, at a cost of $45m., of a 350-km transmission line to Harare, which was completed in January 1998. In November 1994 an agreement was signed with Norway securing $24.5m. to finance the project. The new line allows Zimbabwe to draw 500 MW from Cahora Bassa—about 25% of the dam's installed capacity. In May 2000 it was reported that the Zimbabwe Electricity Supply Authority had defaulted on its payments to HCB, eventually offering food and agricultural products in a barter arrangement. Plans for the construction of further lines to supply Malawi and Swaziland were also being pursued following the signing of agreements between Mozambique and those countries in 1994. In Febuary 2000 electricity supplies from Cahora Bassa were disrupted for three months because of flood damage to the power lines.

The 240-km lake that has been created with the dam reaches the Zambian border, and grandiose plans have been made to irrigate 1.5m. ha in this otherwise economically backward salient of Mozambique. Tete could be developed as an iron and steel industrial centre, and the Zambezi made navigable from Tete to the sea.

Other main hydroelectric plants are on the Revuè river, west of Beira at Chicamba Real and Mavúzi. Further south, on the Limpopo, is the dam which helps to irrigate the *colonato*. Another dam at Massingir was expected to increase the irrigation potential of the Limpopo. However, the Massingir dam has been empty since soon after its completion in 1977, owing to the discovery of defects. In 1988 a French company was contracted to undertake preventive maintenance on the dam, which was subsequently rehabilitated. A dam at Corumana, costing US $250m., was inaugurated in July 1989; the dam's 15-MW power station, financed by Sweden and Norway at a cost of $20m., opened in 1990. Mozambique is connected to the South African grid, and by early 1988, in the absence of regular power supplies from Cahora Bassa, was importing an estimated 1,500m. kWh annually from South Africa, costing R15m. per year and absorbing almost 10% of Mozambique's annual export earnings. Since then imports have fallen to around 500m. kWh. In 1991 an agreement was signed with South Africa and Swaziland to build three dams for power generation and irrigation in the joint Komati river basin. In 1996 the state electricity company announced that it was to invest $60m. over a period of three years in the rehabilitation and expansion of the country's electricity grid. The majority of the financing was to be provided by Scandinavian countries. Domestic demand for electricity has grown from 118 MW in 1977 to 235 MW in 1998. The number of consumers increased from 62,000 to 186,208 in the same period. Plans were under review in the mid-1990s for the construction of the Mepandua Ncua hydroelectric power station at a site in the Zambezi valley, some 70 km downstream of Cahora Bassa. The plant, which was expected to have a generating capacity of between 2,000 MW and 2,500 MW, was projected to cost some US $1,500m., with a further $500m. for the construction of transmission lines linking it to the South African grid. It was envisaged that the station would be completed by 2007.

There is also a coal-fired power station in Maputo with a capacity of 60 MW, which is supplied by imports of coal from South Africa. A new turbine, donated by France, was installed at the Maputo station in 1991. It is estimated that 400,000 tons of timber are used annually as fuel wood in Mozambique.

An electricity consortium, MOTRACO, was created in November 1998 to provide electricity to the Mozal aluminium smelter at Beloluane, near Maputo (see below). The consortium was to provide Mozal with 435 MW once the smelter became operational. MOTRACO consists of the state electricity company, EDM, and its counterparts in South Africa, ESKOM, and Swaziland, SEB. The construction of a 300-km power line from South Africa to Beloluane was to be completed by November 1999.

INDUSTRY

Industries are mainly devoted to the processing of primary materials, and Mozambique remains dependent on South African industrial products. About 47% of Mozambican manufacturers are located in and around Maputo, although the government is encouraging decentralization towards Beira and northern Mozambique. Under the colonial administration, investments from Portugal, South Africa, Italy and the UK established export-oriented industries. Food processing formed the traditional basis of this sector, with sugar refining, cashew- and wheat-processing predominating. However, textile production and brewing gained in importance during the 1980s. Other industries include the manufacture of cement, fertilizers and agricultural implements. Cotton spinning and weaving are undertaken at Chimoio, Maputo, and in Nampula province.

The cement industry is operating at a reduced level, producing 179,000 metric tons in 1996, compared with 611,000 tons in 1973. Cement exports reached 192,000 tons in 1978 but dropped dramatically, to 70,000 tons, in 1982, and to a negligible level in 1986. A programme to rehabilitate the cement plant at Matola, enabling it to produce 400,000 tons a year, was expected to be completed by the end of 1993, with finance provided by the World Bank, European Development Bank, France, Norway, Sweden and Denmark. In 1994 the Portuguese company CIMPOR purchased a 51% share of Cimentos de Moçambique for US $20m. The construction sector expanded by 7% in 1993. A US $4m. ammonia plant in Sofala province, a joint venture between the Empresa Nacional de Hidrocarbonetos (Mozambique), Scimitar Production Limited (Canada) and Zarara Petroleum Resources (UAE) started production in late 1997. In 1995 the MacMahon and Beira breweries were sold for $14m. to South African Breweries, and in May 1997 the brewery Fábrica de Cervejas Reunidas was purchased by the Portuguese company Empresa de Cerveja da Madeira for $4.5m. The new owners have undertaken a substantial investment programme, enhancing the quality and range of products. Following the contraction of the industrial sector by an annual average of 8.4% during 1980–86, official sources estimated that industrial output increased by 6% in 1987, owing partly to restructuring of the sector under the PRE and partly to increased imports of raw materials. In 1988 industrial output increased by 5.1%, according to the government. Under the PRE, resources were to be focused on industries with high domestic added value, and on import-substitution products. Government control of prices was relaxed in several industrial sectors in 1987. During 1990–98 industrial GDP increased by an estimated annual average of 8.5%.

Other secondary industries produce glass, ceramics, paper, tyres and railway carriages. The 1983–85 State Plan aimed to encourage small-scale industries, placing emphasis on the production of basic consumer goods and of import substitutes, using local materials. In 1990 the International Development Associa-

tion (IDA) provided US $38m. for the rehabilitation and promotion of small- and medium-scale enterprises.

In July 1998 construction began on the Mozal aluminium smelter at Beloluane, near Maputo. The principal investors are the South African mining conglomerate Gencor, through its British subsidiary Billiton (49% of the equity), the Japanese corporation Mitsubishi (26%) and the South African Industrial Development Corporation (25%). Of the total cost of US $1,300m., $800m. will be raised in loans, from sources including the World Bank. The smelter began production in June 2000, with an initial output capacity of 250,000 metric tons per year, which was expected to double following the completion of the second phase of the project, making it one of the largest smelters world-wide.

In September 1998 an agreement was signed for the long-awaited anchor project for the natural gas field at Pande. The US corporation Enron and the Industrial Development Corporation (IDC) of South Africa announced plans to use the gas in the Maputo Iron and Steel Project (MISP), which would produce some 4m. tons of steel slabs per year using South African iron ore. The plans envisaged an investment of US $2,500m., which would make it by far the largest single investment in Mozambique. Construction of the factory was expected to begin within two years. A framework agreement for the project was signed with the Mozambique government in April 1999 and construction of the factory was expected to commence within two years. However, the project remained highly controversial, with questions remaining regarding the source of the 67m. litres per day of water necessary to run the factory. In October 1999 the project suffered a set-back when IDC pulled out, citing its overexposure to the steel industry as a reason. In May 2000 Enron, that was to hold a 50% stake in MISP, announced five new equity partners, including Duferro (Switzerland), Kobe Steel (Japan), Midrex (USA), Voest-Alpine (Austria) and Techint (Italy). The initial scope of the project was reduced from 4m. tons to 2m. tons per year, at a cost of $1,100m. In late October 1999 Johannesburg Consolidated Investments (JCI) of South Africa signed an agreement with the Mozambican government to construct a similar, direct-reduced iron foundry in the port of Beira, in the central province of Sofala. The $800m. plant, backed by the Mitsubishi Corporation of Japan, will use the natural gas from the SASOL-operated Temane field. The project will also include a dedicated deep-water port north of Beira and a 100-sq km industrial zone. In 2000 a $2m. car assembly plant was expected to begin operation. Run by a Mozambican company, SIR Grupo, it aims to produce 300 Fiat Unos per year, representing some 10% of the country's annual car purchases.

TRANSPORT

Prior to independence Mozambique derived much of its income from transit charges on goods carried between Zimbabwe, Zambia, Malawi, Swaziland and South Africa and its ports. Railways play a dominant part in this middle-man economy. In 1987 Mozambique had 3,131 km of track, excluding the Sena Sugar Estates railway (90 km), which served only the company's properties. The end of the war precipitated a rapid increase in rail traffic. Passenger traffic escalated from 26m. passenger-km in 1992 to 403m. passenger-km in 1997. Freight traffic also increased, to a lesser extent, from 616m. ton-km in 1992 to 899m. ton-km in 1997. Main lines are: from Maputo, the Maputo–Ressano Garcia line to the South African border, the Maputo–Goba line to the Swaziland border, and the Maputo–Chicualacuala line to the Zimbabwe border (the Limpopo rail link) in the south; from Beira, the Beira–Mutare line to the Zimbabwe border, the Trans-Zambézia line to the Malawi border, and the Tete line. In the north the main route is the Nacala–Malawi line, with a branch-line to Lichinga. All these lines are intended primarily to export the products of land-locked countries, and secondarily to transport Mozambican goods. During the war the whole of Mozambique's rail network was subject to frequent disruption by Renamo guerrilla sabotage.

Most of the international lines are controlled by international conventions, since their effective functioning is vital to Mozambique's neighbours. Revenue from the Beira and Maputo lines was highly profitable to the Mozambican treasury. In 1980 the Harare–Beira line was reopened but, owing to lack of maintenance, the port of Beira could no longer accommodate vessels exceeding 5,000 tons.

In 1983 Mozambique secured several grants for making improvements to the railway network, including the rehabilitation of the vital 450-km rail link between the Moatize coalfields and Beira port.

In October 1986 a short-term programme to reinstate the 'Beira Corridor', linking Zimbabwe to the Beira harbour, was initiated, at a cost of more than US \$300m., financed mainly by the Netherlands, Scandinavia and the USA. A major project to rebuild the transport network in the corridor was announced in May 1987, under which Western European countries were to provide most of the \$589m. cost. In 1987 there was an increase of 25% in traffic through the 'Beira Corridor', although the turnover in the transport sector overall declined by 8%, owing to continued disruption by Renamo and a decline in South African traffic. The rehabilitation of the Limpopo railway, which began in 1986, was completed in early 1993, at a cost of some \$200m.

In December 1992 the government announced the proposed restructuring of the administration of the Beira, Maputo and Nacala transport corridors, with a view to encouraging private-sector involvement in investment and management. In June 1997 the government invited contractors to tender for private concessions to operate Maputo port and the three railways linking it with South Africa, Swaziland and Zimbabwe. The state ports and railway company, Empresa Nacional dos Portos e Caminhos de Ferro de Moçambique (CFM), were to retain a 33% stake in the companies. The operators were to have a 51% stake, while the remaining 16% was to be open to other investors. It was envisaged that the new operators would take over in 1998. However, negotiations with foreign companies had failed to produce agreement on management contracts for the port or any of the three railway lines by early 2000. Similar divestments involving the Beira and Nacala transport corridors were initiated in 1998.

In May 1999 a consortium headed by CFM was given approval to purchase the privatized Malawi Railways. CFM is partnered by the Sociedade de Desenvolvimento do Corredor de Nacala (SDCN–Nacala Corridor Development Company), which consists of US, French and Mozambican private companies. Payment, of some US \$20m., was to be made over a period of 20 years. The assets of the rail company will belong to the consortium, although the task of upgrading the infrastructure will remain the duty of the Malawian government, with World Bank funding. Traffic in the 'Nacala Corridor' increased by 8.7% in 1998, with traffic to Malawi increasing by 11% and internal traffic increasing by 5%. In late February 2000 an agreement was signed transferring the management of the port of Nacala and the 550-km railway line to Malawi to the SDCN.

In July 2000 the Mozambique minister of transport and communications, Tomás Salomão, announced plans to establish a Nacala Development Corridor (NDC), based on the railway line linking the Mozambican port of Nacala with Malawi; Zambia was expected to join the project, extending it into its own territory. The NDC was expected to be launched in September 2000.

This railway-dominated country lacks good roads. In 1996 there were only an estimated 30,400 km of roads and tracks. Unfortunately, the main roads are penetration lines toward the border and are grossly insufficient for Mozambique's purposes. Attempts are being made to construct a paved road from the Tanzanian border to the south. Most of the northern provinces are lacking in roads. There is a bridge across the Zambezi river at Tete, on the Zimbabwe–Malawi route, and a tarred road links Malawi to Maputo via Tete. Prior to the end of hostilities in 1992 the poor security situation all but halted normal road transport to and from most cities, and it was necessary to organize military guards for convoys. A major programme, supervised by the Southern African Development Co-ordination Conference (SADCC, now the Southern African Development Community–SADC), was under way in 1989 to improve the road links between Mozambique and neighbouring countries. UN agencies are helping to fund a programme to rehabilitate roads within the country. In April 1994 the IDA announced a credit of US \$188m. towards an \$814.6m. programme to rehabilitate the country's roads. The five-year programme, covering 3,450 km of main roads, 11,700 km of unasphalted roads and 3,200 Bailey bridges, was also to receive finance from the African Development Bank, EU, USA, France, Germany and Kuwait. The floods in February 2000 caused serious set-backs to the programme. Several sections of the only north–south route were destroyed, as well as a number of bridges over the main Save and Limpopo rivers.

The main ports are Maputo (the second largest port in Africa, with its annexe at Matola), Beira, Nacala and Quelimane. Maputo and Beira ports exist chiefly as outlets for South Africa, Swaziland, Zimbabwe, Zambia, Malawi and the Democratic Republic of the Congo. However, because of the security situation, most of their potential traffic has been re-routed to the South African ports of Durban, East London and Port Elizabeth. The total freight traffic handled by Mozambique's ports was 6.2m. tons of cargo in 1994, increasing to an estimated 7.6m. tons in 1998. Maputo has an excellent, multi-purpose harbour and rehabilitation of its facilities, which aimed to increase the port's annual handling capacity from 7m. tons to 12m. tons, was completed in 1989. The coal terminal at Maputo port, which has a handling capacity of 6m. tons per year, has been rented for a period of 15 years to the South African company CMR Engineers and Project Managers. The sugar terminal reopened in June 1995 following four years of inactivity. In February 1996 the terminal was leased to a private consortium, Mozambique International Port Services (MIPS), that, by the end of 1998, had renovated most of its facilities in a US \$7.5m.-investment programme. In November 1999, following 18 months of negotiations, an agreement was finally signed between CFM and the Maputo Port Development Consortium (MPDC), transferring the management of the port to the private sector. MPDC, led by a British company, Mersey Docks, has a 15-year lease of the facility and is expected to invest some \$50m. in rehabilitating and upgrading its facilities in order to quadruple its present throughput. CFM is also planning a new deep-water port 70 km south of Maputo in partnership with a UK-based company, Porto Dobela Developments. The \$515m. development is considered controversial as it is located within the limits of a nature reserve, and may also be seen as competing for trade with the port of Maputo. CFM and Mozal plan to spend US \$70m. on the expansion of Matola mineral port, situated outside Maputo. The first phase of the rehabilitation of Beira port, which included a joint terminal for petroleum and 'roll on, roll off' traffic and an increase in the capacity of the coal terminal, was completed in 1987, increasing its overall capacity by one-third, to 3.2m. tons per year. The second phase of the rehabilitation, which included the deepening of the entrance channel, was expected to raise capacity to 5m. tons per year on completion. Goods traffic handled at Beira in 1991 totalled 2.4m. tons, compared with 1.8m. tons in 1987.

In May 1996 the governments of Mozambique and South Africa launched the Maputo Development Corridor (MDC) initiative. The project included the rehabilitation of the Maputo–Ressano Garcia railway line, the construction of a toll road between Maputo and Witbank, in South Africa, and improvements to Maputo harbour. Construction of the 440-km toll road, which was scheduled to take three years at a cost of US \$400m., began in June 1998. In March 1999 it was announced that construction of the road was a year ahead of schedule. In March 2000, following the floods which destroyed the old road from Maputo to the South African border, the unfinished road was officially opened to traffic.

International air transport is operated by the state-owned LAM, and domestic routes by TTA. There are 16 airports, of which three are international. During 1983–93 most provincial capitals were accessible from Maputo only by air; however, the restoration of civil order and the rehabilitation of the road network has considerably lessened dependence on internal air transport. In August 1990 LAM agreed to buy one Boeing 767 and one 737 and to lease a further 767 and two 737 aircraft. All three of the leased aircraft were returned in early 1995. Despite opposition from within the ruling party, sustained pressure from the World Bank led the government to agree to transfer LAM and TTA to private-sector ownership. The latter was privatized in May 1997. Efforts to privatize LAM suffered a setback when the restricted tender, apparently won by a consortium led by the Portuguese airline TAP, was cancelled following renewed opposition from within the ruling party. In 1996 LAM incurred operating losses of US \$1.1m., an improvement over the previous year's losses of \$6.7m. In 1998 LAM recorded a profit of \$248,000; the strongest growth was in regional traffic. The government strategy of preserving LAM's monopoly on lucrative routes until 2003 was to be tried in court by TTA, in an effort to open up the domestic market. A \$4.7m.-

rehabilitation programme was planned for Maputo airport. The project included the rebuilding of the terminal to increase handling capacity to 1m. passengers a year. In mid-1999 both Air Mauritius and Ethiopian Airlines announced their intention to launch international services to Mozambique from their respective countries.

TOURISM

A highly profitable activity during the pre-independence period, tourism relied on the influx of Rhodesians and South Africans to Beira and the southern beaches. Gorongosa Park, half-way between Zimbabwe and Beira, was also a great attraction. However, by 1978 organized tourist travel had ceased. In 1984 Frelimo received a South African delegation for talks on a resumption of tourism, and in that year a joint-venture tourism company was established with South Africa in order to develop tourism on Inhaca island. In the event, hopes of a resumption of South African tourism in 1984 proved to be premature, and, except on coastal islands and in the immediate vicinity of Maputo, the security situation hampered any improvement in this highly volatile sector. Some hotels were rehabilitated during the late 1980s, and since the 1992 peace agreement South African tourism has increased rapidly and a number of South African operated camping sites have been established on beaches in the south of the country.

The government hopes that nature and game reserves will develop into a major tourist attraction. A controversial game reserve is being developed in Maputo province by an entrepreneur from the USA, James Blanchard, with a 9.7% stake belonging to the Mozambican state. Following Blanchard's death and a lack of investment, the government cancelled the contract in early 2000. Gongorosa game reserve is being rehabilitated, and there are plans for the extension of South Africa's Kruger National Park into Mozambique. In April 1998 the government announced plans for the development of the 22,000-sq km Niassa reserve in the far north of the country. The reserve was to be managed by a new company with 51% state ownership and 49% private ownership. In 1996 private investment in the tourism sector totalled US $60m. In that year, according to figures released by the Empresa Nacional de Turismo, 550,000 tourists visited Mozambique.

In March 1998 Mozambique, South Africa and Swaziland announced the US $121m. Lubombo Spatial Development Initiative with the purpose of attracting tourists to the sparsely inhabited area of their common borders. The project includes vast transnational parks. Ministers from the three countries agreed to work together to attract international funding. By the end of the 1990s tourism was the fastest growing sector of the Mozambique economy. It was estimated to contribute over US $32m. annually to the budget. Recognizing the importance of the industry, a post of minister for tourism was created for the first time following the 1999 general election. With the help of an EU grant, a firm of Danish consultants was preparing a comprehensive tourist development plan, identifying the five areas of greatest potential.

TRADE AND GOVERNMENT FINANCE

Prior to the advent of peace, Mozambique's severe balance-of-payments problem was accentuated by high defence spending (which was projected to account for 35% of budget expenditure in 1994), much of it in already scarce foreign exchange, and by the drastic decline in tourism. Mozambique has also suffered from adverse movements in the terms of trade. Exports cover only a small proportion of the country's imports: 24.0% in 1995 rising to 32.1% in 1996. In 1998 the total value of exports was US $249.9m., with imports valued at $746.2m. Mozambique has a diversified set of trading partners. In 1998 the principal sources of imports were South Africa (37.9%), Portugal (5.8%), the USA (5.0%) and Japan (5.0%). In that year the principal markets for exports were Zimbabwe (19.2%), South Africa (17.3%), Spain (14.9%), Portugal (7.8%), India (6.6%) and the USA (6.0%).

Agreements on the rescheduling of Mozambique's debts, covering more than US $400m. of repayments and arrears repayable in the period up to December 1988, were signed in May and June 1987 with Western official and commercial creditors, in order to reduce repayments on the country's external debt. Despite the 1987 reschedulings, the cost of debt-servicing in 1989 exceeded 200% of the value of Mozambique's exports of goods and services. In June 1990 Western official and commercial creditors agreed a further rescheduling of the country's debts. In March 1993 a restructuring of bilateral debt resulted in $180m. of the $440m. Mozambique was due to pay its official creditors over the next two years being written off. In November 1996 the 'Paris Club' of official creditors agreed to cancel or reschedule debt-servicing obligations of some $600m. Mozambique's total external public debt was estimated by the World Bank at $5,991m. at the end of 1997, of which $5,430m. was long-term public debt. In that year the cost of debt-servicing was equivalent to 18.6% of the total value of exports of goods and services. According to the World Bank, under the terms of the HIPC debt-reduction initiative, which took effect in June 1999 (see above), the debt-servicing ratio was to fall to 8% by 2001. On 1 June 1999 the government introduced value added tax, replacing the existing sales tax. The introduction of the new tax was a prerequisite to the implementation of debt reduction under the HIPC initiative.

Government finances improved considerably in the years following the General Peace Agreement, owing to improvements in economic opportunities and performance, favourable weather conditions, and reduced expenditure on defence and security. In 1999 total revenue was 6,208,000m. meticais, while expenditure totalled 11,102,000m. meticais.

In April 2000 the Mozambique government presented the 2000 budget to the assembléia da república. It included an 80% increase in expenditure on health care, and a 21% increase in expenditure on education; expenditure on agriculture was expected to increase by 13%. The cost of debt-servicing represented 0.7% of GDP in 1999 and was expected to stand at 0.4% in 2000. As a consequence of the HIPC initiative, debt-servicing was expected to decrease from US $94.1m. to $26.9m. Expenditure was projected at 14,476,000m. meticais and revenue (excluding grants) at 7,295,000m. meticais.

Statistical Survey

Source (unless otherwise stated): Instituto Nacional de Estatística, Comissão Nacional do Plano, Avda Ahmed Sekou Touré 21, CP 493, Maputo; tel. (1) 491054; fax (1) 493547; internet www.ine.gov.mz.

Area and Population

AREA, POPULATION AND DENSITY

Area (sq km)	799,380*
Population (census results)	
1 August 1980	11,673,725†
1 August 1997	
Males	7,714,306
Females	8,384,940
Total	16,099,246
Population (official estimates at mid-year)	
1999	16,840,654
2000	17,242,240
Density (per sq km) at mid-2000	21.6

* 308,641 sq miles. The area includes 13,000 sq km (5,019 sq miles) of inland water.

† Excluding an adjustment for underenumeration. This was estimated to have been 3.8%, and the adjusted total was 12,130,000.

PROVINCES (at 1 July 2000)

Province	Area (sq km)	Population	Density (per sq km)
Cabo Delgado	82,625	1,465,537	17.7
Gaza	75,709	1,203,294	15.9
Inhambane	68,615	1,256,139	18.3
Manica	61,661	1,137,448	18.4
City of Maputo . . .	300	1,018,938	3,396.5
Maputo province . . .	26,058	933,951	35.8
Nampula	81,606	3,265,854	40.0
Niassa	129,056	870,544	6.7
Sofala	68,018	1,453,928	21.4
Tete	100,724	1,319,904	13.1
Zambézia	105,008	3,316,703	31.6
Total	799,380	17,242,240	21.6

PRINCIPAL TOWNS (population at 1997 census)

Maputo (capital) . . .	989,386	Beira	412,588
Matola	440,927	Nampula . . .	314,965

BIRTHS AND DEATHS (UN estimates, annual averages)

	1980–85	1985–90	1990–95
Birth rate (per 1,000) . . .	45.8	45.6	45.1
Death rate (per 1,000) . . .	20.2	18.7	17.4

Expectation of life (UN estimates, years at birth, 1990–95): 48.1 (males 46.3; females 49.9).

Source: UN, *World Population Prospects: The 1998 Revision.*

1999: Registered live births 733,356 (birth rate 43.5 per 1,000); Registered deaths 335,915 (death rate 19.9 per 1,000).

ECONOMICALLY ACTIVE POPULATION
(persons aged 12 years and over, 1980 census)

	Males	Females	Total
Agriculture, forestry, hunting and fishing	1,887,779	2,867,052	4,754,831
Mining and quarrying . . }	323,730	23,064	346,794
Manufacturing . . .			
Construction. . . .	41,611	510	42,121
Commerce	90,654	21,590	112,244
Transport, storage and communications . . .	74,817	2,208	77,025
Other services* . . .	203,629	39,820	243,449
Total employed . . .	2,622,220	2,954,244	5,576,464
Unemployed	75,505	19,321	94,826
Total labour force . . .	2,697,725	2,973,565	5,671,290

* Including electricity, gas and water.

Source: ILO, *Yearbook of Labour Statistics.*

1991 (estimates, '000 persons): Agriculture 6,870; Industry 766; Services 798; Total labour force 8,434 (Source: UN Economic Commission for Africa, *African Statistical Yearbook*).

Mid-1998 (estimates in '000): Agriculture, etc. 7,941; Total 9,799 (Source: FAO, *Production Yearbook*).

Agriculture

PRINCIPAL CROPS ('000 metric tons)

	1996	1997	1998
Rice (paddy)	139	180	191
Maize	947	1,042	1,124
Sorghum	249	262	318
Potatoes*	73	74	75
Sweet potatoes* . . .	58	59	60
Cassava (Manioc) . . .	4,734	5,337	5,639†
Pulses	141	153	191†
Groundnuts (in shell) . .	117	126	143
Sunflower seed* . . .	14	14	15
Cottonseed†	34	48	60
Cotton (lint)†	17	24	30
Coconuts*	440	440	450
Copra	74*	74*	76†
Vegetables and melons* . .	167	173	180
Sugar cane	320*	279	369
Oranges*	16	17	18
Mangoes*	33	34	35
Bananas*	85	86	87
Papayas*	43	44	45
Other fruits*	183	188	193
Cashew nuts	65†	43	52
Tea (made)	2*	2	2
Tobacco (leaves) . . .	3†	3†	3*
Jute and jute-like fibres* . .	5	5	5
Sisal*	1	1	1

* FAO estimate(s).   † Unofficial figure(s).

Source: FAO, *Production Yearbook*.

LIVESTOCK (FAO estimates, '000 head, year ending September)

	1996	1997	1998
Asses	20	21	22
Cattle	1,270	1,290	1,300
Pigs	172	174	176
Sheep	120	122	123
Goats	384	386	388

Chickens (FAO estimates, million): 23 in 1996; 23 in 1997; 24 in 1998.

Source: FAO, *Production Yearbook*.

LIVESTOCK PRODUCTS (FAO estimates, '000 metric tons)

	1996	1997	1998
Beef and veal	37	38	38
Goat meat	2	2	2
Pig meat	12	13	13
Poultry meat	28	29	29
Cows' milk	58	59	60
Goats' milk	10	10	10
Hen eggs	12	12	12
Cattle hides	5	5	5

Source: FAO, *Production Yearbook*.

Forestry

ROUNDWOOD REMOVALS ('000 cubic metres)

	1995	1996	1997
Sawlogs, veneer logs and logs for sleepers	77	77	77
Other industrial wood	1,066	1,099	1,128
Fuel wood	17,324	17,324	17,324
Total	18,467	18,500	18,529

Source: FAO, *Yearbook of Forest Products*.

SAWNWOOD PRODUCTION ('000 cubic metres, incl. railway sleepers)

	1995	1996*	1997*
Coniferous (softwood)	13	13	13
Broadleaved (hardwood)	29	29	29
Total	42	42	42

* FAO estimates.
Source: FAO, *Yearbook of Forest Products*.

Fishing

('000 metric tons, live weight)

	1995	1996	1997
Inland waters:			
Freshwater fishes	2.0	1.9	1.7
Dagaas	3.1	5.6	9.8
Indian Ocean:			
Marine fishes	10.0	15.9	14.5
Shrimps	10.7	10.0	11.4
Other crustaceans	0.8	1.0	1.5
Molluscs	0.2	0.5	0.7
Sea cucumbers	0.0	0.1	0.0
Total catch	26.9	34.9	39.6

Source: FAO, *Yearbook of Fishery Statistics*.

Mining

('000 metric tons)

	1990	1991	1992
Coal	122.2	112.0	27.0
Bauxite	6.6	7.9	9.3
Salt (unrefined)	46.9	45.3	22.8

Source: Ministry of Mineral Resources.
Bauxite ('000 metric tons): 6 in 1993; 10 in 1994; 11 in 1995; 11 in 1996 (Source: UN, *Industrial Commodity Statistics Yearbook*).

Industry

SELECTED PRODUCTS ('000 metric tons, unless otherwise indicated)

	1994	1995	1996
Margarine	0.5	1.0	—
Wheat flour	40	39	38
Raw sugar*	21	34	32
Beer ('000 hl)	118	244	374
Cigarettes (million)	343	106	250
Footwear ('000 pairs)	87	29	n.a.
Cement	62	146	179
Electric energy (million kWh)†	490	563	560

* FAO estimates.
† Estimates.
Source: UN, *Industrial Commodity Statistics Yearbook*.

Finance

CURRENCY AND EXCHANGE RATES

Monetary Units
100 centavos = 1 metical (plural: meticais).

Sterling, Dollar and Euro Equivalents (28 April 2000)
£1 sterling = 23,584.2 meticais;
US $1 = 15,040.0 meticais;
€1 = 13,663.8 meticais;
100,000 meticais = £4.240 = $6.649 = €7.319.

Average Exchange Rate (meticais per US $)
1997 11,543.6
1998 11,874.6
1999 12,775.1

BUDGET ('000 million meticais)

Revenue*	1997	1998	1999
Taxation	4,235	4,946	5,734
Taxes on income	879	951	867
Domestic taxes on goods and services	2,389	2,866	3,638
Customs duties	812	951	1,046
Other taxes	155	178	183
Non-tax revenue	388	365	474
Total	4,623	5,311	6,208

Expenditure†	1997	1998	1999
Current expenditure‡	4,272	5,269	6,035
Compensation of employees	1,445	2,076	2,502
Other goods and services	1,334	1,838	1,838
Interest on public debt	530	458	475
Transfer payments	750	897	1,220
Other purposes	302	—	—
Capital expenditure§	4,816	4,641	5,067
Total	9,088	9,910	11,102

* Excluding grants received ('000 million meticais): 3,705 in 1997; 3,818 in 1998; 5,408 in 1999. Also excluded is unallocated revenue ('000 million meticais): 139 in 1997.
† Excluding net lending ('000 million meticais): 410 in 1997; 298 in 1998; 492 in 1999. Also excluded is unallocated expenditure ('000 million meticais): 27 in 1998; 578 in 1999.
‡ Including adjustments relating to preceding or following periods ('000 million meticais): −89 in 1997.
§ Including adjustments relating to preceding or following periods ('000 million meticais): 1,062 in 1997.

Sources: Banco de Moçambique and IMF, *Republic of Mozambique: Statistical Annex* (August 1999).

INTERNATIONAL RESERVES (US $ million at 31 December)

	1997	1998	1999
IMF special drawing rights . .	0.05	0.06	0.05
Reserve position in IMF . . .	0.01	0.01	0.01
Foreign exchange	517.29	608.43	653.93
Total	517.35	608.50	654.01

Source: IMF, *International Financial Statistics.*

MONEY SUPPLY ('000 million meticais at 31 December)

	1997	1998	1999
Currency outside banks . .	1,544.1	1,649.7	2,174.2
Demand deposits at commercial banks.	3,283.0	3,894.7	4,693.0
Total money (incl. others) . .	4,901.7	5,613.0	6,994.4

Source: IMF, *International Financial Statistics.*

COST OF LIVING
(Consumer Price Index for Maputo; base: 1995=100)

	1997	1998	1999
All items	156.3	157.1	160.3

Source: IMF, *International Financial Statistics.*

NATIONAL ACCOUNTS
National Income and Product ('000 million meticais at current prices)

	1984	1985	1986
Domestic factor incomes* . . .	95.7	137.2	146.3
Consumption of fixed capital . .	4.0	4.0	4.0
Gross domestic product (GDP) at factor cost . . .	99.7	141.2	150.3
Indirect taxes	9.8	6.9	8.7
Less Subsidies	0.4	0.5	0.5
GDP in purchasers' values .	109.1	147.6	158.4
Net factor income from abroad .	0.3	0.2	0.6
Gross national product . .	109.4	147.8	159.0
Less Consumption of fixed capital .	4.0	4.0	4.0
National income in market prices	105.4	143.8	155.0

* Compensation of employees and the operating surplus of enterprises.
Source: UN, *National Accounts Statistics.*

Expenditure on the Gross Domestic Product
('000 million meticais at current prices)

	1996	1997	1998
Government final consumption expenditure	2,454.8	3,222.6	3,925.8
Private final consumption expenditure	31,016.9	35,782.4	38,421.1
Increase in stocks . . .	247.9	492.1	—
Gross capital formation . .	5,901.4	7,073.2	10,160.2
Special public services . .	149.9	143.8	158.1
Total domestic expenditure .	39,771.0	46,714.1	52,665.2
Exports of goods and services . .	4,828.7	5,124.1	5,043.7
Less Imports of goods and services .	12,289.1	11,712.0	14,151.8
GDP in purchasers' values . .	32,310.5	40,126.2	43,557.1

Gross Domestic Product by Economic Activity
('000 million meticais at current prices)

	1996	1997	1998
Agriculture and livestock . . .	9,357.2	11,087.3	12,163.7
Fishing	1,682.2	1,547.7	1,652.9
Mining	77.2	109.5	118.7
Manufacturing	3,040.6	3,687.3	3,702.3
Electricity and water . . .	103.2	178.4	488.3
Construction	2,105.9	2,458.5	3,288.8
Trade	7,165.7	9,085.5	9,544.2
Restaurants and hotels . .	275.6	345.7	315.2
Transport and communications .	3,740.4	4,643.5	4,792.9
Public administration and defence	706.1	990.0	1,351.8
Education	431.2	573.0	673.5
Health	127.5	172.6	189.8
Other services	3,027.6	3,690.3	4,287.0
Special public services* . .	149.9	143.8	158.1
Sub-total	31,990.3	38,713.1	42,727.0
Import duties	670.2	812.2	951.1
Statistical discrepancy . .	−350.1	600.9	−121.1
Total	32,310.4	40,126.2	43,557.1

* Current expenditures from investment projects.

BALANCE OF PAYMENTS (US $ million)

	1996	1997	1998
Exports of goods f.o.b. . . .	226.1	230.0	244.6
Imports of goods f.o.b. . . .	−704.4	−684.0	−735.6
Trade balance	−478.3	−454.0	−491.0
Exports of services . . .	253.2	278.7	286.2
Imports of services . . .	−319.0	−328.6	−396.2
Balance on goods and services .	−544.1	−503.9	−601.0
Other income received . . .	61.0	63.6	46.3
Other income paid . . .	−162.1	−168.2	−187.8
Balance on goods, services and income	−645.2	−608.5	−742.5
Current transfers received . .	224.7	312.9	313.2
Current balance	−420.5	−295.6	−429.3
Direct investment from abroad .	72.5	64.4	212.7
Other investment assets . .	—	—	19.0
Other investment liabilities .	162.5	117.8	68.7
Net errors and omissions . .	−238.3	−364.8	−263.8
Overall balance . . .	−423.8	−478.2	−392.7

Source: IMF, *International Financial Statistics.*

MOZAMBIQUE

External Trade

PRINCIPAL COMMODITIES (US $'000)

Imports c.i.f.	1995	1996
Vegetable products	101,956	101,810
Cereals	66,438	74,409
Products of milling industry	20,856	20,397
Animal and vegetable fats and oils	22,265	20,792
Food products, beverages and tobacco	34,184	44,700
Sugar and sugar confectionery	15,672	20,143
Mineral products	84,463	111,863
Salt, sulphur, earths and stone, plastering material, lime and cement	10,996	17,723
Mineral fuels, mineral oils and products of their distillation	73,370	92,469
Chemical industry products	70,430	59,110
Organic chemicals	16,912	3,619
Pharmaceutical products	26,474	21,041
Rubber and plastic products	20,073	25,053
Paper and products, printing and publishing	25,136	19,860
Textile products	21,328	24,833
Metal and metal products	46,958	77,319
Articles of iron and steel	30,242	42,290
Machinery, equipment, electrical machinery	122,463	150,091
Nuclear reactors, boilers, machinery and mechanical appliances	67,241	92,034
Electrical machinery and equipment	55,222	58,057
Transport equipment	131,000	95,822
Vehicles other than railway or tramway rolling-stock	108,963	90,804
Ships, boats and floating structures	17,951	2,374
Total (incl. others)	726,986	782,646

Exports f.o.b.	1996	1997	1998
Cashew nuts	17,200	14,200	19,100
Shrimps, prawns, etc.	70,300	85,100	72,600
Raw cotton	26,800	25,200	22,300
Sugar	12,800	12,800	8,400
Copra	3,700	4,600	5,000
Timber	9,800	13,800	11,000
Total (incl. others)	226,100	230,600	249,900

Source: IMF, *Republic of Mozambique: Statistical Annex* (August 1999).

PRINCIPAL TRADING PARTNERS (US $'000)

Imports c.i.f.	1995	1996
Australia	1,697	10,270
Belgium	9,900	8,098
Brazil	5,891	13,624
Canada	11,962	10,584
Denmark	11,538	11,918
France	23,804	34,750
Germany	24,072	20,672
Hong Kong	10,596	5,429
India	23,701	35,794
Italy	24,128	32,681
Japan	36,790	31,041
Malawi	670	10,734
Netherlands	17,090	15,903
Norway	4,761	12,017
Pakistan	8,020	1,887
Portugal	65,725	49,322
South Africa	188,159	259,725
Spain	23,661	9,895
Swaziland	23,326	10,254
United Arab Emirates	5,234	11,379
United Kingdom	26,514	18,241
USA	49,897	32,627
Zimbabwe	30,705	30,578
Total (incl. others)	726,986	782,646

1997 (US $ million): France 20.6; Germany 18.5; India 23.6; Japan 34.5; Portugal 46.5; South Africa 310.9; United Kingdom 15.6; USA 39.4; Zimbabwe 17.7; **Total** (incl. others) 760.2.
1998 (US $ million): France 18.3; Germany 12.4; India 22.9; Japan 32.9; Portugal 43.4; South Africa 282.5; United Kingdom 13.6; USA 36.5; Zimbabwe 16.5; **Total** (incl. others) 746.2.

Exports f.o.b.	1994	1995	1996
Belgium	n.a.	2,904	3,476
Canada	n.a.	3,124	736
France	n.a.	7,476	1,326
Hong Kong	n.a.	1,766	1,975
India	16,788	4,534	26,778
Indonesia	n.a.	781	3,105
Japan	19,430	24,820	17,244
Malawi	n.a.	2,606	1,393
Netherlands	n.a.	3,151	3,513
Portugal	14,612	14,575	17,471
South Africa	23,627	41,057	43,792
Spain	34,041	36,373	47,619
Tanzania	n.a.	114	3,957
United Kingdom	n.a.	783	3,001
USA	13,990	9,526	25,803
Zimbabwe	5,441	7,943	9,828
Total (incl. others)	155,444	174,303	226,084

1997 (US $ million): India 13.3; Japan 19.3; Portugal 20.6; South Africa 40.2; Spain 42.6; USA 26.5; Zimbabwe 9.5; **Total** (incl others) 230.1.
1998 (US $ million): India 16.2; Japan 12.8; Portugal 19.1; South Africa 42.5; Spain 36.6; USA 14.8; Zimbabwe 47.3; **Total** (incl. others) 245.9.

Transport

RAILWAYS (traffic)

	1984	1985	1986
Freight carried ('000 metric tons)	3,698.6	2,899.5	2,949.3
Freight ton-km (million)	536.3	289.6	303.3
Passengers carried ('000)	5,296.0	6,723.0	6,619.0
Passenger-km (million)	284.1	225.4	263.6

1987: Passenger-km 105m.; Freight ton-km 353m.
1988: Passenger-km 75m.; Freight ton-km 306m.

Source: UN, *Statistical Yearbook*.

1989: Passenger-km 73.5m.; Freight ton-km 402.2m.
1990: Passenger-km 78.9m.; Freight ton-km 421.4m.
1991: Passenger-km 61.0m.; Freight ton-km 306.7m.
1992: Passenger-km 26.0m.; Freight ton-km 616.0m.
1993: Passenger-km 71.3m.; Freight ton-km 648.9m.
1994: Passenger-km 123.5m.; Freight ton-km 655.0m.
1995: Passenger-km 312.0m.; Freight ton-km 892.7m.
1996: Passenger-km 350.4m.; Freight ton-km 982.8m.
1997: Passenger-km 403.1m.; Freight ton-km 899.2m.
1998 (preliminary figures): Passenger-km 155.0m.; Freight ton-km 860.9m.

(Source: IMF, *Republic of Mozambique: Statistical Annex* (August 1999)).

ROAD TRAFFIC (motor vehicles in use at 31 December)

	1994	1995*	1996*
Passenger cars	30,977	25,740	4,900
Lorries and vans	10,035	7,520	7,520

* Estimates.
Source: International Road Federation, *World Road Statistics*.

SHIPPING

Merchant Fleet (registered at 31 December)

	1996	1997	1998
Number of vessels	96	127	124
Total displacement ('000 grt)	44.8	38.7	35.3

Source: Lloyd's Register of Shipping, *World Fleet Statistics*.

International Sea-borne Freight Traffic ('000 metric tons)

	1989	1990	1991*
Goods loaded	2,430	2,578	2,800
Goods unloaded	3,254	3,379	3,400

* Estimates.

Sources: UN, *Monthly Bulletin of Statistics*; UN Economic Commission for Africa, *African Statistical Yearbook*.

Total Freight Handled ('000 metric tons): 6,224 in 1992; 6,053 in 1993; 6,167 in 1994; 7,508 in 1995; 8,405 in 1996; 8,960 in 1997; 7,606 in 1998 (preliminary figure) (Source: IMF, *Republic of Mozambique: Statistical Annex* (August 1999)).

CIVIL AVIATION (traffic on scheduled services)

	1994	1995	1996
Kilometres flown (million) . .	5	3	3
Passengers carried ('000) . .	221	168	163
Passenger-km (million) . .	443	290	260
Total ton-km (million) . .	52	32	27

Source: UN, *Statistical Yearbook*.

1997: Passenger-km 291.7m.; Freight ton-km 5.5m.
1998: (preliminary figures): Passenger-km 311.7m.; Freight ton-km 5.9m.

Communications Media

	1994	1995	1996
Radio receivers ('000 in use) . .	580	660	700
Television receivers ('000 in use) .	55	60	80
Telephones ('000 main lines in use)	57	60	60
Telefax stations (number in use) .	7,182	n.a.	7,200
Daily newspapers:			
Number	2	3	2
Average circulation ('000) . .	81	130	49

Non-daily newspapers (1996): 4 (estimated average circulation 160,000).
Periodicals (1988): 5 (average circulation 2,263,000).
Book Production (1984): 66 titles (including 37 pamphlets); 3,490,000 copies (including 360,000 pamphlets).
1997 ('000 in use): Radio receivers 730; Television receivers 90.
Source: mainly UNESCO, *Statistical Yearbook*.

Education

(1997, unless otherwise indicated)

	Institutions	Teachers	Students
Pre-primary*†	n.a.	n.a.	45,100
Primary	6,025	32,670	1,899,531
Secondary	75	1,555	51,554
Technical	25	565	12,001
Higher‡	3	954	7,156

* 1986 figures; data refer to initiation classes.
† Source: UNESCO, *Statistical Yearbook*.
‡ Public education only.

Directory

The Constitution

The Constitution came into force on 30 November 1990, replacing the previous version, introduced at independence on 25 June 1975 and revised in 1978. Its main provisions, as amended in 1996, are summarized below.

GENERAL PRINCIPLES

The Republic of Mozambique is an independent, sovereign, unitary and democratic state of social justice. Sovereignty resides in the people, who exercise it according to the forms laid down in the Constitution. The fundamental objectives of the Republic include:

The defence of independence and sovereignty;

the defence and promotion of human rights and of the equality of citizens before the law; and

the strengthening of democracy, of freedom and of social and individual stability.

POLITICAL PARTICIPATION

The people exercise power through universal, direct, equal, secret, personal and periodic suffrage to elect their representatives, by referenda and through permanent democratic participation. Political parties are prohibited from advocating or resorting to violence.

FUNDAMENTAL RIGHTS AND DUTIES OF CITIZENS

All citizens enjoy the same rights and are subject to the same duties, irrespective of colour, race, sex, ethnic origin, place of birth, religion, level of education, social position or occupation. In realizing the objectives of the Constitution, all citizens enjoy freedom of opinion, assembly and association. All citizens over 18 years of age are entitled to vote and be elected. Active participation in the defence of the country is the duty of every citizen. Individual freedoms are guaranteed by the State, including freedom of expression, of the press, of assembly, of association and of religion. The State guarantees accused persons the right to a legal defence. No Court or Tribunal has the power to impose a sentence of death upon any person.

STATE ORGANS

Public elective officers are chosen by elections through universal, direct, secret, personal and periodic vote. Legally-recognized political parties may participate in elections.

THE PRESIDENT

The President is the Head of State and of the Government, and Commander-in-Chief of the armed forces. The President is elected by direct, equal, secret and personal universal suffrage on a majority vote, and must be proposed by at least 10,000 voters, of whom at least 200 must reside in each province. The term of office is five years. A candidate may be re-elected on only two consecutive occasions, or again after an interval of five years between terms.

THE ASSEMBLY OF THE REPUBLIC

Legislative power is vested in the Assembly of the Republic. The Assembly is elected by universal direct adult suffrage on a secret ballot, and is composed of 250 Deputies. The Assembly is elected for a maximum term of five years, but may be dissolved by the President before the expiry of its term. The Assembly holds two ordinary sessions each year.

THE COUNCIL OF MINISTERS

The Council of Ministers is the Government of the Republic. The Prime Minister assists and advises the President in the leadership of the Government and presents the Government's programme, budget and policies to the Assembly, assisted by other ministers.

LOCAL STATE ORGANS

The Republic is administered in provinces, municipalities and administrative posts. The highest state organ in a province is the provincial government, presided over by a governor, who is answerable to the central Government. There shall be assemblies at each administrative level.

THE JUDICIARY

Judicial functions shall be exercised through the Supreme Court and other courts provided for in the law on the judiciary, which also subordinates them to the Assembly of the Republic. Courts must safeguard the principles of the Constitution and defend the rights and legitimate interests of citizens. Judges are independent, subject only to the law.

Note: In October 1998 the Government published draft amendments to the Constitution that envisaged significant changes to the political system. These included a reduction in presidential powers and concomitant increase in those of the Prime Minister and the legislature. However, in September 1999 the draft amendments failed to secure the two-thirds' majority in the legislature necessary for approval, owing to opposition by Renamo deputies. As the political system cannot be altered during a legislative term, the opportunity for such major constitutional amendments would not arise again until 2005.

The Government

HEAD OF STATE

President of the Republic and Commander-in-Chief of the Armed Forces: JOAQUIM ALBERTO CHISSANO (took office 6 November 1986; elected President 27–29 October 1994; re-elected 3–5 December 1999).

COUNCIL OF MINISTERS
(August 2000)

Prime Minister: Dr PASCOAL MANUEL MOCUMBI.

Minister of Foreign Affairs and Co-operation: Dr LEONARDO DOS SANTOS SIMÃO.

Minister of National Defence: Gen. (retd) TOBIAS DAI.

Minister of Planning and Finance: LUÍSA DIOGO.

Minister of Justice: JOSÉ IBRAIMO ABUDO.

Minister of the Interior and Minister in the President's Office, with responsibility for Defence and Security Affairs: ALMERINO DA CRUZ MARCOS MANHENJE.

Minister of State Administration: JOSÉ CHICHAVA.

Minister of Agricultural and Rural Development: HÉLDER MONTEIRO MUTEIA.

Minister of Fisheries: CADMIEL MUTHEMBA.

Minister of Industry and Trade: CARLOS ALBERTO MORGADO.

Minister of Mineral Resources and Energy: CASTIGO LANGA.

Minister of Transport and Communications: TOMÁS AUGUSTO SALOMÃO.

Minister of Education: ALCIDO EDUARDO NGUENHA.

Minister of Health: FRANCISCO SONGANE.

Minister of Culture: MIGUEL COSTA MKAÍMA.

Minister of Environmental Co-ordination: JOHN WILLIAM KACHAMILA.

Minister of Labour: MÁRIO LAMPIÃO SEVENE.

Minister of Public Works and Housing: ROBERTO COSTLEY-WHITE.

Minister of Youth and Sport: JOEL MATIAS LIBOMBO.

Minister of Women's Affairs and Social Welfare Co-ordination: VIRGÍLIA SANTOS MATABELE.

Minister in the Presidency with responsibility for Parliamentary and Diplomatic Affairs: FRANCISCO CAETANO MADEIRA.

Minister of Tourism: FERNANDO SUMBANE JÚNIOR.

Minister of Veterans' Affairs: ANTÓNIO HAMA THAY.

Minister of Higher Education, Science and Technology: LÍDIA MARIA RIBEIRO ARTHUR BRITO.

MINISTRIES

Office of the President: Avda Julius Nyerere 1780, Maputo; tel. (1) 491121; fax (1) 492065.

Office of the Prime Minster: Praça da Marinha Popular, Maputo; tel. (1) 426861; fax (1) 426881.

Ministry of Agriculture and Fisheries: Praça dos Heróis Moçambicanos, CP 1406, Maputo; tel. and fax (1) 460055.

Ministry of Culture, Youth and Sports: Avda Patrice Lumumba 1217, CP 1742, Maputo; tel. (1) 420068; fax (1) 429700.

Ministry of Education: Avda 24 de Julho 167, 9° andar, Maputo; tel. (1) 492006; fax (1) 492160.

Ministry of Environmental Co-ordination: Avda Acordos de Lusaka 2115, CP 516, Maputo; tel. (1) 466245; fax (1) 4685849; internet www.sdnp.mz/ambiente.

Ministry of Foreign Affairs and Co-operation: Avda Julius Nyerere 4, Maputo; tel. (1) 490222; fax (1) 494070; e-mail minec@zebra.vem.mz; internet www.mozambique.mz/governo/minec.

Ministry of Health: Avdas Eduardo Mondlane e Salvador Allende, CP 264, Maputo; tel. (1) 427131; fax (1) 427133.

Ministry of Industry, Commerce and Trade: Avda 25 de Setembro 86, Maputo; tel. (1) 427204; fax (1) 421305.

Ministry of the Interior: Avda Olof Palme 46/48, Maputo; tel. (1) 420130; fax (1) 420084.

Ministry of Justice: Avda Julius Nyerere 33, Maputo; tel. (1) 491613; fax (1) 494264.

Ministry of Labour: Avda 24 de Julho 2351-2365, CP 281, Maputo; tel. (1) 427051; fax (1) 421881.

Ministry of Mineral Resources and Energy: Avda Fernão de Magalhães 34, Maputo; tel. (1) 429615; fax (1) 427103.

Ministry of National Defence: Avda Mártires de Machaua 280, Maputo; tel. (1) 492081; fax (1) 491619.

Ministry of Planning and Finance: Praça da Marinha Popular, CP 272, Maputo; tel. (1) 425071; fax (1) 420137.

Ministry of Public Works and Housing: Avda Karl Marx 268, Maputo; tel. (1) 420543; fax (1) 421369.

Ministry of State Administration: Rua da Rádio Moçambique 112, Maputo; tel. (1) 426666; fax (1) 428565; internet www.sdnp.org.mz/mae.

Ministry of Tourism: Maputo.

Ministry of Transport and Communications: Avda Mártires de Inhaminga 336, Maputo; tel. (1) 420223; fax (1) 431028.

Ministry of Women's Affairs and Social Welfare Co-ordination: Maputo.

PROVINCIAL GOVERNORS
(August 2000)

Cabo Delgado Province: JOSÉ PACHECO.

Gaza Province: ROSÁRIO MUALEIA.

Inhambane Province: AIRES ALY.

Manica Province: SOARES NHACA.

Maputo Province: ALFREDO NAMITETE.

Nampula Province: ABDUL RAZAK.

Niassa Province: DAVID SIMANGO.

Sofala Province: FELÍCIO ZACARIAS.

Tete Province: TOMÁS MANDLATE.

Zambézia Province: LUCAS CHOMERA.

City of Maputo: JOÃO BAPTISTA COSMÉ.

President and Legislature

PRESIDENT

Presidential Election, 3–5 December 1999

	Votes	% of votes
JOAQUIM ALBERTO CHISSANO (Frelimo) . . .	2,338,333	52.29
AFONSO MACACHO MARCETA DHLAKAMA (Renamo—União Eleitoral)	2,133,655	47.71
Total*	4,471,988	100.00

* Excluding 320,795 blank votes and 141,569 spoilt votes.

ASSEMBLÉIA DA REPÚBLICA
Chairman: EDUARDO MULEMBUE.

General Election, 3–5 December 1999

	Votes	% of votes	Seats
Frente de Libertação de Moçambique (Frelimo)	2,005,713	48.54	133
Resistência Nacional Moçambicana—União Eleitoral (Renamo—UE) .	1,603,811	38.81	117
Partido do Trabalho (PT) . . .	111,139	2.69	—
Partido Liberal e Democrático de Moçambique (Palmo)	101,970	2.47	—
Partido Social, Liberal e Democrático (Sol)	83,440	2.02	—
União Moçambicana de Oposição (UMO)	64,117	1.55	—
União Democrática (UD) . . .	61,122	1.48	—
Total (incl. others)*	4,132,323	100.00	250

* Excluding 462,666 blank votes and 238,772 spoilt votes.

Political Organizations

Aliança Democrática de Moçambique (ADM): f. 1994; Co-ordinator JOSÉ PEREIRA BRANQUINHO.

*Aliança Independente de Moçambique (Alimo): f. 1998; Sec.-Gen. ERNESTO SERGIO.

Confederação Democrática de Moçambique (Codemo): f. 1991; Leader DOMINGOS CARDOSO.

Congresso Independente de Moçambique (Coinmo): Pres. VÍTOR MARCOS SAENE; Sec.-Gen. HILDA RABECA TSININE.

*Frente de Ação Patriótica (FAP): f. 1991; Pres. JOSÉ CARLOS PALAÇO; Sec.-Gen. RAUL DA CONCEIÇÃO.

Frente de Libertação de Moçambique (Frelimo): Rua Pereiro do Lago, Maputo; f. 1962 by merger of three nationalist parties; reorg. 1977 as a 'Marxist-Leninist vanguard party'; in July 1989 abandoned its exclusive Marxist-Leninist orientation; Chair. JOAQUIM ALBERTO CHISSANO; Sec.-Gen. MANUEL TOMÉ.

*Frente Unida de Moçambique—Partido de Convergência Democrática (Fumo—PCD): Sec.-Gen. JOSÉ SAMO GUDO.

*Movimento Nacionalista Moçambicana—Partido Moçambicano da Social Democracia (Monamo—PMSD): Sec.-Gen. Dr MÁXIMO DIOGO JOSÉ DIAS.

Partido Agrário de Moçambique (PAM): f. 1991.

Partido Comunista de Moçambique (Pacomo): f. 1995.

Partido do Congresso Democrático (Pacode): Leader VASCO CAMPIRA MAMBOYA ALFAZEMA.

*Partido de Convenção Nacional (PCN): obtained legal status in 1992; Chair. LUTERO CHIMBIRIMBIRI SIMANGO; Sec.-Gen. Dr GABRIEL MABUNDA.

Partido Democrático de Libertação de Moçambique (Padelimo): based in Kenya; Pres. JOAQUIM JOSÉ NIOTA.

Partido Independente de Moçambique (Pimo): f. 1993; Leader YAQUB SABINDY; Sec.-Gen. MAGALHÃES BRAMUGY.

Partido Internacionalista Democrático de Moçambique (Pidemo): f. 1993; Leader JOÃO KAMACHO.

*Partido Liberal e Democrático de Moçambique (Palmo): obtained legal status 1993; Chair. MARTINS BILAL; Sec.-Gen. ANTONIO MUEDO.

Partido Nacional de Obreiros e Camponêses (Panaoc): Leader ARMANDO SIUEIA.

Partido Patriótico Independente de Moçambique: f. 1995; breakaway faction of Pimo.

*Partido Popular de Moçambique (PPM).

Partido Progressivo e Liberal de Moçambique (PPLM): f. 1992; Pres. NEVES SERRANO.

Partido de Progresso do Povo Moçambicano (PPPM): f. 1991; obtained legal status 1992; Pres. Dr PADIMBE MAHOSE KAMATI ANDREA; Sec.-Gen. CHE ABDALA.

*Partido Renovador Democrático (PRD): obtained legal status 1994; Pres. MANECA DANIEL.

Partido Revolucionário do Povo Socialista Unido de Moçambique (Prepsumo): f. 1992.

Partido Social Democrático (PSD): Leader CARLOS MACHEL.

Partido de Todos os Nativos Moçambicanos (Partonamo): f. 1996; Leader MUSSAGY ABDUL REMANE.

Partido do Trabalho (PT): f. 1993; breakaway faction of PPPM; Pres. MIGUEL MABOTE; Sec.-Gen. LUÍS MUCHANGA.

Partido Social, Liberal e Democrático (Sol): breakaway faction of Palmo; Leader CASIMIRO MIGUEL NHAMITHAMBO.

* Partido de Unidade Nacional (PUN).

* Partido Verde de Moçambique (PVM): Leader BRUNO SAPEMBA.

Regedores e Camponeses de Moçambique (Recamo): f. by ARONE SIJAMO.

*Resistência Nacional Moçambicana (Renamo): also known as Movimento Nacional da Resistência de Moçambique (MNR); f. 1976; fmr guerrilla group, in conflict with the Govt between 1976 and Oct. 1992; obtained legal status in 1994; Pres. AFONSO MACACHO MARCETA DHLAKAMA; Sec.-Gen. JOÃO ALEXANDRE.

União Democrática (UD): f. 1994; Gen. Sec. JOSÉ CHICUARRA MASSINGA; coalition comprising:

Partido Nacional Democrático (Panade): obtained legal status 1993; Leader JOSÉ CHICUARRA MASSINGA.

Partido Nacional de Moçambique (Panamo): Pres. MARCOS JUMA.

União Democrática de Moçambique (Udemo): f. 1987 as the mil. wing of Unamo, from which it broke away in 1991; adopted present name in 1992; Leader GIMO PHIRI.

União Moçambicana de Oposição (UMO): electoral alliance comprising three parties incl.:

Partido Democrático de Moçambique (Pademo): f. 1991; obtained legal status in 1993; Co-ordinator WEHIA MONAKACHO RIPUA; Gen. Sec. GIMO GUINDILA.

União Nacional Moçambicana (Unamo): f. 1987; breakaway faction of Renamo; social democratic; obtained legal status 1992; Pres. CARLOS ALEXANDRE DOS REIS; Sec.-Gen. FLORENCIA JOÃO DA SILVA.

* Member of coalition of eleven opposition parties formed in July 1999 to contest December presidential and legislative elections as **Renamo—União Eleitoral**.

Diplomatic Representation

EMBASSIES AND HIGH COMMISSIONS IN MOZAMBIQUE

Algeria: Rua de Mukumbura 121–125, CP 1709, Maputo; tel. (1) 492070; fax (1) 490582; Ambassador: ABDELHAMID BOUBAZINE.

Angola: Avda Kenneth Kaunda 783, Maputo; tel. (1) 493691; fax (1) 493930; Ambassador: ANTÓNIO JOSÉ CONDESSE DE CARVALHO.

Australia: Avda Julius Nyerere 794, Maputo; tel. (1) 497329.

Brazil: Avda Kenneth Kaunda 296, CP 1167, Maputo; tel. (1) 492388; fax (1) 490986; Ambassador: HÉLDER MARTINS DE MORAIS.

Bulgaria: Avda do Zimbabwe 864–868, CP 4689, Maputo; tel. (1) 491476; fax (1) 491755; Ambassador: IVAN MARINOV SOKOLARSKI.

Canada: Avda Julius Nyerere 1128, Maputo; tel. (1) 492623; fax (1) 492667; e-mail canembas@ecanada.uem.mz; High Commisioner: ROBERTO CARR-RIBEIRO.

China, People's Republic: Avda dos Mártires da Machava 1309; CP 4668, Maputo; tel. (1) 491560; fax (1) 491196; Ambassador: MI SHIHENG.

Congo, Democratic Republic: Rua A.W. Bayly 2, Maputo; tel. (1) 491854; Ambassador: W'EBER M. B. ANGELO.

Congo, Republic: Avda Kenneth Kaunda 783, CP 4743, Maputo; tel. (1) 490142; Ambassador: EMILIENNE BOTOKA.

Cuba: Avda Kenneth Kaunda 492, CP 387, Maputo; tel. (1) 492444; fax (1) 493673; Ambassador: EVELINO DORTA GONZÁLEZ.

Denmark: Avda 24 de Julho 1500, CP 4588, Maputo; tel. (1) 303413; fax (1) 303526; e-mail dkembmoz@mail.tropical.co.mz; Ambassador: PETER JUL LARSEN.

Egypt: Avda Mao Tse Tung 851, CP 4662, Maputo; tel. (1) 491118; fax (1) 491489; Ambassador: SOAD MAHMOUD SHALABY.

Finland: Avda Julius Nyerere 1128, Maputo; tel. (1) 490518; fax (1) 491662; Ambassador: ILARI RANTAKARI.

France: Avda Julius Nyerere 2361, CP 4781, Maputo; tel. (1) 490444; fax (1) 491727; e-mail ambfrmoz@virconn.com; Ambassador: DIDIER DESTREMAU.

Germany: Rua Damião de Góis 506, CP 1595, Maputo; tel. (1) 492714; fax (1) 492888; Ambassador: HELMUT RAU.

Holy See: Avda Julius Nyerere 882, CP 2738, Maputo; tel. (1) 491144; fax (1) 492217; e-mail namoz.secret@teledata.mz; Apostolic Nuncio: Most Rev. JULIUSZ JANUSZ, Titular Archbishop of Caorle.

India: Avda Kenneth Kaunda 167, CP 4751, Maputo; tel. (1) 492437; fax (1) 492364; e-mail hcimpto@hcoi.uem.mz; High Commissioner: Dr JASPAL SINGH.

Iran: Avda Mártires da Machava 1630, Maputo; tel. (1) 490700; fax (1) 492005; Ambassador: ABDUL ALI TAUAKALI.

Ireland: Rua Dom João IV 213, Maputo; tel. (1) 491440; fax (1) 493023; Chargé d'affaires a.i.: EDWARD JUSTIN CARROLL.

Italy: Avda Kenneth Kaunda 387, CP 976, Maputo; tel. and fax (1) 492046; Ambassador: UGO GABRIELE DE MOHR.

Korea, Democratic People's Republic: Rua da Kaswende 167, Maputo; tel. (1) 491482; Ambassador: RYANG GUI RAK.

Libya: Rua Pereira Marinho 274, CP 4434, Maputo; tel. (1) 490662; fax (1) 492450; Ambassador: AIAD SALAH ASHAWISH.

Malawi: Avda Kenneth Kaunda 75, CP 4148, Maputo; tel. (1) 491468; fax (1) 490224; High Commissioner: OWEN B. BINAULI.

Mauritius: Maputo; Ambassador: RAJ VIRAHSAWMY.

Netherlands: Rua de Mukumbura 285, CP 1163, Maputo; tel. (1) 490031; fax (1) 490429; e-mail nlgoumao@nedawos.uem.mz; Ambassador: ROELAND VAN DE GEER.

Nigeria: Avda Kenneth Kaunda 821, CP 4693, Maputo; tel. (1) 490105; fax (1) 490991; High Commissioner: ISAIAH JACKSON UDOYEN.

Norway: Avda Agostinho Neto 620, CP 828, Maputo; tel. (1) 429411; fax (1) 429410; e-mail ambassade-maputo@mpm.norad.telemax.no; Ambassador: SIGURD ENDRESEN.

Portugal: Avda Julius Nyerere 720, CP 4696, Maputo; tel. (1) 490431; fax (1) 491172; e-mail cculmapa@mail.tropical.co.mz; Ambassador: ANTÓNIO VALENTE.

Romania: Rua da Gorongosa 59, CP 4648, Maputo; tel. and fax (1) 492999; e-mail valeriu@zebra.uem.mz; Chargé d'affaires a.i.: VALERIU NICOLAE.

Russia: Avda Agostinho Neto 1103, CP 4666, Maputo; tel. (1) 420091; fax (1) 428714; e-mail embrus@mail.tropical.co.mz; Ambassador: VYACHESLAV B. KRYLOV.

Saudi Arabia: Rua João de Barros 124, Maputo; tel. (1) 490098; fax (1) 494705; Ambassador: ALI MAHMOUD EMBAREK.

South Africa: Avda Eduardo Mondlane 41, Maputo; tel. (1) 493030; fax (1) 493029; High Commissioner: MANGISI C. ZITHA.

Spain: Rua Damião de Góis 347, CP 1331, Maputo; tel. (1) 492025; fax (1) 492055; Ambassador: JOSÉ EUGÉNIO SALARICH.

Swaziland: Avda do Zimbabwe 608, CP 4711, Maputo; tel. (1) 492451; fax (1) 492117; High Commissioner: JOHN MSHWESHWE DUBE.

Sweden: Avda Julius Nyerere 1128, CP 338, Maputo; tel. (1) 490091; fax (1) 490056; e-mail maputo-amb@sida.se; Ambassador: ERIK ABERG.

Switzerland: Avda Julius Nyerere 1213, CP 135, Maputo; tel. (1) 492432; fax (1) 491339; Ambassador: CATHERINE KRIEK POLEJACK.

Tanzania: Avda Mártires da Machava 852, Maputo; tel. (1) 490110; fax (1) 41228; High Commissioner: Maj.-Gen. MARTIN N. MWAKALINDILE.

United Kingdom: Avda Vladimir I. Lénine 310, CP 55, Maputo; tel. (1) 420111; fax (1) 421666; High Commissioner: BERNARD JONATHAN EVERETT.

USA: Avda Kenneth Kaunda 193, CP 783, Maputo; tel. (1) 492797; fax (1) 490114; Ambassador: SHARON WILKINSON (designate).

Zambia: Avda Kenneth Kaunda 1286, CP 4655, Maputo; tel. (1) 492452; fax (1) 491893; High Commissioner: Maj.-Gen. BELLON BESTINGS CHISUTA.

Zimbabwe: Avda Mártires da Machava 1623, CP 743, Maputo; tel. (1) 490404; fax (1) 492237; e-mail maro@isl.co.mz; High Commissioner: JOHN ROBERT MAYOWE.

Judicial System

The Constitution of November 1990 provides for a Supreme Court and other judicial courts, an Administrative Court, courts-martial, customs courts, maritime courts and labour courts. The Supreme Court consists of professional judges, appointed by the President of the Republic, and judges elected by the Assembly of the Republic. It acts in sections, as a trial court of primary and appellate jurisdiction, and in plenary session, as a court of final appeal. The Administrative Court controls the legality of administrative acts and supervises public expenditure.

President of the Supreme Court: MÁRIO MANGAZE.

Attorney-General: JOAQUIM MADEIRA.

Religion

There are an estimated 5m. Christians and 4m. Muslims, as well as a small Hindu community. Many inhabitants follow traditional beliefs.

CHRISTIANITY

In 1975 educational and medical facilities that had hitherto been administered by churches were acquired by the State. In June 1988 the Government announced that these facilities were to be returned.

Conselho Cristão de Moçambique (Christian Council of Mozambique): Avda Ahmed Sekou Touré 1822, Maputo; tel. (1) 425102; fax (1) 421968; f. 1948; 22 mems; Pres. Rt Rev. BERNARDINO MANDLATE; Gen. Sec. Rev. LUCAS AMOSSE.

The Roman Catholic Church

Mozambique comprises three archdioceses and nine dioceses. At 31 December 1998 adherents represented some 16.1% of the total population.

Bishops' Conference: Conferência Episcopal de Moçambique, Secretariado Geral, Avda Paulo Samuel Kankhomba 188, CP 286, Maputo; tel. (1) 490766; fax (1) 492174; f. 1982; Pres. Rt Rev. FRANCISCO JOÃO SILOTA, Bishop of Chimoio.

Archbishop of Beira: Most Rev. JAIME PEDRO GONÇALVES, Cúria Arquiepiscopal, CP 544, Beira; tel. (3) 322313; fax (3) 327639.

Archbishop of Maputo: Cardinal ALEXANDRE JOSÉ MARIA DOS SANTOS, Paço Arquiepiscopal, Avda Eduardo Mondlane 1448, CP 258, Maputo; tel. (1) 426240; fax (1) 421873.

Archbishop of Nampula: Most Rev. MANUEL VIEIRA PINTO, Paço Arquiepiscopal, CP 84, Nampula; tel. (6) 213025; fax (6) 214194.

The Anglican Communion

Anglicans in Mozambique are adherents of the Church of the Province of Southern Africa. There are two dioceses in Mozambique. The Metropolitan of the Province is the Archbishop of Cape Town, South Africa.

Bishop of Lebombo: Rt Rev. DINIS SALOMÃO SENGULANE, CP 120, Maputo; tel. (1) 405364; fax (1) 401093; e-mail libombo@zebra.uem.mz.

Bishop of Niassa: Rt Rev. PAULINO TOMÁS MANHIQUE, Missão Anglicana de Messumba, Metangula, CP 264, Lichinga, Niassa.

Other Churches

Baptist Convention of Mozambique: Avda Maguiguane 386, CP 852, Maputo; tel. (1) 26852; Pres. Rev. BENTO BARTOLOMEU MATUSSE.

Free Methodist Church: Pres. Rev. LUÍS WANELA.

Presbyterian Church of Mozambique: Avda Ahmed Sekou Touré 1822, CP 21, Maputo; tel. (1) 421790; fax (1) 428623; 100,000 adherents; Pres. of Synodal Council Rev. MARIO NYAMUXWE.

Other denominations active in Mozambique include the Church of Christ, the Church of the Nazarene, the Reformed Church in Mozambique, the United Congregational Church of Mozambique, the United Methodist Church of Mozambique, and the Wesleyan Methodist Church.

ISLAM

Islamic Congress of Mozambique: represents Sunni Muslims; Chair. HASSANE MAKDÁ.

Islamic Council of Mozambique: Leader Sheikh ABOOBACAR ISMAEL MANGIRÁ.

The Press

DAILIES

Correio da Manha: Avda Filipe Samuel Magaia 528, CP 1756, Maputo; tel. (1) 305322; fax (1) 305321; Dir REFINALDO CHILENGUE.

Diário de Moçambique: Avda 25 de Setembro 1509, 2° andar, CP 2491, Beira; tel. and fax (3) 427312; f. 1981; under state management since 1991; Dir EZEQUIEL AMBRÓSIO; Editor FARUCO SADIQUE; circ. 16,000.

Imparcial Fax: Avda Emilia Daússe 389, CP 2517, Maputo; tel. (1) 308797; fax (1) 308796; e-mail imparcial@emilmoz.com; newssheet by subscription only, distribution by fax; Dir MIGÉIS LOPES JUNIOR.

Mediafax: Avda Amílcar Cabral 1049, CP 73, Maputo; tel. (1) 429180; fax (1) 428799; e-mail mediafax@virconn.com; internet www.sadirectory.co.za/mediacoop; f. by co-operative of independent journalists Mediacoop; news-sheet by subscription only, distribution by fax and internet.

Metical: Avda Mártires da Machava 1002, CP 4371, Maputo; tel. (1) 497385; fax (1) 497387; e-mail metical@zebra.uem.mz; f. 1997; news-sheet, distribution by fax; Editor CARLOS CARDOSO.

Notícias: Rua Joaquim Lapa 55, CP 327, Maputo; tel. (1) 420119; fax (1) 420575; f. 1926; morning; under state management since 1991; Dir BERNARDO MAVANGA; Editor HILÁRIO COSSA; circ. 33,000.

WEEKLIES

Campeão: Avda 24 de Julho 3706, CP 2610, Maputo; tel. and fax (1) 401810; sports newspaper; Dir RENATO CALDÉIRA; Editor ALEXANDRE ZANDAMELA.

Correio Semanal: Avda Filipe Samuel Magaia 528, CP 1756, Maputo; tel. (1) 305322; fax (1) 305312; Dir REFINALDO CHILENGUE.

Demos: Avda Mohamed Siad Barre, CP 2457, Maputo; tel. (1) 401420; fax (1) 401420; Dir VIRGÍLIO MABOTA; Editor PALMIRA VELASCO.

Desafio: Rua Joaquim Lapa 55, Maputo; tel. (1) 305437; fax (1) 305431; Dir ALMIRO SANTOS; Editor BOAVIDA FUNJUA.

Domingo: Rua Joaquim Lapa 55, CP 327, Maputo; tel. (1) 431026; fax (1) 431027; f. 1981; Sun.; Dir JORGE MATINE; Editor MOISES MABUNDA; circ. 25,000.

Savana: c/o Mediacoop, Avda Amílcar Cabral 1049, CP 73, Maputo; tel. (1) 429180; fax (1) 428799; e-mail mediafax@virconn.com; internet www.sadirectory.co.za/mediacoop; f. 1994; Dir KOK NAM; Editor SALOMÃO MOYOANA.

Tempo: Avda Ahmed Sekou Touré 1078, CP 2917, Maputo; tel. (1) 26191; f. 1970; magazine; under state management since 1991; Dir ROBERTO UAENE; Editor ARLINDO LANGA; circ. 40,000.

PERIODICALS

Agricultura: Instituto Nacional de Investigação Agronómica, CP 3658, Maputo; tel. (1) 30091; f. 1982; quarterly; publ. by Centro de Documentação de Agricultura, Silvicultura, Pecuária e Pescas.

Aro: Avda 24 de Julho 1420, CP 4187, Maputo; f. 1995; monthly; Dir POLICARTO TAMELE; Editor BRUNO MACAME, Jr.

Arquivo Histórico: CP 2033, Maputo; tel. (1) 421177; fax (1) 423428; f. 1987; Editor MARIA INÊS NOGUEIRA DA COSTA.

Boletim da República: Avda Vladimir I. Lénine, CP 275, Maputo; govt and official notices; publ. by Imprensa Nacional da Moçambique.

Moçambique–Novos Tempos: Avda Ahmed Sekou Touré 657, Maputo; tel. (1) 493564; fax (1) 493590; f. 1992; Dir J. MASCARENHAS.

Mozambiquefile: c/o AIM, Rua da Radio Moçambique, CP 896, Maputo; tel. (1) 430795; fax (1) 421906; e-mail aim@aimmpto.uem.mz; internet www.sortmoz.com/aimnews; monthly; Dir RICARDO MALATE; Editor PAUL FAUVET.

Mozambique Inview: c/o Mediacoop, Avda Amílcar Cabral 1049, CP 73, Maputo; tel. (1) 429180; fax (1) 428799; e-mail mediafax@virconn.com; internet www.sadirectory.co.za/mediacoop; f. 1994; two a month; Editor GIL LAURICIANO.

Novos Tempos: monthly; Renamo-owned.

Portos e Caminhos de Ferro: CP 276, Maputo; English and Portuguese; ports and railways; quarterly.

Revista Médica de Moçambique: Instituto Nacional de Saúde, Ministério da Saúde e Faculdade de Medicina, Universidade Eduardo Mondlane, CP 264, Maputo; tel. (1) 420368; fax (1) 431103; e-mail mdgedge@malarins.uem.mz; f. 1982; 4 a year; medical journal; Editor MARTINHO DGEDGE.

NEWS AGENCIES

Agência de Informação de Moçambique (AIM): Rua da Rádio Moçambique, CP 896, Maputo; tel. (1) 430795; fax (1) 421906; e-mail aim@aimmpto.uem.mz; internet www.sortmoz.com/aimnews; f. 1975; daily reports in Portuguese and English; Dir RICARDO MALATE.

Foreign Bureaux

Agence France-Presse (AFP): CP 4650, Maputo; tel. (1) 422940; fax (1) 422940; Correspondent RACHEL WATERHOUSE.

Agência Lusa de Informação (Portugal): Avda Ho Chi Min 111, Maputo; tel. (1) 427591; fax (1) 421690; Bureau Chief CARLOS LOBATO.

Agenzia Nazionale Stampa Associata (ANSA) (Italy): Maputo; tel. (1) 430723; fax (1) 421906; Correspondent PAUL FAUVET.

Reuters (UK) is also represented in Mozambique.

Publishers

Arquivo Histórico: CP 2033, Maputo; tel. (1) 421177; fax (1) 423428; Dir INÊS NOGUEIRA DA COSTA.

Editora Minerva Central: Rua Consiglieri Pedroso 84, CP 212, Maputo; tel. (1) 22092; f. 1908; stationers and printers, educational, technical and medical textbooks; Man. Dir J. F. CARVALHO.

Empresa Moderna Lda: Avda 25 de Setembro, CP 473, Maputo; tel. (1) 424594; f. 1937; fiction, history, textbooks; Man. Dir LOUIS GALLOTI.

Instituto Nacional do Livro e do Disco: Avda 24 de Julho 1921, CP 4030, Maputo; tel. (1) 34870; govt publishing and purchasing agency; Dir ARMÉNIO CORREIA.

Government Publishing House

Imprensa Nacional de Moçambique: CP 275, Maputo; tel. (1) 423383.

Broadcasting and Communications

TELECOMMUNICATIONS

Empresa Nacional de Telecomunicações de Moçambique: Rua da Sé 2, CP 25, Maputo; tel. (1) 431921; fax (1) 431944; e-mail rfernandes@tdm.mz; internet www.tdm.mz; f. 1993; Chair. and Man. Dir RUI JORGE LOURENÇO FERNANDES.

BROADCASTING

Radio

Rádio Moçambique: Rua da Rádio 2, CP 2000, Maputo; tel. (1) 421814; fax (1) 421816; e-mail caprimoe@zebra.uem.mz; f. 1975; programmes in Portuguese, English and vernacular languages; Chair. MANUEL FERNANDO VETERANO.

By January 1995 the Government had issued licences to 13 private radio stations. Of those, only three were broadcasting at that time.

Rádio Terra Verde: frmly Voz da Renamo; owned by former rebel movement Renamo; transmitters in Maputo and Gorongosa, Sofala province.

Rádio Miramar: owned by Brazilian religious sect, the Universal Church of the Kingdom of God.

Television

Rádio Televisão Klint (RTK): Avda Agostinho Neto 946, Maputo; tel. (1) 422956; fax (1) 493306; Dir CARLOS KLINT.

Televisão de Moçambique (TVM): Avda Julius Nyerere 942, CP 2675, Maputo; tel. (1) 493452; fax (1) 491059; f. 1981; Pres. ANTÓNIO JÚLIO BOTELHO MONIZ; Dir ANABELA ANDRIANO POULOS.

Finance

(cap. = capital; res = reserves; dep. = deposits; m. = million; brs = branches; amounts in meticais, unless otherwise stated)

BANKING

Central Bank

Banco de Moçambique: Avda 25 de Setembro 1695, CP 423, Maputo; tel. (1) 428151; fax (1) 429718; e-mail pam@bancomoc.vem.mz; internet www.bancomoc.mz; f. 1975; bank of issue; cap. and res 373,736m., dep. 5,516,021m. (Dec. 1997); Gov. ADRIANO AFONSO MALEIANE.

Commercial Banks

Banco Austral: Avda 25 de Setembro 1184, CP 757, Maputo; tel. (1) 428125; fax (1) 424122; f. 1977; frmly Banco Popular de Desenvolvimento (BPD); 80% transferred to private ownership in 1997; total assets 1,970,208m. (Dec. 1998); Chair. OCTAVIO FILIANO MUTHEMBA; CEO KOONJAMBU MUGANTHAN; 193 brs and agencies.

Banco Comercial e de Desenvolvimento de Moçambique (BCDM): Maputo; f. 2000.

Banco Comercial e de Investimentos (BCI): Edif. John Orr's, Avda 25 de Setembro 1465, Maputo; tel. (1) 307777; fax (1) 307152; e-mail bcimoz@teledata.mz; f. 1996; 60% owned by Caixa Geral de Depósitos (Portugal); total assets US $42.3m. (Dec. 1998); Chair. Dir ABDUL MAGID OSMAN; Man. Dir MANUAL JORGE MENDES FIGUEIRA; 5 brs.

Banco Comercial de Moçambique: Avda 25 de Setembro 1800, CP 865, Maputo; tel. (1) 307490; fax (1) 307545; e-mail bcmdri@teledata.cprm.net; f. 1992 to take over commercial banking activities of Central Bank; 51% transferred to private ownership in 1996; total assets 5,188,651m. (Dec. 1998); Pres. Dr MANUEL COUTINHO DE ORTIGÃO RAMOS; Gen. Man. NATALINO BRUNO DE MORAIS; 53 brs and agencies.

Banco Internacional de Comercio, SARL: Avda 24 de Julho 3549, 2° andar, Maputo; tel (1) 404080; fax (1) 400745; f. 1998; total assets 26.7m. (Dec. 1998); Dirs JOSEPHINE SIVARETNAM, HARITH HARUN.

Banco Internacional de Moçambique, SARL (BIM): Avda Zedequias Mananhela 478, CP 2657, Maputo; tel. (1) 429390; fax (1) 429389; f. 1995; 25% owned by Banco Comercial Português SA, 25% by Banco Português do Atlântico; 25% by International Finance Corpn; cap. and res 253,493m., dep. 1,686,656m. (Dec. 1998); Chair. Dr MÁRIO FERNANDES DA GRAÇA MACHUNGO; Man. Dir Dr JOSÉ ALBERTO DE LIMA FÉLIX.

Banco de Investimento: Avda Armando Tivane 625, Maputo; tel (1) 499100; f. 1998; 50% owned by Banco Internacional de Moçambique; total assets 41.6m. (Dec. 1998); Dir Dr MÁRIO FERNANDES DA GRAÇA MACHUNGO.

Banco Standard Totta de Moçambique, SARL: Praça 25 de Junho 45, CP 1119, Maputo; tel. (1) 423041; fax (1) 426967; e-mail bstmcred@teledata.mz; f. 1966; 55% owned by Banco Totta e Açores,

SA; total assets 2,066,660m. (Dec. 1998); Man. Dir ANTÓNIO MEIRELES MOITA; 24 brs.

Creditcoop–Cooperativa de Crédito e Investimento, SARL: Rua Joaquim Lapa 37, CP 4725, Maputo; tel. (1) 307294; fax (1) 421372; e-mail credicoop@mail.tropical.co.mz; f. 1994; cap. 1,000m. (1994); Dir JACINTO VELOSO.

Foreign Banks

Banco de Fomento, SARL (Portugal): Avda Julius Nyerere 1016, CP 4233, Maputo; tel. (1) 494010; fax (1) 494401; e-mail bfe.moc@teledata.mz; frmly Banco de Fomento e Exterior SA, name changed as above 1998; total assets 687.8m. (Dec. 1998); Pres. ARTUR SANTOS SILVA; Man. Dir MANUEL REGALADO.

BNP Nedbank (Moçambique), SARL: Avda 25 de Setembro 1230, 1° andar, CP 1445, Maputo; e-mail bnpnedbank@bnpnedbank.co.mz; f. 1999; 50% owned by Banque Nationale de Paris, 50% by Nedcor Bank Ltd; Man. Dir LIONEL MARTIN.

ULC Moçambique, SARL: Rua da Imprensa 256, 7° andar, CP 4447, Maputo; tel. (1) 300451; fax (1) 431290; e-mail ulcmoz@mail.tropical.co.mz; 44.3% owned by ULC Holdings Ltd, 27.8% by EDFUND; total assets US $1.8m. (Dec. 1998); Chair. ANTÓNIO BRANCO; Gen. Man. VICTOR VISEU.

União Comercial de Bancos (Moçambique), SARL: Avda Friedrich Engels 400, Maputo; tel. (1) 495221; fax (1) 498675; f. 1999; 81.25% owned by Mauritius Commercial Bank Group; Chair. PHILIPPE ALAIN FORGET; Gen. Man. DENIS MOTET.

DEVELOPMENT FUND

Fundo de Desenvolvimento Agrícola e Rural: CP 1406, Maputo; tel. (1) 460349; fax (1) 460157; f. 1987 to provide credit for small farmers and rural co-operatives; promotes agricultural and rural development; Sec. EDUARDO OLIVEIRA.

STOCK EXCHANGE

Bolsa de Valores de Moçambique: Avda 25 de Setembro 1230, Prédio 33, 5° andar, Maputo; tel. (1) 308826; fax (1) 310559; Chair. Dr JUSSUB NURMAMAD.

INSURANCE

In December 1991 the Assembléia da República approved legislation terminating the state monopoly of insurance and reinsurance activities.

Companhia de Seguros de Moçambique: Avda 25 de Setembro 1800–17, CP 616, Maputo; tel. (1) 429696; fax (1) 430020; e-mail impar@zebra.uem.mz; f. 1992; Pres. INOCÊNCIO A. MATAVEL; Gen. Man. MANUEL BALANCHO.

Empresa Moçambicana de Seguros, EE (EMOSE): Avda 25 de Setembro 1383, CP 1165, Maputo; tel. (1) 422095; fax (1) 424526; f. 1977 as state insurance monopoly; took over business of 24 fmr cos; privatization pending in 1999; cap. 150m.; Gen. Dir VENÂNCIO MONDLANE.

Seguradora Internacional de Moçambique: Maputo; tel. (1) 430959; fax (1) 430241; e-mail simseg@zebra.uem.mz; Pres. MÁRIO FERNANDES DA GRAÇA MACHUNGO.

Trade and Industry

GOVERNMENT AGENCIES

Centro de Promoção de Investimentos (CPI): Rua da Imprensa 332, CP 4635, Maputo; tel. (1) 422530; fax (1) 422604; encourages foreign investment and jt ventures with foreign firms; evaluates and negotiates investment proposals.

Empresa Nacional de Hidrocarbonetos de Moçambique (ENHM): Avda Fernão de Magalhães 34, CP 2904, Maputo; tel. (1) 460083; controls concessions for petroleum exploration and production; Dir MÁRIO MARQUES.

Instituto para a Promoção de Exportações (IPEX): Avda 25 de Setembro 1008, 3° andar, CP 4487, Maputo; tel. (1) 307257; fax (1) 307256; e-mail ipex@teledata.mz; internet www.ipexport.org; f. 1990 for the promotion and co-ordination of national exports abroad; Pres. Dr FELISBERTO FERRÃO.

Unidade Técnica para a Reestruturação de Empresas (UTRE): Rua da Imprensa 256, 7° andar, CP 4350, Maputo; tel. (1) 426514; fax (1) 421541; e-mail utre@teledata.mz; internet www.utre.com; implements restructuring of state enterprises; Dir MOMADE JUMAS.

CHAMBER OF COMMERCE

Câmara de Comércio de Moçambique: Rua Mateus Sansão Muthemba 452, CP 1836, Maputo; tel. (1) 491970; fax (1) 492211; f. 1980; Pres. CARLOS KLINT; Sec.-Gen. MANUEL NOTIÇO.

INDUSTRIAL AND TRADE ASSOCIATIONS

Companhia de Desenvolvimento Mineiro (CDM): Avda 24 de Julho 1895, 1°–2° andares, CP 1152, Maputo; tel. (1) 429170; fax (1) 428921; exports marble, tantalite, asbestos anthophylite, beryl, bentonite, agates, precious and semi-precious stones; Dir LUÍS JOSSENE.

Empresa Distribuidora de Equipamento Eléctrico e Electrónico e Componentes (INTERELECTRA): Avda Samora Machel 162, CP 1159, Maputo; tel. (1) 427091; fax (1) 420723; electrical equipment and components; Dir FRANCISCO PAULO CUCHE.

Empresa Estatal de Importação e Exportação de Medicamentos (MEDIMOC): Avda Julius Nyerere 500, 1° andar, CP 600, Maputo; tel. (1) 491211; fax (1) 490168; internet www.medimoc@zebra.uem.mz; f. 1977; pharmaceuticals, medical equipment and supplies; Gen. Dir RENATO RONDA; 230 employees.

Empresa Moçambicana de Importação e Exportação de Produtos Químicos e Plásticos (INTERQUIMICA): Rua de Bagamoyo 333, CP 2268, Maputo; tel. (1) 423168; fax (1) 21229; chemicals, fertilizers, pesticides, plastics, paper; Dir AURÉLIO RICARDO CHIZIANE.

Empresa Nacional de Carvão de Moçambique (CARBOMOC): Rua Joaquim Lapa 108, CP 1773, Maputo; tel. (1) 427625; fax (1) 424714; f. 1948; mineral extraction and export; transfer to private ownership pending; Dir JAIME RIBEIRO.

Empresa Nacional de Petróleos de Moçambique (PETROMOC): Praça dos Trabalhadores 9, CP 417, Maputo; tel. (1) 427191; fax (1) 430181; f. 1977 to take over the Sonarep oil refinery and its associated distribution co; state directorate for liquid fuels within Mozambique, incl. petroleum products passing through Mozambique to inland countries; Dir MANUEL PATRÍCIO DA CRUZ VIOLA.

ENACOMO, SARL (Empresa Nacional de Comércio): Avda Samora Machel 285, 1° andar, CP 698, Maputo; tel. (1) 430172; fax (1) 427754; f. 1976; imports, exports, acquisition, investment; Man. Dir CARLOS PACHECO FARIA.

Lojas Francas de Moçambique (INTERFRANCA): Rua Timor Leste 106, CP 1206, Maputo; tel. (1) 425199; fax (1) 431044; music equipment, motor cars, handicrafts, furniture; Gen. Dir CARLOS E. N. RIBEIRO.

Riopele Têxteis de Moçambique, SARL: Rua Joaquim Lapa 21, CP 1658, Maputo; tel. (1) 31331; fax (1) 422902; textiles; Dir CARLOS RIBEIRO.

UTILITIES

Electricity

Electricidade de Moçambique (EDM): Avda Agostinho Neto 70, CP 2447, Maputo; tel. (1) 490636; fax (1) 491048; internet www.mozambique.mz/electricity/index.htm; f. 1977; 100% state-owned; production and distribution of electric energy; Pres. VICENTE VELOSA; Dir FERNANDO RAMOS JULIÃO; 2,700 employees.

Water

Direcção Nacional de Águas: Maputo.

MAJOR COMPANIES

Comércio Grossista de Produtos Alementares (COGROPA): Avda 25 de Setembro 874–896, CP 308, Maputo; tel. (1) 428655; fax (1) 420153; food supplies; transfer pending to private ownership; Dir ANTÓNIO BAPTISTA DO AMARAL.

Companhia da Zambézia, SARI: Avda Samora Machel 245, 4° andar, CP 617, Maputo; tel. (1) 420639; fax (1) 421507; f. 1892; agriculture; Dirs JOSÉ MENTO VEDOR, JOÃO FORTE, CARLOS DE MATOS.

Companhia Industrial de Cordoaria de Moçambique (CICOMO), SARL: Avda Zedequias Manganhela 520, 4° andar, CP 4113, Maputo; tel. (1) 427272; fax (1) 305211; manufacture and sale of acrylic fibre; Pres. JOSÉ MANUEL DA SILVA JOSÉ DE MELLO.

Companhia Industrial do Monapo, SARL: Avda do Trabalho 2106, CP 1248, Maputo; tel. (1) 400290; fax (1) 401164; animal and vegetable oils and soap; CEO CARMEN RAMOS.

Companhia Siderurgica de Moçambique (CSM), SARL: Avda Nuno Alvares 566, CP 441, Maputo; tel. (1) 401281; fax (1) 400400; steel; Tech. Man. HERLANDER PEDROSO.

Construtora do Tâmega: Avda Zedequias Manganhela 520, CP 1238, Maputo; tel. (1) 430885; fax (1) 425282; f. 1946; civil engineering and construction; Chair. JOAQUÍM DA MOTA; Man. Dir JOAQUÍM CORDEIRO; 1,450 employees.

Empresa de Construções Metálicas (ECOME): Avda das Indústrias-Machava, CP 1358, Maputo; tel. (1) 752282; agricultural equipment; Dir JUSTINO LUCAS.

Empresa de Gestão e Assistência Técnica ao Equipamento Agrícola (MECANAGRO): Avda das FPLM 184, CP 2727, Maputo; tel. (1) 460016; agricultural machinery; Dir RAGENDRA DE SOUZA.

Empresa Metalúrgica de Moçambique, SARL: Avda de Moçambique 1500; CP 1316, Maputo; tel. (1) 475189; fax (1) 475149; f. 1951; metallurgical products; Dir JOAO GARROCHINHO.

Empresa Moçambicana de Malhas (EMMA), SARL: Avda Zedequias Manganhela 488, CP 2663, Maputo; tel. (1) 423112; textiles; Admin. AMADE OSSUMANE.

Empresa Moçambicana de Chá (EMOCHÁ): Avda Zedequias Manganhela 250, CP 4123, Maputo; tel. (1) 424779; fax (1) 417585; tea production; transfer pending to private ownership; Dir MARCOS BASTOS.

Empresa Nacional de Calçado e Têxteis (ENCATEX): Avda 24 de Julho 2969, CP 67, Maputo; tel. (1) 731258; footwear and textiles; Dir SOVERANO BELCHIOR.

Empresa Provincial (AVICOLA) EE: Avda 25 de Setembro 1676, CP 4202, Maputo; tel. (1) 34738; Dir MÁRIO BERNARDO.

Fábricas Associadas de Óleos (FASOL), SARL: Avda de Namaacha, CP 1128, Maputo; tel. (1) 723186; oils; transfer pending to private ownership; Dir CARLOS COSTA.

Forjadora, SARL—Fábrica de Equipamentos Industriais: Avda de Angola 2850, CP 3078, Maputo; tel. (1) 465537; fax (1) 465211; metal structures; Man. Dir JORGE MORGADO.

Indústria Moçambicana de Aço (IMA), SARL: Avda 24 de Julho 2373, 12° andar, CP 2566, Maputo; tel. (1) 421141; fax (1) 423446; f. 1970; steel; Dir MANUEL JOSÉ SEREJO.

Mabor de Moçambique: CP 2341, Maputo; tel. (1) 470551; fax (1) 470227; e-mail mabormoc@virconn.com; f. 1979; manufacture of tyres; Chair. Dr H. GAMITO; Dir L. F. RODRIGUES; 610 employees.

Moçambique-Industrial, SARL: Rua Aruangua 39, 1° andar, CP 432, Beira; tel. (3) 322123; fax (3) 325347; vegetable oils and soap; Dir JOSÉ BARROS CARDOSO.

Química-Geral, SARL: Língamo-Matola, CP 15, Maputo; tel. (1) 424713; fertilizers; Dir ALFREDO BADURU.

Sociedade Agrícola de Tabacos: CP 713, Maputo; tel. (1) 496011; fax 491397; production of cigarettes; Gen. Man. J. F. MEINTJES.

Texlom, SARL: Avda Filipe Samuel Magaia 514, CP 194, Maputo; textiles; Dir JOSÉ AUGUSTO TOMO PSICO.

Vidreira de Moçambique, SARL: Talhão 757, Machava, CP 590, Maputo; tel. (1) 750353; fax (1) 750371; e-mail vidreira@teledata.mz; 45% govt-owned; production of glass; Chair. CARLOS MOREIRA DA SILVA; Gen. Man. CARLOS NEVES.

TRADE UNIONS

Freedom to form trade unions, and the right to strike, are guaranteed under the 1990 Constitution.

Confederação de Sindicatos Livres e Independentes de Moçambique (CONSILMO): Sec.-Gen. JEREMIAS TIMANE.

Organização dos Trabalhadores de Moçambique—Central Sindical (OTM—CS) (Mozambique Workers' Organization—Trade Union Headquarters): Rua Manuel António de Sousa 36, Maputo; tel. (1) 426477; fax (1) 421671; f. 1983 as trade union fed. to replace fmr production councils; officially recognized in 1990; 200,000 mems (1993); Pres. JOAQUIM FANHEIRO; Sec-Gen. AUGUSTO MACAMO.

Sindicato Nacional dos Trabalhadores Agro-Pecuários e Florestais (SINTAF): Avda 25 de Setembro 1676, 1° andar, Maputo; tel. (1) 431182; Sec.-Gen. EUSÉBIO LUÍS CHIVULELE.

Sindicato Nacional dos Trabalhadores da Aviação Civil, Correios e Comunicações (SINTAC): Avda 25 de Setembro 1509, 2° andar, No 5, Maputo; tel. (1) 30996; Sec.-Gen. MANUEL SANTOS DOS REIS.

Sindicato Nacional dos Trabalhadores do Comércio, Banca e Seguros (SINTCOBASE): Avda Ho Chi Min 365, 1° andar, CP 2142, Maputo; tel. (1) 426271; Sec.-Gen. AMÓS JÚNIOR MATSINHE.

Sindicato Nacional dos Trabalhadores da Indústria do Açúcar (SINTIA): Avda das FPLM 1912, Maputo; tel. (1) 460108; f. 1989; Sec.-Gen. ALEXANDRE CÂNDIDO MUNGUAMBE.

Sindicato Nacional dos Trabalhadores da Indústria Alimentar e Bebidas (SINTIAB): Avda Eduardo Mondlane 1267, CP 394, Maputo; tel. (1) 424709; fax (1) 424123; Gen. Sec. SAMUEL FENIAS MATSINHE.

Sindicato Nacional dos Trabalhadores da Indústria de Cajú (SINTIC): Rua do Jardim 574, 1° andar, Maputo; tel. (1) 475300; Sec.-Gen. BOAVENTURA MONDLANE.

Sindicato Nacional dos Trabalhadores da Indústria de Construção Civil, Madeira e Minas (SINTICIM): Avda 24 de Julho 2341, 5° andar dt°, Maputo; tel. (1) 421159; Sec.-Gen. JEREMIAS TIMANA.

Sindicato Nacional dos Trabalhadores da Indústria Hoteleira, Turismo e Similares (SINTHOTS): Avda Eduardo Mondlane 1267, CP 394, Maputo; tel. (1) 420409; Sec.-Gen. ALBERTO MANUEL NHAPOSSE.

Sindicato Nacional dos Trabalhadores da Indústria Metalúrgica, Metalomecânica e Energia (SINTIME): Avda Samora Machel 30, 6° andar, No 6, CP 1868, Maputo; tel. (1) 428588; fax (1) 421671; Sec.-Gen. RUI BENJAMIM COSTA.

Sindicato Nacional dos Trabalhadores da Indústria Química, Borracha, Papel e Gráfica (SINTIQUIGRA): Avda Karl Marx 414, 1° andar, CP 4433, Maputo; tel. (1) 421553; Sec.-Gen. JOAQUIM M. FANHEIRO.

Sindicato Nacional dos Trabalhadores da Indústria Têxtil Vestuário, Couro e Calçado (SINTEVEC): Avda do Trabalho 1276, 1° andar, CP 2613, Maputo; tel. (1) 426753; fax (1) 421671; Sec.-Gen. PEDRO JOAQUIM MANDJAZE.

Sindicato Nacional dos Trabalhadores da Marinha Mercante e Pesca (SINTMAP): Rua Joaquim Lapa 4, 22-5° andares, No 6, Maputo; tel. (1) 421148; Sec.-Gen. DANIEL MANUEL NGOQUE.

Sindicato Nacional dos Trabalhadores dos Portos e Caminhos de Ferro (SINPOCAF): Avda Guerra Popular, CP 2158, Maputo; tel. (1) 420531; Sec.-Gen. DINIS EFRAIME FRANCISCO NHANGUMBE.

Sindicato Nacional dos Trabalhadores dos Transportes Rodoviários e Assistência Técnica (SINTRAT): Avda Paulo Samuel Kankhomba 1568, 1° andar, 14, Maputo; tel. (1) 402390; Sec.-Gen. ALCANO HORÁCIO MULA.

Sindicato Nacional de Jornalistas (SNJ): Avda 24 de Julho, 231, Maputo; tel. (1) 492500; fax (1) 492031; f. 1978; Sec.-Gen. HILÁRIO M. E. MATUSSE.

Transport

The 'Beira Corridor', where rail and road links and a petroleum pipeline run from Manica, on the Zimbabwean border, to the Mozambican port of Beira, forms a vital outlet for the land-locked southern African countries, particularly Zimbabwe. The development of this route is a major priority of the Southern African Development Community (SADC). Rail and road links also run from Ressano Garcia in South Africa to the port at Maputo, and from Malawi to the port of Nacala. Following the General Peace Agreement in 1992, rehabilitation of the transport network, which had been continually disrupted by guerrilla attacks and sabotage, began, funded principally by SADC. In December the Government announced the proposed restructuring of the administration of the Beira, Maputo and Nacala transport corridors, with a view to encouraging private-sector involvement in investment and management. In January 2000 the Empresa Nacional dos Portos e Caminhos de Ferro de Moçambique (CFM) signed an agreement with a consortium, led by South African, Portuguese and US companies, entitled the Nacala Corridor Development Company, granting it the concession to manage the port of Nacala and the Nacala–Malawi railway. Negotiations concerning the granting of similar concessions for the Maputo and Beira transport corridors, as well as for other principal railway lines, were proceeding with private contractors in 2000. The development of these corridors is expected to have a significant impact on the economies of both Mozambique and its neighbouring countries.

In February 2000 much of the country's infrastructure in the southern and central provinces was devastated as the result of massive flooding. Railway lines, roads and bridges suffered considerable damage. In March the Government estimated the cost of reconstruction at US $250m.

RAILWAYS

In 1997 the total length of track was 3,123 km. The railways are all state-owned. There are both internal routes and rail links between Mozambican ports and South Africa, Swaziland, Zimbabwe and Malawi. During the hostilities many lines and services were disrupted by Renamo guerrilla operations. Improvement work on most of the principal railway lines began in the early 1980s. The rehabilitation of the 534-km Limpopo railway, linking Chicualacuala, at the Zimbabwe border, with the port of Maputo, was completed in March 1993. In September 1993 it was announced that the implementation of plans, initiated in 1990 but later disrupted, to rehabilitate the railway linking the port of Beira with the coal-mining centre of Moatize had resumed. However, in early 1997 the Government indicated that the rehabilitation of the line, which would cost in excess of US $300m., was dependent on attracting foreign investors to the coal mines of Moatize who would meet the cost of repairs. In late 1999 the World Bank approved a loan of $100m. to help finance reconstruction of the line. Negotiations with Spain, Australia and Canada were continuing in an effort to secure the remaining funding. In November 1993, following the rehabilitation of some 533 km of the 610-km railway linking the port of Nacala with Blantyre, in Malawi, the completed section, which runs from Nacala to Cuamba in Niassa province, was reopened. In June 1996 the rehabilitation of the remaining 77-km section, linking Cuamba with Entre-Lagos on the Malawian border, was completed. In November 1999 the 200-

km branch line from Cuamba to Lichinga was reopened. In 1996 rehabilitation of the Goba railway, linking Mozambique and Swaziland, which began in 1993, was completed.

Empresa Nacional dos Portos e Caminhos de Ferro de Moçambique (CFM): Praça dos Trabalhadores, CP 2158, Maputo; tel. (1) 427173; fax (1) 427746; Chair. RUI FONSECA; comprises four separate systems linking Mozambican ports with the country's hinterland, and with other southern African countries, including South Africa, Swaziland, Zimbabwe and Malawi:

> **CFM—Sul:** Praça dos Trabalhadores, CP 2158, Maputo; tel. (1) 427173; fax (1) 427746; lines totalling 1070 km linking Maputo with South Africa, Swaziland and Zimbabwe, as well as Inhambane–Inharrime and Xai–Xai systems; Exec. Dir: A.F. MANAVE.

> **CFM—Norte:** CP 16, Nampula; tel. (6) 212927; fax (6) 212034; lines totalling 914 km including link between port of Nacala with Malawi; management concession awarded to Nacala Corridor Development Company (a consortium 67% owned by South African, Portuguese and US companies) in January 2000.

> **CFM—Zambézia:** CP 73, Quelimane; tel. (4) 212502; fax (4) 213123; 145-km line linking Quelimane and Mocuba; Dir O.J. JAIME.

> **CFM—Central:** CP 472, Beira; tel. (3) 325200; fax (3) 326997; lines totalling 994 km linking Beira with Zimbabwe and Malawi, as well as link to Moatize (awaiting rehabilitation, see above); Exec. Dir J.A. FELIPE.

ROADS

In 1996 there were an estimated 30,400 km of roads in Mozambique, of which 5,685 km were paved. In 1991 a major programme, supervised by the SADCC (now SADC), was in progress to improve the road links between Mozambique and neighbouring countries. In 1994 the Government announced a five-year road rehabilitation programme to reopen 11,000 km of roads closed during the hostilities, and to upgrade 3,000 km of paved roads and 13,000 km of secondary and tertiary roads. The programme, which was to cost an estimated US $24,000m., was to be financed mainly by international donors and the World Bank. In 1998 the Government announced a further programme, again financed by international donors, to be implemented from 1999. The programme aimed to increase the percentage of roads in 'good' or 'reasonable' condition from 39% to 70%. However, owing to the widespread destruction caused by the February 2000 flooding (see above) much of this reconstruction work would have to be repeated.

SHIPPING

The principal ports are Maputo, Beira, Nacala and Quelimane, handling an estimated 7.6m. tons of cargo in 1998. The modernization and expansion of the port of Beira was completed in 1994. The construction of a new petroleum terminal doubled the port's capacity, thus facilitating the transportation of petroleum products along the 'Beira Corridor' to Zimbabwe. Rehabilitation of the port of Maputo was completed in 1989, as part of the SADCC (now SADC) transport programme. In mid-1999 plans were announced for the construction of a new deep-water port at Ponta Dobela, 70 km south of Maputo. The port, which was to form part of a special economic zone, was to receive a minimum investment of US $515m., and was expected eventually to handle 30m. tons of goods, principally minerals, per year. A private consortium, Porto Dobela Developments Ltd, was to hold a 60% share of the port's ownership, with the remaining 40% held by CFM. In January 2000 management of the port facilities at Nacala was awarded to a private consortium, the Nacala Corridor Development Company (see above). Negotiations concerning the granting of similar concesions for the ports of Maputo and Beira were proceeding in 2000.

Empresa Nacional dos Portos e Caminhos de Ferro de Moçambique (CFM): Praça dos Trabalhadores, CP 2158, Maputo; tel. (1) 427173; fax (1) 427746; Port Dir ALBERTO ELIAS.

Agência Nacional de Frete e Navegação (ANFRENA): Rua Consiglieri Pedroso 396, CP 492, Maputo; tel. (1) 428111; fax (1) 427822; Dir FERDINAND WILSON.

Companhia Nacional de Navegação: CP 2064, Maputo.

Companhia Portuguesa de Transportes Marítimos: Avda Samora Machel 239, CP 2, Maputo; tel. (1) 426912.

Empresa Moçambicana de Cargas (MOCARGO): Rua Consiglieri Pedroso 430, 1°–4° andares, CP 888, Maputo; tel. (1) 431022; fax (1) 421438; f. 1984; shipping, chartering and road transport; Man. Dir MANUEL DE SOUSA AMARAL.

Manica Freight Services, SARL: Praça dos Trabalhadores 51, CP 557, Maputo; tel. (1) 426024; fax (1) 424595; e-mail achothia@manica.co.mz; international shipping agents; Man. Dir A. Y. CHOTHIA.

Navique, SARL: Rua de Bagamoyo 366, CP 145, Maputo; tel. (1) 423118; fax (1) 426310; Chair. DANIEL C. LAMPIAO; Man. Dir JORGE DE SOUSA COELHO.

CIVIL AVIATION

There are 16 airports, of which three are international airports.

Aerocondor Moçambique: Beira.

Empresa Nacional de Transporte e Trabalho Aéreo, EE (TTA): Aeroporto Internacional de Maputo, CP 2054, Maputo; tel. (1) 465292; fax (1) 465484; scheduled services to 35 domestic points; also operates air taxi services, agricultural and special aviation services; privatized in 1997; Dir ESTEVÃO ALBERTO JUNIOR.

Linhas Aéreas de Moçambique (LAM): Aeroporto Internacional de Maputo, CP 2060, Maputo; tel. (1) 465137; fax (1) 735601; f. 1980; operates domestic services and international services within Africa and to Europe; privatization of 51% share pending in 2000; Chair. and Dir-Gen. JOSÉ RICARDO ZUZARTE VIEGAS.

Sociedade de Transportes Aéreos, SARL: CP 665, Maputo; tel. (1) 742366; fax (1) 491763; e-mail dido@mail.tropical.co.mz; f. 1991; airline and aircraft charter transport services; Chair. ROGÉRIO WALTER CARREIRA; Man. Dir JOSÉ CARVALHEIRA.

Tourism

Tourism, formerly a significant source of foreign exchange, ceased completely following independence, and was resumed on a limited scale in 1980. There were 1,000 visitors in 1981 (compared with 292,000 in 1972 and 69,000 in 1974). In 1984 a joint-venture company was established with South Africa in order to develop tourism on Inhaca island. With the successful conduct of multi-party elections in 1994 and the prospect of continued peace, there was considerable scope for development of this sector. By mid-1998 some 138 tourism projects, involving investment totalling US $900m., had been approved. In July 1997 there were some 1,200 hotel beds in Mozambique.

Empresa Nacional de Turismo (ENT): Avda 25 de Setembro 1203, CP 2446, Maputo; tel. (1) 421794; fax (1) 421795; e-mail entur@virconn.com; internet www.entur.imoz.com; f. 1985; hotels and tourism; Man. Dir GILDO NEVES.

Defence

According to the final report, issued in December 1994, of the ceasefire commission (established under the General Peace Agreement (GPA) to supervise the implementation of truce regulations), a combined total of only 11,579 government and Renamo troops (from a total of 91,691 troops registered at assembly points) had enlisted in the Forças Armadas de Defesa de Moçambique (FADM). In November 1997 legislation was approved providing for the reintroduction of compulsory military service, which had been suspended under the GPA. It was envisaged that the strength of the FADM, which stood at less than 11,000 in late 1996, would be increased to 15,000. In late 1998 the ministry of national defence announced plans to recruit an additional 3,000 conscripts into the armed forces in 1999. The total strength of the FADM was to be defined by government policy, and the figure of 30,000 envisaged in the GPA would not necessarily be observed. By the end of March 1995 all troops and police belonging to the UN Operation in Mozambique (ONUMOZ), stationed in the country to facilitate the pacification and electoral processes, had withdrawn. After that date only a small unit of ONUMOZ officials remained in the country.

Defence Expenditure: Budgeted at 1,200,000m. meticais in 1999.

Commander-in-Chief of the Armed Forces: Pres. JOAQUIM ALBERTO CHISSANO.

Chief of General Staff: Gen. LAGOS LIDIMO.

Deputy Chief of General Staff: Lt-Gen. MATEUS NGONHAMO.

Education

At independence, between 85%–95% of the adult population were illiterate. In the early 1980s there was a major emphasis on campaigns for adult literacy and other adult education. By 1995, according to estimates by UNESCO, 59.9% of the adult population were illiterate (males 42.3%; females 76.7%). Education is officially compulsory for seven years from the age of seven. Primary schooling begins at seven years of age and lasts for seven years, comprising a first cycle of five years and a further cycle of two years. Secondary schooling, which begins at 14 years of age, lasts for five years and comprises a first cycle of three years and a further cycle of two years. The number of children receiving primary education increased from 634,000 in 1973 to 1,495,000 in 1979; the total declined to

1,199,476 in 1992, owing to the security situation, but recovered to 1,899,531 in 1997. As a proportion of the school-age population, the total enrolment at primary and secondary schools increased from 30% in 1972 to 52% in 1979, but declined to the equivalent of 32% in 1995 (males 38%; females 27%). In that year enrolment at primary schools was equivalent to 40% of children in the relevant age-

group (males 45%; females 35%), while secondary enrolment was equivalent to 6% of children in the relevant age-group (males 7%; females 5%). There were 7,156 students in higher education in 1997. Expenditure on education by all levels of government in 1990, including foreign aid received for the purpose, was 72,264m. meticais (12.0% of total government expenditure).

Bibliography

Abrahamsson, H., and Nilsson, A. *Mozambique: The Troubled Transition from Socialist Construction to Free Market Capitalism.* London, Zed Books, 1995.

Armon, J., et al. (Eds). *Accord: The Mozambique Peace Process in Perspective.* London, Conciliation Resources, 1998.

Azevedo, M. *Historical Dictionary of Mozambique.* Metuchen, NJ, Scarecrow Press, 1991.

Berman, E. *Managing Arms in Peace Processes: Mozambique.* New York, United Nations, 1996.

Bhagavan, M. R. *Some Aspects of International Development in Mozambique.* Stockholm, Swedish International Development Authority, 1977.

Birmingham, D. *Frontline Nationalism in Angola and Mozambique.* London, James Currey, 1992.

Cann, J. P. *Counter-insurgency in Africa: The Portuguese Way of War 1961–1974.* Greenwood Press, Westport, CT, 1997.

Chan, S. *War and Peace in Mozambique.* Basingstoke, Macmillan, 1998.

Chingono, M. F. *Conspicuous Destruction: War, Famine and the Reform Process in Mozambique.* New York, Human Rights Watch, 1992.

The State, Violence and Development: The Political Economy of War in Mozambique, 1975–1992. Aldershot, Avebury, 1996.

Chissano, J. A. *Peace and Reconstruction.* Harare, Southern African Research and Documentation Centre, 1997.

Davies, R. *South African Strategy Towards Mozambique in the Post-Nkomati Period: A Critical Analysis of Effects and Implications.* Uppsala, Scandinavian Institute for African Studies, 1985.

Egerö, B. *Mozambique: A Dream Undone. The Political Economy of Democracy, 1975–1984.* Uppsala, Scandinavian Institute for African Studies, 1987.

Finnegan, W. A. *A Complicated War: The Harrowing of Mozambique.* Berkeley, University of California Press, 1992.

Geffray, C. *La Cause des Armes au Mozambique–Anthropologie d'une guerre civile.* Paris, Editions Karthala, 1990.

Hanlon, J. *Apartheid's Second Front: South Africa's War Against its Neighbours.* Harmondsworth, Penguin, 1986.

Peace Without Profit: How the IMF Blocks Rebuilding in Mozambique. London, James Currey, 1996.

Harris, P. *Work, Culture and Identity: Migrant Labourers in Mozambique and South Africa, c.1860–1910.* Johannesburg, University of the Witwatersrand Press; London, James Currey, 1994.

Henriksen, T. H. *Mozambique: A History.* London, Rex Collings; Cape Town, David Philips, 1978.

Revolution and Counterrevolution: Mozambique's War of Independence 1964–74. Westport, CT, Greenwood Press, 1983.

Hermele, K. *Land Struggles and Social Differentiation in Southern Mozambique: A Case Study of Hokwe, Limpopo 1950–1987.* Uppsala, Scandinavian Institute for African Studies, 1988.

Hoile, D. *Mozambique: A Nation in Crisis.* London, Claridge Press, 1989.

Mozambique: Propaganda, Myth and Reality. London, Mozambique Institute, 1991.

Mozambique: Resistance and Freedom: A Case for Reassessment. London, Mozambique Institute, 1994.

Hoile, D. (Ed.). *Mozambique 1962–1993: A Political Chronology.* London, Mozambique Institute, 1994.

Hume, C. *Ending Mozambique's War: The Role of Mediation and Good Offices.* Washington, DC, United States Institute of Peace Press, 1994.

Isaacman, A., and Isaacman, B. *Mozambique from Colonialism to Revolution, 1900–82.* Boulder, CO, Westview Press, 1983.

Konczacki, Z. A., Parpart, J. L., and Shaw, T. M. (Eds). *Studies in the Economic History of Southern Africa.* Vol. I. London, Cass, 1990.

Macqueen, N. *The Decolonization of Portuguese Africa: Metropolitan Revolution and the Dissolution of Empire.* Harlow, Longman, 1997.

Marshall, J. *War, Debt and Structural Adjustment in Mozambique: The Social Impact.* Ottawa, North-South Institute, 1992.

Mazula, B. *Mozambique: Elections, Democracy and Development.* Maputo, Manila, 1996.

Miech-Chatenay, M. *Mozambique: The Key Sectors of the Economy.* Paris, BIDOI, 1986.

Mozambique 1991: The New Phase. Montréal, CIDMAA, 1991.

Minter, W. *Apartheid's Contras: An Inquiry into the Roots of War in Angola and Mozambique.* London, Zed Press, 1994.

Mondlane, E. *The Struggle for Mozambique.* London and Baltimore, MD, Penguin Books, 1969, and London, Zed Press, 1983.

Newitt, M. *A History of Mozambique.* Bloomington, Indiana University Press; London, Hurst, 1993.

Newitt, M. D. D. *Portugal in Africa: The Last Hundred Years.* London, Hurst, 1981.

Núñez, B. *Dictionary of Portuguese-African Civilization.* Vol. I. London, Hans Zell, 1995.

Pélissier, R. *Naissance du Mozambique.* 2 vols. France, Editions Pélissier, 1984.

Penvenne, J. M. *African Workers and Colonial Racism: Mozambican Strategies and Struggles in Lourenço Marques, 1877–1962.* London, James Currey, 1995.

Quarterly Economic Review of Tanzania and Mozambique. London, Economist Intelligence Unit, 1978.

Rotberg, R. I., et al (Eds). *South Africa and its Neighbours: Regional Security and Self-Interest.* Lexington, Lexington Books, 1985.

Saul, J. (Ed.). *A Difficult Road: The Transition to Socialism in Mozambique.* New York, Monthly Review Press, 1985.

Seiler, J. (Ed.). *Southern Africa Under the Portuguese Coup.* Boulder, CO, Westview, 1980.

Slater, M. *Mozambique.* London, New Holland, 1997.

Sogge, D. *Hammer and Hoe: Local Industries under State Socialism in Mozambique.* The Hague, Institute of Social Studies, 1985.

Torp, J. E. *Mozambique: Politics, Economics, Society.* London, Pinter, 1989.

United Nations. *The United Nations and Mozambique, 1992–1995.* New York and Geneva, United Nations Publications, 1995.

Vail, L., and White, L. *Capitalism and Colonialism in Mozambique.* London, Heinemann Educational, 1995.

Verdier, I. (Ed.). *Mozambique: 100 Men in Power.* Paris, Indigo Publication Group, 1996.

Vines, A. *No Democracy Without Money: The Road to Peace in Mozambique (1981–1992).* London, Catholic Institute for International Relations, 1994.

Renamo Mozambique. London, James Currey; Bloomington, Indiana University Press, 1994.

Renamo: From Terrorism to Democracy in Mozambique. USA and Canada, World Press, 1995.

Renamo: Terrorism in Mozambique. 2nd Edn. London, James Currey, 1996.

Waterhouse, R. *Mozambique: Rising from the Ashes.* Oxford, OXFAM, 1996.

Wuyts, M. E. *Peasants and Rural Economy in Mozambique.* Maputo, Centro Estudos Africanos, 1978.

Money and Planning for Socialist Transition: The Mozambican Experience. Aldershot, Gower, 1989.

Young, T., and Hall, M. *Confronting Leviathan: Mozambique Since Independence.* London, Hurst, 1997.

NAMIBIA

Physical and Social Geography

A. MacGREGOR HUTCHESON

The Republic of Namibia, lying across the Tropic of Capricorn, covers an area of 824,292 sq km (318,261 sq miles). It is bordered by South Africa on the south and south-east, by Botswana on the east and Angola on the north, while the narrow Caprivi Strip, between the two latter countries, extends Namibia's boundaries to the Zambezi river and a short border with Zambia.

The Namib Desert, a narrow plain 65–160 km wide and extending 1,600 km along the entire Atlantic seaboard, has a mean annual rainfall of less than 100 mm; long lines of huge sand dunes are common and it is almost devoid of vegetation. Behind the coastal plain the Great Escarpment rises to the plateau which forms the rest of the country. Part of the Southern African plateau, it has an average elevation of 1,100 m above sea-level but towards the centre of the country there is a rise to altitudes of 1,525–2,440 m. A number of mountain masses rise above the general surface throughout the plateau. Eastwards the surface slopes to the Kalahari Basin and northwards to the Etosha Pan. Much of Namibia's drainage is interior to the Kalahari. There are no perennial rivers apart from the Okavango and the Cuando, which cross the Caprivi Strip, and the Orange, Kunene and Zambezi, which form parts of the southern and northern borders.

Temperatures of the coastal areas are modified by the cool Benguela Current, while altitude modifies plateau temperatures (cf. Walvis Bay: January 19°C, July 14.5°C; and Windhoek (1,707 m): January 24°C, July 14°C). Average annual rainfall varies from some 50 mm on the coast to 550 mm in the north. Most rain falls during the summer, but is unreliable and there are years of drought. Grasslands cover most of the plateau; they are richer in the wetter north but merge into poor scrub in the south and east.

Most of the population (enumerated at 1,409,920 at the census of October 1991 and estimated at 1,643,000 at mid-1996) reside on the plateau. Figures for the density of population (2.0 inhabitants per sq km at mid-1996) are misleading, as the better-watered northern one-third of the plateau contains more than one-half of the total population and about two-thirds of the African population, including the Ovambo (the largest single ethnic group), Kavango, East Caprivians and Kaokovelders.

Almost the entire European population (80,000 in 1988, including the European population of Walvis Bay, an exclave of South Africa which was ceded to Namibia in March 1994) are concentrated in the southern two-thirds of the plateau, chiefly in the central highlands around Windhoek, the capital, together with the other main ethnic groups, the Damara, Herero, Nama, Rehoboth and Coloured. Excluding ports and mining centres in the Namib and small numbers of Bushmen in the Kalahari, these regions are largely uninhabited.

Namibia possesses scattered deposits of valuable minerals, and its economy is dominated by the mining sector. Of particular importance are the rich deposits of alluvial diamonds, which are exploited by surface mining, notably in the area between Oranjemund and Lüderitz. Operations at the Oranjemund mine are, however, expected to decline progressively in the years after 2003, and new diamond fields off-shore have been developed with much success. Uranium ore (although of a low grade) is mined open-cast at Rössing, 39 km north-east of Swakopmund, which is the world's largest open-pit uranium oxide complex. There is another, smaller uranium deposit about 80 km south of Rössing, which is thought to be of a higher grade. Tin, copper, rock salt, lead and zinc are also mined, and Namibia is believed to have significant reserves of coal, iron ore and platinum, although these have yet to be assessed. Other minerals currently produced or awaiting exploitation include vanadium, manganese, gold, silver, tungsten (wolfram), cadmium and limestone. There are also considerable reserves of offshore natural gas.

Despite the limitations imposed by frequent drought, agriculture is a significant economic activity. With the help of water from boreholes, large areas are given over to extensive ranching. Rivers, notably the Orange, Kunene and Okavango, are potential water resources for irrigation and hydroelectric power, while swamps, such as those situated in the Caprivi Strip, could be drained to enhance arable output.

Namibia possesses potentially the richest inshore and deepwater fishing zones in tropical Africa as a consequence of the rich feeding provided by the Benguela Current. Measures are being taken to counter the effects of decades of over-fishing by both domestic and foreign fleets.

Recent History

CHRISTOPHER SAUNDERS

HISTORICAL BACKGROUND

South West Africa (SWA), declared a German protectorate in 1884, was occupied by South African forces following the outbreak of the First World War. Following the war, the League of Nations awarded South Africa a mandate to administer the territory. In 1925 the South African government granted limited self-government to the territory's white inhabitants. No trusteeship agreement was concluded after the Second World War, and the refusal of the UN in 1946 to agree to South Africa's request to annex SWA marked the beginning of a protracted dispute. In 1949 South Africa granted the territory's white voters representation in the South African parliament. In 1950 the International Court of Justice (ICJ) ruled that South Africa was not competent to place the territory under the UN trusteeship system, nor able to alter the legal status of the territory unilater-

ally. In 1966 the UN General Assembly voted to terminate South Africa's mandate and to assume responsibility for the territory; a 'Council for South West Africa' was appointed in 1967, and in the following year the UN resolved that the territory should be renamed Namibia. The South African government, however, refused to relinquish the territory's administration to the UN.

Political resistance was, meanwhile, taking hold within the territory. In 1957 the Ovamboland People's Congress was formed. It was subsequently renamed the Ovamboland People's Organisation, and in 1960 the South West Africa People's Organisation (SWAPO). Its leaders included Sam Nujoma and Herman (later Andimba) Toivo ja Toivo. From 1963 SWAPO meetings were effectively banned, although it remained technically a legal organization. In 1966 SWAPO's military wing, the People's

Liberation Army of Namibia (PLAN), began an armed insurgency. In 1968 SWAPO restyled itself as the South West Africa People's Organisation of Namibia.

In 1971 the ICJ ruled that South Africa's presence in Namibia was illegal and that it should withdraw immediately, and in December 1973, the UN General Assembly recognized SWAPO as the 'authentic representative of the people of Namibia', and appointed the first UN commissioner for Namibia to undertake 'executive and administrative tasks'.

South Africa's unsuccessful intervention in Angola in the second half of 1975 set the scene for the escalation of the Namibian armed struggle. With support from the pro-SWAPO government in Angola, PLAN was able to establish bases close to the borders of Namibia. South Africa reacted to this threat by greatly expanding counter-insurgency forces in the territory. South Africa, meanwhile, began to take initiatives on the political front. In September 1975 a constitutional conference was convened to discuss the territory's future. The Turnhalle conference, as it became known, designated 31 December 1978 as the target date for Namibian independence, and in March 1977 it produced a draft constitution for a pre-independence interim government. This constitution, providing for 11 ethnic administrations, was denounced by the UN and SWAPO, which issued its own constitutional proposals based on a parliamentary system with universal adult suffrage.

THE UN 'CONTACT GROUP'

In order to persuade South Africa to reject the Turnhalle proposals in favour of a plan which would be acceptable to the UN, a 'contact group' comprising the five Western members of the UN Security Council was established. From April 1977 the 'contact group' held talks with both the South African government and SWAPO beginning in April 1977. In September of that year South Africa appointed an administrator-general for Namibia, and the territory's representation in the South African parliament was terminated. By April 1978 the 'contact group' was able to present proposals for a settlement providing for UN-supervised elections, a reduction in the numbers of South African troops from Namibia and the release of political prisoners. These proposals were accepted by South Africa in late April and by SWAPO in July. The proposals were then incorporated into UN Security Council Resolution 435 of 28 September 1978. South Africa insisted on holding its own election for a Namibian constituent assembly in the territory in December; this was rejected by the international community, which, however, declined to impose sanctions in protest at the action. With SWAPO boycotting the election, 41 of the 50 seats were won by the Democratic Turnhalle Alliance (DTA), a conservative coalition of the ethnic groups involved in the conference. Its leader, Dirk Mudge, became chairman of a ministerial council which was granted limited executive powers. A separate South West African Territory Force (SWATF) was established in 1980, although control of defence and security matters and external affairs was retained by the South African government.

In January 1981 the UN convened a conference in Geneva, Switzerland, which was attended by SWAPO, South Africa, the DTA and other internal parties. The UN 'contact group' and the 'front-line' states (Angola, Botswana, Mozambique, Tanzania, Zambia and Zimbabwe) were present as observers. South Africa and the internal parties could not agree on a cease-fire date and the implementation of the UN plan. It was apparent that the South African prime minister, P. W. Botha, believed that SWAPO was communist-controlled and that it therefore could not be allowed to come to power. The DTA, for its part, required more time to establish itself as a credible alternative to SWAPO; the South African government, meanwhile, hoped that the newly-elected Reagan administration in the USA would be sympathetic to South African policy.

Under US chairmanship, the 'contact group' resumed consultations with South Africa and SWAPO during 1981. In July 1982 constitutional guidelines were agreed to by the two parties, which provided that the post-independence constitution should include a bill of rights and be approved by two-thirds of the members of a constituent assembly. Although South Africa and SWAPO were unable to agree on whether the election should be conducted wholly on the basis of proportional representation, the UN secretary-general was able to report that all other points

at issue had been resolved. By then, however, a more formidable obstacle to the implementation of the UN plan had arisen. South Africa now insisted that the Cuban troops withdraw from Angola. This concept, known as 'linkage', was initiated in 1981 by the US government, which viewed the war in Namibia and southern Angola as a buffer against Soviet expansionism. This view was not shared by the other members of the 'contact group', particularly France, which eventually left the group in December 1983. The USA then continued the negotiations alone.

Within the territory, the DTA was seriously weakened in early 1982 by the effective loss of support from the Ovambo (the largest ethnic group in Namibia) other than SWAPO. After several months of dispute with the South African government over the future role of the DTA, Mudge resigned as chairman of the ministerial council in January 1983, and the council itself was automatically dissolved. The administrator-general, in turn, dissolved the national assembly, and assumed direct rule of Namibia on behalf of the South African government.

ARMED CONFLICT

During the early 1980s security operations by South African forces, augmented by the locally-recruited SWATF, led to a severe escalation in human rights abuses in Ovamboland and in the Kavango and Caprivi regions. Meanwhile, South Africa conducted extensive raids across the frontier into southern Angola. In February 1984 a cease-fire agreement was concluded in Lusaka, Zambia, following talks between South African and US government officials. Under the terms of the agreement, a joint commission was established to monitor the withdrawal of South African troops from Angola, and Angola undertook to permit neither SWAPO nor Cuban forces to move into the areas vacated by South African troops. SWAPO declared that it would abide by the agreement, but made it clear that it would continue PLAN operations until a cease-fire was established in Namibia as the first stage in the implementation of Resolution 435. US negotiators continued, meanwhile, to aim at achieving a regional accord, in which a settlement in Namibia along the lines of Resolution 435 would be counterbalanced by a removal of the Cuban troops from Angola. In November 1984, in response to US proposals, President dos Santos of Angola suggested a timetable for the withdrawal of Cuban troops from the south of Angola. South African withdrawal from Angola was completed in April 1985, but soon afterwards South Africa established an interim internal government in Namibia.

TRANSITIONAL GOVERNMENT AND POPULAR RESISTANCE

After the dissolution of the DTA ministers' council in January 1983, there was a political hiatus until an informally-constituted Multi-Party Conference (MPC) began to meet in November of that year. At that time, its membership extended beyond the DTA to include the Damara Council, the Rehoboth Liberation Front, the SWAPO–Democrats (SWAPO–D, a breakaway faction of SWAPO), the right-wing National Party of South West Africa (SWANP) and the Herero-dominated South West African National Union (SWANU). SWAPO, however, refused to join, and denounced the MPC as 'another South African puppet show'. In October 1984 the MPC called for an all-party meeting by 31 December of that year, failing which it would negotiate unilaterally with Pretoria for independence.

The credibility of the MPC was not high, owing to the past history of the DTA, the corruption and mismanagement of ethnic authorities under the control of MPC member parties, its failure to attract any Ovambo party, and its readiness to deal with South Africa. Aware of the lack of support for the MPC, the South African government sought to involve at least part of SWAPO in an internal settlement. In March 1984 it released Toivo ja Toivo, who had been imprisoned in South Africa since 1968. A number of SWAPO activists who had been detained since 1978 were also freed. In May 1984 formal talks were held in Lusaka between the administrator-general, SWAPO and the internal parties, under the joint chairmanship of President Kaunda of Zambia and the administrator-general. SWAPO, however, insisted on the implementation of Resolution 435, and the talks ended in failure. The members of the MPC then proceeded with their own plans.

On 17 June 1985 the South African government installed a 'Transitional Government of National Unity' (TGNU) in Windhoek, pending independence, although the arrangement was condemned in advance by the contact group governments and was declared 'null and void' by the UN secretary-general. This interim government consisted of a cabinet and a national assembly. Neither was elected, with appointments made from among the constituent parties of the MPC. A 'bill of rights', drawn up by the MPC, prohibited racial discrimination, and a constitutional council was established, under a South African judge, to prepare a constitution for an independent Namibia. South Africa retained responsibility for foreign affairs, defence and internal security. The administrator-general used his power of legislative veto on several occasions. From 1985 a series of rallies by SWAPO and its youth league were disrupted by the police. In July 1986, however, the courts ruled that SWAPO was entitled to hold public meetings, because the violent overthrow of the state was not an integral part of its programme.

MOVES TOWARDS INDEPENDENCE

In early 1987 Angola secured US agreement to the participation of Cuba in discussions, nominally as part of the Angolan delegation, and in January 1988 Angola and Cuba accepted, in principle, the US demand for a complete withdrawal of Cuban troops from Angola, this being conditional on the implementation of the UN independence plan for Namibia. In March proposals for the withdrawal of all Cuban troops were rejected by South Africa as 'insufficiently detailed'. However, South Africa agreed to participate in tripartite negotiations with Angola and Cuba, with the USA acting as mediator.

At these negotiations, which began in London, United Kingdom, in May 1988, South Africa agreed to implement Resolution 435, providing that a timetable for the withdrawal of Cuban troops could be agreed. By mid-July the participants in the negotiations had accepted a document containing 14 'essential principles' for a peaceful settlement, and in early August it was agreed that the implementation of Resolution 435 would begin on 1 November. South African troops were withdrawn from Angola by the end of August. The November deadline was not met, however, owing to disagreement on an exact schedule for the evacuation of Cuban troops. In mid-November these arrangements were agreed in principle, although their formal ratification was delayed until mid-December, owing to South African dissatisfaction with verification procedures.

On 22 December 1988 South Africa, Angola and Cuba signed a formal treaty designating 1 April 1989 as the implementation date for Resolution 435. Another treaty was signed by Angola and Cuba, requiring the evacuation of all Cuban troops from Angola by July 1991. A further agreement established a joint commission to monitor the implementation of the trilateral treaty. Under the terms of Resolution 435, South African forces in Namibia were to be confined to their bases, and their numbers reduced to 1,500 by 1 July 1989; all South African troops were to have been withdrawn from Namibia one week after the election. A multinational UN observer force, the UN Transition Assistance Group (UNTAG), was to monitor the South African withdrawal and supervise the election.

IMPLEMENTATION OF THE UN INDEPENDENCE PLAN

According to the original proposals regarding Resolution 435, UNTAG was to be composed of 7,500 troops; in February 1989, following disagreement within the UN Security Council over the cost of the operation, it was announced that the number was to be 4,650, with a further 500 police and about 1,000 civilian observers. The UNTAG force began to arrive during February 1989. At the end of that month the TGNU was formally disbanded, and on 1 March the national assembly voted to dissolve itself: from then until independence the territory was governed by the administrator-general, Louis Pienaar, in consultation, from 1 April, with the special representative of the UN secretary-general, Martti Ahtisaari.

The scheduled implementation of Resolution 435 was disrupted by large-scale movements, beginning on 1 April 1989, of PLAN troops into Ovamboland. The South African government obtained Ahtisaari's agreement to the release from base of its forces, and more than 300 PLAN troops were reportedly killed in the subsequent fighting. The origins of the sudden and unanticipated conflict apparently lay in differing interpretations of the terms of the UN peace plan; SWAPO, excluded from the 1988 negotiations, relied on provisions under Resolution 435 for the confinement to base of PLAN combatants located within the territory on 1 April 1999, and it was widely claimed that the insurgents had intended to report to UNTAG officials. On 9 April the joint commission produced conditions for an evacuation of the PLAN forces; meanwhile, Sam Nujoma, president of SWAPO, ordered a withdrawal of PLAN forces to Angola. At a meeting of the joint commission on 19 May, the cease-fire was certified to be in force. In June most racially discriminatory legislation was repealed, and an amnesty was granted to Namibian refugees and exiles: by late September nearly 42,000 refugees, including Nujoma, had returned to Namibia. Meanwhile, South Africa completed its troop reduction ahead of schedule.

The pre-independence election was conducted peacefully in the second week of November 1989; more than 95% of the electorate voted. The 72 seats in the constituent assembly were contested by candidates from 10 political parties and alliances: representatives of seven parties and fronts were elected. SWAPO received 57.3% of all votes cast and won 41 seats, thus obtaining a majority of the seats in the assembly but failing to achieve the two-thirds' majority that would have allowed SWAPO to draft the constitution without recourse to wider consultation. It was widely believed that SWAPO would have fared better had evidence not emerged during the election campaign of the torture and death in its camps in Angola of numerous people whom SWAPO had detained—as alleged by South Africa during the war. The DTA, with 28.6% of the votes, won 21 seats. The election was pronounced 'free and fair' by the special representative of the UN secretary-general. Following the election, the remaining South African troops left Namibia, and SWAPO bases in Angola were disbanded.

SWAPO IN GOVERNMENT

In February 1990 the constituent assembly adopted unanimously a draft constitution, which provided for a multi-party political system, based on universal adult suffrage, with an independent judiciary and a 'bill of rights'. Executive power was to be vested in a president who was permitted to serve a maximum of two five-year terms, while a 72-member national assembly was to have legislative power. The constituent assembly subsequently elected Nujoma as Namibia's first president. On 21 March 1990 Namibia became independent: the constituent assembly became the national assembly, and the president and his cabinet (headed by Hage Geingob, hitherto chairman of the constituent assembly) took office.

Following independence, Namibia became a member of the UN, the Organization of African Unity and the Commonwealth. Full diplomatic relations were established with many states, and partial diplomatic relations with South Africa. In May 1990 Angola and Namibia agreed to form a joint commission to monitor their common border. However, relations became strained in February 1991 when Angolan aircraft bombed a northern Namibian village; the Angolan government claimed that it had attacked covert destabilization bases sponsored by South Africa, and promised to pay compensation to the Namibian government. With the resumption of the civil war in Angola in late 1992, the Namibian government remained concerned over the security of its northern border. Instability in South Africa also threatened to affect Namibia; the government was, therefore, much relieved when South Africa's first democratic election took place peacefully in April 1994.

In March 1990 Namibia became a full member of the Southern African Customs Union (having previously been a *de facto* member of that organization) and a member of the South African Development Co-ordination Conference (SADCC), which sought to reduce the dependence of southern African states on South Africa. In August 1992 Namibia joined the other SADCC members in recreating the organization as the Southern African Development Community (SADC), to which South Africa was admitted in August 1994.

In April 1990 a team of British military advisers arrived in Namibia to assist in training the new Namibian Defence Force, comprising former members of both PLAN and the SWATF. In

September several ex-members of the national police force and of the disbanded pre-independence paramilitary force, Koevoet, were charged with high treason, following the discovery of a weapons cache. The appointment, in October, of the former SWAPO head of security, Maj.-Gen. Solomon Hawala, as commander of the army caused protest among opposition groups, owing to allegations that he had been implicated in the torture and detention of dissidents prior to Namibia's independence. Although the opposition in the national assembly continued to raise the matter from time to time, the government refused to agree to an investigation of events that took place during the struggle for independence. Allegations of past violations of human rights by SWAPO have remained a sensitive political issue.

The disclosure by the South African government in July 1991 that it had provided some R100m. in funding to the DTA and other anti-SWAPO political parties during the 1989 election campaign added to the DTA's post-independence problems. In November 1991 the DTA, formerly a coalition of ethnically-based interests, reorganized itself as a single party, but its support continued to dwindle. In late November and early December 1992 the first elections were held for the country's 13 regional councils and 48 local authorities. SWAPO won nine regional councils while the DTA won only three (in the remaining council there was no clear majority). SWAPO thus secured control of the newly-established second house of parliament, the national council, which comprised two members from each regional council; it began work in May 1993. In June Dirk Mudge, the leading figure in the DTA, resigned from the national assembly and subsequently retired from public life. The DTA repeatedly publicized examples of alleged maladministration and financial extravagance (the most controversial example being the purchase of a presidential aircraft during a period of severe drought), but these efforts failed to revitalize popular support for the DTA.

Walvis Bay, the 1,124-sq km enclave that contains the region's only deep-water port facilities, had remained under South African jurisdiction after Namibian independence. Negotiations between the South African and Namibian governments led to the announcement in August 1992 that a Walvis Bay Joint Administration Authority (JAA) would be established, comprising an equal number of representatives from each country. The JAA began operating in November that year. In August 1993, following pressure from the African National Congress of South Africa (ANC), South Africa's multi-party negotiating forum resolved to transfer sovereignty of Walvis Bay to Namibia. Some white residents of the enclave resorted unsuccessfully to legal action in an attempt to block the transfer. The work of the JAA was completed in February 1994, and from the beginning of March the enclave was formally incorporated into Namibia.

Namibia's first post-independence presidential and legislative elections took place on 7–8 December 1994, and resulted in overwhelming victories for Nujoma and SWAPO. Nujoma was elected for a second term as president, securing 76.3% of the votes cast; his only challenger was Mudge's successor as president of the DTA, Mishake Muyongo. SWAPO secured 53 of the elective seats in the national assembly, obtaining 73.9% of the valid votes cast. The DTA retained 15 seats (with 20.8% of the votes), and the coalition United Democratic Front two. The remaining two seats were won by the Democratic Coalition of Namibia (DCN, an alliance of the National Patriotic Front and the German Union) and the Monitor Action Group. SWANU, which had been a founder member of the DCN in August, but subsequently withdrew to contest the elections in its own right, failed to secure representation in the legislature. Although SWAPO thus had a two-thirds' majority in the national assembly, Nujoma gave assurances that no amendments would be made to the constitution without prior approval by national referendum. The success of Nujoma and SWAPO was, in part, attributed to the popularity of land reform legislation recently approved by the national assembly.

Nujoma was sworn in for his second presidential term on 21 March 1995. The previous day, as part of a major reorganization of cabinet portfolios, he assumed personal responsibility for home affairs and the police, in what was interpreted as an attempt to curb an increase in crime and discontent within the police force. Geingob remained as prime minister, with Hendrik

Witbooi, previously minister of labour, public services and manpower development, as his deputy.

In March 1996 the publication of *Namibia: The Wall of Silence*, a book by German Pastor Siegfried Groth, a former SWAPO supporter, describing the detention and torture of people by the organization during the 1980s, caused much controversy. Nujoma publicly denounced the book as an attempt to discredit SWAPO, and accused its promoters of endangering national reconciliation. Nujoma and his party were, in turn, accused of failing to admit to, and apologize for, the alleged human rights violations in the SWAPO camps in Angola. SWAPO subsequently published a book, entitled *Their Blood Waters Our Freedom*, listing about 8,000 SWAPO supporters who had died during the war. However, a 'breaking the wall of silence' committee continued to accuse the party of failing to acknowledge the alleged atrocities in its camps. When the South African truth and reconciliation commission (see the chapter on South Africa) requested permission to conduct hearings in Namibia in 1997, it was refused, on the grounds that the public discussions might hinder Namibia's own search for reconciliation.

In May 1997, at SWAPO's second party congress since independence, the most intensive debate was on land reform, with the congress urging the government to expedite measures in that area. An important resolution endorsing the proposal that Nujoma should seek re-election for a third term as president was justified on the grounds that Nujoma had initially been chosen by the constituent assembly, and had only once been elected president on a popular mandate. Witbooi, who had been vice-president of the party since 1983, was re-elected to the post, defeating a challenge by Geingob. The minister of fisheries and marine resources, Hifikepunye Pohamba, replaced Moses Garoëb as secretary-general of the party. In a minor reshuffle of the cabinet in December, Pohamba was appointed minister without portfolio.

Increasing discontent with the SWAPO government was reflected in the outcome of local elections conducted in February 1998. Only 34% of the registered voters participated in the ballot, the lowest figure since independence. Voter participation was particularly low in the north of the country, traditionally an area of strong support for SWAPO. The ruling party retained control of 27 of the 45 councils contested, but lost two to its nearest rival, the DTA, which won nine.

Critics continued to accuse SWAPO of autocratic practices and various abuses of power. Investigations into allegations of corruption were protracted, and the government often failed to punish those involved. The proposed purchase of a new presidential aircraft prompted much criticism in 1997, which, however, the government was able to disregard. Both the press and the judiciary were attacked by SWAPO supporters who opposed their independence, while efforts to establish new anti-SWAPO parties attracted little popular support. The dominant trend was to increase the concentration of power in the SWAPO élite.

REGIONAL CONCERNS

In March 1993 the Angolan insurgent movement União Nacional para a Independência Total de Angola (UNITA) alleged that members of the Namibian Defence Force had crossed the border into southern Angola to assist Angolan government forces in offensives against UNITA. The Namibian authorities denied any involvement in the Angolan civil conflict, but a section of the border with Angola was closed from September 1994, following an attack, attributed by the Namibian authorities to UNITA, in which Namibian nationals were killed. In 1996 it was announced that some 1,000 members of a special field force of the Namibia police, created in 1995 to provide employment for former PLAN troops, were to be deployed along the Okavango river on the Angolan border to deter possible UNITA attacks. In August 1996 Namibian and Angolan officials agreed on further measures to increase border security.

In 1996 Namibia and Botswana referred their dispute over the demarcation of their joint border on the Chobe river (specifically, the issue of the sovereignty of the sparsely inhabited island of Kasikili-Sedudu) for adjudication by the ICJ. In December 1997 a new dispute began concerning two further islands, Situngu and Luyondo, when Botswanan soldiers allegedly harvested crops planted on the islands by Namibian villagers. In May 1998 the two countries signed an accord establishing a joint technical commission to demarcate their joint border on the Chobe river.

Following the change of government in South Africa, President Mandela visited Namibia in August 1994 and indicated the possible cancellation of Namibia's pre-independence debt to South Africa (estimated at N\$ 826.6m. in 1990), which Namibia was to have repaid with interest in annual instalments during 1995–2012. Shortly before Namibia's elections in December 1994, Nujoma again met Mandela in South Africa, and the South African president announced that the entire debt would be cancelled. However, when technical experts from the two countries met to discuss the practicalities, they were unable to agree. The issue was given priority during Nujoma's first state visit to South Africa in May 1996, and by August of that year it was reported that the difficulties had been resolved. Legislation providing for the cancellation of the debt was subsequently adopted by the South African parliament. When he addressed the South African parliament on his state visit to Cape Town, Nujoma appealed for South African investment in Namibia; however, few such funds were forthcoming.

In August 1998, apparently without first consulting his cabinet, or the legislature, President Nujoma ordered the dispatch of Namibian troops in support of President Laurent-Désiré Kabila of the Democratic Republic of the Congo (DRC) against rebel forces supported by Uganda and Rwanda. Within weeks almost 2,000 Namibian troops were fighting in the DRC alongside troops from Angola, Zimbabwe (and, at that time, Chad), helping to secure the Matadi corridor from Kinshasa to the sea. However, the military involvement in the DRC was not popular within Namibia. Within six months the cost of the operation was in excess of N \$100m. Although Nujoma asserted that Namibian involvement was an act of solidarity and support for the territorial integrity of the DRC in the face of external aggression, many observers considered that he hoped participation in the war might mean that Namibia would be well-placed to benefit from future mineral exploitation in the DRC. There were also rumours that the authorities were concealing the number of Namibians who had died in the conflict. In May 1999 Geingob conceded that the government had not given adequate information, and later that month the national assembly was informed that 17 Namibians had been killed in the DRC, including five in a helicopter collision in January, in which Nujoma's personal pilots died. Meanwhile, Nujoma played a prominent role in efforts towards a negotiated settlement, undertaking numerous visits to other countries of the region, and helping persuade Kabila to enter talks with the rebels, and Uganda to withdraw from the DRC. He continued to deny that there were any Namibian troops supporting the Angolan government against UNITA, but stated that, if requested, Namibia would assist under the auspices of SADC. In April Namibia signed a regional defence pact with Angola, the DRC and Zimbabwe, providing for mutual assistance in the event of aggression against any of the signatories.

Relations with Botswana were further complicated from late 1998, when refugees began entering that country from Caprivi. Beginning in October a stream of refugees fled to Botswana, citing police harassment, after a man was reportedly killed at a secret military training base which the Namibian government alleged was being used by the secessionist Caprivi Liberation Movement (CLM). The people of Caprivi had long sought closer links with their neighbours to the east, believing that the government in Windhoek was ignoring the development of their region because they did not support SWAPO. It emerged that the leading refugee figure was Mishake Muyongo, who had been forced out of SWAPO in 1980 because of disagreement regarding the Caprivi issue, and had later become leader of the DTA. In August 1998 the DTA's executive had in turn announced the suspension of Muyongo as party president, and dissociated the party from Muyongo's overt support for the secession of the Caprivi Strip. With 14 other members of the CLM, he sought, and was granted, asylum by the Botswana government in February 1999. Nujoma, who had at first sought the extradition of the refugees so that they could be tried as terrorists, made a state visit to Botswana in March 1999, during which he agreed with President Mogae that the secessionist leaders could be accorded refugee status, on condition that they be resettled in a third

country; the remaining refugees, who by then numbered some 2,500 (including many San Bushmen), would be able to return without fear of punishment or persecution. This agreement was subsequently ratified by the two countries and the office of the UN High Commissioner for Refugees. Muyongo and another leader of the movement, Boniface Mamili (a chief of the Mafwe) were granted political asylum in Denmark.

In early August 1999, however, an unanticipated attack by members of what was styled the Caprivi Liberation Army (CLA) on the regional capital of Caprivi, Katima Mulilo, resulted in 12 deaths. The Namibian government imposed a state of emergency in Caprivi, and was offered support by Zimbabwe and Zambia against the separatists. The CLA, which had bases in western Zambia, was said to have close links with the separatist Barotse Patriotic Front in that country. It was widely suspected that UNITA had given the CLA military training and supported the attack because of the Namibian government's close ties with the MPLA government in Angola. Muyongo, stated to be the leader of the CLA, announced from Denmark that the episode marked the beginning of a war against the Namibian authorities, whom, he reasserted, had acted against the interests of the people of the region. Although the state of emergency was revoked in late August, human rights groups in Namibia produced evidence that Namibian troops had committed acts of brutality against those believed to support the rebels.

Tensions in the region of the Namibia-Angola border escalated from late 1999, after the two countries began joint patrols targeting UNITA, and the Namibian government authorized the Angolan armed forces to launch attacks against UNITA from Namibian territory. UNITA responded by launching sporadic attacks on Caprivi. By June 2000, when a curfew was imposed along the Kavango river on the north-eastern border with Angola, more than 50 Namibians had been killed in cross-border raids by the Angolan rebels. At their March 1999 meeting, Presidents Nujoma and Mogae confirmed that Namibia and Botswana would each respect the judgment of the ICJ regarding sovereignty of Kasikili-Sedudu. In December 1999 the judgment was finally made in Botswana's favour. The two countries then established a joint commission to settle the remaining disputes in the Chobe river area, and agreed that its decisions would be binding on both governments. Still unresolved was the issue of Namibia's border with South Africa: Namibia and South Africa disagreed as to whether the boundary followed the centre point of the Orange river, as well as to where the boundary line ran out to sea (and thus to diamond deposits).

RECENT POLITICAL DEVELOPMENTS

In October 1998 the exceptional amendment to the constitution, allowing Nujoma to seek a third presidential term, was approved by the requisite two-thirds' majority in the national assembly, having received the support of SWAPO's members; the amendment was similarly endorsed by the national council in November. Of some concern was the increased apathy among voters, apparent in the regional council elections held in December when turn-out by voters was only about 30%. SWAPO won a majority in 11 of the 13 regional councils, thereby increasing its representation in the national council from 19 to 22 seats.

The first real challenge to SWAPO's dominance emerged with the establishment in March 1999 of a new political party under a former senior SWAPO official, Ben Ulenga. A member of the PLAN who had served a long prison sentence under the apartheid regime on Robben Island, and later become Namibia's best-known trade union leader, Ulenga resigned from his post as Namibia's high commissioner to the United Kingdom in August 1998, in protest against SWAPO's decision to alter the constitution to allow Nujoma to seek a third term as president. Ulenga also opposed Namibia's involvement in the conflict in the DRC, and was critical of the SWAPO government's failure adequately to address the issue of unemployed former combatants. Ulenga did not initially resign from SWAPO, although he was suspended from its central committee; in October he formed a 'consultative forum', with a view to establishing a new party. When the Congress of Democrats (CoD) was formed, it appealed to those disenchanted with SWAPO rule, among them unemployed ex-combatants, members of the labour movement, intellectuals critical of Nujoma's autocratic style of government, and members of SWANU who thought the new party might represent a more effective opposition. Unlike the DTA, it was not tainted with a history of collaboration with South Africa under apartheid. Apparently concerned as to the CoD's prospects in the presidential and general election due in late 1999, Nujoma swiftly appointed two key figures from the labour movement as deputy ministers, and the government set aside N \$255m. in the 1999/2000 budget for the social integration of about 9,000 former combatants, who were to be offered employment in the public service. A number were given posts in the police, and a national youth service scheme was also proposed.

During the general election campaign, a SWAPO spokesman claimed that Ulenga had revealed details of SWAPO's military organizations to his South African captors in the 1970s. Ulenga rejected the allegations and called for a full judicial inquiry. In accordance with tradition, the president nominated the first 30 of SWAPO's candidates for the assembly, but provoked an outcry when the initial list omitted five ministers, including the influential minister of trade and industry, Hidipo Hamutenya, the person thought most likely to succeed Nujoma as president. In October 1999 Ignatius Shixwameni, a deputy minister and former leader of the Namibian National Students Organization, who had often clashed with Nujoma, resigned from the government and from SWAPO, accusing the party of being concerned with self-enrichment. Shixwameni subsequently joined the CoD. There were indications that the CoD, which in its campaign emphasized the failure of the Nujoma administration adequately to address the issues of unemployment, wealth distribution and land reform, together with institutionalized corruption and the

excessive centralization of power in the hands of the president, would present the first serious challenge to the incumbent SWAPO regime since independence. None the less, the elections resulted in an overwhelming victory for Nujoma and SWAPO, with Ulenga and the CoD apparently winning support at the expense of the DTA. In the presidential election Nujoma was returned for a third (and final) term of office with 76.8% of the votes cast, while Ulenga took 10.5% and Katuutire Kaura (Muyongo's successor as president of the DTA) 9.6%. SWAPO won 55 of the elective seats in the national assembly, with 76.1% of the votes cast (thus ensuring that it retained the two-thirds' majority enabling it to amend the constitution): the CoD and the DTA each won seven seats (taking, respectively, 9.9% and 9.5% of the total votes cast).

Geingob was reappointed prime minister in a reorganization of the cabinet announced by Nujoma in mid-March 2000. The functions of the ministries of foreign affairs and of information and broadcasting were, notably, merged (under Theo-Ben Gurirab), as were those of the ministry of justice and office of the attorney-general (under Ngarijutuke Tjiriange). Hifikepunye Pohamba relinquished his post as minister without portfolio, although he remained secretary-general of SWAPO.

By 1999 more than 150,000 of Namibia's population of some 1.7m. were infected with the HIV virus. In April Namibia accepted the SADC decision to make AIDS a notifiable disease. In the same month, the government abandoned plans for legislation, modelled on that in South Africa, to legalize abortion within the first three months of pregnancy (and under certain other conditions). A draft bill had been issued for public consultation in 1996, but opposition from church leaders had proved so strong that the government conceded defeat on the issue.

Economy
DONALD L. SPARKS
Revised for this edition by MAREK GARZTECKI

INTRODUCTION

With a gross domestic product (GDP) per caput of US \$2,250 in 1997, Namibia is relatively prosperous in the African context. This comparative wealth reflects a large and fairly diversified mining sector, producing diamonds, uranium and base metals. Despite frequent drought, large ranches generally provide significant exports of beef and karakul sheepskins. Yet the economy is highly extractive and poorly integrated. About 90% of the goods that Namibia produces are exported, and about 90% of the goods that are used in the country, including about one-half of the food, are imported. Furthermore, the figure for GDP per caput disguises an extreme inequality in income distribution—the average income for the white minority is significantly higher than that for the mass of the black population. The reason for this imbalance lies in the economic structure that was imposed by colonial history. The ranches were established as settlers displaced Africans on two-thirds of the viable farmland. From the African 'reserves' came a stream of migrant workers, on whose low wages the development of the early mines and ranches depended. In the diamond and uranium mines, where profits have been high and the wage bill a small proportion of costs, the situation has changed, and these enterprises now pay the highest wages in the country. Elsewhere, particularly on the ranches, wages remain extremely low.

During the early 1980s Namibia experienced a deep economic recession, intensified by war, severe drought and low world prices for the country's mineral products and for karakul pelts. In real terms, output per head declined by more than 20% over the period 1977–84, representing a fall of about one-third in real purchasing power. The impact of the recession was partly masked by a rapid expansion in state expenditure in the early 1980s, as South Africa tried to buy support for the Democratic Turnhalle Alliance (DTA) and an internal settlement. There were some benefits from this spending. For example, a high-quality road network was built in the north, albeit for military

purposes. From the mid-1980s, however, there was a modest economic recovery. GDP increased by 3% in 1986, compared with a decline of 0.8% in 1985, and there were further increases in 1987 and 1988. GDP declined by 0.6% in 1989. This sluggish rate of growth was due to a number of factors, including depressed international prices for Namibia's mineral exports, a corresponding decline in mining production, and the poor performance of the South African economy (in the period prior to and since independence the Namibian and South African economies have remained closely linked). Real GDP increased by 5.1% in 1991, and by 3.5% in 1992, owing primarily to higher diamond output and increases in the output of the fishing and construction sectors. GDP grew by 6.6% in 1994, after a decline of 2.0% in 1993, by 3.6% in 1995, by 2.1% in 1996 and by 2.4% in 1997. The rate of growth increased slightly to 2.6% in 1998 and an estimated 3.9% in 1999, with considerable advancement in the fishing and manufacturing sectors partially offset by the adverse impact of the Asian economic crisis on the mining sector.

FINANCE

During the 1980s South Africa was an important source of public finance for Namibia, its annual contribution rising from R40m. (12% of total revenue) in 1981 to R469.2m. (30% of total revenue) in 1987. South Africa contributed R308m. in 1988 and 1989, and made its final contribution, of R83m., in 1990. The South African government ceased acting as guarantor of Namibian loans in 1990. Following independence Namibia began to receive financial assistance from the international donor community. Official development assistance (ODA) declined from R125m. in 1991 to R90m. in 1992. However, total aid disbursements increased by nearly 50% (from N \$282m. to N \$421m.) from 1990 to 1992. ODA accounts for about 75% of aid. In July 1990 international donors pledged assistance of US \$696m. for the period 1990–93; Germany was the largest bilateral donor, agreeing to provide US \$186m. The USA and

Scandinavian countries are the other major bilateral donors. Namibia is not permitted to borrow on concessionary terms from the International Development Association, owing to the country's high level of income per head, despite the fact that this is unevenly distributed throughout the population (see above).

Namibia's budget account was characterized by a succession of deficits during the 1980s. Following independence, the government aimed to increase expenditure on health and education. The first post-independence budget, for the financial year 1990/91, produced a surplus of R200m. The 1997/98 budget was received with approval by Namibia's business community owing to its resistance of major expenditure increases and provision for firm commitments on greater transparency in government fiscal operations. Although the government was considering the replacement of the current indirect taxes by a value-added tax (VAT), it pledged that VAT would not be introduced until 1999 at the earliest. Total budget expenditure in 1998/99 reached N $6,800m., 19.2% higher than the previous year. The increase in spending was the result of substantial increases in civil service salaries, larger planned principal and interest payments on domestic debt and increased spending on higher education (education alone accounted for 26% of total expenditure). Over one-third of total expenditure for 1998/99 was to be financed by tax increases, with the general sales tax on goods to rise from 8% to 10%, and additional sales duty on alcoholic beverages and tobacco to increase by 5%–10%. Company tax was to rise by 5% (excluding companies in the mining sector). Thus the budget deficit for 1998/99 increased by 10%, to N $745m., equivalent to 4.3% of nominal GDP. The trend continued with the budget for 1999/2000, which envisaged total expenditure of N $7,751m. and revenue of N $6,952m. In January 2000 an additional budget was tabled providing for a 3% increase in overall expenditure (to N $8,009m.), as a result primarily of the costs of Namibia's intervention in the conflict in the Democratic Republic of the Congo (see Recent History) and increased interest payments on the government's domestic debt. Taking into account higher than expected tax receipts and a N $57m. increase in external grant aid, the 1999/2000 budget deficit was projected at N $881m., representing 4.5% of projected GDP.

The central bank reaffirmed that Namibia's policy was to move towards full exchange control liberalization in conjunction with the South African Reserve Bank. Since 1996 South African nationals and residents have been entitled to hold foreign-currency accounts in South Africa or to transfer limited funds overseas. Namibia applied for IMF Article VIII status, thus providing for eventual full current-account convertibility. The South African parliament finally approved its debt-cancellation agreement with Namibia, more than two years after South Africa's president announced that Namibia's pre-independence bilateral debt would be cancelled; the writing-off liabilities totalled N $1,200m. The conclusion of the debt-cancellation agreement reduced Namibia's outstanding external public debt by 85%, to some N $200m., which represented less than 2% of Namibia's GDP. However, Namibia's external debt situation may not be as favourable as official figures indicate. The government has undertaken increased foreign borrowing in recent years, with non-rand-denominated loans rising from only N $16m. in 1991 to N $132m. in 1993. These were mainly on highly concessionary terms, but, after the expiry of the initial grace period, repayments of debt principal were to start falling due within the following years. Namibia's total debt in 1997 was N $405m. Total debt increased to N $685m. in 1998 (of which N $502m. was public and N $183m. private), although this was due more to the depreciation of the Namibian dollar and drawing down existing loans rather than to contracting of new lending.

The new Namibian Stock Exchange (NSX) continued to expand. The market value of shares traded on the exchange increased substantially establishing NSX as sub-Saharan Africa's second largest stock exchange in capital value, although 98% of it was provided by dual-listed shares in South African firms, and trading volumes, while on the increase, remained relatively modest. From April 1998 dual-listing was permitted with all other stock exchanges of the Southern African Development Community (SADC). NSX added two new listings in 1998: Gendor Holdings, a deep-sea fishing company, and the major South African insurance company Samlan. Another large South African insurance company, Old Mutual, a diamond-mining company, Trans Hex, and the Nedcor Investment Bank were listed on NSX in 1999, adding N $51,000m. to the total market capitalization. Although no new domestic company was listed during that period, the cross-listings in addition to strong gains in the share price of Namibian Minerals Corporation (Namco) and Namibian Breweries Ltd (Nambrew) lifted the market by 44% to a high of N $267,000m. in July 1999. Namibia is continuing its efforts to establish itself as a leading offshore financial centre in the region. The new investment regime will allow investors to bypass some restrictions on foreign-exchange transactions imposed by the South African Reserve Bank with which Namibia had hitherto been obliged to comply as a member of the Common Monetary Area. Both the Namibian dollar and the South African rand, to which it is linked at parity, declined in value by some 20% in 1998 and further depreciation was anticipated in 1999–2000.

The annual rate of inflation was 9.9% in 1995, compared with 10.8% in 1994. The rate declined further, to 8.0%, in 1996. The Consumer Price Index (CPI) recorded only changes in prices in the capital, Windhoek; however, a new measurement, which was to come into force in 1996, was to cover prices throughout the economy. The annual rate of inflation was 8.9% in 1997, slowing to 6.2% in 1998 and then rising again to 8.6% in 1999. The South African central bank's sustained policy of monetary restraint effectively curbs inflation in Namibia (as Namibia's fiscal policies are virtually controlled by South Africa). For example, the 1995 lending rate reached a high of 19%, with a consequent restraining influence on inflation. By the first quarter of 2000 the central bank's interest rate had fallen to 11.75%, from a high of 21.25% in the third quarter of 1999, while the prime lending rate offered by the commercial banks stood at 16.5%, with further interest rate cuts expected in the latter part of 2000.

Unemployment remains a serious problem for Namibia, both in the light industrial sector (manufacturing, for example) and in urban areas in general, and there are serious concerns as to how jobs will be found for recent school-leavers. At the end of the 1990s unemployment stood at around 38%, with some estimating the figure to be even higher.

MINERALS AND MINING

Namibia is mineral-rich. It is the world's leading producer of gem-quality diamonds, traditionally accounting for some 30% of total world output. In addition, Namibia has the world's largest uranium mine, and significant reserves of tin, lithium and cadmium. Namibia is Africa's second largest producer of zinc, its third largest producer of lead and fourth largest source of copper. Other important minerals include hydrocarbons, tungsten, vanadium, silver, gold, columbite/tantalite, germanium and beryl. Under the Minerals (Prospecting and Mining) Act, which came into operation in early 1994, the government has taken action to diversify the mining sector; amendments to the Act were under preparation in the first half of 1999.

In 1980 mining accounted for about one-half of Namibia's GDP, but had declined to 13.0% in 1997. The total value of mineral exports reached R1,645m. in 1986 and totalled R1,543m. in 1988, accounting for 73% of total export earnings. Minerals accounted for an estimated 59.9% of total exports in 1997. In 1998 the total value of exported minerals stood at N $3,463m., with mining and quarrying accounting for 12.6% of GDP. Employment in the sector declined from 21,000 in 1977 to 7,700 in 1998.

Diamonds form a key component of Namibia's economy. Diamond mining contributed 70.1% of the sector's GDP in 1997. Diamonds are the principal mineral export, accounting for an estimated 30.4% of export revenue in 1998. The ownership of Namibia's most important diamond mine, centred on Oranjemund, underwent a significant reorganization in late 1994, when a new operating company, Namdeb Diamond Corpn (owned in equal shares by the government and De Beers Centenary AG), acquired the diamond assets of Consolidated Diamond Mines (CDM), the De Beers subsidiary that had previously held sole exploitation rights to Namibian alluvial diamond deposits. About 98% of the diamonds recovered in Namibia are of gem quality, and under the new arrangements these stones continue to be marketed by De Beers through the Central Selling

Organisation (CSO). Production at Oranjemund is, however, expected to decline progressively after 2003, and the exploitation of an offshore diamond field, extending 300 m from the coast, is proceeding. In 1998 offshore recoveries of gem-quality stones accounted for about one-half of Namibia's diamond output. In 1993 marine exploration concessions were granted to a new privately-financed venture, Namco. Concession rights held by Namco cover three offshore areas totalling almost 2,000 sq km, containing an estimated 80m. carats of gem-quality diamonds. Commercial recoveries began in late 1995. Namco reached its production target of 150,000 carats at the end of 1998, following the commencement in April of commercial operations in the northern sector of its Lüderitz Bay concession, and forecast output for 2000 at 400,000 carats. By October 1999, furthermore, Namco had acquired a 92.5% stake in the South African-based Ocean Diamond Mining Holdings Ltd, and thus had become the world's second largest marine diamond-mining company. In November Namco was granted a second 15-year mining licence in Hottentot Bay, estimated to contain some 650,000 carats. Namibia's total output of diamonds, which reached 1.55m. carats in 1992, fell to 1.14m. carats in 1993, but recovered to 1.31m. carats in 1994 and 1.38m. carats in 1995. Production increased to 1.40m. carats in 1996, owing to an increase in both onshore and offshore recoveries by Namdeb and De Beers Marine (Debmarine) respectively. Namdeb was expanding operations inland at Auchas, and was conducting a feasibility study at the similar upstream Deaberas prospect. In 1997 a weakening of the world diamond market resulted in smaller than envisaged increases in Namibian output. Namdeb's production increased by only 0.1% in 1997, compared to 1.0% in 1996, owing in part to the effect of adverse weather conditions on coastal operations. Despite the decline in the global diamond market in 1997–98, Namdeb's output increased by 3.5%, to some 1.4m. carats, in 1998. In 1999 Debmarine's recoveries increased to some 500,000 carats. The company continues to invest in additional capital equipment, with the launching of a new, N 260m. mining vessel in 1999. Namibia's total output of diamonds was estimated at 1.55m. carats in 1999. In April 1998 President Nujoma signed an agreement with Russia providing for co-operation in mining and prospecting. Under the terms of the agreement the Russian mining company RAO Almazy Rossii-Sakha will be permitted to operate in Namibia. Meanwhile, Diamond Fields International (DFI) of Canada was expected to commission a full feasibility study of its Lüderitz offshore concession, in preparation to become Namibia's third marine producer. A new Diamond Act, to succeed the legislation in force since 1939, was approved by the Namibian parliament in mid-1999; the legislation allows individuals to apply for licences to trade in, import or export diamonds, subject to criminal penalties for unauthorized dealing.

Retail jewellery sales world-wide declined by only 3% in 1998, compared to a fall of 5% in 1997. Furthermore, the US market accounts for 46% of total sales and shows no signs of weakening. Thus, the recovery of the Asian economies is expected to increase demand. In an obvious sign of the market's renewed strength in late 1999 the CSO revealed its purchase of the stockpile accumulated by Namdeb. In addition, export quotas imposed on its contracted producers were removed. The move was expected to increase diamond sales in 1999 well beyond US $500m. Namibia's first diamond cutting and polishing factory was inaugurated by NamGem, a subsidiary of Namdeb, in mid-1998.

The huge, although low-grade, Rössing uranium mine, which is the world's largest single producer of uranium, came into production in 1976. After an initial period of profitability for its owner, the Rio Tinto-Zinc group, the mine suffered from the depression in the uranium market. The Rössing mine's uranium is sold by means of long-term contracts to European Union (EU) countries, Japan and Taiwan, but the persistently weak 'spot' price of uranium has forced renegotiations of the contract prices. In 1986 it was reported that uranium from Rössing was contributing about 16% of Namibia's GDP. As a result of the continuing decline in world uranium prices, Rössing reduced its output to 2,500 metric tons in 1991. Production continued to decline, owing to a reduction in world-wide demand, with output of 1,973 tons in 1992, the lowest output since the mine began operations. Rössing began to deliver uranium to Electricité de France under a long-term contract for 5,000 tons of uranium

oxide annually until 2002. As a result of higher international demand, the 'spot' price of uranium increased in 1995. Namibia produced 2,472 tons of uranium in 1994, 2,579 tons in 1995 and 2,884 tons in 1996, of which virtually all emanated from Rössing. Rössing's plans to expand production to reach full capacity (4,500 tons) suffered following a downturn in the 'spot' price of uranium in the second half of 1997. Production in 1998, at 3,257 tons, was some 5% lower than in 1997. However, revenues increased by 7%, to US $154m., owing to stronger world prices. Production in 1999, at an estimated 3,171 tons, was some 2.6% lower than in the previous year. In an effort to increase the mine's profitability, its owners announced a reduction in its 1,200-strong work-force of one-sixth, to be implemented by the end of 2000. It was expected that the mine would continue production at 75% of its capacity pending an upturn in the uranium market, expected between 2001 and 2003.

Namibia's principal metals producer, Tsumeb Corpn Ltd (TCL), which operated three base-metal mines and a major copper smelter and lead refinery, was placed in provisional liquidation by the owner, Gold Fields Namibia, in August 1998. Subsequent bids to acquire Tsumeb, whose assets were valued at N 180m., failed to prevent a liquidation order, issued by the high court in March 1999, and Tsumeb's mineral rights reverted to the Namibian government. The Australian-managed Metals and Mining Corpn of Namibia (MMN) and a local consortium, Namibian Mining and Processing, were negotiating with the government in mid-1999 to acquire Tsumeb's former operations. While for most of 1999 the MMN appeared to be the front-runner, it was a local consortium, Ongopolo Mining and Processing, formed by trade unionists and former TCL managers, that by mid-2000 was emerging as the likely new owner. Meanwhile, Australia's Copper Mines and Metals (CMM, formerly Great Fitzroy Mines) suspended development of the Haib copper mine and on-site refinery pending an improvement in world prices. The mine had been due to commence production in 1999, with projected output of 115,000 tons of copper cathode. The biggest operating cost component was to be power, and Haib's 200-MW projected annual requirement was to make it Namibia's single largest electricity consumer. Supplies initially would be derived from South Africa's power grid, but Haib's development strengthened the case for the planned expansion in domestic generating capacity. Imcor Zinc (Pty) Ltd, a subsidiary of South Africa's state-controlled Iron and Steel Corpn (ISCOR), has been one of the very few companies to have undertaken significant prospecting for base metals in recent years, increasing capacity at the Uis tin mine by 30% and at the Rosh Pinah zinc/lead mine by 25%. Output at Rosh Pinah increased by 4% in 1998, to 55,600 tons of concentrates. A new company, Rosh Pinah Zinc Corpn, was established in May 1999 as a joint venture between ISCOR and PE Minerals, which holds the mineral rights to the mine. Work on the nearby Skorpion zinc project, by Anglo American Corpn of South Africa, was due to commence in 2000, with production scheduled from 2002. Proven reserves of 18m. tons of high-grade zinc were to be exploited at an estimated cost of US $280m. in an open-cast mine and on-site refinery.

A variety of other minerals are already mined on a small scale. The most significant of these is salt, of which 502,000 metric tons were produced in 1998. Namibia is the primary source of industrial salt for the whole of southern Africa. TCL is investigating small gold prospects, and the Navacheb gold mine in central Namibia, a joint Anglo American and CDM venture, began production in 1990, with total revenue reaching R60m. in 1992. Namibia has considerable offshore reserves of natural gas. The most recent estimates are of as much as 560,000m. cu m of natural gas in the Kudu field off Lüderitz. Exploration rights for the offshore Kudu gas fields are held by a consortium led by Shell, which plans to pipe gas to power stations to be constructed in Namibia and South Africa. Exploration for onshore and offshore reserves of petroleum is proceeding.

AGRICULTURE AND FISHING

War, drought, overgrazing and unscientific farming methods have had an adverse effect on the agricultural sector. The contribution of agriculture and fisheries to GDP, however, increased from 7.3% in 1986 to 12.2% in 1998. Agricultural GDP increased by an average of 2.9% in 1990–98, with growth in the fishing sector generally offsetting poorer performances in other areas of agriculture. An estimated 42.8% of Namibia's labour force were employed in the agricultural sector in 1998.

Namibia has a fragile ecology, and most of the land can support only livestock. The major agricultural activities are the processing of meat and other livestock products, and more than 90% of commercial agricultural output comprises livestock production. The most important agricultural product is beef (beef production represents some 87% of Namibia's gross non-fishing agricultural income). Ostrich farming was an expanding sector in the early 1990s, mainly in the south of the country. In early 2000 flooding caused extensive damage to ostrich farms. The only large-scale commercial arable farming is in the *karstveld* around Tsumeb, and on the Hardap irrigation scheme in the south. In the southern half of Namibia farming is based on karakul sheep, but international fashion markets for karakul pelts slumped in the 1980s: in 1990 the value of exports of karakul pelts was equivalent to only one-half of their value in 1980. Subsistence crops include beans, potatoes and maize. Although output of maize was high in 1991, the severe drought conditions of 1991/92 devastated output. In May 1992 President Nujoma appealed to the international donor community for drought relief aid. The total maize crop for 1992/93 was 32,000 tons, a considerable increase on the previous year (when the yield reached only 13,000 tons), but still below normal levels of about 35,000 tons. The agricultural sector in Namibia remains precarious, despite higher than usual amounts of rainfall in the northern part of the country during early 1995. Output was even lower than in 1994 because commercial and communal farmers planted less cereals. Rainfall in 1997 was higher than average (most dams received substantial inflows), and the situation regarding both crops and livestock was more favourable than at the start of 1996. In early 1997 President Nujoma warned of the prospect of another devastating drought and pledged that the government's Emergency Management Unit (EMU) would take appropriate measures to ensure food security. According to the EMU's preliminary assessments, some 231,000 Namibians required drought relief. The country usually imports about half of its cereals requirement, but in the drought-free years it is able to provide some 70% of local demand. In an effort to diversify agricultural production, seedless-grape plantations are being developed on the banks of the Orange river bordering South Africa. Exports of the grapes to the EU reached 2,100 tons in 1998/99 and were expected to increase tenfold by 2003, making them the second largest source of agricultural export earnings (after beef).

Colonial history bequeathed Namibia three different agricultural sectors: about 4,000 large commercial ranches, almost all white-owned; 20,000 African stock-raising households, compressed into central and southern reserves; and 120,000 black families practising mixed farming on just 5% of the viable farmland in the far north. At the time of Namibia's independence about 50% of the country's commercial farms were owned by absentee landlords, and the possible redistribution of such land was an important political issue. In mid-1991 a national land reform conference rejected calls for radical land expropriations and the abolition of freehold ownership. Nevertheless, the conference did make recommendations for reform, including bans on foreign ownership of agricultural land and on purchases of large tracts of land. In 1992 the government proposed the redistribution of 7.3m. ha of farmland owned by absentee landowners or otherwise underutilized, representing almost one-quarter of the 32m. ha owned by commercial (mostly white) farmers at independence. The Namibian government, through the Agricultural Bank of Namibia, began to grant low-interest loans to farmers in 1994. By 1999 very little farm land had been purchased by the government for redistribution, primarily because the allocated budget, totalling N $20m., had proved inadequate. The government was facing increasing pressure to take possession of commercial farmland without paying full compensation—a development that would require an amendment of the constitution, which stipulates that market prices be paid for land.

Because of the cold, nutrient-rich Benguela current, Namibia has potentially one of the richest fisheries in the world. Prior to independence, however, Namibia received no tax or licence

fees from fishing because the illegal occupation of the territory deprived it of an internationally recognized fishing zone within the usual limit of 200 nautical miles (370 km). There are, in fact, two separate fisheries off Namibia—inshore and offshore. The inshore fishery, for pilchard, anchovy and rock lobster, is controlled by Namibian and South African companies, based at Lüderitz and Walvis Bay. During the mid-1980s, however, persistent over-fishing left stocks severely depleted, and in March 1990 the new Namibian government requested foreign fleets to cease fishing Namibia's coastal waters, pending an assessment of fish stocks. Following independence the Namibian authorities enforced a 370-km Exclusive Economic Zone (EEZ), thereby achieving considerable success in restocking its waters. Under licensing arrangements implemented in 1992, 25 deep-sea trawlers were authorized to fish within Namibian coastal waters. Revenue from exports of fish and fish products provided an estimated 17.5% of total export earnings in 1997, rising steeply to 28.5% in 1998. Government revenue from fishing quota levies was projected at N 70m. in 1998/99. Fish stocks have recovered substantially since independence, and many foreign commercial companies are pressing the government to increase the annual 30,000-ton interim catch limit. Namibia's freezer-trawler hake fleet has increased to some 70 vessels, three times the number in 1991, while the number of foreign-owned ships licensed to fish in Namibian waters has fallen to about a dozen. The fishing industry went into decline in 1993, with output falling by 33% in 1996. Production subsequently recovered with average annual growth of 28% recorded in 1997–98. Onshore fish processing has increased the sector's value added. Thus, landings declined by 4% in 1997, to 488,100 tons, but export earnings increased by some 24%, to N $1,564m. In 1997 scientific surveys indicated a recovery in the pilchard stock, and the government approved a small catch quota for that year's season. The 25,000-ton total allowable catch (TAC), announced by the minister of fisheries and marine resources, was 5,000 tons more than that of 1996. The marked recovery in stocks of pilchard, hake and horse mackerel has prompted the government to increase TACs for the major species. There was a 30% reduction in the TAC for pilchard, from 65,000 tons in 1998 to 45,000 tons in 1999, and a 25% reduction in that for orange roughy over the same period. However, this was more than compensated for by the white fish catch. The TAC for hake, the most valuable of species landed, increased from 165,000 tons in 1998 to 195,000 and 210,000 tons in 1999 and 2000, respectively. While the TAC for mackerel stood unchanged at 375,000 tons in 1998 and 1999, it was raised to 410,000 tons for 2000.

Several companies reported losses for 1995; Namibian Fishing Industries (Namfish), one of the largest pelagic operators, incurred a loss of N $10.5m., and a planned merger with its associated company, Namibian Sea Products, was consequently postponed. A 1997 financial aid package for the industry was to cost the government some N $50m. in revenue during 1997/98, but was expected to reduce the chances of industry bankruptcies. However, recovered stocks and strong exports meant that a number of Namibia's largest fishing companies showed better financial results in 1998. Namfish recorded a net profit of N $21m. in the first six months of 1998, compared with a loss of N $5m. in 1997, while Sea Harvest Namibia made a profit of N $4m. in the year to September 1998, compared with a loss of N $9m. in the previous year. These increases were reflected in the fish-processing sector, resulting in considerable gains overall in the manufacturing sector in 1998 and 1999.

The fishing industry is an important source of employment, and there is considerable scope for job creation in the sector, particularly in fish-processing. Indeed, since independence the number of workers in this industry has increased from 6,000 to 9,000, and the fishing industry could soon replace mining as the largest source of private-sector employment. A fish-processing plant is under construction at Lüderitz. The factory, which will cost R18m. to construct, will provide 250 new jobs. While the two largest pelagic companies, United Fishing Enterprises (UFE) and Etosha Fisheries, operated their canneries in Walvis Bay at near-capacity levels in the 1998 season, there were reports in mid-2000 that UFE was considering suspending production owing to an oversupply of canned fish. The Kuwaiti government was to finance a N $6m. feasibility study for the construction of a new harbour at Mowe Bay, some 440 km north of Walvis Bay, for the expansion of the fishing industry. A N \$150m. investment in rehabilitating the fishing fleet and building a fish-processing plant has been planned for Walvis Bay.

OTHER SECTORS

Namibia's manufacturing sector is extremely small. It provided an estimated 16.3% of GDP in 1998, and consists mainly of processing fish, minerals and meat for export, and production of basic consumer products, such as beer and bread: food products account for about 70% of all goods produced in Namibia. During 1990–97 manufacturing GDP increased, in real terms, by an estimated annual average of 3.9%. Manufacturing output was severely affected by lower fish-processing levels in 1996 with sectoral GDP declining by 6.5% in that year, but its contribution to GDP increased in 1997, with a partial recovery in fish production and the initiation of additional plants in the export processing zone (EPZ): manufacturing GDP increased by 8.0% in 1997. The development of the manufacturing sector has been limited by fluctuations in the supply of cattle and fish, by the small domestic market, by the high cost of energy and transport, and by the lack of an educated entrepreneurial class. Furthermore, Namibia's traditional dependence on South Africa for most manufactured goods has resulted in the underdevelopment of the sector. There are 278 manufacturing firms, mostly located in or near the main urban centres.

The Export Processing Zone Act was approved in 1995, establishing an EPZ in Walvis Bay and allowing others to follow. Seven companies were approved for EPZ status in 1995. The largest of these, Purity Manganese, announced plans to construct a N \$30m. industrial pipe-manufacturing facility. Although the government has banned strikes in the EPZ, all other labour legislation was in force from 1996. The German KFW development bank has financed a N \$12m. strategic development plan for Walvis Bay and Lüderitz harbour. In 1997 the European Commission granted N \$32m. (US \$7.2m.) to develop the EPZ project and to strengthen Namibia's capacity to attract investment and expand foreign trade. Funding was reserved for EPZ infrastructure and services, investment promotion and the establishment of a Namibian Exporters' Association. In the Walvis Bay EPZ, the N \$30m. German-owned Namibia Press and Tools vehicle-components plant, which opened in 1996, was to be expanded. A further four new companies began projects in the EPZ in 1997, including a US \$25m. distillery owned by Rockwood-Heinz (France/USA). Global Textiles and Chinese Friendship Co., both clothing manufacturers, were scheduled to begin operations in 1998. However, the EPZ's incentives have failed to attract substantial investment in non-traditional manufacturing capacity. While some factories in Oshikango's EPZ, near the Angolan border, are advancing, in Walvis Bay, along the coast, several factories have closed and other EPZ projects have been postponed. In fact, only three EPZ factories were operating there in 1999. Namtex, the first EPZ operation which began in 1996, reduced its operations and now produces garments only for the domestic market, while Global Textiles and the Italian-backed MN Construction have actually closed down. A study by the trade union-affiliated Labour Resource and Research Institute claimed that by April 1999 only nine companies were operating in the EPZ. It estimated total investment in the zone at N \$130m., half the figure given by the EPZ promotional agency, the Offshore Development Company (ODC). The ODC dismissed the study as incomplete and predicted that 4,000 new jobs would be created in the zone thanks to an incoming investment of N \$7,000m.

Construction contributed only an estimated 2.9% of GDP in 1997. Following the 1993–94 expansion in commercial and residential property developments, growth in the GDP of the construction sector slowed to 2.8% in 1995. Expansion of 7.2% in 1996 was followed by a decline of 11.0% in 1997, and the sector remained depressed in 1998. However, an increase in capital spending prior to the 1999 elections and gradual reductions in interest rates were expected to boost the construction industry in that year.

The electricity and water sectors (which represented an estimated 3.0% of GDP in 1997) are somewhat more integrated and extensive than might be expected. The principal mines and

towns are linked in a national grid, which can be fed by the 120-MW Van Eck power station outside Windhoek, the hydroelectric station at Ruacana (which has a generating capacity of up to 320 MW) on the Kunene river, and the 45-MW Paratus scheme at Walvis Bay. There is a link to the system operated by South Africa's Electricity Supply Commission (ESKOM), and the Zambia Electricity Supply Corpn provides electricity to the Caprivi region. The Oranjemund diamond mine, however, draws its supply directly from ESKOM, and is not connected to the Namibian grid. In 1991 Namibia and Angola signed an agreement on the further development of the Kunene river as a source of energy. The planned Epupa hydroelectric scheme, on the Kunene river, continues to attract controversy. Fears have been expressed that the dam will disrupt the area's ecology and displace the Himba people. A 30-month study, costing N \$4.8m. began in mid-1995. In 1999 the Namang consortium of consultants submitted its final report, concluding that there would be significant environmental consequences, but that the dam would none the less be the most efficient, and least expensive, method of increasing Namibia's electricity generating capacity. There is, however, a significant difference in approach between the two governments which may delay the project indefinitely. While Namibia prefers the construction of a reservoir at Epupa Falls, at an estimated cost of N \$539m., Angola favours a smaller, slightly more costly, but less ecologically damaging site at Baynes Mountains. Electricity sales to domestic consumers decreased by 0.5% in 1993, despite an increase of 17% in the number of customers. In that year, municipalities consumed more electricity than the mines for the first time. Drought led to a 49m. kWh reduction in hydroelectric power exports, to 204m. kWh in 1993. Owing to low water levels in the Kunene river, only one of the three turbines at the Ruacana hydroelectric station was operating in 1996. For this reason, the Namibia Power Corpn (Nampower) increased electricity rates by 8.5% for large users, and by 3.5% for smaller users. In 1996/97 Nampower imported electricity costing N \$60m. from ESKOM to cover the shortfall from Ruacana. Lower electricity imports were expected in 1998/99 and charges had been reduced under a new tariff agreement between the two utilities. Work began in 1999 on a second power interconnector to the South African grid, at a cost of N \$870m.; this is to be Namibia's largest post-independence construction project.

Mines and towns in Namibia's white-inhabited areas are also the main places served by the long-distance water supply. Windhoek and its surrounding mines are supplied from a number of dams, which came under severe pressure in the recent drought. Rössing, Walvis Bay and Swakopmund draw their water from boreholes in a series of dry river-beds. Both the Tsumeb and coastal underground reserves are under strain, and the long-term plan is to connect the two systems together, and to draw water from the Okavango river in the extreme north of the country. In November 1987 the former interim government and South Africa signed an agreement on the use of water from the Orange river, which forms the border between Namibia and South Africa. Construction of southern Africa's first sea water desalination plant at Walvis Bay was expected to begin in 1998, at a cost of some N \$90m. The principal customers were to be the Rössing uranium mine and EPZ developments at Walvis Bay.

Tourism is playing an increasingly important role in the economy. Some 282,000 tourists visited Namibia in 1991, contributing R32m. to the economy. By 1998 tourist numbers had increased to 559,674. Receipts totalled US \$336m. in 1997. In 1995 a new N \$60m. hotel and entertainment complex was built in Swakopmund, housing Namibia's first casino and employing 700 people in the hospitality sector. Owing to increasing pressure from church leaders, the government has announced the establishment of a new special commission to determine the effects of the casinos and gambling houses act. The minister of environment and tourism was concerned that the government had insufficient resources to monitor the numerous legal (not to mention illegal) gambling establishments, which rapidly came into existence following their legalization in 1995. In 1997 TransNamib was to commence a new twice-weekly 'desert express' rail service linking Windhoek and Swakopmund. The government has also promoted the development of 'eco-tourism' in Namibia. The Namibian government appears to intend to introduce a liberalized air policy, with the minister responsible for transport deciding not to object to a proposal by Kalahari Express Airlines (KEA) that services operate between Windhoek, Cape Town and Johannesburg, despite strong criticism from Air Namibia, the state airline. In 1998 Air Namibia signed a co-operation agreement with a German airline, LTU, under which joint flights were to be operated to Frankfurt, Dusseldorf and Munich. Air Namibia is to be transferred to majority (70%) private ownership. The airline registered a loss of N $49m. in 1997, and the government provided a N $20m. guarantee to assist in raising new capital. Air Namibia has notably encountered increased operating costs and additional competition from German airlines on its main international route to Frankfurt. In 1999 it entered a partnership agreement with South African Airways to co-ordinate flight schedules to ease interconnections between each airline's flights. Also in 1999 Air Namibia added a fourth weekly flight to London, United Kingdom. Quickjet, a new locally-owned airline, was denied authorization to commence operations from Windhoek's Eros Airport.

The newly-completed Trans-Kalahari highway is an important development for regional trade and economic integration. The highway provides a link between Walvis Bay and South Africa's important Gauteng industrial area. However, until Walvis Bay's harbour development programme is completed the port is likely to remain underutilized. Currently Walvis Bay attracts only a 1% share of container traffic to southern Africa because it is too shallow. A project to deepen the port to 12.8m began in February 2000. When completed, it should enable Walvis Bay to receive container vessels with a capacity of 2,200–2,400 tons, allowing the port to attract at least some of the business currently using the South African ports of Cape Town and Durban.

FOREIGN TRADE

Namibia's principal trade partners have included the United Kingdom, South Africa, Switzerland, Germany, Japan and the USA. Namibia's exports and imports have continued to grow since 1993. Exports amounted to US $1,343m. in that year, US $1,351m. in 1994, US $1,400m. in 1995, US $1,374m. in 1996, US $1,359m. in 1997, US $1,278m. in 1998, and an estimated US $1,450m. in 1999. Imports amounted to US $1,310m. in 1993, US $1,423m. in 1994, US $1,649m. in 1995, US $1,631m. in 1996, US $1,615m. in 1997, US $1,451m. in 1998, and an estimated US $1,500m. in 1999. In 1998 Namibia sold 43% of its exports (mostly diamonds) to the United Kingdom, 26% to South Africa, 14% to Spain and 8% to France. Principal exports in that year were diamonds (US $389m.), processed fish (US $365m.), other manufactures (US $232m.), other minerals (incl. uranium) (US $187m.) and live animals and animal products (US $102m.). Namibia's principal imports in 1997 were food, live animals, beverages and tobacco (US $404m.), machinery and electrical goods (US $251.3m.), vehicles and transport equipment (US $246.1m.), chemicals and related products (US $188m.), textiles, clothing and footwear (US $126m.) and metals and metal products (US $126m.). By far its main supplier in that year was South Africa (which accounted for 84% of all imports). Namibia's visible trade deficit was US $127.1m. in 1996, US $271.7m. in 1997, and US $172.6m. in 1998. The current account surplus was US $115.8m. in 1996, US $90.4m. in 1997, and US $161.8m. in 1998. Namibia's foreign exchange reserves reached a record level of US $250m. by the end of 1997, an increase of almost one-third on the previous year's level, mainly as a result of rising uranium sales in 1997; reserves strengthened still further in 1998 and 1999, reaching US $260m. and US $305m., respectively.

ECONOMIC PROSPECTS

Namibia will continue to be economically dominated by neighbouring South Africa for the near future. Namibia is part of the Common Monetary Area (CMA), with Lesotho, South Africa and Swaziland, and a member (with Botswana, Lesotho, South Africa and Swaziland) of the Southern African Customs Union (SACU). At independence, Namibia used the South African rand as its currency, as it still does. However, in 1993 Namibia

created its own central bank and issued its own currency, the Namibian dollar, at par with the rand. In 1999 the average exchange rate was US $1 = 6.11 rand/N $. Namibia has no plans of withdrawing from the CMA in the foreseeable future. In 1999 South Africa introduced a 14% VAT on all trade with other members of SACU, maintaining that this was necessary to redress the lack of VAT payments by South African importers. South Africa is also leading moves to restructure SACU. Moreover South Africa's free-trade agreement with the EU, signed in early 1999, will no doubt reduce tariff revenue for the customs area. Since the smaller members of SACU are so heavily dependent of these revenues, it is thought that the EU may devise a method of compensation for their losses. South Africa is the source of some 90% of Namibia's imports; in addition, South Africa has significant control over Namibia's transport infrastructure, as Namibia's only external rail links are with South Africa. In 1993 Namibia and South Africa agreed to establish joint customs control over Walvis Bay—which handles about 90% of Namibia's sea-borne trade. Although the enclave of Walvis Bay was transferred to Namibia in 1994, the port facilities (owned by a South African parastatal, Portnet) were not ceded. In late 1995, however, the harbour assets at Walvis Bay were formally transferred to Namibia, after the government paid N $30m. for the facilities (considerably below the N $66m. asked by Portnet).

At independence Namibia became a member of the Southern African Development Co-ordination Conference (SADCC), which in 1992 was reorganized as SADC.

The SWAPO government has professed commitment to a mixed economy. Its first Five-Year Development Plan (NDP1), for 1995–2000, envisages increased diversification and growth. In September 1990 Namibia joined the IMF. In December of that year liberal legislation on foreign investment was introduced, and in 1993 a programme of incentives for private-sector investment in manufacturing was announced. The incentives include tax relief, cash grants and low-interest loans for export promotion. In 1999 the government reversed increases in rates of income and corporate taxation which had been introduced in 1998. The reductions were to be accompanied by measures to broaden the tax base, including a new VAT and the closing of tax 'loopholes'. None the less, the progression of government revenue will probably stagnate, or even decline, because of lower diamond exports and the expected reduction in Namibia's corporate tax rate from 40% to 35%.

Namibia's abundant mineral reserves and rich fisheries are expected to form the basis of the nation's future economic prosperity. The economy may be expected to expand, with GDP growth of 4.5% in 2000, owing to a number of factors—for example, in the mining sector increased output of offshore diamonds and a potential resumption of copper mining at Tsumeb could increase the sector's contribution to GDP by at least 5%. Quotas for fish catches are likely to be expanded substantially, and increased catches will have a concomitant beneficial effect on manufacturing. It will be necessary to expand the severely underdeveloped manufacturing sector; at independence most of the country's essential requirements were imported. The development of the impoverished northern region of the country remains a priority. Economic advance has hitherto been accomplished primarily by the extractive industries and has not yet filtered through to the wider economy in terms of increased employment, more equitable income distribution or higher per caput incomes. None the less, Namibia has moved from colonial rule to independence with relatively little social or economic upheaval, and, indeed, with public economic policies and a physical infrastructure that should lead to long-term development and growth.

Namibia's economic progress also depends on political factors. Military involvement in the Democratic Republic of the Congo has forced the government to revise upwards its budgetary expenditure for two successive years, thereby increasing the budgetary deficit. Active engagement in the Angolan civil war has also had a negative effect on the tourism industry, hitherto one of the most promising growth sectors of the economy. There is a real danger that the consequences of involvement in these conflicts may undermine Namibia's stability and economic prospects.

Statistical Survey

Area and Population

AREA, POPULATION AND DENSITY*

Area (sq km)	824,292†
Population (census results)	
May 1981	1,033,196
21 October 1991	
Males	686,327
Females	723,593
Total	1,409,920
Population (official estimates at mid-year)	
1994	1,546,000
1995	1,594,000
1996	1,643,000
Density (per sq km) at mid-1996	2.0

* Including data for Walvis Bay, sovereignty over which was transferred from South Africa to Namibia with effect from March 1994. Walvis Bay has an area of 1,124 sq km (434 sq miles) and had a population of 20,800 in 1981.

† 318,261 sq miles.

ETHNIC GROUPS (population, 1988 estimate)

Ovambo	623,000	Caprivian	. . . .	47,000
Kavango	117,000	Bushmen	. . . .	36,000
Damara	94,000	Baster.	. . . .	31,000
Herero	94,000	Tswana	. . . .	7,000
White .	80,000	Others.	. . . .	12,000
Nama .	60,000	**Total**	. . . .	**1,252,000**
Coloured	51,000			

PRINCIPAL TOWN

Windhoek (capital), population 147,056 at 1991 census (Source: UN, *Demographic Yearbook*).

BIRTHS AND DEATHS (UN estimates, annual averages)

	1980–85	1985–90	1990–95
Birth rate (per 1,000). . .	40.5	39.4	37.5
Death rate (per 1,000) . .	13.6	12.2	10.7

Expectation of life (UN estimates, years at birth, 1990–95): 58.5 (males 57.2; females 59.9).

Source: UN, *World Population Prospects: The 1998 Revision*.

ECONOMICALLY ACTIVE POPULATION
(persons aged 10 years and over, 1991 census)

	Males	Females	Total
Agriculture, hunting, forestry and fishing	99,987	89,942	189,929
Mining and quarrying . .	13,837	849	14,686
Manufacturing	10,773	12,111	22,884
Electricity, gas and water. .	2,826	148	2,974
Construction.	18,137	501	18,638
Trade, restaurants and hotels. .	19,678	18,142	37,820
Transport, storage and communications	8,003	1,319	9,322
Financing, insurance, real estate and business services . .	5,180	3,367	8,547
Community, social and personal services	3,664	2,163	5,827
Activities not adequately defined .	39,224	44,490	83,714
Total employed	**221,309**	**173,032**	**394,341**
Unemployed	57,263	41,976	99,239
Total labour force . . .	**278,572**	**215,008**	**493,580**

Source: ILO, *Yearbook of Labour Statistics*.

Agriculture

PRINCIPAL CROPS ('000 metric tons)

	1996	1997	1998
Wheat	3	6	3
Maize	19	50	15
Millet	57	108	35
Sorghum	8	10	2
Roots and tubers* . . .	230	240	250
Pulses*	8	8	7
Vegetables*	9	9	8
Fruit*	10	10	9

* FAO estimates.

Source: FAO, *Production Yearbook*.

LIVESTOCK ('000 head, year ending September)

	1996	1997	1998
Horses	57	57	53
Mules*	7	7	7
Asses*	70	71	69
Cattle	1,990	2,055	2,192
Pigs.	19	17	15
Sheep	2,198	2,429	2,086
Goats	1,786	1,821	1,710

Poultry (million)*: 2 in 1996; 2 in 1997; 2 in 1998.

* FAO estimates.

Source: FAO, *Production Yearbook*.

LIVESTOCK PRODUCTS (FAO estimates, '000 metric tons)

	1996	1997	1998
Beef and veal	46	50	55
Mutton and lamb . . .	6	9	5
Goat meat	5	5	5
Pig meat	2	2	2
Poultry meat	3	3	3
Other meat	3	4	4
Cows' milk	71	74	79
Hen eggs	2	2	2
Wool:			
greasy.	2	2	2
scoured	1	1	1
Cattle hides	5	6	7
Sheepskins	1	1	1
Goatskins	1	1	1

Source: FAO, *Production Yearbook*.

Forestry

Separate figures are not yet available. Data for Namibia are included in those for South Africa.

Fishing*

('000 metric tons, live weight)

	1995	1996	1997
Cape hakes (Stokvisse) . . .	118.9	115.0	116.9
Alfonsinos	0.9	1.8	10.4
Orange roughy	6.4	13.4	15.6
Cape monk	9.9	9.0	10.3
Cape horse mackerel (Maasbanker)	52.2	92.3	89.2
Southern African pilchard . .	42.8	1.2	27.9
Southern African anchovy . .	48.0	1.1	2.5
Whitehead's round herring . .	1.9	20.7	5.1
Other fishes (incl. unspecified) .	10.7	11.9	12.5
Total fish	291.7	266.4	290.4
Crustaceans and molluscs . .	0.4	0.5	0.7
Total catch	292.2	267.0	291.1
Inland waters	1.2	1.2	1.5
Atlantic Ocean	291.0	265.8	289.6

* Figures include quantities caught by licensed foreign vessels in Namibian waters and processed in Lüderitz and Walvis Bay. The data exclude aquatic mammals (whales, seals, etc.). The number of South African fur seals caught was: 20,450 in 1995; 20,814 in 1996; 25,783 in 1997.

Source: FAO, *Yearbook of Fishery Statistics.*

Mining

('000 metric tons, unless otherwise indicated)

	1995	1996	1997
Diamonds ('000 carats) . . .	1,381.8	1,402.1	1,416.3
Uranium (metric tons) . . .	2,579.4	2,883.5	3,415.0
Copper	29.8	16.6	16.0
Lead	26.8	8.5	0.5
Zinc	59.2	35.8	40.5
Gold (kilograms)	2,099.0	2,015.0	2,302.0

Source: IMF, *Namibia: Statistical Appendix* (February 1999).

Industry

SELECTED PRODUCTS ('000 metric tons, unless otherwise indicated)

	1994	1995	1996
Unrefined copper (unwrought) .	29.8	29.8	25.1
Refined lead (unwrought)* . .	23.8	26.8	18.8
Refined cadmium (unwrought— metric tons)	19	15	13

Source: US Bureau of Mines in UN, *Industrial Commodity Statistics Yearbook.*

Finance

CURRENCY AND EXCHANGE RATES

Monetary Units
100 cents = 1 Namibian dollar (N $).

Sterling, US Dollar and Euro Equivalents (28 April 2000)
£1 sterling = N $10.6921;
US $1 = N $6.8185;
€1 = N $6.1946;
N $1,000 = £93.53 = US $146.66 = € 161.43.

Average Exchange Rate (N $ per US $)
1997   4.60796
1998   5.52828
1999   6.10948

Note: The Namibian dollar was introduced in September 1993, replacing (at par) the South African rand. The rand remained legal tender in Namibia.

CENTRAL GOVERNMENT BUDGET
(N $ million, year ending 31 March)

Revenue*	1996/97	1997/98†	1998/99‡
Taxation	4,114.0	5,102.5	5,382.5
Taxes on income, profits and capital gains . . .	1,353.9	1,979.1	1,785.7
Individual taxes . . .	847.0	965.9	998.7
Corporate taxes . . .	416.3	939.2	708.0
Mining companies . .	134.7	533.6	261.0
Non-mining companies .	281.6	405.6	447.0
Domestic taxes on goods and services	1,342.0	1,487.2	1,712.5
General sales tax . .	663.8	756.3	885.0
Additional sales duties .	286.8	327.9	354.0
Fuel levies . . .	283.9	315.6	360.0
Fishing quota levies . .	74.0	61.7	70.0
Taxes on international trade and transactions . . .	1,348.7	1,560.4	1,805.2
Other current revenue . .	497.6	485.9	651.1
Entrepreneurial and property income . . .	303.5	300.6	384.0
Royalties on diamond exports .	204.2	198.8	249.9
Administrative fees and charges, non-industrial and incidental sales . . .	183.3	171.7	257.1
Total	4,611.6	5,588.4	6,033.6

Expenditure‡	1996/97	1997/98	1998/99
General public services . .	691.5	789.6	1,024.2
Defence	293.8	415.6	442.6
Public order and safety . .	327.4	371.4	492.2
Education	1,176.4	1,523.6	1,700.6
Health	524.2	611.6	712.6
Social security and welfare . .	275.9	280.7	320.8
Housing and community amenities	330.8	366.2	409.0
Recreational, cultural and religious affairs and services .	129.2	149.2	166.4
Economic affairs and services .	821.9	976.5	1,045.4
Agriculture, forestry, fishing and hunting . . .	365.5	420.5	490.5
Transport and communications .	307.8	409.1	320.3
Other purposes . . .	474.4	209.7	411.7
Total	5,045.3	5,694.2	6,755.5
Current expenditure . . .	4,261.4	4,775.4	5,901.4
Capital expenditure . . .	674.9	846.8	814.4
Net lending	109.1	92.0	39.8

* Excluding grants received from abroad (N $ million): 50.3 in 1996/97; 54.0† in 1997/98; 45.7‡ in 1998/99.
† Preliminary out-turn.
‡ Budget forecasts.
Source: IMF, *Namibia: Statistical Appendix* (February 1999).

INTERNATIONAL RESERVES (US $ million at 31 December)

	1997	1998	1999
IMF special drawing rights . .	0.02	0.02	0.02
Reserve position in IMF . .	0.04	0.05	0.05
Foreign exchange . . .	250.47	260.18	305.42
Total	250.53	260.25	305.49

Source: IMF, *International Financial Statistics.*

MONEY SUPPLY (N $ million at 31 December)

	1997	1998	1999
Demand deposits at deposit money banks	2,562.5	3,315.9	3,370.9
Total money . . .	2,898.1	3,680.9	3,793.6

Source: IMF, *International Financial Statistics.*

COST OF LIVING
(Consumer Price Index for Windhoek; base: 1995 = 100)

	1996	1997	1998
All items	108.0	117.5	124.8

Source: IMF, *International Financial Statistics.*

NATIONAL ACCOUNTS (N $ million at current prices)
National Income and Product

	1995	1996	1997
Compensation of employees . .	5,135	5,727	6,343
Operating surplus . . .	3,400	3,928	4,329
Domestic factor incomes . .	8,536	9,655	10,672
Consumption of fixed capital . .	1,694	2,093	2,230
Gross domestic product (GDP) at factor cost . . .	10,230	11,748	12,902
Indirect taxes	2,025	2,164	2,377
Less Subsidies	156	199	164
GDP in purchasers' values .	12,099	13,712	15,115
Factor income received from abroad	1,370	1,383	1,192
Less Factor income paid abroad .	896	1,066	944
Gross national product . .	12,573	14,029	15,363
Less Consumption of fixed capital .	1,694	2,093	2,230
National income in market prices	10,879	11,936	13,133
Other current transfers from abroad	1,548	1,880	2,047
Less Other current transfers paid abroad	512	544	565
National disposable income .	11,916	13,272	14,614

Source: IMF, Namibia: *Statistical Appendix* (February 1999).

Expenditure on the Gross Domestic Product

	1995	1996	1997
Government final consumption expenditure . . .	3,758	4,292	4,728
Private final consumption expenditure	6,790	7,565	8,240
Increase in stocks . . .	−115	−137	−141
Gross fixed capital formation . .	2,619	3,222	3,126
Total domestic expenditure .	13,052	14,942	15,954
Exports of goods and services .	6,244	7,348	7,954
Less Imports of goods and services	7,197	8,578	8,793
GDP in purchasers' values .	12,099	13,712	15,115

Source: IMF, *Namibia: Statistical Appendix* (February 1999).

Gross Domestic Product by Economic Activity

	1995	1996	1997
Agriculture, hunting, forestry and fishing	1,285	1,420	1,416
Mining and quarrying . . .	1,146	1,654	1,764
Manufacturing	1,611	1,552	1,854
Electricity, gas and water . .	279	373	405
Construction	346	405	392
Trade, restaurants and hotels .	1,056	1,142	1,325
Transport, storage and communications	496	509	609
Finance, insurance, real estate and business services* . .	1,331	1,584	1,768
Government services . . .	2,755	3,177	3,521
Other community, social and personal services . . .	127	143	159
Other services	267	294	319
Sub-total	10,699	12,253	13,531
Less Imputed bank service charge	352	457	493
GDP at basic prices . . .	10,347	11,796	13,038
Import duties	425	454	483
Other taxes on products . . .	1,327	1,462	1,594
GDP in purchasers' values . .	12,099	13,712	15,115

* Including imputed rents of owner-occupied dwellings (N $ million): 580 in 1995; 642 in 1996; 717 in 1997.

Source: IMF, *Namibia: Statistical Appendix* (February 1999).

BALANCE OF PAYMENTS (US $ million)

	1996	1997	1998
Exports of goods f.o.b. . . .	1,403.7	1,343.3	1,278.3
Imports of goods f.o.b. . . .	−1,530.9	−1,615.0	−1,450.9
Trade balance	−127.1	−271.7	−172.6
Exports of services . . .	337.4	380.1	327.0
Imports of services . . .	−580.9	−533.7	−456.9
Balance on goods and services	−370.7	−425.2	−302.4
Other income received . . .	319.2	252.0	226.7
Other income paid . . .	−249.0	−180.6	−165.9
Balance on goods, services and income	−300.5	−353.8	−241.6
Current transfers received . .	437.3	462.2	418.2
Current transfers paid . .	−21.0	−18.0	−14.7
Current balance . . .	115.8	90.4	161.8
Capital account (net) . . .	42.1	33.5	23.8
Direct investment abroad . .	21.7	−0.7	2.2
Direct investment from abroad .	128.7	91.0	96.2
Portfolio investment assets . .	−8.1	−14.6	−11.1
Portfolio investment liabilities .	31.2	26.0	−4.4
Other investment assets . .	−411.2	−289.9	−175.5
Other investment liabilities .	63.8	116.7	−53.1
Net errors and omissions . .	39.1	15.3	15.7
Overall balance . . .	22.9	67.8	55.8

Source: IMF, *International Financial Statistics.*

External Trade

PRINCIPAL COMMODITIES (US $ million)

Imports c.i.f.	1995	1996	1997
Food and live animals . . . } Beverages and tobacco . . . }	332.2	348.7	404.0
Mineral fuels and lubricants . .	87.7	96.3	99.0
Chemicals and related products .	170.1	186.5	188.2
Wood, paper and paper products (incl. furniture) . . .	101.2	89.3	92.2
Textiles, clothing and footwear .	117.4	125.6	126.3
Metals and metal products .	127.4	122.3	126.3
Machinery (incl. electrical) . .	305.2	266.6	251.3
Transport equipment . . .	275.2	274.2	246.1
Total (incl. others)	1,648.4	1,630.9	1,675.0

Exports f.o.b.	1995	1996	1997
Food and live animals . .	483.7	504.6	367.7
Live animals chiefly for food .	133.2	144.2	60.7
Cattle . . .	67.3	94.8	23.9
Sheep and goats . .	59.0	43.5	31.4
Meat and meat preparations .	101.4	82.3	62.5
Beef and veal . . .	83.6	66.0	49.7
Fish, crustaceans and			
molluscs . . .	240.8	271.1	238.0
Mineral products . . .	717.7	773.9	814.2
Diamonds	472.2	524.2	541.4
Copper	65.6	43.5	53.1
Gold	26.9	27.4	45.5
Manufactured products . .	160.2	59.2	154.7
Canned fish, fish meal and fish			
oil	130.1	33.4	111.5
Total (incl. others)* . .	1,399.9	1,374.4	1,359.2

* Total includes exports of diamonds imported from Angola, and exports of merchandise to Angola as barter for diamonds (US $ million) 16.5 in 1995; 17.4 in 1996; 5.2 in 1997.

Source: IMF, *Namibia: Statistical Appendix* (February 1999).

PRINCIPAL TRADING PARTNERS

Imports c.i.f. (US $ million)	1995	1996	1997
Germany	29.7	23.7	33.3
Norway	16.2	3.4	2.9
Russia	13.4	9.5	17.3
South Africa	1,431.7	1,443.4	1,412.7
United Kingdom . . .	25.5	15.8	7.2
USA	22.6	35.9	69.0
Zimbabwe	17.0	18.7	7.1
Total (incl. others) . . .	1,648.6	1,630.9	1,675.0

Source: IMF, *Namibia: Statistical Appendix* (February 1999).

Exports f.o.b. (N $ million)	1993
Belgium	232
Côte d'Ivoire	70
France	87
Germany	140
Japan	411
South Africa	1,153
Spain	258
Switzerland	74
United Kingdom	1,450
USA	51
Total (incl. others)	4,213

Source: Bank of Namibia, Windhoek.

Transport

RAILWAYS

	1994/95	1995/96
Freight (million net ton-km)	1,077	1,082
Passengers carried ('000)	110	124

Source: TransNamib Ltd, Windhoek.

ROAD TRAFFIC (motor vehicles in use at 31 December)

	1994*	1995*	1996
Passenger cars	61,269	62,500	74,875
Buses and coaches . . .	5,098	5,200	n.a.
Lorries and vans	60,041	61,300	59,352
Motorcycles and mopeds . .	1,450	1,480	1,520

* Estimates.

Source: International Road Federation, *World Road Statistics*.

SHIPPING
Merchant Fleet (at 31 December)

	1996	1997	1998
Number of vessels . . .	114	104	105
Displacement (gross registered tons)	58,591	55,263	54,794

Source: Lloyd's Register of Shipping, *World Fleet Statistics*.

Sea-borne Freight Traffic (at Walvis Bay, '000 metric tons)

	1995/96
Goods loaded	1,132
Goods unloaded	644

Source: Namibian Ports Authority, Walvis Bay.

CIVIL AVIATION (traffic on scheduled services)

	1994/95	1995/96
Kilometres flown (million)	6.6	7.2
Passengers carried ('000)	209	227
Passenger-km (million)	718	756
Freight ton-km (million)	26	23

Source: TransNamib Ltd, Windhoek.

Tourism

FOREIGN TOURIST ARRIVALS*

Country of origin	1996	1997	1998
Angola	144,915	158,188	177,316
Botswana	16,011	17,695	19,589
Germany	50,899	54,952	59,632
South Africa	172,544	187,687	209,318
United Kingdom . . .	11,562	12,555	13,992
Total (incl. others) . . .	461,310	502,012	559,674

* Excluding same-day visitors: 63,752 in 1996; 69,162 in 1997.

Tourism receipts (US $ million): 297 in 1996; 336 in 1997.

Source: World Tourism Organization, *Yearbook of Tourism Statistics*.

Communications Media

	1995	1996	1997
Radio receivers ('000 in use) . .	215	225	232
Television receivers ('000 in use) .	39	50	60
Telephones ('000 main lines in use)*	78	86	n.a.
Mobile cellular telephones (subscribers)*	3,500	6,644	n.a.

* Year ending 30 September.

Sources: UNESCO, *Statistical Yearbook*; UN, *Statistical Yearbook*.

Daily newspapers: 4 (average circulation 9,500 copies) in 1997.
Non-daily newspapers: 5 (average circulation 9,100 copies) in 1997.
Source: Ministry of Information and Broadcasting, Windhoek.

Education

(1998)

	Students		
	Males	Females	Total
Primary	200,667	199,658	400,325
Secondary:			
General	54,587	60,560	115,147
Vocational	20	70	90

Pre-primary: 4,579 students (males 2,273; females 2,306) in 1994.
Tertiary: 11,344 students (males 4,440; females 6,904) in 1995.
Source: UNESCO, *Statistical Yearbook*.

Directory

The Constitution

The Constitution of the Republic of Namibia took effect at independence on 21 March 1990. Its principal provisions are summarized below:

THE REPUBLIC

The Republic of Namibia is a sovereign, secular, democratic and unitary State and the Constitution is the supreme law.

FUNDAMENTAL HUMAN RIGHTS AND FREEDOMS

The fundamental rights and freedoms of the individual are guaranteed regardless of sex, race, colour, ethnic origin, religion, creed or social or economic status. All citizens shall have the right to form and join political parties. The practice of racial discrimination shall be prohibited.

THE PRESIDENT

Executive power shall be vested in the President and the Cabinet. The President shall be the Head of State and of the Government and the Commander-in-Chief of the Defence Force. The President shall be directly elected by universal and equal adult suffrage, and must receive more than 50% of the votes cast. The term of office shall be five years; one person may not hold the office of President for more than two terms*.

THE CABINET

The Cabinet shall consist of the President, the Prime Minister and such other ministers as the President may appoint from members of the National Assembly. The President may also appoint a Deputy Prime Minister. The functions of the members of the Cabinet shall include directing the activities of ministries and government departments, initiating bills for submission to the National Assembly, formulating, explaining and assessing for the National Assembly the budget of the State and its economic development plans, formulating, explaining and analysing for the National Assembly Namibia's foreign policy and foreign trade policy and advising the President on the state of national defence.

THE NATIONAL ASSEMBLY

Legislative power shall be vested in the National Assembly, which shall be composed of 72 members elected by general, direct and secret ballots and not more than six non-voting members appointed by the President by virtue of their special expertise, status, skill or experience. Every National Assembly shall continue for a maximum period of five years, but it may be dissolved by the President before the expiry of its term.

THE NATIONAL COUNCIL

The National Council shall consist of two members from each region (elected by regional councils from among their members) and shall have a life of six years. The functions of the National Council shall include considering all bills passed by the National Assembly, investigating any subordinate legislation referred to it by the National Assembly for advice, and recommending legislation to the National Assembly on matters of regional concern.

OTHER PROVISIONS

Other provisions relate to the administration of justice (see under Judicial System), regional and local government, the public service commission, the security commission, the police, defence forces and prison service, finance, and the central bank and national planning commission. The repeal of, or amendments to, the Constitution require the approval of two-thirds of the members of the National Assembly and two-thirds of the members of the National Council; if the proposed repeal or amendment secures a majority of two-thirds of the members of the National Assembly, but not a majority of two-thirds of the members of the National Council, the President may make the proposals the subject of a national referendum, in which a two-thirds' majority is needed for approval of the legislation.

* In late 1998 the National Assembly and National Council approved legislation whereby the Constitution was to be exceptionally amended to allow the incumbent President to seek a third term of office.

The Government

HEAD OF STATE

President and Commander-in-Chief of the Defence Force: Dr SAMUEL DANIEL NUJOMA (took office 21 March 1990; elected by direct suffrage 7–8 December 1994; re-elected 30 November–1 December 1999).

CABINET
(August 2000)

President: Dr SAMUEL DANIEL NUJOMA.

Prime Minister: HAGE GEINGOB.

Deputy Prime Minister: Rev. HENDRIK WITBOOI.

Minister of Home Affairs: JERRY EKANDJO.

Minister of Foreign Affairs, Information and Broadcasting: THEO-BEN GURIRAB.

Minister of Basic Education, Youth and Culture: JOHN MUTORWA.

Minister of Higher Education, Vocational Training, Science and Technology and Sport: NAHAS ANGULA.

Minister of Mines and Energy: JESAYA NYAMU.

Minister of Justice and Attorney-General: Dr NGARIJUTUKE TJIRIANGE.

Minister of Trade and Industry: HIDIPO HAMUTENYA.

Minister of Agriculture, Water and Rural Development: HELMUT ANGULA.

Minister of Defence: ERIKKI NGHIMTINA.

Minister of Finance: NANGOLO MBUMBA.

Minister of Health and Social Services: Dr LIBERTINE AMATHILA.

Minister of Labour: ANDIMA TOIVO YA TOIVO.

Minister of Regional and Local Government and Housing: NICKEY IYAMBO.

Minister of Environment and Tourism: PHILEMON MWALIMA.

Minister of Works, Transport and Communications: MOSES AMWEELO.

Minister of Lands, Resettlement and Rehabilitation: PENDUKENI ITHANA.

Minister of Fisheries and Marine Resources: ABRAHAM IYAMBO.

Minister of Prisons and Correctional Services: MARCO HAUSIKU.

Minister of Women's Development and Child Welfare: NET-UMBO NDAITWAH.

MINISTRIES

Office of the President: State House, Robert Mugabe Ave, PMB 13339, Windhoek; tel. (61) 2707111; fax (61) 221780.

Office of the Prime Minister: Robert Mugabe Ave, PMB 13338, Windhoek; tel. (61) 2879111; fax (61) 230648.

Ministry of Agriculture, Water and Rural Development: cnr Robert Mugabe Ave and Peter Muller St, PMB 13184, Windhoek; tel. (61) 2087111; fax (61) 229961.

Ministry of Basic Education, Youth and Culture: Troskie House, Uhland St, PMB 13186, Windhoek; tel. (61) 2933111; fax (61) 224277.

Ministry of Defence: Private Bag 13307, Windhoek; tel. (61) 2049111; fax (61) 232518.

Ministry of Environment and Tourism: Swabou Bldg, Post St Mall, PMB 13346, Windhoek; tel. (61) 2842111; fax (61) 221930; e-mail tourism@iwwn.com.na; internet www.tourism.com.na.

Ministry of Finance: Fiscus Bldg, John Meinert St, PMB 13295, Windhoek; tel. (61) 2099111; fax (61) 236454.

Ministry of Fisheries and Marine Resources: Metje Behnsen Bldg, PMB 13355, Windhoek; tel. (61) 2053911; fax (61) 233286.

Ministry of Foreign Affairs, Information and Broadcasting: Govt Bldgs, Robert Mugabe Ave, PMB 13347, Windhoek; tel. (61) 2829111; fax (61) 223937; e-mail headquarters@mfa.gov.na; internet www.mfa.gov.na.

Ministry of Health and Social Services: Old State Hospital, Harvey St, PMB 13198, Windhoek; tel. (61) 2039111; fax (61) 227607.

Ministry of Higher Education, Vocational Training, Science and Technology and Sport: Winco Bldg, Stuebel St, PMB 13391, Windhoek; tel. (61) 2706111; fax (61) 253671.

Ministry of Home Affairs: Cohen Bldg, Kasino St, PMB 13200, Windhoek; tel.(61) 2922111; fax (61) 2922185.

Ministry of Justice: Justitia Bldg, Independence Ave, PMB 13248, Windhoek; tel. (61) 2805111; fax (61) 221615.

Ministry of Labour: 32 Mercedes St, Khomasdal, PMB 19005, Windhoek; tel. (61) 2066111; fax (61) 212323.

Ministry of Lands, Resettlement and Rehabilitation: Brendan Simbwaye Bldg, Goethe St, PMB 13343, Windhoek; tel. (61) 2852111; fax (61) 254737.

Ministry of Mines and Energy: 1st Aviation Rd, PMB 13297, Windhoek; tel. (61) 2848111; fax (61) 238643; e-mail info@mme .gov.na; internet www.mme.gov.na.

Ministry of Prisons and Correctional Services: Brendan Simbwaye Bldg, Goethe St, PMB 13323; tel. (61) 2846111; fax (61) 233879.

Ministry of Regional and Local Government and Housing: PMB 13289, Windhoek; tel. (61) 2975111; fax (61) 226049.

Ministry of Trade and Industry: Govt Bldgs, Private Bag 13340, Windhoek; tel. (61) 2837111; fax (61) 220148.

Ministry of Women's Development and Child Promotion: Windhoek.

Ministry of Works, Transport and Communications: Private Bag 13341, Windhoek; tel. (61) 2088111; fax (61) 228560.

President and Legislature

PRESIDENT

Presidential Election, 30 November–1 December 1999

Candidate	% of votes
SAMUEL NUJOMA (SWAPO)	76.8
BEN ULENGA (CoD)	10.5
KATUUTIRE KAURA (DTA)	9.6
JUSTUS GAROEB (UDF)	3.0
Total	**100.0**

NATIONAL ASSEMBLY

Speaker: Dr MOSES TJITENDERO.

General Election, 30 November–1 December 1999

Party	% of votes	Seats
South West Africa People's Organisation of Namibia (SWAPO)	76.1	55
Congress of Democrats (CoD)	9.9	7
Democratic Turnhalle Alliance of Namibia (DTA)	9.5	7
United Democratic Front (UDF)	2.9	2
Monitor Action Group (MAG)	0.7	1
Others	0.9	—
Total	**100.0**	**72**

* In addition to the 72 directly-elected members, the President of the Republic is empowered to nominate as many as six non-voting members.

NATIONAL COUNCIL

Chairman: KANDINDIMA NEHOVA.

The second chamber of parliament is the advisory National Council, comprising two representatives from each of the country's 13 Regional Councils, elected for a period of six years.

Political Organizations

Christian Democratic Action for Social Justice (CDA): Ondwangwa; f. 1982; supported by Ovambos and mems of fmr National Democratic Party; Leader Rev. PETER KALANGULA.

Congress of Democrats (COD): Windhoek; internet http://cod .namweb.com.na; f. 1999; Leader BEN ULENGA; Sec.-Gen. TSUDAO GURIRAB.

Democratic Coalition of Namibia (DCN): Windhoek; f. 1994 as coalition of the National Patriotic Front, the South West African National Union (withdrew from coalition in Nov. 1994) and the German Union; Leader MOSES KATJIUONGUA.

Democratic Turnhalle Alliance of Namibia (DTA): POB 173, Windhoek; f. 1977 as a coalition of ethnically-based political groupings; reorg. as a single party in 1991; Pres. KATUUTIRE KAURA; Chair. PIET JUNIUS; Sec.-Gen. MIKE VENAAN.

Federal Convention of Namibia (FCN): Windhoek; f. 1988; Leader JOHANNES DIERGAARDT; federalist; opposes unitary form of govt for Namibia; an alliance of ethnically-based parties, including:

NUDO–Progressive Party Jo'Horongo: f. 1987; Pres. MBU-RUMBA KERINA.

Rehoboth Bevryde Demokratiese Party (Rehoboth Free Democratic Party or **Liberation Front) (RBDP):** Leader JOHANNES DIERGAARDT; coalition of the **Rehoboth Bevrydings-party** (Leader JOHANNES DIERGAARDT) and the **Rehoboth Democratic Party** (Leader K. G. FREIGANG).

Monitor Action Group (MAG): POB 80808, Olympia, Windhoek; f. 1991; fmrly National Party of South West Africa; Leader KOSIE PRETORIUS.

Namibia Movement for Independent Candidate: Windhoek; f. 1997; Leader JUSTICE KAWADENGE.

Namibia National Democratic Party: Windhoek; Leader PAUL HELMUTH.

Namibia National Front: Windhoek; Leader VEKUII RUKORO.

National Democratic Party for Justice (NDPFJ): f. May 1995 as SWAPO for Justice by fmr mems of SWAPO; reorg. as a political party in Nov. 1996, when it claimed to have 3,000 mems; Pres. NGHIWETE NDJOBA.

South West Africa People's Organisation of Namibia (SWAPO): Windhoek; internet www.swapo.org.na; f. 1957 as the Ovamboland People's Congress; renamed South West Africa People's Organisation in 1960; adopted present name in 1968; Pres. Dr SAMUEL DANIEL NUJOMA; Vice-Pres. Rev. HENDRIK WITBOOI; Sec.-Gen. HIFIKEPUNYE POHAMBA.

South West African National Union (SWANU): Windhoek; f. 1959; Leader HITJEVI VEII.

United Democratic Front (UDF): POB 20037, Windhoek; tel. (61) 230683; fax (61) 237175; f. 1989 as a centrist coalition of eight parties; Nat. Chair. ERIC BIWA; Pres. JUSTUS GAROEB.

Workers' Revolutionary Party: Windhoek; f. 1989; Trotskyist; Leaders WERNER MAMUGWE, HEWAT BEUKES.

The **Caprivi Liberation Army (CLA)**, f. 1998 as the Caprivi Liberation Movement, seeks secession of the Caprivi Strip; conducts mil. operations from bases in Zambia and Angola; political wing operates from Denmark as the Caprivi National Union, led by MISHAKE MUYONGO and BONIFACE MAMILI.

Diplomatic Representation

EMBASSIES AND HIGH COMMISSIONS IN NAMIBIA

Algeria: 111A Gloudina St, Ludwigsdorf, POB 3079, Windhoek; tel. (61) 221507; fax (61) 236376; e-mail ambalg.wkh@iwwn.com.na; Chargé d'affaires a.i.: A. I. BENGUEUEDDA.

Angola: Angola House, 3 Dr Agostinho Neto St, Ausspannpltaz, Private Bag 12020, Windhoek; tel. (61) 227535; fax (61) 221498; Ambassador: Dr GARCIA PIRES.

Botswana: 101 Nelson Mandela Ave, POB 20359, Windhoek; tel. (61) 221942; fax (61) 221948; High Commissioner: TUELENYANA ROSE-MARY DITLHABI-OLIPHANT.

Brazil: 52 Bismarck St, POB 24166, Windhoek; tel. (61) 237368; fax (61) 233389; e-mail orlando@iwwn.com.na; Chargé d'affaires a.i.: JOSÉ FERREIRA-LOPES.

China, People's Republic: 13 Wecka St, POB 22777, Windhoek; tel. (61) 222089; fax (61) 225544; e-mail chinaemb@iafrica.com.na; Ambassador: TANG ZHENQI.

Congo, Republic: 9 Korner St, POB 22970, Windhoek; tel. (61) 257517; fax (61) 240796; Ambassador: A. KONDHO.

Cuba: 31 Omuramba Rd, Eros, POB 23866, Windhoek; tel. (61) 227072; fax (61) 231584; e-mail embacuba@iafrica.com.na; Ambassador: SERGIO GONZÁLEZ GONZÁLEZ.

Egypt: 10 Berg St, POB 11853, Windhoek; tel. (61) 221501; fax (61) 228856; Ambassador: HUSSEIN A. M. WAHBY.

Finland: Sanlam Centre, 5th Floor, POB 3649, Windhoek; tel. (61) 221355; fax (61) 221349; e-mail finland@iafrica.com.na; Ambassador: (vacant).

France: 1 Goethe St, POB 20484, Windhoek; tel. (61) 229021; fax (61) 231436; e-mail frambwdk@iafrica.na; Ambassador: EUGÈNE BERG.

Germany: POB 231, Windhoek; tel. (61) 273100; fax (61) 222981; Ambassador: HARALD N. NESTROV.

Ghana: 5 Nelson Mandela Ave, POB 24165, Windhoek; tel. (61) 221341; fax (61) 221343; High Commissioner: H. MILLS-LUTTERODT.

India: 97 Nelson Mandela Ave, POB 1209, Windhoek; tel. (61) 226037; fax (61) 237320; e-mail hicomind.whk@iwwn.com.na; High Commissioner: PRIPURAN SINGH HAER.

Indonesia: 103 Nelson Mandela Ave, POB 20691, Windhoek; tel. (61) 221914; fax (61) 223811.

Kenya: Kenya House, 5th Floor, 134 Robert Mugabe Ave, POB 2889, Windhoek; tel. (61) 226836; fax (61) 221409; e-mail kenyanet@iwwn.com.na; High Commissioner: BINSAI J. CHEPSONGOL.

Libya: 69 Burg St, Luxury Hill, POB 124, Windhoek; tel. (61) 234454; fax (61) 234471; Chargé d'affaires a.i.: H. O. ALSHAOSHI.

Malawi: 56 Bismarck St, POB 13254, Windhoek; tel. (61) 221391; fax (61) 227056; High Commissioner: A. MNTHAMBALA.

Malaysia: 10 Von Eckenbrecker St, POB 312, Windhoek; tel. (61) 259344; fax (61) 259343; e-mail malhicom@iwwn.com.na.

Mexico: Southern Life Tower, 3rd Floor, 39 Post St Mall, POB 13220, Windhoek; tel. (61) 229082; fax (61) 229180; e-mail escalant @iwwn.com.na.

Netherlands: 2 Crohn St, Private Bag 564, Windhoek; tel. (61) 223733; fax (61) 223732; e-mail nlgovwin@namib.com.na.

Nigeria: 4 Omuramba Rd, Eros Park, POB 23547, Windhoek; tel. (61) 232103; fax (61) 221639; e-mail nignam@namib.com.na; High Commissioner: B. M. HIRSE.

Portugal: 24 Robert Mugabe Ave, POB 443, Windhoek; tel. (61) 237928; fax (61) 237929; e-mail emport@nweb.com.na; Ambassador: MARA DO CARMO ALLEGRO DE MAGALHAÉS.

Russia: 4 Christian St, POB 3826, Windhoek; tel. (61) 228671; fax (61) 229061; e-mail rusembna@iafrica.com.na; Ambassador: VYA-CHESLAV D. SHUMSKIY.

South Africa: RSA House, cnr Jan Jonker and Nelson Mandela Aves, POB 23100, Windhoek; tel. (61) 229765; fax (61) 224140; High Commissioner: B. S. S. MABIZELA.

Spain: 58 Bismarck St, POB 21811, Windhoek; tel. (61) 223066; fax (61) 223046; Ambassador: GERMÁN ZURITA Y SÁENZ DE NAVARRETE.

Sweden: Sanlam Centre, 9th Floor, POB 23087, Windhoek; tel. (61) 222905; fax (61) 222774; e-mail embassy.windhoek@sida.se; Ambassador: GUNILLA HESSELMARK.

United Kingdom: 116 Robert Mugabe Ave, POB 22202, Windhoek; tel. (61) 223022; fax (61) 228895; e-mail Windhoek-PPA@windhoek .mail.fco.gov.uk; High Commissioner: BRIAN DONALDSON.

USA: 14 Lossen St, Ausspannplatz, Private Bag 12029, Windhoek 9000; tel. (61) 221601; fax (61) 229792; Ambassador: GEORGE F. WARD.

Venezuela: Southern Life Tower, 3rd Floor, 39 Post St Mall, Private Bag 13353, Windhoek; tel. (61) 227905; fax (61) 227804; e-mail embaven@iwwn.com.na; Chargé d'affaires: CARLOS FORTMANN.

Zambia: 22 Sam Nujoma Drive, Cnr Mandume Ndemufayo Rd, POB 22882, Windhoek; tel. (61) 37610; fax (61) 228162; High Comm-issioner: CHANDA SOSALA.

Zimbabwe: cnr Independence Ave and Grimm St, POB 23056, Windhoek; tel. (61) 228134; fax (61) 226859; High Commissioner: MARY SIBUSISIWE MUBI.

Judicial System

Judicial power is exercised by the Supreme Court, the High Court and a number of Magistrate and Lower Courts. The Constitution provides for the appointment of an Ombudsman.

Chief Justice: JOHAN STRYDOM.

Religion

It is estimated that about 90% of the population are Christians.

CHRISTIANITY

Council of Churches in Namibia: 8 Mont Blanc St, POB 41, Windhoek; tel. (61) 217621; fax (61) 62786; f. 1978; eight mem. churches; Pres. Bishop HENDRIK FREDERIK; Gen. Sec. NANGULA KATHINDI.

The Anglican Communion

Namibia comprises a single diocese in the Church of the Province of Southern Africa. The Metropolitan of the Province is the Arch-bishop of Cape Town, South Africa.

Bishop of Namibia: Rt Rev. NEHEMIAH SHIHALA HAMUPENBE, POB 57, Windhoek; tel. (61) 238920; fax (61) 225903.

Dutch Reformed Church

Dutch Reformed Church in Namibia: 34 Feldstreet, POB 389, Windhoek; tel. (61) 225073; fax (61) 227287; e-mail ngkn@iafrica .com.na; f. 1898; 22,600 mems in 46 congregations; Sec. Rev. CLEM MARAIS.

Evangelical Lutheran

Evangelical Lutheran Church in Namibia (ELCIN): Moderator Rev. HERMAN OOSTHUISEN; Private Bag 2018, Ondangwa; tel. (56) 24241; fax (56) 240472; e-mail elcinhq@ednweb.com.na; Presiding Bishop Rev. APOLLOS KAULINGE.

Evangelical Lutheran Church (Rhenish Mission Church): POB 5069, Windhoek; tel. (61) 224531; f. 1967; Pres. Bishop HEN-DRIK FREDERIK.

German Evangelical-Lutheran Church in Namibia: POB 233, Windhoek; tel. (61) 224294; fax (61) 221470; e-mail delk@namib net.com; 6,000 mems; Pres. Rev. REINHARD KEDING.

Methodist

African Methodist Episcopal Church: Rev. B. G. KARUAERA, Windhoek; tel. (61) 62757.

Methodist Church of Southern Africa: POB 143, Windhoek; tel. (61) 228921.

The Roman Catholic Church

Namibia comprises one archdiocese, one diocese and one apostolic vicariate. At 31 December 1998 adherents of the Roman Catholic Church in Namibia comprised some 13.5% of the total population.

Bishops' Conference: Namibian Catholic Bishops' Conference, POB 11525, Windhoek; tel. (61) 224798; f. 1996; Pres. Most Rev. BONIFATIUS HAUSHIKU, Archbishop of Windhoek.

Archbishop of Windhoek: Most Rev. BONIFATIUS HAUSHIKU, POB 272, Windhoek; tel. (61) 227595; fax (61) 229836.

Other Christian Churches

Among other denominations active in Namibia are the Evangelical Reformed Church in Africa, the Presbyterian Church of Southern Africa and the United Congregational Church of Southern Africa.

JUDAISM

Windhoek Hebrew Congregation: POB 563, Windhoek; tel. (61) 221070; fax (61) 226444; e-mail steinitz@nweb.com.na.

BAHÁ'Í FAITH

National Spiritual Assembly: POB 20372, Windhoek; tel. and fax (61) 239634; e-mail secretary@nsa.bahai.org.na; mems resident in 215 localities.

The Press

Abacus: POB 22791, Windhoek; tel. (61) 235596; fax (61) 236467; weekly; English; educational; Editor HEIDI VON EGIDY; circ. 31,000.

AgriForum: 114 Robert Mugabe Ave, Private Bag 13255, Windhoek; tel. (61) 237838; fax (61) 220193; e-mail richter@agrinamibia.com.na; monthly; Afrikaans, English; publ. by Namibia Agricultural Union; Editor RICHTER ERASMUS; circ. 5,000.

Allgemeine Zeitung: 49 Stuebel St, POB 2127, Windhoek; tel. (61) 230331; fax (61) 220225; e-mail aznews@iafrica.com.na; f. 1916; daily; German; Editor-in-Chief EBERHARD HOFFMANN; circ. 4,500 (Mon.–Wed.), 5,900 (Thur.–Fri.).

Aloe: POB 59, Windhoek; tel. (61) 2902056; fax (61) 2902006; monthly; English; edited by the Windhoek Municipality; Editor SIMON HOABEB; circ. 45,000.

Namib Times: Seventh St., POB 706, Walvis Bay; tel. (64) 205854; fax (64) 204813; 2 a week; Afrikaans, English, German and Portuguese; Editor PAUL VINCENT; circ. 4,300.

Namibia Brief: Independence Ave, POB 2123, Windhoek; tel. and fax (61) 251044; quarterly; English; Editor CATHY BLATT; circ. 7,500.

Namibia Business Journal: POB 9355, Windhoek; tel. (61) 228809; fax (61) 228009; Editor MILTON LOUW; circ. 4,000.

Namibia Focus: Windhoek; tel. (61) 227182; fax (61) 220226; monthly; English; business; Editor JOHAN ENGELBRECHT; circ. 30,000.

Namibia Review: Turnhalle Bldg, Bahnhof St, PMB 13344, Windhoek; tel. (61) 222246; fax (61) 224937; govt-owned; monthly; Editor ALEX KAURE; circ. 5,000.

Namibia Today: POB 24669, Windhoek; tel. (61) 229150; fax (61) 229150; 2 a week; Afrikaans, English, Oshiherero, Oshiwambo; publ. by SWAPO; Editor KAOMO-VIJINDA TJOMBE; circ. 5,000.

The Namibian: John Meinert St, POB 20783, Windhoek; tel. (61) 236970; fax (61) 233980; e-mail graham@namibian.com.na; daily; English; Editor GWEN LISTER; circ. 11,000.

The Namibian Investor: Private Bag 13340, Windhoek; tel. (61) 2837335; fax (61) 220278; e-mail nic@mti.gov.na; publ. by Namibia Investment Centre; circ. 10,000.

The Namibian Worker: POB 50034, Bachbrecht, Windhoek; tel. (61) 215037; fax (61) 215589; Afrikaans, English, Oshiwambo; publ. by National Union of Namibian Workers; Editor-in-Chief C. R. HAIKALI; circ. 1,000.

New Era: PMB 13364, Windhoek; tel. (61) 234924; fax (61) 235419; govt-owned: 2 a week; English; Editor RAJAH MUNAMAVA; circ. 10,000.

Die Republikein: 49 Stuebel St, POB 3436, Windhoek; tel. (61) 230331; fax (61) 223721; e-mail republkn@iwwn.com.na; f. 1977; daily; Afrikaans, English and German; organ of DTA of Namibia; Editor CHRISTO RETIEF (acting); circ. 12,000 (Mon.–Wed.), 15,000 (Thur.–Fri.).

Tempo: 49 Stuebel St, POB 1794, Windhoek; tel. (61) 225822; fax (61) 223110; f. 1992; weekly; English and German; Editor DES ERASMUS; circ. 11,000.

Visitor: POB 23000, Windhoek; tel. (61) 227182; fax (61) 220226; monthly; English; tourist information; Editor JOHAN ENGELBRECHT; circ. 10,000.

The Windhoek Advertiser: 49 Stuebel St, POB 3436, Windhoek; tel. (61) 230331; fax (61) 225863; e-mail advertsr@iwwn.com.na; f. 1919; daily; English; Editor DEON SCHLECHTER; circ. 5,000 (Mon.–Wed.), 7,000 (Thur.–Fri.).

Windhoek Observer: 49 Stuebel St, POB 2255, Windhoek; tel. (61) 221737; fax (61) 226098; f. 1978; weekly; English; Editor HANNES SMITH; circ. 14,000.

NEWS AGENCIES

Namibia Press Agency (Nampa): POB 61354, Windhoek; tel. (61) 221711; fax (61) 221713; e-mail nampa@iafrica.com.na; Editor-in-Chief MOCKS SHIVUTE.

Foreign Bureaux

Informatsionnoye Telegrafnoye Agentstvo Rossii—Telegrafnoye Agentstvo Suverennykh Stran (ITAR—TASS) (Russia): POB 24821, Windhoek; tel. and fax (61) 232909; Correspondent PAVE MYLTSEV.

Inter Press Service (IPS) (Italy): POB 20783, Windhoek; tel. (61) 226645; Correspondent MARK VERBAAN.

South African Press Association (SAPA): POB 2032, Windhoek; tel. (61) 231565; fax (61) 220783; Representative CARMEN HONEY.

Xinhua (New China) News Agency (People's Republic of China): POB 22130, Windhoek; tel. (61) 226484; fax (61) 226484; Bureau Chief TENG WENYI.

Reuters (UK) is also represented in Namibia.

PRESS ASSOCIATIONS

Journalist Association of Namibia (JAN): Windhoek; tel. (61) 236970; fax (61) 248016; e-mail shirumbu@iafrica.com.na; f. 1992; Chair. DAVID LUSH.

Press Club Windhoek: POB 2032, Windhoek; tel. (61) 231565; fax (61) 220783; Chair. CARMEN HONEY.

Publishers

BAUM Publishers: POB 3436, Windhoek; tel. (61) 225411; fax (61) 224843; Publr NIC KRUGER.

Clarian Publishers: POB 5861, Windhoek; tel. (61) 251044; fax (61) 237251; Publr CATHY BLATT.

ELOC Printing Press: PMB 2013, Oniipa, Ondangwa; tel. and fax (6756) 40211; f. 1901; Rev. Dr KLEOPAS DUMENI.

Gamsberg McMillan Publishers (Pty) Ltd: POB 22830, Windhoek; tel. (61) 232165; fax (61) 233538; Man. Dir HERMAN VAN WYK.

Longman Namibia: POB 9251, Eros, Windhoek; tel. (61) 231124; fax (61) 224019; Publr LINDA BREDENKAMP.

National Archives of Namibia: Eugène Marais St, Private Bag 13250, Windhoek; tel. (61) 2934308; fax (61) 239042; e-mail natarch@natarch.mec.gov.na; internet www.natarch.mec.gov.na; Man. J. KUTZNA.

New Namibia Books (Pty) Ltd: POB 21601, Windhoek; tel. (61) 221134; fax (61) 235279; Publr JANE KATJAVIVI.

Out of Africa Publishers: POB 21841, Windhoek; tel. (61) 221494; fax (61) 221720; Man. VIDA LOCHNER.

PUBLISHERS' ASSOCIATION

Association of Namibian Publishers: POB 21601, Windhoek; tel. (61) 235796; fax (61) 235279; f. 1991; Sec. PETER REINER.

Broadcasting and Communications

TELECOMMUNICATIONS

Telecom Namibia Ltd (Telecom): POB 297, Windhoek; tel. (61) 2019211; fax (61) 248723; f. 1992; state-owned; Chair E. H. T. ANGULA; Man. Dir T. MBERIRUA.

Mobile Telecommunications Ltd (MTC): POB 23051, Windhoek; tel. (61) 249570; fax (61) 249571; f. 1994; cellular telecommunications co; Man. Dir B. GUVE.

Multicom: POB 80425, Windhoek; tel. (61) 264755; fax (61) 264756; f. 1994; Gen. Man. G. VAN WYK.

BROADCASTING

Radio

Namibian Broadcasting Corporation (NBC): POB 321, Windhoek; tel. (61) 2913111; fax (61) 216209; e-mail nbcho@iwwn.com.na; f. 1990; broadcasts on eight radio channels in 11 languages; Dir-Gen. Dr BEN MULONGENI.

Channel 7: POB 20500, Windhoek; tel. (61) 218969; fax (61) 215572; Man. NEAL VAN DEN BERGH.

Katutura Community Radio: POB 22355, Windhoek; tel. (61) 263768; fax (61) 262786; Dir FREDERICK GOWASEB.

Radio Antenna (Radio 99): POB 11849, Windhoek; tel. (61) 223634; fax (61) 230964; f. 1994; Man. Dir MARIO AITA.

Radio Energy (Radio 100): POB 11849, Windhoek; tel. (61) 224947; fax (61) 230964; Man. Dir MARIO AITA.

Television

Namibian Broadcasting Corporation (NBC): POB 321, Windhoek; tel. (61) 2913111; fax (61) 216209; e-mail nbcho@iwwn.com.na; f. 1990; operates national television channel; programmes in English; Dir-Gen. Dr BEN MULONGENI.

Multi Choice Namibia: POB 1752, Windhoek; tel. (61) 222222; fax (61) 227605; commercial television channels; Gen. Man. HARRY AUCAMP.

Finance

(cap. = capital; res = reserves; dep. = deposits; m. = million; brs = branches; amounts in Namibian dollars)

BANKING

Central Bank

Bank of Namibia: 71 Robert Mugabe Ave, POB 2882, Windhoek; tel. (61) 2835111; fax (61) 2835067; e-mail governor.office@bon .com.na; internet www.bon.com.na; f. 1990; cap. and res 562.0m., dep. 572.9m. (Dec. 1998); Gov. Tom ALWEENDO; Deputy Gov. L. S. IPANGELWA.

Commercial Banks

Bank Windhoek Ltd: Bank Windhoek Bldg, 262 Independence Ave, POB 15, Windhoek; tel. (61) 2991122; fax (61) 2991620; e-mail info@bankwindhoek.com.na; internet www.bankwindhoek.com.na; f. 1982; cap. and res 151.2m., dep. 1,829.3m. (March 1999); Chair. J. C. BRANDT; Man. Dir J. L. J. VAN VUUREN; 21 brs.

City Savings and Investment Bank (CSIB): FGI Bldg, 2nd Floor, Post St Mall, Windhoek; tel. (61) 221262; fax (61) 221555; e-mail csib@solarium.iwwn.com.na; f. 1994; Chair. A. MUSHIMBA; CEO H. SULAIMAN.

Commercial Bank of Namibia Ltd: 12–20 Bülow St, POB 1, Windhoek; tel. (61) 2959111; fax (61) 2952079; e-mail service@ c-bank.com.na; internet www.c-bank.com.na; f. 1973; controlled by SND Investment Holdings Ltd; cap. and res 122.7m., dep. 1,507.6m. (Dec. 1999); Chair. G. Z. STEFFENS; Man. Dir UDO REINHOLD; 10 brs.

First National Bank of Namibia Ltd: 209/211 Independence Ave, POB 195, Windhoek; tel. (61) 2992222; fax (61) 225604; f. 1986; cap. and res 235.0m., dep. 2,112.5m. (Sept. 1998); Chair. H. D. VOIGTS; Man. Dir S. H. MOIR; 27 brs and 22 agencies.

Namibian Banking Corporation: Carl List Haus, Independence Ave, POB 370, Windhoek; tel. (61) 225946; fax (61) 223741; Chair. J. C. WESTRAAT; Man. Dir P. P. NIEHAUS; 3 brs.

Standard Bank Namibia Ltd: Mutual Platz, Post St Mall, POB 3327, Windhoek; tel. (61) 2949111; fax (61) 2942555; e-mail info@ standardbank.com.na; internet www.standardbank.com.na; f. 1915; controlled by Standard Bank Investment Corpn; cap. and res 239.7m., dep. 2,771.0m. (Dec. 1999); Chair. C. V. KAURAISA; Man. Dir O. M. TIDBURY; 19 brs.

Agricultural Bank

Agricultural Bank of Namibia: POB 13208, Windhoek; tel. (61) 2074111; fax (61) 2074287; e-mail agribank@iafrica.com.na; f. 1922; cap. 492.7m., dep. 25.9m., total assets 659.2m. (March 1999); Chair. and Man. Dir T. HIJARUNGURU; Gen. Man. J. DANIELS.

Merchant Bank

UAL—Namibia: Windhoek; f. 1997; subsidiary of UAL Merchant Bank Ltd (South Africa); Man. Dir STEVE GALLOWAY.

STOCK EXCHANGE

Namibian Stock Exchange (NSX): Shop 8, Kaiserkrone Centre, Post St Mall, POB 2401, Windhoek; tel. (61) 227647; fax (61) 248531; e-mail heikon@nsx.com.na; internet www.nsx.com.na; f. 1992; Chair. Exec. Cttee FRANCOIS UYS; Gen. Man. HEIKO NIEDERMEIER.

INSURANCE

Allianz Insurance Co of Namibia Ltd: POB 3244, Windhoek; tel. (61) 226897; fax (61) 231070; Man. Dir G. DONBO.

W. Biederlack & Co: Metje-Behnsen Bldg, 2nd Floor, Independence Ave, POB 365, Windhoek; tel. (61) 233177; fax (61) 233178; e-mail biderlac@iafrica.com.na; f. 1990.

Commercial Union Insurance Ltd: Bülow St, POB 1599, Windhoek; tel. (61) 37137.

FGI Namibia Ltd: POB 2516, Windhoek; tel. (61) 225450; fax (61) 229195; f. 1993; short-term insurance; Man. Dir PETER OPPERMAN.

Incorporated General Insurance Ltd: 10 Bülow St, POB 2516, Windhoek; tel. (61) 37453; fax (61) 35647.

Insurance Co of Namibia (INSCON): POB 2877, Windhoek; tel. (61) 223425; fax (61) 233808; short-term insurance; Gen. Dir F. OTTO.

Lifegro Assurance Ltd: Independence Ave, POB 23055, Windhoek; tel. (61) 33068.

Lumley Insurance Group: POB 1011, Windhoek 9000; tel. (61) 224471; fax (61) 234802; f. 1953; Chair. and Man. Dir INGO RIX.

Metropolitan Life Ltd: Goethe St, POB 3785, Windhoek; tel. (61) 239140; fax (61) 248191; Chair. M. L. SMITH; Man. Dir R. A. V. E. FOUCHE.

Mutual and Federal Insurance Co Ltd: Mutual and Federal Centre, 7th Floor, 227 Independence Ave, POB 151, Windhoek; tel. (61) 2077111; fax (61) 2077205; f. 1990; Gen. Man. R. I. SANGER.

Namibia National Insurance Co Ltd: Bülow St, POB 23053, Windhoek; tel. (61) 224539; fax (61) 238737; fmrly Federated Insurance Co Ltd.

Old Mutual Life Assurance Co. (Namibia) Ltd: Mutual Platz, 5th Floor, Post St Mall, POB 165, Windhoek; tel. (61) 2993999; fax (61) 223838; e-mail dkotze@oldmutual.com; internet www .oldmutual.com.na.

Protea Assurance Co Ltd: Windhoek; tel. (61) 225891.

Sanlam Life Assurance Ltd: Bülow St, POB 317, Windhoek; tel. (61) 36680.

Santam Insurance Ltd: Independence Ave, POB 204, Windhoek; tel. (61) 238214; fax (61) 235225; Man. Dir C. J. ENGELBRECHT; Dep. Man. Dir H. OCHSE.

Southern Life Assurance Ltd: Southern Tower, Post Street Mall, POB 637, Windhoek; tel. (61) 234056; fax (61) 231574; Man. Dir L. LOMBAARD.

Trade and Industry

GOVERNMENT AGENCIES

Karakul Board of Namibia—Swakara Fur Producers and Exporters: Private Bag 13300, Windhoek; tel. (61) 237750; fax (61) 236122; e-mail agrapels@agra.com.na.

Meat Board of Namibia: POB 38, Windhoek; tel. (61) 33180; fax (61) 228310; f. 1935; Chair. JOHN LE ROUX; Gen. Man. PAUL STRYDOM.

Meat Corporation of Namibia (MEATCO NAMIBIA): POB 3881, Windhoek; tel. (61) 216810; fax (61) 217045.

Namibian Agronomic Board: POB 5096, Windhoek; tel. (61) 224741; fax (61) 225371; Man. JAH HOFFMANN.

National Petroleum Corporation of Namibia (NAMCOR): Windhoek; Man. Dir SKERF POTTAS.

DEVELOPMENT ORGANIZATIONS

Namibia Development Corporation: 11 Goethe St, Private Bag 13252, Windhoek; tel. (61) 2069111; fax (61) 247841; e-mail info@ ndc.org.na; internet www.ndc.org.na; f. 1993; promotes foreign investment and provides concessionary loans and equity to new enterprises; manages agricultural projects; undertakes feasibility studies; Chair. P. T. DAMASEB; Man. Dir I. I. NAMASEB.

Namibia Investment Centre: Ministry of Trade and Industry, Brendan Simbwaye Sq., Block B, Goethe St, Private Bag 13340, Windhoek; tel. (61) 2837335; fax (61) 220278; e-mail nic@mti .gov.na; Exec. Dir D. NUYOMA.

National Housing Enterprise: POB 20192, Windhoek; tel. (61) 2927111; fax (61) 222301; f. 1983; provides low-cost housing; Chair. I. NGATJIZEKO; CEO A. M. TSOWASEB.

CHAMBERS OF COMMERCE

Chamber of Mines of Namibia (CMIN): POB 2895, Windhoek; tel. (61) 237925; fax (61) 222638; e-mail chammin@nweb.com.na; f. 1979; Pres. KOMBADAYEDU KAPWANGA; Gen. Man. JOHN ROGERS; 61 mems (2000).

Namibia National Chamber of Commerce and Industry (NNCCI): POB 9355, Windhoek; tel. (61) 228809; fax (61) 228009; e-mail nnccihq@iwwn.com.na; f. 1990; Pres. M. SHIKONGO; CEO SAM GEISEB (acting).

Windhoek Chamber of Commerce and Industries: SWA Building Society Bldg, 3rd Floor, POB 191, Windhoek; tel. (61) 222000; fax (61) 233690; e-mail: whkchamber@lianam.lia.net; f. 1920; Pres. H. SCHMIDT; Gen. Man. T. D. PARKHOUSE; 230 mems.

EMPLOYERS' ORGANIZATIONS

Construction Industries Federation of Namibia: 22 Stein St, Klein, POB 1479, Windhoek; tel. (61) 230028; fax (61) 224534; Pres. COBUS VAN WYNGAARDEN.

Electrical Contractors' Association: POB 3163, Windhoek; tel. (61) 37920; Pres. F. PFAFFENTHALER.

Motor Industries Federation of Namibia: POB 1503, Windhoek; tel. (61) 37970; fax (61) 33690.

Namibia Agricultural Union (NAU): Private Bag 13255, Windhoek; tel. (61) 237838; fax (61) 220193; e-mail richter@agrinamibia .com.na; Pres. PIETER GOUWS.

Namibia Chamber of Printing: POB 363, Windhoek; tel. (61) 237905; fax (61) 222927; Sec. S. G. TIMM.

UTILITIES
Electricity

Namibia Power Corporation Ltd (NamPower): NamPower Centre, 15 Luther St, POB 2864, Windhoek; tel. (61) 2054111; fax (61) 232805; e-mail register@nampower.com.na; internet www.nampower.com.na; Chair. M. SHIKONGO; Man. Dir LEAKE S. HANGALA.

Northern Electricity: POB 891, Tsumeb; tel. (67) 222243; fax (67) 222245; private electricity supply co; Man. Dir C. G. N. HUYSEN.

MAJOR COMPANIES

Namdeb Diamond Corporation Ltd: POB 1906, Windhoek; tel. (61) 235061 (Windhoek) and (63) 239111 (Oranjemund); telex 658 (Windhoek) and 440 (Oranjemund); fax (61) 238833 (Windhoek); f. 1994; 50% state-owned, 50% owned by De Beers Centenary AG; operates alluvial diamond mine at Oranjemund; also recovers marine diamonds; Chair. J. O. THOMPSON; Man. Dir I. ZAAMWANI.

Namibia Breweries Ltd (Nambrew): POB 206, Windhoek; tel. (61) 262915; fax (61) 263327; e-mail schuetteh@olfitra.com.na; Chair. K. W. R. LIST; Man. Dir BERJD MASCHE.

Namibian Copper Joint Venture (Pty) Ltd: POB 11978, Windhoek; tel. (61) 238628; fax (61) 226978; development of cathode copper project at Haib; produces 100,000 metric tons per year.

Namibian Minerals Corporation (Namco): 114 Robert Mugabe Ave, POB 24857, Windhoek; tel. (61) 231353; fax (61) 249253; e-mail mwilliams@nam-corp.com; f. 1993; operates three marine diamond concessions covering c.2,000 sq km; Chair. and CEO JOHN ALASTAIR HOLBERTON.

Rosh Pinah Zinc Corpn (RPZC): Private Bag, Rosh Pinah; tel. (63342) 2; fax 145; f. 1999 to succeed Imcor Zinc (Pty) Ltd; owned jtly by South Africa Iron and Steel Corpn (ISCOR) and PE Minerals; mines zinc and lead at Rosh Pinah.

Rössing Uranium Ltd: POB 22391, Windhoek; tel. (61) 2809111; fax 233637; f. 1970; operates an open-cast uranium mine in the Namib desert; began production in 1976 and is the world's largest open-pit uranium mine; Chair. CHARLES V. KAURAISA; Man. Dir ANDREW J. HOPE.

TRADE UNIONS

There are several union federations, and a number of independent unions.

Trade Union Federations

Confederation of Labour: POB 22060, Windhoek.

National Allied Unions (NANAU): Windhoek; f. 1987; an alliance of trade unions, representing c. 7,600 mems, incl. Namibia Wholesale and Retail Workers' Union (f. 1986; Gen. Sec. T. NGAUJAKE; 6,000 mems), and Namibia Women Support Cttee; Pres. HENOCH HANDURA.

Namibia Trade Union (NTU): Windhoek; f. 1985; represents 6,700 domestic, farm and metal workers; Pres. ALPHA KANGUEEHI; Sec.-Gen. BEAU TJISESETA.

Namibia Trade Union Council (NTUC): Windhoek; f. 1981; affiliates include Northern Builders' Asscn.

National Union of Namibian Workers (NUNW): POB 50034, Windhoek; tel. (61) 215037; fax (61) 215589; f. 1972; Pres. PONHELE YA FRANCE; Sec.-Gen. RANGA HAIKAILI; 87,000 mems; affiliates include:

  Mineworkers' Union of Namibia (MUN): f. 1986; Chair. ASSER KAPERE; Pres. JACOB NGHIFINDAKA (acting); Gen. Sec. PETER NAHOLO (acting); 12,500 mems.

  Namibia Food and Allied Workers' Union: f. 1986; Chair. MATHEUS LIBEREKI; Pres. ELIFAS NANGOLO; Gen. Sec. MAGDALENA IPINGE (acting); 12,000 mems.

  Namibia Metal and Allied Workers' Union: f. 1987; Chair. ANDRIES TEMBA; Gen. Sec. MOSES SHIKWA (acting); 5,500 mems.

  Namibia Public Workers' Union: f. 1987; Chair. STEVEN IMMANUEL; Gen. Sec. PETER ILONGA; 11,000 mems.

  Namibia Transport and Allied Workers' Union: f. 1988; Chair. TYLVES GIDEON; Gen. Sec. IMMANUEL KAVAA; 7,500 mems.

Other Unions

Association for Government Service Officials: Windhoek; f. 1981; Chair. ALLAN HATTLE; 9,000 mems.

Namibia Building Workers' Association: Windhoek; Sec. H. BOCK.

Public Service Union of Namibia: POB 21662, Windhoek; tel. (61) 213083; fax (61) 213047; f. 1981; Sec.-Gen. STEVE RUKORO.

Transport
RAILWAYS

The main line runs from Nakop, at the border with South Africa, via Keetmanshoop to Windhoek, Kranzberg, Grootfontein, Tsumeb,

Swakopmund and Walvis Bay. There are three branch lines, from Windhoek to Gobabis, Otjiwarongo to Outjo and Keetmanshoop to Lüderitz. The total rail network covers 2,382 route-km. There are plans for a railway line connecting Namibia with Zambia, as part of a programme to improve transport links among the members of the Common Market for Eastern and Southern Africa.

TransNamib Ltd: TransNamib Bldg, cnr Independence Ave and Bahnhof St, Private Bag 13204, Windhoek; tel. (61) 2981111; fax (61) 2982559; e-mail support@transnamib.com.na; internet www.transnamib.com.na; state-owned; Chair. V. E. GRAIG-MCLAREN; Man. Dir Dr PEINGONDJABI T. SHIPOH.

ROADS

In 1997 the road network comprised 63,258 km of roads, of which 3,959 km were main roads and 9,612 km were secondary roads; about 5,250 km of the network were paved. A major road link from Walvis Bay to Jwaneng, northern Botswana, the Trans-Kalahari Highway, is now complete, while the Trans-Caprivi highway, linking Namibia with northern Botswana, Zambia and Zimbabwe, was nearing completion in the late 1990s. The Government is also upgrading and expanding the road network in northern Namibia.

SHIPPING

The ports of Walvis Bay and Lüderitz are linked to the main overseas shipping routes and handle almost one-half of Namibia's external trade. Walvis Bay is a hub port for the region, serving land-locked countries such as Botswana, Zambia and Zimbabwe.

Namibian Ports Authority (NAMPORT): 13th Road, POB 361, Walvis Bay; tel. (64) 2082201; fax (64) 2082320; e-mail jerome@namport.com.na; internet www.namport.com.na; f. 1994; Chair. DIRK H. CONRADIE; CEO WESSIE WESSELS.

Pan-Ocean Shipping Services Ltd: POB 2613, Walvis Bay; tel. (64) 203959; fax (64) 204199; e-mail kirovg@iafrica.com.na; f. 1995; Man. Dir JÜRGEN HEYNEMANN; Gen. Man. GEORGE KIROV.

CIVIL AVIATION

There are international airports at Windhoek and Walvis Bay, as well as a number of other airports throughout Namibia, and numerous landing strips.

Air Namibia: TransNamib Bldg, cnr Independence Ave and Bahnhof St, POB 731, Windhoek; tel. (61) 223019; fax (61) 221910; e-mail aguibeb@airnamibia.com.na; f. 1959 as Namib Air; state-owned; transfer to majority (70%) private ownership pending; domestic flights and services to Southern Africa and Western Europe; Chair. Dr PETRUS DAMASEB; Man. Dir ANDREUS GUIBEB.

Kalahari Express Airlines (KEA): POB 40179, Windhoek; tel. (61) 245665; fax (61) 245612; e-mail keaadmin@kalahariexpress.com.na; internet www.iwwn.com.na/kea/; f. 1995; domestic and regional flights; Exec. Dir PEINGONDJABI SHIPOH.

Tourism

Nambia's principal tourist attractions are its game parks and nature reserves, and the development of 'eco-tourism' is being promoted. In the late 1990s tourism was one of the fastest growing sectors of the Namibian economy. Government investment in expanding the tourism sector was expected to total N $547m. during 1993–98. Tourist arrivals in Namibia in 1998 totalled 559,674. In 1997 tourism receipts were US $336m.

Namibia Tourism: Private Bag 13346, Capital Bldg, Ground Floor, 272 Independence Ave, Windhoek; tel. (61) 2849111; fax (61) 284-2364; e-mail tourism@iwwn.com.na; internet www.iwwn.com.na/namtour/.

Defence

In August 1999 the Namibian Defence Force numbered an estimated 9,000; there was also a coastguard estimated at 100-strong, attached to the ministry of fisheries and marine resources.

Defence Expenditure: Budgeted at N $559.2m. in 1999/2000 (representing 7.2% of total projected budgetary expenditure for that year), with an additional N $173m. allocated in the supplementary budget for that period.

Commander-in-Chief of the Defence Force: Pres. SAMUEL (SAM) DANIEL NUJOMA.

Chief of Staff of the Defence Force: Maj.-Gen. MARTIN SHALLI.

Commander of the Army: Maj.-Gen. SOLOMON HAWALA.

Education

Education is officially compulsory for 10 years between the ages of six and 16 years, or until pre-primary education has been completed (whichever is the sooner). Pre-primary education was abolished in the state sector in 1995. Primary education generally begins at seven years of age, and lasts for seven years. Secondary education, from the age of 14, lasts for five years. In 1996 enrolment at primary schools included 91% of the relevant age-group, while the comparable ratio for secondary enrolment in that year was 36%. Higher education is provided by the University of Namibia, the Technicon of Namibia, a vocational college and four teacher-training colleges. In 1995 11,344 students were enrolled in tertiary education.

Various schemes for informal adult education are also in operation in an effort to combat illiteracy. At the 1991 census the average rate of adult illiteracy, excluding unemployed persons, was 24.2% (males 22.2%; females 26%). UNESCO estimated average adult illiteracy at 21.6% (males 19.9%; females 23.2%) in 1995. The budget for 1998/99 allocated N $1,700.6m. (25.2% of total government expenditure) to education. Approximately 21% of total expenditure was allocated to education under the draft budget for 1999/2000.

Bibliography

Afro-Asian Peoples' Solidarity Organization. *Namibia: Road to Independence*. Cairo, 1990.

Allison, C., and Green, R. H. *Political Economy and Structural Change: Namibia at Independence*. Brighton, University of Sussex, Institute of Development Studies, 1989.

Amukugo, E. M. *Education and Politics in Namibia: Past Trends and Future Prospects*. Windhoek, Gamsberg Macmillan, 1995.

Arcadi de Saint-Paul, M. *Namibie: Une Siècle d'Histoire*. Paris, Albatron, 1984.

Bley, H. *Namibia under German Rule*. Uppsala, Nordiska Afrikainstitutet, 1997.

Catholic Institute for International Relations. *Land Reform in Namibia*. London, 1995.

Cros, G. *Chroniques Namibiennes: La Dernière Colonie*. Paris, Présence Africaine, 1983.

La Namibie. Paris, Presses Universitaires de France, 1983.

Dale, R. *The UN and the Independence of Namibia: The Longest Decolonization, 1946–1990*. 1994.

Diescho, J. *The Namibian Constitution in Perspective*. Windhoek, Macmillan Gamsberg, 1994.

Du Pisani, A. *SWA/Namibia: The Politics of Continuity and Change*. Johannesburg, Jonathan Ball, 1986.

Duggal, N. K. (Ed.). *Namibia: Perspectives for National Reconstruction and Development*. Lusaka, United Nations Institute for Namibia, 1986.

Frayne, B. *Urbanisation in Post-Independence Windhoek: (With Special Emphasis on Katutura)*. Windhoek, University of Namibia, 1992.

Good, K. *Realizing Democracy in Botswana, Namibia and South Africa*. Pretoria, Africa Institute, 1997.

Green, R. H. *From Sudwesafrika to Namibia: The Political Economy of Transition*. Uppsala, Scandinavian Institute for African Studies, 1981.

Groth, S. *Namibia: the Wall of Silence*. Wiepperthal, Germany, Peter Hammer Verlag, 1995.

Grotpeter, J. J. *Historical Dictionary of Namibia*. Metuchen, NJ, Scarecrow Press, 1994.

Harvey, C., and Isaksen, J. (Eds) *Monetary Independence for Namibia*. Windhoek, NEPRU, 1990.

Hayes, P., Silvester, J., Wallace, M., and Hartmann, W. *Namibia under South African Rule*. London, James Currey Publishers, 1998.

Heribert, W., and Matthew, B. (Eds). *The Namibian Peace Process: Implications and Lessons for the Future*. Freiburg, Arnold-Bergstraesser-Institut, 1994.

Hishongwa, N. *The Contract Labour System and its Effects on Social and Family Life in Namibia*. Windhoek, Gamsberg Macmillan, 1992.

Jezkova, P. *Namibia: New Avenue of Industrial Development*. Vienna, UNIDO, 1994.

Karase, C., and Gutto, S. (Eds). *Namibia: The Conspiracy of Silence*. Harare, Nehanda, 1989.

LeBeau, D. *Namibia: Ethnic Stereotyping in a Post-Apartheid State*. Windhoek, University of Namibia, 1991.

Leys, C., and Saul, J. S. *Namibia's Liberation Struggle: The Two-Edged Sword*. London, James Currey Publishers, 1995.

Lister, S. (Ed.). *Aid, Donors and Development Management*. Windhoek, NEPRU, 1991.

Lush, D. *Last Steps to Uhuru: An Eye-Witness Account of Namibia's Transition to Independence (1988–1992)*. Ibadan, Spectrum Books, 1993.

Mbuende, K. *Namibia: The Broken Shield: Anatomy of Imperialism and Revolution*. Uppsala, Scandinavian Institute for African Studies, 1986.

Omar, G., et al. *Introduction to Namibia's Political Economy*. Cape Town, Southern Africa Labour and Development Research Unit, 1990.

Peltola, P. *The Lost May Day: Namibian Workers' Struggle for Independence*. Uppsala, Finnish Anthropological Society and Nordiske Afrikainstitutet, 1995.

Saunders, C. (Ed.). *Perspectives on Namibia: Past and Present*. Cape Town, Centre for African Studies, 1983.

Singham, A. W. *Namibian Independence: A Global Responsibility*. Westport, Hill, 1985.

Soggot, D. *Namibia: The Violent Heritage*. London, Collings, 1986.

Soiri, I. *Radical Motherhood: Namibian Women's Independence Struggle*. Uppsala, Nordiske Afrikainstitutet, 1996.

Sparks, D. L., and Green, D. *Namibia: The Nation after Independence*. Boulder, CO, Westview Press, 1992.

Totemeyer, G., et al. (Eds). *Namibia in Perspective*. Windhoek, Council of Churches in Namibia, 1987.

Totemeyer, G. *The Reconstruction of the Namibian National, Regional and Local State*. Windhoek, University of Namibia, 1992.

Werner, W. *Land Reform in Namibia: The First Seven Years*. Windhoek, NEPRU, 1997.

Wilmsen, E. N. *Land Filled with Flies: A Political Economy of the Kalahari*. Chicago, University of Chicago Press, 1989.

NIGER

Physical and Social Geography

R. J. HARRISON CHURCH

The land-locked Republic of Niger is the largest state in west Africa. With an area of 1,267,000 sq km (489,191 sq miles), it is larger than Nigeria, its immensely richer southern neighbour, which is Africa's most populous country. The relatively small size of Niger's population, 7,248,100 in September 1988 (according to provisional census results), rising to an officially-estimated 8,361,000 at mid-1993, is largely explained by the country's aridity and remoteness. Population density in 1993 averaged 6.6 persons per sq km. Two-thirds of Niger consists of desert, and most of the north-eastern region is uninhabitable. Hausa tribespeople are the most numerous (some 53% of the population in 1988), followed by the Djerma Songhai (22%), Tuaregs (10%) and Peulhs (10%).

In the north-centre is the partly volcanic Aïr massif, with many dry watercourses remaining from earlier wetter conditions. Agadez, in Aïr, receives an average annual rainfall of no more than about 180 mm. Yet the Tuaregs keep considerable numbers of livestock by moving them seasonally to areas further south, where underground well-water is usually available. South again, along the Niger–Nigerian border, are sandy areas where annual rainfall is just sufficient for the cultivation of groundnuts and millet by Hausa farmers. Cotton is also grown in small, seasonally flooded valleys and depressions.

In the south-west is the far larger, seasonally flooded Niger valley, the pastures of which nourish livestock that have to contend with nine months of drought for the rest of the year. Rice and other crops are grown by the Djerma and Songhai peoples as the Niger flood declines.

Niger thus has three very disparate physical and cultural focuses. Unity has been encouraged by French aid and by economic advance, but the attraction of the more prosperous neighbouring state of Nigeria is considerable. Distances to the nearest ports (Cotonou, in Benin, and Lagos, in Nigeria) are at least 1,370 km, both routes requiring breaks of bulk.

Recent History

PIERRE ENGLEBERT

Revised for this edition by the Editor

Formerly a part of French West Africa, Niger became a self-governing republic within the French Community in December 1958, and proceeded to full independence on 3 August 1960. Control of government passed to the Parti progressiste nigérien (PPN), whose leader, Hamani Diori, favoured the maintenance of traditional social structures and the retention of close economic links with France. Organized opposition, principally by the left-wing nationalist Union nigérienne démocratique (UND, or Sawaba party), had been suppressed since 1959 and the UND leader, Djibo Bakary, was forced into exile.

Niger's valuable reserves of uranium began to be exploited in 1971, but the period 1968–74 was overshadowed by the Sahelian drought. Widespread civil disorder followed allegations that some government ministers were misappropriating stocks of food aid, and in April 1974 Diori was overthrown by the armed forces chief of staff, Lt-Col (later Maj.-Gen.) Seyni Kountché. A Conseil militaire suprême (CMS) was established, with a mandate to distribute food aid fairly and to restore morality to public life. The legislature was replaced by a consultative Conseil national de développement (CND). Although political parties were outlawed, Bakary and other opposition activists were permitted to return to the country.

THE KOUNTCHÉ REGIME

The military government's major preoccupation was planning an economic recovery. Generally amicable relations were maintained with France, and new links were formed with Arab states. Domestically, there was a renewal of political activism following Bakary's return from exile, while personal and policy differences developed within the CMS. Plots to remove Kountché were thwarted in 1975 and again in 1976. Kountché began in 1981 to increase civilian representation in the CMS, and in 1982 preparations were undertaken for a constitutional form of government. A civilian prime minister was appointed in January 1983, and one year later, in January 1984 Kountché established a commission to draft a pre-constitutional document, termed a 'national charter'.

Economic adjustment efforts during this period were impeded by the recurrence of drought in 1984–85 and by the closure of the land border with Nigeria in 1984–86, with the result that Niger's dependence on external financial assistance was increased. Relations with the USA (by now the country's principal source of food aid) assumed considerable importance. Meanwhile, a period of renewed tension between Niger and Libya had fuelled Libyan accusations of the persecution of the light-skinned, nomadic Tuareg population by the Kountché regime. In May 1985, following an armed incident near the Niger–Libya border, all non-Nigerien Tuaregs were expelled. The resultant insecurity apparently prompted the rearrest of Diori; the former president took up residence in Morocco following his release in 1984, where he died in 1989.

The draft 'national charter' was overwhelmingly approved (by some 99.6% of voters) at a national referendum—Niger's first since independence—in June 1987. The charter provided for the establishment of non-elective, consultative institutions at both national and local levels.

SAÏBOU AND THE SECOND REPUBLIC

Kountché died in November 1987, after a year of ill health. The chief of staff of the armed forces, Col (later Brig.) Ali Saïbou, who had assumed the role of acting head of state during Kountché's illness, was formally confirmed in the positions of chairman of the CMS and head of state on 14 November. The new leader promised a continuity of Kountché's ideals and objectives, although he displayed a less austere approach to government. Both Diori and Bakary were received by Saïbou, an appeal was made to exiled Nigeriens to return, and an amnesty was announced for political prisoners. Although the military continued to play a prominent role in government, Oumarou Mamane was reinstated as prime minister in July 1988, and in November a civilian was appointed minister of finance.

A constitutional document (which the CND had been commissioned to draft in mid-1988), which provided for the continued role of the armed forces in what was to be designated the second republic, was endorsed by 99.3% of voters in a national referendum in September 1989. Meanwhile, in August 1988 Saïbou had announced an end to the 14-year ban on all political organizations, with the formation of a new ruling party, the Mouvement national pour une société de développement (MNSD). Saïbou made clear his opposition to the establishment of a multi-party system, but stated that the existence of a single party was not incompatible with the concept of political pluralism. In May 1989 the constituent congress of the MNSD elected a Conseil supérieur d'orientation nationale (CSON) to replace the CMS. As president of the CSON, Saïbou was the sole candidate at a presidential election in December, when he was confirmed as head of state, for a seven-year term, by 99.6% of voters. At the same time a single list of 93 CSON-approved deputies to a new legislative assembly (to succeed the CND) was endorsed by a similar margin. It was subsequently announced that Niger's two remaining political detainees were to be released, to commemorate Saïbou's inauguration as president of the second republic. The post of prime minister was abolished later in December, as part of an extensive reorganization of the council of ministers.

In February 1990 intervention by security forces at a demonstration by university students in Niamey, who had been boycotting classes in protest against proposed education reforms and a reduction in the level of graduate recruitment into the civil service, resulted in three deaths. Saïbou (who had been abroad at the time of the incident) expressed regret at the police action, and announced the appointment of a commission to examine the students' grievances. The ministers of the interior and higher education were dismissed in March, and a prominent industrialist, Aliou Mahamidou, was appointed to the restored post of prime minister; the outgoing minister of the interior was, moreover, among senior figures dismissed from the CSON.

The prospect of political reform, following the announcement in June 1990 that the constitution was to be amended to allow for a pluralist system, failed to end a period of industrial unrest, as the trade union federation, the Union des syndicats des travailleurs du Niger (USTN) demanded the cancellation of unpopular austerity measures. In November a five-day general strike effectively halted production of uranium, closed public buildings and disrupted regional and international air links. Later in the month Saïbou announced that, on the basis of the findings of a constitutional review commission, a multi-party political system would be established. He also announced that less stringent austerity measures would be adopted, in consultation with Niger's external creditors. Interim provision was made for the registration of political parties (the constitution was amended to this effect in April 1991), and it was announced that a national conference would be convened during 1991 to determine the country's political evolution. In January 1991 the USTN announced that it was to end its affiliation with the MNSD.

THE TRANSITION PERIOD

In March 1991 it was announced that the armed forces were to withdraw from political life, and serving military officers were, accordingly, removed from the council of ministers. In July Saïbou resigned as chairman of the Mouvement nationale pour une société de développement–Nassara (as the MNSD had been restyled), in order to distance himself from party politics in preparation for the national conference. He was succeeded as party leader by Col (retd) Tandja Mamadou.

The national conference, convened on 29 July 1991, was initially attended by about 1,200 delegates (representing, among others, the organs of state and some 24 political organizations, together with professional, women's and students' groups). Declaring the conference sovereign, delegates voted to suspend the constitution and to dissolve its organs of state: Saïbou was to remain in office as interim head of state, but his powers were reduced to largely ceremonial functions. The government was deprived of its authority to make financial transactions, and links with external creditors were effectively severed when, in October, the conference voted to suspend adherence to the country's IMF- and World Bank-sponsored programme of eco-

nomic adjustment. The conference had meanwhile assumed control of the armed forces and the police, appointing in September a new armed forces chief of staff and deputy chief of staff. The government was dissolved, and in October the conference appointed Amadou Cheiffou (a regional official of the International Civil Aviation Organization) to head a transitional government pending the installation (scheduled for early 1993) of elected democratic institutions. The conference ended in early November 1991; its chairman, André Salifou (a dean of the University of Niamey), was designated chairman of a 15-member Haut conseil de la République (HCR). This was to function as an interim legislature, and was intended to ensure the transitional government's implementation of conference resolutions, supervise the activities of the head of state, and oversee the drafting of a new constitution.

An atmosphere of national consensus prevailed in the immediate aftermath of the national conference. New austerity measures, and consequent delays in the payment of public-sector salaries, were initially accepted with few signs of discontent. In February 1992, however, junior-ranking members of the armed forces staged a mutiny, demanding not only the payment of salary arrears but also the release of an army captain found responsible by the national conference for the violent suppression of a Tuareg attack on Tchin Tabaraden in May 1990 (see below), as well as the dismissal of senior armed forces officers (including the deputy chief of staff installed by the national conference). The mutineers detained Salifou and the minister of the interior, Mohamed Moussa (himself of Tuareg extraction), and took control of the offices of the state broadcasting media in Niamey. A large public demonstration took place in Niamey to condemn the rebellion, and the USTN and several political parties organized a widely-observed general strike to protest against the military's actions. Order was restored when the government agreed to consider all the mutineers' demands. Weakened by the lack of discipline within the military, the country's precarious financial situation and the continuing Tuareg rebellion in the north, Cheiffou admitted that the transitional government had achieved little in its attempts to address the country's problems. The council of ministers was reorganized later in March, with four ministers dismissed and Moussa transferred to a lesser government post.

Numerous technical difficulties were encountered in the transition process. A constitutional referendum finally took place on 26 December 1992, when the new document was approved by 89.8% of those who voted (56.6% of the electorate: an appeal by Islamic leaders for a boycott of the vote, in view of the secular basis of the constitution, had only limited success). Elections to the new national assembly took place, again after considerable delay, on 14 February 1993, and were contested by 12 of the country's 18 registered political parties. The MNSD was the party winning the greatest number of seats (29) in the 83-member assembly, but was prevented from resuming power by the rapid formation, in the aftermath of the election, of an alliance of parties that was able to form a parliamentary majority. This Alliance des forces de changement (AFC) grouped six parliamentary parties with a total of 50 seats (and was also supported by three parties not represented in the legislature), its principal members being the Convention démocratique et sociale–Rahama (CDS), which held 22 seats in the assembly, the Parti nigérien pour la démocratie et le socialisme–Tarayya (PNDS), with 13 seats, and the Alliance nigérienne pour la démocratie et le progrès social–Zaman Lahiya (ANDPS), with 11 seats. The rate of participation by voters was reported to be somewhat higher than at the time of the constitutional referendum.

The MNSD, which denounced opposition tactics in the legislative elections, was similarly frustrated at the presidential election. At the first round, on 27 February 1993, Tandja Mamadou won the greatest proportion of the votes cast (34.2%). He and his nearest rival, Mahamane Ousmane (the leader of the CDS, who took 26.6% of the first-round votes), proceeded to a second round on 27 March. Ousmane was then elected president by 55.4% of those who voted (just over 35% of the electorate): four of the six other candidates at the first round were members of the AFC, and had urged their supporters to transfer allegiance to Ousmane.

OUSMANE AND THE THIRD REPUBLIC

Mahamane Ousmane, a devout Muslim and the country's first Hausa head of state (his predecessors having been members of the Djerma community), who had consistently expressed his commitment to the principle of a secular state, was inaugurated as president of the third republic on 16 April 1993. Shortly beforehand AFC deputies had elected Moumouni Amadou Djermakoye (the leader of the ANDPS and a first-round candidate for the presidency) as the speaker of the new national assembly. The vote had been boycotted by the MNSD and its allies, protesting that Djermakoye's appointment—in accordance with an agreement made within the AFC prior to the second round of the presidential election—was unconstitutional, and was annulled by the supreme court. Ousmane none the less proceeded to appoint another first-round presidential candidate, Mahamadou Issoufou of the PNDS, to the post of prime minister (again in accordance with a prior AFC arrangement), and in May, in the absence of opposition deputies, Djermakoye was voted in as national assembly speaker.

The incoming president and prime minister were anxious to resume a dialogue with the international financial community, with the aim of securing new credits and debt relief, and the stated task of Issoufou's first council of ministers was to address the country's economic and social crisis. In the absence of significant external assistance, arrears had accumulated in the public and education sectors under the transitional authorities. A period of violent disruption in the education sector prompted the government, in May 1993, to declare the 1992/93 academic year invalid in state secondary schools. Furthermore, despite pledges of emergency financial assistance from France, allowing the payment of public-sector wages outstanding since April, the announcement that arrears accumulated under the transitional authorities could not be paid provoked renewed unrest. A 48-hour strike by USTN members in July was swiftly followed by unrest in the army, as soldiers at Zinder, Tahoua, Agadez and Maradi took local officials hostage and demanded the payment of three months' salary arrears. The USTN organized a 72-hour strike in September, in protest at the government's austerity budget, which included a 24% reduction in wages in the public sector, the imposition of new taxes and an indefinite suspension of the payment of salary arrears. Further strikes were averted when the authorities agreed to suspend implementation of a new law restricting the right to strike, and in October the government and unions reached an agreement whereby public-sector employees would forgo three months' salary arrears in return for lesser wage reductions.

Social tensions were exacerbated following the 50% devaluation, in January 1994, of the CFA franc. In March students who had been campaigning for the payment of grant arrears blocked roads in Niamey, and occupied university buildings and boycotted classes. A government undertaking to pay three months' arrears and to establish a commission to investigate the police actions in relation to the death of a student failed to prevent further violent protests. Later in the month Niamey was effectively paralysed by a 24-hour general strike, organized by the USTN to protest against the recent imposition of the controversial 'right to strike' legislation, and also to demand 30%–50% salary increases to compensate for currency devaluation. A three-day strike followed in April, and the announcement of pay increases of 5%–12% for public-sector employees failed to avert a further 72-hour strike in May. An indefinite strike began in June, but at the end of July the USTN agreed to halt industrial action, pending efforts to achieve a negotiated settlement with the government.

Meanwhile, the MNSD was leading an opposition campaign of civil disobedience, demanding representation in the government proportionate to the percentage of votes won by Tandja Mamadou at the second round of presidential voting in 1993. The arrest of Mamadou and two other opposition leaders in April 1994, after a violent protest resulted in the death of an activist, prompted further demonstrations; numerous arrests ensued (although the three party leaders were released). Following a meeting between Ousmane and representatives of the MNSD in May, the opposition agreed to end its boycott of the national assembly.

In September 1994 the PNDS withdrew from the AFC, and Issoufou resigned as prime minister, in protest against what was perceived as the transfer of some of the prime minister's powers to the president of the republic. Souley Abdoulaye, a member of the CDS, who had hitherto been minister of trade, transport and tourism, was appointed to the premiership. However, his new government did not command a majority in the national assembly, and in October a parliamentary motion of 'no confidence' in the Abdoulaye administration (proposed by the MNSD and the PNDS) was approved by 46 votes to 36. Ousmane dissolved the national assembly, confirming the Abdoulaye government in office pending new elections, which were scheduled for December. Ousmane's decision to dissolve the national assembly, rather than designate a prime minister from the new parliamentary majority, provoked criticism from the labour movement, which claimed that the cost of organizing an early general election would be too great, given the country's economic difficulties. From November the USTN co-ordinated weekly 48-hour strikes.

Financial, technical and logistical difficulties meant that the legislative elections did not take place until 12 January 1995. The results indicated that the MNSD, combining its 29 seats with those of its allies, would be able to form a 43-strong majority group in the national assembly. While Ousmane's CDS increased its representation to 24 seats, the AFC (having lost the support of the PNDS and also that of the Parti progressiste nigérien–Rassemblement démocratique africain) held 40 seats. Abdoulaye resigned as prime minister in early February, but Ousmane declined to accept the new majority's nominee, Hama Amadou (the secretary-general of the MNSD); he appointed instead another member of that party, Amadou Aboubacar Cissé, stating that the latter, as a former official of the World Bank, would be ideally suited to the essential task of negotiating new funding arrangements with external creditors. Cissé was expelled from the MNSD, and the party and its allies announced that they would neither participate in, nor co-operate with, his administration. His position was further undermined by continuing strike action, and by the election of Issoufou to the post of speaker of the national assembly. A parliamentary motion of censure against Cissé was approved by 43 votes to 40, and Ousmane was obliged to accept the majority's nomination of Amadou as prime minister. The new government, appointed in late February, included one member of the AFC: Alitor Mano, of the mainly-Tuareg Union pour la démocratie et le progrès social–Amana (UDPS), was designated minister of agriculture and livestock.

Political and Institutional Conflict

The new government swiftly ended several months of labour unrest, agreeing to cancel the 'right to strike' legislation and to pay two months' salary arrears. Relations between the government and the presidency were, however, less conciliatory, and frequent procedural disputes concerning the prerogatives and competences of the two branches of the executive resulted in much political disruption. Difficulties of 'cohabitation' precipitated an institutional crisis from July 1995, when Ousmane apparently refused to chair a session of the council of ministers at which Amadou's nominations for new senior executives of state-owned organizations (effectively replacing those installed by Ousmane and the AFC government) were to have been adopted. The government ordered the deployment of security forces at the premises of state enterprises, thereby preventing the incumbent executives from performing their duties. Despite the expressed commitment of both Ousmane and Amadou to the principle of defining the respective prerogatives of the president, as elected head of state, and prime minister, as leader of the elected majority, the crisis deepened in subsequent weeks, with the contentious issue of the appointment of state company executives compounded by uncertainty as to Amadou's competence to sign an amnesty decree (for all those involved in the Tuareg conflict—see below). The USTN (which had in August threatened to force the removal from office of both Ousmane and Amadou, should the institutional conflict not be resolved) renewed strike action in October, with two 48-hour stoppages in support of demands for the payment of salary arrears to civil servants and the restitution of sums deducted from wages in reprisal for earlier strikes. The government's draft legislation for the sale of some 30 state and parastatal enterprises was not only a source of concern for the unions, but also exacerbated institutional frictions, as Ousmane expressed concern at what he regarded as the surrender of national institutions. The unresolved issue of salary arrears prompted further industrial action by teachers and civil servants, and in mid-December there were violent demonstrations in Niamey, involving some 2,000 university students who were demanding the payment of one year's grant arrears. Ousmane appealed for the restoration of national cohesion. However, his rejection, in early January 1996, of the government's draft budget (the president expressed concern that a proposed standardized rate of income tax would exacerbate disparities in living standards) precipitated a severe decline in institutional relations. The ensuing political impasse, together with further strike action by public employees and mineworkers opposed to the new tax, and a campaign of civil disobedience by university students in Niamey, raised fears that approval by the IMF of essential new funding might be withheld.

MILITARY TAKEOVER

On 27 January 1996 the elected organs of state were overthrown by the military, under the command of Col (later Brig.-Gen.) Ibrahim Baré Maïnassara (a former aide-de-camp to the late president Kountché, who had been appointed chief of staff of the armed forces in March 1995). The coup leaders, who formed a 12-member Conseil de salut national (CSN), chaired by Maïnassara, asserted that their seizure of power had been necessitated by Niger's descent into political chaos. The CSN suspended the constitution, dissolving the national assembly and other institutions; political parties were suspended, and a state of emergency was imposed. Ousmane, Amadou and Issoufou were placed under house arrest: they were reportedly released at the end of the month, although some restrictions on their movements remained.

The CSN asserted that it had no wish to 'cling to power'. The military immediately pledged its commitment to the pursuit of policies of economic restructuring, with a view to concluding funding arrangements with the IMF and the World Bank, and undertook to consolidate efforts towards the restoration of peace in the north of the country. A national forum was to be convened to consider the revision of the constitution and the electoral code, with the aim of preventing a recurrence of the paralysis of recent months; the forum would also determine a timetable for a swift return to government by democratically elected authorities. The coup was, none the less, generally condemned internationally; Western donors withdrew all non-humanitarian assistance, and negotiations with the IMF were stalled.

In late January 1996 the CSN appointed Boukary Adji, the deputy governor of the Banque centrale des états de l'Afrique de l'ouest (and a former finance minister under Kountché) to the post of prime minister. Adji's transitional government was composed entirely of civilians. Among its members was Salifou (the former chairman of the transitional HCR), who was named minister of state, in charge of higher education and research. The government's stated priorities were economic and financial restructuring and the provision of guarantees of health care, education, food and national security. The CSN, meanwhile, pursued a wide range of contacts; Maïnassara held separate discussions with Ousmane, Amadou and Issoufou at the beginning of February, following which each (although condemning the coup) expressed willingness to co-operate with the new regime in securing a restoration of civilian rule. The USTN received assurances regarding the payment of salaries. The appointment, in early February, of military officers to the governorships of Niger's administrative regions was attributed by the CSN to the need to ensure neutrality in the organization of the elections that would precede a return to constitutional government.

In mid-February 1996 the deposed president, prime minister and speaker of the national asembly signed a joint text, in Maïnassara's presence, that effectively endorsed the legitimacy of the CSN and recognized that the assumption of power by the military had been necessitated by the difficulties that were being experienced in the functioning of the organs of state. A preliminary timetable for a return to civilian rule was subsequently released, culminating in a constitutional referendum, the date for which was revised almost immediately (apparently to coincide with a summit meeting of francophone states in Bordeaux, France), rescheduling the referendum for June and

the completion of the election programme by September. The government of France restored full co-operation by early March.

Two independent consultative bodies were established in late February 1996. It was emphasized that both the advisory Conseil des sages (which elected Saïbou as its chairman) and the co-ordinating committee of the national forum, one of the functions of which was to submit proposals for constitutional changes to the forthcoming forum, would function free from military influence. Each body included former state officials, traditional chiefs, religious leaders and members of the judiciary. The 'national forum for democratic renewal' was convened in Niamey at the beginning of April. Other than the members of the co-ordinating committee and the Conseil des sages, its 700 members included representatives of the dissolved parliament and of workers' and employers' organizations. The forum adopted revisions to the constitution that aimed to guarantee greater institutional stability, essentially by conferring executive power solely on the president of the republic and requiring the prime minister to implement a programme stipulated by the head of state. Amendments were also made to the electoral code and to the charter governing the activities of political organizations. In mid-April a decree was issued bringing forward the date of the constitutional referendum to 12 May: this would enable the presidential poll to take place in July, prior to the commencement of the rainy season. Also in April it was announced that restrictions on the movements of Ousmane, Amadou and Issoufou had been ended, and all three accompanied Maïnassara to northern Niger to celebrate 'national concord day', on the first anniversary of the signing of the peace agreement with the Tuareg movement (see below).

Despite Maïnassara's earlier assurances that he and his associates in the CSN had no personal political ambitions, by May 1996 he had confirmed reports of his intention to seek election to the presidency as a non-partisan candidate. Adji's transitional government was reshuffled shortly afterwards. The constitutional referendum took place, as scheduled, on 12 May. According to the official results, the revised document was approved by 92.3% of voters; an abstention rate of some 65% was, however, recorded. The ban on activities by political organizations was revoked shortly afterwards, and this was followed by the ending of the state of emergency imposed in the aftermath of the *coup d'état*. Ousmane, Issoufou, Mamadou and Djermakoye (Issoufou's predecessor as national assembly speaker) swiftly announced their intention to contest the presidential election. Meanwhile, there was criticism among opposition groups of the appointment by the Conseil des sages of a new high court of justice, which was to be solely responsible for trying cases of high treason and other offences committed by public figures (including past officials) in the exercise of their state duties. This end to the political consensus of recent months was compounded by tensions between the authorities and the electoral supervisory body, the Commission électorale nationale indépendante (CENI), as the government disregarded the latter's recommendations that the presidential election be postponed, owing to delays in the finalization of voters' lists and in the distribution of election materials. The announcement that difficulties in compiling accurate lists meant that it would be impossible to arrange for Nigeriens abroad to vote was, furthermore, condemned by the CENI as a violation both of citizens' rights and of the prerogatives and autonomy of the commission. A new funding arrangement was, in the mean time, concluded with the IMF.

Voting in the presidential election commenced, as scheduled, on 7 July 1996, but was quickly halted in Niamey and in several other areas where preparations were incomplete: polling took place in these areas the following day. Controversy arose when, shortly before the end of voting, the authorities announced the dissolution of the CENI, in response to what they termed its 'obvious and deliberate' obstruction of the electoral process. A new commission, largely comprising senior civil servants, was appointed to collate the election results. The democratic credentials of the CSN were further brought into doubt after Maïnassara's four rivals for the presidency were placed under house arrest. The provisional results of voting, announced by the new commission on 9 July, showed an outright victory for Maïnassara, with some 52.2% of the votes cast; ex-president Ousmane had won 19.8%, and Mamadou 15.7%. Security measures in the capital were reinforced in response to opposition unrest, the closure was ordered of the headquarters of the main opposition parties, and a curfew was imposed in Zinder (Ousmane's birthplace) following violent clashes between police and demonstrators: the ministry of the interior and territorial administration subsequently confirmed that 86 arrests had been made in the post-election period. Meanwhile, the USTN, which asserted that Nigeriens would not tolerate a further *coup d'état*, called a general strike, although this was stated by the authorities to have been poorly observed. The supreme court validated the election results on 21 July, and the release from house arrest of the defeated presidential candidates was announced the following day. All those detained in the aftermath of the election were reported to have been released by the end of the month, and the curfew was ended in Zinder; however, it transpired that Issoufou remained under surveillance.

THE FOURTH REPUBLIC

Maïnassara was installed as president of the fourth republic on 7 August 1996. In his inaugural address, he appealed for national unity as a basis for the forging of lasting economic and social stability, and pledged a continuance of the campaign against corruption, injustice and irresponsibility in public affairs. Issoufou was released from house arrest in mid-August, as was Bazoum (who had also recently been placed under surveillance). A new government, under Boukary Adji, was named later in August: incoming members included former prime minister Souley Abdoulaye, as minister of transport, and Amadou Cissé, who returned from a World Bank posting in Chad to become minister of state for the economy, finance and planning. Members of the CDS, the MNSD and the PNDS who accepted government posts were subsequently expelled from their parties.

There was a significant reversal of foreign policy in late August 1996, when relations were resumed with the People's Republic of China. André Salifou (who, as chairman of the HCR, had opposed the restoration of links with Taiwan in 1992) signed documents to this effect while visiting China in his capacity as minister of state for foreign affairs. Disappointment was expressed at the level and nature of co-operation by Taiwan, which severed links shortly afterwards.

The legislative elections, which had been scheduled to take place in late September 1996, were postponed until 10 November, in order that they might take place in what were termed 'suitable' conditions. In early September a group of eight opposition parties (including the CDS, the MNSD and the PNDS) stipulated several preconditions for their participation in the elections, foremost among them the annulment of the presidential election and the restitution of the CENI. These parties subsequently formed a Front pour la restauration et la défense de la démocratie (FRDD). Later in September the Conseil des sages recommended the further postponement of the legislative elections, pending the resolution of difficulties (including the threatened boycott by the FRDD). Maïnassara asked the government to pursue inter-party negotiations, with mediation by the Conseil des sages, to bring about a reconciliation. In the ensuing talks it emerged that the government was prepared to concede opposition access to the state media and an end to the ban (in force since the presidential election) on public meetings and demonstrations. The government also announced the postponement of the legislative election, to 23 November, and the restoration of the CENI, with the same composition as that which had overseen the 1995 election. The commission's prerogatives were, however, amended, and the FRDD reiterated that it would not participate in the forthcoming poll unless the CENI was reinstated with its original powers and the presidential election was annulled.

In mid-October 1996 a report by a prominent human rights organization, Amnesty International, stated that Niger's human rights situation had worsened since the coup, with the deterioration particularly marked since the presidential election. In response to allegations of arrests, deportations to the north, degrading treatment and intimidation of opposition activists, the denial of press freedom and the harassment of journalists, Maïnassara asserted that there were no political prisoners in Niger, that the press was totally free, and that political organizations enjoyed freedom of association and movement.

The legislative elections, on 23 November 1996, were contested by 11 parties and movements, as well as by independent candidates. The FRDD claimed that its appeal to supporters to boycott the vote had been successful: turn-out was low in all areas other than Dosso (Maïnassara's home province) and Agadez, with polling stations in Niamey almost deserted. However, official figures showed a level of participation similar to that at previous elections. According to official results published by the election commission three days after the poll, the pro-Maïnassara Union nationale des indépendants pour le renouveau démocratique (UNIRD) took 52 of the national assembly's 83 seats. International observers pronounced themselves satisfied with the organization and conduct of the election. (The supreme court later upheld complaints of fraud in three constituencies won by the UNIRD, annulling the results there.)

Following the completion of the constitutional referendum and the presidential and legislative elections, the CSN was formally dissolved on 12 December 1996. A new government was appointed in the following week, with Amadou Cissé as prime minister. Salifou became minister of state, responsible for relations with parliament. The FRDD leaders had rejected an invitation by Maïnassara to join the government, and the deputy leader of the CDS, Jackou Senoussi, was expelled from the party after accepting a ministerial post. The final session of the Conseil des sages took place on 26 December, and the national assembly was inaugurated the following day. Moutari Moussa was elected president of the legislature at the end of the month.

As the first anniversary of the *coup d'état* approached, the government warned that opposition parties were planning 'a genuine campaign of permanent destabilization'. In mid-January 1997 an unauthorized demonstration in Niamey to mark what the opposition termed a 'day of democratic initiative' degenerated into clashes with security forces. Some 62 people were arrested, among them Ousmane, Mamadou and Issoufou (who were initially placed under house arrest but subsequently taken into custody). It was announced that they would be tried by the state security court, which had been restored in the aftermath of the demonstration. Considerable controversy ensued regarding the validity of the court's revival. Neither the constitution nor the penal code made provision for the court, which had been in existence under the Kountché regime; however, the government invoked constitutional provisions whereby, unless specifically repealed, laws in force at the time of the promulgation of the constitution remained valid. Meanwhile, national and international human rights bodies, as well as the governments of France and the USA, expressed concern at the arrests. Violent clashes in Zinder were followed, one week after the 'day of democratic initiative', by a second protest in Niamey to demand the release of the opposition leaders. All were released two days later, reportedly on Maïnassara's direct order, and the president appealed to the Cissé administration and the FRDD to co-operate in forming a government of national unity. However, little progress was made in reconciling the government and opposition. Foremost among the FRDD's preconditions for participation in government was the dissolution of the national assembly and the holding of free and fair elections. Its other demands included guarantees of opposition access to the media, of press freedom and freedom of association; the FRDD also required an end to the privatization programme, to which the government was expressly committed. For its part, the government stated its willingness to negotiate on all issues other than the institutions of the fourth republic, thus precluding fresh elections. (It was noted at this time that opposition actions were being increasingly covered by the official broadcasting and press services, as were statements by the national human rights association.) Several demonstrations proceeded peacefully in February, but in early March police used tear gas to prevent an unauthorized opposition rally from proceeding near the parliament building.

Tensions were, meanwhile, exacerbated by labour unrest in February–March 1997. Strikes involved, most notably, school-teachers, demanding improved pay and conditions, and employees at the state electricity company, protesting against the proposed privatization of the company. The power workers' dispute, which had necessitated the deployment of security forces in order to ensure electricity supplies, was declared illegal by the government, which stated that constitutional guarantees of the right to strike did not extend to some strategic sectors. Following stoppages by customs workers in March, their union was dissolved, since strike action was similarly outlawed in paramilitary sectors. The USTN undertook a 72-hour strike in early April, demanding the payment of salary arrears and the release of power workers detained for acts of sabotage. The strike was reported to have been fully observed in educational establishments, and to have had partial support in other sectors. In mid-April four members of the power workers' union were sentenced to prison sentences of up to two years, having been convicted of sabotage.

Addressing the diplomatic corps at the beginning of April 1997, the minister of foreign affairs warned against interference in Niger's internal affairs. Allegations that members of certain diplomatic missions had taken part in demonstrations and issued statements incompatible with diplomatic ethics were widely assumed to be directed at staff at the US, Canadian and German embassies. Later in April, speaking in Tchin Tabaraden to commemorate 'national concord day', Maïnassara appealed to the opposition to engage in dialogue and reconciliation. In early May, none the less, a three-day general strike by civil servants resulted in the closure of schools and colleges and disruption to hospitals and health centres. Meanwhile, the government and opposition resumed a dialogue; as before, however, little was achieved, with the opposition continuing to demand the dissolution of the national assembly and the authorities reiterating that there was no constitutional provision for the holding of fresh elections before 2001 (the date of the expiry of the national assembly's mandate).

A reorganization of the government in mid-June 1997 was followed by a number of other state appointments. Within the military, Col Moussa Moumouni Djermakoye, hitherto prefect-mayor of Niamey, was designated chief of staff of the armed forces, while Lt-Col Issa Kalagbo was named deputy chief of staff. New military prefects were also appointed to Niger's departments. Earlier in June there had been unrest at military garrisons in northern and eastern Niger, involving soldiers who were demanding the payment of arrears in allowances, and the military commander and prefect of Maradi had been taken hostage by mutineers. However, a government statement on the unrest countered reports that the then deputy chief of staff of the armed forces, who was a member of a delegation dispatched to examine the soldiers' grievances, had been among the hostages. Earlier in June the national assembly had appointed members to the high court of justice; the court's president was to be Moumouni Amadou Djermakoye.

As the first anniversary of Maïnassara's election to the presidency approached, the government announced a nation-wide ban on demonstrations planned for 7–8 July 1997. Security forces were mobilized as demonstrations proceeded none the less in several towns on 8 July, with violent clashes reported in Maradi, Zinder and Tahoua, while in Niamey police surrounded the headquarters of the CDS, PNDS and MNSD, where opposition leaders had taken refuge.

Amnesty International issued a further report in May 1997, urging the government to put an end to violations of human rights now perpetrated by the security forces 'with impunity' and condemning what it alleged were arbitrary arrests, systematic intimidation and unfair trials of opposition members in recent months. In late June the national assembly approved new measures governing the media; strict penalties were stipulated for the publication or distribution of libellous or offensive material. In late October the president of the national human rights league was sentenced to two years' imprisonment, having been convicted, under the new law, of defamation of the head of state; the director of publishing of an independent weekly, *L'Alternative*, also received a custodial sentence. Both were released on bail in December, pending appeal.

In early October 1997 Maïnassara inaugurated an operation aimed at ensuring greater accountability in public life. Meeting with officials of the country's development projects and public and parastatal enterprises, the president denounced the 'unorthodox' manner in which such establishments were being managed. In late November Maïnassara dismissed the entire Cissé government, on the grounds of its failure to address Niger's political, economic and social difficulties: by this time a

resumption of hostilities in the north was compounded by chronic food insecurity as a result of poor harvests, by further labour unrest (the new academic year had already been disrupted by strike action involving teachers who were demanding the payment of salary arrears), and by ongoing political agitation. The FRDD subsequently emphasized that it would not consider participation in a new government until fresh legislative elections were held. Maïnassara appointed Ibrahim Hassane Maiyaki, the minister of foreign affairs and co-operation in the outgoing administration, as prime minister, and named a new council of ministers at the beginning of December. Many members of the previous administration were reappointed, although there were, notably, new ministers of national defence, of justice and human rights, and of finance, economic reform and privatization.

In early January 1998 it was announced that members of a commando unit had been arrested and charged with attempting to eliminate Maïnassara and other senior officials. Four of the alleged commandos made a televised confession in which they stated that they had been operating on the direct orders of Hama Amadou. The former prime minister was arrested, along with Mohamed Bazoum (the minister of foreign affairs in the months following the 1996 coup) and another former minister, Issoufou Assoumane (the leader of the Union des forces populaires pour la démocratie et le progrès–Sawaba). Although all three denied involvement in any conspiracy, Maïnassara stated that Amadou had admitted to having received the alleged commandos at his residence, and to having given one money to purchase a weapon. Several members of the armed forces said to have been involved in the plot were reported to have fled the country. Opposition leaders denounced the arrests: Issoufou accused the government of fabricating a plot in an attempt to divert attention from the country's political, economic and social crisis, while Ousmane urged the authorities to show flexibility with regard to a plot for which the evidence was unconvincing. Bazoum and Assoumane were released within a week; Amadou was released on bail shortly afterwards, charged with forming a militia, criminal conspiracy and illegal possession of weapons.

In late February 1998 soldiers at three military garrisons in the Diffa region, in the extreme south-east, mutinied, taking hostage local military commanders and civilian administrators. The rebels imposed a curfew and seized the local radio station to demand the payment of arrears in salary and other allowances. It was announced that military officials would travel to Diffa to negotiate, and the minister of national defence gave assurances that salary arrears would be paid. (Although the government stated that the mutiny had been provoked entirely by material grievances, it was reported that soldiers who had been engaged in the conflict against Tuareg and Toubou rebels in the north and east were increasingly dissatisfied at the terms of recent peace arrangements with these groups.) The mutiny spread to the north—to Agadez and Arlit—and also to Zinder, with soldiers again capturing military and civilian officials; a director of the uranium-mining company at Arlit was also taken hostage. All the rebellions had been abandoned by the beginning of March (the last to end was the Diffa mutiny), after the government promised payment of two months' salary arrears (four months' pay was outstanding) and, acknowledging that conditions in the north and east were particularly harsh, undertook to establish a minimum standard of living for all military personnel.

Meanwhile, the issue of arrears in non-military sectors provoked renewed strike action and student boycotts in February–March 1998. Negotiations between the government and the unions had consistently failed to reach a compromise: the USTN accused the authorities of laxity in dealing with workers' grievances, while the government denounced the unions' intransigence and politicization.

In February 1998 three parties of the presidential group formed the Alliance des forces démocratiques et sociales (AFDS), which grouped Jackou Senoussi's Parti nigerien pour l'autogestion–al Umat, the Parti pour l'unité nationale et le développement–Salama and the ANDPS. However, the AFDS subsequently protested that it was being marginalized in the political process, complaining that its activities were not being covered by the state media, and in subsequent months the alliance was increasingly associated with the opposition. Meanwhile, the FRDD laid down a number of preconditions for participation at the forthcoming local elections: among their demands were the rehabilitation of the CENI and guarantees of the neutrality of regional administrators and the security forces. Political tensions escalated from April. Clashes in Tahoua between the security forces and FRDD activists, who were demanding Maïnassara's resignation, were followed by violent protests by the FRDD in Maradi and in Zinder, where opposition activists allegedly attacked vehicles and property belonging to the pro-Maïnassara Rassemblement pour la démocratie et le progrès–Djamaa (RDP). A rally by the presidential party proceeded in Maradi under police surveillance, after security reinforcements were flown in from Niamey to help restore order. Opposition protests continued until Maïnassara emphasized his determination to end the political violence; an opposition demonstration that had been scheduled to take place in Niamey at the beginning of May was subsequently banned, although a protest in Zinder proceeded without intervention by the security forces.

In July 1998 it was reported that the government and 11 opposition parties (i.e. the eight FRDD and three AFDS members) had signed a 10-point agreement aimed at ending two years of political crisis and thus facilitating opposition participation in the forthcoming local elections (now scheduled for November). Revisions were outlined to electoral procedures and institutions, as well as to the manner in which senior appointments were made to the supreme court. It was agreed that all political groups should have equal access to the state media, and that freedom to demonstrate should be respected. The government undertook to ensure the political neutrality of the military, traditional chiefs and foreign diplomats accredited to Niger. The president of the CENI was to be appointed by consensus among the country's magistrates, and was to have no voting rights. However, the opposition challenged the appointment by Maïnassara of Lawali Mahamane Danda to head the electoral body. Danda none the less protested his neutrality, and gave assurances that the forthcoming polls would be transparent. The remaining members of the CENI (which was to be composed of representatives of the government, political parties, human rights and journalists' organizations, as well as the defence and security forces) were appointed by presidential decree in mid-September. It was evident, however, that preparations were inadequate to allow the elections to proceed as scheduled, and in early October the CENI duly postponed voting until 7 February 1999.

At a press conference on the eve of the local elections, the minister of the interior, Souley Abdoulaye, reiterated earlier warnings to foreign diplomatic missions to refrain from interfering in Niger's domestic political affairs. The minister furthermore showed a document purportedly giving evidence of an opposition plot aimed at the 'total conquest of power' by the end of July 1999.

Voting in the regional, district and municipal elections took place, according to the revised schedule, on 7 February 1999. Obvious irregularities ranged from the absence, to the destruction, of voting equipment, and the CENI emphasized that it favoured by-elections in affected areas. Full results, which were not released by the supreme court until 7 April, gave the 11 opposition parties a marginal overall majority of seats in those municipal, district and regional assemblies where the elections were deemed valid. Voting was to be rerun at 4,000 polling stations in 21 regional wards and 17 of the country's 72 districts. The FRDD and AFDS denounced Maïnassara as personally responsible for the disruption to votes in those areas, and demanded the president's resignation.

DEATH OF MAÏNASSARA

On 9 April 1999 Maiyaki made a broadcast to the nation, announcing the death of Maïnassara in an 'unfortunate accident' at a military airbase in Niamey. The prime minister urged a calming of the social and political climate, and stated that the defence and security forces would continue to be the guarantors of republican order and national unity. A one-month period of national mourning was decreed. Maiyaki announced the dissolution of the national assembly, as well as the temporary suspension of all party political activity. Despite the official explanation for his death, it was generally perceived that Maï-

nassara had been assassinated by members of his presidential guard, and that a *coup d'état* had taken place. Members of the national assembly initially rejected the dissolution of the legislature, stating that the 1996 constitution remained in force and that its institutions must therefore continue to function. On 11 April 1999, however, the constitution was suspended, and its institutions (including the council of ministers, legislature and supreme court) were duly dissolved. The February local elections were annulled. A military Conseil de réconciliation nationale (CRN), under the chairmanship of Maj. Daouda Mallam Wanké (hitherto head of the presidential guard whose officers had been responsible for Maïnassara's 'accident'), was to exercise executive and legislative authority during a nine-month transitional period prior to the restoration of elected civilian institutions. Wanké immediately signed a 21-point ordinance on interim political authority, which was to function as a constitutional document during the transitional period. A new constitution was to be prepared, for submission to a national referendum, and it was stated that the timetable for the restoration of civilian rule, which envisaged the installation of elected organs of state on 31 December, would be strictly adhered to. Assurances were also given that the CRN had no political ambitions beyond ensuring the restoration of democracy. Maiyaki was reappointed as prime minister, to head the government during the transitional period, and a new council of ministers was named. Ide Niandou, as minister of finance and economic reforms, and Rissa Ag Boula, as minister of tourism and crafts, were, notably, retained from the previous administration. New appointees included the former CENI chairman, Lawali Mahamane Danda, as minister of justice. Moussa Moumouni Djermakoye, who had been succeeded as chief of staff of the armed forces by Lt-Col Soumara Zanguina (and who was believed to have rejected the post of CRN chairman) became minister of national defence. In July, in a government reshuffle described as 'technical' by the CRN, the minister of the interior and territorial administration, Lt-Col Boureima Moumouni, was appointed chief of general staff of the armed forces, while Zanguina became an adviser to the head of state. Niandou was replaced as minister of finance and economic reforms by Seydou Sidibe.

Although the military takeover was condemned by the parties that had supported Maïnassara, the incoming regime was broadly welcomed, in its initial stages, by the FRDD and the AFDS. Niger's creditors, however, strongly denounced the events of 9 April: France announced the immediate suspension of all military and non-humanitarian civilian assistance, while the European Union (EU) announced that it was to review its co-operation with Niger. In subsequent weeks the EU appeared to make the maintenance of assistance conditional upon the commissioning of an independent inquiry into Maïnassara's death. The CRN confirmed in mid-June that such an inquiry would be commissioned, but emphasized that this was in response to a complaint lodged by the late president's family. Other west African governments also denounced the apparent coup, and Wanké embarked on a tour of the region in an effort to explain and secure support for the CRN's actions. In late May 1999 a meeting of ministers responsible for foreign affairs of the Economic Community of West African States (ECOWAS) strongly condemned the military takeover, and emphasized the urgent need for an independent inquiry into Maïnassara's death; however, ministers noted the CRN's expressed commitment to implementing the transition programme, and recognized the need to assist and support Niger in its efforts towards the restoration of constitutional democracy. Meanwhile, Nigeria and Libya, both of which had enjoyed particularly close relations with the Maïnassara regime, condemned the military takeover. It was reported in mid-April that Maiyaki had been forced to leave a summit meeting of the Tripoli-based Community of the Sahel-Saharan States, of which Niger had been a founder member in 1997. However, relations between the CRN and the government of Libya had apparently normalized by the end of 1999. In December, notably, the two countries signed an agreement envisaging the establishment of a joint company to distribute petroleum and liquefied natural gas; it was also agreed to expedite the establishment of a joint company for petroleum exploration and production. The CRN subsequently stated that a report on the circumstances of Maïnassara's death had been lodged with those organizations concerned.

In mid-May 1999 Issaka Souna was appointed to chair the CENI. Shortly afterwards a consultative council of state elders was inaugurated, with the stated tasks of considering options for a draft constitution, restoring national unity, and seeking solutions to the country's acute social and political difficulties. Chaired by Moumouni Amadou Djermakoye, its members included Mahamadou Issoufou, Souley Abdoulaye, Hama Amadou and Amadou Aboubacar Cissé, together with other former state officials, representatives of the religious and civilian communities, and traditional leaders. Indications that the council was to recommend a semi-presidential form of government were criticized by political groups, most notably the RDP, as being likely to result in such institutional paralysis as had provoked the military takeover of January 1996. The trade union movement also condemned a system of this kind as a drain on state resources. (After a brief respite following Maïnassara's death, by mid-1999 civil servants' unions had resumed strike action in support of demands for the payment of wage arrears: some 10 months' remuneration was now outstanding in some sectors.)

Meanwhile, in early May 1999 Maiyaki's former minister of the interior was arrested; at the beginning of June it was reported that the former minister of defence, Yahya Tounkar, was under house arrest after defying a government order confining several ex-ministers to the capital. The arrest was reported in early July of two former government ministers, together with the deputy leader of the RDP and a director of a commercial bank. In August an anti-corruption commission appointed by the CRN announced that it had recovered some 2,000m. francs CFA in state funds misappropriated under former regimes.

THE FIFTH REPUBLIC

The draft constitution of what was to be designated the fifth republic envisaged a balance of powers between the president, government and legislature. The president, who was accorded what were termed 'broad ordinary and arbitral powers', was to be politically liable only in the case of high treason. The government, under an appointed prime minister, was to be responsible to the legislative national assembly, which would be competent to remove the prime minister by vote of censure. The draft document was submitted to a referendum on 18 July 1999 (one week later than first scheduled), when it was approved by 89.57% of those who voted. The rate of participation by voters was, however, only about one-third of the registered electorate. The first round of presidential voting was subsequently set for 3 October, but was revised in mid-August to 17 October; an eventual second round was to take place, in tandem with legislative voting, on 24 November. By late August eight candidates had declared their intention to contest the presidency: ex-president Ousmane, for the CDS; Tandja Mamadou, for the MNSD; Mahamadou Issoufou, for the PNDS; Moumouni Amadou Djermakoye, for the ANDPS; André Salifou, for the Union des patriotes democratiques et progressistes–Shamuwa; and Amadou Djibo Ali, for the Union des nigériens indépendants. The RDP candidature was sought by both Hamid Algabid, the party chairman, and Amadou Cissé, and was referred to the state court for adjudication.

Voting proceeded as scheduled and was considered both by the CENI and by independent observers to have been largely transparent and peaceful. Provisional results issued by the CENI three days after the poll, showed a lead for Mamadou, with 32.30% of the votes cast, followed by Issoufou, with 22.78%, and Ousmane, with 22.52%. The rate of participation by voters was 43.66%. Mamadou and Issoufou thus proceeded to a second round, prior to which each accused the other of preparing to manipulate the vote. Having secured the support notably of Ousmane (whose 'cohabitation' with the MNSD had resulted in the institutional paralysis prior to the 1996 coup), Mamadou was elected president with 58.9% of the votes cast. The rate of participation was, however, only about 39% of the registered electorate. The MNSD was similarly successful in the concurrent elections to the new assemblée nationale, winning 38 of the 83 seats; the CDS took 17, the PNDS 16, the RDP eight and the

ANDPS four. The results of the elections were confirmed by the constitutional court in early December 1999.

Prior to his departure from office, Wanké stated that, despite the enormous difficulties of the CRN's term of office, the outcome of the transition period had been largely positive in terms of reconciling the Nigerien people and restoring what he considered a 'moderate and operational democracy'. Mamadou was inaugurated as president of the Fifth Republic on 22 December 1999. The new head of state pledged his commitment to democracy and respect for human rights, individual freedoms and security; he urged responsibility on the part of the opposition, and warned against practices such as corruption and influence-peddling, which had led to what he termed the country's 'disastrous situation'. Mamadou considered the achievement of political, social and institutional stability to be a prerequisite for Niger's economic and financial recovery. Hama Amadou, the secretary-general of the MNSD, was subsequently appointed prime minister. His government, named in early January 2000, included Ali Badjo Gamatie as minister of finance and economic reforms, Nassirou Sabo as minister of foreign affairs, co-operation and African integration, and Sabiou Dadi Gao as minister of national defence. Mamadou urged the government to act to address 'resolutely' the problem of outstanding salaries, grants and scholarships (some 12–13 months' salaries were now outstanding in many areas of the public sector), and to adopt an emergency financial programme so as to allow the rapid resumption of international assistance. In late January schoolteachers ended a three-month strike; however, new industrial action by university lecturers was subsequently joined by workers from other state sectors.

In early January 2000 the newly-inaugurated assemblée nationale adopted draft amnesty legislation, as provided for in the constitution. The amnesty was opposed by the RDP, and many activists of the party joined a demonstration in mid-February to denounce the legislation and to demand an international enquiry into the death of Maïnassara. In April Amnesty International again urged a reconsideration of the impunity clause, in order that those responsible for political killings might be brought to justice. Meanwhile, the head of the national human rights league announced in January that he had lodged a complaint against Wanké in respect of economic crimes allegedly committed by the outgoing military leader.

Following a visit to France by Tandja Mamadou in January 2000, during which the newly-installed Nigerien president met with President Jacques Chirac and Prime Minister Lionel Jospin, the resumption of French co-operation was formalized with the announcement of exceptional assistance principally to allow payment of outstanding salaries in the public sector. Niger's new minister of foreign affairs, co-operation and African integration visited Washington, DC, in February, and in the following month the USA announced an end to the sanctions imposed after Maïnassara's death; however, the US administration subsequently stated that its former aid programmes in Niger would not be resumed. (Meanwhile, preliminary discussions with the IMF for a new programme of funding commenced in early 2000.)

In March 2000 12 opposition parties, led by the PNDS, formed the Coordination des forces démocratiques coalition. Similarly, 17 parties loyal to the president formed an Alliance des forces démocratiques in July; this consisted mainly of the MNSD and also the CDS.

ETHNIC CONFLICT

As in neighbouring Mali, ethnic unrest was precipitated by the return to Niger, beginning in the late 1980s, of large numbers of Tuareg nomads, who had migrated to Libya and Algeria earlier in the decade to escape the drought. In May 1990 Tuaregs launched a violent attack on the prison and gendarmerie at Tchin Tabaraden, in north-eastern Niger. Reports suggested that the incident reflected Tuareg dissatisfaction that promises, made by Saïbou following his accession to power, regarding assistance for the rehabilitation of returnees to Niger had not been fulfilled (it appeared that funds designated for this purpose had been misappropriated). The alleged brutality of the armed forces in quelling the raid was to provoke considerable disquiet, both within Niger and internationally. In April 1991 44 Tuaregs were acquitted of involvement in the attack on Tchin Tabaraden.

Rebels mounted a renewed offensive in October, and in the months that followed numerous violent attacks were directed at official targets in the north, and clashes took place between Tuareg rebels and the security forces. Many arrests were reported, while Tuareg groups were known to have kidnapped several armed forces members. In early 1992 the transitional government intensified security measures in northern Niger, formally recognizing, for the first time, that there was a rebellion in that area (incidents had hitherto been dismissed as isolated acts of banditry) and acknowledging the existence of a Tuareg movement, the Front de libération de l'Aïr et l'Azaouad (FLAA). In the following month the leader of the FLAA, Rissa Ag Boula, stated that the Tuareg rebels were not seeking to achieve independence, but rather the establishment of a federal system, in which each ethnic group would have its own administrative entity.

A two-week truce, agreed in May 1992 by the government and FLAA, in preparation for peace negotiations, failed. Tuareg attacks resumed in subsequent months, and in August the armed forces launched a major offensive against the Tuareg rebellion in the north. According to official figures, 186 Tuaregs were arrested in late August and early September, both in the north and in Niamey. Among those detained were Mohamed Moussa (who, as minister of the interior, had initiated contacts with Tuareg leaders) and the prefect of Agadez. Military authority was intensified, following renewed Tuareg attacks, by the appointment, in October, of senior members of the security forces to northern administrative posts. In November a commission appointed by the transitional government to consider the Tuareg issue recommended a far-reaching programme of decentralization, according legal status and financial autonomy to local communities. In December the government announced the release from custody of 57 Tuaregs.

In January 1993 five people were killed in a Tuareg attack on an MNSD meeting in the northern town of Abala. Although he escaped injury, the principal target of the attack was said to have been Tandja Mamadou, who had been minister of the interior at the time of the suppression of the Tchin Tabaraden raid. Although Tuareg attacks and acts of sabotage persisted, later in January a further 81 Tuaregs, including Mohamed Moussa, were released from detention. In February 30 people were reported to have been killed in raids by Tuaregs (for which the FLAA denied responsibility) around Tchin Tabaraden. In March, following Algerian mediation, Rissa Ag Boula (who was based in Algeria, despite attempts by the Nigerien authorities to secure his extradition) announced a unilateral truce for the duration of the campaign for the second round of the presidential election. Tuareg representatives in Niamey signed a similar truce agreement (brokered by France). The election of the new organs of state appeared to offer new prospects for dialogue, and in early April the transitional government and the FLAA reached an agreement for an extension of the truce. About 30 Tuareg prisoners were released shortly afterwards, and in mid-April the Tuaregs released their hostages.

President Ousmane and prime minister Issoufou identified the resolution of the Tuareg issue as a major priority, and, although sporadic resistance was reported, the truce accord was largely respected. In June 1993 it was revealed that representatives of the Nigerien government and the Tuaregs had for some time been negotiating in France, and on 10 June a formal, three-month truce agreement was signed in Paris. The accord provided for the demilitarization of the north, and envisaged the instigation of negotiations on the Tuaregs' political demands. Financial assistance was promised to facilitate the return of Tuareg refugees from Algeria, and development funds were pledged for northern areas. A committee was to be established to oversee the implementation of the agreement. However, the Paris accord encountered some opposition within the Tuareg community: a new group, the Armée révolutionnaire de libération du nord-Niger (ARLN), emerged to denounce the accord, and by July a further split was evident between supporters of the truce (led by Mano Dayak, the Tuareg signatory to the agreement), who broke away from the FLAA to form the Front de libération de Tamoust (FLT), and its opponents (led by Rissa Ag Boula), who stated that they could not support any agreement that contained no specific commitment to discussion of the federalist issue. In September the FLT and the Nigerien government agreed to

extend the truce for a further three months. The FLAA and the ARLN refused to sign the accord, but in the following month they joined the FLT in a Coordination de la résistance armée (CRA), with the aim of presenting a cohesive programme in future dealings with the Nigerien authorities. It was indicated that the FLAA and the ARLN would henceforth be more willing to compromise in their demands, and efforts were initiated to arrange new talks.

Unrest continued into 1994, although discreet mediation efforts continued. In the same month the establishment was reported of a further Tuareg movement, the Front patriotique de libération du Sahara (FPLS). In February the CRA, including the FPLS, announced its willingness to attend preliminary talks in Ouagadougou, Burkina Faso, although it declined to sign a new truce agreement with the Nigerien government. France agreed to rejoin the negotiations, and, meeting in Burkina in February, the CRA (which presented a list of the Tuaregs' demands for consideration by the Nigerien authorities) and the government of Niger agreed to full negotiations in Paris in March, with French, Algerian and Burkinabè mediation. None the less, reports of a Tuareg attack on a uranium installation at Arlit, and of the harassment of travellers in the north and east, undermined peace efforts in subsequent weeks. Moreover, the CRA's demands for regional autonomy, and for the establishment of quotas for Tuaregs in government, parliament and in the armed forces, received little support in Niamey, where the authorities and parliamentary opposition were prepared to concede the rehabilitation of the north and greater political decentralization. The proposed Paris negotiations did not take place in March, and a further round of consultations was postponed indefinitely in April. There was an escalation of violence during May, including clashes some 200 km to the north of Agadez between the Nigerien armed forces and a rebel unit of the FPLS, as a result of which as many as 40 deaths were recorded. Negotiations reopened in Paris in June, at which considerable progress was made, but there was renewed unrest in August and September, including attempts by Tuaregs to disrupt power supplies to uranium mines. A grenade attack on a meeting in Agadez of the UDPS resulted in six deaths (Tuareg groups accused government forces of responsibility for the assault). At a meeting in Ouagadougou in late September, none the less, the CRA presented Nigerien government negotiators with what it termed a 'comprehensive and final' plan for a restoration of peace. Formal negotiations resumed in Ouagadougou in early October, with mediation by the Burkinabè president, Blaise Compaoré, as well as representatives of France and Algeria. A new peace accord was signed on 9 October, which, while emphasizing that Niger was 'unitary and indivisible', recognized the right of the people to manage their own affairs. Territorial communities were to have their own elected assemblies or councils, to which would be delegated responsibility for the implementation of economic, social and cultural policies at a regional or local level. The Nigerien government was to take immediate measures to ensure the rehabilitation and development of areas affected by the conflict, and to ensure the elimination of insecurity in the north. Provisions were also to be made to facilitate the return and resettlement of refugees. A renewable three-month truce was to take immediate effect, to be monitored by French and Burkinabè military units. By the time of the conclusion of the Ouagadougou agreement the number of deaths since the escalation of the Tuareg rebellion in late 1991 was officially put at 150.

In January 1995 a commission was established to consider the administrative reorganization of the country. Shortly afterwards representatives of the Nigerien government, the CRA, Algeria, Burkina and France met in Agadez, where they agreed to a three-month renewal of the truce. Despite occasional reports of incidents apparently involving renegade Tuareg units, observers confirmed general adherence to the truce, and a further round of negotiations was scheduled to take place in Ouagadougou in March. The opening of these talks was, however, briefly delayed by a split in the Tuareg movement. Rissa Ag Boula, who in January had withdrawn from the CRA (having repeatedly criticized Dayak's negotiating stance) and refused to participate in the decentralization committee, emerged as the leader of the Tuareg delegation (now renamed the Organisation de la résistance armée, ORA) in Ouagadougou: Dayak and the

FLT initially remained within the ORA, which claimed to accord increased autonomy to each of the six movements now reportedly in existence. In mid-April it was announced that a lasting peace agreement had been reached. The accord, which essentially confirmed the provisions of the October 1994 agreement, provided for the establishment of a special peace committee, to be overseen by representatives of the three mediating countries, whose task would be to ensure the practical implementation of the accord, including the disarming of combatants. Demobilized rebels were to be integrated into the Nigerien military and public sector, and special military units were to be accorded responsibility for the security of the northern regions; particular emphasis was to be placed on the economic, social and cultural development of the north, and the government undertook to support the decentralization process. There was to be a general amnesty for all parties involved in the Tuareg rebellion and its suppression, and a day of national reconciliation was to be instituted in memory of the victims of the conflict. The peace agreement, which envisaged the implementation of its provisions within a period of six months, was formally signed by the Nigerien government negotiator, Mai Maigana, and Rissa Ag Boula in Niamey on 24 April 1995. A cease-fire took effect the following day.

Meanwhile, there was increasing evidence in late 1994 and early 1995 of ethnic unrest in southern and eastern Niger, especially in the Lake Chad region. Clashes (frequently over grazing rights) between settled Toubous and nomadic Peulhs resulted in numerous deaths, many of which were attributed to the Front démocratique du renouveau (FDR)—an organization which emerged in October 1994 to demand increased autonomy for south-eastern regions. It was from the Lake Chad region, regarded as a major centre for weapons-trading (with insecurity near the border with Chad being attributed to the presence in Niger, since the overthrow of President Hissène Habré in late 1990, of several thousand mainly Toubou Chadian refugees), that one of the greatest potential obstacles to national reconciliation seemed to emerge in subsequent months.

Although the ORA expressed concern at the slow implementation of the April 1995 peace agreement, its provisions were gradually enacted: the Comité spécial de la paix (CSP) was inaugurated in May, under the chairmanship of Maigana, and a military observer group, comprising representatives of Burkina and France, was deployed in the north in July. The issue of the amnesty proved more controversial, since the inclusion of Arab militias, which had been established by the transitional authorities in 1992 to act as civilian self-defence units in the north, was opposed by many Tuareg groups. The amnesty decree was, none the less, signed by Hama Amadou in July 1995, and all Tuareg prisoners were reported to have been released shortly afterwards. The peace process was undermined following a clash in the north between Tuaregs and an Arab militia unit, as a result of which a Tuareg leader and at least 12 others were killed. Moreover, there was evidence that Dayak and other Tuareg groups in a revived CRA were making common cause with the FDR in demanding autonomy for their regions. In July at least four deaths were reported following an armed attack, responsibility for which was claimed by the FDR, on a military garrison in the south-east, and in August the FDR accused the armed forces of killing 29 civilians in the Lake Chad region. Despite a threat by Rissa Ag Boula that the ORA would once again take up arms if the implementation of the peace agreement was not accelerated, efforts at reconciliation were evident, and the government stated that the FDR would not be excluded from agreements currently under negotiation. However, talks between representatives of the Tuareg movements and the FDR, which took place in northern Niger in September–October, failed either to reunite the CRA and the ORA, or to establish the principle of the FDR's adherence to the April peace accord. In October clashes in the north-east involving rebel Tuaregs and the armed forces (reportedly the first hostilities since April) were attributed to elements of the CRA. Dayak subsequently stated that the fragmentation of the Tuareg movement represented a major obstacle to a lasting peace, but stipulated that the CRA would not join the peace process until the authorities and the ORA recognized all groups (reportedly six) within the CRA. Meeting in Tahoua in late October, bilateral and international donors pledged some 18,700m. francs CFA in support

of a two-year emergency programme for the development of the north. A programme for the repatriation of an estimated 25,000 refugees from Algeria, Burkina and Libya was also discussed. In November a clash in the Tchin Tabaraden region between government forces and a security unit of the ORA provoked tensions between the signatories to the peace agreement. In December Dayak was killed, together with two other leading CRA members, when the aircraft in which they were (according to later reports) travelling to Niamey, for talks on rejoining the peace process, crashed in northern Niger. The new leader of the FLT (and acting leader of the CRA), Mohamed Akotai, indicated that his movement favoured inter-Tuareg reconciliation and a dialogue with government.

Following the military *coup d'état* of January 1996, Niger's new leadership quickly expressed its commitment to the April 1995 agreement. Maïnassara had previously been involved in the work of the CSP, and the government, the ORA and the CRA all expressed the view that direct contacts between the military and the Tuareg movements would expedite the peace process. The FDR also expressed its willingness to co-operate with the new authorities; in early February, none the less, an armed assault on Dirkou by members of that movement, and an army counter-attack, resulted in the deaths of 11 members of the FDR and of one member of the military. The appointment, later in the month, of an ORA spokesman, Mohamed Aoutchéki, as a special adviser to Maïnassara was said to be indicative of the CSN's wish to accelerate the peace process. In March agreements were signed by the Nigerien authorities, the office of the UN High Commissioner for Refugees (UNHCR) and the governments of Algeria and Burkina, regarding the repatriation of refugees. Shortly afterwards the CRA, including the FDR, affirmed its recognition of the April 1995 agreement, and announced that it would observe a unilateral truce for one month, pending the outcome of negotiations with the authorities. The ORA pledged its support for the involvement of the CRA in the peace process, and in April 1996 the government and the CRA signed an agreement formalizing the latter's adherence to the 1995 accord. In May 1996 the ORA and CRA agreed to establish a joint committee to co-ordinate their activities and represent the interests of the resistance movements in negotiations with the authorities on the implementation of the peace accord.

In July 1996 the CSP and the resistance movements recommended measures aimed at curbing what was termed 'residual banditry' in northern areas. Preliminary agreement was also reached regarding the integration of demobilized fighters into regular military and civilian sectors, although Tuareg leaders expressed some disappointment that the number of fighters to be integrated into the army and paramilitary forces (1,400) was not greater. Discussions continued in August regarding the demobilization and disarmament of the rebel movement, and in September joint peace-keeping patrols of the Nigerien armed forces and former rebels were inaugurated in the north. At the end of the month, however, Rissa Ag Boula, denouncing the inadequacy of arrangements for the reintegration of demobilized fighters, announced that the ORA was no longer bound by the peace treaty. The authorities asserted that this abandonment of the 1995 accord was linked less to concerns regarding the implementation of its provisions than to the arrest of ORA members in connection with the diversion, some months previously, of a large consignment of cigarettes bound for the north. In an apparent gesture of reconciliation, however, the detainees were released at the end of October 1996 and the ORA surrendered the consignment to the authorities. In November it was reported that a new group had emerged, combining movements from both the ORA and the CRA; led by Mohamed Anako, the Union des forces de la résistance armée (UFRA) affirmed its commitment to the peace accord. A meeting between the high commissioner for the restoration of peace and 10 of the reported 12 resistance groups was followed in December by the signing of a protocol for the encampment of some 5,900 former fighters, prior to their disarmament and reintegration into regular armed forces and civilian structures. The ORA, however, remained excluded from this process.

Concerns for the peace process were heightened at the end of 1996 by reports of renewed insecurity, including clashes between renegade fighters and joint patrols. Following a meeting in

Niamey between Maïnassara and Rissa Ag Boula in early January 1997, at which mutual co-operation pledges were made, the ORA leader condemned, especially, recent attacks on tourists in the Aïr region. Having received assurances regarding the implementation of provisions of the 1995 accord, the ORA declared its renewed support; it was announced, moreover, that the FLAA and FLT would establish a joint patrol aimed at combating insecurity and banditry. In early February 1997 the UFRA joined members of the regular armed forces, the CRA and the Comité de vigilance de Tassara (CVT) in a peace-keeping patrol in Agadez. In April Maïnassara signed a decree establishing a commission, under his direct jurisdiction, charged with overseeing the process of encampment and reintegration of former fighters. Chaired by the minister of national defence, the commission was to include representatives of other ministries, the military and paramilitary, the high commissioner for the restoration of peace, all signatories to the 1995 accord, and the CVT.

Some insecurity persisted, none the less, particularly in the east. Violent clashes were reported in late March 1997, involving several hundred soldiers and Toubou rebels: the FDR protested that the operation, which was attributed by the authorities to the need to eliminate isolated groups of armed bandits, was endangering the peace accord. In early June it was announced that Toubous and Arabs of the Forces armées révolutionnaires du Sahara (FARS) had, following negotiations in Chad, agreed to join the peace process. It subsequently appeared that large numbers of armed Toubous had fled to north-eastern Nigeria following the defeat of the FARS; Niger's minister of national defence subsequently proposed the establishment of joint patrols, to involve the armed forces of Niger, Nigeria, Chad and Cameroon, to ensure security in the Lake Chad region. At the beginning of June, meanwhile, the authorities denied reports that, following a military rebellion at the Agadez military barracks, former rebel Tuaregs were besieging the town.

A three-day meeting took place in mid-July 1997 to assess encampment procedures. It was reported that the demobilization and billeting of former fighters, as envisaged in the December 1996 accord, had been completed, and that the incorporation of demobilized groups into the regular armed and paramilitary forces and the civil service was proceeding. Appeals were renewed for external funds to expedite the full application of the peace accord. It was stated that some 11,000 refugees would return from Burkina and Algeria, with UNHCR assistance, by the end of 1997. Shortly after the meeting, however, the FDR announced its withdrawal from the peace process, stating that Nigerien and Chadian military units had attacked one of its bases in the Lake Chad region; the FDR reported that 17 members of the armed forces had been killed in clashes with its fighters. The Nigerien authorities strenuously denied that any engagement had taken place.

A further meeting of the parties to the peace process took place in early September 1997, at which agreement was reached on several areas regarding the integration of former fighters into the armed and security forces. At this time, however, elements of Anako's UFRA, apparently frustrated at the slow progress of the implementation of the peace process, had taken up arms again. Joining with the dissident UFRA was the FARS, which was held by the authorities to be responsible for an attack

on a military post at Madama later in September, as a result of which three soldiers were seriously injured (five members of the military were, furthermore, killed when their vehicle struck a land-mine). Further incidents ensued. A total of 27 deaths resulted from an armed attack on Aderbissanat, in the Agadez region; among the victims were six members of the armed forces and one civilian. Allegations by the Nigerien government that the former Chadian president and rebel leader, Goukouni Oueddei, was rallying Toubou and Tuareg rebels with the aim of forming a 'puppet state' in the Lake Chad region were strenuously denied by Goukouni and by the UFRA.

Meanwhile, the encampment process, which had been scheduled for completion at the end of September 1997, was delayed for several weeks. The conclusion of the disarmament process was officially celebrated in Tchin-Tabaraden in late October. The armed forces subsequently undertook an offensive against positions held by dissident fronts. In late November, following two weeks of talks, a peace accord was signed in Algeria between the Nigerien government, the UFRA and the FARS. The protocol agreement provided for an immediate cease-fire; the entry into force of its other provisions, scheduled for 1 January 1998, was briefly delayed, but the former rebels stated that this did not diminish their commitment to the peace process. In mid-January it was announced that six officers of the police and republican guard who had been taken hostage in the Aderbissanat attack had been released. (Captives taken by the armed forces had already been freed.) In late March the ORA and CRA surrendered their weapons stocks at Agadez. The handover of armaments was attended by Rissa Ag Boula (the head of the ORA had been appointed minister-delegate responsible for tourism in the government named in late 1997) and, on behalf of the CRA, Mohamed Akotai. In his new ministerial capacity, the ORA leader gave assurances of the restoration of security in the north. Voluntary repatriations of Nigerien refugees from Algeria, under the supervision of UNHCR and the Algerian Red Crescent, began in March 1998.

In April 1998 Maiyaki chaired a meeting in Niamey of the peace monitoring and implementation committee, now charged with overseeing the implementation of the April 1995 peace agreement and what was termed the November 1997 Algiers addendum protocol. In June 1988 it was reported that the last units of the UFRA had disarmed at a ceremony near Agadez. Negotiations in Chad resulted in the signing of a peace agreement in August by the government of Niger and the FDR.

Following the death of President Maïnassara, in April 1999, the military CRN gave assurances that the peace process would be continued. Rissa Ag Boula was promoted to the rank of minister in the transitional government, while Mohamed Anako was appointed a special adviser to Wanké. Rissa Ag Boula retained his ministerial post in the new government of Hama Amadou, formed in January 2000. In December 1999, meanwhile, at the third meeting of the commission charged with monitoring adherence to the Algiers addendum accord, the High Commissioner for the Restoration of Peace, Lt-Col Seyni Awa, stated that positive results had been achieved in the areas of encampment of former fighters and de-mining of areas affected by the conflict, while integration operations had been undertaken in the defence and security forces and in public administration.

Economy

EDITH HODGKINSON

During the 1980s and 1990s Niger's economy lost the earlier momentum towards growth and modernization which had resulted from the development of the uranium-mining industry in the 1970s. After a long-term decline in international demand and prices for uranium, the formal economy contracted, both in size and diversity, through until the mid-1990s. However, the traditional rural economy has remained intact, and growth has been noted in informal trade and in small-scale artisanal manufacturing and repair activities. The country is greatly influenced by its economic relations with its southern neighbour, Nigeria. While Niger's official exports and imports have tended to decline since the beginning of the 1990s, substantial unrecorded trade has continued to flourish across the 2,000-km border with Nigeria: fuel smuggled from Nigeria already accounts for at least one-third of Niger's national consumption, according to official estimates. The informal, or 'grey', economy is thus unusually large in Niger, and the World Bank estimates that it represents about 70% of all economic activity.

In 1998, according to estimates by the World Bank, Niger's gross national product (GNP) was equivalent to only US $190 per head, making it one of the world's poorest countries. The UN's human development index, which takes into account life expectancy and conditions in health and education, ranked Niger last among 174 countries in both 1995 and 1996, and second from last in 1998 and 1999—after war-ravaged Sierra Leone. This follows more than two decades of decline or stagnation in GNP per head, as the economy performed very erratically during the 1970s and then contracted in almost every year of the 1980s, owing to a combination of weakening earnings from uranium, drought and economic turmoil in neighbouring Nigeria. There are limited prospects of strong and sustained economic growth, even after the 50% devaluation of the CFA franc in January 1994, which has benefited some other Franc Zone countries, since world prices for uranium, Niger's dominant export, remain depressed and the country otherwise has a very limited range of exportable goods. However, it was hoped that the enhanced flows of aid and measures of debt relief that followed immediately after the devaluation would help achieve the objectives of the development programme for 1994–96. This aimed at economic growth of 4% in 1994 and of more than 5% thereafter. In the event, these targets were not met, with growth in gross domestic product (GDP) averaging 3.4% per year in 1994–96. The potentially very damaging boycott by aid donors after the military coup in January 1996 came to an end relatively rapidly: the signing of an Enhanced Structural Adjustment Facility (ESAF) agreement with the IMF in June of that year was followed by pledges of funding from the World Bank, the African Development Bank, the European Union, France and Japan. The programme supported by the ESAF aimed to achieve average annual GDP growth of 4.5% in 1997–98. Economic performance was slightly below this level (at 3.4%) in 1997, but the target was achieved in 1998. Meanwhile, the disposal of state assets accelerated, with the privatization of three state enterprises in 1998: the textiles company, Société nigérienne des textiles (SONITEXTIL), the dairy, Office du lait du Niger (OLANI), and the cement plant, Société nigérienne de cimenterie (SNC). The electricity utility, the petroleum parastatal and the telecommunications company were all scheduled for sale in 1999. In March 1999 a joint mission of the World Bank and IMF thus reported 'significant progress' in Niger's meeting of commitments under the ESAF (which was due to expire at the end of June). This raised the prospect that another such facility would be accorded, and made Niger eligible for debt reduction under the World Bank's Heavily Indebted Poor Countries (HIPC) initiative. This progress was jeopardized by the assassination of President Ibrahim Baré Maïnassara in April 1999 and his replacement by another military head of state. The country's most important donors—France, the World Bank/IMF and the European Union—all suspended their aid. The decisive verdict delivered in the presidential and legislative elections in the subsequent October/November, in a poll which was deemed both fair and transparent, set the scene for a resumption of aid in early 2000. The new government committed itself to reinstating the programme of public-sector reform and privatization, in the hope of securing a Poverty Reduction and Growth Facility (PRGF) for the IMF, in succession to the ESAF, which had expired in 1999. But popular opposition, particularly from the trade unions, which fear job losses, will remain a significant constraint on the pace of implementation of this programme.

THE TRADITIONAL ECONOMY

Although only a small proportion of Niger's land is capable of supporting settled farming, agriculture and livestock contribute some 40% of GDP, and account for close to 90% of the working population. Principal staple products are millet, maize, sorghum, cow-peas and cassava, all grown mainly for household consumption. Rice is also produced, on the small area that is under modern irrigation, while cotton and groundnuts are the principal cash crops. Until the early 1990s the overall expansion in the production of food crops kept pace with population growth, and Niger became self-sufficient in food grains after the mid-1980s, although distribution problems continued to cause local shortages. In 1993–97, however, the increase in production of cereals failed to keep pace with population growth, mainly as the result of generally inadequate levels of rainfall and very limited irrigation, but also, in 1997/98, owing to infestation by pests. In that year cereal production was only 1.7 metric tons, far below the national requirement (of about 2.28m. tons). Heavy rainfall along the Niger river brought a massive improvement in the crop in 1998/99, to 2.98m. tons, while the 1999/2000 crop was estimated at almost the same level, at 2.83m. tons. All the same, the vagaries of the Sahel climate mean that famine remains an ever-present threat in some regions of Niger.

As food production generally increased, output of groundnuts declined sharply from a peak of 191,307 tons (unshelled) in 1967 to an average of only some 25,000 tons per year in the late 1980s. It has since recovered strongly, to an average of 110,000 tons per year in the mid- and late 1990s. Cotton production has fared similarly, after a strong start—11,133 tons (unginned) in 1975/76, 74% up on the level of six years earlier—mainly as a result of investment in irrigated cultivation. Output declined, to around 2,000–4,000 tons (marketed) per year in the early 1990s, but has recovered strongly since, reaching 15,000 tons in 1997/98, after the sale to Chinese interests of a majority stake in the state textile plant in 1997 and the associated extension of the area under cotton. There has also been greater success in the production of cow-peas, with output averaging 200,000 tons per year by the end of the 1980s and reaching about 450,000 tons annually in the early 1990s. The devaluation has made the crop a profitable export to the Nigerian market. However, the single most important activity in this sector is livestock-rearing, which accounts for some 15% of GDP. Cattle are the second most significant export, in terms of foreign-exchange earnings, after uranium, with a significant—if largely unrecorded—trade across the border with Nigeria. As in the rest of the region, extensive stock-rearing made appreciable progress in the years following independence, stimulated by demand from the highly-populated coastal region and Nigeria. The droughts of the 1970s and early 1980s, however, caused a sharp fall in numbers, either because of death or because of the removal of livestock to neighbouring countries, and the size of the cattle herd declined by two-thirds between 1972 and 1975, and by one-half in the crisis year of 1984. Although the return of better rains has allowed the partial restoration of the herd, livestock numbers remain significantly below pre-drought levels, at some 2.1m. cattle and 10.3m. sheep and goats in 1998. The government has been unable to promote either intensive commercial livestock operations or dairy farming, owing to Niger's ecological conditions. However, the sector did benefit from the strong rise in foreign demand after the 1994 currency devaluation.

With about 90% of cultivable land believed to have been lost to drought in the 20th century, and losses recently averaging 200,000 ha per year, the anti-desertification campaign is a priority for the Nigerien government, and a programme of afforestation and environmental protection is proceeding.

MINING AND POWER

The mining and export of uranium plays a very significant role in Niger's economy, representing an important source of budgetary revenue and, until recently, providing most of the country's foreign exchange earnings (80% in 1992, but declining to only 44% in 1998). Niger now ranks third, after Canada and Australia, of the world's principal producers of uranium, accounting for about one-tenth of total output. However, as demand and prices for uranium have weakened, successive governments have made efforts to encourage the development of the country's other mineral resources, which include cassiterite, coal, phosphates, iron ore, gold and petroleum, although exploitation of few of these has yet been considered economic.

The mining of uranium began in 1971 at Arlit, in the desolate Aïr mountains, reaching 1,982 tons by 1980. The mining company, Société des mines de l'Aïr (SOMAÏR), is under French control; the majority interest is held by the Compagnie générale des matières nucléaires (COGEMA—a subsidiary of the French government's Commissariat à l'énergie atomique) and French private interests, with the Nigerien government's Office nationale des ressources minières du Niger (ONAREM) holding a 33% share. Operating costs at the mine are high, owing to the remoteness of the site, and its output is transported by aircraft or overland to Cotonou, Benin. Production at the country's second uranium mine, at Akouta, was begun in 1978 by a consortium—the Compagnie minière d'Akouta (COMINAK)—of the government, COGEMA, the Japanese Overseas Uranium Resources Development and the Spanish Empresa Nacional del Uranio. Output from the mine reached 2,200 tons in 1980, and total uranium production by Niger reached its peak in 1981 at 4,366 tons. Production subsequently slowed, as world prices plummeted, to a recorded average of 3,070 tons per year in 1990–98 (although this is thought to be an understatement). Most output is sold to equity partners in the mining operations, with France, the principal purchaser, paying a substantial (but reduced) premium over the world price since the early 1990s; Japan operates under a similar arrangement. Niger's earnings from sales of uranium were thus only 43,700m. francs CFA in 1993, one-half of the level recorded in 1986 on volumes that were only 13% lower. While earnings improved strongly (to 78,400m. francs CFA) in 1994, and fell only slightly in the following two years (to an average of 71,100m. francs CFA) before recovering to an average of 76,800m. francs CFA in 1997–98, the currency's devaluation meant that in US dollar terms they declined further. In 1992 only about 8% of the national budget was financed by sales of uranium, compared with 40% in 1979. With uranium demand depressed by the scaling down of nuclear power programmes and by the end of the cold war, Niger suffers from its high costs in relation to other producers. Plans to increase capacity by developing the large deposits at Imourarem, 80 km south of Arlit, have therefore been postponed indefinitely.

There is increasing foreign interest in the potential for the industrial-scale mining of Niger's gold reserves, most of which are located in the Liptako region, near the border with Burkina Faso, and which have been exploited on a small scale since the early 1980s. Surveys of sites at Sirba, Téra and Gourouol, conducted by ONAREM, in co-operation with foreign donors, yielded encouraging results, and by early 1999 ore reserves of 90m. tons had been located at 15 sites under exploration in the Liptako region. Canadian, Ghanaian and South African interests are all active in this sector, with Etruscan and SEMAFO, of Canada, planning to start operations in 2000 at Samira Hill, which was estimated to contain up to 425,000 oz of gold.

Other mineral resources include cassiterite, a tin-bearing ore mined in the Aïr region (with an estimated output, in terms of mineral content, of 70 tons in 1991 but of only 20 tons per year in 1992–94), iron ore at Say (deposits, as yet unexploited, of

some 650m. tons), calcium phosphates (some 2,000 tons per year were produced from open-cast mines at Tahoua until 1984) and gypsum. Coal deposits, estimated at 6m. tons, have been located at Anou-Anaren, to the north-west of Agadez. Production began in 1981, for use in power generation, and now averages some 150,000 tons annually. Deposits of petroleum, located in the south-west, were for a long time not deemed commercially exploitable. Elf Aquitaine, of France, and the US Exxon Corpn began seismic work in 1992 in the previously unexplored Agadem region north of Lake Chad. Reserves there have been estimated at 1m. tons, and Elf and Exxon renewed their licence in 1995, with plans to invest 30,000m. francs CFA over five years. During the first half of 1998 there was a marked increase in oil exploration activity, both at the Lake Chad site and in the far north, near the border with Libya where Hunt Oil began exploratory drilling in late 1999.

Electricity consumption has risen rapidly, reaching 233m. kWh in 1996, with the major consumers being the uranium companies. Domestic generation, which is almost entirely thermal, covers about one-half of demand, and the remainder is met by hydroelectric supplies from Nigeria. Because of the unreliability of the Nigerian supply, there are long-standing plans to build a facility at Kandadji, on the Niger river. A feasibility study, funded by the African Development Bank, was put out for tender in 1999.

MANUFACTURING

As in most other west African countries, manufacturing takes the form of the processing of agricultural commodities and import substitution. The sector's contribution to GDP was about 6% in 1998, with the modern sector accounting for only about one-fifth of this. There is a groundnut oil extraction plant, as well as cotton ginneries, rice mills, flour mills and tanneries. Import substitution has been stimulated by the very high cost of transport. A textile plant (whose annual output reached 5.6m. metres in 1998 after it was taken over by Chinese interests) and a cement works (annual capacity 35,000 tons) are in operation, both under majority private ownership, and there are light industries serving the very limited local market. Activity in the sector remains predominantly small-scale and artisanal, and, in that it draws on local inputs, will have been stimulated by the currency devaluation, which made foreign manufactures correspondingly expensive. The modern sector, which is more dependent on imports, was severely affected by devaluation: several businesses closed down in 1994, with the loss of about 3,000 jobs.

TRANSPORT AND TOURISM

The transport system is still inadequate, despite considerable road development—funded by the World Bank, the European Development Fund and Saudi Arabia—including the 902-km all-weather road between Niamey and Zinder, opened in 1980, and a 651-km 'uranium road' from Arlit to Tahoua, which opened in 1981. In 1996 there were an estimated 10,100 km of classified roads, of which only a small proportion (less than 8%) was paved. There is, at present, no railway: plans to extend the Cotonou–Parakou line from Benin elicited no interest from aid donors, and the scheme was postponed indefinitely in 1989. Most foreign trade is shipped through Cotonou, via the Organisation commune Bénin-Niger des chemins de fer et des transports. The emphasis in transport development is on diversifying and improving access to seaports: a road is being built to Lomé, Togo, via Burkina Faso, and the Agadez–Zinder section (428 km) of the Trans-Sahara Highway has been upgraded. There are international airports at Niamey and Agadez, and four major domestic airports.

The development of tourism was impeded, during the 1990s, by insecurity in the north and east of the country. Tourist arrivals, however, increased from 66,927 in 1996 to 69,000 in 1997, and income from tourism rose from US $17m. to $18m. over the same period. Tourist arrivals had been predicted to reach 100,000 in 2000, but the cancellation of the Niger stages of the Paris–Dakar–Cairo car rally, following threats of terrorist attacks, was a set-back to tourism growth in that year.

FINANCE

As in other countries of francophone west Africa, some foreign aid in the years immediately after independence took the form of subsidies to make up the chronic deficit on the budget. In the late 1970s, however, the current budget registered a substantial surplus because of the rapid rise in government revenues from uranium. These financed about one-third of the current budget, as well as nearly all capital investment. The decline in uranium revenues (reflecting lower prices and output) during the early 1980s transformed the current budget balance from a surplus of 15,200m. francs CFA in 1980/81 to a deficit of 51,880m. francs CFA in 1982/83. With the doubling of Niger's debt-servicing burden over the same period (see below), stringent austerity measures were needed in subsequent years to limit the budget deficit. Current spending was first reduced, in 1983/84, and then held steady, partly as a result of cut-backs in public-sector employment and of the sale to private ownership of some parastatal enterprises, which tended to be a drain on government funds. However, the fiscal imbalance remained substantial, as did the country's dependence on foreign funding: in 1993 40% of government income was in the form of external grants.

The devaluation of the currency in January 1994 generated new funding commitments from France (which pledged 85,000m. francs CFA—sufficient to cover one-half of all budget spending for that year), as well as from the IMF and World Bank. These were, none the less, tied to a requirement of renewed efforts to reduce the budget deficit by means of revenue enhancement and restricting the rise in the public-sector salary bill. The fiscal situation remained very poor during 1995, despite an increase in customs revenue and a reduction of one-seventh in the wage bill. While the fundamental problem in Nigerien public finances is the gross inadequacy of tax revenue (which has been equivalent to only 6%–7% of GDP in recent years), as successive governments have failed to bring most of the economy into the tax 'net', the army-backed regime installed in early 1996 brought with it the prospect of tax increases and enforced cuts in public-sector salaries. Although Maïndassara's regime was unable to implement its planned 40% reduction in civil-service pay, owing to union opposition, in May 2000 further plans were announced for 1,043 civil servants to be given early retirement at the end of the year. However, the previous government did manage to put into place a number of new taxes proposed earlier, including a business-licence tax (to bring the informal sector into the tax system) and a property levy on owner-occupied housing. The programme for 1996–98, supported by the ESAF agreed in mid-1996, aimed to increase tax receipts to more than 10% of GDP in 1997. This was intended to narrow the budget deficit (excluding grants) to 7.3% of GDP in 1998, from 8.6% in 1995 and 12.5% in 1994. This relatively modest improvement in the fiscal balance reflects the need to increase expenditure on education, health care and sanitation, and on the general programme of poverty alleviation. The intention was to accommodate these higher outlays by reducing the public-sector payroll. The 1997 budget envisaged a one-third reduction in the wage bill, largely through redundancies, while fiscal stability was to be improved through privatization of public utilities and divestment of some other government corporate assets. It was intended to sell off 12 public enterprises, including the electricity utility, the petroleum import company and the post office. However, this programme was strongly opposed by the trade unions, and by 1999 only three sales had been completed. The new government of Hama Amadou recommitted Niger to a far-reaching privatization programme, including the telecommunications, electricity and water utilities, and the petroleum products importing company. As a result of the delays in the privatization process, fiscal targets were not met in 1997, when the deficit reached 9.1% of GDP (two percentage points above the aim). The deficit was only held down in 1998, to 7.4% of GDP, by accumulating arrears (notably on wages to public-sector workers), while the 1999 budget envisaged no increase in the government's wage bill, by means of a freeze on both salaries and recruitment. However, in June 1999 trade union pressure forced the transitional government to abandon the scheduled reduction in public-sector employment. This only added to the build up of wage arrears, and the new administration that took office in January 2000 announced that the government was facing a severe financial crisis. It suspended all payments on its domestic debt (Niger was already in default

on its foreign debt) pending the preparation of a new budget. Emergency funding was, however, raised from donors in February to help meet some wage arrears.

FOREIGN TRADE AND PAYMENTS

Exports are only partly recorded, but there was evidently a rise—if erratic—in the 1960s, followed by more sustained growth in later years, as the downturn or stagnation of tradional exports (groundnuts and livestock) was more than offset by the impact of the beginning of uranium production. In 1973 uranium became the major export, and within two years it was accounting for around two-thirds of all export earnings. Uranium earnings were responsible for the rapid rise in export receipts in the late 1970s, and reached a peak of 100,804m. francs CFA in 1980—three times the level of 1977. Imports have, none the less, almost always exceeded exports, although by a less substantial margin than in some countries of francophone west Africa. The rise in uranium earnings was matched by the rise in import spending, reflecting higher petroleum prices and investment in capital equipment for the mining industry. Since 1980 the trade balance has fluctuated widely, but deficits have tended to rise over time, owing to the persistent depression in the uranium market and the severe grain shortfall in the drought years. The devaluation of the CFA franc had a very limited impact on officially recorded exports (although unrecorded earnings, from sales of livestock in particular, were thought to have risen very strongly in 1994), while the contraction in imports, because of their doubling in local-cost terms, was brief, leaving merchandise trade in deficit—estimated at US $35m. in 1998.

With merchandise trade normally in deficit, and the high transportation costs arising from the country's landlocked position, the current account of the balance of payments has been in persistent deficit, restricted to manageable levels only by inflows of official aid. Grants from members of the Organisation for Economic Co-operation and Development and of the Organization of the Petroleum Exporting Countries averaged US $273m. per year in 1994–98, roughly equivalent to Niger's average annual export earnings. This still left the current account in deficit by an average of $167m. over the same period. External borrowing to compensate for the chronic deficit on the current payments account had earlier resulted in a sharp escalation in the foreign debt, from $863m. at the end of 1980 to $1,614m. in 1993. Meanwhile, export earnings declined, with the result that in 1982 Niger's debt-service ratio was equivalent to more than one-half of the country's foreign earnings—an unsustainable burden. With the continuing depression in the world uranium market, Niger's major official creditors agreed in 1983 and in following years to reschedule the country's foreign debt. Together with restructuring arrangements with commercial creditors, this kept the debt-service ratio below its 1982 peak, despite the continued sharp rise in the foreign debt. However, with a debt-service ratio of 41% in 1988, Niger was classified as 'debt-distressed' by the World Bank, and hence at the December rescheduling of debt by the 'Paris Club' of official creditors, the highly concessionary 'Toronto terms' for debt relief were applied. The cancellation by France of debts of $320m. in 1990, further 'Paris Club' rescheduling and a 'buy-back', supported by the World Bank, of $108m. in commercial debt reduced the debt-service radio to 12% of foreign earnings by 1992. However, after the devaluation of the CFA franc in January 1994 doubled the cost in local currency terms of repayment of and interest on debt, exceptional measures of debt relief were required. In March a new agreement with the 'Paris Club', in accordance with the more concessionary 'Trinidad terms', rescheduled 85,000m. francs CFA in debt, and France cancelled one-half of Niger's liabilities. Despite this relief, and another round of rescheduling on even more favourable 'Naples terms' (which effectively allow two-thirds of debt to be written off) following agreement of the ESAF in 1996, Niger's debt remained in the region of $1,590m. in 1995–98. This was equivalent to 55% of GNP, while the debt-service ratio, which had increased to 24% in 1993–94, eased to 18%. The foreign debt is thus now manageable, but only in years of good economic performance. Moreover, with just over one-half of external debt owed to multilateral institutions, which cannot reschedule liabilities, there is limited scope for further restructuring to alleviate the burden. Given that prospects for increasing revenue from exports or from domestic taxation are very modest, while the investment needed to raise basic living conditions to a satisfactory level is substantial, the country will remain highly dependent on external support for the foreseeable future.

Statistical Survey

Source (unless otherwise stated): Direction de la Statistique et de l'Informatique, Ministère des Finances et des Réformes Économiques, BP 720, Niamey; tel. 72-23-74; fax 73-33-71.

Area and Population

AREA, POPULATION AND DENSITY

Area (sq km)	1,267,000*
Population (census results)	
20 November 1977	5,098,427
20 May 1988	
Males	3,590,070
Females	3,658,030
Total	7,248,100
Population (UN estimates at mid-year)†	
1996	9,454,000
1997	9,764,000
1998	10,078,000
Density (per sq km) at mid-1998	8.0

* 489,191 sq miles.
† Source: UN, *World Population Prospects: The 1998 Revision.*

ETHNIC GROUPS (estimated population at 1 July 1972)*

Hausa . . .	2,279,000	Tuareg, etc . .	127,000
Djerma-Songhai	1,001,000	Beriberi-Manga .	386,000
Fulani (Peulh) .	450,000	**Total** . . .	4,243,000

* Provisional figures. Revised total is 4,239,000.

PRINCIPAL TOWNS (population in 1977)

Niamey (capital) .	225,314	Tahoua . . .	31,265
Zinder . . .	58,436	Agadez . . .	20,475
Maradi . . .	45,852	Birni N'Konni .	15,227

1981 (estimates): Niamey 360,000; Zinder 75,000.

BIRTHS AND DEATHS (UN estimates, annual averages)

	1980–85	1985–90	1990–95
Birth rate (per 1,000) . .	59.4	56.1	52.5
Death rate (per 1,000) . .	22.1	20.4	18.9

Expectation of life (UN estimates, years at birth, 1990–95): 46.5 (males 44.9; females 48.1).

Source: UN, *World Population Prospects: The 1998 Revision.*

ECONOMICALLY ACTIVE POPULATION
(persons aged 10 years and over, 1988 census, provisional)

	Males	Females	Total
Agriculture, hunting, forestry and fishing	1,549,600	243,950	1,793,550
Mining and quarrying . . .	4,790	960	5,750
Manufacturing	28,060	35,630	63,690
Electricity, gas and water. .	2,330	60	2,390
Construction.	14,040	390	14,430
Trade, restaurants and hotels. .	95,670	112,700	208,370
Transport, storage and communications . . .	14,400	470	14,870
Financing, insurance, real estate and business services . .	1,400	450	1,850
Community, social and personal services	100,620	29,110	129,730
Activities not adequately defined .	21,250	50,270	71,520
Total employed	1,832,160	473,990	2,306,150
Unemployed	44,210	16,360	60,570
Total labour force . . .	1,876,370	490,350	2,366,720

Source: UN, *Demographic Yearbook.*

Mid-1998 (estimates in '000): Agriculture, etc. 4,236; Total 4,795 (Source: FAO, *Production Yearbook*).

Agriculture

PRINCIPAL CROPS ('000 metric tons)

	1996	1997	1998
Maize	13*	3*	3†
Millet	1,832*	1,713*	1,713†
Sorghum	425*	435*	430†
Rice (paddy)	70†	67*	67†
Sugar cane†	145	145	145
Sweet potatoes† . . .	35	37	37
Cassava (Manioc)† . . .	230	225	230
Onions (dry)†	178	178	178
Tomatoes†	48	50	50
Other vegetables† . . .	40	41	41
Pulses†	459	428	458
Dates†	10	10	9
Other fruit†	38	38	39
Groundnuts (in shell) . .	196*	114*	115†
Cottonseed†	2	2	3
Cotton (lint)*	1	1	1
Tobacco (leaves) . . .	1*	1†	1†

* Unofficial figure(s).   † FAO estimate(s).

Source: FAO, *Production Yearbook.*

LIVESTOCK ('000 head, year ending September)

	1996	1997	1998
Horses*	82	82	82
Asses*	450	450	450
Cattle	2,047	2,089†	2,100*
Camels	386†	392†	392*
Pigs*	39	39	39
Sheep	3,849	4,097†	4,100*
Goats	5,869	6,146†	6,150*

Poultry (million)*: 20 in 1996; 20 in 1997; 20 in 1998.

* FAO estimates. † Unofficial figure.

Source: FAO, *Production Yearbook*.

LIVESTOCK PRODUCTS (FAO estimates, '000 metric tons)

	1996	1997	1998
Beef and veal	35	34	34
Mutton and lamb . . .	14	14	14
Goat meat	23	23	23
Pig meat	1	1	1
Poultry meat	23	23	23
Other meat	20	21	21
Cows' milk	168	168	168
Sheep's milk	15	15	15
Goats' milk	97	97	97
Cheese	14	14	14
Butter	5	5	5
Poultry eggs	9	9	9
Cattle hides	6	6	6
Sheepskins	2	2	2
Goatskins	4	4	4

Source: FAO, *Production Yearbook*.

Forestry

ROUNDWOOD REMOVALS ('000 cubic metres, excluding bark)

	1995	1996	1997
Industrial wood . . .	362	374	387
Fuel wood	5,504	5,693	5,887
Total	5,866	6,067	6,274

Source: FAO, *Yearbook of Forest Products*.

SAWNWOOD PRODUCTION
('000 cubic metres, including railway sleepers)

	1995	1996	1997
Total	4	4	4

Source: FAO, *Yearbook of Forest Products*.

Fishing

('000 metric tons, live weight)

	1995	1996	1997
Total catch	3.5	4.1	6.3

Source: FAO, *Yearbook of Fishery Statistics*.

Mining

('000 metric tons, unless otherwise indicated)

	1994	1995	1996
Salt	3	3*†	3*†
Gypsum	2	2*	2*†
Hard coal	172†	173†	n.a.
Tin (metric tons)‡ . . .	20*†	18	20*†

* Data from the US Bureau of Mines.

† Provisional or estimated figure.

‡ Data refer to the metal content of ore.

Source: UN, *Industrial Commodity Statistics Yearbook*.

Uranium (metal content of ore, metric tons): 2,956 in 1994; 2,974 in 1995; 3,322 in 1996; 3,499 in 1997; 3,516 in 1998 (Source: Banque centrale des états de l'Afrique de l'ouest).

Gold (metal content of ore, metric tons): 0.5 per year in 1994–96 (Source: Gold Fields Mineral Services Ltd, *Gold 1997*).

Industry

SELECTED PRODUCTS ('000 metric tons, unless otherwise indicated)

	1993	1994	1995
Flour	10.5	12.8	8.2
Cement	31.2	29.5	31.3
Soap	7.9	6.8	6.8
Textile fabrics (million metres) .	4.8	3.2	2.4
Beer ('000 bottles) . . .	149.9	n.a.	n.a.
Electric energy (million kWh) . .	146.3	175.0	166.8

Source: IMF, *Niger—Statistical Annex* (October 1997).

Finance

CURRENCY AND EXCHANGE RATES

Monetary Units

100 centimes = 1 franc de la Communauté financière africaine (CFA).

Sterling, Dollar and Euro Equivalents (28 April 2000)

£1 sterling = 1,132.20 francs CFA;

US $1 = 722.02 francs CFA;

€1 = 655.96 francs CFA;

10,000 francs CFA = £8.832 = $13.850 = €15.245.

Average Exchange Rate (francs CFA per US $)

1997   583.67

1998   589.95

1999   615.70

Note: An exchange rate of 1 French franc = 50 francs CFA, established in 1948, remained in force until January 1994, when the CFA franc was devalued by 50%, with the exchange rate adjusted to 1 French franc = 100 francs CFA. This relationship to French currency remained in effect with the introduction of the euro on 1 January 1999. From that date, accordingly, a fixed exchange rate of €1 = 655.957 francs CFA has been in operation.

BUDGET ('000 million francs CFA)

Revenue*	1994	1995	1996†
General budget	50.4	65.9	75.2
Tax revenue	47.1	62.1	68.5
Taxes on income, profits, payroll and work force	12.9	18.1	16.2
Taxes on goods and services	9.7	12.1	11.6
Taxes on international trade and transactions	22.6	29.3	36.9
Import Duties	16.9	24.7	25.9
Export duties	2.8	0.3	0.4
Other taxes	1.9	2.6	3.8
Taxes on property	1.0	—	—
Non-tax revenue	3.3	3.8	6.7
Annexed budgets and special accounts	2.4	2.0	3.8
Total	52.8	67.9	79.0

* Excluding grants received ('000 million francs CFA): 50.3 in 1994; 44.3 in 1995; 50.0 (estimate) in 1996.
† Estimates.

Expenditure*	1993	1994†	1995‡
General budget	107.5	158.5	146.8
Current expenditure	80.7	108.4	102.7
Wages and salaries	40.3	47.4	49.8
Materials and supplies	14.7	28.8	23.7
Subsidies and transfers	13.6	10.8	6.0
Interest payments	10.7	19.8	22.9
Capital expenditure	26.8	50.1	44.1
Annexed budgets and special accounts	2.0	3.8	2.8
Sub-total	109.5	162.3	149.6
Changes in arrears§	−24.6	47.6	−11.4
Adjustment	—	—	5.4
Total	84.9	209.9	143.6

* Excluding net lending (million francs CFA): 4.2 in 1993; 4.1 (provisional) in 1994; 5.5 (estimate) in 1995.
† Provisional.
‡ Estimates.
§ A minus sign indicates an increase in arrears.

Note: Figures for expenditure are preliminary. Revised totals for expenditure and net lending are ('000 million francs CFA): 105.4 (current expenditure 80.7) in 1993; 161.1 (current expenditure 108.4) in 1994; 144.9 (current expenditure 102.1) in 1995.

1996: (estimates, '000 million francs CFA): Expenditure and net lending 131.1 (current expenditure 86.1).

Sources: IMF, *Niger—Background Paper* (August 1996) and *Statistical Annex* (October 1997).

INTERNATIONAL RESERVES (US $ million at 31 December)

	1997	1998	1999
Gold*	3.4	3.3	3.3
IMF special drawing rights	0.2	0.2	1.3
Reserve position in IMF	11.6	12.1	11.7
Foreign exchange	41.5	40.8	26.1
Total	56.7	56.4	42.4

* Valued at market-related prices.
Source: IMF, *International Financial Statistics*.

MONEY SUPPLY ('000 million francs CFA at 31 December)

	1997	1998	1999
Currency outside banks	41.7	24.5	34.1
Demand deposits at deposit money banks*	28.8	32.0	33.9
Checking deposits at post office	2.5	2.7	0.3
Total money (incl. others)*	73.1	59.6	68.8

* Excluding the deposits of public enterprises of an administrative or social nature.
Source: IMF, *International Financial Statistics*.

COST OF LIVING
(Consumer Price Index for Africans in Niamey; base: 1995 = 100)

	1997	1998	1999
All items	108.4	113.3	110.7

Source: IMF, *International Financial Statistics*.

NATIONAL ACCOUNTS ('000 million francs CFA at current prices)
Expenditure on the Gross Domestic Product

	1996	1997	1998*
Government final consumption expenditure	168.6	175.9	182.3
Private final consumption expenditure	816.3	871.6	981.5
Increase in stocks	3.0	3.0	3.0
Gross fixed capital formation	95.2	114.0	129.4
Total domestic expenditure	1,083.1	1,164.5	1,296.2
Exports of goods and services	172.3	175.3	196.6
Less Imports of goods and services	238.6	256.9	284.7
GDP in purchasers' values	1,016.8	1,082.9	1,208.1

Gross Domestic Product by Economic Activity

	1996	1997	1998*
Agriculture, hunting, forestry and fishing	381.7	399.9	488.9
Mining and quarrying	45.8	47.6	49.1
Manufacturing	68.5	73.6	78.1
Electricity, gas and water	20.6	22.1	23.4
Construction	19.3	20.3	24.7
Trade, restaurants and hotels	174.9	188.1	201.2
Transport, storage and communications	57.3	60.6	64.7
Other marketable services†	126.0	135.0	140.8
Non-marketable services	94.9	96.3	96.6
Sub-total	989.0	1,043.5	1,167.5
Import duties	27.8	39.4	40.6
GDP in purchasers' values	1,016.8	1,082.9	1,208.1

* Provisional figures.
† After deduction of imputed bank service charges.

Source: Banque centrale des états de l'Afrique de l'ouest.

BALANCE OF PAYMENTS (US $ million)

	1993	1994	1995
Exports of goods f.o.b.	300.4	226.8	288.1
Imports of goods f.o.b.	−312.1	−271.3	−305.6
Trade balance	−11.7	−44.5	−17.6
Exports of services	36.5	30.4	33.3
Imports of services	−185.6	−149.1	−151.8
Balance on goods and services	−160.9	−163.2	−136.0
Other income received	19.3	15.6	5.8
Other income paid	−30.2	−45.2	−52.9
Balance on goods, services and income	−171.7	−192.8	−183.2
Current transfers received	139.5	115.1	60.6
Current transfers paid	−65.0	−48.5	−29.1
Current balance	−97.2	−126.1	−151.7
Capital account (net)	109.3	88.2	65.3
Direct investment abroad	−5.8	1.8	−7.1
Direct investment from abroad	−34.4	−11.3	7.2
Other investment assets	11.2	22.3	−18.4
Other investment liabilities	−94.4	17.1	−27.8
Net errors and omissions	87.2	−67.8	114.4
Overall balance	−23.9	−75.8	−18.1

Source: IMF, *International Financial Statistics*.

External Trade

PRINCIPAL COMMODITIES ('000 million francs CFA)

Imports f.o.b.	1994	1995	1996*
Consumer goods	108.8	105.1	111.0
Cereals	8.9	9.2	14.4
Petroleum products . .	11.3	9.1	10.5
Intermediate and capital goods .	37.1	31.7	28.2
Total (incl. others) . . .	145.9	136.8	139.2

Exports f.o.b.	1994	1995	1996*
Uranium	78.9	72.6	70.0
Livestock and livestock products .	31.9	21.7	23.8
Live animals . . .	30.3	19.8	21.8
Cow-peas	7.4	7.4	10.5
Total (incl. others) . . .	128.4	139.9	143.4

* Estimates.

Source: IMF, *Niger—Statistical Annex* (October 1997).

PRINCIPAL TRADING PARTNERS (US $ million)*

Imports c.i.f.	1993	1994	1995
Côte d'Ivoire	53	53	65
France	111	94	104
Germany	19	11	13
Italy	14	8	6
Japan	10	8	10
Total (incl. others) . . .	470	462	541

Exports f.o.b.	1993	1994	1995
Côte d'Ivoire	9	10	13
France	130	78	119
Nigeria	5	5	5
Total (incl. others) . . .	234	119	161

* Data are compiled on the basis of reporting by Niger's trading partners.

Source: IMF, *Direction of Trade Statistics Yearbook* in IMF, *Niger—Statistical Annex* (October 1997).

Transport

ROAD TRAFFIC (estimates, motor vehicles in use)

	1994	1995	1996
Passenger cars	38,610	37,620	38,220
Lorries and vans	13,160	14,100	15,200

Source: IRF, *World Road Statistics*.

CIVIL AVIATION (traffic on scheduled services)*

	1994	1995	1996
Kilometres flown (million) . .	2	3	3
Passengers carried ('000) . .	69	74	75
Passenger-km (million) . .	215	223	225
Total ton-km (million) . .	34	36	37

* Including an apportionment of the traffic of Air Afrique.

Source: UN, *Statistical Yearbook*.

Tourism

FOREIGN TOURIST ARRIVALS BY ORIGIN*

	1995	1996	1997
Africa	32,886	33,201	33,676
America	7,408	7,569	7,702
Asia and Oceania . . .	4,286	4,328	4,545
Europe	21,651	21,829	22,060
Unspecified	—	—	1,017
Total	66,231	66,927	69,000

* Figures refer to arrivals in hotels and similar establishments.

Tourism receipts (US $ million): 15 in 1995; 17 in 1996; 18 in 1997.

Source: World Tourism Organization, *Yearbook of Tourism Statistics*.

Communications Media

	1994	1995	1996
Radio receivers ('000 in use) . .	540	620	650
Television receivers ('000 in use) .	44	105	110
Telephones ('000 main lines in use) .	12	14	15
Telefax stations (number in use) .	333	327	300
Daily newspapers			
Number	4	2	1
Average circulation ('000 copies) .	11	4	2
Non-daily newspapers			
Number	n.a.	5	5
Average circulation ('000 copies)	n.a.	15	14

1997 ('000 in use): Radio receivers 680; Television receivers 125.

Books published (first editions, 1991): Titles 5; Copies ('000) 11.

Sources: UNESCO, *Statistical Yearbook*; UN, *Statistical Yearbook*.

Education

(1997/98)

	Insti-tutions	Teachers	Students		
			Males	Females	Total
Pre-primary . .	123	494	5,845	5,919	11,764
Primary . .	3,175	11,545	295,577	186,488	482,065
Secondary*					
General . .	n.a.	5,043	61,514	34,016	95,530
Teacher training .	n.a.	101	1,007	333	1,340
Vocational . .	n.a.	114	661	144	805

* 1996/97 figures.

University level: 232 teachers; 4,513 students in 1991/92.

Source: UNESCO, *Statistical Yearbook*.

Directory

The Constitution

Following the death of President Ibrahim Baré Maïnassara, on 9 April 1999, a military Conseil de réconciliation nationale (CRN) was formed to exercise executive and legislative authority during a transitional period prior to the restoration of elected organs of government. The Constitution of the Fourth Republic, promulgated on 22 May 1996, was suspended, and its institutions—including the Council of Ministers, legislature, Supreme Court and Higher Communication Council—dissolved. Party political activity was suspended, although political organizations were not proscribed. A new Constitution, of what was to be designated the Fifth Republic, was approved by national referendum on 18 July 1999. The Constitution of the Fifth Republic, promulgated on 9 August, envisages a balance of powers between the President, Government and legislative Assemblée nationale. The President, who is elected by universal adult suffrage, is Head of State, and is accorded 'broad ordinary and arbitral powers'. The Government, under a Prime Minister appointed by the President, is responsible to the Assemblée nationale, which is competent to remove the Prime Minister by vote of censure. The Assemblée nationale is similarly elected by direct adult suffrage. The new President and legislature were inaugurated in December 1999.

Enshrined in the Constitution is a clause granting immunity from prosecution for all those involved in the *coups d'état* of January 1996 and April 1999. Legislation to this effect was adopted by the new Assemblée nationale in January 2000.

Among regulatory bodies provided for in the Constitution are the Observatoire national de la communication, responsible for the broadcasting and communications sector, and the Conseil supérieur de la défense nationale, which advises the Head of State on defence matters.

The Government

HEAD OF STATE

President: Col (retd) TANDJA MAMADOU (inaugurated 22 December 1999).

COUNCIL OF MINISTERS
(August 2000)

Prime Minister: HAMA AMADOU.
Minister of Public Health: ASSOUMANE ADAMOU.
Minister of Rural Development: WASSALIKE BOUKARI.
Minister of Equipment and Transport: ABDOU LABO.
Minister of Environment and Desertification: ISSOUFOU ASSOUMANE.
Minister of Water Resources, Spokesperson for the Government: AKOLI DAOUEL.
Minister of Trade and Industry: SEINI OUMAROU.
Minister of Finance and Economic Reforms: ALI BADJO GAMATIE.
Minister of Social Development, Population, Women and Children's Protection: NANA AICHA FOUMAKOYE.
Minister of Promotion of Small and Medium-sized Enterprises: SOULEY HASSANE.
Minister of Tourism and Handicrafts: RISSA AG BOULA.
Minister of the Interior and Territorial Administration: MAHAMA MANZO.
Minister of Foreign Affairs, Co-operation and African Integration: NASSIROU SABO.
Minister of National Defence: SABIOU DADI GAO.
Minister of Planning: BAROUMI MALIKI.
Minister of Justice and Keeper of the Seals, responsible for Relations with Parliament: ALI SIRFI.
Minister of National Education: ARI IBRAHIM.
Minister of Communications: AMADOU el Hadj SALIFOU.
Minister of Higher Education, Research and Technology: AMADOU LAWAL.
Minister of Labour and Administrative Modernization: MIREILLE OSSEY.
Minister of Privatization and Enterprise Restructuring: ALMA OUMAROU.
Minister of Mines and Energy: YAHAYA BAARE.
Minister of Animal Resources: KORONE MAOUDE.

Minister of Youth, Sports and Culture: ISSA LAMINE.

MINISTRIES

All ministries are in Niamey.

Ministry of Agriculture and Livestock: PB 10427, Niamey; tel. 73-31-55.
Ministry of the Civil Service, Labour and Employment: Niamey; tel. 72-25-01.
Ministry of Communications, Culture, Youth and Sports: Niamey; tel. 72-21-39; fax 72-23-36.
Ministry of Equipment and Transport: Niamey; tel. 72-25-01.
Ministry of Finance and Economic Reforms: BP 720, Niamey; tel. 72-23-74; fax 73-59-34.
Ministry of Foreign Affairs and Co-operation: BP 396, Niamey; tel. 72-29-07; fax 73-52-31.
Ministry of the Interior and Territorial Development: Niamey; tel. 72-21-76.
Ministry of Justice: Niamey; tel. 72-20-94.
Ministry of Mines and Energy: BP 11700, Niamey; tel. 73-45-82.
Ministry of National Defence: BP 626, Niamey; tel. 72-20-76.
Ministry of National Education: Quartier Yantala Haut, BP 11897, Niamey; tel. 72-25-26.
Ministry of Privatization and Enterprise Restructuring: Immeuble ex-BDRN, BP 862, Niamey; tel. 73-29-10; fax 73-59-91; e-mail ccpp@intnet.ne.
Ministry of Public Health: BP 623, Niamey; tel. 72-27-82.

President and Legislature

PRESIDENT
Presidential Election; first round, 17 October 1999

Candidate	Votes	% of votes
TANDJA MAMADOU (MNSD)	617,554	32.30
MAHAMADOU ISSOUFOU (PNDS)	435,693	22.78
MAHAMANE OUSMANE (CDS)	430,571	22.52
HAMID ALGABID (RDP)	207,658	10.86
MOUMOUNI AMADOU DJERMAKOYE (ANDPS)	147,979	7.74
ANDRÉ SALIFOU (UPDP)	39,797	2.08
AMADOU DJIBO ALI (UNIU*)	32,947	1.72
Total	**1,912,199**	**100.00**

* Union des Nigériens indépendants unis.

Second round, 24 November 1999

Candidate	% of votes
TANDJA MAMADOU (MNSD)	58.89
MAHAMADOU ISSOUFOU (PNDS)	40.11
Total	**100.00**

ASSEMBLÉE NATIONALE
General Election, 24 November 1999

Party	Seats
MNSD	38
CDS	17
PNDS	16
RDP	8
ANDPS	4
Total	**83**

Political Organizations

The following political organizations were among the most prominent at the time of the presidential and legislative elections of October–November 1999.

Alliance nigérienne pour la démocratie et le progrès social—Zaman Lahiya (ANDPS): Leader MOUMOUNI AMADOU DJERMAKOYE.
Convention démocratique et social—Rahama (CDS): Chair. MAHAMANE OUSMANE.

Front démocratique nigérien—Mountounchi (FDN): f. 1995 by fmr mems of PPN—RDA; Chair. OUMAROU YOUSSOUFOU GARBA; Sec.-Gen. MOHAMED MUDUR.

Mouvement national pour une société de développement—Nassara (MNSD): f. 1988; sole party 1988–90; Chair. Col (retd) TANDJA MAMADOU; Sec.-Gen. HAMA AMADOU.

Parti nigérien pour l'autogestion—al Umat (PNA): f. 1997; Leader JACKOU SENOUSSI.

Parti nigérien pour la démocratie et le socialisme—Tarayya (PNDS): Sec.-Gen. MAHAMADOU ISSOUFOU.

Parti progressiste nigérien—Rassemblement démocratique africain (PPN): associated with the late President Diori; Chair. IDE OUMAROU.

Parti républicain pour les libertés et le progrès au Niger—Nakowa (PRLPN): Chair. ALKA ALAMOU.

Parti social-démocrate nigérien—Alheri (PSDN): Leader KAZELMA OUMAR TAYA.

Parti pour l'unite nationale et le développement—Salama (PUND): Leader AKOLI DAOUEL.

Rassemblement pour la démocratie et le progrès—Djamaa (RDP): party of late Pres. MAÏNASSARA; Chair. HAMID ALGABID; Sec.-Gen. MAHAMANE SOULEY LABI.

Union pour la démocratie et le progrès—Amici (UDP): Leader ABDOULAYE TONDI.

Union pour la démocratie et le progrès social—Amana (UDPS): Chair. MOHAMED ABDULLAHI.

Union des forces populaires pour la démocratie et le progrès—Sawaba (UFPDP): Sec.-Gen. ISSOUFOU ASSOUMANE.

Union des patriotes démocratiques et progressistes—Shamuwa (UPDP): Chair. Prof. ANDRÉ SALIFOU.

Diplomatic Representation

EMBASSIES IN NIGER

Algeria: route des Ambassades-Goudel; BP 142, Niamey; tel. 72-35-83; fax 72-35-93; Ambassador: MADJID BOUGUERRA.

Belgium: BP 10192, Niamey; tel. 73-34-47; fax 73-37-56; Ambassador: FRANK RECKER.

Benin: BP 11544, Niamey; tel. 72-28-60; Ambassador: EMMANUEL NOUROU LAWANI .

Canada: Niamey; Ambassador: SUZANNE LAPORTE.

China, People's Republic: Niamey; Ambassador: JI JINGYI.

Egypt: Nouveau Plateau, Niamey; tel. 73-33-55; Ambassador: Dr SOBHY MOHAMED NAFEH.

France: route de Yantala, BP 10660, Niamey; tel. 72-24-31; fax 72-25-18; Ambassador: ALBERT PAVEC.

Germany: 71 ave du Général de Gaulle, BP 629, Niamey; tel. 72-25-34; fax 72-39-85; e-mail amballny@intnet.ne; Ambassador: ANGELIKA VÖLKEL.

Iran: ave de la Présidence, Niamey; tel. 72-21-98; Chargé d'affaires: MUHAMMAD SHOKRANI.

Libya: Rond-point du Grand Hôtel, POB 683, Niamey; tel. 73-47-92; Chargé d'affaires: AHMAD TAHIR BIN ALI.

Mauritania: Yantala, BP 12519, Niamey; tel. 72-38-93; Ambassador: MOHAMED EL HOUSSEIN OULD HABIBOU ALLAH.

Morocco: ave du Président Lubke, BP 12403, Niamey; tel. 73-40-84; fax 74-14-27; Ambassador: TAHAR NEJJAR.

Nigeria: ave du Général Ibrahim Babangida, Goudel, BP 11130, Niamey; tel. 73-24-10; fax 73-35-00; Chargé d'affaires a.i.: SULEY MOHAMED.

Pakistan: BP 10426, Niamey; tel. 72-35-84; Chargé d'affaires: IRFAN-UR-REHMAN RAJA.

Saudi Arabia: Yantala, BP 339, Niamey; tel. 72-32-15; Ambassador: GHASSAN SAID SADEK RACHACH.

USA: Yantala, BP 11201, Niamey; tel. 72-26-61; Ambassador: BARBRO OWENS-KIRKPATRICK.

Judicial System

The Supreme Court was dissolved following the death of President Ibrahim Baré Maïnassara in April 1999. The Conseil de réconciliation nationale established a State Court as the highest judicial authority pending the restoration of constitutional government: the State Court was composed of the four chambers of the dissolved Supreme Court. The Constitution of the Fifth Republic, promulgated in August 1999, provides for a Constitutional Court.

High Court of Justice: Niamey; competent to indict the President of the Republic and all other state officials (past and present) in relation to all matters of state, including high treason; comprises seven perm. mems and three rotating mems.

Court of State Security: Niamey; competent to try cases not within the jurisdiction of the High Court of Justice; incorporates a martial court.

Court of Appeal: Niamey; court of appeal for judgements of **Criminal** and **Assize Courts** (the latter at Niamey, Maradi, Tahoua and Zinder).

Courts of First Instance: located at Niamey (with sub-divisions at Dosso and Tillabéry), Maradi, Tahoua (sub-divisions at Agadez, Arlit and Birni N'Konni) and Diffa (sub-division at Diffa).

Labour Courts: function at each Court of the First Instance and sub-division thereof.

Religion

It is estimated that some 95% of the population are Muslims, 0.5% are Christians and the remainder follow traditional beliefs.

ISLAM

The most influential Islamic groups in Niger are the Tijaniyya, the Senoussi and the Hamallists.

CHRISTIANITY

Various Protestant missions maintain 13 centres, with a personnel of 90.

The Roman Catholic Church

Niger comprises the single diocese of Niamey, directly responsible to the Holy See. The diocese participates in the Bishops' Conference of Burkina Faso and Niger (based in Ouagadougou, Burkina Faso). At 31 December 1999 there were an estimated 17,500 Roman Catholics in Niger.

Bishop of Niamey: Rt Rev. GUY ROMANO, Evêché, BP 10270, Niamey; tel. 73-30-79; fax 74-10-13.

The Press

L'Alternative: Niamey; weekly; Man. MOUSSA TCHANGARI; Editor-in-Chief FUMAZOU KEITA.

Anfani: rue du Damagaram, BP 2096, Niamey; tel. 74-08-80; fax 74-00-52; e-mail anfani@intnet.ne; f. 1992; weekly; Editor-in-Chief ABDOULAYE IBO DADY; circ. 3,000.

Angam: Niamey; f. 1992; monthly; Dir GRÉMAH BOUKAR.

Le Canard Libéré: Niamey; satirical; Dir ABDOULAYE TIEMOGO; Editor ILLA KANE.

Le Démocrate: BP 11064, Niamey; weekly; independent; f. 1992; Editor-in-Chief ABDOULAYE BOUREIMA TOURE.

Haske: BP 297, Niamey; tel. 74-18-44; fax 73-20-06; f. 1990; weekly; Dir CHEIKH IBRAHIM DIOP.

Haske Magazine: BP 297; tel. 74-18-44; fax 73-20-06; f. 1990; quarterly; Dir CHEIKH IBRAHIM DIOP; circ. 3,000.

Horizon 2001: Niamey; f. 1991; monthly; Dir INOUSSA OUSSEÏNI.

Journal Officiel de la République du Niger: BP 116, Niamey; tel. 72-39-30; fax 72-39-43; f. 1960; fortnightly; govt bulletin; Man. Editor BONKOULA AMINATOU MAYAKI; circ. 800.

Kakaki: Niamey; f. 1991; monthly; Dir SIRAJI KANÉ.

La Marche: Niamey; f. 1989; monthly; Dir ABDOULAYE MOUSSA MASSALATCHI.

Nigerama: Niamey; quarterly; publ. by the Agence Nigérienne de Presse.

Le Paon Africain: BP 10381, Niamey; tel. 75-36-98; f. 1993; weekly; satirical; Dir and Editor MOUSTAPHA DIOP; circ. 3,000.

Le Républicain: BP 12015, Niamey; fax 73-41-42; e-mail lerepublican@intnet.ne; f. 1991; weekly; pro-Tuareg; Dir MAMANE ABOU.

Le Sahel: BP 13182, Niamey; f. 1960; publ. by Office National d'Edition et de Presse; daily; Dir ALI OUSSEÏNI; Editor-in-Chief ALASSANE ASOKOFARE; circ. 5,000.

Le Sahel Dimanche: BP 13182, Niamey; publ. by Office National d'Edition et de Presse; weekly; Dir ALI OUSSEÏNI; Editor-in-Chief ALASSANE Asokofare; circ. 3,000.

Le Soleil: Niamey; Dir MOULAYE ABDOULAYE.

La Tribune du Peuple: BP 2624, Niamey; f. 1993; weekly; Man. Editor IBRAHIM HAMIDOU.

La Voix du Citoyen: Niamey; weekly; independent; Editor ALI SEKOU MAÏNA.

NEWS AGENCIES

Agence Nigérienne de Presse (ANP): BP 11158, Niamey; tel. 740809; f. 1987; state-owned; Dir ABDOURAHMANE ALILOU.

Office National d'Edition et de Presse (ONEP): Niamey; f. 1989; Dir ALI OUSSEÏNI.

Publisher

Government Publishing House

L'Imprimerie Nationale du Niger (INN): BP 61, Niamey; tel. 73-47-98; f. 1962; Dir E. WOHLRAB.

Broadcasting and Communications

REGULATORY AUTHORITY

Observatoire National de la Communication (ONC): Niamey; Chair. KIO OKUDISSÉ.

TELECOMMUNICATIONS

Société Nigérienne des Télécommunications (SONITEL): BP 208, Niamey; tel. 72-29-98; fax 72-24-78; e-mail sonitel@intnet.ne; internet www.intnet.ne; privatization pending.

BROADCASTING

Radio

Office de Radiodiffusion-Télévision du Niger (ORTN): BP 309, Niamey; tel. 72-31-63; state broadcasting authority; Dir-Gen. MAHAMANE ADAMOU; Tech. Dir (Radio and Television) ZOUDI ISSOUF.

La Voix du Sahel: BP 309, Niamey; tel. 72-31-55; f. 1958; govt-controlled radio service; programmes in French, Hausa (Haoussa), Djerma (Zarma), Kanuri, Fulfuldé, Tamajak, Toubou, Gourmantché and Arabic; Dir R. A. KHAMED.

Radio Ténéré FM: Niamey; Editor-in-Chief HADJ BASHIR.

Anfani FM: rue du Damagaram, BP 2096, Niamey; tel. 74-08-80; fax 74-00-52; e-mail anfani@intnet.ne; private radio station broadcasting to Niamey, Zinder, Maradi and Diffa; Dir GRÉMAH BOUCAR.

Sudan FM: Dosso; auth. 2000; private radio station; Dir HIMA ADAMOU.

Television

Office de Radiodiffusion-Télévision du Niger (ORTN): (see Radio).

Télé-Sahel: BP 309, Niamey; tel. 72-31-55; fax 72-35-48; govt-controlled television service; broadcasts daily; Dir-Gen. ABDOU SOULEY.

Télévision Ténéré (TTC): Niamey; auth. 2000; Dir ABIBOU GARBA.

Finance

(cap. = capital; res = reserves; m. = million; brs = branches; amounts in francs CFA)

BANKING

Central Bank

Banque Centrale des Etats de l'Afrique de l'Ouest (BCEAO): rond-point de la Poste, BP 487, Niamey; tel. 72-24-91; fax 73-47-43; HQ in Dakar, Senegal; f. 1962; bank of issue for the mem. states of the Union économique et monétaire ouest-africaine (UEMOA, comprising Benin, Burkina Faso, Côte d'Ivoire, Guinea-Bissau, Mali, Niger, Senegal and Togo); cap. and res 806,918m., total assets 4,084,464m. (Dec. 1998); Gov. CHARLES KONAN BANNY; Dir in Niger ABDOULAYE SOUMANA; brs at Maradi and Zinder.

Commercial Banks

Bank of Africa—Niger: Immeuble Sonara II, BP 10973, Niamey; tel. 73-36-20; fax 73-38-18; e-mail bofafrni@intnet.ne; f. 1994 to acquire assets of Nigeria International Bank Niamey; 42.5% owned by African Financial Holding; cap. and res 2,887m., total assets 24,439m. (Dec. 1998); Chair. PAUL DERREMAUX; Man. Dir KHALED SUCCARI (acting).

Banque Commerciale du Niger (BCN): rond-point Maourey, BP 11363/881, Niamey; tel. 73-39-15; fax 73-21-63; f. 1978; owned by private Nigerien (50%) and Libyan (50%) interests; cap. and res 950m. (Sept. 1993); Chair. and Man. Dir CHEICK MOHAMED METRI.

Banque Internationale pour l'Afrique au Niger (BIA—Niger): ave de la Mairie, BP 10350, Niamey; tel. 73-31-01; fax 73-35-95; f. 1980; 35% owned by Groupe Belgolaise SA (Belgium); cap. and res 3,528m., total assets 48,891m. (Dec. 1997); Chair. AMADOU HIMA SOULEY; Man. Dir DANIEL HASSER; 5 brs.

Banque Islamique du Niger pour le Commerce et l'Investissement (BINCI): ave de la Mairie, BP 12754, Niamey; tel. 73-27-30; fax 73-48-25; e-mail binci@intnet.ne; f. 1983; fmrly Banque Masraf Faisal Islami, restructured 1994—96; 33% owned by Dar al-Maal al-Islami (DMI Trust), 33% by Islamic Development Bank; cap. and res 1,415m., total assets 6,051m. (Dec. 1998); Chair. ABDERRAOUF BENESSAÏAH; Man. Dir JUNAID IQBAL.

Ecobank Niger: angle blvd de la Liberté et rue des Bâtisseurs, BP 13804, Niamey; tel. 73-71-81; fax 73-72-03; e-mail ecobank@intnet.ne; owned by Ecobank Transnational Inc. and subsids (operating under the auspices of the Economic Community of West African States); cap. 1,250m.; Man. Dir JOSEPH K. AGBEMEHIN.

Société Nigérienne de Banque (SONIBANQUE): ave de la Mairie, BP 891, Niamey; tel. 73-45-69; fax 73-46-93; f. 1990; 25% owned by Société Tunisienne de Banque; cap. and res 4,222m., total assets 30,446m. (Dec. 1998); Dir-Gen. CHAKIB SIALA.

Development Banks

Caisse de Prêt aux Collectivités Territoriales (CPCT): route de Torodi, BP 730, Niamey, tel. 72-34-12; f. 1970; 100% state-owned (94% by collectivités territoriales); part-privatization pending; cap. and res 1,146m., total assets 3,513m. (Dec. 1995); Chair. BRIGI RAFINI; Man. Dir IBRAHIM KOMMA.

Crédit du Niger (CDN): 11 blvd de la République, BP 213, Niger; tel. 72-27-01; fax 72-23-90; f. 1958; 54% state-owned, 20% owned by Caisse Nationale de Sécurité Sociale; cap. and res 1,121m., total assets 3,037m. (Sept. 1998); Chair. ABOU KANÉ; Man. Dir MOUDOUR MOHAMED.

Fonds d'Intervention en Faveur des Petites et Moyennes Entreprises Nigériennes (FIPMEN): Immeuble Sonara II, BP 252, Niamey; tel. 73-20-98; f. 1990; state-owned; cap. and res 124m. (Dec. 1991); Chair. AMADOU SALLA HASSANE; Man. Dir IBRAHIM BEIDARI.

Savings Bank

Caisse Nationale d'Epargne (CNE): BP 11778, Niamey; tel. 73-24-98; total assets 2,437m. (Sept. 1993); Chair. IDI GADO; Man. Dir BACHIR MALLAM MATO.

STOCK EXCHANGE

Bourse Régionale des Valeurs Mobilières (BRVM): c/o Chambre de Commerce et d'Industrie du Niger, Place de la Concertation, BP 13299, Niamey; tel. 73-66-92; fax 73-46-68; f. 1998; national branch of BRVM (regional stock exchange based in Abidjan, Côte d'Ivoire, serving the member states of UEMOA); Man. IDRISSA S. MAGAGIS.

INSURANCE

Agence Nigérienne d'Assurances (ANA): place de la Mairie, BP 423, Niamey; tel. 72-20-71; f. 1959; cap. 1.5m.; owned by L'Union des Assurances de Paris; Dir JEAN LASCAUD.

Société Civile Immobilière des Assureurs de Niamey: BP 423, Niamey; tel. 73-40-71; fax 73-41-85; f. 1962; cap. 14m.; Dir MAMADOU TALATA DOULLA.

Société Nigérienne d'Assurances et de Réassurances 'Leyma' (SNAR—LEYMA): ave du Général de Gaulle, BP 426, Niamey; tel. 73-55-26; f. 1973; cap. 345m.; Pres. AMADOU OUSMANE; Dir-Gen. MAMADOU MALAM AOUAMI.

Union Générale des Assurances du Niger (UGAN): rue de Kalley, BP 11935, Niamey; tel. 73-54-06; fax 73-41-85; f. 1985; cap. 500m.; Pres. PATHÉ DIONE; Dir-Gen. MAMADOU TALATA; 7 brs.

Trade and Industry

GOVERNMENT AGENCIES

Caisse de Stabilisation des Prix des Produits du Niger (CSPPN): BP 480, Niamey; price control agency for Nigerien goods; Dir IBRAHIM KOUSSOU.

Cellule de Coordination de la Programme de Privatisation: Immeuble ex-BDRN, BP 862, Niamey; tel. 73-29-10; fax 73-29-58; responsible for co-ordination of privatization programme; Co-ordinator IDÉ ISSOUFOU.

Office des Eaux du Sous-Sol (OFEDES): BP 734, Niamey; tel. 73-23-44; govt agency for the maintenance and development of wells and boreholes; Dir ADOU ADAM.

Office du Lait du Niger (OLANI): BP 404, Niamey; tel. 73-23-69; f. 1971; govt agency for development and marketing of milk products; Pres. Dr ABDOUA KABO; Dir MAHAMADOU HAROUNA.

Office National de l'Energie Solaire (ONERSOL): BP 621, Niamey; tel. 73-45-05; govt agency for research and development, commercial production and exploitation of solar devices; Dir ALBERT WRIGHT.

Office National des Ressources Minières du Niger (ONAREM): BP 12716, Niamey; tel. 73-59-26; f. 1976; govt agency for exploration, exploitation and marketing of all minerals; Dir-Gen. OUSMANE GAOURI.

Office des Produits Vivriers du Niger (OPVN): BP 474, Niamey; govt agency for developing agricultural and food production; Dir ADAMOU SOUNA.

Riz du Niger (RINI): BP 476, Tillabéry, Niamey; tel. 71-13-29; f. 1967; cap. 825m. francs CFA; 27% state-owned; development and marketing of rice; Pres. YAYA MADOUGOU; Dir-Gen. OUSMANE DJIKA.

Société Nigérienne de Produits Pétroliers (SONIDEP): BP 11702, Niamey; tel. 73-33-34; f. 1977; govt agency for the distribution and marketing of petroleum products; cap. 1,000m. francs CFA; Man. Dir ADAMOU NAMATA.

DEVELOPMENT ORGANIZATION

Mission Française de Coopération: BP 494, Niamey; tel. 72-20-66; administers bilateral aid from France; Dir JEAN BOULOGNE.

CHAMBERS OF COMMERCE

Chambre de Commerce et d'Industrie du Niger: place de la Concertation, BP 209, Niamey; tel. 73-22-10; f. 1954; comprises 80 full mems and 40 dep. mems; Sec.-Gen. SAMA OUMAROU IBRAHIM.

Chambre de Commerce, d'Agriculture, d'Industrie et d'Artisanat du Niger, Antenne d'Agadez: BP 201, Agadez; tel. 44-01-61.

Chambre de Commerce, d'Agriculture, d'Industrie et d'Artisanat du Niger, Antenne de Diffa: BP 91, Diffa; tel. 54-03-92; f. 1988.

Chambre de Commerce, d'Agriculture, d'Industrie et d'Artisanat du Niger, Antenne de Maradi: BP 79, Maradi; tel. 41-03-66; fax 41-10-32.

Chambre de Commerce, d'Agriculture, d'Industrie et d'Artisanat du Niger, Antenne de Tahoua: BP 172, Tahoua; tel. 61-03-84; f. 1984; Sec. ILYESS HABIB.

Chambre de Commerce, d'Agriculture, d'Industrie et d'Artisanat du Niger, Antenne de Zinder: BP 83, Zinder; tel. 51-00-78.

INDUSTRIAL AND TRADE ORGANIZATIONS

Centre Nigérien du Commerce Extérieur (CNCE): place de la Concertation, BP 12480, Niamey; tel. 73-22-88; fax 73-46-68; f. 1984; promotes and co-ordinates all aspects of foreign trade; Dir AÏSSA DIALLO.

Société Nationale de Commerce et de Production du Niger (COPRO-Niger): BP 615, Niamey; tel. 73-28-41; fax 73-57-71; f. 1962; monopoly importer of foodstuffs; cap. 1,000m. francs CFA; 47% state-owned; Man. Dir DJIBRILLA HIMA.

EMPLOYERS' ORGANIZATIONS

Syndicat des Commerçants Importateurs et Exportateurs du Niger (SCIMPEXNI): Niamey; tel. 73-34-66; Pres. ANDRÉ BEAUMONT; Sec.-Gen. C. SALEZ.

Syndicat National des Petites et Moyennes Entreprises et Industries Nigériennes (SYNAPEMEIN): Niamey; Pres. El Hadj ALI SOUMANA; Sec.-Gen. BOUBACAR ZEZI.

Syndicat Patronal des Entreprises et Industries du Niger (SPEIN): BP 415, Niamey; tel. 73-24-01; fax 73-45-26; f. 1945; Pres. AMADOU OUSMANE.

UTILITIES

Electricity

Société Nigérienne d'Electricité (NIGELEC): BP 11202, Niamey; tel. 72-26-92; fax 72-32-88; f. 1968; 95% state-owned; partial transfer to private ownership pending; production and distribution of electricity; Dir-Gen. AHMADOU MAYAKI.

MAJOR COMPANIES

The following are among the largest companies in terms of either capital investment or employment.

Compagnie Minière d'Akouta SA (COMINAK): BP 10545, Niamey; tel. 73-45-86; fax 73-28-55; f. 1975; cap. 3,500m. francs CFA; 34% owned by Cie générale des matières nucléaires (COGEMA) (France), 31% by ONAREM (Niger govt), 25% by Overseas Uranium Resources Development (Japan), 10% by Empresa Nacional del Uranio (Spain); mining and processing of uranium at Akouta; Chair. BOUKAR MAÏ MANGA; Man. Dir H. PELLO.

Office National des Produits Pharmaceutiques et Chimiques (ONPPC): BP 11585, Niamey; tel. 73-27-81; fax 73-23-74; f. 1962; cap. 440m. francs CFA; state-owned; Dir Dr MAIDANA SAIDOU DJER-MAKOYE.

Société des Brasseries et Boissons Gazeuses du Niger (BRANIGER): BP 11245, Niamey; tel. 72-20-88; f. 1967; cap. 1,428m. francs CFA; mfrs of ice and soft drinks at Niamey and Maradi; Chair. ALPHONSE DENIS; Dir M. TRAVERSA; 300 employees.

Société d'Exploitation des Produits d'Arachides du Niger (SEPANI): BP 8, Magaria; f. 1970; cap. 405m. francs CFA; 33% state-owned; production of groundnut oil at Magaria; Dir MAURICE CHAINE.

Société des Mines de l'Aïr (SOMAÏR): BP 12910, Niamey; tel. 72-35-31; fax 72-29-33; f. 1968; cap. 4,349m. francs CFA; 56.9% owned by COGEMA (France), 33% by ONAREM; uranium mining at Arlit; Dir-Gen. HUGUES BLANCHERE; Dir at Arlit IBRAHIM COURMO.

Société Minière du Niger (SMDN): BP 12443, Niamey; tel. 73-45-82; f. 1941; cap. 36m. francs CFA; 71% state-owned, 10% owned by Benin govt; cassiterite mining at El Mecki and Tarrouadji; Chair. AMANI ISSAKA; Man. Dir MAMADOU SAADOU.

Société Minière de Tassa N'Taghalgué (SMTT): BP 10376, Niamey; tel. 73-36-66; f. 1979; cap. 10,500m. francs CFA; 33% owned by ONAREM, 33% by COGEMA (France), 33% by Kuwait Foreign Trading, Contracting and Investment Co; owns uranium-mining rights at Taza (leased to SOMAÏR in 1986); Chair. Minister of Mines and Energy; Man. Dir MICHEL HAREL.

Société Nigérienne du Charbon d'Anou Araren (SONICHAR): BP 51, Agadez; tel. 44-02-48; fax 44-03-49; f. 1975; cap. 19,730m. francs CFA; 61% state-owned, 10% owned by the Islamic Development Bank, 24% by COMINAK, SMTT and SOMAÏR; exploitation of coal reserves at Anou Araren and generation of electricity; Chair. MAHAMADOU HALILOU; Man. Dir AMADOU DIOFFO; 375 employees.

Société Nigérienne de Cimenterie (SNC): BP 03, Malbaza; tel. 01-02; f. 1963; privatized 1998; cap. 1,300m. francs CFA; 77% by SCANLEM International SNC; production and marketing of cement at Malbaza; Chair. SAIDOU MAMANE; Man. Dir ABOUBACAR KADA LABO; 163 employees.

Société Nigérienne d'Exploitation des Ressources Animales (SONERAN): Niamey; tel. 73-23-75; f. 1968; cap. 270m. francs CFA; 99.9% state-owned; production and export of fresh and processed meat; ranch of 110,000 ha; Man. Dir MOUCTARI MAHAMANE FALALOU.

Société Nouvelle Nigérienne des Textiles (SONITEXTIL): route de Kolo, BP 10735, Niamey; tel. 73-25-11; f. 1978; cap. 1,000m. francs CFA; textile complex at Niamey; 27% state-owned; Chair. SAIDOU MAMANE; Man. Dir ROGER HUBER; 830 employees.

Unimo-Industrie et Chimie: BP 71, Maradi; tel. 41-00-56; f. 1978; cap. 710m. francs CFA; mfrs of foam rubber; Dir ASSAD GHASSAN.

TRADE UNION FEDERATIONS

Confédération des Syndicats Libres des Travailleurs du Niger (CSLTN): Niamey; f. 1993; 4 affiliates.

Union des Syndicats des Travailleurs du Niger (USTN): Bourse du Travail, BP 388, Niamey; tel. and fax 73-52-56; f. 1960; Sec.-Gen. El Hadj MAHAMANE MANSOUR; 28,000 mems in 37 affiliated unions.

Transport

ROADS

Niger is crossed by highways running from east to west and from north to south, giving access to neighbouring countries. A road is under construction to Lomé, Togo, via Burkina Faso, and the 428-km Zinder–Agadez road, scheduled to form part of the Trans-Sahara highway, has been upgraded. Niger and Algeria appealed jointly in mid-1998 for international aid to fund construction of the trans-Sahara highway, development of which was suspended in the mid-1990s because of the conflict in northern Niger.

In 1996 there were an estimated 10,100 km of classified roads, including 3,620 km of main roads and 3,320 km of secondary roads. Only about 800 km of the total network were paved.

Société Nationale des Transports Nigériens (SNTN): BP 135, Niamey; tel. 72-24-55; fax 73-47-07; f. 1961; operates passenger and freight road-transport services; 49% state-owned; Dir AHMADOU MAYAKI.

RAILWAYS

Organisation Commune Bénin-Niger des Chemins de Fer et des Transports (OCBN): BP 38, Niamey; tel. 73-27-90; f. 1959; 50% owned by Govt of Niger, 50% by Govt of Benin; manages the Benin-Niger railway project (begun in 1978). There are as yet no railways in Niger.

INLAND WATERWAYS

The River Niger is navigable for 300 km within the country. Access to the sea is available by a river route from Gaya, in south-western Niger, to the coast at Port Harcourt, Nigeria, between September and March. Port facilities at Lomé, Togo, are used as a commercial outlet for land-locked Niger, and an agreement providing import facilities at the port of Tema was signed with Ghana in November 1986.

Niger-Transit (NITRA): Zone Industrielle, BP 560, Niamey; tel. 73-22-53; fax 73-26-38; f. 1974; 48% owned by SNTN; customs agent, freight-handling, warehousing, etc.; manages Nigerien port facilities at Lomé, Togo; Pres. OUMAROU ALI BEÏOLI; Man. Dir SADE FATIMATA.

Société Nigérienne des Transports Fluviaux et Maritimes (SNTFM): Niamey; tel. 73-39-69; river and sea transport; cap. 64.6m. francs CFA; 99% state-owned; Man. Dir BERTRAND DEJEAN.

CIVIL AVIATION

There are international airports at Niamey (Hamani Diori) and Agadez, and major domestic airports at Arlit, Diffa, Tahoua and Zinder.

Air Afrique: BP 11090, Niamey; tel. 73-30-10; see under Côte d'Ivoire; Dir in Niamey MALLÉ SALL.

Air Inter Niger: Agadez; f. 1997 to operate services to Tamanrasset (Algeria).

Nigeravia SA: BP 10454, Niamey; tel. 73-30-64; fax 74-18-42; e-mail nigavia@intnet.ne; f. 1991 as Trans-Niger Aviation; operates domestic and regional services; Man. Dir JEAN SYLVESTRE.

Société Nigérienne des Transports Aériens (SONITA): Niamey; f. 1991; cap. 50m. francs CFA; owned by private Nigerien (81%) and Cypriot (19%) interests; operates domestic and regional services; Man. Dir ABDOULAYE MAIGA GOUDOUBABA.

Tourism

The Aïr and Ténéré Nature Reserve, covering an area of 77,000 sq km, was established in 1988. Tourism was hampered by insecurity in the north and east during the 1990s. However, the number of foreign arrivals at hotels and similar establishments increased from 66,927 in 1996 to 69,000 in 1997, and income from tourism rose from US $17m. to $18m. over the same period.

Direction du Tourisme et de l'Hôtellerie: BP 480, Niamey; tel. 73-61-38; fax 73-61-39; Dir IBRAHIM BOUBACAR.

Société Nigérienne d'Hôtellerie (SONHOTEL): BP 11040, Niamey; tel. 73-23-87; f. 1977; state-owned hotel corpn; Dir-Gen. HABI ABDOU.

Defence

In August 1999 Niger's armed forces totalled 5,300 men (army 5,200; air force about 100). Paramilitary forces numbered 5,400 men, comprising the gendarmerie (1,400 men), the republican guard (2,500) and the national police force (1,500). Conscription is selective and lasts for two years.

Defence Expenditure: Budgeted at 17,000m. francs CFA in 1999.

Chief of General Staff of the Armed Forces: Lt-Col BOUREIMA MOUMOUNI.

Education

Education is available free of charge, and is officially compulsory for eight years from seven to 15 years of age. Primary education begins at the age of seven and lasts for six years. Secondary education begins at the age of 13 years and comprises a four-year cycle followed by a further three-year cycle. Primary enrolment in 1997 was equivalent to only 29% of children in the appropriate age-group (boys 36%; girls 23%). The Government aimed to increase the rate of primary enrolment to 35% by 1999. Secondary enrolment in 1996 was equivalent to only 7% of the relevant age-group (boys 9%; girls 5%). The Abdou Moumouni Diop University, at Niamey, was inaugurated in 1973, and the Islamic University of West Africa, at Say, was opened in January 1987. Expenditure on education (excluding tertiary education) by the central Government in 1997 represented 12.8% of total government spending. Adult illiteracy at the time of the 1988 census averaged 89.1% (males 83.1%; females 94.6%). In 1995, according to UNESCO estimates, the adult illiteracy rate averaged 86.6% (males 79.4%; females 93.4%).

Bibliography

Abdourhame, B. *Crise institutionnelle et démocratisation au Niger.* Talance Cedex, Université de Bordeaux IV, 1997.

Asiwaju, A. I. et al., and Barkindo, B. M. *The Nigerian-Niger Transborder Co-operation.* Lagos, Malthouse Press, 1993.

Beckwith, C., and Van Offelen, M. *Nomads of Niger.* London, Collins, 1984.

Bernus, E. *Touaregs, un peuple du désert.* Paris, Editions Robert Laffont, 1996.

Charlick, R. B. *Niger: Personal Rule and Survival in the Sahel.* Boulder, CO, Westview Press, 1991.

Clair, A. *Le Niger indépendant.* Paris, ATEOS, 1966.

Decalo, S. *Historical Dictionary of Niger.* 3rd Edn. Metuchen, NJ, Scarecrow Press, 1996.

La Documentation Française. *Bibliographie sommaire de la République du Niger.* Paris, 1969.

La République du Niger. Paris, 1973.

Donaint, P., and Lancrenon, F. *Le Niger.* Paris, Presses universitaires de France, 1972.

Grégoire, E. *Les Alhazi de Maradi.* Paris, Editions Ostrom, 1986.

Harrison Church, R. J. *West Africa.* 8th Edn, London, Longman, 1979.

Keenan, J. *The Tuareg.* London, Allen Lane, 1978.

Klotchkoff, J.-C. *Le Niger aujourd'hui.* Paris, Editions Jeune Afrique, 1982.

Lund, C. *Law, Power and Politics in Niger: Land Struggles and the Rural Code.* Uppsala, Nordiska Africainstitutet, 1998.

Ramir, S. *Les Pistes de l'oubli: Touaregs au Niger.* Paris, Editions du Félin, 1991.

Raynault, G. (Ed.). *Projet de développement rural de Maradi. Le développement rural de la région au village.* Bordeaux, Groupe de recherche interdisciplinaire pour le développement, 1988.

Rimmer, D. *The Economies of West Africa.* London, Weidenfeld and Nicolson, 1984.

Séré de Rivières, E. *Histoire du Niger.* Paris, Berger-Levrault, 1966.

NIGERIA

Physical and Social Geography

AKIN L. MABOGUNJE

The Federal Republic of Nigeria covers an area of 923,768 sq km (356,669 sq miles) on the shores of the Gulf of Guinea, with Benin to the west, Niger to the north, Chad to the north-east, and Cameroon to the east and south-east. The population was enumerated at 88,514,501 at the census of November 1991, increasing to an estimated 97,223,521 at mid-1995. Population density in 1995 averaged 105.2 persons per sq km.

Nigeria became independent on 1 October 1960, and in 1968 adopted a new federal structure comprising 12 states. A federal capital territory was created in 1979. The number of states was increased to 19 in 1976, to 21 in 1987, to 30 in 1991, and to 36 in 1996.

PHYSICAL FEATURES

The physical features of Nigeria are of moderate dimensions. The highest lands are along the eastern border of the country and rise to a maximum of 2,040 m above sea-level at Vogel Peak, south of the Benue river. The Jos plateau, which is located close to the centre of the country, rises to 1,780 m at Shere Hill and 1,698 m at Wadi Hill. The plateau is also a watershed, from which streams flow to Lake Chad and to the rivers Niger and Benue. The land declines steadily northward from the plateau; this area, known as the High Plains of Hausaland, is characterized by a broad expanse of level sandy plains, interspersed by rocky dome outcrops. To the south-west, across the Niger river, similar relief is represented in the Yoruba highlands, where the rocky outcrops are surrounded by forests or tall grass and form the major watershed for rivers flowing northwards to the Niger and southwards to the sea. Elsewhere in the country, lowlands of less than 300 m stretch inland from the coast for over 250 km and continue in the trough-like basins of the Niger and Benue rivers. Lowland areas also exist in the Rima and Chad basins at the extreme north-west and north-east of the country respectively. These lowlands are dissected by innumerable streams and rivers flowing in broad sandy valleys.

The main river of Nigeria is the Niger, the third longest river of Africa. Originating in the Fouta Djallon mountains of north-east Sierra Leone, it enters Nigeria for the last one-third of its 4,200 km course. It flows first south-easterly, then due south and again south-easterly to Lokoja, where it converges with its principal tributary, the Benue. From here the river flows due south until Aboh, where it merges with the numerous interlacing distributaries of its delta. The Benue rises in Cameroon, flows in a south-westerly direction into the Niger, and receives on its course the waters of the Katsina Ala and Gongola rivers. The other main tributaries of the Niger within Nigeria are the Sokoto, Kaduna and Anambra rivers. Other important rivers in the country include the Ogun, the Oshun, the Imo and the Cross, many of which flow into the sea through a system of lagoons. The Nigerian coastline is relatively straight, with few natural indentations.

CLIMATE

Nigeria has a climate which is characterized by relatively high temperatures throughout the year. The average annual maximum varies from 35°C in the north to 31°C in the south; the average annual minimum from 23°C in the south to 18°C in the north. On the Jos plateau and the eastern highlands altitude moderates the temperatures, with the maximum no more than 28°C and the minimum sometimes as low as 14°C.

The annual rainfall total decreases from over 3,800 mm at Forcados on the coast to under 650 mm at Maiduguri in the north-east of the country. The length of the rainy season ranges from almost 12 months in the south to under five months in the north. Rain starts in January in the south and moves gradually across country. June, July, August and September are the rainiest months country-wide. In many parts of the south, however, there is a slight break in the rains for some two to three weeks in late July and early August. No such break occurs in the northern part of the country, and the rainy season continues uninterrupted for three to six months.

SOILS AND VEGETATION

The broad pattern of soil distribution in the country reflects both the climatic conditions and the geological structure; heavily leached, reddish-brown, sandy soils are found in the south, and light or moderately leached, yellowish-brown, sandy soils in the north. The difference in colour relates to the extent of leaching the soil has undergone.

The nutrient content of the soil is linked to the geological structure. Over a large part of the northern and south-western areas of the country the geological structure is that of old crystalline Basement complex rocks. These are highly mineralized and give rise to soils of high nutrient status, although variable from place to place. On the sedimentary rocks found in the south-east, north-east and north-west of the country the soils are sandy and less variable but are deficient in plant nutrient. They are highly susceptible to erosion.

The vegetation displays clear east-west zonation. In general, mangrove and rain forests are found in the south, occupying about 20% of the area of the country, while grassland of various types occupies the rest. Four belts of grassland can be identified. Close to the forest zone is a derived savannah belt, which is evidently the result of frequent fires in previously forested areas. This belt is succeeded by the Guinea, the Sudan and the Sahel savannah northwards in that order. The height of grass and density of wood vegetation decrease with each succeeding savannah belt.

RESOURCES

Although nearly 180,000 sq km of Nigeria is in the forest belt, only 23,000 sq km account for most of its timber resources. These forests are mainly in Ondo, Bendel and Cross River States. Nigeria exports a wide variety of tropical hardwoods, and internal consumption has been growing rapidly.

Cattle, goats and, to a lesser extent, sheep constitute important animal resources. Most of the cattle are found in the Sudan grassland belt in the far north. Poultry and pigs are increasing in importance.

Coastal waters are becoming important fishing grounds. Traditionally, however, major sources of fish have been Lake Chad in the extreme north-east, the lagoons along the coast, the creeks and distributaries of the Niger delta and the various rivers in the country.

Mineral resources are varied, although considerable exploration remains to be carried out. Tin and columbite are found in alluvial deposits on the Jos Plateau. Nigeria was, until 1968, Africa's main producer of tin, but output has since declined. Extensive reserves of medium-grade iron ore exist, and iron and steel production is being developed.

Fuel resources include deposits of lignite and sub-bituminous coal, exploited at Enugu since 1915; however, total reserves are small. More significant are the petroleum reserves, estimates of which alter with each new discovery in the offshore area. The oil produced, being of low sulphur content and high quality, is much in demand on the European and US markets. Since Libya restricted production in 1973, Nigeria has been Africa's leading producer of petroleum. Natural gas is also found in abundance, and has been undergoing development since the mid-1980s.

POPULATION

The Nigerian population is extremely diverse. There are more than 500 spoken languages, and well over 250 ethnic groups, some numbering fewer than 10,000 people. Ten groups, notably Hausa-Fulani, Yoruba, Ibo, Kanuri, Tiv, Edo, Nupe, Ibibio and Ijaw, account for nearly 80% of the total population. Much of the population is concentrated in the southern part of the country, as well as in the area of dense settlement around Kano

in the north. Between these two areas is the sparsely populated Middle Belt.

Urban life has a long history in Nigeria, with centres of population such as Kano (mid-1975 estimate 399,000), Zaria (224,000), Ife (176,000) and Benin (136,000) dating from the Middle Ages. Recent economic development, however, has stimulated considerable rural-urban migration and led to the phenomenal growth of such cities as Lagos, Ibadan, Kaduna and Port Harcourt. In December 1991 the federal capital was formally transferred to Abuja; however, a number of government departments and non-government institutions have remained in the former capital, Lagos.

Recent History

RICHARD SYNGE

The territory that now comprises the Federal Republic of Nigeria (excluding the segment once part of the former German protectorate of Kamerun, see below) was colonized by the United Kingdom during the second half of the 19th century and the first decade of the 20th century. Much of the administration remained under the control of traditional rulers, supervised by the colonial authorities. In 1947 the United Kingdom introduced a new Nigerian constitution, establishing a federal system of government, based on three regions: Eastern, Western and Northern. The federal arrangement sought to reconcile regional and religious tensions, and to accommodate the interests of Nigeria's diverse ethnic groups: mainly the Ibo (in the east), the Yoruba (in the west) and the Hausa and Fulani (in the north). The Northern Region, whose inhabitants were mainly Muslims, contained about one-half of Nigeria's total population.

Politically, the Eastern Region was dominated by the National Council for Nigeria and the Cameroons (NCNC), led by Dr Nnamdi Azikiwe, with mainly Ibo support. The leading political entity in the Western Region was the Action Group (AG), led by Obafemi Awolowo and dominated by educated Yoruba. The largest region in the country, the Northern Region, was dominated by the Northern People's Congress (NPC). The NPC represented the traditional and mercantile Hausa-Fulani élite; its nominal leader was the premier of the Northern Region, the sardauna of Sokoto, Ahmadu (later Sir Ahmadu) Bello. The NPC's political (and subsequently parliamentary) spokesman was Abubakar (later Sir Abubakar) Tafawa Balewa, a former schoolteacher (who became the first federal prime minister in 1957).

In 1954 the federation became self-governing, and, following elections to a federal legislature in 1959 in which the NPC obtained the largest representation, a bicameral federal parliament was formed in January 1960.

On 1 October 1960, as scheduled, the Federation of Nigeria achieved independence, initially as a constitutional monarchy, with Tafawa Balewa as prime minister and minister of foreign affairs. In June 1961 the northern section of the neighbouring UN Trust Territory of British Cameroons, formerly part of the German protectorate of Kamerun, was incorporated into Nigeria's Northern Region as the province of Sardauna. In October 1963 the country was renamed the Federal Republic of Nigeria, remaining a member of the Commonwealth. Azikiwe took office as Nigeria's first (non-executive) president.

MILITARY INTERVENTION AND CIVIL WAR, 1966–76

Nigeria's regional rivalries were reflected in the federal armed forces; most of the quota of personnel recruited from the North came from the Middle Belt of the Northern Region and were opposed to the NPC and to Hausa-Fulani dominance. Ibo from the Eastern Region formed the majority of the officer corps, and this provoked intense distrust from other ethnic groups. In January 1966 Tafawa Balewa's government was overthrown by junior (mainly Ibo) army officers; Balewa was killed, together with a number of other ministers. Maj.-Gen. Johnson Aguiyi-Ironsi, the c-in-c of the army and an Ibo, took control of the government. The coup was followed by anti-Ibo riots, and in

late May many people were killed when violence erupted in most of the major cities of the north, and in July Aguiyi-Ironsi was killed in a counter-coup by northern troops. Power was transferred to the chief-of-staff of the army, Lt-Col (later Gen.) Yakubu Gowon, a Christian northerner. Gowon restored some degree of discipline to the armed forces, and attempted to revive the federal system, appointing a military governor for each region.

Ibo still living in the North began to return to the Eastern Region after the counter-coup of July 1966, and in late September and early October those who remained in the North were massacred by northern army elements. The military governor of the Eastern Region, Lt-Col Chukwuemeka Odumegwu-Ojukwu, under pressure from senior Ibo civil servants, announced the secession of the Eastern Region, and in May 1967 proclaimed its independence as the 'Republic of Biafra'. In July federal forces launched a massive attack and naval blockade, and in the ensuing civil war between 500,000 and 2m. 'Biafran' civilians died, mainly from starvation, before the surrender of 'Biafran' forces in January 1970.

Following the collapse of 'Biafra', Gowon implemented a strategy of reconciliation, which was seriously impeded by the failure of the national population census, conducted in 1973, to produce credible results; the census purported to show a near-doubling of the population in the three northern states (Kano, North-Eastern and North-Western), while that of the Yoruba heartland of Western State was reported to have declined. In October 1974 Gowon announced that the return to civilian rule, scheduled for 1976, had been indefinitely postponed, on the grounds that a government plan for socio-economic reconstruction had not been fulfilled. However, in July 1976 Gowon was forcibly 'retired' and was succeeded as head of government by Brig. (later Gen.) Murtala Ramat Muhammed.

FROM OBASANJO TO SHAGARI AND THE SECOND REPUBLIC, 1976–83

Muhammed was assassinated in February 1976 by disaffected army officers, who demanded the reinstatement of Gen. Gowon. Power was transferred to Muhammed's deputy, Lt-Gen. (later Gen.) Olusegun Obasanjo, the chief-of-staff of the armed forces. As head of state, Obasanjo pledged to fulfil his predecessor's programme for the return to civilian rule by October 1979. During 1976 legislation to reform the structure of local government was introduced, and a constituent assembly (CA) was created in August 1977 to draft the new constitution. This was duly promulgated in September 1978. It envisaged an executive presidency, and a separation of powers between executive, legislative and judicial branches of government. To win the presidential election, a candidate would need to obtain an outright majority of the national vote, and also to win at least 25% of the votes in at least 12 states. Executive governors were to be appointed to each state.

The ending of the state of emergency in September 1978 was accompanied by the lifting of the ban on formal activity by political parties. By November more than 50 political groupings had emerged. In the event, however, of the 19 associations that applied for registration, only five received approval by the Federal Election Commission (FEDECO).

The best prepared of the five parties was the Unity Party of Nigeria (UPN), led by Chief Obafemi Awolowo, a prominent member of Gowon's junta and of the Yoruba community. The National Party of Nigeria (NPN) included such veteran NPC politicians as Alhaji Shehu Shagari (later selected as its presidential candidate). The People's Redemption Party (PRP), the northern-based opposition to the NPN, was led by Alhaji Aminu Kano. The fourth party, the Nigerian People's Party (NPP), chose ex-president Azikiwe as its presidential candidate. The Greater Nigeria People's Party (GNPP), a breakaway faction of the NPP, was formed by Alhaji Waziri Ibrahim. At elections to the new bicameral national assembly, and for state assemblies and state governors, which took place in July 1979, the NPN received the most widespread support, securing 37% of the seats in the house of representatives, 36% in the state assemblies, and 38% in the senate, and winning seven of the 19 state governorships. In the presidential election, which took place in August, Shagari obtained the mandatory 25% of the vote in 12, rather than 13, of the 19 States. Following legal debate on this point, the supreme court upheld the election of Shagari. On 1 October military rule ended, the new constitution came into force, and Shagari was sworn in as president of the Second Republic.

By the early 1980s it was widely believed in Nigeria that the federal democracy was a façade, which allowed NPN politicians, dominated by a powerful political community in Kaduna, to distribute contracts and rewards in order to ensure their own continuation in power. In order to reinforce its power on the federal legislature, the NPN formed an alliance with Azikiwe's NPP, which, however, was dissolved in July 1981. The NPP then established a coalition, known as the Progressive Parties' Alliance (PPA), with the UPN, the major opposition party, thereby engendering further realignments in the parties that had fought the 1979 elections. The PRP and the GNPP split, with some of their members joining the PPA, while others themselves with the government.

In 1982, in preparation for the elections of the following year, FEDECO was reconstituted and given extensive powers. FEDECO subsequently approved the National Advance Party (NAP), led by the radical Lagos lawyer, Tunji Braithwaite. As campaigning began, the NPN used its entrenched position and financial influence to ensure its return to office. In May the government granted a pardon to Odumegwu-Ojukwu, the former 'Biafran' leader, who returned to Nigeria after more than 12 years in exile, and later aligned himself with the NPN. Later that year the PPA became divided over the issue of choosing a presidential candidate; eventually, Awolowo was selected as the UPN candidate, and Azikiwe as the NPP candidate.

The elections, which were contested by the six political parties, took place in August–September 1983. In the presidential poll Shagari was returned for a second term, receiving more than 12m. votes, or 47% of the total votes cast. The NPN attained a decisive majority in the elections to the senate (60 seats out of 96) and the house of representatives (264 seats out of 450), and won 13 of the 19 state governorships. However, allegations of widespread electoral malpractice on the part of the NPN resulted in litigation and a reinforcement of the belief that the elections had been won by means of misconduct on a vast scale. On 1 October Shagari was sworn in for a second term as president.

THE RETURN OF MILITARY RULE

Buhari and the SMC, 1983–85

On 31 December 1983 Shagari was deposed in a bloodless military coup, led by Maj.-Gen. Muhammadu Buhari, a former military governor of Borno and federal commissioner for petroleum during 1976–78. All political parties were banned, FEDECO was dissolved, and all bank accounts were temporarily 'frozen'. Several high-ranking military personnel were replaced, and prominent NPN members and politicians (including Shagari) were arrested. The new military regime, which was identified with the government of Gen. Muhammed, received widespread popular support. The structure of the new regime, similar to that of the military governments of 1975–79, comprised a reconstituted SMC, headed by Buhari. A national council of states, with a federal executive

council, and state executive councils, presided over by military governors, were subsequently established.

In February 1984 the SMC issued a decree which empowered the government to enact laws that could not be challenged in the courts. Further legislation effectively prohibited the publication of information unfavourable to the government. In April it was announced that special tribunals were to be established to try those under arrest, and, *in absentia*, those who had fled the country; it became evident that the special tribunals were designed to recover assets which had been misappropriated by the civilian administration. By July a number of former governors had been sentenced for corruption and fiscal irregularities. The authorities subsequently stated that there was no schedule for a return to civilian rule, and prohibited all debate on the political future of Nigeria. There were subsequent widespread rumours of a coup attempt by junior officers and reports of open dissension within the SMC.

Babangida and the AFRC, 1985–93

In August 1985 Buhari's regime was deposed in a peaceful military coup, led by Maj.-Gen. (later Gen.) Ibrahim Babangida, the army chief-of-staff, who was named as the new head of state. The SMC was replaced by a 28-member armed forces ruling council (AFRC) which, unlike the SMC, solely comprised military personnel. The post of chief-of-staff at supreme military headquarters was replaced by that of chief of the general staff within the AFRC, a position that carried no responsibility for actual control of the armed forces. A national council of ministers was formed, together with a reconstituted national council of state. There was a redistribution of all state governorships, and Buhari's ministers were removed. Following the abolition of the decree on press censorship, a number of journalists were released, together with detainees from the Shagari government. In September Babangida, with the support of Maj.-Gen. Sani Abacha, the chief of the army staff, removed some 40 senior officers, who were placed in detention.

In October 1985 Babangida declared a state of national economic emergency and assumed extensive interventionist powers over the economy. In December Babangida suspended negotiations with the IMF, a move that received widespread popular support, but caused dissension among certain members of the AFRC, and within the army command. On 20 December the AFRC suppressed a coup attempt by disaffected army officers. In February 1986 13 of the 14 named conspirators were convicted and executed.

In January 1986 Babangida announced that the armed forces would transfer power to a civilian government on 1 October 1990. In May, amid protests from the Nigerian Bar Association, the AFRC extended the period of detention without trial from three to six months. In June sanctions were introduced against public officials convicted of corruption, which included the withdrawal of their passports for five years and the 'freezing' or confiscation of their assets. In July Shagari and his former vice-president were released from detention, although they were subsequently banned for life from political activity.

In February 1986 Babangida announced that Nigeria's application for full membership of the Organization of the Islamic Conference (OIC) had been accepted; ensuing unrest among the non-Muslim sector of the population reflected alarm at increasing 'Islamization' in the country. In May about 15 people, mostly students, were shot dead by police during demonstrations at the Ahmadu Bello University, in Zaria, and a ban was imposed on further demonstrations. Babangida subsequently established a national commission to examine the advisability of Nigeria's membership of the OIC.

In March 1987 violent clashes broke out between Muslim and Christian youths at Kafanchan, in southern Kaduna State, which were reported to have resulted in some 30 deaths. A curfew was imposed, and an estimated 1,000 people were arrested. In April the AFRC formed an advisory council on religious affairs (ACRA), comprising Muslim and Christian leaders, to investigate the causes of the violence, and the authorities issued decrees banning religious organizations in schools and universities. However, sporadic outbreaks of student unrest continued in late 1987 and early 1988.

In July 1987, after receiving recommendations from the political bureau, the AFRC announced that power was to be transferred to a civilian government in 1992, two years later than envisaged. Political parties would remain banned during the transitional period, although elections for local government authorities were to be contested on a non-party basis by the end of 1987. A constituent assembly, which was to draft a new constitution, was to be established in 1988, and, following the promulgation of the constitution, further local and state elections were to be held in 1990, at which time the registration of two political parties was to be permitted. Elections for a bi-cameral federal legislature and for the presidency were to follow in 1992.

In August 1987 the AFRC established a programme to promote political education, in preparation for the transition to civilian rule. In September the number of states was increased from 19 to 21. In the same month the AFRC proscribed all categories of former politicians and its own membership from contesting elections in 1992. In addition, the AFRC inaugurated a constitutional review committee to examine proposals for a new constitution, and a national electoral commission (NEC) to supervise future elections. On 12 December local government elections were contested by some 15,000 non-party candidates; however, inadequate preparations for the elections by the NEC resulted in confusion, violence and allegations of electoral fraud and corruption. The NEC annulled the results in 312 local government wards, where further elections took place on 26 March 1988. Babangida subsequently announced that the new constitution would be promulgated in 1989, and proposed that an enlarged constituent assembly should debate the terms of the constitution. Accordingly, in April 1988 local government councillors elected 450 members to the constituent assembly. The AFRC later nominated a further 117 members, to represent various interest groups. Abuja, the future federal capital, was designated as the seat of the new assembly.

At the first session of the constituent assembly in June 1988, it was announced that the new constitution, which was to be modelled on that of 1979, would contain provisions prohibiting groups or individuals from usurping the government by force, and would ensure that all political change was effected by democratic means. Additionally, the constituent assembly was to draft and ratify the new constitution by the end of the year, rather than by May 1989, as originally envisaged. However, debate over the new draft constitution threatened to founder on the issue of religion. Muslims demanded the inclusion of Shari'a courts in the constitution, but in November 1988 further debate on this topic was banned by Babangida, as the progress of the assembly's work was being severely impeded. The AFRC postponed the date of submission of the draft constitution from January to March 1989, and threatened to dissolve the assembly unless it completed its task by the revised date. In January 1989 the assembly ratified the decision that, under the new constitution, a civilian president was to be elected for a six-year term, and was to declare all personal assets and liabilities before taking office.

In February 1989 Babangida reduced membership of the AFRC from 29 to 19, reportedly in order to reduce the power of the armed forces during the transitional period leading to civilian rule. In March electoral legislation was amended to allow the AFRC to decide which of the political groupings recommended by the NEC were to be registered as the two legally permitted political parties when legislation prohibiting political activity was revoked later that year. The constituent assembly presented the draft constitution in early April.

In early May 1989 the ban on political parties was lifted, and the constitution was promulgated. The constitution was to enter into force on 1 October 1992, when a civilian government would be installed. Elections for the government of the Third Republic were to be contested by only two registered political parties, which were to be selected by the AFRC from the register compiled by the NEC. To be eligible for registration, a political party was to be founded on national policy-making (and not be allied to any ethnic or religious grouping), and be democratically organized. Six political parties subsequently emerged, and by the beginning of July this number had risen to approximately 40. However, only 13 parties succeeded in fulfilling the registration requirements by the stipulated date of 15 July. In the same month all local government councils were dissolved, pending the election of new councillors in late 1989.

In October 1989, following the recommendation by the NEC of six of the 13 associations to the AFRC, Babangida announced that the AFRC had decided to dissolve all 13 of the political associations, on the grounds that they lacked distinctive ideologies, and were allied to discredited civilian politicians. In their place the AFRC created two new political parties, the Social Democratic Party (SDP) and the National Republic Convention (NRC). The announcement provoked widespread criticism. Local elections, scheduled for December, were immediately postponed until early 1990, and the NEC announced that delays might be expected in the planned transition to civilian rule. In December the NEC published the draft constitutions and manifestos of the SDP and the NRC. In the same month Babangida carried out a major cabinet reshuffle, in which he assumed the defence portfolio, while his closest associate, Lt-Gen. Sani Abacha, the chief of the army staff, was appointed chairman of the joint chiefs of staff.

In April 1990 junior army officers seized the headquarters of the Federal Radio Corpn and attacked the presidential residence. The leader of the attempted coup, Maj. Gideon Orkar, claimed to be acting on behalf of Nigerians in the centre and south of the country, who, he alleged, were under-represented in the government. The coup attempt was suppressed within 24 hours, and Orkar was arrested, together with about 300 other military personnel, and more than 30 civilians. A number of journalists perceived as critical of the government were also detained. In July Orkar and a number of other prisoners were convicted by a military tribunal, on charges of conspiracy to commit treason; later that month 42 prisoners, including Orkar, were executed. Nine other defendants were imprisoned. In September there were a further 27 executions in connection with the attempted coup.

The election of officials from the SDP and NRC to local government councils was held in May 1990. In July more than 44,000 delegates, representing the two political parties, elected party executives for each state. The administration of the SDP and NRC was transferred from government-appointed administrative secretaries to elected party officials in early August. In the same month Chief Tom Ikimi, a southerner, was elected chairman of the NRC, while Baba Kingibe, a northerner, was installed as chairman of the SDP. (It was widely believed that the NRC received most support from the north of the country, and the SDP from the south.)

Later in August 1990 Babangida extensively reshuffled the government, replacing nine ministers and abolishing the position of chief of general staff, whose incumbent, Vice-Adm. Augustus Aikhomu, was subsequently appointed to the newly-created post of vice-president. Babangida also announced that the presidency would be restructured in order to prepare for the transition to civilian rule, and that the size of the armed forces would be substantially reduced. In early September, in an attempt to restrict military influence in the government, three ministers were obliged to retire from the armed forces, leaving the minister of defence, Lt-Gen. Sani Abacha, as the only serving military officer in the council of ministers. 12 military state governors were replaced, and 21 civilian deputy governors were appointed to each state, pending gubernatorial elections, scheduled for 1991.

Legislation was introduced in November 1990 providing for an 'open ballot' system, which was designed to minimize electoral malpractice in the forthcoming elections. In December local government elections took place in some 440 areas, although only an estimated 20% of registered voters participated. 2,934 candidates representing the SDP were elected as councillors, with a further 232 elected to chair local councils, while 2,588 NRC candidates were elected as councillors, with 208 elected as chairmen. In January 1991 the government announced that state subsidies being provided to the NRC and SDP would end in September. Primary elections, which were to be preceded by a three-stage registration process for candidates, were scheduled for 24 August.

At this time the government was also confronted by manifestations of ethnic discontent and religious conflict. In October 1990 the Movement for the Survival of the Ogoni People (MOSOP) was formed to co-ordinate opposition to the exploitation of petroleum reserves in the territory of the Ogoni ethnic group (Ogoniland), in the south-central Rivers State, by the

Shell Petroleum Development Co of Nigeria. Following demonstrations, organized by MOSOP, in protest at alleged environmental damage caused by petroleum production, some 80 Ogonis were killed by security forces. In April 1991 a number of demonstrations by Muslims in the northern state of Katsina, in protest against the publication of an article considered to be blasphemous, culminated in violence. In the same month some 130 people, mainly Christians, were killed in riots in Bauchi and other predominantly Muslim states, where Christians proposed to slaughter pigs in a local abattoir that was also used by Muslims. It was later reported that some 120 Muslims had been killed by government troops, which had been sent to the region to suppress the riots. In October demonstrations by Muslims took place at Kano, in the north, in protest against a tour of the state by a Christian preacher (following a decision by the authorities to refuse a Muslim leader permission to visit the area). More than 300 people were reported to have been killed in subsequent clashes between Muslims and Christians, which were suppressed by the army.

In late 1991 violence erupted in Taruba, in the east, as a result of a long-standing land dispute between the Tiv and Jukun ethnic groups. The conflict continued in subsequent months, and by March 1992 up to 5,000 people were reported to have been killed. In January demonstrations in Katsina by Muslim fundamentalists demanding the imposition of Shari'a law were forcibly suppressed. In February some 30 people were killed in the northern state of Kaduna in clashes between the Hausa ethnic group (which was predominantly Muslim) and the Kataf (mainly Christian).

In June 1991 the NRC and SDP selected some 144,950 delegates to stand in the primary elections, for the gubernatorial and state assembly elections. In early September the government created nine new states, increasing the size of the federation to 30 states, in an attempt to ease ethnic tensions prior to the elections. However, violent demonstrations took place in several states where the government had failed to comply with demands to create a new state in the region, or where there was discontent at the relocation of the state capital. As a result of these protests, the government announced that the primary elections (which had already been postponed from August to September) would take place on 19 October, and would be followed by state assembly and gubernatorial elections on 14 December. It was confirmed, however, that the transition to civilian rule would be completed on 1 October 1992, as scheduled. Military administrators were subsequently appointed for the nine newly-created states, pending the gubernatorial elections.

On 19 October 1991 primary elections took place to select candidates for the forthcoming gubernatorial and state assembly elections. In November, however, following allegations of electoral fraud on the part of both the NRC and the SDP, results were annulled in nine states, and 12 candidates were disqualified; new elections were held in these states in early December. Controversy over the election results led to increased divisions within both parties, especially within the SDP.

In December 1991 the seat of federal government was formally transferred from Lagos to Abuja, which was to be administered by a municipal council. In the gubernatorial and state assembly elections, which took place on 14 December, the SDP gained a majority in 16 state assemblies, while the NRC won control of 14; however, NRC candidates were elected as governors in 16 of the 30 states, many of which were situated in the south-east of Nigeria, where the SDP had previously received more support. Both the SDP and the NRC subsequently disputed the election results in a number of states, on the grounds of voting irregularities. In the same month 11 former ministers, who had contravened the disqualification of former office-holders from contesting elections, were arrested. They were, however, released later in December, and the ban was lifted. (Only Babangida and officials convicted of criminal offences were henceforth prohibited from taking part in elections.) In early January 1992 the new state governors were inaugurated.

In mid-January 1992 Babangida formed a new 20-member national council of ministers, in which a number of portfolios were reallocated. In the same month the government announced that elections for a bicameral national assembly, comprising a 593-member house of representatives and a 91-member senate, would take place on 7 November, and would be followed by

a presidential election on 5 December. Primary elections for presidential candidates were to take place between 2 May and 20 June, while the selection of candidates to contest the legislative elections was scheduled for 4 July. The formal installation of a civilian government and the promulgation of the new constitution were to take place on 2 January 1993, rather than on 1 October 1992, as previously planned. Later in January 1992 Babangida rejected demands by former politicians for the establishment of a government of national consensus.

In February 1992 disputed election results in the states of Edo, Jigawa and Abia were annulled, and the state governors removed from office. However, the validity of the elections of the governors of Edo and Jigawa was later upheld on appeal. Later in February the government promulgated legislation empowering state governors to appoint commissioners (local ministers) without the approval of the state assemblies. In March, following discussions between the NEC, the NRC and the SDP, legislative elections were scheduled for 4 July, earlier than envisaged. The selection of candidates for the legislature was to commence on 23 May, while primary elections for presidential candidates were to take place between 1 August and 15 September. (The presidential election was to take place on 5 December, as originally scheduled.) Later in March legislation that allowed the NEC to disqualify electoral candidates deemed to be unfit to hold office was introduced.

In early May 1992 widespread rioting in protest at sharp increases in transport fares (resulting from a severe fuel shortage) culminated in a number of demonstrations demanding the resignation of the government, which were violently suppressed by the security forces; several people were reported to have been killed. An alliance of 25 organizations opposed to the government, known as the Campaign for Democracy (CD), which had been formed six months earlier, attributed the unrest to widespread discontent at increasing economic hardship. Later in May further rioting broke out in Lagos, following the arrest of the chairman of the CD, Dr Beko Ransome-Kuti, who had accused the government of provoking the violence in order to delay the transition to civilian rule. In the same month some 300 people were reported to have been killed in renewed violence between the Hausa and the Kataf in Kaduna; a curfew was briefly imposed in that state, and some 250 people were arrested. The government subsequently banned all associations with a religious or ethnic base; a security force, to be known as the national guard, was also to be established in order to reduce the role of the army in riot control.

Extensive government changes were carried out in early June 1992, in which the influential minister of finance and economic planning, Alhaji Abubakar Alhaji, was replaced. Later in June a number of human rights activists, including Ransome-Kuti, were released, pending their trial later that year, on charges of conspiring to incite the riots in May.

In elections to the national assembly, which took place on 4 July 1992, the SDP gained a majority in both chambers, securing 52 seats in the senate and 314 seats in the house of representatives, while the NRC won 37 seats in the senate and 275 seats in the house of representatives. However, the formal inauguration of the national assembly, scheduled for 27 July, was subsequently postponed until 2 January 1993, owing to the AFRC's insistence that it retain supreme legislative power until the installation of a civilian government. Primary elections to select an NRC and an SDP presidential candidate commenced on 1 August 1992, but were suspended, owing to widespread electoral irregularities; results in states where elections had taken place were annulled. Further polls to select presidential candidates took place on 12, 19 and 26 September. By the end of the second round of voting four leading candidates had emerged: Gen. (retd) Shehu Musa Yar'Adua and Chief Olu Falae (SDP), and Alhaji Umaru Shinkafi and Malam Adamu Ciroma (NRC). However, 10 of the original 23 aspirants (including Falae) withdrew from the third and final stage of polling, alleging fraudulent practices. Reports of irregularities were widely believed, and the participation rate in the poll was significantly low. Nevertheless, Yar'Adua claimed to have won the SDP nomination, while Shinkafi and Ciroma were to contest a final poll for the NRC candidacy on 10 October.

On 6 October 1992, however, the AFRC summarily suspended the results of all three stages of the presidential primaries, pending an investigation by the NEC into the alleged incidents of voting irregularities. Despite the AFRC's reaffirmation of its pledge to transfer power to a civilian president by 3 January 1993, widespread suspicion that it intended to extend military rule subsequently increased. Later in October 1992 Babangida cancelled the presidential primaries, following a report by the NEC confirming that malpractice had occurred.

In November 1992 Babangida announced that the presidential election (scheduled for 5 December) was to be postponed until 12 June 1993, and the transition to civilian rule until 27 August. All 23 aspirants who had contested the discredited primaries in September 1992 were disqualified as presidential candidates. Under the new arrangements, the AFRC was to be replaced on 2 January 1993 by a national defence and security council (NDSC), and the council of ministers by a civilian transitional council. The national assembly, however, was to be inaugurated on 5 December, as scheduled. Babangida also announced a new programme for the installation of an elected civilian president: the restructured parties were each to nominate a new presidential candidate at a series of congresses, conducted at ward, local government, state and national level; the results of the rescheduled presidential election were to be announced during June.

In December 1992 the bicameral national assembly was formally convened in the new federal capital of Abuja. Although it had been planned as a legislature for the postponed civilian administration, the national assembly was obliged to submit legislation for approval by the AFRC. On 2 January 1993 the NDSC and transitional council were duly installed. The 14-member NDSC was chaired by Babangida, and included the vice-president, the chief of defence staff, the service chiefs, and the inspector-general of police. The transitional council, which comprised 29 members, was to be responsible for federal administration, but was accountable to the NDSC. Its chairman, Chief Ernest Shonekan (a prominent businessman), was officially designated as head of government.

Following the registration of party voters in January 1993, some 300 aspirants to the presidency emerged, including Gowon and Ojukwu (the principal protagonists in the 'Biafran' civil war). The NEC subsequently reviewed candidates in view of the NDSC's criteria. Following party congresses at ward level on 6 February, at local government level on 20 February, and at state level on 6 March, the number of candidates was reduced to 62. (Gowon was defeated at the local government congress on 20 February, while Ojukwu was disqualified by the NEC.)

National party congresses took place, as scheduled, during 27–29 March 1993: the NRC selected Alhaji Bashir Othman Tofa, an economist and businessman, to contest the presidential election, while Chief Moshood Kashimawo Olawale Abiola, a wealthy publisher, emerged as the SDP presidential candidate. In April Abiola chose Baba Kingibe (a former chairman of the SDP) as his vice-presidential candidate, and Tofa selected Dr Sylvester Ugoh, who had served in the Shagari administration. Later that month both Tofa and Abiola began to campaign throughout the country. Meanwhile, a number of informal organizations with diverse agendas emerged; the Association for a Better Nigeria (ABN) demanded the extension of military rule for a further four years, on the grounds of political instability.

In early June 1993 the ABN leadership obtained an interim injunction in the Abuja high court prohibiting the presidential election from taking place, pending the results of its appeal for the extension of military rule until 1997. However, the NEC rejected the injunction as invalid and stated that the election would take place, as scheduled. The rate of participation in the presidential election on 12 June was relatively low, owing, in part, to the confusion occasioned by the Abuja court action, but international monitors throughout Nigeria reported that it had been conducted relatively peacefully. Two days later, initial results, released by the NEC, indicated that of the 6.6m. votes cast in 14 of the 30 states the SDP had secured 4.3m. and the NRC 2.3m. In 11 of the 14 states (including Tofa's home state of Kano), Abiola had obtained the majority of votes. Shortly afterwards, however, the NEC announced that the remaining results would not be released until further notice, following a further injunction, secured by the ABN, that prohibited the promulgation of the results; several other applications were

presented in a number of courts, in an attempt to delay or suspend the electoral process. Widespread confusion followed, and protests were voiced that the NDSC (principally through the ABN, which was believed to have connections with Babangida) had deliberately sabotaged the elections. Later in June the CD promulgated election results, which indicated that Abiola had won the majority of votes in 19 states, and Tofa in 11 states. Significantly, Tofa did not challenge these results. The NDSC subsequently attracted increasing domestic and international criticism.

Finally, on 23 June 1993, the NDSC declared the results of the election to be invalid, halted all court proceedings pertaining to the election, suspended the NEC, and repealed all decrees relating to the transition to civilian rule. New electoral regulations were introduced that effectively precluded Abiola and Tofa from contesting a further presidential poll. Babangida subsequently announced that the election had been marred by corruption and other irregularities, but insisted that he remained committed to the transition on 27 August; in order to meet this schedule, a reconstituted NEC was to supervise the selection of two new presidential candidates by the SDP and NRC. Abiola, however, continued to claim, with much popular agreement, that he had been legitimately elected to the presidency. The United Kingdom subsequently announced that it was to review its bilateral relations with Nigeria, and imposed a number of military sanctions, while the USA immediately suspended all assistance to the government.

In early July 1993 a demonstration, organized by the CD, led to rioting, prompted by resentment at political developments, in conjunction with long-standing economic hardship. Order was subsequently restored, after security forces violently suppressed protests; however, sporadic unrest was reported throughout the country. The NDSC provisionally announced that a new presidential election was to take place on 14 August in order to fulfil the pledge to transfer power on 27 August, prompting general disbelief. The SDP declared that it intended to boycott an electoral process that superseded its victory on 12 June. Later in July the NDSC proscribed five national publishing groups, including Concord Press, which was owned by Abiola, and detained a number of supporters of democracy.

'Interim National Government'

At the end of July 1993 Babangida announced that an interim national government (ING) was to be established, on the grounds that there was insufficient time to permit the scheduled transition to civilian rule on 27 August. A committee, comprising officials of the two parties and senior military officers, headed by Aikhomu, was subsequently established to determine the composition of the ING. Abiola immediately declared his opposition to the proposed administration, and stated his intention of forming a 'parallel government'. (He subsequently fled abroad, following alleged death threats, and attempted to solicit international support for his claim to the presidency.) In August the CD continued its campaign of civil disobedience in protest at the annulment of the election, appealing for a three-day general strike (which was widely observed in the south-west of the country, where Abiola received most popular support). Several prominent members of the CD were arrested, in an attempt to prevent further protests, while additional restrictions were imposed on the press. Later in August Babangida announced his resignation, reportedly as a result of pressure from prominent members of the NDSC, notably the secretary of defence, Gen. Sani Abacha. On 27 August a 32-member interim federal executive council, headed by Shonekan, was installed; the new administration, which included several members of the former transitional council, was to supervise the organization of local government elections later that year and a presidential election in early 1994, while the transitional period for the return to civilian rule was extended to 31 March 1994. (Shonekan was later designated as head of state and commander-in-chief of the armed forces.) Supporters of democracy criticized the inclusion in the ING of several members of the former NDSC (which had been dissolved), including Abacha, who was appointed to the new post of vice-president, and the proposed establishment of two predominantly military councils as advisory bodies to the president.

At the end of August 1993 the CD staged a further three-day strike, while the Nigerian Labour Congress (NLC) and the National Union of Petroleum and Natural Gas Workers (NUPENG) also announced industrial action in support of the installation of a civilian administration, headed by Abiola. The combined strike action resulted in a severe fuel shortage and widespread economic disruption. Following the establishment of the ING, Shonekan pledged his commitment to the democratic process, and, in an effort to restore order, initiated negotiations with the NLC and effected the release of several journalists and prominent members of the CD, including Ransome-Kuti, who had been arrested in July. In early September the NLC and NUPENG provisionally suspended strike action, after the ING agreed to consider their demands.

In September 1993 a series of military appointments, which included the nomination of Lt-Gen. Oladipo Diya to the office of chief of defence staff, effectively removed supporters of Babangida from positions of influence within the armed forces, thereby strengthening Abacha's position. Diya, who had reportedly opposed the annulment of the presidential election, subsequently declared that military involvement in politics would cease. In the same month Abiola returned to Lagos, amid popular acclaim. Later in September the NRC and SDP agreed to a new timetable, whereby local government elections and a presidential election would take place concurrently in February 1994. The CD subsequently announced the resumption of strike action in support of demands for the installation of Abiola as president; an ensuing demonstration by supporters of the CD in Lagos was violently dispersed by security forces, and Ransome-Kuti, together with other prominent members of the CD, was arrested. In October the SDP (which had previously demonstrated limited support for Abiola, as a result of dissension within the party) demanded that he be inaugurated as president, and refused to participate in the new elections. In the same month Shonekan established a committee to investigate the circumstances that had resulted in the annulment of the presidential election.

In early November 1993 the president of the senate, a strong supporter of Abiola, was removed. Shortly afterwards the high court in Lagos State ruled in favour of an application by Abiola, declaring the establishment of the ING to be invalid under the terms of the 1979 constitution (whereby the president of the senate was to act as interim head of state). In the same month the ING dissolved the government councils, prior to local elections, and withdrew state subsidies on petroleum products. The resultant dramatic increase in the price of fuel prompted widespread anti-government demonstrations, and the NLC announced the resumption of strike action. Meanwhile, the proposed revision of the electoral register was undermined by the refusal of supporters of the SDP to participate, and it became clear that the new schedule for the transition to civilian rule could not be met.

Abacha and the PRC, 1993–98

On 17 November 1993, following a meeting with senior military officials, Shonekan announced his resignation as head of state, and immediately transferred power to Abacha (confirming widespread speculation that Abacha had effectively assumed control of the government following Babangida's resignation). On the following day Abacha dissolved all organs of state and bodies that had been established under the transitional process, replaced the state governors with military administrators, prohibited political activity (thereby proscribing the NRC and the SDP), and announced the formation of a provisional ruling council (PRC), which was to comprise senior military officials and the principal members of a new federal executive council (FEC). He insisted, however, that he intended to relinquish power to a civilian government, and pledged to convene a conference with a mandate to determine the constitutional future of the country. Restrictions on the media were suspended, and the ban that had been imposed on certain publishing groups in July was revoked. Ensuing demonstrations by supporters of democracy were suppressed by security forces (although protests were generally limited). On 21 November Abacha introduced legislation that formally restored the 1979 constitution and provided for the establishment of the new government organs. In an apparent attempt to counter domestic and international criticism, several prominent supporters of Abiola, including Kingibe, and four former members of the ING were appointed to the PRC and FEC, which were installed on 24 November. Abacha subsequently removed 17 senior military officers, who were believed to be loyal to Babangida. In the same month discussions between Abacha and Abiola took place, while the NLC agreed to abandon strike action after the government acted to limit the increase in the price of petroleum products.

In December 1993 controversy arose over the mandate of the proposed constitutional conference, which, Abacha stated, was not to include the issue of devolution of federal government powers. The CD dismissed the conference plan as an attempt to legitimize the new administration. In the same month the United Kingdom announced that member countries of the European Union (EU) were to impose further sanctions against Nigeria, including restrictions on the export of armaments.

In April 1994 the government announced its proposals for the establishment of the national constitutional conference (NCC): some 273 delegates were to be elected in May, while 96 delegates were to be nominated by the government from a list of eligible citizens submitted by each state. The national constitutional conference was to be convened at the end of June, and was to submit recommendations, including a new draft constitution, to the PRC in late October. A further stage in the transitional programme was to commence in mid-January 1995, when the ban on political activity was to end. In May 1994, however, a new pro-democracy organization, comprising former politicians, retired military officers and human rights activists, the National Democratic Coalition (NADECO), demanded that Abacha relinquish power by the end of that month and urged a boycott of the NCC. Later in May, however, elections duly took place at ward, and subsequently at local government, level to select the 273 conference delegates; the boycott was widely observed in the south-west of the country, and a low level of voter participation was reported. In the same month Ken Saro-Wiwa, the leader of MOSOP, was arrested in connection with the deaths of four Ogoni electoral candidates. At the end of May Abiola announced his intention of forming a government of national unity by 12 June (the anniversary of the presidential election). Violent anti-government protests followed the expiry of the date stipulated by NADECO for the resignation of the military administration.

In early June 1994 members of the former senate (including its president) were detained on charges of treason, after the senators reconvened and declared the government to be illegal. A number of prominent opposition members, including Ransome-Kuti, were also arrested, after the CD urged a campaign of civil disobedience, which received the support of NADECO. (Ransome-Kuti was subsequently charged with treason.) Following a symbolic ceremony, in which Abiola was publicly inaugurated as president and head of a parallel government, a warrant was issued for his arrest on charges of treason; the authorities alleged that he intended to organize an uprising to remove the military administration from power. Later in June security forces arrested Abiola (who had emerged from hiding to attend a rally in Lagos), prompting protests from pro-democracy organizations and criticism from the governments of the United Kingdom and the USA. Further demonstrations in support of demands for an immediate suspension of military rule and the installation of Abiola as president ensued, while NUPENG threatened to initiate strike action unless the government agreed to release Abiola.

At the initial session of the NCC, which was convened on schedule at the end of June 1994, Abacha pledged to relinquish power on a date that would be determined by the conference. (The conference subsequently established committees to consider a number of contentious issues, including that of the annulment of the presidential election in 1993.) In early July the minister of justice was charged with contempt of court, after the government failed to comply with two orders from the high court in Abuja to justify the continued imprisonment of Abiola, who had challenged the legality of his detention. Shortly afterwards, a special high court that had been appointed by the government formally indicted Abiola for 'treasonable felony.'

In early July 1994 NUPENG initiated strike action in support of dual demands for Abiola's release and installation as president, and an increase in government investment in the petroleum industry; the strike was subsequently joined by the senior petroleum workers' union, the Petroleum and Natural Gas Senior Staff Association (PENGASSAN). Government troops distributed fuel in an attempt to ease the resultant national shortage, while it was reported that senior officials of NUPENG and PENGASSAN had been arrested. By mid-July members of affiliate unions in a number of sectors had joined the strike action, resulting in an effective suspension of economic activity in Lagos and other commercially significant regions in the south-west of the country. Later in July union officials suspended negotiations with the government, on the grounds that the authorities had failed to release the secretary-general of NUPENG from detention. At the end of July it was reported that some 20 people had been killed, when security forces violently suppressed anti-government demonstrations. In early August the NLC initiated an indefinite general strike in support of NUPENG; following the suppression of further anti-government protests, in which about five demonstrators were killed, however, the NLC suspended strike action after two days to allow negotiations with the government to proceed.

In early August 1994 Abiola's trial was adjourned, pending a ruling regarding a defence appeal that the high court in Abuja had no jurisdiction in the case of an offence that had allegedly been committed in Lagos. Abiola (who was reported to be in poor health) refused to accept bail, since the stipulated conditions required him to refrain from political activity. The court finally decided that it had the necessary jurisdiction, although the presiding judge withdrew from the trial. In the same month the authorities banned the national newspaper, *The Guardian*, following the publication of a report suggesting that divisions existed within the government as to whether to proceed with the charges against Abiola. Later in August Abacha replaced the senior officials of NUPENG and PENGASSAN, and ordered petroleum workers to end strike action. Although a number of union members failed to comply, the effects of the strike soon began to recede: in early September the union officials who had been dismissed suspended the strike action, on the grounds of the widespread hardship that would result from its effects on the economy. In the same month Abacha promulgated legislation that extended the period of detention without trial to three months and prohibited legal action challenging government decisions. The minister of justice was subsequently dismissed, after protesting that he had not been consulted regarding the new legislation. In mid-September the state military administrators were reshuffled. Later that month Abacha reconstituted the PRC, which was enlarged from 11 to 25 members, all of whom were senior military officials.

In late September 1994 Wole Soyinka, a prominent critic of the government (who had received the Nobel Prize for Literature in 1986), legally challenged the legitimacy of the Abacha regime at the federal high court. In the following month the court ruled that Abiola's detention was illegal and awarded him substantial financial compensation. Nevertheless, Abiola remained in detention pending the outcome of other legal action before the federal court of appeal in Kaduna.

In October 1994 the NCC adopted constitutional proposals providing for a 'rotational presidency', whereby the office would be held alternately by northerners and southerners; other elective posts, including state governorships, were to be held successively, for a transitional period, by representatives of the territorial districts. In addition, the NCC envisaged a power-sharing arrangement, whereby any political party that secured a minimum of 10% of the seats in the legislature would be guaranteed representation in the government. Under a proposed transitional timetable, a new constitution was to be adopted by March 1995, the ban on political activity was to be rescinded, and multi-party elections were to take place at local and national level in 1996, prior to the installation of a new government in January 1997. In October 1994 Abacha replaced the minister of finance, who had supported the programme of economic liberalization that had been abandoned by the government in January. In November the NCC adopted further constitutional recommendations, providing for the creation of three vice-presidents and the establishment of a federal council of traditional rulers, which would function in an advisory capacity.

In December 1994 the NCC accepted a proposal that the government relinquish power on 1 January 1996, on the grounds

that a prolonged transitional period would result in a further deterioration of the economy; it was agreed that the PRC would draft a new transitional timetable in accordance with the decisions of the conference. In January 1995 Abacha announced the adoption of a new programme of economic reforms, which was designed to secure the approval of the International Monetary Fund (see Economy). In the same month the NCC, which had been scheduled to complete preparations for a draft constitution in October 1994, adjourned until March 1995, prompting increasing impatience that its protracted deliberations were serving to prolong the tenure of the military administration. The trial of Saro-Wiwa and a further 14 MOSOP activists, on charges of complicity in the murder of the four Ogoni traditional leaders, commenced in mid-January 1995; the defendants were to challenge the legitimacy of the special military tribunal, which had been appointed by the government. In February the federal court of appeal dismissed Abiola's legal action challenging the jurisdiction of the high court in Abuja.

In March 1995 some 150 military officials were arrested, apparently in response to widespread disaffection within the armed forces. The authorities subsequently confirmed reports (which had initially been denied) of a coup conspiracy. (However, opponents of the Abacha regime claimed that it had fabricated a coup attempt, with the aim of suppressing dissent within the armed forces.) Reports that about 80 members of the armed forces had been summarily executed were officially denied. However, the arrest of the former head of state, Gen. (retd) Olusegun Obasanjo and his former deputy, Maj.-Gen. (retd) Shehu Musa Yar'Adua, together with other prominent critics of the government, prompted international protests. In mid-March Abacha reconstituted the FEC, whose 36 members included a number of civilians who were believed to favour an extended period of military rule.

In April 1995 the NCC endorsed the constitutional proposals that had been approved in late 1994. At the end of that month, however, the conference adopted a motion reversing its previous decision that a civilian government be installed on 1 January 1996, on the grounds that the requisite timetable was untenable. The NCC subsequently undertook the incorporation of the necessary amendments to the constitutional recommendations, which were to be submitted for approval by the government. The trial of Saro-Wiwa (which had been suspended while he received medical treatment) resumed in late May. At the end of that month a curfew was imposed in Kano, following ethnic clashes in which five people were killed. In early June it was reported that a number of pro-democracy campaigners had been arrested, following a bomb attack at an official function in Kwara State, in which three people were killed. In the same month about 40 people, including several civilians, were arraigned before a special military tribunal in connection with the alleged coup attempt in March; it was reported that Obasanjo and Yar'Adua had also been secretly charged with conspiring to overthrow the government. Further arrests of pro-democracy activists took place later in June, in an effort by the government to pre-empt protests on the anniversary of the annulled presidential election; nevertheless, a one-day general strike, supported by the CD, was widely observed.

In June 1995 the NCC formally presented proposals for a draft constitution to Abacha, who rescinded the ban on political activity. The PRC was to approve the constitutional recommendations within a period of three months, whereupon Abacha was to announce, on 1 October, a programme for transition to civilian rule. (A number of political organizations subsequently emerged.) At the end of June reports emerged that the military tribunal had sentenced Obasanjo to 25 years' imprisonment for his alleged involvement in the coup attempt, while Yar'Adua and a further 13 military officers had received the death penalty. Numerous international protests and appeals for clemency ensued. Despite indications that the Nigerian government would yield to these pressures, at the end of July a military council ratified the death sentences, which were subject to confirmation by the PRC. Eventually, in early October the PRC commuted the death sentences and reduced the terms of imprisonment. The capital charges against Abiola were not withdrawn. Concurrently, Abacha announced a three-year programme for transition to civilian rule, whereby a new president was to be inaugurated on 1 October 1998, following elections at local, state and national level; the duration of the transitional period was received with international disapproval. New constitutional provisions, which generally accorded with the recommendations of the NCC and were to be formally adopted later in 1995, included the restoration of a multi-party system (whereby any party attaining 10 seats or more in the national assembly would be proportionately represented in the FEC), the division of the country into six regions (and the allocation, in rotation, of the presidency and other principal executive and legislative offices to these regions for a period of 30 years), and the establishment of a national judicial council and constitutional court.

At the end of October 1995 Saro-Wiwa and a further eight Ogoni activists were sentenced to death by the special military tribunal; six other defendants, including the deputy president of MOSOP, were acquitted. Although the defendants were not implicated directly in the incident, the nine convictions were based on the premise that the MOSOP activists had effectively incited the killings. An international campaign (led by Saro-Wiwa's son) against the convictions, and numerous appeals for clemency, ensued (although the Nigerian opposition criticized a number of foreign governments, notably that of South Africa, for favouring a diplomatic approach rather than the imposition of sanctions against Nigeria). However, on 10 November (the same day as a Commonwealth summit meeting, which was to discuss, *inter alia*, events in Nigeria, was convened in Auckland, New Zealand) the nine convicted Ogonis were executed, prompting immediate condemnation by the international community. Nigeria was suspended from the Commonwealth, and threatened with expulsion if the government failed to restore democracy within a period of two years; only The Gambia voted against the suspension. Later that month the EU reaffirmed its commitment to existing sanctions that had been imposed in 1993 (notably an embargo on the export of armaments and military equipment to Nigeria), and extended visa restrictions to civilian members of the administration; the EU also announced the suspension of development co-operation with Nigeria. The governments of the USA, South Africa and the EU member nations recalled their diplomatic representatives from Nigeria in protest at the executions. The Nigerian government condemned the imposition of sanctions as an international conspiracy to overthrow the administration, and, in turn, withdrew its diplomatic representatives from the USA, South Africa and the EU member countries. Additional security forces were dispatched to Ogoniland to deter any protests against the executions while a further 19 Ogonis were charged with complicity in the May 1994 murders.

In early December 1995 Abacha approved the establishment of a number of committees, including the national electoral commission of Nigeria (NECON), to implement the transitional programme. Later in December a Commonwealth Ministerial Action Group (CMAG) comprising eight member countries' ministers with responsibility for foreign affairs, which had been established at the summit meeting in November, met to discuss further measures to be taken if the Nigerian government failed to restore democratic government, and announced that five of the ministers were to visit Nigeria to initiate negotiations with the military regime. (The diplomatic representatives who had been withdrawn following the executions in November subsequently returned to Lagos, in order to facilitate the Commonwealth mission.) The UN general assembly adopted a resolution condemning the executions (although countries that abstained from voting included two members of the CMAG, Ghana and Malaysia).

In January 1996 the government announced that the Commonwealth ministerial delegation would only be granted permission to visit Nigeria if the organization undertook to investigate alleged violations of human rights perpetrated in other countries, and demanded that the decision to suspend Nigeria be reviewed. In the same month two minor bomb attacks were reported in northern Nigeria, at Kano and Kaduna. A government minister subsequently accused Wole Soyinka of complicity in the incidents, on the grounds that the instigator of one of the bombings had apparently been in possession of one of Soyinka's works. At the end of January the government announced that the new constitution would be formally adopted in 1998, upon the completion of the transitional period.

In February 1996 the 19 Ogonis who remained in detention pending their trial appealed to the Commonwealth for assistance in securing their release. In the same month the South African administration denied accusations by Nigeria that it had assisted exiled opponents of the government. In March a UN mission was dispatched to Nigeria (at the latter's request) to investigate the trial and execution of the nine Ogoni activists in 1995. (However, the government continued to refuse to receive the Commonwealth ministerial delegation.) Also in March 1996 local government elections, which were contested on a non-party basis, took place as part of the transitional programme; although opposition leaders had urged a boycott, NECON claimed that a high level of voter participation had been recorded. In April the UN investigative mission visited Ogoniland, where sizeable anti-government demonstrations had taken place; it was reported that Ogoni activists and other opposition representatives were prevented from meeting the delegation. Later that month, following the government's continued refusal to enter into negotiations with the CMAG regarding human rights issues and the restoration of democracy, the Commonwealth proposed to adopt a number of sanctions against Nigeria. In May the PRC was reorganized, following the removal of a number of senior military officials.

In early June 1996 Abiola's wife, Kudirat, who had been a prominent critic of the administration, was killed by unidentified assailants. Although the authorities conducted an investigation of the crime, widespread speculation that the government had ordered the killing increased general hostility towards the regime. The university at Ibadan was temporarily closed, following a demonstration, led by students, in protest at the alleged assassination. Abiola's son and a number of his other immediate relatives were subsequently arrested, apparently on suspicion of complicity in the murder. Four members of NADECO were also detained in connection with the incident. Later in June Nigerian officials met the CMAG in an attempt to avert the threatened imposition of sanctions against Nigeria; shortly before the discussions took place, the government released a number of political prisoners, and promulgated legislation regarding the registration of political parties, in an apparent effort to conciliate critics. The Nigerian delegation demanded that Nigeria be readmitted to the Commonwealth in exchange for the government's adoption of the programme for transition to civilian rule by October 1998. The Commonwealth rejected the programme as unsatisfactory, but remained divided regarding the adoption of consequent measures. It was finally agreed that the Commonwealth would suspend the adoption of sanctions, but that the situation would be reviewed at a further meeting of the CMAG, which was scheduled for September. Canada, however, announced its opposition to this decision and unilaterally imposed a number of sanctions (similar to those already adopted by the EU), including the suspension of military co-operation, the introduction of visa restrictions for members of the administration and their relatives and the cessation of sporting connections.

New restrictive legislation governing the formation of political parties was promulgated in June 1996. At the end of September five of the 15 political organizations that had applied for registration were granted legal status. NADECO condemned the disqualification of the remaining 10 parties, which were subsequently dissolved by decree; it was widely believed that the associations that had been granted registration were largely sympathetic towards the military administration. In early October Abacha announced the creation of a further six states, increasing the total size of the federation to 36 states. At the same time he announced the establishment of a committee of economic representatives, chaired by the former head of state, Chief Ernest Shonekan, which was to draft the government's future policy for economic development (see Economy).

At the end of September 1996 it was agreed that the Commonwealth ministerial delegation would visit Nigeria, despite the continued insistence of the military authorities that it would not be permitted access to opposition activists or political prisoners. The Canadian minister of foreign affairs accused other members of the CMAG of adopting a conciliatory stance towards the Nigerian administration. The Canadian representative subsequently withdrew from the delegation, which visited Nigeria in November, after two Canadian security officials were refused entry visas. Later in November the EU renewed its sanctions against Nigeria for a further six months. In December the Nigerian government rejected a UN resolution criticizing its alleged violations of human rights. In February 1997 a planned mission to Nigeria by the UN Human Rights Commission was abandoned, after the government refused to allow it access to political detainees. In the same month a meeting of the CMAG failed to reach a decision regarding sanctions; Nigerian opposition movements were invited to submit evidence of human rights' violations to the group. The ministerial group was subsequently to prepare recommendations for submission to a Commonwealth summit meeting in October.

A bomb attack in Lagos in December 1996 was widely interpreted as an attempt to assassinate the state administrator, who was a close associate of Abacha. In February 1997 Abacha attributed delays in the holding of local government elections (which had been rescheduled for March) to a further series of bomb attacks in Lagos, in which, it was reported, about six people had been killed and 40 injured; he also indicated that he intended to contest the presidential election in 1998. International observers, including a US monitoring group, declared that the local government elections, which took place accordingly in mid-March, had been conducted peacefully; it was reported that the United Nigerian Congress Party had secured the highest number of seats in the municipal councils. In the same month, after repeatedly accusing NADECO of responsibility for the bomb attacks, the government charged Soyinka and a further 15 pro-democracy activists, including several NADECO leaders, of treason in connection with the incidents. (Soyinka and a further three of the accused were charged *in absentia*.) In March 1997 the Canadian government suspended its diplomatic representation in Nigeria.

In early 1997 escalating tension between the Ijaw and Itsekiri ethnic groups in the town of Warri, south-west of Nigeria, severely disrupted Shell's petroleum-mining operations in the region. In March a demonstration by members of the Ijaw ethnic group in Warri, in protest at the relocation of local government headquarters from Ijaw to Itsekiri territory, precipitated violent clashes. Protesters seized Shell installations and took about 100 employees of the enterprise hostage, in an attempt to force the government to accede to their demands. A curfew was subsequently imposed in the region in an attempt to restore order. By mid-April it was reported that about 90 people had been killed in the disturbances, while the disruption in petroleum production had contributed to a national fuel shortage, effectively suspending the transportation system in much of the country. The government dispatched armed forces to the region in an attempt to quell the unrest. In early May it appeared that a peace settlement had been reached, following a meeting between leaders of the Ijaw and Itsekiri communities. However, the abduction and killing of two Ijaw in Warri precipitated a resumption in hostilities, and further attacks on Shell installations ensued. Later in May the authorities established a commission of inquiry, which was to investigate the cause of the clashes and submit recommendations for restoring order in the region.

In April 1997 Abacha issued a decree empowering himself to replace the mayors who had been elected in March and to dissolve local municipal councils if he considered that they were acting contrary to national interests. In the same month the UN Human Rights Commission voted in favour of appointing a special investigator for Nigeria, in view of continued violations of human rights by the authorities. In May some 22 pro-democracy and human rights organizations, including MOSOP and the CD, formed a loose alliance, the United Action for Democracy (UAD), with the aim of campaigning for the restoration of democracy in Nigeria. UAD announced that the organization would participate in the forthcoming elections providing that Abacha did not seek re-election to the presidency, and adopted a programme of demands, which included the release of political detainees, the formation of a government of national unity and the convening of a sovereign national conference. It was reported that UAD planned to organize a nationwide campaign of civil disobedience, with one-day general strikes, to force Abacha to relinquish power. Also in May a total of four people were killed in a further series of bomb attacks, which took place in Lagos, Ibadan and Onitsha (in Anambra State). NADECO denied reiterated claims by the authorities that the organization was responsible for the attacks.

In July 1997 the authorities announced a new electoral timetable: elections to the state assemblies were to take place on 6 December, followed by elections to the national assembly on 25 April 1998, and presidential and gubernatorial elections on 1 August of that year (despite previous indications that the gubernatorial elections were to be held in late 1997). Although it was confirmed that the new elected organs of government would be installed by 1 October 1998, the rescheduling of the gubernatorial elections was criticized by opposition groups, which voiced concern that the transfer to democratic rule would not be completed on the stipulated date. The absence from the forthcoming presidential election of any of the most prominent second and third republic politicians had by early 1997 been assured by NECON's failure to recognize the parties supported by these figures. Of the five legal parties, only the GDM encouraged its members to seek presidential nomination, prompting competition between a lawyer, Tunji Braithwaite, and a former inspector-general of police, Mohammed Dikko Yusufu. Meanwhile, the most prominent of the registered parties, the UNCP (led by a former minister, Isa Mohammed) deferred consideration of its presidential candidate until the final period of the transition. The UNCP proved to be the most successful party in the state assembly elections of 6 December, in which it won control of 29 of the 36 state assemblies, with a total of 637 of the 990 contested seats; the other four parties accused the UNCP of extensive electoral malpractice.

A CMAG report on Nigeria, which was prepared prior to a summit meeting of Commonwealth heads of government in October 1997, criticized the government's record of human rights and the inadequacies of the planned transition to civilian rule. However, at the summit meeting which took place in Edinburgh, United Kingdom, the member governments postponed for a further year the threat of more severe economic sanctions and Nigeria's expulsion from the organization, reiterating demands that democracy be restored by 1 October 1998. The Nigerian government had succeeded in increasing its standing with Commonwealth members by pressurizing the military junta in Sierra Leone, to agree to the restoration to power of the democratically-elected government of President Ahmed Tejan Kabbah. The apparent relaxation of the Commonwealth's policy on Nigeria was condemned by NADECO and other opponents of the government, but NADECO's influence was reduced by the death in October 1997 of its leader, Chief Michael Ajasin. The opposition was further demoralized by the death in detention of Yar'Adua in December, and the reported ill health of other prisoners, including Obasanjo and Ransome-Kuti. Abacha reinforced his authority by dismissing his entire cabinet on 17 November (the fourth anniversary of his seizure of power), although many prominent members of that government were subsequently reinstated.

In December 1997 it was reported that an assassination attempt had been staged at Abuja airport against Abacha's deputy, Lt-Gen. Oladipo Diya, who was known to favour the military's complete withdrawal from the government. Diya was subsequently arrested and charged with planning the violent overthrow of the government, together with several other senior officials and a number of civilians. A special military tribunal was established in Jos, and in February 1998 it commenced proceedings against some 30 defendants. At the opening session Diya claimed the charges against him had been fabricated by military leadership. In April Diya and five others were sentenced to death; a further four defendants were sentenced to life imprisonment, while five received shorter custodial terms and 15 were acquitted. Appeals for clemency were made by foreign governments and by prominent individuals within Nigeria.

Throughout 1997 and early 1998 disputes between neighbouring communities in different parts of the country resulted in sporadic clashes. Fighting erupted in August 1997 between the Ife and Modakeke communities, following the relocation of a local government headquarters, and more than 100 people were killed in further disturbances in early 1998. There were also violent clashes between Ijaw and Urhobo communities in Bayelsa State in March, in which more than 30 people were killed.

In early March 1998 the government's political and commercial supporters increased pressure for Abacha to be re-elected as a civilian president. A rally was staged in Abuja, in which thousands of people from around the country were transported to the capital by a group known as Youths Earnestly Ask for Abacha (YEAA); the organization's leader, Daniel Kanu, admitted that its activities were financed by the government. Despite these repressive measures, the UAD initiated a further series of opposition protests, and reiterated its demands for a transfer of power to a transitional government of national unity and the holding of a sovereign national conference.

The five registered political parties, having met in February 1998 to consider the adoption of Abacha as a consensus candidate, all proceeded to nominate Abacha during special government-funded conventions, which took place in mid-April. The UNCP was the first to adopt Abacha's candidacy, followed in rapid succession by the other four parties, although Braithwaite and Yusufu, who had both continued to campaign for the GDM's presidential nomination, protested at Abacha's adoption by the party in a highly controversial voting process. Following the adoption of Abacha by the official parties, the UAD urged a boycott of the legislative elections of 25 April. The widespread public disillusionment of Nigerians with the Abacha government's political programme was reflected by the observance of the boycott throughout the country; in many regions the voter turnout was estimated to be as low as 1%. The political atmosphere became increasingly volatile from the end of April when some 10 people were killed in bomb attacks in Ife and Lagos (for which no organization claimed responsibility). In the course of anti-government protests, which took place in early May, violent clashes between demonstrators and the security forces resulted in the deaths of at least seven people and the arrest of numerous others. A number of opposition members were subsequently detained without charge after these events. Attempts at constructing a united pro-democracy alliance intensified during May with the formation of a Joint Action Committee of Nigeria (JACON), comprising a total of 45 groups which opposed the military government. JACON endorsed further protests and urged members of the armed forces not to fire at demonstrators.

Abubakar and Transition, 1998–99

On 8 June 1998 Abacha died unexpectedly from undetermined causes in the presidential residence in Abuja. Senior military officers, including the chief of defence staff, Maj.-Gen. Abdulsalami Abubakar and the chief of army staff, Maj.-Gen. Ishaya Bamaiyi, rapidly asserted their authority, and Abubakar was designated as Abacha's successor. The regime pledged to continue the Abacha government's transition to civilian rule. The UAD responded by urging continued protests against the military government.

Abubakar (who was promoted to the rank of general) was formally installed as head of state on 9 June 1998. The secretary-general of the Commonwealth subsequently announced that the sanctions imposed against Nigeria would remain in force until democratic elections took place. In early July, following discussions with UN officials, the new authorities agreed to release Abiola from detention. Upon his release, however, Abiola, who had been met by a US government delegation, collapsed, and subsequently died. Violent rioting ensued, amid widespread speculation that the authorities were responsible for Abiola's death. Although a subsequent autopsy indicated that he had died of heart failure, it was reported that neglect of his health during his period in detention had contributed to his collapse. Later in July Abubakar, who had ordered the release of a number of political prisoners, announced that the transition to civilian rule would be completed on 29 May 1999 (rather than 1 October 1998). The government annulled the results of the elections that had previously been conducted, and dissolved the five authorized political parties, NECON and other electoral bodies. In early August a new 31-member federal executive council, which included a number of civilians, was appointed to remain in office pending the formal transition to civilian rule; an independent national electoral commission (INEC) was also established. Later that month INEC announced that local government elections would take place on 5 December 1998 and state legislative elections on 9 January 1999, followed by elec-

tions to a bicameral national legislature on 20 February and a presidential election on 27 February. On 7 September 1998 the government published the draft constitution that had been submitted by the NCC in June 1995.

Abubakar also initiated a process of intensive discussions with opposition groupings, including those who had been most critical of military rule. Some prominent activists, such as leaders of JACON, refused to accept any continuation of military rule. Most NADECO leaders similarly began by insisting on the immediate formation of a government of national unity and the holding of a sovereign national conference, but by August 1998 it was apparent that several prominent NADECO supporters had decided to accept the transition programme as proposed by the military. Abubakar also continued to release political prisoners and to urge Nigerians to return from exile (an appeal that eventually prompted the return from Nigeria of Wole Soyinka and the MOSOP leader, Ledum Mitee, in October, although others chose to remain abroad).

The renewed process of transition to civilian rule progressed during August 1998, with strong indications from most northern political leaders that they would accede to demands from southern activists that the next president should be from the south of the country. When INEC commenced proceedings at the end of August numerous political groupings applied for registration. The leading party to emerge was the People's Democratic Party (PDP), which was established by a group of northern politicians who had urged Abacha not to seek re-election in March, but which also built on the political structure formerly established by Shehu Musa Yar'Adua and used funds provided by other retired generals. The All People's Party (APP) was formed by a coalition of associations that had received considerable support during Abacha's rule. By contrast, the Alliance for Democracy (AD) was formed by a grouping of politicians who had been associated with NADECO and were committed to a political restructuring of the country. Of the 29 parties that applied for registration, nine were approved by INEC in late October. Soon afterwards Obasanjo, who had been released from detention in June, announced that he was joining the PDP and that he hoped to become the party's candidate for the presidency.

After sanctions by the Commonwealth, the EU, the USA and other nations were ended (see below), Nigeria was able to secure significant international assistance for the organization of its elections. At local government elections, which took place on 5 December 1998, when the PDP gained control of about 60% of local municipal councils. INEC ruled that only the PDP, APP and AD had received the requisite number of votes at these local elections to be allowed to contest the elections at state and federal level in January and February 1999. At the state legislative elections, which took place on 9 January, the PDP secured the highest number of votes except in the south-west where the AD had its base, while the APP received most support in the Middle Belt and in various parts of the north; the PDP won 21 of the 36 governorships. After the state elections the AD and APP agreed to establish an electoral alliance to contest the federal legislative elections, and to present a joint presidential candidate.

Although the 19 detained Ogoni activists were released in September 1998, violent protests in the Niger Delta region intensified throughout the year and into 1999. The protests were most intense in areas inhabited by the Ijaw ethnic group and were staged in support of demands for compensation from the government and the petroleum companies, in addition to clashes with other ethnic groups, such as the Itsekiri and Ilaje. At times, Nigeria's daily petroleum production was seriously affected by occupations of petroleum installations, and by abductions of oil workers. Such actions intensified after the adoption by Ijaw activists in December of the 'Kaiama Declaration', which demanded the departure of all petroleum companies from the region. In January 1999 there were sharp clashes between troops and armed activists and the security situation deteriorated particularly in the Ijaw-dominated Bayelsa State, where, as a result, the elections taking place in the rest of the country were postponed.

At the party conventions in February 1999 Obasanjo was nominated to contest the presidential election on behalf of the PDP (defeating Alex Ekwueme), with Atiku Abubakar as vice-presidential candidate, while the AD–APP alliance adopted Olu Falae of the AD as its presidential candidate and the APP's Umaru Shinkafi as his running mate. There was a perceptible decline in public interest by the time of the elections to the national assembly on 20 February, in which only 40% of the electorate participated. At the legislative elections the PDP secured 208 seats in the 360-member house of representatives and 60 seats in the 109-member senate; the AD took 76 seats in the house of representatives and 20 in the senate, while the APP won 69 seats in the house of representatives and 24 in the senate. (Elections for the remaining seven seats in the house of representatives and five in the senate were postponed, owing to continued unrest in the Niger Delta region.) On 27 February 1999 Obasanjo was elected to the presidency, with 62.8% of votes cast. Voting irregularities were reported, and Falae submitted a legal challenge to the electoral results (which was subsequently rejected by the Court of Appeal).

RETURN TO CIVILIAN GOVERNMENT

In the transitional period prior to the installation of civilian rule on 29 May 1999, the outgoing administration approved a new constitutional framework based on the 1979 constitution (which Obasanjo's government had adopted) and also issued decrees designed to reinforce economic liberalization. The new constitution was formally promulgated on 5 May. Obasanjo was inaugurated as president on 29 May, when the constitution came into effect; on taking office he announced that anti-corruption legislation would be presented to the national assembly and that all contracts awarded since the begining of 1999 would be reviewed. He also initiated a major reorganization of military officers, appointing Rear-Adm. Ibrahim Ogohi as chief of defence staff, Maj.-Gen. Victor Malu as chief of army staff and Air Vice-Marshal Isaac Alfa as chief of air staff. On 3 June the inaugural session of the national assembly took place. President Obasanjo's administration was subsequently formed with the aim of accommodating people with political experience and achieving full representation of the 36 states. After it had been approved by the national assembly in June 1999, the new federal cabinet included several members of former military and civilian governments, including Gen. (retd) Theophilus Danjuma as minister of defence, Adamu Ciroma as minister of finance and Bola Ige (a member of the opposition AD) as minister of power and steel. Obasanjo also appointed advisers, including Gen. (retd) Aliyu Mohammed, Rilwanu Lukman (the OPEC secretary-general) and Phillip Asiodu, who had longstanding influence on government policy. The president acted promptly to remove from the armed forces all officers who had held political positions under recent previous governments, in order to restore a better ethnic balance among military commanders by allowing promotion of officers from southern and Middle Belt states rather than those from the northern states. Danjuma (whose assumption of responsibility for the armed forces placed severe strain on his health) also announced that troop numbers in the army would be significantly reduced. A further early innovation of the Obasanjo government was the establishment of a commission to investigate human rights' violations during previous administrations; its remit was eventually extended to cover every government since the first coup of 1966.

One apparent effect of the return to civilian government was an upsurge in the levels of inter-ethnic violence, at first in Warri, where about 200 people were killed in early June 1999 during fighting between three rival communities, and then in the following month, with violent clashes between Hausa and Yoruba communities in the Lagos area and later in Kano. The emergence of these hostilities prompted immediate suspicions that powerful interest groups who had previously benefited from military rule were intent on exacerbating ethnic tension and thereby subverting the introduction of democratic rule.

Following its inauguration in early June 1999, the new national assembly based in Abuja initially encountered unfamiliar procedural and ethical difficulties. The first speaker of the house of representatives, Salisu Buhari, was exposed as having misled the chamber about his age and educational qualifications and was forced to resign. A similar scandal later forced the first senate president, Evans Enwerem, to be replaced in November by Chuba Okadigbo, a former political adviser to the Shehu Shagari administration. A potential challenge to the new consti-

tution arose with the proposed adoption of Muslim Shari'a law as the state legal system for substantial parts of the north. Zamfara was the first state to take this measure with the proclamation of Shari'a by its governor, Ahmed Sani Yerimah. These moves were denounced by human rights and Christian groups as unconstitutional and an infringement of legal rights and of freedom of worship. Despite pressure for a legal challenge to the anticipated Shari'a proclamations, President Obasanjo did not declare it to be unconstitutional, indicating by his failure to condemn the state's action that he did not intend to alienate powerful northern interests, and particularly those strongly represented in the PDP.

In October 1999 the government investigations resulted in murder charges being brought against Mohammed Abacha, the late ruler's son, and several former senior military officers. Among the murders cited was the assassination of Kudirat Abiola in 1996 and the suspected murder of Shehu Musa Yar' Adua in detention in December 1997. The new series of arrests included those of two retired generals, Ishaya Bamaiyi and Jeremiah Useni, the former inspector-general of police, Ibrahim Coomassie, and Abacha's head of security, Hamza al-Mustapha. Also in October the government succeeded in persuading the Swiss government to order banks to freeze the accounts of Mohammed Abacha, other members of the Abacha family and several senior officials in the former government, and also confiscated many residences acquired by these officials during the Abacha era.

Trouble in the Niger Delta region again erupted in November 1999, when the army was sent into Bayelsa State to respond to the killing of several policemen by young Ijaw militants in the town of Odi. Armed troops burnt the town to the ground, killing large numbers of inhabitants and forcing many to flee. The government justified the action as necessary to restore order, but the massacre was condemned by human rights' groups. Later in the same month there was a further eruption of anti-Hausa violence in Lagos State, this time with the clear involvement of the militant Yoruba group, the Odua People's Congress (OPC). The killings continued for some days, and a total of about 100 people were believed to have died. The authorities took suppressive measures against the OPC, arresting a number of suspected supporters.

In view of increasing tensions around the country, there were renewed demands for the convening of a sovereign national conference (a proposal that had the nominal support of both NADECO and the AD). However, such demands were not supported in the national assembly; most federal legislators felt that such a conference would act as a platform for extremism and that they themselves had the power to undertake any necessary revisions of the constitution. The demands for a sovereign conference were not made with equal commitment in different parts of the country and tended to be led by the more militant associations, such as the OPC and the Ijaw Youth Congress. Other ethnic or regional organizations, such as those representing Middle Belt and south-eastern opinion, preferred to urge the establishment of a nationwide confederation on the basis of regions. Among the new groups to emerge at this time was the previously-unknown Movement for the Actualization of the Sovereign State of Biafra (MASSOB), although this did not receive the support of the most prominent Igbo politicians; MASSOB leaders' declaration of Biafran independence in May 2000 was widely ignored. The government's proposed solution to the crisis in the Niger Delta was to introduce a Niger Delta Development Commission (NDDC) and to increase the allocation to the petroleum-producing states to 13% of the federal budget. However, after disagreements between the executive and the national assembly, the president vetoed amendments to the NDDC bill, although in May the assembly eventually overruled the veto and approved the bill. There were also difficulties over the adoption of the budget for 2000, which was similarly delayed until May.

The anticipated adoption of Shari'a law in a number of northern states, including Sokoto, Kebbi, Katsina, Kano and Yobe, caused increasing religious tensions from December 1999 onwards. In Ilorin, Kwara State, 14 churches were burnt by suspected Islamic fundamentalists, prompting Christian leaders to demand the arrest of those responsible. After news that the application of Shari'a had commenced in Zamfara in

February 2000, Christians in the town of Kaduna staged a demonstration against the possible introduction of Islamic law in their state, but skirmishes with Muslims rapidly escalated into widespread violence, in which more than 1,000 people were killed and property was destroyed in the city from late February into early March. Revenge attacks against Muslims also occurred in southern cities, notably in Aba, Abia State. A decision at the end of February by northern state governors to suspend the application of Shari'a was too late to prevent much of the violence. There was also a recurrence of the violence in Kaduna in May, in which an estimated 150 people were killed. In that month state governments which had adopted Shari'a law agreed to revert back to the penal code. In June, however, the governor of Kano State proclaimed the introduction of Shari'a law, but delayed its implementation until the Muslim period of Ramadan (beginning in November).

REGIONAL RELATIONS

Nigeria has taken a leading role in African affairs and is a prominent member of the Economic Community of West African States (ECOWAS) and other regional organizations. The Nigerian government contributed a significant number of troops to the ECOWAS Monitoring Group (ECOMOG), which was deployed in Liberia from August 1990 in response to the conflict between government forces and rebels in that country (see chapter on Liberia). In early 1998, following the installation of a democratically-elected civilian government in Liberia, a number of ECOMOG forces were withdrawn from the country. However, some 6,000 ECOMOG troops, including a substantial Nigerian contingent, remained in the country, and were to assist in the reconstruction of the security forces. In 1993 Nigerian troops were dispatched to Sierra Leone, in response to a formal request by the Sierra Leonean government for military assistance to repulse attacks by the rebel Revolutionary United Front in that country. Following a military coup in Sierra Leone in May 1997, the Nigerian government increased its military strength in the Sierra Leonean capital, Freetown, and subsequently launched attacks against supporters of the new junta. In February 1998 Nigerian troops succeeded in gaining control of Freetown, and ousting the coup leaders. In March the democratically-elected Sierra Leonean president, Alhaji Ahmed Tejan Kabbah, was formally reinstalled. However, the Nigerian contingent suffered heavy casualties, particularly during a concerted rebel assault on Freetown in January 1999 (in which about 800 troops were killed). Nigerian military and political leaders favoured ordering a withdrawal of Nigerian troops from Sierra Leone at the earliest possible moment; in response to the apparent progress being made in political negotiations between Sierra Leone's government and rebels in early 1999, however, it was envisaged that the Nigerian contingent (then numbering 15,000) would remain in the country until peace was restored. Following a UN Security Council decision in October 1999 to authorize the deployment of the UN Mission in Sierra Leone (UNAMSIL), ECOMOG was formally withdrawn in April 2000, to be replaced by UNAMSIL. However, in response to the taking hostage of UN troops by rebels and subsequent British military intervention to stablize the situation in Sierra Leone, West African leaders agreed to provide renewed support, and authorized the deployment of 3,000 troops, mainly Nigerians (see chapter on Sierra Leone). A number of ECOMOG troops from Nigeria were transferred to UNAMSIL control at the end of April. In late August members of the US armed forces arrived in Nigeria to assist in the training of some 4,000 Nigerian troops, who were to reinforce the UNAMSIL contingent in Sierra Leone.

In mid-1993 the United Kingdom, together with other European nations and the USA, imposed military sanctions against Nigeria, in response to the suspension of the scheduled transition to civilian rule. Further sanctions were adopted in late 1995 (see above). In May 1997 the Nigerian government imposed an indefinite ban on flights from the United Kingdom, after Nigerian-registered aircraft were banned from British airports on the grounds that they failed to meet safety standards. After the death of Abacha, Nigeria's relations with the United Kingdom, the USA, the EU and the Commonwealth improved rapidly. In September 1998 Canada restored full diplomatic

relations, and in October the Commonwealth announced the lifting of sanctions against Nigeria. At the final transition to civilian rule on 29 May 1999 Nigeria was automatically readmitted as a full member of the Commonwealth.

In 1991 the Nigerian government claimed that Cameroonian security forces had annexed several Nigerian fishing settlements in Cross River State (in south-eastern Nigeria), following a longstanding border dispute, based on a 1913 agreement between Germany and the United Kingdom that ceded the Bakassi peninsula in the Gulf of Guinea (a region of strategic significance) to the German protectorate of Kamerun; Cameroon's claim to the region was upheld by an unratified agreement in 1975. Subsequent negotiations between Nigerian and Cameroonian officials in an effort to resolve the dispute achieved little progress. In December 1993 some 500 Nigerian troops were dispatched to the region, in response to a number of incidents in which Nigerian nationals had been killed by Cameroonian security forces. Later that month the two nations agreed to establish a joint patrol at the disputed area, and to investigate the cause of the incidents. In February 1994, however, the Nigerian government increased the number of troops deployed in the region. Later in February Cameroon announced that it was to submit the dispute for adjudication by the UN, the OAU, and the International Court of Justice (ICJ), and requested military assistance from France. Subsequent reports of clashes between Cameroonian and Nigerian forces in the region prompted fears of a full-scale conflict between the two nations. In March Cameroon agreed to enter into bilateral negotiations with Nigeria (without the involvement of international mediators) to resolve the issue. Later that month, however, a proposal by the Nigerian government that a referendum be conducted in the disputed region was rejected by Cameroon. In June the heads of state of the two nations met at an OAU summit meeting in Tunis, Tunisia, and agreed to establish a joint committee to achieve a resolution to the dispute. However, a meeting to discuss the issue, which was scheduled to take place in July, was postponed, owing to the unrest in Nigeria. In September 10 members of the Cameroonian armed forces were killed in further confrontations.

In February 1996 renewed hostilities between Nigerian and Cameroonian forces in the Bakassi region resulted in several casualties. Later that month, however, Nigeria and Cameroon agreed to refrain from further military action, and delegations from the two countries resumed discussions, with mediation by the Togolese president, in an attempt to resolve the dispute. In March the ICJ ruled that Cameroon had failed to provide sufficient evidence to support its contention that Nigeria had provoked the border conflict, and ordered both nations to cease military operations, to withdraw troops to former positions, and to co-operate with a UN investigative mission that was to be dispatched to the region. In April, however, clashes continued, with each government accusing the other of initiating the attacks. Although tension in the region remained high, diplomatic efforts to avoid further conflict increased in May; in that month a Cameroonian delegation visited Nigeria, while Abacha accepted an invitation to attend an OAU summit meeting, which was convened in Yaoundé in July. The UN investigative mission visited the Bakassi region in September. In December, however, the Nigerian authorities claimed that Cameroonian troops had resumed attacks in the region. In May 1997 the Cameroonian government denied further allegations by Nigeria that it had initiated hostilities; it was reported that the UN had requested that the Togolese president continue mediation efforts. Cameroon accused Nigeria of further attacks in December, and in February 1998; on the latter occasion it claimed that seven members of its armed forces had been killed in the fighting. Cameroon at the same time denied Nigerian accusations that it was amassing 5,000 troops to launch an attack in the Bakassi region. When the ICJ hearings formally opened in March, Nigeria submitted preliminary objections, on the grounds that the international court had no jurisdiction since the two countries had agreed to settle the dispute through bilateral discussions. In June, however, the ICJ ruled that it had jurisdiction to resolve the dispute (although a final decision on the issue was not expected for several months).

Economy

LINDA VAN BUREN

Despite considerable agricultural and mineral resources, Nigeria is ranked by the World Bank as a low-income country, and is among the 13 poorest countries in the world on the basis of per-capita income. According to World Bank estimates, Nigeria's gross national product (GNP) per head was US $320m., compared with $300m. in 1998. During 1990–98, it was estimated, GNP per head increased, in real terms, at an average annual rate of 0.4%, while the population increased by an annual average of 3.3%. Nigeria's gross domestic product (GDP) increased, in real terms, by an annual average of 2.1% in 1990–99; however, GDP growth fell from 3.8% in 1997 to 1.8% in 1998, while a decline in GDP of 1.7% was estimated in 1999.

Statistical assessments of the Nigerian economy are subject to wide margins of error, as a result of the lack of reliable data. The census of November 1991 recorded a total of 88,514,501 inhabitants, and the population was officially estimated at 97,223,521 inhabitants at mid-1995. Unofficial estimates of the population at mid-2000 varied from 112.2m. to 117m. inhabitants.

The development of the petroleum industry, which began in the late 1950s and gained momentum in the late 1960s and 1970s, radically transformed Nigeria from an agriculturally-based economy to a major oil exporter. Increased earnings from petroleum exports generated high levels of real economic growth, and by the mid-1970s Nigeria ranked as the dominant economy in sub-Saharan Africa and as the continent's major exporter of petroleum. Following the decline in world petroleum prices after 1981, however, the government became increasingly over-extended financially, with insufficient revenue from petroleum to pay the rising cost of imports or to finance major development projects. The decline in Nigeria's earnings of foreign exchange led to an accumulation of arrears in trade debts and to import shortages, which, in turn, resulted in a sharp fall in economic activity, with most of Nigerian industry struggling to operate without essential imported raw materials and spare parts. A series of poor harvests, an overvalued currency and a widening budget deficit compounded the problem. The Buhari government responded to the crisis by implementing a range of severe austerity measures in 1984 and 1985, including further cuts in public expenditure, and rigid restrictions on credit and the availability of foreign exchange.

The Babangida military government, which took power in August 1985, continued its predecessor's policies of austerity and monetary control. Babangida declared a state of economic emergency, under which the import of rice and maize was banned, and a national recovery fund was created. However, the dramatic fall in international prices for petroleum in 1986, together with reduced output in all sectors (except agriculture), kept the economy in the depths of recession. In July 1986 the Babangida government announced a two-year structural adjustment programme (SAP), which aimed at expanding non-petroleum exports, reducing the import of goods which could be manufactured locally, achieving self-sufficiency in food and increasing the role of the private sector. The SAP included the abolition of import licences and a reduction in import duties. One of its principal features, however, was the creation, in September, of two rates for foreign exchange transactions; a first 'tier', which the government used for foreign debt-servicing and other specified outgoings, and a second-tier foreign exchange market (SFEM) for commercial transactions. SFEM rates were determined by means of auctions of available foreign exchange, conducted by the Central Bank of Nigeria (CBN). In July 1987 the two-tier exchange mechanism was replaced by fortnightly auctions at a unitary foreign exchange market (FEM). In January 1991 the auction system was replaced; the CBN was henceforth to fix the rate in consultation with leading commercial banks. The government also permitted the establishment of bureaux de change, which were to sell as much as US $30,000 of foreign exchange at market rates that represented a variable premium over the official CBN rate. Dual exchange rates continued to attract criticism from donor and creditor institutions until they were finally abolished on 1 January 1999 (see below).

In early 1988 the government issued a list of 110 state enterprises to be privatized or partially commercialized. A special technical committee was established to implement the programme, which was to involve the Nigerian Railway Corpn, the National Electric Power Authority (NEPA), and the telecommunications conglomerate, NITEL. (Plans for NITEL's privatization were still underway in 1999.) By the end of 1992 90 of the 120 enterprises scheduled for privatization, including 12 commercial banks in which the government had a shareholding, had been sold, while the transfer to private ownership of Nigeria Airways and the Nigerian National Shipping Line was also envisaged. In 2000, however, the privatization of most of these enterprises had still not taken place.

Measures undertaken under the SAP with the aim of attracting private capital from abroad proved largely unsuccessful; investors were deterred by the country's reputation for corruption, and by the government's failure to control expenditure. The budget deficit began to expand rapidly, reaching the equivalent of 11.4% of GDP in 1988 and increasing to more than 12% of GDP in subsequent years. Economic instability was also reflected in a persistently high rate of inflation, which increased from an annual average of 24.0% in 1986–91, to 44.6% in 1992, to 57.2% in 1993, and to 72.8% in 1995; it was reported that in the year to March 1996 the prices of major commodities, such as garri (cassava flour), rice and beans had increased by 100%. Thereafter, official figures indicated that inflation had declined to 29.4% in 1996, to 14.1% in 1997, and to 10.5% in 1998. Inflation was estimated at 13.8% in 1999, although other sources estimated the rate at more than 20%. Public-sector salary and petrol price increases in mid-2000 were expected to result in a significant rise in the rate of inflation in that year. Interest rates were estimated at 26% upwards in June 2000. The SAP was abandoned in 1994, following a severe deterioration in political and economic conditions in the early 1990s.

In 1994 the Abacha government introduced a fixed exchange rate of ₦22.00 = US $1, and selective import controls, but these policies proved unsuccessful and were replaced in 1995 with a return to earlier adjustment policies, allowing the naira to float more freely, and adopting new measures that favoured foreign investment. However, the government's actions were often contrary to official policy, reflecting a desire to impose administrative and sectional control of both the petroleum industry and the banking system.

The political instability in the 1990s severely impeded the ability of successive governments to implement economic policies and also adversely affected international confidence in the economy. The international community took punitive measures against Nigeria (see Recent History), with detrimental effects on the economy. After the transition to civilian rule on 29 May 1999 and the subsequent ending of sanctions, lending was gradually resumed. The World Bank's International Development Association (IDA) in May 2000 extended US $55m. in project aid for primary education and $20m. in programme aid for Nigeria's Economic Management Capacity Building efforts; both loans were over a period of 35 years including 10 years' grace. The European Union in March 2000 pledged 75m. euro of programme aid, and Japan in December 1999 allocated $50m. to Nigeria for education, water resources, and science and technology.

AGRICULTURE

Until Nigeria attained independence in 1960, agriculture was the most important sector of the economy, accounting for more than one-half of GDP and for more than three-quarters of export earnings. However, with the rapid expansion of the petroleum industry, agricultural development was neglected, and the sector entered a relative decline. Between the mid-1960s and the mid-1980s, Nigeria moved from a position of self-sufficiency in basic foodstuffs to one of heavy dependence on imports. Under-investment, a steady drift away from the land to urban centres, increased consumer preference for imported foodstuffs (particularly rice and wheat) and outdated farming techniques continued to keep the level of food production well behind the rate of population growth. After experiencing growth rates of 8%–10% per annum during the early 1970s, the increase in agricultural production declined to around 4% per annum towards the end of the decade. The slow growth continued into the 1980s, and the effects of drought and the government's austerity programme resulted in a severe 9.4% fall in agricultural output in 1983. However, a succession of good harvests, higher producer prices, reductions in cereal imports and a resurgence of public and private investment in crop production resulted in a sharp recovery in production in 1984, with food output reaching 7%. Agriculture was the only sector to show any significant expansion in 1986, when, owing to further record harvests of rice and maize, overall agricultural production increased by 2.1%. In 1997 agriculture (including hunting, forestry and fishing) contributed an estimated 45% of GDP, and employed 36.1% of the labour force. Overall growth of the sector was estimated as negligible in 1999 and 2000. The cassava harvest grew by 1.1% to 33.1m. metric tons in 1999, while the 1999 yam harvest of 25.1m. tons was 1.2% greater than in 1998. The 1999 cereal crop varied, with sorghum increasing by 18.9% and maize by 12.7%, but millet declining by 8.4%.

Traditional smallholder farmers, who use simple techniques of production and the bush-fallow system of cultivation, account for around two-thirds of Nigeria's total agricultural production. The number of state farms is relatively small, and of decreasing importance. Since 1986 many of the loss-making parastatal bodies have been closed down or sold to the private sector. Subsistence food crops (mainly sorghum, maize, yams, cassava, rice and millet) are grown in the central and western areas of Nigeria, and are traded largely outside the cash economy. Of a total cereal crop of 23.2m. metric tons in 1999, sorghum represented the principal share of 8.4m. tons, followed by maize (5.8m. tons), millet (5.4m. tons) and paddy rice (3.4m. tons). Cash crops (mainly groundnuts, followed by oil palm, palm kernels, karite nuts, cotton, cashew nuts, coconuts, cocoa, rubber, kola nuts, sesame seed and coffee) are cultivated in the mid-west and north of the country. Production of groundnuts in shells increased by 10% to 2.8m. tons in 1999, but the harvest of seed cotton declined by 43% to an estimated 200,000 tons in that year. Output of cocoa beans remained constant at 145,000 tons, as did production of green coffee, at only 4,000 tons. Six federal commodity marketing boards were formally abolished in 1987; their dissolution, combined with a devalued naira, contributed to an increase in producer prices and output. Owing to these measures, production of cash crops increased considerably in 1988.

Among the agricultural crops, only cocoa makes any significant contribution to exports, but Nigeria's share of the world cocoa market has been substantially reduced in recent years, owing to ageing trees, low producer prices, black pod disease, smuggling and labour shortages. Moreover, the abolition of the Cocoa Marketing Board in 1987 led to poor quality control and fraudulent trading practices, which adversely affected the market reputation of Nigerian cocoa. The government subsequently reintroduced licences for marketers of cocoa and improved inspection procedures. Recent emphasis has been placed on encouraging domestic cocoa-processing to provide higher-value products for export. According to the International Cocoa Organization, cocoa production in Nigeria fell from 165,000 metric tons to 110,000 tons in the period 1988/89–1991/92, recovering to 145,000 tons in 1992/93, and to 155,000 tons in 1997/98, before declining to 145,000 in 1998/99.

The production and export of oil palm products has declined dramatically. The world's leading exporter of palm oil until overtaken by Malaysia in 1971, Nigeria is now heavily dependent on imports in order to satisfy domestic needs. As in other cash-crop sectors, output of palm products has suffered from labour shortages, inefficient traditional harvesting methods, lack of vital inputs and low levels of capital investment. A sharp reduction in imports and large-scale replanting in eastern Rivers State did, however, result in a substantial

increase in production during the mid-1980s. Trade liberalization and the exchange rate policy also contributed to the improvement in palm oil production after 1987. Most of the surplus output has been used for import substitution, with some increase in exports of palm products. According to FAO estimates, palm kernel production increased from 350,000 metric tons in 1986 to 565,000 tons in 1999. Nigeria is by far the largest producer of palm kernels and oil palm in Africa, and is the third-largest producer in the world (after Malaysia and Indonesia). Substantial investments in oil-milling facilities were made to produce vegetable oil for domestic use. Palm oil production reached 965,000 tons in 1993, but declined to 852,000 tons in 1995, and to 810,000 tons in 1997, before recovering to 847,000 tons by 1999.

In 1990 Nigeria overtook Liberia as the largest rubber producer in Africa. Production rose from 55,000 metric tons in 1986 to 152,000 tons in 1990 and to 155,000 tons in 1991, but then began to decline to 129,000 tons in 1992, and to 90,000 tons per year in 1997–99. Benefits from a replanting programme in the eastern states have yet to materialize, and local demand from the tyre and footwear industries continues to outstrip domestic supply.

Production of raw cotton increased to 276,000 metric tons in 1990 (compared with 187,000 tons in 1989), owing, in part, to considerable public and private investment in the sector. Incentives for local textile companies and higher tariffs on imported cotton stimulated local production, although the textile manufacturers prefer the higher quality of legally or illegally imported cotton from neighbouring countries. In 1997 the government agreed to purchase 400,000 bales of excess cotton from farmers. In 1998 Nigeria produced 348,000 tons of seed cotton, but output declined sharply in 1999, by 43%, when the crop of 200,000 tons of seed cotton yielded 57,000 tons of cotton lint and 135,000 tons of cottonseed. Production of other cash crops in 1999 included 405,000 tons of soya beans, 98,000 tons of wheat (about the same level as the previous year, but an increase of 48%, compared with 1997), 675,000 tons of sugar cane, 152,000 tons of cashew nuts (this tree crop expanded rapidly in the late 1990s), 355,000 tons of karite nuts, 881,000 tons of pineapples, 751,000 tons of papayas, 731,000 tons of mangoes, 719,000 tons of okra (an increase of 13% compared with the 1998 crop), 801,000 tons of tomatoes, 738,000 tons of peppers, 225,000 tons of carrots, 80,000 tons of ginger and 9,200 tons of tobacco leaves.

According to the FAO, output of beef and veal reached 294,000 metric tons in 1997, while the output of goat meat was estimated at 130,000 tons. In 1997 Nigeria's national herd comprised 20m. cattle and 14m. sheep. In 1996 15.3m. sheep and goats, 5.9m. pigs and 2.8m. cattle were slaughtered, producing 183,000 tons of sheep and goat meat, 258,000 tons of pork and 221,000 tons of beef. Output of poultry meat was estimated at 168,000 tons in 1995. Production of all types of meat totalled 1.0m. tons in 1997. Nigeria's annual fish catch declined in the 1980s, owing to shortages of trawlers and nets, and the cancellation of industrial fishing licences. According to the FAO, the marine fish catch totalled 230,402 tons in 1998, with herring, sardines and anchories predominating. The total freshwater catch amounted to 123,949 tons in 1998.

Some 20% of the land area is forested, but exports of timber (mostly obeche, abura and mahogany) are relatively small. Nigeria's annual output of timber declined by 8% in the period 1982–84, and deforestation, particularly in the Niger delta area, remains a considerable problem. Following the removal of a ban on specific timber exports, timber production increased to 99m. cu m in 1988, and then to 100.1m. cu m in 1989. About 12% of the country's total land area is threatened by the encroaching Sahara desert in the north, and a National Committee on Arid Zone Afforestation has been established as part of the anti-desertification programme. In June 1989 it was announced that the government was to share the cost of a $135m. afforestation project with the World Bank. Nevertheless, more trees are felled for fuelwood than for any other use. Industrial roundwood removals in 1998 amounted to 9.4m. cu m, whereas 8.9m. cu m were felled for fuelwood. Fuelwood is still the main source of domestic energy, and accounts for more than 60% of commercial primary energy consumption.

Both the Buhari and Babangida governments made agricultural development and food self-sufficiency key components of their overall economic strategy. Agriculture, arguably the most successful element of the structural adjustment programme, exhibited sharp increases in food crop production and a rise in commodity exports. The increase in agricultural production was attributed to three policy initiatives: the devaluation of the naira, which promoted commodity exports and discouraged cheap food imports; the abolition of the state-controlled commodity boards and removal of restrictions on agricultural pricing; and the imposition of an import ban on wheat, maize and barley. Attention was focused on the smallholder farmer, who produces some 90% of food consumed in Nigeria.

Apart from maize, most of the corporate investment in agriculture since 1986 has centred on oil palm and cotton, reflecting the relative success of the vegetable oil and textile industries in the use of local raw materials. The Land Use Decree, introduced in 1978, stipulated that land be vested in the state governors, who would hold it in trust for all Nigerians. The government agreed to amend the Decree, in response to protests from smallholder farmers, who claimed that the Decree discriminated against them. In addition to the problem of land availability, the other key issues facing the agricultural sector are environmental degradation, inadequate storage facilities and transport, leading to massive post-harvest losses (assessed at 40% of total production in 1996), lack of research and training facilities for the transfer of new technologies, and the absence of credit facilities for smallholder farmers. Nigeria's resources are not fully exploited, and many parts of the country remain very poorly developed. Inadequate provision of economic infrastructure such as power, water supply, roads and telecommunications, especially in the rural areas, has proved an impediment to both agricultural and industrial investment. The 1997 budget included a ₦4,300m. allocation to the Family Economic Advancement Programme (FEAP), which aimed to allocate resources to enterprises in rural areas. The initiative envisaged the establishment of viable rural small-scale industries, which would be provided with locally-produced machinery and equipment to produce garri, palm-kernel oil, palm oil, other vegetable oils, pottery and garments.

PETROLEUM

Nigeria has more than 3,000m. metric tons of proven petroleum reserves, and experts believe that further exploration might double that amount. The first commercial discoveries of petroleum were made in 1956 in the Niger River delta region. Exports began in 1958, and production advanced rapidly, until output was disrupted by the outbreak of the 'Biafra' civil war in 1967. By the early 1970s the petroleum industry had become the dominant sector of the Nigerian economy and the major determinant of the country's economic growth. In 1986 the petroleum sector accounted for around 18% of GDP, more than 97% of total export earnings and over 70% of all government revenues. Nigeria's proven reserves were estimated at 2,126m. tons in December 1995. A five-year investment programme, initiated in 1991, aimed to increase petroleum output capacity to 2.5m. barrels per day (b/d). Output was estimated at 2.01m. b/d at December 1996. The 1997 federal budget was based on an output of 1.79m. b/d earning an average US $17 per barrel. By mid-1998, however, the international price of petroleum had declined to $13–$14 per barrel, the lowest level for 12 years; consequently, the 1999/2000 budget was based on a price of just $9 per barrel. In June 1999 the price per barrel stood at $14.72. The price increased to $32 per barrel by June 2000, creating expectations of relaxations of previous budgetary constraints (see below). Following disturbances at the ports of Bonny and Forcados, however, in July Royal Dutch Shell increased the international price of petroleum to a level of $19.9 for a barrel of Brent Blend (a close alternative to Nigeria's Bonny Light), owing to market perceptions that Nigeria would be unable to maintain supply levels. A member of the Organization of Petroleum Exporting Countries (OPEC), Nigeria accounted for 7.7% of the organization's petroleum production in 1996. In March 1998 it was decided that members of OPEC would agree to remove 1.24m. b/d from the international market in an effort to halt the decline in prices; in June they removed a further 1.36m. b/d from the market, for a total official supply reduction

of 2.6m. b/d. Since Libya restricted output in 1973, Nigeria has been Africa's leading petroleum-producing country. Being of low sulphur content and high quality, its petroleum is much in demand on the European market. Nigeria's two main types of petroleum are Bonny Light and Forcados.

Revenues from exports of petroleum, which are shared in decreasing proportions between federal, state and local governments, have largely determined the pace of Nigeria's economic development. Successive governments based their five-year plans on predicted earnings from petroleum. In the 1990s foreign exchange revenue from sales of petroleum has been virtually the sole means of meeting the country's import needs and debt-servicing commitments, and the size of these earnings varies widely from year to year. According to IMF estimates, earnings rose to $8,500m. in 1989, and to $10,600m. in 1990. By 1995 these earnings had fallen to $7,001m., and they had declined further, to $5,276m., by 1998.

Production costs for Nigerian petroleum are up to seven times as high as those in the Middle East, but the Nigerian product's low sulphur content places it at the upper end of OPEC's price scale. The Niger delta remains Nigeria's main petroleum-producing region, containing more than 200 oilfields, the largest of which is Forcados Yorki. The USA is the major market for Nigeria's petroleum, taking, on average, around one-half of all exports; in 1997 the USA imported 461,611 barrels of Nigerian crude petroleum, valued at US $6,100m. Spain, Germany, France, Portugal and the United Kingdom are also important customers.

In 1971 the state-owned Nigerian National Oil Corpn (NNOC) was formed to be a participant in the operations of the foreign petroleum companies. In 1977 the NNOC was merged with the ministry of petroleum resources to form the Nigerian National Petroleum Corpn (NNPC), which gradually increased its equity stake in all operating companies, except Ashland. In 1979 the NNPC nationalized BP's interests in Nigeria, in retaliation for BP's participation in an oil-swapping agreement which led indirectly to the shipment of Nigerian petroleum to South Africa. (In 1992 the government sold the nationalized BP interests to Shell, Elf-Aquitaine and other private enterprises.) Agreements governing the petroleum producing companies' terms of operation were not officially signed until 1984, after being effective for more than 10 years. The NNPC had a 60% interest in the operations of Agip-Phillips, Elf-Aquitaine, Gulf, Mobil, Texaco and Pan Ocean, and had an 80% share in Shell (which accounts for one-half of total production). In November 1984 the rules governing the operation of the equity contracts, under which foreign companies extract Nigerian petroleum, were revised in an attempt to increase production and exploration. Companies in partnership with the NNPC were permitted to extract more than their contracted amount of petroleum on the basis of a government-determined 'allowable' production rate. Additionally, companies could also buy, on equity terms, any of the petroleum that the NNPC was unable to sell, while reimbursing the NNPC for production costs. New 'incentive' agreements were signed with international petroleum companies in 1986, guaranteeing producers a profit margin of around US $2 per barrel. In July 1991 a new memorandum of understanding (MOU) between the NNPC and its foreign production partners was signed, which guaranteed minimum profit margins to foreign joint-venture operators, depending on their level of capital investment and cost efficiency. The MOU detailed a new five-year plan for exploration and production, with incentives for capital investment in the sector, and guaranteed a profit margin of $2.3 per barrel, on the condition that technical operating costs did not exceed $2.5 per barrel. The minimum guaranteed margin was to increase to $2.5 per barrel if capital investment exceeded $1.5 per barrel, with total operating costs at less than $3.5 per barrel. The MOU also provided bonuses for companies that increased their reserves by more than their annual production in any given year, thereby adding to net reserves. Also in 1991 the NNPC and the foreign petroleum companies signed joint-venture agreements for the new oilfields allocated by the government; these agreements defined procedures for making capital spending decisions, stipulated the foreign companies' obligations to train Nigerian nationals, and allowed the NNPC to become the operator of fields when it chose. In 1993 all major enterprises operating in Nigeria—Shell, Mobil, Chevron, Agip,

Texaco and Elf Aquitaine—initiated new development programmes, while BP and Statoil, the Norwegian state-owned petroleum company, signed a new agreement with the government. The petroleum industry suffered a decline in 1994, as a direct consequence of Nigeria's increasing political and economic instability. After government mismanagement of the NNPC's accounts, the company could no longer meet its financial obligations to the petrolum companies, and the majority of new drilling work was suspended. This did not at first affect ongoing production facilities, and petroleum output remained at almost 2m. b/d in the first half of 1994, but production began to decline after petroleum workers commenced long-term strike action in July. At the end of that month Shell reported that its production had declined by about one-third (the company's previous output level had been approximately 1m. b/d), while petroleum prices increased to more than $18 per barrel. Following the end of strike action in September, production quickly recovered to close to former levels, although the petroleum producing companies remained dissatisfied with the large amounts of money owed to them by the NNPC for past running costs and development work. Unrest continued in early 1997, when protesters occupied flow stations belonging to Shell Petroleum Development Co and held 127 Shell employees hostage. Operations at several stations were suspended, but were subsequently resumed. Increased output from the new offshore Ngo field and from Qua Ibo enabled Nigeria to increase its output level to 2.27m. b/d in late 1996. In mid-1995 the government indicated that continuing criticism from the British administration (see Recent History) would endanger Shell and BP interests in Nigeria. In 1996 the Nigerian government claimed that 150,000 barrels of petroleum were unaccounted for each day, and introduced a new inspection scheme, in addition to existing measures, which would be financed by a 1% levy on non-petroleum commodities and a 0.15% levy on petroleum exports. The principal petroleum enterprises immediately demanded that the levy be abolished. Nigeria is capable of maintaining output at a level of 2.5m. b/d. Elf Aquitaine's offshore Ofon field entered into production on 24 December 1997, and the Amenam field was scheduled to commence production in mid-2003, at a rate of 100,000 b/d. The US enterprise, Conoco, commenced production at its deep-water offshore Ukpokiti field in 1997; output had reached 20,000 b/d by January 1998.

In March 1988 the government announced that the NNPC was to be restructured by division into three sections, responsible for operations, for corporate services and for national petroleum investment management services. Eleven subsidiaries of the NNPC were to be established, each concentrating on a particular area, such as refining, development, engineering and petrochemicals. The marketing of petroleum was also reorganized in order to eliminate intermediate marketers. Under the new scheme, only the NNPC and local and foreign petroleum companies involved in production or exploration would be permitted to market petroleum. Investment in maintenance, capital equipment and exploration had fallen in recent years, owing to difficulties in funding. By virtue of its equity ownership in the various petroleum companies, the government has been responsible for about 75% of total investment in the industry.

In early 1993 the IMF increased pressure on the government to reduce subsidies on petroleum products into the domestic market, which were estimated to cost ₦63,000m. in 1992, and maintained the official petrol price at ₦0.70 per litre—one of the cheapest in the world. In August, despite initial reluctance (owing to concern that the measure would prompt renewed unrest), the government partially removed subsidies on domestic fuel, with the introduction of a new grade of petrol, at a cost of ₦7.50 per litre. Shortages of refined fuel were widespread in 1994, obliging the Nigerian government to import petrol products. It was reported that imports of refined fuel cost $800m. in 1995. Nevertheless, as a result of the unrest, a new fuel crisis occurred in April 1997, when shortages of refined petroleum products were widespread. The NNPC in March 1996 claimed that the two refineries at Port Harcourt and at Kaduna were fully operational, but in May 1999 maintenance work was continuing at both installations. The contract for the repair and refurbishments of the 125,000 b/d Warri refinery was finally awarded by the outgoing military government in the same month to a consortium of US,

Canadian and Dutch companies. In 1999 the official price for a litre of petrol was ₦11.0, but the black-market price was in excess of ₦100.0. Shortages throughout the country continued, and further large-scale imports of petrol, diesel fuel, kerosene and other refined petroleum products were required. The civilian Obasanjo government announced in May 2000 that, of the country's four refineries, only one, at Port Harcourt, was operating at more than 50% capacity. Another increase in official retail prices on 1 June 2000 brought the pump price per litre up by 50%, from ₦20 to ₦30 for petrol, from ₦19 to ₦29 for diesel, and from ₦17 to ₦27 for kerosene. Government subsidization of petroleum products for the domestic market reportedly amounted to $192m. in the first quarter of 2000 alone. Smuggling is a problem; despite discontent with the increase in price, in neighbouring countries petrol is sold for the equivalent of ₦45 per litre and higher.

Controversially, Nigeria has agreements with the governments of Chad and Benin, with negotiations in progress in mid-2000 for one with Niger, for these countries to sell Nigerian petroleum products at Nigerian prices, on condition that the products will not be sold beyond those countries' borders. Critics of the agreements argued that until the Nigerian government was able to provide an adequate supply of refined petroleum products for its own citizens, it should not place further demand on that supply by allowing non-Nigerians to compete for it.

In October 1996 it was announced that the government was to divest a major part of its average 57% share in the joint-venture petroleum partnerships with Shell, Chevron, Mobil, Texaco, Elf Aquitaine and Agip, and to enter into production-sharing arrangements instead. However, subsequent diplomatic disagreements with the USA in particular, prompted criticism over the prospect of foreign nationals owning Nigerian petroleum. In February 1997 the government announced that a committee would be set up to advise on the matter. The Deep Offshore and Inland Basin Production Sharing Contracts Decree was promulgated in March 1999, prompting a number of announcements concerning new investment in petroleum exploration and development. Shell proposed a five-year project, at an estimated cost of US $8,500m.; the enterprise planned to develop four major offshore oilfields, including the 350,000 b/d Bonga field and two large shallow-water offshore fields, which would enable Nigeria to increase petroleum output from just under 2m. b/d in February 1999 to 2.6m., and would generate $20,000m. over a 25-year period. In January 2000 Shell announced plans to drill a further two development wells and two sidetrack wells in its shallow-water Ima oilfield, near the Bonny terminal. The Ima field, discovered in 1994 and brought into production in 1996, had produced 11m. barrels by January 2000 from 10 wells and contained estimated reserves of 15–30m. barrels. The new wells were expected to double Ima's output by 6,000–8,000 b/d.

With increased participation from the private sector, greater emphasis is being placed on gas—both liquefied petroleum gas (LPG) and liquefied natural gas (LNG)—and on increasing the capacity of the country's petroleum refineries to enable the export of higher-value petroleum products (in addition to meeting the demands of the domestic market). Until the completion of the 60,000 b/d petroleum refinery at Port Harcourt in 1965, Nigeria exported its entire output of crude petroleum. A second refinery, with a capacity of 100,000 b/d (later expanded to 125,000 b/d), was constructed in 1978 at Warri, in Bendel State, and a third inland refinery, at Kaduna, was partly operational by 1981. The Kaduna refinery has a capacity of 100,000 b/d, and is divided into two units: one uses the light Nigerian crude, while the second unit, which was not finally commissioned until 1983, uses heavier imported crudes. Both units were out of action in 1998, but one resumed production in March 1999. The NNPC owns the Warri and Kaduna refineries, and has an 80% share in the original refinery at Port Harcourt. A fourth refinery was completed in March 1989 at Alesa Eleme (near Port Harcourt), thereby increasing Nigeria's installed refining capacity to 157,680 b/d. Nevertheless, in 2000 Nigeria continued to export most of its output as crude petroleum, and was obliged to import refined petroleum products to supply its own large domestic market.

Development of an integrated petrochemicals industry has been a main priority of successive governments. Construction of a number of processing units at the refineries in Warri and Kaduna was completed in 1987. The units use feedstock from the refineries to produce benzene, carbon black and polypropylene. The construction of a larger petrochemicals complex at Alesa-Eleme, at a projected cost of US $1,000m., was completed in 1996. By May 1999 it had generated 12,270m. in revenue from the sale of its products to the USA, the United Kingdom, the Netherlands, Egypt and Asia.

NATURAL GAS

Besides its petroleum resources, Nigeria possesses the largest deposits of natural gas in Africa. Proven reserves are assessed at more than 2,800,000m. cu m, most of which is located with petroleum deposits in and around the Niger delta. Probable gas reserves were estimated at a further 1,800,000m. cu m. Production in 1990 was estimated at 27,600m. cu m, of which 77% was flared. Of the gas that was consumed, some 75% was bought by the National Electric Power Authority (NEPA). In a bid to curtail the wasteful flaring of gas, the government issued a decree penalizing petroleum companies for this practice. Although the decree, which came into force in January 1985, affected only 69 of the 155 petroleum-producing fields, many of the large operators began to install gas re-injection facilities. Some 18,000m. cu m of gas was flared each year, at a market cost of over US $4,000m., according to petroleum companies; domestic consumption was estimated at just 3,000m. cu m per year. Utilization of gas increased substantially when the Warri associated gas project, under which 17m. cu m per day was piped from the Niger Delta to Igbin power station, near Lagos, came into operation in 1990. Nevertheless, the flaring of gas was a major source of contention between the Ogoni ethnic group and Shell (see Recent History). In 1996 the Shell Petroleum Development Co of Nigeria Limited awarded a £320m. contract for a new gas-processing plant at Soku in Rivers State. The plant was to enable Shell to flare less gas in the Niger Delta and was to supply the LNG plant, which was under construction at Bonny Island (see below). The plant at Soku, when completed, was to be capable of delivering 12.7m. cu m of gas per day.

Nigeria's most ambitious scheme to utilize flared gas was to construct a gas liquefaction plant, with a daily capacity of at least 45m. cu m, on the Bonny River. To implement the plan to produce LNG, the Bonny LNG consortium, comprising the NNPC (which held a 69% share), Phillips, Shell, BP, Agip and Elf Aquitaine, was formed in 1978. The project received an early boost in 1980, when a consortium of European gas distributors signed a 20-year agreement to buy 23m. cu m per day, starting in 1984. However, the viability of the project hinged on the sale of a further 23m. cu m per day to four US distributors. Negotiations with the US government over access broke down in 1980. Market uncertainties continued to surround the project, and, when the outline of the government's 1981–85 Development Plan deferred investment in the scheme until the late 1980s, the Bonny LNG consortium was dissolved. A scaled-down version of the flared gas project was revived by the Buhari military government in 1985. In 1988 the Babangida government considered a new US $2,000m. scheme to construct a pipeline from gas fields in eastern Nigeria to the LNG plant at Bonny. In May 1989 a joint-venture agreement was signed to implement the scheme. In March 1999 Elf Aquitaine confirmed that the expansion of the Bonny Island LNG plant was to proceed and that a long-awaited third train would be built. The first two trains were under construction, at a cost of $3,700m.; the first train entered production in September 1999, and the second in October. Spain's Enagas was to purchase 70% of the output. Construction of the $1,800m. third train was estimated to be 20% implemented as of 31 March 2000, with completion due by the end of 2002. The proposed construction of two more trains was to depend on market forces, pending the results of a study to be completed by the end of 2001. The entry into production of the third train would raise the plant's capacity from 7,400m. to 11,000m. cu m of gas per year. The scheme was to use gas associated with oilfields in the Niger Delta which at the time was being flared, and was also to produce 1m. tons of LPG

(butane and propane). The Nigerian Liquefied Natural Gas Co is owned 49% by the NNPC, 25.6% by Shell Gas Nigeria, 15% by Elf Aquitaine Gaz's affiliate, Cleag Ltd, and 10.4% by Italy's Agip International.

Meanwhile, Chevron began developing the $1,000m. Escravos facility to manufacture liquid fuels from natural gas. This scheme would have the dual advantage of supplying fuel to the region and reducing the wasteful flaring of natural gas. Phase One of this project entered into production in 1997, supplying primarily the domestic Nigerian market, but also producing some liquefied petroleum gas for export; a shipment of 30,000 metric tons, valued at $4.5m., was exported to the USA in September 1997. In late 1997 Escravos was producing 130m. cu ft of dry gas, more than 8,000 barrels of liquefied petroleum gas and natural-gas liquids, and 2,000 barrels of condensate per day. In April 1998 South Africa's Sasol joined forces with Chevron for a feasibility study to assess the suitability of Sasol's gas-to-liquids (GTL) technology at Escravos, and in June 1999 Sasol and Chevron agreed to proceed with Phase Two of the Escravos scheme. The output of Phase Two, due to enter into production by the end of 2000, is allocated for regional distribution via the West African Gas Pipeline (WAGP). Nigeria, Benin, Togo and Ghana signed a memorandum of understanding in respect of the WAGP in early August 1999, and later that month a consortium comprising Chevron and Shell, led by Chevron, signed a joint-venture agreement with the national petroleum companies of the four signatory countries. The $420m., 620-mile pipeline is to begin at Nigeria's Escravos and then run westward along the Atlantic coast, supplying all four countries en route and ending in Ghana. A second phase was due to come on stream in 1999. The NNPC in 1996 acquired a new route for the gas-distribution pipeline linking with the aluminium smelter plant in Akwa Ibom State. There were also plans by the NNPC to use flared gas to fuel an export-orientated $400m. methanol plant, with a daily output of 2,000–2,500 tons. Discussions were held between the NNPC, Penspen, a UK company, and Mannesman, a German company, on a joint-venture agreement for the project.

Other schemes which are aimed at utilizing the country's gas reserves include the National Fertilizer Company gas-fed fertilizer plant (commissioned in April 1987) at Onne, the Warri refinery extension and the Delta steel plant at Aladja. Gas is also planned to be used as a feedstock for the second phase of the NNPC chemicals complex near Port Harcourt. The NNPC agreed to a price rise of 269% (from ₦1.52 to ₦5.24 per 1,000 cu ft) in April 1989. A new comprehensive gas development policy, offering incentives for companies investing in gas production, distribution and consumption, was released by the NNPC in 1990. The policy provisions also supported the commercialization of LNG production for export and for domestic consumption, the establishment of gas companies distributing to domestic and industrial consumers, and viable projects, aimed at substituting gas for existing fuels.

COAL AND OTHER MINERALS

Nigeria possesses substantial deposits of lignite, but the country has yet to exploit their full potential. Deposits of bitumen near Akure were developed under the government's Bitumen Implementation Project, and the first deliveries of crude bitumen were due to commence in 1999. Coal is mined by the Nigerian Coal Corpn (NCC), and is used mainly by the railway, by traditional metal industries and for the generation of electricity. Coal production declined from a peak of 940,000 metric tons in 1958 to 144,000 tons in 1986, and to 86,700 tons in 1992. The 1996 budget allocated ₦211m. to the NCC for the completion of a rehabilitation programme. There are long-term plans to exploit the Lafia/Obi coal deposits for use at the Ajaokuta steel complex. Reserves are estimated at more than 270m. tons. The Obasanjo government announced plans to revitalize Nigeria's mineral resources other than petroleum, in an attempt to diversify the country's export base. In March 2000 the minister of state for solid minerals development pledged to revive the coal sector, and stated that the Nigeria Coal Corpn had been allowed by previous governments to deteriorate to the point that it was operating with virtually no revenue base, while depending purely on loans from the federal government for the payment of salaries and maintenance. *Nigerian Weekly* reported that initial exports of 200,000 tons of coal in the first quarter of 2000 were expected to earn ₦144m.

Nigeria's output of tin concentrates has been in decline since the late 1960s, and these exports have reflected the depressed conditions in world tin prices since the late 1980s. Production increased from 208,000 metric tons in 1994 to 357,000 tons in 1995, but then declined to 150,000 tons in 1996. The country has two tin smelters, with a combined capacity well in excess of total ore production. Columbite is mined near Jos, but output has fallen steadily since the mid-1970s, to 47 tons in 1989. The Nigerian Mining Corpn was allocated ₦211.5m. in the 1996 budget to co-operate with the private sector in the development of Nigeria's deposits of bentonite, gypsum (in Bauchi State), kaolin (in Plateau State), rock salt, barytes (at three locations in Nasarawa State), phosphates, talc, manganese, copper, gold and tin. In March 2000 the Obasanjo government reconfirmed its commitment to revitalize the mining for export of barytes, kaolin, bitumen and gold. Nigeria also mines modest amounts of gemstones.

Extensive deposits of iron ore have been discovered in Itakpe, Ajabanoko and Shokoshoko—all in Kwara State. Mining operations at Itakpe started in 1984, with the long-term aim of supplying most of the requirements of the Ajaokuta and Delta steel complexes. More than 180,000 metric tons of iron ore had been mined by early 1986. The construction of a US $250m. beneficiation plant at Itakpe began in December 1992; the plant was projected to process 5m. tons of iron ore into a concentrated form for the Ajaokuta steel complex. In 1995 work was completed on the establishment of a river port at Ajaokuta, which was to enable the transportation of iron ore for the steel complex. An aluminium smelter at Ikot Abasi came on stream in 1991, with an installed capacity of 90,000 tons per year, but in its first seven years of operation it produced only 36,000 tons of aluminium ingots.

MANUFACTURING AND CONSTRUCTION

Industrial development has mainly taken the form of import substitution of consumer goods, although, during the 1970s, greater emphasis was placed on the production of capital goods and on assembly industries. In 1983 textiles, beverages, cigarettes, soaps and detergents together accounted for 60% of total manufacturing output. Investment in manufacturing has come mostly from the government and from foreign multinational companies. Private-sector investment in manufacturing was small, and was centred on industries which were shielded from competition by import barriers.

Manufacturing has traditionally been heavily reliant on imported raw materials and components. Efforts to lessen that reliance have been largely unsuccessful. According to the Manufacturers' Assoc of Nigeria (MAN), up to 60% of all the raw materials that local industry used in 1985 were imported. Manufacturing was thus extremely vulnerable to disruption if imports were restricted, as they were from 1980 onwards. Imports of raw materials declined, on average, by 10% per year over the period 1982–85. The combination of import restrictions, overpricing and industrial disputes favoured cheaper foreign goods and encouraged smuggling and black-marketeering. Import licensing was abolished in September 1986, in tandem with the introduction of the SFEM, and tariffs were reduced. However, the resultant sharp devaluation of the naira increased import costs and hence production costs. A new tariff structure, introduced in 1988, aimed to protect local industries from external competition, while encouraging domestic competition to stimulate efficiency. Nevertheless, a number of non-profitable state-owned industries placed a huge burden on government finances, and were to be targeted for privatization or liquidation under new reforms.

Total production from the manufacturing sector declined by more than one-third between 1982 and 1985, while the level of capital expenditure fell by over 50%. The most severely affected branches of the sector were: commercial vehicles, chemicals, metals, textiles, sugar, plastics and paper. Manufacturing accounted for 8% of total GDP in 1980, but for only 5% of the total in 1995, according to the World Bank. Manufacturers asserted that inadequate development funds and the government's stringent fiscal policy had constrained the sector,

which was estimated to be operating at only 25% of its capacity in 1987. Capacity utilization in the manufacturing sector was still only 29.4% in the first half of 1997, declining to 27.8% in the first half of 1998. After the return to civilian rule, a slight improvement was recorded, but energy shortages, the high cost of credit and low purchasing power in the domestic market subsequently continued to constrain the sector, and capacity utilization in the second half of 1999 was only 3.1%.

In the 1980s many manufacturers placed their hopes on the success of the government-backed local sourcing programme, under which all existing industries were actively encouraged to utilize more local raw materials. Various tax and investment incentives were introduced, and a National Raw Materials Development Council and a Raw Materials Data Bank were established. A new tariff structure, to benefit manufacturing based on local resources, was drawn up, although its viability was seriously constrained by the poor state of the country's infrastructure and by the high cost of local materials and parts. Total manufacturing output was estimated at US $2,971m. in 1994. In 1996 growth of manufacturing output was estimated at 0.7%, and the average rate of industrial capacity utilization was 32.5% (compared with 29.3% in 1995). Despite successive governments' efforts to encourage industrial dispersal, most manufacturing plants are still based in Lagos State. The Agbara industrial estate, in Ogun State, has attracted some industries away from Lagos, although most of the heavily import-based companies are reluctant to move, owing to the fact that around 70% of all industrial materials are still handled at ports in Lagos State.

The creation of an integrated iron and steel industry has been a high priority of successive development plans. In January 1982 the Delta steel complex at Aladja, in Bendel State, was formally opened. The complex, which has a capacity of 1m. metric tons per year and operates the direct reduction system, supplies billets and wire rods to three steel-rolling mills at Oshogbo, Katsina and Jos. Each of the three mills has an initial annual capacity of 210,000 tons of steel products. The Ajaokuta Steel Co opened the first light section mill in 1983, and the rolling mill for the production of steel wire rods in 1984, but output was sporadic, owing to shortages of imported billets and to difficulties in obtaining supplies from the Delta complex. In 1996 Nigeria's steel companies were reported to be operating at just 10% of their installed capacity, owing to mismanagement and lack of foreign exchange. Delta Steel asked the civilian Obasanjo government for a cash investment in 1999, but the 2000 budget allocated less than one-fifth of the requested amount. Nigeria's annual steel requirements reached 6m. tons by 1990; however, Nigeria's total steel production in 1996 amounted to just 20,000 tons. There were plans at least to double the capacity of the first stage of the Ajaokuta complex. Construction costs, originally estimated at US $1,400m., exceeded $3,000m. at the end of 1989, and had increased to $8,000m. by 1997. A 20-year contract with a Russian firm, Tyazhpromexport, for the plant equipment and technology, which had been criticized by the World Bank, was terminated in December 1996. However, the 1997 federal budget allocated ₦6,600m. for the completion of the project, confirming the government's intention to continue with the Ajaokuta project. In early 1992 a second stage of the project was initiated. The Iwopin Paper Mill and the rehabilitation of damaged sections of Jebba Paper Mill were completed in 1995, but a number of projects remained unfinished in 1986, as a result of financial difficulties. The Aluminium Smelter Co of Nigeria (ALSCON) entered into production in 1997 in Akwa Ibom State. With an installed capacity of 193,000 tons per annum, ALSCON exported about 24,000 tons of aluminium per year in 1998. ALSCON (of which 70% was owned by the Nigerian government and 30% by German and American interests) was fuelled by gas from Shell's plants at Alakiri and Obigbo North, and, owing in part to an inadequate supply of gas, failed to ever use more than one-fifth of its capacity. In June 1999 the project suspended operations.

Manufacturers using raw materials from local sources were at a strong advantage after the economic reforms of 1986. By 1990 locally sourced operations achieved relatively high levels of capacity utilization: tyres (64%), leather products (63%), beer and stout (59%), textiles (54%) and industrial chemicals

(49%). One of the most successful industrial sub-sector projects was the nitrogenous fertilizer plant at Onne, owned by the National Fertilizer Corpn of Nigeria (NAFCON), which was established in 1987; at full capacity it produced 400,000 metric tons per year of urea and 300,000 tons per year of compound fertilizer. Overall capacity utilization increased from an estimated 33% in 1989 to more than 60% in 1992. The NAFCON plant was temporarily closed in March 1996 to allow major maintenance work, and it was reported that the plant was deteriorating, not only from age but also as a result of the pressure to produce quantities beyond its design capacity.

The assembly of motor vehicles in Nigeria is dominated by Peugeot in passenger cars, and by Mercedes in commercial vehicles. Local demand remains well above supply, but the cost of components and the difficulties in obtaining import licences have reduced output. Government plans to transfer Nigeria's vehicle-assembly plants to private ownership were suspended in early 1993, since it was believed that the prevailing economic recession would reduce their value.

Various government programmes that were aimed at national self-sufficiency in food allowed for the steady growth of agro-business during the 1970s. Sugar refining, textiles, brewing, rubber, fertilizers, edible oils, footwear, paper, cigarettes and general food-processing industries were among the most significant. However, the expansion and modernization of plants was cut short by the onset of economic recession in 1982. The large brewing industry has continued to flourish, although in 1987 it suffered from a ban on imports of malted barley, imposed with the aim of stimulating local barley production. Funding was arranged in 1995 to increase the working capital of the Nigeria Sugar Corpn and a number of other enterprises. In 1988 Firestone opened a new tyre-manufacturing plant in Bendel State, bringing the number of tyre manufacturers in Nigeria to three. With enlarged capacity at Dunlop Nigeria's plant in Lagos, it was estimated that local manufacturers would be able to meet about 60% of domestic demand.

Activity in the construction sector has declined in recent years. Output fell by 50% in value from 1981 to 1985. The construction sector suffered from serious constraints on growth, following the introduction of the structural adjustment programme in 1986 and further reductions in public sector projects. The construction of a federal capital at Abuja was formally completed in 1991. (However, the expansion of the private sector at Abuja subsequently proved to be slow.) The creation of nine new states in 1991 necessitated several new infrastructure projects, and ongoing investment in the energy sector of some $1,000m. a year has also benefited the sector. In 1999 the decision to construct the WAGP (see above) created expectations of new jobs in the sector. However, road construction, and the rehabilitation of railways, airports and seaports virtually ceased in the late 1980s.

In March 1988 changes were made to regulations concerning foreign investment in Nigeria. The 1972 Nigerian Enterprises Promotion Decree, which was strengthened and extended in 1977, involved three categories of business. The first (Schedule I) had to be 100% Nigerian-owned and covered more than 50 enterprises, including printing, rice-milling, advertising, road haulage, bus services, taxis and tyre retreading. The second category (Schedule II) had to be 60%-owned by Nigerian interests and included breweries, department stores and supermarkets, wholesale distribution, banking, insurance, construction and furniture manufacture. All other enterprises, including food-processing (Schedule III), had to be 40% Nigerian-held. By the mid-1980s the decree was being selectively relaxed in order to encourage foreign private investment in neglected areas, such as large-scale agribusiness and manufacturing based on local resources. From March 1988 foreign investors were allowed to increase their holdings in Schedule I enterprises to 20%, and in Schedule III enterprises to 80%. Schedule II enterprises were to be allowed to enter joint ventures with foreign companies. Under a 1989 decree, foreign companies are permitted to own 100% of any new venture, except for enterprises in banking, oil prospecting, insurance and mining. The government in February 1996 stated its intention of encouraging private-sector competition in sectors, such as power and telecommunications, previously monopolized by NEPA and NITEL, and pledged that, 'apart from exceptional circumstances', it would not fund these enterprises after December 1996. In 2000, however, their privatization was yet to be effected. The largest government agency in industrial development is the Nigerian Industrial Development Bank, which, in the 1990s, has centred its activities on directing multilateral funding into private-sector projects in intermediate and capital goods manufacturing, food processing and other agriculture-related industries. Legislation, introduced in 1995, was aimed at stimulating foreign investment by guaranteeing the unconditional transferability of funds through an authorized dealer in freely convertible currency for debt-service payments, dividends and proceeds of sales of assets, although new investments were still required to be processed through the Nigeria Stock Exchange and new companies still had to receive the approval of the Investment Promotion Commission. A new Export Processing Zone (EPZ) at Calabar in Cross River State aimed to attract investors in 14 sectors, including electrical products, electronics, textiles, wood, food-processing, pharmaceuticals, cosmetics, rubber and plastics. By mid-1997 ₦2,500m. had been spent on the EPZ at Calabar, including the construction of an airport and improvements to the port, and in mid-1999 construction was reported to be near completion. A minimum capital investment of US $500,000 was required for companies to be established in the zone. Plans for another EPZ at Port Harcourt, in Rivers State, were underway. In 1997 the Abacha government announced that henceforth all contracts entered into in Nigeria were to be denominated in naira alone, whereas previously some contracts had been denominated both in foreign currency for the offshore portions and in naira for the onshore components.

POWER

Nigeria had 6,040 MW of installed electricity-generating capacity in June 2000; therefore, if power stations were able to operate at full capacity, they would be able to meet the national demand, assessed at about 5,200 MW. Owing to 'system constraints', however, power installations were operating at only about 25% of their capacities, and consequently were able to meet less than 1,600 MW of the national power requirement. The principal supplier of electricity in Nigeria is the state-owned NEPA, which was formed in 1973 by the merger of the Niger Dams Authority and the Electricity Corpn of Nigeria. Although NEPA was allocated for privatization in the 1990s, it remained government-owned in 2000, and amid yet another series of power blackouts and 'load shedding' in the first half of 2000, the Obasanjo government suspended NEPA's management and formed a commission to resolve the crisis. Power-generation facilities include the 1,320-MW Chinese-built thermal power station at Egbin, in Lagos State (fuelled with natural gas piped from the Escravos field, but with most of its units out of action in 1998); the Kainji hydroelectric installation (capacity 760 MW, using eight turbines, all of which were inoperative in 1998); the gas- and oil-fuelled thermal installations at Afam, in Rivers State (742 MW, using 18 units, several of which were not producing in 1998) and at Sapele, in Delta State (696 MW); and the coal-fuelled thermal plant on the Oji River (150 MW). The oil-fuelled power stations were reported to be operating at just 32% of capacity in November 1998. The national grid in theory supplied electricity to 43% of all Nigerians in 1999, and NEPA has set a target of bringing mains electricity to 85% of the population by 2010 (which would require a large capital investment to fund 16 proposed new power plants and 14,500 km of new transmission lines, as well as ancillary services). Plans are under consideration for the construction of new installations at Onitsha, Kaduna, Makurdi, Oron, Katsina and Mambilla. In practice, however, it was estimated that to rehabilitate the country's thermal stations would require ₦45,000m., while the 1998 budget allocated ₦3,000m. for all electricity rehabilitation. While electricity generation was once viewed as a 'strategic' industry where foreigners were not welcome, the civilian Obasanjo government in 1999 invited overseas investment, particularly on 'build, own and operate' terms, known as BOO. Examples of proposed BOO projects were a 350-MW gas-fuelled power station in River State and a power plant in Ondo State, both in the negotiation stage with US companies in 2000.

The country's manufacturers lost nearly two-thirds of working hours from power cuts during 1997, and official sources cited unreliable electricity supplies as one of the principal factors impeding growth in the manufacturing sector. Total electricity generated in the late 1980s was about 10,000m. kWh per year, of which about 50% was supplied by hydroelectric plants; in 1995 total electricity generated was 14,810m. kWh.

TRANSPORT

In comparison with most other west African states, Nigeria has a well-developed transport system. However, congestion, lack of maintenance, and poor planning have resulted in services that are unreliable and often dangerous. The rehabilitation of the transport infrastructure formed a major element of the three-year rolling Investment Plan, announced in January 1990, and the civilian Obasanjo in 1999 ordered extensive port reforms.

Approximately 95% of all traffic in goods and passengers travel by road, most of it to and from the major ports. In 1996 the road network totalled 193,198 km., including 2,044 km of motorways, 30,054 km of main roads and 30,500 km of secondary roads; some 37,000 km were paved. In the 1980s the government's main concern was to repair existing roads, rather than to build new ones. Road safety standards in Nigeria are virtually non-existent, and driving licences are distributed indiscriminately. On average, around 30,000 accidents are reported each year, with the loss of over 8,000 lives. In 1995 about 46,000 passenger cars and 7,000 commercial vehicles were registered in Nigeria.

The railway network covers 3,505 km. The two main narrow-gauge lines run from Lagos to Nguru and from Port Harcourt to Kaura Namoda, with extensions from Kafanchan, through Jos, to Maiduguri, and from Minna to Baro. A new 52-km railway line for iron ore traffic has been constructed between the Ajaokuta steel complex and Itakpe. Despite medium-term expansion plans, the Nigerian Railway Corpn (NRC) reduced services and jobs in 1989; this led to a series of strikes and further operating difficulties. A programme to rehabilitate the railway network, at a projected cost of ₦17,000m., was announced in 1993. In 1997 the China Civil Engineering Co-operative Corpn was under contract to rehabilitate Nigeria's railway system, with the provision of technology, locomotives and 70 passenger carriages, which were to be built by China's Sifang Rolling Stock Plant. Nigeria's railway network accounted for 161m. passenger-km and 108,000 ton-km in 1995.

There are two international airports, at Ikeja (Lagos) and Kano, and 11 domestic airports. A new airport at Abuja under construction in the late 1990s was to have 10 terminals, three of which were to handle international traffic, while the other seven were to serve the domestic market. Murtala Muhammad International Airport in Lagos received new cargo-handling equipment, valued at US $4m., in May 2000. Domestic air fares increased by 25% in that month, reflecting the higher cost of aviation fuel. The parastatal Nigeria Airways' domestic monopoly was ended in the early 1980s, and several private charter airlines commenced operations. International traffic is dominated by foreign airlines. Successive military governments put increasing pressure on Nigeria Airways to improve its standard of service and to reduce its costs, but the carrier continued to incur substantial financial losses. Owing to Nigeria Airways' difficulties, it was announced that private airlines would be allowed to offer international services if they satisfied safety requirements. In early 1993 the Babangida government entered negotiations to sell some 40% of its equity in Nigeria Airways to a foreign airline; control of international services was to be transferred to the private sector, while domestic services were to remain state-owned. The number of passengers on domestic flights declined to 556,000 in 1991 (compared with 621,000 in 1990), while the number of passengers on international routes increased to 187,000 (compared with 160,000 in 1990); 548,000 airline passengers were carried on domestic routes in 1995. In April 1996 only 28 of the 85 aircraft intended for use on

domestic routes in the country were operative. Sanctions forced Nigeria Airways to cease operating its New York–Lagos route in 1993, and in 1997 the carrier closed its New York office. In March 1997 the government announced a 4.0% increase in domestic air fares; in June 2000 the civilian government introduced price increases of 25% on domestic routes.

Nigeria's principal seaports for general cargo are Apapa, Tin Can Island (both of which serve Lagos), Port Harcourt, Warri, Sapele and Calabar. The main ports for petroleum shipments are Bonny and Burutu. After steadily declining since 1982, port utilization increased in the early 1990s, as a result of the rise in import and export volumes. In 1992 a report released by the West African Shipowners Operations Committee indicated that Nigeria's ports charged disproportionately high rates to shipping lines (some 230% above the average rate for west Africa), and that their turnaround times were longer, owing to poor maintenance of equipment. In the budget for 2000 extensive reforms to Nigeria's port procedures were envisaged. The mandatory pre-shipment inspection of all imports, and the Professional Import Duty Administration system, introduced in 1996, were abolished. The state-owned Nigerian National Shipping Line handled only 3.3% of non-petroleum shipments (totalling 10.2m. metric tons) in 1991 and went into liquidation. Its fixed assets and its seven general cargo vessels were to be sold in 1996 to settle its debts and those of a newly-acquired 6,800-ton vessel. A new national shipping line, the Nigeria Unity Line (NUL), was created, to operate services between Europe and Nigeria. Its initial destination in Europe was Antwerp, in Belgium, but Tilbury, in London, and one French port were to be added, as well as West African ports, such as Abidjan and Dakar. Nigeria's commercial fleet comprised 479,000 gross registered tons in 1995. A ₦329.9m. dredging of the Rivers Niger and Benue was completed in 1997.

TRADE

Nigeria, as a petroleum exporter, traditionally operates a visible trade surplus. Export revenue fluctuates according to the international price of petroleum; the volume of exports depends more on quota arrangements than on technical capacity, since Nigeria has the capacity to produce significantly more crude petroleum than it exports at present (see above). Visible exports increased by 6.3% from US $15,903m. in 1997 to $16,900m. in 1998, while imports increased by 14.4% from $6,732m. in 1997 to $7,700m. in 1998. The visible trade surplus increased marginally, from $9,171m. in 1997 to $9,200m. in 1998, but then declined sharply to $4,300m. in 1999. Heavy deficits on the services, other income and capital accounts resulted in the 1999 current account moving into sharp deficit, at $2,617.3m. A marked deterioration in the overall balance of payments occurred when, following a $1,728m. surplus in the first half of 1998, a $734.5m. deficit in the first half of 1999 was registered. Foreign-exchange reserves fell from $7,100m. at the end of 1998 to $4,778m. at 30 June 1999. Only an upturn in the international petroleum price halted the decline, resulting in an increase in external resrves to $5,327m. at 31 December 1999, enough to cover about eight months of visible imports or about five months of imports of goods and services.

Following the introduction, in September 1986, of the SFEM, foreign exchange for trade was made available by the central bank at weekly auctions. This initially resulted in an effective 60% devaluation of the naira. However, as the auction mechanism of the SFEM removed the need for import controls, the licensing of imports was abolished. At the same time the government introduced further measures, which abolished the 30% import levy, reduced import duties, reformed the tariff structure and reduced the list of prohibited imports. The devaluation of the naira, through the currency auction system introduced in 1986, was accompanied by a series of trade liberalization measures, designed to expand the export base. In July 1987 the military government terminated the SFEM, merging the first- and second-tier exchange rates but retaining the auction mechanism, whereby a unitary rate would be determined by fortnightly auctions of available foreign exchange, conducted by the CBN. Under the new arrangement, the naira initially fell by 6.3% against the US dollar, to ₦3.95 = US $1, and reached ₦4.61 = US $1 in May 1988. It was expected that the rate would continue to weaken in the short term, unless the government substantially increased its official funding of the market. In January 1989 the Interbank Foreign Exchange Market (IFEM) was established, in accordance with IMF recommendations, to provide a unified exchange rate for the naira, to be fixed on a daily basis. Exchange rate policy in 1992 and 1993 vacillated between a return to the auction mechanism (which had previously been suspended) and a more managed system. In January 1994 the Abacha government abandoned the auction system, replacing it with occasional allocations of foreign exchange to banks at a fixed rate of ₦22.0 = US $1. The autonomous market for foreign exchange, which had stimulated exports of non-petroleum commodities, was abolished and all foreign exchange entering the country was to be surrendered to the CBN. These policies were again reversed in 1995, with the introduction of the Autonomous Foreign Exchange Market (AFEM). In June 1996 a dual exchange rate was in operation, with the official rate established by the government at a fixed ₦22.0 = US$1 and the market rate allowed to fluctuate and amounting to ₦85.0 = US $1. Although the Abacha government acknowledged the long-term aim of unifying the two rates, it was emphasized in February 1997 that it would continue to maintain a dual exchange-rate system. During 1996 the official exchange rate continued to be fixed at ₦22.0 = US $1, while the market rate remained stable at about ₦80.0 = US $1. In the first half of 1998 the official rate was ₦80.0 = US $1, and the market rate was about ₦320.0 = US $1. In early May 1999 the naira depreciated by 5.1%, but, following the transition to civilian rule later that month, it remained stable, and by June the currency's official exchange rate was ₦94.4 = US $1. In mid-2000 the rate stood at ₦96.63 = US $1. The federal government abolished the dual exchange rate on 1 Janaury 1999 in favour of the interbank foreign exchange market (IFEM).

The principal exports in 1998 were crude petroleum and other petroleum products, cocoa, rubber and wood. The principal imports in that year were refined petroleum products, food, machinery and manufactured goods.

In 1993 Nigeria's principal source of imports was Germany (16.2%); other major suppliers were the United Kingdom, the USA and France. The principal market for exports (45.3%) in that year was the USA; other significant purchasers were Spain, the Netherlands and Italy.

DEBT

Following the sharp rise in government revenues from petroleum and the launching of several large-scale capital-intensive projects during the late 1970s, external borrowing increased dramatically. Although state borrowing was severely restricted during the 1980s and the level of federal government borrowing was reduced, the external debt rose to ₦12,000m. by late 1983. More than one-half of the outstanding debt consisted of medium-term loans from the international capital market at 'floating' interest rates, most of which were incurred during the late 1970s. The net result was a heavy concentration of maturity dates at a time when real interest rates were high and when Nigeria's earnings of foreign currency were declining. Despite the successful refinancing of some US $2,000m. of the trade debt and of $6,000m. of the short-term debt during the course of 1984, Nigeria's total external loan commitments in October 1985 amounted to ₦21,000m., of which ₦3,146m. was in the form of 'open-account' uninsured trade debts. In 1986 debt-servicing alone was expected to cost $3,400m. With the decline in earnings of foreign exchange from petroleum exports, the debt-servicing ratio would have risen to about 47% of total exports, well above the 30% level that the government had set as its target.

From April 1986 Nigeria obtained successive 90-day moratoria on repayments of debt principal to commercial creditors, but it became clear that a rescheduling would be needed. However, the Babangida government declared that it would not seek a loan from the IMF, which was a precondition of rescheduling by the Paris and London 'Clubs' (comprising Western governments and commercial bank creditors respectively). A further problem arose when Nigeria defaulted on the first repayments of debt principal totalling US $1,500m.,

resulting from promissory notes issued for pre-1984 short-term trade debts. However, a compromise with the IMF was reached, as part of the government's structural adjustment plan, whereby Nigeria agreed to accept 'enhanced surveillance' by the IMF. In November 1986 Nigeria reached agreement with its commercial bank creditors on the rescheduling of $1,500m. of medium-term debts and $2,000m. of arrears on letters of credit, and on the provision of a new commercial loan of $320m. In December the 'Paris Club' of creditor governments agreed to a 10-year rescheduling of medium- and long-term debts, accumulated before the end of 1983, and to a four-year rescheduling of short-term debts accumulated since that date; the amount rescheduled was reported to total $7,500m.

In November 1987, following protracted negotiations, Nigeria reached an agreement with its commercial bank creditors on the rescheduling of US $1,550m. of medium-term debts falling due in 1986–87, and $2,350m. of arrears on letters of credit. A new commercial loan of $320m., to be disbursed in instalments from February 1988, was also agreed but was not implemented, owing to the government's failure to secure a renewal of the IMF endorsement of its economic strategy in January 1988. In the same month foreign exporters agreed to reschedule (over 22 years) repayments on $4,000m. of promissory notes representing a portion of the trade debts incurred since 1984 (estimated by creditors to total $9,800m.). In 1988 Nigeria's total debt was estimated at $29,000m. In September another agreement was reached with the creditor banks, to reschedule $5,200m. of debt falling due between January 1988 and December 1991. Repayment of $2,700m. of medium-term debt was to be extended over 20 years, and repayment of $2,500m. in letters of credit over 12 years, with repayment to begin after a three-year period of grace. Both this agreement and the disbursement of loans by various bilateral donors and the World Bank were dependent on Nigeria's gaining approval for its recovery programme from the IMF. This took place in January 1989, and the rescheduling agreement was signed in London in March. During 1986 the World Bank increased its lending to Nigeria to more than $800m., including a major loan of $452m., approved in October. Support from the IMF and World Bank for the reform programme continued in 1987, but was suspended in 1988, following differences of opinion over policy and performance. New adjustment credits were approved by the World Bank in 1989 and 1990, but ceased entirely in 1991, after it emerged that the Babangida government could not account for petroleum revenue amounting to about $2,500m. that Nigeria should have earned during the Gulf War. The World Bank and the IMF were also discouraged by the government's continuing failure to control budgetary spending and its reluctance to raise domestic fuel prices to cover the costs of refining and distribution.

The size of Nigeria's external debt continued to increase in the late 1980s; in 1990 total foreign debt was US $34,089m. and the debt-servicing ratio as a percentage of goods and services was estimated at 34%. According to government estimates, debt-servicing was expected to average $4,200m. a year—about one-third of projected export revenue—until 1997, which implies a financing gap of some $2,500m. over that period. These projections, and the limitations on economic growth and investment that they imply, formed the basis of the Nigerian claim for a 30-year rescheduling of its commercial debt. At the end of 1991 Nigeria's total foreign debt was $34,497m., compared with $2,060m. at the end of 1984. Total external debt declined to $32,531m. by the end of 1993, of which $28,237m. was long-term public debt. In that year the cost of debt-servicing was equivalent to 29.4% of the value of exports of goods and services. Total external debt amounted to $33,485m. at the end of 1994, with a debt-servicing ratio of 18.5% of the value of exports of goods and services. At the end of 1995 Nigeria's total debt was estimated at $32,585m., of which 66.5% was owed to the 'Paris Club', 13.5% to other multilateral donors, 9.7% on promissory notes and 6.3% to the 'London Club'. Debt-servicing arrears for 1995 amounted to US $1,124m. The Nigerian government allocated $2,000m. for external debt-servicing payments in the 1997 budget (the same level of debt-servicing that it had paid in each of the preceding six years). In February 1997 the Abacha government declared that it had succeeded in reducing external debt to $28,060m. at the end of 1996 without further debt rescheduling. The reduction, it was claimed, was achieved primarily through the Debt Conversion Programme, in which Nigeria repurchased some of its debt stock from third parties; Abacha was later (posthumously) to attract severe criticism over his alleged role in this arrangement. In early May 1999, during the final period of the transitional Abubakar military regime, an auction summary of the Debt Conversion Programme was published which indicated that, over the 10-year duration of the programme, 406 participants had successfully redeemed their debts. Of these, 295 reportedly invested the proceeds in the Nigerian economy, including 164 in manufacturing, 67 in agriculture, 23 in construction, and others in such sectors as hotels, tourism projects, mining exploration and financial services. Nevertheless, debt-servicing payments due in 1997 were $4,980m., and, with accumulated arrears from 1996 and earlier included, Nigeria's total debt-servicing bill in 1997 was estimated at $16,104m. The federal government in April 1997 denied claims by external creditors that Nigeria's debt totalled $48,000m., rather than $28,060m; the World Bank estimated the total at $31,407m. Debt-servicing payments were equivalent to 40% of exports in the first half of 1999, and in 2000 the Obasanjo government was negotiating with the Paris Club regarding debt-rescheduling.

Nigerian proposals to convert commercial debt into 30-year bonds, serviced at a 3% interest rate, were discussed at a series of meetings between creditor bank representatives and Nigerian finance officials in 1990. Negotiations, led by the minister of finance, Olu Falae, were suspended in August, when Falae was replaced by Alhaji Abubakar Alhaji. A new accord was reached with the IMF in January 1991, which facilitated the conclusion of negotiations to reschedule the commercial and official debt. The rescheduling of Nigeria's $5,800m. bank debt allowed the government to repurchase as much as 60% of the debt, while the banks were given the option of exchanging the remainder for 30-year bonds at a 6.25% interest rate. The 'Paris Club' agreed to reschedule all development and aid loans that were due before March 1992 for a period of 20 years with 10-years' grace, and also guaranteed commercial debts for a period of 15 years with an eight-year period of grace. Although Nigeria is defined by the World Bank as a low-income country, it was not accorded the debt concessions for which it applied. In 1992 Nigeria's finance ministry officials under the Babangida government initiated a series of negotiations for the renewal of Nigeria's stand-by facility with the IMF (the previous facility had expired in April) and a series of development credits with the World Bank, in an effort to reschedule and to reduce the 'Paris Club' debt, which was the principal burden on the government finance. In May 1993 efforts by the transitional council to obtain a new arrangement with the IMF (which was a precondition to the rescheduling of Nigeria's external debt on concessionary terms) ended in failure, owing to lack of agreement over the exchange rate policy and the proposed removal of subsidies on domestic fuel. Negotiations on further loans from the IMF and World Bank continued under the Abacha government in 1996 and 1997. The federal government's domestic debt burden also increased in the second half of the 1990s, from N341,800m. in December 1994 to N537,000m. in December 1998, and to N680,000m. in December 1999.

The liberalization of the financial sector in the 1980s resulted in a proliferation of banks, from 51 in 1986 to 119 in 1992. By the mid-1990s, however, it was evident that some of these banks were financially instable. The Nigeria Deposit Insurance Co revealed evidence that violations of banking regulations had taken place in a number of institutions. Several banks failed, and other seemed on the point of doing so. In September 1995 the Abacha government initiated measures to rescue several banks. By February 1997 eight banks had been offered for privatization; two of these, the National Bank and the African Continental Bank, attracted investor interest, but purchasers were still being sought for the remaining six. In January 1998 the CBN revoked the licences of 13 commercial banks and 13 merchant banks. During 1997 and 1998 a further 31 financial institutions went into receivership or liquidation. By November 1998 it was reported that 57 of the 89 banks then operating in Nigeria had failed to meet the new minimum capitalization requirement of N500m., due to come into effect on 1 January 1999. In May 2000, of the 179 'first-tier' companies quoted on the Lagos Stock Exchange, 24 were banks and 19 were insurance companies.

PUBLIC FINANCE

Since the early 1970s, the channelling of earnings from petroleum exports, import and excise duties and other forms of revenue from taxation through the federal, state and local governments has been the main impetus of economic activity in Nigeria. After a period in the late 1970s and early 1980s of inflationary domestic policies, the government was faced with serious internal financial difficulties. Budgets in the early 1990s were characterized by overly-ambitious targets that subsequently proved to have been unattainable. Budgetary deficits in most years were larger than those projected, and were equivalent to between 8% and 13% of GDP. In 1995, however, total revenue was projected at N350,660m. and total expenditure at N351,160m., and the Abacha government claimed to have achieved a budgetary surplus of N1,000m. (equivalent to 0.6% of GDP). Value-added tax, introduced in January 1994, increased revenue by N8,600m. in 1994 and by N21,000m. in 1995. The government pledged to pay US $2,000m. of the external debt-servicing costs of $4,400m. which fell due in 1995, and to end the system of dedicated accounts, into which at least $12,000m. of revenue was directed between 1988 and 1994. The 1996 budget required total expenditure of N124,222m., of which N76,745m. was recurrent and N47,477m. capital, and envisaged a budgetary surplus of N19,000m. (equivalent to 1.2% of GDP). Revenue projections were based on a petroleum price of US $16 per barrel and an official exchange rate of N22.0 = US $1. The 1997 budget, announced on 18 January 1997, required N99,000m. in recurrent expenditure and N88,693m. in capital expenditure. The N260,000m. budget for 1998 projected a fiscal deficit of N5,000m., and stipulated that the states would be allocated the largest share of revenue from VAT. Government targets for 1998 included GDP growth of 5.5% and an inflation rate of 9%. The 1999 budget confirmed that the previous 1998 budget revenue projection of N216,336m. from petroleum had not been achieved, largely because the international price of petroleum had declined sharply from US $17 per barrel in December 1997 (when the 1998 budget was being drafted) to just $11; the achieved revenue figure was N134,440m., only 62% of the projected amount. In view of the downward trend, the 1999 budget was based on a petroleum price of $9 per barrel, a level that proved to be overly pessimistic after the petroleum price began to increase again. At an exchange rate of N86 = US $1, revenue from petroleum and gas in 1999 was projected at N214,000m., with total gross revenue estimated at N146,700m. Compared with total expenditure of N211,000m., the budgetary deficit of N152,300m. was equivalent to 4.7% of projected GDP, near the limit tolerated by the IMF and the World Bank; the deficit was quantified in the budget speech as N34,100m. The adoption of the 2000 budget, announced by the new civilian Obasanjo government in November 1999, with projected total expenditure of N470,000m., was to be impeded by dissension in the national assembly, bringing the legislative branch of the federal government into direct conflict with the executive branch. President Obasanjo presented a revised version, at N570,000m., in January 2000, but this too was to undergo protracted scrutiny. The national assembly finally approved a N677,000m. budget in May 2000, and submitted it to Obasanjo for ratification. Among numerous issues of contention was the Petroleum Profit Tax; Obasanjo claimed that in the final version of the budget, as adopted by the legislators, this tax was overestimated by US $650m. The legislators, for their part, raised their own allocation from the N5,600m. (which Obasanjo had originally proposed) to N20,000m. In an attempt to avoid a repetition of this confrontational and protracted situation, Obasanjo introduced greater transparency into the budgeting exercise, implementing the concept of 'core revenue', whereby, for 2001 and beyond, 'budget call circulars' to ministries would specify in advance the levels of current and capital expenditure to be allocated to each ministry.

In November 1996 Gen. Abacha established the Vision 2010 Committee, chaired by a former head of state, Chief Ernest Shonekan; the committee of 172 members (later increased to 194) included the minister of finance, a further nine ministers, members of the armed forces and representatives from a number of civilian fields. The Vision 2010 Committee was to devise strategies to achieve sustained annual GDP growth of 6%–10%, to keep inflation down to not more than 3%–5% per annum by the year 2010, and to attain a high level of employment. The civilian Obasanjo government introduced its own 1999–2001 National Rolling Plan, which would 'draw inspiration from' the broad objectives of Vision 2010. The main priority in the rolling plan was to diversify the productive base of the economy through enhanced capacity utilization in industry, increased agricultural productivity and accelerated development in the gas and solid minerals sector.

The Obasanjo government, like all the predecessing administrations, faces a formidable challenge in addressing the problems inherent in the Nigerian economy. Among his first acts as the new president, Obasanjo suspended all contracts entered into by the outgoing Abubakar regime between 1 January 1999 and the transition date of 29 May 1999, which included 11 contracts involving offshore petroleum concessions; these contracts were to be reviewed by an official panel. He also announced a revision of the 1999 budget, which had been proposed by the Abubakar regime. Meanwhile, the return to civilian rule provided for a resumption of negotiations with bilateral and multilateral donors and creditors. A resumption of agreements with them, however, was expected to be much more difficult to accomplish. In March 1999 the IMF warned the incoming Obasanjo government that the success of discussions with the 'Paris Club' on the rescheduling of debt arrears was dependent on compliance

with the terms of agreed arrangements. In the first few weeks of President Obasanjo's tenure, issues of agreement as well as disagreement with the IMF became apparant. Obasanjo rapidly introduced measures to eliminate corruption, in accordance with IMF demands, declaring in his inaugural address to the national assembly in Abuja in June that the former federal tender board and the ministerial tender board were to be revived and that, in future, all government contracts were to be processed through these two boards. However, there appeared to be disagreement on the issues of privatization and debt. Progress in the privatization of the Nigerian Telecommunications PLC and other parastatals, originally proposed in 1988, has been continually delayed, while Obasanjo has declared that no more privatization measures are to take place until a thorough audit of assets has been effected; the duration of an audit might well become an issue of contention between the IMF and the new civilian government. Although both the IMF and the Obasanjo administration acknowledge that Nigeria has an unsustainably large debt burden, the IMF is unlikely to view this as the first priority and will require progress on other issues before any 'Paris Club' rescheduling takes place. Meanwhile, Obasanjo's government is obliged to address the severe crises in the petroleum-refining and power-generating sectors, which are causing hardships throughout the monetary economy and were significantly depressing manufacturing activity. In accordance with IMF conditions, Obasanjo reduced the subsidy on refined petroleum products, causing a 50% increase in the pump price of petrol in June 2000. This measure precipitated a general strike, which continued despite the introduction of a 118% increase in the national minimum wage. Nevertheless, the naira, which had lost 5.1% of its value in a single week in the final period of the Abubakar military regime, exhibited a remarkable stability in the first year of the civilian era, demonstrating at least some confidence in the new government.

Statistical Survey

Source (unless otherwise stated): Federal Office of Statistics, 7 Okotie-Eboh St, SW Ikoyi, Lagos; tel. (1) 2682935.

Area and Population

AREA, POPULATION AND DENSITY

Area (sq km)	923,768*
Population (census results, 28–30 November 1991)	
Males	44,544,531
Females	43,969,970
Total	88,514,501
Population (official estimates at mid-year)	
1993	93,265,251
1994	95,223,821
1995	97,223,521
Density (per sq km) at mid-1995	105.2

* 356,669 sq miles.

STATES (census of November 1991)*

	Population	Capital
Abia	2,297,978	Umuahia
Adamawa	2,124,049	Yola
Akwa Ibom	2,359,736	Uyo
Anambra	2,767,903	Awka
Bauchi	4,294,413	Bauchi
Benue	2,780,398	Makurdi
Borno	2,596,589	Maiduguri
Cross River	1,865,604	Calabar
Delta	2,570,181	Asaba
Edo	2,159,848	Benin City
Enugu	3,161,295	Enugu
Imo	2,485,499	Owerri
Jigawa	2,829,929	Dutse

— continued	Population	Capital
Kaduna	3,969,252	Kaduna
Kano	5,632,040	Kano
Katsina	3,878,344	Katsina
Kebbi	2,062,226	Birnin Kebbi
Kogi	2,099,046	Lokoja
Kwara	1,566,469	Ilorin
Lagos	5,685,781	Ikeja
Niger	2,482,367	Minna
Ogun	2,338,570	Abeokuta
Ondo	3,884,485	Akure
Osun	2,203,016	Oshogbo
Oyo	3,488,789	Ibadan
Plateau	3,283,704	Jos
Rivers	3,983,857	Port Harcourt
Sokoto	4,392,391	Sokoto
Taraba	1,480,590	Jalingo
Yobe	1,411,481	Damaturu
Federal Capital Territory . .	378,671	Abuja
Total	88,514,501	

* In October 1996 the Government announced the creation of six new states: Bayelsa, Ebonyi, Ekiti, Gombe, Nassarawa and Zamfara.

PRINCIPAL TOWNS (estimated population at 1 July 1975)

Lagos (federal capital)*	1,060,848	Ado-Ekiti	213,000
Ibadan	847,000	Kaduna	202,000
Ogbomosho	432,000	Mushin	197,000
Kano	399,000	Maiduguri	189,000
Oshogbo	282,000	Enugu	187,000
Ilorin	282,000	Ede	182,000
Abeokuta	253,000	Aba	177,000
Port Harcourt	242,000	Ife	176,000
Zaria	224,000	Ila	155,000
Ilesha	224,000	Oyo	152,000
Onitsha	220,000	Ikere-Ekiti	145,000
Iwo	214,000	Benin City	136,000

* Federal capital moved to Abuja in December 1991.

BIRTHS AND DEATHS (UN estimates, annual averages)

	1980–85	1985–90	1990–95
Birth rate (per 1,000)	47.3	44.3	41.1
Death rate (per 1,000)	18.3	16.7	15.4

Expectation of life (UN estimates, years at birth, 1990–95): 49.6 (males 48.1; females 51.2).

Source: UN, *World Population Prospects: The 1998 Revision*.

ECONOMICALLY ACTIVE POPULATION
(sample survey, '000 persons aged 14 years and over, September 1986)

	Males	Females	Total
Agriculture, hunting, forestry and fishing	9,800.6	3,458.4	13,259.0
Mining and quarrying	6.8	—	6.8
Manufacturing	806.4	457.3	1,263.7
Electricity, gas and water	127.0	3.4	130.4
Construction	545.6	—	545.6
Trade, restaurants and hotels	2,676.6	4,740.8	7,417.4
Transport, storage and communications	1,094.7	17.2	1,111.9
Financing, insurance, real estate and business services	109.8	10.3	120.1
Community, social and personal services	3,939.5	962.6	4,902.1
Activities not adequately defined	597.1	147.8	744.9
Total employed	19,704.1	9,797.8	29,501.9
Unemployed	809.8	453.8	1,263.6
Total labour force	20,513.9	10,251.6	30,765.5

Note: Figures are based on a total estimated population of 98,936,800, which may be an overestimate.

Source: ILO, *Yearbook of Labour Statistics*.

Agriculture

PRINCIPAL CROPS ('000 metric tons)

	1996	1997	1998
Wheat	41	66	98*
Rice (paddy)	3,122	3,268	3,268†
Maize	5,667	5,354	5,858*
Millet	5,681	5,902	5,926*
Sorghum	7,084	7,297	7,516*
Potatoes	99	103	103†
Sweet potatoes†	40	40	40
Cassava	31,418	30,409	30,409†
Yams	23,201	19,566	19,566†
Taro (Coco yam)	2,492	1,832	1,832†
Pulses†	1,550	1,600	1,600
Soybeans	322	361	361†
Groundnuts (in shell)	2,278	2,531	2,531†
Sesame seed†	65	60	60
Cottonseed†	225	230	115
Cotton (lint)	116	90*	55*
Coconuts†	150	150	150
Palm kernels	548	548†	548†
Tomatoes	569	570†	570†
Green peppers†	970	970	970
Carrots†	175	175	175
Sugar cane	615	620†	620†
Citrus fruits†	2,200	2,200	2,200
Mangoes†	500	500	500
Pineapples	800	800†	800†
Plantains†	1,685	1,675	1,675
Papayas†	500	500	500
Other fruit (excluding melons)	1,400	1,400†	1,400†
Cashew nuts†	25	25	25
Cocoa beans*	165	145	145
Tobacco (leaves)†	9	9	9
Natural rubber (dry weight)	116	90*	55*

* Unofficial figure(s).   † FAO estimate(s).

Source: FAO, *Production Yearbook*.

LIVESTOCK ('000 head, year ending September)

	1996	1997	1998
Horses*	204	204	204
Asses*	1,000	1,000	1,000
Cattle	18,680	19,610	19,610*
Camels*	18	18	18
Pigs*	7,400	7,600	7,600
Sheep*	14,000	14,000	14,000
Goats*	24,500	24,500	24,500

Poultry (million)*: 125 in 1996; 126 in 1997; 126 in 1998.

* FAO estimate(s).

Source: FAO, *Production Yearbook*.

LIVESTOCK PRODUCTS ('000 metric tons)

	1996	1997	1998*
Beef and veal	280	294	297
Mutton and lamb*	62	74	82
Goat meat*	156	166	180
Pig meat*	278	287	315
Poultry meat*	170	171	172
Other meat*	100	100	100
Edible offals*	87	88	n.a.
Cows' milk*	380	380	380
Butter and ghee*	9	9	9
Cheese*	7	7	7
Poultry eggs*	325	350	350
Cattle hides*	35	36	36
Sheepskins*	11	14	15
Goatskins*	24	26	28

* FAO estimates.

Source: FAO, mainly *Production Yearbook*.

Forestry

ROUNDWOOD REMOVALS
('000 cubic metres, excluding bark)

	1995	1996	1997
Sawlogs, veneer logs and logs for sleepers	5,984	6,200	6,200
Other industrial wood	2,279	2,279	2,279
Fuel wood	102,790	105,828	108,908
Total	111,053	114,307	117,387

Source: FAO, *Yearbook of Forest Products.*

SAWNWOOD PRODUCTION
('000 cubic metres, including railway sleepers)

	1989	1990	1991
Coniferous (softwood)	6	6	—
Broadleaved (hardwood)	2,706	2,723	2,723
Total	2,712	2,729	2,723

1992–97: Annual production as in 1991.

Source: FAO, *Yearbook of Forest Products.*

Fishing

('000 metric tons, live weight)

	1995	1996	1997
Inland waters	117.9	89.5	110.5
Tilapias	9.1	10.1	8.4
Upsidedown catfishes	9.7	4.5	5.1
Characins	8.8	7.1	7.6
Bagrid catfish	4.0	8.5	5.0
North African catfishes	—	2.7	8.6
Other torpedo-shaped catfishes	20.7	8.5	10.2
Other freshwater fishes (incl. unspecified)	60.6	44.5	60.6
Nile perch	5.0	3.7	4.2
Atlantic Ocean	231.6	248.5	255.2
Sea catfishes	12.6	12.7	9.9
West African croakers	9.3	14.5	8.5
Sardinellas	76.6	104.5	99.9
Bonga shad	15.1	4.6	28.0
Sharks, rays, skates, etc.	6.5	8.4	6.6
Other marine fishes (incl. unspecified)	90.8	87.1	77.5
Palinurid spiny lobsters	1.5	1.1	8.3
Southern pink shrimp	14.7	12.1	13.0
Other marine crustaceans	4.5	3.5	3.5
Total catch	349.5	338.0	365.7

Source: FAO, *Yearbook of Fishery Statistics.*

Mining

('000 metric tons, unless otherwise indicated)

	1994	1995	1996
Hard coal*	50	50	50
Crude petroleum	91,045	92,157	92,805
Natural gas (petajoules)	178	174	175*
Tin concentrates (metric tons, metal content)	208	357	150

* Provisional or estimated figure(s).

Source: UN, *Industrial Commodity Statistics Yearbook.*

1997 ('000 metric tons): Crude petroleum 101,375 (Source: UN, *Monthly Bulletin of Statistics*).

Industry

SELECTED PRODUCTS ('000 metric tons, unless otherwise indicated)

	1994	1995	1996
Palm oil*	837	860	776
Wheat flour	265	251	561
Raw sugar*	35	35	35
Wine ('000 hectolitres)	75	68	n.a.
Beer ('000 hectolitres)	1,561	1,461	n.a.
Cigarettes (million)	338	256	n.a.
Footwear, excl. rubber ('000 pairs)	1,182	1,255	n.a.
Plywood (cubic metres)*	72,000	72,000	72,000
Wood pulp*	7	7	7
Paper and paperboard*	55	57	57
Phosphatic fertilizers†	28	n.a.	n.a.
Jet fuels‡	30	30	30
Motor spirit—petrol	1,675	1,718	1,700
Kerosene	799	649	650
Gas-diesel (distillate fuel) oil	1,413	1,767	1,770*
Residual fuel oils	1,257	1,312	1,310
Liquefied petroleum gas‡	60	55	60
Cement	1,275	1,573	n.a.
Crude steel§	58‡	36‡	20
Tin metal—unwrought (metric tons)	316	259	175§
Electric energy (million kWh)‡	14,790	14,810	14,820

* Data from the FAO.
† Production in terms of phospheric acid.
‡ Provisional or estimated figure(s).
§ Data from the US Bureau of Mines.

Source: mainly UN, *Industrial Commodity Statistics Yearbook.*

1997 ('000 metric tons): Palm oil 810; Raw sugar 35 (FAO estimate).
1998 ('000 metric tons, FAO estimates): Palm oil 810; Raw sugar 35.
Source (for 1997 and 1998): FAO, *Production Yearbook.*

Finance

CURRENCY AND EXCHANGE RATES

Monetary Units
100 kobo = 1 naira (₦).

Sterling, Dollar and Euro Equivalents (28 April 2000)
£1 sterling = 156.61 naira;
US $1 = 99.87 naira;
€1 = 90.73 naira;
1,000 naira = £6.385 = $10.013 = €11.021.

Average Exchange Rate (naira per US $)
1997   21.886
1998   21.886
1999   92.338

Note: The information on average rates prior to 1999 refers to the mid-point exchange rate of the Central Bank of Nigeria. There is, in addition, an autonomous foreign exchange market (AFEM). The AFEM rate became the principal rate in January 1999.

FEDERAL BUDGET (₦ million)*

Revenue†	1995	1996	1997‡
Distribution from Federation Account	73,524	81,056	97,262
Share of value-added tax (VAT)	7,433	10,746	12,000
Independent revenue§	19,121	3,407	13,000
Profits from autonomous foreign exchange market	79,645	103,190	90,247
First-charge deductions from federation revenue	98,260	108,344	113,520
External debt-servicing	43,860	44,000	44,000
National priority projects	15,400	13,192	16,280
Nigerian National Petroleum Corporation (NNPC) cash calls and priority projects	39,000	51,152	53,240
Transfer from Petroleum Trust Fund (PTF) for Petroleum Special Trust Fund (PSTF)	20,460	41,935	38,000
PSTF independent revenue	5,192	7,322	11,601
Total (incl. others)‖	317,671	368,405	384,603

Expenditure¶	1995	1996	1997‡
Recurrent expenditure . . .	154,893	146,518	149,805
General administration. . .	16,903	26,302	37,908
Defence	6,598	11,902	13,343
Internal security . . .	5,257	8,919	10,082
Agriculture and water resources	1,510	1,818	2,421
Construction	1,699	608	—
Transport and communications .	1,081	1,199	2,185
Other economic services . .	1,628	2,216	3,188
Education	9,746	11,667	12,983
Health	3,321	3,175	4,702
Other social and community services	754	2,845	3,645
Interest payments due . .	70,568	60,066	48,824
Other transfers** . . .	35,828	15,801	10,524
Capital expenditure . . .	67,706	109,280	162,517
General administration. . .	9,271	9,565	33,656
Defence	2,763	3,784	3,778
Internal security . . .	1,304	1,515	3,095
Agriculture and water resources	2,414	3,895	4,976
Manufacturing, mining and quarrying	4,146	3,114	4,146
Transport and communications .	2,511	8,619	1,018
Special projects . . .	26,000	16,280	16,280
Other economic services . .	8,060	3,954	2,702
Education	2,426	3,216	3,303
Health	1,312	1,660	2,016
Housing	4,818	2,831	4,467
Other social and community services	659	950	736
Transfers	2,004	49,899	82,345
Total	222,599	255,798	312,322

* Figures refer to the operations of the Federal Government, the 'first charges' and the Petroleum Special Trust Fund (PSTF).
† Figures for government revenue refer to federally retained revenue. This includes 48.5% of total distributed revenue of the Federation Account, more than half of which consists of proceeds from the operations of the NNPC and foreign petroleum companies. The remainder of Federation Account revenue is allocated to state governments (24%), local governments (20%) and five special funds (7.5%). The Federal Government retains 20% of federally collected VAT.
‡ Figures are provisional.
§ Including loan repayments and proceeds from the privatization or commercialization of state enterprises.
‖ Including loans, grants and aid received (₦ million): 2,000 in 1996; 2,000 (provisional) in 1997.
¶ Figures exclude the operations of extrabudgetary accounts. Including supplementary and extrabudgetary outlays, total expenditure (in ₦ million) was: 249,057 in 1995; 294,304 in 1996; 398,859 (provisional) in 1997.
** Including pensions, gratuities, grants, subventions and losses from transactions in foreign exchanges.

Source: IMF, *Nigeria: Selected Issues and Statistical Appendix* (August 1998).

INTERNATIONAL RESERVES (US $ million at 31 December)

	1994	1995	1996
Gold*	1	1	1
IMF special drawing rights . .	—	1	1
Foreign exchange . . .	1,386	1,443	4,075
Total	1,387	1,444	4,076

* National valuation of gold reserves (687,000 troy ounces in each year).
Source: IMF, *International Financial Statistics*.

MONEY SUPPLY (₦ million at 31 December)

	1997	1998	1999
Currency outside banks . . .	123,645	156,734	186,456
Demand deposits at commercial banks.	131,887	150,977	209,899
Total money (incl. others) . .	276,564	333,082	400,826

Source: IMF, *International Financial Statistics*.

COST OF LIVING
(Consumer Price Index for rural and urban areas; base: 1990 = 100)

	1994	1995	1996
Food (incl. beverages) . .	379.9	653.7	850.8
Clothing (incl. footwear) . .	362.5	653.5	870.0
Rent, fuel and light . . .	513.0	895.6	1,162.2
All items (incl. others) . .	403.2	687.9	901.0

Source: ILO, *Yearbook of Labour Statistics*.
1997: Food 923.5; All items 975.4.
1998: Food 984.6; All items 1,075.5.
Source: (for 1997 and 1998): UN, *Monthly Bulletin of Statistics*.

NATIONAL ACCOUNTS (₦ million at current prices)
National Income and Product*

	1992	1993	1994
Compensation of employees . .	59,100	74,546	81,048
Operating surplus . . .	468,880	604,200	808,817
Domestic factor incomes . .	527,980	678,746	889,865
Consumption of fixed capital .	16,351	17,240	18,629
Gross domestic product (GDP) at factor cost. . . .	544,331	695,986	908,494
Indirect taxes	5,762	5,689	6,042
Less Subsidies	284	202	202
GDP in purchasers' values . .	549,809	701,473	914,334
Factor income received from abroad	2,799	1,338	1,170
Less Factor income paid abroad .	67,203	74,900	66,878
Gross national product (GNP) .	485,405	627,911	848,626
Less Consumption of fixed capital .	16,351	17,240	18,629
National income in market prices	469,053	610,671	829,997
Other current transfers from abroad	15,240	21,386	13,164
Less Other current transfers paid abroad	2,560	3,592	2,211
National disposable income .	481,733	628,465	840,950

* Figures are provisional.
Source: UN, *National Accounts Statistics*.

Expenditure on the Gross Domestic Product

	1996	1997	1998
Government final consumption expenditure	143,090	171,770	214,710
Private final consumption expenditure	2,367,960	2,379,560	2,817,080
Increase in stocks . . . }	172,490	295,100	283,290
Gross fixed capital formation . }			
Total domestic expenditure .	2,683,540	2,846,430	3,315,080
Exports of goods and services .	852,820	1,239,860	839,100
Less Imports of goods and services	−712,420	−1,101,840	−1,313,040
Statistical discrepancy . . .	—	−44,950	−3,990
GDP in purchasers' values . .	2,823,940	2,939,500	2,837,150
GDP at constant 1990 prices .	308,840	318,504	326,005

Source: IMF, *International Financial Statistics*.

Gross Domestic Product by Economic Activity (at factor cost)

	1996	1997	1998*
Agriculture, hunting, forestry and fishing	841,457	953,549	1,060,759
Mining and quarrying	1,196,978	1,104,831	737,927
Manufacturing	132,554	144,107	146,489
Electricity, gas and water.	2,006	2,038	2,112
Construction.	16,042	18,776	24,526
Trade, restaurants and hotels.	360,382	396,629	442,707
Transport, storage and communications	63,081	72,538	80,916
Finance, insurance, real estate and business services	89,807	99,925	136,660
Government services.	21,043	21,361	36,603
Other community, social and personal services	17,108	21,244	27,776
Total	2,740,458	2,834,999	2,716,617

Source: IMF, *Nigeria: Statistical Appendix* (January 2000).

BALANCE OF PAYMENTS (US $ million)

	1997	1998	1999
Exports of goods f.o.b.	15,207	8,971	12,876
Imports of goods f.o.b.	−9,501	−9,211	−8,588
Trade balance	5,706	−240	4,288
Exports of services	786	884	980
Imports of services	−4,712	−4,166	−3,476
Balance on goods and services	1,781	−3,552	1,792
Other income received	258	333	240
Other income paid	−3,404	−2,624	−2,818
Balance on goods, services and income	−1,365	−5,813	−786
Current transfers received	1,920	1,574	1,301
Current transfers paid	−4	−5	−9
Current balance	552	−4,244	506
Capital account (net).	−49	−54	−48
Direct investment from abroad	1,539	1,051	1,005
Portfolio investment assets	9	51	50
Portfolio investment liabilities	−76	−59	−39
Other investment assets .	−2,183	−332	−3,319
Other investment liabilities .	286	792	−1,699
Net errors and omissions .	−62	−77	7
Overall balance	15	−2,873	−3,538

Source: IMF, *International Financial Statistics*.

External Trade

PRINCIPAL COMMODITIES
(₦ million)

Imports c.i.f.	1993	1994	1995*
Food and live animals	13,912.9	16,585.8	76,819.1
Crude materials (inedible) except fuels	4,306.4	5,636.0	27,576.1
Chemicals	28,322.6	40,578.8	172,678.8
Basic manufactures	39,751.1	35,909.0	152,324.9
Machinery and transport equipment	70,226.9	50,240.4	180,557.6
Miscellaneous manufactured articles	6,293.9	7,246.2	27,094.8
Total (incl. others)	165,629.4	161,027.0	656,572.2

Exports f.o.b.	1993	1994	1995*
Mineral products.	213,803.7	200,826.9	728,648.3
Crude petroleum	213,778.8	200,710.2	728,265.3
Total (incl. others)	218,801.1	206,059.2	748,368.1

* Figures are provisional. A unitary exchange rate of ₦70.3632=US $1 was used as a conversion factor in 1995.

Sources: Central Bank of Nigeria, Lagos, and Federal Office of Statistics.

PRINCIPAL TRADING PARTNERS (US $ '000)*

Imports c.i.f.	1989	1990	1991
Belgium-Luxembourg	122,006	143,671	160,020
Brazil	106,404	175,801	179,085
China, People's Repub.	86,591	128,230	189,776
France	271,611	394,209	440,375
Germany	591,509	644,589	881,035
Hong Kong	52,447	96,415	126,287
India	45,141	67,082	85,003
Italy	185,040	193,827	297,904
Japan	231,902	257,434	401,280
Korea, Repub.	39,543	53,977	80,463
Netherlands	132,990	207,208	298,537
Spain	44,609	59,463	55,258
Switzerland	79,522	115,829	142,016
United Kingdom	556,105	739,417	2,324,956
USA	420,123	373,963	563,039
Total (incl. others)	3,419,079	4,317,921	7,114,360

Exports f.o.b.	1989	1990	1991
Brazil	82,307	9,423	125,754
Canada	16,275	117,584	150,988
Côte d'Ivoire	192,737	224,270	298,050
France	349,424	292,856	497,179
Germany	335,879	591,369	918,662
Ghana	171,746	224,694	189,966
Italy	340,367	298,146	935,714
Netherlands	651,942	933,627	878,331
Portugal	244,797	282,531	134,992
Spain	862,201	939,451	2,070,045
United Kingdom	142,533	298,914	148,715
USA	4,343,233	5,551,527	6,011,690
Total (incl. others)	8,145,435	10,241,646	12,827,941

* Imports by country of production; exports by country of last consignment.

Source: UN, *International Trade Statistics Yearbook*.

Transport

RAILWAYS (traffic)

	1993	1994	1995
Passenger-km (million)	55	220	161
Freight ton-km (million)	162	141	108

Source: UN, *Statistical Yearbook*.

ROAD TRAFFIC (estimates, '000 motor vehicles in use)

	1994	1995	1996
Passenger cars	773	773	773
Lorries and vans	606	606	606

Source: IRF, *World Road Statistics*.

SHIPPING

Merchant Fleet (registered at 31 December)

	1996	1997	1998
Number of vessels	288	293	293
Displacement ('000 grt)	447.2	452.3	451.9

Source: Lloyd's Register of Shipping, *World Fleet Statistics*.

International Sea-borne Freight Traffic
(estimates, '000 metric tons)

	1991	1992	1993
Goods loaded	82,768	84,797	86,993
Goods unloaded	10,960	11,143	11,346

Source: UN Economic Commission for Africa, *African Statistical Yearbook*.

CIVIL AVIATION (traffic on scheduled services)

	1994	1995	1996
Kilometres flown (million) . .	5	6	4
Passengers carried ('000) . .	665	548	221
Passenger-km (million) . .	993	819	273
Total ton-km (million) . .	109	81	30

Source: UN, *Statistical Yearbook*.

Tourism

ARRIVALS BY NATIONALITY*

Country	1994	1995	1996
Benin	90,211	130,225	162,003
Cameroon	6,453	39,651	44,127
Chad	2,916	32,555	35,051
France	1,750	21,294	25,490
Germany	6,312	19,950	24,863
Ghana	24,316	70,272	84,970
Italy	20,210	25,718	27,024
Liberia	151	39,671	44,421
Niger	108,124	213,271	255,704
Sudan	201	18,875	25,973
Togo	19,113	35,612	14,023
Total (incl. others) . . .	327,189	1,030,739	1,230,155

* Figures refer to arrival at frontiers of visitors from abroad. Excluding same-day visitors (excursionists), the total number of tourist arrivals (in '000) was: 214 in 1994; 665 in 1995; 822 in 1996; 611 in 1997.

Tourism receipts (US $ million): 34 in 1994; 54 in 1995; 85 in 1996; 118 in 1997. Source: World Tourism Organization, *Yearbook of Tourism Statistics*.

Communications Media

	1994	1995	1996
Radio receivers ('000 in use) . .	21,300	22,000	22,700
Television receivers ('000 in use) .	n.a.	6,100	6,500
Telephones ('000 main lines in use)	369	405	n.a.
Mobile cellular telephones (number in use)	12,800	13,000	13,000
Book production (titles)* . . .	1,008	1,314	n.a.
Daily newspapers			
Number	27	27	25
Average circulation ('000 copies)†	1,950	1,950	2,740

* Including pamphlets.
† Estimates.

1997 ('000 in use): Radio receivers 23,500; Television receivers 6,900.

Sources: UNESCO, *Statistical Yearbook*; UN, *Statistical Yearbook*.

Education

(1994)

	Institutions	Teachers	Students		
			Males	Females	Total
Primary . . .	38,649	435,210	9,056,367	7,134,580	16,190,947
Secondary . .	6,162*	152,596	2,419,782	2,031,547	4,451,329
Teacher-training† .	135	4,531	n.a.	n.a.	108,751
Technical and vocational† .	240	5,115	n.a.	n.a.	89,536
Higher education .	133*	19,601‡	n.a.	n.a.	383,488*

* 1993 figure.
† 1987 figures.
‡ 1989 figure.

Sources: Federal Ministry of Education, Lagos; UNESCO, *Statistical Yearbook*.

Directory

The Constitution

The Constitution of the Federal Republic of Nigeria was promulgated on 5 May 1999, and entered into force on 31 May. The main provisions are summarized below:

PROVISIONS

Nigeria is one indivisible sovereign state, to be known as the Federal Republic of Nigeria. Nigeria is a Federation, comprising 36 States and a Federal Capital Territory. The Constitution includes provisions for the creation of new States and for boundary adjustments of existing States. The Government of the Federation or of a State is prohibited from adopting any religion as a state religion.

LEGISLATURE

The legislative powers of the Federation are vested in the National Assembly, comprising a Senate and a House of Representatives. The 109-member Senate consists of three Senators from each State and one from the Federal Capital Territory, who are elected for a term of four years. The House of Representatives comprises 360 members, representing constituencies of nearly equal population as far as possible, who are elected for a four-year term. The Senate and House of Representatives each have a Speaker and Deputy Speaker, who are elected by the members of the House from among themselves. Legislation may originate in either the Senate or the House of Representatives, and, having been approved by the House in which it originated by a two-thirds majority, will be submitted to the other House for approval, and subsequently presented to the President for assent. Should the President withhold his assent, and the bill be returned to the National Assembly and again approved by each House by a two-thirds majority, the bill will become law. The legislative powers of a State of the Federation will be vested in the House of Assembly of the State. The House of Assembly of a State will consist of three or four times the number of seats that the State holds in the House of Representatives (comprising not less than 24 and not more than 40 members).

EXECUTIVE

The executive powers of the Federation are vested in the President, who is the Head of State, the Chief Executive of the Federation and the Commander-in-Chief of the Armed Forces of the Federation. The President is elected for a term of four years and must receive not less than one-quarter of the votes cast at the election in at least two-thirds of the States in the Federation and the Federal Capital Territory. The President nominates a candidate as his associate from the same political party to occupy the office of Vice-President. The Ministers of the Government of the Federation are nominated by the President, subject to confirmation by the Senate. Federal executive bodies include the Council of State, which advises the President in the exercise of his powers. The executive powers of a State are vested in the Governor of that State, who is elected for a four-year term and must receive not less than one-quarter of votes cast in at least two-thirds of all local government areas in the State.

JUDICIARY

The judicial powers of the Federation are vested in the courts established for the Federation, and the judicial powers of a State in the courts established for the State. The Federation has a Supreme Court, a Court of Appeal and a Federal High Court. Each State has a High Court, a Shari'a Court of Appeal and a Customary Court of Appeal. Chief Judges are nominated on the recommendation of a National Judicial Council.

LOCAL GOVERNMENT

The States are divided into 768 local government areas. The system of local government by democratically-elected local government councils is guaranteed, and the Government of each State will ensure their existence. Each local government council within the State will participate in the economic planning and development of the area over which it exercises authority.

Federal Government

HEAD OF STATE

President and Commander-in-Chief of the Armed Forces: Gen. (retd) OLUSEGUN OBASANJO (inaugurated 29 May 1999).

Vice-President: Alhaji ATIKU ABUBAKAR.

CABINET
(August 2000)

Minister of Finance: Alhaji ADAMU CIROMA.
Minister of Foreign Affairs: Alhaji SULE LAMIDO.
Minister of Health: Dr TIM MENAKAYA.
Minister of Industry: STEVEN AKIGA.
Minister of Information: Chief DAPO SARUMI.
Minister of Internal Affairs: Chief S. M. AFOLABI.
Minister of Justice and Attorney-General: Chief BOLA IGE.
Minister of Labour and Productivity: Alhaji MUSA GWADABE.
Minister of Police Affairs: Maj.-Gen. DAVID JEMIBEWON.
Minister of Power and Steel: Dr OLUSEGUN AGAGU.
Minister of Agriculture and Rural Development: Alhaju SANI ZANGO DAURA.
Minister of Commerce in Africa: Eng. MUSTAPHA BELLO.
Minister of Communications: Alhaji MOHAMMED ARZIKA.
Minister of Defence: Gen. THEOPHILUS (YAKUBU) DANJUMA.
Minister of Education: Prof. TUNDE ADENIRAN.
Minister of the Environment: HASSAN ADAMU.
Minister of the Federal Capital Territory: Alhaji IBRAHIM BUNO.
Minister of Aviation: KEMA CHIKWE.
Minister of Tourism and Culture: ALABO TONYE GRAHAM-DOUGLAS.
Minister of Science and Technology: Chief EBITIMI BANIGO.
Minister of Solid Minerals: KANU G. AGABI.
Minister of Transport: Chief OJO MADUEKWE.
Minister of Water Resources: MUHAMMADU BELLO KALIEL.
Minister of Sports and Social Development: DAMISI SANGO.
Minister in the Presidency with responsibility for Civil Service Matters: Alhaji BELLO USMAN.
Minister in the Presidency with responsibility for Co-operation and Integration in Africa: Prof. JERRY GANA.
Minister in the Presidency with responsibility for Economic Matters: VINCENT OGBULAFOR.
Minister in the Presidency with responsibility for Inter-Governmental Affairs: Alhaji IBRAHIM UMAR KIDA.
Minister in the Presidency with responsibility for the Special Budget: Eng. DANIEL CHUKE.
Minister of State for Transport: Alhaji ISAH YUGUDA.
Minister of State for Works and Housing: GARBI MADAKI ALI.
Minister of State for Womens' Affairs and Youth Development: Dr BEKKY K. IGWEH.

MINISTRIES

Office of the Head of State: New Federal Secretariat Complex, Shehu Shagari Way, Central Area District, Abuja; tel. (9) 5233536.
Ministry of Agriculture and Rural Development: Area 1, Secretariat Complex, Garki, Abuja; tel. (9) 2341931.
Ministry of Aviation: New Federal Secretariat Complex, Shehu Shagari Way, Central Area District, Abuja; tel. (9) 5232132.
Ministry of Commerce: Federal Secretariat, PMB 88, Garki, Abuja.
Ministry of Communications: New Federal Secretariat Complex, Shehu Shagari Way, Central Area District, Abuja; tel. (9) 5237135.
Ministry of Defence: Area 7, Garki, Abuja.
Ministry of Education: New Federal Secretariat Complex, Shehu Shagari Way, Central Area District, Abuja; tel. (9) 5232800; fax (9) 619904.
Ministry of the Environment: Abuja.
Ministry of the Federal Capital Territory: FCT Secretariat Complex, Area 11, Abuja; tel. (9) 2431295.
Ministry of Finance: Olusegun Obasanjo Way, Garki, Abuja; tel. (9) 2343783.

Ministry of Foreign Affairs: Zone 3, Wuse District, Abuja; tel. (9) 5290185.
Ministry of Health: New Federal Secretariat Complex, Shehu Shagari Way, Central Area District, Abuja; tel. (9) 523490.
Ministry of Industry: Area 1, Secretariat Complex, Garki, Abuja; tel. (9) 2341590.
Ministry of Information: Radio House, Herbert Macaulay Way, Garki, Abuja; tel. and fax (9) 2344106.
Ministry of Internal Affairs: Area 1, Secretariat Complex, Garki, Abuja; tel. (9) 2341934.
Ministry of Justice: New Federal Secretariat Complex, Shehu Shagari Way, Central Area District, Abuja; tel. (9) 5235208.
Ministry of Labour and Productivity: New Federal Secretariat Complex, Shehu Shagari Way, Central Area District, Abuja; tel. (9) 5235580.
Ministry of Police Affairs: New Federal Secretariat Complex, Shehu Shagari Way, Central Area District, Abuja.
Ministry of Power and Steel: New Federal Secretariat Complex, Shehu Shagari Way, Central Area District, Abuja; tel. (9) 5237064.
Ministry of Science and Technology: New Federal Secretariat Complex, Shehu Shagari Way, Central Area District, Abuja; tel. (9) 5233397.
Ministry of Solid Minerals: New Federal Secretariat Complex, Shehu Shagari Way, Central Area District, Abuja; tel. (9) 5235830.
Ministry of Sports and Social Development: Abuja.
Ministry of Tourism and Culture: Radio House, Herbert Macaulay Way, Garki, Abuja.
Ministry of Transport: New Federal Secretariat Complex, Shehu Shagari Way, Central Area District, Abuja; tel. (9) 5237050.
Ministry of Water Resources: Area 1, Secretariat Complex, Garki, Abuja; tel. (9) 2342372.
Ministry of Works and Housing: Radio House, Herbert Macaulay Way, Garki, Abuja; tel. (9) 2346892; fax (9) 2340174.

President and Legislature

PRESIDENT

Election, 27 February 1999

Candidate	Votes	% of votes
Gen. (retd) OLUSEGUN OBASANJO (People's Democratic Party)	18,738,154	62.78
SAMUEL OLUYEMISI FALAE (Alliance for Democracy/All People's Party)	11,110,287	37.22
Total*	29,848,441	100.00

* Excluding 397,316 invalid votes.

NATIONAL ASSEMBLY

Speaker of the House of Representatives: Alhaji GHALI UMAR NA'ABA.

Speaker of the Senate: CHUKA OKADIGBO.

General Election, 20 February 1999

Party	House of Representatives No. of votes	Seats	Senate No. of votes	Seats
People's Democratic Party	13,289,938	215	13,917,193	66
All People's Party*	7,364,763	70	7,453,227	23
Alliance for Democracy*	2,918,614	66	3,015,827	19
Total†	23,573,315	360	24,386,247	109

* The All People's Party and Alliance for Democracy contested the elections in coalition.
† Following a by-election in March 1999, six of the nine remaining seats in the House of Representatives were secured by the People's Democratic Party and three by the Alliance for Democracy. The remaining seat in the Senate was secured by the People's Democratic Party.

Political Organizations

Following the death of the military Head of State in June 1998, the existing officially-authorized political parties were dissolved. The Government established a new independent national electoral commission, which provisionally approved nine political organizations, of which three were subsequently granted registration.

Alliance for Democracy (AD): e-mail alliance@afrikontakt.com; internet www.afrikontakt.com/alliance; f. late 1998; contested 1999 elections in alliance with the APP; Chair. Chief Ayo Adebanjo (acting).

All People's Party (APP): internet www.appnigeria.org; f. late 1998; contested 1999 elections in alliance with the AD; Leader Alhaji Yusuf Garbah Ali.

People's Democratic Party (PDP): f. late 1998 by fmr opponents of the Govt of Gen. Sani Abacha; supports greater federalism; party of Pres., Gen. (retd) Olusegun Obasanjo; Chief Barnabas Gemade; Sec. Okwesilieze Nwodo.

The following political pressure groups were active in early 2000:

Ijaw Youth Congress (IYC): f. 1999; Pres. Felix Tuodolo.

Movement for the Actualization of the Sovereign State of Biafra (MASSOB): f. 1999; Leader Ralph Uwazurike.

Movement for the Survival of the Ogoni People (MOSOP): f. 1990 to organize opposition to petroleum production in Ogoni territory; Leader Ledum Mitee.

O'odua People's Congress (OPC): f. 1994; Yoruba nationalist organization; Pres. Frederick Faseun.

Diplomatic Representation

EMBASSIES AND HIGH COMMISSIONS IN NIGERIA

Algeria: Plot 203, Etim Inyang Crescent, POB 7288, Lagos; tel. (1) 612092; fax (1) 2624017; Ambassador: El-Mihoub Mihoubi.

Angola: 5 Kasumu Ekomode St, Victoria Island, POB 50437, Lagos; tel. (1) 2611135; Ambassador: B. A. Sozinho.

Argentina: 93 Awolowo Rd, SW Ikoyi, POB 51940, Lagos; tel. (1) 2682797; Ambassador: Nicarohicio Bosso.

Australia: 2 Ozumba Mbadiwe Ave, Victoria Island, POB 2427, Lagos; tel. (1) 2618875; fax (1) 2618703; High Commissioner: H. Brown.

Austria: Fabac Centre, 3B Ligali Ayorinde Ave, POB 1914, Lagos; tel. (1) 2616081; fax (1) 2617639; Ambassador: Dr Wilfried Almos-lechner.

Belgium: 1A Murtala Muhammed Dr., Ikoyi, POB 149, Lagos; tel. (1) 2691507; fax (1) 2691444; Ambassador: Christiaan van Driessche.

Benin: 4 Abudu Smith St, Victoria Island, POB 5705, Lagos; tel. (1) 2614411; Ambassador: Patrice Houngavou.

Brazil: 257 Kofo Abayomi St, Victoria Island, POB 1931, Lagos; tel. (1) 2610135; fax (1) 2613394; e-mail nigbrem@intracom5.com; Ambassador: Carlos Alfredo Pinto da Silva.

Bulgaria: 3 Louis Farrakhan Crescent, Victoria Island, PMB 4441, Lagos; tel. (1) 2611931; fax (1) 2619879; Ambassador: (vacant).

Burkina Faso: 15 Norman Williams St, Ikoyi, Lagos; tel. (1) 2681001; Chargé d'affaires a.i.: Adolphe T. Benon.

Cameroon: 5 Elsie Femi Pearse St, Victoria Island, PMB 2476, Lagos; tel. (1) 2612226; Chargé d'affaires a.i.: Prosper Fomba Ngom.

Canada: 4 Idowu Taylor St, Victoria Island, POB 54506, Ikoyi Station, Lagos; tel. (1) 2692195; fax (1) 2692919; High Commissioner: Ian Ferguson.

Central African Republic: Plot 137, Ajao Estate, New Airport, Oshodi, Lagos; Ambassador: Jean-Paul Mokodopo.

Chad: 2 Goriola St, Victoria Island, PMB 70662, Lagos; tel. (1) 2622590; fax (1) 2618314; Ambassador: Dr Issa Hassan Khayar.

China, People's Republic: 19A Taslim Elias Close, Victoria Island, POB 5653, Lagos; tel. (1) 2612586; Ambassador: Lu Fengding.

Colombia: 43 Raymond Njoku Rd, Ikoyi, Lagos; tel. (1) 615342; Chargé d'affaires: Dr Bernardo Echeverri.

Côte d'Ivoire: 3 Abudu Smith St, Victoria Island, POB 7780, Lagos; tel. (1) 2610936; Ambassador: Désiré Amon Tanoe.

Cuba: Plot 935, Idejo St, Victoria Island, POB 328, Victoria Island, Lagos; tel. (1) 2614836; Ambassador: Giraldo Mazola.

Czech Republic: 2 Alhaji Masha Close, Ikoyi, POB 1009, Lagos; tel. (1) 2683207; fax (1) 2683175; Ambassador: Evzen Vacek.

Denmark: 4 Louis Farrakhan Crescent, Victoria Island, POB 2390, Lagos; tel. (1) 2611503; fax (1) 2610841; Ambassador: Lars Blinken-berg.

Egypt: 81 Awolowo Rd, Ikoyi, POB 538, Lagos; tel. (1) 2612922; Ambassador: Fuad Yusuf.

Equatorial Guinea: 7 Bank Rd, Ikoyi, POB 4162, Lagos; tel. (1) 2683717; Ambassador: A. S. Dougan Malabo.

Ethiopia: Plot 97, Ahmadu Bello Rd, Victoria Island, PMB 2488, Lagos; tel. (1) 2613198; fax (1) 2615055; Chargé d'affaires a.i.: Negga Beyenne.

Finland: 13 Louis Farrakhan Crescent, Victoria Island, POB 4433, Lagos; tel. (1) 2610916; fax (1) 2613158; Ambassador: Heikki Lat-vanen.

France: 32 Odi St, off Aso Drive, Maitama, Abuja; tel. (9) 5235506; e-mail ambafrance.abj@micro.com.ng; Ambassador: Philippe Peltier.

Gabon: 8 Norman Williams St, POB 5989, Lagos; tel. (1) 2684673; Ambassador: E. Agueminya.

Gambia: 162 Awolowo Rd, SW Ikoyi, POB 873, Lagos; tel. (1) 682192; High Commissioner: Omar Secka.

Germany: 15 Louis Farrakhan Crescent, Victoria Island, POB 728, Lagos; tel. (1) 2611011; fax (1) 2611173; e-mail 106655.2050@compuserve.com; Ambassador: (vacant).

Ghana: 21–25 King George V Rd, POB 889, Lagos; tel. (1) 2630015; fax (1) 2630338; High Commissioner: John K. Tettegah.

Greece: Plot 1397, 9B Tiamiyu Savage St, Victoria Island, POB 1199, Lagos; tel. (1) 2614852; fax (1) 2611412; Ambassador: Haris Karabarbounis.

Guinea: 8 Abudu Smith St, Victoria Island, POB 2826, Lagos; tel. (1) 2616961; Ambassador: Komo Beavogui.

Holy See: 9 Anifowoshe St, Victoria Island, POB 2470, Lagos; tel. (1) 2614441; fax (1) 2618635; e-mail nunclag@infoweb.abs.net; Apostolic Nuncio: Most Rev. Osvaldo Padilla, Titular Archbishop of Pia.

Hungary: 9 Louis Solomon Close, Victoria Island, POB 3168, Lagos; tel. (1) 2613551; fax (1) 2613717; Ambassador: János Balassa.

India: 107 Awolowo Rd, SW Ikoyi, POB 2322, Lagos; tel. (1) 2681297; High Commissioner: Satinder Kumber Uppal.

Indonesia: 5 Anifowoshe St, Victoria Island, POB 3473, Marina, Lagos; tel. (1) 2614601; fax (1) 2613301; e-mail indlgs@infoweb.abs.net; Ambassador: Susanto Ismodirdjo.

Iran: 1 Alexander Ave, Ikoyi, Lagos; tel. (1) 2681601; Ambassador: Muhammad Ali Qanizadeh-Ezabadi.

Iraq: Plot 708A, Adeola Hopewell St, Victoria Island, POB 2859, Lagos; tel. (1) 610389; fax (1) 618633; Ambassador: Taha Shuker Mahmoud.

Ireland: 34 Kofo Abayomi St, Victoria Island, Lagos; tel. (1) 2615224; Ambassador: (vacant).

Israel: Abuja; Ambassador: Gadi Golan.

Italy: 12 Louis Farrakhan Crescent, Victoria Island, POB 2161, Lagos; tel. (1) 2621046; fax (1) 2619881; Ambassador: Giovanni Ger-mano.

Jamaica: Plot 77, Samuel Adedoyin Ave, Victoria Island, POB 75368, Lagos; tel. (1) 2611085; fax (1) 2610047; High Commissioner: Robert Miller (acting).

Japan: 24–25 Apese St, Victoria Island, PMB 2111, Lagos; tel. (1) 2614929; fax (1) 2614035; Ambassador: Takahisa Sasaki.

Kenya: 53 Queen's Drive, Ikoyi, POB 6464, Lagos; tel. (1) 2682768; High Commissioner: Dr I. E. Maluki.

Korea, Democratic People's Republic: 31 Akin Adesola St, Victoria Island, Lagos; tel. (1) 2610108; Ambassador: Kil Mun Yong.

Korea, Republic: Plot 934, Idejo St, Victoria Island, POB 4668, Lagos; tel. (1) 2615353; Ambassador: Chai Ki-Oh.

Lebanon: Plot 18, Louis Farrakhan Crescent, Victoria Island, POB 651, Lagos; tel. (1) 2614511; Ambassador: M. Salame.

Liberia: 3 Idejo St, Plot 162, off Adeola Odeku St, Victoria Island, POB 70841, Lagos; tel. (1) 2618899; Ambassador: Prof. James Tapeh.

Libya: 46 Raymond Njoku Rd, SW Ikoyi, Lagos; tel. (1) 2680880; Chargé d'affaires a.i.: Ibrahim al-Bashar.

Malaysia: 205 Abiola Segun-Ajayi St, Victoria Island, POB 3729, Lagos; tel. (1) 619415; fax (1) 612741; High Commissioner: Ilankovan Kolandavelu (acting).

Mauritania: 1A Karimu Giwa Close, SW Ikoyi, Lagos; tel. (1) 2682971; Ambassador: Mohamed M. O. Weddady.

Morocco: Plot 1318, 27 Karimu Katun St, Victoria Island, Lagos; tel. (1) 2611682; Ambassador: Saad Eddine Taieb.

Namibia: Victoria Island, PMB 8000, Lagos.

Netherlands: 24 Ozumba Mbadiwe Ave, Victoria Island, POB 2426, Lagos; tel. (1) 2613005; fax (1) 617605; Ambassador: B. R. Körner.

Niger: 15 Adeola Odeku St, Victoria Island, PMB 2736, Lagos; tel. (1) 2612300; Ambassador: Alhaji Mahamang Dado Mansour.

Norway: 3 Anifowoshe St, Victoria Island, PMB 2431, Lagos; tel. (1) 2618467; fax (1) 2618469; e-mail ambassade.lagos@ud.dep.telemax.no; Ambassador: Fred H. Nomme.

Pakistan: 4 Molade Okoya-Thomas St, Victoria Island, POB 2450, Lagos; tel. (1) 613909; fax (1) 614822; High Commissioner: Zafar A. Hilaly.

Philippines: Plot 152, No 302, off 3rd Ave, Victoria Island, Lagos; tel. (1) 2614048; Ambassador: Mukhtar M. Muallam.

Poland: 10 Idejo St, Victoria Island, POB 410, Lagos; tel. (1) 2614634; Ambassador: Kazimierz Gutkowski.

Portugal: Plot 1677, Olukunle Bakare Close, Victoria Island, Lagos; tel. (1) 2619037; fax (1) 2616071; Ambassador: FILIPE ORLANDO DE ALBUQUERQUE.

Romania: Plot 1192, off Olugbosi Close, Victoria Island, POB 72928, Lagos; tel. (1) 2617806; fax (1) 2618249; Chargé d'affaires a.i.: EMIL RAPCEA.

Russia: 5 Louis Farrakhan Crescent, Victoria Island, POB 2723, Lagos; tel. (1) 2613359; fax (1) 2615022; Ambassador: LEV PARSHIN.

Saudi Arabia: Plot 347H, off Adetokunbo Ademola Crescent, Wuse 2, Abuja; (9) 4131880; fax (9) 4134906; Ambassador: ANWAR A. ABD-RABBUH.

Senegal: 14 Kofo Abayomi Rd, Victoria Island, PMB 2197, Lagos; tel. (1) 2611722; Ambassador: CHERIF Y. DIAITE.

Sierra Leone: 31 Waziri Ibrahim St, Victoria Island, POB 2821, Lagos; tel. (1) 2614666; High Commissioner: JOSEPH BLELL.

Slovakia: POB 1290, Lagos; tel. (1) 2621585; fax (1) 2612103; e-mail obeo.sk@micro.com.ng; Ambassador: (vacant).

Somalia: Plot 1270, off Adeola Odeka St, POB 6355, Lagos; tel. (1) 2611283; Ambassador: M. S. HASSAN.

South Africa: 4 Maduike St, Ikoyi, Lagos; tel. (1) 2693842; fax (1) 2690448; High Commissioner: S. G. NENE.

Spain: 21C Kofo Abayomi Rd, Victoria Island, POB 2738, Lagos; tel. (1) 2615215; fax (1) 2618225; Ambassador (vacant).

Sudan: 2B Kofo Abayomi St, Victoria Island, POB 2428, Lagos; tel. (1) 2615889; Ambassador: AHMED ALTIGANI SALEH.

Switzerland: 7 Anifowoshe St, Victoria Island, POB 536, Lagos; tel. (1) 2613918; Ambassador: HANSPETER STRAUCH.

Syria: 25 Kofo Abayomi St, Victoria Island, Lagos; tel. (1) 2615860; Chargé d'affaires a.i.: MUSTAFA HAJ-ALI.

Tanzania: 45 Ademola St, Ikoyi, POB 6417, Lagos; tel. (1) 2613594; High Commissioner: Maj.-Gen. MIRISHO SAM HAGAI SARAKIKYA.

Thailand: 1 Ruxton Rd, Old Ikoyi, POB 3095, Lagos; tel. (1) 2681337; Ambassador: N. SATHAPORN.

Togo: 96 Awolowo Rd, SW Ikoyi, POB 1435, Lagos; tel. (1) 2617449; Ambassador: FOLI-AGBENOZAN TETTEKPOE.

Trinidad and Tobago: 3A Tiamiyu Savage St, Victoria Island, POB 6392, Marina, Lagos; tel. (1) 2612087; fax (1) 612732; High Commissioner: Dr HAROLD ROBERTSON.

Turkey: 3 Okunola Martins Close, Ikoyi, POB 56252, Lagos; tel. (1) 2691140; fax (1) 2693040; e-mail turkemb@infoweb.abs.net; Ambassador: ÖMER SAHINKAYA.

United Kingdom: Shehu Shangari Way, Maitama, Abuja; tel. (9) 5232010; fax (9) 5233552; High Commissioner: Sir GRAHAM BURTON.

USA: 2 Walter Carrington Crescent, Victoria Island, Lagos; tel. (1) 2610050; fax (1) 2619856; Ambassador: WILLIAM H. TWADDELL.

Venezuela: 35B Adetokunbo Ademola St, Victoria Island, POB 3727, Lagos; tel. (1) 2611590; fax (1) 2617350; Ambassador: ALFREDO ENRIQUE VARGAS.

Yugoslavia: 7 Maitama Sule St, SW Ikoyi, PMB 978, Lagos; tel. (1) 2680238; Chargé d'affaires a.i.: DORBEJOG KAHANSKI.

Zambia: 11 Keffi St, SW Ikoyi, PMB 6119, Lagos; High Commissioner: B. N. NKUNIKA (acting).

Zimbabwe: 10A Tiamiyu Savage St, POB 50247, Victoria Island, Lagos; tel. (1) 2619328; High Commissioner: GIFT PUNUNGUE (acting).

Judicial System

Supreme Court: Three Arms Complex, Central District, PMB 308, Abuja; tel. (9) 2346594; consists of a Chief Justice and up to 15 Justices, appointed by the President, on the recommendation of the National Judicial Council (subject to the approval of the Senate). It has original jurisdiction in any dispute between the Federation and a State, or between States, and hears appeals from the Federal Court of Appeal.

   Chief Justice: MUHAMMADU LAWAL UWAIS.

Court of Appeal: consists of a President and at least 35 Justices, of whom three must be experts in Islamic (Shari'a) law and three experts in Customary law.

Federal High Court: consists of a Chief Judge and a number of other judges.

Each State has a **High Court,** consisting of a Chief Judge and a number of judges, appointed by the Governor of the State on the recommendation of the National Judicial Council (subject to the approval of the House of Assembly of the State). If required, a state may have a **Shari'a Court of Appeal** (dealing with Islamic civil law) and a **Customary Court of Appeal. Special Military Tribunals** have been established to try offenders accused of crimes such as corruption, drug-trafficking and armed robbery; appeals against

rulings of the Special Military Tribunals are referred to a **Special Appeals Tribunal**, which comprises retired judges.

Religion

ISLAM

According to the 1963 census, there were more than 26m. Muslims (47.2% of the total population) in Nigeria.

Spiritual Head: Alhaji MOHAMED MACCIDO, the Sultan of Sokoto.

CHRISTIANITY

The 1963 census enumerated more than 19m. Christians (34.5% of the total population).

Christian Council of Nigeria: 139 Ogunlana Drive, Surulere, POB 2838, Lagos; tel. (1) 836019; f. 1929; 12 full mems and seven assoc. mems; Pres. Rt Rev. Dr S. A. FALEYE; Gen. Sec. C. O. WILLIAMS.

The Anglican Communion

Anglicans are adherents of the Church of the Province of Nigeria, comprising 61 dioceses. Nigeria, formerly part of the Province of West Africa, became a separate Province in 1979; in 1997 it was divided into three separate provinces. The Church had an estimated 10m. members in 1990.

Archbishop of Province I and Bishop of Lagos: Most Rev. JOSEPH ADETILOYE, Archbishop's Palace, 29 Marina, POB 13, Lagos; tel. (1) 2635681; fax (1) 2631264.

Archbishop of Province II and Bishop of the Diocese on the Niger: Most Rev. JONATHAN ARINZECHUKWU ONYEMELUKWE, Bishops-court, POB 42, Onitsha.

Archbishop of Province III and Bishop of Abuja: Most Rev. PETER JASPER AKINOLA, Archbishop's Palace, POB 212, ADCP, Abuja; fax (9) 5230986; e-mail abuja@anglican.skannet.com.ng.

General Secretary: Ven. SAMUEL B. AKINOLA, 29 Marina, POB 78, Lagos; tel. (1) 2635681; fax (1) 2631264.

The Roman Catholic Church

Nigeria comprises nine archdioceses, 32 dioceses, three Apostolic Vicariates and one Apostolic Prefecture. At 31 December 1998 the total number of adherents represented an estimated 10% of the population.

Catholic Bishops' Conference of Nigeria: 6 Force Rd, POB 951, Lagos; tel. (1) 2635849; (1) fax 2636680; e-mail cathsecl@infoweb.abs.net; f. 1976; Pres. Most Rev. Dr ALBERT KANENE OBIEFUNA, Archbishop of Onitsha.

Catholic Secretariat of Nigeria: 6 Force Rd, POB 951, Lagos; tel. (1) 2635849; fax (1) 2636680; e-mail cathsecl@infoweb.abs.net; Sec.-Gen. Rev. Fr MATTHEW HASSAN KUKAH.

Archbishop of Abuja: Most Rev. JOHN O. ONAIYEKAN, Archdiocesan Secretariat, Block 64, Area 2, Section II, POB 286, Garki, Abuja; tel. and fax (9) 2340661.

Archbishop of Benin City: Most Rev. PATRICK E. EKPU, Archdiocesan Secretariat, POB 35, Benin City, Edo; tel. (52) 253787; fax (52) 255763.

Archbishop of Calabar: Most Rev. BRIAN D. USANGA, Archdiocesan Secretariat, PMB 1044, Calabar, Cross River; tel. (87) 222176; fax (87) 221407.

Archbishop of Ibadan: Most Rev. FELIX ALABA JOB, Archdiocesan Secretariat, 8 Latosa Rd, PMB 5057, Ibadan, Oyo; tel. (22) 2413544; fax (22) 2414855.

Archbishop of Jos: Most Rev. GABRIEL G. GANAKA, Archdiocesan Secretariat, 20 Joseph Gomwalk Rd, POB 494, Jos, Plateau; tel. (73) 42878; fax (73) 456880.

Archbishop of Kaduna: Most Rev. PETER YARIYOK JATAU, Archbishop's House, Tafawa Balewa Way, POB 248, Kaduna; tel. (62) 236076; fax (62) 240026.

Archbishop of Lagos: Most Rev. ANTHONY OLUBUNMI OKOGIE, Archdiocesan Secretariat, 19 Catholic Mission St, POB 8, Lagos; tel. and fax (1) 2633841.

Archbishop of Onitsha: Most Rev. ALBERT KANENE OBIEFUNA, Archdiocesan Secretariat, POB 411, Onitsha, Anambra; tel. (46) 210444; fax (46) 214537.

Archbishop of Owerri: Most Rev. ANTHONY J. V. OBINNA, Archdiocesan Secretariat, POB 85, Owerri, Imo; tel. (83) 230115; fax (83) 230760.

Other Christian Churches

Brethren Church of Nigeria: c/o Kulp Bible School, POB 1, Mubi, Adamawa; f. 1923; 100,000 mems; Gen. Sec. Rev. ABRAHAM WUTA TIZHE.

Church of the Lord (Aladura): Anthony Village, Ikorodu Rd, POB 308, Ikeja, Lagos; tel. (1) 4964749; f. 1930; 1.1m. mems; Primate Dr E. O. A. ADEJOBI.

Lutheran Church of Christ in Nigeria: POB 21, Numan, Adamawa; 575,000 mems; Pres. Rt Rev. Dr DAVID L. WINDIBIZIRI.

Lutheran Church of Nigeria: Obot Idim Ibesikpo, Uyo, Akwa Ibom; tel. and fax (85) 201848; f. 1936; 370,000 mems; Pres. Rev. S. J. UDOFIA.

Methodist Church Nigeria: Wesley House, 21–22 Marina, POB 2011, Lagos; tel. (1) 2631853; 483,500 mems; Patriarch Rev. SUNDAY COFFIE MBANG.

Nigerian Baptist Convention: Baptist Bldg, PMB 5113, Ibadan; tel. (2) 412146; 500,000 mems; Pres. Rev. DAVID H. KARO; Gen. Sec. Dr SAMUEL T. OLA AKANDE.

Presbyterian Church of Nigeria: 26–29 Ehere Rd, Ogbor Hill, POB 2635, Aba, Imo; tel. (82) 222551; f. 1846; 130,000 mems; Moderator Rt Rev. Dr A. A. OTU; Synod Clerk Rev. UBON B. USUNG.

The Redeemed Church of Christ, the Church of the Foursquare Gospel, the Qua Iboe Church and the Salvation Army are prominent among numerous other Christian churches active in Nigeria.

AFRICAN RELIGIONS

The beliefs, rites and practices of the people of Nigeria are very diverse, varying between ethnic groups and between families in the same group. In 1963 about 10m. persons (18% of the total population) were followers of traditional beliefs.

The Press

DAILIES

Abuja Times: Daily Times of Nigeria Ltd, 2 Hasper Crescent, Wuse Zone 7, PMB 115 Gaski, Abuja, tel. (1) 4900850; f. 1992; Editor CLEMENT ILOBA.

Daily Champion: Isolo Industrial Estate, Oshodi-Apapa, Lagos; Editor EMEKA OMEIHE.

Daily Express: Commercial Amalgamated Printers, 30 Glover St, Lagos; f. 1938; Editor Alhaji AHMED ALAO (acting); circ. 20,000.

Daily Sketch: Sketch Publishing Ltd, Oba Adebimpe Rd, PMB 5067, Ibadan; tel. (2) 414851; f. 1964; govt-owned; Chair. RONKE OKUSANYA; Editor ADEMOLA IDOWU; circ. 64,000.

Daily Star: 9 Works Rd, PMB 1139, Enugu; tel. (42) 253561; Editor JOSEF BEL-MOLOKWU.

Daily Times: Daily Times of Nigeria Ltd, New Isheri Rd, Agidingbi, PMB 21340, Ikeja, Lagos; tel. (1) 4900850; f. 1925; 60% govt-owned; Editor OGBUAGU ANIKWE; circ. 400,000.

The Democrat: 9 Ahmed Talib Ave, POB 4457, Kaduna South, tel. (62) 231907; f. 1983; Editor ABDULHAMID BABATUNDE; circ. 100,000.

Evening Times: Daily Times of Nigeria Ltd, New Isheri Rd, Agidingbi, PMB 21340, Ikeja, Lagos; tel. (1) 4900850; Man. Dir Dr ONUKA ADINOYI-OJO; Editor CLEMENT ILOBA; circ. 20,000.

The Guardian: Rutam House, Isolo Expressway, Isolo, PMB 1217, Oshodi, Lagos; tel. (1) 524111; internet www.ngrguardiannews.com; f. 1983; Publr ALEX IBRU; Editor EMEKA IZEZE; circ. 80,000.

National Concord: Concord House, 42 Concord Way, POB 4483, Ikeja, Lagos; f. 1980; Editor NSIKAK ESSIEN; circ. 200,000.

New Nigerian: Ahmadu Bello Way, POB 254, Kaduna; tel. (62) 201420; f. 1965; govt-owned; Chair. Prof. TEKENA TAMUNO; Editor (vacant); circ. 80,000.

Nigerian Chronicle: Cross River State Newspaper Corpn, 17-19 Barracks Rd, POB 1074, Calabar; tel. (87) 224976; fax (87) 224979; f. 1970; Editor UNIMKE NAWA; circ. 50,000.

Nigerian Herald: Kwara State Printing and Publishing Corpn, Offa Rd, PMB 1369, Ilorin; tel. and fax (31) 220506; f. 1973; sponsored by Kwara State Govt; Editor RAZAK EL-ALAWA; circ. 25,000.

Nigerian Observer: The Bendel Newspaper Corpn, 18 Airport Rd, POB 1143, Benin City; tel. (52) 240050; f. 1968; Editor TONY IKEAKANAM; circ. 150,000.

Nigerian Standard: 5 Joseph Gomwalk Rd, POB 2112, Jos; f. 1972; govt-owned; Editor SALE ILIYA; circ. 100,000.

Nigerian Statesman: Imo Newspapers Ltd, Owerri-Egbu Rd, POB 1095, Owerri; tel. (83) 230099; f. 1978; sponsored by Imo State Govt; Editor EDUBE WADIBIA.

Nigerian Tide: Rivers State Newspaper Corpn, 4 Ikwerre Rd, POB 5072, Port Harcourt; f. 1971; Editor AUGUSTINE NJOAGWUANI; circ. 30,000.

Nigerian Tribune: African Newspapers of Nigeria Ltd, Imalefalafi St, Oke-Ado, POB 78, Ibadan; tel. (2) 2313410; fax (2) 2317573; f. 1949; Editor FOLU OLAMITI; circ. 109,000.

Post Express: 7 Warehouse Rd, PMB 1186, Apapa, Lagos; tel. (1) 5453351; fax (1) 5453436; e-mail postexpress@nova.net.ng; internet www.postexpresswired.com; Publr Chief S. ODUWU; Man. Dir Dr STANLEY MACEBUH.

The Punch: Skyway Press, Kudeti St, PMB 21204, Onipetsi, Ikeja; tel. (1) 4963580; f. 1976; Editor GBMEIGA OGUNLEYE; circ. 150,000.

Vanguard: Kirikiri Canal, PMB 1007, Apapa; e-mail vanguard@linkserve.com.ng; f. 1984; Editor FRANK AIGBOGUN.

SUNDAY NEWSPAPERS

Sunday Chronicle: Cross River State Newspaper Corpn, PMB 1074, Calabar; f. 1977; Editor-in-Chief ETIM ANIM; circ. 163,000.

Sunday Concord: Concord House, 42 Concord Way, POB 4483, Ikeja, Lagos; f. 1980; Editor DELE ALAKE.

Sunday Herald: Kwara State Printing and Publishing Corpn, PMB 1369, Ilorin; tel. (31) 220976; f. 1981; Editor CHARLES OSAGIE (acting).

Sunday New Nigerian: Ahmadu Bello Way, POB 254, Kaduna; tel. (62) 235221; fax (62) 212464; Editor (vacant).

Sunday Observer: PMB 1334, Bendel Newspapers Corpn, 18 Airport Rd, Benin City; f. 1968; Editor T. O. BORHA; circ. 60,000.

Sunday Punch: Kudeti St, PMB 21204, Ikeja; tel. (1) 4964691; fax (1) 4960715; f. 1973; Editor DAYO WRIGHT; circ. 150,000.

Sunday Sketch: Sketch Publishing Co Ltd, PMB 5067, Ibadan; tel. (2) 414851; f. 1964; govt-owned; Editor OBAFEMI OREDEIN; circ. 125,000.

Sunday Standard: Plateau Publishing Co Ltd, Owerri-Egbu Rd, PMB 1095, Owerri; tel. (83) 230099; f. 1978; sponsored by Imo State Govt; Editor EDUBE WADIBIA.

Sunday Sun: PMB 1025, Okoro House, Factory Lane, off Upper Mission Rd, New Benin.

Sunday Tide: 4 Ikwerre Rd, POB 5072, Port Harcourt; f. 1971; Editor AUGUSTINE NJOAGWUANI.

Sunday Times: Daily Times of Nigeria Ltd, New Isheri Rd, Agidingbi, PMB 21340, Ikeja, Lagos; tel. (1) 4900850; f. 1953; 60% govt-owned; Editor DUPE AJAYI; circ. 100,000.

Sunday Tribune: POB 78, Oke-Ado, Ibadan; tel. (2) 2310886; Editor WALE OJO.

Sunday Vanguard: PMB 1007, Apapa; Editor DUPE AJAYI.

WEEKLIES

Albishir: Triumph Publishing Co Ltd, Gidan Sa'adu Zungur, PMB 3155, Kano; tel. (64) 260273; f. 1981; Hausa; Editor ALIYU UMAR (acting); circ. 15,000.

Business Times: Daily Times of Nigeria Ltd, New Isheri Rd, Agidingbi, PMB 21340, Ikeja, Lagos; tel. (1) 4900850; f. 1925; 60% govt-owned; Editor GODFREY BAMAWO; circ. 22,000.

Gboungboun: Sketch Publishing Co Ltd, New Court Rd, PMB 5067, Ibadan; tel. (2) 414851; govt-owned; Yoruba; Editor A. O. ADEBANJO; circ. 80,000.

The Independent: Bodija Rd, PMB 5109, Ibadan; f. 1960; English; Roman Catholic; Editor Rev. F. B. CRONIN-COLTSMAN; circ. 13,000.

Irohin Imole: 15 Bamgbose St, POB 1495, Lagos; f. 1957; Yoruba; Editor TUNJI ADEOSUN.

Irohin Yoruba: 212 Broad St, PMB 2416, Lagos; tel. (1) 410886; f. 1945; Yoruba; Editor S. A. AJIBADE; circ. 85,000.

Lagos Life: Guardian Newspapers Ltd, Rutam House, Isolo Expressway, Isolo, PMB 1217, Oshodi, Lagos; f. 1985; Editor BISI OGUNBADEJO; circ. 100,000.

Lagos Weekend: Daily Times of Nigeria Ltd, New Isheri Rd, Agidingbi, PMB 21340, Ikeja, Lagos; tel. (1) 4900850; f. 1965; 60% govt-owned; news and pictures; Editor SAM OGWA; circ. 85,000.

The News: Lagos; independent; Editor-in-Chief JENKINS ALUMONA.

Newswatch: 3 Billingsway Rd, Oregun, Lagos; tel. (1) 4960950; fax (1) 4935654; f. 1985; English; Editor-in-Chief DAN AGBESE.

Nigerian Radio/TV Times: Nigerian Broadcasting Corpn, POB 12504, Ikoyi.

Sporting Records: Daily Times of Nigeria Ltd, New Isheri Rd, Agidingbi, PMB 21340, Ikeja, Lagos; tel. (1) 4900850; f. 1961; 60% govt-owned; Editor CYRIL KAPPO; circ. 10,000.

Tempo: 26 Ijaiye Rd, PMB 21531, Ogba, Ikeja, Lagos; tel. (1) 920975; fax (1) 4924998; e-mail ijc@linkserve.com.ng; news magazine.

Times International: Daily Times of Nigeria Ltd, 3–7 Kakawa St, POB 139, Lagos; f. 1974; Editor Dr HEZY IDOWU; circ. 50,000.

Truth (The Muslim Weekly): 45 Idumagbo Ave, POB 418, Lagos; tel. (1) 2668455; f. 1951; Editor S. O. LAWAL.

ENGLISH LANGUAGE PERIODICALS

Afriscope: 29 Salami Saibu St, PMB 1119, Yaba; monthly; African current affairs.

The Ambassador: PMB 2011, 1 peru-Remo, Ogun; tel. (39) 620115; quarterly; Roman Catholic; circ. 20,000.

Benin Review: Ethiope Publishing Corpn, PMB 1332, Benin City; f. 1974; African art and culture; 2 a year; circ. 50,000.

Headlines: Daily Times of Nigeria Ltd, New Isheri Rd, Agindingbi, PMB 21340, Ikeja, Lagos; f. 1973; monthly; Editor ADAMS ALIU; circ. 500,000.

Home Studies: Daily Times Publications, 3–7 Kakawa St, Lagos; f. 1964; two a month; Editor Dr ELIZABETH E. IKEM; circ. 40,000.

Insight: 3 Kakawa St, POB 139, Lagos; quarterly; contemporary issues; Editor SAM AMUKA; circ. 5,000.

Journal of the Nigerian Medical Association: 3–7 Kakawa St, POB 139, Apapa; quarterly; Editor Prof. A. O. ADESOLA.

Lagos Education Review: Faculty of Education, University of Lagos Akoka, Lagos; tel. (1) 820448; fax (1) 822644; f. 1978; 2 a year; African education; Editor M. N. OKENIMKPE.

The Leader: 19A Assumpta Press Ave, Industrial Layout, PMB 1017, Owerri, Imo; tel. (83) 230932; fortnightly; Roman Catholic; Editor Rev. KEVIN C. AKAGHA.

Management in Nigeria: Plot 22, Idowu Taylor St, Victoria Island, POB 2557, Lagos; tel. (1) 615105; fax (1) 614116; e-mail nim@rd.nig.com; quarterly; journal of Nigerian Inst. of Management; Editor DELE OSUNDAHUNS; circ. 25,000.

Marketing in Nigeria: Alpha Publications, Surulere, POB 1163, Lagos; f. 1977; monthly; Editor B. O. K. NWELIH; circ. 30,000.

Modern Woman: 47–49 Salami Saibu St, Marina, POB 2583, Lagos; f. 1964; monthly; Man. Editor TOUN ONABANJO.

The New Nation: 52 Iwaya Rd, Onike, Yaba, Surulere, POB 896, Lagos; tel. (1) 5863629; monthly; news magazine.

Nigeria Magazine: Federal Dept of Culture, PMB 12524, Lagos; tel. (1) 5802060; f. 1927; quarterly; travel, cultural, historical and general; Editor B. D. LEMCHI; circ. 5,000.

Nigerian Businessman's Magazine: 39 Mabo St, Surulere, Lagos; monthly; Nigerian and overseas commerce.

Nigerian Journal of Economic and Social Studies: Nigerian Economic Society, c/o Dept of Economics, University of Ibadan; tel. (2) 8101701; fax (2) 8100079; f. 1959; 3 a year; Editor Prof. A. H. EKPO.

Nigerian Journal of Science: University of Ibadan, POB 4039, Ibadan; publ. of the Science Asscn of Nigeria; f. 1966; 2 a year; Editor Prof. L. B. KOLAWOLE; circ. 1,000.

Nigerian Medical Journal: 3 Kakawa St, POB 139, Lagos; monthly.

Nigerian Radio/TV Times: Broadcasting House, POB 12504, Lagos; monthly.

Nigerian Teacher: 3 Kakawa St, POB 139, Lagos; quarterly.

Nigerian Worker: United Labour Congress, 97 Herbert Macaulay St, Lagos; Editor LAWRENCE BORHA.

The President: New Breed Organization Ltd, Plot 14 Western Ave, 1 Rafiu Shitty St, Alaka Estate, Surulere, POB 385, Lagos; tel. (1) 5802690; fax (1) 5831175; fortnightly; management; Chief Editor CHRIS OKOLIE.

Quality: Ultimate Publications Ltd, Oregun Rd, Lagos; f. 1987; monthly; Editor BALA DAN MUSA.

Radio-Vision Times: Western Nigerian Radio-Vision Service, Tele-vision House, POB 1460, Ibadan; monthly; Editor ALTON A. ADEDEJI.

Savanna: Ahmadu Bello University Press Ltd, PMB 1094, Zaria; tel. (69) 50054; f. 1972; 2 a year; Editor AUDEE T. GIWA; circ. 1,000.

Spear: Daily Times of Nigeria Ltd, New Isheri Rd, Agidingbi, PMB 21340, Ikeja, Lagos; tel. (1) 4900850; f. 1962; monthly; family magazine; Editor COKER ONITA; circ. 10,000.

Technical and Commercial Message: Surulere, POB 1163, Lagos; f. 1980; 6 a year; Editor B. O. K. NWELIH; circ. 12,500.

Today's Challenge: PMB 2010, Jos; tel. (73) 52230; f. 1951; 6 a year; religious and educational; Editor JACOB SHAIBY TSADO; circ. 15,000.

Woman's World: Daily Times of Nigeria Ltd, New Isheri Rd, Agidingbi, PMB 21340, Ikeja, Lagos; monthly; Editor TOYIN JOHNSON; circ. 12,000.

VERNACULAR PERIODICALS

Abokiyar Hira: Albah International Publishers, POB 6177, Bompai, Kano; f. 1987; monthly; Hausa; cultural; Editor BASHARI F. FOUKBAH; circ. 35,000.

Gaskiya ta fi Kwabo: Ahmadu Bello Way, POB 254, Kaduna; tel. (62) 201420; f. 1939; 3 a week; Hausa; Editor ABDUL-HASSAN IBRAHIM.

NEWS AGENCIES

News Agency of Nigeria (NAN): Area 1, 29 Benue Crescent, PMB 7006, Garki, Abuja; tel. (9) 2341189; fax (9) 2343196; e-mail abuja@nan.nan.com.ng; internet www.nan.com.ng; f. 1978; Man. Dir Mallam WADA ABDULLAHI MAIDA; Editor-in-Chief DAVE IGIEWE.

Foreign Bureaux

Agence France-Presse (AFP): 26B Keffi St, SW Ikoyi, PMB 2448, Lagos; tel. (1) 2683550; fax (1) 2682752; Bureau Chief GÉRARD VANDENBERGHE.

Informatsionnoye Telegrafnoye Agentstvo Rossii— Telegrafnoye Agentstvo Suverennykh Stran (ITAR—TASS) (Russia): 401 St, POB 6465, Victoria Island, Lagos; tel. (1) 617119; Correspondent BORIS VASILIEVICH PILNIKOV.

Inter Press Service (IPS) (Italy): c/o News Agency of Nigeria, PMB 12756, Lagos; tel. (1) 5801290; Correspondent REMI OYO.

Pan-African News Agency (PANA): c/o News Agency of Nigeria, National Arts Theatre, POB 8715, Marina, Lagos; tel. (1) 5801290; f. 1979.

Xinhua (New China) News Agency (People's Republic of China): 161A Adeola Odeku St, Victoria Island, POB 70278, Lagos; tel. (1) 2612464; Bureau Chief ZHAI JINGSHENG.

Publishers

Africana-FEP Publishers Ltd: Book House Trust, 1 Africana-FEP Drive, PMB 1639, Onitsha; tel. (46) 410669; f. 1973; study guides, general science, textbooks; Man. Dir RALPH O. EKPEH.

Ahmadu Bello University Press: PMB 1094, Zaria; tel. (69) 50054; f. 1974; history, Africana, social sciences, education, litera-ture and arts; Man. Dir Alhaji SAIBU A. AFEGBUA.

Albah International Publishers: 100 Kurawa, Bompai-Kano, POB 6177, Kano City; f. 1978; Africana, Islamic, educational and general, in Hausa; Chair. BASHARI F. ROUKBAH.

Alliance West African Publishers: Orindingbin Estate, New Aketan Layout, PMB 1039, Oyo; tel. (85) 230798; f. 1971; educational and general; Man. Dir Chief M. O. OGUNMOLA.

Aromolaran Publishing Co Ltd: POB 1800, Ibadan; tel. (2) 715980; f. 1968; educational and general; Man. Dir Dr ADEKUNLE AROMOLARAN.

Daar Communications Ltd: Communication Village, AIT Rd, Off Lagos–Abeokuta Expressway, Ilapo Village, Alagbado, Lagos; tel. (1) 2644814; fax (1) 2644817; broadcasting and information services; Man. Dir. KENNY OGUNGBE.

Daystar Press: Daystar House, POB 1261, Ibadan; tel. (2) 8102670; f. 1962; religious and educational; Man. PHILLIP ADELAKUN LADOKUN.

ECWA Productions Ltd: PMB 2010, Jos; tel. (73) 52230; f. 1973; religious and educational; Gen. Man. Rev. J. K. BOLARIN.

Ethiope Publishing Corpn: Ring Rd, PMB 1332, Benin City; tel. (52) 243036; f. 1970; general fiction and non-fiction, textbooks, reference, science, arts and history; Man. Dir SUNDAY N. OLAYE.

Evans Brothers (Nigeria Publishers) Ltd: Jericho Rd, PMB 5164, Ibadan; tel. (2) 2414394; fax (2) 2410757; f. 1966; general and educational; Chair. Dr A. O. OJORA; Man. Dir B. O. BOLODEOKU.

Fourth Dimension Publishing Co Ltd: 16 Fifth Avenue, City Layout, PMB 01164, Enugu; tel. (42) 459969; fax (42) 456904; e-mail nwankwov@infoweb.abs.net; f. 1977; periodicals, fiction, verse, educational and children's; Chair. ARTHUR NWANKWO; Man. Dir V. U. NWANKWO.

Gbabeks Publishers Ltd: POB 37252, Ibadan; tel. (62) 2315705; f. 1982; educational and technical; Man. Dir TAYO OGUNBEKUN.

Heinemann Educational Books (Nigeria) Ltd: 1 Ighodaro Rd, Jericho, PMB 5205, Ibadan; tel. (2) 2412268; fax (2) 2411089; e-mail info@heinemannbooks.com; f. 1962; educational, law, medical and general; Chair. AIGBOJE HIGO; Man. Dir AYO OGUNIYI.

Heritage Books: 2–8 Calcutta Crescent, Gate 1, POB 610, Apapa, Lagos; tel. (1) 871333; f. 1971; general; Chair. NAIWU OSAHON.

Ibadan University Press: Publishing House, University of Ibadan, PMB 16, IU Post Office, Ibadan; tel. (2) 400550; f. 1951; scholarly, science, law, general and educational; Dir F. A. ADESANOYE.

Ilesanmi Press Ltd: Akure Rd, POB 204, Ilesha; tel. 2062; f. 1955; general and educational; Man. Dir G. E. ILESANMI.

John West Publications Ltd: Plot 2, Block A, Acme Rd, Ogba Industrial Estate, PMB 21001, Ikeja, Lagos; tel. (1) 4925459; f. 1964 general; Man. Dir Alhaji L. K. JAKAUDE.

Kolasanya Publishing Enterprise: 2 Epe Rd, Oke-Owa, PMB 2099, Ijebu-Ode; general and educational; Man. Dir Chief K. OSUN-SANYA.

Literamed Publications Ltd (Lantern Books): Plot 45, Alausa Bus-stop, Oregun Industrial Estate, Ikeja, PMB 21068, Lagos; tel. (1) 4962512; fax (1) 4972217; e-mail literamed@cyberspce.net.ng; general; Man. Dir O. M. LAWAL-SOLARIN.

Longman Nigeria Ltd: 52 Oba Akran Ave, PMB 21036, Ikeja, Lagos; tel. (1) 4978925; fax (1) 4964370; f. 1961; general and educational; Man. Dir J. A. OLOWONIYI.

Macmillan Nigeria Publishers Ltd: Ilupeju Industrial Estate, 4 Industrial Ave, POB 264, Yaba, Lagos; tel. (1) 4962185; f. 1965; educational and general; Exec. Chair. J. O. EMMANUEL; Man. Dir Dr A. I. ADELEKAN.

Minaj Systems Ltd: Ivie House, 4–6 Ajose Adeogun St, POB 70811, Victoria Island, Lagos; tel. (1) 2621168; fax (1) 2621167; e-mail minaj@minaj.com; broadcasting, printing and publishing; Chair. Chief MIKE NNANYE I. AJEGBO.

Nelson Publishers Ltd: 8 Ilupeju By-Pass, Ikeja, PMB 21303, Lagos; tel. (1) 4961452; general and educational; Chair. Prof. C. O. TAIWO; Man. Dir R. O. OGUNBO.

Northern Nigerian Publishing Co Ltd: Gaskiya Bldg, POB 412, Zaria; tel. (69) 32087; f. 1966; general, educational and vernacular texts; Man. Dir H. HAYAT.

NPS Educational Publishers Ltd: Trusthouse, Ring Rd, off Akinyemi Way, POB 62, Ibadan; tel. (2) 316006; f. 1969; academic, scholarly and educational; CEO T. D. OTESANYA.

Nwamife Publishers: 10 Ibiam St, Uwani, POB 430, Enugu; tel. (42) 338254; f. 1971; general and educational; Chair. FELIX C. ADI.

Obafemi Awolowo University Press Ltd: Obafemi Awolowo University, Ile-Ife; tel. (36) 230284; f. 1968; educational, scholarly and periodicals; Man. Dir AKIN FATOKUN.

Obobo Books: 2–8 Calcutta Crescent, Gate 1, POB 610, Apapa, Lagos; tel. (1) 5871333; f. 1981; children's books; Editorial Dir BAKIN KUNAMA.

Ogunsanya Press Publishers and Bookstores Ltd: SW9/1133 Orita Challenge, Idiroko, POB 95, Ibadan; tel. (2) 310924; f. 1970; educational; Man. Dir Chief LUCAS JUSTUS POPO-OLA OGUNSANYA.

Onibonoje Press and Book Industries (Nigeria) Ltd: Felele Layout, Challenge, POB 3109, Ibadan; tel. (2) 313956; f. 1958; educational and general; Chair. G. ONIBONOJE; Man. Dir J. O. ONIBONOJE.

Pilgrim Books Ltd: New Oluyole Industrial Estate, Ibadan/Lagos Expressway, PMB 5617, Ibadan; tel. (2) 317218; educational and general; Man. Dir JOHN E. LEIGH.

Spectrum Books Ltd: Sunshine House, 1 Emmanuel Alayande St, Oluyole Estate, PMB 5612, Ibadan; tel. and fax (2) 2312705; e-mail joopberkhout@micro.com.ng; internet www.spectrum.safari .com.ng; f. 1978; educational and fiction; Man. Dir JOOP BERKHOUT.

University of Lagos Press: University of Lagos, POB 132, Akoka, Yaba, Lagos; tel. (1) 825048; e-mail library@rcl.nig.com; university textbooks, monographs, lectures and journals; Man. Dir S. BODUNDE BANKOLE.

University Press Ltd: Three Crowns Bldg, Eleyele Rd, Jericho, PMB 5095, Ibadan; tel. (2) 2411356; fax (2) 2412056; e-mail unipress@skar.net.com; f. 1978; associated with Oxford University Press; educational; Man. Dir WAHEED O. OLAJIDE.

University Publishing Co: 11 Central School Rd, POB 386, Onitsha; tel. (46) 210013; f. 1959; primary, secondary and university textbooks; Chair. E. O. UGWUEGBULEM.

Vanguard Media Ltd: Vanguard Ave, off Mile 2/Apapa Expressway, Kirikiri Canal; tel. (1) 5871200; fax (1) 5872662; e-mail vanguard@linkserve.com.ng; Publr SAM AMUKA.

Vista Books Ltd: 59 Awolowo Rd, POB 282, Yaba, Lagos; tel. (1) 2681656; fax (1) 2685679; f. 1991; general fiction and non-fiction, arts, children's and educational; Man. Dir Dr T. C. NWOSU.

West African Book Publishers Ltd: Ilupeju Industrial Estate, 28-32 Industrial Ave, POB 3445, Lagos; tel. (1) 4977700; fax (1) 4970294; f. 1967; textbooks, children's, periodicals and general; Dir F. B. OMO-EBOH.

Government Publishing House

Government Press: PMB 2020, Kaduna; tel. 213812.

PUBLISHERS' ASSOCIATION

Nigerian Publishers Association: Book House, NPA Permanent Secretariat, Jericho G.R.A., POB 2541, Ibadan; tel. (2) 2413396; f. 1965; Pres. S. B. BANKOLE.

Broadcasting and Communications

TELECOMMUNICATIONS

Nigerian Communications Commission (NCC): Plot 19, Aguata Close, Garki 2, Abuja; tel. (9) 2344589; internet www.ncc.gov.ng; f. 1992 as an independent regulatory body for the supply of telecommunications services and facilities.

Intercellular Nigeria Ltd: UBA House, 57, Marina, PMB 80078, Victoria Island, Lagos; tel. (1) 4703010; fax (1) 2643014; e-mail

hq@intercellular-ng.com; f. 1993; internet and international telephone services; Pres. BASHIR EL-RUFAI.

Motophone Ltd: C. & C. Towers, Plot 1684, Sanusi Fafumwa St, Victoria Island, Lagos; tel. (1) 2624168; fax (1) 2620079; e-mail motophone@hyperia.com; f. 1990; Man. Dir ERIC CHAMCHOUM.

Multi-Links Telecommunication Ltd: 231 Adeola Odeku St, Victoria Island, POB 3453, Marina, Lagos; tel. (1) 7740000; fax (1) 2622452; e-mail ccu@multilink.com; f. 1994; Man. Dir C. K. RAMANI.

Nigerian Mobile Telecommunications Ltd (M-TEL): 3 M-Tel St, off Mal. Aminu Kano Crescent, Wuse 2, Abuja; tel. (9) 5237801; fax (9) 409066; f. 1996; Man. Dir Eng. ISMAILA MOHAMMED.

Nigerian Telecommunications (NITEL): 2 Bissau St, off Herbert Macaulay Way, Wuse Zone 6, Abuja; tel. (9) 5233021; Man. Dir Dr EMMANUEL OJEBA.

Telnet (Nigeria) Ltd: Plot 242, Kofo Abayomi St, Victoria Island, POB 53656, Falomi Ikoyi, Lagos; tel. (1) 2611729; fax (1) 2619945; f. 1985; telecommunications engineering and consultancy services; Man. Dir Dr BURIAN CAREW.

BROADCASTING

Regulatory Authority

National Broadcasting Commission: Lagos; Dir-Gen. Mallam DANLADI BAKO.

Radio

Federal Radio Corporation of Nigeria (FRCN): Area 11, Garki, PMB 55, Abuja; tel. (9) 2345915; fax (9) 2345914; f. 1976; controlled by the Fed. Govt and divided into five zones: Lagos (English); Enugu (English, Igbo, Izon, Efik and Tiv); Ibadan (English, Yoruba, Edo, Urhobo and Igala); Kaduna (English, Hausa, Kanuri, Fulfulde and Nupe); Abuja (English, Hausa, Igbo and Yoruba); Dir-Gen. ITYOHEGH.

Voice of Nigeria (VON): Radio House, Herbert Macaulay Way, Area 10, Garki, Abuja; tel. (9) 2344017; fax (9) 2346970; f. 1990; controlled by the Fed. Govt; external services in English, French, Arabic, Ki-Swahili, Hausa and Fulfulde; Dir-Gen. TAIWO ALIMI.

Menage Holding's Broadcasting System Ltd: Umuahia, Imo; commenced broadcasting Jan. 1996; commercial.

Ray Power 100 Drive: Abeokuta Express Way, Ilapo, Alagbado, Lagos; tel. (1) 2644814; fax (1) 2644817; commenced broadcasting Sept. 1994; commercial; Chair. Chief RAYMOND DOKPESI.

Television

Nigerian Television Authority (NTA): Television House, Ahmadu Bello Way, Victoria Island, PMB 12036, Lagos; tel. (1) 2615949; f. 1976; controlled by the Fed. Govt; responsible for all aspects of television broadcasting; Chair. IFEANYINWA NZEAKOR; Dir-Gen. Alhaji MOHAMMED IBRAHIM.

NTA Aba/Owerri: Channel 6, PMB 7126, Aba, Abia; tel. (83) 220922; Gen. Man. GODWIN DURU.

NTA Abeokuta: Channel 12, PMB 2190, Abeokuta, Ogun; tel. (39) 242971; f. 1979; broadcasts in English and local languages; Gen-Man. VICTOR FOLIVI.

NTA Abuja: PMB 55, Garki, Abuja; tel. (9) 2345915.

NTA Akure: PMB 794, Akure; tel. (34) 230351; Gen. Man. JIBOLA DEDENUOLA.

NTA Bauchi: PMB 0146, Bauchi; tel. (77) 42748; f. 1976; Man. MUHAMMAD AL-AMIN.

NTA Benin City: West Circular Rd, PMB 1117, Benin City; Gen. Man. J. O. N. EZEKOKA.

NTA Calabar: 105 Marion Rd, Calabar; Man. E. ETUK.

NTA Enugu: Independence Layout, PMB 01530, Enugu, Anambra; tel. (42) 335120; f. 1960; Gen. Man. G. C. MEFO.

NTA Ibadan: POB 1460, Ibadan, Oyo; tel. (2) 713238; Gen. Man. JIBOLA DEDENUOLA.

NTA Ikeja: Tejuosho Ave, Surulere.

NTA Ilorin: PMB 1478, Ilorin; tel. and fax (31) 224196; Gen. Man. VICKY OLUMUDI.

NTA Jos: PMB 2134, Jos; Gen. Man. M. J. BEWELL.

NTA Kaduna: POB 1347, Kaduna; tel. (62) 216375; f. 1977; Gen. Man. Alhaji BELLO ABUBAKAR.

NTA Kano: PMB 3343, Kano; tel. (64) 640072; Gen. Man. BELLO ABU-BAKAR.

NTA Lagos: Ahmadu Bello Way, Victoria Island, PMB 12005, 12036, Ikaji, Lagos; tel. (1) 2622082; fax (1) 2626239; Dir-Gen. BEN MURRAY-BRUCE.

NTA Maiduguri: PMB 1487, Maiduguri; Gen. Man. M. M. MAIL-AFIYA.

NTA Makurdi: PMB 2044, Makurdi.

NTA Minna: TV House, PMB 79, Minna; tel. (66) 222941; Gen. Man. M. C. DAYLOP.

NTA Port Harcourt: PMB 5797, Port Harcourt; Gen. Man. JON EZEKOKA.

NTA Sokoto: PMB 2351, Sokoto; tel. (60) 232670; f. 1975; Gen. Man. M. B. TUNAU.

NTA Yola: PMB 2197, Yola; Gen. Man. M. M. SAIDU.

Finance

(cap. = capital; p.u. = paid up; res = reserves; dep. = deposits; m. = million; brs = branches; amounts in naira unless otherwise stated)

BANKING

In 1998 there were a total of 1,106 deposit banks (including 1,015 community banks) operating in Nigeria. There were also some 1,805 other financial institutions at that time.

Central Bank

Central Bank of Nigeria: Samuel Ladoke Akintola Way, PMB 0187, Garki, Abuja; tel. (1) 2660100; f. 1958; bank of issue; cap. and res 6,908.8m., dep. 168,187m. (1995); Gov. Chief JOSEPH SANUSI; 18 brs.

Commercial Banks

Afribank Nigeria Ltd: 94 Broad St, PMB 12021, Lagos; tel. (1) 2663608; fax (1) 2666327; f. 1969 as International Bank for West Africa Ltd; cap. and res 1,625.9m., dep. 26,459.8. (Dec. 1997); Chair. B. B. VERR; Man. Dir JOHN EDOZIEN; 130 brs.

African Continental Bank Ltd: 148 Broad St, PMB 2466, Lagos; tel. (1) 2664833; f. 1947; cap. and res 24.5m., dep. 1,845.1m. (1989); Chair. Chief J. O. IRUKWU; Man. Dir E. A. EZEKWE; 919 brs.

African International Bank Ltd: 42–44 Warehouse Rd, PMB 1040, Apapa, Lagos; tel. (1) 5870389; fax (1) 5877174; f. 1979; cap. and res 190.5m., dep. 1,397.4m. (1990); acquired assets of Bank of Credit and Commerce International (Nigeria) Ltd; Chair. Alhaji MAMMAN DAURA; Man. Dir Alhaji ABDULLAHI MAHMOUD; 47 brs.

Bank of the North Ltd: Ahmadu Bello House, 2 Zaria Rd, POB 211, Kano; tel. (64) 660290; f. 1959; cap. and res 500m. (1996), dep. 5,259.3m. (1995); Chair. Alhaji MUHAMMAD LUGGA; Man. Dir Alhaji MOHAMMED BULAMA; 83 brs.

Chartered Bank Ltd: Plot 1619, Danmole St, POB 73069, Victoria Island, Lagos; tel. (1) 2620380; fax (1) 2615094; cap. 220.8m. (Dec. 1996), dep. 3,704.7m. (Dec. 1995); Chair. Lt-Gen. (retd) M. I. WUSHISHI; Man. Dir O. OLAGUNDOYE.

Citibank Nigeria: Commerce House, 1 Idowu Taylor St, Victoria Island, POB 6391, Lagos; tel. (1) 2622000; fax (1) 2618916; f. 1984; cap. and res 3,457.8m., dep. 14,369.7m. (Dec. 1998); Chair. Chief CHARLES S. SANKEY; Man. Dir MICHEL ACCAD; 13 brs.

Citizens International Bank Ltd: Ahmadu Bello Way, Plot 130, Victoria Island, Lagos; tel. (1) 2601030; fax (1) 2615138; f. 1990; cap. and res 786.5m., dep. 5,340.9m. (1997); Chair. JOY D. IFEGWU.

Commercial Bank (Crédit Lyonnais Nigeria) Ltd: Elephant House, 214 Broad St, PMB 12829, Lagos; tel. (1) 2665594; fax (1) 2665308; f. 1983; cap. p.u. 120m.(1995), dep. 1,700m. (1993); Chair. ALLISON A. AYIDA; Man. Dir R. CESSAC; 21 brs.

Crown Merchant Bank Ltd: 8 Idowu Taylor St, Victoria Island, Lagos; tel. (1) 2613728; fax (1) 2615545; cap. and res 43.6m., dep. 275.8m. (1991); Man. Dir ORE S. A. ONAKOYA.

Ecobank Nigeria Ltd: 2 Ajose Adeogun St, Victoria Island, POB 72688, Lagos; tel. (1) 2615242; fax (1) 2616568; e-mail ecobank@ linkserve.com.ng; cap. 534.0m., res 717.7m., dep. 6,251.7m. (Dec. 1998); Chair. OTUNBA A. OJORA; Man. Dir OLADISUN HOLLOWAY.

Eko International Bank: cnr Nnamdi Azikiwe and Alli Balogun Sts, PMB 12864, Lagos; tel. (1) 2600350; fax (1) 2665176; cap. and res 306m., dep. 2,335.8m. (Dec. 1996); Chair. J. O. EMANUEL; Man. Dir OLATUNDE FASINA; 9 brs.

Equity Bank of Nigeria Ltd: Kingsway House, 107–113 Broad St, Lagos; tel. (1) 2665142; fax (1) 2660235; e-mail itequity@ equitybank.com.ng; f. 1988 as Meridien Equity of Nigeria Ltd; name changed 1995; cap. 515.3m., res 42.9m., dep. 2,313.0m., Man. Dir SAM O. OBAZE.

Federal Savings Bank: 23 Awolowo Rd, Ikoyi, PMB 12512, Lagos; tel. (1) 2690739; fax (1) 2690397; e-mail fsbcsu@link serve.com.ng; f. 1974; cap. 139.1m. (March 1997), dep. 1,590.8m. (March 1995); Chair. Alhaji A. O. G. OTTITI; Man. Dir MOHAMMED HAYATU-DEEN.

First Bank of Nigeria Plc: Samuel Asabia House, 35 Marina, POB 5216, Lagos; tel. (1) 2665900; fax (1) 2665933; e-mail fbn@ firstbank-nig.com.ng; internet www.firstbank-nig.com.ng; f. 1894 as Bank of British West Africa; cap. and res 520.3m., dep. 84,531.2m.

(March 1999); Chair. UMARU ABDUL MUTALLAB; CEO and Man. Dir CHRISTIAN IFEANYICHUKWU ADIMORAH; 291 brs.

Habib Nigeria Bank Ltd: 7–9 Bank Rd, PMB 2180, Kaduna; tel. (62) 235140; fax (62) 234584; cap. and res 866.2m., dep. 6,132m. (Dec. 1997); Chair. MAL MUSA BELLO; Man. Dir Alhaji FALALU BELLO; 65 brs.

Investment Banking and Trust Co Ltd (IBTC): Wesley House, 21–22 Marina, PMB 12557, Lagos; tel. (1) 2626520; fax (1) 2626541; e-mail ibtc@infoweb.abs.net; internet www.ibtc-lagos.com; f. 1989; cap. and res 2,208.1m., dep. 3,345.0m. (March 1999); Chair. DAVID DANKARO; Man. Dir ATEDO A. PETERSIDE.

Lion Bank of Nigeria: 34 Ahmadu Bello Way, PMB 2126, Jos, Plateau; tel. (73) 452223; fax (73) 454602; f. 1987; cap. and res 151.1m., dep. 1,732.6m. (March 1998); CEO PAUL Y. LUGUJA.

Magnum Trust Bank: 67 Marina, PMB 12933, Lagos; tel. (1) 2640060; fax (1) 2640069; f. 1991; cap. and res 64.4m., dep. 225.5m. (June 1995); Chair. Dr P.N.C. OKIGBO; Man. Dir JEAN-GEO PASTOURET.

Nigeria Universal Bank Ltd: Yakubu Gowon Way, POB 1066, Kaduna; tel. (62) 230048; fax (62) 235024; f. 1974; owned by Katsina and Kaduna State Govts; cap. 50m. (1994), dep. 447m. (1992); Chair. Alhaji MUHAMMADU HAYATUDDINI; Man. Dir Alhaji USMAN ABUBAKAR; 27 brs.

Owena Bank (Nigeria) Ltd: Engineering Close, PMB 1122, Victoria Island, Lagos; tel. (1) 2622579; fax (1) 2620761; 30% owned by Ondo State Govt; cap. and res 86m., dep. 1,956.9m. (Dec. 1997); Chair. ADE OJO; Man. Dir SEGUN AGBETUYI.

People's Bank of Nigeria: 33 Balogun St, PMB 12914, Lagos; tel. (1) 2664241; fax (1) 2664631; f. 1989; state-owned; cap. p.u. 230m. (Dec. 1991); Chair. Chief E. A. O. OYEYIPO; Man. Dir HAMRA IMAM.

Savannah Bank of Nigeria Ltd: 62–66 Broad St, POB 2317, Lagos; tel. (1) 2600470; fax (1) 2647332; f. 1976; cap. 1,338.3m., dep. 4,876m. (March 1997); Chair. MARTIN I. IKEDIASHI; 70 brs.

Société Générale Bank (Nigeria) Ltd: Sarah House, 13 Martins St, PMB 12741, Lagos; tel. (1) 2661834; fax (1) 2663731; f. 1977; cap. and res 128.3m., dep. 1,599.3m. (Dec. 1994); Chair. Dr EBENEZER A. IKOMI; Man. Dir G. A. OYENOLA; 35 brs.

Trade Bank plc: 2 Ilofa Rd, PMB 1496, Ilorin; tel. (31) 220062; fax (31) 223532; f. 1987; cap. and res 580m., dep. 3,157.2m. (Dec. 1997); Chair. Maj.-Gen. (retd) ABDULLAHI MOHAMMED; Man. Dir SAMUEL EREOLA KOLAWOLE.

Tropical Commercial Bank Ltd: 72B Murtala Mohammed Way, POB 4636, Kano; tel. (64) 640050; fax (64) 644506; 15% state-owned; cap. p.u. 184.8m. (Feb. 1997), res 764.7m., dep. 37,151m. (Dec. 1996); CEO LAWAN ZAKARIA GANA.

Union Bank of Nigeria Ltd: 40 Marina, PMB 2027, Lagos; tel. (1) 2665441; fax (1) 2663822; f. 1969 as Barclays Bank of Nigeria Ltd; cap. and res 6,124m., dep. 59,310m. (Sept. 1997); Chair. Prof. GREEN ONYEKABA NWANKWO; Man. Dir Alhaji MOHAMMAD IMAM YAHAYA; 255 brs.

United Bank for Africa (Nigeria) Ltd: UBA House, 57 Marina, POB 2406, Lagos; tel. (1) 2644651; fax (1) 2644722; f. 1961; cap. and res 5,036.4m., dep. 48,858m. (March 1998); Chair. HAKEEM BELO-OSAGIE; Man. Dir and CEO Mallam ABBA KYARI; 204 brs.

Universal Trust Bank of Nigeria Ltd: 4/6 Ajose Adeogun St, Victoria Island, POB 52160, Lagos; tel. (1) 2622035; fax (1) 615874; f. 1985; cap. 216.1m. (Dec. 1996), dep. 3.3m. (1994); Chair. Lt-Gen. T. Y. DANJUMA; Man. Dir Alhaji I. O. SULAIMON; 31 brs.

Wema Bank Ltd: 27 Nnamdi Azikiwe St, Tinubu; tel. (1) 2668105; fax (1) 2669508; e-mail info@wemabank.com; internet www .wemabank.com; f. 1945; cap. 519.2m., res 956.1m., dep. 13,497.3m. (March 1999); 75 brs.

Merchant Banks

Fidelity Union Merchant Bank Ltd: Savannah House, 62-66 Broad St, Lagos; tel. (1) 2601960; fax (1) 2636868; e-mail fidelity@ alpha.linkserve.com; f. 1988; cap. 537.6m., res 241.8m., dep. 2,689.1m. (June 1998); Chair. Chief VICTOR I. ODILI; CEO NEBOLISA O. ARAH.

First City Merchant Bank Ltd: Primrose Tower, 17A Tinubu St, POB 9117, Lagos; tel. (1) 2665944; fax (1) 2665126; e-mail caf@ fcmb-ltd.com; internet www.fcmb-ltd.com; f. 1983; cap. 500m., res 518.6m. (Dec. 1998), dep. 4,678.7m. (1999); Chair. and CEO OTUNBA M. O. BALOGUN.

First Interstate Merchant Bank (Nigeria) Ltd: Unity House, 37 Marina, Victoria Island, POB 72295, Lagos; tel. (1) 2600500; fax (1) 2640678; cap. and res 77.8m., dep. 391.7m. (March 1997); Chair. Prof. A. L. MABOGUNJE.

Industrial Bank Ltd (Merchant Bankers): Plot 1637, Adeto-kunbo Ademola St, Victoria Island, PMB 12637, Lagos; tel. (1) 2622454; fax (1) 2619024; e-mail indbank@industrialbank.com.ng; cap. p.u. 60.1m. (Dec. 1993); Chair. Dr SAMUEL ADEDOYIN.

International Merchant Bank (Nigeria) Ltd: IMB Plaza, 1 Akin Adesola St, Victoria Island, PMB 12028, Lagos; tel. (1) 2612204; fax

(1) 2612216; f. 1974; cap. and res 661.1m., dep. 1,154.1m. (June 1997); Chair. Maj.-Gen. MOHAMMED SHUWA (retd); Man. Dir EDWIN CHINYE; 5 brs.

Merchant Banking Corpn (Nigeria) Ltd: 16 Keffi St, S W Ikoyi, POB 53289, Lagos; tel. (1) 2690261; fax (1) 2690767; e-mail mbcnig@linkserve.com.ng; f. 1982; cap. and res 808.7m., dep. 2,495.2m. (March 1998); Chair. Dr M. A. MAJEKODUNMI; Man. Dir FUNKE OSIBODU.

NAL Merchant Bank: NAL Towers, 20 Marina, PMB 12735, Lagos; tel. (1) 2600420; fax (1) 2633294; e-mail infonal@nalbank.com.ng; internet www.nal.com.ng; f. 1960; cap. and res 2,252.2m., dep. 3,699.1m. (March 1999); Chair. Alhaji E. Y. ABDULLAHI; Man. Dir Dr SHAMSUDDEEN USMAN; 6 brs.

New Africa Merchant Bank Ltd: 4 Waff Rd, PMB 2340, Kaduna; tel. (62) 235276; fax (62) 237311; cap. and res 118.7m., dep. 253.1m. (Dec. 1995); Chair. Alhaji SAMAILA MAMMAN; Man. Dir Mallam UMAR YAHAYA.

Nigerian-American Merchant Bank Ltd: Boston House, 10–12 Macarthy St, PMB 12759, Lagos; tel. (1) 2600360; fax (1) 2637568; f. 1979; affiliate of First National Bank of Boston (USA); cap. and res 741.8m., dep. 1,038m.(Dec. 1997); Chair. Alhaji IBRAHIM DAMCIDA; Man. Dir OSARO ISOKPAN; 3 brs.

Nigeria Intercontinental Merchant Bank Ltd: Plot 999C, Intercontinental Plaza, Danmole St, Victoria Island, POB 80150, Lagos; tel. (1) 2622940; fax (1) 2622981; internet www.nimb.com.ng; cap. p.u. 252.9m. (Dec. 1996); Chair. RAYMOND C. OBIERI; Man. Dir ERASTUS B. O. AKINGBOLA.

Rims Merchant Bank Ltd: Kingsway Bldg, 2nd Floor, 51–52 Merina, POB 73029, Lagos; tel. (1) 2662105; fax (1) 2669947; f. 1988; cap. and res 69.3m., dep. 617.8m. (1992); Chair. Alhaji A. IBRAHIM OFR'SAN; CEO EMMANUEL OCHOLI.

Stanbic Merchant Bank Nigeria Ltd: 188 Awolowo Rd, Ikoyi, POB 54746, Lagos; tel. (1) 2690402; fax (1) 2692469; f. 1983 as Grindlays Merchant Bank of Nigeria; cap. 500m., res 124.9m., dep. 1,088.4m. (Sept. 1998); Chair. Dr MATTHEW TAWO MBU; Man. Dir STEPHEN JOHN CALEY.

Development Banks

Federal Mortgage Bank of Nigeria: Plot 124, Moshood Abiola Rd, Area 2, PMB 2273, Garki, Abuja; tel. and fax (9) 2344124; f. 1977; loans to individuals and mortgage institutions; cap. p.u. 150m. (1992), dep. 463.8m. (1991); Chair. Alhaji H. B. KOLO; Man. Dir Alhaji KASSIM MUSA BICHI; 61 brs.

Nigerian Agricultural and Co-operative Bank Ltd (NACB): Hospital Rd, PMB 2155, Kaduna; tel. (62) 201000; fax (62) 210611; f. 1973; for funds to farmers and co-operatives to improve production techniques; cap. p.u. 500m., dep. 4,455.4m. (1992); Chair. Alhaji SULE LAMIDO; Man. Dir Prof. M. B. AJAKAIYE; 38 brs.

Nigerian Bank for Commerce and Industry (NBCI): Bankers' House, Plot 19C Adeola Hopewell, Victoria Island, POB 4424, Lagos; tel. (1) 2616194; fax (1) 2614202; f. 1973; govt bank to aid indigenization and development of small and medium-sized enterprises; cap. p.u. 200m. (1990); Admin. UBADIGBO OKONKWO; 19 brs.

Nigerian Industrial Development Bank Ltd: NIDB House, 63–71 Broad St, POB 2357, Lagos; tel. (1) 2663495; fax (1) 2667074; f. 1964 to provide medium and long-term finance to industry, manufacturing, non-petroleum mining and tourism; encourages foreign investment in partnership with Nigerians; cap. 1,000m., res 292.7m. (Dec. 1997); Man. Dir Alhaji SAIDU YAYA KASIMU; 6 brs.

Bankers' Association

Chartered Institute of Bankers of Nigeria: 19 Adeola Hopewell St, POB 72273, Victoria Island, Lagos; tel. (1) 2615642; fax (1) 2611306; Chair. JOHNSON O. EKUNDAYO; CEO A. A. ADENUBI.

STOCK EXCHANGE

Securities and Exchange Commission (SEC): Mandilas House, 96–102 Broad St, PMB 12638, Lagos; f. 1979 as govt agency to regulate and develop capital market and to supervise stock exchange operations; Dir-Gen. GEORGE A. AKAMIOKHOR.

Nigerian Stock Exchange: Stock Exchange House, 2–4 Customs St, POB 2457, Lagos; tel. (1) 2660287; fax (1) 2668724; e-mail nse@linkserve.com.ng; f. 1960; Pres. PASCAL DOZIE; Dir-Gen. HAYFORD ALILE; 6 brs.

INSURANCE

In December 1994 there were some 134 insurance companies operating in Nigeria. Since 1978 they have been required to reinsure 20% of the sum insured with the Nigeria Reinsurance Corporation.

Insurance Companies

African Alliance Insurance Co Ltd: 112 Broad St, POB 2276, Lagos; tel. (1) 2664398; fax (1) 2660943; e-mail alliance@infoweb

.abs.net; f. 1960; life assurance and pensions; Man. Dir OPE OREDUGBA; 30 brs.

African Insurance Co Ltd: 134 Nnamdi Azikiwe St, Idumota, POB 274, Lagos; tel. (1) 2661720; f. 1950; all classes except life; Area Man. N. E. NSA; 4 brs.

Aiico International Insurance (AIICO): AIICO Plaza, Plot PC 12, Afribank St, Victoria Island, POB 2577, Lagos; tel. (1) 2610651; fax (1) 2617433; e-mail info@aiicoplc.com; internet www.aiicoplc.com; CEO M. E. HANSEN.

Ark Insurance Group: Glass House, 11A Karimu Kotun St, Victoria Island, POB 3771, Marina, Lagos; tel. (1) 2615826; fax (1) 2615850.

Continental Reinsurance Co Ltd: Reinsurance House, 11th Floor, 46 Marina, POB 2401, Lagos; tel. (1) 2665350; fax (1) 2665370; e-mail crcl@cyberspace.net.ng; CEO ADEYEMO ADEJUMO.

Great Nigeria Insurance Co Ltd: 47–57 Martins St, POB 2314, Lagos; tel. (1) 2662288; fax (1) 2668056; f. 1960; all classes; Man. Dir M. A. SIYANBOLA.

Guinea Insurance Co Ltd: Guinea insurance House, 21 Nnandi Azikiwe St, POB 1136, Lagos; tel. (1) 2665201; f. 1958; all classes; CEO AYO BAMMEKE.

Industrial and General Insurance Co Ltd: Plot 741, Adeola Hopewell St, POB 52592, Falomo, Lagos; tel. (1) 2613534; fax (1) 614922; CEO REMI OLOWUDE.

Kapital Insurance Co Ltd: 116 Hadeja Rd, POB 2044, Kano; tel. (64) 645666; fax (64) 636962; CEO Alhaji M. G. UMAR.

Law Union and Rock Insurance Co of Nigeria Ltd: 88–92 Broad St, POB 944, Lagos; tel. (1) 2663526; fax (1) 2664659; fire, accident and marine; 6 brs; ; CEO S. O. AKINYEMI.

Leadway Assurance Co Ltd: NN 28–29 Constitution Rd, POB 458, Kaduna; tel. (62) 200660; fax (62) 236838; f. 1970; all classes; Man. Dir OYEKANMI ABIODUN HASSAN-ODUKALE.

Lion of Africa Insurance Co Ltd: St Peter's House, 3 Ajele St, POB 2055, Lagos; tel. (1) 2600950; fax (1) 2636111; f. 1952; all classes; Man. Dir G. A. ALEGIEUNO.

Mercury Assurance Co Ltd: 17 Martins St, POB 2003, Lagos; tel. (1) 2660216; general; Man. Dir S. N. C. OKONKWO.

National Insurance Corpn of Nigeria (NICON): 5 Customs St, POB 1100, Lagos; tel. (1) 2640230; fax (1) 2666556; f. 1969; all classes; cap. 200m.; Man. Dir Alhaji MOHAMMED U. A. KARI; 28 brs.

N.E.M. Insurance Co (Nigeria) Ltd: 22A Borno Way, Ebute, POB 654, Lagos; tel. (1) 5861920; all classes; Chair. T. J. ONOMIGBO OKPOKO; Man. Dir J. E. UMUKORO.

Niger Insurance Co Ltd: 47 Marina, POB 2718, Lagos; tel. (1) 2664452; fax (1) 2662196; all classes; CEO A. K. ONIWINDE; 6 brs.

Nigeria Reinsurance Corpn: 46 Marina, PMB 12766, Lagos; tel. (1) 2667049; fax (1) 2668041; all classes of reinsurance; Man. Dir O. OSOKA.

Nigerian General Insurance Co Ltd: 1 Nnamdi Azikiwe St, Tirubu Square, POB 2210, Lagos; tel. (1) 2662552; f. 1951; all classes; Chair. Prince SOLAGBADE D. ARAOYE; Man. Dir A. F. KILADEJO; 15 brs.

Phoenix of Nigeria Assurance Co Ltd: Mandilas House, 96–102 Broad St, POB 12798, Lagos; tel. (1) 2661160; fax (1) 2662883; e-mail phoenixassce@alpha.linkserve.com; f. 1964; all classes; cap. 10m.; Chair. A. A. OJORA; Man. Dir A. A. AKINTUNDE; 5 brs.

Prestige Assurance Co (Nigeria) Ltd: 54 Marina, POB 650, Lagos; tel. (1) 2661213; fax (1) 2664110; all classes except life; Chair. Alhaji S. M. ARGUNGU; Man. Dir K. C. MATHEW.

Royal Exchange Assurance (Nigeria) Group: New Africa House, 31 Marina, POB 112, Lagos; tel. (1) 2663120; fax (1) 2664431; all classes; Chair. Alhaji MUHTAR BELLO YOLA; Man. Dir JONAH U. IKHIDERO; 6 brs.

Summit Insurance Co Ltd: Summit Centre, 9 Bishop Aboyade Cole, Victoria Island, POB 52462, Falomlo, Ikoyi, Lagos; tel. (1) 687476; fax (1) 615850; Man. Dir O. O. LADIPO-AJAYI.

Sun Insurance Office (Nigeria) Ltd: Unity House, 37 Marina, POB 2694, Lagos; tel. (1) 2661318; all classes except life; Man. Dir A. T. ADENIJI; 6 brs.

United Nigeria Insurance Co (UNIC) Ltd: 53 Marina, POB 588, Lagos; tel. (1) 2663201; fax (1) 2664282; f. 1965; all classes except life; CEO E. O. A. ADETUNJI; 17 brs.

Unity Life and Fire Insurance Co Ltd: 25 Nnamdi Azikiwe St, POB 3681, Lagos; tel. (1) 2662517; fax (1) 2662599; all classes; Man. Dir R. A. ODINIGWE.

Veritas: NIGUS House, Plot 1412, Victoria Island, Lagos; tel. (1) 2610485; fax (1) 2633688; all classes; Man. Dir SAIDU USMAN.

West African Provincial Insurance Co: 27–29 King George V Rd, POB 2103, Lagos; tel. (1) 2636433; fax (1) 2633688; all classes except life; Man. Dir C. O. IDOWU SILVA.

Insurance Association

Nigerian Insurance Association: Nicon House, 1st Floor, 5 Customs St, POB 9551, Lagos; tel. (1) 2640825; f. 1971; Chair. J. U. IKHIDERO.

Trade and Industry

GOVERNMENT AGENCIES

Corporate Affairs Commission: FCT Area 2, Abuja; tel. (9) 2342916.

National Council on Privatisation: Bureau of Public Enterprises, NDIC Bldg, Constitution Ave, Central Business District, PMB 442, Garki, Abuja; tel. (9) 5237405; fax (9) 5237396; e-mail bpegen@micro.com.ng; internet www.bpe.gov.ng.

Nigeria Export Processing Zones Authority: Radio House, Fourth Floor, Herbert Macaulay Way, PMB 037, Garki, Abuja; tel. (9) 234060; fax (9) 2343061; e-mail info@nepza.com; internet www.nepza.com.

DEVELOPMENT ORGANIZATIONS

Benin–Owena River Basin Development Authority: 24 Benin-Sapele Rd, PMB 1381, Obayantor, Benin City; tel. (52) 254415; f. 1976 to conduct irrigation; Gen. Man. Dr G. E. OTEZE.

Chad Basin Development Authority: Dikwa Rd, PMB 1130, Maiduguri; tel. (76) 232015; f. 1973; irrigation and agriculture-allied industries; Chair. MOHAMMED ABALI; Gen. Man. Alhaji BUNU S. MUSA.

Cross River Basin Development Authority: 32 Target Rd, PMB 1249, Calabar; tel. (87) 223163; f. 1977; Gen. Man. SIXTUS ABETIANBE.

Department of Petroleum Resources: 7 Kofo Abayomi St, Victoria Island, Lagos.

Federal Capital Development Authority: Abuja; govt agency for design, construction and management of Abuja; Perm. Sec. Alhaji ABUBAKAR KOKO.

Federal Institute of Industrial Research, Oshodi (FIIRO): Murtala Muhammed Airport, Bilnd Centre St, Oshodi, Ikeja, PMB 21023, Lagos; tel. (1) 900121; fax (1) 4525880; f. 1956; plans and directs industrial research and provides tech. assistance and information to industry; specializes in foods, minerals, textiles, natural products and industrial intermediates; Dir Prof. S. A. ODUNFA.

Industrial Training Fund: Federal Secretariat, 8th Floor, Miango Rd, PMB 2199, Jos, Plateau; tel. and fax (73) 461887; e-mail dp@itf-nigeria.com; internet www.itf-nigeria.com; f. 1971 to promote and encourage skilled workers in trade and industry; Dir-Gen. Prof. OLU E. AKEREJOLA.

Kaduna Industrial and Finance Co Ltd: Investment House, 27 Ali Akilu Rd, PMB 2230, Kaduna; tel. (62) 240751; fax (62) 240754; e-mail kifc@skannet.com; f. 1989; provides development finance; Chair. (vacant); Man. Dir Alhaji DAHIRU MOHAMMED.

Kwara State Investment Corpn: 109–112 Fate Rd, PMB 1344, Ilorin, Kwara; tel. (31) 220510.

Lagos State Development and Property Corpn: 1 Town Planning Way, Ilupeju, Lagos; tel. (1) 4972243; e-mail isdpc@isdpc.com; internet www.isdpc.com; f. 1972; planning and development of Lagos; Gen. Man. O.R. ASHAFA.

New Nigerian Development Co Ltd: 18/19 Ahmadu Bello Way, Ahmed Talib House, PMB 2120, Kaduna; tel. (62) 236251; fax (62) 235482; e-mail nndc@skannet.com.ng; f. 1949; owned by the Govts of 16 northern States; investment finance; 7 subsidiaries, 36 assoc. cos; Chair. Alhaji ABDULLAHI IBRAHIM.

Niger Delta Basin and Rural Development Authority: 21 Azikiwe Rd, PMB 5676, Port Harcourt; f. 1976.

Nigerian Enterprises Promotion Board: 15–19 Keffi St, S.W. Ikoyi, Lagos; tel. (1) 2680929; f. 1972 to promote indigenization; Chair. MINSO GADZAMA.

Nigerian Livestock and Meat Authority: POB 479, Kaduna.

Northern Nigeria Investments Ltd: 4 Waff Rd, POB 138, Kaduna; tel. (62) 239654; fax (62) 230770; f. 1959 to identify and invest in industrial and agricultural projects in 16 northern States; cap. p.u. 20m.; Chair. Alhaji ABUBAKAR G. ADAMU; Man. Dir GIMBA H. IBRAHIM.

Odu'a Investment Co Ltd: Cocoa House, PMB 5435, Ibadan; tel. (2) 417710; fax (2) 413000; f. 1976; jtly owned by Ogun, Ondo and Oyo States; Man. Dir Alhaji R. S. ARUNA.

Plateau State Water Resources Development Board: Jos; incorporates the fmr Plateau River Basin Devt Authority and Plateau State Water Resources Devt Board.

Projects Development Institute: 3 Independence Layout, POB 609, Enugu; tel. (42) 451593; fax (42) 457691; f. 1974; promotes the establishment of new industries and develops industrial projects utilizing local raw materials; Dir L. K. NWOSU (acting).

Raw Materials Research Development Council: Plot 427, Aguiyi, Ironsi St, Maitama, Abuja; tel. (9) 5237417.

Rubber Research Institute of Nigeria: PMB 1049, Benin City; tel. (52) 254792; f. 1961; conducts research into the production of rubber and other latex products; Dir Dr M. M. NADOMA.

Trans Investments Co Ltd: Bale Oyewole Rd, PMB 5085, Ibadan; tel. (2) 416000; f. 1986; initiates and finances industrial and agricultural schemes; Gen. Man. M. A. ADESIYUN.

CHAMBERS OF COMMERCE

Nigerian Association of Chambers of Commerce, Industry, Mines and Agriculture: 15A Ikorodu Rd, Maryland, PMB 12816, Lagos; tel. and fax (1) 4964737; Pres. Chief M. O. ORIGBO; Dir-Gen. L. O. ADEKUNLE.

Aba Chamber of Commerce and Industry: UBA Bldg, Ikot Expene Rd/Georges St, POB 1596, Aba; tel. (82) 225148; f. 1971; Pres. KALU NNANA KALU.

Abeokuta Chamber of Commerce and Industry: 29 Kuto Rd, Ishabo, POB 937, Abeokuta; tel. (39) 241230; Pres. Chief S. O. AKINREMI.

Abuja Chamber of Commerce and Industry: Wuse, PMB 86, Garki, Abuja; tel. (9) 52341887; Pres. Alhaji ABDULLAHI ADAMU.

Adamawa Chamber of Commerce and Industry: c/o Palace Hotel, POB 8, Jimeta, Yola; tel. (75) 255136; Pres. Alhaji ISA HAMMAN-YERO.

Akure Chamber of Commerce and Industry: 57 Oyemekun Rd, POB 866, Akure; tel. (34) 242540; f. 1984; Pres. Alhaji A. A. AYEGBUSI.

Awka Chamber of Commerce and Industry: 220 Enugu Rd, POB 780, Awka; tel. (45) 550105; Pres. Lt-Col (retd) D. ORUGBU.

Bauchi Chamber of Commerce and Industry: 96 Maiduguri Rd, POB 911, Bauchi; tel. (77) 42620; f. 1976; Pres. Alhaji MAGAJI MU'AZU.

Benin Chamber of Commerce, Industry, Mines and Agriculture: 10 Murtala Muhammed Way, POB 2087, Benin City; tel. (52) 255761; Pres. C. O. EWEKA.

Benue Chamber of Commerce, Industry, Mines and Agriculture: 71 Ankpa Qr Rd, PMB 102344, Makurdi; tel. (44) 32573; Chair. Col (retd) R. V. I. ASAM.

Borno Chamber of Commerce and Industry: Grand Stand, Ramat Sq., off Central Bank, PMB 1636, Maiduguri; tel. (76) 232832; Pres. Alhaji ZANNA BUKAR UMORU MANDARA.

Calabar Chamber of Commerce and Industry: Desan House Bldg, 38 Ndidem Iso Rd, POB 76, Calabar, Cross River; tel. (87) 221558; 92 mems; Pres. Chief TAM OFORIOKUMA.

Enugu Chamber of Commerce, Industry and Mines: International Trade Fair Complex, Abakaliki Rd, POB 734, Enugu; tel. (42) 330575; f. 1963; Dir S. C. NWAEKEKE.

Franco-Nigerian Chamber of Commerce: Plot 24, Afribank St, POB 70001, Victoria Island, Lagos; tel. (1) 2621423; fax (1) 2621422; e-mail fncci@nova.net.ng; f. 1985; Chair. AKIN LAGUDA; Pres. AKIN AKINBOLA.

Gongola Chamber of Commerce and Industry: Palace Hotel, POB 8, Jimeta-Yola; tel. (75) 255136; Pres. Alhaji ALIYU IBRAHIM.

Ibadan Chamber of Commerce and Industry: Commerce House, Ring Rd, Challenge, PMB 5168, Ibadan; tel. (2) 317223; Pres. JIDE ABIMBOLA.

Ijebu Chamber of Commerce and Industry: 51 Ibadan Rd, POB 604, Ijebu Ode; tel. (37) 432880; Pres. DOYIN DEGUN.

Ikot Ekpene Chamber of Commerce and Industry: 47 Aba Rd, POB 50, Ikot Ekpene; tel. (85) 400153; Pres. G. U. EKANEM.

Kaduna Chamber of Commerce, Industry and Agriculture: 24 Waff Rd, POB 728, Kaduna; tel. (62) 211216; fax (62) 214149; Pres. Alhaji MOHAMMED SANI AMINU.

Kano Chamber of Commerce, Industry, Mines and Agriculture: Zoo Rd, POB 10, Kano City, Kano; tel. (64) 666936; fax (64) 667138; Pres. MAL. U. J. KIRU.

Katsina Chamber of Commerce and Industry: 1 Nagogo Rd, POB 92, Katsina; tel. (65) 31014; Pres. ABBA ALI.

Kwara Chamber of Commerce, Industry, Mines and Agriculture: 208 Ibrahim Taiwo Rd, POB 1634, Ilorin; tel. (31) 221069; Pres. W. O. ODUDU.

Lagos Chamber of Commerce and Industry: Commerce House, 1 Idowu Taylor St, Victoria Island, POB 109, Lagos; tel. (1) 613898; fax (1) 610573; f. 1885; 900 mems; Pres. KOLA DAISI.

Niger Chamber of Commerce and Industry: Trade Fair Site, POB 370, Minna; tel. (66) 223153; Pres. Alhaji U. S. NDANUSA.

Nnewi Chamber of Commerce and Industry: 31A Nnobi Rd, POB 1471, Nnewi; f. 1987; Pres. Chief C. M. IBETO.

Osogbo Chamber of Commerce and Industry: Obafemi Awolowo Way, Ajegunle, POB 870, Osogbo, Osun; tel. (35) 231098; Pres. Prince VICTOR ADEMLE.

Owerri Chamber of Commerce and Industry: OCCIMA Secretariat, 123 Okigwe Rd, POB 1640, Owerri; tel. (83) 234849; Pres. Chief BONIFACE N. AMAECHI.

Oyo Chamber of Commerce and Industry: POB 67, Oyo; Pres. Chief C. A. OGUNNIYI.

Plateau State Chambers of Commerce, Industry, Mines and Agriculture: Shama House, 32 Rwang Pam St, POB 2092, Jos; tel. (73) 53918; f. 1976; Pres. Chief M. E. JACDOMI.

Port Harcourt Chamber of Commerce, Industry, Mines and Agriculture: Alesa Eleme, POB 585, Port Harcourt; tel. (84) 239536; f. 1952; Pres. Chief S. I. ALETE.

Remo Chamber of Commerce and Industry: 7 Sho Manager Way, POB 1172, Shagamu; tel. (37) 640962; Pres. Chief S. O. ADE-KOYA.

Sapele Chamber of Commerce and Industry: 144 New Ogorode Rd, POB 154, Sapele; tel. (54) 42323; Pres. P. O. FUFUYIN.

Sokoto Chamber of Commerce and Industry: 12 Racecourse Rd, POB 2234, Sokoto; tel. (60) 231805; Pres. Alhaji ALIYU WAZIRI BODINGA.

Umahia Chamber of Commerce: Aba Rd, Umahia; tel. (88) 220055; Pres. Dr LEVI I. NWOKEAFOR.

Uyo Chamber of Commerce and Industry: 141 Abak Rd, POB 2960, Uyo, Akwa Ibom; Pres. Chief DANIEL ITA-EKPOTT.

Warri Chamber of Commerce and Industry: Block 1, Edewor Shopping Centre, Warri/Sapele Rd, POB 302, Warri; tel. (53) 233731; Pres. MOSES F. OROGUN.

INDUSTRIAL AND TRADE ASSOCIATIONS

Nigerian Export Promotion Council: Zone 2, Block 312, Wuse, PMB 133, Abuja; tel. (9) 5230930; fax (9) 5230931; f. 1976.

Nigerian Marketing Association: 25 Eric Moore Close, Surulere, Lagos.

Union of Importers and Exporters: POB 115, Ibadan; f. 1949; Chair. E. A. SANDA.

EMPLOYERS' ORGANIZATIONS

Association of Advertising Practitioners of Nigeria: 3 William St, off Sylvia Crescent, POB 50648, Anthony Village, Lagos; tel. (1) 4970842.

Chartered Institute of Bankers: Plot PC 19, Adeola Hopewell St, POB 72273, Victoria Island, Lagos.

Institute of Chartered Accountants of Nigeria: Plot 16, Professional Layout Centre, Idowu Taylor St, Victoria Island, POB 1580, Lagos; tel. (1) 2622394; fax (1) 2610304; e-mail info.ican@ican.org.ng; f. 1965; CEO and Registrar P. O. OMOREGIE.

Institute of Personnel Management of Nigeria: IPM House, IPM Ave, Ikeja, POB 5412, Lagos.

Nigeria Employers' Consultative Association: Commercial House, 1–11 Commercial Ave, POB 2231, Yaba, Lagos; tel. (1) 800360; fax (1) 860309; f. 1957; Pres. Chief R. F. GIWA.

Nigerian Institute of Architects: 2 Idowu Taylor St, Victoria Island, POB 178, Lagos; tel. (1) 2617940; fax (1) 2617947; f. 1960; Pres. Chief O. C. MAJOROH.

Nigerian Institute of Building: 1B Market St, Oyingbo, Ebute-Metta, POB 3191, Marina, Lagos; f. 1970; Pres. S. T. OYEFEKO.

Nigerian Institution of Estate Surveyors and Valuers: Flat 2B, Dolphin Scheme, Ikoyi, POB 2325, Lagos; tel. (1) 2685981; Pres. W. O. ODUDU.

Nigerian Society of Engineers: National Engineering Centre, 1 Engineering Close, POB 72667, Victoria Island, Lagos; tel. and fax (1) 2617315; Pres. Dr O. AJAYI.

Pharmaceutical Society of Nigeria: 52A Ikorodu Rd, Fadeyi, Lagos.

STATE PETROLEUM COMPANY

Nigerian National Petroleum Corpn (NNPC): NNPC Towers, Herbert Macaulay Way, Central District, Abuja; tel. (9) 5232717; fax (9) 5234760; f. 1977; reorg. 1988; holding corpn for fed. govt interests in petroleum cos; proposals for transfer to private sector announced in Nov. 1998; 11 operating subsidiaries; Man. Dir JACKSON GAIUS-OBASEKI.

UTILITIES

Electricity

National Electric Power Authority (NEPA): Plot 1071, Area 3, Garki, Abuja; tel. (1) 5231938; f. 1972 by merger of the Electricity Corpn of Nigeria and the Niger Dams Authority; Man. Dir (vacant).

Gas

Nigerian Liquefied National Gas Co: C. and C. Towers, Plot 1684, Sanusi Fafunwa St, Victoria Island, PMB 12774, Marina, Lagos; tel. (1) 2624190; fax (1) 2617146; Man. Dir STEVE J. OLLER-EARNSHAW.

MAJOR COMPANIES

The following are some of the largest companies in terms either of capital investment or employment.

African Petroleum Ltd: AP House, 54–56 Broad St, POB 512, Lagos; tel. (1) 2600050; fax (1) 2635290; cap. ₦72m.; fmrly BP Nigeria Ltd; markets lubricants, fuel oil, automotive gas oil, motor spirits, liquefied petroleum gas and kerosene; CEO GANA ABBA.

African Timber and Plywood (AT & P): PMB 4001, Sapele; f. 1935; a division of UAC of Nigeria Ltd and an assoc. co of UAC International Ltd, London; loggers and mfrs of plywood, particleboard, flushdoors, lumber and machined wood products; Gen. Man. L. HODGSON.

Ajaokuta Steel Co Ltd: PMB 1000, Ajaokuta, Kwara; tel. (58) 400450; fax (58) 400168; CEO M. M. INUWA.

Bhn: Asogun Rd, Km 15, Badagry Expressway, POB 109, Apapa, Lagos; tel. (1) 5453057; fax (1) 5451398; e-mail bhnplc@tolaram .nig.com; cap. p.u. ₦8.1m.; formerly Blackwood Hodge; earth-moving, construction, irrigation, mining and agricultural equipment; Chair. Chief RASHEED GBADAMOSI.

Chemical and Allied Products Co Ltd: POB 1004, 24 Commercial Rd, Apapa, Lagos; tel. (1) 803220; fax (1) 5874840; mfrs of paints, pesticides and pharmaceuticals, distributors of chemicals, dyestuffs, explosives, plastic raw materials and associated products; Chair. D. M. OMOLAYOLE.

Delta Steel Co Ltd: Ovwian-Aladja, POB 1220, Warri; tel. (53) 621001; fax (53) 621012; f. 1979; state-owned; operates direct-reduction steel complex with eventual annual capacity of 1m. tons; Chair. TUNJI AROSANYIN; Man. Dir TIM C. EFOBI.

Guinness (Nigeria) Ltd: Oba Akran Ave, Ikeja, PMB 1071, Lagos State; tel. (1) 4971560; fax (1) 4970560; f. 1950; cap. p.u. ₦25m.; brewers; breweries in Ikeja (700,000 hl), Ogba (700,000 hl) and Benin (900,000 hl); Chief R. A. ALABI.

Henry Stephens Group: Head Office: 90 Awolowo Rd, SW Ikoyi, POB 2480, Lagos; tel. (1) 603460; subsidiary cos include:

  Gilco (Nigeria) Ltd: 292 Apapa Rd, Apapa; import and export.

  Henry Stephens Engineering Co Ltd: 2 Ilepeju By-Pass, Ikeja, PMB 21386, Lagos; tel. (1) 901460; fax (1) 2690758; for construction machinery, motors and agricultural equipment.

  Nigerian Maritime Services: 13–15 Sapele Rd, Apapa, PMB 1013, Lagos; tel. (1) 873018; f. 1964; Chair. Prof. AYO OGUNSHEYE; Gen. Man. W. P. D. DAVSON.

IBRU: 33 Creek Rd, PMB 1155, Apapa, Lagos; tel. (1) 876634; agricultural equipment, machinery and service; fishing and frozen fish distribution, civil and agricultural engineering; Man. Dir O. IBRU.

A. G. Leventis Group: Iddo House, Iddo, POB 159, Lagos; tel. (1) 800220; fax (1) 860574; activities include wholesale and retail distribution, vehicle assembly, food production and farming, manufacture of glass, plastics, beer, technical and electrical equipment, property investment and management; Chair. A. H. AHMADU; Man. Dir. J. OKE.

Lever Brothers (Nigeria) Ltd: 15 Dockyard Rd, POB 15, Apapa, Lagos; tel. (1) 5803300; fax (1) 5803711; f. 1923; cap. ₦112.0m.; mfrs of detergents, edible fats and toilet preparations; Chair. and CEO R. F. GIWA.

Mandilas Group Ltd: 96–102 Broad St, POB 35, Lagos; tel. (1) 2663220; fax (1) 2662605; e-mail mandilas@micro.com.ng; subsidiaries include Mandilas Enterprises Ltd, Mandilas Travel Ltd, Norman Industries Ltd, Electrolux-Mandilas Ltd, Phoenix of Nigeria Assurance Co Ltd, Sulzer Nigeria Ltd, Mandilas Ventures Ltd, Original Box Co Ltd; Chair. T. A. MANDILAS.

Mobil Oil Nigeria: PMB 12054, 1 Lekki Express Way, Victoria Island, Lagos; tel. (1) 2621640; fax (1) 2621733; offshore petroleum production; Chair. DUKE KEISER.

National Oil and Chemical Marketing Co Ltd: 38–39 Marina, PMB 2052, Lagos; tel. (1) 2665880; fax (1) 2662802; f. 1975 (fmrly Shell Nigeria Ltd); 40% state-owned; Man. Dir O. O. OJO; 650 employees.

Nigerian Breweries Ltd: 1 Abebe Village Rd, Iganmu, POB 545, Lagos; tel. (1) 5801340; fax (1) 2646624; f. 1946; also facilities at Aba, Kaduna, Ibadan and Enugu; Chair. and Man. Dir FELIX OHIWEREI; 3,683 employees.

Nigerian Cement Co Ltd (NIGERCEM): Nkalugu, POB 331, Enugu; tel. and fax (42) 253829; f. 1954; Chair. Chief S. N. ANYANWU; Man. Dir Dr OZO NWEKE OZO.

Nigerian Coal Corpn: PMB 01053, Enugu; tel. (42) 335314; f. 1909; operates four mines; Gen. Man. F. N. UGWU.

Nigerian Engineering and Construction Co Ltd (NECCO): Km 14, Badagry Expressway (opp. International Trade Fair Complex), PMB 12684, Lagos; tel. (1) 5880591; building, civil mechanical and electrical engineers, furniture makers and steel fabricators; Chair. EHIOZE EDIAE.

Nigerian Metal Fabricating Ltd: POB 23, Kano; tel. (64) 632427; fax (64) 634677; part of Cedar Group; mfrs of aluminium household utensils, brassware and silverware; also light engineers.

Nigerian Mining Corpn: Federal Secretariat, 7th Floor, PMB 2154, Jos; tel. (73) 462867; fax (73) 463276; f. 1972; exploration, production, processing and marketing of minerals; nine subsidiaries and eight assoc. cos; CEO YOHANNA B. KWA.

Nigerian National Petroleum Corpn (NNPC): Herbert McCauley Way, Central Area, Abuja; tel. (9) 5234761; fax (9) 5234760; f. 1977; reorg. 1988; holding corpn for fed. govt interests in petroleum cos; 11 operating subsidiaries; Man. Dir DALHATU BAYERO.

Nigerian National Supply Co Ltd: 29 Burma Rd, PMB 12662, Apapa, Lagos; state-owned import org.; Chair. Brig. J. I. ONOJA; Gen. Man. Maj. A. DAHIRU.

Nigerian Oil Mills Ltd: POB 342, Kano; tel. (64) 632427; fax (64) 634677; import and production of vegetable oil products.

Nigerian Paper Mill Ltd: POB 1648, Lagos; also at Jebba; tel. (1) 613803; fax (1) 619400; Chair. O. OMOTOSHO.

Nigerian Sugar Co Ltd: PMB 65, Bacita Estate, Jebba; tel. 641035; f. 1961; cap. ₦79.4m.; growers of sugar cane and mfrs of cane sugar and allied products; Chair. Alhaji IBRAHIM AHMED; Man. Dir SULEIMAN ABDULLAHI; 5,600 employees.

Nigerian Textile Mills Ltd: Oba Akran Ave, Industrial Estate, PMB 21051, Ikeja; tel. (1) 4978850; fax (1) 4962011; f. 1960; cap. ₦40m.; spinners, weavers and finishers; Chair. Prof. S. O. BIOBAKU; Man. Dir Alhaji S. DANGOTE; 2,700 employees.

Nigerian Tin Mining Co Ltd: PMB 2036, Jos; tel. (73) 80634; f. 1986 by merger of Amalgamated Tin Mines of Nigeria Ltd and five other mining cos operating on the Jos plateau; owned by Nigerian Mining Corpn and fmr non-national shareholders in the above five cos; cap. p.u. ₦9.5m.; production of tin concentrate from alluvial tin ore and separation of columbite, zircon and monazite; Chair. E. A. IFATUROTI; Gen. Man. Alhaji M. ADAMU.

Nigerian Tobacco Co Ltd: POB 137, Lagos; tel. (1) 2690471; fax (1) 2690470; f. 1951; cap. ₦200m.; mfrs of tobacco products; Chair. OLUDOLAPO IBUKUN AKINKUGBE; Man. Dir PAUL KIRKHAM; 696 employees.

Phillips Oil Co (Nigeria) Ltd: Plot 853, 19 Bishop Aboyade-Cole St, Victoria Island, PMB 12612, Lagos; tel. (1) 2615656; fax (1) 2615663; petroleum exploration and production; Man. Dir M. O. TAIGA.

Port Harcourt Refining Co Ltd: Alesa Eleme, POB 585, Port Harcourt, Rivers State; tel. (84) 239536; fax (84) 239537; e-mail phrchet@linkserve.com.ng; f. 1965; Man. Dir MANSUR AHMED.

PZ Industries Ltd: Planning Office Way, Ilupeju Industrial Estate, Ikeja, PMB 21132, Lagos; tel. (1) 4973460; fax (1) 4962076; fmrly Paterson Zochonis Nigeria Ltd; soaps, detergents, toiletries, pharmaceuticals and confectionery; factories at Ikorodu, Aba and Ilupeju; Chief K. B. JAMODU; Man. Dir N. KOSMAS.

SCOA Nigeria Ltd: 67 Marina, POB 2318, Lagos; tel. (1) 2667977; fax (1) 2669642; cap. ₦44.8m.; vehicle assembly and maintenance, distribution and maintenance of heavyweight engines, industrial air-conditioning and refrigeration, home and office equipment, textiles, tanning, general consumer goods, mechanized farming; Chair. H. AGBAMU.

Shell Petroleum Development Co of Nigeria Ltd: Freeman House, 21–22 Marina, PMB 2418, Lagos; tel. (1) 2601600; fax (1) 2636864; internet www.shellnigeria.com; the largest petroleum operation in Nigeria; carries out onshore and offshore exploration and production; 55% govt-owned; Man. Dir B. H. ANDERSON.

Tate Industries: 47–48 Eric Moore Rd, Iganmu Industrial Estate, POB 1240, Lagos; tel. (1) 801930; fax (1) 833488; sugar, invert syrup, PVC pipes, plastic goods, stationery; Chair. Dr A. L. CIROMA.

Texaco Nigeria Ltd: 241 Igbosere Rd, POB 166, Lagos; tel. (1) 2600540; fax (1) 2630647; internet www.texaco.com; f. 1913; petroleum marketing; Chair. J. R. HAWN.

Texaco Overseas (Nigeria) Petroleum Co: 36 Gerrard Rd, Ikoyi, POB 1986, Lagos; tel. (1) 680070; fax (1) 682520; offshore petroleum mining; Man. Dir R. BUCARAM.

Triana Ltd: 18–20 Commercial Rd, PMB 1064, Apapa, Lagos; tel. (1) 5803040; fax (1) 5876161; e-mail triana@alpha.linkserve.com; f. 1970; shipping, clearing and forwarding, warehousing, air-freighting; Man. Dir M. P. AGUBA.

UAC of Nigeria Ltd: Niger House, 1-5 Odunlami St, POB 9, Lagos; tel. (1) 2663010; fax (1) 2662628; fmrly United Africa Co; divisions include brewing, foods, electrical materials, packaging,

business equipment, plant hire, timber; Man. Dir BASSEY U. NDIOKHO.

The West African Portland Cement Co Ltd: Elephant House, 237–239 Ikorodu Rd, POB 1001, Lagos; tel. (1) 4901060; fax (1) 4970704; f. 1959; production and sale of cement and decorative materials; cap. p.u. ₦60.3m.; Chair. Dr M. PONNLE.

TRADE UNIONS

Federation

Nigerian Labour Congress (NLC): 29 Olajuwon St, off Ojuelegba Rd, Yaba, POB 620, Lagos; tel. (1) 5835582; f. 1978; comprised 29 affiliated industrial unions in 1999; Pres. ADAMS OSHIOMHOLE.

Principal Unions

Amalgamated Union of Public Corporations, Civil Service, and Technical and Recreational Services Employees: 9 Aje St, PMB 1064, Yaba, Lagos; tel. (1) 5863722; Sec.-Gen. SYLVESTER EJIOFOR.

Maritime Workers' Union of Nigeria.

National Union of Chemical, Footwear, Rubber, Leather and Non-Metallic Workers.

National Union of Journalists: Lagos; Pres. LANRE OGUNDIPE; Sec. MOHAMMED KHALID.

National Union of Petroleum Workers and Natural Gas (NUPENG): Lagos; Sec.-Gen. FRANK KOKORI.

National Union of Printing, Publishing and Paper Products Workers.

Nigerian Union of Civil Engineering, Construction, Furniture and Woodworkers: 51 Kano St, Ebute Metta, PMB 1064, Lagos; tel. (1) 5800263.

Nigerian Union of Mine Workers: 95 Enugu St, POB 763, Jos; tel. (73) 52401.

Petroleum and Gas Senior Staff Association of Nigeria (PENGASSAN): Lagos; Leader MILTON DABIBI.

Steel and Engineering Workers' Union of Nigeria.

Transport

RAILWAYS

There are about 3,505 km of mainly narrow-gauge railways. The two principal lines connect Lagos with Nguru and Port Harcourt with Maiduguri.

Nigerian Railway Corporation: Plot 739, Zone A6, Panama St, off IBB Way, Maitama, Abuja; tel. (9) 5231912; f. 1955; restructured in 1993 into three separate units: Nigerian Railway Track Authority; Nigerian Railways; and Nigerian Railway Engineering Ltd; Admin. GREG IHIKUE.

ROADS

In 1996 the Nigerian road network totalled 193,198 km, including 2,044 km of motorways, 30,054 km of main roads and 30,500 km of secondary roads; some 37,000 km were paved.

Nigerian Road Federation: Ministry of Transport and Aviation, Joseph St, PMB 21038, Ikoyi, Lagos; tel. (1) 2652120.

INLAND WATERWAYS

Inland Waterways Department: Ministry of Transport, Joseph St, PMB 21038, Ikoyi, Lagos; tel. (1) 2652120; responsible for all navigable waterways.

SHIPPING

The principal ports are the Delta Port complex (including Warri, Koko, Burutu and Sapele ports), Port Harcourt and Calabar; other significant ports are situated at Apapa and Tin Can Island, near Lagos. The main petroleum ports are Bonny and Burutu.

National Maritime Authority: Michael Okpara St, Plot 1970, Wuse, Zone 5, Abuja; tel. (9) 5237016; fax (9) 5237015; f. 1987; Dir-Gen. Alhaji BUBA GALADIMA.

Nigerian Ports Authority: 26–28 Marina, PMB 12588, Marina, Lagos; tel. (1) 2600620; fax (1) 26303306; e-mail telnpo@infoweb .abs.net; internet www.nigeria-ports.com; f. 1955; Man. Dir Mallam BELLO GWANDO.

Nigerian Green Lines Ltd: Unity House, 15th Floor, 37 Marina, POB 2288, Lagos; tel. (1) 2663303; 2 vessels totalling 30,751 grt; Chair. Alhaji W. L. FOLAWIYO.

Nigerian Unity Line: Development House, 21 Wharf Rd, POB 326, Apapa, Lagos; tel. (1) 5804240; fax (1) 5870260; f. 1995, following the dissolution of the Nigerian National Shipping Line; govt-owned.

Association

Nigeria Shipping Federation: NPA Commercial Offices, Block 'A', Wharf Rd, POB 107, Apapa, Lagos; f. 1960; Chair. (vacant); Gen. Man. D. B. ADEKOYA.

CIVIL AVIATION

The principal international airports are at Lagos (Murtala Muhammed Airport), Kano, Port Harcourt, Calabar and Abuja. There are also 14 airports for domestic flights. In early 1997 a two-year programme to develop the airports at Lagos, Abuja, Port Harcourt and Kano was announced.

Federal Airport Authority of Nigeria: Murtala Muhammed Airport, PMB 21607, Ikeja, Lagos; tel. (1) 4900800; Man. Dir PETER IGBINEDION.

Principal Airlines

General and Aviation Services (Gas) Air Nigeria: Plot 5A, Old Domestic Airport, Ikeja, Lagos; tel. (1) 4933510; fax (1) 4962841; domestic and international cargo services; Pres. S. K. S. OLUBADEWO.

Kabo Air: 6775 Ashton Rd, POB 3439, Kano; tel. (64) 639591; fax (64) 645172; f. 1981; domestic services and international charters; Dir SHITU ADAMU.

Nigeria Airways: Airways House, Ikeja, PMB 136, Lagos; tel. (1) 4900470; fax (1) 2777675; f. 1958; scheduled domestic and services to Europe, the USA, West Africa and Saudi Arabia; Man. Dir Alhaji SHEHU MALAMI.

Okada Air: 17B Sapele Rd, Benin City; tel. (19) 241054; f. 1983; domestic and international charter passenger services, domestic scheduled services; Chair. Chief GABRIEL O. IGBINEDION.

Tourism

Potential attractions for tourists include fine coastal scenery, dense forests, and the rich diversity of Nigeria's arts. Including excursionists, a total of 1,230,155 tourists visited Nigeria in 1996. In 1997 receipts from tourism amounted to US $118m.

Nigerian Tourism Development Corporation: Zone 4, PMB 167, Abuja; tel. (9) 5230418; fax (9) 5230962; Chair. S. A. ALAMATU; Dir Alhaji S. M. JEGA.

Defence

In August 1999 the total strength of the armed forces was 94,000 men: the army totalled 79,000 men, the navy 5,500 and the air force 9,500. Military service is voluntary. In late 1999 the government announced that the strength of the armed forces was to be reduced to about 50,000.

Defence Expenditure: Budgeted at ₦7,023m. in 1995.

Commander-in-Chief of the Armed Forces: Gen. (retd) OLUSEGUN OBASANJO.

Chief of Defence Staff: Rear-Adm. IBRAHIM OGOHI.

Chief of Army Staff: Maj.-Gen. VICTOR MALU.

Chief of Naval Staff: Rear-Adm. VICTOR OMBU.

Chief of Air Staff: Air Vice-Marshal ISAAC ALFA.

Education

Education is partly the responsibility of the state governments, although the federal government has played an increasingly important role since 1970. Primary education begins at six years of age and lasts for six years. Secondary education begins at 12 years of age and lasts for a further six years, comprising two three-year cycles. Education to junior secondary level (from six to 15 years of age) is free and compulsory. In 1994 total enrolment at primary schools was equivalent to 98% of children in the relevant age-group (109% of boys; 87% of girls), while the comparable ratio for secondary enrolment was only 33% (36% of boys; 30% of girls). In 1993 383,488 students were enrolled in 133 higher education institutions. Estimated expenditure on education in 1997 was ₦16,286m., equivalent to 5.2% of total expenditure in the federal budget. According to UNESCO estimates, the rate of adult illiteracy in 1995 averaged 43.5% (males 33.9%; females 52.7%).

Bibliography

Adalemo, I. A., et al. (Eds). *Giant in the Tropics: A Compendium.* Lagos, Gabumo, 1993.

Adamokekun, L. *The Fall of the Second Republic.* Ibadan, Spectrum Books, 1985.

Adejumobi, S., and Momah, A. (Eds) *The Political Economy of Nigeria under Military Rule, 1984–1993.* Nigeria, Southern Africa Printing and Publishing House, 1995.

   The Enigma of Military Rule in Africa. Harare, SAPES Books, 1995.

Akpan, N. U. *The Struggle for Secession 1966–1970.* London, Frank Cass, 1972.

Aniagolu, A. N. *The Making of the 1989 Constitution of Nigeria.* Ibadan, Spectrum Books, 1993.

Anyanwu, U. D., and Aguwa, J. C. U. (Eds). *The Igbo and the Tradition of Politics.* Enugu, Fourth Dimension, 1993.

Asiegbu, J. U. J. *Nigeria and its British Invaders 1851–1920.* Lagos, Nok Publishers International, 1984.

Ate, B. E., and Akinterinwa, B.A. (Eds). *Nigeria and its Immediate Neighbours: Constraints and Prospects of Sub-Regional Security in the 1990s.* Lagos, Nigerian Institute of International Affairs, 1992.

Ayeni, V., and Soremekun, K. (Eds). *Nigeria's Second Republic.* Lagos, Daily Times Publications, 1988.

Babatope, E. *Murtala Muhammed: A Leader Betrayed.* Enugu, Roy and Ezete Publishing Co, 1986.

   The Abacha Regime and the 12 June Crisis. London, Beacons Books, 1995.

Bangura, Y. *Intellectuals, Economic Reform and Social Change: Constraints and Opportunities in the Formation of a Nigerian Technocracy.* Dakar, CODESRIA, 1994.

Clarke, P. B. *West Africans at War 1914–18, 1939–45: Colonial Propaganda and its Cultural Aftermath.* London, Ethnographica, 1986.

Crowder, M. *The Story of Nigeria.* 4th Edn. London, 1978.

Cruise O'Brien, D. B., Dunn, J., and Rathbone, R. (Eds). *Contemporary West African States.* Cambridge University Press, 1989.

Diamond, L. (Ed.). *Transition without End: Nigerian Politics and Civil Society under Babangida.* Boulder, CO, Lynne Rienner Publishers, 1997.

Ekundare, R. O. *An Economic History of Nigeria 1860–1960.* London, Methuen, 1973.

Ekwe-Ekwe, H. *Conflict and Intervention in Africa: Nigeria, Angola and Zaire.* London, Macmillan, 1990.

Enwerem, I. M. *Dangerous Awakening: The Politicization of Religion in Nigeria.* Ibadan, FRA, 1996.

Essien, E. *Nigeria Under Structural Adjustment.* Fountain Publications (Nigeria) Ltd, 1990.

Forrest, T. *Politics and Economic Development in Nigeria.* Boulder, CO, Westview Press, 1993.

   The Advance of African Capital: The Growth of Nigerian Private Enterprise. Charlottesville, VA, University Press of Virginia, 1994.

Graf, W. D. *The Nigerian State: Political Economy, State, Class and Political System in the Post-Colonial Era.* London, James Currey, 1988.

Hayward, M. F. *Elections in Independent Africa.* Boulder, CO, Westview Press, 1987.

Honey, R. and Okafor, S. I. (Eds). *Hometown Associations: Indigenous Knowledge and Development in Nigeria.* London, Intermediate Technology Publications, 1998.

Ihonvbere, J. O. *Nigeria: The Politics of Adjustment and Democracy.* New Brunswick, NJ, Transaction, 1993.

Ikoku, S. G. *Nigeria's Fourth Coup d'Etat.* Enugu, Fourth Dimension, 1985.

Ikpuk, J. S. *Militarism of Politics and Neo-colonialism: The Nigerian Experience 1966–1990.* London, Janus Publishing Co, 1995.

Iweriebor, E. E. G. *Radical Politics in Nigeria, 1945–1950: The Significance of the Zikist Movement.* Zaria, Ahmadu Bello University Press, 1996.

Kastfelt, N. *Religion and Politics in Nigeria: A Study in Middle Belt Christianity.* London, British Academic Press, 1994.

Khan, S. A. *Nigeria: The Political Economy of Oil.* New York, Oxford University Press, 1994.

King, M. C. *Basic Currents of Nigerian Foreign Policy*. Baltimore, Harvard University Press, 1996.

Kirk-Greene, A. H. M., and Rimmer, D. *Nigeria Since 1970: A Political and Economic Outline*. London, Hodder and Stoughton, 1981.

Kukah, M. H. *Religion, Politics and Power in Northern Nigeria*. Ibadan, Spectrum Books, 1993.

Mbadiwe, K. O. *Rebirth of a Nation*. Oxford ABC, Enugu, Fourth Dimension Publishing, 1991.

Momah, S., and Momah, A. (Eds). *Political Economy of Nigeria under Military Rule, 1894–1993*. Harare, SAPES Books, 1995.

Nnoli, O. *Ethnicity and Development in Nigeria*. Aldershot, Avebury, 1995.

(Ed.). *Dead-End to Nigerian Development: An Analysis of the Political Economy of Nigeria 1979–1989*. Dakar, CODESRIA, 1993.

Nwabueze, B. O. *Military Rule and Constitutionalism in Nigeria*. Ibadan, Spectrum Books, 1992.

Nwabueze, B. O., and Akinola, A. (Eds). *Military Rule and Social Justice in Nigeria*. Ibadan, Spectrum Books, 1993.

Nwankwo, A. A. *The Nationalities Question in Nigeria: The Class Foundation of Conflicts*. Enugu, Fourth Dimension, 1990.

Nigeria: The Political Transition and the Future of Democracy. Enugu, Fourth Dimension, 1993.

Obasanjo, O. *My Command: An Account of the Nigerian Civil War 1967–1970*. London, Heinemann, 1981.

Obichere, B. (Ed.). *Studies in Southern Nigerian History*. London, Frank Cass, 1980.

Odole, Chief M. A. F. *Ife: The Genesis of the Yoruba Race*. Ijeka, John West, 1986.

Ogbondah, C. W. *Military Regimes and the Press in Nigeria, 1968–1993; Human Rights and National Development*. Lanham, MD, University Press of America, 1993.

Ogwu, U. J., and Olaniyan, R. O. (Eds). *Nigeria's International Economic Relations: Dimensions of Dependence and Change*. Lagos, Nigerian Institute of International Affairs, 1990.

Okigbo, P. N. C. *National Development Planning in Nigeria, 1900–1992*. Portsmouth, NH, Heinemann, 1989.

Olanrewaju, S. A., and Falola, T. (Eds). *Rural Development Problems in Nigeria*. Aldershot, Avebury, 1992.

Olowu, D., and Soremekun, K. *Governance and Democratisation in Nigeria*. Ibadan, Spectrum Books, 1995.

Olowu, D., Ayo, S. B., and Akande, B. *Local Institutions and National Development in Nigeria*. Ile-Ife, Obafemi Awolowo University Press, 1991.

Olukoshi, A. O. (Ed.). *The Politics of Structural Adjustment in Nigeria*. London, James Currey, 1993.

Olupona, J. (Ed.) *Religion and Peace in Multi-Faith Nigeria*. Ile-Ife, Obafemi Awolowo University Press, 1992.

Onyemelukwe, J. O. C., and Filani, M. O. *Economic Geography of West Africa*. London, Lagos, New York, Longman, 1983.

Osaghae, E. E. *Crippled Giant: Nigeria Since Independence*. London, Hurst, 1998.

Otobo, D. *The Trade Union Movement in Nigeria*. Lagos, Malthouse Press, 1995.

Peel, J. D. Y. *Ijeshas and Nigerians: The Incorporation of a Yoruba Kingdom*. Cambridge University Press, 1983.

Peters, J. *The Nigerian Military and the State*. London, Tauris, 1997.

Rimmer, D. *The Economies of West Africa*. London, Weidenfeld and Nicolson, 1984.

Sklar, R. L. *Nigerian Political Parties: Power in an Emergent African Nation*. New York and Lagos, Nok Publishers, 1983 (reissue).

Smith, R. S. *Kingdoms of the Yoruba*. 3rd Edn. London, James Currey, 1988.

Synge, R. *Nigeria, the Way Forward*. London, Euromoney Books, 1993.

Umoren, J. A. *Democracy and Ethnic Diversity in Nigeria*. Lanham, MD, University Press of America, 1996.

Vogt, M. A., and Ekoko, A. E. (Eds). *Nigeria in International Peace Keeping, 1960–1992*. Lagos, Malthouse Press, 1993.

Wright, S. *Nigeria: Struggle for Stability and Status*. Boulder, CO, Westview Press, 1999.

Zwingini, J. S. *Capitalist Development in an African Economy: The Case of Nigeria*. Ibadan, UP PLC, 1992.

RÉUNION

Physical and Social Geography

Réunion is a volcanic island in the Indian Ocean lying at the southern extremity of the Mascarene Plateau. Mauritius lies some 190 km to the north-east and Madagascar about 650 km to the west. The island is roughly oval in shape, being about 65 km long and up to 50 km wide; the total area is 2,507 sq km (968 sq miles). Volcanoes have developed along a north-west to south-east angled fault; Piton de la Fournaise (2,624 m) most recently erupted in March 1998. The others are now extinct, although their cones rise to 3,000 m and dominate the island. The heights and the frequent summer cyclones help to create abundant rainfall, which averages 4,714 mm annually in the uplands, and 686 mm at sea-level. Temperatures vary greatly according to altitude, being tropical at sea-level, averaging between 20°C (68°F) and 28°C (82°F), but much cooler in the uplands, with average temperatures between 8°C (46°F) and 19°C (66°F), owing to frequent winter frosts.

The population of Réunion has more than doubled since the 1940s, reaching 597,828 at the March 1990 census. During 1990–97 the population increased at an average rate of 1.7% per year. According to official estimates, the population was 706,300 at 1 January 1999, giving a population density of 281.7 inhabitants per sq km. In 1998 38.3% of Réunion's population was under 20 years of age, while 52.4% of the population was aged between 20 and 59 years. The capital is Saint-Denis, with 121,999 inhabitants at the March 1990 census. Other major towns include Saint-Paul, with 71,669 inhabitants, and Saint-Pierre and Le Tampon, with 58,846 and 47,593 inhabitants, respectively, in 1990. The population is of mixed origin, including people of European, African, Indian and Chinese descent.

Recent History

Revised for this edition by the Editor

Réunion (formerly known as Bourbon) was first occupied in 1642 by French settlers expelled from Madagascar, and was governed as a colony until 1946, when it received full departmental status. In 1974 it became an overseas department with the status of a region. Réunion administers the small and uninhabited Indian Ocean islands of Bassas da India, Juan de Nova, Europa and the Iles Glorieuses, which are also claimed by Madagascar, and Tromelin, which is also claimed by both Madagascar and Mauritius. In 1997 Réunion became the administrative centre for the French Southern and Antarctic Territories. Since 1973 Réunion has been the headquarters of French military forces in the Indian Ocean.

In 1978 the Organization of African Unity adopted a report recommending measures to hasten the independence of the island, and condemned its occupation by a 'colonial power'. However, this view attracted little popular support in Réunion; although the left-wing political parties on the island advocated increased autonomy (amounting to virtual self-government), few people were in favour of complete independence.

In 1982 the French government proposed a decentralization plan, envisaging the dissolution of the general and regional councils in the overseas departments and the creation in each department of a single assembly, to be elected on the basis of proportional representation. However, this proposal received considerable opposition in Réunion and the other overseas departments, and the plan was eventually abandoned. Revised legislation on decentralization in the overseas departments was approved by the French national assembly in December.

In the elections to the French national assembly, which took place in March 1986 under a system of proportional representation, the number of deputies from Réunion was increased from three to five. The Parti Communiste Réunionnais (PCR) won two seats, while the Union pour la Démocratie Française (UDF), the Rassemblement pour la République (RPR) and a newly-formed right-wing party, France-Réunion-Avenir (FRA), each secured one seat. In the concurrent elections to the regional council, the centre-right RPR-UDF alliance and FRA together received 54.1% of the votes cast, winning 18 and eight of the 45 seats respectively, while the PCR won 13 seats.

In September 1986 the French government's plan to introduce a programme of economic reforms was opposed by the left-wing parties, which demanded that the overseas departments should receive social parity with metropolitan France through the introduction of similar levels of taxation and benefits. In October Paul Vergès, the PCR secretary-general and a deputy to the French national assembly, accused France of instituting 'social apartheid' in the overseas departments, and referred his complaint to the European parliament in Strasbourg. In October 1987 Vergès and the other PCR deputy, Elie Hoarau, resigned from the national assembly, in protest against the government's proposals. Their seats were taken by Laurent Vergès, Paul Vergès's son, and Claude Hoarau, the PCR mayor of Saint-Louis.

In the second round of the French presidential election, which took place in May 1988, François Mitterrand, the incumbent president and a candidate of the Parti Socialiste (PS), received 60.3% of the votes cast in Réunion. At the ensuing general election for the French national assembly in June, the system of single-member constituencies was reintroduced. As in the previous general election, the PCR won two of the Réunion seats, while the UDF, the RPR (these two parties allying to form the Union du Rassemblement du Centre) and the FRA each won one seat. In July the PCR renewed its criticism of the continuing allocation of lower levels of benefits and revenue to the overseas departments, despite a previous undertaking by Mitterrand to institute a uniform policy for the overseas departments and metropolitan France.

In the elections for the newly-enlarged 44-member general council in September and October 1988, the PCR and the PS won nine and four seats respectively, while other left-wing candidates won two seats. The UDF secured six seats and other right-wing candidates 19, but the RPR, which had previously held 11 seats, won only four.

The results of the municipal elections in March 1989 represented a slight decline in support for the left-wing parties. Nevertheless, for the first time since the 1940s, a PS candidate, Gilbert Annette, became mayor of Saint-Denis. At Saint-Pierre the incumbent mayor and PCR deputy to the French national assembly, Elie Hoarau, unilaterally declared himself the winner, discounting 1,500 votes which had been secured by two minor lists. The result was therefore declared invalid by the administrative tribunal. This incident led to a rift between the PS and the PCR, and, when a fresh election in that municipality was held in September, Elie Hoarau was unable to form an alliance. Hoarau was, however, re-elected mayor, securing just over 50% of the votes cast.

In September 1990, following the restructuring of the RPR under the new local leadership of Alain Defaud, a number of right-wing movements, including the UDF and the RPR, announced the creation of an informal alliance, known as Union pour la France (UPF), to contest the regional elections in 1992. During a visit to Réunion in November the French minister for overseas departments and territories announced a series of proposed economic and social measures, in accordance with the undertakings on parity given by Mitterrand in 1988 (see above). However, these measures were criticized as insufficient by right-wing groups and by the PCR.

In March 1990 violent protests took place in support of a popular, but unlicensed, island television service, Télé Free-DOM, following a decision by the French national broadcasting commission, the Conseil supérieur de l'audiovisuel (CSA), to award a broadcasting permit to a rival company. In February 1991 the seizure by the CSA of Télé Free-DOM's broadcasting transmitters prompted further violent demonstrations in Saint-Denis. Some 11 people were killed in ensuing riots, and the French government dispatched police reinforcements to restore order. The violence was officially ascribed to widespread discontent with the island's social and economic conditions, and a parliamentary commission was established to ascertain the background to the riots.

A visit to Réunion in March 1991 by the French prime minister, Michel Rocard, precipitated further rioting. In the same month the commission of enquiry attributed the riots in February to the inflammatory nature of television programmes, which had been broadcast by Télé Free-DOM in the weeks preceding the disturbances, and blamed the station's director, Dr Camille Sudre, who was also a deputy mayor of Saint-Denis. However, the commission refuted allegations by right-wing and centrist politicians that the PCR had orchestrated the violence. Later in March President Mitterrand expressed concern over the outcome of the enquiry, and appealed to the CSA to reconsider its policy towards Télé Free-DOM. In April, however, the CSA indicated its continued opposition to Télé Free-DOM.

In March 1992 the mayor of Saint-Denis, Gilbert Annette, expelled Sudre, who was one of the deputy mayors, from the majority coalition in the municipal council, after Sudre presented a list of independent candidates to contest regional elections later that month. In the elections to the regional council, which took place on 22 March, Sudre's list of candidates secured 17 seats, while the UPF obtained 14 seats, the PCR nine seats and the PS five seats. In concurrent elections to the general council (which was enlarged to 47 seats), right-wing candidates secured 29 seats, maintaining a substantial majority, although the number of PCR deputies increased to 12, and the number of PS deputies to six; Boyer retained the presidency of the council. Shortly after the elections, Sudre's independent candidates (known as Free-DOM) formed an alliance with the PCR, whereby members of the two groups held a majority of 26 of the 45 seats in the regional council. Under the terms of the agreement, Sudre was to assume the presidency of the regional council, and Paul Vergès the first vice-presidency. On 27 March, with the support of the PCR, Sudre was elected as president of the regional council by a majority of 27 votes. The UPF and the PS rejected Sudre's subsequent offer to join the Free-DOM-PCR coalition. The PS subsequently appealed against the results of the regional elections, on the grounds that, in contravention of regulations, Sudre's privately-owned radio station, Radio Free-DOM, had campaigned on his behalf prior to the elections.

Following his election as president of the regional council, Sudre announced that Télé Free-DOM was shortly to resume broadcasting. However, the CSA maintained that if transmissions were resumed Télé Free-DOM would be considered to be illegal, and would be subject to judicial proceedings. Jean-Paul Virapouillé, a deputy to the French national assembly, subsequently proposed the adoption of legislation which would legalize Télé Free-DOM and would provide for the establishment of an independent media sector outside the jurisdiction of the CSA. In April 1992 Télé Free-DOM transmitters were returned, and at the end of May broadcasting was resumed (without the permission of the CSA).

In June 1992 Sudre, Vergès and the former president of the regional council, Pierre Lagourgue, met President Mitterrand to submit proposals for economic reforms, which would establish greater parity between the island and metropolitan France. In early July, however, the French government announced increases in supplementary income, which were substantially less than had been expected, prompting widespread discontent on the island.

In September 1992 the French government agreed to an economic programme that had been formulated by the regional council. In the same month the PCR advocated a boycott of the French referendum on the ratification of the Treaty on European Union, which was to be conducted later that month, in protest at the alleged failure of the French government to recognize the needs of the overseas departments. At the referendum only 26.3% of the registered electorate voted, of whom 74.3% approved the ratification of the treaty. Later that month Boyer and Lagourgue were elected as representatives to the French senate. (The RPR candidate, Paul Moreau, retained his seat.) In October an investigation into allegations that leading politicians had misappropriated funds and obtained contracts by fraudulent means was initiated. In December increasing discontent with living standards and economic conditions on the island led to renewed rioting at Saint-Denis and at the town of Le Port.

In March 1993 Sudre announced that he was to contest Virapouillé's seat on behalf of the Free-DOM-PCR alliance in the forthcoming elections to the French national assembly. At the elections, which took place in late March, Sudre was defeated by Virapouillé in the second round of voting, while another incumbent right-wing deputy, André Thien Ah Koon, who contested the elections on behalf of the UPF, also retained his seat. The number of PCR deputies in the assembly was reduced from two to one (Vergès), while the PS and RPR each secured one of the remaining seats.

In May 1993 the results of the regional elections in March 1992 were annulled, and Sudre was prohibited from engaging in political activity for one year, on the grounds that programmes broadcast by Radio Free-DOM prior to the elections constituted political propaganda. Sudre subsequently selected his wife, Margie, to assume his candidacy in fresh elections to the regional council. In the elections, which took place in June 1993, the Free-DOM list of candidates, headed by Margie Sudre, secured 12 seats, while the UDF obtained 10, the RPR eight, the PCR nine and the PS six seats. Margie Sudre was subsequently elected as president of the regional council, with the support of the nine PCR deputies and three dissident members of the PS, by a majority of 24 votes.

In April 1993 several prominent businessmen were arrested in connection with the acquisition of contracts by fraudulent means, while a number of members of the principal political organizations, including Boyer and Pierre Vergès, the mayor of Le Port and a member of the PCR, were also implicated in malpractice. Both Boyer and Vergès subsequently fled, following investigations into their activities, and warrants were issued for their arrest. In August Boyer, who had surrendered to the security forces, was placed in detention, pending his trial on charges of corruption. (Joseph Sinimalé, a member of the RPR, temporarily assumed the office of president of the general council.) In the same month the mayor of Saint-Paul and vice-president of the general council, Cassam Moussa, was also arrested and charged with corruption.

In January 1994 Jules Raux, a deputy mayor of Saint-Denis who was also the local treasurer of the PS, was arrested on charges of financial corruption, and in February two municipal councillors from Saint-Denis were arrested on suspicion of involvement in the affair. In the same month a French citizen (who was believed to have connections with members of the Djibouti government) was arrested on Réunion and charged with having transferred the funds that were alleged to have been illegally obtained to Djibouti. In March Annette, who was implicated in the affair, resigned as mayor of Saint-Denis, and was subsequently charged with corruption. Boyer was tried and sentenced to four years' imprisonment, while Moussa received a term of two years. In the same month Pierre Vergès (who remained in hiding) resigned as mayor of Le Port.

At elections to the general council, which took place in March 1994, the PCR retained 12 seats, while the number of PS deputies increased to 12 (despite adverse publicity attached to associates of Annette within the PS). The number of seats held by the RPR and UDF declined to five and 11 respectively (compared with six and 14 in the incumbent council). The RPR and UDF subsequently attempted to negotiate an alliance with the PCR; despite long-standing inter-party dissension, however, the PCR and PS established a coalition within the general council, thereby securing a majority of 24 of the 47 seats. In April a member of the PS, Christophe Payet, was elected president of the general council by a majority of 26 votes, defeating Sinimalé; the right-wing parties (which had held the presidency of the council for more than 40 years) boycotted the poll. The PS and PCR signed an agreement, whereby they were to control the administration of the general council jointly, and indicated that centrist deputies might be allowed to enter the alliance. In July Boyer's prison sentence was reduced on appeal to a term of one year.

In November 1994 an official visit to Réunion by Edouard Balladur, the French prime minister (and declared candidate for the presidential election in 1995), provoked strike action in protest at his opposition to the establishment of social equality between the overseas departments and metropolitan France. Jacques Chirac, the official presidential candidate of the RPR, visited the island in December 1994, when he was endorsed by the organ of the PCR, *Témoignages*, after declaring his commitment to the issue of social equality. In the second round of the presidential election, which took place in May 1995, the socialist candidate, Lionel Jospin, secured 56% of votes cast on Réunion, while Chirac won 44% of the votes (although Chirac obtained the highest number of votes in total); the PCR and Free-DOM had advised their supporters not to vote for Balladur, because of his opposition to the principle of social equality. Following Chirac's election to the French presidency, Margie Sudre was nominated minister of French language and culture, prompting concern among right-wing elements on Réunion. In August Pierre Vergès was sentenced *in absentia* to 18 months' imprisonment; an appeal was rejected in July 1996. In September 1995 the mayor of Salazie, who was a member of the RPR, was also charged with corruption. Following a period of enforced exile in Réunion following a coup attempt in September 1995, the Comoran president, Saïd Mohamed Djohar, returned to the Comoros in January 1996, agreeing to retain only symbolic presidential powers. In November 1995 Boyer lost an appeal against his 1994 conviction and was expelled from the French senate.

With effect from the beginning of 1996 the social security systems of the overseas departments were aligned with those of metropolitan France. In February 1996 Alain Juppé, the prime minister, invited more than 300 representatives from the overseas departments to Paris to participate in discussions on social equality and development; participants came from political parties, trade unions and other associations. The main issue uniting all the political representatives from Réunion was the need to align the salaries of civil servants on the island with those in metropolitan France. Several trade unionists declared themselves willing to enter into negotiations, on the condition that only new recruits would be affected. The French government remained undecided. President Chirac's visit to Réunion in March coincided with the 50th anniversary of France's establishment of overseas departments. The main issues that the president addressed during his visit were unemployment, the reinforcement of social policy, and equality with metropolitan France. Paul Vergès, joint candidate of the PCR and the PS, was elected to the French senate on 14 April 1996, securing 51.9% of the votes cast. Fred K/Bidy won 40.0% of the votes, failing to retain Eric Boyer's seat for the RPR. In the by-election to replace Paul Vergès, which took place in September, Claude Hoarau, the PCR candidate, was elected with 56.0% of the votes cast, while Margie Sudre obtained 44.0%. A new majority alliance between Free-DOM, the RPR and the UDF was subsequently formed in the regional council, with the re-election of its 19-member permanent commission in October.

In October 1996 the trial of a number of politicians and business executives, who had been arrested in 1993–94 on charges of corruption, took place, after three years of investigations. Gilbert Annette and Jules Raux were convicted and, in December of that year, received prison sentences, although

Annette's sentence was reduced on appeal in December 1997. Jacques de Châteauvieux, the chairman of Groupe Sucreries de Bourbon (principally concerned with the production and exportation of sugar), was found guilty of bribery, and was also jailed. Two senior executives from the French enterprise, Compagnie Générale des Eaux, were given suspended sentences, although the public prosecutor subsequently appealed for part of the sentences to be made custodial. Some 20 others were also found guilty of corruption. Pierre Vergès surrendered to the authorities in December and appeared before a magistrate in Saint-Pierre, where he was subsequently detained; in February 1997 he was released by the court of appeal. Also in December 1996 voting on the regional budget for 1997 was postponed three times, as a result of the abstention of eight Free-DOM councillors, led by the first vice-president of the regional council, Jasmin Moutoussamy, who demanded the dismissal of Gilbert Payet, a sub-prefect and special adviser to Sudre, and greater delegation of power to the vice-presidents. They also objected to Sudre's alliance with the RPR-UDF majority. In late March 1997 the regional budget was eventually adopted, although Sudre and many right-wing councillors abstained from voting because of the opposition's insistence on a number of amendments, most significantly on the composition of the council's permanent commission, in which it had no representation. Following the vote, Sudre suspended the session to allow for discussion between the political organizations.

Meanwhile, civil servants and students protested violently against a French government proposal, made earlier in March 1997, to undertake reform of the civil service, including a reduction in the incomes of new recruits to bring them closer to those in metropolitan France. Senator Pierre Lagourgue was chosen to mediate between the French government and the civil servants' trade unions, but strike action and demonstrations continued into April, leading to violent clashes with the security forces.

Four left-wing candidates were successful in elections to the French national assembly held in May and June 1997. Claude Hoarau (PCR) retained his seat and was joined by Huguette Bello and Elie Hoarau, also both from the PCR, and Michel Tamaya (PS), while André Thien Ah Koon, representing the RPR-UDF coalition, was re-elected.

In February 1998 the PCR (led by Paul Vergès), the PS and several right-wing mayors presented a joint list of candidates, known as the Rassemblement, to contest forthcoming elections. In the elections to the regional council, which took place on 15 March, the Rassemblement secured 19 seats, while the UDF obtained nine seats and the RPR eight, with various left-wing candidates representing Free-DOM winning five. Vergès was elected president of the regional council on 23 March, with the support of the deputies belonging to the Rassemblement and Free-DOM groups. In concurrent elections to an expanded 49-member general council, right-wing candidates (including those on the Rassemblement's list) secured 27 seats, while left-wing candidates obtained 22 seats, the PCR and the PS each winning 10 seats. At the end of the month Jean-Luc Poudroux, of the UDF, was elected president of the general council, owing to the support of two left-wing deputies.

In October 1998 Réunion's three PCR deputies to the French national assembly proposed legislation providing for the division of the island into two departments, with Saint-Pierre joining Saint-Denis as a departmental town. In March 1999 it was reported that Claude Hoarau had been given a one-year suspended prison sentence for his participation in demonstrations organized by the PCR in mid-1996 and early 1997. In June 1999 Michel Tamaya and Claude Lise, a senator from Martinique, completed an official six-month review of administrative structures in the overseas departments. They presented 70 proposals for the government's consideration, including a clarification of the division of responsibilities between the region and the department. In December, whilst attending the heads of state summit of the Indian Ocean Commission (IOC, see p. 152) on the island, President Chirac announced that he supported the proposed creation of a second department on Réunion, a move supported by all local politicians. In March 2000 the French secretary of state for overseas departments and territories declared that Réunion was to be divided into two departments,

Réunion South and Réunion North, as of 1 January 2001. However, both the proposed date and the geographical division of the island were rejected by the PS, although it stated that it remained in favour of the creation of a second department. The president of the UDF, Jean-Paul Virapoullé, expressed his opposition to the proposals. Demonstrations both for and against the division of the island took place in March 2000. It was subsequently agreed that the proposals would not be effected

until 1 January 2002, and changes were made to the initial plans regarding the geographical division of the island. However, on 15 June 2000 the creation of a second department was rejected by the French senate by 203 votes to 111.

In January 1986 France was admitted to the IOC, owing to its sovereignty over Réunion. Réunion was given the right to host ministerial meetings of the IOC, but is not eligible to occupy the presidency, owing to its non-sovereign status.

Economy

Revised for this edition by the Editor

As a result of its connection with France, Réunion's economy is relatively developed, especially in comparison with its sub-Saharan African neighbours. Réunion's gross national product (GNP) in 1995 was estimated at 29,200m. French francs, equivalent to about 44,300 francs per head. In 1990–97, according to World Bank estimates, Réunion's population increased at an average annual rate of 1.7% per year. The population density remained very high, averaging 281.7 inhabitants per sq km at 1 January 1999. In 1995 Réunion's gross domestic product (GDP) totalled 42,577m. French francs, equivalent to 64,303 francs per head. In 1988–94 GDP increased, in real terms, at an average rate of 3.4% per year. GDP grew by 1.5% in 1994 and by 6.3% in 1995.

The economy has traditionally been based on agriculture, which engaged an estimated 3.8% of the employed labour force in 1998, and contributed 3.4% of GDP in 1995. According to the FAO, agricultural production increased at an average rate of 1.3% per year during 1990–98. It increased by 4.6% in 1997, but decreased by 5.1% in 1998. Sugar cane is the principal crop and has formed the basis of the economy for over a century. In 1998 sugar accounted for 58.9% of export earnings. Only 17.1% of the land area was cultivated in 1998, mainly because of the volcanic nature of the soil but also owing to increasing urbanization; however, 59.1% of the arable land was used for sugar plantations in that year. The cane is grown on nearly all the good cultivable land up to 800 m above sea-level on the leeward side of the island, except in the relatively dry north-west, and up to 500 m on the windward side. Although the volcanic soil is fertile, the quality and yield are not as high as in Mauritius, and the modernization of agricultural practices is hindered in part by archaic restrictions on land tenure. Sugar cane harvests entered a decline in the early 1970s, owing to drought, ageing plants, rising production costs and inefficient harvesting techniques and transport systems. In 1974 a modernization plan was put into effect, and by 1976 production had begun to reflect both higher yields and an increase in the land used for sugar cultivation. By 1981, when the plan ended, average annual production of raw sugar had risen to 247,000 metric tons, despite several tropical storms. In 1986 state aid of 45 French francs per ton of sugar was given directly to farmers for the first time. In 1989 sugar production declined to 170,965 tons, compared with 252,230 tons in 1988 (as a result of damage caused by a further cyclone), but had increased to 226,700 tons by 1992. In subsequent years the sugar industry was adversely affected by increasing urbanization, which resulted in a decline in the area of agricultural land. By 1998, however, production of both raw sugar (222,000 tons) and sugar cane (1,675,000 tons) had recovered significantly. The French-owned sugar producer, Quartier, announced the closure of one of its refineries in 1995, owing to unprofitability; only two refineries (Gol, owned by Quartier, and Bois Rouge, owned by the local producer, Groupe Sucreries de Bourbon) remained on Réunion.

Geraniums, vetiver and ylang-ylang are grown for the production of aromatic essences. Exporters of oil of geranium and vetiver have experienced difficulty in competing with new producers whose prices are much lower. In 1985 measures were introduced to increase the output of oil of geranium; output had increased to 25.4 metric tons by 1991, but declined to 14.7 tons in 1992 and to 6.3 tons in 1998. Output of vetiver totalled 12.1

tons in 1987, but subsequently declined to only 0.2 ton in 1998, and has become insignificant as an export crop. Vanilla is produced for export in the south-east; production totalled 132.8 tons in 1987, but declined to 31.2 tons in 1990; however, output increased to 116.5 tons in 1992. An agreement between Réunion, Madagascar and the Comoros concerning price and export quotas on vanilla ended in 1992; in early 1995, however, negotiations regarding a new agreement between Réunion and the Comoros commenced. None the less, in 1998 vanilla remained insignificant as an export crop. Tobacco cultivation (introduced at the beginning of the century) produced a crop of 192.8 tons in 1988. Unfavourable climatic conditions intervened in the 1989/90 crop year, however, and the sector was further adversely affected by cyclone damage, which destroyed 115 of the island's 400 tobacco drying sheds; production declined sharply, to 107.8 tons in 1990, to 73.3 tons in 1991, and to 22 tons in 1992. A variety of vegetables and fruits is grown, and the island is self-sufficient in cattle and pigs. Overall, however, substantial food imports are necessary to supply the dense population.

Although fish are not abundant off Réunion's coast, the commercial fishing industry is an important source of income and employment, especially in the deep-sea sector. The largest fishing vessels make voyages lasting several months, to catch spiny lobsters (langoustes) that breed in the cold waters near Antarctica. In an attempt to preserve resources of langoustes, the fishing quota for 1989 was reduced, and the total catch declined to 1,725 metric tons, increasing slightly to 1,731 tons in 1990. The total catch increased substantially thereafter, reaching 5,882 tons by 1997.

Industry (including mining, manufacturing, construction and power) contributed 12.0% of GDP in 1995, and employed an estimated 13.7% of the working population in 1993. The principal branch of manufacturing is food-processing, particularly the production of sugar and rum. Other significant sectors include the fabrication of construction materials, mechanics, printing, metalwork, textiles and garments, and electronics. In January 1989 there were a total of 958 industrial enterprises in Réunion, 89.6% of which employed fewer than 20 salaried staff; by January 1998 the number of industrial enterprises had increased to 2,566, with a further 2,983 engaged in construction activities. In early 1999 it was announced that a Singaporean textiles group, Tolarem, was to establish a subsidiary on the island, creating some 283 jobs.

No mineral resources have been identified on Réunion. Imports of petroleum products accounted for 5.4% of the value of total imports in 1998. Energy is derived principally from thermal and hydroelectric power, which constituted 64% and 36%, respectively, of total electricity production (1,566.2m. kWh) in that year. Bagasse (a by-product of sugar cane) is used to fuel thermal power installations.

Services (including transport, communications, trade and finance) contributed 84.6% of GDP in 1998, and employed 71.7% of the working population in 1993. The public sector accounts for about one-half of employment in the services sector. The development of tourism is actively promoted, and it is hoped that increased investment in this sector will lead to higher receipts and will help to reduce the trade deficit, as well as providing new jobs. In 1988 Réunion received aid from the European Community (EC, now the European Union–EU) to stimulate the sector. Tourist arrivals subsequently increased considerably, rising by an average of 9.2% per year in 1990–97. In 1998 400,000 tourists visited Réunion (an increase of 7.0% compared with 1997), and revenue from tourism increased to 1,563m. French francs. Of the total number of visitors in that year, 79.7% were from France, 10.0% from Mauritius, and 2.6% from Madagascar. The tourism sector contributed only 3%–4% of GDP in 1993.

In 1997 the principal source of imports was France (63.5%), which was also the principal market for exports (72.1%). Other major trading partners included Bahrain, Japan, Italy and Belgium-Luxembourg. In 1998 the main imports were road and rail vehicles, solid mineral fuels and petroleum products, and pharmaceutical products. The principal export in that year was sugar. There is a substantial trade deficit, which is partly financed by aid from France and receipts from expatriates. In 1996 Réunion recorded a trade deficit of 13,143.0m. francs, which declined slightly, to 13,011.4m. francs, in 1997, but increased again, to 14,095.0m. francs, in 1998. The contribution of exports to GDP declined from 12% at the beginning of the 1970s to 2% in 1992, owing partly to a decline in world sugar prices, and stood at an estimated 7.4% in 1995. In 1998 the volume of goods passing through the ports increased, exceeding 3m. metric tons for the first time, principally as a result of a rise in imports. At the ports the tonnage of goods handled increased at an average annual rate of 5.1% in 1990–98. Fuel imports were boosted by the growing number of motor vehicles and a greater number of direct flights from Réunion.

The close connection with France protects the island from the dangers inherent in the narrowness of its economic base. Nevertheless, unemployment and inflation, compounded after 1974 by a number of bankruptcies among small sugar planters, have been the cause of major social and economic problems. The rise in the cost of imported fertilizers and of labour has exceeded the rise in the price of sugar. The annual rate of inflation averaged 2.4% in 1990–98; consumer prices increased by 1.3% in 1998. In March 2000 an estimated 36.5% of the labour force were unemployed. Since 1980 the government has invested significant sums in a series of public works projects in an effort to create jobs and to alleviate the high level of seasonal unemployment following the sugar cane harvest. However, large numbers of workers emigrate in search of employment each year, principally to France. In 1998 the state budgetary deficit was estimated at 8,048.9m. French francs.

The French government has increased its infrastructural spending in Réunion, particularly on improvements to health services, housing, electricity supply and communication facilities for low-income families. In 1979 an estimated 75% of the population received welfare payments from France, and direct subsidies averaged 25% higher per recipient in Réunion than in metropolitan France. In January 1989 legislation which established a guaranteed minimum income was introduced. In January 1990 a French government commission, appointed in 1989 to examine the economic condition of the overseas departments, published a report containing 58 proposals for the rectification of social and economic shortcomings, and recommended an improvements programme to be phased over two three-year stages. In November 1990 the French government announced measures aimed at establishing parity of the four overseas departments with metropolitan France in social and economic programmes. The reforms included the standardization by 1992 of minimum wage levels in Réunion with those operating in the other three overseas departments. It was envisaged that minimum wages in the overseas departments would be equal with those in metropolitan France by 1995, although this was to be achieved by way of trade union negotiations with employers rather than by government wage guarantees.

In April 1991 representatives of the four overseas departments in the French national assembly and senate formed an interparliamentary group to safeguard and promote the agricultural economies of these territories. In July 1992, however, the French government announced an increase in minimum income of 3.3%, and in family allowance of 20% (far less than required to establish parity with metropolitan France). In September the regional council adopted an economic development programme, known as the emergency plan, which provided for the creation of an export free zone (EFZ). Under the emergency plan, the French government would subsidize wages and some employer's contributions of companies operating within the EFZ. By 1993 levels of family allowance in the overseas departments had reached parity with those in force in metropolitan France, as envisaged. In early 1994, however, the French government indicated that it intended to give priority to the reduction of unemployment rather than the standardization of minimum wage levels, and announced a programme of economic and social development for the overseas departments, whereby approximately one-third of the unemployed population were to be involved in community projects, enterprises were to receive incentives to engage the unemployed, and a number of economic sectors that had been disadvantaged by international competition were to be exempted from certain taxes. In June the regional council drafted a five-year development plan, at a projected cost of 10,000m. French francs, of which 4,900m. francs were to be financed by the EU: these funds were principally designated to support export initiatives and to improve infrastructure and the environment; allocations were also made to the tourism sector.

In 1996 a committee, established to compare incomes and prices in Réunion with those in metropolitan France, reported that the gross disposable income per inhabitant in Réunion was only 57% of the average income per inhabitant in metropolitan France. The average net salary for state employees was, however, found to be 51% higher on the island, as a result of various benefits, some dating back to colonial times. The disparity between prices for many consumer goods was emphasized, with minimum prices in Réunion being as much as three times the French level. The island's political organizations were united in their insistence that civil servants' salaries and benefits should be reduced, thereby releasing funds that could be used to create more employment. Reactions from trade unions were mixed, and the French government, although willing to hold discussions, delayed making any decision on this politically sensitive issue. In March 1997, however, civil servants and their trade unions were angered by the French government's proposal to reduce the entrance-level salaries to the civil service (see Recent History).

Despite attempts to create more jobs on Réunion, its rate of unemployment remained the highest of all the French departments in 1997. Youth unemployment was of particular concern, with 62% of those under 25 years of age unemployed in that year. In November 1997 the French government and the authorities on Réunion signed an agreement that was designed to create nearly 3,500 jobs for young people over a period of three years. Part of Saint-Denis was designated as a 'special urban zone' in January 1997, with fiscal incentives on offer to companies establishing themselves in the area; by January 1998 some 240 companies had been attracted to the zone. In early 1995 the minimum wage level in Réunion was about 14% below that in metropolitan France. However, by 1 January 1996 the minimum wage on Réunion was equal to that in metropolitan France, having increased on average by 23% since the end of 1993.

Although the economy progressed in 1998, sustained largely by tourism, economists identified Réunion's need to expand external trade, notably with other IOC members, if the island's economy was to continue to prosper. In May 2000 the French government announced that it had agreed to equalize the minimum taxable wage in the overseas departments with that of metropolitan France, within a period of three years; the current minimum taxable wage in Réunion is 20% lower than that of metropolitan France. This measure was approved by the French senate in June.

Statistical Survey

Source (unless otherwise indicated): Institut National de la Statistique et des Etudes Economiques, Service Régional de la Réunion, 15 rue de l'Ecole, 97490 Sainte-Clotilde; tel. 29-51-57; fax 29-76-85.

AREA AND POPULATION

Area: 2,507 sq km (968 sq miles).

Population: 515,798 (males 252,997, females 262,801) at census of 9 March 1982; 597,828 (males 294,256, females 303,572) at census of 15 March 1990; 706,300 at 1 January 1999.

Density (1 January 1999): 281.7 per sq km.

Principal Towns (population at census of 15 March 1990): Saint-Denis (capital) 121,999; Saint-Paul 71,669; Saint-Pierre 58,846; Le Tampon 47,593.

Births and Deaths (provisional figures, 1998): Registered live births 13,550 (birth rate 19.3 per 1,000); Registered deaths 3,805 (death rate 5.4 per 1,000).

Economically Active Population (persons aged 15 years and over, 1990 census): Agriculture, hunting, forestry and fishing 11,141; Mining, manufacturing, electricity, gas and water 11,295; Construction 16,563; Wholesale and retail trade 17,902; Transport, storage and communications 7,250; Financing, insurance, real estate and business services 3,005; Other services (incl. activities not adequately defined) 79,097; Total employed 146,253 (males 90,526, females 55,727); Unemployed 86,108 (males 45,889, females 40,219); Total labour force 232,361 (males 136,415, females 95,946). Figures exclude persons on compulsory military service. Source: International Labour Office, *Yearbook of Labour Statistics*.

Mid-1998 (estimates in '000): Agriculture, etc. 11; Total labour force 279. Source: FAO, *Production Yearbook*.

AGRICULTURE, ETC.

Principal Crops (FAO estimates, '000 metric tons, 1998): Sugar cane 1,675 (unofficial figure); Raw sugar 222 (unofficial figure); Maize 17; Vegetables 60; Fruit 36. Source: FAO, *Production Yearbook*.

Livestock (FAO estimates, '000 head, year ending September 1998): Cattle 26; Pigs 87; Sheep 2; Goats 31; Chickens 11,000. Source: FAO, *Production Yearbook*.

Livestock Products (FAO estimates,'000 metric tons, 1998): Beef and veal 1; Pig meat 11; Poultry meat 17; Cow's milk 14; Eggs 5. Source: FAO, *Production Yearbook*.

Forestry ('000 cubic metres): Roundwood removals: 36 in 1995; 36 in 1996; 36 in 1997. Source: FAO, *Yearbook of Forest Products*.

Fishing (metric tons, live weight): Total catch 5,173 in 1996; 5,883 in 1997; 6,363 in 1998.

INDUSTRY

Production (metric tons, 1998): Oil of geranium 6.25; Oil of vetiver root 0.24; Tobacco 22.0 (1992); Vanilla 116.5 (1992); Ginger 95.0 (1992); Pimento 405.6 (1992); Rum (hl) 68,169; Electric energy (million kWh) 1,566.

FINANCE

Currency and Exchange Rates: 100 centimes = 1 French franc. *Sterling, Dollar and Euro Equivalents* (28 April 2000): £1 sterling = 11.3220 francs; US $1 = 7.2202 francs; €1 = 6.5596 francs; 1,000 French francs = £88.32 = $138.50 = €152.45. *Average Exchange Rate* (French francs per US dollar): 5.8367 in 1997; 5.8995 in 1998; 6.1570 in 1999. Since the introduction of the euro, with French participation, on 1 January 1999, a fixed exchange rate of €1 = 6.55957 francs has been in operation.

Budget (million francs, 1998): *State Budget:* Revenue 7,432.1, Expenditure 15,481.0; *Regional Budget:* Revenue 2,118, Expenditure 2,090; *Departmental Budget:* Revenue 4,624, Expenditure 4,300.

Money Supply (million francs at 31 December 1996): Currency outside banks 4,050; Demand deposits at banks 7,469; Total money 11,519.

Cost of Living (Consumer Price Index for urban areas, average of monthly figures; base: 1990 = 100): 117.7 in 1996; 119.3 in 1997; 120.8 in 1998. Source: UN, *Monthly Bulletin of Statistics*.

Expenditure on the Gross Domestic Product (million francs at current prices, 1995): Government final consumption expenditure 19,010; Private final consumption expenditure 27,209; Increase in stocks −262; Gross fixed capital formation 7,467; *Total domestic expenditure* 53,424; Exports of goods and services 3,167; *Less* Imports of goods and services 14,014; *GDP in purchasers' values* 42,577.

Gross Domestic Product by Economic Activity (million francs at current prices, 1995): Agriculture, forestry and fishing 1,392; Mining, manufacturing, electricity, gas and water 3,101; Construction 1,761; Wholesale and retail trade 6,140; Transport and communications 1,753; Finance and insurance 1,926; Real estate 2,669; Owner-occupied dwellings 2,767; Public administration 3,322; Other marketable services 5,228; Other non-market services 10,435; *Subtotal* 40,494; *Less* Imputed bank service charge 1,760; *GDP at basic prices* 38,734; Taxes on products, *less* subsidies on products 3,843; *GDP in purchasers' values* 42,577.

EXTERNAL TRADE

Principal Commodities (million francs, 1998): *Imports c.i.f.:* Agricultural products 437; Solid mineral fuels and petroleum products 824; Ceramic materials 403; Parachemical products 595; Pharmaceutical products 835; Metal manufactures 556; Industrial equipment 511; Electrical equipment 370; Electronic equipment 510; Road and rail vehicles 2,248; Meat and meat preparations 509; Milk and milk products 347; Preserves 309; Cereal preparations 446; Threads and hosiery products 350; Clothing 434; Manufactured wood products 320; Furnishings 324; Paper and cardboard 440; Printed matter 358; Plastic products 330; Total (incl. others) 15,310. *Exports f.o.b.:* Sugar 715.5; Capital equipment 212.3; Intermediate goods 43.7; Rum 30.5; Consumer goods 29.2; Total (incl. others) 1,214.9.

Principal Trading Partners (million francs, 1996): *Imports c.i.f.:* Bahrain 519.4; Belgium-Luxembourg 302.0; France (metropolitan) 9,348.2; Germany 466.0; Italy 515.6; Japan 299.0; South Africa 291.5; Total (incl. others) 14,251.5. *Exports f.o.b.:* Belgium-Luxembourg 56.8; France (metropolitan) 759.3; Japan 56.1; Madagascar 34.1; Mauritius 36.2; Mayotte 48.7; United Kingdom 26.6; Total (incl. others) 1,071.2.

TRANSPORT

Road Traffic (1 Jan. 1999): Motor vehicles in use 234,578.

Shipping: *Merchant Fleet* (total displacement at 31 December 1992): 21,000 grt (Source: UN, *Statistical Yearbook*); *Traffic* (1998): Vessels entered 885; Freight unloaded 2,597,300 metric tons; Freight loaded 467,900 metric tons; Passenger arrivals 20,147; Passenger departures 22,189.

Civil Aviation (1998): Passenger arrivals 677,487; Passenger departures 674,651; Freight unloaded 15,060 metric tons; Freight loaded 7,270 metric tons.

TOURISM

Tourist Arrivals (by country of residence, 1998): France (metropolitan) 318,600, Mauritius 39,800, Madagascar 10,200, EU countries (excl. France) 8,600; Total (incl. others) 400,000.

Tourism Receipts (million francs): 1,331 in 1996; 1,455 in 1997; 1,563 in 1998.

COMMUNICATIONS MEDIA

Radio Receivers (1997): 173,000 in use. Source: UNESCO, *Statistical Yearbook*.

Television Receivers (1997): 127,000 in use. Source: UNESCO, *Statistical Yearbook*.

Telephones (main lines at 31 Dec. 1997): 250,000.

Telefax Stations (1991): 1,906 in use. Source: UN, *Statistical Yearbook*.
Mobile Cellular Telephones (Sept. 1999): 85,000 subscribers.
Book Production (1992): 69 titles (50 books; 19 pamphlets). Source: UNESCO, *Statistical Yearbook*.
Daily Newspapers (1996): 3 (estimated average circulation 55,000 copies). Source: UNESCO, *Statistical Yearbook*.
Non-daily Newspapers (1988, estimates): 4 (average circulation 20,000 copies). Source: UNESCO, *Statistical Yearbook*.

EDUCATION

Pre-primary (1998/99): Schools 176; teachers 1,336 (1986); pupils 43,137.

Primary (1998/99): Schools 353; teachers 3,917 (1986); pupils 77,976.

Secondary (1998/99): Schools 111; teachers 6,479; pupils 95,132.

University: (1998/99): Teaching staff 283; students 8,882.

Directory

The Government
(August 2000)

Prefect: JEAN DAUBIGNY, Préfecture, Place du Barachois, 97405 Saint-Denis Cédex; tel. 40-77-77; fax 41-73-74.
President of the General Council: JEAN-LUC POUDROUX (UDF), Hôtel du Département, 2 rue de la Source, 97400 Saint-Denis; tel. 90-30-30; fax 90-39-99.
Deputies to the French National Assembly: HUGUETTE BELLO (PCR), CLAUDE HOARAU (PCR), ELIE HOARAU (PCR), MICHEL TAMAYA (PS), ANDRÉ THIEN AH KOON (RPR-UDF).
Representatives to the French Senate: EDMOND LAURET (RPR), LILIAN PAYET (MDLFT), PAUL VERGÈS (PCR).

GOVERNMENT OFFICES

Direction du Développement Économique et de l'Économie Solidaire: ave de la Victoire, 97488 Saint-Denis Cédex; tel. 90-31-90; fax 90-39-89.
Direction du Développement Local: ave de la Victoire, 97488 Saint-Denis Cédex; tel. 90-36-36; fax 90-39-94.
Direction de l'Environnement: 60 rue Fénélon, 97488 Saint-Denis Cédex; tel. 90-24-00; fax 90-39-48.
Direction des Finances: ave de la Victoire, 97488 Saint-Denis Cédex; tel. 90-39-39; fax 90-39-92.
Direction de l'Informatique: 19 route de la Digue, 97488 Saint-Denis Cédex; tel. 90-32-90; fax 90-32-99.
Direction des Infrastructures Départementales: 1 rue Charles Gounaud, 97488 Saint-Denis Cédex; tel. 41-56-52; fax 90-39-94.
Direction de la Logistique: 2 rue de la Source, 97488 Saint-Denis Cédex; tel. 90-31-38; fax 90-39-91.
Direction du Patrimoine: 6b rue Rontaunay, 97488 Saint-Denis Cédex; tel. 90-86-86; fax 90-86-90.
Direction de la Presse et de la Communication: 42 rue du Général de Gaulle, 97488 Saint-Denis Cédex; tel. 21-86-30; fax 21-39-45.
Direction de la Promotion Culturelle et Sportive: 18 rue de Paris, 97488 Saint-Denis Cédex; tel. 90-35-35; fax 20-26-03.
Direction de la Promotion de l'Enfance, de la Famille et de la Santé: 2 rue de la Source, 97488 Saint-Denis Cédex; tel. 90-33-33; fax 90-39-96.
Direction des Resources Humaines: 2 rue de la Source, 97488 Saint-Denis Cédex; tel. 90-37-37; fax 90-34-90.
Direction des Transports: 34 rue Notre Dame de la Source, 97488 Saint-Denis Cédex; tel. 20-38-08; fax 41-72-88.
Direction de la Vie Éducative: ave de la Victoire, 97488 Saint-Denis Cédex; tel. 90-31-31; fax 90-39-98.

REGIONAL COUNCIL

Hôtel de la Région Pierre Lagourgue, ave René Cassin, Moufia BP 7190, 97719 Saint-Denis Messog 09; tel. 48-70-00; fax 48-70-71; e-mail region.reunion@cr-reunion.fr.

President: PAUL VERGÈS (PCR).

Election, 15 March 1998

Party	Seats
Le Rassemblement*	19
UDF	9
RPR	8
Free-DOM	5
Réunion France Europe	4
Total	**45**

* An alliance comprising the PCR, the PS and the MDLFT (a right-wing group).

Political Organizations

Front National (FN): Saint-Denis; f. 1972; extreme right-wing; Leader ALIX MOREL.
Mouvement des Radicaux de Gauche (MRG): Saint-Denis; f. 1977; advocates full independence and an economy separate from, but assisted by, France; Pres. JEAN-MARIE FINCK.
Mouvement pour l'Egalité, la Démocratie, le Développement et la Nature: affiliated to the PCR; advocates political unity; Leader RENÉ PAYET.
Mouvement pour l'Indépendance de la Réunion (MIR): f. 1981 to succeed the fmr Mouvement pour la Libération de la Réunion; grouping of parties favouring autonomy.
*****Parti Communiste Réunionnais (PCR):** 21 bis rue d l'Est, 97400 Saint-Denis; f. 1959; Pres. PAUL VERGÈS; Sec.-Gen. ELIE HOARAU.
*****Parti Socialiste (PS)–Fédération de la Réunion:** 18 ave Stanislas Gimart, 97490 Saint-Denis; tel. 29-04-19; left-wing; Sec.-Gen. JEAN-CLAUDE FRUTEAU.
Rassemblement des Démocrates pour l'Avenir de la Réunion (RADAR): Saint-Denis; f. 1981; centrist.
Rassemblement des Socialistes et des Démocrates (RSD): Saint-Denis; Sec.-Gen. DANIEL CADET.
Rassemblement pour la République (RPR): 6 bis blvd Vauban, BP 11, 97400 Saint-Denis; tel. 20-21-18; Gaullist; Pres. EDMOND LAURET; Sec.-Gen. TONY MANGLOU.
Réunion France Europe: Saint-Denis.
Union pour la Démocratie Française (UDF): Saint-Denis; f. 1978; centrist; Pres. JEAN-PAUL VIRAPOULLÉ.
Les Verts Réunion: 13 allée Terrasses, 97400 Saint-Denis.

* In the March 1998 regional elections the PCR, the PS and the MDLFT (a right-wing group) presented a joint list of candidates, known as the Rassemblement.

Judicial System

Cour d'Appel: Palais de Justice, 166 rue Juliette Dodu, 97488 Saint-Denis; tel. 40-58-58; fax 21-95-32; Pres. JEAN CLAUDE CARRIÉ.

There are two **Tribunaux de Grande Instance**, one **Cour d'Assises,** four **Tribunaux d'Instance**, two **Tribunaux pour Enfants** and two **Conseils de Prud'hommes.**

Religion

A substantial majority of the population are adherents of the Roman Catholic Church. There is a small Muslim community.

CHRISTIANITY
The Roman Catholic Church

Réunion comprises a single diocese, directly responsible to the Holy See. At 31 December 1998 there were an estimated 590,000 adherents, equivalent to some 92.2% of the population.

Bishop of Saint-Denis de la Réunion: Mgr GILBERT AUBRY, Evêché, 36 rue de Paris, BP 55, 97461 Saint-Denis; tel. 94-85-70; fax 94-85-73.

The Press

DAILIES

Journal de l'Ile de la Réunion: 357 rue du Maréchal Leclerc, BP 166, 97463 Saint-Denis Cédex; tel. 90-46-76; fax 90-46-04; internet www.jir.fr; f. 1956; Dir BRUNO HERVIEU; circ. 35,000.

Quotidien de la Réunion: BP 303, 97712 Saint-Denis Cédex 9; tel. 92-15-15; fax 28-43-60; f. 1976; Dir MAXIMIN CHANE KI CHUNE; circ. 30,000.

PERIODICALS

Al-Islam: Centre Islamique de la Réunion, BP 437, 97459 Saint-Pierre Cédex; tel. 25-45-43; fax 35-58-23; f. 1975; 4 a year; Dir SAÏD INGAR.

Cahiers de la Réunion et de l'Océan Indien: 24 blvd des Cocotiers, 97434 Saint-Gilles-les-Bains; monthly; Man. Dir CLAUDETTE SAINT-MARC.

L'Economie de la Réunion: c/o INSEE, 15 rue de l'Ecole, BP 13 Le Chaudron, 97408 Saint-Denis; tel. 48-89-00; fax 48-89-89; 6 a year; Dir RENÉ JEAN; Editor-in-Chief COLETTE PAVAGEAU.

L'Eglise à la Réunion: 18 rue Montreuil, 97469 Saint-Denis; tel. 41-56-90; Dir P. FRANÇOIS GLÉNAC.

L'Enjeu: Saint-Denis; tel. 21-75-76; fax 41-60-62; Dir BLANDINE ETRAYEN; Editor-in-Chief JEAN-CLAUDE VALLÉE; circ. 4,000.

Le Journal de la Nature: 97489 Saint-Denis; tel. 29-45-45; fax 29-00-90; Dir J. Y. CONAN.

Le Memento Industriel et Commercial Réunionnais: 80 rue Pasteur, 97400 Saint-Denis; tel. 21-94-12; fax 41-10-85; e-mail memento@oceanes.fr; f. 1970; monthly; Dir CATHERINE LOUAPRE POTTIER; Editor GEORGES-GUILLAUME LOUAPRE POTTIER; circ. 10,000.

974 Ouest: Montgaillard, 97400 Saint-Denis; monthly; Dir DENISE ELMA.

La Réunion Agricole: Chambre d'Agriculture, 24 rue de la Source, BP 134, 97463 Saint-Denis Cédex; tel. 21-25-88; fax 21-06-17; e-mail chambagri.cda-97@wanadoo.fr; f. 1967; monthly; Dir JEAN-YVES MINATCHI; Chief Editor BÉATRICE TEVANÉE; circ. 8,000.

Télé 7 Jours Réunion: 6 rue Montyon, BP 405, 93200 Saint-Denis; weekly; Dir MICHEL MEKDOUD; circ. 25,000.

Témoignage Chrétien de la Réunion: 21 bis rue de l'Est, BP 192, 97465 Saint-Denis; weekly; Dir RENÉ PAYET; circ. 2,000.

Témoignages: 21 bis rue de l'Est, BP 192, 97465 Saint-Denis; tel. 21-13-07; f. 1944; publ. of the PCR; weekly; Dir ELIE HOARAU; circ. 6,000.

Visu: 97712 Saint-Denis Cédex 9; tel. 90-20-60; fax 90-20-61; weekly; Editor-in-Chief GUY LEBLOND; circ. 53,000.

Broadcasting and Communications

TELECOMMUNICATIONS

Cegetel: Saint-Denis; sole cellular telephone operator on Réunion; 93,000 subscribers.

BROADCASTING

Société Nationale de Radio-Télévision Française d'Outre-mer (RFO): 1 rue Jean Chatel, 97716 Saint-Denis Cédex; tel. 40-67-67; fax 21-64-84; internet www.rfo.fr; home radio and television relay services in French; operates two television channels; Chair. ANDRÉ-MICHEL BESSE; Dir ALBERT-MAX BRIAND.

Radio

Radio Free-DOM: BP 666, 97473 Saint-Denis Cédex; tel. 41-51-51; fax 21-68-64; f. 1981; privately-owned radio station; Dir Dr CAMILLE SUDRE.

In February 1998 there were a total of 44 authorized radio stations broadcasting in Réunion.

Television

Antenne Réunion: 33 chemin Vavangues, 97490 Sainte-Clotilde; tel. 48-28-28; fax 48-28-29; f. 1991; broadcasts 10 hours daily; Dir THIERRY MICHAUT.

Canal Réunion: 35 chemin Vavangues, 97490 Sainte-Clotilde; tel. 29-02-02; fax 29-17-09; subscription television channel; broadcasts a minimum of 19 hours daily; Chair. DOMINIQUE FAGOT; Dir JEAN-BERNARD MOURIER.

TV-4: 8 chemin Fontbrune, 97400 Saint-Denis; tel. 52-73-73; broadcasts 19 hours daily.

TV Sud: 10 rue Aristide Briand, 97430 Le Tampon; tel. 57-42-42; commenced broadcasting in 1993; broadcasts 4 hours daily.

Other privately-owned television services include TVB, TVE, RTV, Télé-Réunion and TV-Run.

Finance

(cap. = capital; res = reserves; dep. = deposits; m. = million; brs = branches; amounts in French francs)

BANKING
Central Bank

Institut d'Emission des Départements d'Outre-mer: 4 rue de la Compagnie, 97400 Saint-Denis Cédex; tel. 90-71-00; fax 21-41-32; Dir GUY DEBUYS.

Commercial Banks

Banque Française Commerciale Océan Indien (BFCOI): 60 rue Alexis de Villeneuve, BP 323, 97468 Saint-Denis Cédex; tel. 40-55-55; fax 20-09-07; Chair. PHILIPPE BRAULT; Dir PHILIPPE LAVIT D'HAUTEFORT; 8 brs.

Banque Nationale de Paris Intercontinentale: 67 rue Juliette Dodu, BP 113, 97463 Saint-Denis; tel. 40-30-30; fax 41-39-09; e-mail bnpipmv@guetali.fr; f. 1927; Chair. MICHEL PEBEREAU; Man. Dir JEAN TABARIES; 11 brs.

Banque de la Réunion, SA: 27 rue Jean Chatel, 97711 Saint-Denis Cédex; tel. 40-01-23; fax 40-00-61; internet www .banquedelareunion.fr; f. 1849; cap. 121.0m., res 475.3m., dep. 4,632m. (Dec. 1998); Pres. SERGE ROBERT; Gen. Man. CHRISTIAN GODEFROY; 12 brs.

Caisse Régionale de Crédit Agricole Mutuel de la Réunion: parc Jean de Cambiaire, cité des Lauriers, BP 84, 97462 Saint-Denis Cédex; tel. 40-81-81; fax 40-81-40; f. 1949; affiliate of Caisse Nationale de Crédit Agricole; Chair. CHRISTIAN DE LA GIRODAY; Dir ERIC PRADEL.

Development Bank

Banque Populaire Fédérale de Développement: 33 rue Victor MacAuliffe, 97400 Saint-Denis; tel. 21-18-11; Dir OLIVIER DEVISME; 3 brs.

INSURANCE

More than 20 major European insurance companies are represented in Saint-Denis.

Trade and Industry

DEVELOPMENT ORGANIZATIONS

Association pour le Développement Industriel de la Réunion: 8 rue Philibert, BP 327, 97466 Saint-Denis Cédex; tel. 94-43-00; fax 94-43-09; e-mail adir@guetali.fr; f. 1975; 190 mems; Pres. MAURICE CERISOLA.

Chambre d'Agriculture de la Réunion: 24 rue de la Source, BP 134, 97463 Saint-Denis Cédex; tel. 21-25-88; fax 21-06-17; e-mail chambagri.cda-97@wanadoo.fr; Pres. JEAN-YVES MINATCHY; Dir-Gen. FATMA BADAT.

Direction de l'Action Economique: Secrétariat Général pour les Affaires Economiques, ave de la Victoire, 97405 Saint-Denis; tel. 40-77-10; fax 40-77-01.

Jeune Chambre Economique de Saint-Denis de la Réunion: 25 rue de Paris, BP 1151, 97483 Saint-Denis; f. 1963; 30 mems; Chair. JEAN-CHRISTOPHE DUVAL.

Société de Développement Economique de la Réunion—SODERE: 26 rue Labourdonnais, 97469 Saint-Denis; tel. 20-01-68; fax 20-05-07; f. 1964; Chair. RAYMOND VIVET; Man. Dir ALBERT TRIMAILLE.

CHAMBERS OF COMMERCE

Chambre d'Agriculture: 24 rue de la Source, BP 134, 97463 Saint-Denis Cédex; tel. 21-25-88; fax 21-06-17.

Chambre de Commerce et d'Industrie de la Réunion: 13 rue Pasteur, 97400 Saint-Denis Cédex; tel. 94-20-00; fax 94-22-90; internet www.reunion.cci.fr; f. 1830; Pres. ROGER ROLAND.

Chambre de Métiers: 42 rue Jean Cocteau, 97490 Sainte-Clotilde; tel. 21-04-35; fax 21-68-33; internet www.cm-reunion.fr.

INDUSTRIAL AND TRADE ASSOCIATIONS

Fedération Réunionnaise du Bâtiment et des Travaux Publics: BP 108, 97462 Saint-Denis Cédex; tel. 41-70-87; fax 21-55-07; Pres. J. M. LE BOURUELLEC.

Syndicat des Exportateurs d'Huiles Essentielles, Plantes Aromatiques et Medicinales de Bourbon: Saint-Denis; tel. 20-10-23; exports oil of geranium, vetiver and vanilla; Pres. RICO PLOENIÈRES.

Syndicat des Fabricants de Sucre de la Réunion: BP 284, 97466 Saint-Denis Cédex; tel. 90-45-00; fax 41-24-13; e-mail prestsuc@groupemace.com; Chair. XAVIER THIEBLIN.

Syndicat des Producteurs de Rhum de la Réunion: BP 284, 97466 Saint-Denis; tel. 90-45-00; fax 41-24-13; e-mail prestsuc@groupemace.com; Chair. XAVIER THIEBLIN.

MAJOR COMPANIES

Coopérative d'Achats des Détaillants Réunionnais (CADRE) SA: 3 rue Simone Morin, Zone Industrielle les Tamarins, 97420 Le Port; tel. 42-93-93; fax 42-92-50; Chair. DAVID SOUI MINE.

Établissements Jules Caille: 31 rue Jean Chatel, BP 23, 97400 Saint-Denis; tel. 21-12-30; fax 21-63-77; f. 1919; agent for Peugeot motors; Chair. JACQUES CAILLE; Dir GASTON CAILLE.

Établissements Ravate: 131 rue Maréchal Leclerc, 97400 Saint-Denis; tel. 21-06-63; fax 41-26-63; trades in construction materials, wood, hardware; Chair. ISSOP RAVATE; Dir ADAM RAVATE.

Groupe Sucreries de Bourbon (SB): 2 chemin Bois Rouge, BP 2, 97438 Sainte-Marie; tel. 53-46-02; fax 53-06-33; holding co for nine subsidiaries; producing, refining and exporting sugar; also interests in shipping, fishing and food retailing; Chair. JACQUES DE CHÂTEAUVIEUX.

Renault Réunion: 11 blvd du Chaudron, 97490 Sainte-Clotilde; tel. 29-54-62; retails motor vehicles and parts; Chair. REGIS PICOT; Man. M. COSTANTINI.

Société Réunionnaise de Produits Pétroliers (SRPP): BP 2015, 97824 Le Port Cédex; tel. 42-07-11; fax 42-11-34; storage and retail of petroleum; Chair. ROBERT LAUROUA; Dir XAVIER CALLOT.

TRADE UNIONS

Confédération Générale du Travail de la Réunion (CGTR): 144 rue du Général de Gaulle, BP 1132, 97482 Saint-Denis Cédex; Sec.-Gen. GEORGES MARIE LEPINAY.

Réunion also has its own sections of the major French trade union confederations, **Confédération Française Démocratique du Travail (CFDT), Force Ouvrière (FO), Confédération Française de l'Encadrement** and **Confédération Française des Travailleurs Chrétiens (CFTC).**

Transport

ROADS

A route nationale circles the island, generally following the coast and linking the main towns. Another route nationale crosses the island from south-west to north-east linking Saint-Pierre and Saint-Benoît. In 1994 there were 370 km of routes nationales, 754 km of departmental roads and 1,630 km of other roads; 1,300 km of the roads were bituminized.

SHIPPING

In 1986 work was completed on the expansion of the Port de la Pointe des Galets, which was divided into the former port in the west and a new port in the east (the port Ouest and the port Est). In 1998 some 3.1m. tons of freight were loaded and discharged at the two ports.

Compagnie Générale Maritime (CGM): 1 rue Jesse Owens, BP 2007, 97822 Le Port Cédex; tel. 55-10-10; fax 43-23-04; e-mail gmc-cgm@stor.fr; shipping agents; Dir HENRI FELCE.

Réunion Maritime: f. 1991; consortium of 15 import cos; freight only.

Shipping Mediterranean Co: Le Port.

Société de Manutention et de Consignation Maritime (SOMACOM): BP 7, Le Port; shipping agents.

Société Réunionnaise de Services Maritimes: Zac 2000, BP 2006, 97822 Le Port Cédex; tel. 55-17-55; fax 55-17-58; freight only; Man. BERNARD LEGROS.

CIVIL AVIATION

Réunion's international airport, Roland Garros-Gillot, is situated 14 km from Saint-Denis. A programme to develop the airport was completed in 1994, and in 1997 work commenced on the extension of its terminal, at a cost of some 175m. French francs. The Pierrefonds airfield, near Saint-Pierre, commenced operating as an international airport in December 1998, serving daily flights to Mauritius, following its development at an estimated cost of nearly 50m. French francs. An extension to the runway was planned for 2000 to enable flights to Madagascar.

Air Austral: Zone Aéroportuaire, Aéroport de la Réunion Roland Garros, 97438 Sainte-Marie, BP 611, 97473 Saint-Denis; tel. 93-10-10; fax 29-28-95; internet www.air-austral.com; f. 1975; subsidiary of Air France; scheduled regional services; Dir-Gen. GÉRARD ETHEVE.

Air Outre-Mer: Saint-Denis; f. 1990; scheduled services to Paris; Chair. RENÉ MICAUD.

Tourism

Tourism is being extensively promoted. Réunion's attractions include spectacular scenery and a pleasant climate. In 1997 the island had 49 hotels with a total of 1,810 rooms. In 1998 400,000 tourists visited Réunion, and revenue from tourism totalled 1,563m. French francs.

Comité du Tourisme de la Réunion (CTR): BP 615, 97472 Saint-Denis Cédex; tel. 21-00-41; fax 21-00-21; e-mail ctr@la-reunion-tourisme.com; internet www.la-reunion-tourisme.com; Pres. MARGIE SUDRE.

Délégation Régionale au Commerce, à l'Artisanat et au Tourisme: Préfecture de la Réunion, 97400 Saint-Denis; tel. 40-77-58; fax 50-77-15; Dir RENAUD FERRAND.

Office du Tourisme: 48 rue Sainte-Marie, 97400 Saint-Denis; tel. 41-83-00; fax 21-37-76; Vice-Pres. YASMINA HATIA.

Defence

Réunion is the headquarters of French military forces in the Indian Ocean. In August 1999 there were 2,200 troops stationed on Réunion and Mayotte, the French Overseas Collectivité Territoriale in the Comoros archipelago.

Education

Education is modelled on the French system, and is compulsory for 10 years between the ages of six and 16 years. Primary education begins at six years of age and lasts for five years. Secondary education, which begins at 11 years of age, lasts for up to seven years, comprising a first cycle of four years and a second of three years. For the academic year 1998/99 there were 43,137 pupils enrolled at 176 pre-primary schools, 77,976 at 353 primary schools and 95,132 at 111 secondary schools (comprising 69 collèges and 42 lycées). There is a university, with several faculties, providing higher education in law, economics, politics, and French language and literature, and a teacher-training college. In 1995, according to UNESCO estimates, the illiteracy rate among the population over 15 years of age averaged 15.2% (males 17.5%; females 13.0%).

Bibliography

Bunge, F. M. (Ed.). *Indian Ocean: Five Island Countries.* Washington, DC, American University, 1983.

Cornu, H. *Paris et Bourbon, La politique française dans l'Océan indien.* Paris, Académie des Sciences d'Outre-mer, 1984.

Defos du Rau, J. *L'Ile de la Réunion. Étude de géographie humaine.* Institut de Géographie, Bordeaux, 1960.

Lavaux, C. *La Réunion: du battant des lames au sommet des montagnes.* Montligeon, 1975.

Leguen, M. *Histoire de l'Ile de la Réunion.* Paris, Editions L'Harmattan, 1979.

Leymarie, P. *Océan indien, nouveau coeur du monde.* Paris, Editions Karthala, 1983.

Prudhomme, C. *Histoire religieuse de la Réunion.* Paris, Editions Karthala, 1984.

Scherer, A. *La Réunion.* Paris, Presses Universitaires de France, 1980.

Service Régional de la Réunion. *Panorama de l'économie de la Réunion 1983.* Saint-Denis, Institut National de la Statistique et des Etudes Economiques, 1984.

Références bibliographiques dans les domaines démographique, économique et social sur la Réunion. Saint-Denis, Institut National de la Statistique et des Etudes Economiques, 1984.

Liste d'addresses des établissements commerciaux, industriels et artisanaux. Saint-Denis, Institut National de la Statistique et des Etudes Economiques, 1984.

Toussaint, A. *Histoire des Iles Mascareignes.* Paris, Berger-Levrault, 1972.

RWANDA

Physical and Social Geography

PIERRE GOUROU

The Rwandan Republic, like the neighbouring Republic of Burundi, is distinctive both for the small size of its territory and for the density of its population. Covering an area of 26,338 sq km (10,169 sq miles), Rwanda had an enumerated population of 7,142,755 at the census of 15 August 1991, with a density of 271 inhabitants per sq km. However, political and ethnic violence during 1994 was estimated to have resulted in the death or external displacement of 35%–40% of the total population. Prior to these events, the population had been composed of Hutu (about 85%), Tutsi (about 14%) and Twa (1%). The official languages are French, English (which is widely spoken by the Tutsi minority) and Kinyarwanda, a Bantu language with close similarities to Kirundi, the main vernacular language of Burundi.

It seems, at first sight, strange that Rwanda has not been absorbed into a wider political entity. Admittedly, the Rwandan nation has long been united by language and custom and was part of a state that won the respect of the east African slave-traders. However, other ethnic groups, such as the Kongo, Luba, Luo and Zande, which were well established in small territorial areas, have not been able to develop into national states. That Rwanda has been able to achieve this is partly the result of developments during the colonial period. While part of German East Africa, Rwanda (then known, with Burundi, as Ruanda-Urundi) was regarded as a peripheral colonial territory of little economic interest. After the First World War it was entrusted to Belgium under a mandate from the League of Nations. The territory was administered jointly with the Belgian Congo, but

was not absorbed into the larger state. The historic separateness and national traditions of both Rwanda and Burundi have prevented their amalgamation, although both countries participate, with the Democratic Republic of the Congo, in the Economic Community of the Great Lakes Countries.

Although the land supports a high population density, physical conditions are not very favourable. Rwanda's land mass is very rugged and fragmented. It is part of a Pre-Cambrian shelf from which, through erosion, the harder rocks have obtruded, leaving the softer ones submerged. Thus very ancient folds have been raised and a relief surface carved out with steep gradients covered with a soil poor in quality because of its fineness and fragility. Rwanda's physiognomy therefore consists of a series of sharply defined hills, with steep slopes and flat ridges, which are intersected by deep valleys, the bottoms of which are often formed by marshy plains. The north is dominated by the lofty and powerful chain of volcanoes, the Virunga, whose highest peak is Karisimbi (4,519 m) and whose lava, having scarcely cooled down, has not yet produced cultivable soil.

The climate is tropical, although tempered by altitude, with a daily temperature range of as much as 14°C. Kigali, the capital (117,749 inhabitants in 1978), has an average temperature of 19°C and 1,000 mm of rain. Altitude is a factor which modifies the temperature (and prevents sleeping sickness above about 900 m), but such a factor is of debatable value for agriculture. Average annual rainfall (785 mm) is only barely sufficient for agricultural purposes, but two wet and two relatively dry seasons are experienced, making two harvests possible.

Recent History

THOMAS OFCANSKY

HUTU ASCENDANCY

Rwanda, in common with its southern neighbour Burundi, was not an artificial creation of colonial rule. When they were absorbed by German East Africa in 1899, they had been established kingdoms for several centuries. In 1916, during the First World War, the area was occupied by Belgian forces. From 1920 Rwanda formed part of Ruanda-Urundi, administered by Belgium under a League of Nations mandate and later as a UN Trust Territory. In 1961 it was decided by referendum to replace Rwanda's monarchy with a republic, to which full independence was granted on 1 July 1962. Political life in the new republic was dominated by its first president, Grégoire Kayibanda, and the governing party, the Mouvement démocratique républicain (MDR), also known as the Parti de l'émancipation du peuple Hutu (Parmehutu). Tensions between the majority Hutu (comprising about 85% of the population) and their former overlords, the Tutsi (14%), which had sporadically erupted into serious violence during 1963–65, recurred in late 1972 and early 1973. In July the minister of defence and head of the national guard, Maj.-Gen. Juvénal Habyarimana, deposed Kayibanda, proclaimed a second republic and established a military government under his leadership. In 1975 a new ruling party, the Mouvement révolutionnaire national pour le développement (MRND), was formed. A referendum in December 1978 approved a new constitution, aimed at returning the country to normal

government in accordance with an undertaking by Habyarimana in 1973 to end the military regime within five years. An unsuccessful coup attempt took place in April 1980, and elections to the legislature, the Conseil national du développement (CND), were held in December 1981 and in December 1983; in the same month Habyarimana was re-elected president.

From 1982 cross-border refugee problems began to affect Rwanda's relations with Uganda. In October Rwanda closed its border with Uganda after an influx of 45,000 refugees, most of whom were Rwandan exiles fleeing Ugandan persecution. A further 32,000 refugees collected in camps on the Ugandan side of the border. In March 1983 Rwanda agreed to resettle more than 30,000 refugees, but Ugandan persecution of ethnic Rwandans continued, and in December thousands crossed into Tanzania. In November 1985 it was reported that 30,000 ethnic Rwandan refugees had been repatriated to Uganda. In 1986 the UN High Commissioner for Refugees (UNHCR) reported that there were about 110,000 registered Rwandan refugees living in Uganda, while an even greater number of refugees were believed to have settled in Uganda without registering with UNHCR. In July the central committee of the MRND issued a declaration that Rwanda would not allow the return of large numbers of refugees, since the country's economy was incapable of sustaining such an influx. In the same year President Museveni of Uganda announced that Rwandans who had been resident in Uganda for more than 10 years would automatically be entitled to Ugandan citizenship. In January 1987 a Ugandan government minister visited Rwanda for discussions concerning the problem of border security, and in February 1988 Habyarimana visited Uganda for talks with President Museveni. A subsequent joint communiqué confirmed that relations between the two countries had improved. A resurgence of ethnic tensions in Burundi led to the flight, in August 1988, of an estimated 80,000 refugees, mainly Hutu, into Rwanda. With assistance from the international community, the Rwandan authorities were able to cater for their needs. By June 1989 all but approximately 1,000 of the refugees had been repatriated to Burundi.

At a presidential election held in December 1988, Habyarimana, as sole candidate, secured 99.98% of the votes cast. Elections for the CND were held in the same month, and the government was reshuffled in January 1989. During 1989 economic conditions deteriorated sharply, as the combined effects of soil degradation, population pressure and crop disease affected harvests. In addition, a sharp fall in world coffee prices, combined with a low output of poor-quality beans, led to serious balance-of-payments and budgetary problems. The introduction of an economic austerity programme in December added to public discontent. In early July 1990 Habyarimana conceded that political reform was needed and announced that a national commission would be appointed. The Commission nationale de synthèse (CNS) was duly established in September with a mandate to make recommendations for political renewal. However, these measures did little to alleviate the acute sense of political crisis.

REBEL INVASION AND POLITICAL UPHEAVAL

On 1 October 1990 an estimated force of 10,000 guerrillas, representing the exiled, Tutsi-dominated Front patriotique rwandais (FPR, or Inkotanyi), crossed the border from Uganda into north-eastern Rwanda, where they swiftly occupied several towns. Numerically, the troops were dominated by Tutsi refugees, but also included significant numbers of disaffected elements of Uganda's ruling National Resistance Army (NRA, now the Uganda People's Defence Force—UPDF). The invasion force was reported to have been led by Maj.-Gen. Fred Rwigyema, a former Ugandan deputy minister of defence. In response to a request for assistance by Habyarimana, Belgian and French paratroopers were dispatched to Kigali to protect foreign nationals and to secure evacuation routes, but in the event did not engage in combat. However, a contingent of troops sent by Zaire (now the Democratic Republic of the Congo, DRC) assisted the small Rwandan army in turning back the FPR some 70 km from Kigali. During the first week of hostilities an estimated 8,000 people throughout Rwanda were arrested and imprisoned, of whom the vast majority were Tutsi. However, in only a few cases was there any evidence of complicity with the invaders and almost all were released in April 1991, while those convicted were subsequently released under an amnesty introduced in November.

Internationally, the FPR successfully presented itself as a democratic and multi-ethnic movement seeking to depose a corrupt and incompetent regime, with the result that the Belgian government encountered increasing pressure to terminate military aid to Habyarimana. Visits were paid to the region by the Belgian prime minister and other senior ministers with the aim of securing a cease-fire, to be followed by a regional conference on the Rwandan refugee problem. In October 1990 a summit meeting at Mwanza, Tanzania, was attended by the presidents of Rwanda, Uganda and Tanzania, who agreed in principle to the holding of a regional conference. Although numerous other bilateral contacts took place, there was no direct dialogue between the Rwandan government and the FPR. Despite the obvious frailty of the agreements, Belgium decided to extricate itself from the crisis and by 1 November had withdrawn its troops from Rwanda. Their departure coincided with a statement by the Rwandan government that victory had been achieved and that the invaders had fled to Uganda. The FPR, however, now began to attack border areas in the north and north-west from bases within Uganda, raising accusations, denied by Uganda, that the country was actively aiding the FPR. The conflict continued throughout 1991 and into 1992, as the FPR made frequent guerrilla forays into Rwanda. Thousands of casualties were reported on both sides while many civilians

resident in the border region were killed and as many as 100,000 were displaced. Increasing racial tension, exacerbated by the war, resulted in a series of unprovoked attacks upon Tutsis, and prompted accusations of government involvement, particularly in the Bugesera region. In late July 1992 it was reported that a cease-fire had been negotiated, providing for the establishment of a 'neutral area'. The cease-fire arrangements were to be overseen by a 50-member African military monitoring team.

Regional refugee problems came once again to the fore in early 1992, when the presidents of Rwanda, Burundi and Zaire met in an attempt to resolve border difficulties arising from the flight of Hutu refugees from Burundi into Rwanda and Zaire. The three presidents agreed to intensify border controls and to work together to facilitate the voluntary return of refugees to their country of origin. Further bilateral talks between Rwanda and Burundi sought to consolidate this agreement.

The political reform process, initiated before the conflict, was accelerated by the FPR invasion. The CNS published its report and a draft constitution in March 1991, following widespread public discussion of proposals put forward by the commission in December 1990. In June 1991 the new constitution, providing for the legalization of political parties, entered into force. Full freedom of the press was declared, leading to the establishment of a number of magazines and newspapers critical of government policy. In April 1992, following a series of unsuccessful attempts to negotiate a transitional government, the composition of a broadly-based coalition government, incorporating four opposition parties (the revived MDR, the Parti social-démocrate–PSD, the Parti libéral–PL and the Parti démocratique chrétien–PDC), together with the Mouvement républicain national pour la démocratie et le développement–MRNDD (the new party name adopted by the MRND in April 1991), was announced. The cabinet was to be headed by Dismas Nsengiyaremye of the MDR as prime minister, a post established by the new constitution. It was also announced that multi-party elections for municipalities, the legislature and for the presidency would take place before April 1993. In late April 1992, to comply with the new constitutional prohibition of participation in the political process by the armed forces, Habyarimana relinquished his military title and functions.

Renewed dialogue was initiated between the new transitional government and FPR representatives in May 1992, and formal discussions were conducted in Paris during June. Further negotiations, in Arusha, Tanzania, in July, resulted in an agreement on the implementation of a new cease-fire, to take effect from the end of July, and the creation of an OAU-sponsored military observer group (GOM), to comprise representatives from both sides, together with officers drawn from the armed forces of Nigeria, Senegal, Zimbabwe and Mali. However, subsequent negotiations in Tanzania, during August, September and October, failed to resolve outstanding problems concerning the creation of a 'neutral zone' between the Rwandan armed forces and the FPR (to be enforced by the GOM), the incorporation of the FPR in a future combined Rwandan national force, the repatriation of refugees, and the demands of the FPR for full participation in a transitional government and legislature.

A resurgence in violence followed the breakdown of negotiations in early February 1993, resulting in the deaths of hundreds on both sides. An estimated 1m. civilians fled southwards and to neighbouring Uganda and Tanzania, in order to escape the fighting, as the FPR advanced as far as Ruhengeri and seemed, for a time, poised to occupy Kigali. The actions of the FPR were denounced by Belgium, France and the USA. French reinforcements were dispatched to join a small French military contingent, stationed in Kigali since October 1990 in order to protect French nationals. Meanwhile, the commander of the GOM declared that the group had inadequate manpower and resources to contain the FPR front line, and requested the deployment of an additional 400 troops from the OAU.

In late February 1993 the government accepted FPR terms for a cease-fire in return for an end to attacks against FPR positions and on Tutsi communities, and the withdrawal of foreign troops. Although fighting continued with varying intensity, new peace negotiations were convened in March, in Arusha. In late March the French government began to withdraw its troops.

Negotiations conducted during April 1993 failed to produce a solution to the crucial issue of the structure of future unitary Rwandan armed forces. In the same month, the five participating parties in the ruling coalition agreed to a three-month extension of the government's mandate, in order to facilitate the achievement of a peace accord. Significant progress was made during fresh talks between the government and the FPR in the northern town of Kinihira, during May, when a timetable for the demobilization of 19,000-strong security forces was agreed. Later in the month further consensus was reached on the creation of a 'neutral zone'. In June agreement was concluded on a protocol for the repatriation of all Rwandan refugees resident in Uganda, Tanzania and Zaire, including recommendations that compensation should be made available to those forced into exile more than 12 years ago. In late June the UN Security Council approved the creation of UN Observer Mission Uganda-Rwanda (UNOMUR), to be deployed on the Ugandan side of the border for an initial period of six months, in order to ensure that no military supply lines would be maintained for the FPR.

In July 1993, with improved prospects for a prompt resolution of the conflict, Habyarimana met representatives of the five political parties represented in the government and sought a further extension to the mandate of the coalition government. However, the prime minister's insistence that the FPR should be represented in any newly-mandated government exacerbated existing divisions within the MDR, prompting Habyarimana to conclude the agreement with a conciliatory group of MDR dissidents, including the education minister, Agathe Uwilingiyimana, who was elected to the premiership. The council of ministers was reshuffled to replace the disaffected MDR members.

On 4 August 1993 a peace accord was formally signed by Habyarimana and Col Alex Kanyarengwe of the FPR, in Arusha. A new transitional government, to be headed by a mutually-approved prime minister (later named as the MDR moderate faction leader, Faustin Twagiramungu), would be installed by 10 September. Multi-party general elections were to take place after a 22-month period, during which the FPR would join the political mainstream and participate in a transitional government and national assembly. In mid-August the curfew in Kigali was lifted, and military road-blocks were removed from all but three northern prefectures. By the end of the month, however, the prime minister was forced to make a national appeal for calm, following reports of renewed outbreaks of violence in Kigali and Butare. The failure to establish a transitional government and legislature by 10 September was attributed by the government and the FPR to the increasingly fragile security situation, and both sides urged the prompt dispatch of a neutral UN force to facilitate the implementation of the accord. Meanwhile, relations between the government and the FPR deteriorated, following the rebels' assertion that the government had infringed the terms of the accord by attempting to dismantle and reorganize those government departments assigned to the FPR under the terms of the agreement.

UN INTERVENTION

On 5 October 1993 the UN Security Council adopted Resolution 872, endorsing the recommendation of the UN secretary-general for the creation of UN Assistance Mission to Rwanda (UNAMIR), to be deployed in Rwanda for an initial period of six months, with a mandate to monitor observance of the cease-fire, to contribute to the security of the capital and to facilitate the repatriation of refugees. UNAMIR, which was to incorporate UNOMUR and GOM, was formally inaugurated on 1 November, and was to comprise some 2,500 personnel when fully operational. In early December 1993, in compliance with the stipulations of the Arusha accord, the French government announced the withdrawal of its military contingent in Kigali, and in mid-December the UN declared that it was satisfied that conditions had been sufficiently fulfilled to allow for the introduction of the transitional institutions by the end of the month.

In late December 1993 a 600-strong FPR battalion was escorted to the capital by UNAMIR officials (as detailed in the Arusha accord), in order to ensure the safety of FPR representatives selected to participate in the transitional government and legislature. However, dissension within a number of political parties had obstructed the satisfactory nomination of represen-

tatives to the transitional institutions, forcing a further postponement of their inauguration. On 5 January 1994 Juvénal Habyarimana was invested as president of a transitional government, for a 22-month period, under the terms of the Arusha accord. (Habyarimana's previous term of office, in accordance with the constitution, had expired on 19 December 1993.) The inauguration of the transitional government and legislature, scheduled for the same day, was again postponed when several major participants failed to attend. While government spokesmen identified the need to resolve internal differences within the MDR and the PL as the crucial expedient for the implementation of the new government and legislature, a joint statement, issued by the PSD, the PDC and factions of the MDR and the PL, accused the president of having abused the terms of the Arusha accord by interfering in the selection of prospective ministers and deputies. This charge was reiterated by the FPR in late February, when it rejected a list of proposed future gubernatorial and legislative representatives (tentatively agreed following several days of discussions between the president, the prime minister and the five participating parties of the current administration) as having been compiled as the result of a campaign of intimidation and manipulation by the president in order to secure the participation of his own supporters, and thereby prolong his political influence. The FPR insisted that a definitive list of each party's representatives in the future transitional institutions had been approved by the constitutional court in January. In March the prime minister-designate, Faustin Twagiramungu, declared that he had fulfilled his consultative role as set out in the Arusha accord, and announced the composition of a transitional government, in an attempt to accelerate the installation of the transitional bodies. However, political opposition to the proposed council of ministers persisted, and Habyarimana insisted that the list of proposed legislative deputies, newly presented by Agathe Uwilingiyimana, should be modified to include representatives of additional political parties, including the reactionary Coalition pour la défense de la république (CDR, whose participation was strongly opposed by the FPR, owing to its alleged failure to accept the code of ethics for the behaviour of political parties which proscribed policies advocating tribal discrimination), prompting a further postponement of the formation of a transitional administration.

Meanwhile political frustration had erupted into violence in late February 1994, with the murder of the minister of public works and energy, Félicien Gatabazi of the PSD, who had actively supported the Arusha agreement and the transitional administration. Hours later, the CDR leader, Martin Bucyana, was killed, in apparent retaliation, by an angry mob of PSD supporters, provoking a series of violent confrontations resulting in some 30–40 deaths.

In April 1994 the UN Security Council (which in February had warned that the UN presence in Rwanda might be withdrawn in the absence of swift progress in the implementation of the Arusha accord) agreed to extend UNAMIR's mandate for four months, pending a review of progress made in implementing the accord, to be conducted after six weeks.

COLLAPSE OF CIVIL ORDER

On 6 April 1994 the presidential aircraft, returning from a regional summit meeting in Dar es Salaam, Tanzania, was fired upon, above Kigali airport, and exploded on landing, killing all 10 passengers, including Habyarimana. The president of Burundi, Cyprien Ntaryamira, two Burundian cabinet ministers, the chief of staff of the Rwandan armed forces, and a senior diplomat were among the other victims. In Kigali the presidential guard immediately initiated a brutal campaign of retributive violence against political opponents of the late president, although it remained unclear who had been responsible for the attack on the aircraft, and UNAMIR officials attempting to investigate the site of the crash were obstructed by the presidential guard. As politicians and civilians fled the capital, the brutality of the political assassinations was compounded by attacks on the clergy, UNAMIR personnel and members of the Tutsi tribe. Hutu civilians were forced, under pain of death, to murder their Tutsi neighbours, and the mobilization of the Interahamwe, or unofficial militias (allegedly affiliated to the MRNDD and the CDR), apparently committed to the massacre of government opponents and Tutsi civilians, was encouraged by the presidential guard (with support from some factions of the armed forces) and by inflammatory broadcasts from Radio-Télévision Libre des Mille Collines in Kigali. The prime minister, Agathe Uwilingiyimana, the president of the constitutional court, the ministers of labour and social affairs and of information, and the chairman of the PSD were among the prominent politicians murdered, or declared missing and presumed dead, within hours of the death of Habyarimana.

On 8 April 1994 the speaker of the CND, Dr Théodore Sindikubwabo, announced that he had assumed the office of interim president of the republic, in accordance with the provisions of the 1991 constitution. The five remaining participating political parties and factions of the government selected a new prime minister, Jean Kambanda, and a new council of ministers (drawn largely from the MRNDD) from among their ranks. The legality of the new administration was immediately challenged by the FPR, which claimed that the constitutional right of succession to the presidency of the speaker of the CND had been superseded by Habyarimana's inauguration, in January, as president under the terms of the Arusha agreement. (However, Félicien Ngango, who had been nominated to lead the transitional national assembly, and therefore became next in line to the presidency, had been murdered by the presidential guard.) The legitimacy of the new government (which had fled to the town of Gitarama to escape escalating violence in the capital) was subsequently rejected by factions of the PL and MDR (led by Faustin Twagiramungu), and by the PDC and the PSD (which in May announced that they had allied themselves as the Democratic Forces for Change).

FPR Offensives and the Refugee Crisis

In mid-April 1994 the FPR resumed military operations from its northern stronghold, with the stated intention of relieving its beleaguered battalion in Kigali, restoring order to the capital and halting the massacre of civilians. Grenade attacks and mortar fire intensified in the capital, prompting the UN to mediate a fragile 60-hour cease-fire, during which small evacuation forces from several countries escorted foreign nationals out of Rwanda. Belgium's UNAMIR contingent of more than 400 troops was also withdrawn, having encountered increasing hostility as a result of persistent rumours of Belgian complicity in the attack on Habyarimana's aircraft, and of providing logistical support to the FPR, which were emphatically denied by the Belgian government.

In late April 1994 the government embarked upon a diplomatic offensive throughout Europe and Africa, seeking to enhance the credibility of the government through international recognition of its legitimacy. However, these efforts achieved only limited success (notably in France, Egypt and Togo), and the FPR's continued refusal to enter into dialogue with the 'illegal' administration proved a major obstacle to attempts, undertaken by the UN and the presidents of Tanzania and Zaire, to sponsor a new cease-fire agreement in late April and early May.

As the violent political crusade unleashed by the presidential guard and the Interahamwe (described by Amnesty International as a well-trained militia numbering some 30,000) gathered momentum, the militia's identification of all members of the Tutsi tribe as political opponents of the state promoted tribal polarization, resulting in an effective pogrom. Reports of mass Tutsi graves and unprovoked attacks on fleeing Tutsi refugees, and on those seeking refuge in schools, hospitals and churches, provoked unqualified international condemnation and outrage, and promises of financial and logistical aid for an estimated 2m. displaced Rwandans (some 250,000 had fled across the border to Tanzania in a 24-hour period in late April 1994) who were threatened by famine and disease in makeshift camps. By late May attempts to assess the full scale of the humanitarian catastrophe in Rwanda were complicated by unverified reports that the FPR (which claimed to control more than one-half of the country) was carrying out retaliatory atrocities against Hutu civilians. However, unofficial estimates indicated that between 200,000–500,000 Rwandans had been killed since early April.

On 21 April 1994, in the context of intensifying violence in Kigali, and the refusal of the Rwandan armed forces to agree

to the neutral policing of the capital's airport (subsequently secured by the FPR), the UN Security Council resolved to reduce significantly its representation in Rwanda to 270 personnel, a move which attracted criticism from the government, the FPR, international relief organizations and the international community in general. However, on 16 May, following intense international pressure and the disclosure of the vast scale of the humanitarian crisis in the region, the UN Security Council approved Resolution 917, providing for the eventual deployment of some 5,500 UN troops with a revised mandate, including the policing of Kigali's airport and the protection of refugees in designated 'safe areas'. In late May the UN secretary-general criticized the failure of the UN member nations to respond to his invitation to participate in the enlarged force (only Ghana, Ethiopia and Senegal had agreed to provide small contingents). Further UN-sponsored attempts to negotiate a cease-fire failed in late May and early June, and the FPR made significant territorial gains in southern Rwanda, forcing the government to flee Gitarama and seek refuge in the western town of Kibuye.

In early June 1994 the UN Security Council adopted Resolution 925, whereby the mandate of the revised UN mission in Rwanda (UNAMIR II) was extended until December 1994. However, the UN secretary-general continued to encounter considerable difficulty in securing equipment and armaments requested by those African countries which had agreed to participate. By mid-June the emergence of confirmed reports of retributive murders committed by FPR members (including the massacres, in two separate incidents in early June, of 22 clergymen, among them the Roman Catholic archbishop of Kigali) and the collapse of a fragile truce (negotiated at a summit meeting of the Organization of African Unity, OAU, in Tunis, Tunisia) prompted the French government to announce its willingness to lead an armed police action, endorsed by the UN, in Rwanda. Although the French government insisted that the French military presence (expected to total 2,000 troops) would maintain strict political neutrality, and operate, from the border regions, in a purely humanitarian capacity pending the arrival of a multinational UN force, the FPR was vehemently opposed to its deployment, citing the French administration's maintenance of high-level contacts with representatives of the self-proclaimed Rwandan government as an indication of political bias. While the UN secretary-general welcomed the French initiative, and tacit endorsement of the project was contained in Resolution 929, approved by the Security Council in late June, the OAU expressed serious reservations regarding the appropriateness of the action. On 23 June a first contingent of 150 French marine commandos launched 'Operation Turquoise', entering the western town of Cyangugu, in preparation for a large-scale operation to protect refugees in the area. By mid-July the French had successfully relieved several beleaguered Tutsi communities, and had established a temporary 'safe haven' for the displaced population in the south-west, through which a massive exodus of Hutu refugees began to flow, encouraged by reports (disseminated by supporters of the defeated interim government) that the advancing FPR forces were seeking violent retribution against the Hutu. An estimated 1m. Rwandans sought refuge in the border town of Goma, in Zaire (now the Democratic Republic of the Congo, DRC), while a similar number attempted to cross the border elsewhere in the south-west. The FPR had swiftly secured all major cities and strategic territorial positions, but had halted its advance several kilometres from the boundaries of the French-controlled neutral zone, requesting the apprehension and return for trial of those responsible for the recent atrocities. (At the end of June the first report of the UN's special rapporteur on human rights in Rwanda—appointed in May—confirmed that as many as 500,000 Rwandans had been killed since April, and urged the establishment of an international tribunal to investigate allegations of genocide; in early July the UN announced the creation of a commission of enquiry for this purpose.)

The FPR Takes Power

On 19 July 1994 Pasteur Bizimungu, a Hutu, was inaugurated as president for a five-year term. On the same day the FPR announced the composition of a new government of national unity, to be headed by Faustin Twagiramungu as prime minister. The majority of cabinet posts were assigned to FPR members (including the FPR military chief Maj.-Gen. Paul Kagame, who became minister of national defence and also assumed the newly-created post of vice-president), while the remainder were divided among the MDR, the PL, the PSD and the PDC. The new administration urged all refugees to return to Rwanda and issued assurances that civilian Hutus could return safely to their homes. The prime minister identified the immediate aims of the administration as the restoration of peace and democracy, the reactivation of the economy and the repatriation of refugees. Identity cards bearing details of ethnic origin were to be abolished forthwith. The new government declared its intention to honour the terms of the Arusha accord within the context of an extended period of transition. However, the MRNDD and the CDR were to be excluded from participation in government.

The FPR victory and the new administration were promptly recognized by the French government, which urged the new Rwandan government to assume responsibility for relief operations. In return, Twagiramungu was reported to have expressed his appreciation for the humanitarian and stabilizing nature of the French operation. The French government announced its intention to begin a reduction in personnel by the end of July 1994, with a view to complete withdrawal by the end of August. In mid-July France began to equip a force of 500 troops drawn from Senegal, the Republic of the Congo, Chad, Niger and Guinea-Bissau, to assist the French contingent and facilitate the eventual transfer of responsibility to a UN force. The claims of the former government were seriously undermined by the recognition by the European Union (EU) of the new Rwandan government of national unity in mid-September 1994.

Meanwhile, conditions in refugee camps in Zaire had continued to deteriorate, as hunger and cholera became more widespread. By the end of July 1994, despite an intensification of international relief efforts in the region, at least 2,000 refugees were dying each day, adding to a refugee camp death toll already in excess of 20,000. Non-government relief agencies were highly critical of the inadequate and overdue nature of the international response to the crisis. In late July Bizimungu met the presidents of Zaire and Tanzania, and concluded agreements on the disarmament and gradual repatriation of refugees.

Amid persistent rumours that the Rwandan armed forces were attempting to regroup and rearm in Zaire in preparation for a counter-offensive strike against the FPR, on 20 August 1994 the UN began to deploy some 2,500 UNAMIR II forces, largely drawn from Ghana and Ethiopia, in the security zone (which was redesignated 'zone four'). On the following day French troops began to withdraw from the area (the final contingent left on 20 September), prompting hundreds of thousands of Hutu refugees sheltering within the zone to move to Zairean border areas. An estimated 500,000 refugees remained at camps in the former security zone at the end of August, as the first Rwandan government officials were assigned to customs and immigration and army recruitment duties in the region.

In early August 1994 the prime minister, Faustin Twagiramungu, had declared the country technically bankrupt, accusing the former government of having fled to Zaire with Rwanda's exchange reserves. (New banknotes were subsequently printed in order to invalidate the former currency.) Twagiramungu stressed that economic recovery could only be achieved following the return to their farms and workplaces of the country's displaced population. The government suffered a further financial setback in October, when the minister of foreign affairs and co-operation, Jean-Marie Ndagijimana, was reported to have absconded, while abroad, with government funds.

In November 1994 a multi-party protocol of understanding was concluded, providing for a number of amendments to the terms of the August 1993 Arusha accord relating to the establishment of a transitional legislature. The most notable of the new provisions was the exclusion from the legislative process of members of those parties implicated in alleged acts of genocide during 1994. A 70-member national transitional assembly, whose membership included five representatives of the armed forces and one member of the national police force, was installed on 12 December. On 5 May 1995 the new legislature announced its adoption of a new constitution based on selected articles of the 1991 constitution, the terms of the August 1993 Arusha

accord, the FPR's victory declaration of July 1994 and the November multi-party protocol of understanding.

In July 1999 Rwanda announced the end of the five-year transitional government and its replacement by a four-year national unity government. The new transitional period was to allow the government to complete the national reconciliation process, restore internal security, improve the economy and social services, and establish a democratic system. Critics rejected the unilateral extension of political power and claimed that the government's action revealed its undemocratic and dictatorial nature. In August 1999 the US-based International Strategic Studies Association (ISSA) released a statement which indicated that there was evidence that Rwanda was moving into a period of growing chaos which was likely to be followed by another genocide and total civil war. The ISSA justified its prediction by pointing to a report by a former FPR official and journalist (editor of the news magazine, *Le Tribun du Peuple*), Jean-Pierre Mugabe, who currently lives in exile in the USA, published in the April 1999 issue of *Defense and Foreign Affairs Strategic Policy*, which outlined massive corruption and diversion of aid funds by Kagame and other senior FPR officials. Mugabe also said that political and economic power was concentrated in the hands of the APR *Akazu* (clan). In June a radio debate on the Mugabe article developed into an anti-Kagame diatribe. A few weeks later students at the University of Butare established a movement which demanded the restoration of the monarchy. Critics also claimed that Kagame was adept at creating an appearance of democracy to legitimize his dictatorship.

On 20 August 1999 the legislature, the transitional national assembly, endorsed a cabinet decision to create a national security force, which was to unite the national gendarmerie, communal police, and judicial police. According to the legislature, the existence of three separate units was expensive and inefficient.

The increasingly harsh and dictatorial policies of the Kagame regime has prompted an increasing number of prominent figures to flee Rwanda. A notable case involved the popular speaker of the transitional national assembly, Kabuye Sebarenzi, who pressed for good government and official accountability. After moving from the FPR to the Liberal Party (LP) and drawing attention to government ministers accused of corruption, Sebarenzi's fortunes gradually waned. In December 1999 the LP president, Pio Mugabo, postponed the vote for a new president, reportedly on orders from Kagame. Sebarenzi had been expected to win the election, which would have improved his chances of winning the election for the national presidency. In early January 2000 the transitional national assembly forced Sebarenzi's resignation on fabricated charges of official misconduct, organizing genocide survivors against the government, and supporting the 'army of the king'. Also in January Sebarenzi, who feared that the government would assassinate him, fled to Uganda, then to Europe, and finally to the USA. On 23 March President Pasteur Bizimungu resigned and subsequently relocated to the USA. Kagame served as provisional president until 17 April, when members of the legislature and the government elected, by 81 votes to five, Kagame as the first Tutsi president since Rwanda gained independence from Belgium in 1962. Kagame, who was to serve for the remainder of the transition period which expired in 2003, promised to facilitate political decentralization, expedite the trials of some 125,000 genocide suspects, and conduct elections at the commune level.

Corruption affects all levels of government. In October 1999 a legislative commission of inquiry convicted several government ministers of corruption. Charles Ntakirutinka, (minister of communications), Anatase Gasana (minister in the president's office), and Marc Rugenera (minister of commerce, industry, and tourism) had participated in a vehicle-procurement fraud in 1997. A further parliamentary commission of inquiry discovered that, while minister of education in 1995, the prime minister, Pierre-Célestin Rwigyema, had diverted funds from a World Bank education programme almost exclusively to his home town of Gitarama. Some of these officials subsequently resigned. However, there has been no prosecution or resignation of FPR members accused of corruption.

Refugee Repatriation Problems

In late 1994 Hutu refugees within Rwanda and in neighbouring countries were continuing to resist the exhortations of the UN and the new Rwandan administration to return to their homes, despite the deteriorating security situation in many camps which had forced the withdrawal of a number of relief agencies. Hutu militia were reported to have assumed control of several camps, notably Katale in Zaire and Benaco in Tanzania, where it was reported that a state of near lawlessness existed. Reports also emerged that Hutu civilians intending to return to their homes were subjected to violent intimidation by the militia. It was further alleged that male Hutu refugees were undergoing enforced military training in preparation for a renewed armed conflict. In early November the UN secretary-general appealed to the international community for contributions to a 12,000-strong force to police the refugee camps. By late January 1995, however, the UN had abandoned attempts to raise the force, having failed to secure a commitment from member countries for the provision of equipment or personnel for such a mission. A compromise agreement was subsequently concluded with Zairean troops for the supervision of camps in Zaire. At the end of November 1994 the UNAMIR II mandate was extended for a further six months, and in June 1995, at the request of the Rwandan government, the strength of the force was reduced from 5,586 to 2,330 personnel (to be further reduced by September), and the six-month mandate was again renewed.

The reluctance of many refugees to return to their homes was also attributed to persistent allegations that the Tutsi-dominated FPR armed forces (the Armée patriotique rwandaise, APR) were conducting a systematic campaign of reprisals against returning Hutu civilians. In an address to the UN General Assembly in early October 1994, President Bizimungu denied these allegations (presented by investigating officers of UNHCR) and insisted that the government should not be held responsible for what a UN inquiry, conducted earlier in the month, had concluded were frequent but individual acts of retaliation. In late August Bizimungu had announced the execution of two FPR members, following their court martial for involvement in violent acts of reprisal. It was reported that some 50–70 FPR members were awaiting trial for similar offences. In February 1995 the UN Security Council adopted Resolution 977, whereby Arusha was designated the venue for the International Criminal Tribunal for Rwanda (ICTR). The six-member tribunal was inaugurated in late June for a four-year term. It was reported that the tribunal intended to investigate allegations made against some 400 individuals (many of them resident outside of Rwanda) of direct involvement in the planning and execution of a series of crimes against humanity perpetrated in Rwanda during 1994. At a national level, preliminary hearings against an estimated 35,000 Rwandan nationals, imprisoned in Kigali on similar charges, began in early 1995, but were immediately suspended owing to lack of funds. In mid-1995 reports emerged of severely overcrowded conditions in Rwandan prisons, where diseases such as malaria, pneumonia and dysentery were resulting in as many as 300 deaths each week. Meanwhile, lack of finance and personnel had resulted in the virtual collapse of Rwanda's judicial system, and it was estimated that the majority of suspects had been imprisoned without formal charge. The prosecutor's office in Kigali also estimated that as many as 20% of prisoners could be innocent individuals denounced by others who sought to acquire their land and property. The supreme court was established in October.

The ICTR began formal proceedings in late November 1995. The tribunal's first indictment, against eight unnamed individuals implicated in massacres committed on four sites in Kibuye between April and June 1994, was published in December. Exhumation of bodies at the sites was begun in January 1996 in order to assist the prosecutions. In the same month the ICTR cited three further suspects (two former mayors and a former cabinet minister) accused of involvement in massacres in Butare. The Belgian government, which had detained the suspects in mid-1995, agreed to co-operate fully in their extradition to face charges. However, members of the Rwandan government have expressed frustration with the slow prosecution of individuals. Consequently, in February 1996, the prime minister announced the creation of special courts within the country's existing judicial system. Under these arrangements, Rwanda's chief supreme court prosecutor was to oversee investigations in each of the country's 10 districts, and establish three-member judicial panels in each district to consider cases. The latter were to be drawn from some 250 lay magistrates who were to receive a four-month legal training course. Additionally, 320 judicial police inspectors, all of whom have received a three-month training course, will compile dossiers on those detained on suspicion of having committed genocide. Newly established assessment commissions were to review possible detentions on the basis of available evidence.

International scepticism regarding the government's programme of refugee repatriation increased in early 1995, following a series of uncompromising initiatives to encourage the return of internally displaced Rwandans (including the interruption of food supplies to refugee camps), culminating in the forcible closure of the camps through military intervention. An attempt to dismantle the Kibeho camp in southern Rwanda, in late April, provoked widespread international condemnation after APR troops opened fire on refugees amid confusion arising from the activities of some hostile elements within the camp and a sudden attempt by large numbers of refugees to break through the military cordon. While the government stated that the number of fatalities (many as a result of suffocation) from the ensuing panic was 338, independent witnesses estimated as many as 5,000 deaths. The report of an international enquiry into the incident, published in mid-May, concluded that the massacre had not been premeditated but that the armed forces had employed excessive force in their response to the situation. The commission also estimated the number of fatalities to be far in excess of the official total.

In August 1995, in response to requests made by the Rwandan government, the UN Security Council voted to suspend the arms embargo to Rwanda (imposed against the previous administration in May 1994) for one year, in order to allow the government to safeguard against the threat of a military offensive to be launched by Hutu extremists encamped in neighbouring countries. In April 1996 the UN Security Council had unanimously voted to investigate alleged illegal shipments of weapons to the former Forces armées rwandaises (FAR) in eastern Zaire. Under the August UN directive, weapons could be purchased only for use by the APR and could be imported only through specified entry points. In September the Security Council adopted Resolution 1013, which created a commission of enquiry to examine allegations that ex-FAR personnel were receiving military training to destabilize Rwanda; to investigate reports of illegal arms-trafficking throughout the Great Lakes region; and to recommend ways to end this trade. Despite this action, weapons were reported to be readily available in the region, since a number of nations, such as Bulgaria, the People's Republic of China, South Africa and Zaire (all of which were allegedly involved in the illegal arms trade), refused to co-operate with the UN commission of enquiry. As a result, the commission's final report failed to make any specific accusations regarding the countries involved. However, the commission's findings did implicate Zaire in an illegal arms sale, conducted in June 1994, whereby weapons were shipped from Seychelles to Goma for distribution to the former FAR. The Seychelles government, which co-operated fully with the commission of enquiry, denied any knowledge of the transaction. In March 1996 the Rwandan government urged the UN Security Council to increase its efforts to end regional arms-trafficking and to consider the imposition of diplomatic and other sanctions against governments that failed to co-operate with the commission of enquiry. Consequently, in April 1996, the UN Security Council adopted Resolution 1053, which urged all Central African states to observe the arms embargo against former FAR troops and to ensure that their territories were not used as a base for armed groups to launch cross-border raids into Rwanda.

In December 1995 the UN Security Council unanimously adopted Resolution 1029, which extended the mandate of UNAMIR until 8 March 1996. Under the terms of the mandate the UNAMIR contingent was reduced by one-third, leaving 1,200 troops and 200 military observers and staff to assist in the repatriation of Rwandan refugees from neighbouring countries. This resolution also adjusted UNAMIR's mandate, authorizing it to attempt actively to facilitate national reconciliation and to encourage refugees to repatriate voluntarily. In addition, UNAMIR was mandated henceforth to perform monitoring tasks to help to re-establish stability and to restore confidence in the Rwandan government. On 19 April 1996 the last member of the UN peace-keeping contingent left Rwanda. Many Rwandans remained critical of the UN's performance during and following the 1994 genocide, and welcomed the termination of UNAMIR operations. In April 1996 the Rwandan government accepted the establishment of a UN Office for Rwanda (UNOR), to comprise a special representative to the UN secretary-general, aided by UN officials and local staff. The UNOR was expected to serve as a small co-ordinating, advocacy and advisory office, while the UNOR special representative will continue to co-ordinate UN activities in Rwanda and to facilitate the repatriation of Rwandan refugees.

By mid-August 1995 the security situation in refugee camps along the Zairean border had deteriorated to such an extent that the Zairean government initiated a programme of forcible repatriation. Some 15,000 Rwandans were deported in a number of days, prompting widespread international concern for their welfare. Later in the month in Geneva, at a meeting with UNHCR, the prime minister of Zaire, Kengo Wa Dondo, agreed to entrust the repatriation process to UNHCR officials until the end of 1995, after which time the Zairean government would resume the forcible return of all remaining refugees. In early September a formal agreement was concluded between UNHCR and the Zairean government for a more regulated and bilateral approach to the refugee crisis. An APR attack on the village of Kanama, near the border with Zaire, some days later, resulted in the deaths of more than 100 civilians (including the local mayor) and did little to reassure returning refugees of the safety of such an undertaking. The Rwandan minister of national defence, Maj.-Gen. Paul Kagame, attributed the atrocity to an exaggerated response by frustrated army elements to repeated anti-government activities in the area, perpetrated by armed militias from camps in Zaire. Kagame declared his intention to bring to justice those responsible for the massacre (separate government and military investigations into the incident were inaugurated during September) and later in the month, following a further meeting of representatives of UNHCR, Rwanda and Zaire in Geneva, further commitments were made by both governments to improve security conditions on both sides of the border. Following a subsequent APR attack on a suspected rebel base on the island of Iwawa, in Lake Kivu, in early November, a UN mission verified government claims that there had been no civilian casualties. The UN officials estimated the number of dead at 25, while Rwandan defence ministry sources reported the deaths of more than 100 militiamen, and the discovery of a large weapons cache, allegedly amassed in preparation for an attack on the mainland to be launched from Lake Kivu. (In June Amnesty International claimed that dealers based in the United Kingdom were organizing the illegal supply, to members of the former Rwandan armed forces and the Interahamwe militia based at camps in Zaire, of consignments of armaments purchased in Eastern Europe.) At a conference of the Great Lakes Countries, convened in Cairo, Egypt, in late November, and attended by the presidents of Burundi, Rwanda, Uganda and Zaire and by a Tanzanian presidential envoy, the member nations recognized the need to disarm and demilitarize displaced groups within their borders that threatened the security of neighbouring nations. President Mobutu of Zaire also indicated (and in December confirmed) that the forcible return of remaining refugees in early 1996 was no longer a realistic objective. The conference also accepted the Rwandan president's assertion that the participation of UNAMIR forces in peacekeeping operations in Rwanda was no longer necessary, but urged the Rwandan government to accept the extension of a revised, three-month mandate for the forces to provide assistance in the refugee repatriation process.

During 1995 UNHCR assisted in the repatriation of 240,388 Rwandan refugees from neighbouring countries. The Rwandan authorities were reported to have detained a small number of these returnees, on suspicion that they had participated in the 1994 genocide or had committed other related crimes. Despite the large number of returnees, by February 1996 little progress had been made in repatriating displaced Rwandans who still remained in Zaire. A new initiative, endorsed by UNHCR, was launched early in that month. Zairean troops, deployed at the Kibumba camp in eastern Zaire, sought to encourage the return of refugees by dismantling the unofficial commercial zones that had been established in the camp. However, the difficulties of the initiative were further compounded by the publication in a French newspaper, at the end of February, of reports (based on alleged first-hand accounts) detailing violent acts of reprisal committed by the FPR against fleeing and returning refugees, which had claimed the lives of some 100,000 Hutus since April 1994. These allegations were strenuously denied by the Rwandan government, while UNHCR sources were unable to confirm or deny the alleged scale of the slaughter, owing to lack of evidence.

During the course of 1996 more than 1.3m. refugees were repatriated, and by the end of that year the number of Rwandan refugees in neighbouring countries had fallen to 257,000 from an estimated 1,684,645 in March. In particular, Tanzania, with the support of UNHCR, initiated a policy of forced repatriation of all Rwandan refugees. This provoked criticism from Amnesty International and Human Rights Watch, Africa, as UNHCR's charter states a commitment to voluntary repatriation, and many refugees moved further east into Tanzania as a result. However, these were turned back by the Tanzanian authorities, and by the end of 1996 an estimated 475,000 refugees had returned from that country to Rwanda. Within Rwanda itself, however, there were reported to be about 20,000 refugees from Zaire and Burundi. A programme for the Return of Qualified Rwandan Nationals, sponsored by the EU, began in February 1996, with the aim of encouraging skilled Rwandan refugees to return home. As a result of the mass influx of refugees, the Rwandan government, together with the UN World Food Programme (WFP) and other relief agencies, distributed food aid to the returnees in an attempt to avert a humanitarian crisis. In August 1997 the WFP announced the completion of this distribution programme, and stated its intention to help to construct houses for the repatriated refugees. In late 1996, owing to the deterioration of the security situation in eastern Zaire, pressure for UN-sponsored international intervention in the region increased, and Canada agreed to lead an international military force with the dual aim of securing Goma airport and establishing a secure humanitarian corridor between Rwanda and Zaire. However, the subsequently high level of refugee repatriations rendered these arrangements unnecessary.

During a visit to Rwanda in December 1997, the UNHCR stated that the Rwandan government lacked a commitment to a national reconciliation policy. Rwandan officials rejected this finding. However, after several site visits, the US Committee for Refugees (USCR) concluded that several Rwandan government policies intended to heal ethnic animosities were, in fact, aggravating them, particularly the practice of making Hutu returnees attend re-education camps before they could qualify for certain jobs or school placements.

By early 1998, some 43,000 Rwandan refugees remained in neighbouring countries, of whom 30,000 were in the DRC, 10,000 in Uganda, 2,000 in Burundi and 1,000 in the Central African Republic. An estimated 50,000 Rwandans were internally displaced. Rwanda received approximately 28,000 refugees (25,000 from the DRC and 3,000 from Burundi) at that time. During 1997, an estimated 200,000 Rwandan refugees were repatriated, giving rise to several reintegration problems. According to the WFP, many returning refugees arrived home in poor health and showed signs of malnutrition. Consequently, most returnees received food assistance for up to six months. Rwandan security officials arrested approximately 30,000 new and old returnees during the year, increasing the country's prison population to as much as 130,000. In April 1998, the WFP announced that the number of Rwandans facing food shortages had increased to more than 360,000. Some 600,000 people arrived at refugee camps in the north-west in December, owing to increased instability. More than 2,200 refugees returned from the DRC in January 1999, and there was further refugee movement in that month as some 5,400 Rwandan refugees entered Tanzania. In early 1999 the government initiated a resettlement programme, with the aim of rehousing the displaced in the north-west into 'cluster settlements'; those resettled were to construct their own dwellings. About 300,000 people, predominantly Hutus, were resettled in early 1999. Concerns about the programme were raised owing to the enforced nature of the resettlement, and as to the ability of the government to secure the foreign financial assistance necessary for its success.

HUMAN RIGHTS ISSUES

By 2000 Rwanda had one of the worst human rights' records in Africa, which the government justified by claims that such excesses have resulted from its efforts to prevent another genocide. According to Rwandan authorities, a variety of rebel groups presented a continued threat to security. Most of the incidents involving these groups were minor. In late 1999, for example, several insurgent groups, operating from bases in the Democratic Republic of Congo (DRC), infiltrated the north-western prefectures of Gisenyi and Ruhengeri, stole food from farmers, and clashed with Rwandan troops in Kidaho and Nyamutera communes. A more serious confrontation occurred in December, when rebels, known locally as *abacengezi*, launched a raid into Tamira, in Gisenyi prefecture, killing 312 civilians.

By early 2000 Kigali had succeeded in ending most rebel activity which had emanated from north-west Rwanda and areas of eastern DRC. However, various international human rights organizations, such as Amnesty International and Human Rights Watch, questioned Rwanda's excessive use of force against these insurgents. In restoring order to these areas, the APR killed tens of thousands of people, many of whom were civilians. Government troops also forced hundreds of thousands of others to move into 'protected villages'. By late 1999 94% of the population of Kilbungo, 60% of the population of Mutara, and 40% of the population of the prefecture surrounding Kigali had been moved into such villages, with the police arresting anyone who resisted. Despite government pledges to provide adequate care for the inhabitants, most villages lacked basic services such as water, schools, and health care.

Owing to the 'protected villages' being located far away from the inmate's farms, agricultural production dropped. By early 2000 farmers from Ruhengeri prefecture were cultivating less than 60% of available arable land. As a result, more than 500,000 people became dependent on foreign food aid. Some 60% of the population of the north-western prefectures was malnourished as compared to 40% in the rest of the country. The government also took harsh measures against anyone suspected of anti-gouvernement sympathies. In mid-1999, for example, the authorities claimed that the organization known as the 'army of the king' posed a serious threat to the country's security. This group supposedly supported the restoration of Kigeli V Ndahindurwa, the Rwandan king (*umwami*), who was overthrown by the Hutu-led revolution, which began in 1959, and was driven into exile in 1961. In late November 1999 security forces in Kigali arrested about 200 people and charged them with being members of the 'army of the king'. The security forces then handed the suspects over to the department of military intelligence (DMI), which reportedly released them after they had confessed to unspecified crimes. A further government tactic to suppress dissent involved the revival of the local defence forces, which had existed during the 1994–95 period. This minimally-trained 7,000-member force, armed with guns or machetes, searched neighbourhoods for people suspected of 'anti-government activity'. Assassination and torture are also means regularly used against suspected opponents of the Kagame regime.

There have also been numerous government attempts to suppress press activity. Following the departure of the speaker of the legislature, Kabuye Sebarenzi, from Rwanda, Deo Mushaidi, the president of the Rwandan Journalists Association (RJA), published a special issue of a popular journal, *Imboni*, in which he rejected government accusations that Sebarenzi had belonged to the 'army of the king'. The authorities confiscated the journal and arranged the removal of Mushaidi as president of the RJA. In early April 2000 Mushaidi, fearing arrest or assassination, fled from Rwanda to Burundi. The Kalgame regime has harassed journalists from the locally-produced Rwanda Newsline and the Agence France Presse for writing articles critical of the FPR. The authorities also criticized the Association for the Defense of Human Rights and Public Liberties (ADL) for publishing critical reports about the government's 'protected villages' scheme.

The APR's record in eastern DRC has alarmed many international human rights' organizations owing to consistently credible reports of executions, rapes, forcible removal of people, and other abuses. An increasing number of people from North and South Kivu, especially those who do not belong to the pro-FPR Banyarwanda group, stongly oppose the APR, owing to its harsh treatment of local populations. Many have joined the anti-Rwandan Mai-Mai militia to combat the APR and its Banyarwanda allies. In May 2000 Human Rights Watch released a report, entitled *Eastern Congo Ravaged*, which outlined the excesses committed by the APR in the DRC. At about the same time Amnesty International published the report, *Democratic Republic of Congo: Killing Human Decency*, which indicated that the APR had killed 'hundreds or even thousands' of unarmed civilians in part of North Kivu since 1998. In particular, Amnesty International pointed to the APR's killing of 74 civilians, in a church at Kailenge county of Walikale territory.

Rwanda's relations with the International Criminal Tribunal for Rwanda (ICTR) continued to experience difficulties. In November 1999 the government suspended co-operation with the ICTR after the Appeal Chamber in the Hague annulled the indictment and ordered the release of the genocide suspect, Jean-Bosco Barayagwiza, who had co-founded the anti-Hutu radio station, *Radio Télévision Libre des Mille Collines*, and had led the *Coalition pour la Défense de la République* (CDR), an extremist party whose supporters participated in the 1994 genocide. Rwanda withheld a visa for the UN Prosecutor, Carla del Ponte, but in early December 1999 decided to lift the ban. Rwanda's relations with the ICTR became more normal after the Appeals Chamber reversed its decision at the end of March 2000, which allowed the ICTR to continue its prosecution of Barayagwiza.

In April 2000 Amnesty International released a report about the slow process of justice in Rwanda. According to the publication's findings, an estimated 125,000 detainees remained in prison and detention centres awaiting trial for their role in the 1994 genocide. Amnesty International believed that conditions in these prisons and detention centres 'constituted cruel, inhuman and degrading treatment'. To make matters worse, the government still had not fulfilled its pledge to release prisoners against whom there was no evidence. Instead, the Rwandan authorities repeatedly have extended the period of pre-trial detention in contravention of international law. To relieve the pressure on courts, the Rwandan government initiated a legal system, known as *gacaca*, which supposedly is based in a traditional model of participative justice, to deal with the majority of genocide cases. However, Amnesty International believed that *gacaca* would fail to meet international fair trial standards unless amendments were made to the draft law.

REGIONAL CONCERNS

The APR has also been militarily active in the DRC. In July 1997 Kagame admitted that the APR had played a major role in the overthrow of President Mobutu of Zaire. By early 1998, Rwanda had stationed some 3,000 APR personnel in the DRC, to counter the presence of Interahamwe militias and former FAR soldiers. However, the APR presence failed not only to stop cross-border raids, but also to end propaganda broadcasts by radio stations in the eastern DRC. In July DRC President Kabila replaced his army chief of staff (a Rwandan) with a DRC national and ordered all Rwandan troops to leave the DRC. In August relations between Rwanda and the DRC deteriorated sharply, following accusations by the DRC of Rwandan involvement in a rebellion in the eastern DRC. Rwanda initially denied involvement; it later conceded that it had provided logistical support to the rebels but maintained that the rebellion was internally driven. Kabila, however, maintained that Rwanda, together with Uganda, had invaded the DRC and consequently refused to negotiate with the rebels at a number of regional peace conferences. Differences between Rwanda and Uganda became evident by early 1999 and while both countries admitted to minor disagreements over tactics, they denied allegations of a serious rift. During 1999 Rwanda rejected a number of peace accords (which Uganda supported) and indicated that it would maintain a military presence in the DRC as long as ex-FAR and Hutu militia (which, it claimed, were trained by the DRC) threatened its borders. In mid-1999 there were continued reports of clashes between Rwandan and Ugandan troops in the DRC, and in April Uganda recalled temporarily its ambassador to Rwanda following an incident during which a number of Ugandan soldiers died when the Rwandan army opened fire on demonstrators in the DRC. In May divisions within the Rassemblement congolaise pour le démocratie (RCD) resulted in the creation of two factions within the DRC rebel movement; Rwanda and Uganda now support different factions, further emphasizing the differences between them.

In mid-August 1999 there was a clash between the APR and Uganda People's Defence Force (UPDF) units in Kisangani, which resulted in hundreds of casualties. On 17 August Kagame met the Ugandan president, Yoweri Museveni, in the Ugandan town of Mweya; the discussions resulted in a suspension of the fighting but tensions between the two countries continued. Both sides issued conflicting reports about what had happened at Kisangani and blamed the other for starting hostilities. In early May 2000 Uganda attacked Rwandans in Kisangani. The incident occurred after the UPDF had occupied the Kapalata military camp, despite Rwandan protests, and had deployed an additional 700 troops to Kisangani. On 14 May Kagame and Museveni met in the northern Tanzanian city of Mwanza to defuse tensions between their two countries. The Tanzanian president, Benjamin Mkapa, chaired the negotiations. On 12 May the Kenyan President, Daniel arap Moi, arrived in Kigali and met with Kagame to explore means of normalizing Rwandan–Ugandan relations. (Moi's visit was the first since the 1994 genocide.) Relations between Kigali and Nairobi had been strained largely since Hutu extremists suspected of participating in the genocide had sheltered in Kenya. After Kagame became president, Moi authorized the arrest of at least six genocide suspects by the ICTR. Shortly after the clash in early May, a team of UN observers were deployed in Kisangani to prevent additional clashes. Nevertheless, tensions remained high between APR and UPDF units in that city. In early June Rwandan and Ugandan forces again clashed in Kisangani, with the latter withdrawing from the city.

There are at least two factors that have contributed to these confrontations. Rwanda and Uganda support competing factions of the *Rassemblement Congolais pour la Démocratie* (RCD), a rebel group active in eastern DRC. The Rwandan government supported the removal of the pro-Uganda RCD faction, led by Ernest Wamba dia Wamba, from Kisangani, which would allow the pro-Rwanda RCD–Goma faction, led by Emile Illunga, to establish a presence in the city. On a broader level, Rwanda and Uganda have pursued different goals in the DRC. Rwanda's focus is on eliminating all military elements associated with the Habyarimana regime. The Ugandan government, on the other hand, aims to facilitate the emergence of an effective local government in eastern DRC. Disagreements between the APR and the UPDF over the control of business opportunities in the DRC and which side would dominate the looting of the DRC's mineral wealth also contributed to the clashes.

During 1999 international criticism of Rwandan involvement in the conflict escalated. However, no organization or country was willing to take decisive action against the Kagame regime. For example, the EU claimed that the war was disrupting much of eastern and central Africa and threatened to end aid to the parties to the conflict. In the event, however, the EU only suspended assistance for a short time. The EU and the UN repeatedly condemned armaments-trafficking to the region, but by mid-2000 had failed to devise any policies to prevent illicit imports into eastern and central Africa. In July 1999 the EU announced that Rwanda bore much of the responsibility for ending the DRC war but did not condemn Kigali for any of the massacres in eastern DRC attributed to its troops.

During 1995 and 1996 relations between Rwanda and France continued to experience difficulty. However, both countries have remained committed to improving relations. In September 1995 President Bizimungu held talks with the French secretary of state for emergency humanitarian affairs, Xavier Emmanuelli, during his fact-finding mission to Rwanda. The two officials announced a commitment to co-operate in restructuring the judicial system. Emmanuelli also pledged aid for the rehabilitation of the health, education and agriculture sectors. France pledged further funding in March 1996. During 1997 and 1998 relations with France remained strained as a result of France's

policy towards Rwanda during the 1994 genocide. Following several French newspaper reports and international criticism concerning allegations that France had supplied weapons to the Hutu-led government during the genocide, a parliamentary committee was established to investigate France's activities both prior to and at the time of the genocide. The committee presented its report in December 1998. It cleared France of any direct complicity in the genocide, although it conceded that 'Operation Turquoise' both delayed the accession to power of the FPR, and facilitated the escape of Hutu extremist forces into the DRC. The report laid the blame for the genocide with the international community as a whole—and particularly with the USA (which had blocked the deployment of a UN force in Rwanda). Rwanda rejected the committee's findings, claiming that the inquiry had been established to absolve France of any blame and had therefore reached its expected conclusion. In March 1999 the UN Security Council approved a proposal for the establishment of a commission of inquiry into the actions of the UN prior to and during the genocide.

The USA has remained committed to facilitating the process of national reconciliation and reconstruction in Rwanda. To this end, the US government provided an array of assistance to Kigali, during the 1994 and 1995 financial years, amounting to some US $557.6m. in assistance to various UN agencies, non-governmental organizations (NGO) and international bodies administering relief programmes in Rwanda. Two US department of justice prosecutors and four US investigators were also assigned to assist the work of the ICTR in Rwanda. In August 1997 Rwandan–US relations were revealed to have been closer than previously known, when it was reported that there had been a near-continuous US military presence in Rwanda since 1995. In late 1997 the USA promised nearly $4m. in aid: $1.7m. for the APR's demobilization scheme, $1.2m. for education and $1m. for various democratization programmes. Rwanda's increasing influence both regionally and internationally was demonstrated in June 1998, when it agreed, along with the USA, to mediate in a border dispute between Ethiopia and Eritrea. However, by mid-1998 this initiative had failed to produce any positive results. In mid-1999 the USA was the only country providing military aid to Rwanda. The USA maintains that such aid is necessary to facilitate regional stability and that it provides only non-lethal military equipment and training to help Rwanda rebuild its civilian and military judicial systems, establish FPR civil affairs mobile training units, enhance the FPR's demining capabilities and improve basic military training. The USA also plans to support a number of other initiatives, including training programmes for Rwandans at military schools in the USA, and for air force and naval personnel in Rwanda, and further programmes to improve police investigative techniques. Many African countries remain convinced that the USA also supplies armaments to Rwanda, despite repeated denials by the US government.

In 1998 the issue of foreign arms shipments to Rwanda during the 1994 genocide resurfaced. The former French minister of co-operation, Bernard Debré, alleged that the missiles used to shoot down President Habyarimana's plane were probably of US origin, and had entered Rwanda via Uganda. (Rwanda, Uganda and the USA all strenuously denied this accusation.) On 9 April 1998 the UN Security Council reactivated the four-member International Commission of Inquiry into illegal arms sales to Rwanda. China, which has long been active in arms sales throughout east Africa, supported the action and urged the commission to end arms trafficking to Rwanda. A few months earlier, the UN had released the commission's October 1996 report, which had been completed prior to its dissolution. That document showed the extent of international involvement in the proliferation of arms in Rwanda and the Great Lakes region. The commission implicated, among others, the Seychelles government, a former Rwandan minister (who is currently awaiting trial at the ICTR), a South African arms broker, and the Banque Nationale de Paris in possible violations of the arms embargo. By 15 May 1998 Belgium and Japan had donated about US $140,000 to the commission, which also received subsequent financial pledges from several other sources, including France, Germany, the United Kingdom, Sweden and the USA. In November 1998 the UN International Commission of Inquiry released its report which indicated that Hutu rebels fighting in the Great Lakes region were selling drugs to finance weapons purchases. The commission also found that ex-FAR officers continued their recruitment and fund-raising activities in Kenya in order to purchase arms intended for use against Rwanda. However, the commission failed to address adequately the question of weapons acquisitions by the Rwandan government. The commission repeated an earlier recommendation for the creation of mechanisms to monitor and ensure the implementation of Security Council resolutions. The report also criticized the attitude of the DRC government which, although initially favourable, changed following the August 1998 rebellion; the DRC failed to invite the commission to visit the DRC despite requests that it do so. The commission estimated that there were some 5,000–8,000 ex-FAR and Interahamwe militia in the northern DRC and 10,000 in the south, and that these numbers were growing.

INTERNATIONAL RELATIONS

Despite Rwanda's increasingly poor record in the areas of governance and human rights, the government retained the support of much of the international community. During 1999 foreign aid accounted for about 45% of Rwanda's budget. Major donors included the World Bank (US $75m. for economic reforms and a further $5m. for another programme), the United Kingdom ($70m. of unrestricted funding over a ten-year period), Netherlands ($6.7m. for education and civil service reform), and the USA ($10m. to support justice, $3m. of which was for a public relations campaign to win popular support for *gacaca* (a term used for local justice mechanism). In July 1999 Austria, Belgium, Denmark, and Norway announced that they would increase their support to Rwanda. In December, Rwanda and South Africa concluded an agreement which pledged both nations to co-operate in the areas of agriculture, control of drug-trafficking, culture, education, and trade.

On 15 January 2000 Charles Josselin, the French minister for overseas co-operation, visited Rwanda (the first time since the FPR seized power in 1994 that a French cabinet minister had made a visit to the country). Josselin refused to apologize for France's role in the 1994 genocide and urged Rwanda to focus on present and future co-operation rather than the past. On 7 April 2000 (the sixth anniversary of the start of the genocide) the Belgian prime minister visited Rwanda and apologized for his country's refusal to intervene to prevent the killings. He also announced that Belgium would fund a $3m. health services programme.

On 3 June 2000 Presidents Kagame and Kabila met for the first time in Eldoret, Kenya. The two leaders pledged their commitment to the Lusaka Accords and promised to co-operate to promote peace, security, and stability in Central Africa. However, Kagame reportedly indicated to Kabila that a Rwanda–DRC *rapprochement* depended on Kinshasa's willingness to end the threat posed by former Forces Armée Rwandaise troops and the Interahamwe militia who participated in the 1994 genocide. Kabila made no commitment on this issue.

Since the 1994 genocide, Rwanda's attitude toward the UN had been less than cordial. However, in December 1999 there was an improvement in relations after the UN released the results of an independent report, commissioned by Sec.-Gen. Kofi Annan, which indicated that the UN and its members states failed Rwanda by ignoring that the genocide was being planned, refusing to act once the genocide was underway, and abandoning the Rwandan people when they most needed protection. In a statement that accompanied the release of the report, Anan expressed deep remorse on behalf of the UN. Questions about the UN's role in Rwanda reemerged in March 2000, when the National Post, a Canadian newspaper, revealed the existence of a UN document, which indicated that the APR had shot down the aircraft carrying President Halbyarimana, an incident which precipitated the genocide. The Kagame regime rejected the report, while other pro-APR elements questioned its authenticity. However, a subsequent investigation revealed that the document was genuine. The UN handed the document over to the International Criminal Tribunal for Rwanda (ICTR) for further action. As of mid-2000 the ICTR had yet to take any action on the document. This incident, together with a March 1999 report by Human Rights Watch, which suggested that the UN had concealed a report about a counter-genocide by the APR in north-west Rwanda, prompted some UN critics to demand the release of all UN documents associated with the 1994 genocide and its aftermath. (As of mid-2000 the UN had failed to act on these demands.) In March 2000 Canada's ambassador to the UN, Robert Fowler, released a report indicating that Rwanda and several other nations had violated a UN armaments embargo against the Angolan insurgent group, the Uniao Nacional para Independencia Total de Angola (UNITA). According to the report, Rwanda allowed UNITA to arrange diamond sales and to meet armaments traffickers in Kigali. Kagame reacted to these accusations by describing the report as 'outrageous', and by threatening to take legal action against the UN. Fowler refused to withdraw the report.

Economy

FRANÇOIS MISSER

Rwanda has two main physical handicaps to economic development: the extreme population density and the distance from the sea. The population problem with its concomitant effect on food resources, is aggravated by soil erosion caused by leaching and other natural factors. In 1996, according to estimates by the World Bank, Rwanda's gross national product (GNP), measured at average 1994–96 prices, was US $1,268m., equivalent to $190 per head. Rwanda's level of GNP per head is one of the lowest in the world. During 1990–96, it was estimated, GNP per head decreased, in real terms, at an average annual rate of 8.2%. Rwanda's gross domestic product (GDP) decreased in real terms, by an annual average of 5.7% in 1990–97. During 1994, it was estimated, Rwanda's GDP contracted by some 57%, from $1,359m. to $585m. In 1995 a 25% recovery was recorded, and in 1996 GDP was $1,330m., according to World Bank figures. In 1997 GDP was estimated to have increased by 12%, to $1,590m. GDP increased by 9% in 1998. Preliminary estimates of a 7.6% increase of GDP for 1999 were revised to 4% in the last quarter of that year, owing to the adverse effects of low coffee and tea prices on the international market, and of a sharp increase in petrol prices. The government's three-year programme of rehabilitation and reconciliation for 1996–98 aimed to restore the economy to the level of its 1990 achieve-

ments by 1998. However, by the end of 1998 the government estimated that the production represented 85% of the potential of 1993. In 1990–96 the average annual rate of inflation was 21.1%. Although inflation in 1996 had declined to 9%, from a high of 64% in 1994, inflation again increased to an estimated 17% in 1997, owing mainly to food price rises which were caused by large numbers of returning refugees, as well as security problems in some food producing regions. In 1998 inflation declined to 7%, largely owing to an 11% increase in food production. According to government estimates, the inflation rate decreased further, to below 3% in 1999.

AGRICULTURE

The agricultural sector accounted for about 51% of Rwanda's GDP in 1994, and engaged an estimated 91% of the labour force (mainly at subsistance level in 1994). Agriculture's share of GDP was estimated to have decreased to 37% in 1995, before increasing slightly to 40% in 1996. About 95% of the total value of agricultural production is provided by subsistence crops. While these have failed to meet the needs of the population, the annual increase in production of subsistence crops broadly kept pace with the population growth until 1977. Since then the area of land annually made available for subsistence crops has increased only marginally and, moreover, crop yields are declining in many areas, owing to erosions and the traditional intensive cultivation methods used. (The problem of erosion was exacerbated during 1990–1994 by the felling by displaced Rwandans of trees for timber and charcoal). This resulted in the late 1980s in increasing strains on food production, and consequently to severe food shortages. Attempts to increase the yield of small farm plots have included a recent initiative to cultivate climbing beans. In late 1989 and early 1990 many parts of the country, in particular the south, were affected by famine, following drought and crop failure. Subsequently, the government had recourse to emergency food aid to avert widespread starvation.

The principal food crops are bananas (the single most important, with production of about 2.3m. tons in 1997), sweet potatoes, potatoes, cassava, beans, sorghum, rice, maize and peas, in descending order of importance. The cereals production was 182,000 tons in 1996 and 189,000 tons in 1997. However, owing to increased insecurity in the north-western part of the country, the beans output decreased from 189,000 tons in 1996 to 150,000 tons in 1997. By early 1999 the improvement of the security situation, combined with larger supplies of fertilizers, was expected to prompt a rise of both beans and potatoes production. A land reform project, aiming at freezing the dismantlement of agricultural plots and the transformation of marshes and swamps into suitable land for agriculture, might also contribute to an increase in food production in subsequent years. However, in 1998, despite an overall increase of food production, there were still occurrences of famine in some areas of the country, such as the southern province of Gikongoro, where 400 persons died of malnutrition during the five first months of the year. The lack of agricultural inputs was one of the main causes of this tragedy.

The major cash crop is coffee, exports of which provided 7,209m. Rwanda francs (60.2% of total export earnings) in 1991, compared with 12,569m. Rwanda francs (82% of total export earnings) in 1986. In dollar terms, revenue decreased from US $85m. in 1988 to $42m. in 1993 and to $17m. in 1994. However, a rise in world coffee prices and an increase in production contributed to receipts of $48m. (78% of total export revenue) in 1995. Revenue from coffee fluctuates considerably, and in the late 1980s declined sharply because of the combined effects of a low level of production, declining international prices and the weakness of the US dollar in relation to the currencies of Rwanda's other major trading partners. Even prior to the catastrophic political events of 1994, it had seemed unlikely that Rwanda would fully benefit from the resurgence in world prices at the end of 1993. The volume of production has been dwindling for several years, partly owing to price instability. Reduced revenues have also forced farmers to abandon the purchase and introduction of pesticides and fertilizers. The impact of the political and humanitarian crisis was considerable and production declined from 28,135 metric tons in 1992–93 to 1,994 metric tons in 1993–94. Output for 1994–95 was 21,041 tons, equivalent to some 50%–60% of annual production in the late 1980s. Unfavourable climatic conditions and a shortage of manpower led to a further decrease, to 15,667 tons in 1995–96. In 1996–97 output reached 21,051 tons, but, according to government projections, it was unlikely to exceed 22,500 tons by 1998. Indeed, the government has prioritized agricultural diversification in its three-year investment programme of rehabilitation and reconciliation. In 1995, however, the price payable to growers for parchment coffee was increased, reflecting the government's continuing commitment to provide incentives to producers.

The government liberalized the processing, marketing and exports of coffee which enabled farmers to receive higher prices without resorting to subsidies. In mid-1998 the government announced plans to progressively remove the remaining taxes on coffee exports and to sell three of its coffee factories, in order to accelerate the recovery of the sector. However, despite these efforts, coffee exports dropped to 14,800 tons in 1997 and declined further to 13,000 tons in 1998. According to Bank of Rwanda statistics, exports amounted to 12,887 tons for the first nine months of 1999, showing a slight increase compared to the 1998 figure for the same period. Meanwhile, owing to a sharp decline in international prices, export revenue decreased by

40.7%, from 13,650m. Rwanda francs (approximately US $45.5m.) in 1997 to 8,101m. Rwanda francs in 1998 (approximately $27m.). A further decrease of export revenue was projected in 1999, despite government efforts to encourage the trade by suppressing the tax on coffee exports. However, export figures do not entirely reflect the critical situation of the sector, owing to the importance of the smuggling of Burundian coffee to Rwanda, where producers are offered higher prices. One of the main problems, as the government acknowledged, is that average yields of about 300 kg/ha are three to four times lower than in the other countries of the region.

Prior to 1994, the government had attempted to diversify the crops grown for export through the Office des Cultures Industrielles du Rwanda (OCIR), established in 1964. This concentrated its efforts on tobacco, cotton, pyrethrum, quinquina, forestry and, pre-eminently, tea. Rwanda's output of made tea has increased steadily in recent years, rising from 2,522 tons in 1972 to 8,669 tons in 1984, and to 13,546 tons in 1991. Exports of tea earned 2,796.6m. Rwanda francs, or 23.4% of total export earnings in 1991, and this percentage increased to 32.3% in 1992. However, production declined to 10,493 metric tons in 1993, and export earnings decreased to $16m. (equivalent to 23.5% of the value of total exports), following the occupation of the lucrative Mulindi plantations by forces of the Front patriotique rwandais (FPR). In 1993–1994 production collapsed to just 4,902 metric tons, largely owing to the adverse effects of the war and to the former government's removal to the Congo of the Cyangugu tea factory. Production in 1994–1995 increased to 5,346 tons, still considerably below the government's target for 1998 of 13,500 tons (1991 production levels). However, in 1995–96 there was a spectacular increase, to 8,322 tons, and this rose further to 12,938 tons in 1996–97. Estimates for 1997–98 indicated another good harvest. Exports amounted to 12,396 tons in 1997 and increased by 16.9% in 1998 to 15,124 tons. In 1999 the level of tea exports was similar to the 1998 figure, with a total of 10,240 tons for the first nine months of that year. However, export revenue from tea fluctuated considerably, increasing from 5,040m. Rwanda francs in 1997 (approximately US $16.8m.) to 7,154m. Rwanda francs in 1998 (approximately $23.8m.). Projections for 1999 were, however, of only 6,000m., a decline of 16.2%, compared with the 1998 figure, owing to a sharp decrease in international prices during that year. This trend annihilated the effects of an increase of the producer price in 1998 which had been designed to encourage the peasants, initiated by the government which simultaneously decided to privatize the tea estates and factories. In November 1994 the European Union (EU) allocated ECU 20m. to Rwanda for the rehabilitation of the coffee and tea sectors. The four tea plantations of Mulindi, Shagasha, Kitabi and Mata (which together account for 80% of the national production) were expected to be among the first beneficiaries of these funds. The African Development Bank (ADB) also pledged $2.2m. for the rehabilitation of export agriculture. By November 1995, however, the EU had disbursed only $6.5m. of the allocated funds. An agricultural diversification programme was aided by the EU. In addition, the European Development Fund (EDF), together with the FAO and the World Bank, is involved in aiding the creation of local farming communes (*paysannats*). In late 1993 the International Development Association (IDA) approved a $15m. loan to contribute to the finance of agricultural research projects and the transformation of existing research institutes in Rwanda. Prior to the political events of 1994, it was envisaged that the full implementation of the research development programme would generate an annual increase in the sector's growth of some 4%. In 1990–96, however, the sector declined by an annual average of 8.4%, compared with annual growth of 0.5% in 1980–90. The success of a proposal to diversify agricultural exports through the sale of 'karamasenge' bananas to Europe was likely to be dependent on the success of a marketing campaign to promote the superior quality of the fruit against more competitively priced and more accessible central American fruits.

By July 1994 the sector was in extreme crisis and the majority of the country's livestock had disappeared (although some cattle were introduced by refugees returning from Uganda). Limited livestock-vaccination programmes were undertaken by the FAO and smaller agencies in the north-east, but the main problem remains the overstocking of cattle (and the consequent environment strain) in this region, while livestock numbers are hopelessly insufficient elsewhere in the country. An FAO-World Food Programme report estimated that food production in 1994 amounted to just 45% of the 1993 yield. It was also estimated that hundred of hectares of natural forests had been damaged by displaced persons and that support systems for agriculture were almost completely destroyed. Food aid requirements (mainly grain and pulses) were estimated at more than 150,000 metric tons in 1994 and 116,000 tons in 1995. During the two seasons following the war 10,000 metric tons of beans, maize, vegetable and other seeds, together with 700,000 hoes, were distributed to some 690,000 households. It was estimated that 62% of farmers received seeds, while some 72% received tools. A conference of potential donors, sponsored by the UN Development Programme (UNDP), was convened in Geneva during January 1995, at which pledges of financial assistance totalling US $587m. were made, including a substantial share for agriculture recovery programmes. By the end of 1995 pledges amounted to $1,260m., of which $189.5m. was to be allocated to the agriculture sector. At the same time, however, disbursements amounted to just $28.6m., slowed, in part, by the suspension of aid channelled through the government in the months following the April 1995 massacre of displaced persons by security forces at the Kibeho refugee camp. Disputes involving land tenure were still common in mid-1997, and discouraged farmers from making long-term investments. However, by the end of 1996 part of the $500m. pledged to facilitate the return of refugees had been allocated to basic rural and agricultural infrastructures. A programme of reform was also announced at this time. The government intended to encourage a system of population regroupment known as *Imidugu* (grouped habitat), which was believed to reduce social and economic costs by enabling shared use of expensive items and the maximization of water supplies. In 1997 the FAO and the government distributed seeds to approximately 2.3m. persons, including many returnees. The food deficit in that year was 179,000 tons and decreased slightly to 158,000 tons in 1998. Apart from the continuing insecurity in the north-western part of the country, which particularly affected until 1998 production of beans and potatoes, some 150,000 persons suspected to have participated in the 1994 genocide remained in prison and were therefore unable to contribute to food production. According to FAO estimates, food production in 1997 was 3.9m. tons, a decline of 14% compared with 1984, while the population has increased by 40% in the same period. By late 1999, after an 11% increase of the food production owing to the improvement of the security situation in the north-western part of the country, the authorities were again projecting an increase of the food deficit owed to the drought which was affecting most parts of the country. In order to avert this threat in the future and not to rely exclusively on rain water, the government planned to encourage the development of irrigation schemes using the country's underground water resources. The situation was also aggravated owing to the competition of foreign imports which has undermined efforts to develop domestic rice production schemes, according to the ministry of agriculture. In March 1998 the African Development Fund disbursed US $1.4m. to finance a feasibility study on the improvement of soil conservation and the utilization of marshes in order to enable the farmers to benefit from new arable land. The World Bank also planned to finance two projects (one in agriculture and one in rural water) for a total of $25m. in 2000. It also considered the provision of assistance to the agricultural sector during 2001.

INDUSTRY AND MINING

The industrial sector followed the usual pattern for the less developed African states, and food-based industries predominated, with the major companies prior to 1994 being BRALIRWA–SOBOLIRWA, the Rwandan subsidiary of a Dutch brewery, the Régie Sucrière de Kibuy, sugar plant and the OVIBAR factory producing banana wine and liquors. In 1995 manufacturing accounted for an estimated 14% of GDP, while in the same year the industrial sector accounted for 21% of GDP.

By July 1994 the country's political turmoil had suspended economic activity in the sector. Factories and plants (where production had been virtually halted by power shortages earlier in the year) were looted, destroyed or abandoned. By early

October 1994 the BRALIRWA plant had resumed production. In 1994 manufacturing accounted for an estimated 3% of GDP, while industry provided 9% of GDP in the same year. In 1995, although only 40% of enterprises had resumed production, manufacturing was estimated to have recovered sufficiently to provide 12.5% of GDP, with industry accounting for 16.3%. Government officials claimed that the slow disbursement of some US $72.9m. in international donor aid, allocated to the trade and industry sectors (only $5.4m. had been activated by the end of 1995), together with competition from tax-free imports of goods such as soap and plastics, had seriously hindered the recovery of the sector. By June 1997 69% of the companies existing before April 1994 had resumed their activities. The industrial output grew by 18% in 1996 and by 30% in 1997. However, sectoral growth was hampered by the lack of investment and lack of basic infrastructure. In 1998 the sector was hindered by several factors, including excessive prices for water and energy supplies, insufficient use of installed capacities and competition from cheaper imported products; BRALIRWA and the Utexerwa textile plants, for example, reduced production by 40%. Despite this situation, the government resisted requests to increase customs duties or impose quotas but instead was considering in early 1999 the provision of cheaper electricity and water for industry. By the end of 1998 perspectives were improving for BRALIRWA, which obtained a contract, valued at 1,000m. Rwanda francs, for the supply of Primus beer to the neighbouring Democratic Republic of Congo (DRC)—formerly Zaire. An additional difficulty for the manufacturing sector was the transport cost increase of imported inputs as a result of the decision of Kenya and Uganda to limit the maximum weight per axle of trucks transiting on their respective road networks. The Rwandan government was also concerned with smuggling of alcoholic beverages, petroleum products and cigarettes. In order to curb these practices, the government, assisted by customs agents, announced its intention of introducing in 2000 new legislation, providing not only for the seizure of smuggled goods, but also of the vehicles which were used to transport them. By late 1999 the government also announced plans to create export processing zones along the Congolese border in Cyangugu and other cities which could bring added value to products imported from the DRC. The Banque Rwandaise de Développement financed the first cut flowers exports project in 1999, allocating to this effect $2m. to the Highland Flowers company, based in Nyacyonga.

Cassiterite (a tin-bearing ore) is Rwanda's principle mineral resource (exports of tin ore and concentrates were valued at 320m. Rwanda francs in 1991), followed by wolframite (a tungsten-bearing ore), and small, known quantities of beryl, colombotantalite, and gold. While tin concentrates (about 1,500 tons) were the third-largest export earner in 1985, high transport costs and the sharp decline in international tin prices resulted in the sector becoming virtually inactive in the late 1980s. At the end of 1985 Géomines, the Belgian company with a 51% shareholding in the Rwandan mining company, SOMIRWA, went into liquidation; SOMIRWA itself was declared insolvent a few months later. A tin-processing plant, constructed at the cost of 1,000m. Rwanda francs in Karuruma near Kigali, had never operated at more of 20% of capacity, and the profitability of SOMIRWA's other operations had also been poor. Plans for other foundries were consequently suspended. Despite the insolvent state of the company, the government's annual maintenance costs for SOMIRWA's installations had continued to exceed 70m. Rwanda francs. In 1992 the Régie Ministre mining concern was established, with state involvement, and began to exploit the SOMIRWA mines in an artisanal capacity. However, the company was reported to be operating on an annual deficit of some 50m. Rwanda francs. In 1996 the government announced its decision to privatize the company. From 1992 the SOMIRWA smelter resumed activity for six months of the year, processing cassiterite supplied by the ALICOM gold concern. Some efforts were made with EU support to stimulate the artisanal tin sector, and the UNDP provided some funds towards an increase in gold production. Mining activities were resumed at a modest level in 1988 by artisans regrouped in COOPIMAR, an independent co-operative offering managerial and commercial support. In 1992, a new company, Saphirs du Rwanda, began exploration for sapphires. In 1996 Rwanda exported 330 tons of cassiterite, 43 tons of wolfram and 96 tons of columbo-tantalite. In 1997 exports of cassiterite amounted to 327 tons, whereas Rwanda exported 63 tons of wolfram and 224 tons of columbo-tantalite, for a total of 1,130m. Rwanda francs. In 1998 Rwanda exported 187 tons of cassiterite, 122 tons of wolfram and 197 tons of columbo-tantalite. During the first nine months of 1999 exports amounted to 389 tons of cassiterite, 60 tons of wolfram and 255 tons of columbo-tantalite. The increase of both cassiterite and columbo-tantalite exports is attributed to the increase of the smuggling from the DRC, by Rwandan and Burundian traders, from the areas controlled by the Rwandan army. Indeed, in 1995 (the last year during which Zaire maintained sovereignty of its entire territory) Rwandan columbo-tantalite exports amounted to only one-quarter of the 1998 figure. The IMF also estimated that Rwanda's exports of gold and diamonds amounted to US $30m. for the first half of 1998, confirming suspicions that these precious minerals were from the DRC. Indeed, on he one hand, Rwanda does not mine diamonds and on the other hand, Belgian statistics for 1998 show a dramatic rise of gold imports from Rwanda raised from an annual average of $15m. during 1990–1993 to $35m. in 1997, the first year of Rwanda's military presence in the eastern part of the DRC. By early 1996 the Rwandan government introduced a request to obtain a grant from the Sysmin, the EU special financing facility, to relaunch the artisanal exploitation of tin and other minerals. By early 1997 a Belgian company established in Burundi initiated talks with the Rwandan government in order to open a gold refining plant in Kigali which would process imports from the DRC. In mid-1998 the government announced plans to revise the mining code before 2001 to attract investors.

Another important mineral to be exploited is natural gas, which was discovered beneath Lake Kivu on the border with the DRC. Reserves of an estimated 60,000m. cu m (about one-half of which are in the DRC) are believed to be among the largest in the world. Two pilot installations, funded by the EU, produce gas, but here again the small size of the potential market casts doubt on the likely profitability of large-scale processing. However, the national electricity and gas company, Electrogaz, hopes to receive Belgian funding for a programme to increase its daily output of gas from 5,000 cu m to 25,000 cu m. In October 1997 the governments of Rwanda, Uganda and of the DRC agreed to finance a joint feasibility study to exploit the gas reserves of the Lake Kivu. In September 1999 the Banque Rwandaise de Développement announced plans to submit a project for the establishment of a further pilot installation to process the Lake Kivu gas resources to the European Investment Bank, the Commonwealth Development Corporation, the International Finance Corporation and the Arab Bank for Economic Development in Africa. Government plans to privatize Electrogaz (of which state monopoly was abolished in June) have attracted interests from Franco-Canadian and Franco-Belgian consortia. In February 1999 the South African oil company, Engen, purchased the local subsidiaries of British Petroleum and Fina (Belgium) and took over 25% of the petrol distribution market in Rwanda. In August Shell Oil acquired for $2.1m. the Petrorwanda distribution corporation.

POWER AND COMMUNICATIONS

Rwanda's electricity needs are supplied almost entirely from hydroelectric sources, as the land relief is ideal for power generation. According to studies undertaken by the Rwanda-Burundi-Zaire tripartite organization, Enérgie des Pays des Grands Lacs (EGL), the Ruzizi river alone offers a total 500-MW potential, of which only a fraction is being used currently. Rwanda imports more than one-half (54% in 1990) of its total electricity requirements. In early 1994 the European Investment Bank, together with French and German credit institutions, pledged more than US $1m. to help rehabilitate the Ntaruka power station, which had been damaged by Front patriotique rwandais (FPR) guerillas, and the project was completed in 1998. By October 1994, as a result of the catastrophic sequence of political events, the Mukungwa power station alone was supplying Kigali, Ruhengeri and Gisenyi with insufficient amounts of electricity. By early 1995, however, following the EU's allocation of ECU 5m. for the rehabilitation of the power sector, the situation had improved vastly, and Butare, Gitarama and all areas of Kigali

were receiving adequate power supplies. Further reconstruction enabled the Gibira and Gisenyi power stations and also the Gatsasa thermal installation to resume production. A new 15-MW power station, supplied by Canada, was installed at Gikondo, near Kigali, by January 1996, but one-third of the country's total requirements were still not being met. In April 1997 it was announced that a feasibility study would be conducted into the possibility of aligning the power grids in Rwanda and in Uganda in order to lessen Rwanda's deficit. The Ntaruka diesel-power station, completed in 1998, was expected to help reduce the deficit; in 1997 15 MW (of a total consumption of 39 MW) were provided by the neighbouring countries. Also in early 1996 the government announced partial privatization plans for Electrogaz, which was to entrust management of network exploitation to private interests. Similar divestment was envisaged for the national water company. In June 1998 Electrogaz signed a technical cooperation agreement with the South African parastatal, Eskom. In 1998 the production of electricity increased from 72m. to 111m. Kwh. Reserves of peat are being assessed as an additional source of energy, mainly for homes and small factories in rural areas. Since the mid-1980s the Rwandan government has also expressed its commitment to the development of *biogas* in the rural areas.

Internal communications in Rwanda are operated almost exclusively along the relatively well-developed road system (13,173 km in 1990), as there are no railways nor navigable waterways (except Lake Kivu). Asphalted highways link Rwanda with Burundi, Uganda, Zaire and Tanzania. They also connect the principal towns. Tarmac roads extend to just over 1,000 km, which, given the small size of the country, is one of the highest densities in Africa. In early 1999 the works financed by the IDA for the asphaltation of the 91-km Gitarama–Kibuye road were completed. Moreover, the World Bank agreed to disburse an additional $10m. by the end of 1998 for the construction of roads to connect the nearby villages to the Gitarama–Kibuye road in order to facilitate the transport of crops. Rwanda's external trade is heavily dependent on the ports of Mombasa, Dar es Salaam and Matadi, and about 80% of Rwandan exports and imports pass through Uganda and Kenya. Insecurity caused by the war in the north of Rwanda led to the closure of the northern transport 'corridor' through Uganda. With the Gatuna and Kagitumba roads unavailable, most traffic has had to be diverted to the difficult and unreliable route through Tanzania. In 1992 several projects had been approved by the EU and the World Bank to improve road links between eastern Zaire and western Uganda, hoping to facilitate the passage of Rwandan trade across the border with Zaire, and thereby bypass the troubled border with Uganda. Following the FPR victory in July 1994, however, the northern transport 'corridor' was immediately reopened. In January 1997 the EU approved funding to upgrade the main road in and around Kigali. By the end of 1997 the EU had committed a total ECU 34.5m. to rehabilitate 200 km of roads and the national airport of Kanombe and the project had already commenced.

By that time some 500 army soldiers were deployed permanently to protect one of the principal roads of the country, between the prefectures of Gisenyi and Ruhengeri, from rebel attacks. By mid-1998 the government announced plans to strengthen the management of the Road Fund and increasingly contract out road maintenance. Furthermore, the government announced plans to encourage the establishment of truck cooperatives in rural areas to improve the distribution of agriculture produce. Feasibility studies have been conducted for a railway network to link Uganda, Rwanda, Burundi and Tanzania. The Rwandan business community showed a renewed interest in early 2000, dispatching a delegation to the railway terminal of Isaka (Tanzania) to discuss with the local authorities and the Tanzania Railway Corporation plans to make a greater use of this central corridor, combining a 500-km road link from Kigali to Isaka (500 km) and the railway line from Isaka to the port of Dar es Salaam (1,300 km). In April 2000 Burundi, Rwanda and Tanzania expressed their renewed intention to seek funds to build the railway link between Isaka and Kigali with a possible extension to Burundi. This project became an even higher priority of the Rwandan authorities in June for both economic and political reasons. Indeed, transport costs have increased sizeably on the northern corridor (Kigali-Kampala-Mombasa), owing to the Ugandan and Kenyan governments' decision to limit the maximum weight per axle of the trucks transiting through their territory. However, tensions also derived from the military clashes between the Ugandan and the Rwandan armies in Kisangani, DRC, in early June, have contributed to a dramatic decline in traffic through the northern corridor between Uganda and Rwanda and prompted the Rwandan government and businessmen to seek alternative routes of access to the Indian Ocean. Prior to the escalation of hostilities in April 1994, a number of international airlines, most prominently Sabena and Air France, operated services to Kigali, while the small national carrier, Air Rwanda (scheduled for privatization), operated domestic passenger and cargo services and international cargo flights to Burundi, Kenya, Tanzania, Uganda, the DRC and destinations in Europe. Only Sabena has resumed flights since the FPR took power in July 1994, although the airport is to be upgraded to meet international standards with the aid of the EU. In early 1998 the national carrier, Air Rwanda, announced plans to buy shares in Alliance Air, a regional carrier owned jointly by the Tanzanian and Ugandan states, and by South African Airways; the creation of a new company, to be known as Air Alliance Rwanda (AAR), was announced simultaneously. Jointly-owned by the Rwandan government (51%) and Alliance Air (49%), AAR was to replace Air Rwanda and offer direct flights from Kigali to Johannesburg, Entebbe, Nairobi, Dar es Salaam and Lumbumbashi. By mid-1998 the government announced it would adopt a regulatory framework to supervise the participation of private companies in the telecommunications sector and to finalize the privatization of Rwandatel. In late 1999 the government announced that the privatization of the national telecommunication company would take place during 2000. Meanwhile, the private mobile cellular telephone corporation MTN-Rwandacell announced the extension of its Global System for Mobile Communications (GSM) network, which would henceforth cover three-quarters of Rwanda's territory.

DEVELOPMENT PLANNING

The DRC, Burundi and Rwanda, the members of the Economic Community of the Great Lakes Countries (CEPGL), agreed to form a joint development bank in 1978, and to co-operate in the development of a transport system and the construction of a hydroelectric power station (the Ruzizi-II project) on the Rwanda–Congo border, the exploitation of methane gas deposits beneath Lake Kivu and the promotion of a fishing industry. The bank was formerly established in 1980, with it headquarters at Goma, in the DRC. Since the change of regime in the DRC, all the CEPGL states have expressed their desire for continuing regional co-operation.

The government has sought unsuccessfully to limit the overall budget deficit, which reached 19.2% of GDP in 1993, compared with 9% in 1989, despite an 11% increase in tax revenue and a 25% decline in capital expenditure until 1992 (project implementation slowed, owing to escalating hostilities), and notwithstanding the government's failure to finance adequately the social contingency fund agreed under the terms of its adjustment programme. Budget expenditure increased in order to finance the war and internal security, and to support producer prices for coffee. The situation deteriorated further in 1993, with revenue declining by an estimated 6%, while expenditure increased by an estimated 5%. By the end of October 1993 foreign reserves were estimated to be insufficient to sustain imports for one week.

The overall budget deficit amounted to 16% of GDP by the end of 1994, and to 12.5% by the end of 1995. By 1997 the budget deficit had decreased to 10% of GDP but an increase, to 13.5%, was expected in 1998, following a temporary acceleration of government investment, and the high costs of structural reforms. Although IMF projections indicated a further decrease by 2000, owing to improved savings and a stabilization of government investments, estimates for 1999 project a budgetary deficit of 16.4% of GDP. Furthermore, the high level of military expenditure (about one-third of current expenditure in 1997, despite a demilitarization programme which commenced in that year) was a matter of concern for the donors, particularly compared with the share of the social sectors, which declined from 38% to 18% between 1985 and 1995. In November 1998

the government pledged to limit military expenditure to 4% of GDP and civil service salaries to 3.6% of GDP. In that year the government announced plans for some 3,600 redundancies within the civil service and for the sale of up to one-half of its vehicles in an effort to reduce expenditure. The government also announced plans to increase substantially taxes on beer, petrol, soft drinks, cigarettes, wines and spirits, in an attempt to balance the 1999 budget. At the end of 1997 Rwanda's external debt was US $1,111m., of which $994m. was long-term public debt. Debt-service payments made in that year were equivalent to 13.3% of the value of export of goods and services. By the end of 1999 the external debt was estimated at $1,200m.

In 1999 a primary budget deficit (before grants) of 4,500m. Rwanda francs was recorded instead of a projected surplus of 5,900m. francs due to lower than expected tax receipts. This was owed to the decrease of earnings from coffee, pyrethrum and skins and hides exports, despite the good performance of the tea sector. The 2000 budget of 168,900m. Rwanda francs (including foreign funding which amounted to 53.7% of the total) is 2,000m. Rwanda francs lower than the budget of the previous year. In order to balance the 2000 budget, the government decided to maximise its earnings, by introducing a value-added tax on the 1 July of that year and by accelerating the privatization process. Apart from the telecoms company, Rwandatel, the Office des Cultures Industrielles du Rwanda (OCIR), tea plants and plantations have been listed among the assets which are to be privatized, alongside with STIR (international transport), Sodeparal (agricultural products), Soporiz (rice) and the water, electricity and gas corporation, Electrogaz. The state also plans divestment from three banks (Banque Commerciale du Rwanda, Banque Rwandaise de Développement and Banque de Kigali), the tobacco corporation, Tabarwanda, the flour mill, Etiru, the coffee company, Rwandex, the Bralirwa brewery, the printing company, Imprisco, and the travel agency, Amirwanda. Despite the concerns expressed by the donors, defence still remained a priority of the national budget in 2000, absorbing 18.6% of total expenditure. However, the government confirmed its decision to create 3,600 redundancies and to stop new recruitments of civil servants. The new prime minister, Bernard Makuza, expressed in April 2000 the government's commitment to curb corruption, following the resignation of his predecessor and parliamentary investigations into embezzlement charges concerning several ministers of the previous government.

Rwanda's heavy dependence on foreign assistance (equivalent to as much as 90% of public investment in recent years) has made the economy vulnerable to civil and political instability. By the end of 1995 external assistance was equivalent to 172.5% of imports or to US $56 per caput. Of the $587m. pledged by donors at the UNDP-sponsored conference, convened in Geneva in January 1995, only $69m. had been disbursed by June, largely as a result of the Kibeho refugee camp massacre and the government's failure to accept a broader political and ethnic base. In that month, however, the EU and other donors began the resumption of aid disbursements and subsequent pledges brought the total amount to $1,260m., out of which $404m. (32%) had been spent by the end of 1995. With such transfers, by the end of 1995 foreign reserves increased to the value of 3.7 months of imports, compared to that of 1.3 months in 1994. Delays to aid disbursements were not only prompted by security issues, but also by disagreements between the World Bank and the government over the assignment of a procurement of commodities and technical assistance, under the World Bank Emergency Recovery Credit. Other delaying factors were the government's limited capacity to absorb aid, due to its own limited technical and administrative staff and its unwillingness to accept foreign technical assistance. In June 1996, at a second donors conference held in Geneva, additional funds of $617m. were pledged, although, in effect, according to some participants at the meeting, the new money made available amounted to only $240m. Indeed, the EU attached very stringent conditions for the disbursement of its funds, which were unlikely to be met by the government in the short term. Such conditions included appropriate measures for the repatriation of the refugees in Zaire and in Tanzania and the improvement of the judicial system. In late 1996 accusations were raised that external aid had been used by the Habyarimana government to purchase weapons. It was also alleged that bank transfers, again used to purchase armaments had been allowed, even during the geno-cide.

In 1995, principally as a result of external assistance funds, a surplus on the current account of the balance of payments of US $65m. was registered. By May 1998 the IMF was projecting the current account deficit at the equivalent of 18% of GDP during the 1998–2000 period. Financial requirements during 1998–2001 were projected at $1,600m.; this total was expected to be met through capital grants ($465m.), project loans ($235m.) and from non-budgetary transfers (humanitarian assistance—$450m.). The remainder was expected to be covered through IMF disbursements, debt relief from the Paris Club and refinancing and assistance from both multilateral and bilateral creditors. In July 1998 it was announced that the 'Paris Club' had agreed to restructure Rwanda's bilateral debt (currently around $181m.), reducing it by up to 67%. In June of that year Rwanda obtained a $250m. quick disbursement loan from the World Bank to support the government's 1998–2000 reform programme. It was aimed at backing the country's efforts in the areas of health, education, national reconciliation, reform of the administration and at contributing to the fund for the survivors of the genocide. Furthermore, the IMF approved in June a three-year loan amounting to $95m. under the Enhanced Structural Adjustment Facility (ESAF). A trust fund of $41.7m., managed by the World Bank, was established during that meeting to help Rwanda manage its external debt. According to the IMF, Rwanda has made substantial progress in rebuilding its severely damaged infrastructure since 1994; most internally displaced people have been settled, macroeconomic stability has been restored and key structural reforms have been initiated. However, Rwanda's administrative and institutional capacity in the public sector remained weak. Increased amounts of concessional external assistance would, therefore, be required in the long term to finance higher social expenditure and ensure sustained human resource development. In 2000 91.7% of Rwanda's public investment budget was to be financed by foreign aid.

In 2000, despite criticisms of Rwanda's involvement in the DRC war, donors continued to provide economic and financial support to Rwanda. In January the European Investment Bank was considering plans to expand the Mombasa-Eldoret-Kampala oil pipeline to Kigali. In March 2000 the European Commission announced that it would allocate 110m. euros to Rwanda under the country's national indicative programme of the fourth Lomé convention. The remaining 47m. euros would be disbursed according to the use of the first tranche. Three-quarters of the programme were allocated to poverty alleviation projects, whereas the remainder would concern projects aiming at promoting good governance and justice. Meanwhile, the World Bank announced that it would provide assistance during 2000 through two projects, one in agriculture and one in rural water for a total of $25m. The World Bank was planning to disburse an additional amount of $125m. for four projects in 2001: one in agriculture, one in human resources development, one in trade and private sector development and a leveraged insurance facility for trade (LIFT), a regional facility to guarantee investment against sovereign, but not exchange rate risk. In addition, in early 2000 China announced a grant of Yuan 20m. (approximately US $2.5m.) for agriculture, road construction and education projects.

FOREIGN TRADE

In April 1976 Rwanda's economy came almost to a standstill, as the result of a blockade imposed by President Amin of Uganda in a dispute with neighbouring Kenya. Amin's ban on heavy vehicles from neighbouring countries from using Uganda's roads in 1977, contributed to increasing petrol prices, resulted in further hardship and strengthened the government's determination to find alternative outlets. Road transport on routes through Uganda was further disrupted by civil disorder during 1984 and 1985, and in 1986 a series of major initiatives was taken in order to assure Rwanda's vital trade links through Uganda. The October 1990 guerrilla invasion again showed the extreme vulnerability of Rwanda's geographical position. Both trade and road communications with Uganda and Kenya virtually ceased as a result of the hostilities. The FPR victory in July 1994 improved this situation considerably and the Ugandan border,

with ready access to the port of Mombasa, was reopened immediately.

Rwanda has long been experiencing a trade deficit, which stood at US $69m. in 1986 and deteriorated in 1987 to the extent that it exceeded the total of export earnings (which covered only 36% of imports). This imbalance appeared unlikely to be rectified in the foreseeable future (despite an increase in international coffee prices), owing to war damage inflicted on the economic infrastructure, the death and displacement of a vast number of the working population. In 1994 coffee production amounted to only 7% of the 1993 total, whereas production of tea represented only 43% of the previous year's crop. In 1995 the situation improved considerably, with output of coffee and tea at 75% and 50% of 1993 production levels, respectively. However, the trade deficit for 1995 was estimated at US $173m. (or $250m. including exports and imports of non-factor services). Export earnings covered 26% of imports, compared with 6.9% in 1994 and 43% in 1985. In 1996 export earnings amounted to $91m. and represented 23.8% of the value of imports ($382m.). Coffee and tea accounted respectively for 38% and 8.2% of the value of exports in 1996, while the trade deficit amounted to $291m. In 1997 export earnings amounted to $88m. and covered 30% of imports, bringing the trade deficit to $205m. Coffee accounted for 50.2% of the value of total exports, followed by tea (21.5%), re-exportations (8.6%, possibly of Zairian gold smuggled into Rwanda), hides and skins (5.0%) and mineral products (4.1%). In 1998 export earnings dropped to $82m. and covered only 25% of the value of imports, while the trade deficit rose again to $244m. In September 1999 total export earnings were 16,028m. Rwanda francs (equivalent to $53.4m.) and amounted to 25.7% of the value of import bill (62,200 Rwanda francs—$207m.) for the first nine months of that year. In 1998 Rwanda's principal suppliers were respectively Kenya, with 22% of total imports, followed by Belgium (20.3%), the United Arab Emirates (5.9%), Tanzania (5.3%), Germany (4.1%), Uganda (3.8%) and Japan (3.7%). Rwanda's principal export destinations in 1998 were Kenya (72.6%), followed by Belgium (5.6%), Tanzania (3.5%), Switzerland (2.6%), Burundi (2.6%), Uganda (2%), the United Kingdom (1.8%) Russia (1.7%) and South Africa (1.4%). In 2000, however, these percentages were likely to change substantially because of the much greater use by Rwandan traders of the central corridor to Dar-es-Salaam (Tanzania) at the expanse of the northern corridor via Uganda to the Kenyan port of Mombasa. However, hopes have been expressed that the restoration of peace might facilitate the implementation of a free trade zone for Burundi and Rwanda (as envisaged by Presidents Ndadaye and Habyarimana in October 1993) to encourage the bilateral exchange of goods and services and to enhance the sales of Rwandan cement and Burundian glass in the respective neighbouring country. As well as increased investments in the cash crops, the government's 1996–1998 three-year rehabilitation programme also envisaged the creation of free export zones to promote trade by 1998. Liberalization of the coffee sector and the foreign exchange regime were also planned during 1996–1998.

According to statistics presented by the Belgian office of foreign trade, Rwanda also exported 538m. Belgian francs (some US $18m.) of precious stones and minerals in 1992, an amount which decreased to 523m. Belgian francs in 1993 and 133m. in 1994. Mining experts have suggested that these revenues, which do not feature in official Rwandan statistics, are derived from the re-export (possibly smuggled) of Congolese gold. Total exports to Belgium fell to 30m. Belgian francs in 1995, and increased only to 50m. Belgian francs in 1996, as a result of the closure of the Congolese border during those years. In 1997 the Congolese business association complained to the DRC government about the significant level of smuggling of Congolese gold and coffee to Rwanda. The Banque Nationale de Belgique estimated that gold exports from Rwanda amounted to Belgian francs 1,300m. in 1997 and to Belgian francs 1,084m. in 1998. In addition, according to IMF estimates, Rwandan gold and diamond exports amounted to $30m. in the first half of 1998. These figures, which indicated an intensification of the smuggling of precious minerals out of the DRC, prompted the UN security council to launch an investigation into the looting of the DRC resources by the warring parties.

STRUCTURAL ADJUSTMENT

One area of concern for the government was the low level of fiscal revenue, which was only 7% of GDP in 1995, compared with 12% in 1990, and which was equivalent to only 36% of total expenditure. In the 1996–1998 three-year programme the government aimed to curtail public expenditure. One of the challenges for the new authorities will be the application of stricter budgetary control and greater discipline in this area. Other problems facing the present government included the rationalization of the fiscal administration, the prioritization of long-term development expenditures and the restructuring, and in some cases the privatization, of state-owned companies. By mid-1996 the administration announced its intention to reform the taxation system by abolishing tax exemptions previously extended to new companies, and by increasing measures to suppress practices such as under-invoicing of import bills and smuggling, although a new tax on turnover provoked much criticism, including strike action, since companies demanded that the government return to the previous tax on profits. It was hoped that annual state receipts would increase from 322,500m. to 40,800m. Rwanda francs by 1998. However, in the event receipts registered a decline of 3,500m. Rwanda francs.

An agreement on a three-year programme of reforms was concluded with the IMF at a donors meeting in Stockholm, Sweden, in early June 1998. Both the IMF and the World Bank agreed loans with the Rwandan government, which expressed confidence that it would secure the additional funding for the programme's implementation. Rwanda committed itself to con-

tain the growth of public expenditure and improving the revenue to GDP ratio by strengthening tax administration, broadening the tax base and introducing a value-added tax on 1 July 2000. The tax advantages afforded to foreign investors remained the only point of controversy, as the government favoured the establishment of export processing areas in preference to adopting such measures. The 2000 budget was reduced by 2,000,000m. Rwandan francs, compared to 1999. Measures to curb customs fraud were adopted by late 1999, including the seizure of smuggled goods and of the vehicles which were used to transport them. In addition, the government announced a reduction of military expenditures to 3.2% of GDP for 2000, whereas 3,647 redundancies were eliminated during 1999. As a result of measures to increase the recovery of taxes, the government expected that tax receipts would amount to 7.2% of GDP in 2000. In April 1999 the World Bank afforded a $75m. loan to finance the programme of economic reforms. These funds are intended to help strengthen the capacity building in the administration, to help the government's launch of a privatization programme and to initiative several infrastructure projects. In May the EU decided to allocate 68m. euros to support Rwanda's budget. The EU programme aimed to avert the effects of the structural adjustment on the most vulnerable part of the population. However, despite donors' efforts, the government warned about a decline of the foreign assistance, with only one-half of the amounts pledged since 1994 being effectively disbursed by early 1999. In 2000, however, the EU announced the signature of a five-year programme of co-operation with Rwanda, with financing of 157m. euros.

Statistical Survey

Source (unless otherwise stated): Office rwandais d'information, BP 83, Kigali; tel. 75724.

Area and Population

AREA, POPULATION AND DENSITY

Area (sq km)	26,338*
Population (census results)	
15–16 August 1978	4,830,984
15 August 1991†	
Males	3,487,189
Females	3,677,805
Total	7,164,994
Population (UN estimates at mid-year)‡	
1996	5,475,000
1997	5,962,000
1998	6,604,000
Density (per sq km) at mid-1998	250.7

* 10,169 sq miles.
† Provisional results. The revised total is 7,142,755.
‡ Source: UN, *World Population Prospects: The 1998 Revision.*

PREFECTURES (1991 census)

	Area (sq km)	Population*	Density (per sq km)
Butare	1,830	765,910	418.5
Byumba	4,987	779,365	159.2
Cyangugu	2,226	517,550	232.5
Gikongoro	2,192	462,635	211.1
Gisenyi	2,395	728,365	304.1
Gitarama	2,241	849,285	379.0
Kibungo	4,134	647,175	156.5
Kibuye	1,320	472,525	358.0
Kigali	3,251 {	921,050 }	355.2
Kigali-Ville		233,640 }	
Ruhengeri	1,762	765,255	434.3
Total	**26,338**	**7,142,755**	**271.2**

* Source: UN, *Demographic Yearbook.*

PRINCIPAL TOWNS (population at 1978 census)

Kigali (capital) . . . 117,749		Ruhengeri 16,025
Butare . . . 21,691		Gisenyi 12,436

BIRTHS AND DEATHS (UN estimates, annual averages)

	1980–85	1985–90	1990–95
Birth rate (per 1,000) . . .	50.4	45.1	43.6
Death rate (per 1,000) . . .	18.6	16.5	42.9

Expectation of life (years at birth, 1990–95): 23.5 (males 22.9; females 24.0).

Source: UN, *World Population Prospects: The 1998 Revision.*

ECONOMICALLY ACTIVE POPULATION
(persons aged 14 years and over, official estimates at January 1989)

	Males	Females	Total
Agriculture, hunting, forestry and fishing	1,219,586	1,612,972	2,832,558
Mining and quarrying . . .	4,652	40	4,692
Manufacturing	32,605	12,483	45,088
Electricity, gas and water . .	2,445	116	2,561
Construction	37,674	563	38,237
Trade, restaurants and hotels .	61,169	18,857	80,026
Transport, storage and communications . . .	6,796	536	7,332
Financing, insurance, real estate and business services . .	2,202	926	3,128
Community, social and personal services	89,484	30,537	120,021
Activities not adequately defined .	5,392	4,021	9,413
Total employed	**1,462,005**	**1,681,051**	**3,143,056**

Source: ILO, *Yearbook of Labour Statistics.*

Mid-1998 (estimates, '000 persons): Agriculture, etc. 3,190; Total labour force 3,518 (Source: FAO, *Production Yearbook*).

Agriculture

PRINCIPAL CROPS ('000 metric tons)

	1996	1997	1998
Maize	67*	78*	78†
Sorghum	104*	130*	130†
Potatoes*	96	96	135
Sweet potatoes†	950	1,000	1,000
Cassava (Manioc)†	250	250	250
Yams†	4	4	4
Taro (Coco yam)*	39	47	32
Dry beans	105*	100†	120†
Dry peas	12†	8*	10*
Groundnuts (in shell)†	8	8	8
Plantains	2,105	2,248*	2,248†
Coffee (green)*	20	14	13
Tea (made)	6†	10*	10†

* Unofficial figure(s).   † FAO estimate(s).

Source: FAO, *Production Yearbook*.

LIVESTOCK (FAO estimates, '000 head, year ending September)

	1996	1997	1998
Cattle	475	500	500
Pigs	82	84	80
Sheep	260	270	270
Goats	950	980	980

Source: FAO, *Production Yearbook*.

LIVESTOCK PRODUCTS (FAO estimates, '000 metric tons)

	1996	1997	1998
Beef and veal	11	14	14
Goat meat	3	3	3
Pig meat	2	2	2
Other meat	10	10	10
Cows' milk	84	88	88
Goats' milk	14	14	14
Poultry eggs	2	2	2
Cattle hides	2	2	2

Source: FAO, *Production Yearbook*.

Forestry

ROUNDWOOD REMOVALS ('000 cubic metres, excluding bark)

	1990	1991	1992
Sawlogs, veneer logs and logs for sleepers	20	20	60
Other industrial wood	208	208	208
Fuel wood	5,353	5,392	5,392
Total	5,581	5,620	5,660

1993–97: Annual output assumed to be unchanged since 1992.

Source: FAO, *Yearbook of Forest Products*.

SAWNWOOD PRODUCTION

('000 cubic metres, including railway sleepers)

	1990	1991	1992
Total	8	8	36

1993–97: Annual output assumed to be unchanged since 1992.

Source: FAO, *Yearbook of Forest Products*.

Fishing

(FAO estimates, '000 metric tons, live weight)

	1995	1996	1997
Total catch (freshwater fishes)	3.3	3.0	3.1

Source: FAO, *Yearbook of Fishery Statistics*.

Mining*

(metric tons)

	1995	1996	1997
Tin concentrates	247.0	330.0	453.0
Tungsten concentrates	19.2	62.3	42.0
Columbo-tantalite	53.9	97.0	250.0

* Figures refer to the metal content of ores and concentrates.

Source: IMF, *Rwanda—Statistical Appendix* (October 1998).

Natural gas: about 1 million cubic metres per year.

Industry

SELECTED PRODUCTS

	1995	1996	1997
Beer ('000 hectolitres)	491	596	767
Soft drinks ('000 hectolitres)	137	184	248
Cigarettes (million)	40	129	253
Soap ('000 metric tons)	5	7	8
Cement ('000 metric tons)	36	42	61
Electric energy (million kWh)	54	71	110

Source: IMF, *Rwanda—Statistical Appendix* (October 1998).

Finance

CURRENCY AND EXCHANGE RATES

Monetary Units
100 centimes = 1 franc rwandais (Rwanda franc).

Sterling, Dollar and Euro Equivalents (28 April 2000)
£1 sterling = 582.5 Rwanda francs;
US $1 = 371.5 Rwanda francs;
€1 = 337.5 Rwanda francs;
1,000 Rwanda francs = £1.717 = $2.692 = €2.963.

Average Exchange Rate (Rwanda francs per US $)

1997   301.53
1998   312.31
1999   333.94

Note: Since September 1983 the currency has been linked to the IMF special drawing right (SDR). Until November 1990 the mid-point exchange rate was SDR 1 = 102.71 Rwanda francs. In November 1990 a new rate of SDR 1 = 171.18 Rwanda francs was established. This remained in effect until June 1992, when the rate was adjusted to SDR 1 = 201.39 Rwanda francs. The latter parity was maintained until February 1994, since when the rate has been frequently adjusted. In March 1995 the Government introduced a market-determined exchange rate system.

BUDGET ('000 million Rwanda francs)

Revenue*	1996	1997	1998†
Tax revenue	36.2	54.9	62.6
Taxes on income and profits .	10.0	14.2	17.8
Company profits tax . .	6.6	9.3	12.7
Individual income tax .	2.7	4.3	4.0
Domestic taxes on goods and services	14.4	21.9	28.5
Excise taxes	7.9	12.3	13.8
Turnover tax . . .	5.0	7.5	12.2
Road fund . . .	1.5	2.1	2.5
Taxes on international trade .	11.5	18.5	15.8
Import taxes . . .	10.7	13.5	13.7
Export taxes . . .	0.3	4.3	1.6
Non-tax revenue	3.2	3.1	3.4
Total	**39.4**	**58.1**	**66.0**

Expenditure‡	1996	1997	1998†
Current expenditure . . .	55.9	64.0	75.3
General public services . .	14.4	17.7	27.5
Defence	22.6	23.3	27.2
Social services . . .	10.0	13.9	14.7
Education	8.1	11.9	11.1
Health	1.4	1.5	2.6
Economic services . .	2.0	1.3	2.5
Energy and public works .	1.0	0.3	1.0
Interest on public debt . .	6.9	6.8	5.7
Capital expenditure . . .	39.4	46.1	42.3
Sub-total	**95.3**	**110.1**	**117.6**
Adjustment for payment arrears§ .	-9.4	-1.6	22.2
Total	**85.9**	**108.5**	**139.8**

* Excluding grants received ('000 million Rwandan francs): 31.4 in 1996; 37.8 in 1997; 33.0 in 1998 (estimate).
† Estimates.
‡ Excluding lending minus repayments ('000 million Rwanda francs): 0.0 in 1996; −0.5 in 1997; -0.2 in 1998.
§ Minus sign indicates increase in arrears.

Source: IMF, *Rwanda: Recent Economic Developments* (January 2000).

INTERNATIONAL BANK RESERVES (US $ million at 31 December)

	1997	1998	1999
IMF special drawing rights . .	26.50	24.44	14.46
Foreign exchange . . .	126.84	144.31	159.72
Total	**153.34**	**168.75**	**174.18**

Source: IMF, *International Financial Statistics*.

MONEY SUPPLY (million Rwanda francs at 31 December)

	1997	1998	1999
Currency outside banks . .	20,635	22,865	21,501
Demand deposits at deposit money banks	34,523	31,509	37,009
Total money (incl. others) . .	**55,746**	**55,291**	**59,237**

Source: IMF, *International Financial Statistics*.

COST OF LIVING
(Consumer Price Index for Kigali; base: 1990 = 100)

	1988	1989	1991
Food	92.5	95.2	113.6
Fuel and light	98.9	97.1	114.2
Clothing.	99.7	99.4	120.8
Rent	92.2	92.9	100.0
All items (incl. others) . .	**95.1**	**96.0**	**119.6**

1992: Food 121.6; All items 131.0.
1993: All items 147.2.
Source: ILO, *Yearbook of Labour Statistics*.

All items: (base: 1995 = 100): 107.4 in 1996; 120.3 in 1997; 127.8 in 1998; 124.7 in 1999 (Source: IMF, *International Financial Statistics*).

NATIONAL ACCOUNTS
(million Rwanda francs at current prices)
National Income and Product*

	1987	1988	1989
Compensation of employees . .	42,530	45,050	46,970
Operating surplus . . .	102,920	105,310	116,250
Domestic factor incomes .	**145,450**	**150,360**	**163,220**
Consumption of fixed capital . .	11,080	12,360	14,540
Gross domestic product (GDP) at factor cost. . . .	**156,530**	**162,720**	**177,760**
Indirect taxes . . .	14,910	15,460 ⎫	12,460
Less Subsidies	—	250 ⎬	
GDP in purchasers' values . .	**171,440**	**177,930**	**190,220**
Factor income from abroad . .	800	690	750
Less Factor income paid abroad .	3,540	4,260	2,980
Gross national product (GNP) .	**168,700**	**174,360**	**187,990**
Less Consumption of fixed capital .	11,080	12,360	14,540
National income in market prices	**157,620**	**162,000**	**173,450**
Other current transfers from abroad	6,290	7,120	6,470
Less Other current transfers paid abroad	2,010	1,950	1,810
National disposable income .	**161,900**	**167,170**	**178,110**

* Figures are rounded to the nearest 10 million francs.

Expenditure on the Gross Domestic Product*

	1997	1998	1999
Government final consumption expenditure . . .	49,900	54,500	61,200
Private final consumption expenditure	529,000	590,000	540,800
Increase in stocks . . ⎫			
Gross fixed capital formation . ⎬	84,500	99,500	114,300
Total domestic expenditure .	**663.400**	**744,000**	**716,300**
Exports of goods and services .	44,000	35,000	36,500
Less Imports of goods and services	143,000	147,000	117,100
GDP in purchasers' values . .	**561,600†**	**632,000**	**635,700**

* Figures are rounded to the nearest 100 million francs.
† Including adjustment.
Source: IMF, *International Financial Statistics*.

Gross Domestic Product by Economic Activity

	1995	1996	1997
Agriculture, hunting, forestry and fishing	126,787	156,806	205,133
Mining and quarrying . . .	81	135	195
Manufacturing	46,477	60,387	88,374
Electricity, gas and water. . .	1,382	1,653	2,019
Construction.	20,441	27,498	35,836
Trade, restaurants and hotels. .	56,992	68,526	87,568
Transport, storage and communications . . .	16,519	18,549	22,087
Public administration . . .	16,508	19,188	22,586
Other services	43,706	46,130	57,455
Sub-total	**328,893**	**401,051***	**521,253**
Indirect taxes	18,784	25,934	40,359
GDP in purchasers' values . .	**347,677**	**426,985**	**561,612**

* Incl. statistical discrepancy.
Source: IMF, *Rwanda—Statistical Appendix* (October 1998).

BALANCE OF PAYMENTS (US $ million)

	1996	1997	1998
Exports of goods f.o.b. . . .	61.7	93.2	64.5
Imports of goods f.o.b. . . .	−218.5	−278.2	−262.6
Trade balance	−156.8	−185.0	−198.1
Exports of services . . .	21.5	51.2	47.2
Imports of services . . .	−149.7	−198.3	−219.3
Balance on goods and services	−284.9	−332.1	−370.2
Other income received . .	5.4	8.0	8.8
Other income paid . . .	−18.8	−24.8	−17.3
Balance on goods, services and income	−298.3	−348.9	−378.7
Current transfers received . .	293.9	311.6	252.6
Current transfers paid . . .	−4.1	−24.9	−16.9
Current balance . . .	−8.5	−62.2	−143.0
Direct investment from abroad .	2.2	2.6	7.1
Portfolio investment assets . .	−0.1	—	n.a.
Other investment assets . .	−13.6	1.2	0.8
Other investment liabilities . .	36.3	43.0	−23.1
Net errors and omissions . .	4.1	45.9	29.7
Overall balance . . .	20.3	30.5	−128.4

Source: IMF, *International Financial Statistics*.

External Trade

PRINCIPAL COMMODITIES (million Rwanda francs)

Imports c.i.f.	1989	1990	1991
Consumer goods	7,610.7	n.a.	10,819.7
Food	2,323.8	2,673.0	4,366.9
Clothing	1,143.4	554.0	915.9
Mineral fuels and lubricants	3,850.5	3,689.2	4,913.1
Capital goods . . .	6,909.9	4,826.2	6,725.8
Transport equipment . .	1,832.5	901.8	1,322.2
Machinery and tools . .	3,969.5	2,496.0	4,260.6
Semi-manufactures . . .	8,329.3	7,999.0	16,015.9
Construction materials . .	1,570.0	1,316.1	1,486.5
Total (incl. others) . . .	26,700.4	23,057.4	38,474.5

Exports f.o.b.	1996	1997
Coffee	13,201	13,650
Tea	2,845	5,872
Cassiterite	249	295
Tungsten	36	40
Columbo-tantalite . . .	385	795
Hides and skins	975	1,379
Pyrethrum extract . . .	92	1,024
Quinquina bark	15	32
Total (incl. others) . . .	34,377	27,709

Sources: Banque Nationale du Rwanda; Ministère des Finances et de l'Economie; Ministère du Commerce, de l'Industrie et du Tourisme.

1994 (US $ million): *Imports c.i.f.:* Capital goods 36.0; Intermediate goods 22.8; Energy products 23.6; Food 218.1; Total (incl. others) 458.7. *Exports f.o.b.:* Coffee 17.4; Tea 5.8; Cassiterite and tin 0.5; Hides and skins 1.2; Pyrethrum and quinquina 0.3; Total (incl. others) 32.2.
1995 (US $ million): *Imports c.i.f.:* Capital goods 49.8; Intermediate goods 41.1; Energy products 21.8; Food 56.3; Total (incl. others) 238.2. *Exports f.o.b.:* Coffee 38.8; Tea 3.8; Cassiterite and tin 0.9; Hides and skins 2.2; Pyrethrum and quinquina 0.4; Total (incl. others) 50.4.
1996 (US $ million): *Imports c.i.f.:* Capital goods 54.1; Intermediate goods 54.7; Energy products 26.7; Food 50.6; Total (incl. others) 257.0. *Exports f.o.b.:* Coffee 43.2; Tea 9.3; Cassiterite and tin 0.8; Hides and skins 3.2; Pyrethrum and quinquina 0.3; Total (incl. others) 62.0.
1997 (US $ million): *Imports c.i.f.:* Capital goods 61.7; Intermediate goods 70.5; Energy products 32.0; Food 53.5; Total (incl. others) 342.9. *Exports f.o.b.:* Coffee 45.3; Tea 20.6; Cassiterite and tin 0.4; Hides and skins 2.2; Pyrethrum and quinquina 0.8; Total (incl. others) 93.0.
1998 (estimates, US $ million): *Imports c.i.f.:* Capital goods 60.7; Intermediate goods 68.5; Energy products 34.8; Food 49.3; Total (incl. others) 323.1. *Exports f.o.b.:* 26.7 ; Tea 22.9; Cassiterite and tin 0.4; Hides and skins 2.2; Pyrethrum and quinquina 0.8; Total (incl. others) 62.4.

Source: IMF, *Rwanda: Recent Economic Developments* (January 2000).

PRINCIPAL TRADING PARTNERS (million Rwanda francs)

Imports	1993	1994	1995
Belgium-Luxembourg . . .	7,702.7	2,631.1	8,257.5
Burundi	592.8	259.5	1,331.8
Canada	756.3	306.4	677.7
Denmark	613.2	127.7	2,721.1
France	3,152.2	1,192.0	2,000.2
Germany	2,875.4	841.4	3,278.0
Italy	1,106.6	2,631.1	1,135.6
Japan	4,647.5	1,205.7	2,476.5
Kenya	4,593.9	2,357.6	14,843.2
Netherlands	2,749.2	774.8	1,640.4
Singapore	534.4	12.4	262.9
Switzerland	784.1	139.0	1,053.5
Tanzania	4,110.8	1,361.0	3,781.1
Uganda	2,207.3	1,694.7	3,022.7
United Kingdom	1,290.8	608.9	1,486.7
USA	2,835.0	942.1	2,345.6
Total (incl. others) . . .	40,620.2	17,127.7	50,650.8

Exports	1993	1994	1995
Belgium-Luxembourg . . .	1,989.3	483.8	2,019.2
Burundi	86.3	99.5	802.0
Denmark	59.5	n.a.	124.5
France	67.3	16.1	538.4
Germany	2,393.1	423.9	1,128.4
Italy	268.9	63.2	386.5
Kenya	46.1	253.2	167.4
Netherlands	1,324.8	216.3	3,623.6
Switzerland	32.4	41.8	1,979.1
Uganda	66.1	923.2	198.3
United Kingdom	827.3	304.1	949.3
USA	25.3	131.5	98.3
Zaire	84.3	35.1	161.0
Total (incl. others) . . .	7,309.2	3,002.1	12,205.4

Source: Banque Nationale du Rwanda, Kigali.

Transport

ROAD TRAFFIC (motor vehicles in use at 31 December)

	1989	1990	1991
Motor cycles and scooters . . .	8,202	8,054	8,207
Passenger cars	8,135	9,255	10,217
Other vehicles	11,692	9,150	8,670
Total	28,029	26,459	27,094

Source: Banque Nationale du Rwanda, Kigali.

CIVIL AVIATION (traffic on scheduled services)

	1992	1993	1994
Passengers carried ('000) . . .	9	9	9
Passenger-km (million) . . .	2	2	2

Source: UN, *Statistical Yearbook*.

Tourism

	1995	1996	1997
Tourist arrivals ('000) . . .	1	1	1
Tourism receipts (US $ million) .	2	4	17

Source: World Tourism Organization, *Yearbook of Tourism Statistics*.

Communications Media

	1994	1995	1996
Radio receivers ('000 in use) . .	520	525	550
Telephones ('000 main lines in use)	15*	15*	15
Daily newspapers (number) . .	1	1	1

Telefax stations (number in use, 1992): 481.

1997: Radio receivers ('000 in use) 601.

* Provisional or estimated figure.

Sources: UN, *Statistical Yearbook,* and UNESCO, *Statistical Yearbook.*

Education

(1991/92, unless otherwise indicated)

	Insti-tutions	Teachers	Pupils		
			Males	Females	Total
Primary . . .	1,710	18,937	556,731	548,171	1,104,902
Secondary . .	n.a.	3,413	52,882	41,704	94,586
Tertiary* . .	n.a.	646	2,750	639	3,389

* Figures are for 1989/90.

Source: UNESCO, *Statistical Yearbook.*

Directory

The Constitution

On 10 June 1991 a series of amendments to the Constitution in force since 19 December 1978 received presidential assent. The document, as amended, provided, *inter alia*, for a multi-party polit-ical system, the separation of the functions of the executive, judiciary and legislature, the limitation of presidential tenure to a maximum of two consecutive five-year terms of office, the establishment of the office of Prime Minister, freedom of the press, and the right of workers to withdraw their labour. On 5 May 1995 the Transitional National Assembly introduced a new Constitution based on selected articles of the 1991 Constitution, the August 1993 Arusha peace accord, the FPR victory declaration of July 1994 and the multi-party protocol of understanding concluded in November 1994 (see Recent History).

The Government

HEAD OF STATE

President: Maj.-Gen. PAUL KAGAME (took office 22 April 2000).

COUNCIL OF MINISTERS
(September 2000)

A coalition council of national unity, comprising the Mouvement démocratique républicain (MDR), the Front patriotique rwandais (FPR), the Parti social-démocrate (PSD), the Parti libéral (PL), and the Parti démocratique islamique (PDI).

Prime Minister: BERNARD MAKUZA (MDR).

Minister of Defence and National Security: Col. EMMANUEL HABYARIMANA.

Minister for Local Government and Social Affairs: DÉSIRÉ NYANDWI (PSD).

Minister for Internal Affairs: THEOBALD RWAKA GAKWAYA.

Minister for Foreign Affairs and Regional Co-operation: ANDRÉ BUMAYA (PDI).

Minister for Finance and Economic Planning: Dr DONALD KAB-ERUKA (FPR).

Minister for Agriculture, Animal Resources and Forestry: Dr EPHRAIM KABAYIJA (FPR).

Minister of Education: EMMANUEL MUDIDI (FPR).

Minister of Energy, Water and Natural Resources: MARCEL BAHUNDE.

Minister of Public Works, Transport and Communications Protection: JEAN DE DIEU NTIRUHUNGWA (MDR).

Minister for Commerce, Industry and Tourism: Dr ALEXANDRE LYAMBABAJE.

Minister of Lands, Human Resettlement and Environment: Prof. LAURENT NKUSI.

Minister for Justice and Institutional Relations: JEAN DE DIEU MUCYO.

Minister for Public Service and Labour: SYLVIE ZAINAB KAYITESI.

Minister of Health: Dr EZECHIAS RWABUHIHI (FPR).

Minister of Gender and Women in Development: ANGELINE MUGANZA.

Minister of Youth and Sports: FRANÇOIS NGARAMBE (FPR).

MINISTRIES

Office of the President: BP 15, Kigali; tel. 75432.

Ministry of Agriculture, Animal Resources and Forestry: BP 621, Kigali; tel. 75324.

Ministry of Commerce, Industry and Tourism: BP 2378, Kigali; tel. 74725.

Ministry of Education: BP 624, Kigali; tel. 85422.

Ministry of Finance and Economic Planning: BP 158, Kigali; tel. 75410.

Ministry of Foreign Affairs and Regional Co-operation: BP 179, Kigali; tel. 75257.

Ministry of Health: BP 84, Kigali; tel. 77910; e-mail sgsante@rwandatel1.rwanda1.com.

Ministry of Internal Affairs: BP 446, Kigali; tel. 86708.

Ministry of Justice: BP 160, Kigali; tel. 866626.

Ministry of Local Government and Social Affairs: BP 790, Kigali; tel. 73481.

Ministry of the Public Service and Labour: BP 403, Kigali; tel. 86578.

Ministry of Public Works, Transport and Communications Protection: BP 24, Kigali; tel. 86649.

Ministry of Youth and Sports: BP 1044, Kigali; tel. 75861.

President and Legislature

PRESIDENT

On 17 April 2000 an electoral college, comprising members of the legislature and the Government, appointed the Chairman of the Front patriotique rwandais, Maj.-Gen. PAUL KAGAME, as President by 81 votes; his only opponent, CHARLES MURIGANDE, received five votes.

LEGISLATURE

The multi-party protocol of understanding in November 1994 agreed to a number of amendments to the August 1993 Arusha accord relating to the establishment of a transitional legislature. The new provisions excluded from all legislative processes members of those parties implicated in alleged acts of genocide during 1994.

A 70-member Transitional National Assembly was installed on 12 December 1994.

Speaker of the Transitional National Assembly: VINCENT BIRUTA.

Political Organizations

Coalition pour la défense de la République (CDR): Kigali; f. 1992; operates an unofficial Hutu militia known as Impuza-mugambi; banned by FPR in 1994 from participation in transitional Govt and legislature.

Front patriotique rwandais (FPR): f. 1990; also known as Inkot-anyi; comprises mainly Tutsi exiles, but claims multi-ethnic support; commenced armed invasion of Rwanda from Uganda in Oct. 1990; took control of Rwanda in July 1994; Chair. Maj.-Gen. PAUL KAGAME; Vice-Chair. PASTEUR BIZIMUNGU; Sec.-Gen. CHARLES MURIGANDE.

Mouvement démocratique républicain (MDR): Kigali; banned 1973–91; fmrly also known as Parti de l'émancipation du peuple

Hutu (Parmehutu), dominant party 1962–73; Chair. PIERRE CÉLÉSTIN RWIGYEMA; Exec. Sec. Dr CHRISTIAN MARARA.

Mouvement républicain national pour la démocratie et le développement (MRNDD): BP 1055, Kigali; f. 1975 as the Mouvement révolutionnaire national pour le développement (MRND); sole legal party until 1991; adopted present name in April 1991; draws support from hard-line Hutu elements; Chair. MATHIEU NGIRUMPATSE; operates unofficial militia known as Interahamwe (Leader ROBERT KADJUGA); banned by FPR in 1994 from participation in transitional Govt and legislature.

Parti démocrate chrétien (PDC): BP 2348, Kigali; tel. 76542; fax 72237; f. 1990; Leader JEAN NEPOMUCÈNE NAYINZIRA.

Parti démocratique islamique (PDI): Kigali; f. 1991.

Parti démocratique rwandais (Pader): Kigali; f. 1992; Sec. JEAN NTAGUNGIRA.

Parti écologiste (Peco): Kigali; f. 1992.

Parti libéral (PL): BP 1304, Kigali; tel. 77916; fax 77838; f. 1991; split into two factions in late 1993–early 1994: pro-MRNDD faction (led by JUSTIN MUGENZI and AGNÈS NTAMBYARIRO); anti-MRNDD faction (led by PROSPER HIGIRO, JOSEPH MUSENGIMANA and ESDRA KAYIRANGA).

Parti progressiste de la jeunesse rwandaise (PPJR): Kigali; f. 1991; Leader ANDRÉ HAKIZIMANA.

Parti républicain rwandais (Parerwa): Kigali; f. 1992; Leader AUGUSTIN MUTAMBA.

Parti social-démocrate (PSD): Kigali; f. 1991 by a breakaway faction of the MRND.

Parti socialiste rwandais (PSR): BP 827, Kigali; tel. 76658; fax 83975; f. 1991; workers' rights.

Le Peuple en Armes pour Libérer le Rwanda (Palir): Kigali; opposition grouping; in existence since 1996; armed wing L'Armée de Libération du Rwanda (Alir).

Rassemblement travailliste pour la démocratie (RTD): BP 1894, Kigali; tel. 75622; fax 76574; f. 1991; Leader EMMANUEL NIZEYIMANA.

Union démocratique du peuple rwandais (UDPR): Kigali; f. 1992; Pres. VINCENT GWABUKWISI; Vice-Pres. SYLVESTRE HUBI.

Other political organizations have been formed by exiled Rwandans and operate principally from abroad; these include:

Forces de résistance pour la démocratie (FRD): Brussels, Belgium; f. 1996 by moderate Hutu exiles; seeks return of Rwanda to UN Trust Territory status; Leader FAUSTIN TWAGIRAMUNGU.

Rassemblement pour le retour des réfugiés et la démocratie au Rwanda (RDR): Brussels, Belgium; f. 1995 by fmr supporters of Pres. Habyarimana; prin. org. representing Hutu refugees; Chair. FRANÇOIS NSABAHIMANA.

Union du peuple rwandais (UPR): Brussels, Belgium; f. 1990; Hutu-led; Pres. SILAS MAJYAMBERE; Sec.-Gen. EMMANUEL TWAGILIMANA.

Diplomatic Representation

EMBASSIES IN RWANDA

Belgium: rue Nyarugenge, BP 81, Kigali; tel. 75554; fax 73995; Ambassador: JEAN LINT.

Burundi: rue de Ntaruka, BP 714, Kigali; tel. 75010; Chargé d'affaires a.i.: CHARLES NSABIMANA.

Canada: rue Akagera, BP 1177, Kigali; tel. 73210; fax 72719; Ambassador: BERNARD DUSSAULT.

China, People's Republic: ave Député Kayuku, BP 1345, Kigali; tel. 75415; Ambassador: SHEN JIANKUAN.

Congo, Democratic Republic: 504 rue Longue, BP 169, Kigali; tel. 75289; Ambassador: (vacant).

Egypt: BP 1069, Kigali; tel. 82686; fax 82686; Ambassador: SAMEH SAMY DARWISH.

France: 40 ave Député Kamuzinzi, BP 53, Kigali; tel. 75225; Ambassador: JEAN-CLAUDE BROCHENIN.

Germany: 8 rue de Bugarama, BP 355, Kigali; tel. 75222; fax 77267; Ambassador: JOHANNA KÖNIG.

Holy See: 49 ave Paul VI, BP 261, Kigali (Apostolic Nunciature); tel. 75293; fax 75181; e-mail nuntrw@rwandatel1.rwanda1.com; Apostolic Nuncio: Most Rev. SALVATORE PENNACCHIO, Titular Archbishop of Montemarano.

Kenya: BP 1215, Kigali; tel. 82774; Ambassador: PETER KIHARA MATHANJUKI.

Korea, Democratic People's Republic: Kigali; Ambassador: RI KWANG ROK.

Libya: BP 1152, Kigali; tel. 76470; Secretary of the People's Bureau: MOUSTAPHA MASAND EL-GHAILUSHI.

Russia: 19 ave de l'Armée, BP 40, Kigali; tel. 75286; fax 74818; e-mail ambruss@rwandatel1.rwanda1.com; Ambassador: STANISLAV AKHMEDOV.

United Kingdom: Parcelle 1131, Blvd de l'Umuganda, Kacyiru, BP 576, Kigali; tel. 84098; fax 82044; Ambassador: GRAEME N. LOTEN.

USA: blvd de la Révolution, BP 28, Kigali; tel. 75601; fax 72128; Ambassador: GEORGE STAFFORD.

Judicial System

The judicial system comprises a Supreme Court, 12 Tribunals of First Instance and 143 Provincial Tribunals. Each type of court has a Public Prosecutor's Office. As well as these ordinary courts, specialized courts, such as military courts, can be created by law. The Supreme Court directs and co-ordinates the activities of all the Courts and Tribunals. It is divided into five sections, each of which is headed by a Vice-President, who, with the President of the Court, constitute its directorate.

In early 2000 a system of Gacaca (participatory) justice was established as a sixth section of the Supreme Court. Trials were to be conducted by councils in the communities in which they were committed and it was hoped that this system of justice would both alleviate pressure on the existing justice system, by reducing the number of detainees awaiting trial, and aid the process of reconciliation within Rwanda.

It was estimated that three-quarters of Rwanda's judges were killed during the violent political events of 1994.

SUPREME COURT

Chair of the Supreme Court: SIMON RWAGASORE.

Presiding Judge: BALTHAZAR KANOBANA.

Religion

AFRICAN RELIGIONS

About one-half of the population hold traditional beliefs.

CHRISTIANITY

Union des Eglises Rwandaises: BP 79, Kigali; tel. 85825; fax 83554; f. 1963; fmrly Conseil Protestant du Rwanda.

The Roman Catholic Church

Rwanda comprises one archdiocese and eight dioceses. At 31 December 1998 the estimated number of adherents represented about 47% of the total population.

Bishops' Conference: Conférence Episcopale du Rwanda, BP 357, Kigali; tel. 75439; f. 1980; Pres. (vacant).

Archbishop of Kigali: Most Rev. THADDÉE NTIHINYURWA, Archevêché, BP 715, Kigali; tel. 75769; fax 76371.

The Anglican Communion

The Church of the Province of Rwanda, established in 1992, has nine dioceses.

Archbishop of the Province and Bishop of Kigali: Most Rev. EMMANUEL MBONA KOLINI, BP 61, Kigali; tel. and fax 73213; e-mail sonja914@compuserve.com.

Provincial Secretary: Canon JOSIAS SENDEGEYA, BP 2487, Kigali; tel. 87566; fax 73213.

Other Protestant Churches

Eglise Baptiste: Nyantanga, BP 59, Butare; Pres. Rev. DAVID BAZIGA; Gen. Sec. ELEAZAR ZIHERAMBERE.

There are about 250,000 other Protestants, including a substantial minority of Seventh-day Adventists.

BAHÁ'Í FAITH

National Spiritual Assembly: BP 652, Kigali; tel. 75982.

ISLAM

There is a small Islamic community.

The Press

Bulletin Agricole du Rwanda: OCIR—Café, BP 104, Kigali-Gikondo; f. 1968; quarterly; French; Pres. of Editorial Bd Dr AUGUSTIN NZINDUKIYIMANA; circ. 800.

L'Ere de Liberté: BP 1755, Kigali; fortnightly.

Etudes Rwandaises: Université Nationale du Rwanda, Rectorat, BP 56, Butare; tel. 30302; f. 1977; quarterly; pure and applied science, literature, human sciences; French; Pres. of Editorial Bd CHARLES NTAKIRUTINKA; circ. 1,000.

Hobe: BP 761, Kigali; f. 1955; monthly; children's interest; Kinyarwanda; circ. 95,000.

Imboni: BP 694, Kigali; tel. 74520; fortnightly.

Ingoboka: BP 635, Kigali; fortnightly.

Inkingi: BP 969, Kigali; tel. 77626; fax 77543; monthly.

Inkoramutima: Union des Eglises Rwandaises, BP 79, Kigali; tel. 85825; fax 83554; quarterly; religious; circ. 5,000.

Intaremara: BP 83, Kigali; fortnightly.

Kaberinka: BP 83, Kigali; tel. 76182; fortnightly.

Kinyamateka: 5 blvd de l'OUA, BP 761, Kigali; tel. 76164; f. 1933; fortnightly; economics; circ. 11,000.

La Lettre du Cladho: BP 3060, Kigali; tel. 74292; monthly.

The New: BP 635, Kigali; tel. 73409; fax 74166; monthly.

Nouvelles du Rwanda: Université Nationale du Rwanda, BP 117, Butare; every 2 months.

Nyabarongo—Le Canard Déchaîné: BP 1585, Kigali; tel. 76674; monthly.

Le Partisan: BP 1805, Kigali; tel. 73923; fortnightly.

La Patrie–Urwatubyaye: BP 3125, Kigali; tel. 72552; monthly.

La Relève: Office Rwandais d'Information, BP 83, Kigali; tel. 75665; f. 1976; monthly; politics, economics, culture; French; Dir CHRISTOPHE MFIZI; circ. 1,700.

Revue Dialogue: BP 572, Kigali; tel. 74178; f. 1967; bi-monthly; Christian issues; Belgian-owned; circ. 2,500.

Rwanda Libération: BP 398, Kigali; tel 77710; monthly; Dir and Editor-in-Chief ANTOINE KAPITENI.

Revue Medicale Rwandaise: Ministry of Health, BP 84, Kigali; tel. 76681; f. 1968; quarterly; French.

Revue Pédagogique: Ministry of Education, BP 622, Kigali; tel. 85697; quarterly; French.

Rwanda Renaître: BP 426, Butare; fortnightly.

Rwanda Rushya: BP 83, Kigali; tel. 72276; fortnightly.

Le Tribun du Peuple: BP 1960, Kigali; tel. 82035; bi-monthly; owner JEAN-PIERRE MUGABE.

Ukuri Gacaca: BP 3170, Kigali; tel. 73327; monthly.

Umucunguzi: Gisenyi; f. 1998; organ of Palir; Kinyarwanda and French; Chief Editor EMILE NKUMBUYE.

Umuhinzi-Mworozi: OCIR—Thé, BP 104, Kigali; f. 1975; monthly; circ. 1,500.

Umusemburo—Le Levain: BP 117, Butare; monthly.

Urunana: Grand Séminaire de Nyakibanda, BP 85, Butare; tel. 30793; f. 1967; 3 a year; religious; Pres. THOMAS NAHIMANA; Editor-in-Chief ALEXANDRE KABERA.

NEWS AGENCIES

Agence Rwandaise de Presse (ARP): 27 ave du Commerce, BP 83, Kigali; tel. 75735; f. 1975.

Office Rwandais d'Information (Orinfor): BP 83, Kigali; tel. 75724; Dir JOSEPH BIDERI.

Foreign Bureau

Agence France-Presse (AFP): BP 83, Kigali; tel. 72997; Correspondent MARIE-GORETTI UWIBAMBE.

Publishers

Editions Rwandaises: Caritas Rwanda, BP 124, Kigali; tel. 5786; Man. Dir Abbé CYRIAQUE MUNYANSANGA; Editorial ALBERT NAMBAJE.

Implico: BP 721, Kigali; tel. 73771.

Imprimerie de Kabgayi: BP 66, Gitarama; tel. 62252; fax 62254; f. 1932; Dir THOMAS HABIMANA.

Imprimerie de Kigali, SARL: 1 Blvd de l'Umuganda, BP 956, Kigali; tel. 82032; fax 84047; e-mail impkig@rwandatel1.rwanda1.com; f. 1980; Dir THÉONESTE NSENGIMANA.

Imprimerie URWEGO: BP 762, Kigali; tel. 86027; Dir JEAN NSENGIYUNVA.

Pallotti-Presse: BP 863, Kigali; tel. 74084.

Government Publishing Houses

Imprimerie Nationale du Rwanda: BP 351, Kigali; tel. 76214; fax 75820; f. 1967; Dir JUVÉNAL NDISANZE.

Régie de l'Imprimerie Scolaire: BP 1347, Kigali; tel. 85695; fax 85695; e-mail imprisco@rwandatel1.rwanda1.com; f. 1985; Dir CELESTIN KAYITARE.

Broadcasting and Communications

TELECOMMUNICATIONS

Rwandatel: Kigali; majority state-owned; provides national telecommunications service.

MTN Rwandacell: Telecom House, Blvd de l'Umuganda, Kigali; f. 1998; provides mobile cellular telephone services; CEO FRANÇOIS DU PLESSIS.

BROADCASTING
Radio

Radio Rwanda: BP 83, Kigali; tel. 75665; fax 76185; f. 1961; state-controlled; daily broadcasts in Kinyarwanda, Swahili, French and English; Dir of Programmes DAVID KABUYE.

Deutsche Welle Relay Station Africa: Kigali; daily broadcasts in German, English, French, Hausa, Swahili, Portuguese and Amharic.

Television

Télévision rwandaise (TVR): Kigali; fax 75024; transmissions reach more than 60% of national territory.

Finance

(cap. = capital; res = reserves; dep. = deposits; m. = million; brs = branches; amounts in Rwanda francs)

BANKING
Central Bank

Banque Nationale du Rwanda: BP 531, Kigali; tel. 75249; fax 72551; e-mail nbank@rwandatel1.rwanda1.com; f. 1964; bank of issue; cap. 2,000m., res 4,574m., dep. 47,481m. (Dec. 1999); Gov. FRANÇOIS MUTEMBEREZI; Vice-Gov. Dr LAUREAN RUTAYISIRE.

Commercial Banks

Banque de Commerce, de Développement et d'Industrie (BCDI): BP 3268, Kigali; tel. 74143; fax 73790; cap. and res 982.0m., total assets 17,875.7m. (Dec. 1998); Pres. and Dir Gen. ALFRED KALISA.

Banque Commerciale du Rwanda, SA: BP 354, Kigali; tel. 75591; fax 73395; e-mail bcr@rwandatel1.rwanda1.com; internet www .bcr-rwanda.com; f. 1963; 44.5% state-owned; cap. and res 1,854m., total assets 40,154m. (Dec. 1998); Pres. FAUSTIN MUSARE; Gen. Man. JOHN MADDER; 5 brs.

Banque à la Confiance d'Or (BANCOR): ave du Commerce, BP 2509, Kigali; tel. and fax 75761; cap. and res 335.5m., total assets 1,391.5m. (Dec. 1998); Pres. ABID ALAM; Gen. Man. MANZUR ALAM.

Banque Continentale Africaine (Rwanda), SA (BACAR): 20 blvd de la Révolution, BP 331, Kigali; tel. 74456; fax 73486; e-mail bacar@rwandatel1.rwanda1.com; f. 1983; cap. and res 391.8m., total assets 9,602.7m. (Dec. 1998); Pres. VALENS KAJEGUHAKWA; Dir-Gen. EUSTACHE NDAYISABYE; 3 brs.

Banque de Kigali, SA: 63 ave du Commerce, BP 175, Kigali; tel. 76931; fax 73461; e-mail bkigi10@calva.com; f. 1966; cap. and res 1,063.9m. , total assets 34,304.1m. (Dec. 1998); Pres. PIUS NDAYAMBAJE; Gen. Man. MICHEL DEUCUYPER; 6 brs.

Caisse Hypothécaire du Rwanda (CHR): BP 1034, Kigali; tel. and fax 76796; cap. 237.5m., total assets 455.5m. (Dec. 1998); Pres. CLAUDINE ZANINKA; Gen. Man. FRANÇOIS NDUWUMWE.

Development Banks

Banque Rwandaise de Développement, SA (BRD): BP 1341, Kigali; tel. 75079; fax 73569; e-mail jbrd@rwandatel1.rwanda1.com; f. 1967; 56% state-owned; cap. and res 2,693.6m., total assets 6,615.0m. (Dec. 1998); Pres. EDITH GASANA.

Union des Banques Populaires du Rwanda (Banki z'Abaturage mu Rwanda): BP 1348, Kigali; tel. 73559; fax 73579; e-mail ubpd@rwandatel1.rwanda1.com; f. 1975; cap. 136.1m., dep. 4,919.9m. (Dec. 1993); Pres. INNOCENT KAYITARE; 145 brs.

INSURANCE

Société Nationale d'Assurances du Rwanda (SONARWA): BP 1035, Kigali; tel. 73350; fax 72052; e-mail sonarwa@rwandatel1 .rwanda1.com; f. 1975; cap. 500m.; Dir-Gen. HOPE MURERA.

Société Rwandaise d'Assurances, SA (SORAS): BP 924, Kigali; tel. 73716; fax 73362; f. 1984; cap. 201m.; Dir-Gen. (Admin.) CHARLES MHORANYI.

Trade and Industry

GOVERNMENT AGENCIES

Central Tender Board: Kigali; f. 1998 to promote effective and efficient procurement.

Centre for Investment Promotion: Kigali; f. 1998.

Rwanda Revenue Authority: Kigali; f. 1998 to maximize revenue collection; Commissioner-Gen. EDWARD LARBI SIAW.

DEVELOPMENT ORGANIZATIONS

Coopérative de Promotion de l'Industrie Minière et Artisanale au Rwanda (COOPIMAR): BP 1139, Kigali; tel. 82127; fax 72128; Dir DANY NZARAMBA.

Institut de Recherches Scientifiques et Technologiques (IRST): BP 227, Butare; tel. 30396; fax 30939; Dir-Gen. CHRYSOLOGUE KARANGWA.

Institut des Sciences Agronomiques du Rwanda (ISAR): BP 138, Butare; tel. 30642; fax 30644; for the development of subsistence and export agriculture; Dir MUNYANGANIZI BIKORO; 12 centres.

Office des Cultures Industrielles du Rwanda–Café (OCIR–Café): BP 104, Kigali; tel. 75600; fax 73992; e-mail ocircafe@ rwandatel1.rwanda1.com; f. 1978; development of coffee and other new agronomic industries; operates a coffee stabilization fund; Dir ANASTASE NZIRASANAHO.

Office des Cultures Industrielles du Rwanda–Thé (OCIR–Thé): BP 1344, Kigali; tel. 75956; fax 73943; development and marketing of tea; Dir JEAN BOSCO IYADEMA.

Office National pour le Développement de la Commercialisation des Produits Vivriers et des Produits Animaux (OPROVIA): BP 953, Kigali; tel. 82946; fax 82945; privatization pending in 1999; Dir DISMAS SEZIBERA.

Office du Pyrèthre du Rwanda (OPYRWA): BP 79, Ruhengeri; tel. 46306; fax 46364; f. 1978; cultivation and processing of pyrethrum; post-war activities resumed in Oct. 1994; current production estimated at 30% pre-war capacity; Dir SYLVAIN NZABAGAMBA.

Régie d'Exploitation et de Développement des Mines (REDEMI): BP 2195, Kigali; tel. 73632; fax 73625; f. 1988 as Régie des Mines du Rwanda; privatization pending 1999; state org. for mining tin, columbo-tantalite and wolfram; Man. Dir MARCEL BAHUNDE MIVUMBI.

Riziculture du Rwanda: Kigali; development and cultivation of rice; privatization pending; activities suspended in December 1997.

INDUSTRIAL ASSOCIATIONS

Association des Industriels du Rwanda: BP 39, Kigali; tel. and fax 75430; Pres. YVES LAFAGE; Exec. Sec. MUGUNGA NDOBA.

Federation of the Rwandan Private Sector Associations: Kigali; f. 1999; to represent interests of private sector; Exec. Sec. PIPIAN HAKIZABERA.

UTILITIES

Electrogaz: POB 537, Kigali; tel. 72392; fax 73802; state-owned water, electricity and gas supplier; Dir JOSEPH MUJENGA.

MAJOR COMPANIES

BRALIRWA: BP 131, Kigali; tel. 82995; fax 85693; f. 1959; mfrs and bottlers of beer in Gisenyi and soft drinks in Kigali.

Cimenterie du Rwanda (CIMERWA): Kigali; f. 1984; mfrs of cement; post-war activities resumed in Aug. 1994; 1995 production estimated at 60% of pre-war capacity.

Kabuye Sugar Works SARL: BP 373; Kigali; tel. 75468; fax 72865; f. 1969, privatized 1997; production of sugar to resume March 1998.

MIRONKO Plastic Industries: Kigali; tel. 76231; plastic wares.

Office de la Valorisation Industrielle de la Banane du Rwanda (OVIBAR): BP 1002, Kigali; tel. 85857; f. 1978; mfrs of banana wine and juice; post-war activities resumed in Dec. 1994; 1995 production estimated at only 1% of pre-war capacity; activities suspended; Dir ALOYS MUTAGANDA.

Rwanda Paints: BP 222, Kigali; tel. 75745; Admin. RAPHAËL RUZINDANA.

Rwandex Chillington: BP 356, Kigali; tel. 74736; produces agricultural equipment; Dir Gen. J. F. T. HAZEL.

RWANDEX CAFE: BP 356, Kigali; tel. 73968; Dir Gen. ALAIN VIGNERON.

Savonnerie de Kicukiro (SAKIRWA): BP 441, Kigali; tel. 72678; fax 75450; e-mail hram@rwandatel.1.rwanda1.com; soap and washing powders; edible oil refinery; Chair. H. RAMJI.

Société emballage–Rwanda: BP 1009, Kigali; tel. 75705; export of fruit and fruit products; production of soya- and cereal-based foods since 1997.

Société Industrielle du Rwanda: BP 338, Kigali; tel. 76613; Pres. F. X. MIRONKO.

Société Rwandaise d'Allumettes (SORWAL): BP 689, Butare; tel. 30028; Dir GABRIËL GAKUBA.

Société Rwandaise pour la Production et la Commercialisation du Thé (SORWATHE), SARL: Kigali; tel. 75461; f. 1978; tea; Dir ALLES.

Sulfo-Rwanda Industries, SA: BP 90, Kigali; tel. 75353; fax 74573; f. 1964; soap, cosmetics, plastic products, confectionery, mineral water; Chair. and Man. Dir TAJDIN HUSSAIN JAFFER; Gen. Man. VINOD THARAMAL.

TABARWANDA: BP 650, Kigali; tel. 85539; e-mail tbr@ rwandatel1.rwanda1.com; produces cigarettes; Dir PIE MUGABO.

Tôlerie Industrielle du Rwanda (TOLIRWA): BP 521, Kigali; tel. 72129; produces sheet metal; Dir Gen. JAFFER.

TRADE UNIONS

Centrale d'Education et de Coopération des Travailleurs pour le Développement/Alliance Coopérative au Rwanda (CECOTRAD/ACORWA): BP 295, Kigali; f. 1984; Pres. ELIE KATABARWA.

Centrale Syndicale des Travailleurs du Rwanda: BP 1645, Kigali; tel. 85658; fax 84012; e-mail cestrav@rwandatel1.rwanda1 .com; Sec.-Gen. FRANÇOIS MURANGIRA.

Transport

RAILWAYS

There are no railways in Rwanda, although plans exist for the eventual construction of a line passing through Uganda, Rwanda and Burundi, to connect with the Kigoma–Dar es Salaam line in Tanzania. Rwanda has access by road to the Tanzanian railways system.

ROADS

In 1990 there were 13,173 km of roads, of which 5,200 km were main roads. Around 954 km of roads were paved in 1993 and it was planned that the total length of this network would increase to 1,085 km by 1995. There are road links with Uganda, Tanzania, Burundi and the Democratic Republic of the Congo. Internal conflict during 1994 caused considerable damage to the road system, and to the destruction of several important bridges. In 1997 Rwanda received a US $45m. loan to be used for road improvement.

Office National des Transports en Commun (ONATRACOM): BP 609, Kigali; tel. 75564; Dir (vacant).

INLAND WATERWAYS

There are services on Lake Kivu between Cyangugu, Gisenyi and Kibuye, including two vessels operated by ONATRACOM.

CIVIL AVIATION

The Kanombe international airport at Kigali can process up to 500,000 passengers annually. There is a second international airport at Kamembe, near the border with the Democratic Republic of the Congo. There are airfields at Butare, Gabiro, Ruhengeri and Gisenyi, servicing internal flights.

Alliance Express Rwanda (ALEX): BP 808, Kigali; tel. 75492; fax 72562; f. 1998 to succeed fmr Air Rwanda as national carrier; 51% owned by Alliance Air (jtly owned by Govts of Uganda and South Africa and by South African Airways), 49% state-owned; domestic and regional passenger and cargo services; Chair. JUVENAL UWILINGIYIMANA.

Rwanda Airlines: BP 3246, Kigali; tel. 77564; fax 77669; f. 1998; privately-owned; operates one passenger aircraft; Chair. CHARLES NGARAMBE.

Tourism

Attractions for tourists include the flora and fauna of the national parks, Lake Kivu and fine mountain scenery. In 1996, when there were an estimated 1,000 foreign visitors to Rwanda, total receipts from tourism were estimated at US $1m.

Office rwandais du tourisme et des parcs nationaux (ORTPN): BP 905, Kigali; tel. 76515; fax 76512; f. 1973; govt agency.

Defence

In August 1999 the total strength of the army was estimated at 30,000–40,000 and there was a 7,000-strong paramilitary gendarmerie. An estimated 7,000 former government troops dispersed during recent fighting in the Democratic Republic of the Congo; a number of these have returned with associated Interahamwe militias.

Defence Expenditure: Estimated at 31,000m. Rwanda francs in 1997.

Chief of Staff of the Army: Brig-Gen. KAYUMBA NYAMWASA.

Education

Primary education, beginning at seven years of age and lasting for seven years, is officially compulsory. Secondary education, which is not compulsory, begins at the age of 15 and lasts for a further six years, comprising two equal cycles of three years. Schools are administered by the state and by Christian missions. In 1991 the enrolment at primary schools included an estimated 76% of children in the relevant age-group, but the comparable ratio for secondary enrolment was only 8%. In 1995, according to estimates by UNESCO, the average rate of adult illiteracy was 39.5% (males 30.2%; females 48.4%). Rwanda has a university, with campuses at Butare and Ruhengeri, and several other institutions of higher education, but some students attend universities abroad, particularly in Belgium, France or Germany. In 1991/92 there were 1,104,902 pupils enrolled at primary schools and 94,586 pupils enrolled at secondary schools, including agricultural and technical vocational schools. In 1989/90 an estimated 3,389 students were receiving higher education. In 1997 an estimated 10.4% of total government expenditure was allocated to education.

Bibliography

Abdulai, N. (Ed.). *Genocide in Rwanda: Background and Current Situation.* London, Africa Research and Information Centre, 1994.

Adelman, H., and Suhrke, A. (Eds). *The Path of a Genocide: The Rwanda Crisis from Uganda to Zaire.* Piscataway, NJ, Transaction Publishers, 1999.

Braekman, C. *Rwanda: Histoire d'un genocide.* Paris, Fayard, 1994.

Brauman, R. *Devant le mal. Rwanda, un génocide en direct.* Paris, Arléa, 1994.

Chrétien, J. P. *Rwanda, les Médias du génocide.* Paris, Editions Karthala, 1995.

Destexhe, A. *Rwanda and Genocide in the Twentieth Century.* London, Pluto Press, 1994.

Dorsey, L. *Historical Dictionary of Rwanda.* Lanham, MD, Scarecrow Press, 1999.

Dupaquier, J.-F. (Ed.). *La justice internationale face au drame rwandais.* Paris, Editions Karthala, 1996.

Guichaoua, A. (Ed.). *Les crises politiques au Burundi et au Rwanda (1993–1994).* Paris, Editions Karthala, 1995.

Harroy, J.-P. *Rwanda: de la féodalité à la démocratie: 1955–62.* Paris, Académie des Sciences d'Outre-mer.

d'Hertefelt, M., and de Lame, D. *Société, Culture et Histoire du Rwanda.* Tervuren, 1987.

Kagame, A. *Un abrégé de l'ethno-histoire du Rwanda.* Butare, Editions universitaires du Rwanda, 1972.

Kamukama, D. *Rwanda Conflict: Its Roots and Regional Implications.* Kampala, Fountain Publishers, 1993.

Keane, F. *Season of Blood: A Rwandan Journey.* London, Viking.

McCullum, H. *The Angels Have Left Us: The Rwanda Tragedy and the Churches.* Geneva, World Council of Churches.

Minear, L., and Guillot, P. *Soldiers to the Rescue: Humanitarian Lessons from Rwanda.* Paris, OECD, 1996.

Misser, F. *Vers un nouveau Rwanda?—Entretiens avec Paul Kagame.* Brussels, Editions Luc Pire, 1995.

Omaar, R. *Rwanda: Death, Despair and Defiance.* London, African Rights, 1994.

Prunier, G. *The Rwanda Crisis 1959–1964: History of a Genocide.* London, Hurst, 1995.

Reyntjens, F. *Pouvoir et droit au Rwanda: Droit public et évolution politique 1916–1973.* Tervuren, Musée royal de l'Afrique centrale, 1985.

L'Afrique des grands lacs en crise. Paris, Editions Karthala, 1994.

Sirven, P., Gotanegre, J.-F., and Prioul, G. *Géographie du Rwanda.* Brussels, Editions A. de Boeck, 1974.

Sparrow, J. *Under the Volcanoes: Rwanda's Refugee Crisis.* Geneva, Federation of Red Cross and Red Crescent Societies, 1994.

Vanderlinden, J. 'La République rwandaise', in *Encyclopédie politique et constitutionnelle.* Paris, Berger-Levrault, 1970.

Vidal, C. *Sociologie des passions—Côte d'Ivoire, Rwanda.* Editions Karthala, 1991.

Waller, D. *Rwanda: Which Way Now?* Oxford, Oxfam, 1993.

Willame, J.-C. *Aux sources de l'hécatombe rwandaise.* Paris, L'Harmattan, 1995.

ST HELENA
(WITH ASCENSION AND TRISTAN DA CUNHA)
Physical and Social Geography

St Helena, a rugged and mountainous island of volcanic origin, lies in the South Atlantic Ocean, latitude 16° S, longitude 5° 45' W, 1,131 km south-east of Ascension and about 1,930 km from the south-west coast of Africa. The island is 16.9 km long and 10.5 km broad, covering an area of 122 sq km (47 sq miles). The highest elevation, Diana's Peak, rises to 823 m above sea-level. The only inland waters are small streams, few of them perennial, fed by springs in the central hills. These streams and rainwater are sufficient for domestic water supplies and a few small irrigation schemes.

The cool South Atlantic trade winds are continuous throughout the year. The climate is sub-tropical and mild: the temperature in Jamestown, on the sea-coast, is 21°C–29°C in summer and 18°C–24°C in winter. Inland it is some 5°C cooler. Annual rainfall varies from 200 mm to 760 mm in the centre of the island.

The most recent census was held on 22 February 1987, when the total population was enumerated at 5,644. In mid-1994 the population was estimated to have risen to 6,472, giving a density of 53.0 inhabitants per sq km.

Jamestown, the capital, is the only town and had a population of 1,413 at the 1987 census.

The language of the island is English and the majority of the population belong to the Anglican communion.

St Helena has one of the world's most equable climates. Industrial pollution is absent from the atmosphere, and there are no endemic diseases of note. The island is of interest to naturalists for its rare flora and fauna; there are about 40 species of flora that are unique to St Helena.

Recent History

Revised by the Editor

The then uninhabited island of St Helena was discovered on 21 May 1502 by a Portuguese navigator, João da Nova, who named it in honour of Saint Helena, whose festival falls on that day. The existence of the island appears to have remained unknown to other European nations until 1588, when it was visited by the British navigator, Capt. Thomas Cavendish. In 1633 the Dutch formally claimed St Helena but made no attempt to occupy it. The British East India Co first established a settlement there in 1659, in order that the island might serve as a distant outpost from which to protect England's trade interests. The island was captured and briefly held by the Dutch in 1673. In that year a charter to occupy and govern St Helena was issued by King Charles II to the East India Co. In this charter the king confirmed the status of the island as a British outpost, and bestowed full rights of British citizenship on all those who settled on the island and on their descendants in perpetuity (see below). During 1815–21 the British government temporarily assumed direct control of the island, owing to the exile there at Longwood House of Napoleon Bonaparte. In 1834 control over the island's affairs was transferred on a permanent basis from the British East India Co to the British government. However, St Helena was administered by the foreign and colonial office (and classified as a colony), and not, as might have been expected, given its continuing use as a British outpost, by the war office or the admiralty. Its importance as a port of call on the trade route between Europe and India ceased with the opening of the Suez canal in 1869.

Temporary revivals in St Helena's importance as an outpost and as a place of exile occurred during the Zulu and Anglo-Boer wars and during the First and Second World Wars. However, further periods of economic depression followed. It has been alleged that efforts to render the island economically self-supporting overlook the fact that the island was originally occupied, not as a colony, but as a strategic base, which, given its isolation and lack of resources, never could be fully independent financially and would require substantial assistance on a permanent basis.

In 1968 a South African concern, the South Atlantic Trading and Investment Co, acquired ownership of Solomon & Co (St Helena) Ltd, the local trading company. However, in view of the latter's dominant role in the island's economy, the British government decided in 1974 to take full control of the enterprise. At the general election held in 1976, all but one of the 12 members elected to the legislative council strongly supported a policy of maintaining close economic links with the United Kingdom. This policy has been advocated by almost all members of the legislative council brought to office at subsequent elections (normally held every four years) up to and including that of July 1997.

In October 1981 the governor announced the appointment of a commission to review the island's constitution. The commission reported in 1983 that it was unable to find any proposal for constitutional change that would command the support of the majority of the islanders. In 1988, however, the government obtained the introduction of a formal constitution to replace the order in council and royal instructions under which St Helena was governed. This constitution entered into force on 1 January 1989.

St Helena's persistently high rate of unemployment (estimated at 20% in 1997) has resulted in widespread reliance on welfare benefit payments and a concurrent decline in living standards for the majority of the population. Underlying social discontent was expressed in two protest marches held in Jamestown during 1996, followed in April 1997 by an incident involving alleged arson attacks on police vehicles and a bus at Longwood. In the same month, the governor (who exercises full executive and legislative authority in St Helena) refused to accept the nomination of a prominent critic of government policy to the post of director of the department of social welfare. Two members of the executive council (which acts in an advisory capacity) resigned in protest at the action of the governor, who announced that elections to the legislative council would take place in July. Following the elections, held on 9 July, the governor agreed to the nomination as chairman of the education committee of the candidate he had previously refused to nominate to the social welfare directorate. The newly elected legislative council became the first in which members were to receive a fixed salary to serve on a full-time basis, relinquishing any other paid employment during their term of office.

Owing to the limited range of economic activity on the island, St Helena is dependent on development and budgetary aid from the United Kingdom. Since 1981, when the United Kingdom adopted the British Nationality Act, which effectively removed the islanders' traditional right of residence in Britain, opportunities for overseas employment have been limited to contract work, principally in Ascension and the Falkland Islands. In 1992 an informal 'commission on citizenship' was established by a number of islanders to examine St Helena's constitutional relationship with the United Kingdom, with special reference to the legal validity of the 1981 legislation as applied to St Helena. In April 1997 the commission obtained a legal opinion from a former acting attorney-general of St Helena to the effect that the application of the Act to the population of St Helena was in contravention of the royal charter establishing British sovereignty in 1673. The commission indicated that it intended to pursue the matter further. In July 1997 private legislation was introduced in the British parliament to extend full British nationality to 'persons having connections with' St Helena. In the following month the British government indicated that it was considering arrangements under which islanders would be granted employment and residence rights in the United Kingdom. In February 1998, following a conference held in

London of representatives of the British Dependent Territories, it was announced that a review was to take place of the future constitutional status of these territories, and of means whereby their economics might be strengthened. It was subsequently agreed that the operation of the 1981 legislation in relation to St Helena would also be reviewed. As an immediate measure to ameliorate the isolation of St Helena, the British government conceded permission for civilian air landing rights on Ascension Island, which, with the contemplated construction of a small airstrip on St Helena, could facilitate the future development of the island as a tourist destination. In March 1999 the British government published draft legislation proposing that full British nationality, including the right of abode in the United Kingdom, was to be restored to the population of St Helena and its dependencies, under the reorganization of the British Dependent Territories as the United Kingdom Overseas Territories. However, this had still not been implemented in July 2000, when the citizens took their case to the United Nations Committee on Decolonisation, in pursuit of British passports, a new constitution, and with a request for administration as a Crown dependency rather than as a colony.

Economy

Revised by the Editor

St Helena's principal crops are potatoes and vegetables. In the past the islanders grew formio (New Zealand flax), used in the manufacture of flax fibre (hemp). However, at the end of 1965 the market price of hemp fell sharply and production ceased in 1966.

Since 1979/80 increased benefits have been made available to private farmers in a major effort to encourage greater local production, local utilization and farming efficiency. Grants, loans (of capital and labour) and free technical assistance have been offered and an increasing number of full-time smallholders are taking advantage of the scheme. Two major irrigation schemes using butyl-lined reservoirs have been completed. Following a notable rise in food production in the early 1980s, more land is being rented or leased from the government for this purpose. The Agricultural Development Authority farmed approximately one-half the arable area and one-third of the grazing areas during 1975–96. Commonage grazing areas are now made available by government to private stock owners on a per caput per mensem basis. Individuals hold land either in fee simple or by lease. Immigrants require a licence to hold land. Crown land may be leased on conditions approved by the governor.

A major reafforestation programme was begun during the mid-1970s, aimed at replacing flax and fostering land reclamation. A sawmill/timber treatment plant, opened in 1977, produces a proportion of the timber needed for construction and fencing requirements, but most timber continues to be imported. No mineral resources have been identified.

Fish of many kinds are plentiful in the waters around St Helena, and a fisheries corporation was formed in 1979 to exploit this resource. A freezing/storage unit, built in 1977, is capable of storing 20 metric tons, allowing fish to be frozen for export as well as the local market. A drying and salting plant was built at Rupert's Bay in 1981 to process skipjack for export and a deep-sea fishing/survey vessel was acquired in 1982. Fish exports, which commenced in 1979, comprise tuna, skipjack and dried salted skipjack. In 1989 147 tons of fish were exported, mainly to the United Kingdom and South Africa, with a value of £125,842; in 1995 fish exports totalled 226 metric tons, and export revenue from this source amounted to £430,070. A small quantity of coffee is the only other commodity exported.

Unemployment is a serious problem, and a large proportion of the labour force (the employed population numbered 2,416 in April 1991) is forced to seek employment overseas, principally

on Ascension and the Falkland Islands. The rate of unemployment in St Helena was estimated at 20% in 1997, but was officially stated to have fallen to about 14% in the late 1990s. In March 1999 725 St Helenians were working on Ascension.

The main imports, by value, are foodstuffs, liquor, timber, motor spirit, fuel oils, animal feed, building materials, motor vehicles and parts, machinery and parts. Total imports for 1990/91 were valued at £5,774,351, of which 60.3% were supplied by the United Kingdom and 38.6% by South Africa.

In 1996/97 St Helena received about £8m. in British aid. Budget revenue (including budgetary aid of £3.56m.) totalled £10.46m. in 1995/96, and expenditure in that year balanced at £10.46m.

The St Helena Growers' Co-operative Society is the only such association on the island. It is both a consumers' and a marketing organization, and provides consumer goods, such as seeds, implements and feeding stuffs, to its members, and markets their produce, mainly vegetables, locally, to visiting ships and to Ascension Island. The local market is limited and is soon over-supplied, and this, together with the decrease in the number of ships calling over recent years, has inhibited the growth of this enterprise.

The only port in St Helena is Jamestown, which is an open roadstead with a good anchorage for ships of any size.

There is no airport or airstrip on St Helena and no railway, although a proposal was pending from the St Helena Leisure Corporation Ltd (Sheko) in 2000, for the construction of a small airport and the establishment of an airline. There are 98 km of all-weather roads, and a further 20 km of earth roads, which are used mainly by animal transport and are usable by motor vehicles only in dry weather. All roads have steep gradients and sharp curves.

In 1978, with the establishment of the St Helena Shipping Co, the St Helena government assumed responsibility for the operation and maintenance of a charter vessel, which carries cargo and passengers four times a year between Avonmouth, in the UK, and Cape Town, in South Africa, with calls at the Canary Islands, Ascension Island and St Helena, and to Tristan da Cunha once a year. The vessel currently operating this service entered operation in 1990. The St Helena Shipping Co receives an annual subsidy of more than £1m. from the British government. There is a bulk fuel farm at Rupert's Valley, which is supplied at approximately 3-month intervals with fuel from Europe.

Statistical Survey

AREA AND POPULATION

Area: 122 sq km (47 sq miles).

Population: 5,147 (males 2,514; females 2,633) at census of 31 October 1976; 5,644 (males 2,769; females 2,875) at census of 22 February 1987; 6,472 (males 3,324; females 3,148) at mid-1994 (official estimate).

Density (mid-1994): 53.0 per sq km.

Principal Town: Jamestown (capital), population 1,413 (1987 census).

Births and Deaths (1996): Registered live births 59; Registered deaths 44.

Economically Active Population (1987 census): Agriculture, hunting, forestry and fishing 137; Mining and quarrying 5; Electricity, gas and water 52; Construction 1,130; Trade, restaurants and hotels 302; Transport, storage and communications 216; Financing, insurance, real estate and business services 455; Community, social and personal services 156; Activities not adequately defined 63; Total employed 2,516 (males 1,607, females 909); Unemployed 281 (males 52, females 229); Total labour force 2,797 (males 1,659, females 1,138). Source: UN, *Demographic Yearbook*.

April 1991: Total employed 2,416.

AGRICULTURE, ETC.

Livestock (1994): Cattle 673; Sheep 1,051; Pigs 622; Goats 1,203; Poultry 8,814.

Fishing (metric tons, live weight, including Ascension and Tristan da Cunha): Total catch 818 in 1995; 726 in 1996; 847 in 1997. Figures include catches of rock lobster from Tristan da Cunha during the 12 months ending 30 April of the year stated. Source: FAO, *Yearbook of Fishery Statistics*.

FINANCE

Currency and Exchange Rate: 100 pence (pennies) = 1 St Helena pound (£). *Sterling, Dollar and Euro Equivalents* (28 April 2000):

£1 sterling = St Helena £1; US $1 = 63.77 pence; €1 = 57.94 pence; £100 = $156.81 = €172.60. *Average Exchange Rate* (US $ per £): 1.6377 in 1997; 1.6564 in 1998; 1.6182 in 1999. Note: The St Helena pound is at par with the pound sterling.

Budget (1995/96): *Revenue* £10,459,011 (including budgetary aid of £3,560,000); *Expenditure* £10,458,241.

Cost of Living (Consumer Price Index; base: 1990 = 100): 122.8 in 1994; 128.2 in 1995; 134.0 in 1996. Source: UN, *Monthly Bulletin of Statistics*.

EXTERNAL TRADE

Principal Commodities: *Imports* (1990/91): £5,774,351 (including food and drink £1,154,568, tobacco £107,273, motor spirits and fuel oils £423,824, animal feed £123,403, building materials £477,298, motor vehicles and parts £355,562, electrical equipment, other machinery and parts £757,090); *Exports* (1995): fish £430,070; coffee n.a. Trade is mainly with the United Kingdom and South Africa.

TRANSPORT

Road Traffic (1995): 1,663 vehicles in use.

Shipping (1995): Vessels entered 141; Merchant fleet (31 December 1998): 1 vessel (displacement 789 grt).

COMMUNICATIONS MEDIA

Radio Receivers ('000 in use, 1997): 3. Source: UNESCO, *Statistical Yearbook*.

Television Receivers ('000 in use, 1997): 2. Source: UNESCO, *Statistical Yearbook*.

Telephones ('000 main lines in use, 1995): 2. Source: UN, *Statistical Yearbook*.

EDUCATION

Primary (1997): 5 schools; 32 teachers; 404 pupils.

Intermediate (1997): 3 schools; 31 teachers; 303 pupils.

Secondary (1997): 1 school; 47 teachers; 446 pupils.

Directory

The Constitution

The St Helena Constitution Order 1988, which entered into force on 1 January 1989, replaced the Order in Council and Royal Instructions of 1 January 1967. Executive and legislative authority is reserved to the British Crown, but is ordinarily exercised by others in accordance with provisions of the Constitution. The Constitution provides for the office of Governor and Commander-in-Chief of St Helena and its dependencies (Ascension Island and Tristan da Cunha). The Legislative Council for St Helena consists of the Speaker, three *ex-officio* members (the Chief Secretary, the Financial Secretary and the Attorney-General) and 12 elected members; the Executive Council is presided over by the Governor and consists of the above *ex-officio* members and five of the elected members of the Legislative Council. The elected members of the legislature choose from among themselves those who will also be members of the Executive Council. Although a member of both the Legislative Council and the Executive Council, the Attorney-General does not vote on either. Members of the legislature provide the Chairmen and a majority of the members of the various Council Committees. Executive and legislative functions for the dependencies are exercised by the Governor.

The Government

(August 2000)

Governor and Commander-in-Chief: David J. Hollamby.

Chief Secretary: Michael Clancy.

Financial Secretary: Matthew Young.

Chairmen of Council Committees:

Agriculture and Natural Resources: (vacant).

Education: Robert M. Robertson.

Employment and Social Services: William E. Drabble.

Public Health: Eric W. George.

Public Works and Social Services: Stedson W. George.

GOVERNMENT OFFICES

Office of the Governor: The Castle, Jamestown; tel. 2555; fax 2598; e-mail ocs@helanta.sh.

Office of the Chief Secretary: The Castle, Jamestown; tel. 2555; fax 2598; e-mail ocs@helanta.sh.

Political Organizations

There are no political parties in St Helena. Elections to the Legislative Council, the latest of which took place in July 1997, are conducted on a non-partisan basis.

Judicial System

The legal system is derived from English common law and statutes. There are four Courts on St Helena: the Supreme Court, the Magistrate's Court, the Small Debts Court and the Juvenile Court. Provision exists for the St Helena Court of Appeal, which can sit in Jamestown or London.

Chief Justice: B. W. Martin (non-resident).

Attorney-General: Kurt De Freitas.

Sheriff: G. P. Musk.

Magistrates: J. Beadon, D. Bennett, D. Clarke, J. Corker, L. Crowie, J. Flagg, P. Francis, B. George, E. W. George, I. George, C. Lawrence, H. Legg, G. P. Musk, G. Sim, J. Thomas, D. Wade, C. Yon, P. Yon.

Religion

The majority of the population belongs to the Anglican Communion.

CHRISTIANITY
The Anglican Communion

Anglicans are adherents of the Church of the Province of Southern Africa. The Metropolitan of the Province is the Archbishop of Cape Town, South Africa. St Helena forms a single diocese.

Bishop of St Helena: Rt Rev. JOHN SALT, Bishopsholme, POB 62, St Helena; tel. 4471; fax 4330; e-mail bishop@helanta.sh; diocese f. 1859; has jurisdiction over the islands of St Helena and Ascension.

The Roman Catholic Church

The Church is represented in St Helena, Ascension and Tristan da Cunha by a Mission, established in August 1986. There were an estimated 87 adherents in the islands at 31 December 1998.

Superior: Rev. Fr ANTON AGREITER (also Prefect Apostolic of the Falkland Islands); normally visits Tristan da Cunha once a year and Ascension Island two or three times a year; Vicar Delegate Rev. Fr JOSEPH WHELAN, Sacred Heart Church, Jamestown; tel. and fax 2535.

Other Christian Churches

The Salvation Army, Seventh-day Adventists, Baptists, New Apostolics and Jehovah's Witnesses are active on the island.

BAHÁ'Í FAITH

There is a small Bahá'í community on the island.

The Press

St Helena News: St Helena News Media Board, Broadway House, Jamestown; tel. 2612; fax 2802; e-mail sthelena.news@helanta.sh; internet www.sthelena.gov.sh/sthelena; f. 1986; govt-sponsored; weekly; Editor JOHN DRUMMOND; circ. 1,300.

Broadcasting and Communications

TELECOMMUNICATIONS

Cable & Wireless PLC: The Moon, Jamestown; tel. 2200; e-mail webmaster@helanta.sh.

BROADCASTING

Cable & Wireless PLC: The Moon, Jamestown; tel. 2200; provides a two channel television service 24 hours daily from five satellite channels.

St Helena Radio: St Helena Information Office, Broadway House, Jamestown; tel. 4669; fax 4542; e-mail radio.sthelena@helanta.sh; govt service providing broadcasts for 81 hours weekly; local programming and relays of BBC World Service programmes; Station Man. ANTHONY D. LEO.

Finance

BANK

Government Savings Bank: Jamestown; tel. 2345; total deposits (31 March 1996): £8,782,269.

INSURANCE

Royal and SunAlliance Insurance Group PLC: Agents: Solomon & Co (St Helena) PLC, Jamestown; tel. 2523; fax 2423.

Trade and Industry

GOVERNMENT AGENCY

St Helena Development Agency: POB 117, Jamestown; tel. 2920; fax 2166; e-mail shda@helanta.sh.

CHAMBER OF COMMERCE

St Helena Chamber of Commerce: Jamestown.

CO-OPERATIVE

St Helena Growers' Co-operative Society: Jamestown; tel. and fax 2511; vegetable marketing; also suppliers of agricultural tools, seeds and animal feeding products; 108 mems (1999); Chair. STEDSON FRANCIS; Sec. PETER W. THORPE.

Transport

There are no railways or airfields in St Helena. Proposals were pending in 2000 for the construction of a small airfield.

ROADS

In 1995 there were 98 km of bitumen-sealed roads, and a further 20 km of earth roads, which can be used by motor vehicles only in dry weather. All roads have steep gradients and sharp bends.

SHIPPING

St Helena Line Ltd: Jamestown; mailing address: Curnow Shipping, 48/50 Killigrew St, Falmouth, Cornwall, TR11 3AP, United Kingdom; tel. (1326) 211466; fax (1326) 212808; e-mail admin@curnow-shipping.co.uk; internet www.curnow-shipping.co.uk; operates two-monthly passenger/cargo services by the RMS *St Helena* to and from the United Kingdom, calling at the Canary Islands, Ascension Island and Cape Town, South Africa, and occasionally at Tristan da Cunha; also operates programme of shuttle services between St Helena and Ascension Island; Man. Dir ANDREW BELL.

Tourism

Although St Helena possesses flora and fauna of considerable interest to naturalists, as well as the house (now an important museum) in which the French Emperor Napoleon I spent his final years in exile, the remoteness of the island, which is a two-day sea voyage from Ascension Island, has inhibited the development of tourism. Following the opening of air facilities on Ascension Island to civilian visitors, it is hoped that proposals to construct a small airfield on St Helena will proceed, thus increasing the island's accessibility to the limited number of visitors that can currently be accommodated.

Education

Education is compulsory and free for all children between the ages of five and 15 years, although power to exempt after the age of 14 can be exercised by the Education Committee. The standard of work at the secondary comprehensive school is orientated towards 'GCSE' and 'Advanced' Level requirements of the United Kingdom. During the second half of the 1980s, the educational structure was reorganized from a two-tier to a three-tier comprehensive system, for which a new upper-school building was constructed. Free part-time further education classes at London University 'GCSE' and 'Advanced' Level certificate standard are available. The adult literacy rate is 97%.

There is a free public library in Jamestown, financed by the government and managed by a committee, and a mobile library service in the country districts.

ASCENSION

The island of Ascension lies in the South Atlantic Ocean (7° 55′ S, 14° 20′ W), 1,131 km north-west of St Helena. It was discovered by a Portuguese expedition on Ascension Day 1501. The island was uninhabited until the arrival of Napoleon, the exiled French emperor, on St Helena in 1815, when a small British naval garrison was placed there. Ascension remained under the supervision of the British admiralty until 1922, when it was made a dependency of St Helena.

Ascension is a barren, rocky peak of purely volcanic origin, which was previously destitute of vegetation except above 450 m on Green Mountain (which rises to 875 m). The mountain supports a small farm producing vegetables and fruit. Since 1983 an alteration has taken place in the pattern of rainfall in Ascension. Total average annual rainfall has increased and the rain falls in heavy showers and is therefore less prone to evaporation. Grass, shrubs and flowers have grown in the valleys. These plants survived the dry periods experienced in 1987 and 1990. Some topsoil has been produced by the decay of previous growth and root systems. The island is famous for green turtles, which land there from December to May to lay their eggs in the sand. It is also a breeding ground of the sooty tern, or wideawake, vast numbers of which settle on the island every 10 months to lay and hatch their eggs. All wildlife except rabbits and cats is protected by law. Shark, barracuda, tuna, bonito and other fish are plentiful in the surrounding ocean. Following the decision by the British government in February 1998 to open airfield facilities on Ascension to civilian flights, a modest eco-tourism sector is being developed.

The population in March 1999 was 1,103 (excluding British military personnel), of whom 750 were St Helenians. The majority of the remainder were expatriate civilian personnel of Merlin Communications International (MCI), which operates the BBC Overseas World Service relay station; Cable and Wireless PLC, which provides international communications services and operates the 'Ariane' satellite tracking station of the European Space Agency; the US military base; and staff providing the island's common services. The island is an important communications centre. The BBC operates a relay station on the island, and a local broadcasting station has been established. Ascension does not raise its own finance; the costs of administering the island are borne collectively by the user organizations, supplemented by income from philatelic sales. Some revenue, which is remitted to the St Helena administration, is derived from fishing licences.

In 1942 the US government, by arrangement with the British government, established an air base, which it subsequently reoccupied and extended by agreement with the British government in 1956, in connection with the extension of the long-range proving ground for guided missiles, centred in Florida. A further agreement in 1965 allowed the USA to develop tracking facilities on the island in support of the National Aeronautics and Space Administration's 'Apollo' space programme. This operation was terminated in 1990.

Facilities on Ascension underwent rapid development in 1982 to serve as a major staging post for British vessels and aircraft on their way to the Falkland Islands, and the island has continued to provide a key link in British supply lines to the South Atlantic.

Area: 88 sq km (34 sq miles).

Population (March 1999): 1,103 (St Helenians 725, UK nationals 124, US nationals 254).

Budget (estimates for year ending 31 March 1999): Net expenditure £1,455,000.

Government: The Government of St Helena is represented by an Administrator. Two advisory groups, one comprising senior managers of resident organizations, and one comprising their employees' representatives, assist the Administrator.

Administrator: GEOFFREY FAIRHURST, The Residency, Georgetown, Ascension; tel. 6311; fax 6152; e-mail administrator@atlantis.co.ac; internet www.ascension-island.gov.ac.

Magistrate: GEOFFREY FAIRHURST.

Justices of the Peace: Mrs A. GEORGE, S. A. YOUDE, G. F. THOMAS, A. FOWLER, Mrs J. PETERS, Miss C. PARKER.

Religion: Ascension forms part of the Anglican diocese of St Helena, which normally provides a resident chaplain who is also available to minister to members of other denominations. There is a Roman Catholic chapel served by visiting priests, as well as a small mosque.

Transport (1998): *Road vehicles:* 830. *Shipping:* ships entered and cleared 105. The St Helena Line Ltd (q.v.) serves the island with a two-monthly passenger/cargo service between Cardiff, in the United Kingdom, and Cape Town, in South Africa. A vessel under charter to the British Ministry of Defence visits the island monthly on its United Kingdom–Falkland Islands service. A US freighter from Cape Canaveral calls at three-month intervals. *Air services:* A twice-weekly Royal Air Force Tristar service between the United Kingdom and the Falkland Islands transits Ascension Island both southbound and northbound. There is a weekly US Air Force military service linking the Patrick Air Force Base in Florida, USA, with Ascension Island, via Antigua.

Tourism: Small-scale eco-tourism is encouraged, although accommodation on the island is limited and all visits require written permission from the Administrator. Access is available by twice-weekly flights operated from the United Kingdom by the Royal Air Force (see above), and by the RMS *St Helena* (see St Helena—Shipping).

TRISTAN DA CUNHA

Tristan da Cunha lies in the South Atlantic Ocean, 2,800 km west of Cape Town, South Africa and 2,300 km south-west of St Helena. Also in the group are Inaccessible Island, 37 km west of Tristan; the three Nightingale Islands, 37 km south; and Gough Island (Diego Alvarez), 425 km south. Tristan is volcanic in origin and nearly circular in shape, covering an area of 98 sq km (38 sq miles) and rising in a cone to 2,060 m above sea-level. The climate is typically oceanic and temperate. Rainfall averages 1,675 mm per annum on the coast. The island provides breeding-grounds for albatrosses, rock-hopper penguins and seals, and a number of unique species, including the flightless land rail.

The British navy took possession of the island in 1816 during Napoleon's residence on St Helena, and a small garrison was stationed there. When the garrison was withdrawn, three men, headed by Cpl William Glass, elected to remain and became the founders of the present settlement. Because of its position on a main sailing route the colony thrived until the 1880s, but with the replacement of sail by steam a period of decline set in. No regular shipping called and the islanders suffered at times from a shortage of food. Nevertheless, attempts to move the inhabitants to South Africa were unsuccessful. The islanders were engaged chiefly in fishing and agricultural pursuits.

The United Society for the Propagation of the Gospel has maintained an interest in the island since 1922, and in 1932 one of its missionary teachers was officially recognized as honorary commissioner and magistrate. In 1938 Tristan da Cunha and the neighbouring uninhabited islands of Nightingale, Inaccessible and Gough were made dependencies of St Helena, and in 1950 the office of administrator was created. The administrator is also the magistrate. The island council was established in 1952.

In 1942 a meteorological and wireless station was built on the island by a detachment of the South African defence force and was manned by the Royal Navy for the remainder of the war. The coming of the navy reintroduced the islanders to the outside world, for it was a naval chaplain who recognized the possibilities of a crayfish industry on Tristan da Cunha. In 1948 a Cape Town-based fishing company was granted a concession to fish the Tristan da Cunha waters.

On 10 October 1961 a volcanic cone, thought to have been long extinct, erupted close to the settlement of Edinburgh and it was necessary to evacuate the island. The majority of the islanders returned to Tristan da Cunha in 1963. The administration was fully re-established, and the island council re-formed. The population in December 1996 was 288, including 6 expatriates.

The island is remote, and regular communications are restricted to about six calls each year by vessels from Cape Town (usually crayfish trawlers), an annual visit from a British vessel, the RMS *St Helena*, from Cape Town and the annual call by a South African vessel with supplies for the island and the weather station on Gough Island. There is, however, a wireless station on the island which is in daily contact with Cape Town. A local broadcasting service was introduced in 1966 and a closed-circuit television system operated between 1983 and 1989, when it was replaced by a video lending-library. In 1969 electricity was extended to all of the islanders' homes, and in the same year a radio-telephone service was established. A satellite system, which provides direct dialling for telephone and fax facilities, was installed in 1992, and radio telex was installed at the island radio station in 1994.

The island's major source of revenue derives from a royalty for the crayfishing concession, supplemented by income from the sale of postage stamps and other philatelic items, and handicrafts. The fishing industry and the administration employ all of the working population. Some 20 power boats operating from the island land their catches to a fish freezing factory built by the Atlantic Islands Development Corpn, whose fishing concession was transferred in January 1997 to a new holder, Premier Fishing (Pty) Ltd, of Cape Town. Premier also operates two large fishing vessels exporting the catch to the USA, France and Japan.

Estimated expenditure for the 1999/2000 financial year was £691,559 and revenue was estimated at £533,214. Development aid from the United Kingdom ceased in 1980, leaving the island financially self-sufficient. The United Kingdom, however, has continued to supply the cost of the salaries and passages of the administrator, a doctor and visiting specialists (a dentist every two years and an optician every two years).

Area: Tristan da Cunha 98 sq km (38 sq miles); Inaccessible Island 10 sq km (4 sq miles); Nightingale Island 2 sq km (¾ sq mile); Gough Island 91 sq km (35 sq miles).

Population (December 1999): 295 (including 11 expatriates) on Tristan; there is a small weather station on Gough Island, staffed, under agreement, by personnel employed by the South African Government.

Fishing (catch, metric tons, year ending 30 April): Tristan da Cunha rock lobster 344 in 1994/95; 327 in 1995/96; 321 in 1996/97. Source: FAO, *Yearbook of Fishery Statistics.*

Budget (estimates for 1999/2000): Revenue £533,214; Expenditure £691,559.

Government: The Administrator, representing the Government of St Helena, is assisted by an Island Council of eight elected members (of whom at least one must be a woman) and three appointed members, which has advisory powers in legislative and executive functions. The member receiving the largest number of votes at elections to the Council is appointed Chief Islander. The Council's advisory functions in executive matters are performed through 11 committees of the Council dealing with the separate branches of administration. The most recent election was held in October 1997.

Administrator: BRIAN P. BALDWIN, The Residency, Tristan da Cunha; tel. (satellite) 874-1445434; fax (satellite) 874-1445435; e-mail hmg@cunha.demon.co.uk.

Legal System: The Administrator is also the Magistrate and Coroner.

Religion: Adherents of the Anglican church predominate on Tristan da Cunha, which is within the Church of the Province of Southern Africa, and is under the jurisdiction of the Archbishop of Cape Town, South Africa. There is also a small number of Roman Catholics.

Transport: The St Helena Line Ltd (q.v.), the *MV Hanseatic,* and *MS Explorer* and the SA *Agulhas* each visit the island once each year, and two lobster concession vessels each make three visits annually, remaining for between two and three months. Occasional cruise ships also visit the island. There is no airfield.

Tourism: Permission from the Administrator and the Island Council is required for visits to Tristan da Cunha. Facilities for tourism are limited, although some accommodation is available in island homes.

Bibliography

Blackburn, J. *The Emperor's Last Island: A Journey to St Helena.* London, Secker and Warburg, 1992.

Blakeston, O. *Isle of Helena.* London, Sidgwick and Jackson, 1957.

Booy, D. M. *Rock of Exile: A Narrative of Tristan da Cunha.* London, Dent, 1957.

Castell, R. *St Helena: Island Fortress.* Old Amersham, Bucks, Byron Publicity Group, 1977.

Christopherson, E., et al. *Tristan da Cunha* (trans. R. L. Benham). London, Cassell, 1940.

Christopherson, E. (Ed.) *Results of the Norwegian Scientific Expedition to Tristan da Cunha, 1937–1938,* 16 parts. Oslo University Press, 1940–62.

Cohen, R. (Ed.) *African Islands and Enclaves.* London, Sage Publications, 1983.

Crawford, A. *Tristan da Cunha and the Roaring Forties.* Edinburgh, Charles Skilton, 1982.

Cross, T. *St Helena: with chapters on Ascension and Tristan da Cunha.* Newton Abbot, David and Charles, 1981.

Day, A. (Ed.) *St Helena, Ascension and Tristan da Cunha* (World Bibliographical Series, Vol. 197). Santa Barbara, ABC-Clio, 1997.

Falk-Ronne, A. *Back to Tristan.* London, Allen and Unwin, 1967.

Gosse, P. *St Helena, 1502–1938.* London, Thomas Nelson, 1990 (reissue).

Hart-Davis, D. *Ascension: The Story of a South Atlantic Island.* London, Constable, 1972.

Hughes, C. *Report of an enquiry into conditions on the Island of St Helena . . . (and) observations by the St Helena Government on Mr Hughes' report.* London, 1958.

Mackay, M. M. *Angry Island: The Story of Tristan da Cunha (1506–1963).* London, Barker, 1963.

Martineau, G. *Napoleon's St Helena.* London, John Murray, 1968.

Munch, P. A. *Crisis in Utopia: The Ordeal of Tristan da Cunha.* New York, Cromwell, 1971.

The St Helena Research Group. *A Strategic Profile of St Helena, 2000 Edition* (Strategic Planning Series). Icon Group International Inc, 2000.

Thompson, J. A. K. *Report on a Visit to Ascension Island.* St Helena Government Printer, 1947.

SÃO TOMÉ AND PRÍNCIPE

Physical and Social Geography

RENÉ PÉLISSIER

The archipelago forming the Democratic Republic of São Tomé and Príncipe is, after the Republic of Seychelles, the smallest independent state in Africa. Both the main islands are in the Gulf of Guinea on a south-west/north-east axis of extinct volcanoes. The boundaries take in the rocky islets of Caroço, Pedras and Tinhosas, off Príncipe, and, south of São Tomé, the Rôlas islet, which is bisected by the line of the Equator. The total area of the archipelago is 1,001 sq km (386.5 sq miles), of which São Tomé occupies an area of 854 sq km.

São Tomé is a plantation island where the eastern slopes and coastal flatlands are covered by huge cocoa estates (roças) formerly controlled by Portuguese interests, alongside a large number of local smallholders. These plantations have been carved out of an extremely dense mountainous jungle which dominates this equatorial island. The highest point is the Pico de São Tomé (2,024 m), surrounded by a dozen lesser cones above 1,000 m in height. Craggy and densely forested terrain is intersected by numerous streams. The coast of Príncipe is extremely jagged and indented by numerous bays. The highest elevation is the Pico de Príncipe (948 m). Both islands have a warm and moist climate, with an average yearly temperature of 25°C. Annual rainfall varies from over 5,100 mm on the south-western mountain slopes to under 1,020 mm in the northern lowlands. The dry season, known locally as gravana, lasts from June to September.

The total population was 117,504 at the census of 4 August 1991, when São Tomé had 112,033 inhabitants and Príncipe 5,471. The population was estimated by the United Nations at 141,000 in mid-1998, giving a density of 140.9 inhabitants per sq km. During 1990–98, according to the World Bank, the population increased by an annual average of 3.0%. The capital city is São Tomé, with an estimated 45,700 inhabitants in 1994. It is the main export centre of the island. Inland villages on São Tomé are mere clusters of houses of native islanders. Príncipe has only one small town of about 1,000 people, Santo António.

The native-born islanders (forros) are the descendants of imported slaves and southern Europeans who settled in the 16th and 17th centuries. Intermarriage was common, but subsequent influxes of Angolan and Mozambican contract workers until about 1950 re-Africanized the forros. Descendants of slaves who escaped from the sugar plantations from the 16th century onwards, who formed a formidable maroon enclave in the south of São Tomé and became known as Angolares, are now mainly fishermen.

The widespread exodus of skilled Portuguese plantation administrators, civil servants and traders during the period just prior to independence in July 1975, together with the departure of most of the Angolan and Mozambican workers and the repatriation of more than 10,000 São Tomé exiles from Angola, caused considerable economic dislocation, whose impact continues to be felt.

Recent History

GERHARD SEIBERT

São Tomé and Príncipe were colonized by Portugal in the 16th century. A nationalist group, the Comité de Libertação de São Tomé e Príncipe, was formed in 1960 and became the Movimento de Libertação de São Tomé e Príncipe (MLSTP) in 1972, under the leadership of Dr Manuel Pinto da Costa. Following the military coup in Portugal in April 1974, the Portuguese government recognized the right of the islands to independence, although negotiations were delayed until September. In December Portugal appointed a transitional government which included members of the MLSTP, which was recognized as the sole legitimate representative of the people. At elections for a constituent assembly held in July 1975, the MLSTP won all 16 seats. Independence as the Democratic Republic of São Tomé and Príncipe took effect on 12 July, with Pinto da Costa as president and Miguel Trovoada as prime minister. The constitution promulgated in November effectively vested absolute power in the president and the political bureau of the MLSTP. Radical socialist policies were introduced, and any activity deemed contrary to MLSTP directives was viewed as treason.

MLSTP GOVERNMENT

During 1976–82 serious ideological as well as personal divisions arose within the MLSTP, and a number of prominent members who favoured a more moderate approach to social, economic and agrarian reforms were forced into exile. In March 1978 Angolan soldiers were brought to the islands, following an alleged attempt to overthrow the government. In March 1979 Dr Carlos da Graça, a former minister of health who had left

for Gabon in 1977, was tried in absentia and sentenced to 24 years' imprisonment. In April 1979 Trovoada was dismissed as prime minister. In September he was arrested, accused of complicity in the census riots of the previous month and detained without trial until 1981, when he was permitted to leave the islands. In December 1981 rioting broke out on Príncipe, where food shortages had led to agitation for that island's autonomy. During 1982 Leonel d'Alva, a former prime minister and minister of foreign affairs, fled to exile in Cape Verde, and Daniel Daio, the minister of defence and national security, was removed from office.

In its foreign relations, São Tomé and Príncipe avoided any formal commitment to the Eastern bloc, although close economic ties existed with the People's Republic of China and the German Democratic Republic. Cuba and the USSR provided the regime with military advisers. Gabon, the islands' nearest mainland neighbour, viewed these developments with disquiet, and relations consequently deteriorated. However, the republic extended the range of its international contacts by joining the International Monetary Fund (IMF) in 1977, acceding to the Lomé Convention in 1978 and participating in the foundation of the francophone Communauté économique des états de l'Afrique central (CEEAC) in 1983. The bulk of the country's trade continued to be transacted with Western Europe, and relations with Portugal remained generally cordial.

In 1985, confronted by the threat of the complete collapse of the economy, Pinto da Costa began to abandon economic ties with the Eastern bloc in favour of capitalist strategies. Trade agreements with Eastern bloc countries were allowed to lapse, and Pinto da Costa and his ministers made extensive visits to Western Europe and North America to solicit support for measures of economic liberalization. The two main Western nations seeking to exert influence in the country were Portugal and France; however, trade with Portugal was much more substantial than with France, and negotiations concerning São Tomé's admission to the Franc Zone were eventually inconclusive. The USA accredited its first ambassador to São Tomé in 1985, and provided the country with a limited amount of military aid.

Political Change

In October 1987 the central committee of the MLSTP announced major political and constitutional changes, including the election by universal suffrage of the head of state, and of members of the national people's assembly by secret ballot, as well as the admission of different political currents within the party. In January 1988 the post of prime minister was reintroduced, to which Celestino Rocha da Costa, the former minister of education, labour and social security, was appointed. Da Graça, who had been pardoned in 1985, was appointed minister of foreign affairs. However, Miguel Trovoada, who had been invited to return from exile, remained in France, stating that he regarded the changes as insufficient. By 1987 three small overseas opposition groups were already in existence: the Frente de Resistência Nacional de São Tomé e Príncipe (FRNSTP), the Acção Democrática Nacional de São Tomé e Príncipe (ADNSTP) and the União Democrática Independente de São Tomé e Príncipe (UDISTP). In March 1988 Afonso dos Santos, a former member of the FRNSTP, led an expedition of 44 men from his headquarters in Cameroon, in an attempt to invade São Tomé and seize power. The operation was poorly executed and the invaders were captured. In September 1989 dos Santos was sentenced to 22 years' imprisonment and other defendants received custodial sentences.

Increasingly concerned by the country's economic problems, and encouraged by a progressive faction within the party, the MLSTP embarked, in late 1989, on a transition to full multiparty democracy. In August 1990, in a national referendum, 72% of the electorate approved the introduction of the new constitution, proposed by the MLSTP central committee, which provided for a multi-party political system, and a maximum of two five-year terms of office for the president. At the MLSTP party congress, held in October 1990, da Graça succeeded Manuel Pinto da Costa as secretary-general. In addition, the party's name was amended to the Movimiento de Libertação de São Tomé e Príncipe–Partido Social Democrata (MLSTP–PSD). Also in that year dos Santos, who had been granted an amnesty, founded the Frente Democrata Cristã (FDC); also, the Coligação Democrática de Oposição (CODO), a merger of the three opposition groups formerly in exile, was formed, under the leadership of Albertino Neto. However, the major challenge to the ruling party came from the Partido de Convergência Democrática–Grupo de Reflexão (PCD–GR), a coalition of former MLSTP dissidents, independents and young professionals, under the leadership of Leonel d'Alva.

At elections to the new national assembly, held on 20 January 1991, the MLSTP–PSD secured only 30.5% of the total votes and 21 seats, while the PCD–GR obtained 54% of the votes and 33 seats; CODO took the one remaining seat. In February a transitional government, headed by Daniel Daio, was installed, pending the forthcoming presidential election; President Pinto da Costa confirmed his decision not to run in the election. The MLSTP–PCD did not present an alternative candidate, and two of the three remaining candidates subsequently withdrew from the election. On 3 March Miguel Trovoada, the sole remaining contender, was elected president, receiving 82% of the votes cast. Trovoada took office the following month and officially inaugurated the PCD–GR government, headed by Daio.

THE TROVOADA PRESIDENCY

In early 1992 a political crisis erupted when co-operation between the government and the presidency began to break down. The PCD–GR, which wished to limit the extent of powers granted to the president under the constitution of September 1990, attempted to introduce a constitutional amendment limit-

ing the presidential powers. Meanwhile, widespread popular dissatisfaction followed the imposition in June 1991 of stringent austerity measures that had been imposed by the IMF and the World Bank as preconditions for economic assistance. These measures, which included a 40% devaluation of the currency and a substantial increase in petroleum prices, had contributed to a sharp decline in the islanders' living standards. Following two mass demonstrations held in April 1992 to protest against the austerity programme, Trovoada dismissed the Daio government, citing as his main reason the 'institutional disloyalty' of the prime minister, who had publicly blamed the president for the country's economic plight and attendant political unrest. The PCD–GR, which initially condemned Trovoada's actions as an 'institutional coup', was invited to designate a new prime minister. In May Norberto Costa Alegre (the minister of economy and finance in the former administration, who had been instrumental in the negotiation of the structural adjustment measures) replaced Daio as prime minister and formed a new administration.

On 6 December 1992, in the first local elections to be held since independence, the PCD–GR suffered a considerable reverse, obtaining only 15 of the total of 61 seats and failing to gain outright control of any of the seven districts. Conversely, the MLSTP–PSD won 38 seats and gained control of five districts. The newly formed Acção Democrática Independente (ADI) won the remaining eight seats and secured control of one district. However, the government refused to accede to opposition demands that it resign, form a government of national unity or call new legislative elections.

In February 1993 Daio resigned as secretary-general of the ruling PCD–GR, and in April was replaced, in an interim capacity, by the more moderate João do Sacramento Bonfim. Opposition expectation that the appointment of Bonfim would facilitate political dialogue, and perhaps lead to the formation of a government of national unity, proved unfounded; in November four opposition parties issued a joint statement accusing the government of authoritarianism and incompetence, and, in turn, were accused of fomenting instability.

In April 1994 the national assembly began discussion of a draft bill providing local autonomy for the island of Príncipe. Its proposals, which were approved later that year, included provision for the creation of a regional assembly and a five-member regional government.

In early 1994 relations between the government and the presidency again began to deteriorate. In April Trovoada publicly dissociated himself from government policy. In June political tension increased when the PCD–GR accused Trovoada of systematic obstruction of the government's programme. The same month opposition parties petitioned the president to dismiss the government and to appoint foreign auditors to investigate the management of public funds under its term of office. On 2 July 1994 Trovoada dismissed the Alegre administration citing 'institutional conflict' as the justification for the decision. Moreover, the president accused the ruling party of ignoring presidential vetoes and of attempting to replace the semi-presidential system with a parliamentary regime without executive powers for the head of state. On 4 July Trovoada appointed Evaristo do Espírito Santo de Carvalho (the minister of defence and security in the outgoing administration) as prime minister. The PCD–GR, which refused to participate in the new government, subsequently expelled Carvalho from the party. An interim administration, comprising eight ministers, took office on 9 July. On the following day, in an attempt to resolve the political crisis, Trovoada dissolved the national assembly and announced that a legislative election would be held on 2 October.

This election resulted in a decisive victory for the MLSTP–PSD, which secured 27 seats, one short of an absolute majority. The PCD–GR and the ADI each obtained 14 seats. The level of voter participation, which was as low as 52%, was believed to reflect public disillusionment at the failure of democracy immediately to realize expectations of a transformation in the country's social and economic prospects. In late October 1994 da Graça was appointed prime minister and subsequently announced his intention to form a government of national unity with those parties represented in the legislature. However, both the ADI and the PCD–GR rejected the proposal.

The council of ministers that took office in late October thus was comprised almost entirely of members of the MLSTP–PSD.

Social and Economic Problems

In early February 1995 the government appealed for international aid to mitigate the economic effects of the imminent return of some 6,000–7,000 Santomeans from Gabon, from where all immigrants who had not by that month legalized their status were to be expelled. In the event some 1,500 migrant workers were forced to return to São Tomé. In April about 50 returnees attempted to occupy the prime minister's office in protest at the alleged disappearance of foreign funds intended to support their reintegration.

In mid-February 1995 the government announced that a general salary increase, of 64%–90%, for public- and private-sector employees would be introduced at the end of the month, in an effort to assuage increasing social tension caused by the constantly rising cost of living. Later that month, with the aim of securing the release of suspended funds from the World Bank, the government announced the introduction of austerity measures, including a 25% increase in fuel prices, the dismissal of some 300 civil servants, and an increase in interest rates.

In March 1995 the first elections to a new seven-member regional assembly and five-member regional government were conducted on Príncipe, which had been granted local autonomy by the national assembly in 1994. The elections resulted in victory for the MLSTP–PSD, which won an absolute majority. The ADI and the PCD–GR did not themselves offer candidates, but instead supported a local opposition group. The new regional government began functioning in April. At the end of March 1995, a privatization agreement with an Angolan commercial enterprise, the Mello Xavier Group, provoked a wave of protest in the country. The agreement provided for Mello Xavier to assume control of the Porto Alegre cocoa estate and gave the Angolan company priority in the privatization of a further four non-agricultural enterprises. In addition, the government was to grant Mello Xavier a concession for offshore banking. Both Trovoada and the opposition parties strongly rejected the agreement, and, in the light of the protest, Mello Xavier did not pursue the original agreement. In early 1996 Mello Xavier finally acquired the management contract for the Porto Alegre estate.

In early June 1995 the police assumed control of the national radio station following several days of strike action by employees of the station in support of salary increases of up to 300%. In the wake of the dispute the government suspended a 350% salary increase awarded earlier to bank employees, and created a commission to review state administration salaries. Social unrest continued in the following months with teachers and doctors striking in support of demands for increased salaries and improved working conditions. In June the minister of planning and finance, Carlos Quaresma Batista da Sousa, relinquished the post and assumed fully the position of governor of the central bank, a post which he had held in an acting capacity since December 1994. The finance portfolio was assumed by the minister of economic affairs, Joaquim Rafael Branco.

Coup Attempt

On 15 August 1995 a group of some 30 soldiers, led by five junior officers of the armed forces, seized control of the presidential palace. Trovoada was detained at the headquarters of the armed forces, da Graça was placed under house arrest and a curfew imposed. The insurgents cited widespread corruption and political incompetence as justification for the coup. São Tomé's principal aid donors, including the USA and Portugal, immediately condemned the coup and demanded the reinstatement of constitutional order under penalty of the withdrawal of development assistance. Confronted by both international pressure and the lack of professionals to establish a military regime, the five-member military commission, headed by Lt Manuel Quintas de Almeida, abandoned its initial proposal to establish a junta of national salvation and began negotiations with Trovoada, the government and political parties. Talks were mediated by an Angolan delegation, led by the Angolan minister of foreign affairs, Dr Venâncio da Silva Moura. Six days after the initial coup attempt, the military insurgents and the government signed a 'memorandum of understanding', providing for the reinstatement of Trovoada and the restoration of constitutional order. In return, the government gave an undertaking to restructure the armed forces, and the national assembly granted a general amnesty to all those involved in the coup. Following the coup attempt, Alberto Paulino was replaced as minister of defence by Capt. Carlos Carneiro Paquete da Silva. In early September da Silva's appointment as c-in-c of the army prompted a protest by the officers who had promoted the coup, on the grounds that it contravened the 'memorandum of understanding'. As a consequence, da Silva was replaced in that role by Capt. António do Nascimento. In a national address that month Trovoada expressed his wish to form a government of national unity in order to establish a more stable foundation for government. In addition, he acknowledged the high level of corruption prevalent in São Tomé and the rising incidence of crime.

Consensus Government

At the end of December 1995 Armindo Vaz d'Almeida was appointed prime minister, at the head of the government of national unity. The new administration, which took office in early January 1996, included six members of the MLSTP–PSD, four members of the ADI and one of the PDSTP–CODO. The PCD–GR, however, refused to participate in the new government. In February 1996, at the request of the national electoral commission, the forthcoming presidential election, which had been scheduled for early March, was postponed pending the finalization of the electoral rolls. In March the date of the election was set for 30 June, and in early April the national assembly approved the extension of the existing presidential mandate by a further five months. At the congress of the MLSTP–PSD, held in March, Pinto da Costa was selected as the party's official candidate in the forthcoming presidential election, while Francisco Fortunato Pires was appointed secretary-general of the party. In April Trovoada declared his candidacy for the presidential election, in which he was supported by the ADI and the PDSTP–CODO.

At the presidential election of 30 June 1996 no candidate secured an absolute majority. Consequently, a second ballot, between the two leading candidates, was conducted on 21 July, at which Trovoada won 52.74% of the votes, defeating Pinto da Costa, who secured 47.26% of the votes. In late July da Costa, who had initially acknowledged Trovoada's victory, contested the results of the election, claiming that irregularities had occurred in the registration process. In early August the supreme court declared that it was unable to adjudicate on the appeal made by Pinto da Costa, and recommended that the government seek international legal arbitration. However, on 20 August Pinto da Costa withdrew his challenge and Trovoada was confirmed as president. In mid-September the Vaz d'Almeida administration was dissolved, following its defeat in a confidence motion in the national assembly. The motion had been proposed by Vaz d'Almeida's own party, the MLSTP–PSD, which accused the government of inefficiency and corruption, and had received the support of the PCD–GR. Vaz d'Almeida remained as prime minister in a caretaker capacity, pending the appointment of a successor. In late October the MLSTP–PSD and the PCD–GR signed an accord providing for the establishment of a nine-member coalition government. In mid-November, following Trovoada's refusal earlier that month to appoint Fortunato Pires as prime minister, the president appointed Raúl Wagner da Conceição Bragança Neto, assistant secretary-general of the MLSTP–PSD, to the position. The new coalition government, which included five members of the MLSTP–PSD, three members of the PCD–GR and one independent, was inaugurated later that month. The ADI had refused to participate in the new administration.

In July 1996 São Tomé and Príncipe was among the five lusophone African countries which, together with Portugal and Brazil, formed the Comunidade dos Países de Língua Portuguesa (CPLP), a Portuguese-speaking commonwealth seeking to achieve collective benefits from co-operation in technical, cultural and social matters.

In mid-August 1996 demonstrators blockaded roads in the capital in protest at the shortage of energy and water supplies. The demonstration had been prompted by reports that the government had spent US $500,000 of state funds, derived from a structural adjustment credit disbursed in January, on luxury cars for government ministers. Several injuries resulted as riot police were deployed to disperse the demonstrators.

In December 1996 the Bragança administration accused the former government of Vaz d'Almeida of corrupt practices, including embezzlement and the illegal diversion of public funds. Earlier that month Vaz d'Almeida had been expelled by the MLSTP–PSD, having declined the party's request that he volunteer his resignation. In mid-December the MLSTP–PSD and the PCD–GR presented the national assembly with a proposal for a revision of the constitution. The proposal, which aimed to redefine the extent of the powers invested in the president, included provision for the establishment of a state council which would have to be consulted before the president could dissolve the legislature. In addition, the president would no longer direct foreign policy. Whilst Trovoada recognised the need for a review of the constitution, he favoured a strengthening of the presidential powers and advocated the replacement of the existing semi-presidential system with a presidential regime.

In April 1997, as part of an initiative to promote national reconciliation and political stability, Trovoada held discussions with former president Pinto da Costa. In order to end the continuous political struggle between the presidency and the government, Trovoada proposed the creation of a unity forum for national reconciliation to debate the country's problems.

In April 1997 an increase of some 140% in fuel prices, and a concomitant rise in the prices of transport, food and consumer goods, precipitated violent popular protests in São Tomé city. Hundreds of anti-government demonstrators blockaded roads, and the security forces were deployed to quell rioting. In that month the government announced a 200% salary increase for the public sector. The announcement was criticized by the IMF, which stressed that the increase would hinder efforts to control the budget deficit, and recommended that the government postpone the increase, pending a rationalization of the civil service (which would entail the dismissal of some 1,000 employees).

Following Trovoada's unilateral decision in May 1997 to establish diplomatic relations with Taiwan, in July the People's Republic of China (PRC) suspended diplomatic relations with São Tomé, ceased all development co-operation, and demanded the repayment, within 90 days, of bilateral debts amounting to US $17m. In exchange for diplomatic recognition, Taiwan promised São Tomé $30m. in development aid over a three-year period. Trovoada declared that, in view of the economic condition of São Tomé, the Taiwanese aid could not be rejected. By contrast, the government declared that the aid promised by Taiwan could not compensate for the loss of the long-standing co-operation enjoyed with the PRC. Since 1975 the PRC had granted donations totalling $32.7m., as well as providing interest-free loans totalling $18.7m. Consequently, the government refused to accept $4.3m. in aid offered by Taiwan and prohibited its officials from receiving the four high-ranking diplomats appointed to represent Taiwan in São Tomé. In October, in order to avoid an open conflict with Trovoada, the government withdrew its opposition to the diplomatic recognition of Taiwan and subsequently accepted the Taiwanese development aid. In January 1998 Taiwan's ambassador presented his credentials to Trovoada.

In mid-March 1998 the country's 3,750 civil servants organized an indefinite strike in support of demands for the payment of salary arrears; when, in September 1997, the government had agreed to increase civil servants' salaries by 200%–300%, it had promised to pay the new salaries retroactively for the first six months of that year, but subsequently failed to do so. The strike ended after three days, when the government produced a schedule for the payment of the arrears. In May 1998 members of the armed forces at São Tomé international airport prevented the minister of finance and planning, Acácio Elba Bonfim, from leaving the country. The troops detained Bonfim, who was on his way to attend a meeting of the African Development Bank, to demand the payment of promised salary increases. The situation was resolved following renewed promises of payment by the prime minister and the minister of defence and internal security.

The Prime Ministership of Pósser da Costa

At an extraordinary congress of the MLSTP–PSD held in May 1998, the former president and party leader, Manuel Pinto da Costa, was elected unopposed as president of the party. (The ruling party of Angola, the Movimento Popular de Libertação de Angola (MPLA) had made the resumption of financial support for the MLSTP–PSD conditional on Pinto da Costa's election; following his defeat in the 1996 presidential election, the MPLA had ceased payments, creating serious problems for the MLSTP–PSD). New party statutes were approved, creating the position of party president, together with three vice-presidential posts. The party's national council was enlarged from 95 to 120 members and it subsequently elected three vice-presidents: Dionísio Dias, the party's parliamentary leader, became vice-president for party affairs, Guilherme Pósser da Costa, a former minister of foreign affairs, was appointed vice-president for parliamentary affairs, and Damião Vaz d'Almeida, the president of the regional government of Príncipe, was elected vice-president for issues related to Príncipe. The former secretary-general of the party, Francisco Fortunato Pires, refused to assume any leading position within the party and declared the new leadership structure to be unsuitable.

At a legislative election held on 8 November 1998 (postponed from October owing to delays in the electoral process) the MLSTP–PSD secured a majority, with 31 seats, while the ADI won 16 seats and the PCD obtained the remaining eight seats. The level of voter participation was 64.7%, considerably lower than at the 1996 presidential election, but higher than at the 1994 legislative election. In December 1998 Pósser da Costa was appointed prime minister. However, the MLSTP–PSD accused Trovoada of interfering in areas outside his jurisdiction when, later that month, he vetoed Pósser da Costa's initial nominations for the council of ministers. A revised council of ministers was finally installed on 5 January 1999. At the instigation of the IMF, the number of ministries was limited to nine; responsibility for international co-operation was assumed by the ministry of finance and planning, while the portfolios of agriculture, fishing, industry, tourism and trade were combined in a single ministry, of the economy. At his inauguration Pósser da Costa promised to re-establish the authority of the state, reinforce the law, restore macroeconomic stability and combat mass poverty. On 18 March the national assembly approved the government's programme.

In July 1999 a new ministry of public administration and labour was created as part of a reorganization of the council of minsters, following the resignation of Alberto Paulino as minister of foreign affairs: Paolo Jorge Rodrigues do Espírito Santo was appointed as his replacement, and Paulino was appointed minister of justice and minister adjunct to the prime minister. In August an amendment to the electoral law was passed by the national assembly, granting citizens of Comunidade dos Países de Lingua Portuguesa (CPLP) member states who had been resident in São Tomé and Príncipe for longer than two years the right to vote in local, legislative and presidential elections.

In January 2000 an estimated 3,500 civil servants and public-sector workers demanded an increase in the minimum wage from 40,000 dobras to 600,000 dobras. The government had earlier offered a minimum wage of 120,000 dobras, in accordance with IMF recommendations not to increase the total expenditure on salaries by more than 7%. The public-sector unions subsequently scaled down their demands to 350,000 dobras. In late February negotiations between the two parties broke off without an agreement. In April, however, the unions accepted the government's proposal to increase the minimum wage to 170,000 dobras, and a pledge to resume wage negotiations in August of that year.

In mid-April 2000 the minister of foreign affairs and co-operation, Paulo Jorge do Espírito Santo, resigned, following rumours of disagreements with President Trovoada; he was replaced by the former deputy secretary of the CPLP, Joaquim Rafael Branco. The minister of justice, Alberto Paulino, took on the additional portfolio of minister of public administration and labour, while the youth and sports portfolios were integrated into the ministries of education and health respectively.

Financial Scandal

In March 1999 the governor of the central bank, Carlos Quaresma, was dismissed for his alleged involvement in corrupt financial practices. The allegations arose following the detention in Brussels, Belgium, two months earlier of three men who had attempted to sell falsified Santomean treasury bonds worth US $500m. The bonds bore the signature of Quaresma, who allegedly had links with the men concerned. Maria do Carmo Trovoada Silveira was appointed to replace Quaresma. The government subsequently appointed a commission comprising the ministers of planning, finance and co-operation and of justice and parliamentary affairs, to conduct an inquiry into the case. In their report, released in mid-March, the commission concluded that the bonds had been issued illegally and the case was referred to the attorney-general for investigation. Quaresma, meanwhile, denied all allegations of corruption and declared that the deal had been intended to finance development projects in the country and that former prime ministers Vaz d'Almeida and Bragança, and President Trovoada, had been completely aware of the proceedings. Trovoada immediately denied these allegations. In late March the minister of planning, finance and co-operation, Afonso da Graça Varela da Silva, resigned; he was replaced by Adelino Castelo David. In mid-April the Belgian authorities issued an international warrant of arrest against Quaresma. In May the national assembly lifted Quaresma's parliamentary immunity to allow him to be questioned by the office of the attorney-general. Quaresma was detained in October 1999, but in March 2000, following the discovery of a document signed by the former prime minister Armindo Vaz d'Almeida ordering the issue of the treasury bonds, he was released by the supreme court. Vaz d'Almeida denied the allegations, stating that the document had been falsified. In April the former director of the foreign exchange department of the central bank, Leonel Vagante, was accused of tranferring government money from a French account into his own private account, allegedly to help finance the sale and purchase of motor vehicles. In May Vagante was sentenced to 18 years' imprisonment, and was ordered to pay 5.5m French francs to the government in compensation.

REGIONAL RELATIONS

In November 1999 São Tomé and Príncipe became a founder of the seven-member Gulf of Guinea Commission; it was hoped that the commission would assist in solving inter-state conflicts within the region. In January 2000 37 Santomean soldiers took part in an international military manoeuvre, known as 'Gabon 2000', which included military personnel from seven other central African countries; technical assistance was offered by eight western nations. The military exercise was part of the French-inspired Programme for the Reinforcement of African Capacities for Peace Maintenance (RECAMP), which, it was hoped, would help to establish a capacity for intra-African peace-keeping interventions. There were also plans for the CPLP member states to establish a peace-keeping force.

Economy

GERHARD SEIBERT

The economy of São Tomé and Príncipe, which is based almost exclusively on the export of cocoa, has experienced a long period of decline since independence in 1975. The sudden loss of protected markets in Portugal and the mass exodus of skilled personnel were compounded by the negative effects of systematic nationalizations and the relentless fall in the world price of cocoa after 1979. According to estimates by the World Bank, São Tomé's GDP increased, in real terms, by an annual average of 1.0% in 1985–95. Real GDP growth in 1996 was 1.2%, 1.0% in 1997 and 2.5% in both 1998 and 1999. The government target for 2000 was 3.0%. GDP growth was projected to increase to 4.0% by 2002. During 1990–98, it was estimated, gross national product (GNP) per head declined, in real terms, at an average annual rate of 1.0%. Over the same period the population increased by an average of 3.0% per year. In 1998 some 26.3% of GDP was derived from the primary sector, 11.4% from the secondary sector, and 62.3% from the tertiary sector, the latter figure mainly reflecting the considerable size of the bureaucracy.

The Marxist economic policies implemented during the decade following independence contributed to the country's economic deterioration. President Pinto da Costa decided at independence to nationalize virtually all enterprises of any size. The government also took a monopoly of foreign trade, and controlled prices and distribution through a network of 'people's shops'. São Tomé became a member of the International Monetary Fund (IMF) and the World Bank in 1977, and introduced a new currency unit, the dobra, to replace the Portuguese escudo at par. The dobra became increasingly overvalued, placing considerable strain on the balance of payments, but the government refused to devalue the currency.

In 1985, confronted by the threat of economic collapse, the president initiated a process of economic liberalization. Foreign companies were invited to bid for management contracts for the state farms, and a cautious process of privatization of the non-agricultural sector was begun. In 1986, the 'people's shops' were leased to private traders, a new investment code was promulgated to attract foreign capital, and a donors' conference was held. Following discussions during 1986 with the World Bank and the IMF, the government widened the scope of its reforms with the introduction in 1987 of a three-year structural adjustment programme (SAP). This aimed to reduce the large trade and budget deficits, to increase agricultural production, to stimulate exports, and to increase foreign earnings from tourism and fishing. The SAP included measures to restructure the public investment programme and unprofitable public enterprises, to liberalize prices, and to improve incentives for investment by the private sector. The SAP received financial support from the World Bank and the African Development Bank (ADB).

The first step in the SAP was taken in July 1987, when the government devalued the dobra by 54.75%, and increased duties on local and imported consumer goods by between 15% and 150%. Price controls were abolished on many goods, and wages were increased by 10%–30% to compensate for the higher prices. Reductions in government spending were announced and taxes were raised. Foreign trade was liberalized with the abolition of the monopoly of the state enterprise, Ecomex, over the import and export of goods. In 1988 the dobra was again devalued, by about 20%, and the prices of consumer goods and fuels were raised by 60%–100%. In an attempt to compensate for the steep increase in prices, the wages of workers in the agricultural sector and agro-based industries were increased by 15%. The value of the dobra drifted downwards towards parallel rates, while further adjustments to controlled prices were made to bring these rates closer to market levels. Public sector wages were raised periodically, but did not keep pace with the cost of living. In recognition of these reforms, a donors' meeting in Geneva in 1989 pledged new loans and a rescheduling of debts, and in June the IMF approved a three-year SDR 2.8m. structural adjustment facility (SAF). The resultant structural adjustment programme, however, began to lose momentum in 1990, as the government subordinated economic concerns to its own survival. The IMF suspended payments under the SAF, and the World Bank threatened to do the same. The budget deficit increased to $4.5m., and inflation reached 47%. Additionally, the gap between official and parallel rates of exchange widened, and foreign exchange reserves were severely depleted.

The priority of the government since 1991 has been a return to fiscal and economic austerity in accordance with the IMF and World Bank guidelines. The currency was repeatedly devalued and by June 1993 the dobra was trading officially at approximately US $1 = 425 dobras, while 'black market' rates stood at about US $1 = 600 dobras. This was outside the 15% margin between official and parallel market rates demanded by the IMF. By mid-1992 the IMF indicated that enough progress had been made for payments under the SAF to be resumed. This was a precondition to addressing the probblem of the country's high level of external debt, estimated at $215m. at the end of 1991. In 1993 the total external debt stood at $254m., of which $225.8m. was long-term debt. In that year total external debt per caput was some $2,100, while GDP per caput, measured at average 1991–93 prices, was only $330. In the 1994 budget 13,000m. dobras, of a projected total expenditure of 18,000m. dobras, were set aside for external debt financing.

In early 1994 the World Bank threatened to suspend structural adjustment credits due to delays in the implementation of agreed economic adjustment measures. Subsequently São Tomé failed to qualify for an IMF enhanced structural adjustment facility (ESAF). However, despite its criticism of the slow pace of the restructuring of public enterprises, a World Bank mission indicated in June that it would recommend the release of US $10m. in structural adjustment credits.

In 1994 the current account of the balance of payments, which had recorded a surplus equivalent to 1.3% of GDP in 1991–93, registered a deficit equivalent to 9.6% of GDP. Inflation increased from 20% in 1993 to 40% in 1994. By September 1994 none of the public finance targets set by the IMF had been met. Owing principally to the shortfall of contributions from state enterprises, only 71% of projected receipts of 4,400m. dobras were realized. Current expenditure (excluding interest payments on debt) totalled 3,700m. dobras, representing 83.1% of total projected expenditure for the nine-month period, while only 5.4% of 2,900m. dobras in programmed interest payments on the external debt had been paid. Instead of a surplus of 1,040m. dobras, as scheduled by the IMF for the 1994 national budget, by September the deficit (excluding interest payments on debt) had already reached 442.4m. dobras. In order to reverse the negative trend, in December 1994 the government increased fuel prices by some 30%. In addition the official and free market exchange rates were unified. Successive devaluations of the currency implemented during 1994 totalled some 50%.

In 1995, following negotiations with a joint mission of the IMF and the World Bank, the government announced a series of austerity measures aimed at facilitating the disbursement of a third tranche of credit (US $3.2m.) under the SAF. The measures included a further increase in fuel prices and the dismissal of 300 civil servants. In addition, the privatization of state-owned companies was to be expedited, salary increases for the public sector limited to 30% and the interest base rate increased from 35% to 50%. With the implementation of successive increases in fuel prices in March and September 1995, the government succeeded in facilitating the release of the structural adjustment credit of $3.2m., which was disbursed in early 1996. Further increases in fuel prices were imposed in February and May 1996. In mid-1996 the government announced a series of measures aimed at stemming the rapid depreciation of the currency and at reducing the annual rate of inflation from 48% to about 25% by the end of the year. The measures included efforts to prevent widespread tax evasion.

In January 1997 a parliamentary commission of enquiry into the implementation of the 1996 budget revealed several instances of fiscal impropriety. The commission accused the government of Armindo Vaz d'Almeida of exceeding the budget limits defined by fiscal legislation. In September 1996 the government had illegally borrowed 13,500m. dobras from the central bank to finance the budget deficit. Unofficial extra-budgetary expenditure by the treasury totalled 4,274m. dobras.

In February 1997 the World Bank issued an ultimatum to São Tomé, threatening the withdrawal of support if the country should fail to implement the necessary measures to qualify for the Heavily Indebted Poor Countries (HIPC) initiative. The ultimatum followed a review of the country's public finances, conducted by a World Bank mission in December 1996, which had observed increasing macro-economic imbalances. By October 1996 the current fiscal balance (excluding donations) had reached a deficit of 7,800m. dobras, compared with a targeted surplus for the year of 4,400m. dobras. The deficit resulted from low revenues, owing to tax evasion, the exemption of import duties on 73% of all imports, and excessive public spending. The World Bank urged the government to take immediate measures to increase fiscal discipline and to combat corruption.

In May 1997 the IMF advised the government to take urgent measures to curb inflation and to stem the rapid devaluation of the currency. It was envisaged that measures aimed at containing the budgetary deficit within 1% of GDP, including restrictions on expenditure and strengthened financial discipline, would reduce the annual rate of inflation from 51.7% in 1996 to 40% in 1997. In October the government liquidated the savings bank Caixa Nacional de Poupança e Crédito (CNPC), which had become insolvent, owing largely to mismanagement and fraudulent practices. By the end of its mandate, in March 1998, the liquidation commission had succeeded in recovering only some 700m. dobras of total outstanding liabilities of 4,000m. dobras, much of which was owed by prominent politicians and businessmen. In November 1997 the World Bank estimated the fiscal deficit at 1,200m. dobras, excluding a credit of 8,000m. dobras from the central bank for the liquidation of the CNPC. In early 1999 the government announced its intention vigorously to pursue the repayment of loans granted by the CNPC; debtors who failed to repay their loans were to be denied access to other bank credits and have legal action taken against them. Expenditure on civil service salaries increased from 15.1% of total government spending in 1996 to 21.7% in 1997. In late 1997 the World Bank granted a loan of US $415,000 to strengthen the government's preparation and execution of the budget. In turn, the IMF stipulated that the government reduce annual expenditure on salaries to below 5,000m. dobras, present a timetable for a reduction of civil service employees by 1,000, and limit monetary financing of the budget to 6,500m. dobras, as well as take measures to reduce the fiscal deficit, increase revenue and improve the customs service. However, in April 1998 the annual IMF mission to São Tomé found that government expenditure had risen, owing to salary increases, while revenue had remained low. The performance of the customs service had deteriorated and excessive tax exemptions had not been reduced. In addition, as the result of extra-budgetary spending, monetary financing of the budget was as high as 12,300m. dobras. The government had done nothing to reduce the civil service or to improve the management of state companies. As a result, the IMF announced that São Tomé would not qualify for debt cancellation under the HIPC.

As a consequence of vigorous adjustment measures imposed by the IMF, the country's economic and fiscal performance improved considerably in 1998. In that year there was a surplus in the primary budget (excluding externally financed capital outlays) equivalent to 0.7% of GDP, compared with a deficit of 2.2% in 1997. The average annual inflation rate was reduced from 68.5% in 1997 to 42.3% in 1998, while the differential between the official rate of exchange of the dobra and the 'black market' rate was narrowed from 6.5% in 1996 to less than 1% in 1998. Private investment increased to the equivalent of 18.4% of GDP in 1998, while gross national savings amounted to 21% of GDP in the same year. Owing to measures aimed at improving the tax administration, including the reinforcement of the tax audit department, in 1998 government revenues increased to 54,500m. dobras (equivalent to 19.4% of GDP), exceeding budget projections by more than 9,500m. dobras. However, owing to excessive exemptions and to fraudulent practices within the customs office, revenues from import and export tax were considerably lower than projected. Despite stricter budgetary controls primary expenditure exceeded projections by 7,600m. dobras, mainly owing to government investments and an increase in public sector wages. However, as a result of the primary budget surplus, the government succeeded in settling all its domestic payment arrears in 1998 and in meeting its external debt service requirements with regard to its multilateral creditors. Growth in money supply in 1998 was 16.3%, less than nominal GDP growth. The sale of petroleum concession rights and of shares in the fuel company ENCO contributed to a limited increase in net government bank credit. Following the reduction in inflation, the central bank reduced its reference interest rate from 55% to 29.5% in November 1998, and again to 24.5% in February 1999, and finally to 19% in May. The measure was expected to encourage investment and in turn lead to greater economic growth. In 1999 the government assured the IMF of its intention to consolidate the progress made in the pre-

vious year. Among its targets for 1999 the government intended
to reduce inflation to 10%, limit the external current account
deficit (excluding official transfers) to 63% of GDP, achieve real
GDP growth of 2.5%, and increase the primary budget surplus to
2.8% of GDP. In addition the government announced that it was
to reduce the civil service and refrain from increasing public-
sector wages in 1999. In that year the government was to negotiate with the IMF in an effort to secure an ESAF, the successful
implementation of which might facilitate debt relief under the
HIPC initiative.

In March 1999 the government presented a memorandum of
economic and financial policies outlining its objectives and economic policies for 1999–2002. The three-year programme included
the development of a more prudent fiscal policy aimed at broadening the tax base, prioritizing expenditure on infrastructure and
the social sector, the creation of a social programme to reduce
poverty and improve educational and health services, the implementation of a tight monetary policy (including a reduction in
inflation and an increase in international reserves), and the introduction of accelerated structural reforms in an attempt to boost
private-sector development and achieve sustainable economic
growth. Inflation was expected to decrease from 13% in 1999 to
5% in 2000 and 3% in 2001, and the deficit on the external account
(excluding official transfers) was to be restricted to 62% and 66%
of GDP in 2000 and 2002 respectively, as a result of new petroleum
investments (private investments were projected to increase from
14% of GDP in 1999 to 31% of GDP in 2002). The primary fiscal
surplus was expected to increase from 1.3% of GDP in 1999 to
2.3% of GDP in 2000 and 5% of GDP in 2002, enabling the government to allocate more funds to the health and education sectors.
Following the introduction of a new customs tariff in February
2000, revenue (excluding grants) was expected to increase by
16.5% in 2000 to 75,000m. dobras (20.4% of GDP, compared with
19.3% of GDP in 1999). The government hoped to control public
spending by reducing expenditure on salaries (this accounted for
7.5% of GDP in 1999), and subsequently announced a reduction
in the number of civil servants in the first half of 2000. Other
current expenditure on goods and services was expected to decrease from 3.8% of GDP in 1999 to 2.9% of GDP in 2000. Spending
on education was projected to increase from 14% of total primary
expenditure in 1999 (7.9% of GDP) to 15.9% in 2000 (8.5% of GDP).
The central bank announced its intention to reduce inflation and
raise gross international reserves to $17.5m., as well as reducing
the differential between the official and parallel exchange rates
from 1.5% in 1999 to below 1% in 2000; money supply was
expected to grow by 5% in 2000, in line with the planned rate of
inflation. The government committed itself to good governance,
and to combating fraud and corruption. The accounts of the central bank and of all public enterprises were to be audited by independent, external auditors. There was a projected deficit of $31m.
(62% of GDP, compared with 57% in 1999) in 2000 on the current
account of the balance of payments.

In April 2000 the government presented an interim Poverty
Reduction Strategy Paper (PRSP) for 2000–2002. According to
the document, at least 40% of the local population live below the
poverty line, while some 33% are considered to live in extreme
poverty, with an income sufficient to cover only one-half of the
minimum household food requirements. In an attempt to reduce
poverty levels, the government announced its intention to
improve infrastructure and access to education, training and
health services, strengthen basic institutions and develop their
capacity to deliver public services, and increase income-generating opportunities and employment creation. In late April the
IMF granted São Tomé and Príncipe a three-year Poverty Reduction and Growth Facility (PRGF, formerly ESAF), worth some
$8.9m. Disbursements were to take place in seven semi-annual
loans, with the first one (some $1.3m.) available immediately.
The government's three-year programme (see above) was to be
monitored and evaluated on a yearly basis by the IMF; the successful implementation of the programme was a precondition for
future debt reduction within the framework of the HIPC initiative. In May the Paris Club group of donors agreed to reduce the
interest on São Tomé and Príncipe's external debt by 95% until
2003, which was worth an estimated $26m.

AGRICULTURE

Agriculture (including forestry and fishing) contributed an estimated 23.3% of GDP and employed 39.6% of the economically active
population in 1997. At independence, São Tomé inherited a plantation economy dominated by cocoa and partially protected from
international price movements by a guaranteed home market.
Most land was farmed by 29 large Portuguese-owned enterprises.
In 1975 the government nationalized all landholdings of over
200 ha and grouped them into 15 state enterprises, two of them
on Príncipe. They covered over 80% of the cultivable land area.
The nationalization of the estates led to the exodus of many of
the skilled agricultural personnel. Equipment on the plantations
ceased to function through poor maintenance and lack of spare
parts. Wages fell in real terms, and food for the labourers was in
short supply, leading to a fall in employment and productivity.
Portuguese consumers turned to cheaper sources of supply, especially as the overvaluation of the dobra raised the prices of São
Tomé produce. The state farms incurred substantial deficits and,
within a decade, were brought to the point of financial collapse.

In 1985, the government initiated a policy of partial privatization. Ownership of the estates was kept in the hands of the state,
but foreign aid was sought to rehabilitate the plantations and
foreign companies were invited to tender for management contracts of 15–20 years' duration. Privatization proceeded slowly
under this system, and was confined to the prime land in the
north-east of São Tomé island.

By the early 1990s, the strategy of estate management contracts was in crisis. Managers complained that the contracts,
which gave the government a right of supervision over major
decisions and specified that 80% of all profits went to the state,
denied them effective control. Critics pointed out that the state
took the risk of major losses, and alleged that the foreigners were
merely collecting their management fee from aid money and were
doing little to rehabilitate the estates. Declining cocoa prices soon
stifled the optimism of the late 1980s. In 1991 the two Portuguese
companies that had managed the Agua-Izé estate since 1987
announced that they were to withdraw. Faced with falling cocoa
prices and the aftermath of a two-month strike in late 1990, the
Portuguese managements had wished to break up the 5,000-ha
estate into smallholdings, retaining only the central processing
facilities. When the government refused to allow this, the companies declared that their losses had become excessive and that
they were giving up the management contract by mutual agreement. In 1992 the United Nations Development Programme
(UNDP) announced that it would provide US $3.5m. to rehabili-
tate the estate over the period 1993–95. In mid-1993, on the advice
of the World Bank, the government began the process of replacing
management contracts with long leases. Companies gained managerial autonomy (subject to maintaining the value of the assets
entrusted to them by the state), obtained control over the size of
their labour force, were no longer able to finance investments with
public funds, and had to pay the government rents commensurate
with their economic performance.

The alternative strategy of breaking up the estates into
smallholdings has been pursued since 1985. About 10,000 ha of
land were distributed to small farmers during 1985–89, although
in a rather arbitrary manner and without any cohesive support
programme. The government viewed these areas as suitable only
for domestic food production, rather than for cash crops for export.
The authorities were unwilling to grant full freehold tenure and
in 1989, only one-third of the distributed land was under cultivation. At the instigation of the World Bank, which was providing
finance of US $17.2m. for the process of land reform, the govern-
ment announced that some 20,000 ha of land would be
transferred to smallholders between 1993–98. Land distributed
to smallholders since 1985 which had not been cultivated would
be repossessed and redistributed by the state. In January 1995
the government signed an agreement with the UNDP providing
financing of $3.4m. for a five-year project to support smallholder
agriculture. In March a six-year national programme for the support and promotion of family agriculture was established with
financing of 51.1m. French francs, from the Caisse française de
développement and the International Fund for Agricultural Development. In May the International Development Association
(IDA) granted a loan of $9.8m. for the development of the small-
holder sector.

By mid-1996 the Agua-Izé, Ponta Figo and Milagrosa estates had been liquidated and their land redistributed to former workers and to medium-sized enterprises. A further five estates were to be completely dismantled as part of the redistribution programme.

A parliamentary commission of enquiry, established in November 1996 to investigate the process of land distribution, reported in January 1997 that since late 1994 land distribution to medium-sized enterprises had become increasingly irregular. Land was distributed directly by the government of Carlos da Graça and Armindo Vaz d'Almeida, without consulting the national committee for land distribution or observing the pertinent legislation. According to the enquiry, proceeds derived from the sale of state property at the former estates of Milagrosa, Mesquita, Colonia Açoriana and Agua-Izé were not transferred to the treasury.

By the end of 1997 a total of 3,927 smallholders had received 9,672 ha of former plantation lands as part of the land reform. Two estates, Ribeira Peixe and Santa Catarine, were distributed entirely to former plantation workers. By that time a total of 112 medium-sized enterprises had received 5,170 ha in plots of between 10 and 222 ha. The owners of these enterprises were politicians, civil servants and traders, most of whom lacked agricultural experience. Outside the framework of the recent reform, another 5,721 ha had already been distributed to 56 medium-sized enterprises prior to 1992. According to the law, some 75% of the 20,000 ha of land to be distributed was to be allocated to smallholders. By the end of 1998 the government had distributed a total of 17,964 ha as part of its land distribution programme, of which 24.5% was to medium-sized enterprises and 75.5% to small farmers. A further 2,276 ha were expected to be distributed by the end of the programme in June 1999. Altogether nine state-owned plantations have been dissolved and their lands distributed, while six estates have remained intact and are managed under long-term operating leases. The workers of these privately managed estates have demanded equal benefits from the land distribution programme. The government intends to fully privatize the six state-owned estates and rationalize the land tenure system by December 1999 with the aim of encouraging agricultural investment and increasing production.

Since independence, cocoa has regularly accounted for well over 90% of exports by value. Cocoa covered 61% of the cultivated area on the 15 large estates in 1986. Production fell from some 11,500 metric tons in 1973 to around 4,000 tons a year in the 1980s, and export earnings from cocoa fell by 67% between 1979 and 1988. In 1985 the islands' cocoa trees were 30 years old on average, and some were much older. Black pod disease has spread because of a lack of phytosanitary treatment, and soil fertility has declined with the lack of fertilizer application. As cocoa prices fell still further in the early 1990s, production drifted down to a low point of 3,193 tons in 1991. Output then increased to 4,305 tons in 1993. Although prices had risen during 1993, production fell in 1994 to 3,392 tons. Cocoa exports declined from 4,400 tons in 1995 to 3,200 tons in 1996, and 3,187 tons in 1997. Cocoa production was an estimated 3,300 tons in 1998. In 1997 the World Bank disclosed that the investment of some US $40m. in the rehabilitation of six privately managed cocoa estates, financed by multilateral creditors, had been a failure. With an average cocoa yield of only 170 kg per ha, the productivity of these estates remained far below expectations. Low yields were caused in part by an infestation of the insect *Heliothrips rubrocintus*, which affected 40% of the cocoa crop. The World Bank blamed the government's poor provision of agricultural services for the spread of the infestation. In 1996 cocoa still accounted for 96.6% of exports, illustrating the failure of the government's export diversification programme. In 1998 the government launched a campaign to control infestation by *Heliothrips rubrocintus*. However, in early 1999 the government recognized that the cocoa and coffee rehabilitation programmes had failed and announced a shift in policy favouring smallholder agriculture and local food production.

The islands' principal secondary crops are copra, coffee and palm oil and kernels. In 1986 coconut palms covered 23% of the cultivated area on the 15 state-owned estates, and copra was the country's only export of any significance apart from cocoa. In 1987 less than 2,000 metric tons of copra were exported,

compared with over 5,000 tons in 1973. By 1997 production of copra had fallen to only an estimated 433 tons. Oil palms accounted for 10% of the cultivated area on the estates in 1986 and coffee for 3%, but exports of these commodities ceased altogether in the latter half of the 1980s. Coffee output increased from 14 tons in 1992 to an estimated 45 tons in 1997. Exports of cocoyam (also known as taro, or matabala), plantain and citrus fruit to Gabon were also targeted for development. In October 1999 the government adopted an agricultural policy charter, the Carta de Política e Desenvolvimento Rural, which, it hoped, would provide an integrated strategy for the entire sector. The charter emphasizes production, diversification, private-sector involvement, and the full participation of the rural population. Efforts were made to diversify into production of crops including ylang-ylang, pepper, vanilla and other aromatic plants, fruits, vegetables, flowers and tubers. The government also announced its intention to adopt a privatization programme for large estates which had hitherto only been assigned to private companies under long-term operating leases. The programme was to be funded by the World Bank and was expected to commence in mid-2000.

Self-sufficiency in basic food crops has eluded the government since independence, despite the high fertility of the islands' volcanic soils, the long growing season, the variety of microclimates, and abundant rainfall. The apportionment of centrally-fixed planning targets for food production among the nationalized estates proved unsuccessful, and by the mid-1980s the country was estimated to be importing 90% of its food requirements. The emphasis after 1985 was on developing smallholder agriculture on the fringes of the great estates. By 1992 it was estimated that imports of food had fallen to around 45% of consumption. The only surviving large-scale food project is the oil palm plantation at Ribeira Peixe. Since the early 1980s, the European Community (EC, now the European Union—EU) has been providing funds to plant 610 ha of high yielding oil palms and to establish a publicly-owned palm oil factory on the 1,500-ha Ribeira Peixe estate in the south-east of São Tomé island. By 1992 the project was producing about 80,000 litres of oil a month and was able to meet the country's internal requirements. The greatest obstacles to self-sufficiency in food are the virtual absence of a smallholder tradition, due to the plantation economy and the impossibility of growing wheat for a population increasingly accustomed to eating bread and other wheat-based products. Average food consumption in the country is 300 metric tons per month, comprising mainly local food crops including plantain, bread-fruit, matabala (taro), cassava, sweet potatoes and vegetables. According to local statistics, annual plantain production increased from 10,250 tons in 1992 to 34,596 tons in 1997. Annual matabala production increased from 5,000 tons in 1992 to 20,964 tons over the same period.

The livestock sector has been seriously affected by the decline in veterinary services since independence. Pork has traditionally been the main source of animal protein, but all 30,000 pigs in the islands had to be slaughtered in 1979 after an outbreak of African swine fever. With the help of foreign donors production was restored to pre-1979 levels by 1986, but swine fever recurred on São Tomé island in 1992 and pork production decreased from 220 tons in 1992 to 34 tons in 1995. However, by 1996 pig stocks had recovered and numbered an estimated 25,337 head; pork production in that year reached 264 metric tons. Chicken and egg production were also badly affected by disease in 1993 when chicken production fell to 100 tons, eventually recovering to 188 tons by 1996. Egg production, however, continued to fall, from 2m. in 1992 to 1.6m. in 1994 and 1995. Goats are widely reared, and are sometimes exported to Gabon. In 1996 there were 46,604 head of goat and sheep, and 102 tons of goat- and sheep-meat were produced. The islands are free of tsetse fly, but cattle have been badly affected by bovine tuberculosis. Beef production increased, however, from 12 tons in 1992 to 24 tons in 1995. In late 1999 the ADB granted São Tomé US $3.8m. to finance the Projecto de Apoio ao Desenvolvimento Pecuário (Project for the Support of Livestock Development), which aimed to rehabilitate all infrastructures necessary for the sustainable development of livestock production, including the renovation of pig stalls at Água Izé and Nova Olinda, and the abattoir on São Tomé.

Similar difficulties have beset the fishing sector, a priority area for economic diversification. In the early 1990s fishing was the second largest source of foreign exchange, due principally to revenue from fishing licences, and employed some 10% of the economically active population. A state-owned fishing company, Empesca, was formed at independence. Its two modern trawlers had on-board freezing facilities, and cold store facilities were installed at the port of Neves on São Tomé island. In June 1978, the government established an exclusive economic zone around the islands of 370 km (200 nautical miles), although the trawlers actually spent most of their time fishing in Angolan waters. The industrial catch rose to just over 2,500 metric tons in 1984, but subsequently lack of maintenance on the trawlers led to a rapid decrease. The industrial catch in 1988 was only one ton. Empesca was then reconstituted as a joint venture, but refitting the trawlers proved more difficult than originally expected. Subsequently, industrial fishing ceased to contribute to the total fishing catch. In 1990 the government and the Feliciaggi group (France) established another joint venture, Africa Fishing. Since then the company has not presented any accounts to the government and the whereabouts of the two trawlers has been subject to speculation. In 1997 the IMF requested that the government privatize its 49% share of Africa Fishing. In the long term, the government is basing its hopes for the fishing industry on the tuna resources of the area, and it is estimated that tuna catches could reach 17,000 tons a year without affecting stocks. Since the 1985 reforms, the main emphasis of foreign donors has been on upgrading artisan fishing, which significantly increased the total catch. The EC, Japan and Canada have provided funds for this purpose. However, the total catch by artisan fishermen decreased from 3,572 tons in 1990 to 2,312 tons in 1997. In 1995 there were some 1,850 artisan fishing boats in the country, of which 754 were motorized. A fish-processing plant, the Sociedade Nacional de Comércio e Pesca (SNCP), financed with US $2m. of private capital, began operations in September 1995 in Ribeira Funda, some 20 km from the capital. Production was mainly destined for export. In 1996 São Tomé renewed, for a further three-year period, its fishing agreement with the EU, in return for a grant of ECU 2.1m. In May 1999 the agreement was again renewed for three years. Under the terms of the protocol, 76 European boats are permitted to catch 8,500 tons of tuna annually in return for €1.9m. Of this amount half is to be used to finance the training of personnel, improvement of the fisheries department and to support artisan fishermen. In addition, European ship owners have to pay the government for an annual fishing licence and a fee per ton of fish caught. In January 2000 the EU placed an embargo on the import of fish from São Tomé and Príncipe as the country's sanitary control system did not meet the EU's requirements for fish-exporting countries. The embargo was a set-back for the government, which had given priority to the fishing sector in an attempt to attract foreign investment.

São Tomé and Príncipe's considerable forestry resources have been neglected, although it was estimated in 1984 that two-thirds of the country's energy consumption came from fuelwood and most housing is of wooden construction. Colonial legislation for the protection of forests was replaced by a new law in 1979, but it was not enforced and no barriers were placed to the uncontrolled cutting of trees. A commission was set up in 1988 to study the problems of forest preservation and reafforestation, and it began by drawing up a national forest inventory with foreign assistance. This revealed that 29% of the country was still covered in primary forest (*obó*), mainly in the inaccessible south-western quadrant of both islands. Some 245 sq km on São Tomé island and 45 sq km on Príncipe were identified as needing to be demarcated as 'ecological reserves', in areas where commercial agriculture is uneconomic. In addition, the inventory noted the existence of 30,000 ha of secondary forest, largely on abandoned plantation land and 32,000 ha of 'shade forest', covering commercial crops. The resources exploitable on a sustainable basis outside the 'ecological reserves' were estimated at between 70,000 and 105,000 cu m of construction wood and between 43,000 and 65,000 cu m of fuelwood per year. However, it was also estimated that the country needed 20,000 cu m of fuelwood for dry-processing cocoa, copra and other commercial crops, and a further 140,000 cu m for domestic purposes. In 1990 São Tomé was included in a Central African forest conservation project, financed by the EC, which was intended to lead to the demarcation and enforcement of forest reserves covering 32%

of the total land area. Although a provisional code of forest regulations was issued in 1993, the current programme of land distribution to smallholders has led to increasing deforestation, with the new occupants arbitrarily felling trees. Local observers fear serious ecological consequences. With the assistance of the UN Environment Programme, the government formulated legislation, which was approved by the national assembly in 1998, concerning management of the environment in order to address increasing problems of this kind. In 2000 the government announced its intention formally to adopt a National Strategy for the Protection of the Environment and Sustainable Development, which aimed to improve the control and conservation of the country's natural environment.

MANUFACTURING AND SERVICES

Industry, including construction and public utilities, accounted for an estimated 11.4% of GDP in 1998 and employed 15.8% of the economically active population in 1997. The secondary sector comprises some 50 small- and medium-sized enterprises and several hundred microenterprises. Of the 25 manufacturing companies in existence at independence in 1975, 12 had closed down completely by 1993, eight were functioning well below capacity, and five had been rehabilitated and expanded. Three new enterprises had been created. Apart from a printing workshop, beer, soft drinks, spirits, bread, vegetable oil, soap, sawn wood, furniture, ceramics, bricks and garments are produced. Industry is generally confined to production for the local market, but garments are exported to Angola. Many basic manufactured products are still imported, especially from Portugal. The government aims to develop food processing and the production of construction materials. All industrial companies were originally scheduled for privatization by the end of 1993. By early 1995 ten non-agricultural public enterprises had been privatized, liquidated or placed under foreign management. In October 1996 the government liquidated the insurance company A Compensadora. In mid-1997 the government announced the sale of its minority shares in three enterprises: the brick manufacturer Cerámica de São Tomé (in which it held a 40% share), the clothing manufacturer Confecções Agua Grande Lda (35%), and the construction materials supplier Cunha Gomes SA (30%). In November 1998 the government liquidated the pharmaceutical company Empresa Nacional de Medicamentos, and the slaughterhouse Empresa de Transformação de Carnes. Those enterprises to remain under state control were the palm oil manufacturer EMOLVE, the water and electricity utility Empresa de Água e Electricidade (EMAE), the ports administration ENAPORT, the airport administration company ENASA, the telecommunications company CST (49%) and the airline Air São Tomé e Príncipe (35%), all of which were to be transformed into limited-liability companies. In September 2000 the government announced that the privatization of the state television and radio station had been postponed. As part of a new reform and privatization programme, the government announced the adoption of a financial restructuring plan for EMAE, to be implemented by mid-2000. At the instigation of the IMF, the accounts of EMAE, ENAPORT and ENASA were to be submitted annually to external auditors.

In May 1997 the government granted a South African enterprise, the Western African Development Corporation (WADCO), a 50-year concession to establish a free-trade zone at Príncipe island's deep-water Agulhas Bay. In September the government appointed an eight-member office for the establishment and development of free-trade zones. It was expected that interested companies would be able to apply for concessions from mid-1998. WADCO claimed to have received requests for concessions for fish-processing, telecommunications, aviation services, ship repair, agro-industries, construction and offshore banking for the 50 sq km zone. The regional government of Príncipe has claimed 60% of the central government's share of the proceeds, which have been estimated at US $100,000 for the first year. In late 1998 the government approved legislation on free-trade and offshore activities which provides for the establishment of a Free-trade Zone Authority (Autoridade de Zonas Francas) to control such activities. Owing to delays the government did not appoint the members of this body until May 1999. At that time WADCO had not yet begun commercial activities within the Agulhas Bay free zone, but was preparing a pre-survey draft of a detailed general project proposal. However, in January 2000 WADCO postponed the launching of the Agulhas Bay Corporation Free Zone, due to the deteriorating investor climate.

ENERGY

There are no mineral resources on the islands, but offshore prospecting for hydrocarbons since the late 1980s has produced encouraging preliminary findings. In May 1997 the government signed an accord with the US Environmental Remediation Holding Corpn (ERHC) and the South African Procura Financial Consultants (PFC) concerning the exploration and exploitation of petroleum, gas and mineral reserves in São Tomé's territory. The agreement, which was valid for 25 years, provided for an initial payment to the government of US $5m. ERHC and PFC were then to finance the evaluation of the petroleum reserves, and a petroleum company was to be established with the government, from which the state would receive 40% of the revenue. In November the government submitted details of the country's 370-km Exclusive Economic Zone (EEZ), drafted by the ERHC, to the UN and the Gulf of Guinea Commission. In March 1998 São Tomé approved a law establishing the boundaries of the EEZ, which was presented to the UN Law of the Sea Commission in May. In April the ERHC claimed that significant quantities of petroleum had been discovered in Santomean waters. The drilling of a test well was to be conducted in late 1998. Subsequently, the company announced that the sale of petroleum concessions could begin before the end of 1998. In addition, the ERHC announced the establishment of an offshore logistics centre in São Tomé. According to the ERHC, Jugobanka a.d., Beograd (Yugoslavia) had agreed to provide finance of US $50m. for the logistics centre. Nevertheless, there have been some doubts that the ERHC will succeed in raising the $20m. funding necessary to begin petroleum exploration in São Tomé. By mid-1998 the ERHC had paid the government only $2m. of the initial payment of $5m. provided for in the May 1997 agreement. In July 1998 the government and ERHC established a joint venture petroleum company, Sociedade Nacional de Petróleos de São Tomé e Príncipe (STPETRO), with the government holding 51% of the shares. In September STPETRO and Mobil signed a technical assistance agreement to survey 22 deep-water blocks within an 18-month period. In January 1999 Schlumberger Geco/Prakla began a seismic survey of Mobil's concession area. In February ERHC signed an agreement with the London-based Technology and Communications International Corpn (TCI) to establish the Logistics Centre for offshore petroleum activities in São Tomé. Following sustained financial problems and high losses, in April an investment group acquired a 51% stake in ERHC. In the same month, the new majority shareholders, led by São Tomé's principal investor, South African businessman Christian Hellinger, replaced the company's board. In May, the São Tomé government appointed Hellinger's Island Oil Exploration Co to obtain finance for the Logistic Centre within a period of six months. Subsequently, Hellinger, ERHC, TCI, and the Norwegian SIMEX joined forces to establish and finance the Logistics Centre. The investors intend to obtain the necessary financing, estimated at $50m., from multilateral creditors. The project competes with similar support facilities for the petroleum sector planned by WADCO as part of the free-trade zone on Príncipe. There have been concerns about possible disputes regarding the delimitation of maritime borders with neighbouring countries. In June 1999 President Trovoada and the president of Equatorial Guinea, Teodoro Obiang Nguema Mbasogo, signed a bilateral agreement on the delimitation of the two countries' maritime borders. In late April 2000, negotiations with Nigeria ended without an agreement on maritime boundaries between the two countries. The main obstacle had been Nigeria's refusal to agree to the Santomean proposal, which bases the boundary on equidistance from the continent. The next round of talks was scheduled for the end of May 2000. In March 1999 the government assured the IMF of transparency in all future operations concerning petroleum exploration activities and promised to consult the Bretton Woods institutions in all its negotiations with petroleum companies. Petroleum products were imported from Angola at concessionary rates after independence, but are now being supplied at commercial prices. At the request of the World Bank, in early 1998 the government sold a 49% share of the state fuel

company, ENCO, of which 40% was acquired by the Angolan petroleum company SONANGOL and 9% by local investors. In May ENCO increased fuel prices by 20%.

In June 1999 the government and Mobil signed an agreement on the partitioning of São Tomé's future petroleum production. Further negotiations on the matter took place in September 1999 and March 2000.

In October 1999 the government rescinded the agreement with ERHC (signed in 1997), on the grounds that the company had not met a number of financial and other commitments included in the contract. The president of ERHC, Geoffrey Tirman, subsequently accused STPETRO's president, Carlos 'Ito' Gomes, of corruption; Tirman claimed that following his refusal to provide Gomes with incentives, Gomes obstructed negotiations with the government. Gomes denied the allegations, and in turn accused Tirman of committing irregularities. In a video recording broadcast by local television in January 2000, Tirman publicly presented his apologies to Prime Minister Guilhermo Pósser da Costa. ERHC had earlier embarrassed the government by lodging a request for arbitration at the Paris-based International Chamber of Commerce, without prior warning. During that time ERHC was subject to an investigation by the US Securities and Exchange Commission (SEC), due to missing accounting records. ERHC also failed to submit its latest annual report, arguing that it did not have the funds to pay the audit fees. ERCH subsequently declared its insolvency to the SEC and raised the possibility of commencing bankruptcy procedures. Despite the uncertainties over the future of ERHC, the government resumed negotiations with the company in March.

In October 1999 the government replaced the Comissão Nacional de Petróleo (National Petroleum Committee) by an inter-ministerial commission. In late October ENCO raised fuel prices by some 12%, citing the increased international petroleum prices as a reason. In February 2000 ENCO raised the prices of petrol, diesel and petroleum by 45%, 35% and 11% respectively.

In 1997 some 73% of electricity generation was derived from thermal sources, and 27% from hydroelectric sources. The capital city's recently rehabilitated generators still rely on fuel oil, and power cuts have become increasingly frequent as fuel prices have risen sharply. A project aimed at increasing, by 50%, the fuel storage capacity of the state fuel company, with finance of 20.6m. French francs from the Caisse (now Agence) française de developpement, was concluded in late 1995 and was expected to help curb problems arising from erratic supplies. In 1991 the public company responsible for electricity and water supplies, Empresa de Água e Electricidade (EMAE), which had become much criticized for its inefficiency, was handed over to a French company to manage. In 1995, in the light of the French company's failure to improve the energy supply, the government declined to renew the management contract. In 1996, with the installation of a new electricity generator with a capacity of 1,200 kw, EMAE succeeded in reducing the energy deficit by 40%. A comprehensive energy plan was scheduled for the end of 1993, and the entire electricity and water distribution systems were to be replaced from 1994. Between 1993 and 1996 the government invested US $13.5m. in EMAE. However, owing to poor financial and technical management, in 1996 the company still required government subsidies totalling $402,000, equivalent to almost 1% of GDP. In the budget for 1999 the government planned to curb this expenditure to the equivalent of 0.6% of GDP.

TRANSPORT, TOURISM AND COMMUNICATIONS

The asphalted road network of some 250 km suffered serious deterioration following independence, although a repair programme financed by foreign aid began in 1989, and by 1995 most roads outside of the capital had been repaired with donor funds of almost US $10m. However, until 1997 the government failed to provide for any expenditure on road maintenance, while the minimum annual expenditure necessary for routine road repairs was estimated at $300,000. Foreign donors are also upgrading three of the country's ports, although São Tomé city lacks a natural deep-water harbour and has been losing traffic to the better-endowed port of Neves, which handles petroleum imports and industrial fishing. Joint ventures were established in 1989 to replace the inefficient state enterprises for maritime communications and telecommunications. In late 1993 a new airline, Air São Tomé e Príncipe, began operations. The company is managed by TAP-Air Portugal which also holds a 40% share of the capital. The government of São Tomé holds a 35% share while the French companies Golfe International Air Service and Mistral Voyages hold 24% and 1% respectively. In April 1999 the new Portuguese director-general of Air São Tomé e Príncipe announced that the company was technically bankrupt. Owing to competition from Air Gabon the company has incurred heavy losses on its flight to Libreville, while the rental of a Russian LET 410 aircraft, following an accident involving the company's single Twin Otter in 1997, resulted in an additional financial burden. Consequently, the company has reduced its flights to Libreville and increased those to Príncipe. In 1990 a telecommunications company, Companhia Santomense de Telecomunicações (CST), was established as a joint venture between the state (49%) and the Portuguese Rádio Marconi (51%). In November 1996 CST installed the first experimental internet link in the archipelago. In March 1997 the internet service was officially launched. In April 1999 Rádio Marconi threatened to withdraw from the CST if the government did not revise legislation, approved in 1998, regarding free-trade zones which placed CST's monopoly in jeopardy by liberating the local telecommunications sector. In July 1999 CST completed the digitalization of the telecommunications system. Also in that month the Swedish internet provider Bahnhof AB purchased the country's principal domain, 'st', from the government. The company hoped that the government would attract foreign enterprises, through the provision of fiscal incentives, to use the internet services available at relatively low prices.

The improvement in communications has been of great importance in sustaining efforts to develop tourism. The islands benefit from spectacular volcanic mountains and craters, unpeopled beaches, unique bird life and flora, and have ample potential for game-fishing. However, the high rainfall during most of the year limits the duration of the tourist season, and the sea is usually dangerous to bathe in because of strong currents. Nevertheless, the first modern tourist hotel was completed in 1986 with a capacity of 50 beds, and it has attracted a modest current of tourists, mainly European expatriates and wealthy Gabonese. The Bombom luxury tourist complex on Príncipe island, which caters particularly for game-fishing, and the Santana tourist complex south of São Tomé city, also with emphasis on marine activities, were opened in late 1992. Renovation of the colonial Pousada Boa Vista, financed by TAP-Air Portugal, was completed in mid-1993. In August 1997 ESTA Hotel Management, a subsidiary of TAP-Air Portugal, withdrew from the management of the Pousada Boa Vista, which had recorded considerable losses, owing to a low occupation rate. In 1998 the Pousada Boa Vista was placed under private management. In 1994 a new hotel, the Marlin Beach Hotel, was opened near the airport. In late 1995 the government leased the Miramar Hotel, for a period of 20 years, to a group of German investors, São Tomé Invest SA. The hotel, which had been renovated at a cost of US $2.5m., reopened in June 1997. Although tourism has been identified as a growth sector for many years, failure to develop has confined its contribution to GDP to only 3%.

In May 1992 the government and Voice of America (VOA) signed an agreement providing for the establishment of a radio relay station at Pinheira, on São Tomé island. The agreement is for a duration of 30 years, and, since 1994, has provided São

Tomé with an annual revenue of US $210,000. Broadcasts to some 25m. listeners throughout Africa began in 1996. In early 1997 VOA began local transmissions on FM. In 1994 the government and Radio France Internationale signed an agreement allowing for the installation of a relay station. Broadcasting began in June 1995. In the same month Rádio Televisão Portuguesa Internacional began relaying television broadcasts to the archipelago. In 1996 the Lisbon-based Rádio Difusão Portuguesa-África (RDP-África) began local transmissions of their daily radio programmes on FM. In August 1999 the government approved the establishment of a retransmission station by Africa Pay Television (APTV) in São Tomé. In April 2000 the local bishop, Abílio Ribas, announced that the diocese of São Tomé and Príncipe was to launch its own radio station, Rádio Jubilar, funded by Portuguese sources, which was to provide moral, civic and Portuguese-language education.

FOREIGN TRADE AND PAYMENTS

Because of the overwhelming importance of the cocoa plantations, the islands' economic life is entirely dependent on external markets. Until 1980, the trade balance was usually positive because of the small value of imports. However, since then low world cocoa prices and low cocoa production, combined with the higher cost of food imports, have led to a continuing trade deficit. The deficit reached a record total of US $21.5m. in 1991, and stood at $13.9m. in 1997. Shortages of essential supplies, especially fuel, have become more frequent. Portugal is the country's main supplier of goods, accounting for 26.3% of total imports in 1997, although there are considerable fluctuations from year to year. Most other imports come from Western Europe and East Asia. Since the mid-1980s, São Tomé has sold its cocoa mainly to Germany and the Netherlands. In 1997 the Netherlands accounted for 50.9% of total exports.

São Tomé is reputed to be one of the largest recipients per caput of international aid. In 1990 net foreign aid was equivalent to US $200 per caput. UNDP, the World Bank, the EU, Portugal, France, Italy, Sweden, Canada, Japan, the People's Republic of China and Arab countries have been especially prominent as donors. However, the institutional weakness of the country and the lack of co-ordination between donors has led to problems in the efficiency with which aid is utilized. The influx of aid has helped to deal with the deficit on the current account, but it has distorted prices. Total external debt stood at US $260.7m. at the end of 1997, of which $226.8m. was long-term public debt. Total bilateral debt stood at $107m. at the end of 1996. The major bilateral creditors were Portugal ($30.5m) and Angola ($24.8m.). According to the IMF, total external debt stood at $274.3m. at the end of 1998. According to UN figures, in 1993 São Tomé received official development assistance of $378 per caput, the highest level of any developing country. According to the UNDP, in 1998 São Tomé received total official development assistance of $20.7m., a 54.5% decrease on the previous year. Technical co-operation represented 39.4% of the total, investment projects 53.4% and food aid 6.2%. Multilateral donors provided $8.2m. (58.9% less than in 1997), while bilateral donors allocated $12.5m. (a decrease of 51.1%). The principal donor countries were France (providing 24.4% of the total), Portugal (15.3%) and Taiwan (11.5%). Agriculture, forestry and fishing accounted for 21.5% of the total, while economic management, social development and development administration absorbed 17.2%, 14.8% and 13.8% respectively. At the end of 1999 total external debt was estimated at $290m.

Statistical Survey

Sources (unless otherwise stated): Banco Central de São Tomé e Príncipe, Praça da Independência, CP 13, São Tomé; tel. 21901; e-mail bcentral@cstome.net; Direcção de Estatística, São Tomé; Ministry of Planning, Finance and Co-operation, Largo Alfândega, CP 168, São Tomé; tel. 21083; fax 22790.

AREA AND POPULATION

Area: 1,001 sq km (386.5 sq miles).

Population: 96,611 (males 48,031; females 48,580) at census of 15 August 1981; 116,998 (males 57,837; females 59,161) at census of 4 August 1991; 141,000 in mid-1998 (UN estimate).

Density (1998): 140.9 per sq km.

Births and Deaths (1995): Registered live births 4,070 (birth rate 32.14 per 1,000); Registered deaths 1,031 (death rate 8.14 per 1,000).

Expectation of Life (years at birth, 1995): 64.9.

Economically Active Population (1997): Agriculture 12,796; Fishing 1,938; Industry, electricity, gas and water 2,417; Public works and civil construction 3,474; Trade, restaurants and hotels 5,335; Financing, insurance, real estate and business services 207; Transport, storage and communications 2,819; Public administration 3,287; Other activities 4,972; Total employed 37,245.

AGRICULTURE, ETC.

Principal Crops (metric tons, 1998): Bananas 16,000 (FAO estimate); Bread-fruit 1,800 (1996); Cabbages 950 (1996 estimate); Cassava 3,000 (FAO estimate); Cocoa 3,000 (provisional figure); Coconuts 29,000 (FAO estimate); Coffee 45 (1997); Copra 433 (1997); Maize 4,000 (FAO estimate); Matabala (Taro) 11,000 (FAO estimate); Palm kernels 2,000 (FAO estimate); Tomatoes 5,000 (1996 estimate). Source: partly FAO, *Production Yearbook*, and IMF, *São Tomé and Príncipe: Statistical Appendix* (September 1998).

Livestock ('000 head, year ending September 1998, FAO estimates): Cattle 4; Sheep 3; Goats 5; Pigs 2; Poultry 80 (1994). Source: Ministério da Agricultura e Desenvolvimento Rural.

Livestock Products (estimates, metric tons unless otherwise indicated, 1995): Beef 24; Pork 34; Mutton and goat meat 32; Poultry meat 118; Eggs 1.6 (million); Milk 1.5 ('000 litres, 1994); Honey 1.5. Source: mainly Ministério da Agricultura e Desenvolvimento Rural.

Forestry ('000 cubic metres): Roundwood removals 9 in 1989; 1990–97 annual production as in 1989. Source: FAO, *Yearbook of Forest Products*.

Fishing ('000 metric tons, live weight): Total catch 2.8 in 1995 (FAO estimate); 2.9 in 1996 (FAO estimate); 3.3 in 1997. Source: FAO, *Yearbook of Fishery Statistics*.

INDUSTRY

Production (metric tons, unless otherwise indicated, 1997): Bread and biscuits 3,768 (1995); Soap 261.1 (1995); Beer (litres) 529,400 (1995); Palm oil 1,183; Electric energy (million kWh) 22.8. Source: partly IMF, *São Tomé and Príncipe: Statistical Appendix* (September 1998).

FINANCE

Currency and Exchange Rates: 100 cêntimos = 1 dobra (Db). *Sterling, Dollar and Euro Equivalents* (31 January 2000): £1 sterling = 11,934.2 dobras; US $1 = 7,350.0 dobras; €1 = 7,196.4 dobras; 100,000 dobras = £8.379 = $13.605 = €13.896. *Average Exchange Rate* (dobras per US $): 4,552.5 in 1997; 6,883.2 in 1998; 7,119.0 in 1999.

Budget (million dobras): 1997: *Revenue:* Taxation 21,236 (Consumption taxes 4,186; Import taxes 4,701; Export taxes 1,874; Other taxes 10,475); Other current revenue 10,009 (Transfers from enterprises 2,058); Total 31,245, excl. grants (55,528). *Expenditure:* Current expenditure 55,675 (Personnel costs 11,709; Goods and services 7,004; Interest on external debt 22,356; Transfers 8,892; Defence 1,630; Other current expenditure 3,488; Redeployment fund 596); Capital 84,499; Total 140,174. Source: IMF, *São Tomé and Príncipe: Statistical Appendix* (September 1998).

International Reserves (US $ million at 31 December 1999): Foreign exchange 10.88; Total 10.88. Source: IMF, *International Financial Statistics*.

Money Supply (million dobras at 31 December 1999): Currency outside banks 20,920; Demand deposits at commercial banks 27,187; Total money 49,441. Source: IMF, *International Financial Statistics*.

Cost of Living (Consumer Price Index; base: 1996 = 100): 72.7 in 1995; 100.0 in 1996; 168.2 in 1997. Source: IMF, *São Tomé and Príncipe: Statistical Appendix* (September 1998).

Gross Domestic Product by Economic Activity (estimates, million dobras at current prices, 1997): Agriculture, forestry and fishing 46,682; Manufacturing, electricity, gas and water 7,875; Construction 29,469; Trade and transport 37,508; Public administration 44,669; Financial institutions 15,134; Other services 18,664; *Total* 200,000. Source: IMF, *São Tomé and Príncipe: Statistical Appendix* (September 1998).

Balance of Payments (estimates, US $ million, 1997): Exports of goods f.o.b. 5.3; Imports of goods f.o.b. –19.2; *Trade balance* –13.9; Exports of services 7.1; Imports of nonfactor services –22.1; *Balance on goods and services* –28.9; Other income (net) –4.8; *Balance on goods, services and income* –33.7; Private unrequited transfers (net) 0.8; Official unrequited transfers (net) 31.3; *Current balance* –1.6; Direct investment (net) 0.4; Other long-term capital (net) 2.3; Short-term capital (incl. net errors and omissions) –0.4; *Overall balance* 0.8. Source: IMF, *São Tomé and Príncipe: Statistical Appendix* (September 1998).

EXTERNAL TRADE

Principal Commodities (US $ million, 1997): *Imports c.i.f.*: Food and live animals 4.7; Petroleum and petroleum products 4.8; Capital goods 7.0; Total (incl. others) 24.0. *Exports f.o.b.*: Cocoa 4.59; Total (incl. others) 5.34. Source: IMF, *São Tomé and Príncipe: Statistical Appendix* (September 1998).

Principal Trading Partners (US $ million, 1997): *Imports c.i.f.*: Angola 1.6; Belgium 1.4; France 4.3; Gabon 0.2; Germany 0.4; Japan 0.8; Portugal 6.3; Total (incl. others) 24.0. *Exports f.o.b.*: Germany 0.3; Netherlands 2.7; Portugal 0.3; Total (incl. others) 5.3. Source: IMF, *São Tomé and Príncipe: Statistical Appendix* (September 1998).

TRANSPORT

Road Traffic (registered vehicles, 1994): Light vehicles 4,581; Heavy vehicles 561; Motor cycles 815; Tractors 299.

Shipping: *International Freight Traffic* (estimates, metric tons, 1992): Goods loaded 16,000; Goods unloaded 45,000. *Merchant Fleet* (registered at 31 December 1998): Number of vessels 10; Total displacement 10,242 grt. Source: Lloyd's Register of Shipping, *World Fleet Statistics*.

Civil Aviation (traffic on scheduled services, 1996): Passengers carried ('000) 23; Passenger-km (million) 9; Total ton-km (million) 1. Source: UN, *Statistical Yearbook*. (1992) Passengers carried 29,975; Freight 297,422 metric tons.

TOURISM

Tourist Arrivals: 6,160 in 1995; 6,436 in 1996; 4,924 in 1997. Source: World Tourism Organization, *Yearbook of Tourism Statistics*.

Tourist Arrivals by Country (1997): Angola 336, Cape Verde 110, France 996, Gabon 289, Germany 165, Portugal 1,700, Spain 238.

Tourism Receipts (US $ m): 2 in 1995; 2 in 1996; 2 in 1997. Source: World Tourism Organization, *Yearbook of Tourism Statistics*.

Hotels (1997): 11.

COMMUNICATIONS MEDIA

Radio Receivers (1997): 38,000 in use. Source: UNESCO, *Statistical Yearbook*.

Television Receivers (1997): 23,000 in use. Source: UNESCO, *Statistical Yearbook*.

Non-daily Newspapers and Periodicals (1999): Titles 4; Estimated average circulation 500 copies.

Telephones (1997): 2,864 lines in use. Source: Companhia Santomense de Telecomunicações.

Telefax Stations (1996): 173 in use. Source: Companhia Santomense de Telecomunicações.

EDUCATION

Pre-primary (1989): 13 schools; 116 teachers; 3,446 pupils (males 1,702; females 1,744).
Primary (1997): 69 schools; 638 teachers; 20,502 pupils (1996).
General Secondary (1997): 10 schools; 415 teachers; 12,280 pupils.

Teacher Training: 10 teachers (1983); 188 students (males 74; females 114) (1987).
Vocational Secondary (1989): 18 teachers; 101 students (males 68; females 33).

Source: mainly UNESCO, *Statistical Yearbook*.

Directory

The Constitution

The Constitution came into force on 10 September 1990 as the result of a national referendum, in which 72% of the electorate voted in favour of a draft that had been introduced by the Central Committee of the Movimento de Libertação de São Tomé e Príncipe and approved in March 1990 by the Assembleia Popular Nacional. The following is a summary of its main provisions:

The Democratic Republic of São Tomé and Príncipe is a sovereign, independent, unitary and democratic state. There shall be complete separation between Church and State. Sovereignty resides in the people, who exercise it through universal, direct and secret vote, according to the terms of the Constitution.

Legislative power is vested in the Assembleia Nacional, which comprises 55 members elected by universal adult suffrage. The Assembleia Nacional is elected for four years and meets in ordinary session twice a year. It may meet in extraordinary session on the proposal of the President, the Council of Ministers or of two-thirds of its members. The Assembleia Nacional elects its own President. In the period between ordinary sessions of the Assembleia Nacional its functions are assumed by a permanent commission elected from among its members.

Executive power is vested in the President of the Republic, who is elected for a period of five years by universal adult suffrage. The President's tenure of office is limited to two successive terms. He is the Supreme Commander of the Armed Forces and is accountable to the Assembleia Nacional. In the event of the President's death, permanent incapacity or resignation, his functions shall be assumed by the President of the Assembleia Nacional until a new president is elected.

The Government is the executive and administrative organ of State. The Prime Minister is the Head of Government and is appointed by the President. Other ministers are appointed by the President on the proposal of the Prime Minister. The Government is responsible to the President and the Assembleia Nacional.

Judicial power is exercised by the Supreme Court and all other competent tribunals and courts. The Supreme Court is the supreme judicial authority, and is accountable only to the Assembleia Nacional. Its members are appointed by the Assembleia Nacional. The right to a defence is guaranteed.

The Constitution may be revised only by the Assembleia Nacional on the proposal of at least three-quarters of its members. Any amendment must be approved by a two-thirds' majority of the Assembleia Nacional.

Note: In 1994 the Assembleia Nacional granted political and administrative autonomy to the island of Príncipe. Legislation was adopted establishing a seven-member regional assembly and a five-member regional government; both are accountable to the Government of São Tomé and Príncipe.

The Government

HEAD OF STATE

President and Commander-in-Chief of the Armed Forces: MIGUEL DOS ANJOS DA CUNHA LISBOA TROVOADA (took office 3 April 1991; re-elected 21 July 1996).

COUNCIL OF MINISTERS
(August 2000)

Prime Minister: GUILHERME PÓSSER DA COSTA.
Minister Adjunct to the Prime Minister and Minister of Justice, Labour, Public Administration and Parliamentary Affairs: ALBERTO PAULINO.
Minister of Foreign Affairs and Co-operation: JOAQUIM RAFAEL BRANCO.
Minister of Defence: Lt-Col JOÃO QUARESMA VIEGAS BEXIGAS.
Minister of Planning and Finance: ADELINO SANTIAGO CASTELO DAVID.

Minister of the Economy: MARIA DAS NEVES CEITA BATISTA DE SOUSA.
Minister of Education, Youth and Culture: PEREGRINO DO SACRAMENTO DA COSTA.
Minister of Infrastructure and Natural Resources: LUÍS ALBERTO CARNEIRO DOS PRAZERES.
Minister of Health and Sports: ANTÓNIO SOARES MARQUES DE LIMA.
Minister of Internal and Territorial Administration: MANUEL DA CRUZ MARÇAL LIMA.

Government of the Autonomous Region of Príncipe
(August 2000)

President: DAMIÃO VAZ D'ALMEIDA.
Secretary for Social Affairs: ZEFERINO VAZ DOS SANTOS DOS PRAZERES.
Secretary for Infrastructure and Environment: OZÓRIO UMBELINA.
Secretary for Economic Affairs: SILVESTRE UMBELINA.
Secretary for Finance: EPIFÁCIO CASSANDRA.

MINISTRIES

Office of the Prime Minister: Praça Yon Gato, CP 302, São Tomé; tel. 22890; fax 21670.
Ministry of Defence: Avda 12 de Julho, CP 427, São Tomé; tel. 21092.
Ministry of the Economy: Largo Alfândega, São Tomé; tel. 21083; fax 22790; e-mail economia@cstome.net.
Ministry of Education, Youth and Culture: Rua Misericórdia, CP 41, São Tomé; tel. 21398; fax 21466.
Ministry of Foreign Affairs and Co-operation: Avda 12 de Julho, CP 111, São Tomé; tel. 22309; fax 22597.
Ministry of Health and Sports: Avda Patrice Lumumba, CP 23, São Tomé; tel. 22290; fax 21306.
Ministry of Infrastructure and Natural Resources: Avda 12 de Julho, CP 47, São Tomé; tel. 22714; fax 22347.
Ministry of Internal and Territorial Administration: Avda 12 de Julho, CP 130, São Tomé; tel. 22648.
Ministry of Justice and Parliamentary Affairs: Avda 12 de Julho, CP 4, São Tomé; tel. 23263; fax 22256.
Ministry of Planning, Finance and Co-operation: Largo Alfândega, CP 168, São Tomé; tel. 22105; fax 22683.
Ministry of Public Administration and Labour: São Tomé.

President and Legislature

PRESIDENT

Presidential Election, First Ballot, 30 June 1996

Candidate	Votes	% of votes
MIGUEL TROVOADA	15,344	41.38
MANUEL PINTO DA COSTA	13,627	37.75
ALDA BANDEIRA	5,970	16.10
CARLOS DA GRAÇA	1,973	5.32
ARMINDO TOMBA	168	0.45
Total	**37,082**	**100.00**

Second Ballot, 21 July 1996

Candidate	Votes	% of votes
MIGUEL TROVOADA	19,885	52.74
MANUEL PINTO DA COSTA	17,818	47.26
Total	**37,703**	**100.00**

SÃO TOMÉ AND PRÍNCIPE

Directory

ASSEMBLEIA NACIONAL

General Election, 8 November 1998

	Seats
Movimento de Libertação de São Tomé e Príncipe—Partido Social Democrata	31
Acção Democrática Independente	16
Partido de Convergência Democrática—Grupo de Reflexão	8
Total	**55**

Political Organizations

Acção Democrática Independente (ADI): São Tomé; f. 1992; Leader CARLOS AGOSTINHO DAS NEVES.

Aliança Popular—Partido Trabalhista (AP—PT): São Tomé; f. 1993; Leader ANACLETO ROLIN.

Frente Democrata Cristã—Partido Social da Unidade (FDC—PSU): São Tomé; f. 1990; Pres. SABINO DOS SANTOS.

Movimento de Libertação de São Tomé e Príncipe—Partido Social Democrata (MLSTP—PSD): São Tomé; f. 1972 as MLSTP; adopted present name in 1990; sole legal party 1972–90; Pres. MANUEL PINTO DA COSTA.

Partido de Convergência Democrática—Grupo de Reflexão (PCD—GR): São Tomé; f. 1990; Pres. ALDA BANDEIRA.

Partido CODÓ (CODÓ): São Tomé; f. 1990 as Partido Democrático de São Tomé e Príncipe—Coligação Democrática da Oposição; renamed as above June 1998; Leader MANUEL NEVES E SILVA.

Partido Popular do Progresso (PPP): São Tomé; f. 1998; Leader JOÃO GUADALUPE VIEGAS DE CEITA.

União Nacional para Democracia e Progresso—Grupo Bóia-Fria (UNDP—GBF): São Tomé; f. 1998; Leader PAIXÃO LIMA.

Diplomatic Representation

EMBASSIES IN SÃO TOMÉ AND PRÍNCIPE

Angola: Avda Kwame Nkrumah 45, São Tomé; tel. 22206; fax 21563; Chargé d'affaires: PEDRO FERNANDO MAVUNZA.

China (Taiwan): Avda Marginal de 12 de Julho, CP 839, São Tomé; tel. 23529; fax 21376; e-mail rocstp@cstome.net; Ambassador: PEDRO YEN-CHU HSIANG.

Gabon: Rua Damão, São Tomé; tel. 21280; Ambassador: HENRI MBIRA NZE.

Portugal: Avda Marginal de 12 de Julho, CP 173, São Tomé; tel. 22470; fax 21190; Ambassador: MÁRIO DE JESUS SANTOS.

Judicial System

Judicial power is exercised by the Supreme Court of Justice and the Courts of Primary Instance. The Supreme Court is the ultimate judicial authority.

President of the Supreme Court: PASCOAL DAIO.

Religion

More than 90% of the population are Christians, almost all of whom are Roman Catholics.

CHRISTIANITY

The Roman Catholic Church

São Tomé and Príncipe comprises a single diocese, directly responsible to the Holy See. At 31 December 1998 there were an estimated 104,753 adherents in the country, representing about 82% of the population. The bishop participates in the Episcopal Conference of Angola and São Tomé (based in Luanda, Angola).

Bishop of São Tomé e Príncipe: Rt Rev. ABÍLIO RODAS DE SOUSA RIBAS, Centro Diocesano, CP 104, São Tomé; tel. and fax 23455.

The Press

Diário da República: Cooperativa de Artes Gráficas, Rua João Devs, CP 28, São Tomé; tel. 22661; f. 1836; official gazette; Dir OSCAR FERREIRA.

Jornala Vitrina: CP490, São Tomé; tel. 21150; fax 21666; f. 1999; Dir MANUEL BARROS.

Notícias: Avda 12 de Julho, CP 112, São Tomé; tel. 22087; fax 21973; f. 1991; state-owned; Dir CARLOS DUARTE.

O País: Avda Amílcar Cabral, CP 361, São Tomé; tel. 23833; fax 21989; e-mail iucai@cstome.net; f. 1998; Dir FRANCISCO PINTO DA SILVEIRA RITA.

O Parvo: CP 535, São Tomé; tel. 21031; f. 1994; Editor ARMINDO CARDOSO.

Tribuna: Praça Yon Gato, CP 19, São Tomé; tel. and fax 23295; f 1998; Dir LEONEL MENDES.

NEWS AGENCY

STP-Press: Avda Marginal de 12 de Julho, CP 112, São Tomé; tel. 23431; fax 21365; f. 1985; operated by the radio station in asscn with the Angolan news agency, ANGOP; Dir MANUEL DÊNDE.

Broadcasting and Communications

TELECOMMUNICATIONS

Companhia Santomense de Telecomunicações, SARL (CST): CP 141, São Tomé; tel. 22226; fax 22500; e-mail cst@cstome.net; f. 1989 by Govt of São Tomé (49%) and Rádio Marconi SA (Portugal; 51%) to facilitate increased telecommunications links and television reception via satellite; in March 1997 CST introduced internet services; Rádio Marconi's shares subsequently assumed by Portugal Telecom SA; Pres. of Admin. Bd JOSÉ MANUEL BRIOSA E GALA; Administrator-Delegate JOSÉ MANUEL MAMEDE DA COSTA.

BROADCASTING

Portuguese technical and financial assistance in the establishment of a television service was announced in May 1989. Transmissions commenced in 1992, and the service currently broadcasts seven days a week. In 1995 Radio France Internationale and Rádio Televisão Portuguesa Internacional began relaying radio and television broadcasts, respectively, to the archipelago. In 1997 Voice of America, which had been broadcasting throughout Africa since 1993 from a relay station installed on São Tomé, began local transmissions on FM.

Radio

Rádio Nacional de São Tomé e Príncipe: Avda Marginal de 12 de Julho, CP 44, São Tomé; tel. 23293; fax 21365; e-mail rnstp@cstome.net; f. 1958; state-controlled; home service in Portuguese and Creole; Dir ARTUR PINHO.

Television

Televisão Santomense (TVS): Bairro Quinta de Santo António, CP 393, São Tomé; tel. 21493; fax 21942; state-controlled; Dir VICTOR CORREIA.

Finance

(cap. = capital; m. = million)

BANKING

Central Bank

Banco Central de São Tomé e Príncipe (BCSTP): Praça da Independência, CP 168, São Tomé; tel. 22407; fax 22501; e-mail bcentral@cstome.net; f. 1992 to succeed fmr Banco Nacional de São Tomé e Príncipe; bank of issue; Gov. MARIA DO CARMO TROVOADA SILVEIRA.

Commercial Banks

Banco Comercial do Equador (BCE): Rua de Moçambique, CP 361, São Tomé; tel. 21898; fax 21989; e-mail bce@cstome.net; f. 1995; Dir AGOSTINHO DA SILVEIRA RITA.

Banco Internacional de São Tomé e Príncipe (BISTP): Praça da Independência, CP 536, São Tomé; tel. 21445; fax 22427; e-mail bistp@cstome.net; f. 1993; 33% govt-owned, 30% owned by Banco Totta e Açores, SA (Portugal), 22% by Banco Nacional Ultramarino (Portugal), 15% by BCSTP; cap. US $1.8m. (1998); Exec. Cttee MANUEL MARQUÊS COSTA OLIVEIRA, ACÁCIO ELBA BONFIM, JOÃO CARLOS AGUIAR CRISTOVÃO.

INSURANCE

Instituto de Segurança Social: Rua Soldado Paulo Ferreira, São Tomé; tel. 21382; e-mail inss@cstome.net; f. as Caixa de Previdência dos Funcionários Públicos, adopted present name 1994; insurance fund for civil servants; Pres. of Admin. Bd ALBINO GRAÇA DA FONSECA; Dir JUVENAL DO ESPÍRITO SANTO.

957

Trade and Industry
DEVELOPMENT ORGANIZATION
Instituto para o Desenvolvimento Económico e Social (INDES): Travessa do Pelourinho, CP 408, São Tomé; tel. 22491; fax 21931; e-mail indes@cstome.net; f. 1989 as Fundo Social e de Infrastructuras, adopted present name 1994; channels foreign funds to local economy; Dir HOMERO JERÓNIMO SALVATERRA.

CHAMBER OF COMMERCE
Câmara do Comércio da Indústria e Agricultura (CCIA): CP 527, Rua de Moçambique, São Tomé; tel. 22723; Pres. ANTONIO DE BARROS AMARAL AGUIAR.

UTILITIES
Electricity and Water
Empresa de Água e Electricidade (EMAE): Avda Água Grande, CP 46, São Tomé; tel. 22351; fax 22488; e-mail emae@cstome.net; f. 1979; state electricity and water co.

TRADE UNIONS
Organizacão Nacional de Trabalhadores de São Tomé e Príncipe (ONTSTP): Rua Cabo Verde, São Tomé; tel. 22431; Sec.-Gen. JOÃO TAVARES.

União Geral dos Trabalhadores de São Tomé e Príncipe (UGSTP): Avda Kwame Nkrumah, São Tomé; tel. 22443; Sec.-Gen. COSTA CARLOS.

Transport
RAILWAYS
There are no railways in São Tomé and Príncipe.

ROADS
In 1996 there were an estimated 320 km of roads, of which 218 km were asphalted.

SHIPPING
The principal ports are at São Tomé city and at Neves on São Tomé island. In 2000 plans were proceeding to construct a deep-water port at Agulhas Bay on Príncipe island.

Companhia de Navegação e Transportes Marítimos: CP 49, São Tomé; tel. 22278; fax 21311; shipping and freight forwarding.

Transportes e Serviços Marítimos: CP 11, António do Príncipe; tel. 21057; fax 22447; shipping and freight forwarding.

CIVIL AVIATION
The international airport is at São Tomé. A US $16m. modernization project, including a runway extension, and a new control tower, was financed mainly by the African Development Bank and completed in 1992.

Air São Tomé e Príncipe: Avda Marginal de 12 de Julho, CP 45, São Tomé; tel. 21976; fax 21375; e-mail astp@cstome.net; f. 1993; owned by Govt of São Tomé (35%), TAP-Air Portugal, SA (40%), Golfe International Air Service (France) (24%) and Mistral Voyages (France) (1%); operates domestic service between the islands of São Tomé and Príncipe and international connection to Libreville (Gabon); Pres. RAÚL BRAGANÇA WAGNER NETO; Dir-Gen. SÉRGIO LOPES.

Tourism
The islands benefit from spectacular mountain scenery, unspoilt beaches and unique species of flora and wildlife. Although still largely undeveloped, tourism is currently the sector of the islands' economy attracting the highest level of foreign investment. However, the high level of rainfall during most of the year limits the duration of the tourist season, and the expense of reaching the islands by air is also an inhibiting factor. There were 4,924 tourist arrivals in 1997, when receipts totalled some US $2m. In 1996 there were nine hotels and nine guest houses, with a total of 520 beds.

Defence
In 1995 the armed forces were estimated to number some 600. Military service, which is compulsory, lasts for 30 months. In 1992 a reorganization was initiated of the islands' armed forces and the police into two separate police forces, one for public order and another for criminal investigation. However, in December 1993, following increasing pressure from the military high command, parliament approved the new legal status of the armed forces, maintaining their role as military defenders of the nation. In late 1996 restructuring of the armed forces resumed, with technical assistance from Portugal.

Commander-in-Chief of the Armed Forces: Pres. MIGUEL DOS ANJOS DA CUNHA LISBOA TROVOADA.

Chief of General Staff of the Armed Forces: Lt-Col ANTÓNIO DO NASCIMENTO.

Defence Expenditure: Budgeted at 1,630m. dobras (excl. capital expenditure) in 1997.

Education
Primary education is officially compulsory for a period of four years between seven and 14 years of age. Secondary education lasts for a further seven years, comprising a first cycle of five years and a second cycle of two years. In 1997 the country had 69 primary schools. In 1996 primary schools had a total enrolment of 20,280 pupils. In 1997 there were 10 secondary schools, with a total enrolment of 12,280 pupils. In 1995 there was one vocational training centre in the country. In 1991 the average rate of adult illiteracy was 26.8% (males 14.8%; females 38.1%). In 1995 21.2% of the public investment programme was spent on education. Two secondary schools, financed by the OPEC Fund for International Development, and a teacher-training college, the Instituto Superior Politécnico, were completed in 1997.

Bibliography

ABP. Zeitschrift zur portugiesischsprachigen Welt. *Beiträge zum Symposium 'São Tomé und Príncipe', 7.4.1995 in der Universtat zu Köln*, no 1/1996.

Ambrósio, A. *Subsidios para a história de São Tomé e Príncipe.* Lisbon, Livros Horizonte, 1984.

Associação Industrial Portuguesa (AIP), *Guia de Oportunidades para as Empresas Industriais Portuguesas em S. Tomé e Príncipe.* Lisbon, 1996.

Bredero, J. T., Heemskerk, W., and Toxopeus, H. *Agriculture and Livestock Production in São Tomé and Príncipe (West Africa).* Wageningen, Foundation for Agricultural Plant Breeding, 1977.

Caldeira, A. M. *Mulheres, Sexualidade e Casamento no Arquipelago de S. Tomé e Príncipe (Seculos XV a XVII).* Lisbon, Edições Cosmos, 1999.

da Cruz, C. B. *São Tomé e Príncipe: do colonialismo à independência.* Lisbon, 1975.

Economist Intelligence Unit. *Congo, São Tomé & Príncipe, Guinea-Bissau, Cape Verde, Country Report.* London, quarterly.

Congo, São Tomé & Príncipe, Guinea-Bissau, Cape Verde, Country Profile. London, annual.

Espírito Santo, C. *Contribuição para a história de São Tomé e Príncipe.* Lisbon 1979.

A Coroa do Mar. Editorial Caminho, Lisbon, 1998.

European Union. 'São Tomé and Príncipe: The Last Card in the Pack', in *The Courier*, No 168, March–April 1998.

Eyzaguirre, P. B. 'The Independence of São Tomé e Príncipe and Agrarian Reform', in *Journal of Modern African Studies*, April 1989.

'The Ecology of Swidden Agriculture and Agrarian History in São Tomé', in *Cahiers d'Etudes africaines*, Vol. XXVI, No 101–102, 1986.

'Competing Systems of Land Tenure in an African Plantation Society', in Downs, R.E., and Reyna, S.P. (Eds), *Land and Society in Contemporary Africa.* Hanover, NH: University Press of New England, 1988.

Ferraz, L. I. *The Creole of São Tomé.* Johannesburg, Witwatersrand University Press, 1979.

'São Tomé and Príncipe: Combating Cocoa Colonialism', in *Africa Report*, January 1986.

Garfield, R. *A History of São Tomé Island 1470–1655: The Key to Guinea.* New York, Edwin Mellen Press, 1992.

Henriques, I. C. *São Tomé e Príncipe: A Invenção de uma Sociedade.* Lisbon, Vega Editora, 2000.

Hodges, T., and Newitt, M. *São Tomé and Príncipe: From Plantation Colony to Microstate.* Boulder, CO, Westview Press, 1988.

International Monetary Fund. *São Tomé and Príncipe—Recent Economic Developments and Selected Issues.* Washington, DC, IMF, 1997.

Jones, P. J., Burlison, J. P., and Tye, A. *Conservação dos ecossistemas florestais da República Democrática de São Tomé e Príncipe.* Gland and Cambridge, UICN, 1991.

Macqueen, N. *The Decolonization of Portuguese Africa: Metropolitan Revolution and the Dissolution of Empire.* Harlow, Longman, 1997.

Mantero, F. *A Mão d'Obra em S. Thomé e Príncipe.* Lisbon, 1910.

Mata, I. *Emergência e Existência de uma Literatura. O Caso Santomense.* ALAC–África, Literatura, Arte e Cultura, Linda-a-Velha (Portugal), 1993.

Diálogo com as Ilhas. Sobre Cultura e Literatura de São Tomé e Príncipe. Edições Colibri, Lisbon, 1998.

Nascimento, A. 'Conflitos de europeos em S. Tomé e Príncipe', in *Revista Internacional de Estudos Africanos,* No 12–13, Lisbon, 1990.

'A crise braçal de 1875 em S. Tomé', in *Revista Crítica de Ciências Sociais,* No 34, Coimbra, 1992.

'Cabindas em S. Tomé', in *Revista Internacional de Estudos Africanos,* No 14–15, Lisbon, 1991.

'Conflitos locais e soberania portuguesa no Príncipe nas décadas de 1820 e 1830', in *Mare Liberum,* No 10, Lisbon, 1995.

'Conflitos raciais durante a República (1910–1926)—Um campo de luta: a imprensa dos naturais', in *Africa,* No 16–17, São Paulo, 1993–1994.

'Duas figuras, duas elites e duas épocas em S. Tomé: Jacinto Carneiro de Sousa e Almeida e Augusto Gamboa', in *Revista Internacional de Estudos Africanos,* No 16–17, Lisbon, 1992–1994.

'Hegemonia das roças versus instituição municipal na ilha do Príncipe nos primeiros anos da República', in *O Município no Mundo Português,* CEHA, Funchal, 1998.

'Humberto Delgado versus isolamento de S. Tomé e Príncipe', in Delgado I., Pacheco, C. and Faria, T. (Eds), *Huberto Delgado as Eleições de 58,* Vega, Lisbon, 1998.

A Liga dos Interesses Indígenas, in Arquipélago–História, 2nd series, Vol. III, Ponta Delgada 1999.

'A marginalidade social e política do protestantismo em São Tomé e Príncipe (do último quartel de oitocentos a meados de novecentos)', in *Lusotopie, Enjeux contemporains dans les espaces lusophones,* Vol. 1998.

'Salubridade, urbanismo e ordenamento social em S. Tomé', in *Construção e ensino da História de Africa.* Lisbon, 1994.

'S. Tomé e Príncipe nos séculos XIX-XX: os estudos pós-independência', in Vieira, Alberto. *Guia de História das Ilhas do Atlântico.* Funchal, 1995.

'Recolonização, mutações demográficas e afluxo de degredados a S. Tomé no século XIX', in *História das Ilhas do Atlântico,* 2 vols. Funchal, 1997.

'O Recrutamento de Serviçais Moçambicanos para as Roças de São Tomé e Príncipe (1908–1921), in *Actas do Seminário "Moçambique: Navegações, Comércio e Técnicas".* Lisbon, Comissão Nacional para as Comemoracões dos Descobrimentos Portugueses, Lisbon, 1998.

'A sedição de 1931 em S. Tomé', in *História,* No. 01 (Ano XX), Lisbon, 1998.

'S. Tomé e Príncipe', in Alexandre, V. and Dias, J., *O Império Africano 1825–1890,* Estampa, Lisboa, 1998.

Corporações religiosas de ilheus em São Tomé e Príncipe do liberalismo à Republica, in *Estudos Afro-Asiáticos,* No 35, Rio de Janeiro, Universidade Candido Mendes, 1999.

das Neves, C. A. *São Tomé e Príncipe na Segunda Metade do Século XVIII.* Região Autónoma da Madeira, 1989.

Núñez, B. *Dictionary of Portuguese–African Civilization.* Vol. I. London, Hans Zell, 1995.

Oliveira, J. E. *A Economia de São Tomé e Príncipe.* Lisbon, Instituto de Investigação Científica Tropical, 1993.

Pélissier, R. *Le Naufrage des Caravelles (1961–75).* Orgeval, Editions Pélissier, 1979.

Explorar. Voyages en Angola et autres lieux incertains. Orgeval, Editions Pélissier, 1980.

Programa dos Nações Unidas para o Desenvolvimento (PNUD/UNDP), *Relatório do Desenvolvimento Humano São Tomé e Príncipe 1998.* São Tomé, 1998.

Romana, H. A. C. B. *São Tomé e Príncipe. Elementos para uma Análise Antropológica das suas Vulnerabilidades e Potencialidades.* Instituto Superior de Ciências Sociais e Políticas, Universidade Técnica de Lisboa, 1997.

da Rosa, L.C. *Die lusographe Literatur der Inseln São Tomé und Príncipe: Versuch einer literaturgeschichtlichen Darstellung.* TFM/Domus Editoria Euroaea, Frankfurt am Main, 1994.

Schümer, M. *São Tomé und Príncipe, Ausbruch aus der Isolation.* Bonn, Forschungsinstitut der Deutschen Gesellschaft für Auswärtige Politik eV, 1987.

Seibert, G. 'A política num micro-estado: São Tomé e Príncipe, ou os conflitos pessoais e políticos na génese dos partidos políticos', in *Lusotopie, Enjeux contemporains dans les espaces lusophones,* Vol. 1995.

'São Tomé e Príncipe: Military Coup as a Lesson?', in *Lusotopie, Enjeux contemporains dans les espaces lusophones,* Vol. 1996.

'Le massacre de février à São Tomé raison d'être du nationalisme santoméen', in *Lusotopie, Enjeux contemporains dans les espaces lusophones,* Vol. 1997.

Comrades, Clients and Cousins. Colonialism, Socialism and Democratization in São Tomé and Príncipe. CNWS Publications, Leiden University, 1999.

Shaw, C. S. *São Tomé and Príncipe.* Clio Press (World Bibliographical Series, vol. 172), Oxford, 1994.

Tenreiro, F. *A Ilha de São Tomé, Memórias da Junta de Investigações do Ultramar,* Lisbon, 1961.

Torp, E., Denny, L. M., and Ray, D. I. (Eds). *Mozambique and São Tomé and Príncipe: Politics, Economics and Society.* New York, Pinter, 1989.

de Unzueta y Yuste, A. *Islas del Golfo de Guinea (Elobeyes, Corisco, Annobón, Príncipe y Santo Tomé).* Madrid, Instituto de Estudios Políticos, 1945.

SENEGAL

Physical and Social Geography

R. J. HARRISON CHURCH

The Republic of Senegal, the most westerly state of Africa, covers an area of 196,722 sq km (75,955 sq miles). The population was 6,896,808 at the census of May 1988, and was estimated at 9,278,617 (47.2 persons per sq km) at mid-1999. The southern border is first with Guinea-Bissau and then with Guinea on the northern edge of the Primary sandstone outcrop of the Fouta Djallon. In the east the border is with Mali, in the only other area of bold relief in Senegal, where there are Pre-Cambrian rocks in the Bambouk mountains. The northern border with Mauritania lies along the Senegal river, navigable for small boats all the year to Podor and for two months to Kayes (Mali). The river has a wide flood plain, annually cultivated as the waters retreat. The delta soils are saline, but dams for power, irrigation and better navigation are being built or proposed. The commissioning in 1985 of the Djama dam has considerably improved navigability at the Senegal river delta. The Manantali scheme, completed in 1988, will eventually extend the all-year navigability of the river from 220 km to 924 km, as far as Kayes, in Mali.

The Gambia forms a semi-enclave between part of southern Senegal and the sea, along the valley of the navigable Gambia river. This has meant that, since the colonial delimitation of the Gambia–Senegal borders in 1889, the river has played no positive role in Senegal's development and that the Casamance region, in the south, was isolated from the rest of Senegal until the opening of the Trans-Gambian highway in 1958.

The Cap Vert (Cape Verde) peninsula, on which the capital, Dakar, stands, is of verdant appearance, resulting from exposure to south-westerly winds, and thus contrasts with the yellow dunes to the north. Basalt underlies much of Dakar, and its harbour was constructed in a sandy area east of (and sheltered by) the basaltic plateau. South of the peninsula, particularly in Casamance, the coast is a drowned one of shallow estuaries.

Apart from the high eastern and south-eastern borderlands most of the country has monotonous plains, which in an earlier period were drained by large rivers in the centre of the country. Relic valleys, now devoid of superficial water, occur in the Ferlo desert, and these built up the Sine Saloum delta north of The Gambia. In a later dry period north-east to south-west trending sand dunes were formed, giving Senegal's plains their undulating and ribbed surfaces. These plains of Cayor, Baol, and Nioro du Rip are inhabited by Wolof and Serer cultivators of groundnuts and millet. The coast between Saint-Louis and Dakar has a broad belt of live dunes. Behind them, near Thiès, calcium phosphates are quarried (aluminium phosphates are also present) and phosphatic fertilizer is produced.

Although Senegal's mineral resources are otherwise relatively sparse, there are potentially valuable reserves of gold, in the south-east (production of which began in mid-1997), as well as deposits of high-grade iron ore, in considerable quantity, in the east. Reserves of natural gas are exploited offshore from Dakar, and there is petroleum off the Casamance coast.

Senegal's climate is widely varied, and the coast is remarkably cool for the latitude (Dakar 14° 38′ N). The Cap Vert peninsula is particularly breezy, because it projects into the path of northerly marine trade winds. Average temperatures are in the range 18°C–31°C, and the rainy season is little more than three months in length. Inland both temperatures and rainfall are higher, and the rainy season in comparable latitudes is somewhat longer. Casamance lies on the northern fringe of the monsoonal climate. Thus Ziguinchor (12° 35′ N) has four to five months' rainy season, with average annual rainfall of 1,626 mm, nearly three times that received by Dakar. The natural vegetation ranges from Sahel savannah north of about 15°N, through Sudan savannah in south-central Senegal, to Guinea savannah in Casamance, where the oil palm is common.

Recent History

PIERRE ENGLEBERT

Revised for this edition by RICHARD SYNGE

Following three centuries of French rule, Senegal became a self-governing member of the French Community in 1958. The Mali Federation with Soudan (now Mali) was formed in April 1959 and became independent in June 1960. However, the incompatibility of the two leaderships undermined the federation, which collapsed after only two months. The Republic of Senegal was proclaimed on 5 September, with Léopold Sédar Senghor, the founder of the Union progressiste sénégalaise (UPS), as its first president. His prime minister, the socialist Mamadou Dia, attempted, despite French opposition, to introduce comprehensive national planning. Senghor reversed this policy, and assumed the premiership himself after Dia was convicted in 1962 of plotting a *coup d'état* and sentenced to life imprisonment. A new constitution, strengthening the powers of the president, was approved in a referendum in March 1963. Later in the year the UPS won a decisive victory in elections to the national assembly, and other parties were either outlawed or absorbed into the UPS, which by 1966 was the sole legal party.

In 1970 the office of the prime minister was revived and assigned to a young provincial administrator, Abdou Diouf. Elections in January 1973 returned both Senghor and the UPS with substantial majorities, but student unrest ensued and in 1976 Senghor announced the creation of a three-party system, comprising the UPS (later renamed the Parti socialiste, PS), the recently founded Parti démocratique sénégalais (PDS) and a Marxist-Leninist party. Several other unofficial opposition parties were subsequently formed. At elections in February 1978 the PS won 83 of the 100 seats in the national assembly, while Senghor overwhelmingly defeated the PDS leader, Abdoulaye Wade, in the presidential election. In December a fourth political grouping, the right-wing Mouvement républicain sénégalais, was officially recognized.

DIOUF'S LEADERSHIP

A period of economic decline and resultant austerity measures, in conjunction with intense pressure for political reform, led to Senghor's resignation in December 1980. Diouf assumed the presidency in January 1981 (also becoming secretary-general of the PS), and undertook to reorganize the political system, by removing restrictions on political activity, and allowing the official registration of previously unofficial parties.

In August 1981, following a *coup d'état* in The Gambia, Diouf despatched Senegalese troops to restore the deposed president, Sir Dawda Jawara, to power. Senegalese forces were subsequently asked to remain, and Diouf and Jawara swiftly established a confederation of the two states, with co-ordinated policies in defence, foreign affairs and economic and financial matters. An agreement establishing the Senegambian confederation came into effect in February 1982. Diouf was designated permanent president of a joint council of ministers, and a confederal assembly was established. However, The Gambia resisted attempts by Senegal to proceed towards the full political and economic integration of the two countries.

In February 1983 Diouf led the PS to a clear victory in presidential and legislative elections. Diouf received 83.5% of the votes cast, and the PS candidates for the national assembly secured 111 seats, with 79.9% of the votes. The PDS won eight seats, and the Rassemblement national démocratique only one. Disputing the results, the government's opponents resolved to boycott the assembly, although most had taken their seats by the end of the year.

The PS consistently benefited from opposition disunity; a boycott by 12 of the country's 15 registered parties contributed to the success of the PS in municipal and rural elections in November 1984. In September 1985 the government banned an alliance of five opposition parties, on the grounds of unconstitutionality. Wade and the leader of the Ligue démcratique–Mouvement pour le parti du travail (LD–MPT), Abdoulaye Bathily, had been among alliance members detained for several days in August, on charges of 'unauthorized demonstration'. The emergence of a PDS splinter group, the Parti démocratique sénégalais–Rénovation (PDS–R), under the leadership of Serigne Diop, was announced in June 1987, following a period of defections and resignations from Wade's party.

Classes at the University of Dakar were boycotted in early 1987 by students who were protesting against the late payment of grants and poor living conditions. The student demonstrations were followed by an unprecedented (and illegal) strike by police forces in April, which led to the dismissal of the minister of the interior and the suspension from duty of more than 6,000 police officers. By August nearly 5,000 police officers had been reinstated, with the main antagonists permanently dismissed.

Preliminary results of the February 1988 presidential and legislative elections indicated decisive victories for both Diouf and the PS. The PDS, which had long demanded reform of the electoral code, alleged that fraud had been widespread, and rioting erupted in the Dakar region. A state of emergency was declared, public gatherings were banned and educational establishments closed. Abdoulaye Wade and Amath Dansokho, the leader of the Marxist-Leninist Parti de l'indépendance et du travail (PIT), were arrested, together with other opposition activists. The official results allocated 73.2% of the votes cast in the presidential election to Diouf, and 25.8% to Wade (there were three other candidates). In the legislative election, the PS returned 103 deputies to the national assembly, and the PDS 17. Trials began in April for incitement to violence and attacks on the internal security of the state. Dansokho and five others were acquitted, but in May Wade received a one-year suspended prison sentence, while three other PDS activists received prison terms of between six months and two years. However, Diouf swiftly terminated the state of emergency, and all those who had been convicted of involvement in the post-election violence were included in a presidential amnesty later in the month.

Secondary school pupils (who had been boycotting classes since October 1987) and university students failed to return to classes after the elections. In October 1988 a programme for the rehabilitation of the national education system was announced, and in the following month the government agreed to the students' demands for improved welfare provisions, and gave assurances regarding the independence of the University of Dakar, now renamed the Cheikh Anta Diop University. The 1988/89 academic year was, none the less, disrupted by a three-month strike by academic staff in early 1989, and by continuing protests by students concerning academic and welfare issues.

In March 1989 Wade, who had left for France in mid-1988, following the failure of attempts by the government and opposition to establish multi-party commissions to consider Senegal's political, economic and social problems, returned, asserting that Diouf had agreed to his demands that a transitional government of national unity be established (in which the PDS leader was to hold a prominent position) pending new presidential and legislative elections; the president, however, denied that such an agreement existed. In October the national assembly approved a series of electoral reforms, in accordance with the recommendations of a PS committee appointed earlier in the year. Changes to the electoral code were said to ensure a fair system of voter registration; a new system of proportional representation (within administrative departments) was to be introduced for legislative elections, and opposition parties were to be granted access to the state media. Also approved was a 'national democratic charter', governing the activities of political parties, and a controversial new labour code. The reforms were approved in the absence of PDS deputies, who were boycotting legislative sessions in protest against what they alleged was partial and selective media coverage of parliamentary debates.

Wade returned to Senegal in February 1990, after a further absence of more than six months. Although the PDS leader stated that he no longer disputed Diouf's victory in the 1988 elections, he demanded that, in view of the deteriorating economic and social conditions in Senegal, the electorate be allowed to choose new leaders. A series of days of action were subsequently organized by the opposition parties. Many parties boycotted municipal and rural elections in November 1990 (at which the PS reportedly received the support of 70% of voters), claiming that Senegal's electoral code still permitted widespread malpractice.

Constitutional Concessions

In March 1991 the national assembly approved several constitutional amendments, notably the restoration of the post of prime minister. It was also agreed that opposition parties would, henceforth, be allowed to participate in government. Accordingly, in April Habib Thiam was restored to his former post as premier. His government included four representatives of the PDS, among them Wade, as minister of state, and Ousmane Ngom (the party's parliamentary leader), who became minister of labour and professional training; Amath Dansokho also joined the new administration as minister of housing and town planning. In September the national assembly adopted a series of amendments to the electoral code, in accordance with recommendations that had been made by a national commission established in May. Under the amended code, presidential elections would henceforth take place, in two rounds if necessary (the new regulations stipulated that the president would have to be elected by at least one-quarter of registered voters, and by an absolute majority of the votes cast), every seven years, and the president would be limited to a maximum of two terms of office. Elections to the presidency would no longer coincide with legislative elections, which would continue to take place at five-yearly intervals. The amendments also included the lowering of the age of eligibility to vote from 21 to 18 years of age. A major reform of the organs of the judiciary was, meanwhile, implemented in May, as a result of which the supreme court was abolished and its functions divided between three new bodies: a constitutional council, a council of state and a court of higher appeal.

In October 1992 Wade (who had already declared his intention to contest the 1993 presidential election) and his three PDS colleagues resigned from the council of ministers, stating that they had been excluded from the governmental process. In subsequent months Wade protested that the PS retained privileged access to the state-owned media, and alleged that the government was attempting to hinder the registration of certain categories of voter prior to the presidential and legislative elections.

The presidential election, which took place on 21 February 1993, was contested by eight candidates. Despite some irregularities, voting was reported to be well-ordered in most areas, although there were serious incidents in the Casamance region (see below). The opposition denounced preliminary results, which indicated that, while Wade had enjoyed considerable success in Dakar and in the nearby manufacturing town of Thiès, Diouf had won a majority of the overall votes. Disagreements within the electoral commission (a body comprising a presiding magistrate and representatives of the candidates) delayed the process of determining the official outcome of the election, and eventually prompted the resignation of the president of the constitutional council. It was not until 13 March that the council was able to confirm that Diouf had been re-elected by 58.4% of the votes cast (51.6% of the electorate had voted). Wade secured 32.0% of the votes, with none of the other candidates obtaining more than 2.9%. Diouf announced that the electoral code was to be modified, with the immediate aim of avoiding similar delays in announcing the results of the forthcoming legislative elections.

Post-election Unrest

Elections to the national assembly took place on 9 May 1993, and on 14 May the electoral commission (now required to submit the results to the constitutional council within five days) announced that the PS had won 84 of the assembly's 120 seats. The PDS, with considerable support in urban areas, took 27 seats, the remainder being divided between three other parties and one electoral alliance. Participation by voters was only 40.7%. Shortly after the announcement of the results the vice-president of the constitutional council, Babacar Seye, was assassinated. Although an organization styling itself the 'Armée du peuple' claimed responsibility, Wade (who had recently declared that he had no confidence in the supposed impartiality of Seye and the council) and three other PDS leaders were detained for three days in connection with the murder. The PDS protested that its opponents were plotting to discredit the party, and suggested that attempts to implicate Wade in the assassination may have been orchestrated by those who sought to prevent any *rapprochement* of Diouf and the opposition leader. The official results of the legislative elections were confirmed by the constitutional council on 24 May. Meanwhile, four people suspected of involvement in Seye's murder were arrested: among those detained were Samuel Sarr, a close associate of Wade, and a PDS deputy, Mody Sy.

Wade and the PDS were excluded from Habib Thiam's new government, which was formed in June 1993. Dansokho, who had supported Diouf's presidential campaign, retained his position in the council of ministers, while the LD–MPT leader, Abdoulaye Bathily (himself a candidate for the presidency), was appointed minister of the environment and nature conservation. Other new appointments included Serigne Diop of the PDS–R, as minister of employment and professional training, and Papa Ousmane Sakho, hitherto the national director of the Banque centrale des états de l'Afrique de l'ouest, as minister of the economy, finance and planning.

In July 1993 six PDS and LD–MPT deputies were briefly detained after security forces intervened at a violent demonstration in Dakar, organized to demand the release of Mody Sy—who, it was alleged, had been tortured while in custody. A descent into social crisis followed. Citing the need to reduce the budget deficit in order to secure vital economic support from the international financial community, in August the government announced wide-ranging austerity measures. Trade unions and the political opposition denounced, especially, the proposed 15% reduction in salaries in the public sector, and in September, following the failure of attempts to reach a compromise, a 24-hour general strike, organized by the Confédération nationale des travailleurs sénégalais (CNTS), was widely observed. Diouf postponed the imposition of the measures, pending further negotiations with the CNTS and other unions. However, the talks again failed, and the salary cuts were imposed in October. Two 72-hour general strikes were organized, with only partial success, by trade unions later in October. In the same month Wade was charged with complicity in the assassination of Seye; Wade's wife and a PDS deputy were also charged with 'complicity in a breach of state security'. None was detained, although Mody Sy, Sarr and three others remained in custody in connection with the murder. A PDS motion expressing 'no confidence' in the government was defeated in the national assembly, and the party announced a boycott of parliamentary sessions, in protest against what it considered to be biased coverage by the state media of the vote.

In November 1993 Ousmane Ngom and Landing Savané, the leader of And Jëf–Parti africain pour la démocratie et le socialisme (AJ–PADS), were among those detained following a protest in Dakar to demand the cancellation of the austerity measures. The action coincided with a demonstration, at which further arrests were made, to appeal for the release of Moustapha Sy, the leader of an Islamist youth movement, Dahira Moustarchidine wal Moustarchidate, who had recently been arrested after having criticized the government (and who had also reportedly claimed to know the circumstances and authors of Seye's assassination). Ngom, Savané and more than 80 others were convicted of participating in an unauthorized demonstration, and received six-month suspended prison sentences. In January 1994 Moustapha Sy was sentenced to one year's imprisonment.

Diouf was widely regarded as a principal architect of the 50% devaluation, in January 1994, of the CFA franc, and the opposition accused the president of responsibility for resultant hardships. (Government measures to compensate for the devaluation included the cancellation of the previous year's wage reductions and 10% increase, effective from April, in salaries.) A demonstration in Dakar in February, organized by opposition parties grouped in a Coordination des forces démocratiques (CFD), degenerated into serious rioting throughout the capital, as a result of which eight people (including six police officers) were killed. Dahira Moustarchidine wal Moustarchidate, identified by the authorities as being implicated in much of the violence, was outlawed, and the government stated that it regarded the CFD (which the authorities stressed was an unauthorized organization) as responsible for the unrest. Wade, Savané and more than 70 others were subsequently detained and charged with attacks on state security. Opposition activists alleged that some of the accused had been tortured while in custody (as a result of which one detainee had died), and Wade and Savané instigated a hunger strike, in support of their demands for access to proper legal procedures (they were not formally charged before a court for several weeks). In May charges against Wade and his associates (including Mody Sy and Samuel Sarr) in connection with the murder of Babacar Seye in May 1993 were dismissed on the grounds of insufficient evidence, although Wade and Savané, awaiting trial in connection with the post-devaluation violence, were not released from custody. Sarr and Mody Sy, who also remained in detention pending an appeal by the prosecution, began a hunger strike in June, and were subsequently released on bail. Wade, Savané and four others, also refusing food, were provisionally released in July. Legal proceedings against them and 140 others implicated in the February riots were dismissed later in July, again on the grounds of insufficient evidence. In September 24 alleged members of Dahira Moustarchidine wal Moustarchidate received prison sentences of between six months and two years for their part in the violence. Shortly beforehand Moustapha Sy had been granted a presidential pardon and released from custody. In October three of those accused of Seye's murder were convicted and sentenced to between 18 and 20 years' imprisonment, with hard labour; the fourth defendant was acquitted.

In August 1994 the 1993/94 academic year at Cheikh Anta Diop University was declared invalid, following almost three months of disruption by students who were protesting against proposed reforms of the higher education system.

During the latter part of 1994 both the government and opposition expressed their desire to restore a national consensus. In January 1995 Diouf and Wade held their first private meeting since the PDS leader's departure from the council of ministers in 1992, and in February 1995 Wade was formally invited to rejoin the government. Thiam named a new council of ministers in March: Wade was designated minister of state at the presidency, while four other PDS members, including Ngom (as minister of public health and social action), were also appointed to the new administration. Djibo Ka, a long-serving government member who recently, as minister of the interior, had been associated with the legal proceedings against Wade and other opposition leaders, left the government. In September Dansokho and the minister-delegate responsible for planning, also a member of the PIT, were dismissed from the council of ministers, shortly after their party had issued a statement effectively denouncing the poor governance of Senegal.

In August 1995 the government announced that municipal and local elections, scheduled for November, would, for reasons of economy, be postponed by one year to coincide with regional voting. However, opposition groups attributed the decision to delay the elections to difficulties within the PS itself. There were subsequent reports that the conduct of internal elections for PS officials throughout the country was at times resulting in severe violence. In late March 1996 the 13th congress of the PS overwhelmingly elected Diouf to the new post of party chairman. The post of secretary-general, hitherto held by Diouf, was abolished and a new position of executive secretary created: Ousmane Tanor Dieng, the minister of state responsible for presidential affairs and services, was elected to this post. Critics of the PS leadership denounced a lack of debate prior to the implementation of the changes.

Elections and Political Sequels

In January 1996 Diouf announced that a senate was to be established as a second chamber of the legislature. Local organs of government would thereby be afforded greater representation within the country's legislative framework, as part of a programme of regionalization for which legislation was approved by the national assembly in February. The abolition of independent candidatures for municipal, rural and regional elections prompted widespread criticism, and in subsequent months opposition activists accused the PS of manipulating voters' lists, alleging that likely opposition voters had been removed from electoral registers while the names of potential PS supporters had appeared on lists after the revision process had formally ended. It was claimed, moreover, that only by the establishment of an independent electoral commission could the credibility of the elections be ensured.

Following consultations in July 1996, which involved the minister of the interior, Abdourahmane Sow, and representatives of some 20 political parties, it was announced that adjustments would be considered to certain aspects of the electoral code, although the government remained disinclined to consider the opposition's principal demands regarding independent candidatures and an autonomous commission. In mid-September the PDS, AJ–PADS and the LD–MPT announced the formation of an electoral coalition, with a view to presenting joint candidates to challenge the PS at the regional, rural and municipal elections. Within the government there was marked antipathy between the PS and the PDS and LD–MPT, prompting Ousmane Tanor Dieng to issue a formal warning to Wade and Bathily, in early October, that they must either cease their criticism or leave the government. Political tensions were heightened later in October when the PDS accused the ministry of the interior of stockpiling 1m. voting cards (in addition to the 3m. to be issued to eligible voters) that could be used fraudulently: Sow stated that the additional cards had been ordered to cover 'unforeseen circumstances'.

Elections for some 44,000 regional, municipal and rural councillors took place on 24 November 1996. Logistical and administrative difficulties were widespread, and necessitated a rerun of voting at about 100 polling stations in Dakar three days later. Opposition parties demanded that all the elections be annulled, alleging official complicity in the chaos that had been especially evident in areas where support for the PS was considered doubtful. The official results confirmed an overwhelming victory for the PS, which won control of the country's 10 regions, of all the main towns (including those in which the PDS had polled well in the 1993 presidential and legislative elections), and in the vast majority of rural communities. The opposition continued to dispute the election results, despite the failure of legal challenges to the outcome in certain areas. None the less, the PDS resolved, at an extraordinary session in February 1997, to remain in the government, and the party was among 19 opposition groups that joined the PS in a 'cellular commission' to examine the issue of establishing an independent electoral commission (to which the PS had hitherto been strongly opposed). The commission began its deliberations in late March.

Tensions were, however, revived in early March 1997, when the PS issued writs for defamation against representatives of 12 parties (including the PDS and LD–MPT), in respect of

allegations that the success of the PS in the local elections was attributable to the complicity of the authorities and to the misappropriation, for the purpose of organizing unfair elections, of foreign assistance. The opposition denounced the defamation suits as an attempt by the government to distract attention from the country's genuine economic, social and political difficulties. After a month of discussions, the 'cellular commission' succeeded in drafting a constitutional bill, to be submitted to Diouf, defining the legal framework for a nine-member electoral body. In May, however, the opposition withdrew from the commission, alleging that the PS was unwilling entirely to relinquish control of the electoral process.

Meanwhile, the education sector suffered several months of severe disruption from early 1997, as a strike by teachers, whose principal demands included the withdrawal of recent changes to pension and retirement provisions, was accompanied by protests by secondary school pupils and students at Cheikh Anta Diop University, who feared that the academic year might be declared invalid as a result of their teachers' actions. Classes finally resumed in late June. In mid-August Diouf announced the creation of an electoral verification body, which would be responsible for ensuring the conduct of elections in accordance with the law. The new Observatoire national des élections (ONEL) was to operate under the aegis of the ministry of the interior, and its nine members were to be appointed by the president, after consultations, from among magistrates, lawyers, university graduates, media practitioners and human rights activists. Although the proposed new body fell short of the opposition's demands for a fully independent electoral commission, legislation to amend the electoral law providing for the ONEL's creation was overwhelmingly approved by the national assembly at the end of August. In September Diouf appointed the ONEL's members, and nominated Gen. (retd) Mamadou Niang as the body's chairman. Shortly afterwards the 19 opposition parties created a coalition, entitled the Directoire national pour l'alternance, in order to demand further clarification regarding the ONEL's mandate. The coalition further resolved to undertake joint action to challenge the hegemony of the PS.

In late 1997 serious divisions within the ruling party emerged with the creation of a dissident grouping within the PS by former minister of the interior Djibo Ka and other senior party members. This split was reported to have resulted, at least in part, from personal rivalry between Ka and the PS chairman, Ousmane Tanor Dieng. Ka pledged continuing allegiance to Diouf, but his Mouvement pour le renouveau démocratique (MRD), as the breakaway faction was called, strongly criticized the power structures of the PS. Discussions aimed at achieving reconciliation with the dissidents were initiated by the president of the national assembly, Cheikh Abdoul Khadre Cissokho, in early November. However, in response to indications that the MRD was intending to present an independent list of candidates in the 1998 legislative elections, 11 of its leading members, including Ka, were suspended from the PS for three months. At the end of November Diouf announced that the legislative elections were to be held on 24 May 1998.

In January 1998 Gen. Mamadou Seck was appointed chief of staff of the armed forces following the retirement of Maj.-Gen. Lamine Cissé. In a reorganization of the council of ministers in mid-January Diouf appointed Cissé minister of the interior, thus giving him responsibility for the organization of the forthcoming elections. Sow, hitherto minister of the interior, was allocated the portfolio of the ministry of town planning and housing.

In February 1998 the PDS filed an appeal to the constitutional council to overturn legislation providing for the increase in the number of deputies in the national assembly from 120 to 140 members. Wade claimed that the proposed enlargement of the legislature would place an unnecessary added strain on the country's already limited resources. Wade's party, along with several other opposition parties, had abstained in the vote concerning the assembly enlargement proposals. The council annulled the proposed increase on procedural grounds: this was the first time that the council had ruled against a decision of the legislature. Opposition parties also condemned a threefold increase in the deposit required from candidates or parties seeking elected office. In March, however, the national assembly voted again to increase the number of deputies. Wade, who had hitherto resisted pressure from his party to resign from his ministerial position (along with the other PDS members in the government) prior to the elections, announced in late March that the PDS had withdrawn from the government; at the start of April he refused to attend a state function given in honour of US President Clinton. Meanwhile, in early March Ka and his associates had submitted a separate list of candidates for the elections and at the end of the month they resigned from the PS. The list was submitted under the name Union pour le renouveau démocratique (URD); the URD formed an electoral alliance with the Mouvement de la gauche démocratique, the Union pour le socialisme et la démocratie and the Jëf Jël party. The URD alliance was to present candidates in each of Senegal's 31 regions, with Ka himself to head the alliance's national list. Having left the party Ka denounced the PS for allegedly perpetrating corruption and electoral fraud and publicly apologized for his own mistakes during his time in public office.

In mid-April 1998 opposition parties demanded greater transparency regarding the registration lists of voters, alleging that there were discrepancies between the list submitted to the ONEL and that at the ministry of the interior. In late May six PDS supporters were reported to have been wounded by unidentified gunmen following a party rally in Thiès at which Wade had presided. Nevertheless, the legislative elections which took place on 24 May were reported to have proceeded in a generally peaceful atmosphere except in Casamance (see below). The elections were contested by a total of 18 parties and coalitions and were widely regarded as the fairest to have been conducted so far in Senegal, thanks largely to the monitoring role of the ONEL. In the immediate aftermath of the elections the PDS and six other opposition parties accused the PS of electoral fraud on a massive scale and appealed to the constitutional council to annul the election results in the worst-affected areas. These appeals were rejected by the council, which issued definitive results on 8 June. The PS retained 93 seats in the enlarged assembly, with 50.19% of the valid votes cast, while the number of PDS deputies was reduced to 23 (the party took 19.16% of the votes); Djibo Ka's URD, in alliance with Jëf Jël, secured 11 seats, with 13.21% of the votes. Eight further groups won representation on the basis of national lists: only the PS (58), the PDS (10) and the Jëf Jël–URD alliance (two) secured seats by majority voting within departments. The rate of participation by voters was only 39% of the registered electorate.

In mid-June 1998 Ousmane Ngom, hitherto deputy leader of the PDS, resigned from the party and announced the establishment of the Parti libéral du Sénégal (PLS). Ngom resigned in protest following a reorganization of the party leadership in which Wade had demoted Ngom to the post of permanent secretary. In mid-July the PDS established the Alliance des forces pour le changement, together with five other opposition parties including AJ–PADS, the Convention des démocrates et des patriotes and the PIT. The members of the new alliance declared their intention to field a single candidate in the next presidential election, to be held in 2000. The URD subsequently announced that it was to form a parliamentary alliance with the LD–MPT, who had announced that they would not participate in the new government.

In early July 1998 Thiam resigned as prime minister; he was replaced by Mamadou Lamine Loum, recently appointed minister of the economy, finance and planning. Loum appointed a council of ministers which contained only one minister not drawn from the PS: Serigne Diop, secretary-general of the PDS–R, hitherto minister of communications, was appointed minister of justice, keeper of the state seals. Jacques Baudin was appointed minister of foreign affairs and Senegalese abroad in the place of Moustapha Niasse, who was reportedly disillusioned with the direction of the PS. In mid-August Lamine Loum presented his government's general policy statement to the national assembly. Following the presentation, Djibo Ka unsuccessfully sought a motion of no confidence, citing rising unemployment and unnecessary privatizations as causes for concern.

In late August 1998 the national assembly voted to revise the constitution to remove the clause restricting the president to a maximum of two terms of office, on the grounds that the present limitation encouraged premature competition among the political classes, and consequent instability. The requirement that the president be elected by over 25% of all registered voters was also removed, since the PS claimed that the constant expansion of the electoral register made the 25% rule almost impossible to enforce. The opposition parties unanimously agreed to boycott the vote on the reforms, and, at a joint news conference, the leaders of all the opposition parties condemned the reforms, describing them as a constitutional *coup d'état*. The opposition agreed, however, not to boycott the presidential elections.

In October 1998 Diouf was invited to speak at the French national assembly, the first such invitation accorded to a head of state from sub-Saharan Africa. Trade union officials and the leaders of seven opposition groups agreed to send a delegation to Paris to protest against Diouf's alleged manipulation of the constitution. Abdoulaye Wade of the PDS criticized the French authorities for tacitly offering support to Diouf in his campaign for re-election in 2000. Wade also denounced the infringement of the constitution, widespread electoral fraud, increasingly authoritarian government, and the handling of the conflict in Casamance. Labour leaders also protested at the imprisonment of 25 members of the electricity workers' union, including their leader Mademba Sock, following protests in July against the privatization of SENELEC, the state electricity company.

On 24 January 1999 Senegal held elections to the newly created senate, in which 45 of the 60 senators were to be elected by members of the national assembly, together with local, municipal and regional councillors. Twelve senators were to be chosen by the president, and three were to be elected by Senegalese resident abroad. Only the PS, the PLS, and a coalition of the PIT and AJ–PADS contested the elections. The main opposition parties had called for a boycott of the elections, describing the new chamber as unnecessary and costly, and accusing the government of attempting to manipulate the elections. The government, however, repeated its belief that the creation of a second chamber would improve the representation of local government areas, thereby completing the policy of decentralization. The PS won all 45 seats contested, with 91.3% of the votes cast. The 12 senators nominated by Diouf included two opposition leaders, Marcel Bassène of the PLS and Majhemouth Diop of the Parti africain de l'indépendance, the only opposition representatives in the senate. On 5 February the constitutional court confirmed the election results, despite an appeal lodged by the AJ–PADS–PIT coalition against the vote-counting techniques used, and the senate's first session began on 15 February.

Presidential Election

In March 1999 a left-wing alliance of the AJ–PADS, the PIT, the PDS and the LD–MPT agreed to nominate Wade as their joint candidate in the presidential election scheduled for 2000; Wade had resigned his seat in the national assembly the previous July in order to concentrate on the presidential election. In the same month Talla Sylla, the leader of Jëf Jël, was sentenced to six months in prison for having denounced the head of state at an illegal rally held in October 1998. Sylla was also banned from voting or participating in elections for a period of five years; he had been planning to contest the presidential election.

In late April 1999 the PDS decided to boycott the national assembly, accusing the government of seeking to manipulate the electoral register for the presidential election. The PDS claimed that many of the registers in areas in which it enjoyed strong support had been lost. The government admitted that about 600 of the estimated 8,400 voter registers used for the 1998 legislative elections were missing, but offered to reconstitute and update these lists in the presence of the opposition parties. Wade called for experts from France and the USA to help compile a reliable electoral register.

In May 1999 the court of appeal ordered Mademba Sock, the leader of the electricity workers' union, and two colleagues, to pay compensation to SENELEC following their July 1998 strike. The court also upheld the prison sentences imposed upon the men in connection with the strike. Sock later indicated that he would appeal. In late June a two-day general strike was announced, after negotiations broke down between the unions, the government, and employers' associations on improvements in salaries and conditions of employment. The strike was widely observed, and, following intensive negotiations, an agreement was reached with the government, whereby a commission was to be formed to investigate the possibility of establishing a social security fund and a health insurance scheme. A commission was also formed to investigate possible improvements to employee benefits, and a mandatory retirement age of 60 years.

In June and July 1999 demonstrations took place at the offices of the ONEL in protest at the appointment in May of Gen. Amadou Dieng as chairman. The opposition, led by Djibo Ka, had claimed that Dieng actively supported the re-election of Diouf, a charge denied by Dieng, who none the less subsequently resigned. In late July Louis Pereira de Carvalho, a magistrate and former head of the council of state, was appointed in his place.

In mid-June 1999 Moustapha Niasse, the former minister of foreign affairs and Senegalese abroad, and currently the UN special representative in the Great Lakes region, announced his intention of contesting the presidential election. Niasse also published a document criticizing the policies of Diouf and the PS and accusing them of corruption; he was immediately expelled from the PS, of which he was a founder member. Niasse, who was reportedly supported by several influential religious leaders, subsequently applied for permission to form his own party, the Alliance des forces de progrès. At the end of July Djibo Ka announced that he too was to contest the presidential election, although Ka acknowledged the need for the opposition to support a single candidate in the second round of the election.

Campaigning for the February 2000 presidential election began in earnest with Wade's return to Senegal at the end of October 1999 after a year of voluntary exile. With Diouf apparently weakened by the desertion of his former allies, Wade quickly succeeded in winning an endorsement from influential members of the Islamic Mouride brotherhood. By December the main candidates for the election consisted of Diouf, Wade, Moustapha Niasse and Djibo Ka, although there were also four other candidates, including the trade unionist Mademba Sock. Much of the campaigning centred on opposition accusations that the PS intended to manipulate the election, and there were persistent complaints about what were perceived to be false voter cards, which differed slightly in colour from the usual white cards. The campaigning was, however, largely peaceful, despite continuing disturbances in Casamance (see below).

In the presidential election, held on 27 February 2000, Diouf failed to win an overall majority, and Diouf and Wade therefore proceeded to a second round of voting. The three most successful candidates were Diouf with 41.3%, Wade with 31.0% and Niasse with 16.8%. Overall turn-out was estimated at 61.0% and the ONEL described the poll as 'free and transparent'. In the following weeks, Wade succeeded in gathering the support of Niasse and of the other opposition candidates, with the exception of Djibo Ka, who lent his support to Diouf. Wade profited from his endorsement by almost all the other candidates, and at the second round of the election, held on 19 March, he gained a substantial victory, winning 58.5% of the vote, to Diouf's 41.5%. Turn-out was provisionally estimated at 60.1%. Both the victory for the 73-year-old political veteran and Diouf's dignified acceptance of defeat were acclaimed internationally as an example of a peaceful transition in Africa. Western countries were quick to congratulate Wade and to offer support for his government, which was sworn in in April, with Niasse as prime minister and Maj.-Gen. Mamadou Niang as minister of the interior.

Early in his tenure, Wade declared his priorities to be restoring peace in Casamance, applying the principle of transparency to the administration, and guaranteeing the independence of the judiciary. He also promised to reform the agricultural sector, to attract foreign investment and to solve the country's youth unemployment problems. However, with the PS remaining the largest party in the national assembly and the senate, there remained the prospect of a legislative crisis. In May 2000 Wade promised to submit his preferred constitutional revisions to a referendum, with a view to calling new legislative elections early in 2001. However, in mid-May 2000 the PS criticized what they perceived to be the new government's lack 'of a clear programme and orientation, the lack of coherence and vision'.

The opening session of the national assembly in June 2000 was complicated by the defection from the URD of a number of deputies who had been alienated by Djibo Ka's support for Diouf

in the second round of the presidential election. In a move fiercely attacked in the press as undemocratic, the PS subsequently 'lent' the URD a number of socialist deputies in order that the URD could continue to be registered as a group within the assembly. In July the PS itself was affected by several important defections, including that of the president of the senate, Abdoulaye Diack, as well as two other senators, a member of the national assembly and a mayor, who transferred their allegiance to Wade's PDS. It was widely believed that Diack's defection to the PDS would delay the abolition of the senate, which Wade had previously proposed.

SEPARATISM IN CASAMANCE

For many years there has been separatist sentiment among Diola communities in the southern region of Casamance, which is virtually cut off from the rest of Senegal by the enclave of The Gambia, and the emergence since the early 1980s of the Mouvement des forces démocratiques de la Casamance (MFDC) has presented the Senegalese authorities with considerable security difficulties.

After demonstrations in the regional capital, Ziguinchor, in December 1982, several leaders of the MFDC were detained without trial. A more serious demonstration in December 1983 was suppressed by force, reportedly resulting in more than 100 deaths. Casamance was divided into two administrative regions, Ziguinchor and Kolda, in 1984. In January 1986 a leading Casamance independence campaigner was sentenced to life imprisonment, while other demonstrators received prison sentences ranging from two to 15 years; further arrests were made in October. However, almost 100 detainees were provisionally released in April 1987, and a further 320 separatists reportedly benefited under the conditions of the May 1988 presidential amnesty.

The MFDC initiated an offensive in 1990 with a series of attacks, most of which were directed at administrative targets in the Casamance region. Tensions escalated when military reinforcements were dispatched to the region, and in September 1990 a military governor was appointed for Casamance. A prominent human rights organization, Amnesty International, issued several reports expressing concern at events in Casamance, although allegations of the torture and summary executions of suspected separatists were investigated and subsequently refuted by the Senegalese government. By April 1991 at least 100 people were said to have been killed as a result of violence in the region, while more than 300 Casamançais had been transported to Dakar to await trial for sedition. Among those in detention was the president of the MFDC, Abbé Augustin Diamacouné Senghor. In that month renewed action by separatists violated a truce that had apparently been negotiated by leaders of the MFDC and the new Thiam government. In May Diouf announced the immediate release of more than 340 detainees (including Diamacouné Senghor) who had been arrested in connection with the unrest in Casamance. This facilitated the conclusion, at talks in Guinea-Bissau, of a cease-fire agreement by representatives of the Senegalese government and the MFDC. In June the military governor was replaced by a civilian (as part of the demilitarization of the region that had been envisaged in the cease-fire accord). An amnesty was ratified by the national assembly later in June, benefiting some 400 Casamançais (including separatists released in the previous month). In December, however, a PS deputy and a local village chief were assassinated near Ziguinchor, although MFDC leaders denied involvement in the killings.

In January 1992 a peace commission (the Comité de gestion de la paix en Casamance), comprising government representatives and members of the MFDC, was established, with mediation by Guinea-Bissau. However, a resurgence of violence during July and August prompted the government to redeploy armed forces in the region: this further exacerbated tensions, and gave rise to MFDC protests that the 'remilitarization' of Casamance was in contravention of the cease-fire agreement. The death of a police officer, in July, was followed in August by a violent clash near Ziguinchor, in which, according to official figures, 50 separatist rebels and two members of the armed forces were killed. Evidence emerged of a split within the MFDC: the so-called 'Front nord' and the MFDC vice-president, Sidi Badji, appealed to the rebels to lay down their arms, while the 'Front sud', based in areas of dense forest near the border with Guinea-Bissau, and led by Diamacouné Senghor (himself now based in Guinea-Bissau), appeared determined to continue the armed struggle. Negotiations between representatives of the Senegalese government and the MFDC achieved little, and in October 32 people were killed when separatist rebels attacked a fishing village near the Cap-Skirring tourist resort, causing local residents and tourists to flee the region. Following the deaths of two Senegalese soldiers in December, the army instigated a major security operation, launching air attacks on supposed rebel bases along the border with Guinea-Bissau (see below).

Indications in advance of the 1993 presidential and legislative elections that MFDC rebels would seek to prevent voting in Casamance prompted Diouf to begin his electoral campaign in the province. His visit, in January, proceeded amid strict security measures, following the recent deaths of seven aid workers to the south-east of Ziguinchor. About 30 people were reported to have been killed in rebel attacks on voters on the day of the presidential election. Army reinforcements were dispatched to Casamance in March, following further clashes. In April Diamacouné Senghor (who had returned to Senegal in March, having apparently been expelled from Guinea-Bissau) reportedly expressed a willingness to negotiate with the Senegalese government. Shortly afterwards, however, at least 100 rebels and three members of the armed forces were killed in a clash near the border with Guinea-Bissau. In late April the Senegalese authorities confirmed their willingness to observe a truce, stating that the military would henceforth act only in a defensive capacity, and gave assurances regarding the continuation of negotiations and the resumption of economic initiatives in Casamance. A period of relative calm followed, and in July a cease-fire agreement was signed, which envisaged the release of Casamançais prisoners, and made provision for the return of those who had fled the region. Guinea-Bissau was to act as a guarantor of the agreement, and the government of France was to be asked to submit an historical arbitration regarding the Casamance issue: the Senegalese authorities had consistently refuted MFDC assertions that documents from the colonial era indicated that France favoured independence for Casamance. Later in July 256 Casamançais were released from detention. At the time of the conclusion of the new cease-fire, the total number of casualties of the conflict was uncertain, since the Senegalese authorities had not given details of military operations in Casamance for some months; however, it was believed that in the year preceding the Ziguinchor accord between 500 and 1,000 people had been killed and many hundreds injured, while humanitarian organizations estimated that 25,000–30,000 people might have fled to The Gambia and Guinea-Bissau, or to other regions of Senegal. In December 1993 France issued its judgment that Casamance had not existed as an autonomous territory prior to the colonial period, and that independence for the region had been neither demanded nor considered at the time of decolonization.

Casamance was widely regarded as being among the regions of Senegal that benefited most from the devaluation of the CFA franc at the beginning of 1994. Tourists returned to the region, and the fishing sector flourished, while several donor-sponsored development initiatives were undertaken with the aim of enhancing the region's economic potential. From early 1995, however, renewed violence near the border with Guinea-Bissau indicated a re-emergence of divisions between the northern and southern factions of the MFDC. Rebels in the south were reportedly frustrated at the slow progress of the dialogue between the MFDC and the authorities, and accused the Senegalese armed forces of violating the provisions of the Ziguinchor accord. At least 20 soldiers were reported to have been killed in military operations in southern Casamance in early 1995, and there were believed to have been heavy casualties among the rebels and among the civilian population. Following the disappearance in April of four French tourists in the Basse-Casamance region, more than 1,000 élite troops were deployed in southern Casamance, and were assisted in their search by French reconnaissance aircraft. In subsequent weeks the aim of the operation appeared increasingly to be to dislodge MFDC dissidents from the border region. Both factions of the MFDC denied any involvement in the abduction of the tourists, and Diamacouné Senghor accused the Senegalese army of responsi-

bility for the disappearances. The MFDC leader was placed under house arrest in Ziguinchor in late April, and his four fellow-members of the movement's 'political bureau' were transported to Dakar and imprisoned. In June MFDC rebels announced an end to their cease-fire, again accusing the government forces of violating the 1993 accord. Although Diamacouné Senghor appealed to the separatists not to break the truce, by early September 60 deaths had been reported among the rebels, the armed forces and the civilian population in the south-west. In the most serious incident at this time, in late July at least 23 soldiers were killed in an ambush as they advanced on what was stated by the armed forces to be a rebel base near Babanda. The army claimed to have regained control of this area (which the MFDC rebels denied having occupied) by mid-August.

In September 1995 Thiam established a Commission nationale de paix (CNP), headed by a Casamance-born former minister of foreign affairs, Assane Seck. Members of the commission travelled to Ziguinchor in late September, where they reportedly sought a dialogue with Diamacouné Senghor (who remained under house arrest) and the MFDC's four other political leaders (who were returned to Ziguinchor and placed under house arrest there in mid-October). During October, none the less, renewed rebel attacks on government forces were accompanied by a major army offensive in the south-western border region—apparently in an effort to reinforce security prior to the forthcoming tourist season. By the end of the month it was reported that about 100 separatists and nine members of the armed forces had been killed, and that three rebel bases near the border with Guinea-Bissau had been destroyed. In late November military sources disclosed that some 51 rebels and six members of the armed forces had been killed in a clash in the border region. Representatives of the armed forces asserted that an intensification of anti-rebel operations had been prompted by a recent series of armed attacks on civilians.

Meanwhile, the CNP was reported to be seeking to arrange a meeting between those members of the MFDC who wished to secure a peace accord and those whose supporters were in direct conflict with the armed forces. In November 1995 the MFDC's representative in Europe, Mamadou Sane N'Krumah, indicated the organization's willingness to enter negotiations with the government if Diamacouné Senghor and his four associates were released from house arrest. In December, following discussions with representatives of the government and the CNP, Diamacouné Senghor made a televised appeal to the MFDC rebels to lay down their arms. He proposed that preliminary talks between his organization and the CNP take place in early January 1996, to be followed by peace negotiations, in a neutral country, three months later. The members of the MFDC 'political bureau' were released from house arrest at the end of December 1995; it was also reported that the CNP had secured the release of 50 of some 150 suspected separatists detained in recent months. Salif Sadio, reported as the MFDC military leader, confirmed observance of a truce in early January 1996. The preliminary discussions between the MFDC and the CNP took place as scheduled in that month, at which Diamacouné Senghor presented his organization's requirements for the conduct of peace talks.

In mid-February 1996 it was announced that the office of the UN High Commissioner for Refugees (UNHCR) was to supervise the voluntary movement of some 20,000–30,000 refugees from the conflict in Casamance, who were currently encamped at several locations along the border with Guinea-Bissau, to two sites within that country. At the end of February Amnesty International denounced detentions without trial, the use of torture and summary executions in Senegal, with specific reference to the conflict in Casamance. The organization condemned incidents of the abuse of human rights by both the armed forces and the MFDC, and considered that the torture of detainees in Senegal was widespread and 'officially tolerated'. The Diouf government strongly denied the allegations.

While there was considerable optimism regarding the commitment of the government and the MFDC to the peace process, it emerged in early April 1996 that Diamacouné Senghor and his associates were unwilling to attend the formal opening of peace talks in Ziguinchor. The MFDC leaders based their refusal to attend on the grounds that a request that they be issued with passports, to enable them to travel to Europe for discussions with 'exiled' members of the movement, had not been fulfilled, and also that Diamacouné Senghor had stipulated that negotiations be conducted abroad. The peace talks were postponed indefinitely, and in late April there were reports of renewed tensions in the region. Diouf visited Ziguinchor in May (his first visit to Casamance since the 1993 election campaign): he expressed his commitment to the pursuit of peace, stating that the ongoing process of administrative decentralization would afford greater autonomy to regional structures, but reiterated that it was a 'permanent and historical' fact that Casamance was an integral part of Senegal.

In early July 1996, following the deaths of three soldiers outside Ziguinchor, the armed wing of the MFDC warned all those 'unfamiliar' with the southern Casamance region not to enter the territory. At his inauguration in mid-July, however, the new chief of general staff of the Senegalese armed forces, Maj.-Gen. Lamine Cissé, asserted that the military would be denied access to no part of Senegalese territory. In late August there was renewed optimism regarding the likely resumption of negotiations between a united MFDC and the authorities, following discussions in Ziguinchor between Diamacouné Senghor and Diouf's personal chief of staff. There were few reports of unrest until March 1997, when more than 40 rebels and two members of the armed forces were killed in clashes near the border with Guinea-Bissau. The MFDC denied that it had ended its cease-fire, stating that it would investigate these incidents. In that month four representatives of the MFDC had been permitted to travel to France, where they had spent three weeks meeting with representatives of the movement based in Europe. A delegation of the MFDC made a further visit to France in early July, and members of the external wing made a reciprocal visit to Ziguinchor shortly afterwards: the two wings expressed their desire to establish a harmonized position in preparation for future negotiations with the authorities. Sane N'Krumah did not personally attend the talks in Ziguinchor, despite a specific request by Diamacouné Senghor that he do so, stating that he feared for his safety should he enter Senegal. While both the Senegalese authorities and the MFDC leadership appeared committed to reviving the peace process, several incidents in the Ziguinchor region in July and August were attributed by the Senegalese authorities to separatists, and a clash between members of the armed forces and a rebel group in mid-August reportedly resulted in the deaths of 25 soldiers. In early September the armed forces launched a new offensive aimed at dislodging the rebel forces from positions around Ziguinchor. The separatists were reported to have sustained heavy losses and to have abandoned some of their bases in the area. There was evidence that separatist fighters were targeting rebels who had given up the armed struggle, as violence was reported in so-called 'pacified areas' both north and south of Ziguinchor.

The Senegalese army renewed its offensive in early October 1997, targeting rebel bases in areas south-west of Ziguinchor. As many as 3,000 troops were involved in what was the largest army operation in Casamance since the 1995 cease-fire. Rebels were reported to have retreated northwards, establishing encampments in the Kolda region; others, particularly the injured, fled across the border into Guinea-Bissau. In mid-October 1997 it was estimated that over 300 people, many of whom were civilians, had lost their lives since the resumption of hostilities in July. Salif Sadio, the MFDC's military leader, stated that the organization remained committed to the peace process begun in late 1995, but maintained that its forces were justified in defending themselves against armed attack. The MFDC's political leadership was also reported to be prepared to pursue peace talks with the government. Violence persisted, none the less, and in late October it was reported that 18 soldiers and 80 rebels had been killed in violent confrontations near the border with Guinea-Bissau. After a relative lull in November a series of attacks in the area of the Front nord stronghold of Bignona in late December, in which more than 10 people were killed, marked a spread of the violence to the north of the province. Resumption of the peace process was complicated by the divisions within the MFDC which were reported to be deepening.

In early September 1997 some 2,000 refugees arrived in The Gambia, fleeing the new upsurge in hostilities in Casamance; around 20,000 people were reported to have sought refuge from

the conflict in Guinea-Bissau between November and the end of the year. In a communiqué issued in France in early January 1998, the MFDC alleged that some 3,000 members of Guinea-Bissau's armed forces were massing along the border in preparation for an attack on rebel bases in Casamance, in a joint operation with 4,000 Senegalese soldiers. Both Senegal and Guinea-Bissau denied that they were preparing for a joint offensive, and the government of Guinea-Bissau stated that it had sent some reinforcements to the border region to safeguard its citizens and territorial integrity. Shortly afterwards it was reported that 10 alleged rebels had been killed, and 40 captured, by the Guinea-Bissau armed forces in an operation (conducted in accordance with a security agreement reached by the military chiefs of Senegal, Guinea-Bissau and The Gambia in October 1997) against rebels suspected of hiding in refugee camps.

In mid-January 1998 Diamacouné Senghor appealed to MFDC supporters to cease fighting and urged them to desist from laying anti-personnel mines. Armed confrontations between MFDC factions (particularly between the northern and southern fronts) had increased, as had attacks on civilians. The MFDC leader indicated that his organization would be prepared to abandon its demand for independence, on condition that the government institute measures to ensure greater economic and social development in Casamance. (The government had for some time asserted that its regionalization programme could serve as a basis for negotiations regarding greater autonomy for Casamance.) In subsequent weeks there was relative calm, although clashes in the north and around Bignona reportedly resulted in some 15 deaths by the end of February. In early March there were reports of 50 rebels having been killed as they attempted to ambush an army base in a village east of Ziguinchor; the government asserted that this figure was grossly exaggerated. Security operations in advance of the legislative elections resulted in the deaths of some 30 rebels in May, and six civilians were killed by rebels on the day before the election. Further violence was reported as voting proceeded, and two soldiers who were transporting votes were reportedly killed. Fear of violence was thought to have deterred many Casamançais from voting. Election results from 15 polling stations in Bignona were annulled by the constitutional council. Separatist and government forces were involved in violent clashes in mid-June at Kantene, south-east of Ziguinchor. In early July military sources in Dakar stated that MFDC fighters were being dispatched to reinforce insurgents in the internal conflict in Guinea-Bissau: the leaders of the rebellion had been dismissed from senior positions in the Guinea-Bissau armed forces for allegedly smuggling arms to the Casamançais separatists (see below).

In August 1998 the army shelled rebel positions and villages, which had allegedly sheltered rebels, on both sides of the border with Guinea-Bissau. The armed forces reported that seven soldiers and 43 rebels had been killed in the clashes, although the MFDC claimed that the majority of the victims were civilians. In the same month 13 civilians were killed when their bus hit a land-mine. In mid-October separatists ambushed another civilian bus, killing four people, and attacked an army checkpoint. In November fighting was again reported in the area around Ziguinchor.

In an address on New Year's Day 1999 Diouf stated that any negotiations must take place within the framework of the Senegalese state, a precondition rejected by the MFDC, who further declared that there could be no negotiations while many of their leaders remained under house arrest. Later in the month Diouf visited Ziguinchor and made a passionate appeal for peace in the region. During his visit he also held talks with Diamacouné Senghor. In February, in a move seen as a response to the improved atmosphere in the region following Diouf's visit, the Senegalese authorities released 123 rebels from detention. None the less, sporadic violence continued in February and March.

In early April 1999 the MDFC reportedly disarmed its fighters, although some factions refused to participate. In late April a delegation of the various factions of the MFDC, led by Diamacouné Senghor, visited Banjul, The Gambia, in an attempt to arrive at a common stance prior to negotiations with the Senegalese government. The rebel delegation also held talks with President Jammeh of The Gambia. The MFDC, however, advised the estimated 8,000 refugees from the conflict present in The Gambia that they should not return to the area until the situation was calmer, and at the end of April rebel attacks were again reported in the area around Ziguinchor. In early May Diamacouné Senghor wrote to members of the MFDC asking them to cease their attacks and to respect the peace process. In the same month the government promised a large-scale investment programme for Casamance. However, in late May elements of the MFDC launched a series of mortar attacks on Ziguinchor. Diamacouné Senghor blamed the attacks on MFDC dissidents, whom he accused of seeking to sabotage the peace process.

In late June 1999 talks between the various MFDC factions began in Banjul, although several leaders of military and exiled factions of the MFDC did not attend, claiming that Diamacouné Senghor was effectively a hostage of the Senegalese government. Around 50 observers attended the talks, including Gen. Ansumane Manè, the leader of the rebels in Guinea-Bissau, and two Senegalese ministers. At the meeting Léopold Sagna was confirmed as the head of the armed forces of the MFDC in place of the reportedly more radical Salif Sadio. In its final communiqué the MFDC reiterated its commitment to peace and to negotiations with the government, although it condemned the conduct of the Senegalese army and called for its immediate withdrawal from Casamance. The Senegalese authorities subsequently acceded to the MFDC conference's demand that Diamacouné Senghor be freed from house arrest; his movements, however, remained restricted, allegedly to guarantee his safety. In early June, during a brief visit to Senegal, the UN Secretary-General, Kofi Annan, suggested that improving relations between the two sides meant that international intervention in the Casamance region would not be necessary. However, with continuing sharp disagreements in MFDC ranks, the resumption of peace talks remained stalled until the end of 1999, and attacks by MFDC militants continued.

On 26 December 1999 a new cease-fire was agreed at a meeting between the MFDC and the government held in Banjul, The Gambia. For their part, the Senegalese authorities promised to review the MFDC's demand to be recognized as a political party and to consider lifting restrictions on freedom of movement. However, the cease-fire did not last and clashes escalated in February and March 2000, when there was also an increase in incidents along the common border with Guinea-Bissau. The MFDC leadership condemned the escalation of the violence, which it blamed on MFDC dissidents and on bandits.

Following his election as president in early March 2000, Abdoulaye Wade announced that he was to continue the negotiations begun under Diouf, but that his preference was to conduct direct dialogue with the MFDC. Wade, who declared that he would allow Diamacouné Senghor full freedom of movement, also issued a call for calm in the region. However, further clashes were subsequently reported between the security forces and rebels, while relations with The Gambia deteriorated after Wade publicly denounced Libya's provision of arms to both The Gambia and Guinea-Bissau. In protest, the Gambian government briefly suspended the regular meetings it had been hosting between the Senegalese authorities and the MFDC. These, however, resumed in June. In May, at a meeting with Wade, the president of Guinea-Bissau, Kumba Yala, indicated his desire to preserve good relations with Senegal and his country's neutrality in the Casamance question. In late August, at a further meeting between the two heads of state, it was agreed that Senegal and Guinea-Bissau would undertake joint military border patrols in order to curb the movement of rebel troops.

REGIONAL AND INTERNATIONAL RELATIONS

From 1989 onwards Senegal's traditional policy of peaceful coexistence with neighbouring countries was severely undermined by a series of regional disputes. Senegal's relations with both The Gambia and Guinea-Bissau have in recent years been dominated by issues relating to the conflict in the southern Casamance region, which also led large numbers of displaced persons to seek refuge in neighbouring countries. Senegal maintains good relations with France, which maintains a military presence in Senegal, and with the USA, which has provided training for Senegalese troops involved in peace-keeping missions. (During the 1990s the Senegalese armed forces were active in peace-keeping activities world-wide, the majority under

the auspices of the UN.) Senegal also receives significant financial support from Taiwan, with which diplomatic links have been maintained since 1996.

Relations with Mauritania

In April 1989 the deaths of two Senegalese farmers, following a disagreement with Mauritanian livestock-breeders regarding grazing rights in the border region between the two countries, precipitated a crisis that was fuelled by long-standing ethnic and economic rivalries. Mauritanian nationals residing in Senegal were attacked, and their businesses ransacked (the retail trade in Senegal had hitherto been dominated by an expatriate community of mainly light-skinned Mauritanians, estimated to number about 300,000), and Senegalese nationals in Mauritania suffered similar attacks. By early May it was believed that several hundred people, mostly Senegalese, had been killed. Operations to repatriate nationals of both countries were undertaken with international assistance, and Senegal granted asylum to black Mauritanians who feared official persecution. Despite international mediation efforts, and the expressed commitment of both Senegal and Mauritania to the principle of a negotiated settlement of the dispute, Senegal's insistence on the inviolability of the border as defined at the time of French colonial rule, together with Mauritanian demands that its nationals be compensated for their losses, remained among the main impediments to a solution. Diplomatic relations were severed in August. Renewed outbreaks of violence were reported in late 1989, while in early 1990 attempts at mediation were thwarted by military engagements in the border region, as a result of which several deaths were reported. Relations deteriorated further in late 1990, when the Mauritanian authorities accused Senegal of complicity in an alleged attempt to overthrow the Taya government (an accusation denied by the Diouf administration). In January and February 1991 incidents were reported in which Mauritanian naval vessels had opened fire on Senegalese fishing boats, apparently in Senegal's territorial waters, and in March several deaths were reported to have resulted from a military engagement, on Senegalese territory, between members of the two countries' armed forces, following an incursion by Senegalese troops into Mauritania. Further diplomatic initiatives resulted, in July, in a meeting in Guinea-Bissau of the foreign ministers of Senegal and Mauritania, at which they agreed in principle to the reopening of the Mauritania–Senegal border and to a resumption of diplomatic relations.

Diplomatic links, at ambassadorial level, were finally restored in April 1992, and the process of reopening the border began in May. None the less, the issues of border demarcation and the status of Mauritanian refugees in Senegal remained to be resolved. Further tensions were reported in September 1993, when the Mauritanian authorities announced that Senegalese nationals would henceforth be required to fulfil certain criteria, including currency exchange formalities, before being allowed to remain in (or enter) Mauritania. In December 1994, however, the governments of Senegal and Mauritania agreed new co-operation measures, including efforts to facilitate the free movement of goods and people between the two countries. In January 1995, moreover, the governments of Senegal, Mauritania and Mali undertook to co-operate in resolving joint border issues and in combating extremism, arms-smuggling and drugs-trafficking. In October the Mauritanian authorities gave assurances that Mauritanian refugees in Senegal (estimated to number some 66,000), were free to return home. In January 1996, none the less, several hundred Mauritanian refugees took part in protests to denounce the Mauritanian authorities' arrangements for their return, and to demand that their repatriation be organized under UNHCR auspices. The ongoing insecurity in eastern Senegal also remained a concern, and in May 1998 the ministers of the interior of Mauritania, Mali and Senegal met to discuss border security, following reports of increased cross-border banditry in the region. The unrest was blamed by the Senegalese press on the continued presence of an estimated 60,000 Mauritanian refugees, and in September the refugees announced that the Senegalese authorites were no longer issuing them with travel documents. The refugees requested that the Senegalese government negotiate an acceptable settlement with Mauritania, which they claimed was attempting to compel them to return home without any guarantees as to their safety. However, the re-establishment of good relations with Mauritania remained a priority of the Senegalese government, and in May 1999 the two countries signed an agreement on the joint exploitation of fisheries, while in August Senegal, Mauritania and Mali agreed to establish a joint operational force in order to combat the ongoing insecurity in the border region.

In early June 2000 a new and potentially dangerous dispute broke out between the two countries after Mauritania accused Senegal of threatening its interests by relaunching an irrigation programme in the fossil valleys area of the river Senegal. Claiming that the project would deprive its own lands of water, and that Senegal was pursuing 'hegemony over its neighbours', Mauritania instructed Senegalese nationals to leave the country within 15 days. Of the 345,000 Senegalese resident in Mauritania, some 25,000 returned home before the order was subsequently cancelled on 10 June after a conciliatory telephone conversation between President Wade and his Mauritanian counterpart. Wade immediately visited Nouakchott and announced that he would cancel the irrigation project as it was no longer in line with Senegal's national water development programme. It was later suggested that the crisis was engineered by Mauritania as a warning to Wade to discontinue the formerly cordial relationship between his party, the PDS, and black Mauritanian liberation movements based in Senegal.

Relations with Guinea-Bissau

A dispute with Guinea-Bissau regarding the sovereignty of a maritime zone that is believed to contain reserves of petroleum, together with valuable fishing grounds, has caused tensions between the two countries. In July 1989 an international arbitration panel (to which the issue had been referred in 1985) judged the waters to be part of Senegalese territory. However, the government of Guinea-Bissau refused to accept the judgment, and referred the matter to the International Court of Justice (ICJ). Moreover, the Vieira government accused Senegal of repeated violations of both Guinea-Bissau's maritime borders and airspace during April 1990, and in the following month several skirmishes involving Senegalese and Guinea-Bissau troops occurred in the border region. The situation was exacerbated by Senegalese allegations that Guinea-Bissau was allowing members of the MFDC to train on its territory. None the less, meetings between representatives of the two countries culminated, in late May, in the signing of an accord whereby each country undertook to refrain from harbouring organizations hostile to the other and to maintain troops at a 'reasonable distance' from the border. In November 1991 the ICJ ruled that the delimitation of the maritime border, as agreed by the French and Portuguese colonial powers in April 1960, remained valid, thereby confirming Senegal's sovereignty over the disputed zone, and Senegal and Guinea-Bissau signed a treaty recognizing this judgment in February 1993.

Although Guinea-Bissau (together with France) played an important role in the formulation of the 1991 cease-fire agreement between the Senegalese government and the MFDC, relations were again strained in late 1992. In December an offensive by the Senegalese armed forces against MFDC strongholds close to the border with Guinea-Bissau (some reports suggested that MFDC bases within Guinea-Bissau had been targeted) resulted in the deaths of two nationals of that country. The Vieira government formally protested at Senegalese violations of Guinea-Bissau's airspace, and reiterated that, as a guarantor of the 1991 accord, it was not assisting the rebels. Although Senegal apologized for the incident, a further violation was reported in January 1993. None the less, Guinea-Bissau was again active in efforts to bring about a new cease-fire agreement between the Senegalese authorities and the MFDC in mid-1993. In October of that year, moreover, the two countries signed a major 20-year agreement regarding the joint exploitation and management of fishing and petroleum resources in their maritime zones.

Renewed operations by the Senegalese military against MFDC rebels in southern Casamance, from early 1995, again affected relations with Guinea-Bissau. In March Diouf visited Guinea-Bissau to discuss joint security issues and to apologize for two recent attacks perpetrated by the Senegalese armed forces on villages in Guinea-Bissau during February. In April

Guinea-Bissau temporarily deployed as many as 500 troops near the border with Senegal, as part of attempts to locate four missing French tourists: the government of Guinea-Bissau subsequently announced that it was satisfied that the tourists were not on its territory, and reiterated that it was not harbouring separatists (although reports persisted of sightings of the French nationals, apparently with MFDC members, in Guinea-Bissau). In May, following the withdrawal of its troops from the border region, Guinea-Bissau pledged assistance in the establishment of an enduring settlement between the Senegalese authorities and the MFDC. The October 1993 treaty on the joint exploration of maritime wealth was ratified in December 1995: fishing resources were to be shared equally between the two countries, while Senegal was to benefit from a majority share (85%) of petroleum deposits. A joint agency (to be based in Dakar, and headed by Guinea-Bissau's ambassador to Senegal) for the management of common resources was formally established during a visit to Guinea-Bissau by Diouf in February 1996. Meanwhile, during bilateral contacts in 1995–96 the two countries pledged co-operation in matters of joint defence and security, while the government of Guinea-Bissau continued to give assurances that it was not assisting MFDC rebels.

In late January 1998 it was announced that the authorities in Guinea-Bissau had intercepted a consignment of armaments destined for MFDC rebels, and that some 15 officers of the Guinea-Bissau armed forces had been arrested and suspended from duty, including the head of the armed forces, Brig. (later Gen.) Ansumane Manè. The government of Guinea-Bissau again reiterated that the country was not assisting rebels in Casamance, and President Vieira again expressed his willingness to act as a mediator between the Senegalese government and the MFDC. In June, however, troops loyal to Manè rebelled against Vieira, and civil war broke out in Guinea-Bissau. Senegalese troops subsequently intervened in support of the forces loyal to Vieira. Senegal's armed forces in Guinea-Bissau, who were reinforced to number more than 2,500, appeared to be at the forefront of military operations aimed at crushing the rebellion in late June and in the first half of July. Senegal's involvement became the subject of controversy, with Guinea-Bissau refugees accusing Senegalese troops of brutality against civilians; the mutineers demanded the departure of foreign forces before they entered peace negotiations with the government. Senegal was also criticized for closing its borders, thus preventing the international medical charity, Médecins sans frontières, from crossing into Guinea-Bissau to bring humanitarian assistance to casualties of the civil conflict. In mid-July Diouf announced that 'aid corridors' into Guinea-Bissau had been established. Refugees from Guinea-Bissau, many of whom had been turned back from the Senegalese border, were reported, none the less, to be entering Senegal in the area of southern Casamance controlled by the MFDC. In late July the Guinea-Bissau insurgents signed a cease-fire agreement with the government, having apparently abandoned their precondition that foreign troops must leave the country before negotiations could take place.

In November 1998 the two sides in the conflict arrived at an agreement, brokered in Abuja, Nigeria, by the Economic and Monetary Community of West African States (ECOWAS). The agreement provided for new elections and for the withdrawal of foreign troops. It was envisaged that the West African peacekeeping force ECOMOG would replace the mainly Senegalese forces present in Guinea-Bissau. In December the first Senegalese troops departed, and the final 800 Senegalese soldiers withdrew in mid-March. President Vieira of Guinea-Bissau subsequently visited Dakar to thank Senegal for its intervention in this crisis. In accordance with the agreement, ECOMOG troops were deployed on the Guinea-Bissau side of the border with Casamance, while Senegal strengthened its own presence in the border area.

In May 1999, however, following a dispute over the disarmament of the presidential guard, fighting again broke out in Guinea-Bissau and Vieira was overthrown. A military junta was installed, pending new elections. Senegal declared itself 'surprised and disappointed' by events; the new government in Guinea-Bissau was, however, reported to be anxious to normalize relations with Senegal, its most powerful neighbour, and in late June the acting president of Guinea-Bissau, Malam

Bacai Sanha, visited Dakar to hold talks with Diouf. Talks apparently centred on the conflict in Casamance, while the new regime in Guinea-Bissau was also reported to have requested Senegal's support for its efforts to repair its relations with the international community.

Tensions between the two countries resurfaced in April 2000, when an armed group, reportedly composed of members of the MFDC operating from within Guinea-Bissau, attacked a Senegalese border post. The Senegalese government later denied reports that its armed forces had entered Guinea-Bissau and killed civilians, whilst undertaking reprisals against the rebels. In late April the regional military commanders of both countries agreed to close the border temporarily for reasons of security. Wade later assured Guinea-Bissau that the border incidents would not be repeated. However, in the following month Wade publicly stated that he feared the prospect of an invasion by forces from Guinea-Bissau, and called upon France to supply Senegal with military equipment in order to strengthen the country's position. Wade also requested that UN military observers be sent to the border area. The government of Guinea-Bissau continued to deny supporting the MFDC rebels, although it was widely believed that support for the MFDC was a source of tension between the president and the military junta. In July residents of the southern Senegalese district of Kolda again closed the border between the two countries in order to protest at the theft of cattle by armed groups operating from Guinea-Bissau. In August the revision was announced of the agreement on the joint exploitation of petroleum resources; henceforth Guinea-Bissau was to receive 20% rather than 15% of the revenue generated. President Koumba Yala of Guinea-Bissau subsequently downplayed the previous border disturbances and announced the creation of an agenda of joint military activity in order to co-ordinate security in the border area. Later in that month residents of the Kolda district again briefly closed the border in order to demand swifter restitution for the losses suffered in the cross-border raids.

Relations with The Gambia

In August 1989 the Diouf government announced the withdrawal of 1,400 Senegalese troops from The Gambia, apparently in protest at a request by Jawara that his country be accorded more power within the Senegambian confederal agreement (and also, it seemed, in response to The Gambia's alleged lack of

commitment to combating cross-border smuggling, as well as to Senegal's continuing dispute with Mauritania). Later in that month Diouf stated that, in view of The Gambia's reluctance to proceed towards full political and economic integration with Senegal, the functions of the confederation should be suspended, and the two countries should endeavour to formulate more attainable co-operation accords. The confederation was formally dissolved in September. The Jawara government subsequently accused Senegal of imposing customs and travel regulations that were unfavourable to Gambian interests, and of preventing supplies of important commodities from entering The Gambia via Senegal. Relations remained strained during 1990, and in October of that year the Diouf government accused the Gambian authorities of allowing members of the MFDC to operate from Gambian territory. By January 1991, none the less, relations had improved sufficiently to permit the foreign ministers of the two countries to sign a bilateral treaty of friendship and co-operation. However, Senegal's abrupt, unilateral decision to close the Senegalese–Gambian border in September 1993, apparently to reduce smuggling between the two countries, again strained relations, although negotiations subsequently took place between representatives of Senegal and The Gambia, in an attempt to minimize the adverse effects of the closure on The Gambia's regional trading links. Following the *coup d'état* in The Gambia in July 1994, Jawara was initially granted asylum in Senegal; in subsequent months, however, it was widely believed that Senegal's failure openly to condemn the suspension of constitutional rule by the military regime in The Gambia had influenced the generally muted regional response to Jawara's overthrow. Despite the presence in Senegal of prominent opponents of the Gambian military regime, in January 1996 the two countries signed an agreement aimed at increasing bilateral trade and at minimizing cross-border smuggling. The agreement was signed on behalf of Senegal by Diouf, who was visiting The Gambia for the first time since the coup in that country. A further accord, concluded in April 1997, was to facilitate the trans-border movement of goods destined for re-export. In June the two countries agreed to take joint measures to combat insecurity, illegal immigration, arms-trafficking and drugs-smuggling. In early 1998 Jammeh offered to act as a mediator between the Senegalese government and the MFDC. Jammeh subsequently hosted regular meetings between the government and the MFDC.

Economy

EDITH HODGKINSON

Revised for this edition by the Editor

Senegal retains some of the economic advantages derived from its leading position in pre-independence French West Africa. In 1998 Senegal's gross national product (GNP) was equivalent to US $520 per head, one of the highest levels in west Africa. However, its economic performance has often been disappointing. Growth in the gross domestic product (GDP)—averaging only 2.3% per year in 1970–80, before improving slightly, to 2.8% annually, in 1980–94—has barely kept pace with the rate of population growth (estimated at 2.7% per year in 1980–97). In 1999 the population was officially estimated at 9.3m. The World Bank put total GDP at $5,770m. in 1993. Nominal GDP fell to $3,911m. in 1994, because of the 50% devaluation of the CFA franc in January of that year; however, it increased, in real terms, by 2.0% (having declined by 0.4% in 1993).

The Senegalese economy responded positively to the 1994 devaluation and the accompanying government reform programme, with real GDP growth rates estimated at 5.2%, 5.0% and 5.7% in 1996, 1997 and 1998 respectively. The major sources of foreign exchange—tourism, fishing and phosphates—responded particularly favourably to the change in relative prices and the liberalization of factor markets. However, economic performance was badly affected by the frequent shortages of

electricity experienced during 1999, and the Senegalese authorities were therefore obliged to revise their estimates of growth for that year to 5% or lower. (Improvements in the country's electricity supply and transport infrastructure are regarded as central to the country's long-term economic prospects.) None the less, the recent development of agricultural exports and growth in the tourism and fishing sectors, together with the government's plans to develop reserves of gold and offshore petroleum, indicate the capability of the Senegalese economy successfully to maintain current levels of growth. Abdoulaye Wade, who was elected president in March 2000, indicated his intention to continue the process of economic reform and liberalization begun by his predecessor.

Senegal's economy is none the less vulnerable to competition in almost all areas of productive activity, and remains highly dependent on comparatively large inflows of foreign financial assistance. The agricultural base of the economy has been eroded by periodic droughts and the gradual desertification of large tracts of land. The agricultural sector's contribution to GDP declined from 24% in 1970 to 19.3% in 1998, according to World Bank figures. Following a substantial drift of population from rural to urban areas, approximately 44% of the country's total population is urban, of whom about one-half live in the overcrowded Dakar region. As the role of the public sector has declined, as part of the economic reform programme, unemployment is growing—an estimated 25% of the active population in Dakar were unemployed in 1992. Agriculture continues to be the predominant sector for employment, engaging some 74.4% of the total labour force in 1998.

Fishing, phosphate-mining and tourism have developed to rival groundnuts and groundnut products as the principal sources of foreign exchange. The importance of these sectors has been further enhanced as a result of the devaluation of the CFA franc, although many of Senegal's more import-dependent industrial activities have suffered payments' difficulties. Senegal's industrial base, which was comparatively well-developed at independence, is threatened by competing industrial investment in the west African region, particularly in Côte d'Ivoire. Many Senegalese industries have been protected by monopoly rights and tax concessions, and there is much excess capacity. Since 1995, the government has pursued a policy of gradually dismantling artificial protection barriers and promoting market-orientated incentives, in the face of considerable resistance from entrenched interest groups (particularly trade unions and organized élites). Most sectors demonstrated some recovery during the period 1995–97, although the overall situation remains fragile. The services sector, including government services, trade and transport, is calculated to have contributed about 60% of GDP in 1996, 1997 and 1998. With the prevailing difficulties in both agriculture and industry, economic activity has been conducted increasingly outside the formal sectors.

Following the devaluation of the currency, Senegal received significant financial support from the IMF, the World Bank, France and other external donors. The government undertook to accelerate its economic reforms, including the elimination of subsidies on some food commodities and the privatization of agricultural marketing, industrial units and some public utilities, such as the supply of drinking water. An ambitious privatization programme was adopted for the period 1994–97, with 22 major state-owned companies offered for sale and restructuring; it was intended that the state should withdraw from all commercial activity by the end of 2000. However, Senegalese state companies are highly unionized, and recent privatization proposals have resulted in serious disruption in some sectors and delays to the programme, as has the difficulty of finding suitable purchasers.

AGRICULTURE

The principal food crops are millet, sorghum, rice and maize. Groundnuts are the leading cash crop, but the area under cultivation has declined in recent years. Annual groundnut harvests now average around 600,000 metric tons, compared with more than 900,000 tons per year in the 1960s. There has been a long-term shift from cash to food crop cultivation, a process that is generally believed to be responsible for a decline in the real income of the rural population.

In an attempt to stimulate marketing through official channels, groundnut purchasing was opened to private traders in 1985/86 and producer prices were increased sharply. Improved weather conditions in the following years resulted in a strong rise in output, to 844,045 metric tons, in 1989/90. After late rains, production in 1990/91 contracted to 702,584 tons; output remained at a similar level (728,368 tons) in 1991/92, before declining to 578,498 tons in 1992/93. There has since been some recovery: with output rising to 631,300 tons in 1993/94, to 718,000 tons in 1994/95, and to 827,000 tons in 1995/96. However, poor rainfall resulted in a decline in the groundnut crop in 1996/97, to an estimated 626,000 tons. Production was provisionally estimated to have declined further in 1997/98, to 545,000 tons. The government is continuing more closely to link its producer prices to international price trends, and, as part of structural adjustment efforts, has almost abandoned its policy of providing inputs (such as seed and fertilizer) to farmers of groundnuts and other agricultural products. One result has been the reversal of smuggling trends, with a significant portion of the Gambian crop reaching Senegalese markets in the early 1990s.

The government has attempted to reduce dependence on groundnuts by diversifying cash and food crops, in particular by expanding cotton, rice, sugar and market-garden produce.

Production of unginned cotton rose very rapidly, from only 698 metric tons in 1965 to 51,176 tons by 1992/93. Production regressed to 38,800 tons in 1993/94 and to 28,800 tons in 1994/95, partly reflecting a reduction in the planted area, although there was some improvement, to 31,400 tons in 1995/96, to 38,400 tons in 1996/97 and an estimated 40,000 tons in 1997/98, as the producer price (and the area under cultivation) increased. Sugar is produced at the Richard Toll complex in the north, near Saint-Louis. Output, all of which is for domestic consumption, has risen steadily since 1979, and totalled an estimated 85,000 tons in 1997/98.

Output of rice has fluctuated widely, and, at an annual average of 186,000 metric tons since the beginning of the 1990s, falls far short of domestic demand (some 500,000 tons annually). The shortfall is met by cheap imports of rice from the Far East; however, this seriously jeopardizes the viability of local produce, which in the past attracted a state subsidy of 50–60 francs CFA per kilo. A number of small- and medium-scale projects, supported by foreign aid, have so far been largely unsuccessful in extending the area under irrigation for rice, although the completion of the Manantali project (see below) is expected to have a great impact on output levels and production costs in the future. Market gardening was begun in 1971, and, following initial difficulties, exports from this sector are viewed as having considerable potential, although Senegal's price competitiveness compared with other African producers is declining. The traditional food sector has suffered sharp set-backs from repeated droughts, but the overall production level has risen. Output of millet and sorghum averaged 650,000 tons per year in the mid-1970s, but fell to 351,800 tons in 1983/84, because of drought. Production has since rebounded, to average about 675,000 tons per year in 1990/91–1997/98; favourable weather conditions produced harvests of 794,100 tons and 734,400 tons in 1995/96 and 1996/97 respectively. Output of maize, which reached a record 146,500 tons in 1985/86, declined to 123,327 tons in 1988/89, recovered slightly, to 133,147 tons in 1990/91, before falling back to 114,561 tons in 1992/93. A good crop of 138,300 tons was produced in 1993/94, but has since fallen, to only 88,600 tons in 1996/97 and an estimated 60,300 tons in 1997/98.

In recent drought years concessionary grain supplies have amounted to more than 100,000 metric tons annually, while apparent consumption levels per head have been declining. The attainment of food self-sufficiency remains a major priority. Of great relevance to this objective is the enormous increase in irrigated land which is due to result from the completion of the Manantali dam in Mali. The combined benefits of the anti-salt barrage at Diama and of the Manantali dam are expected to provide newly-irrigated land totalling 240,000 ha in Senegal over the next 25 years. (However, a World Bank report has criticized the project's immediate impact on traditional farming methods, which rely on annual floods.) In the short term, it is hoped to stabilize rice imports at 340,000 tons a year, while promoting the increased cultivation and consumption of millet and sorghum. In late July 1998 the president of the Conseil national des ruraux warned of the threat of serious food shortages arising from the late arrival of the rains.

Food crops are supplemented by output from fishing. This sector has considerable potential and, including processing, has in some years accounted for about 4% of GDP and more than 25% of merchandise exports. Annual catches averaged 307,000 metric tons during 1988–92, with output rising to an estimated 507,000 tons in 1997. Small-scale fishing continues to predominate, with about 45,000 fishers providing some 60%–70% of the total national catch and about 45% of fish exports although the political insecurity in the Casamance region (the main fishing area) has at times adversely affected the sector. Industrial fishing is practised both by national and foreign operators. It has been estimated that the fishing sector as a whole provides the livelihood for as many as 400,000 people, including those engaged in local canning factories. Senegal's contribution to the international fish market remains very small, however.

Since 1979 regular fishing agreements have been concluded with the European Community (now European Union—EU), for which Senegal receives financial compensation of about £7.5m. annually, and part of the catch made by EU vessels is landed for processing locally. Some 78 EU boats were licensed to fish in Senegal in 2000. Concern has, however, been expressed that industrial fishing activities by EU vessels are not only depleting Senegal's fish stocks but also undermining the traditional fishing sector. There is also concern that Senegal is unable effectively to police its coastal waters, and thereby prevent illegal fishing by foreign vessels. In May 1999 Senegal concluded an agreement with Mauritania on the long-term management of the two countries' fish resources. Senegal also faces increasing competition from Côte d'Ivoire, which has eroded Senegal's share of the French market, and following the devaluation of its currency in 1998 Thailand also began to encroach on European markets hitherto supplied by Senegal. This increased competition, combined with a sharp decline in fish prices, led to the closure, in October 1998, of three Dakar canning factories.

From 1986 fish overtook groundnuts to become Senegal's principal export, with an average value of US \$225m. per year during 1991–96; the number of fish export firms increased from 25 in 1994 to 55 in 1997. In 1997 the value of Senegal's exports of fish and fish products (112,147 tons) increased by 4.4%, compared with 1996, to 165,000m. francs CFA. In 1998 their value was estimated at 170,700m. francs CFA.

Livestock is a significant sector of the traditional economy (although less important than in most other countries of this area), and is the base for the dairy and meat-processing industries. In 1998 numbers of cattle were estimated by the FAO at 2.9m., sheep and goats at 7.8m., pigs at 320,000 and horses at 506,000.

MINING

The mining sector's contribution to GDP has been estimated at less than 1% of GDP in recent years. However, including processed derivatives, the sector is the country's second largest source of merchandise export earnings. Mining in Senegal is dominated by the extraction of phosphates: reserves of calcium phosphates are estimated at 100m. metric tons, while there are reserves of 50m.–70m. tons of aluminium phosphates. Senegal accounts for about 1.5% of world output and 3% of world exports of phosphates. The Cie sénégalaise des phosphates de Taïba (CSPT, 50% state-owned) and the Société sénégalaise des phosphates de Thiès (SSPT, fully privatized in March 1998) have been the two companies extracting phosphates, which are then processed by Industries chimiques du Sénégal (ICS), in which the Senegalese government has a 33% stake. The merger of the activities of the CSPT and the ICS was announced in September 1996, and was expected to result in a twofold increase in the production of chemical fertilizers over the next seven years. The new company took the name ICS. The CSPT has been the principal producer of calcium phosphates, although the SSPT has modest reserves of some 2m.–3m. tons of lower-quality chalk phosphates at Lam Lam. In 1981 1.8m. tons of calcium phosphates were produced (compared with 198,000 tons in 1960). Output of calcium phosphates, which increased from 1.8m. tons in 1985 to 2.3m. tons in 1992, subsequently declined from 1.7m. tons in 1993 to 1.5m. tons in 1996. Production recovered to 1.6m. tons in 1997. Exports to countries of the EU have fallen, partly because of the high cadmium content of Senegalese phosphates, although EU funding has been provided to finance plant to remove the chemical. Expansion is planned both at existing facilities and at new ones at Tobène, while a plant for the recovery of phosphates from tailings has been constructed at the ICS fertilizer complex, with World Bank support, which will increase the life of the mine through the utilization of lower-quality deposits. There are also unexploited deposits at Semmé, estimated to contain 60m. tons of calcium phosphates. Plans to exploit further the country's reserves of phosphates were impeded in the late 1980s by low international prices (development of the Semmé deposits would cost an estimated US \$110m.). Conditions in European and south-east Asian markets remained unfavourable in the early 1990s, but from 1994 the ICS benefited from an increase in international prices for phosphoric acid in conjunction with enhanced competitiveness arising from the devaluation of the CFA franc. In 1997 ICS achieved net profits of 15,000m. francs CFA, compared with 8,000m. francs CFA in 1996.

Reserves of aluminium phosphates have been exploited by the SSPT. Output fluctuated widely in the 1970s and 1980s, with a peak of 405,000 metric tons in 1974, a halving of that figure in subsequent years, and a slight recovery, to 366,000

tons, in 1985. Concerns regarding the environmental consequences of the use of aluminium phosphates have since adversely affected the international market for this commodity, and Senegal's aluminium phosphates are no longer sold in their natural state. Most of SSPT's production is now processed locally into clinker, with the production of aluminium phosphates reduced to an estimated 37,300 tons in 1997.

Some 330m. metric tons of high-grade iron ore have been located at Falémé, in the east, but development would require new sources of electricity (the installation of the hydroelectric plant at the Manantali dam could provide such a source), a new, 740-km rail link to Dakar and new port facilities. The persistent over-supply in the world iron-ore market caused the target initial output to be halved, to 6m. tons per year. A gradual increase is then projected, to reach 12m. tons. At the lower capacity, the project, including transport investment, would require funding of some US \$700m., but adequate financial support is still being sought. Gold deposits (estimated to contain 30 tons of metal) have been discovered at Sabodala, in the south-east, and the Société minière de Sabodala, a joint venture by the Senegalese government and French official interests (with Australian participation from 1993), began production in May 1997. Several other foreign companies, including South Africa's Anglo American Corpn and Randgold, as well as Samax of the United Kingdom and several Canadian interests, have been awarded gold exploration permits in south-eastern Senegal. In late 1998 the government ordered the closure of the country's principal gold mining works at Sabodala, owing to a dispute with Eximcor, the company responsible for mining operations. It was reported that Eximcor's contract to mine for gold had expired in October 1997 and had not been renewed. In July the company's director had been accused of attempting illegally to export gold from the country. Production at the Sabodala works amounted to 100 kg in 1997. Exploration for diamonds is also in progress. Commercially-viable reserves of titanium were discovered in 1991: workable ores are estimated at some 10m. tons.

Deposits of petroleum, estimated at 52m.–58m. metric tons, have been located in the Dôme Flore field, off the Casamance coast, but the development of these reserves (which are overwhelmingly of heavy oil) was long regarded as economically unfeasible. Disagreement with Guinea-Bissau regarding sovereignty of waters in this region was a further obstacle to their development. In mid-1995, none the less, the two countries signed an agreement envisaging joint co-operation in prospecting for petroleum in adjoining territorial waters, and exploration rights were subsequently awarded to US interests, operating in partnership with the Société nationale des pétroles du Sénégal (PETROSEN). A small offshore natural gas deposit, of 50m. cu m, at Diam Niadio, near Rufisque, was developed to fuel the Cap des Biches power station, but output was only some 42,000 cu m per day, and production ceased in late 1992. However, a much larger source has been located nearby, and was supplying the Cap des Biches plant in mid-1993. In early 1997 PETROSEN announced the discovery of a major natural gas deposit, with reserves estimated at 10,000m. cu m, in the Thiès region. The deposit could be exploited for the production of electricity over a 30-year period. The development of peat deposits, in the Niayès area, is being examined with external financial support. It was hoped that these would provide fuel for electricity generation (a 20–30 MW station) and also substitute for firewood as domestic fuel. After a period of inactivity, the project was revived in 1990. The government adopted a new petroleum code and a new mining code in 1997 and 1998 respectively, in an attempt to encourage the further exploitation of Senegal's mineral resources. The incentives include generous exploration rights if a deposit is located, while there is no requirement for government equity participation.

POWER AND WATER

The high cost of electricity and poor quality of service delivery, compared to its regional neighbours and comparable economies, has long been a constraint on Senegal's industrial development. The average cost of electricity was US \$0.11 per kWh in Senegal during 1995–96, compared to \$0.07 in Côte d'Ivoire and Thailand. Electric power is supplied from six thermal stations, with a total installed capacity of 231 MW. The rehabilitation of existing capacity forms part of a project currently being implemented at a cost of more than $84m. This includes the construction by General Electric of the USA of the 56-MW power station at Cap des Biches. The power station, which will cost $65m., represents the biggest ever US investment in Senegal. Electricity from the station will be sold to SENELEC. Work began in 1982 on the Manantali hydroelectric plant, on the Senegal river, in a joint scheme with Mali and Mauritania, under the auspices of the Organisation pour la mise en valeur du fleuve Sénégal (OMVS). Construction was completed in March 1988, but the installation of generators has been delayed by arguments among the three OMVS members regarding the distribution of electricity and the routeing of power lines. Agreement was apparently reached in late 1995, and the plant is now targeted to begin production in 2001. The scheme should eventually provide total generating capacity of 200 MW, of which Senegal will have a 30% share. In an attempt to improve efficiency the government adopted legislation in January 1998 providing for the privatization of the monopoly energy producer-distributor, SENELEC. In late 1998 Hydro-Quebec International of Canada and its French partner, Elvo (a subsidiary of Suez Lyonnaise des Eaux) acquired a 34% stake in SENELEC at a cost of $66m., thereby becoming SENELEC's strategic partner. The government retained a 41% share in the utility. Hydro-Quebec subsequently proposed increasing SENELEC's capital base in order to provide much needed new financing for the company. If agreed, Hydro-Quebec would increase its ownership to 51% of SENELEC.

Dakar suffers from a water deficit estimated at 100,000 cu m in May 1999. In that month the government pledged to reduce the deficit to 60,000 cu m by July. This was to be accomplished by bringing 11 boreholes into operation, and by utilizing a factory facility in the Thiès region. The cost of this and other planned improvements in the supply of water to the capital has been estimated at 150,000m. francs CFA.

MANUFACTURING

Senegal has the most developed manufacturing sector in francophone west Africa after Côte d'Ivoire, with production accounting for 15% of GDP in 1997. The main activity is light industry (most of which is located in or near Dakar), transforming basic local commodities and import substitution to satisfy domestic demand. The agro-industrial sector mainly comprises oil mills, sugar refineries, fish-canning factories, flour mills and drinks, dairy-products and tobacco industries, which together account for 40% of total value added. Extractive industries (mainly the processing of phosphates) constitute the second most important branch of industrial activity. The manufacturing of textiles, leather goods and chemicals are also important, while subsidiary activities include paper and packaging and the manufacture of wood products and building materials. Senegal's textiles industry is well equipped and is potentially the most important in black francophone Africa, but has performed badly hitherto. The immediate, short-term impact of devaluation was, moreover, detrimental, as cotton was sold for higher prices abroad, leaving the domestic industry short of raw materials. The chemicals industry (soap, paints, insecticides, plastics, pharmaceuticals and a petroleum refinery) is aimed at import substitution, as are nearly all the metalworking, engineering and electrical plants (including three shipyards, and truck and bicycle assembly plants).

In line with the emphasis on the processing of raw materials, ICS built plants to produce sulphuric acid (625,000 metric tons per year), phosphoric acid (475,000 tons), ammonium phosphate (250,000 tons) and triple superphosphate (250,000 tons). Production started in 1984, with 180,000 tons of the fertilizer output to be sold in the Senegalese and Malian markets, and the rest to be exported, mainly to other west African markets, eventually representing earnings of up to 24,000m. francs CFA per year. The total cost of this complex, including related infrastructure, was US $312m., making it the single most important industrial project in Senegal. Funds have been contributed by the African Development Bank (ADB), the European Investment Bank (EIB), the International Finance Corpn, France and Arab agencies, including the Arab Bank for Economic Development in Africa, while the governments of Nigeria, Côte d'Ivoire, Cameroon and India have equity shares in ICS. The annual

capacity of the cement plant at Rufisque was expanded from 380,000 to 800,000 tons by the end of 1983, at a cost of 16,000m. francs CFA (with France and the EIB contributing loans), and further expansion is planned. In addition, the petroleum refinery's annual capacity has since expanded to 1.4m. tons.

The government introduced a New Industrial Policy in 1986, with the purpose of improving the competitiveness of Senegalese companies and encouraging the development of activities generating high value-added, while reducing the role of the state. There were two strands to this policy: firstly, to reduce and harmonize customs tariffs with those of competitors in the Union économique et monétaire ouest-africaine (UEMOA) and to remove quantitative restrictions on imports; and, secondly, to restructure enterprises and to improve the economic and regulatory environment by reducing the cost of key inputs, including labour. However, within three years the programme was effectively abandoned. As cheap imports flooded the market, through formal and informal channels, the government decided in 1989 to restore customs tariffs to their previous high levels. The reduction of costs and enactment of an enabling environment were never implemented, largely because of resistance to labour law reforms from the trade unions.

There has been a decline in output in many industrial subsectors since 1986, although the production of phosphates, water and electricity have shown overall increases, and there has been resilience in output of petroleum products, soap, fertilizers and cement. Most has been achieved in those industries that have not been directly affected by the industrial reforms introduced after 1986. The decline was particularly severe in light manufacturing industries such as textiles and shoes, which were vulnerable to competition from imported goods.

After the devaluation of the currency, new measures were undertaken in an attempt to stimulate private-sector participation in industry. Import licensing was abolished, and the government made further commitments to end the effective monopolies enjoyed by a few large companies, to reduce the rigidity of the statutory labour code, and to privatize several state-owned companies and parastatals—including SONACOS, the main groundnut-oil producer. However, the government's rejection in 1996 of several unacceptably low offers for state enterprises was endorsed by the World Bank. Performance in the manufacturing sector since the devaluation has been uneven, with some sectors (such as food-processing and electronics) suffering a decline in output as protective barriers have been reduced. Although initially slow to respond, investment has increased since the devaluation; the ratio of gross domestic investment to GDP increased from 13.1% during 1991–93 to 18.7% in 1997 (however, even this rate is below the 20% rate, or more, expected to sustain growth rates in excess of the target of 5%). Loans for private-sector development and small and medium-sized enterprises were awarded by the International Development Association (the World Bank's concessionary lending agency) and the ADB.

In mid-1998 it was reported that a higher council for industry had been established and charged with the elaboration of a coherent economic strategy. Delegates to the council were to include representatives of ministerial departments, of the private sector and of employers' organizations. Later in 1998 it was reported that the Senegalese Confederation of Employers was in the process of restructuring and intended to construct a 'private industrial property' comprising storage depots, an administrative centre, a customs area and a power station. Investment in the project was to amount to some 2,000m. francs CFA.

TRANSPORT INFRASTRUCTURE

Industrial development has been stimulated by, and has in turn boosted, the port at Dakar. Container-handling facilities were increased from 29,000 metric tons to more than 100,000 tons when a new terminal was inaugurated in 1988, and the extension of container facilities was completed in 1993. The port handles some 6m. tons of freight per year. Improvements to the fishing port at Dakar have also been carried out. There were proposals to construct a naval repair yard, to service bulk oil carriers, but plans were scaled down because of a downturn in the tanker market, and a smaller-scale dock, able to handle vessels up to 60,000 tons, entered service in 1981. In that year more than 400 ships were serviced. Completion of the Manantali project will eventually extend the all-year navigability of the Senegal river, currently just 220 km, to 924 km, as far as Kayes in Mali.

Senegal possesses a good road network. In 1996 there were an estimated 14,576 km of classified roads, of which about 3,361 km were surfaced. In mid-1986, as part of the economic adjustment programme, the government suspended virtually all new road-building projects, concentrating instead on financing the maintenance of existing roads. None the less, a 163-km road between Dialakoto and Kédougou, the construction of which was financed by regional donor organizations, was inaugurated in March 1996. The rail infrastructure is also well-developed, with 1,225 km of track, although only 70 km of this is two-way and the network would benefit from modernization. The two main lines run from Dakar to Kidira, from the west to the east and across the border with Mali to Bamako, and from Dakar, via Thiès, to Saint-Louis in the north, near the border with Mauritania. In late 1995 the governments of Senegal and Mali agreed to establish, with a view to privatization, a joint company to operate the Dakar–Bamako line.

There is an international airport at Dakar, which handles about 850,000 passengers and 24,000 metric tons of freight annually; in addition there are three other major airports and about 15 smaller airfields. A second airport for the capital is to be constructed at Keur Massar (about 30 km east of Dakar), at an estimated cost of US $200m., with capacity for 2.5m. passengers annually. Meanwhile, facilities at Cap-Skirring and Ziguinchor are being upgraded, with the aim of improving direct access to the Casamance region. In accordance with the government's overall strategy in the transport sector, Air Sénégal, the national carrier, was partially privatized in 1999, with Royal Air Maroc taking a 51% stake. The company was later renamed Air Sénégal International.

In March 1999 it was reported that the World Bank had committed 55,000m. francs CFA in support of Senegal's transport programme for 1999–2000. Key projects of the programme are the construction of new phosphate terminals at Dakar port and the development of Kaolack and Ziguinchor ports. The World Bank was also to fund the lengthening of runways at Saint-Louis airport and at Dakar international airport. Also in March 1999 the government announced that it would invest 2,000m. francs CFA in a project to build and renovate roads in the Louga region.

COMMUNICATIONS

In mid-1997 the national telecommunications company, SON-ATEL, was partially privatized, with France Câbles et Radio, a subsidiary of France Telecom, purchasing 33% of the company's capital. A further 10% of shares in the company were sold to SONATEL employees at a discounted rate, while a further 17% of the company's value was offered to institutions and the general public. Following the recapitalization of the company in 1999, France Câbles et Radio increased its share in SONATEL to 42%.

In July 1998 it was announced that Millicom International Cellular, based in Luxembourg, had been awarded a 20-year licence to construct Senegal's second mobile phone network. Senegal's other mobile network is managed by SONATEL. Mobile subscribers were reported to number 16,000 in October 1998, compared with 7,000 at the beginning of the year. SON-ATEL aimed to increase the number of subscribers to 20,000 by the end of 1998.

TOURISM

Tourism has grown in importance since the early 1970s, and it now ranks as one of the country's major sources of foreign earnings. In 1998 gross earnings from tourism reached 100,100m. francs CFA, and visitor arrivals were estimated to total 392,500. Senegal has about 16,500 hotel beds of international tourist standard, and Dakar is of considerable importance as an international conference centre. The sector, which provides 4,500 direct and 15,000 indirect jobs, contributed almost 3% of GDP in 1995. The devaluation of the CFA franc improved the competitiveness of tourism in Senegal, hitherto regarded as a high-cost destination, and Senegal has declared its intention of attracting 1m. tourists by 2005. However, further violence

in Casamance and the failure to secure an enduring peace settlement in the region, where much tourist activity is traditionally located, could prevent the further development of the sector.

INVESTMENT AND FINANCE

Despite overall economic difficulties, the level of investment increased steadily in the 1960s, from the rather low figure of 9% of GDP in 1961 to 17% in 1971, although it had fallen back to about 13% by the early 1990s as Senegal's economic structure became increasingly uncompetitive. Public investment has accounted for the majority of total gross investment (69% in 1990), with government borrowing—both internal and external—increasing, as budgetary revenue declined. Gross domestic savings have also tended to be low, averaging around 5.6% of GDP during 1991–93. Since 1994, gross investment and domestic saving rates have risen, however, averaging 17.3% and 11.5% respectively during 1994–97.

Considerable progress was made, under the austerity programmes of the early 1980s, in reducing the budget deficit, which declined from 8.2% of annual GDP in 1982/83 to 3.8% of GDP in 1987/88. However, the economic situation was severely undermined in 1988/89 by Senegal's dispute with Mauritania, while the implementation of 'liberalization' policies, such as the reduction in customs tariffs, has also affected the level of government revenue. As a result, the budget deficit nearly doubled in 1988/89, to 30,900m. francs CFA, compared with 16,800m. francs CFA in the previous year. The deficit widened further, to 46,400m. francs CFA in 1989/90. However, estimates for 1990/91 indicated that improvements in revenue collection and restraints on expenditure led to an initial surplus in government finances (on a commitment basis) of 31,200m. francs CFA. However, the overall deficit in that year, on a cash basis, was only 400m. francs CFA, reflecting the implementation of a programme to pay off arrears. In the equivalent period of 1991/92 there was a surplus, on a commitment basis, of 3,700m. francs CFA; this budgetary period was extended to the end of 1992, so that subsequent financial years were to coincide with the calendar year. The increasing overvaluation of the currency had a negative impact on government revenues, resulting in a fiscal deficit of 47,200m. francs CFA in 1993 (equivalent to 3.0% of GDP in that year). Although the subsequent fiscal reforms restrained the budget deficit to about 1.9% of GDP in 1994 (on a commitment basis), the deficit on a cash basis continued to widen, reaching 9.9% of GDP, or 200,000m. francs CFA, in that year (owing to the payment of considerable accumulated arrears). None the less, continued fiscal austerity has continued to improve the budgetary position, and the cash deficit narrowed to 2.9% of GDP in 1995. Provisional figures indicate that the overall fiscal deficit (on a cash and commitment basis) has continued to decline, with the budget almost balancing in 1996 and a small surplus expected for 1997. Excluding foreign grants, the fiscal deficit was reduced from 6.1% of GDP in 1994 to 1.1% in 1997. One of the main aims of the government's policy is to eliminate the budget's reliance on sizeable foreign grants.

In December 1997 the national assembly approved a public investment programme for 1998–2000 requiring some 928,000m. francs CFA. Budget proposals for 1998 envisaged that revenue and expenditure would balance at 479,000m. francs CFA, an increase of 8.5% compared with the previous year. In January 1999 the national assembly approved a public investment programme for 1999–2001 requiring 969,000m. francs CFA. Of this total, the government was to provide 321,000m. francs CFA, while the remainder was to take the form of foreign grants, subsidies and loans. Budget proposals for 1999 envisaged that revenue and expenditure would balance at 490,000m. francs CFA. In May 1999 the government announced plans to invest 114,000m. francs CFA in the Casamance region over a five-year period. The aim was to initiate an emergency programme to counter the effects of regional instability.

Since independence, Senegal has benefited from the consistent support of Western donors, who have been keen to assist the country's relatively stable, conservative governments. Donors have always recognized that Senegal is poorly-endowed with natural resources, and external aid and funding have been forthcoming. Moreover, relations with both the World Bank and the IMF have generally remained good.

In 1987 the consultative group of aid donors pledged funds of US $1,800m. to support the public investment programme and to provide payments support for 1987–90. Throughout the period of the economic reform programme the IMF accorded stand-by and structural adjustment facilities. In November 1988 an Enhanced Structural Adjustment Facility (ESAF), of SDR 145m. over three years, was approved. However, attempts in mid-1993 to reduce current expenditure—in accordance with creditors' demands that the problem of the public-sector deficit, of some 180,000m. francs CFA, be addressed—principally by means of reductions in civil servants' salaries prompted considerable domestic disquiet. In March 1994 Senegal was the first Franc Zone member to reach agreement with the IMF on new funding (a stand-by credit of $67m.), following the devaluation of the CFA franc, and a new ESAF, of SDR 138.8m., was approved in August 1994. Almost all the new assistance pledged by multilateral and bilateral donors was conditional upon the government's continued adherence to the programme of reforms. Principal among the donors of new loans were the World Bank, the ADB and France. In July 1995 the consultative group of donors, expressing broad satisfaction at the progress of adjustment measures hitherto, pledged $1,500m. over a two-year period. Senegal was granted another three-year ESAF, with a value of $142m., in April 1998. Subsequently, the major donors (including the World Bank, the EU and France) committed almost $2,000m. in aid pledges to support Senegal's 1998–2000 economic programme.

FOREIGN TRADE AND PAYMENTS

Senegal's foreign trade and current-account balance have consistently been in deficit, with the size of the former varying in response to the groundnut crop. Since the mid-1970s, however, the fluctuations have tended to narrow, as exports have stabilized at higher levels, reflecting the expansion, first, of exports of phosphates (to an average of 22,000m. francs CFA per year during the 1980s) and, later, of fishery products (an average of 18,000m. francs CFA per year in 1978–80, rising to 55,000m. francs CFA in 1990, and to 120,400m. francs CFA in 1994—the year of the currency devaluation). The very strong rise in imports in the early 1980s, as petroleum prices rose, the food deficit widened, and purchasing power was maintained through foreign borrowing, resulted in a trade deficit of 130,000m. francs CFA in 1985. The 1985–92 adjustment programme aimed to increase export earnings by 12.9% annually, with exports of fish and chemical products from the ICS complex rising strongly, while import growth was to be held to an average 9.8% per year. This was still to leave Senegal with a substantial trade deficit; in the event the restrictive reform programme and an overvalued exchange rate led to the value of merchandise exports declining by an annual average of 0.7% during 1985–92, while that of imports declined by an average of 1.7% per year. Exports in 1989–93 averaged 228,000m. francs CFA annually, compared with imports averaging 316,000m. francs CFA per year. The trade deficit in 1994 was 128,300m. francs CFA (equivalent to about US $350m. or 8% of GDP). In nominal CFA franc terms the value of both imports and exports increased substantially following the 50% devaluation of the currency in January. Exports increased by 119%, to 439,100m. francs CFA, while the increase in expenditure on imports was limited to 84%, at 567,400m. francs CFA. The value of exports increased by 10.1% in 1995, by 4.3% in 1996, by 7.9% in 1997 and by an estimated 5.8% in 1998, to 575,700m. francs CFA. The corresponding annual increases in the value of imports were 9.3% in 1995, 4.5% in 1996, 7.6% in 1997 and an estimated 6.5% in 1998, to 743,400m. francs CFA. In US dollar terms exports have continued to expand, rising from $736.8m. in 1993 to $819m. in

1994, and $993m. in 1995. In 1995 the trade deficit stood at $249.6m.

The chronic deficits on foreign trade and on imports and exports of services are to some degree offset on the current account by inward cash transfers, consisting mainly of official development grants. The current-account deficit remained relatively stable during the 1980s and early 1990s: it fell from 122,400m. francs CFA in 1985 to a low point of 49,300m. francs CFA in 1990, but regressed somewhat, to 79,000m. francs CFA in 1993 (equivalent to 5% of GDP). A sharp narrowing of the trade deficit and a surge in official development assistance in 1994 resulted in a small current-account surplus, of 1,800m. francs CFA, or US $3.2m., in that year. However, the surplus was not sustained, and a current-account deficit of 12,700m. francs CFA, or $58m., was recorded for 1995, while the government estimated a deficit of some 32,400m. francs CFA (around 7% of GDP) in 1996; both were largely attributable to the decline in the level of foreign official transfers, which fell from $641m. in 1994 to $506m. in 1996. According to official sources, Senegal recorded a current-account deficit of 41,900m. francs CFA in 1997, and of an estimated 64,700m. francs CFA in 1998.

Since the late 1970s, the government has had increasing recourse to external borrowing, and outstanding external long-term debt increased from US $1,114m. in 1980 to $2,071m. in 1985 and to $3,861m. in 1998. Commercial bank debt is negligible following a World Bank initiated 'buy-back' of 'London Club' debt (at 16% of its face value) in December 1996. The rise in debt-servicing payments, which reached 29% of total foreign earnings in 1980, was restricted by a series of debt-rescheduling agreements by the 'Paris Club' of Western official creditors, linked to the IMF-backed austerity programme. None the less, the debt-service ratio reached a record level of 32.4% in 1987, before easing to 28.6% in 1989, to 20.5% in 1990, and to 8.4% in 1993. Subdued export performance in 1994, in conjunction with the clearing of some servicing arrears and the effects of devaluation (which resulted in the doubling, in local-currency terms, of the external debt), meant that the debt-service ratio was 15.1% in 1994, rising to 17.3% in 1995. Since 1988, reschedulings of debt by the 'Paris Club' have been made in accordance with the exceptional terms formulated at the summit meeting of industrialized nations that had been held in Toronto in 1988. Further substantial debt relief, including cancellations and reschedulings in accordance with the 'Trinidad terms' (devised in 1990), was approved by the 'Paris Club' in March 1994, while France agreed to cancel one-half of Senegal's bilateral debt. Even more concessionary relief, involving some 87,000m. francs CFA of debt, was granted by official creditors in early 1995, in accordance with the new 'Naples terms', which allow the cancellation or rescheduling of as much as 67% of public debt.

According to criteria devised by the World Bank and IMF under the Heavily Indebted Poor Countries initiative (HIPC), Senegal's debt was considered sustainable in early 1998; however, in mid-2000 the IMF and the International Development Association (IDA) announced that Senegal was in fact eligible for debt relief under the newly-revised terms of the expanded HIPC initiative, since Senegal's external debt exceeded 150% of the value of exports and 250% of the value of fiscal revenue. The IMF and IDA subsequently annouced a debt-relief programme for Senegal, which, with the support of Senegal's other creditors, would be equivalent to some US $800m. The debt relief provided by the IDA was equivalent to a 50% reduction in Senegal's obligations to the IDA over the following nine years, while the relief provided by the IMF was equivalent to 20% of obligations to the IMF over the following seven years. Full assistance was, however, to be made dependent on the government's continued implementation of macroeconomic reform and the introduction of a comprehensive poverty reduction strategy.

Statistical Survey

Source (unless otherwise stated): Direction de la Prévision et de la Statistique, Ministère l'Economie, des Finances et du Plan, Immeuble Peytavin, BP 4017, Dakar; tel. 821-96-99; fax 822-41-95.

Area and Population

AREA, POPULATION AND DENSITY

Area (sq km)	196,722*
Population (census results)†	
16 April 1976	5,085,388
27 May 1988	
Males	3,353,599
Females	3,543,209
Total	6,896,808
Population (official estimates at mid-year)	
1997	8,802,304
1998	9.037.906
1999	9,278,617
Density (per sq km) at mid-1999	47.2

* 75,955 sq miles.
† Figures refer to the *de jure* population. The *de facto* population at the 1976 census was 4,907,507, and at the 1988 census was 6,773,417.

POPULATION BY ETHNIC GROUP (at 1988 census)

Ethnic group	Number	%
Wolof	2,890,402	42.67
Serere	1,009,921	14.91
Peul	978,366	14.44
Toucouleur	631,892	9.33
Diola	357,672	5.28
Mandingue	245,651	3.63
Rural-Rurale	113,184	1.67
Bambara	91,071	1.34
Maure	67,726	1.00
Manjaag	66,605	0.98
Others	320,927	4.74
Total	**6,773,417**	**100.00**

Source: UN, *Demographic Yearbook*.

REGIONS AND PRINCIPAL TOWNS
(de jure population at 1988 census)

	Area (sq km)	Popu-lation	Density (per sq km)	Population of capital*
Dakar . . .	550	1,488,941	2,707.2	1,375,067
Diourbel . . }	33,547 {	619,245 }	33.1 {	n.a.
Louga . . }		490,077 }		n.a.
Fatick . .	7,935†	509,702	64.2	n.a.
Kaolack . .	16,000†	811,258	50.7†	150,961
Kolda . .	21,000†	591,833	28.2†	n.a.
Saint-Louis . .	44,127	660,282	15.0	113,917
Tambacounda . .	59,602	385,982	6.5	n.a.
Thiès . .	6,601	941,151	142.6	175,465
Ziguinchor . .	7,300†	398,337	54.6†	124,283
Total . .	**196,722**	**6,896,808**	**35.1**	

* Each region has the same name as its capital.
† Figures are approximate.
Note: The city of Dakar is the national capital.
Principal towns (official estimates at mid-1994): Dakar 1,641,358; Thiès 216,381; Kaolack 193,115; Ziguinchor 161,680; Saint-Louis 132,499.
Source: UN, *Demographic Yearbook*.

BIRTHS AND DEATHS (UN estimates, annual averages)

	1985–90	1990–95	1995–2000
Birth rate (per 1,000) . . .	45.5	42.2	40.0
Death rate (per 1,000) . . .	17.7	14.8	13.0

Expectation of life (UN estimates, years at birth, 1990–95): 50.4 (males 48.3; females 52.6).
Source: UN, *World Population Prospects: The 1998 Revision*.

ECONOMICALLY ACTIVE POPULATION

Mid-1998 (estimates in '000): Agriculture, etc. 2,958; Total 3,978 (Source: FAO, *Production Yearbook*).
Unemployed (general survey, Feb.-March 1999): 157,063 (males 99,892; females 57,171).

Agriculture

PRINCIPAL CROPS ('000 metric tons)

	1996	1997	1998*
Rice (paddy)	149	174	174
Maize	89	60	60
Millet	601	426	426
Sorghum	133	118	118
Potatoes	6	8*	8
Cassava (Manioc) . . .	36	37	47
Pulses	21	33	33
Groundnuts (in shell) . .	588	506	506
Cottonseed*	24	33	33
Cotton (lint)* . . .	20	27	27
Palm kernels* . . .	5	5	5
Tomatoes	30	30*	30
Dry onions	77	65*	65
Green beans	7	7*	7
Watermelons	220	261	261
Other vegetables* . . .	44	45	45
Mangoes	78	77*	77
Oranges	31†	30*	30
Bananas	9	9*	9
Other fruit*	21	21	21
Coconuts*	5	5	5
Sugar cane*	885	883	883

* FAO estimate(s).   † Unofficial figure.
Source: FAO, *Production Yearbook*.

LIVESTOCK ('000 head, year ending September)

	1996	1997	1998*
Cattle	2,835*	2,913	2,913
Sheep	4,450*	4,239	4,239
Goats	3,300*	3,572	3,572
Pigs*	320	320	320
Horses*	504	506	506
Asses*	372	376	376
Camels*	7	8	8

Poultry (million): 42* in 1996; 44 in 1997; 44* in 1998.
* FAO estimate(s).
Source: FAO, *Production Yearbook*.

LIVESTOCK PRODUCTS (FAO estimates, '000 metric tons)

	1996	1997	1998
Beef and veal	46	47	47
Mutton and lamb	15	14	14
Goat meat	14	15	15
Pig meat	7	8	8
Horse meat	7	7	7
Poultry meat	60	62	64
Other meat	6	5	5
Cows' milk	104	105	105
Sheep's milk	17	15	15
Goats' milk	14	15	15
Poultry eggs	32	33	33
Cattle hides	9	9	9
Sheepskins	3	3	3
Goatskins	3	3	3

Source: FAO, *Production Yearbook*.

Forestry

ROUNDWOOD REMOVALS ('000 cubic metres, excluding bark)

	1995	1996	1997
Sawlogs, veneer logs and logs for sleepers	40	40	40
Other industrial wood	679	697	715
Fuel wood	4,266	4,457	4,563
Total	4,985	5,194	5,318

Source: FAO, *Yearbook of Forest Products*.

SAWNWOOD PRODUCTION ('000 cubic metres, incl. railway sleepers)

	1995	1996	1997
Total (all broadleaved)	23	23	23

Source: FAO, *Yearbook of Forest Products*.

Fishing

('000 metric tons, live weight)

	1995	1996	1997
Freshwater fishes	37.4	49.3	82.6
Flatfishes	10.5	8.1	8.0
Sea catfishes	3.9	4.5	10.2
Grunts, sweetlips, etc.	4.2	13.0	14.0
West African croakers	2.5	9.0	8.5
Round sardinellas	116.8	142.5	152.7
Madeiran sardinellas	64.7	108.2	114.8
Bonga shad	17.3	17.8	17.1
Other marine fishes (incl. unspecified)	69.2	59.3	71.6
Total fish	333.3	412.3	479.5
Gastropods	7.5	6.7	5.2
Other crustaceans and molluscs	17.8	17.4	22.3
Total catch	358.6	436.3	507.0

Note: Figures cover the artisanal Senegalese fishery, the industrial Senegalese tuna fishery, the industrial Senegalese and French trawler fishery, and the industrial Senegalese sardine fishery.

Source: FAO, *Yearbook of Fishery Statistics*.

Mining

('000 metric tons)

	1996	1997	1998
Calcium phosphates	1,376.8	1,589.2	1,519.2
Aluminium phosphates	77.5	8.7	21.2
Fuller's earth (attapulgite)	78.0	81.6	65.3
Salt (unrefined)	113.4	122.0	138.0

Industry

PETROLEUM PRODUCTS (estimates, '000 metric tons)

	1993	1994	1995
Jet fuel	92	92	93
Motor spirit (Petrol)	117	118	118
Kerosene	17	17	18
Gas-diesel (Distillate fuel) oils	294	295	295
Residual fuel oils	225	226	226
Lubricating oils	3	3	3
Liquefied petroleum gas	3	3	3

Source: UN, *Industrial Commodity Statistics Yearbook*.

SELECTED OTHER PRODUCTS
('000 metric tons, unless otherwise indicated)

	1996	1997	1998
Sugar cubes	36.8	39.2	42.2
Tobacco products (tons)	1,566	1,556	1,816
Groundnut oil—crude	91.4	38.1	49.8
Vegetable oil—refined	95.4	89.2	103.4
Canned tuna	19.8	14.3	18.7
Footwear ('000 pairs)	695.0	739.9	712.5
Cotton yarn (tons)	1,452	1,272	1,107
Soap	38.2	40.5	38.6
Paints and varnishes (tons)	3,069	2,656	2,972
Cement	810.2	853.9	846.5
Metal cans (million)	128.9	132.8	n.a.
Electricity (million kWh)	1,109.9	1,214.5	1,304.1

Nitrogenous fertilizers (estimated nitrogen content, '000 metric tons, year ending 30 June): 24 in 1993/94; 12 in 1994/95.
Phosphate fertilizers (estimated phosphoric acid content, '000 metric tons): 42 in 1994.

Finance

CURRENCY AND EXCHANGE RATES

Monetary Units
100 centimes = 1 franc de la Communauté financière africaine (CFA).

Sterling, Dollar and Euro Equivalents (28 April 2000)
£1 sterling = 1,132.20 francs CFA;
US $1 = 722.02 francs CFA;
€1 = 655.96 francs CFA;
10,000 francs CFA = £8.832 = $13.850 = €15.245.

Average Exchange Rate (francs CFA per US $)
1997	583.67
1998	589.95
1999	615.70

Note: An exchange rate of 1 French franc = 50 francs CFA, established in 1948, remained in force until January 1994, when the CFA franc was devalued by 50%, with the exchange rate adjusted to 1 French franc = 100 francs CFA. This relationship to French currency remained in effect with the introduction of the euro on 1 January 1999. From that date, accordingly, a fixed exchange rate of €1 = 655.957 francs CFA has been in operation.

BUDGET ('000 million francs CFA)

Revenue*	1995	1996	1997
Tax revenue	330.3	369.3	401.1
Taxes on income and property .	80.1	85.0	94.3
Individual	44.5	45.8	53.7
Corporate	24.4	26.3	29.0
Capital income . . .	6.1	6.4	4.9
Taxes on goods and services (excl. petroleum)	119.9	135.8	158.7
Value-added tax on domestic goods	56.0	68.2	82.8
Value-added tax on imported goods	38.6	42.1	48.1
Taxes on imports (excl. petroleum)†	97.0	115.8	108.7
Taxes on petroleum products .	33.2	32.7	39.4
Non-tax revenue	35.9	25.0	31.1
Société Africaine de Raffinage .	21.9	20.1	7.5
Total	**366.2**	**394.3**	**432.2**

Expenditure	1995	1996	1997
Current expenditure . . .	316.6	312.6	317.6
General public services . .	81.3	81.4	88.4
National defence . . .	36.6	39.6	40.2
Education	76.9	79.5	82.0
Health	16.7	17.2	16.0
Social and community services .	4.8	5.0	12.6
Economic services . . .	8.0	7.6	10.7
Unallocable	92.3	82.3	67.7
Interest on government debt .	64.5	55.9	58.6
Capital expenditure . . .	117.7	127.6	147.5
Domestically financed . .	35.7	41.6	57.5
Externally financed . .	82.0	86.0	50.0
Treasury special accounts (net)‡ .	4.2	−1.3	−0.2
Treasury correspondents (net)‡ .	6.2	9.2	7.5
Sub-total	**444.7**	**448.1**	**472.4**
Adjustment for payments arrears§	60.4	0.0	0.0
Total	**505.1**	**448.1**	**472.4**

* Excluding grants received ('000 million francs CFA): 73.5 in 1995; 47.7 in 1996; 30.0 in 1997.
† Including customs duties, fiscal duties, stamp duties and surtaxes.
‡ Additions to expenditure are deficits, while deductions are surpluses.
§ Positive figures indicate a reduction in arrears.

Source: IMF, *Senegal — Statistical Appendix* (January 1999).

INTERNATIONAL RESERVES (US $ million at 31 December)

	1997	1998	1999
Gold*	8.9	8.5	8.6
IMF special drawing rights .	0.5	0.5	2.5
Reserve position in IMF . .	1.8	1.9	1.9
Foreign exchange . . .	383.9	428.4	398.5
Total	**395.1**	**439.3**	**411.5**

* Valued at market-related prices.

Source: IMF, *International Financial Statistics*.

MONEY SUPPLY ('000 million francs CFA at 31 December)

	1997	1998	1999
Currency outside banks . .	142.3	158.5	179.4
Demand deposits at deposit money banks	196.3	234.0	255.9
Checking deposits at post office .	4.0	4.1	3.9
Total money (incl. others) . .	**343.2**	**397.0**	**439.8**

Source: IMF, *International Financial Statistics*.

COST OF LIVING (Consumer price index, Dakar. Base: 1995 = 100)

	1997	1998	1999
All items	104.6	105.8	106.6

Source: IMF, *International Financial Statistics*.

NATIONAL ACCOUNTS ('000 million francs CFA at current prices)
Expenditure on the Gross Domestic Product

	1996	1997	1998*
Government final consumption expenditure	256.7	259.0	278.3
Private final consumption expenditure	1,815.1	1,933.7	2,069.7
Gross fixed capital formation . .	413.7	477.1	545.5
Total domestic expenditure .	**2,485.5**	**2,669.8**	**2,893.5**
Exports of goods and services . .	812.1	868.4	913.3
Less Imports of goods and services	947.2	1,013.9	1,079.3
GDP in purchasers' values .	**2,350.4**	**2,524.3**	**2,727.5**

* Provisional figures.

Source: Banque centrale des états de l'Afrique de l'ouest.

Gross Domestic Product by Economic Activity

	1996	1997	1998*
Agriculture, hunting, forestry and fishing	486.0	489.9	525.2
Mining and quarrying . . } Manufacturing	379.9	407.9	444.9
Electricity, gas and water . .	46.9	50.4	53.8
Construction and public works .	109.8	126.0	142.4
Trade, restaurants and hotels .	580.3	648.8	700.1
Transport, storage and communications . . .	250.9	285.7	306.4
Other marketable services . .	271.3	289.7	320.7
Government services . . .	193.6	192.8	199.4
Non-profit services to households .	31.7	33.1	34.6
GDP in purchasers' values .	**2,350.4**	**2,524.3**	**2,727.5**

* Provisional figures.

Source: Banque centrale des états de l'Afrique de l'ouest.

BALANCE OF PAYMENTS (US $ million)

	1995	1996	1997
Exports of goods f.o.b. . .	993.3	998.0	904.6
Imports of goods f.o.b. . .	−1,242.9	−1,264.0	−1,176.0
Trade balance	**−249.6**	**−275.9**	**−271.5**
Exports of services . . .	512.5	378.6	371.7
Imports of services . . .	−578.2	−395.8	−391.7
Balance on goods and services	**−315.3**	**−293.1**	**−291.5**
Other income received . .	87.2	81.3	67.9
Other income paid . . .	−211.5	−154.1	−139.8
Balance on goods, services and income	**−439.6**	**−366.0**	**−363.4**
Current transfers received .	284.7	244.3	258.8
Current transfers paid . .	−89.6	−77.8	−80.3
Current balance . . .	**−244.5**	**−199.5**	**−184.9**
Capital account (net) . . .	187.0	169.2	96.0
Direct investment abroad . .	3.3	−3.0	0.5
Direct investment from abroad .	31.7	8.4	176.4
Portfolio investment assets . .	−0.4	−25.8	−19.6
Portfolio investment liabilities .	4.0	−4.8	−8.1
Other investment assets . .	−6.2	−70.8	−22.1
Other investment liabilities . .	11.8	91.6	77.1
Net errors and omissions . .	−19.6	8.0	−9.2
Overall balance	**−32.9**	**−26.8**	**106.1**

Source: IMF, *International Financial Statistics*.

External Trade

PRINCIPAL COMMODITIES (distribution by SITC, US $ million)

Imports c.i.f.	1993	1994	1995
Food and live animals	293.7	174.5	317.1
Dairy products and birds' eggs	70.4	39.6	34.4
Milk and cream	63.3	35.3	30.5
Milk and cream, preserved, concentrated or sweetened	61.9	34.3	29.3
Fish, crustaceans and molluscs	13.4	7.9	0.9
Fresh, chilled or frozen fish	12.7	6.7	0.1
Cereals and cereal preparations	126.1	76.6	195.9
Wheat and meslin (unmilled)	35.2	31.6	53.9
Rice	80.7	41.0	132.4
Rice, broken	80.6	41.0	132.4
Vegetables and fruit	24.4	11.8	19.5
Coffee, tea, cocoa and spices	22.8	12.1	17.0
Crude materials (inedible) except fuels	45.9	33.9	40.8
Mineral fuels, lubricants, etc.	103.9	168.8	122.4
Petroleum, petroleum products, etc.	103.4	157.7	122.1
Crude petroleum oils, etc.	84.1	35.8	88.6
Refined petroleum products	16.9	119.4	30.5
Animal and vegetable oils, fats and waxes	63.9	34.5	67.4
Fixed vegetable oils and fats	62.2	32.1	56.0
Fixed vegetable oils, 'soft', crude, refined or purified	45.8	24.1	50.6
Rape, colza and mustard oils	24.1	20.9	30.0
Chemicals and related products	134.1	114.7	170.3
Inorganic chemicals	11.4	10.7	29.0
Inorganic chemical elements, oxides and halogen salts	7.7	7.5	25.5
Medicinal and pharmaceutical products	45.0	32.7	36.1
Medicaments (incl. veterinary)	41.2	28.4	31.9
Artificial resins, plastic materials, etc.	22.4	23.5	36.2
Polymerization and copolymerization products	18.0	19.6	30.6
Basic manufactures	175.5	132.7	212.6
Paper, paperboard, etc.	29.1	22.4	36.0
Textile yarn, fabrics, etc.	24.3	16.3	35.6
Iron and steel	51.9	42.7	58.7
Universals, plates and sheets, of iron or steel	24.0	17.4	21.3
Machinery and transport equipment	252.4	161.8	221.3
Machinery specialized for particular industries	44.0	25.0	35.9
Civil engineering and contractors' plant and equipment	26.5	8.8	12.6
Construction and mining machinery	21.7	6.3	8.5
General industrial machinery, equipment and parts	44.3	30.3	41.2
Electrical machinery, apparatus, etc.	47.8	31.2	48.8
Road vehicles and parts (excl. tyres, engines and electrical parts)	79.9	42.6	66.9
Passenger motor cars (excl. buses)	37.2	18.0	24.1
Miscellaneous manufactured articles	55.5	44.2	54.1
Total (incl. others)	1,139.2	876.8	1,224.4

Exports f.o.b.	1993	1994	1995
Food and live animals	176.3	63.5	21.3
Fish, crustaceans and molluscs	143.6	42.9	9.8
Fresh, chilled or frozen fish	57.0	21.5	8.6
Fresh, chilled, frozen, salted or dried crustaceans and molluscs	15.4	10.6	0.0
Prepared or preserved fish, crustaceans and molluscs	66.9	8.4	0.2
Fish (incl. caviar)	48.3	2.2	0.2
Feeding stuff for animals (excl. unmilled cereals)	13.6	13.6	6.3
Oil-cake, etc.	11.9	12.5	5.1
Groundnut cake	11.4	12.4	5.0
Crude materials (inedible) except fuels	103.4	63.0	104.6
Textile fibres (excl. wool tops) and wastes	27.4	19.0	33.5
Cotton	27.2	19.0	33.5
Raw cotton (excl. linters)	27.2	19.0	33.5
Crude fertilizers and crude minerals	64.9	29.8	51.6
Crude fertilizers	51.2	16.7	43.3
Natural calcium phosphates, etc.	51.2	16.7	43.3
Minerals fuels, lubricants, etc.	87.4	73.0	80.0
Petroleum, petroleum products, etc.	86.9	72.6	79.4
Refined petroleum products	86.4	72.4	78.9
Motor spirit (gasoline) and other light oils	33.6	31.8	35.2
Spirit-type jet fuel	28.5	27.3	30.9
Gas oils (distillate fuels)	28.6	23.1	22.4
Animal and vegetable oils, fats and waxes	34.4	74.1	55.7
Fixed vegetable oils and fats	34.4	74.0	54.4
Fixed vegetable oils, 'soft', crude, refined or purified	34.3	74.0	54.2
Groundnut (peanut) oil	33.7	73.8	53.8
Chemicals and related products	103.8	109.4	209.7
Inorganic chemicals	56.7	71.4	119.7
Inorganic chemical elements, oxides and halogen salts	56.6	71.3	119.5
Inorganic acids and oxygen compounds of non-metals	55.4	69.4	118.9
Phosphorus pentoxide and phosphoric acids	55.3	69.3	118.9
Manufactured fertilizers	26.8	21.2	63.6
Basic manufactures	44.2	23.4	27.9
Paper paperboard and manufactures	14.6	7.6	13.7
Metal containers for storage and transport	12.7	4.8	4.2
Casks, drums, cans, boxes, etc., of iron, steel or aluminium	12.5	4.7	4.2
Machinery and transport equipment	39.3	25.5	13.5
Machinery specialized for particular industries	13.8	3.6	3.2
Miscellaneous manufactured articles	13.5	11.4	11.8
Total (incl. others)	605.1	444.4	530.8

Source: UN, *International Trade Statistics Yearbook*.

PRINCIPAL TRADING PARTNERS (US $ million)*

Imports c.i.f.				1996	1997	1998
Belgium-Luxembourg	.	.	.	37.6	45.6	59.7
Brazil	.	.	.	30.1	19.9	16.3
China, People's Repub.	.			31.0	25.2	28.7
Côte d'Ivoire	.	.	.	36.5	31.5	39.6
France (incl. Monaco)	.			392.9	371.7	538.0
Gabon	.	.	.	15.3	1.2	13.3
Germany	.	.	.	90.8	44.9	67.5
India	.	.	.	90.4	47.0	49.5
Italy	.	.	.	46.5	39.9	56.1
Japan	.	.	.	40.7	36.4	51.4
Netherlands	.	.	.	42.3	32.9	42.3
Nigeria	.	.	.	76.6	87.6	92.1
Spain	.	.	.	57.1	53.7	56.9
Thailand	.	.	.	43.6	35.5	83.6
United Kingdom	.	.	.	25.9	22.0	31.6
USA	.	.	.	69.7	58.4	86.3
Total (incl. others)	.	.	.	1,409.0	1,209.3	1,574.7

Exports f.o.b.				1996	1997	1998
Belgium-Luxembourg	.	.	.	28.5	26.1	27.8
Benin	.	.	.	16.8	15.8	15.0
Cameroon	.	.	.	36.1	29.6	32.3
Côte d'Ivoire	.	.	.	57.1	57.4	60.8
France (incl. Monaco)	.	.	.	117.7	98.2	107.6
Gabon	.	.	.	38.0	37.1	38.7
Gambia	.	.	.	12.7	12.2	16.1
Germany	.	.	.	5.6	8.8	2.6
Guinea	.	.	.	10.2	9.2	11.8
India	.	.	.	110.7	101.3	143.0
Italy	.	.	.	73.6	50.0	58.4
Japan	.	.	.	9.9	9.7	9.5
Korea, Repub.	.	.	.	8.9	8.5	8.9
Mali	.	.	.	48.7	37.0	42.5
Mauritania	.	.	.	15.5	14.8	21.4
Netherlands	.	.	.	12.4	9.5	10.6
Spain	.	.	.	42.1	36.0	38.3
United Kingdom	.	.	.	12.6	6.7	2.5
Total (incl. others)	.	.	.	853.1	710.9	811.5

* Imports by country of production; exports by country of last consignment.

Transport

RAILWAYS (estimated traffic)

			1996	1997	1998
Passenger-km (million)	.	.	103.4	78.3	63.4
Freight ton-km (million)	.	.	474.3	446.4	435.2

ROAD TRAFFIC (motor vehicles in use)

			1994	1995	1996
Passenger cars	.	.	76,092	79,219	85,488
Buses and coaches	.	.	9,362	9,699	10,359
Lorries and vans	.	.	21,211	22,307	24,040
Road tractors	.	.	2,142	2,251	2,383
Motor cycles and mopeds	.	.	3,241	3,679	4,062

Source: IRF, *World Road Statistics*.

SHIPPING

Merchant Fleet (vessels registered at 31 December)

			1996	1997	1998
Number of vessels	.	.	189	198	198
Total displacement ('000 grt)	.		50	51	51

Source: Lloyd's Register of Shipping, *World Fleet Statistics*.

International Sea-borne Freight Traffic ('000 metric tons)

			1996	1997	1998
Goods loaded	.	.	3,788.4	4,062.5	4,544.9
Goods unloaded	.	.	2,243.8	2,064.1	1,844.3

CIVIL AVIATION (traffic on scheduled services)*

			1994	1995	1996
Km flown (million)	.	.	2	3	3
Passengers carried ('000)	.	.	113	120	124
Passenger-km (million)	.	.	227	235	238
Total ton-km (million)	.	.	36	38	38

* Including an apportionment of the traffic of Air Afrique.
Source: UN, *Statistical Yearbook*.

Tourism

	1996	1997	1998
Tourist arrivals ('000) . .	322.1	358.7	392.5
Tourism receipts ('000 million CFA francs) . .	77.8	91.8	100.1

Communications Media

	1994	1995	1996
Radio receivers ('000 in use) . .	945	1,000	1,200
Television receivers ('000 in use) .	297	320	350
Telephones ('000 main lines in use) .	72	82	95
Mobile cellular telephones (subscribers)	98	122	1,412
Daily newspapers			
Number	3	3	1
Average circulation ('000 copies)	48	48	45
Non-daily newspapers			
Number	6	6	n.a.
Average circulation ('000 copies)	37	37	n.a.

1997: Radio receivers ('000 in use) 1,240; Television receivers ('000 in use) 361.

1998 (October): Mobile cellular telephones (subscribers) 16,000.
Source: mainly UNESCO, *Statistical Yearbook*; UN, *Statistical Yearbook*.

Education

(1997/98, unless otherwise indicated)

	Institu-tions	Teachers	Students Males	Students Females	Students Total
Pre-primary . .	270	995	9,816	10,064	19,880
Primary . . .	3,884	14,887	562,958	463,612	1,026,570
Secondary					
General . .	480	6,219*	95,614	79,506	175,120
Teacher training .	n.a.	n.a.	495	94	589
Vocational .	9	n.a.	2,910	1,705	4,615
Tertiary† . .	n.a.	641	17,427	6,342	23,769

* 1996/97 figure.
† Data refer solely to the Cheikh Anta Diop University.

Directory

The Constitution

The Constitution of the Republic of Senegal was promulgated on 7 March 1963, and was most recently amended in August 1998. The main provisions are summarized below:

PREAMBLE

Affirms the Rights of Man, liberty of the person and religious freedom. National sovereignty belongs to the people who exercise it through their representatives or by means of referendums. There is universal, equal and secret suffrage for adults of 18 years of age and above. French is the official language.

THE PRESIDENT

The President of the Republic is elected by direct universal suffrage for a seven-year term and no limits are imposed upon his subsequent attempts to be re-elected. The President holds executive power and, as Commander of the Armed Forces, is responsible for national defence. The President of the Republic appoints the Prime Minister. He may, after consultation with the President of the Assemblée nationale, with the Prime Minister and with the appropriate organ of the judiciary, submit any draft law to referendum. In circumstances where the security of the State is in grave and immediate danger, he can assume emergency powers and rule by decree. The President of the Republic can be impeached only on a charge of high treason or by a secret ballot of the Assemblée nationale carrying a three-fifths' majority.

THE PRIME MINISTER

The Prime Minister is appointed by the President of the Republic, and, in turn, appoints the Council of Ministers in consultation with the President.

THE LEGISLATURE

Legislative power is vested in the Assemblée nationale, which is elected by universal direct suffrage for a five-year term, and in the Sénat, which is elected by the deputies of the Assemblée nationale, and by regional, municipal and local councillors. Additional senators are appointed by the President, and others are elected by Senegalese abroad. The Assembly discusses and votes legislation and submits it to the President of the Republic for promulgation. The President can direct the Assembly to give a second reading to the bill, in which case it may be made law only by a three-fifths' majority. The President of the Republic can also call upon the Constitutional Council to declare whether any draft law is constitutional and acceptable. Legislation may be initiated by either the President of the Republic or the Assemblée nationale. Should the Presidency fall vacant, the President of the legislature is automatic successor to the Head of State. A motion expressing 'no confidence' in the Government can be considered if it has been endorsed by one-tenth of the members of the Assembly.

LOCAL GOVERNMENT

Senegal is divided into 10 regions, each having a governor and an elected local assembly. It is further divided into 48 communes and 320 rural communities.

POLITICAL PARTIES

There is no limit to the number of political parties.

AMENDMENTS

The President of the Republic and Deputies to the Assemblée nationale may propose amendments to the Constitution. Draft amendments are adopted by a three-fifths' majority vote of the Assemblée nationale. Failing this, they are submitted to referendum.

Amendments to clauses concerning the election of the President were adopted in 1998.

The Government

HEAD OF STATE

President: ABDOULAYE WADE (took office 1 April 2000).

COUNCIL OF MINISTERS
(August 2000)

Prime Minister: MOUSTAPHA NIASSE.

Minister of Mines, Handicrafts and Industry: LANDING SAVANÉ.

Minister of Energy and Water Resources: ABDOULAYE BATHILY.

Minister of Town Planning and Housing: AMATH DANSOKHO.

Minister of Equipment and Transportation: MADIEYNA DIOUF.

Minister of the Economy and Finances: MAKHTAR DIOP.

Minister of Agriculture and Stockbreeding: PAPE DIOUF.

Minister of Foreign Affairs and Senegalese Abroad: CHEIKH TIDIANE GADIO.

Minister of Armed Forces: YOUBA SAMBOU.

Minister of Justice, Keeper of the Seals: MAME MADIOR BOYE.

Minister of the Interior: Maj.-Gen. MAMADOU NIANG.

Minister of Higher Education: MADIOR DIOUF.

Minister of Planning: OUMAR KHASSIMOU DIA.

Minister of National Education, Technical and Vocational Training: KANSOUMBALY NDIAYE.

Minister of Health: ABDOU FALL.

Minister of Family Affairs and National Solidarity: AMINATA TALL.

Minister of Territorial Administration and Decentralization: KHADIDJATOU FALL DIALLO.

Minister of Trade: KHOURAÏCHI THIAM.

Minister of the Civil Service, Labour and Employment: YÉRO DE.

Minister of Fisheries: OUMAR SARR.

Minister of the Environment: LAMINE BA.

Minister of Culture and Communication: MAMADOU DIOP.

Minister of Tourism: NDIAWAR TOURE.

Minister of Sports and Leisure: JOSEPH NDONG.

Minister of Youth: MODOU FADA DIAGNE.

Minister of African Integration: AMADOU SARR.

Minister in charge of Relations with the Assemblies: HAOUA DIA THIAM.

Minister-delegate at the Ministry of the Economy and Finances in charge of the Budget: ABDOULAYE DIOP.

Minister-delegate at the Ministry of National Education, Technical and Vocational Training in charge of Literacy, Technical and Vocational Training: BÉCAYE DIOP.

MINISTRIES

Office of the President: ave Léopold Sédar Senghor, BP 168, Dakar; tel. 823-10-88.

Office of the Prime Minister: Building Administratif, ave Léopold Sédar Senghor, Dakar; tel. 823-10-88; fax 822-55-78.

Ministry of Agriculture and Stockbreeding: Building Administratif, ave Léopold Sédar Senghor, Dakar; tel. 823-10-88; fax 821-32-68.

Ministry of the Armed Forces: Building Administratif, ave Léopold Sédar Senghor, BP 176, Dakar; tel. 823-10-88; fax 823-63-38.

Ministry of the Civil Service, Labour and Employment: Building Administratif, ave Léopold Sédar Senghor, BP 403, Dakar; tel. 823-10-88; fax 823-74-29.

Ministry of Communications: Immeuble République, Dakar; tel. 823-10-65; fax 821-41-04.

Ministry of Culture: Building Administratif, ave Léopold Sédar Senghor, Dakar; tel. 823-10-88; fax 822-16-38.

Ministry of the Economy and Finances: Immeuble Peytavin, BP 4017, Dakar; tel. 821-96-99; fax 822-41-95.

Ministry of Energy and Water Resources: 122 bis ave André Peytavin, BP 4037, Dakar; tel. 822-96-26; fax 822-55-94; e-mail memisen@sonatel.senet.net; internet www.primature.sn/memi.

Ministry of the Environment: Bloc Calmette, Dakar; tel. 821-11-26; e-mail mepn@syfed.refer.sn; internet www.refer.org/sngal_ct/cop/mepn.

Ministry of Equipment and Transportation: Ex-Camp Lat Dior, Dakar; tel. 823-83-51; fax 823-82-79.

Ministry of Family Affairs and National Solidarity: 3 rue Béranger Ferraud, BP 4050, Dakar; tel. 823-69-19; fax 823-66-73; e-mail mfef@primature.sn; internet www.primature.sn/mfef.

Ministry of Foreign Affairs and Senegalese Abroad: 1 place de l'Indépendance, Dakar; tel. 823-42-84; fax 823-84-88.

Ministry of Health: Building Administratif, ave Léopold Sédar Senghor, Dakar; tel. 823-10-88; fax 822-26-90.

Ministry of the Interior: place Washington, Dakar; tel. 823-42-84; fax 821-05-42; internet www.mint.sn.

Ministry of Justice: Building Administratif, ave Léopold Sédar Senghor, BP 784, Dakar; tel. 823-10-88; fax 823-27-27.

Ministry of Mines, Handicrafts and Industry: Dakar.

Ministry of National Education, Technical and Vocational Training: 8 rue Calmette, BP 4025, Dakar; tel. 821-71-80; fax 821-12-28; internet www.primature.sn/men.

Ministry of Territorial Administration and Decentralization: rue Emile Zola, Dakar; tel. 822-98-06; fax 822-97-64.

Ministry of Tourism: 23 rue Calmette, BP 4049, Dakar; tel. 823-65-02; fax 822-94-13; e-mail mtta@primature.sn; internet www.primature.sn/tour.

Ministry of Town Planning and Housing: Building Administratif, BP 4028, Dakar; tel. 823-10-88; fax 822-26-90.

Ministry of Trade: Building Administratif, ave Léopold Sédar Senghor, Dakar; tel. 823-10-88.

Ministry of Youth: Bloc Madeleine, Dakar; tel. 822-26-01.

President and Legislature

PRESIDENT

Presidential Election, First Ballet, 27 February 2000

Candidate	Votes	% of votes
ABDOU DIOUF (PS)	690,886	41.33
ABDOULAYE WADE (PDS)	517,642	30.97
MOUSTAPHA NIASSE (AFP)	280,085	16.76
DJIBO KA (URD)	118,487	7.09
IBA DER THIAM (CDP)	20,133	1.20
OUSSEYNOU FALL (PRS)	18,676	1.12
CHEIKH ABDOULAYE DIÈYE (FSD)	16,216	0.97
MADEMBA SOCK (FRAP)	9,318	0.56
Total	**1,671,443**	**100.00**

Second Ballot, 19 March 2000

Candidate	Votes	% of votes
ABDOULAYE WADE (PDS)	969,332	58.49
ABDOU DIOUF (PS)	687,969	41.51
Total	**1,657,301**	**100.00**

ASSEMBLÉE NATIONALE

President: CHEIKH ABDOUL KHADRE CISSOKHO (PS).

General Election, 24 May 1998

Party	Votes	% of votes	Seats
PS	616,847	50.19	93*
PDS	235,470	19.16	23†
Alliance Jëf Jël–URD	162,374	13.21	11‡
AJ–PADS	60,760	4.94	4
LD–MPT	48,445	3.94	3
CDP	24,579	2.00	1
FSD	16,445	1.34	1
PDS–R	12,978	1.06	1
PIT	10,899	0.89	1
RND	8,220	0.67	1
Bloc des centristes Gaïndé	7,517	0.61	1
Others	24,589	2.00	—
Total	**1,229,123**	**100.00**	**140**

* Including 58 seats won by majority voting within departments.
† Including 10 seats won by majority voting within departments.
‡ Including 2 seats won by majority voting within departments.

SÉNAT

President: ABDOULAYE DIACK (PDS).

Senatorial Election, 24 January 1999*

Party	Votes	% of votes	Seats
PS	9,840	91.32	45
Alliance AJ–PADS–PIT	609	5.65	—
PLS	326	3.03	—
Total	**10,775**	**100.00**	**45†**

* The 45 elective members of the Sénat are voted for by members of the Assemblée nationale and local municipal and regional councillors.
† The total membership of the Sénat is 60, including 12 members appointed by the President, and three members elected by Senegalese abroad.

Advisory Council

Conseil Economique et Social: 25 ave Pasteur, BP 6100, Dakar; tel. 823-40-88; fax 822-86-10; internet www.conseil-eco.sn; f. 1964; Pres. FAMARA IBRAHMA SAGNA; Sec.-Gen. MAMADOU DIA.

Political Organizations

The following parties were among the most prominent at the time of the 2000 presidential election.

Alliance des forces de progrès (AFP): f. 1999; Leader MOUSTAPHA NIASSE.

Alliance Jëf-Jël (AJJ): Dakar; fmrly Alliance pour le Progrès et la Justice; name changed 2000; Pres. TALLA SYLLA.

And Jëf–Parti africain pour la démocratie et le socialisme (AJ–PADS): BP 12025, Dakar; tel. 822-54-63; e-mail ajsavmar@sonatel.senet.net; internet www.ajpads.org; f. 1991 by merger of And Jëf–Mouvement révolutionnaire pour la démocratie nouvelle, Organisation socialiste des travailleurs and Union pour la démocratie populaire; progressive reformist; Sec.-Gen. LANDING SAVANÉ.

Bloc des centristes Gaïndé: Leader PAUL DIAZ.

Convention des démocrates et des patriotes (CDP): 96 rue 7, Bopp, Dakar; f. 1992; Sec.-Gen. Prof. IBA DER THIAM.

Front de rupture pour une alternative populaire (FRAP): Dakar.

Front pour le socialisme et la démocratie (FSD): Leader CHEIKH ABDOULAYE DIÈYE.

Ligue démocratique–Mouvement pour le parti du travail (LD–MPT): BP 10172, Dakar Liberté; tel. 825-67-06; fax 827-43-00; regd 1981; social-democrat; Sec.-Gen. ABDOULAYE BATHILY.

Mouvement de la gauche démocratique (MGD): Dakar; f. 1997 as breakaway from PIT; Leader SAMBA DIOULDE THIAM.

Mouvement pour le socialisme et l'unité (MSU): Villa no 54, rue 4, Bopp, Dakar; f. 1981 as Mouvement démocratique populaire; socialist; Sec.-Gen. MAMADOU DIA; Co-ordinator-Gen. BAMBA N'DIAYE.

Parti africain des écologistes–Sénégal (PAES): Ecole Normale Germaine Legoff, Dakar; Sec.-Gen. ABOUBACRY DIA.

Parti africain de l'indépendance (PAI): BP 820, Dakar; f. 1957, reorg. 1976; Marxist; Sec.-Gen. MAJHEMOUTH DIOP.

Parti africain pour l'indépendance des masses (Pai–M): 440, Cité Abdou Diouf Guédiawaye, Dakar; tel. 834-75-90; f. 1982; social democratic; Sec.-Gen. ALY NIANE.

Parti démocratique sénégalais (PDS): 5 blvd Dial Diop, Dakar; f. 1974; liberal democratic; Sec.-Gen. Me ABDOULAYE WADE; Dep. Sec.-Gen. IDRISSA SECK.

Parti démocratique sénégalais–Rénovation (PDS–R): 343 Gibraltar II, Dakar; regd 1987; breakaway group from PDS; Sec.-Gen. SERIGNE DIOP.

Parti de l'indépendance et du travail (PIT): BP 5612, Dakar Fann; regd 1981; Marxist-Leninist; Sec.-Gen. AMATH DANSOKHO.

Parti libéral du Sénégal (PLS): Dakar; f. 1998 by breakaway faction of PDS; Leader OUSMANE NGOM.

Parti pour la libération du peuple (PLP): 4025 Sicap Amitié II, Dakar; f. 1983 by RND dissidents; neutralist and anti-imperialist; Sec.-Gen. Me BABACAR NIANG; Asst Sec.-Gen. ABDOULAYE KANE.

Parti populaire sénégalais (PPS): Clinique Khadim Diourbel, Dakar; regd 1981; populist; Sec.-Gen. Dr OUMAR WANE.

Parti républicain sénégalais (PRS): Dakar; Leader OUSSEYNOU FALL.

Parti socialiste du Sénégal (PS): Maison du Parti, ave Cheikh Amadou Bamba, Rocade Fann, Bel Air, BP 12010, Dakar; e-mail ps@telecomplus.sn; internet www.telecomplus.sn.ps; f. 1958 as Union progressiste sénégalaise, reorg. 1978; democratic socialist; Chair. ABDOU DIOUF; Exec. Sec. OUSMANE TANOR DIENG.

Rassemblement national démocratique (RND): Villa no 29, Cité des Professeurs, Fann Résidence, Dakar; f. 1976, legalized 1981; progressive; Sec.-Gen. MADIOR DIOUF.

Union démocratique sénégalaise—Rénovation (UDS—R): Villa no 273, Ouagou Niayes, Dakar; f. 1985 by PDS dissidents; progressive nationalist; Sec.-Gen. MAMADOU PURITAIN FALL.

Union pour le renouveau démocratique (URD): Dakar; f. 1998 by breakaway faction of PS; Leader DJIBO KA.

Union pour le socialisme et la démocratie (USD): Dakar; Leader DOUDOU SARR.

Diplomatic Representation

EMBASSIES IN SENEGAL

Argentina: 34–36 blvd de la République, BP 3343, Dakar; tel. 821-51-71; Ambassador: HÉCTOR TEJERINA.

Austria: 24 blvd El Hadji Djily Mbaye, BP 3247, Dakar; tel. 822-38-86; fax 821-03-09; e-mail ambaut@telecomplus.sn; Ambassador: MICHAEL BRUNNER.

Bangladesh: Immeuble Kébé, Appts 11–12, 7e étage, ave André Peytavin, BP 403, Dakar; tel. 821-68-81; Ambassador: M. D. MANI-RUZZAMAN MIAH.

Belgium: route de la Petite Corniche-Est, BP 524, Dakar; tel. 822-47-20; fax 821-63-45; Ambassador: PHILIPPE DE CLERCK.

Brazil: Immeuble Fondation Fahd, 4e étage, blvd Djily Mbaye, angle rue Macodou Ndiaye, BP 136, Dakar; tel. 823-14-92; fax 823-71-81; e-mail embdakar@telecomplus.sn; Ambassador: RICARDO C. DO N. BORGES.

Cameroon: 157–9 rue Joseph Gomis, BP 4165, Dakar; tel. 821-33-96; Ambassador: EMMANUEL MBONJO EJANGUE.

Canada: Immeuble Daniel Sorano, 45 blvd de la République, BP 3373, Dakar; tel. 823-92-90; fax 823-87-49; Ambassador: JACQUES BIL-ODEAU.

Cape Verde: Immeuble El Fahd, BP 2319, Dakar; tel. 821-18-73; Ambassador: VÍCTOR AFONSO GONÇALVES FIDALGO.

Congo, Democratic Republic: Fann Résidence, 16 rue Léo Fro-bénius, Dakar; tel. 825-19-79; Ambassador: KALENGA WA BELABELA.

Congo, Republic: Mermoz Pyrotechnie, BP 5243, Dakar; tel. 824-83-98; Ambassador: CHRISTIAN GILBERT BEMBET.

Côte d'Ivoire: 2 ave Albert Sarraut, BP 359, Dakar; tel. 821-01-63; Ambassador: Prof. ALASSANE SALIF NDIAYE.

Czech Republic: rue Aimé Césaire, Fann Résidence, BP 3253, Dakar; tel. 825-77-82; fax 824-14-06; Chargé d'affaires: OTTO HOLUBÁŘ.

Egypt: Immeuble Daniel Sorano, 45 blvd de la République, BP 474, Dakar; tel. 821-24-75; fax 821-89-93; Ambassador: MOHAMED ABDEL-RAHMAN DIAB.

Ethiopia: 18 blvd de la République, BP 379, Dakar; tel. 821-98-90; fax 821-08-05; Ambassador: MOHAMED HASSEN KAHIN.

France: 1 rue Amadou Assane Ndoye, BP 4035, Dakar; tel. 823-91-81; fax 822-18-05; Ambassador: JEAN DE GLINIASTY.

Gabon: Villa no 7606 Mermoz, BP 436, Dakar; tel. 824-09-95; fax 825-98-26; Ambassador: SIMON OMBEGUE.

Gambia: 11 rue de Thiong, BP 3248, Dakar; tel. 821-44-76; Ambassador: Col (retd) ANTOUMAN SAHO.

Germany: 20 ave Pasteur, angle rue Mermoz, BP 2100, Dakar; tel. 823-48-84; fax 822-52-99; Ambassador: Dr ELEONORE LINSMAYER.

Guinea: point E, rue 7, angle B&D, BP 7123, Dakar; tel. 824-86-06; fax 82-55-94; Chargé d'affaires a.i.: AMIR SAMPIL.

Guinea-Bissau: Point E, rue 6, BP 2319, Dakar; tel. 821-59-22; Ambassador: PIO GOMES CORREIA.

Holy See: rue Aimé Césaire, angle Corniche-Ouest, Fann Résidence, BP 5076, Dakar; tel. 824-26-74; fax 824-19-31; Apostolic Nuncio: Most Rev. JEAN-PAUL GOBEL, Titular Archbishop of Galazia in Campania.

India: 1e étage, 5 ave Carde, BP 398, Dakar; tel. 822-58-75; fax 822-35-85; e-mail indiaemb@telecomplus.sn; Ambassador: JAWAHAR LAL.

Indonesia: 126 ave Cheikh Anta Diop, à côté de l'ENEA, BP 5859, Dakar; tel. 825-73-16; fax 825-58-96; e-mail ambitsen@telecomplus.sn; Ambassador: UTOJO YAMTOMO.

Israel: 3 place de l'Indépendance, BP 2096, Dakar; tel. 823-35-61; fax 823-64-90; Ambassador: DORON GRASSMAN.

Italy: rue Alpha Hachamiyou Tall, BP 348, Dakar; tel. 822-05-78; fax 821-75-80; e-mail ambitsen@telecomplus.sn; Ambassador: PAOLO GUIDO SPINELLI.

Japan: blvd Martin Luther King, Corniche-Ouest, BP 3140, Dakar; tel. 823-91-41; fax 823-73-51; Ambassador: TAKESHI NAKAMURA.

Korea, Republic: Immeuble Fayçal, BP 3338, Dakar; tel. 822-58-22; Ambassador: KIM IL-KUN.

Kuwait: blvd Martin Luther King, Dakar; tel. 824-17-23; Ambassador: ABDERRAHAMANE AHMAD AL-BAKR.

Lebanon: 18 blvd de la République, BP 234, Dakar; tel. 822-09-20; Ambassador: NAJI ABDOU ASSI.

Mali: 46 blvd de la République, BP 478, Dakar; tel. 823-48-93; Ambassador: MOHAMED ALI BATHILY.

Mauritania: Fann Résidence, Corniche-Ouest, Dakar; tel. 825-98-07; fax 825-72-64; Ambassador: MALIFOND OULD DADDAH.

Morocco: ave Cheikh Anta Diop, BP 490, Dakar; tel. 824-69-27; fax 825-70-21; Ambassador: DRISS ENNAHDI ELIDRISSI.

Netherlands: 37 rue Kléber, BP 3262, Dakar; tel.823-94-83; fax 821-70-84; e-mail nlgovdak@telecomplus.sn; Ambassador: JOS VAN AGGELEN.

Nigeria: Point E, rue 1, angle Fa, BP 3129, Dakar; tel. 821-69-22; fax 825-81-36; Chargé d'affaires a.i.: O. A. D. NWAOBASI.

Pakistan: Stelle Mermoz, Villa no. 7602, BP 2635, Dakar; tel. 824-61-35; fax 824-61-36; e-mail parepdkr@telecomplus.sn; Ambassador: SAJJAD ASHRAF.

Poland: Fann Résidence, angle Corniche-Ouest, BP 343, Dakar; tel. 824-23-54; fax 824-95-26; Chargé d'affaires a.i.: JANUSZ MROWIEC.

Portugal: 5 ave Carde, BP 281, Dakar; tel. 823-58-22; fax 823-50-96; Ambassador: FERNANDO PINTO DOS SANTOS.

Romania: Point E, blvd de l'Est, angle rue 4, Dakar; tel. and fax 825-19-13; Chargé d'affaires: IONEL ILIE.

Russia: ave Jean-Jaurès, angle rue Carnot, BP 3180, Dakar; tel. 822-48-21; fax 821-13-72; e-mail consru@telecomplus.sn; Ambassador: VALERIONAS BALTROUNAS.

Saudi Arabia: 33 rue Kléber, BP 3109, Dakar; tel. 822-23-67; Ambassador: AHMED BIN MOHAMED BAYARI.

South Africa: 12 ave Albert Sarraut, BP 21010, Dakar-Ponty; tel. 823-65-81; fax 821-48-78; Ambassador: (vacant).

Spain: 45 blvd de la République, BP 2091, Dakar; tel. 821-30-80; fax 821-68-45; Ambassador: JOSÉ MARÍA OTERO.

Switzerland: rue René Ndiaye, angle rue Seydou Nourou Tall, BP 1772, Dakar; tel. 823-05-90; e-mail swiemdkr@metissacana.sn; Ambassador: INGRID APELBAUM PIDOUX.

Syria: Point E, rue 1, angle blvd de l'Est, BP 498, Dakar; tel. 821-62-77; Chargé d'affaires a.i.: HILAL AL-RAHEB.

Thailand: Fann Résidence, 10 rue Léon Gontran Damas, BP 3721, Dakar; tel. 825-70-95; fax 824-84-58; e-mail thaidkr@telcomplus.sn; Ambassador: PICHAI PONG RAET.

Tunisia: rue El Hadj Seydou Nourou Tall, BP 3127, Dakar; tel. 823-47-47; fax 823-72-04; Ambassador: ALI HACHANI.

Turkey: ave des Ambassadeurs, Fann Résidence, BP 6060, Etoile, Dakar; tel. 824-58-11; fax 825-69-77; Ambassador: SENBIR TÜMAY.

United Kingdom: 20 rue du Dr Guillet, BP 6025, Dakar; tel. 823-73-92; fax 823-27-66; e-mail britemb@telecomplus.sn; Ambassador: ALAN BURNER.

USA: ave Jean XXIII, BP 49, Dakar; tel. 823-42-96; fax 822-29-91; Ambassador: HARRIET L. ELAM-THOMAS.

Zimbabwe: Fann Résidence, BP 15153, Dakar; tel. 825-03-25; fax 825-89-59; Ambassador: CHIMBIDZAYI EZEKIEL SANYANGARE.

Judicial System

In 1992 the Cour Suprême was replaced by three judicial bodies. The Conseil Constitutionnel verifies that legislation and international agreements are in accordance with the Constitution. It decides disputes between the Executive and the Legislature, and determines the relative jurisdictions of the Conseil d'Etat and the Cour de Cassation. The Conseil d'Etat judges complaints brought against the Executive. It also supervises the public accounts, and resolves electoral disputes. The Cour de Cassation is the highest court of appeal, and regulates the activities of subordinate courts and tribunals.

Conseil Constitutionnel: Dakar; internet www.rapide-pana.com/demo/conseil; 5 mems; Pres. YOUSSOUPHA NDIAYE.

Conseil d'Etat: Pres. OUSMANE CAMARA; Sec.-Gen. DOUDOU NDIR.

Cour de Cassation: Procurator-Gen. ANDRÉSIA VAZ; Sec.-Gen. MOUSTAPHA TOURÉ.

Religion

At the time of the 1988 census almost 94% of the population were Muslims, while some 4% professed Christianity (the dominant faith being Roman Catholicism); a small number followed traditional beliefs.

ISLAM

There are four main Islamic brotherhoods active in Senegal: the Tidjanes, the Mourides, the Layennes and the Qadiriyas.

Grand Imam: El Hadj MAODO SYLLA.

Association pour la coopération islamique (ACIS): Dakar; f. 1988; Pres. Dr THIERNAO KÁ.

National Association of Imams: Dakar; f. 1984; Pres. El Hadj MAODO SYLLA.

CHRISTIANITY

The Roman Catholic Church

Senegal comprises one archdiocese and five dioceses. At 31 December 1998 there were an estimated 601,089 adherents of the Roman Catholic Church, representing about 6.8% of the total population.

Bishops' Conference: Conférence des Evêques du Sénégal, de la Mauritanie, du Cap-Vert et de Guinée-Bissau, BP 941, Dakar; tel. 836-33-09; fax 836-16-17; f. 1973; Pres. Most Rev. THÉODORE-ADRIEN SARR, Archbishop of Dakar.

Archbishop of Dakar: Most Rev. THÉODORE-ADRIEN SARR, Arch-evêché, ave Jean XXIII, BP 1908, Dakar; tel. 823-69-18.

The Anglican Communion

The Anglican diocese of The Gambia, part of the Church of the Province of West Africa, includes Senegal and Cape Verde. The Bishop is resident in Banjul, The Gambia.

Protestant Church

Eglise Protestante du Senegal: 65 rue Wagane Diouf, BP 22390, Dakar; tel. 821-55-64; fax 821-71-32; f. 1862; Pastor ETITI YOMO DJERIWO.

BAHÁ'Í FAITH

National Spiritual Assembly: BP 1662, Dakar; tel. 824-23-59; registered 1975; mems resident in 363 localities.

The Press

NEWSPAPERS

Le Matin: Dakar; daily; independent.

Réveil de l'Afrique Noire: Dakar; f. 1986; daily.

Le Soleil: Société sénégalaise de presse et de publications, route du Service géographique, BP 92, Dakar; tel. 832-46-92; fax 832-03-81; e-mail lesoleil@primature.sn; internet www.primature.sn/lesoleil; f. 1970; daily; publ. by PS; Man. Dir ALIOUNE DRAME; Editor MAMADOU KASSE; circ. 45,000.

Sud Quotidien: Immeuble Fahd, 18 rue Raffenel, BP 4130, Dakar; tel. 822-53-93; fax 822-52-90; e-mail info@sudonline.sn; internet www.sudonline.sn; daily; fmrly Sud Hebdo; Editor ABDOULAYE NDIAGA SYLLA; circ. 30,000.

Wal Fadjri (The Dawn): Dakar; tel. 824-35-71; e-mail walf@telecomplus.sn; internet www1.telecomplus.sn/walf; f. 1984; Islamic daily; Exec. Dir MBAYE SIDY MBAYE; circ. 15,000.

PERIODICALS

Afrique Economique: Dakar; f. 1975; monthly; Editor ASSANE SECK; circ. 10,000.

Afrique Médicale: 10 rue Abdou Karim Bourgi, BP 1826, Dakar; tel. 823-48-80; fax 822-56-30; f. 1960; monthly; review of tropical medicine; Editor JOËL DECUPPER; circ. 7,000.

Afrique Nouvelle: 9 rue Paul Holle, BP 283, Dakar; tel. 822-51-22; f. 1947; weekly; development issues; Roman Catholic; Dir RENÉ ODOUN; circ. 15,000.

Amina: BP 2120, Dakar; monthly; women's magazine.

Bingo: 17 rue Huart, BP 176, Dakar; f. 1952; monthly; illustrated; Editor E. SOELLE; circ. 110,750.

Le Cafard Libéré: 10 rue Tolbiac, angle autoroute, 3e étage, Dakar; tel. 822-84-43; f. 1987; weekly; satirical; Editor ABDOULAYE BAMBA DIALLO; circ. 12,000.

Combat pour le Socialisme: Dakar; f. 1987; politics; circ. 10,000.

Construire l'Afrique: BP 3770, Dakar; tel. 823-07-90; fax 824-19-61; f. 1985; six a year; African business; Dir and Chief Editor CHEIKH-OUSMANE DIALLO.

Le Démocrate: 5 blvd Dial Diop, Dakar; f. 1974; monthly; publ. by PDS.

Ethiopiques: BP 2035, Dakar; tel. and fax 821-53-55; f. 1974; two a year; literary and philosophical review; publ. by Fondation Léopold Sédar Senghor.

Fippu: Dakar; f. 1987; quarterly; feminist; Dir FATOUMATA SOW.

Journal Officiel de la République du Sénégal: Rufisque; f. 1856; weekly; govt journal.

Momsareew: BP 820, Dakar; f. 1958; monthly; publ. by PAI; Editor-in-Chief MALAMINE BADJI; circ. 2,000.

L'Observateur Africain: 29 rue Paul Holle, BP 2824, Dakar; f. 1971; monthly; Dir ALIOUNE DIOP.

L'Ouest Africain: rue Carnot, BP 2047, Dakar; news and current affairs; weekly.

Le Politicien: 95 ave Georges Pompidou, Dakar; f. 1977; fortnightly; satirical.

Promotion: Ancienne Maison des Artistes Plasticiens, Colobane, BP 1676, Dakar; tel. 821-70-23; f. 1972; weekly; Dir BOUBACAR DIOP; circ. 5,000.

Le Rénovateur: BP 12172, Dakar; monthly; publ. by PDS—R.

Sénégal d'Aujourd'hui: 58 blvd de la République, BP 4027, Dakar; monthly; publ. by Ministry of Culture; circ. 5,000.

Sopi (Change): 5 blvd Dial Diop, Dakar; f. 1988; weekly; publ. by PDS; Dir of Publishing JOSEPH NDONG.

Le Témoin: 56 rue Raffenal, Dakar; f. 1990; weekly; Editor-in-Chief MAMADOU OUMAR NDIAYE.

Unir Cinéma: 1 rue Neuville, BP 160, Saint Louis; f. 1973; six a year; African cinema review.

L'Unité Africaine: Maison du Parti, ave Cheikh Amadou Bamba, Rocade Fann, Bel Air, BP 12010, Dakar; f. 1974; monthly; publ. by PS.

Xareli (Struggle): BP 12136, Dakar; tel. 822-54-63; fortnightly; publ. by AJ–PADS; circ. 7,000.

NEWS AGENCIES

Agence de Presse Sénégalaise: 72 blvd de la République, BP 117, Dakar; tel. 821-14-27; f. 1959; govt-controlled; Dir AMADOU DIENG.

PANA-Presse SA: BP 4056, Dakar; tel. 824-13-95; fax 824-13-90; e-mail quoiset@sonatel.senet.net; internet www.rapide-pana.com; f. 1979 as Pan-African News Agency, restructured as majority privately-owned (75%) co in 1997; operates under OAU auspices providing news service to 130 countries; Co-ordinator-Gen. BABACAR FALL.

Foreign Bureaux

Agence France-Presse (AFP): Immeuble Maginot, 7e étage, BP 363, Dakar; tel. 823-21-92; fax 822-16-07.

Xinhua (New China) News Agency (People's Republic of China): Villa 1, 2 route de la Pyrotechnie, Stele Mernoz, BP 426, Dakar; tel. 823-05-38.

ANSA (Italy), IPS (Italy), ITAR—TASS (Russia), Reuters (UK) and UPI (USA) are also represented in Dakar.

PRESS ORGANIZATION

Syndicat des Professionnels de l'Information et de la Communication du Sénégal: 20 rue Mohammed V, BP 21722, Dakar; tel. 821-78-01; fax 822-17-61.

Publishers

Africa Editions: BP 1826, Dakar; tel. 823-48-80; fax 822-56-30; f. 1958; general, reference; Man. Dir JOËL DECUPPER.

Agence de Distribution de Presse: km 2.5, blvd du Centenaire de la Commune de Dakar, BP 374, Dakar; tel. 832-02-78; fax 832-49-15; e-mail adpresse@telecomplus.sn; f. 1943; general, reference; Man. Dir PHILIPPE SCHORP.

Altervision: BP 3770, Dakar; tel. 823-07-90; fax 824-19-61; f. 1985; business; Dir-Gen. CHEIKH-OUSMANE DIALLO.

Centre Africain d'Animation et d'Echanges Culturels Editions Khoudia: BP 5332, Poste de Fann, Dakar; tel. 21-10-23; fax 21-51-09; f. 1989; fiction, education, anthropology; Dir AISSATOU DIA.

Editions Juridiques Africaines (EDJA): 18 rue Raffenel, BP 2875, Dakar; tel. 821-66-89; fax 823-60-72; f. 1986; law.

Editions Sahel: 9 rue Thiong, BP 3683, Dakar; tel. 21-21-64; f. 1982; Dir NIANE IDRISSA.

Editions des Trois Fleuves: blvd de l'Est, angle Cheikh Anta Diop, BP 123, Dakar; tel. 825-79-23; fax 825-59-37; f. 1972; general non-fiction; luxury edns; Dir GÉRARD RAZIMOWSKY; Gen. Man. BERTRAND DE BOISTEL.

Enda Editions (Environmental Development Action in the Third World): 54 rue Carnot, BP 3370, Dakar; tel. 822-98-90; fax 823-51-

57; e-mail editions@enda.sn; internet www.enda.sn/editions/accueil.htm; f. 1972; third-world environment and development; Dir GIDEON PRINSLER OMOLU; Exec. Sec. JACQUES BUGNICOURT.

Grande imprimerie africaine: 9 rue Amadou Assane Ndoye, Dakar; tel. 822-14-08; fax 822-39-27; f. 1917; law, administration; Man. Dir CHEIKH ALIMA TOURÉ.

Institut fondamental d'Afrique noire (IFAN): BP 206, Dakar; scientific and humanistic studies of black Africa.

Librairie Clairafrique: 2 rue El Hadji Mbaye Guèye, BP 2005, Dakar; tel. 822-21-69; fax 821-84-09; f. 1951; politics, law, sociology, anthropology, literature, economics, development, religion, school books.

Nouvelles éditions africaines du Sénégal (NEAS): 10 rue Amadou Assane Ndoye, BP 260, Dakar; tel. 822-15-80; fax 822-36-04; e-mail neas@telecomplus.sn; f. 1972; general; Dir-Gen. JACQUES DE LONGEVILLE.

Per Ankh: Dakar; co-operative publishing venture.

Société africaine d'édition: 16 bis rue de Thiong, BP 1877, Dakar; tel. 821-79-77; f. 1961; African politics and economics; Man. Dir PIERRE BIARNES.

Société d'édition 'Afrique Nouvelle': 9 rue Paul Holle, BP 283, Dakar; tel. 822-38-25; f. 1947; information, statistics and analyses of African affairs; Man. Dir ATHANASE NDONG.

Société nationale de Presse, d'édition et de publicité (SONA-PRESS): Dakar; f. 1972; Pres. OBEYE DIOP.

Sud-Communication: BP 4100, Dakar; operated by a journalists' co-operative; periodicals.

Government Publishing House

Société sénégalaise de presse et de publications (SSPP): route du Service géographique, BP 92, Dakar; tel. 832-46-92; fax 832-03-81; f. 1970; 62% govt-owned; Pres. and Man. Dir ALIOUNE DRAME.

Broadcasting and Communications

TELECOMMUNICATIONS

Bernabé Sénégal: km 2.5 blvd du Centenaire de la Commune de Dakar, Dakar; tel. 823-59-45; fax 823-34-20.

Excaf Carrefour Afrique: Domaine Industrielle, rue 14 Prolongée, Dakar; tel. 824-24-24; fax 824-21-91.

Multicom: rue Abdou Karim Bourgi, Dakar; tel. 823-27-81; fax 824-21-89; f. 1999; Dir AMINATA DIAGNE.

Sentel Sénégal GSM: ave Nelson Mandela angle ave Moussé Diop. BP 146, Dakar; tel. 675-42-02; fax 823-18-73; mobile cellular telephone operator; 75% owned by Millicom International Cellular (Luxembourg), 25% by Senegalese private investors; Gen. Man. YOUVAL ROSH.

Société Nationale des Télécommunications du Sénégal (SONATEL): 6 rue Wagane Diouf, BP 69, Dakar; tel. 823-10-23; fax 822-14-92; f. 1985, restructured 1997–98; 33% owned by France Câbles et Radio, who manage SONATEL's cellular telephone service; Man. Dir CHEIKH TIDIANE MBAYE.

Télécom Plus SARL: 20 rue Amadou Assane Ndoye, BP 21100, Dakar; tel. 839-97-00; fax 823-46-32; telecommunications products and services.

BROADCASTING

Regulatory Authority

Haut Conseil de la Radio Télévision: Dakar; f. 1991; Pres. BABACAR KEBE.

Radio

Société Nationale de Radiodiffusion-Télévision Sénégalaise (RTS): Dakar; tel. 821-78-01; fax 822-34-90; e-mail dgrts@telecomplus.sn; internet www.primature.sn/rts; f. 1972; fmrly Office de Radiodiffusion-Télévision du Sénégal; state broadcasting co; broadcasts in French, Portuguese, Arabic, English and six vernacular languages from Dakar, Saint-Louis, Ziguinchor, Tambacounda and Kaolack; Man. Dir GUILA THIAM; Tech. Dir SEYDOU DIALLO; Dir of Radio IBRAHIM SANÉ.

FM 94: Dakar; 20 hours of local broadcasts daily.

Nostalgie 90.3 FM: Dakar; internet www.metissacana.sn/nostalgie; broadcasts in French and Wolof; Administrator AÏDA WAGUE.

Oxy-Jeunes: Dakar; f. 1999; community radio station.

Sud FM: Immeuble Fahd, 5e étage, BP 4130, Dakar; tel. 822-53-93; fax 822-52-90; e-mail info@sudonline.com; internet www.sudonline.com; f. 1994; operated by Sud-Communication; Man. Dir CHERIF EL-WAHIB SEYE.

Wal Fadjri FM: Dakar; tel. 824-35-71; e-mail walf@telecomplus.sn; internet www1.telecomplus.sn/walf; f. 1997; Islamic broadcaster; Exec. Dir MBAYE SIDY MBAYE.

Broadcasts by the Gabonese-based Africa No. 1 and by Radio France International are received in Dakar.

Television

Société Nationale de Radiodiffusion-Télévision du Sénégal (RTS): (see radio); Dir of Television BABACAR DIAGNE.

Canal Horizons Sénégal: 31 ave Albert Sarrant, BP 1390, Dakar; tel.823-50-50; fax 823-30-30; f. 1990; private coded channel; 18.8% owned by RTS and Société Nationale des Télécommunications du Sénégal, 15% by Canal Horizons (France); Man. Dir JACQUES BARBIER DE CROZES.

Finance

(cap. = capital; res = reserves; m. = million; brs = branches; amounts in francs CFA)

BANKING
Central Bank

Banque Centrale des Etats de l'Afrique de l'Ouest (BCEAO): ave Abdoulaye Fadiga, BP 3108, Dakar; tel. 839-05-00; fax 823-93-35; e-mail akangni@bceao.int; internet www.bceao.int; National HQ: blvd du Général de Gaulle, angle Triangle Sud, BP 3159, Dakar; tel. 823-53-84; fax 823-57-57; f. 1962; bank of issue for mem. states of the Union économique et monétaire ouest africaine (UEMOA, comprising Benin, Burkina Faso, Côte d'Ivoire, Guinea-Bissau, Mali, Niger, Senegal and Togo); cap. and res 806,918m., total assets 4,084,464m. (Dec. 1998); Gov. CHARLES KONAN BANNY; Dir in Senegal SEYNI NDIAYE; brs at Kaolack and Ziguinchor.

Commercial Banks

Banque Internationale pour le Commerce et l'Industrie du Sénégal (BICIS): 2 ave Léopold Sédar Senghor, BP 392, Dakar; tel. 839-03-90; fax 823-37-07; e-mail bicis@bicis.sn; internet www.bicis.sn; f. 1962; 28% owned by Société Financière pour les Pays d'Outre-Mer, 25% state-owned, 22% owned by Banque Nationale de Paris; cap. and res. 6,469m., total assets 150,510m. (Dec. 1998); Pres. SERIGNE LAMINE DIOP; Dir-Gen. AMADOU KANE; 13 brs.

Citibank NA: 2 place de l'Indépendance, BP 3391, Dakar; tel. 849-11-11; fax 823-88-17; internet www.citicorp.com; f. 1975; total assets 79,515m. (Dec. 1998); Chair. JOHN REED; Dir-Gen. MICHAEL GROSSMAN.

Compagnie Bancaire de l'Afrique Occidentale (CBAO): 2 place de l'Indépendance, BP 129, Dakar; tel. 839-96-96; fax 823-20-05; f. 1853; e-mail cbaonet@telecomplus.sn; 65% owned by Mimran Group; 10% state-owned; cap. 2,640m., res 6,054m., dep. 89,259m. (Dec. 1998); Pres. JEAN-CLAUDE MIMRAN; Dir-Gen. ARISTIDES O. ALCANTARA; 8 brs.

Compagnie Ouest Africaine de Crédit Bail (Locafrique): 11 rue Galandou Diouf, BP 292, Dakar; tel. 822-06-47; fax 822-08-94; e-mail cfoa.senegal@ns.arc.sn; cap 1,157m., total assets 2,166m. (Dec. 1998); Pres. ANDRÉ BOURUET-AUBERTOT.

Crédit Lyonnais Sénégal (CLS): blvd El Hadji Djily Mbaye, angle rue Huart, BP 56, Dakar; tel. 823-10-08; fax 823-84-30; f. 1989; 95% owned by Crédit Lyonnais (France); 5% state-owned; cap. 2,000m., total assets 79,604m. (Dec. 1998); Pres. BERNARD NORMAND; Dir-Gen. JEAN-CLAUDE DUBOIS; 1 br.

Crédit National du Sénégal (CNS): 7 ave Léopold Sédar Senghor, BP 319, Dakar; tel. 823-34-86; fax 823-72-92; f. 1990 by merger; 87% state-owned; cap. 1,900m., total assets 2,032m. (Dec. 1996); Pres. ABDOU NDIAYE.

Ecobank Sénégal: 8 ave Léopold Sédar Senghor, BP 9095 CD, Dakar; tel. 823-47-00; fax 823-47-07; e-mail ecobank@sentoo.sn; Pres. BIRIMA MAHENTA FALL; Dir-Gen. AYAO AMOUSSOU-KPETO.

Société Générale de Banques au Sénégal SA (SGBS): 19 ave Léopold Sédar Senghor, BP 323, Dakar; tel. 839-55-00; fax 823-90-36; e-mail sgbs@telecomplus.sn; f. 1962; 38% owned by Société Générale (France); 38% owned by private Senegalese investors; cap. and res 9,120m., total assets 212,940m. (Dec. 1998); Chair. IDRISSA SEYDI; Dir-Gen. BERNARD LABADENS; 11 brs.

Development Banks

Banque de l'Habitat du Sénégal (BHS): blvd du Général de Gaulle, BP 229, Dakar; tel. 839-33-33; fax 823-80-43; internet www.earth2000.com/BHS; f. 1979; 9.1% state-owned; cap. 1,650m., total assets 60,132m. (Dec. 1998); Pres. MAMADOU NDONG; Man. Dir OUSMANE DIÈNE; 1 br.

Banque Sénégalo-Tunisienne (BST): 97 ave Peytavin, BP 4119, Dakar; tel. 823-75-76; fax 823-62-30; f. 1986; 42% owned by Compagnie Africaine pour l'Investissement; cap. and res 2,100m., total assets 9,091m. (Dec. 1998); Pres. MAMADOU TOURÉ; Gen. Man. ABDOUL MBAYE.

Caisse Nationale de Crédit Agricole du Sénégal (CNCAS): 45 ave Albert Sarraut, BP 3890, Dakar; tel. 839-36-36; fax 821-26-06; e-mail cncas@telecomplus.sn; f. 1984; 23.9% state-owned; cap. 5,807m. (Dec. 1997); Admin. OUSMANE NOËL MBAYE; Dir-Gen. SAMCIDINE DIENG; 4 brs.

Société Financière d'Equipement (SFE): 2e étage, Immeuble Sokhna Anta, rue Dr Thèze, BP 252, Dakar; tel. 823-66-26; fax 823-43-37; 37% owned by Compagnie Bancaire de l'Afrique Occidentale; cap. 675m., total assets 7,929m. (Dec. 1998); Pres. ARISTIDES O. ALCANTARA; Dir-Gen. MAMADOU SENE.

Islamic Bank

Banque Islamique du Senegal (BIS): Immeuble Fayçal, rue Huart & A.A. Ndoye, BP 3381, Dakar; tel. 829-99-20; fax 822-49-48; e-mail bis@telecomplus.sn; f. 1983; 44% owned by Dar al-Maal al-Islami, 33% by Islamic Development Bank, 22% state-owned; cap. 2,706m., total assets 10,017m. (Dec. 1998); Chair. ABDERRAOUF BENESSAÏAH; Gen. Man. JUNAID IQBAL.

Banking Association

Association Professionnelle des Banques et des Etablissements Financiers du Sénégal (APBEF): c/o CBAO, 2 place de l'Indépendance, BP 129, Dakar; tel. 823-10-00; Pres. ABDOUL MBAYE.

STOCK EXCHANGE

Bourse Régionale des Valeurs Mobilières (BRVM): BP 22500, Dakar; tel. 821-15-18; fax 821-15-06; f. 1998; national branch of BRVM (regional stock exchange based in Abidjan, Côte d'Ivoire, serving the member states of UEMOA); Man. OUSMANE SANE.

INSURANCE

Les Assurances Conseils Dakarois A. Gueye et cie: 20 rue Mohamed V, BP 2345, Dakar; tel. 822-69-97; fax 822-86-80.

Assurances Générales Sénégalaises (AGS): 43 ave Albert Sarraut, BP 225, Dakar; tel. 823-49-94; fax 823-37-01; f. 1977; cap. 2,990m.; Man. Dir A. SOW.

AXA Assurances Sénégal: 5 place de l'Indépendance, BP 182, Dakar; tel. 849-10-10; fax 823-37-01; f. 1977; Man. Dir M. ALTOUNIAN.

Compagnie d'Assurances-Vie et de Capitalisation (La Nationale d'Assurances-Vie): 7 blvd de la République, BP 3853, Dakar; tel. 822-11-81; fax 821-28-20; f. 1982; cap. 80m.; Pres. MOUSSA DIOUF; Man. Dir BASSIROU DIOP.

Compagnie Sénégalaise d'Assurances et de Réassurances (CSAR): 5 place de l'Indépendance, BP 182, Dakar; tel. 823-27-76; fax 823-46-72; f. 1972; cap. 945m.; 49.8% state-owned; Pres. MOUSTAPHA CISSÉ; Man. Dir MAMADOU ABBAS BA.

SA Capillon V-Assurances: 5 ave Léopold Sédar Senghor, BP 425, Dakar; tel. 822-90-26; f. 1951; cap. 10m.; Pres. and Man. Dir GILLES DE MONTALEMBERT.

Gras Savoye Sénégal: 15 blvd de la République, BP 9, Dakar; tel. 823-51-51; fax 823-44-72; correspondent co. of the Forbes Group; Dir MAURICE MOYAL.

Mutuelles Sénégalaises d'Assurance et de Transport (MSAT): 2 rue Malenfant, BP 370, Dakar; tel. 822-29-38; fax 823-42-47; f. 1981; all branches; Dir MOR ATJ.

La Nationale d'Assurances: 5 ave Albert Sarrault, BP 3328, Dakar; tel. 822-10-27.

Nouvelle Société Inter-Africaine de Courtage de Réassurances (Nouvelle SIACRE): 3 ave Albert Sarraut, BP 3135, Dakar; tel. 821-71-38; fax 823-83-91; f. 1977; cap. 50m.; Dir DEMBA SAMBA DIALLO.

La Sécurité Sénégalaise (ASS): Gare Routière, BP 2623, Dakar; tel. 823-75-95; f. 1984; cap. 100m.; Pres. LOBATT FALL; Man. Dir MBACKE SENE.

Société Africaine d'Assurances: ave Léopold Sédar Senghor, angle Victor Hugo, BP 508, Dakar; tel. 823-64-75; fax 823-44-72; f. 1945; cap. 9m.; Dir CLAUDE GERMAIN.

Société Nationale d'Assurances Mutuelles (SONAM): 6 ave Léopold Sédar Senghor, BP 210, Dakar; tel. 823-10-03; fax 820-70-25; f. 1973; cap. 1,464m.; Pres. ABDOULAYE FOFANA; Man. Dir DIOULDÉ NIANE.

Société Sénégalaise de Courtage et d'Assurances (SOSECODA): 16 ave Léopold Sédar Senghor, BP 9, Dakar; tel. 823-54-81; fax 821-54-62; f. 1963; cap. 10m.; 55% owned by SONAM; Man. Dir A. AZIZ NDAW.

Société Sénégalaise de Réassurances SA (SENRE): 6 ave Léopold Sédar Senghor, angle Carnot, BP 386, Dakar; tel. 822-80-89; fax 821-56-52; cap. 600m.

Insurance Association

Syndicat Professionel des Agents Généraux d'Assurances du Sénégal: 43 ave Albert Sarraut, BP 1766, Dakar; Pres. URBAIN ALEXANDRE DIAGNE; Sec. JEAN-PIERRE CAIRO.

Trade and Industry

GOVERNMENT AGENCIES

Société de Développement Agricole et Industriel (SODAGRI): Immeuble Fondation Fahd, 9e étage, blvd Djily Mbaye, angle Macodou Ndiaye, BP 222, Dakar; tel. 821-04-26; fax 822-54-06; cap. 120m. francs CFA; agricultural and industrial projects; Dir-Gen. YOUSSOU DIALLO.

Société de Développement des Fibres Textiles (SODEFITEX): km 4.5, blvd du Centenaire de la Commune de Dakar, BP 3216, Dakar; tel. 832-47-80; f. 1974; 70% state-owned, 30% owned by Cie Française pour le Développement des Fibres Textiles; responsible for planning and development of cotton industry; cap. 750m. francs CFA; Dir-Gen. BACHIR DIOP.

Société de Développement et de Vulgarisation Agricole (SODEVA): 92 rue Moussé Diop, BP 3234, Dakar; tel. 823-16-78; fax 821-01-53; f. 1968; cap. 100m. francs CFA; 55% state-owned; development of intensive farming methods and diversified livestock breeding; Dir-Gen. PAPA OUSMANE DIALLO.

Société d'Exploitation des Ressources Animales du Sénégal (SERAS): km 2.5, blvd du Centenaire de la Commune de Dakar, BP 14, Dakar; tel. 832-31-78; fax 832-06-90; f. 1962; cap. 619.2m. francs CFA; 28.5% state-owned; livestock development; Dir-Gen. MAMADOU LO.

Société Nationale d'Aménagement et d'Exploitation des Terres du Delta du Fleuve Sénégal et des Vallées du Fleuve Sénégal et de la Falémé (SAED): route de Khor, BP 74, Saint-Louis; tel. 961-15-33; fax 961-14-63; f. 1965; cap. 2,500m. francs CFA; state-owned; controls the agricultural development of 30,000 ha around the Senegal river delta; Pres. and Man. Dir SIDY MOCTAR KEITA.

Société Nationale d'Etudes et de Promotion Industrielle (SONEPI): derrière Résidence Seydou Nourou Tall, ave Bourguiba Prolongée, BP 100, Dakar; tel. 825-21-30; fax 824-65-65; f. 1969; cap. 150m. francs CFA; 28% state-owned; promotion of small and medium-sized enterprises; Chair. and Man. Dir HADY MAMADOU LY.

Société Nouvelle des Etudes de Développement en Afrique (SONED–AFRIQUE): Immeuble SONACOS, 32–36 rue du Dr Calmette, BP 2084, Dakar; tel. 823-94-57; fax 823-42-31; f. 1974; cap. 98m. francs CFA; 61% state-owned; Pres. El Hadj IBRAHIMA NDAO; Man. Dir RUDOLPH KERN.

DEVELOPMENT ORGANIZATIONS

Agence Française de Développement (AFD): 15 ave Mandéla, BP 475, Dakar; tel. 823-11-88; fax 823-40-10; e-mail afddkn@telecomplus.sn; fmrly Caisse Française de Développement; Dir in Senegal ALAIN CÉLESTE.

Centre International du Commerce Extérieur du Sénégal: route de l'Aéroport, BP 8166, Dakar-Yoff, Dakar; tel. 827-54-66; fax 827-52-75; e-mail cices@metissacana.sn; Sec.-Gen. AMADOU SY.

Mission Française de Coopération: BP 2014, Dakar; administers bilateral aid from France; Dir FRANÇOIS CHAPPELLET.

CHAMBERS OF COMMERCE

Chambre de Commerce, d'Industrie et d'Agriculture de la Région de Dakar: 1 place de l'Indépendance, BP 118, Dakar; tel. 823-71-89; fax 823-93-63; e-mail cciad@telecomplus.sn; internet www.tpsnet.org/francais/cciad/accueil.htm; f. 1888; Pres. MAMADOU LAMINE NIANG; Sec.-Gen. MBAYE NDIAYE.

Chambre de Commerce, d'Industrie et d'Agriculture de la Région de Diourbel: BP 7, Diourbel; tel. 971-12-03; fax 971-38-49; e-mail mamandiaye@hotmail.com; f. 1969; Pres. ALIOU DIOP; Sec.-Gen. MAMADOU NDIAYE.

Chambre de Commerce de la Région de Fatick: BP 66, Fatick; tel. 949-51-27; Sec.-Gen. SEYDOU NOUROU LY.

Chambre de Commerce et d'Industrie de la Région du Kaolack: BP 203, Kaolack; tel. 941-20-52; Pres. IDRISSA GUÈYE; Sec.-Gen. AROHA TRAORÉ.

Chambre de Commerce d'Industrie et d'Agriculture de la Région de Kolda: BP 23; Kolda; tel. 996-12-30; fax 996-10-68; Sec.-Gen. YAYA CAMARA.

Chambre de Commerce de la Région de Louga: BP 26, Louga; tel. 967-11-14; Pres. El Hadj AMADOU BAMBA SOURANG; Sec.-Gen. SOULEYMANE N'DIAYE.

Chambre de Commerce, d'Industrie et d'Agriculture de la Région de Saint-Louis: rue Bisson Nord, BP 19, Saint-Louis;

tel. 961-10-88; f. 1879; Pres. El Hadj Momar Sourang; Sec.-Gen. Massamba Diop.

Chambre de Commerce, d'Industrie et d'Agriculture de la Région de Tambacounda: BP 127, Tambacounda; tel. 981-10-14; Pres. Djiby Cissé; Sec.-Gen. Tenguella Ba.

Chambre de Commerce, d'Industrie et d'Agriculture de la Région de Thiès: ave Lamine-Guèye, BP 3020, Thiès; tel. 951-10-02; f. 1883; 38 mems; Pres. El Hadj Alioune Palla M'Baye; Sec.-Gen. Abdoul Khadre Camara.

Chambre de Commerce, d'Industrie et d'Artisanat de la Région de Ziguinchor: BP 26, Ziguinchor; tel. 991-13-10; f. 1908; Pres. Youssouf Seydi; Sec.-Gen. Mamadi Diatta.

EMPLOYERS' ASSOCIATIONS

Chambre des Métiers de Dakar: route de la Corniche Ouest, Soumbedioune, Dakar; tel. 821-79-08.

Confédération Nationale des Employeurs du Sénégal: 41 rue A. Assane Ndoye, Dakar; tel. 821-76-62.

Confédération Sénégalaise du Patronat (CSP): Dakar; Pres. Mansour Cama.

Conseil National de Jeunes Dirigeants d'Entreprises du Sénégal: 2e étage, 36 rue Wagane Diouf, Dakar; tel. 822-46-96.

Conseil National du Patronat du Sénégal: 7 rue Jean Mermoz, Dakar; tel. 821-58-03.

Groupement Professionnel de l'Industrie du Pétrole du Sénégal (GPP): rue 6, km 4.5, blvd du Centenaire de la Commune de Dakar, BP 479, Dakar; tel. and fax 832-29-03; Pres. Jean-Denis Royère; Sec.-Gen. Jean-Pierre Noël.

Organisation des Commerçants, Agriculteurs, Artisans et Industriels: 71 ave Lamine Gueye, Dakar; tel. 823-67-94.

Rassemblement des Opérateurs Economiques du Sénégal: Quartier Mermoz, Dakar; tel. 822-87-26.

Syndicat des Commerçants Importateurs, Prestataires de Services et Exportateurs de la République du Sénégal (SCIMPEX): 2 rue Parent, angle ave Abdoulaye Fadiga, BP 806, Dakar; tel. and fax 821-36-62; f. 1943; Pres. Jacques Conti; Sec.-Gen. Maurice Sarr.

Syndicat Patronal de l'Ouest Africain des Petites et Moyennes Entreprises et des Petites et Moyennes Industries: 41 blvd Djily Mbaye, BP 7015, Dakar; tel. 821-35-10; fax 823-37-32; f. 1937; Pres. Babacar Seye; Sec.-Gen. Moctar Niang.

Syndicat Professionnel des Entrepreneurs de Bâtiments et de Travaux Publics du Sénégal: ave Abdoulaye Fadiga, BP 593, Dakar; tel. 823-43-73; f. 1930; 130 mems; Pres. Christian Virmaud.

Syndicat Professionnel des Industries du Sénégal (SPIDS): ave Abdoulaye Fadiga, angle Thann, BP 593, Dakar; tel. 823-43-73; fax 822-08-84; f. 1944; 110 mems; Pres. Donald Baron; Sec. Gen. Philippe Barry.

Union des Entreprises du Domaine Industriel de Dakar: SODIDA, rue 14 prolongée et rue Bourguiba, Dakar; tel. 825-67-39.

Union Nationale des Chambres de Métiers: Zone Industrielle SODIDA, ave Bourguiba, Dakar; tel. 825-05-88.

Union Nationale des Commerçants et Industriels du Sénégal: 3 rue Valmy et Faidherbe, Dakar; tel. 826-15-19.

UTILITIES
Electricity

Société Nationale d'Electricité (SENELEC): 28–30 rue Vincens, BP 93, Dakar; tel. 839-30-30; fax 823-82-46; e-mail senelecd@senelec.sn; f. 1983; 41% state-owned; 34% owned by Hydro-Quebec International and Elvo; Chair. A. Aziz Ndao; Man. Dir Abdourahmane Ndir.

Gas

Société Sénégalaise des Gaz: BP 2062, Dakar; tel. 832-82-12; fax 823-59-74.

Water

Société Nationale des Eaux du Sénégal (SONES): 97 ave André Peytavin, BP 400, Dakar; tel. 821-28-65; f. 1972; water works and supply; owned by Saur; Pres. Abdoul Magib Seck; Man. Dir Bernard Debenest.

MAJOR COMPANIES

The following are some of the largest companies in terms of either capital investment or employment.

BP Sénégal SA: rue 6, km 4.5, blvd du Centenaire de la Commune de Dakar, BP 59, Dakar; tel. 823-10-80; fax 832-90-65; f. 1951; cap. 3,000m. francs CFA; 99.99% owned by BP Africa Ltd (UK); import, storage and distribution of petroleum products, mfrs of lubricating oil; Man. Dir Ferdinand da Costa.

CarnaudMetalbox Sénégal: route du Service géographique, Hann Village, BP 3850, Dakar; tel. 832-32-32; fax 832-37-25; e-mail cmbsen@sonatel.senet.net; f. 1959; cap. 900m. francs CFA; 72% owned by CarnaudMetalbox (France); mfrs of metal packaging; Chair. Guido Spaas; Man. Dir Maurice Prangère.

Compagnie Commerciale Industrielle du Sénégal (CCIS): route du Front de Terre, angle Service géographique, BP 137, Dakar; tel. 832-33-44; fax 832-68-22; f. 1972; cap. 1,969.6m. francs CFA; mfrs of PVC piping and plastic for shoes; Man. Dir Nayef Derwiche.

Compagnie Sucrière Sénégalaise (CSS): BP 49, Richard Toll; tel. 963-33-20; fax 963-31-47; f. 1970; cap. 13,586m. francs CFA; growing of sugar cane and refining of cane sugar; Chair. and Man. Dir Robert Mimran.

Les Grands Moulins de Dakar (GMD): ave Félix Eboué, BP 2068, Dakar; tel. 839-97-97; fax 832-89-47; e-mail gmd@sonatel.senet.net; f. 1946; cap. 1,180m. francs CFA; production of flour and animal food; Chair. Robert Mimran; Dir Jean-Claude Beguinot; 280 employees.

Industrial Drip Irrigation System (Senegal) (IDIS): BP 2031, Dakar; tel. 832-28-86; fax 832-91-92; f. 1976; cap. 405m. francs CFA; subsidiary of CSS; mfrs of plastic pipes; Chair. Jean-Claude Mimran.

Industries Chimiques du Sénégal (ICS): km 18, blvd du Centenaire de la Commune de Dakar, BP 3835, Dakar; tel. 834-01-22; fax 834-08-14; e-mail mdiop@telecomplus.sn; f. 1976; restructured by merger with Cie Sénégalaise des Phospates de Taïba in 1996; cap. 55,300m. francs CFA; 52% state-owned; mining of high-grade calcium phosphates, production of sulphuric and phosphoric acid, fertilizer factory at M'Bao; Chair. and Man. Dir Djibril Ngom; 570 employees.

Lesieur Afrique (Dakar): place Amílcar Cabral, BP 236, Dakar; tel. 823-10-66; f. 1942; cap. 1,796m. francs CFA; groundnut-shelling plant (annual capacity: 350,000 metric tons) and vegetable oil refining plant (capacity: 30,000 tons) at Dakar; Man. Dir Mambaye Diaw.

Manufacture de Tabacs de l'Ouest Africain (MTOA): km 2.5, blvd du Centenaire de la Commune de Dakar, BP 76, Dakar; tel. 849-25-00; fax 849-25-55; e-mail mtoa@telecomplus.sn; f. 1951; cap. 3,129.6m. francs CFA; mfrs of tobacco products; Chair. Pierre Imbert; Gen. Man. Henri Luquet; 300 employees.

Mobil Oil Sénégal: BP 227, Dakar; tel. 832-18-92; fax 832-80-59; marketing and sale of petroleum and petroleum products; Man. Dir Richard Willems.

Les Moulins Sentenac SA (MS): 50 ave du Président Lamine Guèye, BP 451, Dakar; tel. 839-90-00; fax 823-80-69; e-mail sentenac@telecomplus.senet.net; f. 1943; cap. 1,056m. francs CFA; milling, production of wheat and millet flour and other food products and of livestock feed; Chair. Donald Baron.

Nestlé Senegal: km 14, blvd du Centenaire de la Commune de Dakar, BP 796, Dakar; tel. 834-05-75; fax 834-17-02; f. 1961; cap. 1,620m. francs CFA; mfrs of sweetened and unsweetened condensed milk and culinary products; Man. Dir Jean-Marie Mauduit.

La Rochette Dakar (LRD): km 13.7, blvd du Centenaire de la Commune de Dakar, BP 891, Dakar; tel. 34-01-24; fax 834-28-26; f. 1946; cap. 500m. francs CFA; mfrs of paper and cardboard packaging; Chair. and Man. Dir Adel Salhab.

Mobil Oil Sénégal: BP 227, Dakar; tel. 832-03-79; marketing and distribution of petroleum and gas.

Sénégal–Pêche, SA: Môle 10, Nouveau Quai de Pêche, BP 317, Dakar; owned by China Nat. Fisheries Corpn.

Shell Sénégal: BP 144, Dakar; tel. 849-37-37; fax 832-87-30; marketing and distribution of petroleum and gas; Dir-Gen. Sow Sadio.

Société Africaine de Raffinage (SAR): 15 blvd de la République, BP 203, Dakar; tel. 834-02-07; fax 834-07-62; f. 1961; cap. 1,000m. francs CFA; petroleum refinery at M'Bao.

Société des Brasseries de l'Ouest Africain (SOBOA): route des Brasseries, BP 290, Dakar; tel. 832-01-90; fax 832-54-69; f. 1928; cap. 820m. francs CFA; mfrs of beer and soft drinks; Man. Dir Pierre Traversa.

Société de Conserves Alimentaires du Sénégal (SOCAS): 50 ave du Président Lamine Guèye, BP 451, Dakar; tel. 823-94-04; fax 823-80-69; e-mail socas@sonatel.senet.net; f. 1963; cap. 726m. francs CFA; cultivation of tomatoes and other food crops, mfrs of tomato concentrate and other preserves at Savoigne; Chair. and Man. Dir Donald Baron.

Société Industrielle Moderne des Plastiques Africains (SIMPA): 50 ave du Président Lamine Guèye, BP 451, Dakar; tel. 823-43-25; fax 821-80-69; f. 1958; cap. 551m. francs CFA; mfrs of injection-moulded and extruded plastic articles; Chair. and Man. Dir Raymond Gaveau.

Société Industrielle de Papeterie au Sénégal (SIPS): km 11, route de Rufisque, BP 1818, Dakar; tel. 834-09-29; fax 834-23-03; f. 1972; cap. 750m. francs CFA; mfrs of paper goods; Chair. Omar

ABDEL KANDER GHANDOUR; Man. Dirs ALI SALIM HOBALLAH, RIAD BOUKA-
ROUM.

Société Minière de Sabodala (SMS): 7 rue Mermoz, BP 268,
Dakar; tel. 821-95-60; fax 823-38-64; e-mail gapeina@cyg.sn; f. 1982;
cap. 1,875m. francs CFA; 49.4% state-owned; 50.6% owned by
BRGN-La Source; exploration and exploitation of gold mines in
Sabodala region; Pres. NAKHA KEITA; Dir Gen. ALAIN GUY PREIRA.

**Société Nationale de Commercialisation des Oléagineux du
Sénégal (SONACOS):** Immeuble SONACOS, 32–36 rue du Dr
Calmette, BP 639, Dakar; tel. 823-10-52; fax 823-88-05; f. 1975; cap.
4,800m. francs CFA; 80% state-owned; transfer pending to majority
private ownership; processing of groundnuts and groundnut products; Pres. and Man. Dir ABDOULAYE DIOP.

Société Nationale des Pétroles du Sénégal (PETROSEN): 19
rue Parchappe, Immeuble Façyal, POB 2076, Dakar; tel. 822-04-44;
fax 822-83-40; e-mail petrosen@sonatel.senet.net; f. 1981; 90% state-
owned; exploration and exploitation of hydrocarbons; Man. Dir.
OUSMANE NDIAYE.

Société Nouvelle des Salins du Sine Saloum (SNSSS): BP 200,
Kaolack; tel. 941-10-13; fax 941-16-29; f. 1965; cap. 723m. francs
CFA; 49% state-owned; production and marketing of sea-salt; Chair.
AMADOU LY; Man. Dir HENRI DUNESME.

Société de Produits Industrielles et Agricoles (SPIA): 56 ave
Faidherbe, BP 3806, Dakar; tel. 821-43-78; fax 821-66-37; f. 1980;
cap. 640m. francs CFA; mfrs of plant-based medicines at Louga;
Chair. DJILLY MBAYE; Man. Dir CHEIKH DEMBA NAMARA.

**Société Sénégalaise d'Engrais et de Produits Chimiques
(SSEPC):** km 13, blvd du Centenaire de la Commune de Dakar, BP
656, Dakar; tel. 834-02-79; f. 1958; cap. 727m. francs CFA; mfrs of
fertilizers, insecticides and livestock feed; Chair. BERNARD PORTAL;
Man. Dir PAUL SASPORTES.

Société Sénégalaise des Phosphates de Thiès (SSPT): 39 ave
Jean XXIII, BP 241, Dakar; tel. 823-32-83; fax 823-83-84; e-mail
miller@telecomplus.sn; f. 1948; cap. 1,000m. francs CFA; owned by
TOLSA SA (Spain); production of phosphates and attapulgite, mfrs
of phosphate fertilizers; Chair. MÍREN LARREA; Man. Dir EDUARDO
MILLER MENDEZ.

**Société de Teinture, Blanchiment, Apprêts et d'Impressions
Africaines (SOTIBA-SIMPAFRIC):** km 9.5, blvd du Centenaire
de la Commune de Dakar, BP 527, Dakar; tel. 834-03-78; fax
834-52-68; f. 1951; cap. 2,600m. francs CFA; owned jtly by UB
International (India) and CBAO; bleaching, dyeing and printing of
textiles; Chair. and Man. Dir SERIGNÉ NDIAYE BOUNA; 1,100
employees.

Société Textile de Kaolack (SOTEXKA): 57 ave Georges Pompidou, BP 4101, Dakar; tel. 821-89-99; fax 821-23-01; f. 1977; cap
8,628m. francs CFA; 63% state-owned; transfer pending to private
ownership; textile and garment-assembling complex; Man. Dir
ABDOURAHMANE TOURÉ.

TRADE UNIONS

Collectif National des Pêcheurs Sénégalais (CNPS): BP 3211,
Dakar; tel. 832-11-74; fax 832-11-75; e-mail credetip@sonatel
.senet.net; f. 1987; represents workers in the fishing industry; Sec.-
Gen. DAO GAYE; 10,000 mems.

**Confédération Nationale des Travailleurs Sénégalais
(CNTS):** 15 rue Escarfait, BP 937, Dakar; f. 1969; affiliated to PS;
Sec.-Gen. MADIA DIOP; 120,000 mems.

Confédération des Syndicats Autonomes (CSA): Dakar; organization of independent trade unions.

SUTELEC: Dakar; electricity workers' union.

**Syndicat National des Professionnels de l'Information et de
la Communication du Sénégal (SYNPICS):** Dakar; information
and communication workers' union; Sec. Gen. ALPHA SALL.

Union Démocratique des Travailleurs du Sénégal (UDTS):
Dakar; Dep. Gen. Sec. MA LAMINE NDIAYE.

**Union Nationale des Commerçants et Industriels du Sénégal
(UNACOIS):** Dakar.

**Union Nationale des Syndicats Autonomes du Sénégal
(UNSAS):** Dakar; Sec.-Gen. MADEMBA SOCK.

Transport

RAILWAYS

There are 1,225 km of main line including 70 km of double track.
One line runs from Dakar north to Saint-Louis (262 km), and the
main line runs to Bamako (Mali). All the locomotives are diesel-
driven. The rehabilitation and expansion of the railway network
(which is in a poor state of repair) is proceeding, and responsibility
for the operation of rolling-stock was transferred to a Canadian
company, under a two-year contract, from late 1994. In late 1995

the Governments of Senegal and Mali agreed to establish, with a
view to privatization, a joint company to operate the
Dakar–Bamako line.

Société Nationale des Chemins de Fer du Sénégal (SNCFS):
BP 175, Cité Ballabey, Thiès; tel. 951-10-13; fax 951-13-93; state-
owned; Pres. ALIEU DIENE DRAME; Man. Dir IBRAHIMA NIANG.

ROADS

In 1996 there were 14,576 km of roads, of which 3,361 km were
main roads and 1,194 km were secondary roads. About 4,300 km of
the network were paved. A 162.5-km road between Dialakoto and
Kédougou, the construction of which (at a cost of some 23,000m.
francs CFA) was largely financed by regional donor organizations,
was inaugurated in March 1996. The road is to form part of an
eventual transcontinental highway linking Cairo (Egypt) with the
Atlantic coast, via N'Djamena (Chad), Bamako (Mali) and Dakar.
In 1999 new highways were completed in the east of Senegal, linking
Tambacounda, Kidira and Bakel.

Comité Executif des Transports Urbains de Dakar (CETUD):
route du Front de Terre, Dakar-Hann; tel. 832-47-42; fax 832-47-
44; e-mail cetud@telecomplus.sn; regulates the provision of urban
transport in Dakar; Pres. OUSMANE THIAM.

Dakar-Bus: Colobane, Dakar; f. 1999 following the privatization of
SOTRAC; operates public transport services within the city of
Dakar; owned by RATP (France), Transdev (France), Eurafric-
Equipment (Senegal), Mboup Travel Agency (Senegal) and Senegal
Tours (Senegal).

Société des Transports Bourdier: km 4, blvd du Centenaire de
le Commune de Dakar, Dakar; tel. 832-33-78.

Tous Transports Transafricains: km 2.5, blvd du Centenaire de
la Commune de Dakar, Dakar; tel. 832-97-74.

Transport AKF: km 18, blvd du Centenaire de la Commune de
Dakar, Dakar; tel. 834-02-64.

INLAND WATERWAYS

Senegal has three navigable rivers: the Senegal, navigable for three
months of the year as far as Kayes (Mali), for six months as far as
Kaédi (Mauritania) and all year as far as Rosso and Podor, and the
Saloun and Casamance. Senegal is a member of the Organisation
de mise en valeur du fleuve Gambie and of the Organisation pour
la mise en valeur du fleuve Sénégal, both based in Dakar. These
organizations aim to develop navigational facilities, irrigation and
hydroelectric power in the basins of the Gambia and Senegal Rivers
respectively.

SHIPPING

The port of Dakar is the second largest in west Africa, after Abidjan
(Côte d'Ivoire), and the largest deep sea port in the region, serving
Senegal, Mauritania, The Gambia and Mali. It handled more than
6m. metric tons of international freight in 1998. The port's facilities
include 40 berths, 10 km of quays, and also 53,000 sq m of warehousing and 65,000 sq m of open stocking areas. There is also a
container terminal with facilities for vessels with a draught of up
to 11m. In September 1998 the World Bank agreed to finance
improvements to the secondary regional ports of Senegal.

**Compagnie Sénégalaise de Navigation Maritime (COSE-
NAM):** rue le Dantec, angle Huart, BP 683, Dakar; tel. 821-57-66;
fax 821-08-95; f. 1979; 26.1% state-owned, 65.9% owned by private
Senegalese interests, 8.0% by private French, German and Belgian
interests; river and ocean freight transport; Pres. ABDOURAHIM AGNE;
Man. Dir SIMON BOISSY.

Conseil Sénégalais des Chargeurs: 57 ave Georges Pompidou,
Dakar; tel. 822-43-62.

Dakar-marine: port de Dakar, Dakar; responsible for Senegalese
shipyards; owned by Dakarnave, a subsidiary of Lisnave International, Portugal; Administrator FREDERICO SPANGER.

Maersk Line Sénégal: km 3.5, blvd du Centenaire de la Commune
de Dakar; Dakar; tel. 832-16-16.

SDV: 8–10 allée Robert Delmas, BP 164, Dakar; tel. 823-56-82; fax
821-45-47; f. 1936; fmrly Union Sénégalaise d'Industries Maritimes;
shipping agents, warehousing; Pres. GASTON GUILLABERT.

**Société pour le Développement de l'Infrastructure de Chan-
tiers Maritimes du Port de Dakar (DAKAR-MARINE):** blvd de
l'Arsenal, BP 438, Dakar; tel. 823-36-88; fax 823-83-99; f. 1981;
privately-controlled; operates facilities for the repair and maintenance of supertankers and other large vessels; Man. YORO KANTE.

Société Maritime Casamançaise: 4 rue Joris, Dakar; tel. 821-
52-19.

Société Nationale de Port Autonome de Dakar (PAD): 21 blvd
de la Libération, BP 3195, Dakar; tel. 823-45-45; fax 823-36-06; e-
mail pad@sonatel.senet.net; f. 1865; state-operated port authority;
Pres. El Hadj MALICK SY; Man. Dir Col ALIOUNE BADARA NIANG.

SOCOPAO-Sénégal: 47 ave Albert Sarraut, BP 233, Dakar; tel. 823-10-01; fax 823-56-14; f. 1926; warehousing, shipping agents, sea and air freight transport; Man. Dir GILLES CUCHE.

TransSene: 1 blvd de l'Arsenal, face à la gare ferroviaire, Dakar; tel. 821-81-81.

Yenco Shipping: Fondation Fahd, blvd Djily Mbaye, Dakar; tel. 821-27-26.

CIVIL AVIATION

The international airport is Dakar-Léopold Sédar Senghor. There are other major airports at Saint-Louis, Ziguinchor and Tambacounda, in addition to about 15 smaller airfields. Facilities at Ziguinchor and Cap-Skirring were being upgraded during the mid-1990s, with the aim of improving direct access to the Casamance region. In 1998 the Islamic Development Bank agreed to fund a new international airport at Tobor, Casamance. In 2000 work began to extend the runway at Saint-Louis in order to accommodate larger aircraft. Construction is also planned of a second international airport for the capital, at Keur Massar.

Direction de l'aviation civile (DAC): Dakar-Léopold Sédar Senghor, Dakar; civil aviation authority; Dir ABABACAR DIOP.

African West Air: Dakar—Léopold Sédar Senghor, Dakar; tel. 822-45-38; fax 822-46-10; f. 1993; services to western Europe and Brazil; Man. Dir J. P. PIEDADE.

Air Afrique: place de l'Indépendance; BP 3132, Dakar; tel. 839-42-00; fax 823-89-37; see under Côte d'Ivoire; Dir at Dakar MAHAMAT BABA ABATCHA.

Air Sénégal International: BP 8010, Dakar-Léopold Sédar Senghor, Dakar; tel. 820-09-13; fax 820-00-33; internet www.primature.sn/tour/airsen.htm; f. 1971 as Air Sénégal; name changed 2000; 51% owned by Royal Air Maroc, 49% state-owned; domestic and international services; Gen. Man. IBRAHIMA FAYE.

Tourism

Senegal's attractions for tourists include six national parks (one of which, Djoudj, is listed by UNESCO as a World Heritage Site) and its fine beaches. The island of Gorée, near Dakar, is of considerable historic interest as a former centre for the slave-trade. In 1993 the number of foreign tourist arrivals declined dramatically, largely as a result of the suspension of tourist activity in the Casamance region in that year. The sector recovered strongly from 1995 onwards, and in 1997 visitor arrivals of 358,700 were recorded; receipts from tourism in that year were 91,800m. francs CFA. In 1998 visitor arrivals again increased, to 392,500; receipts from tourism were estimated at 100,100m. francs CFA. Senegal has announced its intention of attracting 1m. tourists per annum by 2005.

Ministry of Tourism: 23 rue Calmette, BP 4049, Dakar; tel. 823-65-02; fax 822-94-13; e-mail mtta@primature.sn; internet www.primature.sn/tour.

Defence

In August 1999 Senegal's active armed forces comprised a land army of 11,000 (mostly conscripts), a navy of 600, and an air force of 400. There is also a 5,800-strong paramilitary gendarmerie. Military service is by selective conscription and lasts for two years. France and the USA provide technical and material aid, and in August 1999 there were 1,200 French troops stationed in Senegal.

Defence Expenditure: Estimated at 43,000m. francs CFA in 1999.

Chief of Defence Staff: Col BABACAR GAYE.

Education

Primary education, which usually begins at seven years of age, lasts for six years and is officially compulsory. In 1997 primary enrolment included 71% of children in the relevant age-group (males 78%; females 65%). The 1995–2008 Educational and Training Plan aims to increase overall levels of pupil enrolment by 5% annually, with special emphasis on female education. Secondary education usually begins at the age of 13, and comprises a first cycle of four years and a further cycle of three years. In 1997 secondary enrolment was equivalent to only 16% of children in the relevant age-group (males 20%; females 12%). Dakar's Université Cheikh Anta Diop specializes in local studies. The Université Gaston-Berger, at Saint-Louis, was established in 1990. Construction of a pan-African university began at Sebikotane, near Dakar, in 1996. Since 1981 the reading and writing of national languages has been actively promoted. The 1988 census recorded a rate of adult illiteracy of 73.1% (males 63.1%; females 82.1%), while the government estimated an adult illiteracy rate of 73% in 1997. Current expenditure on education in 1996 was 88,518m. francs CFA (representing 3.4% of gross national product).

Bibliography

Adedeji, A., Senghor, C., and Diouf, A. *Towards a Dynamic African Economy*. Ilford, Frank Cass Publishers, 1989.

Barry, B. *Le royaume du Waalo: le Sénégal avant la conquête*. Paris, Karthala, 1985.

Berthlémy, J.-C., et al. *Growth in Senegal: A Lost Opportunity*. Paris, OECD, 1996.

Boone, C. *Merchant Capital and the Roots of State Power in Senegal*. Cambridge, Cambridge University Press, 1992.

Clark, A. F., and Phillips, L. C. *Historical Dictionary of Senegal*. 2nd Edn. Metuchen, NJ, Scarecrow Press, 1994.

Coulon, C. *Le Marabout et le Prince: Islam et Pouvoir en Sénégal*. Paris, Editions A. Pedone, 1981.

Crowder, M. *Senegal: A Study in French Assimilation Policy*. London, 1967.

Cruise O'Brien, D. B., Dunn, J., and Rathbone, R. (Eds.). *Contemporary West African States*. Cambridge, Cambridge University Press, 1989.

Cruise O'Brien, D. B. 'Sénégal: la démocratie a l'épreuve', in *Politique Africaine*, No. 45. Paris, 1992.

Cruise O'Brien, R. (Ed.). *The Political Economy of Underdevelopment: Dependence in Senegal*. London, Sage Publications, 1979.

Delgado, C., Jammeh, S. (Eds). *Political Economy of Senegal Under Structural Adjustment*. New York, Praeger, 1991.

Dia, M. *Mémoires d'un militant du tiers-monde*. Paris, Publisud, 1986.

Diagne, A. *Abdou Diouf, le maître du jeu*. Dakar, Agence Less Com, 1996.

Diarassouba, V. C. *L'Evolution des structures agricoles du Sénégal*. Paris, Editions Cujas, 1968.

Diop, A.-B. *La société Wolof*. Paris, Editions Karthala, 1983 (reissue).

Diop, M. *Histoire des classes sociales dans l'Afrique de l'ouest: Vol. 2: Le Sénégal*. Paris, Editions Maspero, 1972.

Diop, M. C. (Ed.). *Senegal: Essays in Statecraft*. Dakar, CODESA, 1993.

Diouf, M. *Sénégal, les ethnies et la nation*. Paris, UN Research Institute for Social Development, Forum du Tiers-Monde and l'Harmattan, 1994.

Dumont, P. *Le français et les langues africaines du Sénégal*. Paris, Editions Karthala, 1983.

Duruflé, G. *L'ajustement structurel en Afrique (Sénégal, Côte d'Ivoire, Madagascar)*. Paris, Editions Karthala, 1987.

Eades, J., and Dilley, R. *Senegal*. Santa Barbara, CA, ABC Clio, 1993.

Fatton, R., Jr. *The Making of a Liberal Democracy. Senegal's Passive Revolution, 1975–1985*. Boulder, CO, Westview Press, and London, Lynne Rienner Publishers, 1987.

Gagnon, G. *Coopératives ou autogestion: Sénégal, Cuba, Tunisie*. Paris, Presses de l'Université de Montréal, 1976.

Gellar, S. *Senegal: An African Nation between Islam and the West*. London, Gower, 1983.

Gersovitz, M., and Waterbury, J. (Eds). *The Political Economy of Risk and Choice in Senegal*. London, Frank Cass, 1987.

Harrison Church, R. J. *West Africa*. 8th Edn. London, Longman, 1979.

Harvey, C., and Robinson, M. *The Design of Economic Reforms in the Context of Economic Liberalization: The Experience of Mozambique, Senegal and Uganda*. Brighton, Institute of Development Studies, 1995.

Hayward, M. F. *Elections in Independent Africa*. Boulder, CO, Westview Press, 1987.

Hesseling, G. *Histoire politique du Sénégal*. Paris, Editions Karthala, 1983.

Hymans, J. L. *Léopold Sédar Senghor*. Edinburgh University Press, 1972.

Johnson, G. W. *Naissance du Sénégal contemporain*. Paris, Editions Karthala, 1991.

Lewis Renaud, L. *Women at the Crossroads: A Prostitute Community's Response to AIDS in Urban Senegal*. Amsterdam, Gordon and Breach Publishers, 1997.

Linares, O. *Power, Prayer and Production: The Jola of Casamance*. Cambridge, Cambridge University Press, 1993.

Makédonsky, E. *Le Sénégal, La Sénégambie*. Paris, L'Harmattan, 1987.

Milcent, E., and Sordet, M. *Léopold Sédar Senghor et la naissance de l'Afrique moderne*. Paris, Editions Seghers, 1969.

Pfefferman, G. *Industrial Labor in the Republic of Senegal*. New York, Praeger, 1968.

Pison, G. (Ed.). *Population Dynamics of Senegal*. Washington, DC, National Academy Press, 1995.

Rimmer, D. *The Economies of West Africa*. London, Weidenfeld and Nicolson, 1984.

Rocheteau, G. *Pouvoir financier et indépendance économique en Afrique noire. Le cas du Sénégal*. Paris, Editions Karthala, 1983.

Saint-Martin, Y.-J. *Le Sénégal sous le second empire*. Paris, Editions Karthala, 1989.

Sene, M., and Ricou, M.-J. *Le Sénégal*. Centre d'Information du Sénégal, 1974.

Senghor, L. S. *Liberté I, Négritude et Humanisme; Liberté II, Nation et voie africaine du socialisme*. Editions du Seuil, 1964 and 1971.

Snipe, T. *Arts and Politics in Senegal, 1960–1996*. Lawrenceville, NJ, Africa World Press Inc, 1997.

Sweeney, P. (Ed.). *The Gambia and Senegal*. London, APA, 1996.

Vengroff, R., and Johnston, A. *Decentralization and the Implementation of Rural Development in Senegal*. Lewiston, NY, Edwin Mellen Press, 1988.

Villalon, L. *Islamic Society and State Power in Senegal*. Cambridge, Cambridge University Press, 1995.

Wade, A. *Un destin pour l'Afrique*. Paris, Editions Karthala, 1992.

Waterbury, J. *The Political Economy of Risk and Choice in Senegal*. Ilford, Frank Cass Publishers, 1987.

Zarour, C. *La Coopération arabo-sénégalaise*. Paris, L'Harmattan, 1989.

SEYCHELLES

Physical and Social Geography

The Republic of Seychelles comprises a scattered archipelago of granitic and coralline islands, lying about 1,600 km east of continental Africa and ranging over some 1m. sq km of the western Indian Ocean. The exact number of islands is unknown, but has been estimated at 115, of which 41 are granitic and the remainder coralline. The group also includes numerous rocks and small cays. At independence in June 1976, the Aldabra Islands, the Farquhar group and Desroches (combined area 28.5 sq km, or 11 sq miles), part of the British Indian Ocean Territory (see p. 229) since 1965, were reunited with the Seychelles, thus restoring the land area to 308 sq km (119 sq miles). Including the Aldabra lagoon, the country's area is 454 sq km (175.3 sq miles).

The islands take their name from the Vicomte Moreau de Séchelles, controller-general of finance in the reign of Louis XV of France. The largest of the group is Mahé, which has an area of about 148 sq km (57 sq miles) and is approximately 27 km long from north to south. Mahé lies 1,800 km due east of Mombasa, 3,300 km south-west of Bombay, and 1,100 km north of Madagascar. Victoria, the capital of Seychelles and the only port of the archipelago, is on Mahé. It is the only town in Seychelles of any size and had a population of 24,324 (including suburbs) at the census of August 1987. The islanders have a variety of ethnic origins—African, European, Indian and Chinese. In 1981 Creole (Seselwa), the language spoken by virtually all Seychellois, replaced English and French as the official language. The total population was enumerated at 74,331 at the August 1994 census, and at 78,846 at mid-1998, giving a density of just over 173 persons per sq km.

The granitic islands, which are all of great scenic beauty, rise fairly steeply from the sea and Mahé has a long central ridge which at its highest point, Morne Seychellois, reaches 912 m. Praslin, the second largest island in the group, is 43 km from Mahé and the other granitic islands are within a radius of 56 km. The coral islands are reefs in different stages of formation, rising only marginally above sea-level.

For islands so close to the Equator, the climate is surprisingly equable. Maximum shade temperature at sea-level averages 29°C, but during the coolest months the temperature may fall to 24°C. There are two seasons, hot from December to May, and cooler from June to November while the south-east trade winds are blowing. Rainfall varies over the group; the greater part falls in the hot months during the north-west trade winds and the climate then tends to be humid and somewhat enervating. The mean annual rainfall in Victoria is 2,360 mm and the mean average temperature nearly 27°C. All the granitic islands lie outside the cyclone belt.

Recent History

Revised for this edition by the Editor

The archipelago now forming the Republic of Seychelles was occupied by French settlers in 1770. Following its capture in 1811 by British naval forces, Seychelles was formally ceded by France to Britain in 1814. The islands were administered as a dependency of Mauritius until 1903, when Seychelles became a separate crown colony.

During the 1960s political activity was focused on the socialist-orientated Seychelles People's United Party (SPUP), led by Albert René, and the centre-right Seychelles Democratic Party (SDP), led by James (later Sir James) Mancham, who became the islands' chief minister in 1970. The SPUP sought full independence for the islands, while the SDP favoured a form of economic integration with the United Kingdom. This option was not acceptable to the British government, and in 1974 the SDP adopted a pro-independence policy. The two parties formed a coalition government in 1975, and the independent Republic of Seychelles, with Mancham as president and René as prime minister, was proclaimed on 29 June 1976.

SINGLE-PARTY GOVERNMENT

In June 1977 supporters of the SPUP staged an armed coup while Mancham was absent in Britain, and installed René as president. René claimed that Mancham had intended to postpone the 1979 elections (a charge that Mancham denied), but there is little doubt that the ex-president's extravagant lifestyle and capitalist philosophy had displeased many of the islanders. The SDP had intended to develop Seychelles as a financial and trading centre and placed great emphasis on the tourist industry. The SPUP considered the development of agriculture and fishing to be as important as tourism to the economy, and planned to ensure a more equitable distribution of wealth.

A new constitution was promulgated in 1979. The SPUP, now redesignated the Seychelles People's Progressive Front (SPPF), was declared the sole legal party, and legislative and presidential elections were held to legitimize the new political order. The government's socialist programme, however, led to discontent, particularly among the islands' small middle class. Two plots to overthrow René were suppressed in 1978, and a third and more serious attempt, involving South African mercenaries, was thwarted in 1981. In 1982 the government put down both an army mutiny and a further coup plot. In 1983 another attempt to depose René was quelled. This sustained anti-government activism was blamed by the government on pro-Mancham exile groups, although Mancham denied any involvement in the conspiracies. Dissent within the SPUP itself was evident, however, in the enforced resignations of two government ministers; Dr Maxime Ferrari, the minister of planning and external relations, left the islands in 1984, and two years later the minister of youth and defence, Col Ogilvy Berlouis, was removed from office after the discovery of another alleged conspiracy against the government.

During the mid-1980s there was a series of violent attacks upon, and disappearances of, exiled opponents of the SPPF. Notable among these was the murder in London in 1985 of Gérard Hoarau, a former government official and leader of the Mouvement pour la Résistance. In 1987 an elaborate plan to overthrow the Seychelles government was discovered by police in the United Kingdom, together with a co-conspiracy to abduct leading members of the African National Congress of South Africa (ANC), who were based in London.

Until the early 1990s, exiled opposition to René remained split among a number of small groups based principally in London. In July 1991 five of these parties, including the Rassemblement du Peuple Seychellois pour la Démocratie (subsequently renamed the Seychelles Christian Democrat Party, SCDP), founded by Dr Maxime Ferrari, established a coalition, the United Democratic Movement (UDM), under Ferrari's leadership, while ex-president Mancham rallied his supporters in a 'Crusade for Democracy'.

During 1991 the René government came under increasing pressure from France and the United Kingdom, the islands' principal aid-donors, to return Seychelles to a democratic political system. Internally, open opposition to the SPPF was voiced by the newly-formed Parti Seselwa (PS), led by a Protestant clergyman, Wavel Ramkalawan. In August Maxime Ferrari returned from exile to organize support for the UDM, and in November René invited all political dissidents to return to the islands. In December the minister of tourism and transport, Jacques Hodoul, left the government and subsequently formed the Seychelles Movement for Democracy.

RESUMPTION OF MULTI-PARTY POLITICS

In December 1991 the SPPF conceded its political monopoly, and agreed that, from January 1992, political groups numbering at least 100 members could be granted official registration, and that multi-party elections would take place in July for a constituent assembly, whose proposals for constitutional reform would be submitted to a national referendum, with a view to holding multi-party parliamentary elections in December. In April Mancham returned from exile to lead the New Democratic Party (NDP).

Elections for a 20-seat commission to draft a new constitution took place in July 1992. The SPPF won 58.4% of the votes, while the NDP received 33.7%. The PS, which took 4.4% of the votes, was the only other political party to obtain representation on the commission. The commission, which comprised 11 representatives from the SPPF, eight from the NDP (now renamed the Democratic Party, DP) and one from the PS, completed its deliberations in October. In September, however, the DP withdrew its delegation, on the grounds that the SPPF had allegedly refused to permit a full debate of reform proposals. It also expressed objections that the commission's meetings had been closed to the public and news media. Following publication of the draft constitution, the DP focused its opposition on proposed voting arrangements for a new national assembly, whose members were to be elected on a basis of one-half by direct vote and one-half by proportional representation. The latter formula was to reflect the percentage of votes obtained by the successful candidate in presidential elections,and was intended to ensure that the president's party would secure a legislative majority. Other sections of the proposed constitution, relating to social issues, were strongly opposed by the Roman Catholic Church, to which more than 90% of the islanders belong.

The draft constitution, which required the approval of at least 60% of voters, was endorsed by only 53.7% and opposed by 44.6% at a referendum held in November 1992. A second constitutional commission, whose meetings were opened to the public, began work in January 1993 on proposals for submission to a further referendum, which was to be held later in the year. In April René reshuffled the council of ministers.

In May 1993 the second commission unanimously agreed on a new draft constitution, in which a compromise plan was reached on the electoral formula for a new national assembly. With the joint endorsement of René and Mancham, the draft constitution was submitted to a national referendum in June, at which voters approved the constitutional plan by 73.9% to 24.0%. Opponents of the new constitutional arrangements comprised the PS, the Seychelles National Movement (SNM) and the National Alliance Party (NAP). At the presidential and legislative elections that followed in July, René received 59.5% of the vote, against 36.7% for Mancham and 3.8% for Philippe Boullé, the United Opposition candidate representing the PS, the SCDP, the SNM and the NAP. In the legislative elections, the SPPF secured 21 of the 22 seats elected by direct vote, and the DP one seat. Of the 11 additional seats allocated on a proportional basis, the SPPF received a further seven seats, the DP three seats and the PS one seat. Immediately following the elections, René, whose decisive victory was widely attributed to his promise of increased expenditure on social programmes, carried out an extensive reshuffle of the council of ministers.

Socio-Economic Transition

Following the 1993 elections, the government began to promote a gradual transition from socialism to free-market policies, aimed at maximizing the country's potential as an 'offshore' financial and business centre. State-owned port facilities were transferred to private ownership in 1994, when plans were also announced for the creation of a duty-free international trade zone to provide transhipment facilities. Arrangements also proceeded during 1995 for the privatization of government activities in tourism, agriculture and tuna-processing. The economic liberalization, accompanied by diminished levels of aid and the consequent pressure to reduce budgetary deficits, led the government to announce, in February 1995, that some state-funded welfare services were to be reduced.

In early 1995 tensions developed within the opposition DP, whose only directly-elected MP, Christopher Gill, sought to remove Mancham from the party leadership on the grounds that the former president was insufficiently vigorous in opposing the policies of the René government. Gill was suspended from the DP in June, and subsequently formed a breakaway 'New Democratic Party' with the aim of restructuring the DP under new leadership. The official registration of active political organizations, affording them corporate status, led to the formal amalgamation of the PS, the SNM, the SCDP and the NAP as a single party, the United Opposition (UO), under the leadership of Wavel Ramkalawan of the former PS.

In the furtherance of its efforts to promote Seychelles as an international 'offshore' financial centre, the government introduced, in November 1995, an Economic Development Act (EDA), under whose provisions investors of a minimum US $10m. would receive immunity in Seychelles from extradition or seizure of assets. It was feared in international financial circles, however, that the operation of the EDA would make Seychelles a refuge for the proceeds of drugs-trafficking and other crimes. Protest was led by the United Kingdom, France and the USA, and in February 1996 the EDA was described by the Financial Action Task Force, the investigative branch of the 'Group of Seven' leading industrial countries, as a 'serious threat to world financial systems.' Within Seychelles, aspects of the EDA were criticized by Mancham. The government, while refusing to rescind the EDA, established an Economic Development Board under the chairmanship of René, to vet potential EDA investors. In April the government introduced legislation aimed at preventing the use of the EDA for 'laundering' illicit funds. Full implementation of the EDA provisions, however, had still not taken place by early 1998. Meanwhile, it was disclosed in April 1997 that 243 foreign nationals had obtained Seychelles passports, in return for individual payments of $25,000, under an Economic Citizenship Programme (ECP) introduced in the previous year to attract foreign investors to the republic. It was claimed, however, by opposition groups that many of the grantees had never visited the islands, and that the names of some of these absentee citizens had been added to electoral lists. In early 1998 the minister of foreign affairs stated that the ECP in its existing form was 'finished', but that consideration was being given to a new citizenship scheme to be linked to investment in the Seychelles economy.

In July 1996 the SPPF introduced a series of constitutional amendments, creating the post of vice-president, to which James Michel, the minister of finance, communications and defence and a long-standing political associate of René, was appointed in August. The constitutional changes also provided for revisions in constituency boundaries, which were generally interpreted as favouring SPPF candidates in future legislative elections. Measures were also implemented whereby the number of directly-elected members of the national assembly was to be increased from 22 to 25, and the number of seats allocated on a proportional basis reduced from 11 to a maximum of 10.

The 1998 Elections

Following the 1993 elections, effective opposition to the government came increasingly to be led by Ramkalawan's UO, as the DP opted to pursue a policy of 'reconciliation' and 'nonconfrontation' with the SPPF. In November 1997, ahead of the presidential and legislative elections due to take place before mid-1998, Mancham rejected proposals by Ramkalawan for the creation of an electoral alliance.

In January 1998 René announced that the elections would be held in March, and that he was to seek the second of a maximum of three consecutive five-year terms as president permitted under the 1993 constitution. The outcome of the elections provided the SPPF with a decisive victory. René obtained 66.7% of the presidential ballot (compared with 59.5% in the previous election), while his party secured 30 of the 34 seats in the enlarged national assembly. Ramkalawan, with 19.5% of the presidential vote (compared with 3.8% for the UO candidate in the 1993 election), substantially exceeded support for Mancham, who received 13.8% (as against 36.7% in 1993). In the national assembly the UO increased its representation from one seat to three seats, with the DP losing three of the four seats previously held. Mancham, who lost his seat, announced his temporary withdrawal from active politics. The UO, which consequently emerged as the principal parliamentary opponent of the SPPF, boycotted a number of debates in protest at allegedly partisan coverage of legislative proceedings by the Seychelles Broadcasting Corpn, and has accused the speaker of the national assembly of authoritarian conduct. In July 1998 the party changed its name to the Seychelles National Party. Further criticism of the government's alleged intolerance of political opposition was voiced in the same month by the Anglican bishop of Seychelles, who claimed that local administrations controlled by the SPPF neglected the needs of inhabitants who did not support the government. In December 1999 a reallocation of government portfolios was announced, although it brought no new ministers into the administration. Proposals to amend the 1993 constitution were being finalized in April 2000 by René, under which the president would be empowered to declare a presidential election at any time following the completion of one year in office. This proposal was interpreted by some observers as an attempt by René to ensure the eventual succession to a candidate of his own choice.

EXTERNAL RELATIONS

Seychelles, a member of the Commonwealth, the African Development Bank, the Common Market for Eastern and Southern Africa (COMESA), the Organization of African Unity and the Southern African Development Community (SADC), has traditionally pursued a policy of non-alignment in international affairs.

In 1983 Seychelles, Madagascar and Mauritius agreed to form an Indian Ocean Commission (IOC) with the aim of increasing regional co-operation. The first such agreement under the IOC was signed by the three countries in January 1984. Comoros joined the IOC in 1985. In early 1986 Seychelles withdrew its objections to the admission to membership of France (as the representative of Réunion) despite its reluctance to recognize permanent French sovereignty over Réunion, and disagreements over the demarcation of regional tuna-fishing rights. Relations with France improved in 1987, despite Seychelles' opposition to the accession of France to the presidency of the IOC. France signed three new economic assistance agreements with Seychelles during that year, and the French minister of co-operation visited the islands and opened an electricity generator that had been provided by the French government. In June 1990 President Mitterrand of France visited Seychelles in the course of an Indian Ocean tour.

In 1988 Seychelles established diplomatic relations with the Comoros and with Mauritius, and an agreement was made with the latter to co-operate in health matters. In 1989 diplomatic relations were established with Morocco, Madagascar and Côte d'Ivoire, and in 1990 with Kenya. During 1992 formal relations were established with Israel and South Africa, and in 1998 Seychelles proposed to establish a diplomatic mission in Malaysia to expand its relations in Asia and Oceania. Libya opened a diplomatic mission in Seychelles in January 2000.

During the 1980s President René actively pursued initiatives for the creation of an Indian Ocean 'peace zone' and the demilitarization of the British Indian Ocean Territory (see p. 229), which includes the atoll of Diego Garcia. Until 1983, Seychelles allowed limited use of its naval facilities to warships of all nations, but only on condition that an assurance was issued that they were not carrying nuclear weapons. Neither the British nor the US governments would agree to this condition, and their refusal to do so caused their respective naval fleets to be effectively banned from using Seychelles port facilities. It is thought that this embargo lost Seychelles a considerable amount of foreign exchange, and that this may have been one reason for the lifting of the guarantee requirement in September 1983. Seychelles continues, theoretically, to refuse entry to ships carrying nuclear weapons.

In 1986 Seychelles and the USA renegotiated an agreement, originally signed in 1976 and renewed in 1981, which allowed the USA to maintain a satellite tracking station on Mahé. In 1988 the USA increased its annual level of economic support to US $3m., exclusive of the $4.5m. paid annually in rental fees for the satellite tracking facilities. Direct economic aid to Seychelles, however, was reduced by the US government in 1993 to $1m. annually, and in October 1996 the station was closed (its dismantlement finally commenced in mid-2000). The US diplomatic mission in Victoria was closed in 1996, also as a cost-saving measure.

Economy

DONALD L. SPARKS

Revised for this edition by the Editor

In 1998, according to estimates by the World Bank, Seychelles' gross national product (GNP), measured at average 1996–98 prices was US $505m., equivalent to $6,420 per head. During 1990–98, it was estimated, GNP per caput increased, in real terms, at an average annual rate of 1.4%. Over the same period, the population increased at an average annual rate of 1.7%. Seychelles' gross domestic product (GDP) increased, in real terms, at an average annual rate of 3.2% in 1990–98. Real GDP rose by 4.7% in 1996, by 4.3% in 1997 and by an estimated 2.3% in 1998. Following the political changes that took place in 1993, the government has introduced a number of important reforms in the economy, notably towards encouraging the greater involvement of the private sector in tourism, industry and agriculture.

AGRICULTURE AND FISHERIES

As the area of cultivable land is limited to about 6,000 ha of Seychelles' total land area and the soil is often poor, it is unlikely that the republic will ever become self-sufficient in agriculture.

The islands are heavily dependent on imported food, which, together with drink and tobacco, accounted for 22.8% of the total import bill in 1998, although this proportion is being slowly reduced. The government is seeking to stimulate greater self-sufficiency in vegetables, fruit, meat and milk. There are a number of large farms and about 650 small farms and numerous smallholdings, about one-half of them run by 'part-time' farmers. In 1993, in accordance with the government strategy for reduced state involvement in the economy, the ministry of agriculture withdrew from the management of its five state-owned farms, whose profitability had been overtaken by the increasing cost of subsidies and poor productivity. These farms are being subdivided into small plots and leased to private individuals, and the ministry of agriculture is now to concentrate on stressing increased extension services to small farmers in its continuing attempts to stimulate food production. The transfer of government-owned agricultural land to smallholder farmers was proceeding in the late 1990s. In addition, the African Development Bank (ADB) has provided substantial financial assistance to an integrated agricultural development project to develop roads and irrigation facilities. Agriculture, forestry and fishing was estimated to have contributed 3.8% of GDP in 1998, and accounted for 5.7% of total employment in that year.

The main exports from this sector have traditionally been coconuts (especially for copra), frozen fish and cinnamon (exported as bark). In 1987, the first year of its production, canned tuna became the most significant export commodity; in 1996 canned tuna was estimated to account for almost 85% of total merchandise exports (excluding re-exports). Minor export crops include patchouli, vanilla, tea and limes. Cup copra is processed locally into oil, and the by-product made into animal feed. However, by the early 1990s, exports of copra, which in the late 1960s were about 6,000 tons per year, had fallen to only 10% of 1968 levels, mainly as a result of competition for land from food crops, together with high labour costs, which lessened their competitiveness in world markets. The value of copra exports declined by an average of 40.7% per year between 1990 and 1994, and totalled only SR 300,000 in 1995. Exports of this commodity were halted indefinitely from 1996. In the late 1980s exports of cinnamon bark, traditionally an important export item, fell to about one-third of 1986 totals, and remained depressed in the early 1990s. However, exports subsequently recovered; the value of cinnamon bark exports increased by an average of 55.5% per year between 1990 and 1994, and stood at SR 4.7m. in 1996, declining again to an estimated SR 2.7m. in 1998. Tea is grown for domestic consumption, and there is a small surplus for export. Output ranged from 225–250 tons annually in the early 1990s. The government is encouraging the production of bananas, mangoes and avocados. Seychelles is self-sufficient in eggs and poultry, and there has been a large increase in the number of pigs, although animal feed has to be imported. The islands possess a fruit and vegetable canning plant and an integrated poultry unit.

Seychelles expected to be self-sufficient in timber by the year 2000. A reafforestation scheme, with new plantings of 100 ha per year, was started to provide timber for the sawmill established in 1979 at Grande Anse by the Seychelles Timber Co (SEYTIM).

Seychelles' per caput consumption of fish is one of the highest in the world, at 85 kg per year. The local catch, by largely traditional methods (the recorded catch was 4,645 metric tons in 1996 and 5,344 tons in 1997), satisfied domestic demand, leaving a small surplus for export as frozen fish. Until relatively recently, there was little exploitation of the islands' abundant marine resources. A modern fishing industry, operated by the Fishing Development Co (FIDECO), is concentrating on industrial tuna fishing through joint-venture operations, including the Société Thonière de Seychelles (of which 49% is owned by French interests), which has two freezer ships, and a tuna canning plant at Victoria that began operation in 1987 as a joint venture between the governments of Seychelles and France. In 1995 the US multinational foods group H. J. Heinz acquired a 60% interest in the tuna-canning factory. The government retained a 40% holding in the company, which was reorganized as the Indian Ocean Tuna Co and has established Seychelles as the largest centre for tuna processing in the Indian Ocean. In 1997 production at the cannery was averaging 160 tons per day, compared with 58 tons per day prior to the Heinz take-over. Heinz planed to invest some US $20m. to increase production to 300–400 tons per day by 2000. About 99% of tuna produced at the factory is exported to Europe through the port at Victoria, which has become the principal centre in the Indian Ocean for tuna transhipment.

In 1978 Seychelles declared an exclusive economic zone (EEZ), extending 370 km (200 nautical miles) from the coast, to curtail the activities of large foreign fleets, which until then had been freely catching almost 24,000 metric tons per year of deep-sea tuna. Since 1979, when Seychelles began to enforce its control over the EEZ, agreements have been concluded with several foreign governments. The most important of these is with the European Union (EU), which, under arrangements covering 1999–2000, has the right to operate 38 purse-seiners and 13 longliners within the EEZ. These licences were expected to yield SR 23m. to the government. Additional revenue is derived from supplying vessels at Victoria and through leasing the newly expanded port facilities to foreign vessels. An indigenous fleet of 10 purse-seiners is under construction, the first of which was

launched in 1991. Seychelles' first tuna-seiner, with a capacity of 250 tons, began operations in late 1991. Assistance in expanding the fishing industry sector has been forthcoming from Japan, France, the United Kingdom and the ADB. In 1991 Seychelles joined Mauritius and Madagascar to form a tuna fishing association. A study on the potential for prawn fishing estimated that the annual catch could total 8 tons. About 3 tons of prawns per year are currently imported, mainly for the tourist industry. In 1999 a Chinese company was licensed to catch 100 tons annually of grouper, destined for the Asian gourmet food market. There is also future potential for Seychelles to exploit its rich stock of marine algae, for use in the manufacture of fertilizers, adhesives, beverages and medicines. Exports of canned tuna, fresh and frozen fish contributed 82.2% of the total value of merchandise exports (excluding re-exports) in 1994, and by 1998 production of canned tuna had reached 18,939 tons.

TOURISM

The economy is heavily dependent on tourism, which in 1998 provided 13.8% of total GDP. However, it has been estimated that more than 60% of gross earnings from tourism leaves the country as payment for imported food and other goods, and by way of remittances to tour operators.

The tourism industry began in 1971 with the opening of Mahé international airport. In that year there were only 3,175 visitors; however, by 1981 the number had risen to 60,425. In November of that year, however, the arrival by commercial airline from South Africa of a group of mercenaries, seeking to oust the government, had a highly deleterious effect on tourism. These factors, combined with an army rebellion in August 1982, led to a fall in arrivals: the final figure for 1982 was 47,280 visitors. By 1990, however, the number of tourist arrivals had recovered to 103,900. The Gulf War caused arrivals to decline to about 90,000 in 1991, although 1992 and 1993 both brought a strong recovery, to more than 116,000 visitors in the latter year. Arrivals of tourists and business visitors totalled 109,901 in 1994, to 120,717 in 1995, when receipts from this source totalled SR 471m. Tourism receipts rose to SR 531m. in 1996, when there were 130,955 visitors, and to SR 612m. in 1997; in that year there were some 4,600 hotel beds. Tourist arrivals in 1998, however, declined by almost 1.4% on 1997, to 128,258. The majority of the visitors were from EU countries.

Seychelles has developed an extensive network of international air links. Air France flies three times each week from Paris to Seychelles, in conjunction with Air Seychelles. In 1991 Air Seychelles began weekly scheduled flights to Johannesburg. Air Seychelles also operates international services to London, Paris, Frankfurt, Rome, Singapore and Mumbai (Bombay). These are joint marketing arrangements with Kenya to promote combined tour programmes.

Since the mid-1980s the government has rehabilitated and improved existing tourist facilities, and developed new attractions, including a craft village, a national aquarium and historical sites. However, care has been taken to control the development of tourism in order to protect both the natural and the social environments, and the emphasis on promoting tourism on a year-round basis has been aimed at restricting visitor numbers to under 4,000 at any one time. The government has estimated the islands' maximum tourist capacity, without detriment to the environment, at 200,000 visitors annually. It is hoped to attract an increasing proportion of visitors interested in the ecological aspects of the archipelago, and to this end attention was focused in the late 1990s on the tourism potential of the outlying islands. Meanwhile, a conglomerate based in Dubai, in the United Arab Emirates, purchased land near Victoria with a view to constructing a marina village, to include yachting facilities, a golf course, a conference centre and a 320-room hotel. Despite concerns that this type of development is inconsistent with Seychelles' ethos of sustainable tourism, the ministry of finance affirmed that it would welcome as many as 15 further hotel developments on a similar scale by 2000. Since 1993 the government has divested itself of most of its parastatal holdings in the tourism sector, and foreign investment has been actively sought. A series of new taxes on the tourism industry, introduced by the government, includes a hotel licence fee, which is levied according to the number of beds per hotel and was estimated to have contributed additional revenue of SR 23m. in 1997.

MINERALS

The islands' sole mineral export is guano (of which 6,000 metric tons were exported in 1990). The government is investigating the possibility of processing local coral into lime for a cement factory. There may also be potential for exporting Seychelles granite, of which small quantities were exported in 1982. India has collaborated in surveys for polymetallic nodules in the EEZ.

In 1977 the government signed a petroleum exploration agreement, covering an offshore concession area of 16,000 sq km, with a consortium including Amoco of the USA, which later acquired sole control. In 1982 Amoco Seychelles signed a new agreement, covering five more offshore wells in addition to those already drilled. Other concessions are held by Elf-Aquitaine of France and Santa Fe Industries of the USA. An exploration promotion programme was launched by the government in 1985. In 1987 the government signed an agreement with Enterprise Oil Exploration, a British company, which obtained exclusive rights to explore an offshore area south-east of Mahé and to develop any viable fields. Exploratory drilling proved unsuccessful, however, and was discontinued in 1995. Other petroleum companies have subsequently expressed interest in conducting exploration operations, and the Seychelles government has received technical assistance and funding from Norway to further offshore exploration activities.

INFRASTRUCTURE AND MANUFACTURING

The network of roads is generally good and an improvement programme is proceeding. In 1998 there were 397 km of roads, of which 343 km were paved. Most surfaced roads are on Mahé and Praslin. The international airport on Mahé has been expanded, its runway has been strengthened to take Boeing 747s, and a new domestic terminal has been built. There are airstrips on several outlying islands.

Seychelles' major infrastructural project, the Mahé east coast development plan, includes the modernization and expansion of Victoria port and the construction of a new road linking Victoria to the airport. The World Bank agreed in 1985 to lend US $6.2m. for dredging work, quayside paving and rehabilitation of roads on Mahé. The total cost of the scheme was projected to be $40m.–$42m., of which $12m. was to be spent on the fisheries development project. As well as the World Bank, the ADB, the Banque Arabe pour le Développement Economique en Afrique (BADEA) and the Kuwait Fund have provided finance for the east coast project. The commercial port can accommodate vessels of up to 214 m in length, but there is only one berth. Additional berthing capacity is planned, with some facilities for containerization, and possibly a repair dock. In early 1999 the government announced plans for a major land reclamation project on Mahé, costing an estimated $100m. and encompassing a new harbour and anchorage for cruise ships.

The Seychelles Electricity Corpn was set up in 1980 as a parastatal organization which was to finance its own recurrent costs. The extension of electricity supply to the islands of Mahé, Praslin and La Digue has been completed. Power supplies are generated entirely from petroleum. In 1998 mineral fuels accounted for 8.9% of the value of total imports. (However, the vast majority of fuel imports are re-exported, mainly as bunker sales to visiting ships and aircraft—exports of refined petroleum products contributed 21.8% of total export earnings in 1996.) Studies have been conducted on the use of windmills, solar and wave power for electricity generation.

The recurring problem of water shortages should eventually be eased by the completion of the Baie Lazare water supply scheme, in the south of Mahé, with the capacity to supply 18,000 people in the Victoria area. A project to extend La Digue's water supply to 80% of the population, from the existing level of 50%, began in 1988. Funds for this scheme, which was estimated to cost SR 8m. were provided by France and the USA.

Several small industries have been established, none of which have an unfavourable impact on the environment. These include brewing, plastic goods, salt, coconut oil, cinnamon essence distilling, soft drinks, detergents, cigarettes, soap, boat building, furniture, printing and steel products, together with animal feed, meat and fish processing, dairy products, paints, television

assembly, and handicrafts for the tourist industry. However, the tuna-canning factory (see above) remains pre-eminent in the industrial sector. A series of incentives was introduced in 2000 to aid small businesses; these included the creation of an Export Development and Promotion Facility and an Export Marketing Fund, as well as a Small Business Finance Fund. Also, as part of a new trade tax concession, export businesses were to be able to claim a full refund of trade tax.

TRADE, FINANCE AND PLANNING

Seychelles traditionally sustains a substantial visible trade deficit. However, this deficit is partly offset by earnings from tourism and by capital inflows in the form of aid and private investment. According to the IMF, in 1992 the current account deficit stood at a manageable US $6.9m., rising to $38.82m. in 1993 before declining to $25.88m. in 1994, increasing to $53.92m. in 1995, and then declining to $20.08m. in 1996. The current account deficit rose in 1997, however, to $63.2m. Seychelles' total external debt was US $186.7m. at the end of 1998, of which $145.1m. was long-term public debt. In that year the cost of debt-servicing was equivalent to 5.7% of the value of exports of goods and services. Reserves of foreign exchange, which declined steadily during the late 1980s and first half of the 1990s, totalled $20.6m. in 1996, recovering to $25.2m. in 1997, before decreasing again, to $21.6m., in 1998. In 1996 Seychelles' main suppliers of imports were the USA (accounting for 28.9% of the total), the United Kingdom (12.2%), the Southern African Customs Union (comprising Botswana, Lesotho, Namibia, South Africa and Swaziland, and accounting for 11.4%) and Singapore (10.2%). Seychelles' principal export markets in that year were the USA (37.3% of total exports), the United Kingdom (9.2%), Singapore (9.2%) and France (7.8%).

Following the installation in 1994 of a democratically-elected government in South Africa, there has been an increasing level of trade with (as well as investment from) that country. In 1993 Seychelles joined the Preferential Trade Area for Eastern and Southern Africa (PTA, which in 1994 became the Common Market for Eastern and Southern Africa–COMESA) and should benefit from the clearing house function which facilitates the use of member countries' currencies for regional transactions. This will reduce the pressure on foreign exchange resources, particularly from trade with Mauritius, another COMESA member.

In 1996 legislation came into effect under which it became compulsory to remit all foreign currency earnings to local banks. In January 1997 the existing foreign exchange allocation system was abandoned and commercial banks assumed control of the allocation of foreign currency. Recipients of foreign exchange may claim up to 20% of their earnings in foreign exchange, but the amount allocated is decided on a discretionary basis by the commercial bank concerned. In May 1999 the government also announced that visitors would have to pay their hotel accounts in some form of foreign exchange when checking out (including cash, credit cards and traveller's cheques), to ensure a greater flow of foreign exchange into the banking system.

Government spending increased dramatically following independence in 1976, as the new administration expanded its provision of social services and raised its levels of defence spending. British grant support ended in 1979. Revenue deficits expanded steadily between 1984 and 1986. In 1987 the government introduced an austerity budget, restricting public spending, and reduced the deficit to 3.8% of GDP. The deficit rose to nearly 10% of GDP in 1989, but fell to 1.0% in 1994 before rising to 2.8% of GDP in 1995. It was estimated that the deficit could be as great as 19.4% of GDP in 1998, owing to declining revenue (with the postponement of the divestment of several state assets) and the costs of repairing infrastructural damage, caused by a heavy storm in August 1997. In response, the government announced that economic austerity measures were to be introduced.

Seychelles receives development aid from a wide variety of sources, including the World Bank, the EU (particularly France), and other Western European countries the ADB, the Arab Bank for Economic Development in Africa, the USA, India, Canada, Arab countries and funds and the People's Republic of China. By 1997 Seychelles had received a total of ECU 17.6m.

from various European Development Funds (EDF) since its accession to the first Lomé Convention in 1976.

The Seychelles rupee, previously tied to sterling, was linked to the IMF Special Drawing Right (SDR) in November 1979. In March 1981 the mid-point exchange rate was set at SDR 1 = 7.2345 Seychelles rupees. This remained in effect until February 1997, when the fixed link with the SDR was ended.

The government has been generally successful in controlling inflation. The annual rate of inflation averaged 1.3% in 1990–98; consumer prices declined by 0.9% in 1996, before rising by 0.7% in 1997 and by 2.6% in 1998.

Trade between Seychelles and other members of the Indian Ocean Commission (IOC, see Recent History) accounts for only 2%–3% of the country's total official trade, owing principally to Seychelles' high import duties. Seychelles is a member of African Development Bank, the Southern African Development Community (SADC) and COMESA, and of the IOC. Application has been made for membership of the Indian Ocean Rim Association for Regional Co-operation (IOR–ARC) and the World Trade Organization (WTO).

ECONOMIC PROSPECTS

Government control of key economic sectors was exercised through the Seychelles National Investment Corpn, set up in 1979, rather than by way of open nationalization. Since 1991 the government has, apart from transport and public utilities, transferred most of its interests to private-sector investors, and is now actively encouraging foreign investment, both public and private, particularly in tourism, farming, fisheries and small-scale manufacturing. There is, however, an official preference for joint ventures where foreign investors are concerned. Taxed profits can be freely repatriated. Certain aspects of the Economic Development Act (EDA), introduced in 1995 to assist in establishing Seychelles as a centre for international 'offshore' finan-cial services, attracted intense criticism, on the grounds that they could provide a shelter for illegally obtained funds (see Recent History). The government has, however, established procedures for vetting investors bringing more than US $10m. to Seychelles under EDA provisions. Meanwhile, Seychelles' desire to become an international business centre has gained momentum. Measures to promote the development of an international business centre for financial services, trading and transhipment commenced in 1995 with the formation of the Seychelles International Business Authority (SIBA) as the regulatory authority. By early 1999 about 3,000 international companies had been incorporated in the country, operating from the proposed Seychelles International Trade Zone (SITZ), for which a site was under development in 2000 on reclaimed land near Port Victoria. A major constraint, however, on the expansion of manufacturing activity in the SITZ is posed by shortages of skilled and unskilled labour. Legislation introduced in early 1997 aimed to increase the appeal of the 'offshore' sector by facilitating taxation agreements with other countries. The legislation was specifically aimed at establishing Seychelles as a major financial centre serving the Far East.

In 1993 the government created the National Economic Consultative Committee, with a membership including business leaders as well as members of the political opposition. In 1994, with the implementation of the Investment Promotion Act, the government offered a range of incentives to stimulate increased private-sector investment in tourism, agriculture, manufacturing and services. As many of the highly skilled Seychellois professional people (many of whom left the islands during the period of single-party rule) return to Seychelles, and as political changes translate into genuine economic reform, the republic may well be within reach of further rises in per caput incomes and an extended period of sustained economic growth and development.

Statistical Survey

Source (unless otherwise stated): Information and Telecommunications Division, POB 321, Victoria; tel. 324161; fax 321006.

AREA AND POPULATION

Area: 455.3 sq km (175.8 sq miles), incl. Aldabra lagoon (145 sq km).

Population: 68,598 at census of 17 August 1987; 74,331 (males 37,128, females 37,203) at census of 26 August 1994; 78,846 (official estimate) at mid-1998.

Density (mid-1998): 173.2 per sq km.

Principal Town: Victoria (capital), estimated population 60,000 (incl. suburbs) in 1994.

Births and Deaths (registered in 1998): Live births 1,412 (birth rate 17.9 per 1,000); Deaths 570 (death rate 7.2 per 1,000). Source: Management and Information Systems Division, Government of Seychelles.

Expectation of Life (years at birth, 1981–85): Males 65.26; Females 74.05. Source: UN, *Demographic Yearbook*.

Economically Active Population: 1987 census (persons aged 12 years and over): Employed 24,293; Unemployed 4,442; Total labour force 28,735 (Source: UN, *Demographic Yearbook*). June 1989 (persons aged 15 years and over): Total labour force 29,494 (males 16,964, females 12,530).

Employment (1998): Agriculture, hunting, forestry and fishing 1,698; Manufacturing and construction 7,003; Restaurants and hotels 3,791; Transport, distribution and communications 5,805; Other services 11,389; Total 29,686. Figures exclude self-employed persons, unpaid family workers and employees in private domestic services. Source: Management and Information Systems Division, Government of Seychelles.

AGRICULTURE, ETC.

Principal Crops (metric tons, 1997): Coconuts 4,000*; Vegetables 2,000*; Bananas 2,000*; Tea (green leaf) 270†; Cinnamon bark (exports) 220†. (*FAO estimate. †Provisional figure.) Source: mainly FAO, *Production Yearbook*.

Livestock (FAO estimates, '000 head, year ending September 1998): Cattle 1; Pigs 18; Goats 5. Source: FAO, *Production Yearbook*.

Livestock Products (FAO estimates, '000 metric tons, 1998): Pig meat 1; Poultry meat 1; Hen eggs 3. Source: FAO, *Production Yearbook*.

Fishing (metric tons, live weight): Total catch 3,982 in 1995; 4,645 in 1996; 5,344 in 1997. Source: FAO, *Yearbook of Fishery Statistics*.

MINING AND INDUSTRY

Mining (1990): Guano 6,000 metric tons (exports). Source: UN Economic Commission for Africa, *African Statistical Yearbook*.

Industrial Production (1997): Tinned fish 40,600 metric tons; Beer 64,800 hectolitres; Soft drinks 82,900 hectolitres; Cigarettes 70 million; Electric energy 148 million kWh (provisional). Source: IMF, *Seychelles: Statistical Annex* (September 1998).

Electric Energy (1998): 159 million kWh. Source: Management and Information Systems Division, Government of Seychelles.

FINANCE

Currency and Exchange Rates: 100 cents = 1 Seychelles rupee (SR). *Sterling, Dollar and Euro Equivalents* (28 April 2000): £1 sterling = 8.834 rupees; US $1 = 5.634 rupees; €1 = 5.118 rupees; 100 Seychelles rupees = £11.32 = $17.75 = €19.54. *Average Exchange Rate* (Seychelles rupees per US $): 5.0263 in 1997; 5.2622 in 1998; 5.3426 in 1999. Note: In November 1979 the value of the Seychelles rupee was linked to the IMF's special drawing right (SDR). In March 1981 the mid-point exchange rate was set at SDR 1 = 7.2345 rupees. This remained in effect until February 1997, when the fixed link with the SDR was ended.

Budget (SR million, 1998): *Revenue:* Taxation 966.2 (Taxes on income, etc. 164.9, Social security contributions 119.9, Domestic taxes on goods and services 92.2, Import duties 575.0); Other current revenue 413.4 (Entrepreneurial and property income 202.1, Administrative fees and charges, non-industrial and incidental sales 162.4); Capital revenue 41.2; Total 1,420.8, excl. grants received (24.8). *Expenditure:* General public services 272.0; Defence 55.5; Public order and safety 68.1; Education 164.9; Health 141.3; Social security and welfare 267.2; Housing and community amenities 6.2; Recreational, cultural and religious affairs and services 18.3; Economic affairs and services 116.7 (Agriculture, forestry, fishing and hunting 29.7, Transport and communications 34.6); Other purposes 814.4 (Interest payments 288.9); Total 1,924.6 (Current 1,509.9, Capital 414.7), excl. lending minus repayments (−517.6). Note: Figures represent the consolidated accounts of the central Government, covering the operations of the Recurrent and Capital Budgets and of the Social Security Fund. Source: IMF, *Government Finance Statistics Yearbook*.

International Reserves (US $ million at 31 December 1999): IMF special drawing rights 0.04; Foreign exchange 30.31; Total 30.35. Source: IMF, *International Financial Statistics*.

Money Supply (SR million at 31 December 1999): Currency outside banks 248.0; Demand deposits at commercial banks 823.3; Total money (incl. others) 1,078.5. Source: IMF, *International Financial Statistics*.

Cost of Living (Consumer Price Index; base: 1995 = 100): 99.5 in 1997; 102.1 in 1998; 108.6 in 1999. Source: IMF, *International Financial Statistics*.

Expenditure on the Gross Domestic Product (SR million at current prices, 1998): Government final consumption expenditure 847.0; Private final consumption expenditure 1,603.9; Increase in stocks 56.0; Gross fixed capital formation 1,100.0; *Total domestic expenditure* 3,607.0; Exports of goods and services 2,045.5; *Less* Imports of goods and services 2,525.8; *GDP in purchasers' values* 3,126.7. Source: IMF, *International Financial Statistics*.

Gross Domestic Product by Economic Activity (SR million at current prices, 1997): Agriculture, hunting, forestry and fishing 109.8; Mining and manufacturing 355.7; Electricity, gas and water 57.6; Construction 218.5; Restaurants and hotels 248.0; Transport, distribution and communications 823.8; Finance, insurance, real estate and business services 286.0; Government services 371.0; Other services 65.1; *Sub-total* 2,535.5; Import duties 309.7; *Less* Imputed bank service charge 137.8; *GDP in purchasers' values* 2,707.4. Source: IMF, *Seychelles: Statistical Annex* (September 1998).

Balance of Payments (US $ million, 1997): Exports of goods f.o.b. 115.21, Imports of goods f.o.b. −302.71, *Trade balance* −187.51; Exports of services 241.22, Imports of services −119.34, *Balance on goods and services* −65.62; Other income received 6.31, Other income paid −17.96, *Balance on goods, services and income* −77.28; Current transfers received 27.13, Current transfers paid −13.09, *Current balance* −63.24; Direct investment abroad −9.95, Direct investment from abroad 54.41, Portfolio investment assets 0.08, Portfolio investment liabilities −0.04, Other investment assets −16.83, Other investment liabilities 21.89, Net errors and omissions 8.44, *Overall balance* −5.23. Source: IMF, *International Financial Statistics*.

EXTERNAL TRADE

Principal Commodities (distribution by SITC, US $ '000, 1996): *Imports c.i.f.*: Food and live animals 58,157 (Dairy products and birds' eggs 7,337, Fish and fish preparations 18,829, Cereals and cereal preparations 12,259, Vegetables and fruit 9,477); Mineral fuels, lubricants, etc. 11,395 (Refined petroleum products 10,318); Chemicals and related products 16,178; Basic manufactures 50,608 (Non-metallic mineral manufactures 8,223, Metal containers for storage and transport 7,367); Machinery and transport equipment 166,141 (Power-generating machinery and equipment 10,269, General industrial machinery, equipment and parts 11,385, Telecommunications and sound equipment 14,097, Other electrical machinery, apparatus, etc. 10,733, Road vehicles and parts 13,482, Aircraft, associated equipment and parts 93,330); Miscellaneous manufactured articles 27,418; Total (incl. others) 346,723. *Exports f.o.b.*: Food and live animals 40,783 (Fish, crustaceans and molluscs 39,761); Mineral fuels, lubricants, etc. 30,469 (Refined petroleum products 30,445); Machinery and transport equipment 64,309 (Electrical machinery, apparatus, etc. 11,210, Aircraft, associated

equipment and parts 50,872); Total (incl. others) 139,354. Source: UN, *International Trade Statistics Yearbook*.

Principal Trading Partners (US $ '000, 1996): *Imports c.i.f.*: France 26,879; Germany 7,841; India 9,063; Italy 13,943; Japan 8,228; Singapore 35,209; Southern African Customs Union* 39,366; United Kingdom 42,467; USA 100,363; Yemen 9,287; Total (incl. others) 346,723. *Exports f.o.b.*: France 10,804; Germany 7,856; Italy 6,631; Singapore 12,768; United Kingdom 12,834; USA 52,039; Yemen 29,427; Total (incl. others) 139,354. * Comprising Botswana, Lesotho, Namibia, South Africa, Swaziland. Source: UN, *International Trade Statistics Yearbook*.

TRANSPORT

Road Traffic (estimates, motor vehicles in use, 1996): Passenger cars 7,120; Lorries and vans 1,980. Source: International Road Federation, *World Road Statistics*.

Shipping: *Merchant Fleet* (registered at 31 December 1998): Vessels 16; Total displacement 17,699 grt (Source: Lloyd's Register of Shipping, *World Fleet Statistics*); *Sea-borne Freight Traffic* (1998): Freight ('000 metric tons): Loaded 47; Unloaded 636 (Source: Management and Information Systems Division, Government of Seychelles).

Civil Aviation (traffic on scheduled services, 1996): Kilometres flown 8 million; Passengers carried 373,000; Passenger-km 784 million; Total ton-km 94 million. Source: UN, *Statistical Yearbook*.

TOURISM

Foreign Tourist Arrivals: 130,955 in 1996; 130,070 in 1997; 128,258 in 1998.

Arrivals by Country of Residence (1998): France 25,229; Germany 18,992; Italy 20,773; Mauritius 2,730; Réunion 2,235; South Africa 4,457; Switzerland 5,254; USSR (former) 2,573; United Kingdom 15,943; USA 5,050; Total (incl. others) 128,258.

Tourism Receipts (US $ million): 97 in 1995; 108 in 1996; 122 in 1997.

Source: World Tourism Organization, *Yearbook of Tourism Statistics*.

COMMUNICATIONS MEDIA

Radio Receivers (1997): 42,000 in use. Source: UNESCO, *Statistical Yearbook*.

Television Receivers (1997): 11,000 in use. Source: UNESCO, *Statistical Yearbook*.

Telephones (1999): 19,635 main lines in use. Source: Management and Information Systems Division, Government of Seychelles.

Telefax Stations (1999): 581 in use. Source: Management and Information Systems Division, Government of Seychelles.

Mobile Cellular Telephones (1999): 16,316 subscribers. Source: Management and Information Systems Division, Government of Seychelles.

Book Production (1980): 33 titles (2 books, 31 pamphlets).

Daily Newspapers (1996): 1 (average circulation 3,000 copies). Source: UNESCO, *Statistical Yearbook*.

Non-daily Newspapers (1996): 3 (average circulation 7,000 copies). Source: UNESCO, *Statistical Yearbook*.

EDUCATION

Pre-primary (1996): 35 schools; 180 teachers; 3,262 pupils.

Primary (1996): 26 schools; 577 teachers; 9,886 pupils.

Secondary

General (1996): 598 teachers; 8,151 pupils.

Teacher-training (1996): 27 teachers; 237 pupils.

Vocational (1996): 64 teachers; 711 pupils.

Source: UNESCO, *Statistical Yearbook*.

Directory

The Constitution

The independence Constitution of 1976 was suspended after the coup in June 1977 but reintroduced in July with substantial modifications. A successor Constitution, which entered into force in March 1979 was superseded by a new Constitution, approved by national referendum on 18 June 1993.

The President is elected by popular vote simultaneously with elections for the National Assembly. The President fulfils the functions of Head of State and Commander-in-Chief of the armed forces and may hold office for a maximum period of three consecutive five-year terms. The Assembly, elected for a term of five years, consists of 34 seats, of which 25 are filled by direct election and nine are allocated on a proportional basis. Constitutional amendments, introduced in July 1996, provided for an Assembly of 25 directly elected seats and a maximum of 10 proportionally allocated seats. There is provision for an appointed Vice-President. The Council of Ministers is appointed by the President and acts in an advisory capacity to him. The President also appoints the holders of certain public offices and the judiciary.

The Government

HEAD OF STATE

President: FRANCE ALBERT RENÉ (assumed power 5 June 1977; elected President 26 June 1979, re-elected 18 June 1984, 12 June 1989, 23 July 1993 and 22 March 1998).

Vice-President: JAMES MICHEL.

COUNCIL OF MINISTERS
(August 2000)

President and Minister of Internal Affairs, Defence and Legal Affairs: FRANCE ALBERT RENÉ.

Vice-President and Minister of Finance and Transport: JAMES MICHEL.

Minister of Foreign Affairs, Planning and the Environment: JÉRÉMIE BONNELAME.

Minister of Industry and International Trade: PATRICK PILLAY.

Minister of Local Government and Sports: SYLVETTE FRICHOT.

Minister of Health: JAQUELINE DUGASSE.

Minister of Housing and Land Use: JOSEPH BELMONT.

Minister of Tourism and Civil Aviation: SIMONE DE COMARMOND.

Minister of Social Affairs and Manpower Development: WILLIAM HERMINIE.

Minister of Culture and Information: RONNY JUMEAU.

Minister of Education: DANNY FAURE.

Minister of Agriculture and Marine Resources: ERNESTA DOLOR.

Minister of Public Administration: NOELLIE ALEXANDER.

MINISTRIES

Office of the President: State House, Victoria; tel. 224391; fax 224200.

Ministry of Agriculture and Marine Resources: Independence House, POB 166, Victoria; tel. 224030; fax 225245.

Ministry of Education: POB 48, Mont Fleuri; tel. 224777; fax 224859; e-mail edups@seychelles.net.

Ministry of Finance and Information: Central Bank Bldg, POB 313, Victoria; tel. 225252; fax 225265.

Ministry of Foreign Affairs: POB 656, Mont Fleuri; tel. 224688; fax 224845; e-mail mfapesey@seychelles.net.

Ministry of Health: POB 52, Victoria; tel. 388000; fax 224792; e-mail mohprs@seychelles.net.

Ministry of Housing and Land Use: Independence House, Victoria; tel. 224030; fax 225182; e-mail mcd@seychelles.net.

Ministry of Industry and International Trade: International Conference Centre, POB 648, Victoria; tel. 225060; fax 225086; e-mail minind@seychelles.net.

Ministry of Local Government and Sports: Oceangate House, Victoria; tel. 225477; fax 225262.

Ministry of Public Administration: National House, POB 56, Victoria; tel. 383000; fax 224936; e-mail psam@seychelles.net.

Ministry of Social Affairs and Manpower Development: Unity House, POB 190, Victoria; tel. 323991; fax 321880; e-mail psmesa@seychelles.net.

Ministry of Tourism and Civil Aviation: Independence House, Independence Ave, POB 92, Victoria; tel. 225313; fax 224035; e-mail mtca@seychelles.net.

President and Legislature

PRESIDENT

Election, 22 March 1998

Candidate	Votes	% of total
FRANCE ALBERT RENÉ (SPPF) . . .	31,048	66.7
WAVEL RAMKALAWAN (UO)	9,098	19.5
JAMES MANCHAM (DP)	6,427	13.8

NATIONAL ASSEMBLY

Speaker: FRANCIS MACGREGOR.

Election, 22 March 1998

Party	Number of votes	% of votes	Seats*
Seychelles People's Progressive Front	28,610	61.7	30
United Opposition†	12,084	26.1	3
Democratic Party . . .	5,609	12.1	1

* The Assembly consists of 34 seats, of which 25 were filled by direct election and nine by allocation on a proportional basis.

† Name changed to Seychelles National Party in July 1998.

Political Organizations

Democratic Party (DP): POB 169, Mont Fleuri; tel. 224916; fax 224302; f. 1992; successor to the Seychelles Democratic Party (governing party 1970–77); Leader JAMES MANCHAM; Sec.-Gen. DANIEL BELLE.

Mouvement Seychellois pour la Démocratie: Mont Fleuri; tel. 224322; fax 224460; f. 1992; Leader JACQUES HODOUL.

Seychelles National Party (SNP): Arpent Vert, Mont Fleuri, POB 81, Victoria; tel. and fax 224124; e-mail snp2003@hotmail.com; f. 1995 as the United Opposition, comprising the fmr mem. parties of a coalition formed to contest the 1993 elections; adopted present name in 1998; Leader Rev. WAVEL RAMKALAWAN; Sec. ROGER MANCIENNE.

Seychelles People's Progressive Front (SPPF): POB 91, Victoria; tel. 224455; fax 225351; fmrly the Seychelles People's United Party (f. 1964), which assumed power in 1977; renamed in 1978; sole legal party 1978–91; Pres. FRANCE ALBERT RENÉ; Sec.-Gen. JAMES MICHEL.

Diplomatic Representation

EMBASSIES AND HIGH COMMISSIONS IN SEYCHELLES

China, People's Republic: POB 680, St Louis; tel. 266808; fax 266866; Ambassador: HOU GUIXIN.

France: Immeuble Arpent Vert, POB 478, Victoria; tel. 224523; fax 225248; Ambassador: MARCEL SURBIGUET.

India: Le Chantier, POB 488, Victoria; tel. 224489; fax 224810; e-mail hicomind@seychelles.net; internet www.seychelles.net/hicomind; High Commissioner: R. O. WALLANG.

Libya: Victoria.

Russia: Le Niol, POB 632, Victoria; tel. 266590; fax 266653; Ambassador: GENNADII I. FEDOSOV.

South Africa: British-American Insurance Bldg, 4th Floor, Pope Hennessy St, POB 908, Victoria; tel. 226925; fax 226936.

United Kingdom: Oliaji Trade Centre, POB 161, Victoria; tel. 225225; fax 225127; e-mail bhcsey@seychelles.net; High Commissioner: JOHN W. YAPP.

Judicial System

The legal system is derived from English Common Law and the French Code Napoléon. There are three Courts, the Court of Appeal, the Supreme Court and the Magistrates' Courts. The Court of Appeal hears appeals from the Supreme Court in both civil and criminal cases. The Supreme Court is also a Court of Appeal from the Magistrates' Courts as well as having jursidiction at first instance. The Constitutional Court, a division of the Supreme Court, determines matters of a constitutional nature, and considers cases bearing on civil liberties. There is also an industrial court and a rent tribunal.

Chief Justice: VIVEKANAND ALLEEAR.

President of the Court of Appeal: EMMANUEL AYOOLA.

Justices of Appeal: ANNEL SILUNGWE, A. PILLAY, G. P. S. DE SILVA, K. P. MATADEEN.

Puisne Judges: RANJAN PERERA, D. KARUNAKARAN, N. JUDDOO.

Attorney-General: ANTHONY F. FERNANDO.

Religion

Almost all of the inhabitants are Christians, of whom more than 90% are Roman Catholics and about 8% Anglicans.

CHRISTIANITY

The Anglican Communion

The Church of the Province of the Indian Ocean comprises six dioceses: four in Madagascar, one in Mauritius and one in Seychelles. The Archbishop of the Province is the Bishop of Antananarivo, Madagascar.

Bishop of Seychelles: Rt Rev. FRENCH CHANG-HIM, POB 44, Victoria; tel. 224242; fax 224296; e-mail angdio@seychelles.net.

The Roman Catholic Church

Seychelles comprises a single diocese, directly responsible to the Holy See. At 31 December 1998 there were an estimated 70,380 adherents in the country, representing more than 90% of the total population.

Bishop of Port Victoria: Rt Rev. XAVIER BARONNET, Bishop's House, Olivier Maradan St, POB 43, Victoria; tel. 322152; fax 324045.

The Press

L'Echo des Iles: POB 138, Victoria; tel. 322620; monthly; French, Creole and English; Roman Catholic; Editor P. SYMPHORIEN; circ. 2,800.

The People: Maison du Peuple, Revolution Ave, Victoria; tel. 224455; owned by the SPPF; monthly; Creole, French and English; circ. 1,000.

Popsport: Premier Bldgs, POB 485, Victoria; tel. 323158.

Regar: Arpent Vert, Victoria; tel. 224507; fax 224987; opposition political weekly.

Seychelles Nation: Information and Telecommunications Division, POB 321, Victoria; tel. 324161; fax 321006; govt-owned; Mon.–Sat.; English, French and Creole; Chief Editor RENÉ MORRELL; circ. 3,500.

Seychelles Review: POB 29, Victoria; tel. 323700; monthly.

Seychellois: POB 32, Victoria; f. 1928; publ. by Seychelles Farmers Asscn; quarterly; circ. 1,800.

NEWS AGENCY

Seychelles Agence de Presse (SAP): Victoria Rd, POB 321, Victoria; tel. 224161; fax 226006.

Broadcasting and Communications

TELECOMMUNICATIONS

Cable and Wireless (Seychelles) Ltd: Mercury House, Francis Rachel St, POB 4, Victoria; tel. 284000; fax 322777; e-mail cws@seychelles.net; internet www.cws.seychelles.net.

Seychelles Telecom: Victoria; 80% owned by private investors, 10% by Govt of Seychelles; provides fixed-line and satellite telephone and internet services.

BROADCASTING

Radio

Seychelles Broadcasting Corpn (SBC): Hermitage, POB 321, Victoria; tel. 224161; fax 225641; e-mail sbcadmin@seychelles.net; f. 1983, reorg. as independent corpn in 1992; programmes in Creole, English and French; Man. Dir IBRAHIM AFIF.

FEBA Radio (Far East Broadcasting Association): POB 234, Mahé; tel. 282000; fax 242146; Christian programmes; Dir HUGH BARTON.

SBC Radio: Union Vale, POB 321, Victoria; tel. 224161; fax 324015; e-mail sbcadmin@seychelles.net; f. 1941; programmes in Creole, English and French; Programme Man. MARGUERITE HERMITTE.

Television

Seychelles Broadcasting Corpn (SBC): (see Radio).

SBC TV: Hermitage, POB 321, Mahé; tel. 224161; fax 225641; e-mail sbcadmin@seychelles.net; f. 1983; programmes in Creole, English and French; Head of Production RICHARD RAMASWAMY.

Finance

(cap. = capital; res = reserves; dep. = deposits; m. = million; brs = branches; amounts in Seychelles rupees)

BANKING

Central Bank

Central Bank of Seychelles (CBS): Independence Ave, POB 701, Victoria; tel. 225200; fax 224958; e-mail cbs@seychelles.net; f. 1984; bank of issue; cap. and res 11m., dep. 739.1m. (Dec. 1997); Chair. NORMAN WEBER; Gen. Man. FRANCIS CHANG-LENG.

National Banks

Development Bank of Seychelles: Independence Ave, POB 217, Victoria; tel. 224471; fax 224274; e-mail dbs.md@seychelles.net; f. 1978; 55.5% state-owned; cap. and res 82.1m., dep. 7.6m. (Dec. 1997); Chair. ANTONIO LUCAS; Man. Dir R. TOUSSAINT.

Seychelles International Mercantile Banking Corporation Ltd (Nouvobanq): Victoria House, State House Ave, POB 241, Victoria; tel. 225011; fax 224670; e-mail simbc@seychelles.net; f. 1991; 78% state-owned, 22% by Standard Chartered Bank (UK); cap. and res 103m., dep. 850m. (1999); Chair. CONRAD BENOITON; Pres. AHMAD SAEED; 1 br.

Seychelles Savings Bank Ltd: Kingsgate House, POB 531, Victoria; tel. 225251; fax 224713; f. 1902; state-owned; term deposits, savings and current accounts; cap. and res 7.8m. (Dec. 1992); Man. Dir ROGER TOUSSAINT; 4 brs.

Foreign Banks

Bank of Baroda (India): Srinivas Complex, Albert St, POB 124, Victoria; tel. 323038; fax 324057; f. 1978; Man. K. N. SUVARNA.

Banque Française Commerciale Océan Indien–BFCOI (France): Albert St, Victoria; tel. 323096; fax 322676; f. 1976; Man. HENRI ALLAIN D'OFFAY; 3 brs.

Barclays Bank PLC (United Kingdom): Independence Ave, POB 167, Victoria; tel. 224101; fax 224678; f. 1959; Seychelles Dir M. P. LANDON; 3 brs and 4 agencies.

Habib Bank Ltd (Pakistan): Frances Rachel St, POB 702, Victoria; tel. 224371; fax 225614; f. 1976; Man. JAVED IQBAL SHEIKH.

INSURANCE

H. Savy Insurance Co Ltd: Maison de la Rosière, 2nd Floor, Victoria; tel. 322272; fax 321666; all classes.

State Assurance Corporation of Seychelles (SACOS): Pirate's Arms Bldg, POB 636, Victoria; tel. 225000; fax 224495; f. 1980; state-owned; all classes of insurance; Exec. Chair. ANTONIO LUCAS.

STOCK EXCHANGE

Proposals for the establishment of a stock exchange in Victoria were pending in 2000.

Trade and Industry

GOVERNMENT AGENCIES

Seychelles Fishing Authority: POB 449, Fishing Port, Victoria; tel. 224597; fax 224508; e-mail sfaseze@seychelles.net; Man. Dir RIAZ AUMEERUDY.

Seychelles Marketing Board (SMB): Latanier Rd, POB 634, Victoria; tel. 224444; fax 224735; f. 1984; state trading org. for food production and processing, fisheries development and toiletries; transfer to private sector of agro-industries subsidiaries announced in 1992; Chair. FRANCE ALBERT RENÉ; CEO MUKESH VALABHJI.

DEVELOPMENT ORGANIZATIONS

Seychelles Agricultural Development Co Ltd (SADECO): POB 172, Victoria; tel. 375888; f. 1980; Gen. Man. LESLIE PRÉA (acting).

Seychelles Industrial Development Corporation (SIDEC): POB 537, Victoria; tel. 323151; fax 324121; promotes industrial development and manages leased industrial sites; CEO MAXWELL JULIE.

Seychelles International Business Authority (SIBA): POB 991, Victoria; tel. 380800; fax 380888; e-mail siba@seychelles.net; internet www.siba.net; f. 1995 to supervise registration of companies, transhipment and 'offshore' financial services in an international free trade zone covering an area of 23 ha near Mahé International Airport; Man. Dir CONRAD BENOITON.

CHAMBER OF COMMERCE

Seychelles Chamber of Commerce and Industry: Ebrahim Bldg, 2nd Floor, POB 1399, Victoria; tel. 323812; fax 321422; e-mail scci@seychelles.net; Chair. BASIL SOUNDY; Sec.-Gen. MONICA CHETTY.

EMPLOYERS' ORGANIZATION

Federation of Employers' Associations of Seychelles: POB 214, Victoria; tel. 224710; Chair. BASIL SOUNDY.

UTILITIES
Electricity

Public Utilities Corporation (Electricity Division): Unity House, POB 34, Victoria; tel. 322444; fax 321020.

Water

Public Utilities Corporation (Water and Sewerage Division): Unity House, POB 34, Victoria; tel. 322444; fax 325612.

MAJOR COMPANIES

Amalgamated Tobacco Co (Seychelles) Ltd: POB 679, Victoria; tel. 373118; fax 373322; Man. Dir R. LATIMER; Gen. Man. J. HIPWAYE.

Indian Ocean Tuna Co: POB 676, Victoria; tel. 282500; fax 224628; e-mail r.weber@heinz.com.sc; fmrly Conserveries de l'Océan Indien; reorg. 1995; H. J. Heinz owns 60% and Seychelles Govt 40%; tuna-processing; largest private-sector employer in Seychelles, with c. 2,000 employees; Man. Dir RADLEY WEBER.

Seychelles Breweries: Victoria; sole producer of beer and soft drinks; Chair. DAVID HAMPSHIRE.

Seychelles National Oil Co: Maison du Peuple, POB 230, Victoria; tel. 225182; fax 225177; e-mail snoc@seychelles.net; f. 1984; Man. Dir EDDIE BELLE.

Seychelles Petroleum Co Ltd: POB 222, Victoria; tel. 224240; fax 224456; f. 1985; distributing fuel and lubricants; state-owned; Chair. NORMAN WEBER; Exec. Dir GUY ADAM.

Seychelles Timber Co (SEYTIM): Grand Anse, Mahé; tel. 278343; logging, timber sales, joinery and furniture; operates sawmill at Grande Anse.

United Concrete Products (Seychelles) Ltd (UCPS): POB 382, Victoria; tel. 373100; fax 373142; manufactures concrete products; Exec. Dir J. ALBERT; Gen. Man. S. PAYET.

TRADE UNION

Seychelles Federation of Workers' Unions: Maison du Peuple, Latanier Rd, POB 154, Victoria; tel. 224455; fax 225351; f. 1978 to amalgamate all existing trade unions; affiliated to the Seychelles People's Progressive Front; 25,200 mems; Pres. OLIVIER CHARLES; Gen. Sec. BERNARD ADONIS.

Transport
RAILWAYS

There are no railways in Seychelles.

ROADS

In 1998 there were 397 km of roads, of which 343 km were tarmac roads. Most surfaced roads are on Mahé and Praslin.

SHIPPING

Privately-owned ferry services connect Victoria, on Mahé, with the islands of Praslin and La Digue. At 31 December 1998 Seychelles' merchant fleet numbered 16 vessels, totalling 17,699 grt.

Port and Marine Services Division, Ministry of Environment and Transport: POB 47, Mahé Quay, Victoria; tel. 224701; fax 224004; e-mail ports@seychelles.net; Dir-Gen. (Port of Victoria) SAM ANDRADE.

Allied Agencies Ltd: POB 345, Victoria; tel. 224441; fax 224226; shipping agents.

Aquarius Shipping Agency Ltd: POB 865, Victoria; tel. 225050; fax 225043.

Hunt, Deltel and Co Ltd: Victoria House, POB 14, Victoria; tel. 380300; fax 225367; e-mail hundel@seychelles.net.

Mahé Shipping Co Ltd: Maritime House, POB 336, Victoria; tel. 380500; fax 380538; e-mail maheship@seychelles.net; shipping agents; Chair. Capt. G. C. C. ADAM.

Harry Savy & Co: POB 20, Victoria; tel. 322120; fax 321421; shipping agents.

Seychelles Shipping Line Ltd: POB 977, Providence, Victoria; tel. 373655; fax 373185; e-mail gondwana@seychelles.net; f. 1994; operates freight services between Seychelles and Durban, South Africa; Chair. SELWYN GENDRON; Man. Dir HASSAN OMAR.

Union Trading Co Ltd: POB 475, Victoria; tel. 322708.

CIVIL AVIATION

The international airport is located at Pointe Larue, 10 km from Victoria. There are airstrips on several outlying islands.

Air Seychelles: Victoria House, POB 386, Victoria; tel. 381000; fax 224305; e-mail airseymd@seychelles.net; f. 1979; operates scheduled internal flights from Mahé to Praslin; also charter services to Bird, Desroches and Denis Islands and to outlying islands of the Amirantes group; international services to Europe, Far East, East and South Africa; Chair. NORMAN WEBER; CEO Capt. DAVID SAVY.

Tourism

Seychelles enjoys an equable climate, and is renowned for its fine beaches and attractive scenery. There are more than 500 varieties of flora and many rare species of birds. Most tourist activity is concentrated on the islands of Mahé, Praslin and La Digue, although the potential for ecological tourism of the outlying islands received increased attention in the late 1990s. It is government policy that the development of tourism should not blight the environment, and strict laws govern the location and construction of hotels. In 1998 the government indicated that up to 200,000 visitors (although not more than 4,000 at any one time) could be accommodated annually without detriment to environmental quality. Receipts from tourism totalled an estimated SR 612m. in 1997, when there were 4,600 hotel beds and 130,070 tourist and business arrivals; most visitors (78.6% in 1997) are from Europe. Tourist arrivals in 1998 totalled 128,258.

Compagnie Seychelloise de Promotion Hotelière Ltd: POB 683, Victoria; tel. 224694; fax 225291; e-mail cosproh@seychelles.net; promotes govt-owned hotels.

Seychelles Tourism Marketing Authority: POB 1262, Victoria; tel. 620000; fax 620620; e-mail stma@seychelles.net; Chair. FRANCIS SAVY; Dir-Gen. ALAIN VOLCERE.

Defence

In August 1999 the army numbered 400 men, including a coastguard of 200. Paramilitary forces comprised a 250-strong national guard.

Defence Expenditure: Budgeted at SR 56m. in 1999.

Commander-in-Chief of Seychelles Armed Forces: Col LEOPOLD PAYET.

Education

Education is free and compulsory for children between six and 16 years of age. A programme of educational reform, based on the British comprehensive schools system was introduced in 1980. The language of instruction in primary schools is English. The duration of primary education is six years, while that of general secondary education is five years (of which the first four years are compulsory), beginning at 12 years of age. Pre-primary and special education facilities are also available. About 90% of secondary school students undergo one year of voluntary residential National Youth Training Service, whose abolition was pending in the near future. Seychelles Polytechnic had 1,847 students in 1999. A number of students study abroad, principally in the United Kingdom. In 1992 the average rate of adult illiteracy was officially estimated at 12%, and it is intended by the government to eradicate illiteracy by 2020. Government expenditure on education in 1998 was SR 164.9m., or about 8.6% of total expenditure.

Bibliography

Barclays Bank International. *Seychelles: Economic Survey*. London, William Lea, 1972.

Benedict, B. *People of the Seychelles*. London, HMSO, 1966.

Benedict, M., and Benedict, B. *Men, Women and Money in Seychelles*. Berkeley, University of California Press, 1982.

Bennett, G., and Bennett, P.R. *Seychelles* (World Bibliographical Series). Santa Barbara, ABC-Clio, 1993.

Bradley, J. T. *History of Seychelles*. Victoria, Clarion Press, 1940.

Central Bank of Seychelles. *Quarterly Review*. Victoria, Central Bank of Seychelles.

Cohen, R. (Ed.) *African Islands and Enclaves*. London, Sage Publications, 1983.

Doyle, S., Ewing, D., Kelly, R.C., Youngblood, D. *Seychelles Country Review 2000*. Houston, CountryWatch.com, 1999.

Franda, M. *Quiet Turbulence in the Seychelles: Tourism and Development*. Hanover, NH, American Field Staff Reports, Asia Series No. 10, 1979.

The Seychelles. Boulder, CO, Westview Press, 1981.

Gabby, R., and Ghosh, R. N. *Seychelles Marketing Board: Economic Development in a Small Island Economy*. Singapore, Academic Press International, 1992.

International Monetary Fund. *Seychelles—Recent Economic Developments*. Washington, DC, IMF, 1996.

Lee, C. *Seychelles: Political Castaways*. London, Hamish Hamilton, 1976.

Leymarie, P. *Océan indien, nouveau coeur du monde*. Paris, Editions Karthala, 1983.

Lionnet, G. *The Seychelles*. Newton Abbot, David and Charles, 1972.

Mancham, Sir J. R. *Paradise Raped: Life, Love and Power in the Seychelles*. London, Methuen, 1983.

Island Splendour. London, Methuen, 1984.

Maubouche, R., and Hadjitarkhani, N. *Seychelles Economic Memorandum*. Washington, DC, World Bank, 1980.

Scarr, D. *Seychelles since 1770: History of a Slave and Post-Slavery Society*. New Jersey, Africa World Pres Inc., 2000.

Skerrett, J., and Skerrett, A. *Seychelles*. London, APA, 1994.

Thomas, A. *Forgotten Eden*. London, Longman, 1968.

Toussaint, A. *History of the Indian Ocean*. London, Routledge and Kegan Paul, 1966.

USA International Business Publications. *Seychelles Country Study Guide* (World Country Study Guide). 2000.

Webb, A. W. T. *Story of Seychelles*. Seychelles, 1964.

World Bank. *Seychelles' Economic Memorandum*. Washington, DC, World Bank, 1980.

SIERRA LEONE

Physical and Social Geography

PETER K. MITCHELL

The Republic of Sierra Leone, which covers an area of 71,740 sq km (27,699 sq miles), rises from the beaches of the south-west to the broad plateaux of the Atlantic/Niger watershed at the north-eastern frontier. Despite the general horizontal aspect of the landscapes, developed over millennia upon largely Pre-Cambrian structures there are a number of abrupt ascents to older uplifted erosion surfaces—most impressively along sections of a major escarpment, 130 km inland, separating a western lowland zone (c. 120 m above sea-level) from the country's more elevated interior half (c. 500 m). Incised valleys, interspersed by minor waterfalls, carry drainage south-westwards; only locally or along a coastal sedimentary strip do rivers flow through open terrain.

A geologically recent submergence of major floodplains, particularly north of Cape St Ann, has brought tide-water into contact with the rocky margins of the ancient shield, impeding up-river navigation. Water-borne trade has found compensation in sheltered deep-water anchorages, notably off Freetown, the principal port and capital, where a line of coastal summits rising to almost 900 m above sea-level facilitates an easy landfall.

Intrusive gabbros form the peninsular range; elsewhere, isolated blocks or hill groups consist of rock-bare granites or the metamorphic roots of long-vanished mountain chains, which provide mineral deposits: iron, chromite, gold, rutile and bauxite. Reserves of kimberlite in the southern high plateaux are approaching exhaustion. The pipes and dikes of kimberlite may provide the basis for future deep mining.

Differences in seasonal and regional incidence of humidity and rainfall are important. Prolonged rains (May to October, with heaviest rains from July to September) are bracketed by showery weather with many squally thunderstorms, such spells beginning earlier in the south-east. Consequently, the growing season is longest here (although total rainfall—over 5,000 mm locally—is greater along the coast) and the 'natural' vegetation is tropical evergreen forest; the cultivation of cash crops such as cocoa, coffee, kola and oil-palm is successful in this area, and the more productive timber areas, though limited, are concentrated here. The savannah-woodlands of the north-east have less rain (1,900–2,500 mm), a shorter period for plant growth and a dry season made harsh by harmattan winds, with

cattle-rearing, groundnuts and tobacco as potential commercial resources. Semi-deciduous forest occupies most intervening areas, but long peasant occupation has created a mosaic of short-term cropland, fallow regrowth plots and occasional tracts of secondary forest.

Permanent rice-lands have been created from mangrove swamp in the north-west, and much encouragement is being given to the improvement of the many small tracts of inland valley swamp throughout the east. Such innovation contrasts with a widespread bush-fallowing technique, giving low yields of rain-fed staples, normally rice, but cassava (especially on degraded sandy soils) and millet in the north. Sierra Leone's agricultural sector is able to provide most of the country's food requirements.

Sierra Leone's third national census, which was held in December 1985, enumerated 3,515,812 inhabitants, representing a population density of 49 inhabitants per sq km. However, there was believed to have been underenumeration, and the census total was subsequently adjusted to 3.7m. At mid-1998, according to UN estimates, Sierra Leone had 4,568,000 inhabitants and a population density of 61.7 inhabitants per sq km.

Traditional *mores* still dominate, in spite of the Westernizing influences of employment in mining, of education and of growing urbanization. A large proportion of the population follows animist beliefs, although there are significant Islamic and Christian communities. Extended family, exogamous kin-groups and the paramount chieftaincies form a social nexus closely mirrored by a hierarchy of hamlet, village and rural centre: 29,000 non-urban settlements including isolated impermanent homesteads. The towns, however, are expanding. Greater Freetown had almost 470,000 inhabitants at the 1985 census, while Koindu, the centre of the Kono diamond fields, had about 82,000 inhabitants; in 1985 there were, in total, 10 towns with more than 10,000 people. Diamond mining has attracted settlers to many villages in the mining areas. At the end of 1999 more than 85% of the population were receiving assistance from the Office of the UN High Commissioner for Refugees.

The official language of the country is English, while Krio (Creole), Mende, Limba and Temne are also widely spoken.

Recent History

CHRISTOPHER CLAPHAM

Revised for this edition by RICHARD SYNGE

In 1896 a British protectorate was proclaimed over the hinterland of the coastal colony of Sierra Leone, which had been under British administration since 1787. In 1951, following the introduction of a constitution, elections were won by the Sierra Leone People's Party (SLPP), led by Dr (later Sir) Milton Margai, who became chief minister in 1953 and prime minister in 1958. On 27 April 1961 Sierra Leone became an independent state within the Commonwealth. The SLPP retained power in elections in 1962. Sir Milton died in 1964 and was succeeded as prime minister by his half-brother, Dr (later Sir) Albert Margai. The main opposition party, the All-People's Congress (APC), led by Dr Siaka Stevens, gained a parliamentary majority at general elections in 1967, but was prevented from taking power by a military coup. Following an army mutiny in April 1968, a civilian

government was restored, with Stevens as prime minister. A period of political instability followed, culminating in an attempted military coup in March 1971, which was suppressed with the aid of troops from neighbouring Guinea. In April a republican constitution was introduced, with Stevens as executive president. The SLPP offered no candidates in the 1973 general elections, and Stevens, as sole candidate, was elected to a further presidential term. In 1978 the APC was constitutionally established as the sole legal party, upon which a number of prominent supporters of the SLPP joined the APC and received ministerial posts. The government encountered increasing opposition in 1981, following a scandal involving government officials and several cabinet ministers in the misappropriation of public funds. Stevens temporarily assumed the additional post of minister of finance in December, following a second financial scandal implicating senior officials. Amid serious outbreaks of violence, a general election took place in May 1982 and a new government was formed, in which the finance ministry was reorganized.

THE MOMOH PRESIDENCY, 1985–92

In April 1985 Stevens announced that he was to leave office upon the expiry of his existing mandate later that year. At a conference of the APC in August, Maj.-Gen. Joseph Saidu Momoh, a cabinet minister and the commander of the armed forces, was nominated as sole candidate for the presidency and for the leadership of the party. In October Momoh received 99% of votes cast in a presidential election, and was inaugurated as president on 28 November. Although retaining his military affiliation, Momoh installed a civilian cabinet, which included several members of the previous administration. Elections to the house of representatives took place in May 1986; 335 candidates (all APC members) contested the 105 elective seats. About half of the incumbent representatives, including four cabinet ministers, were replaced.

Momoh's initial popularity receded in 1986, owing to his administration's failure to revive the deteriorating economy. In March the government announced that it had foiled an attempted coup; more than 60 people were arrested (of whom 18 were later charged). In early April the first vice-president, Francis Minah, was arrested and subsequently charged with treason. In October Minah and 15 others were sentenced to death for plotting to assassinate Momoh and to overthrow the government. Minah and five others were executed in October 1989; the remaining death sentences were commuted to life imprisonment.

In 1987 Momoh initiated measures to combat financial corruption in the public sector. In July the minister of agriculture, natural resources and forestry resigned, after allegations of accountancy irregularities in the distribution of domestic sugar supplies, and was later ordered by Momoh to make financial restitution. In August and September a deputy minister and a number of senior officials in the civil service and the Bank of Sierra Leone were charged with financial malpractice. In November, following a series of strikes by workers in the public sector, which resulted from the government's inability to pay their salaries, Momoh declared a state of emergency in the economy, announced measures to prevent hoarding of currency and essential goods, and intensified the campaign against smuggling. Under the new measures, corruption was redefined as a criminal offence, and people accused of any crime could be tried *in absentia*. Severe penalties were introduced for the publication of 'defamatory' articles in newspapers, and government censorship was imposed. In November a number of ministers were removed in a cabinet reshuffle, which was apparently prompted by accusations of official corruption. At a conference of the APC in January 1989, during which an official code of conduct for political leaders and public servants was adopted, Momoh was re-elected unopposed as secretary-general of the party. In December a new minister of finance took office, following allegations of corruption in the finance ministry.

During early 1990 there was widespread popular support for the restoration of a multi-party system; this was initially rejected by Momoh, although he emphasized that he would continue to encourage broadly-based participation in the one-party state. In mid-August, however, Momoh conceded the necessity of electoral reforms, and announced an extensive review of the constitution. The central committee of the APC approved a number of proposed amendments to the constitution, and in November Momoh appointed a 30-member national constitutional review commission.

In March 1991 the commission submitted a draft constitution, which provided for the restoration of a plural political system. The revised constitution stipulated that the president was to be elected by a majority of votes cast nationally and by at least 25% of the votes cast in more than one-half of the electoral districts. The maximum duration of the president's tenure of office was to be limited to two five-year terms. The president was to appoint the cabinet, which was to include one vice-president, rather than two. Legislative power was to be vested in a bicameral legislature, elected by universal adult suffrage for a term of five years. The government subsequently accepted the majority of the commission's recommendations. The proposed formation of an upper legislative chamber was rejected; instead, the government approved the establishment of a 22-member state advisory council, which was to comprise 12 paramount chiefs (one from each district) and 10 presidential appointees. In early June the government presented the draft constitution to the house of representatives, and announced that the parliamentary term, which was due to end that month, was to be extended for a further year, owing to the disruption caused by the conflict between government forces and Liberian rebels in the south of the country. The general elections, which were scheduled for May, were also to be postponed for a year to allow time for the transition to a plural political system.

In mid-July 1991 the minister of social affairs, rural development and youth, Musa Kabia, resigned, following disputes within the APC over the new constitution. Ten members of the house of representatives, including Kabia, were temporarily suspended from the APC for alleged activities contrary to the interests of the party. In August the house of representatives approved the new constitution, subject to endorsement by a national referendum, which was to be conducted at the end of that month. However, political activity by parties other than the APC remained illegal until the new constitution took effect. (Following the publication of the constitution in March, some 10 opposition movements had emerged.) At the national referendum, which was conducted during 23–30 August, the new constitution was approved by 60% of voters, with 75% of the electorate participating. The new constitution was promulgated in September (although the constitution of 1978 also remained officially in force).

In late September 1991 six newly-created political associations established an alliance, known as the United Front of Political Movements (UNIFOM), and demanded that the government give way to an interim administration. In the same month the government announced that the minister of national development and economic planning, Sheka Kanu, had been dismissed. Shortly afterwards the first vice-president, Abubakar Kamara, and the second vice-president, Salia Jusu-Sheriff, resigned from both the APC and the government. On 23 September Momoh announced the formation of a new 18-member cabinet, which retained only seven members of the previous government. In late September legislation was introduced to provide for the registration of political associations; a number of political parties, including the APC, were subsequently granted legal status. In December Momoh and leaders of the registered political parties agreed to co-operate in the establishment of a multi-party system.

MILITARY GOVERNMENT, 1992–96

On 29 April 1992 members of the armed forces seized a radio station in Freetown and occupied the presidential offices. Their leader, Capt. Valentine Strasser, subsequently declared that the government had been replaced by a five-member military junta. Momoh sought assistance from the Guinean government, which dispatched troops to Freetown, and more than 100 people were killed in the ensuing violence. Momoh fled to Guinea, and Strasser announced the formation of a national provisional ruling council (NPRC). Strasser affirmed the NPRC's commitment to the introduction of a multi-party system, pledged to end the conflict in the country and assured the Economic Community of West African States (ECOWAS) of the continued participation of Sierra Leone in the ECOWAS Monitoring Group (ECOMOG), which had been engaged since August 1990 in peace-keeping operations in Liberia (see below). The NPRC suspended both the constitutions of 1991 and 1978, dissolved the house of representatives, imposed a state of emergency and curfew, and temporarily closed the country's air, sea and land borders.

On 1 May 1992 the NPRC (which comprised 18 military officers and four civilians) was formally convened under Strasser's chairmanship. On 3 May the NPRC appointed a 19-member cabinet, which retained two members of the Momoh administration. All political activity was suspended, and it was subsequently reported that some 55 people, including members of the former cabinet, had been arrested. On 6 May Strasser was sworn in as head of state. Later that month the government established a commission of inquiry to investigate the activities of members of the former regime.

In early July 1992 Strasser reorganized the cabinet; three members of the armed forces were replaced by civilians, and it was decreed that civilian cabinet ministers were not to hold membership of the NPRC. Later in the month, however, Strasser introduced extensive measures that were designed to reduce the role of the armed forces in government administration: the NPRC was officially designated the supreme council of state, and the cabinet was to be replaced by a council of secretaries, headed by a chief secretary of state, which was to be responsible for the management of the government, subject to the authority of the NPRC. The chairman and deputy chairman of the NPRC were no longer to be involved in government administration (although Strasser retained his defence portfolio in the council of secretaries). Each secretary of state was to assume responsibility for a ministry (henceforth known as a department). The three members of the NPRC who had been removed from the cabinet earlier that month were appointed as principal liaison officers, who were each allocated a number of departments in which they were to supervise government administration. (However, the NPRC was henceforth principally concerned with the suppression of the civil conflict.) In the same month the government introduced legislation which imposed severe restrictions on the media and authorized state censorship. John Benjamin, hitherto the secretary of state in the office of the chairman, became chief secretary of state.

In August 1992 Strasser announced the establishment of an advisory council, which, among other functions, was to review the provisions of the 1991 constitution. In early September 1992 Capt. Solomon Musa, the deputy chairman of the NPRC, became the acting head of state during Strasser's absence in the United Kingdom to obtain medical treatment for injuries sustained during counter-insurgency operations in the south-east of the country (see below). In November about 30 people, who were alleged to be supporters of Momoh, were arrested and charged with subversion. In early December Strasser reorganized the council of secretaries, replacing the two remaining members of the Momoh administration. In the same month Musa was appointed chief secretary of state. Later in December, in an apparent attempt to regain public support, the government established a 15-member advisory council, which was to formulate a programme for transition to civilian rule.

In late December 1992 the government announced that it had foiled a coup attempt by a group known as the Anti-Corruption Revolutionary Movement (which included former members of the army and security forces). Among those reported to have been killed by security forces was the alleged instigator of the plot, Sgt Lamin Bangura. Shortly afterwards nine of those accused of involvement in the conspiracy were tried by a military tribunal, and, together with 17 prisoners who had been convicted in November on charges of treason, were summarily executed. In January 1993 the United Kingdom announced the suspension of economic aid to Sierra Leone, in protest at the executions. Later that month, in an apparent attempt to allay further accusations of human rights violations, the military regime released several former members of the Momoh government, who had been detained since May 1992. In mid-January 1993, however, the government imposed further press restrictions.

In February 1993 the commissions of inquiry that had been established in May 1992 published reports containing evidence of corruption on the part of former members of the Momoh administration. In April 1993 Strasser promised that all political prisoners would be released and announced that a programme providing for a return to civilian government by 1996 had been adopted. He also stated that measures were being taken to reduce the powers of the security services. In a government reorganization in July, Musa was replaced as deputy chairman of the NPRC and chief secretary of state by Capt. Julius Maada Bio, ostensibly on the grounds that false allegations against him had proved detrimental to the stability of the administration. Musa (who was widely blamed for the repressive measures undertaken by the government) took refuge in the Nigerian high commission in Freetown, amid widespread speculation regarding his dismissal, and subsequently sought refuge in the United Kingdom. Also in July a number of political prisoners were released. In September the government expropri-

ated the assets of several former politicians, including Momoh, in accordance with the findings of the commissions of inquiry that had investigated their activities. In October a former minister in the Stevens administration, Dr Abbas Bundu, was appointed secretary of state for foreign affairs and international co-operation.

Transitional Arrangements

In late November 1993 Strasser announced a two-year transitional programme, which provided for the installation of a civilian government by January 1996. In December 1993, in accordance with the transitional programme, a five-member interim national electoral commission (INEC), under the chairmanship of Dr James Jonah (the assistant secretary-general of the UN, in charge of political affairs), was established to organize the registration of voters and the demarcation of constituency boundaries, in preparation for the forthcoming local government elections. In the same month the national advisory council submitted several constitutional proposals (which included a number of similar provisions to the 1991 constitution), stipulating that: executive power was to be vested in the president, who was to be required to consult with the cabinet (except in the event of a national emergency), and was to be restricted to a tenure of two four-year terms of office; only Sierra Leonean nationals of more than 40 years of age were to qualify to contest a presidential election (thereby precluding Strasser and the majority of members of the NPRC, on the grounds of age); the president was to be elected by a minimum of 50% of votes cast nationally, and at least by 25% of the votes cast in each of the four provinces; the legislature was to comprise a house of representatives, which was to be elected by universal adult suffrage for a term of five years, and a 30-member upper chamber, the senate, which was to include a number of regional representatives and five presidential nominees.

At the end of December 1993 the government ended the state of emergency that had operated since April 1992 (although additional security measures remained in force). In March 1994 the authorities introduced further legislation regulating the registration of newspapers, which effectively prevented a number of independent publications from renewing their licences. In April 13 senior members of the armed forces were dismissed, following criticism of the government's failure to end the civil conflict (see below), and rumours of complicity between military officers and the rebels. In May 20 former members of the Momoh government were arrested, after failing to pay compensation for funds that they had misappropriated during their service. In early August Strasser reorganized the council of secretaries (which subsequently included nine civilians). In a further reshuffle in September, the three regional secretaries of state were replaced. Later that month the attorney-general and secretary of state for judicial affairs, Franklyn Kargbo, resigned in protest at the death sentence imposed on an elderly military official, who had been convicted by military tribunal on charges of collaborating with the rebels; Kargbo fled into exile, and was subsequently granted political asylum in the United Kingdom.

In October 1994 a draft constitution was submitted to the NPRC. In November, in accordance with the transitional programme, a five-member national commission for civil education was established to inform the public regarding the principles of the new constitution. However, an increase in rebel activity (see below) prevented the organization of district council elections, which had been scheduled to take place later that month, and was expected to impede the further implementation of the transitional programme.

In January 1995 Strasser reorganized the council of secretaries. In March Musa was apparently ordered to retire from the armed forces, after Strasser rejected his proposal for the installation of a transitional civilian government. Later that month the council of secretaries was reorganized to allow principal military officials in the government to assume active functions within the armed forces (following the advance of rebel forces towards Freetown); Lt-Col Akim Gibril became chief secretary of state, replacing Maada Bio, who was appointed chief of the defence staff. In late April, on the third anniversary of the NPRC coup, Strasser announced that the ban on political activity would be lifted and that a national consultative conference was to be convened to discuss the transitional process. He further indicated that elections would take place by the end of the year, with the installation of a civilian president and government in January 1996, in accordance with the provisions of the transitional programme. The ban on political parties was formally rescinded on 21 June. The insurgent Revolutionary United Front (RUF, see below) refused to participate in the political process, however, although about 15 parties were subsequently granted registration. The government subsequently announced that 56 former government officials, including ex-president Momoh, would be banned from holding public office for a period of 10 years, on the grounds of their alleged misuse of public funds while in office. The replacement of the chief of staff of the armed forces and of two ministers (including Bundu) was widely interpreted as indicative of divisions within the NPRC.

The Fall of Strasser

In October 1995, while Strasser was abroad, a coup attempt was thwarted by government forces; seven military officers were subsequently arrested in connection with the incident. In early December it was announced that the presidential and legislative elections were to take place concurrently on 26 February 1996. In January 1996, however, Strasser was deposed by military officers, led by Bio, in a bloodless coup. Bio, who assumed the office of head of state, announced that the coup had been instigated in response to efforts by Strasser to remain in power. (It was reported that Strasser had indicated that he intended to amend restrictions on the age of prospective candidates to enable himself to contest the elections.) Strasser (who had been expelled to Guinea) claimed, however, that the new military administration planned to delay the transition to civilian government. A reconstituted supreme council of state and council of secretaries were formed, and, following a meeting of the new military leadership, and representatives of the political parties and the INEC, it was announced that the elections would proceed as scheduled. The RUF indicated that it was prepared to enter into negotiations with the new government, and declared a temporary cease-fire to allow voter registration to proceed throughout the country.

RETURN OF THE SLPP

On 26 February 1996 presidential and legislative elections, which were contested by 13 political parties and were monitored by international observers, took place as scheduled. However, some 27 people were killed in attacks by armed groups, particularly in Bo and parts of Freetown, which were generally attributed to efforts by the RUF to disrupt the electoral process; voting was consequently extended for a further day. The reconstituted SLPP secured 36.1% of votes cast in the legislative elections, while its presidential candidate, Ahmed Tejan Kabbah, also received most support, with 35.8% of votes. Seven of the political parties, including the National Unity Party (which had supported Bio), demanded that the results be annulled, owing to the disruption of the elections in several regions caused by the civil violence. Since none of the candidates had achieved the requisite majority of 55% of the votes, a second round of the presidential election, which took place on 15 March, was contested by Kabbah and the candidate of the United National People's Party (UNPP), John Karefa-Smart (who had obtained 22.6% of votes cast in the first round): Kabbah was elected president by 59.5% of the votes. Later in March seats in the new 80-member parliament were allocated on a basis of proportional representation, with the SLPP securing 27, the UNPP 17, the People's Democratic Party 12 and the reconstituted APC only five; the 12 provincial districts were represented in the legislature by paramount chiefs. Kabbah was inaugurated on 29 March, when the military government officially relinquished power to the new civilian administration. In April Kabbah appointed a cabinet, which was subsequently approved by parliament. In July the national assembly adopted legislation that formally reinstated the constitution of 1991.

In September 1996 Kabbah ordered the compulsory retirement of some 20 officers, including Strasser and Bio, from the armed forces. Shortly afterwards it was reported that a plot against the government had been discovered by senior military officers. Later that month the government announced that a

team of specialists from Nigeria was to assist the armed forces in the investigation of the planned coup attempt. About 17 members of the armed forces were arrested, of whom nine were subsequently charged with involvement in the conspiracy. In November Kabbah carried out a government reorganization, in which a number of ministries were amalgamated. Following reports of a further plot to overthrow the government in January 1997, Kabbah announced that the Nigerian investigative mission had concluded that former members of the NPRC administration had instigated the coup conspiracy of the previous September.

REIMPOSITION OF MILITARY RULE

On 25 May 1997 dissident members of the armed forces, led by Maj. Johnny Paul Koroma, seized power, deposing Kabbah, who fled to Guinea. Koroma claimed that the coup, which prompted international condemnation, was in response to the government's failure to implement a peace agreement with the RUF, reached in November 1996 (see below). (The coup leaders were believed to have connections with members of the former NPRC, many of whom, it was reported, planned to return to Sierra Leone.) The Nigerian government demanded that the junta relinquish power, and increased its military strength in Freetown. The new authorities imposed a curfew in Freetown, following widespread violent looting by armed factions; most foreign nationals were evacuated. In early June Nigerian forces initiated a naval bombardment of Freetown in an effort to force the new military leaders to resign. However, forces loyal to the coup leaders, assisted by RUF members, succeeded in repelling Nigerian attacks; it was reported that about 62 people were killed in the fighting. Some 300 Nigerian troops were taken hostage, but were subsequently released. Koroma announced the establishment of a 20-member armed forces revolutionary council (AFRC), with himself as chairman and the RUF leader, Foday Sankoh, as vice-chairman (*in absentia*); the AFRC (which was not internationally recognized as the legitimate government) included a further three members of the RUF and several civilians. All political activity, the existing constitution and government bodies were suspended, although Koroma pledged that democratic rule would be restored, following new elections. Nigeria reiterated that it intended to reinstate the ousted government with the support of ECOWAS, and a further two Nigerian warships were dispatched to the region; further clashes between Nigerian troops and supporters of the new military leaders occurred at the international airport at Lungi.

In mid-June 1997 the AFRC announced that it had suppressed a coup attempt, following the arrest of 15 people, including several senior military officers. In the same month it was reported that troops supporting the junta had repulsed an attack by the traditional fighters known as Kamajors (see below), who remained loyal to Kabbah, at the town of Zimmi, 250 km southeast of Freetown. On 17 June Koroma was formally installed as the self-proclaimed head of state. However, despite appeals from Koroma, civilians continued to observe a campaign of civil disobedience, which had been organized by the labour congress in protest at the coup. In the same month members of the disbanded legislature, who had met in defiance of the ban on political activity, proposed a peace agreement, under which a government of national unity representing all political parties and the RUF would be established, and ECOMOG and UN forces would be deployed throughout the country.

By early July 1997 the new military government had become completely isolated by the international community. The Commonwealth ministerial action group which had been established to respond to unlawful activities by member states) suspended Sierra Leone from meetings of the Commonwealth, pending the restoration of constitutional order and the reinstatement of a democratically-elected government. The UN security council also condemned the coup, and expressed support for ECOWAS efforts to resolve the situation. The effective imposition of an ECOWAS embargo against Sierra Leone, enforced through the naval blockade and occupation of Lungi airport by Nigerian troops, resulted in increasing shortages of food, crude petroleum and other essential commodities. Meanwhile, a four-nation committee, comprising representatives of Nigeria, Côte d'Ivoire, Guinea and Ghana, which had been established by ECOWAS to monitor a return to constitutional rule, urged the government to relinquish power during a series of negotiations with an AFRC delegation.

In mid-July 1997, in an apparent effort to consolidate power, Koroma formed a cabinet, known as the council of secretaries, comprising representatives of the RUF and the army, together with a number of civilians. Later that month, following further reports of clashes between Kamajors and government forces in the south of the country, AFRC representatives and the ECOWAS committee, meeting in Abidjan, Côte d'Ivoire, agreed to an immediate cease-fire; negotiations were to continue, with the aim of restoring constitutional order. However, Nigeria subsequently accused the AFRC of violating the cease-fire, while further clashes between the Kamajors and the AFRC forces were reported at Zimmi. Renewed skirmishes between Nigerian and AFRC troops also occurred at Lungi airport, following an attempt by forces loyal to the junta to locate a clandestine radio station, which had allegedly been established by supporters of Kabbah. At the end of July continuing discussions between the ECOWAS committee and AFRC representatives in Abidjan were abandoned, after Koroma insisted that he retain power for a tenure of four years, and refused to restore the constitution and to end the ban on political activity. It was reported that the minister of defence in the AFRC cabinet, who had headed the delegation, had subsequently defected in Abidjan. Later in August former members of the RUF (which had been reconstituted as a government security force, known as the People's Army) clashed with civilians, after suppressing a protest against the coup. At the end of August the ECOWAS members agreed to impose a total embargo on all supplies of petroleum products, armaments and military equipment to the military junta, and they sought the endorsement of the UN in strengthening these sanctions. The UN Security Council subsequently approved the adoption of sanctions against Sierra Leone. The ECOMOG military presence at Lunghi airport was increased, and a base was established at Jui, on the principal road linking Freetown to the rest of the country. ECOMOG enforced the economic blockade on Freetown by launching aerial bombardments against merchant ships in the port. During September there was an escalation of hostilities between the AFRC's forces and ECOMOG, resulting in numerous deaths; thousands of Freetown residents subsequently fled from the capital.

Amid increasing ECOMOG military pressure and mounting popular resistance, the military junta apparently acceded to ECOWAS demands that the AFRC relinquish power by 22 April 1998, as part of an agreement which also provided for the imposition of a ceasefire, and the disarmament and demobilization of combatant forces. However, subsequent major disagreements over the terms of the accord prompted further confrontations between the AFRC and ECOMOG. Despite Koroma's demands that ECOMOG begin to withdraw its forces as a precondition for his adherence to the agreement, ECOMOG's Nigerian forces were strengthened. There was no progress on the disarmament programme, which had been scheduled to begin in December.

RESTORATION OF CIVILIAN GOVERNMENT

International efforts to restore Kabbah to power intensified during January 1998, when the United Kingdom appointed a former ambassador to Angola, John Flynn, to co-operate with the UN and ECOWAS officials to this end. According to subsequent reports in the British media, Kabbah contracted a British military consultancy, Sandline International, to undertake the supply of armaments, and to provide military support and training, both to Sierra Leonean forces loyal to the ousted government and to ECOMOG. Following armed clashes near the ECOMOG base at Jui (16 km outside Freetown) at the end of January, the ECOMOG task force commander, Col Maxwell Khobe, ordered a final offensive against the capital in early February. The presidential mansion was captured after several days of fighting, and full control of Freetown was achieved by mid-February; it was estimated that about 100 people had been killed during the operation. Following the seizure of the capital, ECOMOG ended the military embargo and opened Lunghi airport to commercial traffic. A special task force was established to supervise government activities and to expedite the delivery of humanitarian aid. International donors pledged to provide emergency food and medical supplies, and mine-clearance exper-

tise. The Kamajor forces initially seized Bo and Koindu in mid-February; however, intensive fighting for control of the area ensued, while violence and looting continued in many parts of the country. Some AFRC officers were quickly captured by ECOMOG, while others fled to the northern region; Koroma was reported to have taken refuge in a village in the south-east of the country. Many refugees, including RUF activists, fled into Liberia. Nigerian troops undertook most of the operations to suppress continuing rebel activity, ousting the RUF from Kenema and forcing AFRC troops to surrender in Makeni. ECOMOG only finally gained control of Bo in late February, but fighting continued in the surrounding countryside for some weeks thereafter. On 10 March Kabbah returned to Freetown and was formally inaugurated; he subsequently appointed a cabinet (which included a number of members of his previous administration). Although international donors pledged substantial support, the stability of Kabbah's government was initially dependent on the continued presence of the ECOMOG forces, then numbering 7,000 (principally Nigerians, but also including Ghanaians and Guineans). In mid-April Kabbah appointed Khobe as chief of national security. During April the reinstated government charged a total of 59 people, including the former president, Joseph Momoh, with treason and collaboration with the AFRC.

In May 1998 government and ECOMOG troops continued to launch attacks against rebel forces, which remained in control of Kailahun District and part of Kono District. In that month the British high commissioner, Peter Penfold, was temporarily withdrawn from the country, amid controversy in the United Kingdom over the alleged complicity of the British government in contraventions of the UN arms embargo. (Sierra Leoneans subsequently staged public demonstrations in support of Penfold.) In late July the UN Security Council adopted a resolution establishing a 70-member United Nations Observer Mission in Sierra Leone (UNOMSIL); the force, which had an initial mandate to remain in the country for a six-month period, was to monitor the security situation, and the disarmament of former combatants based in secure regions of the country. In August 16 people were convicted and sentenced to death for their involvement in the May 1997 coup. After appeals for clemency, their sentences were reviewed but in October 24 former members of the armed forces were executed, after having been convicted of collaborating with the ousted junta. At the end of October Sankoh, who had in July been returned from detention in Nigeria, was convicted and sentenced to death for treason and murder, owing to his support for the May 1997 coup, but launched an appeal. In November a further 15 civilians were sentenced to death for treason, and ex-President Momoh received a 10-year prison sentence.

The death sentence imposed on Sankoh prompted an upsurge in attacks by RUF forces, in alliance with former AFRC members, after October 1998. There were increased reports of atrocities being perpetrated against civilians as the rebels began the systematic recruitment and abduction of minors, both to act as combatants and to transport ammunition and goods. Fighting spread rapidly in the eastern diamond district of Kono and in northern areas of the country. ECOMOG launched further air attacks in November. The RUF issued a general threat of retaliation if Sankoh was harmed. Despite a rapid reinforcement of the ECOMOG contingent to 15,000 troops, and the deployment of Kamajors, the rebels seized Koindu in the east and the northern town of Makeni, before advancing into Lunsar and Waterloo, closer to Freetown. Fighting subsequently erupted throughout the capital in early January 1999; the rebels attacked civilians and forced them to flee towards the city centre, thus securing cover for a rapid advance. Over a period of three weeks an estimated 5,000 people were killed in Freetown, including thousands of civilians and hundreds of ECOMOG troops and RUF rebels, while many thousands of city residents were assaulted or multilated. A subsequent investigation by a human rights organization concluded that these widespread abuses were authorized at a high level within the RUF's command structure. The investigation also identified violations of human rights committed by ECOMOG forces, especially with regard to their policy of summary execution of captured rebels.

As the rebels withdrew from the city they set alight buildings, causing widespread destruction. ECOMOG was eventually able to restore a semblance of order to Freetown, but in view of an implied threat of a complete withdrawal by the Nigerian forces, which had lost an estimated 800 men in the fighting, there was a renewed international initiative for negotiations with the RUF (including Sankoh) and the Sierra Leonean government. With mediation by the UN, the OAU, the Commonwealth, the United Kingdom and the USA, the discussions began in Lomé, Togo, following a UN-supervised release of Sankoh in April 1999. In May the Sierra Leonean government and the RUF signed a cease-fire agreement, although violations were subsequently reported. Continuing negotiations on the proposed participation of the RUF in a transitional administration followed. In early July the government and the RUF reached a power-sharing agreement, after the government acceded to rebel demands that Sankoh be appointed vice-president, with responsibility for the mineral resources industry, and the RUF be allocated a further eight cabinet posts. The accord provided for the release of civilians who had been abducted by the rebels, and the disarmament and reintegration into the armed forces of former combatants; the RUF was to be reconstituted as a political organization. However, the UN High Commissioner for Refugees and human rights organizations objected to a general amnesty for perpetrators of human rights violations granted under the provisions of the peace agreement. In early August former supporters of the AFRC junta kidnapped some 34 members of ECOMOG and UNOMSIL (including five British nationals) who had been attempting to mediate the release of several hundred Sierra Leonean civilians (mainly minors), who had been abducted by the rebels. The dissidents issued demands for the extension of the amnesty to supporters of the former junta and the release of Koroma, who, they believed, had been detained by the RUF. Following negotiations between the Sierra Leonean authorities and the rebels, with the assistance of British mediators, the ECOMOG and UNOMSIL hostages were released.

In the months that followed the Lomé agreement (which remained highly controversial on account of its implied amnesty for the RUF leadership) the international response was cautious, and there were prolonged negotiations regarding the most appropriate level of UN support required to uphold the agreement. However, the emphasis on a combination of peace-keeping and disarmament was maintained in discussions under the auspices of the UN. In Freetown the uncertainties surrounding the RUF's commitment to complying with the agreement were reflected in the prolonged delay in the return from Liberia of both Foday Sankoh and Johnny Paul Koroma, whose mutual alliance was by now under severe strain. Eventually arriving in the capital in early October 1999, Sankoh issued a prepared apology for atrocities committed during the war, but under questioning from journalists, he continued to deny most accusations that had been levelled against the RUF. Negotiations ensued on the composition of the government, in which the former AFRC junta had expected to be allocated senior posts. Sankoh was eventually ceded powers equivalent to those of a vice-president, as well as the chairmanship of a new commission for strategic resources, national reconstruction and development, while four RUF members were allocated government positions, with the AFRC effectively excluded from participation in the new administration. During November the RUF clashed with AFRC supporters in the north of the country; Sankoh's RUF forces took control of the towns of Makeni and Lunsar, previously held by the AFRC.

The political climate was already highly uncertain by the time the UN Security Council eventually approved the UN Mission to Sierra Leone (UNAMSIL) on 22 October 1999, and tension increased as the UN peace-keeping force, at first mainly comprising troops from Commonwealth countries, began to arrive and be deployed in the country during November. UNAMSIL, as first approved, was to consist of 6,000 troops, who were to join the remaining 5,000-strong Nigerian ECOMOG contingent. In accordance with the Lomé agreement, the RUF was registered as a political party during November, but Sankoh showed little inclination to modify the aggressive culture of the movement or to oblige it to adhere to the disarmament timetable, which was considerably behind schedule (see below). In January 2000 the UN Secretary-General, Kofi Annan, described the peace in Sierra Leone as very fragile and asked the Security

Council to increase the size of UNAMSIL to 11,000 troops, to allow for the complete replacement of ECOMOG.

In February 2000 the RUF's resistance to the full deployment of the UN force escalated into direct confrontation. The first serious crisis occurred when heavily-armed RUF fighters prevented much more lightly-armed Indian and Ghanaian peace-keeping troops from being deployed in the east of the country. In a further incident the armaments of the Guinean contingent were seized. In response to these direct threats from the RUF, the UN increased its co-operation with, and support for, the Sierra Leone army, the AFRC and the Kamajors. By the end of April, when the ECOMOG force was formally withdrawn, the RUF had prepared an offensive against UNAMSIL contingents. In early May about 500 peace-keeping troops were taken hostage in different parts of the country, prompting the British government to undertake emergency military support, both to the Sierra Leone government and to the UN mission (see below). A renewed RUF attempt to advance on Freetown was successfully repelled and Sankoh, after a brief disappearance, was arrested and detained on behalf of the government on 17 May. The Kabbah government proceeded to clarify its conditions for the continuation of the Lomé peace agreement, and issued direct demands that the RUF cease its aggressive actions and withdraw its forces from Kono mining district. It rejected ECOWAS proposals that Sankoh be sent to a third country to face trial, and requested the establishment of a special UN court to try him for war crimes, on the grounds that the Sierra Leonean authorities lacked the necessary resources.

CIVIL CONFLICT AND REGIONAL CONCERNS

Following the outbreak of civil conflict in Liberia in December 1989 (see Recent History of Liberia), an estimated 125,000 Liberians took refuge in Sierra Leone. Some 500 Sierra Leonean troops joined ECOMOG, which was dispatched to Liberia in August 1990. In November 1990 Charles Taylor, the leader of the principal Liberian faction, the National Patriotic Front of Liberia (NPFL), threatened to attack the international airport at Lungi, north of Freetown, which was used as a base for ECOMOG offensives against rebel strongholds. In March 1991 repeated border incursions by Liberian rebels, reported to be members of the NPFL, resulted in the deaths of several Sierra Leoneans. The Sierra Leone government subsequently deployed 2,150 troops on the Liberian border, and, in early April, attacked rebel bases in Liberian territory. The government alleged that the rebel offensive had been instigated by Charles Taylor, in an attempt to force Sierra Leone's withdrawal from ECOMOG, and also accused the government of Burkina Faso of assisting the rebels. Although the NPFL denied involvement, it was reported that members of a Sierra Leonean guerrilla movement, known as the Revolutionary United Front (RUF), led by Foday Sankoh, had joined forces with the NPFL in attacks against government army positions. In mid-1991 Sierra Leonean troops, assisted by military units from Nigeria and Guinea, initiated a counter-offensive against the rebels, and succeeded in recapturing several towns in the east and south of the country. Government forces were also assisted by some 1,200 Liberian troops, who had fled to Sierra Leone in September 1990, while a number of other countries, including the United Kingdom and the USA, provided logistical support to Sierra Leone. In September 1991 former supporters of the Liberian president, Samuel Doe, known as the United Liberation Movement of Liberia for Democracy (ULIMO), initiated attacks from Sierra Leone against NPFL forces in north-western Liberia. The Sierra Leone government denied allegations by Taylor that Sierra Leonean troops were involved in the offensive. In October clashes between ULIMO and the NPFL continued in the Mano River Bridge area on the border with Liberia. In December Momoh claimed that, contrary to the terms of a peace agreement, which had been signed between the Liberian interim government and the NPFL at the end of October (see Recent History of Liberia), the NPFL had continued its offensive in Sierra Leone; it was reported that the NPFL had regained control of several villages near the border with Liberia.

In January 1992 discussions took place in the Liberian capital, Monrovia, under the auspices of ECOWAS, between members of the Sierra Leone government and leaders of the Liberian factions, in an attempt to resolve the conflict. In May ECOMOG began to establish units along the border between Sierra Leone and Liberia, in accordance with the terms of the October peace agreement; however, the deployment of troops was impeded by renewed ULIMO forays into Liberia. In the same month the RUF (which was reported to have gained control of territory in the south of the country) rejected appeals by the government to end the civil conflict, and demanded that all foreign troops be withdrawn from Sierra Leone as a precondition to the cessation of hostilities. In early 1993 the RUF became militarily disadvantaged by the reduction of logistical support from the NPFL, after ULIMO gained control of the greater part of western Liberia (see Recent History of Liberia); by April it was reported that only Kailahun District in the extreme east of Sierra Leone, near the border with Liberia, and Pujehun District in the south of the country remained under the control of rebel forces. Later that year government forces advanced within Kailahun District, regaining control of the significant diamond-mining town of Koindu, 250 km east of Freetown, in November. In January 1994 the government claimed that it had regained control of further rebel bases in Pujehun District and the town of Kenema near the border with Liberia. Later that year fighting in the south and east of Sierra Leone intensified, and in April it was reported that the RUF, which had been joined by disaffected members of the armed forces, had initiated attacks in the north of the country.

During July and August 1994 government troops initiated offensives against rebel bases in the region of Kenema, following reports that the RUF were exploiting diamond reserves in the area in order to finance their activities. Later in 1994 reports emerged of an increase in insurgent activity, with widespread looting and killing by unidentified armed groups. In early November the RUF seized two British members of a voluntary relief organization, following an attack against the northern town of Kabala. Strasser subsequently renewed his offer of negotiations; however, the RUF rejected the conditions stipulated by the government, which included the declaration of an immediate cease-fire and the release of the two British prisoners. The RUF leadership insisted that the United Kingdom suspend military assistance to the Strasser regime as a precondition to the release of the two hostages, and further demanded that the British authorities recognize the RUF as a political organization and provide it with armaments and medical supplies. The British government denied claims by the RUF that it was supplying armaments to the Strasser regime.

In January 1995 the RUF gained control of the mining installations owned by the Sierra Leone Ore and Metal Co (SIEROMCO) and Sierra Rutile Ltd, and seized a number of employees of the two enterprises, including eight foreign nationals. Later in January seven Roman Catholic nuns (who were Italian and Brazilian nationals), together with a number of Sierra Leonean citizens, were abducted, following an attack by the RUF against the north-western town of Kambia. In the same month the RUF threatened to kill the British hostages if the Sierra Leonean authorities executed an officer, who had been convicted by military tribunal of collaborating with the rebels. In early February Sankoh indicated that the RUF was prepared to negotiate with the government, and invited the International Committee of the Red Cross (ICRC) to mediate in the discussions. Later that month, however, the RUF rejected appeals by the UN and the OAU that peace negotiations be initiated, and demanded that all foreign troops assisting the government be withdrawn as a precondition to discussions. In mid-February government forces (which had succeeded in recapturing the Sierra Rutile mining installations) launched an offensive against a principal rebel base in the Kangari region, east of Freetown. Meanwhile, continued atrocities perpetrated against civilians were increasingly attributed to 'sobels', disaffected members of the armed forces who engaged in acts of looting, banditry and indiscriminate killing. By mid-February some 900,000 civilians had been displaced as a result of the increase in the civil conflict, of which about 185,000 had fled to Guinea, 90,000 to Liberia and some 500,000 had settled around the capital.

In February 1995 the Sierra Leone government (which had ordered the total mobilization of the armed forces to repulse rebel attacks) engaged 58 Gurkha mercenaries, who had previously served in the British army, prompting further concern regarding the safety of the British hostages in Sierra Leone.

In March government forces regained control of the mining installations owned by SIEROMCO and the principal town of Moyamba, 100 km south-east of Freetown (which had been captured by the RUF earlier that month). Later that month the rebels released the seven nuns who had been abducted in January. Despite the successful counter-offensives by government forces, by April it was reported that the RUF had advanced towards Freetown and had initiated a series of attacks against towns in the vicinity (including Songo, which was situated only 35 km east of Freetown), apparently prior to besieging the capital. The government of Guinea announced that it was to provide additional troops to assist government operations against the RUF. Later in April the 10 remaining foreign nationals who had been seized by the RUF, together with six Sierra Leoneans, were released to the ICRC. (It was reported, however, that the rebels continued to hold a number of Sierra Leonean civilians as hostages.) At the end of April the RUF rejected an unconditional offer by Strasser to initiate peace negotiations.

In May 1995 government forces initiated a number of counter-attacks, and succeeded in recapturing Songo. The governments of Guinea and Nigeria dispatched additional troops to Sierra Leone, while it was reported that mercenaries recruited from South Africa were assisting the authorities with military training and logistics. Later in May Strasser requested that ECOWAS mediate in negotiations between the RUF and the government; however, the RUF rejected the initiative and reiterated its demands that all foreign troops leave the country as a precondition to negotiations. By the end of June government forces had regained control of diamond-mining areas in the eastern Kono District, and part of Bo District, in a successful counter-offensive which was generally attributed to the assistance of the mercenaries. In early September the RUF requested that civilian groups mediate in discussions between the rebel movement and the government; this proposal was subsequently abandoned, however, and large numbers of civilians were killed in further RUF offensives against towns in Bo District (which were recaptured by government forces in early October). Sankoh indicated that humanitarian organizations would be prevented from operating in territory controlled by the RUF, while increasing reports of massacres and other violations of human rights perpetrated by the rebels against the civilian population emerged. In November the RUF regained control of Kailahun, and a further 10 towns in Moyamba District. In December an OAU mission conducted negotiations with RUF representatives in Abidjan, Côte d'Ivoire.

Following the replacement of Strasser by Bio at the head of a new military administration in January 1996 (see above), the RUF withdrew its earlier preconditions to negotiations. The Ivorian head of state subsequently offered to mediate in discussions, and RUF and government delegations met for the first time in February, in Abidjan. Nevertheless, in response to the refusal of Bio to accede to the RUF's request for a postponement of multi-party elections pending a peace agreement, the rebels abandoned a cease-fire in early February and subsequently launched a series of attacks in various parts of the country, killing large numbers of civilians, in an apparent attempt to undermine the electoral process. After the elections took place, however, the government announced in March that the RUF had agreed to a cease-fire; at a meeting between Sankoh and Bio in Yamoussoukro later that month, the RUF agreed to observe the cease-fire for a period of two months and to continue negotiations with the newly-elected civilian government. Following discussions between Sankoh and the new president, Ahmed Kabbah, which took place in April, the government and RUF reaffirmed their commitment to a permanent cessation of hostilities, and announced the establishment of three joint committees, which would consider issues regarding the demobilization of rebel forces. However, Sankoh continued to refuse to recognize the legitimacy of the new government, and demanded that a transitional administration be installed pending further elections. In the same month the RUF released some 250 civilian hostages. At continuing negotiations in May, agreement was reached on a number of issues, although the RUF demanded that the mercenaries be withdrawn from the country as a precondition to the demobilization of its forces. Despite the official cease-fire, sporadic attacks by the RUF were subsequently reported. Additional clashes occurred later that year between government forces and the Kamajors (traditional fighters reconstituted as an auxiliary defence force), who had proved highly successful in repelling rebel attacks, apparently prompting resentment from members of the armed forces. At further discussions between the government and the rebel leadership in July, Sankoh demanded that members of the RUF be allocated government posts as a precondition to the cessation of hostilities.

In November 1996 Kabbah demanded that the RUF relinquish armaments within a period of two weeks, threatening that government forces would resume military operations. At the end of that month Kabbah and Sankoh signed a peace agreement in Abidjan, whereby RUF forces were to be demobilized and the movement was to be reconstituted as a political organization (although members were not to be granted ministerial portfolios), while all foreign troops were to be withdrawn from the country and replaced with foreign observers. A national commission for the consolidation of peace was subsequently established to monitor the peace settlement. By February 1997 all foreign mercenaries had left Sierra Leone in accordance with the agreement, while the repatriation of Sierra Leonean refugees from Liberia had commenced. However, at the end of that month (when the implementation of the peace agreement was scheduled for completion) it was reported that members of the RUF had repeatedly violated the peace agreement and had failed to report to designated centres for disarmament. In March members of the political wing of the RUF issued a declaration that Sankoh had been removed as leader of the organization, owing to his opposition to the peace process; Sankoh was accused of provoking further unrest and failing to attend scheduled discussions with UN officials and members of the national commission for the consolidation of peace regarding the implementation of the peace accord. Later that month, however, RUF forces loyal to Sankoh kidnapped members of the movement who had supported his replacement, together with the Sierra Leonean ambassador to Guinea; the faction issued demands for the release of Sankoh, who had been detained in Nigeria earlier that month (being reportedly in possession of armaments). In May Sankoh (who remained in Nigeria) announced his support for a military coup which ousted the civilian government (see above). A makeshift alliance between the RUF and the new military authorities was established, and the RUF was subsequently reconstituted as a security force, known as the People's Army. During the period of military intervention from May 1997 until February 1998, the links between Liberia's new president, Charles Taylor, and both the military junta and the RUF were a cause of concern to ECOMOG and to Nigeria. Taylor uttered frequent criticisms of the ECOMOG strategy, and there were reports that Liberia was helping the AFRC to rearm. When ECOMOG took Freetown in February 1998, Taylor objected to its forces' incursions into Liberian airspace to apprehend fleeing members of the junta. In April the ECOMOG task force commander, Col Khobe, alleged that the NPFL was training forces to support rebel activity in Sierra Leone. At a meeting in Abuja in July, however, Kabbah and Taylor agreed to a number of measures to improve security and co-operation between the two countries. The RUF successfully intensified activity at the end of 1998, with the assistance of armaments from Liberia and Burkina Faso. As the RUF prepared to stage its January 1999 assault on Freetown, Liberian troops were stationed at the joint border with the stated intention of preventing escalated military operations in Sierra Leone. At the height of the fighting in Freetown, Kabbah publicly accused Taylor of supporting the offensive.

Nigeria's continued commitment to protecting the government of Sierra Leone was called into question in January 1999, when the military head of state, Gen. Abdulsalami Abubakar, indicated that he hoped to withdraw the contingent from Sierra Leone by May. Following peace negotiations, which commenced in Togo in May, the RUF and Sierra Leonean government reached a power-sharing agreement. The new Nigerian civilian administration subsequently announced that a phased withdrawal of some of its troops from Sierra Leone would take place; this commenced in early September.

ECOMOG and the UN were engaged in a complicated transition of their respective responsibilities during the second half of 1999. The scheduled departure of ECOMOG's Nigerian forces was repeatedly delayed while the UN Security Council debated the size of the force that was to replace them. Eventually, on 22 October 1999 the establishment of a 6,000-strong UN Mission in Sierra Leone (UNAMSIL) was authorized, to comprise six infantry battalions and a helicopter-borne reaction force. In view of the slow arrival and deployment of these troops, Nigeria continued to delay the withdrawal of its forces. The first UNAMSIL troops to arrive were from Kenya, followed by Indian and a substantial contingent of Nigerian troops.

RUF hostility to the proposed disarmament of its fighters was increased by the UN decision not to pay for surrendered armaments. Sankoh's instruction to his combatants not to demand compensation for armaments was ignored. Sankoh's associates also reacted with antagonism to the prospect of being charged with crimes committed during the earlier war. These developments contributed to the increasing strain on the cease-fire between government and rebels, just as the UNAMSIL force was beginning to be deployed around the country. The disarmament process, which had been scheduled to end in December, did not proceed as planned, with most RUF combatants refusing to relinquish their weapons and some being rearmed through supply lines from Liberia, especially after the joint border between the two countries was opened in November. By early December only 2,500 out of an estimated 45,000 former combatants had surrendered any armaments. The rate of disarmament accelerated only in those areas that were controlled by the AFRC; by early 2000 12,000 combatants had complied, while a further 33,000 RUF combatants still held armaments (some of which were newly-supplied) and aggressively enforced their control of the territory that they effectively held, particularly in the diamond-mining areas in the east. In January there were confrontations between ECOMOG and RUF forces, and these were followed in February by the RUF's refusal to allow Indian and Ghanaian UNAMSIL forces to be deployed in the east of the country.

In January 2000 the UN Secretary-General, Kofi Annan, urged the UN Security Council to increase UNAMSIL to 11,000 troops, to assist the mission to consolidate the tenuous peace. Nigeria at the same time agreed to suspend the progressive withdrawal of its ECOMOG troops from Sierra Leone, on the understanding that many of them would be transferred to UNAMSIL control at the end of April. While the RUF became increasingly aggressive it was also undergoing division between Sankoh's loyalists and those of Sam Bockarie and other leaders operating from bases in Liberia. The RUF's refusal to disarm was in April condemned by the other militias, in particular the AFRC and the Kamajors, who pledged to force the rebel movement's followers to surrender their weapons. The formal ending of the ECOMOG mission on 30 April was accompanied by a severe loss of control by UNAMSIL, under its force commander, Gen. Vijay Jetley of India. The deployment of newly-arrived Jordanian troops was almost cancelled as a result of unconfirmed rumours of an RUF advance on Freetown. At the same time the leadership of the Sierra Leone army was also thrown into confusion by the unexpected death in April of the Nigerian chief of staff, Brig.-Gen. Maxwell Khobe.

By the end of April 2000 the disarmament process had accounted for 23,000 former combatants, of which only 5,000 were from the RUF. It was consequently estimated that about 20,000 armed RUF were still capable of moving freely around the country. The UN force at this stage amounted to only 8,500 troops, many of them on unarmed monitoring duties. At the beginning of May the RUF clashed with the UN forces at a number of locations around the country, and after a few days some 500 UN troops were reported missing, presumed kidnapped. This development prompted the British government to start preparations for a rescue mission, on behalf of both the UN and the Sierra Leone armed forces. On 8 May the United Kingdom dispatched a force of 800 paratroopers, with strong air force and naval support. After first securing the airport, the British forces were deployed throughout Freetown and surrounding areas in time to prevent an RUF offensive against Waterloo, near the capital, on 11 and 12 May. British helicopters transported Jordanian peace-keepers to defensive positions, while army experts assisted the UN in preparing new military tactics. The British forces also commenced emergency retraining of the Sierra Leone army.

In mid-May 2000 British forces declared Freetown to be secure and it was reported that the RUF had commenced the release of some of its hostages through Liberia. For their part, ECOWAS leaders urged the UN to expand its peace-keeping mandate to allow the use of force, whereupon Nigeria campaigned to be allowed to retain the military leadership of the peace-keeping exercise in Sierra Leone, but also demanded international assistance to be able to undertake the task. After further deliberations, ECOWAS defence chiefs agreed to resume sending troops to the country, but under a changed command structure that would reflect the military role played by Nigeria and would expand the mandate from peace-keeping to peace enforcement. In mid-May the UN Security Council approved a further increase in the size of UNAMSIL, to 13,000, by immediately deploying 3,000 West African and 800 Bangladeshi troops.

On 22 May 2000, while government forces and the Kamajors engaged the RUF at Lunsar, many of the Zambian and other peace-keeping troops who had been held hostage for three weeks were released, following mediation by the Liberian president, Charles Taylor. The rebels were reported to have demanded the freedom of Sankoh in return for releasing the hostages, but this proposal was not accepted. In mid-June most of the British forces were withdrawn after a visit by the secretary of state for foreign and Commonwealth affairs, Robin Cook, who promised continued British involvement in training the Sierra Leone

army and to support an increase in the UN presence to 16,500 peace-keeping troops. About 250 British troops subsequently remained in the country. In early July the UN Security Council adopted a resolution, proposed by the United Kingdom, for an international embargo on the purchase of diamonds mined from RUF-controlled regions. Later that month some 233 peace-keeping personnel (mainly Indian) held hostage by the RUF at Kailahun were rescued in a military operation, staged by UNAMSIL with the endorsement of the UN Security Council. Meanwhile, increasing divisions in the pro-government forces were reported. In late August one of the most notorious of the militia groups supporting the former AFRC junta, the West Side Boys (WSB), abducted 11 British military personnel and one member of the Sierra Leone army. The WSB subsequently issued a number of demands, including the release from detention of their leader, as a precondition to freeing the hostages. Five of the British personnel were released a few days later, but additional British troops were dispatched to Sierra Leone following the failure of negotiating officials to secure an agreement over the remaining hostages. In early September about 150 British troops attacked the WSB base, and succeeded in freeing the remaining hostages; one British serviceman and 25 WSB members were killed during the rescue mission. Later that month the Indian government announced that the Indian contingent, numbering 3,073, was gradually to be withdrawn from UNAMSIL. On 20 September the UN Security Council extended the mandate of UNAMSIL to the end of the year; meanwhile, Annan continued efforts to generate support for the strengthening of the UN operation to number about 20,500.

Economy

LINDA VAN BUREN

Sierra Leone's economy was poorly developed, even prior to the civil conflict of the 1990s. Gross national product (GNP) per caput amounted to only US $180 in 1995 and to $200 in 1996, according to estimates by the World Bank. By 1998 GNP per head had declined further, to $140. In 1998 the World Bank ranked Sierra Leone as one of the eight poorest countries in the world. The lack of progress in infrastructural development has rendered large areas of the country untouched by monetization or by the valorization of formal trade. A majority of the population survive by subsistence agriculture and by informal trading activities, which, however, suffered much disruption owing to the civil conflict. Poor implementation of economic policies has meant that modernization projects have failed, while political instability, the associated activities of rebel groups, and economic isolation after the coup in May 1997 have caused severe disruption to the traditional economy, as well as to the few mining operations that provided high earnings of foreign exchange. In 1997 the estimated gross domestic product (GDP) was $849.9m., of which agriculture contributed 39%, services 34% and industry 27%, and manufacturing contributed 6% (only marginally more than in 1980). By 1998 GDP had declined to $671.6m., a decline of 21%, in real terms. For many years, the Sierra Leone economy was affected by high inflation, which averaged 61.6% annually in 1985–95. Although some success was achieved in reducing inflation, with the rate declining steadily from 26.0% in 1995, to 23.1% in 1996, and to 14.9% in 1997, it subsequently increased to 35.5% in 1998. During 1985–95, it was estimated, GNP per head declined, in real terms, at an average annual rate of 3.6%. Sierra Leone's GDP declined by an estimated 10% in 1995, and, following a return to positive growth of 5% in 1996, GDP contracted by 17.6% in 1997 (the year of the military coup). Real GDP growth was only 0.8% in 1998, and GDP was estimated to have contracted by 8.1% in 1999.

The economy became export-orientated early in the colonial period, when emphasis was placed on the production of primary commodities for overseas industrial markets which were also the principal suppliers of the country's import requirements. Favourable terms of trade in the 1950s, in conjunction with an expansion in the diamond industry, resulted in a rapid increase

in incomes, allowing imports and government expenditure to rise sharply. Increasing government expenditure, together with slow export and revenue growth in the early 1960s, led to a financial crisis, which was exacerbated in the mid-1960s by an overly ambitious programme of investment in plantations and oil-palm mills by the Sierra Leone Produce Marketing Board (SLPMB), the sole exporter of the country's crops.

By the 1980s there was a high rate of inflation, an acute shortage of foreign exchange and heavy external debt, while the country's natural mineral resources remained underutilized. Official revenue from exports (particularly diamonds) was adversely affected by smuggling, which was encouraged by government policies on price controls and the exchange rate. In 1986 the Momoh government implemented an economic reform programme, based on IMF recommendations, which included the introduction of a 'floating' exchange rate, the elimination of government subsidies on rice and petroleum, the liberalization of trade, and increases in producer prices with the aim of encouraging self-sufficiency in rice and other foods. In 1988, however, the IMF withdrew its support for the programme, declaring Sierra Leone ineligible for assistance until arrears in repayments were received. In 1989 the government announced measures to increase revenue from the mining sector and to reorganize loss-making state-owned companies, and adopted an IMF-approved three-year structural adjustment programme. Further lending was postponed, however, owing to the IMF's concern at the government's continued failure to reduce expenditure or to control debt arrears.

Internal unrest since 1991 has impeded government efforts to achieve economic stability, although the Strasser regime that assumed power in April 1992 agreed to implement the final stage of the IMF-endorsed economic programme, which aimed to tighten controls over the money supply, to develop a foreign-exchange market and to improve the management of the country's natural resources. The government also aimed to continue the implementation of structural reforms, including the reduction of civil-service employees and privatization measures. Under an agreement with the IMF, Sierra Leone was able to accumulate 'rights' through its progress during the economic programme, which could then be used as the first disbursement of debt arrears under successive IMF-supported structural-adjustment programmes. In March 1994 Sierra Leone became eligible to receive new credits from the IMF (see below). An extensive privatization programme involving 19 enterprises (including the Sierra Leone Petroleum Refining Co) was initiated in that month; it was announced that a certain percentage of shares would be reserved for Sierra Leone citizens, while the state would also place shares on the international market. The civil conflict, which had affected mainly the southern and eastern regions of the country, escalated in early 1995, forcing the closure of the bauxite and rutile mining operations, which formed the principal sources of official export earnings. Major long-term foreign investors withdrew from the country. With the disruption of nearly all export activity, Sierra Leone became increasingly dependent on the small amounts of foreign assistance that were available from the International Development Association (IDA) and the European Union (EU), as well as on emergency humanitarian aid. Following the coup in May 1997, the UN World Food Programme (WFP) commenced the limited distribution of emergency food aid. However, members of the armed factions intercepted and diverted emergency food supplies, severely hindering the WFP's efforts to distribute aid. During the nine-month period from May 1997 to February 1998 more than 2m. Sierra Leoneans were internally and externally displaced, economic and social infrastructure was virtually destroyed, and the financial system severely disrupted. In mid-1998 the WFP reported that Sierra Leone's food stocks were very low. Some 35,000 internally displaced and vulnerable civilians received WFP emergency food aid in May and June 1998. However, a further 130,000 people who were isolated near the border with Guinea were reported to be in urgent need of emergency assistance. The WFP provided relief food supplies to 200,000 Sierra Leonean civilians affected by the civil conflict in May 2000 alone. In June the WFP reported that fighting had delayed its efforts to supply relief food to 16,000 displaced civilians at Lungi, and to 14,000 at Port Loko.

AGRICULTURE AND FISHING

Sierra Leone's economy is predominantly agricultural; in 1998 the sector employed 63.3% of the economically active population. Some 70 different crops have been cultivated in the country, but only a few (mainly coffee, cocoa, palm kernels and piassava, a fibre crop) have been exported, and these were produced by fewer than 10% of the country's farmers. Prior to the civil conflict, about three-quarters of farmers were engaged in the cultivation of the staple food crop, rice, but production was insufficient to satisfy domestic demand, and the shortfalls were offset by imports (accounting for about 25% of annual consumption in recent years). The harvest of paddy rice declined from 405,000 metric tons in 1994 to 284,000 tons in 1995, but, according to FAO estimates, had recovered to 328,310 tons in 1998. Output declined by 24.7%, to 247,235 tons in 1999. Total cereal production was estimated at 279,832 tons in 1999, a decline of 25%, compared with 373,010 tons in 1998; rice constituted 88% of the total. In contrast, Sierra Leone's domestic requirements for rice are estimated at about 530,000 tons per annum. The Momoh government opened the rice-import trade to the private sector in 1989, with demand determining selling prices, except for the official subsidy on supply to the security forces. However, the ultimate success of moves towards privatization depended crucially on the response of investors to the new opportunities being provided, as well as the prevailing political, economic and security environment. As fierce civil conflict continued, the effects on agricultural production were devastating, with production of all major food and cash crops suffering. The sorghum crop, estimated at 24,000 tons in 1994, had declined to 17,500 tons by 1998, and to 17,200 tons in 1999. Even worse affected was the millet crop, which declined from 26,000 tons in 1994 to 16,500 tons in 1998, and to just 4,725 tons in 1999, according to FAO estimates. The cassava crop decreased by 17%, from 289,200 tons in 1998 to 239,597 tons in 1999. The 1995 output of plantains, amounting to 27,860 tons, was about the same as that of the previous year; production was estimated at 26,000 tons in 1997, and at a similar amount in 1998 and 1999. Production of groundnuts in shells declined from 35,400 tons in 1998 to 29,010 tons in 1999, a decline of 18%. The coffee crop decreased by 50%, from 30,700 tons in 1998 to 15,350 tons in

1999. Output of cocoa beans fell from 13,000 tons in 1998 to 10,920 tons in 1999, a decline of 16%. Production of palm kernels declined by 30%, from 31,000 tons in 1998 to 21,700 tons in 1999. The only crop to register an increase in 1999 was maize, with the 1999 harvest of 8,772 tons 2% greater than the output of 8,600 tons in 1998.

Since 1993 Sierra Leone's fishing sector, particularly marine fisheries, has been seriously affected by the civil conflict. The total catch was 62,046 metric tons in 1995, 61,200 tons in 1996, and 62,782 tons in 1997. Of the 1997 total catch, saltwater fishing accounted for 77%. Overfishing by foreign vessels within Sierra Leone's coastal waters (including the continental shelf of some 25,000 sq km) is believed to have depleted the available stocks of sardinellas and other common species. It was estimated that illegal fishing deprived the government of some US $30m. per year in revenue in the mid-1990s.

MINING

Mining, which began in Sierra Leone in the 1930s, was, prior to the civil conflict, the second most important commodity-producing sector and the main source of foreign exchange. During the civil conflict, with severe disruption to the agricultural sector as well as to most mining operations, the matter of which side had access to Sierra Leone's diamonds became an issue of military importance. Throughout the first half of 2000 increasing international acknowledgement of this factor emerged. A World Bank report, published in June 2000 and entitled *Economic Causes of Civil Conflict and Their Implications for Policy*, studied 47 civil wars in various areas of the world between 1960 and 1999. This study concluded that the primary cause motivating rebel groups to attempt to seize power was not that of political, ethnic or religious differences, but the desire to gain control of lucrative economic resources (in Sierra Leone, diamond reserves). The diamonds sold on the open market by rebel groups became known as 'conflict diamonds'. On 5 July 2000 the UN Security Council imposed an international embargo on the sale of rough diamonds from Sierra Leone. The UN directly stated that the reason for doing so was to halt the flow of funds to the RUF rebels, who were then in control of most of the country's alluvial diamond-mining areas. Under the embargo, which was to continue for a period of 18 months, it was declared illegal to buy any diamond from Sierra Leone unless it was accompanied by a certificate of origin from the legal government. Until such a certification system could be put into effect, it would be illegal to purchase any diamonds from Sierra Leone. However, the embargo did not specifically name Liberia as a conduit for the illicit sale of Sierra Leone diamonds, primarily owing to the fact that the Liberian president, Charles Taylor, was then involved in sensitive negotiations to release UN peace-keeping personnel held by the RUF in Kailahun.

Sierra Leone's mining sector contributed 16% of GDP and 84% of export earnings in 1984. Diamonds, for many years the principal export commodity of Sierra Leone, have long attracted widespread illicit trafficking, despite large expenditures on security. Alluvial diamond mining was carried out by numerous small prospectors, while larger-scale mining operations were conducted by the Sierra Leone Selection Trust (SLST), in which the government-controlled National Diamond Mining Co (NDMC, also known as DIMINCO) held a majority share. This enterprise, however, was adversely affected by management, financial and technical problems, and by 1992 its production made only a negligible contribution to foreign-exchange receipts. By 1995 the NDMC had ceased operations. The marketing of Sierra Leone diamonds was subsequently conducted by the Government Gold and Diamond Office (GGDO). Legal exports of diamonds declined from 2m. carats in 1970 to 395,000 carats in 1980, to 132,000 carats in 1989, and to 31,929 carats, with a value of US $3.3m., in 1996. Following the coup of May 1997, fighting continued in the region of the diamond-mining areas, followed by large-scale looting and destruction of equipment. Mining companies carried out emergency evacuations of their foreign staff, and production ceased. After the return to civilian government in March 1998, some mining companies announced their intention to resume production. However, the new civilian government under President Kabbah announced in April 1998 that all foreign nationals would be banned from gold-mining areas, while in May it was proclaimed that all diamond mining in the country was to cease until a new mining policy could be promulgated. Rex Diamond Mining Corpn of South Africa, which had withdrawn from the country following the coup in May 1997, announced that it planned to resume mining in Sierra Leone and added that the civilian government's proclamation about the mining sector did not affect the company's position. In 1995 mercenaries were recruited via a private South African concern to recapture the Kono diamond-mining areas held by RUF rebels, and by August the province had reportedly been recovered. Security in the diamond-mining areas was again a priority after March 1998. An agreement regarding a kimberlite project had been reached with a South African-linked company, Branch Energy, which was to control 60%, with 30% allocated to the government and 10% to the public. The project was intended to absorb many former employees of the NDMC. However, a legal dispute occurred in 1995 over the leases for the kimberlite pipes at Koidu, previously held by Sunshine Mining until the government assigned the rights to Branch Mining. Output from the Koidu pipe was projected at 250,000 carats per year, with reserves estimated at 2.4m. carats.

In response to uncertainties in the organization of both the production and the marketing of Sierra Leone's diamonds, operators had increasingly turned to the black market, even prior to the civil conflict of the late 1990s. In early 1994, in an effort to reduce illicit trade, the Strasser government offered informants rewards of up to 40% of the value of anything recovered. This offer resulted in the recovery in June of that year of a particularly large (172-carat) diamond, which obtained US $2.8m. for the government from its sale by public auction. In August 1994 the government granted a South African enterprise, De Beers Consolidated Mines Ltd, a concession to explore 15,800 sq km off the coast of Sierra Leone. In May 1996 illicit exports of diamonds were estimated to cost the country $200m. per year.

Sierra Leone's second most important mineral export was formerly iron ore, which was mined by the foreign-owned Sierra Leone Development Co (DELCO). In the early 1970s, when the mine's ore output averaged 2m. metric tons annually, the company experienced serious technical difficulties and a depressed market for iron ore, and operations were suspended during 1975–81. The government-owned Marampa Iron Ore Co was formed in 1981, with the help of an Austrian loan and with management provided by Austro-Mineral. Exports resumed in 1983, but the new company encountered administrative, technical and financial difficulties, and it suspended operations in October 1985. A project to recover scrap metal from the mine began in 1988; new investors were sought to reopen the mine, which was reported to have ore deposits with an iron content of 69%.

The Sierra Leone Ore and Metal Co (SIEROMCO), a subsidiary of Alusuisse of Switzerland, began mining bauxite at Mokanji in 1964. Exports averaged 631,000 metric tons per year in 1972–79, but declined to 576,000 tons in 1983. Export levels increased sharply to an average of 1.7m. tons per year in 1984–88, but declined to 1.6m. tons in 1989 and to 1.3m. tons in 1992. Production amounted to 735,000 tons in 1994, but in January 1995 RUF forces seized the mine site, obliging SIEROMCO to suspend all operations. Government forces regained control in February, but the company did not resume production. Looters subsequently inflicted damage estimated at US $30m., and in September 1996 the company announced its withdrawal from the country, owing to the cost that the resumption of operations would involve.

Rutile (titanium dioxide), an essential ingredient of paint pigment, was first exported by Sherbo Minerals in 1967, but the company became bankrupt in 1971 and closed its alluvial mine near the town of Bonthe. The mine was taken over the following year by Sierra Rutile, a US-owned company. Production was resumed in 1980, and exports rose from 21,000 metric tons in that year to 148,000 tons in 1992. A major rehabilitation of rutile production facilities was announced in 1992, for which external finance exceeding US $13m. was obtained. Prior to the disruption resulting from the civil conflict, Sierra Leone was, after Australia, the world's second-largest producer of rutile, and the Sierra Rutile reserves are reported to be the largest and highest-grade natural rutile resource in the world. Australia's Consolidated Rutile bought a 50% interest in Sierra Rutile in

1994 and undertook, in partnership with the US Nord Resources Corpn, to continue expansion of the mining activity and to increase production to 190,000 tons per year by 1996, with investment amounting to $72m. In 1993 rutile provided 57% of Sierra Leone's official mineral export earnings, which totalled $108m. In the year to June 1994 rutile production was 144,000 tons, but in January 1995 all production was suspended when RUF forces overran the mining operation. After the rebels were driven out in February, the company took renewed steps to secure the property but was unable to resume production. In September 1996 Sierra Rutile indicated that the IMF and the World Bank had pledged $18m. towards the reopening of the mine, which was projected to cost a total of $80m. However, the coup in May 1997 disrupted those plans, and Nord Resources applied for US $15.7m. in compensation under insurance provisions of the US government's Overseas Private Investment Corpn. After an initial payment of $1m., the remaining $14.2m. was paid in May 1998. Nord Resources used the compensation to restructure Sierra Rutile's $34.2m. debt to various development banks (half of which was guaranteed by Nord Resources, as a 50% partner in Sierra Rutile). In August Nord Resources indicated that it had been negotiating with the Kabbah government in preparation for the resumption of Sierra Rutile operations.

No significant investment has been made in the gold industry, although some corporate interest had been shown in this activity prior to the civil conflict. Gold mining was principally carried out by petty diggers, and most of the production in the 1990s was believed to have been smuggled out of the country. Foreign nationals were banned from gold-mining areas in April 1998.

Mining policy, under the IMF-supported economic reform measures, aimed to encourage reputable companies to participate in mining and exporting minerals, but progress in this direction has been slow, owing to the magnitude of investment involved, bureaucratic restrictions and other official practices deterring potential investors, and the civil conflict. In the early 1990s the government revised its agreements with SIEROMCO and Sierra Rutile in a renewed effort to raise the companies' contributions to government revenue. A new mining policy, introduced in 1994, involved the imposition of a 2.5% royalty on precious mineral exports and a range of licence fees related to the size of mining operations. There was provision for foreign nationals to form companies, and it was proposed that there would be assistance in the provision of security of tenure for artisanal mining activity. In May 1998 the civilian government announced that a new mining policy was to be drafted.

MANUFACTURING, TRADE AND TRANSPORT

With the introduction in 1960 of the Development Ordinance, Sierra Leone adopted a policy of industrial development using an import-substitution strategy. Under the Ordinance, the government extended generous tax incentives, which included duty-free importation of equipment and raw materials and tax 'holidays', and established an industrial estate at Wellington, near Freetown, with basic services and an employment exchange. At first the prospects for this sector were good, as the country began to produce alcoholic and non-alcoholic beverages, cigarettes and several other goods which had been principal imports. By the late 1970s, however, the manufacturing sector had suffered as a result of the extensive shortages of foreign exchange, unreliable electricity and water supplies, poor telecommunications and rising costs of imported raw materials. By the late 1990s the sector comprised mainly palm-oil production and other agro-based industries, textiles and furniture-making. The sector was severely affected by the 1997 coup, which forced most manufacturers to shut down; widespread looting and destruction of factories occurred during the nine-month period in government of the junta. The damage was so extensive that many companies were unlikely ever to reopen after peace was restored. However, one that did resume operations was Sierra Leone Breweries, in April 1998.

High priority was accorded to road construction in the 1970s, especially after the closure in 1971 of the 292-km narrow-gauge government railway. The country had 11,700 km of roads in 1996, including 1,390 km of main roads and 1,630 km of secondary roads; however, only about 1,284 km of the network was paved, and most of the network was in a poor state of repair even before the renewed fighting of 1997 and 1998. Inland waterways and coastal shipping are important features of internal transport. There are almost 800 km of established routes for launches, which include the coastal routes from Freetown northward to the areas served by the Great and Little Scarcies rivers and southward to the important seaport of Bonthe. The services and facilities of the international airport at Lungi, north of Freetown, were improved, with financial assistance from the UNDP, but the civil conflict subsequently disrupted services. Services have remained—for financial, security and other reasons—subject to periods of disruption.

EXTERNAL TRADE AND PAYMENTS

Sierra Leone is heavily dependent on foreign trade. Total exports were US $42m. in 1995, less than one-fifth of the level in 1980, and represented a decline of 48% compared with the previous year. They covered less than one-third of total 1995 imports, which amounted to $135m., leaving a visible trade deficit of $93m., compared with $73m. in 1994. The World Bank estimated Sierra Leone's exports of goods and services at $12m. in 1996. The principal markets for Sierra Leone's exports in 1996 were the USA and Belgium (each accounting for 20%), followed by Spain (13%), the United Kingdom (6%), and other European Union (EU) countries. The principal source of imports in 1996 was Côte d'Ivoire, followed by the EU countries and India. The principal exports in 1994 were rutile, diamonds and bauxite; however, the civil conflict severely affected exports, with a complete suspension of rutile and bauxite production in early 1995. These commodities have been absent from the export list since then. Owing to extensive smuggling of diamonds, the contribution of minerals to total exports declined from 77.2% in 1981 to 69% in 1989, rising to 85% in 1990 (rutile 52%, bauxite 18%, diamonds 9%) and increasing considerably to 93% in 1992 (reflecting the disruption of cocoa and coffee farming, owing to guerrilla activity in producing areas), before falling to 84% in 1994 (rutile 48%, diamonds 22%, bauxite 14%), and then collapsing as the civil conflict escalated. The contribution of agricultural commodities to exports increased from 21% in 1981 to 28% in 1984, but declined to 21% in 1989, 10% in 1990 (coffee 5%, cocoa 4%), 6% in 1992 (coffee 2%, cocoa 3%), and to 5% in 1994 (coffee 2%, cocoa 3%). Imports have traditionally been dominated by manufactured goods. However, even before the civil conflict created severe food shortages in the country, Sierra Leone had become more dependent on imports of food (mainly rice), which in 1990–92 accounted for one-third of total imports; in the same period manufactures accounted for 35%, and mineral fuels and lubricants 18%. The residue consisted of semi-processed materials, beverages and chemicals. In 1994 machinery and transport equipment accounted for 58% of total imports, while food and live animals represented 17%, basic manufactures 6%, chemicals 6%, and mineral fuels and lubricants 4%. According to the IMF, exports (as denominated in US dollars) declined by 16% in 1997 and by 26.2% in 1998, while imports (also as denominated in US dollars) declined by 56.1% in 1997, before increasing by 4.9% in 1998.

Unfavourable terms of trade since the early 1970s, in conjunction with the dramatic increases in crude-oil prices in the 1970s, resulted in increasing import costs. As a result, large deficits on the current account of the balance of payments were incurred, equivalent to 4.2% of GDP in 1979/80, 9.1% of GDP in 1981/82, 7.5% of GDP in 1983/84 and 6% of GDP in 1990/91. The current-account balance (excluding official transfers) registered deficits of US $161.6m. in 1996, $27.5m. in 1997, $60.8 in 1998, and a provisional $62.4m. in 1999; a deficit of $122.4m. was projected for 2000. Owing to a shortage of foreign exchange, the Momoh government, in the early 1990s, mortgaged the future export earnings of the SLPMB, in order to finance the country's essential imports, especially of rice and petroleum, and (before the exchange rate was 'floated' in April 1990) bought foreign currencies at rates in excess of its own official rates. The ratio of scheduled external debt-servicing charges to exports of goods and non-factor services was 54% in 1995, 38.3% in 1996, 30.7% in 1997, 47.8% in 1998 and 57.5% in 1999, with 51.9% projected for 2000, according to IMF figures. As a result of its protracted foreign-exchange crisis (see below), Sierra Leone has a poor record of servicing its foreign debt and has had little access to loans at concessionary rates. Total public debt was equivalent

to 69% of GDP in 1980/81, 127% in 1990/91, 187.3% in 1994/95, and 181.5% in 1999. External debt totalled US $1,243m. at the end of 1998, of which $944m. was long-term public debt. The period covered by the most recent rescheduling by the 'Paris Club' of Western official creditors expired in December 1997, while the military junta was still in power. Gross international reserves, which had dropped to $4m. in 1989, had recovered to $35m. in 1995, enough to cover about 3.6 months' worth of imports; at 31 December 1999 they totalled $49m., sufficient to cover the value of 2.3 months of imports. During the period of the military junta in 1997–98 private-sector banks closed, leaving only the two state banks, Commercial Bank and the National Development Bank, in operation. Three private-sector banks reopened in March 1998 when civilian rule resumed, but a dispute arose immediately over interest paid on deposits or charged on overdrafts during the nine-month closure. Barclays Bank and Standard Chartered Bank, which together hold 70% of all deposits in the commercial-bank sector, and Union Trust Bank came under pressure to moderate their policies, after they announced that they would pay no interest on deposits during the closure, while at the same time charging 22% interest on any overdrafts during the period. They subsequently agreed to pay interest on deposits for the period (Barclays was to pay 3%, Standard Chartered 7% and Union Trust 8%), and to reduce or forgo the interest charged on overdrafts if the overdrafts were paid back in full within one month of reopening.

PUBLIC FINANCE

The civilian government under Kabbah announced its first budget in June 1998. The budget, which covered the period from 17 February to 31 December 1998, projected total expenditure of Le 113,100m. and total revenue at Le 79,100m., leaving a budgetary deficit of Le 34,000m. The international donor community was to be requested to cover this deficit, equivalent to about US $22m., at a conference, which was scheduled to take place in mid-July in London. Successive government budgets had been in almost continuous deficit during the previous three decades; the deficit on a commitment basis increased from 2.5% of GDP in 1976/77 to 12.7% in 1979, to 16.8% in 1986/87, and to 18% in 1991/92, when the actual deficit (including grants) was Le 26,000m., compared with a projected deficit of Le 14,000m. The 1998 primary fiscal deficit was equivalent to 12.8% of GDP in 1998, and to 17.4% in 1999, according to the IMF.

Negotiations between the government and multilateral donors resulted in the adoption, in 1986, of a structural-adjustment programme, under which the Momoh government agreed, among other things, to 'float' the exchange rate, to remove all subsidies on rice and petroleum, to liberalize trade, to increase producer prices and to repay US $3m. in arrears to the IMF. The IMF promised financial support of SDR 50.36m. over a three-year period. Meanwhile, the 'Paris Club' rescheduled Sierra Leone's immediate debt obligations. The 1986 programme ended prematurely when the IMF withdrew its financial support in 1988, stating that the government had not met the agreed conditions. In the same year Sierra Leone was declared ineligible to use IMF resources and was under threat of suspension from membership of the Fund for failing to service its foreign debt and for not implementing IMF-approved economic reforms. In December 1989 the government adopted an IMF-monitored three-year reform programme covering the period 1990/91 to 1992/93. In conjunction with these measures, import and export licensing was abolished for all commodities in December 1989. The leone was devalued by 85% in January 1990 and was 'floated' in April 1990, with the result that it depreciated rapidly. The currency's value weakened to Le 755.22 = US $1 in 1995 and Le 981.48 = US $1 in 1997, and by June 1999 the exchange rate was Le 1,600 = US $1. A revaluation in December 1999 brought the rate to Le 190.30 = US $1, and the exchange rate averaged Le 197.05 = US $1 in January–June 2000. Revenue measures introduced in December 1989 included sharp increases in excise duties on tobacco, beer, petroleum products and a new tax (in the form of an excise duty) on petroleum products. A 'freeze' was imposed on civil-service recruitment (except for essential services) in order to limit expenditure; the exercise of deleting the names of non-existent or 'ghost' workers from the payroll, initiated in July 1988, was pursued more vigorously, while a new retrenchment exercise, designed to reduce civil-service employment levels (estimated at some 75,000) by about 30% before the end of 1992/93, was introduced in early 1991. (However, the IMF still urged a review of civil service and pension payrolls in the first quarter of 1999.) All official subsidies were terminated in 1991, except those on rice for the security forces. In the financial sector, interest rates on treasury bills and on commercial-bank loans were raised substantially in an attempt to attract savers. However, the high rate of inflation only continued to deter saving, with the price of a 50kg bag of rice in Freetown increasing from Le 8,000 in June 1994 to Le 15,000 in October 1995. The price of a bag of rice increased to Le 18,000 shortly before the May 1997 coup, reached Le 60,000 during the time that the junta was in power, and then in April 1998 was reduced by the civilian government to Le 31,000. By mid-2000 thousands of civilians, who had hitherto managed to survive by growing their own crops, had been displaced by the civil conflict and had become dependent on emergency relief from the WFP.

In March 1994 the IMF announced the resumption of credit to Sierra Leone and approved loans totalling SDR 116m. (then equivalent to about US $163m.), following the payment of the country's outstanding debt arrears, which was facilitated by loans from France, Norway and the USA. Of the total credit, SDR 88.8m. was to be provided under a three-year enhanced structural adjustment facility (ESAF), and a further SDR 27m. was to come from a one-year structural adjustment facility, which was to support the Strasser government's economic and financial reform programme for 1994–96. Contrary to the recommendations of a joint delegation of the World Bank and the IMF, however, the budget for 1994/95 awarded a salary increase of 20% to public-sector workers. Performance during the 1994/95 fiscal year again fell short of expectations, with the budget deficit increasing to 7.3% of GDP. The minister of finance attributed the loss of export revenue and damage to agricultural production to the civil conflict, and announced a short-term budget for the remainder of 1995 in which income and expenditure were to be balanced at Le 75,300m. The fiscal year was henceforth to coincide with the calendar year. A donors' conference, which was convened in Geneva in September 1996, pledged $212m. towards the first part of a $1,000m. programme of recovery measures under the Kabbah government; Canada,

France, Germany, Italy, India and Japan pledged loans. The peace agreement signed in July 1999 in Lomé, Togo, resulted in a number of 'post-conflict' aid pledges, notably US $21m. from the IMF in December 1999, a $25m. allocation from the World Bank in the same month to fund the community reintegration and rehabilitation project, and a further $30m. credit from the World Bank in February 2000, in support of the Kabbah government's national rehabilitation and recovery programme.

ECONOMIC PROSPECTS

The protracted civil conflict throughout the 1990s resulted in the cumulative and severe deterioration of the economy. Agricultural activity, both in food and cash crops, was sharply reduced, leaving the mining sector to generate essential foreign exchange, until production in that sector was also severely disrupted. In 1995 the two most lucrative mining operations were also suspended; the Sierra Leone Ore and Metal Co ceased bauxite production permanently, while rutile mining was suspended, pending an improvement in the security situation. Only diamond mining continued, but, although several major deposits were discovered (indicating that Sierra Leone's diamond resources might be of international distinction), the sector was adversely affected by smuggling, rebel attacks and controversy over South African mercenaries brought in to maintain security in the region. In May 1998 the civilian government halted diamond mining altogether, pending the adoption of a new mining policy. International condemnation of the May 1997 coup resulted in the imposition of an ECOWAS blockade (see Recent History). Even the distribution of emergency food aid to civilians was disrupted by the activities of armed groups and by lack of co-operation from the military junta, which in July 1997 ordered the International Red Cross to cease all operations in Sierra Leone. After the Kabbah government was restored in March 1998, the fragile Lomé peace accord of July 1999 was followed by a resumption of rebel activity, and by mid-2000 it had become evident that whoever had access to the revenue from the one remaining exportable commodity, diamonds, would have a formidable source of funding for military operations. Although the UN responded by imposing a total embargo on the purchase of Sierra Leonean diamonds, it remained unclear how effectively this ban could be enforced. Moreover, unless peace was restored, large numbers of Sierra Leonean citizens would remain unable to resume their usual economic activities.

Statistical Survey

Source (unless otherwise stated): Central Statistics Office, Tower Hill, Freetown.

Area and Population

AREA, POPULATION AND DENSITY

Area (sq km)	71,740*
Population (census results)†	
8 December 1974	2,735,159
14 December 1985	
Males	1,746,055
Females	1,769,757
Total	3,515,812
Population (UN estimates at mid-year)‡	
1996	4,289,000
1997	4,420,000
1998	4,568,000
Density (per sq km) at mid-1998	61.7

* 27,699 sq miles.

† Excluding adjustment for underenumeration, estimated to have been 10% in 1974 and 9% in 1985. The adjusted total for 1974 (based on a provisional total of 2,729,479 enumerated) is 3,002,426.

‡ Source: UN, *World Population Prospects: The 1998 Revision*.

PRINCIPAL TOWNS (population at 1985 census)

Freetown (capital) .	384,499	Kenema . . .	52,473
Koindu . . .	82,474	Makeni . . .	49,474
Bo	59,768		

BIRTHS AND DEATHS (UN estimates, annual averages)

	1980–85	1985–90	1990–95
Birth rate (per 1,000) . .	48.9	48.9	49.1
Death rate (per 1,000) . .	28.5	27.2	29.8

Expectation of life (UN estimates, years at birth, 1990–95): 34.1 (males 32.7; females 35.6).

Source: UN, *World Population Prospects: The 1998 Revision*.

ECONOMICALLY ACTIVE POPULATION
(sample survey, '000 persons, 1988/89)

	Males	Females	Total
Agriculture, etc.	551.2	673.3	1,224.5
Industry	235.9	98.9	334.8
Services	198.4	223.0	421.4
Total	985.5	995.2	1,980.7

Mid-1998 (estimates in '000): Agriculture, etc. 1,075; Total economically active population 1,699 (Source: FAO, *Production Yearbook*).

Agriculture

PRINCIPAL CROPS ('000 metric tons)

	1996	1997	1998
Maize	9	9	9
Millet	21	22*	22
Sorghum	21	22*	22
Rice (paddy)	392	411*	411
Sweet potatoes	47	50*	50
Cassava (Manioc)	281	310*	310
Taro (Coco yam)*	3	3	3
Tomatoes	32*	27	27
Dry broad beans*	1	1	1
Citrus fruit*	75	75	75
Mangoes	5*	13	13
Palm kernels*	30	29	29
Palm oil	46*	51	51
Groundnuts (in shell)	36*	38	38
Coconuts	2*	3	3
Coffee (green)	25*	31	31
Cocoa beans	10*	13	13

* FAO estimate(s).

Source: FAO, *Production Yearbook*.

LIVESTOCK (FAO estimates, '000 head, year ending September)

	1996	1997	1998
Cattle	390	400	400
Pigs	50	50	50
Sheep	340	350	350
Goats	185	190	190

Poultry (FAO estimates, million): 6 in 1996; 6 in 1997; 6 in 1998.
Source: FAO, *Production Yearbook*.

LIVESTOCK PRODUCTS (FAO estimates, '000 metric tons)

	1996	1997	1998
Beef and veal	6	6	6
Poultry meat	9	9	9
Other meat	5	5	6
Cows' milk	17	17	17
Poultry eggs	7	7	7

Source: FAO, *Production Yearbook*.

Forestry

ROUNDWOOD REMOVALS ('000 cubic metres, excl. bark)

	1995	1996	1997
Sawlogs, veneer logs and logs for sleepers	4	4	4
Other industrial wood*	120	120	120
Fuel wood	2,978	3,050	3,141
Total	3,102	3,174	3,265

* Annual output assumed to be unchanged since 1980.
Source: FAO, *Yearbook of Forest Products*.

SAWNWOOD PRODUCTION
('000 cubic metres, incl. railway sleepers)

	1995	1996	1997
Total	5	5	5

Source: FAO, *Yearbook of Forest Products*.

Fishing

('000 metric tons, live weight)

	1995	1996*	1997
Freshwater fishes	15.0	14.5	14.5
Sardinellas	7.7	7.7	7.7
Bonga shad	21.7	21.7	21.8
Other marine fishes (incl. unspecified)	17.4	17.1	21.8
Crustaceans and molluscs	0.3	0.3	2.9
Total catch	62.3	61.3	68.7

* FAO estimates.
Source: FAO, *Yearbook of Fishery Statistics*.

Mining

('000 metric tons, unless otherwise indicated)

	1993	1994	1995
Bauxite*	1,165	735	280
Ilmenite*	62.9	47.4	n.a.
Rutile concentrates	150	144	n.a.
Diamonds ('000 metric carats)*	158	255	213
Salt ('000 bags)	360	166	n.a.

* Data from the US Bureau of Mines.
Source: partly UN, *Industrial Commodity Statistics Yearbook*.

Industry

SELECTED PRODUCTS
(estimates, '000 metric tons, unless otherwise indicated)

	1993	1994	1995
Jet fuels	16	15	16
Motor spirit (petrol)	28	27	28
Kerosene	7	8	8
Distillate fuel oils	67	67	68
Residual fuel oils	50	52	53
Electric energy (million kWh)	233	237	241

Source: UN, *Industrial Commodity Statistics Yearbook*.

Finance

CURRENCY AND EXCHANGE RATES
Monetary Units
    100 cents = 1 leone (Le).

Sterling, Dollar and Euro Equivalents (28 April 2000)
    £1 sterling = 3,021.4 leones;
    US $1 = 1,926.8 leones;
    €1 = 1,750.5 leones;
    10,000 leones = £3.310 = $5.190 = €5.713.

Average Exchange Rate (leones per US $)
    1997   981.48
    1998   1,563.62
    1999   1,804.20

BUDGET (Le million, year ending 30 June)

Revenue*	1994/95	1995/96	1996/97
Tax revenue	59,462	66,428	82,708
Taxes on income, profits and capital gains.	10,092	10,809	14,568
Individual taxes . . .	4,686	5,365	6,020
Taxes on corporate income	4,842	4,756	7,849
Taxes on payroll and workforce .	109	111	200
Domestic taxes on goods and services	23,166	20,866	28,113
Sales tax	2,824	2,631	2,738
Excise duties . . .	15,479	14,058	21,024
Taxes on international trade and transactions	26,083	34,624	39,742
Import duties . . .	25,715	34,187	39,222
Other taxes	12	18	85
Other current revenue . .	2,281	3,285	2,790
Entrepreneurial and property income	100	260	301
Administrative fees and charges, non-industrial and incidental sales . . .	881	960	430
Total	61,743	69,713	85,498

Expenditure	1994/95	1995/96	1996/97
Current expenditure . . .	82,534	101,251	108,305
Expenditure on goods and services	39,426	44,922	55,906
Wages and salaries . .	22,150	24,956	28,321
Interest payments . . .	12,582	16,055	17,932
Subsidies and other current transfers	30,526	40,274	34,467
Capital expenditure . . .	25,481	32,178	34,988
Sub-total	108,015	133,429	143,293
Adjustment	−703	−5,262	—
Total	107,312	128,167	143,293

* Excluding grants received (Le million): 5,734 in 1994/95; 8,529 in 1995/96; 9,495 in 1996/97.

Source: IMF, *Government Finance Statistics Yearbook*.

INTERNATIONAL RESERVES (US $ million at 31 December)

	1997	1998	1999
IMF special drawing rights . .	11.2	10.4	20.8
Foreign exchange . . .	27.3	33.7	17.0
Total	38.5	44.1	37.8

Source: IMF, *International Financial Statistics*.

MONEY SUPPLY (Le million at 31 December)

	1997	1998	1999
Currency outside banks . . .	57,260	61,492	84,462
Demand deposits at commercial banks.	24,494	25,875	47,800
Total money (incl. others) . .	83,611	89,744	135,725

Source: IMF, *International Financial Statistics*.

COST OF LIVING
(Consumer Price Index for Freetown; base: 1995 = 100)

	1997	1998	1999
All items	141.5	191.8	257.2

Source: IMF, *International Financial Statistics*.

NATIONAL ACCOUNTS
(Le million at current prices, year ending 30 June)

National Income and Product

	1992/93	1993/94	1994/95*
Compensation of employees . .	86,503.1	107,650.3	138,658.6
Operating surplus . . .	313,873.8	352,605.6	467,380.1
Domestic factor incomes .	400,376.9	460,255.8	606,038.7
Consumption of fixed capital . .	30,097.2	35,104.2	41,907.3
Gross domestic product (GDP) at factor cost .	430,474.1	495,360.0	647,946.1
Indirect taxes, *less* subsidies . .	36,713.4	48,351.0	62,443.2
GDP in purchasers' values .	467,187.5	543,711.0	710,389.3
Factor income received from abroad / *Less* Factor income paid abroad	−66,914.8	−70,237.5	−84,216.0
Gross national product (GNP) .	400,272.7	473,473.5	626,173.3
Less Consumption of fixed capital	30,097.2	35,104.2	41,907.3
National income in market prices	370,175.5	438,369.3	584,265.9
Other current transfers received from abroad / *Less* Other current transfers paid abroad	11,483.0	12,438.6	15,067.8
National disposable income	381,658.5	450,807.9	599,333.7

* Provisional figures.

Expenditure on the Gross Domestic Product

	1996/97	1997/98	1998/99
Government final consumption expenditure . . .	85,312	109,577	121,441
Private final consumption expenditure	671,197	839,100	976,431
Increase in stocks . . .	−2,414	361	−11,010
Gross fixed capital formation .	13,152	40,772	64,643
Total domestic expenditure .	767,247	989,810	1,151,505
Exports of goods and services .	114,154	148,400	308,235
Less Imports of goods and services	−64,505	−103,207	−233,068
GDP in purchasers' values .	816,995*	1,035,003	1,226,672
GDP at constant 1989/90 prices	67,139	67,224	59,407

* Including adjustment.

Source: IMF, *International Financial Statistics*.

Gross Domestic Product by Economic Activity

	1992/93	1993/94	1994/95*
Agriculture, hunting, forestry and fishing	162,194.6	188,884.1	275,327.5
Mining and quarrying . .	98,615.8	96,748.8	119,229.2
Manufacturing	39,567.0	47,816.7	61,475.3
Electricity, gas and water . .	469.8	757.3	2,816.8
Construction	4,655.4	12,544.4	15,788.2
Trade, restaurants and hotels .	69,139.9	77,251.0	98,270.1
Transport, storage and communications . . .	37,056.5	50,047.1	61,267.5
Finance, insurance, real estate and business services . . .	15,947.0	17,988.0	14,732.2
Government services . . .	14,500.0	17,884.0	19,844.9
Other community, social and personal services . . .	8,998.3	9,769.0	12,308.9
Sub-total	451,144.3	519,690.4	681,060.6
Import duties	18,994.0	27,410.0	32,942.0
Less Imputed bank service charge	2,950.8	3,389.8	3,612.3
GDP in purchasers' values .	467,187.5	543,711.0	710,389.3

* Provisional figures.

BALANCE OF PAYMENTS (US $ million)

	1993	1994	1995
Exports of goods f.o.b. . . .	118.3	116.0	41.5
Imports of goods f.o.b. . . .	−187.1	−188.7	−168.1
Trade balance	−68.8	−72.7	−126.7
Exports of services . . .	58.5	100.2	86.8
Imports of services . . .	−61.5	−107.6	−91.8
Balance on goods and services	−71.9	−80.1	−131.7
Other income received . .	2.3	1.5	0.7
Other income paid	−5.6	−57.0	−21.4
Balance on goods, services and income . . .	−75.2	−135.7	−152.3
Current transfers received .	19.1	47.5	35.3
Current transfers paid . .	−1.7	−0.9	−9.5
Current balance . . .	−57.8	−89.1	−126.5
Capital account (net) . . .	0.1	0.1	—
Direct investment from abroad	−7.5	−2.9	−1.7
Other investment assets . .	−14.6	−0.8	15.6
Other investment liabilities .	71.2	−21.8	47.8
Net errors and omissions . .	16.1	55.1	19.3
Overall balance . . .	7.5	−59.5	−45.6

Source: IMF, *International Financial Statistics.*

External Trade

PRINCIPAL COMMODITIES (Le million)

Imports	1992	1993	1994
Food and live animals . . .	30,347	75,286	31,855
Beverages and tobacco . .	664	5,169	2,419
Crude materials (inedible) except fuels	1,735	4,356	3,010
Mineral fuels, lubricants, etc. . .	10,407	6,529	6,776
Animal and vegetable oils and fats	1,898	3,008	1,424
Chemicals	5,328	18,235	10,459
Basic manufactures . . .	21,650	20.003	11,146
Machinery and transport equipment	24,366	63,151	106,395
Miscellaneous manufactured articles	4,722	26,223	8,922
Total (incl. others) . . .	101,672	222,697	183,550

Exports	1992	1993	1994
Coffee	1,351.0	1,301.3	1,549
Cocoa beans	1,053.1	2,115.9	1,704
Palm kernels	6.9	—	—
Bauxite	19,408.3	13,764.5	9,687
Piassava	50.1	49.9	51
Diamonds	15,360.0	11,089.3	15,075
Rutile	32,878.6	32,461.7	32,454
Other items	4,764.4	6,048.3	6,185
Re-exports	161.9	246.2	1,224
Total	75,034.3	67,077.3	67,930

1995 (US $ million): *Imports c.i.f.* 136.3 (Food and live animals 54.0; Mineral fuels, lubricants, etc. 23.7; Chemicals and related products 10.6; Basic manufactures 11.3; Machinery and transport equipment 20.0); *Exports f.o.b.* 76.1 (Aluminium ore 11.2; Other non-ferrous ore 27.7; Pearls, precious and semi-precious stones 19.7; Special transactions 7.6).
Source: UN, *International Trade Statistics Yearbook.*

PRINCIPAL TRADING PARTNERS (Le million)

Imports	1992	1993	1994
Belgium	5,828	5,889	4,377
China, People's Repub. . .	4,986	8,160	4,794
Côte d'Ivoire	1,315	1,762	4,026
France	2,440	14,639	2,525
Germany	8,750	19,564	5,578
Hong Kong	325	7,465	5,536
Indonesia	261	4,377	6,838
Italy	8,896	4,618	2,019
Japan	6,256	6,521	3,715
Netherlands	6,015	40,506	26,050
Pakistan	2,678	1,719	1,626
Switzerland	881	9,647	855
United Kingdom . . .	6,809	43,680	10,453
USA	23,295	19,960	78,288
Total (incl. others) . . .	101,672	222,697	183,550

Exports	1992	1993	1994
Belgium	25,770	54	11,412
Germany	1,060	2,486	1,328
Guinea	1,315	817	1,331
Netherlands	5,307	1,201	2,815
Switzerland	7,546	486	215
United Kingdom . . .	5,567	5,988	11,767
USA	13,832	17,564	30,431
Total (incl. others) . . .	75,034	67,077	67,930

Transport

ROAD TRAFFIC (motor vehicles in use at 31 December)

	1994	1995	1996*
Passenger cars	34,288	20,860	17,640
Buses and coaches . . .	1,103	933	890
Goods vehicles	11,201	10,081	10,000
Motorcycles	10,977	9,879	10,120

* Estimates.
Source: International Road Federation, *World Road Statistics.*

SHIPPING

Merchant Fleet (registered at 31 December)

	1996	1997	1998
Number of vessels . . .	56	55	52
Displacement (gross registered tons)	19,361	19,181	18,792

Source: Lloyd's Register of Shipping, *World Fleet Statistics.*

International Sea-borne Freight Traffic
(estimates, '000 metric tons)

	1991	1992	1993
Goods loaded	1,930	2,190	2,310
Goods unloaded	562	579	589

Source: UN Economic Commission for Africa, *African Statistical Yearbook.*

CIVIL AVIATION (traffic on scheduled services)

	1994	1995	1996
Passengers carried ('000) . .	14	14	15
Passenger-km (million) . .	23	23	24
Total ton-km (million) . .	2	2	2

Source: UN, *Statistical Yearbook.*

Tourism

	1994	1995	1996
Tourist arrivals ('000) . . .	72	38	46
Tourism receipts (US $ million)	10	6	10

1997: Tourist arrivals 48,000.

Source: World Tourism Organization, *Yearbook of Tourism Statistics*.

Communications Media

	1994	1995	1996
Radio receivers ('000 in use) . .	1,025	1,050	1,080
Television receivers ('000 in use) .	48	49	51
Telephones ('000 main lines in use)	16	17	17
Telefax stations (number in use)*	800	1,000	1,700
Daily newspapers			
Number	1	1	1
Average circulation ('000 copies)	10	20	20

* Twelve months beginning 1 April of year stated.

1997 ('000 in use): Radio receivers 1,120; Television receivers 53.

Sources: UNESCO, *Statistical Yearbook*, and UN, *Statistical Yearbook*.

Education

(1992/93)

	Institu-tions	Teachers	Pupils		
			Males	Females	Total
Primary . . .	1,643	10,595	157,781	109,644	267,425
Secondary:					
General . .	167	4,313	41,831	29,069	70,900
Vocational .	38	459	3,237	2,249	5,486
Teacher					
training .	6	250	1,339	931	2,270
Higher . . .	1	1,130	2,005	566	2,571

Source: Central Statistics Office and the former Department of Education, Freetown.

Directory

The Constitution

Following the transfer of power to a democratically-elected civilian administration on 29 March 1996, the Constitution of 1991 (which had been suspended since April 1992) was reinstated. The Constitution provided for the establishment of a multi-party system, and vested executive power in the President, who was to be elected by the majority of votes cast nationally and by at least 25% of the votes cast in each of the four provinces. The maximum duration of the President's tenure of office was limited to two five-year terms. Legislative power was vested in a unicameral 80-member Parliament, elected by universal adult suffrage for a five-year term. The President was to appoint the Cabinet, subject to approval by the Parliament. The parties that had secured a minimum of 5% of votes in the legislative elections were allocated seats on a system of proportional representation, while 12 Paramount Chiefs also represented the provincial districts in the legislature. Members of the Parliament were not permitted concurrently to hold office in the Cabinet.

The Government

HEAD OF STATE

President and Commander-in-Chief of the Armed Forces: Alhaji AHMED TEJAN KABBAH (took office 29 March 1996; reinstated 10 March 1998)

Vice President: Dr ALBERT JOE DEMBY.

CABINET
(August 2000)

Minister of Finance: Dr JAMES O. C. JONAH.

Minister of Foreign Affairs and International Co-operation: Dr SAMA S. BANYA.

Minister of Justice: SOLOMON E. BEREWAH.

Minister of Development and Economic Planning: Dr KADIE SESAY.

Minister of Trade and Industry: MIKE LAMIN.

Minister of Education, Youth and Sports: Dr ALPHA T. WURIE.

Minister of Safety and Security: CHARLES MARGAI.

Minister of Agriculture, Forestry and Marine Resources: OKERE ADAMS.

Minister of Health and Sanitation: Dr IBRAHIM I. TEJAN-JALLOH.

Minister of Transport and Communications: MOMOH PUJEH.

Minister of Energy and Works: ALIMAMY PAOLO BANGURA.

Minister of Works and Maintenance: Dr S. U. M. JAH.

Minister of Mineral Resources: Alhaji MOHAMED S. DEEN.

Minister of Labour and Industrial Relations: ALPHA TIMBO.

Minister of Rural Development and Local Government: J. B. DAUDA.

Minister of Information and Broadcasting: Dr JULIUS SPENCER.

Minister of Social Welfare, Gender and Children's Affairs: SHIRLEY GBUJAMA.

Minister of Lands, Housing, Country Planning and the Environment: PETER VANDY.

Minister of Political and Parliamentary Affairs: ABU A. KOROMA.

Minister of Tourism and Culture: A. B. S. JOMO-JALLOH.

Minister of State of Presidential Affairs: MOMODU KOROMA.

Minister of State of Public Affairs: DOMINIC NGOMBU.

Minister of the Southern Region: FODAY SESAY.

Minister of the Northern Region: IBRAHIM SESAY.

Minister of the Eastern Region: S. R. FILLIE-FABOE.

MINISTRIES

All ministries are in Freetown.

Ministry of Agriculture, Forestry and the Environment: Youyi Bldg, Freetown.

Ministry of Education, Youth and Sport: New England, Freetown; tel. (22) 240846.

Ministry of Energy and Works: New England, Freetown; tel. (22) 240101.

Ministry of Finance, Development and Economic Planning: Secretariat Bldg, George St, Freetown; tel. (22) 226911.

Ministry of Foreign Affairs and International Co-operation: Gloucester St, Freetown; tel. (22) 224778.

Ministry of Health and Sanitation: Youyi Bldg, 4th Floor, Brookfields, Freetown; tel. (22) 241500.

Ministry of Information, Communications, Tourism and Culture: Youyi Bldg, 8th Floor, Brookfields, Freetown; tel. (22) 240034.

Ministry of Justice: Guma Bldg, Lamina Sankoh St, Freetown; tel. (22) 226733.

Ministry of Mineral Resources: Youyi Bldg, 5th Floor, Brookfields, Freetown; tel. (22) 241500.

Ministry of Trade, Industry and Transport: Ministerial Bldg, George St, Freetown; tel. (22) 225211.

President and Legislature

PRESIDENT

Presidential Election, First Ballot, 26–27 February 1996

Candidate	Votes	% of votes
AHMED TEJAN KABBAH (SLPP) . . .	266,893	35.8
JOHN KAREFA-SMART (UNPP) . . .	168,666	22.6
THAIMU BANGURA (PDP) . . .	119,782	16.1
Dr JOHN KARIMU (NUP) . . .	39,617	5.3
EDWARD MOHAMMED TURAY (APC) . . .	38,316	5.1
ADU AIAH KOROMA (DCP) . . .	36,779	4.9
ABASS CHERNOR BUNDU (PPP) . . .	21,557	2.9
AMADU M.B. JALLOH (NDA) . . .	17,335	2.3
EDWARD JOHN KARGBO (PNC). . .	15,798	2.1
DESMOND LUKE (NUM) . . .	7,918	1.1
ANDREW VICTOR LUNGAY (SDP) . . .	5,202	0.7
ANDREW TURAY (NPP) . . .	3,925	0.5
MOHAMED YAHYA SILLAH (NADP) . . .	3,723	0.5
Total . . .	**745,511**	**100.0**

Second Ballot, 15 March 1996

Candidate	Votes	% of votes
AHMED TEJAN KABBAH (SLPP) . . .	608,419	59.5
JOHN KAREFA-SMART (UNPP) . . .	414,335	40.5
Total . . .	**1,022,754**	**100.0**

PARLIAMENT

Speaker: SHEKU MOHAMED KUTUBU.

General Election, 26–27 February 1996

Party	Votes	% of votes	Seats
SLPP . . .	269,486	36.1	27
UNPP . . .	161,618	21.6	17
PDP . . .	114,409	15.3	12
APC . . .	42,443	5.7	5
NUP . . .	39,280	5.3	4
DCP . . .	35,624	4.8	3
PPP . . .	21,354	2.9	0
NDA . . .	20,105	2.7	0
PNC . . .	19,019	2.5	0
NUM . . .	8,884	1.2	0
SDP . . .	5,900	0.8	0
NADP . . .	4,653	0.6	0
NPP . . .	3,989	0.5	0
Total . . .	**746,764**	**100.0**	**68***

* A further 12 seats were allocated to Paramount Chiefs, who represented the 12 provincial districts.

Political Organizations

A ban on political activity was rescinded in June 1995. Some 15 political parties have subsequently been granted registration.

All-People's Congress (APC): 39 Siaka Stevens St, Freetown; f. 1960; sole authorized political party 1978–91; merged with the Democratic People's Party in 1992; reconstituted in 1995; Leader EDWARD TURAY.

Coalition for Progress Party (CPP): Leader GEREDINE SARHO.

Democratic Centre Party (DCP): Leader ADU AIAH KOROMA.

National Alliance Democratic Party (NADP): Leader MOHAMED YAHYA SILLAH.

National Democratic Alliance (NDA). Leader AMADU M.B. JALLOH.

National People's Party (NPP): Leader ANDREW TURAY.

National Republican Party (NRP).

National Unity Movement (NUM): Leader DESMOND LUKE.

National Unity Party (NUP): Leader Dr JOHN KARIMU.

People's Democratic Party (PDP): Leader THAIMU BANGURA.

People's National Convention (PNC): Leader EDWARD JOHN KARGBO.

People's Progressive Party (PPP): Leader ABASS CHERNOR BUNDU.

Sierra Leone People's Party (SLPP): in opposition during 1968–78; largest parl. party, following elections in Feb. 1996; party of Pres. Kabbah.

Social Democratic Party (SDP): Leader ANDREW VICTOR LUNGAY.

United National People's Party (UNPP): Leader AHMED TAYLOR-KAMARA.

Diplomatic Representation

EMBASSIES AND HIGH COMMISSIONS IN SIERRA LEONE

China, People's Republic: 29 Wilberforce Loop, Freetown; tel. (22) 231797; Ambassador: QU WEMING.

Côte d'Ivoire: 1 Wesley St, Freetown; tel. (22) 223983; Chargé d'affaires a.i.: EDO VAN AS.

Egypt: 174C Wilkinson Rd, POB 652, Freetown; tel. (22) 231499; Ambassador: MOHAMED ABDEL SALAM MOUSSA.

Gambia: 6 Wilberforce St, Freetown; tel. (22) 225191; High Commissioner: (vacant).

Germany: Santanno House, 10 Howe St, POB 728, Freetown; tel. (22) 222511; fax (22) 226213; Chargé d'affaires a.i.: CONRAD J. FISCHER.

Ghana: Freetown; High Commissioner: Lt-Col (retd) EBENEZER KOFI ANUKU TSEDE.

Guinea: 4 Liverpool St, Freetown; tel. (22) 223080; Ambassador: CHARLES EMMANUEL DE STEFAN.

Holy See: 23 Jomo Kenyatta Rd, PMB 526, Freetown; tel. (22) 242131; fax (22) 240509; Apostolic Nuncio: Most Rev. ANTONIO LUCIBELLO, Titular Archbishop of Thurio.

Italy: 32A Wilkinson Rd, POB 749, Freetown; tel. (22) 230995; Ambassador: RANIERI FORNARI.

Korea, Republic: 22 Wilberforce St, POB 1383, Freetown; tel. (22) 224269; Ambassador: KIM CHANG-SOK.

Lebanon: 22 Wilberforce St, POB 727, Freetown; tel. (22) 223513; Ambassador: Dr FAWAZ FAWAD.

Liberia: 30 Brookfields Rd, POB 276, Freetown; tel. (22) 240322; Ambassador: MACDONALD BOWEN.

Nigeria: 37 Siaka Stevens St, Freetown; tel. (22) 224202; fax (22) 224219; High Commissioner: MUHAMMED CHADI ABUBAKAR.

United Kingdom: Spur Rd, Wilberforce, Freetown; tel. (22) 232563; fax (22) 228169; e-mail bhc@sierratel.sl; High Commissioner: DAVID ALAN JONES.

USA: Walpole and Siaka Stevens Sts, Freetown; tel. (22) 226481; fax (22) 225471; Ambassador: JOSEPH H. MELROSE, Jr.

Judicial System

The Supreme Court: The ultimate court of appeal in both civil and criminal cases. In addition to its appellate jurisdiction, the Court has supervisory jurisdiction over all other courts and over any adjudicating authority in Sierra Leone, and also original jurisdiction in constitutional issues.

Chief Justice: DESMOND LUKE

Supreme Court Justices: C. A. HARDING, AGNES AWUNOR-RENNER.

The Court of Appeal: The Court of Appeal has jurisdiction to hear and determine appeals from decisions of the High Court in both criminal and civil matters, and also from certain statutory tribunals. Appeals against its decisions may be made to the Supreme Court.

Justices of Appeal: S. C. E. WARNE, C. S. DAVIES, S. T. NAVO, M. S. TURAY, E. C. THOMPSON-DAVIS, M. O. TAJU-DEEN, M. O. ADOPHY, GEORGE GELAGA KING, Dr A. B. Y. TIMBO, VIRGINIA A. WRIGHT.

High Court: The High Court has unlimited original jurisdiction in all criminal and civil matters. It also has appellate jurisdiction against decisions of Magistrates' Courts.

Judges: FRANCIS C. GBOW, EBUN THOMAS, D. E. M. WILLIAMS, LAURA MARCUS-JONES, L. B. O. NYLANDER, A. M. B. TARAWALLIE, O. H. ALGHALLI, W. A. O. JOHNSON, N. D. ALHADI, R. J. BANKOLE THOMPSON, M. E. T. THOMPSON, C. J. W. ATERE-ROBERTS (acting).

Magistrates' Courts: In criminal cases the jurisdiction of the Magistrates' Courts is limited to summary cases and to preliminary investigations to determine whether a person charged with an offence should be committed for trial.

Local Courts have jurisdiction, according to native law and custom, in matters which are outside the jurisdiction of other courts.

Religion

A large proportion of the population holds animist beliefs, although there are significant numbers of Islamic and Christian adherents.

ISLAM

In 1990 Islamic adherents represented an estimated 30% of the total population.

Ahmadiyya Muslim Mission: 15 Bath St, Brookfields, POB 353, Freetown; Emir and Chief Missionary KHALIL A. MOBASHIR.

Kankaylay (Sierra Leone Muslim Men and Women's Association): 15 Blackhall Rd, Kissy, POB 1168, Freetown; tel. (22) 250931; f. 1972; 500,000 mems; Pres. Alhaji IBRAHIM BEMBA TURAY; Lady Pres. Haja ISATA KEBE; Vice-Pres. Haja SERAY SILLAH.

Sierra Leone Muslim Congress: POB 875, Freetown; Pres. Alhaji MUHAMMAD SANUSI MUSTAPHA.

CHRISTIANITY

Council of Churches in Sierra Leone: 4A King Harman Rd, Brookfields, POB 404, Freetown; tel. (22) 240568; fax (22) 241109; e-mail ccsl@sierratel.sl; f. 1924; 17 mem. churches; Pres. Rev. MOSES B. KHANU; Gen. Sec. ALIMAMY P. KOROMA.

The Anglican Communion

Anglicans in Sierra Leone are adherents of the Church of the Province of West Africa, comprising 12 dioceses, of which two are in Sierra Leone. The Archbishop of the Province is the Bishop of Koforidua, Ghana.

Bishop of Bo: Rt Rev. SAMUEL SAO GBONDA, MacRobert St, POB 21, Bo, Southern Province.

Bishop of Freetown: Rt Rev. JULIUS O. PRINCE LYNCH, Bishopscourt, Fourah Bay Rd, POB 128, Freetown.

Baptist Churches

Sierra Leone Baptist Convention: POB 64, Lunsar; Pres. Rev. JOSEPH S. MANS; Sec. Rev. N. T. DIXON.

The Nigerian Baptist Convention is also active.

Methodist Churches

Methodist Church Sierra Leone: Wesley House, George St, POB 64, Freetown; tel. (22) 222216; autonomous since 1967; Pres. of Conf. Rev. GERSHON F. H. ANDERSON; Sec. Rev. CHRISTIAN V. A. PEACOCK; 26,421 mems.

United Methodist Church: Freetown; Presiding Bishop T. S. BANGURA; 36,857 mems.

Other active Methodist bodies include the African Methodist Episcopal Church, the Wesleyan Church of Sierra Leone, the Countess of Huntingdon's Connexion and the West African Methodist Church.

The Roman Catholic Church

Sierra Leone comprises one archdiocese and two dioceses. At 31 December 1998 there were an estimated 137,967 adherents in the country, representing about 3.0% of the total population.

Inter-territorial Catholic Bishops' Conference of The Gambia, Liberia and Sierra Leone: Santanno House, POB 893, Freetown; tel. (22) 228240; fax (22) 228252; f. 1971; Pres. Rt Rev. GEORGE BIGUZZI, Bishop of Makeni.

Archbishop of Freetown and Bo: Most Rev. JOSEPH HENRY GANDA, Santanno House, POB 893, Freetown; tel. (22) 224590; fax (22) 224075.

Other Christian Churches

The following are represented: the Christ Apostolic Church, the Church of the Lord (Aladura), the Evangelical Church, the Missionary Church of Africa, the Sierra Leone Church and the United Brethren in Christ.

AFRICAN RELIGIONS

There is a diverse range of beliefs, rites and practices, varying between ethnic and kinship groups.

The Press

DAILY

Daily Mail: 29–31 Rawdon St, POB 53, Freetown; tel. (22) 223191; f. 1931; state-owned; Editor AIAH MARTIN MONDEH; circ. 10,000.

PERIODICALS

African Crescent: 15 Bath St, POB 353, Brookfields, Freetown; Editor MAULANA-KHALIL A. MOBASHIR.

The Catalyst: Christian Literature Crusade Bookshop, 35 Circular Rd, POB 1465, Freetown; tel. (22) 224382; Editor Dr LEOPOLD FOULLAH.

Concord Times: 139 Pademba Rd, Freetown; 3 a week; Editor DOROTHY GORDON.

Leonean Sun: 49 Main Rd, Wellington, Freetown; tel. (22) 223363; f. 1974; monthly; Editor ROWLAND MARTYN.

Liberty Voice: 139 Pademba Rd, Freetown; tel. (22) 242100; Editor A. MAHDIEU SAVAGE.

New Breed: Freetown; weekly; independent; Man. Editor (vacant).

New Citizen: 5 Hanna Benka-Coker St, Freetown; tel. (22) 241795; Editor I. BEN KARGBO.

The New Globe: 49 Bathurst St, Freetown; tel. (22) 228245; weekly; Man. Editor SAM TUMOE; circ. 4,000.

The New Shaft: 60 Old Railway Line, Brookfields, Freetown; tel. (22) 241093; 2 a week; independent; Editor FRANKLIN BUNTING-DAVIES; circ. 10,000.

Progress: 1 Short St, Freetown; tel. (22) 223588; weekly; independent; Editor FODE KANDEH; circ. 7,000.

Sierra Leone Chamber of Commerce Journal: Sierra Leone Chamber of Commerce, Industry and Agriculture, Guma Bldg, 5th Floor, Lamina Sankoh St, POB 502, Freetown; tel. (22) 226305; fax (22) 228005; monthly.

Unity Now: 82 Pademba Rd, Freetown; tel. (22) 227466; Editor FRANK KPOSOWA.

The Vision: 60 Old Railway Line, Brookfields; tel. (22) 241273; Editor SIAKA MASSAQUOI.

Weekend Spark: 7 Lamina Sankoh St, Freetown; tel. (22) 223397; f. 1983; weekly; independent; Editor ROWLAND MARTYN; circ. 20,000.

Weekly Democrat: Freetown; Editor JON FORAY.

NEWS AGENCY

Sierra Leone News Agency (SLENA): 15 Wallace Johnson St, PMB 445, Freetown; tel. (22) 224921; fax (22) 224439; f. 1980; Man. Dir ABOU KARIM DIALLO.

Publishers

Njala University Publishing Centre: Njala University College, PMB, Freetown; science and technology, university textbooks.

Sierra Leone University Press: Fourah Bay College, POB 87, Freetown; tel. (22) 22491; fax (22) 224439; f. 1965; biography, history, Africana, religion, social science, university textbooks; Chair. Prof. ERNEST H. WRIGHT.

United Christian Council Literature Bureau: Bunumbu Press, POB 28, Bo; tel. (32) 462; books in Mende, Temne, Susu; Man. Dir ROBERT SAM-KPAKRA.

Government Publishing House

Government Printer: New England, Freetown; tel. (22) 241146.

Broadcasting and Communications

TELECOMMUNICATIONS

Sierra Leone Telecommunications Co (SIERRATEL): 7 Wallace Johnson St, POB 80, Freetown; tel. (22) 222804; fax (22) 224439.

BROADCASTING

Sierra Leone Broadcasting Service: New England, Freetown; tel. (22) 240403; f. 1934; state-controlled; programmes mainly in English and the four main Sierra Leonean vernaculars, Mende, Limba, Temne and Krio; weekly broadcast in French; television service established 1963; Dir-Gen. JEANA BANDATOMO.

Finance

(cap. = capital; res = reserves; dep. = deposits; m. = million; brs = branches; amounts in leone)

BANKING

Central Bank

Bank of Sierra Leone: Siaka Stevens St, POB 30, Freetown; tel. (22) 226501; fax (22) 224764; f. 1964; cap. and res 167,207.8m., dep. 47,790.0m. (June 1996); Gov. STEVE SWARAY (acting); Dep. Gov. YVONNE GIBRIL; 1 br.

Other Banks

National Development Bank Ltd: Leone House, 6th Floor, 21–23 Siaka Stevens St, Freetown; tel. (22) 226791; fax (22) 224468; f. 1968; 99% state-owned; provides medium- and long-term finance and tech. assistance to devt-orientated enterprises; cap. 1,604.3m., total assets 5,183.6m. (Dec. 1995); Chair. MOHAMED M. TURAY; Man. Dir CHRISTIAN J. SMITH; 3 brs.

Rokel Commercial Bank of Sierra Leone Ltd: 25–27 Siaka Stevens St, POB 12, Freetown; tel. (22) 222501; fax (22) 222563; f. 1971; cap. and res 2,319.1m., dep. 19,093.0m. (Dec. 1995); Chair. AUGUSTUS D. A. M'CORMACK; Man. Dir EMYR LLOYD-DAVIES; 9 brs and agencies.

Sierra Leone Commercial Bank Ltd: 29–31 Siaka Stevens St, Freetown; tel. (22) 225264; fax (22) 225292; e-mail slcb@sierratel.sl; f. 1973; state-owned; cap. and res 5,794.5m., dep. 21,754.3m. (Dec. 1998); Chair. I. I. MAY-PARKER; Man. Dir A. KAKAY; 7 brs.

Standard Chartered Bank Sierra Leone Ltd: 9 and 11 Lightfoot-Boston St, POB 1155, Freetown; tel. (22) 225021; fax (22) 225760; f. 1971; cap. and res 542.4m., total assets 34,394.3m. (Dec. 1998); Chair. LLOYD A. DURING; CEO ROY DEWAR; 12 brs.

Union Trust Bank Ltd: Lightfoot Boston St, PMB 1237, Freetown; tel. (22) 226954; fax (22) 226214; e-mail utb@sierratel.sl; fmrly Meridien BIAO Bank Sierra Leone Ltd; adopted present name in 1995; cap. 439.8m., total assets 7,057.8m. (Dec. 1998); Chair. S. B. NICOL-COLE; Man. Dir S. J. B. ANTHONY.

INSURANCE

Aureol Insurance Co Ltd: Kissy House, 54 Siaka Stevens St, POB 647, Freetown; tel. (22) 223435; fax (22) 229336; f. 1987; Chair. LLOYD A. DURING; Man. Dir S. G. BENJAMIN.

National Insurance Co Ltd: 18–20 Walpole St, PMB 84, Freetown; tel. (22) 223892; fax (22) 226097; f. 1972; state-owned; Chair. J. T. SARJAH-WRIGHT; CEO A. N. YASKEY.

New India Assurance Co Ltd: 18 Wilberforce St, POB 340, Freetown; tel. (22) 226453; fax (22) 222494; Man. Dir V. KRISHNAN.

Reliance Insurance Trust Corporation Ltd: 24 Siaka Stevens St, Freetown; tel. (22) 225115; fax (22) 228051; f. 1985; Chair. S. S. DEEN; Man. Dir E. B. KOROMA.

Sierra Leone Insurance Co Ltd: 31 Lightfoot Boston St, POB 836, Freetown.

Trade and Industry

GOVERNMENT AGENCY

Government Gold and Diamond Office (GGDO): c/o Bank of Sierra Leone, Siaka Stevens St, Freetown; tel. (22) 222600; fax (22) 229064; f. 1985; govt regulatory agency for diamonds and gold; combats illicit trade; Chair. Alhaji M. S. DEEN.

CHAMBER OF COMMERCE

Sierra Leone Chamber of Commerce, Industry and Agriculture: Guma Bldg, 5th Floor, Lamina Sankoh St, POB 502, Freetown; tel. (22) 226305; fax (22) 228005; f. 1961; 215 mems; Pres. Alhaji MOHAMED MUSA KING.

EMPLOYERS' ORGANIZATIONS

Sierra Leone Employers' Federation: POB 562, Freetown; Chair. DONALD C. SMYTHE-MACAULAY; Exec. Officer A. E. BENJAMIN.

Sierra Leone Chamber of Mines: POB 456, Freetown; tel. (22) 226082; f. 1965; mems comprise the principal mining concerns; Pres. D. J. S. FRASER; Exec. Officer N. H. T. BOSTON.

UTILITIES
Electricity

Sierra Leone Electricity Corporation: Freetown; supplies all electricity in Sierra Leone.

Water

Guma Valley Water Co: Guma Bldg, 13/14 Lamina Sankoh St, POB 700, Freetown; tel. 25887; f. 1961; responsible for all existing water supplies in Freetown and surrounding villages, including the Guma dam and associated works.

MAJOR COMPANIES

Aureol Tobacco Co Ltd: Wellington Industrial Estate, POB 109, Freetown; tel. (22) 223435; fax (22) 263138; f. 1959; cigarette mfrs; Chair. Prof. K. KOSO-THOMAS; Man. Dir A. D. A. M'CORMACK; 75 employees.

Bata Shoe Co Sierra Leone Ltd: Wallace Johnson St, POB 111, Freetown; footwear mfrs and distributors. Assoc. Co:

Plastic Manufacturing Sierra Leone Ltd: Wilkinson Rd, POB 96, Freetown; footwear mfrs.

Chanrai Sierra Leone Ltd: Wellington Industrial Estate, POB 57, Freetown; tel. (22) 263292; fax (22) 263305; f. 1893; importers of motor spares, air-conditioners, refrigerators, building materials, textiles and provisions; mfrs of soaps and polyethylene bags; Dir R. K. LAKHANPAL; 115 employees.

The Diamond Corporation (West Africa) Ltd: 25–27 Siaka Stevens St, POB 421, Freetown; purchase and export of diamonds; Dir S. L. MATTURI.

Rokel Leaf Tobacco Development Co Ltd: POB 29, Makeni; f. 1974; production of leaf tobacco; Chair. J. T. SHORT.

Sierra Leone Breweries Ltd: POB 721, Freetown; tel. (22) 263384; fax (22) 263118; f. 1961; brewing and marketing of Guinness stout and Star lager; Gen. Man. P. P. SUTTON; Man. Dir O. A. SMITH.

Sierra Leone National Petroleum Co: NP House, Cotton Tree, POB 277, Freetown; tel. (22) 225040; fax (22) 226892; petroleum products; CEO VINCENT LAMIN KANU.

Sierra Leone Ore and Metal Co (SIEROMCO): POB 725, Freetown; tel. (22) 226777; fax (22) 227276; mining of bauxite; operations suspended since 1995; Chair. K. WOLFENSBERGER; Man. Dir JAMES WESTWOOD.

Sierra Leone Petroleum Refining Co Ltd: PMB, Kissy Dockyard, Freetown; 50% state-owned; operates a refinery.

Sierra Rutile Ltd: PMB, Freetown; tel. and fax (22) 228144; f. 1971; jtly-owned by US and Australian interests; mining of rutile and ilmenite (titanium-bearing ores); CEO BRIAN CALVER; 1,600 employees.

UAC of Sierra Leone Ltd: 6-8 Blackhall Rd, Freetown; fmrly United Africa Co; mfrs agents: construction, mining, marine, agriculture and power plants; Chair. LLOYD A. DURING; Man. Dir VICTOR G. THOMAS.

TRADE UNIONS

Artisans', Ministry of Works Employees' and General Workers' Union: 4 Pultney St, Freetown; f. 1946; 14,500 mems; Pres. IBRAHIM LANGLEY; Gen. Sec. TEJAN A. KASSIM.

Sierra Leone Labour Congress: 35 Wallace Johnson St, POB 1333, Freetown; tel. (22) 226869; f. 1966; c. 51,000 mems in 19 affiliated unions; Pres. H. M. BARRIE; Sec. Gen. KANDEH YILLA.

Principal affiliated unions:

> **Clerical, Mercantile and General Workers' Union:** 35 Wallace Johnson St, Freetown; f. 1945; 3,600 mems; Pres. M. D. BENJAMIN; Gen. Sec. M. B. WILLIAMS.

> **Sierra Leone Association of Journalists:** Freetown; Pres. SIAKA MASSAQUOI.

> **Sierra Leone Dockworkers' Union:** 165 Fourah Bay Rd, Freetown; f. 1962; 2,650 mems; Pres. D. F. KANU; Gen. Sec. A. C. CONTEH.

> **Sierra Leone Motor Drivers' Union:** 10 Charlotte St, Freetown; f. 1960; 1,900 mems; Pres. A. W. HASSAN; Gen. Sec. ALPHA KAMARA.

> **Sierra Leone Teachers' Union:** Regaland House, Lowcost Step—Kissy, POB 477, Freetown; f. 1951; 18,500 mems; Pres. FESTUS E. MINAH; Sec.-Gen. A. O. TIMBO.

> **Sierra Leone Transport, Agricultural and General Workers' Union:** 4 Pultney St, Freetown; f. 1946; 1,600 mems; Pres. S. O. SAWYERR-MANLEY; Gen. Sec. S. D. KARGBO.

> **United Mineworkers' Union:** 35 Wallace Johnson St, Freetown; f. 1944; 6,500 mems; Pres. H. M. BARRIE; Gen. Sec. S. D. GBENDA.

Also affiliated to the Sierra Leone Labour Congress: **General Construction Workers' Union, Municipal and Local Government Employees' Union, Sierra Leone National Seamen's Union.**

Transport

RAILWAYS

There are no passenger railways in Sierra Leone.

Marampa Mineral Railway: Delco House, POB 735, Freetown; tel. (22) 222556; 84 km of track linking iron ore mines at Marampa (inactive since 1985) with Pepel port; Gen. Man. SYL KHANU.

ROADS

In 1996 there were an estimated 11,700 km of classified roads, including 1,390 km of main roads and 1,630 km of secondary roads; about 1,287 km of the total network was paved. In 1993 the Government announced a seven-year road rehabilitation programme, which, at an estimated cost of US $100m., was to be financed by the World Bank.

Sierra Leone Road Transport Corpn: Blackhall Rd, POB 1008, Freetown; tel. (22) 250442; fax (22) 250000; f. 1965; state-owned; operates transport services throughout the country; Gen. Man. DANIEL R. W. FAUX.

INLAND WATERWAYS

Established routes for launches, which include the coastal routes from Freetown northward to the Great and Little Scarcies rivers and southward to Bonthe, total almost 800 km. Although some of the upper reaches of the rivers are navigable only between July and September, there is a considerable volume of river traffic.

SHIPPING

Freetown, the principal port, has full facilities for ocean-going vessels.

Sierra Leone National Shipping Co Ltd: 45 Cline St, POB 935, Freetown; tel. (22) 250881; fax (22) 223222; f. 1972; state-owned; shipping, clearing and forwarding agency; representatives for foreign lines; Gen. Man. PAUL K. NIELSEN.

Sierra Leone Ports Authority: Queen Elizabeth II Quay, PMB 386, Cline Town, Freetown; tel. (22) 250111; fax (22) 250616; f. 1965; parastatal body, supervised by the Ministry of Trade, Industry and Transport; operates the port of Freetown; Gen. Man. Capt. P. E. M. KEMOKAI.

Sierra Leone Shipping Agencies Ltd: Deep Water Quay, Clinetown, POB 74, Freetown; tel. (22) 250882; fax (22) 250400; f. 1949; Man. Dir I. HEDEMANN.

UMARCO (Freetown) Ltd: POB 417, Freetown; shipping agents; Gen. Man. R. HUGHES.

CIVIL AVIATION

There is an international airport at Lungi.

Directorate of Civil Aviation: Dept of Transport and Communications, Ministerial Bldg, 5th Floor, George St, Freetown; tel. (22) 222106; Dir T. T. A. VANDY.

Sierra National Airlines: Leone House, 25 Pultney St, POB 285, Freetown; tel. (22) 222075; fax (22) 222026; f. 1982; state-owned; operates domestic and regional services, and a weekly flight to Paris, France; Pres STANLEY A. PALMER.

Tourism

The main attractions for tourists are the coastline, the mountains and the game reserves. In 1994, when an estimated 72,000 tourists visited Sierra Leone, receipts from this source totalled US $10m. In 1997, according to official estimates, tourist arrivals numbered 48,000. However, civil conflict has effectively suspended tourist activity.

National Tourist Board: International Conference Centre, Aberdeen Hill, POB 1435, Freetown; tel. (22) 272520; fax (22) 272197; f. 1990; Gen. Man. CECIL J. WILLIAMS.

Defence

In August 1999 active members of the armed forces of the Republic of Sierra Leone numbered about 3,000; a three-year programme for the restructuring of the armed forces, with the assistance of a 90-member team of British military advisers, had been announced. In October 1999 the UN Security Council adopted a resolution establishing the UN Mission in Sierra Leone (UNAMSIL), which was to supervise the implementation of a peace agreement between the Government and rebel forces, signed in July of that year. In early May 2000 about 500 members of UNAMSIL were taken hostage by the rebel Revolutionary United Front. The British Government subsequently dispatched a military task force to the region; at mid-June about 250 British troops remained in the country temporarily to train new members of the Sierra Leone armed forces. At the end of July UNAMSIL numbered 12,474 military personnel, including 260 military observers, and had a maximum authorized strength of 13,000. After a rebel militia group took a number of British military personnel hostage in August, further British troops were dispatched to Sierra Leone (see Recent History).

Defence Expenditure: Estimated at Le 26,000m. in 1998.

Commander-in-Chief of the Armed Forces: Alhaji AHMED TEJAN KABBAH.

Chief of Staff of the Army: Col TOM CAREW.

Education

Primary education begins at five years of age and lasts for seven years. Secondary education, beginning at the age of 12, also lasts for a further seven years, comprising a first cycle of five years and a second cycle of two years. In 1987 tuition fees for government-funded primary and secondary schools were abolished. In 1990 primary enrolment was equivalent to 50% of children in the appropriate age-group (boys 60%; girls 41%), while the comparable ratio for secondary enrolment was 17% (boys 22%; girls 13%). There is one university, which comprises six colleges; in 1992/93 2,571 students were enrolled in higher education. Budgetary expenditure on education and social welfare by the central government in the financial year 1990/91 was estimated at Le 2,775.1m. (11.7% of total spending). In 1995, according to UNESCO estimates, adult illiteracy averaged 68.5% (males 54.6%; females 81.8%).

Bibliography

Allie, Joe. *A New History of Sierra Leone.* London, Macmillan, 1990.

Cartwright, J. R. *Politics in Sierra Leone 1947–67.* Toronto, 1970.

  Political Leadership in Sierra Leone. Toronto, 1978.

Clapham, C. *Liberia and Sierra Leone: An Essay in Comparative Politics.* Cambridge University Press, 1976.

Clarke, J. I. *Sierra Leone in Maps.* London, 1966.

Conteh-Morgan, E., and Dixon-Fyle, M. *Sierra Leone at the End of the Twentieth Century: History, Politics and Society.* Berne, Peter Lang, 1999.

Cruise O'Brien, D. B., Dunn, J., and Rathbone, R. (Eds). *Contemporary West African States.* Cambridge University Press, 1989.

Daramy, S. B. *Constitutional Developments in the Post-Colonial State of Sierra-Leone 1961–1984.* Lewiston, Edwin Mallen, 1993.

Fashole Luke, D. *Labour and Parastatal Politics in Sierra Leone: A Study in African Working-class Ambivalence.* Lanham, MD, University Press of America, 1984.

Funna, S. M. 'Structure and Performance of the Sierra Leone Economy: 1971–81', in *Sierra Leone Studies at Birmingham, 1983.* Birmingham University Press, 1984.

Fyle, C. M. *The History of Sierra Leone: A Concise Introduction.* London, 1981.

  (Ed.) *The State and Provision of Social Services in Sierra Leone Since Independence.* Dakar, CODESRIA, 1993.

Greenhalgh, P. *West African Diamonds: An Economic History 1919–83.* Manchester University Press, 1985.

Gwynne-Jones, D. R. G., et al. *A New Geography of Sierra Leone.* Longman, 1978.

Harrell-Bond, B., Howard, A. M., and Skinner, D. E. *Community Leadership and the Transformation of Freetown, 1801–1976.* Leiden, 1978.

Hayward, M. F. *Elections in Independent Africa.* Boulder, CO, Westview Press, 1987.

International Labour Organisation. *Ensuring Equitable Growth: A Strategy for Increasing Employment, Equity and Basic Needs Satisfaction in Sierra Leone.* Addis Ababa, 1981.

Koroma, A. K. *Sierra Leone: Agony of a Nation.* Freetown, Afro Media, 1996.

Luke, D. F., and Riley, S. P. *Economic Decline and the New Reform Agenda in Africa: The Case of Sierra Leone.* Manchester, University of Manchester Press, 1991.

Makannah, T. J. (Ed.). *Handbook of the Population of Sierra Leone.* Freetown, Toma Enterprises, 1996.

Reno, W. *Corruption and State Politics in Sierra Leone.* Cambridge University Press, 1995.

Richards, P. *Fighting for the Rain Forest: War, Youth and Resources in Sierra Leone.* Oxford, James Currey, 1996.

Rimmer, D. *The Economies of West Africa.* London, Weidenfeld and Nicolson, 1984.

Stevens, S. *What Life Has Taught Me.* London, Kensal Press, 1984.

Thomas, A. C. *The Population of Sierra Leone: An Analysis of Population Data*. Freetown, Fourah Bay College, 1983.

Thompson, B. *The Constitutional History and Law of Sierra Leone, 1961–1995*. Lanham, MD, University Press of America, 1997.

Turay, E. D. A., and Abraham, A. *The Sierra Leone Army: A Century of History*. London, Macmillan, 1988.

Weeks, J. *Development Strategy and the Economy of Sierra Leone*. New York, St Martin's Press, 1992.

Wyse, A. *The Krio of Sierra Leone: An Interpretive History*. London, Hurst, 1989.

Zack-Williams, A. *Tributors, Supporters and Merchant Capital: Mining and Underdevelopment in Sierra Leone*. Aldershot, Avebury, 1995.

SOMALIA

Physical and Social Geography

I. M. LEWIS

The Somali Democratic Republic covers an area of 637,657 sq km (246,201 sq miles). It has a long coastline on the Indian Ocean and the Gulf of Aden, forming the 'Horn of Africa'. To the north, Somalia faces the Arabian peninsula, with which it has had centuries of commercial and cultural contact. To the north-west, it is bounded by the Republic of Djibouti, while its western and southern neighbours are Ethiopia and Kenya. The country takes its name from its population, the Somali, a Muslim Cushitic-speaking people who stretch far beyond its present frontiers into these neighbouring states.

Most of the terrain consists of dry savannah plains, with a high mountain escarpment in the north, facing the coast. The climate is hot and dry, with an average annual temperature of 27°C, although temperate at higher altitudes and along the coast during June–September, with annual rainfall rarely exceeding 500 mm in the most favourable regions. Only two permanent rivers—the Juba and Shebelle—water this arid land. Both rise in the Ethiopian highlands, but only the Juba regularly flows into the sea. The territory between these two rivers is agriculturally the richest part of Somalia, and constitutes a zone of mixed cultivation and pastoralism. Sorghum, millet and maize are grown here, while along the rivers, on irrigated plantations, bananas (the mainstay of Somalia's exports) and citrus fruits are produced. This potentially prosperous zone contains remnants of Bantu groups—partly of ex-slave origin—and is also the home of the Digil and Rahanwin, who speak a distinctive dialect and are the least nomadic element in the population. Of the other Somali clans—the Dir, Isaaq, Hawiye and Darod, primarily pastoral nomads who occupy the rest of the country—the Hawiye along the Shebelle valley are the most extensively engaged in cultivation. A small subsidiary area of cultivation (involving Dir and Isaaq) also occurs in the north-west highlands.

In this predominantly pastoral country, permanent settlements are small and widely scattered, except in the agricultural regions, and for the most part are tiny trading centres built around wells. There are few large towns. Mogadishu, the capital, which dates from at least the 10th century as an Islamic trading post, had an estimated population of 500,000 in 1981. The other main centres are Kismayu (population 70,000 in 1981) and Berbera (65,000 in 1981), the main southern and northern ports respectively. The northern town of Hargeysa (population 70,000 in 1981) was declared the capital of the secessionist 'Republic of Somaliland' in 1991.

According to the results of a census taken in February 1975, the population of Somalia was 3,253,024 (excluding adjustment for underenumeration). The February 1986 census recorded a total of 7,114,431. According to UN estimates, the mid-year population in 1998 was 9,237,000. Important demographic changes have taken place in recent years, beginning with the serious drought which affected the north of the country in 1974–75 and led to the resettlement of large numbers of people in the south. During 1980–88 successive influxes of refugees from Ethiopia created a serious refugee problem before repatriations began in 1990. Of greatest consequence, however, has been the dislocation of Somalia's population during the civil unrest that began in the late 1980s. In early 1993 it was estimated that three-quarters of the population had been internally displaced by civil conflict; by late 1997 there were an estimated 250,000 internally displaced Somalis. In late 1998 there were an estimated 470,950 Somali refugees outside the country, of whom about 195,400 were resident in Ethiopia and 164,700 in Kenya. There were reports in early 1999 of an influx of Somali refugees into Yemen, bringing the number of Somali refugees in that country to some 65,000.

Recent History

THOMAS OFCANSKY

Based on an earlier article by PATRICK GILKES

Britain declared a protectorate over northern Somalia in 1886, with the aim of safeguarding the trade links of its colony Aden and excluding other interested powers (especially France). With the latter objective in mind, Italy established a colony in southern regions in the same period Italian Somaliland became, with Eritrea, a base for the Italian conquest of Ethiopia in 1936. The Italian colony was captured by British forces in 1941 and placed under military administration. Although Italy subsequently renounced all rights to Italian Somaliland, in 1950 it became the UN Trust Territory of Somalia, placed under Italian administration for a 10-year transitional period prior to independence. The British protectorate meanwhile had reverted to civilian rule, while most of the Somali areas in Ethiopia had been returned to Ethiopian administration.

The trust territory's first general election on the basis of universal adult suffrage was held in March 1959, when 83 of the 90 seats in the legislative assembly were won by the Somali Youth League (SYL). Britain, meanwhile, prepared its protect-orate for self-government. British Somaliland became independent on 26 June 1960, and on 1 July, having secured its own independence, the former Italian Somaliland united with the former British Somaliland as the independent Somali Republic. The president of the southern legislative assembly was proclaimed head of state and the two legislatures merged to form a single assembly in Mogadishu. A coalition government was formed by the SYL and the two leading northern political parties, with Dr Abd ar-Rashid Ali Shirmake, a leading SYL politician and a member of the Darod clan, as the first prime minister. Shirmake's government, constituting a balance of northern and southern members representative of the main clans, set the pattern of Somali political life for the next decade.

The problems of merging the administrative systems of the two former colonies were offset to an extent by the shared Somali culture and by the presence of clans straddling the old colonial boundaries. Internal harmony was further encouraged, at the price of external conflict, by the commitment of all political leaders to a policy of extending the boundaries of the state to include Somali communities in Ethiopia, French Somaliland (now Djibouti) and northern Kenya. Accordingly, liberation movements were established for these areas. In the 1964 elections the SYL secured a majority of seats in the assembly. However, a split within the SYL's Darod leadership, leading to the appointment of a new Darod prime minister, Abd ar-Razak Hussein, left the party seriously divided and culminated in the election as president in 1967 of Shirmake, who formed a new government with Mohamed Ibrahim Egal (a northerner from the Isaaq clan) as prime minister. Acknowledging the failure so far of its efforts to promote Somali unification, the government, through Zambian mediation, reached agreement with Ethiopia and Kenya to negotiate a lasting frontiers settlement.

With external pressure on the republic diminished, the smaller constituent units of the traditional political structure returned to the fore, with an upsurge of divisive tribalism. The 1969 legislative elections were contested by more than 1,000 candidates, representing 68 political parties and the most important lineages and sub-lineages of the Somali clan system. With the resources of the state at its disposal, and with considerable manipulation of the electoral arrangements, the SYL again secured victory, and Egal was reappointed premier. Following the formation of the customary clan-coalition government, all but one of the members of the assembly joined the ruling party. Because of the prevailing political fragmentation, however, the government and the assembly were in reality no longer representative of the public at large. Discontent was aggravated by the increasingly autocratic style of both the president and prime minister, and by the latter's efforts to provide political and administrative posts for northerners.

THE SIAD BARRE REGIME, 1969–91

In October 1969 Shirmake was assassinated in the course of factional violence. When it became clear that the assembly would elect a new president supported by Egal, the army seized control in a bloodless coup. A supreme revolutionary council (SRC), which comprised army and police-officers, announced that it had acted to preserve democracy and justice and to eliminate corruption and tribalism (clanism) and that the country had been renamed the Somali Democratic Republic to symbolize these aims. The president of the SRC, Maj.-Gen. Mohamed Siad Barre, became head of state.

Siad Barre swiftly assumed personal control of the government, introducing a policy of 'scientific socialism'. The Somali Revolutionary Socialist Party (SRSP) was established in 1976 under Soviet influence, although it operated more as a mechanism for control than as an ideological vehicle. Most key sections of the economy were brought under government control. In 1975 land was nationalized: farmers received holdings on 50-year renewable leases from the state, but from the outset the system was subject to manipulation and corruption. (Subsequent efforts to recover land became a significant element in inter-clan conflict after 1991.) A mass literacy campaign was launched, building on the adoption of Somali as the official language in 1972, using a modified Roman alphabet.

Somalia suffered from severe drought in the mid-1970s, although a programme of resettlement, accomplished with the help of a massive Soviet airlift, relocated some 140,000 people to farming colonies in the agricultural south and experimental fishing settlements along the coast. During this period, the army's dependence on Soviet equipment and training greatly increased Soviet influence in Somalia. The USSR acquired a variety of military facilities, notably at the northern port of Berbera. Somalia nevertheless emphasized its traditional links by joining the Arab League in 1974, when Siad Barre also acted as chairman of the Organization of African Unity (OAU). Ethiopia's revolutionary transformation to military socialism in September 1974 at first seemed to offer the prospect of an acceptable accommodation for Somali aspirations to self-determination in the Ogaden. These hopes were soon extinguished, however, and as internal chaos spread in Ethiopia, Somalia saw an opportunity to reactivate claims to the Ogaden and the Somali-speaking regions of Ethiopia. In 1976 Siad Barre restructured the Western Somali Liberation Front (WSLF) and allowed it to operate inside Ethiopia. The Ogaden, the main clan in the

Ogaden region and within the WSLF, represented a crucial element of Barre's clan support.

New urgency was given to Somalia's intentions by preparations for Djibouti's independence in June 1977 (both Somalia and Ethiopia had an interest in the strategic port of Djibouti and its rail link to Addis Ababa via Dire Dawa—passing through Somali inhabited areas), and by Soviet overtures to Ethiopia's Col Mengistu after he took power in February. Despite Soviet attempts to dissuade him, Siad Barre's forces invaded Ethiopia, unofficially, in July 'in support of the WSLF'. Within three months Somali troops had overrun the Ogaden region and reached Harar. The USSR began to supply Ethiopia with weapons; in November Somalia abrogated its treaty of friendship with the Soviet Union and expelled 6,000 Soviet advisers and experts. Somalia obtained some financial assistance from Saudi Arabia, but hopes of Western assistance were largely frustrated, and by March 1978 the Soviet and Cuban-led counter-attack had re-established Ethiopian control in the main centres of the Ogaden and the Somali government announced the withdrawal of its forces.

Defeat in the Ogaden war and the break with the USSR led to a gradual strengthening of links with the USA, stemming from US strategy in the Persian (Arabian) Gulf, following the Soviet intervention in Afghanistan in 1979. A defence agreement, announced in 1980, permitted the use by US military personnel of the air and naval facilities at Berbera. The USA provided Somalia with substantial amounts of aid during the 1980s, but remained hesitant about supplying it with military aid as long as Somali forces continued to operate in Ethiopia. The US administration also expressed reservations regarding renewed Somali links with Libya after 1985.

The Ethiopian government's recovery of the Ogaden and its response to continued guerrilla operations as well as Somali army incursions (together with prevailing drought conditions), resulted in the flight, to Somalia, of hundreds of thousands of refugees. Food aid from Western relief agencies became a significant factor in the Somali economy. There was considerable disagreement over refugee numbers, with government estimates of as many as 1.5m., in contrast to a figure of 400,000 quoted by some relief agencies. The failure of rains in 1985–86, and the recurrence of famine in 1987, led to further refugee movements. A compromise refugee figure of 800,000 was accepted for the provision of food relief in the later 1980s.

Military defeat, shifts in alliance and ideology, as well as famine and the influx of refugees, had considerable impact on internal politics. Opposition movements began to appear, notably the Somali Salvation Democratic Front (SSDF), a largely Majerteen-supported group, and the Somali National Movement (SNM), whose support was primarily drawn from the northern Isaaq clan. The Majerteen are a Darod clan living largely in the north-east. Both movements received Ethiopian support. The SSDF took control of two small central Somali towns near the border in 1981 but virtually collapsed with internal divisions in the mid-1980s. In 1988, after a meeting in which Siad Barre and Mengistu agreed to restore diplomatic relations, withdraw troops from border areas, and end support for each other's dissidents, the SNM were ordered to leave their Ethiopian bases. This precipitated a premature guerrilla offensive. In May the SNM seized Burao and captured most of Hargeysa, in the north. They were promptly ousted by a full-scale armed government response under the command of Gen. Mohamed Siad 'Morgan' (a son-in-law of the president). His uncompromising operations included the systematic bombardment of Hargeysa (by South African mercenary pilots), resulting in an estimated 40,000 deaths and the flight of around 400,000 refugees into Ethiopia. The brutal suppression of the insurgency resulted in far greater support for the SNM within the Isaaq and other northern clans than it had ever managed to achieve by its own efforts. Siad Barre's response to political and economic difficulty was to tighten his own control, although he allowed the introduction of a new constitution with an elected assembly, within the single-party system, in 1979. However, the assembly's lack of power was underlined in late 1984 when it effectively transferred all government powers to the president. Although seriously injured in an automobile accident in May 1986, Siad Barre (as sole candidate) was re-elected president for a further seven-year term. In 1987 Siad Barre reluctantly agreed to the creation of the post of prime minister, which was occupied by Gen. Mohamed Ali Samatar, formerly first vice-president and defence minister.

Siad Barre's temporary incapacitation in 1986 precipitated a struggle for the succession within his own Marehan clan and significantly weakened the government's position. The main claimants were his eldest surviving son, Gen. Maslah, and his cousin, Abd ar-Rahman Jama Barre, a veteran foreign minister; their rivalry divided the clan and also the armed forces. Economic difficulties were also increasing, as remittances from Somalis working in the Persian (Arabian) Gulf region declined in the aftermath of the Iran-Iraq war and then during the 1990–91 conflict in that region; international aid also declined, as a result of concern over the regime's human rights record.

With the collapse of the economy, Siad Barre no longer had the resources to continue the manipulation of clan rivalries, which he had ruthlessly employed to ensure his political survival, and opposition continued to grow. In early 1989 a group of Hawiye notables established the United Somali Congress (USC), in exile, in Rome, Italy. The USC included a guerrilla wing, operating from Ethiopia, commanded by Gen. Mohamed Farah 'Aidid'. (The Hawiye are the dominant group in Mogadishu and are particularly prominent in commercial and intellectual life.) Hawiye opposition was also expressed through the 'Manifesto' movement in Mogadishu which produced a declaration, in June 1990, appealing for the resignation of Siad Barre, the establishment of a transitional government to organize democratic elections, and the immediate abolition of all security structures. Siad Barre's response was to arrest about half of the signatories, including the country's highly respected first president, Aden Abdullah Osman. In turn, the 'Manifesto' group began to nurture a military wing, although it was widely considered to be a part of the USC. The arrest of a number of Muslim religious leaders, accused of supporting various opposition elements, led to demonstrations in Mogadishu in July 1989. These were ruthlessly suppressed by the security police, with reports of as many as 1,500 dead and injured, including one instance in which 46 people, all northerners, were summarily executed. During 1989 the government also lost the support of the Ogaden clan, which, together with the Dolbuhunta, had been the main supporters of Siad Barre's Marehan clan. Following the dismissal and arrest of the Ogadeni minister of defence, Ogadeni army deserters established the Somali Patriotic Movement (SPM) in the south. This gained considerable support from the Ogaden who had long considered that the Marehan, as the president's clan, had been able to expand their grazing at the expense of the Ogaden in the Juba valley. In response to mounting military and civil opposition, the government made some conciliatory gestures, but they were largely dismissed as superficial exercises.

In August 1989 Siad Barre announced that opposition parties would be allowed to contest elections, scheduled to take place before the end of 1990, and additionally offered to relinquish power. One effect of this was to encourage the creation of political parties within those major clans that had yet to evolve a political identity. In January 1990 the president dismissed his government, castigating the prime minister, Gen. Samatar, for the government's poor performance. However, Siad Barre failed to persuade any opposition figures to join the administration, and was forced to reappoint Samatar.

A renewed military offensive in the north in early 1990 was largely successful in its aims, with the government temporarily recapturing a couple of towns from the SNM. Significantly, much of the fighting was carried out by clan militia, armed by the government. In July, following the appearance of the 'Manifesto' group, the government announced a constitutional referendum for October to be followed by elections in February 1991. Samatar was dismissed in September and replaced by Mohamed Hawadle Madar, an Isaaq from the north. A month later it was announced that the multi-party system would take immediate effect, and Siad Barre relinquished the post of secretary-general of the SRSP, in accordance with the provisions of the new constitution, which proscribed the president's maintenance of additional official responsibilities. However, by late 1990 the government retained little authority outside Mogadishu. The army, its administration and command structure in decay owing to the over-promotion of untrained Marehan, had

virtually disintegrated. Indeed, its clan support was essentially confined to the Marehan which was itself divided on the wisdom of continued support for Siad Barre, some believing that the fortunes of the president had become too closely allied to those of the clan. In November widespread fighting erupted in Mogadishu when Siad Barre attempted to exploit an inter-clan dispute in order to attack the Hawiye. A full-scale uprising followed indiscriminate shelling of Hawiye areas of the city; USC guerrillas arrived in force and steadily advanced on the government's positions. Urgent efforts to form an acceptable government, headed by Umar Arteh Ghalib, an Isaaq and a former minister, and an announcement by Siad Barre that he would relinquish power in exchange for a cease-fire, were ignored. Offers by Egypt and Italy to mediate in the conflict were rejected. On 27 January 1991 Siad Barre fled with the remnants of his army, and the USC took power.

DESCENT TO CIVIL WAR

On announcing its take-over the USC urged all opposition forces to participate in a national reconciliation conference. However, on 29 January 1991, the USC unexpectedly appointed one of the 'Manifesto' group, Ali Mahdi Mohamed, a government minister in the 1960s, as interim president. The USC emphasized that it did not intend to form a permanent government, but other political groups saw the move as an attempt to pre-empt their participation, despite the appointment of non-Hawiye to government. In February Umar Arteh Ghalib was appointed prime minister at the head of a new government; other appointments included Gen. Mohamed Abshir, of the Majerteen clan. Umar Arteh, however, was considered to have compromised his position by his acceptance of the premiership shortly before Siad Barre's overthrow, and was unpopular with the SSDF and the SNM. The majority of government posts were allocated to Hawiye clan members, in particular those from the 'Manifesto' group.

In the north the SNM, which expelled the remnants of Siad Barre's forces in January–February 1991, convened a series of clan elders' meetings which led to the declaration of an independent 'Republic of Somaliland' in May. The SNM elected its chairman, Abd ar-Rahman Ahmed Ali 'Tur', as president. The secession was denounced by the USC and by the Mogadishu government. In the south, fighting erupted between the USC and elements from the Darod clan as Siad Barre tried to rally support under a Somali National Front (SNF). The move split one Darod clan, the Ogaden, and its political group, the SPM. One faction co-operated with the SNF and forces raised by Gen. Mohamed Siad 'Morgan', who led several advances of SNF forces towards Mogadishu during 1991. The other section of the SPM, led by Col Ahmed Omar Jess, united with the USC to block any attempt by Siad Barre to return. The southern port of Kismayu changed hands several times during the year. Much of the fighting was on a clan basis, between Hawiye (USC) and Darod (SNF or SPM), or between sub-clans of the Ogaden, which supported different factions of the SPM.

In June 1991 President Gouled of Djibouti sponsored the first of two reconciliation conferences. The conference was chaired by ex-president Aden Abdullah Osman, and included delegations from the USC, the Somali Democratic Movement (SDM, a Rahanwin organization), the SSDF (Majerteen), and the SPM (Ogaden). Although the SNM refused to attend a second meeting or participate in a transitional government for all Somalia, two additional groups, the Somali Democratic Alliance (Gadabursi), and the United Somali Front (Issa), took part in the second conference, convened in July. An agreement was negotiated, committing all those attending to resist the forces of Siad Barre, implement a general cease-fire, respect national unity, readopt the 1960 constitution, and recognize Ali Mahdi's two-year mandate as interim president. Much discussion was devoted to dividing ministerial portfolios equitably among the clan groups. The Darod groups (the SSDF and the SPM) wanted a Darod prime minister, while others requested a northerner, although not Umar Arteh. Other major difficulties arose concerning Darod demands for the return of property seized after Siad Barre's overthrow. Darod and Isaaq clans were estimated to have owned as much as 60% of land and property in Mogadishu before 1989. Most was looted in 1991 and appropriated by Hawiye, who were reluctant to return it. The issues of property and blood debt for deaths in the fighting have since remained highly contentious, and unresolved, problems.

The Mogadishu government's difficulties were compounded during 1991 by a major split in the USC, between the factions led by Ali Mahdi and by Gen. Mohamed Farah 'Aidid' who had been the main USC guerrilla leader. These factions had different origins, but more importantly, they also represented different sub-clans within the Hawiye—Ali Mahdi being from the Abgal, a prominent group in and around Mogadishu; and Gen. Aidid being from the Habr Gidir, who comprise a significant element of the more rural, pastoral Hawiye, living in the central regions of the country. The Abgal provided much of the support for the 'Manifesto' group while the Habr Gidir comprised most of the Hawiye guerrilla forces. Many Habr Gidir felt that the 'Manifesto' politicians had benefited undeservedly, after coming late to the struggle and doing little fighting. Aidid made it clear he felt he had a better claim to the presidency than Ali Mahdi. In July, at the third congress of the USC, he was elected USC chairman, affording him a significant power base. When Ali Mahdi failed to award ministerial posts to Aidid's supporters in the reshuffle that followed the Djibouti conferences, confrontation seemed inevitable.

The first clash occurred in September 1991, when four days of fighting resulted in heavy casualties. More serious hostilities erupted in November and lasted until March 1992, when a cease-fire was eventually negotiated. Both sides were exhausted, with food supplies short and no international body prepared to intervene until hostilities ceased. Stores of ammunition were also depleted. By then at least 30,000 people had died and thousands more had been injured, with Mogadishu in disarray and divided between the two sides. The struggle was complicated by two other Hawiye clan militias in Mogadishu, the Hawadle and the Murasade. The Hawadle, in possession of the airport, originally supported Gen. Aidid, the Murasade, in control of the port, backed Ali Mahdi.

The March 1992 cease-fire was organized by the UN, which had first investigated the possibility of a UN peace-keeping force being sent to Somalia early in the year. In January a resolution was adopted unanimously by the UN Security Council, imposing an arms embargo on Somalia, requesting humanitarian aid and urging the parties to cease hostilities. By the end of the month, hundreds of thousands of people displaced by the conflict were reported by the International Committee of the Red Cross to be in danger of starvation, and thousands of refugees from Somalia were continuing to cross the border into Kenya. Following the March cease-fire a UN technical team arrived to act in a supervisory capacity. In April the UN Security Council approved the establishment of a 'UN Operation in Somalia' (UNOSOM) and the dispatch of 50 observers to Mogadishu. Mohammed Sahnoun, an Algerian diplomat, appointed by the UN secretary-general as his representative in Somalia, arrived in Mogadishu in May to establish a UN presence. Deployment of the UN observers was slow, partly because Gen. Aidid temporarily suspended co-operation with the UN, alleging that UN aid flights to Mogadishu had been used to supply arms and funding for supporters of Ali Mahdi. The cease-fire monitors eventually arrived in July. A further UN Security Council resolution approved an urgent airlift of food aid to Somalia, the dispatch of a technical team and 48 military observers to assess the situation in preparation for deploying 500 UN peace-keeping troops. Agreement was finally reached with Aidid on the presence of UN peace-keeping forces and the first elements of a Pakistani battalion arrived in Mogadishu in September. The UN also approved the dispatch of a further 3,000 troops to Somalia, although this was opposed by Aidid.

The UN's gradual involvement during 1992 failed to interrupt continuing fighting. Although the cease-fire in Mogadishu held, forces loyal to Siad Barre attempted to recapture the capital. These forces advanced to within 30 km of Mogadishu, only to be halted by Gen. Aidid's forces in a battle at Afgoi in April. Aidid capitalized upon his victory by repulsing Siad Barre's forces, and Siad Barre himself, initially to Garba Harre, where Siad Barre had been based since his overthrow, and then on into Kenya. Siad Barre was refused political asylum in Kenya, and in May he moved to Nigeria, where he died in exile in January 1995. Following his victory over Siad Barre's forces, in May 1992 Aidid's troops, in alliance with Omar Jess of the SPM

faction, recaptured the port of Kismayu from the forces of Gen. 'Morgan'. 'Morgan' and his supporters also fled into Kenya. Aidid's military successes and his efforts to establish administrative control of the whole of southern Somalia, generated considerable opposition. He himself formed a coalition, the Somali National Alliance (SNA), comprising his own USC, a faction of the SPM, a faction of the SDM, and the Southern Somali National Movement, a political group of non-Darod clans to the south of Mogadishu. In response to this and to Aidid's recent victories, Ali Mahdi strengthened his links with opponents of Aidid, notably the SSDF, the other SPM faction, and the SNF. After mid-1992 the SNF, although a largely Marehan organization, disassociated itself from Siad Barre, while allying itself with 'Morgan', who became one of its main military commanders. In October Aidid's opponents, led by 'Morgan' and Gen. Ahmed Warsame of the SNF, recaptured Bardera, a strategic southern town and advanced towards Kismayu.

The escalation of fighting in October 1992 underlined the serious nature of food shortages in rural areas, particularly in the areas around Bardera. With the country in a state of anarchy, aid agencies encountered difficulties in ensuring the security of relief supplies and of their own personnel, and many were forced to hire armed guards from local clans for their protection. There were growing differences of opinion between the UN, which wished to secure a general cease-fire with the aid of peace-keeping forces, in order to protect relief supplies from looting, and the relief agencies which identified an urgent need to maximize food distribution as quickly as possible. By mid-1992 it had become apparent that a major humanitarian crisis had arisen in and around Bardera and Baidoa in the south of the country, largely owing to the destruction of food stocks in the area by the forces of Siad Barre in the months before and after their last attack on Mogadishu in April. The failure of Aidid's efforts to establish control in the area contributed to the severity of the problem. It was subsequently estimated that some 300,000 people may have died from starvation in this period. The UN's slow response to the humanitarian crisis was widely criticized. At a conference in Geneva in October, convened for the launch of the UN's 100-Day Programme for Somalia (a relief programme requesting more food aid, and the provision of basic health services—but including the rehabilitation of civil society), Sahnoun denounced the competence of UN agencies; he also questioned the continued lack of operations in Somalia of the World Health Organization. Sahnoun advocated local reconciliation and a gradual approach to a national reconciliation conference, and was resistant to the idea of any rapid deployment of UN peace-keeping forces. His criticism of senior UN officials, and his disagreement with the UN secretary-general over future policy, forced his resignation later in the month.

INTERNATIONAL INTERVENTION

Deteriorating conditions in Somalia in the latter part of 1992 prompted a response from the US government. In November President Bush, who had earlier authorized a US airlift to assist in food distribution, offered up to 30,000 US troops to ensure food deliveries to those in need, and to prevent looting. The offer was a cause for concern among many aid workers in Somalia, who felt that since the death toll had already slowed significantly, and food distribution had improved considerably, intervention on such a scale was unnecessary. The US proposition, however, coincided with the aim of UN secretary-general, Boutros Boutros-Ghali, to increase the UN's capacity to intervene in such crisis situations, and the UN welcomed the offer. It was suggested that an additional motivation for the US offer of intervention might have been the emergence of an Islamic political group in June in Somalia. A number of towns in the north-east had been temporarily seized by the al-Ittihad al-Islam party. While they were quickly expelled by the SSDF, Islamic groups continued to gain prominence in several other areas of the country, prompting US concern at the possibility of the spread of Iranian influence in Somalia, Kenya and Ethiopia.

Following the (albeit brief) convergence of UN and US interests, the first US troops of the Unified Task Force (UNITAF) landed at Mogadishu in early December 1992 as part of 'Operation Restore Hope'. Contingents from 21 countries, including

France, Belgium, Saudi Arabia, Zambia, Canada, Morocco and Australia participated. UNITAF forces were deployed throughout Somalia over the next few weeks, entering Baidoa and Kismayu in mid-December. Under pressure from UNITAF, Gen. Aidid and Ali Mahdi held peace talks, and on 27 December announced that they had signed a 'reconciliation agreement'. The scope and aims of UNITAF's operation, however, were both ill-defined and controversial. The US administration was determined to limit the activity of its forces to protecting the flow of aid. The UNITAF commander, a US officer, made it clear that he would not be prepared to enforce disarmament on a substantive scale. The UN wanted the role of UNITAF to include complete disarmament of the rival factions and the establishment of security in the country, which it argued could not be achieved without full-scale disarmament of the factions and indeed of bandits, whose activities remained a considerable threat to security. UNITAF forces did carry out some seizures of weapons and the US claimed that the military task of restoring security had been completed by early February 1993, allowing the free movement of relief aid throughout Somalia. Nevertheless, violent incidents continued as the US administration negotiated the withdrawal of its forces and the transfer of operations to a multinational peace-keeping force under direct UN command. The strength of UNITAF (some 38,300 men in mid-January 1993) had been reduced to 24,000 by early February, although there was disappointment among US officials at the poor level of UN preparedness for any transfer. One of the main areas of conflict remained Kismayu, where the forces of Gen. 'Morgan' and those of Omar Jess's faction of the SPM were in conflict at the end of February. Clashes continued in March, prompting the US to dispatch marines in an attempt to restore order and reinforce US and UN troops already deployed there.

Meanwhile, negotiations continued among the factions on proposed peace talks, which were scheduled to be held in Addis Ababa, Ethiopia, in March 1993. The national reconciliation conference was attended by representatives of 15 leading factions; members of the SNM from the self-declared 'Republic of Somaliland' (see below) were present with observer status. The conference nearly collapsed at the outset when Gen. Aidid's supporters were ousted from Kismayu by Gen. 'Morgan' despite the presence of UN forces there. However, in late March, the leaders reached a compromise agreement, to form a 74-member transitional national council as the supreme authority in Somalia, with a mandate to hold elections within two years. The council was to have three representatives from each of the 18 proposed administrative regions of Somalia (inclusive of 'Somaliland'), five from Mogadishu and one from each of the 15 signatory factions to the agreement. The agreement committed the factions to disarmament within 90 days and required the peace-keeping forces of the UN to administer the cease-fire by taking sanctions against violators. On the day preceding the signing of the agreement, the UN Security Council adopted Resolution 813, authorizing the deployment of UNOSOM II to replace UNITAF, and instructing it to use whatever means necessary to uphold peace, disarm combatants and protect relief workers. UNOSOM II, the largest peace-keeping operation to be dispatched under UN auspices, was also the first such operation to engage in peace enforcement without the consent of parties in the relevant country. The creation of UNOSOM II followed proposals made by the UN secretary-general in March, that operations in Somalia should be transferred to a multinational force of 28,000 men on 1 May. In March a retired US admiral, Jonathan Howe, was appointed as special representative of the secretary-general in Somalia, with a mandate to oversee the transition from UNITAF to UNOSOM II.

UNOSOM II, under the command of Gen. Çevik Bir of Turkey, formally took control of the peace-keeping operation on 4 May 1993, with more than 30 countries contributing to a force which numbered some 30,000 at full strength. UNOSOM II inherited a series of difficulties from UNITAF and from US policies. The view that 'Somaliland' should be considered part of Somalia complicated UNOSOM's dealings with the north, while failure to disarm the militias and the factions meant that violent confrontation was difficult to prevent. UNITAF's acceptance of politicians and warlords as key negotiators rather than making serious efforts to widen the basis of political consultancy, meant that the existing political structures, responsible for the pre-

vious two years of anarchy, were reinforced. This also resulted in the promotion of personal conflicts at the expense of understanding clan hostilities. UNOSOM took this a stage further by taking sides and effectively declaring war on Gen. Aidid, after US advisers had decided that he was the one figure with no future role in negotiations, owing to his independent attitude towards UNITAF and towards the UN's presence in Somalia. A legacy inherited by UNOSOM II was the independence of the US Rapid Deployment Force which remained under direct US command. It was this unit which was responsible for a series of attacks against Aidid in Mogadishu, during 1993. Conflict began in June in Mogadishu when fighting between Aidid's SNA and UNOSOM left 24 Pakistani soldiers dead and 50 wounded. There were several hundred Somali casualties. The next day the UN Security Council condemned the 'unprovoked attack' on the Pakistani force and demanded the arrest and punishment of those responsible. Adm. Howe made it clear that he believed Aidid was responsible for the attack and, in response, UNOSOM forces launched a series of attacks on the SNA. These failed in their main objective of seizing Aidid, and also provoked hostile reactions in Mogadishu. In one attack, Pakistani soldiers fired on a crowd of civilians, killing 20 and injuring 50 others. The UN issued a warrant for Aidid's arrest on charges of war crimes, while US helicopters attacked Aidid's home in Mogadishu, destroying ammunition dumps. Increasingly violent operations, which sought to disarm the SNA and arrest Aidid, continued over the next few months. One of the worst incidents occurred in July when US helicopters attacked a suspected pro-Aidid command centre, resulting in 50–100 Somali fatalities, and the murder, in retaliation, of four foreign journalists by enraged Somali crowds. The attack revealed clear divisions within UNOSOM's command structure. Italy, providing the third largest contingent, urged a suspension of military operations to defuse tension and promote dialogue. There were claims that UNOSOM's original humanitarian mission had been sacrificed to US government preoccupations with capturing Aidid. The Italian view was echoed by aid agencies, the OAU and even by the UN's own department of humanitarian affairs. However, the secretary-general insisted that initiatives for disarmament should continue. Italy was asked to withdraw its commander in Somalia amid allegations that he was obeying Italian government orders rather than those of UN commanders, and unilaterally negotiating with Aidid. A compromise agreement was eventually arrived at, whereby Italian troops in Mogadishu were to be redeployed elsewhere in the country.

UNOSOM continued to ignore all criticism of its actions, and in August 1993 the death of four US soldiers in another clash led to the dispatch of an élite US military unit to Mogadishu to reinforce efforts to capture Gen. Aidid. Embarrassingly, four days after the rangers' arrival in Mogadishu in August, they mistakenly raided a UN compound and briefly arrested several UN employees. Subsequent US operations were more successful and some senior members of the SNA were detained, though no warrants had been issued, raising questions about the legality of the detentions. UNOSOM claimed preventive detention was permissible under its mandate, and there was no obligation to allow access to lawyers. Human rights organizations strongly criticized UNOSOM's arguments. Criticism was also levelled at UNOSOM's refusal to provide figures for Somalis killed as a result of its operations. In two further clashes, in September, Somali casualties, including many civilians, were estimated at 500 dead and wounded. On 3 October an effort by US soldiers to seize Aidid's supporters in a heavily-populated district led to an all-night battle in which there were 19 UNOSOM fatalities, and at least 200 Somalis were killed and more than 700 injured. The incident provoked renewed scrutiny of UNOSOM operations, which had become increasingly characterized by indiscriminate military action and damage to non-military installations.

The events of 3 October 1993 prompted an immediate change in US policy, encouraged by massive popular support for the withdrawal of their troops. Although President Clinton's response was to dispatch reinforcements to the area, he made it clear that the US would promote a political rather than military solution to the conflict with Aidid. Following the release of two servicemen captured on 3 October and Aidid's declaration of a unilateral cease-fire in mid-October, UNOSOM abandoned demands for Aidid's arrest. Efforts were subsequently concentrated on a political settlement, although the last of the SNA political detainees held by UNOSOM were only released in early 1994 after an independent inquiry into the reasons for their detention.

Another UNOSOM objective during 1993 was the rehabilitation of local government through the establishment of district and regional councils, as detailed in the Addis Ababa conference of March 1993. However, local observers were again critical of the methods employed by UNOSOM, claiming that council members were often imposed or excluded (particularly in the case of SNA members) by UN officials. It was suggested that the local administration rehabilitation programme had been precipitately implemented, and had failed to address the problem of refugee resettlement.

Another reconciliation conference, convened in Addis Ababa in December 1993, was again attended by faction leaders. No agreement was reached between the four factions of Aidid's SNA and the 11 factions comprising Ali Mahdi's Somali Salvation Alliance. However, at an affiliated humanitarian conference convened simultaneously, it was made clear that UNOSOM intended to link further aid and assistance to political stability. This had the effect of encouraging local clan and regional agreements, some of which were concluded under UNOSOM auspices, while others were independently negotiated. The first of several regional conferences had been the Jubaland peace conference which took place in Kismayu during May–August 1993. Discussions included recommendations for a cease-fire and for the forcible encampment of militia forces. Negotiations also covered the creation of district councils, of local police and security forces, the rehabilitation of roads and the return of property (though the question of ownership was left undefined). However, this conference and a subsequent Kismayu meeting, convened in June 1994, failed to produce any binding agreement between the Majerteen-Harti and the Ogaden (both Darod—the major clan in the region), nor for an equitable division of resources with other claimants. Indeed the Ogaden elders did not attend the meeting in June, owing to preoccupation with their own efforts to achieve Ogaden unity. UNOSOM's reaction to elders' conferences was inconsistent. While it supported the Jubaland peace conferences, UNOSOM was accused of having attempted to sabotage a successful conference organized by Aidid in May 1993 to settle conflicts between the Hawiye and Majerteen clans in central Somalia. It was also suggested that UNOSOM's negative attitude to the continued independence of 'Somaliland', during meetings with clans from the north-east at Garowe in late 1993, undermined considerable progress in inter-clan co-operation proceeding from discussions which took place in Engavo between August and November, at which UNOSOM was not officially represented.

The decision of the US, and most European contingents, to withdraw from Somalia by March 1994 meant that the UN's mandate had to be revised. Although both India and Pakistan increased their contingents, UNOSOM no longer had sufficient personnel to carry out its larger mission. In February 1994 the UN Security Council revised UNOSOM's mandate, authorizing a progressive reduction of troops to a maximum of 22,000, effectively ending UNOSOM's programme of disarmament of Somali factions, in favour of the protection of ports, airports and roads. In May the UN Security Council voted to extend UNOSOM's mandate for four months (rather than six, as requested by the secretary-general), and in November the Security Council extended UNOSOM's mandate to a final date of 31 March 1995, by which time the whole operation was to have been withdrawn. There was growing alarm at the cost of UNOSOM, with daily running costs of US $2.5m., while the cost of the deployment of US troops in Somalia between December 1992 and March 1994 was estimated at $1,200m.

There was also considerable consternation in early 1994 at the failure of Somali faction leaders to make further political progress. Meetings in Nairobi, Kenya, in March had resulted in another agreement between Aidid and Ali Mahdi to establish a government, but by the end of July there had been five postponements, and no meeting, because of disagreements over the timing and location of future meetings. Aidid's return to Mogadishu in May did not improve prospects for peace. Renewed conflict erupted between factions of the Hawiye clan and there

were indications that Aidid was encountering dissension within his own clan and political organization. Aidid's Habr Gidir and the Hawadle clan disputed control of the airport, and their conflict extended north to Beled Weyne in late July where the Habr Gidir took control. UNOSOM subsequently evacuated its troops from the region after the entire 168-strong Zimbabwe contingent was disarmed by Aidid's forces.

In September 1994 clashes betweeen UN troops and Somali militias were reported, in which several Somalis were killed. In October fierce fighting erupted in the Bermuda area of Mogadishu, this time betwen Ali Mahdi's Abgal clan and the Murusade clan, although the two groups had previously been in alliance (there were rumours that Gen. Aidid had engineered the estrangement). Hostilities continued sporadically into January 1995 (resulting in as many as 200 fatalities), in which month the two clans brokered a peace agreement. As the deadline for UNOSOM's departure approached, the competition for control of installations currently in UN hands, in particular the port and airport, became the focus of factional hostility.

In late November 1994 UN forces began to withdraw from positions outside Mogadishu in the first stages of UNOSOM's departure. In December Harti and Marehan clansmen fought for control of Kismayu port in the wake of the UN's withdrawal from that town. 'Operation United Shield', to ensure the safe evacuation of the UN troops and civilian personnel, as well as most of the equipment brought in under UNOSOM, was organized and led by the USA. The USA stationed several thousand marines in warships off the Somali coast in December, and in early 1995 they were joined by a multinational force of naval and air force units (comprising some 10,000 armed personnel) in order to protect departing UN employees (by early 1995 some 136 members of UNOSOM had been killed since the beginning of the operation).

In early February 1995 UN troops left their compound in Mogadishu, which had served as UNOSOM's headquarters, and withdrew to positions in the port and airport. In mid-February thousands of SNA supporters demonstrated against the return of US forces, although Aidid gave assurances that they would not be attacked. Even though Aidid and Ali Mahdi reached agreement on joint management of the port and airport, as well as a cessation of hostilities, including the removal of weapons from the streets of the capital during the UN withdrawal, in late February fighting was reported around both the port and airport areas. The combatants in the airport area appeared to be rival factions of the Habr Gidir sub-clan, with some supporting Aidid and others his former aide, Osman Hassan Ali 'Ato'. At the end of February 1,800 US and 400 Italian marines landed on Mogadishu's beaches, and command of the remaining 2,400 UN troops and of the whole operation was passed from the UN to the US commander. The marines secured the port and airport, and evacuated the last UN soldiers in an operation the execution of which was designed to minimize casualties, although several Somalis were killed and more injured as they threatened US positions. The departure of the last UN personnel in March (almost one month ahead of schedule) was closely followed by that of the US and Italian marines themselves. Somali looters overran the airport, but armoured cars from Aidid's faction, reportedly accompanied by UN-trained police-officers, took control of the area. Ali Mahdi's Abgal clansmen gained control of the eastern section of the airport and skirmishes were reported between the two sides. Aidid and Ali Mahdi subsequently agreed on the reopening of the port and set out detailed terms for the 'technical peace committee' that was to administer the port and airport; however, the terms of the agreement were promptly violated by both sides and fighting for control of the crucial sites was resumed. In May the heaviest fighting since the UN withdrawal was reported in the Bermuda area of Mogadishu.

RESURGENCE OF MILITIA RIVALRY

Significant divisions within the SNA became more apparent in June 1995, following an attempt, made by a group of disaffected party members, to replace Gen. Aidid with Ali 'Ato' as chairman of the party. SNA members loyal to Aidid immediately broadcast a rejection of the legitimacy of the actions of the Ali 'Ato' faction and announced the expulsion of the faction from the SNA. In mid-June a reconciliation conference convened in southern

Mogadishu by representatives of 15 pro-Aidid factions, elected Aidid president of the Republic of Somalia for a three-year term. Five vice-presidents, representing the interests of distinct clans, were also elected, and the composition of a comprehensive cabinet was subsequently announced. However, Aidid's presidency and mandate to govern were immediately rejected in a joint statement issued by Ali Mahdi and Ali 'Ato'. Although Aidid announced a weapons collection programme in Mogadishu in August, many militias refused to comply and continued to clash with pro-Aidid factions. In September Aidid's forces occupied the south-western city of Baidoa, reportedly in an attempt to seize food supplies. The capture of Baidoa was widely considered to be the most significant military development since Aidid's forces were ejected from the port of Kismayu in 1993. More than 20 foreign aid workers, captured during the battle for Baidoa, were subsequently released unharmed by Aidid's followers. In October it was reported that Aidid had lost control of the airport at Balidogle (some 90 km south-west of Mogadishu) to Ali 'Ato' forces. In the same month a joint committee representing the interests of supporters of Ali Mahdi and those of Ali 'Ato' was established to consider the future of banana exports (a crucial source of revenue) in the context of Aidid's increasingly effective stranglehold on all operations at the port of Mogadishu. (Some goods were being imported through the neighbouring natural harbour at Ceel Macaan.) The committee announced that it would extend a ban on all banana exports from the port of Mogadishu for as long as all revenues were diverted into Aidid's war efforts. Ships attempting to dock at the port were subsequently shelled by the committee's supporters, while Aidid's gunboats returned fire in an attempt to secure the safe passage of merchant vessels. Fighting between Gen. Aidid's supporters and those loyal to Ali 'Ato' intensified in early 1996, resulting in Aidid's capture of Hoddur in January and the deaths of 120 people in Mogadishu and southern Somalia in April alone.

Meanwhile, Gen. Aidid attempted to prevent the spread of Islamic fundamentalism in Somalia, which he perceived as a threat to his power. In May 1995 Sheikh Abbas bin Omar, the leader of the Islamic organization Jihad al-Islam, threatened to launch a holy war against Aidid and Ali Mahdi if they failed to reach an accommodation within two months. He also claimed that Jihad al-Islam maintained offices in Kenya, Sudan, Yemen and Pakistan. Despite the threats, no Muslim uprising was reported. After the departure of the international peace-keepers, 17 men, based in north Mogadishu, formed the Shari'a Implementation Club (SIC) which sought to enforce Shari'a (Islamic) law throughout Somalia. In June SIC spokesman Mohamed Hassan Ahmed announced that more than 200 military volunteers had joined his organization. In February 1996 gunmen loyal to Aidid killed three people and wounded four others at the residence of an Islamic cleric.

Sporadic fighting between Aidid's followers and those of Ali Mahdi and Ali 'Ato' continued during May–August 1996. In July more than 90 people were killed and some 350 were wounded during clashes between rival factions in Mogadishu. Gen. Aidid was wounded during the skirmishes, and on 1 August he died as a result of his injuries. Despite initial hopes that Aidid's demise might precipitate peace negotiations, on 4 August one of Aidid's sons, Hussein Mohamed Aidid (a former US marine and hitherto Aidid's chief of security), was elected interim president by the SNA leadership council. Hussein Aidid (who was subsequently elected chairman of the SNA) pledged to continue his father's struggle, and factional fighting quickly resumed.

The Rahanwin Resistance Army (RRA) captured Hoddur in August 1996, and in the following months the RRA clashed with pro-Aidid forces on several occasions. In addition, there was fighting in the port of Kismayu, when warring factions in the SNF clashed as a result of disagreements over the allocation of fees collected from ships using the port. Hostilities also continued in Mogadishu. In October Ali 'Ato', Hussein Aidid and Ali Mahdi attended negotiations in Nairobi, under the auspices of Kenya's president, Daniel arap Moi, during which they agreed, *inter alia*, to cease hostilities. Nevertheless, in late October the cease-fire was broken, and fighting intensified in the following months.

In December 1996 representatives of some 26 Somali factions (notably not including the SNA) held protracted talks in Sodere, Ethiopia, under the auspices of the Ethiopian government and the Intergovernmental Authority on Development (IGAD). The conference culminated, in January 1997, in the creation of a 41-member national salvation council (NSC), with an 11-member executive committee and a five-member joint chairmanship committee, to act as an interim government charged with drafting a transitional charter and holding a national reconciliation conference. Hussein Aidid condemned the establishment of the NSC, insisting that he was the legitimate president of Somalia.

In January 1997 the NSC drew attention to the fact that payments for many shipments of weapons were being made with revenue earned by the country's banana industry, and urged the European Union (EU) to refrain from supporting individuals who had secured illegal banana concessions and their parent companies abroad. The NSC also appealed to the international community to enforce arms sanctions against Somalia. The NSC's second ordinary session ended in Addis Ababa in July. The council urged the EU to impose a temporary ban on banana imports from Somalia and appealed for international assistance to help finance the national reconciliation conference, scheduled to be held in Boosaaso, northern Somalia, in November.

International mediation efforts continued, and in March 1997 representatives of Somali factions participated in talks in Cairo, Egypt, under the auspices of the Egyptian government and the Arab League. In May Ali 'Ato' and Hussein Aidid reaffirmed their commitment to the Nairobi agreement during a meeting in San'a, Yemen. Later in the month Ali Mahdi and Aidid signed a reconciliation agreement in Cairo; however, Aidid maintained that he would not attend the national reconciliation conference in Boosaaso, as he opposed the Ethiopian-supported peace initiative.

There was a steady deterioration in security after March 1994 with an increase in banditry, abductions of aid workers and attacks on UNOSOM personnel. The World Food Programme suspended operations in Kismayu in April, after persistent threats to its employees. In the same month US $2.6m. of UN personnel salaries were stolen from the organization's compound in Mogadishu. The creation of an 8,000-strong police force by the end of June was one of UNOSOM's more successful initiatives. However, the force was insufficiently equipped to deal effectively with the factions. UNOSOM's problems were compounded by an outbreak of cholera early in the year. By the time it had been contained (mid-year) more than 1,000 people had died and 27,000 had been affected. In late 1993 the UN had established a commission of inquiry to investigate the violent exchanges which had resulted in the deaths of more than 100 peace-keeping troops and several thousand Somalis (the SNA claimed at the beginning of 1994 that 13,000 Somalis had been killed by UNOSOM). The report, which was extensively leaked prior to its publication, attributed responsibility for some atrocities to Gen. Aidid's forces, but was also highly critical of UNOSOM methods. Among prominent criticisms were those of inadequate training and equipment, and a lack of co-ordination between military and civilian elements. UNOSOM was also accused of having underestimated Somali military capacity, and political advisers were said to have lacked expertise and to have been insensitive to Somali culture. The US was criticized for its 'premature' withdrawal and for its insistence on retaining command of its own troops. The report suggested that the UN should consider compensation for innocent Somali victims of the conflict. It also concluded that UNOSOM, rather than providing assistance for Somalia, as was intended, 'tried to impose a political solution' inconsistent with the UN mandate. In June 1995 the UN disclosed that of the $70.3m. requested by the organization for emergency relief and short-term rehabilitation projects, only $13.1m. had been contributed to date.

PEACE PROCESS AND EMERGING PROBLEMS

Despite considerable support for the peace process during 1997–99, serious domestic problems cast doubt on Somalia's ability to re-establish stability and re-create a nation state system.

In December 1997 Egypt announced that 26 Somali faction leaders, including Hussein Aidid and Ali Mahdi, had signed a peace agreement in Cairo. The pact was a precursor of a national reconciliation conference, which was charged with electing a 13-member presidential council, a premier and a 189-seat legislature. Ethiopia rejected the Cairo accord on the grounds that it failed to include all members of the NSC.

In April 1998 Ali Mahdi, Ali 'Ato', Mohamed Qanyare Afrah and Hussein Aidid met in Nairobi to discuss the establishment of a joint administration for Mogadishu. Kenya, as a member of the IGAD, organized the talks, which focused on power-sharing and the reopening of Mogadishu's air and sea ports. The four leaders met with President Moi and publicly appealed for international financial assistance to fund the reconciliation conference. After returning to Somalia, Ali Mahdi and Aidid announced their intention to establish a joint administration in the capital; however, progress in achieving their objective remained slow.

In spite of efforts to restore stability, inter-clan fighting continued in Mogadishu, Kismayu, around Baidoa, in Gedo region, and in numerous other towns and villages in southern Somalia. As a result of continued clashes in Mogadishu, the UN and several humanitarian organizations frequently suspended or curtailed operations in the capital and elsewhere.

During 1998–99 armed clashes continued unabated throughout Somalia. In Gedo region fighting increased after the collapse of the August 1998 el-Ade peace pact between the SNF and al-Ittihad. The SNF, moreover, split into two warring factions, one led by the uncompromising Haji, and the other by the more moderate Ali Nur, who had been one of Haji's deputies. Each faction controlled three districts in Gedo region and battled for control of Bardhere district. In April 1999, Ali Nur was assassinated, most probably by forces loyal to Omar Haji.

In August 1998 Mogadishu's principal faction leaders (including Ali Mahdi, Hussein Aidid and Qanyare Afrah) formed the Banaadir administration for the capital and its environs. Ali Mahdi and Aidid were designated as its two chairmen, and a 29-member regional supreme council (incorporating other faction representatives) and a body of governors (including managers for the port and airport) were established. One of the administration's main aims was to reopen Mogadishu's port and airport. Ali 'Ato', Muse Sudi Yalahow and Hussein Haji Bod immediately rejected the new administration, claiming it was 'non-representative'. Nevertheless, Egypt, Italy and Libya provided aid to the Banaadir administration, enabling the regional supreme council to unveil plans for the establishment of a 6,000-strong police force, with the help of US $800,000 and some arms from Libya. However, when the administration held a police graduation ceremony in December 1998, there were only an estimated 2,000 officers, all of whom were former militiamen. Within months the police force had disbanded as a result of the Banaadir administration's failure to pay them. Meanwhile, battles between rival militias continued in Mogadishu, and there were reports of attacks on relief organizations, ships and convoys.

In late December 1999 five Mogadishu faction leaders Hussein Aidid, Ali 'Ato', Qanyare Afrah, Hussein Haji Bod and Ali Mahdi (who was in exile and represented by an aide—Mahdi returned to Mogadishu in February 2000) agreed to establish a new government in the city. The faction leaders, all of whom belonged to the Hawiye clan, believed that this agreement would eventually lead to the creation of a national government. Libya pledged financial aid to help implement the scheme; however, the plan never materialized. Later in December 1999 armed gunmen, supposedly loyal to Jama Mohamed Furuh, occupied the port of Mogadishu. Furuh, who had been in charge of security at the port prior to its closure in 1995, then denounced the new authority and called on Aidid to relinquish his position as its leader. Islamic elements in Mogadishu also opposed the new authority. Local businessmen hired militias that had been created by Mogadishu's Islamic courts to provide security in and around the capital. In November 1999 these local businessmen had provided food rations and paid nearly 600 militiamen about US $30 each for their services; in early December 1999 the militias dismantled roadblocks throughout Mogadishu.

A further complication arose in December 1999 when the Ethiopian-supported RRA established a regional administration in the central Bay region. Mohamed Ali Aden Qalinleh assumed the position of governor, while other senior RRA personnel took positions in the government. By early 2000, a new military force called the Rahanwin Salvation Army (RSA) had emerged. On 8 February the RSA, which reportedly received support from Hussein Aidid, captured the town of Bur Acaba from the RRA. The following month, a clash between the RRA and a joint RSA-Digil Salvation Army (DSA) force left some 30 people dead.

The security situation remains uncertain throughout much of southern Somalia. Fighting in and around the port of Kismayo occurred regularly in late 1999. In September militiamen killed more than 30 people and wounded more than 50 others. The clash involved the Ayr sub-clan of Habr Gidir and a group of Ogaden fighters. Ironically, both belonged to the Juba Valley Alliance, which had earlier in the year expelled forces loyal to Gen. 'Morgan' from Kismayo. In the same month a battle in Garbaharrey, the capital of the Gedo region, between the Ethiopian-supported faction of the SNF and the main SNF group resulted in at least 27 deaths. The main SNF group, led by Omar Haji Masalleh, succeeded in expelling the breakaway faction from the town. The defeated forces retreated to the Ethiopian-controlled town of Luq. At about the same time, a combined force from the RRA and the DSA launched an unsuccessful attack on the town of Qoryole, which was controlled by troops loyal to Aidid. There were at least nine deaths and 14 people were wounded. Inter-clan fighting continued into 2000. In early February hundreds of people arrived in Mogadishu and Merca after fleeing from clashes between the RRA and the local Islamic court militia in the Kurtunwarey district. Similar confrontations occurred in Qoryole and Arrile. These and scores of similar incidents not only threatened civilians but also thwarted development efforts. Public disgust with the faction leaders provoked a large-scale anti-war demonstration in Mogadishu at the end of September 1999. Protesters also encouraged all Somalis to support the peace proposals made by President Gelleh of Djibouti.

DJIBOUTI PEACE CONFERENCE

In March 1998 the IGAD conceived the idea of holding a Somali national peace conference. Many observers were sceptical of this plan as there had already been 12 conferences sponsored by the US, UN, Ethiopia and Egypt since the collapse of the Somali state in 1991. Nevertheless, President Gelleh of Djibouti's recommendation that a national reconciliation conference in Djibouti be staged in late April 2000 and early May, to be attended by up to 1,500 delegates from various cross-sections of Somali society, was accepted. Under the plan they would elect members to a new national legislature to be based in Mogadishu, who would, in turn, elect a president. The president would be responsible for choosing a prime minister, subject to the approval of the members of the legislature, who would lead a transitional government for a period of no longer than two years, during which time a national constitution would be drawn up and a date for elections would be selected.

On 2 May 2000 the 'consultative' phase of the Somali national reconciliation conference opened in Arta, about 25 miles south of Djibouti town, with some 400 delegates, representing various Somali clans and political and armed groups, in attendance. Both 'Somaliland' and 'Puntland' refused to attend because they did not want to be reunited with the turbulent south. 'Puntland's' decision provoked some protests from groups which supported the peace conference. Demonstrations occurred in the regional capital of Garoe, Boosaaso, and in Qardho in the Bari region. Mogadishu's major faction leaders were divided in their attitudes toward the reconciliation conference. Hussein Aidid, Qanyare Afrah and Ali 'Ato' rejected any participation, while Haji Bod and Ali Mahdi both expressed their support for the reconciliation conference. In mid-June the second phase of the reconciliation conference, which aimed to create new Somali institutions, commenced. By this stage it was reported that the number of delegates attending the conference had risen to around 900. A draft proposal produced in early July provided for the Somali Republic to adopt a federal system, after a three-year period, comprising 18 regional administrations. The capital of the country was to be Mogadishu. Futhermore, it was announced that the Somali transitional national assembly would consist of 225 members, of whom 25 would be women. In mid-July the proposal was adopted by a comprehensive majority and the process of electing members to the assembly began. By late July a commission appointed by the peace conference participants to apportion the parliamentary seats had submitted its report. Each of the four major clans, Dir, Hawiye, Darod and Oigil and Mirifle, was to receive 44 seats in the new Somali parliament and an alliance of small clans was allocated a total of 24 seats; the remaining 25 seats were reserved for women from the four major clans and the alliance of small clans, each of which would receive five seats. Nevertheless, disagreements between clans and sub-clans over the distribution of the parliamentary seats continued. Gelleh intervened and proposed the appointment of 20 extra members of the assembly, thus increasing the number to 245. The proposal was accepted and on 13 August the Somali transitional national assembly held its inaugural session, which was attended by 166 members. The transitional national assembly subsequently elected Abdallah Deerow Issaq, a former head of the political wing of the RRA, to the post of speaker. On 26 August Abdulkasim Salad Hassan, a member of the Hawiye clan, who had held several ministerial positions in the Siad Barre administration, was elected president of Somalia by the members of the transitional national assembly. Hassan obtained 145 of the 245 votes, thus defeating his nearest rival, Abdallah Ahmed Adow, who gained 92. Hassan was sworn in as president the following day at a ceremony attended by the Ethiopian prime minister, Meles Zenawi, the Sudanese president, Omar Hassan Ahmad al-Bashir, and the president of Eritrea, Issaias Afewerki. Upon his return to Mogadishu in early September, Hassan appealed for aid to assist with the rebuilding of Somalia. In mid-September Hassan met with Hussein Aidid in Sirte (Surt), Libya. Following discussions, an agreement of national reconciliation was signed, under the terms of which the SNA pledged its support for the Hassan regime.

EXTERNAL RELATIONS

Historically, relations between Somalia and Kenya have been close. After the downfall of the Siad Barre regime the Kenyan government declined to express its support for any particular Somali faction striving for power. However, in July 1995 Kenyan police detained Ali 'Ato', who had been in Nairobi to participate at a conference. Kenyan President Moi personally expressed regrets at the arrest when Ali 'Ato' was released the following day. Ali 'Ato' returned to Nairobi in August to attend a meeting sponsored by the Organization of the Islamic Conference (OIC), resulting in the release of a communiqué urging Gen. Aidid to renounce violence and to support the national reconciliation process. In June 1996 Kenya hosted a European Commission-financed conference regarding political decentralization for Somalia, which was attended by some 30 Somali intellectuals. In October President Moi hosted negotiations between Hussein Aidid, Ali Mahdi and Ali 'Ato', and additional discussions between the faction leaders were held in Nairobi in April 1998. After Ethiopia and Eritrea started sending arms to opposing Somali factions, the security situation along the border with Kenya deteriorated. In June 1999 some 400 Somali militiamen loyal to the pro-Aidid SNF faction attacked a small military camp and police patrol base at Amuma, and stole rifles, ammunition and communications equipment. Kenya immediately increased its military presence in the area and President Moi warned the raiders that if they did not return the goods they would face military action. The commander of the SNF faction, Gen. Omari Haji Mohamed, returned unconditionally all the stolen items and indicated that his troops had mistaken the Kenyans for an opposing SNF faction. Despite the quick resolution of the incident, Kenya closed its border with Somalia to prevent the further influx of Somali refugees and defeated militiamen. Additionally, five Kenyan navy ships, including three fast-attack craft, continued to patrol the Kenya–Somalia border where they had been deployed after the Somali attack. Moi imposed a ban on all flights into Somalia, but later eased this restriction because of protests from the UN and traders who export qat to Somalia. In April 2000 Kenya reopened its border with Somalia.

Somali-Ethiopian relations have been defined largely by the Ogaden, a Somali-inhabited region in Ethiopian territory. Since the 1977–78 war between Somalia and Ethiopia regarding the Ogaden, conditions along the common border have been unstable. After the outbreak of the Eritrean-Ethiopian border conflict in mid-1998, rival Somali factions received increasingly large consignments of weapons from the two warring countries, which sought to secure Somali allegiance to their respective causes. In January 1999 the pro-Ethiopian RRA and the DSA accused Eritrea of sending five plane-loads of weapons to Hussein Aidid to arm Ethiopian dissidents. They claimed that the weapons arrived at Balidogle and were then distributed to Aidid. According to Ethiopia, Eritrea wanted to arm Ethiopian opposition groups such as the Ogaden National Liberation Front and the Oromo Liberation Front (OLF) through Aidid in order to create tensions in the Somali-dominated Ogaden region of eastern Ethiopia. Eritrea was also accused of providing aid to al-Ittihad al-Islam, which had clashed with Ethiopian troops in the past. The DSA accused Aidid of training ethnic Ethiopian Oromos in the Qoryole district of Somalia's Lower Shebelle region. Additionally, Aidid used some of the Eritrean-supplied arms to settle scores with his enemies in the Bay and Bakool regions of south-western Somalia. In February an unidentified vessel unloaded more arms and ammunition to Aidid at the port of Merca, south of Mogadishu. There was another Eritrean arms shipment in May. All these shipments violated UN Security Council Resolution 751, which placed an arms embargo on Somalia in 1992. There also were reports that Eritrea had agreed to train 200 of Aidid's militiamen. Growing concern about the activities of Eritrean-supported Somali militias prompted Ethiopia to launch cross-border raids into Somalia against faction leaders and militias loyal to Aidid. In June 1999 a 3,000-man joint Ethiopian–RRA force, supported by armoured vehicles, occupied Baidoa and conducted operations against the OLF and forces loyal to Aidid. The operation consolidated the establishment of a Luq-Belatwein-Baidoa buffer zone. Shortly afterwards some 500 Ethiopian troops deployed from Luq temporarily occupied the town of Garba Harre in Gedo region. Notwithstanding, Aidid, his allies and Ethiopian rebel groups remained active, not least because of the steady influx of Eritrean military aid. In September 1999 Hussein Aidid complained to the UN secretary-general that Ethiopia had been providing weapons to the RRA, the Somali Patriotic Movement headed by Gen. 'Morgan', and to President Egal of 'Somaliland'. In October 1999 Aidid, who had been receiving Eritrean military aid, concluded an agreement with the Ethiopian authorities, whereby he curtailed the activities of the Eritrean-supported OLF, which had been fighting a guerrilla war against Ethiopia. Egyptian and Libyan representatives monitored the disarming of OLF personnel, the closure of the OLF office in Mogadishu, and the expulsion of nine OLF leaders. In August 1999 Ethiopian troops announced that they had captured an undisclosed number of al-Ittihad fighters in the Gedo region. The following month, Ethiopian soldiers, operating in alliance with the RRA and the DSA, occupied the town of Dinsoor in the Bay region. In early January 2000 hundreds of Ethiopian troops with armoured personnel carriers, artillery and tanks launched a cross-border raid into Somalia. The force surrounded the town of Goldogob in the central Mugud region. According to town elders, the Ethiopians were searching for members of the al-Ittihad group that is reportedly active in the Ogaden region of Ethiopia. By mid-2000 the Ethiopian strategy had resulted in some successes. The RRA had consolidated its presence in the Bay and Bakool regions; Aidid and his anti-Ethiopian allies were in disarray; the Hawadle militia in the Hiran region had become a staunch ally and the SNF appeared to be reuniting.

REFUGEES AND HUMANITARIAN AFFAIRS

In early 2000 there was a total of 426,000 Somalis seeking refuge or asylum in other countries. Of those, it was estimated that 170,000 were in Ethiopia and 160,000 in Kenya, with smaller numbers of Somali refugees and asylum seekers in Libya, Tanzania, Yemen, Djibouti, Uganda and various European states. There are also an additional 20,000 Somalis who live in Yemen but are not recognized as refugees. Approximately 350,000 Somalis are currently internally displaced. An estimated 25,000 Somali refugees were repatriated during 1999, primarily to northern Somalia.

On 20 June 2000 the US Agency for International Development (USAID) released a report indicating that more than

750,000 Somalis were affected by drought conditions. According to a UN estimate, the most vulnerable group is the agro-pastoralists who are dependent on rain-fed crops that were not scheduled to be harvested until August 2000. Up to 450,000 others are displaced owing to clan warfare. Thus, the total number of food dependent Somalis is 1.2m.

During late April–mid-May 2000 heavy rainfall alleviated some pasture and water shortages, but also caused flash floods in parts of the country. Such rains could increase the potential for outbreaks of disease. The northern Gedo and Bakool regions face the most extreme threats of water and food shortages. In May 2000 the World Food Programme and CARE reported that total food distribution amounted to 3,077 tons through emergency food aid, food for work programmes, and support to social institutions. Nevertheless, poor road conditions and chronic insecurity continue to hamper relief efforts in many parts of Somalia.

Health conditions remain poor throughout Somalia. In the Bakool region UNICEF recorded malnutrition rates in children under five of 30% in the town of Rabule and 22% in Oddur. The rate at Baardheere in the Gedo region was 24%. Cholera had broken out in the Bay and Bakool regions. Meanwhile, in February 2000 the Belgian chapter of Médecins sans Frontières (MSF) resumed operations in Kismayo. MSF–Belgium had withdrawn all its expatriates in June 1999, and terminated all activity in December, because of clashes between the SNF and SPM.

THE 'REPUBLIC OF SOMALILAND'

The 'Great Conference of the Northern Peoples', convened in May 1991, entrusted the SNM with the task of forming a government and drafting a constitution for the 'Republic of Somaliland'. From the outset the SNM was divided on the issue of independence. Several SNM leaders had expressed opposition to secession from Somalia. In addition, clan divisions arose over the distribution of ministerial portfolios and the allocation of resources. These divisions rendered the government virtually inoperative. However, the major problem for the government, headed by President Ahmed Ali 'Tur', was a shortage of resources. Without international recognition it proved extremely difficult to attract aid, and this in turn meant the government had no means to settle the claims of ex-guerrilla fighters, nor could it afford to demobilize them. Only assistance from non-governmental organizations (NGOs) enabled the government to begin the work of repairing the war-damaged infrastructure of the region, and some progress was made in the removal of mines (it has been estimated that there are about 2m. such devices to be cleared).

Progress in reconstruction was hampered by clan fighting that broke out in Burao in January 1992, and in Berbera twice during the year. The conflict, between Isaaq sub-clans (the Habr Yunis, the clan of President 'Tur', and the Habr Awal) was exacerbated by the grievances of the guerrillas and by government inactivity. Peace negotiations initiated by clan elders brought the conflict to an end in October, though the key economic port of Berbera remained outside government control. With the SNM leadership divided, political power passed into the hands of the national council of elders, who met at Boroma during February–May 1993 in a national reconciliation conference attended by 150 elders from all 'Somaliland' clans, with support from another 150 advisers and observers. Following the SNM's failure to establish a constitution and an effective government, the meeting formulated a national peace charter and a transitional structure of government. This was to comprise a council of elders (an upper house), an elected constituent assembly and an executive council (council of ministers). On 5 May Mohamed Ibrahim Egal (a former prime minister of Somalia during the 1960s), from the Habr Awal clan, was elected president, defeating the incumbent president, Ahmed Ali 'Tur', by 97 votes to 24. However, Egal's election failed to resolve clan differences. In June, following the announcement of Egal's cabinet, the Habr Yunis clan claimed that the appointments were calculated to foment clan rivalry and that assembly seats had been unjustly distributed. Habr Yunis opposition continued, and a clan conference in June 1994 rejected Egal's government. (Ahmed Ali 'Tur' had publicly renounced secession early in the year.)

'Somaliland' leaders continued to express concern at their relationship with the UN and consistently made clear their opposition to the deployment of UN peace-keeping forces in their territory. Demonstrations against the possible deployment in the region of UNOSOM II forces took place in Hargeysa in April 1993. Adm. Howe, as special representative of the UN secretary-general, visited 'Somaliland' after Egal's election and pledged UN support for reconstruction. However, the UN stance at regional and political conferences indicated that it would continue to consider 'Somaliland' as part of Somalia. By mid-1994 the 'Republic of Somaliland' had made no progress in its attempts to achieve international recognition. In July Egal, following an invitation from President Mubarak to visit Egypt, expressed the hope that international attitudes were changing. However, a few weeks later he intimated that the solution for 'Somaliland' might be to reconsider the 1960 independence agreement and adopt a fresh approach to federation. Meanwhile, influential Western nations identified the region's lack of political and civil stability as reasons for their refusal to recognize an independent 'Somaliland', denying the aid and investment necessary to address the region's problems.

In February 1994 Egal announced that a referendum would be organized in the north-western region, in order to ascertain the level of popular support for an independent 'Somaliland'. By mid-2000, however, no such referendum had taken place. In August 1994 Egal expelled UN representatives from 'Somaliland', accusing them of interfering in the country's internal affairs. This was apparently precipitated by talks held between the new UN special representative to Somalia, James Victor Gbeho (appointed in July), and Ahmed Ali 'Tur', who was courted by both the UN and Gen. Aidid following his disavowal of secession for 'Somaliland'. In October and November there were violent confrontations in Hargeysa between military units remaining loyal to Egal and those defecting to support Ahmed Ali 'Tur'. By mid-December it was estimated that three-quarters of the population of Hargeysa had fled, many thousands of them seeking refuge in Ethiopia. Rebel militias continued to launch attacks on government positions in Hargeysa during 1995, although their success was difficult to ascertain. Fighting spread to other parts of 'Somaliland', and in April government forces were in armed conflict with fighters from the Garhadji clan who had recently formed an alliance with Issa militiamen belonging to the anti-secessionist United Somali Front (USF). Fighting between rival factions of the SNM continued south of Hargeysa airport in August. In addition, clashes between 'Somaliland' government forces and Issa militias were reported in August and November near the border with Djibouti. In January 1996 more than 60 people were killed during fighting near Burao between troops loyal to Egal and militias apparently supporting Gen. Aidid's aim to become president of a unified Somalia. Instability within the territory led the EU to postpone new rehabilitation projects. Egal had retaliated by banning all EU activities in 'Somaliland'; however, in June 1995 the two sides reached an accommodation allowing the EU to resume operations.

Despite Egal's obviously weakened position he persevered with the introduction of a new currency for the territory, the 'Somaliland shilling', which was completed by the end of January 1995. In August 1995 four subcommittees were established to draft a new constitution for 'Somaliland'. A provisional document comprising 183 articles was published in March 1996. In late 1996 the third congress of 'Somaliland' communities began deliberations on the adoption of a constitution and the selection of a new president for the 'Republic of Somaliland'. On 16 February 1997 the congress approved the constitution, which would be effective for a three-year interim period, prior to ratification by public referendum. On 23 February Egal was re-elected (by an electoral college) president of 'Somaliland' for a five-year term. However, opposition to the Egal regime continued to mar efforts to create a national polity. Although the anti-Egal United Somali Party and the USF merged into the Northern Somali Alliance in March, the new grouping did little to weaken Egal or to present a viable alternative to his government. Meanwhile, in an attempt to defend the republic's national security, Egal supported the acquisition of new equipment for the 15,000-strong armed forces. During 1996 the military's logistics capabilities were improved by the purchase of numerous vehicles, including tanks. In addition, Egal used diplomacy to facilitate the stabilization process, meeting the Edagale community, an Isaaq sub-clan, in January 1997 to review security issues. The two sides had been at odds since clashes betweeen them erupted in 1994 and 1996. The 120-man Edagale team, led by Sultan Mohamed Abdullahi Galal, pledged to support national reconciliation.

In March 1997 Egal demanded that the UN and its agencies recognize the 'Republic of Somaliland' and appoint a UN resident representative in Hargeysa. He indicated that any agency that refused to meet these demands would have to terminate its activities in the region within three weeks. By mid-2000, however, 'Somaliland' had not received official international recognition and the UN agencies remained in place.

In August 1997 an Eritrean delegation visited Hargeysa, ostensibly to brief the 'Somaliland' leadership about the IGAD summit in Nairobi and the Sodere peace process. Other sources suggested that the delegation wished to determine if there were any Islamist groups based in 'Somaliland'. Relations with Djibouti remained tense, largely because Egal believed that President Gouled had failed to take adequate action against Issa militia units campaigning for part of western 'Somaliland' to be transferred to Djibouti. Additionally, Egal maintained that Djibouti, by supporting a united Somalia, had obstructed his efforts to gain international recognition for 'Somaliland'. Egal opposed the Sodere peace conference in Ethiopia in early 1997, fearing that the establishment of an internationally recognized provisional government in Somalia would hinder the recognition of 'Somaliland'. He therefore supported the third congress of 'Somaliland' communities when it refused to join the NSC.

In December 1997 President Egal offered his resignation to parliament; however, in a joint session, the house of representatives and the house of elders voted to reject the offer. Observers suggested that Egal had proposed resigning in an attempt to rally support and increase his powers in parliament. It was reported that in May 1999 Egal agreed to allow the establishment of political parties in 'Somaliland', provided that they were not based on religion or clan-based politics. New parties were to be permitted to participate in forthcoming civic elections, and also in presidential elections.

The issue of returning refugees to 'Somaliland' became a serious concern in April 1998 when the office of the UN High Commissioner for Refugees (UNHCR) appealed for US $24m. to finance the repatriation and resettlement of all Somali refugees in Africa and the Middle East. Although President Egal opposed the mass repatriation of Somalis because of the republic's economic problems, he agreed to allow UNHCR to repatriate 40,000 citizens in 1997 and 60,000 in 1998. However, 'Somaliland' lacked adequate humanitarian programmes to care for the returnees, and as a result UNHCR repatriated only some 11,000 refugees to 'Somaliland' in 1997, mainly from the Hartishek camps in Ethiopia. By mid-1998 another 8,000 refugees had settled in the north-west. UNHCR anticipated that an additional 60,000 refugees would return from Ethiopia to 'Somaliland' later in the year, and that some 16,500 would resettle from other countries. UNHCR indicated that the 'Somaliland' authorities agreed to resettle some 100,000 refugees by the end of 1998.

In December 1997 the minister of foreign affairs of 'Somaliland', Mahmoud Salah Fagadeh Nour, visited several countries in the Horn of Africa, including Eritrea, where he persuaded President Issaias Afewerki to act as mediator between 'Somaliland' and Ethiopia. During his visit to Ethiopia he informed government officials that the Ethiopian authorities had alienated the Egal regime by providing weapons to some of the republic's Dolbuhunta sub-clans on the pretext of dissuading al-Ittihad from launching cross-border raids into Ethiopia. The Ethiopian authorities subsequently agreed to deal only with the 'Somaliland' government, and not with clans and sub-clans. Fagadeh reviewed plans to resurface the highway from Dire Dawa to Berbera port in an attempt to promote bilateral trade, while he also concluded a joint security agreement with Ethiopia to combat al-Ittihad and to open liaison bureaux in Dire Dawa and Jijiga. Several months later President Egal visited Ethiopia, France and Italy. In Addis Ababa Egal convinced Ethiopian Prime Minister Meles Zenawi to abandon his support for the Sodere peace process in exchange for Egal's pledge to resolve the warlord problem in 'Somaliland' by convening a conference

in Hargeysa to negotiate a peace agreement without the presence of the military. Egal also sought to persuade the Italian and French governments to terminate their support for the Sodere accord.

In late 1997 'Somaliland' and Djibouti concluded an accord whereby the latter agreed to grant official recognition to the Egal regime and to give certain concessions to members of the Isaaq clan living in Djibouti. In exchange, 'Somaliland' promised to repatriate some 20,000 Issa refugees from the Djiboutian townships of Ali Adde, Assamo and Hol Hol. The repatriation programme began in February 1998.

In July 1998 Egal ordered Dominik Lagenbacher, the most senior UN official in Somalia, and Paul Knight, the UN Development Programme's representative to 'Somaliland', to leave the republic immediately. The officials were accused of sabotaging the flow of international aid into 'Somaliland'.

Relations between 'Somaliland' and Egypt remained tense during 1998 because of the latter's decision to hold a peace conference for Somalia's warring factions in late 1997, which Egal refused to attend. Egal claimed that Egypt had secured the agreement by promising to help southern Somalia's clans to regain 'Somaliland' by force. In his view, this amounted to a 'declaration of war'. In early 1999 Egal visited Egypt in an attempt to improve bilateral relations. The Egyptian authorities urged Egal to maintain Somali unity, but Egal argued that he intended to wait for reconciliation in southern Somalia and the re-establishment of a government before the matter of national reconciliation could be discussed.

In late 1998 a consortium of Danish NGOs received funding to carry out a mine clearing project in 'Somaliland'. According to the mine clearing agency of 'Somaliland', Somalia imported as many as 8m. landmines prior to 1987. Between 2.5m. and 2.8m. were laid in what became 'Somaliland'.

'Somaliland' has maintained cordial relations with Libya, as reflected by President Egal's visit to Tripoli in October 1999, which resulted in the signing of an investment and trade agreement. Under the terms of the agreement Libya pledged to rehabilitate Berbera's cement factory, a maize farming project and a spaghetti factory. 'Somaliland' also agreed to export camels to Libya. In late November 1999 a seven-man Libyan delegation visited 'Somaliland'.

'Somaliland'–Djibouti relations experienced considerable tension, largely owing to President Egal's refusal to participate in the Somali national reconciliation conference. In late November 1999 President Egal closed the border with Djibouti. Shortly thereafter, 'Somaliland's' interior minister, Ahmad Adam Umar, accused Djibouti of organizing a demonstration in Borama for people opposed to 'Somaliland's' self-declared independence from Somalia. At around the same time there were two explosions near a Hargeisa compound occupied by humanitarian organizations; in late December there was a further explosion at the UNDP headquarters in Hargeisa. Many in 'Somaliland' believed that these bombings were carried out in order to pressurize Egal into attending the Djibouti-sponsored reconciliation conference. In December 1999 the two countries agreed to normalize relations and reopen their common border. However, 'Somaliland' and Djibouti remained divided over the peace conference. In February 2000 Egal announced that 'Somaliland' would go to war if attempts were made to unite it with Somalia. The 'Somaliland' parliament subsequently issued a decree, which stated it would be an act of treason to attend the Djibouti peace conference. In April 2000 Djibouti closed the 'Somaliland' liaison office and deported its representative.

In November 1999 the 'Somaliland' 'navy' seized five Yemeni fishing boats and arrested 67 crewmen for illegal fishing in 'Somaliland' waters. However, six days later the police released the fishermen.

'PUNTLAND' REGIONAL ADMINISTRATION

In May 1998 delegates from three north-eastern regions of Somalia met in Garowe to establish a single administration for the area, modelled on the self-declared 'Republic of Somaliland'. They named the region 'Puntland' or 'Land of Frankincense', one of its main exports, and designated Garowe as its capital. These discussions came in the wake of the December 1997 Cairo peace agreement which, it was claimed, failed to accord the region sufficient importance. In July the delegates elected Col

Abdullahi Yussuf Ahmed, a former leader of the SSDF, as president, and Mohamed Abdi Hashi as deputy president. According to Abdullahi Yussuf, 'Puntland' supported the unity and territorial integrity of Somalia, advocating the re-establishment of a federal government in Somalia. The conference also endorsed the creation of a 69-member parliament and a nine-member cabinet. The cabinet, appointed in August, nominated the members of the supreme court in September, subject to parliamentary approval. In February 1999 Abdullahi Yussuf presided over the graduation of 500 police-officers, who joined some 700 police-officers already on duty. 'Puntland' planned to establish local and frontier police forces. Meanwhile, cases of piracy in the region escalated.

'Puntland' quickly gained regional stature. In September 1998 a German delegation visited President Abdullahi Yussuf to discuss ways to repatriate Somali refugees living in Germany. The president indicated that a repatriation programme would be impossible as long as there was instability in 'Puntland'. A Danish delegation also visited the region, and in December an Ethiopian special envoy arrived in Garowe to assume the position of ambassador. At about the same time Abdullahi Yussuf visited Libya, which had been one of the SSDF's major benefactors during the early 1990s. He continued on to Egypt, where he argued that instead of sponsoring national reconciliation conferences, the Egyptian authorities should support existing de facto regional states like 'Puntland'. While in Cairo, Abdullahi Yussuf also met with Arab League officials who promised to consider providing aid to 'Puntland'. In March 1999 a Libyan delegation of diplomats and businessmen arrived in 'Puntland' to explore the possibility of enhancing co-operation in the fishing, livestock and agricultural sectors.

Although more stable than many parts of southern Somalia, 'Puntland' experienced some security problems. In early February 2000 'Puntland' asked Ethiopia for military aid to use against al-Ittihad in the Mudug region. The following month competing clans clashed in the town of Haradhere in the Mudug region. The fighting claimed at least 12 lives.

'Puntland's' search for donor funds has been only marginally successful. In April 2000 Denmark granted US $3m. through the United Nations Development Programme to finance the renovation and expansion of the power generation capacity of the Boosaaso power plant. 'Puntland's' transport sector suffered a series of setbacks during 1999. In August President Yussuf dismissed 18 officials who worked at the air and sea ports of Garoweh, Galkayo and Boosaaso. According to the government, the 18 caused the loss of some $1.8m. through mismanagement and incompetence. At about the same time, a UN official indicated that it had become increasingly difficult to find donor funds to repair the airfields in Galkayo and Boosaaso.

In September 1999 'Puntland' and 'Somaliland' clashed over the status of the eastern Sool region. In mid-December 1999 'Somaliland' resolved the problem by terminating its support for Sool's regional administration because of mismanagement of various development programmes. However, in late December there was another confrontation in Las Anod, the regional capital, after 'Somaliland' troops tried to expel a 300-man 'Puntland' force.

In November 1999 the Food and Agriculture Organization (FAO) issued an appeal for food assistance for some 50,000 drought-affected people. However, the international aid effort foundered after the 'Puntland' government expelled three UN workers for 'unsatisfactory services'. The UN reacted by suspending its activities in 'Puntland'. In mid-February 2000 'Puntland' issued a circular that prohibited all political activities until June 2001, when the two-year transition period is scheduled to end. According to Ahmad M. Egal, the director-general for international relations, the government made its move to avert civil war, social unrest, and to ensure that law and order are maintained. In March 2000 construction started on the East African University in Boosaaso. The university, which is funded by the 'Puntland' government and local businessmen, is scheduled to be completed by 2001. The university will consist of lecture halls, offices, student and teacher living quarters, a mosque, and a service center.

Economy

THOMAS OFCANSKY

AGRICULTURE

Somalia's long history of civil unrest (which intensified following the overthrow of Siad Barre in 1991), together with erratic climatic conditions, have undermined the traditional agricultural base of the economy. Agricultural production in 1991–92 was estimated at just 5%–10% that of 1987–88, although an increase in rainfall contributed to more encouraging forecasts for 1992–93.

Since independence in 1960, Somalia's economic growth has failed to keep pace with the rise in the country's population, which has been expanded by the influx of refugees. Over the period 1985–95 the population increased by an annual average of 1.9%. In 1990, according to estimates by the World Bank, Somalia's gross national product (GNP), measured at average 1988–90 prices, was US $946m., equivalent to $150 per head. During 1980–90, it was estimated, GNP grew, in real terms, at an average annual rate of 1.1%, while real GNP per head declined by 2.3% per year in the period 1985–93. Over the period 1990–98 the population increased by an annual average of 2.2%. In 1990 agriculture contributed 66% of gross domestic product (GDP) and the sector engaged an estimated 72.0% of the labour force in 1998. During 1980–90 agricultural GDP increased by an annual average of 3.3%; in 1991, however, output declined by 8.8%.

The economy is traditionally based, principally on the herding of camels, sheep, goats and cattle (the latter mainly in the southern regions), which still provide for the subsistence needs of about 75% of the population and furnish a substantial export trade in live animals, skins, clarified butter and canned meat. After independence, exports of these items rose dramatically

and, until 1988, outstripped the other main export, bananas, which accounted for 40.3% of the total value of exports in that year. In 1989 livestock products accounted for about 49% of GDP.

Exports of livestock products accounted for about 67% of Somalia's total export earnings in 1988. The livestock sector was severely affected by drought in the mid-1970s and in 1984/85. In March 1985 the government requested emergency international assistance for a US $51m. programme to construct 120 water reservoirs in the north, but by the middle of the year it was estimated that up to 30% of Somalia's livestock faced death from drought. A six-year programme to control livestock diseases, based in Hargeysa, was launched in 1986 with support from the International Fund for Agricultural Development. In April 1989 Italy's official aid programme financed a $37m. joint venture between the Italian company Giza and the Somali government to operate a 14,000 ha farm, whose livestock was to be exported to the Arabian peninsula. In 1990 the African Development Fund approved a $24.4m. loan to help finance cattle-breeding and fishing projects; in November 1990 the Islamic Development Bank (IDB) also expressed willingness to assist Somalia in increasing its livestock exports. A significant loss of livestock, suffered as a result of famine and civil conflict in the early 1990s, was reported to have been largely recovered by mid-1995—when large quantities of livestock were being exported to the states of the Persian (Arabian) Gulf region.

Bananas are grown on plantations along the Juba and Shebelle rivers. Output increased by more than 70% in the first five years after independence, but declined steadily from 1972, when production totalled 188,500 metric tons, to 75,000 tons in 1986, but rose to 116,000 tons in 1989. Bananas, which, with livestock, form the backbone of Somalia's exports, earned 2,469m. Somali shillings in 1987 and 3,992m. Somali shillings in 1988 (equivalent to some 40% of total export earnings in that year). A decision in 1983 to sell the majority of shares in the National Banana Board—which controlled exports after 1970—to the private sector led to optimism about a revival in production, as did the October 1985 agreement by Italy, the major importer, to abolish tax on bananas imported from Somalia, and the continuing efforts to improve agricultural technology. By May 1995 exports of bananas also had recovered from the adverse effects of famine and civil war. Reports suggested that exports to the European Union (EU) for 1994 had exceeded the quota recommended by the terms of the Lomé Convention. However, concern was expressed that the most productive plantations, in the lower Shebelle region, were controlled by competing Itabr Gidir clansmen, channelling revenues into their war efforts. Exports of bananas were expected to total 27,000 tons in 1995. In early 1999 an Italian-based fruit company, Evergreen, abandoned attempts to revitalize Somalia's once lucrative banana industry after it failed to secure EU technical aid to help rebuild its operations in the Juba valley.

Other fruits, chiefly for local consumption, are grown on plantations in the same area. Sugar cane is a significant crop, and a number of rehabilitation schemes are under way with the aim of making the country self-sufficient in sugar, with a small surplus available for export. To this end, a second sugar factory was built as part of the Juba sugar estate development, established in 1977. Production of cotton more than doubled, with output of seed (unginned) cotton reaching about 7,000 tons per year in the 1980s, but there is still insufficient locally-grown cotton to meet the demands of the textile factory at Balad, and the balance must be imported. Large-scale expansion of this factory made it, by 1979, one of the best-equipped textile mills in Africa, but by late 1984 a major rehabilitation was needed, and by 1985 output had fallen to just 30% of capacity. In 1983 Somalia overtook Ethiopia to become the world's leading producer of incense, selling more than 2,000 tons annually.

The area between the rivers, of which at present only some 700,000 ha of an estimated potential of 8.2m. ha are under cultivation, also provides the subsistence maize and sorghum crops of the southern Somali. The full utilization of this fertile belt, envisaged in development plans, could eventually satisfy the grain needs of the domestic market and provide a subsidiary export crop. Experiments in rice cultivation, assisted by the People's Republic of China (PRC), may eventually enable Somalia to dispense with costly imports of this grain. Government agricultural programmes since the early 1980s have promoted 'self-help' programmes in the villages, with the aim of enabling Somalia to achieve self-sufficiency in basic foodstuffs. In 1985 Somalia became self-sufficient in maize and sorghum, but has not managed to maintain this achievement. A spectacular advance in sorghum production in 1994, from 80,000 tons to 252,000 tons, was largely attributed to increased rainfall and the 'low-value' nature of the crop, making it unattractive to looters. The country's potential as a producer of grain has been affected by the imbalance caused by imports of food (of which about one-half was food aid), which increased by an annual average of 8% in 1980–84. Three vast new agricultural settlement schemes in southern Somalia, for the victims of the 1974–75 drought, offered scope for increased production. However, the heavy influx of refugees during the late 1980s, together with the civil war, posed serious economic problems, despite aid from the office of the UN High Commissioner for Refugees (UNHCR) and other international organizations. Although crop production in 1996 was reported to have increased by 50% compared with the previous year, output was still some 37% lower than it had been prior to the civil war. In 1998 total cereal production was estimated at 160,000-170,000 tons, the lowest annual yield since 1993.

One of the largest agricultural schemes, at Afgoi-Mordile, was reactivated in 1985, after being suspended since the late 1970s. It provides for bananas, grapefruit, papaya and vegetables to be grown by a joint Libyan–Somali company, with rice, maize and sesame seed being produced by smallholders over a total of 2,500 ha. The planned Bardera dam, on the Juba river, is regarded as a vital step towards self-sufficiency in food, and has received priority in development planning. The dam is intended to fulfil three separate functions: flood control, irrigation and power supply. It will irrigate a minimum of 175,000 ha of agricultural land, and, by providing power for Mogadishu, should enable the cost of petroleum imports to be reduced by 20%. Finance was to come from the European Development Fund (EDF), the IDB, Abu Dhabi, France, Italy, Saudi Arabia and Germany. Under the public investment programme announced in 1987, the project was to be allocated US $106m. during the period 1987–90, with the total cost estimated at $317m. and completion scheduled for 1992. By 1990, however, work had yet to start and estimated costs had risen to $780m.

FISHING

Before 1972 fishing along the Somali coast was mainly a small-scale subsistence activity. By 1980 it was coming to be regarded as one of the country's leading priorities. During the 1974–75 drought some 12,000 nomads were settled and organized in fishing co-operatives, which have shown considerable promise. There were 4,000 full-time and 10,000 part-time fishermen in 21 co-operatives in 1981. The annual fish catch doubled between 1975 and 1980, reaching 10,000 tons per year. However, fish is still a negligible part of the Somali diet. Originally organized with Soviet assistance, the industry was hampered in 1977 by the expulsion of Soviet advisers and the withdrawal of their trawlers from the projects. The industry is currently receiving aid from the EU and other Western sources. In 1979 Somalia helped to found a joint Arab fisheries company, created under the auspices of the Arab League. Agreement was reached with Italy, in 1980, on a joint fishing venture in which the Italians were to provide four trawlers as well as training and technology. The FAO identified the Hafuna region as one of excellent potential for sardine fishing. The World Bank lent US $13.5m. to develop traditional fishing on the north-east coast, while Japan constructed two cold chambers and two fish markets for Mogadishu. In 1986 the PRC provided a further $17m. for fisheries development. Under the 1987–89 public investment programme, the sector was allocated $88m., of which almost one-half was to be spent on upgrading and expanding the fishing fleet. In 1988 Somalia's potential annual catch of fish was assessed at 200,000 tons and potential revenue at $26m. per year; however, according to estimates by the FAO, the actual annual catch for that year was only 18,200 tons. It was estimated that the total catch subsequently declined, and was 15,000 tons in 1996. In north-east Somalia fishermen currently export about 600 tons of lobster tails and some $800,000 worth of shark fins annually. Sardines are also exported.

Illegal fishing by foreign ships increased after the collapse of the Somali nation state. According to local sources, more than 200 foreign vessels were known to have conducted illegal fishing operations along Somalia's coastline. The ships, mainly from India, Italy, Japan, the Republic of Korea, Pakistan, Spain and Yemen, extract as much as 420 tons of fish on each occasion. As a result Somali fishermen, with the help of motor boats donated by local non-governmental organizations (NGO), often attack the ships, fining the captain and holding the crew to ransom. However, some Somali warlords undercut the fishermen by selling fishing rights to foreign companies. For example, the Middle East Trading Co, which was established in 1996 by Ali Mahdi Mohamed, Osman Hassan Ali 'Ato' and Gen. Mohamed Siad Hersi 'Morgan', sells licences for tuna fishing in exchange for foreign currency, some of which undoubtedly is spent on weapons and military supplies. Hussein Mohamed Aidid has a similar company, Samico. 'Puntland' was also considering establishing a licensing company.

MINERALS AND INDUSTRIAL PRODUCTS

Petroleum exploration has so far proved disappointing. Since the mid-1940s more than 60 exploratory wells have been sunk, but by early 1986 only one-third of the concessions on offer were under contract to European or North American oil companies for exploration. Plans to start oil exploration off Somalia's Indian Ocean coast were announced by Mobil Corpn and Pecten, the US subsidiary of Shell, in 1990, but postponed as the civil war intensified later in that year. The government of the 'Republic of Somaliland' made contacts with a number of international oil companies during 1991–92 and an exploration agreement for a block between Hargeysa and Burao was reported to have been signed with US-based Alliance Resources. However, the company failed to take up its permit, and other companies, while expressing interest, appeared reluctant to commit themselves until 'Somaliland' had obtained international recognition. In April 1979 a petroleum refinery, jointly developed with Iraq, went into operation with a throughput of 10,000 barrels per day. Somalia assumed ownership of the refinery in 1984. Production of petroleum products, which has been hindered by the irregularity of supplies of crude oil and by technical problems, amounted to 227,000 tons in 1983, 143,000 tons in 1984 and 156,000 tons in 1985. However, production declined to 44,000 tons in 1987, and to just 30,000 tons in 1988. The construction of a petroleum refinery in Mogadishu, with finance provided by two Saudi Arabian firms and Somali entrepreneurs, has been pending for some time. Petroleum accounted for about one-third of total expenditure on imports in 1988. There were reports in late 1998 that US companies had begun prospecting for petroleum around Boorama in north-western Somalia.

Somalia's mineral resources include salt, limestone, gypsum, gold, silver, nickel, copper, zinc, lead, manganese, uranium and iron ore. Iron ore reserves estimated at 170m. tons have been located in the Bur region, and deposits of uranium ore exist to the west of Mogadishu. Work began in 1984 on their development, although currently depressed conditions in world uranium markets suggest that their economic potential lies in the long term. Somalia contains some of the world's largest gypsum deposits, near Berbera. The mining sector contributed only 0.3% of GDP in 1988.

Industry is small in scale and mostly based on agriculture: meat- and fish-processing, textiles and leather goods. In 1974–77 employment in the industrial sector increased by 20% and gross output by 65%. In 1991 the sector employed an estimated 10.5% of the labour force, and in 1988 contributed 8.6% of GDP. Manufacturing GDP decreased by an average of 1.7% annually during 1980–90. In 1988 the sector contributed almost 5% of GDP. More than 80% of enterprises were formerly state-owned, but the government subsequently gave priority to plans to attract private investment. The country's first pharmaceuticals factory, built mainly with Italian aid, was completed in 1984, but has yet to enter into production. In 1986 the Italian government proposed renovating the factory, and operating it as a joint venture. France has agreed to finance the inauguration of the Berbera cement works (with a capacity of 200,000 tons per year), which lay idle for more than a year, after its completion in 1985, because of foreign exchange problems. Opportunities for further development under the 1987–89 public investment programme were limited. Manufacturing was allocated only US $84m., the bulk of which was to go to the Juba sugar estate and factory. In 1989 a hide and skin processing plant (financed by the Italian government) was completed in Mogadishu.

PUBLIC FINANCE

Despite the rise in exports after independence, imports, and the country's external debt, also increased. From 1969 the government made vigorous attempts to increase the country's self-sufficiency. In 1988 Somalia recorded a budget deficit of 10,009.4m. Somali shillings. A provisional budget for 1991 was projected to balance at 268,283.2m. Somali shillings. The country's total external debt was US $2,643m. at the end of 1997, of which $1,918m. was long-term public debt. In 1990 (when the long-term debt totalled $1,926m.) the cost of debt-servicing was equivalent to 11.7% of the value of exports of goods and services.

The current deficit on the balance of payments increased sharply after the Ogaden war and continued to increase until 1980. Despite a stabilization programme adopted in 1980 with the help of a US $14m. stand-by credit from the IMF, loans of $9m. from OPEC and of $47m. from the Arab Monetary Fund were required to offset balance-of-payments deficits. In July 1981 a further stand-by credit of $46.6m. was granted by the IMF in support of a new fiscal policy, involving the introduction of a two-tier exchange rate, with a 'parallel' rate (representing a 50% devaluation of the Somali shilling) for exports. The two-tier exchange rate was abolished after one year and a further IMF stand-by credit was granted. The government sought to liberalize the economy by abolishing the state trading companies and introducing strict measures to control currency.

The economy showed some encouraging signs of revival during 1981–83, but deteriorated badly in 1984. An IMF stand-by credit

expired in January 1984, and negotiations for an extension of these arrangements collapsed over Somali reluctance to undertake a further currency devaluation. The Somali economy passed through 1984 without IMF support and with the additional handicap of a huge trade deficit, resulting from the ban on livestock exports to Saudi Arabia. Inflation reached 100%, and the 'black market' thrived. The government eventually agreed to a 32% devaluation of the Somali shilling in September, and to a further 29% devaluation, with the introduction of a two-tier exchange rate, in January 1985. An IMF stand-by credit of US $54.7m. was duly announced, as part of a programme which included a further liberalization of the economy, especially in the import/export sector, and a reduction of price controls. However, disbursements were suspended after just a few weeks, because of a major dispute over Somalia's exchange rate policy.

In December 1985 the Somali shilling was again devalued, by about 50%, and in early 1986 the IMF resumed lending to Somalia, after the central bank agreed to the introduction of a system whereby the currency's value would be determined by means of fortnightly auctions of available foreign exchange. The auctions began in September 1986, assisted by a 'soft' loan of US $50m. from the International Development Association (IDA), and by balance-of-payments support from the USA and Italy. Shortages of funds led to the suspension of the auctions in January 1987, but they were resumed in February, after the USA and Italy agreed to make additional contributions. In June, after the government had acted to clear $29m. of arrears owed to the IMF, loans totalling SDR 53.9m. were approved by the IMF, of which SDR 33.15m. was to be drawn over the next 20 months under a stand-by arrangement, while the remainder was to be available over the next three years under the Fund's Structural Adjustment Facility. In July the 'Paris Club' of Western official creditors agreed to reschedule $170m. of Somali government debt over a 20-year period. However, debt principal and interest due to be repaid in 1987 and 1988 ($138m. and $146m. respectively) remained substantially in excess of Somalia's forecast export earnings in those years, while outstanding arrears were estimated at $100m.

In September 1987 it was announced that the system of auctioning foreign currency by the central bank was to be abandoned and that there would be a return to a fixed rate of exchange, set at 100 Somali shillings = US $1. This reversal of financial policy was believed to have been prompted by a 14% depreciation of the Somali shilling which had occurred between August and September, and by protests at rising prices. Since the continuation of the foreign exchange auctions had been one of the principal conditions of Somalia's agreement with the IMF in June, the IMF suspended disbursement of the loans, and the World Bank also suspended the remaining $10m. of a credit of $50m. for agricultural adjustment.

In February 1988 a committee was established by the government to review Somalia's relationship with the IMF and other Western financial institutions; however, talks held with the IMF in March foundered on the government's reluctance to readopt the auction system to determine the value of the Somali shilling. In May the IMF declared Somalia to be ineligible for further borrowing, owing to its overdue financial obligations to the Fund, which totalled SDR 26.8m. In June, in an effort to resume negotiations with the IMF, the government effected a 45% devaluation of the Somali shilling and in July it was reported that Somalia had signed an economic and financial agreement with the IMF, under the terms of which it undertook to repay its debts to the Fund with livestock, fish and other natural resources. A further devaluation of the Somali shilling, of about 20%, took place in August, and in January 1989 the government indicated that the foreign exchange auctions would be resumed on a monthly basis in March. The government also introduced significant reforms in both the agricultural and financial sectors, with the liberalization of the trade in hides and skins and veterinary pharmaceuticals, together with plans to permit the opening of foreign banks and the abolition of the state monopoly of insurance. These measures facilitated the adoption in mid-1989 of an IMF-supported structural adjustment programme. This, however, did little to help the government solve its financial problems. In September a Somali government delegation visited the IMF headquarters in Washington, DC, to discuss debt arrears and to seek eligibility for fresh loans. The delegation failed in its mission, however, despite an attempt on the part of the IMF to form a support group to raise resources to pay Somalia's US $100m. arrears. Of the seven largest donor countries, only Italy agreed to provide further lending to clear arrears, although this was made conditional on the participation of other members of the support group in financing the debt. The government's financial position continued to deteriorate during 1990, owing to growing instability and donors' reluctance to provide support because of concern about the government's human rights record. There were hopes, however, that Somalia might benefit from a new initiative by the IMF, the rights accumulation programme, allowing countries in arrears to the Fund to accumulate borrowing rights by implementing an adjustment programme and making regular interest payments. In 1991 the annual rate of inflation was estimated at more than 100%; it was estimated to have averaged 45.7% annually during 1980–88.

In the absence of government-led initiatives for economic reform, an 'unconventional economy' regulated by clans and sub-clans evolved, fuelled by workers' remittances from abroad (often in the form of foreign exchange and household goods and appliances), unrecorded sales of livestock and the cultivation and sale of qat (a mild stimulant). The response of international relief and assistance organizations to the humanitarian crisis in Somalia has contributed to this economy, with clans competing for revenues proceeding from the provision of equipment and accommodation for foreign personnel, the sale of food supplies looted from aid deliveries, and—prior to the arrival of the Unified Task Force (UNITAF) in December 1992—the exaction of protection money from relief organizations.

FOREIGN AID AND DEVELOPMENT, 1960–91

During 1960–69 Somalia received a substantial amount of foreign aid, chiefly from Italy, the USA and the USSR, but without producing any proportionate return. During 1963–70 the government launched a series of plans to improve the country's resources. Although the plans proved too ambitious, much was accomplished during those years, notably in road-building, the construction of ports at Berbera (with aid from the USSR) and Kismayu (with US aid), the building of schools, and a large hospital at Mogadishu, financed by the European Community (EC, now the European Union—EU). Few projects for livestock management and agricultural development had successfully progressed beyond the planning stage by 1969.

Under the Siad Barre regime, many of these projects became operational. The government initially sought to encourage 'self-help' rural development projects (e.g. in school-building or well-digging) which produced good results before 1969. The policy was to develop the Somali economy along socialist lines, although private enterprise on a small scale was encouraged, and to aim for self-sufficiency, particularly in food production.

The 1974–78 Five-Year Plan was delayed, since resources had to be diverted for drought relief in 1974–75. In April 1976 the World Bank issued a US $8m. loan to help to repair the effects of the drought.

Some 50% of the expenditure of 7,104m. Somali shillings envisaged in the 1979–81 Development Plan was to finance projects carried forward from the previous Five-Year Plan. Of this budget, 35.4% was allocated to agriculture and fisheries, 18% to economic infrastructure and 7.4% to education. There was a new emphasis on the needs of small producers rather than large-scale schemes. The 1982–86 Plan envisaged overall expansion in real GDP of 27% over five years, equivalent to an annual average growth of 4.6%. During 1980–87, GDP increased by an estimated 2.2%. The 1982–86 Plan attracted declarations of intent totalling US $1,200m. from a donors' meeting in October 1983. However, many projects had to be deferred when the economy was severely dislocated by the problems over livestock exports. Under the 1987–91 Plan, GDP growth was expected to average 5%.

At the consultative group meeting with aid donors in April 1987, pledges, at US $835m., fell short of the $1,025m. which the government had sought for its 1987–89 public investment programme. Total project aid, at $720m. over three years, would cover only 70% of the public investment programme for 1987–89.

Until 1977 the major source of aid was the USSR, together with the PRC, the EDF, UN specialized agencies, the IDA and the Federal Republic of Germany. Since 1974 Arab states have also been very important contributors, especially Libya, the United Arab Emirates (UAE) and Saudi Arabia, which reportedly supplied considerable military aid in the war with Ethiopia. In 1987 bilateral discussions were reported to have taken place with the Arab funds to reschedule Somalia's external debt. After Siad Barre's visits to Abu Dhabi, in early 1989, the United Arab Emirates reportedly provided substantial financial aid to Somalia. Following the 1980 agreement permitting US forces to use Somalia's military bases, the USA became a major donor. Its support was particularly important for Somalia's transport systems, which were among Africa's poorest.

In 1985 work finished on a US-sponsored US $37.5m. project to double the number of berths at Berbera port and to deepen its harbour, which handles a large volume of cattle exports. Soon afterwards, a $42m. development of Kismayu port began, designed to equip it to handle livestock in addition to bananas. The USA also provided finance for the expansion of the runway at Mogadishu airport. US aid, which was suspended in 1988 because of the Somali government's alleged abuses of human rights and the protracted civil war, was resumed in 1989 following the release of more than 200 political prisoners in January. In May the USA supplied 6,536 tons of edible oil worth $5m. and in June signed a grant agreement worth $15.1m. A further $36.3m. of aid for 1988/89 remained blocked because of the continuing conflict in the north. In February 1990 the US suspended all financial aid for 1990/91 in protest at Somalia's 'long pattern of human rights abuses'. During that financial year the USA was to provide only $750,000 for some projects already in progress. A more traditional benefactor is Italy, which in 1985 offered more than $200m. in special assistance from its emergency aid fund for Africa, mostly for the construction of a road linking Garowe to Boosaaso, to provide access to the isolated north-east. In 1989 Italy financed the reconstruction and expansion of Mogadishu airport.

In October 1988 the EDF provided ECU 5m. for a programme to improve Somalia's satellite communications links with Europe and the Gulf states. Somalia received a further ECU 15m. in December for specific imports in the agriculture, industry and transport sectors. A US $83m. project to improve and expand Somalia's telecommunications network, due to be completed in 1991, was financed by Italy, the African Development Bank (ADB) and Japan. In July 1988 Japan also donated $6.5m. in financial aid, cancelled its Somalia debt and pledged to increase its aid disbursements. In early 1989 the Japanese government provided an additional 350m. yen in food aid and in March promised a further 900m. yen to support Somalia's economic recovery programme. In July the EDF granted $54m. for the construction of a 230-km road between Gelib and Bardera. The road was intended to provide access to the fertile Juba valley, which was to be developed following the completion of the Bardera dam project, originally scheduled for 1992. A further grant, of ECU 16m., to fund the purchase of oil imports, was provided by the EU, which also donated ECU 2m. in aid to cattle breeders for the purchase of veterinary drugs.

In March 1989 a three-year agreement was signed with the IMF, under the terms of which US $260,000 were to be allocated by the Fund to development projects in the agriculture, livestock and fisheries sectors during 1989–91. In August the World Bank released the first $20m. of a $70m. loan provided for agricultural development. Of the overall credits disbursed through the IDA over the two-year period, $44.5m. was allocated to finance imports of goods and materials for both the private and public sectors, and $16.5m. for fuel purchases. In early 1990 the IDA pledged $26.1m. towards a seven-year $32.5m. education project; the share of education in the national budget had fallen from 10% in 1980 to only 1.9% in 1988. In late 1990 the IDA allocated $18.5m. for rehabilitation work on the country's road network and telecommunications infrastructure and Mogadishu's water supply.

FOREIGN TRADE

Somalia's foreign trade deficit (which is almost entirely financed by foreign aid) increased to around US $300m. in 1987; only an increase in official transfers in that year prevented the current account deficit from rising far above the 1986 level of $88m. Despite a considerable narrowing of the trade deficit in 1988, to $157.6m., the trade gap widened to $278.6m. in the following year, with the deficit on the current account of the balance of payments increasing from $98.5m. to $156.7m. Total external debt amounted to $2,635m. at the end of 1998, of which $1,886m. was long-term public debt. In February 1993 the Arab Monetary Fund suspended Somalia's membership because of arrears totalling $113.9m. at the end of 1991.

ECONOMIC INFRASTRUCTURE IN POST-BARRE SOMALIA

In 1989–90 the economy deteriorated rapidly, largely owing to the continuing civil strife in many parts of the country. Severe shortages of food, fuel and medical supplies were reported following the overthrow of the Siad Barre government in January 1991, with many aid agencies reluctant to return to the country. Fighting in agricultural regions in mid-1991 was reported to have severely disrupted production, and, as fighting intensified in late 1991 and early 1992, agriculture, and domestic and foreign trade all virtually halted and large numbers of people were displaced from their homes. By July 1992 the UN estimated that 1.5m. people were in immediate danger of starvation, with a further 4.5m. at risk; cereal import needs were assessed at about 480,000 tons. At that time, almost 1m. Somalis were refugees. As a result of the extended civil conflict, considerable damage was inflicted on the infrastructure, telecommunications and electricity and water supplies of many urban areas, notably the capital. Large-scale reconstruction and the exploitation of Somalia's underdeveloped resources (including large areas of uncultivated arable land between the Juba and Shebelle rivers, and rich fishing grounds along the country's coastline) were expected to be hampered by unwieldy foreign debt, in the unlikely event of the prompt negotiation of a durable peace accord. In 1993–94 the UN became Somalia's largest employer and introduced a significant amount of foreign currency; the withdrawal of the UN operation in early 1995 resulted in the loss of hundreds of jobs in Somalia and of the country's principal source of income.

Despite continuing insecurity in Mogadishu and other parts of the country, the UNITAF peace-keeping operation, which arrived in December 1992, was successful in facilitating the distribution of food aid. By late January 1993, relief workers were feeding 1m. people daily at 1,000 centres throughout the country. Nevertheless, pockets of famine persisted in rural areas, particularly in the south. In March the FAO estimated that 1m. people would continue to require food aid throughout 1993; the FAO also estimated that 300,000 people had died of hunger-related causes during 1992, although other sources estimated the total to be as high as 500,000. A UN-sponsored conference of donors in Addis Ababa in March pledged US $130m. towards the reconstruction of Somalia, although this fell short of the UN's target of $166m., already revised downwards from $253m. The programme aimed to re-establish administrative infrastructure, repatriate refugees, restore livestock herds and restart primary education. Donors warned that Somalis needed to restore stability and security if aid was to continue. Improving conditions in rural areas and good rains in early 1993 allowed agricultural activity to resume, with good harvests and even the resurgence of small-scale exports of livestock and fruit.

In March 1995 it was reported that more than 500,000 people in southern Somalia were in imminent danger of dying of starvation and disease, and urgently required food and medical aid. In June the European Community Humanitarian Office (ECHO) announced that it had approved a grant of ECU 350,000 for medical aid and for a survey on food requirements. In July the International Committee of the Red Cross (ICRC) provided emergency food aid, seeds and fishing equipment to more than 9,000 families in southern Somalia. In August ECHO pledged an additional US $441,000 to support ICRC's activities in southern Somalia and in Somali refugee camps in Kenya. In September the EU announced it would provide ECU 505,000 to fund food and medical aid in Mogadishu. A further ECU 1m. was made available in October to relieve the acute food shortages in the Juba valley. Relief agencies funded programmes in disease control, education, farming, water chlorination, and the repair of roads, hospitals and schools. (By November 1995 health facilities in Somalia included 21 hospitals, 470 health centres

and 99 out-patient dispensaries.) However, despite the advances made by relief agencies, the UN Co-ordination Team (meeting in Kenya in August 1995) indicated that it was not food supplies that were lacking, but the resources for most people to purchase them.

In mid-1996 the EU announced plans to fund a modernization project for the port of Boosaaso, providing trained personnel and adequate equipment to develop the port's capabilities. It was anticipated that the scheme would improve the prospects of the 100,000 local inhabitants. The EU also announced a two-year US $60m. rehabilitation programme for Somalia, encompassing 115 projects to advance humanitarian aid, infrastructure, education and health services. The EU subsequently pledged ECU 600,000 to rehabilitate wells in Nugaal Province and ECU 1.5m. for a measles vaccination programme, food and medical aid for war victims. It also allocated ECU 47m. to improve the social, agricultural, private and public sectors.

During 1996 a combination of continued warfare, drought, floods and internal displacement made approximately 1m. Somalis dependent on emergency food aid. In some areas of southern Somalia malnutrition rates reached 22%, although by November the national malnutrition rate totalled 7%. Ten UN agencies and 32 international NGOs were active in the country in 1996, but relief operations continued to be hampered by violence, banditry and the lack of law enforcement. Three of Somalia's Red Crescent Society workers died in August as the result of shelling in Mogadishu, and in October relief agencies temporarily suspended non-emergency aid deliveries to Mogadishu to protest at kidnappings of their employees. In late 1996 UN agencies launched an appeal for US $100m. to sustain their humanitarian operations in Somalia. In August 1996 UNHCR appealed for $5m. to cover a funding shortage for the repatriation and rehabilitation of returnees. UNHCR also continued to provide aid to some 500,000 Somalis who have returned to their homes in recent years, and to work on a variety of returnee projects in southern Somalia, including the improvement of infrastructure, the construction of water wells and programmes to develop health services, sanitation, education, agriculture, livestock and small businesses. In December the UN announced that more than $46m. of donor aid would be required to avoid a crisis similar to that of 1991/92, which claimed at least 300,000 lives. Assistance was needed to finance emergency food shipments, rehabilitation projects, international repatriation programmes and improved security. Meanwhile, civil unrest contributed to a sharp deterioration in public health.

In early 1997 the US government released a study indicating that a serious food emergency might occur later in the year. The report suggested that some 58,000 tons of cereals might be required to avert a catastrophe, especially in the Bay and Bakool regions. In April the EU announced that it would provide ECU 3.7m. in humanitarian aid for victims of conflict in Somalia. The assistance, which was to be managed by ECHO, would allow the ICRC and several NGOs to undertake an eight-month feeding programme and a health care project. In June the UN World Food Programme (WFP) appealed for US $2m. to help pay for food distribution in drought-affected areas of southern Somalia, where a crop failure had left 360,000 Somalis short of food. The WFP subsequently distributed 3,240 tons of food to vulnerable Somalis in 78 locations in the Bay, Bakool, Hiran, Lower Juba, Middle Juba, and Lower Shebelle regions.

In October 1996 a group of Somali businessmen opened the Barakat Bank of Somalia in Mogadishu. With an initial capital of US $2m., the bank intends to specialize in small loans to Somali merchants, foreign currency exchange, and currency exchanges abroad. The bank aimed gradually to establish 90 branches in Somalia. In early 1997 the Somali-Malaysian Commercial Bank opened in Mogadishu, with capital of $4m.

During 1997 and 1998 some of the most fertile agricultural regions in Somalia suffered from drought, serious flooding, or both. Floods in late 1997 left up to 250,000 southerners homeless. Weather-related problems and the lack of employment opportunities led to some malnutrition in Mogadishu and other communities. In addition, political insecurity often hampered international relief efforts. Countries and organizations that donated aid to flood victims included the USA, Italy, Japan, the UN and the EC.

In July 1998 the WFP reported that Somalia's grain harvest would reach a five-year low, creating concern within the aid community that food would be in short supply in the months ahead. It was anticipated that the maize and sorghum harvests would be reduced by some 50% as a result of floods. The flood waters, which engulfed the agriculturally rich Juba and Shebelle river areas, left communities with broken river embankments, destroyed irrigation schemes, heavily silted soil, extensive weed growth and infestations by rats, crickets and other pests. Abnormally low rains following the floods made it more difficult for crops to mature. In late 1998 the FAO and several humanitarian organizations warned of a looming famine in Somalia. According to the FAO, at least 700,000 people faced food shortages, while some 300,000 others were at risk of starvation, primarily in the Bay and Bakool areas. The FAO indicated that Somalia required about 125,000 tons of food aid through at least July 1999. Appeals were made to the international community for US $67.5m. to furnish aid to the most vulnerable populations. The UN and other humanitarian agencies pledged to work in southern Somalia and other parts of the country to avert a disaster. By mid-1999 the presence of international humanitarian workers in Somalia had increased to its highest level in five years. However, the poor security situation in southern Somalia posed a threat to relief activities and food shipments.

In July 1999 a continued deterioration in the food situation prompted the Somalia Aid Co-ordination Body, which includes UN agencies and NGOs, to issue an appeal for more than US $17m. for southern Somalia for the period July–December 1999. The predictions for the pending harvest were extremely poor. The sorghum belt of Bay, Bakool and Gedo were under the greatest threat, with poor prospects also in Hiran, and in Middle and Lower Shebelle. A notable contributory factor to the emergency was the influx of additional Somali currency into the country, which resulted in serious inflation and a four-fold increase in fuel prices. According to UN estimates, by mid-1999 the number of people at risk of starvation had increased to 1m. There also were some 300,000 displaced persons. During late 1999 the food situation worsened further following an upsurge in inter-clan fighting, which disrupted food production activities and prevented aid reaching civil war and drought victims. The FAO estimated that some 1.6m. Somalis did not have access to humanitarian agencies' assistance and efforts to reach them were further hindered by the escalation of violence against humanitarian workers. Earlier in 1999 the sixth consecutive poor cereals harvest, as a result of adverse weather, the destruction of the agricultural infrastructure, pests and the continuous displacement of the population, had led the UN to launch a Consolidated Inter-Agency Appeal for Somalia, which hoped to raise $50.6m. in 2000. Donor contributions to the fund the previous year had, however, only reached $35m. of the requested $64m.

The continuation of factional fighting during 1998–2000 led many NGOs and other humanitarian agencies to re-evaluate their presence in Somalia. In September 1998 the ICRC announced that it had terminated its programme of sending expatriates to Somalia and reduced its activities. The subsequent suspension of all non-emergency assistance and some emergency aid threatened the lives of displaced persons living in camps in Mogadishu. Medicine and food shortages also adversely affected the health sector. Militiamen exacerbated the humanitarian situation by 'taxing' relief shipments.

Despite these problems, there have been some economic improvements. The re-establishment of security in many regions stimulated a revival of livestock and fruit exports, although some shipments were disrupted by the closure of Mogadishu port and by the temporary ban by Saudi Arabia and other Middle Eastern countries on the importation of Somali livestock. The north-eastern town of Boosaaso has become a major point of entry for goods into Somalia, and the fishing and livestock sectors have expanded throughout the relatively stable north-east, thanks largely to Boosaaso's tax-free environment. As of late 1997 there were 14 aviation companies with 62 aircraft operating out of Boosaaso, compared to one aviation firm with three aircraft prior to the war. Additionally, businessmen have established a modern communications centre in the town, and clinics, schools and a post office are also in operation. Notwith-

standing, Boosaaso's wealth has yet to benefit the majority of people who continue to live in slums and cannot afford the cost of such services.

THE 'REPUBLIC OF SOMALILAND'

The relative stability of the self-proclaimed 'Republic of Somaliland', following its secession in 1991, contributed to an improvement in the economy of that territory, with an estimated increase in GNP per head of 20% in 1991–94. The Egal administration introduced tax, banking and customs systems in late 1993, and a new currency, the Somaliland shilling, in late 1994. However, during 1994 the 'Somaliland' government was placed increasingly under threat by rebels from the armed forces, which, together with the refusal of the international community to recognize the territory's independence, jeopardized the republic's future prosperity. Furthermore, during 1995 the annual rate of inflation reached as much as 400% in some parts of the territory, resulting in a five-fold increase in the price of basic foodstuffs. In September Egal announced a comprehensive programme to control inflation and to improve the republic's economy. Traders and wholesalers were obliged to maintain a minimum deposit of 10m. Somaliland shillings (US $125,000) in the state bank, where foreign organizations working in the territory were obliged to exchange their currencies. The disparity between the official and unofficial exchange rates in 'Somaliland' led some foreign organizations to announce in early 1996 that, as a result of the new regulations, they would be reviewing their activities in the territory. In February Egal banned the use of foreign currencies in 'Somaliland', with the exception of the Ethiopian birr and the Djibouti franc. Penalties for violating the measures included lengthy terms of imprisonment. In addition, Egal sought to reduce inflation by requiring banks to hold auctions of US dollars, and by establishing a ministerial committee to supervise exchange rates. Meanwhile, budgetary expenditure for 1996 was projected at 3,252m. Somaliland shillings.

The pursuit of international aid for projects in 'Somaliland' remained a priority of Egal's government. In February 1996 the EU agreed to finance the reconstruction of Berbera port; under the terms of the project, local contractors would upgrade the port's security, infrastructure and cargo-handling facilities. The improvements were expected to increase livestock exports through the port (some 3m. head in 1995). Activity at Berbera port is central to the economy of the 'Republic of Somaliland', as it provides considerable employment and generates much-needed convertible currency. Notable exports include camels, while there are also plans to increase the trade in frankincense and myrrh. It was estimated that in 1996 'Somaliland' exported 500,000 sheep to Saudi Arabia (its principal petroleum supplier). In January 1997 the Intergovernmental Authority on Development (IGAD) announced a project (estimated to cost US $18m.) to improve communications between Berbera and several other East African ports. Meanwhile, the EU agreed to fund the reconstruction of several roads, and an Italian relief agency, Cooperazione Internazionale, was to rehabilitate Berbera's water system. In September 1998 an IDB delegation arrived in Hargeysa to consider developing the veterinary, education and water sectors in 'Somaliland'. In December a British company, Digital Exchange Products, announced that it had been appointed by Somaliland Telecommunications Corporation to reinstall a telecommunications system (destroyed during the civil war) and to design and maintain a website for the 'Somaliland' government. In October 1998 the UN Conference on Trade and Development embarked on a programme to rehabilitate the port of Berbera and to train Somalis to become port managers, mechanics, cargo-handlers and clerks. The programme also included the port of Boosaaso. In May 1999 the EU granted 'Somaliland' $1m. to finance water projects and to train staff in water management and in the maintenance of water installations.

In late 1995 the fishing industry in 'Somaliland' was assisted by the resumption of operations of the Somali Highseas Fishing Co after it concluded an agreement with the tribal chief of the Osman Mahmoud sub-clan of the Majerteen, who allegedly had allowed pirates to operate in the Red Sea. Notwithstanding, reports of piracy continued.

In October 1997 the house of representatives passed a US $9m. budget for the six-month period ending December 1997. The new budget established salaries for assembly members, government workers and soldiers. In early 1998 the council of ministers approved a $23m. budget for that year. In December the deputy minister of finance presented the budget for 1999, which amounted to more than 40,000m. Somaliland shillings. Some 33,000m. shillings were allocated to pay the salaries and allowances of civil servants and the army, while 4,000m. shillings was set aside for the various ministries.

In February 1998 President Egal protested to the World Health Organization about Saudi Arabia's decision to suspend livestock imports from 'Somaliland' for fear that the animals suffered from the Rift Valley fever which had broken out in Kenya. The ban devastated the economy, which depends on livestock sales for foreign exchange earnings amounting to some US $100m. annually. The export of goats reportedly declined from 1m. head in March 1997 to 481,000 in March 1998, while sheep exports fell from 1.2m. head in April 1997 to about 514,000 in April 1998. In November 1998 Saudi Arabia and the UAE lifted the livestock ban. A few months later the FAO reported that the republic's livestock were healthy and free of disease, particularly Rift Valley fever.

In April 1998 'Somaliland' concluded agreements with the US-based Collins Engineering Co and British-American Energy to rehabilitate power stations throughout the republic. The companies agreed to complete a US $23m. project on the 25 MW power station at Hargeysa before rehabilitating other facilities.

In late 1999 the EU began using the port of Berbera for food aid bound for Ethiopia. According to the EU, the shipment of 16,670 tons of food aid constituted a pilot project to assess 'Somaliland's' suitability as a transhipment point. The use of Berbera was necessary owing to congestion at the port of Djibouti, the main supply route into Ethiopia. In January 2000 Egal approved a plan for Total Red Sea, the local subsidiary of the French oil company, to assume management responsibility for the port of Berbera's oil storage facilities.

Compared to the war-torn south, 'Somaliland's' economy has experienced relative stability. In January 2000 a delegation from Saudi Arabia visited President Egal in Berbera to explore ways to improve livestock trade between the two countries. On 26 March 2000 Egal announced that the 2000 budget would balance at $26m. This was an increase over the previous year and was attributed to increased revenue collection at Berbera, which remains the government's main source of income.

'PUNTLAND'

The regional administration of 'Puntland' was established in mid-1998, incorporating the areas of Bari and Nugaal, and parts of Mudug, Sanaag and Sool regions. The main economic activity of 'Puntland' is cattle rearing, while frankincense is one of the region's principal exports.

In December 1998 a drought crippled the economic viability of 'Puntland'. Officials appealed to the UN and foreign governments and relief agencies for food and medical supplies for the populations of Mudug and Nugaal regions, both of which were suffering from severe drought. To make matters worse, some 200,000 displaced people from southern Somalia sought refuge in 'Puntland'. Some 900,000 were facing starvation and famine, out of an estimated 2.4m. people in 'Puntland'. In April 1999 'Puntland' declared a state of emergency. At about the same time, the WFP announced the arrival at Boosaaso port of a shipment of 335 tons of food aid for 'Puntland'. The food, donated by the EU, was part of a 1,400 ton consignment to feed some 100,000 famine victims. Oxfam also warned that the situation had become 'acute' in Nugaal and Mudug because of water shortages. Oxfam, in co-operation with other humanitarian agencies, planned to transport 1,500 tanker-loads of water to key grazing areas over a six-week period. Meanwhile, UNICEF launched a US $1.3m. appeal for drought-stricken areas of northern Somalia.

Statistical Survey

Sources (unless otherwise stated): Economic Research and Statistics Dept, Central Bank of Somalia, Mogadishu, and Central Statistical Dept, State Planning Commission, POB 1742, Mogadishu; tel. (1) 80385.

Area and Population

AREA, POPULATION AND DENSITY

Area (sq km)	637,657*
Population (census results)†	
7 February 1975	3,253,024
February 1986 (provisional)	
Males	3,741,664
Females	3,372,767
Total	7,114,431
Population (UN estimates at mid-year)‡	
1996	8,467,000
1997	8,821,000
1998	9,237,000
Density (per sq km) at mid-1998	14.5

* 246,201 sq miles.
† Excluding adjustment for underenumeration.
‡ Source: UN, *World Population Prospects: The 1998 Revision*.

PRINCIPAL TOWNS (estimated population in 1981)

Mogadishu (capital)	500,000
Hargeysa	70,000
Kismayu	70,000
Berbera	65,000
Merca	60,000

BIRTHS AND DEATHS (UN estimates, annual averages)

	1980–85	1985–90	1990–95
Birth rate (per 1,000) . .	51.8	51.7	52.1
Death rate (per 1,000) . .	22.0	20.3	25.1

Expectation of life (UN estimates, years at birth, 1990–95): 39.3 (males 38.5; females 40.1).

Source: UN, *World Population Prospects: The 1998 Revision*.

ECONOMICALLY ACTIVE POPULATION
(estimates, '000 persons, 1991)

	Males	Females	Total
Agriculture, etc.	1,157	1,118	2,275
Industry	290	46	336
Services	466	138	604
Total labour force	1,913	1,302	3,215

Source: UN Economic Commission for Africa, *African Statistical Yearbook*.

Mid-1998 (estimates in '000): Agriculture, etc. 2,859; Total labour force 3,969 (Source: FAO, *Production Yearbook*).

Agriculture

PRINCIPAL CROPS ('000 metric tons)

	1996	1997	1998*
Maize	142†	128	121
Sorghum	145*	153	108
Rice (paddy)	2*	2	2
Cassava (Manioc)*	50	52	52
Pulses*	14	13	11
Groundnuts*	3	3	3
Sesame seed	23†	24†	21
Sugar cane*	210	180	190
Grapefruit*	19	19	17
Bananas*	55	55	53
Vegetables*	74	74	68

* FAO estimate(s).   † Unofficial figure.
Source: FAO, *Production Yearbook*.

LIVESTOCK (FAO estimates, '000 head, year ending September)

	1996	1997	1998
Cattle	5,400	5,600	5,300
Sheep	13,800	14,000	13,500
Goats	12,800	13,000	12,500
Pigs	4	5	4
Asses	20	21	19
Mules	20	20	18
Camels	6,200	6,300	6,100

Poultry (million): 3 in 1996; 3 in 1997; 3 in 1998.
Source: FAO, *Production Yearbook*.

LIVESTOCK PRODUCTS (FAO estimates, '000 metric tons)

	1996	1997	1998
Cows' milk	570	580	540
Goats' milk	400	410	390
Sheep's milk	440	450	430
Beef and veal	54	59	64
Mutton and lamb	29	30	30
Goat meat	31	31	31
Poultry eggs	2	3	2
Cattle hides	10	11	12
Sheepskins	6	6	6
Goatskins	5	5	5

Source: FAO, *Production Yearbook*.

Forestry

ROUNDWOOD REMOVALS ('000 cubic metres, excl. bark)

	1995	1996	1997
Sawlogs, veneer logs and logs for sleepers*	28	28	28
Other industrial wood	80	83	86
Fuel wood	8,917	9,228	9,600
Total	9,025	9,339	9,714

* Annual output assumed to be unchanged since 1975.
Source: FAO, *Yearbook of Forest Products*.

SAWNWOOD PRODUCTION ('000 cubic metres, incl. railway sleepers)

	1995	1996	1997
Total (all broadleaved)	14	14	14

Source: FAO, *Yearbook of Forest Products*.

Fishing

(FAO estimates, '000 metric tons, live weight)

	1995	1996	1997
Freshwater fishes	0.3	0.3	0.3
Marine fishes	15.0	14.8	14.5
Spiny lobsters	0.4	0.4	0.4
Marine molluscs	0.6	0.6	0.5
Total catch	16.3	16.0	15.7

Source: FAO, *Yearbook of Fishery Statistics*.

Mining

	1993	1994	1996*
Salt (estimates, '000 metric tons)†	1	1	2

* Data for 1995 unavailable.
† Data from the US Bureau of Mines.
Source: UN, *Industrial Commodity Statistics Yearbook*.

Industry

SELECTED PRODUCTS
('000 metric tons, unless otherwise indicated)

	1986	1987	1988
Sugar*	30.0	43.3	41.2
Canned meat (million tins)	1.0	—	—
Canned fish	0.1	—	—
Pasta and flour	15.6	4.3	—
Textiles (million yards)	5.5	3.0	6.3
Boxes and bags	15.0	12.0	5.0
Cigarettes and matches	0.3	0.2	0.1
Petroleum products	128	44	30
Electric energy (million kWh)†	253	255‡	257‡

Sugar (unofficial estimates, '000 metric tons)*: 21 in 1996; 18 in 1997; 19 in 1998.
Electric energy (provisional figures, million kWh)†: 268 in 1993; 271 in 1994; 272 in 1995.

* Data from FAO.
† Source: UN, *Industrial Commodity Statistics Yearbook*.
‡ Provisional figure.

Finance

CURRENCY AND EXCHANGE RATES
Monetary Units
100 cents = 1 Somali shilling (So. sh.).

Sterling, Dollar and Euro Equivalents (28 April 2000)
£1 sterling = 15,053.8 Somali shillings;
US $1 = 9,600.0 Somali shillings;
€1 = 8,721.6 Somali shillings;
100,000 Somali shillings = £6.643 = $10.417 = €11.466.

Average Exchange Rate (Somali shillings per US $)
1987   105.18
1988   170.45
1989   490.68

Note: A separate currency, the 'Somaliland shilling', was introduced in the 'Republic of Somaliland' in January 1995. The exchange rate was set at US $1 = 80 'Somaliland shillings' in July 1995.

CURRENT BUDGET (million Somali shillings)

Revenue	1986	1987	1988
Total tax revenue . . .	8,516.4	8,622.4	12,528.1
Taxes on income and profits .	1,014.8	889.7	1,431.0
Income tax	380.5	538.8	914.8
Profit tax	634.3	350.9	516.2
Taxes on production, consumption and domestic transactions . . .	1,410.4	1,274.2	2,336.4
Taxes on international transactions . .	6,091.2	6,458.5	8,760.6
Import duties . . .	4,633.2	4,835.2	6,712.1
Total non-tax revenue . .	6,375.2	8,220.4	7,623.4
Fees and service charges .	274.1	576.1	828.8
Income from government property	633.4	656.4	2,418.9
Other revenue	5,467.2	6,987.9	4,375.7
Total	14,891.6	16,842.8	20,151.5

Expenditure	1986	1987	1988
Total general services . .	11,997.7	19,636.7	24,213.6
Defence	2,615.9	3,145.0	8,093.9
Interior and police . . .	605.0	560.7	715.4
Finance and central services .	7,588.3	14,017.8	12,515.6
Foreign affairs . . .	633.0	1,413.9	2,153.1
Justice and religious affairs .	248.5	290.2	447.0
Presidency and general administration . . .	93.0	148.0	217.4
Planning	189.0	24.9	24.3
National Assembly . .	25.0	36.2	46.9
Total economic services . .	1,927.6	554.1	600.3
Transportation . . .	122.2	95.2	94.5
Posts and telecommunications .	94.3	76.7	75.6
Public works . . .	153.9	57.5	69.8
Agriculture	547.2	59.4	55.3
Livestock and forestry . .	459.0	89.5	109.9
Mineral and water resources .	318.8	85.2	93.1
Industry and commerce .	131.0	45.1	43.9
Fisheries	101.2	45.5	58.2
Total social services . .	1,050.5	900.1	930.8
Education	501.6	403.0	478.1
Health	213.8	203.5	255.2
Information	111.5	135.0	145.8
Labour, sports and tourism .	139.6	49.3	51.7
Other	84.0	109.3	—
Total	14,975.8	21,091.0	25,744.7

1989 (estimates): Budget to balance at 32,429m. Somali shillings.
1990 (estimates): Budget to balance at 86,012.0m. Somali shillings.
1991 (estimates): Budget to balance at 268,283.2m. Somali shillings.

CENTRAL BANK RESERVES (US $ million at 31 December)

	1987	1988	1989
Gold*	8.3	7.0	6.9
Foreign exchange . . .	7.3	15.3	15.4
Total	15.6	22.3	22.3

* Valued at market-related prices.

Source: IMF, *International Financial Statistics*.

MONEY SUPPLY (million Somali shillings at 31 December)

	1987	1988	1989
Currency outside banks . .	12,327	21,033	70,789
Private-sector deposits at central bank	1,771	1,555	5,067
Demand deposits at commercial banks	15,948	22,848	63,971
Total money	30,046	45,436	139,827

Source: IMF, *International Financial Statistics*.

COST OF LIVING
(Consumer Price Index for Mogadishu; base: 1985 = 100)

	1986	1987	1988
Food	123.6	161.4	319.8
Beverages and tobacco . . .	117.5	155.5	249.3
Clothes	119.2	153.4	271.3
Rent	131.5	169.5	250.6
Water, fuel and power . .	156.0	203.2	222.8
Transport and petrol . . .	130.2	155.4	260.1
Miscellaneous items . . .	121.5	140.9	253.0
All items	125.8	161.2	292.9

NATIONAL ACCOUNTS

Expenditure on the Gross Domestic Product*
(estimates, million Somali shillings at current prices)

	1988	1989	1990
Government final consumption expenditure	33,220	58,530	104,760
Private final consumption expenditure	240,950	481,680	894,790
Increase in stocks . . .	14,770	n.a.	n.a.
Gross fixed capital formation . .	44,780	134,150	240,030
Total domestic expenditure .	333,720	674,360	1,239,580
Exports of goods and services .	7,630	8,890	8,660
Less Imports of goods and services	49,430	57,660	58,460
GDP in purchasers' values .	291,920	625,580	1,189,780

* Figures are rounded to the nearest 10m. Somali shillings.

Source: UN Economic Commission for Africa, *African Statistical Yearbook*.

Gross Domestic Product by Economic Activity
(million Somali shillings at constant 1985 prices)

	1986	1987	1988
Agriculture, hunting, forestry and fishing	54,868	59,378	61,613
Mining and quarrying . .	291	291	291
Manufacturing	4,596	4,821	4,580
Electricity, gas and water . .	77	62	57
Construction	3,289	3,486	2,963
Trade, restaurants and hotels .	8,587	9,929	8,599
Transport, storage and communications . .	6,020	6,153	5,873
Finance, insurance, real estate and business services . .	3,743	4,095	3,890
Government services . . .	1,631	1,530	1,404
Other community, social and personal services . . .	2,698	2,779	2,863
Sub-total	85,800	92,524	92,133
Less Imputed bank service charges	737	748	748
GDP at factor cost . . .	85,064	91,776	91,385
Indirect taxes, *less* subsidies . .	5,301	4,250	3,262
GDP in purchasers' values .	90,365	96,026	94,647

GDP at factor cost (estimates, million Somali shillings at current prices): 249,380 in 1988; 500,130 in 1989; 923,970 in 1990 (Source: UN Economic Commission for Africa, *African Statistical Yearbook*).

BALANCE OF PAYMENTS (US $ million)

	1987	1988	1989
Exports of goods f.o.b. .	94.0	58.4	67.7
Imports of goods f.o.b. .	−358.5	−216.0	−346.3
Trade balance .	−264.5	−157.6	−278.6
Imports of services .	−127.7	−104.0	−122.0
Balance on goods and services .	−392.2	−261.6	−400.6
Other income paid .	−52.0	−60.6	−84.4
Balance on goods, services and income .	−444.2	−322.2	−485.0
Current transfers received .	343.3	223.7	331.2
Current transfers paid .	−13.1	—	−2.9
Current balance .	−114.0	−98.5	−156.7
Investment liabilities .	−22.8	−105.5	−32.6
Net errors and omissions .	39.0	22.4	−0.8
Overall balance .	−97.9	−181.7	−190.0

Source: IMF, *International Financial Statistics*.

External Trade

PRINCIPAL COMMODITIES (million Somali shillings)

Imports*	1986	1987	1988
Foodstuffs .	1,783.3	3,703.6	1,216.1
Beverages and tobacco .	298.1	183.6	6.2
Textiles, household goods .	156.0	304.1	115.5
Medicinal and chemical products .	89.2	133.9	97.9
Manufacturing raw materials .	230.0	626.9	661.4
Fertilizers .	1.8	238.0	2,411.4
Petroleum .	2,051.0	3,604.2	3,815.9
Construction materials .	981.4	2,001.9	307.8
Machinery and parts .	1,098.3	1,203.6	957.1
Transport equipment .	1,133.8	1,027.6	195.2
Agricultural machinery .	4.2	62.7	113.4
Total (incl. others) .	8,443.4	13,913.7	11,545.5

* Figures cover only imports made against payments of foreign currencies. The total value of imports in 1986 was 20,474 million Somali shillings.

Exports	1986	1987	1988
Livestock .	4,420.3	7,300.0	3,806.5
Bananas .	1,207.2	2,468.8	3,992.3
Fish .	45.2	70.4	291.8
Hides and skins .	294.0	705.2	492.0
Myrrh .	43.6	229.9	252.8
Total (incl. others) .	6,372.5	10,899.9	9,914.1

1992 (estimates, US $ million): Imports 150; Exports 80.

PRINCIPAL TRADING PARTNERS ('000 Somali shillings)

Imports	1980	1981	1982
China, People's Repub. .	46,959	40,962	89,772
Ethiopia .	43,743	146,853	155,775
Germany, Fed. Repub. .	104,117	430,548	214,873
Hong Kong .	5,351	13,862	3,972
India .	41,467	19,638	4,801
Iraq .	2,812	67,746	402
Italy .	756,800	662,839	1,221,146
Japan .	28,900	54,789	48,371
Kenya .	86,515	105,627	198,064
Saudi Arabia .	120,208	160,583	82,879
Singapore .	18,569	15,592	73,652
Thailand .	19,296	40,527	106,474
United Kingdom .	172,613	935,900	238,371
USA .	201,662	141,823	154,082
Total (incl. others) .	2,190,627	3,221,715	3,548,805

Exports	1980	1981	1982
Djibouti .	6,640	3,209	2,458
Germany, Fed. Repub. .	11,376	1,956	20,086
Italy .	107,661	58,975	77,870
Kenya .	2,425	6,929	4,211
Saudi Arabia .	583,768	803,631	1,852,936
United Kingdom .	1,233	—	3,169
USA .	1,301	—	6,970
Yemen, People's Dem. Repub. .	3,182	—	—
Total (incl. others) .	844,012	960,050	2,142,585

Source: the former Ministry of Planning, Mogadishu.

1986: *Imports* (estimates, million Somali shillings) USA 1,816; Japan 836; China, People's Repub. 553; United Kingdom 773; France 341; Germany, Fed. Repub. 1,481; Total (incl. others) 8,443; *Exports* (estimates, million Somali shillings) USA 5; China, People's Repub. 4; United Kingdom 31; France 27; Germany, Fed. Repub. 11; Total (incl. others) 6,373. (Source: UN Economic Commission for Africa, *African Statistical Yearbook*.)

Transport

ROAD TRAFFIC (estimates, '000 motor vehicles in use)

	1994	1995	1996
Passenger cars .	2.8	2.0	1.0
Commercial vehicles .	7.4	7.3	6.4

Source: International Road Federation, *World Road Statistics*.

SHIPPING

Merchant Fleet (registered at 31 December)

	1996	1997	1998
Number of vessels .	22	22	22
Total displacement ('000 grt) .	13.9	11.4	11.4

Source: Lloyd's Register of Shipping, *World Fleet Statistics*.

International Sea-borne Freight Traffic ('000 metric tons)

	1989	1990	1991
Goods loaded .	325	324	n.a.
Goods unloaded .	1,252*	1,118	1,007*

* Estimate.

Source: UN Economic Commission for Africa, *African Statistical Yearbook*.

CIVIL AVIATION (traffic on scheduled services)

	1989	1990	1991
Kilometres flown (million) .	3	3	1
Passengers carried ('000) .	89	88	46
Passenger-km (million) .	248	255	131
Freight ton-km (million) .	8	9	5

Source: UN, *Statistical Yearbook*.

Tourism

	1995	1996	1997
Tourist arrivals ('000) .	10	10	10

Source: World Tourism Organization, *Yearbook of Tourism Statistics*.

Communications Media

	1994	1995	1996
Radio receivers ('000 in use) . .	375	400	450
Television receivers ('000 in use) .	120	124	129
Telephones ('000 main lines in use)*	15	15	15
Daily newspapers . . .	1	1	2

* Provisional.

Sources: UNESCO, *Statistical Yearbook*; UN, *Statistical Yearbook*.

Education

(1985)

	Institutions	Teachers	Pupils
Pre-primary	16	133	1,558
Primary	1,224	10,338	196,496
Secondary			
General	n.a.	2,149	39,753
Teacher training	n.a.	30*	613*
Vocational.	n.a.	637	5,933
Higher	n.a.	817†	15,672†

* Figures refer to 1984.   † Figures refer to 1986.

Source: UNESCO, *Statistical Yearbook*.

1990 (UN estimates): 377,000 primary-level pupils; 44,000 secondary-level pupils; 10,400 higher-level pupils.

1991: University teachers 549; University students 4,640.

Directory

The Constitution

The Constitution promulgated in 1979 and amended in 1990 was revoked following the overthrow of President Siad Barre in January 1991. Proposals to reinstate the independence Constitution of 1960 were subsequently abandoned. A preparatory commission for a Transitional National Council, formed in March 1993, presented a draft transitional national charter in November 1993, providing the constitutional framework for the country during a two-year transitional period.

The Government

(August 2000)

In August 2000, following the successful completion of the Somali national reconciliation conference, which commenced in Arta, Djibouti in May, a transitional Somali national assembly, comprising 245 members was established; the assembly held its inaugural session on 13 August. On 26 August the transitional national assembly elected Abdulkasim Salad Hassan to the post of President. It was proposed that following a three-year interim period the Somali Republic would adopt a federal system of government, which would comprise 18 regional administrations.

Representatives of the self-proclaimed 'Republic of Somaliland' announced in February 1997 the promulgation of a three-year interim constitution, together with the re-election (by an electoral college) of Mohamed Ibrahim Egal as the territory's President.

MINISTRIES

Office of the President: People's Palace, Mogadishu; tel. (1) 723.

Ministry of Agriculture: Mogadishu; tel. (1) 80716.

Ministry of Civil Aviation and Transport: Mogadishu; tel. (1) 23025.

Ministry of Commerce: Mogadishu; tel. (1) 33089.

Ministry of Defence: Mogadishu; tel. (1) 710.

Ministry of Finance and Economy: Mogadishu; tel. (1) 33090.

Ministry of Foreign Affairs: Mogadishu; tel. (1) 721.

Ministry of Health: Mogadishu; tel. (1) 31055.

Ministry of Higher Education and Culture: POB 1182, Mogadishu; tel. (1) 35042.

Ministry of Industry: Mogadishu.

Ministry of Information and National Guidance: POB 1748, Mogadishu; tel. (1) 20947.

Ministry of the Interior: Mogadishu.

Ministry of Justice and Islamic Affairs: Mogadishu; tel. (1) 36062.

Ministry of Labour, Youth and Sports: Mogadishu; tel. (1) 33086.

Ministry of National Planning: POB 1742, Mogadishu; tel. (1) 80384.

Ministry of Public Works: Mogadishu; tel. (1) 21051.

Ministry of Telecommunications: Mogadishu; tel. (1) 29005.

Political Organizations

The majority of Somalia's political organizations have split into two factions, with one aligned to the Somali National Alliance (SNA) and the other to the Somali Salvation Alliance (SSA).

Islamic Party (Hizb al-Islam): radical Islamist party; Chair. Sheikh AHMAD QASIM.

Islamic Union Party (al-Ittihad al-Islam): aims to unite ethnic Somalis from Somalia, Ethiopia, Kenya and Djibouti in an Islamic state.

Northern Somali Alliance (NSA): f. 1997 as alliance between the United Somali Front and the United Somali Party.

United Somali Front (USF): f. 1989; represents Issas in the north-west of the country; Chair. ABD AR-RAHMAN DUALEH ALI; Sec.-Gen. MOHAMED OSMAN ALI.

United Somali Party (USP): opposes the SNM's declaration of the independent 'Republic of Somaliland'; Leader MOHAMED ABDI HASHI.

Rahanwin Resistance Army: guerrilla force active around Baidoa; Chair. ISAAQ MALAAQ IBRAHIM.

Somali Democratic Alliance (SDA): f. 1989; represents the Gadabursi ethnic grouping in north-west; opposes the Isaaq-dominated SNM and its declaration of an independent 'Republic of Somaliland'; Leader MOHAMED FARAH ABDULLAH.

Somali Democratic Movement (SDM): represents the Rahanwin clan; movement split in early 1992, with this faction in alliance with Ali Mahdi Mohamed; Leader ABDULKADIR MOHAMED ADAN.

Somali Eastern and Central Front (SECF): f. 1991; opposes the SNM's declaration of the independent 'Republic of Somaliland'; Chair. HIRSI ISMAIL MOHAMED.

Somali National Alliance (SNA): f. 1992 as alliance between the Southern Somali National Movement (which withdrew in 1993) and the factions of the United Somali Congress, Somali Democratic Movement and Somali Patriotic Movement given below; Chair. HUSSEIN MOHAMED AIDID.

Somali Democratic Movement (SDM): represents the Rahanwin clan; Chair. ADAM UTHMAN ABDI: Sec.-Gen. Dr YASIN MA'ALIM ABDULLAHI.

Somali Patriotic Movement (SPM): f. 1989; represents Ogadenis (of the southern Darod clan); Chair. GEDI UGAS MADHAR.

United Somali Congress (USC): f. 1989; overthrew Siad Barre in 1991; party split in mid-1991, and again in mid-1995; Chair. OSMAN HASSAN ALI 'ATO'.

Somali National Front (SNF): f. 1991; guerrilla force active in southern Somalia, promoting Darod clan interests and seeking restoration of SRSP Govt; a rival faction (led by OMAR Haji MASALEH) is active in southern Somalia; Leader Gen. MOHAMED SIAD HERSI 'MORGAN'.

Somali National Movement (SNM): Hargeysa; f. 1981 in London; conducted guerrilla operations in north and north-west Somalia, with early support from Ethiopia, until 1991; support drawn mainly from nomadic Isaaq clan; in May 1991 declared independent 'Republic of Somaliland' with the capital at Hargeysa; mems hold a majority of ministerial portfolios in 'Govt of Somaliland'; Chair. HASAN ISA JAMA.

Somali Patriotic Movement (SPM): f. 1989 in southern Somalia; represents Ogadenis (of the Darod clan) in southern Somalia; this faction of the SPM has allied with the SNF in opposing the SNA; Chair. Gen. ADEN ABDULLAHI NOOR ('GABIO').

Somali People's Democratic Union (SPDU): f. 1997; breakaway group from the SSDF; Chair. Gen. MOHAMED JIBRIL MUSEH.

Somali Revolutionary Socialist Party (SRSP): f. 1976 as the sole legal party; overthrown in Jan. 1991; conducts guerrilla operations in Gedo region, near border with Kenya; Sec.-Gen. (vacant); Asst Sec.-Gen. AHMED SULEIMAN ABDULLAH.

Somali Salvation Democratic Front (SSDF): f. 1981, as the Democratic Front for the Salvation of Somalia (DFSS), as a coalition of the Somali Salvation Front, the Somali Workers' Party and the Democratic Front for the Liberation of Somalia; operates in cen. Somalia, although a smaller group has opposed the SNA around Kismayu in alliance with the SNF; Chair. MOHAMED ABSHIR MONSA.

Somali Solidarity Party: Mogadishu; f. 1999; Chair. ABD AR-RAHMAN MUSA MOHAMED; Sec.-Gen. SA'ID ISA MOHAMED.

Southern Somali National Movement (SSNM): based on coast in southern Somalia; Chair. ABDI WARSEMEH ISAR.

United Somali Congress (USC): f. 1989 in cen. Somalia; overthrew Siad Barre in Jan. 1991; party split in 1991, with this faction dominated by the Abgal sub-clan of the Hawiye clan, Somalia's largest ethnic group; Leader ABDULLAHI MA'ALIN; Sec.-Gen. MUSA NUR AMIN.

United Somali Congress–Somali National Alliance (USC–SNA): f. 1995 by dissident mems of the SNA's USC faction; represents the Habr Gidir sub-clan of the Hawiye; Leader OSMAN HASSAN ALI 'ATO'.

Unity for the Somali Republic Party (USRP): f. 1999; the first independent party to be established in Somalia since 1969; Leader ABDI NUR DARMAN.

In November 1993 interim President Ali Mahdi Mohamed was reported to have assumed the leadership of the **Somali Salvation Alliance (SSA),** a new coalition of 12 factions opposed to Gen. Aidid, including the Somali African Muki Organization (SAMO), the Somali National Union (SNU), the USF, the SDA, the SDM, the SPM, the USC (pro-Mahdi faction), the SSDF, the Somali National Democratic Union (SNDU), the SNF and the SSNM. In May 1994 the SNU announced its intention to leave the alliance and join the SNA.

Diplomatic Representation

EMBASSIES IN SOMALIA

Note: Following the overthrow of Siad Barre in January 1991, all foreign embassies in Somalia were closed and all diplomatic personnel left the country. Some embassies were reopened, including those of France, Sudan and the USA, following the arrival of the US-led Unified Task Force (UNITAF) in December 1992; however, nearly all foreign diplomats left Somalia in anticipation of the withdrawal of the UN peace-keeping force, UNOSOM, in early 1995.

Algeria: POB 2850, Mogadishu; tel. (1) 81696.

Bulgaria: Hodan District, Km 5, off Via Afgoi, POB 1736, Mogadishu; tel. (1) 81820.

China, People's Republic: POB 548, Mogadishu; tel. (1) 20805.

Cuba: Mogadishu.

Djibouti: Mogadishu.

Egypt: Via Maka al-Mukarama Km 4, POB 76, Mogadishu; tel. (1) 80781; Ambassador: MAHMOUD MUSTAFA.

Ethiopia: POB 368, Mogadishu.

France: Corso Primo Luglio, POB 13, Mogadishu; tel. (1) 21715.

Germany: Via Mahamoud Harbi, POB 17, Mogadishu; tel. (1) 20547.

India: Via Jigjiga, Shingani, POB 955, Mogadishu; tel. (1) 21262.

Iran: Via Maka al-Mukarama, POB 1166, Mogadishu; tel. (1) 80881.

Iraq: Via Maka al-Mukarama, POB 641, Mogadishu; tel. (1) 80821.

Italy: Via Alto Giuba, POB 6, Mogadishu; tel. (1) 20544; Chargé d'affaires: FRANCESCO SCIORTINO.

Kenya: Via Mecca, POB 618, Mogadishu; tel. (1) 80857.

Korea, Democratic People's Republic: Via Km 5, Mogadishu; Ambassador: KIM RYONG SU.

Kuwait: First Medina Rd, Km 5, POB 1348, Mogadishu.

Libya: Via Medina, POB 125, Mogadishu; Ambassador: MOHAMED ZUBEYD.

Nigeria: Via Km 5, Mogadishu; tel. (1) 81362.

Oman: Via Afgoi, POB 2992, Mogadishu; tel. (1) 81658.

Pakistan: Via Afgoi, Km 5, POB 339, Mogadishu; tel. (1) 80856.

Qatar: Via Km 4, POB 1744, Mogadishu; tel. (1) 80746.

Romania: Via Lido, POB 651, Mogadishu.

Saudi Arabia: Via Benadir, POB 603, Mogadishu; tel. (1) 22087.

Sudan: Via Maka al-Mukarama, POB 552, Mogadishu; Chargé d'affaires a.i.: ALI HASSAN ALI.

Syria: Via Medina, POB 986, Mogadishu.

Turkey: Via Km 6, POB 2833, Mogadishu; tel. (1) 81975.

United Arab Emirates: Via Afgoi, Km 5, Mogadishu; tel. (1) 23178.

United Kingdom: Hassan Geedi Abtow 7/8, POB 1036, Mogadishu; tel. (1) 20288.

USA: Via Afgoi, Km 5, POB 574, Mogadishu; tel. (1) 39971.

Yemen: Via Km 5, POB 493, Mogadishu.

Yugoslavia: Via Mecca, POB 952, Mogadishu; tel. (1) 81729.

Zimbabwe: Mogadishu.

Judicial System

Constitutional arrangements in operation until 1991 provided for the Judiciary to be independent of the executive and legislative powers. Laws and acts having the force of law were required to conform to the provisions of the Constitution and to the general principles of Islam.

Supreme Court: Mogadishu; the court of final instance in civil, criminal, administrative and auditing matters; Chair. Sheikh AHMAD HASAN.

Military Supreme Court: Mogadishu; f. 1970; tried mems of the armed forces.

National Security Court: Mogadishu; heard cases of treason.

Courts of Appeal: Mogadishu; sat at Mogadishu and Hargeysa, with two sections, General and Assize.

Regional Courts: There were eight Regional Courts, with two sections, General and Assize.

District Courts: There were 84 District Courts, with Civil and Criminal Divisions. The Civil Division had jurisdiction over all controversies where the cause of action had arisen under Shari'a (Islamic) Law or Customary Law and any other Civil controversies where the matter in dispute did not involve more than 3,000 shillings. The Criminal Division had jurisdiction with respect to offences punishable with imprisonment not exceeding three years, or fine not exceeding 3,000 shillings, or both.

Qadis: Districts Courts of civil jurisdiction under Islamic Law.

In September 1993, in accordance with Resolution 865 of the UN Security Council, a judiciary re-establishment council, composed of Somalis, was created in Mogadishu to rehabilitate the judicial and penal systems.

Judiciary Re-establishment Council (JRC): Mogadishu; Chair. Dr ABD AL-RAHMAN Haji GA'AL.

Following the withdrawal of the UN peace-keeping force, UNOSOM, in early 1995, most regions outside of Mogadishu reverted to clan-based fiefdoms where Islamic (*Shari'a*) law (comprising an Islamic Supreme Council and local Islamic high courts) prevailed. In October 1996 Ali Mahdi Mohamed endorsed a new Islamic judicial system under which appeals could be lodged on all sentences passed by Islamic courts, and no sentence imposed by the courts could be implemented prior to an appeal court ruling. In August 1998 the Governor of the Banaadir administration announced the application of *Shari'a* law in Mogadishu and its environs thenceforth.

Religion

ISLAM

Islam is the state religion. Most Somalis are Sunni Muslims.

Imam: Gen. MOHAMED ABSHIR.

CHRISTIANITY

The Roman Catholic Church

Somalia comprises a single diocese, directly responsible to the Holy See. At 31 December 1998 there were an estimated 100 adherents.

Bishop of Mogadishu: (vacant); POB 273, Ahmed bin Idris, Mogadishu; tel. (1) 20184.

The Anglican Communion

Within the Episcopal Church in Jerusalem and the Middle East, the Bishop in Egypt has jurisdiction over Somalia.

The Press

The Country: POB 1178, Mogadishu; tel. (1) 21206; f. 1991; daily.

Dalka: POB 388, Mogadishu; f. 1967; current affairs; weekly.

Heegan (Vigilance): POB 1178, Mogadishu; tel. (1) 21206; f. 1978; weekly; English; Editor MOHAMOUD M. AFRAH.

Horseed: POB 1178, Mogadishu; tel. (1) 21206; weekly; in Italian and Arabic.

Huuriya (Liberty): Hargeysa; daily.

Jamhuuriya (The Republic): Hargeysa; independent; daily; Editor-in-Chief MAHMOUD ABDI SHIDE; circ. 2,500.

Al Mujeehid: Hargeysa; weekly.

New Era: POB 1178, Mogadishu; tel. (1) 21206; quarterly; in English, Somali and Arabic.

Qaran (Nation): Mogadishu; financial information; daily; in Somali; Editor ABDULAHI AHMED ALI; circ. 2,000.

Riyaaq (Happiness): Boosaaso.

Sahan (Pioneer): Boosaaso; Editor MUHAMMAD DEEQ.

Somalia in Figures: Ministry of National Planning, POB 1742, Mogadishu; tel. (1) 80384; govt statistical publ.; 3 a year; in English.

Xiddigta Oktobar (October Star): POB 1178, Mogadishu; tel. (1) 21206; in Somali; daily.

Other periodicals, published in Mogadishu at irregular intervals, include *Ayaamaha* and *Xog Ogaal*.

NEWS AGENCIES

Horn of Africa News Agency: Mogadishu; f. 1990.

Somali National News Agency (SONNA): POB 1748, Mogadishu; tel. (1) 24058; Dir MUHAMMAD HASAN KAHIN.

Foreign Bureaux

Agence France-Presse (AFP) (France): POB 1178, Mogadishu; Rep. MOHAMED ROBLE NOOR.

Agenzia Nazionale Stampa Associata (ANSA) (Italy): POB 1399, Mogadishu; tel. (1) 20626; Rep. ABDULKADIR MOHAMOUD WALAYO.

Publishers

Government Printer: POB 1743, Mogadishu.

Somalia d'Oggi: Piazzale della Garesa, POB 315, Mogadishu; law, economics and reference.

Broadcasting and Communications

TELECOMMUNICATIONS

Ministry of Telecommunications: Mogadishu; tel. (1) 29005; Dir-Gen. HASSAN MOHAMED ELMI.

Somaliland Telecommunications Corporation: Hargeysa; Dir MOHAMED ARWO.

BROADCASTING
Radio

Holy Koran Radio: Mogadishu; f. 1996; religious broadcasts in Somali.

Radio Awdal: Boorama, 'Somaliland'; operated by the Gadabursi clan.

Radio Banaadir: Mogadishu; f. 2000; serves Mogadishu and its environs.

Radio Free Somalia: f. 1993; operates from Galacaio in north-eastern Somalia; relays humanitarian and educational programmes.

Radio Gaalkayco: operates from Puntland.

Radio Hargeysa, the Voice of the 'Republic of Somaliland': POB 14, Hargeysa; tel. 155; serves the northern region ('Somaliland'); broadcasts in Somali, and relays Somali and Amharic transmission from Radio Mogadishu; Dir of Radio IDRIS EGAL NUR.

Radio HornAfrique: Mogadishu; f. 1999; commercial independent station broadcasting music and programmes on social issues; Dir AHMAD ABDI SALAN Haji ADAN.

Radio Mogadishu, Voice of the Masses of the Somali Republic: southern Mogadishu; f. 1993 by supporters of Gen. Aidid after the facilities of the fmr state-controlled radio station, Radio Mogadishu (of which Gen. Aidid's faction took control in 1991), were destroyed by UNOSOM; broadcasts in Somali, Amharic, Arabic, English and Swahili; Chair. FARAH HASAN AYOBOQORE.

Radio Mogadishu, Voice of Somali Pacification: Mogadishu; f. 1995 by supporters of Osman Hassan Ali 'Ato'; broadcasts in Somali, English and Arabic; Dir-Gen. MUHAMMAD DIRIYEH ILMI.

Radio Mogadishu, Voice of the Somali Republic: northern Mogadishu; f. 1992 by supporters of Ali Mahdi Mohamed; Chair. FARAH HASSAN AYOBOQORE.

Voice of Peace: POB 1631, Addis Ababa, Ethiopia; f. 1993; aims to promote peace and reconstruction in Somalia; receives support from UNICEF and the OAU.

Some radio receivers are used for public address purposes in small towns and villages.

Television

A television service, financed by Kuwait and the United Arab Emirates, was inaugurated in 1983. Programmes in Somali and Arabic are broadcast for three hours daily, extended to four hours on Fridays and public holidays. Reception is limited to a 30-km radius of Mogadishu.

Somali Television Network (STN): Mogadishu; f. 1999; broadcasts 22 channels in Somali, English, French, Indian, Italian and Arabic; Man. Dir ABURAHMAN ROBLEY ULAYEREH.

Television HornAfrique: Mogadishu; f. 1999; broadcasts 6 channels in Somali and Arabic; CEO ALI IMAN SHARMARKEH.

Finance

(cap. = capital; res = reserves; m. = million; brs = branches; amounts in Somali shillings unless otherwise stated)

BANKING
Central Bank

Central Bank of Somalia (Bankiga Dhexe ee Soomaaliya): Corso Somalia 55, POB 11, Mogadishu; tel. (1) 725; f. 1960; bank of issue; cap. and res 132.5m. (Sept. 1985); Gov. OMAR AHMED OMAR; Gen. Mans MOHAMED MOHAMED NUR, BASHIR ISSE ALI.

A central bank (with 10 branches) is also in operation in Hargeysa (in the self-proclaimed 'Republic of Somaliland').

Commercial Bank

Commercial Bank of Somalia: Via Primo Luglio, POB 203, Mogadishu; tel. (1) 22861; f. 1990 to succeed the Commercial and Savings Bank of Somalia; state-owned; cap. 1,000m. (May 1990); 33 brs.

Private Banks

Barakat Bank of Somalia: Mogadishu; f. 1996; cap. US $2m.; Chair. AHMED NUR ALI JUMALE.

Somali-Malaysian Commercial Bank: Mogadishu; f. 1997; cap. US $4m.

Development Bank

Somali Development Bank: Via Primo Luglio, POB 1079, Mogadishu; tel. (1) 21800; f. 1968; state-owned; cap. and res 2,612.7m. (Dec. 1988); Pres. MOHAMED MOHAMED NUR; 4 brs.

INSURANCE

Cassa per le Assicurazioni Sociali della Somalia: POB 123, Mogadishu; f. 1950; workers' compensation; Dir-Gen. HASSAN MOHAMED JAMA; 9 brs.

State Insurance Co of Somalia: POB 992, Mogadishu; f. 1974; Gen. Man. ABDULLAHI GA'AL; brs throughout Somalia.

Trade and Industry

DEVELOPMENT ORGANIZATIONS

Agricultural Development Corpn: POB 930, Mogadishu; f. 1971 by merger of fmr agricultural and machinery agencies and grain marketing board; supplies farmers with equipment and materials and purchases growers' cereal and oil seed crops; Dir-Gen. MOHAMED FARAH ANSHUR.

Livestock Development Agency: POB 1759, Mogadishu; Dir-Gen. HASSAN WELI SCEK HUSSEN; brs throughout Somalia.

Somali Co-operative Movement: Mogadishu; Chair. HASSAN HAWADLE MADAR.

Somali Oil Refinery: POB 1241, Mogadishu; Chair. NUR AHMED DARAWISH.

Water Development Agency: POB 525, Mogadishu; Dir-Gen. KHALIF Haji FARAH.

CHAMBER OF COMMERCE

Chamber of Commerce, Industry and Agriculture: Via Asha, POB 27, Mogadishu; tel. (1) 3209; Chair. MOHAMED Haji IBRAHIM EGAL.

TRADE ASSOCIATION

National Agency of Foreign Trade: POB 602, Mogadishu; major foreign trade agency; state-owned; brs in Berbera and over 150 centres throughout Somalia; Dir-Gen. JAMA AW MUSE.

UTILITIES

Water Development Agency: POB 525, Mogadishu; Dir-Gen. KHALIF Haji FARAH.

TRADE UNION

General Federation of Somali Trade Unions: POB 1179, Mogadishu; Chair. MOHAMED FARAH ISSA GASHAN.

Transport

RAILWAYS

There are no railways in Somalia.

ROADS

In 1996 there were an estimated 22,100 km of roads, of which some 11.8% were paved.

SHIPPING

Merca, Berbera, Mogadishu and Kismayu are the chief ports.

At 31 December 1998 Somalia's merchant fleet totalled 22 vessels, with a combined displacement of 11,438 grt.

An EU-sponsored development project for the port of Berbera (in 'Somaliland') was announced in February 1996. It was reported that the port of Mogadishu, which had been largely closed since 1995, was to be reopened in early 2000.

Somali Ports Authority: POB 935, Mogadishu; tel. (1) 30081; Port Dir MOHAMED JUMA FURAH.

Juba Enterprises Beder & Sons Ltd: POB 549, Mogadishu; privately-owned.

National Shipping Line: POB 588, Mogadishu; tel. (1) 23021; state-owned; Gen. Man. Dr ABDULLAHI MOHAMED SALAD.

Puntland Shipping Service: Boosaaso.

Shosman Commercial Co Ltd: North-Eastern Pasaso; privately-owned.

Somali Shipping Corporation: POB 2775, Mogadishu; state-owned.

CIVIL AVIATION

Mogadishu has an international airport. There are airports at Hargeysa and Baidoa and six other airfields. It was reported that a daily service had been inaugurated in April 1994 between Hargeysa (in the self-declared 'Republic of Somaliland') and Nairobi, Kenya. Mogadishu international airport (closed since 1995) was officially reopened in mid-1998, but continuing civil unrest limited services significantly.

Somali Airlines: Via Medina, POB 726, Mogadishu; tel. (1) 81533; fax (1) 80489; f. 1964 (suspended operations in 1991); state-owned; operates internal passenger and cargo services and international services to destinations in Africa, Europe and the Middle East; Pres. MOHAMOUD MOHAMED GULAID.

Defence

Of total armed forces of 64,500 in June 1990, the army numbered 60,000, the navy 2,000 and the air force 2,500. In addition, there were 29,500 members of paramilitary forces, including 20,000 members of the people's militia. Following the overthrow of the Siad Barre regime in January 1991, there were no national armed forces; Somalia was divided into areas controlled by different armed groups, which were based on clan, or sub-clan, membership. In March 1994 the UN announced that 8,000 former Somali police-officers had been rehabilitated throughout the country, receiving vehicles and uniforms from the UN. Following the UN withdrawal from Somalia in early 1995, these police-officers ceased receiving payment, and their future and their hitherto neutral stance appeared uncertain. Although a police force was established in the Banaadir region (Mogadishu and its environs) in late 1998, there were reports that it had disbanded by mid-1999. The total armed forces of the self-proclaimed 'Republic of Somaliland' were estimated to number 12,900 in August 1998.

Education

All private schools were nationalized in 1972, and education is now provided free of charge. Despite the introduction of the Somali script in 1972, the level of literacy remains low. According to estimates by UNESCO, the average rate of adult illiteracy declined from 83.1% in 1985 to 75.9% (males 63.9%; females 86.0%) in 1990. Primary education, lasting for eight years, is officially compulsory for children aged six to 14 years. However, the total enrolment at primary schools of children in this age-group declined from 14% (boys 18%; girls 10%) in 1980 to only 8% (boys 11%; girls 6%) in 1985. Secondary education, beginning at the age of 14, lasts for four years but is not compulsory. In 1985 enrolment of children at secondary schools included 3% (boys 4%; girls 2%) of those in the relevant age-group. In 1985 enrolment at primary and secondary schools was equivalent to 10% of the school-age population (boys 13%; girls 7%). Current expenditure on education in the 1988 budget was 478.1m. Somali shillings (equivalent to 1.9% of total current spending). Following the overthrow of Siad Barre's government in January 1991 and the ensuing internal disorder, Somalia's education system collapsed. In January 1993 a primary school was opened in the building of Somalia's only university, the Somali National University in Mogadishu (which had been closed in early 1991). The only other schools operating in the country were a number under the control of fundamentalist Islamic groups and some that had been reopened in the 'Republic of Somaliland' in mid-1991.

Bibliography

Africa Watch. *A Government at War with its Own People*. New York, Africa Watch, 1990.

Ahmed, A. J. (Ed.). *The Invention of Somalia*. Lawrenceville, KS, Red Sea Press, 1995.

Aidid, M. F., and Ruhela, S. P. (Eds). *The Preferred Future: Development in Somalia*. New Delhi, Vikas Publishing House, 1993.

Beachey, R. *The Warrior Mullah: The Horn Aflame 1892–1920*. London, Bellew Publishing, 1990.

Besteman, C., and Cassanelli, L. V. (Eds). *The Struggle for Land in Southern Somalia: The War Behind the War*. Boulder, CO, and Oxford, Westview Press, 1996.

Bongartz, M. *The Civil War in Somalia: Its Genesis and Dynamics*. Uppsala, Scandinavian Institute for African Studies, 1991.

Cassanelli, L. V. *The Shaping of Somali Society: Reconstructing the History of A Pastoral People, 1600–1900*. Philadelphia, Pennsylvania University Press, 1982.

Castagno, M. *Historical Dictionary of Somalia*. Metuchen, NJ, Scarecrow Press, 1975.

Clarke, W., and Herbst, J. (Eds). *Learning from Somalia: The Lessons of Armed Humanitarian Intervention*. Boulder, CO, Westview Press, 1997.

Contini, P. *The Somali Republic: An Experiment in Legal Integration*. 1969.

DeLong, K., and Tuckey, S. *Mogadishu: Heroism and Tragedy*. Westport, CT, and London, Praeger, 1994.

de Waal, R., and de Waal, A. *Somalia: Crimes and Blunders*. London, James Currey Publishers, 1995.

Drysdale, J. *Whatever Happened to Somalia?*. London, Haan Associates, 1994.

Dualeh, H.A. *From Barre to Aidid: The Story of Somalia and the Agony of a Nation*. Nairobi, Stellagraphics, 1994.

Ghalib, J.M. *The Cost of Dictatorship. The Somali Experience*. New York and Oxford, Lilian Barber Press, 1995.

Hashim, A. B. *The Fallen State: Dissonance, Dictatorship and Death in Somalia*. Lanham, MD, University Press of America, 1997.

Hess, R. L. *Italian Colonialism in Somalia*. 1966.

Hirsch, J.L., and Oakley, R.B. *Somalia and 'Operation Restore Hope': Reflections on Peacemaking and Peacekeeping*. Washington, DC, United States Institute of Peace Press, 1995.

Issa-Salwe, A.M., and Cissa-Salwe, C. *The Collapse of the Somali State*. London, Haan Associates, 1994.

Laitin, D.D., and Saïd, S.S. *Somalia: Nation in Search of a State*. Boulder, CO, Westview Press, 1987.

Lewis, I. M. *A Modern History of Somalia: Nation and State in the Horn of Africa*. Boulder, CO, Westview Press, 1988.

Blood and Bone: The Call of Kinship in Somali Society. Trenton, NJ, Red Sea Press, 1994.

Saints and Somalis: Popular Islam in a Clan-Based Society . Lawrencville, NJ, Red Sea Press, 1998.

Lyons, T., and Samatar, A.I. *Somalia: State Collapse, Multilateral Intervention and Strategies for Political Reconstruction.* Washington, DC, Brookings Institution, 1995.

Makinda, S.M. *Seeking Peace from Chaos: Humanitarian Intervention in Somalia.* Boulder, CO, Lynne Rienner Publishers, 1993.

Metz, H.C. (Ed.). *Somalia: A Country Study.* Washington, DC, US Government Printing Office, 1993.

Morin, D. *Littérature et politique en Somalie.* Talenco Cedex, Université Montesquieu—Bordeaux IV, 1997.

Mubarak, J.A. *From Bad Policy to Chaos in Somalia: How an Economy Fell Apart.* Westport, CT, and London, Praeger, 1996.

Omar, M.O. *Somalia: A Nation Driven to Despair.* New Delhi, Somali Publications, 1996.

Pankhurst, E.S. *Ex-Italian Somaliland.* New York, Philosophical Library, 1951.

Sahnoun, M. *Somalia: The Missed Opportunities.* Washington, DC, United States Institute of Peace Press, 1994.

Salih, M. A. M., and Wohlgemuth, L. (Eds) *Crisis Management and the Politics of Reconciliation in Somalia.* Uppsala, Scandinavian Institute for African Studies, 1994.

Samatar, A.I. (Ed.). *The Somali Challenge: From Catastrophe to Renewal?* Boulder, CO, Lynne Rienner, 1994.

Samatar, S.S. *Somalia: A Nation in Turmoil.* London, Minority Rights Group, 1991.

Simons, A. *Networks of Dissolution: Somalia Undone.* Boulder, CO; Oxford, Westview Press, 1995.

Stevenson, J. *Losing Mogadishu: Testing US Policy in Somalia.* Annapolis, MD, Naval Institute Press, 1995.

United Nations, Dept of Public Information. *The United Nations and Somalia 1992–1996.* New York, United Nations, 1996.

SOUTH AFRICA

Physical and Social Geography

A. MacGREGOR HUTCHESON

The Republic of South Africa occupies the southern extremity of the African continent and, except for a relatively small area in the northern Transvaal, lies poleward of the Tropic of Capricorn, extending as far as latitude 34° 51′ S. The republic covers a total area of 1,219,080 sq km (470,689 sq miles) and has common borders with Namibia on the north-west, with Botswana on the north, and with Zimbabwe, Mozambique and Swaziland on the north-east. Lesotho is entirely surrounded by South African territory, lying within the eastern part of the republic.

PHYSICAL FEATURES

Most of South Africa consists of a vast plateau with upwarped rims, bounded by an escarpment. Framing the plateau is a narrow coastal belt. The surface of the plateau varies in altitude from 600 m to 2,000 m above sea-level, but is mostly above 900 m. It is highest in the east and south-east and dips fairly gently towards the Kalahari Basin in the north-west. The relief is generally monotonous, consisting of undulating to flat landscapes over wide areas. Variation is provided occasionally by low ridges and *inselberge* (or *kopjes*) made up of rock more resistant to erosion. There are three major sub-regions:

(i) the High Veld between 1,200 m and 1,800 m, forming a triangular area which occupies the southern Transvaal and most of the Free State;

(ii) a swell over 1,500 m high, aligned WNW–ESE, part of which is known as the Witwatersrand, rising gently from the plateau surface to the north of the High Veld and forming a major drainage divide; and

(iii) the Middle Veld, generally between 600 m and 1,200 m, comprising the remaining part of the plateau.

The plateau's edges, upwarped during the Tertiary Period, are almost everywhere above 1,500 m. Maximum elevations of over 3,400 m occur in the south-east in Lesotho. From the crests the surface descends coastwards by means of the Great Escarpment which gives the appearance of a mountain range when viewed from below, and which is known by distinctive names in its different sections. An erosional feature, dissected by seaward-flowing rivers, the nature of the escarpment varies according to the type of rock which forms it. Along its eastern length it is known as the Drakensberg; in the section north of the Olifants river fairly soft granite gives rise to gentle slopes, but south of that river resistant quartzites are responsible for a more striking appearance. Further south again, along the KwaZulu/Natal–Lesotho border, basalts cause the Drakensberg to be at its most striking, rising up a sheer 1,800 m or more in places. Turning westwards the Great Escarpment is known successively as the Stormberg, Bamboes, Suurberg, Sneeuberg, Nieuwveld, and Komsberg, where gentle slopes affording access to the interior alternate with a more wall-like appearance. The Great Escarpment then turns sharply northwards through the Roggeveld mountains, following which it is usually in the form of a simple step until the Kamiesberg are reached; owing to aridity and fewer rivers the dissection of this western part of the escarpment is much less advanced than in the eastern (Drakensberg) section.

The Lowland margin which surrounds the South African plateau may be divided into four zones:

(i) The undulating to flat Transvaal Low Veld, between 150 m and 600 m above sea-level, separated from the Mozambique coastal plain by the Lebombo mountains in the east, and including part of the Limpopo valley in the north;

(ii) The south-eastern coastal belt, a very broken region descending to the coast in a series of steps, into which the rivers have cut deep valleys. In northern KwaZulu/Natal the republic possesses its only true coastal plain, some 65 km at its widest;

(iii) The Cape ranges, consisting of the remnants of mountains folded during the Carboniferous era, and flanking the plateau on the south and south-west. On the south the folds trend E–W and on the south-west they trend N–S, the two trends crossing in the south-western corner of the Cape to produce a rugged knot of mountains and the ranges' highest elevations (over 2,000 m). Otherwise the Cape ranges are comparatively simple in structure, consisting of parallel anticlinal ridges and synclinal valleys. Narrow lowlands separate the mountains from the coast. Between the ridges and partially enclosed by them, e.g. the Little Karoo, is a series of steps rising to the foot of the Great Escarpment. The Great Karoo, the last of these steps, separates the escarpment from the Cape ranges; and

(iv) The western coastal belt is also characterized by a series of steps, but the slope from the foot of the Great Escarpment to the coast is more gentle and more uniform than in the south-eastern zone.

The greater part of the plateau is drained by the Orange river system. Rising in the Drakensberg within a short distance of the escarpment, as do its two main perennial tributaries the Vaal and the Caledon, the Orange flows westward for 1,900 km before entering the Atlantic Ocean. However, the western part of its basin is so dry that it is not unknown for the Orange to fail to reach its mouth during the dry season. The large-scale Orange River Project, a comprehensive scheme for water supply, irrigation and hydroelectric generation, aids water conservation in this western area and is making possible its development. The only other major system is that of the Limpopo, which rises on the northern slopes of the Witwatersrand and drains most of the Northern Province to the Indian Ocean. Apart from some interior drainage to a number of small basins in the north and north-west, the rest of the republic's drainage is peripheral. Relatively short streams rise in the Great Escarpment, although some rise on the plateau itself, having cut through the escarpment, and drain directly to the coast. With the exception of riparian strips along perennial rivers most of the country relies for water supplies on underground sources supplemented by dams. None of the republic's rivers are navigable.

CLIMATE AND NATURAL VEGETATION

Except for a small part of the Northern Province the climate of South Africa is subtropical, although there are important regional variations within this general classification. Altitude and relief forms have an important influence on temperature and on both the amount and distribution of rainfall, and there is a strong correlation between the major physical and the major climatic regions. The altitude of the plateau modifies temperatures and because there is a general rise in elevation towards the Equator there is a corresponding decrease in temperature, resulting in a remarkable uniformity of temperature throughout the republic from south to north (cf. mean annual temperatures: Cape Town, 16.7°C; and Pretoria, 17.2°C). The greatest contrasts in temperature are, in fact, between the east coast, warmed by the Mozambique Current, and the west coast, cooled by the Benguela Current (cf. respectively, mean monthly temperatures: Durban, January 24.4°C, July 17.8°C; and Port

Nolloth, January 15.6°C, July 12.2°C). Daily and annual ranges in temperature increase with distance from the coast, being much greater on the plateau (cf. mean annual temperature range: Cape Town, 8°C; Pretoria, 11°C).

The areas of highest annual rainfall largely coincide with the outstanding relief features, over 650 mm being received only in the eastern third of South Africa and relatively small areas in the southern Cape. Parts of the Drakensberg and the seaward slopes of the Cape ranges experience over 1,500 mm. West of the Drakensberg and to the north of the Cape ranges there is a marked rain-shadow, and annual rainfall decreases progressively westwards (cf. Durban 1,140 mm, Bloemfontein 530 mm, Kimberley 400 mm, Upington 180 mm, Port Nolloth 50 mm). Virtually all the western half of the country, apart from the southern Cape, receives less than 250 mm and the western coastal belt's northern section forms a continuation of the Namib Desert. Most of the rain falls during the summer months (November to April) when evaporation losses are greatest, brought by tropical marine air masses moving in from the Indian Ocean on the east. However, the south-western Cape has a winter maximum of rainfall with dry summers. Only the narrow southern coastal belt between Cape Agulhas and East London has rainfall distributed uniformly throughout the year. Snow may fall occasionally over the higher parts of the plateau and the Cape ranges during winter, but frost occurs on an average for 120 days each year over most of the interior plateau, and for shorter periods in the coastal lowlands, except in KwaZulu/Natal, where it is rare.

Variations in climate and particularly in annual rainfall are reflected in changes of vegetation, sometimes strikingly, as between the south-western Cape's Mediterranean shrub type, designed to withstand summer drought and of which the protea—the national plant—is characteristic, and the drought-resistant low Karoo bush immediately north of the Cape ranges and covering much of the semi-arid western half of the country. The only true areas of forest are found along the wetter south and east coasts—the temperate evergreen forests of the Knysna district and the largely evergreen subtropical bush, including palms and wild bananas, of the eastern Cape and KwaZulu/Natal, respectively. Grassland covers the rest of the republic, merging into thorn veld in the north-western Cape and into bush veld in the Northern Province.

MINERAL RESOURCES

South Africa's mineral resources, outstanding in their variety, quality and quantity, overshadow all the country's other natural resources. They are mainly found in the ancient Pre-Cambrian foundation and associated intrusions and occur in a wide curving zone which stretches from the Northern Province through the Free State and Northern Cape to the west coast. To the south of this mineralized zone, one of the richest in the world, the Pre-Cambrian rocks are covered by Karoo sedimentaries which generally do not contain minerals, with the exception of extensive deposits of bituminous coal, the republic's only indigenous mineral fuel. These deposits occur mainly in the eastern Transvaal High Veld, the northern Free State and northern KwaZulu/Natal, mostly in thick, easily worked seams fairly near to the surface. In the mid-1980s reserves were estimated to exceed 110,000m. tons, of which 58,000m. tons were considered to be economically extractable by current technology. Coal is of particular importance to South Africa because of relatively

low production elsewhere in the continent south of the Equator, and South Africa's current dependence on imported petroleum.

The most important mineral regions are the Witwatersrand and the northern Free State, producing gold, silver and uranium; the diamond areas centred on Kimberley, Pretoria, Jagersfontein and Koffiefontein; and the Transvaal bushveld complex containing multiple occurrences of a large number of minerals, including asbestos, chrome, copper, iron, magnesium, nickel, platinum, tin, uranium and vanadium. In the Northern Cape important deposits of manganese, iron ore and asbestos occur in the Postmasburg, Sishen and Kuruman areas, while in the north-western Cape reserves of lead, zinc, silver and copper are being exploited. This list of occurrences and minerals is by no means exhaustive, and prospecting for new mineral resources is continuing. In 1988 exploitable petroleum deposits were discovered near Hondeklip Bay, off the western Cape coast, and a substantial reserve of gas and petroleum was discovered south-west of Mossel Bay, off the south coast of the Cape.

ETHNIC GROUPS AND POPULATION

Five major ethnic groups make up South Africa's multiracial society. The 'Khoisan' peoples—Bushmen, Hottentots and Bergdamara—are survivors of the country's earliest inhabitants. The negroid Bantu-speaking peoples fall into a number of tribal groupings. The major groups are formed by the Nguni, comprising Zulu, Swazi, Ndebele, Pondo, Tembu and Xhosa on the one hand, and by the Sotho and Tswana on the other. The European or 'white' peoples, who once dominated the political and social organization of the republic and continue to exercise considerable economic influence, are descended from the original 17th-century Dutch settlers in the Cape, refugee French Huguenots, British settlers from 1820 onwards, Germans, and more recent immigrants from Europe and ex-colonial African territories. The remainder of the population comprises Coloureds (people of mixed race) and Asians, largely of Indian origin. At the October 1996 census the total population was 40,583,573. The adjusted population at the previous census, held in March 1991, was 37,944,018. At mid-1999 the total population was estimated to be 43,054,306. At mid-1998 the estimated ethnic composition of the total population was: Africans 77.0%; Europeans (Whites) 10.7%; Coloureds 8.8%; and Asians 2.6%. The official languages are Afrikaans, English, isiNdebele, Sesotho sa Leboa, Sesotho, siSwati, Xitsonga, Setswana, Tshivenda, isiXhosa and isiZulu.

The overall density of the population was 33.3 inhabitants per sq km at the census of October 1996, but its distribution is extremely uneven. It is generally related to agricultural resources, more than two-thirds living in the wetter eastern third of the republic and in the southern Cape. The heaviest concentrations are found in the Witwatersrand mining area—the Johannesburg Metropolitan Area had 1,916,061 people at the 1991 census—and in and around the major ports of Cape Town (2,350,137 in 1991) and Durban (1,137,378). Europeans have a widespread geographical distribution, but more than 80% reside in towns. Relatively few Africans are resident in the western Cape, and, while an increasing number are moving to the large black townships on the periphery of the major urban centres, more than 60% continue to reside in those rural areas which comprised the former tribal reserves. These extend in a great horseshoe along the south-eastern coast and up to the Northern Province and then south-westwards to the north-eastern Cape. The Coloured population are mainly resident in the Cape, and the Asian population is concentrated largely in KwaZulu/Natal and the Witwatersrand.

Recent History

CHRISTOPHER SAUNDERS

Based on an earlier article by J. D. OMER-COOPER

HISTORICAL BACKGROUND

European interest in the area that now comprises the Republic of South Africa dates from 1652; agricultural settlements were created by arrivals of white immigrants, principally from the Netherlands, Germany, Britain and France. The expansion of British influence in the Cape after 1795, and the territory's eventual annexation by Britain in 1806, resulted in increasing friction between the British authorities at the Cape and the Dutch (Afrikaner, or Boer) frontier farmers. Following the abolition of slavery in 1834, many Afrikaner farmers embarked upon a northward trek to establish an independent polity. Britain subsequently annexed Natal (KwaZulu), while permitting the creation of two Boer republics, the Orange Free State (OFS) and the South African Republic of Transvaal. The rapid development of gold-mining in the Transvaal after 1886, together with the emergence of the South African Republic as the most powerful state in the region, were perceived by British interests as a threat to their paramountcy; the consequent exertion of pressure on the Transvaal and the OFS provoked the Anglo–Boer War of 1899–1902. At its conclusion, the Boer republics passed under effective British control, and on 31 May 1910 the Union of South Africa was formally declared a dominion under the British crown.

The Union constitution gave the franchise to white males only, except in the Cape, where the existing voting rights were retained and protected. The two Afrikaner parties in the ex-republics amalgamated with the Cape's South Africa Party to form the national South Africa Party (SAP). Led by two Boer generals, Louis Botha and Jan Smuts, the SAP formed the first government of the new Union. The pro-imperial and pro-capitalist attitudes of the two leaders, however, antagonized many poorer rural Afrikaners. In 1912 the SAP split, and Gen. J. B. M. Hertzog founded the National Party (NP). In the same year members of the African élite, under the chairmanship of Pixley Seme, established the South African Native National Congress, soon renamed the African National Congress (ANC). In order to coerce African peasants into migrant labour for mine owners and white farmers, the 1913 Land Act denied Africans the right to buy land outside the Native Reserves, or to lease white-owned land. Following the First World War of 1914–18, the former German colony of South West Africa (Namibia) was entrusted to South African administration as a League of Nations mandated territory. The NP, realigned with the SAP, emerged victorious from parliamentary elections held in 1933, after which the two parties formally merged as the United Party (UP). Hertzog, the prime minister, was then able, by means of the 1936 Land Act, to extend the 1913 Act to the Cape. Coloured voters' rights in the Cape were, however, retained. The fusion of the NP with the SAP prompted a small group of extreme Afrikaner nationalist deputies, under Daniel Malan, to form a 'purified' NP.

APARTHEID

As South Africa approached the 1948 election, many Afrikaner farmers, badly affected by the loss of low-cost African labour to the towns, and Afrikaner workers fearful of black competition, found apartheid attractive. The NP secured a narrow parliamentary majority. Daniel Malan formed a government and commenced putting apartheid into practice. In 1954 Malan was replaced by the hard-line J. G. Strydom, who died in 1958 and was succeeded by Hendrik Verwoerd, apartheid's chief architect and leading ideologue.

According to the doctrine of apartheid, each race and nation was to be kept apart so that each was to develop to the full along its own inherent lines. Each racial group was to have its own territorial area within which to develop its unique cultural personality. Of the areas envisaged for the African peoples, the overwhelming majority, however, were the poverty-stricken Native Reserves, comprising little more than 13% of the national territory. The period 1948–59 saw the introduction of a series of interrelated laws and measures aimed at restructuring South African society to conform to apartheid doctrine. The Population Registration Act provided for the classification of the entire population on the basis of race. Inter-racial marriages were forbidden and the Immorality Act, banning sexual relations between whites and blacks, was extended to include relations between whites and coloureds. Urban segregation was intensified by the Group Areas Act, which provided for the designation of particular residential areas for specific races. Existing provisions for the reservation of categories of employment for particular races were strengthened. Race segregation in public places, trains and buses, post-offices, hospitals and even ambulances was introduced wherever it had not been previously practised. The Separate Amenities Act gave legislative sanction for this and stated that the amenities provided for different races need not be of equal standard. The Bantu Education Act removed black education from the care of the ministry of education to that of native affairs. In 1959 the Extension of University Education Act removed the right of non-white students to attend the previously open universities of Cape Town and the Witwatersrand. To strengthen its hand against radical opposition the government introduced the Suppression of Communism Act, banned the South African Communist Party (SACP), and decreed that persons named as communists could be subjected to a wide range of restrictions.

The repressive policies of the NP compelled the ANC to employ the tactics of mass civil disobedience, for which its Youth Wing had been pressing. An alliance was formed between the ANC and the South African Indian Congress (SAIC). In 1959 members of the PAC, led by Robert Sobukwe, formed the exclusively black Pan-Africanist Congress (PAC).

The need to improve South Africa's international standing and defuse internal African opposition was made strikingly evident in March 1960, when police in Sharpeville opened fire on a crowd of unarmed blacks who were surrounding the police station in response to a PAC demonstration, leaving 67 dead and many more injured. The Sharpeville massacre aroused international indignation to an unprecedented degree, South Africa sustained a net outflow of foreign investment capital, and appeals for military, economic and sporting boycotts began to be given serious attention. In 1961, following a referendum among white voters in October 1960, South Africa became a republic, and was obliged to leave the Commonwealth.

In response to further demonstrations within South Africa in protest at the Sharpeville massacre, the government banned both the ANC and the PAC. In 1961 the ANC formed a military wing, Umkhonto we Sizwe (MK—'Spear of the Nation'). Under the leadership of Nelson Mandela, it aimed to force the government to negotiate by attacking white-owned property, while avoiding harm to people. Some leaders of both movements escaped abroad to organize an armed liberation struggle. Mandela was detained in 1962 and sentenced to life imprisonment on charges of sabotage in 1964, but remained a focus for opposition to apartheid.

The government, however, modified its formerly overtly racist doctrine. Territorial segregation was now to be rationalized on the grounds that the Native Reserves constituted the historic 'homelands' (Bantustans) of different African nations. The 'homelands' were to be led to self-government under constitutions giving scope to the elective principle but with the balance of power in the hands of government-appointed chiefs. Transkei was accorded 'self-government' under such a system in 1963. Ciskei, Bophuthatswana, Lebowa, Venda, Gazankulu, Qwaqwa and KwaZulu followed in the early 1970s. The first steps towards this new version of apartheid were taken under the leadership of Verwoerd, but in September 1966 he was assassinated in the house of assembly, and was succeeded by J. B. Vorster.

The replacement of explicit racism by separate nationality as a rationale for the denial of civil rights to blacks gave new urgency to reducing the settled African population in white areas. Stricter controls were imposed to prevent Africans acquiring permanent residence in urban areas. Wherever possible, jobs performed by settled blacks were transferred to migrant labour. A massive campaign was launched to rid the white areas of 'surplus Bantu' and force them into the overcrowded 'homelands'. During 1960–70 more than 1.5m. people were forcibly resettled.

These measures, more drastic than those of the first phase of apartheid, required more ruthless repression to enforce them. The powers of the security police were massively extended. In 1968 the state security services were centralized under the authority of the Bureau of State Security (BOSS). Reports of the widespread use of torture were given credence by the lengthening lists of those who died in police custody.

South Africa's control over South West Africa (Namibia) had been a subject of international criticism ever since the territory had been entrusted to South Africa as a League of Nations mandated territory. In 1964, despite the opposition of the UN which had assumed responsibility for the mandate, the South African government developed a scheme for the introduction of formal apartheid in the territory. In 1966 the UN General Assembly resolved to revoke South Africa's mandate and place the territory under direct UN administration. This was confirmed by the Security Council in 1968 and South Africa was ordered to withdraw its forces. South Africa refused to co-operate or to admit UN authorities to the country. The apartheid plan was embodied in the 1968 Development of Self-Government for Native Nations in South West Africa Act.

INTERNAL PRESSURES FOR CHANGE

In the 1970s the South African government endeavoured to confer formal independence on the 'Bantustans'. Transkei accepted this status in 1976, Bophuthatswana in 1977, Venda in 1979 and Ciskei in 1981. All remained dependent on South African financial support and their 'independence' was not internationally recognized. The imposition of 'independence' was resisted by KwaNdebele and, still more determinedly, by KwaZulu under the leadership of Chief Mangosuthu Buthelezi, who used the political immunity conferred by his position to attack the apartheid system. He attempted to transform Inkatha, the Zulu cultural movement that he had founded, into a national political force and to consolidate an alliance with Coloured and Indian political movements. His activities aroused suspicion among supporters of the ANC and other radical political groups, who felt that he had compromised his political integrity by participating in the 'homeland' system.

In June 1976 the agglomeration of segregated African townships to the south-west of Johannesburg known as Soweto (South-West Townships) erupted in the most serious racial violence in South Africa since the establishment of the Union. It began with a protest by school children at being forced to use Afrikaans as the medium of instruction for some of their school subjects. Police opened fire on the demonstrators, prompting rioting, which spread not only to other black townships around the Rand and Pretoria but to Natal and the Cape, where Coloured and Indian youths joined in. Repeatedly and violently repressed, the disturbances were not brought under control until the end of the year. Thousands of young people were arrested but many others escaped across the borders to join the liberation movements. The ANC proved far more successful than the PAC in attracting this cadre of prospective freedom fighters, thus consolidating its political hold over the loyalties of the majority. In October 1977 18 'black consciousness' organizations were suppressed and 50 of their leaders detained. International opinion was further incensed to learn that a prominent activist, Steve Biko, had been arrested and died from injuries suffered while in police custody.

The parliamentary majority of the NP was considerably strengthened at the November 1977 general election. Following the dissolution of the UP, the Progressive Party, which was reconstituted as the Progressive Federal Party (PFP), became the official parliamentary opposition. In 1978 Vorster

announced his intention to resign as prime minister and seek election to the mainly ceremonial post of state president. In September Vorster was succeeded as prime minister by P. W. Botha, hitherto the minister of defence. In November, however, Mulder resigned from the new government. He was also forced out of the NP, and formed the National Conservative Party (NCP). In June 1979 Vorster had to resign in disgrace from his new position as president.

Botha altered the balance of influence within the state security network in favour of the armed forces, as opposed to the police. The BOSS was abolished and replaced by a more modest organization. The state security council became the main decision-making organ, with the roles of the NP and parliament increasingly reduced. Racial job restrictions were abolished and trade union rights further extended. Africans with urban rights of residence could now move freely from one town to another. Restrictions on multiracial sports were reduced and the laws against interracial marriage and extra-marital sexual relations were repealed. The ineffective senate was abolished and replaced by a president's council made up of nominated Coloureds and Indians along with white nominees. It proposed the establishment of a tricameral parliament, comprising separate houses for whites, Coloureds and Indians. The need for some political representation for the black population resident in the towns was recognized, but the intention of including them in the central parliament denied. The reforms precipitated a conflict with hardliners in the NP. Treurnicht challenged the prime minister but was defeated. In March 1982 he founded the Conservative Party of South Africa (CPSA), which absorbed the NCP.

Following the departure of Treurnicht and his followers from the NP, Botha proceeded to implement his constitutional plan. In November 1983 the creation of a tricameral legislature was approved by a referendum restricted to white voters. Elections for the Coloured house of representatives and the Indian house of delegates followed in August 1984, and in September the electoral college chose P. W. Botha as the country's first executive president. Meanwhile, in August 1983, a number of groups opposed to apartheid, many with church affiliations and with multiracial memberships, formed the United Democratic Front (UDF) to promote the rejection of the constitutional plan, on the grounds of its failure to provide representation for the black majority. The UDF won strong support from Coloured voters, only 18% of whom participated in the election. Indian participation was even lower.

The introduction of the new constitution catalysed a rebellion in the black townships which exceeded the scale of the 1976 Soweto upheaval. It was supported by strikes, notably in the economically crucial mining industry. The Congress of South African Trade Unions (COSATU), a federation of black trade unions that were politically aligned with the ANC, was formed in December 1984, and demanded the abolition of pass restrictions, the withdrawal of foreign investment and the release of Nelson Mandela. The township rebellion escalated dramatically when, on 21 March 1985 (the 25th anniversary of the Sharpeville massacre), the police opened fire on an unarmed African procession in Uitenhage, killing 20 and wounding many more. In July the government declared a state of emergency in 36 magisterial districts, but the violence continued to increase. Black policemen, community councillors and suspected informers were killed in growing numbers. Continuing throughout 1985 and much of 1986, the disturbances encouraged conflicts between sections of the black communities. These divisions were especially acute in Natal where members of the mainly rural Zulu-supported Inkatha movement, led by Buthelezi (chief minister of the KwaZulu 'homeland' since 1976), became involved in escalating hostilities with ANC supporters, who were mainly urban-based Zulu and Xhosa speakers from southern Natal.

On 12 June 1986 the government extended the state of emergency to cover the whole country. As many as 24,000 people, many of them children, were detained without trial. Disturbances in the townships continued into 1987 but, with army units largely replacing the police and with massive injections of funds for house-building and improved services, they gradually subsided. The upheavals aroused international opinion against South Africa still further. European banks suspended new lending and the European Community (EC, now the European

Union—EU) and the USA introduced a number of economic sanctions.

Among Afrikaner intellectuals, professionals and businessmen and within the NP itself, opinion was already growing that apartheid would have to be abandoned and an accommodation reached with an effective African leadership. While liberal Afrikaner opinion was moving towards this view, a proliferation of movements on the extreme right expressed the growing desperation of the poorer sections of the white community at the erosion of their privileged position. A paramilitary organization, the Afrikaanse Weerstandsbeweging (AWB), founded in 1977 and led by Eugene Terre'Blanche, now attracted a mass following, and actively recruited among the police forces within whose ranks it had many sympathisers.

General elections for the white house of parliament in 1987 resulted in a partial realignment of forces. The NP emerged with a secure majority but a considerably reduced vote. The CPSA obtained more seats than the PFP and became the official opposition. In 1989 the PFP, augmented by two small splinter groups and a number of other individual members who broke away from the National Party, was reconstituted as the Democratic Party (DP).

During the 1980s South Africa's continued occupation of Namibia resulted in frequent clashes between guerrillas of the South West Africa People's Organisation of Namibia (SWAPO) and South African troops (see chapter on Namibia). In 1971 the International Court of Justice had declared South Africa's presence in Namibia to be illegal and the UN had, in 1973, recognized SWAPO as the 'authentic representative of the Namibian people'. Following the collapse of the semi-autonomous internal administration, South Africa resumed direct rule of Namibia in January 1983. In February 1984 South Africa and Angola agreed on a cease-fire along the Angola–Namibia border, and established a joint commission to monitor the withdrawal of South African troops from Angola. In May 1988 negotiations began between Angola, Cuba and South Africa, with the USA acting as mediator. On 22 December 1988 Angola, Cuba and South Africa signed a formal treaty designating 1 April 1989 as the commencement date for the process leading to Namibian independence, as well as a treaty requiring all 50,000 Cuban troops to be withdrawn from Angola by July 1991. Elections were held in Namibia in November 1989, and independence for the former South African territory was achieved on 21 March 1990, under a SWAPO-controlled government.

THE ABANDONMENT OF APARTHEID

The resolution of the Namibian issue re-focused attention on political conditions within South Africa. Liberal whites, including influential Afrikaners, initiated direct contact with the ANC, at a meeting held in Dakar, Senegal, in July 1987. In spite of Botha's disapproval, further contacts followed. In January 1989 Botha withdrew from official duties on the grounds of ill health and, in early February, he relinquished the NP leadership to F. W. de Klerk. Before finally retiring from office, Botha had a meeting with Nelson Mandela, thus effectively recognizing the ANC leader's position as the potential alternative head of government. Botha relinquished the presidency, with some unwillingness, in mid-August. Prior to the September parliamentary election, de Klerk, still the acting head of state, gave little indication of any radical intentions. At the election, the CPSA and the liberal DP both made considerable gains. The NP retained a clear majority, however, and de Klerk was confirmed as state president.

During 1989 international and internal pressures on the government increased. The greater part of the NP and the Afrikaner intellectual élite was already convinced that apartheid was unsustainable and that the ANC must be accepted as a negotiating partner. The ANC, after losing its facilities in Angola, had no military bases from which to operate. In the USA President Bush initiated a more active approach towards democratic change in South Africa. During 1989 informal meetings were held in the United Kingdom of representatives of the ANC, the NP, a number of African states and of the USA and USSR. In September US officials indicated that if no move to release Mandela had taken place within six months President Bush would assent to an extension of economic sanctions.

Addressing the three houses of parliament on 2 February 1990, President de Klerk made the dramatic announcement that Nelson Mandela would be released and that the ban had been lifted on the ANC, the PAC, the SACP and 33 other organizations, including the UDF. It was the government's intention to open negotiations with black leaders, with a view to devising a new constitution based on universal franchise. Equality of all citizens, regardless of race, was to be guaranteed by an independent judiciary, and protection for individual rights entrenched.

On 11 February 1990 Nelson Mandela was released after 27 years in prison. ANC refugees soon began to return from exile. However, the ANC faced major problems in bringing the spontaneous loyalties of the great majority of the black population within a disciplined organizational framework, and urged the continuation of sanctions until the abandonment of apartheid had become demonstrably irreversible.

By the end of 1990 the remnants of traditional social segregation had largely disappeared and people of all races were making common use of beaches, swimming baths, hospital wards, railway carriages, hotels and restaurants. In October the Separate Amenities Act was formally repealed. A beginning of school desegregation had also been made, as white schools could, with the consent of parents, admit a proportion of children of other races. The CPSA protested bitterly and the AWB held demonstrations threatening a violent struggle against black rule. It was unable, however, to attract crowds large enough to give it much political credibility.

ANC and government members met in May 1990 to discuss conditions for the opening of full constitutional negotiations, and again in August, when the ANC agreed to the formal suspension of its guerrilla activities. The ANC favoured the election by universal franchise of a constituent assembly to draw up the new constitutional order, while the government instead favoured a multi-party conference giving each party an equal voice. In January 1991 the government agreed to a proposal by the ANC that a multi-party conference should determine the procedures for drawing up a new constitution. Prospects of expeditious constitutional negotiations were threatened, however, by continuing and expanding violence between followers of Inkatha and those of the ANC.

On 1 February 1991 de Klerk again took the initiative in an address to parliament by announcing that all the remaining legislation enshrining apartheid, including the Group Areas Act and the Population Registration Act, was to be repealed. By the end of June this legal revolution was complete. The NP even changed its own constitution to open membership to all races, and began to attract significant numbers of Indian and Coloured, as well as smaller numbers of African members. The EC and the USA abandoned most economic sanctions, despite ANC appeals. Contacts between South Africa and black African states multiplied and trade was expanded, although Commonwealth countries voted to maintain sanctions for the present. The ANC supported the abandonment of international boycotts for those sports which accepted genuine non-racial management and participation. In July 1991 the International Olympic Committee agreed to South Africa's readmission.

In early July 1991, at its national congress, the ANC elected a new national executive, successfully fusing new elements with 'old guard' members. Mandela became president, with the hitherto leader of the national union of mineworkers, Cyril Ramaphosa, as secretary-general. The ANC published preliminary constitutional proposals, which included a bicameral legislature (with the lower house elected by proportional representation) and a bill of rights. The government's suggestions, issued in September, had much in common with these but included provisions for a collegial presidency and a constitutional role for the upper house which appeared to build in a white veto, and were rejected by the ANC. At a secret meeting held in February 1992 the government and ANC agreed on the release of political prisoners, the return of exiles and the formal abandonment by the ANC of armed struggle.

CONSTITUTIONAL NEGOTIATIONS

The main obstacle impeding constitutional negotiations, however, was the continuing violence between Inkatha and ANC supporters and the suspicion that elements of the state security forces were involved. In early April 1991 the ANC threatened to withdraw from negotiations if the government failed to take effective action to stop the violence, and demanded the dismissal of the minister of defence, Magnus Malan, and the minister of law and order, Adriaan Vlok. In July it was admitted that secret payments had been made from government funds to Inkatha during 1989–90, and Malan and Vlok were demoted to minor cabinet posts. Suspicions of official complicity in the violence were not fully dispelled, however, and the ANC insisted on the formation of an interim government in which it would be represented during the finalization of constitutional negotiations.

The multi-party conference on procedures for drafting the new constitution, the Convention for a Democratic South Africa (CODESA), met on 20 December 1991.The commencement of constitutional discussions intensified the hostility of the extreme right and, after losing a parliamentary by-election to the CPSA, de Klerk called a referendum of white voters for 17 March 1992. Despite demonstrations and campaigning by the far right the government achieved a more than two-thirds majority in support of continuing negotiations towards a democratic constitution. The CODESA talks were resumed, but the government insisted on provisions that appeared to give it a veto. The talks became deadlocked and the ANC called for a campaign of non-violent mass action by its supporters to put pressure on the government. Then, on 17 June, a number of residents of the settlement of Boipatong, including women and children, were massacred, apparently by Inkatha supporters who had allegedly been brought to the scene by police trucks. The ANC broke off negotiations with the government, and demanded effective action to stop the violence, including the disbandment of groups involved in covert operations. The ANC was invited to resume constitutional negotiations, but refused to do so unless the government modified its insistence on a veto in the constitution-making procedure. During July 1992 mounting criticism of the activities of the security forces and a public outcry at the rising number of deaths in police custody strengthened the ANC's resolve to continue its campaign of mass action. In mid-July President de Klerk announced the dissolution of a number of police and army units. In late July the UN Security Council, acting upon a request by Nelson Mandela, sent a UN special representative to South Africa on a fact-finding mission. As a result of the visit, the UN recommended the establishment of an independent investigation into the activities of the security forces and, in mid-August, the Security Council authorized the deployment of UN observers in South Africa to monitor political violence.

In early August 1992 the ANC, SACP and COSATU joined forces to organize an unprecedented level of mass action against the government, involving political rallies and a two-day general strike. Shortly afterwards the PAC met the government to discuss the possibility of introducing an alternative negotiating forum to the suspended CODESA. In mid-August talks between the ANC and the government on the resumption of constitutional negotiations failed, as the government refused to meet the demands articulated in June by the ANC. In late August the government announced a major restructuring of the police force and the authorization of an independent body, the Goldstone Commission (established in October 1991), to investigate alleged police complicity in serious crimes.

In early September 1992 the armed forces of the nominally independent 'homeland' of Ciskei fired on a procession of ANC supporters, killing 28 people and wounding about 200 others. The ANC blamed the South African government for complicity in the massacre, and demanded the removal of the Ciskei 'head of state'. President de Klerk agreed to conduct an enquiry into the incident, and in mid-September it was announced that legislation was to be introduced to reintegrate 'homeland' security forces and educational bodies into the South African system. Measures to reduce the 'independence' of the 'homelands' were also promised.

While formal talks between the ANC and the government were suspended, informal contacts continued, and in mid-September 1992 the ANC announced its agreement to a summit meeting between Mandela and de Klerk. This resulted in a 'record of understanding', which allowed for the resumption of full bilateral negotiations. In November the ANC announced

its acceptance of a proposal (originating from the SACP and sponsored by Chris Hani, a leading militant radical in the ANC and the general secretary of the SACP) that an interim government of national unity should be formed, which would include the major parties that had won seats in the constituent assembly. The interim government would hold office for a five-year period, during which the constituent assembly would act as the interim legislature, while also finalizing the new constitution. The government welcomed this idea and proposed a number of procedural steps, including the resumption of multi-party talks in order to discuss the formation of a transitional executive committee (which was to have control over key ministries), to set the date for the election of the constituent assembly and to draft an interim constitution under which the proposed interim government of national unity and the constituent assembly would function. The ANC accepted the procedural programme, but rejected the government's suggested timetable, pressing for elections for the constituent assembly to be held before the end of 1993. In response to initial reports of the Goldstone Commission, de Klerk took the strong measure of dismissing several high-ranking officers. Gen. Constand Viljoen, a former head of the army, and a committee of former generals subsequently began to take a major overt role in the leadership of the white extreme right.

With substantial agreement between the two main negotiating partners achieved, the multi-party negotiating forum was reconvened in April 1993. Buthelezi, who protested vigorously at the bilateral agreements between the government and the ANC, initiated meetings between representatives of Inkatha, a number of 'homeland'-based movements and the CPSA. This led to the formation of the Concerned South Africans Group (COSAG), including Inkatha, Bophuthatswana, Ciskei, KwaZulu and the CPSA, to act as a pressure group at the negotiating forum, in favour of extreme regional autonomy. In early April, however, on the eve of the talks, Hani was assassinated by a white right-wing extremist; several members of the CPSA were implicated in the affair, and three of them were subsequently charged in connection with the murder which was believed to be part of a right-wing plot to disrupt the constitutional negotiations. At this time a series of random terrorist attacks against whites began, which were alleged to be the work of the Azanian People's Liberation Army (APLA—the military wing of the PAC). In early May an alliance was established of right-wing organizations (which included the CPSA and the AWB), known as the Afrikaner Volksfront (AVF), to co-ordinate opposition to the negotiating process.

In June 1993, shortly before the date of the elections (provisionally scheduled for 27 April 1994) was due to be confirmed, armed right-wing extremists staged a violent protest, occupying the negotiating centre. The ANC criticized the failure of the security forces to prevent the attack; some 25 members of the AWB were later arrested. At the end of June the negotiating forum reached an agreement whereby the future constitution was to be drafted by a constituent assembly. In early July, despite continuing opposition from COSAG, the forum confirmed the election date. Inkatha and the CPSA subsequently withdrew from the negotiating forum in protest at the rejection of demands for full regional autonomy.

In late July the draft interim constitution was presented to the negotiating forum. This document embodied major compromises by both the main negotiating partners. Its regional proposals provided for some measure of federalism, but were insufficient to enable de Klerk to persuade Buthelezi to resume participation in the talks. The CPSA proclaimed the proposals had put an end to all possibility of further negotiations. At this time political violence between supporters of Inkatha and those of the ANC in the Rand and Natal escalated again. In August substantial army contingents moved into East Rand townships to restore control.

TOWARDS DEMOCRATIC ELECTIONS

In late September 1993 parliament approved legislation authorizing the formation, from late October, of a transitional executive council to oversee procedures. Immediately afterwards, in response to an appeal by Mandela to the UN, the USA and Commonwealth countries withdrew all economic sanctions against South Africa.

During November 1993 the forum completed details of an interim constitution, which was approved by the tricameral parliament in December. The national territory was re-divided into nine regions: Western Cape, Eastern Cape, Northern Cape, Orange Free State (renamed 'Free State' in June 1995), North-West, KwaZulu/Natal, Eastern Transvaal (subsequently renamed Mpumalanga), Northern Transvaal (renamed 'Northern Province' in June 1995) and PWV (Pretoria, Witwatersrand and Vereeniging—subsequently renamed 'Gauteng'). The former 'homelands', including those purported to be 'independent', disappeared as distinct entities and were absorbed into one or more of the new regions. Each of the new regions was provided with an elected assembly, to be chosen by proportional representation, and a regional government with extensive local authority and autonomy.

The central parliament was to comprise a house of assembly of 400 members, all elected by proportional representation but on a basis of one-half from national and one-half from regional lists. There was to be an upper house of 90 members chosen by the regional assemblies. The executive would be headed by an executive president, to be chosen by parliament, and at least two executive vice-presidents. Under the terms of the agreement on a government of national unity, any party obtaining 20% of the national vote would be entitled to one of the vice-presidential positions. In the event that only one party achieved this total, the second position would go to any grouping with the second largest support. Any party receiving 5% or more of the vote would be entitled to a position in the national cabinet. The national and regional assemblies and governments were to function within the limitations of a justiciable interim bill of rights. The interim parliament was to function as the national legislature for a maximum period of five years, and was also to act as a constituent assembly charged with the responsibility for drafting the definitive new constitution for the country within the first two years. The adoption of constitutional clauses by the constituent assembly was to require a two-thirds majority.

The forum did not succeed in winning the assent of Buthelezi, the AVF and the representatives of Bophuthatswana and the Ciskei. They now formed a new alliance—the Freedom Front (FF)—and threatened to boycott the April 1994 elections. The intensity of the violence between Inkatha and supporters of the ANC in Natal and the African townships on the Rand escalated further. After repeated attempts at negotiations, Buthelezi was persuaded to register the Inkatha Freedom Party (IFP) for the election before reverting to demanding postponement and threatening a boycott. Negotiations between Mandela, de Klerk and the AVF were somewhat more productive. The AVF was offered the possibility of the subsequent creation of an Afrikaner 'boerestaat', given sufficient support and provided that such a state would remain part of South Africa and subject to the provisions of the bill of rights. Viljoen agreed to register the movement for the elections. However, Terre'Blanche and the more militant of his AWB supporters rejected the offer and threatened civil war if the election proceeded.

During March 1994 the killings in Natal and KwaZulu continued; the declaration of a state of emergency in the area and the dispatch of troops failed to bring the violence to an end. Buthelezi's followers mounted repeated armed demonstrations; on 30 March this resulted in violent clashes at ANC headquarters in Johannesburg, in which about 53 people were killed.

In mid-March 1994, however, the militant section of the Afrikaner extreme right suffered a severe reverse. The Bophuthatswana army and police mutinied against the highly unpopular government of Chief Mangope, who was forced to flee from the 'homeland'. Over 2,000 Afrikaner extremists then invaded the Bophuthatswana capital, Mmabatho, with the intention of restoring Mangope and securing all or part of the area for the 'boerestaat'. Bophuthatswana armed forces attacked them, however, and de Klerk dispatched units of the South African army, who swiftly restored order, oversaw the departure of the remaining white militants, established an interim administration and effectively reintegrated the 'homeland' into South Africa. Later in March members of the armed forces were also deployed in Ciskei, following the resignation of the 'homeland's' military ruler in response to a strike by reformist members of the security forces. By early April Buthelezi's isolated situation

was becoming increasingly evident and he was under great pressure from many of his own supporters who wished to participate in the elections. He finally agreed that the IFP would contest the elections in return for the enhancement of the status of the Zulu monarchy by the transfer of extensive state lands to a trust in the name of the Zulu monarch, King Goodwill Zwelithini. These issues were only resolved, and the IFP's participation assured, on 21 April 1994. (In the mean time, the election timetable had been amended in the light of practical considerations to commence on 26 April.) Since the IFP had missed the deadline for the registration of candidates and Inkatha names were not on the ballot papers which had already been printed, additional strips were required to be attached to ballot papers during the voting procedure.

With the IFP's last-minute participation, the long-running bloody conflict in Natal and the Rand townships subsided. In a last desperate attempt to abort the election and prevent the transition to majority rule, members of the white extreme right conducted a bombing offensive, in which about 21 people were killed. The violence failed, however, in its purpose of disrupting the election, merely serving to illustrate the isolation and impotence to which the movement (30 of whose members were subsequently arrested) had been reduced. By this stage the security forces had decisively aligned themselves in support of constitutional order.

The election, involving 19 political parties, commenced on 26 April 1994, as scheduled, and continued for three days. The logistical difficulties of organizing an election on this scale for the first time, compounded by the complex procedures which were exacerbated by the need to affix the Inkatha strips to voting ballots during the actual proceedings, resulted in much frustration and long delays. (Organizational failures were especially severe in the KwaZulu area, resulting in the extension of the voting period there for an extra day.) Despite this, blacks and whites voted together without conflict.

The various electoral problems resulted in abundant opportunities for errors as well as election fraud and in spite of the presence of UN and Commonwealth observers, the precise results in many areas remain distinctly dubious. The overall outcome of the election was, however, clear beyond doubt. The ANC gained an overwhelming majority at national level, although just short of the two-thirds majority which would have enabled it to rewrite the constitution unilaterally. It also gained control of all but two of the nine regional assemblies. The NP was the only other grouping to top 20% of the poll. It also gained control of the Western Cape regional assembly. Inkatha trailed well behind the leaders with just over 10% of votes, but was credited with a 51% victory in KwaZulu/Natal. The constitutional wing of the AVF achieved significant support, but less than the 5% needed for a place in the cabinet. The PAC, with its radical africanist approach, received less than 2% of the vote.

THE NEW GOVERNMENT

On 9 May 1994 the national assembly elected Mandela as president, and on the following day he was inaugurated as head of state at a ceremony which was attended by a large number of international dignitaries. In accordance with the interim constitution (which had taken effect on 27 April), an interim government of national unity was formed, in which the ANC, the NP and the IFP were represented in proportion to the number of seats that they had won in the election. Mbeki and de Klerk both became deputy presidents, while the former minister of finance, Derek Keys, was re-appointed to that position, and Buthelezi was allocated the portfolio of home affairs. Cyril Ramaphosa, the secretary-general of the ANC, remained outside the cabinet, but was selected to preside over the constitutional assembly, which comprised the national assembly and the senate. In accordance with the interim constitution, all the former 'homelands' were reincorporated into South Africa, which was henceforth divided into nine (replacing the previous four) provinces, each with its own legislature and executive. The interim government of national unity focused on the maintenance of stability and the promotion of economic growth, with initial emphasis laid on a reconstruction and development programme (RDP), which included an undertaking to construct 1m. homes in a period of five years, and to extend basic educational and health facilities to all. In June 1994 Keys announced he was to resign the finance portfolio for personal reasons, prompting a loss in international business confidence. Mandela acted swiftly to reassure the business community by appointing an Afrikaner banker, Christo Liebenberg, in his place.

Following the installation of a democratic government, South Africa was admitted into the OAU, the Commonwealth and the SADC, and resumed its seat in the general assembly of the UN. The arms embargo that the UN had imposed in 1977 was finally removed. South Africa's standing in the Commonwealth was acknowledged by a visit by the British prime minister, John Major, in September 1994, and subsequently by a royal visit from Queen Elizabeth II in March 1995. In return, Mandela made a state visit to the United Kingdom in July 1996.

The government planned to finance the RDP through savings on security-related expenses and increased revenue resulting from economic growth, while Japan and other countries provided sizeable contributions to the programme. Implementation of the RDP proved much more difficult than the government had anticipated, however. In early 1996 it was announced that the separate ministry for the RDP was to be abolished, and the programme was transferred to the office of Mbeki. By then, fewer homes had been constructed than in the last decade of the apartheid government, largely owing to bureaucratic difficulties. Joe Slovo, the first minister of housing in the interim government of national unity, died in January 1995. The government's schemes to provide electricity and clean water to those without these services were initially among its most successful, but unemployment remained very high in the townships, and many communities continued to refuse to pay for services and rents, despite the efforts of the government's campaign to persuade them to do so. It was evident that the alleviation of poverty was dependent on economic growth, while economic growth required substantial foreign investment, which was not forthcoming.

Following Liebenberg's resignation from the post of minister of finance in March 1996 and his replacement by Trevor Manuel, who had been an activist politician in the 1980s, there was a further loss in international business confidence, exacerbated by rumours that Dr Christian Stals, the governor of the South African Reserve Bank, was to resign (which in the event proved unfounded). In June 1996 Manuel announced that the government had approved a new macro-economic plan for growth, employment and redistribution (GEAR), which laid particular emphasis on the privatization of state assets and the gradual removal of exchange controls.

The principal critics of GEAR were the ANC's two alliance partners, COSATU and the SACP, which objected to the way it had been adopted without consultation and debate, and predicted that it would mean fewer rather than more jobs, at least in the short term. This criticism, together with COSATU's support for industrial action to demand improved working conditions, increased the concern of foreign investors regarding the influence which the alliance partners had on the ANC. Although the GEAR strategy was intended to stimulate the labour market, Tito Mboweni, the minister of labour, promoted a number of measures supported by COSATU, which appeared unlikely to help to create new jobs. Exchange controls were partially removed in June 1997, but there was little progress in privatization, owing, in part, to COSATU's opposition. GEAR was intended to generate 400,000 new jobs annually by the year 2000; however, more than 100,000 jobs in the formal economy were lost in both 1996 and 1997, and few new ones were created.

Mandela remained aware of a possible threat from right-wing extremists and continued efforts to appear reconciliatory towards this element. The FF, which had participated in the election, was allowed to establish a 'volkstaat council', which was to debate the issue of self-determination for right-wing Afrikaners. Various plans were proposed (one concerning Pretoria, another a region principally located in the Northern Cape), but none of these was practicable, and Mandela insisted that he would not consider a new structure based on racial criteria. Many Afrikaners opposed the downgrading of Afrikaans from one of two official languages to one of 11, which was reflected, for example, in the great reduction in the use of Afrikaans in television broadcasting. Both Afrikaners and English-speaking whites resented 'affirmative action' (discrimination in favour of Africans) in job appointments. However, there was no significant protest by whites against the new system, and the extreme right-wing threats of armed resistance receded after the election in April 1994.

The integration of the various armed forces into the new South African National Defence Force (SANDF) proceeded without difficulty, after an incident in late 1994 in which some 3,000 former members of the MK protested at what they claimed to be discriminatory treatment. Mandela ordered them to return to barracks, or be dismissed, and some 2,000 were subsequently discharged. (The commander of the former defence forces, Gen. George Meiring, had been reappointed head of the SANDF.) In March 1998, however, he was obliged to resign, following the release of a military report regarding a conspiracy to overthrow the government, which was subsequently proved to be a fabrication. He was succeeded by Siphiwe Nyanda, a former MK guerilla commander. Thus, a process of transformation emerged, with power beginning to shift from whites to blacks.

KwaZulu/Natal (where the IFP commanded a majority) was the first province to draft its own constitution, which was accepted unanimously by the local legislature in March 1996. The Western Cape, which was dominated by the NP, also decided to draft its own constitution. However, the provinces had been granted limited powers under the new system of government, and the constitutional court eventually rejected the KwaZulu/Natal constitution, which provided for a devolution of powers from central to provincial government. In KwaZulu/Natal the conflict between supporters of the IFP and the ANC (in which an estimated 20,000 people had been killed since the mid-1980s) continued sporadically, increasing prior to the adoption of the provincial constitution, and to local elections, but declining again in mid-1996, owing, in part, to mediation by Mbeki. However, relations between the ANC and the IFP subsequently improved. Buthelezi, who was minister of home affairs, abandoned his demands for devolution for KwaZulu/Natal and no longer insisted that the matter of provincial powers be referred to international mediation. Mandela responded by inviting him to be acting president on a number of occasions.

Local elections were held successfully in November 1995, except in Western Cape (as a result of boundary disputes) and in KwaZulu/Natal (owing to the persistent violence). The postponed elections in Western Cape took place in May 1996, with the NP increasing its share of votes cast, compared with the election in April 1994. The election in KwaZulu/Natal took place relatively peacefully in June; the IFP secured 44.5% of votes cast, although support for the ANC increased, especially in the urban areas, compared with the general election.

A number of communities began increasingly to use vigilante methods in response to the police force's apparent inability to combat an increase in violent crime. In Western Cape an Islamist vigilante group, known as People Against Gangsterism and Drugs (PAGAD), patrolled the streets and openly carried weapons. The increase in crime prompted demands for the restoration of the death penalty, which the constitutional court had, in June 1995, ruled to be unconstitutional. Mandela maintained, however, that the death penalty would not be reintroduced. Continued corruption within the police force and the use of old methods of policing were among the reasons for the government's inability to combat successfully the increase in crime. The process of transforming the police into a force that was regarded by the public as legitimate and credible was hindered by evidence which emerged about the measures that had, during the period of apartheid, been used against opponents of that system. A number of members of the former police force were placed on trial, notably, Col Eugene de Kock, the former head of a clandestine police base near Pretoria. After proceedings lasting 18 months, de Kock was convicted in 1996 on 89 charges of murder and other crimes. In another trial, which came to an end in that year, Gen. Magnus Malan, the former minister of defence, and prominent officials in the former armed forces were acquitted of complicity in a massacre, perpetrated in KwaZulu in 1987 by commandos who had been trained in Namibia. As a result of such trials, and the proceedings of the truth and reconciliation commission, much was revealed of the illicit activities which had been employed during apartheid and the transitional period.

CONSTITUTIONAL AND POLITICAL DEVELOPMENTS

Following intense negotiations within the constitutional assembly, a final draft of the new constitution was submitted shortly before the expiry of the deadline stipulated in the interim constitution. Since none of the parties favoured a constitutional referendum, a number of concessions were made on significant outstanding issues. On 8 May 1996 parliament approved the final version of the constitution, with the NP voting in favour; only the representatives of the small African Christian Democratic Party voted against the draft, while, despite its recognition of the right of communities to self-determination, the FF abstained. (The IFP had withdrawn from the constitutional assembly, owing to the government's failure to fulfil its pre-election pledge of international mediation.) The new constitution was subsequently referred to the constitutional court for confirmation that it accorded with the constitutional principles that had been established in negotiations prior to the 1994 election. In September the court returned sections of the constitution to the constitutional assembly, which was to reconvene to consider the court's objections. The court subsequently ratified the constitution, which was signed by Mandela at Sharpeville on 10 December 1996, and entered into force on 4 February 1997. The new constitution provided for the establishment of a 'commission for the promotion and protection of the rights of cultural, religious and linguistic communities', while a national council of provinces replaced the existing senate, increasing the influence of the provinces on central government policy.

Although members of parliament agreed in 1996 to a code of conduct requiring disclosure of their financial assets, widespread evidence of corruption, particularly within the government, continued to prompt criticism, and concern for future stability. In August Bantu Holomisa, the former ruler of Traskei and a deputy minister, claimed, at a hearing of the truth and reconciliation commission that part of a donation, which a hotel owner, Sol Kerzner, had made in 1989 to the government of Transkei, in order to secure casino rights, had been used by Stella Sigcau, also an ANC minister. Holomisa further alleged that Mbeki had also received funds from Kerzner for personal use. Holomisa was removed from his post and was subsequently expelled from the ANC for indiscipline.

Following the approval of the draft constitution, the NP announced that it was to leave the government of national unity from the end of June 1996, to form a parliamentary opposition. Although Buthelezi continued to assert his differences with the ANC, the IFP remained in the government of national unity. Efforts by Mandela to persuade the PAC to join the government were unsuccessful. After the NP ministers left the cabinet, their portfolios were allocated to ANC members and de Klerk became the official leader of the opposition. The NP had been restyled as a non-racial party, but continued to receive almost all its support from the white and Coloured communities. Roelf Meyer, who had played a significant role in the negotiations of 1992–93 and (as secretary-general of the party) was the designated successor to de Klerk, became increasingly concerned with the NP's inability to attract black voters. Following his suggestion that the NP disband and re-form as part of a realigned opposition, he was obliged to resign from the party. He subsequently formed the New Movement Process, and developed close links with Holomisa (after the latter's expulsion from the ANC). Meyer and Holomisa together established a new political party, the United Democratic Movement (UDM), in September 1997. By mid-1998 Holomisa had become leader of the party, with Meyer his deputy and a former ANC activist from Natal, Sifiso Nkabinde, as secretary-general. The UDM began to attract significant support, most notably in the former 'independent homeland' of Transkei. Meanwhile, de Klerk had been the subject of increasing criticism from Western Cape members of his party, who accused him of having betrayed the Afrikaner community in the constitutional negotiations. In August 1997 he unexpectedly resigned as leader of the NP, on the grounds that this was in the interests of the party. A number of senior members of the IFP also resigned at this time, including its most prominent white member, Walter Felgate, who accused Buthelezi of administering the party undemocratically. In September the leadership of the NP passed to its secretary-general, Marthinus van Schalkwyk.

Mandela's announcement that he would resign as ANC leader at the end of 1997, and would not serve a second term as president, was received with concern. At the ANC congress in December 1997 Mandela resigned from the presidency of the party, and was succeeded by Mbeki, who was elected unopposed. Jacob Zuma (hitherto the party chairman) was elected deputy president at the congress. Although Mandela remained active as head of state, Mbeki was already effectively in control of government administration. In July 1998, on his 80th birthday, Mandela married Graça Machel (the former wife of the president of Mozambique, Samora Machel).

THE TRUTH AND RECONCILIATION COMMISSION

In 1995, following protracted disputes regarding its method of operating, parliament approved the establishment of a truth and reconciliation commission (TRC), and in December of that year 17 members were appointed to the commission by Mandela. Desmond Tutu (whose term of office as Anglican archbishop of Cape Town ended in 1996) became chairman of the TRC. The commission began by conducting public hearings throughout the country, at which former victims of human rights' violations gave evidence. The TRC's amnesty committee considered applications by perpetrators of such abuses, and from August 1996 began to grant amnesty to those who had appeared before it and given a full account of their actions. Considerable interest was aroused when Janusz Walus and Clive Derby-Lewis, who had been convicted of the murder of Chris Hani, testified before the TRC. After the mandate of the commission had been extended from December 1993 to 10 May 1994 (as requested both by the FF and the PAC), large numbers of applications for amnesty were received. Following some 8,000 applications by the stipulated date in May, it was decided that the amnesty committee would continue to function after the TRC itself had completed its reports. The commission's reparations committee was to recommend how surviving victims could, within the means of the government, be compensated for their suffering.

From August 1996 the TRC heard representations from political parties. Although de Klerk formally apologized for the policy of apartheid, he denied that he or other members of the previous government had ordered or condoned illegal activities. The ANC admitted responsibility for some violations of human rights, committed by its members in the 1980s, asserting that these were justified in the context of the struggle against apartheid. However, Buthelezi refused to co-operate with the TRC, claiming that he had already apologized for acts of violence perpetrated by IFP supporters. In May 1997 the NP suspended participation in the commission and threatened legal action against Tutu, after he accused de Klerk of responsibility for human rights' violations. Although the legal action was abandoned, and relations improved when van Schalkwyk replaced de Klerk as the leader of the NP, many in the NP remained deeply suspicious of the TRC, which they regarded as biased towards the ANC. The decision by the TRC's amnesty committee to grant amnesty to 37 leading ANC politicians, including Mbeki, prompted strong criticism; the TRC later announced that it was to review its decision. The only former cabinet minister to apply for amnesty, Adriaan Vlok, claimed that de Klerk had known of human rights' violations. P. W. Botha, having refused to testify, was brought before a court, which in August 1998, following considerable delays, sentenced him to a fine of R10,000, with the alternative of 12 months' imprisonment, for being in contempt of the TRC. However, Botha subsequently won an appeal against the conviction, on the technical grounds that the TRC's subpoena was invalid since the commission's mandate had temporarily expired. In 1998 some of the most horrifying revelations before the TRC concerned the apartheid regime's clandestine project to produce a chemical and biological weapons capability; it was claimed that pharmaceutical substances had been developed with specific properties to incapacitate blacks.

In late October 1998 Tutu submitted the extensive TRC report to Mandela. De Klerk had won a legal challenge preventing the release of a section in the report concerning his role in human rights violations, but the ANC failed in an attempt to delay the publication of the report, on the grounds that it 'criminalized' its role in the struggle against apartheid. Although the main work of the TRC had ended, some 2,000 amnesty applications remained to be considered, and the deliberations of the amnesty committee continued throughout 1999. A number of members of APLA were granted amnesty for random killings of whites, but the members of the security forces who murdered Steve Biko in 1977 were refused amnesty, on the grounds that the killing was not politically motivated. The amnesty applications of the two right-wing extremists who killed Chris Hani in 1993 were also rejected, as they were judged not to have made full disclosure. In early August Vlok, Eugene de Kock and other members of the former security forces were granted amnesty for bombing the offices of the South African Council of Churches in 1988. As the amnesty hearings continued, there were demands for the proceedings to be suspended, on the grounds that they were costing too much, and not helping to achieve reconciliation, but Tutu, Mandela and others rejected any suggestion that a general amnesty might be granted to perpetrators of abuses. One of the most serious failings of the TRC was its inability to investigate thoroughly the numerous human rights' violations which South Africans had committed in neighbouring countries (being unable to demand testimony relating to such acts because it could not guarantee indemnity from prosecution in those countries).

FOREIGN POLICY UNDER MANDELA

Following Mandela's assumption of office, it became evident that the new government intended to maintain cordial relations with regimes which were regarded with disapproval by the USA and other Western countries, but which had provided substantial support to the ANC during the apartheid era, most notably those of Iran, Cuba and Libya. Nevertheless, South Africa's links with the USA strengthened following the transition to democratic rule. The two nations established a joint commission, chaired by Mbeki and the US vice-president, Albert Gore. South Africa was the location for a number of important international meetings, and Mandela's personal stature, in addition to the success of the country's transition to democracy, enhanced South Africa's prestige internationally. These meetings included the Non-Aligned Movement summit, which South Africa hosted in Durban in August 1998, and the Commonwealth heads of government meeting, also held in Durban, in October 1999.

Following a prolonged debate, the EU in March 1996 agreed on a framework for negotiations with South Africa on the proposed establishment of a joint 'free-trade area'. It was another three years before the EU and South Africa reached agreement on a comprehensive free-trade agreement in the final months of the Mandela administration, although details of the accord were not finalized until well into the Mbeki presidency, delaying its implementation. In November 1996 Mandela announced that South Africa would transfer diplomatic recognition from Taiwan to the People's Republic of China, with effect from the end of 1997. Taiwan immediately severed diplomatic relations, announced the suspension of most of its aid projects in South Africa, and banned South African Airways from flying to the Taiwanese capital, Taipeh. The South African decision was influenced by the return of Hong Kong to Chinese rule in 1997, and by its aim to secure a permanent seat on an enlarged UN Security Council.

In November 1995 Mandela attracted international criticism for failing to intervene effectively to prevent the execution in Nigeria of the Ogoni activist, Ken Saro-Wiwa, and eight others. He had rejected the proposed imposition of sanctions, in favour of a more conciliatory approach, as a means of exerting pressure on the Nigerian military regime. Following the executions, Mandela denounced the Nigerian government and supported Nigeria's suspension from the Commonwealth. After becoming chairman of the SADC in September 1996, he pursued a more active foreign policy, frequently intervening personally in an effort to resolve regional problems. In early 1997 Mandela was involved in intensive diplomatic activity which was aimed at ending the civil war in Zaire (now the Democratic Republic of the Congo, DRC), meeting both the then Zairean rebel leader, Laurent Kabila, and the Zairean president, Mobutu Seso Seko. Mandela also sought to mediate in the dispute over Indonesia's annexation of East Timor in 1976, and in the continuing civil war in Southern Sudan. However, South Africa was subject to criticism for continuing to supply armaments to governments accused of human rights' violations, such as those of Rwanda and Indonesia; negotiations on a proposed sale of arms to Syria were suspended in response to protests by the US government in early 1997.

In February 1998 it was announced that South Africa and the USA were to normalize their defence trade agreement (thereby allowing South African armaments companies to trade with their US counterparts for the first time). In March the US president, Bill Clinton, made an official visit to South Africa. In August two people were killed and about 27 injured in a bomb attack on a US restaurant in Cape Town. A supporter of an organization styled Muslims Against Global Oppression (MAGO) claimed to have carried out the bombing, apparently in retaliation for US air attacks on Sudan and Afghanistan (although MAGO officially denied responsibility for the incident). Several members of PAGAD were subsequently arrested in connection with the bombing. In January 1999 supporters of MAGO demonstrated in protest at British and US air attacks on Iraq during the visit to South Africa of the British prime minister, Tony Blair; protesters were violently dispersed by the security forces.

THE 1999 GENERAL ELECTION

In the later years of the Mandela presidency Mbeki increasingly assumed responsibility for government administration, and accumulated power in the office of deputy president. One of his major achievements was to contribute to the restoration of relative peace in KwaZulu/Natal, and to improve relations between the ANC and Inkatha. Although he lacked Mandela's personal charisma, he proved himself to be a competent campaigner for the ANC in the 1999 election.

Much concern was expressed as to whether the independent electoral commission would be able to conduct a well-organized and 'free and fair' election, especially when it insisted that only voters with coded identity documents would be permitted to register. That decision was upheld by the constitutional court and, in the event, the first voter registration to take place in democratic South Africa proceeded relatively smoothly. Nor was the election campaign in the first half of 1999 marred by any significant new violence, even in regions, such as Richmond in KwaZulu/Natal, where incidents of violence had taken place in the preceding year. With considerable support from Mandela, the ANC conducted a skilful campaign, urging voters to award it a decisive mandate to continue with the process of change and transformation. The various opposition parties failed either to unite or to capitalize on the failure of the government to fulfil its pledges during its five-year tenure in office. The NP, which had been reconstituted as the New National Party (NNP), under van Schalkwyk, lost Coloured support to the ANC and white support to the DP, which under the leadership of Tony Leon maintained the importance of denying the ANC a two-thirds majority, to prevent it from being able to change the constitution without support from other political parties. For his part, Mbeki pledged that he had no plans for constitutional changes, even if the ANC obtained the requisite parliamentary majority.

On 2 June 1999 almost 17m. voters participated in the elections, which, contested on the same proportional representation system as in 1994, were judged to be substantially 'free and fair' by domestic and international observers. The ANC obtained 266 seats, narrowly failing to secure a two-thirds' majority in the national assembly. Support for the opposition fragmented, with the NNP winning only 28 seats. The DP was the main beneficiary of this, increasing representation in the national assembly from seven to 38 seats (thus becoming the official opposition). In the Western Cape province no party won a majority of the seats and, after much negotiating, the NP and DP formed a coalition, to prevent the ANC, which had obtained the largest number of votes, from gaining power. The IFP reached an agreement with the ANC which allowed it continued control of the province of KwaZulu/Natal, where Lionel Mtshali remained premier. At national level the IFP, which won 34 seats in the national assembly, entered into a coalition with the ANC, and Buthelezi (who was rumoured to have aimed to secure the office of deputy president until it was rendered largely ceremonial by the creation of a new ministerial post at the presidency) remained minister of home affairs. Jacob Zuma, a close associate of Mbeki, became deputy president. As a result of the coalition, the ANC achieved much more than a two-thirds' majority in the legislature. The UDM, led by Holomisa, did not gain as much support as expected in the election, winning only 14 seats in the national assembly, but it became the main opposition to the ANC in the province of Eastern Cape.

THE MBEKI PRESIDENCY

On 16 June 1999 Mbeki was formally inaugurated as president; he announced a new cabinet, which was larger than Mandela's, despite a prior commitment to a more rationalized government structure. There were a number of unexpected appointments, but the two principal economic ministers, Trevor Manual with the finance portfolio and Alec Erwin as minister of trade and industry, were retained in their posts (a clear indication that Mbeki had no wish to alter the macroeconomic strategies on which the Mandela government had embarked). The GEAR policy, in which he had taken a leading role, had proved successful in restraining government expenditure, and lowering the country's budgetary deficit. Mbeki was able to announce, soon after taking office, that 20% of South African Airways had been sold to Swissair, and he pledged that the privatization of other parastatal companies would proceed with more urgency than hitherto. The first major challenge to Mbeki's government was economic, however. When the Bank of England announced in May that it was to sell part of its gold holdings on the open market, the international price of gold declined dramatically and fell further when the first sale took place in June. If the price of gold were to remain at such a low level, a number of South Africa's 16 major gold mines would have to close, jeopardizing a further 80,000 jobs, in addition to the 100,000 jobs that had been lost in the industry in the preceding few years. In July public sector workers took strike action in large numbers in support of a demand of a 10% increase in wages. The government offered them a rise of 6%, which was just less than the rate of inflation. COSATU, which supported the strike, had helped the ANC to reach its large majority in the election the previous month, but there was now much speculation that a dissolution of the alliance between the ANC government and its allies, COSATU and the SACP, was inevitable, especially if Mbeki attempted to renege on the government's concessions to the trade unions, to provide for greater flexibility in the labour market. In mid-2000 the minister of labour proposed amendments aimed at rendering the government's labour regime more attractive to foreign investors; COSATU subsequently opposed such changes vehemently.

One of Mbeki's main aims in foreign policy was to secure a peaceful settlement in the DRC. He assisted in the arrangement of a cease-fire there in June 1999, and subsequently endeavoured to persuade the rebels to observe it. In August 2000 South Africa was preparing to contribute troops to a future peace-keeping force in the DRC. In the Angolan conflict, the South African government had for some time made efforts to prevent any supplies reaching UNITA from its territory, but found this difficult to enforce. Under Mbeki, South Africa appeared to be aiming to continue, and further links with states such as Libya and Iraq. Nevertheless, Mbeki had developed close associations with the US vice-president, Al Gore (with whom he had co-chaired the meetings of the South Africa–US bi-national commission). With Mandela out of office, Mbeki had to demonstrate that South Africa would continue to take a significant role in international affairs. Mandela remained active, and took a leading role in trying to bring about peace in Burundi.

As chairman of the Non-Aligned Movement and leader of an important developing country, President Thabo Mbeki endeavoured to promote the case for economic justice on behalf of poorer countries to the developed world, and at many international fora emphasized the importance of debt relief and the elimination of global poverty. However, his international stature was severely tarnished in early 2000 owing to his handling of two major issues: Zimbabwe and AIDS. When land invasions began in neighbouring Zimbabwe, and were supported by President Mugabe, Mbeki was urged to condemn what was happening there. Not only did he fail to criticize Mugabe, but it took a long time for him to state that land occupations would not be allowed to take place in South Africa. Identifying land inequalities as a major issue to be addressed, he said he preferred to use 'quiet diplomacy' with Mugabe, to influence him to hold a free and fair election and to deal with the land issue peacefully. In May 2000 Mbeki attempted to raise funds internationally to pay for land transfers in Zimbabwe. Many foreign investors understood from this that the situation in Zimbabwe might occur in South Africa in the future, and that Mbeki might not stand firm on the rule of law. The programme for the restitution and reform of land in South Africa was indeed proceeding exceedingly slowly, mainly as a result of an extremely cumbersome bureaucratic process. Of the more than 60,000 claims for restitution lodged, only a few hundred had been decided by 2000. An estimated 86% of all rural land remained in the hands of approximately 60,000 white commercial farmers, while some 14m. Africans struggled to survive on the remaining 14%. Some critics urged Mbeki to abandon talk of South Africa playing a role in the rebirth of Africa, and instead to distance himself from the tragedies unfolding elsewhere on the continent and assert the claim that South Africa was a different case.

It was on AIDS that Mbeki was most severely criticized by the media because of statements he made in support of dissident scientists who questioned whether HIV was linked to AIDS, and promoting the idea that an indigenous cure might be found for the disease. Substantial amounts of money were spent on a conference to discuss the scientific evidence of the link between HIV and AIDS, and the president refused to back down when he addressed the international conference on AIDS which met in Durban in July 2000. There was widespread support for his view that AIDS must be considered in the context of poverty in Africa, but his statements served to divert attention from the problem of AIDS in South Africa, where an estimated 4.2m. people were infected with HIV. The Mbeki government refused to provide anti-retroviral drugs, even for pregnant women, arguing that a system of monitoring would be required which South Africa could not afford and that the drugs themselves were too expensive. The ministry of health campaigned for multi-national pharmaceutical companies to lower the prices of anti-AIDS drugs, or to allow generic alternatives to be used. But by mid-2000 the government had yet to present a coherent and co-ordinated plan to combat AIDS, and did not appear to take the crisis seriously enough.

The AIDS pandemic was expected to lead to an increase in crime, which was already at very high levels. While some categories of crime had declined, the underfunded police seemed incapable of detaining many offenders, including those responsible for a series of bomb blasts in the Western Cape, widely thought to be the work of radical elements within PAGAD. The bombs, planted at Cape Town's waterfront, one of its main beaches, its airport (in July 2000) and outside a shopping centre (in August) adversely affected foreign tourism. Cape Town's economy was also damaged by a continuing territorial dispute between the two main minibus taxi companies and a bus company, which had resulted in a number of deaths. An elite anti-crime unit, known as the Scorpions, had been formed in September 1999, but by mid-2000 it was still too early to measure its effectiveness. Meanwhile, in May 2000, Allan Boesak, a prominent former anti-apartheid activist, began a three-year prison sentence after being convicted in March 1999 of using donor funds fraudulently for personal gain.

Crime and the impact of events in Zimbabwe contributed to an increase in white emigration in 1999–2000. Another main factor was legislation that required all companies and organizations to set targets for making their work-force more representative of the demographics of the country. Many young white males had no prospect of employment. Mbeki and some members of his government seemed to view the situation in racial terms, despite the ANC's commitment to non-racialism. The Human Rights Commission, which held controversial hearings on racism in the media in April 2000, claimed that it was trying to confront racism, but white liberals criticized the commission and the government for heightening racial tensions by the emphasis they placed on race. In the SANDF, where integration of the various armies had proceeded relatively smoothly, there were high profile cases of blacks killing white officers. In the universities there was much debate about the need for transformation, and in mid-2000 a task team presented a major report to the government, which proposed a differentiated system of higher education. A more serious crisis was in the secondary schools, many of which provided an extremely poor level of education; the minister of education, Kader Asmal, was widely praised when he abandoned some of the outcomes-based curriculum announced by his predecessor.

The amnesty committee of the TRC continued to arouse controversy, especially with its decision, in June 2000, to grant amnesty to Craig Williamson and other former members of the security forces for the murders of Ruth First, Jeanette Schoon and other political activists in the 1980s. Details of some of the most extreme crimes of the apartheid era emerged in the trial of Wouter Basson, head of the secret chemical and biological warfare programme in 1982–92, which commenced in October 1999 in Pretoria (and was expected to last up to three years). Hundreds of captured SWAPO guerrillas, it emerged, had been thrown from planes, some of them still alive, into the sea off the Namibian coast. Despite evidence of such atrocities, the government refused to publish the TRC's recommendations regarding compensation for victims, and reparations remained an unresolved issue.

The alliance formed by the DP and the NNP in the Western Cape in June 1999, to keep the ANC out of power there, helped lead in mid-2000 to the establishment of a wider Democratic Alliance (DA), which linked the two parties nationally, under the vigorous leadership of Tony Leon, with Marthinus van Schalkwyk as his deputy. The DP claimed that it had not weakened its liberal principles, but there were few Africans in the new alliance, and the ANC was able to present the DA as an anti-African front. The more multi-racial UDM seemed to fall apart, ahead of the municipal elections, which were scheduled to take place in November 2000. The elections were to replace the more than 800 existing local government structures with 284 new municipalities; and the main urban centres were to become uni-cities, each under one authority. The ANC, meanwhile, remained in a loose alliance with the IFP. As there were no longer any significant ideological divisions between them, a merger seemed possible in the future. In KwaZulu Natal this alliance brought relative stablity, although the chiefs (*inkosi*), who were now paid by the government, feared that the new local government system would reduce their powers, and sought unsuccessfully to challenge the demarcation of the new structures.

The government had, meanwhile, allocated some R30,000m. to purchase arms, primarily from the United Kingdom and Sweden, despite criticism that the weapons were not necessary. The armaments were justified in part by the promised 'offsets', which were supposed to bring foreign capital into the country and create jobs; whether or not these would materialize remained to be seen. Controversy over the arms-procurement programme persisted throughout the first half of 2000; by June four official investigations into the purchases had been initiated.

The record of the Mbeki presidency by mid-2000 was mixed. Mbeki had established a specialist unit to deal with violent offences, and some success had been achieved in combating crime, but many attributed the scale of crime to the apartheid-era culture of non-compliance with the law, which would take a long time to dispel. The government realized that it had to accelerate the provision of jobs, housing, education and health care, while maintaining fiscal discipline. Electricity and clean water were provided for large sectors of the population which had not had them before, and many new health clinics were opened in the rural areas. Not all of the new schemes proved sustainable, however, and some of the money spent was dissipated in various kinds of corruption. A special investigative unit, established by the Mandela administration, uncovered much corruption, but was threatened with disbandment by the government, which disliked its public image. The Mbeki government failed to set a strong example, and resources continued to be wasted through a mixture of inexperience, lack of expertise, mismanagement and corrupt practices. As a result of a lack of capacity in many ministries, budgets were often not spent, even on poverty relief.

In the 1990s South Africa moved from conflict to a new democracy, with the new freedoms protected in the constitution and in the existence of a number of bodies designed to restrict the power of government. A considerable black middle class had come into existence; however, many more blacks had experienced little or no improvement to their lives. As the country entered the 21st century, the greatest task before the government was to create the conditions in which these continuing inequalities in society could be minimized.

Economy

LINDA VAN BUREN

The South African economy has exhibited a fundamental strength, stability and resilience in the post-apartheid era. Even when threatened by weak international prices for one of its key commodities, gold, the outflow of investment resources which some had predicted simply did not occur. However, as the Thabo Mbeki administration surveys the economic challenges of the new millennium, the signs are clear that merely maintaining the current level of performance will not be enough. Growth is positive, but moderate, and stronger growth will be needed in order to create many more jobs in a nation where one-quarter of the labour force is unemployed. Foreign investment could play a major role in job creation. When exchange controls were partially relaxed, an outward flow of capital was avoided; however, inflows of investment have been modest, and insufficient to create large numbers of new positions. A reduction in the rate of unemployment could be one of the best ways of countering the country's high crime rate, which was a major topic of discussion in 1999 and 2000. Both the government and the private sector have introduced job-creation schemes and initiatives such as Black Economic Empowerment, as well as various training and skills programmes. At the end of any training course, however, a worker will still need to find employment, and his chances will be limited if growth remains moderate.

NATURAL RESOURCES

Although South Africa's diverse climate permits the cultivation of a wide range of crops, only 13% of the land surface is suitable for arable farming, largely owing to inadequate or erratic rain-

fall, and only 11% of the total land area, or 132,000 sq km, was under major crops in 1996, according to the World Bank. Topographic difficulty is the main factor limiting the extent of irrigation, although the ambitious Orange River Project is expected eventually to increase the total irrigated area by about 300,000 ha, or 37.5%. The completion of the project's Gariep and Vanderkloof dams considerably increased the area under irrigation in the Orange River valley. Despite improvements in farming methods and conservation techniques in the 1980s and the 1990s, South Africa remains a relatively poor crop-raising country. This situation also imposes limits on animal husbandry, for which South Africa is better suited, although even here, the carrying capacity of the land is fairly low by international standards. Nevertheless, owing to a high degree of specialization, experience and advanced methods, along with considerable capital investment, certain branches of farming, such as the fruit and wool sectors, continue to make a substantial contribution to the economy and to exports in particular.

It is in mineral deposits, though, that South Africa's greatest wealth lies. The discovery, first, of diamonds and then, more importantly, of gold, during the latter part of the 19th century, formed the basis of the country's modern economic development. A huge complex of heavy and light industry, based initially on the gold-mining sector, grew up in the interior, although South Africa's share in the volume of world gold production (excluding the former USSR) declined from 70% in 1980 to 21% in 1996, owing to a fall in the average grade of ore mined and to increases in output in other parts of the world. Nevertheless, in 1999 South Africa remained the largest gold producer in the world, supplying 19% of the world total; South Africa has five of the 12 largest gold mines and seven of the 20 largest gold-mining companies in the world, including the largest, Anglo American Corporation, which alone accounted for 11.9% of the international market in 1998. The country also has abundant deposits of many other important minerals. The production of minerals other than gold accounted for 50% of the total value of mining output in 1999; 44 different minerals were commercially exploited. There are huge reserves of coal, with a pit-head price which is probably the lowest in the world, and also large reserves of iron ore. In 1996 South Africa possessed more than three-quarters of the world's reserves of manganese ore (81%), more than two-thirds of the world's chromium (68%), and more than one-half of world reserves of platinum-group metals (56%), as well as 45% of the world's vanadium, 40% of its gold and vermiculite, 37% of its alumino-silicates, 26% of its zirconium-group minerals, 17% of its titanium minerals, 12% of its fluorspar and 11% of its coal. In addition, it is a major producer of copper, lead, zinc, antimony and uranium.

South Africa's long coastline has few natural harbours, but close to its shores are some of the richest fishing areas in the world. The catch includes Southern African anchovy, Cape hakes, Southern African pilchard, Cape horse mackerel and Whitehead's round herring. The total catch increased from 520,300 metric tons in 1994 to 574,400 tons in 1995, but declined to 436,300 tons in 1996 before recovering to 509,400 tons in 1997.

POPULATION

The chief characteristic of South Africa's population, and the one that dominates its society, is the great racial, linguistic and cultural heterogeneity of its people, with Africans, Asians, Europeans and mixed-race citizens making up the population.

At the March 1985 census the total population (excluding the former 'independent homelands') was enumerated as 23,385,645. The total population at the October 1996 census was 40,583,573, and in mid-1999 the total population was estimated at 43,054,306. People are no longer officially classified according to race, as they were during apartheid, but, in order to gain some idea of the figures involved, in the 1996 census South Africans were invited to classify themselves. The result was that 77% of those enumerated described themselves as African, 11% as white, 9% as coloured and 3% as Asian.

The occupational distribution of the economically active population at the 1996 census was as follows: of the 9,113,847 persons aged 15–65 years who were in employment, 1,580,684 worked in community, social and personal services (17.3%), 1,119,973 in manufacturing (12.3%), 1,098,051 in wholesale and retail trade (12.0%), 1,053,103 in private households (11.6%), 814,350 in agriculture, hunting, forestry and fishing (8.9%), 680,156 in financial, insurance, real estate and business services (7.5%), 555,129 in construction (6.1%), 541,546 in mining and quarrying (5.9%), and 483,652 in transport, storage and communications (5.3%). The most drastic structural change in the economy has been an apparently sharp decline in the proportion of the population engaged in agriculture (28% at the 1970 census).

NATIONAL INCOME

Gross domestic product (GDP) increased by an annual average of 5.9% between 1960 and 1970, an increase rivalling that of Japan. At the same time GDP per caput increased by 2.9% per annum. This rate fell sharply in the 1970s, however, with real GDP growing at an average of only 3.9% (and about 1% per caput) per annum in the period 1970–80. This was followed by an exceptionally high increase of nearly 8% in real GDP in 1980, caused largely by the high price of gold in that year. During the 1980s real GDP growth slowed to an average of only 1.0% per year in 1980–90. A decline in real growth rates of GDP were recorded in 1982, 1983, 1985 and 1990. With the population increasing at an annual average rate of 2.6% in that decade, income per head was in decline. In 1998, according to estimates by the World Bank, South Africa's gross national product (GNP), measured at average 1996–98 prices, was US $136,868m., equivalent to $3,310 per head. During 1990–98, it was estimated, GNP per head declined, in real terms, by an annual average of 0.1%, while the population increased by an annual average of 2.3%. GDP increased, in real terms, by an annual average of 1.9% in 1990–98. Real GDP increased by 2.5% in 1997 and by

0.6% in 1998, according to revised figures, and by 1.2% in 1999. GDP was forecast to grow by some 3% in 2000, but in the first quarter of the year, partly owing to heavy flooding which damaged agriculture, an increase of only 0.9% was recorded.

Despite an improvement in the racial distribution of personal income in recent years, income remains very unevenly distributed in South Africa. It was estimated in 1988 that the 13% of South Africans who were white received about 54% of total personal income, while the 76% of South Africans classified as Africans received only 36%. In 1988 the differential in earnings per employee between whites and Africans in the manufacturing sector was 3.5:1, increasing to 5:1 in mining and quarrying. The greatest differential was to be found between those residing in metropolitan areas (white and black) and the rural former 'homelands' (mainly black), estimated to be 18:1 in 1985. The October 1996 census indicated that 54% of South Africans resided in urban areas overall, but the percentage varied widely among provinces: Gauteng province was 97% urbanized, while only 11% of the population of the Northern province lived in urban areas. In 1992 the average monthly income per head was R1,572 for whites, R523 for Asians, R325 for Coloureds, and R165 for black Africans.

The contribution to national income of the three main productive sectors—manufacturing, mining and agriculture—has changed markedly over the years. Manufacturing steadily increased its relative position, overtaking mining as the leading sector during the Second World War. By 1995 manufacturing contributed 24% of GDP at factor cost, mining and quarrying 7% and agriculture only 5%. The services sector contributed 64% of GDP in that year, the highest proportion in Africa, and in 2000 it was the services sector that was expected to grow the fastest.

INVESTMENT AND SAVING

Since the discovery of diamonds and gold in the 19th century, foreign investment has played a vital role in developing these industries and the economy in general. From 1984 until the accession of the Mandela administration, foreign investment was strongly in a negative direction. At first this outflow was attributed to speculative movements against the currency, brought on by a large balance-of-payments deficit and a weakening rand. However, with a deepening recession and the serious political disturbances that erupted in 1985, accompanied by the refusal of foreign banks to defer repayment of short-term loans, negative short-term capital movements reached record levels. Further deterioration was avoided only by the reintroduction, in September 1985, of the two-tier (financial and commercial) system of exchange rates for foreign investors. In the same month the government also declared a moratorium on repayments of debt principal on foreign loans until the end of the year (later extended until the end of March 1986), although interest payments were to continue. In October 1985 negotiations began with creditor banks on rescheduling the country's short-term debt, and in March 1986 the negotiations resulted in a one-year interim agreement whereby South Africa was to make a series of payments of 5% of debts due before the end of June 1987. In March 1987 it was announced that a further agreement had been reached with creditor banks, allowing a three-year rescheduling of US $13,000m. of foreign debt.

At the end of May 2000 South Africa's government debt totalled R400,952m., equivalent to US $57,879m., or about $1,350 per person. Of the total, a relatively small amount, R28,560m., was foreign debt; nevertheless, this was equivalent to more than $4,000m. With a level of foreign borrowing which has been especially low for a country at South Africa's level of development, many predicted that this situation would change after South Africa, following its political transition, gained access to institutions such as the World Bank and was more favourably treated by the international financial community. These fears proved unfounded in the first few years after President Mandela's inauguration in May 1994. After an initial increase of 11.5% in total long-term debt, from the US $12,963m. in 1994, most of which the Mandela government inherited, to $14,459m. in 1995, the level of total long-term debt actually declined thereafter, according to World Bank estimates. The first World Bank loan to post-apartheid South Africa—and indeed the first lending from the Bank to the country in 30

years—was a \$46m. Industrial Competitiveness and Job Crea-
tion funding repayable over 15 years after three years' grace.

MANUFACTURING INDUSTRY

Unlike its counterparts in the rest of Africa, South Africa's
manufacturing industry is the largest of the productive sectors
of the national economy, measured in terms of contribution to
GDP. In 1993 it contributed R81,167m. to GDP at factor cost,
employing 1,438,409 (more than 75% of the work-force being
non-white) in 1992. In 1999 the manufacturing sector contributed an estimated 18.2% of GDP, and in 1998 employed about
1,385,000 (equivalent to 14.7% of the employed labour force).
Manufacturing exports increased by as much as 20% in 1996.
GDP in the manufacturing sector declined by 1.8% in 1998,
but increased by 0.6% in the first quarter of 1999. Seasonally
adjusted manufacturing indices (1995 = 100) indicated that, in
April 2000, the value of manufacturing output was 99.3 and the
volume of manufacturing output was 97.8.

The mining industry, except for a limited number of industries
servicing it, did not, at first, stimulate local manufacturing to
any extent. As the mining industry favoured cheap imports,
little protection was offered to local manufacturers. It was only
in 1925 that an active policy of protecting local industry was
first adopted. As a consequence, industry grew significantly in
the latter half of the 1920s, particularly in the production of
consumer goods. That period also saw the foundation of heavy
industry under state auspices, with the establishment of the
Iron and Steel Corpn of South Africa (ISCOR) in 1928. By 1939
net industrial output was double the 1929 level, and expansion
continued in the post-war period. Industrial progress in the
1960s was particularly rapid. Its contribution to GDP, at factor
cost, increased by an average of 10.2% per annum between
1961–70, the physical volume of production by 8.5% per annum
and employment by 6.1% per annum, indicating increases in
productivity over the same period. Real growth was slower in
the 1970s, with the physical volume of production increasing
by an average of only 2.9% per annum, while employment
increased by 2.6% annually. Industrial GDP declined by an
annual average of 1.1% in 1980–90, but increased at an annual
average rate of 0.4% in 1990–98.

Industry is heavily concentrated in four industrial areas (Gauteng, Western Cape, Durban-Pinetown and Port Elizabeth-Uit-
enhage), accounting for more than 75% of net industrial output
and employment. More than 50% of the country's industry is
now located in Gauteng alone, and the tendency has been for
this concentration to increase at the expense of the ports and
the rural areas. Largely to stem the flow of blacks to 'white'
industrial areas, the state attempted, from 1960, to decentralize
industrial location to proclaimed border areas near to the former
'independent homelands'. Financial assistance in the form of
tax concessions, loans, reduced railway rates, exemption from
wage regulation etc. was granted to industrialists in these areas.
Between 1960 and 1980, tax and interest concessions (including
rental concessions) amounting to R222.8m. were given, and
181,198 jobs (of which 142,061 were for blacks) were created in
border areas. The government introduced in 1982 a revised
Regional Industrial Development Programme (RIDP), which
provided substantial relocation incentives to industrialists,
including wage subsidies, training grants, transport rebates,
housing subsidies and soft loans. Over the period 1982–90 about
450,000 jobs were created in the target areas at an average cost
(in 1990 prices) of R18,000 per job—for a massive total cost of
R8,100m. It was felt, however, that the policy had failed in its
primary purpose of job creation, as most of the jobs would have
existed somewhere else in the absence of relocation incentives,
at no cost to the taxpayer. Uneconomic location decisions were
encouraged by this policy, as was confirmed by a study which
concluded that between 34% and 42% of firms would be unprofitable if incentives were withdrawn.

In the post-apartheid era, a new RIDP was adopted in 1991,
which shifted the emphasis away from decentralized industrial
development in rural areas to broader regional development.
Incentives were to be performance-linked and therefore more
cost-effective. In April 1995 RIDP incentives were in the form
of an establishment grant for the first two years, a profit-based
incentive for the following three years and a relocation incentive
for foreign firms. In addition, a Simplified Regional Industrial

Development Programme (SRIDP) offered incentives to manufacturers, processors and assemblers whose total investment
did not exceed R2.5m.

Metal Products and Engineering

This comprises the largest sector of industry (including basic
metals, metal products, machinery and transport equipment),
employing about 500,000 workers in 2000. The steel industry
is the most important branch of this sector, with production of
crude steel valued at R12,593m. in 1992, R13,476m. in 1993
and R14,070m. in 1994. The industry is dominated by ISCOR,
the transfer of which from state to private-sector ownership
was completed in November 1989. In 1997 ISCOR operated 10
ore mines and four steel mills, while a fifth, at a projected cost
of US \$1,550m., entered production in 1998 at Saldanha Bay.
In addition, a \$280m. ISCOR stainless-steel plant was under
construction in Pretoria. There were six other steel-producing
companies in the private sector. Owing to favourable costs of
location, raw materials and labour, and an efficient scale of
production, South African steel is among the cheapest in the
world. In November 1998 ISCOR announced a joint venture
with Lime Sales Ltd to mine dolomite at Bridgetown, on the
Berg River; the project was expected to supply 228,000 metric
tons per annum of dolomite to Saldanha Steel. Three manganese
plants were being upgraded in 1997, at Sasolburg, Meyerton
and Witbank, and Gencor was also rehabilitating its Impala
platinum refinery, at a cost of \$100m. The aluminium enterprise
ALUSAF—owned 45% by Gencor and 20% by the Industrial
Development Corpn (IDC)—commissioned its Hillside
aluminium smelter in April 1997, five months earlier than
scheduled. The total cost of the project was finally estimated at
R6,000m.; it had already achieved full production in June 1996,
and its output reached 636,000 tons in its first year. ALUSAF's
production cost, at \$750 per metric ton, was one of the lowest
in the world. An estimated 490,000 tons of its output was to be
exported, of which 230,000 tons was to be sold under long-term
contracts.

The motor industry is another important branch of the engineering sector. The transport-equipment industry employed
91,000 workers and produced 206,600 passenger cars and 93,600
commercial vehicles in 1992; this sector is a major contributor
to South Africa's exports. The volume of production in the motor-
vehicle subsector increased by 5.1% in 1993 and by 6.8% in
1994. The vast majority of new cars contain at least 66% local
content by weight, thereby qualifying for special tariff rates as
'locally manufactured' models. In common with this industry in
other developing countries, vehicle manufacturing faces the
problem of rising costs with increasing local content, because of
the lack of those economies of scale which are enjoyed in the
major producing countries. With its potential market size of
over 40m. people, South Africa would offer better opportunities
to achieve economies of scale if incomes were more evenly
distributed and a larger proportion of the population could
afford to buy basic luxuries such as automobiles.

Food, Beverages and Tobacco

Industries processing local farm produce were among the first
to develop in South Africa. While this sector has expanded and
contributes significantly to exports, its relative position declined
from 32% of the net value of manufacturing output in 1925 to
17% in 1963. Food, beverages and tobacco accounted for 19.3% of
the value of manufacturing output in November 1994, compared
with 20.7% for the whole year in 1993, when combined output
in these sub-sectors amounted to R44,367.2m. In 1986 the gross
value of output of these industries was R18,193m. (21% of the
total for all manufacturing industry), and in 1992 they employed
197,300 workers (13.7% of the manufacturing industry labour
force). This subsector experienced difficulties in 1993, when
volume output declined by 12.6% in beverages, by 2.7% in
food and by 1.0% in tobacco. In 1994, however, both food and
beverages recovered, by 4.6% and 3.1% respectively; only tobacco
remained in decline, and that downturn continued in subsequent
years, owing to a marked decline in global demand. In 1997
South African Breweries embarked on the construction of a new
US \$175m. brewery at East London. In a major example of new
inward foreign investment, the US company, Coca-Cola, in 1995
joined South African Bottling Co in a \$400m. venture, which

was aimed not only at the South African market but also at those of other African countries. The country's wine industry experienced a rapid growth in exports in the late 1990s; in 1999 exports were projected to increase by 12%, to 130m. litres, of which 40% went to the United Kingdom.

Clothing and Textiles

The clothing industry, which was well established before the Second World War, now supplies 90% of local demand, and employed 113,500 workers in 1992. The textile industry (other than clothing) was essentially a post-war development; it now meets 60% of the country's textile needs, and employed 82,600 workers in 1992. In November 1994 textiles, wearing apparel and footwear contributed 7% of the value of manufacturing output, up from 6.7% for the whole of 1993, when combined output from these sub-sectors was R14,411.9m. Output of non-clothing textiles increased by 5.6% in 1994 in terms of volume, while that of clothing grew by 3.0% and that of footwear declined by 1.5%. The local textile industry was adversely affected in the 1990s by mass illegal imports of textile products, which continued in 2000. Some 20,000 jobs in the sector were lost between 1996–99.

Chemicals

This industry had an early beginning, with the manufacture of explosives for the gold mines. The Modderfontein factory, near Johannesburg, is now one of the world's largest privately owned explosives factories. Production of fertilizers is also a significant branch of this industry. However, the most important development in the late twentieth century was the establishment by the state-owned South African Coal, Oil and Gas Corpn (SASOL) of its first oil-from-coal plant (SASOL 1), which began production in the northern Orange Free State in 1955. Based on cheap, low-grade coal with a high ash content, this establishment was, until the commissioning of SASOL 2 and SASOL 3, the largest plant of its kind in the world. Besides producing a small but significant percentage of South Africa's petrol requirements, the development of synthetic fuel production led to the establishment of a huge petrochemical complex capable of manufacturing about 110 products, some of which, like coal-tar products, were only by-products of a coal-using process. Because of the absence of local supplies of natural mineral oil, attempts at a petroleum embargo and the huge rise in world petroleum prices in 1973, it was decided in 1974 to build SASOL 2 with 10 times the capacity of SASOL 1. SASOL was privatized in 1979. Production at SASOL 2, which had a capital cost of R2,400m., reached full capacity in 1982. Following the change of government in Iran in 1979 and the consequent loss by South Africa of its main source of supply of crude petroleum, it was decided to build SASOL 3, almost an exact copy of SASOL 2, at a capital cost of R3,200m. This plant began operation in 1983, and reached full production in 1985. The three plants in full production provided about 40% of South Africa's fuel requirements, and a fourth plant was planned. Part of the huge capital cost of these plants was provided by private-sector investment, but the government also invested heavily in the schemes. In the post-apartheid and post-sanctions era, when international prices for crude petroleum were low and the commodity could easily be imported, the giant SASOL scheme became less significant, prompting the government to reconstitute its relationship with the hydrocarbons sector. In 1995 SASOL negotiated an agreement whereby the government would purchase its output at US$17 per barrel until 1 July 1999, when the price was to fall to $16 per barrel. This arrangement appeared more attractive to the government when international prices for crude petroleum were higher, at an average $19.20 per barrel in 1997, but by March 1998 a barrel of crude petroleum on the open market could be bought for just $11.60. A government report on energy in June proposed a sweeping liberalization of the hydrocarbons sector, with the government subsidies to SASOL and Mossgas to be removed completely by 2000. Government controls over the import and export of crude petroleum were to end, with the result that SASOL would be free to market its output directly to the public by establishing its own retail network and also would be allowed to export its product, while at the same time other enterprises would be allowed to import crude petroleum and sell it in competition on the South African market. In April

1997 SASOL announced a co-operation agreement with Statoil of Norway, under which the two companies were to convert South African natural gas to synthetic crude petroleum. In June SASOL also commissioned a new acetic acid plant at Secunda; the R167m. plant had the capacity to produce 16,000 metric tons per year of acetic acid and 7,000 tons per year of propionic acid. SASOL announced in June 2000 that it was to build four new chemical plants in Sasolburg at a cost of R1,430m.; due to enter production in 2003, they are to produce 'world-scale' crude acrylic acid, normal-butyl acrylate, ethyl acrylate and glacial (high-purity) acrylic acid. Output is forecast at 80,000 tons per annum of crude acrylic acid. In addition, another plant in Sasolburg is expected to come on stream in 2002, producing 150,000 tons of normal butanol per year. The chemical industry employed 120,800 workers in 1992. In November 1994 industrial chemicals and chemical products (excluding petroleum) contributed 11.3% of the value of manufactured output, down from 13.2% for the whole of 1993, when these two sub-sectors' combined output was R28,237.5m. Production of industrial chemicals, in terms of volume, declined by 2.9% in 1993, but increased by 2.3% in 1994, while that of non-industrial chemicals declined by 0.2% in 1993, but increased by 1.8% in 1994.

AGRICULTURE

Reference has already been made to the declining role of agriculture as a source of income in the South African economy. The effect of recurrent drought can be seen in the dramatic fluctuations in production of maize—the staple food of the African population and the most important single item in South African farming. From a record output of 13.6m. metric tons in the 1981/82 season, production fell to only 3.4m. metric tons during the 1983/84 drought, resulting in maize imports of 2.4m. tons in that year. Again, from a peak of 11.7m. tons in 1989/90, output fell to 2.9m. tons in the disastrous drought of 1992/93, necessitating imports of 4.5m. tons at a cost of R2,570m. Maize production amounted to 9.7m. tons in 1993, 13.2m. tons in 1994, 4.8m. tons in 1995, 10.2m. tons in 1996 and 10.1m. tons in 1997. Maize production totalled 7.2m. tons in 1998/99 and 9.8m. tons in 1999/2000, according to the crop estimates committee of the national department of agriculture. Output in 2000/2001 was expected to be reduced by flooding and excessive rainfall in the early part of the year. The damp conditions led to infestation by diplodia, a fungal disease affecting maize. In 1999/2000 South Africa also produced 1.56m. tons of wheat (down from 1.79m. tons in 1998, which represented a sharp decline from the 2.29m. tons harvested in 1997), 299,400 tons of sorghum (a steep decline of 47.9% from 1998/99), 90,800 tons of barley (a 58% decline), 22,394 tons of oats, 11,000 tons of millet, 3,000 tons of rye and 2,900 tons of paddy rice. The total cereal harvest fluctuated in the 1990s, declining from 15.9m. tons in 1994 to 7.4m. tons in 1995; the figure for 1999 was 9.6m. tons.Wool, although prone to wide fluctuations in price, is one of South Africa's most important agricultural exports (along with maize, fruit and cane sugar). The country grows a wide range of cash crops, both for domestic consumption and for the export market. Fruit growers produce apples, pears, peaches, apricots, nectarines, plums, quinces, cherries, strawberries and other berries, table grapes, mangoes, avocados, pineapples, papayas, various melons, figs, passion fruits, bananas and all types of citrus fruits. Principal vegetables grown are asparagus, beans, cabbages, carrots, cauliflower, chillies, cucumbers, lettuce, mushrooms, onions, peas, pulses of many types, pumpkins, squashes and tomatoes. Agricultural products contributed R9,857.6m. to exports in 1994 (10.9% of the total). Following the abandonment of sanctions, exports of wine and of various fruits and vegetables to Europe increased dramatically. The low overall productivity of farming, relative to other sectors, was also reflected in the fact that, although engaging about 10.0% of the employed labour force in 1998, it contributed only 3.7% of GDP in 1999, owing principally to poor crop yields obtained by large numbers of inefficient African subsistence farmers in the former 'homelands'. However, even commercial farms, which were relatively efficient, obtained comparatively low yields by international standards. In maize farming, for example, yields per ha were only 38% of those in the USA; according to the FAO, South Africa's average maize yield in 1994 (a year not affected by drought) was 3,308 kg per ha, compared with 8,685 kg per ha in the USA. GDP in the agricultural sector declined by 3.1% in 1998, while figures for the first quarter of 2000 indicated a pronounced decline.

MINING

Despite having given way to manufacturing as the leading sector, mining is still of great importance in external trade. The sector contributed an estimated 6.5% of GDP in 1998. In 1993 total sales of minerals amounted to R50,219.4m., of which 63.5% was exported. In 1994 total exports of minerals amounted to R53,526.3m. (an increase of 6.6% compared with 1993). Mining and quarrying employed a total work-force of 541,546 in 1996. However, the continuing low international price for gold in the late 1990s resulted in major structural changes in the sector (see below).

South Africa is the world's leading gold producer. Since the Second World War new gold mines in the Free State, Far West Rand, Klerksdorp and Evander areas not only have replaced output from the worked-out mines on the old Rand but also have greatly increased total production. In the absence of new discoveries, however, gold output was expected to continue the decline that began in the early 1970s, after a record 1,000 metric tons in 1970. This was largely a result of a policy by the industry of lowering the grade of ore mined as the price rises. (Unless there is a compensating increase in tonnage milled when the average grade of ore mined is lowered, output falls.) From the late 1980s, however, the industry came under pressure from declines in both the US dollar and rand price of gold and continued increases in costs, forcing several economically marginal mines to close. Gold production amounted to 613.7 tons, valued at R19,512.6m., in 1992, rising to 619.9 tons, valued at R23,239.3m., in 1993. Net gold exports generated R22,229m. in 1993, R22,661m. in 1994 and R51,900m. in 1998. Having remained well below US $350 per oz throughout 1992, the price of gold began to rise in 1993, briefly exceeding $400 per oz in mid-1993. In August 1996 the world gold price stood at $387 per oz; by July 1997, however, it had declined to $316 per oz, prompting concern that several unprofitable gold mines might be closed. In 1996 South Africa's production of gold fell below 500 tons for the first time since 1956. In December 1997 a government report announced a major liberalization of the gold-marketing sector. Whereas previously all gold producers were required to hand over any newly mined gold to the South African Reserve Bank within 30 days, under the new policy producers were to be allowed to market their output directly to foreign buyers. The international gold price, already at an alarmingly low level, declined still further in 1999, when stocks were sold on the market. The IMF, in an agreement supported by the USA, the United Kingdom and Japan, proposed to sell part of its 103m.-oz reserves to enable it to provide additional concessionary loans to highly-indebted developing countries and to fund debt-relief. These proposals divided the African gold-producing countries from the non-producers (even though some of those who were to receive the benefits from the sale were themselves gold exporters). In May 1999, moreover, the Bank of England announced plans to sell 415 tons of gold, with 125 tons to be divested in 1999, in five auctions of 25 tons each. By late July 1999, following the first auction, the international gold price had declined to US $252.90 per oz. In comparison the average cost of producing gold for many companies had been $347 per oz in 1997 and $305 per oz in 1998. Of the 37 gold-mining companies in South Africa in 1990, only 10 were still operating in 1999, and industry sources predicted that, as a result of further mergers and consolidations, the number would be reduced to four by 2001. In addition to some 300,000 mining jobs which had already been lost since 1987, six mining companies proposed in July 1999 to dismiss a further 11,700 employees. By July 2000 the world gold price had recovered moderately, to $283.50 per oz. Although the industry welcomed the halt in the price decline, the strong upsurge that was needed to boost profits continued to be elusive.

The output of other minerals rapidly gained in importance after the Second World War. Gold accounted for about 80% of South Africa's mineral production in 1946 but for only 50% by 1993. There has been a great expansion in the output of uranium, platinum, palladium, nickel, copper, coal, antimony, diamonds, vanadium, asbestos, iron ore, fluorspar, chromium,

manganese and limestone, to name only the most important. In 1992 South Africa's output of chromium ore, at 3.36m. metric tons, was a close second, in terms of world production, to Kazakhstan's 3.6m. tons. Sales of platinum-group metals generated earnings of R6,600m. in 1995. When it was reported that the Impala platinum refinery had been affected by strike action in 1997, the international price of platinum increased from US $445 to $460 per oz; in 1998 the price fell below $400, but platinum performed well in late 1999 and 2000, and was selling at $552.20 in July 2000. These minerals are prominent in South Africa's exports, earning R10,177m. in 1990. A new underground copper mine at Phalaborwa, which was undertaken by Palabora Mining Co at a projected cost of R1,500m., was due to enter into production in the year 2002. Anglo American, whilst selling off its non-core sectors in 1999 and 2000, announced in May 2000 a new R700m. expansion at its Black Mountain mine at Aggeneys in the Northern province. The mine, which Anglo had purchased from Goldfields of South Africa and Phelps Dodge in July 1998, produces zinc, lead and copper. The new expansion involves the sinking of a new vertical shaft to a depth of 1,750m, which should extend the life of the mine to 2013. A feasibility study was in progress in mid-2000 into Anglo's proposed Gamsberg zinc project; if the R1,500m. project is approved, Gamsberg would become the largest integrated zinc mine and refinery in the world and would create 1,000 permanent jobs during its expected 25-year life span, in addition to an estimated 5,000 jobs during the construction phase.

Diamonds were traditionally the country's second most important export commodity after gold, but by the 1980s they had been overtaken by coal. South African diamond production had been conducted for some time at five mine locations. A sixth mine, Venetia, discovered in 1980 and opened in 1992, was expected during the 1990s to become South Africa's largest-producing diamond mine. Output in 1993 was 9.8m. carats, compared with 10m. carats in 1992 and 8.2m. carats in 1991. Production in 1994 was 10.2m. carats, declining to 9.1m. carats in 1995. In 1996 the Venetia mine accounted for about 41% of South Africa's output of 10.2m. carats. In 1997 South African diamond production declined to 9.8m. carats. In April of that year, Benguela Concessions and Moonstone Diamonds completed a project to exploit marine diamonds off South Africa's Atlantic coast. In February 1999 exports of South African diamonds were temporarily suspended, pending the resolution of a dispute over the method used to value the gems, and over regulations for exemption from a 15% export duty.

The coal-mining industry, which stagnated for many years owing to low prices and slow growth, acquired renewed vigour after the petroleum crisis in 1973. Exports grew rapidly, helped by the opening of the new rail link and coal terminal at Richards Bay in northern KwaZulu/Natal, which by 1987, with the completion of Phase III of the export programme, had increased its capacity to 44m. metric tons per annum. However, the increase in international sanctions and especially a fall in international prices had a particularly adverse effect on this industry. Exports fell from 44.9m. tons, earning R3,127m. in 1986, to 42.6m. tons, valued at R2,294m., in 1987. The decline in exports led coal producers to lay off some 3,000 workers, mostly black Africans. By 1991, with the recovery of international prices for coal and the removal of sanctions by most of the countries which had traditionally been South Africa's major export markets for coal, exports increased significantly, with shipments of 50.1m. tons earning R4,300m. in foreign exchange. In 1993 total production of coal was 183m. tons, valued at R9,674.4m. In 1994 output was 197m. tons, valued at R10,427m., an increase of 7.4% in volume terms. In 1996 exports of coal increased to 61.7m. tons, generating income of R8,000m. The industry employed 76,200 workers in 1992. In late June 2000 Anglo Coal initiated a study into the development of the Kriel South coal reserves in Mpumalanga; if the project were to go ahead, it could enter production in 2004, with output of between 9m. and 10m. tons per annum.

South Africa is the continent's leading producer of iron ore, and exports, to Japan in particular, also became important in the late 1980s, despite declining world demand for steel. A railway line from the high-grade deposits of the Sishen area, in the northern Cape, carries iron ore to Saldanha Bay. As a result of falling demand, South Africa's exports of iron ore declined from a peak of 14.7m. tons in 1980 to 8.8m. tons in 1986. Despite persistently depressed market conditions, export volume recovered to 15.5m. tons in 1990. In 1991, when shipments declined to 14.9m. tons, this export earned R772.1m. Production of iron ore amounted to 32.3m. tons, valued at R1,327m., in 1994. In May 1996 the IDC announced that it was conducting a feasibility study into the construction of a R2,500m. iron-ore reduction plant in Northern Province.

Only two major mineral products—petroleum and bauxite—have not been found in economic quantities. However, in February 1985 the Southern Oil Exploration Corpn (SOEKOR), a government-owned company which had been involved since 1965 in an intensive search for petroleum deposits, announced that a recent discovery offshore at Mossel Bay, off the south coast of Cape Province, had yielded a daily output of 2,600 barrels of light crude and 1m. cu ft of natural gas. While the petroleum potential of this field was thought to be limited, the natural gas reserves were estimated to be substantial, about 30,000m. cu m. In 1987 the government decided to proceed with the establishment of a plant to convert this natural gas into liquid fuel, at a cost of R5,500m. This plant was designed to supply 10% of South Africa's liquid fuel requirements when it came into operation in 1992. SOEKOR announced in May 1997 that Petrol SA Ltd and Phillips Petroleum of the USA were to explore an area of the Indian Ocean, off South Africa's east coast. Other participants in the venture, for which Phillips was the operator, with a 40% share, were Pan Canadian Petroleum (Africa) Ltd of Canada (20%), Energy Africa Bredasdorp (Proprietary) Ltd of South Africa (20%), and SASOL (20%). Phillips was to spend US $8m. in gathering seismic data and was to drill at least one exploratory well over the four-year period of the lease (which could be extended for up to two subsequent periods of three years each).

TRANSPORT AND COMMUNICATIONS

With no navigable rivers, South Africa's transport system is entirely dependent on its rail and road network, with air transport playing a small but increasing role. The state-owned railways covered 31,400 route-km in 1996 (about one-third of all the railway track length in sub-Saharan Africa); some 87% of the rail network is electrified, and the system was computerized in 1980. In the year to 31 March 1989 total freight traffic was 174.2m. metric tons, and 579.5m. passenger journeys were made. Spoornet, which operates the railway, came under pressure to reduce costs in the 1990s, and began to curtail its workforce. In mid-1999 it announced that it was to dismiss more than one-half of its remaining employees, with the further loss of 27,000 jobs. The number of people employed in the transport, storage and communications sectors increased from 483,652 in 1996 to some 552,000 in 1998. In 1999 and 2000 the government was proceeding with plans to construct the country's first new railway line in 15 years, and the transport sector was forecast to grow at a faster rate than the economy as a whole. South African harbours handled 136.5m. tons of cargo in 1995/96. The Richards Bay coal terminal handled 58.7m. tons of coal exports in 1996. Plans, announced in August 1997, to construct a new US $146m. dry dock and a R500m. container terminal were aimed at developing Richards Bay into a principal transhipment port. Safmarine and Unicorn, the two largest shipping companies, are both in the private sector. In 1999 Portnet was divided into two entities, the port authority and the port operators, and two ancillary divisions were sold. Transnet Ltd, which controls the national railways, harbours, and oil pipelines, was the largest commercial undertaking in South Africa, employing 168,419 people in 1990. On 6 August 1993 the country's nine major airports were placed under the management of The Airports Company Ltd, which was 100% owned by the government but was nevertheless operating the airports on a commercial basis. The national carrier is South African Airways (SAA), but the sector was deregulated in 1990, and the airline is now exposed to competition, both on domestic and on international routes, from other private-sector carriers. More than 20 private-sector airlines provided 80 routes to 50 towns in South Africa in 1996. Following the end of apartheid, SAA began to expand services to the rest of Africa. Swissair purchased a 20% share in the carrier in 1999, at a cost of

R1,400m., in the second-largest privatization exercise at that time; a further 40% of SAA was to be sold by 2000.

An extensive road network serves the country, with an estimated 331,265 km of classified roads in 1995. About 41.5% of the network was paved. In 1999 there were 1,049,086 registered passenger motor vehicles, 364,398 load vehicles, 31,506 motor cycles and 32,195 special vehicles. Private long-distance road haulage was for many years restricted by government legislation designed to protect the railways.

Telecommunications are fairly extensively developed, with 4.3m. telephone lines in use in 1996. In 1997 Telkom, the state telecommunications company, and Telecom Malaysia revealed plans for the construction of a US $360m. Indian Ocean undersea cable, which would link Cape Town to Penang, Malaysia, via Port Louis, Mauritius. Telkom was offered for privatization in 1997, in the hope that the sale of part of its equity would generate revenue amounting to about R5,000m. In March 1997 the sale of a 30% stake in Telkom for R5,600m. was completed, in the country's largest privatization exercise. The government's ambitious R16,000m. Vision 2000 scheme proposed to extend the telecommunications network to a far greater proportion of the population by installing 12m. new telephone lines, at a cost of R6,000m., by the year 2000.

POWER AND WATER

Electricity

In 1993 South Africa consumed 174,581m. kWh of electricity, with a per capita consumption equal to that of Western Europe. In South Africa, however, only 15m. people, or 37% of the population, had access to electricity in their homes. Since 1994 1.5m. households have been connected to the national grid. Most of the national supply (97% in 1995) was generated by the state-controlled Electricity Supply Commission (ESKOM) via a national grid system which came into operation in 1973. Coal, owing mainly to its low cost, is the main source of fuel for power generation (78% in 1993). South Africa's electricity is among the cheapest in the world (US $0.079 per kWh in 1990). Nearly one-half of the country's coal production is used for electricity production. Some peak-load power is now being provided by the hydroelectric stations of the Orange River Project. The first nuclear power station to be constructed in South Africa, Koeberg, was commissioned by ESKOM in 1976. It was built at Duynefontein, between Cape Town and Saldanha Bay, by a French consortium. The plant was damaged in a sabotage attack in 1982, but began operating in 1984 when the first of its two 920-MW units was connected to the national grid and reached full generating capacity two months later. The second unit came into operation in 1985. With both units in full operation, the plant has a generating capacity of 1,842 MW, representing about 10% of South Africa's total capacity. In February 1985, however, the Koeberg plant was temporarily closed, following the discovery of defects. In 1993 nuclear generation supplied the equivalent of only 2.3m. metric tons of coal, or 1.7% of the total. In 1988 South Africa finalized an agreement with Mozambique and Portugal to restore electricity supplies from the Cahora Bassa dam, in Mozambique; the supplies had been interrupted since 1983 by the destruction of power lines in Mozambique linking the dam to the South African grid. Reconstruction work on the power lines was scheduled to begin in August 1993, with the aim of achieving a full resumption of electricity supply to South Africa by 1996. ESKOM entered a new agreement in 1998 to buy 900 MW of power from Cahora Bassa. In 1995 ESKOM exported electricity to Botswana, Lesotho, Mozambique, Namibia, Swaziland and Zambia, and was engaged in discussions with authorities in a number of other African countries. Exports of electricity by ESKOM earned R8,000m. in 1996 (an increase of 7.7% compared with 1995). However, under a 1998 agreement, South Africa was also to import power from Zambia via Zimbabwe (for which the Zimbabwe government was also to be paid a fee).

Water

Water supply is increasingly becoming a problem for the future location of industry. The Vaal river, which is the main source of water supply for the large concentration of manufacturing industry and mining in Gauteng and the northern Free State, is nearing the limit of its capacity. Even with planned increases in supply to the Vaal from the Tugela basin in KwaZulu/Natal, it is unlikely that this river will meet future requirements after the end of the century. It is likely, therefore, that KwaZulu/Natal with its much greater water supply will have a higher rate of growth of industry than Gauteng in the future. In March 1988 South Africa and Lesotho signed the final protocols for the Highlands Water Project (HWP); the arrangements were reconfirmed in the mid-1990s after South Africa's change of leadership. At a projected cost of US $3,770m., the HWP proposed the diversion of water from Lesotho's rivers for export to South Africa. The prospective throughput of water was projected at 77 cu m per second by the time the scheme is completed in the year 2017, although at the end of the $2,500m. Phase 1A, planned for late 1998, the rate was to be about 18 cu m per second. The first water deliveries flowed in 1997, and South Africa made the first annual royalty payment, of R110m. At full completion, the scheme would provide South Africa with 2,428m. cu m of water annually. About 75% of the cost of Phase 1A was raised in southern Africa (including some 57% from banks), with diversified external sources providing the balance, including $110m. from the World Bank in 1989. The commercial segment of the debt was to be met from royalty payments on water purchases by South Africa. Phase 1B, with a total projected cost of $1,100m., was also to be funded largely from South African capital and money markets and from the water users ($825m. in all, also equivalent to 75%). Phase 1B received the necessary backing to proceed; however, some observers doubted that the remaining five proposed dams would ever be built. The water treaty negotiated with South Africa covered the legal framework of the project and the pricing and volume of water to be sold. One of the most contentious aspects of the treaty was the control of water delivery. There was strong concern, both in Lesotho and among its neighbours, that unless the Lesotho government controlled delivery, the country would be even more dependent on South Africa, which could delay the transfer of water payments as a form of leverage. The treaty addresses part of the problem, with South Africa due to pay monthly royalties in cash, regardless of water delivered, plus a unit cost component based on each cu ft of water delivered. In 1997 the Rand Water Board planned to construct a second reservoir, at a cost of R100m., which was located at Klipriviersberg, south of Johannesburg, and was to serve Johannesburg and Gauteng. In 1999 the government had identified 1,020 water supply projects, at various stages of planning or execution, which were aimed at supplying 25 litres of drinkable water per person per day to every community by 2004. The water sector was also chosen to provide jobs in some of the country's poorest communities.

FOREIGN TRADE

South Africa is highly dependent on international trade. The value of merchandise imports f.o.b. was R301,500m. in 1998, while the value of visible exports c.i.f. was R269,800m., leaving a visible trade deficit of R31,700m. Despite rapid industrialization, with the encouragement of import-replacement industries by protective tariffs and comprehensive direct import control machinery in operation from 1948 to the late 1990s, imports as a rule are not a much smaller proportion of national income than their average of 24% in the 1930s; in recent years, however, they have been significantly below average and below the level of exports, including gold, owing to the need to finance capital repayments overseas. The composition of imports, however, has changed considerably over the years. Whereas in 1910 food, drink, clothing and textiles constituted 46% of total imports, these consumer goods are usually only a small fraction today (10% in 1998), with intermediate and capital goods making up the bulk of imports. In 1968 about 92% of imports were manufactured, whereas only 38% of exports were in this category, and even here a large proportion of exports classified as manufactured were lightly processed agricultural and mineral products. The country remains heavily dependent, therefore, on agriculture and mining (gold in particular) to pay for imports.

The United Kingdom, traditionally South Africa's main trading partner, slipped down the rankings in the 1990s. In 1996 the United Kingdom's share as a supplier of South Africa's imports (11.5%) was surpassed by Germany (15.0%) and the USA (12.9%); Japan supplied 7.8%. The principal market for

South African exports was the United Kingdom (13.2%); other important purchasers were the USA (9.6%), Japan (8.6%) and Germany (5.6%). In 1994 exports to all African countries were nearly R8,632m. (9.6%), while imports were only R2,354m. (3.0%). The chief African markets for exports in 1996 were Zimbabwe (5.3%), Mozambique (2.4%) and Zambia (1.8%). The only substantial supplier of imports to South Africa was Zimbabwe (1.0%). On 29 August 1994 South Africa became a member of the Southern African Development Community (SADC). After four years of negotiations, South Africa and the European Union finally signed a Free Trade Agreement in March 1999. The development was not well received by the Common Market for Eastern and Southern Africa (COMESA), however, which threatened to challenge the agreement if it was found to be to the detriment of COMESA members (who included most of the other members of SADC). The USA also complained that the accord would render its exports to South Africa less competitive.

With import controls established in the late 1940s and strict exchange control regulations imposed in 1961 (after the massive outflow of foreign capital following the political disturbances of 1960), South Africa was generally able to protect itself against disruptions to the balance of payments on both current and capital accounts. In favourable times during the apartheid era, these regulations were relaxed but not abolished. They were again stringently applied after the political disturbances which commenced in the second half of 1984, but despite massive outflows of foreign capital in 1985–93, the balance-of-payments position and reserves remained fairly steady, although South Africa was forced to draw heavily upon its reserves of gold and foreign exchange during 1988 in order to fulfil foreign debt commitments for that year. This was achieved only by large surpluses on the balance of trade, offsetting the outflows of capital. With the widespread abandonment of international sanctions on trade and investment from 1991, a more favourable climate for South Africa's balance of payments was forecast. The year-end figures for 1994 confirmed that the flow of capital could indeed be reversed: South Africa achieved a net inflow of short-term capital of R1,430m. as well as a net inflow of long-term capital of R3,780m., totalling a net capital inflow of R5,210m. The current account of the balance of payments remained in deficit between 1995 and 1999, with shortfalls of US $2,204m. in 1995, $1,881m. in 1996, $2,273m. in 1997, $1,936m. in 1998 and $464m. in 1999. (Prior to 1998 trade data refer to the Southern African Customs Union, which includes Botswana, Lesotho, Namibia, South Africa and Swaziland.)

FINANCE

The South African currency is the rand, issued by the South African Reserve Bank. The 'commercial' rand's link with the dollar was freed and allowed to float in 1979, and non-residents were allowed to buy 'security' rands at a discount for direct investment purposes. In 1983 the 'security' rand was abolished and merged with the commercial rand for non-residents. Owing to the outbreak of political disturbances in the second half of 1984, the rand depreciated sharply against the US dollar and all other major currencies, falling from R1 = US $0.80 in early 1984 to R1 = US $0.42 in January 1985. Despite measures taken by the Reserve Bank to curtail speculation against the rand, the escalation of violence generated a lack of confidence in the country, politically, and a further flight of capital led the value of the rand to fall to R1 = US $0.35 by August 1985. Coupled with the unwillingness of foreign banks to reschedule short-term loans, a moratorium on debt repayments was imposed in September 1985, together with the reintroduction of the two-tier system of exchange control on foreign investors. In March 1987, however, an agreement was reached with foreign creditor banks allowing a three-year rescheduling of $13,000m. of outstanding debt. In August 1994 the commercial rand stood at R1 = US $0.28 and the financial rand at R1 = US $0.18, while the discount on the financial rand was 20.59%, reflecting the continued outflow of foreign capital. By March 1995, however, the outflow had been reversed (see above), and the then minister of finance, Christo Liebenberg, announced the abolition of the financial rand and the termination of the dual exchange-rate system. Following speculation regarding government policy and the fact that the exchange rate had become overvalued, the rand depreciated by 17% against a number of trade-weighted currencies and by 18% against the US dollar between mid-February and the end of May 1996. The exchange rate stood at R4.33 = US $1 in July 1996 and at R4.67 = US $1 in August 1997. By July 1999 it had declined to R6.08 = US $1. The rand was considered to be sufficiently stable for the government in the 1997/98 budget to relax exchange controls for South African residents (although not for those who had emigrated and who still had assets blocked in the country). No sudden outflow of funds ensued. The exchange rate weakened to R7.02 = US $1 in May 2000, but recovered to R6.82 = US $1 by late July 2000.

Public finance is conducted along orthodox lines, although there has been a steady trend for public spending to grow as a proportion of GDP, despite repeated attempts to prevent further increases in real terms. In 1991/92 expenditure was 29.7% of GDP, compared with 25.5% in 1977/78. From 1994 economies in outlays on defence expenditure have been more than offset by large increases in social expenditure on housing, health and education for the African population, which, together with the weak performance of the economy, led to stagnating revenues and spiralling deficits. The first post-election budget, presented in June 1994, essentially followed the conservative tradition of previous budgets. The planned 6.5% increase in expenditure to R135,100m. was below the current rate of inflation so that the fiscal deficit was forecast to shrink substantially to some 6.6% of GDP. The outturn of the 1994/95 budget, however, showed total estimated expenditure to have been R140,004.9m., and attributed the larger figure to higher inflation (9% in 1994) than had been forecast a year earlier. Nevertheless, the 1994/95 budget deficit was stated to be R28,500m., or 6.4% of the latest estimate of GDP. The 1995/96 budget proposals, announced on 15 March 1995, projected total expenditure at R123,248.3m. (an increase of 9.5% on actual 1994/95 expenditure) and total revenue and grants at R124,191.0m. (an increase of 11.3% on actual 1994/95 revenue), leaving a projected deficit of R29,057.3m., equivalent to 5.8% of projected GDP. In 1994/95 a special budget of R2,500m. for post-apartheid reconstruction was to be financed by budgetary restrictions elsewhere, with small savings being made in such areas as forestry, transport and foreign affairs. Initially the cost of defence, previously a source of economizing, was to rise owing to the absorption of ex-guerrillas into a single force. The total cost of transition—the dismantling of the old state and the creation of a new one—was estimated to be some R4,000m. in 1994 alone (the election itself cost nearly R1,000m.). The short-term costs were to be met by a non-recurring levy of 5% on individuals and companies with an annual taxable income of over R50,000. At the same time the company tax rate was reduced from 40% to 35%, although the dividends tax increased from 15% to 25% to compensate for the difference. The 1996/97 budget projected total expenditure at R173,700m. (an increase of 10.4% compared with the revised estimate of the previous year), and total revenue at R144,900m., leaving a budgetary deficit of R28,800m. (or 5.1% of GDP). The 1997/98 budget was described by leading private-sector bankers as 'conservative'; it projected expenditure at R186,700m. and revenue at R161,900m., leaving a deficit of R24,800m. (4% of projected GDP). This budget provided for the Growth, Employment and Redistribution strategy, known as GEAR. The government also opted for a system of three-year rolling budgets. The 1998/99 budget required spending of R201,000m. (a 6% increase compared with the revised 1997/98 expenditure); 60% of this amount was allocated to social services. The 1999/2000 budget, announced in February 1999, introduced tax reductions valued at R5,000m., including an unexpected reduction in company tax, from 35% to 30%. The 2000 budget forecast spending of R17,535m. and revenue of R16,792m., leaving a deficit of R743m., a sizeable improvement over the previous year's shortfall of R2,345m.

The combined fixed investment of public authorities and public corporations was 29% of total gross fixed investment in 1993. Although still officially committed to a basically private-enterprise economic system, the state under white rule became increasingly involved, through the IDC, in a whole new range of commercial activities, in addition to traditional infrastructure and public utility enterprises. The post-apartheid government, however, committed itself to a programme of privatization of public enterprises. The 1997/98 budget emphasized the gov-

ernment's commitment to the privatization programme, which was to be accelerated. Emphasis was placed on deregulation, liberalization and the removal of subsidies, even in such principal sectors as gold mining and oil-from-coal production. Although this policy was in agreement with IMF and World Bank principles, it has also contributed to greater unemployment, and to popular discontent.

ECONOMIC OUTLOOK

South Africa undoubtedly achieved remarkable economic development in the 1960s, with one of the highest growth rates in the world during that decade. The results of that development, however, were very unevenly distributed, with the 'homelands' remaining as wretched and overpopulated as ever. Growth in the 1970s was much slower, owing partly to instability of the world economy in this period and partly to the effects of the disturbances following the Soweto riots in June 1976. These factors had a particularly discouraging effect on foreign investment in South Africa. After a short-lived boom in 1979 and 1980, growth in the 1980s was even slower than in the 1970s, averaging only 1.4% per annum in real terms over the decade, and therefore resulting in a fall in real income per head. Factors that contributed to this poor performance included unfavourable commodity prices in international markets (in particular a weakening of the price of gold), drought in 1983 and 1984, the damaging effect of political instability in causing a net outflow of foreign investment and low overall investment in the economy in the late 1980s and early 1990s, and the effect of sanctions on foreign trade in some markets such as coal exports.

Between the first quarter of 1989 and the first quarter of 1993 real GDP fell by 4%, creating South Africa's longest recession of the 20th century. International recession, as well as severe drought and the volatility of the political climate, were all contributory factors. The most serious manifestation of the recession was the decline in investment, which was equivalent to only 15% of GDP in 1992 and had been well below earlier levels (24% on average during 1982–85) since the late 1980s. A low level of investment undermined the economy's future ability to generate growth and absorb work-seekers. Following the establishment of the ANC administration, a major reversal of the flow of investment took place. In 1994 South Africa achieved a record net inflow of foreign investment of R821m., while in 1995 this figure increased almost fivefold, to R3,900m. Disinvestment, in contrast, was less than R50m. per year in 1994 and 1995.

More than 300,000 jobs were lost in mining, and over 60,000 in manufacturing in the 1990s. The Reserve Bank estimated that from the first quarter of 1989 (the beginning of the recession) to the third quarter of 1993, employment in the formal non-agricultural sectors fell by some 410,000. During this period 8% of workers were declared redundant. Unemployment figures continued to rise even with recovery in the second half of 1993. The employment situation had, however, been weak for much longer. Whereas in the period 1963–70 numbers employed in the non-agricultural sectors of the economy increased at an average annual rate of 4.2%, well in excess of the rate of population increase, this fell to 2.7% in the period 1970–78, barely equal to the increase in population. A major structural change in the South African economy after the abolition of all forms of influx control was a huge migration to the large towns. Disguised unemployment in the rural areas was increasingly registered as overt unemployment in the urban areas. However, there were also positive signs of a big increase in the size of the 'informal' sector, assisted by the removal of most of the petty restrictions that had previously hampered this sector. According to an official survey, open unemployment amounted to 32% of the labour force (about 4.6m.) at October 1994. Government assessments estimated the rate of unemployment at 25.2% in mid-2000. Most of the unemployed were blacks, among whom unemployment was more than 40%; one-half of these lived in rural areas. In 1995 employment increased by only 0.6%, while the labour force grew by 2.5%; unemployment increased by some 280,000 in that year. A significant two-year wage contract between the Chamber of Mines and the National Union of Mineworkers, which was announced in July 1997, established strict linkages between productivity and wage increases; gold production was to increase by 90 metric tons in 1997, and this higher level was to be sustained in 1998. If this target was reached, the lowest-paid, least-skilled workers would receive a 25% rise in wages, which would effectively amount to a minimum wage of R1,000 per month for official work and R1,150 per month for unofficial work. However, this was implemented at a time when the international price of gold increasingly declined, falling below the cost of production, despite companies reducing their costs by about 12% in a single year. In 1999 mining unions supported the managements of the gold-mining companies in their efforts to prevent the IMF and others from selling their gold reserves on the world market, adding further downward pressure on the international gold price. Another initiative, which sought to create jobs for black South Africans, was the Black Economic Empowerment scheme, in which major companies such as Telkom gave preference to black-run suppliers for their purchases. A skills levy imposed on companies was due to rise from 0.5% of a company's total payroll to 1% in April 2001. This levy was expected to generate R1,000m. per annum to fund 25 sectoral education and training authorities aimed at improving the skills levels of black employees; details of how these funds would be allocated were awaited in late July 2000. A quota system was also in force to achieve 'employment equity', which required that 80% of a company's work-force be black, 54% be female and 5% have disabilities.

Following the election in April 1994, the new government acted to address the prevailing negative investor sentiment, with a number of prudent financial and structural policies. These included a programme of progressive fiscal-deficit reduction, the constitutional guarantee of the independence of the reserve bank, plans for trade liberalization in a number of areas including gold and fuel, measures to begin to redress social imbalances under the GEAR strategy, availability of funding to help small and medium-sized firms to become established in a number of sectors, from fishing to forestry to horticulture to manufacturing, the reform of labour legislation to reduce tension in industrial relations, and a commitment to a progressive elimination of capital controls. The impact of these extensive policies was reflected in the strong increase in investor confidence during 1994 and 1995 and in subsequent years. Much was to depend on the government's success in fostering the creation of new jobs and in narrowing the earnings gap between the lowest-paid and the highest-paid workers. Government efforts have resulted in 900 community-based projects, creating some 40,000 jobs; nevertheless, many more thousands of jobs are lost in the sectors of mining, transport and manufacturing, while every year the number of unemployed increases. The 'informal sector' can provide some employment, in what the government refers to as 'income-earning opportunities'. The first year of the Mbeki administration, 1999, posed even more challenges than any of the previous five years. The government must endeavour to redistribute wealth more evenly, in a way that is effective, without deterring potential private-sector investors, whose funds are badly needed. However, even more importantly, South Africa's economic planners must find a way to increase the country's wealth. Through all means possible, the Mbeki administration will have to create sustainable jobs in large numbers. New investment, both by local companies and by foreign enterprises, will be an essential element of any strategy to achieve that end.

Statistical Survey

Source (unless otherwise indicated): Central Statistical Service, Steyn's Arcade, 274 Schoeman St, Private Bag X44, Pretoria 0001; tel. (12) 3108911; fax (12) 3223374; e-mail info@statssa.pwv.gov.za; internet www.statssa.gov.za.

Area and Population

AREA, POPULATION AND DENSITY*

Area (sq km) .	1,219,080†
Population (census results)	
7 March 1991	37,944,018
9 October 1996	
Males	19,520,887
Females	21,062,685
Total	40,583,573
Population (official estimates at mid-year)	
1997	41,226,700
1998	42,130,500
1999	43,054,306
Density (per sq km) at mid-1999	35.3

* Excluding data for Walvis Bay (area 1,124 sq km or 434 sq miles, population 23,641 in 1970), sovereignty over which was transferred from South Africa to Namibia on 1 March 1994.
† 470,689 sq miles.

ETHNIC GROUPS (estimates, 30 June 1999)

	Number	% of total
Africans (Blacks) .	33,239,879	77.20
Europeans (Whites) .	4,538,727	10.54
Coloureds .	3,792,631	8.81
Asians .	1,092,254	2.54
Other and unspecified .	390,815	0.91
Total .	**43,054,306**	**100.00**

* Figures have been estimated independently, so the total is not the sum of the components. The data have not been adjusted to take account of the 1996 census results.

POPULATION BY PROVINCE (estimates, 30 June 1999)

KwaZulu/Natal .	8,924,643
Gauteng* .	7,807,273
Eastern Cape .	6,658,670
Northern Province† .	5,337,267
Western Cape .	4,170,971
North-West .	3,562,280
Mpumalanga‡ .	3,003,327
Free State§ .	2,714,654
Northern Cape .	875,222
Total .	**43,054,306**

* Formerly Pretoria-Witwatersrand-Vereeniging.
† Formerly Northern Transvaal.
‡ Formerly Eastern Transvaal.
§ Formerly the Orange Free State.

PRINCIPAL TOWNS (population at 1991 census)

	City Proper	Metropolitan Area
Cape Town* .	854,616	2,350,157
Durban .	715,669	1,137,378
Johannesburg .	712,507	1,916,061
Pretoria* .	525,583	1,080,187
Port Elizabeth .	303,353	853,205
Umlazi .	299,275	n.a.
Roodepoort .	162,632	870,066
Pietermaritzburg .	156,473	228,549
Germiston .	134,005	n.a.
Bloemfontein* .	126,867	300,150
Boksburg .	119,890	n.a.
Benoni .	113,501	n.a.
East London .	102,325	270,127
Kimberley .	80,082	167,060
Springs .	72,647	700,906
Vereeniging .	71,255	773,594

* Pretoria is the administrative capital, Cape Town the legislative capital and Bloemfontein the judicial capital.

BIRTHS AND DEATHS (UN estimates, annual averages)

	1980–85	1985–90	1990–95
Birth rate (per 1,000) . . .	31.8	30.6	29.0
Death rate (per 1,000) . . .	11.1	10.3	9.8

Source: UN, *World Population Prospects: The 1998 Revision.*

October 1994 (household survey): Birth rate 23.4 per 1,000; Death rate 9.4 per 1,000.

Expectation of life (UN estimates, years at birth, 1990–95): 59.0 (males 54.8; females 63.6) (Source: UN, *World Population Prospects: The 1998 Revision*).

IMMIGRATION AND EMIGRATION

	1996	1997	1998
Immigrants			
Africa	1,601	1,201	1,200
Europe	2,315	1,494	1,614
Asia	1,137	1,118	1,284
Americas	257	218	203
Oceania	86	56	61
Total (incl. others and unspecified)	5,407	4,103	4,371
Emigrants			
Africa	1,223	1,410	1,502
Europe	3,198	2,962	3,138
Asia	402	410	399
Americas	1,786	1,432	1,383
Oceania	3,035	2,671	2,513
Total (incl. others and unspecified)	9,708	8,946	9,031

ECONOMICALLY ACTIVE POPULATION
(household survey, '000 persons aged 15 to 65 years, October 1998)*

	Males	Females	Total
Agriculture, hunting, forestry and fishing	674	261	935
Mining and quarrying . .	422	13	435
Manufacturing	912	473	1,385
Electricity, gas and water . .	93	20	113
Construction	518	30	548
Trade, restaurants and hotels .	968	819	1,787
Transport, storage and communications . . .	454	97	552
Financing, insurance, real estate and business services . .	535	319	855
Community, social and personal services	863	985	1,848
Private households . . .	109	663	772
Activities not adequately defined	77	48	125
Unspecified	21	15	36
Total employed . . .	5,647	3,743	9,390
Unemployed	1,548	1,614	3,163
Total labour force . . .	7,195	5,358	12,553

* Figures have been assessed independently, so that totals are not always the sum of the component parts.

Agriculture

PRINCIPAL CROPS ('000 metric tons)

	1996	1997	1998
Maize	10,171	10,136	7,574
Sorghum	536	432	319
Wheat	2,712	2,294	1,469
Barley	176	182	146
Oats	36	36	35*
Dry beans	63	63	52
Cottonseed	69	44	64
Cotton (lint)	40	25	37
Sugar cane	20,951	22,155	24,460
Tobacco (leaves)	22	27	32
Potatoes	1,592	1,581	1,584
Sweet potatoes . . .	46	48	47*
Soybeans	80	120	201
Groundnuts (in shell) . . .	216	158	108
Sunflower seed	784	463	584
Cabbages	205	207	205*
Tomatoes	452	445	445*
Pumpkins, squash and gourds	313	331	330*
Onions (dry)	279	316	320*
Carrots	103	103	100*
Watermelons	51	55	50*
Apples	617	519	515*
Grapefruit and pomelo . .	125	128	125*
Grapes	1,411	1,439	1,273
Lemons and limes . . .	87	93	88*
Oranges	890	962	900*
Peaches and nectarines . .	173	251	240*
Pears	227	284	275*
Bananas	165	206	200*
Mangoes	24	30	25*
Avocados	54	45	43*
Apricots	55	72	65*
Pineapples	134	144	140*

* FAO estimate.

Source: FAO, *Production Yearbook.*

LIVESTOCK ('000 head, year ending September)

	1996	1997	1998
Cattle	13,389	13,667	13,800
Pigs	1,603	1,617	1,641
Sheep	28,934	29,187	29,980*
Goats	6,674	6,644	7,000*
Horses†	250	255	260
Mules†	14	14	14
Asses†	210	210	210

* Unofficial figure.
† FAO estimates.

Chickens (FAO estimates, million): 60 in 1996; 59 in 1997; 59 in 1998.

Source: FAO, *Production Yearbook.*

LIVESTOCK PRODUCTS ('000 metric tons)

	1996	1997	1998
Beef and veal	480	490	676*
Mutton and lamb* . . .	117	119	120
Goat meat*	37	37	39
Pig meat	128	127	127*
Poultry meat*	454	444	445
Cows' milk	2,592	2,720	2,800*
Butter	7	14	14*
Cheese	40	36	36*
Hen eggs	290	285	285*
Wool:			
greasy	62	54	54*
clean*	37	32	33
Cattle hides (fresh)* . .	70	74	90
Sheepskins (fresh) . . .	21	16	17*

* FAO estimate(s).

Source: FAO, *Production Yearbook.*

Forestry

(including Namibia)

ROUNDWOOD REMOVALS ('000 cubic metres, excl. bark)

	1993	1994	1995
Sawlogs, veneer logs and logs for sleepers	4,155	4,374	5,432
Pulpwood	8,806	10,166	10,166
Other industrial wood . .	2,193	2,578	2,578
Fuel wood	7,210	7,120	7,156
Total	22,364	24,238	25,332

1996–97: Annual output as in 1995.

Source: FAO, *Yearbook of Forest Products*.

SAWNWOOD PRODUCTION

('000 cubic metres, incl. railway sleepers)

	1993	1994	1995
Coniferous (softwood) . .	1,251	1,365	1,439
Broadleaved (hardwood) . .	132	134	135
Total	1,383	1,499	1,574

1996–97: Annual output as in 1995 (FAO estimates).

Source: FAO, *Yearbook of Forest Products*.

Fishing

('000 metric tons, live weight)

	1995	1996	1997
Freshwater and diadromous fishes	0.8	0.9	0.9
Cape hakes (Stokvisse) . . .	137.7	155.2	141.1
Cape horse mackerel (Maasbanker)	10.3	32.0	31.2
Southern African pilchard . .	115.2	105.2	117.0
Whitehead's round herring . .	76.9	47.1	92.2
Southern African anchovy . .	170.3	40.7	60.1
Snoek (Barracouta) . . .	15.3	12.4	11.1
Silver scabbardfish . . .	4.9	3.2	2.0
Chub mackerel	4.7	4.2	8.0
Other marine fishes (incl. unspecified)	27.6	25.3	40.1
Total fish	563.7	426.2	503.7
Crustaceans	3.0	1.8	1.9
Cape Hope squid . . .	7.0	7.5	3.7
Other molluscs	0.7	0.8	0.1
Total catch*	574.4	436.3	509.4

* Excluding aquatic plants ('000 metric tons): 6.3 in 1995; 6.2 in 1996; 6.4 in 1997. Also excluded are crocodiles. The number of Nile crocodiles captured was: 14,805 in 1995; 2,280 in 1996; 13,322 in 1997.

Source: FAO, *Yearbook of Fishery Statistics*.

Mining

('000 metric tons, unless otherwise indicated)

	1996	1997	1998
Hard coal	206,211	206,269	224,385
Crude petroleum ('000 barrels) .	n.a.	3,744	6,549
Natural gas	n.a.	1,485.5	1,486.1
Iron ore: gross weight . .	30,830	33,225	32,965
gmetal content*[1] .	19,115	20,600	20,400
Copper ore (metric tons)[2] . .	152,062	153,469	165,661
Nickel ore (metric tons)[3] . .	33,861	34,849	36,679
Lead concentrates (metric tons)[2]	88,613	83,114	84,128
Zinc ore (metric tons)[2] . .	76,853	71,062	69,630
Manganese ore: gross weight .	3,240	3,120	3,044
metal content*[1] .	1,380	1,320	1,300
Chromium ore: gross weight .	4,914.3	6,143.0	6,479.6
Vanadium ore (metric tons)[2] .	17,095	16,103	18,954
Zirconium concentrates (metric tons)*[1]	260,000	265,300	300,000
Antimony concentrates (metric tons)[1,2]	5,137	3,415	4,243
Cobalt ore (metric tons)[2] . .	247.2	317.8	296.4
Silver ore (kilograms)[2] . .	168,689	144,004	144,482
Uranium ore (metric tons)[2,4] .	1,436	1,100	962
Gold (kilograms)[2] . . .	498,250	490,101	464,216
Platinum-group metals (kilograms)[2,5] . . .	188,636	196,597	200,143
Kaolin	150.6	122.8	90.9
Magnesite—crude[1] . . .	71.4	76.7	74.3
Natural phosphates[1] . . .	2,655	2,732	2,739
Fluorspar—Fluorite[6] . . .	201.9	207.0	228.6
Salt—unrefined	289.9	326.8	356.1
Diamonds ('000 metric carats)[7] .	9,955	10,086	10,756
Gypsum—crude	340.7	396.9	485.7
Asbestos	56.9	50.0	27.2
Mica (metric tons) . . .	1,515	1,423	1,556
Talc (metric tons) . . .	16,397	21,055	20,296

* Provisional or estimated figures.
[1] Data from the US Geological Survey.
[2] Figures relate to the metal content of ores or concentrates.
[3] Nickel content of matte and refined nickel.
[4] Data from the Uranium Institute (London).
[5] Comprising platinum, palladium, rhodium, ruthenium, iridium and osmium. According to estimates by the US Geological Survey, the totals included (in kg): Platinum 105,400 in 1996, 115,861 in 1997, 116,483 in 1998; Palladium 52,600 in 1996, 55,675 in 1997, 56,608 in 1998.
[6] Acid, metallurgical and ceramic grade.
[7] According to the US Geological Survey, production in 1996 comprised 5.67 million carats of industrial diamonds and 4.28 million carats of gem diamonds.

Source (unless otherwise indicated): Department of Minerals and Energy, Pretoria.

1999 (provisional, '000 metric tons, unless otherwise indicated): Hard coal 220,323; Manganese ore (estimated metal content) 1,270; Zirconium concentrates 400; Antimony concentrates 6; Gold (metric tons) 449.5; Platinum-group metals (metric tons) 224.9 (Platinum 131.0, Palladium 63.6); Magnesite 75; Natural phosphates 2,900; Asbestos 20.1 (Sources: US Geological Survey; UN, *Monthly Bulletin of Statistics*; Chamber of Mines of South Africa).

Industry

SELECTED PRODUCTS
('000 metric tons, unless otherwise indicated)

	1997	1998	1999
Wheat flour	1,956	1,905	1,814
Sugar—refined	1,120	1,151	1,032
Wine ('000 hectolitres)[1]	247	218	n.a.
Cotton yarn—incl. mixed	84.4	74.1	76.1
Woven cotton fabrics (million sq metres)	275	223	224
Footwear ('000 pairs)	35,486	29,581	24,926
Mechanical wood pulp[2]	370	370	370
Chemical wood pulp[2]	914	1,360	1,360
Newsprint paper	957	1,230	1,249
Other printing and writing paper	773	n.a.	n.a.
Other paper and paperboard[2]	1,130	1,292	1,292
Synthetic rubber	62.3	62.9	63.0
Rubber tyres ('000)	9,232	9,853	10,654
Nitrogenous fertilizers	1,508	1,839	1,176
Phosphate fertilizers	643	557	632
Motor spirit—petrol (million litres)[3]	10,114	10,042	10,253
Kerosene (million litres)[3]	1,033	1,214	1,193
Jet fuel (million litres)[3]	2,300	2,156	2,587
Distillate fuel oils (million litres)[3]	6,971	6,550	7,174
Lubricating oils (million litres)[3]	312	310	283
Petroleum bitumen—asphalt*	278	242	229
Cement	7,891	7,676	8,197
Pig-iron[4]	6,192	6,000*	n.a.
Crude steel[4]	8,311	8,500*	n.a.
Refined copper—unwrought[4]	127*	123*	n.a.
Colour television receivers ('000)	280	273	226
Passenger motor cars—assembled ('000)	285.4	216.9	234.5
Lorries—assembled ('000)	132.3	117.1	113.0
Electric energy (million kWh)[5]	187,507	187,516	190,120

* Estimate(s).
[1] Natural and sparkling wines.
[2] Including data for Namibia.
[3] Excluding data for Transkei, Bophuthatswana, Venda and Ciskei.
[4] Source: US Geological Survey.
[5] Electricity available for distribution.

Sources: Central Statistical Service, Pretoria; National Productivity Institute, Pretoria; UN, *Monthly Bulletin of Statistics*; FAO, *Yearbook of Forest Products*.

Finance

CURRENCY AND EXCHANGE RATES

Monetary Units
100 cents = 1 rand (R).

Sterling, Dollar and Euro Equivalents (28 April 2000)
£1 sterling = 10.6921 rand;
US $1 = 6.8185 rand;
€1 = 6.1946 rand;
1,000 rand = £93.53 = $146.66 = €161.43.

Average Exchange Rate (rand per US $)
1997	4.60796
1998	5.52828
1999	6.10948

BUDGET (million rand, year ending 31 March)

Revenue	1997/98	1998/99*	1999/2000*
Income taxes:			
Gold mines	333	230	228
Other mines	1,349	1,500	1,450
Other companies	19,696	20,000	20,000
Individuals	68,342	76,400	86,200
Value-added tax	40,096	43,600	46,540
Customs duty	6,056	6,200	6,100
Excise duty	8,007	8,338	9,095
Fuel levy	12,091	13,600	15,162
Other revenue	12,757	16,553	18,725
Sub-total	168,728	186,421	203,500
Less Transfers to neighbouring countries	5,237	5,577	7,197
Total	163,491	180,845	196,302

Expenditure	1997/98	1998/99*	1999/2000*
Defence	11,079	10,348	10,742
Police, prisons and law courts	18,385	20,893	21,779
Education	44,794	45,369	47,841
Health	26,704	27,875	29,928
Other social services	24,304	23,844	24,865
Economic services	18,614	17,928	19,040
Interest on public debt	38,820	42,669	44,483
Other expenditure	21,857	22,125	24,887
Total	204,558	211,051	223,564

* Provisional.

Source: mainly Department of Finance, Pretoria.

INTERNATIONAL RESERVES (US $ million at 31 December)

	1997	1998	1999
Gold*	1,048	1,034	1,020
IMF special drawing rights	9	185	288
Foreign exchange	4,790	4,171	6,065
Total	5,847	5,390	7,373

* National valuation, based on market prices.

Source: IMF, *International Financial Statistics*.

MONEY SUPPLY (million rand at 31 December)

	1997	1998	1999
Currency outside banks	17,327	18,510	22,663
Demand deposits at deposit money banks	155,065	194,873	233,223
Total (incl. others)	173,335	213,532	256,075

Source: IMF, *International Financial Statistics*.

COST OF LIVING (Consumer Price Index; base: 1995 = 100)

	1997	1998	1999
Food	116.1	123.3	129.3
Housing	121.3	130.7	131.9
All items (incl. others)	116.6	124.6	131.1

NATIONAL ACCOUNTS (million rand at current prices)

National Income and Product

	1997	1998*	1999*
Compensation of employees . .	338,744	371,361	399,956
Operating surplus	189,822	198,813	213,101
Domestic factor incomes . .	528,566	570,174	613,057
Consumption of fixed capital .	87,155	94,686	103,517
Gross domestic product (GDP) at factor cost	615,721	664,860	716,574
Indirect taxes	76,084	84,218	91,895
Less Subsidies	8,138	8,498	7,354
GDP in purchasers' values .	683,666	740,581	801,115
Factor income received from abroad	6,013	7,256	8,627
Less Factor income paid abroad .	20,808	23,936	26,049
Gross national product . .	668,871	723,901	783,693
Less Consumption of fixed capital	87,155	94,686	103,517
National income in market prices	581,716	629,215	680,176
Current transfers received from abroad	641	334	404
Current transfers paid abroad .	−3,970	−4,412	−6,066
Statistical discrepancy . .	516	−2,406	−3,802
National disposable income	578,903	622,731	670,712

* Figures are provisional.

Expenditure on the Gross Domestic Product

	1997	1998	1999
Government final consumption expenditure	135,599	146,800	154,066
Private final consumption expenditure	431,072	464,760	501,334
Increase in stocks . . .	−1,464	−4,602	1,983
Gross fixed capital formation .	111,279	122,088	119,698
Statistical discrepancy . .	−516	2,406	3,802
Total domestic expenditure	675,970	731,452	780,883
Exports of goods and services . .	168,415	190,088	203,571
Less Imports of goods and services	160,719	180,959	183,339
GDP in purchasers' values .	683,666	740,581	801,115
GDP at constant 1995 prices .	585,263	588,935	596,180

Gross Domestic Product by Economic Activity

	1997	1998*	1999*
Agriculture, forestry and fishing .	25,280	25,648	26,634
Mining and quarrying . .	40,524	44,244	47,139
Manufacturing	124,604	128,561	132,640
Electricity, gas and water. .	20,386	22,479	23,785
Construction (contractors) .	19,386	20,681	20,918
Wholesale and retail trade, catering and accommodation .	85,858	89,266	95,211
Transport, storage and communication . . .	57,732	64,995	73,146
Finance, insurance, real estate and business services . .	109,601	124,295	140,632
Government services . . .	106,792	116,435	123,782
Other community, social and personal services . . .	17,374	19,394	22,108
Other producers (non-profit institutions and domestic servants)	17,803	19,880	22,060
GDP at basic prices . .	625,340	675,878	728,055
Taxes on products . . .	63,713	70,656	77,502
Less Subsidies on products .	5,389	5,953	4,442
GDP in purchasers' values .	683,666	740,581	801,115

* Figures are provisional.

BALANCE OF PAYMENTS (US $ million)

	1997*	1998	1999
Exports of goods f.o.b. . . .	31,171	29,234	28,361
Imports of goods f.o.b. . . .	−28,848	−27,216	−24,611
Trade balance	2,324	2,018	3,751
Exports of services . . .	5,334	5,292	4,959
Imports of services . . .	−6,003	−5,471	−5,395
Balance on goods and services	1,655	1,839	3,314
Other income received . .	1,298	1,319	1,412
Other income paid . . .	−4,502	−4,348	−4,264
Balance on goods, services and income	−1,549	−1,190	462
Current transfers received . .	138	60	66
Current transfers paid . . .	−862	−806	−993
Current balance . . .	−2,273	−1,936	−464
Capital account (net) . . .	−192	−56	−43
Direct investment abroad . .	−2,324	−1,590	−1,118
Direct investment from abroad .	3,811	550	1,376
Portfolio investment assets . .	−4,587	−5,575	−5,128
Portfolio investment liabilities .	11,327	9,967	13,482
Other investment assets . .	−1,983	−694	−1,343
Other investment liabilities .	1,887	2,237	−3,171
Net errors and omissions . .	−1,070	−1,984	364
Overall balance	4,596	920	3,955

* Including Botswana, Lesotho, Namibia and Swaziland.

Source: IMF, *International Financial Statistics.*

External Trade

Figures refer to the Southern African Customs Union, comprising South Africa, Namibia, Botswana, Lesotho and Swaziland. Trade between the component territories is excluded.

PRINCIPAL COMMODITIES (distribution by SITC, US $ million)

Imports f.o.b.	1994	1995	1996
Food and live animals . . .	868.9	1,232.6	1,245.6
Crude materials (inedible) except fuels . . .	695.7	996.3	950.7
Mineral fuels, etc. . . .	79.0	2,238.3	2,572.8
Petroleum and products . .	48.6	2,194.2	2,484.6
Chemicals and related products	2,632.7	3,250.1	3,178.0
Organic chemicals . . .	700.1	892.1	783.7
Plastic materials, etc. . .	489.0	670.6	581.5
Basic manufactures . . .	3,078.8	3,696.9	3,493.2
Textile yarn, fabrics, etc. . .	651.9	736.7	675.5
Non-metallic mineral manufactures . . .	705.3	652.3	691.2
Machinery and transport equipment	10,202.5	11,989.6	10,209.9
Power-generating machinery and equipment. . . .	485.8	592.0	562.8
Machinery specialized for particular industries . .	1,401.2	1,746.0	1,945.2
General industrial machinery, equipment and parts . .	1,439.1	1,861.3	1,896.7
Office machines and automatic data-processing equipment .	1,162.4	1,332.3	1,333.0
Telecommunications and sound equipment. . . .	863.9	1,037.9	1,158.8
Other electrical machinery, apparatus, etc.. . .	1,396.7	1,617.2	1,491.7
Road vehicles and parts* . .	2,658.6	2,992.5	1,196.1
Passenger motor vehicles (excl. buses)	927.0	1,064.0	482.6
Lorries and specialized motor vehicles	564.0	677.8	111.4
Parts and accessories for cars, buses, lorries, etc.* . .	1,002.7	985.7	428.5
Miscellaneous manufactured articles . . .	1,867.1	2,187.8	2,559.6
Professional, scientific and controlling instruments and apparatus	558.0	633.0	669.8
Total (incl. others)	21,109.6	26,744.6	26,872.5

* Data on parts exclude tyres, engines and electrical parts.

	1994	1995	1996
mals . . .	1,909.0	1,795.6	2,137.9
t . . .	800.3	899.8	868.1
esh or dried	545.4	581.6	483.6
Crude materials (inedible) except fuels . . .	1,995.4	2,803.8	2,524.1
Pulp and waste paper	371.0	613.6	346.9
Crude fertilizers and minerals	222.2	255.9	207.8
Metalliferous ores and metal scrap	927.4	1,382.2	1,407.4
Ores and concentrates of base metals	557.1	810.7	832.7
Mineral fuels, lubricants, etc.	1,368.0	2,508.5	2,549.8
Coal, coke and briquettes .	1,296.1	1,610.7	1,525.8
Coal, lignite and peat . .	1,289.9	1,606.6	1,525.6
Chemicals and related products	1,623.6	1,963.9	2,123.8
Inorganic chemicals . . .	706.0	826.6	838.8
Inorganic chemical elements, oxides, etc.	379.2	591.3	581.3
Oxides of zinc, iron, lead, etc.	206.2	351.8	361.8
Basic manufactures . .	6,586.7	7,403.9	8,093.8
Paper, paperboard and manufactures . . .	348.3	450.8	458.0
Non-metallic mineral manufactures . . .	2,844.7	2,500.1	3,044.5
Pearls, precious and semi-precious stones, unworked or worked	2,692.9	2,326.7	2,862.2
Diamonds (except sorted industrial diamonds) .	2,687.4	2,319.9	2,854.1
Iron and steel . . .	2,133.0	2,791.8	2,429.9
Pig-iron, etc. . . .	806.5	1,232.8	1,056.4
Ferro-alloys . . .	750.2	1,141.2	963.2
Ingots and other primary forms	502.1	499.4	517.6
Universals, plates and sheets	463.3	574.1	419.6
Non-ferrous metals . .	470.4	620.0	1,053.8
Machinery and transport equipment . . .	1,865.4	2,476.5	2,633.1
General industrial machinery, equipment and parts . .	317.8	474.6	534.0
Road vehicles and parts* . .	634.8	921.2	826.3
Miscellaneous manufactured articles . . .	684.9	945.3	1,017.3
Non-monetary gold (excl. ores and concentrates) . .	13.8	187.2	242.4
Total (incl. others) . . .	25,621.6	28,226.3	23,468.9

* Excluding tyres, engines and electrical parts.

Source: UN, *International Trade Statistics Yearbook*.

PRINCIPAL TRADING PARTNERS (US $ million)*

Imports f.o.b.	1994	1995	1996
Australia	297.3	450.1	668.3
Belgium-Luxembourg . . .	508.2	609.1	544.8
Canada	299.8	278.3	226.5
China, People's Repub. . .	360.5	509.1	577.2
France	779.0	1,044.4	918.0
Germany	3,626.8	4,411.5	4,041.8
Hong Kong	410.6	447.9	435.0
Iran	13.8	1,206.9	1,229.4
Italy	837.7	1,094.8	1,184.2
Japan	2,217.8	2,719.0	2,098.4
Korea, Repub. . . .	303.4	411.3	542.2
Kuwait	0.2	165.0	383.3
Netherlands	530.4	628.0	681.6
Singapore	275.9	322.8	327.7
Sweden	232.2	408.9	448.9
Switzerland	520.2	648.4	685.6
United Kingdom	2,455.3	2,934.7	3,094.6
USA	2,390.4	3,158.0	3,479.0
Zimbabwe	281.6	268.8	277.8
Total (incl. others) . . .	21,109.6	26,744.6	26,872.4

Exports f.o.b.	1994	1995	1996
Angola	87.1	123.1	353.2
Australia	186.5	289.0	384.5
Belgium-Luxembourg . . .	727.3	899.7	840.0
China, People's Repub. . .	163.0	289.5	187.8
France	281.8	358.7	428.2
Germany	987.7	1,402.1	1,307.5
Hong Kong	418.5	566.7	611.0
Israel	303.4	387.1	394.1
Italy	494.4	669.4	625.4
Japan	1,169.5	1,799.7	2,022.4
Korea, Repub. . . .	489.2	577.9	667.9
Mozambique	388.4	617.6	565.2
Netherlands	591.3	855.6	785.5
Singapore	128.9	315.4	391.6
Spain	339.6	466.6	634.9
Switzerland	1,703.8	1,153.4	805.4
United Kingdom	1,654.0	2,347.8	3,107.0
USA	1,238.1	2,145.0	2,256.7
Zambia	317.8	377.5	417.2
Zimbabwe	678.0	1,254.3	1,248.0
Total (incl. others) . . .	25,621.5	28,226.3	23,468.8

* Imports by country of production; exports by country of last consignment.

Source: UN, *International Trade Statistics Yearbook*.

Transport

RAILWAYS (traffic, year ending 31 March)*

	1990/91	1991/92	1992/93
Passenger-km (million) . . .	103,781	89,466	71,573
Freight ton-km (million) . . .	85,524	88,586	89,716

* Including Namibia.

Source: UN, *Statistical Yearbook*.

Freight ton-km (million): 89,706 in 1993/94; 96,597 in 1994/95; 96,565 in 1995/96; 96,421 in 1996/97; 100,342 in 1997/98; 99,199 in 1998/99; 96,618 in 1999/2000.

ROAD TRAFFIC (registered motor vehicles)

	1999
Heavy load vehicles	61,478
Heavy passenger motor vehicles	47,989
Light load vehicles	302,920
Light passenger motor vehicles	1,001,097
Motor cycles	31,506
Special vehicles	32,195
Total (incl. others)	1,479,826

SHIPPING

Merchant Fleet (vessels registered at 31 December)

	1996	1997	1998
Number of vessels . . .	182	189	192
Displacement ('000 grt) . . .	371.4	382.6	383.7

Source: Lloyd's Register of Shipping, *World Fleet Statistics*.

International Sea-borne Freight Traffic (metric tons)*

	1998	1999
Goods loaded	125,692,659	125,601,802
Goods unloaded	23,489,480	21,341,965

* Excl. petroleum products.

Source: PORTNET, Johannesburg.

CIVIL AVIATION (traffic on scheduled services)

	1994	1995	1996
Kilometres flown (million) . .	96	98	121
Passengers carried ('000) . . .	5,802	6,396	7,183
Passenger-km (million) . . .	12,352	14,496	15,957
Total ton-km (million) . . .	1,374	1,551	1,747

Source: UN, *Statistical Yearbook.*

Tourism

FOREIGN TOURIST ARRIVALS
(number of visitors by region of origin)

	1996	1997	1998
Africa	3,606,757	3,284,138	3,676,810
Europe	771,166	782,093	875,851
Asia.	157,969	149,439	163,904
Americas	169,579	188,980	208,500
Oceania	73,680	57,696	64,200
Total (incl. others and unspecified)	4,944,430	4,638,934	5,170,096

Communications Media

	1995	1996	1997
Radio receivers ('000 in use) . .	13,100	13,400	13,750
Television receivers ('000 in use)	4,500	5,000	5,200
Telephones ('000 main lines in use)	3,926	4,259	n.a.
Telefax stations (number in use)*	100,000	100,000	n.a.
Mobile cellular telephones (subscribers)	535,000	953,000	n.a.
Daily newspapers			
Number	17	17	17
Average circulation ('000)* . .	1,201	1,288	1,185*
Book production (titles) . . .	5,418	n.a.	n.a.

* Estimates.

Sources: Central Statistical Service, Pretoria; UNESCO, *Statistical Yearbook*; UN, *Statistical Yearbook.*

Education

(1999)*

	Institutions	Teachers	Students
Pre-primary	1,150	4,112	97,159
Primary.	14,897	159,432	5,578,978
Secondary	4,197	94,219	3,037,390
Combined	3,903	52,824	1,820,823
Intermediate and middle . .	393	5,262	150,719
ABET centres†	1,328	8,816	188,191
ISEN centres‡	339	5,444	68,099
Colleges of education . . .	66	2,723	22,408
Technical colleges . . .	139	4,963	126,487
Universities	21	n.a.	330,100
Technikons	15	n.a.	190,120

* Figures for public and independent institutions.

† Adult basic education and training.

‡ Education for learners with special needs.

Directory

The Constitution

Following multi-party negotiations (see Recent History), the interim Constitution of the Republic of South Africa was ratified on 22 December 1993, and officially came into effect on 27 April 1994; it was to remain in force pending the adoption of a new constitution. The new Constitution was adopted by the Constitutional Assembly (comprising the National Assembly and the Senate) on 8 May 1996, and entered into force on 4 February 1997. The main provisions of the new Constitution are summarized below:

FOUNDING PROVISIONS

The Republic of South Africa is one sovereign democratic state founded on the following values: human dignity, the achievement of equality and advancement of human rights and freedoms; non-racialism and non-sexism; supremacy of the Constitution and the rule of law; universal adult suffrage, a national common voters' roll, regular elections, and a multi-party system of democratic government, to ensure accountability, responsiveness and openness. There is common South African citizenship, all citizens being equally entitled to the rights, privileges and benefits, and equally subject to the duties and responsibilities of citizenship.

BILL OF RIGHTS

Everyone is equal before the law and has the right to equal protection and benefit of the law. The state may not unfairly discriminate directly or indirectly against anyone on one or more grounds, including race, gender, sex, pregnancy, marital status, ethnic or social origin, colour, sexual orientation, age, disability, religion, conscience, belief, culture, language and birth. The rights that are enshrined include: protection against detention without trial, torture or any inhuman form of treatment or punishment; the right to privacy; freedom of conscience; freedom of expression; freedom of assembly; political freedom; freedom of movement and residence; the right to join or form a trade union or employers' organization; the right to a healthy and sustainable environment; the right to property, except in the case of the Government's programme of land reform and redistribution, and taking into account the claims of people who were dispossessed of property after 19 June 1913; the right to adequate housing; the right to health care, food and water and social security assistance, if needed; the rights of children; the right to education in the official language of one's choice, where this is reasonably practicable; the right to use the language and to participate in the cultural life of one's choice, but not in a manner inconsistent with any provision of this Bill of Rights; access to state information; access to the courts; the rights of people who have been arrested or detained; and the right to a fair trial.

CO-OPERATIVE GOVERNMENT

Government is constituted as national, provincial and local spheres of government, which are distinctive, interdependent and inter-related. All spheres of government and all organs of state within each sphere must preserve the peace, national unity and indivisibility of the Republic; secure the well-being of the people of the Republic; implement effective, transparent, accountable and coherent government for the Republic as a whole; respect the constitutional status, institutions, powers and functions of government in the other spheres; not assume any power or function except those conferred on them in terms of the Constitution.

PARLIAMENT

Legislative power is vested in a bicameral Parliament, comprising a National Assembly and a National Council of Provinces. The

National Assembly has between 350 and 400 members and is elected, in general, by proportional representation. National and provincial legislatures are elected separately, under a 'double-ballot' electoral system. Each provincial legislature appoints six permanent delegates and nominates four special delegates to the 90-member National Council of Provinces, which is headed by a Chairperson, who is elected by the Council and has a five-year term of office. Parliamentary decisions are generally reached by a simple majority, although constitutional amendments require a majority of two-thirds.

THE NATIONAL EXECUTIVE

The Head of State is the President, who is elected by the National Assembly from among its members, and exercises executive power in consultation with the other members of the Cabinet. No person may hold office as President for more than two terms. Any party that holds a minimum of 80 seats in the National Assembly (equivalent to 20% of the national vote) is entitled to nominate an Executive Deputy President. If no party, or only one party, secures 80 or more seats, the party holding the largest number of seats and the party holding the second largest number of seats in the National Assembly are each entitled to designate one Executive Deputy President from among the members of the Assembly. The President may be removed by a motion of no-confidence or by impeachment. The Cabinet comprises a maximum of 27 ministers. Each party with a minimum of 20 seats in the National Assembly (equivalent to 5% of the national vote) is entitled to a proportional number of ministerial portfolios. The President allocates cabinet portfolios in consultation with party leaders, who are entitled to request the replacement of ministers. Cabinet decisions are reached by consensus.

JUDICIAL AUTHORITY

The judicial authority of the Republic is vested in the courts, which comprise the Constitutional Court; the Supreme Court of Appeal; the High Courts; the Magistrates' Courts; and any other court established or recognized by an Act of Parliament. (See Judicial System.)

PROVINCIAL GOVERNMENT

There are nine provinces: Eastern Cape, Free State (formerly Orange Free State), Gauteng (formerly Pretoria-Witwatersrand-Vereeniging), KwaZulu/Natal, Mpumalanga (formerly Eastern Transvaal), Northern Cape, Northern Province (formerly Northern Transvaal), North-West and Western Cape. Each province is entitled to determine its legislative and executive structure. Each province has a legislature, comprising between 30 and 80 members (depending on the size of the local electorate), who are elected by proportional representation. Each legislature is entitled to draft a constitution for the province, subject to the principles governing the national Constitution, and elects a Premier, who heads a Cabinet. Parties that hold a minimum of 10% of seats in the legislature are entitled to a proportional number of portfolios in the Cabinet. Provincial legislatures are allowed primary responsibility for a number of areas of government, and joint powers with central government in the principal administrative areas.

LOCAL GOVERNMENT

The local sphere of government consists of municipalities, with executive and legislative authority vested in the Municipal Council. The objectives of local government are to provide democratic and accountable government for local communities; to ensure the provision of services to communities; to promote social and economic development, and a safe and healthy environment; and to encourage the involvement of communities and community organizations in the matters of local government. The National Assembly is to determine the different categories of municipality that may be established, and appropriate fiscal powers and functions for each category. Provincial Governments have the task of establishing municipalities, and of providing for the monitoring and support of local government in each province.

STATE INSTITUTIONS SUPPORTING CONSTITUTIONAL DEMOCRACY

The following state institutions are designed to strengthen constitutional democracy: the Public Protector (whose task is to investigate any conduct in state affairs, or in the public administration in any sphere of government, that is alleged or suspected to be improper); the Human Rights Commission; the Commission for the Protection and Promotion of the Rights of Cultural, Religious and Linguistic Communities; the Commission for Gender Equality; the Auditor-General; and the Electoral Commission.

TRADITIONAL LEADERS

The institution, status and role of traditional leadership, according to customary law, are recognized, subject to the Constitution. A traditional authority that observes a system of customary law may function subject to any applicable legislation and customs. National and provincial legislation may provide for the establishment of local or provincial houses of traditional leaders; the National Assembly may establish a national council of traditional leaders.

The Government

HEAD OF STATE

President: THABO MBEKI (inaugurated 16 June 1999).
Deputy President: JACOB ZUMA.

CABINET
(August 2000)

The Government comprises representatives of the African National Congress of South Africa (ANC) and the Inkatha Freedom Party (IFP).

Minister of Agriculture and Land Affairs: THOKO DIDIZA (ANC).

Minister of Arts, Culture, Science and Technology: BEN NGUBANE (IFP).

Minister of Communications: IVY MATSEPE-CASABURRI (ANC).

Minister of Correctional Services: BEN SKOSANA (IFP).

Minister of Defence: PATRICK LEKOTA (ANC).

Minister of Education: KADER ASMAL (ANC).

Minister of Environmental Affairs and Tourism: MOHAMMED VALLI MOOSA(ANC).

Minister of Finance: TREVOR MANUEL (ANC).

Minister of Foreign Affairs: NKOSAZANA DLAMINI-ZUMA (ANC).

Minister of Health: MANTO TSHABALALA-MSIMANG (ANC).

Minister of Home Affairs: MANGOSUTHU BUTHELEZI (IFP).

Minister of Housing: SANKIE MTHEMBI-MAHANYELE (ANC).

Minister of Intelligence: PENUEL MADUNA (acting, ANC).

Minister of Justice and Constitutional Development: PENUEL MADUNA (ANC).

Minister of Labour: MEMBATHISI MDLADLANA (ANC).

Minister of Minerals and Energy: PHUMZILE MLAMBO-NGCUKA (ANC).

Minister of Provincial and Local Government: SYDNEY MUFAMADI (ANC).

Minister of Public Enterprises: JEFF RADEBE (ANC).

Minister of Public Service and Administration: GERALDINE FRASER-MOLEKETI (ANC).

Minister of Public Works: STELLA SIGCAU (ANC).

Minister of Safety and Security: STEVE TSHWETE (ANC).

Minister of Social Development: ZOLA SKWEYIYA (ANC).

Minister of Sport and Recreation: NGCONDE BALFOUR (ANC).

Minister of Trade and Industry: ALEC ERWIN (ANC).

Minister of Transport: DULLAH OMAR (ANC).

Minister of Water Affairs and Forestry: RONNIE KASRILS (ANC).

Minister at the Presidency: ESSOP PAHAD (ANC).

MINISTRIES

The Presidency: Union Bldgs, West Wing, Government Ave, Pretoria 0001; Private Bag X1000, Pretoria 0001; tel. (12) 3191500; fax (12) 3238246; e-mail president@po.gov.za; internet www.gov.za/president/index.html.

Ministry of Agriculture and Land Affairs: 184 Jacob Mare Bldg, cnr Jacob Mare and Paul Kruger Sts, Pretoria 0002; Private Bag X844, Pretoria 0001; tel. (12) 3235212; fax (12) 3211244; sanitaG@nda.agric.za; internet www.nda.agric.za.

Ministry of Arts, Culture, Science and Technology: Oranje Nassau Bldg, 188 Schoeman St, Pretoria 0002; Private Bag X727, Pretoria 0001; tel. (12) 3378378; fax (12) 3242687; e-mail frans@dacsts.pwv.gov.za; internet www.dacst.gov.za.

Ministry of Communications: Nkululeko House, Iparioli Office Park, 339 Duncan St, 0083 Hatfield, Pretoria; tel. (12) 4278111; fax (12) 3626915; e-mail nowjoan@doc.org.za; internet www.doc.gov.za/index.html.

Ministry of Correctional Services: Poyntons Bldg, West Block, cnr Church and Schubart Sts, Pretoria 0002; Private Bag X853, Pretoria 0001; tel. (12) 3238198; fax (12) 3234111; internet www.dcs.pwv.gov.za.

Ministry of Defence: Armscor Bldg, Block 5, Nossob St, Erasmusrand 0181; Private Bag X427, Pretoria 0001; tel. (12) 3556119; fax (12) 3470118; e-mail webmaster@mil.za; internet www.mil.za

Ministry of Education: 123 Schoeman St, Magister Bldg, Pretoria 0002; Private Bag X603, Pretoria 0001; tel. (12) 3260126; fax (12) 3235989; e-mail webmaster@educ.pwv.gov.za; internet www .education.pwv.gov.za.

Ministry of Environmental Affairs and Tourism: Fedsure Forum Bldg, North Tower, cnr Van der Walt and Pretorius Sts, Private Bag X447, Pretoria 0001; tel. (12) 3103611; fax (12) 3220082; e-mail vmoosa@ozone.pwv.gov.za; internet www.environment .gov.za.

Ministry of Finance: 240 Vermeulen St, Pretoria 0002; Private Bag X115, Pretoria 0001; tel. (12) 3238911; fax (12) 3233262; e-mail info@finance.pwv.gov.za.; internet www.finance.gov.za.

Ministry of Foreign Affairs: Union Bldgs, East Wing, Government Ave, Pretoria 0002; Private Bag X152, Pretoria 0001; tel. (12) 3510005; fax (12) 3510253.

Ministry of Health: 2027 Civitas Bldg, cnr Andries and Struben Sts, Pretoria 0002; Private Bag X399, Pretoria 0001; tel. (12) 3284773; fax (12) 3255526; e-mail mnwbd@hltrsa2.pwv.gov.za; internet www.health.gov.za.

Ministry of Home Affairs: 1005 Civitas Bldg, cnr Andries and Struben Sts, Pretoria 0002; Private Bag X741, Pretoria 0001; tel. (12) 3268081; fax (12) 3216491.

Ministry of Housing: 240 Walker St, Sunnyside, Pretoria 0002; Private Bag X644, Pretoria 0001; tel. (12) 4211311; fax (12) 3418513.

Ministry of Intelligence: Embassy House, Third Floor, cnr Edmund St and Bailey Crescent, Arcadia, Pretoria 0083; POB 56450, Arcadia 0007; tel. (12) 3236738; fax (12) 3230718.

Ministry of Justice and Constitutional Development: Presidia Bldg, 8th Floor, cnr Pretorius and Paul Kruger Sts, Pretoria 0002; Private Bag X276, Pretoria 0001; tel. (12) 3238581; fax (12) 3111708.

Ministry of Labour: Laboria Bldg, Schoeman and Paul Kruger Sts, Pretoria 0002; Private Bag X499, Pretoria 0001; tel. (12) 3226532; fax (12) 3201942; internet www.labour.gov.za.

Ministry of Minerals and Energy: DRC Synod Centre, cnr Andries and Visagie Sts, Pretoria 0002; Private Bag X646, Pretoria 0001; tel. (12) 3228695; fax (12) 3228699; e-mail gavin@ mepar.wcape.gov.za; internet www.dme.gov.za.

Ministry of Provincial Affairs and Local Government: 87 Hamilton St, Arcadia, Pretoria 0083; Private Bag X802, Pretoria 0001; tel. (12) 3340600; fax (12) 3340604; e-mail editor@dso .pwv.gov.za; internet www.local.gov.za.

Ministry of Public Enterprises: Infotech Bldg 401, 1090 Arcadia St, Hatfield, Pretoria 0083, Private Bag X15, Hatfield 0028; tel. (12) 3427111; fax (12) 3427226; internet www.dpe.gov.za.

Ministry of Public Service and Administration: Transvaal House, cnr Vermeulen and van der Walts Sts, Pretoria 0002; Private Bag X884, Pretoria 0001; tel. (12) 3147911; fax (12) 3286565; e-mail info@dpsa.pwv.gov.za; internet www.gcis.gov.za.

Ministry of Public Works: Central Government Bldg, cnr Bosman and Vermeulen Sts, Pretoria 0002; Private Bag X890, Pretoria 0001; tel. (12) 3241510; fax (12) 3256380; e-mail imochaliban @pwdmail.pwv.gov.za; internet www.publicworks.gov.za.

Ministry of Safety and Security: Wachthuis, 7th Floor, 231 Pretorius St, Pretoria 0002; Private Bag X463, Pretoria 0001; tel. (12) 3392800; fax (12) 3392819; internet www.gcis.gov.za.

Ministry of Social Development: Hallmark Bldg, Vermeulen St, Pretoria 0002; Private Bag X885, Pretoria 0001; tel. (12) 3284600; fax (12) 3257071; e-mail welso57@welspta.pwv.gov.sa; internet www.welfare.gov.za.

Ministry of Sport and Recreation: Oranje Nassau Bldg, 3rd Floor, 188 Schoeman St, Pretoria; Private Bag X869, Pretoria 0001; tel. (12) 3211781; fax (12) 3218493; e-mail zonika@sport1 .pwv.gov.za; internet www.dsr.gov.za.

Ministry of Trade and Industry: House of Trade and Industry, 11th Floor, Prinsloo St, Pretoria 0002; Private Bag X274, Pretoria 0001; tel. (12) 3227677; fax (12) 3227851; e-mail alec@dti.pwv.gov.za; internet www.dti.pwv.gov.za.

Ministry of Transport: Forum Bldg, cnr Struben and Bosman Sts, Pretoria 0002; Private Bag X193, Pretoria 0001; tel. (12) 3093131; fax (12) 3283194; e-mail mabasam@ndot.pwv.gov.za; internet www.transport.gov.za.

Ministry of Water Affairs and Forestry: Residensie Bldg, 185 Schoeman St, Pretoria 0002; Private Bag X313, Pretoria 0001; tel. (12) 3387500; fax (12) 3284254; e-mail zan@dwaf-par.wcape.gov.za; internet www.dwaf.pwv.gov.za.

Legislature

PARLIAMENT

National Council of Provinces

Chairman: PATRICK LEKOTA.

The National Council of Provinces (NCOP), which replaced the Senate under the new Constitution, was inaugurated on 6 February 1997. The NCOP comprises 90 members, with six permanent delegates and four special delegates from each of the nine provinces.

National Assembly

Speaker: Dr FRENE NOSHIR GINWALA.

General Election, 2 June 1999

Party	Votes	% of votes	Seats
African National Congress	10,600,838	66.36	266
Democratic Party	1,526,244	9.55	38
Inkatha Freedom Party	1,371,436	8.58	34
New National Party	1,097,998	6.87	28
United Democratic Movement	546,705	3.42	14
African Christian Democratic Party	228,908	1.43	6
Freedom Front	127,188	0.80	3
United Christian Democratic Party	125,273	0.78	3
Pan-Africanist Congress of Azania	113,114	0.71	3
Federal Alliance	86,672	0.54	2
Minority Front	48,276	0.30	1
Afrikaner Eenheidsbeweging	46,286	0.29	1
Azanian People's Organization	27,255	0.17	1
Abolition of Income Tax and Usury Party	10,611	0.07	—
Government by the People Green Party	9,188	0.06	—
Socialist Party of Azania	9,060	0.06	—
Total	15,975,052	100.00	400

Provincial Governments

(August 2000)

EASTERN CAPE

Premier: Rev. MAKENKHESI STOFILE (ANC).
Speaker of the Legislature: MKHANGELI MATOMELA (ANC).

FREE STATE

Premier: ISABELLA WINKIE DIREKO (ANC).
Speaker of the Legislature: J. MAFEREKA (ANC).

GAUTENG

Premier: MBHAZIMA SHILOWA (ANC).
Speaker of the Legislature: FIROZ CACHALIA (ANC).

KWAZULU/NATAL

Premier: LIONEL MTSHALI (IFP).
Speaker of the Legislature: Chief BONGA MDLETSHE (IFP).

MPUMALANGA

Premier: NDAWENI MAHLANGU (ANC).
Speaker of the Legislature: S. W. LUBISI (ANC).

NORTHERN CAPE

Premier: MANNE DIPICO (ANC).
Speaker of the Legislature: ETHNE PAPENFUS (DP).

NORTHERN PROVINCE

Premier: NGOAKO RAMATHLODI (ANC).
Speaker of the Legislature: ROBERT MALAVI (ANC).

NORTH-WEST

Premier: POPO MOLEFE (ANC).
Speaker of the Legislature: JOHANNES SELAPEDI (ANC).

WESTERN CAPE

Premier: GERALD MORKEL (NNP).
Speaker of the Legislature: WILLEM DOMAN (NNP).

Political Organizations

African Christian Democratic Party (ACDP): POB 3578, Cape Town 8000; tel. (21) 246591; fax (21) 241307; e-mail webmaster@ acdp.org.za; internet www.acdp.org.za; f. 1993; Leader Rev. KENNETH MESHOE.

African National Congress of South Africa (ANC): 51 Plein St, Johannesburg 2001; POB 61884, Marshalltown 2107; tel. (11) 3307000; fax (11) 3360302; e-mail info@anc.org.za; internet www .anc.org.za; f. 1912; in alliance with the South African Communist Party (SACP) and the Congress of South African Trade Unions (COSATU); governing party since April 1994; Pres. THABO MBEKI; Deputy Pres. JACOB ZUMA; Sec.-Gen. KGALEMA MOTLANTHE.

Afrikaner Eenheidsbeweging (AEB) (Unity Movement): Pretoria; right-wing movement.

Afrikaner Weerstandsbeweging (AWB) (Afrikaner Resistance Movement): POB 274, Ventersdorp 2710; tel. (18) 2642005; fax (18) 2642032; f. 1973; extreme right-wing paramilitary group; Leader EUGENE TERRE'BLANCHE; Sec.-Gen. PIET 'SKIET' RUDOLPH.

Azanian People's Organization (AZAPO): Kopanong Centre 3, cnr Luthuli and Main Rds, Dobsonville; POB 4230, Johannesburg 2000; tel. (11) 9881255; fax (11) 9883925; f. 1978 to seek the establishment of a unitary, democratic, socialist republic; excludes white mems; Pres. MOSIBUDI MANGENA; Nat. Chair. NKOSI MOLALA; Sec.-Gen. JAIRUS KGOKONG.

Blanke Bevrydingsbeweging (BBB) (White Protection Movement): f. 1987; extreme right-wing activist group; Leader Prof. JOHAN SCHABORT.

Boerestaat Party (Boer State Party): POB 3456, Randburg 2125; tel. and fax (11) 7081988; f. 1988; seeks the reinstatement of the Boer Republics in a consolidated Boerestaat; Leader (vacant).

Cape Democrats: f. 1988; white support; liberal.

Conservative Party of South Africa (CPSA): 203 Soutpansberg Rd, Rietondale, Pretoria; Private Bag X847, Pretoria 0001; tel. (12) 3291220; fax (12) 3291229; e-mail kp@kp.co.za; internet www.kp.co.za; f. 1982 by fmr mems of the National Party; seeks the establishment of a separate Afrikaner state as part of a South African confed.; Leader Dr FERDINAND HARTZENBERG; Dep. Leader Dr WILLIE SNYMAN.

Democratic Alliance (DA): f. 2000 by opposition parties, including the Democratic Party and the New National Party, to contest that year's municipal elections; Leader ANTHONY (TONY) LEON; Dep. Leader MARTHINUS VAN SCHALKWYK; Chair. JOE SEREMANE.

Democratic Party (DP): 123 Louis Botha Ave, Fellside, Johannesburg; POB 46400, Orange Grove 2119; tel. (11) 4832743; fax (21) 4615276; e-mail democrat@dp.org.za; internet www.dp.org.za; f. 1989 by merger; supports the implementation of a democratic, multiracial society by peaceful means; Leader ANTHONY (TONY) LEON; Exec. Dir GREG KRUMBOCK.

Democratic Reform Party (DRP): f. 1988; Coloured support; Leader CARTER EBRAHIM.

Democratic Workers' Party (DWP): Cape Town; f. 1984 by breakaway faction of the People's Congress Party; mainly Coloured support; Leader DENNIS DE LA CRUZ.

Federal Alliance: POB 767, Saxonwold 2132, Pretoria; tel. (11) 4029551; fax (11) 4027282; e-mail media@federalalliance.org.za; internet www.federalalliance.org.za; f. Sept. 1998 by fmr Pres. of the South African Rugby Football Union; Pres. LOUIS LYUT.

Federal Independent Democratic Alliance (FIDA): POB 10528, Johannesburg 2000; tel. (11) 4034268; fax (11) 4031557; f. 1987; black support; centrist; Leader JOHN GOGOTYA.

Freedom Front (FF/VF): Constantia Park Centre, cnr Gen. Louis Botha Ave and Douglas Scholtzst, Constantia Park, POB 74693, Lynnwood Ridge 0040; tel. (12) 9330230; fax (12) 9930242; e-mail vryheidsfront@vryheidsfront.co.za; internet www.vryheidsfront .co.za; f. 1994 as a right-wing electoral alliance; included some mems of the CPSA; Leader Gen. (retd) CONSTAND VILJOEN; Chief Sec. PIET UYS.

Freedom Party: Coloured support; Leader ARTHUR BOOYSEN.

Herstigte Nasionale Party (HNP) (Reconstituted National Party): 1043 Pretorius St, Hatfield, POB 1888, Pretoria 0001; tel. (12) 3423410; fax (12) 3423417; e-mail info@hnp.org.za; internet www.hnp.org.za; f. 1969 by fmr mems of the National Party; advocates 'Christian Nationalism'; Chair. WILLEM MARAIS; Gen. Sec. L. J. VAN DER SCHYFF.

Inkatha Freedom Party (IFP): Albany House North, 4th Floor, Albany Grove, POB 4432, Durban 4000; tel. (31) 3074962; fax (31) 3074964; internet www.ifp.org.za; f. as Inkatha Movement, a liberation movement with mainly Zulu support; reorg. in 1990 as a multiracial political party; represented in Govt; Leader Chief MANGOSUTHU GATSHA BUTHELEZI; Nat. Chair. BEN NGUBANE (acting); Sec.-Gen. ZAKHELE KHUMALO.

Justice and Freedom Alliance (JAFA): Johannesburg; f. Sept. 1997; CEO BARRY NILSSON.

Minority Front: Durban; Indian support; formed political alliance with ANC in June 1999; Leader AMICHAND RAJBANSI.

National People's Party: Private Bag X54330, Durban 4000; Indian support; Leader AMICHAND RAJBANSI.

New Freedom Party of Southern Africa: 15 Eendrag St, Bellville 7530; Coloured support.

New National Party (NNP): POB 1698, Cape Town 8000; tel. (21) 4615833; fax (21) 4615329; e-mail info@natweb.co.za; internet www.natweb.co.za; f. 1912 as National Party; ruling party 1948–94; opened membership to all racial groups in 1990; represented in interim Govt of Nat. Unity, following 1994 elections, withdrew in June 1996 to form the official opposition; adopted present name in 1999; Leader MARTHINUS VAN SCHALKWYK; Exec. Dir RENIER SCHOEMAN.

New Solidarity: POB 48687, Qualbert 4078; tel. (11) 3055692; fax 3011077; f. 1989; Indian support; Leader Dr J. N. REDDY.

Die Orangjewerkers: seeks to establish several small, self-governing white states; Leader HENDRIK FRENSCH VERWOERD.

Pan-Africanist Congress of Azania (PAC): SAAU/SALU Bldg, 15th Floor, 316 Andries St, Pretoria 0001; POB 13412, The Tramshed 0126; tel. (12) 3206243; fax (12) 3201509; e-mail azania@ pac.org.za; internet www.paca.org.za; f. 1959; Pres. Rev. STANLEY MOGOBA; Sec.-Gen. MICHAEL MUENDANE.

Progressive Independent Party (PIP): Indian support; Leader FAIZ KHAN.

South African Communist Party (SACP): Cosatu House, 3rd Floor, 1 Leyds St, Braamfontein; POB 1027, Johannesburg 2000; tel. (11) 3393621; fax (11) 3396880; e-mail sacp@wn.apc.org; internet www.sacp.org.za; f. 1921, reorg. 1953; supports ANC; Chair. CHARLES NQAKULA; Gen. Sec. BLADE NZIMANDE.

Transvaal Indian Congress: f. 1902, reactivated 1983; Pres. Dr ESSOP JASSAT.

United Christian Democratic Party: Johannesburg; f. 1986; multiracial; Pres. LUCAS MANGOPE.

United Democratic Movement: f. 1997; multiracial support; demands effective measures for enforcement of law and order; Pres. BANTU HOLOMISA; Deputy Pres. ROELF MEYER.

United Democratic Reform Party: POB 14048, Reigerpark 1466; f. 1987 by merger; mainly Coloured and Indian support; Leader JAKOBUS (JAC) ALBERT RABIE; Nat. Chair. NASH PARMANAND.

Workers' Organization for Socialist Action (WOSA): Cape Town; f. 1990; Chair. Dr NEVILLE ALEXANDER; Gen. Sec. C. BRECHER.

Other political parties that contested the 1999 elections included the Abolition of Income Tax and Usury Party, the Government by the People Green Party, and the Socialist Party of Azania.

Diplomatic Representation

EMBASSIES AND HIGH COMMISSIONS IN SOUTH AFRICA

Algeria: 950 Arcadia St, POB 57480, Hatfield, Pretoria 0083; tel. (12) 3425074; fax (12) 3426479; Ambassador: SAÏD KITOUNI.

Angola: 1030 Schoeman St, POB 8685, Hatfield, Pretoria 0001; tel. (12) 3420049; fax (12) 3427039; Ambassador: M. A. DUARTE RODRIGUES.

Argentina: 200 Standard Plaza, 440 Hilda St, POB 11125, Hatfield, Pretoria 0083; tel. (12) 433527; fax (12) 433521; Ambassador: PEDRO R. HERRERA.

Australia: 292 Orient St, Arcadia, Pretoria 0083; Private Bag X150, Pretoria 0001; tel. (12) 3423740; fax (12) 3428442; e-mail australia@new.co.za; internet www.australia.co.za; High Commissioner: DAVID M. CONNOLLY.

Austria: 1109 Duncan St, Brooklyn 0181; POB 95572, Waterkloof 0145; tel. (12) 462483; fax (12) 461151; Ambassador: Dr F. PALLA.

Bangladesh: 410 Farenden St, Sunnyside, Pretoria 0002; tel. (12) 3432105; fax (12) 3435222; e-mail bangladoot@global.co.za; High Commissioner: A. T. KARIM.

Belgium: 625 Leyds St, Muckleneuk, Pretoria 0002; tel. (12) 443201; fax (12) 443216; Ambassador: L. TEIRLINCK.

Botswana: 24 Amos St, Colbyn, POB 57035, Arcadia 0007; tel. (12) 3424761; fax (12) 3421845; High Commissioner: O. J. TEBAPE.

Brazil: 201 Leyds St, Arcadia 0083; POB 3269, Pretoria 0001; tel. (12) 3411712; fax (12) 3417547; Ambassador: O. AGRIPINO MAIA.

Bulgaria: 1071 Church St, Hatfield 0083; POB 26296, Arcadia 0007; tel. (12) 3423720; fax (12) 3423721; Ambassador: PETKO DRAGANOV.

Burundi: 1315 Church St, POB 12914, Hatfield, Pretoria 0083; tel. (12) 3424881; fax (12) 3424885; Chargé d'affaires a.i.: S. BARUT-WANAYO.

Canada: 1103 Arcadia St, cnr Hilda St, Hatfield, Pretoria 0028; tel. (12) 4223000; fax (12) 4223052; internet www.canada.co.za; High Commissioner: LUCIE EDWARDS.

Chile: Campus Centre 1102, 5th Floor, Burnett St, Hatfield 0083; POB 12672, Pretoria 0028; tel. (12) 3421511; fax (12) 3421658; e-mail chile@iafrica.com; Ambassador: JORGE HEINE.

China, People's Republic: 972 Pretorius St, Arcadia 0083, Pretoria; tel. (12) 3424194; fax (12) 3424244; e-mail info@chinese-embassy.co.za; internet www.chinese-embassy.co.za; Ambassador: WANG XUEXIAN.

Colombia: First National Bank Bldg, 3rd Floor, 1105 Park St, Pretoria 0083; tel. (12) 3420211; fax (12) 3420216; e-mail emcolsf@mweb.co.za; Ambassador: FRED ERIK JACOBSEN.

Congo, Democratic Republic: 791 Schoeman St, POB 28795, Sunnyside 0132, Arcadia 0083; tel. (12) 3441478; fax (12) 3441510; Ambassador: EMMANUEL DUNGIA.

Congo, Republic: 960 Arcadia St, Arcadia, Pretoria; POB 40427, Arcadia 0007; tel. (12) 3425508; fax (12) 3425510. Ambassador: D. MANU-MAHOUNGU.

Côte d'Ivoire: 795 Government Ave, POB 13510, Hatfield, Arcadia 0083; tel. (12) 3426913; fax (12) 3426713; Ambassador: K. BALLOU.

Croatia: 1160 Church St, Colbyn, Pretoria 0083; POB 11335, Hatfield 0028; tel. (12) 3421206; fax (12) 3421819; Ambassador: Dr VERA TADIĆ.

Cuba: 45 Mackenzie St, Brooklyn 0181; POB 11605, Hatfield 0028; tel. (12) 3462215; fax (12) 3462216: Ambassador: ANGEL DALMAU.

Czech Republic: 936 Pretorius St, Arcadia 0083; POB 3326, Pretoria 0001; tel. (12) 433601; fax (12) 432033; e-mail pretoria@embassy.mzv.cz; internet www.icon.co.za; Ambassador: Dr PAVEL VOŠALÍK.

Denmark: Sanlam Centre, 8th Floor, cnr Andries and Pretorius Sts, POB 2942, Pretoria 0002; tel. (12) 3220595; fax (12) 3220596; e-mail rde@icon.co.za; Ambassador: ALF JÖNSSON.

Egypt: 270 Bourke St, Muckleneuk 0002; POB 30025, Sunnyside 0132; tel. (12) 3431590; fax (12) 3431082; Ambassador: M. M. KHATTAB.

Eritrea: 1281 Cobham Rd, POB 11371, Queenswood 0186; tel. (12) 3331302; fax (12) 3332330; Chargé d'affaires a.i.: TEKESTE G. ZEMUY.

Estonia: 16 Hofmeyer St, Cape Town 7530; tel. (21) 9133850.

Ethiopia: 47 Charles St, Bailey's Muckleneuk, Brooklyn 0181; POB 11469, Hatfield 0028; tel. (12) 3463542; fax (12) 3463687; Ambassador: AMAN HASSEN.

Finland: 628 Leyds St, Muckleneuk, Pretoria 0002; POB 443, Pretoria 0001; tel. (12) 3430275; fax (12) 3433095; Ambassador: TAPANI BROTHERUS.

France: 807 George Ave, Arcadia 0083; POB 4619, Pretoria 0001; tel. (12) 4297000; fax (12) 4297029; e-mail capamba@iafrica.com; internet www.france.co.za; Ambassador: TRISTAN D'ALBIS.

Gabon: Southern Life Plaza, cnr Festival and Schoeman Sts, POB 9222, Hatfield, Pretoria 0083; tel. (12) 3424376; fax (12) 3424375; Ambassador: J. EHOUMBA.

Germany: 180 Blackwood St, Arcadia 0083; POB 2023, Pretoria 0001; tel. (12) 4278900; fax (12) 3439401; Ambassador: HARALD GANNS.

Ghana: 1038 Arcadia St, POB 12537, Hatfield, Pretoria; tel. (12) 3425847; fax (12) 3425863; e-mail glcom27@icon.co.za; High Commissioner: KWESI BAAH-BOAKYE (acting).

Greece: 1003 Church St, Arcadia, Pretoria 0083; tel. (12) 437351; fax (12) 434313; Ambassador: I. THEOPHANOPOULOS.

Guinea: 336 Orient St, POB 13523, Arcadia, Pretoria 0083; tel. (12) 3428465; fax (12) 3428467; Ambassador Dr O. SYLLA.

Holy See: 800 Pretorius St, Arcadia, Pretoria 0083; tel. (12) 3443815; fax (12) 3443595; e-mail nunziosa@iafrica.com; Chargé d'affairs a.i.: Rev. ALBERTO ORTEGA.

Hungary: 959 Arcadia St, Hatfield, Pretoria 0083; POB 27077, Sunnyside 0132; tel. (12) 433030; fax (12) 433029; e-mail hunem@cis.co.za; Ambassador: Dr LÁSZLÓ PORDÁNY.

India: 852 Schoeman St, Arcadia 0083; POB 40216, Arcadia 0007; tel. (12) 3425392; fax (12) 3425310; e-mail hcipta@iafrica.com; High Commissioner: HARSH K. BHASIN.

Indonesia: 949 Schoeman St, Arcadia 0083; POB 13155, Hatfield 0028; tel. (12) 3423350; fax (12) 3423369; e-mail indonemb@lantic.co.za; Ambassador: R. ISKANDAR.

Iran: 1002 Schoeman St, Hatfield 0083; POB 12546, Hatfield 0028; tel. (12) 3425880; fax (12) 3421878; Ambassador: Hojatoleslam MUHAMMAD SHARIF MAHDAVI.

Ireland: First Floor, Delheim Suite, Tulbagh Park, 1234 Church St, Colbyn 0083, POB 4174, Pretoria 0001; tel. (12) 3425062; fax (12) 3424752; Ambassador: HUGH SWIFT.

Israel: 3rd Floor, 339 Hilda St, Hatfield, Pretoria 0083; POB 3726, Pretoria 0001; tel. (12) 3422693; fax (12) 3421442; e-mail embofisr @iafrica.com; Ambassador: U. OREN.

Italy: 796 George Ave, Arcadia, Pretoria 0083; tel. (12) 435541; fax (12) 435547; e-mail ambpret@iafrica.com; Ambassador: RENATO VOLPINI.

Japan: Sanlam Bldg, 2nd Floor, 353 Festival St, Hatfield 0083; POB 11434, Hatfield 0028; tel. (12) 3422100; fax (12) 433922; Ambassador: A. HATAKENAKA.

Jordan: 209 Festival St, Hatfield 0083; POB 55755, Arcadia 0007; tel. (12) 3428026; fax (12) 3427847; e-mail embjord@embjord.co.za; internet www.embjord.co.za; Ambassador: S. BAK.

Kenya: 302 Brooks St, Menlo Park 0081; POB 35954, Menlo Park 0102; tel. (12) 3622249; fax (12) 3622252; High Commissioner: (vacant).

Korea, Republic: Greenpark Estates, Block 3, 27 George Storrar Drive, Groenkloof 0181; POB 939, Groenkloof 0027; tel. (12) 462508; fax (12) 461158; Ambassador: Y. S. KIM.

Kuwait: 890 Arcadia St, Pretoria 0001; Private Bag X920, Arcadia 0083; tel. (12) 3420877; fax (12) 3420876; e-mail safarku@global.co.za; Ambassador: DHARI AL-AJRAN.

Lebanon: 7 Sixteenth Ave, POB 2150, Lower Houghton, Johannesburg 2198; tel. (11) 4831106; fax (11) 4831810; Chargé d'affaires a.i.: CHARBEL STEPHAN.

Lesotho: West Tower Momentum Centre, 6th Floor, 343 Pretorius St, POB 55817, Pretoria 0002; tel. (12) 3226090; fax (12) 3220376; High Commissioner: L. R. MOKOSE.

Libya: 900 Church St, Arcadia, POB 40388, Pretoria 0083; tel. (12) 3423902; fax (12) 3423904; Ambassador: Dr. A. A. AL-ZUBEDI.

Malawi: 770 Government Ave, Arcadia, Pretoria 0083; POB 11172, Hatfield 0028; tel. and fax (12) 3420146; High Commissioner: J. J. CHIKAGO.

Malaysia: 1007 Schoeman St, Arcadia, Pretoria 0083; POB 11673, Hatfield 0028; tel. (12) 3425990; Fax (12) 437773; High Commissioner: A. K. B. M. DEEN.

Mali: Infotech Bldg, Suite 402, 1090 Arcadia St, Pretoria 0083; tel. (12) 3427464; fax (12) 3420670; e-mail malipta@iafrica.com; Ambassador: (vacant).

Mauritius: 1163 Pretorius St, Hatfield, Pretoria 0083; tel. (12) 3421283; fax (12) 3421286; e-mail mhcpta@mweb.co.za; High Commissioner: MAHEN KUNDASAMY.

Mexico: 1 Hatfield Sq., 3rd Floor, 1101 Burnett St, POB 9077, Hatfield, Pretoria 0083; tel. (12) 3622822; fax (12) 3621380; e-mail embamexza@mweb.co.za; Ambassador: IGNACIO VILLASEÑOR ARANO.

Morocco: 799 Schoeman St, POB 12382, Arcadia, Pretoria 0083; tel. (12) 3430230; fax (12) 3430613; Ambassador: SAÏD BENRYANE.

Mozambique: 199 Beckett St, Arcadia, Pretoria 0083; POB 40750, Pretoria 0001; tel. (12) 3437840; fax (12) 3436714; High Commissioner: Lt-Gen. ARMANDO ALEXANDRE PANGUENE.

Myanmar: 23 Amos St, Colbyn, Pretoria 0083; tel. (12) 3420706; fax (12) 3422039; e-mail euompta@global.co.za; Ambassador: U HLA MYINT OO.

Namibia: 702 Church St, Pretoria 0083; tel. (12) 3445992; fax (12) 3445998; High Commissioner: S. N. KAUKUNGUA.

Netherlands: 825 Arcadia St, Pretoria; POB 117, Pretoria 0001; tel. (12) 3443910; fax (12) 3439950; e-mail nlgovpre@cis.co.za; internet www.dutchembassy.co.za; Ambassador: H. R. R. V. FROGER.

New Zealand: Block C, Hatfield Gardens, 1110 Arcadia St, Hatfield, Pretoria 0083; Private Bag X17, Hatfield 0028; tel. (12) 3428656; fax (12) 3428640; e-mail nzhc@global.co.za; High Commissioner: RENE WILSON.

Nigeria: 138 Beckett St, Arcadia, POB 27332, Pretoria 0083; tel. (12) 3432021; fax (12) 3431668; High Commissioner: Alhaji SHEHU MALAMI OFR.

Norway: Sancardia, 7th Floor, 524 Church St, Arcadia, Pretoria 0084; POB 9843, Pretoria 0001; tel. (12) 3234790; fax (12) 3234789; Ambassador: P. Ø. GRIMSTAD.

Oman: Export House, 3rd Floor, cnr Maude and West Sts, Johannesburg 2196; tel. (11) 8840999; fax (11) 8836569.

Pakistan: 97 Charles St, Brooklyn, Pretoria 0181; tel. (12) 3464605; fax (12) 467824; e-mail pakistan@icon.co.za; High Commissioner: SHAFKAT SAEED.

Paraguay: 189 Strelitzia Rd, POB 95774, Waterkloof Heights, Pretoria 0181; tel. (12) 3471047; fax (12) 3470403; Ambassador: Chargé d'affaires a.i.: VÍCTOR AQUINO FORNERA.

Peru: Infotech Bldg, Suite 202, 1090 Arcadia St, Hatfield, Pretoria 0083; tel. (12) 3422390; fax (12) 3424944; e-mail emperu@iafrica.com; Ambassador: JUAN JOSÉ MEIER.

Philippines: Southern Life Plaza, 1st Floor, cnr Schoeman and Festival Sts, Pretoria 0083; tel. (12) 3426920; fax (12) 3426666; e-mail philemb@mweb.co.za; Ambassador: ELOY R. BELLO, III.

Poland: 14 Amos St, Colbyn, Pretoria 0083; tel. (12) 432631; fax (12) 432608; Ambassador: (vacant).

Portugal: 599 Leyds St, Muckleneuk, Pretoria 0002; POB 27102, Sunnyside 0132; tel. (12) 3412340; fax (12) 3413975; e-mail port.caba@iafrica.com; Ambassador: FERNANDES PEREIRA.

Romania: 117 Charles St, Brooklyn 0181; POB 11295, Pretoria 0011; tel. (12) 466941; fax (12) 466947; e-mail romembsa@global .co.za; Chargé d'affaires a.i.: DUMITRU NEAGU.

Russia: POB 6743, Pretoria 0001; tel. (12) 3621337; fax (12) 3620116; Ambassador: VADIM B. LUKOV.

Rwanda: 35 Marais St, Brooklyn, POB 55224, Pretoria 0181; tel. (12) 460709; fax (12) 460708; Ambassador: Dr B. KARENZI.

Saudi Arabia: 711 Duncan St, Pretoria 0083; POB 13930, Hatfield 0028; tel. (12) 3624230; fax (12) 3624239; Chargé d'affaires a.i.: Dr. S. M. ZEDAN.

Seychelles: Pretoria; High Commissioner: PETER SINON.

Singapore: 173 Beckett St, Arcadia, Pretoria 0083; POB 11809, Hatfield 0028; tel. (12) 3434371; fax (12) 3433083; High Commissioner: H. HOCHSTADT.

Slovakia: 930 Arcadia St, Pretoria 0083; POB 12736, Hatfield 0028; tel. (12) 3422051; fax (12) 3423688; Ambassador: LADISLAV VLAŠIČ.

Spain: 169 Pine St, POB 1633, Arcadia, Pretoria 0083; tel. (12) 3443875; fax (12) 3434891; Ambassador: MIGUEL ANGEL CARRIEDO MONPIN.

Sri Lanka: 410 Alexander St, Brooklyn, Pretoria 0181; tel. (12) 467690; fax (12) 467702; e-mail srilanka@global.co.za; internet www.srilanka.co.za; High Commissioner: GAMINI MUNASINGHE.

Sudan: 1187 Pretorius St, Hatfield, Pretoria 0083; POB 25513, Monumentpark 0105; tel. (12) 3424538; fax (12) 3424539; e-mail embassy@sudani.co.za; internet www.sudani.co.za; Ambassador: N. A. M. IDRIS.

Swaziland: 715 Government Ave, POB 14294, Arcadia, Pretoria 0007; tel. (12) 3441910; fax (12) 3430455; High Commissioner: M. J. N. HLOPHE.

Sweden: 1 Parioli Bldg, 1166 Park St, POB 13477, Hatfield 0028; tel. (12) 4266400; fax (12) 4266464; e-mail sweden@iafrica.com; Ambassador: B. HEINEBÄCK.

Switzerland: 818 George Ave, Arcadia, Pretoria 0083; POB 2289, Pretoria 0001; tel. (12) 436707; fax (12) 436771; e-mail swiempre@cis.co.za; Ambassador: ROBERT MAYOR.

Tanzania: 822 George Ave, Arcadia, Pretoria 0083; POB 56572, Arcadia 0007; tel. (12) 3424393; fax (12) 434383; High Commissioner: AMI MPUNGWE.

Thailand: 840 Church St, Eastwood, Pretoria 0083; POB 12080, Hatfield 0028; tel. (12) 3425470; fax (12) 3424805 Ambassador: B. SOTIPALALIT.

Tunisia: 850 Church St, Arcadia, Pretoria; POB 56535, Arcadia 0007; tel. (12) 3425282; fax (12) 3426284; Ambassador: MONCEF BENATTIA.

Turkey: 1067 Church St, Hatfield, Pretoria 0083; POB 56014, Arcadia 0007; tel. (12) 3426053; fax (12) 3426052; Ambassador: K. ÖZGÜVENÇ.

Uganda: Infotech Bldg, Suite 402, 1090 Arcadia St, Pretoria 0083; POB 12442, Hatfield 0083; tel. (12) 3426031; fax (12) 3426206; High Commissioner: Prof. E. RUGUMAYO.

Ukraine: 398 Marais St, Brooklyn, Pretoria 0181; POB 57291, Arcadia 0007; tel. (12) 461946; fax (12) 461944; Ambassador: L. M. GURYANOV.

United Arab Emirates: 980 Park St, Arcadia, Pretoria 0083; POB 57090, Arcadia 0007; tel. (12) 3427736; fax (12) 3427738; Ambassador: ALI T. AL-SUWAIDI.

United Kingdom: 255 Hill St, Arcadia, Pretoria 0083; tel. (12) 4831200; fax (12) 4831302; e-mail britain@icon.co.za; internet www.britain.org.za; High Commissioner: Dame MAEVE FORT.

USA: 877 Pretorius St, Pretoria 0083; POB 9536, Pretoria 0001; tel. (12) 3421048; fax (12) 3422244; internet www.usembassy.state.gov/southafrica; Ambassador: DELANO E. LEWIS, Sr.

Venezeula: 474 Hatfield Gables South, Hilda St, Pretoria 0083; POB 11821, Hatfield 0028; tel. (12) 3626593; fax (12) 3626591; Ambassador: Dr VICENTE VALLENILLA.

Yemen: 1063 Pretorius St, Hatfield, Pretoria 0083; POB 13343, Hatfield 0028; tel. (12) 3428650; fax (12) 3428653; e-mail ghamdan@tta.lia.net; Chargé d'affaires a.i.: ALI MOHAMED AL-THAUR.

Yugoslavia: 163 Marais St, Brooklyn, Pretoria; POB 13026, Hatfield 0028; tel. (12) 465626; fax (12) 4660023; Chargé d'affaires a.i.: O. DŽUVEROVIĆ.

Zambia: Sanlam Centre, 353 Festival St, POB 12234, Pretoria 0083; tel. (12) 3421541; fax (12) 3424963; High Commissioner: J. M. KABINGA.

Zimbabwe: 798 Merton St, Arcadia, Pretoria 0083; POB 55140, Arcadia 0007; tel. (12) 3425125; fax (12) 3425126; High Commissioner: N. P. MOYO.

Judicial System

The common law of the Republic of South Africa is the Roman-Dutch law, the uncodified law of Holland as it was at the time of the secession of the Cape of Good Hope in 1806. The law of England is not recognized as authoritative, though the principles of English law have been introduced in relation to civil and criminal procedure, evidence and mercantile matters.

The Constitutional Court consists of a President, Deputy President and nine other judges. Its task is to ensure that the executive, legislative and judicial organs of government adhere to the provisions of the Constitution. It has the power to reverse legislation that has been adopted by Parliament. The Supreme Court of Appeal comprises a Chief Justice, Deputy Chief Justice and a number of judges of appeal, and is the highest court of appeal in all but constitutional matters. There are also High Courts and Magistrates' Courts. A National Director of Public Prosecutions is the head of the prosecuting authority and is appointed by the President of the Republic. A Judicial Service Commission makes recommendations regarding the appointment of judges and advises central and provincial government on all matters relating to the judiciary.

THE SUPREME COURT

Chief Justice: (vacant).

THE CONSTITUTIONAL COURT

President: ARTHUR CHASKALSON.

Religion

Some 80% of the population profess the Christian faith. Other religions that are represented are Hinduism, Islam, Judaism and traditional African religions.

CHRISTIANITY

The South African Council of Churches: Khotso House, 62 Marshall St, POB 4921, Johannesburg 2000; tel. (11) 4921380; fax (11) 4921448; f. 1936; 26 mem. churches; Pres. Dr K. MGOJO; Gen. Sec. HLOPHE BAM.

The Anglican Communion

Most Anglicans in South Africa are adherents of the Church of the Province of Southern Africa, comprising 23 dioceses (including Lesotho, Namibia, St Helena, Swaziland and two dioceses in Mozambique). The Church had more than 2m. members in 1988.

Archbishop of Cape Town and Metropolitan of the Province of Southern Africa: Most Rev. NJONGONKULU WINSTON HUGH NDUNGANE, 16–20 Bishops Court Drive, Claremont 7708; tel. (21) 7612531; fax (21) 7614193; e-mail archbish@iafrika.com.

The Dutch Reformed Church (Nederduitse Gereformeerde Kerk–NGK)

In 1996 the Dutch Reformed Churches in South Africa consisted of the Dutch Reformed Church with 1,288,837 (mainly white) mems, the Uniting Reformed Church with 1,216,252 (mainly Coloured and black) mems, and the Reformed Church in Africa with 2,386 Indian mems. All congregations were desegregated in 1986.

General Synod: POB 4445, Pretoria 0001; tel. (12) 3228900; fax (12) 3223803; e-mail ngkdrc@mweb.co.za; Moderator Prof. P. C. POTGIETER; Scribe Rev. J. C. CARSTENS; CEO Dr W. J. BOTHA.

The Lutheran Churches

Lutheran Communion in Southern Africa (LUCSA): POB 7170, Bonaero Park 1622; tel. (11) 9731873; fax (11) 3951615; f. 1991; co-ordinating org. for the Lutheran churches in southern Africa, incl. Angola, Botswana, Malawi, Mozambique, Namibia, South Africa, Swaziland, Zambia and Zimbabwe; 1,618,720 (1999); Pres. Bishop P. J. ROBINSON; Exec. Dir Rev. B. C. KHUMALO.

Evangelical Lutheran Church in Southern Africa (ELCSA): POB 7231, 1622 Bonaero Park; tel. (11) 9731853; fax (11) 3951888; f. 1975 by merger of four non-white churches; the largest Lutheran church in southern Africa; Pres. Bishop A. J. FORTUIN; Gen. Sec. Rev. T. MAKGATO; 624,567 mems.

Evangelical Lutheran Church in Southern Africa (Cape): 240 Long St, Cape Town 8001; tel. (21) 244932; fax (21) 249618; Pres. Bishop NILS ROHWER; 4,521 mems.

Evangelical Lutheran Church in Southern Africa (Natal–Transvaal): POB 7095, Bonaero Park 1622; tel. (11) 9731851; fax (11) 3951862; e-mail elksant@elksant.co.za; Pres. Bishop D. R. LILJE.

Moravian Church in Southern Africa: POB 24111, Lansdowne 7780; tel. (21) 6962926; fax (21) 6963887; f. 1737; Pres. W. M. MAJIKIJELA; 50,000 mems (1997).

The Roman Catholic Church

South Africa comprises four archdioceses, 21 dioceses and one Apostolic Prefecture. At 31 December 1998 there were an estimated

3,052,915 adherents in the country, representing about 6.5% of the total population.

Southern African Catholic Bishops' Conference (SACBC): Khanya House, 140 Visagie St, Pretoria 0002; POB 941, Pretoria 0001; tel. (12) 3236458; fax (12) 3266218; e-mail sacbelib@wn .apc.org; internet www.cnwinfo.co.za; f. 1951; mems representing South Africa, Botswana and Swaziland; Pres. Rt Rev. LOUIS NDLOVU, Bishop of Manzini (Swaziland); Sec.-Gen. Rev. Fr BUTI TLHAGALE.

Archbishop of Bloemfontein: Most Rev. BUTI JOSEPH TLHAGALE, Archbishop's House, 7A Whites Rd, Bloemfontein 9300; POB 362, Bloemfontein 9300; tel. (51) 4481658; fax (51) 4472420; e-mail bfnarch@mweb.co.za.

Archbishop of Cape Town: Most Rev. LAWRENCE HENRY; Cathedral Place, 12 Bouquet St, Cape Town 8001; POB 2910, Cape Town 8001; tel. (21) 4622317; fax (21) 4619330; e-mail catholic@intekom.co.za.

Archbishop of Durban: Most Rev. WILFRID NAPIER, Archbishop's House, 154 Gordon Rd, Durban 4001; POB 47489, Greyville 4023; tel. (31) 3031417; fax (31) 231848.

Archbishop of Pretoria: Most Rev. GEORGE DANIEL, Archbishop's House, 125 Main St, Waterkloof 0181; POB 17245, Groenkloof, Pretoria 0027; tel. (12) 462048; fax (12) 462452.

Other Christian Churches

In addition to the following Churches, there are a large number of Pentecostalist groups, and more than 4,000 independent African Churches (with 8,563,000 members in 1994).

African Gospel Church: POB 32312, 4060 Mobeni; tel. (31) 9074377; Moderator Rev. F. D. MKHIZE; Gen. Sec. O. MTOLO; 100,000 mems.

Afrikaanse Protestantse Kerk (Afrikaans Protestant Church): POB 11488, Hatfield 0028; tel. (12) 3621390; fax (12) 3622023; e-mail apkskkan@lantic.net; f. 1987 by fmr mems of the Dutch Reformed Church (Nederduitse Gereformeerde Kerk) in protest at the desegregation of church congregations; c. 53,000 mems.

Apostolic Faith Mission of South Africa: POB 890197, Lyndhurst 2106; tel. (11) 7868550; fax (11) 8871182; f. 1908; Gen. Sec. Pastor M. G. MAHLABO; 136,000 mems.

Assemblies of God: POB 51065, Musgrave 4062, tel. (31) 231341; fax (31) 231342; f. 1915; Chair. Rev. ISAAC HLETA; Gen. Sec. Rev. C. P. WATT; 300,000 mems.

Baptist Union of Southern Africa: Private Bag X45, Wilropark 1731; tel. (11) 7685980; fax (11) 7685983; e-mail busa@icon.co.za; f. 1877; Pres. Rev. G. D. MATABOGE; Gen. Sec. Rev. T. G. RAE; 49,354 mems.

Black Dutch Reformed Church: POB 137, Bergvlei 2012; Leader Rev. SAM BUTI; c. 1m. mems.

Church of England in South Africa: POB 185, Gillitts 3603; tel. (31) 7652876; fax (31) 7655150; e-mail noel.wright@pixie.co.za; internet www.cesa.co.za; 207 churches; Bishops: Rt Rev. J. BELL, Rt Rev. J. NGUBANE, Rt Rev. F. RETIEF, Rt Rev. M. MORRISON.

Evangelical Presbyterian Church in South Africa: POB 31961, Braamfontein 2017; tel. (11) 3391044; Gen. Sec. Rev. S. NGOBE; Gen. Sec. Rev. J. S. NGOBE; Treas. Rev. H. D. MASANGU; 60,000 mems.

The Methodist Church of Southern Africa: Methodist Connexional Office, POB 50216, Musgrave 4062; tel. (31) 2024214; fax (31) 2017674; e-mail methodist@mweb.co.za; internet www.users .club.co.za/mco; f. 1883; Pres. Bishop H. M. DANDALA; Sec. Rev. ROSS A. J. OLIVER; 696,353 mems.

Nederduitsch Hervormde Kerk van Afrika: POB 2368, Pretoria 0001; tel. (12) 3228885; fax (12) 3227907; e-mail skribaat@pixie .co.za; Chair. Prof. T. F. J. DREYER; Gen. Sec. Dr S. P. PRETORIUS; 193,561 mems.

Nederduitse Gereformeerde Kerk in Afrika: Portland Place, 37 Jorissen St, 2017 Johannesburg; tel. (11) 4031027; 6 synods (incl. 1 in Swaziland); Moderator Rev. S. P. E. BUTI; Gen. Sec. W. RAATH; 350,370 mems.

Presbyterian Church of Africa: POB 54840, Umlazi 4031; tel. (31) 9072366; f. 1898; 8 presbyteries (incl. 1 in Malawi and 1 in Zimbabwe); Chief Clerk Rev. S. A. KHUMALO; 1,231,000 mems.

Reformed Church in South Africa (Die Gereformeerde Kerke): POB 20004, Noordbrug 2522, Potchefstroom; tel. (148) 2973986; fax (148) 2931042; f. 1859; Prin. Officer H. S. J. VORSTER; 158,973 mems.

Seventh-day Adventist Church: POB 468, Bloemfontein 9300; tel. (51) 4478271; fax (41) 4488059; Pres. Pastor V. S. WAKABA; Sec. Pastor B. H. PARKERSON; 150,000 mems.

United Congregational Church of Southern Africa: POB 61305, Marshalltown 2107; tel. (11) 8366537; fax (11) 8369249; f. 1799; Gen. Sec. Rev. S. M. ARENDS; 234,451 mems.

Uniting Presbyterian Church of Southern Africa: POB 96188, Brixton 2019; tel. (11) 8371258; fax (11) 8371653; e-mail assembly@ presbyterian.org.za; f. 1897; Moderator Rt Rev. C. W. LEEUW; Gen. Sec. and Clerk of the Assembly Rev. A. RODGER; 130,000 mems.

Zion Christian Church: Zion City, Moria; f. 1910; South Africa's largest black religious group, with c. 4m. mems; Leader Bishop BARNABAS LEKGANYANE.

JUDAISM

There are about 100,000 Jews in South Africa, and about 200 organized Jewish communities.

South African Jewish Board of Deputies: POB 87557, Houghton 2041; tel. (11) 4861434; fax (11) 6464940; e-mail sajbod@iafrica.com; f. 1903; the representative institution of South African Jewry; Pres. MARLENE BETHLEHEM; Chair. RUSSELL GADDIN; Nat. Dir YEHUDA KAY.

BAHÁ'Í FAITH

National Spiritual Assembly: 10 Acorn Lane, Houghton Estate, Houghton 2198; POB 2142, Houghton 2041; tel. (11) 4872077; fax (11) 4871809; e-mail nsa.sec@pixie.co.za; internet www .bahai.org.za; f. 1956; 11,000 mems resident in 320 localities; Sec. SHOHREH RAWHANI.

The Press

In December 1993 legislation was adopted that provided for the establishment of an Independent Media Commission, which was to ensure the impartiality of the press.

Government Communication and Information System (GCIS): Midtown Bldg, cnr Vermeulen and Prinsloo Sts, Pretoria; Private Bag X745, Pretoria 0001; tel. (12) 3142911; fax (12) 3233831; e-mail hildadj@gcis.gov.za; internet www.gov.za; govt agency.

Press Ombudsman of South Africa: POB 47221, tel. (11) 7884837; fax (11) 7884990; e-mail pressombudsman@ombudsman .org.za; Ombudsman E. H. LINNINGTON.

DAILIES
Eastern Cape

Die Burger (Oos-Kaap): 52 Cawood St, POB 525, Port Elizabeth 6001; tel. (41) 5036111; fax (41) 5036138; e-mail dbokaap@burger .naspers.co.za; f. 1937; morning; Afrikaans; Editor LEON VAN DER VYVER; circ. 23,849.

Cape Times: Newspaper House, 122 St George's St, POB 56, Cape Town 8000; tel. (21) 4884911; fax (21) 4884744; f. 1876; morning; English; Editor RYLAND FISHER; circ. 53,000.

Daily Dispatch: 35 Caxton St, POB 131, East London 5200; tel. (43) 7022000; fax (43) 7435159; e-mail gavinst@ dispatch.co.za; internet www.dispatch.co.za; f. 1872; morning; English; Editor Prof. G. STEWART; circ. 39,000.

Eastern Province Herald: Newspaper House, 19 Baakens St, POB 1117, Port Elizabeth 6000; tel. (41) 5047911; fax (41) 554966; f. 1845; morning; English; Editor RIC WILSON; circ. 30,000 (Mon.–Fri.), 25,000 (Sat.).

Evening Post: Newspaper House, 19 Baakens St, POB 1121, Port Elizabeth 6000; tel. (41) 5047911; fax (41) 554966; f. 1950; evening; English; Editor NEVILLE WOUDBERG; circ. 19,000.

Free State

Die Volksblad: 79 Voortrekker St, POB 267, Bloemfontein 9300; tel. (51) 473351; fax (51) 306949; f. 1904; morning; Afrikaans; Editor PAUL MARAIS; circ. 28,000 (Mon.–Fri.), 23,000 (Sat.).

Gauteng

Beeld: 32 Miller St, POB 5425, Johannesburg 2000; tel. (11) 4064600; fax (11) 4064643; f. 1974; morning; Afrikaans; Editor WILLIE KÜHN; circ. 111,958 (Mon.–Fri.), 81,000 (Sat.).

Business Day: 4 Biermann Ave, Rosebank 2196; tel. (11) 2803000; fax (11) 2805505; e-mail busday@tml.co.za; internet www.bday .co.za; f. 1985; morning; English; financial; Editor JIM JONES; circ. 41,000.

The Citizen: POB 7712, Johannesburg 2000; tel. (11) 4022900; fax (11) 4026862; f. 1976; morning; English; Editor M. A. JOHNSON; circ. 14,000 (Mon.–Fri.), 108,000 (Sat.).

The Pretoria News: 216 Vermeulen St, Pretoria 0002; tel. (12) 3255382; fax (12) 3257300; e-mail ptanews@ptn.independent.co.za; f. 1898; morning; English; Editor A. DUNN; circ. 25,500 (Mon.–Fri.), 14,000 (Sat.).

Sowetan: 61 Commando Rd, Industria West, POB 6663, Johannesburg 2000; tel. (11) 4714000; fax (11) 4748834; e-mail swtnedit@ sowetan.co.za; internet sowetan.co.za; f. 1981; Mon.–Fri.; English; Editor Z. AGGREY KLAASTE; circ. 225,000.

The Star: 47 Sauer St, POB 1014, Johannesburg 2000; tel. (11) 6339111; fax (11) 8368398; f. 1887; English; Editor PETER J. SULLIVAN; circ. 162,316 (Mon.–Fri.), 135,203 (Sat.).

Transvaaler: 28 Height St, Doornfontein, POB 845, Johannesburg 2000; tel. (11) 7769111; fax (11) 4020037; afternoon; Afrikaans; Editor G. JOHNSON; circ. 40,000.

KwaZulu/Natal

The Daily News: 18 Osborne St, Greyville 4001, POB 47549, Greyville 4023; tel. (31) 3082911; fax (31) 3082715; internet www.iol .co.za; f. 1878; Mon.-Fri., afternoon; English; Editor K. NYATSUMBA; circ. 77,500.

Mercury: 18 Osborne St, Greyville, POB 950, Durban 4001; tel. (31) 3082300; fax (31) 3082333; e-mail pather@nn.independent.co.za; f. 1852; morning; English; Editor D. WIGHTMAN; circ. 42,000.

Natal Witness: 244 Longmarket St, POB 362, Pietermaritzburg 3200; tel. (33) 3551111; fax (33) 3551122; internet www.witness .co.za; f. 1846; morning; English; Editor J. CONYNGHAM; circ. 28,000.

Northern Cape

Diamond Fields Advertiser: POB 610, Kimberley 8300; tel. (53) 8326261; fax (53) 8321141; e-mail johandp@dfa.independent .co.za; morning; English; Editor KEVIN RITCHIE; circ. 8,000.

North-West

Rustenburg Herald: 28 Steen St, POB 2043, Rustenburg 0300; tel. (14) 5928329; fax (14) 5921869; e-mail mailbag@rtbherald.co.za; f. 1924; English and Afrikaans; Editor C. THERON; circ. 11,000.

Western Cape

Die Burger: 40 Heerengracht, POB 692, Cape Town 8000; tel. (21) 4062222; fax (21) 4062913; f. 1915; morning; Afrikaans; Editor E. DOMMISSE; circ. 105,841 (Mon.–Fri.), 97,881 (Sat.).

Cape Argus: 122 St George's St, Cape Town POB 56, Cape Town 8000; tel. (21) 4884911; fax (21) 4884075; f. 1857; English; independent; Editor MOEGSIEN WILLIAMS; circ. 85,000.

WEEKLIES AND FORTNIGHTLIES

Eastern Cape

Imvo Zabantsundu (Black Opinion): 35 Edes St, POB 190, King William's Town 5600; tel. (433) 23550; fax (433) 33865; f. 1884; weekly; English and Xhosa; Editor W. MNYIKIZO; Gen.Man. WILL FERREIRA; circ. 31,000.

Weekend Post: POB 1141, Port Elizabeth 6000; tel. (41) 5047911; fax (41) 554966; English; Editor N. M. WOUDBERG; circ. 38,000.

Free State

Vista: POB 1027, Welkom 9460; tel. (57) 3571304; fax (57) 3552427; e-mail avaneck@volksblad.com; internet www.perskorfs.co.za; f. 1971; 2 a week; English and Afrikaans; Editor P. GOUWS; circ. 34,368 (Tues. and Thurs.)

Gauteng

African Jewish Newspaper: Johannesburg 2000; tel. (11) 6468292; f. 1931; weekly; Yiddish; Editor LEVI SHALIT.

Die Afrikaner: POB 1888, Pretoria 0001; tel. (12) 3423410; fax (12) 3423417; f. 1970; Wednesday; organ of Herstigte Nasionale Party; Editors Dr J. L. BASSON, J. J. VENTER; circ. 10,000.

Benoni City Times en Oosrandse Nuus: 28 Woburn Ave, POB 494, Benoni 1500; tel. (11) 8451680; fax (11) 4224796; English and Afrikaans; Editor HILARY GREEN; circ. 32,000.

City Press: POB 3413, Johannesburg 2000; tel. (11) 4021632; fax (11) 4026662; f. 1983; weekly; English; Editor-in-Chief KHULU SIBIYA; circ. 259,374.

Finance Week: Private Bag 78816, Sandton 2146; tel. (11) 4440555; fax (11) 4440424; f. 1979; Editor S. MURRAY; circ. 15,000.

Financial Mail: 4 Biermann Ave, Rosebank, Johannesburg 2196; tel. (11) 2803000; fax (11) 2805800; weekly; English; Editor PETER BRUCE; circ. 33,000.

The Herald Times: POB 31015, Braamfontein 2017; tel. (11) 8876500; weekly; Jewish interest; Man. Dir R. SHAPIRO; circ. 5,000.

Mail and Guardian: 7 Quince Rd, Media Mill, 2092 Milpark, POB 91667, Auckland Park 2006; tel. (11) 7277000; fax (11) 7277111; e-mail ceo@mg.co.za; CEO GOVIN REDDY; Editor PHILIP VAN NIEKERK; circ. 33,023.

Mining Week: Johannesburg; tel. (11) 7892144; f. 1979; fortnightly; Editor VAL PIENAAR; circ. 10,000.

Die Noord-Transvaler: POB 220, Ladanna, Pietersburg 0704; tel. (152) 931831; fax (152) 932586; weekly; Afrikaans; Editor A. BUYS; circ. 12,000.

Noordwes Gazette: POB 515, Potchefstroom 2520; tel. (18) 2930750; e-mail pherald@iafrica.com; weekly; English and Afrikaans; Editor H. STANDER; circ. 35,000.

Northern Review: 16 Grobler St, POB 45, Pietersburg 0700; tel. (152) 2959167; fax (152) 2915148; weekly; English and Afrikaans; Editor R. S. DE JAGER; circ. 10,300.

Potchefstroom and Ventersdorp Herald: POB 515, Potchefstroom 2520; tel. (18) 930750; fax (18) 2943916; e-mail pherald@ iafrica.com; f. 1908; 1 a week; English and Afrikaans; Editor H. STANDER; Man. A. COERTZEN; circ. 5,000 (Fri.).

Rapport: POB 8422, Johannesburg 2000; tel. (11) 4022620; fax (11) 4026163; internet www.naspers.co.za/rapport; weekly; Afrikaans; Editor IZAK DE VILLIERS; circ. 353,000.

South African Industrial Week: Johannesburg; Man. Editor W. MASTINGLE; circ. 19,000.

Springs and Brakpan Advertiser: POB 138, Springs 1560; tel. (11) 8121600; fax (11) 8121908; f. 1916; English and Afrikaans; Editor CATHY GROSVENOR; circ. 13,000.

Sunday Times: POB 1742, Saxonwold 2132; tel. (11) 2805102; fax (11) 2805111; internet www.suntimes.co.za; English; Editor MIKE ROBERTSON; circ. 458,000.

Vaalweekblad: 27 Ekspa Bldg, D.F. Malan St, POB 351, Vanderbijlpark 1900; tel. (16) 817010; fax (16) 810604; weekly; Afrikaans and English; Editor W. J. BUYS; circ. 16,000.

Vrye Weekblad: 153 Bree St, Newtown, Johannesburg 2001; tel. (11) 8362151; fax (11) 8385901; f. 1988; weekly; Afrikaans; Editor MAX DU PREEZ; circ. 13,000.

KwaZulu/Natal

Farmers' Weekly: POB 32083, Mobeni 4060; tel. (31) 422041; fax (31) 426068; f. 1911; weekly; agriculture and horticulture; Editor M. FISHER; circ. 17,000.

Ilanga: 128 Umgeni Rd, POB 2159, Durban 4000; tel. (31) 3094350; fax (31) 3093489; e-mail edilanga@nn.independent.co.za; f. 1903; 2 a week; Zulu; Editor S. NGOBESE; circ. 117,000.

Independent On Saturday: 18 Osborne St, Greyville 4001, POB 47549, Greyville 4023; tel. (31) 3082500; fax (31) 3082355; e-mail satmail@nn.independent.co.za; internet www.nn .independent.co.za; f. 1878; English; Editor CYRIL MADLALA; circ. 77,500.

Keur: POB 32083, Mobeni 4060; tel. (31) 4508100; fax (31) 426068; f. 1967; Afrikaans; Editor GERHARD BURGER; circ. 54,398.

Ladysmith Gazette: POB 10019, Ladysmith 3370; tel. (36) 6376801; fax (36) 6372283; f. 1902; weekly; English, Afrikaans and Zulu; Editor DIANA PROCTER; circ. 7,000.

Personality: POB 32083, Mobeni 4060; tel. (31) 422041; fax (31) 426068; weekly; Editor DAVID MULLANY; circ. 65,000.

Post: 18 Osborne St, Greyville 4000, POB 733, Durban 4000; tel. (31) 3082400; fax (31) 3082427; e-mail post@nn.independent.co.za; internet www.nn.independent.co.za; f. 1935; weekly; English; general; Editor BRIGLALL RAMGUTHEE; circ. 42,203.

Rooi Rose: POB 2600, Suite 192, Houghton 2041; tel. (11) 8890600; fax (11) 8890975; e-mail rooirose@iafrica.com; Afrikaans; fortnightly; women's interest; Editor J. KRUGER; circ. 145,000.

Sunday Tribune: 18 Osborne St, POB 47549, Greyville 4023; tel. (31) 3082911; fax (31) 3082715; e-mail pdavis@nn.independent.co.za; f. 1937; English; weekly; Editor PETER DAVIS; circ. 113,000.

Umafrika: POB 11002, Mariannhill 3601; tel. (31) 7002720; fax (31) 7003707; e-mail umafrika@futuredbn.co.za; f. 1911; weekly; Zulu and English; Editor M. J. KHUZWAYD; circ. 60,000.

Northern Cape

Die Gemsbok: POB 60, Upington 8800; tel. 27017; fax 24055; English and Afrikaans; Editor D. JONES; circ. 8,000.

Western Cape

Eikestadnuus: 44 Alexander St, POB 28, Stellenbosch 7600; tel. (2231) 72840; fax (2231) 99538; weekly; English and Afrikaans; Editor R. GERBER; circ. 7,000.

Fair Lady: Naspers Bldg, 9th Floor, 40 Heerengracht, Foreshore, Cape Town, POB 1802, Cape Town 8000; tel. (21) 4062204; fax (21) 4062930; e-mail fimag@fairlady.com; fortnightly; English; Editor ALICE BELL; circ. 100,952.

Huisgenoot: 40 Heerengracht, POB 1802, Cape Town 8000; tel. (21) 4062115; fax (21) 4062937; f. 1916; weekly; Afrikaans; Editor WILLIE KÜHN; circ. 488,000.

Sarie: POB 1802, Cape Town 8000; tel. (21) 4062203; fax (21) 4062913; fortnightly; Afrikaans; women's interest; Editor A. ROSSOUW; circ. 227,000.

South: 6 Russel St, Castle Mews, Woodstock 7925; POB 13094, Sir Lowry Rd 7900; tel. (21) 4622012; fax (21) 4615407; weekly; black interest; Editor Dr GUY BERGER; circ. 25,000.

The Southern Cross: POB 2372, Cape Town 8000; tel. (21) 455007; fax (21) 453850; f. 1920; weekly; English; Roman Catholic; Editor M. SHACKLETON; circ. 10,000.

Tyger-Burger: 40 Heerengracht, POB 2271, Cape Town 8000; tel. (21) 4062121; fax (21) 4062913; weekly; Afrikaans and English; Editor ABIE VON ZYL.

Weekend Argus: 122 St George's Mall, POB 56, Cape Town 8000; tel. (21) 4884911; fax (21) 4884075; f. 1857; Sat. and Sun.; English; Editor CHRIS WHITFIELD; circ. 120,000.

You Magazine: 40 Heerengracht, POB 7167, Cape Town 8000; tel. (21) 4062116; fax (21) 4062937; f. 1987; weekly; English; Editor-in-Chief ANDRIES VAN WYK; circ. 316,252.

MONTHLIES

Free State

Wamba: POB 1097, Bloemfontein; educational; publ. in seven vernacular languages; Editor C. P. SENYATSI.

Gauteng

Centre News: Johannesburg; tel. (11) 5591781; English; publ. by R.J.J. Publications; circ. 30,000.

The Mail of Rosebank News: Johannesburg; tel. (11) 3391781; English; publ. by R.J.J. Publications; circ. 40,000.

Nursing News: POB 1280, Pretoria 0001; tel. (12) 3432315; fax (12) 3440750; f. 1978; magazine of the Democratic Nursing Org.; English and Afrikaans; circ. 76,000.

Pace: POB 48985, Roosevelt Park 2129; tel. (11) 8890600; fax (11) 8805942; Man. Editor FORCE KOSHANI; circ. 131,000.

Postal and Telkom Herald: POB 9186, Johannesburg 2000; tel. (11) 7255422; fax (11) 7256540; f. 1903; English and Afrikaans; Staff Assen (Workers' Union); Editor F. A. GERBER; circ. 13,000.

Technobrief: POB 395, Pretoria 0001; tel. (12) 8414078; fax (12) 8413789; e-mail vmuskett@csir.co.za; internet www.csir.co.za; f. 1991; publ. by the Council for Scientific and Industrial Research (CSIR); Editor VENE MUSKETT; circ. 8,000.

Telescope: POB 925, Pretoria 0001; tel. (12) 3217121; fax (12) 3114031; e-mail mudzwim@telkom.co.za; f. 1970; English, Afrikaans and vernacular languages; telecom staff journal; Editor MOSES MUDZWITI; circ. 60,000.

KwaZulu/Natal

Bona: POB 32083, Mobeni 4060; tel. (31) 422041; fax (31) 426068; f. 1956; English, Sotho, Xhosa and Zulu; Editor R. BAKER; circ. 263,000.

Living and Loving: POB 32083, Mobeni 4060; tel. (31) 422041; fax (31) 426068; English; Editor ANGELA STILL; circ. 113,000.

Tempo: POB 16, Pinetown 3600; tel. (31) 7013225; fax (31) 7012166; f. 1984; weekly; Afrikaans; Editor Dr HILDA GROBLER; circ. 7,000.

World Airnews: POB 35082, Northway, Durban 4065; tel. (31) 5641319; fax (31) 5637115; e-mail tom@airnews.co.za; f. 1973; aviation news; Editor T. CHALMERS; circ. 13,500.

Your Family: POB 473016, Parklands 2121; tel. (11) 8890600; fax (11) 8890642; e-mail yourfamily@caxton.co.za; f. 1973; English; cooking, crafts, DIY; Editor PATTI GARLICK; circ. 216,000.

Western Cape

Boxing World: Unit 17, Park St, POB 164, Steenberg 7945; tel. 7015070; fax 7015863; Editor BERT BLEWETT; circ. 10,000.

Car: POB 180, Howard Place 7450; tel. (21) 5311391; (21) fax 5313333; e-mail johnw@rsp.co.za; Editor J. WRIGHT; circ. 130,000.

Drum: POB 784696, Sandton 2146; tel. (11) 7837227; fax (11) 7838822; f. 1951; English; Editor BARNEY COHEN; circ. 135,850 in southern Africa.

Femina: 21 St. John's St, POB 3647, Cape Town 8001; tel. (21) 4623070; fax (21) 4612500; e-mail femina@assocmags .co.za; Editor JANE RAPHAELY; circ. 88,421.

Finance Week: Sandton Court, 2nd Floor, Fredman Drive, Sandton; POB 786466, Sandton 2146; tel. (11) 8847676; fax (11) 8840851; Afrikaans and English; Publisher G. L. MARAIS; circ. 21,910.

Learning Roots: POB 1161, Cape Town 8000; tel. (21) 6968414; fax (21) 6968346; f. 1980; newsletter for black schools in the Western Cape; circ. 50,000.

Nursing RSA Verpleging: Private Bag XI, Pinelands 7430; tel. (21) 5312691; fax (21) 5314126; f. 1986; professional nursing journal; Editor LILLIAN MEDLIN; circ. 10,000.

Reader's Digest (South African Edition): POB 2677, Cape Town 8000; tel. (21) 254460; fax (21) 4191090; English; Editor-in-Chief W. PANKHURST; circ. 371,000.

South African Medical Journal: Private Bag XI, Pinelands 7430; tel. (21) 5313081; fax (21) 5314126; e-mail multimedia@samedical .co.za; f. 1926; publ. by the Medical Assen of South Africa; Editor Prof. DANIEL J. NCAYIYANA; circ. 20,000.

Die Unie: POB 196, Cape Town 8000; tel. (21) 4616340; fax (21) 4619238; e-mail saou@new.co.za; f. 1905; educational; publ. by the South African Teachers' Union; Editor A. P. J. BOTHA; circ. 7,200.

Die Voorligter: POB 1444, Cape Town 8000; tel. (21) 259233; fax (21) 255522; f. 1937; journal of the Dutch Reformed Church of South Africa; Editor Dr F. M. GAUM; circ. 84,000.

Woman's Value: POB 1802, Cape Town 8000; tel. (21) 4062205; fax (21) 4062929; e-mail valmay@womansvalue.com; internet www.womansvalue.24.com; English; Editor ALICE BELL; circ. 146,000.

Wynboer: K. W. V. Van SA Bpk, POB 528, Suider-Paarl 7624; tel. (21) 8073267; fax (21) 8631562; e-mail ridderd@kwv.co.za; f. 1931; viticulture and the wine and spirit industry; Editor HENRY HOPKINS; circ. 8,750.

QUARTERLIES

Gauteng

The Motorist/Die Motoris: POB 31015, Braamfontein 2017; tel. (11) 8876500; fax (11) 8876551; f. 1966; journal of the Automobile Assen of SA; Editor MICHAEL WANG; circ. 184,000.

South African Journal of Economics: 4-44 EBW Bldg, University of Pretoria, Pretoria 0002; tel. (12) 4203525; fax (12) 3625266; e-mail saje@hakuna.up.ac.za; internet www.essa.org.za; f. 1933; English and Afrikaans; Man. Editor Prof. D. J. J. BOTHA.

Vuka SA: POB 1758, Pretoria 0001; tel. (12) 3226404; fax (12) 3207803; f. 1952; publ. by the Foundation for Education, Science and Tech.; Editor CHARLES KING; circ. 5,000.

Western Cape

New Era: Cape Town 8000; tel. (2721) 7975101; fax (2721) 7627424; f. 1884; Editor ELLISON KAHN; circ. 3,000.

South African Law Journal: POB 30, Cape Town 8000; tel. (2721) 7975101; fax (2721) 7627424; f. 1884; Editor ELLISON KAHN; circ. 3,000.

NEWS AGENCIES

South African Press Association: Cotswold House, Greenacres Office Park, cnr Victory and Rustenburg Rds, Victory Park; tel. (11) 7821600; fax (11) 7821591; internet www.sapa.org.za; f. 1938; 40 mems; Chair. S. P. JORDAAN; Man. W. J. H. VAN GILS; Editor MARK A. VAN DER VELDEN.

Foreign Bureaux

Agence France-Presse (AFP): Nixdorf Centre, 6th Floor, 37 Stanley Ave, Milpark; POB 3462, Johannesburg 2000; tel. (11) 4822170; fax (11) 7268756; Bureau Chief MARC HUTTEN.

Agenzia Nazionale Stampa Associata (ANSA) (Italy): POB 32312, Camps Bay, Cape Town 8040; tel. (21) 7903991; fax (21) 7904444; Correspondent LICINIO GERMINI.

Associated Press (AP) (USA): 15 Napier St, Richmond, Johannesburg 2092; tel. (11) 7267022; fax (11) 7267834; Bureau Chief JOHN DANISZEWSKI.

Central News Agency (Taiwan): Kine Centre, 1st Floor, 141 Commissioner St, Johannesburg 2001; tel. (11) 3316654; fax (11) 3319463; Chief CHANG JER SHONG.

Deutsche Presse-Agentur (dpa) (Germany): 96 Jorrisen St, POB 32521, Braamfontein 2017; tel. (11) 4033926; fax (11) 4032849; Chief Dr ARNO MAYER.

Informatsionnoye Telegrafnoye Agentstvo Rossii—Telegrafnoye Agentstvo Suverennykh Stran (ITAR—TASS) (Russia): 1261 Park St, Atfield, Pretoria; tel. (12) 436677; fax (12) 3425017; Bureau Chief YURII K. PICHUGIN.

Inter-Press Service (IPS) (Italy): POB 30764, Braamfontein 2017, Johannesburg; tel. (11) 4034967; fax (11) 4032516; e-mail ipsjnb@wn.apc.org; Correspondent GUMISAI MUTUME.

Kyodo News (Japan): Mentone Center, 3rd Floor, 1 Park Rd, Richmond, Johannesburg 2092; tel. (11) 4826524; fax (11) 4826534; e-mail isoya@global.co.za; Rep. NAOHITO ISOYA.

Reuters Ltd (UK): Surrey House, 7th and 8th Floors, 35 Rissik St, Johannesburg; Man. CHRIS INWOOD.

United Press International (UPI) (USA): Nedbank Centre, 2nd Floor, POB 32661, Braamfontein 2017; tel. (11) 4033910; fax (11) 4033914; Bureau Chief PATRICK COLLINS.

Agencia EFE (Spain) is also represented.

PRESS ASSOCIATIONS

Newspaper Association of Southern Africa: Nedbank Gardens, 5th Floor, 33 Bath Ave, Rosebank 2196, Johannesburg; POB 47180, Parklands 2121; tel. (11) 4471264; fax (11) 4471289; e-mail na@ printmedia.org.za; f. 1882; represents 27 urban daily, weekly and independent nat. newspapers; Pres. J. L. MALHERBE; Exec. Dir G. LANGMEAD.

Print Media SA: POB 47180, Parklands 2121; tel. (11) 4471264; fax (11) 4471289; e-mail printmediasa@printmedia; f. 1995, following the restructuring of the Newspaper Press Union of Southern Africa; represents all aspects of the print media (newspapers and magazines); 680 mems; Pres. C. RAMAPHOSA; Exec. Dir G. LANGMEAD.

Publishers

Acorn Books: POB 4845, Randburg 2125; tel. (11) 8805768; fax (11) 8805768; e-mail acorbook@iafrica.com; f. 1985; Africana, general, natural history.

Albertyn Publishers (Pty) Ltd: Andmar Bldg, Van Ryneveld St, Stellenbosch 7600; tel. (21) 8871202; fax (21) 8871292; f. 1971; encyclopaedias; Editorial Man. S. CARSTENS.

BLAC Publishing House: POB 17, Athlone, Cape Town; f. 1974; general fiction, poetry; Man. Dir JAMES MATTHEWS.

Jonathan Ball Publishers: POB 33977, Jeppestown 2043; tel. (11) 6222900; fax (11) 6223553; fiction, reference, bibles, textbooks, general. Subsidiary:

> **A. Donker (Pty) Ltd:** POB 33977, Jeppestown 2043; tel. (11) 6222900; fax (11) 6223553; Africana, literature, history, academic.

Bible Society of South Africa: POB 6215, Roggebaai 8012; tel. (21) 212040; fax (21) 4194846; f. 1820; Gen. Sec. Dr D. TOLMIE.

Book Promotions (Pty) Ltd: POB 5, Plumstead 7800; tel. (21) 7060949; fax (21) 7060940; e-mail enquiries@bookpro.co.za; Man. Dir. R. MANSELL.

Book Studio (Pty) Ltd: POB 121, Hout Bay 7872.

Books of Africa (Pty) Ltd: POB 10, Muizenberg 7950; tel. (21) 888316; f. 1947; biography, history, Africana, art; Man. Dir T. V. BULPIN.

Brenthurst Press (Pty) Ltd: POB 87184, Houghton 2041; tel. (11) 6466024; fax (11) 4861651; e-mail orders@brenthurst.co.za; internet www.brenthurst.org.za; f. 1974; Southern African history.

Butterworth Publishers (Pty) Ltd: POB 4, Mayville 4058; tel. (31) 2683111; fax (31) 2683100; internet www.butterworths.co.za; law, tax, accountancy; Man. Dir WILLIAM J. LAST.

Clever Books: POB 13186, Hatfield 0028; tel. (12) 3423263; fax (12) 432376; e-mail inl0631@mweb.co.za; f. 1981; Propr J. STEENHUISEN.

College of Careers/Faircare Books: POB 10207, Caledon Sq., Cape Town 7905; tel. (21) 4614411; f. 1946; general, educational; Man. Dir MICHAEL IRVING.

CUM Books: POB 1599, Vereeniging 1930; tel. (16) 214781; fax (16) 211748.

Da Gama Publishers (Pty) Ltd: MWU Bldg, 6th Floor, 19 Melle St, Braamfontein 2017; tel. (11) 4033763; fax (11) 4031263; travel; Publr DERMOT SWAINE.

Digma Publications: POB 95466, Waterkloof 0145; tel. (11) 3463840; fax (11) 3463845.

Dreyer Printers and Publishers: POB 286, Bloemfontein 9300; tel. (51) 4479001; fax (51) 4471281.

Educum Publishers: POB 3068, Halfway House 1685.

Eksamenhulp: POB 55555, Arcadia 0007.

Fisichem Publishers: Private Bag X3, Matieland 7602; tel. (21) 8870900; fax (21) 8839635; e-mail fisichem@iafrica.com.

Flesch, W. J., & Partners: 4 Gordon St, Gardens, POB 3473, Cape Town 8000; tel. (21) 4617472; fax (21) 4613758; e-mail sflesch@iafrica.com; f. 1954; Prin. Officer S. FLESCH.

Fortress Books: POB 189, Rondebosch 7700; tel. and fax (21) 7884927; e-mail fortress@iafrica.com; f. 1973; military history, biographies, financial; Man. Dir I. UYS.

T. W. Griggs & Co: 341 West St, Durban 4001; tel. (31) 3048571; Africana.

F.J.N. Harman Publishers: Menlo Park; tel. (12) 469575; f. 1981; educational; Man. Dir F. J. N. HARMAN.

HAUM: Prima Park 4 and 6, cnr Klosser and King Edward Rds, Porow 7500; tel. (21) 926123; f. 1894; Man. C. J. HAGE. Subsidiaries include:

> **Kagiso Publishers:** POB 629, Pretoria 0001; tel. (12) 3284620; fax (12) 3284705; school textbooks and other materials for schools and tertiary institutions in all 11 official South African languages; Man. Dir L. M. MABANDLA.

> **University Publishers & Booksellers (Pty) Ltd:** POB 29, Stellenbosch 7599; tel. (21) 8870337; fax (21) 8832975; f. 1947; educational; Man. Dir B. B. LIEBENBERG.

Heinemann Publishers (Pty) Ltd: POB 781940, Sandown, Sandton 2146; tel. (11) 7848619; fax (11) 7848360; educational; incl. imprints Lexicon, Isando and Centaur; Man. Dir K. KROEGER.

Home Economics Publishers: POB 7091, Stellenbosch 7599; tel. (21) 8864722; fax (21) 8864722.

Human and Rousseau (Pty) Ltd: POB 5050, Cape Town 8000; tel. (21) 4233911; fax (21) 4265744; e-mail humanhk@human

rousseau.com; internet www.humanrousseau.com; f. 1959; English, Afrikaans, Xhosa and Zulu; general adult and children's trade books; Gen. Man. C. T. BREYTENBACH.

Incipit Publishers: POB 28754, Sunnyside, Pretoria 0132; tel. and fax (12) 463802; f. 1987; music; Man. MARIANNE FEENSTRA.

Juta and Co Ltd: POB 14373, Kenwyn 7790, Cape Town; tel. (11) 7975101; fax (11) 7627424; e-mail books@juta.co.za; internet www.juta.co.za; f. 1853; academic, educational, law, electronic; CEO R. J. WILSON.

Klipbok Publishers: POB 170, Durbanville 7550; tel. and fax (21) 9762293; f. 1979; prose, poetry, drama.

Knowledge Unlimited (Pty) Ltd: POB 781337; Sandton 2146; tel. (11) 6521800; fax (11) 3142984; children's fiction, educational; Man. Dir MIKE JACKLIN.

Konsensus Publishers: 213 Orion St, Waterkloof 0180.

Lemur Books (Pty) Ltd: POB 1645, Alberton 1450; tel. (11) 9072029; fax (11) 8690890; e-mail lemur@mweb.co.za; military, political, history, hunting, general; Man. Dir F. STIFF.

Lovedale Press: Private Bag X1346, Alice; tel. (040) 6531135; fax (040) 6531871; f. 1841; Gen. Man. Rev. B. NTISANA.

Lux Verbi: POB 1822, Cape Town 8000; tel. (21) 4215540; fax (21) 4191865; e-mail luxverbi.publ@kingsley.co.za; religion; CEO H. S. SPIES; Editor-in-Chief D. FOURIE.

Macdonald Purnell (Pty) Ltd: POB 51401, Randburg 2125; tel. (11) 7875830; South African flora, fauna, geography and history; Man. Dir E. ANDERSON.

Marler Publications (Pty) Ltd: POB 27815, Sunnyside, Pretoria 0132; tel. (12) 573770; f. 1987; educational; Man. Dir C. J. MULLER.

Maskew Miller Longman (Pty) Ltd: Howard Drive, Pinelands 7405, POB 396, Cape Town 8000; tel. (21) 5317750; fax (21) 5314049; f. 1983; educational and general; CEO M. A. PEACOCK.

Methodist Publishing House: POB 13128, Woodstock, Cape Town 7915; tel. (21) 4483640; fax (21) 4483716; e-mail methpub@iafrica.com; internet www.methbooks.co.za; religion and theology; Gen. Man. D. R. LEVERTON.

Nasionale Boekhandel: POB 122, Parow 7500; tel. (21) 5911131; fiction, general, educational, academic; English, Afrikaans and several African languages; Man. Dir P. J. BOTMA.

Nasou—Via Afrika: POB 5197, Cape Town 8000; tel. (21) 4063313; fax (21) 4062922; e-mail nasouhk@nasou.com; educational; Gen. Man. D. H. SCHROEDER.

Oudiovista Productions (Pty) Ltd: Parow; tel. (21) 5911131; Man. Dir P. J. BOTMA.

Oxford University Press: POB 12119, Cape Town 7463; tel. (21) 5954400; fax (21) 5954430; e-mail oxford@oup.co.za; f. 1914; Man. Dir KATE McCALLUM.

Perskor Publishers: POB 3068, Halfway House 1685 tel. (11) 3153647; fax (11) 3152757; e-mail vlacberg@icon.co.za; f. 1940; general and educational; Sr Gen. Man. G. DE BEER.

David Philip Publishers (Pty) Ltd: POB 23408, Claremont 7735; tel. (21) 644136; fax (21) 643358; e-mail dpp@iafrica.com; f. 1971; general, academic, literature, reference, fiction; Man. Dir BRIDGET IMPEY.

Pretoria Boekhandel: POB 23334, Innesdale, Pretoria 0031; tel. (12) 761531; f. 1971; Prin. Officer L. S. VAN DER WALT.

Random House SA (Pty) Ltd: POB 2263, Parklands 2121; tel. (11) 4843538; fax (11) 4846180; e-mail mail@randomhouse.co.za; f. 1966; Man. Dir S. JOHNSON.

Ravan Press (Pty) Ltd: POB 145, Randburg 2125; tel. (11) 7897636; fax (11) 7897653; e-mail ipuseng@hodder.co.za; f. 1972; political, sociological, fiction, business studies, gender, history, autobiography, biography, educational; Man. Dir DAVID LEA.

Saayman and Weber (Pty) Ltd: POB 673, Cape Town 8000; f. 1980.

Sasavona Publishers and Booksellers: Private Bag X8, Braamfontein 2017; tel. (11) 4032502; fax (11) 3397274; Northern Sotho, Tshwa, Tsonga, Tswana, Venda and Zulu; Man. A. E. KALTENRIEDER.

Shuter and Shooter (Pty) Ltd: 230 Church St, Pietermaritzburg 3201; POB 109, Pietermaritzburg 3200; tel. (33) 3946830; fax (33) 3427419; e-mail dryder@shuter.co.za; internet www.shuter.co.za; f. 1921; educational, general and African languages; Man. Dir D. F. RYDER.

The Struik Publishing Group (Pty) Ltd: POB 1144, Cape Town 8000; tel. (21) 4624360; fax (21) 4619378; Dirs G. STRUIK, A. D. L. CRUZEN, M. C. H. JAMES, C. M. HANLEY, N. D. PRYKE, J. D. WILKINS, J. L. SCHOEMAN, A. S. VERSCHOYLE.

Study Aids Ltd: 13 Darrock Ave, Albemarle Park, Germiston 1401; study aids.

Hans Strydom Publishers: Private Bag 10, Mellville 2109.

Sunray Publishers: 96 Queen St, Durban 4001; tel. (31) 3052543.

Tafelberg Publishers Ltd: 28 Wale St, Cape Town 8000; tel. (21) 4241320; fax (21) 4242510; e-mail tafelberg@tafelberg.com; internet www.tafelberg.com; f. 1950; juvenile, fiction and non-fiction, arts and crafts, nature and tourism; Gen. Man. J. P. VAN ZYL.

Thomson Publications: Johannesburg 2123; tel. (11) 7892144; fax (11) 7893196; f. 1948; trade and technical; Man. Dir JOE M. BRADY.

UCCSA Publications Dept: POB 31083, Braamfontein 2017; tel. (11) 8360065; f. 1946; Gen. Man. W. WESTENBORG.

University of Natal Press: Private Bag X01, Scottsville 3209; tel. (33) 2605226; fax (33) 2605801; e-mail books@press.unp.ac.za; internet www.unpress.co.za; Publr GLENN COWLEY.

Van der Walt and Son, J. P. (Pty) Ltd: POB 123, Pretoria 0001; tel. (12) 3252100; fax (12) 3255498; f. 1947; general; Man. Dir C. J. STEENKAMP.

Chris van Rensburg Publications (Pty) Ltd: POB 29159, Mellville 2109; tel. (31) 7264350; yearbooks, general; Man. Dir. C. C. VAN RENSBURG.

Van Schaik, J. L. Publishers: POB 12681, Hatfield 0028; tel. (12) 3422765; fax (12) 433563; e-mail mbothae@jlvanscaik.com; f. 1914; educational, general, religion; English, Afrikaans and vernaculars; Gen. Man. E. WESSELS.

Waterkant Publishers: POB 4539, Cape Town 8000; tel. (21) 215540; fax (21) 4191865; f. 1980; Exec. Chair. W. J. VAN ZIJL.

Witwatersrand University Press: PO Wits, Johannesburg 2050; tel. (11) 4845910; fax (11) 4845971; e-mail wup@iafrica.com; internet www.wits.ac.za; f. 1922; academic; Head PAT TUCKER.

PUBLISHERS' ASSOCIATION

Publishers' Association of South Africa: POB 116, St James, Cape Town 7946; tel. (21) 7827677; fax (21) 7827679; e-mail pasa@iafrica.com; internet www.icon.co.za; f. 1992; Chair. KATE MCCALLUM; Admin. P. CLAYTON.

Broadcasting and Communications

TELECOMMUNICATIONS

South African Telecommunications Regulatory Authority (SATRA): 164 Katherine St, Sandton 2146; Private Bag X1, Marlboro 2063; tel. (11) 3218200; fax (11) 3218551; e-mail estag@satra.gov.za; internet www.satra.org.za.

Mobile Telephone Network: PMB 9955, Sandton 2146; tel. (11) 3016000; fax (11) 3016111.

Telkom SA Ltd: Private Bag X74, Pretoria 0001; tel. (12) 3111028; fax (12) 3114031; internet www.telkom.co.za; f. 1991; Chair. E. D. MOSENEKE; CEO SIZWE NXASANA.

BROADCASTING
Regulatory Authority

Independent Broadcasting Authority: Pinmill Farm, 164 Katherine St, Sandton 2146; tel. (22) 7220000; fax (11) 4441919; e-mail info@lba.org.za; internet www.lba.org.za; f. 1993; Chair. S. M. MATABANE; CEO HARRIS GXAWENI (suspended May 1997).

RADIO

South African Broadcasting Corporation (SABC)–Radio: Private Bag X1, Auckland Park 2006; tel. (11) 7143407; fax (11) 7142635; e-mail mbathah@sabc.co.za; internet www.sabc.co.za; Chair. Prof. PAULUS ZULU; CEO CHARLOTTE MAMPANE.

Domestic Services

Radio South Africa; Afrikaans Stereo; Radio 5; Radio 2000; Highveld Stereo; Good Hope Stereo; Radio Kontrei; RPN Stereo; Jacaranda Stereo; Radio Algoa (regional services); Radio Lotus (Indian service in English); Radio Metro (African service in English); Radio Lebowa; Radio Ndebele; Radio Sesotho; Setswana Stereo; Radio Swazi; Radio Tsonga; Radio Xhosa; Radio Zulu.

External Service

Channel Africa Radio: POB 91313, Auckland Park 2006; tel. (11) 7142255; fax (11) 7142546; e-mail africancan@channel.africa.org; f. 1966; SABC's external service; broadcasts 217 hours per week in English, French, Kiswahili, Portuguese and several African languages; Exec. Editor HANS-DIETER WINKENS.

TELEVISION

South African Broadcasting Corporation (SABC)–Television: Private Bag X41, Auckland Park 2006; tel. (11) 7149111; fax (11) 7145055; internet www.sabc.co.za; transmissions began in 1976; operates television services in seven languages over three channels; English and Afrikaans programmes on Channel one (TV1); Channel two (CCV-TV) broadcasts in English, Northern and Southern Sotho, Tswana, Xhosa and Zulu; Channel three (NNTV) broadcasts documentaries, educational programmes and sport; Chair. Prof. PAULUS ZULU; CEO MOLEFE MOKGATLE.

Finance

(cap. = capital; auth. = authorized; res = reserves; dep. = deposits; m. = million; brs = branches; amounts in rand)

BANKING
Central Bank

South African Reserve Bank: 370 Church St, POB 427, Pretoria 0001; tel. (12) 3133911; fax (12) 3133197; e-mail info@gwise.resbank .co.za; internet www.resbank.co.za; f. 1921; cap. and res 2,300.6m., dep. 10,764.7m. (March 1999); Gov. TITO MBOWENI; Dep. Govs T. T. THAHANE, J. H. CROSS; 7 brs.

Commercial Banks

ABSA Bank Ltd: ABSA Towers, 19th Floor, 170 Main St, Johannesburg 2001; tel. (11) 3504000; fax (11) 3504009; e-mail groupsec@absa.co.za; internet www.absa.co.za; cap. 3,476m. (March 1999); Chair. Dr DANIE CRONJE; Man. Dir E. R. BOSMAN; 726 brs.

African Bank Limited: 56 Marshall St, Johannesburg 2001; POB 61352, Marshall 2107; tel. (11) 9741156; fax (11) 9741100; e-mail afribank@afribank.co.za; f. 1975; cap. 1,600.0m., res 1,116.7m. (Dec. 1998); Chair. Dr N. H. MOTLANA; Man. Dir C. J. BEAZLEY.

Albaraka Bank Ltd: POB 4395, Durban 4000, KwaZulu/Natal; tel. (31) 3072972; fax (31) 3052631; e-mail albaraka@icon.co.za; f. 1989; cap. and res 31.4m., dep. 249.2m. (June 1997); Chair. Dr S. J. MALAIKAH; CEO E. E. VAWDA.

BOE Bank Ltd: NBS Kingsmead, 90 Ordnance Rd, Durban 4001; tel. (31) 3641111; fax (31) 3642900; internet www.boe.co.za; cap. and res 2,980m. (Oct. 1998); Chair. W. J. MCADAM.

BOE Bank Holdings Ltd: NBS Kingsmead, 90 Ordnance Rd, Durban 4001, KawZulu/Natal; tel. (31) 3641111; fax (31) 3642900; e-mail info@nbs.co.za; internet www.nbs.co.za; f. 1997 by merger of NBS Bank Ltd and Boland Bank PKS, BOE Investment Bank Ltd, and BOE Private Bank Ltd, and BOE Private Bank; cap. and res 1,078m. (Sept. 1999); Chair. W. J. MCADAM; Man. Dir T. A. BOARDMAN.

FirstRand Bank Ltd: 1 First Place, 6th Floor, BankCity, Johannesburg 2001; POB 1153, Johannesburg 2000; tel. (11) 3712111; fax (11) 3712257; internet www.fnb.co.za; First National Bank of Southern Africa and Rand Merchant Bank merged July 1999; f. 1971; cap. 3,500m., res 5,087.1m., dep. 86,767.8m. (Sept. 1998); Chair. T. N. CHAPMAN; Man. Dir V. W. BARTLETT; 1,360 brs.

Habib Overseas Bank Ltd: Oriental Plaza, Fordsburg 2092; tel. (11) 8347441; fax (11) 8347446; e-mail habib@gobal.co.za; internet www.habibsons.com; f. 1990; cap. 11m., dep. 97.1m. (Dec. 1998); Chair. MOHAMMAD HASSAN HABIB; Man. Dir ANJUM ZAHEER; 4 brs.

International Bank of Southern Africa Ltd: Sunnyside Ridge Bldg, 3rd Floor, 32 Princess of Wales Terrace, Parktown, Johannesburg 2193, Gauteng; tel. (11) 6443300; fax (11) 6431122; e-mail bsa@internationalbank.co.za; f. 1990 as Commercial Bank of Namibia S.A.; cap. 64.1m., dep. 1,340.1m. (Dec. 1998); Chair. GUENTAR ZENO STEFFENS; Man. Dir NIGEL ERNEST PALMER.

Investec Bank Ltd: 100 Grayston Drive, Sandown, Sandton 2196; tel. (11) 2867000; fax (11) 2867777; internet www.investec.com; f. 1974; cap. 12m., res 4,928m., dep. 104,132m. (March 1999); Chair. HUGH HERMAN.

Meeg Bank Ltd: POB 232, Bank of Transkei Bldg, 60 Sutherland St, Umtata; tel. (471) 311367; fax (471) 22546; f. 1977; cap. and res 34.8m., dep. 392.6m. (March 1996); formerly Bank of Transkei; name changed Oct. 1998; Chair. E. R. BOSMAN; Man. Dir. E. G. KALTENBRÜNN; 5 brs.

Mercantile Bank Ltd: Mercantile Lisbon House, 142 West St, Sandown, Gauteng 2196; tel. (11) 3020300; fax (11) 3020700; e-mail fcoelho@mercantile.co.za; internet www.mercantile.co.za; f. 1965; cap. and res 283.1m. dep. 2,445.8m. (March 1998); Chair. H. V. VORSTER; Man. Dir D. P. COHEN.

Nedcor Bank: 100 Main St, Johannesburg, Gauteng 2001; POB 1144, Johannesburg 2000; tel. (11) 6307111; fax (11) 6302465; e-mail nedcorir@icon.co.za; internet www.nedcor.co.za; f. 1988; cap. 20m., res 5,780m., dep. 88,347m. (Dec. 1998); Chair. C. F. LIEBENBERG; CEO RICHARD C. M. LAUBSCHER; 317 brs.

The South African Bank of Athens Ltd: Bank of Athens Bldg, 116 Marshall St, Johannesburg 2001; POB 7781, Johannesburg 2000; tel. (11) 8321211; fax (11) 8381001; f. 1947; associated with National Bank of Greece; cap. 4.1m., res 55.2m., dep. 353.9m. (Dec. 1998); Chair. T. KARATZAS; Man. Dir D. PAPANIKOLAOU; 14 brs.

The Standard Bank South Africa Ltd: Standard Bank Centre, 5 Simmonds St, Johannesburg, Gauteng 2000; tel. (11) 6369111; fax (11) 6365617; internet www.standardbank.co.za; f. 1862; cap.

51.5m., res 6,816.4m., dep. 116,860.5m. (Dec. 1998); Chair. Dr CONRAD B. STRAUSS; CEO JACKO H. MAREE; 997 brs.

Merchant Bank

UAL Merchant Bank Ltd: UAL Gardens, 1 Newton Ave, Killarney, Johannesburg; tel. (11) 4801000; fax (11) 4801525; cap. 6.0m., total assets 5,830.1m. (Sept. 1997); Chair. R. C. M. LAUBSCHER.

Savings Banks

British Kaffrarian Savings Bank Society: POB 1432, King William's Town 5600; tel. (433) 21478; f. 1860; dep. 28.8m.; CEO D. E. DAUBERMANN.

Pretoria Bank Ltd: Woltemade Bldg, POB 1393, Pretoria; cap. 601,250; dep. 7.6m.; Chair. M. D. MARAIS; Gen. Man. I. W. FERREIRA.

Staalwerkersspaarbank: 417 Church St, POB 1747, Pretoria; cap. 240,630; dep. 2.5m.; Chair. and Man. Dir L. J. VAN DEN BERG.

Investment Banks

Investec Bank Ltd: 100 Grayston Drive, Sandton City 2146; tel. (11) 2867000; fax (11) 2867777; e-mail crosenberg@investec.co.za; internet www.investec.com; f. 1974; cap. 12m., res 4,928m., dep. 104,132m. (March 1999); Chair. H. S. HERMAN; CEO S. KOSEFF; 5 brs.

Nedcor Investment Bank Ltd: 1 Newtown Ave, Killarney 2193; POB 582, Johannesburg 2000; tel. (11) 4801000; fax (11) 4801525; f. 1955 as Union Acceptances Limited; cap. 6m., total assets 15,976.2m. (Dec. 1998); Chair. R. C. M. LAUBSCHER; 2 brs.

Development Bank

Development Bank of Southern Africa (DBSA): 1258 Lever Rd, Midrand, POB 1234, Halfway House 1685; tel. (11) 3133911; fax (11) 3133086; e-mail thandim@dbsa.org; internet www.dbsa.org; cap. and res 6,131.4m., dep. 1,573.2m. (March 1998); f. 1983; Chair. Prof. W. NKUHLU; CEO Dr IAN GOLDIN.

Discount Houses

Discount House Merchant Bank Ltd: 66 Marshall St, Johannesburg 2001; POB 61574, Marshalltown 2107; tel. (11) 8367451; fax (11) 8369636; f. 1957; cap. 18.8m.; Exec. Chair. C. J. H. DUNN; Man. Dir M. R. THOMPSON.

Interbank Ltd: 108 Fox St, POB 6035, Johannesburg; tel. (11) 8344831; fax (11) 8345357; f. 1971; cap. 15.5m., dep. 564m. (1990); Chair. A. KELLY; Man. Dir M. SWART.

The National Discount House of South Africa Ltd: Loveday House, 1st Floor, 15 Loveday St, Johannesburg; tel. (11) 8323151; f. 1961; auth. cap. 10m., dep. 357.1m. (1987); Chair. M. MACDONALD; Man. Dir G. G. LUND.

Bankers' Association

Banking Council of South Africa: 17 Harrison St, 10th Floor, POB 61674, Marshalltown 2107; tel. (11) 3703500; fax (11) 8365509; e-mail banking@banking.org.za; internet www.banking.org.za; f. 1993; 15,000 mems; CEO R. S. K. TUCKER.

STOCK EXCHANGE

Johannesburg Stock Exchange: 17 Diagonal St, POB 1174, Johannesburg 2000; tel. (11) 3772200; fax (11) 8387106; e-mail pr@jse.co.za; f. 1887; in late 1995 legislation was enacted providing for the deregulation of the Stock Exchange; automated trading commenced in June 1996; Exec. Pres. R. M. LAUBSER.

INSURANCE

ACA Insurers Ltd: 35 Symons Rd, Auckland Park; tel. (11) 7268900; f. 1948; Man. Dir L. G. Y. NEMORIN.

Aegis Insurance Co Ltd: Aegis Insurance House, 91 Commissioner St, Johannesburg; tel. (11) 8367621; fax (11) 8384559; Man. Dir B. H. SEACH.

African Mutual Trust & Assurance Co Ltd: 34 Church St, POB 27, Malmesbury; f. 1900; Chief Gen. Man. R. A. L. CUTHBERT.

Allianz Insurance Ltd: Allianz House, 13 Fraser St, Johannesburg 2001; POB 62228, Marshalltown 2107; tel. (11) 2804300; fax (11) 2804309; Chair. D. DU PREEZ; Man. Dir Dr U. F. DELIUS.

Anglo American Life Assurance Co Ltd: Life Centre, 45 Commissioner St, POB 6946, Johannesburg 2000; Exec. Chair. Dr Z. J. DE BEER; Man. Dir Dr M. BERNSTEIN.

CGU Holdings Ltd: CGU House, 26 Loveday St, POB 3555, Johannesburg 2000; tel. (11) 4911911; fax (11) 8382600; internet www.cgu.co.za; f. 1964; Chair. J. C. ROBBERTZE; Man. Dir R. R. McWANLESS.

Credit Guarantee Insurance Corpn of Africa Ltd: 31 Dover St, POB 125, Randburg 2125; tel. (11) 8897000; fax (11) 8861027; e-mail info@cgic.co.za; internet www.creditguarantee.co.za; f. 1956; Chair. C. J. OOSTHUIZEN; Man. Dir C. T. L. LEISEWITZ.

Fedsure Life Assurance Ltd: Fedsure House, 1 de Villiers St, POB 666, Johannesburg 2000; tel. (11) 3326500; fax (11) 4921102;

e-mail fedsure@fedsure.co.za; internet www.fedsure.co.za; f. 1944; Chair. J. A. BARROW; Man. Dir MORRIS BERNSTEIN.

I. G. I. Insurance Co Ltd: 162 Anderson St, POB 8199, Johannesburg 2000; tel. (11) 3351911; fax (11) 290491; f. 1954; Chair. I. M. A. LEWIS; Man. Dir P. S. DENNISS.

Liberty Life Association of Africa Ltd (LibLife): Liberty Life Centre, 1 Ameshoff St, Johannesburg 2001; POB 10499, Johannesburg 2000; tel. (11) 4083911; fax (11) 4082109; internet www.liberty.co.za; f. 1958; Chair. D. E. COOPER; CEO ROY ANDERSEN.

Metropolitan Life Ltd: 7 Coen Steytler Ave, Foreshore, Cape Town; POB 2212, Bellville 7535; tel. (21) 9405911; fax (21) 9405730; internet www.metropolitan.co.za; Chair. D. E. MOSENEKE; Man. Dir P. R. DOYLE.

Momentum Life Assurers Ltd: Momentum Park, 267B West Ave, Centurion 0157; POB 7400, Centurion 0046; tel. (12) 6718911; fax (12) 6636288; internet www.momentum.co.za; f. 1967; Chair. LAURIE DIPPENAAR; Man. Dir HILLIE P. MEYER.

Mutual & Federal Insurance Co Ltd: Mutual Federal Centre, 19th Floor, 75 President St, Johannesburg 2001; POB 1120, Johannesburg 2000; tel. (11) 3749111; fax (11) 3742652; f. 1970; Chair. M. J. LEVETT; Man. Dir B. CAMPBELL.

Old Mutual (South African Mutual Life Assurance Society): Mutualpark, Jan Smuts Drive, POB 66, Cape Town 8001; tel. (21) 5099111; fax (21) 5094444; internet www.oldmutual.com; f. 1845; Chair. MIKE J. LEVETT; Man. Dir G. S. VAN NIEKERK.

Protea Assurance Co Ltd: Protea Assurance Bldg, Greenmarket Sq., POB 646, Cape Town 8000; tel. (21) 4887911; fax (21) 4887110; Man. Dir A. L. TAINTON.

The Rand Mutual Assurance Co Ltd: POB 61413, Marshalltown 2107; tel. (11) 4976600; fax (11) 8344150; f. 1894; Chair. P. J. EUSTACE; Man. Dir A. J. E. FIVAZ.

Santam Ltd: Santam Head Office, 1 Sportica Crescent, Bellville 7530, POB 3881, Tyger Valley 7536; tel. (21) 9157000; fax (21) 9140700; internet www.santam.co.za; f. 1918; Chair. M. H. DALING; Man. Dir L. VERMAAK.

South African Eagle Insurance Co Ltd: Eagle House, 70 Fox St, Johannesburg 2001; POB 61489, Marshalltown 2107; tel. (11) 3709111; fax (11) 8365541; internet www.saeagle.co.za; Chair. D. W. WHITE; CEO N. V. BEYERS.

South African National Life Assurance Co Ltd (SANLAM): 2 Strand Rd, Bellville, POB 1, Sanlamhof 7532; tel. (21) 9479111; fax (21) 9478066; e-mail chairman@sanlam.co.za; f. 1918; Chair. MARINUS DALING.

South African Trade Union Assurance Society Ltd: Capital Alliance Life Ltd, 162 Anderson St, Johannesburg 2000; tel. (11) 3301000; fax (11) 3301013; f. 1941; Chair. E. VAN TONDER; Gen. Man. A. SUMNER.

Standard General Insurance Co Ltd: Standard General House, 12 Harrison St, POB 4352, Johannesburg 2000; tel. (11) 8362723; fax (11) 8344935; f. 1943; Man. Dir Dr M. DEYSEL.

Swiss Re Southern Africa Ltd: Swiss Park, 10 Queens Rd, Parktown, POB 7049, Johannesburg 2000; tel. (11) 4895600; fax (11) 4844448; f. 1950; Chair. and Man. Dir L. KEEL.

UBS Insurance Co Ltd: United Bldgs, 6th Floor, cnr Fox and Eloff Sts, Johannesburg; Chair. P. W. SCEALES; Gen. Man. J. L. S. HEFER.

Westchester Insurance Co (Pty) Ltd: Mobil Court, POB 747, Cape Town 8000; tel. (21) 4034000.

Association

The South African Insurance Asscn: POB 30619, Braamfontein 2017; tel. (11) 4038150; e-mail saia@iafrica.com; f. 1973; represents short-term insurers; CEO BARRY SCOTT.

Trade and Industry

DEVELOPMENT ORGANIZATIONS

Industrial Development Corporation of South Africa Ltd (IDCSA): 19 Fredman Drive, POB 784055, Sandton 2146; tel. (11) 2693000; fax (11) 2693116; e-mail idc@idc.co.za; internet www.idc.co.za; f. 1940; Chair. C. H. WIESE; Gen. Man. M. MACDONALD.

The Independent Development Trust: 129 Bree St, Cape Town 8001, POB 16114, Vlaeberg 8018; tel. (21) 238030; fax (21) 238401; f. 1990; finances health and rural devt, housing and urban devt, micro-enterprises, education, school and clinic-building projects; Chair. Dr MAMPHELA RAMPHELE.

National Productivity Institute: POB 3971, Pretoria 0001; tel. (12) 3411470; fax (12) 441866; e-mail npiinfo@cis.co.za; internet www.npi.co.za; f. 1968; Exec. Dir Dr Y. DLADLA.

CHAMBER OF COMMERCE

South African Chamber of Business (SACOB): JCC House, 3rd Floor, Empire Rd, Milpark, Johannesburg; POB 91267, Auckland Park 2006; tel. (11) 3589743; fax (11) 3589773; e-mail econo@sacob.co.za; internet www.sacob.co.za; f. 1990 by merger of Asscn of Chambers of Commerce and Industry and South African Federated Chamber of Industries; 70 chambers of commerce and industry are mems; Pres. HUMPHREY KHOZA; Dir-Gen. R. W. K. PARSONS; CEO KEVIN WAKEFORD.

CHAMBERS OF INDUSTRIES

Bloemfontein Chamber of Trade and Industry: POB 87, Kellner Heights, Bloemfontein 9300; tel. (51) 473368; fax (51) 475064.

Cape Chamber of Commerce and Industry: Cape Chamber House, 19 Louis Gradner St, Foreshore, Cape Town 8001; tel. (21) 4184300; fax (21) 4181800; f. 1994; Pres. DENIS SKEATE; 3,800 mems.

Durban Chamber of Commerce and Industry: POB 1506, Durban 4000; tel. (31) 3013692; fax (31) 3045255; e-mail chambers@iafrica.com; internet www.durban.org.za/chamber; Dir G. W. TYLER; 7,000 mems.

Johannesburg Chamber of Commerce and Industry: JCC House, 6th Floor, Empire Road, Milpark; Private Bag 34, Auckland Park 2006; tel. (11) 7265300; fax (11) 4822000; e-mail jcci@cis.co.za; internet www.jcci.co.za; Pres. M. LEOKA; 5,000 mems.

Northern Transvaal Chamber of Industries: Showground Office, Souttter St, Pretoria 0183; tel. (12) 3271487; fax (12) 3271501; f. 1929; Exec. Dir R. A. BUITENDAG; 289 mems (secondary industries).

Pietermaritzburg Chamber of Industries: POB 637, Pietermaritzburg 3200; tel. (331) 452747; fax (331) 944151; f. 1910; Dir R. J. ALLEN; 300 mems.

Port Elizabeth Regional Chamber of Commerce and Industry: Chamber House, 22 Grahamstown Rd, Port Elizabeth 6001, POB 2221, North End 6056; tel. (41) 4844430; fax (41) 4871851; e-mail info@pechamber.org.za; internet www.pechamber.org.za; f. 1995; CEO A. DA COSTA; 1,100 mems.

Wesvaal Chamber of Business: POB 7, Klerksdorp 2570; tel. (18) 4627401; fax (18) 4627402; e-mail chamber@gds.co.za; Pres. J. McENDOO.

INDUSTRIAL AND TRADE ORGANIZATIONS

Building Industries Federation South Africa: POB 1619, Halfway House 1685; tel. (11) 3151010; fax (11) 3151644; e-mail bifsa@bifsa.org.za; internet www.bifsa.org.za; f. 1904; 5,000 mems.

Chamber of Mines of South Africa: Chamber of Mines Bldg, 5 Hollard St, POB 61809, Marshalltown 2107; tel. (11) 4987100; fax (11) 8341884; e-mail webmaster@bullion.org.za; internet www.bullion.org.za; f. 1889; Pres. RICK MENELL.

Clothing Federation of South Africa: Cambridge Place, Crosskeys House, Kirkby Rd, Bedford Gardens, POB 75755, Gardenview 2047; tel. (11) 6228125; fax (11) 6228316; e-mail clofed@clofed.co.za; internet www.clofed.co.za; Dir P. L. THERON.

FOSKOR Ltd: POB 1, Phalaborwa 1390; tel. (15) 7892910; fax (15) 7892070; e-mail foskor.msmail@foskor.co.za; Man. Dir P. J. GREYLING.

Grain Milling Federation: Johannesburg; f. 1944; Sec. J. BARENDSE.

Industrial Rubber Manufacturers' Association of South Africa: POB 91267, Auckland Park 2006; tel. (11) 4822524; fax (11) 7261344; f. 1978; Chair. Dr D. DUNCAN.

Master Diamond Cutters' Association of South Africa: S.A. Diamond Centre, Suite 511, 240 Commissioner St, Johannesburg 2001; tel. (11) 3341930; fax (11) 3341933; e-mail diam@pixie.co.za; f. 1928; 76 mems.

Motor Industries' Federation: POB 2940, Randburg 2125; tel. (11) 7892542; fax (11) 7894525; f. 1910; Dir W. FOURIE; 7,800 mems.

National Association of Automobile Manufacturers of South Africa: Nedbank Plaza, 1st Floor, cnr Church and Beatrix Sts, Pretoria 0002; POB 40611, Arcadia 0007; tel. (12) 3232003; fax (12) 3263232; e-mail naamsa@iafrica.com; f. 1935; Dir N. M. W. VERMEULEN.

National Chamber of Milling, Inc: Braamfontein; tel. (11) 4033739; f. 1936; Dir Dr J. B. DE SWARDT.

National Textile Manufacturers' Association: POB 1506, Durban 4000; tel. (31) 3013692; fax (31) 3045255; f. 1947; Sec. PETER McGREGOR; 9 mems.

Plastics Federation of South Africa: 18 Gazelle Rd, Corporate Park, Old Pretoria Rd, Midrand, Private Bag X68, Halfway House 1685; tel. (11) 314-4021; fax (11) 314-3764; f. 1979; Exec. Dir W. NAUDÉ; 3 mems.

Printing Industries Federation of South Africa: Printech Ave, Laser Park, POB 1084, Honeydew 2040; tel. (11) 7943810; fax (11) 7943964; e-mail pifsa@pifsa.org; internet www.pifsa.org; f. 1916; CEO C. W. J. SYKES.

SOEKOR (Pty) Ltd: POB 307, Parow 7500; tel. (21) 9383911; fax (21) 9383144; f. 1965; responsible for all offshore petroleum and natural gas prospecting in South Africa; CEO M. J. HEÜSER.

South African Brewing Industry Employers' Association: Private Bag 34, Auckland Park 2006; tel. (11) 7265300; f. 1927; Sec. L. I. GOLDSTONE; 2 mems.

South African Cement Producers' Association: POB 168, Halfway House 1685; tel. (11) 3150300; fax (11) 3150584; e-mail graham@onci.org.za.

South African Dairy Foundation: POB 72300, Lynnwood Ridge 0040; tel. (2712) 3485345; fax (2712) 3486284; f. 1980; Sec. S. L. VAN COLLER; 59 mems.

South African Federation of Civil Engineering Contractors: POB 644, Bedfordview 2008; tel. (11) 4551700; fax (11) 4551153; f. 1939; Exec. Dir R. R. VALENTE; 230 mems.

South African Foreign Trade Organization (SAFTO): POB 782376, Sandton 2146; tel. (11) 8833737; fax (11) 8836569; e-mail safto@apollo.is.co.za; f. 1963; Chair. W. C. VAN DER MERWE; CEO J. J. SCHEEPERS; 1,500 mems.

South African Fruit and Vegetable Canners' Association (Pty) Ltd: Canning Fruit Board Bldg, 258 Main St, POB 6175, Paarl 7622; tel. (21) 8711308; fax (21) 8725930; f. 1953; Gen. Man. P. S. BUYS; 12 mems.

South African Inshore Fishing Industry Association (Pty) Ltd: POB 2066, Cape Town 8000; tel. (21) 251500; f. 1953; Chair. W. A. LEWIS; Man. S. J. MALHERBE; 4 mems.

South African Lumber Millers' Association: Private Bag X686, Isando 1600; tel. (11) 9741061; fax (11) 9749779; e-mail jmort@salma.org.za; internet www.salma.org.za; f. 1941; Exec. Dir J. H. MORTIMER; 88 mems.

South African Oil Expressers' Association: Cereal Centre, 6th Floor, 11 Leyds St, Braamfontein 2017; tel. (11) 7251280; f. 1937; Sec. Dr R. DU TOIT; 14 mems.

South African Paint Manufacturers' Association: POB 751605, Gardenview, Johannesburg 2047; tel. (11) 4552503; fax (11) 4552502; e-mail sapma@mweb.co.za; internet www.mbendi.co.za.

South African Petroleum Industry Association (SAPIA): Cape Town; represents South Africa's six principal petroleum cos; Chair. FRED PHASWANA.

South African Sugar Association: 170 Flanders Drive, POB 700, Mount Edgecombe 4340; tel. (31) 5087000; fax (31) 5087199; e-mail mukeshtri@sasa.org.za; internet www.sugar.org.za; Exec. Dir M. K. TRIKAM.

South African Wool Board: POB 2191, Port Elizabeth 6056; tel. (41) 544301; fax (41) 546760; f. 1946; 12 mems: nine appointed by wool-growers and three by the Minister of Agriculture; Chair. H. F. PRINSLOO; CEO Dr J. W. GIESELBACH.

South African Wool Textile Council: POB 2201, North End, Port Elizabeth 6056; tel. (41) 4845252; fax (41) 4845629; e-mail woolexsa@iafrica.com; Sec. BEATTY-ANNE STARKEY.

Steel and Engineering Industries Federation of South Africa (SEIFSA): POB 1338, Johannesburg 2000; tel. (11) 8336033; fax (11) 8381522; e-mail angelique@seifsa.co.za; internet www.seifsa.co.za; f. 1943; Exec. Dir. B. ANGUS; 40 affiliated trade asscns representing 2,443 mems.

Sugar Manufacturing and Refining Employers' Association: 170 Flanders Drive, POB 1000, Mount Edgecombe 4300; tel. (31) 5087300; fax (31) 5087310; e-mail sasmal@sasa.org.za; f. 1947; Chair. C. H. KYLE.

UTILITIES
Electricity

Electricity Supply Commission (ESKOM): POB 1091, Johannesburg 2000; tel. (11) 8008111; fax (11) 8004390; internet www.eskom.co.za; f. 1923; state-controlled; CEO A. J. MORGAN.

Gas

SASOL Gas: POB 4211, Randburg 2125; tel. (11) 8897600; fax (11) 8897955; internet www.sasol.com/gas; f. 1964; Gen. Man. G. J. STRAUSS.

Water

Umgeni Water: 310 Burger St, Pietermaritzburg 3201; tel. (331) 3411111; fax (331) 3411167; internet www.umgeni.co.za/contact.html.

Water Research Commission: POB 824, Pretoria; tel. (12) 3300342; fax (12) 3312565; e-mail wrcit@wrc.org.za; internet www.wrc.org.za.

MAJOR COMPANIES

The following are among the leading companies in South Africa.

AECI Ltd: Private Bag X21, Gallo Manor 2052; tel. (11) 8068700; fax (11) 8068701; internet www.aeci-hq.co.za; f. 1924; cap. and res R1,886m., sales R8,646m. (Dec. 1998); mfrs of explosives, industrial and agricultural chemicals, paints, synthetic yarns and plastic raw materials; Chair A. J. Trahar; Man. Dir L. C. van Vught; 15,700 employees.

Alpha Ltd: 94 Rivonia Rd, POB 781868, Sandton 2146; tel. (11) 7801000; fax (11) 8833000; internet www.alphaltd.co.za; f. 1934; cap. and res R1,122.8m., sales R1,967.2m. (Dec. 1997); major producer of cement, stone aggregates, lime, industrial minerals and ready-mixed concrete, with extensive interests in manufacture of paper sacks and fertilizers; Chair. Basil E. Hersov; Man. Dir Johan G. Pretorius; 4,583 employees.

Barlow Ltd: POB 782248, Sandton 2146; tel. (11) 4451000; fax (11) 4443643; e-mail barlowpr@barlows.co.za; internet www.barlows.com; f. 1902; cap. R749m., sales R20,835m. (Sept. 1999); international industrial corpn involved in marketing and distribution of several leading brands on behalf of principals; products include machines, engines, lift trucks, trenching equipment and motor vehicles; also manufactures and distributes its own products, which include cement, lime, paper sacks, coatings, steel tubes, photonics and laboratory equipment; financial services operation; Chair. W. A. M. Clewlow; CEO. A. J. Phillips; some 11,000 employees (South Africa).

CNA Gallo Ltd: POB 9380, Johannesburg 2000; tel. (11) 4822600; fax (11) 7261374; cap. R930m.; core businesses of the group are the CNA and Literary Group chains of retail stores and manufacture and distribution of gramophone records, music cassettes, compact discs and video cassettes, and music publishing; activities of support subsidiaries and associate cos include manufacture and sale of greeting cards and stationery, general book publishing, freight forwarding and clearing, business training and film production and distribution; Chair. D. D. B. Band.

Consolidated Frame Textiles Ltd: POB 207, New Germany 3620; tel. (31) 7051370; fax (31) 7054420; e-mail framexec@iafrica.com; f. 1933; mfrs of fabrics for clothing and textile industries; Chair. R. Sable; Man. Dir W. Simeoni.

ICS Holdings Ltd: Harrowdene Office Park, Bldg 4, Western Service Rd, Woodmead, POB 783854, Sandton 2146; tel. (11) 8045780; fax (11) 8044173; e-mail info@icsholdings.co.za; f. 1902; cap. R10.7m.; processes and distributes red meat, poultry and meat products, milk and milk products, ice cream, fish; Chair. R. A. Williams; Man. Dir R. V. Smither; 14,400 employees.

Illovo Sugar Ltd: POB 194, Durban 4000; tel. (31) 5084300; e-mail kswann@illovo.co.za; internet www.illovosugar.com; f. 1891; cap. and res R1,053.6m., sales R3,799.2m. (Sept. 1999); Africa's largest sugar producer (annual output of some 1.2m. metric tons of raw and refined sugar in South Africa); downstream producer of syrup, furfural and its derivatives, ethyl alcohol, lactulose and dextron; agricultural, manufacturing and other interests in six southern African countries; Man. Dir D. G. MacLeod; 22,000 permanent employees.

Irvin and Johnson Ltd: 70 Prestwhich St, Cape Town 8001; POB 1628, Cape Town 8000; tel. (21) 4029200; fax (21) 4029282; f. 1910; cap. and res R895.8m., sales R2,752.0m. (June 1999); trawler operators; processors, distributors and exporters of frozen fish; Sec. C. Schoeman; 8,000 employees.

LTA Ltd: Private Bag X030, Kempton Park 1620; tel. (11) 9235000; fax (11) 3973422; f. 1889; cap. and res R330.4m., sales R3,581m. (Dec. 1998); holding co; active in all aspects of the construction industry, incl. building, civil and electrical engineering, steel reinforcing and earthworks, open-cast mining, property development and process engineering; Chair. C. V. Campbell Man. Dir P. F. Crowley; 15,000 employees.

Malesela Technologies (Pty) Ltd: Steel Rd, Peacehaven, POB 1643, Vereeniging; tel. (16) 4508200; fax (16) 4233406; e-mail info@mtech.co.za; internet www.mtech.co.za; cap. R20m. (June 2000); mfr of copper and aluminium conductor and associated products; Chair. M. K. Madungandaba; 354 employees.

Nampak Ltd: 114 Dennis Rd, Athol Gardens, POB 784324, Sandton 2146; tel. (11) 4447418; fax (11) 4444794; e-mail webmaster@nampak.co.za; internet www.nampak.co.za; f. 1968; cap. and res R3,202.7m., sales R7,942.9m. (Sept. 1999); mfrs of packaging in various forms based on paper, paper board, metal, glass and plastics; there are subsidiaries in the service area and fields allied to packaging; Chair. Brian Connellan; Man. Dir Trevor Evans; 15,345 employees.

Premier Group Ltd: POB 412157, Craighall 2024; tel. (11) 2800900; fax (11) 2800930; e-mail premierg@webware.co.za; f. 1913; cap. and res R2,636.2m., sales R16,802.5m. (April 1997); holding co of Premier Food Industries Ltd, Bonnita Holdings Ltd, Metro Cash and Carry Ltd, United Pharmaceutical Holdings (Proprietary) Ltd and Teltron Ltd; activities of operating companies include wheat and maize mills, bakeries, edible oils, fats, margarine and derivatives, animal feed factories, poultry and crop farms, sugar and cotton processing, retail liquor outlet, music companies, bookshops, distribution and wholesaling division, stationery division, and pharmaceutical divisions both manufacturing and wholesale; Chair. Douglas Band; 37,201 employees.

Pretoria Portland Cement Co Ltd: POB 3811, Johannesburg 2000; tel. (11) 4881700; fax (11) 7263537; e-mail invest@ppc.co.za; internet www.ppc.co.za; f. 1892; cap. and res R1,492.5m., sales R1,886.5m. (Sept. 1999); mfrs and distributors of cement, lime and limestone products, paper sacks and other containers; also mines and markets gypsum; Chair. W. A. M. Clewlow; Group Man. Dir J. E. Gomersall; 3,179 employees.

Protea Holdings Cape (Pty) Ltd: POB 3839, Cape Town 8000; tel. (21) 512357; f. 1963; Man. Dir A. Wolfaardt; 100 employees.

SAPPI Ltd: POB 31560, Braamfontein 2017; tel. (11) 4078111; fax (11) 3391846; internet www.sappi.com; f. 1936 as South African Pulp and Paper Industries Ltd; cap. and res R12,701m., sales R22,710m. (Sept. 1998); eight pulp and paper mfg and processing subsidiaries; Exec. Chair. Eugene van As; 25,000 employees.

SASOL Ltd: POB 5486, Johannesburg 2000; tel. (11) 4413111; fax (11) 7885092; e-mail sasolltd@sasol.com; internet www.sasol.com; f 1950; cap. and res R15,131m., sales R19,180m. (June 1999); group of cos operating the world's largest complex of oil-from-coal petrochemical installations; produces c. 120 products; Chair. Paul du P. Kruger; CEO Pieter Cox; 24,300 employees.

The South African Breweries PLC: 2 Jan Smuts Ave, POB 1099, Johannesburg; tel. (11) 4071700; fax (11) 3391830; internet www.sabplc.com; f. 1895; cap. and res US $1,703m., sales US $6,184m. (March 1999); largest non-mining industrial group in sub-Saharan Africa; brewing and marketing of beer; mfrs, wholesalers and retailers of furniture, footwear, domestic appliances, plate glass, textiles, natural fruit juices and soft drinks; discount department, food and fashion chain stores; also owns and operates hotels; Non-Exec. Chair. J. M. Kahn; CEO Graham Mackay; 50,000 employees.

Stewarts and Lloyds Export: POB 1137, Johannesburg 2000; tel. (11) 4933000; fax (11) 4931440; f. 1902; cap. R12m.; export trading co; also mfrs and distributors of industrial metal products, e.g. steel tubing and fittings, valves, diesel engines and generators, pumps, irrigation equipment. Export Man. P. Kemp; 10,000 employees.

L. Suzman Ltd: 2 Elray St, Raedene POB 2188, Johannesburg 2192; tel. (11) 4851020; fax (11) 6401325; f. 1889; cap. R2.1m.; wholesale distribution of tobacco products and other consumer products; operates 26 brs in South Africa; Chair. P. R. S. Thomas; Man. Dir C. J. van der Walt; 1,000 employees.

The Tongaat-Hulett Group Ltd: POB 3, Tongaat, KwaZulu/Natal 4400; tel. (322) 994000; fax (322) 923333; e-mail info@tongaat.co.za; internet www.tongaat.co.za; f. 1892 as Huletts Corpn; cap. R4.9m.; divisions operating in sugar cane growing and processing, food production and processing, textiles manufacture, building materials, aluminium products, speciality starches, property administration; Chair. Dr C. J. Saunders; Man. Dir C. M. L. Savage; 17,000 employees.

Mining Companies

Anglo American Corporation of South Africa Ltd: 44 Main St, Johannesburg; POB 61587, Marshalltown 2107; tel. (11) 6389111; fax (11) 6382455; f. 1917; wholly-owned subsidiary of Anglo American plc; group sales US $19,245m. (1999); mining and natural resource group; a world leader in gold, platinum group metals and diamonds, with significant interests in coal, base and ferrous metals, industrial minerals, forestry and financial services; Non-Exec. Chair. Julian Ogilvie Thompson; CEO Tony Trahar.

AngloGold Ltd: 55 Marshall St, POB 62117, Marshalltown 2107; internet www.anglogold.co.za; cap. and res R21,680m. (Dec. 1998); world's largest gold producer; Chair. Nicholas F. Oppenheimer; CEO Robert M. Godsell; 93,000 employees.

Anglovaal Mining Ltd: POB 1885, Saxonwold 2132; tel. (11) 2830000; fax (11) 2830007; internet www.avmin.co.za; f. 1933; cap. and res R3,125m., sales R2,489m. (June 1999); mining, financial and industrial group with divisions operating in precious metal and base mineral mining and beneficiation, fishing, food and rubber production, packaging, construction, engineering, electronics, information technology, textiles; Chair. Kennedy Maxwell; CEO Rick Menell; 70,000 employees.

De Beers Consolidated Mines Ltd: 36 Stockdale St, POB 616, Kimberley 8300; tel. (53) 8394111; fax (53) 8394210; internet www.edata.co.za; cap. and res R23,349m., sales R15,957m. (Dec. 1998); group of diamond mining cos and allied interests; reorg. 1990, when foreign interests were transferred to De Beers Centenary AG

(Switzerland); Chair. NICHOLAS F. OPPENHEIMER; Man. Dir GARY RALFE; 14,000 employees.

Gencor Ltd: Postnet Suite 222, Private Bag X30500, Houghton 2041; tel. (11) 6476200; fax (11) 4841654; e-mail johan@gencor.co.za; f. 1895; fmrly General Mining Union Corpn; cap. and res R3,674m., sales R2,261m. (June 1998); diversified group with investments in several cos, incl. GENMIN, which administers mines producing coal, platinum, ferro-alloys, and ENGEN, which has interests in petroleum refining and retail petrol sales; Chair. J. M. MCMAHON.

Gold Fields of South Africa Ltd: Postnet Suite 252, Private Bag X30500, Houghton 2041; tel. (11) 6442460; fax (11) 4840639; internet www.goldfields.co.za; cap. and res R1,342m., sales R200m. (June 1999); includes five gold-producing cos, platinum, coal and base metals; Chair. J. P. RUPERT; Man. Dir IAN COCKERILL.

JCI Gold Ltd: Consolidated Bldg, cnr Fox and Harrison Sts, Johannesburg 2001, POB 590, Johannesburg 2000; tel. (11) 3739111; fax (11) 4921070; f. 1889; cap. and res R1,555.5m., sales R100.4m. (March 1999); mining house with major investments in gold, ferrochrome, coal and base metals; Chair. Prof. W. L. NKUHLU; CEO J. BROWNRIGG.

Palabora Mining Co Ltd: POB 65, Phalaborwa 1390; tel. (15) 7803135; fax (15) 7812708; e-mail postmaster@pmc.rtsa.co.za; internet www.palabora.co.za; cap. and res R736.9m., sales R1,866.1m. (Dec. 1997); 39% held by Rio Tinto-Zinc Corpn; mining of copper, with by-products of magnetite, zirconia metals, uranium oxide, anode slimes, nickel sulphate, sulphuric acid and vermiculite; copper refining; Chair. F. FENWICK; Man. Dir J. G. DEYZEL.

Rand Mines Ltd: 5 Handel Rd, Ormonde, Johannesburg; POB 78861, Sandton 2146; tel. (11) 4961777; fax (11) 4961260; cap. and res exceed R718.4m.; 74.4% held by Barlow Rand Ltd; mining of coal, mineral exploration, property development, management and financial services; Chair. and Man. Dir J. C. HALL; 52,212 employees.

Randgold and Exploration Co Ltd: POB 82291, Southdale 2135; tel. (11) 8370706; fax (11) 8372396; e-mail haddond@randgold.co.za; internet www.randgold.co.za; f. 1992 to acquire gold-mining interests of Rand Mines Ltd; cap. and res R310.8m., sales R309.2m. (March 1999); mineral exploration and devt; Chair. ROGER KEBBLE.

TRADE UNIONS

In 1994 the number of registered unions totalled 213, with a membership that represented about 24% of the economically active population. In addition there were an estimated 65 unregistered unions, with a membership of about 510,000.

Trade Union Federations

Congress of South African Trade Unions (COSATU): COSATU House, 4th Floor, 1–5 Leyds St, Braamfontein, POB 1019, Johannesburg 2000; tel. (11) 3394911; fax (11) 3396940; e-mail cosatu@wn.apc.org; internet www.cosatu.org.za; f. 1985; 18 trade union affiliates representing c. 2m. mems; Pres. WILLIE MADISHA; Gen. Sec. ZWELINZIMA VAVI.

Principal affiliates include:

Chemical Workers' Industrial Union: Dalbridge 4014; tel. (11) 259510; fax (11) 256680; Pres. D. GUMEDE; Gen. Sec. R. CROMPTON.

Construction and Allied Workers' Union: POB 1962, Johannesburg 2000; tel. (11) 294321; fax (11) 3371578; Pres. D. NGCOBO; Gen. Sec. L. MADUMA.

Food and Allied Workers' Union: POB 234, Salt River 7925; tel. (21) 6379040; fax (21) 6383761; Pres. ERNEST THERON; Gen. Sec. MANDLA GXANYANA.

Health and Allied Workers' Union: POB 47011, Greyville 4023; tel. (11) 3063993; Gen. Sec. S. NGCOBO.

National Education, Health and Allied Workers' Union: 56 Marshall St, Marshalltown, POB 10812, Johannesburg 2000; tel. (11) 8332902; fax (11) 8343416; Pres. VUSI NHLAPO; Gen. Sec. FIKILE MAJOLE.

National Union of Metalworkers of South Africa (NUMSA): 153 Bree St, Newtown, POB 260483, Johannesburg 2001; tel. (11) 8322031; fax (11) 8384092; e-mail dumisan@numsa.org.za; Pres. M. TOM; Gen. Sec. PETER DANTJE; 232,000 mems (1996).

National Union of Mineworkers: POB 2424, Johannesburg 2000; tel. (11) 8337012; e-mail jmotlatsi@num.org.za; internet www.num.org.za; Pres. JAMES MOTLATSI; Gen. Sec. GWEDE MANTASHE; 350,000 mems.

Paper, Printing, Wood and Allied Workers' Union: POB 3528, Johannesburg 2000; tel. (11) 3317721; fax (11) 3313750; e-mail ppwawu@wn.apc.oyg; Pres. P. DYANI; Gen. Sec. B. MTHOMBENI.

Post and Telecommunications Workers' Association: POB 260100, Excom 2023; tel. (11) 234351; Pres. K. MOSUNKULU; Gen. Sec. V. A. KHUMALO.

Southern African Clothing and Textile Workers' Union: POB 18359, Dolbridge 4014; tel. (31) 3011391; fax (31) 3017050;

e-mail sactwudb.apc.org; Pres. A. NTULI; Gen. Sec. J. NGCOBO; 185,000 mems.

South African Railways and Harbours Workers' Union: POB 8059, Johannesburg 2000; tel. (11) 8343251; fax (11) 8344664; Pres. J. LANGA; Gen. Sec. M. SEBEKOANE.

Transport and General Workers' Union: POB 9451, Johannesburg 2000; tel. (11) 3319321; fax (11) 3315418; Pres. A. NDLOVU; Gen. Sec. R. HOWARD.

Federation of Unions of South Africa (FEDUSA): POB 2096, Northcliff 2115, Pretoria; tel. (11) 4765188; fax (11) 4765131; e-mail fedusa@fedusa.org.za; internet www.fedusa.org.za; Gen. Sec. CHEZ MILANI.

National Council of Trade Unions (NACTU): Lekton House, 7th Floor, 5 Wanderers St, POB 10928, Johannesburg 2000; tel. (11) 3368031; fax (11) 3337625; f. 1986; fed. of 22 African trade unions; Pres. JAMES MDLALOSE; Gen. Sec. CUNNINGHAM MCGUKAMU.

Principal affiliates include:

Building, Construction and Allied Workers' Union: POB 96, Johannesburg 2000; tel. (11) 236311; Pres. J. SEISA; Gen. Sec. V. THUSI.

Hotel, Liquor and Catering Trade Employees' Union: POB 1409, Johannesburg 2000; tel. (11) 234039; Pres. E. NKOSI (acting); Gen. Sec. K. KEELE (acting).

Metal and Electrical Workers' Union of South Africa: POB 3669, Johannesburg 2000; tel. (11) 8369051; fax (11) 8369002; e-mail mewusa@cis.co.za; f. 1989; Pres. RUSSELL SABOR; Gen. Sec. ZITHULELE CINDI.

National Union of Farm Workers: POB 10928, Johannesburg 2000; tel. (11) 333054; fax (11) 337625; Pres. E. MUSEKWA; Gen. Sec. T. MOLETSANE.

National Union of Food, Beverage, Wine, Spirits and Allied Workers: POB 5718, Johannesburg 2000; tel. (11) 3335561; fax (1) 3333480; Pres. M. L. KWELEMTINI; Gen. Sec. L. SIKHAKHANE.

National Union of Public Service Workers: POB 10928, Johannesburg 2000; tel. (11) 232812; Pres. K. NTHUTE; Gen. Sec. S. RADEBE.

South African Chemical Workers' Union: POB 236, Johannesburg 2000; tel. (11) 8386581; fax (11) 8386622; Pres. W. THUTHANI; Gen. Sec. O. H. NDABA.

Steel, Engineering and Allied Workers' Union of South Africa: POB 4283, Johannesburg 2001; tel. (11) 3364865; fax (11) 294869; Pres. G. MABIDIKAMA; Gen. Sec. N. RAMAEMA.

Transport and Allied Workers' Union of South Africa: POB 4469, Johannesburg 2000; tel. (11) 296851; fax (11) 3375481; Pres. A. MAHLATJIE; Gen. Sec. RANDALL HOWARD.

South African Confederation of Labour: POB 19299, Pretoria West 0117; tel. (12) 793271; 7 mems; Pres. I. J. ELS; Sec. L. N. CELLIERS.

South African Independent Trade Unions Confederation—SAITUCO: f. 1995 by 14 independent trade unions that opposed the new draft legislation on labour relations; Pres. PIET SKHOSANA; Gen. Sec. THEMBA NCALO.

Transport

Most of South Africa's railway network and the harbours and airways are administered by the state-owned Transnet Ltd. There are no navigable rivers. Private bus services are regulated to complement the railways.

Transnet Ltd: 8 Hillside Rd, Parktown, Johannesburg; POB 72501, Parkview 2122; tel. (11) 4887055; fax (11) 4887511; e-mail sakim@transnet.co.za; internet www.tnet.co.za; Chair. Prof. LOUISE A. TAGER; Man. Dir SAKI MACOZOMA.

RAILWAYS

With the exception of commuter services, the South African railways system is operated by Spoornet Ltd (the rail division of Transnet). The network comprised 31,400 track-km in 1996, of which 16,946 km was electrified. Extensive rail links connect Spoornet with the rail networks of neighbouring countries.

Spoornet: Paul Kruger Bdg, 30 Wolmarans St, Private Bag X47, Johannesburg 2001; tel. (11) 7735090; fax (11) 7733033; internet www.spoornet.co.za; CEO A. S. LE ROUX.

ROADS

In 1995 there were 331,265 km of classified roads, including 1,142 km of motorways, 59,900 km of main roads and 147,828 km of secondary roads. Some 41.5% of the network was paved.

South African National Roads Agency Ltd: POB 415, Pretoria 0001; tel. (12) 4266000; fax (12) 3421320; internet www.nra.co.za;

f. 1998; responsible for design, construction, management and maintenance of national road network; CEO Nazir Alli.

SHIPPING

The principal harbours are at Richards Bay, Cape Town, Port Elizabeth, East London, Durban and Saldanha Bay. The deep-water port at Richards Bay has been extended and its facilities upgraded. Both Richards Bay and Saldanha Bay are major bulk-handling ports, while Saldanha Bay also has an important fishing fleet.

More than 30 shipping lines serve South African ports. At the end of 1998 South Africa's merchant fleet had a total displacement of 383,739 grt.

PORTNET: POB 72501, Johannesburg; tel. (11) 2424019; fax (11) 2424027; e-mail webmaster@portnet.co.za; internet www.portnet .co.za; manages all seven commercial ports; Gen. Mans Gert de Beer, Pumi Sithole, Sylvester Haanyama.

South African Maritime Safety Authority: SAMSA, POB 13186, Hatfield 0028; tel. (12) 3423049; fax (12) 3423160; e-mail samsa@ iafrica.com; advises the Govt on matters connected with sea transport to, from or between South Africa's ports, incl. safety at sea, and prevention of pollution by petroleum; CEO Capt. B. R. Watt.

CIVIL AVIATION

Civil aviation is controlled by the Minister of Transport. The Chief Directorate: Civil Aviation Authority at the Department of Transport is responsible for licensing and control of domestic and international air services. The Airports Company owns and operates South Africa's nine principal airports, of which three (at Johannesburg, Cape Town and Durban) are classified as international airports.

Civil Aviation Authority (CAA): 281 Middle St, Nieu Muckleneuk, Pretoria; tel. (12) 3465566; fax (12) 3465979; e-mail mail@ caa.co.za; internet www.caa.gov.za; CEO Trevor Abrahams.

South African Airways (SAA): Airways Park, Jones Rd, Private Bag X13, Johannesburg 1627; tel. (11) 9781111; fax (11) 9781106; internet www.flysaa.com; f. 1934; 80% state-owned; internal passenger services linking all the principal towns; international services to Africa, Europe, N and S America and Asia; CEO and Pres. Coleman Andrews.

COMAIR Ltd: POB 7015, Bonaero Park 1622; tel. (11) 9210111; fax (11) 9733913; e-mail comair.co.za; f. 1946; scheduled domestic, regional and international services; Chair. D. Novick; Man. Dir P. van Hoven.

Airlink Airline: POB 7529, Bonaero Park 1622; tel. (11) 3953333; fax (11) 3951076; f. 1992; internal and external scheduled services and charters; flights; Man. Dirs Rodger Foster, Barrie Webb.

Safair (Pty) Ltd: POB 938, Kempton Park 1620; tel. 9280000; fax 3951314; internet www.safair.co.za; f. 1969; subsidiary of Safmarine Aircraft Charters and Leasing; aircraft charters, leasing, engineering and maintenance services; Chair. W. G. Lynch; CEO R. J. Boёttger.

Air Cape (Pty) Ltd: POB D.F. Malan Airport, Cape Town 7525; tel. (21) 9340344; fax (21) 9348379; scheduled internal passenger services and charters, engineering services and aerial surveys; Chair. Dr P. van Aswegen; Gen. Man. G. A. Nortje.

Tourism

Tourism is an important part of South Africa's economy. The chief attractions for visitors are the climate, scenery and wildlife reserves. Tourist receipts provided an estimated US $2,100m. in foreign exchange in 1996. In 1998 5,170,096 tourists visited South Africa.

South African Tourism Board (SATOUR): 442 Rigel Ave South, Erasmusrand 0181, Private Bag X164, Pretoria 0001; tel. (12) 4826200; fax (12) 3478753; e-mail jhb@satour.com; internet www .za.satour.com; f. 1947; 13 overseas brs; Exec. Dir Stella du Plessis.

Defence

In August 1999 the South African National Defence Force (SANDF) totalled about 82,400: army 58,600, navy 5,500, air force 10,900 and a medical corps numbering 6,000. In addition, there was a paramilitary force within the police service numbering 129,300. The SANDF comprised members of the former South African armed forces, together with personnel from the former military wings of the ANC and the Pan-Africanist Congress, and the former 'homelands'. In early 2000 the Government announced plans to reduce the SANDF to number about 70,000.

Defence Expenditure: Budgeted at R10,742m. in 1999/2000.

Chief of the South African National Defence Force: Gen. Siphiwe Nyanda.

Education

School attendance is compulsory for children of all population groups between the ages of seven and 16 years. From 1991 state schools were permitted to admit pupils from all races, and in 1995 the right to free state education for all population groups was introduced. In 1996 total enrolment at primary schools included 94% of pupils in the relevant age-group (males 93%; females 95%), while the comparable ratio for secondary education was 51% (males 46%; females 57%). During the 1980s universities, which were formerly racially segregated, began to admit students of all races. In 1999 there were 21 universities and 15 'technikons' (tertiary education institutions offering technical and commercial vocational training). In 1995, according to estimates by UNESCO, the rate of adult illiteracy averaged 16.7% (males 15.9%; females 17.5%). The budget for 1999/2000 allocated R47,841m. (21.4% of total expenditure) to education.

Bibliography

Abedian, I., and Standish, P. (Eds). *Economic Growth in South Africa: Selected Policy Issues*. Cape Town, Oxford University Press, 1992.

Abel, R. L. *Politics by Other Means: Law in the Struggle Against Apartheid, 1980–1994*. London, Routledge, 1995.

Adam, H. et al. *Comrades in Business: Post-Liberation Politics in South Africa*. Cape Town, Tafelberg, 1997.

African National Congress. *The Reconstruction and Development Programme*. Johannesburg, Umanyano Publications, 1994.

Asmal, K., Asmal, L., and Robert, R. S. *Reconciliation Through Truth: A Reckoning of Apartheid's Criminal Governance*. Cape Town, David Philip, 1996.

Barnard, N., and Du Toit, J. *Understanding the South African Macro-Economy*. Pretoria, Van Schaik, 1992.

Beinart, W. *Twentieth-Century South Africa*. Cape Town, Oxford University Press, 1994.

Bloomberg, C. *Christian Nationalism and the Rise of the Afrikaner Broederbond in South Africa, 1918–1948*. Bloomington, Indiana University Press, 1989.

Bond, P. *Commanding Heights and Community Control: New Economics for a New South Africa*. Johannesburg, Ravan Press, 1991.

Callinicos, L. *People's History of South Africa*. Johannesburg, Ravan Press. 3 vols. 1981–93.

Cameron, T., and Spies, S. B. (Eds). *Illustrated History of South Africa*. 3rd Edn. Gauteng, Halfway House, Southern Book Publishers, 1996.

Central Statistical Services, *South African Statistics*. Pretoria, Government Printer, biennial.

Christopher, A. J. *South Africa*. London, Longman, 1982.

Cloete, J. J. N. *Accountable Government and Administration for the Republic of South Africa*. Pretoria, Van Schaik, 1996.

Cole, K. (Ed.). *Sustainable Development for a Democratic South Africa*. London, Earthscan, 1994.

Davenport, T. R. H. *South Africa: A Modern History*. 4th Edn. London, Macmillan, 1991.

Davies, R., O'Meara, D., and Dlamini, S. *The Struggle for South Africa: A Reference Guide to Movements, Organizations and Institutions*. 2 vols. London, Zed Books, 1984.

De Beer, J., and Lourens, L. *Local Government: The Road to Democracy*. Midrand, Educum Publishers, 1995.

De Ville, J., and Steytler, N. (Eds). *Voting in 1999: Choosing an Electoral System*. Durban, Butterworth Publishers, 1996.

Du Pre, R. H. *Separate but Unequal: The 'Coloured' People of South Africa: A Political History*. Johannesburg, Jonathan Ball, 1994.

Du Toit, P. *State Building and Democracy in Southern Africa: Botswana, Zimbabwe and South Africa*. Washington, DC, US Institute of Peace Press, 1995.

Elphick, R., and Giliomee, H. (Eds). *The Shaping of South African Society, 1652–1820.* Cape Town, Longman, 1979.

Falkena, H. B. *Fundamentals of the South African Financial System.* Gauteng, Halfway House, Southern Book Publishers, 1993.

(Ed.). *South African Financial Institutions.* Gauteng, Halfway House, Southern Book Publishers, 1992.

Faure, M., and Lane, J. E. (Eds). *South Africa: Designing New Political Institutions.* London, Sage Publications, 1996.

Gastrow, S. *Who's Who in South African Politics.* 5th Edn. Johannesburg, Ravan Press, 1995.

Hain, P. *Sing the Beloved Country: The Struggle for the New South Africa.* London, Pluto Press, 1996.

Hall, M. *The Changing Past: Farmers, Kings and Traders in Southern Africa, 1800–1860.* Cape Town, Philip, 1987.

Hammond-Tooke, D. *The Roots of Black South Africa: An Introduction to the Traditional Culture of the Black People of South Africa.* Johannesburg, Jonathan Ball, 1993.

Heyns, S. *Parliamentary Pocketbook.* Cape Town, Institute for Democracy in South Africa, 1996.

Hodge, T. *South African Politics since 1994.* Cape Town, David Philip, 1999.

James, W., et al. (Eds). *Now That We Are Free: Coloured Communities in a Democratic South Africa.* Rondebosch, Institute For a Democratic South Africa, 1996.

Johnson, R. W., and Schlemmer, L. (Eds). *Launching Democracy in South Africa: The First Open Election, April 1994.* New Haven, Yale University Press, 1996.

Joyce, P. *Concise Dictionary of South African Biography.* Cape Town, Francolin, 1999.

Keegan, T. *Colonial South Africa and the Origins of Racial Order.* Cape Town, David Philip, 1996.

Konczacki, Z. A., and Konczacki, J. M. (Eds). *An Economic and Social History of South Africa.* London, Frank Cass, 1980.

Konczacki, Z. A., Parpart, J. L., and Shaw, T. M. (Eds). *Studies in the Economic History of Southern Africa.* Vol. II. London, Frank Cass, 1991.

Laband, J. P. C. *Rope of Sand: The Rise and Fall of the Zulu Kingdom in the Nineteenth Century.* Johannesburg, Jonathan Ball, 1995.

Le May, G. H. L. *The Afrikaners: An Historical Interpretation.* Oxford, Blackwell Publishers, 1995.

Lipton, M. *Capitalism and Apartheid: South Africa 1910–1984.* Aldershot, Hampshire, Maurice Temple Smith/Gower, 1985.

Marais, H. *South Africa: Limits to Change—The Political Economy of Transformation.* London, Zed Books, 1998.

Marks, S., and Trapido, S. *The Politics of Race, Class and Nationalism in Twentieth Century South Africa.* London and New York, Longman, 1987.

Marsh, R. *With Criminal Intent: The Changing Face of Crime in South Africa.* Kenilworth, Ampersand Press, 1999.

Mayekiso, M. *Township Politics: Civic Struggles For a New South Africa.* New York, Monthly Review Press, 1996.

Maylam, P. *History of the African People of South Africa.* Cape Town, David Philip, 1986.

Meli, F. *South Africa Belongs To Us: A History of the ANC.* London, James Currey; Cape Town, Philip; Bloomington, Indiana University Press, 1989.

Musiker, N., and Musiker, R. *Historical Dictionary of Greater Johannesburg.* Lanham, MD, Scarecrow Press, 1999.

Nattrass, N., and Ardington, E. (Eds). *Political Economy of South Africa.* Cape Town, Oxford University Press, 1990.

Nicholson, J. (Ed.). *User's Guide to the South African Economy.* Durban, Y Press, 1994.

Nuttall, T., et al. *From Apartheid to Democracy: South Africa 1948–1994.* Pietermaritzburg, Shuter and Shooter, 1998.

Oden, B., et al. *The South African Tripod: Studies on Economics, Politics and Conflict.* Uppsala, Nordiska Afrikainstitutet, 1994.

O'Meara, D. *Forty Lost Years: The Apartheid State and the Politics of the National Party.* Johannesburg, Ravan Press, 1996.

Omer-Cooper, J. D. *History of Southern Africa.* 2nd Edn. Cape Town, Philip, 1994.

Pakenham, T. *The Boer War.* London, Weidenfeld and Nicolson, 1979; Johannesburg, Jonathan Ball, 1992 (reprint).

Pampallis, J. *Foundations of the New South Africa.* London, Zed Books; Cape Town, Maskew Miller Longman, 1991.

Pollock, N. C., and Agnew, S. *An Historical Geography of South Africa.* London, Longman, 1963.

Preston-Whyte, E., and Rogerson, C. (Eds). *South Africa's Informal Economy.* Cape Town, Oxford University Press, 1991.

Ramphela, M. *The Affirmative Action Book: Towards an Equity Government.* Rondebosch, Institute for a Democratic South Africa, 1995.

Reader's Digest. *Illustrated History of South Africa.* 3rd Edn. Cape Town, 1994.

Reynolds, A. (Ed.). *Election '94 South Africa: The Campaigns, Results and Future Prospects.* Cape Town, David Philip, 1994.

Rogerson, C., and McCarthy, J. (Eds). *Geography in a Changing South Africa: Progress and Prospects.* Cape Town, Oxford University Press, 1992.

Roux, A. *Everyone's Guide to the South African Economy.* 4th Edn. Wynberg, Sandton, Zebra Books, 1996.

Saunders, C., and Southey, N. *Dictionary of South African History.* Cape Town, David Philip, 1998.

Schrire, R. (Ed.). *Wealth or Poverty: Critical Choices for South Africa.* Cape Town, Oxford University Press, 1992.

Seegers, A. *The Military in the Making of Modern South Africa.* London, Taurus, 1997.

Simon, D. (Ed.). *South Africa in Southern Africa: Reconfiguring the Region.* Athens, Ohio, Ohio University Press, 1998.

Simons, H. J., and Simons, R. E. *Class and Colour in South Africa, 1850–1950.* Harmondsworth, Middlesex, Penguin Books, 1969.

Smollan, R. *Black Advancement in the South African Economy.* Johannesburg, Macmillan Boleswa, 1993.

South African Institute of Race Relations. *South African Survey.* Johannesburg, annual.

Sparks, A. *Tomorrow is Another Country: The Inside Story of South Africa's Road to Change.* New York, Hill and Wang, 1995.

Thompson, L. *The Unification of South Africa 1902–1910.* Oxford, Clarendon Press, 1960.

History of South Africa. New Haven, Yale University Press, 1990.

United Nations. *United Nations and Apartheid 1984–1994.* New York and Geneva, United Nations Publications, 1995.

Vosloo, W. B. (Ed.). *Entrepreneurship and Economic Growth.* Pretoria, Human Sciences Research Council, 1994.

Wentzel, J. *The Liberal Slideaway.* Johannesburg, South African Institute of Race Relations, 1995.

Wilson, M., and Thompson, L. (Eds). *The Oxford History of South Africa.* Oxford, Clarendon Press, 1969–71.

History of South Africa to 1870. (Revised Edn of Vol. 1 of *The Oxford History of South Africa.*) Cape Town, David Philip, 1982.

SUDAN

Physical and Social Geography

J. A. ALLAN

THE NILE

The River Nile and its tributaries form the basis of much of the economic activity of Sudan, and of most of the future activity that is now envisaged. The river traverses diverse landscapes, from the relatively humid tropical forest in the south to the arid deserts in the north. The Republic of Sudan has a total area of 2,505,813 sq km (967,500 sq miles), and the Nile waters which enter Sudan just south of Juba either evaporate or flow 3,000 km until they reach Lake Nubia on the Egyptian border. Even those which flow down the Blue Nile travel 2,000 km. The distances are vast, and the remoteness of places on the Nile system, not to speak of those in the deserts, savannah and swamps of the rest of the country, explains much of the character of Sudan's land use. The other important factor is climate, which influences vegetation and, more significantly, affects the seasonal flow of the Nile tributaries.

The Blue Nile is the main tributary, both in the volume of water which it carries (four-sevenths of the total average flow of the system) as well as in the area of irrigated land, of which it supports over 40% of the present area and 70% of potential irrigable land. The Blue Nile and other east-bank tributaries are sustained by monsoon rains over the Ethiopian highlands which cause the river to flood at the end of July, reach a peak in August and remain high through September and the first half of October. The Atbara, another seasonal east-bank tributary, provides a further one-seventh of the flow in the system, and the remaining two-sevenths come from the White Nile. The sustained flow of the White Nile arises firstly because its main source is Lake Victoria, which regulates the flow, and secondly because the swamps of the Sudd and Machar act as a reservoir, absorbing the irregular stream flow from the south while discharging a regular flow, much reduced by evaporation, in the north.

The River Nile is an international river system, and Sudan depends on river flows from seven other states. Sudan does not yet use all of the 18,500m. cu m of annual flow agreed with Egypt in 1959 as its share of the total average flow at Aswan of 84,000m. (Egypt receives 55,500m. cu m, while 10,000m. cu m are assumed to evaporate annually from Lake Nasser/Nubia). In anticipation of future additional demand by upstream states such as Ethiopia, and in view of Egypt's rising demand for water, Sudan and Egypt jointly embarked in 1978 on the construction of the Jonglei Canal project, which will eventually conserve some 4,000m. cu m of the 33,000m. cu m of water lost annually through evaporation in the Sudd swamp. The Machar swamps will also yield water at a rate as yet undetermined, but likely to be about 4,000m. cu m per year (3,240m. cu m at Aswan).

PHYSICAL FEATURES AND CLIMATE

Sudan is generally a flat, featureless plain reflecting the proximity to the surface of the ancient Basement rocks of the African continent. The Basement is overlain by the Nubian Sandstone formation in the centre and north-west of the country, and by the Umm Ruwaba formation in the south. These formations hold groundwater bodies which are of agricultural significance. No point in the country is very high above sea-level. Elevations rise to 3,187 m on Mt Kinyeti, near the Uganda border, and to 3,071 m on Jabel Marrah, an extinct volcano, in west central Sudan near the frontier with Chad. Some idea of the level character of the landscape is provided by the small amount of the fall in the Blue Nile, which starts its 2,000-km flow through Sudan at 500 m above sea-level at the Ethiopian border and formerly flowed past Wadi Halfa (now flooded) at an elevation

of 156 m. It now flows into Lake Nubia at 180 m above sea-level. The White Nile, as it emerges from Uganda, falls some 600 m between the border and Khartoum, a distance of 1,700 km, but falls only 17 m in the last 700 km from entering the southern clay plains.

Average temperatures and rainfall change steadily from month to month, except where the effect of the Ethiopian highlands disturbs the east-west trend in the climatic belts in the south-east. The north of Sudan is a desert, with negligible rainfall and high average daily temperatures (summer 35°C, winter 20°C). Low temperatures occur only in winter. Rainfall increases steadily south of Khartoum (200 mm per year), reaching over 1,000 mm per year at the southern border. Rainfall varies from year to year, especially in the north, and is seasonal. In the south it falls in the period April–October; the rainy season is progressively shorter towards the north, where it lasts only from July until August. Potential evaporation approaches 3,000 mm per year in the north and is always over 1,400 mm per year, even in the humid south.

VEGETATION AND SOILS

The soil resources of Sudan are rich in agricultural potential. Their exploitation, however, depends on the availability of the limiting factor, water, and only a small proportion of the clay plains of central and east Sudan are currently farmed intensively. Clay soils also occur in the south, being deposits of the White Nile and Sobat streams. Recent alluvium provides a basis for productive agriculture in the narrow Nile valley north of Khartoum. Elsewhere, in the west and north the soils are sandy, with little agricultural potential, except in the dry valleys, which generally contain some soil moisture.

Vegetation is closely related to the climatic zones. From the desert in the north vegetation gradually improves through semi-arid shrub to low woodland savannah characterized by acacia and short grasses. Progressively higher rainfall towards the south promotes trees and shrubs as well as herbs, while the more reliably watered rangeland of the Bahr al-Arab provides an important seasonal resource for the graziers from the poor pastures of Darfur and Kordofan. The flooded areas of the Sudd and Machar and environs support swamp vegetation and grassland. On the uplands of the southern border, rainfall is sufficient to support tropical rain forest.

During 1984–85 and again in the early 1990s large areas of Sudan were affected by drought, and it was estimated that thousands of people faced starvation, particularly in the western provinces of Darfur and Kordofan.

POPULATION

The population of Sudan was enumerated at 24,940,683 at the census held in April 1993, compared with 20,594,197 in February 1983 and 14,113,590 in April 1973. According to official estimates, the population increased at an annual average rate of 2.3% in 1990–98. According to UN estimates, the population was 28,292,000 at mid-1998. At the 1983 census about 71% of the population resided in rural areas, 18% in urban and semi-urban areas and the remaining 11% were nomadic. The population is concentrated in Khartoum province and the Central Region, where population densities were, respectively, 55 and 28 per sq km in 1973, compared with 3.6–6.8 per sq km elsewhere. Agricultural development in the two most populous regions created employment opportunities and this led to the doubling of these populations during 1956–1973, compared with rises of between zero and 50% elsewhere. There are local concentrations of population in the Nuba mountains and higher densities than average in better-farmed parts of the Southern and Darfur Regions.

The ethnic origin of the people of Sudan is mixed, and the country is still subject to significant immigration by groups from Nigeria and Chad, such as the Fulani. In the south the Nuer, the Dinka and the Shilluki are the most important of the Nilotic peoples. The Arab culture and language predominate in the north, which includes the most populous provinces and the capital, Khartoum. The South is predominantly Christian and this cultural difference, added to the ethnic separateness and its extreme remoteness, has been expressed in economic backwardness and a tendency to political distinctness, which have been the main cause of persistent unrest in Southern Sudan.

The capital, Khartoum, had an estimated population of 924,505 at the 1993 census. It is the main administrative,

commercial and industrial centre of the country. The neighbouring city of Omdurman had 228,778 inhabitants, thus creating, with Khartoum, a conurbation of some 1.2m. inhabitants. As communications are very poor and since Khartoum is at least 1,000 km away from 80% of the country, the influence that the capital exerts on the rest of the country is small. The relatively advanced character and general success of much of the irrigated farming on the east-central clay plains has led to a predominance of investment there and to the misguided impression that the success of the east-central plains could be transferred to other parts of the country where the resources are unfortunately much less favourable. Much of Sudan is so dry for part of each year that the only possible way to use the land and vegetation resources is by grazing, and tribes such as the Bagara traverse the plains and plateaux of Darfur and Kordofan in response to the availability of fodder.

Recent History

THOMAS OFCANSKY

The British military conquest of the Sudan was completed during 1896–98. A nominally Anglo-Egyptian administration governed the territory until 1924, when the British government introduced a system of 'Indirect Rule' through tribal chiefs, and Egyptian involvement effectively ceased. Nationalist movements, which began to mobilize in the mid-1930s, exerted pressure for increased Sudanese participation in government in preparation for full independence. In 1953 elections were held, resulting in a victory for the National Unionist Party (NUP), whose leader, Ismail al-Azhari, became the first Sudanese prime minister in January 1954. On 19 December 1955 the Sudan parliament unanimously declared the country to be an independent republic. Britain and Egypt were left with no choice but to recognize this independence, which formally took effect on 1 January 1956.

Soon after independence, Azhari's government was replaced by an unstable coalition of the Mahdist-supported Umma Party (UP) and the People's Democratic Party (PDP), the political organ of a rival religious fraternity, the Khatmiyya, with Abdallah Khalil, the UP secretary, as prime minister. After an indecisive election in February 1958, a military coup in November 1958 by Gen. Ibrahim Abboud won the support of civilian politicians with assurances that the junta aimed merely to restore stability and would relinquish power when this was achieved. The Abboud regime had some success in the economic sphere, but the extent of military involvement in government and allegations of corruption created growing discontent. The government also pursued a military solution to the problem of the predominantly Christian South, where its operations against the *Anya Nya* rebels forced thousands of Southerners to flee to neighbouring countries. In 1964 Abboud transferred power to a transitional government which was formed with representatives from all parties, including for the first time, the Sudanese Communist Party (SCP) and the Muslim Brotherhood. Its conciliatory approach to the Southern issue proved unsuccessful, however, and following elections held in June 1965, a coalition government was formed by the UP and the NUP, with the UP's Muhammad Ahmad Mahgoub as prime minister and Azhari as permanent president of the committee that acted as collective head of state.

The new government faced serious rebel activity in the South and large numbers of Southerners were killed by government troops. The government itself became increasingly right-wing, and in late 1965 the SCP was banned. A split meanwhile developed within the UP, with the more moderate members rallying around the party president, Sadiq al-Mahdi, in opposition to the prime minister. Mahgoub resigned in July 1966 and al-Mahdi was elected prime minister at the head of another UP–NUP coalition, which collapsed in May 1967. Mahgoub again became prime minister. However, domestic problems were neglected by the new government, which severed diplomatic relations with the USA and Britain following the Arab-Israeli

war in June and developed closer relations with the Eastern bloc. Faced by worsening violence in the South and growing divisions within the coalition, the government survived only a little over a year, until it was overthrown in a bloodless coup, led by Col Gaafar Muhammad Nimeri, in May 1969.

THE NIMERI REGIME, 1969–85

Nimeri's first two years in power were characterized by the adoption of socialist policies and the forging of an alliance between the new military leadership and the SCP. The foundations for a one-party state were laid with the formation of the Sudanese Socialist Union (SSU), and the country was renamed the Democratic Republic of the Sudan. Internal opposition was ruthlessly suppressed. The government declared its commitment to regional administrative autonomy for the South and set up a ministry for southern affairs. It developed closer relations with the Eastern bloc and followed a policy of militant support for the Palestinian cause. However, the announcement in November 1970 that presidents Nimeri, Qaddafi and Sadat had decided to unite Sudan, Libya and Egypt as a single federal state proved unacceptable to the communists, who staged a military coup, led by Maj. Hashim al-Ata, which resulted in the temporary overthrow of Nimeri in July 1971. With popular support, Nimeri was restored to power within three days. A purge of communists followed and 14 people were executed.

The attempted coup was followed by a cooling of relations with the Eastern bloc and led to a surge in the personal popularity of Nimeri, who won the first presidential election in Sudanese history in October 1971. The SSU became the sole legal political party. The Addis Ababa Agreement, signed in March 1972 between the government and the *Anya Nya* rebels, appeared to establish the basis for a settlement by introducing regional autonomy for the three Southern provinces. A regional people's assembly was established in Juba with representatives in the national people's assembly and a higher executive council (HEC) of its own.

The leaders of the traditional parties and their largely right-wing supporters, excluded from involvement in politics, organized themselves into a National Front (NF) which operated as a largely external opposition to the regime. Supported at various times by Libya, Iraq, Saudi Arabia and Ethiopia, the NF made several attempts to overthrow Nimeri. However, as the ideological differences between the government and the NF diminished, attempts at reconciliation began. During 1977–78 large numbers of political detainees were released and many exiled members of the NF, including al-Mahdi, returned to Sudan, some to take up government posts.

Sudan's relations with Egypt, normally close, became strained in the early 1980s, partly because of Sudan's desire to preserve close links with the rest of the Arab world at a time when Egypt was increasingly isolated by its signing of the Camp David accord with Israel. The assassination of President Sadat of

1093

Egypt in October 1981, and growing fears of Libyan attempts to destabilize the Nimeri regime, reinforced the feeling of need in the two regimes for closer co-operation. In October 1982 this culminated in the signing of a charter of integration between Egypt and Sudan, a 10-year agreement providing for political and economic integration and close co-operation in foreign policy, security and development. However, the charter was greeted with scepticism by many Sudanese and with opposition by Southern leaders who feared it would lead to a diminution of their role.

Prolonged discussions about decentralization led to the adoption in January 1980 of a plan whereby Sudan was to be divided into five regions (Northern, Eastern, Central, Kordofan and Darfur) in addition to Khartoum and the South, which would continue to enjoy a special status and administrative structure. However, relations between the government and the South were again deteriorating. A decision to sub-divide the South into three sub-regions to avoid the domination of one ethnic group (the Dinka), eventually implemented in May 1983, was opposed by many Southerners, who feared it would weaken their collective position *vis-à-vis* the North. Southern resentment was further aroused by the decision that petroleum from the newly-discovered oilfields astride the traditional boundaries of the two regions would not be refined locally but exported via a pipeline to Port Sudan, and by fears that the Jonglei Canal project would benefit Northerners and Egypt but have an adverse effect on the Southern population.

A major factor in the deepening crisis was the adoption by the Nimeri regime, after September 1983, of certain aspects of Islamic Shari'a law, followed by the introduction, after April 1984, of martial law. Despite the general popularity, in principle, of Islamization among the Northern Muslim majority, and regardless of official assurances that non-Muslims would not be adversely affected, many Southern Sudanese were now alienated to the point of armed insurrection. Commonly known as *Anya Nya II*, the revitalized rebel groups were organized into political and military wings, the Sudan People's Liberation Movement (SPLM) and Sudan People's Liberation Army (SPLA) respectively. During 1983–84, the rebels engaged government forces in a series of battles, especially in Upper Nile and Bahr al-Ghazal.

Meanwhile, Nimeri's commitment to Islamization continued to attract some support among the mainly Muslim population of the North. The harsher penalties of the new legal code were enforced regardless of, and even contrary to, the teachings of the Shari'a itself. Corruption, which was inconsistent with the principles of the Shari'a, continued to proliferate within the ruling élite. No effective action was taken to institutionalize the principle of consultation (shura) in government, and it was proposed that Nimeri be given even greater powers than he had previously exercised. Prominent among the burgeoning opposition was Sadiq al-Mahdi, who viewed Nimeri's Islamization policies as a gross distortion of Islamic principles. Relations between Nimeri and Hassan at-Turabi's faction of the Muslim Brotherhood deteriorated, both because the Brotherhood was ignored in the formulation of Islamization policies and because it was potentially a formidable contender for political power, although formally allied to the regime since 1977.

As the country sank deeper into economic disarray, Nimeri's dependence on his Western allies (especially the USA), and their influence over him, increased. Eventually he was persuaded not only to acquiesce to the wishes of the IMF in the removal of food subsidies and the further devaluation of the currency, but also to consent to participate in the evacuation from Ethiopia to Israel of several thousand Falasha Jews, an action which contravened Sudan's commitments as a member of the Arab League. By February 1985 disillusionment with the regime and its policies, both internal and external, was rapidly crystallizing. At this late juncture, Nimeri moved to deal with the Muslim Brotherhood by putting its leaders on trial for sedition and, by so doing, alienated his last vestiges of popular support. Public sentiment was also being rapidly alienated by the government's failure to deal with the effects of the prolonged drought and the problems created by the continued influx of refugees from Ethiopia, Chad and Uganda. Nimeri reacted to this situation by adopting a conciliatory stance. The state of emergency was lifted, and the operation of the special courts was suspended,

while an offer was made to revoke the redivision of the South if a majority of Southerners desired it. Nimeri also reshuffled the council of ministers and presidential council. Among those appointed in March 1985 was Lt-Gen. Abd ar-Rahman Swar ad-Dahab, receiving the posts of minister of defence and c-in-c of the armed forces.

MILITARY COUP

Public discontent with Nimeri's regime reached its culmination in March 1985, exacerbated by substantial increases in the price of food and fuel, and Khartoum was immobilized by a general strike. On 6 April, while Nimeri was visiting the USA, he was deposed in a bloodless military coup, led by Lt-Gen. Swar ad-Dahab. A state of emergency was declared, and a transitional military council (TMC) was appointed. After two weeks of negotiations with the various organizations which had worked for Nimeri's downfall, a 15-member council of ministers, including three non-Muslim Southerners, was announced. Dr Gizuli Dafallah, a trade unionist who had been a prominent organizer of the general strike, was appointed prime minister. The council of ministers was to be responsible to the TMC during a 12-month transitional period prior to the holding of free elections, scheduled for April 1986. Hundreds of Nimeri's officials were arrested, and the SSU was dissolved.

In response to the coup, the SPLM initially declared a cease-fire, but presented the new regime with a series of demands concerning the Southern Region. Swar ad-Dahab offered various concessions to the South, including the cancellation of the redivision and the reinstatement of the Southern HEC in Juba, with Maj.-Gen. James Loro, a member of the TMC, as its interim president. The SPLM rejected these terms, broke off negotiations with the TMC, and resumed hostilities. The civil war in the South continued throughout 1985, with many Southern towns under siege. In an attempt to reach agreement with the SPLM, a conference was held in March 1986 in Addis Ababa, Ethiopia, between the SPLM and the National Alliance for Salvation (NAS), a semi-official alliance of trade unionists and politicians who supported the government. The SPLM insisted that the retention of the Shari'a remained a major obstacle to national unity; the NAS agreed to abolish the Shari'a and, in response to another of the rebels' demands, to end military links with Libya and Egypt; however, these measures were not implemented by the TMC before the April 1986 election.

Despite these difficulties, Swar ad-Dahab promised a return to civilian rule after a 12-month interim period. A transitional constitution was signed in October 1985; under its provisions, numerous political groupings began to emerge in preparation for the forthcoming general election. In December the name of the country was changed to 'the Republic of Sudan', thus restoring the official designation to its pre-1969 form.

The TMC's foreign policy during its 12-month rule reversed Nimeri's strongly pro-Western stance. While advocating a policy of non-alignment, the TMC sought to improve relations with Ethiopia, Libya and the USSR, to the concern of Sudan's former allies, Egypt and the USA. A military co-operation agreement was signed with Libya in July 1985, and diplomatic relations were quickly restored between Sudan, Libya and Ethiopia. Relations also improved with Iran, which had been one of the main adversaries of Nimeri's government. In November links with Egypt were reaffirmed. Relations with the USA, already viewed with suspicion (owing to the US government's former support for Nimeri), were further strained after an attack on Libya by US aircraft in April 1986.

CIVILIAN COALITIONS AND REGIONAL UNREST

More than 40 political parties participated in the general election held in April 1986. As expected, no single party won an outright majority of seats in the assembly, but Sadiq al-Mahdi's UP won the largest number (99), followed by the Democratic Unionist Party (DUP), formed in 1968 by a merger of the PDP and the NUP and now led by Osman al-Mirghani (63 seats), and the National Islamic Front (NIF) of Dr Hassan at-Turabi (with 51 seats). The newly elected assembly was, however, unable to agree on the composition of the new government; following protracted negotiations over the allocation of portfolios, a broadly-based administration was formed in May. The council of ministers comprised of a coalition of the UP and the

DUP, with, in addition, four portfolios allocated to Southern parties. Sadiq al-Mahdi became prime minister and minister of defence. He urged the Southern rebels to negotiate a peaceful settlement, and promised that Shari'a law would be abolished and the state of emergency lifted. In foreign policy, al-Mahdi undertook to maintain the non-aligned policy of the TMC, which was dissolved in preparation for the return to civilian rule. Swar ad-Dahab relinquished the posts of head of state (being replaced by a six-member supreme council, installed in May) and of military c-in-c.

In an attempt to make the new government acceptable to the Southerners, a special portfolio, the ministry of peace and unity, had been created for a member of the NAS, and Col John Garang, leader of the SPLM, had been offered a post in the council of ministers. However, the SPLM refused either to recognize or take part in the new government. Tensions in the South continued to worsen; in early 1986 the SPLM launched a new offensive, and captured the town of Rumbek. In July, however, al-Mahdi and Garang held direct talks for the first time, in Addis Ababa, but the only result was an agreement to maintain contacts. Further negotiations, held in August, between the NAS and the SPLM ended abruptly when the SPLM shot down a Sudan Airways aircraft, killing 60 civilians on board. The SPLM launched a new offensive, with the aim of recapturing the four strategic Southern towns of Juba, Wau, Malakal and Bentiu. Although al-Mahdi attempted a new peace initiative in April, with a suggestion to the SPLM of a two-week cease-fire, by May the military situation in the South had become so unstable that it appeared possible that the government might consent to the outright secession of three Southern provinces.

In May 1987 al-Mahdi asked the supreme council to dissolve his coalition government, citing as his reasons alleged incompetence on the part of certain ministers, lack of progress in addressing the country's serious economic problems, and divisions within the council of ministers. These disagreements arose from widening divisions within the DUP, where contending factions of liberals and religious traditionalists had led al-Mahdi during April to enter into secret negotiations with the opposition NIF, with a view to forming a new coalition. In the event, neither the NIF nor the UP were willing to participate in a single administration, and al-Mahdi's reconstructed council of ministers, announced in June, differed little from the outgoing administration. Following the formation of the new council of ministers, al-Mahdi stated that the coalition parties had agreed on mutually acceptable guidelines for the conduct of government policy, with special reference to the abrogation of religiously-based legislation unacceptable to the South. Progress was also to be made on the long-delayed convening of a constitutional conference. On the former point, it was stated that laws based on a 'Sudanese legal heritage' would replace those unacceptable to non-Muslims, who would be exempted from Islamic punishments and the system of *zakat* (alms) taxation. Such a compromise, however, was rejected by the SPLM, which continued to demand the total abrogation of Shari'a law as a precondition to peace negotiations, while the fundamentalist NIF restated its demand that the Islamic code be applied to the country as a whole. In late July the government imposed a 12-month state of emergency, aimed at resolving the country's worsening economic crisis. In August the DUP temporarily withdrew from the coalition government, after the party's proposed candidate for a vacancy on the supreme council had been rejected by the UP. However, efforts to replace the coalition with an all-party government of national unity were unsuccessful, and in October the UP and the DUP agreed to form a joint administration once again, the NIF having elected to remain in opposition.

In September 1987 representatives of Southern Sudanese political parties met in Nairobi, Kenya; they issued a joint appeal for all Sudanese political forces to join the peace efforts, and requested that the government should convene a national constitutional conference. However, the conflict in the South continued unabated. In November SPLM forces, allegedly with Ethiopian assistance, captured the town of Kurmuk, near the border with Ethiopia. Although the capture of this town was of little strategic significance, it was nevertheless regarded as damaging to government morale, as the SPLA had previously confined itself to the South. Kurmuk was recaptured by

government forces in December, and in the same month the government entered into secret peace negotiations in London with representatives of the SPLM. Although no agreement was reached, the SPLM was reported to have abandoned its demand for the abrogation of Islamic law as a precondition for talks. In December al-Mahdi announced that a number of provisions of Shari'a law had been repealed, and that preparations were being made to replace those remaining in force with a new legal code.

In January 1988 representatives of the government and 17 political parties signed a 'transitional charter' which aimed to define Sudan's political structure pending a proposed constitutional conference. The 'transitional charter' stressed Sudan's commitment to multi-party democracy; stipulated that the government of the South would be in accordance with the 1972 system of autonomous regional government; and requested the government to replace Shari'a law with an alternative legal system before the constitutional conference was convened.

In April 1988 al-Mahdi requested the supreme council to dissolve his coalition government, following a vote by the national assembly in favour of the formation of a new 'government of national unity'. In order to expedite its formation, al-Mahdi resigned as prime minister on 16 April. On 27 April he was re-elected to a further two-year term, obtaining 196 of 222 votes cast by the 260-member national assembly. In early April, during negotiations on the formation of a new government, the UP, the DUP and the NIF had agreed to proceed with the implementation of an Islamic legal code within two months of taking office. Following his re-election as prime minister, al-Mahdi declared that, while the precise nature of the relationship between the state and religion should be established at the proposed constitutional conference, the Muslim majority had the right to choose laws that governed Muslims in so far as they did not infringe upon the rights of non-Muslims.

The formation of a new 27-member 'government of national unity', comprising members of the UP, the DUP, the NIF and a number of Southern Sudanese political parties, was completed in May 1988. Al-Mahdi announced that the new government would deal with the critical economic and security problems facing the country. Few observers, however, expected the new administration to be able to resolve the problem of the war in the South, especially since the fundamentalist NIF had joined the coalition on condition that a 'replacement' Shari'a code be introduced within 60 days of its formation.

In November 1988 representatives of the SPLM met senior members of the DUP and reached agreement on proposals to end the civil war. In December, however, a state of emergency was again declared amid reports that a military coup had been attempted (see below). The DUP withdrew its six ministers from the coalition government, following a request by al-Mahdi that the national assembly convene a national constitutional conference, without the agreement between the SPLM and the DUP being incorporated into his proposal.

In February 1989 Dr Hassan at-Turabi, the leader of the NIF, was appointed deputy prime minister. This appointment, while strengthening the position of the NIF in the government, reduced the likelihood of an early solution to the war in the South. In late February al-Mahdi threatened to resign as prime minister unless senior army officers allowed him to form a new government and to work for peace in the South. However, the army refused to guarantee that it would not intervene if necessary to arrest Sudan's continued perceived drift towards Libya and to expedite negotiations to end the war in the South. In March al-Mahdi agreed to form a new, broadly-based government which would begin negotiations with the SPLM. Thirty political parties and 17 trade unions had previously signed an agreement endorsing the peace agreement drawn up by the DUP and the SPLM in November 1988. However, the NIF refused to endorse the agreement (which called for the suspension of Islamic laws as a prelude to the negotiation of a peace settlement to the civil war), and was excluded from the new government formed on 23 March 1989. Peace negotiations between a government delegation and the SPLM commenced in Ethiopia in April. In early May the SPLM proclaimed a 45-day cease-fire, but by mid-June negotiations had become deadlocked.

MILITARY RULE AND CIVIL WAR

By late 1988 there were signs of widespread discontent in military circles at the government's continuing lack of progress in resolving the civil conflict. A coup attempt in December, promoted by supporters of ex-president Nimeri, was quickly suppressed, but subsequent political manoeuvres by al-Mahdi (see above) did little to allay the increasing frustration of senior army officers. On 30 June 1989 a bloodless *coup d'état*, led by Brig. (later Lt-Gen.) Omar Hassan Ahmad al-Bashir, removed al-Mahdi's government and formed a 15-member Revolutionary Command Council for National Salvation (RCC), which declared its primary aim to be the resolution of the Southern conflict. Al-Bashir rapidly dismantled the civilian ruling apparatus; the constitution, national assembly and all political parties and trade unions were abolished, a state of emergency was declared, and civilian newspapers were closed. About 30 members of the former government were detained, including al-Mahdi, although three of the ex-ministers were included in the new 21-member cabinet which was announced in early July. Its composition included 16 civilians, of whom four were Southerners, as well as several members who were understood to be sympathetic towards Islamic fundamentalism. Internationally, the RCC regime received immediate diplomatic recognition from Chad, Egypt, Libya, the People's Democratic Republic of Yemen and Saudi Arabia, and the new government was generally welcomed as a potentially stabilizing influence in the region.

The SPLA response to the coup was cautious. Al-Bashir declared a one-month unilateral cease-fire on 5 July 1989 and offered an amnesty to those opposing the Khartoum government 'for political reasons'. In an effort to restart negotiations, al-Bashir requested Ethiopia, Egypt and Kenya to act as mediators. At the same time, however, the government's announcement of proposals for a national referendum on Shari'a law alienated the SPLA, which demanded its suspension as a precondition for talks. Peace negotiations were, however, renewed in Ethiopia in August. By this time the SPLM's terms for a negotiated settlement to the conflict included the immediate resignation of the RCC prior to the establishment of an interim government, which would represent the SPLM, the banned political parties and other groupings; and the new regime's proximity to the fundamentalist NIF had become apparent. The negotiations immediately foundered on the issue of Shari'a law. Col Garang was invited to attend a government-sponsored peace conference in Khartoum in early September, but declined to do so while the curfew and the state of emergency remained in force. Further peace negotiations began in Kenya at the beginning of December, but quickly collapsed over the issue of Shari'a law. By the end of January 1990 the SPLM, which had been achieving significant military advances after resuming hostilities in October 1989, was preparing a full-scale assault on the important garrison town of Juba. In March President Mobutu of Zaire held talks, separately, with both al-Bashir and Col Garang, in an unsuccessful attempt to reactivate peace negotiations.

A number of coup attempts were reported during 1990 as was growing internal unrest. An opposition government-in-exile was formed in January 1991 by Col Garang and a former c-in-c of the army, Lt-Gen. Fatih Ahmed Ali. A cabinet reshuffle followed in late January, in which al-Bashir created three new ministries and redesignated several existing departments. At the beginning of February, al-Bashir signed a decree introducing a new penal code, based, like its predecessor, on Shari'a law. (Although the earlier Islamic penal code had remained in force, the punishments it prescribed had not been applied since the overthrow of Nimeri in 1985.) The code, which was to take effect from 22 March 1991, was not to apply, for the present, in the three Southern regions of Equatoria, Upper Nile and Bahr al-Ghazal. This exemption, however, appeared to cover only five of the code's 186 articles, and it was stated that the code would be applicable to non-Muslim Sudanese residents in the North, notably the estimated 2m. refugees who had fled to the Khartoum area from the civil war in the South.

A new administrative structure for the provinces was introduced in February 1991. According to the government, the changes would be conducive to greater regional autonomy—an issue in the civil war. The previous 18 administrative regions were replaced with nine states, which were in turn sub-divided into 66 provinces and 281 local government areas. Each of the nine new states was to have its own governor, deputy governor and cabinet of ministers, and was to assume responsibility for local administration and the collection of some taxes. The central government retained control over foreign policy, military affairs, the economy and the other main areas of administration. The SPLA rejected the measures as inadequate.

Renewed indications of dissent within the regime emerged following the execution of 20 army officers in April 1991 for their alleged involvement in a coup attempt. Faisal Abu Salih, the minister of the interior and a member of the RCC, together with another RCC member, Brig.-Gen. Uthman Ahmed Hassan, were subsequently dismissed. At the end of April, al-Bashir announced the immediate release of all the country's political prisoners. Human rights organizations subsequently claimed, however, that at least 60 of the government's opponents remained in detention. Among those released was the former prime minister, Sadiq al-Mahdi, who had been under house arrest. A one-month amnesty for all opponents of the government was declared, and was further renewed in June without limit on time. The announcements coincided with the holding, in Khartoum between 29 April–2 May, of a national conference on Sudan's political future, attended by some 1,600 delegates chosen by the regime. Following this conference, al-Bashir announced, on 29 June, that a political system based on Libyan-style 'people's congresses' was to be introduced.

In May 1991 Col Garang marked the eighth anniversary of the start of the civil war by inviting the government to take part in peace negotiations. The government responded by stating that it was willing at any time to discuss terms for a settlement, but it reiterated its view that the administrative reforms introduced in February already represented a considerable degree of compromise. Rebel forces remained in control of most of Southern Sudan. The overthrow, on 21 May, of the Ethiopian government led by Mengistu Haile Mariam had implications for the SPLA, which had in the past enjoyed Ethiopian support; armed clashes within Ethiopia between SPLA forces and those of the new Ethiopian regime were reported in late May. On 29 May the Sudanese government declared its recognition of, and support for, the new Ethiopian government.

International efforts to achieve a peace settlement within Sudan gained renewed momentum in mid-1991. In mid-June the government announced that it would consider proposals made by the US government, providing for the partial withdrawal of government forces from Southern Sudan, the withdrawal of the SPLA forces from government-held areas and the declaration of Juba, the Southern capital, as an 'open' city. On 14 June the SPLA endorsed the government's suggestion that the Nigerian head of state, Ibrahim Babangida, should act as a mediator. However, this diplomatic progress coincided with a new government offensive against the SPLA. At the beginning of July, following further initiatives by the USA, Garang was reported to have agreed to begin unconditional peace negotiations with the government. However, in August 1991, as part of a cabinet reshuffle, which was carried out during the absence abroad of al-Bashir, a prominent Islamic fundamentalist, Tayib Ibrahim Muhammad Khair, was appointed governor of the Southern province of Darfur. This appointment was viewed as unlikely to improve the prospects of a definitive peace settlement in the immediate future.

An alleged coup attempt in late August 1991, resulted in the arrest of 10 army officers and a number of civilians and was officially ascribed to unspecified 'foreign powers'. Subsequent official statements alleged that those implicated included members of the National Democratic Alliance (NDA, a grouping formed in 1989 by the SPLA and some of the other former political parties, including the UP and the DUP) and the previously unknown organization, *Ana al-Sudan* ('I am Sudan'). The NDA claimed at the end of September that some 70 people had been arrested and that the former prime minister, Sadiq al-Mahdi, had been among those interrogated. The subsequent trial by a military court of 15 people accused of involvement in the coup attempt, resulted in death sentences for 10 army officers, commuted in December to life imprisonment.

Reports of a split within the SPLA, circulated from Khartoum at the end of August 1991, were immediately denied by Garang. Three SPLA field commanders—Riek Mashar Teny-Dhurgon, Lam Akol and Kerubino Kuanyin Bol—claimed to have taken over the leadership of the SPLA and accused Garang of dictatorial behaviour. The dissidents were reported to favour a policy of secession for the South, whereas the aim of Garang and his supporters, based at Kapoeta, remained a united, secular state. The split was also along ethnic lines, with the Dinka supporting Garang and the Nuer the breakaway faction. The SPLA's divisions led to a postponement of the first round of peace talks due to be held under the auspices of the OAU in Abuja, Nigeria, at the end of October. Fierce fighting between the two SPLA factions was reported in November and resulted in the massacre of several thousand civilians in the southern towns of Bor and Kongor before a cease-fire was negotiated in mid-December. At the end of November the government announced a one-month amnesty for rebels who wished to surrender.

Proposals for constitutional reform were announced by al-Bashir on 1 January 1992. A 300-member transitional parliament was to be appointed, with full legislative functions and the power to veto decisions of the RCC. The parliament, which convened for the first time on 24 February, included—as well as all members of the RCC (excluding al-Bashir), state governors and representatives of the army and police—former members of the banned UP and DUP, and former aides to ex-president Nimeri, reflecting the government's desire to broaden its support in the wake of the introduction of an unpopular programme of economic austerity measures. There were reports of widespread political unrest in February, with demonstrations against the new economic policies and the reported arrest of a number of army officers who were alleged to be planning an attack on the military leadership. A further alleged coup attempt was reported to have been foiled in mid-April.

The government, while still declaring its willingness to take part in peace talks, launched a new military offensive against the SPLA in late February 1992. With the SPLA weakened by its internal divisions and the loss of Ethiopian support, the town of Pochala, on the Ethiopian border and held by the SPLA since 1985, was captured in March. During April 1992 the towns of Bor, Kongor, Yirol, Pibor and Mongalla also fell to government forces. In late April Col Garang claimed that the government offensive had been halted and that the towns lost by the SPLA had been in the hands of the dissident faction, which he accused of defecting to the government. However, on 1 May government forces were reported to have captured a larger rebel camp at Bahr al-Ghazal in western Sudan, followed on 12 May by Liria, on the road east from Juba to Garang's Torit headquarters. On 28 May, Kapoeta, near the Kenyan border, also fell to government forces. Strengthened by its military successes and by Kenya's reported agreement to stop supporting the SPLA, the government announced its willingness to participate in peace talks. These discussions were convened in Abuja on 26 May by President Babangida of Nigeria, the then OAU chairman, and were attended by a government delegation and two from the SPLA: one representing Col Garang's faction, the other the dissident group based at Nasir and led by Lam Akol. The talks concluded on 5 June, with an agreement by all parties to continue 'peaceful negotiations' at a future date, although there was no mention of a cease-fire. The final communiqué referred to Sudan as a 'multi-ethnic, multi-lingual, multi-cultural and multi-religious country' but a demand by the two SPLA factions for a referendum on self-determination for the South was withdrawn at government insistence.

The government's military offensive continued to make progress in Southern Sudan, with the opening, for the first time in seven years, of a river passage to Juba in mid-June 1992 and of the railway to Wau later in the month. On 12 July the government announced the capture of Torit, near the Ugandan border, which had been Col Garang's headquarters and the last major town in rebel hands. Garang himself was reported to have escaped to Kajo Kaji, closer to the Ugandan border, shortly before the fall of Torit and the SPLA quickly mounted a counter-attack on the town. Eager to re-establish its credibility after a series of setbacks, the rebel movement launched a new offensive as the rainy season started, mounting an attack on Juba and attempting to disrupt government supply lines to the newly-recaptured Southern towns. There were indications that the two rebel factions had achieved a measure of reconciliation since the Abuja meeting, enabling them to offer a united response to the government advance. The shelling of Juba led to the

suspension of relief flights to the city and by mid-August the city's 300,000 people were reported to be close to starvation. Meanwhile, the SPLA claimed that government troops had massacred 900 civilians in the city. Conflicting reports emerged about fighting around Malakal, the capital of Upper Nile province, with the Nasir faction of the SPLA claiming to have captured the town from government forces in early October.

Evidence of divisions between the RCC leadership and the NIF over the continued military domination of the government emerged in early 1993. In statements that he later retracted at-Turabi declared that he expected the RCC to resign and to transfer power to a transitional assembly. In mid-January a cabinet reshuffle disbanded three ministries and created two new ones, and in February the minister of foreign affairs, Ali Sahloul, was replaced by Hussein Suleiman Abu Salih.

Contacts between the government and the various rebel factions took place in Uganda and Kenya during February 1993, with a view to resuming the peace process following unsuccessful attempts to do so in 1992. Col Garang announced a unilateral cease-fire on 17 March, in honour of the Muslim holiday of Id al-Fitr, and aimed at providing a favourable atmosphere for the peace talks, a gesture to which the government responded with its own announcement of a cease-fire two days later. Garang also urged the establishment of safety zones to allow the delivery of food supplies to starving people. However, at the end of March fighting was reported at Kongor between Garang's forces and the 'Forces of Unity' faction of the SPLA, led by William Nyuon.

Peace talks between the government and the faction of the SPLA led by Col Garang resumed in Abuja in April 1993. After preliminary discussions on 8 April, at which it was agreed to continue to observe a cease-fire, the two sides met again for substantive talks on 26 April. Meanwhile, in Nairobi, talks were also taking place between a government delegation and SPLA–United, an alliance formed in early April between the Nasir faction, the 'Forces of Unity' and a faction led by Kerubino Kuanyin Bol. The Abuja talks adjourned on 18 May, having made little progress on the main issues dividing the parties. Although the government claimed the talks would resume in June, the SPLA said they had been a failure and that the cease-fire was at an end. The Nairobi talks, after a break in early May, resumed during 7–26 May and ended with agreement on the concept of a unified federal state and on the rights of state governments to introduce laws supplementary to federal legislation—allowing the implementation of Shari'a law in the North, but not in the South. No agreement was reached, however, on the length of the period of transition before the holding of a referendum on future divisions of power.

The collapse of the Abuja negotiations was quickly followed by allegations of cease-fire violations from both the government and rebel factions, and in July 1993 the faction of the SPLA led by Col Garang announced that it had launched a major offensive after attacks by government troops, aided by rival SPLA factions. In August government forces attacked SPLA-held towns near the Ugandan border in an offensive aimed at cutting supply routes to rebel forces in Southern and Western Sudan. They were reported to have gained control of the town of Morobo and to have blocked the road route for relief supplies to Bahr al-Ghazal and Western Equatoria. Also in August, the Nuba people were reported to be threatened by government forces in central Sudan. Independent observers urged the UN to establish 'safe havens' for refugees and to extend its Operation Lifeline Sudan to the Nuba mountains. In early September the SPLA was reported to have checked the advance of the government forces in Southern Sudan.

A reshuffle of the cabinet in July 1993 was regarded as having strengthened the position of the NIF within the government, and as a further step towards the establishment of a civilian administration. On 19 October al-Bashir announced political reforms in preparation for presidential and legislative elections to be held in 1994 and 1995 respectively. The RCC had been dissolved three days previously—after it had appointed al-Bashir as president and as head of a new civilian government. Cabinet ministers were requested to remain in office until elections took place. Al-Bashir appointed a new minister of defence—a portfolio that he had formerly held himself—and a new vice-president. Western observers regarded the dissolution of the RCC as reinforcing the position of the NIF within the government during the transition to civilian rule. At the end of October the cabinet was reshuffled. In early February 1994, by constitutional decree, Sudan was redivided into 26 states instead of the previous nine. The executive and legislative powers of each state government were to be expanded, and Southern states were expected to be exempted from Shari'a law.

At the beginning of 1994 the civil war in Southern Sudan remained in stalemate. As in previous years, the government's 1993–94 Southern offensive involved the deployment of army and Popular Defence Force (PDF) units from sizeable garrisons in Juba and Wau, largely along main roads, to locations along the borders with Zaire (now the Democratic Republic of the Congo, DRC) and Uganda. The objective was to capture border towns such as Tambura and Nimule, which the rebels used as transhipment points to bring troops, weapons and other supplies into the war zone from bases in Zaire and Uganda. Rebel forces, which remained divided into warring factions, suffered from a lack of arms and ammunition. As a result, government troops made some minimal advances. In June 1994 army units recaptured Kajo Kaji and opened a land route between Renk in Sobat state and the Upper Nile regional capital of Malakal, for the first time in some 10 years.

On 13 July 1994 a restructuring of the cabinet was announced, in which Lt-Col at-Tayeb Ibrahim Muhammad Khair was appointed minister of the interior. In late October al-Bashir announced the start of a dual offensive to sever the SPLA's supply lines from Uganda and Zaire before the next government offensive. The president also announced that his goal was to liberate Southern Sudan from the SPLA and, at the same time, to pursue efforts to negotiate with the rebels. The offensive did not proceed as planned, however, and army and PDF units suffered several defeats in the area of Mangall and Terakeka, north of Juba. By mid-December the fighting was taking place primarily around the government-held town of Kapoeta. The government acknowledged that its forces had suffered another military defeat east of Torit, on the supply route to Kapoeta. According to Col Garang, the SPLA had killed more than 1,000 government troops. By January 1995 there were reports that rebel forces had surrounded Kapoeta, and had captured part of the town. On 25 March, in spite of these losses, government forces managed to capture Nasir, a stronghold of the South Sudan Independence Movement (SSIM) near the Ethiopian border. On 31 March, however, the SSIM captured intact an armoured military convoy of government forces at the town of Lafon. This development was significant in that the Sudanese government had previously provided support to the SSIM. With the SSIM now in conflict with the government, a reconciliation between the SSIM commander, Dr Riek Mashar Teny-Dhurgon, and Col Garang became more likely. Indeed, on 27 April the two commanders signed the Lafon Declaration, which provided for a cease-fire and a cessation of hostilities between their forces; reunification; reintegration of military forces; and a general amnesty. In early February the cabinet was reshuffled, the pattern of changes suggesting a reinforcement of the Islamic character of the government.

An unexpected development in the Southern conflict occurred on 27 March 1995, when former US president Jimmy Carter persuaded the Sudanese government to declare a unilateral two-month cease-fire and to offer the rebel groups an amnesty if they surrendered their weapons. Three days later the SPLA also declared a two-month cease-fire and requested the deployment of international observers to monitor the truce. Finally, on 3 April, the SSIM issued a cease-fire declaration. On 27 May the Sudanese government extended its cease-fire for two months. However, it soon became apparent that the army was continuing to conduct military operations. Four days prior to the extension of the government cease-fire, the SSIM claimed that government forces had launched a new offensive in Latjor state, which brought the number of government violations of the Carter-mediated cease-fire to 21. On 4 June army units temporarily entered Pariang in Upper Nile province, which had been under the control of the SPLA for 12 years. It was also reported that the government was preparing another dry season offensive in Southern Sudan.

During 15–23 June 1995 a conference took place in Asmara, Eritrea, of groups and parties opposed to the government. The conference, hosted by the Eritrean People's Front for Democracy and Justice (PFDJ) and organized by the Asmara-based NDA, was attended, among others, by representatives of the DUP, the UP, the SCP and the SPLA. At its conclusion the conference issued a communiqué in which opposition leaders pledged (once the al-Bashir regime had been ousted) to support the right of self-determination for all Sudanese peoples, based on the results of future referendums; and to establish a decentralized government for a four-year interim period. The communiqué also envisaged the future separation of religion and politics and the abolition of Shari'a law. The creation of a government-in-exile was announced and the conference was also reported to have achieved a *rapprochement* between the SPLA and the other opposition groups: the NDA announced details of a forthcoming military campaign to be undertaken by its military wing in alliance with, among others, Col Garang's faction of the SPLA.

In August 1995 a cabinet reshuffle was announced. The DUP claimed that ministers who were dismissed had been involved in planning the attempted assassination of President Mubarak of Egypt in June (see below). Later in August President al-Bashir announced that legislative and presidential elections which had been scheduled to take place in 1994 and 1995, respectively, would now be held in 1996. Political prisoners who were released in a government amnesty on 24-25 August 1995 included the UP leader, Sadiq al-Mahdi, who had been placed under arrest in May for having alleged that state funds were being misused.

In September 1995 the government imposed strict security measures in response to rioting in Khartoum. Some reports suggested that the disturbances had been provoked by the arrest of student demonstrators in the city earlier in the month, but the government blamed the SCP for fomenting the unrest. In the same month the government issued a formal denial of any responsibility for the attempted assassination of Egypt's President Mubarak in June.

In November 1995, having begun a new offensive in late October, Col Garang's SPLA forces were reported to be advancing on the Southern town of Juba. The retreat of government forces which this provoked appeared to be regarded as more serious than other, similar retreats in the past: the government declared a mass mobilization, urging all sectors of the population to defend the country. On 11 November the government claimed that its forces had inflicted a major defeat on the SPLA and on Ugandan and Eritrean forces allied with it. The governments of Uganda and Eritrea denied the involvement of their forces in the fighting. By late 1996 the SPLA claimed to have taken control of all of Western Equatoria, all of the rural regions of Eastern Equatoria and 13 towns in central Equatoria.

The first legislative and presidential elections to be held in Sudan since 1989 took place during 6-17 March 1996. Some 5.5m. of Sudan's 10m. eligible voters were reported to have participated in the election of 275 deputies to a new, 400-seat national assembly. The remaining 125 deputies had been appointed at a national conference in January. Representatives of opposition groups and parties alleged that electoral malpractice had been widespread and that many voters had been intimidated into participating. In the presidential election al-Bashir (opposed by some 40 candidates, none of them representatives of the principal opposition groups and parties) obtained 75.7% of the total votes cast, and formally commenced a five-year term of office on 1 April. On the same day Dr Hassan at-Turabi, the secretary-general of the NIF, was unanimously elected president of the national assembly.

Rumours of an attempted *coup d'état* in late March 1996 prejudiced the newly-constituted regime's claim that the elections signified the beginning of a new period of stability and reconciliation, as did reports of serious unrest in Khartoum in early April and the decision not to appoint a new cabinet until it became clear whether the UN would impose sanctions on Sudan for its failure to comply with the terms of Resolution 1044 (see below).

A unilateral cease-fire declared by the government throughout Southern Sudan on 3 March 1996 did not lead to a cessation of hostilities there. Col Garang's faction of the SPLA ignored it, attacking towns close to the Sudanese-Ethiopian border, one of which was only a short distance from the Roseires dam and thus provoked speculation that an attack on this key installation might be imminent. However, another peace agreement concluded by the government and the SSIM in February—initially in order to facilitate the provision of emergency food aid to areas of need in Southern Sudan—appeared, in April, to culminate in a substantial breakthrough in the Southern conflict. On 10 April the government, the SSIM and the SPLA–United signed an agreement—described as a 'political charter for peace'—under which they pledged to preserve Sudan's national unity and to take joint action to develop those areas of the country which had been affected by the civil war. The charter also provided for the holding of a referendum as a 'means of realizing the aspirations of Southern citizens' and affirmed that Shari'a law would be the basis of future legislation. Other opposition groups, however, rejected the charter. On 17 April Sudan's first vice-president was reported to have invited Garang to sign the charter on behalf of the faction of the SPLA under his control, and there was speculation that this was part of an attempt to form a new government of national unity. However, the new cabinet, announced on 21 April, retained the military, Islamic cast of its predecessor.

In June 1996 the NDA issued an ultimatum to the government, urging it to relinquish power without further bloodshed. It predicted that its fall was, in any case, imminent and announced plans for a popular uprising for which it forecast support among the armed forces. In the same month anti-government demonstrations by student supporters of the NDA were reported to have taken place in Khartoum, followed by similar agitation in Omdurman. Renewed demonstrations were reported to have taken place in Khartoum in early September.

In late August 1996 opponents of the government based in Cairo, Egypt, claimed that 11 military officers had been executed for having taken part in a conspiracy to occupy government facilities in Port Sudan. In October, however, the government denied that any of the conspirators had been executed. In early October al-Bashir appointed eight deputies to the national assembly to represent constituencies in the South, where, owing to the civil war, it had not been possible to hold elections in March. In December Sadiq al-Mahdi fled to Eritrea, subsequently claiming that he had left Sudan to avoid becoming a government hostage.

In January 1997 the government was reported to be seeking assistance from Egypt, after its forces suffered a series of defeats at the hands of an alliance of various rebel forces. Sudan claimed that Ethiopia was lending active support to the rebels and appealed to the UN Security Council to intervene. In late January rebel forces were reported to be advancing on the Southern city of Damazin; and in February government forces were reported to have lost control of all but a few Southern towns to rebel forces.

In March 1997 reports indicated that the Sudanese People's Armed Forces (SPAF) were rounding up young men in Khartoum for military service, and at the end of May al-Bashir announced that all male secondary school-leavers would be subject to compulsory military service. Various international human rights organizations maintained that the SPAF were assigning young men to combat units against their will, although the government claimed that in such cases non-combative duties were assigned. On 21 April a peace agreement was concluded between the government and six of the Southern factions. In this agreement self-determination was promised for the Southern states, as was, after a four-year transitional period, a referendum on independence. The SPLA refused to sign, claiming that the pact was devised in such a way as to divide and weaken the Southern opposition. In the same month, the southern rebels came within 40 km of Juba, the Southern capital, although they lacked the capabilities to seize the town. In the north-east the situation was less clear, as the NDA was exaggerating its military gains, although it did advance towards its target, the Roseires dam. This exaggeration undermined its credibility and masked its ineffective action, which alienated the SPLA and Eritrea—its principal ally. This led the Eritrean government to advocate the creation of a replacement 'Progressive Alliance', but by mid-1997 no such grouping had been formed. Although the SPLA and the NDA carried out some successful military offensives during 1997 and 1998, neither grouping came close to scoring a decisive military victory over the SPAF, and in late 1997 al-Bashir sought to improve the SPAF's efficiency and performance by reshuffling the senior military leadership. The issue of mili-

tary conscription remained to the fore during 1997. Despite protests which followed the escape of 72 students from Khartoum international airport (who were to be airlifted to the South), the government warned that conscription would be rigorously enforced. On 2 April 1998 hundreds of military recruits sought to escape from a military camp south-east of Khartoum; however, the boat on which they were travelling capsized, drowning at least 55 recruits, and leaving another 260 missing. On 8 April al-Bashir responded both to this incident and to public opinion by substituting new conscription arrangements, under which students were to be allowed to delay compulsory military service until after their graduation from university.

In early August 1997, in accordance with the terms of the peace treaty, the Southern States Co-ordination Council (SSCC) was established; Dr Riek Mashar Teny-Dhurgon, leader of the SSIM, was appointed its chairman. Dr Lam Akol, leader of the SPLA–United, signed a peace agreement with the government in September and returned to Khartoum in the following month. (The SPLA–United is the third largest of the Southern insurgent groups, and controls northern Upper Nile state.) In early 1998 Riek Mashar announced that the six Southern rebel factions which had made peace with the government had agreed to unify their troops with his Southern Sudan Defence Force (SSDF). Unification of the former factions' troops leaves two armed organizations, the SPAF and the SSDF, operating in the South, which was expected to facilitate the war against the SPLA. Discontent among Southern politicians became evident in February when many of them threatened to rejoin rebel ranks unless they received positions in the proposed state governments; four were already expected to have done so, including Maj.-Gen. Kerubino Kuanyin Bol, one of the founders of the SPLA.

On 12 February 1998 the first vice-president, Zubair Muhammad Salih, was among 13 people who died when their aircraft crashed during a tour of the front line. Ali Osman Muhammad Taha was appointed first vice-president, and Dr Mustafa Osman Ismail assumed his responsibilities as minister of foreign affairs. In early March al-Bashir announced a cabinet reshuffle in which a new ministry, for international co-operation and investment, was created. Also as part of the reshuffle, a number of former rebel leaders were appointed to the cabinet, including Dr Lam Akol as minister of transport. In late March the supreme council for peace, which had been created in 1994, was dissolved; its responsibilities and functions were assumed by the SSCC.

In October 1997 a 277-member constitutional committee was formed to draft a new constitution. This document was approved by the national assembly in April 1998 and then submitted to al-Bashir. A referendum on the new constitution was held during 1–20 May; results, announced in late June, showed that 96.7% of voters were in favour of the constitution, which came into force on 1 July 1998. Under its terms, executive power was vested in the council of ministers, which was appointed by the president but responsible to the national assembly. Legislative power was vested in the national assembly. The constitution also contained guarantees of freedoms of thought and religion, and the right to political association, provided that such associations complied with the law. At the end of October the minister of irrigation and water resources, Sharif at-Tuhami, resigned. Although the minister of justice had issued a statement exonerating him of any wrongdoing, at-Tuhami had been linked to a corruption case involving contracts for his son's business. Fighting continued in the South in November, and in that month a state of emergency was declared in Darfur region and in Northern Kordofan. Opposition radio reported in December that 84 government soldiers had been killed in the continuing SPLA offensive in the Nuba Mountains.

New political laws approved in November 1998 provided for the establishment of an independent election commission, to prepare guidelines for elections and referendums, and of a constitutional court, and for the legalization of political associations. In January 1999 the age of eligibility to vote was reduced to 17 years. Registration of political parties began in that month; all parties were required to have 100 founding members, none of whom was to have a criminal record. The first registration documents were issued in early February. At that time it was reported that a ban had been imposed preventing all media reports of opposition parties. In late January, meanwhile, it was reported that the government had introduced a new code requiring all women to wear Islamic dress, regardless of their religious affiliation.

Clashes were reported between the government and rebels in early January 1999, during which the rebels claimed to have captured seven soldiers and to have killed a further 48. In mid-January it was announced that the government had agreed to extend the cease-fire for a further three months, although bombing raids were reported in the Southern town of Yei at the end of the month. During a statement on the progress of the peace talks and the civil war, al-Bashir announced his opinion that Southern secession was preferable to the continuation of war. In March a minor ministerial reorganization was carried out. Four new ministers entered the government including Lt-Gen. Abd ar-Rahman Sir al-Khatim as minister of defence; Dr Nafie Ali Nafie, former minister of agriculture and forestry, was appointed to the new role of presidential adviser on peace affairs.

In early 1999 it was announced that elections would be held in mid-1999 for the state legislative assemblies. However, the opposition claimed that this schedule would not give the new parties time to prepare themselves for elections. In April voting was postponed in the South until November, as adverse weather conditions would impede the movement of citizens, and thus their ability to register and to vote. Elections in the northern and central states were to be completed in early June. On 9 May al-Bashir granted an amnesty to ex-president Nimeri. Two days later a licence was granted to Nimeri's followers to form a political party called the Alliance of the People's Working Forces. On 22 May Nimeri returned to Khartoum. During that month the opposition claimed a series of victories in the South and on 31 May Col Garang of the SPLA, Sadiq al-Mahdi of the UP and Mubarak al-Mahdi of the NDA held closed meetings in Kampala, Uganda, to discuss several issues regarding their armed campaign against the government.

In February 1999 the Dinka and the Nuer peoples began talks, brokered by the New Sudan Council of Churches and supported by the SPLA. The talks aimed to end the long-standing rivalry between the two tribes and resulted in the signing of a peace and reconciliation agreement known as the 'Wunlit Dinka-Nuer Covenant'. The covenant granted an amnesty for offences committed before 1 January 1999, allowed freedom of movement across lines of conflict, and encouraged the development of inter-community commerce and services. The covenant also appealed to the SPLA and the SSDF 'to endorse, embrace and assist in implementation of this covenant and its resolutions'.

Instability continued in Western Darfur during 1999. In January tribal clashes between Arab nomadic cattle traders and African Masalit farmers resulted in some 300 deaths; at least 70 villages were burned during the battle. In April 10 people were sentenced to death by hanging and crucifixion for their part in initiating the hostilities and later that month the national assembly extended the state of emergency in Western Darfur for three months in order to complete peace arrangements. On 5 June the two sides signed an agreement which settled their differences over water, grazing and land rights. The accord included provisions to demarcate cattle routes away from Masalit land, share water resources, and create mechanisms to resolve future conflicts. Western Darfur state agreed to pay some US $60,000 to the Masalit and US $2,400 to the Arab tribes as compensation for the damages and deaths.

President al-Bashir gradually sought to steer Sudan away from its hard-line, isolationist domestic foreign policies. Among other things, he sought reconciliation with northern opposition groups which had relocated to Eritrea. In November 1999 al-Bashir and UP leader al-Mahdi met for talks in Djibouti; al-Mahdi had previously met with at-Turabi in Geneva. The Djibouti meeting ended with a joint declaration which envisaged a federal system of government and the holding of a referendum within four years to allow southerners to choose between the division of the country or unity with decentralized powers. The Government later announced it would accept the result of such a referendum. The agreement was welcomed by many parties; however, the NDA responded by stating that it would escalate the war in the south, not end it. SPLA leader John Garang later condemned and disavowed the Djibouti agreement.

During 1999 there were increasing reports of rivalry between al-Bashir and at-Turabi, particularly following the introduction of a bill in the national assembly which sought to curb the power of the president by removing his power to appoint and dismiss state governors. Consideration of the draft legislation was repeatedly delayed, but a vote was scheduled to be held in mid-December in which the national assembly was widely expected to approve it.

On 12 December 1999 al-Bashir set Sudan on a new course by declaring a three-month state of emergency and suspending the national assembly. Al-Bashir announced that he had taken these measures in order to end the 'duality' in the administration. An emergency order suspended some articles of the 1998 constitution, although provincial councils and governors were to continue working. At-Turabi accused al-Bashir of having carried out a *coup d'état*, although a legal challenge, mounted against the measures, was rejected by the Constitutional Court in February. On 24 January 2000 al-Bashir announced the formation of a new government and appointed new governors in 25 of the 26 states. Ten ministers were replaced; and 15 were retained, including those with responsibility for external relations, the interior and defence; the ministry of public services was abolished and the international co-operation functions of the ministry of international co-operation and investment were transferred to the ministry of finance and national economy while its investment functions were assigned to the ministry of national industry. In early February al-Bashir stated that the dissolution of the national assembly was irrevocable and relocated several senior army officers in order to prevent a possible coup. In March al-Bashir extended the state of emergency from three to 12 months. In April it was reported that presidential elections were planned for October. Observers interpreted the announcement as yet another step to curb at-Turabi's power. Most opposition parties, including the UP, indicated that they would boycott any elections prior to the convening of a national conference to discuss the problems in Sudan. In March the UP had announced its decision to suspend its membership of the NDA. Relations had deteriorated after December 1999 when al-Mahdi initiated independent talks with al-Bashir following the dissolution of the national assembly. On 6 May al-Bashir took a further step against at-Turabi by suspending him as secretary-general of the ruling National Congress. According to al-Bashir this action would help to unify the National Congress and preserve the country's security. Despite his removal, at-Turabi still enjoyed considerable support within the National Congress, the Muslim Brotherhood, the Sudanese People's Armed Forces, the People's Defence Force and various other Islamic militias. In late June at-Turabi responded to his dismissal by creating a new political party called the Popular National Congress (PNC). In mid-July al-Bashir effected a government reshuffle following the defection of two ministers to the PNC. Notably, Maj.-Gen. Bakri Hassan Salih was appointed minister of defence, replacing Gen. Abd ar-Rahman Sir al-Khatim, who became minister of cabinet affairs.

Regional Peace Initiatives

In September 1993 the Intergovernmental Authority on Drought and Development (IGADD, now IGAD—see below), under the chairmanship of President Moi of Kenya, sought to mediate an end to the civil war in Southern Sudan. Two months later, the IGADD convened its first meeting with the warring Sudanese parties in Kampala, Uganda. Further meetings followed during 1994–1995. The IGADD mediation committee comprised two sections: a committee of the heads of state of Eritrea, Ethiopia, Kenya, and Uganda; and a standing committee composed of their ministers. The IGADD believed that the civil war in Southern Sudan was a regional rather than a national conflict.

At its May 1994 meeting, the IGADD adopted a Declaration of Principles, which gave priority to national unity, but also acknowledged the right of self-determination for all Sudanese people. The SPLA and the SSIM immediately accepted the Declaration of Principles, but the Sudanese government opposed it. Eventually, the government agreed to discuss the principles in question and to make any objections it had on specific points. The right of self-determination and a proposed separation between religion and the state proved to be the most contentious issues. Neither government nor rebel negotiators could devise a compromise which avoided using the terms 'self-determin-ation' and 'secularism'; however, all parties agreed to attend another IGADD-sponsored meeting.

In July 1994 the warring parties met in Nairobi, Kenya, and continued to debate the terms 'self-determination' and 'secularism'. As during the May meeting, the rebel groups were willing to accept the terms. The government's position, however, was that secularism was out of the question; indeed, it wanted Islamic law to apply not only throughout Sudan but also the rest of Africa. The government also rejected the term 'self-determination', which it regarded as a ploy for partitioning the country; and expressed its preference for 'shuttle diplomacy', rather than the face-to-face sessions adopted by the IGADD. Finally, it sought support for its own internal peace process instead of IGADD mediation.

On 7 September 1994 the latest round of IGADD-sponsored peace negotiations collapsed in Nairobi, after al-Bashir reiter-ated the aforementioned terms. The government subsequently sought a new mechanism for the talks, which would have involved it in separate meetings with the SPLA and the SSIM. Although the negotiations which it had sponsored were effec-tively stalled, the IGADD remained engaged in the peace pro-cess. After convening another session of talks in January 1995, the IGADD called attention to the need for co-operation between itself, the OAU and the international community, led by the UN. However, this did nothing to relieve the deadlock in the negotiations.

In mid-1995 those countries designated as the Friends of IGADD, at a meeting chaired by the Netherlands minister of co-operation, Jan P. Pronk, and attended by delegates from Canada, the United Kingdom, Italy, the Netherlands, Norway, and the USA, sought to persuade the IGADD to resume its work as mediator in the Sudanese civil war. On 17–18 May 1995 Pronk visited Nairobi and Khartoum in order to persuade the warring parties to extend a previously declared cease-fire, which was due to expire on 28 May 1995. The Kenyan president eventually convinced al-Bashir, the SPLA, and the SSIM to extend the cease-fire by two months. Despite this achievement, military action continued in Southern Sudan, the army cap-turing the town of Pariang on 4 June 1995.

Meanwhile, the Friends of IGADD continued to advocate a longer cease-fire, the introduction of joint surveillance patrols assisted by international monitors, and a new round of IGADD-sponsored peace talks. Pronk promised that Western countries would finance the surveillance patrols and supply technical equipment, and that they would help to establish a secretariat in Nairobi for the IGADD peace-talks committee. Although it had reservations about some members of the Friends of IGADD, especially the USA, Canada and the United Kingdom, Sudan subsequently approved the Friends of IGADD peace initiative.

In March 1996 al-Bashir attended an IGADD conference in Nairobi at which the mandate of the IGADD was expanded to include regional economic co-operation and the co-ordination of political and social policies. President Moi of Kenya's chairman-ship was extended for a further year and it was agreed to change the organization's name to the Intergovernmental Authority on Development (IGAD).

In early July 1997 IGAD announced that the Sudanese gov-ernment had agreed to accept the 1994 Declaration of Principles (see above) as a framework for peace. However, the government declared that it did not consider the declaration to be binding, but merely a basis for future discussions. The SPLA, on the other hand, felt that it could not resume peace negotiations without such a binding agreement. At the end of August al-Bashir attended talks convened by President Mandela of South Africa (see below). In October 1997 a further round of IGAD-sponsored peace talks was held in Nairobi, under the Declar-ation of Principles. The talks were adjourned without agreement after two weeks, although the government and the SPLA issued a joint communiqué in which they acknowledged that a military solution could not bring stability to Southern Sudan. The next round of talks was scheduled for April 1998 and talks opened on 4 May. It was later reported that during the talks both sides had agreed on the need for a referendum on Southern self-determination and on a time-scale within which it should be held. Considerable differences still remained, however, and it was agreed that a further round of talks would be held three

months later in Addis Ababa, Ethiopia. Both sides also stated that a cessation of fighting was unlikely in the near future. In mid-July, however, the SPLA issued a unilateral three-month cease-fire to allow relief operations to combat the famine. The government responded with a one-month cease-fire, which it later extended for an unspecified period. During talks held in August, no progress was made, and the next round of negoti-ations was scheduled to take place in six months' time. The talks, eventually scheduled for 20 April 1999, were postponed by the government at the beginning of that month following the deaths of three government officials and a Sudanese aid worker who had been taken hostage by the SPLA; at that time the government suspended all contacts with the rebels through IGAD. The rebels, however, claimed that the four had been killed in cross-fire during a rescue attempt by government forces, despite ongoing negotiations for their release, and that the government was, in fact, seeking an alternative mediator to IGAD. Attempts to reschedule the talks were unsuccessful.

The IGAD peace process remained moribund during 1999–2000 despite donor efforts to 'invigorate' the talks by establishing a Nairobi-based IGAD secretariat headed by senior Kenyan diplomat Daniel Mboya. Funding and organizational problems, coupled with the intransigence of the warring parties, have prevented the secretariat from making any meaningful accomplishments. In January 2000 IGAD unsuccessfully sought to translate the Declaration of Principles, which supposedly will allow southern Sudanese to hold a referendum to determine whether they want to be independent or part of a confederal Sudan, into a formal agreement. The SPLA and the government participated in another round of IGAD-sponsored talks in April in Nairobi but no progress was made. A further round of discus-sions was due to be held in mid-May; however, early that month the SPLA announced that it had suspended its participation in the peace negotiations in protest at the government's alleged continued bombing of civilian targets. It reaffirmed its commit-ment to the unification of the IGAD process and the joint Egyptian-Libyan initiative (see below), but did not indicate on what conditions it would resume talks. In June the SPLA announced it would rejoin the peace talks and in that month President al-Bashir declared a general amnesty for all opponents of the government; however, it was rejected by a number of opposition groups, including the SPLA. Later in June al-Bashir proposed a national forum of all political forces and national leaders, which was to attempt to negotiate an end to the country's civil war.

In August 1999 Egypt and Libya proposed a five-point peace initiative which envisaged a cease-fire and a national reconcilia-tion conference, which would welcome all parties, including the NDA, which had been excluded from the IGAD process. In January 2000 the Libyan and Egyptian foreign ministers visited Sudan and held talks with al-Bashir, during which they dis-cussed recent developments in Sudan; at the end of the meeting they stressed that the joint Egyptian-Libyan peace initiative would continue. In May 2000 SPLA leader Col Garang informed the Egyptian minister of foreign affairs that he favoured com-bining the Egyptian-Libyan peace initiative with the IGAD process. However, by mid-2000 Egypt and Libya had still not been successful in their attempts to persuade IGAD to join their initiative largely owing to opposition by Kenya and the USA. Similarly, there has been no progress with the proposal that Egypt and Libya co-ordinate their efforts with IGAD.

The other major cause of instability in southern Sudan con-cerns tribal fighting between the many groups in the region. The New Sudan Council of Churches (NSCC) has sponsored several 'people-to-people' meetings in an attempt to end this instability. During 8–15 May 2000 the NSCC sponsored the East Bank Nilotic People-to-People Peace and Reconciliation Conference, which was held in Liliir, Bor County in the Upper Nile region. The meeting sought to establish peace amongst the Anyuak, Dinka (Bor and Padang), Jie, Kachipo, Murle (Boma) and Nuer (Gawaar and Lou). The Gawaar-Nuer, however, refused to participate in the conference owing to opposition from an Upper Nile faction. Despite these efforts, factional fighting amongst these various groups was reported to be responsible for a greater number of deaths than the clashes between the Sudanese government and the SPLA. Nevertheless, the NSCC's initiatives have won widespread praise and are popular with many Western countries which view them as an important complement to the IGAD peace process.

FOREIGN RELATIONS

Owing to the strong influence of the NIF on Sudanese politics after the al-Bashir regime came to power, the status of Sudan's relations with any particular country since 1989 has been determined by the extent to which it opposes or supports Sudan's determination to spread radical Islamic fundamentalism throughout eastern Africa and the Middle East. Sudan's closest allies include Iraq, Iran and, interestingly (because the alliance is not based solely on economic interest), France. Relations with neighbouring countries, such as Uganda, Eritrea, Ethiopia, Kenya and Egypt, are characterized either by acrimony or co-operation, often related to the civil war being waged in Southern Sudan. The People's Republic of China (PRC), South Africa and Russia have all pursued economic opportunities in Sudan. The USA, meanwhile, has condemned Sudan in the strongest terms for its alleged role in the organization of international terrorism and has actively sought the international isolation of the al-Bashir regime.

Sudan's alleged involvement in the attempted assassination of President Mubarak of Egypt in June 1995 provoked international outrage. In January 1996 the UN Security Council accused Sudan of supporting terrorism, condemned the attempt on President Mubarak's life and unanimously approved Resolution 1044, demanding that Sudan immediately extradite three Islamists implicated in the attack. On 28 April the Security Council adopted Resolution 1054, imposing sanctions on Sudan (with effect from 10 May 1996) for its failure to comply with Resolution 1044. Under the sanctions, the number of Sudanese diplomatic personnel serving abroad was to be reduced, and international organizations were requested not to hold conferences in the country. The Security Council stated that the sanctions would remain in force until Sudan complied with Resolution 1044, ceased its support for terrorism and conducted its foreign relations in accordance with the charters of the UN and the OAU. On 16 August, in view of Sudan's continued failure to comply with Resolution 1044, the Security Council adopted a resolution (to take effect three months from that date) which would ban all international flights operated by Sudan Airways. However, by mid-1997 the air embargo had still not been implemented, owing to concerns over its humanitarian implications.

Sudan's support for Iraq's invasion of Kuwait in 1990 was a cause of increasing international isolation for the country from the second half of 1990, alienating foreign aid donors, as well as contributing to internal tensions. As a result of this support Sudan and Iraq now have particularly close relations. In April 1994 al-Bashir held talks with an Iraqi envoy and restated Sudan's support for the lifting of the UN trade embargo on Iraq. In June Sudan and Iraq signed a technical co-operation agreement and Iraq also agreed to help Sudan exploit its petroleum reserves and to train Sudanese technicians.

A rift developed between Sudan and Iran because of the former's support of Iraq during the 1990–91 Gulf crisis. Since then, however, relations have gradually improved. In June 1994 the head of the Sudan judiciary, Jallal Ali Lutfi, met the speaker of the Iranian parliament, Ali Akbar Nateq Nouri, and the President of Iran, Hashemi Rafsanjani, and expressions of mutual support were exchanged. In October, a delegation from the Iranian Majlis visited Khartoum in order to explore ways of improving relations between Iran and Sudan. In November 1995 the secretary-general of the Iran supreme council for national security was reported to have visited Sudan in order to assess the country's military requirements. Iran was later reported to have agreed to supply Sudan with armoured vehicles, heavy artillery and radar equipment. An agreement concluded in May 1996 expanded the scope of Sudanese-Iranian co-operation.

Relations between Sudan and France experienced a dramatic improvement in August 1994, when French security officials left Khartoum on a French military aircraft with the Venezuelan-born terrorist Illich Ramirez Sanchez, better known as 'Carlos the Jackal', in their custody. The Sudanese government claimed that its co-operation in the extradition proved that Sudan did not sponsor terrorism but this assertion failed to

impress the USA which kept Sudan on its list of nations accused of sponsoring terrorism. In return for Sudan's co-operation, the French government reportedly financed the purchase of four Airbus planes and interceded on Sudan's behalf with the IMF and the UN. In addition, France provided security assistance to Sudan for use in the war against the SPLA. In October, in order to promote trade between Sudan and France, a Franco-Sudanese council on economic affairs was established in the Franco-Arab chamber of commerce in Paris. There have also been reports of French interest in obtaining additional petroleum exploration concessions in Southern Sudan, and in resuming work on the Jonglei Canal and the international airport at Juba. In late 1995 and early 1996 French companies successfully pursued Sudanese contracts in the fields of mining, telecommunications and power. Nevertheless, France observed the UN diplomatic sanctions imposed on Sudan in April (see above).

The USA has been one of the severest critics of the present Sudanese government. On 1 April 1994 Madeleine Albright, the US ambassador to the UN, visited Khartoum, and warned President al-Bashir that Sudan faced further international isolation unless it took immediate steps to improve its human rights record. She also accused the government of blocking food relief shipments to Southern Sudan, and indicated that Sudan would remain on the US list of state sponsors of terrorism. Sudanese officials denied these accusations, defended the country's human rights record and maintained that the USA had failed to produce any evidence that Sudan harboured international terrorists.

In January 1996 the USA announced that it was transferring all of its diplomatic personnel from Khartoum to Nairobi, Kenya, owing to its doubts about the Sudanese government's ability to guarantee their security. In April a Sudanese diplomat was expelled from the USA for alleged involvement in terrorist activities and espionage. In November the USA offered US $20m. in military aid to Uganda, Ethiopia and Eritrea, which, despite denials by the USA, Sudan believed to be intended to assist the Sudanese opposition forces.

In November 1997 the USA imposed severe economic sanctions on Sudan; humanitarian, diplomatic, journalistic and UN activities were, however, exempt. On 10 December US secretary of state Madeleine Albright held talks in Kampala with Col Garang and three representatives from the NDA. On 21 April 1998 the UN Commission on Human Rights adopted a resolution introduced by the US, which called on Sudan to improve its human rights record and to allow the UN special rapporteur access to all areas of the country. Despite its opposition to the Sudanese government, the USA provided more than US $39m. for humanitarian relief operations in Southern Sudan.

On 21 August 1998, following bomb attacks on US embassies in Nairobi, Kenya, and Dar es Salaam, Tanzania, the USA launched a missile attack on a factory complex near Khartoum, which the US government claimed to be a chemical weapons installation with terrorist links. The Sudanese authorities, however, stated that the site comprised a factory producing standard pharmaceutical goods. Sudan offered to open the site to international inspection, and withdrew its diplomatic mission from the USA. Following a statement of support for the US action by the British government, its ambassador to Sudan was asked to leave the country. The British diplomatic mission left Sudan on 28 August.

In late 1998 the Sudanese government arranged for an inspection of the factory ruins; the team, headed by an American, found no traces of chemical weapon compounds. Salah Idris, the owner of the factory, asked an international security company to examine the US allegations. The company's report indicated that there was no evidence of a link with terrorists and the report concluded that the plant produced only pharmaceutical products. Nevertheless, the USA stood by its decision to bomb the plant. In early November the USA announced that the sanctions imposed on Sudan in 1997 would be extended for another year owing to Sudan's support of terrorism, its poor human rights record and the lack of religious freedom in Southern Sudan. However, in early 1999 the sanctions were eased to allow food and medicinal imports. In May the USA announced that it would unfreeze assets of some US $24m.

belonging to Salah Idris which had been frozen at the time of the bombing. This announcement occurred shortly before a lawsuit, filed by Idris to achieve the return of his assets, was due to be heard. Idris asserted that this action indicated his innocence although the USA claimed that it was unable to fight the lawsuit as this would jeopardize its intelligence sources. In mid-1999 relations between Sudan and the USA remained strained, although negotiations with the United Kingdom had resulted in an agreement for the return of diplomats from each country. In August Idris filed a further lawsuit against the US government demanding compensation of $30m. for the attack on his factory. However, while US law allows individuals to sue the government, it was believed that the government would plead sovereign immunity.

Relations between Sudan and Uganda remain poor, largely because of Uganda's support of the SPLA and Sudan's links to Ugandan rebel groups, such as the Lord's Resistance Army (LRA) and the West Nile Bank Front (WNBF). For many years Sudan has tried to dissuade Uganda from giving aid to the SPLA by bombing targets in Northern Uganda. In May 1994 al-Bashir met President Yoweri Museveni of Uganda in Vienna, Austria, ostensibly to attempt to improve relations between the two countries. Museveni was reported to have promised to try to persuade Col Garang to participate in peace talks, while al-Bashir pledged to end Sudan's support of the LRA. Despite these mutual assurances, relations between the two countries failed to improve. After Sudanese armed forces attacked targets in Northern Uganda in April 1995 Uganda severed diplomatic relations with Sudan. Shortly thereafter representatives from the two countries met in Tripoli, Libya, to try to resolve their differences. However, the talks collapsed after the Sudanese-supported LRA massacred 250 civilians at Atiak, a town in northern Uganda. In June Presidents al-Bashir and Museveni met in Blantyre, Malawi, and agreed to restore diplomatic relations 'gradually' and to establish a multilateral border-monitoring group and a permanent joint ministerial team. In spite of this progress Uganda demanded that Sudan dismantle LRA camps at Paloteka and Parajok and a WNBF camp at Morobo—all in Southern Sudan. When Sudan failed to respond to this demand the Blantyre agreement collapsed, although Uganda claimed it was committed to a peaceful resolution of the dispute between the two nations. In July the former US president, Jimmy Carter, who was visiting Sudan, announced that Sudan and Uganda had agreed to cross-border monitoring of each other's activities. Under the terms of the envisaged agreement, Sudan was to deploy an army unit in northern Uganda to ensure that the SPLA did not engage in the cross-border trafficking of arms. Uganda was to undertake similar action. In October, however, Sudan accused Uganda of providing military support to Garang's faction of the SPLA. Uganda responded by accusing Sudan of providing similar assistance to the LRA. A further deterioration of relations in December was so serious that it prompted speculation that the two countries were on the brink of open war. President Museveni threatened to take military action against Sudan if it did not eradicate units of the LRA which had allegedly launched cross-border raids on Ugandan territory from Sudan, causing the displacement of some 5,000 Ugandan civilians. Some observers suggested that Uganda's threat of military action signalled an alliance of Sudan's southern and eastern neighbours against the al-Bashir regime. The extent of the rift was emphasized by Museveni's expression of support for the secession of Southern Sudan if the north of the country continued to treat the South unjustly. He had previously been a staunch opponent of secession. In April 1996 the Ugandan government alleged that Sudanese armed forces had carried out artillery attacks against targets in Uganda and condemned the aggression; and in July claimed that the Sudanese government was co-ordinating a military campaign waged by Christian fundamentalist rebels with the aim of destabilizing northern Uganda. In September, however, following mediation by President Rafsanjani of Iran, Sudan and Uganda were reported to have agreed to restore diplomatic relations, dependent upon each side undertaking to cease its support for rebel factions operating from the other's territory, and to participate in an international committee (also comprising Iran, Libya and Malawi) to monitor the agreement.

In November there were reports that a peace agreement had been signed, although Uganda later denied this.

In February 1997, in response to protests about its deployment of troops on the Sudan-Uganda border, Uganda denied accusations that it intended to invade Sudan; it claimed that the troops had been deployed solely to prevent Ugandan rebel fighters leaving that country. In late April Sudan denied allegations that its forces had invaded northern Uganda and at the end of the month Dr Riek Mashar Teny-Dhurgon, the chairman of the SSCC, visited Uganda to discuss relations between the two countries prior to the forthcoming IGAD summit. Talks held in Kenya in May achieved little progress in easing tension, and the planned IGAD summit was later cancelled owing to a concurrent OAU summit. In August al-Bashir claimed to have been denied transit through Ugandan airspace and at the end of the month President Mandela of South Africa convened talks between the two countries, although the SPLA was not represented. Relations between Sudan and Uganda appeared to have improved in May 1998 when Uganda released 42 Sudanese prisoners of war; five days later, Sudan released two Ugandan prisoners of war. In May 1999 the Sudanese minister of foreign affairs stressed the country's readiness to restore and normalize relations with Uganda and to accept dialogue as the means to resolve any problems, although Sudanese military intervention in the Democratic Republic of the Congo (DRC) in support of its government further strained relations between Sudan and Uganda, which has been supporting anti-government forces in the DRC.

Sudan's relations with Eritrea have also been marred by repeated border incidents, and deteriorated in December 1993, when Eritrean security forces killed 20 members of the Sudanese-supported Eritrean Islamic Jihad (EIJ) after its units had infiltrated into western Eritrea from bases in eastern Sudan. The EIJ, an Islamic fundamentalist group, reportedly aims to overthrow the Eritrean government. Over the following months, there were numerous other low-level EIJ cross-border raids into western Eritrea. During 1994 Sudan and Eritrea made at least two diplomatic efforts to resolve their differences. In April an Eritrean delegation arrived in Khartoum, and held discussions with a Sudanese counterpart with the aim of improving relations between the two countries. A joint statement, issued at the end of the talks, committed Sudan and Eritrea to take the steps necessary to stabilize the border region. In August Sudan and Eritrea also signed an agreement under which each undertook not to intervene in the internal affairs of the other; and to ban terrorist activities in their territories. Despite this accord, the EIJ continued to raid locations in western Eritrea. In December 1994 Eritrea severed diplomatic relations with Sudan, largely because of Sudan's continued support for the EIJ. President Afewerki of Eritrea stated that relations would not be restored until Sudan had severed its ties with the EIJ. The Sudanese government denied that it had provided any aid to the EIJ.

On 27 December 1994 Eritrea sponsored a meeting between various Sudanese opposition groups, which resulted in a 'Declaration of Political Agreement'. The signatories included the SPLA, the UP, the DUP, and the Sudanese Allied Forces (SAF), which had split from the Egyptian-based Legitimate High Command owing to the latter's inability to launch military operations against Sudanese government forces. While stressing national unity, the Declaration acknowledged the possibility of independence for Southern Sudan and expressed support for the IGADD-sponsored peace negotiations (see above). On 31 December negotiations between Sudan and Eritrea, sponsored by Yemen, ended in failure. In January 1995 Sudan demanded that Eritrea withdraw from the IGADD peace committee, which also included Ethiopia, Kenya, and Uganda. A further deterioration in relations occurred after a conference of the Sudanese opposition, organized by the NDA, was held in Asmara in June (see above). In October the national assembly endorsed a report by the Sudanese security and national defence committee which recommended — with reference to Eritrea — the strengthening of defence facilities and a firm response to military provocation. On 7–12 October the NDA held a conference in Asmara. Among the conclusions reached at the conference was that the al-Bashir regime was responsible for the sanctions imposed on the country by the UN. Attention was also drawn to the threat which Iranian support for the al-Bashir regime allegedly posed to regional stability. The NDA urged regional instutions and governments to support the Sudanese people's struggle against the al-Bashir regime.

In June 1997 Sudan accused Eritrea of supporting the SCP's terrorist activities. Shortly thereafter, Sudan denied Eritrean accusations that it had been plotting to assassinate the Eritrean president. At this time there were numerous reports of an Eritrean military build-up along the joint border. In January 1998 Sudan announced that its forces had repelled a surprise attack by Eritrean soldiers on a Sudanese border post. Sudan also claimed that Eritrea was massing troops along the border for a larger attack; Eritrea denied these accusations. After the outbreak of the Eritrean-Ethiopian border dispute, Sudan again claimed that Eritrean troops had launched a cross-border raid into eastern Sudan. In November 1998 Eritrea and Sudan agreed to explore the possibility of improving relations and following negotiations, mediated by Qatar, they signed the Doha Agreement in May 1999 which provided for a restoration of diplomatic relations, the formation of joint committees to resolve any differences and a cessation of hostile propaganda between the two countries. However, by mid-1999, Sudan and Eritrea had yet to re-establish diplomatic relations and in June Sudan accused Eritrea of breaking the agreement following talks which Eritrea held with the Sudanese opposition.

Until late 1995 Sudan enjoyed relatively harmonious links with Ethiopia. Indeed, during the 1994–95 period, most contact between the two countries was focused on improving co-operation. In September 1995, however, Ethiopia accused Sudan of harbouring three terrorists implicated in the attempted assassination of President Mubarak of Egypt in June and announced that it would close some Sudanese diplomatic facilities in the country and all non-governmental organizations connected with Sudan. In January 1996 Sudan complained to the UN Security Council about alleged Ethiopian aggression and in April Sudan claimed that Ethiopian government forces had collaborated with the SPLA in attacks on two towns in South Eastern Sudan in which many civilians had been killed. Ethiopia denied both allegations. In June Ethiopia's President Zenawi accused Sudan of attempting to destabilize the region after Sudanese armed forces had allegedly carried out cross-border raids on Ethiopian territory in May. In January 1997 the University of Khartoum closed to allow its students to join the forces fighting Ethiopia. Relations failed to improve in 1997, although in January 1998 Sudan's chief of external intelligence and minister of state in the president's office, Qutbi al-Mahdi, made a third clandestine visit to Addis Ababa which, according to various press reports, succeeded in making relations less acrimonious. A further improvement occurred after Sudan issued a statement of support for Ethiopia in its border dispute with Eritrea. Diplomatic contacts between Sudan and Ethiopia increased in 1998 and in October Ethiopian Airlines resumed flights between Addis Ababa and Khartoum. In May 1999 Presidents Bashir and Zenawi met in Djibouti where they discussed regional problems, the Eritrea-Ethiopia border conflict, and Somalia. They also explored ways to improve further relations between their two countries.

The Kenyan government has sought to maintain good relations with all of the opposing forces in Sudan. The SPLA and most of the other Sudanese rebel factions have maintained a strong presence in Nairobi, which has also served as headquarters for the UN-administered Operation Lifeline Sudan (OLS). The president of Kenya serves as chairman of the IGADD's committee of heads of state and has played a major role in peace negotiations between the Sudanese government and the rebels. A rift developed between Sudan and Kenya in early 1995, when the SPLA claimed that the Islamic Party of Kenya, an unregistered political party which is active largely in Mombasa, was engaging in subversive activities against the Kenyan government from a base in Sudan. The Sudanese government denied the accusation. On 25 May Presidents al-Bashir and Moi issued a joint communiqué committing their countries to the IGADD peace process. The two presidents met again, in Nairobi, in February 1996, noted the excellent state of relations between their countries and reiterated their commitment to the IGADD-sponsored peace process.

Sudan is opposed to what it regards as Egypt's illegal occupation of the Halaib triangle, a small wedge of territory located along the Sudan-Egypt border. In July 1994 Sudan announced that it had sent memoranda to the UN Security Council, the OAU and the Arab League explaining the nature of the Halaib triangle dispute. According to the memorandum, there had been more than 39 military and administrative incursions into Sudanese territory since Sudan had complained about similar incidents in May 1993. In September Sudan accused Egypt of having attacked Challal port, in the disputed Halaib region. Egypt denied the charge and retaliated by temporarily suspending the ferry service between Aswan and Wadi Halfa. In late October the NIF leader, Hassan at-Turabi, justified the use of force by Egyptian Islamist militants, claiming that such activity was an expression of revolt against a government that did not grant freedom of expression. In response, the Egyptian government alleged that Sudan supported international terrorism. In November Sudan claimed that Egypt's President Mubarak had 'violated Arabism for the benefit of the Jews'. On 30 September Egypt had expelled two Sudanese diplomats on charges of threatening state security. In January 1995 Egypt rejected a Sudanese request to place the Halaib triangle dispute before the 61st ordinary session of the OAU foreign ministers' council being held in Addis Ababa.

On 26 June 1995 Sudan's relations with Egypt suffered a further setback after an unsuccessful assassination attempt was made on President Mubarak, on his arrival in Addis Ababa to attend the annual OAU conference. The Egyptian government immediately accused Sudan of complicity in the attack and during the following weeks relations deteriorated sharply. Egypt immediately strengthened its control of the Halaib triangle and in July, in contravention of an agreement concluded with Sudan in 1978, imposed visa and permit requirements on Sudanese nationals visiting or resident in Egypt. Relations between the two countries deteriorated further in September, when the OAU accused Sudan of direct involvement in the attempted assassination, and in December when it demanded that Sudan should immediately extradite three individuals wanted in connection with the attack. In February 1996 Sudan introduced permit requirements for Egyptian nationals resident in Sudan. Egypt has opposed the imposition of more stringent, economic sanctions on Sudan by the UN (see above), however, on the grounds that they would harm the Sudanese people more than the government.

During 1997 and 1998 Sudanese-Egyptian relations appeared to improve. In January 1998 the two countries agreed to resume river traffic along the Nile after a four-year interruption, and to form two joint committees, one including senior trade officials and the other comprising businessmen, to study investment opportunities. Shortly afterwards, both countries pledged to work towards a peaceful resolution of the dispute over the Halaib triangle. There was also to be increased co-operation between the Sudanese and Egyptian security services. In May 1998 Sudan was reported to have agreed to return Egyptian property assets which it had seized in 1992. Despite these developments, Egypt continued to maintain good relations with the Sudanese opposition. On 30 November 1997, Col Garang met with President Mubarak; Egyptian officials also held discussions with former prime minister al-Mahdi and NDA chairman Osman al-Mirghani. In early 1998 the NDA convened a meeting in Cairo to examine ways of overthrowing the al-Bashir regime. In August 1998 Egypt hosted a further NDA summit during which Egyptian officials held a meeting with the rebel leaders. In late October 1998 a joint Sudanese-Egyptian technical committee met in Khartoum to review aspects of the Nile waters issue including a number of proposed dam projects. During 1998 Sudan accused Egypt of harassing Sudanese citizens in the disputed Halaib triangle although Egypt denied the accusations. In March 1999 the two countries began to explore ways to improve relations, and in June it was reported that diplomatic relations were soon to be upgraded.

Sudan and Libya have traditionally maintained very close relations. In March 1990, for example, they signed a 'declaration of integration' which provided for the merging of the two countries. The declaration of integration was not realized and the increasingly Islamic fundamentalist character of the Sudanese regime after 1989 meant that the two countries could no longer be counted as natural allies. However, the Libyan leader, Col Qaddafi, was reported on various occasions to have attempted to mediate between the al-Bashir regime and its more hostile neighbours, notably Uganda in 1996. Trade links remain strong and the expulsion by Libya, in late 1995, of thousands of Sudanese expatriate workers did not, apparently, detract from the two countries' commitment to eventual integration, reiterated in May 1996.

In February 1996 Sudan, Chad and the Central African Republic (CAR) announced that they had concluded a so-called 'triangle agreement' in order to improve border security and promote greater co-operation. Among other things, the three countries agreed to reinforce military units stationed along their common borders and to co-ordinate future security operations. In December 1997 ministers of foreign affairs from Sudan, Chad, the CAR and a representative from Niger agreed to create an organization for regional and international co-operation. In 1997 Sudan was one of the founding members of the Community of the Sahel-Sahara States, which has its headquarters in Tripoli, Libya.

Recent Initiatives to Improve Foreign Relations

Following al-Bashir's declaration of a state of emergency in December 1999, Sudan embarked on a campaign to repair its foreign relations throughout the world. Khartoum took several steps to assuage international concerns about its relationship to terrorism. In April 2000, for example, the council of ministers approved a draft anti-terrorism bill which provided for the execution or life imprisonment of anyone convicted of a terrorist act. In May Sudan ratified the Arab Agreement on Combating Terrorism. In Eastern Africa, Sudan focused on ending its disputes with Eritrea, Ethiopia and Uganda.

In December 1999 Sudan and Uganda concluded an agreement under the terms of which both countries pledged to disarm terrorists, respect one another's borders, exchange prisoners of war, free abductees taken by the insurgent LRA, stop rebel activity on each side of their common border, and offer amnesties to those who renounce the use of force. In January 2000 Sudan released 58 people who had been abducted by the LRA, while Uganda freed 72 Sudanese prisoners of war. Despite this exchange and several follow-on meetings between Sudanese and Ugandan officials, relations between the countries have yet to stabilize largely because the LRA has been excluded from all talks. Continued LRA activities in northern Uganda prompted President Museveni to announce in May that if Khartoum failed to control the LRA, Ugandan troops would be deployed to southern Sudan to combat the rebels.

Sudan also took steps to resolve its differences with Eritrea and Ethiopia. In January 2000 Sudan and Eritrea restored diplomatic relations and agreed to reopen the land route between the two countries and to adopt procedures for issuing travel permits to those wanting to cross the common border. In the same month the Eritrean government also ordered the NDA to evacuate the Sudanese embassy in Asmara, which it had been using as a headquarters. In February President al-Bashir and President Issaias Afewerki of Eritrea met in Khartoum, and declared that they would not allow opposition groups located in their respective countries to launch cross-border raids. Also in February Sudan Airways resumed flights to Asmara. However, by mid-2000 Sudanese-Eritrean relations had once again begun to deteriorate, when in July the Sudanese government accused Eritrea of helping the NDA rebels to plan an offensive in eastern Sudan.

In November 1999 and January 2000 Sudan and Ethiopia conducted talks which resulted in the reopening of their common border. The Sudanese authorities also agreed to allow Ethiopia to use Port Sudan as an import and export terminal. Additionally, the two countries agreed to improve road links, reactivate a joint ministerial committee, and install telephone lines between their respective capitals. Ethiopia indicated that it would no longer demand the repatriation of those suspected of launching the failed assassination attempt against Egypt's President Mubarak in Addis Ababa in 1995.

Sudan also repaired relations with several European powers. In September 1999, for example, Sudan and the United Kingdom exchanged ambassadors, marking an end to the enmity that had existed between the two nations since the 1998 US missile

strike against Khartoum. In July 2000 Sudan's minister of external relations, Mustafa Osman Ismail, met the British secretary of state for foreign and commonwealth affairs, Robin Cook, in London. The two officials discussed ways to facilitate the southern Sudanese peace process, increase respect for human rights, and the state of relations between Sudan and the United Kingdom. In addition, Cook agreed to visit Sudan in the near future. Ismail also visited France and Germany where he held talks with government officials about increasing economic co-operation and facilitating the southern Sudanese peace process. In October 1999 the EU issued a statement which indicated its willingness to enter into a 'critical dialogue' with Sudan in order to foster peace in the south, facilitate democracy and respect for human rights, combat terrorism, and improve relations with neighbouring countries. In November 1999 the EU sent a delegation to Sudan for the first time since 1996.

Sudan's relations with the Arab world continued to improve during 1999–2000. For example, Sudanese-Egyptian relations began to improve after Presidents al-Bashir and Mubarak met during the OAU summit in July 1999. Following al-Bashir's dissolution of parliament in December 1999, the two countries re-established full diplomatic relations and pledged to resolve their dispute over the Halaib issue amicably. In early April 2000 al-Bashir visited Cairo and met President Mubarak on the occasion of an Africa-Europe summit. In mid-April Egypt appointed a new ambassador to Sudan. This was the first time that Egypt had had an ambassador to Sudan since the assassination attempt, which had reportedly involved Sudanese elements, on Mubarak in 1995. The two countries also agreed to take steps to establish an Egyptian-Sudanese joint committee. Sudan and Egypt subsequently reached an agreement about Khartoum's US $70m. debt to Cairo. Afterwards, Egypt abandoned the 10% levy on exports from Sudan. In September 2000 the Sudanese and Egyptian ministers of foreign affairs held the first session of the Egyptian-Sudanese Commission for 10 years. The two countries expressed their commitment to further bilateral economic development.

In November 1999 Sudan and Iran took steps to improve their relations when both countries agreed to resolve the problem of the US $400m. debt owed by Sudan to Iran. As of early 2000, however, no progress had been made on this issue. In late 1999 Sudan and Kuwait restored diplomatic relations, which had been severed as a result of the Sudanese authorities' support for the 1990 Iraqi invasion of Kuwait. In May 2000 Sudan and Tunisia restored relations and exchanged diplomatic representation following meetings between Sudanese and Tunisian officials in Egypt and Cuba. Sudanese-Syrian relations received a boost in August 1999, when the Syrian authorities offered to invest in Sudan's oil industry. In January 2000 the two countries signed a series of agreements regarding agriculture, animal resources, humanitarian affairs, investment, tourism, trade and transport. The two countries also established a board for Sudanese and Syrian businessmen. In March 2000 al-Bashir met Algerian President Abdelaziz Bouteflika to attempt to repair relations which had been tense since 1993, when Algeria had accused Sudan of supporting Islamic guerrillas in Algeria.

Sudanese-US relations remained strained over a variety of issues, including Sudan's poor human rights record, its reported relationship to international terrorism, and the ongoing southern civil war. In July 1999 the US senate tabled a resolution which called on the administration of President Bill Clinton to support political and material support to the SPLA and NDA. As of mid-2000, however, neither opposition group had received such aid. Nevertheless, there were some minor improvements in relations between the two countries. In July 1999 the US authorities eased sanctions against Sudan to allow US companies to sell food, medicine and medical equipment to Sudan. At about the same time, the US house of representatives approved a resolution condemning Khartoum for 'committing genocide in southern Sudan'. In October 1999 the US secretary of state, Madeleine Albright, visited Kenya, where she met Col Garang and announced an extension (from three to five years) of the Sudan Transitional Assistance for Rehabilitation (STAR). This programme provides democratization training to various southern Sudanese groups. Congressional efforts to pressure the US authorities into providing military aid to the SPLA failed. In August 1999 the USA appointed a special envoy to Sudan to focus on improving human rights, facilitating the delivery of humanitarian aid, and supporting the IGAD-sponsored peace negotiations. In June 2000 the USA and Sudan agreed to postpone the decision regarding the lifting of US sanctions against Sudan until after the US presidential election in November 2000.

Sudan's relations with Canada remained controversial owing to the role that a private Canadian company, Talisman, plays in helping to exploit Sudan's petroleum reserves. In February 2000 the Canadian government published a report which concluded that petroleum production activities were exacerbating the civil war in southern Sudan. However, despite exhortations by the Canadian authorities that Canadian companies should be 'good corporate citizens', a second Canadian company (Melut Petroleum Company, which is owned by the Canadian firm Fosters) concluded a petroleum deal with Sudan. Despite concerns regarding the al-Bashir regime, Canada decided to renew diplomatic relations with Sudan.

FOOD AID AND REFUGEE PROBLEMS

The population of Sudan has suffered from both natural disasters and the civil war in recent years. In March 1994 the SPLA and the SPLA–United concluded an agreement under which they undertook to deliver food aid to all those in need of it, regardless of their locations; to ensure that humanitarian aid benefited civilians rather than military personnel; and to carry out all humanitarian actions with the full knowledge of all parties. Despite this pledge, both factions continued to obstruct the famine relief process. In early April, for example, the government, the SPLA, and the SPLA–United concluded an agreement under the auspices of the IGADD, which provided for the safe shipment of food to Southern Sudanese war zones. According to the Sudanese government, the agreement collapsed when Col Garang refused to sign the final document. As a result, relief activities came to a halt throughout many parts of Southern Sudan. Nevertheless, the government succeeded in delivering some relief food to areas under its control. By mid-1994 the UN estimated that about 1.3m. Sudanese required emergency food aid. The situation in Southern Sudan subsequently improved, however, and in January 1995, the UN resident co-ordinator in Sudan announced that better security in some areas had allowed people to acquire food on their own rather than rely on humanitarian aid. In September the Sudan Relief and Rehabilitation Association (SRRA)—the humanitarian wing of the SPLA—convened a conference to discuss the operations of the UN-administered OLS. A subsequent meeting in November was attended by representatives of the SPLA, of various UN agencies, human rights organizations and donor countries. In December the UN announced that it would carry out a comprehensive review of the OLS, scheduled for completion in late 1996. In late 1995 the UN also concluded an assessment which indicated that in 1996 at least 4.25m. Sudanese would require some form of relief assistance. Of these, some 3.6m. were located in the South and some 300,000 in camps outside Khartoum.

In January 1996 a meeting of donor nations in Geneva, Switzerland, approved the establishment of the UN Inter-Agency Consolidated Appeal for Sudan in order to assist in the co-ordination of relief activities. In the same month an FAO/World Food Programme (WFP) assessment team, working in conjunction with the OLS, estimated that at least 2.1m. Sudanese would require food aid during 1996. However, the Sudanese minister of agriculture claimed that international food aid was unnecessary as the country produced enough food to feed the population, and rejected the UN's assessment. In February, nevertheless, the UN requested its members to provide US $107.6m. in aid for Southern Sudan, in particular the war-afflicted provinces of Bahr al-Ghazal, Jonglei and Upper Nile.

In mid-1998 the FAO estimated that more than 1.2m. Sudanese were in need of food and non-food aid. However, international relief efforts were hampered by the war. In February 1998 the government suspended OLS air operations in Bahr al-Ghazal and Lakes regions on security grounds. This was the largest regional flight suspension since OLS operations began. Limited air operation resumed later that month and were extended on 31 March. In April many aid agencies were warning of widespread famine in the south if immediate action

was not taken, but by mid-year the OLS had succeeded in gaining only 7% of the US $109.3m. that it had requested for its emergency operations in Bahr al-Ghazal. In August 1998 the OLS announced that Sudan was facing its worst humanitarian aid crisis in 10 years, with up to 2.6m. people at risk throughout the country. In response to the crisis, the OLS launched its most comprehensive humanitarian operation since its formation and urged other humanitarian organizations to join the relief effort. In mid-1999 the government and the SPLA held a meeting of the Technical Committee on Humanitarian Assistance in Oslo, Norway. Both sides renewed their commitment to a humanitarian cease-fire in Bahr el-Ghazal and to security protocols for the railway and roads used by OLS. The government and the SPLA also agreed to take steps to protect OLS personnel and property.

During 1995 UNHCR repatriated some 15,000 Eritreans, while a further 25,000 were reported to have returned to their homes without assistance. UNHCR claimed that it was providing aid to some 250,000 Eritrean refugees. UNHCR originally aimed to repatriate some 60,000 Ethiopian refugees in 1995. However, lack of funds and increased tension between Sudan and Ethiopia caused this figure to be reduced to about 7,000. In late January 1997 Eritrea refused to sign an agreement designed to facilitate the repatriation of refugees from Sudan to Eritrea on the grounds that its conclusion would have constituted diplomatic recognition of the al-Bashir regime. In December 1995 the Ethiopian government complained to UNHCR that the Sudanese authorities were arresting, torturing and killing Ethiopian refugees. UNHCR subsequently agreed to finance the voluntary repatriation of Ethiopian refugees. In January 1997 UNHCR reported that Sudanese were crossing into Ethiopia at a daily rate of 80 in order to escape violence and famine in Sudan.

By early 2000 the US Committee for Refugees estimated that there were some 423,000 Sudanese refugees in seven neighbouring countries (180,000 in Uganda; 70,000 in Ethiopia; 65,000 in Kenya; 50,000 in the DRC, 35,000 in the CAR; 20,000 in Chad; and 3,000 in Egypt). There also were about 4m. internally displaced Sudanese, which amounts to the largest displaced population in the world. It was also estimated that Sudan hosted some 363,000 refugees (320,000 from Eritrea; 30,000 from Ethiopia; 5,000 from Uganda; 5,000 from Chad; and 3,000 from the DRC). Following the outbreak of the latest round of fighting in the Eritrean-Ethiopia war in mid-2000, at least 70,000 Eritreans sought refuge in Sudan.

Famine continued to plague vast areas of Sudan during 1999–2000. In August 1999 the OAU granted US $5m. to help the country recover from the drought. Despite this and other regional and international aid, the number of Sudanese in need of assistance continued to increase. By June 2000 there were an estimated 2.8m. food-dependent people in Sudan, some 61,700 of whom were affected by drought conditions. The remainder of the population was internally displaced or affected by the southern Sudanese civil war. The influx of some 85,000 Eritrean refugees into eastern Sudan from war-torn Eritrea exacerbated this situation. Although there had been good rainfall in many areas, food insecurity continued to exist in parts of Eastern Equatoria, Bahr al-Ghazal and Upper Nile. According to the US Agency for International Development, these areas will continue to require food aid until at least September 2000. In mid-2000 the WFP issued an appeal for $58m. to feed up to 1.7m. people.

The SPLA has hampered the international relief in southern Sudan by imposing restrictions on NGOs. The SRRA ordered some 60 NGOs working in southern Sudan to sign a memorandum of understanding by 1 March 2000 or to terminate their activities. Under the terms of the memorandum, NGOs would have to submit project proposals, operating budgets, progress reports and financial statements to the SRRA office in Nairobi for scrutiny. At least 11 major NGOs withdrew from southern Sudan rather than sign the memorandum, which gave the SPLA control over the nature and scope of relief activities in southern Sudan.

In early August 2000 the Sudanese government informed the UN that all aid flights to southern Sudan would have to depart from Khartoum. The decision provoked outrage among relief agencies which feared that attempts by the Sudanese authorities to control the flow of aid could destroy the UN-sponsored aid programme. A few days later Médecins sans Frontières, an international aid agency, announced the suspension of its operations in the southern province of Bahr al-Gazal following a wave of bomb attacks by government aircraft, which narrowly missed one of its health centres. Later in August the UN suspended relief flights in southern Sudan for a one-week period after one of its compounds was bombed.

HUMAN RIGHTS ISSUES

Many different sources have alleged, and documented, the widespread denial of human rights in Sudan. In addition to atrocities committed in connection with the fighting in the South, these include the denial by the government of civil liberties such as the freedom of association, the freedom of speech and the suppression of opposition political activity. While the most significant reports have concentrated on abuses allegedly committed by the government and the armed forces, many of the rebel factions in conflict with the government in Southern Sudan have been similarly accused.

In October 1994 the UN special rapporteur on human rights for Sudan presented a report to the UN General Assembly which claimed that the Sudanese government had engaged in indiscriminate aerial bombardment of civilian targets in Southern Sudan; recruited minors for military service; and interfered with the delivery of food relief shipments. It also alleged that all of the combatants in Sudan had used land mines. In December the UN General Assembly's social, humanitarian and cultural committee adopted a resolution which censured the Sudanese government for these abuses and for arresting individuals who had met UN human rights personnel. The Sudanese government rejected the report's findings as 'outrageous, repetitive, untruthful and politicized'.

On 25 January 1995 Amnesty International launched a six-month campaign against human rights violations in Sudan. According to that organization, the Sudanese government had purged the civil service, trade unions, the judiciary, and educational institutions of elements opposed to it; and had virtually destroyed all political opposition in the country. Amnesty International also accused the Sudanese rebel movements of widespread human rights' violations, and, in order to stop them, recommended the establishment of an international civilian monitoring group.

In November 1995 the UN special rapporteur on human rights for Sudan reported that there had been a substantial increase in reported abductions, and cases of torture and rape perpetrated, mainly, by the Sudanese security forces. He also expressed his concern at an increase in 'slavery, servitude and forced labour'. After a visit to Sudan in August 1996 he reported that there had been no improvement in the human rights situation there since the presentation of his first official report to the UN General Assembly. In April the UN had published a report which included Sudan in a list of countries allegedly guilty of using physical and psychological torture on prisoners. In May the US-based Human Rights Watch (Africa) accused the government of permitting the enslavement of women and children captured by its forces in the South as spoils of war. Representatives of Sudan's Roman Catholic community—and of other Christian minorities—have also documented alleged human rights' violations.

The government has denied all of the allegations detailed above. In mid-1996, however, it continued to restrict the freedom of representatives of human rights organizations to investigate allegations of violations; and, in some instances, to deport them. In 1998, according the US government's annual report on human rights, Sudan's human rights record remained 'extremely poor'. Some of the more serious problems included the absence of political freedoms, extra-judicial killings and disappearances, harsh prison conditions and the harassment of government opponents. The report also alleged that discrimination persisted against religious and ethnic minorities, as did child labour and slavery. Sudan was stated to be reluctant to co-operate with international human rights agencies. The SPLA was also accused of continuing to commit human rights abuses, such as extra-judicial executions, arbitrary detention, forced conscription and occasional arrests without charge of foreign relief workers. The US government repeated these accusations in its 1999 report.

In October 1999 the Zurich-based Christian Solidarity International (CSI) announced that it had bought the freedom of 4,300 black slaves in Sudan during the 1–6 October 1999 period. This brought the number of slaves it had bought since 1995 to 15,447. The organization paid about $50 per head to Arab slave middlemen. Such claims elicited criticism from numerous sources. In February 2000, for example, John Harker, the Canadian special envoy to Sudan, issued a report that was sceptical of CSI's work. Among other things, he claimed that the organization allowed the SPLA to use fraudulent slave redemptions to raise money for buying arms and ammunition.

In September 1999 the Sudanese authorities temporarily suspended three Khartoum dailies for publishing articles critical of the civil war and various government policies.

In May 2000 the Sudanese minister of justice, Ali Muhammad Osman Yassin, announced that he intended to stop abductions of rural women and children allegedly committed by Arab tribesmen. The official made the announcement at a conference which included humanitarian groups such as Save The Children Fund-UK and UNICEF, European diplomats, and more than 100 tribal leaders from victimized African tribes such as the Dinka as well as Arab clans like the Muraheel, who were accused of abducting women, children and livestock as they escorted government trains through southern rebel areas. Also in May the Sudanese authorities released 563 female prisoners, the first group to be freed under a presidential pardon. The pardon covered women sentenced by public order courts and did not apply to those who had been jailed for financial crimes. In early June the pro-government European-Sudanese Public Affairs Council dismissed the findings of an Amnesty International report entitled *Sudan: The Human Price of Oil*. The report detailed various human rights violations by the Sudanese People's Armed Forces, the Popular Defence Forces and other government-allied militias in the region of the oilfields of Western Upper Nile State. Violations included forcible displacement of civilians from petroleum-producing areas, aerial bombing and strafing of villages, destruction of crops and seizure of livestock, and the torture, rape and killing of civilians. The report also noted that much of the suffering in the region was caused by inter-fighting between the various rebel factions. The Public Affairs Council claimed that Amnesty International had failed to produce conclusive evidence that foreign petroleum companies were involved in abuses and had ignored ample evidence of serious human rights violations by the SPLA in petroleum-producing areas.

Economy

THOMAS OFCANSKY

Sudan is primarily an agricultural and pastoral country, with about 63% of the economically active population engaged in the agricultural sector—the majority in essentially subsistence production. Industry is mostly agriculturally-based and accounted for an estimated 14.0% of gross domestic product (GDP) in 1997 (compared with 2% in the early 1960s). A major expansion of rain-fed production, which provides most staple foods and some export crops, in the 1970s helped to generate vigorous economic growth. By the early 1980s, however, the progressively deteriorating rainfall in the west and east of Sudan began to reduce production, and the contribution of agriculture to GDP declined sharply. Nevertheless, agriculture has remained the largest single component of GDP, accounting for an estimated 41% of GDP in 1999; agriculture is also the source of virtually all of Sudan's earnings of foreign exchange.

In 1998, according to estimates by the World Bank, Sudan's gross national product (GNP), measured at average 1996–98 prices, was US $8,224m., equivalent to $290 per head. During 1990–98, it was estimated, GNP per head increased, in real terms, at an average annual rate of 3.6%. During that period the population increased at an average annual rate of 2.3%. According to World Bank estimates, Sudan's GDP increased by an annual average of 0.4% in 1980–90 and by 8.0% in 1990–98.

Until the early 1970s Sudan's trade deficit was minimal despite a steady growth of imports, thanks to high domestic production and good world prices for cotton (the crop which has dominated Sudan's exports since the late 1920s). After 1971, however, there was a dramatic decline in cotton production, which was only partially compensated for in terms of earnings by a major expansion to rain-fed exports (notably of sorghum). Despite some recovery in cotton production after 1982, total export earnings have continued to decline, owing to drought and poor world prices. In 1999, despite a fall in the value of cotton exports, the value of Sudanese exports rose to US $780m., compared with $595.7m. in 1998. The value of imports in 1999 amounted to $1,412.2m.

Prospects for the economy remained bleak in the early 1990s, with production of cotton and sorghum (which accounted for over 47% of total exports in 1988) fluctuating. In 1999 the visible trade deficit amounted to US $475.9m. In that year the deficit on the current account of the balance of payments was $465.2m. The phasing-out of subsidies on many basic commodities and the devaluation of the Sudanese pound in 1991 and 1992 led to a sharp increase in inflation. During 1985–95 the average annual rate of inflation was 83%, but in 1996 the rate of inflation averaged 133%. Consumer prices increased by an average of 47% in 1997 and by 17% in 1998.

The deterioration in Sudan's economic position in the 1970s was a result of the policies pursued by the Nimeri government. Encouraged by the willingness of Western and Arab states to channel vast amounts of concessionary and commercial finance into Sudan, the regime embarked upon a grandiose development programme which emphasized new, capital-intensive projects, such as the Kenana sugar complex and an ambitious road-building programme, at the expense of traditional, irrigated infrastructure and the railways which produced and transported the bulk of Sudan's cotton and other exports. By 1980, such policies, combined with the heavy borrowing involved and growing mismanagement, inefficiency and corruption in the public sector (which controlled some 60% of productive capacity), had brought the economy to the verge of collapse and burdened the country with a level of foreign debt which is now the prime obstacle to economic recovery.

Attempts to resolve Sudan's economic crisis began in 1978 and for the next five years consisted of repeated debt reschedulings and donor aid, underpinned by the IMF, World Bank-sponsored austerity measures and structural adjustment programmes aimed at restoring some balance to the external account by stimulating the production of export crops. After 1981 the new policies, especially towards the irrigated sector,

began to have an effect. However, the Islamization, in 1983, of economic policies and the legal code, in an attempt to suppress growing popular opposition to Nimeri's government and to the fall in living standards associated with the austerity programmes, brought this improvement to an abrupt end. This dislocation of the domestic economy alienated foreign donors and creditors, leading to the suspension of several important rehabilitation schemes and the collapse of the vital support programme of debt relief and economic aid. By exacerbating civil unrest in the South, Islamization also created security uncertainties, which led to the suspension of activity, in 1984, on two projects that had been viewed as vital to Sudan's long-term recovery: the Jonglei canal scheme and the exploitation of the country's petroleum reserves.

The situation remained little changed for the first two years following the overthrow of Nimeri in April 1985, with drought compounding the problems of political instability and continuing civil conflict in the South. Various programmes aimed at attracting multilateral and bilateral loans were initiated by the al-Mahdi government, but all eventually lapsed (see below). Following the June 1989 coup, the military regime of Lt-Gen. al-Bashir introduced strict measures in its attempt to ameliorate the economic situation, and government economic policies have since attempted—with little success—to achieve food self-sufficiency, stricter control of the budget and a reduction of the government deficit through the privatization of state enterprises. In mid-1995 the economy remained handicapped by high inflation, a huge external debt (US $17,603m. at the end of 1995), an acute shortage of 'hard' currencies and declining foreign aid. In mid-1997 it appeared that Sudan had resolved its dispute with the IMF over the management of its debt to the Fund. In November, however, economic sanctions were imposed by the USA for Sudan's alleged involvement in terrorist activities. At the end of 1998 Sudan's external debt had decreased slightly, to $16,843m.

On 1 March 1999 the Sudanese pound was replaced by the Sudanese dinar, equivalent to 10 Sudanese pounds. It was anticipated that this move would help Sudan to control inflation. The pound was withdrawn from circulation on 31 July 1999.

AGRICULTURE

Approximately one-third of Sudan's total area of about 2.5m. sq km is considered to be suitable for some form of agriculture. Of this, about 84m. ha is potential arable land and the remainder pastoral. Only about 15%, however, of the available arable area is cropped, reflecting the critical role of water availability in the development of the sector. The vast majority of settled cultivation has, until recently, been limited to the permanent watercourses of the Blue and White Niles and their tributaries in north-central Sudan. It is these areas which, within the framework of Sudan's 2m. ha of irrigation schemes, have been the focus of modern, commercial agriculture—producing the major export crop, cotton, as well as vital import substitutes such as sugar and wheat.

In contrast, some 60% of Sudan's area is occupied by the 11% of the population (enumerated at 25m. in the June 1993 census) who are fully or partly nomadic—combining cultivation of subsistence crops and some cash crops with seasonal migration, with their herds, along well-defined routes, determined by the location of sources of drinking water during the wet and dry seasons.

The rainlands account for virtually all output of the staple grains—sorghum, millet and wheat—as well as of meat, milk and some vegetable products, and output in normal rainfall years has usually been enough for self-sufficiency. Livestock have also been an important export, as have other rain-fed products such as sesame seed, gum arabic and groundnuts. According to FAO estimates, the rate of growth of agricultural production declined in the 1980s, and revived to an average annual growth rate of 7.2% in the period 1990–98. In 1998 cereal production, including maize, millet and sorghum, totalled a record 6.5m. tons.

In January 1985 Sudan was included on the UN list of 10 most severely drought-affected countries. With Sudan's annual food deficit estimated by the FAO at over 1m. metric tons, excluding some 900,000 tons of food aid pledged after late 1984, it was feared the country was facing a famine disaster paralleling that afflicting Ethiopia. Nearly all the deficit was subsequently pledged, mainly by the USA, but transport difficulties hampered distribution to the most severely affected areas in Darfur and Kordofan. The establishment, in June and July, of an EC-co-ordinated airlift came too late to prevent the death, from starvation, of thousands of people.

In 1986 famine also became a major problem in the South, where inadequate rains and the disruptions caused by the civil war created major food shortages. The civil war caused relief efforts to be constantly interrupted during 1987 and 1988, and the problem of distribution, both of local surpluses and food aid, has remained acute. In September 1988 it was stated that the levels of malnutrition and the percentage of those dying from starvation among the thousands of refugees from the civil war in the South were the worst hitherto recorded world-wide. In March 1989 the government endorsed a UN-sponsored proposal to call a one-month cease-fire in the war in the South in order to facilitate the supply of 170,000 metric tons of food and medical supplies to victims of the conflict. 'Operation Lifeline Sudan' (OLS) was launched in April and its first phase ended in October 1989. After a four-month delay, the second phase of OLS got under way in early April 1990 after the government and the insurgent Sudan People's Liberation Army (SPLA) ended their opposition to relief flights. The 1990 programme of 'OLS' aimed to transport 100,000 tons of relief supplies by air, road, river and rail. The World Food Programme maintained airlifts of food under 'OLS' from Uganda to the South in 1990 and 1991.

The consequences of the drought made a significant impact on livestock exports, which had been a major source of overseas earnings in the early 1980s. The national herd was estimated to have fallen by about one-third during the drought years, although by the early 1990s overseas sales of cattle, sheep, goats and camels were estimated by the FAO to have contributed about 18% of the total value of exports, compared with 17% in the mid-1980s. In 1996 the proportion fell to 12.5%.

Almost 12% of Sudan's area is classified as forest land, but a minimal amount is under commercial plantations, largely fuel-wood developments in the central region. Exploitation of the natural forest is also predominantly limited to fuel wood, other than gum arabic, which is by far the most important forest product. Until the 1970s Sudan was the world's largest single producer of edible gum, accounting for some 92% of production, but this was reduced to about 80% with the advent of new producers and artificial substitutes and with it the importance of gum in exports. In 1987 this commodity benefited from a consumer reaction against artificial substitutes, and gum arabic regained its place as Sudan's second most important export after cotton, accounting for 22% of total exports. In 1990 exports of gum arabic amounted to 40,000 metric tons, worth US $62m. However, by 1997 the value of exports of gum arabic was estimated at $27.0m., about 4.5% of the total value of exports. In 1998 earnings from this source fell to $23.7m., about 4.0% of the total value of exports; however, in 1999 they rose to $26.4m., about 3.4% of the total value of exports.

Sesame, which is also used locally as a source of vegetable oil, has pursued a similar trend in production and exports. Sesame was the third most important export crop in 1988, when the harvest exceeded 300,000 metric tons. Output subsequently declined, however, with production totalling only 83,000 tons in 1990 before recovering to an average of about 120,000 tons annually during 1991–93. In 1999 exports of sesame seed represented 16.3% of the total value of Sudan's exports.

Groundnuts were until recently Sudan's second most important cash crop, and in 1993 the country was the fourth largest producer in Africa, after Nigeria, Senegal and Zaire. Groundnuts are grown both under rain-fed conditions in the far west and in the irrigated areas, and have major local use as a source of food and oil, as well as being a key export crop. Groundnut output has fluctuated considerably, but the trend

since the mid-1970s has been downwards, as a result of low producer prices, falling world prices, problems related to aflatoxin disease in the west, and drought. In the late 1980s the area under groundnuts totalled 1.2m. feddans (1 feddan = 4,201 sq m). Production, which totalled 218,000 metric tons in 1989, fell to 123,000 tons in 1990, before recovering to 714,000 tons in 1994. Production increased further to 738,000 tons in 1995, to 815,000 tons in 1996 and to 1,051,000 tons in 1997; however, in 1998 production decreased to 800,000 tons.

Of the 2m. ha of land under irrigation, about 50% is in the Gezira scheme, which is located between the Blue and White Niles. First developed by the British in the 1920s, the Gezira is now the world's largest farming enterprise under one management—the parastatal Sudan Gezira Board. The remaining irrigated land is also predominantly under publicly-administered schemes: the small-scale farmer pump schemes on the Blue, White and main Niles; the New Halfa scheme developed in the 1960s on the Gash river to resettle people displaced by the Aswan high dam flooding; and the Rahad scheme, on the Blue Nile, inaugurated in 1977. Although these schemes account for over 60% of Africa's total irrigated area, they represent less than 50% of Sudan's estimated potential.

Expansion into new areas has been limited by capital costs, and by the terms of agreements with Egypt governing the use of the Nile waters. By the late 1970s Sudan was close to drawing its full quota of 20,500m. cu m per year and began, in joint venture with Egypt, construction of the Jonglei canal in Southern Sudan. This scheme aimed at conserving, by the construction of a 360-km canal, some 4,000m. cu m of the 33,000m. cu m of water lost annually through evaporation in the Sudd swamp. The additional yield was to have been divided equally between the two countries, enabling Sudan to develop an additional 12,600 ha on the west bank of the Nile and reclaim up to 1.5m. ha of potential agricultural land. Work began in 1978 but had to be suspended in 1984, with 250 km completed, following attacks on construction workers by the SPLA. The persistence of civil conflict in the South has effectively delayed any substantial progress towards completing this scheme.

The irrigated sector normally accounts for 40%–70% of export earnings, reflecting the fact that the major irrigated crop is cotton. The main types of cotton grown in Sudan are medium-staple Akala variety (which accounted for about 75% of total production in 1996/97); long-staple Barakat (24%); and long-medium staple Shambat B (less than 1%). A small amount of rain-fed short-staple cotton is also grown.

The share of cotton in Sudan's total exports declined from 65% in 1979 to less than 45% in 1980, partly as a result of government policies which emphasized the development of wheat and other new crops, and the expansion of the mechanized rain-fed sector. A reversal of official policy in mid-1979, under IMF pressure to improve export crop production, brought the start of a large-scale rehabilitation programme for the irrigated sector, which was focused on the Gezira scheme. Gezira currently provides more than one-half of Sudan's cotton output, which totalled 520,000 bales in 1996/97 (compared with around 1.3m. bales in 1970/71). In that year the total area under cotton was 290,000 ha, compared with 324,000 ha in the early 1980s. In 1997 overseas sales of cotton represented 17.8% of the total value of Sudan's exports; however, this figure declined to 16.0% in 1998 and to just 5.8% in 1999.

The development of sugar production began in the 1960s to reduce the cost of Sudan's single most expensive import commodity after petroleum. The largest of the parastatal sugar enterprises, the Kenana Scheme, was officially opened in 1981, and played a major role in eliminating Sudan's sugar import costs in 1986. However the development of the sugar sector has been variously impeded by drought, inadequate provision for recurrent expenditure and technical and managerial problems. Shortfalls in sugar production have occurred, as in 1988/89, when output fell short of domestic demand by 200,000 metric tons. Production amounted to 450,000 tons in 1995, 460,000 tons in 1996 and 500,000 tons in 1997. In early 1999 plans were announced for the construction of a US $500m. sugar production facility in the White Nile region. Commercial production is to begin in 2003, when 75,000 tons of sugar are to be exported from total production of 150,000 tons. The majority of the finance is expected to be provided by the Chinese government. Sugar output in Sudan in 1998/99 was expected to be 603,000 tons. Sudan exports some 185,000 tons each year, worth some US $70m. in foreign exchange.

Wheat, Sudan's other major irrigated crop, is also an import substitute, although attempts to increase irrigated domestic production have had very limited success owing to the unsuitability of the climate south of the Egyptian border area. This causes yields to be very low.

The agricultural sector showed some signs of improvement as the 1999/2000 cotton crop was estimated to be 71,000 metric tons, compared with 47,000 tons the previous year. Additionally, the Sudanese authorities' decision to lift export taxes on cotton was expected to boost prospects for the cotton sector and facilitate the redevelopment of the country's textile industry.

The sugar industry also showed signs of growth as domestic production reached 695,000 metric tons in 1998/99 and was expected to increase to more than 900,000 tons in 1999/2000. Moreover, Sudan and the People's Republic of China agreed to build a sixth sugar plant, which would further boost production.

Prospects for sorghum, however, are poor. In January 2000 the FAO announced that the harvest would probably be down by as much as 50% owing to depredations by insects and other problems. As a result, sorghum prices increased and the government announced that it was considering the imposition of a ban on sorghum exports to ensure that domestic supply is adequate.

INDUSTRY

The ginning of cotton encouraged the beginning of industry in Sudan in the early 20th century. With the expansion of cotton production, the number of ginning factories has increased, with the Gezira Board alone operating the world's largest single ginning complex. The country is not yet self-sufficient in basic cotton cloth, however, owing to a disparity between spinning and weaving capacity. Cotton seeds are partly decorticated, while exports of cotton-seed oil and oil-cake are increasing. Groundnuts are also partly processed, with oil and cake dominating exports of groundnut products. Minerals (copper, iron, mica, chromite and, most recently, gold), which constitute less than 1% of exports, are exported in the crudest form.

With the exception of enterprises producing cement, soap, soft drinks and vegetable oils, large-scale manufacturing of import substitutes started in Sudan only after 1960. This is reflected in the manufacturing sector's contribution to GDP, which totalled only an estimated 8.6% in 1999. State involvement expanded dramatically after the 1971 nationalizations. A shift in emphasis towards a more mixed economy followed the overthrow of Nimeri in 1985, but the trend towards 'privatization' gained new momentum in 1988 as part of the medium-term economic recovery programme approved by the IMF and the World Bank. Plans were announced to privatize two agricultural schemes, as well as the four state-owned commercial banks and some new industrial concerns. At the same time, plans were announced to rehabilitate existing public sector concerns, and in March 1989 the government initiated a programme for the rehabilitation and modernization of the cotton-spinning sector.

Average annual industrial growth declined from 3.1% between 1965–80 to 2.5% during the period 1980–90. The amount of idle capacity in the textile and food industries has been of particular concern as Sudan has imported many goods which it could produce itself. At the time of the military coup of June 1989 it was estimated that many factories were operating at only 5% of capacity.

The military government proclaimed an 'open-door' policy to the private sector. It announced in April 1990 that private local and foreign investors would be invited to purchase loss-making state corporations. The National Economic Salvation Programme, unveiled in June, named several parastatal bodies in the agricultural sector and many others in the industrial, hotel and transport and communication sectors which would be sold or reorganized as joint ventures. Further privatization plans were announced by the minister of finance in July 1991.

In March 1992, in an attempt to attract foreign investment, the government announced that it would establish four free-trade zones: at Port Sudan, Juba, Janaynat (in western Sudan) and at Melot (in central Sudan).

In July 1999 Sudan announced that work was progressing on the Red Sea Free Trade Zone between Port Sudan and the port of Suwakin, which will be accessible by a road linking the coast with Khartoum. The project, which eventually will encompass a 600 sq km area, began with a 26 sq km zone, which encompasses warehouse, industrial and commercial areas. Investors are from a variety of countries, including Qatar, Saudi Arabia and the United Arab Emirates (UAE). Additional investors are being approached in Chad, India, Kenya, the Republic of Korea and Romania. In January 2000 a co-operation agreement was signed between the Red Sea Free Trade Zone and the Free Trade Zone of Jebel Ali, UAE. Under its terms, the UAE pledged to help Sudan to establish free zone areas at all of Sudan's border areas, linking trade between East Asia and Africa via Sudan, to increase marketing and shipping activities, and exchange manpower and technical information. A similar agreement was also signed with Saudi Arabia's Jeddah Free Trade Zone. In February the Sudan authorities officially opened the Red Sea Free Trade Zone.

MINERALS

Since 1973 a number of international companies have shown an interest in exploring for petroleum. More than 80% of available concessions were allocated by 1983, but to date Chevron, a subsidiary of the US company Standard Oil, is the only exploration company to have made any commercial discoveries. These were identified in south-western Sudan, and were forecast to have an eventual production capacity of 190,000 barrels per day (b/d). In early 1984 attacks by the SPLA on Chevron's oilfield operations compelled the company to suspend all operations, and associated plans to construct an oil-export pipeline were also subsequently abandoned. Chevron had continued until early 1986 to carry out some small-scale exploratory drilling in its concession areas outside the South, but neither the Nimeri regime nor the al-Mahdi government accepted security problems as a justification for Chevron and other foreign concessionaires suspending their exploration operations in the South. However, following representations from the government, Chevron agreed to resume drilling on a limited basis in southern Kordofan, but this programme had to be postponed in April 1988 as the civil war spread into the province. During 1988 a number of companies, including Amoco and Conoco of the USA, were reported to have expressed interest in drilling in a previously unallocated area near the Libyan border. Chevron estimated that its concession area, comprising in mid-1990 about 100 wells in western Sudan, had around 1,000m. barrels of reserves, of which around 270m. barrels were recoverable with present technology. The only other international oil company operating in the country is Sun International, which began exploratory drilling at an oil well in its Nile block in November 1989. According to the Institute of Petroleum, Sudan's total proven reserves of petroleum exceeded 3,000m. barrels at the end of 1996. Reserves of natural gas off the coast of Suakin, 30 km from Port Sudan, have been estimated by Chevron to total 70m. barrels of condensate and 3,000,000m. cu ft of natural gas.

During the early 1990s, the government appeared to be renewing its efforts to develop the petroleum sector without the assistance of western companies. In June 1992 al-Bashir announced that Chevron had transferred its concessions in Southern Sudan to a local enterprise, Concorp. In August Concorp announced that the Muglad well had begun production at a rate of 600 b/d of crude petroleum, adding that a refinery capable of processing some 20,000 b/d of crude was to be constructed at Muglad. Sudan has pursued a dispute with Egypt over exploration rights in the Halaib triangle, on the Red Sea coast. In December 1992 Sudan signed an agreement with Iraq to co-operate in petroleum exploration.

As part of its strategy to escape international isolation, Sudan is seeking to become a modest exporter of crude oil. To achieve this goal, the government concluded an agreement with a Canadian entrepreneur, Arakis Energy, which has acquired a number of the petroleum fields in Southern Sudan previously abandoned by Chevron. (Total of France also retains concessions in petroleum.) However the success of any future scheme would require substantial financial investment as well as technical assistance. According to Arakis Energy, investment of US $300m.–$400m. would be required to build a pipeline from

Southern Sudan's petroleum fields to Port Sudan; and of a further $100m. for operational expenses (other construction estimates are as high as $1,300m.). Arakis has so far unsuccessfully sought funding from Italy, Japan, the Republic of Korea and Russia, although in 1995 a Saudi Arabian investment group acquired a 43% interest in Arakis. In August 1995 Arakis' shareholders were reported to have concluded a $750m. arrangement with a Saudi Arabian financier to fund the pipeline project, but this collapsed one month later and Arakis was subsequently reported to be seeking financing for the project from French and Asian sources. It appeared likely, however, that any effective development of the scheme would have to await the settlement of the conflict in Southern Sudan. In January 1997 China was granted the right to exploit Sudan's largest oilfield with proven oil reserves at 220m. tons. In March it was awarded a contract to build a refinery in Khartoum with a capacity of 50,000 b/d.

Sudan has pursued other opportunities to develop its petroleum industry. In June 1995 Sudan and the People's Republic of China established a joint venture to explore for petroleum. Sudan was to provide 30% of the finance for the company, while China agreed to provide the remaining 70% and to train Sudanese technicians. China subsequently agreed to make Sudan a grant of US $15m. for the exploitation of its petroleum reserves. In October 1995 the Qatar General Petroleum Corpn agreed to participate in a joint venture with Sudan's Concorp to exploit petroleum reserves in central Sudan, while the French bank Paribas was reported to be involved in discussions with the Sudanese ministry of finance and the Bank of Sudan regarding a $25m. rehabilitation scheme for the oil refinery at Port Sudan. In March 1997 an agreement was signed with four international companies — from Malaysia, Canada, China and Sudan — allowing for shared petroleum production and the construction of a $1,000m. pipeline which will transport petroleum to Port Sudan.

The development of the petroleum industry remained an important objective in 1997 and 1998. Arakis began production in the Heglig field in 1997, and continued both exploration activities and its plans for the construction of a pipeline. Company estimates for the Heglig and Unity fields show combined in-place resources of 1,200m. barrels. In July Sudan and Iraq concluded a pact for petroleum exploration, construction of refineries and training of Sudanese technicians. More significantly, a consortium, comprising the Qatari Gulf Petroleum and the Sudanese companies Concorp and National Oil Co, has established a presence in the Adar-Yale field, which reportedly has reserves of 40m. barrels. Current output, according to consortium officials, is 5,000 b/d—a rate which is expected to double after the completion of a $30m. project to drill five new wells. Some petroleum analysts are, however, sceptical about the long-term viability of Sudan's production capabilities. Apart from the harsh operating environment, and repeated SPLA threats against employees and facilities, much of the petroleum is of questionable value. In mid-September the government announced various improvements in the transportation sector which would facilitate the movement of petroleum until the completion of the pipeline, and in early 1998 President al-Bashir announced that income from petroleum exports would be used for development, particularly reconstruction in the South. In May the China National Petroleum Co (CNPC) and the Sudanese ministry of mining and energy started work on the Port Sudan refinery which is to be completed in late 1999. In 1998 it became clear that Arakis lacked the capital to continue its operations. At the end of the year, however, Talisman Energy, a Canadian firm, finalized its take-over of Arakis. Talisman subsequently agreed a partnership with CNPC and Sudapet to develop the Heglig and Unity oil fields and to construct the pipeline from the southern oil fields to Port Sudan. On 31 May 1999 the 1,610-km oil pipeline was inaugurated. The line, which has a capacity of 150,000 b/d, links Southern Kordofan's Heglig petroleum field with a loading terminal at Port Sudan, via a petroleum refinery being built at al-Jayli, 30 km north of Khartoum. The pipeline has been largely financed by Chinese, Malaysian, Argentine, Canadian and British companies. Although Sudan's revenue from petroleum exports will be modest, production should meet domestic fuel requirements, thus saving some US $250–$350m. annually on imports. However, the pipeline is still threatened by attack from the SPLA.

In an effort to prevent this, in May 1999, Sudan deployed the first contingent of a volunteer petroleum protection brigade whose remit was to defend the pipeline and other petroleum facilities. In late August Sudan began exporting crude petroleum from this facility, which has a storage capacity of 2m. barrels. Officials expect that the terminal's capacity will rise to 3.2m. barrels with the use of reserve reservoirs. Petroleum production increased from 140,000 b/d in September 1999 to 155,000 b/d in November and to 180,000 b/d in January 2000. It was estimated that by the end of 2000 production would have reached about 200,000 b/d. Reports by the Greater Nile Petroleum Operating Company and Sweden's International Petroleum Company indicate that Sudan's total petroleum reserves may exceed 1,000m. barrels. In June 2000 Sudan commenced exporting refined petroleum products from a newly-inaugurated refinery located on the outskirts of Khartoum. Later that month the government announced a 27% reduction in the price of benzine and a 17% reduction in the prices of gasoline and kerosene. The refinery is expected to refine 50,000 b/d of crude petroleum.

Sudan's other known mineral resources include marble, mica, chromite and gypsum. Gold deposits in the Red Sea hills have been known since Pharaonic times, and there are uranium reserves on the western borders with Chad and the Central African Republic. Until recently, only the chromite deposits in the Ingessana Hills near the Ethiopian border were exploited on a substantial scale by the state-owned Sudan Mining Co, which produces 10,000-15,000 metric tons a year for export. The known reserves exceed 1m. tons of high-quality chromite. In November 1988 it was reported that Northern Quarries and Mines (UK) was planning to develop an iron ore and gypsum mine in the Fodikwan area. These deposits were discovered in 1910 but were not exploited on a large scale until the 1960s. About 83,000 metric tons of ore were exported before political disturbances disrupted work. It is now estimated that there are four or five deposits in the Fodikwan area, with reserves of more than 500m. tons of ore. It was planned to resume the commercial extraction of iron ore in the first half of 1990, after a break of more than 20 years. In recent years Sudan has benefited from a resurgence of interest among foreign companies in reworking gold deposits in the Red Sea hills, which, using new processing technology, have a high recoverable gold content. Gold production at the Hassai mine, which is carried out by a joint Sudanese-French venture, reached an estimated 1.6 tons in 1993 and was expected to advance to 4 tons in 1994. British and Irish mining interests have also become involved in developing the country's gold-mining sector. In late 1996 the Ariab mining company announced that it had mined 3 metric tons of gold to the year ending August 1996. In 1998 it mined 5 tons of gold and estimated that there were reserves of a further 25 tons. Sudan's offshore sea-bed is known to be rich in precious minerals, as well as copper, zinc and iron, and plans are under consideration for these to be exploited jointly with Saudi Arabia.

FOREIGN TRADE AND BALANCE OF PAYMENTS

More than 90% of Sudan's export earnings are from primary agricultural products. Cotton remains the dominant export, although its share of earnings has declined from 65% in the late 1970s to 5.8% in 1999, reflecting both a decline in cotton production and world prices and rising output of other agricultural products, such as sorghum and livestock. Petroleum and its products have historically dominated imports, and in 1999 accounted for 13.0% of the import total. Other major imports are machinery and transport equipment, which together accounted for 34.7% of imports in 1999, and wheat and other foodstuffs, which accounted for 19.5%.

The dominant position of petroleum imports is illustrated by Saudi Arabia's position as Sudan's leading supplier, accounting for 15.5% of imports in 1998. Other important suppliers in that year were the People's Republic of China, France and the United Kingdom. In recent years Saudi Arabia has also emerged as Sudan's single largest export market (24.4% in 1998). Other major purchasers in that year were Italy, the United Kingdom, Germany and Egypt. In November 1997 the USA imposed trade and financial sanctions on Sudan as a result of the latter's sponsorship of terrorism. This halted bank loans, shipment of US technology, and Sudanese exports to the USA. Sudanese government assets in the USA were 'frozen'. In 1996, the USA had provided 4.6% of Sudan's imports and had purchased 2.1% of its exports. Libya, with Saudi Arabia, provided Sudan with substantial amounts of essentially 'free' petroleum in 1985/86, but subsequent attempts to develop barter arrangements (exchanging oil for livestock and other agricultural products) proved less successful. Libya's role as Sudan's main supplier of oil came to an end in 1992, however, owing to Sudan's failure to maintain payments. Talks in April 1993 failed to resolve the issue and the government announced that it would continue to purchase its petroleum requirements on the spot market. However, a lack of foreign exchange subsequently led to severe fuel shortages.

Sudan has had a deficit on the current account of its balance of payments since independence in 1956, but the deficits were relatively insignificant until the mid-1970s, when government policies resulted in escalating deficits on the balance of trade and rising debt-service requirements. By 1995, despite a number of IMF agreements, austerity programmes and currency devaluations during the 1980s, the current account deficit stood at US $499.9m. This increased to $828.1m. in 1997 and to $956.5m. in 1998; however, the deficit was reduced to $465.2m. in 1999.

FOREIGN AID

Since 1971 the majority of foreign aid has come from Western sources, with the exception of the People's Republic of China. Arab aid, led by Saudi Arabia and Kuwait, has also been substantial.

Assistance from the USA increased dramatically during the 1970s, in accordance with US assessments of Sudan's strategic importance, and by the mid-1980s the USA was the largest single donor to Sudan, which as a recipient was second only to Egypt in Africa. Owing to the identification in Sudan of the US government as a major supporter of President Nimeri, the USA's relations with the military regime that succeeded him, and subsequently the elected coalition government, were initially strained, particularly as Sudan began to improve its relations with Libya. From March 1986 a number of aid programmes were suspended and with effect from March 1990, the USA banned all new economic and military aid to the country under a law prohibiting all but humanitarian assistance to non-elected governments that have not moved towards democracy within eight months of taking power.

Substantial infrastructural aid was received from Japan during the early 1990s and the EC (European Community, now the European Union—EU) is also an important donor. The most important of the multilateral agencies has been the World Bank. Its loans, which are granted on generous terms, have included $80m. toward the Gezira scheme, together with a $50m. credit for agricultural inputs, and $60m. for the sugar rehabilitation project. However, Sudan's substantial and increasing arrears on repayments meant that not only the USA, but also the United Kingdom and Saudi Arabia, among other bilateral donors, have suspended disbursements on aid programmes at various times since 1984.

Efforts to reschedule Sudan's foreign debt and thereby enable the government to maintain Sudan's repayment obligations both to the 'Paris Club' of Western official creditors and the 'London Club' of commercial creditors were unsuccessfully pursued through the 1980s. By March 1989, however, there had been no improvement in Sudan's external financial situation. Sudan's debt liabilities (including principal and interest) in 1988/89 were estimated at $980m., more than twice the country's projected export earnings. However, the 1988/89 budget provided only $100m. for debt repayment. By early 1990 Sudanese government debt was being traded at just two US cents to the dollar in the inter-bank secondary debt market—the lowest rate applied to any developing country's debt.

The al-Bashir government opened talks with the IMF in mid-May 1990, after being given until July to begin settling debt arrears to the Fund of US $1,150m.—the largest in Africa—or face expulsion. Sudan's total foreign debt exceeded $13,000m. by mid-1990, one-quarter of which was then due for repayment. Denmark, the USA and France agreed to cancel outstanding debts, although in September the IMF adopted a Declaration of Non-co-operation regarding Sudan, noting that the country had remained in arrears in its financial obligations to the Fund since July 1984. It was also pointed out that Sudan had made payments to other creditors while failing to discharge its obligations to the

IMF, thus ignoring the preferred creditor status that members are expected to give to the Fund.

In October 1991 the government announced the reduction of subsidies on a number of basic commodities, including sugar and petrol, which resulted in immediate rises in consumer prices of 65%–75%. To mitigate the effect, a wage rise of £S300 a month was awarded to government employees and grants were made available to low-paid workers. Later in October the Sudanese pound was devalued by 70%, to a rate of £S15 = US $1, with the abolition of the previous two-tier rate. The devaluation was welcomed by the IMF.

An IMF mission visited Khartoum in January 1992 for consultations with the government. In February a rigorous programme of economic reforms and austerity measures was announced by the minister of finance, Abd ar-Rahim Hamdi, who denied, however, that the measures had resulted from pressure from the IMF. The reforms included the floating of the pound, which resulted in an immediate devaluation of 83%. Measures taken to reduce the budget deficit included increases of 30% in import and export duties, and reductions of 10% and 60% respectively in recurrent and capital spending. Further cuts in commodity subsidies were announced, although these were accompanied by increases in allowances to poor families. In his announcement, Hamdi stated that the government was spending £S8,700m. annually on wheat and flour subsidies alone, and that this could not continue. However, the subsidy cuts led to a doubling of the price of petrol, a 50% rise in sugar prices and a halving of the size of a standard loaf of bread and were greeted by demonstrations in Khartoum and Omdurman which were dispersed by police with tear gas. A further doubling of fuel prices was announced in April, in anticipation of UN economic sanctions against Libya, which had been supplying Sudan with 100,000 tons of petroleum a month at a special rate. By late July Sudan was suffering increasing fuel shortages, blamed by the government on difficulties in transporting fuel from Port Sudan, and a rationing system was introduced. With inflation running at an annual rate of around 120%, the government announced that basic consumer goods would be sold through co-operatives at controlled prices.

Sudan's continuing debt arrears to the World Bank, totalling US $1,142m., led it to suspend new lending at the end of 1992 and, in April 1993, to withhold the financing of 15 existing projects, including the Gezira rehabilitation scheme (see above). With Sudan's arrears to the IMF standing at $1,600m., in August 1993 the Fund suspended the country's voting rights—the first time such action had been taken against a member nation.

In February 1994 Sudan's arrears to the Fund were estimated to be the largest ever recorded, at US $1,700m. In the same month the Executive Board of the IMF was reported to have voted to commence proceedings to withdraw Sudan's membership of the Fund. Withdrawal proceedings were suspended in July, however, after the government undertook to reform the economy; they were later postponed until January 1995, allowing the government time to develop debt management policies and economic reforms. In November 1994 Sudan and the IMF conducted a series of successful discussions concerning the status of economic reforms. Sudanese officials claimed that the IMF was impressed with Sudan's foreign exchange policy, which had stabilized the Sudanese pound. The IMF also agreed with the government's forecast of GDP growth of about 7% in fiscal 1994/95 as a result of improved agricultural performance. Sudan had also begun to prepare to implement a structural adjustment programme and had lifted the ban on imports of consumer goods. The government promised to increase taxes by raising petroleum prices, customs duties, airport tax, and sales tax on new vehicles; and to repay some $35m. to the Fund by the end of 1995. In January 1995 the IMF announced that it had decided not to recommend Sudan's expulsion from the Fund, and that it had lifted a ban on technical aid to Sudan. In March IMF representatives arrived in Khartoum to assess the progress of Sudan's economic reform programme. There was to be a further review in mid-1995, when the IMF would decide on whether to initiate a rights accumulation programme (RAP). In April the minister of finance reaffirmed Sudan's commitment to meeting all of the IMF targets, including a reduction of the inflation rate and an increase in export revenue. In June, however, the governor of the Bank of Sudan indicated that a further dispute with the IMF had arisen owing to a request by the Fund to extend its review of Sudan's economy from three to six months, during which time Sudan would remain ineligible for loans. Sudan considered such an extension unnecessary in view of the satisfaction with the economic reform programme which the Fund had expressed in November 1994. In August 1995 the IMF renewed its threat to expel Sudan from the Fund after its executive directors had failed to reach agreement with the Sudanese minister of finance on the monthly amount by which Sudan should reduce its arrears of $1,700m. The IMF was reported to be seeking repayment in monthly instalments of $7m., to which the government responded by offering to repay at a monthly rate of $4m. The dispute over the level of Sudan's monthly repayments appeared to have been resolved in May 1996, when an agreement with the IMF was reported to have been concluded. However, no details of the agreement were published and in July 1996 further negotiations with the IMF were reported to be deadlocked over this and other issues. In March 1997 Sudan avoided expulsion from the IMF by agreeing to a series of economic reforms intended to increase growth and cut inflation. Sudan's progress was to be monitored monthly, and any failure to comply would result in expulsion. Both the Arab Monetary Fund and the Arab Fund for Economic and Social Development (AFESD) decided to freeze Sudan's membership in 1997, as a result of the government's inability to clear its arrears. In April 1999, however, Sudan announced that it was seeking to rejoin both organizations and to reschedule its debt to them. In January 1998 the Bank of Sudan announced measures designed to promote development, reduce inflation, stabilize the exchange rate, and support macroeconomic liberalization. Shortly afterwards, an IMF mission arrived in Sudan to compile a report on the implementation of economic reforms. On 14 April the IMF praised Sudan's economic reforms and approved its 1998–2003 economic programme, which aims to achieve an annual GDP growth rate of 6%, to reduce inflation to 5% by 2000, to increase private savings and to encourage investment. The IMF also announced its intention to open a branch office in Khartoum to strengthen relations with the Sudanese government. In June 1999 the IMF announced that Sudan had reduced its debt arrears to US $1,540m. from $1,570m. in 1997 and praised its efforts in reducing inflation which declined to 8% in 1998 from 32% in 1997 and 133% in 1996. In early 1999 Sudan authorized businesses to open bank accounts in euros, the new currency of the EU, in an effort to facilitate trade with EU countries. In August the IMF rescinded the Declaration of Non-co-operation that had been in force since 1990 (see above).

In August 1999 the IMF lifted its nine-year sanction against Sudan following the latter's efforts to reduce its arrears and implement economic reforms. Sudan, which still owes the IMF US $1,300m., repaid some $58m. in 1998 and about $25m. during the first eight months of 1999. In May 2000, in accordance with an IMF-approved Structural Adjustment Programme, Sudan introduced a value-added tax (VAT), which represented 10% of the value of transactions involving goods and services in the country, and exempted capital goods from import duties. The Sudanese government also plans to expand its privatization programme in the agro-industrial, communications and transport sectors. The performance of the privatized Sudan Telecommunications Company (SUDATEL) suggests that the IMF strategy may be paying some dividends. In April 2000 SUDATEL reported that its 1999 earnings totalled $55m. According to its five-year plan, SUDATEL plans to invest $620m. and increase the number of its subscribers to 1.5m. In August 2000 Sudan regained full membership and voting rights in the IMF.

In March 2000 Sudan signed two concessionary loan agreements worth US $114m. with the AFESD. The 25-year loans carry an interest rate of 3% and a seven-year grace period. Sudan plans to use the loans to finance highways out of Khartoum and to upgrade an existing dam which stores Nile flood waters for irrigation. At about the same time, Sudan arranged a $16m. loan from the Islamic Development Bank to fund several water and research projects. Furthermore, the OPEC Fund for International Development provided $10m. for upgrades to Sudan's power sector. On 18 April 2000 Sudan announced that it had rejoined the AFESD after coming to an agreement about the issue of its arrears, which amounted to $214m.

PUBLIC FINANCE, PLANNING AND DEVELOPMENT

The Sudanese government, like governments in many other less-developed countries, has historically depended heavily on indirect taxes, especially import duties, for its main source of revenue. Since the late 1970s, however, the share of indirect taxes in total revenue has declined in parallel with the economy, reflecting the cut-backs in imports that have been imposed in continuing attempts to reduce the balance-of-payments deficit.

Government finances experienced serious disruption from 1984 onwards as a result of the changes in regime, in 1985 and 1989, and of a collapse of imports and of exports. The government had expected taxes on imports and exports to provide more than 50% of estimated revenue. The impact of the Gulf crisis, particularly the rise in oil prices and the decline in remittances from Sudanese workers in the Gulf, compelled the government to introduce an emergency supplementary budget in January 1991, and in July the minister of finance and economic planning reported that the 1990/91 budget had raised a current account surplus of £S400m. instead of the anticipated deficit of £S705m. Military spending dominated the budget for 1993/94, rising by more than 100% to £S41,070m. The budget also allocated £S150,000m. to debt repayment, and increased subsidies on bread and petroleum prices by 13% and 19% respectively. With inflation rising to an annual rate of 105% in July 1993, further measures to protect consumers were taken in August, including the reintroduction of subsidies on some essential commodities and of price controls on other goods. In that year a deficit of £S224,500m. was recorded, with revenue of £S131,900m. and expenditure of £S356,400m. The budget for 1996 (1 January-31 December) projected revenue of £S679,600m., while it was estimated that expenditure would amount to £S2,377,100m. Actual budget out-turn showed revenue of £S629,500m. and expenditure of £S2,722,100m. in that year. In 1997 revenue of £S1,086,000m. was recorded, and expenditure was £S3,386,000m., resulting in a deficit of £S2,300.000m. Tax on tobacco was raised to 70% from 50%. The 1998 budget, announced in December 1997, projected revenue at £S1,758,000m., expenditure at £S1,936,000m., thus resulting in an estimated deficit of £S178,000m. The budget provided for increased current, and development, spending and a reduction in some taxation. Actual budget out-turn showed revenue of £S1,569,000m. and expenditure of £S3,949,900m. in that year. The 1999 budget resulted in a deficit of 20,500m. Sudanese dinars from revenue of 206,700m. Sudanese dinars and expenditure of 227,200m. Sudanese dinars. A further reduction in some forms of taxation was also envisaged.

Following the disappointing course of development programmes in the 1970s, there were no further attempts to implement a co-ordinated planning policy until the introduction, in 1987, of an economic recovery programme. This was successfully completed and was succeeded in 1988 by a three-year medium-term recovery programme, the priorities of which were the reform of the exchange rate and trade policy, the reduction of the budget deficit and subsidies, the promotion of exports and a privatization programme. The military government formed in July 1989 by Lt-Gen. al-Bashir presented a three-year National Economic Salvation Programme (NESP) to coincide with the 1990/91 budget. Efforts to reform the economy were to include a reallocation of resources towards agriculture and other productive sectors, and a refinement of the Investment Encouragement Act to create a more conducive investment climate for the local and foreign private sector. Measures to attract investment included the removal of the government monopoly in all areas except petroleum exploitation, as well as liquidation with full or part privatization of government parastatals. Other measures announced included a review of the banking system, export liberalization and price decontrol, and introduction of a 'social solidarity' system to cushion the effects of economic restructuring for low-income groups. In August 1990 the government announced that it was implementing four measures under the NESP: cuts in government expenditure; increases in tax revenues; a reduction in imports; and wage freezes and widespread job cuts. In May 1991 the government announced that, in order to encourage production, it was lifting restrictions on the price of farm products.

After the suspension of parliament on 12 December 1999, the government passed its 2000 budget by decree. The budget, which was in line with the IMF's economic restructuring plan, emphasized economic stability and liberalization and promised to reduce inflation, accelerate privatization, ease trade restrictions, and achieve a 6.5% growth rate. It was projected that revenue would total 298,000m. Sudanese dinars and that expenditure would amount to 335,000m. Sudanese dinars; an increase of 34% compared with the previous year. The commencement of exports of crude petroleum led the minister of finance to predict a 68% rise in the value of exports from 1999. In January 2000 the Sudanese authorities announced subsidy cuts on several basic goods. This action resulted in a 20% increase in petrol and diesel prices and a 30% increase in the price of beef, chicken and other foodstuffs. To allay complaints about the subsidy cuts by trade unions, the al-Bashir regime pledged to implement a 15% pay rise for public-sector workers.

POWER, TRANSPORT AND COMMUNICATIONS

Sudan's publicly operated generating capacity in the mid-1980s was about 1,000 MW, of which about 53% was hydroelectricity and the remainder thermally generated. Some 83% of the total was accounted for by the Blue Nile grid, centred on the Roseires and Sennar hydroelectric schemes. However, because of problems related to shortages of spare parts, siltation at the dams and fluctuations in river levels, actual output was less than 50% of this level. These problems with the public supply led to a major growth in private generation. Estimated at a total 177 MW in 1982, including some 70 MW generated by the sugar schemes (of which some 50 MW came from Kenana), self-generated capacity is since estimated to have grown by some 50%, with a particularly large growth in the number of private household and company generators in the main urban areas to combat the frequent power cuts.

The growth in private generation also reflects Sudan's highly irregular electricity consumption patterns, with Khartoum and the central region accounting for 87% of total consumption and the south and west only 2%. Sectorally, industry accounts for 39% and residential customers 37%. The completion of new thermal units in 1982, at Dongola, el-Fasher, Shendi and Wau, redressed the balance somewhat, and work is also under way to complete the long-delayed Juba power station and construct new stations at Karima and Nyala. In 1986 the Power III electricity scheme was completed, almost doubling generating capacity in the Blue Nile grid. A new 60-MW thermal power station at Khartoum North came on stream in May 1985. In 1986 work began to add a 40-MW extension to the adjacent Burri thermal power station, and in 1988 work was due to begin on the first of two 40-60 MW units at Khartoum North. Finance for subsequent projects to enhance Sudan's thermal power capacity has been forthcoming from Germany, Japan, the USA, the Netherlands and Saudi Arabia. In addition, the African Development Bank has promoted a study on power generation and desalination in Port Sudan which would determine the feasibility of a project to supply Port Sudan, Suakin and the surrounding areas with drinking water and electricity. In April 1997 the Islamic Development Bank (IDB) agreed a US $22m. loan to raise the height of the Roseires dam on the Blue Nile. This project will increase water storage and power generating capacity. The IDB also agreed a $1.44m. loan for the construction of 13 health centres. In 1998 a Sudanese-Russian trade agreement provided for the construction of a hydroelectric dam on the river Nile, and China agreed to contribute 75% of the necessary funding for a $300m. dam, expected to produce electricity and sufficient water to irrigate 400,000 ha. In April 1999 a French delegation visited Sudan to explore the possibility of investing in electricity generation and distribution. The delegation signed agreements with Sudan's National Electricity Corpn to train workers and rehabilitate power stations. Companies from the United Kingdom, China and Iran have also expressed an interest in the development of the electricity sector in Sudan. In August 1999 the Sudanese government announced that it was to seek foreign investors to finance an ambitious programme of dam construction, which envisages harnessing the Nile to generate electricity. Under the plan, 10 dams are scheduled to be built on the Blue Nile, White Nile and Atbara River by 2010.

Although Sudan still depends heavily on railways for transport, the road network has played an increasingly important role since 1980. More than 48,000 km of tracks are classed as 'motorable'; there were more than 3,160 km of main roads and 739 km of secondary roads in 1985. The completion in 1980 of a 1,190-km highway between Khartoum and Port Sudan encouraged a rapid increase in the number of road haulage firms and as a result road transport now accounts for over 60% of internal haulage traffic. Only a few of the road projects planned received financing after 1983. By 1997, work had been completed on a 270-km road linking Jaili with Atbara, as part of a project to provide an alternative route from Khartoum to the coast and work on a 510-km road from Omdurman to Dongola began in mid-1992. In the same year Iran agreed to assist in the construction of the road from Kosti to Malakal and Juba. Also in progress in 1992 were studies for a road from Gedaref to Doka and Gullalat, linking eastern Sudan with Ethiopia, and for the rehabilitation of the road from Port Sudan to Gedaref. In January 1997, al-Bashir inaugurated the second phase of the Challenge Highway which is expected to link eastern and northern Sudan. He also laid the foundation stone for the third phase of the Atbara-Hayya road. In 1997 a German company agreed to construct a 250-km road between southern Kordofan and northern Darfur, and in January 1998 it was reported that the Kuwait Development Fund had agreed to finance a US $415m. road to link Sudan to Chad. In early 1999 Sudan announced plans to rehabilitate the 126-km road linking Khartoum and Wad Medani. The project was estimated to cost US $11m. A company based in the United Arab Emirates was to finance 62% of the project, in return for a 20-year monopoly on all services on the road.

The total length of railway operated by the Sudan Railways Corporation (SRC) in 1997 was 4,784 route-km. The main line runs from Wadi Halfa, on the Egyptian border, to al-Obeid, via Khartoum. Lines from Atbara and Sinnar connect with Port Sudan. There are lines from Sinnar to Damazine on the Blue Nile (227 km) and from Aradeiba to Nyala in the south-western province of Darfur (689 km), with a 445-km branch line from Babanousa to Wau in Bahr al-Ghazal province. The Sudan Gezira Board also operated 1,400 km of railway in 1994, serving the country's cotton plantations. In July 1989, shortly after the military coup, it was estimated that railways and ports were operating at less than 20% of capacity. Shortages of spare parts and the impact of import controls on the rehabilitation requirements of track and rolling stock have considerably hampered the country's railway system. The rehabilitation of both lines and rolling stock was announced in September 1997, in order to facilitate the transportation of petroleum. In May 1999 the SRC announced plans to privatize its passenger and cargo services by the end of 2001. Under this proposal, the SRC would retain the responsibility for the management of the rails, the stations and signalling equipment.

Although Sudan has about 4,068 km of navigable river, with some 1,723 km open throughout the year, river transport has, until recently, been minimal. The waterway which is most frequently used in the 1,435-km section of the White Nile route between Karima and Dongola. Since 1981 the government has been attempting to remedy past neglect, and foreign assistance has been sought to upgrade the rivers through dredging, improving quays and providing navigation aids.

Following the reopening of the Suez Canal in 1975, work began on modernizing and enlarging the facilities at Sudan's principal port, Port Sudan. Work on the project, financed by the World Bank and the United Kingdom, started in 1978. It will increase cargo-handling capacity to 13m. tons per year, and container, 'roll on, roll off' and new deep-water berths are being added. The first phase was completed in 1982, and a revised second phase began in 1983. The port at Suakin has the capacity to handle about 1.5m. tons of cargo annually.

Sudan Airways, the national carrier, operates internal and international services. It connects Khartoum with 20 internal points as well as with Europe, the Middle East and Africa. Plans originally announced in 1983, to transfer the airline to private-sector ownership were deferred following the coup in April 1985, but revived in 1991. Following considerable delays, a US $40m. contract, financed by the Saudi Fund for Development and the IDB, to build an international airport in Port Sudan was finalized in 1990. A programme has been implemented to restore runways at regional airports which had been damaged by drought, and by the early 1990s most of the work to improve

Juba airport had been completed. In June 1999 plans were announced for the construction of a new international airport 25 km east of Khartoum at a cost of US $750m. The new airport was to have two runways and was to replace the existing airport which would continue to be used for internal flights. At that time three companies had submitted tenders for the project and the contract was expected to be awarded in the near future.

Sudan has a fixed telephone network of some 99,000 lines. A mobile telephone network for Khartoum State was inaugurated in February 1997, and it was expected that this would later be expanded to cover other states. In early 1997 three contracts were signed with a French company, Alcatel, concerning the provision of equipment for an ARABSAT ground station, operated by the Arab Satellite Communications Organization (an agency of the Arab League), and the improvement of both the domestic and international exchanges in Khartoum. In February 1999 SUDATEL launched its second expansion plan, which aimed to increase the number of subscribers from 180,000 to 1,500,000 by 2003. The programme was expected to cost some US $620m.

Statistical Survey

Source (unless otherwise stated): Department of Statistics, Ministry of Finance and National Economy, POB 700, Khartoum; tel. (11) 777003.

Area and Population

AREA, POPULATION AND DENSITY

Area (sq km)	2,505,813*
Population (census results)†	
1 February 1983	20,594,197
15 April 1993‡	
Males	12,518,638
Females	12,422,045
Total	24,940,683
Population (UN estimates at mid-year)§	
1996	27,160,000
1997	27,718,000
1998	28,292,000
Density (per sq km) at mid-1998	11.3

* 967,500 sq miles.
† Excluding adjustments for underenumeration, estimated to have been 6.7% in 1993.
‡ Provisional result.
§ Source: UN, *World Population Prospects: The 1998 Revision*.

PROVINCES (1983 census, provisional)*

	Area (sq miles)	Population	Density (per sq mile)
Northern	134,736	433,391	3.2
Nile	49,205	649,633	13.2
Kassala	44,109	1,512,335	34.3
Red Sea	84,977	695,874	8.2
Blue Nile . . .	24,009	1,056,313	44.0
Gezira	13,546	2,023,094	149.3
White Nile . . .	16,161	933,136	57.7
Northern Kordofan . . .	85,744	1,805,769	21.1
Southern Kordofan . . .	61,188	1,287,525	21.0
Northern Darfur . .	133,754	1,327,947	9.9
Southern Darfur . .	62,801	1,765,752	28.1
Khartoum	10,883	1,802,299	165.6
Eastern Equatoria . .	46,073	1,047,125	22.7
Western Equatoria . .	30,422	359,056	11.8
Bahr al-Ghazal . .	52,000	1,492,597	28.7
Al-Bohayrat . . .	25,625	772,913	30.2
Sobat	45,266	802,354	17.7
Jonglei	47,003	797,251	17.0
Total	967,500	20,564,364	21.3

* In 1991 a federal system of government was inaugurated, whereby Sudan was divided into nine states, which were sub-divided into 66 provinces and 281 local government areas. A constitutional decree, issued in February 1994, redivided the country into 26 states.

PRINCIPAL TOWNS (population at 1993 census)

Omdurman . .	1,271,403	Nyala	227,183
Khartoum (capital) .	947,483	El-Gezira . . .	211,362
Khartoum North .	700,887	Gedaref . . .	191,164
Port Sudan . .	308,195	Kosti . . .	173,599
Kassala . . .	234,622	El-Fasher . . .	141,884
El-Obeid . .	229,425	Juba	114,980

Source: UN, *Demographic Yearbook*.

BIRTHS AND DEATHS (UN estimates, annual averages)

	1980–85	1985–90	1990–95
Birth rate (per 1,000) . . .	43.5	36.9	34.9
Death rate (per 1,000) . . .	15.8	14.0	13.9

Expectation of life (UN estimates, years at birth, 1990–95): 50.9 (males 49.6; females 52.4).

Source: UN, *World Population Prospects: The 1998 Revision*.

ECONOMICALLY ACTIVE POPULATION*
(persons aged 10 years and over, 1983 census, provisional)

	Males	Females	Total
Agriculture, hunting, forestry and fishing	2,638,294	1,390,411	4,028,705
Mining and quarrying . . .	5,861	673	6,534
Manufacturing	205,247	61,446	266,693
Electricity, gas and water . .	42,110	1,618	43,728
Construction	130,977	8,305	139,282
Trade, restaurants and hotels . .	268,382	25,720	294,102
Transport, storage and communications	209,776	5,698	215,474
Financing, insurance, real estate and business services . .	17,414	3,160	20,574
Community, social and personal services	451,193	99,216	550,409
Activities not adequately defined .	142,691	42,030	184,721
Unemployed persons not previously employed	387,615	205,144	592,759
Total	4,499,560	1,843,421	6,342,981

* Excluding nomads, homeless persons and members of institutional households.

Mid-1998 (estimates in '000): Agriculture, etc. 6,950; Total 11,056 (Source: FAO, *Production Yearbook*).

Agriculture

PRINCIPAL CROPS ('000 metric tons)

	1996	1997	1998
Wheat	527	642	597
Maize	54	52	55*
Millet	440	648	1,122
Sorghum (Durra)	4,179	3,159	4,891
Potatoes	14†	14*	15*
Sweet potatoes*	8	9	9
Cassava (Manioc)*	10	10	10
Yams*	133	134	135
Dry beans	8	11	12*
Dry broad beans	83†	80*	85*
Other pulses	73	76	78*
Groundnuts (in shell)	815	1,104	800
Castor beans	2†	1†	1*
Sesame seed	416	281	165
Cottonseed	157	150	99
Tomatoes*	235	238	240
Pumpkins, etc.*	65	65	66
Aubergines	109†	110*	110*
Onions (dry)	56†	57*	57*
Melons*	25	26	26
Water melons*	135	138	140
Dates*	168	174	175
Sugar cane	5,076	5,500*	5,850*
Oranges*	16	16	17
Lemons and limes*	58	57	58
Grapefruit*	65	64	65
Mangoes*	184	185	190
Bananas*	70	70	71
Cotton lint	100†	87†	106*

* FAO estimate(s).   † Unofficial figures.

Source: FAO, *Production Yearbook*.

LIVESTOCK ('000 head, year ending September)

	1996	1997	1998
Horses*	24	25	25
Asses*	680	700	720
Cattle	31,669	33,103	34,584
Camels	3,039†	3,050*	3,100*
Sheep	37,202	39,835	42,363
Goats	35,216	36,037	37,346

Poultry (million): 40 in 1996; 40* in 1997; 41* in 1998.

* FAO estimate(s).   † Unofficial figure.

Source: FAO, *Production Yearbook*.

LIVESTOCK PRODUCTS ('000 metric tons)

	1996	1997	1998
Beef and veal	226	230*	235*
Mutton and lamb	130	133*	135*
Goat meat	113	115*	116*
Poultry meat*	37	38	38
Other meat	71	73*	75*
Cows' milk*	2,880	2,928	2,952
Sheep's milk	410	435	461
Goats' milk	1,064	1,107	1,151
Butter and ghee*	15	15	15
Cheese*	114	91	91
Poultry eggs*	41	41	42
Wool:			
greasy*	39	42	44
clean*	20	21	22
Cattle hides*	47	48	48
Sheepskins*	19	20	21
Goatskins*	22	22	22

* FAO estimate(s).

Source: FAO, *Production Yearbook*.

Forestry

ROUNDWOOD REMOVALS ('000 cubic metres)

	1995	1996	1997
Sawlogs, veneer logs and logs for sleepers	110	110	110
Other industrial wood	2,003	2,064	2,092
Fuel wood	13,507	13,803	14,111
Total	15,620	15,959	16,313

Source: FAO, *Yearbook of Forest Products*.

Gum arabic ('000 metric tons, year ending 30 June): 24 in 1993/94; 27 in 1994/95; 25 in 1995/96. Source: IMF, *Sudan—Recent Economic Developments* (March 1997).

Fishing

(metric tons, live weight)

	1995	1996	1997
Nile tilapia	10,000	10,500	11,000
Other freshwater fishes	30,000	30,000	31,000
Marine fishes	4,000	4,500	5,000
Total catch	44,000	45,000	47,000
Inland waters	40,000	40,500	42,000
Indian Ocean	4,000	4,500	5,000

Source: FAO, *Yearbook of Fishery Statistics*.

Mining

	1994	1995	1996
Salt (unrefined) ('000 metric tons)*	75	75	50
Chromium ore ('000 metric tons)†	7*	13	4*
Gold ore (kilograms)*†	3,000	3,700	3,700

* Estimate(s).

† Figures refer to the metal content of ores.

Source: UN, *Industrial Commodity Statistics Yearbook*.

Industry

PETROLEUM PRODUCTS (estimates, '000 metric tons)

	1994	1995	1996
Motor spirit (petrol)	95	98	98
Aviation gasoline	5	5	5
Naphtha	23	23	24
Jet fuels	88	90	88
Kerosene	25	25	26
Gas-diesel (distillate fuel) oils	325	327	328
Residual fuel oils	318	318	320
Liquefied petroleum gas	6	7	7

Source: UN, *Industrial Commodity Statistics Yearbook*.

SELECTED OTHER PRODUCTS

	1997	1998	1999
Flour ('000 metric tons)	324	310	532
Raw sugar ('000 metric tons)	500	610	622
Vegetable oils ('000 metric tons)	90	120	100
Soft drinks (million bottles)	276	n.a.	n.a.
Textiles (million metres)	33	n.a.	n.a.
Footwear (million pairs)	24	33	48
Cigarettes (metric tons)	1,138	122	n.a.
Rubber tyres ('000)	60	207	173
Cement ('000 metric tons)	288	206	267

Source: IMF, *Sudan—Statistical Annex* (April 1998 and July 2000).

Finance

CURRENCY AND EXCHANGE RATES

Monetary Units
100 piastres = 1 Sudanese dinar.

Sterling, Dollar and Euro Equivalents (28 April 2000)
£1 sterling = 402.45 dinars;
US $1 = 256.65 dinars;
€1 = 233.17 dinars;
1,000 Sudanese dinars = £2.485 = $3.896 = €4.289.

Average Exchange Rate (Sudanese dinars per US $)
1997   157.57
1998   200.80
1999   252.55

Note: On 1 March 1999 the Sudanese pound (£S) was replaced by the Sudanese dinar, equivalent to £S10. The pound was withdrawn from circulation on 31 July 1999. Some of the figures in this Survey are still in terms of Sudanese pounds.

CENTRAL GOVERNMENT BUDGET
('000 million Sudanese dinars)

Revenue	1997	1998	1999
Tax revenue	90.9	126.4	153.3
Taxes on income and profits .	21.7	31.2	36.1
Personal income tax . .	2.1	4.1	3.0
Business profit tax . .	6.2	8.7	22.9
Remittances from expatriate Sudanese	4.0	4.7	5.4
Taxes on goods and services .	21.1	25.9	32.8
Excise duties . . .	21.1	21.3	24.7
Sales taxes	–	4.6	8.1
Taxes on international trade and transactions . . .	48.2	69.3	84.4
Import duties . . .	24.3	35.5	53.8
Export tax	3.3	1.2	1.8
Consumption tax. . .	9.9	17.1	18.4
Non-tax revenue* . . .	16.4	30.4	53.4
Fees and charges on public services	6.3	9.5	9.4
Public enterprise profits, interest, rent and dividends .	5.5	8.0	14.1
Receipts from sales of public enterprises	0.1	n.a.	n.a.
Total	107.3	156.9	206.7

Expenditure	1997	1998	1999
Current expenditure . . .	109.8	155.3	195.0
Wages and salaries. . .	37.5	57.3	80.4
Goods and services. . .	45.8	31.2	37.9
Ministries	n.a.	n.a.	n.a.
Defence	n.a.	19.8	24.3
Current transfers . . .	4.7	8.9	12.8
Interest paid . . .	10.1	13.9	20.2
Capital expenditure and net lending	9.3	15.6	32.2
Development expenditure .	9.3	15.6	32.2
Foreign expenses . .	2.6	3.4	6.5
Local expenses . . .	6.7	12.2	25.7
Total	119.1	170.9	227.2

* Excluding price differential on oil, sugar and cement.

Source: IMF, *Sudan — Statistical Appendix* (July 2000).

INTERNATIONAL RESERVES (US $ million at 31 December)

	1996	1997	1998
Foreign exchange . . .	106.8	81.6	90.6
Total	106.8	81.6	90.6

Source: IMF, *International Financial Statistics*.

MONEY SUPPLY (£S '000 million at 31 December)

	1996	1997	1998
Currency outside banks . .	444.39	584.94	821.40
Demand deposits at deposit money banks	309.21	413.51	469.38
Total money	753.59	998.45	1,290.78

Source: IMF, *International Financial Statistics*.

COST OF LIVING
(Retail Price Index; estimates; base: 1970 = 100)

	1991	1992	1993
Food	27,279.9	40,756.2	60,889.8
Clothing	19,054.6	28,696.2	43,216.5
Rent	21,501.4	31,650.1	46,588.9
Housing	24,778.9	36,895.8	54,937.8
Other goods and services . .	22,852.3	34,027.1	54,937.8
All items	25,167.5	37,474.4	55,794.4

Source: UN Economic Commission for Africa, *African Statistical Yearbook*.

All items (Index for middle-income households in the Greater Khartoum area at December; base: January 1995 = 100): 59.4 in 1994; 100.0 in 1995; 232.8 in 1996; 341.4 in 1997; 399.8 in 1998.

Source: IMF, *International Financial Statistics*.

NATIONAL ACCOUNTS
Expenditure on the Gross Domestic Product
(estimates, '000 million Sudanese dinars at current prices)

	1997	1998	1999
Government final consumption expenditure	91.3	88.5	118.3
Private final consumption expenditure	1,465.9	1,882.2	2,172.6
Gross fixed capital formation . .	210.7	259.1	318.7
Total domestic expenditure .	1,767.9	2,229.8	2,609.6
Exports of goods and services . .	98.4	122.4	205.7
Less Imports of goods and services	255.4	393.9	383.8
GDP in purchasers' values . .	1,676.9	2,062.1	2,536.3
GDP at constant 1981/82 prices*	1,201.9	1,262.1	1,338.2

* Million Sudanese dinars.

Source: IMF, *Sudan — Statistical Appendix* (July 2000).

Gross Domestic Product by Economic Activity
(estimates, '000 million Sudanese dinars at current prices)

	1997	1998	1999
Agriculture and forestry . . .	745.7	841.6	1,040.3
Mining and quarrying . . .	4.2	5.5	20.9
Manufacturing and handicrafts .	100.7	177.4	217.3
Electricity and water. . .	14.3	16.1	19.0
Construction. . . .	73.1	132.5	156.8
Trade, restaurants and hotels. .	260.5	405.9	492.0
Transport and communications .	150.5	116.3	142.3
Other services	266.0	290.8	354.1
GDP at factor cost . . .	1,677.0	2,062.1	2,536.3

Source: IMF, *Sudan — Statistical Appendix* (July 2000).

BALANCE OF PAYMENTS (US $ million)

	1997	1998	1999
Exports of goods f.o.b. . . .	594.2	595.7	780.1
Imports of goods f.o.b. . . .	−1,421.9	−1,732.2	−1,256.0
Trade balance	−827.7	−1,136.5	−475.9
Exports of services . . .	31.5	15.8	81.6
Imports of services . . .	−172.8	−204.0	−275.3
Balance on goods and services .	−969.0	−1,324.7	−669.6
Other income received . .	16.9	13.7	19.1
Other income paid . . .	−5.3	−10.6	−123.2
Balance on goods, services and income	−957.4	−1,321.6	−773.7
Current transfers received . .	439.1	731.8	702.2
Current transfers paid . .	−309.8	−366.7	−393.7
Current balance . . .	−828.1	−956.5	−465.2
Capital account (net) . .	n.a.	−54.2	−22.9
Direct investment from abroad .	97.9	370.7	370.8
Investment assets . . .	n.a.	−78.5	−38.4
Investment liabilities. . .	97.1	41.2	102.9
Net errors and omissions . .	651.2	750.5	167.6
Overall balance . . .	18.1	73.2	114.8

Source: IMF, *International Financial Statistics.*

External Trade

PRINCIPAL COMMODITIES (US $ million)

Imports c.i.f.	1997	1998	1999
Foodstuffs	237.9	263.7	275.7
Wheat flour . . .	60.8	59.0	51.2
Tea	32.2	36.3	37.9
Animal and vegetable oils .	1.7	4.7	9.9
Crude materials . . .	324.1	307.5	237.2
Petroleum	292.7	255.7	183.9
Chemicals . . .	189.9	157.0	113.9
Pharmaceuticals . .	38.7	49.2	44.1
Fertilizers . . .	47.4	10.6	2.2
Insecticides . . .	2.9	1.6	1.6
Basic manufactures . .	292.6	592.1	236.9
Machinery and equipment .	269.7	348.2	358.3
Transport equipment . .	173.2	192.7	131.8
Automobiles . . .	19.5	29.5	30.4
Trucks . . .	38.0	86.4	45.1
Spare parts for automobiles .	65.7	31.1	22.0
Total (incl. others) . . .	1,579.7	1,924.7	1,412.2

Exports f.o.b.	1997	1998	1999
Cotton	105.6	95.6	44.9
Groundnuts (incl. oil and oilcake) .	68.1	63.5	5.4
Sesame seed (incl. oilcake) .	118.3	105.1	127.3
Sorghum	0.0	5.4	27.8
Gum arabic . . .	27.0	23.7	26.4
Sugar	28.9	29.3	14.8
Livestock . . .	78.3	120.3	114.3
Sheep and lambs . .	71.0	97.8	101.1
Hibiscus	17.6	10.7	19.1
Yarn	11.0	9.4	7.6
Watermelon seeds . .	14.7	8.2	12.8
Hides and skins . . .	22.8	20.2	3.9
Gold	47.2	43.7	55.3
Total (incl. others) . .	594.2	595.7	780.0

Source: IMF, *Sudan—Statistical Appendix* (July 2000).

PRINCIPAL TRADING PARTNERS (US $ million)

Imports c.i.f.	1994	1995	1996
Austria	17.6	9.7	2.3
Bangladesh . . .	25.5	11.1	13.5
Belgium-Luxembourg . .	55.2	52.0	11.6
Canada	4.9	2.8	13.0
China, People's Repub. .	30.0	31.1	46.9
Djibouti	23.0	0.0	0.0
Egypt	68.8	63.6	30.3
France	73.0	86.7	57.5
Germany	50.0	72.3	48.6
Greece	6.7	12.5	8.7
Hungary	0.2	24.7	8.9
India	31.2	17.9	34.2
Indonesia . . .	17.9	8.0	12.5
Iran. . . .	37.1	8.4	55.9
Italy	21.2	20.6	25.5
Japan	77.7	114.3	59.7
Kenya	18.5	9.8	18.2
Korea, Repub. . .	22.8	16.9	20.7
Libya	48.5	25.4	6.7
Malaysia . . .	17.9	30.4	16.2
Netherlands . . .	51.4	41.5	24.5
Poland	21.5	5.7	4.9
Romania	45.1	15.3	30.9
Saudi Arabia . . .	242.3	65.7	103.0
Southern African Customs Union*	0.2	7.8	12.9
Sweden	16.8	8.8	9.1
Switzerland . . .	14.0	30.0	11.7
Turkey	33.0	23.5	18.9
United Arab Emirates . .	54.5	40.8	40.9
United Kingdom . . .	129.1	74.3	71.8
USA	70.1	122.6	91.6
Yemen	5.8	0.4	12.8
Zimbabwe . . .	n.a.	15.3	15.9
Total (incl. others) . .	1,486.0	1,184.9	1,072.8

Exports f.o.b.	1994	1995	1996
Bangladesh	4.2	3.7	0.9
Belgium-Luxembourg . .	8.6	47.4	1.7
China, People's Repub. . .	45.7	50.2	22.2
Djibouti	0.6	1.5	3.1
Egypt	9.1	20.3	14.4
France	204.0	50.8	4.5
Germany	10.4	27.5	6.7
Greece	3.9	2.7	5.6
Hong Kong . . .	0.8	0.2	3.3
India	10.4	11.8	0.9
Italy	0.0	50.9	15.8
Japan	14.7	39.0	12.2
Jordan	7.2	16.0	12.4
Korea, Dem. People's Repub. .	11.6	1.2	0.0
Korea, Repub. . . .	5.3	1.4	4.0
Lebanon	0.0	16.0	5.3
Libya	16.2	0.3	2.5
Netherlands . . .	5.5	6.6	6.1
Norway	0.0	8.5	n.a.
Romania	n.a.	8.5	0.0
Saudi Arabia . . .	81.0	95.1	54.8
Somalia	7.5	n.a.	3.9
Switzerland . . .	1.7	16.0	0.3
Syria	4.7	1.9	2.9
Thailand	20.3	40.9	12.8
Tunisia	4.0	2.6	1.7
Turkey	2.9	12.1	3.6
United Arab Emirates . .	1.9	27.3	12.4
United Kingdom . . .	25.4	38.6	41.0
USA	16.9	56.2	5.2
Yemen	4.1	7.4	3.9
Total (incl. others) . .	394.9	685.2	273.1

* Comprising Botswana, Lesotho, Namibia, South Africa and Swaziland.

Source: UN, *International Trade Statistics Yearbook.*

Transport

RAILWAY TRAFFIC*

	1991	1992	1993
Freight ton-km (million) . . .	2,030	2,120	2,240
Passenger-km (million) . . .	1,020	1,130	1,183

* Estimates.

Source: UN Economic Commission for Africa, *African Statistical Yearbook.*

ROAD TRAFFIC* (motor vehicles in use)

	1994	1995	1996
Passenger cars	257,000	263,000	285,000
Lorries, trucks, etc. . . .	43,120	48,000	53,000

* Estimates.

Source: International Road Federation, *World Road Statistics.*

SHIPPING
Merchant Fleet (registered at 31 December)

	1996	1997	1998
Number of vessels . . .	19	19	19
Displacement (grt) . . .	42,114	42,114	43,078

Source: Lloyd's Register of Shipping, *World Fleet Statistics.*

International Sea-borne Freight Traffic (estimates, '000 metric tons)

	1991	1992	1993
Goods loaded	1,290	1,387	1,543
Goods unloaded	3,800	4,200	4,300

Source: UN Economic Commission for Africa, *African Statistical Yearbook.*

CIVIL AVIATION (traffic on scheduled services)

	1994	1995	1996
Kilometres flown (million) . .	13	13	13
Passengers carried ('000) . .	432	497	491
Passenger-km (million) . .	615	681	650
Total ton-km (million) . .	96	121	107

Source: UN, *Statistical Yearbook.*

Tourism

	1995	1996	1997
Tourist arrivals ('000) . .	63	57	30
Tourism receipts (US $ million) .	8	8	4

Source: World Tourism Organization, *Yearbook of Tourism Statistics.*

Communications Media

	1994	1995	1996
Radio receivers ('000 in use) . .	7,050	7,200	7,360
Television receivers ('000 in use) .	2,180	2,240	2,300
Telephones ('000 main lines in use)	64	75	99
Telefax stations (numbers in use) .	5,000	5,800	7,000
Daily newspapers:			
Number	5	5	5
Average circulation ('000 copies)*	620	650	737

Mobile cellular telephones (subscribers): 2,200 in 1996.
1997 ('000 in use): Radio receivers 7,550; Television receivers 2,380.
* Estimates.

Sources: UNESCO, *Statistical Yearbook*, and UN, *Statistical Yearbook.*

Education

(1996/97)

	Institutions	Teachers	Pupils/Students
Pre-primary	7,541	8,897	343,767
Primary	11,158	102,987	3,000,048
Secondary:			
General	n.a.	14,743	379,162
Vocational	n.a.	761	26,421
Universities etc.* . . .	n.a.	2,043	59,824

* Figures refer to 1990/91.

Source: UNESCO, *Statistical Yearbook.*

Directory

The Constitution

Following the coup of 6 April 1985, the Constitution of April 1973 was abrogated. A transitional Constitution, which entered into force in October 1985, was suspended following the military coup of 30 June 1989. In April 1998 a new Constitution was approved by the National Assembly, and presented to President al-Bashir. At a referendum held in June, the new Constitution was endorsed by 96.7% of voters. This Constitution, which entered into force on 1 July 1998, vests executive power in the Council of Ministers, which is appointed by the President but responsible to the National Assembly. Legislative power is vested in the National Assembly. The Constitution guarantees freedom of thought and religion, and the right to political association, provided that such activity complies with the law.

The Government

HEAD OF STATE

President: Lt-Gen. OMAR HASSAN AHMAD AL-BASHIR (took power as Chairman of the Revolutionary Command Council for National Salvation (RCC) on 30 June 1989; appointed President by the RCC on 16 October 1993; elected in March 1996 for a five-year term of office).

First Vice-President: ALI OSMAN MUHAMMAD TAHA.

Second Vice-President: Maj.-Gen. GEORGE KONGOR AROP.

COUNCIL OF MINISTERS

(August 2000)

Prime Minister: Lt-Gen. OMAR HASSAN AHMAD AL-BASHIR.

Deputy Prime Minister: ALI OSMAN MUHAMMAD TAHA.

Minister at the Presidency and Adviser for the President: Maj.-Gen. ABD AR-RAHIM MUHAMMAD HUSSAIN.

Minister of Cabinet Affairs: Gen. ABD AR-RAHMAN SIR AL-KHATIM.

Minister of Defence: Maj.-Gen. BAKRI HASSAN SALIH.

Minister of External Relations: MUSTAFA OSMAN ISMAIL.

Minister of the Interior: Maj.-Gen. EL HADI ABDALLAH.

Minister of Justice: ALI MUHAMMAD OSMAN YASSIN.

Minister of Finance and National Economy: Dr MUHAMMAD KHAIR AZ-ZUBAIR.

Minister of Culture and Information: Dr GHAZI SALAH AD-DIN.

Minister of Federal Relations: IBRAHIM SULAYMAN HASSAN.

Minister of Energy and Mining: Dr AWAD AHMAD AL-JAZ.

Minister of Social Planning: Dr QUTBI AL-MAHDI.

Minister of National Industry and Investment: Dr ABD AL-HALIM ISMAIL ALMUTAFI.

Minister of Agriculture and Forestry: Dr AB AL-HAMID MOUSSA KASHA.

Minister of Foreign Trade: MEKKI ALI BALAIL.

Minister of Higher Education and Scientific Research: Prof. AZ-ZUBAIR BASHIR TAHA.

Minister of Education: ABD AL-BASIT ABD AL-MAGID.

Minister of Roads and Communications: MUHAMMAD TAHIR EILA.

Minister of Tourism and the Environment: Maj.-Gen. (retd) AT-TAGANI ADAM AT-TAHIR.

Minister of Urban Survey and Development: Eng. JOSEPH MALWAL.

Minister of Animal Resources: Dr ABDULLAH MUHAMMAD SIDAHMAD.

Minister of Irrigation and Water Resources: Eng. KAMAL ALI MUHAMMAD SIDAHMAD.

Minister of Manpower: Maj.-Gen. ALISON MANANI MAGAYA.

Minister of Health: ABD AL-GASSIM MUHAMMAD IBRAHIM.

Minister of Transport: Dr LAM AKOL.

Minister of Aviation: SHAMBUL ADCANE.

MINISTRIES

Ministry of Agriculture and Forestry: POB 285, al-Gamaa Ave, Khartoum; tel. (11) 780951.

Ministry of Aviation: Khartoum; tel. (11) 773000.

Ministry of Culture and Information: Khartoum; tel. (11) 771967.

Ministry of Defence: POB 371, Khartoum; tel. (11) 774910.

Ministry of Education: Khartoum; tel. (11) 78900.

Ministry of Energy and Mining: POB 2087, Khartoum; tel. (11) 775595.

Ministry of External Relations: POB 873, Khartoum; tel. (11) 773101: e-mail info@sudmer.com; internet www.sudmer.com.

Ministry of Finance and National Economy: POB 700, Khartoum; tel. (11) 770288.

Ministry of Foreign Trade: Khartoum; tel. (11) 772793.

Ministry of Health: POB 303, Khartoum; tel. (11) 773000.

Ministry of Higher Education and Scientific Research: Khartoum; tel. (11) 789970.

Ministry of the Interior: POB 2793, Khartoum; tel. (11) 776554.

Ministry of Irrigation and Water Resources: POB 878, Khartoum; tel. (11) 77533.

Ministry of Justice: POB 302, An-Nil Ave, Khartoum; tel. (11) 774842.

Ministry of National Industry and Investment: POB 2184, Khartoum; tel. (11) 777830.

Ministry of Roads and Communications: POB 1130, Khartoum 11111; tel. (11) 779493; fax (11) 780507.

Ministry of Tourism and the Environment: POB 300, Khartoum; tel. (11) 462604.

Ministry of Transport: POB 300, Khartoum; tel. (11) 781629.

STATE GOVERNORS
(August 2000)

Bahr al-Jabal: Lt-Col (retd) HENRY JADA ZAKARIA.

Blue Nile: Maj.-Gen. (retd) HADI BUSHRA.

Eastern Equatoria: Col ABDULLAH ALLAH JABU.

Gadarif: Prof. AMIN DAF'ALLAH.

Gezira: SHARIF AHMAD UMAR BADR.

Jonglei: Dr RIAK GAI KOK.

Kassala: IBRAHIM MAHMOUD HAMID.

Khartoum: Dr MAJZOUB AL-KHALIFA.

Lakes: Maj.-Gen. GABRIEL CHOUL YAK.

Northern: BADAWI KHAYR IDRIS.

Northern Bahr al-Ghazal: KUAJ MAKOI MIAR.

Northern Darfur: Maj.-Gen. (retd) Pilot ABDULLAH SAFI AN -NUR.

Northern Kordofan: UTHMAN AL-HADI IBRAHIM.

Red Sea: ABU ALI MAJDHUB ABU ALI.

River Nile: HASSAN SA'D AHMAD.

Sennar: Dr YUNIS ASH-SHARIF AL-HUSSAIN.

Southern Darfur: HIRAYKAH IZZ AD-DIN.

Southern Kordofan: MAJDHUB YUSUF BABIKR.

Unity: (vacant).

Upper Nile: PETER CHARLIMAN.

Warab: MOSES MACHAR.

Western Bahr al-Ghazal: CHARLES JOLO BOBO.

Western Darfur: Eng. UMAR HARUN ABDULLAH.

Western Equatoria: Maj.-Gen. ISAIAH PAUL.

Western Kordofan: JAYLI AHMAD ASH-SHARIF.

White Nile: BADAWI AL-KHAIR IDRIS.

Legislature
NATIONAL ASSEMBLY

On 6–17 March 1996 legislative elections were held in Sudan for the first time since 1989. The new National Assembly, which replaced the transitional legislature appointed by Lt-Gen. al-Bashir in February 1992, comprised 400 seats, of which 275 were elective. The remaining 125 seats had been filled directly at a national conference in January 1996 by representatives of what were described as Sudan's 'modern forces'. Sixty of the elective seats were occupied by candidates who were unopposed. Elections were not held in 10 of the country's Southern constituencies, owing to a lack of security there. All candidates for election to the Assembly campaigned as independent of any party-political allegiance. About 5.5m. of Sudan's 10m. eligible voters were reported to have participated in the legislative elections, and in the presidential election which was held concurrently. In October 1996 deputies were appointed to eight of the 10 vacant seats representing Southern constituencies, where it had not been possible to hold elections in March. The term of the National Assembly is four years.

On 12 December 1999 President al-Bashir suspended the National Assembly.

Political Organizations

National Congress: Khartoum; successor to National Islamic Front and ruling political org.; Pres. Lt-Gen. OMAR HASSAN AHMAD AL-BASHIR.

The right to political association, subject to compliance with the law, was guaranteed in the Constitution approved by referendum in June 1998. (All political organizations had been banned following the military coup of 30 June 1989.) The registration of parties began on 6 January 1999, and by 14 February 32 parties had applied to register. These included:

Alliance of the People's Working Forces: Khartoum; Head GAAFAR MUHAMMAD NIMERI; Acting Sec.-Gen. KAMAL AD-DIN MUHAMMAD ABDULLAH.

Democratic Unionist Party (DUP): Khartoum; Leader OSMAN AL-MIRGHANI; participates in National Democratic Alliance (see below).

Free Sudanese National Party (FSNP): Khartoum; Chair. Fr PHILIP ABBAS GHABBUSH.

Islamic-Christian Solidarity: Khartoum; Founder HATIM ABDULLAH AZ-ZAKI HUSAYN.

Islamic Revival Movement: Khartoum; Founder SIDDIQ AL-HAJ AS-SIDDIQ.

Islamic Ummah Party: Khartoum; Chair. WALI AD-DIN AL-HADI AL-MAHDI.

Muslim Brotherhood: Khartoum; Islamic fundamentalist; Leader Dr HABIR NUR AD-DIN.

Nile Valley Conference: Khartoum; Founder Lt-Gen. (rtd) UMAR ZARUQ.

Popular Masses' Alliance: Khartoum; Founder FAYSAL MUHAMMAD HUSAYN.

Popular National Congress (PNC): Khartoum; f. 2000; Founder HASSAN AT-TURABI.

Socialist Popular Party: Khartoum; Founder SAYYID KHALIFAH IDRIS HABBANI.

Sudan Green Party: Khartoum; Founder Prof. ZAKARAIA BASHIR IMAM.

Sudanese Central Movement: Khartoum; Founder Dr MUHAMMAD ABU AL-QASIM HAJ HAMAD.

Sudanese National Party (SNP): Khartoum; Leader HASAN AL-MAHI; participates in the National Democratic Alliance (see below).

Umma Party (UP): Asmara, Eritrea; tel. (1) 184335; fax (1) 184158; e-mail hq@umma.org; internet www.umma.org; Mahdist party based on the Koran and Islamic traditions; Chair. Dr UMAR NUR AD-

DA'IM; Leader SADIQ AL-MAHDI; withdrew from the National Democratic Alliance (see below) in March 2000.

United Democratic Salvation Front: Khartoum; political wing of the Southern Sudan Defence Force (see below); Chair. Dr RIEK MASHAR TENY-DHURGON.

A number of opposition movements are grouped together in the Asmara-based **National Democratic Alliance (NDA)** (Chair. OSMAN AL-MIRGHANI; Sec. Gen. MUBARAK AL-MAHDI). These include the **Beja Congress**, the **Legitimate Command (LC)**, the **Sudan Alliance Forces (SAF)** (internet www.safsudan.com; f. 1994; Cmmdr-in-Chief Brig. ABD EL-AZIZ KHALID OSMAN), the **Sudan Federal Democratic Alliance (SFDA)** (f. 1994, advocates a decentralized, federal structure for Sudan; Chair. AHMAD DREIGE), the **Sudan People's Liberation Movement (SPLM)** (Leader Dr MANSUR KHALID) and its mil. wing, the **Sudan People's Liberation Army (SPLA)** (Leader Col JOHN GARANG; Sec. Gen. JAMES WANI IGGA). Other opposition groups include the **Liberation Front for Southern Sudan (LFSS)** and a rival faction to the original SPLM, the **Southern Sudan Defence Force (SSDF)** (f. 1997 from several insurgent groups, incl. the **South Sudan Independence Movement (SSIM)** and the **SPLA-United;** Leader RIEK MASHAR TENY-DHURGON).

Diplomatic Representation

EMBASSIES IN SUDAN

Algeria: St 31, New Extension, POB 80, Khartoum; tel. (11) 741954; Ambassador: SALIH BEN KOBBI.

Bulgaria: St 31, Middle Road, New Extension, POB 1690, Khartoum; tel. (11) 743414; Ambassador: T. F. MITEV.

Canada: Khartoum.

Chad: 21, St 17, New Extension, POB 1514, Khartoum; tel. (11) 742545; Ambassador: MBAILAOU BERAL MOÏSE.

China, People's Republic: 93, St 22, POB 1425, Khartoum; tel. (11) 222036; Ambassador: DENG SHAOQIN.

Congo, Democratic Republic: St 13, Block 12CE, New Extension, 23, POB 4195, Khartoum; tel. (11) 742424; Ambassador: MGBAMA MPWA.

Egypt: Al-Gamma St, POB 1126, Khartoum; tel. (11) 772836; Ambassador: MUHAMMAD ASIM IBRAHIM.

Ethiopia: 6, 11A St 3, New Extension, POB 844, Khartoum; Chargé d'affaires a.i.: Dr AWOKE AGONGFER.

France: Amarat, St 3, Plot No. 29, Block 10AE, Burri, POB 377, Khartoum; tel. (11) 225608; Ambassador: MICHEL RAIMBAUD.

Germany: Baladia St, Block No. 8DE, Plot No. 2, POB 970, Khartoum; tel. (11) 777990; fax (11) 777622; Ambassador: Dr WERNER DAUM.

Greece: Sharia al-Gamhouria, Block 5, No. 30, POB 1182, Khartoum; tel. (11) 773155; Ambassador: VASSILIS COUZOPOULOS.

Holy See: Kafouri Belgravia, POB 623, Khartoum (Apostolic Nunciature); tel. (11) 330037; fax (11) 330692; e-mail aponunkrt@email.sudanet.net; Apostolic Nuncio: Most Rev. MARCO DINO BROGI, Titular Archbishop of Città Ducale.

India: 61 Africa Rd, POB 707, Khartoum; tel. (11) 471202; fax (11) 472266; e-mail indemb@sudanet.net; Chargé d'affaires a.i.: Shri A. C. GOGNA.

Iran: House No. 8, Square 2, Mogran, Khartoum; tel. (11) 748843; Chargé d'affaires a.i.: NIMATALLAH GADIR.

Iraq: Khartoum; tel. (11) 745428; Ambassador: NADIM AL-WASSIN.

Italy: St 39, POB 793, Khartoum; tel. (11) 745326; e-mail italsd@usa.net; Ambassador: Dr MAURIZIO BATTAGLINI.

Japan: 24, Block AE, St 3, New Extension, POB 1649, Khartoum; tel. (11) 777668; fax (11) 451600; Ambassador: YOSHINORI IMAGAWA.

Jordan: 25, St 7, New Extension, Khartoum; tel. (11) 743264; Ambassador: MOHAMMED JUMA ASANA.

Kenya: POB 8242, Khartoum; tel. (11) 440386; fax (11) 452265; Ambassador: (vacant).

Korea, Republic: House 2, St 1, New Extension, POB 2414, Khartoum; tel. (11) 451136; fax (11) 452822; Ambassador: SAE DON CHANG.

Kuwait: Africa Ave, near the Tennis Club, POB 1457, Khartoum; tel. (11) 781525; Chargé d'affaires: FAISAL AL-MALIFIE.

Lebanon: Khartoum; Ambassador: NASR AJAJ BAZANA.

Libya: 50 Africa Rd, POB 2091, Khartoum; Secretary of People's Bureau: GUMMA AL-FAZANI.

Morocco: 32, St 19, New Extension, POB 2042, Khartoum; tel. (11) 743223; Ambassador: MOHAMMED KAMLICHI.

Netherlands: St 47, House No. 6, POB 391, Khartoum; tel. (11) 471200; fax 471204; Ambassador: A. H. HUITZING.

Nigeria: St 17, Sharia al-Mek Nimr, POB 1538, Khartoum; tel. (11) 779120; Ambassador: IBRAHIM KARLI.

Oman: St 1, New Extension, POB 2839, Khartoum; tel. (11) 745791; Ambassador: MOSLIM EBIN ZAIDAN AL-BARAMI.

Pakistan: House No. 94, Block 16, ar-Riyadh, POB 1178, Khartoum; tel. (11) 742518; Ambassador: DHAFRALLA SHIEK.

Poland: 73 Africa Rd, POB 902, Khartoum; tel. (11) 744248; Chargé d'affaires a.i.: WALDEMAR POPIOLEK.

Qatar: St 15, New Extension, POB 223, Khartoum; tel. (11) 742208; Chargé d'affaires a.i.: HASSAN AHMED ABDULLAH ABU HINDI.

Romania: Kassala Rd, Plot No. 172–173, Kafouri Area, POB 1494, Khartoum North; tel. (11) 613445; Chargé d'affaires a.i.: GHEORGHE GUSTEA.

Russia: B1, A10 St, New Extension, POB 1161, Khartoum; Ambassador: VALERII Y. SUKHIN.

Saudi Arabia: St 11, New Extension, Khartoum; tel. (11) 741938; Ambassador: SAYED MOHAMMED SIBRI SULIMAN.

Somalia: St 23–25, New Extension, POB 1857, Khartoum; tel. (11) 744800; Ambassador: MUHAMMAD Sheikh AHMED.

Switzerland: Amarat, Street 15, POB 1707, Khartoum; tel. (11) 451010; fax (11) 452804; Chargé d'affaires a.i.: GIANBATTISTA MONDADA.

Syria: St 3, New Extension, POB 1139, Khartoum; tel. (11) 744663; Ambassador: MOHAMMED AL-MAHAMEED.

Turkey: 31, St 29, New Extension, POB 771, Khartoum; tel. (11) 451197; fax (11) 472542; e-mail trembkh@email.sudanet.net; Ambassador: Dr ALI ENGIN OBA.

United Arab Emirates: St 3, New Extension, POB 1225, Khartoum; tel. (11) 744476; Ambassador: ABDULLAH MATAR KHAMIS.

United Kingdom: St 10, off Baladia St, POB 801, Khartoum; tel. (11) 777105; fax (11) 776457; e-mail british@sudanmail.net; Ambassador: RICHARD MAKEPEACE.

USA: Khartoum; Chargé d'affaires: DONALD TEITLEBAUM.

Yemen: St 11, New Extension, POB 1010, Khartoum; tel. (11) 743918; Ambassador: ABD AS-SALAM HUSSEIN.

Yugoslavia: St 31, 49A, POB 1180, Khartoum 1; tel. (11) 741252; Ambassador: VLADIMIR PETKOVSKI.

Judicial System

Until September 1983 the judicial system was divided into two sections, civil and Islamic, the latter dealing only with personal and family matters. In September 1983 President Nimeri replaced all existing laws with Islamic (Shari'a) law. Following the coup in April 1985, the Shari'a courts were abolished, and it was announced that the previous system of criminal courts was to be revived. In June 1986 the Prime Minister, Sadiq al-Mahdi, reaffirmed that the Shari'a law was to be abolished. It was announced in June 1987 that a new legal code, based on a 'Sudanese legal heritage', was to be introduced. In July 1989 the military Government established special courts to investigate violations of emergency laws concerning corruption. It was announced in June 1991 that these courts were to be incorporated in the general court administration. Islamic law was reintroduced in March 1991, but was not applied in the Southern states of Equatoria, Bahr al-Ghazal and Upper Nile.

Chief Justice: HAFEZ ASH-SHEIKH AZ-ZAKI.

Religion

The majority of the Northern Sudanese population are Muslims, while in the South the population are principally Christians or animists.

ISLAM

Islam is the state religion. Sudanese Islam has a strong Sufi element, and is estimated to have more than 15m. adherents.

CHRISTIANITY

Sudan Council of Churches: Inter-Church House, St 35, New Extension, POB 469, Khartoum; tel. (11) 742859; f. 1967; 12 mem. churches; Chair. Most Rev. PAOLINO LUKUDU LORO (Roman Catholic Archbishop of Juba); Gen. Sec. Rev. CLEMENT H. JANDA.

Roman Catholic Church

Latin Rite

Sudan comprises two archdioceses and seven dioceses. At the end of 1998 the estimated number of adherents represented about 9% of the total population.

Sudan Catholic Bishops' Conference: General Secretariat, POB 6011, Khartoum; tel. (11) 2250759; fax (11) 703518; f. 1971; Pres. Most Rev. PAOLINO LUKUDU LORO, Archbishop of Juba.

Archbishop of Juba: Most Rev. PAOLINO LUKUDU LORO, Catholic Church, POB 32, Juba, Equatoria State; tel. 20388; fax 20755.

Archbishop of Khartoum: Most Rev. GABRIEL ZUBEIR WAKO, Catholic Church, POB 49, Khartoum; tel. (11) 782174; fax (11) 783518.

Maronite Rite

Maronite Church in Sudan: POB 244, Khartoum; Rev. Fr YOU-SEPH NEAMA.

Melkite Rite

Patriarchal Vicariate of Egypt and Sudan: Patriarcat Grec-Melkite Catholique, 16 rue Daher, 11271 Cairo, Egypt; tel. (2) 5905790; Protosyncellus: Most Rev. PAUL ANTAKI, Titular Archbishop of Nubia; Vicar in Sudan: Fr GEORGE BANNA, POB 766, Khartoum; tel. (11) 776466.

Syrian Rite

Syrian Church in Sudan: Under the jurisdiction of the Patriarch of Antioch; Protosyncellus: Rt Rev. JOSEPH HANNOUCHE, Bishop of Cairo.

Orthodox Churches

Coptic Orthodox Church

Metropolitan of Khartoum, Southern Sudan and Uganda: Rt Rev. ANBA DANIAL, POB 4, Khartoum; tel. (11) 770646; fax (11) 785646; e-mail metaous@email-sudan.net.

Bishop of Atbara, Omdurman and Northern Sudan: Rt Rev. ANBA SARABAMON, POB 628, Omdurman; tel. (11) 550423; fax (11) 556973.

Greek Orthodox Church: POB 47, Khartoum; tel. (11) 772973; Metropolitan of Nubia: Archbishop DIONYSSIOS HADZIVASSILIOU.

The Ethiopian Orthodox Church is also active.

The Anglican Communion

Anglicans are adherents of the (Episcopal) Church of the Province of the Sudan. The Province, with 24 dioceses and about 1m. adherents, was established in 1976.

Archbishop in Sudan: Most Rev. JOSEPH BIRINGI, POB 110, Juba; tel. (11) 20065.

Other Christian Churches

Evangelical Church: POB 57, Khartoum; c. 1,500 mems; administers schools, literature centre and training centre; Chair Rev. RADI ELIAS.

Presbyterian Church: POB 40, Malakal; autonomous since 1956; 67,000 mems (1985); Gen. Sec. Rev. THOMAS MALUIT.

Society for International Ministries (SIM): Dir R. WELLING, POB 220, Khartoum; tel. (11) 472790; fax (11) 467213; e-mail postmast@simkhar.sim.org; f. 1937.

The Africa Inland Church, the Sudan Interior Church and the Sudanese Church of Christ are also active.

The Press

DAILIES

Press censorship was imposed following the 1989 coup.

Abbar al-Youm: Khartoum; tel. (11) 779396; daily; Editor AHMED AL-BALAL AT-TAYEB.

Al-Anbaa: Khartoum; tel. (11) 466523; f. 1998; Editor-in-Chief NAJIB ADAM QAMAR AD-DIN.

Al-Nasr: Khartoum; tel. (11) 772494; Editor Col YOUNIS MAHMOUD.

Ar-Rai al-Akhar: Khartoum; tel. (11) 777934; daily; Editor MOHI AD-DIN TITTAWI.

Ar-Rai al-Amm: Khartoum; tel. (11) 778182; e-mail info@rayaam.net; internet www.rayaam.net; daily; Editor SALAH MUHAMMAD IBRAHIM.

Sudan Standard: Ministry of Culture and Information, POB 2651, Khartoum; daily; English.

Al-Wan: Khartoum; tel. (11) 775036; e-mail alwaan@cybergates.net; internet www.alwaan.com/alwaan; daily; independent; pro-government; Editor HOUSSEN KHOGALI.

PERIODICALS

Al-Guwwat al-Musallaha (The Armed Forces): Khartoum; f.1969; publs a weekly newspaper and monthly magazine for the armed forces; Editor-in-Chief Maj. MAHMOUD GALANDER; circ. 7,500.

New Horizon: POB 2651, Khartoum; tel. (11) 777913; f. 1976; publ. by the Sudan House for Printing and Publishing; weekly; English; political and economic affairs, development, home and international news; Editor AS-SIR HASSAN FADL; circ. 7,000.

Sudanow: POB 2651, Khartoum; tel. (11) 777913; f. 1976; publ. by the Sudan House for Printing and Publishing; monthly; English; political and economic affairs, arts, social affairs and diversions; Editor-in-Chief AHMED KAMAL ED-DIN; circ. 10,000.

NEWS AGENCIES

Sudan News Agency (SUNA): Sharia al-Gamhouria, POB 1506, Khartoum; tel. (11) 775770; e-mail suna@sudanet.net; internet www.sudanet.net/suna.htm; Dir-Gen. ALI ABD AR-RAHMAN AN-NUMAYRI.

Sudanese Press Agency: Khartoum; f. 1985; owned by journalists.

Foreign Bureaux

Middle East News Agency (MENA) (Egypt): Dalala Bldg, POB 740, Khartoum.

Xinhua (New China) News Agency (People's Republic of China): No. 100, 12 The Sq., Riad Town, POB 2229, Khartoum; tel. (11) 224174; Correspondent SUN XIAOKE.

The Iraqi News Agency and the Agence Arabe Syrienne d'Information (Syria) also have bureaux in Khartoum.

Publishers

Ahmad Abd ar-Rahman at-Tikeine: POB 299, Port Sudan.

Al-Ayyam Press Co Ltd: POB 363, Aboulela Bldg, United Nations Sq., Khartoum; f. 1953; general fiction and non-fiction, arts, poetry, reference, newspapers, magazines; Man. Dir BESHIR MUHAMMAD SAID.

As-Sahafa Publishing and Printing House: POB 1228, Khartoum; f. 1961; newspapers, pamphlets, fiction and govt publs.

As-Salam Co Ltd: POB 944, Khartoum.

Claudios S. Fellas: POB 641, Khartoum.

Khartoum University Press: POB 321, Khartoum; tel. (11) 776653; f. 1964; academic, general and educational in Arabic and English; Man. Dir ALI EL-MAK.

Government Publishing House

El-Asma Printing Press: POB 38, Khartoum.

Broadcasting and Communications

TELECOMMUNICATIONS

A mobile telephone network for Khartoum State was inaugurated in 1997.

Ministry of Roads and Communications: (see Ministries, above); regulatory body; Sec.-Gen. Eng. AWAD E. WIDAA.

Posts and Telegraphs Public Corporation: Khartoum; tel. (11) 770000; fax (11) 772888; regulatory body; Dir-Gen. AHMAD AT-TIJANI ALALLIM.

Sudan Telecom Co (Sudatel): POB 11155, Khartoum; tel. (11) 773930; fax (11) 451111; service provider for Sudan; Gen. Man. ABD AL-AZIZ OSMAN.

BROADCASTING

Radio

Sudan National Broadcasting Corporation: POB 572, Omdurman; tel. (11) 552100; state-controlled service broadcasting daily in Arabic, English, French and Swahili; Dir-Gen. SALAH AD-DIN AL-FADHIL USUD.

Voice of Sudan: e-mail sudanvoice@umma.arg; active since 1995; run by the National Democratic Alliance; Arabic and English.

Television

An earth satellite station operated on 36 channels at Umm Haraz has much improved Sudan's telecommunication links. A nation-wide satellite network is being established with 14 earth stations in the provinces. There are regional stations at Gezira (Central Region) and Atbara (Northern Region).

Sudan Television: POB 1094, Omdurman; tel. 550022; f. 1962; state-controlled; 60 hours of programmes per week; Head of Directorate HADID AS-SIRA.

Finance

(cap. = capital; res = reserves; dep. = deposits;
m. = million; brs = branches; amounts in Sudanese pounds,
unless otherwise indicated)

BANKING

All domestic banks are controlled by the Bank of Sudan. Foreign banks were permitted to resume operations in 1976. In December 1985 the government banned the establishment of any further banks. It was announced in December 1990 that Sudan's banking system was to be reorganized to accord with Islamic principles. In May 2000 the Bank of Sudan issued new policy guidelines under which Sudan's banks were to merge into six banking groups to improve their financial strength and international competitiveness; the mergers should be fully implemented by 2002.

Central Bank

Bank of Sudan: Gamaa Ave, POB 313, Khartoum; tel. (11) 778064; fax (11) 780273; e-mail cbank@sudanet.net; f. 1960; bank of issue; cap. and res 496,057m., dep. 324,337,523m. (Dec. 1997); Gov. MAHDI EL-FAKI EL-SHEIKH; 9 brs.

Commercial Banks

Al-Baraka Bank: Al-Baraka Tower, Sharia al-Kasr, POB 3583, Khartoum; tel. (11) 780688; fax (11) 778948; internet www.albaraka .com; f. 1984; investment and export promotion; cap. and res 445.8m., total assets 63,613.4m. (Dec. 1998); Chair. MUSA ABD AL-AZIZ SHADADA; 33 brs.

Al-Shamal Islamic Bank: POB 10036, 11111 Khartoum; tel. (11) 773111; fax (11) 773585; e-mail shib@sudanet.net; f. 1990; cap. 494.2m., res 704.9m., dep. 11,692m. (Dec. 1999); Chair. ADIL ABDEL JALEEL BATARJI; Gen. Man. MOHAMMED SHEIKH MOHAMMED; 15 brs.

Bank of Khartoum Group: 8 Gamhouria Ave, POB 1008, Khartoum; tel. (11) 772880; fax (11) 781120; f. 1913; absorbed National Export/Import Bank and Unity Bank in 1993; cap. and res 4,457.7m., total assets 121,308.2m. (1995); Chair. and Gen. Man. OMAR TAHA ABU SAMRA; 118 brs.

National Bank of Sudan: Kronfli Bldg, Al-Qasr Ave, POB 1183, Khartoum; tel. (11) 778154; fax (11) 779497; f. 1982; cap. 39.2m. (Dec. 1991); Chair. BASHIR AL-BAKRI; 13 brs in Sudan, 2 abroad.

Omdurman National Bank: POB 11522, Khartoum; tel. (11) 770400; fax (11) 770392; f. 1993; cap. 5,000m., res 3,842m., dep. 107,417m. (Dec. 1998); Chair. HASSAN YAHYA; 16 brs.

Sudan Commercial Bank: Al-Qasr Ave, POB 1116, Khartoum; tel. (11) 779836; fax (11) 774194; e-mail scb.ho@sudanet.net; f. 1960; cap. and res 1,554.1m., total assets 36,951.9m. (Dec. 1996); Chair. ET-TAYB ELSOBEID BADR; 19 brs.

Sudanese French Bank: Zubair Basha St, POB 2775, Khartoum; tel. (11) 776542; fax (11) 771740; e-mail sfbankb@sudanet.net; f. 1978 as Sudanese Investment Bank; cap. 1,013m., res 21,414m., dep. 148,624m. (Dec. 1998); Chair. Dr ABBAS MUSTAFA OSMAN; 19 brs.

Tadamon Islamic Bank: Baladia Ave, POB 3154, Khartoum; tel. (11) 771505; fax (11) 773840; e-mail tadamon@sudanmail.net; f. 1981; cap. and res 14,677m., total assets 302,834m. (Dec. 1998); Pres. ET-TIGANI HASSAN HILAL; 20 brs.

Foreign Banks

Blue Nile Bank Ltd: Zubeir Pasha Ave, POB 984, Khartoum; tel. (11) 778925; f. 1983; cap. 31.9m., total assets 197.2m. (Dec. 1991); jtly controlled by the Govts of Sudan and the Repub. of Korea; Chair. CHAN SUP LEE.

Faisal Islamic Bank (Sudan) (Saudi Arabia): Ali Abdel Latif Ave, POB 2415, Khartoum; tel. (11) 781848; fax (11) 780193; f. 1977; cap. 117.7m., total assets 16,490m. (Dec. 1993); Chair. Prince MUHAMMAD AL-FAISAL AS-SAUD.

Habib Bank (Pakistan): Baladia St, POB 8246, Khartoum; tel. (11) 781497; fax (11) 781497; f. 1982; cap. and res 13.8m., total assets 27.3m. (Dec. 1987); Gen. Man. BAZ MUHAMMAD KHAN.

Mashreq Bank PSC (United Arab Emirates): Baladia St, POB 371, Khartoum; tel. (11) 772969; fax (11) 772743; Man. MUHAMMAD KHEDIR AL-ARAKI.

National Bank of Abu Dhabi (United Arab Emirates): Atbara St, POB 2465, Khartoum; tel. (11) 774870; f. 1976; cap. and res 16.9m., total assets 12.5m. (Dec. 1987); Man. GAAFAR OSMAN.

Saudi Sudanese Bank: Baladia St, POB 1773, Khartoum; tel. (11) 776700; fax (11) 81836; f. 1986; Saudi Arabian shareholders have a 60% interest, Sudanese shareholders 40%; cap. and res 3,276.5m., dep. 30,713.4m. (Dec. 1996); Chair. Sheikh MAHFOUZ SALIM BIN MAH-FOUZ.

Development Banks

Agricultural Bank of Sudan: POB 1363, Khartoum; tel. (11) 779410; fax (11) 778296; f. 1957; cap. and res 5,741m., total assets 106,098m. (Dec. 1997); provides finance for agricultural projects; Chair. and Gen. Man. HAGO GASM AS-SEED; 40 brs.

Islamic Co-operative Development Bank (ICDB): POB 62, Khartoum; tel. (11) 780223; fax (11) 777715; f. 1983; cap. and res 4,162m., total assets 53,077m. (Dec. 1998); Chair. USTAZE ABDELGLIL AN-NAZER ELKARORI; 6 brs.

Nilein Industrial Development Bank: United Nations Sq., POB 1722, Khartoum; tel. (11) 771984; fax (11) 780776; e-mail nidbg@ sudan.net; internet www.nidb.com; f. 1993 by merger; provides tech. and financial assistance for private-sector industrial projects and acquires shares in industrial enterprises; cap. and res 1,210m. S. dinars, total assets 1,996m. S. dinars (Dec. 1999); Chair. Dr SABIR MUHAMMAD EL-HASSAN; Man. Dir IBRAHIM ADAM HABIB; 40 brs.

NIMA Development and Investment Bank: Hashim Hago Bldg, As-Suk al-Arabi, POB 665, Khartoum; tel. (11) 779496; fax (11) 781854; f. 1982 as National Devt Bank, name changed as above 1998; 90%-owned by NIMA Groupe, 10% private shareholders; finances or co-finances economic and social development projects; cap. 4,000m., res 106m. (Dec. 1998); Dir-Gen. SALIM EL-SAFI HUGIR; 6 brs.

Sudanese Estates Bank: Baladia St, POB 309, Khartoum; tel. (11) 777917; fax (11) 779465; f. 1967; mortgage bank financing private-sector urban housing development; cap. and res 1,700m., total assets 9,500m. (Dec. 1994); Chair. Eng. MUHAMMAD ALI EL-AMIN; 6 brs.

Sudanese Saving Bank: POB 159, Khartoum; tel. (11) 772000; f. 1974; cap. 10m., total assets 1,613.4m. (Dec. 1991); Chair. MANSOUR AHMAD ESH-SHEIKH; 22 brs.

STOCK EXCHANGE

Sudanese Stock Exchange: Al-Baraka Tower, 5th Floor, POB 10835, Khartoum; tel. (11) 776235; fax (11) 776134; f. 1995; Chair. HAMZA MOHAMED JENAWI; 27 mems.

INSURANCE

African Insurance Co (Sudan) Ltd: Muhammad Hussein Bldg, Al-Baladiya Ave, POB 149, Khartoum; f. 1977; fire, accident, marine and motor; Gen. Man. AN-NOMAN AS-SANUSI.

Blue Nile Insurance Co (Sudan) Ltd: POB 2215, Khartoum; Gen. Man. MUHAMMAD AL-AMIN MIRGHANI.

General Insurance Co (Sudan) Ltd: El-Mek Nimr St, POB 1555, Khartoum; tel. (11) 780616; fax (11) 772122; f. 1961; Gen. Man. ABD AL-FATTAH MUHAMMAD SIYAM.

Islamic Insurance Co Ltd: Al-Faiha Commercial Bldg, POB 2776, Khartoum; tel. (11) 772656; f. 1979; all classes.

Khartoum Insurance Co Ltd: POB 737, Khartoum; tel. (11) 778647; f. 1953; Chair. MUDAWI M. AHMAD; Gen. Man. ABD AL-MENIM AL-HADARI.

Middle East Insurance Co Ltd: POB 3070, Khartoum; tel. (11) 772202; f. 1981; fire, marine, motor, general liability; Chair. AHMAD I. MALIK; Gen. Man. ALI AL-FADL.

Sudanese Insurance and Reinsurance Co Ltd: Sharia al-Gamhouria, Nasr Sq., POB 2332, Khartoum; tel. (11) 770812; f. 1967; Gen. Man. IZZ AD-DIN AS-SAID MUHAMMAD.

United Insurance Co (Sudan) Ltd: Makkawi Bldg, Sharia al-Gamhouria, POB 318, Khartoum; tel. (11) 776630; fax (11) 770783; f. 1968; Dir-Gen. MUHAMMAD ABDEEN BABIKER.

Trade and Industry

GOVERNMENT AGENCIES

Agricultural Research Corporation: POB 126, Wadi Medani; tel. (511) 42226; fax (511) 43213; e-mail arcsudan@sudanet .net; f. 1967; Dir-Gen. Prof. SALIH HUSSEIN SALIH.

Animal Production Public Corporation: POB 624, Khartoum; tel. (11) 778555; Gen. Man. Dr FOUAD RAMADAN HAMID.

General Petroleum Corporation: POB 2986, Khartoum; tel. (11) 771554; f. 1976; Chair. Dr OSMAN ABDULWAHAB; Dir-Gen. Dr ABD ER-RAHMAN OSMAN ABD ER-RAHMAN.

Gum Arabic Co: POB 857, Khartoum; tel. (11) 777288; fax (11) 451336; f. 1969; Chair. OMER EL-MUBARAK ABU ZEID; Gen. Man. SULAYMAN MUHAMMAD AHMAD.

Industrial Production Corporation: POB 1034, Khartoum; tel. (11) 771278; Chair. OMER TAHA ABU SAMRA; Dir-Gen. OSMAN TAMMAM; incorporates:

    Cement and Building Materials Sector Co-ordination Office: POB 2241, Khartoum; tel. (11) 774269; Dir T. M. KHOGALI.

    Food Industries Corporation: POB 2341, Khartoum; tel. (11) 775463; Dir MUHAMMAD AL-GHALI SULIMAN.

    Leather Trading and Manufacturing Co Ltd: POB 1639, Khartoum; tel. (11) 778187; f. 1986; Man. Dir IBRAHIM SALIH ALI.

Oil Corporation: POB 64, Khartoum North; tel. (11) 332044; Gen. Man. BUKHARI MAHMOUD BUKHARI.

Spinning and Weaving General Co Ltd: POB 765, Khartoum; tel. (11) 774306; f. 1975; Dir MUHAMMAD SALIH MUHAMMAD ABDALLAH.

Sudan Tea Co: POB 1219, Khartoum; tel. (11) 781261.

Sudanese Mining Corporation: POB 1034, Khartoum; tel. (11) 770840; f. 1975; Dir IBRAHIM MUDAWI BABIKER.

Sugar and Distilling Industry Corporation: POB 511, Khartoum; tel. (11) 778417; Man. MIRGHANI AHMAD BABIKER.

Mechanized Farming Corporation: POB 2482, Khartoum; Man. Dir AWAD AL-KARIM AL-YASS.

National Cotton and Trade Co Ltd: POB 1552, Khartoum; tel. (11) 80040; f. 1970; Chair. ABD EL-ATI A. MEKKI; Man. Dir ABD AR-RAHMAN A. MONIEM; Gen. Man. ZUBAIR MUHAMMAD AL-BASHIR.

Port Sudan Cotton Trade Co Ltd: POB 590, Port Sudan; POB 590, Khartoum; Gen. Man. SAID MUHAMMAD ADAM.

Public Agricultural Production Corporation: POB 538, Khartoum; Chair. and Man. Dir ABDALLAH BAYOUMO; Sec. SAAD AD-DIN MUHAMMAD ALI.

Public Corporation for Building and Construction: POB 2110, Khartoum; tel. (11) 774544; Dir NAIM AD-DIN.

Public Corporation for Irrigation and Excavations: POB 619, Khartoum; tel. (11) 780167; Gen. Sec. OSMAN AN-NUR.

Public Corporation for Oil Products and Pipelines: POB 1704, Khartoum; tel. (11) 778290; Gen. Man. ABD AR-RAHMAN SULIMAN.

Rahad Corporation: POB 2523, Khartoum; tel. (11) 775175; financed by the World Bank, Kuwait and the USA; by 1983 300,000 ha had been irrigated and 70,000 people settled in 15,000 tenancies; Man. Dir HASSAN SAAD ABDALLA.

The State Trading Corporation: POB 211, Khartoum; tel. (11) 778555; Chair. E. R. M. TOM.

Automobile Corporation: POB 221, Khartoum; tel. (11) 778555; importer of vehicles and spare parts; Gen. Man. DAFALLA AHMAD SIDDIQ.

Engineering Equipment Corporation: POB 97, Khartoum; tel. (11) 773731; importers and distributors of agricultural, engineering and electronic equipment; Gen. Man. IZZ AD-DIN HAMID.

Gezira Trade and Services Co: POB 215, Khartoum; tel. (11) 772687; fax (11) 779060; f. 1980; importer of agricultural machinery, spare parts, electrical and office equipment, foodstuffs, clothes and footwear; exporter of oilseeds, grains, hides and skins and livestock; provides shipping insurance and warehousing services; agents for Lloyds and P and I Club.

Khartoum Commercial and Shipping Co: POB 221, Khartoum; tel. (11) 778555; import, export and shipping services, insurance and manufacturing; Gen. Man. IDRIS M. SALIH.

Silos and Storage Corporation: POB 1183, Khartoum; stores and handles agricultural products; Gen. Man. AHMAD AT-TAIEB HARHOOF.

Sudan Cotton Co Ltd: POB 1672, Khartoum; tel. (11) 771567; fax (11) 770703; e-mail sccl@sudanet.net; f. 1970; exports raw cotton; Chair. ABBAS ABD AL-BAGI HAMMAD; Dir-Gen. ABDIN M. ALI.

Sudan Gezira Board: POB 884, HQ Barakat Wadi Medani, Gezira Province; tel. 2412; Sales Office, POB 884, Khartoum; tel. 740145; responsible for Sudan's main cotton-producing area; the Gezira scheme is a partnership between the Govt, the tenants and the board. The Govt provides the land and is responsible for irrigation. Tenants pay a land and water charge and receive the work proceeds. The Board provides agricultural services at cost, technical supervision and execution of govt agricultural policies relating to the scheme. Tenants pay a percentage of their proceeds to the Social Development Fund. The total potential cultivable area of the Gezira scheme is c. 850,000 ha and the total area under systematic irrigation is c. 730,000 ha. In addition to cotton, groundnuts, sorghum, wheat, rice, pulses and vegetables are grown for the benefit of tenant farmers; Man. Dir Prof. FATHI MUHAMMAD KHALIFA.

Sudan Oilseeds Co Ltd: Parliament Ave, POB 167, Khartoum; tel. (11) 780120; f. 1974; 58% state-owned; exporter of oilseeds (groundnuts, sesame seeds and castor beans); importer of foodstuffs and other goods; Chair. SADIQ KARAR AT-TAYEB; Gen. Man. KAMAL ABD AL-HALIM.

DEVELOPMENT CORPORATIONS

Sudan Development Corporation (SDC): 21 al-Amarat, POB 710, Khartoum; tel. (11) 472151; fax (11) 472148; f. 1974 to promote and co-finance development projects with special emphasis on projects in the agricultural, agri-business, and industrial sectors; cap. p.u. US $200m.; Man. Dir Dr MUHAMMAD KHIER AHMED EL-ZUBIER; affiliates:

Sudan Rural Development Co Ltd (SRDC): POB 2190, Khartoum; tel. (11) 773855; fax (11) 773235; e-mail srdfc@hotmail;

f. 1980; SDC has 27% shareholding; cap. p.u. US $20m.; Gen. Man. EL-AWAD ABDALLA H. HIJAZI (designate).

Sudan Rural Development Finance Co (SRDFC): POB 2190, Khartoum; tel. (11) 773855; fax (11) 773235; f. 1980; Gen. Man. OMRAN MUHAMMAD ALI.

CHAMBER OF COMMERCE

Sudan Chamber of Commerce: POB 81, Khartoum; tel. (11) 772346; f. 1908; Pres. SAAD ABOU AL-ELA; Sec.-Gen. HAROUN AL-AWAD.

INDUSTRIAL ASSOCIATION

Sudanese Industries Association: Africa St, POB 2565, Khartoum; tel. (11) 773151; f. 1974; Chair. FATH AR-RAHMAN AL-BASHIR; Exec. Dir A. IZZ AL-ARAB YOUSUF.

UTILITIES

Public Electricity and Water Corporation: POB 1380, Khartoum; Dir Dr YASIN AL-HAJ ABDIN.

CO-OPERATIVE SOCIETIES

There are about 600 co-operative societies, of which 570 are officially registered.

Central Co-operative Union: POB 2492, Khartoum; tel. (11) 780624; largest co-operative union operating in 15 provinces.

MAJOR COMPANIES

The following are among the larger companies, either in terms of capital investment or employment.

Aboulela Cotton Ginning Co Ltd: POB 121, Khartoum; tel. (11) 770020; cotton mills.

AGIP (Sudan) Ltd: POB 1155, Khartoum; tel. (11) 780253; f. 1959; cap. £S15.8m.; distribution of petroleum products; Pres. E. CAMPOLI; Gen. Man. G. BARONIO; 187 employees.

Bata (Sudan) Ltd: POB 88, Khartoum; tel. (11) 732240; f. 1950; cap. £S1.7m.; mfrs and distributors of footwear; Man. Dir A. A. ALI; 1,065 employees.

The Blue Nile Brewery: POB 1408, Khartoum; f. 1954; cap. £S734,150; brewing, bottling and distribution of beer; Man. Dirs IBRAHIM ELYAS, HUSSEIN MUHAMMAD KEMAL, OMER AZ-ZEIN SAGAYROUN; 336 employees.

The Central Desert Mining Co Ltd: POB 20, Port Sudan; f. 1946; cap. £S150,000; prospecting for and mining of gold, manganese and iron ore; Dirs ABD AL-HADI AHMAD BASHIR, ABOU-BAKR SAID BASHIR; 274 employees.

Cotton Textile Mills Ltd: POB 203, Khartoum; tel. (11) 731414; f. 1976; yarns and fabrics; Man. ABDEL MAROUF ZEINELABDEEN.

Kenana Sugar Co Ltd: POB 2632, Khartoum; tel. (11) 224703; f. 1971; financed by Sudan govt and other Arab nations; 18,000 employees; Man. Dir OSMAN ABDULLAH AN-NAZIR.

Maxim Co Ltd: POB 1785, Khartoum; tel. (11) 780904; telex (11) 22360; iron and steel foundries.

TRADE UNIONS

All trade union activity was banned following the 1989 coup. The following organizations were active prior to that date.

Federations

Sudan Workers Trade Unions Federation (SWTUF): POB 2258, Khartoum; tel. (11) 777463; includes 42 trade unions representing c. 1.75m. public-service and private-sector workers; affiliated to the Int. Confed. of Arab Trade Unions and the Org. of African Trade Union Unity; Pres. MUHAMMAD OSMAN GAMA; Gen. Sec. YOUSUF ABU SHAMA HAMED.

Sudanese Federation of Employees and Professionals Trade Unions: POB 2398, Khartoum; tel. (11) 773818; f. 1975; includes 54 trade unions representing 250,000 mems; Pres. IBRAHIM AWADALLAH; Sec.-Gen. KAMAL AD-DIN MUHAMMAD ABDALLAH.

Transport

RAILWAYS

The total length of railway in operation in 1997 was 4,784 route-km. The main line runs from Wadi Halfa, on the Egyptian border, to al-Obeid, via Khartoum. Lines from Atbara and Sinnar connect with Port Sudan. There are lines from Sinnar to Damazine on the Blue Nile (227 km) and from Aradeiba to Nyala in the south-western province of Darfur (689 km), with a 445-km branch line from Babanousa to Wau in Bahr al-Ghazal province.

Sudan Railways Corporation: POB 65, Atbara; tel. 2000; f. 1875; Gen. Man. OMAR MUHAMMAD NUR.

ROADS

Roads in northern Sudan, other than town roads, are only cleared tracks and often impassable immediately after rain. Motor traffic on roads in the former Upper Nile province is limited to the drier months of January–May. There are several good gravelled roads in Equatoria and Bahr al-Ghazal provinces which are passable all the year, but in these districts some of the minor roads become impassable after rain. Rehabilitation of communications in southern Sudan is hampered by the continuing hostilities in the area.

Over 48,000 km of tracks are classed as 'motorable'; there were 3,160 km of main roads and 739 km of secondary roads in 1985. A 1,190-km tarmac road linking the capital with Port Sudan was completed during 1980. In 1996, according to World Bank estimates, some 36.3% of Sudan's roads were paved. By 1997 a 270-km road linking Jaili with Atbara had been completed, as part of a scheme to provide an alternative route from Khartoum to the coast.

National Transport Corporation: POB 723, Khartoum; Gen. Man. MOHI AD-DIN HASSAN MUHAMMAD NUR.

Public Corporation for Roads and Bridges: POB 756, Khartoum; tel. (11) 770794; f. 1976; Chair. ABD AR-RAHMAN HABOUD; Dir-Gen. ABDOU MUHAMMAD ABDOU.

INLAND WATERWAYS

The total length of navigable waterways served by passenger and freight services is 4,068 km, of which approximately 1,723 km is open all year. From the Egyptian border to Wadi Halfa and Khartoum navigation is limited by cataracts to short stretches but the White Nile from Khartoum to Juba is almost always navigable.

River Transport Corporation (RTC): POB 284, Khartoum North; operates 2,500 route-km of steamers on the Nile; Chair. ALI AMIR TAHA.

River Navigation Corporation: Khartoum; f. 1970; jtly owned by Govts of Egypt and Sudan; operates services between Aswan and Wadi Halfa.

SHIPPING

Port Sudan, on the Red Sea, 784 km from Khartoum, and Suakin, are the only commercial seaports.

Axis Trading Co Ltd: POB 1574, Khartoum; tel. (11) 775875; f. 1967; Chair. H. A. M. SULIMAN.

Red Sea Shipping Corporation: POB 116, Khartoum; tel. (11) 777688; Gen. Man. OSMAN AMIN.

Sea Ports Corporation: Port Sudan; tel. 2910; f. 1906; Gen. Man. MUHAMMAD TAHIR AILA.

Sudan Shipping Line Ltd: POB 426, Port Sudan; tel. 2655; and POB 1731, Khartoum; tel. (11) 780017; f. 1960; 10 vessels totalling 54,277 dwt operating between the Red Sea and western Mediterranean, northern Europe and United Kingdom; Chair. ISMAIL BAKHEIT; Gen. Man. SALAH AD-DIN OMER AL-AZIZ.

United African Shipping Co: POB 339, Khartoum; tel. (11) 780967; Gen. Man. MUHAMMAD TAHA AL-GINDI.

CIVIL AVIATION

Civil Aviation Authority: Khartoum; tel. (11) 772264; Dir-Gen. Brig. MAHGOUB MUHAMMAD MAHDI.

Air West Express: POB 10217, Khartoum; tel. (11) 452503; fax (11) 451703; f. 1992; passenger and freight services to destinations in Africa; Chair. SAIF M. S. OMER.

Azza Transport: POB 11586, Khartoum; tel. (11) 779717; fax (11) 770408; f. 1993; charter and dedicated freight; Man. Dir Dr GIBRIL I. MOHAMED.

Sudan Airways Co Ltd: POB 253, SDC Bldg Complex, Amarat St 19, Khartoum; tel. (11) 747953; fax (11) 747978; f. 1947; internal flights and international services to Africa, the Middle East and Europe; Chair. Col SALIH AD-DIN MUHAMMAD AHMAD KARRAR.

Sudanese Aeronautical Services (SASCO): POB 8260, El Amarat, Khartoum; tel. (11) 7463362; fax (11) 4433362; fmrly Sasco Air Charter; chartered services; Chair. M. M. NUR.

Trans Arabian Air Transport (TAAT): POB 1461, Africa Street, Khartoum; tel. (11) 451568; fax (11) 451544; f. 1983; dedicated freight; services to Africa, Europe and Middle East; Man. Dir Capt. EL-FATI ABDIN.

Tourism

Public Corporation of Tourism and Hotels: POB 7104, Khartoum; tel. (11) 781764; f. 1977; Dir-Gen. Maj.-Gen. EL-KHATIM MUHAMMAD FADL.

Defence

In August 1999 the armed forces comprised: army an estimated 90,000, including an estimated 20,000 conscripts, navy an estimated 1,700, air force 3,000. A paramilitary Popular Defence Force included 15,000 active members and 85,000 reserves. Military service is compulsory for males aged 18–30 years and lasts for up to 36 months.

Defence Expenditure: Budgeted at US $430m. for 1999.

Commander-in-Chief of the People's Armed Forces: Lt-Gen. OMAR HASSAN AHMAD AL-BASHIR.

Education

The government provides free primary education from the ages of six to 13 years. Secondary education begins at 14 years of age and lasts for up to three years. The average rate of illiteracy in the population aged 15 years and over was estimated by UNESCO at 49.2% (males 36.5%; females 61.7%) in 1995, compared with 67.6% (males 55.5%; females 79.0%) in 1983. In 1996 the total enrolment at primary and secondary schools was equivalent to 44% of children in the appropriate age-groups (47% of boys; 40% of girls). About 15% of current government expenditure in 1985 was for primary and secondary education. Pupils from secondary schools are accepted at the University of Khartoum, subject to their reaching the necessary standards. (The University of Khartoum was closed in January 1997 to allow students to join the armed forces.) The Khartoum branch of Cairo University was appropriated and renamed Nilayn University by the Sudanese government in 1993. There are three universities at Omdurman. Omdurman Islamic University; Omdurman Ahlia University; and Ahfad University for Women. New universities were opened at Juba and Wadi Medani (University of Gezira) in 1977. There is also a University of Science and Technology in Khartoum.

Bibliography

Abdel-Rahim, M. *Imperialism and Nationalism in the Sudan: A Study in Constitutional and Political Developments 1899–1956.* Oxford University Press, 1969.

Abdel-Rahim, M., et al. *Sudan since Independence.* London, Gower, 1986.

Africa Watch. *War in South Sudan: The Civilian Toll.* New York, Africa Watch, 1993.

African Rights. *Facing Genocide: The Nuba of Sudan.* London, African Rights, 1995.

Albino, O. *The Sudan: A Southern Viewpoint.* London, Oxford University Press, 1970.

Alier, A. *Southern Sudan: Too Many Agreements Dishonoured.* Exeter, Ithaca Press, 1990.

Amnesty International. *The Ravages of War: Political Killings and Humanitarian Disaster.* New York, Amnesty International, 1993.

An-Náim, A.A., and Kok, P.N. *Fundamentalism and Militarism: A Report on the Root Causes of Human Rights Violations in the Sudan.* New York, The Fund for Peace, 1991.

Arkell, A. J. *History of Sudan from Earliest Times to 1821.* 2nd Edn. London, Athlone Press, 1961.

Barbour, K. M. *The Republic of the Sudan: A Regional Geography.* University of London Press, 1961.

Beasley, I., and Starkey, J. (Eds). *Before the Winds Change: Peoples, Places and Education in the Sudan.* Oxford, Oxford University Press, 1991.

Beshir, M. O. *The Southern Sudan: Background to Conflict.* C. Hurst, London, 1968, New York, Praeger, 1968.

Revolution and Nationalism in the Sudan. New York, Barnes and Noble, 1974.

(Ed.) *Sudan: Aid and External Relations, Selected Essays.* University of Khartoum, Graduate College Publications No. 9, 1984.

Brown, R. P. C. *Public Debt and Private Wealth: Debt, Capital Flight and the IMF in Sudan.* Basingstoke, Macmillan (in association with the Institute of Social Studies), 1992.

Burr, J. M., and Collins, R. O. *Requiem for the Sudan: War, Drought and Disaster Relief on the Nile.* Boulder, CO, Westview Press, 1995.

Collins, R. O. *Shadows in the Grass: Britain in the Southern Sudan 1918–1956.* Yale University Press, 1983.

Craig, G. M. (Ed.) *Agriculture of the Sudan.* Oxford, Oxford University Press, 1991.

Daly, M. W. *Imperial Sudan.* New York, Cambridge University Press, 1991.

Daly, M. W., and Sikainga, A. A. *Civil War in the Sudan.* London, British Academic Press, 1993.

Deng, F. M. *War of Visions: Conflict of Identities in the Sudan.* Washington, DC, Brookings Institution, 1995.

Doornbos, M., Cliffe, L., Ahmed, A. G. M., and Markakis, J. (Eds). *Beyond Conflict in the Horn: The Prospects of Peace and Development in Ethiopia, Somalia, Eritrea and Sudan.* Lawrenceville, KS, Red Sea Press, 1992.

El-Affendi, A. *Turabi's Revolution: Islam and Power in Sudan.* London, Grey Seal Books, 1991.

Eprile, C. L. *War and Peace in the Sudan 1955–1972.* Newton Abbot, David and Charles, 1974.

Fluehr-Lobban, C., Fluehr-Lobban, R.A., and Voll, J. *Historical Dictionary of the Sudan.* 2nd Edn. Metuchen, NJ, Scarecrow Press, 1992.

Fukui, K., and Markakis, J. (Eds). *Ethnicity and Conflict in the Horn of Africa.* London, James Currey, 1994.

Garang, J. *The Call for Democracy in Sudan* (Ed. Khalid, M.). 2nd Edn. London, Kegan Paul International, 1992.

Gurdon, C. (Ed.). *The Horn of Africa.* London, University College London Press, 1994.

Hill, R., and Hogg, P. *A Black Corps d'Elite.* East Lansing, Michigan State University Press, 1995.

Hodgkin, R. A. *Sudan Geography.* London, 1951.

Holt, P. M., and Daly, M. W. *The History of the Sudan from the Coming of Islam to the Present Day.* 4th Edn. London and New York, Longman, 1988.

Hurst, H. E., and Philips, P. *The Nile Basin.* 7 vols. London, 1932–38.

International Monetary Fund. *Sudan—Recent Economic Developments.* Washington, DC, International Monetary Fund, 1995.

Johnson, D. H. *The Root Causes of Sudan's Civil Wars.* London, James Currey, 1995.

Karrar, A. S. *The Sufi Brotherhoods in the Sudan.* London, Hurst, 1992.

Katsuyoshi, F., and Markakis, J. *Ethnicity and Conflict in the Horn of Africa.* London, James Currey, 1994.

Keen, D. *The Benefits of Famine: A Political Economy of Famine and Relief in Southwestern Sudan, 1983–1989.* Princeton, NJ, Princeton University Press, 1994.

Khalifa, M. E. *Reflections on the Sudanese Political System.* Khartoum, Sudan House, 1995.

Kibreab, G. *People on the Edge: Displacement, Land Use and the Environment in the Gedaref Region, Sudan.* London, James Currey, 1996.

Mackie, I. *Trek into Nuba.* Edinburgh, Pentland Press, 1994.

Metz, H. C. (Ed.). *Sudan: A Country Study.* Washington, DC, US Government Printing Office, 1991.

Minority Rights Group. *Sudan: Conflict and Minorities.* London, Minority Rights Group, 1995.

Niblock, T. *Class and Power in Sudan: The Dynamics of Sudanese Politics 1898–1985.* Albany, State University Press of New York, 1987.

Nyaba, P. A. *The Politics of Liberation in South Sudan: An Insider's View.* Kampala, Fountain Publishers, 1997.

O'Ballance, E. *The Secret War in the Sudan 1955–1972.* London, Faber and Faber, 1977.

Oduho, J., and Deng, W. *The Problem of the Southern Sudan.* Oxford University Press, 1963.

Prendergast, J. *Sudanese Rebels at a Crossroads: Opportunities for Building Peace in a Shattered Land.* Washington, DC, Center of Concern, 1994.

Prunier, G. *From Peace to War: The Southern Sudan (1972–1984).* Hull, University of Hull, 1986.

Rone, J., et al. (Eds). *Civilian Devastation: Abuses by the Parties in the War in Southern Sudan.* New York, Human Rights Watch, 1994.

Ruay, D. D. A. *The Politics of Two Sudans: The South and the North, 1921–1969.* Uppsala, Nordiska Afrikainstitutet, 1994.

Santi, P., and Hill, R. (Eds). *The Europeans in the Sudan 1834–1878.* Oxford University Press, 1980.

Sidahmed, A. S. *Politics and Islam in Contemporary Sudan.* Richmond, Curzon Press, 1996.

Sikainga, A. A. *Slaves into Workers: Emancipation and Labor in Colonial Sudan.* Austin, University of Texas Press, 1996.

Simone, T. A. M. *In Whose Image?* Chicago, University of Chicago Press, 1994.

Sylvester, A. *Sudan under Nimeri.* London, Bodley Head, 1977.

Thomas, G. F. *Sudan: Struggle for Survival, 1984–1993.* London, Darf, 1993.

Voll, J. O. (Ed.). *Sudan: State and Society in Crisis.* Bloomington, Indiana State University Press, 1991.

Wai, D. *The African-Arab Conflict in the Sudan.* New York, Africana Publishing Co, 1981.

Woodward, P. *Sudan 1898–1989: The Unstable State.* Boulder, CO, Lynne Rienner, 1990.

SWAZILAND

Physical and Social Geography

A. MacGREGOR HUTCHESON

The Kingdom of Swaziland is one of the smallest political entities of continental Africa. Covering an area of only 17,363 sq km (6,704 sq miles), it straddles the broken and dissected edge of the South African plateau, surrounded by South Africa on the north, west and south, and separated from the Indian Ocean on the east by the Mozambique coastal plain.

PHYSICAL FEATURES

From the High Veld on the west, averaging 1,050 to 1,200 m in altitude, there is a step-like descent eastwards through the Middle Veld (450 to 600 m) to the Low Veld (150 to 300 m). To the east of the Low Veld the Lebombo Range, an undulating plateau at 450–825 m, presents an impressive westward-facing scarp and forms the fourth of Swaziland's north–south aligned regions. Drainage is by four main systems flowing eastwards across these regions: the Komati and Umbeluzi rivers in the north, the Great Usutu river in the centre, and the Ngwavuma river in the south. The eastward descent is accompanied by a rise in temperature and by a decrease in mean annual rainfall from a range of 1,150–1,900 mm in the High Veld to one of 500–750 mm in the Low Veld, but increasing again to about 850 mm in the Lebombo range. The higher parts, receiving 1,000 mm, support temperate grassland, while dry woodland savannah is characteristic of the lower areas.

RESOURCES AND POPULATION

Swaziland's potential for economic development in terms of its natural resources is out of proportion to its size. The country's perennial rivers represent a high hydroelectric potential and their exploitation for irrigation in the drier Middle Veld and Low Veld has greatly increased and diversified agricultural production. Sugar, however, is the dominant industry and has traditionally been the principal export commodity. Other major crops include cotton (in terms of the number of producers, this is the most important cash crop), maize, tobacco, rice, vegetables, citrus fruits and pineapples. The well-watered High Veld is particularly suitable for afforestation and over 120,000 ha (more than 100 plantations) have been planted with conifers and eucalyptus since the 1940s, creating the largest man-made forests in Africa.

Swaziland is also rich in mineral wealth. Once a major exporter of iron ore, this industry ceased with the exhaustion of high-grade ores, although considerable quantities of lower-grade ore remain. World demand for Swaziland's exports of chrysolite asbestos has declined in recent years as the result of health problems associated with this mineral. Coal holds the country's most important mineral potential, with reserves estimated at 250m. tons. Coal is currently mined at Mpaka, mostly for export, and further reserves have been identified at Lobuka. The exploitation of anthracite deposits at Maloma began in 1993. Gold and diamond deposits are being exploited in the north-west of the country. Other minerals of note are cassiterite (a tin-bearing ore), kaolin, talc, pyrophyllite and silica.

Nearly one-half of the population live in the Middle Veld, which contains some of the best soils in the country. This is Swaziland's most densely peopled region, with an average of 50 inhabitants per sq km, rising to more than 200 per sq km in some rural and in more developed areas. The total population of Swaziland (excluding absentee workers) was enumerated at 980,722 at the census of 1997. Preliminary results of this census indicated that nearly 50% of the population is under 15 years of age.

A complex system of land ownership, with Swazi and European holdings intricately interwoven throughout the country, is partly responsible for considerable variations in the distribution and density of the population. Only about 40% of the country was under Swazi control at the time of independence in 1968, but this proportion steadily increased in subsequent years, as non-Swazi land and mineral concessions were acquired through negotiation and purchase. The Swazi Nation, to which most of the African population belongs, has now regained all mineral concessions.

Recent History

RICHARD LEVIN

Revised for this edition by HUGH MACMILLAN

Swaziland, which emerged as a cohesive nation in the early 19th century, became a British protectorate following the Boer War in 1903 and in 1907 became one of the high commission territories. A preoccupation of King Sobhuza II during his 61-year reign, which began in 1921, was the recovery of lands granted to settlers and speculators in the late 19th century.

Moves towards the restoration of independence in the early 1960s were accompanied by a growth in political activity. The Ngwane National Liberatory Congress (NNLC), an African nationalist party formed in 1962 and led by Dr Ambrose Zwane, advocated independence on the basis of universal adult suffrage and a constitutional monarchy. Royalist interests formed the rival Imbokodvo National Movement, which won all seats in the new house of assembly in the pre-independence elections in April 1967. The independence constitution vested legislative authority in a bicameral parliament with a large proportion of its membership nominated by the king. Formal independence followed on 6 September 1968.

The 14-year post-independence rule of Sobhuza was characterized by stability and a significant expansion of the economy as investment flowed in, much of it from South Africa. Growing reliance on South African capital, along with Swaziland's membership of the Southern African Customs Union, produced an increasing dependence on South Africa and severely restricted the country's economic and political choices. During this period the royal authorities acquired a significant material base in the economy, through their control of the Tibiyo Taka Ngwane and Tisuka Taka Ngwane, royal corporations which managed the investment of mineral royalties. Politically, the king extended his influence on executive and legislative decisions through his indirect control of the country's traditional 'tinkhundla', local authorities each grouping a small number of chieftaincies. In 1973 Sobhuza decreed a suspension of the constitution and a formal ban on party political activity. By the time of Sobhuza's diamond jubilee in 1981, the authority of the Swazi monarchy was absolute. Sobhuza's death in August 1982 precipitated a prolonged and complex power struggle both within the royal family and among contending factions of the liqoqo, a traditional advisory body which Sobhuza had sought to establish as the supreme council of state. By early 1983, however, supporters of the regent, Queen Ntombi Laftwala, mother of the 14-year-old heir apparent, Prince Makhosetive, had emerged as the group most likely to ensure an orderly succession and to overcome fractious and corrupt elements within the liqoqo, whose powers were substantially curtailed in 1985.

ACCESSION OF MSWATI III

Prince Makhosetive was crowned as King Mswati III in April 1986. The young king moved quickly to assert his authority. The liqoqo was disbanded in May and the cabinet reshuffled. In October Sotsha Dlamini, a former assistant commissioner of police, was appointed as prime minister. Despite the faction-alism and personal intrigue within the royal family, both the king and the new prime minister indicated a determination to eliminate corruption from the administration. In the absence of democratic institutions and public accountability, however, corruption thrived. In September 1987 parliament was dissolved in preparation for elections to be held in November, one year ahead of schedule. In November the electoral college duly appointed 40 members of the house of assembly (none of whom had previously been members). Of the 10 additional members nominated by the king, eight were former MPs. The new house of assembly and King Mswati each appointed 10 members of the senate. A new cabinet, appointed in late November, included Sotsha Dlamini, as prime minister, and three members of the previous cabinet. The low turn-out at the polls for the election of the electoral college was widely interpreted as an indication of growing dissatisfaction among the Swazi population with the tinkhundla system. The limited impact of Swazi voters on the composition of government was evident in the fact that it was the king's nominated members in both houses who were installed as cabinet ministers. Developments within parliament reflected public discontent when, in October 1988, a majority of the members of the upper house supported a motion demanding a comprehensive review of the legislative structure. The prime minister strongly opposed the motion on the grounds that it would be 'un-Swazi' to challenge an established traditional institution. King Mswati has voiced the opinion that political stability in the kingdom can best be achieved through the maintenance of the tinkhundla, as guardians of 'unity and democracy'. Opposition to the tinkhundla, perceived as potential challenges to their own authority, has been expressed by some of the traditional chiefs, and in 1989 about 40 of their number advocated the introduction of direct elections to parliament. In January 1990 the founder and former leader of the NNLC, Dr Ambrose Zwane, in his first public address since the party's suppression in 1973, also urged the introduction of a system of direct legislative elections.

RE-EMERGENCE OF PUDEMO

In July 1989 the king dismissed Sotsha Dlamini for 'disobedi-ence' and replaced him as prime minister with Obed Dlamini, a founder member and former secretary-general of the Swaziland Federation of Trade Unions (SFTU). This appointment was viewed as an attempt to allay labour unrest which had led to recent strikes in the banking and transport systems. The second half of 1989, however, witnessed an escalation in labour dis-putes, which affected several sectors; disaffection was also expressed by students, prompting the king to order the closure of the university for one month from the end of September. These manifestations of discontent, together with a more broadly-based popular opposition of political and civic organiza-tions, began to pose a serious challenge to the continuance of royal hegemony. Until late 1989 open criticism of Mswati's maintenance of autocratic rule had been restricted to sporadic appearances of anti-liqoqo pamphlets linked to the People's United Democratic Movement (PUDEMO), an organization which had been formed during the regency. PUDEMO returned to prominence in 1990 with the distribution of new pamphlets which advocated a constitutional monarchy rather than de-

manding a republican system. PUDEMO criticized the king for his alleged excesses, condemned corruption and called for democratic reform, thus encapsulating public criticism of the tinkhundla.

In mid-July 1990 the police moved to suppress PUDEMO, arresting about 20 people, of whom 11 were variously charged with treason, sedition, or conspiring to form a political party. By the end of October, all the accused had been released. In the following month, however, police and army units violently dispersed a peaceful protest held at the university, injuring up to 300 of those involved in the demonstration. The government promised to appoint a judicial commission of enquiry into the events, although this was not carried out until March 1991. Shortly after the violence, the minister of justice, Reginald Dhladhla, was replaced by Zonkhe Khumalo, a former deputy prime minister who had earlier been implicated in a financial scandal surrounding the royal investment fund, Tisuka Taka Ngwane. Early in 1991 Dhladhla's dismissal was raised in parliament by Dzingalive Dlamini, who asserted that a 'secret group' within the kingdom's power structure was taking major decisions. In March Dzingalive Dlamini briefly fled the country, fearing arrest and indefinite detention by the authorities. Diplo-matic activity by a number of countries, notably the USA, led to Dlamini's return and to the release of Mfanasibili and five PUDEMO detainees.

By mid-1991 there appeared to be widespread public support for the PUDEMO activists and their cause, and in the second half of the year the organization began to establish civic struc-tures in order to advance its objectives through legal organiza-tions. The most prominent of these were the Swaziland Youth Congress (SWAYOCO) and the Human Rights Asscn of Swazi-land (HUMARAS). The king finally agreed to review the tink-hundla, and established a commission, which became known as the vusela ('greeting') committee, to conduct a series of public forums throughout the country in order to elicit popular opinion on political reforms. Prince Masitsela, a cabinet minister under King Sobhuza II during the 1970s, was appointed chairman of the vusela. There was widespread criticism of the political system as well as of the composition of the vusela itself. At the tinkhundla review meeting held in Mbabane, speakers de-manded the abolition of the system, asserting that it was undemocratic and promoted corruption and nepotism, since it provided no system of accountability. In Manzini the meeting of the vusela planned for early November was cancelled, fol-lowing a demonstration march by supporters of PUDEMO and SWAYOCO. The non-violent march was dispersed by the police, who arrested 19 people for staging an illegal demonstration.

In the months following this event, SWAYOCO was involved in a number of confrontations with the police over its right to engage in peaceful protest and community welfare activities, as increasingly militant Swazi youth seized the initiative in the campaign for democracy. Divisions began to emerge within the government concerning its response to the activities of SWAYOCO, with royal advisory council members, in particular, advocating that the youth congress be suppressed. These influences were resisted by more moderate forces, led by the prime minister, who asserted that political and social change in Swaziland was inevitable.

PUDEMO's activities, meanwhile, were also intensified. In the second half of 1991 the organization's national executive committee rejected the process of review by the vusela com-mittee, and set out five demands whose fulfilment was deemed necessary to create conditions conducive to democratic transi-tion. These included the establishment of an interim govern-ment, the suspension of the effective state of emergency, the holding of a constitutional referendum, and the establishment of a constituent assembly to determine a new and appropriate constitution for Swaziland. These demands were officially ignored, but in February 1992, when the king announced the establishment of a second vusela committee (Vusela 2), he included a member of PUDEMO and a member of HUMARAS among the commissioners.

A further two opposition movements, the Swaziland United Front and the Swaziland National Front, subsequently re-emerged. In February 1992 PUDEMO declared itself a legal opposition party, in contravention of the prohibition of political associations. Kislon Shongwe was named as president, and, among other members of the party executive, Mandla Hlatsh-wako was appointed national organizer. In a decree, published at the beginning of April, setting out the terms of reference of Vusela 2, the king appointed Hlatshwako as one of the commissioners. The terms of reference of Vusela 2 included a study of the submissions made by Vusela 1, receiving further submissions in camera from any Swazi, examining shortcomings in the existing system of voting and investigating ways in which customary and modern political institutions could be integrated. Following protracted negotiations with the commission over its function and influence, Hlatshwako withdrew from the committee, on the grounds that the purpose of Vusela 2 appeared to be to sustain the tinkhundla rather than to democratize. HUMARAS also rejected Vusela 2 as a waste of resources. HUMARAS president Sam Mkhombe, also a commissioner, was dismissed as president of the organization, having ignored HUMARAS demands that he should resign from Vusela 2.

PRESSURE FOR REFORM

In October 1992 the king approved a number of proposals, which had been submitted by Vusela 2. Under new amendments to the electoral system, the house of assembly (which was redesignated as the national assembly) was to be expanded to 65 deputies (of whom 55 were to be directly elected by secret ballot from candidates nominated by the tinkhundla, and 10 appointed by the king), and the senate to 30 members (of whom 10 were to be selected by the national assembly and 20 appointed by the king); in addition, detention without trial was to cease, and a new constitution, which incorporated the amendments, enshrining an hereditary monarchy and confirming the fundamental rights of the individual and the independence of the judicial system, was to be drafted. However, opposition groups protested at the committee's failure to recommend the immediate restoration of a multi-party political system; the issue was to be postponed until the forthcoming elections in order to determine the extent of public support.

PUDEMO announced its opposition to the electoral reforms, and demanded that the government organize a national convention to determine the country's constitutional future. King Mswati subsequently dissolved parliament, one month prior to the expiry of its term of office, and announced that he was to rule by decree, with the assistance of the cabinet (which was redesignated as the council of ministers), pending the adoption of the new constitution and the holding of parliamentary elections. A third committee (Vusela 3) was established to inform the population about the forthcoming amendments to the electoral system. Later in October 1992 the king announced that elections to the national assembly were to take place in the first half of 1993. At a series of public meetings, which were convened by Vusela 3 from December 1992, doubts regarding the viability of the reformed electoral system were expressed; in early 1993, in response to public concern, it was announced that legislation preventing the heads of the tinkhundla from exerting undue influence in the nomination of candidates had been introduced.

In December 1992 an informal alliance of organizations that advocated democratic reform (principally comprising HUMARAS, PUDEMO and SWAYOCO), known as the Convention for a Full Democratic Swaziland, was formed. In the same month PUDEMO rejected a proposal by SWAYOCO that a 'Vusela Resistance Movement' be established, to impede the implementation of economic reforms by disrupting essential services. In early 1993, in response to attempts by the opposition to impede the elections, the government moved to suppress political gatherings. In March more than 50 opposition activists, including leaders of PUDEMO and SWAYOCO, were arrested and charged in connection with the organization of illegal political meetings. Although those arrested were subsequently released on bail, legal restrictions prevented them from participating in opposition activity, thereby effectively undermining efforts to co-ordinate a campaign in protest at the elections. Despite the opposition's failure to organize an official electoral boycott, however, a low level of voter registration appeared to reflect public response to the proposed reforms.

The first round of elections to the expanded national assembly, which was contested by 2,094 candidates nominated by the tinkhundla, took place on 25 September 1993. At the end of September the king repealed the legislation providing for deten-tion without trial for a period of 60 days. The second round of parliamentary elections, which took place on 11 October, was contested by the three candidates in each tinkhundla who had obtained the highest number of votes in the first poll; the majority of members of the former cabinet (which had been dissolved in late September), including Obed Dlamini, failed to secure seats in the national assembly. (The king subsequently appointed an acting prime minister, with responsibility for all ministerial portfolios, pending the formation of a new cabinet.) Shortly afterwards, Mfanasibili questioned the loyalty to the king of the elected parliamentary deputies, and claimed that certain elements planned to transfer executive power to the prime minister and redesignate the head of state as a constitutional monarch. Later in October the king nominated a further 10 deputies to the national assembly, which elected 10 of its members to the senate; the king subsequently appointed the remaining 20 senators, who included Obed Dlamini and Bhekimpi. In early November the former minister of works and construction, Prince Jameson Mbilini Dlamini, who was regarded as a traditionalist, was appointed prime minister, and a new cabinet (which included Nxumalo, in the office of deputy prime minister) was formed.

In February 1994, following a report by the US department of state that described the parliamentary elections as 'undemocratic', the government claimed that the majority of the Swazi people were opposed to the establishment of a multi-party political system. It was announced, however, that the king was to appoint a five-member committee, comprising representatives of state organs and non-governmental organizations, to draft a new constitution, and a national policy council, which was to prepare a manifesto of the Swazi people. In March elections to the tinkhundla, which were scheduled to take place later that month in accordance with the reforms, were postponed, owing to lack of preparation. (The heads of the tinkhundla had previously been appointed by the king.)

In early 1995 there were outbreaks of arson and incendiary attacks on the property of government officials, and on the parliament and high court buildings. Although crude in execution, these attacks were the first manifestations for almost 20 years of overt political violence against established authority. Simultaneously, the focus of opposition shifted from unauthorized political organizations to the trade union movement. On 13–14 March the SFTU brought the economy to a standstill with a general strike, staged in protest at the government's failure to respond to a set of 27 demands which had been put forward in January of the previous year. Although the demands of the SFTU focused on labour issues, the strike was clearly part of the wider political context. In July a second general strike was narrowly averted following government threats, including an announcement by the king, that the proposed strike would provoke a violent official response. Allegations of official malfeasance continued, meanwhile, to heighten political discontent. The ministers of information and finance were dismissed from their posts in February, on the grounds of alleged corrupt conduct. In May the new minister of finance, Derrick von Wissel, asked the central bank to take over the state-owned Swaziland Development and Savings Bank after the discovery of possible irregularities in loans to prominent public figures. In August the senate approved a motion supporting a statement, made by the king during a visit to South Africa, to the effect that the Swazi population was not in favour of a multi-party system. In November, however, a conference of political organizations (including PUDEMO and SWAYOCO) and the SFTU urged Mswati to leave the country for a temporary period of exile, pending the establishment of a multi-party democracy.

In January 1996 PUDEMO announced that a campaign of protests and civil disobedience would be initiated, following the government's failure to respond to demands for the installation of a multi-party system and for the adoption of a constitution that would restrict the monarch to a symbolic role in government. Strike action, which was scheduled by the SFTU for later that month, was declared to be illegal by the authorities. However, an attempt by the government to have the industrial action pronounced illegal in the high court was rejected, and the indefinite general strike was staged as planned, despite the arrest of three senior SFTU officials (who were subsequently released, following a further legal ruling). Demonstrations by

SFTU members were firmly suppressed by security forces, leading to violent clashes in which three people were reported to have been killed. The SFTU refused to enter into negotiations with the government, demanding that the prohibitions on political activity and restrictions on trade unions be revoked prior to discussions. At the end of January the king accused the SFTU membership of attempting to overthrow the monarchy and demanded that they abandon industrial action, threatening to order his traditional warriors to suppress the strike. The SFTU subsequently suspended its industrial action to allow negotiations with the government to proceed. In February the SFTU threatened to resume strike action, but again agreed to a postponement pending negotiations, after the king announced that the process of drafting a new constitution would begin later that year, and that the legislation prohibiting political activity would also be reviewed. In March PUDEMO recommended that a 'government of national unity' be installed to supervise the transitional process. During early May the king indicated that a 'people's parliament', comprising a series of consultative meetings between citizens and government leaders, had been initiated to solicit public opinion regarding constitutional reform, leading to the formation of a committee to prepare proposals for a draft constitution for submission to a referendum. The European Union (EU) offered to assist in this exercise. At the same time the king removed Mbilini from the office of prime minister, and announced that he would appoint his successor in consultation with the Swaziland national council. (Nxumalo assumed the duties of acting prime minister pending the appointment.)

In late July 1996, following an emergency meeting (attended by Nxumalo and the heads of state of Mozambique, Botswana, Zimbabwe and South Africa) to discuss Swaziland's political situation, King Mswati appointed a constitutional review commission, comprising chiefs, political activists and unionists, to collate submissions from the Swazi people and subsequently draft proposals for a new constitution. (The commission subsequently received substantial funds from international donors.) At the same time, Dr Barnabas Sibusiso Dlamini, an executive director of the IMF and a former finance minister, was appointed prime minister. In August PUDEMO expressed its dissatisfaction with the composition of the constitutional review commission under the chairmanship of the king's brother, Prince Mangaliso, and appealed for South African and other regional and international support in expediting the constitutional review.

In early November 1996 the council of ministers was reorganized, and four ministers were dismissed. Derrick von Wissel, who as minister of finance had attempted to recover debts owed to the central bank by several senior establishment figures, resigned after he was transferred to the tourism portfolio. (He subsequently became governor of the central bank.) Later that month teachers and civil servants withdrew from pay negotiations with the government.

General Strike and Civil Disorder

In early December 1996 the prime minister announced that a 'task force', composed of workers, employers and government representatives, had discussed the SFTU's 27 demands of January 1994, and that the implementation of the recommendations outlined in the resulting report was to be overseen by the labour advisory board. In mid-January 1997, however, the SFTU claimed that there had been no response to its demands for democratic reform, and resolved to begin indefinite strike action from early February. Meanwhile, the president of PUDEMO, Mario Masuku, declared that Swaziland's leaders were not committed to change, and withdrew from the constitutional review commission. At the end of January the four main leaders of the SFTU were arrested and were subsequently charged with intimidating bus owners into joining the forthcoming strike; it was believed that the arrests had been made at the behest of the Swaziland national council. The strike, declared illegal by the government, proceeded as planned, however, and was apparently observed by approximately one-half of the labour force, with particular support from workers in agriculture and forestry. Several SFTU and PUDEMO members were arrested at a meeting to assess the first day of the strike, although they were released without charge shortly afterwards. Some days later, PUDEMO reportedly distributed a pamphlet containing threats to attack and assassinate journalists whose coverage of the strike favoured the government. Violent clashes with the security forces resulted in serious injuries to a few strikers. A number of southern African leaders expressed concern at the length of the dispute, and a 10-member international delegation of trade unionists threatened to organize a blockade of the kingdom, following inconclusive talks with the government. The SFTU leaders declined the government's offer to release them on condition that they end the strike; their trial began, but was dismissed in late February, owing to lack of evidence. At the beginning of March commercial activity was disrupted by a one-day blockade of the Swazi border, initiated by the Congress of South African Trade Unions (COSATU), which had asserted its support for the SFTU throughout the strike. The SFTU urged workers to support the blockade, although it decided to suspend the strike shortly afterwards, as the government had agreed to commence negotiations. However, it was resolved to continue industrial action on the first two days of each month until the SFTU's 27 demands, made in 1994, had been met. It was subsequently announced that Mswati was reviewing King Sobhuza's 1973 decree. In early April 1997 the SFTU postponed a further blockade, in order to allow the government adequate time to review the situation.

In late May 1997 Nxumalo warned that he believed a violent revolution would take place, unless a referendum was held to ascertain whether Swazis wished to retain the present political system or to establish a multi-party democracy. In early June the king appealed to the nation to contribute to the constitutional debate. Shortly afterwards South Africa offered assistance in the preparation of the constitution, in response to a request from the king. In July, however, differences were emerging within the commission, with a number of members having threatened to resign.

In mid-October 1997 the SFTU called a country-wide strike in support of its demands for democratic reform, after talks with the government failed to produce any agreement. Support for the strike was low, however, with workers apparently disillusioned, given the failure of previous strike action to achieve any significant progress. Teachers none the less resolved to continue with separate industrial action in support of pay demands.

In late October 1997 there was further evidence of civil unrest, when a reported 2,000 demonstrators gathered at Matsapha Airport to await the return of the king from a meeting of Commonwealth heads of government; armed paramilitary police intervened, firing tear-gas in an attempt to disperse the crowd. The following day the government banned a further demonstration at the airport, which had been scheduled to coincide with the arrival of Prince Charles, heir to the British throne. Meanwhile, the SFTU and other protesters demanded the recall from Swaziland of the British high commissioner, who was accused of colluding with the king and interfering in domestic affairs.

In late November 1997 the national assembly decided to postpone discussions on controversial government proposals for the establishment of a media council, which had been condemned by human rights groups and journalists who felt that they should have been consulted during the preparation of the proposals. The government had dismissed the criticism, insisting that the intention was to regulate the activities of the press, not to interfere with its freedom. By December three members of the constitutional review commission had resigned, amid reports of increasing public discontent with the commission's apparent lack of progress and calls for its dissolution. In early April 1998 the council of ministers was reshuffled, with the notable departure of Nxumalo, who was appointed to chair a new Swaziland Investment Promotion Authority. In May the government established an anti-corruption unit, to work independently from the police, following reports of increasing corruption in the public sector.

Elections and Labour Unrest

In mid-August 1998 King Mswati dissolved the national assembly in preparation for elections due to take place in October. Opposition groups, however, urged voters to boycott the elections, in the absence of the immediate legalization of political parties. Some 350 candidates were nominated by the tinkhundla to contest the 55 elective seats in the assembly.

Voting took place on 16 October. The authorities attributed a low turn-out to heavy rains, which had made many polling stations inaccessible, and a second day of voting was arranged for 24 October; however, overall participation remained low. A new cabinet, again with Sibusiso Dlamini as prime minister, was appointed in mid-November. Only three ministers were elected members of the national assembly. A new senate and Swaziland National Council were, meanwhile, formed. On the day of the ceremony to swear in the new cabinet a powerful bomb exploded in the building in which the offices of the deputy prime minister, Arthur Khoza, were located, killing one person and seriously injuring two others. The prime minister later denied reports that he had received a letter warning him about the bomb. Officials linked the attack to another bomb explosion, in late October, near a bridge outside the capital, shortly after the king's motorcade had crossed the bridge. Police subsequently seized documents purportedly detailing the manufacture of explosive devices from a house occupied by SWAYOCO. The SFTU leader, Jan Sithole, and members of PUDEMO were subsequently questioned in connection with the dynamiting of the bridge.

In January 1999 the Swazi authorities deregistered the country's biggest labour union, the Swaziland Agriculture, Plantation and Allied Workers' Union, on the grounds that it had failed to submit annual financial reports for inspection. In April the NNLC, PUDEMO and the SFTU united to form the Swaziland Democratic Alliance (SDA). The NNLC leader Obed Dlamini was elected chairman. The formal launch of the Alliance was to have been on 11 April, to coincide with the end of the Southern African Development Community (SADC) labour conference in Mbabane. However, following warnings from the police that the proposed inauguration, which had been rescheduled for 19 April, was illegal and would not be permitted to take place, the executive of the SDA met and cancelled the event. The SADC labour conference was also the focus of pro-democracy demonstrations by some 2,000 workers in Mbabane and by a larger group, comprised mainly of public-sector workers, in Manzini. Protests were swiftly suppressed by riot police. Dissatisfaction was restricted chiefly to urban areas, among civil sevants, and among sugar-cane plantation workers in the south of the country.

Towards the Millennium

As the millennium approached, there continued to be uncertainty as to the future political dispensation. King Mswati's statement at the opening of parliament in 1999 that the constitutional review commission, established in 1996, would report before the end of the year was later rescinded. He gave a similar assurance at the opening of parliament in February 2000, although the chairman of the commission, Mangaliso Dlamini, had earlier indicated that it would not report before 2002. However, in June 2000 the commission claimed that it would be ready to present a draft constitution to the King in October. It became clear in the later months of 1999 that uncertainty was having a paralysing effect on the government itself. in a number of instances, such as the industrial relations bill, there were long delays in the enactment of legislation. In other instances, such as the swazi administration order, it was announced that legislation that had been enacted by parliament, or decreed by the King, would be held in abeyance. While real power rested with the King, and a small group of close advisers within the traditionalist Swaziland National Council, they had to take some account of the views of the more technocratic and modernizing elements in the council of ministers, led by Dlamini, as well as of internal and external pressures.

Apart from the political dispensation, labour relations remained the most contentious issue. The industrial relations bill, which had been presented to parliament in 1998, was not finally approved by the King until 29 May 2000. It was only then approved as a result of pressure from the USA and the International Labour Organization (ILO), which threatened to impose sanctions unless the bill were passed. It was, however, only approved after amendments by the Swaziland National Council, which limited the right to strike and which were likely to make the legislation unacceptable to the ILO. In November 1999 nine members of the executive of the Swaziland National Association of Teachers were detained for five hours at a police station in Mbabane before a meeting with two senior princes and representatives of the Swaziland National Council, Princes Matsitsela and Tfohlongwane. According to the teachers' spokesman, Phineas Magagula, they were then 'interrogated' by the princes about a peaceful demonstration which had paraded through the streets of Mbabane with a coffin representing a new and 'unworkable' system of continuous assessment which had recently been introduced. The princes were most critical of the singing by the teachers of the South African national anthem, Nkosi Sikele' iAfrika, which they described as revolutionary and insulting to the King.

There were also long delays in the enactment of the media council bill, which was first pressented to parliament in 1997 and which remained subject to discussion three years later. The bill would provide for the licensing of journalists, and for fines and imprisonment for journalistic offenders. It was, nevertheless, the press itself which provided the most dramatic news story of 1999. The editor of the Sunday edition of *The Times of Swaziland*, Bheki Makhubu, was detained in early October and charged with defamation under a colonial ordinance. He had already been suspended by the management of the newspaper following a series of articles that were critical of King Mswati's choice of Senteni Masango, who was portrayed as wild and irresponsible, as one of two new royal fiancées. Particular offence was caused in royal circles by the publication of a photograph of the fiancées taken at the university graduation of one of the King's six wives, LaMbikiza. The caption referred to Miss Masango as a 'dropout'. Makhubu had caused further offence by the publication of an article in a South African newspaper, in which he claimed that he was motivated by the wish to defend King Msawati against the threat of HIV/AIDS. The prime minister attempted to distance the government from Makhubu's arrest, referring to Swaziland's 'independent judicial system.' It later emerged that the minister of public service and information, Ephraim Magwagwa Mdluli, was himself suing Makhubu and *The Times of Swaziland* for R1.5m. following the publication of an article which alleged that he was having an affair with a senior civil servant. The editor of the government-owned *Swaziland Observer*, Lathu Jonga, expressed his unease concerning the minister's intention of introducing a new defamation law.

The press provided another major news story in March 2000 when the government suddenly closed its own newspaper, the *Swaziland Observer*. The newspaper had been founded in 1981 by the royal trust fund, Tibiyo TakaNgwane, as an alternative to the long-established *Times of Swaziland*. The *Swaziland Observer* had been seen as a government mouthpiece, and was run at a loss, but it had recently increased its circulation under the editorship of Lathu Jonga who had adopted a more independent stance and had published articles about government corruption and scandals. It was widely believed that allegations concerning a disagreement over ambassadorial expenditure between the Prime Minister Dlamini and the Minister of Foreign Affairs and Trade, Albert Shabangu, contributed to the government's action. Dlamini, however, denied that the government was responsible for the closure of the newspaper. The secretary-general of the Swaziland Federation of Trade Unions, Jan Sithole, described the closure of the newspaper as a violation of press freedom and labour laws. He claimed that employees were given no notice of the closure and that they were not provided for in terms of retrenchment settlements in line with their legal rights. In addition, the Media Institute of Southern Africa and the Human Rights Association of Swaziland both criticized the closure of the newspaper.

There was little evidence in the later months of 1999 or the first half of 2000 of overt activity by the newly-formed SDA or its main constituent parts, PUDEMO or the NNLC. They appeared to continue to pursue a policy of not organizing marches or demonstrations within Swaziland before the achievement of legal recognition. There was, however, a demonstration by 50 members of PUDEMO at the Commonwealth heads of state and government meeting in Durban, South Africa, in November 1999. The PUDEMO president, Mario Masuku, demanded the expulsion of Swaziland from the Commonwealth, alleging political repression and human rights abuses. The government, in turn, accused the opposition of having been responsible for a bomb explosion at a development centre at

Mahlanya, the timing of which coincided with the Commonwealth conference. There was speculation that the attack might have been carried out by a group known as the Black Tigers, which claimed to have executed a similar attack on the deputy prime minister's office in Mbabane almost a year previously.

When King Mswati opened parliament on 11 February 2000 he did so in the absence of the speaker of the national assembly, Mgabhi Dlamini, whose earlier arrest for stealing manure from the royal cattle-byre had aroused international media interest. It was presumed that he had sought the manure for medicinal purposes. In his speech to parliament, the king identified the stimulation of foreign investment, the alleviation of poverty and the effort to remove corruption as priorities for his government. In addition to the industrial relations bill, there was a substantial backlog of legislation, including an income tax bill, which was intended to encourage foreign investment by reducing corporation tax, and measures relating to corruption, the stock exchange and land reform. The rejection by parliament during the latter half of 1999 of a public health bill, which included measures relating to HIV/AIDS, was regarded by some as symbolizing the failure of the country to come to terms with the epidemic. HIV/AIDS is believed to have infected between one-quarter and one-third of the adult population in Swaziland.

In April 2000 Prime Minister Dlamini announced details of the Millennium Project. Recalling that King Mswati had earlier declared 2000 to be 'the Year of Delivery', Dlamini promised that feasibility studies for a number of projects, including a new international airport, a new large hotel, a theme park, a convention centre and new industrial centres in each of the four regions, would be completed by July 2000. The Millennium Project was inaugurated in addition to the 25-year national development strategy, which was announced by King Mswati in September 1999, although only after a delay of some months and the deletion of clauses relating to human rights and the recognition of political parties. The Millennium Project also complemented the prime minister's own economic and social reform agenda, which accompanied the publication of the new strategy. Taken together, these three initiatives provide some indication that the government of King Mswati, although still reluctant to come to terms with the need for political reform, is taking steps to deal with the economic crisis, which has resulted from stagnant foreign investment, wide-scale unemployment and endemic poverty.

EXTERNAL RELATIONS

After achieving independence in 1968 Swaziland joined a number of international organizations, including the Commonwealth, the United Nations and the Organization of African Unity (OAU). It later also became a member of the Southern African Development Community (SADC). During the Cold War, Swaziland adopted a conservative position with regard to international relations and maintained close links with the United Kingdom and the USA. It also maintained diplomatic relations with Israel and Taiwan and received substantial development assistance from those countries. With the end of the Cold War, Swaziland came under increasing pressure from the USA to move towards the establishment of a multi-party democracy. The relocation, from Swaziland to Botswana, of the regional office of the United States Agency for International Development and the withdrawal of the US Peace Corps from the kingdom were announced in 1996. These moves were widely seen as signifying US disapproval of the slow pace of political reform in the country.

As a small and land-locked country, Swaziland's most important bilateral relationships have been with its two neighbours, South Africa and Mozambique. From the mid-1950's until shortly before Swaziland's independence in 1968, South Africa saw the country as the potential nucleus of a Swazi 'bantustan' ('homeland'). Conversely, King Sobhuza II harboured the ambition of reclaiming from South Africa areas in the eastern Transvaal and northern Natal that were separated from the Swazi kingdom in the 19th century. The achievement of independence by Mozambique in 1975 created a situation in which the exiled African National Congress (ANC) of South Africa was able to use Swaziland as a corridor for the movement of recruits from South Africa and for the infiltration of guerrilla fighters.

This posed a threat to South Africa's security and provided the basis for negotiations between the governments of Swaziland and South Africa about a possible 'land deal.' South Africa offered to transfer to Swaziland the KaNgwane 'Bantustan' in the Transvaal and the Ingwavuma district in northern Natal (the acquisition of the latter area would have afforded Swaziland direct access to the sea) in exchange for the imposition of more stringent restrictions on the activities of the ANC. The first step in these negotiations was the conclusion in February 1982 of a secret security agreement between the two countries. Within weeks, the ANC's representative, Stanley Mabizela, was deported from Swaziland, and both his successor and his wife were assassinated. Sobhuza's death in August 1982 removed the only obstacle to an all-out offensive on the ANC, and by the end of that year the first of a series of round-ups and 'voluntary deportations' of alleged ANC members had occurred. However, as a result of legal obstacles and strong opposition, both in white and black political circles, in South Africa, the proposals for the land transfer were finally abandoned in 1984. Despite this, Swazi security forces continued to harass the ANC.

In 1984, within days of the signing of the Nkomati Accord between South Africa and Mozambique, the Swazi government revealed the existence of its security agreement with South Africa. The systematic suppression of ANC activities intensified, and open collaboration between the two countries led to gun battles in Manzini as speculation increased that this policy was being orchestrated by a South African trade mission which was established in Mbabane in 1984. In January 1985 the Swazi prime minister defended his government's close relationship with South Africa and implied that the attacks against the ANC would continue. The ANC responded by creating a sophisticated underground network in Swaziland, as conflict within Swazi territory between itself and South Africa intensified. This conflict escalated in 1986, and in June, July and August armed raids by South African security personnel resulted in a number of ANC deaths in border areas and in Manzini. Increased public outrage at these activities led the Swazi prime minister publicly to accuse South Africa of responsibility and to condemn the August raid as an 'illegal act of aggression', the first open attack on South African policies by a Swaziland government. Nevertheless South African covert security forces continued to carry out operations within Swaziland, in which ANC activists were abducted or murdered. The era of political reform within South Africa that followed the release of Nelson Mandela in February 1990 brought a general improvement in relations between the two countries, and in late 1993 formal diplomatic relations were established.

In 1995 South African press criticism of the absolute monarchy in Swaziland, the only country in southern Africa not to have adopted a multi-party democratic system, strained relations between the two neighbours. The king paid a state visit to South Africa in mid-1995 and was received by President Mandela, who recalled King Sobhuza's role in the early years of the ANC. These events went some way towards improving relations, but international pressure for constitutional reform continues to mount. The establishment of a constitutional review commission, in July 1996, was welcomed by the governments of the UK, Botswana, Tanzania and South Africa. In April of that year the South African government announced that it had rejected a long-standing claim by Swaziland to a region in Mpumalanga Province (formerly Eastern Transvaal). During 1996–97 prominent South African organizations, including the ANC and COSATU, expressed support for the SFTU's demands for political reform, prompting the Swazi government to protest at interference in its domestic affairs. In October 1997 the South African Broadcasting Corpn's coverage of strike action organized by the SFTU was condemned as being inaccurate and biased by the Swazi government; its broadcasts in Swaziland were subsequently suspended.

During the prolonged period of civil unrest within Mozambique, considerable numbers of Mozambicans crossed into Swaziland in search of food and employment, an influx which was linked by Swazi police to an increase in armed crime, and resulted in several mass arrests in urban areas. A sizeable 'unofficial' population of Mozambicans gathered in urban areas; these Mozambicans, many of whom were highly skilled workers, were perceived as a threat to the jobs of Swazi urban residents.

The presence of Mozambican refugees in rural areas also caused tension, owing to a shortage of land to accommodate them. The officially-maintained refugee settlement camps were crowded and, in the absence of sufficient co-operative agricultural facilities, were heavily dependent on food rations. In June 1990 the governments of Swaziland and Mozambique signed an extradition agreement providing for the repatriation of alleged criminals and illegal immigrants, which was designed to reduce the incidence of smuggling between the two countries. In 1992, however, tension at the border with Mozambique increased, following reports of raids against Swazi farms by members of the Mozambican armed forces. Following the ratification of a Mozambican peace accord in October 1992, an agreement, which was signed by the governments of Swaziland and Mozambique and the UN high commissioner for refugees in August 1993, provided for the repatriation of some 24,000 Mozambican nationals resident in Swaziland; in October 500 Mozambican refugees returned from Swaziland under the programme. In December the number of Swazi troops deployed at the border with Mozambique was increased, following clashes between Swazi and Mozambican forces in the region. Mozambique subsequently protested at alleged border incursions by members of the Swazi armed forces. In early 1994 discussions took place between Swazi and Mozambican officials to seek mutually satis-

factory arrangements for the joint patrol of the border, and in 1995 it was announced that the Mhlumeni border post, closed since the 1970s, would re-open as the second official transit point between the two countries. In September 1997, during the first visit to Swaziland made by a Mozambican prime minister, the governments of both countries signed a further extradition agreement, with the aim of reducing cross-border crime.

In recent years an area of conflict, and co-operation, between Swaziland, South Africa and Mozambique has been the use of the water resources of the Nkomati River. The apparently excessive use of the river for hydro-electric projects and irrigation schemes in South Africa and Swaziland has severely reduced the flow of water into Mozambique and led that country to take a claim for compensation to the International Court of Justice in The Hague, Netherlands. In 1995 the Swedish government provided funds, through the Swedish International Development Agency (SIDA), for the establishment of the Inkomati Shared River Basin Initiative (ISRBI). This resulted in the presentation in March 2000 of a proposed scheme for fair and equal access to the water of the river by the three countries to the Second World Water Security Forum at The Hague. Mozambique's representative on the ISRBI stated that this plan might encourage the country to withdraw its claim for compensation.

Economy
GRAHAM MATTHEWS
Revised for this edition by MAREK GARZTECKI

Swaziland has one of the continent's highest per caput income levels, although it is, after The Gambia, the smallest state in mainland Africa. In 1998, according to World Bank estimates, the kingdom's gross national product (GNP), measured at average 1996–98 prices, was US $1,384m., equivalent to $1,400 per caput: enough to rank Swaziland as a 'middle income' economy. The World Bank estimates real GNP per caput to have declined at an average of 0.1% per annum in 1990–98, while the population increased at an average annual rate of 3.6% during the same period. Since independence there has been diversification of the economy away from early dependence upon agriculture and mining. According to national estimates, manufacturing contributed the largest share of gross domestic product (GDP) with 32.0% in 1996/97. Manufacturing also accounted for some 18% of formal employment in 1994. After government services, which contributed 20.0% in 1996/97, the other main sectors' contributions to GDP were agriculture and forestry 18.2%, trade, restaurants and hotels 8.8%, transport and communications 5.3%, construction 4.9% and financial and business services 4.6%. Despite its relative diversification and wealth, however, Swaziland has not escaped the extremes of income distribution familiar elsewhere in Africa. More than two-thirds of the resident population comprises families earning generally poor incomes from smallholder cashcropping or subsistence agriculture on Swazi Nation Land (SNL), where the average land holding was just 1.35 ha in 1991. Moreover, the condition of the rural poor has been largely unimproved by periods of rapid growth since independence.

The most recent period of accelerated growth began with the record sugar crop of 1986 and continued until the regional drought broke the pattern with its disastrous effects upon rainfed agriculture in 1992. In 1985–89 the average annual rate of GDP growth was 9.4%, while population growth averaged 3.7% per year over the same period. Swaziland's 'open' economy (exports of goods and services accounted for 81.4% of GDP in 1995/96) was severely affected by the depressed commodity prices and drought in the early 1980s; 'Cyclone Domoina', which battered the kingdom in 1984, also took its toll. Finally, the initial impact of the currency's decline during 1983–85 was additionally damaging and led to a period of rapid inflation, among other problems. During 1990–95, according to the IMF, GDP increased, in real terms, by an annual average of 2.6%. Regional recession and drought cut agricultural value added by

20% in 1992/93, although improved construction and manufacturing figures cushioned the blow and the economy grew marginally by 1.2%. In 1993/94 real GDP expanded by 3.8%, when the beneficial demand-side effects of improved growth in South Africa were offset by the agricultural sector's slow recovery from the drought and a drift back across the border of capital previously relocated from South Africa. Real GDP increased by 3.0% in 1995, by 3.6% in 1996, by 3.7% in 1997, by 2.7% in 1998 and by an estimated 3.1% in 1999 as a result of strong growth in the manufacturing sector. Two new plants, producing buses and textiles, came into operation. Although bad climatic conditions resulted in slower growth in the agricultural sector, cotton output was the best for three years, production increasing from 16,197 metric tons in 1996/97 to 16,888 tons in 1997/98. The agricultural sector will probably drive economic growth in 2000–2001, providing the rain pattern remains positive. However, the rate of growth during the 1990s barely kept pace with the rate of population expansion. Real incomes per caput have been stagnant as a result.

Swaziland's development has been dominated by its relation to South Africa, the dominant regional power. South African capital and imports, the Southern African Customs Union (SACU), the South African labour market and the Common Monetary Area (CMA, successor to the Rand Monetary Area) have shaped the economy and restricted the scope for independent economic policy. However, a consistent determination to maintain an investment climate attractive to foreign business and a policy of accepting the dominance of its powerful neighbour has brought Swaziland a rate of post-independence capital formation not achieved in most African states. In the late 1980s the kingdom benefited as foreign and South African companies relocated to Swaziland. In the early 1990s, however, Swaziland experienced the negative repercussions of political uncertainty and economic recession in South Africa. In the immediate aftermath of the installation of a democratically elected government in South Africa in 1994, there were mixed implications for Swaziland, such as the likelihood of a renegotiation of SACU to the country's disadvantage. Nevertheless, in the longer term, regional reintegration in the post-apartheid era should be of net benefit to the Swazi economy.

Tourism has stagnated as a result of the expanding South African tourist industry and Swaziland's failure to become more attractive to tourist visitors, by refusing to extend the opening of the main border with South Africa. In addition, the region is becoming increasingly competitive and the economy must further diversify if the necessary jobs are to be created. In February 1997 the government presented the economic and social reform agenda (ESRA), prepared in consultation with the IMF and the World Bank, which aimed to accelerate economic growth, reduce the level of unemployment and encourage investment in the private sector. However, long-term prospects for investment in Swaziland could depend on a satisfactory political settlement, in view of strike action which disrupted economic activity in 1996 and early 1997 (see Recent History). In a survey of economic freedom, published in 1998, Swaziland ranked number one of the 37 sub-Saharan countries reviewed. Criteria used to compile the report included levels of government intervention, inflation, barriers to foreign investment and levels of protection of private property.

The national currency is the lilangeni (plural: emalangeni) introduced in 1974. The terms of the Trilateral Monetary Agreement, signed with South Africa and Lesotho to form the CMA in 1986, allowed the Swazi authorities the option of determining the lilangeni's exchange rate independently. Under the amended Multilateral Monetary Agreement (signed in early 1992 to formalize Namibia's *de facto* membership) this freedom is maintained but the currency has remained pegged at par to the South African rand. Although they are formally no longer legal tender, rand notes still circulate freely in the kingdom. In 1999 the exchange rate was US $1 = E6.11.

As a member of the CMA, Swaziland was affected by South Africa's decision in 1997 to relax further its controls on the availability of foreign exchange. The limits on capital investment by companies in the Southern African Development Community (SADC) region have also been relaxed, and thus Swaziland will have to become more competitive if it is to attract further capital and investment from South Africa. Progress on the renegotiation of the SACU agreement slowed in 1997, as South Africa needed to address a number of additional pressing international economic issues, including accession to the Lomé Convention, the proposed free-trade agreement with the European Union (EU), and the SADC trade protocol revisions. In 1999 South Africa launched a 14% value-added tax (VAT) on exports and imports to and from the other members of SACU. Swaziland is concerned about the delays that trucks will experience at the border, although South African customs officials have guaranteed that the delay will be minimal. Despite the disagreement between the SACU members over the introduction of VAT, there was progress in late 1998 on the renegotiation of the SACU agreement. Receipts from SACU represent about one-half of total government recurrent revenue. The recent signing of the South African-EU free-trade agreement is likely to have a negative impact on Swaziland's revenue from SACU. However, SACU is expected to negotiate arrangements with the EU to compensate the smaller SACU members for any revenue losses.

In 1998 the Lebombo Spatial Development Initiative (SDI) was launched. The SDI is a joint E600m. project by the governments of South Africa, Swaziland and Mozambique to attract investment to eastern Swaziland, southern Mozambique and parts of the South African provinces of Mpumalanga and Kwa-Zulu/Natal. Potential projects for Swaziland include tourism and agricultural developments, and road improvements from the southern border with KwaZulu/Natal. In June 1998 a passenger rail service was introduced from Durban, South Africa, to Maputo, the capital of Mozambique, through Swaziland.

In its 1998 annual report, the IMF commended the Swazi government for the country's recent economic stability but expressed concern about failing GDP growth. The IMF urged that the privatization programme be expedited, infrastructure be improved and the banking system be more tightly supervised. It was also concerned about expanding and diversifying the government's revenue base and keeping government expenditure under firmer control.

AGRICULTURE AND FORESTRY

Although the agricultural sector accounts for a declining share of GDP (an estimated 18.2% in 1996/97), it remains the backbone of the economy, employing some 34.9% of the labour force in mid-1998. Agro-industry continues to contribute the majority of

manufacturing value added; the sector provided about 25% of formal employment in 1995; and the bulk of the population is still engaged in subsistence agriculture or small-scale cash cropping on SNL. Some 56% of the total land area is SNL, where traditional subsistence farming is conducted on land held by the monarchy, access to which is managed by the Swazi aristocracy and local chiefs. However, more than one-half of all SNL is designated as Rural Development Areas, and cash cropping of rain-watered crops, particularly maize and cotton, contribute significantly to total agricultural production when climatic conditions are favourable. In 1994/95 total SNL crop production represented 2.4% of GDP. Smallholders' rain-fed crops were most severely affected by the drought in 1992 (when this sub-sector's share of GDP fell to just 0.9%). The remainder of the land, the Title Deed Land (TDL), comprises individual tenure farms, owned by commercial companies, wealthy Swazis and white settlers. The principal agricultural commodities are sugar (of which Swaziland is continental Africa's second largest exporter), maize, citrus fruits, pineapples (for canning) and cotton. Livestock-rearing is an important sub-sector of the economy, particularly on SNL.

Sugar is the dominant agricultural export, providing 13% of domestic export earnings in 1997, with a value of US $126m. and $106m. in 1998. Following exceptionally good weather conditions, production of raw sugar reached 506,349 metric tons in 1986/87, an increase of 33.8% over the 1985/86 season, raising this commodity's share of export receipts to almost 40% in that year. However, production declined to around 440,000 tons in 1987/88 and 1988/89, before increasing to 475,140 tons in 1989/90, the largest part of which was sold to the EU (147,170 tons), mostly under the quota terms of the Lomé Convention. Other important customers were the USA and Canada. Output stabilized in the late 1990s, reaching 471,000 tons in 1996, 476,000 tons in 1997, 475,000 tons in 1998 and a projected 485,000 tons in 1999. There were fears, however, that the unseasonal weather in January–March 2000 had seriously affected the growth of sugar cane, as it was stunted by the lack of sunshine during the growing period. Meanwhile, since 1987 increased quantities have been sold and refined locally, with the establishment of Coca-Cola's soft drink concentrate plant, Cadbury's confectionery factory and a new refinery. Soft drink concentrates became Swaziland's major export in 1996, with sales of US $170m. more than doubling, to $384m., in 1998. Coca-Cola's wholly-owned subsidiary, Conco, increased its sales by 20% (in volume terms) in 1997. This is Coca-Cola's only concentrate plant in southern Africa, and about 70% of its syrup is sold to South Africa, with the remainder going to 16 other countries in the region. Conco is Swaziland's largest privately-owned foreign exchange earner. Local sales of raw sugar amounted to an estimated 43% of production in 1994/95, as new local refining capacity was added. There are three sugar mills in the country, in which the Swazi Nation has substantial shareholdings. The sugar industry was adversely affected by the industrial action which disrupted economic activity across the country in 1996 and 1997. In February 1997 Ubombo Ranches, Swaziland's only producer of refined white sugar, lost four weeks of factory maintenance work, off-crop sugar refining and preparatory work for the milling season. In terms of production, 12,000 tons of white sugar, worth E24m., were lost. In 1998 Swaziland's sugar exports increased by 5.6%, with 55% going to preferential markets in the EU and the USA, and the remainder to the domestic and SACU markets. Domestic consumption rose by 15.3% in 1997/98, owing to the growth of the soft drinks and confectionery manufacturing industries. In 1998 the sugar associations of Swaziland and South Africa signed an agreement ending a three-year dispute over the export of Swazi sugar to South Africa. Swaziland regained access to South Africa's specialist sugar export terminal in Durban and to research and experimental facilities. Many Swazis remain resentful, however, that the country is not allowed to sell its sugar freely to the South African market (as they feel it should be able to, under the SACU agreement).

Rain-fed maize production on SNL, where the bulk of the crop is raised, was severely affected by the drought of the early 1980s, and again in 1992. However, with improved rainfall and increased plantings in response to the import of unpopular yellow maize, this smallholder harvest recovered to 83,800 metric tons in 1983/84, from 29,900 tons the previous year. Thereafter about 100,000 tons were produced annually, with the harvest attaining a record 125,800 tons in 1990/91, until drought returned in 1992. The 1991/92 crop was estimated to have fallen to just 45,600 tons, against annual consumption needs of 116,000 tons. A partial recovery followed over the subsequent two seasons (84,500 tons in 1992/93 and 88,800 tons in 1993/94), but poor rains cut production again in 1994/95, when output fell to 76,000 tons, against annual needs of 123,100 tons. In 1995/96, however, the harvest was an estimated 107,575 tons. The 1998/99 harvest of 113,000 tons failed to meet domestic requirements of 137,000 tons. A further sharp decrease was expected following the catastrophic rains and the devastation caused by 'Cyclone Eline' at the beginning of 2000. By May of that year the market prices for fresh produce rose steeply following reports that maize crops had also been destroyed in some areas.

An increase in livestock slaughterings in the early 1980s was the result of increased offtake brought about by drought and did not represent sustainable growth in output. A similar pattern emerged in 1992 with the recurrence of drought. The national cattle herd declined to 614,000 head in 1984, but had recovered to number 740,000 in 1991. Numbers slaughtered rose to 65,606 in 1992, although herd numbers rose to 753,000 head. In the wake of the drought, cattle mortality rose to 11% in 1993 and the herd declined to 607,000. Numbers recovered to 626,000 in 1994 before declining to 597,000 in 1995, but increasing to 646,000 in 1996. Supported by the role of cattle as a store of wealth in customary society, at this level the national herd represents a significant environmental problem in terms of the overgrazing of SNL. Factory slaughterings virtually ceased, following the collapse of the Swaziland Meat Corpn in 1988. They recovered with the operation's relaunch as Swaziland Meat Industries in late 1989 but the company collapsed again in early 1992, although the abattoir at Matsapha was re-opened later that year. Frozen and canned meat is exported to the EU under quota.

In 1984 Swaziland's production of citrus fruit (oranges and grapefruit) declined dramatically to 43,000 metric tons following the devastation wreaked by 'Cyclone Domoina'. In the following year there was a mixed performance, with grapefruit production recovering strongly (a rise of 18%) but a further small decline in the orange harvest due to root-rot problems and trees coming to the end of their productive lives. By 1987, however, the citrus industry had recovered and total production increased to 82,700 tons. Steadier output in the range of 66,000–72,000 tons was achieved annually through the early 1990s. In 1994 the first fruits of recent new plantings combined with favourable weather conditions (there was no repeat of the hail damage of 1993) to produce a bumper harvest of 104,100 tons. In the following year output declined to 80,000 tons, but export earnings were sustained at E56m. Production declined further, to 68,000 tons in 1996, and to an estimated 60,000 tons in 1997.

In the main, sturdy low-level pineapple plants were undamaged by the 1984 cyclone. The crop and fruit-canning production were thus unaffected; 43,431 metric tons of pineapple were harvested, almost matching the substantial 1983 crop, and 23,350 tons were canned. Subsequent production levels have fluctuated. In 1991 the total crop declined to 31,567 tons, owing to poor rainfall, while cannery output decreased to 14,600 tons. During 1992/93 adverse weather and world market conditions threatened the survival of the country's sole processing plant, Swazican, as export unit prices fell while costs rose. In 1992 cannery output was 14,709 tons, falling to 11,934 tons in 1993. In 1994 output rose to 13,806 tons, and 1,885 tons of jam were produced in addition. The total crop declined to 13,000 tons in 1995, and to 8,000 tons in 1996. The company continues to restructure and diversify away from the traditional dependence upon pineapple. Sales of citrus and canned fruit fell drastically in 1998, to US $30m., compared with $133m. in 1996.

Smallholders on SNL grow most of the kingdom's cotton. The diversification of certain of the sugar estates into raising an irrigated crop and the rapid expansion of the area planted to cotton by SNL farmers combined to raise output from 9,000 metric tons of seed cotton in 1982/83 to a record 32,538 tons in 1988/89. In 1989/90 the crop fell to 26,000 tons owing to adverse weather conditions. A similar quantity was produced in the following year, but production was hindered by drought in 1991/92, when output fell to 5,879 tons. Production has since remained depressed, with 10,000 tons in 1992/93, 7,500 tons in 1993/94 and 6,183 tons in 1994/95. By 1996 output had recovered to some 9,000 tons, according to FAO estimates. In 1997 output of seed cotton rose further, to 16,000 tons.

At December 1993 Swaziland had 98,153 ha of planted forest, representing 6% of the country's total land area. Of the total, more than half was devoted to supplying the kingdom's main forestry industry, the Usutu pulp mill which produces unbleached wood pulp. The mill is Swaziland's third largest source of export earnings. Wood pulp production was consistent at 170,000–180,000 metric tons throughout the 1980s until boiler problems reduced the figure to 147,000 tons in 1989 and 142,000 tons in 1990. A recovery to above 158,000 tons was recorded in 1991, and the company has produced at or around 170,000 tons annually since then. In 1994 170,800 tons were produced, when improved world market conditions led the mill owners to approve an E224m. expansion plan which is to raise annual capacity to 220,000 tons. Production of wood pulp in 1995 was 170,857 tons, when strong international prices took export earnings to US $122m., equal to sugar earnings. Wood and wood products earned a further $25m. in export revenue in that year, rising to $83m. in 1996, but declining to $75m. in 1998. After South Africa, Far Eastern markets are the principal importers of Swazi wood pulp products. Of the remaining area planted to timber, 27,331 ha was for sawlogs in 1991; a further 12,331 ha (mostly gum) was planted for mine timber. The kingdom has three saw mills supplying a small but diversified timber products industry, and pine shelving of Swazi manufacture is sold in the British market, in 'kit' form. Difficulties experienced by the Usutu Pulp Co, owing to a decline in orders from markets in Asia, had been alleviated to some extent by mid-1998. The parent South African company, Sappi International, agreed to buy the pulp, and production at the group's South African mills was reduced in order to satisfy the Swaziland government. Although closure and job losses have been averted, the company is operating at a loss and is delaying the purchase of new machinery and the maintenance of forest access roads. The company's surplus pulp will now be taken by Sappi as a result of agreements with customers in Thailand, Taiwan and the Republic of Korea. In 1998 the company lost an estimated E70m. because of a fall in demand in the company's major markets in South-East Asia.

MINING

Mining and quarrying have represented a declining proportion of GDP overall since independence, although the kingdom is relatively rich in mineral resources. From 10% in the 1960s, the sector's contribution fell to only 1.3% in 1993/94 as a result of the closure of one of the country's three commercial mines. By 1993/94 the opening of a new coal mine raised the sector's contribution to 1.9% of GDP; its share was 2.0% in 1994/95, but declined to 1.4% in 1995/96 with revenue at E86.88m. By 1997/98 its share in GDP had fallen to 1.0%, worth E19m. at factor cost. The asbestos mine remained the major contributor to this sector, accounting for E46.5m. in 1996. The poor performance was due to reduced output at the Maloma colliery (which, at 62,000 tons, was worth only E8.25m.) and to the phasing-out of the diamond mine, which closed at the end of 1996. In addition to the three exported minerals, quarry stone is produced to meet the needs of the local construction industry. Iron ore and (on a smaller scale) gold have been significant export minerals in the past, but neither has been mined for more than a decade. Asbestos was the first mineral product to be exploited in the country on a large scale. The Havelock mine was developed in the 1930s, and it was not until 1962 that it was overtaken by the sugar industry as the territory's leading export earner. Since then, however, the identification of health problems associated with asbestos and the depletion of reserves have resulted in the decline of this sub-sector. A steady 30,000–40,000 metric tons were exported annually for decades, but production declined to 22,804 tons in 1988. In 1989 development of the new Far West ore-body returned output to 27,291 tons and this figure rose to 35,938 tons in 1990. Beset with financial and labour problems the mine went into provisional liquidation in early 1991, when output fell to just 13,888 tons, but was subsequently reopened under new ownership, and output recovered to 33,862 tons in 1993. Production fell to 26,988 tons in 1994, recovering a little to 27,914 tons in 1995. By 1998 asbestos production stood at 27,693 tons, but, owing to falling world prices, its value decreased by 11% to E57m. Plans by a Taiwanese company to mine green chert (used in Asia for jewellery, tiles and ornaments) in the Malolotja Nature Reserve in north-western Swaziland were under attack in 1999. An environmental impact study has suggested that the project would be damaging to the reserve; it has been argued that it would be better to develop tourism rather than mining. The mine, should it start operations, would produce 300 tons per annum over a 12-year lifespan.

Coal holds the country's most important mineral potential, with reserves estimated at 1,000m. metric tons. Production at Emaswati Coal's Mpaka mine fell from 165,122 metric tons in 1989 to 122,502 tons in 1991, as the result of strikes and a cave-in during the year. Mpaka's potential capacity has been consistently under-utilized, and in 1992 the mine closed, owing to lack of consumer demand (potential local users have failed to adapt existing facilities to burn coal). Output in that year consequently fell to 100,200 tons. A second coal-mine, near Maloma, came on stream in late 1993: its output brought total coal production to 227,700 tons in 1994, declining to 171,666 tons in 1995, as the company prepared to shift from open-cast operations to underground workings. By 1997, however, output at Maloma had increased to some 200,000–240,000 tons per year. In 1998 production more than doubled, to 410,000 tons, and the government was considering the feasibility of reopening the Mpaka mine.

Production of mainly industrial-quality diamonds began at the Dokolwako mine in 1984. Output rose steadily to 72,676 carats in 1988, before the open pit operation encountered poorer ground and production fell to 55,264 carats in 1989 and 42,488 carats in 1990. A recovery to 57,420 carats in 1991 coincided with weakening world prices. After a fall to 50,547 carats in 1992, output rose to 61,686 carats in 1993 but declined to an estimated 52,800 carats in 1994, when sales earned E24m. Earnings rose marginally to E25.4m. in 1995. Recovery in the global economy strengthened demand, but the mine's longer-term future is uncertain.

MANUFACTURING

Excluding the processing of agricultural and forestry products, the majority of Swaziland's manufacturing is based at the Matsapha industrial estate. Prior to the new investment in the sector in the latter part of the 1980s, four-fifths of manufacturing's value added derived from agro-industries of various kinds, ranging from sugar, timber and wood-pulp mills to fruit, cotton and meat-processing plants. Manufacturing contributes about 35% of GDP annually, to the value of E508m. at factor cost. In 1984 the Swaziland Chemical Industries fertilizer factory ceased operations, as a combined result of drought conditions and South Africa's adjustment of SACU tariffs. At the end of 1984 the Finnish-owned Salora Swaziland television factory was closed, following its take-over by a South African firm. As a result, the kingdom lost combined exports of E44m., and real manufacturing value added fell slightly in 1985. As a result of industrial action in early 1997, a shortage of sugar supplies from the country's three mills led to the depletion of stocks in the sugar-based industries, which were obliged to import at a higher price from South Africa. Major agro-industrial companies were estimated to have lost E100m. during the strike.

One of the most serious impediments to the growth of manufacturing in Swaziland was the policy of incentives being offered by the South African government and its 'homelands' administrations in their efforts to attract and decentralize industry. Subsequently, however, conditions for investment in Swaziland were made more attractive, and more competitive when compared with the situation in neighbouring states. In 1985 the government introduced a programme of incentives for investment and also embarked upon a promotion exercise to advertise the benefits of Swaziland to industrialists. In 1996, however, the government put an end to the five-year tax-exempt period offered to investors in Swaziland; studies had apparently shown that this incentive had little effect on potential investors. In 1987 the effective replacement of the National Indus-

trial Development Corpn of Swaziland by the Swaziland Industrial Development Co (SIDC) was also a watershed in the history of manufacturing in the kingdom. The SIDC has since established itself as an effective catalyst of industrial development.

Despite these developments within the kingdom, arguably the single most important factor in the improved fortunes of the manufacturing sector in the late 1980s was renewed unrest in South Africa in 1986 and the imposition of international sanctions against that country in the aftermath of its suppression under a state of emergency. It was against this background that Coca-Cola relocated its regional concentrate plant to Swaziland in 1987. This single decision added some 5% to real value added in manufacturing by 1988. Sanctions against South Africa also brought less welcome 'investment' interest to Swaziland. It was reported that a number of South African products were being exported from the kingdom with false 'Made in Swaziland' labels. Several companies, mainly foreign textile concerns, were formally instructed to cease this practice in 1988, but the problem only began to ease as South African domestic reform brought the progressive removal of sanctions after 1990.

Since the late 1980s there has been encouraging diversification of the manufacturing sector, and Swaziland now ranks among the most industrialized of African economies. The pace of investment has slowed in the 1990s, however, as a combined result of drought, regional recession, labour unrest and a drift back to post-apartheid South Africa of earlier relocations. Natex Swaziland (successor to an earlier national textile company) has been installing the capacity for a vertically-integrated national cotton and textile industry, but once again a South African adjustment of SACU tariffs now threatens an important industry in the kingdom. With its protective tariff shield removed the company has been struggling for survival since 1992. Several smaller factories producing knitwear, footwear, gloves, refrigerators, office equipment, beverages, confectionery, pine furniture, safety glass and bricks were established during the investment boom, creating many new jobs. Refrigerators have become an important source of export earnings for Swaziland, with sales of US $54m. in 1996. Formal employment grew strongly over the five years to 1990, when the total in formal employment reached an estimated 92,000. Employment has since stagnated, the total being 91,873 in 1994. In 1996 there were high levels of retrenchment in the manufacturing sector and relatively low levels of new investment. The result was a rate of job creation of less than 1% per year. In 1997 the number of people in formal employment fell to 88,182. The problem of unemployment, therefore, is serious and growing, especially among young people: 54% of the jobless are under 25 years of age and a further 29% are aged between 25 and 34. In 1997 and 1998, according to ministry of labour statistics, 448 and 1,287 workers were made redundant, respectively, bringing the estimated unemployment rate to 45%. Almost one-third of the job losses were in the manufacturing sector, caused by the severe difficulties that several large companies were facing. The losses at Langa National Brickworks, a joint Swazi-UK concern, threatened the future of 500 workers. The Sharma Group of India plans to sell the tissue division of Swazi Paper Mills to South Africa's Nampak Group; this would result in about 300 job losses. Also, Natex, one of Swaziland's largest employers and its leading textile producer, may have to close, or almost certainly reduce its workforce because of slack demand in South Africa and competition from Asia. On a more positive note, however, Fridgemaster Limited reported a profit of E400,000 for the first half of 1998. Also, the Fridgemaster factory was to increase production in 1999 to supply US-based General Electric for its new line of products for African markets; a further 200 workers were to be employed, increasing the workforce to 1,500. However, by mid-1999 the company had become embroiled in a dispute with the authorities, which questioned the high number of deaths among its staff. Denying the accusation that these were due to toxic chemicals used in the manufacturing process, the company put the blame on AIDS, which was apparently responsible for the death of one worker per month. Because of the controversy, Fridgemaster threatened to locate its planned new stove factory in Botswana. There was more positive news regarding new investment from Taiwan, following an agreement on double taxation signed by the two countries in September 1998.

South Africa's decision to recognize the People's Republic of China greatly benefited Swaziland. Taiwan has suspended new investment in South Africa, and is reducing its trade and commercial ties with that country. Much Taiwanese investment, originally intended for South Africa, is now expected to be relocated to Swaziland, and the kingdom has been consolidating its economic ties with Taiwan, with the prime minister paying a visit there in 1997 to discuss new investment projects. These included a E12m. Taiwanese nylon-casting operation and a jumper manufacturer, Gold Investment, which was planning to employ an additional 300 workers to cater for a planned increase in its exports to the USA. An even larger expansion was announced by Tuntex Swaziland, a textile producer, including almost trebling its current workforce of 1,050 employees; this will make it the country's largest private employer. Another Taiwanese-owned company, Sunny Way, was also planning to relocate its agricultural and woven bags plant from South Africa to Swaziland in 2000. An electrical appliance assembly plant at Matsapha was expected to be built in 2000. Despite persistent reports that some companies were contemplating leaving Swaziland for more stable conditions, there was no indication that any major company was seriously considering relocation. On the contrary, a number of new enterprises have announced plans to locate in the country. Afinita Motor Corporation, a bus assembly plant, opened in 1997 with South African investment, and by 1999 was planning to double its monthly production. As a result of the King's visit to Asia in 1998, a Malaysian company decided to establish a computer assembly plant in Swaziland. The confectionery industry is also expanding. Unfortunately, however, although the level of foreign direct investment grew by 17% in 1998, to E2,300m., most of the growth was attributed to the reinvestment of earnings. The 1998/99 annual report by the Central Bank of Swaziland concluded that the country has not received any major foreign investment in recent years, and that a more investor-friendly environment and improved infrastructure were needed.

Swaziland's nascent financial sector experienced a major setback in 1998 with the voluntary liquidation of the Swaziland Business Growth Trust (SBGT). The SBGT—previously funded by the United States Agency for International Development—was undercapitalized and unable to collect repayments on loans made to the small business sector.

POWER, TRANSPORT AND COMMUNICATIONS

The country has a comparatively well-developed and maintained physical infrastructure, but the Swaziland Electricity Board (SEB) still imports from South Africa most of the power it supplies, and the proportion has risen steadily during the recent period of historically low rainfall. In 1995 imports, of 597 GWh, amounted to 85% of total supply of 705 GWh. The 20-MW capacity Luphohlo-Ezulwini hydroelectric station, completed under drought conditions in 1983/84, represents the largest part of domestic installed capacity of 50 MW. The link to the South African grid had a capacity of 96 MW, with new capacity planned. Delays and engineering problems elevated the cost of the Luphohlo scheme far beyond budget, but it was the subsequent slump in the exchange value of the lilangeni which burdened the SEB with unserviceable foreign loans. In July 2000 Swziland's electricity grid was connected to the 400-kV 'Motraco' line delivering power from South Africa's Camden plant to the newly-built Mozal aluminium smelter in Maputo, Mozambique. This will replace the more expensive, smaller lines previously used. The SEB was also investigating the possibility of drawing power from the Cahora Bassa Hydroelectric plant in central Mozambique. Such a project would probably take several years and a massive capital outlay would have to be realized, especially if it was to involve constructing a direct power line through Mozambican territory.

'Cyclone Domoina' destroyed large parts of Swaziland's transport and communications infrastructure in 1984, bringing down major bridges and ruining large sections of the road network. Rehabilitation costs in 1984 were estimated at E60m., and substantial provisions of international aid were forthcoming. The 1995/96 season brought unusually heavy rains once more, but flood damage was modest as compared with that of a decade

earlier. The cost of road repairs following 'Cyclone Eline' in February 2000 was put provisionally at E53m., with additional funding needed for the restoration of the damaged infrastructure, including the railway lines. Swaziland Railways was also expected to lose an additional E2.5m., as a result of international trains being diverted from its territory during March–May.

The kingdom's first railway line was built during 1962–64 to connect the Ngwenya iron ore mine in the far west of the country, via the then railhead across the eastern border at Goma, to the port of Maputo (then Lourenço Marques) and so to its Japanese customers. Long disused west of the Matsapha industrial estate, the line was finally taken up in 1995. A southern link via Lavumisa and connecting to the South African port of Richards Bay was completed in 1978, while a northern link, crossing the border near Mananga and running to the South African town of Komatipoort, was opened in 1986. These lines established a direct link between the eastern Transvaal and the Natal ports, integrating the Swazi lines into the South African network. In the year to March 1995 the northern link carried 3.3m. tons of transit traffic, which represented 78% of all tonnages hauled by the Swaziland Railway Board. In June 1998 a rail service was launched to carry passengers from Durban, South Africa, to Maputo, Mozambique, via Swaziland. In that year Swaziland was also studying the feasibility of linking its rail network to Mpumalanga province in South Africa. This route could compete with existing lines between South Africa and Mozambique, and add alternatives to Durban. The Italian government has announced financial support to help rehabilitate Swaziland's east–west line. By mid-1999 the Swaziland Railway had invested E15.8m. in purchasing materials for the rehabilitation of the east–west line to Maputo, in addition to E12.2m. already spent on upgrading the southern link to Lavumisa. In 1999 the government terminated its annual subsidies to the Royal Swazi National Airways Corpn. Swazi Airlink, a new joint-venture company with Airlink, a subsidiary of South African Airways, was scheduled to commence operations in 1999/2000.

The kingdom's road network is comparatively well developed. In 1996 there were an estimated 3,810 km of roads. About 28.2% of the road network was paved in 1994. Road projects have dominated the capital expenditure programmes of recent development plans and in 1991 work began on the rebuilding of the kingdom's main road artery connecting the capital, Mbabane, to Manzini, via Matsapha. The highway was completed in 1999, behind schedule and well over budget. By the end of 1999 a large-scale infrastructure investment programme was in place. It included resurfacing and upgrading the main road from Manzini to Lomahasha on the Mozambican border. A new E21m. bridge and approach roads over the Komati river have already been completed. Several other roads are also being upgraded, including Siteki to Mhlumeni in the east of the country, Nhlangano to Lavumisa in the south and Luvengo to Sicunusa in the west.

Much of Swaziland can now be reached telephonically by dialling directly; a satellite link was inaugurated in 1983 allowing the kingdom's subscribers to bypass South Africa when contacting Europe and North America. At the end of 1994 Swaziland had 18,605 telephone exchange connections. The Swaziland Posts and Telecommunications Corpn (SPTC) introduced new telephone codes in late 1998 to include area codes as a prefix for the existing numbers. This would bring Swaziland into line with most international telephone exchange systems. The level of internet use, with more than 2,000 subscribers in 1998, is considered high by African standards. The fastest growing service was the mobile operator MTN Swaziland, a SPTC joint venture. In the planned reform of the state-owned sector, the SPTC was to be broken up into separate postal and telecommunications companies in preparation for their future privatization. An estimated 95% of the population have access to two radio stations operated by the Swaziland Broadcasting and Information Service. One television channel is run by the Swaziland Television Broadcasting Corpn. There are two national daily newspapers, one of which is privately owned.

TOURISM

Tourism in Swaziland was largely depressed during the early 1980s, owing primarily to the economic recession in South Africa (whence the majority of the tourists come; 63% in 1993), together with strong competition from new hotel complexes in the South African 'homelands'. There were significant improvements after 1985, when the total number of arrivals was stimulated by growth in the number of business visitors as well as by renewed tourist interest. Since 1992 regional recession has depressed the sector once more, although some encouragement has been provided by an increase in arrivals from Mozambique following increased stability in the border region.

Facilities in the central Ezulwini valley (the heart of the Swazi tourism industry) are dominated by the South African Sun International chain. A new hotel complex, owned by the government but managed by Protea of South Africa, was opened in Piggs Peak in 1986. Visitor arrivals rose to 287,796 in 1990, but thereafter stagnated. In 1994 an improvement in the industry's fortunes was reflected in a 24% increase in tourist arrivals at hotels compared with the previous year (reaching 335,933). In 1995 arrivals declined to 299,822, but receipts from tourism increased to a total of US $48m. The peaceful political transition in South Africa was the principal cause of the recovery. In 1996 tourist arrivals increased to 314,921, but receipts from tourism decreased to $38m. In 1997 arrivals increased further, to 322,000, and receipts rose to $40m. It was hoped that with the drafting of the tourism bill, which was to be presented to parliament in 2000, the government would finally adopt a comprehensive policy to develop the tourism sector.

BALANCE OF PAYMENTS

Swaziland's balance-of-payments position improved considerably after the mid-1980s. From the latter part of 1983 until the end of 1985 the value of the lilangeni fell sharply. In terms of the IMF's 'basket' of major currencies, the special drawing right (SDR), the lilangeni exchange rate was SDR 0.78 = E1 at the end of 1983, but had declined to SDR 0.36 = E1 two years later (the decline against the surging US dollar being even more precipitous). This raised the local currency value of commodity exports sold on world markets, albeit at depressed prices in real terms. However, import prices rose sharply. Most imports are supplied by or via South Africa, and the shared currency devaluation fuelled inflation in both countries; the South African index of the cost of imported goods rose by 24% in 1985. The initial impact of this was a widening of the trade deficit in lilangeni terms, but a narrowing in real terms. Distortions further down the external accounts included a sudden rise in the burden of the service of external debt and substantial real valuation losses on reserves held in South Africa. However, as the currency stabilized and exports rose strongly, following the record sugar crop of 1986, the trade deficit of the balance of payments fell from US $95.9m. in 1985 to $18.6m. As a result, the current account moved into surplus for the first time since 1977, and, with new investment supporting capital inflows, the overall balance-of-payments position was also in surplus, signalling the beginning of a sustained period of rising foreign reserves. This improved performance was reversed after 1992, as wider trade deficits and outflows of short-term capital (related to trade credit and pension-fund investments in South Africa) brought about a decline in external reserves. The lilangeni, which is at par with the rand, fell to record lows in 1998 against the US dollar. This devaluation will affect Swaziland's exports in world markets, but could help to offset the weaker currencies in the East Asian countries. Furthermore, sugar exports are unlikely to be negatively affected as contracts with the EU generally are fixed, while most of the rest goes to South Africa in the form of soft drinks concentrate which will not be affected by foreign exchange fluctuations.

In 1999, according to IMF figures, a trade deficit of an estimated US $110.8m. was recorded (imports $1,052m., exports $941.3m.), compared with $116.5m. in 1998. In 1996 Swaziland's principal exports were edible concentrates, sugar, wood pulp, refrigerators and cotton yarn. Principal imports in that year included machinery and transport equipment, manufactured goods, chemicals and chemical products, food products, fuels and lubricants. The major destination for Swaziland's exports in 1997 were South Africa, accounting for 74% of the total, followed by the EU (12.3%), Mozambique (5.2%) and the USA (2.4%). South Africa was also the principal source of imports (82.9%); other suppliers included the EU, Japan and the USA.

Over 1986–92 the current account recorded consistent surpluses, which peaked at US $65.9m. in 1990. In 1993, however, Swaziland recorded a current-account deficit of $63.7m. According to IMF figures, the current account recorded a surplus of $9.0m. in 1997, a deficit of $16.8m. in 1998 and a surplus of $17.2m. in 1999. Service debits have been augmented by the transfer of dividends and profits from foreign-owned businesses. Official unrequited transfers also make a significant contribution. Apart from grant aid from abroad, these flows comprise SACU transfers over and above the reimbursement of the duty raised on Swaziland's own trade and production. SACU receipts are expected to contribute a declining share of balance-of-payments and budgetary income as a result of the ongoing renegotiation of the customs union agreement. None the less, the major source of government revenue continues to be SACU receipts, which accounted for 50.3% of 1998/99 revenue estimates, a decline from the 1997/98 share, which was 55.6%, and an estimated 53% of the revenue in 2000.

The recovery in capital flows in the mid-1980s was very marked. Supported in the early 1980s by the activities of the official sector (the government borrowing abroad), the capital account recorded, after 1985, strong net private inflows as political and commercial considerations combined to bring about the relocation of manufacturing capacity from South Africa or attracted new investment to Swaziland. Private inflows peaked at E170m. in 1989. New investment flows have since declined, but increased private-sector drawings on foreign loans and reinvestment of profits have maintained the surplus on long-term capital inflows. According to the Central Bank of Swaziland, the rate of growth of foreign direct investment (FDI) declined from 1992–98. The major reasons were political uncertainty in South Africa and industrial/political unrest in Swaziland. Total FDI stock declined in 1997, but was estimated to have risen again in 1998, by 3.1%, reflecting increased Taiwanese investment. Government budget surpluses in the five years to 1991/92 led to net redemptions of foreign debt (meaning public sector outflows), but this trend has since reversed. The overall position strengthened considerably after 1986, and by the end of 1992 official holdings of foreign reserves had increased to E912m. Holdings fell over 1993–94 (the first decrease in seven years) to stand at E846m. at the end of 1994. The total rose again to E995m. in 1995, representing a comfortable 16 weeks' import cover. The estimated value of foreign reserves in 1999 amounted to E2,321m. (US $380m.).

PUBLIC FINANCE

Swaziland's public finances are characterized by a heavy dependence upon receipts from South Africa from the SACU revenue pool. Over and above the revenue raised in customs and excise duty on the kingdom's own trade and excisable production, these include cash compensation for the distorting effects of high import tariffs which protect South African producers' dominance of the Swazi market. With the installation of a government in South Africa which no longer needs to buy goodwill in the region, the future of these receipts is uncertain and the customs union agreement is being renegotiated. A sales tax was introduced in 1984 to lessen the dependence upon SACU receipts. Its tighter application increased revenue from this source from the 1986/87 (April–March) fiscal year, but it still represented less than a quarter of the contribution of customs union receipts in 1995/96. Overall receipts stagnated in the early 1990s as a result of the general economic downturn. Compounded by the wasteful growth of current expenditure and improved capital budget implementation, this trend took the government's finances into deficit again in 1992/93. Capital spending previously peaked with the internationally-backed reconstruction effort which followed the cyclone damage of 1984, but the general inability of the authorities to spend their investment budget is a structural problem characteristic of the administrative inefficiencies inherent in the dichotomous nature of Swaziland's governance. Finally, there has been significant net lending to public sector industries, some inefficiently run and others struggling with foreign debt, following the sharp decline in the exchange rate during the mid-1980s. In 1989 a public enterprise unit was formed within the finance ministry, charged with reviewing the performance of the public sector companies and advising on future policy in their regard. As a result, an improved performance has been achieved by this sector, although this too has been compromised by the general downturn in the economy since 1992.

In late 1995 a programme for the reform of public enterprises was introduced, and in 1996 an extensive reform of the tax system was initiated, as part of the government's continuing austerity programme. The government intends to establish a non-discriminatory tax regime in which investors in all sectors are subject to the same rate of tax. In June 1999 the corporate tax rate was reduced from 37.5% to 30%, the same as South Africa's. Earlier in that year an additional petrol tax of 7 cents per litre was proposed. The government also announced that it wanted to diversify its revenue base, especially given probable cuts in SACU customs receipts.

The budgets of the early 1980s were introduced against a background of chronic public finance problems, successive (often large) deficits and growing domestic and external debt. However, the economy's buoyancy in the late 1980s and early 1990s turned the deficits into persistent, large and embarrassing surpluses since the effects of the record sugar crop of 1986 entailed a near doubling of direct taxation receipts in 1987/88. In 1987 the finance minister tabled a budget projecting an E24m. deficit; the 1986/87 deficit of E49m. had represented 4.8% of GDP. In the event, company tax delivered E73m. rather than the budgeted E35m. in 1987/88, while personal taxes also came in well above expectations as formal sector employment grew strongly in the boom conditions. Current expenditure was held almost exactly to budget, while net lending was greater than expected at E14m. and the capital budget was 13% underspent at E66m. The result was a surplus, the first since 1980/81, of E22m.

The pattern was repeated over the next five years. The finance ministry's routine revisions of the budget projections in July and December/January of each fiscal year showed higher than expected revenue, tight control of recurrent outgoings and underspending of the capital budget. In 1988/89 the original projection was of an E9.5m. deficit; the eventual surplus for the year was E59m. (3.8% of GDP). In 1989/90 an E1m. deficit was expected; the result was an E85m. surplus (some 5.0% of GDP). In 1990/91 the surplus was only contained at E1m. by the introduction of an E165m. Capital Investment Facility (CIF) established to save from the surplus and so reduce it. In 1991/92 a budgeted E7m. deficit was, in effect, eventually recorded as a surplus of E21m. (E100m. having been diverted by the CIF). One response to this trend was for the authorities to ease the personal tax burden. The government also embarked upon a programme of accelerated debt redemption.

The 1992/93 financial year was a turning-point in the kingdom's public finances. Growth in revenue slowed to 9% (a decline, in real terms, given inflation of some 13%), while expenditure increased by 17%. This latter increase reflected civil service pay and benefits increases, as well as improvements in capital budget implementation. An overall deficit of E42m. was recorded. The 1993/94 budget projected an E120m. deficit. In the event, an E171m. shortfall was recorded. The first signs that the tide was about to turn once more came in 1994/95, when the final deficit turned out at less than that budgeted, albeit still larger, at E198m. (equivalent to 5.2% of GDP), than in 1993/94. Although the 1995/96 budget showed a surplus of E68m., the country's macroeconomic situation deteriorated and the 1996/97 budget resulted in a deficit of E217m. Revenue was revised downwards as a result of the late implementation of sales tax reforms. Furthermore, estimated recurrent expenditure was higher than originally budgeted because of additional allocations for the Swaziland Development and Savings Bank. In 1997/98, according to projected figures, there was an estimated overall budgetary surplus of E0.7m. The budget for 1998/99 resulted in a small deficit of E7.1m., although it was projected to increase to E244m. in 1999/2000. Government personnel costs, at E919.8m., are the largest single expenditure item, representing 53.3% of recurrent expenditure in 1998/99 (up from 50.1% two years previously). Education continued to receive a large portion of the budget (25.2%), followed by law and order (17.5%). Given the falling exchange rate against major currencies, the debt burden was expected to double in 1998/99, resulting in higher interest payments and increased debt-service obligations. In the mean time, the debt burden remained modest. Total external debt stood at US $250.7m. at the end of 1998 (compared with $368.2m. at the end of 1997), of which $222.5m. was long-term public debt. In that year the cost of debt-servicing was equivalent to 2.1% of the value of exports of goods and services. In 1990–98 the average annual rate of inflation was 9.5%; consumer prices increased by 7.1% in 1997, by 8.2% in 1998, and by 6.1% in 1999. During 1998–99 the CMA countries experienced high interest rates. The South African Reserve Bank had to raise interest rates to help strengthen the value of the rand, which was depressed because of uncertainty over the impending change in power in South Africa. All CMA members keep their interest rates roughly aligned, and the prime lending rate of commercial banks in South Africa and Swaziland was 14% on 31 July 1999.

Statistical Survey

Source (unless otherwise stated): Central Statistical Office, POB 456, Mbabane.

AREA AND POPULATION

Area: 17,363 sq km (6,704 sq miles).

Population (excluding absentee workers): 494,534 (males 231,861, females 262,673) at census of 25 August 1976; 681,059 (males 321,579, females 359,480) at census of 25 August 1986; 980,722 at 1997 census.

Density (1997): 56.5 per sq km.

Ethnic Groups (census of August 1986): Swazi 661,646; Other Africans 14,468; European 1,825; Asiatic 228; Other non-Africans 412; Mixed 2,403; Unknown 77; Total 681,059.

Principal Towns (population at census of August 1986): Mbabane (capital) 38,290; Manzini 18,084.

Births and Deaths (UN estimates, 1990–95): Average annual birth rate 40.2 per 1,000; average annual death rate 9.1 per 1,000. Source: UN, *World Population Prospects: The 1998 Revision.*

Expectation of Life (UN estimates, years at birth, 1990–95): 57.8 (males 55.4; females 60.0). Source: UN, *World Population Prospects: The 1998 Revision.*

Economically Active Population (persons aged 12 years and over, census of August 1986): Agriculture, hunting, forestry and fishing 30,197; Mining and quarrying 5,245; Manufacturing 14,742; Electricity, gas and water 1,315; Construction 7,661; Trade, restaurants and hotels 12,348; Transport, storage and communications 7,526; Financing, insurance, real estate and business services 1,931; Community, social and personal services 32,309; Activities not adequately defined 3,156; Total employed 116,430 (males 79,528, females 36,902); Unemployed 43,925 (males 25,663, females 18,262); Total labour force 160,355 (males 105,191, females 55,164). Source: UN, *Demographic Yearbook.*

Mid-1997 (estimates in '000): Agriculture, etc. 116; Total labour force 325.

Mid-1998 (estimates in '000): Agriculture, etc. 118; Total labour force 338.

Source: FAO, *Production Yearbook.*

AGRICULTURE

Principal Crops ('000 metric tons, 1998): Rice (paddy) 1*; Maize 107; Potatoes 6*; Sweet potatoes 2*; Pulses 7*; Cottonseed 11*; Cotton (lint) 6; Oranges 31; Grapefruit 25; Pineapples 8*; Sugar cane 3,886.

* FAO estimate.

Livestock (FAO estimates, '000 head, year ending September 1998): Horses 1; Asses 15; Cattle 650; Pigs 30; Sheep 25; Goats 435.

Livestock Products ('000 metric tons, 1998): Beef and veal 13*; Goat meat 3*; Cows' milk 38; Cattle hides 2*.

* FAO estimate.

Source: FAO, *Production Yearbook.*

FORESTRY

Roundwood Removals ('000 cubic metres, 1997): Sawlogs, veneer logs and logs for sleepers 260; Pulpwood 604; Fuel wood 560; Total 1,424.

Sawnwood Production ('000 cubic metres, 1997): 75.

Source: FAO, *Yearbook of Forest Products.*

FISHING

Total Catch (FAO estimates, metric tons, live weight): 60 in 1995; 60 in 1996; 65 in 1997. Source: FAO, *Yearbook of Fishery Statistics.*

MINING

Production (estimates, 1994): Coal 227,700 metric tons; Asbestos 27,000 metric tons; Quarrystone 211,500 cubic metres; Diamonds 52,800 carats. Source: partly IMF, *Swaziland—Recent Economic Developments* (April 1997).

INDUSTRY

1995: Electric energy 425m. kWh; **1996:** Wood pulp 200,000 metric tons; Raw sugar 472,000 metric tons. Source: UN, *Industrial Commodity Statistics Yearbook.*

FINANCE

Currency and Exchange Rates: 100 cents = 1 lilangeni (plural: emalangeni). *Sterling, Dollar and Euro Equivalents* (28 April 2000): £1 sterling = 10.6921 emalangeni; US \$1 = 6.8185 emalangeni; €1 = 6.1946 emalangeni; 1,000 emalangeni = £93.53 = \$146.66 = €161.43. *Average Exchange Rate* (US \$ per lilangeni): 0.21724 in 1997; 0.18246 in 1998; 0.16370 in 1999. Note: The lilangeni is at par with the South African rand.

Budget (provisional, million emalangeni, year ending 31 March 1998): *Revenue:* Taxes on net income and profits 529; Taxes on property 3; Taxes on goods, services and international trade 1,351 (Receipts from Southern African Customs Union 1,007, Sales tax 255, Road levy and oil tax 0); Other current revenue 135; Total 2,018, excl. grants received (47). *Expenditure:* Current expenditure 1,544 (Wages and salaries 797, Other purchases of goods and services 475, Interest payments 28, Subsidies and other current transfers 244); Capital expenditure 310; Total 1,850, excl. lending minus repayments (−4). Source: IMF, *Swaziland—Statistical Appendix* (February 1999).

International Reserves (US \$ million at 31 December 1999): IMF special drawing rights 3.33; Reserve position in IMF 8.99; Foreign exchange 363.61; Total 375.93. Source: IMF, *International Financial Statistics.*

Money Supply (million emalangeni at 31 December 1999): Currency outside banks 136.95; Demand deposits at commercial banks 525.72; Total money (incl. others) 662.69. Source: IMF, *International Financial Statistics.*

Cost of Living (Retail Price Index, excluding rent, for low-income wage-earners' families in Mbabane and Manzini; base: 1995 = 100): 114.0 in 1997; 123.3 in 1998; 130.8 in 1999. Source: IMF, *International Financial Statistics.*

Expenditure on the Gross Domestic Product (million emalangeni at current prices, 1996/97): Government final consumption expenditure 1,185.8; Private final consumption expenditure 3,072.6; Increase in stocks 47.2; Gross fixed capital formation 1,530.1; *Total domestic expenditure* 5,835.7; Exports of goods and services 4,265.2; *Less* Imports of goods and services 4,858.4; *GDP in purchasers' values* 5,245.5. Source: IMF, *Swaziland—Statistical Appendix* (February 1999).

Gross Domestic Product by Economic Activity (million emalangeni in current purchasers' values, 1996/97): Agriculture and forestry 766.8; Mining and quarrying 44.6; Manufacturing 1,350.2; Electricity, gas and water 57.5; Construction 206.0; Trade, restaurants and hotels 372.1; Transport and communications 221.9; Finance, insurance, real estate, etc. 194.6; Government services 843.6; Other non-marketable services 69.9; Owner-occupied dwellings 93.7; *Sub-total* 4,220.9; *Less* Imputed bank service charge 137.9; *GDP at factor cost* 4,083.0; Indirect taxes, *less* subsidies 1,159.5; *GDP in*

purchasers' values 5,242.5. Source: IMF, *Swaziland—Statistical Appendix* (February 1999).

Balance of Payments (US \$ million, 1999): Exports of goods f.o.b. 941.3; Imports of goods f.o.b. −1,052.1; *Trade balance* −110.8; Exports of services 71.8; Imports of services −173.2; *Balance on goods and services* −212.2; Other income received 173.6; Other income paid −78.7; *Balance on goods, services and income* −117.3; Current transfers received 239.6; Current transfers paid −105.0; *Current balance* 17.2; Direct investment abroad −0.2; Direct investment from abroad 32.6; Portfolio investment assets −0.4; Portfolio investment liabilities −0.9; Other investment assets −89.4; Other investment liabilities 23.4; Net errors and omissions 39.2; *Overall balance* 21.5. Source: IMF, *International Financial Statistics.*

EXTERNAL TRADE

Principal Commodities (US \$ million, 1996): *Imports c.i.f.:* Food and live animals 172; Beverages and tobacco 25; Inedible crude materials 50; Mineral fuels, lubricants 135; Chemicals and chemical products 172; Manufactures classified by material 168; Machinery and transport equipment 312; Miscellaneous manufactured articles 107; Total (incl. others) 1,168. *Exports f.o.b.:* Sugar 146; Wood pulp 56; Wood and wood products 28; Canned fruits 13; Edible concentrates 180; Cotton yarn 40; Refrigerators 79; Paper products 27; Total (incl. others) 878. Figures refer to domestic exports, excluding re-exports (19). Source: IMF, *Swaziland—Statistical Appendix* (February 1999).

Principal Trading Partners ('000 emalangeni): *Imports* (year ending 31 March 1993): France 1,552.2; Netherlands 10,726.9; South Africa 2,428,294.0; Switzerland 7,499.6; United Kingdom 75,117.8; Total (incl. others) 2,587,338.5. *Exports* (excl. re-exports, 1991): South Africa 804,103.7; United Kingdom 56,561.3; Total (incl. others) 1,711,539.0.

TRANSPORT

Railways (traffic estimates, million, 1991): Passenger-km 1,210 (1988); Freight net ton-km 2,910. Source: UN Economic Commission for Africa, *African Statistical Yearbook.*

Total freight ('000 metric tons, 1993): 4,203.

Road Traffic (estimates, motor vehicles in use, 31 December 1997): Passenger cars 31,882; Buses and coaches 3,495; Lorries and vans 29,277; Motorcycles and scooters 2,727 (1996). Source: International Road Federation, *World Road Statistics.*

Civil Aviation (traffic on scheduled services, 1996): Kilometres flown 1 million; Passengers carried 54,000; Passenger-kilometre 57 million; Total ton-kilometre 5 million. Source: UN, *Statistical Yearbook.*

TOURISM

Tourist Arrivals (at hotels): 299,822 in 1995; 314,921 in 1996; 322,000 in 1997. Source: World Tourism Organization, *Yearbook of Tourism Statistics.*

Tourism Receipts (US \$ million): 48 in 1995; 38 in 1996; 40 in 1997. Source: World Tourism Organization, *Yearbook of Tourism Statistics.*

COMMUNICATIONS MEDIA

Radio Receivers (1997): 155,000 in use.

Television Receivers (1997): 21,000 in use.

Daily Newspapers (1996): 3.

Source: UNESCO, *Statistical Yearbook.*

Telephones (year ending 31 March 1996): 21,000 main lines in use.

Telefax Stations (year ending 31 March 1996): 1,012 in use. Source: UN, *Statistical Yearbook.*

EDUCATION

Primary (1997): Institutions 529; Teachers 6,094; Students 205,829.

General Secondary: Institutions 165 (1994); Teachers 2,954; Students 57,330 (1996).

Teacher Training (1993/94): Institutions 3; Teachers 88; Students 924.

Technical and Vocational Training (1993/94): Institutions 2; Teachers 140; Students 2,034.

University Education (1996/97): Institution 1; Teachers 257; Students 3,438.

Directory

The Constitution

The Constitution of 13 October 1978 vests supreme executive and legislative power in the hereditary King (Ngwenyama—the Lion). Succession is governed by traditional law and custom. In the event of the death of the King, the powers of Head of State are transferred to the constitutional dual monarch, the Queen Mother (Indlovukazi—Great She Elephant), who is authorized to act as Regent until the designated successor attains the age of 21. The Constitution provides for a bicameral legislature, comprising a House of Assembly and a Senate. The functions of the Libandla are confined to debating government proposals and advising the King. Executive power is exercised through the Cabinet (later redesignated the Council of Ministers), which is appointed by the King. The Swaziland National Council (Libandla), which comprises members of the royal family, and is headed by the King and Queen Mother, advises on matters regulated by traditional law and custom. The Constitution affirms the fundamental rights of the individual.

Following a number of amendments to the electoral system, which were approved by the King in October 1992, the House of Assembly (which was redesignated as the National Assembly) was expanded to 65 deputies (of whom 55 are directly elected from candidates nominated by traditional local councils, known as Tinkhundla, and 10 appointed by the King), and the Senate to 30 members (of whom 20 are appointed by the King and 10 elected by the National Assembly). Elections to the National Assembly are conducted by secret ballot, in two rounds of voting; the second round of the elections is contested by the three candidates from each of the Tinkhundla who secure the highest number of votes in the first poll. In July 1996 the King appointed a commission to prepare proposals for a draft constitution, which would subsequently be submitted for approval by the Swazi people.

The Government

HEAD OF STATE

HM King Mswati III (succeeded to the throne 25 April 1986).

COUNCIL OF MINISTERS
(August 2000)

Prime Minister: Dr Barnabas Sibusiso Dlamini.

Deputy Prime Minister and Minister of Foreign Affairs and of Trade: Arthur R. V. Khoza.

Minister of Justice and Constitutional Development: Chief Maweni Simelane.

Minister of Finance: John Carmichael.

Minister of Home Affairs: Prince Sobandla Dlamini.

Minister of Education: Rev. Abednego Ntshangase.

Minister of Agriculture and Co-operatives: Roy Fanourakis.

Minister of Broadcasting and Information: Magwagwa Mdluli.

Minister of Enterprise and Employment: Lufto Dlamini.

Minister of Economic Planning and Development: Majozi Sithole.

Minister of Health and Social Welfare: Dr Phetsile Dlamini.

Minister of Public Service and Information: Mntonzima Dlamini.

Minister of Public Works and Transport: Prince Guduza Dlamini.

Minister of Natural Resources and Energy: Ephraim Magwagwa Mdluli.

Minister of Tourism and Communications: Dr George Soze Vilakati.

Minister of Housing and Urban Development: Stella Lukhele.

MINISTRIES

Office of the Prime Minister: Government House, POB 395, Mbabane; tel. 4042251; fax 4043943; e-mail ppcu@realnet.co.sz.

Office of the Deputy Prime Minister: POB 433, Swazi Plaza, Mbabane; tel. 4042723; fax 4044085.

Ministry of Agriculture and Co-operatives: POB 162, Mbabane; tel. 4042731; fax 4044700; e-mail moac-hq@realnet.co.sz.

Ministry of Broadcasting and Information: POB 338, Mbabane; tel. 4043521; e-mail nhlanhla@realnet.co.sz.

Ministry of Defence: Mbabane; tel. 5185774; e-mail defence1@realnet.co.sz.

Ministry of Economic Planning and Development: POB 602, Mbabane; tel. 4043765; fax 4042157.

Ministry of Education: POB 39, Mbabane; tel. 4042491; fax 4043880.

Ministry of Enterprise and Employment: POB 451, Mbabane; tel. 4043201; fax 4044711.

Ministry of Finance: POB 443, Mbabane; tel. 4048148; fax 4043187; e-mail minfin@realnet.co.sz.

Ministry of Foreign Affairs and Trade: POB 518, Mbabane; tel. 4042661; fax 4042669.

Ministry of Health and Social Welfare: POB 5, Mbabane; tel. 4042431; fax 4042092; e-mail minhealth@realnet.co.sz.

Ministry of Home Affairs: POB 432, Mbabane; tel. 4042941; fax 4044303.

Ministry of Housing and Urban Development: POB 1832, Mbabane; tel. 4041739; fax 4045290; e-mail minhouse@realnet.co.sz.

Ministry of Justice and Constitutional Development: POB 924, Mbabane; tel. 4046010; fax 4043531.

Ministry of Natural Resources and Energy: POB 57, Mbabane; tel. 4046244; fax 4042436.

Ministry of Public Service and Information: POB 338, Mbabane; tel. 4042761; fax 4042774.

Ministry of Public Works and Transport: POB 58, Mbabane; tel. 4042321; fax 4042364.

Ministry of Tourism and Communications: POB 58, Mbabane; tel. 4046420; fax 4046438; e-mail mintour@realnet.co.sz; internet www.mintour.gov.sz.

Legislature

SENATE

There are 30 senators, of whom 20 are appointed by the King and 10 elected by the National Assembly.
President: Muntu Msawane.

NATIONAL ASSEMBLY

There are 65 deputies, of whom 55 are directly elected from candidates nominated by the Tinkhundla and 10 appointed by the King. The latest elections to the National Assembly took place on 16 and 24 October 1998.
Speaker: (vacant).

Political Organizations

Party political activity was banned by royal proclamation in April 1973, and formally prohibited under the 1978 Constitution. Since 1991, following indications that the Constitution was to be revised, a number of political associations have re-emerged.

Imbokodvo National Movement (INM): f. 1964 by King Sobhuza II; traditionalist movement, which also advocates policies of development and the elimination of illiteracy; Leader (vacant).

Ngwane National Liberatory Congress (NNLC): Ilanga Centre, Martin St, Manzini; tel. 5053935; f. 1962, by fmr mems of the SPP; advocates democratic freedoms and universal suffrage, and seeks abolition of the Tinkhundla electoral system; Pres. Obed Dlamini; Sec.-Gen. Dumisa Dlamini.

Confederation for Full Democracy in Swaziland: f. 1992 as an alliance of orgs advocating democratic reform; includes:

People's United Democratic Movement (PUDEMO): POB 4588, Manzini; tel. and fax 5054181; f. 1983; seeks constitutional limitation of the powers of the monarchy; affiliated orgs include the Human Rights Asscn of Swaziland and the Swaziland Youth Congress (SWAYOCO—Pres. Bongani Masuku; Sec.-Gen. Temangcamane Maseko); Pres. Mario Masuku; Sec.-Gen. Thulani Maseko.

Swaziland National Front (SWANAFRO): Mbabane; Pres. Elmond Shongwe; Sec.-Gen. Glenrose Dlamini.

Swaziland Progressive Party (SPP): POB 6, Mbabane; tel. 2022648; f. 1929; Pres. J. J. Nquku.

Swaziland United Front (SUF): POB 14, Kwaluseni; f. 1962 by fmr mems of the SPP; Leader Matsapa Shongwe.

Diplomatic Representation

EMBASSIES AND HIGH COMMISSIONS IN SWAZILAND

China (Taiwan): Embassy House, Warner St, POB 56, Mbabane; tel. 4042379; fax 4046688; Ambassador: Enti Liu.

Mozambique: Princess Drive, POB 1212, Mbabane; tel. 4043700; fax 4043692; High Commissioner: PAULO TEMBE.

South Africa: The New Mall, 2nd Floor, Plasmall St, POB 2597, Mbabane; tel. 4044651; fax 4046944; High Commissioner: WALTER LOUW.

United Kingdom: Lilunga House, Gilfillan St, Private Bag, Mbabane; tel. 4042582; fax 4042585; e-mail enquiries@mbabane.mail.fco.gov.uk; High Commissioner: NEIL HOOK.

USA: Central Bank Bldg, Warner St, POB 199, Mbabane; tel. 4046442; fax 4045959; Ambassador: ALAN R. MCKEE.

Judicial System

Swaziland's legal system operates on a dual basis, comprising both traditional Swazi National Courts as well as Constitutional Courts. The latter are based on Roman-Dutch law and comprise a High Court (which is a Superior Court of Record) with subordinate courts in all the administrative districts. The Court of Appeal sits at Mbabane. The Constitutional Courts are headed by a Chief Justice, subordinate to whom are judges and magistrates. There is also an Industrial Court.

There are 17 Swazi National Courts, including two Courts of Appeal and a Higher Court of Appeal, which have limited jurisdiction in civil and criminal cases. Their jurisdiction excludes non-Swazi nationals. The Constitutional Courts have the final ruling in the event of any conflict between the two legal systems.

Chief Justice: S. SAPIRE.

Religion

About 60% of the adult Swazi population profess Christianity. Most of the remainder hold traditional beliefs. There is also a small Muslim community.

CHRISTIANITY

Council of Swaziland Churches: Mandlenkosi Ecumenical House, 142 Esser St, Manzini; POB 1095, Manzini; tel. 5053931; fax 5055841; f. 1976; 10 mem. churches; Chair. Rev. S. J. NXUMALO; Gen. Sec. MARIA MBELU.

League of African Churches: POB 230, Lobamba; asscn of 48 independent churches; Pres. ISAAC DLAMINI.

Swaziland Conference of Churches: 175 Ngwane St, POB 1157, Manzini; tel. 5055259; fax 5054430; e-mail cmediac@iafrica.sz; f. 1929; Pres. Rev. NICHOLAS NYAWO; Gen. Sec. JOHANNES V. MAZIBUKO.

The Anglican Communion

Swaziland comprises a single diocese within the Church of the Province of Southern Africa. The Metropolitan of the Province is the Archbishop of Cape Town, South Africa.

Bishop of Swaziland: Rt Rev. LAWRENCE BEKISIA ZULU, POB 118, Mbabane; tel. 4043624; fax 4046759; e-mail anglicanchurch@iafrica.sz.

The Roman Catholic Church

The Roman Catholic Church was established in Swaziland in 1913. For ecclesiastical purposes, Swaziland comprises the single diocese of Manzini, suffragan to the archdiocese of Pretoria, South Africa. At 31 December 1998 there were an estimated 50,160 adherents in Swaziland, equivalent to about 5.1% of the total population. The Bishop participates in the Southern African Catholic Bishops' Conference (based in Pretoria, South Africa).

Bishop of Manzini: Rt Rev. LOUIS NCAMISO NDLOVU, Bishop's House, Sandlane St, POB 19, Manzini; tel. 5056900; fax 5056762; e-mail bishop@iafrica.sz.

Other Christian Churches

Church of the Nazarene: POB 1460, Manzini; tel. 5054732; f. 1910; 7,649 adherents (1994).

The Evangelical Lutheran Church in Southern Africa: POB 117, Mbabane; tel. 4046453; f. 1902; Bishop R. SCHIELE; 2,800 adherents in Swaziland (1994).

Lutheran Development Service: POB 388, Mbabane; tel. 4042562; fax 4043870; e-mail lds@realnet.co.sz.

Mennonite Central Committee: POB 329, Mbabane; tel. 4042805; fax 4044732; f. 1971; Co-ordinators JON RUDY, CAROLYN RUDY.

The Methodist Church in Southern Africa: POB 218, Mbabane; tel. 4042658; f. 1880; 2,578 adherents (1992).

United Christian Church of Africa: POB 253, Nhlangano; tel. 2022648; f. 1944; Pres. Rt Rev. JEREMIAH NDZINISA; Founder and Gen. Sec. Dr J. J. NQUKU.

The National Baptist Church, the Christian Apostolic Holy Spirit Church in Zion and the Religious Society of Friends (Quakers) are also active.

BAHÁ'Í FAITH

National Spiritual Assembly: POB 298, Mbabane; tel. 5052689; f. 1960; mems resident in 153 localities.

ISLAM

Ezulwini Islamic Institute: Al Islam Dawah Movement of Swaziland, POB 133, Ezulwini; c. 3,000 adherents (1994).

The Press

The Nation: Mbabane; f. 1997; monthly; independent news magazine; Editor BHEKI MAKHUBU.

The Swazi News: Sheffield Rd, POB 156, Mbabane; tel. 4042520; fax 4042438; f. 1983; weekly; English; owned by *The Times of Swaziland*; Editor KIMBER FRASER; circ. 18,000.

Swaziview: Mbabane; tel. 4042716; monthly magazine; general interest; circ. 3,500.

The Times of Swaziland: Sheffield Rd, POB 156, Mbabane; tel. 4042520; fax 4042438; f. 1897; English; Mon.–Fri.; also monthly edn; Editor MASHUMI THWALA; circ. 18,000.

Publishers

Apollo Services (Pty) Ltd: POB 35, Mbabane; tel. 4042711.

GBS Printing and Publishing (Pty) Ltd: POB 1384, Mbabane; tel. 5052779.

Jubilee Printers: POB 1619, Matsaka; tel. 5184557; fax 5184558.

Longman Swaziland (Pty) Ltd: POB 2207, Manzini; tel. 5053891.

Macmillan Boleswa Publishers (Pty) Ltd: POB 1235, Manzini; tel. 5184533; fax 5185247; Man. Dir T. BALL.

Swaziland Printing & Publishing Co Ltd: POB 28, Mbabane; tel. 4042716; fax 4042710; e-mail veares@iafrica.sz.

Whydah Media Publishers Ltd: Mbabane; tel. 4042716; f. 1978.

Broadcasting and Communications

TELECOMMUNICATIONS

Posts and Telecommunications Corporation: POB 125, Mbabane; tel. 4042341; fax 4043130; f. 1986; Man. Dir ALFRED S. DLAMINI; Gen. Man. MZWANDILE R. MABUZA.

BROADCASTING

Radio

Swaziland Broadcasting and Information Service: POB 338, Mbabane; tel. 4042763; fax 4042774; f. 1966; broadcasts in English and siSwati; Dir T. MAKAMA.

Swaziland Commercial Radio (Pty) Ltd: POB 1586, Alberton 1450, South Africa; tel. (11) 4344333; fax (11) 4344777; e-mail cicade@icon.co.za; privately-owned commercial service; broadcasts to southern Africa in English and Portuguese; music and religious programmes; Man. Dir A. DE ANDRADE.

Trans World Radio: POB 64, Manzini; tel. 5052781; fax 5055333; internet www.icon.co.za/~ttatlow/Welcome.htm; f. 1974; religious broadcasts from five transmitters in 30 languages to southern, central and eastern Africa and to the Far East; Pres. THOMAS J. LOWELL.

Television

Swaziland Television Authority: POB A146, Swazi Plaza, Mbabane; tel. 4043036; fax 4042093; f. 1978; state-owned; broadcasts seven hours daily in English; colour transmissions; Gen. Man. DAN S. DLAMINI.

Finance

(cap. = capital; res = reserves; dep. = deposits; m. = million; brs = branches; amounts in emalangeni)

BANKING

Central Bank

Central Bank of Swaziland: POB 546, Mbabane; tel. 4043221; fax 4045417; e-mail research@realnet.co.sz; internet www.centralbank.sz/; f. 1974; bank of issue; cap. and res 9.4m., dep. 364.4m. (March 1998); Gov. M. G. DLAMINI; Dep. Gov. S. G. MDLULI.

Commercial Banks

First National Bank of Swaziland Ltd: Sales House Bldg, 2nd Floor, POB 261, Mbabane; tel. 4044501; fax 4044735; e-mail keith@fnbswz.co.sz; f. 1988; fmrly Meridien Bank Swaziland Ltd; cap. and res 5.6m., dep. 11.9m. (Sept. 1991); Chair. J. MOSES; Man. Dir R. A. PAWSON; 7 brs and 1 agency.

Nedbank (Swaziland) Ltd: Swazi Plaza, POB 68, Mbabane; tel. 4043351; fax 4044060; e-mail nedbank@iafrica.sz; f. 1974; fmrly Standard Chartered Bank Swaziland Ltd; 30% state-owned; cap. and res 30.0m., total assets 493.7m. (Dec. 1998); Chair. A. R. B. SHABANGU; Man. Dir A. R. SOUTHEY; 4 brs and 1 agency.

Development Banks

Standard Bank Swaziland Ltd: Standard House, 1st Floor, Swazi Plaza, POB A294, Mbabane; tel. 4046587; fax 4045899; e-mail StandardBankSwaziland@iafrica.sz; f. 1988; fmrly Stanbic Bank Swaziland, present name since 1997; merged with Barclays Bank of Swaziland in Jan. 1998; 10% state-owned; cap. and res 44.7m., total assets 1,153.1m. (Dec. 1998); Chair. A. D. B. WRIGHT; Man. Dir W. G. PRICE; 6 brs.

Swaziland Development and Savings Bank: Engungwini House, Allister Miller St, POB 336, Mbabane; tel. 4042551; fax 4042550; f. 1965; state-owned; taken over by central bank in 1995; cap. and res –1.7m., total assets 254m. (Dec. 1999); Chair. G. P. DLAMINI; Man. Dir A. F. DIXON (acting); 8 brs.

Financial Institution

Swaziland National Provident Fund: POB 1857, Manzini; tel. 5053731; fax 5054377; total assets 290m. (June 1996).

STOCK EXCHANGE

Swaziland Stock Market: c/o Swaziland Stockbrokers Ltd, Dhlan'Ubeka House, 2nd Floor, Walker St, POB 2818, Mbabane; tel. 4046163; fax 4044132; f. 1993; Chair. Dr MICHAEL MATSEBULA; CEO ANDREW MCGUIRE.

INSURANCE

Although the state-controlled Swaziland Royal Insurance Corporation (SRIC) operates as the country's sole authorized insurance company, cover in a number of areas not served by SRIC is available from several specialized insurers. In early 1998 the Government was preparing legislation terminating the monopoly of the SRIC and providing for its transfer to private-sector ownership.

Insurance Companies

AON Swaziland Insurance Brokers (Pty) Ltd: POB 222, Mbabane; tel. 4043226; fax 4046412; e-mail theopheiffer/ars/sz/aon@aonemea; f. 1970; Man. Dir THEO W. PHEIFFER.

Associated Insurance Brokers (Pty) Ltd: POB 1216, Manzini M200; tel. 5056543; fax 5053831; e-mail kdukes@iafrica.sz; Man. Dir K. DUKES.

Swaziland Employee Benefit Consultants (Pty) Ltd: POB 3159, Mbabane; tel. 4044776; fax 4046413; e-mail sebc@iafrica.co.sz; specialized medical cover.

Swaziland Royal Insurance Corporation (SRIC): Liluga House, Gilfillan St, POB 917, Mbabane; tel. 4043231; fax 4046415; e-mail sric@iafrica.sz; 51% state-owned; sole auth. insurance co since 1974; reorg. pending in 1998; Gen. Man. Z. R. MAGAGULA.

Tibiyo Insurance Brokers: Swazi Plaza, POB 1072, Mbabane; tel. 4042010; fax 4045035; Man. Dir D. T. BAKER.

Insurance Association

Insurance Brokers' Association of Swaziland (IBAS): Swazi Plaza, POB A32, Mbabane; tel. 4042929; f. 1983; four mems.

Trade and Industry

GOVERNMENT AGENCY

Swaziland Investment Promotion Authority: POB 4194, Mbabane; tel. 4041982; fax 4043374; f. 1998; Chair. Dr SISHAYI S. NXUMALO.

DEVELOPMENT ORGANIZATIONS

National Industrial Development Corporation of Swaziland (NIDCS): POB 866, Mbabane; tel. 4043391; fax 4045619; f. 1971; state-owned; administered by Swaziland Industrial Development Co; Admin. Dir P. K. THAMM.

Small Enterprise Development Co (SEDCO): POB A186, Swazi Plaza, Mbabane; tel. 4042811; fax 4040723; e-mail sedco@iafrica.sz;

f. 1970; govt devt agency; supplies workshop space, training and expertise for 120 local entrepreneurs at seven sites throughout the country.

Swaziland Industrial Development Co (SIDC): Dhlan'Ubeka House, 5th Floor, cnr Tin and Walker Sts, POB 866, Mbabane; tel. 4044010; fax 4045619; e-mail sidc@iafrica.sz; internet www.realnet.co.sz; f. 1986; 34.9% state-owned; finances private-sector projects and promotes local and foreign investment; cap. E24.1m., total assets E178.4m. (June 1999); Chair. A. R. SHABANGU; Gen. Man. E. T. GINA.

Swaki (Pty) Ltd: Liqhaga Bldg, 4th Floor, Nkoseluhlaza St, POB 1839, Manzini; tel. 5052693; fax 5052001; jtly owned by SIDC and Kirsh Holdings; comprises a number of cos involved in manufacturing, services and the production and distribution of food (especially maize).

Tibiyo Taka Ngwane (Bowels of the Swazi Nation): POB 181, Kwaluseni; tel. 5184390; fax 5184399; f. 1968; nat. devt agency, with investment interests in all sectors of the economy; participates in domestic and foreign jt investment ventures; total assets: E 420m. (1996); Man. Dir A. T. DLAMINI; Gen. Man. C. N. MAMBA.

CHAMBERS OF COMMERCE

Sibakho Chamber of Commerce: POB 2016, Manzini; tel. 5057347.

Swaziland Chamber of Commerce and Industry: POB 72, Mbabane; tel. 4044408; fax 4045442; Sec. HARVEY BIRD.

INDUSTRIAL AND TRADE ASSOCIATIONS

National Agricultural Marketing Board: POB 1713, Mbabane; tel. 5185211; fax 5184088.

National Maize Corporation: POB 158, Manzini; tel. 5052261; fax 5052265.

Swaziland Citrus Board: Sokhamila Bldg, Cnr. Johnston/Walker Sts, H100, Mbabane; tel. 4044266; fax 4043548; f. 1969.

Swaziland Commercial Board: POB 509, Mbabane; tel. 4042930; Man. Dir J. M. D. FAKUDZE.

Swaziland Cotton Board: POB 230, Manzini; tel. 5052775; Gen. Man. T. JELE.

Swaziland Dairy Board: POB 1789, Manzini; tel. 5184411; fax 5185313.

EMPLOYERS' ORGANIZATIONS

Building Contractors' Association of Swaziland: Mbabane; tel. 4045566.

Swaziland Association of Architects, Engineers and Surveyors: Swazi Plaza, POB A387, Mbabane; tel. 4042309.

Swaziland Institute of Personnel and Training Managers: c/o UNISWA, Private Bag, Kwaluseni; tel. 5184545; fax 5185276.

Employers' Federation

Federation of Swaziland Employers: POB 777, Mbabane; tel. 2022768; fax 4046107; f. 1964; 376 mems; Pres. R. SEAL; Exec. Dir E. HLOPHE.

UTILITIES

Electricity

Swaziland Electricity Board: POB 258, Mbabane; tel. 4042521; fax 4042335; statutory body; f. 1963.

Water

Water Services Corporation: POB 20, Mbabane; tel. 4045584; fax 4045355; state authority.

MAJOR COMPANIES

Bromor Foods (Swaziland) (Pty) Ltd: Matsapha Industrial Estate, POB 1638, Matsapha; tel. 5184554; fax 5184510; f. 1986; mfrs of soft drink concentrates and confectionery.

Cadbury Swaziland (Pty) Ltd: POB 679, Matsapha; tel. 5186168; fax 5186173; f. 1989; mfrs of confectionery; Gen. Man. FRANK PHILLIPS.

Master Fridge Ltd: POB 1604, Matsapha; tel. 5184186; fax 5184069; f. 1993; mfrs of domestic refrigerators and freezers; Exec. Dirs CHARLES H. PALMER, CHARLES H. PALMER Jr., BRONWEN F. PHILLIPS.

GMH Manufacturing (Pty) Ltd: POB 503, Matsapha; tel. 5185386; f. 1990; manufacture, preparation and packaging of food-related products.

Mantenga Craft: POB 364, Eveni; tel. 4161136; fax 4161040; e-mail mantengacraft@iafrica.sz; internet www.mantenga.com; handcrafts.

Natex Swaziland Ltd: Matsapha Industrial Sites, POB 359, Manzini; tel. 5186133; fax 5186029; e-mail natex@africaonline.co.sz; f. 1987; textiles; Man. Dir A. N. KUMAR.

Neopac Swaziland Ltd: Matsapha Industrial Sites, POB 618, Manzini; tel. 5186204; fax 5184277; f. 1968; mfrs of corrugated containers for agriculture and industry; Man. Dir WILLIE HORSBURGH.

Ngwane Mills (Pty) Ltd: Matsapha Industrial Sites, POB 1169, Manzini; tel. 5185011; fax 5185112; f. 1992; flour and related products.

Spintex Swaziland (Pty) Ltd: POB 6, Matsapha; tel. 5186166; fax 5186038; mfrs of cotton and poly-cotton combed yarns, sewing thread, core yarns, lycra core yarns and open-end yarns; Man. Dir PETER RIDING.

Swazi Paper Mills Ltd: POB 873, Mbabane; tel. 4086024; fax 4086091; e-mail spm@realnet.co.sz; f. 1987; Swaziland's largest privately-owned concern; produces paper and paper products; Man. Dir P. SHARMA.

Swazi Timber Products Ltd: POB 2313, Manzini; tel. and fax 5086312; f. 1987.

Swaziland Brewers Ltd: POB 100, Matsapha; tel. 5186033; fax 5186309; f. 1976; annual production of 250,000 hl of beer; Group Man. Dir M. B. MANYATSHE.

Swaziland Laminated Timbers (Pty) Ltd: POB 4, Piggs Peak; tel. 4371344; fax 4371386; mfrs of pine furniture.

Swaziland Meat Industries Ltd: POB 446, Manzini; tel. 5184165; fax 5184418; e-mail simunvemeats@smi.co.sz; f. 1965; operates an abattoir and deboning plant at Matsapha to process beef for local and export markets; Gen. Man. J. C. WILLIAMS.

Swaziland Safety Glass: Matsapha Industrial Estate, POB 3058, Manzini; tel. 5085366; fax 5085361; f. 1990; mfrs of glass for transport industry; Man. Dir BRIAN BROOKS.

Swaziland Sugar Association: POB 445, Mbabane; tel. 4042646; fax 4045005; e-mail info@ssa.co.sz; internet www.realnet.co.sz/ssa; f. 1967; responsible for all sugar storage, transport and sales; CEO Dr M. MATSEBULA.

Ubombo Sugar Ltd: POB 23, Big Bend; tel. 3636511; fax 3636330; f. 1958; produces raw and refined sugar; Man. Dir E. WILLIAMS.

Usutu Pulp Co Ltd: Private Bag, Mbabane; tel. 4026010; fax 4026025; mfrs of unbleached Kraft pulp; Pres. I. FORBES.

YKK Zippers (Swaziland) (Pty) Ltd: POB 1425, Mbabane; tel. 5184188; fax 5184182; f. 1977; mfrs of zip fasteners; Man. Dir J. CHUNG.

CO-OPERATIVE ASSOCIATIONS

Swaziland Central Co-operatives Union: POB 551, Manzini; tel. 5052787; fax 5052964.

There are more than 123 co-operative associations, of which the most important is:

Swaziland Co-operative Rice Co Ltd: handles rice grown in Mbabane and Manzini areas.

TRADE UNIONS

The following trade unions are recognized by the Department of Labour:

The Association of Lecturers and Academic Personnel of the University of Swaziland, the Building and Construction Workers Union of Swaziland, Swaziland Commercial and Allied Workers' Union, Swaziland Conservation Workers' Union, Swaziland Electricity Supply, Maintenance and Allied Workers' Union, Swaziland Engineering, Metal and Allied Workers' Union, Swaziland Hotel, Catering and Allied Workers' Union, Swaziland Manufacturing and Allied Workers' Union, Swaziland Mining, Quarrying and Allied Workers' Union, Swaziland National Association of Civil Servants, Swaziland National Association of Teachers, Swaziland Post and Telecommunications Workers' Union, Swaziland Transport Workers' Union, Swaziland Union of Financial Institutions and Allied Workers, University of Swaziland Workers' Union, Workers Union of Swaziland Security Guards, Workers' Union of Town Councils.

Trade Union Federations

Swaziland Federation of Labour: mems include workers from the banking sector and mems of the Swaziland Manufacturing and Allied Workers' Union.

Swaziland Federation of Trade Unions (SFTU): Mbabane; f. 1973; prin. trade union org. since mid-1980s; mems from public and private sectors, incl. agricultural workers; 83,000 mems; Pres. RICHARD NXUMALO; Sec.-Gen. JAN SITHOLE.

Staff Associations

Three staff associations exist for employees whose status lies between that of worker and that of management:

The Nyoni Yami Irrigation Scheme Staff Association, the Swazican Staff Association and the Swaziland Electricity Board Staff Association.

Transport

Buses are the principal means of transport for many Swazis. Bus services are provided by private operators who are required to obtain annual permits for each route from the Road Transportation Board, which also regulates fares.

RAILWAYS

The rail network, which totalled 297 km in 1998–99 provides a major transport link for imports and exports. Railway lines connect with the dry port at Matsapha, the South African ports of Richards Bay and Durban in the south, the South African town of Komatipoort in the north and the Mozambican port of Maputo in the east. Goods traffic is mainly in wood pulp, sugar, molasses, coal, citrus fruit and canned fruit. In June 1998 the Trans Lebombo rail service was launched to carry passengers from Durban to Maputo via Swaziland. The service was terminated in May 2000, owing to insufficient demand.

Swaziland Railway Board: Swaziland Railway Bldg, cnr Johnston and Walker Sts, POB 475, Mbabane; tel. 4047211; fax 4047210; e-mail ceo@iafrica.sz; f. 1962; Chair. B. A. G. FITZPATRICK; CEO G. J. MAHLALELA.

ROADS

In 1996 there were an estimated 3,810 km of roads, including 1,360 km of main roads and 1,610 km of secondary roads. About 28.2% of the road network was paved in 1994. The rehabilitation of about 700 km of main and 600 km of district gravel-surfaced roads began in 1985, financed by World Bank and US loans totalling some E18m. In 1991 work commenced on the reconstruction of Swaziland's main road artery, connecting Mbabane to Manzini, via Matsapha.

Ministry of Public Works and Transport: POB 58, Mbabane; tel. 4042321; fax 4042364; Prin. Sec. EVART MADLOPHA; Sr Roads Engineer A. MANANA.

Roads Department: POB 58, Mbabane; tel. 4042321; e-mail mopwt_rd@realnet.co.sz.

SHIPPING

Royal Swazi National Shipping Corporation Ltd: POB 1915, Manzini; tel. 5053788; fax 5053820; f. 1980 to succeed Royal Swaziland Maritime Co; owns no ships, acting only as a freight agent; Gen. Man. M. S. DLAMINI.

CIVIL AVIATION

Swaziland's only airport is at Matsapha, near Manzini, about 40 km from Mbabane. In mid-1997 the government initiated a three-year programme to upgrade the airport.

African International Airways (AIA): Suite 108, Development House, Swazi Plaza, POB 569, Mbabane; tel. 4043875; fax 4043876; e-mail ams@global.co.za; f. 1985; operates cargo services; Chair. PATRICK CORBIN; Man. Dir MARTIN LONGMORE.

Airlink Swaziland: POB 939, Matsapha Airport, Manzini; tel. 5186146; fax 5186156; f. 1999; frmrly Royal Swazi National Airways Corpn; joint venture between SA Airlink of South Africa and the Swazi government; scheduled passenger services to destinations in Africa.

Air Swazi Cargo: Dhlan'Ubeka House, Walker St, POB 2869, Mbabane; tel. 4045575; fax 4045003; charter services for freight to destinations in Africa and Europe; Man. BRIAN PARMENTER.

Tourism

Swaziland's attractions for tourists include game reserves and magnificent mountain scenery. In 1992 268,071 tourist arrivals were registered at hotels; the total number of visitors to Swaziland was 1,568,198. A total of 322,000 arrivals at hotels was recorded in 1997. Receipts from tourism in that year totalled US $40m.

Hotel and Tourism Association of Swaziland: POB 462, Mbabane; tel. 4042218.

Ministry of Tourism and Communications: POB 58, Mbabane; tel. 4046420; fax 4046438; e-mail mintour@realnet.co.sz; internet www.mintour.gov.sz; Tourism Officer SIMEONE SIMELANE.

Defence

The Umbutfo Swaziland defence force, created in 1973, totalled 2,657 regular troops in November 1983. There is also a paramilitary police force. Compulsory military service of two years was introduced in 1983.

Defence Expenditure: Budgeted at E94.3m. for 1994/95 (including public safety).

Education

Education is not compulsory in Swaziland. Primary education begins at six years of age and lasts for seven years. Secondary education begins at 13 years of age and lasts for up to five years, comprising a first cycle of three years and a second of two years. In 1996 some 95% of children in the relevant age-group (boys 95%; girls 95%) were enrolled at primary schools, while secondary enrolment was equivalent to 54% of children in the appropriate age-group (boys 55%; girls 54%). Higher education is provided by the University of Swaziland, with campuses in Luyengo and in Kwaluseni, and a number of other institutions of higher education. At the 1986 census the rate of adult illiteracy averaged 32.7% (males 30.3%; females 34.8%). According to estimates by UNESCO, the rate of adult illiteracy in 1995 averaged 24.0% (males 22.4%; females 25.3%). The 1999/2000 budget allocated E764.2m., representing 27.1% of total expenditure, on education and training.

Bibliography

Bischoff, P.-H. *Swaziland's International Relations and Foreign Policy: A Study of a Small African State in International Relations.* Berne, P. Lang, 1990.

Booth, A. R. *Historical Dictionary of Swaziland.* Metuchen, NJ, Scarecrow Press, 1975.

Swaziland: Tradition and Change in a Southern African Kingdom. Boulder, CO, Westview Press, 1983; London, Gower Publishers, 1984.

Daniel, J., and Stephen, M. F. (Eds). *Historical Perspectives on the Political Economy of Swaziland.* Kwaluseni, University of Swaziland, 1986.

Davies, R. H., et al. (Eds). *The Kingdom of Swaziland: A Profile.* London, Zed Press, 1985.

Forster, S. and Nsibande, B. S. (Eds). *Swaziland: Contemporary Social and Economic Issues.* Aldershot, Ashgate Publishing Ltd, 2000.

Funnell, D. C. *Under the Shadow of Apartheid: Agrarian Transformation in Swaziland.* Aldershot, Avebury, 1991.

Gillis, D. H. *The Kingdom of Swaziland.* Westport, CT, Greenwood Publishing Group, 1999.

International Monetary Fund. *Swaziland—Recent Economic Developments.* Washington, DC, IMF, 1997.

Konczacki, Z. A., et al. (Eds). *Studies in the Economic History of Southern Africa.* Vol. II. London, Cass, 1991.

Leliveld, A. *Social Security in Developing Countries: Operation and Dynamics of Social Security Mechanisms in Rural Swaziland.* Amsterdam, Thesis Publishers, 1994.

Matsebula, J. S. *A History of Swaziland.* 2nd Edn. Cape Town, Maskew Miller, Longmans, 1988.

Okpalmba, Chuks, et al. (Eds). *Human Rights in Swaziland: The Legal Response.* Kwaluseni, University of Swaziland, 1997.

Rose, L. L. *The Politics of Harmony: Land Dispute Strategies in Swaziland.* Cambridge, Cambridge University Press, 1992.

Schwager, D. *Swaziland.* Mbabane, Websters, 1984.

Simelane, N. C. (Ed.). *Social Transformation: The Swaziland Case.* Dakar, CODESRIA, 1995.

TANZANIA

Physical and Social Geography

L. BERRY

PHYSICAL FEATURES AND CLIMATE

The 945,087 sq km (364,900 sq miles) of the United Republic of Tanzania (incorporating mainland Tanganyika and a number of offshore islands, including Zanzibar, Pemba, Latham and Mafia) have a wide variety of land forms, climates and peoples. The country includes the highest and lowest points in Africa—the summit of Mt Kilimanjaro (5,895 m above sea-level) and the floor of Lake Tanganyika (358 m below sea-level). The main upland areas occur in a northern belt—the Usambara, Pare, Kilimanjaro and Meru mountains; a central and southern belt—the Southern highlands, the Ugurus and the Ulugurus; and a north–south trending belt, which runs southwards from the Ngorongoro Crater. The highest peaks are volcanic, although block faulting has been responsible for the uplift of the plateau areas. Other fault movements have resulted in the depressed areas of the rift valleys; Lakes Tanganyika, Malawi, Rukwa, Manyara and Eyasi occupy part of the floor of these depressions. Much of the rest of the interior comprises gently sloping plains and plateaux, broken by low hill ranges and scattered isolated hills. The coast includes areas with wide sandy beaches and with developed coral reefs, but these are broken by extensive growth of mangroves, particularly near the mouths of the larger rivers.

With the exception of the high mountain areas, temperatures in Tanzania are not a major limiting factor for crop growth, although the range of altitude produces a corresponding range of temperature regimes from tropical to temperate. Rainfall is variable, both from place to place and time to time, and is generally lower than might be expected for the latitude. About one-fifth of Tanzania can expect with 90% probability more than 750 mm of rainfall annually, and only about 3% normally receives more than 1,250 mm. The central third of the country is semi-arid (less than 500 mm), with evaporation exceeding rainfall in nine months of the year. For much of Tanzania most rain falls in one rainy season, December–May, though two peaks of rainfall in October–November and April–May are found in some areas. Apart from the problem of the long dry season over most parts of the country, there is also a marked fluctuation in annual rainfall from one year to the next, and this may be reflected in the crop production and livestock figures.

The surplus water from the wetter areas drains into the few large perennial rivers. The largest of these, the Rufiji, drains the Southern highlands and much of southern Tanzania. With an average discharge of 1,133 cu m per second, it is one of the largest rivers in Africa, and has major potential for irrigation and hydroelectric power development. The Ruvu, Wami and Pangani also drain to the Indian Ocean. The Pangani has already been developed for hydroelectric power, which supplies Arusha, Moshi, Tanga, Morogoro and Dar es Salaam. Apart from the Ruvuma, which forms the southern frontier, most other drainage is to the interior basins, or to the Lakes Tanganyika, Victoria and Malawi.

The most fertile soils in Tanzania are the reddish-brown soils derived from the volcanic rocks, although elsewhere *mbuga* and other alluvial soils have good potential. The interior plateaux are covered with tropical loams of moderate fertility. The natural vegetation of the country has been considerably modified by human occupation. In the south and west-central areas there are large tracts of woodland covering about 30% of the country, while on the uplands are small but important areas of tropical rain forest. Clearly marked altitudinal variations in vegetation occur around the upland areas and some distinctive mountain flora is found. Tanzania has set aside about one-third of its land for national parks and game and forest reserves.

POPULATION AND RESOURCES

In mid-1998, according to United Nations estimates, Tanzania had a population of 32,102,100, of whom about 800,000 resided in Zanzibar. Most of the country's inhabitants are of African origin, although people of Indian and Pakistani ancestry comprise a significant component of the urban population. Tanzania is one of the least urbanized countries of Africa. According to official estimates, the population of the principal towns at mid-1985 was: Dar es Salaam (1,096,000), Mwanza (252,000), Tabora (214,000), Mbeya (194,000) and Tanga (172,000). There are more than 120 ethnic groups in Tanzania, of which the largest are the Sukuma and the Nyamwezi. None, however, exceeds 10% of the total population.

Traditionally, the main features of the pattern of population distribution have been, firstly, sharp variations in density, with a number of densely populated areas separated from each other by zones of sparse population; secondly, the comparatively low density of population in most of the interior of the country; and, thirdly, the preponderance in rural areas of scattered individual homesteads. Since the late 1960s, however, the majority of the rural population have been settled in nucleated villages. The highest population densities, reaching over 250 per sq km, occur on the fertile lower slopes of Mt Kilimanjaro and on the shores of Lake Malawi. Most other upland areas have relatively high densities, as does the area south of Lake Victoria known as Sukumaland.

Agriculture, which employs about four-fifths of the economically active population, is geared in large part towards subsistence farming. The main cash crops are coffee, cotton, cashew nuts, cloves (Zanzibar's principal export, cultivated mainly on the island of Pemba), tobacco, tea, sisal, pyrethrum, coconuts, sugar, cardamom and groundnuts. Exports of cut flowers commenced in the mid-1990s. Tanzania's mineral resources include diamonds, other gemstones, gold, salt, phosphates, coal, gypsum, kaolin, tin, limestone and graphite, all of which are exploited. There are also reserves of nickel, silver, copper, cobalt, lead, soda ash, iron ore, tungsten, pyrochlore, magnesite, niobium, titanium, vanadium, uranium and natural gas.

Dar es Salaam is the main port, the dominant industrial centre, and the focus of government and commercial activity, although the administrative functions of the capital city are scheduled to be transferred to Dodoma by 2005. Dar es Salaam has been growing at a substantial rate and attempts are being made to decentralize industrial development to other centres. Arusha has also been growing rapidly in recent years, partly because of its importance to tourism.

Considerable variation in the pattern of development occurs within Tanzania. In some areas agriculture is becoming much more orientated towards cash crops. In such a large country distance to market is an important factor, and in successive development plans major attempts have been made to improve the main and subsidiary communication networks. The TanZam road and Tazara railway are an important addition, leaving only the far west and the south-east without good surface links to the rest of the country.

Recent History

GRAHAM MATTHEWS

Revised for this edition by the Editor

European interest in the area that now forms the United Republic of Tanzania was attracted in the 17th century by the mercantile opportunities of the Omani-controlled caravan trade from Zanzibar into the eastern Congo and Buganda. British trading interests on the island and its then extensive coastal possessions expanded rapidly after 1841. Zanzibar declared its independence from Oman in 1856, and its mainland areas were acquired by Britain and Germany between 1886–90, when a British protectorate was established over the islands of Zanzibar and Pemba.

Mainland Tanganyika was declared a German protectorate in 1885. In 1920, following the defeat of Germany in the First World War, Tanganyika was placed under a League of Nations mandate, with the United Kingdom as the administering power, and in 1946 became a UN trust territory, still under British administration. The politicization of indigenous Africans began in 1929 with the formation of the Tanganyika African Association, which evolved in 1954 into the Tanganyika African National Union (TANU), under the leadership of Julius Nyerere.

THE NYERERE PERIOD, 1959–85

TANU won decisive victories in general elections held in 1959 and 1960, when Nyerere became chief minister. Nyerere duly became prime minister when internal self-government was granted in May 1961. Full independence followed on 9 December. In January 1962 Nyerere resigned as prime minister; he was succeeded by Rashidi Kawawa. In December Tanganyika became a republic, with Nyerere returning to power as the country's first president, having been elected in the previous month. Kawawa became vice-president.

Zanzibar (together with the neighbouring island of Pemba and several smaller islets), became an independent sultanate in December 1963. The sultan was overthrown in an armed uprising in January 1964, following which a republic was declared and the Afro-Shirazi Party (ASP) took power. In April Nyerere signed an act of union with the new government of Zanzibar. The leader of the ASP, Abeid Karume, became the United Republic's first vice-president as well as chairman of the ruling supreme revolutionary council of Zanzibar. The union was named Tanzania in October.

A new constitution, introduced in July 1965, provided for a one-party state (although, until 1977, TANU and the ASP remained the respective official parties of mainland Tanzania and Zanzibar, and co-operated in affairs of state). In September 1965 Nyerere was returned to power in the first one-party election. Nyerere was re-elected president in 1970, 1975 and 1980. Early in 1967, TANU adopted a programme of socialism and self-reliance, known as the Arusha Declaration. Party leaders were required to divest themselves of private sources of income; rural development was to come not through large farms but community (*ujamaa*) villages; the small urban sector was not to exploit the countryside and the education system was to be completely reorganized in order to serve the mass of the population rather than to train a privileged few. Commercial banks and many industries were immediately nationalized, but the rest of the programme was much more difficult to implement, as it ran counter to existing trends of social change. The national assembly voted in June 1975 to incorporate the fundamental principles of socialism and self-reliance into the constitution.

In Zanzibar, Karume survived two coup plots, in 1967 and 1971, but was assassinated in April 1972. His successor, Aboud Jumbe, reorganized the islands' government in that month by extending the powers of the ASP. Despite its incorporation into Tanzania, Zanzibar retained a separate administration, which ruthlessly suppressed all opposition.

In 1972 Kawawa was reappointed to the revived post of prime minister, relieving Nyerere of some of his responsibilities. In February 1977 TANU and the ASP merged to form the Chama

Cha Mapinduzi (CCM–Revolutionary Party), of which Nyerere was elected chairman and Jumbe vice-chairman. A government reshuffle followed, in which Kawawa was replaced as prime minister by Edward Sokoine. In April the national assembly adopted a permanent constitution for Tanzania, providing for the election of 10 Zanzibari representatives to the assembly. In October 1979 the supreme revolutionary council of Zanzibar adopted a separate constitution, governing Zanzibar's internal administration, with provisions for a popularly-elected president and a legislative house of representatives elected by delegates of the CCM.

At a general election in October 1980 about one-half of the members of the national assembly, including several ministers, lost their seats, in what was seen as a protest against Tanzania's parlous economic condition and bureaucratic inefficiency. Constitutional amendments were adopted in October 1984, limiting the president's tenure of office to two five-year terms and strengthening the powers of the national assembly.

Following the discovery of a coup plot against the union government in January 1983, nine people were sentenced to terms of life imprisonment in December 1985. (All those convicted eventually received a presidential pardon in October 1995.) A political crisis arose in Zanzibar in early 1984 as a result of growing dissatisfaction with the union and calls for greater autonomy for the islands. Jumbe and three of his ministers resigned in January, and in April Ali Hassan Mwinyi, the islands' former minister of natural resources and tourism, was elected president of Zanzibar (thus also becoming vice-president of Tanzania). Mwinyi, a supporter of the union, made sweeping changes to Zanzibar's supreme revolutionary council. A new, more liberal, constitution for the islands was introduced in January 1985, providing for the house of representatives to be directly elected by universal suffrage and for the introduction of a Commonwealth legal system.

At his retirement, in November 1985, Nyerere was succeeded by Mwinyi, who had been elected in the previous month with 96% of the valid votes cast; thus was established a pattern of alternate mainland and Zanzibari presidents of the United Republic. Idris Abdul Wakil (formerly speaker of the Zanzibar house of representatives) was elected president of Zanzibar to replace Mwinyi. After taking office in November, Mwinyi appointed Joseph Warioba, previously minister of justice, as prime minister and first vice-president.

THE MWINYI PRESIDENCY, 1985–95

The change of president coincided with a worsening economic crisis (see below) which forced the new administration to alter the direction of its economic policy. Greater encouragement was given to the private sector, and acceptance of proposals from the International Monetary Fund (IMF) on budgeting, agricultural reform and management of the shilling persuaded donors to sponsor the country with large disbursements of aid.

Nyerere, who described Tanzania's new economic policy as 'unplanned retreats from socialism', was re-elected chairman of the CCM for a further five-year term in October 1987. His re-election also represented a victory for Rashidi Kawawa (who was himself re-elected almost unanimously as secretary-general of the party) and for other socialist radicals and militants who looked to Nyerere to strengthen the party and to act as a counterbalance against Mwinyi's controversial economic reforms. Two prominent 'liberal-modernists' failed to secure re-election to the CCM's central committee: Seif Sharrif Hamad, the chief minister of Zanzibar (who subsequently also lost this office), and Cleopa Msuya, the minister of finance, who was closely involved in negotiations with the IMF. However, Mwinyi was re-elected vice-chairman of the party, and in December 1987 he dismissed three cabinet ministers who were perceived to oppose his liberalization policies. The cabinet was again reshuffled in early 1989; among the new appointees were three ministers of state considered to be sympathetic to Islamic fundamentalism, thus redressing a perceived predominance of Christian influence in the cabinet.

In February 1990 the CCM initiated a campaign against corruption among government officials. In March an extensive reshuffle of the cabinet took place: Mwinyi dismissed seven ministers who had allegedly opposed plans for economic reform and presided over corrupt or irresponsible ministries. The president's position was further consolidated in August when, following the resignation of Nyerere, he was appointed chairman of the CCM.

In October 1990 concurrent parliamentary and presidential elections were held in Zanzibar. Wakil did not stand for re-election as president and chairman of the supreme revolutionary council; the sole presidential candidate, Dr Salmin Amour, was elected as Wakil's successor by 97.7% of the votes cast. At the end of October national parliamentary and presidential elections took place. Mwinyi, the sole candidate in the presidential election, was re-elected for a second term, receiving 95.5% of the votes cast. At the elections to the 216 directly elective seats in the 291-member Tanzanian national assembly, 33 delegates lost their seats. Following the elections Warioba was replaced as prime minister by John Malecela.

In December 1991 a presidential commission (inaugurated in March to consider electoral reform) published recommendations for the establishment of a plural political system. In February 1992 proposed constitutional amendments to this effect were ratified by a special congress of the CCM, which stipulated that, in order to protect national unity, all new political organizations should command support in both Zanzibar and mainland Tanzania, and should be free of tribal, religious and racial bias. In May both the United Republic's constitution and the Zanzibar constitution were duly amended to implement these changes.

Mwinyi reallocated cabinet portfolios in late May 1992. Several political organizations were officially registered from mid-1992; however, the government continued to impose restrictions on opposition activities.

At the beginning of 1993 it emerged that the Zanzibar government had unilaterally arranged for the islands to join the Organization of the Islamic Conference (OIC). This action infringed both the 1964 articles of union and the 1977 union constitution, whereby the United Republic was established as a secular state and the Zanzibar administration was denied any separate competence in foreign affairs, which was the exclusive responsibility of the union government. In an atmosphere of worsening inter-religious communalism, predominantly Christian mainlanders demanded the resignation of Mwinyi (a Muslim and a Zanzibari). In February 1993 a parliamentary commission ruled that Zanzibar's OIC membership was unconstitutional. In a cabinet reshuffle the minister of foreign affairs, Ahmed Hassan Diria (a Zanzibari and close presidential adviser), was transferred to a lesser post.

In August 1993 Zanzibar withdrew from membership of the OIC, but significant damage had been done to relations between the mainland and the islands. In the same month, during the budget debate in the national assembly, a group of 55 mainland MPs successfully sponsored a private member's bill (the so-called 'G55 motion') providing for the establishment of a third level of government within the union to administer the mainland separately from Zanzibar. The legislation was passed unanimously, despite intense opposition from Nyerere, who denounced both the national assembly and the CCM for abandoning a basic tenet of party policy (a commitment to maintaining and enhancing the union) without obtaining a consensus of the entire CCM membership. As a result of Nyerere's intervention, the G55 motion was referred for approval by the CCM membership, which was prevailed upon to reject it. The national assembly eventually rescinded the motion in August 1994.

Nyerere continued to exert his influence with the publication, in November 1994, of a controversial short book in which he accused Malecela, the prime minister, and Horace Kolimba, the CCM secretary-general, of 'poor leadership', particularly over the OIC affair and the G55 motion. Later in the month a wider political crisis was precipitated when foreign donors began to suspend aid disbursements in protest at official connivance in

widespread tax evasion. In December Mwinyi responded to these pressures by dismissing Malecela, Kolimba and Kighoma Ali Malima, the minister of finance, from their posts. Cleopa Msuya, hitherto the minister of industry and trade and previously prime minister during 1980–83, was appointed to the premiership.

In July 1995 the CCM convened a special national conference to select a candidate to contest the presidential election which was due to take place (concurrently with legislative elections) in October. Once again Nyerere's influence was evident. At his behest the list of candidates was restricted to three: Msuya, Lt-Col Jakaya Kikwete, the minister of finance, and Benjamin Mkapa, the minister of science, technology and higher education. Mkapa, who was widely believed to have been Nyerere's first choice from the outset, was eventually nominated.

Opposition and Division

Between July 1992 (when the CCM-appointed registrar of political parties began work) and mid-1996 more than a dozen opposition movements were officially recognized. However, when the CCM fought its first multi-party by-election, in a Zanzibari constituency, in April 1993 the poll was boycotted by all but one of the newly-registered parties, and the CCM won by default.

In January 1993 the anti-Asian speeches of the leader of the unregistered Democratic Party, Rev. Christopher Mtikila, provoked a number of attacks on Asian residents and their businesses in Dar es Salaam. In early April young Muslim radicals took to the streets in a series of attacks on pork butchers (Islam considers the meat unclean). These outbreaks of violence reflected separate but overlapping divisions that had long been contained within Tanzanian society: that between black African and Asian Tanzanians; and that between Christianity and Islam. Set alongside the crisis in the union itself, these completed a picture of deepening divisions in a state that had once been taken as a model of African nation-building.

In February 1994 the CCM won the third by-election of the multi-party era. In a significant judgment delivered in August, the high court asserted a new-found independence when it upheld the petition of the opposition Chama Cha Demokrasia na Maendeleo (Chadema) that the seat had been won by unfair means. The CCM's authority was further challenged in February 1995, when Augustine Mrema, the minister of home affairs, precipitated his own dismissal from the cabinet and, soon after, joined the opposition National Convention for Construction and Reform (NCCR–Mageuzi). In June, following allegations of personal financial irregularities, the minister of industry and trade (and former minister of finance), Kighoma Ali Malima, was forced to resign from the government. Malima defected to the opposition National Reconstruction Alliance (NRA), briefly leading the party until his death in August.

THE 'THIRD PHASE' GOVERNMENT

In October 1995 multi-party legislative elections were held for the first time, concurrently with presidential elections, both in Zanzibar (see below) and throughout the Tanzanian union. The CCM achieved a convincing majority at the national legislative elections, winning 186 of the 232 elective seats in the national assembly, while the Civic United Front (CUF), a party favouring Zanzibari autonomy (see below), secured 24 seats, NCCR–Mageuzi 16, and both Chadema and the United Democratic Party (UDP) took three seats. The ballots in seven constituencies in Dar es Salaam were cancelled and restaged in November, owing to apparent administrative inefficiency. Benjamin Mkapa was elected national president, winning 61.8% of the votes cast. President Mkapa was inaugurated in November; Omar Ali Juma (hitherto the chief minister of Zanzibar) was appointed vice-president. Mkapa appointed Frederick Sumaye (formerly minister of agriculture) as prime minister; many long-standing ministers were not reappointed to their posts. The opposition refused to participate in the new administration (known as the 'third phase' government) in protest at alleged electoral fraud by the CCM.

In his election campaign Mkapa had promised a crusade against corruption in high public office, and in January 1996 he appointed a special presidential commission, under the chairmanship of the former prime minister, Joseph Warioba, to carry out a full investigation of the matter. At a special congress of the CCM, held in June, Mkapa was elected party chairman, and there were many new appointees to the party's central committee. (In order to secure the support of the Zanzibari wing of the CCM at the party elections, Mkapa refrained from taking a firm line in the dispute over the re-election of Dr Amour as Zanzibari president—see below.) During June the allegedly corrupt Dar es Salaam city council was disbanded. In September a parliamentary select committee investigating bribery allegations against the minister of finance, Simon Mbilinyi, published a report recommending that he be made accountable for having illegally granted tax exemptions. Mbilinyi resigned. Meanwhile, in October 1996, Mrema unexpectedly won a parliamentary by-election for NCCR–Mageuzi in a Dar es Salam constituency; although his campaign had focused on financial impropriety in government, Mrema had recently been accused of having presented false evidence to the parliamentary select committee on corruption in order to undermine the government's credibility. In December the Warioba commission issued a report asserting that corruption was widespread in the public sector; Dr Juma Alifa Ngasongwa, minister of natural resources and tourism, subsequently resigned.

In May 1997 a faction of NCCR–Mageuzi, led by the party's secretary-general, Mabere Marando, attempted to oust Mrema from the party chairmanship, reportedly after the latter ordered an investigation into the disappearance of substantial sums of money belonging to the organization. In June the high court banned an NCCR–Mageuzi special congress from taking place, purportedly in order to prevent violent confrontation between the opposing factions. Following allegations that the state security forces were not independent of CCM interests, and that the harassment of the government's political opponents was a regular occurrence, reports emerged in August that certain political groupings had formed their own private militias.

At the CCM congress held in November 1997 Mkapa and Dr Amour were re-elected as, respectively, party chairman and vice-chairman. The congress assigned the mainland vice-chairmanship to John Malecela, the previously disgraced former prime minister. During the congress Mkapa confirmed the government's commitment to encouraging private investment and privatization and to promoting production co-operatives. He did not, however, announce decisive action against the widespread corruption among government officials that had been identified in the Warioba report.

In mid-February and early April 1998 violent clashes erupted at the Mwembechai mosque in Dar es Salaam, during which three people were killed; some government ministers accused unidentified Islamic states of agitating the unrest. In early August a powerful bomb exploded outside the US embassy in Dar es Salaam (concurrently with a similar attack at the US mission in Nairobi, Kenya); 11 people were killed in Dar es Salaam and some 86 were injured. The attacks were believed to have been co-ordinated by international Islamic terrorists led by a Saudi Arabian dissident, Osama bin Laden, and, in mid-August, the USA retaliated by launching air strikes against targets associated with bin Laden in Afghanistan and Sudan. Following extensive enquiries by Tanzanian investigators and US federal agents, two suspects were charged with murder by the Tanzanian authorities in mid-September in connection with the Dar es Salaam atrocity. Meanwhile, the USA was strongly criticized for having underestimated the potential security threat posed to its East African embassies.

In July 1998 a committee was appointed by the government to assess public opinion on constitutional reform. In early September Mkapa reorganized the cabinet, following the recent nullification of the election to the national assembly in 1995 of two ministers and the resignation, in August 1998, of the minister of state in the president's office, Hassy Kitine, who was alleged to have financed medical treatment abroad for his wife using state funds. (By-elections held in July 1999 to fill the ensuing two vacant seats in the national assembly were narrowly won by the CCM; the results were, however, strongly contested by the CUF, which contended that the polls had been conducted unfairly.) In late April 1999 Mrema and his faction of NCCR-Mageuzi defected to the Tanzania Labour Party (TLP). Mrema initially assumed the chairmanship of the TLP; in mid-

May, however, he was banned by the high court from holding any official post in the party.

THE OCTOBER 2000 ELECTIONS

In June 1999 six opposition parties that were not represented in the national assembly formed the Outside Parliament Political Parties Organization, under the chairmanship of Emmanuel Makaidi, leader of the National League for Democracy (NLD). Other parties represented in the union included the NRA, the Tanzania Democratic Alliance Party (TADEA), the Popular National Party (PONA), the Union for Multi-Party Democracy of Tanzania (UMD) and the United People's Democratic Party (UPDP).

There was speculation that the death, in October 1999, of former President Nyerere might lead to increased pressure for a restructuring of the United Republic. This was, to some extent, reinforced by the release, in the same month, of the report of the committee charged with assessing public opinion on constitutional reform. While it found that some 96.25% of Zanzibaris and 84.97% of mainland Tanzanians favoured a 'two-tier' government for the United Republic, the committee itself recommended the establishment of a 'three-tier' system. In so doing it was adjudged by President Mkapa to have exceeded its mandate. In February 2000 the national assembly approved draft legislation to amend the constitution in accordance with the citizens' recommendations as reported by the committee. Among these recommendations was one that the president should henceforth be elected by a majority vote. Opposition deputies declared that they would prevent the enactment of the proposed legislation, if necessary by resorting to legal action.

In late May 2000 candidates for the presidential elections scheduled for October were announced. President Mkapa was the sole CCM candidate for the presidency of Tanzania, and he would be opposed by the CUF chairman, Ibrahim Lipumba. In August Naila Jiddawi left the CUF and became the presidential candidate for NCCR-Mageuzi, thus becoming Tanzania's second female candidate. CCM candidates for the presidency of Zanzibar included: the island's chief minister, Gharib Bilali, who announced his intention to stand after the United Republic vice-president, Juma, said he would not seek to succeed Amour; Aman Abeid Karume, the son of the first vice-president of the United Republic; the Tanzanian deputy minister of finance, Abdisalaam Issa Khatibu; and the Zanzibari minister of finance, Amina Salim Ali, the first female candidate to stand for such election. Seif Sharrif Hamad announced his decision to run a second time for the presidency of Zanzibar. The CUF and Chadema agreed to present joint candidates in both presidential elections in order to provide a more robust challenge to the CCM. The plan to form a united opposition had originally included the UDP, but the latter withdrew from the alliance when it was confirmed that the constitution barred the presidential running mate from being drawn from a different party. In the event of a victory for this alliance, a member of Chadema was to be appointed prime minister. The UDP chairman, John Cheyo, declared that he would stand for the Tanzanian presidency. An alliance between the TLP and the UPDP was also planned, but was postponed until August 2000.

Opposition parties regularly expressed concerns that election procedures were designed to ensure that the CCM remained in power. However, the National Electoral Commission (NEC) announced various measures in an attempt to guarantee free and fair elections: polling booths were to be introduced, replacing voting in the open; ballot boxes were to be transparent; and NEC division offices were not to be used as polling stations, nor division officers appointed as returning officers, owing to many NEC staff having their own political interests. In August 2000, when announcing its list of candidates for the parliamentary elections, the CCM removed 40 incumbent deputies, including at least five at ministerial level, some of whom had been suspected of malpractice during the pre-selection voting exercise. There were also concerns that biased reporting would appear in the media during the election campaigning. In July the media agreed new guide-lines, which urged journalists to report objectively during the elections; it was reported that media coverage of the elections was to be monitored by a Tanzanian non-governmental organization (NGO), the Legal and Human Rights Centre. However, in the same month the publicly-funded media was accused of broadcasting pro-government propaganda by a human rights group, ARTICLE 19.

In late July 2000 seven parties agreed on a code of conduct during a joint meeting with the NEC. The code barred politicians from using prayer meetings or places of worship to carry out political campaigns, and banned religious leaders from using their positions to campaign for political parties of candidates during prayer sessions. It also prohibited the carrying of weapons, including traditional ones, to political gatherings or in polling stations. Other rules stated that parties with their own mass media organs should not use them to discredit other political parties or their candidates. The parties that accepted the code of conduct were the CCM, NCCR-Mageuzi, TADEA, the UMD, PONA, the TPP and the UPDP. The CUF, Chadema, the TLP and the UDP set preconditions to their signing the code, including a demand that the government should sign the agreement first. A further two parties rejected the code of conduct completely. The CUF complained that voter registration centres were located in centres belonging to the CCM, such as the houses of 'sheshas' (local administrative officials such as the village chief) who were known to be committee members of the CCM. The CUF also opposed voter registration centres in military bases, claiming that soldiers should register and vote in civilian centres. The CUF suggested that registration centres should, instead, be located in schools, and claimed that the opposition should have been involved in the process of choosing locations for the centres. There were reported incidents, in the north-western region of the mainland, of police breaking up rallies organized by the CUF and Chadema, on the grounds that the official campaigning period had not begun. The CUF and Chadema protested, however, that the rallies were part of their campaign to mobilize people to register as voters.

TENSIONS IN ZANZIBAR

In early 1988 tension began to increase in Zanzibar, reflecting rivalries between the inhabitants of the main island and those of the smaller island of Pemba, between Zanzibar's African and Arab populations, and between supporters and opponents of unity with the mainland.

In January 1988 President Wakil suspended the supreme revolutionary council and assumed control of the armed forces, having accused a group of dissidents, including members of the supreme revolutionary council, of conspiring to overthrow his government. These allegations clearly signalled a power struggle within the Zanzibar administration, in which the Pembans have long regarded themselves as under-represented. The chief minister, Seif Sharrif Hamad (a Pemban), was dismissed, together with five other ministers, who were mostly Pembans favouring policies of economic liberalization. All were subsequently expelled from the CCM, and in May 1989 Hamad was arrested for allegedly being in possession of secret government documents and for attending an 'illegal meeting' in Pemba.

Wakil's reshuffle of the revolutionary council was widely interpreted as a triumph for the supporters of the former Afro-Shirazi Party. Omar Ali Juma, a senior government official, was appointed as the new chief minister. Restrictions were subsequently imposed on the Zanzibari press. In December 1989 about 4,000 troops were dispatched to Zanzibar from the mainland, in response to renewed reports that a coup was being plotted.

Although no coup attempt materialized, strong undercurrents of discontent remained in evidence on Zanzibar and Pemba. The islands, whose links with the Arab Gulf stretch back to the ninth century, depended significantly on Oman for financial and development aid which had not been forthcoming from the Tanzanian mainland. In addition, certain religious and other groups began to perceive an erosion of traditional cultural values. From the late 1980s the value to Zanzibar of the union has come increasingly under question, and dissident groups such as the Movement for Democratic Alternative (MDA) and the smaller, religiously-based group on Pemba, the Bismillah Party, became active even before multi-party politics were officially sanctioned in 1992.

In the immediate prelude to the multi-party era, opposition in Zanzibar coalesced around the Kamati ya Mageuzi Huru (Kamahuru), led by Shaaban Mloo. In order to comply with the requirement that all political movements should function throughout Tanzania, Kamahuru merged in 1992 with the mainland-based Chama Cha Wananchi to form the CUF.

At the October 1995 multi-party elections to the house of representatives the CCM secured 26 of the 50 elective seats, while the CUF, campaigning for increased Zanzibari autonomy, took 24 seats, including every constituency on Pemba. The Zanzibar electoral commission credited Amour with victory by a narrow margin at the presidential election, attributing 50.2% of the votes to the incumbent president and 49.8% to Hamad who represented the CUF. Rejecting Nyerere's advice to form a government of national unity with the opposition, Amour appointed a new supreme revolutionary council, with Dr Mohamed Gharib Bilali as chief minister. However, the CUF refused to accept the election result, alleging that the ballot had been rigged in Amour's favour, and demanded that the contest be restaged. Meanwhile, the newly-elected CUF delegates refused to take up their seats in the house of representatives.

In February 1996 the Zanzibari government banned demonstrations by the CUF in southern Pemba; allegations persisted that numerous abuses of human rights were being perpetrated by the authorities against supporters of the CUF. Mkapa's failure to intervene in the islands' affairs was attributed in part to his need for the support of Zanzibari members of the CCM at the party elections in June. During 1996 external donors began to suspend aid disbursements to Zanzibar, in view of the continuing political deadlock between the islands' administration and the CUF. There were signs of a *rapprochement* in January 1997, when representatives of the mainland branch of the CUF reportedly agreed to recognize the legitimacy of the Amour administration and urged fellow members to cease political confrontation with the Zanzibari government. During December 1997 and early January 1998, however, 17 members of the CUF were arrested on suspicion of conspiring to overthrow the Amour government (these included several members of the house of representatives whose parliamentary immunity had not, at that stage, been properly lifted). From January CUF members refused to attend sessions of the house of representatives in protest; consequently, in February all CUF deputies were officially suspended from the house for 10 days as a punitive measure. During January the secretary-general of the Commonwealth, Chief Emeka Anyaoku, visited Zanzibar and offered to mediate between the two sides, presenting proposals for a peaceful solution, including a cessation of confrontational statements, freedom of action for political parties and a return to parliament by those who had boycotted its proceedings. Both sides, however, had difficulties in accepting this initiative. Chief Anyaoku subsequently appointed a special envoy, Dr Moses Anafu, to continue mediation efforts. Meanwhile, the government repeatedly castigated the CUF for its supposedly close links with foreign interests and sought to justify its continued harassment of the party's members on the islands by claiming that Zanzibar was being destabilized by an 'external plot'. In early May the UN secretary-general, Kofi Annan, declared the full support of his organization for the Commonwealth's ongoing mediation efforts. During that month a member of a CUF delegation that had been negotiating with Dr Anafu was arrested on suspicion of treason. Treason charges against the 18 CUF members who had been detained in 1997 and 1998 were finally presented in February 1999. The Zanzibari CCM, meanwhile, came under considerable pressure from senior mainland CCM officials to reach an agreement with the CUF, while that party's leadership eventually resigned itself to accepting Amour's tenure of the presidency until the end of his term of office in 2000. A mutual accord (witnessed by Chief Anyaoku) was finally concluded in early June 1999. CUF deputies took up the 24 seats which they had boycotted, in return for promises of constitutional, judicial and electoral reform intended to ensure free and fair elections. However, in May 2000 the CCM reneged on the agreement, claiming that any reforms would have to wait until after the elections scheduled for October 2000.

In January 2000 45 deputies of the mainland CCM were reported to have petitioned the Zanzibari president to have withdrawn the charges against the 18 CUF members being tried for treason. By that time the court proceedings had already been adjourned several times and, two days prior to the deputies' appeal, the Zanzibari attorney-general had been dismissed after he had ordered the arrest of two more leading members of the

CUF, including Mloo, the party's secretary-general. Nevertheless, in February President Amour declared that the trial would not be abandoned. Later in the same month the national executive committee of the CCM rejected a proposal to amend the Zanzibari constitution in order to allow President Amour to serve a third term of office. The president had earlier appeared to indicate that he would seek re-election after his second term of office concluded in October.

In April 2000 the 18 members of CUF who had been awaiting trial on treason charges since their detention in 1997 and 1998 were refused bail. International donors, who were continuing to withhold aid, expressed their concern over the situation and over President Mkapa's refusal to intervene. In a further worsening of relations Hamad was also detained by police and charged in May with assault and violent robbery; his trial was adjourned until June. In the same month the Zanzibari government charged the CUF with a total of 114 criminal acts, including alleged terrorism. The CUF claimed this was part of a premeditated campaign to discredit them, but President Mkapa denied this and other allegations that members of the CUF were being persecuted. A court case began in mid-August to establish whether or not Zanzibar is a sovereign state within the United Republic, such that a breach of allegiance to it could amount to treason. The result of the case would determine whether or not the trial of the 18 CUF members for treason could continue. In July five of the 18 were nominated as candidates in the Zanzibar parliamentary elections of October, but, as they had not received bail by August, they were not able to register as voters and would, therefore, be unable to stand.

Tension grew when the CUF declared that it would answer any violence against its supporters during the coming election campaign. President Mkapa condemned the CUF's position, and said that he would not hesitate to use the government's security apparatus to prevent bloodshed. There were frequent clashes between CCM and CUF members during the voter registration procedure in Zanzibar, and, on occasion, the police intervened by firing tear gas and rubber bullets. Mloo, now the CUF deputy chairman, accused the CCM of transporting its supporters from the mainland to the island so that they could register to vote in Zanzibar, in contravention of electoral regulations.

In mid-August 2000 the army deployed troops in Zanzibar. In a statement to the press the ministry of defence said this was in line with their constitutional responsibility to improve the security of the region during the elections. Opposition parties remained sceptical, however, and believed that the government was using the army to increase the number of voters in the region in order to help the CCM win the election; however, the ministry of defence insisted that the army would not be involved in politics. It was reported that security forces were detaining over 120 members, agents and candidates of the CUF. Ibrahim Lipumba, the CUF candidate for the Tanzanian presidency, claimed that this was part of a CCM strategy to suppress the opposition's chances of success in the elections. He also claimed that over 7,000 CUF supporters had been barred from registering to vote. President Mkapa assured the public that the government had established the right environment for a peaceful election. He said that the government would not allow anybody to cause 'chaos and insecurity' and would not tolerate campaigns of intimidation or provocation aimed at denying people their right to take part in the elections.

FOREIGN RELATIONS

Tanzania's relations with neighbouring Burundi deteriorated in 1973, when many thousands of refugees poured into Tanzania, and Tanzanian border villages were raided by Burundi troops. Trouble also arose with Uganda in 1973, when Gen. Amin, of whom President Nyerere had been a persistent critic, accused Tanzania of plotting against his regime; supporters of ex-president Obote had attempted an invasion of Uganda from Tanzanian territory in September 1972.

Following the collapse of the East African Community (EAC) in 1977, Tanzania's strained relations with Uganda worsened. Renewed border fighting was reported in October 1978, and in the following month Uganda announced the annexation of Tanzania's bordering Kagera region. Ugandan troops withdrew after pressure from the OAU but border fighting continued. Then, in January 1979, a Tanzania-based invasion force entered

Uganda. The force, comprising approximately 20,000 members of the Tanzanian defence forces and 1,200 members of the Uganda National Liberation Front (UNLF), rapidly gained control of Uganda's southern region. Amin's army capitulated and an interim UNLF government was proclaimed in April. Tanzania's intervention, which led to the second Obote presidency, was condemned by the OAU as a violation of territorial integrity, despite Nyerere's claim to have acted in response to Ugandan aggression. However, in July 1999 Uganda reportedly agreed to pay compensation for costs incurred during the operation to defeat Amin.

In mid-2000 there was a border dispute between Tanzania and Uganda over a stretch of land 115 km by 300 metres. Beacons used to mark the border had been removed during the 1978–79 fighting between the Tanzania and Uganda. Negotiations in the border town of Mutukula were postponed when an agreement on how to proceed could not be reached, but resumed a few months later. It was widely believed that a peaceful settlement to the dispute would be reached.

In October 1993 a failed coup attempt in Burundi sent a wave of refugees into Tanzania's Kigoma and Kagera regions. Their numbers were subsequently far exceeded by the massive and sudden influx of Rwandans which followed the outbreak of civil war in that country in April 1994 and the renewed offensive by the Uganda-based Front patriotique rwandais (FPR). By March 1995 further influxes of both Rwandan and Burundian refugees, combined with Tanzanian frustration at the international community's perceived preoccupation with the Zairean refugee camps, resulted in the controversial closure by Tanzania of its border with Burundi. The International Criminal Tribunal for Rwanda, authorized by the UN to try Rwandan nationals accused of direct participation in the genocide perpetrated in that country in 1994, was inaugurated in June 1995 in Arusha. In early 1996 ex-president Nyerere mediated in peace talks between the warring parties in Burundi; these failed, however, and in July the democratically elected Hutu government was overthrown in a Tutsi-led military coup. The Mkapa administration subsequently imposed economic sanctions against the new Burundi regime, in co-operation with other regional governments. Relations remained uneasy, owing both to the presence of Burundian rebels in northern Tanzania (which the Buyoya regime accused the Mkapa administration of supporting) and to the increasing number of Burundians seeking refuge in Tanzania throughout 1996 and 1997. In October 1997 the Burundian government protested to the UN over alleged Tanzanian acts of aggression at the two countries' common border; Tanzania, however, strongly denied the claims. Renewed peace talks beween the Burundi government and opposition parties, again with Nyerere as mediator, were convened in Arusha during 1998 and 1999. The regional economic sanctions that were imposed against the Burundi regime in 1996 were suspended in January 1999. Following the death of Nyerere, Nelson Mandela became the chief mediator in the Arusha peace negotiations. The negotiations were deadlocked for a while, with the 19 Burundian parties involved rejecting the inclusion of external personnel in the intra-Burundian consultation sessions. Another area of contention was the naming of the transitional government. However, by late August 2000 the negotiations had succeeded and President Buyoya signed the peace accord. All but four parties signed the accord on the same day; a further party signed the agreement in September, while the remaining three said that they wanted a clear cease-fire before they would sign. However, there were reports of continued fighting and increasingly intense rebel attacks along Tanzania's border with Burundi. The agreement also contained provisions for the repatriation of refugees. It was estimated that Tanzania was accommodating 540,592 refugees from Burundi; meanwhile further refugees were still entering Tanzania to escape the ongoing fighting.

In December 1996 some of the Rwandan refugees remaining in Tanzania returned to their homeland, following the threat of forcible repatriation by the Tanzanian government. In March 1997 the Tanzanian authorities appealed for international assistance in coping with the remaining refugees (an estimated 200,000 Burundians and 250,000 Zaireans). In June 1997 it was agreed to repatriate some 100,000 refugees to the Democratic Republic of the Congo (DRC, as Zaire had been renamed in the previous month). At the end of December the office of the United Nations high commissioner for refugees estimated that some 74,300 refugees from the DRC remained in Tanzania. In August 2000, president Mkapa said he believed that the Lusaka peace accord could bring peace to the DRC, but at the same time urged the DRC, Rwanda and Uganda to renegotiate the agreement so that it could be implemented more smoothly. The government of the DRC announced plans to cancel visa requirements for Tanzanians wishing to travel to the DRC in an effort to promote closer social and economic ties between the two countries.

In November 1993 the presidents of Tanzania, Uganda and Kenya signed a protocol on renewed co-operation among their countries. In March 1996 the three leaders formally inaugurated the Secretariat of the Permanent Tripartite Commission for East African Co-operation, which aimed to revive the EAC. A treaty for the re-establishment of the EAC (providing for the creation of a free trade area (with the eventual introduction of a single currency), for the development of infrastructure, tourism and agriculture within the Community, and for the establishment of a regional legislative assembly and regional

court) was initially expected to be ratified by the three heads of state in July 1999. The conclusion of the treaty was, however, postponed, pending the completion of negotiations concerning several unresolved trade issues. In July Tanzania announced that it was to withdraw from the Common Market for East and Southern Africa (COMESA). The EAC Treaty was signed by Presidents Mkapa, Moi (Kenya) and Museveni (Uganda) in Arusha in November 1999. However, Tanzania postponed ratification of the treaty, initially until after the elections in October 2000. In early 2000 Tanzanian MPs expressed doubts over the country's readiness to join the EAC. They feared, in particular, that Kenyan goods would flood the Tanzanian market, and that Tanzanian industries would not be able to compete. Nevertheless, Tanzania ratified the treaty, and it came into force in July. According to the agreed plan of action, a customs union was to be formed 18 months after the signing of the Treaty. Tanzania formally withdrew from COMESA in September, claiming that it was too expensive to remain a member of both COMESA and the EAC; it was, however, to remain a member of the Southern African Development Community (SADC).

Economy
LINDA VAN BUREN

Following independence in 1961 Tanzania, under the leadership of Julius Nyerere, embarked on a socialist path that placed more emphasis on the alleviation of illiteracy, poverty and disease than on the productive sectors. The landmark Arusha Declaration of 1967 envisaged the elimination of these ills by means of a programme of socialism and self-reliance. At the time, a large proportion of the population was either nomadic or dispersed in widely scattered homesteads. By 1974, however, the majority of the rural population had been settled into planned and permanent villages (*ujamaa vijijini*). The main objective of villagization was originally to raise output through collectivization and larger-scale farming methods; however, from an agronomic viewpoint, the results were largely unsuccessful, with ineffective management and shortages of materials contributing to low levels of crop production. The emphasis was gradually moved from the agricultural to the social benefits, with the *ujamaa* villages envisaged as centres for social and infrastructural services. The government also pursued a policy of nationalizing important economic sectors, particularly major industries and distribution and marketing. However, more than a decade of severe economic decline brought the country to a condition of economic collapse by 1985, when President Nyerere voluntarily left office. In order to obtain continuing aid from international donors, the new Mwinyi government adopted a more pragmatic approach to economic planning. By the late 1990s efforts to restructure Tanzania's state-owned concerns were under way on a large scale, with privatization for many of them as the stated intention. The humanitarian aims of the Arusha Declaration had not been fully achieved and, indeed, by the 1990s, Tanzania performed significantly worse than its northerly neighbour Kenya, even in comparisons based on national education and health statistics.

NATIONAL INCOME AND DEVELOPMENT PLANNING

In 1998, according to official estimates, the nominal gross domestic product (GDP) of mainland Tanzania was Ts. 5,631,500m., equivalent to US $8,651m. GDP per caput amounted to $262 in 1998. During 1990–97, according to World Bank estimates, GNP per caput, in real terms, declined by an annual average of 0.9%; however, in the second half of the 1990s GDP growth per head was positive, albeit modest, rising to a provisional 1.8% in 1999. In 1998 agriculture contributed 44.8% of GDP on the mainland and 41.5% of GDP in Zanzibar. Manufacturing contributed 7.4% on the mainland and 4.9% in Zan-

zibar. These percentages show little change from those in 1965, when agriculture contributed 46% and manufacturing 8%. Inflation has afflicted the Tanzanian economy for decades, but after hitting peaks of 44% in 1986 and 34.1% in 1994, the Mkapa government gained control of inflation, with the annual average rate steadily declining, from 28.4% in 1995 to 12.8% in 1998. In 1999, for the first time in 22 years, Tanzania achieved an inflation rate of less than 10%, with an annual average of 7.9%.

With the Arusha Declaration, President Nyerere placed Tanzania's economic and social policies firmly along a line of 'African socialism', rejecting both Western capitalism and the ideology of the extreme left. A succession of five-year development plans (the first commencing in 1964 and abandoned in 1966) were undermined by the country's lack of foreign exchange; the fourth and last, announced in 1981, was soon replaced by a national economic survival programme. The balance-of-payments problem had become so acute by early 1982 that Nyerere suspended all new development projects and launched a three-year structural-adjustment programme (SAP), which was prepared jointly by the ministry of planning and economic affairs and advisers from the World Bank. This aimed to stimulate the productive sectors (particularly the main export crops), to curtail government spending and to relax price controls.

A new three-year Economic Recovery Programme (ERP), announced by the Mwinyi government in June 1986, provided for some downward adjustment of the shilling's official exchange rate and further producer-price rises in the first year. The target of 4.5% average annual GDP growth was over-ambitious, but positive growth was achieved, at 3.6% in 1986, 3.9% in 1987, 5.1% in 1988 and 3.6% in 1989. The Mwinyi government launched a second three-year phase of the recovery programme, the Economic and Social Action Plan (ESAP), in January 1990. It aimed to continue the ERP policies but also to alleviate the social costs of adjustment measures, and achieved GDP growth of 3.2% in 1990, 3.7% in 1991 and 3.6% in 1992. GDP continued to grow in subsequent years under the Mkapa government, by 2.6% in 1995, 4.1% in 1996, 4.0% in 1997, 3.4% in 1998 and 4.8% in 1999.

AGRICULTURE

The agricultural sector is the mainstay of Tanzania's economy, providing a livelihood for more than 80% of the economically active population, contributing 44.8% of GDP (on the mainland) and accounting for 51.5% of export earnings in 1999. Subsistence farming accounted for 44.2% of total agricultural output in the same year. No more than about 8% of the country's land area is cultivated, and only about 3% of the cultivated land is irrigated, yet the growing of field crops heavily dominates the agricultural sector as a whole. The northern and south-western areas are the most fertile, receiving the highest rainfall. The main food crop is maize, and others include cassava, paddy rice, sorghum, plantains, sweet potatoes, potatoes, beans and millet. In 1999, following intensive efforts to revitalize the cashew-nut sector, this tree crop overtook coffee as Tanzania's main export crop, earning $98.94m., compared to $76.62m. for green coffee beans. The main reason for the change in ranking was a 52% increase in the dollar price for cashew nuts in 1999 compared to the previous year, while at the same time the price for coffee fell by 17%; the export volume for both crops in fact declined. Other important export crops were tobacco, cotton, tea, sisal and cloves (from Zanzibar).

During the 1980s, successive increases in producer prices for all the major crops were diluted by the weakness of the shilling, but new foreign-exchange support from international aid donors led to better availability of imported agricultural inputs and contributed to improved harvests. In 1990 the World Bank's International Development Association (IDA) approved a US $200m. credit to support an agricultural adjustment programme, which aimed to make agricultural marketing more efficient. In 1991 legislation was adopted to end the state monopoly over agricultural marketing, permitting private traders to market crops alongside co-operatives; implementation of the legislation was particularly slow regarding the marketing of cotton. Government agencies continued to dominate the official marketing of agricultural produce in the mid-1990s. In January 1998 the World Bank approved a further $21.8m. credit for the Tanzanian agricultural sector. Agricultural output increased, according to the FAO, at an average annual rate of 2.9% during 1984–89, and by an average rate of 3.7% per year in 1990–97. Official Tanzanian figures indicated that agriculture grew by 1.9% in 1998 and by 4.0% in 1999.

Tanzania's cashew-nut sector experienced a revival during the 1990s. Production of cashew nuts fell from 145,000 metric tons in 1973–74 to only 7,400 tons in 1990, partly because of low producer prices, long delays in payments to growers, disease, poor husbandry and lack of imported inputs, but also partly because growers were moved away from their trees to *ujamaa* villages. Efforts to revitalize the sector included the creation of the Cashew Nut Industry Development Fund (CIDEF). Among other measures, in 1998 CIDEF arranged a $100m. overdraft facility from Exim Bank to overcome the cash-flow problem that often made it impossible to make timely payments to producers for their crop. Output of cashew nuts rose steadily during the 1990s to 90,000 tons in 1997, 93,200 tons in 1998 and 106,500 tons in 1999 (according to FAO estimates). The total annual processing capacity is nominally just over 100,000 tons, but the country's 10 processing factories were built mostly in the mid-1970s (ironically, just as the growers were being moved away) and are badly in need of updating. A CIDEF source reported in June 2000 that the level of breakage of the kernels during processing at these old factories was 'more than 50%', at great cost, because cashew nuts are among the most expensive nuts on the world market, and consumers paying high prices for them expect to get whole nuts, not broken pieces. Even more wastefully, in some previous years, the whole crop was exported raw in order to earn foreign exchange quickly. Southern raw nuts, selling at about Ts. 527 per kg f.o.b. in November 1997, traditionally fetch about 40% more than northern raw nuts, which were selling at Ts. 372 per kg f.o.b. in November 1997. In the 1999/2000 season cashew nuts exported from Tanzania fetched, on average, $1,055 per ton, up 6.6% from the previous season's $989.50 per ton, according to figures from the Cashewnut Board of Tanzania (known as the Cashewnut Authority of Tanzania until the reform of the crop-purchasing authorities). Exports of cashew nuts grew steadily from 7,400 tons in 1990, earning $5.6m., to a record 164,680 tons in 1998, with a value of $107.32m.

Coffee is grown mainly by some 400,000 smallholders, mostly in the Kilimanjaro region; it accounted for 49% of export earnings in 1986, but this share had fallen to 21% by 1990, 17% in 1998 and 14% in 1999. A record crop of 67,300 tons was produced in 1980/81, but since then output has fluctuated.

Coffee production was estimated at 38,000 tons in 1998, but increased to 46,600 tons in 1999. Unfortunately, this 23% rise in volume coincided with a 17% decline in the global price, encouraging producers to withhold a proportion of their stocks from the market; the volume of Tanzania's exports actually declined by 7% in 1999. Tanzania's total coffee exports in the 1990s ranged from 37,000 tons in 1994 to 64,000 tons in 1996. Tanzania is a member of the International Coffee Organization (ICO). The fall in world prices from 1989, following the collapse of the ICO quota arrangements, affected robustas more severely than arabicas, which make up about 75% of Tanzania's coffee output. During the mid-1990s African and Latin American producers implemented schemes to withhold a proportion of their output from global markets, resulting in an improvement in world coffee prices and prospects and, consequently, a revival in Tanzania's export revenue from coffee (which reached $142.6m. in 1995). Coffee, however, is a highly cyclical commodity, and Tanzania's coffee earnings fell to $108.74m. in 1998 and to a disappointing $76.62m. in 1999. Buyers expressed concern in the mid-1990s that the declining quality of Tanzanian coffee was leading to a reduction in foreign demand.

In 1997 8.2m. coffee seedlings were distributed to farmers to stimulate production. In April 1998 the government admitted that some coffee-processing plants were operating below capacity and acknowledged that the use of fewer inputs and irregular payments to farmers had contributed to a decline in coffee harvests. A 'coffee input voucher scheme' was announced, whereby farmers were to receive a Ts. 50 voucher for each kg of arabica delivered, over and above the coffee payment; the vouchers could then be used to purchase fertilizers and pesticides. Much of the 23% production increase of 1999 was attributed to this and other measures to develop the coffee sector. In 1999 a metric ton of Tanzanian green coffee beans fetched, on average, $2,012.78.

Tobacco production increased significantly during the early 1990s. Although output declined from 19.1m. kg in 1975/76 to 10.7m. kg in 1998/89, production recovered to 17.1m. kg in 1992 before soaring to successive records of 24m. kg in 1993, 27m. kg in 1995, 37.8m. kg in 1998 and 39m. kg of tobacco leaves in 1999. Exports of tobacco rose from 5.8m. kg in 1990 to 24.9m. kg in 1996 and to 27.9m. kg in 1997, before falling to 26.35m. kg in 1998 and to 21.35m. kg in 1999. In 1999 the annual average price for 1 kg of Tanzanian tobacco leaves was $2.03.

Cotton production fluctuated during the 1990s. Output of cotton lint amounted to 31,467 tons in 1999, compared with 85,118 tons in 1989. A major rehabilitation programme began in the late 1980s, funded by the Netherlands, which sought to improve the performance of the cotton sector and which placed particular emphasis on the ginneries and transport infrastructure. The United Kingdom and the European Investment Bank (EIB) also funded rehabilitation schemes during the 1980s. Smallholders grow most of the cotton crop. Some 400,000 ha were under cotton in 1997, the majority in the Mwanza region, but by 1999 the figure had declined by 43%, to 250,000 ha. In May 2000 the Tanzania Cotton Lint and Seed Board admitted that growers in Arusha, Kilimanjaro and Coast regions still had large stocks of the previous season's crop on their hands, as the 20 or so buyers in the market had little interest in it in view of the prevailing low level of global prices. Tanzania's exports of cotton dwindled from 86,290 tons in 1997 to 37,290 tons in 1998 and to just 27,990 tons in 1999, while the price fetched for Tanzanian lint declined from $1,695.60 per ton in 1995 to $1,277.04 per ton in 1998 and to $1,009.42 in 1999. The 1999 crop of 104,891 tons of seed cotton yielded 31,467 tons of cotton lint and 73,423 tons of cottonseed. Tanzanian cotton growers face fierce competition from overseas in an era when protective measures are increasingly disapproved of and have, in any case, proved largely ineffective. Tanzania's average yield per hectare under cotton deteriorated from 675 kg in 1995 to 420 kg in 1999, compared to a global average of 1,700 kg per ha. Private-sector investment in the country's cotton ginneries improved efficiency and doubled output of ginned cotton in the mid-1990s. Local textile mills bought nearly 74,000 bales in 1989/90, but in the 1990s cheap imports of textile products from Asia flooded many African markets, including Tanzania, selling at prices below the cost of locally-produced cotton.

Tea production recovered after private-sector investment in the late 1980s and 1990s. The output of made tea rose from 8,492 tons in 1970 to about 25,000 tons in 1999. Export volume remained fairly stable during the 1990s, declining slightly from a peak of 22,120 tons in 1998 to 21,390 tons in 1999. Revenue from those exports has fluctuated more; Tanzanian tea fetched an annual average $1,139.24 per ton in 1999, for a total revenue from tea of $24.37m. The Tanzania Tea Authority (TTA) accounts for about one-quarter of tea output. Brooke Bond Liebig Tanzania is the largest producer, accounting for 40% of total output. The UK-based Lonrho group bought back into the Mufindi and Luponde tea estates, which it had owned before nationalization; the TTA retained a 25% holding in both companies. The estates are being rehabilitated, and some are producing organic teas, which command high prices. Lonrho announced in 1991 that it would invest $5.6m. in a five-year programme aimed at doubling yields at the Mufindi estates to 3,000 kg per ha and extending the planted area from 730 to 1,000 ha. In 1988 the East Usambara Tea Co was formed, with the UK-based Commonwealth Development Corpn (CDC) taking a 60% interest and the TTA the remainder. The company acquired two TTA estates in Tanga region.

Production of sisal was just over 250,000 tons in 1964, but output fell drastically when more than one-half of the estates were nationalized in 1976; only on the remaining privately owned estates was production maintained at a fairly steady level. Marketing was undertaken by the Tanzania Sisal Development Board (TSDB). In 1986 the Mwinyi government began to dispose of many of its 37 estates to private interests, and indeed, the entire privatization campaign which was to follow began with the coutry's sisal estates. By 1989 only about one-third of annual production came from TSDB estates, and in 1992 the government announced its intention to return all its estates to the private sector. World prices for sisal recovered in the late 1980s from the very low levels of the 1970s, as the product began to compete successfully with synthetic substitutes, particularly in some specialized uses. Output, which declined to 30,000 tons in 1987, recovered to 36,000 tons in 1991, when new plantings reached maturity. However, production slumped to 17,000 tons in 1994, before recovering to 30,000 tons in 1999. Renewed world demand is encouraging investment in sisal, and several foreign groups have bought estates or started joint ventures with the TSDB, which was transferred to private-sector control in April 1998. Tanzania exported 15,400 tons of sisal in 1999, earning $7.26m. in export revenue.

Cloves, cultivated mainly on Pemba, are the main export of Zanzibar, providing about 80% of the islands' foreign-exchange earnings. Zanzibar, once the world's largest clove producer, ranked only third in 1999 behind Indonesia and Madagascar. When Indonesia, the world's largest consumer, became self-sufficient in cloves in 1983, Zanzibar had to compete for much smaller markets in India, Thailand, Singapore and the Netherlands. Compared with up to 20,000 tons per year in the mid-1960s, output had fallen to 5,800 tons by 1990 and to only 1,575 tons in 1995. Insufficient profit incentives were blamed on the sector's poor performance. Together with low producer prices, the industry suffered the effects of smuggling, tree diseases and, in early 1997, fires (the result of prolonged drought), which destroyed thousands of clove trees. Nevertheless, production increased in the late 1990s; output increased to 5,000 tons in 1998 and then doubled to 10,000 tons in 1999. A clove distillery on Pemba produces clove-stem oil for export. Alternative export crops now being encouraged, and increasingly widely grown on the islands, include tobacco, rubber, cardamom, nutmeg, vanilla and peppermint. In 1995 seaweed became the second-largest source of foreign exchange for Zanzibar, with production at 4,975 tons.

Other cash crops include sugar cane, copra, groundnuts, oil-palm fruits, sunflower seeds, sesame seeds, cocoa beans, soya beans and pyrethrum. Tanzania's output of sugar cane was 1.35m. tons in 1999, according to the FAO, and the five sugar factories produced about 120,000 tons of sugar, while local demand is about 415,000 tons per year. Despite this deficit, Tanzania exports 10,000 tons per year to the EU countries. The smuggling of cheaper foreign sugar into Tanzania was widespread in the late 1990s. By May 2000 the government banned the import of sugar into all but the three largest ports

in a bid to stem the practice. In 1999 Tanzania produced 74,000 tons of groundnuts in shells, 62,000 tons of oil-palm fruits, 34,000 tons of sunflower seeds, 42,037 tons of sesame seeds, 3,692 tons of cocoa beans and 2,044 tons of soya beans. Production of pyrethrum, cultivated mainly in the Southern Highlands, declined from about 6,000 tons per year in the 1960s to just 460 tons in 1994/95. Nevertheless, world prices did improve in the late 1990s, and the government made efforts to reorganize the industry; the Tanzania Pyrethrum Board raised prices in line with higher world prices and supplied free seeds to growers. As a result, production of dried pyrethrum flowers increased from 1,300 tons in 1998 to about 4,000 tons in 1999. A project is under way to rehabilitate the Arusha processing factory. Fresh fruit and vegetables and flowers are potentially important export crops, and small quantities are being air-freighted to European markets. This non-traditional trade has been stimulated by the encouragement of private enterprise, but it is still severely constrained by many factors, including the very limited chilled storage facilities at Dar es Salaam international airport. In 1999 Tanzania produced 190,000 tons of mangoes, 75,000 tons of pineapples, 751,601 tons of bananas and plantains, 23,000 tons of chick-peas, 255,000 tons of beans, 27,000 tons of dry peas, 139,359 tons of tomatoes, 54,000 tons of dry onions and 2,000 tons of garlic. Exports of cut flowers earned about US $5m. in 1996. Honey and beeswax produced by Tabora Beekeepers' Co-operative are being exported in small quantities, after a gap of some years. Grapes are cultivated in central Tanzania, with output totalling 13,000 tons in 1999; some local wine is also produced.

Tanzania is one of Africa's largest cattle producers, with an estimated national herd of 14m. head in 1999; epidemics of lung disease and rinderpest threatened stocks in the mid-1990s. The country's resources of commercial species of timber, including camphor wood, podo and African mahogany, are exploited. Fishing, on both a commercial and subsistence basis, contributed about 2.4% of GDP in 1997. In 1997 the total fish catch was 352,530 tons. The 107,000-ton freshwater catch, included Nile perch and tilapia from inland waters; other species included shad, redfish, sardines and tuna from the Indian Ocean. The African Fishing Co, the country's first deep-sea fishing company, was licensed in 1997, with authorization to run six vessels for deep-sea trawling. The Deep Sea Fishing Act, promulgated in May 1998, imposed tighter controls on the monitoring of Tanzania's fish stocks. In May 1998 two new deep-sea fishing vessels entered service, increasing the Tanzanian fleet to four, out of a total of 14 vessels licensed to fish the country's coastal waters in the 1998 fishing season. Tanzania also produced modest amounts of prawns, molluscs and sea urchins.

During 2000, as in the early 1990s, severe food shortages were experienced in some areas. The World Food Programme estimated in June 2000 that more than 1m. Tanzanians in nine districts, mainly in the central and north-eastern parts of the country, were at risk from drought following poor rainfall. The smuggling of Tanzanian grain into Kenya in pursuit of higher prices exacerbated the situation, but the biggest problem was the inability of the authorities to transport maize within Tanzania from areas of surfeit to areas of deficit. In addition, an estimated 30%–40% of all crops are lost through post-harvest pest infestation and other damage. Maize output fell from 2.75m. tons in 1998 to 2.46m. tons in 1999. In 1999 Tanzania also harvested 676,000 tons of paddy rice (down 16% from 810,800 tons in 1998), 561,030 tons of sorghum, 194,372 tons of millet and 82,373 tons of wheat (down 36% from 129,000 tons in 1998). In May 1998, the wholesale price of maize varied by a wide margin from region to region, as market forces in the liberalization era reflected major differences in supply: a 100-kg bag cost Ts. 14,500 in Morogoro region, but only Ts. 6,000 in Moshi region.

INDUSTRY AND POWER

According to estimates by the World Bank, the average annual growth rate of industrial production was 2.6% in 1970–80 and 3.4% in 1980–90. Many factories closed down or suspended operations for long periods during the 1980s. Industries suffered from rising costs of fuel and other imports and from a severe lack of foreign exchange to pay for raw materials, machinery, equipment and spares, as well as from frequent interruptions to the water and electricity supply. A few signs of improvement appeared from 1986, mainly as more foreign exchange became available through the IMF and various aid donors. By mid-1990, most factories were operating at 20%–40% of capacity, and a few had reached 70%. Industrial output increased by an annual average of 9.7% during 1990–94. The sector's growth rate slowed to just 0.4% in 1995, and interruptions to the supply of power in the late 1990s also hindered manufacturing output.

The industrial sector is based on the processing of local commodities (with agro-industrial companies manufacturing beet sugar, sisal twine and cigarettes) and on import substitution. However, the government is seeking to encourage the production of manufactured goods for export, in order to lessen dependence on agricultural commodities, and some industrial goods—textiles, clothing, footwear, tyres, batteries, transformers, switch gear, electric cookers, bottles, cement and paper—are exported to neighbouring countries. According to Bank of Tanzania figures, revenue from exports of manufactured goods peaked in 1996 at $122.8m., and then began a steady decline until, in 1999, exports of Tanzanian manufactured goods earned only $32.31m., the lowest level for eight years. High production costs and reliance on imported content remain a barrier to international competitiveness.

The principal industries, after food processing, are textiles, brewing and cigarettes. Other industrial activities include oil refining, fertilizer production, rolling and casting milling, metalworking, vehicle assembly, fruit canning, engineering (spares for industrial machinery and for vehicles), railway wagon assembly, and the manufacture of pulp and paper, paperboard, cement, soft drinks, gunny bags, glassware, ceramics, hoes, pharmaceutical products, oxygen, carbon dioxide, bricks and tiles, lightbulbs, electrical goods, wood products, machine tools, footwear and disposable hypodermic syringes.

With protective barriers in place aimed at increasing textile output to a target of 61.1m. sq m of cloth in 1990, Tanzania's textile mills produced 47.5m. sq m in the first six months of the year alone, compared with 38.9m. sq m in the whole of 1988. But protective barriers, costly and difficult to enforce at the best of times, met with increasing global disapproval in the 1990s, and when they were removed in the early 1990s, at least two textile companies found themselves in severe financial difficulty. Then too, much cheaper manufactured textile products from Asia flooded onto the market, and demand for locally-manufactured textiles fell sharply just as the costs rose steeply. The National Bicycle Co reopened in 1990, after closing down in 1982 owing to lack of foreign exchange. In 1996, the government's share in the company was privatized, and the $1.8m. investment by Avon Cycles of India was backed by the World Bank's Multilateral Investment Guarantee Agency (MIGA). There are three cement plants, at Mbeya, at Wazo Hill near Dar es Salaam, and at Tanga. After several years of severe cement shortage, rehabilitation of the plants, mainly with Danish and Swedish assistance, allowed production to increase in 1989 to 700,000 tons, meeting domestic needs of about 580,000 tons and allowing exports of 70,000 tons, with the remainder held as stock; combined capacity in 1997 was about 1m. tons per year. Finnish Valmet tractors, Swedish Scania trucks and Italian Fiat tractors are among the vehicles assembled. Southern Paper Mills' US $260m. pulp- and paper-mill at Mgololo (in Mufindi district, on the Tazara railway line) commenced production in 1985. It was envisaged that the nearby Sao Hill forest would eventually supply the mill's timber needs, but, meanwhile, the plant used imported chemical pulp. The eventual target output was 75,000 tons per year, in seven grades of paper, although additional investment was required to attain that level of production; meanwhile, in 1999 the mill's capacity was 60,000 tons per year. Tanzania's domestic demand for paper was estimated at 30,000 tons per year in 1996. In April 1999 the government put its majority shareholding in Southern Paper Mills up for sale, and negotiations began with a US company. It was estimated that the operation would initially require $29m. in capital investment, followed by two further instalments of $10m. towards the rehabilitation and modernization of the paper machines, the bleaching plant and the finishing sections, and in order to expand the rated capacity to the targeted 75,000 tons per year. In 1996 the Kilwa Ammonia Co (KILAMCO) announced that it was to build an ammonia-urea fertilizer plant

at Kilwa Masoka. East African Agro-Industries was formed in 1990 to trawl for Nile perch in Lake Victoria; it is to build a plant near Mwanza airport to process 20–25 tons of fish per day for export. The African Fishing Co (which was licensed in 1997 for deep-sea trawling—see above) had plans to construct processing facilities. The Tanzanian Italian Petroleum Refinery (TIPER), in Dar es Salaam, is jointly owned by Italy's AGIP and the Tanzanian Petroleum Development Corpn (TPDC). It underwent rehabilitation, at a cost of $18m., in 1990–93. The refinery has a capacity of 875,000 tons per year. The IDA has extended a loan of $44m. towards a $104m. petroleum distribution improvement project, which is regarded as a key component of overall infrastructure improvement plans. In 1995 Tanzania Breweries Ltd, which had been taken over by South Africa's Indol, paid a dividend for the first time in 20 years. In September 1997 Kenya Breweries Limited announced plans to invest Ks. 1,500m. in the construction of a new brewery at Moshi, in north-eastern Tanzania. In February 1998 the World Bank's private-sector agency, the International Finance Corpn (IFC), approved a $1m. loan to Maji Masafi Ltd, towards a $2.8m. expansion of its fruit-flavoured drinks plant. The IFC also approved a $450,000 loan to Pallsons Consumer Industries Tanzania (producers of edible oil and cake from sunflower seeds) in January 1999.

During the 1990s the government aimed to sell, restructure or dissolve 395 state-owned companies; the number was later increased to 410. It established the Parastatal Sector Reform Commission (PSRC) to oversee the privatization exercise. Between April 1993 and June 1999, 191 parastatals were privatized or disposed of. The majority were small companies engaged in agro-industrial activities, but mining entities attracted the largest sums of investment money. The two principal obstacles in negotiations with potential investors were the assumption of the often very large debts of these parastatals, and the burden of severance compensation costs for any workers to be dismissed by the new investors as part of a cost-cutting exercise. In mid-1999 there was some concern that the planned revival of the East African Community (EAC—see below), and the proposed subsequent creation of an EAC free trade area, would result in a legalized influx of manufactured goods from Kenya, thereby weakening the less developed Tanzanian manufacturing sector. On the other hand, a number of investors have expressed a greater willingness to invest when there is access to a wider regional market than when there is access to only one national market. In December 1999 the World Bank's IDA approved two instruments in support of Tanzania's private-sector development. The first was of $41.2m. towards the $103.4m., 12-year, three-phase Public Service Reform Programme, aimed at improving sustainable performance by concentrating on core capacity while contracting out non-core activities. The second was a $45.9m. credit to the $76.81m. Privatization and Private Sector Development Project.

Tanzania's total electricity generating capacity was 642 MW in 1997, of which 460 MW was operational, against a national demand of 700 MW. Lack of reliable electricity supply is often identified as the biggest hindrance to manufacturing growth in Tanzania. In 1999 the Tanzania Electricity Supply Co (Tanesco) projected that the country's electricity requirements would rise to 2,312 MW by 2025 and indicated that 1,440 MW of new electricity-generating capacity would be required to meet this demand. Of the total generating capacity in 1999, about two-thirds was supplied by hydroelectric facilities. Expansion of the major Kidatu hydroelectric complex on the Great Ruaha river was completed in the late 1980s. An eight-year investment programme for the power sector was initiated in 1991 and included the $410m. development of the 200-MW Kihansi power station, to be commissioned in 1998; the expansion of the Pangani Falls power station; and the $107m. construction of a 220-kv transmission line from Singida to Arusha. The 112-MW Ubungo power station near Dar es Salaam has four turbines which operate using imported fuel. The national grid was to be extended in a major distribution project, taking electricity from Kidatu to six mainland regions. In 1997 electricity supply to Zanzibar was scheduled to be transferred to Electrogen Ltd, a South African company, via gas-powered generators to be built on the island. Tanesco raised electricity prices by 27% in March 1993 and by a further 71% in July 1993. In 1994 the country's energy consumption, in oil equivalent, was 975m. kg. Total electricity generation in 1995/96 was 1,979m. kWh, according to the Bank of Tanzania. In the mid-1990s the production of electricity was opened to private-sector investment, but in September 1999 only about 2% of output was generated by private-sector operations. In 1997 Independent Power Tanzania Ltd (IPTL), a joint venture between Malaysian and Tanzanian investors, began the construction of a large-scale, 100-MW, $163m. thermoelectric power generation plant at Sala Sala, 18 km north of Dar es Salaam. Work was carried out by Dutch and Finnish contractors. Electricity was to be produced by 10 diesel-fuelled generators, each with a capacity of 10 MW. The first three generators were commissioned in June 1998, followed by four more in July and the remaining three in August. In 1995, at the height of a power-supply crisis, Tanesco contracted to buy 100% of IPTL's output at a price of $5m. per month. However, in April 1998, a dispute arose when the government served a 'default notice' on the Malaysian partner, alleging that the medium-speed diesel generators being installed did not meet the specifications of the contract. IPTL denied the allegation and claimed that the notice was a ploy designed to force a renegotiation of the contract price for the plant's output. Although IPTL is by far the largest private-sector investment in Tanzania's power sector, it is not the first. The Tanganyika Wattle Co in Njombe and the Kiwira coal-powered station in Mbeya had already begun contributing 2.5 MW and 3.96 MW, respectively.

MINERALS

Tanzania's mining sector grew by 17% in 1998 and by 27.4% in 1999 according to the Tanzania Chamber of Mines. Mineral exports earned US $103m. in 1998 (compared with earnings of $27m. in 1990). Exports of gold alone rose from $7.6m. in the year to 30 April 1999 to $53.4m. in the year to 30 April 2000, according to Bank of Tanzania figures, as exports commenced from the Golden Pride mine at Nzega (see below). Expenditure by mining companies on exploration programmes in the country (which totalled about $6m. in 1992) reportedly exceeded $80m. in 1997. Diamonds, gold, salt, various gemstones, phosphates, coal, gypsum, kaolin, limestone, graphite and tin are exploited. Deposits of lead, iron ore, silver, tungsten, pyrochlore, magnesite, nickel, copper, cobalt, soda ash, uranium, niobium, titanium and vanadium have also been identified. Output of diamonds fell from a peak of 988,000 carats in 1967 to 150,000 carats in 1987, but then recovered slightly to 190,000 carats in 1988. A continuing problem is that small-scale diamond prospectors sell their finds outside the Tanzanian buying system. The Mwadui diamond pipe, covering an area of 146 ha in the Shinyanga region, is the world's largest. However, production at the Williamson Mwadui mine, which is 75% owned by the government and 25% by De Beers, began to suffer in the late 1980s from deterioration in diamond grades as well as technical and mine maintenance problems, and output temporarily ceased. Following extensive rehabilitation, operations at Mwadui recommenced in August 1995, and exports were resumed in December. Production totalled 117,000 carats in 1996, 68,969 carats in 1998 and 207,500 carats in 1999. However, resources are almost depleted, and production is continuing primarily in order to repay outstanding debts. In 1993 De Beers Centenary, together with Canadian interests, obtained exploration rights and mining leases covering almost 9,000 sq km. near Mwadui. TANEX, a joint venture between Anglo-American and De Beers, is continuing exploration work.

Gold production virtually ceased in the 1970s, but renewed interest in the 1990s led to a major revitalization. The ministry of energy and mineral resources projected, in June 2000, that Tanzania's annual gold output would reach 40 tons by 2002. Ashanti Goldfields of Ghana and AngloGold brought their joint-venture gold project at Geita into production in June 2000, three months ahead of schedule. Output at Geita is projected at 500,000 ounces per year, at a cost of $180 per ounce. The $48m. Golden Pride gold mine at Lusu, near Nzega, in central Tanzania, began exporting in 1999. Golden Pride is a joint venture between Resolute Resources of Australia and Samax of Canada. Another Canadian company is investing $86m. in a $211m. underground gold mine at Bulyanhulu in Kahama district, which has proven reserves of 3.8m. ounces and is expected

to be capable of producing 180,000 oz of gold annually for 15 years, starting in 2001. Tancan Gold, a Tanzanian-Canadian joint venture, is to mine gold at Matinje in Tabora region. Official gold exports rose as reforms to the official buying mechanism began to take effect in 1991. Official purchases were only 41 kg in 1988, but rose to 3,770 kg in 1991, and to 7,000 kg in 1993. Foreign-exchange earnings declined dramatically in 1995, to $3.2m. from $25.7m. in 1994, largely because financial institutions abandoned a scheme to purchase gold at above the parallel market rate and because the authorities failed to institute proper marketing mechanisms. A programme was under way in 1998 in Mwanza region to train artisanal miners in safe methods of processing gold and other minerals, following an accident near Arusha in which about 100 artisanal tanzanite miners were killed.

Tanzania has extensive reserves of precious and semi-precious stones, and new discoveries are continuing to be made, generating a high level of foreign interest. The Longido ruby mine is the largest in the world, although growth in production has been slow since the mine re-opened in 1994, following a temporary halt in operations. The Umba River Valley yields rubies and sapphires, with particular interest in the gem market centring on a fiery reddish-orange sapphire to rival the famous and increasingly scarce paparadzha sapphire of Sri Lanka. Sapphires have been discovered at Songea, and alluvial deposits at Tunduru have yielded sapphires, tourmalines, alexandrites, chrysoberyls and spinels; nine prospecting licences have been granted. Both Songea and Tunduru have been overrun by illegal prospectors. Deposits of tanzanite, a blue semi-precious stone that was first discovered in the Merelani Hills near Arusha in 1967, and is found nowhere else in the world, have been exploited by unlicensed miners. The government is now attempting to curtail this activity and at the same time is reviving the Tanzania Gemstone Industry enterprise, which buys and processes gemstones.

Large soda ash deposits in Lake Natron are to be used for the production of caustic soda. Salt is produced at coastal salt pans, and is a potential export. The feasibility of extracting salt from Lake Eyasi, 200 km west of Arusha, is being investigated. Romex International of Canada has signed an agreement to develop nickel deposits in the western Ngara district. Tanzania has nickel deposits estimated at 31.4m. tons. In 1992 Canada's Sutton Resources commenced exploration of 26,400 sq km of the Kagera basin, searching for nickel, cobalt, copper, lead, zinc and platinum. In that year a scheme to exploit deposits of nickel, copper and cobalt, which had already been located in the region, was launched, at a projected cost of $750m. The Chinese-built Songwe-Kiwira coal mine in the south-west, which came into production in 1988, has an annual capacity of 100,000 tons, but the coal's high ash content renders it unsuitable for use by the intended major customers, Southern Paper Mills and Mbeya Cement Co. The mine does produce electricity for the national grid. In September 1996 a $2m. rehabilitation of the Kiwira coal mine was announced, which would increase its annual production capacity to 150,000 tons. Coal is mined on a smaller scale at Ilima in the Mbeya region. Iron ore is mined at Chunya. Tin is mined on a small scale near the Congolese border. Graphite deposits in the Merelani Hills, believed to hold significant potential, were being developed in 1997.

Prospecting for petroleum and natural gas has been continuing for many years. In the 1970s there were reports of the discovery of petroleum in the Songo Songo island area, offshore from Kilwa, south of Dar es Salaam; the presence of an estimated 42,890m. cu m of natural gas in the area was later confirmed. The proposed KILAMCO fertilizer plant was to use gas from the field. In 1998 Songas Ltd announced plans to develop the Songo Songo reserves. The $375m. project is funded by a $200m. IDA credit, a $50m. equity investment by TransCanada and Ocelot of Canada and a $37m. European Investment Bank loan, as well as by several smaller equity investments. Songas was to build two gas-processing units on Songo Songo island, a 25-km underwater pipeline to deliver the gas from the island to Somanga, on the mainland, and a 207-km underground pipeline to deliver the gas from Somanga northwards to Dar es Salaam, where it was to supply the existing 122-MW Ubungo power plant (whose four turbines were to be converted to run on gas) and the cement plant at Wazo Hill. The scheme entails several infrastructural developments on Songo Songo island, including the construction of an airstrip. The scheme was due to begin producing gas by 2003 and has a projected lifetime of 20 years. There is a much larger offshore gas field at Kimbiji, 40 km south-east of Dar es Salaam, where recoverable reserves are estimated at 130,000m. cu m. Results of petroleum exploration so far have been disappointing, but a number of international companies have been active, in both on- and offshore areas (in some cases grouped in consortia), including Shell and Esso, Elf Aquitaine, Petrofina, PetroCanada, AGIP, Amoco, Statoil of Norway, Exxon, BP, Broken Hill (Pty) Co, Texaco, the Oil and Natural Gas Commission of India and the Swiss-based International Energy Development Corpn. The Tanganyika Oil Co Ltd announced that it was to drill an exploratory well in 1999 to test the East Lika prospect at the Mandawa Jurassic Salt Basin. Fuel accounted for 7.4% of the import bill in 1998.

TOURISM

Tanzania's tourism sector has aroused more investor interest during the privatization era than any other sector except mining. During the period when the old East African Community (EAC) was active, the tourism sector in Tanzania was an adjunct of the Kenyan tourist industry. Most travellers merely visited Tanzania's tourist attractions on one-day excursions, pre-paid in Kenya. The dissolution of the EAC and the closure of the Kenya–Tanzania border in 1977 led to a fall in visitor arrivals; only 60,218 tourists visited Tanzania in 1983, compared with 178,000 in 1974. Hotels, lodges and access roads were allowed to deteriorate badly. From 1986 onwards, however, the tourism sector began to recover, with the growing recognition of Tanzania's very promising potential as a tourist destination (based on the country's unspoiled beaches and superb game parks, covering one-quarter of its area, as well as its long-term political stability). By 1996 tourist arrivals had reached a record 326,000, according to government figures. Gross receipts from tourism were estimated at $392.4m. in 1997, when the sector overtook coffee to become Tanzania's primary source of foreign exchange. Devaluation of the shilling has benefited tourism, because Tanzania was previously an extremely expensive destination. The sector is co-ordinated by the state-owned Tanzania Tourist Board. Investment has been forth-coming from several local and foreign private companies. Most new investment has been in the so-called 'northern circuit', centred on the Serengeti National Park, the Ngorongoro Crater and Mount Kilimanjaro; the government would like to encourage the development of tourism in the 'southern circuit', which includes the Selous National Park. Zanzibar, which had an estimated 87,000 visitors in the year to June 2000, is expanding and upgrading its tourist facilities, in particular through an agreement signed with the Aga Khan Fund for Economic Development to build two new hotels (one of which was opened in March 1997), develop a tourism centre and repair historic buildings in the old capital. Tourism was projected to contribute 14% of Zanzibar's GDP in 2000/01. In 1998 a British company was preparing to develop a 57 sq km site on Zanzibar's Nungwi peninsula, at a reported cost of $4,000m., with plans for a harbour, an airport, five-star hotels, a mosque and a university. The number of hotel beds in Zanzibar reportedly increased from 3,000 in 1986 to 5,352 in mid-2000.

TRANSPORT AND COMMUNICATIONS

The concentration of Tanzania's population on the periphery of the country, leaving the central part relatively sparsely populated, poses considerable problems in transport and communications.

The Tanzania-Zambia Railway Authority (Tazara) rail line and the Tanzania-Zambia highway, designed to provide an alternative sea outlet to landlocked Zambia, have eased the problem of transportation to the rich Kilombero valley as well as the Iringa and Mbeya regions. The Chinese-built, 1,860-km Tazara line initially experienced financial and technical problems, together with lack of equipment and spare parts. Tazara made its first profit in the June quarter of 1983, although it did not consistently achieve profits until 1988. Following the political changes which took place in South Africa during the early 1990s, Zambia started to make greater use of the much more reliable southern transport routes, creating new problems

for the Tazara line. Traffic levels fell from approximately 1m. tons of freight in 1990 to an estimated 600,000 tons in 1994/95. Tanzania's central railway line and its branches are operated by Tanzania Railways Corpn (TRC). Canada provided finance and technical assistance for TRC's development programme. The IDA agreed in 1991 to lend $76m. for TRC's five-year, $279m. rehabilitation project. There is a rail connection with Kenya, and marine services and ferry services across Lake Victoria link Tanzania to Uganda. TRC also operates ferry links across Lake Tanganyika to the Democratic Republic of the Congo and across Lake Malawi to Malawi. In 1999 TRC was awaiting privatization.

Air Tanzania Corpn (ATC), which was founded in 1977, operates domestic and regional services. ATC has persistently suffered severe financial difficulties and technical problems. The airline has on several occasions had to suspend international flights because of financial problems. In 1992 the government proposed the partial privatization of ATC. Alliance Air was founded in 1994 as a joint venture between ATC, the Ugandan and South African national airlines and the Tanzanian and Ugandan governments, in order to compete with major international airlines. Zanzibar's airport runway has been extended, with aid from Oman, to enable long-haul aircraft to land. In 1998 a British-led consortium won a 25-year contract to handle all airport services at Kilimanjaro International Airport. The East African Development Bank financed an investment of just over $1m. in cold-storage facilities at the airport in the same year. Air Zanzibar started operations in 1990 and aimed mainly to cater for the tourist trade. The Tanzania Harbours Authority's $220m. improvement programme for Dar es Salaam port, including the development of container-handling facilities, received funding from the World Bank, Finland, Denmark, Italy, the Netherlands, Norway, the United Kingdom and the EIB. The project aimed to raise the port's annual throughput capacity from 3m. tons to 7m. tons by the mid-1990s. The new container terminal came into service in 1989, and an inland container depot was developed at Ubungo, 15 km from Dar es Salaam. The number of containers handled in 1990 was 73,000 TEU (20-foot equivalent units), rising to 147,000 TEU per year by 1995. Zambia accounted for over 40% of cargo handled at the port in 1993. In 1999 plans for the privatization of both the Harbours Authority and the National Shipping Agencies Co Ltd were under way.

The road network in Tanzania is in a state of poor repair, despite significant investment in the sector. A 10-year, $650m. integrated road project, funded by the World Bank and several other multilateral and bilateral donors, commenced in 1991. The programme sought to repair and improve 70% of the country's primary roads and to construct 2,828 km of roads and 205 bridges. Nevertheless, in 1999 only about 14% of Tanzania's 85,000 km of roads were said to be in 'good' condition. In a bid to simplify road maintenance, the government set up TanRoads in 1999; a 1997 study found that contractors had to negotiate excessive bureaucracy in order to win a road-construction or -rehabilitation contract and that the negotiation process often took more than three years before any work could commence. In September 1996 it was announced that a feasibility study was to be conducted on the construction of a bridge over the Rovuma river, linking Tanzania and Mozambique. A new international telephone service giving direct-dialling facilities was inaugurated in 1991. A satellite earth station at Mwenge, built in 1979, has been replaced by a new installation supplied by an Italian company, giving access to Atlantic as well as Indian Ocean satellites. Plans to privatize the Tanzanian Telecommunications Co Ltd (TTCL) were announced in 1996 and were reported to be at an advanced stage in early 1999. The telephone network is extremely limited, with fewer than four lines per 1,000 inhabitants in 1996, and often faulty. A new exchange came into operation in Dar es Salaam in 1997. The first cellular network in the capital was inaugurated in 1994.

EXTERNAL TRADE

The leading exports are cashew nuts, coffee beans, tobacco leaves, raw cotton, tea, sisal and gold, with the role of gold expected to increase rapidly. Other exports include fish and prawns, cloves, beans, gemstones, pyrethrum and timber. Industrial exports include textiles, hides, wattle-bark extract and spray-dried instant coffee. Non-traditional exports developed in the 1990s included fresh fruit, vegetables and flowers. Honey exports were resumed in 1989, after a gap of several years. Fluctuating world prices lead to wide variations in coffee's share of Tanzania's total exports. In 1999 manufactures of all types accounted for 6% of total exports, according to the Bank of Tanzania, compared with 11% in 1998, 23% in 1995 and 7% in 1985.

Tanzania's terms of trade were estimated to have declined by 36% between 1972 and 1980 (or by 21.5% if petroleum imports are excluded). They subsequently levelled off, but deteriorated again in the early 1990s and fluctuated throughout the rest of the decade. Official merchandise exports f.o.b. earned $541m. in 1999, down from $576.5m. in 1998 and $719.2m. in 1997. An encouraging feature has been the success of small private exporters, demonstrating how quickly many of them responded to trade-liberalization measures. In 1994 the United Nations Development Programme provided $30m. for a project which aimed to assist and expand small-scale enterprises. Imports also grew with the implementation of the economic recovery programme; official merchandise c.i.f. amounted to $1,630.6m. in 1999, $1,518.5m. in 1998 and $1,394.7m. in 1997. The import bill was expected to increase steadily until at least 2002.

An Open General Licensing (OGL) scheme was introduced in 1988, with aid from the IDA and the United Kingdom, to give small importers access to foreign exchange, which was made available through the National Bank of Commerce and could initially be used only for importing items on an approved list. The scheme was subsequently expanded and altered until any goods were eligible for a licence unless they appeared on a list of excluded items. The original ceiling of $1m. worth of goods a year per importer was discontinued; for any order worth more than $1m., however, the importer was still required to obtain at least three quotations from potential suppliers. Unfortunately the OGL scheme was affected by severe 'leakage' problems. Fiscal audits for 1992 revealed that while the Bank of Tanzania (the central bank) remitted to the Treasury the full counterpart value of foreign exchange disbursed, the commercial banks had failed to turn over to the Bank of Tanzania some Ts. 17,000m. worth of the counterpart funds. This situation, in addition to a lack of disclosure in the allocation of resources, led to a nearly complete withdrawal of donor support. Banking reforms were therefore announced (see below).

In 1962 about 32% of official exports went to the United Kingdom, but by 1991 the UK was outranked consistently by Germany and occasionally also by Japan, the Netherlands, Belgium and India. In 1999 India ranked first with 20.6% of the total, followed by the UK with 17.0%, Japan with 8.0%, Germany with 6.4%, the Netherlands with 5.7%, Singapore with 4.5% and Kenya with 3.8%. The UK's share of Tanzanian imports in 1962 was 29%, but by 1991, although the UK still ranked first as a supplier, its proportion had fallen to 9.1%. In 1996 Kenya overtook the UK as the chief supplier, and in 1998 and 1999 Japan ranked first. Japan's share of the Tanzanian market was 10.9% in 1999, followed by South Africa with 10.4%, the UK with 7.8% and the USA with 6.1%.

Improved relations between Tanzania and its neighbours Kenya and Uganda during the late 1990s, with a view to renewed East African co-operation, opened new possibilities for regional trade. A treaty for the re-establishment of the EAC, providing for the promotion of free trade between the member states (envisaging the eventual introduction of a single currency, as well as the development of infrastructure, tourism and agriculture in the region) was ratified in June 2000 after signature by the Kenyan, Tanzanian and Ugandan heads of state. All three countries were then to introduce legislation in their parliaments before a new EAC Law could be promulgated. In Tanzania, however, the EAC bill was postponed until after the October 2000 elections and was expected to be dealt with by the next parliament in January 2001.

BALANCE OF PAYMENTS AND INTERNATIONAL AID

Tanzania's visible trade account, current account and overall balance of payments were all chronically in deficit throughout the 1990s, and even with growing tourism receipts, the goods and services account has also shown a series of deficits. In 1999 visible exports f.o.b., at $541m., covered less than one-third of the cost of visible imports, at $1,630.6m. c.i.f., producing a visible trade deficit of $1,089.6m. In that year there was also a shortfall on the services account totalling $224.9m. The current account deficit amounted to $861.9m., an improvement on the 1998 shortfall of $946.6m., but well up on the 1997 deficit of $555.1m. Despite inflows to the capital account of $303.1m., the overall balance of payments registered a deficit of $558.8m. before, or $411.3m. after, official transfers. According to the IMF, gross official foreign reserves stood at $775.6m. at 31 December 1999, sufficient to cover 4.1 months' imports of goods and non-factor services. Tanzania's total external debt stood at $7,300m. at 31 January 2000, down from $8,295m. at 31 March 1999. The Bank of Tanzania indicated that more than one-quarter of the debt disbursed during the year to the end of March 1999 was used to support the balance of payments which, in turn, was weakened on account of the $426.5m. owed by Tanzania in debt-servicing payments during the 1998/99 fiscal year. This level of debt-servicing yielded a debt-service ratio equivalent to 33.6% of exports of goods and non-factor services. In addition, the Tanzanian government owed Ts. 919,000m. (about $1,350m.) in domestic debt at the end of March 1999. During that month it paid Ts. 5,900m. in service on this debt, making a negligible impact on the outstanding arrears, which stood at Ts. 107,500m. Debt rescheduling agreements were reached at meetings of the 'Paris Club' of Western official creditors held in September 1986, July 1987, March 1990, July 1992 and December 1996. Under a debt conversion programme inaugurated by the Bank of Tanzania in 1990, foreign private creditors were permitted to convert their claims into equity or into cash to invest in certain sectors, on a basis which reduced the local costs involved in starting a business in Tanzania. In April 2000 the World Bank and the IMF agreed a $1,200m. package of debt-relief assistance for Tanzania; the sums were to be dispersed over a 20-year period and were to cover 69.1% of Tanzania's debt-service obligations to the IDA. Nevertheless, Tanzania still carried a heavy debt burden of $7,300m. at 31 January 2000.

After years of fruitless negotiations, Tanzania finally reached agreement with the IMF in 1986 for a $77m. stand-by facility over 18 months, and $24m. under the Fund's structural adjustment scheme. The IMF demanded the devaluation of the shilling to Ts. 58.90 = US $1 by June 1986. The actual official rate at mid-1986 was Ts. 40.00 = $1. Among other IMF conditions were abolition of the subsidy on the staple food, maize meal (sembe), a 'freeze' on the level of minimum wages, a reduction in the annual budget deficit to Ts. 2,500m., the removal of price controls, and the raising of producer prices by at least 45% in real terms. Prior to the 1986 agreement, the government had already introduced some far-reaching measures, and had proposed graduated moves towards fulfilling the IMF's conditions. It reduced the subsidy on maize meal (at the risk of causing urban unrest), dissolved some parastatal bodies, and reorganized or amalgamated others, cutting back their subsidies in order to force them into greater efficiency.

The negotiations with the IMF were closely linked to parallel talks with the World Bank, which subsequently agreed to lend $50m. in support of the government's ERP with a further $46.2m. from the Special Africa Facility. These agreements cleared the way for a World Bank-sponsored Consultative Group meeting on Tanzania held in Paris in 1986, the first to take place since 1977. Donors strongly endorsed the recovery programme, which required $1,200m. to finance imports in 1986/87. In November 1988 the IMF released the second tranche of a three-year structural-adjustment facility (SAF), following agreement with the government on further devaluation of the shilling, restructuring of export crop and food marketing, reform of the tax system and continued reform of public enterprises. This agreement unblocked funds from other donors. A major devaluation of the shilling in December 1989, to Ts. 190=US $1, persuaded the IMF to release the third and final tranche of the three-year SAF. It also opened the way for a new meeting of the Consultative Group in December 1989, at which donors pledged $865m. towards the country's financing needs of $1,300m. for 1990. The Investment Promotion Centre, established in July 1990, had by the end of that year approved 58 proposed projects, representing total planned investment of $100m.

The exchange rate underwent a series of minor adjustments following the December 1989 devaluation, and by June 1992 it had declined to Ts. 297.68 = US $1. The parallel rate at this date was about Ts. 425 = US $1, indicating that the shilling was still considerably overvalued. The official rate continued to fall, to Ts. 378.6 = US $1 in June 1993, to Ts. 516 = US $1 in June 1994, to Ts. 602 = US $1 in June 1997, to Ts. 653 = US $1 in March 1998, to Ts. 694 = US $1 in May 1999 and to Ts. 797 = US $1 in June 2000.

In November 1994 foreign donors began to suspend aid disbursements in protest at alleged high-level government connivance in widespread tax evasion. In response, the government established a new regulatory body, the Tanzania Revenue Authority (TRA), which became operational in July 1996. During that month, the Consultative Group on Tanzania met in Paris and pledged some $1,200m. in assistance for 1996/97. In February 1997 the TRA enforced a harmonization of import tariffs throughout the country, following donor concerns that the lower rate of duty in Zanzibar encouraged smuggling to the mainland. IMF credit was restored in November 1996, with the approval of a three-year ESAF of $234m., following the implementation of measures to improve revenue collection, to reduce expenditure and to contain inflation. In July 1999 the IMF approved the $39m. final tranche of this ESAF arrangement. The Fund praised the government for having substantially reduced the rate of inflation and set a number of economic targets for 1999, including a further fall in the rate of growth of consumer prices, and GDP growth of 4.3%. In December 1996 the 'Paris Club' agreed to a rescheduling of some $1,700m. in debts. The Consultative Group met again in December 1997 in Dar es Salaam and pledged just under $1,000m. to help meet Tanzania's development needs in 1998. Donors at that meeting commended the Tanzanian government for maintaining positive growth despite the 1996/97 drought, for improving revenue collection, for reducing inflation and for managing the budget more carefully. However, several donors called for a faster pace for reforms and demanded greater transparency in government decision-making, including that affecting new private investments. At a meeting in May 1999 the 'Paris Club' pledged just under $1,000m. towards Tanzania's development requirements in 2000. Donors acknowledged a 'clear increase in the intensity' of the government's efforts to combat corruption. The IDA pledged $40m. in March 1999 towards the $70.2m. Tanzania Tax Administration Project, which aimed to reform tax legislation, expand the tax base and improve revenue collection.

A new investment code was approved by parliament in April 1990; this aimed to encourage both local and foreign investment in the economy. Measures to deregulate the banking sector were introduced during the 1990s. By March 1996 the Bank of Tanzania (in its new role as 'regulator and supervisor' of the banking sector) had licensed eight private commercial banks and four non-bank financial institutions. From April 1991, a number of bureaux de change opened throughout the country, and in 1996 the government announced plans to remove all remaining controls on currency convertibility. It was announced in 1997 that the state-owned National Bank of Commerce (NBC) was to be reorganized into three separate units, dealing with trade, corporate business and micro-finance. The NBC had dominated the banking sector, but had accumulated considerable debts. In April 1998 the IFC invested US $285,000 in the purchase of a 15% equity share in Jubilee Insurance Co of Tanzania Ltd (JICT), which had been incorporated in the 1930s in Kenya. The Insurance Act of November 1996 provided for private-sector participation in the insurance sector, which had been nationalized in 1967. JICT is 40% owned by Jubilee Insurance Kenya, 24% by local Tanzanian investors, 15% by the IFC, 15% by the Aga Khan Fund for Economic Development, 3% by Jubilee Insurance Uganda and 3% by Jubilee Insurance Mauritius. In the 1999/2000 fiscal year a banking licence was granted to Barclays of the UK.

PUBLIC FINANCE

The 1994/95 budget heralded a broadening of the tax base, an increase in customs tariffs from 40% to 50% and further anti-inflationary controls. In July 1994, it was reported that the government had increased by 100% the salaries of all its employees and of those working for parastatal companies. Civil service reforms under the budget included the elimination of 50,000 jobs and the introduction of a mandatory retirement age of 55 years. The 1996/97 budget forecast a deficit of Ts. 68,150m. The 1997/98 budget envisaged total expenditure of Ts. 975,639m., of which Ts. 666,842m. was recurrent expenditure and Ts. 308,776m. development expenditure. Airport and harbour fees were increased, as were fuel prices, while three taxes were eliminated in an attempt to simplify business procedures. Budgetary targets included an annual GDP growth rate of 5.5% and a reduction in the inflation rate to 10% annually by June 1998. Under the 1998/99 budget total expenditure was forecast at Ts. 1,007,786m., while revenues were envisaged to meet only 74% of requirements; the shortfall was to be partly financed by donors. The budget proposals included the introduction of value added tax (at 20%). The 1999/2000 budget set a revenue target of Ts. 810,000m. but, owing to lower receipts from import duties and tax evasion, this target was not met. The 2000/01 budget called for an overhaul of the customs duty structure, abolished the excise duty on 46 items (that is, all items except cigarettes, alcoholic beverages, soft drinks, refined petroleum products and motor vehicles with an engine size above 2,000 cc) and harmonized the levels of withholding tax at 10% on dividends and at 15% on interest income.

CONCLUSION

Evidence that Tanzania's earlier period of economic decline had been arrested became apparent by mid-1987. Two good harvests and the fall in world petroleum prices lessened the potentially threatening inflationary effects of the devaluation of the currency and of other measures introduced in successive budgets. Shortages of essential goods had become less acute, and many services had improved. The Mwinyi and Mkapa governments persevered with the policies formulated in the ERP and approved by the IMF and other donors, albeit less rapidly than the donors wished.

Since the late 1980s the rise in inflation has been tempered, government recurrent expenditure has been reduced, and non-traditional exports have expanded. Nevertheless, the Mkapa administration inherited many economic challenges. Among major problems still facing Tanzania were excessive bureaucracy, continuing corruption, the severe shortage of management and entrepreneurial skills, the lack of access to credit by private businesses, transport congestion and other infrastructural weaknesses, and the low purchasing power of the shilling. As the Mkapa era reached its fifth year, most of these problems remained although measures to cut back on the bureaucracy were seen as encouraging. At best, economic recovery will be a very slow process, with many obstacles to overcome. However, the reform programme was firmly on course in the late 1990s. In 2000 recoveries were under way both in mineral exploitation and in cash-crop performance, the shilling had achieved some stability, investor confidence showed a marked improvement and a major success had been achieved in gaining control of inflation. As a result, in 2000 forecasts for Tanzania's economic future were tinged with some optimism.

Statistical Survey

Source (unless otherwise stated): Economic and Research Policy Dept, Bank of Tanzania, POB 2939, Dar es Salaam; tel. (51) 110946.

Area and Population

AREA, POPULATION AND DENSITY

Area (sq km)	945,087*
Population (census results)	
26 August 1978	17,512,611
28 August 1988	
Males	11,217,723
Females	11,908,587
Total	23,126,310
Population (UN estimates at mid-year)†	
1996	30,700,000
1997	31,417,000
1998	32,102,000
Density (per sq km) at mid-1998	34.0

* 364,900 sq miles. Of this total, Tanzania mainland is 942,626 sq km (363,950 sq miles), and Zanzibar 2,461 sq km (950 sq miles).
† Source: UN *World Population Prospects: the 1998 Revision.*

ETHNIC GROUPS
(private households, census of 26 August 1967)

African . . .	11,481,595	Others . . .		839
Asian . . .	75,015	Not stated . .		159,042
Arabs . . .	29,775	**Total** . . .		11,763,150
European . . .	16,884			

REGIONS (estimated population at mid-1995)

Arusha . .	1,640,399	Mtwara . . .		1,079,495
Dar es Salaam .	1,651,534	Mwanza . . .		2,280,206
Dodoma . . .	1,502,344	Pemba* . . .		322,466
Iringa . . .	1,467,144	Pwani (Coast) . .		774,297
Kagera (Bukoba) .	1,652,991	Rukwa . . .		843,424
Kigoma . . .	1,043,491	Ruvuma . . .		950,649
Kilimanjaro . .	1,345,523	Shinyanga . .		2,151,539
Lindi . . .	784,658	Singida . . .		960,947
Mara . . .	1,178,340	Tabora . . .		1,257,650
Mbeya . . .	1,791,522	Tanga . . .		1,590,381
Morogoro . .	1,525,577	Zanzibar* . . .		456,934

* The island regions of Pemba and Zanzibar comprise the autonomous territory of Zanzibar.

PRINCIPAL TOWNS (estimated population at mid-1985)

Dar es Salaam .	1,096,000	Tanga . . .	172,000
Mwanza . .	252,000	Zanzibar . .	133,000
Tabora . . .	214,000	Dodoma . .	85,000
Mbeya . . .	194,000		

Source: UN, *Demographic Yearbook.*

BIRTHS AND DEATHS (UN estimates, annual averages)

	1980–85	1985–90	1990–95
Birth rate (per 1,000) . .	46.5	45.1	43.2
Death rate (per 1,000) . .	14.9	14.5	14.4

Expectation of life (UN estimates, years at birth, 1990–95): 50.4 (males 49.0; females 51.9).

Source: UN, *World Population Prospects: The 1996 Revision.*

ECONOMICALLY ACTIVE POPULATION (1967 census)

	Males	Females	Total
Agriculture, forestry, hunting and fishing	2,549,688	2,666,805	5,216,493
Mining and quarrying . .	4,918	99	5,017
Manufacturing . . .	85,659	13,205	98,864
Construction	32,755	318	33,073
Electricity, gas, water and sanitary services	5,704	158	5,862
Commerce	71,088	7,716	78,804
Transport, storage and communications . . .	46,121	711	46,832
Other services . . .	169,693	38,803	208,496
Other activities (not adequately defined) . . .	35,574	18,081	53,655
Total labour force . . .	3,001,200	2,745,896	5,747,096

1978 census: Total labour force 7,845,105 (males 3,809,135; females 4,035,970) aged 5 years and over.

Mid-1980 (ILO estimates, '000 persons): Agriculture etc. 8,140 (males 3,787, females 4,353); Industry 431 (males 353, females 78); Services 938 (males 630, females 308); Total 9,508 (males 4,769, females 4,739) (Source: ILO, *Economically Active Population Estimates and Projections, 1950–2025*).

Mid-1998 (estimates in '000): Agriculture, etc. 13,353; Total labour force 16,426 (Source: FAO, *Production Yearbook*).

Agriculture

PRINCIPAL CROPS ('000 metric tons)

	1996	1997	1998
Wheat	78	111	96*
Rice (paddy)	734	551	811
Maize	2,663	1,879	2,750
Millet	367	347*	148*
Sorghum*	609	498	427
Potatoes†	245	240	250
Sweet potatoes . . .	420*	336*	400†
Cassava (Manioc)* . .	5,992	5,704	6,193
Yams†	10	10	10
Dry beans†	280	230	250
Dry peas†	30	22	25
Chick-peas†	30	22	22
Other pulses† . . .	135	101	115
Groundnuts (in shell)† . .	74	72	73
Sunflower seed† . . .	33	32	33
Sesame seed† . . .	27	26	27
Cottonseed	166*	166*	107†
Coconuts†	375	370	340
Copra†	34	34	30
Palm kernels† . . .	7	7	7
Tomatoes†	22	21	22
Onions (dry)† . . .	54	53	54
Other vegetables† . .	979	948	959
Sugar cane†	1,460	1,460	1,060
Citrus fruits† . . .	37	36	37
Mangoes†	188	187	188
Pineapples†	74	73	74
Bananas*	641	603	778
Plantains*	641	603	778
Other fruit	265	259	263
Cashew nuts . . .	82	67	70†
Coffee (green) . . .	52	41	34
Tea (made)	18	22*	27*
Tobacco (leaves) . . .	35	25*	26†
Sisal	30	30*	30†
Cotton (lint)	84	85	54*

* Unofficial figure(s).   † FAO estimate(s).

Source: FAO, *Production Yearbook.*

LIVESTOCK (FAO estimates, unless otherwise indicated, '000 head, year ending September)

	1996	1997	1998
Asses	178	178	178
Cattle*	14,025	14,163	14,302
Pigs	335	335	340
Sheep	3,955	3,955	3,960
Goats	9,682	9,682	9,685

* Unofficial estimates.

Chickens (FAO estimates, million): 25 in 1996; 26 in 1997; 27 in 1998.
Ducks (FAO estimates, million): 1 in 1996; 1 in 1997; 1 in 1998.

Source: FAO, *Production Yearbook*.

LIVESTOCK PRODUCTS ('000 metric tons)

	1996	1997	1998
Beef and veal*	209	211	213
Mutton and lamb*	11	11	11
Goat meat*	24	24	24
Pig meat*	9	9	9
Poultry meat	32	36	36
Other meat	14	14	14
Cows' milk†	585	600	670
Goats' milk*	93	93	93
Butter*	5	5	5
Hen eggs*	50	52	52
Other poultry eggs*	1	1	1
Honey*	25	25	25
Cattle hides*	43	43	43
Sheepskins*	3	3	3
Goatskins*	5	5	5

* FAO estimates.   † Unofficial estimates.

Source: FAO, *Production Yearbook*.

Forestry

ROUNDWOOD REMOVALS
('000 cubic metres, excluding bark)

	1995	1996	1997
Sawlogs, veneer logs and logs for sleepers*	317	317	317
Pulpwood	153	153	153
Other industrial wood	1,708	1,746	1,781
Fuel wood	34,976	35,859	36,668
Total	37,154	38,075	38,919

* Annual output assumed to be unchanged since 1987.

Source: FAO, *Yearbook of Forest Products*.

SAWNWOOD PRODUCTION
(FAO estimates, '000 cubic metres, including railway sleepers)

	1995	1996	1997
Coniferous (softwood)	13	13	13
Broadleaved (hardwood)	11	11	11
Total	24	24	24

Source: FAO, *Yearbook of Forest Products*.

Fishing

('000 metric tons, live weight)

	1995	1996	1997
Tilapias	25.9	25.2	25.1
Mouth-brooding cichlids	12.0	11.6	10.6
Torpedo-shaped catfishes	7.9	7.7	7.8
Other freshwater fishes (incl. unspecified)	62.2	60.5	60.5
Dagaas	50.4	49.0	48.0
Nile perch	155.9	151.6	152.0
Emperors (Scavengers)	6.5	7.3	7.4
Other marine fishes (incl. unspecified)	35.0	38.9	40.9
Other marine animals	4.2	4.7	4.7
Total catch	359.8	356.6	357.0
Inland waters	317.0	308.4	306.8
Indian Ocean	42.8	48.2	50.2

Source: FAO, *Yearbook of Fishery Statistics*.

Mining

	1993	1994	1995
Diamonds ('000 carats)	40.7	22.7	49.1
Gold (kg)	3,370	2,861	320
Salt ('000 metric tons)	83.4	84.3	66.9

Industry

SELECTED PRODUCTS
('000 metric tons, unless otherwise indicated)

	1995	1996	1997*
Sugar	88.0	104.1	116.1
Cigarettes (million)	3.7	3.7	4.7
Beer (million litres)	111.2	125.1	148.3
Textiles (million sq metres)	12.3	33.4	42.7
Cement	796.3	725.8	604.0
Rolled steel	1.6	4.8	13.7
Iron sheets	18.3	6.4	15.2
Aluminium	1.1	0.4	0.1
Petroleum products	398.0	336.3	313.0
Sisal ropes	17.3	11.2	4.9
Paint (million litres)	3.2	5.2	4.9
Electric energy (million kWh)†	1,738	1,782	n.a.

* Provisional figures.
† Estimates from the UN.

Source: IMF, *Tanzania—Statistical Appendix* (April 1999).

Finance

CURRENCY AND EXCHANGE RATES

Monetary Units
100 cents = 1 Tanzanian shilling.

Sterling, Dollar and Euro Equivalents (28 April 2000)
£1 sterling = 1,253.7 Tanzanian shillings;
US $1 = 799.5 Tanzanian shillings;
€1 = 726.3 Tanzanian shillings;
10,000 Tanzanian shillings = £7.976 = $12.508 = €13.768.

Average Exchange Rate (Tanzanian shillings per US $)
1997   612.12
1998   664.67
1999   744.76

BUDGET (million shillings, year ending 30 June)*

Revenue†				1995/96	1996/97	1997/98
Tax revenue	.	.	.	383,800	514,600	566,100
Taxes on imports	.	.		121,200	174,200	180,700
Sales taxes and excises on local						
goods	.	.		104,700	141,700	140,500
Income taxes	.	.		112,300	134,200	149,800
Other taxes	.	.		45,600	64,500	95,200
Non-tax revenue	.	.		64,600	57,500	52,900
Total	.	.	.	**448,300**	**572,100**	**619,100**

Expenditure‡				1995/96	1996/97	1997/98
Recurrent expenditure		.	.	474,600	528,400	567,900
Wages and salaries	.	.		156,100	199,200	218,800
Interest payments	.	.		112,600	111,100	115,900
Other goods and services and						
transfers	.	.	.	205,900	218,100	233,000
Development expenditure‡	.	.		121,400	110,300	197,400
Total	.	.	.	**595,900**	**638,700**	**765,200**

* Figures refer to the Tanzania Government, excluding the revenue and expenditure of the separate Zanzibar Government.
† Excluding grants received (million shillings): 74,600 in 1995/96; 152,400 in 1996/97; 156,400 in 1997/98.
‡ Including lending minus repayments.

INTERNATIONAL RESERVES
(Tanzania mainland, US $ million at 31 December)

			1997	1998	1999
IMF special drawing rights	.	.	0.1	0.4	0.3
Reserve position in IMF	.	.	13.5	14.0	13.7
Foreign exchange	.	.	608.5	584.8	761.5
Total	.	.	**622.1**	**599.2**	**775.5**

Source: IMF, *International Financial Statistics*.

MONEY SUPPLY
(Tanzania mainland, million shillings at 31 December)*

			1997	1998	1999
Currency outside banks	.	.	287,880	307,800	384,860
Demand deposits at					
commercial banks	.	.	205,990	237,720	247,720
Total money	.	.	**493,870**	**545,520**	**632,580**

* Figures are rounded to the nearest 10 million shillings (Source: IMF, *International Financial Statistics*).

COST OF LIVING
(Consumer Price Index for Tanzania mainland; base: December 1994 = 100)

			1995	1996	1997
Food	.	.	115.1	138.6	169.2
Fuel, light and water	.	.	126.5	166.1	212.3
Clothing	.	.	114.2	136.3	153.9
Rent	.	.	106.7	137.4	168.2
All items (incl. others)	.	.	**115.8**	**140.1**	**169.0**

NATIONAL ACCOUNTS
(Tanzania mainland, million shillings at current prices)
National Income and Product (provisional)

		1992	1993	1994
Compensation of employees	.	88,230	119,119	148,194
Operating surplus	.	906,923	1,132,774	1,462,193
Domestic factor incomes	.	**995,153**	**1,251,894**	**1,610,387**
Consumption of fixed capital	.	35,802	36,697	49,542
Gross domestic product (GDP)				
at factor cost	.	**1,030,955**	**1,288,591**	**1,659,929**
Indirect taxes	.	109,442	183,389	260,039
Less Subsidies	.	9,801	67,611	97,398
GDP in purchasers' values		**1,130,596**	**1,404,369**	**1,822,570**
Factor income received from				
abroad	.	2,563	7,934	8,648
Less Factor income paid abroad	.	72,969	67,842	78,173
Gross national product (GNP)	.	**1,060,190**	**1,344,460**	**1,753,045**
Less Consumption of fixed capital		35,802	36,697	49,542
National income in market				
prices	.	**1,024,387**	**1,307,763**	**1,703,504**
Other current transfers from				
abroad (net)	.	282,813	291,673	308,518
National disposable income		**1,307,200**	**1,599,436**	**2,084,022**

Expenditure on the Gross Domestic Product*

		1996	1997	1998
Government final consumption				
expenditure	.	435,330	413,560	433,790
Private final consumption				
expenditure	.	3,130,070	3,968,070	4,641,180
Increase in stocks	.	6,640	8,400	9,910
Gross fixed capital formation	.	620,600	692,400	827,090
Total domestic expenditure*		**4,192,640**	**5,082,430**	**5,911,970**
Exports of goods and services	.	751,160	741,440	1,049,360
Less Imports of goods and services		−1,203,520	−1,208,300	−1,519,090
GDP in purchasers' values		**3,767,640**	**4,708,630**	**5,571,140**
GDP at constant 1992 prices	.	**1,524,680**	**1,578,300**	**n.a.**

* Figures are rounded to the nearest 10 million shillings.
Source: IMF, *International Financial Statistics*.

Gross Domestic Product by Economic Activity
(at factor cost)

		1995	1996	1997*
Agriculture, hunting, forestry and				
fishing	.	1,318,460	1,658,275	2,003,763
Mining and quarrying	.	35,190	38,511	53,515
Manufacturing	.	200,525	254,326	295,272
Electricity, gas and water	.	60,347	65,800	74,599
Construction	.	109,429	132,248	188,123
Trade, restaurants and hotels	.	417,626	493,572	562,760
Transport, storage and				
communications	.	159,771	193,946	219,393
Public administration	.	171,551	200,913	63,957
Other services	.	436,930	551,925	681,974
Sub-total		**2,909,829**	**3,589,516**	**4,143,356**
Less Imputed bank service charge	.	113,187	136,957	138,244
Total	.	**1,796,642**	**3,452,559**	**4,281,600**

* Provisional figures.

BALANCE OF PAYMENTS (US $ million)

	1996	1997	1998
Exports of goods f.o.b.	764.1	715.3	589.5
Imports of goods f.o.b.	−1,213.1	−1,164.4	−1,365.3
Trade balance	**−449.0**	**−449.1**	**−775.9**
Exports of services	608.1	494.1	555.0
Imports of services	−953.4	−797.3	−988.1
Balance on goods and services	**−794.3**	**−752.4**	**−1,209.0**
Other income received	50.3	44.9	35.1
Other income paid	−105.4	−168.2	−173.7
Balance on goods, services and income	**−849.4**	**−875.7**	**−1,347.7**
Current transfers received	370.9	313.6	426.6
Current transfers paid	−32.3	−67.7	−35.5
Current balance	**−510.9**	**−629.8**	**−956.5**
Capital account (net)	191.0	360.6	422.9
Direct investment from abroad	150.1	157.9	172.3
Other investment assets	20.1	−85.0	−50.7
Other investment liabilities	−262.9	−69.3	−44.0
Net errors and omissions	158.6	−31.9	−53.5
Overall balance	**−254.0**	**−297.5**	**−509.4**

Source: IMF, *International Financial Statistics.*

External Trade

PRINCIPAL COMMODITIES (US $ million)

Imports c.i.f.	1995	1996	1997
Capital goods	554.2	501.0	496.3
Transport equipment	209.7	202.7	187.4
Building and construction	49.2	42.5	31.8
Machinery	295.3	255.8	277.1
Intermediate goods	609.0	531.0	490.4
Petroleum and petroleum products	193.8	158.4	187.0
Crude petroleum	115.2	69.9	93.5
Petroleum products	78.6	88.5	93.5
Consumer goods	377.7	361.8	351.0
Food and foodstuffs	44.2	52.7	57.9
Unclassified	0.0	15.0	0.0
Total	**1,540.9**	**1,408.8**	**1,337.7**

Exports f.o.b.	1995	1996	1997
Coffee	142.6	136.1	117.4
Cotton	120.2	125.3	116.5
Tea	23.4	22.5	30.1
Tobacco	27.1	49.2	12.9
Cashew nuts	64.0	97.8	73.4
Minerals	44.9	55.9	92.8
Total (incl. others)	**661.2**	**768.0**	**717.2**

Source: IMF, *Tanzania—Statistical Appendix* (April 1999).

PRINCIPAL TRADING PARTNERS (million shillings)

Imports c.i.f.	1988	1989	1990
Belgium	1,596	4,523	6,408
Canada	1,875	3,232	3,927
China, People's Repub.	1,423	1,854	3,660
Denmark	4,545	4,751	5,621
France (incl. Monaco)	1,084	3,123	8,556
Germany, Fed. Repub.	11,791	14,651	20,059
Hong Kong	670	9,191	1,030
India	1,560	2,757	3,436
Ireland	114	113	5,300
Italy	8,240	13,342	13,391
Japan	8,546	14,244	15,426
Kenya	3,681	4,140	3,533
Netherlands	—	5,905	8,719
Norway	955	1,613	2,485
Singapore	969	2,249	1,764
Sweden	1,893	2,101	6,108
Switzerland	28	2,146	2,249
United Kingdom	1,468	23,912	34,104
USA	1,198	2,141	3,112
Zambia	945	1,197	1,010
Total (incl. others)	**87,893**	**146,705**	**199,260**

Exports	1988	1989	1990
Belgium	1,183	1,481	1,368
France	328	572	613
Germany, Fed. Repub.	4,798	7,422	10,044
Hong Kong	1,302	2,200	2,178
India	2,166	1,298	1,352
Indonesia	235	216	797
Italy	1,637	2,467	2,336
Japan	1,595	2,440	3,140
Kenya	1,102	2,088	2,368
Netherlands	1,974	2,993	4,353
Singapore	869	2,704	2,565
Spain	648	538	968
Switzerland	180	148	1,448
Taiwan	1,409	2,728	3,329
Uganda	341	560	780
United Kingdom	3,432	6,267	8,578
USA	869	1,638	5,495
Zaire	272	802	319
Zambia	393	244	388
Total (incl. others)	**27,041**	**52,777**	**64,571**

Transport

RAILWAYS (estimated traffic)

	1989	1990	1991
Passenger-km (million)	3,630	3,690	3,740
Freight ton-km (million)	1,420	1,470	1,490

Source: UN Economic Commission for Africa, *African Statistical Yearbook.*

ROAD TRAFFIC (estimates, '000 motor vehicles in use)

	1994	1995	1996
Passenger cars	28.0	26.0	23.8
Buses and coaches	78.0	81.0	86.0
Lorries and vans	27.2	27.7	29.7
Road tractors	6.7	6.7	6.6

Source: IRF, *World Road Statistics.*

SHIPPING

Merchant fleet (registered at 31 December)

	1996	1997	1998
Number of vessels . . .	53	56	53
Displacement ('000 grt) . . .	45.2	46.3	35.5

Source: Lloyd's Register of Shipping, *World Fleet Statistics.*

International sea-borne freight traffic (estimates '000 metric tons)

	1988	1989	1990
Goods loaded	1,208	1,197	1,249
Goods unloaded	3,140	3,077	2,721

Source: Government Printer, *Economic Survey 1990.*

CIVIL AVIATION (traffic on scheduled services)

	1994	1995	1996
Kilometres flown (million) . .	3	4	4
Passengers carried ('000) . .	199	236	224
Passenger-km (million) . .	165	189	190
Total ton-km (million) . .	17	20	20

Source: UN, *Statistical Yearbook.*

Tourism

FOREIGN VISITOR ARRIVALS (by country of origin)

	1996	1997	1998
Canada	9,941	10,944	13,900
Germany	15,475	17,036	21,700
Italy	12,152	13,377	16,900
Kenya	61,414	67,610	85,850
Scandinavia	25,405	27,968	35,600
United Kingdom	36,451	40,128	53,900
USA	25,957	28,576	41,200
Zambia	9,224	10,154	12,890
Total (incl. others) . . .	326,188	360,000	482,331

Source: World Tourism Organization, *World Tourism Statistics.*

Communications Media

	1995	1996	1997
Radio receivers ('000 in use)* . .	8,300	8,550	8,800
Television receivers ('000 in use)* .	70	100	103
Telephones ('000 main lines in use)	90	93	n.a.
Mobile cellular telephones (subscribers)	3,500	9,038	n.a.
Daily newspapers:			
Number	3	3	n.a.
Average circulation ('000 copies)*	121	120	n.a.

* Estimates.
Sources: UNESCO, *Statistical Yearbook*; UN, *Statistical Yearbook.*

Education

(1997, unless otherwise indicated, Tanzania mainland)

	Teachers	Pupils
Primary	109,936	4,057,965
General secondary	11,434	225,607
Teacher training colleges	1,062	9,136
Higher*		
Universities	1,168	5,881
Distance-learning institutions . . .	35	2,836
Other institutions	447	4,059

* 1995/96 figures.
Source: UNESCO, *Statistical Yearbook.*

Directory

The Constitution

The United Republic of Tanzania was established on 26 April 1964, when Tanganyika and Zanzibar, hitherto separate independent countries, merged. An interim Constitution of 1965 was replaced, on 25 April 1977, by a permanent Constitution for the United Republic. In October 1979 the Revolutionary Council of Zanzibar adopted a separate Constitution, governing Zanzibar's internal administration, with provisions for a popularly-elected President and a legislative House of Representatives elected by delegates of the then ruling party. A new Constitution for Zanzibar, which came into force in January 1985, provided for direct elections to the Zanzibar House of Representatives. The provisions below relate to the 1977 Constitution of the United Republic, as subsequently amended.

GOVERNMENT

Legislative power is exercised by the Parliament of the United Republic, which is vested by the Constitution with complete sovereign power, and of which the present National Assembly is the legislative house. The Assembly also enacts all legislation concerning the mainland. Internal matters in Zanzibar are the exclusive jurisdiction of the Zanzibar executive, the Supreme Revolutionary Council of Zanzibar, and the Zanzibar legislature, the House of Representatives.

National Assembly

The National Assembly comprises both directly-elected members (chosen by universal adult suffrage) and nominated members (including five members elected from the Zanzibar House of Representatives). The number of directly-elected members exceeds the number of nominated members. The Electoral Commission may review and, if necessary, increase the number of electoral constituencies before every general election. The National Assembly has a term of five years.

President

The President is the Head of State, Head of the Government and Commander-in-Chief of the Armed Forces. The President has no power to legislate without recourse to Parliament. The assent of the President is required before any bill passed by the National Assembly becomes law. Should the President withhold his assent and the bill be repassed by the National Assembly by a two-thirds majority, the President is required by law to give his assent within 21 days unless, before that time, he has dissolved the National Assembly, in which case he must stand for re-election.

The President appoints a Vice-President to assist him in carrying out his functions. The President presides over the Cabinet, which comprises a Prime Minister and other ministers who are appointed from among the members of the National Assembly.

JUDICIARY

The independence of the judges is secured by provisions which prevent their removal, except on account of misbehaviour or incapacity when they may be dismissed at the discretion of the President. The Constitution also makes provision for a Permanent Commission of Enquiry which has wide powers to investigate any abuses of authority.

CONSTITUTIONAL AMENDMENTS

The Constitution can be amended by an act of the Parliament of the United Republic, when the proposed amendment is supported by the votes of not fewer than two-thirds of all the members of the Assembly.

The Government

HEAD OF STATE

President: BENJAMIN WILLIAM MKAPA (took office 23 November 1995).

Vice-President: OMAR ALI JUMA.

CABINET
(August 2000)

President and Commander-in-Chief of the Armed Forces: BENJAMIN WILLIAM MKAPA.

Vice-President: Dr OMAR ALI JUMA.

Prime Minister: FREDERICK SUMAYE.

Ministers of State in the President's Office: JACKSON MAKWETA, NASSORO MALOCHO, WILSON MASILINGI, JUMA MKANGAA, MATEO QUARESI.

Minister of State in the Vice-President's Office: EDWARD LOWASSA.

Ministers of State in the Prime Minister's Office: BAKARI MBONDE, ALI AMEIR MUHAMMED.

Minister of Regional Administration and Local Government: KINGUNGE NGOMBALE MWIRU.

Minister of Foreign Affairs and International Co-operation: Lt-Col JAKAYA MRISHO KIKWETE.

Minister of Home Affairs: MOHAMMED SEIF KHATIB.

Minister of Finance: DANIEL YONA NDHIWA.

Minister of Industry and Trade: IDI SIMBA.

Minister of Communications and Transport: ERNEST NYANDA.

Minister of Agriculture and Co-operatives: WILLIAM KUSILA.

Minister of Health: Dr AARON CHIDUO.

Minister of Education and Culture: Prof. JUMA ATHUMANI KAPUYA.

Minister of Energy and Mineral Resources: Dr ABDALLAH OMAR KIGODA.

Minister of Water and Livestock Development: MUSSA NKHANGAA.

Minister of Natural Resources, Tourism and Environment: ZAKHIA MEGHJI.

Minister of Lands, Housing and Urban Development: GIDEON CHEYO.

Minister of Science, Technology and Higher Education: Dr PIUS NG'WANDU.

Minister of Works: ANNA ABDALLAH.

Minister of Labour and Youth Development: PAUL KIMITI.

Minister of Community Development, Women's Affairs and Children: MARY NAGU.

Minister of Justice and Constitutional Affairs: HARITH BAKARI MWAPACHU.

Minister of Defence and National Service: EDGAR MAOKOLA MAJOGO.

MINISTRIES

All Ministries in Dar es Salaam are to be transferred to Dodoma by 2005.

Office of the President: State House, POB 9120, Dar es Salaam; tel. (51) 116898; fax (51) 113425.

Office of the Vice-President: State House, POB 9120, Dar es Salaam; tel. (51) 116919; fax (51) 110614.

Office of the Prime Minister: POB 980, Dodoma; tel. (61) 20511.

Ministry of Agriculture and Co-operatives: POB 9192, Dar es Salaam; tel. (51) 112323.

Ministry of Community Development, Women's Affairs and Children: Dar es Salaam.

Ministry of Defence: POB 9544, Dar es Salaam; tel. (51) 28291.

Ministry of Education and Culture: POB 9121, Dar es Salaam; tel. (51) 27211.

Ministry of Energy and Mineral Resources: POB 2000, Dar es Salaam; tel. (51) 110414; fax (51) 116719.

Ministry of Finance: POB 9111, Dar es Salaam; tel. (51) 111174; fax (51) 38573.

Ministry of Foreign Affairs and International Co-operation: POB 9000, Dar es Salaam; tel. (51) 111906.

Ministry of Health: POB 9083, Dar es Salaam; tel. (51) 20261.

Ministry of Home Affairs: POB 9223, Dar es Salaam; tel. (51) 112034.

Ministry of Industry and Trade: POB 9503, Dar es Salaam; tel. (51) 27251.

Ministry of Justice and Constitutional Affairs: Dar es Salaam.

Ministry of Labour and Youth Development: POB 2483, Dar es Salaam; tel. (51) 20781.

Ministry of Lands, Housing and Urban Development: POB 9372, Dar es Salaam; tel. (51) 27271.

Ministry of Natural Resources, Tourism and Environment: Dar es Salaam.

Ministry of Regional Administration and Local Government: Dar es Salaam.

Ministry of Science, Technology and Higher Education: Dar es Salaam.

Ministry of Water and Livestock Development: POB 9153, Dar es Salaam; tel. (51) 117153; fax (51) 118075.

Ministry of Works, Communications and Transport: POB 9423, Dar es Salaam; tel. (51) 23235.

SUPREME REVOLUTIONARY COUNCIL OF ZANZIBAR
(August 2000)

President and Chairman: Dr SALMIN AMOUR.

Chief Minister: Dr MOHAMED GHARIB BILALI.

Deputy Chief Minister, Minister of Education: OMAR RAMADHAN MAPURI.

Minister of State for Constitutional and Legal Affairs: IDI PANDU HASSAN.

Minister of the Treasury: AMINA SALIM ALI.

Minister in the President's Office: MOHAMED RAMIYA.

Minister of Planning and Investments: ALI JUMA SHAMHUNA.

Minister of Agriculture: Brig.-Gen. ADAM MURAKANJUKI.

Minister of Information, Tourism, Youth and Cultural Affairs: ISA MOHAMED ISA.

Minister of Transport and Communications: AMAN ABEID KARUME.

Minister of Health: SAID BAKARI JECHA.

Minister of Regional Administration: ALI HAJI ALI.

Minister of Women's and Children's Affairs: ASHA BAKARI.

Minister of Water, Works, Land and Energy: KAMALI PANDU.

Minister of Trade, Industry and Marketing: (vacant).

President and Legislature

PRESIDENT

Election, 29 October 1995

Candidate	Votes	%
BENJAMIN WILLIAM MKAPA	4,026,422	61.8
AUGUSTINE LYATONGA MREMA	1,808,616	27.8
Prof. IBRAHIM HARUNA LIPUMBA	418,973	6.4
JOHN MOMOSE CHEYO	258,734	4.0
Total	**6,512,745**	**100.0**

NATIONAL ASSEMBLY

Speaker: PIUS MSEKWA.

Election, 29 October 1995

Party	Seats*
CCM	186
CUF	24
NCCR—Mageuzi	16
Chadema	3
UDP	3
Total	**232**

* In addition to the 232 elective seats, 37 nominated seats are allocated to women, five to members of the Zanzibar House of Representatives, and one to the Attorney-General.

ZANZIBAR PRESIDENT

Election, 22 October 1995

Candidate						Votes	%
Dr SALMIN AMOUR	.	.	.	.	.	165,271	50.2
SEIF SHARRIF HAMAD	.	.	.	.	.	163,706	49.8
Total	.	.	.	.	.	**328,977**	**100.0**

ZANZIBAR HOUSE OF REPRESENTATIVES

Speaker: PANDU AMIR KIFICHO.

Election, 22 October 1995

Party									Seats*
CCM	.	.	.	.	.	.	.	.	26
CUF	.	.	.	.	.	.	.	.	24
Total	.	.	.	.	.	.	.	.	**50**

* In addition to the 50 elective seats, five seats are reserved for regional commissioners, 10 for presidential nominees, and 10 for women.

Political Organizations

Bismillah Party: Pemba; seeks a referendum on the terms of the 1964 union of Zanzibar with mainland Tanzania.

Chama Cha Demokrasia na Maendeleo (Chadema–Party for Democracy and Progress): Plot No. 922/7, Block 186005, Kisutu St, POB 5330, Dar es Salaam; supports democracy and social development; Chair. EDWIN I. M. MTEI; Sec.-Gen. BOB NYANGA MAKANI.

Chama Cha Haki na Usitawi (Chausta—Party for Justice and Development): Dar es Salaam; f. 1998; Chair. JAMES MAPALALA.

Chama Cha Mapinduzi (CCM—Revolutionary Party of Tanzania): Kuu St, POB 50, Dodoma; tel. (61) 2282; f. 1977 by merger of the mainland-based Tanganyika African National Union (TANU) with the Afro-Shirazi Party, which operated on Zanzibar and Pemba; sole legal party 1977–92; socialist orientation; Chair. BENJAMIN WILLIAM MKAPA; Vice-Chair. Dr SALMIN AMOUR; Sec.-Gen. PHILIP MANGULA.

Civic United Front (CUF): Mtendeni St, Urban District, POB 3637, Zanzibar; tel. (54) 237446; fax (54) 237445; e-mail headquarters @cuftz.org; internet www.cuftz.org; f. 1992 by merger of Zanzibar opposition party Kamahuru and the mainland-based Chama Cha Wananchi; commands substantial support in Zanzibar and Pemba, for which it demands increased autonomy; Sec.-Gen. SEIF SHARIFF HAMAD.

Democratic Party (DP): Dar es Salaam; Leader Rev. CHRISTOPHER MTIKILA.

Movement for Democratic Alternative (MDA): Zanzibar; seeks to review the terms of the 1964 union of Zanzibar with mainland Tanzania; supports democratic institutions and opposes detention without trial and press censorship.

National Convention for Construction and Reform (NCCR—Mageuzi): Plot No. 48, Mchikichi St, Kariakoo Area, POB 5316, Dar es Salaam; f. 1992; Chair. Dr KASSIM MAGUTU; Sec.-Gen., MABERE MARANDO.

*National League for Democracy (NLD): Sinza D/73, POB 352, Dar es Salaam; Chair. EMMANUEL J. E. MAKAIDI; Sec.-Gen. MICHAEL E. A. MHINA.

*National Reconstruction Alliance (NRA): House No. 4, Mvita St, Jangwani Ward, POB 16542, Dar es Salaam; Chair. ULOTU ABUBAKAR ULOTU; Sec.-Gen. SALIM R. MATINGA.

*Popular National Party (PONA): Plot 104, Songea St, Ilala, POB 21561, Dar es Salaam; Chair. WILFREM R. MWAKITWANGE; Sec.-Gen. NICOLAUS MCHAINA.

*Tanzania Democratic Alliance Party (TADEA): Block 3, Plot No. 37, Buguruni Malapa, POB 63133, Dar es Salaam; Pres. FLORA M. KAMOONA; Sec.-Gen. JOHN D. LIFA-CHIPAKA.

Tanzania Labour Party (TLP): Dar es Salaam; Chair. AUGUSTINE LYATONGA MREMA.

Tanzania People's Party (TPP): Mbezi Juu, Kawe, POB 60847, Dar es Salaam; Chair. ALEC H. CHE-MPONDA; Sec.-Gen. GRAVEL LIMO.

United Democratic Party (UDP): Leader JOHN MOMOSE CHEYO.

*United People's Democratic Party (UPDP): Al Aziza Restaurant, Kokoni and Narrow Sts, POB 3903, Zanzibar; Chair. KHALFANI ALI ABDULLAH; Sec.-Gen. AHMED M. RASHID.

*Union for Multi-Party Democracy of Tanzania (UMD): 77 Tosheka St, Magomeni Mapiga, POB 41093, Dar es Salaam; Chair. ABDALLAH FUNDIKIRA.

* Members of the Outside Parliament Political Parties Organization (Chair. EMMANUEL J. E. MAKAIDI).

Diplomatic Representation

EMBASSIES AND HIGH COMMISSIONS IN TANZANIA

Albania: 93 Msese Rd, POB 1034, Kinondoni, Dar es Salaam; Ambassador: MEHDI SHAQIRI.

Algeria: 34 Upanga Rd, POB 2963, Dar es Salaam; Ambassador: (vacant).

Angola: Plot 78, Lugalo Rd, Upanga, POB 20793, Dar es Salaam; tel. (51) 117674; fax (51) 132349; Ambassador: JOSÉ AGOSTINHO NETO.

Belgium: NIC Investment House, 7th Floor, Samora Machel Ave, POB 9210, Dar es Salaam; tel. (51) 112688; fax (51) 117621; Ambassador: BEATRIX VAN HEMELDONCK.

Brazil: IPS Bldg, 9th Floor, POB 9654, Dar es Salaam; tel. (51) 21780; Ambassador: JOSÉ FERREIRA LOPES.

Burundi: Plot No. 10007, Lugalo Rd, POB 2752, Upanga, Dar es Salaam; tel. (51) 38608; Ambassador: (vacant).

Canada: 38 Mirambo St, POB 1022, Dar es Salaam; tel. (51) 112831; fax (51) 112639; High Commissioner: WAYNE HAMMOND.

China, People's Republic: 2 Kajificheni Close at Toure Drive, POB 1649, Dar es Salaam; tel. (51) 667212; Ambassador: XIE YOUKUN.

Congo, Democratic Republic: 438 Malik Rd, POB 975, Upanga, Dar es Salaam; tel. (51) 150282; Ambassador: DUBAKO BETEMA.

Cuba: Plot No. 313, Lugalo Rd, POB 9282, Upanga, Dar es Salaam; Ambassador: A. ROLANDO GALLARDO FERNÁNDEZ.

Denmark: Ghana Ave, POB 9171, Dar es Salaam; tel. (51) 113887; fax (51) 116433; Ambassador: PETER LYSHOLT HANSEN.

Egypt: 24 Garden Ave, POB 1668, Dar es Salaam; tel. (51) 117622; Ambassador: BAHER M. EL-SADEK.

Finland: Mirambo St and Garden Ave, POB 2455, Dar es Salaam; tel. (51) 119170; fax (51) 119173; e-mail finemb@twiga.com; Ambassador: RITRA SOLKKONEN.

France: Ali Hassan Mwinyi Rd, POB 2349, Dar es Salaam; tel. (51) 666021; fax (51) 668435; e-mail ambfrance@africaonline.co.tz; Ambassador: JACQUES MIGOZZI.

Germany: NIC Investment House, Samora Ave, POB 9541, Dar es Salaam; tel. (51) 117409; fax (51) 112944; e-mail german.emb.dar @raha.com; Ambassador: Dr ENNO BARBER.

Guinea: 35 Haile Selassie Rd, POB 2969, Oyster Bay, Dar es Salaam; tel. (51) 68626; Ambassador: M. BANGOURA.

Holy See: Msasani Peninsula, POB 480, Dar es Salaam (Apostolic Nunciature); tel. (51) 600833; fax (51) 600143; e-mail nunzio @cats-net.com; Apostolic Nuncio: Most Rev. LUIGI PEZZUTO, Titular Archbishop of Turris in Proconsulari.

Hungary: Plot 294, Chake Chake Rd, POB 672, Dar es Salaam; tel. (51) 668573; fax (51) 667214; Ambassador: JÁNOS ZEGNAL.

India: POB 2684, Dar es Salaam; tel. (51) 46341; fax (51) 46747; High Commissioner: OM PRAKASH GUPTA.

Indonesia: 299 Ali Hassan Mwinyi Rd, POB 572, Dar es Salaam; tel. (51) 46024; fax (5) 46350; Ambassador: R. CHARIS.

Iraq: Dar es Salaam; tel. (51) 25728; Ambassador: FAWZ ALI AL-BANDER.

Ireland: Plot 1131, Msasani Rd, Msasani Peninsular, POB 9612, Dar es Salaam; tel. (51) 602355; fax (51) 602362; e-mail iremb@ raha.com; Chargé d'affaires a.i.: RONAN CORUIN.

Italy: Plot 316, Lugalo Rd, POB 2106, Dar es Salaam; tel. (51) 115935; fax (51) 115938; e-mail italdipl@cats.net.com; Ambassador: ALFREDO MATACOTTA CORDELLA.

Japan: 1018 Upanga Road, POB 2577, Dar es Salaam; tel. (51) 46356; fax (51) 46360; Ambassador: MITSURU EGUCHI.

Kenya: NIC Investment House, Samora Machel Ave, POB 5231, Dar es Salaam; tel. (51) 112955; fax (51) 113098; High Commissioner: NJUNUNA NGUNJIRI.

Korea, Democratic People's Republic: Plot 460B, United Nations Rd, POB 2690, Dar es Salaam; Ambassador: RO MIN SU.

Libya: Dar es Salaam; Secretary of People's Bureau: BASHIR ABDA AL-DA'IM BASHIR.

Madagascar: Magoret St, POB 5254, Dar es Salaam; tel. (51) 41761; Chargé d'affaires a.i.: RAHDRAY DESIRÉ.

Malawi: IPS Bldg, POB 23168, Dar es Salaam; tel. (51) 37260; High Commissioner: L. B. MALUNGA.

Mozambique: 25 Garden Ave, POB 9370, Dar es Salaam; tel. and fax (51) 116502; High Commissioner: PEDRO DAVANE.

Netherlands: New ATC Town Terminal Bldg, cnr Ohio St and Garden Ave, POB 9534, Dar es Salaam; tel. (51) 118566; fax (51) 112828; e-mail nlgovdar@intafrica.com; Ambassador: B. S. M. BERENDSEN.

Nigeria: 3 Ali Hassan Mwinyi Rd, POB 9214, Oyster Bay, Dar es Salaam; tel. (51) 666000; fax (51) 112828; High Commissioner: SOLOMON A. YISA.

Norway: 160 Mirambo St, POB 2646, Dar es Salaam; tel. (51) 113366; fax (51) 116564; Ambassador: NILS JOHAN JORGENSEN.

Pakistan: 149 Malik Rd, Upanga, POB 2925, Dar es Salaam; tel. (51) 117630; fax (51) 113205; High Commissioner: (vacant).

Poland: 63 Alykhan Rd, POB 2188, Dar es Salaam; tel. (51) 115271; fax (51) 115812; Chargé d'affaires: EUGENIUSZ RZEWUSKI.

Romania: POB 590, Dar es Salaam; Chargé d'affaires a.i.: IOAN BUNEA.

Russia: Plot No. 73, Ali Hassan Mwinyi Rd, POB 1905, Dar es Salaam; tel. (51) 666005; fax (51) 666818; Ambassador: DOKU G. ZAV-GAYEV.

Rwanda: Plot 32, Upanga Rd, POB 2918, Dar es Salaam; tel. (51) 130119; fax (51) 115888; e-mail ambarwa.dsm@raha.com; Ambassador: ZEPHYR MUTANGUHA.

South Africa: Plot 1338/1339, Mwanya Rd, Msaski, POB 10723, Dar es Salaam; tel. (51) 600484; fax (51) 600618; High Commissioner: T. LUJABE RANKOE.

Spain: 99B Kinondoni Rd, POB 842, Dar es Salaam; tel. (51) 666936; fax (51) 666938; Ambassador: LUIS GÓMEZ DE ARANDA VILLÉN.

Sudan: 'Albaraka', 64 Ali Hassan Mwinyi Rd, POB 2266, Dar es Salaam; tel. (51) 117641; fax (51) 115811; Ambassador: CHARLES DE WOL.

Sweden: Mirambo St and Garden Ave, POB 9274, Dar es Salaam; tel. (51) 111235; Ambassador: THOMAS PALME.

Switzerland: POB 2454, Dar es Salaam; tel. (51) 666008; fax (51) 666736; Ambassador: LISE FAVRE.

Syria: POB 2442, Dar es Salaam; tel. (51) 117655; Chargé d'affaires: KANAAN HADID.

United Kingdom: Social Security House, Samora Machel Ave, POB 9200, Dar es Salaam; tel. (51) 117659; fax (51) 112952; e-mail bhc.dar@dar.mail.fco.gov.uk; High Commissioner: BRUCE H. DINWIDDY.

USA: 140 Msese Rd, Kinondoni, POB 9123, Dar es Salaam; tel. (51) 666010; fax (51) 666701; e-mail usembassy-dar2@cats-net.com; Ambassador: Rev. CHARLES STITH.

Viet Nam: 9 Ocean Rd, Dar es Salaam; Ambassador: TRAN MY.

Yemen: 353 United Nations Rd, POB 349, Dar es Salaam; tel. (51) 21722; fax (51) 66791; Chargé d'affaires: MOHAMED ABDULLA ALMAS.

Yugoslavia: Plot 35/36, Upanga Rd, POB 2838, Dar es Salaam; tel. (51) 115891; fax (51) 115893; Ambassador: (vacant).

Zambia: 5–6 Ohio St/City Drive Junction, POB 2525, Dar es Salaam; tel. (51) 118481; High Commissioner: JOHN KASHONKA CHI-TAFU.

Zimbabwe: NIC Life Bldg, 6th Floor, POB 20762, Dar es Salaam; tel. (51) 116789; fax (51) 112913; High Commissioner: J. M. SHAVA.

Judicial System

Permanent Commission of Enquiry: POB 2643, Dar es Salaam; tel. (51) 113690; fax (51) 111533; Chair. and Official Ombudsman Prof. JOSEPH F. MBWILIZA; Sec. A. P. GUVETTE.

Court of Appeal: Consists of the Chief Justice and four Judges of Appeal.

    Chief Justice of Tanzania: BARNABAS SAMATTA.

    Chief Justice of Zanzibar: HAMID MAHMOUD HAMID.

High Court: Its headquarters are at Dar es Salaam but regular sessions are held in all Regions. It consists of a Jaji Kiongozi and 29 Judges.

    Jaji Kiongozi: (vacant).

District Courts: These are situated in each district and are presided over by either a Resident Magistrate or District Magistrate. They have limited jurisdiction and there is a right of appeal to the High Court.

Primary Courts: These are established in every district and are presided over by Primary Court Magistrates. They have limited jurisdiction and there is a right of appeal to the District Courts and then to the High Court.

Attorney-General: ANDREW CHENGE.

Director of Public Prosecutions: KULWA MASSABA.

People's Courts were established in Zanzibar in 1970. Magistrates are elected by the people and have two assistants each. Under the Zanzibar Constitution, which came into force in January 1985, defence lawyers and the right of appeal, abolished in 1970, were reintroduced.

Religion

ISLAM

Islam is the religion of about 98% of the population in Zanzibar and of about one-third of the mainland population. A large proportion of the Asian community is Isma'ili.

Ismalia Provincial Church: POB 460, Dar es Salaam.

National Muslim Council of Tanzania: POB 21422, Dar es Salaam; tel. (51) 34934; f. 1969; supervises Islamic affairs on the mainland only; Chair. Sheikh HEMED BIN JUMA BIN HEMED; Exec. Sec. Alhaj MUHAMMAD MTULIA.

Supreme Muslim Council: Zanzibar; f. 1991; supervises Islamic affairs in Zanzibar.

Wakf and Trust Commission: POB 4092, Zanzibar; tel. (54) 30853; f. 1980; Islamic affairs; Exec. Sec. YUSUF ABDULRAHMAN MUHAMMAD.

CHRISTIANITY

In 1993 it was estimated that about one-half of the mainland population professed Christianity.

Jumuiya ya Kikristo Tanzania (Christian Council of Tanzania): Church House, POB 1454, Dodoma; tel. (61) 321204; fax (61) 324445; f. 1934; Chair. Rt Rev. JOHN ACLAND RAMADHANI (Bishop of the Anglican Church); Gen. Sec. Dr WILSON LWEGANWA MTEBE.

The Anglican Communion

Anglicans are adherents of the Church of the Province of Tanzania, comprising 16 dioceses.

Archbishop of the Province of Tanzania and Bishop of Ruaha: Most Rev. DONALD LEO MTETEMELA, POB 1028, Iringa; fax (64) 2479.

Provincial Secretary: Rev. MKUNGA H. P. MTINGELE, POB 899, Dodoma; tel. (61) 21437; fax (61) 324265; e-mail mmtingele@maf.org.

Greek Orthodox

Archbishop of East Africa: NICADEMUS of IRINOUPOULIS (resident in Nairobi, Kenya); jurisdiction covers Kenya, Uganda and Tanzania.

Lutheran

Evangelical Lutheran Church in Tanzania: POB 3033, Arusha; tel. (57) 8855; fax (57) 8858; 1.5m. mems; Presiding Bishop Rt Rev. Dr SAMSON MUSHEMBA (acting); Exec. Sec. AMANI MWENEGOHA.

The Roman Catholic Church

Tanzania comprises five archdioceses and 24 dioceses. There were an estimated 9,427,921 adherents at 31 December 1999.

Tanzania Episcopal Conference: Catholic Secretariat, Mansfield St, POB 2133, Dar es Salaam; tel. (51) 851075; fax (51) 851133; e-mail tec@cats-net.com; internet www.rc.net/tanzania/tec; f. 1980; Pres. Mgr JUSTIN TETEMU SAMBA, Bishop of Musoma.

Archbishop of Arusha: Most Rev. JOSAPHAT LOUIS LEBULU, Archbishop's House, POB 3044, Arusha; tel. (57) 4362; fax (57) 8004; e-mail angelo.arusha@habori.co.tz.

Archbishop of Dar es Salaam: Cardinal POLYCARP PENGO, Archbishop's House, POB 167, Dar es Salaam; tel. (51) 113223; fax (51) 113204.

Archbishop of Mwanza: Most Rev. ANTHONY MAYALA, Archbishop's House, POB 1421, Mwanza; tel. and fax (68) 501029; e-mail archdiocese-mwanza@sukumanet.com.

Archbishop of Songea: Most Rev. NORBERT WENDELIN MTEGA, Archbishop's House, POB 152, Songea; tel. (65) 602004; fax (65) 602593; e-mail songea-archdiocese@cats-net.com.

Archbishop of Tabora: Most Rev. MARIO EPIFANIO ABDALLAH MGU-LUNDE, Archbishop's House, Private Bag, PO Tabora; tel. (62) 2329; fax (62) 4536.

Other Christian Churches

Baptist Mission of Tanzania: POB 9414, Dar es Salaam; tel. (51) 170130; fax (51) 170127; f. 1956; Admin. FRANK PEVEY.

Christian Missions in Many Lands (Tanzania): German Branch; POB 34, Tunduru, Ruvuma Region; f. 1957; Gen. Sec. KARLGERHARD WARTH.

Moravian Church: POB 377, Mbeya; 113,656 mems; Gen. Sec. Rev. SHADRACK MWAKASEGE.

Pentecostal Church: POB 34, Kahama.

Presbyterian Church: POB 2510, Dar es Salaam; tel. (51) 29075.

BAHÁ'Í FAITH

National Spiritual Assembly: POB 585, Dar es Salaam; tel. (51) 21173; mems resident in 2,301 localities.

OTHER RELIGIONS

Many people follow traditional beliefs. There are also some Hindu communities.

The Press

NEWSPAPERS

Daily

The African: Sinza Rd, POB 4793, Dar es Salaam; e-mail dimba@ africaonline.co.tz; Editor-in-Chief JOHN KULEKANA.

Alasiri: POB 31042, Dar es Salaam; Swahili.

Daily News: POB 9033, Dar es Salaam; tel. (51) 110165; fax (51) 112881; f. 1972; govt-owned; Man. Editor SETHI KAMUHANDA; circ. 50,000.

The Democrat: Dar es Salaam; independent; Editor IDRISS LUGULU; circ. 15,000.

The Guardian: POB 31042, Dar es Salaam; e-mail guardian @ipp.co.tz; Man Dir VUMI URASA; Man. Editor PASCAL SHIJA.

Kipanga: POB 199, Zanzibar; Swahili; publ. by Information and Broadcasting Services.

Majira: POB 71439, Dar es Salaam; tel. (51) 38901; fax (51) 31104; independent; Swahili; Editor THEOPHIL MAKUNGA; circ. 15,000.

Nipashe: POB 31042, Dar es Salaam; Swahili; Editor HAMISI MZEE.

Uhuru: POB 9221, Dar es Salaam; tel. (51) 182224; fax (51) 185065; e-mail uhuru@intafrica.com; 1961; official publ. of CCM; Swahili; Man. Editor SAIDI NGUBA; circ. 100,000.

Weekly

Business Times: POB 71439, Dar es Salaam; tel. (51) 38901; fax (51) 31104; e-mail majira@bcsmedia.com; internet www .bcstimes.com; independent; English; Editor ALLI MWAMBOLA; circ. 15,000.

The Express: cnr Bibi/Maktaba Rd, POB 20588, Dar es Salaam; tel. (51) 119621; independent; English; Editor N. ODHIAMBO; circ. 20,000.

Gazette of the United Republic: POB 9142, Dar es Salaam; tel. (51) 31817; official announcements; Editor H. HAJI; circ. 6,000.

Government Gazette: POB 261, Zanzibar; f. 1964; official announcements.

Kasheshe: POB 31042, Dar es Salaam; Swahili.

Mfanyakazi (The Worker): POB 15359, Dar es Salaam; tel. (51) 26111; Swahili; trade union publ.; Editor NDUGU MTAWA; circ. 100,000.

The Family Mirror: Faru/Nyamwezi St, Karikoo Area, POB 6804, Dar es Salaam; tel. (51) 181331; Editor ZEPHANIAH MUSENDO.

Mzalendo: POB 9221, Dar es Salaam; tel. (51) 182224; fax (51) 185065; e-mail uhuru@intafrica.com; f. 1972; publ. by CCM; Swahili; Man. Editor SAIDI NGABA; circ. 115,000.

Leta Raha: POB 31042, Dar es Salaam; Swahili.

Nipashe Jumapili: POB 31042, Dar es Salaam; Swahili.

Sunday News: POB 9033, Dar es Salaam; tel. (51) 116072; fax (51) 112881; f. 1954; govt-owned; Man. Editor SETHI KAMUCHANDA; circ. 50,000.

Sunday Observer: POB 31042, Dar es Salaam; e-mail guardian@ ipp.co.tz; Man. Dir VUMI URASA; Man. Editor THEO MUSHI.

Taifa Letu: POB 31042, Dar es Salaam; Swahili.

PERIODICALS

The African Review: POB 35042, Dar es Salaam; tel. (51) 43500; 2 a year; journal of African politics, development and international affairs; publ. by the Dept of Political Science, Univ. of Dar es Salaam; Chief Editor Dr. C. GASARASI; circ. 1,000.

Eastern African Law Review: POB 35093, Dar es Salaam; tel. (51) 43254; f. 1967; 2 a year; Chief Editor N. N. N. NDITI; circ. 1,000.

Elimu Haina Mwisho: POB 1986, Mwanza; monthly; circ. 45,000.

Habari za Washirika: POB 2567, Dar es Salaam; tel. (51) 23346; monthly; publ. by Co-operative Union of Tanzania; Editor H. V. N. CHIBULUNJE; circ. 40,000.

Jenga: POB 2669, Dar es Salaam; tel. (51) 112893; fax (51) 113618; journal of the National Development Corpn; circ. 2,000.

Kiongozi (The Leader): POB 9400, Dar es Salaam; tel. (51) 29505; f. 1950; fortnightly; Swahili; Roman Catholic; Editor ROBERT MFUGALE; circ. 33,500.

Kwupe: POB 222, Zanzibar; weekly; Swahili; publ. by Information and Broadcasting Services.

Mlezi (The Educator): POB 41, Peramiho; tel. 30; f. 1970; every 2 months; Editor Fr DOMINIC WEIS; circ. 8,000.

Mwenge (Firebrand): POB 1, Peramiho; tel. 30; f. 1937; monthly; Editor JOHN P. MBONDE; circ. 10,000.

Nchi Yetu (Our Country): POB 9142, Dar es Salaam; tel. (51) 110200; f. 1964; govt publ.; monthly; Swahili; circ. 50,000.

Nuru: POB 1893, Zanzibar; tel. (54) 23253; fax (54) 33457; f. 1992; bi-monthly; official publ. of Zanzibar Govt; circ. 8,000.

Safina: POB 21422, Dar es Salaam; tel. (51) 34934; publ. by National Muslim Council of Tanzania; Editor YASSIN SADIK; circ. 10,000.

Sauti Ya Jimbo: POB 899, Dodoma; tel. (61) 21437; fax (61) 324565; quarterly; Swahili; Anglican diocesan, provincial and world church news.

Sikiliza: POB 635, Morogoro; tel. (56) 3338; fax (56) 4374; quarterly; Seventh-day Adventist; Editor MEL H. M. MATINYI; circ. 100,000.

Taamuli: POB 899, Dar es Salaam; tel. (51) 43500; 2 a year; journal of political science; publ. by the Dept of Political Science, Univ. of Dar es Salaam; circ. 1,000.

Tantravel: POB 2485, Dar es Salaam; tel. (51) 111244; fax (51) 116420; e-mail shfisher@yahoo.com; quarterly; publ. by Tanzania Tourist Board; Editor STEPHEN H. FISHER.

Tanzania Education Journal: POB 9121, Dar es Salaam; tel. (51) 27211; f. 1984; 3 a year; publ. by Institute of Education, Ministry of Education and Culture; circ. 8,000.

Tanzania Trade Currents: POB 5402, Dar es Salaam; tel. (51) 851706; fax (51) 851700; e-mail betis@intafrica.com; bimonthly; publ. by Board of External Trade; circ. 2,000.

Uhuru na Amani: POB 3033, Arusha; tel. (57) 8855; fax (57) 8858; quarterly; Swahili; publ. by Evangelical Lutheran Church in Tanzania; Editor ELIZABETH LOBULU; circ. 15,000.

Ukulima wa Kisasa (Modern Farming): POB 2308, Dar es Salaam; tel. (51) 22335; fax (51) 113260; f. 1955; bimonthly; Swahili; publ. by Ministry of Agriculture and Co-operatives; Editor E. M. K. SABUNI; circ. 15,000.

Wela: POB 180, Dodoma; Swahili.

NEWS AGENCIES

Press Services Tanzania (PST) Ltd: POB 31042, Dar es Salaam; tel. and fax (51) 119195.

Foreign Bureaux

Inter Press Service (IPS) (Italy): 304 Nkomo Rd, POB 4755, Dar es Salaam; tel. (51) 29311; Chief Correspondent PAUL CHINTOWA.

Newslink Africa (UK): POB 5165, Dar es Salaam; Correspondent NIZAR FAZAL.

Rossiyskoye Informatsionnoye Agentstvo—Novosti (RIA—Novosti) (Russia): POB 2271, Dar es Salaam; tel. (51) 23897; Dir ANATOLII TKACHENKO.

Xinhua (New China) News Agency: 72 Upanga Rd, POB 2682, Dar es Salaam; tel. (51) 23967; Correspondent HUAI CHENGBO.

Reuters (UK) is also represented in Tanzania.

Publishers

Central Tanganyika Press: POB 1129, Dodoma; tel. (61) 304180; fax (61) 324565; f. 1954; religious; Man. Rev. JAMES LIFA CHIPAKA.

DUP (1996) Ltd: POB 35182, Dar es Salaam; tel. and fax (51) 410137; e-mail director@dup.udsm.ac.tz; f. 1979; educational, academic and cultural texts in Swahili and English; Dir Dr N. G. MWITTA.

Eastern Africa Publications Ltd: POB 1002 Arusha; tel. (57) 3176; f. 1979; general and school textbooks; Gen. Man. ABDULLAH SAIWAAD.

Inland Publishers: POB 125, Mwanza; tel. (68) 40064; general non-fiction, religion, in Kiswahili and English; Dir S. M. MAGESA.

Oxford University Press: Maktaba Rd, POB 5299, Dar es Salaam; tel. (51) 29209; f. 1969; Man. SALIM SHAABAN SALIM.

Tanzania Publishing House: 47 Samora Machel Ave, POB 2138, Dar es Salaam; tel. (51) 32164; f. 1966; educational and general books in Swahili and English; Gen. Man. PRIMUS ISIDOR KARUGENDO.

Government Publishing House

Government Printer: POB 9124, Dar es Salaam; tel. (51) 20291; Dir JONAS OFORO.

Broadcasting and Communications

TELECOMMUNICATIONS

Tanzania Communications Commission: POB 474, Dar es Salaam; tel. (51) 112576; fax (51) 116664.

Tanzania Telecommunications Co Ltd (TTCL): POB 9070, Dar es Salaam; tel. (51) 110055; fax (51) 113232; e-mail ttcl@ttcl.co.tz; privatization pending in 1999; Man. Dir ASMATH N. MPATWA.

Tri-Telecommunication Tanzania Ltd, MIC Ltd, Vodacom and Zanzibar Telecom Ltd also provide telecommunications services.

BROADCASTING
Radio

Radio Kwizera: N'Gara.

Radio One: POB 4374, Dar es Salaam; tel. (51) 75914; e-mail ipptech@ipp.co.tz; internet www.ippmedia.com.

Radio Tanzania Dar es Salaam (RTD): POB 9191, Dar es Salaam; tel. (51) 860760; fax (51) 865577; f. 1951; state-owned; domestic services in Swahili; external services in English; Dir ABDUL NGARAWA.

Radio Tumaini (Hope): 1 Bridge St, POB 9916, Dar es Salaam; tel. (51) 117307; fax (51) 112594; e-mail tumaini@africaonline.co.tz; broadcasts in Swahili within Dar es Salaam; operated by the Roman Catholic Church; broadcasts on religious, social and economic issues; Dir Fr JEAN-FRANÇOIS GALTIER.

Sauti Ya Tanzania Zanzibar (The Voice of Tanzania Zanzibar): POB 1178, Zanzibar; tel. (54) 31088; fax (54) 31985; f. 1951; state-owned; broadcasts in Swahili on three wavelengths; Dir SULEIMAN JUMA.

Television

Dar Television (DTV): Dar es Salaam; Man. Dir FRANCO TRAMONTANO.

Independent Television (ITV): Dar es Salaam.

Television Zanzibar: POB 314, Zanzibar; tel. (54) 32816; f. 1973; Dir JAMA SIMBA.

Finance

(cap. = capital; res = reserves; dep. = deposits; m. = million; brs = branches; amounts in Tanzanian shillings)

BANKING
Central Bank

Bank of Tanzania (Benki Kuu Ya Tanzania): 10 Mirambo St, POB 2939, Dar es Salaam; tel. (51) 110945; fax (51) 113325; e-mail info@hq.bot-tz.org; internet www.bot.tz.org; f. 1966; bank of issue; cap. and res 34,184m., dep. 182,422m. (June 1998); Gov. and Chair. Dr DAUDI T. S. BALLALI; Dep. Gov. M. H. MBAYE.

Principal Banks

CRDB (1996) Ltd: Azikiwe St, POB 268, Dar es Salaam; tel. (51) 117442; fax (51) 324984; e-mail crdb@ics.dar.sprint.com; internet www.crdb.com; f. as Co-operative and Rural Development Bank in 1984, transferred to private ownership and current name adopted 1996; provides commercial banking services and loans for rural development; cap. 6,932m. (Dec. 1998); Chair JERRY SOLOMON; Man. Dir C. S. KIMEI.

Eurafrican Bank Tanzania Ltd: NDC Development House, cnr Kivukoni Front and Ohio St, POB 3054, Dar es Salaam; tel. (51) 111229; fax (51) 113740; f. 1994; 70% owned by Banque Belgolaise SA (Belgium); other shareholders: International Finance Corpn (IFC) (7%), PROPARCO (3%), Tanzania Development Finance Co (10%), others (10%); cap. 3,500m. (Dec. 1998); Chair. FULGENCE M. KAZAURA; Man. Dir JOHN N. B. LISTER.

Exim Bank (EB): 9 Samora Ave, POB 1431, Dar es Salaam; tel. (51) 119738; fax (51) 119737; e-mail eximbank.tz@cats.net.com; Man. Dir (acting) H. JAFFER.

NBC (1997) Ltd: NBC House, Sokoine Drive, POB 1863, Dar es Salaam; tel. (51) 112082; fax (51) 112887; e-mail nbc97@raha.com; f. 1997, following disbandment of The National Bank of Commerce; state-owned; transfer to private-sector ownership proceeding in 2000; cap. and res 3,222m., dep. 52,173m. (Dec. 1998); Man. Dir GERALD JORDAN; 34 brs.

National Microfinance Bank Ltd (NMB): POB 9213, Dar es Salaam; tel. (51) 118785; fax (51) 110077; e-mail nmb.ltd@raha.com; f. 1997 following disbandment of The National Bank of Commerce; state-owned; transfer to private-sector ownership pending; Chair. IBRAHIM M. KADUMA; Man. Dir JAMES A. N. KARASHANI.

People's Bank of Zanzibar Ltd (PBZ): Gizenga St, POB 1173, Forodhani, Zanzibar; tel. (54) 31118; fax (54) 31121; f. 1966; controlled by Zanzibar Govt; cap. 16m. (June 1991); Chair. MOHAMED ABOUD; Gen. Man. N. S. NASSOR.

Stanbic Bank Tanzania Ltd: Sukari House, cnr Ohio St and Sokoine Drive, POB 72647, Dar es Salaam; tel. (51) 112195; fax (51) 113742; f. 1993; wholly owned by Standard Bank Investment Corpn Ltd (Botswana); cap. and res 12,985m., dep. 65,928m. (Dec. 1998); Chair R. E. NORVAL; Man. Dir I. J. MITCHELL.

Standard Chartered Bank Tanzania Ltd: 1st Floor, NIC Life House, cnr Ohio St/Sokoine Drive, POB 9011, Dar es Salaam; tel. (51) 122125; fax (51) 113775; f. 1992; wholly owned by Standard Chartered Holdings (Africa) BV (Netherlands); cap. 1,000m. (Dec. 1993); Chair. and Man. Dir P. V. DOCHERTY.

Tanzania Development Finance Co Ltd (TDFL): TDFL Bldg, Plot 1008, cnr Upanga Rd/Ohio St, POB 2478, Dar es Salaam; tel. (51) 25091; fax (51) 116418; e-mail tdfl@raha.com; f. 1962; owned by the Tanzania Investment Bank, govt agencies of the Netherlands and Germany, the Commonwealth Development Corpn and the European Investment Bank; cap. and res 1,284m. (Dec. 1996); Chair. H. K. SENKORO; CEO C. I. BUCHANAN.

Tanzania Investment Bank (TIB): cnr Zanaki St and Samora Machel Ave, POB 9373, Dar es Salaam; tel. (51) 115906; fax (51) 113438; e-mail tib-tz@africaonline.co.tz; f. 1970; provides finance, tech. assistance and consultancy, fund administration and loan guarantee for economic devt; 99% govt-owned; cap. 7,642m., total assets 10,404m. (Dec. 1998); Chair. JUMA V. MWAPACHU; Man. Dir WILLIAM A. MLAKI.

Tanzania Postal Bank (TPB): Samora Ave, POB 9300, Dar es Salaam; tel. (51) 115258; fax (51) 114815; e-mail postbank@twiga.com; internet www.africaonline.co.tz/tpbank; f. 1991; dep. 15,715.7m. (1994); Gen. Man. R. D. SWAI; 207 brs.

ulc (Tanzania) Ltd: 1st Floor, Sukari House, cnr Ohio St and Sokoine Drive, Dar es Salaam; tel. (51) 115141. fax (51) 112402; e-mail info@ulc.co.tz; cap. 2,204 (Dec. 1997). Chair BASIL ANDERSON; CEO H. KRUGER.

STOCK EXCHANGE

Dar es Salaam Stock Exchange: POB 75713, Dar es Salaam; tel. (51) 113903; fax (51) 113846; e-mail des@cats-net.com; internet www.darstock.com; f. 1998; Chair. ERNEST MASSAWE; CEO Dr HAMIS KIBORA.

INSURANCE

Jubilee Insurance Co of Tanzania Ltd (JICT): Dar es Salaam; 40% owned by Jubilee Insurance Kenya, 24% by local investors, 15% by the IFC, 15% by the Aga Khan Fund for Economic Devt, 6% by others; cap. US $2m.

National Insurance Corporation of Tanzania Ltd (NIC): POB 9264, Dar es Salaam; tel. (51) 113823; fax (51) 113403; f. 1963; state-owned; all classes of insurance; Chair. Prof. J. L. KANYWANYI; Man. Dir OCTAVIAN W. TEMU; 30 brs.

Trade and Industry
GOVERNMENT AGENCIES

Board of External Trade (BET): POB 5402, Dar es Salaam; tel. (51) 851706; fax (51) 851700; e-mail betis@intafrica.com; f. 1978; trade and export information and promotion, market research, marketing advisory and consultancy services; Dir-Gen. MBARUK K. MWANDORO.

Board of Internal Trade (BIT): POB 883, Dar es Salaam; tel. (51) 28301; f. 1967 as State Trading Corpn, reorg. 1973; state-owned; supervises seven national and 21 regional trading cos; distribution of general merchandise, agricultural and industrial machinery, pharmaceuticals, foodstuffs and textiles; shipping and other transport services; Dir-Gen. J. E. MAKOYE.

Parastatal Sector Reform Commission (PSRC): Sukari House, POB 9252, Dar es Salaam; tel (51) 115482; fax (51) 113065; e-mail masalla@raha.com.

Tanzania Investment Centre (TIC): POB 938, Dar es Salaam; tel. (51) 116328; fax (51) 118253; internet www.cats-net.com/tic; f. 1997; Exec. Dir SAMUEL SITTA.

CHAMBERS OF COMMERCE

Dar es Salaam Chamber of Commerce: Kelvin House, Samora Machel Ave, POB 41, Dar es Salaam; tel. (51) 21893; Exec. Officer I. K. MKWAWA.

Tanzania Chamber of Commerce, Industry and Agriculture: POB 9713, Dar es Salaam; tel. (51) 119436; fax (51) 119437; Pres. C. MWANGIKA.

Zanzibar Chamber of Commerce: POB 1407, Zanzibar; tel. (54) 233083; fax (54) 233349.

DEVELOPMENT CORPORATIONS

Capital Development Authority: POB 1, Dodoma; tel. (61) 324053; f. 1973 to develop the new capital city of Dodoma; govt-controlled.

Economic Development Commission: POB 9242, Dar es Salaam; tel. (51) 112681; f. 1962 to plan national economic development; state-controlled.

National Development Corporation: POB 2669, Dar es Salaam; tel. (51) 112893; fax (51) 113618; f. 1965; state-owned; cap. 21.4m. sh.; promotes progress and expansion in production and investment.

Small Industries Development Organization (SIDO): POB 2476, Dar es Salaam; tel. (51) 151945; fax (51) 152070; f. 1973; promotes and assists development of small-scale enterprises in public, co-operative and private sectors, aims to increase the involvement of women in small businesses; Chair. E. M. K. MSELLA; Dir-Gen. E. B. TOROKA.

Sugar Development Corporation: Dar es Salaam; tel. (51) 112969; fax (51) 30598; Gen. Man. GEORGE G. MBATI.

Tanzania Petroleum Development Corporation (TPDC): POB 2774, Dar es Salaam; tel. (51) 181407; fax (51) 180047; f. 1969; state-owned; oversees petroleum exploration and undertakes autonomous exploration, imports crude petroleum and distributes refined products; Man. Dir YONA S. M. KILLAGANE.

There is also a development corporation for textiles.

INDUSTRIAL AND TRADE ASSOCIATONS

The privatization of various nationalized industries was proceeding in 1999.

Cashewnut Board of Tanzania: POB 533, Mtwara; tel. (59) 333445; fax (59) 333536; govt-owned; regulates the marketing, processing and export of cashews; Chair. GALUS ABEID; Gen. Man. Dr ALI F. MANDALI.

Confederation of Tanzania Industries (CTI): POB 71783, Dar es Salaam; tel. (51) 123802; fax (51) 115414; e-mail cti@raha.com; Dir JUMA MWAPACHU.

National Coconut Development Programme: POB 6226, Dar es Salaam; tel. (51) 74606; fax (51) 75549; e-mail arim@ arim.africaonline.co.tz; f. 1979 to revive coconut industry; processing and marketing via research and devt in disease and pest control, agronomy and farming systems, breeding and post-harvest technology; based at Mikocheni Agricultural Research Inst.; Dir Dr ALOIS K. KULLAYA.

Tanganyika Coffee Growers' Association Ltd: POB 102, Moshi.

Tanzania Association of Floriculture (TAFA): POB 11123, Arusha; tel. (57) 4432; fax (57) 4214; e-mail aru.cut@kabari.co.tz; Sec. MATTHIAS OLE KISSAMBU.

Tanzania Coffee Board (TCB): POB 732, Moshi; tel. (55) 52324; fax (55) 53033; e-mail coffee@eoltz.com; internet www .newafrica.com; Man. Dir LESLIE OMARI.

Tanzania Cotton Lint and Seed Board: Pamba House, Garden Ave, POB 9161, Dar es Salaam; tel. (51) 112555; fax (51) 112894; e-mail tclb@raha.com; f. 1984; regulates the marketing and export of cotton lint; Gen. Man. ALI N. NGONGOLO.

Tanzania Exporters' Association: POB 1175, Dar es Salaam; tel. and fax (51) 460948.

Tanzania Pyrethrum Board: POB 149, Iringa; f. 1960; Chair. Brig. LUHANGA; CEO P. B. G. HANGAYA.

Tanzania Sisal Authority: POB 277, Tanga; tel. (53) 44401; fax (53) 42759; Chair. W. H. SHELLUKINDO; Man. Dir S. SHAMTE.

Tanzania Tea Authority: POB 2663, Dar es Salaam; tel. (51) 116596; fax (51) 23322; Chair. J. J. MUNGAI; Gen. Man. M. FRANCIS L. SHIRIMA.

Tanzania Tobacco Board: POB 227, Mazimbu Rd, Morogoro; tel. (56) 4517; fax (56) 4401; Chair. S. GALINOMA; CEO HAMISI HASANI LIANA.

Tanzania Wood Industry Corporation: POB 9160, Dar es Salaam; Gen. Man. E. M. MNZAVA.

Tea Association of Tanzania: POB 2177, Dar es Salaam; tel. (51) 122033; e-mail trit@twiga.com; f. 1989; Chair. Dr NORMAN C. KELLY; Exec. Dir DAVID E. A. MGWASSA.

Zanzibar State Trading Corporation: POB 26, Zanzibar; tel. (54) 30272; fax (54) 31550; govt-controlled since 1964; sole exporter of cloves, clove stem oil, chillies, copra, copra cake, lime oil and lime juice; Gen. Man. ABDULRAHMAN RASHID.

UTILITIES

Electricity

Tanzania Electric Supply Co Ltd (TANESCO): POB 9024, Dar es Salaam; tel. (51) 112891; fax (51) 113836; e-mail mdtan @intafrica.com; state-owned, division into separate units and subsequent privatization planned; Man. Dir BARUANY LUHANGA.

Gas

Enertan Corpn Ltd: POB 3746, Dar es Salaam.

Songas Ltd: POB 6342, Dar es Salaam; tel. (51) 117313; fax (51) 113614.

Water

Dar es Salaam Water and Sanitation Authority: Dar es Salaam; privatization pending.

National Urban Water Authority: POB 5340, Dar es Salaam; tel. (51) 667505.

MAJOR COMPANIES

The following are some of the largest companies in terms either of capital investment or employment.

Agip (Tanzania) Ltd: cnr Msimbazi Mikunguni St, POB 9540, Dar es Salaam; tel. (51) 180110; fax (51) 181374; e-mail agip@agiptz .intafrica.com; f. 1966; cap. 1,000m. sh.; 50% state-owned; distribution and marketing of petroleum products; Man. Dir GIAN ROMEO; 360 employees.

Aluminium Africa Ltd: POB 2070, Dar es Salaam; tel. (51) 863306; fax (51) 864690; mfrs of aluminium circles, corrugated and plain sheets, galvanized corrugated iron sheets, furniture tubes, steel billets, galvanized pipes, cold rolled steel sheets and coils; CEO S. N. SALGAR.

Friendship Textiles Mill Ltd: POB 20842, Dar es Salaam; tel. (51) 189841; fax (51) 183689; f. 1966; wholly owned by National Textile Corpn; dyed and printed fabric mfrs; 5,400 employees.

Gapco Tanzania Ltd: Mafuta St, Kurasini, POB 9103, Dar es Salaam; tel. (51) 117225; fax (51) 113265; took over operations of Esso Tanzania Ltd (f. 1990); marketing of petroleum products; Man. Dir Y. G. KOTAK; 102 employees.

Mwanza Textiles Ltd: POB 1344, Mwanza; tel. (068) 40466; f. 1966; spinners, weavers, dyers and printers of cotton; 3,901 employees.

National Milling Corporation (NMC): 74/1 Mandela/Nyerere Rd, POB 9502, Dar es Salaam; tel. (51) 860260; fax (51) 863817; f. 1968; stores and distributes basic foodstuffs, owns grain milling establishments and imports cereals as required; Chair. T. SIWALE; Gen. Man. VINCENT M. SEMESI; 1,300 employees.

Songas Ltd: Maarifa House, Ohio St, POB 6342, Dar es Salaam; tel. (51) 117313; fax (51) 113614; e-mail jim_mccardle@songas.com; internet www.songas.com; f. 1998; development of Songo Songo natural gas field; Gen. Man. JIM MCCARDLE.

Southern Paper Mills Co Ltd: POB 1, Mgololo; tel. (64) 2416; fax (64) 2427; paper mfrs.

State Mining Corporation (STAMICO): POB 4958, Dar es Salaam; tel. (51) 150243; fax (51) 153152; e-mail betacomms@ intertanzania.com; f. 1972; provides mineral consultancy and marketing services; engaged in contract drilling and mining; mining interests currently undergoing privatization; Dir-Gen. AUGUSTINE Y. HANGI.

Tanganyika Instant Coffee Co Ltd: POB 410, Bukoba; tel. (66) 20352; fax (66) 20526; e-mail tanica@twiga.com; mfrs and exporters of spray-dried instant coffee powder; Gen. Man. MELKIOR E. KAREGA; 109 employees.

Tanganyika Packers Ltd: POB 60138, Dar es Salaam; tel. (51) 47511; f. 1947; govt-owned; mfrs of corned beef and other food products; 470 employees.

Tanzania Breweries Ltd: POB 9013, Dar es Salaam; tel. (51) 182780; fax (51) 181458; f. 1960; subsidiary of South African Breweries International; manufacture, bottling and distribution of malt beer; Man. Dir A. B. S. KILEWO; 1,266 employees.

Tanzania Cigarette Co Ltd: POB 40114, Dar es Salaam; tel. (51) 860150; fax (51) 865210; e-mail tcc@cats-net.com; f. 1965; 49% state-owned 51% of shares sold to foreign investors in 1995; manufacture and marketing of cigarettes; Chair. and CEO NATWAR GOTECHA; 773 employees.

Tanzania Oxygen Ltd: POB 911, Dar es Salaam; tel. (51) 860047; fax (51) 864041; mfrs of industrial and medical gas; Gen. Man. LAWRACE MASHA.

Tanzania Portland Cement Co Ltd: POB 1950, Dar es Salaam; tel. (51) 630130; fax (51) 116648; e-mail twiga@intafrica.com; f. 1959; jt venture; mfrs of ordinary Portland cement; capacity: 520,000 metric tons per annum; Man. Dir ARNE TVEDT; 650 employees.

Williamson Diamonds Ltd: POB 9470, Dar es Salaam; PO Mwadui, Shinyanga; tel. (68) 762960; fax (68) 762965; e-mail acland @raha.com; f. 1942; State Mining Corpn owns 25% of capital; diamond mining; Man. Dir J. W. B. D. ACLAND; 480 employees.

CO-OPERATIVES

There are some 1,670 primary marketing societies under the aegis of about 20 regional co-operative unions. The Co-operative Union of Tanzania is the national organization to which all unions belong.

Co-operative Union of Tanzania Ltd (Washirika): POB 2567, Dar es Salaam; tel. (51) 23346; f. 1962; Sec.-Gen. D. HOLELA; 700,000 mems.

Department of Co-operative Societies: POB 1287, Zanzibar; tel. (54) 30747; f. 1952; promotes formation and development of co-operative societies in Zanzibar.

Principal Societies

Bukoba Co-operative Union Ltd: POB 5, Bukoba; 74 affiliated societies; 75,000 mems.

Kilimanjaro Native Co-operative Union 1984 Ltd: POB 3032, Moshi; tel. (55) 54410; fax (55) 54204; f. 1984; 88 regd co-operative societies.

Nyanza Co-operative Union Ltd: POB 9, Mwanza.

TRADE UNIONS

Union of Tanzania Workers (Juwata): POB 15359, Dar es Salaam; tel. (51) 26111; f. 1978; Sec.-Gen. JOSEPH C. RWEGASIRA; Dep. Secs-Gen. C. MANYANDA (mainland Tanzania), I. M. ISSA (Zanzibar); 500,000 mems (1991); comprises eight sections:

Agricultural Workers: Sec. G. P. NYINDO.

Central and Local Government and Medical Workers: Sec. R. UTUKULU.

Commerce and Construction: Sec. P. O. OLUM.

Communications and Transport Workers: Sec. M. E. KALUWA.

Domestic, Hotels and General Workers: Sec. E. KAZOKA.

Industrial and Mines Workers: Sec. J. V. MWAMBUMA.

Railway Workers: Sec. C. SAMMANG' OMBE.

Teachers: Sec. W. MWENURA.

Principal Unaffiliated Unions

Organization of Tanzanian Trade Unions (OTTU): Dar es Salaam; Sec.-Gen. BRUNO MPANGAL.

Workers' Department of Chama Cha Mapinduzi: POB 389, Vikokotoni, Zanzibar; f. 1965.

Transport

RAILWAYS

Tanzania Railways Corporation (TRC): POB 468, Dar es Salaam; tel. and fax (51) 110599; f. 1977 after dissolution of East African Railways; privatization pending; operates 2,600 km of lines within Tanzania; also operates vessels on Lakes Victoria, Tanganyika and Malawi; Chair. J. K. CHANDE; Dir-Gen. LINFORD MBOMA.

Tanzania-Zambia Railway Authority (Tazara): POB 2834, Dar es Salaam; tel. (51) 860340; fax (51) 865338; e-mail acistz@ twiga.com; jtly owned and administered by the Tanzanian and Zambian Govts; operates a 1,860-km railway link between Dar es Salaam and New Kapiri Mposhi, Zambia, of which 969 km are within Tanzania; plans to privatize the line, which has incurred heavy losses in recent years, were under consideration in 1999; Chair. SALIM MSOMA; Man. Dir K. MKANDAWIRE; Regional Man. (Tanzania) A. F. S. NALITOLELA.

ROADS

In 1996 Tanzania had an estimated 88,200 km of classified roads, of which 10,400 km were primary roads and 17,900 km were secondary roads. A 1,930-km main road links Zambia and Tanzania, and there is a road link with Rwanda. A 10-year Integrated Roads Programme, funded by international donors and co-ordinated by the World Bank, commenced in 1991: its aim was to upgrade 70% of Tanzania's trunk roads and to construct 2,828 km of roads and 205 bridges, at an estimated cost of US $650m.

The island of Zanzibar has 619 km of roads, of which 442 km are bituminized, and Pemba has 363 km, of which 130 km are bituminized.

INLAND WATERWAYS

Steamers connect with Kenya, Uganda, the Democratic Republic of the Congo, Burundi, Zambia and Malawi. A joint shipping company was formed with Burundi in 1976 to operate services on Lake Tanganyika. A rail ferry service operates on Lake Victoria between Mwanza and Port Bell.

SHIPPING

Tanzania's major harbours are at Dar es Salaam (eight deep-water berths for general cargo, three berths for container ships, eight anchorages, lighter wharf, one oil jetty for small oil tankers up to 36,000 tons, offshore mooring for oil supertankers up to 100,000 tons, one 30,000-ton automated grain terminal) and Mtwara (two deep-water berths). There are also ports at Tanga (seven anchorages and lighterage quay), Bagamoyo, Zanzibar and Pemba. A

programme to extend and deepen the harbour entrance at Dar es Salaam commenced in 1997.

Tanzania Harbours Authority (THA): POB 9184, Dar es Salaam; tel. (51) 110371; fax (51) 32066; privatization pending in 1999; Exec. Chair. J. K. CHANDE; Gen. Man. A. S. M. JANGUO; 3 brs.

Chinese-Tanzanian Joint Shipping Co: POB 696, Dar es Salaam; tel. (51) 113389; fax (51) 5011380; f. 1967; services to People's Republic of China, South East Asia, Eastern and Southern Africa, Red Sea and Mediterranean ports.

National Shipping Agencies Co Ltd (NASACO): POB 9082, Dar es Salaam; f. 1973; state-owned shipping co; reorg. into five operating divisions and removal of monopoly on dealings with foreign shipping cos pending in 1999; Man. Dir D. R.M. LWIMBO.

Tanzania Central Freight Bureau (TCFB): POB 3093, Dar es Salaam; tel. (51) 114174; fax (51) 116697; e-mail tcfb@cats-net.com.

Tanzania Coastal Shipping Line Ltd: POB 9461, Dar es Salaam; tel. (51) 37034; fax (51) 116436; regular services to Tanzanian coastal ports; occasional special services to Zanzibar and Pemba; also tramp charter services to Kenya, Mozambique, the Persian (Arabian) Gulf, Indian Ocean islands and the Middle East; Gen. Man. RICHARD D. NZOWA.

CIVIL AVIATION

There are 53 airports and landing strips. The major international airport is at Dar es Salaam, 13 km from the city centre, and there are also international airports at Kilimanjaro and Zanzibar.

Air Tanzania Corporation: ATC House, Ohio St/Garden Ave, POB 543, Dar es Salaam; tel. (51) 110245; fax (51) 113114; f. 1977; operates an 18-point domestic network and international services to Africa, the Middle East and Europe; Chair. ABBAS SYKES; CEO JOSEPH S. MARANDUS; Dir-Gen. MELKIZEDECK SANARE.

Air Zanzibar: POB 1784, Zanzibar; tel. (54) 32512; fax (54) 33098; f. 1990; operates scheduled and charter services between Zanzibar and destinations in Tanzania, Kenya and Uganda.

Alliance Air: f. 1994; jtly owned by South African Airways, Air Tanzania Corpn, Uganda Airlines Corpn and the Tanzanian and Ugandan Govts; merger with Uganda Airlines Corpn pending; operates regional services and intercontinental routes to Asia, the Middle East and Europe; Chair. ADRIAN SIBO; Man. Dir CHRISTO ROODT.

New ACS Ltd: Peugeot House, 36 Upanga Rd, POB 21236, Dar es Salaam; fax (51) 37017; operates domestic and regional services; Dir MOHSIN RAHEMTULLAH.

Precisionair: POB 70770, Dar es Salaam; tel. (51) 30800; operates domestic and regional services.

Tanzanair: Sheraton Hotel, Dar es Salaam; tel. (51) 843131; operates domestic charter services.

Tourism

Tanzania has set aside about one-quarter of its land area for 12 national parks, 17 game reserves, 50 controlled game areas and a conservation area. Other attractions for tourists include beaches and coral reefs along the Indian Ocean coast, and the island of Zanzibar (which received 86,495 tourists in 1997 and is expanding and upgrading its tourism facilities). Visitor arrivals reached a record 359,096 in 1997, when revenue from tourism was estimated to total US $392.4m.

Tanzania Tourist Board: IPS Bldg, cnr Azikiwe Samora Machel Ave, POB 2485, Dar es Salaam; tel. (51) 111244; fax (51) 116420; e-mail ttb@tanza.net; state-owned; supervises the development and promotion of tourism; Man. Dir PETER J. MWENGUO.

Tanzania Wildlife Corporation: POB 1144, Arusha; tel. (57) 8830; fax (57) 8239; e-mail tawico@marie.gn.apc.org; organizes safaris; also exports and deals in live animals, birds and game-skin products; Gen. Man. DAVID S. BABU.

Zanzibar Tourist Corporation: POB 216, Zanzibar; tel. (54) 238630; fax (54) 233430; e-mail ztc@zanzinet.com; f. 1985; operates tours and hotel services; Gen. Man. ALPHONCE KATEMA.

Defence

In August 1999 the total armed forces numbered 34,000, of whom an estimated 30,000 were in the army, 1,000 in the navy and 3,000 in the air force. Paramilitary forces comprise a 1,400-strong Police Field Force and an 80,000-strong reservist Citizens' Militia.

In mid-1998 troops from Tanzania, Kenya and Uganda participated in a joint military exercise.

Defence Expenditure: Budgeted at Ts. 102,000m. in 1999.

Commander-in-Chief of the Armed Forces: President BENJAMIN WILLIAM MKAPA.

Head of the People's Defence Forces: Gen. ROBERT MBOMA.

Education

Education at primary level is officially compulsory and is provided free of charge. In secondary schools a government-stipulated fee is paid: from January 1995 this was Ts. 8,000 per year for day pupils at state-owned schools and Ts. 50,000–60,000 per year for day pupils at private schools. Villages and districts are encouraged to build their own schools with government assistance. Almost all primary schools are government-owned. Primary education begins at seven years of age and lasts for seven years. Secondary education, beginning at the age of 14, lasts for a further six years, comprising a first cycle of four years and a second of two years. As a proportion of the school-age population, total enrolment at primary and secondary schools rose from 22% in 1970 to 57% in 1980, but was equivalent to only 42% in 1996. Enrolment at primary schools in 1997 included 66% of children in the relevant age-group (males 67%; females 66%). Secondary enrolment in that year was equivalent to only 6% of children in the appropriate age-group (males 6%; females 5%). In 1997 there were 4,057,965 primary pupils and some 225,607 pupils attending secondary schools. There is a university at Dar es Salaam. Tanzania also has an agricultural university at Morogoro, and a number of vocational training centres and technical colleges. In 1995, according to UNESCO estimates, adult illiteracy averaged 32.2% (males 20.6%; females 43.2%), compared with a rate of some 67% in 1967. Education was allocated 23% of expenditure by the central government in 1994.

Bibliography

Angelsen, A., and Fjeldstad, O.-H. *Land Reforms and Land Degradation in Tanzania: Alternative Economic Approaches.* Bergen, CMI, 1995.

Bagachwa, M.S.D. *Financial Integration and Development in Sub-Saharan Africa: A Study of Informal Finance in Tanzania.* London, Overseas Development Institute, 1995.

(Ed.). *Poverty Alleviation in Tanzania: Recent Research Issues.* Dar es Salaam University Press, 1994.

Bagachwa, M. S. D., and Mbelle, A. V. Y. (Eds) *Economic Policy under a Multiparty System in Tanzania.* Dar es Salaam University Press, 1993.

Bennett, N. R. *A History of the Arab State of Zanzibar.* London, Methuen, 1978.

Bryceson, D. F. *Liberalizing Tanzania's Food Trade: Public and Private Faces of Urban Marketing Policy 1939–1988.* Geneva, UN Research Institute for Social Development; Tanzania, Mkuki na Nyota, 1993.

Buchert, L. *Education in the Development of Tanzania, 1919–1990.* London, James Currey Publishers, 1994.

Campbell, H., and Stein, H. *Tanzania and the IMF: The Dynamics of Liberalization.* Boulder, CO, Westview Press, 1990.

Cliffe, L., and Saul, J. *Tanzania Socialism—Politics and Policies: An Interdisciplinary Reader.* 2 vols. Nairobi, East African Publishing House, 1972.

Creighton, C., and Omazi, C. K. (Eds). *Gender, Family and Household in Tanzania.* Brookfield, VT, Ashgate Publishing, 1995.

Drysdale, H. *Dancing with the Dead: A Journey through Zanzibar and Madagascar.* London, Hamish Hamilton, 1991.

Elgstrom, O. *Foreign Aid Negotiations: The Swedish-Tanzanian Aid Dialogue.* Aldershot, Avebury, 1992.

Feierman, S. *Peasant Intellectuals: Anthropology and History in Tanzania.* Madison, University of Wisconsin Press, 1990.

Forster, P. G., and Maghimbi, S. (Eds). *The Tanzanian Peasantry: Economy in Crisis.* Aldershot, Avebury, 1992.

Forster, P., and Maghimbi, S. *The Tanzanian Peasantry: Further Strides.* Brookfield, VT, Ashgate Publishing, 1995.

Gibbon, P. (Ed.). *Liberalized Development in Tanzania: Studies on Accumulation Processes and Local Institutions.* Uppsala, Nordiska Afrikainstitutet, 1995.

Havenik, K. J. *Tanzania: The Limits to Development From Above.* Uppsala, SIAS, 1993.

Hayward, M. F. *Elections in Independent Africa.* Boulder, CO, Westview Press, 1987.

Iliffe, J. *Tanganyika under German Rule, 1905–12.* Cambridge University Press, 1969.

A Modern History of Tanganyika. Cambridge University Press, 1979.

International Monetary Fund. *Tanzania—Statistical Apendix.* Washington, DC, IMF, 1998.

Kahama, C. G., Maliyamkono, L. and Wells, S. *The Challenge for Tanzania's Economy.* London, James Currey Publishers, 1986.

Kaijage, F., and Tibaijuka, A. *Poverty and Social Exclusion in Tanzania.* Geneva, International Labour Organisation, 1996.

Kaniki, M. H. Y. (Ed.). *Tanzania under Colonial Rule.* London, Longman, 1980.

Kikula, I. S. *Policy Implications on Environment: The Case of Villagization in Tanzania.* Uppsala, Nordiska Afrikainstitutet, 1998.

Kimambo, I. N. *Penetration and Protest in Tanzania: The Impact of the World Economy on the Pare, 1860–1960.* London, James Currey Publishers, 1991.

Lange, S. *From Nation-Building to Popular Culture: The Modernization of Performance in Tanzania.* Bergen, CMI, 1995.

Legum, C., and Mmari, G. (Eds). *Mwalimu: The Influence of Nyerere.* London, James Currey Publishers, 1995.

Liebenow, J. G. *Colonial Rule and Political Development in Tanzania.* Nairobi, East African Publishing House, 1972.

Lofchie, M. *Zanzibar: Background to Revolution.* Princeton, New Jersey; London, Oxford University Press, 1965.

Maddox, G., Giblin, J. L., and Kimambo, I. N. (Eds). *Custodians of the Land: Environment and Hunger in Tanzanian History.* London, James Currey Publishers, 1995; Athens, OH, Ohio University Press, 1996.

McHenry, D. E., Jr. *Limited Choices: The Political Struggle for Socialism in Tanzania.* Boulder, CO, Lynne Rienner Publishers, 1994.

Martin, D. *Serengetu Tanzania: Land, People, History.* Harare, APG, 1997.

Mmuya, M. (Ed.). *Functional Dimensions of the Democratization Process: Tanzania and Kenya.* Dar es Salaam University Press, 1994.

Mmuya, M., and Chaligha, A. *Political Parties and Democracy in Tanzania.* Dar es Salaam University Press, 1994.

Mukandala, R., and Othman, H. *Liberalization and Politics: The 1990 Election in Tanzania.* Dar es Salaam University Press, 1994.

Nyerere, J. K. *Freedom and Socialism: A Selection from Writings and Speeches, 1965–67.* Dar es Salaam and London, Oxford University Press, 1968; contains the Arusha Declaration and subsequent policy statements.

Ofcansky, T. P., and Yeager, R. *Historical Dictionary of Tanzania.* Lanham, MD, Scarecrow Press, 1997.

Okema, M. *Political Culture in Tanzania.* Lewiston, Edwin Mellen, 1996.

Othman, H. I. B., and Okema, M. *Tanzania: Democracy in Transition.* Dar es Salaam University Press, 1990.

Pratt, C. *The Critical Phase in Tanzania: 1945–1968.* Oxford University Press, 1980.

Rosch, P. G. *Der Prozess der Strukturanpassung in Tanzania.* Hamburg, Institut für Afrika-Kunde, 1995.

Sheriff, A. *Slaves, Spices and Ivory in Zanzibar: Integration of an East African Commercial Empire into the World Economy, 1770–1873.* London, James Currey Publishers, 1987.

Shivji, I. G. *Law, State and the Working Class in Tanzania.* London, James Currey Publishers, 1986.

Stephens, H. W. *The Political Transformation of Tanganyika: 1920–67.* New York, Praeger; London, Pall Mall, 1968.

Stoecker, H. (Ed.) *German Imperialism in Africa.* London, Hurst Humanities, 1986.

von Freyhold, M. *Ujamaa Villages in Tanzania*. London, Heinemann Educational, 1979.

Wange, S. M., et al. (Eds). *Traditional Economic Policy and Policy Options in Tanzania*. Dar es Salaam, Mkuki Na Nyota Publishers, 1998.

World Bank. *Tanzania: the Challenge of Reforms: Growth, Incomes and Welfare*. Washington, DC, World Bank, 1996.

Yeager, R. *Tanzania: An African Experiment*. 2nd Edn. Boulder, CO, Westview Press, 1989.

TOGO

Physical and Social Geography

R. J. HARRISON CHURCH

The Togolese Republic, a small state of western Africa (bordered to the west by Ghana, to the east by Benin and to the north by Burkina Faso), covers an area of 56,785 sq km (21,925 sq miles), and comprises the eastern two-thirds of the former German protectorate of Togoland. From a coastline of 56 km on the Gulf of Guinea, Togo extends inland for about 540 km. In January 1988 the population was officially estimated to be 3,296,000, giving a density of 58.0 persons per sq km, higher than average for this part of Africa. According to UN estimates, the population numbered 4,397,000, giving a density of 77.4 persons per sq km, at mid-1998. Northern Togo is more ethnically diverse than the south, where the Ewe predominate. The official languages are French, Ewe and Kabiye.

The coast, lagoons, blocked estuaries and Terre de Barre regions are identical to those of Benin, but calcium phosphate, the only commercially-exploited mineral resource, is quarried north-east of Lake Togo. Pre-Cambrian rocks with rather siliceous soils occur northward, in the Mono tableland and in the Togo-Atacora mountains. The latter are, however, still well wooded and planted with coffee and cocoa. To the north is the Oti plateau, with infertile Primary sandstones, in which water is rare and deep down. On the northern border are granite areas, remote but densely inhabited, as in neighbouring Ghana and Burkina Faso. Togo's climate is similar to that of Benin, except that Togo's coastal area is even drier: Lomé, the capital, has an average annual rainfall of 782 mm. Thus Togo, though smaller in area than Benin, is physically, as well as economically, more varied than its eastern neighbour.

Recent History

PIERRE ENGLEBERT

Revised for this edition by the Editor

Togoland, of which the Togolese Republic was formerly a part, became a German protectorate in 1894. The territory was occupied by Anglo-French forces in 1914, and was designated a League of Nations mandate in 1919. France was awarded the larger eastern section, while the United Kingdom administered the west. This partition divided the homeland of the Ewe people of the southern part of the territory, and became a continuing source of internal friction. Ewe demands for reunification were intensified during the UN trusteeship system which took effect after the Second World War. In May 1956 a UN-supervised plebiscite in British Togoland produced, despite Ewe opposition, majority support for a merger with the neighbouring territory of the Gold Coast, then a British colony. The region was transferred to the independent state of Ghana in the following year (see p. 545). In October 1956, in a separate plebiscite, French Togoland voted to become an autonomous republic within the French Community.

Political life in French Togoland was dominated by the Comité de l'unité togolaise, led by Sylvanus Olympio, and the Parti togolais du progrès, led by Olympio's brother-in-law, Nicolas Grunitzky. Following independence on 27 April 1960, Olympio, a campaigner for Ewe reunification, became president.

In January 1963 Olympio was overthrown and killed in a military coup led by Sgt (later Gen.) Etienne (Gnassingbe) Eyadéma, a Kabiye from the north of the country, who invited Grunitzky to return from exile as head of state. Subsequent efforts by Grunitzky to achieve constitutional multi-party government proved unsuccessful, and in January 1967 Eyadéma, by then army chief of staff, assumed power. Political activity remained effectively suspended until the creation in 1969 of the Rassemblement du peuple togolais (RPT), which served as a vehicle for integrating the army into political life. Plots to overthrow Eyadéma were suppressed in 1970 and again in 1977, when the exiled sons of ex-president Olympio were accused of organizing a mercenary invasion. The introduction of a new constitution in 1980 made little impact on Eyadéma's authoritarian style of government, or to the furtherance of the personality cult surrounding the president. Although Olympio's supporters maintained an exiled Mouvement togolais pour la démocratie (MTD), by the mid-1980s Eyadéma's rule had entered a more tranquil phase politically, although the country was experiencing economic difficulties. In 1985 the constitution was amended to allow candidates for election to the assemblée nationale to be adopted without prior approval by the RPT, which, however, remained the only legal political party.

POLITICAL REPRESSION

An unprecedented wave of bomb attacks in Lomé in August 1985 led to the arrest, in September and October, of at least 15 people accused of involvement in the bombings and of distributing subversive literature. When one of the detainees died shortly following his arrest, the exiled MTD claimed that the government had used the pretext of the bomb attacks to unleash a 'wave of repression'. The Togolese government accused the Ghanaian authorities of complicity in the attacks, prompting allegations in the Ghanaian press that the explosions had in fact been detonated by members of Eyadéma's entourage. In 1986 attempts by the human rights organization, Amnesty International, to investigate allegations of torture of political prisoners, were blocked by the government. However, a visiting delegation of French jurists concluded that torture was being used, and condemned the conditions under which political prisoners were being detained. Many of those who had been arrested following the August 1985 bombings were released under a presidential amnesty in January 1986.

In September 1986 19 people were detained following an apparent attempt by what was described as a 'terrorist commando unit' to occupy the Lomé military barracks (which was also the president's home), the RPT headquarters and the national radio station. About 13 people, including six civilians, were reported to have been killed during the attack. The government subsequently accused both Ghana and Burkina Faso of involvement in the alleged coup attempt. The border with Ghana was closed, and 250 French paratroopers were sent briefly to Togo (in accordance with a previously unpublished defence agreement). Some 350 troops from the then Zaïre (now the

Democratic Republic of the Congo) were also dispatched to Togo. In December Eyadéma was re-elected as president for a further seven-year term, reportedly winning 99.95% of votes cast. At trials in the same month 13 people were sentenced to death, and 14 to life imprisonment, for complicity in the events in September. Gilchrist Olympio, son of the former president and the alleged instigator of the attack, was one of three people sentenced to death *in absentia*.

In the aftermath of the alleged coup attempt Eyadéma combined measures to increase his personal security with reforms aimed at apparent political democratization. In October 1987 a national human rights commission, the Commission nationale des droits de l'homme (CNDH), was established, while most of the death sentences imposed in the previous December were commuted. However, the appointment, in December 1988, of the former joint chief of staff of the security forces, Brig.-Gen. (later Maj.-Gen.) Yao Mawulikplimi Amegi, to the position of minister of the interior and security, was regarded as indicative of Eyadéma's preoccupation with national security.

At elections to the assemblée nationale in March 1990, 230 candidates, all of whom declared their allegiance to the RPT, contested the assemblée's 77 seats. Only 18 members of the outgoing legislature were re-elected.

By the close of the 1980s demands for political change were increasingly apparent. In December 1989 two Togolese dissidents, who were allegedly members of an opposition movement, the Convention démocratique des peuples africains du Togo (CDPA–T), were expelled from Côte d'Ivoire. In August of that year Eyadéma stated that he would assent to a multi-party system, if that were the will of the people. However, in May 1990 a national congress of the RPT unanimously rejected the possibility of a return to multi-party politics, but agreed that proposals made by Eyadéma for the separation of the functions of the party and state would be examined at a later date. In late July, during an official visit to the USA, Eyadéma indicated that the process of democratization in Togo would inevitably include the development of a two-party system.

The formation, in August 1990, of the independent Ligue togolaise des droits de l'homme (LTDH) was widely regarded as a direct challenge to the integrity of the official CNDH. In the same month 13 people, allegedly members of the CDPA–T and of an unofficial students' organization, were arrested on suspicion of distributing anti-government tracts. Eleven of the detainees were later released, after they had admitted to having been 'manipulated and used by external organizations hostile to Togo', while two others, Logo Dossouvi and Doglo Agbelenko, remained in detention. An official inquiry was ordered to investigate allegations of the torture of the detainees: the CNDH found that four detainees, including Dossouvi and Agbelenko, had been subjected to torture while in custody. In early October Dossouvi and Agbelenko were convicted of distributing defamatory tracts and inciting the army to revolt, and were sentenced to five years' imprisonment. Violent demonstrations erupted in Lomé during the trial, leading to four deaths. The government claimed that the unrest had been orchestrated by 'international machinations', and many of the 170 people who were arrested in connection with the violence were said to be foreigners. In mid-October Dossouvi and Agbelenko were granted presidential pardons, and clemency was subsequently extended to all those who had been detained during the riots.

THE COLLAPSE OF LEGITIMACY

In October 1990 a commission was established to draft a new constitution, which, it was announced, would be submitted for approval in a national referendum in December 1991. The constitutional commission presented its draft document, which (apparently at Eyadéma's instigation) provided for the establishment of a multi-party political system, at the end of the year. In January 1991 Eyadéma declared an amnesty for all those (including exiles) who had been implicated in political offences other than the September 1986 coup attempt. The sentences of criminal offenders were also reduced, and mandatory contributions to the RPT were abolished. However, such concessions were rejected by Togo's emergent opposition, which demanded that a national conference be convened.

A boycott of classes by university students and secondary school pupils, during the first half of March 1991, provoked violent clashes between striking students and the security forces and supporters of Eyadéma. Meanwhile, several opposition movements formed a co-ordinating organization, the Front des associations pour le renouveau (FAR), to campaign for the immediate introduction of a multi-party political system. Following a meeting between Eyadéma and the leader of the FAR, Yao Agboyibo, an agreement was reached whereby Eyadéma consented to an amnesty for all political dissidents, and agreed to the legalization of political parties and to the organization of a national forum to discuss the country's political evolution.

In early April 1991 further student unrest erupted, prompted by a demonstration in Lomé by pupils at Roman Catholic mission schools in support of their teachers' demands for salary increases. Two deaths were reported following intervention by the security forces. Further deaths resulted from similar action by the security forces in Kévé (to the north-west of Lomé) to disperse a demonstration to demand Eyadéma's resignation. Violent protests broke out in the capital; all educational establishments were closed, and a night-time curfew imposed. The official endorsement, by the assemblée nationale, of legislation regarding the general amnesty and the legalization of political parties was overshadowed by the discovery, in mid-April, of about 26 bodies in a lagoon in Lomé. Opposition allegations that the bodies were those of demonstrators who had been beaten to death by the security forces were denied by the government, which ordered the CNDH to investigate the deaths. Retrieval of the bodies provoked further protests, at which the security forces again intervened. Fearing an ethnic conflict between the Kabiye and Ewe ethnic groups, Eyadéma appealed for national unity, and announced that a new constitution would be introduced within one year, and that multi-party legislative elections would be organized. In May Eyadéma relinquished the defence portfolio to Maj.-Gen. Yao Mawulikplimi Amegi.

The FAR was disbanded in late April 1991, to allow for the establishment of independent political parties. Agboyibo formed his own party, the Comité d'action pour le renouveau (CAR). Numerous other movements obtained official status, and in early May 10 parties (including the CAR) announced the formation of a new political coalition, the Front de l'opposition démocratique (FOD), which was later renamed the Coalition de l'opposition démocratique (COD), to co-ordinate the activities of opposition groups in preparation for the national forum.

Negotiations between the government and the opposition, in preparation for the national forum, took place amid conditions of renewed social and labour unrest. In early June 1991 the FOD organized a widely-observed general strike, in an attempt to force Eyadéma's resignation. Shortly afterwards a rally in the capital that had been organized by the FOD was reportedly disrupted by Kabiye supporters of Eyadéma, while demonstrations in Lomé and Sokodé, in central Togo, were dispersed by the security forces. In mid-June it was announced that the government and the FOD had reached agreement regarding the mandate of what was to be known henceforth as the national conference. (The government's previous insistence that the convention be termed a national forum was widely thought to indicate its desire to limit the competence of the meeting, as sovereign national conferences elsewhere in the region, notably in Benin, had imposed radical political reforms.) The FOD subsequently suspended its industrial action. Shortly afterwards the government announced that ex-presidents Olympio and Grunitzky were to be posthumously rehabilitated. Also rehabilitated was Gilchrist Olympio, who returned to Togo in early July to participate in the national conference.

The national conference was opened, after some delay, on 8 July 1991. It was attended by 700–1,000 delegates (representing, among others, the organs of state and the country's newly legalized political organizations, together with workers', students' and religious leaders). A resolution by the conference, in mid-July, to declare itself sovereign, to suspend the constitution and to dissolve the assemblée nationale prompted the government to boycott the proceedings for one week. Upon their return to the conference, government representatives refused to endorse these resolutions. In late July the conference resolved to sequester the assets of the RPT and its former trade union affiliate, the Confédération nationale des travailleurs du Togo (CNTT), and to create a commission to investigate the finances of these organizations, together with an authority to control the finances of state and parastatal organizations, with the aim of preventing the transfer of state funds abroad. Exit visa requirements were imposed on foreign travel by government ministers.

Meanwhile, renewed allegations had emerged concerning violations of human rights by the Eyadéma regime. In mid-July 1991 the CNDH concluded that the security forces had been responsible for the deaths of at least 20 of those whose bodies had been discovered in mid-April. In late July the national conference heard allegations that a 'death camp' had been established in northern Togo in 1983.

On 26 August 1991 Eyadéma, deprived by the national conference of most of his powers, abruptly suspended the conference. Opposition delegates responded by proclaiming a provisional government under the leadership of Joseph Kokou Koffigoh, a prominent lawyer and the head of the LTDH. The conference also voted to dissolve the RPT and to form an interim legislature, the Haut conseil de la république (HCR). Fearing renewed unrest, Eyadéma hastily signed a decree confirming Koffigoh as transitional prime minister; the conference ended on 28 August.

Koffigoh's council of ministers, appointed in early September 1991, was composed mainly of technocrats who had not previously held political office. The prime minister assumed personal responsibility for defence, and it was envisaged that Eyadéma would remain only nominally head of the military. However, the events of subsequent months were to show that the Kabiye-dominated armed forces looked to Eyadéma for their command. On 1 October a group of soldiers, apparently dissatisfied at the failure of the HCR to sanction pay increases for the lower ranks of the armed forces, seized control of the offices of the state broadcasting service in Lomé. The troops claimed to have dissolved the HCR, and demanded the resignations of Koffigoh and his government, but returned to barracks on Eyadéma's orders. Five people were killed, and about 50 injured, during the incident. Later the same day members of the presidential guard, led by Eyadéma's half-brother, were rumoured to have staged a second rebellion. One week later presidential guards attempted unsuccessfully to abduct Koffigoh. Although Eyadéma condemned the incident, and ordered a return to barracks, the rebels claimed to be supporters of the president. Seven deaths and more than 50 injuries were reported, as demonstrations by civilian supporters of Koffigoh degenerated into looting and violence, which was seemingly exacerbated by ethnic rivalries. Three senior armed forces officers were arrested in early November, in connection with the disturbances.

CONSTITUTIONAL TRANSITION

Work began in October 1991 on drafting the new constitution. The brief political calm ended on 26 November, when the HCR responded to attempts to convene a congress of the RPT by reaffirming the ban on the former ruling party. Clashes between supporters of Eyadéma and Koffigoh, again aggravated by inter-ethnic differences, resulted in further casualties. The military retook the broadcasting headquarters and surrounded government offices, demanding that the transitional authorities be disbanded and that Eyadéma be empowered to nominate a new prime minister. A night-time curfew was imposed, and the borders and main airport were closed. The troops returned to barracks on 30 November, and conciliation talks began. Two days later, however, the military reoccupied strategic positions in the capital, and on the following day captured the prime minister. Following negotiations between Eyadéma and Koffigoh, it was announced that a broadly-based 'government of national unity' (including, it was implied, the RPT) would be appointed. The provisional government that was formed in late December included many members of the outgoing council of ministers, although two key portfolios were allocated to close associates of Eyadéma: Yao Komlavi again became responsible for national security, and Aboudou Assouma was appointed minister-delegate for the armed forces. Also in late December the HCR adopted a 'social contract for a peaceful transition', compiled by Koffigoh, which (among other provisions) restored legal status to the RPT. (Despite the armed forces' earlier demands, the HCR continued to function, although its members were subject to frequent harassment by the military.)

Delays in the transition process prompted sporadic outbreaks of unrest in the early part of 1992. However, the fragility of the political situation was exemplified in early May, when a failed assassination attempt on Gilchrist Olympio, in which the involvement of the armed forces was widely alleged, resulted in the death of another political leader. A subsequent investigation by the International Federation of Human Rights apparently substantiated these allegations. As a result of the unrest, Lomé was effectively paralysed by a two-day general strike, organized by independent trade unions, and some 15,000 people demonstrated in the capital to demand the resignations of Eyadéma and Koffigoh. At the end of the month it was revealed that preparations for the election of democratic institutions were incomplete, and the electoral timetable (already delayed) was abandoned. Tensions were further exacerbated by ethnic unrest involving the Kabiye and Kotokoli communities in central Togo.

Proposals for a new electoral schedule were announced later in July 1992, beginning with a constitutional referendum at the end of August. In the same month the government was reorganized (Aboudou Assouma had been dismissed in mid-June, and one minister had subsequently resigned his post). The political climate deteriorated shortly after the reshuffle, when a prominent opposition leader, Tavio Ayao Amorin, was shot and seriously wounded, and later died. Eyadéma denounced the assassination; none the less, a new opposition coalition, the Collectif de l'opposition démocratique (COD–2), comprising some 25 political organizations and trade unions, organized a widely-observed general strike in Lomé, and violent confrontations took place between protesters and the police.

Disarray among the country's political parties (estimated to number about 40 by mid-1992) contributed to the atmosphere of instability. Many opposition parties had withdrawn support for Koffigoh following what was perceived to be his 'capitulation' in late 1991, and political alliances were frequently formed and disbanded. An attempt to resolve the political crisis was made in late July 1992, when representatives of Eyadéma and of the country's eight leading political parties began a series of meetings. The negotiations made faltering progress in subsequent weeks. Confidence was undermined by an armed attack (in which the complicity of the security forces was rumoured) on a centre for the processing of electoral data, and by an assassination attempt on the minister of equipment and mines. None the less, agreement was reached on opposition access to the state-controlled media and on the extension, until 31 December, of the transitional period. In late August the HCR restored a number of important powers to the president, empowering Eyadéma to preside over the council of ministers and to represent the country abroad, and obliging the prime minister to make government appointments in consultation with the head of state. Moreover, in an important concession to Eyadéma and his supporters, the draft constitution was amended to permit members of the armed forces seeking election to the new democratic organs of state to retain their commissions.

The transitional government was dissolved on 1 September 1992, and a new electoral schedule was announced: a referendum on the new constitution was to take place later in September, local and legislative elections in October and November, and presidential elections in December. In mid-September a new transitional government was formed: Koffigoh remained as prime minister, and 10 parties were reportedly represented in the new administration, but the most influential posts (including the national defence, foreign affairs and justice portfolios) were allocated to members of the RPT. On 27 September the new constitution was approved in a referendum by 98.11% of the votes cast (the rate of participation by voters was about 66%). At the end of the month, however, it was announced that the elections were to be rescheduled yet again. In late October members of the armed forces stormed a meeting of the HCR, holding some of its members hostage and demanding that it authorize the reimbursement of contributions made to the RPT, whose assets had remained 'frozen' since 1991. Although Eyadéma stated that disciplinary measures would be taken against the men involved, the COD–2 successfully organized a general strike in protest at the incident. In November Koffigoh dismissed two ministers (both supporters of the RPT) for their conduct during the attack on the HCR, but his decision was overruled by Eyadéma. In the same month another general strike was organized by the COD–2 and the Collectif des syndicats indépendants labour movement, to support their demands for elections, the neutrality of the armed forces, the formation of a non-military 'peace force', and the bringing to justice of those responsible for the attacks on the HCR. The strike was widely observed, except in the north of Togo (where support for Eyadéma was strongest), and continued during the first half of 1993, causing considerable economic disruption.

In mid-January 1993 Eyadéma dissolved the government, but reappointed Koffigoh as prime minister. The president stated that he would appoint a new 'government of national unity', whose task would be to organize elections as soon as possible. His action provoked protests by the opposition parties, who claimed that, according to the constitution, the HCR should appoint a prime minister since the transition period had now expired. Later in the same month representatives of the French and German governments visited Togo to offer mediation in the political crisis. During their visit at least 20 people were killed when police opened fire on anti-government protesters. Thousands of Togolese (including most opposition leaders who were not already in exile) subsequently fled from Lomé, many taking refuge in Benin and Ghana. In early February discussions took place, under French and German auspices, in Colmar, France, attended by representatives of Eyadéma, the RPT, Koffigoh, the HCR and the COD–2, but these failed when the presidential delegation left after one day. The formation of a new 'crisis government' was announced shortly afterwards: eight new ministers were appointed, but supporters of Eyadéma retained the principal posts. The COD–2 declared that they now regarded Koffigoh as an obstacle to democratization, and in March COD–2 member parties, meeting in Benin, nominated a 'parallel' prime minister, Jean-Lucien Savi de Tové (the leader of the Parti des démocrates pour l'unité).

On 25 March 1993 there was an armed attack on the military camp in Lomé where Eyadéma had his residence: more than 20 people, including the deputy chief of staff of the armed forces, Col Kofi Tepe, were killed during the attack, after which about 110 members of the armed forces fled the country. The government identified Tepe as the principal military organizer of the attack, but declared that it had been instigated by Gilchrist Olympio, with assistance from the Ghanaian authorities.

In early April 1993 the government announced a new electoral timetable, beginning with the presidential election in early June. This was rejected by the opposition, which reiterated that legitimate polls could only be organized following the restoration of a national consensus. A revised schedule, formulated one month later (apparently following secret negotiations in Ouagadougou, Burkina Faso, between Togolese government representatives and members of the COD–2), was similarly rejected by the opposition. A series of bomb attacks on both government and opposition targets in the second half of May was said by the authorities to have been plotted outside Togo by persons who wished to sabotage democratization. The election was modified twice during June, and was abandoned in early July, in anticipation of renewed negotiations in Ouagadougou (talks there in mid-June had failed, when the participants failed to reach agreement on procedures for the organization of elections). In mid-July those meeting in Ouagadougou (including Eyadéma and President Compaoré of Burkina Faso, Koffigoh and members of the transitional government, representatives of the COD–2 and French and German diplomats) set 25 August as the date for the presidential poll. Agreement was reached on both the issue of security during the election campaign (the Togolese armed forces would be confined to barracks, under the supervision of a multinational military team), and also the establishment and functions of an independent national electoral commission to oversee the polling. International observers were also to be invited to monitor the elections.

However, divisions within the opposition were evident (the total number of political parties at this time exceeded 60). Gilchrist Olympio denounced the Ouagadougou accord, protesting that the government had been allowed too much control over the election process and that no provision had been made for the return of refugees in advance of the elections (international human rights organizations estimated the number of people who had fled Togo in recent months at 200,000, most of whom were sheltering in Benin and Ghana, while Olympio put the total number at about 350,000). Shortly after the conclusion of the Ouagadougou agreement, Edem Kodjo, the leader of the

Union togolaise pour la démocratie (UTD), was chosen as the presidential candidate of the COD–2. Four other opposition candidates, including Yao Agboyibo and Gilchrist Olympio, were selected to contest the election. However, the supreme court disallowed Olympio's candidature, on a legal technicality. Meanwhile, the authorities revealed that a warrant for Olympio's arrest, in connection with the March 1993 attack on Eyadéma's residence, had been issued in May. Olympio challenged the legality of the warrant and refused to return from Ghana in the absence of a guarantee of his security by the Togolese authorities.

As the election campaign gained momentum during August 1993, opposition demands, supported by the national electoral commission, that the election be postponed intensified, and Kodjo (widely regarded as Eyadéma's strongest challenger) and Agboyibo effectively withdrew from the election. The COD–2 and Olympio's Union des forces de changement appealed to their supporters to boycott the poll, and US and German observers withdrew from Togo, alleging irregularities in the compilation of voting lists and in electoral procedures. As voting began, on 25 August, the government announced that a coup attempt, plotted by Togolese dissidents in Ghana, had been detected on the eve of polling. Shortly after the poll, it was revealed that at least 15 opposition supporters, arrested in connection with attacks on polling stations in Lomé, had died while in detention (the authorities alleged that the prisoners had been intentionally poisoned by their associates). According to official election results, published in late August, Eyadéma was re-elected president by 96.49% of voters. Only about 36% of the electorate voted in the election.

THE FOURTH REPUBLIC

In September 1993 the COD–2 announced that it would only participate in the forthcoming legislative election if the electoral register was revised, equitable access to state media granted and international observers present. The government subsequently agreed to revise the electoral registers. Eyadéma was sworn in as first president of the fourth republic on 24 September. In November the government announced that the legislative election would take place in two stages in December and January, but both the national electoral commission and the opposition parties declared these dates to be premature, and, following consultation with the international monitoring committee, the government agreed to postpone the first round of the election to 23 January 1994.

In early January 1994 an armed attack on Eyadéma's official residence was reported. As in March 1993, the government alleged that the attack had been organized by Gilchrist Olympio, with Ghanaian support: this was denied both by Olympio and by the Ghanaian government. A total of 67 people were officially reported to have died in the violence. It was claimed by the human rights organization, Amnesty International, that at least 48 summary executions were carried out by the armed forces. On the day after the disturbances the government announced that the election would now take place on 6 February and 20 February 1994, rejecting requests by the CAR and the UTD for a further postponement.

In the legislative election of February 1994, 347 candidates contested 81 seats in the assemblée nationale. Despite the murder of a newly-elected CAR candidate after the first round, and some incidents of violence at polling stations during the second round, international observers expressed themselves satisfied with the conduct of the election. The final result revealed a narrow victory for the opposition, with the CAR winning 36 seats and the UTD seven; the RPT obtained 35 seats and two smaller pro-Eyadéma parties won three. During March Eyadéma consulted the main opposition parties on the formation of a new government. In late March the CAR and the UTD reached agreement on the terms of their alliance and jointly proposed the candidacy of Agboyibo for prime minister (a stipulation of the agreement was that the candidate for prime minister should be a member of the CAR). In rulings issued in late March and early April the supreme court declared the results of the legislative election invalid in three constituencies (in which the CAR had won two seats and the UTD one) and ordered by-elections. The CAR and the UTD refused to attend the new assemblée nationale, in protest at the annulment.

In April Eyadéma nominated Kodjo as prime minister. Kodjo accepted the appointment despite assertions by the CAR that to do so was a violation of the agreement of March 1994 between the two parties on which their parliamentary majority was based. The CAR subsequently announced that it would not participate in an administration formed by Kodjo. On 25 April Kodjo took office, citing his priorities as national reconciliation, the return of refugees, economic recovery, and the integration of the armed forces into democratic life. It was not until late May that he announced the formation of his government, which comprised eight members of the RPT and other pro-Eyadéma parties, three members of the UTD, and eight independents. Kodjo maintained, however, that this was an 'interim' government and that, should the CAR decide to join the government, there would be a reorganization of the cabinet to accommodate it. Shortly beforehand, the CAR had announced (in response to the postponement of the parliamentary by-elections, originally scheduled for May) that it was to end its boycott of the assemblée nationale.

In October 1994 the government announced that an attempted terrorist attack on installations of the Office togolais des phosphates had been thwarted by the security forces. It was alleged that an armed group had infiltrated from Ghana with the intention of destroying a transformer at the phosphate mines in Hahotoé, some 50 km north-east of the capital. The group claimed to have been recruited by Togolese political exiles living in Ghana.

In November 1994 the CAR again withdrew from the assemblée nationale, and indicated that it would return only when agreement had been reached with the government on the conduct of the by-elections, ordered by the supreme court in April and due to be held on 27 November. The CAR's demands included the establishment of a joint electoral commission, the reinforcement of security measures and the entrustment of the electoral process to an independent body, such as the constitutional court. In the light of the dispute, on 25 November the by-elections were postponed. Later that month the CAR informed the speaker of the assemblée nationale that it would resume participation in the legislature only when the government had shown a commitment to reaching a general consensus on the organization of free and fair elections.

Political and Constitutional Manoeuvres

In December 1994 the assemblée nationale declared a general amnesty covering all persons who had been charged with political offences committed before 15 December 1994, including those alleged to have participated in attacks on the presidential residence in March 1993 and January 1994. The release of those held in detention for such offences began later in December.

In March 1995 Amnesty International expressed concern at the lack of effective measures for ensuring the observance of human rights in Togo, and criticized the absence of independent legal inquiry into abuses committed during the period of political transition in 1991–94. In the following month the CAR announced that it was to end its boycott of the assemblée nationale, following an agreement between the government and the major opposition parties. The terms of the agreement provided for the government and the legislative opposition to have equal representation on national, district and local electoral commissions. In June, following five weeks of negotiations with employers and trade unions, the government agreed to pay, by the end of 1996, wage arrears owing to civil servants that had been accumulated during the nine-month general strike of 1992-93. The amount of arrears was estimated to total 13,500m. francs CFA. In August 1995 the CAR, whose return to the assemblée nationale had been postponed pending the resolution of issues relating to the electoral process, officially resumed participation in the legislature. The CAR's eventual return had also been prompted by the approval, in early August, of legislation concerning the independence of the judiciary.

In November 1995 Kodjo implemented a major reorganization of the cabinet, increasing the number of portfolios from 21 to 23. The CAR, which was not represented in the new government, expressed concern at the level of representation of supporters of Eyadéma; of the 13 new members, 11 (including the ministers responsible for foreign affairs and defence) were considered to be close allies of the president.

In March 1996 the German government issued a formal protest and demanded prompt clarification from the Togolese government, following an incident in which a member of staff at the German embassy was shot dead by a military unit at a road-block in the capital.

In April 1996 a legislative deputy of the CAR resigned from the party, thus reducing the CAR's representation in the assemblée nationale to 33 seats. In June the by-elections that had been postponed in November 1994 were finally rescheduled for August 1996. The CAR subsequently issued demands, dismissed by the government, that the by-elections be organized on the basis of the Ouagadougou accord of July 1993, specifically that the polls be conducted in the presence of an international monitoring committee. In May 1996 the CAR announced its withdrawal from the by-elections, owing to the government's failure to adhere to the terms of the Ouagadougou accord. In the same month a legislative deputy of the UTD was dismissed from the party, thus reducing the UTD's representation in the assemblée nationale to five seats.

At by-elections to the assemblée nationale held in August 1996, conducted in the presence of 22 international observers, the RPT won an absolute majority in the three constituencies being contested. As a result of the by-elections, the RPT and its political allies were able to command a legislative majority, thus forcing the resignation of the Kodjo administration. On leaving office, Kodjo criticized the lack of support that his administration had received for the establishment of the institutions enshrined in the constitution of the fourth republic, and in particular the failure to establish a constitutional court, as a result of which constitutional issues were still referred to the supreme court. On 20 August Eyadéma appointed Kwassi Klutse as prime minister. Klutse, a technocrat and the minister of planning and territorial development in the outgoing administration, cited the recovery of the national economy as the priority of the new government. Both the CAR and the UTD refused to participate in a proposed government of national union, and consequently the new cabinet, appointed in late August, comprised, almost exclusively, supporters of Eyadéma.

In October 1996 a further CAR deputy left the party, transferring his allegiance to the RPT. In the following month the Union pour la justice et la démocratie, which held two seats in the legislature, announced that it was to merge with the RPT, thus giving the RPT 41 seats and an overall majority. In December the remaining 32 deputies of the CAR boycotted a vote on the law governing the constitutional court. The CAR abandoned the session following the legislature's rejection of its proposal that the constitutional court be empowered to rule on disputes arising from legislative and presidential elections. In the absence of the CAR and the UTD, which also boycotted the vote, the government's legislation was unanimously approved. The seven members of the new constitutional court were installed in February 1997.

In May 1997 the CAR organized a demonstration in the capital to protest against what it alleged to be manoeuvres by the RPT aimed at stifling the political activities of the opposition. The RPT responded by staging a demonstration on the following day which, according to its organizers, was attended by some 100,000 government supporters. In August a dispute arose between the government and opposition parties concerning a government proposal for the revision of the electoral law. Included in the reforms was a measure to modify the national electoral commission, providing for its chairman to be appointed by the cabinet instead of, as under the existing law, by the president of the court of appeal. The CAR opposed the reforms, proposing instead the establishment of an independent national electoral commission headed by a president who would be appointed by consensus. In September the new electoral code was approved, providing for a national electoral commission comprising nine members, chaired by the president of the court of appeal and including four members appointed by the opposition. The CAR, however, boycotted the legislative session in protest at the government's refusal to reveal the findings of a report by a mission from the European Union (EU) to examine the country's electoral process. Later that month the CAR, the UFC and the Parti pour la démocratie et le renouveau organized a demonstration in the capital, which reportedly received the support of some 12,000 people, in protest at the new electoral law and condemning the government's preparations for the forthcoming presidential election as fraudulent.

In January 1998 students at the country's university in Lomé staged a three-day strike in protest at the excessive force employed by the security forces in dispersing an earlier demonstration by students, held on the university campus, in support of demands for the payment of educational grants. In February Eyadéma reorganized the council of ministers.

Electoral Controversies

In March 1998 the government announced that the presidential election would take place on 7 June. In April the RPT nominated Eyadéma as its presidential candidate. In the same month the leader of the UFC, Gilchrist Olympio, returned from exile in Ghana and announced his candidacy. Following a postponement, the presidential election eventually took place on 21 June amid accusations of harassment and electoral malpractice. On the following day, as early voting figures indicated that Eyadéma might lose the election, the vote count was suspended. On 23 June five members of the national electoral commission, including the chairman, resigned as the result of pressure and intimidation concerning the outcome of the ballot. The vote count was not resumed, and on 24 June the minister of the interior and security, Col Seyi Memene, declared Eyadéma to have won the election with 52.13% of the vote. EU observers expressed serious concern at the suspension of the vote count and called on the Togolese authorities to complete the process. Monitors reported that Olympio had received a greater share of the vote than Eyadéma in much of Lomé, and, according to many observers, all indications were of a victory for Olympio. Supporters of the UFC staged demonstrations in the capital in protest at the results, which they claimed to be fraudulent, prompting the government to impose a ban on all organized protests.

In mid-August 1998 armed attacks on an army post and a police station near the border with Ghana were blamed by the authorities on supporters of Gilchrist Olympio. Olympio, however, speaking from Ghana, accused the government of exploiting the disturbances to attack the opposition, noting that during the disturbances the residence of two UFC leaders and the party headquarters had been ransacked. The PDR also reported that its headquarters in Sokodé and a party official's house in Bafilo had been damaged by explosions.

In September 1998 Klutse announced his new council of ministers. Despite Eyadéma's stated desire for a government of national unity, no opposition figures were willing to be included, and few new appointments were made. In November the government survived a vote of no confidence tabled by the CAR and the UTD in response to the government's economic action programme for 1998/99. In the same month Olympio called on Eyadéma to resign, offering to concede defeat at the June presidential elections and not to stand in future elections, if he did so.

In January 1999 the government announced that the first round of legislative elections would take place on 7 March. In February the opposition parties called for discussions with the government prior to the elections, on the grounds that the issue of the disputed presidential elections should be settled before legislative elections were held. The government, however, insisted that the elections be held in accordance with the time limit imposed by the constitution, although it agreed to postpone the elections until later in March. The government rejected the opposition's suggestion that the constitution should be amended in order to allow the extension of the incumbent assemblée nationale's mandate, and the main opposition parties therefore announced that they would boycott the elections and instruct their supporters not to vote.

Elections took place on 21 March 1999, and were contested by the RPT, by twelve independent candidates, and by two small parties loyal to Eyadéma, the Coordination nationale des forces nouvelles and the Parti pan-africain écologiste. The constitutional court ruled that the RPT had won 77 seats, and that independent candidates had taken two seats, while fresh elections were scheduled in two constituencies. Turnout was estimated at 66%, although the opposition estimated that it was little more than 10%. Despite international criticism, Eyadéma rejected calls for fresh elections, declaring that the opposition

had been afforded ample opportunity to participate. In mid-April Klutse tendered his government's resignation, and in late May Eugene Koffi Adogboli, a former UN official, was appointed prime minister. In June Adogboli appointed a new council of ministers dominated by long-term supporters of Eyadéma.

In April 1999 the editor of the weekly newspaper *Le Reporter*, Romain Koudjodji, was arrested after he had published an article alleging that the security forces had tortured an opposition activist. At his trial in late June Koudjodji was ordered to pay a fine of one million francs CFA and was given a two-month suspended sentence. Following Koudjodji's arrest, the government issued a warning to journalists not to report unsubstantiated slurs on private citizens and on the authorities. In the same month two journalists were released after nine months' detention imposed for 'spreading false news that threatened the honour of the head of state and his wife'.

In May 1999 four international facilitators, representing France, Germany, the EU and La Francophonie arrived in Lomé to hold talks with the government and the opposition. Discussions began in Lomé in mid-July, following an initial meeting in Paris to discuss the security concerns of opposition delegates. Gilchrist Olympio, who had arrived late for talks, citing unresolved security concerns, subsequently demanded that his party, the UFC, should meet government representatives separately, to resolve the issue of the disputed presidential elections. His proposal was rejected as unhelpful and divisive by both the government and the opposition, and Olympio therefore withdrew from discussions and returned to Ghana. The UFC, however, continued to be represented in the discussions. Eyadéma's announcement, reportedly advocated by President Chirac of France, that he would not stand for re-election, and that new legislative elections would be held in 2000, was widely credited with breaking the deadlock in negotiations, and, after the opposition had agreed to accept Eyadéma's victory in the presidential elections, an accord was signed on 29 July by all the parties involved in negotiations, including the UFC. The accord made provision for the creation of an independent electoral body, which was to create a definitive electoral register, and for the creation of a code of conduct to regulate political activity. The accord also called for the dissolution of militias, and the collection of illegally held weapons. The accord, described by Eyadéma as 'turning a fresh page in the history of Togo', was well received in Togo and by the international community.

In early August 1999 the first meeting was held of the 24-member committee, composed equally of opposition and pro-Eyadéma representatives, responsible for the implementation of the accord. At the same time, the government launched a campaign to gather illegal weapons. In early September talks on the mechanism for announcing election results broke down, and several opposition parties withdrew from the discussions. Despite the reservations of the UFC, a compromise agreement was subsequently reached in late September, while in December agreement was reached on a revised electoral code, providing for the establishment of an independent electoral commission. However, the refusal in January 2000 of the RPT-dominated assemblée nationale to adopt the revised electoral code, caused the UFC, the CAR and the Convention démocratique des peuples africains (CDPA) to withdraw from further discussions, claiming that little political will for change existed in government circles. In April, however, Eyadéma obliged the assemblée nationale to accept the new electoral code, and announced that there was now no obstacle to the creation of an independent electoral commission. The three parties therefore returned to negotiations, and preparations continued for the legislative elections, scheduled for later in 2000. The EU, which expressed its satisfaction at the adoption of the electoral code, later offered to provide financial support for the elections.

In January 2000 the government amended legislation regulating the press, introducing terms of imprisonment and substantial fines for those found guilty of violating the press code, as well as the seizure and destruction of the offending publication, and the possible suspension of the publication's future activities. The new regulations were widely condemned as detrimental to the freedom of the press, and the publisher's association subsequently undertook a protest strike. The week-long strike also demanded the release of the director of the weekly newspaper *L'Aurore*, who had been detained by the security forces. In April UFC activists were reported to have attacked a meeting of state media workers, who they accused of systematic disinformation. In the same month the editor of the weekly newspaper *L'Exile* was arrested and charged with slander after publishing a report suggesting that one of Eyadéma's children had been killed in a car accident. Other senior journalists subsequently went into hiding in order, they alleged, to evade arrest.

In April 2000 the committee responsible for implementing the accord began discussions regarding the appointment of an independent electoral commission, and in May the opposition accused the government of delaying the process. The authorities, however, blamed the delays on the opposition parties' temporary withdrawal from discussions in January. The 20 members of the new independent electoral commission were finally named in June, and it was confirmed at the same time that fresh legislative elections would be held later in 2000.

In May 2000 Gilchrist Olympio's cousin, Henry Octavianus Olympio, the minister for human rights and the promotion of democracy, announced that he had survived an attempted assassination attempt. However, in June Olympio was removed from his post, after evidence was discovered which indicated that he had himself engineered the supposed assassination attempt. The portfolios of human rights and the promotion of democracy were subsequently assimilated into that of justice.

In August 2000, after the prime minister had presented his report on his government's activities in the previous year to the assemblée nationale, several deputies, who felt that Adogboli had not met the promises made at the time of his appointment, called for a vote of no confidence in his premiership. Adogboli was overwhelmingly defeated in the vote, and therefore, in accordance with the constitution, he presented his resignation and that of his government to Eyadéma. The resignation of Adogboli, described in the independent press as 'the most mediocre prime minister of the fourth republic', was widely welcomed in Togo. In late August Eyadéma, appointed Kodjo Agbéyomè, hitherto the president of the assemblée nationale, as prime minister, and requested that the current council of ministers expedite their current business in order to permit the appointment of a new administration.

HUMAN RIGHTS ISSUES

In early May 1999 Amnesty International published a report detailing numerous abuses of human rights allegedly committed by the security forces in Togo. The report described Togo as 'ruled by terror', and claimed that hundreds of political opponents of Eyadéma had been killed following the 1998 presidential elections. The government reacted with indignation to the report, and threatened to institute legal proceedings against Amnesty International. In early May four human rights activists, all of whom were members of the opposition CDPA, were detained by the authorities, accused of providing Amnesty with false information. Opposition parties and human rights organizations held a protest march later in the month in order to demand the release of the detainees, while the CDPA declared that it would not participate in reconciliation talks with the government until its members were released. The four men were subsequently released on bail in mid-June. In the same month Amnesty accused the Togolese security forces of the detention and torture of one of their members, Amen Ayodole, a Nigerian who had presented his membership card at the Togolese border as a form of identification. The authorities, however, claimed that Ayodole had been detained on suspicion of drugs-smuggling. In the same month Eyadéma met with a French legal team, led by Jacques Verges, with a view to instituting legal proceedings against Amnesty.

In July 1999 a human rights organization in Benin reported that, following the 1998 presidential elections in Togo, corpses had been discovered on the beaches of Benin. The government of Benin, however, stated that it had received no such intelligence, and called for witnesses to come forward with evidence. Amnesty also appealed for evidence of human rights abuses, which could be presented if Eyadéma was to take the case to court. In late July Eyadéma agreed to the establishment of an international commission of inquiry into the allegations, and he urged the UN and the Organization of African Unity to assist

in the creation of a suitable independent body. A commission of inquiry was subsequently established in June 2000.

FOREIGN RELATIONS

The issue of Ewe reunification has at times led to difficult relations with Ghana. President Nkrumah assisted Togo in its campaign for independence but with the intention of integrating Togo into Ghana. When this objective failed, Nkrumah subjected Togo to constant harassments, through trade embargoes and border closures. Relations improved after the assassination of Olympio, and Nkrumah was the first to recognize the new government. However, relations between the two countries deteriorated as Togo's political crisis of the early 1990s intensified, and the presence of Togolese opposition leaders in Ghana prompted renewed suspicion in Lomé that the Ghanaian authorities were supporting elements that might seek to destabilize the Eyadéma regime. In January 1993 the Ghanaian government criticized Eyadéma and expressed fears of a breakdown in law and order in Togo. In March of that year, and again in January 1994, the Rawlings administration in Ghana refuted allegations made by the Togolese government of Ghanaian complicity in armed attacks on Eyadéma's residence (see above).

By late 1994 relations with Ghana had improved considerably. In November full diplomatic relations, suspended since 1982, were formally resumed, and in the following month Togo's border with Ghana, which had been closed since January 1994, was reopened. In July 1995, following talks between Eyadéma and Rawlings, a communiqué was issued reiterating both countries' adherence to a protocol of non-aggression between Economic Community of West African States (ECOWAS) member states. In addition, agreement was reached providing for the reactivation of the Ghana-Togo joint commission for economic, social and technical co-operation and the Ghana-Togo border demarcation commission. Relations were further strengthened by the two governments' successful co-operation following the August 1998 attacks on Togolese targets. However, in June 1999 the Ghanaian authorities were reported to be investigating allegations of an incursion by Togolese aircraft into Ghanaian airspace, while in August the joint border commission received complaints that Togolese farmers had crossed into Ghanaian territory. A Togolese delegation subsequently visited Ghana to tour the disputed areas. Following the visit, Togo apologized for the incursion into Ghanaian airspace, and both sides expressed their resolve to settle disputes amicably. In November, at a meeting in Lomé, the ministers of the interior of Togo and Ghana called for an atmosphere of calm and understanding to prevail in relations between the two countries.

Relations with Benin have similarly been bedevilled by the problems of smuggling and political activities by exiles, and the border between the two countries has frequently been closed. In March 1993 the Eyadéma regime criticized the government of Benin for allowing Togolese opposition leaders to meet on Beninois territory. Some 100,000 Togolese refugees were believed to be sheltering in Benin in mid-1993. In November 1994, following a visit by the president of Benin in the previous month, the Benin-Togo border demarcation commission, which had been dormant since 1978, resumed its activities. In August 1995 Togo signed an accord with the UN High Commissioner for Refugees, providing for the introduction of a programme of voluntary repatriation of Togolese exiles from Ghana and Benin. By December 1996 some 40,500 Togolese exiles, of an estimated total of 48,000, had reportedly been repatriated from Ghana.

Relations with France, which were frequently strained in the 1980s and early 1990s by the uneasy relationship between the Eyadéma regime and the socialist administration in France, have improved in recent years. The victory of centre-right parties in the French legislative elections of March 1993 prompted speculation that the new government might display a more conciliatory attitude towards the Eyadéma regime, and in June 1994 France announced that it was to resume civil co-operation with Togo. Relations improved further with the election in 1995 of Jacques Chirac as French president, who while remaining supportive of Eyadéma, has sought to encourage political dialogue and increased democratization in Togo. In 1998 the French authorities criticized the lack of opposition participation in the legislative elections, and in June 1999 the French government hosted talks in Paris between the government and opposition groups, which led to an agreement to hold further talks in Lomé in July. In July, while on an official visit to West Africa, Chirac visited Lomé and met the participants in the reconciliation talks. Gilchrist Olympio, however, refused to meet Chirac, accusing him of favouring Eyadéma. Prior to his visit to Togo, Chirac received an open letter from Amnesty International, asking him to exert pressure on Eyadéma to improve Togo's record on human rights, which Amnesty had recently criticized in a published report. Chirac, however, condemned Amnesty's report as a 'manipulation', and vigorously denied accusations of French complicity in Togolese abuses.

From mid-1998 in his capacity as chairman of the authority of heads of state and government of ECOWAS, Eyadéma mediated in the conflict in Guinea-Bissau. A contingent of Togolese troops was sent to Guinea-Bissau as part of the ECOWAS ceasefire monitoring group, and a peace conference was held in Lomé in February. In June, after the failure of the peace agreement, the Togolese contingent withdrew from Guinea-Bissau. Eyadéma has also mediated in the conflict in Sierra Leone. In March

1999 Eyadéma met the rebel leader, Foday Sankoh, in Togo, and in April he hosted talks between the rebel factions, which preceded peace negotiations with the Sierra Leone government in late May. A peace agreement was concluded in Lomé in July, in the presence of Eyadéma and other regional leaders.

In mid-2000 Eyadéma denied UN accusations that Togo had violated UN sanctions on trade in Angolan diamonds produced in rebel held territory. In September, however, the government agreed to ban the sale of Angolan diamonds lacking a certificate of authenticity.

With the escalation of the political crisis in Togo in 1992–93, many of Togo's external creditors, including France, Germany, the USA and the EC (European Community, now the EU), attempted (with limited success) to exert political pressure on Eyadéma and Koffigoh by withdrawing all but the most urgent economic assistance. By March 1995 the majority of Togo's external creditors, with the exception of the EU, had resumed co-operation, although in most cases aid was again suspended following the disputed presidential election in 1998.

Economy

EDITH HODGKINSON

Revised for this edition by the Editor

At independence in 1960, Togo's economy, compared with those of most of its neighbours, was relatively advanced. Moreover, the country possessed the potential for sustained economic growth. In recent years, however, the economy has declined to such an extent that Togo is now classified as a least developed country, and is experiencing difficulties in servicing a foreign debt acquired in earlier, more prosperous, times.

In the years following independence, rates of population growth and urbanization have continued at a high level. The population was estimated at 4,397,000 at mid-1998 (representing a fairly high population density of 77.4 per sq km), of whom 32% were living in urban areas. According to World Bank estimates, annual population growth in 1990–97 averaged 3.0%. In most years there is seasonal migration, of around 100,000 Togolese annually, to neighbouring Ghana. The escalation of the political crisis in late 1992 prompted large numbers of Togolese to flee to Ghana and Benin, and by mid-1993 the population was estimated to have fallen by more than 400,000. Thousands of refugees have since returned.

In 1997, according to estimates by the World Bank, Togo's gross national product (GNP), measured at average 1995–97 prices, was US $1,485m., equivalent to $300 per head. Economic growth, which had eased off in the early 1960s (only just keeping pace with population growth, compared with 1948–60's average annual growth of 5%), accelerated again, to an average of 4.5% per year in 1965–80, as development programmes took effect. However, the severe economic problems which beset the country during the 1980s (see below) reduced growth in gross domestic product (GDP) to an average of 0.5% per year in 1981–90. Compared with the 6.5% average annual growth target set in the 1981–85 Development Plan, GDP is estimated to have fallen each year in 1981–83 because of drought, the slump in phosphate production, the recession in neighbouring economies, and measures of economic adjustment in response to these adverse trends. The end of the drought in 1984 and the upturn in phosphate production caused GDP to increase by 5.5% in that year and by 3.1% in 1985, but growth rates declined again in the following two years, to 2.2% and 1.5% respectively, as a result of lower international prices for the country's major commodities and the impact of fiscal austerity on development expenditure and on overall demand. However, there was an upturn, to 4.7%, in 1988, reflecting increases in both production of and international prices for phosphates and an easing in the financing constraint following the rescheduling of the public debt (see below). The rate of growth declined to 3.2% in 1989, and GDP fell by 1% in 1990, as a result of the decline in the volume of cash crops and other primary commodities, in conjunction with the decline in

world prices for Togo's export commodities. Although the three-year programme of economic reform that was adopted in 1989 (with support from IMF funds) projected average real GDP growth of more than 4% annually, GDP continued to contract: a decline of an estimated 5% in 1991 was followed by falls of 10.5% in 1992 and 13.7% in 1993, as political unrest disrupted agricultural distribution and phosphate production. Foreign aid and investment flows (on which the economy is heavily reliant) also declined dramatically in response to the political unrest, severely weakening the country's fiscal and external payments position. In January 1994 the franc CFA underwent a 50% devaluation, and in mid-year the government adopted a comprehensive adjustment strategy. The resultant increase in economic activity led to real GDP growth of 13.9% in that year, although this represented little more than economic recovery from the disastrous downturns of 1992–93. Further GDP growth of 7.2% was recorded in 1995, owing largely to improved performances in the mining and manufacturing sectors. Growth in these sectors slowed in 1996 but was partially offset by a recovery in the cash-crop sector which contributed to GDP growth of 6%. According to the IMF, real GDP growth was 4.3% in 1997. In 1998 real GDP was estimated to have declined by 1%. It was, however, hoped that a recovery in the agricultural sector and the stabilization of the banking sector would contribute to a return to growth in 1999 and 2000, and that renewed economic growth would enable further economic reform, including the implementation of the delayed privatization programme, and the government's 2000 budget therefore envisaged GDP growth of 3.6% in 1999 and 2000.

AGRICULTURE

Agriculture is by far the dominant economic activity, accounting for 42.1% of GDP and for 61.2% of the working population in 1998. However, after rising rapidly in the mid-1960s, agricultural output grew slowly in the 1970s, and the drought of 1981–83 resulted in an average annual decline in output of 1% in the following five years. In non-drought years Togo is self-sufficient in basic foodstuffs. According to official estimates, the yam crop totalled 630,000 metric tons in 1997/98, while production of manioc was 571,000 tons, maize 452,000 tons, millet and sorghum 223,000 tons and rice 41,000 tons. Food supplies are supplemented by fishing, but Togo's narrow coastline constrains activity, which is mainly artisanal. None the less, modern vessels are used, although the total catch—14,300 tons in 1997—is insufficient to satisfy domestic demand. The livestock sector contributes to—but does not satisfy—the local meat and dairy market. Livestock numbers in 1998, according to FAO figures, were 740,000 sheep, 1.1m. goats, 850,000 pigs and 223,000 cattle.

Production in the cash-crop sector has, on the whole, recovered after the decline recorded in the mid-1970s. The most important contribution has come from cotton, which is now the country's principal export crop. After falling to negligible levels in the second half of the 1970s, output of seed cotton rose strongly, reaching 100,247 tons in 1990/91, reflecting increases in the area under cultivation. However, owing to political disruption, output in 1991/92 declined to an estimated 90,000 tons, contracting further to 65,000 tons in 1992/93, before recovering in 1993/94 to 84,500 tons. Favourable growing conditions and strong world prices resulted in expanding production in 1994/95, when output reached 125,700 tons. In 1995/96 production declined to 102,000 tons, amid fears of soil depletion. In 1997/98, however, production recovered to 176,000 tons, and it was hoped that the harvest would amount to 200,000 tons in 1998/99.

Coffee output fluctuated widely in the 1980s, reaching a low of 2,701 tons in 1983/84, but recovered strongly in 1989/90, reaching a record 16,100 tons (reflecting the improvement in climatic conditions, the impact of replanting programmes, and higher producer prices). Production then declined, by 40%, to 9,653 tons, in 1990/91 before recovering to an estimated 12,000 tons in 1991/92. Coffee production failed to respond to the increase in nominal producer prices following the devaluation of the currency in 1994, and, according to official estimates, declined to some 5,000 tons in 1996. According to the FAO, coffee production amounted to 12,000 tons in 1997. Groundnut production has also fluctuated markedly, from a peak of 19,561 tons in 1986/87 to about 9,000 tons in 1990/91. In 1997/98, according to official estimates, groundnut production totalled 58,000 tons. Similarly, output of shea-nuts (karité nuts) varies enormously, although the bulk goes to subsistence consumption and therefore is not recorded. From a peak of 28,200 tons in 1971/72, output of cocoa beans has since declined, and by the late 1980s averaged less than 9,000 tons a year. According to FAO estimates output has remained low in the 1990s, at about 5,000 tons annually, owing largely to the ageing of cocoa bushes, which consequently produce lower yields. (It must also be borne in mind that production figures are greatly distorted by the smuggling of cocoa from Ghana.)

The government's agricultural development programme has received substantial foreign support, including grants from the European Development Fund (EDF), and France's Fonds d'aide et de coopération (FAC) for the development of coffee, cocoa and cotton production in the south, the most developed area. The World Bank has also provided US $9.5m. for this area, and credits have come from the International Development Association (IDA) for rural development projects, intended to increase the area under cultivation and to introduce cotton, maize, sorghum and groundnut crops. It is also planned to develop irrigated agriculture—rice, sugar cane, fruits and vegetables. The Anié sugar complex, in central Togo, was inaugurated in 1987. The complex has the capacity to refine 60,000 tons of sugar cane annually. Other projects intend to increase self-sufficiency in animal protein by encouraging the rearing of cattle, pigs and poultry.

MINING AND POWER

Traditionally the main stimulus to Togo's exports—and overall economic growth—has come from phosphate mining. Phosphates were discovered in Togo in 1952, and exports began in 1961. Togo's phosphate deposits are the richest in the world, with a mineral content of 81%. Reserves of first-grade ore are estimated at 260m. tons, while there are more than 1,000m. tons of carbon phosphates, which, although of a lower quality, have the advantage of a significantly lower cadmium content (see below). The country now ranks fifth among the world's producers of calcium phosphates, and they accounted for almost half of Togo's domestic export receipts (excluding re-exports) in 1991. However, with the relatively rapid growth of cotton and non-traditional exports since 1994 Togo's dependence on phosphate exports has declined; phosphates accounted for an estimated 30.7% of domestic exports in 1996. Exports of phosphates from the reserves at Akoupamé and Hahoté by the Compagnie togolaise des mines du Bénin (CTMB), subsequently merged into the Office togolais des phosphates (OTP), rose from 199,000

tons in 1962 to 2.6m. tons in 1974. In 1974 the government nationalized the company, in which it previously had a 35% holding. When, in the following year, prices slumped, owing to the energy crisis and a fall in world demand, Togolese phosphate rock's high quality made it more difficult to place on the market, and production fell to 1.1m. tons. Demand subsequently recovered, and production was around 2.9m. tons per year in 1977–80. Additional treatment and recovery plant costing 4,000m. francs CFA, financed by Arab and French interests, brought total annual capacity to 3.6m. tons in 1980, but the downturn in demand for Togo's relatively high-priced ore in 1981 caused the extra capacity to be closed in that year, and production declined to only 2.01m. tons in 1982. There was a subsequent recovery in foreign demand, and output reached 3.36m. tons in 1989, stimulated by the strength of international prices for phosphates; however, production declined by 27% in 1990, to just 2.44m. tons. Following a recovery to 2.96m. tons in 1991, output declined once more, to 2.03m. tons in 1992. With the mine out of operation for much of the first half of 1993, owing to the general strike, output was reduced to only 1.79m. tons in that year. Output recovered in 1994 to 2.12m. tons and increased to 2.59m. tons in 1995, 2.73m. tons in 1996 and 2.63m. tons in 1997. In 1997 OTP exports of phosphates via Lomé port totalled 2.9m. tons, an increase of 33% compared with 1996. Revenue from exports of phosphates was reported to have totalled 57,600m. francs CFA in 1997.

The future development of the phosphate-mining sector may be adversely affected by concerns regarding the high cadmium content of Togolese phosphates. The European Union (EU), which has banned the agricultural use of certain categories of phosphate fertilizers, is to provide the OTP with funds for the research and development of sources of phosphates with a lower cadmium content. After lengthy negotiations with creditors, the government agreed to open the heavily indebted OTP to private ownership, and in 1997 a 38% share in the company's capital was offered for sale.

Togo also possesses extensive limestone reserves (some 200m. tons), utilization of which began in 1981 at a large-scale cement plant run by Ciments de l'Afrique de l'ouest (CIMAO), with an output of 600,000 tons of clinker (one-half of capacity). It was hoped to increase annual output to 1.8m. tons during the 1981–85 Plan period. The governments of Ghana and Côte d'Ivoire, as well as French, British and Canadian interests, participated in the scheme, which cost US $285m. Credits were provided by the World Bank and the European Investment Bank (EIB), but the programme was cut back in 1984 and CIMAO went into liquidation in March 1989. However, the construction industry revived in the following two years, with continued work on the Nangbeto dam (see below) and on offices of the regional central bank and the Economic Community of West African States. Cement production has therefore continued under the Société des ciments du Togo (CIMTOGO), a parastatal organization operated in co-operation with Norwegian interests, with an annual capacity of 780,000 tons. Exploitation of reserves of marble at Gnaoulou and Pagola (estimated at 20m. tons) began in 1970 by the Société togolaise de marbrerie (now restructured and operating, with Norwegian participation, as the Nouvelle société togolaise de marbrerie et de matériaux). In early 1999 it was reported that deposits of petroleum and gas had been discovered in Togolese territorial waters by Petroleum Geo-Service of Norway. Subject to a favourable assessment of the deposits' commercial viability, petroleum production was expected to commence by the end of 1999. Mining and quarrying accounted for 5.6% of GDP in 1997. The GDP of the mining sector increased by an annual average of 3.4% in 1982–91, but declined by an estimated annual average of 3.2% in 1991–95; according to the IMF, mining GDP increased by 9.3% in 1996.

Electricity was, in the past, generated mainly at a thermal plant in Lomé and a small hydroelectric installation at Kpalimé, built with Yugoslav assistance. Togo formerly derived electric power principally from the Akosombo hydroelectric installation in Ghana. Beginning in 1988, however, supplies were enhanced by the 65 MW hydroelectric plant at Nangbeto, on the Mono river, constructed in co-operation with Benin. The project, which cost US $144m., received financial support from multilateral agencies (the IDA, the African Development Bank (ADB), the Arab Bank for Economic Development in Africa, and the OPEC

Fund for International Development) and from Kuwait, France, the Federal Republic of Germany and Canada. The plant has a maximum capacity of 150m. kWh, and also provides irrigation for 43,000 ha of land. Total domestic electricity generation was 35m. kWh in 1996, when a further 349.3m. kWh was purchased from Benin. Total electricity consumption in that year was 263.1m. kWh.

In 1998 Togo experienced a serious shortage of electricity that obliged the Compagnie Energie Electrique du Togo (CEET) to impose rationing of power supplies in and around Lomé. The shortage arose owing to a dispute between Togo and Ghana — on which Togo depends for 70% of its electricity supplies — over the distribution of electricity from Côte d'Ivoire. Togo is seeking to gain greater control over its supply of domestic production facilities. In early 1998 the Banque Ouest-Africaine de Développement (BOAD), the European Union and Germany granted Togo loans in order to alleviate the energy crisis. In August 1999 six companies including Chevron, Royal Dutch Shell, and the Société Togolaise de Gaz concluded arrangements to construct a US $400m. pipeline, which will supply natural gas from Nigeria to Togo, Benin and Ghana. A governmental agreement on the pipeline was reached in February 2000. The pipeline is scheduled for completion in 2002, and it is hoped that it will solve the problem of shortages in the region, which had been expected to become increasingly severe due to receding water levels in Lake Volta, which feeds the Akasombo hydroelectric dam.

In 2000 the management of the CEET was ceded to a consortium consisting of Hydro-Québec of Canada and ELYO of France under a 20-year contract. The government was, however, to retain control of the company.

INDUSTRY

The manufacturing sector is small and relatively undeveloped, accounting for 8.6% of GDP in 1997, but it has shown some expansion in recent years. Manufacturing was, in the past, centred on the processing of agricultural commodities (palm oil extraction, coffee roasting, cassava flour milling, and cotton ginning) and import substitution of consumer goods—textiles, footwear, beverages, confectionery, salt and tyres. During the 1970s, however, major investments were made in a number of heavy industrial schemes, including the CIMAO cement plant (see above) and a petroleum refinery at Lomé with an annual capacity of 250,000 tons, which closed in 1983. A steel works (Société nationale de sidérurgie) with a capacity of 20,000 tons per year started production in 1979, but was liquidated in 1992. An integrated textile mill, which cost 10,000m. francs CFA and has a capacity of 24,000 tons per year, began operations at Kara in 1981, and the expansion of domestic cotton production led to the establishment of two further plants, at Notse and Atakpamé. A new cotton-ginning plant was inaugurated at Talo in January 1991, with a total capacity of 50,000 tons of seed cotton per year. Total investment, of 3,000m. francs CFA, was provided by France and the Banque Ouest-Africaine de Développement. By 1999 Togo had a total cotton-ginning capacity of 150,000 tons, of which 110,000 tons was located in state-owned factories. It was reported in early 1999 that Continental Eagle of the USA planned to construct a new cotton-ginning plant in central Togo, with a capacity of 40,000 tons. At early 1999 some 230,000 Togolese were reported to depend on the cotton sector for their livelihoods. New palm oil mills have been installed, including one with EU funds equivalent to ECU 5.4m., to complement the development of plantations. On the whole, however, the industrialization programme of the late 1970s proved to be an expensive failure, and large-scale projects have not featured in subsequent plans. In order to improve economic efficiency and reduce the fiscal burden of financing unproductive investments, the government has gradually withdrawn from its dominant role in the productive sectors. It has sold (either wholly or partially) or leased a number of state enterprises to the private sector as well as liquidating the most unprofitable ventures. By the end of 1990 the assets of 30 companies had been transferred to private ownership, and 18 others were intended for privatization. Following the resumption of the economic reform programme in 1994, there were renewed efforts to further the privatization process; the government has continued to reduce its holdings in a number of hotels, in cement production and in agri-processing (the most significant privatization being the ongoing divestment of the OTP—see above). Meanwhile, it was expected that manufacturing aimed at export markets would be stimulated by the establishment of a free-trade zone at Lomé, which was inaugurated in 1990. By the end of 1991 15 companies had invested some 56,000m. francs CFA in the zone; most of these, however, suspended operations during 1992–93, owing to the political upheaval. In 1994 the government resumed the promotion of its free-trade zone project, and by mid-1996 some 30 companies were operating in the zone, with a further 20 companies in the process of being established.

TRANSPORT AND TOURISM

Communications are made difficult by the country's long, narrow shape. However, the road network (7,520 km in 1996, of which 2,376 km were paved) is currently being improved, with aid from the EDF, IDA and FAC. The 1981–85 Plan projected investment of 8,000m. francs CFA in this sector, mainly to improve the north-south highway and to develop the east-west route via Kara. Of the US $310m. scheduled for the improvement of the transport infrastructure in 1988–90, $217m. was to be devoted to the rehabilitation and maintenance of the road network. The railways, with 517 km of track, are generally in need of modernization, and two lines, to Palimé and Aného, have been closed to passenger traffic. The port of Lomé handled about 2m. tons of freight per year in the late 1980s and early 1990s, following an increase in its capacity at the beginning of the 1980s, which afforded new facilities for handling minerals and for fishing. However, hopes of attracting a greater volume of regional transit trade from land-locked west African countries such as Mali, Niger, and Burkina Faso have been disappointed because of the recession in these economies in recent years. During the Sahel drought of the early 1980s Lomé served as a major shipment point for food aid, and work began there in 1986 on the first bulk grain trans-shipping facility in west Africa. The level of freight handled declined to 1.8m. tons in 1992 and to 1.1m. tons in 1993, as the political crisis in Togo resulted in the diversion of a large proportion of transit trade to Benin. The level of freight handled stood at 0.9m. tons in 1994, but recovered to 1.3m. tons in 1995 and 1996, and to 1.7m. tons in 1997. In 1995 the Banque Ouest-Africaine de Développement approved a loan of 5,000m. francs CFA to help finance the rehabilitation of the infrastructure at Lomé port. There are international airports at Tokoin, near Lomé, and at Niamtougou, in the north of the country, as well as several smaller airfields.

Tourism, formerly a major source of foreign exchange, suffered from the economic downturn of the 1980s and, above all, from the political crisis of the early 1990s. Visitor numbers, which reached a record 143,000 in 1982, declined to a low of 22,244 in 1993, but recovered to 69,500 in 1998. The privatization of most state-owned hotels was initiated in early 1997, following studies into the restructuring of the sector by the government and the World Bank. In 1997 the hotel sector employed 1,575 people, and in that year the sector's estimated revenue was 7,442,000m. francs CFA, although revenue declined to 5,612,000m. in 1998. In addition to recreational tourism, efforts have been made to promote Togo as an international conference centre, for which the country is reasonably well equipped.

DEVELOPMENT AND FINANCE

In the past, Togo's official investment targets have been attained or even exceeded, but in the late 1970s, as the result of a deterioration in the country's economic situation (owing mainly to a decline in international prices for phosphates), development spending had to be reduced as part of the government's austerity programme. The 1976–80 Plan provided for total investment of 250,600m. francs CFA, of which just over one-third was projected to come from foreign official sources. However, expenditure fell considerably short of these projections and averaged around three-quarters of the original target.

The 1981–85 Plan projected investment, under a priority programme, at the same level as in 1976–80, which meant a reduction of about one-third in real terms, with infrastructure receiving 74,100m. francs CFA, industry 73,400m. and rural development 66,600m. A supplementary 'optional' programme provided for an additional 117,500m. francs CFA in development spending. Foreign aid was expected to cover two-thirds of the programme. In view of Togo's payments difficulties (see below), this latter projection was over-optimistic, while the downturn in phosphate production since 1980, and the budget cuts (see below), meant that the development programme was behind schedule. Reflecting the influence of the IMF, the six-year Development Plan for 1985–90 involved relatively modest targets: an average rise in real GNP of 1.9% per year, and an absence of new investment projects in favour of the maintenance and rehabilitation of existing ones. Proposed spending on national projects was 360,800m. francs CFA (with infrastructure allocated 53% of the total, and rural development 35%), while a further 19,200m. francs CFA was allocated to small-scale local projects, and 88,000m. to support the balance of payments and budgetary operations. Total planned spending was 468,000m. francs CFA, almost 90% of which, it was hoped, was to be covered by foreign sources. By the late 1980s, however, funding at this level had not been procured, rendering the investment target unattainable.

One of the major objectives of the Development Plans has been the strengthening of the government's revenue position. Togo was able to finance a rising capital programme in the 1970s because of the strong expansion in budget revenue, largely owing to higher receipts from phosphate mining and indirect taxation. However, the worsening in the payments situation since 1978 (see below) necessitated recourse to IMF capital support, which required, in turn, an economic stabilization programme (begun in 1979), including a reduction in the growth of spending to an average 5% per year in 1979–81, with development spending down sharply in each year. Fiscal austerity continued in 1982–84, with increases in taxation, further constraints on development spending (which remained well below the rate required under the 1981–85 Plan), and a five-year 'freeze' on public-sector salaries. These trends were scheduled to continue throughout the 1985–90 Plan period, with current spending projected to fall in real terms, as the rise in spending on salaries was kept below the rate of inflation at the same time as tax receipts increased. However, with the ending of the public-sector salary 'freeze' in January 1987, and the deterioration in state marketing finances as a result of lower commodity prices and higher producer prices, the budget deficit almost doubled in 1987, to the equivalent of 6.8% of GDP. However, the proportion was more than halved in 1988, to 3.3%, as a result of higher receipts from taxation (mostly additional import duties), strict controls on current expenditure, and a sharp decline in capital spending. The deficit was little changed in 1989 and 1990, with small increases in revenue in both years, and the primary budget (excluding interest payments) was estimated to have been almost in balance in 1991. However, with the onset of political unrest and suspension of financial support by major external creditors—to put pressure on the regime to democratize—total budget receipts declined considerably, by 8% in 1992 and by 47.4% in 1993. The situation in 1993 was exacerbated by the seven-month general strike (beginning in November 1992), which directly affected both generation and collection of revenue. The government revised its budget revenue forecast for 1993 from 90,000m. francs CFA to 50,000m. francs CFA, although the eventual out-turn was as low as 38,220m. francs CFA. Budget expenditure for 1993 was revised to 93,010m. francs CFA, with the shortfall to be met by drawing on foreign reserves. With the return to work, in the second half of 1993, of civil servants, renewed expenditure on wages, which had been reduced by the general strike, had a detrimental effect on the cash flow position. However, a complete collapse of the fiscal and financial system was avoided. By March 1995 the majority of major external creditors had resumed financial co-operation. In June the government agreed to meet civil servants' claims for wage arrears that had accrued during the general strike and were estimated to total 13,500m. francs CFA. Most arrears were paid by the end of 1996. The draft budget for 1995 balanced revenue and expenditure at 149,500m. francs CFA. The increase in revenue reflected the government's intention to improve methods of tax collection. In July the government introduced value added tax on commercial operations, replacing the general business tax, primarily in order to simplify fiscal management. However, reductions in domestic and external debt arrears, undertaken following pressure from creditors,

resulted in an overall budget deficit of 90,200m. francs CFA in 1995 (equivalent to some 6.4% of GDP). The overall budget deficit in 1996 was reduced to 46,000m. francs CFA, equivalent to 5.8% of GDP. The 1997 budget envisaged revenue of 126,020m. francs CFA and expenditure of 136,444m. francs CFA. Budget estimates for 1998 envisaged a deficit of some 12,170m. francs CFA (revenue 140,950m. francs CFA, expenditure 153,120m. francs CFA). In 1999 Togo planned to reduce the budget deficit to 11,000m. francs CFA. Revenue in that year was forecast at 144,070m. francs CFA, including 62,680m. francs CFA in customs income and 66,410m. francs CFA in tax income. Total expenditure in 1999 was forecast at 155,070m. francs CFA, an increase of 12.6% over actual spending in 1998. Of total expenditure, some 128,780m. francs CFA was allocated for the payment of civil-service salaries. Investment spending, meanwhile, was fixed at 8,500m. francs CFA.

The government's economic programme for 1997–99, supported by programmes from the IMF and World Bank, aimed to achieve sustained and diversified economic growth and a viable external position. Targets for the end of the period included real economic growth of 5.7%, while inflation was to be reduced to 3.5%, from 4.6% in 1996, and the current account deficit cut to 5.8% of GDP, from 8.5% in 1996. Reforms of the tax system and tax administration were to be continued, while expenditure was to be channelled towards the health and education sectors and the rehabilitation and maintenance of infrastructure. In May 1999 the IMF reported that, while the target for real growth in GDP had not been met in 1998 (see above), the average rate of inflation had fallen to 1%, compared with 5.3% in 1997. There had been no improvement in 1997–98 in the current account deficit, which remained equivalent to 7.3% of GDP in those years. In 1999 the IMF forecast that real growth in GDP would resume at a rate of 6.7%, that consumer price inflation would average 2.5% and that the current account deficit would increase slightly, to a figure equivalent to 7.8% of GDP.

FOREIGN TRADE AND PAYMENTS

Togo's chronic deficit on foreign trade worsened after the mid-1970s, as export earnings declined as a proportion of import spending. Despite a continuing rise in phosphate receipts (reflecting the higher volume shipped), export earnings were depressed by adverse fluctuations in cocoa production, while the import bill was rising very rapidly (more than doubling over the period 1976–78). Foreign trade registered a record deficit of US $173.8m. in 1979, with exports financing just under two-thirds of imports. The trade deficit then narrowed substantially (and in 1984 even recorded a modest surplus) as earnings from both phosphates and cocoa improved, while the level of imports was restricted by the economic adjustment programme. In 1986, with the renewed decline in international prices for Togo's export commodities, the trade deficit widened again, to $56.2m. It remained close to this level for the rest of the 1980s, with the impact of generally weak prices for export commodities offset by import restraint resulting from government policies directed at suppressing growth in domestic demand. The situation worsened considerably in 1992 and 1993, as political disorder resulted in a decrease in exports exceeding the concurrent contraction in imports, producing a deficit of $127.7m. and $111.3m. respectively, according to the IMF. However, these figures do not take into account smuggling, the importance of which would have increased substantially during the political unrest. According to IMF figures, the deficit declined to $37.1m. in 1994. In that year the principal source of imports (24.0%) was France; other major suppliers were Germany, Côte d'Ivoire and the USA. The principal market for exports was Canada (which took 17.0% of Togo's exports in that year); other significant purchasers were Bolivia, Indonesia, the Philippines and France. According to IMF figures, the trade deficit was 64,600m. francs CFA in 1995 and an estimated 3,300m. francs CFA in 1996. In 1997, according to the IMF, Togo recorded a visible trade deficit of $30.4m. (imports f.o.b. $455.2m., exports f.o.b. $424.8m.). In that year there was a deficit of $74.5m. on the current account of the balance of payments. In 1998, according to IMF estimates, Togo recorded a visible trade deficit of $31.6m. (imports f.o.b. $446.5m., exports f.o.b. $414.9m.). The deficit on the current account of the balance of payments was estimated at $74.2m. in 1998.

Since the services side of the current payments account normally shows a deficit, it is usually left to grants and loans to cover the shortfall. Togo's receipts of official development assistance (ODA) from non-communist countries and multilateral agencies have tended to be lower, and slightly less concessionary, than those of other countries in francophone west Africa. In 1986–91 the country received an annual average of US $209.4m. In 1991–95 the average declined to $168m., reflecting the impact on donor confidence of the political crisis of 1992–93. In 1991, in order to exert pressure on the Eyadéma administration to proceed towards democratic reform, France, Germany and the USA (the three leading sources of bilateral aid) suspended development aid, while military assistance from the USA and France was suspended in 1992. This contributed to a sharp deterioration in the balance of payments in 1992 and 1993, with a capital deficit of $55m. contributing to a record overall deficit of $187.5m. in 1993. An increase in export receipts and the resumption of foreign aid led to a reduction in the overall deficit to $97.1m. By 1996 ODA flows had increased to $166m., which, according to the World Bank, constituted about 12% of GDP and 85% of gross domestic investment.

Since 1993 the European Union (EU) has confined the aid it grants to Togo to 'vital projects' in disease control, sanitation and education. The bulk of the 7th European Development Fund (EDF) grant — some 31,000m. francs CFA — remains suspended, for instance, although individual EU member states, notably France, have resumed development aid. At mid-1999 there appeared to be no prospect of any resumption of aid in the near future, the EU having decided to continue to withhold its co-operation following alleged irregularities in the June 1998 Togolese presidential elections. Togo has successfully sought aid from other sources. The World Bank is now the country's principal aid donor, providing credits in support of the government's privatization and reform programme. Other significant donors are the Islamic Development Bank (IDB), of which Togo became a member in November 1998, the ADB and the African Development Fund (ADF). In May 1999 the IDA granted Togo 3,000m. francs CFA in support of the government's anti-poverty programme.

The steep rise in foreign borrowing in the late 1970s, stimulated by the commodity price increases which took place in preceding years, brought Togo's external debt to US $1,049m. at the end of 1980 (95.7% of total GNP in that year), of which $896m. was long-term public debt. Debt-rescheduling was necessary in 1979 and again in 1981 and 1983, as exports and GNP contracted and arrears accumulated. In 1982 Togo's reclassification by its official creditors as a least developed country resulted in the cancellation of one-sixth of its outstanding debt to creditor countries. In 1984 and 1985, however, the increase in the exchange value of the US dollar, in which much of Togo's foreign debt is denominated, kept the debt-service ratio at a high level (an estimated 27.3% of foreign earnings in 1985) despite a continued growth in the value of exports. This necessitated the conclusion of further rescheduling agreements, within the context of the austerity programme negotiated with the IMF and scheduled to be continued until the 1990s. Togo clearly could not service its debt at such rates, and further agreements were reached in 1988, under the terms of which the 'Paris Club' of Western official creditors agreed to reschedule all debts due to the end of that year over 16 years, with eight years' grace and with lower interest spreads. More rescheduling of official debt liabilities over a 12-month period followed, in 1989 (covering $76m.), 1990 ($184m.) and 1992, when relief was accorded on payments due on one-half of Togo's total external debt, with creditors taking the option either of cancelling 50% of payments due and rescheduling the remainder over 23 years, with a six-year grace period, or of reducing the interest rate payable on long-term debt so as to reduce the amount due by one-half. These agreements helped to reduce the debt-service ratio, in relation to the value of exports of goods and services, from 15.6% in 1989 to only 6.1% in 1992. However, political uncertainty obstructed further rescheduling agreements, while external debt, which stood at $1,339m. at the end of 1992, remained substantial in relation to the size of the economy, being equivalent to 80.6% of GNP in that year. Moreover, the devaluation of the franc CFA in January 1994 effectively doubled the external debt in local currency terms, and Togo, while it benefited from the French government's cancellation of debt following the devaluation, was unable initially to draw on the special grants and concessionary loans promised by France, the IMF and the World Bank. In September 1994 France resumed financial co-operation with Togo with the release of 26,000m. francs CFA towards economic restructuring and rural development. That month the IMF approved a series of credits, totalling $95m., in support of Togo's 1994–97 economic programme. In February 1995 the 'Paris Club' rescheduled some $237m. of Togo's debt-service obligations. In May France agreed to the cancellation of 17,000m. francs CFA of Togolese debt and to the rescheduling of a further 19,000m. francs CFA. Togo's total external debt was $1,339m. at the end of 1997, of which $1,207m. was long-term public debt. In that year the cost of debt-servicing was equivalent to 8.1% of the value of exports of goods and services.

Statistical Survey

Source (except where otherwise indicated): Direction de la Statistique, BP 118, Lomé; tel. 21-22-87.

Area and Population

AREA, POPULATION AND DENSITY

Area (sq km)	56,785*
Population (census results)	
1 March–30 April 1970	1,997,109
22 November 1981	2,703,250
Population (UN estimates at mid-year)†	
1996	4,172,000
1997	4,284,000
1998	4,397,000
Density (per sq km) at mid-1998	77.4

* 21,925 sq miles.

† Source: UN, *World Population Prospects: The 1998 Revision*.

PRINCIPAL TOWNS
(official estimates in 1997)

Lomé (capital) . . .	700,000	Kpalimé	30,000
Sokodé . . .	51,000	Kara	30,000

BIRTHS AND DEATHS (UN estimates, annual averages)

	1980–85	1985–90	1990–95
Birth rate (per 1,000). . . .	45.0	44.7	44.4
Death rate (per 1,000) . . .	15.8	15.0	15.5

Expectation of life (UN estimates, years at birth, 1990–95): 49.8 (males 48.4; females 51.4).

Source: UN, *World Population Prospects: The 1998 Revision*.

ECONOMICALLY ACTIVE POPULATION
(census of 22 November 1981)

	Males	Females	Total
Agriculture, hunting, forestry and fishing	324,870	254,491	579,361
Mining and quarrying . . .	2,781	91	2,872
Manufacturing	29,307	25,065	54,372
Electricity, gas and water . .	2,107	96	2,203
Construction.	20,847	301	21,148
Trade, restaurants and hotels. .	17,427	87,415	104,842
Transport, storage and communications . . .	20,337	529	20,866
Financing, insurance, real estate and business services . .	1,650	413	2,063
Community, social and personal services . . .	50,750	12,859	63,609
Activities not adequately defined .	14,607	6,346	20,953
Total employed . . .	484,683	387,606	872,289
Unemployed	21,666	7,588	29,254
Total labour force . . .	506,349	395,194	901,543

Mid-1998 (estimates in '000): Agriculture, etc. 1,106; Total 1,816 (Source: FAO, *Production Yearbook*).

Agriculture

PRINCIPAL CROPS ('000 metric tons)

	1996	1997	1998
Rice (paddy).	77	86	87
Maize	388	452	336
Millet	55	49	42
Sorghum	156	152	136
Sweet potatoes	5	6	6*
Cassava (Manioc) . . .	548	596	579
Yams	605	683	694
Taro (Coco yam) . . .	7	11	11*
Dry beans	43	47	24
Other pulses.	6	6	6
Groundnuts (in shell) . . .	55	34	26
Sesame seed*	2	2	2
Cottonseed*	68	86	91
Coconuts*	14	14	14
Copra*	2	2	2
Palm kernels	18	14	14
Tomatoes*	9	9	9
Other vegetables* . . .	151	151	151
Oranges*	12	12	12
Bananas*	16	16	16
Other fruit	21	21	21
Coffee (green)	15	10	13
Cocoa beans	6	6	9
Tobacco (leaves)* . . .	2	2	2
Cotton (lint)	52	65*	69

* FAO estimate(s).

Source: FAO, *Production Yearbook*.

LIVESTOCK ('000 head, year ending September)

	1996	1997	1998
Cattle	217	206	223
Sheep	841	607	740
Pigs*	850	850	850
Goats	1,091	991	1,110
Horses*	2	2	2
Asses*	3	3	3

Poultry (million): 9 in 1996; 6 in 1997; 8 in 1998.

* FAO estimates.

Source: FAO, *Production Yearbook*.

LIVESTOCK PRODUCTS (FAO estimates, '000 metric tons)

	1996	1997	1998
Beef and veal	7	7	7
Mutton and lamb . . .	3	3	3
Goat meat	4	4	5
Pig meat	12	12	12
Poultry meat	7	7	8
Cows' milk	8	8	8
Hen eggs	6	6	6

Source: FAO, *Production Yearbook*.

Forestry

ROUNDWOOD REMOVALS ('000 cubic metres, excluding bark)

	1995	1996	1997
Sawlogs, veneer logs and logs for sleepers	35	35	99
Other industrial wood*	201	212	220
Fuel wood*	2,151	2,223	2,318
Total	2,387	2,470	2,637

Source: FAO, *Yearbook of Forest Products*.

Fishing

('000 metric tons, live weight)

	1995	1996	1997
Tilapias	3.5	3.5	3.5
Other freshwater fishes	1.5	1.5	1.5
Sardinellas	0.4	0.9	1.7
European anchovy	4.8	7.1	4.8
Other marine fishes (incl. unspecified)	1.5	2.1	2.8
Total catch (incl. others)	12.2	15.1	14.3

Source: FAO, *Yearbook of Fishery Statistics*.

Mining

('000 metric tons)

	1995	1996	1997
Calcium phosphates (gross weight)	2,591.2	2,730.7	2,631.4

Source: Banque centrale des états de l'Afrique de l'ouest.

Industry

SELECTED PRODUCTS
('000 metric tons, unless otherwise indicated)

	1996	1997	1998
Wheat flour*	31	n.a.	n.a.
Palm oil*	9	7	7
Cement	402.6	420.2	555.2
Electric energy (million kWh)	384.3	412.7	413.0

* Estimates by the FAO.

Sources: mainly UN, *Industrial Commodity Statistics Yearbook*, and Banque centrale des états de l'Afrique de l'ouest.

Finance

CURRENCY AND EXCHANGE RATES

Monetary Units
100 centimes = 1 franc de la Communauté financière africaine (CFA).

Sterling, Dollar and Euro Equivalents (28 April 2000)
£1 sterling = 1,132.20 francs CFA;
US $1 = 722.02 francs CFA;
€1 = 655.96 francs CFA;
10,000 francs CFA = £8.832 = $13.850 = €15.245.

Average Exchange Rate (francs CFA per US $)
1997   583.67
1998   589.95
1999   615.70

Note: An exchange rate of 1 French franc = 50 francs CFA, established in 1948, remained in force until January 1994, when the CFA franc was devalued by 50%, with the exchange rate adjusted to 1 French franc = 100 francs CFA. This relationship to French currency remained in effect with the introduction of the euro on 1 January 1999. From that date, accordingly, a fixed exchange rate of €1 = 655.957 francs CFA has been in operation.

BUDGET (million francs CFA)

Revenue	1996	1997	1998*
Tax revenue	98,100	115,700	115,400
Direct tax revenue	34,100	34,400	30,100
Taxes on individual income and profits	8,600	11,300	9,900
Taxes on enterprises	6,700	8,400	7,800
Direct contribution of public enterprises	11,400	11,200	6,400
Other direct tax revenue	7,300	3,500	5,900
Indirect tax revenue	64,000	81,300	85,300
Taxes on goods and services	16,800	22,600	26,000
Taxes on international trade	45,500	56,900	57,400
Import duties	37,200	48,100	49,200
Other current revenue	12,300	12,800	12,200
Total	110,400	128,500	127,600

Expenditure	1996	1997	1998*
Current expenditure†	119,600	123,800	133,000
Allocated to ministries	75,300	85,300	96,600
Common expenditures	11,400	6,200	14,600
Scholarships and training	3,700	3,700	3,900
Interest on domestic debt	3,100	2,700	1,000
Contribution to state agencies	1,000	3,900	2,800
Subsidies and transfers	9,600	14,000	12,700
Extrabudgetary and other expenditure	15,600	7,900	9,300
External debt repayments	17,400	17,600	18,100
Investment expenditure	20,800	17,600	35,900
Unclassified expenditure and net lending	—	—	500
Total	157,700	159,000	187,500

* Estimates.
† Incl. adjustment.
Source: IMF, *Togo: Selected Issues* (July 1999).

INTERNATIONAL RESERVES
(US $ million at 31 December)

	1997	1998	1999
Gold*	3.8	3.7	3.7
IMF special drawing rights	—	0.1	0.2
Reserve position	0.3	0.4	0.3
Foreign exchange	118.3	117.3	121.4
Total	122.3	121.5	125.6

* Valued at market-related prices.
Source: IMF, *International Financial Statistics*.

MONEY SUPPLY ('000 million francs CFA at 31 December)

	1997	1998	1999
Currency outside banks	60.3	65.3	79.5
Demand deposits at deposit money banks	60.6	63.5	61.1
Total money (incl. others)	123.3	131.8	144.8

Source: IMF, *International Financial Statistics*.

COST OF LIVING
(Consumer price index, low-income households; base: 1996 = 100)

	1997	1998
Food, beverages and tobacco	108.3	99.0
Clothing and shoes	103.6	108.2
Housing, water, electricity and gas	102.1	103.0
Household supplies and maintenance	102.9	106.3
Transport	117.7	115.6
Entertainment	100.0	101.2
All items (incl. others)	105.3	106.3

Source: IMF, *Togo: Selected Issues* (July 1999).

NATIONAL ACCOUNTS
(million francs CFA at current prices)
Expenditure on the Gross Domestic Product

	1996	1997	1998*
Government final consumption expenditure . . .	98,100	90,200	98,800
Private final consumption expenditure . . .	620,000	754,900	760,600
Increase in stocks . . .	4,400	14,000	−300
Gross fixed capital formation . .	97,800	116,800	127,700
Total domestic expenditure	820,300	975,900	986,800
Exports of goods and services .	237,200	307,300	315,200
Less Imports of goods and services	305,900	407,800	411,400
GDP in purchasers' values . .	751,600	875,400	890,600

* Provisional figures.

Source: Banque centrale des états de l'Afrique de l'ouest.

Gross Domestic Product by Economic Activity

	1996	1997	1998*
Agriculture, hunting, forestry and fishing . . .	305,900	369,700	375,100
Mining and quarrying . .	37,800	48,200	52,100
Manufacturing	69,200	73,600	81,300
Electricity, gas and water. .	27,400	29,300	27,500
Construction. . . .	23,400	25,000	27,200
Trade, restaurants and hotels. .	134,700	155,800	151,100
Transport, storage and communications . .	41,900	47,900	47,300
Other marketable services† . .	56,900	65,300	67,000
Non-marketable services . .	54,400	60,700	62,100
GDP in purchasers' values . .	751,600	875,400	890,600

* Provisional figures.

† After deduction of imputed bank service charges.

Source: Banque centrale des états de l'Afrique de l'ouest.

BALANCE OF PAYMENTS (million francs CFA)

	1996	1997	1998
Exports of goods f.o.b. . .	440.6	422.5	420.3
Imports of goods f.o.b. . .	−567.8	−530.6	−553.5
Trade balance . . .	−127.2	−108.1	−133.2
Export of services . .	116.2	88.5	76.0
Imports of services . .	−201.4	−167.8	−149.2
Balance on goods and services	−212.3	−187.4	−206.4
Other income received . .	45.6	35.0	44.4
Other income paid . .	−72.0	−63.9	−67.7
Balance on goods, services and income . . .	−238.8	−216.3	−229.7
Current transfers received . .	106.8	120.2	101.8
Current transfers paid . .	−21.9	−20.8	−12.2
Current balance . .	−153.9	−116.9	−140.1
Capital account (net). . .	5.6	5.8	6.1
Direct investment abroad . .	−2.8	−2.5	−10.6
Direct investment from abroad .	17.3	21.0	30.2
Portfolio investment assets .	−15.8	8.7	−5.2
Portfolio investment liabilities .	21.7	2.4	11.2
Other investment assets . .	−19.2	−1.6	16.2
Other investment liabilities .	150.1	98.9	72.3
Net errors and omissions . .	−27.9	−2.7	2.7
Overall balance . . .	−24.9	13.1	−17.2

Source: IMF, *International Financial Statistics.*

External Trade

PRINCIPAL COMMODITIES (million francs CFA)

Imports c.i.f.	1996	1997	1998
Consumer goods*	113,000	158,700	169,300
Intermediate goods . .	52,900	55,200	54,600
Petroleum products . .	17,400	24,200	22,600
Capital goods	53,700	59,100	57,000
Total	237,000	297,200	303,500

Exports f.o.b.†	1996	1997	1998
Ginned cotton	49,400	62,900	60,000
Coffee	4,600	18,900	22,300
Cocoa	8,200	14,300	10,500
Phosphate	46,900	64,300	53,900
Total (incl. others) . . .	152,600	203,600	196,900

* Including goods intended for re-export.

† Not including re-exports: 40,000 in 1996; 44,400 in 1997; 47,900 in 1998.

Source: IMF, *Togo: Selected Issues* (July 1999).

PRINCIPAL TRADING PARTNERS (US $ million)

Imports c.i.f.	1992	1993	1994
Belgium-Luxembourg . .	9.5	3.2	6.8
Benin	4.7	5.4	3.3
China, People's Repub. . .	9.5	6.7	5.9
Côte d'Ivoire . . .	11.9	7.5	13.9
Denmark	2.1	1.1	2.8
France (incl. Monaco) . .	134.9	50.1	53.3
Germany	23.1	10.6	21.9
Ghana	4.3	1.8	2.0
Greece	4.5	0.7	1.1
Hong Kong . . .	11.0	8.0	7.4
Italy	10.7	5.2	6.6
Japan	20.5	8.0	7.8
Mauritania . . .	5.2	4.1	11.4
Netherlands	23.8	9.4	11.5
Nigeria . . .	9.9	9.9	5.7
Norway	1.3	1.3	3.3
Pakistan	3.2	2.0	2.0
SACU*	3.6	4.8	3.5
Spain	7.9	2.8	5.9
Thailand	4.4	1.9	0.8
United Kingdom . . .	9.1	3.2	7.5
USA	3.5	11.0	12.2
Total (incl. others) . . .	394.7	179.5	222.0

Exports f.o.b.		1992	1993	1994
Australia	. . . .	1.2	—	3.3
Belgium-Luxembourg	. .	4.2	2.7	3.3
Benin	. . .	6.2	4.4	4.3
Bolivia	. . . .	—	4.2	12.4
Brazil	. . . .	—	7.0	1.6
British Indian Ocean Territory		14.3	2.6	—
Burkina Faso	. . .	4.9	1.4	3.8
Canada	. . . .	56.2	17.9	27.5
France (incl. Monaco)	. .	14.1	6.7	8.1
Germany	. . . .	6.2	2.6	2.6
Ghana	. . . .	4.2	2.3	3.5
Greece	. . . .	3.5	1.5	2.1
India	. . . .	15.6	3.7	2.9
Indonesia	. . .	1.4	4.0	9.2
Italy	. . . .	6.4	2.0	2.5
Morocco	. . .	3.2	2.4	2.8
Netherlands	. . .	10.1	8.9	5.8
Niger	. . . .	3.5	1.1	0.6
Nigeria	. . . .	25.6	8.7	6.2
Pacific Islands (fmr Trust Territory)†	. . .	2.8	0.7	1.7
Philippines	. . .	5.4	9.8	8.8
Poland	. . . .	15.5	1.8	4.0
Portugal	. . .	1.5	1.5	2.9
SACU*	. . . .	—	—	3.6
Spain	. . . .	11.8	0.7	1.6
Thailand	. . . .	12.9	6.6	5.2
Total (incl. others)	. . .	275.0	136.0	162.2

* Southern African Customs Union, comprising Botswana, Lesotho, Namibia, South Africa and Swaziland.
† Now Marshall Islands, Federated States of Micronesia, the Northern Mariana Islands and Palau.
Source: UN, *International Trade Statistics Yearbook*.

Transport

RAILWAYS (estimated traffic)

		1996	1997	1998
Passenger-km (million)	. .	16.5	12.8	35.2
Freight (million ton-km)	. .	49.0	47.9	758.7

Source: Banque centrale des états de l'Afrique de l'ouest.

ROAD TRAFFIC (motor vehicles registered at 31 December)

		1994	1995	1996*
Passenger cars	. . .	67,936	74,662	79,200
Buses and coaches	. .	529	547	580
Goods vehicles	. . .	31,457	32,514	33,660
Tractors (road)	. . .	1,466	1,544	1,620
Motor cycles and scooters	. .	39,019	52,902	59,000

* Estimates.
Source: IRF, *World Road Statistics*.

SHIPPING
Merchant Fleet (registered at 31 December)

		1996	1997	1998
Number of vessels	. .	6	10	9
Total displacement (grt)	. .	1,128	1,764	1,608

Source: Lloyd's Register of Shipping, *World Fleet Statistics*.

International Sea-borne Freight Traffic
('000 metric tons)

Port Lomé		1996	1997	1998
Goods loaded	. . . .	177.0	391.0	324.5
Goods unloaded	. . . .	1,171.3	1,273.7	982.3

Source: Banque centrale des états de l'Afrique de l'ouest.

CIVIL AVIATION (traffic on scheduled services)*

		1994	1995	1996
Km flown (million)	. . .	2	3	3
Passengers carried ('000)	. .	69	74	75
Passenger-km (million)	. .	215	223	225
Total ton-km (million)	. .	34	36	37

* Including an apportionment of the traffic of Air Afrique.
Source: UN, *Statistical Yearbook*.

Tourism

FOREIGN TOURIST ARRIVALS*

		1996	1997	1998
International arrivals	. . .	58,049	92,081	69,458
National arrivals	. . .	23,252	22,594	24,754
Receipts from tourism ('000 million francs CFA	. . .	5,601	7,442	5,612

* Arrivals at hotels and similar establishments.
Source: Direction des Etudes et de la Planification, Ministère du Tourisme et des Loisirs.

Communications Media

	1994	1995	1996
Radio receivers ('000 in use) . .	850	880	910
Television receivers ('000 in use) .	30	50	70
Telephones ('000 main lines in use)	21	22	24
Telefax stations ('000 in use) . .	4	10	16
Daily newspapers			
Number	1	1	1
Circulation ('000 copies) . .	10	10	15

1997: Radio receivers ('000 in use) 940; Television receivers ('000 in use) 73.
Sources: UNESCO, *Statistical Yearbook*; UN, *Statistical Yearbook*.

Education

(1996/97, unless otherwise indicated)

	Institutions	Teachers	Students		
			Males	Females	Total
Pre-primary . . .	232*	469	5,381	5,108	10,489
Primary . . .	3,283†	18,535	502,872	356,702	859,574
Secondary					
General . . .	n.a.	4,736†	124,148	45,030	169,178
Vocational . .	n.a.	653	6,511	2,565	9,076
Tertiary† . . .	n.a.	443	9,894	1,745	11,639

* 1994/95 figures.   † 1995/96 figures.
Source: UNESCO, *Statistical Yearbook*.

Directory

The Constitution

The Constitution that was approved in a national referendum on 27 September 1992 defines the rights, freedoms and obligations of Togolese citizens, and defines the separation of powers among the executive, legislative and judicial organs of state.

Executive power is vested in the President of the Republic, who is elected, by direct universal adult suffrage, with a five-year mandate. The legislature, the Assemblée nationale, is similarly elected for a period of five years, its 81 members being directly elected by universal suffrage. The President of the Republic appoints a Prime Minister who is able to command a majority in the legislature, and the Prime Minister, in consultation with the President, appoints other government ministers. A Constitutional Court is designated as the highest court of jurisdiction in constitutional matters.

The Government

HEAD OF STATE

President: Gen. GNASSINGBE EYADÉMA (assumed power 13 January 1967; proclaimed President 14 April 1967; elected 30 December 1979; re-elected 21 December 1986, 25 August 1993 and 21 June 1998).

COUNCIL OF MINISTERS
(August 2000)

President: Gen. GNASSINGBE EYADÉMA.

Prime Minister: KODJO AGBÉYOMÈ.

Minister of Justice and Keeper of the Seals, Minister of Democracy and the Promotion of the Rule of Law: Gen. SEYI MEMENE.

Minister of Foreign Affairs and Co-operation: JOSEPH KOKOU KOFFIGOH.

Minister of National Defence: Gen. ASSANI TIDJANI.

Minister of Communication and Civic Education: KOFFI PANOU.

Minister of Mines, Energy, Post and Telecommunications: TCHAMDJA ANDJO.

Minister of Technical Education, Vocational Training and Handicrafts: EDO KODJO MAURILLE AGBOBLI.

Minister of National Education and Research: KOFFI SAMA.

Minister of Tourism and Leisure: TANKPADJA LALLE.

Minister of the Environment and Forest Resources: KOFFI ADADE.

Minister of Economic Affairs, Finance and Privatization: ABDOULHAMID SEGOUN TIDJANI DOUROUDJAYE.

Minister of Planning and Development: SINFEITCHEOU PRE.

Minister of the Civil Service, Labour and Employment: BIOSSEY KOKOU TOZOUN.

Minister of Culture, Youth and Sports: HORATIO FREITAS.

Minister of the Interior, Security and Decentralization: Gen. SIZING AKAWILOU WALA.

Minister of Transport and Water Resources: DAMA DRAMANI.

Minister of Health: KONDI CHARLES AGBA.

Minister of Industry, Trade and Free Zone Development: RUDOLPH KOSSIVI OSSEYI.

Minister of Agriculture, Livestock and Fisheries: KOMIKPINE BAMENANTE.

Minister of Social Affairs and Women's Affairs: IRENE ASHIRA AISSAH.

Minister of Town Planning and Housing: HOPE AGBOLI.

Minister-delegate at the Prime Minister's Office in charge of Relations with the Assemblée nationale and the European Union: HODEMINOU DEVO.

Secretary of State at the Prime Minister's Office in charge of the Private Sector: SAIBOU SAMAROU.

Special Adviser to the President of the Republic: BARRY MOUSSA BARQUE.

MINISTRIES

Office of the President: Palais Présidentiel, ave de la Marina, Lomé; tel. 21-27-01; fax 21-18-97; internet www.republicof togo.com.

Ministry of Agriculture, Livestock and Fisheries: ave de Sarakawa, Lomé; tel. 21-56-71.

Ministry of the Civil Service, Labour and Employment: angle ave de la Marina et rue Kpalimé, Lomé; tel. 21-26-53.

Ministry of Communication and Civic Education: Lomé.

Ministry of Culture, Youth and Sports: BP 3193, Lomé; tel. 21-23-52.

Ministry of Economic Affairs, Finance and Privatization: Ancien Palais, ave de la Marina, BP 387, Lomé; tel. 21-23-71; fax 21-76-02.

Ministry of the Environment and Forest Resources: Lomé.

Ministry of Foreign Affairs and Co-operation: place du Monument aux Morts, Lomé; tel. 21-36-01; fax 21-39-79.

Ministry of Health: rue Branly, Lomé; tel. 21-29-83.

Ministry of Industry, Trade and Free Zone Development: rue de Commerce, Lomé; tel. 21-09-09.

Ministry of the Interior, Security and Decentralization: rue Albert Sarraut, Lomé; tel. 21-23-19.

Ministry of Justice: ave de la Marina, rue Colonel de Roux, Lomé; tel. 21-26-53.

Ministry of Mines, Energy, Post and Telecommunications: ave de Sarakawa, Lomé; tel. 21-11-01; fax 21-68-12.

Ministry of National Defence: Lomé; tel. 21-28-91.

Ministry of National Education and Research: rue Colonel de Roux, BP 12175, Lomé; tel. 22-09-83.

Ministry of Planning and Development: Lomé; tel. 21-37-51; fax 21-37-53.

Ministry of Social Affairs and Women's Affairs: Lomé.

Ministry of Technical Education, Vocational Training and Handicrafts: Lomé.

Ministry of Tourism and Leisure: rue du Lac Togo, BP 1289, Lomé; tel. 21-43-13; fax 21-89-27.

Ministry of Transport and Water Resources: Lomé.

President and Legislature

PRESIDENT

Presidential Election, 21 June 1998

Candidate	Votes	% of votes
Gen. GNASSINGBE EYADÉMA	813,313	52.13
GILCHRIST OLYMPIO	532,328	34.12
YAO AGBOYIBO	149,308	9.57
ZARIFOU AYIVA	47,117	3.02
LÉOPOLD GNININVI	12,737	0.82
KWAMI MENSAN JACQUES AMOUZOU	5,460	0.35
Total	**1,560,263**	**100.00**

ASSEMBLÉE NATIONALE

President: FAMBARÉ NATCHABA OUATTARA.

General Election, 21 March 1999

Party	Seats
Rassemblement du peuple togolais (RPT)	79*
Independents	2
Total	**81**

* Including two seats won in by-elections after voting was declared invalid.

Political Organizations

In mid-1993 there were 63 registered political parties. Of those active in mid-2000, the following were among the most influential:

Alliance togolaise pour la démocratie (ATD): Leader: ADANI IFÉ ATAKPAMEVI.

Comité d'action pour le renouveau (CAR): Leader Me YAO AGBOYIBO.

Convention démocratique des peuples africains (CDPA): f. 1991; Leader Prof. LÉOPOLD GNININVI.

Convergence patriotique panafricaine (CPP): BP 12703, Lomé; f. 1999 by merger of the Parti d'action pour la démocratie (PAD), the Parti des démocrates pour l'unité (PDU), the Union pour la démocratie et la solidarité (UDS), and the Union togolaise pour la démocratie (UTD); Pres. EDEM KODJO.

Coordination nationale des forces nouvelles (CFN): f. 1993; Pres. Me JOSEPH KOKOU KOFFIGOH.

Démocratie sociale togolaise (DST): linked to PDT; Leader ABOU DJOBO BOUKARI.

Mouvement du 5 octobre (MO5): radical; Leader BASSIROU AYEVA.

Mouvement nationaliste de l'unité (MNU): f. 1992; Gen. Sec. KOFFITSE ADZRAKO.

Parti pour la démocratie et le renouveau (PDR): f. 1991; Leader ZARIFOU AYIVA.

Parti démocratique togolais (PDT): linked to DST; Leader MBA KABASSEMA.

Parti pan-africain écologiste (PPE): Leader ESSO RAMA LAWANI.

Parti pan-africain socialiste (PPS): radical; Leader FRANCIS AGBOBLI.

Rassemblement du peuple togolais (RPT): place de l'Indépendance, BP 1208, Lomé; tel. 21-20-18; f. 1969; sole legal party 1969–91; Pres. Gen. GNASSINGBE EYADÉMA; Sec.-Gen. VIGNIKO AMEDEGNATO.

Union des forces de changement (UFC): rue Koudadzé, Quartier Lom-Nava, Lomé; e-mail contact@ufc-togo.com; internet www .ufc-togo.com; f. 1992; social-democratic; Leader GILCHRIST OLYMPIO; Sec.-Gen. JEAN-PIERRE FABRE.

Union pour la justice at la démocratie (UJD): supports Pres. Eyadéma; Leader LAL TAXPANDJAN.

Union des libéraux indépendants (ULI): f. 1993 to succeed Union des démocrates pour le renouveau; Leader KWAMI MENSAN JACQUES AMOUZOU.

Union togolaise pour la réconciliation (UTR): Leader BAWA MANKOUBU.

Diplomatic Representation

EMBASSIES IN TOGO

Angola: blvd du 13 Janvier, Boccovi, Lomé; tel. 21-72-11; fax 21-80-51.

Belgium: 165 rue Pelletier Caventou, BP 7643, Lomé; tel. 21-03-23; Ambassador: PIERRE VAESEN.

Brazil: 119 rue de l'OCAM, BP 1356, Lomé; tel. 21-00-58; Chargé d'affaires a.i.: JOSÉ ROBERTO PROCOPIAK.

China, People's Republic: Tokoin-Ouest, BP 2690, Lomé; tel. 21-31-59; Ambassador: JIANG KANG.

Congo, Democratic Republic: 325 blvd du 13 janvier, BP 102, Lomé; tel. 21-51-55; Ambassador: LOKOKA IKUKELE BOMOLO.

Egypt: route d'Aného, BP 8, Lomé; tel. 21-24-43; Ambassador: HUSSEIN EL-KHAZINDAR.

France: 51 rue du Golfe, BP 337, Lomé; tel. 21-25-71; Ambassador: JEAN-FRANÇOIS VALETTE.

Gabon: Tokoin Super-Taco, Lomé; tel. 22-18-93; fax 22-18-92; Ambassador: (vacant).

Germany: blvd de la République, BP 1175, Lomé; tel. 21-23-70; fax 22-18-88; e-mail amballmtogo@bibway.com; Ambassador: Dr DIETER PAPENFUSS.

Ghana: 8 rue Paulin Eklou, Tokoin-Ouest, BP 92, Lomé; tel. 21-31-94; fax 21-77-36; Ambassador: DAVID ANAGLATE.

Guinea: Lomé; tel. 51-74-98; fax 21-81-16.

Israel: 159 rue de l'OCAM, BP 61187, Lomé; tel. 21-79-58; fax 21-88-94; Ambassador: JACOB TOPAZ.

Libya: blvd du 13 janvier, BP 4872, Lomé; tel. 21-40-63; Chargé d'affaires a.i.: AHMED M. ABDULKAFI.

Nigeria: 311 blvd du 13 janvier, BP 1189, Lomé; tel. 21-34-55; Ambassador: VINCENT OKOBI.

Russia: Lomé; tel. 21-35-78.

USA: angle rue Pelletier Caventou et rue Vauban, BP 852, Lomé; tel. 21-29-91; fax 21-79-52; internet usembassy.state.gov/togo; Ambassador: BRENDA BROWN SCHOONOVER.

Judicial System

Justice is administered by the Cour Constitutionnelle (Constitutional Court), the Cour Suprême (Supreme Court), two Cours d'Appel (Appeal Courts) and the Tribunaux de première instance, which hear civil, commercial and criminal cases. There is a labour tribunal and a tribunal for children's rights. In addition, there are two exceptional courts, the Cour de sûreté de l'Etat, which judges crimes against internal and external state security, and the Tribunal spécial

chargé de la répression des détournements de deniers publics, which deals with cases of misuse of public funds.

Cour Constitutionnelle: Lomé; f. 1997; seven mems; Pres. ATSU-KOFFI AMEGA.

Cour Suprême: BP 906, Lomé; tel. 21-22-58; f. 1961; consists of three chambers; judicial, administrative and auditing; Chair. FESSOU LAWSON; Attorney-Gen. KOUAMI AMADOS-DJOKO.

State Attorney: ATARA NDAKENA.

Religion

It is estimated that about 50% of the population follow traditional animist beliefs, some 35% are Christians (mainly Roman Catholics) and 15% are Muslims.

CHRISTIANITY

The Roman Catholic Church

Togo comprises one archdiocese and six dioceses. At 31 December 1998 there were an estimated 1,187,021 adherents in the country, representing about 23.7% of the total population.

Bishops' Conference: Conférence Episcopale du Togo, 10 rue Maréchal Foch, BP 348, Lomé; tel. 21-22-72; fax 22-48-08; statutes approved 1979; Pres. Most Rev. PHILIPPE FANOKO KOSSI KPODZRO, Archbishop of Lomé.

Archbishop of Lomé: Most Rev. PHILIPPE FANOKO KOSSI KPODZRO, Archevêché, 10 rue Maréchal Foch, BP 348, Lomé; tel. 21-22-72; fax 22-48-08.

Protestant Churches

There are about 250 mission centres, with a personnel of some 250, affiliated to European and US societies and administered by a Conseil Synodal, presided over by a moderator.

Directorate of Protestant Churches: 1 rue Maréchal Foch, BP 378, Lomé; Moderator Pastor AWUME (acting).

Eglise Evangélique Presbytérienne du Togo: 1 rue Tokmake, BP 2, Lomé; tel. 21-46-69; fax 22-23-63; Moderator Pastor YAWO FATSÈME AMIOU.

BAHÁ'Í FAITH

National Spiritual Assembly: BP 1659, Lomé; tel. 21-21-99; mems resident in 600 localities.

The Press

DAILY

Togo-Presse: EDITOGO, BP 891, Lomé; tel. 21-37-18; fax 22-14-89; f. 1961; official govt publ.; French, Kabiye and Ewe; political, economic and cultural; circ. 8,000.

PERIODICALS

Abito: Lomé; weekly; independent; Editor PAMPHILE GNIMASSOU.

L'Aurore: BP 270, Lomé; tel. 22-65-41; fax 22-65-89; e-mail aurore37@caramail.com; weekly; independent; Editor-in-Chief ANKOU SALVADOR; circ. 2,500.

Bulletin de la Chambre de Commerce: angle ave de la Présidence, BP 360, Lomé; tel. 21-70-65; fax 21-47-30; monthly; directory of commercial, industrial and agricultural activities.

Bulletin d'Information de l'Agence Togolaise de Presse: 35 rue Binger, Lomé; weekly; publ. by govt information service.

Cité Magazine: 50 ave Pas de Souza, BP 6275, Lomé; tel. and fax 22-67-40; e-mail citemag@cafe.tg; internet www.cafe.tg/citemag; monthly.

Le Citoyen: Lomé; independent.

La Conscience: Lomé; tel. and fax 26-13-70; e-mail laconscience@hotmail.com; Editor KODJO DJISSENOU; circ. 3,000.

Le Combat du Peuple: Lomé; pro-opposition weekly; Dir LUCIEN MESSAN.

Courrier du Golfe: Lomé; f. 1990; independent.

Crocodile: BP 60087, Lomé; tel. 21-38-21; fax 26-13-70; e-mail crocodile.crocodile@caramail.com; pro-opposition; 2 a week; Dir VIGNO KOFFI HOUNKANLY; Editor FRANCIS PEDRO AMAZUN; circ. 5,000.

La Dépêche: BP 20039, Lomé; tel. and fax 21-09-32; e-mail journdep@hotmail.com; bi-monthly; Editor APPOLINAIRE MÈWÈNA-MÈSSÈ ESSO-WE; circ. 3,000.

Les Echos du Matin: Lomé; independent.

Etudes Togolaises: Institut National de la Recherche Scientifique, BP 2240, Lomé; tel. 21-57-39; f. 1965; quarterly; scientific review, mainly anthropology.

L'Eveil du Peuple: Lomé; weekly.

L'Eveil du Travailleur Togolais: BP 163, Lomé; tel. 21-57-39; quarterly; Elrato; publ. by Confédération Nationale des Travailleurs du Togo; Chief Editor M. K. AGBEKA; circ. 5,000.

L'Evénement: Lomé; independent.

L'Exile: Lomé; weekly; independent; Editor HIPPOLYTE AGBOH.

Forum Hebdo: Lomé; weekly; independent; Dir GABRIEL KOMI AGAH (in exile since 1993).

Game su/Teu Fema: 125 ave de la Nouvelle Marche, BP 1247, Lomé; tel. 21-28-44; f. 1997; monthly; Ewe and Kabiye; govt publ. for the newly literate; circ. 3,000.

Journal Officiel de la République du Togo (JORT): EDITOGO, BP 891, Lomé; tel. 21-37-18; fax 22-14-89; government acts, laws, decrees and decisions.

Kpakpa Désenchanté: Lomé; weekly; independent.

Le Miroir du Peuple: Lomé; weekly.

Le Nouveau Combattant: Lomé; f. 1998; weekly; privately-owned.

Le Nouveau Journal: Lomé; weekly; independent; Man. Editor HOUNKALI ELIAS.

Nouvel Echo: Lomé; pro-opposition; weekly.

Observateur Togolais: BP 20740, Lomé; tel. 22-76-06; e-mail observateurtg@usa.net; 2 a month; Editor-in-Chief MICHEL MAZIGUE; Editor KOJO ARRE; circ. 1,500.

La Parole: Lomé; weekly; independent; Dir BERTIN KANGHI FOLY.

Politicos: BP 20312, Lomé; tel. and fax 26-13-70; e-mail politicos@africanet.com; 2 a month; Editor ELVIS KAO; circ. 2,000.

Le Regard: Maison du Journalisme, BP 81213, Lomé; tel. and fax 26-13-70; e-mail leregard@webmails.com; weekly; Editor MIKHAILA SAIBOU; circ. 3,000.

Le Reporter (des Temps Nouveaux): BP 1800, Lomé; tel. and fax 26-18-22; e-mail reporter51@hotmail.com; weekly; independent; Man. Editor ROMAIN ATTISO KOUDJODJI; circ. 3,500.

Le Scorpion Akéklé: Lomé; weekly; independent.

Le Secteur Privé: angle ave de la Présidence, BP 360, Lomé; tel. 21-70-65; fax 21-47-30; monthly; publ. by Chambre de Commerce et d'Industrie du Togo.

Le Temps: Lomé; pro-opposition.

Tingo Tingo: BP 80419, Lomé; tel. 22-17-58; e-mail coted@africanet.com; weekly; independent; Editor ASIONBO AUGUSTIN; circ. 3,500.

Togo-Images: BP 4869, Lomé; tel. 21-56-80; f. 1962; monthly series of wall posters depicting recent political, economic and cultural events in Togo; publ. by govt information service; Dir AKOBI BEDOU; circ. 5,000.

La Tribune des Démocrates: Lomé; weekly; independent; Editor MARTIN NBENOUGOU.

PRESS ASSOCIATION

Union des Journalistes Indépendants du Togo: BP 81213, Lomé; tel. 26-13-00; fax 26-13-70; e-mail maison-du-journalisme@ids.tg; also operates Maison de Presse; Sec.-Gen. GABRIEL AYITÉ BAGLO.

NEWS AGENCY

Agence Togolaise de Presse (ATOP): 35 rue des Media, BP 2327, Lomé; tel. 21-25-07; f. 1975; Dir SESHIE SEYENA BIAVA.

Publishers

Centre Togolais de Communication Evangélique (CTCE): 1 rue de Commerce, BP 378, Lomé; tel. 21-45-82; fax 21-29-67; Dir MARC K. ETSE.

Editions Akpagnon: BP 3531, Lomé; tel. 22-02-44; fax 22-02-44; f. 1979; general literature; Man. Dir YVES-EMMANUEL DOGBÉ.

Les Nouvelles Editions Africaines du Togo (NEA-TOGO): 239 blvd du 13 janvier, BP 4862, Lomé; tel. 21-67-61; fax 22-10-19; e-mail ctce@cafe.tg; general fiction, non-fiction and textbooks; Man. Dir YAWO AGBEKO TSOLENYANU; Editorial Man. TCHOTCHO CHRISTIANE EKUE.

Les Presses de l'Université du Bénin: BP 1515, Lomé; tel. 25-48-44; fax 25-87-84.

Société National des Editions du Togo (EDITOGO): BP 891, Lomé; tel. 21-61-06; f. 1961; govt-owned; general and educational; Pres. BIOSSEY KOKOU TOZOUN; Man. Dir WIYAO DADJA POUWI.

Broadcasting and Communications

TELECOMMUNICATIONS

Société des Télécommunications du Togo (Togo Télécom): ave N. Grunitzky, BP 333, Lomé; tel. 21-44-01; fax 21-03-73; e-

mail contact@togotel.net.tg; internet www.togotel.net.tg; Dir-Gen. KOSSIVI PAUL AYIKOE.

BROADCASTING
Radio

Kanal FM: BP 81190, Lomé; tel. 21-33-74; fax 26-13-70; e-mail kanalfm@hotmail.com; broadcasts in French and Min; Man. DANY KOMLA AYIDA.

Radiodiffusion du Togo (Internationale)–Radio Lomé: BP 434, Lomé; tel. 21-24-93; fax 21-36-73; f. 1953; renamed Radiodiffusion-Télévision de la Nouvelle Marche 1979–91; state-controlled; radio programmes in French, English and vernacular languages; Dir BAWA SEMEDO.

Radiodiffusion du Togo (Nationale): BP 21, Kara; tel. 60-60-60; f. 1974 as Radiodiffusion Kara (Togo); state-controlled; radio programmes in French and vernacular languages; Dir M'BA KPEN-OUGOU.

Radio Liberté: operated by the COD–2 opposition alliance.

Radio Nostalgie 92.5: BP 13836, Lomé; tel. 22-25-41; fax 22-65-47; e-mail nostalgie92-5@yahoo.fr; internet www.netcom.tg/nostalgie; music station; broadcasts in French; Man. THIERRY SALLAH.

Television

Télévision Togolaise: BP 3286, Lomé; tel. 21-53-57; fax 21-57-86; f. 1973; state-controlled; three stations; programmes in French and vernacular languages; Dir MARTIN AHIAVI.

Broadcasting Association

Organisation des Radios et Télévisions Indépendantes (ORTI): BP 81302, Lomé; tel. 21-33-74; e-mail kawokou@syfed.tg.refer.org; RAYMOND AWOKOU KOUKOU.

Finance

(cap. = capital; res = reserves; dep. = deposits; m. = million; br. = branch; amounts in francs CFA)

BANKING
Central Bank

Banque Centrale des Etats de l'Afrique de l'Ouest (BCEAO): ave de Sarakawa, BP 120, Lomé; tel. 21-53-83; fax 21-76-02; HQ in Dakar, Senegal; f. 1962; bank of issue for the mem. states of the Union économique et monétaire ouest-africaine (UEMOA, comprising Benin, Burkina Faso, Côte d'Ivoire, Guinea-Bissau, Mali, Niger, Senegal and Togo); cap. and res 806,918m., total assets 4,084,464m. (Dec. 1998); Gov. CHARLES KONAN BANNY; Dir in Togo AYÉWANOU AGETOHO GBEASOR; br. at Kara.

Commercial Banks

Banque Togolaise pour le Commerce et l'Industrie (BTCI): 169 blvd du 13 janvier, BP 363, Lomé; tel. 21-46-41; fax 21-32-65; f. 1974; 51.5% state-owned, 24.8% owned by Société Financière pour les Pays d'Outre-mer, 23.8% by Banque Nationale de Paris; cap. 1,700m., total assets 44,774m. (Dec. 1998); Pres. ABDOULHAMID SEGOUN TIDJIANI DOUROUDJAYE; Man. Dir YAO PATRICE KANEKATOUA; 8 brs.

Banque Internationale pour l'Afrique au Togo (BIA–Togo): 13 rue de Commerce, BP 346, Lomé; tel. 21-32-86; fax 21-10-19; f. 1965; fmrly Meridien BIAO–Togo; 30% owned by Banque Belgolaise; cap. 3,500m., total assets 42,220m. (Dec. 1998); Pres. BAUDOUIN LEMAIRE; Dir-Gen. JEAN-PIERRE CARPENTIER; 7 brs.

Ecobank–Togo: 20 rue de Commerce, BP 3302, Lomé; tel. 21-72-14; fax 21-42-37; e-mail ecbtogo@ecobank.tg; f. 1988; 80.1% owned by Ecobank Transnational Inc (operating under the auspices of the Economic Community of West African States), 14.0% by Togolese private investors; cap. 2,000m., total assets 51,379m. (Dec. 1998); Pres. OGAMO BAGNAH; Man. Dir K. ABOU KABASSI; 2 brs.

Société Interafricaine de Banques (SIAB): 14 rue de Commerce, BP 4874, Lomé; tel. 21-28-30; fax 21-58-29; f. 1975; fmrly Banque Arabe Libyenne-Togolaise du Commerce Extérieur; 50% state-owned, 50% owned by Libyan Arab Foreign Bank; cap. 5,840m., total assets 2,721m. (Dec. 1998); Vice-Pres. ALI SALAH SAKKAH; Dir-Gen. KHALIFA ACHOUR ETTLUAA.

Union Togolaise de Banque (UTB): blvd du 13 janvier, Nyékonakpoé, BP 359, Lomé; tel. 21-64-11; fax 21-22-06; f. 1964; state-owned; privatization pending; cap. 2,000m., total assets 68,966m. (Dec. 1998); Pres. and Dir-Gen. ALEXIS LAMSEH LOOKY; 11 brs.

Development Banks

Banque Nationale d'Investissement (BNI): 11 ave du 24 janvier, BP 2682, Lomé; tel. 21-62-21; fax 21-62-25; f. 1971; frmly Société Nationale d'Investissement et Fonds Annexes, name changed as above 1997; 33% state-owned; cap. 2,600m., total assets 20,140m. (Dec. 1998); Pres. PALOUKI MASSINA; Dir-Gen. RICHARD K. ATTIPOE.

Banque Ouest-Africaine de Développement (BOAD): 68 ave de la Libération, BP 1172, Lomé; tel. 21-42-44; fax 21-72-69; f. 1973; promotes West African economic development and integration.

Banque Togolaise de Développement (BTD): angle ave des Nîmes et ave Nicolas Grunitzky, BP 65, Lomé; tel. 21-36-41; fax 21-44-56; f. 1967; 43% state-owned, 20% owned by BCEAO, 13% by Banque Ouest Africaine de Développement; cap. 3,065m., total assets 27,019m. (Dec. 1998); Pres. MICHÈLE DÉDÉVI EKUE; Gen. Man. MENSAVI MENSAH; 10 brs.

Savings Bank

Caisse d'Epargne du Togo (CET): 23 ave de la Nouvelle Marché, Lomé; tel. 21-20-47; fax 21-85-83; state-owned; cap. 120m., total assets 11,125m. (Dec. 1998); Pres. DEMBA A. TIGNOKPA; Man. Dir MINDI LAMBONI.

Credit Institution

Société Togolaise de Crédit Automobile (STOCA): 3 rue du Mono, BP 899, Lomé; tel. 21-37-59; fax 21-08-28; e-mail stoca@ids.tg; f. 1962; 93.3% owned by SAFCA; cap. and res 270m., total assets 1,448m. (Dec. 1998); Pres. DIACK DIAWAR; Dir-Gen. ERIC LECLÈRE.

Bankers' Association

Association Professionnelle des Banques et Etablissements Financiers du Togo: Lomé.

STOCK EXCHANGE

Bourse Régionale des Valeurs Mobilières (BRVM): BP 3263, Lomé; tel. 21-23-05; fax 21-23-41; e-mail natcholi@brvm.org; internet www.brvm.org; f. 1998; national branch of BRVM (regional stock exchange based in Abidjan, Côte d'Ivoire, serving the member states of UEMOA); Man. in Togo NATHALIE BITHO ACHOLI.

INSURANCE

Assurances Générales de France (Togo): BP 1349, Lomé; tel. 21-59-58; fax 21-73-58.

CICA–RE/Compagnie Commune de Réassurance des Etats Membres de la CICA: ave du 24 janvier, BP 12410, Lomé; tel. 21-62-69; fax 21-49-64; e-mail cicare@cafe.tg; f. 1981; reinsurance co operating in 12 west and central African states; cap. 1,500m.; Chair. LÉON-PAUL N'GOULAKIA; Gen. Man. DIGBEU KIPRE.

Colina Assurances: BP 1349, Lomé; tel. 21-73-58; fax 21-73-58.

Groupement Togolais d'Assurances (GTA): route d'Atakpamé, BP 3298, Lomé; tel. 25-60-75; fax 25-26-78; f. 1974; 62.9% state-owned; all classes of insurance and reinsurance; Pres. Minister of the Economy and Finance; Man. Dir KOSSI NAMBEA.

Sicar Gras Savoye Togo: 14 ave de la Nouvelle Marché, BP 2932, Lomé; tel. 21-35-38; fax 21-82-11; Dir ALEXANDRE WILSON.

UAT: Immeuble BICI, 169 blvd du 13 Janvier, BP 495, Lomé; tel. 21-10-34; fax 21-87-24.

Trade and Industry

ECONOMIC AND SOCIAL COUNCIL

Conseil Economique et Social: Lomé; tel. 21-53-01; f. 1967; advisory body of 25 mems, comprising five trade unionists, five reps of industry and commerce, five reps of agriculture, five economists and sociologists, and five technologists; Pres. KOFFI GBODZIDI DJONDO.

GOVERNMENT AGENCIES

Direction Générale des Mines et de la Géologie: BP 356, Lomé; tel. 21-30-01; fax 21-31-93; organization and administration of mining in Togo; Dir-Gen. ANKOUME P. AREGBA.

EPZ Promotion Board: BP 3250, Lomé; tel. 21-13-74; fax 21-52-31; promotes the Export Processing Zone at Lomé internationally.

Société d'Administration des Zones Franches (SAZOF): BP 2748, Lomé; tel. 21-07-44; fax 21-43-05; administers and promotes free zones; Dir Gen. YAZAZ EGBARÉ.

Société Nationale de Commerce (SONACOM): 29 blvd Circulaire, BP 3009, Lomé; tel. 21-31-18; f. 1972; cap. 2,000m. francs CFA; importer of staple foods; Dir-Gen. JEAN LADOUX.

Société Nationale d'Investissement et Fonds Annexes (SNI): Lomé; f. 1971; state-owned investment co.; Dir-Gen. KUAKU RICHARD ATTIPOE.

DEVELOPMENT ORGANIZATIONS

Agricultural development is under the supervision of five regional development authorities, the Sociétés régionales d'aménagement et de développement.

Agence Française de Développement: ave de Sarakawa, BP 33, Lomé; tel. 21-04-98; fax 21-79-32; frmly Caisse Française de Développement; Dir M. TYACK.

Association Villages Entreprises: BP 23, Kpalimé; tel. and fax 41-00-62; Dir KOMI AFELETE JULIEN NYUIADZI.

Office de Développement et d'Exploitation des Forêts (ODEF): 15 rue des Conseillers Municipaux, BP 334, Lomé; tel. 21-71-28; fax 21-34-91; f. 1971; develops and manages forest resources; Man. Dir KOFFI AGOGNO.

Office des Produits Agricoles du Togo (OPAT): angle rue Branly et ave no. 3, BP 1334, Lomé; tel. 21-44-71; f. 1964; agricultural development, marketing and exports; Dir-Gen. ABALO KELEM.

Recherche, Appui et Formation aux Initiatives d'Autodéveloppement (RAFIA): BP 43, Dapaong; tel. 70-80-89; fax 70-82-37; Dir NOIGUE TAMBILA LENNE.

Service de Coopération et d'Action Culturelle: BP 91, Lomé; tel 21-21-26; fax 21-21-28; e-mail scac-lome@tg.refer.org; administers bilateral aid from the French Ministry of Foreign Affairs; Dir HENRI-LUC THIBAULT.

Société d'Appui a la Filière Café-Cacao-Coton (SAFICC): Lomé; f. 1992; development of coffee, cocoa and cotton production.

CHAMBER OF COMMERCE

Chambre de Commerce et d'Industrie du Togo (CCIT): angle ave de la Présidence et ave Georges Pompidou, BP 360, Lomé; tel. 21-70-65; fax 21-47-30; e-mail ccit@rdd.tg; f. 1921; Pres. ALEXIS LAMSEH LOOKY; Sec.-Gen. YAZAS EGBARÉ TCHOHOU.

EMPLOYERS' ORGANIZATIONS

Groupement Interprofessionnel des Entreprises du Togo (GITO): BP 345, Lomé; Pres. CLARENCE OLYMPIO.

Syndicat des Commerçants Industriels Importateurs et Exportateurs du Togo (SCINPEXTO): BP 1166, Lomé; tel. 22-59-86; Pres. C. SITTERLIN.

Syndicat des Entrepreneurs de Travaux Publics, Bâtiments et Mines du Togo: BP 12429, Lomé; tel. 21-19-06; fax 21-08-30; Pres. JOSÈPHE NAKU.

UTILITIES
Electricity

Communauté Electrique du Bénin: ave de la Kozah, BP 1368, Lomé; tel. 21-61-32; fax 21-37-64; f. 1968 as a jt venture between Togo and Benin to exploit the energy resources in the two countries; Chair. CODJO DÉLAVA; Man. CYR M'PO KOUAGOU.

Compagnie Energie Electrique du Togo (CEET): 10 ave du Golfe, BP 42, Lomé; tel. 21-27-43; fax 21-64-98; e-mail amarchal@togo-imet.com; f. 1963; in 2000 a 20-year management contract was awarded to ELYO, France and Hydro-Québec International, Canada; production, transportation and distribution of electricity; Man. Dir GEORGES CUBLIER.

Gas

Société Togolaise de Gaz SA (Togogaz): BP 1082, Lomé; tel. 21-44-31; fax 31-55-30; 71% privatization pending.

Water

Régie Nationale des Eaux du Togo (RNET): 53 ave de la Libération, angle rue du Chemin de Fer, BP 1301, Lomé; tel. 21-34-81; fax 21-46-13; e-mail rnetdg@cafe.tg; f. 1964; cap. 252m. francs CFA; state-owned; production and distribution of drinking water; Chair. ANATO AGBOZOUHOUE; Man. Dir KPANDJA I. BINGUITCHA-FARE.

MAJOR COMPANIES

The following are among the country's largest companies in terms of either capital investment or employment:

Amina Togo SA: BP 10230, Lomé; tel. 26-84-04; fax 26-92-72; production of synthetic hair; operates in the Export Processing Zone; South Korean-owned; Man. LEE DAE.

Atlantic Produce: BP 3170, Lomé; tel. 26-76-05; fax 26-28-49; exporter of tropical houseplants; Danish-owned; operates in the Export Processing Zone; Man. M. TINGGARRARD.

Boncomm International Togo: Immeuble TABA, BP 13124, Lomé; tel. 27-94-69; fax 27-08-33; Indian-owned clothing manufacturer; exports to Europe and the USA; operates in the Export Processing Zone; Man. M. SIRINIVAS.

Brasserie BB Lomé SA: 47 rue du Grand Marché, BP 896, Lomé; tel. 21-50-62; fax 21-38-59; f. 1964 as Brasserie du Bénin SA; cap. 2,500m. francs CFA; 25% owned by Castel, France; mfrs of beer and soft drinks at Lomé and Kara; Chair. and Man. Dir JOACHIM HAASE; Dirs ELMAR VAN BOEMMEL, OSCAR BOSSHARD; 523 employees.

CEREKEM Exotic Togo: BP 2082, Lomé; f. 1987; cap. 400m. francs CFA; agro-industrial complex at Adétikopé for cultivation and processing of aromatic plants; Chair. and Man. Dir OLE RASMUSSEN; 400 employees.

Cotonfil: Cacavéli, BP 1481, Lomé; tel. 25-14-45; fax 22-38-44; cotton producer; jt Spanish and Togolese ownership; Man. M. MORA.

Crustafric: BP 2051, Lomé; tel. 27-82-52; fax 27-48-86; processor and exporter of seafood; operates in the Export Processing Zone; Italian-owned; Man. M. INGLEESE.

Industrie Togolaise des Plastiques (ITP): Zone Industrielle, BP 9157, Lomé; tel. 27-49-83; fax 27-15-58; e-mail kkohouvi@itp.cafe.tg; f. 1980; cap. 1,100m. francs CFA; owned by a consortium of private Togolese, Dutch, German and Danish interests; mfr and marketing of moulded articles, etc.; Man. Dir KOKOU KOHOUVI.

Nouvelle Industrie des Oléagineux du Togo (NIOTO): BP 1755, Lomé; f. 1976; cap. 1,000m. francs CFA; majority owned by Société Générale du Golfe de Guinée-Togo; production and marketing of edible plant oils; Man. Dir ANANI ERNEST GASSOU.

Nouvelle Société Togolaise de Marbrerie et de Matériaux (Nouvelle SOTOMA): Zone Portuaire, BP 2105, Lomé; tel. 21-29-22; fax 21-71-32; cap. 500m. francs CFA; exploitation of marble at Gnaoulou and Pagola; Man. Dir K. PEKEMSI.

Office Togolais des Phosphates (OTP): BP 379 et 362, Lomé; tel. 21-39-01; fax 21-71-52; f. 1974; cap. 15,000m. francs CFA; production and marketing of phosphates; Dir-Gen. KPANLOU PATASSE.

Sagefi et PS: route de l'Aéroport, BP 4566, Lomé; tel. 21-55-43; fax 21-64-24; f. 1976; mfrs of electronic equipment; Chair. K. HOFFER.

Société Agricole Togolaise-Arabe-Libyenne (SATAL): 329 blvd du 13 janvier, BP 3554, Lomé; tel. 21-69-18; f. 1978; cap. 1,400m. francs CFA; 50% state-owned, 50% owned by Govt of Libya; production, processing and marketing of agricultural goods; Chair. KATANGA KOFFI WALLA; Man. Dir ASSAID MOHAMED RAAI.

Société des Ciments du Togo (CIMTOGO): Zone Industrielle Portuaire PK 12, BP 1687, Lomé; tel. 21-08-59; fax 21-71-32; f. 1969; cap. 750m. francs CFA; owned by SCANCEM International (Norway); production and marketing of cement and clinker; turnover in 1991: 9,700m. francs CFA; Pres. Minister of Industry, Commerce and Free Zone Development; Man. Dir H. RASMUSSEN.

Société Générale du Golfe de Guinée–Togo (SGGG–TOGO): 7 rue Koumoré, BP 330, Lomé; tel. 21-23-90; fax 21-51-65; f. 1972; cap. 2,744.9m. francs CFA; retail commerce, import-export agency and transportation; Chair. and Man. Dir MATÉ KWAME ABBEY; 309 employees.

Société Générale des Moulins du Togo (SGMT): Zone Industrielle Portuaire, BP 9098, Lomé; tel. 21-35-59; f. 1971; cap. 300m. francs CFA; 45% state-owned; flour milling at Lomé; Chair. KOUDJOLOU DOGO; Man. Dir VASKEN BAKALIAN.

Société Industrielle de Coton (SICOT): BP 12465, Lomé; tel. 27-00-69; fax 27-75-35; ginning and marketing of cotton; Dir-Gen. ENSELME GOUTHON.

Société Nationale pour le Développement de la Palmeraie et des Huileries (SONAPH): BP 1755, Lomé; tel. 21-22-32; f. 1968; cap. 1,320m. francs CFA; state-owned; cultivation of palms and production of palm-oil and palmettoes; Chair. Dr FOLI AMAIZO BUBUTO; Man. Dir ANANI ERNEST GASSOU.

Société Togolaise des Boissons (STB): Zone Industrielle Portuaire, BP 2239, Lomé; tel. 27-58-80; f. 1970; cap. 264m. francs CFA; manufacture, bottling and sale of soft drinks; owned by Castel, France; Chair. PIERRE CASTEL.

Société Togolaise du Coton (SOTOCO): BP 3553, Lomé; tel. 21-05-39; fax 22-49-57; f. 1974 to promote cotton cultivation; Dir-Gen. TCHAMBAKOU AYASSOR.

Société Togolaise et Danoise de Savons (SOTODAS): Zone Industrielle Portuaire, Lomé; tel. 21-52-03; fax 21-52-04; f. 1987; cap. 205m. francs CFA; 40% owned by Domo Kemi (Denmark) 20% by private Togolese interests; mfrs of detergents and cleansers; Man. Dir S. RAZVI.

Société Togolaise de Sidérurgie (STS): route d'Aného, Zone Portuaire, Lomé; tel. 21-10-16; cap. 700m. francs CFA; steel production; Chair. JOHN MOORE; Man. Dir STANLEY CLEVELAND.

Société Togolaise de Stockage de Lomé (STSL): BP 3283, Lomé; tel. 21-50-64; f. 1976; cap. 4,000m. francs CFA; exploitation and commercialization of hydrocarbons; Dir-Gen. M. BLAZJENVICZ.

Sogotel Co Ltd: Chateau d'Eau Be, BP 497, Lomé; tel. 21-05-43; fax 21-10-71; f. 1973; processors of fish and meat; Pres. CLARENCE ANSAH JOHNSON.

Togo et Shell: rue du Lac, BP 797, Lomé; tel. 21-17-51; fax 21-74-15; marketing and sale of petroleum and petroleum products; owned by Royal Dutch Shell.

Togotex International: BP 3511, Lomé; tel. 21-33-25; fax 21-60-49; f. 1990; cap. 2,250m. francs CFA; owned by Cha Chi Ming (Hong Kong); operates textile mills; Pres. CHA CHI MING; Man. Dir JOHN GRIMSHAW.

UAC-Togo SA: 16 rue de Commerce, BP 345, Lomé; tel. 21-28-00; fax 21-59-99; e-mail uac-togo@ids.tg; import-export co; cap. 853.2m. francs CFA; 67% owned by Gamma Holding, Netherlands.

TRADE UNIONS

Collectif des Syndicats Indépendants (CSI): Lomé; f. 1992 as co-ordinating org. for three trade union confederations:

> **Confédération Syndicale des Travailleurs du Togo (CSTT):** Lomé.

> **Groupement Syndical Autonome (GSA):** Lomé.

> **Union Nationale des Syndicats Indépendants du Togo (UNSIT):** Tokoin-Wuiti, BP 30082, Lomé; tel. 21-65-65; fax 25-95-66; f. 1991; 17 affiliated unions.

Confédération Nationale des Travailleurs du Togo (CNTT): 160 blvd du 13 janvier, BP 163, Lomé; tel. 21-57-39; f. 1973; affiliated to RPT until April 1991; Sec.-Gen. DOUEVI TCHIVIAKOU.

Transport

RAILWAYS

Société Nationale des Chemins de Fer du Togo (SNCT): BP 340, Lomé; tel. 21-43-01; fax 21-22-19; f. 1905; restructured under present name in 1995; total length 517 km, incl. lines running inland from Lomé to Atakpamé and Blitta (280 km), and a coastal line, running through Lomé and Aného, which links with the Benin railway system, but which was closed to passenger traffic in 1987 (a service from Lomé to Palimé—119 km—has also been suspended); passengers carried (1997): 152,000, freight handled (1997): 249,900 metric tons; Gen. Man. ROY GEMMELL.

ROADS

In 1996 there were an estimated 7,520 km of roads, of which 2,376 km were paved. The rehabilitation of the 675-km axis road that links the port of Lomé with Burkina Faso, and thus provides an important transport corridor for land-locked West African countries, was considered essential to Togo's economic competitiveness; in 1997 the World Bank provided a credit of US $50m. for the rehabilitation of a severely deteriorated 105-km section of the road between Atakpamé and Blitta. In 1998 Kuwait awarded Togo a loan of 6,000m. CFA francs to improve the Notse-Atakpamé highway. Other principal roads run from Lomé to the borders of Ghana, Nigeria and Benin.

Africa Route International (ARI–La Gazelle): km 9, route d'Atakpamé, BP 4730, Lomé; tel. 25-27-32; fax 29-09-93; f. 1991 to succeed Société Nationale de Transports Routiers; Pres. and Man. Dir BAWA S. MANKOUBI.

SHIPPING

The major port, at Lomé, generally handles a substantial volume of transit trade for the land-locked countries of Mali, Niger and Burkina Faso, although political unrest in Togo has resulted in the diversion of much of this trade to neighbouring Benin. Freight handled at Lomé declined to about 856,600 metric tons (including transit trade) in 1994, compared with some 2m. tons in previous years. In 1995 the Banque ouest-africaine de développement approved a loan of 5,000m. francs CFA to help finance the rehabilitation of the infrastructure at Lomé port. The project aimed to re-establish Lomé as one of the principal transit ports on the west coast of Africa. By 1996 freight traffic had recovered to an estimated 1.3m. tons, and in 1997 it rose to an estimated 1.7m. tons. Further upgrading of the port's facilities, including the computerization of port operations and the construction of a new container terminal, were in progress in 1998 and 1999, largely funded by the private sector. There is another port at Kpémé for the export of phosphates.

Port Autonome de Lomé: BP 1225, Lomé; tel. 27-47-42; fax 27-26-27; e-mail deport@cafe.tg; internet www.togoport.com; f. 1968; Pres. IHOU AGBOBOLI; Man. Dir AWA BELEYI.

Société Ouest-Africaine d'Entreprises Maritimes Togo (SOAEM–TOGO): Zone Industrielle Portuaire, BP 3285, Lomé; tel. 21-07-20; fax 21-34-17; f. 1959; forwarding agents, warehousing, sea and road freight transport; Pres. JEAN FABRY; Man. Dir JOHN M. AQUEREBURU.

Société Togolaise de Navigation Maritime (SOTONAM): place des Quatre Etoiles, rond-point du Port, BP 4086, Lomé; tel. 21-51-73; fax 27-69-38; state-owned; privatization pending; Man. PAKOUM KPEMA.

SOCOPAO–Togo: 18 rue du Commerce, BP 821, Lomé; tel. 21-55-88; fax 21-73-17; f. 1959; freight transport, shipping agents; Pres. GUY MIRABAUD; Man. Dir HENRI CHAULIER.

SORINCO—Marine: 110 rue de l'OCAM, BP 2806, Lomé; tel. 21-56-94; freight transport, forwarding agents, warehousing, etc.; Man. AHMED EDGAR COLLINGWOOD WILLIAMS.

Togolaise d'Armements et d'Agence de Lignes SA (TAAL): 21 blvd du Mono, BP 9089, Lomé; tel. 22-02-43; fax 21-06-09; f. 1992; shipping agents, haulage management, crewing agency, forwarding agents; Pres. and Man. Dir LAURENT GBATI TAKASSI-KIKPA.

CIVIL AVIATION

There are international airports at Tokoin, near Lomé, and at Niamtougou. In addition, there are smaller airfields at Sokodé, Sansanné-Mango, Dapaong and Atakpamé.

Air Afrique: 20 rue de Grand Marché, BP 111, Lomé; tel. 21-20-42; fax 21-69-68; internet www.airafrique-airlines.com; see under Côte d'Ivoire; Man. in Togo OUEDRAOGO DELPHINE.

Air Togo: Lomé; tel. 21-33-10; f. 1963; cap. 5m. francs CFA; scheduled internal services; Man. Dir AMADOU ISAAC ADE.

Peace Air Togo (PAT): Lomé; internal services and services to Burkina Faso and Côte d'Ivoire; Man. Dir M. DJIBOM.

Société aéroportuaire de Lomé: Aéroport de Lomé, BP 10112, Lomé; tel. 26-71-21; fax 26-88-95.

Tourism

Togo's tourist industry collapsed in the wake of the political instability of the early 1990s; occupancy rates in the capital's hotels dropped from 33% in 1990 to 10% in 1993. The tourist industry has, however, recovered in the late 1990s. Some 69,458 foreign tourist arrivals were reported in 1998, when hotel receipts from tourism totalled 5,612,000m. CFA francs. In 1998 occupancy rates were estimated at 20%. In that year there were 2,258 hotel rooms and 4,289 hotel beds available.

Direction des Professions Touristiques: BP 1289, Lomé; tel. 21-56-62; fax 21-89-27; Dir ANATE S. BAGNAH.

Direction de la Promotion Touristique: Ministère du Tourisme et des Loisirs, rue du Lac Togo, BP 1289, Lomé; tel. 21-43-13; fax 21-89-27; Dir FOLEY DAHLEN.

Defence

In August 1999 Togo's armed forces officially numbered about 6,950 (army 6,500, air force 250, naval force 200). Paramilitary forces comprised a 750-strong gendarmerie. Military service is by selective conscription and lasts for two years. Togo receives assistance with training and equipment from France.

Defence Expenditure: Budgeted at 21,000m. francs CFA in 1999.

Chief of the Armed Forces: Gen. GNASSINGBE EYADÉMA.

Chief of General Staff: Col ZAKARI NANDJI.

Education

In 2000, according to UNESCO estimates, the adult illiteracy rate averaged 42.9% (males 27.8%; females 57.4%). Primary education, which begins at six years of age and lasts for six years, is officially compulsory. Secondary education, beginning at the age of 12, lasts for a further seven years, comprising a first cycle of four years and a second of three years. In 1996 enrolment at primary schools included 81% of children in the relevent age-group (93% of boys; 69% of girls). In the same year secondary enrolment was equivalent to only 27% of the appropriate age group (boys 40%; girls 14%). Proficiency in the two national languages, Ewe and Kabiye, is compulsory. Mission schools are important, educating almost one-half of all pupils. The Université du Bénin at Lomé had about 11,000 students in the mid-1990s, and scholarships to French universities are available. Current expenditure on education was an estimated 23,800m. francs CFA in 1995 (16.2% of total expenditure by the central government), and a further 3,700m. francs CFA was allocated to scholarships and training (2.5% of total expenditure).

Bibliography

Ameagbleame, S. *Histoire, littérature et société au Togo.* Frankfurt, IKO Verlag, 1997.

Amenumey, D. *The Ewe Unification Movement: A Political History.* Accra, Ghana University Press, 1989.

Cornevin, R. *Le Togo: des origines à nos jours.* Paris, Académie des sciences d'outre-mer, 1987.

Curkeet, A. A. *Togo: Portrait of a West African Francophone Republic in the 1980s.* Jefferson, McFarland, 1993.

Decalo, S. *Historical Dictionary of Togo.* 2nd Edn. Metuchen, NJ, Scarecrow Press, 1996.

Togo. Paris, ABC-Clio, 1995.

Delval, R. *Les musulmans au Togo.* Paris, Académie des sciences d'outre-mer, 1984.

François, Y. *Le Togo.* Paris, Editions Karthala, 1993.

Harrison Church, R. J. *West Africa.* 8th Edn. London, Longman, 1979.

Heilbrunn, J. *Social origins of national conferences in Benin and Togo,* in The Journal of Modern African Studies, Vol. 31, No. 2, Cambridge, 1993.

Stoecker, H. (Ed.). *German Imperialism in Africa.* London, Hurst Humanities, 1987.

Toulabor, C. *Le Togo sous Eyadéma.* Paris, Editions Karthala, 1986.

Verdier, R. *Le pays kabiyé Togo.* Paris, Editions Karthala, 1983.

UGANDA

Physical and Social Geography

B. W. LANGLANDS

PHYSICAL FEATURES AND CLIMATE

The Republic of Uganda is located on the eastern African plateau, at least 800 km inland from the Indian Ocean, and has a total area of 241,139 sq km (93,104 sq miles), including 44,081 sq km of inland water. There are several large freshwater lakes, of which Lakes Victoria, Edward and Albert are shared with neighbouring states. These lakes and most of the rivers form part of the basin of the upper (White) Nile, which has its origin in Uganda. At the point where the upper Nile leaves Lake Victoria, it is harnessed for hydroelectricity by the Owen Falls dam.

Of the land area (excluding open water), 84% forms a plateau at 900–1,500 m above sea-level, with a gentle downwarp to the centre to form Lake Kyoga. The western arm of the east African rift system accounts for the 9% of the land area at less than 900 m; this includes the lowlands flanking the rift lakes (Edward and Albert) and the course of the Albert Nile at little more than 620 m. Some 5% of the land area lies at an altitude of 1,500-2,100 m, including (in the eastern and western extremities) the shoulders of rift valley structures, and also the foothills of the mountains referred to below; this altitude accommodates some of the most heavily populated regions, as it is free of malaria. Mountains of over 2,100 m occupy the remaining 2% of the land area and these lands are above the limit of cultivation. The highest point is Mt Stanley, 5,109 m, in the Ruwenzori group on the border with the Democratic Republic of the Congo, but larger areas of highland are included in the Uganda portion of the volcanic mass of Mt Elgon, near the Kenyan border.

Geologically the great proportion of the country is made up of Pre-Cambrian material, largely of gneisses and schists into which granites have been intruded. In the west, distinct series of metamorphosed rocks occur, mainly of phyllites and shales, in which mineralized zones contain small quantities of copper, tin, tungsten and beryllium. Deposits of cobalt and nickel have also been identified, and also potentially substantial reserves of gold-bearing ores. Small quantities of gold, tungsten and tin concentrates are currently mined. In the east of the country there are extensive reserves of magnetite, apatite and crystalline limestone. The apatite provides the basis for a superphosphate industry and the limestone for a cement industry.

NATURAL RESOURCES

The economy of Uganda depends upon agriculture and this, in turn, is affected by climate. The country's location, between 1° 30′S and 4°N, gives little variation in temperature throughout the year, affording an equatorial climate modified by altitude. Rainfall is greatest bordering Lake Victoria and on the mountains, where small areas have over 2,000 mm per year. The high ground of the west, the rest of the Lake Victoria zone, and the eastern and north-central interior all have more than 1,250 mm annually. Only the north-east (Karamoja) and parts of the south

(east Ankole) have less than 750 mm. However, total amounts of rain are less significant agriculturally than the length of the dry season. For much of the centre and west there is no more than one month with less than 50 mm and this zone is characterized by permanent cropping of bananas for food, and coffee and tea for cash crops. To the south the dry season increases to three months (June to August); in the north it increases to four months (December to March) and in the north-east the dry season begins in October. Where the dry season is marked, as in the north and east, finger millet provides the staple food and cotton the main cash crop. In the driest parts pastoralism predominates, together with some sorghum cultivation.

Western Uganda, where there is a greater range of different physical conditions, and generally where population densities are below average, shows a diversity of land use, with tropical rain forest, two game parks, ranch lands, fishing, mining and the cultivation of coffee and tea. The north and east is more monotonous, savannah-covered plain with annually sown fields of grain and cotton. Most of the country's coffee comes from the Lake Victoria zone (*robusta*) and Mt Elgon (*arabica*). The economy relies heavily upon smallholding peasant production of basic cash crops.

POPULATION

The latest census, conducted in January 1991, enumerated a population of 16,671,705, giving a density of about 69 inhabitants per sq km. The total at the 1980 census had been 12.6m. In mid-1998 the population was officially estimated to have risen to 21,029,000, producing a density of 87.2 inhabitants per sq km. The population is predominantly rural; at the 1980 census only about 7% of the populace resided in towns of more than 1,000 people. Kampala (population estimated at 458,423 in 1980), the capital and main commercial centre, and Jinja (45,060), an industrial town, are the only urban centres of any significance. The annual birth rate is just under 51 per 1,000 of the population. Average life expectancy at birth in 1990–95 was 37.2 years, according to estimates by the UN. Demographic patterns in the later 1990s and beyond were expected to be significantly affected by the high rate of incidence of the acquired immunodeficiency syndrome (AIDS), which, by the early 1990s, had reportedly reached epidemic proportions in parts of Uganda. According to estimates by the World Bank 9.5% of the adult population were HIV–1 seropositive in 1997.

In 1959 about two-thirds of the population, mainly in the centre and south, were Bantu-speaking, about one-sixth Nilotic-speaking and a further one-sixth Nilo-Hamitic (Paranilotic). In 1969 there were 74,000 people of Indian and Pakistani origin, engaged mainly in commerce, and 9,500 Europeans, mostly in professional services. Since the 1972 expulsions of non-citizen Asians (who comprised the majority of the resident Asian population), both of these totals have fallen substantially.

Recent History

ALAN RAKE

British colonial activity in Uganda, which commenced after 1860, was consolidated in 1891 by a treaty with the kabaka (king) of Buganda, the dominant kingdom. In 1894 Buganda was declared a protectorate, and the same status was subsequently conferred on the kingdoms of Bunyoro, Toro, Ankole and Bugosa. For the next 50 years, debate over the position of Buganda within a future self-governing state inhibited the creation of a united nationalist movement. In 1956 the Democratic Party (DP) was formed, favouring a unitary independent state of Uganda and opposing the ambitions of the Baganda people, who did not wish Buganda's influence to be diminished after independence. The Uganda National Congress (UNC), meanwhile, advocated greater African control of the economy in a federal independent state. In 1958 seven African members of the protectorate's legislative council, including two members of the UNC, joined another faction, led by Dr Milton Obote, to form the Uganda People's Congress (UPC). By 1960 the UPC, the DP (led by Benedicto Kiwanuka) and the Buganda council (lukiiko) were the principal political forces in Uganda.

In 1961, at the first country-wide election to the legislative council, the DP won a majority of the seats. Kiwanuka was appointed chief minister, but he proved to be unacceptable to the ruling élite of Buganda. The Kabaka Yekka (KY, or 'King Alone'), a political party representing the interests of the lukiiko, was formed to ally with the UPC against the DP. Uganda was granted self-government in 1962, with Kiwanuka as prime minister. At pre-independence elections to a national assembly, held in April, the UPC won a majority of seats. The UPC–KY coalition formed a government, led by Obote. The new constitution provided for a federation of four regions—Buganda, Ankole, Bunyoro and Toro—each with considerable autonomy. In October Uganda became independent, within the Commonwealth, and a year later, on 9 October 1963, the country became a republic, with Mutesa II, the kabaka of Buganda, as non-executive president.

OBOTE AND THE UPC

During the first years of independence the UPC–KY alliance was placed under strain by controversy over levels of central government expenditure in Buganda, and over the 'lost counties', two districts of Bunyoro that had been transferred to Buganda in the late 19th century: in a referendum in November 1964 the inhabitants of the two districts voted to return to Bunyoro, but President Mutesa refused to endorse this result. By now, sufficient KY and DP members of the national assembly had defected to the UPC for the alliance to be no longer necessary. The UPC had also gained control of all district councils and kingdom legislatures, except in Buganda. The UPC itself, however, was split between conservative, centrist and radical elements of the party. In February 1966 the national assembly approved a motion demanding an investigation into gold-smuggling, in which Obote, the minister of defence, and the second-in-command of the army, Col Idi Amin Dada, were alleged to be involved. Later in that month Obote led a pre-emptive coup against his opponents within the UPC. Five government ministers were arrested, the constitution suspended, the president deposed and all executive powers transferred to Obote. In April an interim constitution was introduced, withdrawing regional autonomy and introducing an executive presidency. Obote became head of state. In May, when the lukiiko demanded the restoration of Buganda's autonomy, government troops, commanded by Amin, seized the palace of the kabaka (who escaped abroad) and a state of emergency was imposed in Buganda. A new constitution was adopted in September 1967, establishing a unitary republic and abolishing traditional rulers and legislatures. National elections were postponed until 1971.

During the late 1960s the Obote regime came to rely increasingly on detention and armed repression by the paramilitary and intelligence services. Estrangement began to develop, however, between Obote and the army. In December 1969 Obote was wounded in an assassination attempt in Kampala: Amin (still commander of the army) immediately fled to a military base in his home area. In the following month Brig. Pierino Okoya, Amin's most forceful critic in the government, was murdered.

THE AMIN REGIME

In January 1971, while Obote was out of the country, Amin seized power. In February Amin declared himself head of state, promising a return to civilian rule within five years. Many Ugandans believed that Amin would bring about the national cohesion which the UPC had failed to provide, and at first he received substantial support, as well as obtaining ready recognition from Western governments. Amin consolidated his military position by massacring troops and police (particularly those of the Langi and Acholi tribes) who had supported the Obote regime. Soon after taking power Amin suspended political activity and most civil rights. The national assembly was dissolved, and Amin ruled by decree. The jurisdiction of military tribunals was extended to cover the entire population, and several agencies were established to enforce state security. In August 1972 Amin announced the expulsion of all non-citizen Asians (who comprised the majority of the resident Asian population). The order was subsequently extended to include all Asians, and although this was later rescinded, under internal and external pressure, all but 4,000 Ugandan Asians left the country. Most went to the United Kingdom, which severed diplomatic relations and imposed a trade embargo against Uganda. In December all British companies in Uganda were nationalized without compensation.

In September 1972 a group of pro-Obote guerrillas (former members of the army and police who had fled the country when Amin seized power) attempted to oust Amin by an invasion, launched from Tanzania. The attempt was led by David Oyite-Ojok, the former chief of staff, and Yoweri Museveni, another senior officer. In retaliation, Amin's air force bombed Tanzanian towns. The Amin regime was supplied with military aid by Libya and the USSR, and by the end of 1972 virtually all Western aid had ceased. No coherent economic development policy existed, and the country's infrastructure deteriorated. During 1972–75 there were sporadic occurrences of factional fighting within the army, including a coup attempt in March 1974. Attacks on the Langi and Acholi populations were perpetrated by the army between late 1976 and early 1977. In February 1977, after protesting at the massacres, the Anglican archbishop of Uganda and two government ministers were murdered.

In October 1978 Amin sought to divert the attention of the armed forces from internal divisions (which had led to another abortive coup in August) by invading Tanzania, claiming the rightful possession of the Kagera salient. The attempt was unsuccessful and stimulated the Tanzanian government's efforts to remove Amin from power. Political exiles in Tanzania and elsewhere, including Obote, were encouraged by President Nyerere of Tanzania to form a united political front to remove Amin. In January 1979 the Tanzanian armed forces invaded Uganda, assisted by the Uganda National Liberation Army (UNLA), which comprised exiled Ugandan volunteers under the command of Oyite-Ojok and Museveni. They met little resistance from Amin's forces (assisted by 1,500 Libyan troops) and captured Kampala in April. Amin fled the country, eventually taking refuge in Saudi Arabia. (In July 1999 Uganda reportedly agreed to pay compensation to the Tanzanian government for the costs incurred during the operation to remove Amin.)

TRANSITIONAL GOVERNMENTS

A provisional government, the national executive council (NEC), was established in April 1979 from the ranks of the Uganda National Liberation Front (UNLF, a coalition of 18 previously exiled groups), with Dr Yusuf Lule, a former vice-chancellor of Makerere University, as president. When Lule attempted to reshuffle the NEC in June, opposition from within the UNLF forced his resignation. Lule was succeeded by Godfrey Binaisa (a former attorney-general), who was, in turn, overthrown by the military commission of the UNLF in May 1980, after he had decided to allow only UNLF members to stand in parliamentary elections and attempted to dismiss Oyite-Ojok from the command of the UNLA. The military commission was chaired by Paulo Muwanga (an associate of Obote), supported by Oyite-Ojok and with Museveni as vice-chairman.

OBOTE AND OKELLO

The elections held in December 1980 were contested by four parties: the UPC, under Obote; the DP, led by Paul Ssemogerere; the Uganda Patriotic Movement (UPM), a regrouping of the radical faction of the UPC, led by Museveni; and the Conservative Party (CP), a successor to the KY. The UPC gained a majority of seats, and Obote was proclaimed president for the second time in mid-December. The defeated parties complained of gross electoral malpractice by UPC supporters.

The new UPC government did not bring military or political stability to Uganda. Dissatisfaction with the conduct and outcome of the elections caused several factions to initiate guerrilla operations. The three main guerrilla movements were the Uganda National Rescue Front (UNRF), comprising supporters of Amin who were active in the West Nile area, the Uganda Freedom Movement (UFM), led by Balaki Kirya and Andrew Kayiira, and the National Resistance Army (NRA), led by Museveni, with ex-president Lule, now in exile, as chairman of its political wing, the National Resistance Movement (NRM). (Following Lule's death in 1985 Museveni became sole leader of the NRM and NRA.) Meanwhile, hundreds of Obote's opponents, including DP members of the national assembly, were detained, and several newspapers were banned.

The NRA (drawing on disaffected southern Ugandans and defectors from the increasingly disorganized UNLA) began to establish a reputation for military discipline. In March 1983, during a UNLA campaign to combat the NRA, attacks on refugee camps resulted in the deaths of hundreds of civilians, and more than 100,000 people were displaced. The offensive against the NRA was renewed in late 1984, with civilians again suffering the main impact of attacks. In mid-1985 Amnesty International alleged widespread torture and murder of civilians by the security forces.

Meanwhile, tensions were evident within the UNLA between the two main ethnic groups from which the army was recruited, the Acholi and the Langi. Following the death in December 1983 of Oyiti-Ojok, the Langi chief of staff, another Langi was appointed as his replacement. Some 200 Acholi officers were eventually promoted, in compensation.

In July 1985 Obote (a Langi) was overthrown in an Acholi military coup, led by Brig. (later Lt-Gen.) Basilio Okello. (The deposed president was subsequently granted political asylum by Zambia.) A military council, headed by Lt-Gen. (later Gen.) Tito Okello, the commander-in-chief of the army, was established to govern the country, pending elections to be held a year later. In subsequent months, groups which had been in opposition to Obote, with the exception of the NRA/NRM, reached agreement with the new administration, and accepted positions on the military council. An amnesty was declared for exiles who had supported Amin. By the end of August, however, the Okello government was facing serious difficulties. The NRA had occupied the main towns of the west (Fort Portal and Kasese), and by late September southern Uganda, up to the Katonga river, was under its control, while UNLA troops in the southern towns of Mbarara and Masaka remained under siege in their barracks. The discipline of the NRA forces contrasted starkly with the performance of the UNLA, while the NRA's control of southern Uganda, and the region's cash crops, placed an economic stranglehold on the Kampala government.

Against this volatile background, peace talks opened in Nairobi, Kenya, between representatives of the NRA and the Okello government. It soon became apparent, however, that neither side was fully committed to a permanent peace settlement, and the terms of the accord that they eventually signed, in December 1985, were never implemented. Instead of taking up his allotted seat on the military council in Kampala, Museveni returned to south-west Uganda to lead the NRA in a final offensive.

THE MUSEVENI PRESIDENCY

Claiming that law and order had broken down throughout Uganda, NRA troops surrounded Kampala, and took control in January 1986. Museveni was sworn in as president and formed a National Resistance Council (NRC), with both civilian and military members. His cabinet, with Samson Kisekka as prime minister, included members as diverse as Paul Ssemogerere of the DP, Brig. Moses Ali, a former minister under Amin, and Andrew Kayiira of the UFM. Elections were postponed for at least three years. Political parties were not banned, although their activities were officially suspended in March. The defeat of Okello's remaining UNLA troops was officially completed by the end of March. They wreaked havoc in the areas through which they retreated into Sudan.

Museveni announced a policy of national reconciliation. He established a commission to investigate breaches of human rights during the regimes of Amin, Obote and Okello, under whom, he claimed, up to 800,000 Ugandans had been killed. Following an investigation of the activities of the police force, more than 2,500 of its members were dismissed in July 1986. During 1986 the Museveni government developed a system of resistance committees at local and district level; these were to be partly responsible for the maintenance of security and the elimination of corruption.

Lawlessness and banditry remained rife, especially in the north. In March 1986 an armed movement seeking the overthrow of Museveni, the Uganda People's Democratic Movement (UPDM), was formed, with Obote's former prime minister, Eric Otema Allimadi, as chairman. This, together with raids by remnants of the UNLA, chronic problems with armed cattle-rustlers in the north-east and the lack of any basic infrastructure of law and order, prevented Museveni from consolidating his control over Uganda. Although he allowed the return from exile of Prince Ronald Mutebi, the claimant to the throne of Buganda, Museveni refused to restore Uganda's traditional monarchies until stability had returned to the country.

In October 1986 26 people, including Paulo Muwanga, Obote's former vice-president, and Kayiira, had been arrested for treason. Although charges against some of these were later withdrawn, the murder of Kayiira in March 1987 caused the UFM to remove its support for the government. The trial of seven of the 26 who had been arrested began in August 1987, and in the following March three were sentenced to death, while the remaining four were acquitted.

The largest uprising in the period immediately following Museveni's accession to power was led by a charismatic cult leader, Alice Lakwena, whose religious sect attracted both peasant farmers from the Acholi tribe and former soldiers of the UNLA. The rebel 'Holy Spirit Movement', as it became known, engaged the NRA in attacks that were effectively suicidal. In late 1987, after several thousand of the rebels had been killed, the revolt was crushed, and Lakwena fled to Kenya. However, remaining members of the movement subsequently regrouped themselves as the Lord's Resistance Army (LRA), under the leadership of Joseph Kony, Lakwena's nephew.

In conjunction with the use of force to curb dissidence, Museveni also adopted a reconciliatory approach towards opponents of the NRC. In June 1987 an amnesty was declared for insurgents (except those accused of murder or rape), which was subsequently repeatedly extended; by April 1988 Ugandan officials reported that almost 30,000 rebels had surrendered. However, in December 1987, while on a mission to implement the amnesty in Soroti district, Stanislas Okurut, the minister of labour, and two deputy ministers were detained by rebels of the Ugandan People's Army (UPA), led by Peter Otai, a former minister in the Obote administration. The UPA's demands for the release of rebel prisoners in exchange for the ministers were not met; one of the deputy ministers escaped in March 1988, while a clash between NRA troops and the rebels in August led to the death of the other deputy minister and the injuring of Okurut. In early 1988 the NRA held peace talks with the armed wing of the UPDM, the Uganda People's Democratic Army (UPDA). The failure by the commander of the UPDA, Brig. Justin Odong Latek, to endorse the proposed peace agreement led, in May, to his removal. In the following month his successor, Lt-Col John Angelo Okello, signed a peace agreement with the NRC; however, a faction of the UPDA regrouped, under the leadership of Odong Latek, and continued to oppose the government. In mid-1989 the NRC launched a major offensive against guerrilla forces.

Further efforts were made to strengthen the position of the Museveni administration. The president carried out a major cabinet reshuffle in February 1988, in which he increased the number of ministers originating from the north-east of Uganda, where opposition to the government was most prevalent. An abortive mutiny by members of the NRA in April resulted in the detention of some 700 army officers and soldiers. In May the NRC approved legislation validating the NRC as the country's official legislature. In the following month, draft legislation was introduced to prohibit the practice and promotion of sectarianism; other new legislation imposed heavy penalties for revealing military operations and strategies to the 'enemy'. A degree of press censorship was also introduced. It was stressed by Museveni that the prohibition of 'sectarianism' was not aimed at stifling political debate. In October 24 people were arrested and charged with plotting a coup.

Post-Election Reforms

In February 1989 the first national election since 1980 was held. The NRC, which had previously comprised only members nominated by the president, was expanded from 98 to 278 members, to include 210 elected representatives. While a total of 20 ministerial posts were reserved for nominated members of the NRC, 50 were allocated to elected members. As a result of these changes, 10 cabinet ministers and four deputy ministers lost their posts. Following the election, Museveni appointed a constitutional commission to gauge public opinion on Uganda's political future and to draft a new constitution.

In October 1989 (despite opposition from the DP) the NRC approved draft legislation, submitted by the NRM, to extend the government's term of office by five years from January 1990, when its mandate had been due to expire: the NRM justified seeking to extend its rule by claiming that it required further time in which to prepare a new constitution, to organize elections, to eliminate continuing anti-government guerrilla activity, to improve the judiciary, police force and civil service, and to rehabilitate the country's infrastructure. It was announced in January 1990 that several army officers and civilians had been charged with plotting to overthrow the government. In March the NRM extended the ban on party political activity (imposed in March 1986) for a further five years. In February 1990 the minister of culture, youth and sports, Brig. Moses Ali, was dismissed and charged with plotting a *coup d'état*. (Ali was subsequently acquitted of this charge, but in January 1991 was found guilty of illegally possessing ammunition.) In July 1990 Allimadi, the leader of the UPDM, signed a peace accord with the government.

In January 1991 Samson Kisekka was replaced as prime minister by George Adyebo; Kisekka was appointed vice-president and minister of internal affairs. In April Daniel Omara Atubo, the minister of state for foreign affairs and regional co-operation, was arrested, together with two other members of the NRC, and charged with plotting to overthrow the Museveni administration by assisting anti-government rebels; 15 other people (including further members of the NRC) were subsequently detained on similar grounds. At the beginning of April the government initiated a campaign to combat continuing guerrilla activity in northern and eastern districts: by July it was reported that more than 1,500 rebels had been killed and more than 1,000 had been arrested. International observers accused the NRA of committing atrocities during the offensive.

In May 1991 Museveni formally invited all emigré Ugandan Asians, who had been expelled during the Amin regime, to return. This gesture was intended to attract both international approval and investment in the Ugandan economy by expelled Asians who had prospered since leaving Uganda. In July the cabinet was reorganized, with the number of ministries substantially reduced. A report by Amnesty International, which was released in early December, accused the NRA of torturing and summarily executing prisoners during anti-insurgency operations.

In October 1992 the government launched a three-year programme to reduce the size of the NRA by about one-half, in response to pressure from the international donor community.

In December negotiations on the restoration of the Bugandan monarchy commenced between Museveni and the claimant, Prince Ronald Mutebi. Later in the same month the constitutional commission which had been established in 1989 presented its draft constitution to the government. The document, which was officially published in March 1993, was strongly opposed by the UPC and the DP on the grounds that it would increase presidential powers still further. The commission recommended the proscription of party political activity for at least a further seven years and a continuation of 'non-party democracy', under the auspices of a national political movement to which all citizens would belong; a non-party presidential election was envisaged. In April the NRC passed legislation authorizing the establishment of a constituent assembly.

In July 1993 legislation was approved which provided for the restoration of each of Uganda's traditional monarchies; these were, however, to be limited to ceremonial and cultural functions. At the end of that month Mutebi was enthroned as the kabaka of Buganda, and in early August the lukiiko was re-established. A new omukama (king) of Toro, Patrick Olimi Kaboyo, was installed in July, and a new omugabe (king) of Ankole, John Barigye, was installed in November. However, Museveni, although himself an Ankole, refused to recognize the new omugabe, thereby increasing suspicions that his recognition of the kabaka of Buganda and the omukama of Toro was based on short-term political expediency rather than a desire to revive Uganda's traditional monarchies. In June 1994 Museveni agreed to the coronation of Solomon Gafabusa Iguru as omukama of the Bunyoro. Kaboyo died in August 1995, and was succeeded as omukama of Toro in September 1996 by his infant son Oyo Nyimba Iguru. The kingdom of Busoga was restored in February 1996, with Henry Wako Muloki installed as king.

In September 1993 nine army officers, who had been arrested on treason charges between 1988–90, and held without trial, were released. In the same month the government ordered a judicial review of the trials of those sentenced to death in January 1993 by army tribunals which were now officially described as 'illegal and incompetent'. In October Lt-Col James Oponyo, the commander of the UPA in the Teso area in north-eastern Uganda, surrendered to government forces. In January 1994 two other rebel groups, the Ugandan Democratic Alliance (UDA) and the Uganda Federal Army (UFA), also agreed to suspend their guerrilla operations. However, in early 1994 Peter Otai, a former leader of the UPA, formed a new rebel group, known as the Uganda People's Freedom Movement (UPFM).

In March 1994 renewed clashes occurred in northern Uganda between the forces of Joseph Kony's LRA and the government, following the collapse of short-lived negotiations between the two sides which had commenced in January of that year. The rebels, who claimed to be fighting a 'holy war' on behalf of the northern Acholi tribe, carried out ambushes and abductions which prompted the government to dispatch large numbers of security forces to the region.

The return of emigré Asians to reclaim the property which was expropriated by the Amin regime continued in 1994, although the process provoked jealousies and racial antagonism, with indigenous businessmen claiming that they had not been sufficiently compensated. Despite sporadic acts of violence, the government adhered to its compensation policy and extended from October 1993 to April 1994 the deadline for Asians to return and reclaim their expropriated assets.

Political and Constitutional Changes

Elections to the 288-member constituent assembly took place in March 1994, and were accepted by a majority of Ugandans to have been conducted fairly. In a turn-out of 7m. of the total 8m. registered voters, Museveni and the NRM won overwhelming support. Although candidates were officially required to stand on a non-party basis, tacit official tolerance of party campaigning was reflected in the leaders of three parties—the DP, the CP and the UPC—being given access to national radio and television during the weeks prior to the election. Of the 214 elective seats to the constituent assembly the government alliance won an estimated 150 seats, most of which were in Buganda, the Western region and parts of the East, while the opposition (supporters of the UPC and DP) secured most seats in the north and the north-east. Museveni and Kisekka, the vice-president, who indicated that he was to retire from active politics, did not stand. Museveni's most senior government colleagues (including the prime minister, Adyebo and his three deputies) won convincingly. Among five senior ministers who failed to obtain seats, however, was the minister of finance and economic planning, Jehoash Mayanja-Nkangi, and the katikiro (prime minister) of Buganda. The constituent assembly, which also comprised nominated representatives of the armed forces, political parties, trade unions and various special interest groups, was empowered to debate, amend and finally to enact the draft constitution. Amendments to the draft required a two-thirds majority of the assembly; changes that received majority support but less than two-thirds were to be submitted to referendum. The new constitution, under whose terms a national referendum on the future introduction of a multi-party political system was to be staged in 2000, was eventually promulgated in October 1995.

In November 1994 Museveni reshuffled the cabinet, replacing Adyebo as prime minister by Kintu Musoke, hitherto minister of state for security, and appointing Dr Speciosa Wandira Kazibwe, the minister of women's affairs and community development, as vice-president. Brig. Moses Ali rejoined the cabinet. In June 1995 Paul Ssemogerere resigned from his posts of second deputy prime minister and minister of public service, announcing that he intended to prepare a campaign with which to contest the presidential election that was scheduled to take place, with legislative elections, in 1996.

In June 1995 the constituent assembly rejected the immediate restoration of multi-party democracy, claiming that it would exacerbate existing ethnic and religious divisions. Consequently, candidates at the legislative and presidential elections would be required to seek election without official reference to their respective political affiliations. The constituent assembly's decision was strongly opposed by the UPC and other unofficial opposition parties.

It was announced in mid-1995 that defence expenditure would be increased by 40% (despite recent cutbacks) in order to combat continuing insurrection in northern Uganda by rebel groups (including the LRA, see below) which was hampering the economic development of the already impoverished region. Signs of serious tensions in the army were apparent at this time. A military report was published, which detailed deteriorating conditions and equipment, as well as corruption and low morale among soldiers. A number of opposition groups were established during the mid-1990s by Baganda with federalist aspirations.

Preparations for the forthcoming presidential and legislative elections proceeded at a leisurely pace during 1995 and early 1996. The election dates were postponed several times. Registration of the presidential candidates eventually took place in March 1996. The main challenger to Museveni was Paul Ssemogerere, the leader of the DP. While many of Ssemogerere's election rallies were banned, Museveni campaigned with the full backing of the army, police and security forces. The presidential election was held on 9 May; Museveni won convincingly, securing 74.2% of the votes (Ssemogerere took 23.7%). The incumbent president triumphed in most regions, including Buganda and other areas that had traditionally been loyal to the DP. As the unofficial representative of an electoral alliance between the DP and the UPC, Ssemogerere was widely perceived to be associated with the UPC's exiled leader, Dr Milton Obote. This brought Ssemogerere some successes in the north but lost him support in Buganda and in the west. The election, which was declared free and fair by international observers, emphatically legitimized Museveni's presidency. He immediately declared that he would not restore multi-party democracy for at least five years. Legislative elections took place in June. The total membership of the NRC, redesignated the parliament under the new constitution, was reduced from 278 to 276, comprising 214 elected and 62 nominated representatives. In the same month elections were held for new local councils (to replace the resistance committees). In July Museveni appointed an enlarged government, despite disapproval from international creditors, citing the need to achieve a regional balance in his administration.

Nation-wide local elections took place in November 1997. Museveni reorganized the cabinet in May and August 1998. In September five people were killed in a plane crash in the Ruwenzori mountains, near the Uganda–DRC border. It emerged that one of the casualties had been on a gold-buying mission in the DRC for an Israeli company in which Salim Saleh had a major interest. Saleh, at that time Uganda's principal military strategist in the conflict in the DRC, had evidently also taken the opportunity to pursue private business interests there. In December Saleh resigned as minister of state for defence, after admitting 'improper conduct' in connection with the recent privatization of Uganda Commercial Bank. Uganda's criminal investigation department confirmed that it had opened files on Saleh and others, including a further four government ministers. Museveni accepted his half-brother's resignation reluctantly, as he valued Saleh's military guidance in the DRC. Saleh did not, however, abandon his political ambitions, announcing in April 1999 that he intended to stand for the vice-presidency at the elections scheduled for 2001. Saleh's critics reacted strongly, accusing him of attempting to establish a family power base.

In the second half of 1999 campaigning began for the referendum to decide whether Uganda should continue to be governed under the non-party system or revert to pluralism. The opposition parties declared that the Referendum Act (passed in July 1999) was unconstitutional, because it had not secured the necessary majority in the national assembly. Foreign aid donors and the US-based Human Rights Watch organization joined in the criticism, warning that the referendum would not be fair unless political parties were allowed to put their case. Western donors (Belgium, Denmark, the EU, Germany, Japan, Norway, Sweden, the UK and the USA) provided US $3m. to help finance the referendum, but criticized both the government, for not allowing political parties to participate, and the opposition, for threatening an outright boycott.

The referendum campaign became more intense at the beginning of 2000. President Museveni toured the country, putting the case for a continuation of the non-party NRM system. Museveni was expected to win, given that all the main opposition parties had announced their intention to boycott the poll. The opposition parties claimed that the referendum process was rigged against them, and that the government was not funding them adequately. Public apathy was revealed by the low numbers registering to vote, following a series of low participation rates in preceding elections. Though registration and the participation rate were low, the referendum went ahead on 29 June. Electoral monitors from the OAU declared that the referendum had been conducted fairly and peacefully, although the opposition parties continued to claim that the referendum was unfair, and had carried out their threatened boycott of the poll. Museveni said the 'no-party' system was democratic because anyone could compete for political office on individual merit, and justified the NRM on the grounds that Uganda's bloody past had been caused, largely, by the divisive effects of political parties which, according to the president, split underdeveloped countries along ethnic and tribal lines. Museveni won, as expected, receiving 90.7% of the vote; however, only around 45% of the electorate cast their ballots. In September Museveni effected a minor cabinet reshuffle.

Internal Security Concerns

From the mid-1990s the Museveni administration was greatly preoccupied with controlling the mounting (and evidently foreign-backed) insurrections perpetrated by three main rebel groups in northern and western Uganda. Firstly, in the north, the LRA (backed by Sudan) was becoming increasingly disruptive. Museveni took the threat seriously, announcing that the NRA would be re-equipped to fight mobile and modern warfare against the rebels. In July 1996 Museveni appointed his younger half-brother, Maj.-Gen. Salim Saleh, to oversee all military operations in the north. Saleh launched 'Operation Clean', a campaign to rout the rebels; although this had some success initially, the LRA soon resumed its attacks. During 1993–98 the LRA killed as many as 10,000 people, while a further 220,000 sought refuge in protected camps; economic activity in the region was devastated. The group's use of abducted children as soldiers attracted widespread international condemnation. During the late 1990s the authorities introduced a programme to provide a number of protected villages for northerners. However, the government strongly resisted pressure to resume negotiations with the LRA, prompting some speculation that

Museveni (a southerner) might be prepared to profit from the disablement of opposition strongholds in the northern region. In the west, meanwhile, the Uganda People's Defence Forces (UPDF, as the NRA had become) was challenging the serious threat posed by both the West Nile Bank Front (WNBF), led by a former minister of foreign affairs, Col Juma Oris, until his death in action in February 1997, and the Allied Democratic Front (ADF), mainly comprising Ugandan Islamic fundamentalists and former soldiers of the defeated UNLA, assisted by exiled Rwandan Hutu militiamen and by former soldiers from Zaire (which, in May 1997, became the Democratic Republic of the Congo—DRC).

Although WNBF activities subsided in mid-1997 following the killing of several hundred of its members by Sudanese rebels on good terms with the Ugandan government, the ADF (which had been disabled temporarily in the first half of 1997 when its lines of communication were cut owing to the civil war in Zaire) mounted a persistent terror campaign from mid-1997 against western Ugandan targets. In June 1997 some 500 ADF soldiers briefly occupied the town of Bundibugyo, before being dislodged by the UPDF. In October the ADF carried out a series of attacks in the Ruwenzori mountains (where its bases were) and in Kilembe district, prompting the Ugandan and DRC armies to launch a joint military operation against the rebels; the UPDF was reinforced by 50 tanks which it had previously loaned to the former guerrilla army of Laurent-Désiré Kabila, the DRC's new president. Meanwhile the Ugandan military leadership accused Libya and Iran of supporting the ADF: Libya was alleged to have sent 40 tons of military equipment to the rebels, while Iran was suspected of giving them financial aid via an Islamic foundation in South Africa. In October an Israeli envoy (Gideon Ezra, a Likud member and former agent of the Israeli secret intelligence service) visited Kampala and addressed the Ugandan parliament, suggesting co-operation with Israel in combating militant Islamic fundamentalism.

The inability of the UPDF to eliminate the guerrilla threat in the north and west of the country and allegations of corruption concerning some senior army officers increasingly concerned Museveni. In December 1997 the security services established a special task force to investigate allegations that a number of officers had been offered money to carry out an assassination attempt against the president. This led to a major purge of the army in January 1998, when several high-ranking officers were dismissed. Maj.-Gen. Salim Saleh was promoted to minister of state for defence, while the UPDF commander Maj.-Gen. Mugisha Muntu was replaced by Maj.-Gen. Jeje Abubaker Odongo. Museveni also redressed the perceived ethnic imbalance in the army by appointing more non-westerners to top posts. In March 1998 it was reported that Idi Amin, still exiled in Saudi Arabia, had been accused by the Saudi authorities of attempting to organize a shipment of arms to northern Uganda. During April a combination of WNBF guerrillas, former Zairean soldiers and Sudanese government troops were reported to be operating just across the Uganda-DRC border. In June the ADF attacked the Kichwambwa Technical Institute, in the foothills of the Ruwenzori, killing an estimated 80 students and reportedly abducting more than 100 others. Reports subsequently emerged that army troops guarding the college had abandoned their posts and fled during the incident, prompting many citizens in the region to lose confidence in the ability of the state to protect them and consequently seriously impairing Museveni's local popularity. Following the Kichwambwa atrocity the president came under mounting pressure to master the national security crisis, if needs be by abandoning his policy of refusing to negotiate with the guerrillas. His immediate response was to promise disciplinary action against the incompetent soldiers and compensation for the victims of the attack, and to appoint his trusted army chief of staff, Brig. James Kazini, as regional commander for the Ruwenzori area. By early 1999 the ADF had reportedly displaced about 70,000 western Ugandans, while a number of development projects in the region had been suspended and the success of tourism to the Ruwenzori was threatened. There was some evidence that the ADF was receiving arms and equipment from the DRC and by air-drop from Sudan.

At the beginning of March 1999 eight foreign tourists and four Ugandans were kidnapped and murdered at the Bwindi national park in south-western Uganda by Rwandan Hutu Interahamwe guerrillas. The rebels' declared aims were to destabilize Uganda, engender economic chaos and to publicize their cause internationally. All tourists selected for execution were anglophone, evidently in protest at the support of the USA and United Kingdom for the Tutsi regime which took power in Rwanda in 1994. In a joint operation by Ugandan and Rwandan troops, 33 of the Hutu guerrillas were subsequently killed. Museveni argued that the atrocity vindicated his decision to send troops into the DRC in August 1998 to protect Uganda's borders (see below). Action Aid and Médecins Sans Frontières withdrew their representatives from the region following the attacks. In May the USA asked its peace corps workers to leave Uganda, in view of the generally poor security situation. In early April 1999 Museveni reshuffled the cabinet, appointing Prof. Apolo Nsimbambi (hitherto minister of education and sports) as prime minister in place of Kintu Musoke, who had resigned. In May Museveni announced that the UPC leader and former president, Milton Obote, would be permitted to return to Uganda under an amnesty offered to all exiles. Museveni stressed, however, that he was not inviting Obote back. Some 28 prisoners, many of them allegedly former UPC security agents, had been executed in the previous month (despite European Union pleas for clemency) for torturing prisoners to death in 1981. Legislation was enacted in July 1999 providing for the proposed referendum on a plural political system to take place as planned in 2000. Nation-wide campaigning by the government commenced immediately, although most political parties announced that they would boycott the referendum on the grounds that it would be manipulated by the NRM for its own purposes.

The LRA intensified its campaign in the first half of 1999. However, divisions within the guerrilla group were becoming evident at that time. In May Museveni revised his previous insistence on eradicating the LRA solely by military means, issuing an amnesty to the rebels and promising Kony, the LRA leader, a cabinet post should he be democratically elected to government. It was reported at that time that the Sudanese government (which had allegedly been paying Kony a substantial 'salary') was considering withdrawing its assistance to the LRA. In June UNICEF reported that 21,719 people (including 6,652 children) were known to have been abducted by the LRA, in four northern districts, since the inception of its activities, and that it continued to hold 3,703 captives. During May Roman Catholic leaders in the Ruwenzori region offered to mediate between the Ugandan government and the ADF. In addition to the terror campaign it had been conducting in the south-west, the ADF was believed to be mainly responsible for co-ordinating a series of bomb attacks on civilian targets in Kampala that had commenced in 1997 and continued throughout 1998 and the first half of 1999. By mid-1999 it was estimated that 55 people had been killed and at least 183 injured by the attacks. By July more than 120 alleged dissidents had reportedly been arrested and interrogated in connection with the atrocities, prompting a number of protests from human rights organizations. Some 13 of those arrested were charged with terrorism and treason in June. Smith Opon Acak, a former chief of staff under president Obote, was killed in a military operation in July. He had been arrested on treason charges in 1987 and then released later that year, when he had gone into exile in Kenya. He had returned to Uganda to lead a group called the Citizens' Army for Multi-Party Politics (CAMP). The UPDF claimed that he was planning to attack a police post and military barracks in the district of Lira when he was shot.

In December 1999 the national assembly passed a bill granting a general amnesty to all rebels who had been fighting to overthrow the Museveni government and who were prepared to renounce rebellion. This, and the peace agreement with Sudan also signed in December, presented an opportunity to weaken the LRA. There had been faction-fighting in the ranks of the group during the absence of Kony, who had been hospitalized in Khartoum. There were also presistent reports that Kony had ordered the execution of his deputy, Alex Otti-Logony, after a leadership struggle.

Also in December 1999 a faction of the ADF, which was facing its own internal schisms, attacked Katojo prison in Kabarole and released 365 prisoners, including some suspected rebels. Then, in January 2000, the rebels attacked a refugee camp in Bundibuyogo in the west, killing at least 24 people. At this,

Museveni based himself for a week in the Ugandan army camp at Semiliki National Park to direct operations against the ADF. It was the first time that he had involved himself, as president, directly in military operations and it implied some criticism of his commanders, who had been outspoken against amnesty policies towards the rebels. The intensified campaign against the ADF resulted, in March, in the capture of a senior ADF leader, Commander Mwamba, and the surrender of two other senior commanders to the UPDF. At the same time more than 100 civilians were rescued from rebel captivity.

In mid-March 2000 more than 330 bodies were discovered burnt to death in a church at Kanungu in western Uganda. They had been members of a fanatical cult called the Movement for the Restoration of the Ten Commandments of God. Hundreds more bodies were discovered in other mass graves. The sect members had either been killed or persuaded to commit suicide by their leaders. Museveni ordered a full inquiry and warrants were issued for the arrest of the sect leaders, who had gone into hiding.

REGIONAL RELATIONS

During 1987 Uganda's relations with neighbouring Kenya deteriorated, with the Museveni government accusing Kenya of sheltering Ugandan rebels. In March the Kenyan authorities expelled hundreds of Ugandans. When, in October, Uganda stationed troops at the two countries' common border, Kenya threatened to retaliate with force against any attempts by Ugandan military personnel to cross the frontier in pursuit of rebels. In December clashes occurred between Kenyan and Ugandan security forces and the border was temporarily closed. Later in December, discussions between the heads of state of the two countries led to an improvement in relations, and in January 1988 Kenya and Uganda signed a joint communiqué, which provided for co-operation in resolving problems relating to the flow of traffic across the common border. However, several incursions into Kenya by Ugandan troops were subsequently reported. In August 1990 President Moi of Kenya visited Museveni, indicating a renewed *détente* between Uganda and Kenya. Moi made a further visit to Uganda in November 1993, at which a communiqué was signed providing for the exploration of areas of co-operation in both security and trade. In November 1994 the presidents of Uganda, Kenya and Tanzania met in Arusha, Tanzania, and established a permanent commission for co-operation between the three countries, with a view to reviving the defunct East African Community (EAC). Initial progress was hindered, however, by a sudden deterioration in relations between Uganda and Kenya. During early 1995 the Kenyan government protested strongly to the UN, following the granting of refugee status in Uganda to an alleged Kenyan guerrilla leader; the Ugandan authorities subsequently claimed to have deported the Kenyan to a third country (reported to be Ghana). Relations between Uganda and Kenya remained strained until January 1996 when, following the intervention of the newly-elected President Mkapa of Tanzania, Museveni and Moi were publicly reconciled. In March 1996 Museveni, Moi and Mkapa, meeting in Nairobi, Kenya, formally inaugurated the secretariat of the permanent tripartite commission for East African co-operation. Relations between Uganda and Tanzania came under brief strain in December 1997, when the Burundian authorities accused Tanzania of supporting rebel groups active in Uganda, Burundi and Rwanda; the Museveni administration, however, strongly dissociated itself from the allegations, reaffirming its good relations with Tanzania. A treaty for the re-establishment of the EAC, providing for the creation of a free trade area (with the eventual introduction of a single currency), for the development of infrastructure, tourism and agriculture within the community and for the establishment of a regional legislative assembly and regional court) was initially expected to be ratified by the heads of state of Uganda, Kenya and Tanzania in July 1999. The conclusion of the treaty was postponed, pending the completion of negotiations on several unresolved trade issues, but was eventually signed in November.

During 1988 tension arose along Uganda's border with Zaire (now the DRC), owing to a number of attacks by Zairean troops on NRA units; further border clashes occurred in 1992. In November 1996 Ugandan rebels were reportedly operating from within Zaire with the support of Zairean troops. In late 1996

and early 1997 the Ugandan authorities repeatedly denied allegations that Ugandan forces were occupying territory in eastern Zaire; however, it was widely reported that Uganda was supplying armaments and tactical support, if not troops, to Laurent-Désiré Kabila's Alliance des forces démocratiques pour la libération du Congo-Zaïre (AFDL), which overthrew the government of President Mobutu in May 1997. The Museveni administration, however, subsequently withdrew its support from the Kabila regime in the new DRC, as Kabila made no attempt to sever the ongoing supply of arms to Ugandan rebels operating brutal campaigns from the DRC-Uganda border region. When, in August 1998, anti-Kabila elements launched a rebellion from the eastern part of the DRC, Uganda intervened, at first covertly, on the side of the rebels. Soon reports emerged that large numbers of Ugandan and Rwandan troops were massed on key fronts in the eastern border region. Uganda eventually admitted that it had deployed troops in the DRC in co-operation with the Rwandan government, asserting that they were protecting Ugandan and Rwandan interests by creating a 'security zone'. In November the two governments formed a joint military command. The Kabila regime accused Uganda and Rwanda of creating, with the DRC rebels, a Tutsi-dominated alliance with expansionist ambitions; it was also alleged that the DRC's two eastern neighbours were illegally exploiting mineral interests in the area occupied by their forces. From early 1999 the Ugandan government appeared to become increasingly disenchanted with the protracted Congolese civil war. The high level of military expenditure incurred by Uganda's engagement in the conflict was unpopular with the IMF. In addition, the DRC government was threatening to protest against Uganda's military involvement in its internal affairs at the International Court of Justice. Initially Uganda insisted that no peace settlement could be agreed unless Kabila negotiated directly with the rebels. Subsequently, however, the Museveni administration decided to compromise, agreeing that all foreign troops should withdraw swiftly from the DRC, leaving the rebels to make their own peace with Kabila. In April 1999 Museveni met Kabila in Sirte, Libya (without his Rwandan counterpart) and unilaterally signed a cease-fire agreement, which entailed the withdrawal of all Ugandan troops and their replacement by an African peace-keeping force. The Sirte accord was, however, superseded by a comprehensive cease-fire agreement concluded at Lusaka, Zambia in early July by the heads of state of all the countries involved militarily in the civil war in the DRC (Kabila, Museveni and the Rwandan president, as well as the presidents of Angola, Namibia and Zimbabwe, who had entered the conflict in support of the DRC government). Under the Lusaka accord a joint military commission was to be formed to supervise the cease-fire and all foreign troops were to withdraw from the DRC and be replaced by a UN peace-keeping force. Disagreements subsequently emerged, however, over the schedule for the evacuation of the foreign forces, and Uganda continued to station about 16,000 troops in the DRC. Meanwhile, tensions had arisen between Uganda and Rwanda when, in May, the DRC rebel group, the Rassemblement congolais démocratique (RCD), that they had been jointly supporting split into two factions, with the Ugandan and Rwandan governments suspending their co-operation to back rival rebel leaders. In mid-August fighting erupted between Ugandan and Rwandan troops in Kisangani, in the DRC, reportedly following an attempt by the Rwandans to capture the leader of the Ugandan-backed rebel faction. A cease-fire agreement was signed after three days; it was reported that more than 200 people had been killed in the disturbance, including many DRC civilians. In September Museveni transferred leading army commanders from Kisangani to Uganda, in an attempt to reduce tension between Ugandan and Rwandan troops. Further fighting occurred in June 2000 before the UN special representative, Kamel Morjane, reported that Kisangani had been demilitarized and that both the Ugandan and Rwandan factions had agreed to leave the city.

During the late 1980s and early 1990s Sudanese troops reportedly made repeated incursions into Ugandan territory in pursuit of Sudanese rebels, and Sudanese aircraft were alleged to have dropped bombs in northern Uganda on several occasions. In early 1992 nearly 80,000 Sudanese refugees fled to Uganda, followed by a further 50,000 in August 1993. Relations between the two countries deteriorated seriously in 1994, when each government accused the other of harbouring and supporting their respective outlawed guerrilla groups; in April 1995 Uganda severed diplomatic relations with Sudan, accusing several Sudanese diplomats of endangering Ugandan national security. In October 1995 intense fighting between Sudanese rebels and government forces resulted in the displacement of several thousand Ugandans residing in the border region. In November the Ugandan government dispatched troops to protect the area. Subsequent allegations by the Sudanese authorities that Ugandan forces were massing on the two countries' common border in order to invade southern Sudan were strongly denied by the Museveni regime. In the following month, however, Museveni threatened to launch military assaults into Sudan in retaliation for the Sudanese government's alleged continuing support for the LRA. Sudanese troops shelled the border area for three consecutive days in April 1996, provoking strong protest from the Ugandan government. In September 1996 Sudan and Uganda resumed diplomatic relations, and in the following month a preliminary accord was signed in the Iranian capital, Tehran. Relations between the two countries did not improve, however: in September 1996 and in February 1997 it was alleged that Sudanese aircraft had once again attacked northern Uganda, and in April 1997, despite continuing discussions under the auspices of Iran and Libya, the Sudanese authorities claimed that their forces had killed several hundred Ugandan soldiers who had been assisting Sudanese rebels from within Sudan. At the end of August 1997 President Mandela of South Africa mediated a meeting between the Ugandan and Sudanese leaderships, the outcome of which was described as 'positive'. In December, however, the Museveni administration banned a number of Sudanese non-governmental organizations represented in Uganda which were accused of providing assistance to Ugandan rebel groups. The leader of one such organization was charged with treason and deported, having been accused of attempting to recruit exiled Rwandan Hutu soldiers to fight with the LRA. In February 1998 Uganda deployed troops along the Uganda-Sudan border, with the aim of preventing LRA rebels from taking captives over the frontier into Sudan. In September Uganda denied allegations by the Sudanese government that it had made incursions into Sudanese territory and that it had shelled border villages and refugee camps. In May 1999 it was reported that the Sudanese government was re-evaluating its policy towards the LRA. Uganda showed itself prepared to improve relations with its northern neighbour if Sudan ended its support for the LRA. In December Presidents Museveni and Omar al-Bashir met in Nairobi and signed a peace agreement, brokered by the ex-US president, Jimmy Carter. Each country agreed to stop hosting guerrilla groups directed against each other. The two presidents also agreed to resume full diplomatic relations. Analysts concluded that if Uganda fully withdrew its support from the Sudan People's Liberation Army (SPLA), the SPLA would find it difficult to maintain its pressure against the Sudanese government. Similarly, the LRA and ADF would have problems in sustaining their campaign against the Ugandan government without Sudanese support. In January 2000 the Ugandan government released the last group of 72 Sudanese prisoners of war. The Sudanese government announced that it was reopening its embassy in Kampala, which had been closed since 1995. However, the fighting did not stop and the rebels (particularly the ADF) continued their attacks. Museveni became disenchanted with the *rapprochement* with Sudan, and in February 2000 he complained that, while Uganda had returned its prisoners, Sudan had not responded. Sudan had not returned all the children kidnapped by the LRA, nor had it disarmed or disbanded the bandits operating against Uganda.

During the late 1980s an estimated 250,000 Rwandan refugees were sheltering in Uganda. Relations with Rwanda deteriorated in October 1990, following the infiltration of northern Rwanda by an invasion force of some 4,000 Rwandan rebels who had been based in Uganda; their leader, Maj.-Gen. Fred Rwigyema (who was killed by the Rwandan armed forces), was a deputy commander of the NRA and a former Ugandan deputy minister of defence. In November President Museveni dismissed all non-Ugandan members of the NRA. In February 1991 a conference was held on the Rwandan security situation; an amnesty was agreed for all Rwandans who were exiled abroad, and the rebels were urged to observe a cease-fire. Nevertheless, the allegedly Uganda-based Rwandan rebels continued to operate in northern Rwanda during 1991–93. In January 1992 it was reported that 64,000 Ugandans residing near the two countries' common border had been displaced, owing to cross-border shelling by Rwandan troops. In August 1993 the UN Observer Mission Uganda-Rwanda (subsequently disbanded) stationed troops on the Ugandan side of this border to verify that no military assistance reached Rwandan rebels. In May 1994 the Ugandan authorities appealed for emergency assistance, claiming that the corpses of thousands of victims of massacres taking place in Rwanda were contaminating the water supply of districts abutting Lake Victoria. The victory in Rwanda of the Front patriotique rwandais (FPR) in mid-1994 brought about a significant change in bilateral relations; Maj.-Gen. Paul Kagame, Rwandan vice-president and minister of national defence, had previously served in the Ugandan NRA, as had other members of the FPR administration. In August 1995 Museveni made an official visit to Rwanda, and both countries made commitments to enhance economic and social co-operation. In August 1998 Uganda and Rwanda jointly deployed troops in the DRC, although tensions subsequently emerged between the two forces (see above). The Ugandan government has strenuously denied allegations that a military alliance has been formed between the countries with the ultimate aim of extending Tutsi rule as far as Burundi and the DRC. In July 1996 Uganda joined other regional governments in imposing economic sanctions on the military regime in Burundi; these were withdrawn in January 1999.

The Western alliance has been keen to support Uganda against the perceived militant Islamic threat posed by Sudan. In mid-1997 the USA dispatched 59 military staff to Uganda to train a battalion of the UPDF to act as an African peace-keeping force under the African Crisis Response Initiative programme. Critics in the Ugandan parliament speculated that this might be a cover for a force that could potentially be used to destabilize neighbouring African countries. In November 1997 about 20 British army officers arrived to train UPDF members. In late March 1998 President Clinton of the USA made a two-day visit to Uganda, during a tour of six African nations.

Economy

LINDA VAN BUREN

In May 2000 the International Monetary Fund (IMF) observed that 'while Uganda remains one of the poorest countries in the world, the share of the population living in poverty declined to 44% in 1996/97, from 56% in 1992/93'. The Fund also noted that the percentage of Ugandan children of primary-school age who attended school increased from 56% in 1995/96 to 94% in 1998/99. This was no small accomplishment for a country whose real gross domestic product (GDP) per caput had declined by a full 40% between 1971 and 1986, the year in which the government of Yoweri Museveni came to power. Nevertheless, a weakening currency, a worrying budgetary deficit, lower coffee revenues and the remaining high level of poverty indicated that many challenges still lay ahead for Uganda's economic planners.

AGRICULTURE

Agriculture is overwhelmingly the most important sector in this land-locked country. It accounts for some 90% of export earnings, contributes about 50% of GDP when both subsistence and monetary agricultural production are counted and provides a livelihood for an estimated 80% of Uganda's labour force. Nearly two-thirds of government revenue is provided by the agricultural sector, mainly through export duties on coffee, the country's principal export. The development of the whole economy is therefore heavily influenced by the sector's performance. Coffee is, by far, the most important export crop, followed by cotton and tea. Tobacco was also an important crop until the 1970s. Soils are generally fertile and, apart from some parts of the north-east and the north-west, the country has a climate favourable to both field crops and livestock production. Smallholder mixed farming predominates, with estate production confined mainly to tea and sugar cane. Agricultural output was severely affected by the unstable security situation which prevailed during the 1970s and the early 1980s. Under Museveni's presidency, efforts have been made to rehabilitate the sector, although continuing security problems in northern and western regions have slowed the pace of recovery. Growth in agricultural GDP reached 7.8% in 1987/88, but had fallen to 2.7% by 1991/92 and averaged 4.0% per annum in 1990–96.

Coffee

Coffee (mostly robusta) continues to dominate the monetary sector. It is grown by some 2.8m. small-scale farmers. Production fell steadily throughout the 1970s, from a record 3.75m. bags (each of 60 kg) in 1973 to only 1.62m. bags in 1981. Lack of transport and spare parts, and smuggling into Kenya and Zaire (now the Democratic Republic of the Congo, DRC), were the main factors that limited coffee exports during this period.

Following Museveni's assumption of power in January 1986, coffee exports were temporarily halted, with the unfortunate result that Uganda failed to benefit from the prevailing high prices for coffee on the world market. Although exports were resumed later in the year, the total quantity for the 1985/86 coffee year was only 2.4m. bags, leaving substantial unsold stocks. As a result of favourable weather and the introduction by the Coffee Marketing Board (CMB) in August 1987 of advance payments to farmers, Uganda easily fulfilled its International Coffee Organization (ICO) quota for 1987/88 of 2.1m. bags, and additional exports to non-ICO countries raised total exports for the year to 2.7m. bags. In 1988/89 a record 3.1m. bags were exported. However, despite the greatest coffee output for 14 years, export earnings declined to US $160m. in 1989, from $270m. in 1988, owing to a collapse of world prices, following the suspension of ICO quotas. Output reached a low point in 1992, at 1.83m. bags. Effective action to revive the market began in August 1993, when the Inter-African Coffee Organization, of which Uganda is a member, joined Latin American producers in a scheme to withhold 20% of output whenever market prices fell below an agreed limit. By September 1994, market quotations for all grades and origins of coffee had achieved their highest levels since 1986, although they subsequently fell back.

In February 1995, Uganda was among the five African coffee producers which agreed to participate in coffee-price guarantee arrangements under the auspices of the Common Market for Eastern and Southern Africa (COMESA). During the mid-1990s Uganda's coffee output showed a steady and sustained recovery, totalling 2.35m. bags in 1993, 3.4m. bags in 1994 and 3.7m. bags in 1995. Despite the spread of tracheomycosis, a coffee wilt disease (see below), Uganda produced a record coffee crop (4.15m. bags) in the 1995/96 season, and overtook Côte d'Ivoire as Africa's number-one coffee exporter by volume. A further record crop was harvested in 1996/97, when Uganda exported 4.2m. bags, earning some $400m. in revenue. In the six-month period October 1998–March 1999 1.9m. bags were exported, representing an increase of 36% over the 1.4m. bags exported in October 1997–March 1998. However, owing to lower global coffee prices, the rise in the value of exports was much less pronounced. Total production of green coffee rose negligibly from 3.28m. bags in 1998 to 3.3m. bags in 1999.

The CMB, which was the sole purchaser and exporter of coffee during the 1980s, had persistent problems with crop finance, which adversely affected deliveries from farmers. The sector exhibited many of the problems that beset commodity-marketing arrangements in a number of African countries: a state-run commodity marketing board held a statutory monopoly over the purchase of the crop; prices were fixed by the government; and farmers often had to wait for long periods of time for their payments, owing to cash-flow crises at the commodity board. However, unlike many slow privatization programmes in Africa, the coffee sector in Uganda underwent a thorough and fundamental transformation during the 1990s. In 1990 the CMB's monopoly of coffee marketing was abolished. Five coffee co-operatives joined forces to form Union Export Services (UNEX), and by mid-1992 UNEX was handling 20% of coffee sales with the CMB handling the remaining 80%. By the mid-1990s Uganda had 12 coffee-marketing co-operatives and 167 licensed coffee exporters. However, there was fierce competition and the market was unable to sustain that many, so that mergers and take-overs became commonplace. By 1996/97 the number of licensed exporters had fallen by more than one-half, to 76, and, of these, 10 were reportedly accounting for 75% of total coffee exports. Of the 46 Ugandan licensed coffee exporters in 1997/98, only 37 renewed their permits in 1998/99 and, reportedly, only 26 actually exported any coffee. The largest firm accounted for 17.8% of total exports in the latter year, while a further five companies provided more than 50% of the total. The government undertook to reduce the CMB's assets into smaller, more attractive units, in order to accelerate its privatization. However, as of mid-2000, investors interest in the former monopoly's facilities were lukewarm and non-Ugandan backed companies preferred to finance new factory plants. The Uganda Coffee Development Authority (UCDA) was established in 1991, with responsibility for policy-making, as well as for research and development, promotion, the co-ordination of marketing, and quality control. Prior to 1991, growers competed with each other to sell their crop to a single buyer and earned less than 20% of the value their coffee fetched on the world market. However, by 1997, according to the UCDA, growers were receiving between 60% and 70% of total revenue earned. In 1994, in a bid to alleviate the potential 'boom-and-bust' effect of then soaring international coffee prices, the government introduced a coffee stabilization tax; in the 1994/95 financial year, the tax produced revenue of Us. 14,300m. However, some exporters avoided payment of the tax by underselling coffee, at a rate of more than US $6.5m. per month, as a result of which a lower threshold of Us. 1,500m. per kg and a new rate of 25% were introduced from June 1995. This failed to solve the problem, and in June 1996 the unpopular tax was abolished. While the value of coffee exports boomed, farmgate prices paid to coffee growers declined from Us. 1,200 per kg to Us. 600 per kg in the mid-1990s. In 1994 and 1995 the Uganda Investment Authority sought investors in coffee nurseries and enterprises for roasting, packaging, processing, blending and the utilization of coffee by-products. Private-sector coffee nurseries have introduced seedlings with higher yields; the first major crop of these seedlings began to mature in 1995, with more maturing every year thereafter. Coffee wilt disease was reported to have affected trees in 20 of Uganda's 34 coffee-growing districts. The disease is incurable, and affected trees must be uprooted and burned. An estimated 1.5m. Ugandan coffee trees per year were destroyed because of the disease during the late 1990s, but most of the country's 330m. coffee trees have not been affected. The UCDA is responsible for replacing these coffee trees, and conducted research, including cloning techniques, in an attempt to introduce trees that were resistant to the disease. An estimated 20m. new trees per year were being produced. Another feature of the coffee sector in the 1990s was the increased cultivation of arabica trees. During the 1970s, when infrastructural support was virtually non-existent, nearly all output was robusta, owing to its straightforward processing requirements; robusta continued to account for nearly all production throughout the 1980s. The arabica variety, which commands a higher price on the world market, is grown at higher elevations than robusta and is processed using the more sophisticated 'wet' method, which requires far greater organization of the processing infrastructure. During the 1990s the UCDA encouraged the 'wet' processing of coffee, and by October 1997 almost 17% of Uganda's coffee exports by volume were arabica. In 1999 some 10% of Uganda's total coffee production was arabica.

The United Kingdom is Uganda's largest customer for coffee, taking about one-third of the total. The USA, Japan and Germany are also important markets. Most of Uganda's coffee is transported to the Kenyan port of Mombasa by road and rail, although the Museveni government would prefer to effect a transfer to rail freight for all Ugandan trade, in order to reduce costs. In 1999 Kenya imposed an axle load limit on its roads, which led to delays in evacuating Ugandan coffee to Mombasa and doubled the cost of transporting it to port.

Tea

The tea sector experienced a sustained recovery in the 1990s. Prior to the Amin regime and the nationalization of tea plantations in 1972, Uganda was second only to Kenya among African tea producers. However, production declined each year thereafter until 1980, by which time Uganda's tea exports were negligible. In 1980, the British-based company Mitchell Cotts, former owner of three groups of tea estates until these were nationalized by Amin, was invited back to establish a joint venture with the government to own and operate the estates. The Toro and Mityana Tea Co (Tamteco) was formed in 1980, with 51% of the shares owned by the government, and work began on a US $8.8m. programme to rehabilitate the overgrown plantations and near-derelict factories. Tamteco, the main producer of tea, with 2,300 ha under cultivation, was fully privatized in 1995. Other tea producers include Rwenzori Highland Tea Co, which harvested 7.2m. kilos of tea in 1997. The remaining government holdings in tea enterprises are awaiting transfer to the private sector, and investors in processing and packaging plants are being sought. Smallholders, numbering about 1m. and cultivating some 9,500 ha, market their output through the Uganda Tea Growers' Asscn. The Uganda Tea Authority organizes research into growing methods and oversees the sector. Tea estates still face some of the problems that have hindered the sector for decades, such as a shortage of pickers and transport difficulties. The sector has, however, benefited from the success of Uganda's economic reform programme, with higher wages attracting harvest labour. Uganda harvested 6.74m. kg of made tea in 1990, which earned the country $3.57m.; by 1996 output had nearly trebled, to 17.42m. kg, earning $14.98m. Tea production was estimated at 23m. kg in 1999, a decline of 11% from the 25.9m. harvested in 1998.

Cotton

In the early 1970s Uganda ranked third among African cotton producers. However, production decreased from a peak of 467,000 bales (each of 480 lb or 217.7 kg) in 1970 to a low of 10.000 bales in 1987. The causes of the decline were the very low official prices paid to producers and the physical deterioration of

the ginneries during Amin's rule, as well as security problems in the main cotton-growing areas in the north and east of the country. Exports ceased altogether during the 1970s, resuming in 1982. The government initiated the Emergency Cotton Production Programme in 1986. The US $15m. programme was funded by the World Bank, the United Kingdom and other donors. The production target for 1988/89 was 150,000 bales, but actual output was only 44,000 bales. Production reached 105,650 bales in 1989 but then fell back to 101,516 bales in 1992. Thereafter output grew steadily during the 1990s, to 266,422 bales in 1997, before falling back to 207,160 bales in 1998; output amounted to 211,300 bales of seed cotton in 1999, yielding 30,000 tons of cottonseed and 15,400 tons of cotton lint. Exports of cotton earned $14.7m. in 1996, an increase of more than 50% on the previous year's level. The derelict state of the ginneries frequently resulted in stockpiles awaiting ginning, even when harvests were low. Ginneries were privatized during 1995–97, and the ensuing competition, together with the distribution of free high-quality seed by the government in 1996 and the liberalization of seed distribution in 1997, contributed to increased yields. The country has 29 ginneries, of which 27 are double-roller gins. A high proportion of Uganda's output is long-staple cotton, which commands a price premium sometimes as high as 20%.

Other Crops

Tobacco output has frequently been adversely affected by unfavourable weather conditions and recurrent fighting in the West Nile region, where it is grown. Production was estimated at only 100 metric tons in 1981, compared with a peak of 5,000 tons in 1972, but by 1983 exports resumed on a very small scale. Following a rise in producer prices and the implementation of a US $5.5m. rehabilitation programme, production increased to 1,900 tons in 1984. Output fell to 925 tons in 1986, but recovered to about 4,000 tons annually during 1987–89. There was a further recovery in 1992, to 7,285 tons, the largest crop for more than two decades. Production fell back to just under 5,000 tons in 1993, but exceeded 7,000 tons in 1994, when interest-free crop finance was available from British-American Tobacco (BAT). Phillip Morris of the USA was given permission in April 1994 to enter the Ugandan market, thereby breaking a monopoly previously held by BAT. In 1996 exports of tobacco earned $7.4m. The 1999 harvest of tobacco leaves was 7,100 tons.

Production of raw sugar had fallen to only 2,400 metric tons by 1984, compared with a peak of 152,000 tons in 1968. Local demand is estimated at some 215,000 tons per year. Lack of transport and problems with the maintenance of mechanical equipment contributed to this drastic fall in output, but the major cause was the expulsion of the Asian families who ran much of the sugar industry, on three large estates. The Madhvani and Mehta families returned in 1980 to begin the rehabilitation of the estates and factories, in joint-venture companies with the government. The Lugazi sugar complex, 40 km east of Kampala, is now operated by the Uganda Sugar Corpn, which is 51% owned by the government and 49% by the Mehta group. A new refinery, with a capacity of 60,000 tons per year, was opened in 1988. The complex, which included a 9,180-ha plantation, was rehabilitated in a US $90m. project funded by the International Development Asscn (IDA), the African Development Bank (ADB), the Commonwealth Development Corpn (CDC), the Arab Bank for Economic Development in Africa (BADEA), Kuwait and India. In 1993, however, the factory suspended production, owing to competition from sugar which had been smuggled from western Kenya. Despite pledges to curtail it, this smuggling continued throughout the 1990s. A $58m. project to rehabilitate the state-owned Kinyala sugar works was partly financed by Kuwait, BADEA and the Saudi Fund for Development. Once rehabilitated, Kinyala was expected to produce 37,000 tons of sugar per year. In 1985 a branch of the Madhvani family signed an agreement with the government to establish a new company, Kakira Sugar Works (1985). The rehabilitation of the Kakira complex began in 1988, and trial production commenced in the following year. Upon completion of the rehabilitation work, Kakira had an annual capacity of 120,000 tons of cane sugar; in 1997 it produced an estimated 70,000 tons. Uganda's output of raw sugar amounted to some 78,000 tons in 1996, up from 49,300 tons in 1993. The sugar cane harvest amounted to 1.85m. tons in 1997, but fell to 1.55m. tons in 1998; output in 1999 was an estimated 1.6m. tons.

Cocoa production declined significantly during the Amin regime and then slowly recovered during the late 1980s and the 1990s. Exports increased from 100 metric tons in 1982 to 170 tons in 1984 and to 1,396 tons in 1990. Production remained steady at about 1,000 tons per year in 1991-95, and was estimated to have grown to 2,700 tons in 1997 and to 2,800 tons per year in 1998 and 1999. Revenue from cocoa exports amounted to US $442,000 in 1995, soaring to $1.1m. in 1996.

Uganda's staple food crop is matoke, a form of plantain. Output of matoke was 9.3m. metric tons in 1997, 9.32m. tons in 1998 and 9.4m. tons in 1999. Also contributing towards national food requirements in 1999 were 3.4m. tons of cassava, 2.52m. tons of sweet potatoes (up 15.8% on the 1998 output), 780,000 tons of maize, 638,000 tons of finger millet, 454,000 tons of sorghum, 449,000 tons of potatoes (up 17% on the 1998 harvest) and 448,200 tons of various pulses (mainly dry beans, pigeon peas and dry cowpeas). There are three rice-growing projects in the country. The largest, in Olwiny swamp in the north, covers 800 ha and is being implemented with help from China, the ADB and the Islamic Development Bank. A further 680 ha is to be developed for smallholder production. The International Finance Corpn (IFC), an affiliate of the World Bank, announced in March 1999 that it would lend US $2.4m. to Tilda Uganda Ltd for the development of an integrated rice-growing and processing facility at Kibimba, in eastern Uganda. The rice mill was to have a capacity of 5 tons per hour, and was to process rice grown locally by smallholders in addition to that cultivated on the main farm. Uganda produced about 96,000 tons of paddy rice in 1999. Maize cultivation is rapidly expanding, both for subsistence and as a cash crop, although transport problems and the poor state of rural roads hamper the evacuation of crops. In July 2000 crop failures were reported in 30 districts, owing to a combination of drought and civil strife.

Output of groundnuts in shells totalled 153,000 metric tons in 1993, but declined to 134,000 tons in 1997 before recovering to 140,000 tons in 1998 and to 183,000 tons in 1999. Uganda also produced 5,097 tons of groundnut oil in 1995. Production of soya beans grew steadily throughout the 1990s, increasing from 53,000 tons in 1992 to 79,000 tons in 1995, 87,000 tons in 1997, 92,000 tons in 1998 and 101,000 tons in 1999. In 1999 Uganda also harvested about 600,000 tons of sweet bananas, 93,000 tons of simsim (sesame seeds, for a 21% rise on the 1998 harvest), 13,000 tons of tomatoes, 9,000 tons of wheat, 3,200 tons of chickpeas, 2,500 tons of sunflower seeds and 900 tons of castor beans. Small amounts of peppers, ginger, vanilla and allspice were also produced. During the late 1990s investors were being sought to finance the cultivation of horticultural produce, including vanilla, chillies, papayas, asparagus, medicinal plants and fresh flowers. In May 1999 the IDA pledged US $26m. in support of an agricultural education programme in Uganda, which aimed especially to introduce smallholders to new technology.

Beef and dairy cattle are kept by smallholders and on large commercial ranches. The country has good-quality pasture, but the prevalence of several endemic diseases and the armed theft of cattle are persistent problems. The total number of cattle was estimated at 5.4m. in 1998. Following a decline in cattle numbers during the 1980s, the government initiated an artificial-insemination programme to regenerate the herd, with funding from the European Union (EU). The dairy sector is being revitalized in a scheme funded by several UN agencies, the ADB, the European Development Fund (EDF) and Denmark. The project is aimed at improving the processing, collection and transport of dairy produce to urban markets. Dairy cattle account for about one-third of the national cattle herd. Poultry, pigs, sheep, goats and bees are also important. In the mid-1990s, the government invited foreign companies to invest in cattle, sheep and goat ranching; in chicken, peking duck and ostrich farming; in beekeeping; in hide, skin and leather processing; in cattle-horn processing; in preserved-meat processing; and in crocodile farming and processing.

Uganda has an abundance of lakes and rivers, and fishing is an important rural industry in this land-locked country, with considerable scope for further development, particularly in inshore fish farming, eels and freshwater prawns. The total catch amounted to 126,500 tons in 1997, of which 81,419 tons were of tilapia and other cichlid species. In 1989, an Italian company began to develop an integrated fisheries centre at Masese to smoke and dry tilapia and Nile perch. Concerns were raised in 1996 that the country's fish stocks were being depleted, and the licensing of processing factories was suspended (20 were licensed at the time, although not all were operational). In the same year, a fast-growing aquatic plant, water hyacinth, had covered large areas of Lake Victoria and had rendered the main landing at Port Bell inaccessible; a US company was brought in to control the problem. In 1998 Fish and fish products constituted Uganda's second-largest export by value, earning US $40m. and accounting for 7% of total export revenue. This sum, however, was almost 50% lower than the $75.8m. earned from fish exports in 1997. In March 1999 exports of fish to Europe were halted, and a one-month ban on sales of fish in Kampala was imposed, when it emerged that several people had died after consuming fish believed to have been poisoned by herbicides used to control the water-hyacinth problem. A meeting of the EU's Standing Veterinary Committee, scheduled for July 2000, was due to rule on whether the ban on Ugandan fish exports to Europe, then in its 16th month, would be lifted.

Forests and woodland cover some 7.5m. ha of the country. In 1990 the government banned exports of timber, pending the implementation of legislation to regulate the forestry sector. By 1997 production of industrial roundwood had reached 2.24m. cu m, while output of non-coniferous sawnwood recovered significantly, from 20,000 cu m in 1991 to 77,000 cu m in 1993.

INDUSTRY

The main industries involve the processing of the country's agricultural produce, including coffee, cotton, tea, sugar, tobacco, edible oils and dairy products, and grain milling and brewing. There has also been some activity in the areas of vehicle assembly and the manufacture of textiles, steel, metal products, hoes, wheelbarrows, mattresses, cement, soap, shoes, animal feeds, fertilizers, paints, cigarettes and matches. The output of all these industries fell drastically during the 1970s. Much plant and machinery was in a poor state of repair, and shortages of fuel, spare parts and technical and managerial skills also hampered the sector. Another problem was the poor purchasing power of the currency, which encouraged the labour force to avoid wage labour in favour of activities rewarded with food or other consumables.The European Investment Bank (EIB) provided Uganda with a loan of ECU 5.4m. in support of industrial development in 1993. Copper refining was formerly very important, but production ceased during Amin's regime. Efforts to revive the copper-refining sector were under way in 2000.

The rehabilitation of Uganda's industrial sector has proceeded slowly. In 1987 the government claimed that several industries, including grain-milling and the manufacture of hoes, beer, blankets and poultry feed, were operating at more than 50% of capacity. In 1992 industry was estimated to be operating on average at below 30% of capacity. Manufacturing GDP grew an average of 13.9% per year in 1990–97, and by 9.7% in the year to June 1999. This growth was attributable mostly to the food-processing, timber and paper, tobacco, and leather and footwear sectors. Nevertheless, in 1997 manufacturing provided only 8% of GDP and the industrial sector as a whole contributed only 17%. In 2000 the Ugandan government was seeking to encourage private-sector investment in a myriad of manufacturing activities, ranging from packaging materials to fish sausages.

The textile industry is suffering a severe lack of skilled personnel and spare parts, but considerable amounts of aid from the ADB, the EU and Arab funds are helping to establish new ginneries and spinning and weaving mills and are enabling the industry to repair existing plants and equipment. There are four fully integrated textile mills, with a total rated capacity of 66m. linear m of cloth per year. Yarn is also produced. Uganda's largest textile factory, Nyanza Textiles Industries (NYTIL) at Jinja, reopened in 1996 under private management, after several years of dormancy. NYTIL's purchaser was Picfare Ltd, which reportedly paid US $7m., which it had borrowed from the UK's Commonwealth Development Corpn (CDC). In June 1999 a review of NYTIL's performance alleged that some 3.7m. sq m of textiles are smuggled into Uganda every month and concluded that if this were to continue NYTIL Picfare would be forced to close: NYTIL Picfare went into receivership in May 2000.

The country's first vehicle-assembly plant, operated by GM Co, is a joint venture between the local Spear Motors and Peter Bauer of Germany. Capacity is 490 commercial vehicles and 360 trailers per year, with about 40% available for export. In 1983 the British-based Lonrho group resumed production at its Chibuku brewery, which had fallen into disuse after its expropriation by the Amin government. The group also opened negotiations for the repossession of its other expropriated assets in Uganda, including Consolidated Printers, which prints the government-controlled daily *New Vision*, and Printpak (Uganda). Lonrho signed an agreement with the government in 1986, under which it was to construct an oil pipeline from the Kenyan border to Kampala, and participate in the marketing of Ugandan coffee and cotton. In 1989 the Madhvani group began to bring nine of its 10 industrial companies back into production; at that time, only its textile firm, Mulco, was still operating. By 1997 the group was producing tea, beer, cooking oil, sugar, confectionery, steel bars, fencing, cables, matches, bottle tops, glassware, cut flowers, twine and cardboard boxes, and in 1998 it ventured into the assembly of televisions. In addition, in 2000 the company was involved in vehicle distribution and servicing, flour milling, software development, air-charter services, tourism and the distribution of television programming. It was also manufacturing 12,000 tons of soap per annum and producing rhizobium, an agrochemical used to increase yields of leguminous crops. In 1984 Uganda Breweries was returned to its original owners, East African Breweries of Kenya and Ind Coope and City Breweries of the UK. It subsequently started to rehabilitate its Port Bell plant. In 1995, the Madhvani group announced a Us. 9,000m. project to expand its Nile Breweries plant at Jinja, which increased the factory's capacity to 450,000 crates of beer per month; a similar project of expansion at Uganda Breweries was also under way in the mid-1990s. In 1995 the government awarded KW Uganda Ltd a licence to import beer from South Africa, thereby opening the Ugandan beer market to foreign competition. In 1997 Nile Breweries announced a joint venture with South African Breweries, to produce South African brands of beer in Uganda. A local firm, Century Bottling Co, obtained the franchise to produce Coca-Cola in the Ntinda industrial area, outside Kampala. The East African Development Bank and the Uganda Development Bank were major investors in the project. Lake Victoria Bottling Co Ltd produces Pepsi-Cola. A tannery has been opened at Jinja, and it is hoped that Uganda will become self-sufficient in leather goods. Chloride (Uganda) has been expanded and expects eventually to make Uganda self-sufficient in batteries. The country's second pharmaceutical plant, INLEX, opened in 1989.

There are two cement plants, at Tororo (near the Kenyan border) and at Hima (about 500 km to the west), with rated annual capacities of 150,000 tons and 300,000 tons respectively, although in 1995 their combined output was only 84,000 tons. Total domestic requirements are 650,000 tons per year. Some renovation work has been carried out, by a Turkish company at Tororo and by a German company at Hima. In 1995 the Kenya-based Rawal group bought the Hima plant for $20.5m., while the Tororo complex was purchased for $5.7m. by the Kenyan company Corrugated Sheets Ltd.

During 1992-95 the Uganda Investment Authority identified 1,600 new investment projects in agro-processing, tourism, mining, banking and communications. It is seeking investors in radio, television and video assembly and in the manufacture of office equipment, household durables and electrical goods. Other areas in which investment was invited in 2000 were meat processing, tea processing and packaging, fruit-juice processing, cashew nut, honey and vanilla processing, tanning, rice milling, tourism and the production of edible oils, soap, scrap steel, pharmaceuticals and metal products.

MINERALS

The Kilembe copper mines, in western Uganda, which produced about 17,000 metric tons of blister copper in 1970, became inactive in 1979, and the associated smelter at Jinja fell into disrepair. Exports of copper resumed in 1994. Reserves of copper

ore were estimated in 1982 to exceed 4m. tons. Prior to the Amin period, a stockpile of copper pyrites accumulated at the Kilembe mines. The Kasese Cobalt Co, a joint venture between the state-owned Kilembe Mines Ltd, La Source of France and Banff Resources of Canada (which has a 55% interest) aims to extract cobalt from these tailings in a scheme with an estimated cost of US $125m., scheduled to come into operation by the end of 2000; target annual production is 1,000 tons of cobalt. Prior to the Amin period, Uganda exploited substantial deposits of apatite (used in superphosphate fertilizers) at Tororo. Until the 1970s, the country also mined tungsten, beryl, columbo-tantalite, gold, bismuth, phosphate, limestone and tin, mostly on a small scale. Extraction of small quantities of tungsten, tin concentrates and gold has recommenced. Investors were being sought in 2000 to exploit the silica sands at four locations along the Ugandan shore of Lake Victoria, as well as on two islands in the lake; these deposits are said to be suitable for making container glass. In 1996, following the removal of a 5% royalty on the metal, gold was Uganda's second-largest export; an unquantified proportion, however, had allegedly been smuggled into the country from the DRC. In 1996 Branch Energy, a consortium of British and South African mining interests, was prospecting for gold in Karamoja, while Pangea Goldfields of Canada was prospecting for gold near Busia under 12 licences. In 1998 Uganda Gold Mining Ltd was exploring a 55 sq km concession at Kyakiddu, in central Uganda. A study, financed by the World Bank, was made by US and French consultants on a phosphate fertilizer project using phosphate deposits in the Sukulu hills, estimated at 220m.–225m. tons. The study recommended construction of a plant to make single superphosphates, with an initial capacity of 80,000 tons per year. The total cost of the project was to be about $102m. High-grade iron ore deposits at Kigezi have not yet been exploited. A group of 20 Ugandan investors formed a consortium, Muko Iron Ore Development Co (MIDECO), in July 2000 to exploit haematite iron ore in Kabale district, in the south-west, with a view to supplying domestic iron and steel operations. Geological surveys have been carried out in the Lake Albert and Rift Valley areas.

Petroleum exploration has proceeded slowly. In the early 1980s the IDA loaned US $5.1m. for exploration promotion, to attract bids from international oil companies and for consultancy services to evaluate these offers. Initially, there was little interest, and successive changes of government prevented any progress, until in 1987 the Museveni government initiated a Petroleum Exploration Promotion Project. Bidding for exploration rights was opened in 1988. In 1990 Uganda and Zaire (now the DRC) signed an agreement for the joint exploration and exploitation of petroleum reserves beneath Lakes Albert and Edward. Geological surveys in Lake Albert were completed in 1994, and those in the Lake Edward basin were proceeding in 1995. In February 1995 the government awarded a US-affiliated firm, the Uganda General Works and Engineering Co, a licence to exploit reserves in the Lake Albert area. A further exploration licence was awarded in January 1997 to a British company, Heritage Oil and Gas Ltd, which was due to begin test drilling at Semiliki by the end of 2000.

POWER

Electricity is generated at the Owen Falls hydroelectric station at Jinja, which has an installed capacity of 180 MW, of which 30 MW has been exported, under contract, to Kenya since 1955. Plans have been announced to modernize the Owen Falls plant, and to expand its capacity to 380 MW, under a US $282m. programme to rehabilitate the power grid, which received pledges of finance from the IDA and a number of Western European development agencies. In 1993 the Chinese company Sietco was awarded the contract for the principal construction work at the Owen Falls plant; by mid-1996, however, Sietco had departed. The power station was refurbished and restored to full capacity in 1997. Energy consumption per head grew by an annual average of 3.7% in 1980–92, a marked increase over the annual average of –7.0% in 1971–80. However, by the mid-1990s, domestic demand for electricity was considerably in excess of supply, despite price rises amounting to some 300% during 1994–97; after exports of power, barely one-half of Uganda's domestic requirement was being met. With the need for further revenue to install new generators, protracted negotiations were held with Kenya concerning the price of that country's contractual imports from Uganda. An agreement was eventually reached in June 1997. Electricity production was estimated at 1,128m. kWh in 1996. In that year, Uganda imported 58% of its energy requirements and consumed 479,000 tons of petroleum equivalent. The monopoly held by the Uganda Electricity Board (UEB) over electricity supply was removed from September 1996, opening the sector to competition. Companies in all fields were encouraged to establish 'build, own and operate' schemes to provide electricity to meet their own demands, while selling power to others as a means of recouping some of their investment. A new $463m., 250-MW dam at Bujagali Falls, near Jinja, has been proposed by the Madhvani group and AES, of the USA; finance was being sought in 1997, and, despite objections from environmentalists, promoters of the project were pressing ahead in 2000 after winning the approval of the cabinet, parliament and the people living at the proposed site. A 200-MW scheme at Karuma Falls in northern Uganda was scheduled for completion in 2001. In 1999 negotiations were under way with Rwanda and Tanzania concerning the exportation of excess power from these facilities by 2003.

TOURISM

During the 1960s and until 1972, tourism was, after coffee and cotton, the third most important source of foreign exchange. In 1971, there were 85,000 visitors, and receipts were US $27m. Tourism ceased during Amin's rule, with wildlife parks and hotels totally neglected. Under the Obote government, the sector began to be slowly rehabilitated. The number of visitors of all categories rose from 8,622 in 1982 to an estimated 189,000 in 1995 and 220,000 in 1997. Revenue from the tourism sector totalled some $90m. in 1995. In that year there were 29 tour operators in Uganda. The country has eight national parks, and approval was given in 2000 for the creation of a new park in the Kibale forest. The kidnapping and killing by Rwandan Hutu rebels of foreign visitors to Bwindi national park in March 1999 (see Recent History) precipitated a large increase in tourist cancellations.

The state-owned Uganda Hotels Corpn, which is to be transferred to the private sector, owns four hotels. In early 1988 a consortium of Italian companies, led by Viginter, agreed to construct four four-star hotels, in Masaka, Fort Portal, Jinja and Mbale. The 264-room Sheraton Kampala was refurbished by the Yugoslav company Energoprojekt at a cost of $27.5m.; the Sheraton Corpn of the USA subsequently took over its management. The hotel underwent a $4m. renovation in 1996, and Apollo Hotel Corpn, which held an 80% share of the complex overlooking the city, was reported to have reached agreement to sell its holding to a Saudi-Ethiopian company in 1998. In 1995, the 76-room Nile Hotel International announced plans to build a 16-storey, 150-room tower block. The 109-room luxury Grand Imperial Hotel opened in Kampala in October 1995. Finance was being sought in 1998 from private-sector investors for a four-star hotel at Entebbe, a four-star hotel at George National Park, a three-star hotel at Jinja and a three-star hotel at Mount Elgon.

TRANSPORT AND COMMUNICATIONS

The Third Highway Project costing US $32.6m. (with financing by the IDA) was inaugurated in August 1987. It involved the repair of existing surfaced and unsurfaced roads. The road link with Rwanda was to be improved with EU finance, as part of the 'northern corridor' scheme to link the eastern part of the DRC, Rwanda and Uganda with the Kenyan port of Mombasa. The EDF has pledged funding for the second phase of a project to repair Kampala's roads. Other major programmes of road repairs have received financial backing from Germany, under its bilateral aid programme. The government signed an agreement in 1987 with Energoprojekt for the construction of a 250-km road in western Uganda, from Mityana to Fort Portal, as part of the Trans-African Highway. Under a $150m. road rehabilitation project, launched in 1994, some 15 roads were to be improved by mid-1998. In June 1999 the IDA pledged a $91m. credit in support of the first stage of the government's four-phase $360m. Road Sector Development Programme. Under the initial phase of the programme the country's two highest-priority roads (Busunju-Kiboga-Hoima and Karuma-

Oliwiyo-Pakwach-Nebbi-Arua) were to be upgraded and some 1,500 km of feeder roads were to be rehabilitated. The road system suffers not only from weather-related damage but also from neglect and wear and tear from overloaded lorries. Several hundred new lorries were imported, many under barter agreements, in the early 1990s.

India, France and Germany supplied locomotives and rolling stock which were urgently needed by the Uganda Railways Corpn (URC), established following the dissolution of East African Railways. The United Kingdom, France, Italy, Germany and the EU have all assisted with a programme to rehabilitate the railway system, which also forms part of the 'northern corridor'. The URC operates a wagon-ferry service on Lake Victoria between Jinja and the Tanzanian lake port of Mwanza. This provides a much-needed alternative route to the sea, via the Tanzanian ports of Tanga and Dar es Salaam. The URC carried an officially estimated 1m. tons of freight in 1995. In 1996 the company was pursuing a strategy of 'privatization from within', selling off non-core activities such as locomotive maintenance. Following the withdrawal of government subsidies the URC suspended operations on unprofitable lines, retaining just two routes: Kampala-Kasese and Kampala-Jinja-Tororo; the 333-km Kampala-Kasese line was subsequently also closed. In 1999 the East African Railways Development Corpn offered to invest $12.6m. in these two routes, announcing plans to re-open the Kasese line and to carry out repairs and update equipment. In 1998 the URC's workforce was reduced by about 2,000, to 1,900 employees. In mid-1999 the ministry of finance, planning and economic development recommended cutting the workforce further, to 800 employees.

The government established Uganda Airlines Corpn (UAC) in 1976, and the airline inaugurated its first international scheduled service in 1978, between Entebbe and Nairobi. A scheduled passenger and cargo service started operating from Uganda to Rome, Brussels and London in 1980. The airline subsequently introduced new routes, to Cologne, Dubai and Bombay. By 1991, UAC had only a single Fokker F-27 passenger aircraft, and the airline's route coverage had been considerably curtailed. The government appointed a new management team in 1991, and soon afterwards UAC leased an Air Zimbabwe Boeing 737-200. The number of passengers carried by the airline increased from 32,000 in 1992 to 100,000 in 1995. In the latter year, UAC leased a Boeing 737-500 from Ansett of Australia. UAC holds 10% of the equity in Alliance, a joint venture with South African Airways, Air Tanzania Corpn, the Ugandan and Tanzanian governments and private investors. The carrier operates weekly services from London to Johannesburg, South Africa, via Uganda. Plans to privatize UAC were under way in 2000. A $52m. project to modernize Entebbe airport began in 1994, and included the construction of a new passenger terminal.

Kampala's telephone network has been modernized and expanded in a $13m. project, financed mainly by a concessionary loan from France. In 1993 Uganda had only one telephone line per 1,000 inhabitants; by 1998 the ratio had improved to two lines per 1,000. A $52.3m. IDA credit was approved in 1989 to finance part of the $100m. rehabilitation of the Uganda Posts and Telecommunications Corpn (UP & TC), in preparation for its privatization. In 1998 UP & TC was divided into three units, including Uganda Telecom Ltd (UTL). In November 1998 the government invited a consortium comprising German and Swiss interests to start negotiations on the sale of a 51% share in UTL; a bid was submitted by the consortium of $23m. in cash and deferred payments. Mobile telephone services were available in Kampala in 1995 from CelTel Ltd (which had approximately 3,000 customers in 1996), and in 1994, Kenya's Wilken Group received a licence to establish a V-Sat (a small-aperture satellite terminal) to provide voice, data and fax links in remote areas of the country. South African, Swedish, Ugandan and Rwandan interests, grouped together in a consortium known as MTN Uganda Ltd, entered a successful $5.8m. bid for a licence to become the country's Second National Operator (SNO). The consortium committed itself to investing $60m. and providing 89,000 new telephone lines in the first five years, beginning in August 1998. The licence covers a full range of services including fixed lines, international links and cellular services. In April

1998 Uganda had 52,000 fixed telephone lines and about 5,000 cellular subscribers.

EXTERNAL TRADE

Traditionally, Uganda's four leading export commodities were coffee, tea, cotton and copper. However, copper exports dwindled from US \$20.6m. in 1970 to nil by 1979, with the halting of production at Kilembe. Coffee alone for many years provided about 95% of total export earnings. In the 1990s the profile of Uganda's exports began to change. The value of coffee exports declined sharply in 1993, contributing only about 53% of total export revenue. This sharp fall in coffee's share of exports had two main causes: lower world coffee prices and, at the same time, a marked increase in exports of other commodities. By 1996 the principal export commodities were coffee (accounting for 62.5% of the total), gold (6.9%), fish (4.0%) and maize (2.8%). In 1998 coffee accounted for 64% of total revenue, while fish exports (subsequently banned by the EU—see above) ranked second, with 7%. Not only did the proportions change, but the value of total exports also rose strongly and steadily during the mid-1990s. The substantial increase in gold exports (from \$43.9m. in 1994 to \$224,000 in 1996) appeared to be partly attributable to consignments smuggled into the country from the DRC. In the eastern provinces of the DRC the Ugandan shilling was being used as currency in 1997. According to the IMF, total exports amounted to \$200m. in 1992/93, covering 45% of imports (all figures on a free-on-board—f.o.b.—basis), at \$442m., leaving a visible trade deficit of \$242m. In 1993/94 exports climbed to \$253.9m., covering less than 38% of total imports (\$671.6m.), leaving a visible trade deficit of \$417.7m. In 1994/95 exports more than doubled, to \$595.3m., so that even though imports soared to \$1,085.5m., the visible trade deficit rose only slightly, to \$490.2m., and exports covered more than one-half of imports for the first time in years. In 1995/96 exports remained at about the same level, at \$590.3m., while imports increased to \$1,218.3m., producing an enlarged trade deficit of \$628m. In 1996/97 exports rose by 13.7% to \$670.9m., while imports rose by only 2.3% to \$1,246.3m., with the result that the visible trade deficit narrowed to \$575.4m., and exports again covered more than one-half the value of imports, at 53.8%. However, poor weather conditions (excessive rain in some parts of the country and insufficient rain in other regions, blamed on the El Niño phenomenon) led the IMF to make gloomy forecasts for 1997/98: exports were projected at \$519.7m., while imports were expected to reach \$1,334.4m., widening the projected visible trade deficit to \$814.7m. Export revenue in dollar terms f.o.b. grew by 19.8% in 1998/99, but lower receipts for coffee led to slower growth of 6.2% in 1999/2000. At the same time, imports in dollar terms c.i.f. declined by 2.6% in 1998/99 but rose by 9.1% in 1999/2000. Uganda's terms of trade deteriorated by 1.8% in 1997/98, by 6.7% in 1998/99 and by an estimated 3.2% in 1999/2000. The United Kingdom is Uganda's main supplier after Kenya, which provides refined petroleum products and also re-exports goods to Uganda through Mombasa. Other principal suppliers in 1998 were France, Japan, the United Arab Emirates, India and Germany. The main customers for Uganda's exports in 1992 were the United Kingdom, Belgium-Luxembourg, Spain, the USA and France.

In June 1996 Uganda implemented an 80% tariff reduction on trade with other COMESA members, four months ahead of the October 1996 deadline set by COMESA. From July 1996, however, Uganda imposed a 10% surtax on all commodities entering the country from COMESA sources.

EAST AFRICAN COMMUNITY

Uganda was a partner, with Kenya and Tanzania, in the East African Community (EAC), which came into existence in December 1967. The EAC disintegrated, however, as a result of continual disagreements among the partners over financial and political issues. By 1977 the various common services, such as railways, harbours and the airline, had ceased to function, and the EAC had collapsed. In November 1983 agreement was finally reached, after nearly six years of negotiations, on the division of the EAC's assets and liabilities. The final accounts of the EAC, produced by the World Bank, were approved by the three heads of state in July 1986. The surviving EAC institution, the East African Development Bank (based in Kampala), was

given a new charter in August 1980 and gradually expanded its lending programme. In January 1996 the presidents of Uganda, Kenya and Tanzania undertook to co-operate over an initiative to relaunch the EAC. The permanent tripartite commission for East African co-operation was formally inaugurated in March 1996. A treaty for the re-establishment of the EAC, providing for the creation of a free trade area (with the eventual introduction of a single currency) and for the development of infrastructure, tourism and agriculture within the community, was initially expected to be ratified by the Ugandan, Kenyan and Tanzanian heads of state in July 1999. However, the conclusion of the treaty was postponed, pending the completion of negotiations over several unresolved trade issues. The last of the three countries, Tanzania, finally ratified the treaty in June 2000.

PUBLIC FINANCE

Measures under the three-year rehabilitation and development programme for 1987/88–1989/90, announced in May 1987, included the devaluation of the currency by 76.7%, and the introduction of a 'new' Ugandan shilling, equivalent to 100 'old' shillings (the word 'new' soon disappeared from use). The main aim of the rehabilitation programme, to reduce government spending, was echoed in the 1987/88 budget. The budget deficit represented a 42.6% reduction in dollar terms from that of the previous year and was equivalent to only 16.2% of total planned expenditure, projected at Us. 53,200m. (\$886.7m.). The increase in budgetary spending was moderate in real terms, when set against the estimated rate of inflation of 300%. The lifting of import duties on raw materials and industrial equipment and the reduction of interest rates were aimed at encouraging investment in industry.

The shilling was devalued by 60% in July 1988, by 10% in December 1988 and by 17% in March 1989, bringing it to Us. 200 = US \$1. The rate on the parallel market fell to Us. 530 = US \$1 from Us. 420 = US \$1 following the March devaluation. In July 1989 a two-tier foreign-exchange system was reintroduced. The Bank of Uganda (the central bank) was to sell foreign currency to importers at a rate of about Us. 400 = US \$1, undercutting the parallel market rate, which was about Us. 600 = US \$1 at that time. The selling rate was to be adjusted weekly. Five further devaluations reduced the value of the shilling to Us. 620 = US \$1 by end-March 1991.

In February 1992 Uganda re-introduced the auctioning of foreign currency, with the Bank of Uganda auctioning the currency to commercial banks. This arrangement initially yielded an exchange rate of Us. 980 = US \$1. By May 1992, however, inflation was running at 52% over the rate at the beginning of the year, projecting an annual rate of 139%. The government announced the licensing of foreign-exchange bureaux, and by September 1993 79 forex bureaux were in operation, of which 26 were owned by commercial banks and 53 were privately owned. By July 1992 the government claimed that inflation had been brought under control, and in mid-1993 the IMF assessed the annual average rate of inflation at 3%. By June 1993 the shilling had stabilized and was trading at Us. 1,197 = US \$1. In November 1993 the government abandoned the auction of foreign exchange and introduced the Foreign Exchange Inter-Bank Market. By July 1994 the exchange rate had improved to Us. 937 = US \$1, and a year later in July 1995 it stood at Us. 950 = US \$1, exhibiting a degree of stability unknown previously. By September 1996 the currency had weakened to Us. 1,040 = US \$1, showing a relatively mild depreciation of 8.7% over 14 months; thereafter, it was stable for over a year, standing at Us. 1,053 = US \$1 in June 1997 and at Us. 1,080 = US \$1 in October 1997, before depreciating to Us. 1,231 = US \$1 by June 1998. The value of the Ugandan shilling depreciated by 14% in the period January–May 1999; this was attributed to the effects of depressed international coffee prices. In April 1999 the Bank of Uganda intervened by selling \$28m.; the sale of a further \$10m. followed in May. The currency fell from Us. 1,507.12 = US \$1 at the beginning of 2000 to Us. 1,594.19 = US \$1 in July 2000. In the year to April 1997 the IMF estimated that inflation stood at 1.7% on an annual average basis, and it estimated that consumer prices actually fell, by 1.4%, in the year ending June 1998. However, in the year ending June 1999, the inflation rate increased by an annual average of 5.0%. Consumer prices rose by 5.3% in 1999/2000.

In 1999 Uganda, Kenya and Tanzania were considering plans for full currency convertibility.

The 1996/97 budget envisaged total revenue of Us. 824,300m., of which Us. 728,700m. was to be derived from taxes, and total expenditure of Us. 1,233,200m., of which Us. 660,500m. was recurrent. The projected budgetary deficit was forecast at 6.7% of GDP, lower than the actual deficit for 1995/96 (equivalent to 7% of GDP), but higher than the ceiling set by the IMF (5% of GDP). Under the 1996/97 budget, the former sales tax (at 15%) was replaced by a value-added tax (VAT), at an initial rate of 17%. The government was also to pay VAT on its purchases, thereby providing a means for businesses to claim refunds where applicable. Although the new tax was proclaimed a success and company registration was high, traders protested that they felt unable to pass on the increased cost to their customers. The level of taxation in Uganda—reportedly the highest in Africa—gave rise to concern that GDP growth could be stunted. The 1997/98 budget envisaged total revenue of Us. 840,000m., of which Us. 828,000m. was to be derived from taxes; expenditure was to be reduced by some 23%, and civil-service salaries were frozen. With the introduction of free universal primary schooling, education expenditure, in particular on teachers' salaries, was to be a priority. To help defray the cost of this initiative, the World Bank awarded Uganda US $155m. Nevertheless, a revenue shortfall was expected, owing to smuggling and tax evasion. The IMF assessed the actual budgetary deficit to be equivalent to 6.4% of GDP (at factor cost) in 1997/98, while that in 1998/99 was reported to be equivalent to 6.7% of GDP. The 1999/2000 budget, announced in June 1999, heralded a 25% increase in expenditure, owing to higher spending on public-sector salaries and poverty eradication. Expenditure on defence, however, was to be reduced, having been deemed excessively high by the IMF under the 1998/99 budget. According to the IMF, the government agreed to offset the purchase of a presidential aircraft by cuts in defence and other non-wage expenditures.

BALANCE OF PAYMENTS

The current account of the balance of payments carried a deficit of US $434m. before, and $255m. after, official transfers in 1990, improving to a $393m. deficit before, and a $182m. deficit after, official transfers in 1991 and a $346m. deficit before, and a $113m. deficit after, official transfers in 1992. In 1993 the shortfall was $369m. before, and $107m. after, official transfers, and in 1994 the deficit before official transfers amounted to $264m. The IMF assessed Uganda's current-account deficit at 1% of GDP in 1993/94, at 2.7% in 1994/95, at 2.0% in 1995/96, at 0.9% in 1996/97, at 2.2% in 1997/98, at 4.1% in 1998/99 and at an estimated 3.1% in 1999/2000. The overall balance of payments, according to the IMF, registered surpluses of $61.2m. in 1995/96, $107.3m. in 1996/97, $109.2m. in 1997/98 and $47.1m. in 1998/99. However, the overall balance was estimated to have been in deficit by $36.9m. in 1999/2000. End-of-year foreign reserves stood at $28.3m. in 1989 and at $59m. in 1991, enough to cover just four weeks' imports. Foreign reserves strengthened to $146m. by the end of 1993, equivalent to six weeks' imports, and rose to $382m. at the end of 1995, which was reportedly sufficient to cover 4.8 months' imports. According to the IMF, Uganda's gross official reserves increased from $622m. at mid-1997, sufficient to cover 4.5 months' imports, to $751m. at mid-1998 (covering 4.9 months' imports), to $833m. at mid-1999 (covering 5 months' imports) and to $832m. at mid-2000.

Total end-of-year external debt was officially estimated at about US $1,800m. in 1989, $2,830m. in 1991, $2,997m. in 1992, $3,056m. in 1993, $3,473m. in 1994, $3,384m. in 1995 and $3,200m. in 1996. It was reported that Uganda spent 10 times as much on debt-servicing as on health care in 1996. Debt-servicing throughout the 1970s had remained as low as 5% of export earnings, owing to a low level of foreign investment and lending. In 1981, however, the debt-service ratio was about 60%, but subsequently, as export revenue increased more quickly than borrowing, the ratio declined. According to the World Bank, debt-servicing costs, based on payments actually made, amounted to 23.5% of exports of goods and services in 1994/95, 21.8% in 1995/96, 17.9% in 1996/97, 26.7% in 1997/98 and 15.6% in 1998/99. Of the $194.1m. of medium- and long-term debt

due for repayment in 1989, $93.1m. was rescheduled by four members of the 'Paris Club' of Western official creditors and Libya. In July 1993 Uganda repurchased $153m. of commercial debt at a substantial discount. In February 1995 international creditor governments agreed to cancel some two-thirds of Uganda's bilateral government-guaranteed debt. In April 1997 the IMF and the World Bank approved a $338m. debt-relief programme for Uganda, to be released in April 1998; however, it was argued that, because the payments were to be spread over a number of years, actual year-on-year cash savings would be minimal; moreover, the Ugandan government had budgeted for such relief to be disbursed in 1997, and it was feared that plans to introduce universal primary education would be set back. In the end, these concerns were heeded by the Bretton Woods institutions, which opted for a slightly larger package of debt relief and direct assistance for the education programme as well. In March 1998 Uganda became the first country in the world to receive a new World Bank product, in the form of a combination grant-credit. The $155m. facility, offered in support of Uganda's Education Sector Adjustment Operation, consisted of a $75m. grant, which carried no repayment obligation, and an $80m. 'equivalent credit' from the IDA, which carried no interest but must be paid back, on standard terms of 40 years including 10 years' grace. In April 1998 the IMF agreed that Uganda met the requirements for receiving debt relief under its new Initiative for Heavily Indebted Poor Countries (HIPC). The amount of debt relief from all participating external creditors was a nominal $650m., which was assessed by the IMF at $350m. in net present value terms, of which the Fund itself was to contribute $69m. and the World Bank was to provide $160m. The action amounted to a 20% reduction in Uganda's total foreign debt. The HIPC Trust Fund was to purchase and cancel outstanding IDA credits with a face value of $181m. (but with a current value of $84m.) and was to pay debt servicing with a nominal value of $39m. (but an actual value of $52m.) on IDA credits over five years. The IMF also agreed to provide a $69m. grant to cancel part of Uganda's debt-service payments due to the Fund, an amount that was equivalent to about 22% of the country's repayment obligations to the Fund over the next nine years. In February 2000 the IMF and the IDA together agreed to increase Uganda's HIPC relief by an additional sum which brought the total to a nominal $2,000m., or, in net present value (NPV) terms, to $700m., equivalent to 38% of the NPV of total debt outstanding as of 30 June 1999. In September the 'Paris Club' of creditors cancelled $145m. of Uganda's debt under the HIPC initiative.

AID

During the rule of Idi Amin, Uganda experienced a drastic decline in receipts of aid except, after 1974, from Arab countries, in particular Libya. After the overthrow of Amin, several countries and multilateral agencies signed agreements with Uganda to provide official assistance. The World Bank Consultative Group for Uganda met in Paris in May 1982 and in January 1984, and donors gathered in Kampala in March 1986 for the first such meeting after the Museveni administration gained power. The new government presented proposals for a US $160m. programme of emergency relief and rehabilitation, aimed at repairing the damage resulting from five years of civil war. However, international donors waited for the government to formulate its economic policies before pledging any new funds, and the IDA suspended disbursement of part of its committed funds. Discussions with the IMF and the World Bank were resumed in early 1987. Following the introduction of the three-year rehabilitation programme in May 1987 (see below), the IMF agreed to provide $24m. for the first year and then $32m. over the following 24 months, in addition to $20m. from its compensatory financing facility (CFF) fund, in respect of lost export revenue. The World Bank agreed in principle to a $100m. arrangement to support the recovery plan, and a Consultative Group meeting of donors in June 1987 resulted in new commitments amounting to $310m. for the first year of the three-year rehabilitation programme. Also in June 1987 the 'Paris Club' rescheduled $66m. of debts due to be repaid in 1987/88. Non-members of the 'Paris Club' also rescheduled debts of up to $45m. In February 1988 the IMF approved a CFF equivalent to SDR 24.8m. (about $33.7m.), in connection with Uganda's shortfall in export earnings in the year ended September 1987, caused mainly by low world coffee prices in 1987. The Consultative Group committed $550m. in loans and grants for 1989, in addition to existing commitments and $640m. for 1990. The World Bank accorded Uganda $265m. for 1990, of which $125m. represented balance-of-payments support which had been withheld during 1989, pending the implementation of measures to reduce inflation. Disbursement of aid pledged by the international donor community had been slow in the late 1980s but improved after 1990. The Consultative Group pledged $830m. in support for the adjustment programme for 1992/93 and similar amounts for subsequent years. The government's introduction of VAT under the 1996/97 budget, as part of its structural-reform strategy, received the approval of the IMF. At a meeting in Kampala in December 1998 the Consultative Group committed $2,200m. over the three-year period 1998/99–2000/01, of which $830m. was described as 'quick-disbursing budget support'. Although the Consultative Group donors commended the Ugandan government for achieving strong GDP growth (5.5% in the year to June 1998) and low inflation, they expressed concern over the high level of defence spending, continuing corruption, and the poor financial management and procurement practices on some development projects. In March 1999 the IMF suspended the disbursement of a $18m. loan for two months, demanding a firm commitment from the Museveni administration to controlling military expenditure; this had risen significantly following the deployment of Ugandan troops in the DRC in August 1998 (see Recent History). Further discussions centred on the acquisition of a new presidential jet (see above). Nevertheless, the IMF and the World Bank continued their approvals of new lending and debt relief during 1999 and 2000. In December 1999 the IMF agreed a $36.7m. sum in support of the third year of Uganda's three-year arrangement under the IMF's Poverty Reduction and Growth Facility.

ECONOMIC DEVELOPMENT

During 1965–71 Uganda's GDP grew by about 4.2% annually, as a result of the excellent performance of the agricultural sector and the food-processing industry. Uganda's 1971–76 development plan, under Amin, envisaged an annual average growth rate of 5.6%, but, in reality, GDP declined during each year of the plan period. A three-year plan in 1976–79 had little chance of being fulfilled, since the economy was by that time operating at the most basic level. The dire state of the economy was due, in large measure, to ex-president Amin's policies of expulsion of non-citizen Asians and mass expropriations of foreign firms. The disruption that was caused by the war of liberation early in 1979 produced a further fall in output in every sector during that year.

Emergency aid began to arrive in Uganda several months after Amin's overthrow, and large sums of development aid appeared to be waiting for the moment when the country was again in a position to absorb it. However, the nascent economic recovery came to a virtual halt with the May 1980 coup. President Obote announced an economic recovery plan in 1981 which aimed at, among other things, providing greater encouragement and protection for foreign investors. In July 1982 his government ordered a study on the country's parastatal enterprises, to decide which should be sold off to private investors, and to devise means of strengthening the remainder and making them more efficient. Uganda's annual inflation rate, which was 104% in 1980, was reduced to 30% in 1983, the government claimed. However, by the mid-1980s, inflation had increased sharply. After President Museveni came to power in January 1986, he commissioned a report on the economy from Canadian consultants. The Rehabilitation and Development Programme for 1987–90, which was finally announced in May 1987, had the approval of the IMF and the World Bank, and was the first sign that the government was getting to grips with the country's economic problems. The programme included the introduction of a 'new' shilling, to equal 100 'old' shillings, and at the same time devalued the currency by 76%. The programme was replaced by an Economic Recovery Programme for 1988–92, presented to donors in October 1988. Total investment was scaled down to $1,674m., compared with $2,866m. for the previous plan. Projected average annual growth during the period of the programme was 5%; the plan aimed to revive exports and to stimulate non-traditional exports. Of total investment, transport and communications were allocated 27%, social infrastructure 25.7%, agriculture 23.8% and industry and tourism 17.2%. The reorganization of the tax collection system and the diversification of exports were priorities under a three-year economic reform programme (supported by the IMF) that covered the period 1994/95–96/97.

In July 1995 the World Bank put pressure on the Ugandan government to privatize or close 15 commercial banks. All the banks were to raise a minimum capital base of Us. 500m. (for domestic banks) or Us. 1,000m. (for foreign banks) by mid-1997; any bank that failed to do so was to be wound up. All 15 banks reportedly had high levels of 'non-performing loans'; Uganda Commercial Bank (UCB) was in the worst bad-debt situation, with non-performing loans amounting to Us. 105,000m. in 1995. In preparation for privatization, UCB was reduced in size; of its 189 branches in 1993, 50 had been closed and 54 had been put on a part-time basis by 1996. Opponents of UCB's privatization feared that future private-sector owners would close the bank's unprofitable rural network, leaving the banking requirements of large areas of the country unserved. By the end of April 1996, 1,885 non-performing UCB loans totalling Us. 66,900m. had been transferred to a Non-Performing Assets Recovery Trust, and during 1996 the British merchant bank Morgan Grenfell was brought in to advise on the reform and privatization of the bank. It was originally decided that 60% of UCB's equity would be reserved for Ugandan nationals, but in October 1997 49% of UCB's shares were offered to a Malaysian company, and in April 1998 the same company successfully purchased a further 2%, giving it a 51% controlling interest in UCB. However, the Ugandan government subsequently terminated the contract, and in April 1999 the Bank of Uganda placed UCB under statutory management, alleging irregularities in the bank's operations. In 1995 Nile Bank Ltd and Sembule Investment Bank had been placed under the supervision of the Bank of Uganda while undergoing restructuring. Meanwhile, the Bank of Uganda itself had financial difficulties. Its Us. 40,000m. loss in 1993/94 was attributed primarily to currency-conversion operations. However, the bank was also owed money by the government, and was in need of recapitalization. In the June 1996 budget speech it was announced that the government had made an outstanding payment to the central bank and that it planned to pay Us. 60,000m. towards the first phase of the bank's recapitalization. In early 1999 international donors and the IMF requested stricter controls in the banking sector. Several locally-owned banks were placed under the management of the Bank of Uganda or closed in late 1998 and early 1999. The collapse of Greenland Bank, in April 1999, deprived some 100,000 customers of their deposits, including several coffee exporters.

The Expropriated Properties Act, governing the return of (or compensation for) property confiscated during Amin's rule (mainly from Asian owners) came into force in 1983. Unclaimed or unverified property was to be sold to Ugandan nationals or to foreign investors in joint ventures with Ugandans. The government announced further measures in 1991 to benefit dispossessed Asian Ugandans. A new investment code to protect foreign investors was promulgated in 1991. By January 1993, some 524 properties had reportedly been returned to their original owners. In April 1993 responsibility for the Asian-owned entities was entrusted to the Departed Asians' Property Custodian Board (DAPCB). In the mid-1990s, the Asian-controlled Madhvani group rapidly became one of the most active industrial investors in the country.

In early 1995 the government established a privatization unit, and transferred to the ministry of finance and economic planning responsibility for those parastatals which were to be divested. Some 13 former state-owned enterprises had already been privatized in 1994/95, realizing combined gross proceeds of Us. 57,720m. Net proceeds were, however, expected to be at a much lower level, because the government was required to settle the large debts which some of the organizations had accumulated. By the end of June 1998 about one-third of the 140 companies scheduled for privatization were still awaiting disposal. The programme was briefly suspended in 1998, while a parliamentary committee investigated allegations that it was being undermined by corruption and mismanagement.

On the basis of gross national product (GNP) per head (only US $320 in 1997), Uganda is among the 17 poorest countries in the world. Uganda's GNP per caput, in real terms, expanded by an annual average of 4.0% in 1990–96, according to World Bank estimates. During 1990–97 GDP increased, in real terms, by an annual average of 7.4%. GDP grew by 3.4% in 1991/92, 8.3% in 1992/93, 5.3% in 1993/94, 10.5% in 1994/95, 7.8% in 1995/96, 4.5% in 1996/97, 5.4% in 1997/98 and, provisionally, by 7.8% in 1998/99, according to the IMF. The target of 7.8% for 1999/2000 was not met, and GDP grew in that year by 5%.

The Museveni administration's implementation of effective economic recovery plans, supported by the IMF and the World Bank, has been greeted with approval by Uganda's donors and business partners. By mid-1990 the short-term prospects for recovery seemed to be reasonably favourable; there had been a considerable influx of aid, and inflation was greatly reduced. In 1997 the Kampala Stock Exchange was launched, under the supervision of a Capital Markets Authority. The government has made efforts to encourage investment from abroad, in order to reduce Uganda's significant dependence on aid. Although economic growth has been consistent since the early 1990s, obstacles to economic recovery include the cost of combating rebel insurrections (and the loss in tourism receipts envisaged following the murder of several foreign tourists by rebels in March 1999 and the deaths of large numbers of a religious sect),

as well as a continuing reliance on coffee for most of Uganda's export revenue, and hence vulnerability to international commodity prices and weather conditions. These and many other problems will have to be overcome before the country can begin to benefit from its unquestionable advantages: a generally favourable climate, fertile soils and an abundance of natural resources. However, Uganda has another potential resource, for which it was well known in the days before Idi Amin: a relatively well-educated and skilled labour force. Long periods of devastation and insecurity led many Ugandans to fear sending their children to school, so that the education sector, as other sectors, fell into decay. A major initiative to redress this situation was launched in 1997, in the form of the introduction of free primary education for up to four children in every Ugandan family. In the first year after fees were abolished, enrolment nearly doubled, from 2.7m. pupils in 1996 to 5.2m. in 1997. Schools began operating two shifts daily, and a system of community-based school management was introduced, whereby parents and teachers determined each school's budgetary priorities. This is a major undertaking which aims to prepare the nation for a potentially favourable economic future. With the revival of the EAC, that future could include closer co-operation with Kenya and Tanzania, and if good intentions can be translated into action, a market of over 100m. people could open up new opportunities for all three member states.

Statistical Survey

Source (unless otherwise stated): Statistics Department, Ministry of Finance, Planning and Economic Development, POB 8147, Kampala.

Area and Population

AREA, POPULATION AND DENSITY

Area (sq km)	
Land	197,058
Inland water	44,081
Total	241,139*
Population (census results)	
18 January 1980	12,636,179
12 January 1991	
Males	8,185,747
Females	8,485,958
Total	16,671,705
Population (official estimates at mid-year)	
1996	19,848,000
1997	20,438,000
1998	21,029,000
Density (per sq km) at mid-1998	87.2

* 93,104 sq miles. Source: Lands and Surveys Department.

DISTRICTS (population at 1991 census)

Apac	454,504	Kumi	236,694
Arua	637,941	Lira	500,965
Bundibugyo	116,566	Luwero	449,691
Bushenyi	579,137	Masaka	838,736
Gulu	338,427	Masindi	260,796
Hoima	197,851	Mbale	710,980
Iganga	945,783	Mbarara	798,774
Jinja	289,476	Moroto	174,417
Kabale	417,218	Moyo	175,645
Kabarole	746,800	Mpigi	913,867
Kalangala	16,371	Mubende	500,976
Kampala	774,241	Mukono	824,604
Kamuli	485,214	Nebbi	316,866
Kapchorwa	116,702	Ntungamo	289,222
Kasese	343,601	Pallisa	357,656
Kibaale	220,261	Rakai	383,501
Kiboga	141,607	Rukungiri	390,780
Kisoro	186,681	Soroti	430,390
Kitgum	357,184	Tororo	585,574
Kotido	196,006		

PRINCIPAL TOWNS (population at census of 18 August 1969)

Kampala (capital)	330,700	Mbale	23,544
Jinja and Njeru	52,509	Entebbe	21,096
Bugembe planning area	46,884	Gulu	18,170

1980 (provisional census results): Kampala 458,423; Jinja 45,060; Masaka 29,123; Mbale 28,039; Mbarara 23,155; Gulu 14,958.

BIRTHS AND DEATHS (UN estimates, annual averages)

	1980–85	1985–90	1990–95
Birth rate (per 1,000)	49.9	49.9	50.8
Death rate (per 1,000)	18.5	22.0	24.6

Expectation of life (UN estimates, years at birth, 1990–95): 37.2 (males 36.5; females 38.0).

Source: UN, *World Population Prospects: The 1998 Revision*.

ECONOMICALLY ACTIVE POPULATION
(ILO estimates, '000 persons at mid-1980)

	Males	Females	Total
Agriculture, etc.	2,950	2,340	5,290
Industry	222	50	272
Services	353	247	600
Total	**3,525**	**2,637**	**6,162**

Source: ILO, *Economically Active Population Estimates and Projections, 1950–2025*.

Mid-1998 (estimates in '000): Agriculture, etc. 8,125; Total 10,020 (Source: FAO, *Production Yearbook*).

Agriculture

PRINCIPAL CROPS ('000 metric tons)

	1996	1997	1998
Wheat	9	9	9†
Rice (paddy)	82	80	77†
Maize	759	740	750†
Millet	440	502	580†
Sorghum	298	294	350†
Potatoes	318	360	360†
Sweet potatoes	1,548	1,894	1,890†
Cassava (Manioc)	2,245	2,291	2,285†
Dry beans	234	221	220†
Other pulses	125	130	126†
Soybeans	87	87	85†
Groundnuts (in shell)	125	134	130†
Sesame seed	73	73	72†
Cottonseed†	28	29	30
Vegetables and melons	476	488	480†
Sugar cane†	1,450	1,600	1,550
Bananas†	590	590	585
Plantains	9,144	9,303	9,250†
Other fruit	47	48	47†
Coffee (green)	288	220	180†
Tea (made)	17	21	26*
Tobacco (leaves)	6	7*	7†
Cotton (lint)†	13	13	13

* Unofficial figure.   † FAO estimate(s).

Source: FAO, *Production Yearbook*.

LIVESTOCK ('000 head, year ending September)

	1996	1997	1998*
Asses*	18	18	18
Cattle	5,301	5,363	5,370
Sheep	1,920*	1,950†	1,960
Goats	3,550*	3,594	3,600
Pigs	930*	940	950

* FAO estimate(s).   † Unofficial figure.

Poultry (million): 22 in 1996; 22 in 1997; 23 (FAO estimate) in 1998.

Source: FAO, *Production Yearbook*.

LIVESTOCK PRODUCTS ('000 metric tons)

	1996*	1997	1998*
Beef and veal	88	89	89
Mutton and lamb	9	10	10
Goat meat	15	15	15
Pig meat	51	52	53
Poultry meat	35	36	36
Other meat	18	18	17
Cows' milk*	464	469	470
Poultry eggs	18	18	18
Cattle hides*	12	12	12

* FAO estimates.

Source: FAO, *Production Yearbook*.

Forestry

ROUNDWOOD REMOVALS
('000 cubic metres, excl. bark)

	1995	1996	1997
Sawlogs, veneer logs and logs for sleepers	150	150	150
Other industrial wood	1,974	2,031	2,085
Fuel wood	13,814	14,215	14,589
Total	15,938	16,396	16,824

Source: FAO, *Yearbook of Forest Products*.

SAWNWOOD PRODUCTION
('000 cubic metres, incl. railway sleepers)

	1995	1996	1997
Coniferous (softwood)	7	7	7
Broadleaved (hardwood)*	77	77	77
Total	83	83	83

* FAO estimates.

Source: FAO, *Yearbook of Forest Products*.

Fishing

('000 metric tons, live weight)

	1995	1996	1997
Tilapias	83.2	75.0	81.4
African lungfishes	7.7	6.1	7.6
Characins	10.4	12.2	11.7
Naked catfishes	4.9	5.0	4.8
Other freshwater fishes	9.8	15.6	20.9
Nile perch	92.7	81.3	91.7
Total catch	208.8	195.1	218.0

Source: FAO, *Yearbook of Fishery Statistics*.

Mining

(metric tons, unless otherwise indicated)*

	1994	1995	1996
Tin concentrates†	30	30	30
Tungsten concentrates†	12	17	—
Salt—unrefined ('000 metric tons)	5	5	5

* Estimates from the US Bureau of Mines.
† Figures refer to the metal content of concentrates.

Source: UN, *Industrial Commodity Statistics Yearbook*.

Industry

SELECTED PRODUCTS
('000 metric tons, unless otherwise indicated)

	1997	1998	1999
Beer (million litres)	89.6	110.5	117.8
Soft drinks (million litres)	65.4	69.3	80.8
Cigarettes (million)	1,844	1,846	1,602
Sugar	103.2	102.7	126.9
Soap	66.6	72.8	83.8
Cement	289.6	321.3	347.3
Paint (metric tons)	2,355	2,466	2,450
Edible oil and fat ('000 litres)	27,532	28.3	40.5
Animal feed	25.5	15.9	17.5
Footwear ('000 pairs)	1,274	1,471	1,725
Wheat flour	13.2	27.6	21.1
Electricity (million kWh)	1,217.3	1,232.4	1,340.6

Finance

CURRENCY AND EXCHANGE RATES

Monetary Units
100 cents = 1 new Uganda shilling.

Sterling, Dollar and Euro Equivalents (28 April 2000)
£1 sterling = 2,405.8 new Uganda shillings;
US $1 = 1,534.2 new Uganda shillings;
€1 = 1,393.8 new Uganda shillings;
10,000 new Uganda shillings = £4.157 = $6.518 = €7.174.

Average Exchange Rate (new Uganda shillings per US $)
1997   1,083.0
1998   1,240.3
1999   1,454.8

Note: Between December 1985 and May 1987 the official exchange rate was fixed at US $1 = 1,400 shillings. In May 1987 a new shilling, equivalent to 100 of the former units, was introduced. At the same time, the currency was devalued by 76.7%, with the exchange rate set at $1 = 60 new shillings. Further adjustments were implemented in subsequent years. Foreign exchange controls were mostly abolished in 1993.

BUDGET ('000 million new shillings, year ending 30 June)

Revenue*					1994/95	1995/96	1996/97
Tax revenue .	.	.	.	.	486.2	588.8	688.1
Non-tax revenue .	.	.	.	40.4	38.4	43.3
Total	.	.	.	.	**526.6**	**627.2**	**731.4**

Expenditure†				1994/95	1995/96	1996/97
Current expenditure .	.	.	.	493.1	554.0	667.7
Wages and salaries.	.	.	135.5	167.4	227.0
Interest payments .	.	.	53.3	59.0	63.0
Other current expenditure	.	.	287.0	307.9	351.3
Capital expenditure .	.	.	424.7	431.0	476.6
Total	.	.	.	**917.8**	**984.9**	**1,144.3**

* Excluding grants received ('000 million shillings): 248.0 in 1994/95; 248.2 in 1995/96; 292.9 in 1996/97.
† Excluding lending minus repayments ('000 million shillings): 11.3 in 1994/95; 7.2 in 1995/96; 2.0 in 1996/97.

INTERNATIONAL RESERVES (US $ million at 31 December)

		1997	1998	1999
IMF special drawing rights	. .	5.4	5.0	2.3
Foreign exchange	. . .	628.1	720.4	760.8
Total	. . .	**633.5**	**725.4**	**763.1**

Source: IMF, *International Financial Statistics.*

MONEY SUPPLY (million new shillings at 31 December)*

	1997	1998	1999
Currency outside banks . .	240,460	285,880	330,760
Demand deposits at commercial banks. . . .	272,080	326,560	363,060
Total money . . .	**512,530**	**612,440**	**693,820**

* Figures are rounded to the nearest 10 million shillings.
Source: IMF, *International Financial Statistics.*

COST OF LIVING
(Consumer Price Index for all urban households; base: 1990 = 100)

				1994	1995	1996
Food	.	.	.	227.7	238.1	253.7
Clothing.	.		.	164.5	163.8	167.0
Rent*	.	.	.	248.7	284.7	305.1
All items (incl. others)	.	.	228.3	243.3	260.5

* Including fuel and light.
Source: ILO, *Yearbook of Labour Statistics.*

NATIONAL ACCOUNTS
(million new shillings at current prices, year ending 30 June)
Expenditure on the Gross Domestic Product

	1993/94	1994/95	1995/96
Government final consumption expenditure	453,929	504,008	594,881
Private final consumption expenditure	3,730,985	4,447,233	5,154,110
Increase in stocks . . .	2,091	44,692	49,431
Gross fixed capital formation .	641,311	819,893	1,062,422
Total domestic expenditure	**4,828,316**	**5,815,826**	**6,761,982**
Exports of goods and services .	384,788	631,227	734,365
Imports of goods and services .	−850,477	−1,105,522	−1,363,759
GDP in purchasers' values*	**4,366,721**	**5,273,248**	**6,077,035**
GDP at constant 1991 prices	2,572,413	2,868,209	3,150,019

* Including statistical discrepancy (million shillings): 4,094 in 1993/94; −68,282 in 1994/95; −55,554 in 1995/96.

Gross Domestic Product by Economic Activity

	1993/94	1994/95	1995/96
Agriculture, hunting, forestry and fishing	1,998,986	2,401,274	2,519,382
Mining and quarrying . .	13,320	14,801	15,891
Manufacturing . . .	265,353	311,510	397,874
Electricity, gas and water.	45,725	60,239	65,167
Construction. . . .	238,898	290,318	402,317
Trade, restaurants and hotels	493,427	616,472	742,024
Transport, storage and communications . . .	160,408	185,663	213,857
General government services .	180,882	212,046	248,231
Education	174,906	188,340	223,149
Health	58,989	62,948	70,245
Other services . . .	404,966	484,577	622,986
GDP at factor cost . . .	**4,035,860**	**4,828,189**	**5,521,123**
Indirect taxes . . .	330,861	445,059	555,912
GDP in purchasers' values .	**4,366,721**	**5,273,248**	**6,077,035**

Source: Bank of Uganda.

BALANCE OF PAYMENTS (US $ million)

	1995	1996	1997
Exports of goods f.o.b. . .	560.3	639.3	575.6
Imports of goods f.o.b. . .	−926.8	−986.9	−1,042.5
Trade balance . . .	**−366.5**	**−347.6**	**−466.9**
Exports of services . .	104.0	144.7	164.6
Imports of services . . .	−562.7	−674.6	−693.1
Balance on goods and services	**−825.2**	**−877.5**	**−995.4**
Other income received . .	17.7	29.7	40.5
Other income paid . .	−113.3	−79.2	−52.5
Balance on goods, services and income	**−920.8**	**−927.0**	**−1,007.5**
Current transfers received .	581.9	674.7	619.6
Current balance . . .	**−338.9**	**−252.3**	**−387.8**
Capital account (net) . .	48.3	61.4	31.9
Direct investment from abroad	121.2	121.0	175.0
Investment assets . .	−9.9	−37.2	−14.0
Other investment liabilities .	99.4	56.7	139.2
Net errors and omissions . .	28.8	41.3	20.9
Overall balance . . .	**−51.2**	**−9.1**	**−34.8**

Source: IMF, *International Financial Statistics.*

External Trade

PRINCIPAL COMMODITIES (US $ '000)

Imports c.i.f. (by SITC)	1994	1995	1996*
Food and live animals	70,837	90,226	53,951
Cereals and cereal preparations	38,336	39,741	31,696
Sugar, sugar preparations and honey	16,355	26,694	7,540
Crude materials (inedible) except fuels	28,532	37,098	38,469
Textile fibres and waste	19,648	23,421	22,445
Mineral fuels, lubricants, etc.	30,105	16,664	10,890
Petroleum, petroleum products, etc.	29,949	16,254	10,519
Animal and vegetable oils, fats and waxes	35,712	47,047	31,737
Fixed vegetable fats and oils	21,042	27,376	21,899
Chemicals and related products	67,711	105,407	116,839
Medicinal and pharmaceutical products	29,239	40,365	46,372
Basic manufactures	164,022	205,684	161,985
Rubber manufactures	15,937	16,885	17,015
Paper, paperboard, etc.	14,470	20,719	17,508
Textile yarn, fabrics, etc.	28,740	37,599	25,242
Non-metallic mineral manufactures	32,241	41,847	33,267
Iron and steel	44,653	49,439	35,033
Other metal manufactures	20,681	29,086	21,353
Machinery and transport equipment	220,047	327,321	248,519
Machinery specialized for particular industries	25,322	53,062	30,449
General industrial machinery, equipment and parts	20,466	29,614	26,835
Office machines and automatic data-processing machines	19,496	11,856	10,436
Telecommunications and sound equipment	13,739	26,210	16,427
Other electrical machinery, apparatus, etc.	28,838	39,556	32,637
Road vehicles (incl. air-cushion vehicles) and parts (excl. tyres, engines and electrical parts)	94,955	149,055	115,525
Miscellaneous manufactured articles	67,916	78,887	72,002
Clothing and accessories (excl. footwear)	15,614	14,754	12,819
Total (incl. others)	686,465	909,428	735,080

Domestic exports f.o.b.	1994	1995	1996
Traditional export crops	366,847	409,913	435,208
Coffee	343,289	384,122	396,100
Cotton	3,485	9,696	14,659
Tea	11,804	8,698	17,058
Tobacco	8,269	7,397	7,391
Non-traditional exports	93,092	150,592	198,462
Maize	28,666	19,302	17,818
Beans and other legumes	12,900	10,847	15,231
Fish and fish products	10,403	17,541	25,194
Cattle hides	10,549	8,886	7,835
Gold and gold compounds	224	23,197	43,914
Total†	459,939	560,505	633,670

* Provisional figures.
† Includes some re-exports, and therefore overstates the true level.

PRINCIPAL TRADING PARTNERS (US $ '000)

Imports c.i.f.	1994	1995	1996*
Austria	n.a.	10,699	n.a.
Bangladesh	7,275	n.a.	n.a.
Belgium-Luxembourg	15,354	27,474	15,164
Canada	14,360	12,066	11,248
China, People's Repub.	9,216	20,146	9,953
Denmark	13,705	19,306	16,796
France (incl. Monaco)	10,895	25,376	18,997
Germany	30,965	37,261	30,712
Hong Kong	15,893	30,060	21,800
India	46,762	61,448	47,229
Italy	21,891	46,845	22,745
Japan	57,679	99,432	66,332
Kenya	196,883	213,445	157,132
Korea, Repub.	3,389	12,519	6,360
Malaysia	1,786	17,014	18,499
Netherlands	9,583	19,841	10,514
Singapore	6,570	17,336	10,824
South Africa	5,873	27,674	19,445
Switzerland (incl. Liechtenstein)	6,628	7,642	9,309
Tanzania	8,709	11,583	5,082
United Arab Emirates	35,482	61,717	44,437
United Kingdom	91,116	126,922	103,500
USA	30,379	31,478	22,291
Total (incl. others)	686,475	1,047,649	729,410

* Provisional figures.

Exports f.o.b.	1990	1991	1992
Belgium-Luxembourg	16,906	11,392	21,139
France (incl. Monaco)	23,229	24,643	10,912
Germany	8,030	8,813	7,408
Italy	25,207	21,586	7,290
Korea, Repub.	189	329	2,225
Netherlands	8,030	8,813	7,408
Spain	27,183	17,436	15,859
United Kingdom	14,545	30,767	35,557
USA	19,348	19,708	13,961
Total (incl. others)	190,102	196,009	171,353

Source (for exports): UN, *International Trade Statistics Yearbook*.

Transport

RAILWAYS (traffic)

	1994	1995	1996
Passenger-km (million)	35	30	28
Freight ton-km (million)	208	236	187

ROAD TRAFFIC (vehicles in use)

	1994	1995	1996
Passenger cars	24,208	28,941	35,361
Buses and coaches . . .	9,273	11,749	11,878
Lorries and vans	25,733	30,570	36,552
Road tractors	1,541	1,785	2,043

Source: IRF, *World Road Statistics*.

CIVIL AVIATION (traffic on scheduled services)

	1994	1995	1996
Kilometers flown (million) . .	2	2	2
Passengers carried ('000) . .	63	95	100
Passenger-km (million) . .	52	103	110
Total ton-km (million) . .	5	10	11

Source: UN, *Statistical Yearbook*.

Tourism

	1995	1996	1997
Foreign tourist arrivals ('000) .	188	205	227
Tourism receipts (US $ million) .	78	117	135

Source: World Tourism Organization, *Yearbook of Tourism Statistics*.

Communications Media

	1995	1996	1997
Radio receivers ('000 in use) . .	2,300	2,500	2,600
Television receivers ('000 in use) .	250	300	315
Telephones ('000 main lines in use)* .	39	48	n.a.
Telefax stations*	2,500†	3,000†	n.a.
Mobile cellular telephones (subscribers)*	1,747	4,000	n.a.
Book production‡			
Titles	n.a.	288	n.a.
Daily newspapers:			
Number	2†	2	n.a.
Average circulation ('000 copies)	35†	40	n.a.

* Year ending 30 June.
† Estimate.
‡ Not including pamphlets or government publications.

Sources: mainly UN, *Statistical Yearbook*; UNESCO, *Statistical Yearbook*.

Education

(1999)

	Teachers	Students
Primary	109,733	6,591,429
Secondary:		
General	22,599	427,492
Vocational*‡	1,138	17,772
Primary teacher training colleges‡ . .	956	20,728
Higher:		
University	1,134	14,279
Other†‡	1,344	23,994

* Technical schools and institutes.
† Includes secondary teacher training colleges.
‡ 1998 data.

Directory

The Constitution

Following the military coup in July 1985, the 1967 Constitution was suspended, and all legislative and executive powers were vested in a Military Council, whose Chairman was Head of State. In January 1986 a further military coup established an executive Presidency, assisted by a Cabinet of Ministers and a legislative National Resistance Council (NRC). In September 1995 a Constituent Assembly (comprising 214 elected and 74 nominated members) enacted a draft Constitution. The new Constitution was promulgated on 8 October 1995. Under its terms, a national referendum on the introduction of a multi-party political system was to take place in 2000. The referendum produced an overwhelming vote in favour of retaining the existing 'no-party' system. A direct presidential election took place in May 1996, followed in June of that year by legislative elections to the Parliament. This body, comprising 214 elected members and 62 nominated members, replaced the NRC.

The Government

HEAD OF STATE

President: Lt-Gen. YOWERI KAGUTA MUSEVENI (took office 29 January 1986; elected 9 May 1996).

THE CABINET
(September 2000)

President and Minister of Defence: Lt-Gen. YOWERI KAGUTA MUSEVENI.

Vice-President: Dr SPECIOSA WANDIRA KAZIBWE.

Prime Minister: Prof. APOLO NSIMBAMBI.

First Deputy Prime Minister and Minister of Foreign Affairs: ERIYA KATEGAYA.

Second Deputy Prime Minister and Minister of Internal Affairs: Brig. MOSES ALI.

Minister of Parliamentary Affairs: REBECCA KADAGA.

Minister of Disaster Preparedness and Refugees: Maj. TOM BUTINE.

Minister of Agriculture, Animal Industry and Fisheries: KISAMBA MUGERWA.

Minister of Education and Sports: KIDDU MAKUBUYA.

Minister of Energy and Minerals: SYDA BBUMBA.

Minister of Finance, Planning and Economic Development: GERALD SSENDAWULA.

Minister of Health: Dr CRISPUS W. C. B. KIYONGA.

Minister of Justice and Constitutional Affairs: JEHOASH MAYANJA-NKANGI.

Minister of Labour, Gender and Social Development: JANET BALUNZI MUKWAYA.

Minister of Local Government: JABERI BIDANDI-SSALI.

Minister of Public Service: AMANYA NUWE MUSHEGA.

Minister of Tourism, Trade and Industry: Prof. EDWARD RUGUMAYO.

Minister of Water, Lands and Environment: HENRY MUGANWA KAJURA.

Minister of Works, Housing and Communication: JOHN NASASIRA.

Ministers in the Office of the President: APARITE LOKERIS, MURILI MUKASA, BASOGA NSADHU, KWERONDA RUHEMBA.

Minister in the Office of the Vice-President: BETTY OKWIR.

Minister in the Office of the Prime Minister: (vacant).

MINISTRIES

Office of the President: Parliament Bldg, POB 7168, Kampala; tel. (41) 258441; fax (41) 256143; e-mail info@gouexecutive.net; internet www.gouexecutive.net.

Office of the Prime Minister: POB 341, Kampala; tel. (41) 259518; fax (41) 242341.

Ministry of Agriculture, Animal Industry and Fisheries: POB 102, Entebbe; tel. (42) 20752; fax (42) 21042.

Ministry of Defence: Bombo, POB 7069, Kampala; tel. (41) 270331; fax (41) 245911.

Ministry of Education and Sports: Crested Towers, POB 7063, Kampala; tel. (41) 234440; fax (41) 244594; e-mail mine@starcom .co.ug.

Ministry of Energy and Minerals: Amber House, Kampala Rd, Kampala.

Ministry of Finance, Planning and Economic Development: Nile Ave, POB 8147, Kampala; tel. (41) 234700; fax (41) 230163; e-mail finance@starcom.co.ug.

Ministry of Foreign Affairs: POB 7084, Kampala; tel. (41) 258251; fax (41) 258722; e-mail mofa@starcom.co.ug.

Ministry of Health: Kitante Rd, Kampala; tel. (41) 20385.

Ministry of Internal Affairs: Crested Towers, POB 7084, Kampala; tel. (41) 233811; fax (41) 231188.

Ministry of Justice and Constitutional Affairs: POB 7183, Kampala; tel. (41) 233219; fax (41) 254828.

Ministry of Labour, Gender and Social Development: Udyam House, Jinja Rd, POB 7168, Kampala; tel. (41) 258334.

Ministry of Local Government: Uganda House, POB 7037, Kampala; tel. (41) 241763; fax (41) 258127.

Ministry of Public Service: Buganda Rd, POB 7003, Kampala; tel. (41) 254881.

Ministry of Tourism: Parliament Ave, POB 4241, Kampala: tel. (41) 232971; fax (41) 242188.

Ministry of Trade and Industry: POB 7103, Kampala; tel. (41) 258202; fax (41) 245077.

Ministry of Water, Lands and Environment: Kampala.

Ministry of Works, Housing and Communication: POB 10, Entebbe; tel. (42) 20990; fax (42) 20135; e-mail mowto@imul.com.

President and Legislature

PRESIDENT

Election, 9 May 1996

Candidate	Votes	%
Lt-Gen. YOWERI KAGUTA MUSEVENI	4,428,119	74.2
PAUL KAWANGA SSEMOGERERE	1,416,139	23.7
KIBIRIGE MOHAMED MAYANJA	123,290	2.1
Total	5,967,548	100.0

PARLIAMENT

Speaker: FRANCIS AYUME.

The National Resistance Movement, which took office in January 1986, established a National Resistance Council (NRC), initially comprising 80 nominated members, to act as a legislative body. National elections were held on 11–28 February 1989, at which 210 members of an expanded NRC were elected by members of district-level Resistance Committees (themselves elected by local-level Resistance Committees, who were directly elected by universal adult suffrage). The remaining 68 seats in the NRC were reserved for candidates nominated by the President (to include 34 women and representatives of youth organizations and trades unions). Political parties were not allowed to participate in the election campaign. In October 1989 the NRC approved legislation extending the Government's term of office by five years from January 1990, when its mandate was to expire. The Constituent Assembly (see Constitution) extended further the NRM's term of office in November 1994. Under the terms of the Constitution that was promulgated in October 1995, the NRC was to be restyled as the Ugandan Parliament, and a national referendum on the future introduction of a multi-party political system was to be staged in 2000. Legislative elections to the Parliament took place in June 1996 (again officially on a non-party basis). The total membership of the Parliament was reduced from 278 to 276, comprising 214 elected and 62 nominated representatives.

Political Organizations

Political parties were ordered to suspend active operations, although not formally banned, in March 1986. At a referendum on the future restoration of a plural political system, which took place on 29 June 2000, the retention of the existing 'no-party' system was overwhelmingly endorsed by voters.

Bazzukulu ba Buganda ('Grandchildren of Buganda'): Bagandan separatist movement.

Buganda Youth Movement: f. 1994; seeks autonomy for Buganda; Leader STANLEY KATO.

Conservative Party (CP): f. 1979; Leader JEHOASH MAYANJA-NKANGI.

Democratic Party (DP): POB 7098, Kampala; tel. (41) 230244; f. 1954; main support in southern Uganda; seeks a multi-party political system; Pres. PAUL KAWANGA SSEMOGERERE; Sec.-Gen. MARY MUTAGAMBA.

Federal Democratic Movement (FEDEMO): Kampala.

Forum for Multi-Party Democracy: Kampala; Gen. Sec. JESSE MASHATTE.

Movement for New Democracy in Uganda: based in Zambia; f. 1994 to campaign for multi-party political system; Leader DAN OKELLO-OGWANG.

National Resistance Movement (NRM): f. to oppose the UPC Govt 1980–85; also opposed the mil. Govt in power from July 1985 to Jan. 1986; its fmr. mil. wing, the National Resistance Army (NRA), led by Lt-Gen. YOWERI KAGUTA MUSEVENI, took power in Jan. 1986; Chair. Dr SAMSON KISEKKA.

Nationalist Liberal Party: Kampala; f. 1984 by a breakaway faction of the DP; Leader TIBERIO OKENY.

Uganda Democratic Alliance: opposes the NRM Govt; Leader APOLO KIRONDE.

Uganda Democratic Freedom Front: Leader Maj. HERBERT ITONGA.

Uganda Freedom Movement (UFM): Kampala; mainly Baganda support; withdrew from NRM coalition Govt in April 1987; Sec.-Gen. (vacant).

Uganda Independence Revolutionary Movement: f. 1989; opposes the NRM Govt; Chair. Maj. OKELLO KOLO.

Uganda Islamic Revolutionary Party (UIRP): Kampala; f. 1993; Chair. IDRIS MUWONGE.

Uganda National Unity Movement: opposes the NRM Govt; Chair. Alhaji SULEIMAN SSALONGO.

Uganda Patriotic Movement: Kampala; f. 1980; Sec.-Gen. JABERI SSALI.

Uganda People's Congress (UPC): POB 1951, Kampala; internet www.members.home.net/upc; f. 1960; socialist-based philosophy; mainly northern support; ruling party 1962–71 and 1980–85, sole legal political party 1969–71; Pres. Dr APOLO MILTON OBOTE (in exile in Zambia); Nat. Leader Dr JAMES RWANYARARE.

Ugandan People's Democratic Movement (UPDM): seeks democratic reforms; support mainly from north and east of the country; includes mems of fmr govt armed forces; signed a peace accord with the Govt in 1990; Chair. ERIC OTEMA ALLIMADI; Sec.-Gen. EMMANUEL OTENG.

Uganda Progressive Union (UPU): Kampala; Chair. ALFRED BANYA.

The following organizations are in armed conflict with the Government:

Alliance of Democratic Forces (ADF): active since 1996 in south-eastern Uganda; combines Ugandan Islamic fundamentalist rebels, exiled Rwandan Hutus and guerrillas from the Democratic Republic of the Congo; President Sheikh JAMIL MUKULU.

Lord's Resistance Army (LRA): f. 1987; claims to be conducting a Christian fundamentalist 'holy war' against the Govt; forces est. to number up to 6,000, operating mainly from bases in Sudan; Leader JOSEPH KONY; a breakaway faction (LRA–Democratic) is led by RONALD OTIM KOMAKECH.

Uganda National Rescue Front Part Two (UNRF II): based in Juba, Sudan; Leader ALI BAMUZE.

Uganda People's Freedom Movement (UPFM): based in Tororo and Kenya; f. 1994 by mems of the fmr Uganda People's Army; Leader PETER OTAI.

West Nile Bank Front (WNBF): operates in northern Uganda.

Diplomatic Representation

EMBASSIES AND HIGH COMMISSIONS IN UGANDA

Algeria: POB 4025, Kampala; tel. (41) 232918; fax (41) 341015; e-mail ambalgka@imul.com; Ambassador: MOHAMED EL AMINE DERRAGUI.

Austria: POB 7457, Kampala; tel. (41) 235103; fax (41) 235160; Chargé d'affaires: ANTON MAIR.

Burundi: POB 4379, Kampala; tel. (41) 221697; Ambassador: GEORGES NTEZEZIMANA.

China, People's Republic: POB 4106, Kampala; tel. (41) 236895; fax (41) 235087; Ambassador: TAN XINGJIN.

Congo, Democratic Republic: POB 4972, Kampala; tel. (41) 233777; Chargé d'affaires a.i.: BWANAMAZURI KAMONGU.

Cuba: POB 9226, Kampala; tel. (41) 233742; fax (41) 233320; Chargé d'affaires a.i.: ANGEL NICHOLAS.

Denmark: Plot 3, Lumumba Ave, POB 11234, Kampala; tel. (41) 256783; fax (41) 254979; Ambassador: FLEMMING BJORK PEDERSEN.

Egypt: POB 4280, Kampala; tel. (41) 254525; fax (41) 232103; Ambassador: SAMIR ABDALLAH.

Ethiopia: POB 7745, Kampala; tel. (41) 231010; fax (41) 231782; Ambassador: DAWIT KEBEDE.

France: POB 7112, Kampala; tel. (41) 242120; fax (41) 241252; Ambassador: RENÉ ROUDAUT.

Germany: 15 Philip Rd, POB 7016, Kampala; tel. (41) 256767; fax (41) 343136; Ambassador: HANS-JOACHIM HELDT.

Holy See: POB 7177, Kampala (Apostolic Nunciature); tel. (41) 221167; fax (41) 221774; Apostolic Nuncio: Most Rev. CHRISTOPHE PIERRE, Titular Archbishop of Gunela.

India: Plot 11, Kyodondo Rd, Nakaseru, POB 7040, Kampala; tel. and fax (41) 254943; e-mail hicomind@mail.l.starcom.co.ug; High Commissioner: B. S. PRAKASH.

Italy: POB 4646, Kampala; tel. (41) 341786; fax (41) 250448; e-mail ambkamp@imul.com; Ambassador: LUIGI NAPOLITANO.

Kenya: POB 5220, Kampala; tel. (41) 258235; fax (41) 258239; High Commissioner: (vacant).

Korea, Democratic People's Republic: POB 3717, Kampala; tel. (41) 233667; Ambassador: RI KWANG ROK.

Libya: POB 6079, Kampala; tel. (41) 344924; fax (41) 344969; Sec. of People's Bureau: (vacant).

Netherlands: Plot 8A, Kisozi Complex, 4th floor, Nakasero Lane, POB 7728, Kampala; tel. (41) 234427; fax (41) 231861; Chargé d'affaires a.i.: S. E. DE LANG.

Nigeria: 33 Nakasero Rd, POB 4338, Kampala; tel. (41) 233691; fax (41) 232543; High Commissioner: MAMMAN DAURA.

Pakistan: POB 7022, Kampala; tel. and fax (41) 231142.

Russia: 28 Malcolm X Ave, POB 7022, Kampala; tel. (41) 233676; fax (41) 345798; e-mail russemb@imul.com; Ambassador: ALEXANDER A. SADOVNIKOV.

Rwanda: POB 2468, Kampala; tel. (41) 244045; fax (41) 258547; Ambassador: SAGAHUTU MURASHI ISAIE.

Sudan: Nakasero Rd, Kampala; tel. (41) 243518.

Tanzania: POB 5750, Kampala; tel. (41) 257357; High Commissioner: JOSHUA OPANGA.

United Kingdom: 10–12 Parliament Ave, POB 7070, Kampala; tel. (41) 257054; fax (41) 257304; e-mail bhcinfo@starcom.co.ug; High Commissioner: TOM R. V. PHILLIPS.

USA: POB 7007, Kampala; tel. (41) 259795; fax (41) 235306; Ambassador: MARTIN BRENNAN.

Judicial System

Courts of Judicature: POB 7085, Kampala.

The Supreme Court: Mengo; hears appeals from the Court of Appeal, which in turn hears appeals from the High Court. Also acts as a constitutional court.

   Chief Justice: SAMUEL WILLIAM WAKO WAMBUZI.

   Deputy Chief Justice: S. T. MANYINDO.

The High Court: POB 7085, Kampala; tel. (41) 233422; has full criminal and civil jurisdiction. The High Court consists of the Principal Judge and 29 Puisne Judges.

   Principal Judge: J. H. NTABGOBA.

Magistrates' Courts: These are established under the Magistrates' Courts Act of 1970 and exercise limited jurisdiction in criminal and civil matters. The country is divided into magisterial areas, presided over by a Chief Magistrate. Under the Chief Magistrate there are three categories of Magistrates. The Magistrates preside alone over their courts. Appeals from the first category of Magistrates' Court lie directly to the High Court, while appeals from the second and third categories of Magistrates' Court lie to the Chief Magistrate's Court, and from there to the High Court.

Religion

It is estimated that more than 60% of the population profess Christianity (with approximately equal numbers of Roman Catholics and Protestants). About 5% of the population are Muslims.

CHRISTIANITY
The Anglican Communion

Anglicans are adherents of the Church of the Province of Uganda, comprising 27 dioceses. There are about 8m. adherents.

Archbishop of Uganda and Bishop of Kampala: Most Rev. LIVINGSTONE MPALANYI-NKOYOYO, POB 14123, Kampala; tel. (41) 270218; fax (41) 251925; e-mail couab@uol.co.ug.

Greek Orthodox Church

Archbishop of East Africa: NICADEMUS of IRINOUPOULIS (resident in Nairobi, Kenya); jurisidiction covers Kenya, Tanzania and Uganda.

The Roman Catholic Church

Uganda comprises one archdiocese and 18 dioceses. At 31 December 1999 there were an estimated 10,391,024 adherents (an estimated 47.2% of the total population).

Uganda Episcopal Conference: Uganda Catholic Secretariat, POB 2886, Kampala; tel. (41) 268175; fax (41) 268713; f. 1974; Pres. Mgr PAUL L. KALANDA, Bishop of Fort Portal.

Archbishop of Kampala: Cardinal EMMANUEL WAMALA, Archbishop's House, POB 14125, Mengo, Kampala; tel. (41) 270183; fax (41) 345441.

ISLAM

The Uganda Muslim Supreme Council: POB 3247, Kampala; Mufti of Uganda IBRAHIM SAID LUWEMBA; Chief Kadi and Pres. of Council HUSAYN RAJAB KAKOOZA.

BAHÁ'Í FAITH

National Spiritual Assembly: POB 2662, Kampala; tel. (41) 540511; e-mail bahai@starcom.co.ug; mems resident in 2,721 localities.

The Press

DAILY AND OTHER NEWSPAPERS

The Citizen: Kampala; official publ. of the Democratic Party; English; Editor JOHN KYEYUNE.

The Crusader: Kampala Rd, Kampala; Publ. suspended April 1999; Editor GEORGE LUGALAMBI.

The Economy: POB 6787, Kampala; weekly; English; Editor ROLAND KAKOOZA.

Financial Times: Plot 17/19, Station Rd, POB 31399, Kampala; tel. (41) 245798; bi-weekly; English; Editor G. A. ONEGI OBEL.

Focus: POB 268, Kampala; tel. (41) 235086; fax (41) 242796; f. 1983; publ. by Islamic Information Service and Material Centre; 4 a week; English; Editor HAJJI KATENDE; circ. 12,000.

Guide: POB 5350, Kampala; tel. (41) 233486; fax (41) 268045; f. 1989; weekly; English; Editor-in-Chief A. A. KALIISA; circ. 30,000.

The Monitor: POB 12141; Kampala; tel. (41) 231541; fax (41) 251352; e-mail monitor@imul.com; internet www.monitor.co.ug; f. 1992; daily; English; Editor-in-Chief WAFULA OGUTTU; Editor CHARLES ONYANGO-OBBO; circ. 30,000.

Mulengera: POB 6787, Kampala; weekly; Luganda; Editor ROLAND KAKOOZA.

Munnansi News Bulletin: POB 7098, Kampala; f. 1980; weekly; English; owned by the Democratic Party; Editor ANTHONY SGEKWEYAMA.

Munno: POB 4027, Kampala; f. 1911; daily; Luganda; publ. by the Roman Catholic Church; Editor ANTHONY SSEKWEYAMA; circ. 7,000.

New Vision: POB 9815, Kampala; tel. (41) 235846; fax (41) 235221; e-mail nvision@imul.com; internet www.imul.com/vision; f. 1986; official govt newspaper; daily; English; Editor WILLIAM PIKE; circ. 40,000.

Ngabo: POB 9362, Kampala; tel. (41) 42637; f. 1979; daily; Luganda; Editor MAURICE SEKAWUNGU; circ. 7,000.

The People: Kampala; weekly; English; independent; Editor AMOS KAJOBA.

The Star: POB 9362, Kampala; tel. (41) 42637; f. 1980; revived 1984; daily; English; Editor SAMUEL KATWERE; circ. 5,000.

Taifa Uganda Empya: POB 1986, Kampala; tel. (41) 254652; f. 1953; daily; Luganda; Editor A. SEMBOGA; circ. 24,000.

Weekly Topic: POB 1725, Kampala; tel. (41) 233834; weekly; English; Editor JOHN WASSWA; circ. 13,000.

PERIODICALS

Eastern Africa Journal of Rural Development: Dept of Agriculture, Makerere University, POB 7062, Kampala; 2 a year; circ. 800.

The Exposure: POB 3179, Kampala; tel. (41) 267203; fax (41) 259549; monthly; politics.

Leadership: POB 2522, Kampala; tel. (41) 221358; fax (41) 221576; f. 1956; 6 a year; English; Roman Catholic; circ. 7,400.

Mkombozi: c/o Ministry of Defence, Republic House, POB 3798, Kampala; tel. (41) 270331; f. 1982; military affairs; Editor A. OPO-LOTT.

Musizi: POB 4027, Mengo, Kampala; f. 1955; monthly; Luganda; Roman Catholic; Editor F. GITTA; circ. 30,000.

Pearl of Africa: POB 7142, Kampala; monthly; govt publ.

Uganda Confidential: POB 5576, Kampala; tel. (41) 250273; fax (41) 255288; e-mail ucl@swiftuganda.com; internet www .swiftuganda.com/~confidential; f. 1990; monthly; Editor TEDDY SSEZI-CHEEYE.

NEWS AGENCIES

Uganda News Agency (UNA): POB 7142, Kampala; tel. (41) 232734; fax (41) 342259; Dir CRISPUS MUNDUA (acting).

Foreign Bureaux

Inter Press Service (IPS) (Italy): Plot 4, 3rd St, Industrial Area, POB 16514, Wandegeya, Kampala; tel. (41) 235846; fax (41) 235211; Correspondent DAVID MUSOKE.

Newslink Africa (United Kingdom): POB 6032, Kampala.

Rossiiskoye Informatsionnoye Agentstvo — Novosti (RIA—Novosti) (Russia): POB 4412, Kampala; tel. (41) 232383; Correspondent Dr OLEG TETERIN.

Xinhua (New China) News Agency (People's Republic of China): Plot 27, Prince Charles Drive, Kampala; tel. (41) 347109; fax (41) 254951; Chief Correspondent WANG SHANGZHI.

Publishers

Centenary Publishing House Ltd: POB 6246, Kampala; tel. (41) 241599; fax (41) 250427; f. 1977; religious (Anglican); Man. Dir Rev. SAM KAKIZA.

Fountain Publishers Ltd: POB 488, Kampala; tel. (41) 259163; fax (41) 251160; e-mail fountain@starcom.co.ug; f. 1989; general, school textbooks, children's books, academic; Man. Dir JAMES TUMU-SIIME.

Longman Uganda Ltd: POB 3409, Kampala; tel. (41) 42940; f. 1965; Man. Dir M. K. L. MUTYABA.

Uganda Printing and Publishing Corporation: POB 33, Entebbe; tel. (42) 20639; fax (42) 20530; f. 1993; Man. Dir P.A. BAKER.

Broadcasting and Communications

TELECOMMUNICATIONS

CelTel Ltd: POB 6771, Kampala; tel. (41) 230110; fax (41) 230106; e-mail celmail@imul.com; Man. Dir A. K. SSEMMANDA.

MTN Uganda Ltd: POB 24624, Kampala; fax (41) 078212250; internet www.mtn.co.ug; f. 1998.

Starcom: POB 10524, Kampala; tel. (41) 345701; fax (41) 345708.

Uganda Communications Commission: Kampala; f. 1998; regulatory body.

Uganda Telecom Ltd (UTL): POB 7171, Kampala; tel. (41) 258855; fax (41) 345907; f. 1998; state-owned; privatization pending.

BROADCASTING

Radio

91.3 Capital FM: POB 7638, Kampala; tel. (41) 235092; fax (41) 344556; e-mail pquarcoo@capitalfm-ug.com; f. 1993; independent music station broadcasting from Kampala, Mbarara and Mbale; Chief Officers WILLIAM PIKE, PATRICK QUARCOO.

Central Broadcasting Service (CBS): POB 12760, Kampala; tel. (41) 272993; fax (41) 340031; e-mail cbs@imul.com; f. 1996; independent station broadcasting in local languages and English to most of Uganda.

Radio Uganda: POB 7142, Kampala; tel. (41) 257256; fax (41) 256888; f. 1954; state-controlled; broadcasts in 24 languages, including English, Swahili and Ugandan vernacular languages; Commr for Broadcasting JACK TURYAMWIJUKA.

Sanyu Radio: Katto Plaza, Nkrumah Rd, Kampala; f. 1993; independent station broadcasting to Kampala and its environs.

Television

Sanyu Television: Naguru; f. 1994; independent station broadcasting to Kampala and its environs.

Uganda Television (UTV): POB 7142, Kampala; tel. (41) 254461; f. 1962; state-controlled commercial service; programmes mainly in English, also in Swahili and Luganda; transmits over a radius of 320 km from Kampala; five relay stations are in operation, others are under construction; Controller of Programmes FAUSTIN MISANVU.

Finance

(cap. = capital; res = reserves; dep. = deposits; m. = million; brs = branches; amounts in new Uganda shillings unless otherwise indicated).

BANKING

Central Bank

Bank of Uganda: 37–43 Kampala Rd, POB 7120, Kampala; tel. (41) 258441; fax (41) 230878; e-mail info@bou.or.ug; internet www.bou.or.ug; f. 1966; bank of issue; cap. and res 119,003m., dep. 1,558,266m. (June 1997); Gov. CHARLES NYONYINTONO KIKONYOGO; Dep. Gov. Dr LOUIS KASEKENDE.

State Banks

Uganda Commercial Bank Ltd (UCBL): Plot 12, Kampala Rd, POB 973, Kampala; tel. (41) 234710; fax (41) 259012; e-mail ucb@starcom.co.ug; f. 1965; 51% state-owned; operations placed under the control of Bank of Uganda April 1999; cap. and res 117,907m., dep. 194,020m. (Sept. 1997); Chair. I. K. KABANDA; Man. Dir JAYANT HIRANI (acting); 65 brs.

Uganda Development Bank: UDB Towers, 22 Hannington Rd, POB 7210, Kampala; tel. (41) 230446; fax (41) 258571; e-mail udb2mail@swiftuganda.com; f. 1972; state-owned; cap. 11m. (Dec. 1993); Man. Dir JOHN K. TWINOMUSINGUZI.

Commercial Banks

Allied Bank International (Uganda) Ltd: 24 Jinja Rd, POB 2750, Kampala; tel. (41) 236535; fax (41) 230439; e-mail allied@ starcom.co.ug; reorg. in 1996; 35% owned by Banque Belgolaise SA; cap. and res 2,244m. (Dec. 1999); Chair. J. ÉPELU-ÓPIO JUSTINE; Man. Dir J. J. LAING.

Crane Bank Ltd: 20 Kampala Rd, POB 22572, Kampala; tel. (41) 341410; fax (41) 231578; e-mail cranebnk@imul.com; cap. 4,500m., dep. 45,928m. (March 1998); Chair. SAMSON MUWANGUZI; Man. Dir DAVID J. SCHOLTZ.

Gold Trust Bank Ltd: 13 Kimathi Ave, POB 70, Kampala; tel. (41) 231784; fax (41) 231687; f. 1984; cap. and res 1,021m., dep. 14,298m. (Dec. 1997); Chair. MANZUR ALAM; Man. Dir ABID ALAM.

International Credit Bank Ltd: Katto Plaza, Plot 11/13, Nkrumah Rd, POB 22212, Kampala; tel. (41) 342291; fax (41) 230408; f. 1977; cap. and res 2,060m., dep. 9,794m. (June 1996); Chair. THOMAS I. KATTO; Gen. Man. S. BALARAMAN.

Nile Bank Ltd: Spear House, Plot 22, Jinja Rd, POB 2834, Kampala; tel. (41) 346904; fax (41) 257779; e-mail nilebku@ imul.com; f. 1988; cap. and res 3,423.8m., dep. 30,461m. (Dec. 1997); Chair. J. KARIISA-KASA; Man. Dir ANTHONY BENTLEY; 3 brs.

Orient Bank Ltd: Uganda House, Plot 10, Kampala Rd, POB 3072, Kampala; tel. (41) 236012; fax (41) 236066; e-mail orient@starcom .co.ug; internet www.orientbankuganda.com; cap. and res 5,658m., dep. 42,315m. (June 1998); Chair. and Man. Dir RAJNA BIKAS; br in Jinja.

Development Banks

East African Development Bank (EADB): East African Development Bank Bldg, 4 Nile Ave, POB 7128, Kampala; tel. (41) 230021; fax (41) 259763; f. 1967; provides financial and tech. assistance to promote industrial development within Uganda, Kenya and Tanzania, whose Govts each hold 25.46% of the equity, the remaining 23.62% being shared by FMO Netherlands, Deutsche Investitions-und Entwicklungs-GmbH, the African Development Bank and others; regional offices in Nairobi and Dar es Salaam; cap. SDR 27.4m., dep. SDR 43m. (Dec. 1997); Dir (Uganda) E. TUMUSIIME-MUTE-BILE.

Development Finance Co of Uganda Ltd: Rwenzori House, Lumumba Rd, POB 2767, Kampala; tel. (41) 231215; fax (41) 259435; e-mail dfcu@dfc-ug.com; owned by Commonwealth Devt Corpn, Uganda Devt Corpn, Int. Finance Corpn and DEG (25% each); cap. and res 6,953m. (Dec. 1995); Chair. WILLIAM KALEMA; CEO JOHN S. TAYLOR.

Foreign Banks

Bank of Baroda (Uganda) Ltd (India): 18 Kampala Rd, POB 7197, Kampala; tel. (41) 233680; fax (41) 230781; f. 1969; 49% govt-owned; cap. and res 4,643m., dep. 58,678m. (Dec. 1998); Chair. and Man. Dir A. M. RAO; 5 brs.

Barclays Bank of Uganda Ltd (United Kingdom): 16 Kampala Rd, POB 2971, Kampala; tel. (41) 232594; fax (41) 259467; f. 1969; 49% govt-owned, 51% wholly owned by Barclays Bank PLC (UK); cap. and res 10,519m., dep. 82,645m. (Dec. 1998); Chair. and Man. Dir M. GRIFFITHS; 2 brs.

Stanbic Bank Uganda Ltd: 45 Kampala Rd, POB 7131, Kampala; tel. (41) 230811; fax (41) 231116; e-mail stanbic@starcom.co.ug; f. 1906 as National Bank of India, adopted present name 1993; wholly owned by SBIC Africa Holdings Ltd (Botswana); cap. and res 4,511m., dep. 116,548m. (Sept. 1998); Chair. R. E. NORVAL; Man. Dir A. C. KLEINSCHMIDT.

Standard Chartered Bank Uganda Ltd (United Kingdom): 5 Speke Rd, POB 7111, Kampala; tel. (41) 258211; fax (41) 231473; e-mail scbugand@infocom.co.ug; f. 1969; wholly owned by Standard Chartered Holdings (Africa) BV (Netherlands); cap. 2,000m. (Dec. 1997), res 7,191m., dep. 62,294m. (Dec. 1998); Chair. E. A. H. GROAG; Man. Dir W. MATSAIRA.

Tropical Africa Bank Ltd (Libya): Plot 27, Kampala Rd, POB 9485, Kampala; tel. (41) 231990; fax (41) 232296; e-mail tabu1o@calva.com; f. 1972; 50% govt-owned, 50% owned by Libyan Arab Foreign Bank; cap. 7,000m. (Jan. 2000); Chair. EMMANUEL TUMUSIIME-MUTEBILE; Gen. Man. KAMEL M. EL KHALLAS.

STOCK EXCHANGE

Kampala Stock Exchange: East African Development Bank Bldg, Nile Ave, POB 24565, Kampala; tel. (41) 342788; fax (41) 343803; e-mail cma@starcom.co.ug; f. 1997; Chair. LEO KIBIRANGO; CEO JAPHETH KATTO.

INSURANCE

East Africa General Insurance Co Ltd: Plot 14, Kampala Rd, POB 1392, Kampala; tel. and fax (41) 343234; life, fire, motor, marine and accident; Gen. Man. E. MULONDO.

National Insurance Corporation: Plot 3, Pilkington Rd, POB 7134, Kampala; tel. (41) 258001; fax (41) 259925; f. 1964; general and life; Man. Dir S. SEBUUFU.

Pan World Insurance Co Ltd: POB 7658, Kampala; tel. (41) 341618; fax (41) 341593; e-mail pwico@imul.com; Gen. Man. GORDON SENTIBA.

Uganda American Insurance Co Ltd: POB 7077, Kampala; tel. and fax (41) 533781; f. 1970; Man. Dir STAN MENSAH.

Uganda Co-operative Insurance Ltd: Plot 10, Bombo Rd, POB 6176, Kampala; tel. (41) 241836; fax (41) 258231; f. 1982; general; Chair. EPHRAIM KAKURU; Gen. Man. D. S. MASWERE.

Trade and Industry

GOVERNMENT AGENCIES

Capital Markets Authority: East African Development Bank Bldg, 4 Nile Ave, POB 24565, Kampala; tel. (41) 342788; fax (41) 342803; e-mail cma@starcom.co.ug; f. 1996 to develop, promote and regulate capital markets sector; CEO JAPHETH KATTO.

Enterprise Development Unit (EPD): Kampala; oversees privatization programme; Exec. Dir LEONARD MUGANWA.

Export and Import Licensing Division: POB 7000, Kampala; tel. (41) 258795; f. 1987; advises importers and exporters and issues import and export licences; Prin. Commercial Officer JOHN MUHWEZI.

Uganda Advisory Board of Trade: POB 6877, Kampala; tel. (41) 33311; f. 1974; issues trade licences and service for exporters.

Uganda Export Promotion Board: POB 5045, Kampala; tel. (41) 230233; fax (41) 259779; e-mail uepc@starcom.co.ug; internet www.ktp.co.org; f. 1983; provides market intelligence, organizes training, trade exhbns, etc.; Exec. Dir ROBERT K. RUTAAGI.

Uganda Investment Authority: Investment Centre, Plot 28, Kampala Rd, POB 7418, Kampala; tel. (41) 251562; fax (41) 342903; e-mail uia@starcom.co.ug; internet www.ugandainvest.com; f. 1991; promotes foreign and local investment, assists investors, provides business information, issues investment licences; Exec. Dir YOB YOBE OKELLO.

DEVELOPMENT ORGANIZATIONS

Agriculture and Livestock Development Fund: f. 1976; provides loans to farmers.

National Housing and Construction Corporation: Crested Towers, POB 659, Kampala; tel. (41) 257461; fax (41) 258708; e-mail nhcc@imul.com; internet www.nhcc.ug.com; f. 1964; govt agent for building works; also develops residential housing; Chair. Dr COLIN SENTONGO; Gen. Man. M. S. KASEKENDE.

Uganda Industrial Development Corporation Ltd (ULDC): 9–11 Parliament Ave, POB 7042, Kampala; f. 1952; Chair. SAM RUTEGA.

CHAMBER OF COMMERCE

Uganda National Chamber of Commerce and Industry: Plot 17/19 Jinja Rd, POB 3809, Kampala; tel. (41) 258792; fax (41) 258793; e-mail uma@starcom.co.ug; Chair. Pres. BONEY KATATUMBA.

INDUSTRIAL AND TRADE ASSOCIATIONS

CMB Ltd (Coffee Marketing Board): POB 7154, Kampala; tel. (41) 254051; fax (41) 230790; state-owned, privatization pending; purchases and exports coffee; Chair. Dr DDUMBA SSENTAMU; Man. Dir SAM KIGGUNDU.

Cotton Development Organization: POB 7018, Kampala; tel. (41) 232968; fax (41) 232975; Man. Dir JOLLY SABUNE.

Produce Marketing Board: POB 3705, Kampala; tel. (41) 236238; Gen. Man. ESTHER KAMPAMPARA.

Ugandan Coffee Development Authority: Coffee House, Plot 35, Jinja Rd, POB 7267, Kampala; tel. (41) 256940; fax (41) 256994; f. 1991; enforces quality control and promotes coffee exports, maintains statistical data, advises Govt on local and world prices and trains processors and quality controllers; Man. Dir TRESS BUCYANAY-ANDI.

Uganda Importers', Exporters' and Traders' Association: Kampala.

Uganda Manufacturers' Association (UMA): POB 6966, Kampala; tel. (41) 221034; fax (41) 220285; e-mail uma@starcom.co.ug; internet www.uganda.co.ug/uma.htm; promotes mfrs' interests; Chair. JAMES MULWANA.

Uganda Tea Authority: POB 4161, Kampala; tel. (41) 231003; state-owned; controls and co-ordinates activities of the tea industry; Gen. Man. MIRIA MARGARITA MUGABI.

EMPLOYERS' ORGANIZATION

Federation of Uganda Employers: POB 3820, Kampala; e-mail fue@infocom.co.ug; Chair. BRUNO ABALIWANO; Exec. Dir J. KASWARRA.

UTILITIES

Electricity

Uganda Electricity Board: POB 7059, Kampala; tel. (41) 254071; fax (41) 235119; e-mail okumu@infocom.co.ug; f. 1948; privatization pending; Chair. J. E. N. KAGULE-MAGAMBO; 36 brs.

Water

National Water Uganda: POB 7053, Kampala; tel. (41) 256762; fax (41) 258299; f. 1972; privatization pending; Man. Dir WILLIAM T. MUHAIRWE; 12 brs.

MAJOR COMPANIES

The following are some of the largest companies in terms either of capital investment or employment.

African Textile Mills Ltd: POB 242, Mbale; tel. (45) 34373; fax (45) 34549; f. 1968; cap. sh. 12,000m.; textile mfrs; operates one mill; Man. Dir P. R. PATEL; 200 employees.

Blenders Uganda Ltd: POB 3515, Kampala; tel. (41) 259152; fax (41) 232510; tea- and coffee-blending, packaging and distribution; Gen. Man. T. D. MUZITO.

British-American Tobacco (BAT) Uganda 1984 Ltd: POB 7100, Kampala; f. 1928; tel. (41) 243231; jtly owned by the Uganda Govt and BAT London; tobacco mfrs and exporters; Man. Dir PHILIP PAYNE.

Bugirinya United Steel Co: POB 1321, Kampala; tel. (41) 345279; iron and steel producers.

Fina Exploration Uganda Ltd: wholly-owned by Petrofina Ltd (Belgium); petroleum exploration.

International Distillers Uganda Ltd: POB 3221, Kampala; tel. (41) 221111; fax (41) 221903; f. 1964; cap. US $15m.; production of potable spirits; Man. Dir I. H. KINSTON.

Kakira Sugar Works (KSW): POB 121, Jinja; tel. (43) 121475; fax (43) 121475; e-mail madhvani@madhvani.org; jtly owned by Madhvani Group (70%) and Uganda Govt; mfrs of some 70,000 metric tons of sugar annually; joint Man. Dirs MAYUR MADHVANI, MANUBHAI MADHVANI; 7,000 employees.

Kibimba Rice Co Ltd: f. 1977; owned by Tilda Uganda Ltd; rice producer.

Lake Victoria Bottling Co Ltd: f. 1950 as Crown Co Ltd, current name adopted 1992; mfrs of soft drinks.

Lonrho Motors Uganda Ltd: Plot 64/66, 7th St, Industrial Area, POB 353, Kampala; tel. (41) 257819; fax (41) 257818; e-mail iwlmu.lonroug@imul.com; distributors of motor vehicles, tractors, motorcycles and parts.

Mitchell Cotts Uganda Ltd: POB 6641, Kampala; tel. (41) 345117; fax (41) 343121; UK trading group active in tea sector, in which it part-owns the Toro and Mityana Tea Co; instigated a jt venture with the Govt to rehabilitate the tea industry in 1980; also operates freight services; Man. Dir DANNY SSEMWANGA.

Mulco Textiles Ltd: POB 54, Jinja; tel. (43) 120511; fax (43) 130174; e-mail madhvani@madhvani.org; f. 1963; mfrs of cotton textiles.

Nile Breweries Ltd: POB 762, Jinja; tel. (43) 130060; fax (43) 120759; e-mail gkrishnan@nbl.bushnet.net; internet www.nile-beer.com; f. 1951; mem. of Madhvani Group; CEO HENRY RUOD; 500 employees.

Nyanza Textile Industries Ltd (NYTIL): POB 408, Jinja; tel. (43) 20205; fax (43) 20241; f. 1949; owned by Picfare Ltd; textile mfrs; Man. Dir Mr ONEG-OBEL.

Sembale Steel Mill: POB 15182, Kampala; tel. (41) 270147; iron and steel producers.

Steel Corpn of East Africa Ltd: POB 1023, Jinja; tel. (43) 21452; fax (43) 21453.

Tororo Industrial Chemicals and Fertilisers Ltd: POB 254, Tororo; f. 1962; mfrs of single super-phosphate fertilizer, sulphuric acid and insecticide.

Uganda Bata Shoe Co Ltd: 92–94 Fifth St, Industrial area, POB 422, Kampala; tel. (41) 258911; fax (41) 3241380; e-mail batakampala@imul.com; f. 1966.

Uganda Breweries Ltd: POB 7130, Kampala; tel. (41) 220224; fax (41) 220059; produces Bell, Pilsner and Guinness beers for the domestic market; Man. Dir DAVID J. LLOYD; 700 employees.

Uganda Grain Milling Co Ltd: POB 895, Jinja; tel. (43) 120171; fax (43) 120060; millers; Man. Dir A. L. N. MUKASA; 600 employees.

Uganda Metal Products and Enamelling Co Ltd: POB 3151, Kampala; f. 1956; cap. £225,000; mfrs of enamelware, furniture, signs, etc.; 110 employees.

CO-OPERATIVES

In 2000 there were 6,313 co-operative societies, grouped in 34 unions. There is at least one co-operative union in each administrative district.

Uganda Co-operative Alliance: Kampala; co-ordinating body for co-operative unions, of which the following are among the most important:

Bugisu Co-operative Union Ltd: Palisa Rd, Private Bag, Mbale; tel. (45) 33027; f. 1954; processors and exporters of Bugisu arabica coffee; 226 mem. socs; Gen. Man. WOMUTU.

East Mengo Growers' Co-operative Union Ltd: POB 7092, Kampala; tel. (41) 270383; fax (41) 243502; f. 1968; processors and exporters of coffee and cotton; 280 mem. socs; Chair. FRANCIS MUKAMA; Man. JOSEPH SSEMOGERERE.

Kakumiro Growers' Co-operative Union: POB 511, Kakumiro; processing of coffee and cotton; Sec. and Man. TIBIHWA-RUKEERA.

Kimeeme Livestock Co-operative Society: Mwanga II Rd, POB 6670, Kampala; f. 1984; farming and marketing of livestock; Chair. SAMUSI LUKIMA.

Lango Co-operative Union: POB 59, Lira; tel. (473) 79; f. 1956; ginning and exporting of conventional and organic cotton produce; Gen. Man. PATRICK ORYANG.

Masaka Co-operative Union Ltd: POB 284, Masaka; tel. (481) 20260; f. 1951; coffee, dairy farming, food processing, carpentry; 245 primary co-operative socs; Chair. J. M. KASOZI; Gen. Man. EDWARD C. SSERUUMA.

Mubende District Co-operative Union: coffee growers.

Nyakatonzi Growers Co-operative Union: Fort Portal Rd, POB 32, Kasese; tel. (483) 4370; fax (483) 44135; f. 1957; processors and exporters of coffee and cotton; Gen. Man. ADAM BWAMBALE.

South Bukedi Co-operative Union: 6 Busia Rd, POB 36, Tororo; tel. (45) 44327; f. 1952; ginning and export of cotton, manufacturers of edible oil; Gen. Man. GEORGE OBOTH.

South-west Nile Co-operative Union: POB 33, Pakwach, Nebbi, f. 1958; ginning and export of cotton; Gen. Man. PHILIP UPAKRWOTH.

Uganda Co-operative Savings and Credit Society: 62 Parliament Ave, POB 9452, Kampala; tel. (41) 257410; f. 1973; Chair PATRICK KAYONGO.

Uganda Co-operative Transport Union: 41 Bombo Rd, POB 5486, Kampala; tel. (41) 567571; f. 1971; general transport, imports of motor vehicles, vehicle repair and maintenance; Gen. Man. STEPHEN TASHOBYA.

Wamala Growers' Co-operative Union Ltd: POB 99, Mityana; tel. (46) 2036; f. 1968; coffee and cotton growers; 250 mem. socs; Gen. Man. HERBERT KIZITO.

West Mengo Growers' Co-operative Union Ltd: POB 7039, Kampala; tel. (41) 567511; f. 1948; cotton growing and buying,

coffee buying and processing, maize milling; 250 mem. socs; Chair. H. E. KATABALWA MIIRO.

West Nile Tobacco Co-operative Union: Wandi, POB 71, Arua; f. 1965; growing, curing and marketing of tobacco; Gen. Man. ANDAMAH BABWA.

TRADE UNION

National Organization of Trade Unions (NOTU): POB 2150, Kampala; tel. (41) 256295; f. 1973; Chair. E. KATURAMU; Sec.-Gen. MATHIAS MUKASA.

Transport

RAILWAYS

In 1992 there were 1,241 km of 1000-mm-gauge track in operation. A programme to rehabilitate the railway network is under way.

Uganda Railways Corporation: Nasser Rd, POB 7150, Kampala; tel. (41) 254961; fax (41) 344405; f. 1977, following the dissolution of East African Railways; Man. Dir D. C. MURUNGI.

ROADS

In 1985 there was a total road network of 28,332 km, including 7,782 km of main roads and 18,508 km of secondary roads. About 22% of roads were paved. By early 1997 about 60% of main roads (by then totalling some 10,000 km) had been rehabilitated, and it was planned to invest some US $1,500m. in a further 10-year rehabilitation project.

INLAND WATERWAYS

A rail wagon ferry service connecting Jinja with the Tanzanian port of Tanga, via Mwanza, was inaugurated in 1983, thus reducing Uganda's dependence on the Kenyan port of Mombasa. In 1986 the Uganda and Kenya Railways Corporations began the joint operation of Lake Victoria Marine Services, to ferry goods between the two countries via Lake Victoria.

CIVIL AVIATION

The international airport is at Entebbe, on Lake Victoria, some 40 km from Kampala. There are also several small airfields.

Civil Aviation Authority (CAA): Entebbe International Airport, POB 5536, Kampala; tel. (41) 20516; fax (41) 321401; e-mail caa@starcom.ug.com; Man. Dir AMBROSE AKANDONDA.

Principal Airlines

Air Alexander: Entebbe International Airport; f. 1999; operates cargo and passenger services between Entebbe and Kisangani (Democratic Republic of the Congo).

Alliance Air (African Joint Air Service); Impala House, 13 Kimathi Ave, POB 2128, Kampala; tel. (41) 244011; fax (41) 251681; e-mail alliance2@starcom.co.ug; internet www.uganda.co.ug/alliance; f. 1994; jtly owned by South African Airways (40%), Air Tanzania Corpn (10%), Uganda Airlines Corpn (10%), the Ugandan and Tanzanian Govts (30%) and private investors (10%); transfer of control to Uganda Airlines Corpn pending; operates scheduled passenger and cargo services to Africa, Europe, the Middle East and Asia; Chair. ADRIAN SIBO; Man. Dir CHRISTO ROODT.

Dairo Air Cargo Services: 24 Jinja Rd, POB 5480, Kampala; tel. (41) 257731.

Eagle Aviation Uganda Ltd: Entebbe International Airport, POB 7392, Kampala; tel. (41) 344292; fax (41) 344501; e-mail eagle@swiftuganda.com; internet www.eagleuganda.com; f. 1994; domestic services, charter flights to neighbouring countries; Man. Dir Capt. ANTHONY RUBOMBORA.

Inter Air: Nile Ave, POB 22658, Kampala; tel. (41) 255508.

Uganda Airlines Corporation: Airways House, 6 Colville St, POB 5740, Kampala; tel. (41) 232990; fax (41) 257279; f. 1976; state-owned; transfer to private-sector ownership and merger with Alliance Air pending; scheduled cargo and passenger services to Africa, Europe and the Middle East; scheduled cargo and passenger domestic services; Chair. Dr EZRA SURUMA (acting); Gen. Man. BENEDICT MUTYABA.

Tourism

Uganda's principal attractions for tourists are the forests, lakes, mountains and wildlife and an equable climate. A programme to revive the tourist industry by building or improving hotels and creating new national parks began in the late 1980s. There were 227,000 tourist arrivals in 1997 (compared with 12,786 in 1983). Revenue from the sector in 1997 was estimated at US $135m. Unrest in western Uganda during the late 1990s has had a negative impact on tourism.

Ministry of Tourism: Parliament Ave, POB 4241, Kampala; tel. (41) 232971; fax (41) 242188; provides some tourist information.

Uganda Tourist Board: Parliament Ave, POB 7211, Kampala; tel. (41) 342196; fax (41) 342188; e-mail utb@starcom.co.ug; internet www.visituganda.com; Chair. PETER KAMYA; Gen. Man. IGNATIUS NAKISHERO.

Defence

In August 1999 the Uganda People's Defence Forces (UPDF, formerly the National Resistance Army) was estimated to number 30,000–40,000 men, including paramilitary forces (a border defence unit of about 600 men, a police air wing and about 400 marines). Disruptive activity by rebel groups in northern and western Uganda, in conjunction with Uganda's military involvement in the civil war in the Democratic Republic of the Congo from mid-1998, resulted in higher levels of military expenditure during the late 1990s than had initially been envisaged. In July 1997 US military staff arrived in Kampala to train a batalion of the UPDF to act as an African peace-keeping force under the African Crisis Response Initiative programme. The United Kingdom has also provided training to the UPDF. In mid-1998 troops from Uganda, Kenya and Tanzania participated in a joint military exercise.

Defence Expenditure: Budgeted at Us. 177,000m. in 1999/2000.

Commander of the UPDF: Maj.-Gen. JEJE ABUBAKER ODONGO.

Education

Education is not compulsory. Most schools are supported by the government, although a small proportion are sponsored by missions. Traditionally all schools have charged fees. In 1997, however, the government introduced an initiative known as Universal Primary Education (UPE), whereby free primary education was to be phased in for up to four children per family. Primary education begins at six years of age and lasts for seven years. Secondary education, beginning at the age of 13, lasts for a further six years, comprising a first cycle of four years and a second of two years. In 1995 the number of pupils attending government-aided primary and secondary schools was equivalent to 49% of children in the relevant age-group (males 54%; females 44%). In 1995 there were 2,636,409 pupils enrolled at primary schools, and 255,158 pupils attending general secondary schools. However, the numbers of pupils attending primary schools reportedly doubled in 1997, following the instigation of the UPE programme, and by 1999 there were 6,591,429 pupils enrolled in primary schools and 427,492 pupils attending general secondary schools. In addition to Makerere University in Kampala, there is a university of science and technology at Mbarara, and a small Islamic university is located at Mbale. In 1996 enrolment in tertiary education was equivalent to 2% of students in the relevant age-group (males 3%; females 1%). In 1995, according to UNESCO estimates, the average rate of adult illiteracy was 38.1% (males 26.3%; females 49.6%). Education expenditure in the financial year ending 30 June 1997 accounted for approximately 24.9% of government current expenditure.

Bibliography

Ahluwalia, D. P. S. *Plantations and the Politics of Sugar in Uganda.* Kampala, Fountain Publishers, 1995.

Armstrong, J. *Uganda's AIDS Crisis: Its Implications for Development.* Washington, DC, World Bank, 1995.

Hansen, H. B. *Mission, Church and State in a Colonial Setting, Uganda 1890–c.1925.* London, Heinemann Educational, 1984.

Hansen, H. B., and Twaddle, M. (Eds). *Uganda Now.* London, James Currey, 1988.

    Changing Uganda: The Dilemmas of Structural Management Adjustment and Revolutionary Change. London, James Currey, 1991.

    Developing Uganda. Oxford, James Currey, 1998.

Jørgensen, J. J. *Uganda: A Modern History.* Croom Helm, 1981.

Karugire, S. R. *A Political History of Uganda.* London, Heinemann, 1980.

Kasozi, A. B. K. *Social Origins of Violence in Uganda, 1964–1985.* London, University College London Press, 1995.

Langlands, B. W. *Notes on the Geography of Ethnicity in Uganda.* Kampala, 1975.

Langseth, P., and Katotobo, J. (Eds). *Uganda: Landmarks in Rebuilding a Nation.* Kampala, Fountain Publishers, 1993.

Low, D. A., and Pratt, R. C. *Buganda and British Overrule.* London, Oxford University Press, 1960.

Mamdani, M. *Politics and Class Formation in Uganda.* London, Heinemann Educational, 1977.

    Imperialism and Fascism in Uganda. London, Heinemann Educational, 1983.

Martin, D. *General Amin.* London, Faber and Faber, 1974.

Mukholi, D. *A Complete Guide to Uganda's Fourth Constitution: History, Politics and the Law.* Kampala, Fountain Publishers, 1995.

Museveni, Y. K. *Sowing the Mustard Seed: The Struggle for Freedom and Democracy in Uganda.* London, Macmillan, 1997.

Mutibwa, P. *Uganda since Independence: A Story of Unfulfilled Hopes.* London, Hurst, 1992.

Nabudere, D. W. *Imperialism and Revolution in Uganda.* Tanzania Publishing House/Onyx, 1980.

Nzita, R., and Mbaga-Niwampa. *Peoples and Cultures of Uganda.* 2nd edn. Kampala, Fountain Publishers, 1995.

Okoth, G. P., and Muranga, M. (Eds). *Uganda: A Century of Existence.* Kampala, Fountain Publishers, 1995.

Pirouet, M. L. *Historical Dictionary of Uganda.* Metuchen, NJ, Scarecrow Press, 1995.

Robertson, A. F. (Ed.). *Uganda's First Republic: Chiefs, Administrators and Politicians 1967–1971.* Cambridge, African Studies Centre, 1982.

Roth, M., Cochrane, J., and Kisamba-Mugerwa, W. *Tenure Security, Credit Use and Farm Investment in the Rujumbura Pilot Land Registration Scheme, Rukungiri District, Uganda.* Madison, University of Wisconsin, 1993.

Ruzindana, A., et al (Eds). *Fighting Corruption in Uganda.* Kampala, Fountain Publishers, 1998.

Sathymurthy, T.V. *The Political Development of Uganda 1980–86.* Aldershot, Gower Publishers, 1986.

Ssekamnsa, I. C. *History and Development of Education in Uganda.* Kampala, Fountain Publishers, 1997.

Soghayroun, I. E.-Z. *The Sudanese Muslim Factor in Uganda.* Khartoum University Press, 1981.

World Bank. *Uganda: Growing out of Poverty.* Washington, DC, World Bank, 1993.

    The Challenge of Growth and Poverty Reduction. Washington DC, World Bank, 1996.

ZAMBIA

Physical and Social Geography

GEOFFREY J. WILLIAMS

PHYSICAL FEATURES

The Republic of Zambia is a land-locked state occupying elevated plateau country in south-central Africa. Zambia has an area of 752,614 sq km (290,586 sq miles). The country is irregularly shaped, and shares a boundary with eight other countries.

The topography of Zambia is dominated by the even skylines of uplifted planation surfaces. Highest elevations are reached on the Nyika plateau on the Malawi border (2,164 m). Elevations decline westward, where the country extends into the fringe of the vast Kalahari basin. The plateau surfaces are interrupted by localized downwarps (occupied by lakes and swamp areas, such as in the Bangweulu and Lukanga basins), and by the rifted troughs of the mid-Zambezi and Luangwa.

Katangan rocks of upper-Pre-Cambrian age yield the copper ores exploited on the Copperbelt. Younger Karoo sedimentaries floor the rift troughs of the Luangwa and the mid-Zambezi rivers, while a basalt flow of this age has been incised by the Zambezi below the Victoria Falls to form spectacular gorges. Coal-bearing rocks in the Zambezi trough are of this same system. Over the western third of the country there are extensive and deep wind-deposited sands.

The continental divide separating Atlantic from Indian Ocean drainage forms the frontier with the Democratic Republic of the Congo, then traverses north-east Zambia to the Tanzanian border. Some 77% of the country is drained to the Indian Ocean by the Zambezi and its two main tributaries, the Kafue and Luangwa, with the remainder being drained principally by the Chambeshi and Luapula via the River Congo to the Atlantic. Rapids occur along most river courses so that the rivers are of little use for transportation. The country's larger lakes, including the man-made Lakes Kariba and Itezhitezhi, offer possibilities of water use as yet relatively little developed.

Zambia's climatic year can be divided into three seasons: a cool dry season (April–August), a hot dry season (August–November) and a warm wet season (November–April). Temperatures are generally moderate. Mean maximum temperatures exceed 35°C only in southern low-lying areas in October, most of the country being in the range 30°–35°C. July, the coldest month, has mean minima of 5°–10°C over most of the country, but shows considerable variability. Rainfall is highest on the high plateau of the Northern Province and on the intercontinental divide west of the Copperbelt (exceeding 1,200 mm per year). In the south-west and the mid-Zambezi valley, annual mean rainfall is less than 750 mm.

The eastern two-thirds of the country has generally poor soils. Soils on the Kalahari Sands of the west are exceptionally infertile, while seasonal waterlogging of soils in basin and riverine flats makes them difficult to use. Savannah vegetation dominates, with miombo woodland extensive over the plateau, and mopane woodland in the low-lying areas. Small areas of dry evergreen forest occur in the north, while treeless grasslands characterize the flats of the river basins.

RESOURCES AND POPULATION

Zambia's main resource is its land, which, in general, is under-utilized. Although soils are generally poor, altitudinal modifications of the climate make possible the cultivation of a wide range of crops. Cattle numbers are greatest in the southern and central areas, their range being limited by large tsetse-infested areas in the Kafue basin and the Luangwa valley. In the Western Province their numbers are less, but their importance to the local economy is even greater. Subsistence farming characterizes most of the country, with commercial farming focusing along the line of rail. Commercial forestry is important on the Copperbelt, where there are extensive softwood plantations, and in the south-west, where hardwoods are exploited. The main fisheries are located on the lakes and rivers of the Northern Province, with the Kafue Flats, Lukanga and Lake Kariba also contributing significantly. Game parks cover 7.9% of the country.

For many years, the mining of copper has been the mainstay of Zambia's economy, although its contribution has fallen sharply since the mid-1980s, reflecting price fluctuations on international commodity markets. By the mid-1990s the country remained Africa's largest producer, although only the 11th largest in terms of copper output world-wide. It has been estimated that, at current production rates, Zambia's economically recoverable reserves will be virtually exhausted by the year 2010. Cobalt, a by-product of copper mining, has recently gained in significance, and Zambia has been steadily expanding its cobalt production in an attempt to offset falls in copper output. Since the collapse of cobalt output in Zaire (now the Democratic Republic of the Congo) in 1992, Zambia has been the world's leading cobalt-producing country. Lead and zinc are mined at Kabwe, although the reserves of the Broken Hill Mine are nearing exhaustion. Coal, of which Zambia has the continent's largest deposits outside South Africa, is mined in the Zambezi valley, although this industry is in need of re-equipment and modernization. Manganese, silver and gold are produced in small quantities. Deposits of uranium have been located, and prospects exist for the exploitation of iron ore. No petroleum deposits have yet been located. However, Zambia is rich in hydropower, developed and potential.

At mid-1998, according to UN estimates, Zambia's population was 8,781,000, equivalent to 11.7 inhabitants per sq km. This level of population density is low, by African standards, for a state which contains no truly arid area. However, this average figure is misleading, for Zambia is the third most urbanized country in mainland sub-Saharan Africa, with 41% of its population of 5,661,801 at the September 1980 census residing in towns of more than 5,000 inhabitants (42% in 1993, according to World Bank figures). Some 78% of the urban population was, in fact, located in the 10 largest urban areas, all situated on the 'line of rail', extending south from the Copperbelt, through Lusaka, to the Victoria Falls, forming the major focus of Zambia's economic activity. Lusaka is the largest single urban centre, but the Copperbelt towns together constitute the largest concentration of urban population (47.1% of the total). While the increasing rate of population growth for the country as a whole (3.1% per annum in 1990–98) is a problem, the sustained influx to urban areas is even more acute as this growth has not been matched by employment and formal housing provision.

There are no fewer than 73 different ethnic groups among Zambia's indigenous population. Major groups are: the Bemba of the north-east, who are also dominant on the Copperbelt; the Nyanja of the Eastern Province, also numerous in Lusaka; the Tonga of the Southern Province and the Lozi of the west. Over 80 languages have been identified, of which seven are recognized as 'official' vernaculars. English is the language of government.

Recent History

GREGORY MTHEMBU-SALTER

Based on an earlier article by ANDREW D. ROBERTS

The protection of British supremacy at the Cape from encroachment by German and Portuguese interests to the north prompted the occupation by Britain in 1890 of the eastern area south of the Zambezi river, that became Southern Rhodesia (now Zimbabwe). Subsequent treaties with various African chiefs to the north of the Zambezi placed most of the region that subsequently became Northern Rhodesia firmly within the British sphere of influence. By the mid-1930s, following discoveries of vast deposits of copper ores, the large-scale exploitation of the region known as the Copperbelt was firmly established, using Northern Rhodesia as a vast labour reserve. As African trade unions were prohibited, African workers formed 'welfare societies', which by 1951 had emerged as a cohesive political force, the Northern Rhodesia African National Congress, which unsuccessfully opposed federation with Southern Rhodesia. In 1953 Northern Rhodesia became part of the Central African Federation (CAF) with Southern Rhodesia and Nyasaland (now Malawi). In 1958 leadership of the Congress passed to Kenneth Kaunda, whose demands for the dissolution of the CAF and the independence of Northern Rhodesia, under the name of Zambia, led to Kaunda's imprisonment and the banning of the Congress in 1959. On his release, a few months later, Kaunda assumed the leadership of the newly-formed United National Independence Party (UNIP). In 1962, following a massive campaign of civil disobedience, organized by UNIP, the British government introduced a constitution for Northern Rhodesia, which would create an African majority in the legislature. UNIP agreed to participate in the ensuing elections, and formed a coalition government with the remaining supporters of Congress. The CAF was formally dissolved in December 1963 and Northern Rhodesia became independent as the Republic of Zambia on 24 October 1964, with Kaunda as president.

The new republic inherited an economy which was heavily dependent on the massive industrial complex of white-ruled southern Africa. Southern Rhodesia's unilateral declaration of independence in November 1965, and the subsequent imposition of international sanctions, stimulated Zambian efforts to reduce its economic reliance on the south, particularly in relation to fuel, hydroelectric power and rail communications.

UNIP was returned to power at general elections in 1968, although popular support for the party had declined. In 1971 Simon Kapwepwe, a former vice-president of Zambia, left UNIP and formed the United People's Party (UPP). The UPP was suppressed, and in December 1972 Zambia was declared a one-party state. Legislative elections took place in December 1973, and Kaunda was re-elected for a further term of office.

In January 1973 the Rhodesian regime closed the border along the Zambezi to all Zambian exports except copper; the government's subsequent decision to divert copper exports resulted in a severe deterioration in the economy, which was compounded, following the outbreak of civil war in Angola in late 1975, by the closure of the Benguela railway. Between 1974–76, moreover, world copper prices fell, and Zambia's revenues accordingly declined. By the end of the year, there was widespread discontent resulting from high food prices, import restrictions and increasing unemployment. Fears that this unrest was being exploited by external forces prompted Kaunda to declare a state of emergency in January 1976.

In 1978 Kapwepwe rejoined UNIP; as a recognized leader of the Bemba ethnic group (who were traditionally hostile to Kaunda), his support was considered vital for Kaunda at a time of acute internal instability. Disagreement persisted, however, within UNIP over Zambia's economic relations with Rhodesia. In October 1978 rail links with Rhodesia were restored, and an agreement was reached on the shipping of exports via South Africa. Since 1977, however, Zambia had openly harboured members of the Zimbabwe African People's Union (ZAPU) wing of the Patriotic Front, and in 1978 and 1979 Rhodesian forces

attacked ZAPU bases in Zambia and carried out air raids on Lusaka. Zambia continued to suffer severe disruption from Rhodesian bombing until the implementation, in December 1979, of an agreement providing for the internationally recognized independence of Southern Rhodesia, as Zimbabwe, which came into effect in April 1980.

ECONOMIC PROBLEMS AND POLITICAL UNREST

Political dissent increased towards the end of 1980, following a further deterioration in economic conditions. In October several prominent businessmen, government officials and UNIP members allegedly staged a coup attempt. Kaunda claimed that South Africa had supported the plot, but many of those arrested after the incident were ethnic Bemba. In January 1981 the suspension from UNIP of 17 officials of the Mineworkers' Union of Zambia (MUZ) and the Zambia Congress of Trade Unions (ZCTU) prompted a widely-observed strike, and riots.

Despite the introduction of unpopular austerity measures, necessitated by worsening economic problems, Kaunda retained a strong following; in October 1983 he was again re-elected president, receiving, as sole candidate, 93% of the votes cast. In March 1985, following a series of strikes by public-sector employees demanding higher wages, Kaunda took emergency powers to ban strikes in essential services. In an extensive government reorganization in April, Kebby Musokotwane was appointed prime minister, while Alexander Grey Zulu became secretary-general of UNIP. In response to the continuing economic crisis, further austerity measures were imposed in that year, leading to an increase in retail prices, which provoked angry demonstrations in Lusaka in October. Student demonstrations, which began in December, led to the closure of the university in the following May. In December 1986 the removal of the government subsidy on refined maize meal, the staple food, resulted in an increase of 120% in the price of this essential commodity. After violent rioting in the Copperbelt towns of Kitwe and Ndola, the subsidy was restored. Although peace in the region was restored by the end of December, strikes in support for wage increases occurred in early 1987, and in April of that year the government was forced to rescind a 70% increase in the price of fuel, following protests in Lusaka. In May Kaunda announced that an economic austerity programme advocated by the IMF was to be replaced by a government-devised strategy involving greater state controls, and a new minister of finance was appointed.

Meanwhile, the government became increasingly preoccupied with internal security. In April 1987 Kaunda alleged that the South African government, with the assistance of Zambian businessmen and members of the Zambian armed forces, had conspired to destabilize the Zambian government. In the following month a long-standing opponent of Kaunda, Alfred Masonda Chambeshi, was arrested, following allegations in court that he planned to overthrow the government, in collusion with Angolan rebels of the União Nacional para a Independência Total de Angola (UNITA). In July three members of the Zambian air force and a businessman were charged with having engaged in espionage for the South African government. In March 1988 a former South African soldier was sentenced to 50 years' imprisonment on espionage charges, and in June a New Zealand national, also convicted of spying for South Africa, was deported. In October three civilians and six military officers, including Lt-Gen. Christon Tembo, a former commander of the Zambian army, were arrested on suspicion of plotting a coup. (Tembo and a further three military officers were subsequently charged with treason, but were pardoned in July 1990.)

In August 1988, the UNIP central committee was enlarged to include a number of military commanders and industrialists, together with the chairman and secretary-general of the MUZ. In late October presidential and legislative elections took place.

Kaunda, the only candidate, received 95.5% of all votes cast in the presidential election; however, four cabinet ministers lost their seats in the elections to the national assembly. In November Kaunda reorganized the cabinet, merging or abolishing five portfolios, apparently in an attempt to reduce government costs. In March 1989 Kebby Musokotwane, widely considered to be a potential rival to the president, was removed from the post of prime minister and briefly relegated to the ministry of general education, youth and sport, before being transferred to an overseas diplomatic posting; he was succeeded as prime minister by Gen. Malimba Masheke, minister of home affairs and a former minister of defence.

In early 1989 continued unrest among workers and students was reported, and the government threatened to ban trade unions involved in strike action. Increases in the prices of essential goods were implemented in mid-1989, prompting renewed rioting in the Copperbelt region in July. In June 1990 an announcement that the price of maize meal was to increase by more than 100% resulted in severe rioting in Lusaka, in which at least 30 people were reported to have been killed. In the same month the minister of defence, Frederick Hapunda (who was widely believed to favour a multi-party system), was dismissed, while several other prominent state officials were similarly removed from office. On 30 June a junior army officer, Lt Mwamba Luchembe, announced on the state radio that Kaunda had been overthrown by the armed forces. Luchembe was immediately arrested, although he was subsequently pardoned and released. In early July Lt-Gen. Hannaniah Lungu was appointed minister of defence.

In April 1990 the UNIP general conference rejected proposals for the introduction of a multi-party political system in Zambia. In the following month, however, Kaunda announced that a popular referendum on the subject of multi-party politics would be conducted in October of that year, and that proponents of such a system would be permitted to campaign and hold public meetings. Accordingly, in early July the Movement for Multi-party Democracy (MMD), an unofficial alliance of political opponents of the government, was formed, under the leadership of a former minister of finance, Arthur Wina, and the chairman of the ZCTU, Frederick Chiluba. In addition, the ZCTU demanded an end to the existing state of emergency, the creation of an independent body to monitor the referendum, and equal access to the media for both those supporting and those opposing the introduction of a multi-party system. In July 1990, however, Kaunda announced that the referendum was to be postponed until August 1991 to facilitate full electoral registration. Although he welcomed the registration procedure, Wina severely criticized the referendum's postponement and requested that it take place before December 1990. In August 1990 the national assembly proposed the introduction of a multi-party system, to which Kaunda again expressed his opposition. In the following month, however, Kaunda abandoned his opposition to the restoration of a plural political system, and proposed that multi-party presidential and legislative elections be organized, that the national referendum be abandoned, and that a commission be appointed to revise the constitution. Later in September UNIP endorsed the proposals for multi-party elections, which were scheduled for October 1991, and accepted recommendations for the restructuring of the party.

CONSTITUTIONAL TRANSITION

In December 1990 Kaunda formally adopted constitutional amendments, approved by the national assembly earlier that month, which permitted the formation of political parties other than UNIP to contest the forthcoming elections. Shortly afterwards, the MMD was granted official recognition as a political organization; the establishment of a further 11 opposition movements followed in subsequent months. In early 1991 several prominent members of UNIP resigned from the party and declared their support for the MMD, while the ZCTU officially transferred its allegiance to the MMD. In February Kaunda announced that he would permit other members of UNIP to contest the presidential election, despite previous statements to the contrary.

In early June 1991 the constitutional commission presented a series of recommendations, which included the establishment of a bicameral system of parliament, the creation of the post of

vice-president, and the expansion of the national assembly from 135 to 150 members. Kaunda accepted the majority of the proposed constitutional amendments, which were subsequently submitted for approval by the national assembly. However, the MMD rejected the draft constitution, and threatened to boycott the elections in October if the national assembly accepted the proposals. Opposition supporters objected in particular to amendments permitting the appointment of non-elected ministers from outside the national assembly, and the vesting of supreme authority in the president rather than in the national assembly. The government also rejected opposition demands that foreign observers be invited to monitor the elections. In July, following discussions between Kaunda, Frederick Chiluba and delegates from seven other opposition parties, under the chairmanship of the deputy chief justice, Mathew Ngulube, Kaunda agreed to suspend the review of the draft constitution in the national assembly, pending further discussions; it was also decided that state subsidies would be granted to all registered political parties. Subsequent negotiations between the MMD and UNIP resulted in the formation of a joint commission of experts to revise the draft constitution. Later in July, following a meeting of the two parties under the auspices of the constitutional commission, Kaunda conceded to opposition demands that ministers be appointed only from members of the national assembly and that the proposed establishment of a constitutional court be abandoned; presidential powers to impose martial law were also to be rescinded. On 2 August the national assembly formally adopted the new draft constitution, which included these amendments.

In late July 1991 Kaunda's leadership of UNIP was challenged by Enoch Kavindele, a businessman, and member of the central committee of UNIP. In addition, allegations of the misuse of state funds by government officials threatened to increase opposition to Kaunda. Two days prior to UNIP's party congress, however, Kavindele withdrew his canditure, allegedly in the interests of party unity. In early August the party congress re-elected Kaunda as president. However, several prominent party officials, including Alexander Grey Zulu, hitherto secretary-general of the party, refused to contest the elections. Later in August Kaunda agreed to permit foreign observers to monitor the forthcoming elections, in an attempt to counter opposition allegations that UNIP would perpetrate electoral fraud. In addition, Kaunda announced that the armed forces were henceforth disassociated from UNIP, in accordance with the tenets of political pluralism; leaders of the armed forces were obliged to retire from membership of the party's central committee.

In September 1991 the national assembly was dissolved in preparation for the presidential and legislative elections, which were scheduled for 31 October. On the same day Kaunda officially disassociated UNIP from the State; workers in the public sector were henceforth prohibited from engaging in political activity. However, international observers, who arrived in Zambia in September, expressed concern that the elections would not be conducted fairly, on the grounds that the government-owned media and parastatal organizations continued to support UNIP in its electoral campaign, and that the state of emergency remained in force. During October numerous outbreaks of violence were reported; in one incident four supporters of the MMD were killed by members of UNIP. Kaunda warned that UNIP's failure to win the election would provoke a civil conflict, while Chiluba accused Kaunda of amassing troops on the border with Malawi to fight the MMD in the event of its accession to power. Chiluba also claimed that an attempt to assassinate him had been staged, and appealed to the Organization of African Unity (OAU) to deploy peace-keeping forces in Zambia during the election period. In late October Kaunda accused the international observers of involvement in a conspiracy to remove UNIP from power.

THE CHILUBA PRESIDENCY

Contrary to previous indications, international observers reported that the elections, which took place on 31 October 1991, had been conducted fairly. In the presidential election Chiluba, who received 75.79% of votes cast, defeated Kaunda, who obtained 24.21% of the vote. In the legislative elections, which were contested by 330 candidates representing six political parties, the MMD secured 125 seats in the national assembly, while UNIP won the remaining 25 seats; only four members of the previous government were returned to the national assembly. Kaunda's failure to be re-elected to the presidency was attributed to widespread discontent at the deterioration of economic conditions, as a result of the government's continued mismanagement. On 2 November Chiluba was inaugurated as president. Chiluba appointed Levy Mwanawasa, a constitutional lawyer, as vice-president and leader of the national assembly, and formed a new 22-member cabinet. In addition, a minister was appointed to each of the country's nine provinces, which were previously administered by governors. Two days later the government allowed the state of emergency to lapse. During his first month in office Chiluba began to carry out a major restructuring of the civil service and parastatal organizations, as the first step in his programme of economic revival.

Internal 'Conspiracies' and Official Investigations

In December 1991, following a road accident in which Mwanawasa was severely injured, the minister without portfolio, Brig.-Gen. Godfrey Miyanda, was accused of plotting his death. A commission of inquiry was later informed that Miyanda had previously conspired with members of the former government to assassinate Chiluba and to abduct Mwanawasa. It was alleged that after the failure of this plan he had arranged the road accident, in an attempt to kill Mwanawasa, and subsequently to assume the vice-presidency. In March 1992, however, following an investigation, by detectives from the United Kingdom, into the circumstances of the accident, Miyanda was exonerated. Later in December 1991 Kaunda announced that he was to relinquish the leadership of UNIP; a new president was to be elected at a party congress in August 1992. In January 1992 Kaunda denied allegations that he had misappropriated public funds during his tenure of office, and moved to institute legal proceedings against the state, members of the media and leading government officials, following accusations of his complicity in a number of offences. Later in January the minister of defence, Ben Mwila, claimed that UNIP was promoting a coup attempt by former army officers.

In May 1992, amid widespread opposition to government, a dissident faction of academics within the MMD, known as Caucus for National Unity (CNU), emerged. The CNU, which claimed support from several members of the government, requested that Chiluba review his appointment of cabinet ministers and heads of parastatal organizations, to ensure that all ethnic groups were represented. The CNU, together with the Zambia Research Foundation and the Women's Lobby, also advocated the establishment of a constitutional commission to curtail the executive powers of the president and the cabinet. However, Chiluba refused to initiate a review of the constitution, on the grounds of expense. The government was also criticized for its rigid enforcement of the structural adjustment programme supported by the IMF and World Bank, which had resulted in an increase in economic hardship.

In June 1992 a breakaway faction of UNIP formed a new opposition group, the United Democratic Party (UDP). In July, following the rejection by the national assembly of a report that implicated several members of the government in alleged financial malpractice, two cabinet ministers (who were believed to have links with the CNU) resigned in protest at the government's failure to eradicate corruption and to implement democratic reform; Chiluba subsequently reshuffled the cabinet. Later that month the CNU registered as an independent political party, after the resignation of its leader, Dr Muyoba Macwani, from the MMD. At a party congress in late September, Kaunda formally resigned as leader of UNIP, and was replaced by Kebby Musokotwane, hitherto secretary-general of the party. In local government elections which took place in late November, the MMD won the majority of seats. There was, however, a high rate of abstention (the turnout was less than 10% of registered voters); this was widely attributed to disillusionment with the Chiluba administration.

In early March 1993 Chiluba declared a state of emergency, following the discovery of UNIP documents detailing an alleged conspiracy (referred to as the 'Zero Option') to destabilize the government by inciting unrest and civil disobedience. A number of prominent members of UNIP, including Kaunda's three sons,

were subsequently arrested. Musokotwane conceded the existence of the documents, but denied that UNIP officials were involved in the conspiracy, which he attributed to extreme factions within the party. Kaunda, however, claimed that the conspiracy had been fabricated by Zambian security forces, with the assistance of US intelligence services, in an attempt to discredit the opposition. Later that month, following allegations by the Zambian government that Iran and Iraq had financed subversive elements within UNIP, diplomatic relations with the two countries were suspended. Shortly afterwards, the national assembly approved the state of emergency, which was to remain in force for a further three months. Owing to pressure from Western governments, however, Chiluba reduced the maximum period of detention without trial from 28 to seven days.

In April 1993, with the stated intention of eradicating government corruption, Chiluba extensively reshuffled the cabinet. Although four senior ministers were dismissed, a number of ministers who were implicated in alleged malpractice remained in the government. In the same month 15 members of UNIP, who had been arrested in connection with the alleged conspiracy in March, appealed to the high court against their continued detention without trial; seven of the detainees were subsequently released. In May the detention orders on the remaining eight members were revoked; however, they were immediately rearrested and charged with related offences. Later that month the state of emergency was lifted.

Political Realignments

In July 1993 UNIP, the UDP and the Labour Party (LP) established an informal alliance, and advocated a campaign of civil disobedience in protest at the economic austerity measures. In the same month Kaunda announced that he was to retire from political activity. Divisions within the MMD became apparent in August, when 15 members (11 of whom held seats in the national assembly and including several former cabinet ministers) left the party. The rebels accused the government of protecting corrupt cabinet ministers and of failing to respond to numerous reports linking senior party officials with the illegal drugs trade. Their opposition to Chiluba's government was consolidated later in the month by the formation of a new political group, the National Party (NP). An existing organization, the National Party for Democracy, merged with the new party.

In January 1994 two prominent cabinet ministers announced their resignations, following persistent allegations of their involvement in high-level corruption and drugs-trafficking, and increasing domestic and international pressure for the government to take action over the allegations. One of the ministers, Vernon Mwaanga, a founder member of the MMD, who had held the foreign affairs portfolio, had been accused of drugs-trafficking by a tribunal in 1985, although he had not been convicted of the alleged offences. Both ministers denied any misconduct and declared they had resigned pending an official investigation. The resignations were followed by an extensive reorganization of cabinet portfolios, in which a further two ministers were removed. At by-elections for 10 of the 11 vacated seats in the national assembly, which were held in November 1993 and April 1994, the MMD regained five seats, while the NP secured four and UNIP one.

In June 1994 seven opposition parties, including UNIP, formed the Zambia Opposition Front (ZOFRO) to co-ordinate the various groups' activities. In early July Levy Mwanawasa resigned as vice-president, citing long-standing differences with Chiluba, and was replaced by Godfrey Miyanda. In the same month ex-president Kaunda announced that he was considering renouncing political retirement to contest the presidential election in 1996. However, UNIP officials indicated that he would be allowed to resume the leadership of the party only if he were officially elected by members. (Kaunda's decision to return to active politics subsequently led to factional division within UNIP.) In August 1994 Kaunda was allegedly warned against inciting revolt, after he conducted a number of rallies in the Northern Province (where the MMD traditionally attracted considerable support). Later that month the government announced that Kaunda had been placed under surveillance in the interests of national security, following reports that he had received support from foreign diplomatic missions in Zambia.

In October 1994 two deputy government ministers were dismissed, after criticizing the modalities of government plans to privatize the country's principal industrial enterprise, Zambia Consolidated Copper Mines. At a by-election in December UNIP secured the remaining vacant seat in the national assembly. In January 1995 Chiluba dismissed the minister of lands, Dr Chuulu Kalima, on grounds of misconduct; Kalima had apparently accused the president of involvement in a transaction in which a deputy minister had acquired land formerly owned by the University of Zambia. In early February Chiluba ordered members of the government to declare their financial assets and liabilities within a period of two days. In the same month Kaunda was charged with convening an illegal political gathering, after he had addressed a public rally. Later in February the governor of the Bank of Zambia was replaced, following a sharp depreciation in the value of the national currency. In March increasing divisions became evident within the MMD between the Bemba ethnic group (to which Chiluba belonged) and the traditionalist Nsenga; it was reported that MMD factions had circulated pamphlets criticizing Chiluba and Mwanawasa (who remained as vice-president of the MMD). In April a former cabinet minister, Dean Mung'omba, announced that he intended to contest Chiluba's leadership of the MMD. In the same month a pro-Kaunda faction of UNIP indicated that it would challenge the leadership of the incumbent party president, Musokotwane. Later in April the MMD retained two parliamentary seats contested in further partial elections. In late June, at an extraordinary congress of UNIP, Kaunda was elected UNIP president by a large majority. Kaunda's avowed aim on election was to contest the country's presidential election scheduled for 1996; he subsequently demanded that both the presidential and general elections be brought forward to October 1995. It was widely expected, however, that proposed constitutional reforms would include a clause banning any president from a third term of office, and bar candidates from seeking election as president if their parents were not both of Zambian origin (Kaunda's parents were reported to have come from Malawi, of which country Kaunda was subsequently himself alleged to have been a national at the time of his election as president in 1964). In mid-June the leader of the Movement for Democratic Process (MDP), Chama Chakomboka, had also declared his intention of standing in the forthcoming elections.

In mid-July 1995 Chiluba reshuffled the cabinet, appointing a new minister of foreign affairs. Later in that month the minister of home affairs, Chitalu Sampa, warned Kaunda to desist from 'inciting violence' or risk being arrested, following Kaunda's urging of a public campaign of civil disobedience against the government. It appeared, however, that there were growing signs of divisions within UNIP itself when, by the end of August, three opposition MPs had resigned, including the opposition parliamentary leader, Dingiswayo Banda, who defected to the MMD. Banda's defection followed reports of a plot within UNIP, after the election of Kaunda, to have Banda removed as opposition parliamentary leader. Two other UNIP officials also joined the MMD in that month.

In early September 1995 the Munyama Commission on Human Rights, established by Chiluba in 1993 to review allegations of abuses during the Kaunda presidency, alleged that torture and other abuses of human rights had been carried out in cells beneath the presidential residence which were subsequently opened to public inspection. The report further asserted that torture and other violations of human rights were still taking place in Zambia. At by-elections held in 13 constituencies in September and early October 1995, the MMD secured seven seats, and UNIP six. In October the minister of legal affairs announced that Kaunda had not officially relinquished Malawian citizenship until 1970 (and had therefore governed illegally for six years), and that he had not obtained Zambian citizenship through the correct procedures. Later that month, however, following widespread reports that the authorities intended to deport Kaunda, the government ordered the security forces to suspend investigations into his citizenship (apparently owing to fears of civil unrest). In the same month opposition parties criticized the government's failure to establish a constituent assembly to approve the draft constitution. At the end of October much of the Asian population of the southern town of Livingstone fled to Lusaka or neighbouring Zimbabwe, following an outbreak of racial violence prompted by the alleged involvement of two Asian traders in the ritual murder of two minors. (The two Asians were, however, later acquitted of murder.)

Electoral Controversies

In January 1996 seven opposition parties, including UNIP and the NP, established an informal alliance to campaign in favour of democratic elections and the establishment of a constituent assembly to approve the draft constitution by a process of national consensus. In March a parliamentary edict sentenced three journalists to indefinite imprisonment on charges of contempt of parliament. The charges concerned the publication of newspaper articles commenting on criticism by Miyanda in the national assembly of a supreme court ruling that restrictions on public gatherings were unconstitutional. The three journalists subsequently went into hiding (although two of them later surrendered to security forces), while the International Press Institute condemned the convictions, which it declared to be invalid; the edict was later overturned by the high court, and the journalists were released. In early May division emerged within the MMD regarding the draft constitution when the minister of works and supply resigned from office in protest at the amendment barring foreign nationals and those with foreign parentage from contesting the presidency. (The same issue had already prompted the resignation, in February, of the minister of commerce, trade and industry.) The cabinet was reorganized at the end of May. Opposition parties, moreover, demanded that the government abandon the draft constitution and negotiate with them regarding electoral reform. Later that month UNIP deputies withdrew from a parliamentary debate on the draft, which was subsequently approved by a large majority in the national assembly. On 28 May, despite continuing criticism of the new constitution, it was officially adopted by Chiluba. In early June the USA and Norway announced a reduction in aid to Zambia, in protest at the constitutional amendment that effectively procluded Kaunda from contesting the presidential election. Other Western donor governments subsequently announced their decision to review aid disbursements to Zambia in the light of the new constitution. Despite this set-back, Chiluba announced that the forthcoming presidential and legislative elections would be conducted according to the terms of the new constitution, while Kaunda announced that he intended to contest the presidency despite the ban. In the same month eight senior UNIP officials, including the vice-president of the party, were arrested and charged in connection with a series of bomb attacks against official buildings, which were attributed to a clandestine anti-government organization, known as 'Black Mamba'.

In August 1996 Chiluba and Kaunda met for discussions in Lusaka as part of a programme of dialogue between the government and opposition parties. Following Kaunda's decision to boycott a scheduled second round of discussions in September, the government made minor concessions regarding the conduct of forthcoming elections, including assurances that votes would be counted at polling stations and that the electoral commission (appointed by Chiluba) would be independent; UNIP's request that the elections be conducted according to the 1991 constitution was rejected. In mid-October 1996 Chiluba dissolved the national assembly and announced that presidential and legislative elections would take place on 18 November. UNIP, still dissatisfied with the electoral system, announced its intention to boycott the elections and organize a campaign of civil disobedience; by early November a further six political parties had also decided to boycott the elections. There was widespread criticism of the voter registration process (conducted by an overseas computer company), in which fewer than one-half of the estimated 4.6m. eligible voters had been listed. The government ordered the temporary closure of the University of Zambia, after two days of rioting by students who were attempting to force Chiluba to reopen negotiations with the opposition and reach agreement on the electoral process.

The 1996 Elections

Despite appeals for a postponement, the elections took place, as planned, on 18 November 1996, and Chiluba and the MMD were returned to power by a large majority. In the presidential election Chiluba defeated the four other candidates with 72.5% of the valid votes cast. His nearest rival (with only 12.5%) was Dean Mung'omba of the Zambia Democratic Congress (ZADECO), an erstwhile opponent of Chiluba within the MMD. The MMD secured 131 of the 150 seats in the national assembly. Of the eight other parties that finally contested the legislative elections, only the NP (five seats), ZADECO (two seats) and Agenda for Zambia (AZ–two seats) won parliamentary representation, with independent candidates taking the remaining 10 seats. The rate of participation was low. Despite the electoral commission's verdict that the elections had been conducted fairly, allegations of fraud were made by opposition parties and local monitoring groups, which criticized voter registration procedures and accused the MMD of buying votes. The chairmen of two electoral monitoring groups were taken into custody for questioning, but were later released without charge. A former senior official of one of the groups claimed that the monitoring groups had been influenced by donor governments attempting to discredit the elections, and six journalists working in the state media were suspended for allegedly conspiring to undermine the elections.

Chiluba was inaugurated for a second presidential term on 21 November 1996. Amid demands for his resignation and for fresh elections to be held, Chiluba dissolved the cabinet and put the military on alert at the end of the month. In early December a new government was appointed: there were no changes to the main portfolios, except for the appointment of Lawrence Shimba (a professor of law at the University of Zambia) as minister of foreign affairs. Opposition parties continued their campaign of civil disobedience throughout December, although nation-wide marches of solidarity with the government were reported to have been widely supported. Four opposition parties filed petitions with the supreme court challenging Chiluba's citizenship (and therefore his eligibility as president), and accusing the electoral commission of conspiring with the MMD to commit electoral fraud; the petitions were dismissed in early 1997. In response to reports in late December that a senior army commander had been placed under house arrest as a result of rumours of a military takeover, Chiluba warned the media against attempting to incite the security forces to challenge his leadership.

In early February 1997 a human rights report prepared for the US department of state condemned police brutality and prison conditions in Zambia, but claimed that there had been no evidence of significant electoral fraud in the 1996 elections. In the same month an African human rights group released a report, in which it asserted that further investigation was required into the deaths of five opposition politicians during 1995–96. In March 1997 the government established a permanent commission to investigate human rights violations, although opposition parties refused to participate. (In October 1996 the human rights commission established by Chiluba in 1993 had presented its final report, disclosing evidence of the violation of the human rights of political detainees under both Kaunda's and Chiluba's governments.)

In early April 1997 UNIP expelled three central committee officials from the party on disciplinary charges, provoking clashes involving the security forces later that month as the expelled officials and their supporters attempted to gain entry to party headquarters. Also in April the government, in response to public pressure, suspended a proposed bill that was to have increased official control over the media. In early May the MMD retained three parliamentary seats unopposed at by-elections, owing to an opposition boycott.

Internal Tensions

Political tensions intensified in June 1997. The opposition continued with its campaign of civil disobedience. Joint rallies were held, at which voter cards from the November elections were burnt, and in late July security forces intervened to disperse demonstrators at a protest march against the MMD after government vehicles were stoned. In mid-August the government accused the opposition of inciting unrest, as market-traders rioted after their stalls were destroyed by fire; 56 people were arrested in the disturbances. Later that month Kaunda and Chongwe were shot and wounded when the security forces opened fire on an opposition gathering, following the cancella-

tion of a rally in Kabwe, north of Lusaka. Kaunda's subsequent allegation that the shooting was an assassination attempt organized by the government was strongly denied by Chiluba. Two senior police-officers were suspended pending the completion of an investigation. In late September members of Zambia's two civil service trade unions embarked on a planned three-day strike in protest at the government's refusal to implement previously agreed pay awards. The minister of labour and social security maintained that the government could not afford the pay awards and persuaded the industrial court to rule the action illegal; the strike was called off the following day. Relations between the government and trades unions deteriorated further when, in late November, the government announced that all public sector wages would be frozen in 1998 to allow for the government to finance major civil service redundancies, as part of its public sector reform programme. In early March the ZCTU organized a general strike in protest at the wage freeze, but the action soon collapsed after the government threatened participating state employees with dismissal. In June 1999 Zambia's industrial relations court ruled that the wage freeze of 1998 had been illegal, and awarded workers a 10% increase in addition to the 30% increase agreed between the government and civil service unions for 1999. Although the government accepted the ruling, it subsequently announced that it would only pay the increase subject to its being able to locate additional funds. The unions rejected this condition, and in July council workers embarked on a nation-wide strike.

In the early morning of 28 October 1997 rebel officers, led by Capt. Stephen Lungu, briefly captured the national television and radio station from where they proclaimed the formation of a military regime. The attempted coup was suppressed within a few hours by regular military units; 15 people, including Lungu, were arrested during the operation and one man was killed. Allegations by Kaunda that the government had orchestrated the coup in order to be in a position to detain prominent members of the opposition were repeated by other opposition figures after Chiluba declared a state of emergency on 29 October, providing for the detention for 28 days without trial of people suspected of involvement in the attempted coup. Several non-governmental organizations, including the Law Association of Zambia, described the state of emergency as an abuse of human rights. Mung'omba was among 84 people arrested in the immediate aftermath of the coup and in November the high court ordered that he undergo a medical examination to investigate injuries allegedly sustained during interrogation by the police.

Chiluba carried out an extensive cabinet reshuffle in early December 1997. Observers interpreted the transfer to lesser cabinet posts of Miyanda and of Benjamin Mwila, hitherto the minister of defence, as an attempt to forestall the emergence of potential rivals to Chiluba within the MMD. Lt-Gen. Christon Tembo, hitherto the minister of mines and mineral development, replaced Miyanda as vice-president.

On 25 December 1997 Kaunda was arrested under emergency powers and imprisoned, shortly after his return to Zambia from more than two months abroad. Numerous regional and international governments expressed serious concern at the detention of Kaunda, who refused food until the end of the month when he was visited by Julius Nyerere, the former president of Tanzania. On the following day Kaunda was placed under house arrest at his home in Lusaka. He was arraigned in court in January 1998 and in mid-February he was formally notified that he was to stand trial for 'misprision of treason', on the grounds that he had failed to report in advance to the authorities details allegedly known to him of the attempted coup of October 1997. Meanwhile, in late January the national assembly voted to extend the state of emergency for a further three months; Chiluba eventually revoked the state of emergency on 17 March, following pressure from external donors. Three days later, Chiluba effected a minor cabinet reshuffle, most notably dismissing the minister of finance and economic development, Ronald Penza. In late April 80 people who were being detained in connection with the attempted coup, including Kaunda and Mung'omba, were committed to summary trial in the high court. Kaunda was released from detention in early June, after charges against him were withdrawn, apparently owing to lack of evidence. He subsequently announced his intention to retire from active politics, and his resignation as UNIP president in July created a split within the party over the nomination of a replacement. The MMD was also reported to be divided over an eventual successor to Chiluba, despite a recent ban within the party on presidential campaigning, amid strongly denied suggestions that Chiluba might seek a third term of office in 2001, contrary to the constitution. In September 1998 the minister of commerce, trade and industry, Enoch Kavindele, was dismissed following a dispute with the minister of finance and economic development concerning tariff reform. In the subsequent cabinet reshuffle the minister of tourism, Katele Kalumba, was promoted to the home affairs portfolio, while the minister of labour and social security, Newstead Zimba, was appointed to the influential post of minister of information and broadcasting services. In October two senior UNIP officials resigned from their positions in the party, and it was also reported that Kaunda had reversed his decision to withdraw from active politics. Meanwhile, the MMD announced that 14 political parties had been deregistered for failing to meet the required standards for parties.

In November 1998 Penza was murdered at his home in Lusaka. Shortly afterwards five of the six suspects were shot dead by police officers, prompting widespread allegations that the authorities were seeking to conceal the true motive behind the killing; the police claimed that the motive was robbery. The police action, and Chiluba's subsequent approval of legislation providing for Zambia's intelligence service to be armed, were of considerable concern to human rights organizations. In mid-December Mung'omba and Princess Nakatindi Wina, a former minister and the MMD's national chairperson for women, were released from prison, as no witnesses had provided evidence against them since their detention on charges of treason following the failed coup attempt of October 1997.

Long-delayed local government elections were held on 30 December 1998. Fewer than half of the eligible voters had registered, and of these only 27% participated in the vote, according to the electoral commission. The MMD won the majority of the wards contested, securing 880 of the 1,275 seats. UNIP, which had decided to abandon its former policy of boycotting elections, obtained 190 seats, while the newly formed United Party for National Development, established by a former managing director of Anglo-American (Zambia), Anderson Mazoka, gained 28 seats. Opposition parties protested at the use of the controversial electoral register from the 1966 elections, although all parties agreed that the register would be replaced for future elections.

In mid-February 1999 opposition parties demanded the dismissal of Tembo and Mwila, who had been implicated, along with Kavindele, in Angolan claims that Zambia was supporting the Angolan rebel movement, UNITA — allegations which the Zambian authorities strongly denied. On 28 February a number of bombs exploded in Lusaka, one of which seriously damaged the Angolan embassy, killing a security guard. Over the course of the next two days several more explosive devices were discovered and defused. The security forces were placed on full alert and an investigation into the bombings was instigated. In mid-March it was reported that two Zambians had been arrested, and two foreigners deported, in connection with the bombings. In March 12 journalists were arrested and charged with espionage after their newspaper, *The Post,* printed a report claiming that Zambia's military capacity was inferior to that of Angola. In mid-April all 12 were committed to trial by the high court. A minor reorganization of the cabinet was implemented in March.

In late March 1999 the high court delivered its judgment in a case concerning Kaunda's citizenship, declaring him to be stateless. The ruling was based on Kaunda's apparent failure to follow correct procedures to attain Zambian citizenship in 1970. On the day after the ruling Kaunda entered an appeal with the supreme court; later that day he escaped a reported assassination attempt, when a group of armed men opened fire on his car. In April five opposition parties, including ZADECO and AZ, formed a new alliance, which was later named the Zambia Alliance for Progress (ZAP). In June the registrar of societies forced a change in the ZAP's constitution by ruling that it could only be registered if its constituent parties disbanded. The ZAP made the necessary adjustments (ZADECO formally announced its dissolution and that all its members had joined the ZAP) and relaunched itself as an official party

in August; as a result of the requisite changes, however, some of the ZAP's founder members, including AZ, withdrew from the alliance. Following a poor performance at the annual consultative group meeting of Zambia's principal donors, the minister of finance and economic development, Edith Nawakwi, was moved to the ministry of labour and social security by Chiluba in late June and replaced by Dr Katele Kalumba. In November Chiluba demoted Benjamin Mwila to the ministry of energy and water development in a further cabinet reshuffle, after increasingly transparent hints from Mwila that he intended to contest the presidency in 2001. Kaunda's son, Maj. Wezi Kaunda, was shot dead on 3 November outside his Lusaka home. Kaunda later alleged that the murder had been politically motivated, and British detectives subsequently arrived to help with investigations; police sources, however, indicated that they believed Wezi Kaunda had been the victim of an attempted car hijack. It had been widely perceived that Kenneth Kaunda had been grooming his son to succeed him as president of the UNIP. In October Sebastian Zulu, the secretary-general of UNIP had said that he would challenge Wezi Kaunda for the UNIP presidency. Junior doctors went on strike in mid-December in protest at the late payment of salaries and at the lack of basic medical equipment and supplies in hospitals. Despite initial promises to look into their grievances, the government dismissed all 300 of Zambia's junior doctors and prohibited them from leaving the country to seek employment abroad.

Chiluba announced to parliament in January 2000 the creation of District Administrators (DAs) for each province. DAs were subsequently appointed by the government. On 12 March the minister without portfolio, Michael Sata, warned MMD deputies to co-operate with DAs, since the DAs controlled constituency development funds, which play a key role in improving the reputations of parliamentary members with their voters. Opposition parties, on the other hand, accused the DAs of being governors in disguise, and reminded the MMD that it campaigned for their abolition in 1990. By June, most of the DAs had established offices and received new vehicles, despite the fact that in March Mwape Mutakila, the president of the Zambia Allied Union of Local Authority Workers, had warned that elected local government was collapsing because of a lack of funds. Kenneth Kaunda resigned as president of UNIP in late March, shortly before the convocation of an extraordinary party congress, which elected Francis Nkhoma as UNIP's new leader in mid-May. Nkhoma had been governor of the central bank during Kaunda's presidency, but had joined the MMD after its election victory, prior to rejoining UNIP in 1998. Kaunda's son, Tilyenji, was appointed as UNIP's new secretary-general.

In late March 2000 the controversial and drawn-out privatization of Zambia Consolidated Copper Mines Ltd (ZCCM) was completed, with the sale of the remaining assets to a subsidiary of the UK-based Anglo-American Konkola Copper Mines, and to a subsidiary of Canada's First Quantum Minerals (FQM) Mopani Copper Mines. Donors had made new aid to Zambia conditional on the sale of ZCCM, which was reported to have been losing US $1m. per day.

Mwila was expelled from the MMD at a disciplinary hearing in July 2000 after formally declaring his presidential bid in late May. At least 10 other prominent MMD members were also expelled from the ruling party for supporting Mwila. Mwila protested at his expulsion and the allegedly dictatorial behaviour of Chiluba, and later in July more than 1,000 MMD members resigned in support of Mwila. The annual consultative meeting of Zambia's principal donors was held in Lusaka for the first time in mid-July, and provided an opportunity for local civil society and human rights organizations publicly to demand government reforms. Donors rewarded the Zambian government for the sale of ZCCM with fresh aid, but made it conditional on progress with regard to government reform in the build-up to the 2001 general election. Donors stated that they wished to see press freedom, a 'level playing field' for both the ruling party and the opposition in the period preceding the election, and reform of the Public Order Act (which gives the police wide-ranging powers to ban and break up political gatherings); the Zambian government promised that it would strive to address all these issues.

REGIONAL RELATIONS

Relations between Zambia and a newly independent Zimbabwe were initially tense, owing to Kaunda's long-standing support for Robert Mugabe's political rival, Joshua Nkomo. Contacts between the two states were considerably improved, however, following reciprocal state visits in 1981, and the two countries' shared experience as frontline states did much to build closer relations. The MMD government has also enjoyed good relations with its Zimbabwean counterpart, but accuses it of economic protectionism. During Zimbabwe's difficult pre-election period in May and June 2000, Chiluba stood in rhetorical solidarity with the Zimbabwean government, calling on other African leaders to support Mugabe during his 'persecution' by foreign forces; Chiluba's ministers, however, reassured Zambian farmers that their land would neither be invaded nor confiscated, and extended a welcome to any Zimbabwean farmers interested in relocating north.

In 1987 the first state visit to Zambia by the Tanzanian president, Ali Hassan Mwinyi, reinforced economic and technical co-operation between the two countries.

Kaunda assumed a leading role in peace initiatives in southern Africa, and supported both the South West Africa People's Organisation of Namibia (SWAPO), allowing it to operate from Zambian territory, and the African National Congress of South Africa (ANC), which, until its return to South Africa in mid-1990, maintained its headquarters in Lusaka. In 1984 Kaunda was joint chairman of a conference on the issue of Namibian independence, which was held in Lusaka and involved the South African administrator-general in Namibia, together with representatives from SWAPO and some of Namibia's internal political parties. In September 1985 Kaunda was appointed chairman of the 'front-line' states, and in July 1987 he was elected to the chairmanship of the OAU. Owing to Kaunda's support for SWAPO and the ANC, Zambia was frequently subjected to military reprisals by South Africa. In May 1986 an air attack on an alleged ANC base near Lusaka, resulting in two deaths, was carried out by South African defence forces. Intermittent bomb attacks in Lusaka in 1987, 1988 and 1989 were generally viewed as attempts at destabilization by South Africa. Following the initiation of a programme of political reforms in South Africa in 1990, however, the Zambian government envisaged the restoration of diplomatic relations between the two countries. In mid-1993 the South African president, F. W. de Klerk, made an official visit to Zambia (the first by a South African head of state). In 2000 relations with South Africa seemed cordial but not warm. South African president Thabo Mbeki appeared appreciative of Chiluba's efforts to end the war in the Democratic Republic of the Congo (DRC, formerly Zaire—see below), and grateful that Chiluba was not permitting farm invasions like his southern neighbour, Zimbabwean president Robert Mugabe; Mbeki expressed concerns, however, during a visit to Zambia in October 1999 about the latter's role as a conduit for stolen South African goods. South Africa's ruling ANC also resented the MMD's treatment of Kaunda. The Zambian government, meanwhile, condemned the trade imbalance between the two countries, and accused the South African government of doing too little to remove protectionist barriers to Zambian imports.

The Namibian and Zambian authorities have worked together since the 1990s to supress Lozi nationalism. In June 1999 Lozi nationalists from the Caprivi strip in Namibia fled to Zambia seeking asylum. The activists were detained in Lusaka, and were subsequently returned to Namibia by the Zambian government. After Lozi nationalists clashed with Namibian troops in Caprivi in June, Imasiku Mutangelwa, the leader of Zambia's Barotse Patriotic Front (BPF), allegedly declared his support for their actions. A warrant for Mutangelwa's arrest was issued by the Zambian authorities, and Mutangelwa fled to the South African high commission in Lusaka for refuge. He was, however, handed over by the South Africans to the Zambian police.

Zambia's support for the governments of Angola and Mozambique also resulted in retaliatory attacks by UNITA rebels and by Mozambican guerrillas of the Resistência Nacional Moçambicana (Renamo). In May 1986 landmine explosions in the Zambezi district, which killed three people, were reportedly the responsibilty of UNITA; attacks by UNITA rebels continued in the late 1980s and early 1990s. Over the same period, a number

of Zambian civilians were reported to have been killed in repeated raids by members of Renamo, while Zambian troops entered Mozambican territory in pursuit of the rebels. In September 1992 the governments of Zambia and Angola signed a security agreement providing for joint border controls. Following a peace accord, signed by the Mozambican government and Renamo in October of that year, Zambia contributed some 950 troops to a UN peace-keeping force, which was deployed in Mozambique. In May 1993 the Zambian government dispatched troops to the border with Angola, in an attempt to prevent further attacks by UNITA rebels. In July 1994 it was alleged that Zambia was violating UN sanctions against UNITA rebels by supplying arms and oil to the movement. The allegation was rejected by President Chiluba. In early 1996 Zambia contributed some 1,000 troops to the UN Angola Verification Mission. Zambia consistently denied allegations, made by the Angolan government in 1997–98, that it was providing military and logistical support to UNITA. In early 1999, however, tension between the two countries intensified, as the accusations resurfaced and a bomb severely damaged the Angolan embassy in Lusaka (see above). Zambia invited a number of international delegations to investigate the claims, none of which found any evidence to support the allegations. In June, following discussions conducted in Swaziland, with the mediation of King Mswati III, intelligence and security chiefs from Zambia and Angola signed an agreement aimed at resolving their differences. A ministerial meeting was to be held in Swaziland to formalize the agreement, and in November the Angolan minister of foreign affairs, João Bernardo de Miranda, visited Zambia to strengthen relations further. The Angolan government expressed its annoyance, however, that Chiluba refused its request that its troops be allowed to pursue UNITA forces onto Zambian territory. Angolan military aircraft bombed border areas of Zambia's north-western province in early December. The intensification of the Angolan government campaign against UNITA in December and January 2000 caused thousands of Angolans to flee to Zambia as refugees, bringing the total Angolan refugee population in the country to around 170,000. Following military incursions by both Angolan government and UNITA forces into Zambia in early 2000, the Zambian government sent troop reinforcements to the Angolan border. On 10 May the Zambian minister of defence, Chitalu Sampa, accused Angola of launching air and ground attacks on Zambia's western and north-western provinces, and claimed that Angolan government troops had killed a Zambian soldier on Zambian territory. The Angolan government immediately denied that any of its aircraft had crossed into Zambia, and, although it conceded that Angolan and Zambian troops had indeed clashed, it insisted that the incident had taken place on Angolan soil. At the end of the month Chiluba said that although Zambia did not want war it had the capacity to deal with aggression, after which Angolan president José Eduardo dos Santos warned Chiluba to proceed with caution. On 4 June Zambian and Angolan military officials met in Windhoek, Namibia, and on 28 June the bilateral security commission of Zambia and Angola met in Lusaka.

In early March 1997 the Zambian government appealed for international assistance in coping with the influx of refugees fleeing the civil conflict in Zaire; by March some 6,000 Zairean refugees had arrived in Zambia. In January 1998 Zambia and the DRC (as Zaire had been renamed) agreed to establish a joint commission on defence and security. During late 1998 and early 1999 the Zambian government was involved in regional efforts to find a political solution to the conflict in the DRC, after a rebellion was mounted against its government in August 1998; President Chiluba was appointed to co-ordinate SADC and OAU peace initiatives on the crisis. All summits prior to June 1999 had foundered on the refusal of the president of the DRC, Kabila, to negotiate directly with rebel leaders. A summit held in Lusaka in June and July overcame this obstacle and resulted in a cease-fire document that provided a timetable for the withdrawal of foreign forces from the DRC and for political reform in the country. The accord was signed, on 10 July, by Kabila and all the countries involved in the conflict. However, apparently owing to a leadership dispute within one of the rebel groups, the rebel leaders did not sign the agreement until 31

August. The Lusaka agreement has since been hailed as a major diplomatic achievement by Chiluba. However, implementation of the agreement has been fraught with difficulties, set-backs and delays. Chiluba has responded to these with energetic bouts of shuttle diplomacy, but his government lacks the leverage to pressure the belligerents into compromise. The Joint Military Commission (JMC), the implementation structure established by the peace agreement, is based in Lusaka. Meanwhile, thousands of Congolese entered Zambia, fleeing the hostilities, prompting the government to appeal to the international community for immediate assistance to cope with the refugees, which, by then, were reported to number more than 30,000.

Economy

LINDA VAN BUREN

Copper is the mainstay of the Zambian economy. During the 1960s and the early 1970s, the Zambian economy expanded rapidly, owing to high levels of international copper prices. Despite considerable investment in physical and social infrastructure, however, the government of President Kaunda failed to develop other sectors of the economy, and a fall in the level of copper prices in the mid-1970s led to severe economic setbacks for Zambia. Development was subsequently constrained by a shortage of foreign exchange with which to import essential inputs, and by a lack of skilled manpower, a poor transport network and high debt-service obligations. Economic mismanagement during the Kaunda period brought about a further deterioration in domestic conditions, with severe food shortages and a dramatic increase in inflation rates and unemployment. Hopes were high in the early 1990s that an economic recovery would follow the establishment of a new government in 1991 by President Chiluba and the resumption of an IMF-approved austerity programme. Signs of improvement, however, were slow to appear.

AGRICULTURE

Zambia's topography, with its variations in elevation, enables a variety of crops to be grown, although only about 7% of the surface area is under cultivation, while some 40% serves as permanent pasture and 43% is under forest. The government estimates that, of the country's 60m. ha of arable land, only about 15% is currently being exploited. The principal food crop is maize. Other crops are cassava, wheat, millet, vegetables, sugar cane, groundnuts, sweet potatoes, melons, fruits, cotton, sorghum, pulses, soya beans, sunflower seeds and paddy rice. A number of lakes and rivers, particularly those in the Northern Province and at Lake Kariba on the southern border, offer considerable potential for fishing. Zambia has 323,000 sq km of forest land, of which 265,000 sq km is open to exploitation. Commercial forestry is important on the Copperbelt, where there are numerous softwood tree plantations, and in the hardwood areas of the south-west, which are rich in African teak.

Zambia has a few hundred large commercial farms, situated mostly near the railway lines, which account for about 45% of the country's agricultural output. The number of smallholders who cultivate cash crops is increasing, while most subsistence farmers in all parts of the country use traditional methods, without adequate inputs or infrastructural support. Agriculture accounted for 11% of gross domestic product (GDP) in 1970, and for 17% in 1999; the sector employed some 50% of the labour force in that year, according to government estimates. Food production per caput remained virtually static throughout the 1980s, registering a decline of 0.7%. The agricultural sector is frequently affected by drought, but grew at an average annual rate of 2.1% in 1970–80 and at an average annual rate of 3.3% in 1980–91. However, it experienced negative growth of 0.5% in 1990–95, mostly as a result of the 1994/95 drought, which caused the sector to register a decline of 11.3% in 1995. Maize, the staple domestic foodstuff, determines the fortunes of the agricultural sector, and about 17m. 90-kg bags are consumed annually by the local population. After a particularly severe drought in 1991/92, the crop achieved a remarkable recovery, and output reached a record level of 17.8m. bags in 1992/93 before falling back to 8.2m. bags in 1994/95. After a recovery in 1995/96 to 15.7m. bags, output fell back to 10.7m. bags in 1996/97, a year in which drought in some parts of the country, flooding in other parts and a lack of fertilizers at a crucial time in the growing period all combined to damage the maize crop,

leaving Zambia with a 3m.-bag domestic maize deficit for that year. Arrangements were made to import 1.33m. bags of maize from Zimbabwe, but in July 1997 Zimbabwe announced that it could supply only 555,600 bags. South Africa, a source of maize during a previous drought in 1994, was also unable to provide supplies. Moreover, it was discovered that an insect larva had infested some of the country's stored grain in Luapula Province. Grain imports in 1995 cost Zambia an estimated US $100m. and increased the deficit on the current account of the balance of payments. In 1997/98 maize production fell to just 7.2m. bags, the lowest level since 1991/92, owing partly to a 10% lower yield per ha. However, the principal reason for the decline was a 25% reduction in the amount of land planted with maize, from about 600,000 ha in 1997 to about 450,000 ha in 1998. Zambia's maize farmers consistently achieve a substantially higher yield than their counterparts south of the border; in 1999 Zimbabwe's average maize yield was 1,051 kg per ha, whereas Zambia's was 36% higher, at 1,431 kg per ha. In 1998/99 Zambia recorded an estimated 6.5m.-bag maize deficit, necessitating the importation of 2.3m. bags from three South African companies, one of which bought Tanzanian maize with which to fulfil the contract, and 1.6m. bags from Zimbabwe, which itself had to import 6.8m. bags of maize in that year. Zambia produced 9.5m. bags of maize in 1999, a full 34% rise over the previous year's output.

In April 1993 the Zambia National Union of Farmers complained that the basic guaranteed price of K5,000 per 90-kg bag was uneconomic and warned that commercial farmers might abandon the cultivation of maize unless the government were to increase the price to at least K8,000 per bag; the government subsequently agreed to review the price. In the event, in preference to increasing the guaranteed price, the government chose to introduce two types of promissory note. The first, a rediscountable promissory note, allowed farmers to collect, after 15 February 1994, money owed to them on maize that they had produced up to 31 October 1993, together with interest equivalent to the prevailing rate on 182-day treasury bills (at the time, 125% per annum). Farmers could, alternatively, sell the notes to a commercial bank at a discount, or they could use them as collateral on loans or to purchase agricultural inputs such as fertilizers. The farmers' other option was to accept a forward-contract promissory note, guaranteeing a price of K7,500 per 90-kg bag on 15 February 1994, which was intended to reflect the market price plus interest and a storage allowance. The farmers had then to decide whether they would lose or gain by waiting to accept the undertaking to buy on 15 February. The scheme was immediately criticized for being both complicated and costly. According to the FAO, the area planted with maize declined by 23.4% between 1994 and 1995, from 679,355 ha to 520,165 ha. In 1996 the area planted with maize increased to 675,565 ha. Subsequently, however, the area declined to 649,039 ha in 1997 and to 410,372 ha in 1998. A 46% expansion took place in 1999, when the area under maize grew to 598,181 ha. Financial losses, principally resulting from overproduction, continued to pose a problem, and experts advocated a comprehensive strategic maize policy that would assure adequate stocks to meet domestic requirements in times of drought, and sufficient storage for that purpose, while avoiding costly maintenance of excessive stocks. The Chiluba government reacted effectively to the drought in 1991/92, distributing emergency supplies far more efficiently than the governments of neighbouring countries, and subsequently arranging the timely supply of seed to effect a quick recovery. However, its performance in reacting to subsequent droughts was less successful.

Wheat is grown almost exclusively on large commercial farms, usually under irrigation. Production increased from 37,000 metric tons in 1988 to 71,000 tons in 1993 and to a record 89,743 tons in 1999. The country's flour mills require some 140,000 tons per annum to keep the nation supplied with bread. In September 1997 the government imposed a ban on the import of wheat flour, with the stated aim of curtailing the smuggling of 'expired products' into Zambia from unnamed 'neighbouring countries'. The wheat sector was assisted by Canadian agricultural advisers, who maintained that Zambia had the potential to meet much more of its wheat requirement from local production. The Zambian government lifted controls over the producer price of wheat in June 1988, precipitating a dramatic increase in the price, to K370 per 90-kg bag in October (compared with K190 in June). However, liberalization also meant that the National Milling Co (the country's only miller of wheat, although no longer with a statutory monopoly) was free to obtain its wheat at lower prices from elsewhere, notably from South Africa. Zambian farmers also grew 69,617 metric tons of millet and 25,493 metric tons of sorghum in 1999. In 1999 production of paddy rice more than doubled to 14,698 tons, comfortably exceeding the annual domestic demand of some 10,000 tons.

Zambia has about 300,000 cash-crop smallholders, the majority of whom produce cotton and tobacco. Preferring not to commit itself to just one sector, the Mineworkers' Union of Zambia owns the 90,000-ha Mukuba Farm. Smallholders grow most of the nation's cotton crop. Textile factories in the country have required some 12,000 metric tons of cotton lint per annum, and in most years the domestic cotton crop is large enough to meet all of the demand and to allow for cotton exports. However, output declined from 21,000 tons in 1988 to 17,000 tons in 1989, and to 10,000 tons in 1990, even before the 1991/92 drought. Textile companies complained that the best cotton was exported, leaving only lower-quality raw material for the local industry. Another problem was that, following the liberalization of trade, cheap imports reduced demand for local textiles, and therefore the textile companies' demand for local cotton. In 1999 Zambian farmers harvested 23,000 metric tons of seed cotton, yielding 8,200 tons of cotton lint and 14,400 tons of cottonseed. In July 1997 the Zambia Agricultural High Value Crops Asscn was formed, with the aim of encouraging Zambian smallholders to grow high-value cash crops such as cotton, castor-bean seed, simsim (sesame seed) and paprika. The tobacco sector experienced major problems in the 1990s, with reduced yields (owing to drought) in 1983, 1985 and 1992. Yields averaged 1,034 kg per ha annually in 1979–81 and rose to 1,776 kg per ha in 1991. Drought reduced yields to 438 kg per ha in 1992, and the effects were still being felt in 1993, when yields were 514 kg per ha. Yields averaged 1,077 kg per ha in 1996–99. Tobacco price controls were lifted in 1989. Zambia harvested 3,100 metric tons of tobacco leaves in 1999, only about half as much as in 1995. The sugar sector recovered from the 1991/92 drought much more quickly in Zambia than in neighbouring countries. The 1992/93 output totalled 143,204 metric tons, sufficient to cover the national demand of about 93,000 tons and to allow 50,000 tons to be exported, of which 40,000 tons went to Zimbabwe. In 1995/96 the harvest of sugar cane was 1.38m. metric tons, yielding a sugar crop of 150,503 tons, of which 69,887 tons were exported. In 1997/98 the harvest increased to 1.65m. tons, boosting export potential by some 20%; revenue from exports of sugar totalled an estimated US $26m. in 1998. The 1999 harvest was 1.6m. tons of sugar cane. A $63m. rehabilitation and expansion programme, which received new impetus following the privatization of the state sugar company in mid-1995, was expected to increase annual production to 200,000 tons per annum by 2000. To meet this target, output would need to grow by about 5.6% per annum in 1999 and 2000; the sector is on course to meet this goal following production growth of 16% during 1997–98. Tate and Lyle of the United Kingdom acquired a 40% share in Zambia Sugar PLC, which was one of the eight companies whose shares were listed on the Lusaka Stock Exchange in July 1998. The coffee sector, which produces mostly arabica, suffered both from reduced output and from lower international prices in the 1990s. Exports declined from 1,772 metric tons in 1991/92 (year ended 31 March) to 1,675 tons in 1992/93; total production of green coffee was 2,280 tons in 1998 and 2,400 tons in 1999. The horticultural sector experienced strong growth in the 1990s, with the export of fruits and vegetables to Europe. The sector's interests are overseen by the Zambia Export Growers' Asscn (ZEGA) which, among other things, lobbies for affordable air-freight charges. The European Investment Bank extended a $12m. facility to encourage the production and export of vegetables and roses; exports of these crops totalled some $12m. in 1998, and were expected to increase to some $30m. in 2000. The Zambia Horticultural Co (Zamhort) was acquired by Foodcorp of South Africa in 1997. Production of other crops in 1999 amounted to 850,000 tons of cassava, 50,965 tons of groundnuts in shells (a 10% decline from 1998's 56,934 tons), 52,000 tons of sweet potatoes, 24,000 tons of tomatoes, 15,000 tons of pulses (a 20% rise), 10,000 tons of potatoes (a 25% rise), 6,748 tons of sunflower seeds (an 18% increase over the 1998 crop, but still only a fraction of the 21,176 tons produced in 1993), 3,530 tons of citrus fruits, 600 tons of bananas, 600 tons of barley and 450 tons of tea.

About 70% of livestock is owned by traditional farmers. The livestock sector suffered as a result of the drought in 1991/92, when a higher number of animals were slaughtered than in most years; in 1992/93, however, herds began to recover to normal levels. A small amount of beef is generally exported. Foot-and-mouth disease constitutes a problem in some areas of the country. An outbreak of African swine fever in 1992 threatened the destruction of 10,000 pigs and prompted the government to establish a K3,200m. fund to compensate pig farmers for their losses from the disease. Trans-Zambezi Industries, whose shares were quoted on the Lusaka Stock Exchange in 1997, owns 90% of Zambezi Ranching and Cropping, which manages a 100,000-ha holding, the largest ranch in Zambia, grazing some 25,000 head of cattle. The Central Veterinary Research Institute in Chilanga produces livestock vaccines for the local market and for export.

Although rural development was accorded a high priority during the Kaunda period, most of the schemes and programmes yielded disappointing results. Nearly 18% of total development expenditure in 1980 was for agriculture. However, poor organization, lack of skills, inadequate marketing and transport infrastructure, and migration to urban areas all impeded growth. The sector was additionally constrained by low producer prices, late and unreliable payments to farmers for their crops, inefficient marketing and inadequate supply of inputs from the state-owned National Agricultural Marketing Board (NAMBOARD). NAMBOARD maintained a statutory monopoly over all aspects of agricultural marketing until 1986, when private companies and co-operatives were allowed to compete for the first time. For several years after liberalization was introduced, however, farmers continued to face most of these impediments. In 1994 larger-scale traders in agricultural commodities established the Zambian Grain Growers and Marketing Asscn. In that year the government ceased setting minimum support prices for agricultural commodities, allowing prices to be determined entirely by supply and demand. In 1995, in an effort to remedy the lack of effective agricultural credit, the government launched a Pilot Credit Management Scheme and appointed 117 'credit co-ordinators' to distribute seed, fertilizers and other agricultural inputs to farmers. Although agricultural liberalization has produced mixed results, some subsectors, such as horticulture, have benefited significantly. Freshwater fishing in this land-locked country also provides a livelihood for rural Zambians. The total catch amounted to 60,701 metric tons in 1997, including some 10,000 tons of shad and 4,430 tons of tilapia.

MINING

Copper accounted for about 93% of all Zambia's foreign exchange earnings in 1991, but the proportion fell to 68% in 1994 and to 52% in 1996. Other minerals exploited include cobalt (found in association with copper), zinc, lead, gold, silver, selenium, marble, emeralds and amethysts. In 1996 mining and quarrying contributed 10.8% of GDP and engaged some 10% of the total labour force. The mining industry in Zambia was established during the colonial period, with the opening in 1906 of the Broken Hill lead and zinc mine at Kabwe. Copper mining was begun in the 1920s by Zambian Anglo American (later Nchanga Consolidated Copper Mines) and Roan Selection Trust (later Roan Consolidated Mines), which, in 1982, united to form

Zambia Consolidated Copper Mines (ZCCM), in which the government took a 60.3% share. Growth continued after independence in 1964, and by 1969 Zambia had become a leading producer of unrefined copper, with a record output of 747,500 metric tons, accounting for 12% of international production. After the mid-1970s, however, copper output and revenues declined significantly; production dropped from 700,000 metric tons in 1976 to 338,000 tons in 1993 and to 291,000 tons in 1998. Earnings from copper exports declined from US $851m. in 1995 to $567.7m. in 1996. Earnings declined further, to just $430.2m., in 1998, owing to a 14% decrease in the volume of production, and to a 9% decline in copper prices to an average of $1,507 per ton. Early indications for 1999 were not encouraging; the volume of exports fell by 17% in the first quarter of 1999 compared to the first quarter of 1998, from 65,226 tons to 53,925 tons.

ZCCM recorded a gross profit of K31,551m. in the financial year to 31 March 1992, compared with K18,539m. in the previous financial year. However, the company ultimately incurred financial losses during both these years, despite operating at well below capacity at the mining, smelting and refining stages. Ageing capital equipment, shortages of skilled labour, poor maintenance and inadequacy of reinvestment all adversely affected productivity. In 1983 the Kaunda government introduced an export levy in order to compensate for lack of tax revenue during the company's loss-making years. The levy initially contributed 4% of gross sales revenue, but increased to 8% in 1983 and to 10% in 1985. ZCCM resorted to borrowing to cover this export levy and other high costs, with the result that debts accrued. The major purchaser of ZCCM copper is Japan (which accounted for 18% of total exports in 1993), followed by Thailand (12%), and France (10%).

Following Zambia's change of government in 1991, a number of remedial measures, including the proposed transfer of ZCCM to private-sector ownership, were announced. A range of reforms within ZCCM was carried out, and higher production targets for copper were set. Potential bidders' plans for the expansion of productive capacity and a wide-ranging programme of exploration and modernization were an important part of the evaluation of bids. Nevertheless, in 1994 ZCCM experienced 'operational problems' which caused mineral revenue to the government for that year to fall 35% below target. In 1995 'geotechnical problems' were experienced at the Mufilira, Luanshya and Konkola mines. In that year Nchanga operated at a loss, owing to the low grade of ore extracted. Because of these problems, Zambia was unable to benefit from the high level of world copper prices in that year. In 1996 an international consortium, led by Anglo American, opened negotiations with ZCCM to develop the Konkola Deep copper belt, with envisaged investment of US $650m. and production forecast at 180,000 tons of finished copper per annum. Also involved were Falconbridge of Canada, Gencor of South Africa and Western Mining Corpn (WMC) of Australia; however, all three subsequently withdrew from the consortium. In 1996 the government announced its intention to initiate the partial privatization of ZCCM. The conglomerate was originally to be divested as four separate entities, and the process was to be completed by late 1998. After continually reviewing the complicated privatization of this huge conglomerate, it was eventually decided that nine 'packages' of ZCCM assets would be offered, and by February 1997 15 companies had entered 26 bids for them. Konkola is potentially the richest of Zambia's copper mines, possessing reserves of 44.3m. tons, with a copper content of 3.92%, while reserves at Nchonga have a copper content of 3.75% and those at Mufulira a content of 3.16%; Nkana is the largest mine, with 95.5m. tons of reserves, but with a copper content of only 2.3%. AVMIN of South Africa, part of the Anglovaal Minerals group, became the majority shareholder in the Konkola North reserve in 1997, and signed a 'tentative agreement' on the further development of the mine, the cost of which was projected at $500m., and was to undertake an exploratory drilling programme covering 50,000 sq km. Talks for the development of the Nkara and Nchonga divisions were under way in 1999 with a consortium comprising Angloraal, Noranda of Canada, Phelps Dodge of the USA and the Commonwealth Development Corpn. The US company Cyprus Amax Minerals agreed to purchase the rights to develop the Kansanshi mine for $28m.; the total cost of the project was estimated at between $200m. and $300m.

An 85% stake in the Chambeshi copper mine, known as ZCCM (D) or 'D Co', was purchased by China Non-Ferrous Metal Industry (CNMI) in March 1998. ZCCM (B), or 'B Co', comprising the Luanshya facility, was sold to the Binani group of India for $35m. The Chibuluma mine assets were sold to a Canadian-South African consortium led by South Africa's Metorex for $17m. The new owners pledged to invest $34m. in the facility, the production capacity of which was described as 480,000 tons of ore per year. The future ownership of the Nchanga and Nkana divisions, which together accounted for some two-thirds of ZCCM's output, was still unresolved in 1998, after protracted negotiations with potential investors had collapsed. Amid reports in early 1999 that ZCCM's remaining operations were losing $2m. per day, Anglo American, the Chilean state mining company Codelco and the World Bank's private-sector arm, the International Finance Corpn (IFC), teamed up and entered into negotiations over the purchase of Nchanga, Nkana and Konkola (including the Nampundwe pyrite mine). However, by August 1999 Codelco had pulled out, and by September Anglo had also left the negotiating table. On 27 October 1999 agreement in principle was reached for a deal in which 80% of the assets of the Konkola Division (including Konkola Deep), Nampundwe and Nchanga were to be acquired by Anglo's Zambia Copper Investments Ltd (ZCI), in a complicated arrangement that was heavily criticized in the Zambian press. An option for the purchase of the Nkana smelter and refinery within three years was part of the package. Anglovaal Mining (AVMIN) of South Africa acquired the Chambeshi cobalt mine, along with its acid plants and slag heaps, for $50m. in immediate payment and another $45m. over a five-year period; the new owner pledged to invest $70m., with a further contingency investment of $50m. The ZCCM power division was sold in July 1997 to the Copperbelt Energy Consortium, led by British interests. Bids were still being considered in mid-1998 for the Nampundwe Pyrite Mine. In December 1996 First Quantum of Canada acquired the Bwana Mkubwa open-pit copper mine, which had been inoperative since 1984. The move was described as the first private-sector copper project in Zambia for 25 years. In 1999 the World Bank's IFC invested $1m. in the Mpelembe Drilling Co of Zambia, which provides underground mining services to the copper industry and undertakes underground and surface diamond drilling.

Zambian output of cobalt increased from 2,934 tons in 1995 to 4,381 tons in 1998. In 1994 Apollo Enterprises Ltd of Zambia formed a joint venture with Claim Minerals NL of Australia to study and potentially to exploit nickel-sulphide deposits at Munali, 65 km south-west of Lusaka. The site, estimated to contain some 11.69m. tons of ore, is situated close to power, water, road and rail infrastructures. Output of zinc declined from 13,637 tons in 1990 to 13,387 tons in 1991 (owing, in part, to power cuts), and to just 6,459 tons in 1992, while international prices of zinc were low in 1992 and 1993. Production of lead amounted to 2,332 tons in 1992, stimulating revenue of K93m. Output of precious metals totalled 38,902 kg in 1992, stimulating revenue of K286m. Production of zinc and lead at Kabwe was undertaken by the Kabwe division of ZCCM until its closure in 1994. Zambia mines emeralds, aquamarines, amethysts and some diamonds. Two gem companies identified for privatization in 1999 were Kariba Minerals & Kariba Amethyst, an equal joint venture between the Zambian government and Lonrho, and Zambia Emeralds Industries, which arts, polishes and markets emeralds, aquamarines, amethysts, garnets and tourmalines. In the mid-1990s Zambia's emeralds accounted for a significant and growing share of the coloured-gem market, and by 1997 held a dominant position near the top of the market. A new deposit of diamonds was discovered in Western Province in 1992, and it was hoped that investigations would reveal further reserves. Smuggling of gemstones is a major problem; in 1999 the government estimaterd that some 70% of Zambia's emeralds were exported illegally, costing the treasury US $600m. a year in lost revenue. In mid-2000 Rhino Industry and Mining Co was seeking a joint-venture partner to invest $1.5m. in a project to mine emeralds, amethysts and malachite in the North-Western Province. A consortium known as Sable Zinc announced plans to resume zinc production at Kabwe; the project was due to enter production in early 2001, with output projected at 5,000 tons per annum. Petroleum exploration took place in the 1980s, but no significant discoveries have emerged. In April 1995 the government announced plans to sell 27.4% of the shares in Chilanga Cement on the Lusaka Stock Exchange, where the company was one of the 13 listed companies in July 2000. Chilanga exported 146,925 metric tons of cement to Malawi, the Democratic Republic of the Congo (DRC, formerly Zaire) and Burundi, earning $8m., in 1998. Ndola Lime Co, Zambia's only producer of quicklime, crushed limestone and other lime products, was identified for privatization in 1999. Total production levels in the mining sector were declining in the mid-1990s, with output falling by 16.3% in 1994 and by 7.8% in 1995.

INDUSTRY

Zambia's manufacturing sector has experienced a variety of problems, not least a chronic shortage of foreign exchange with which to import raw materials and inputs. The sector was also constrained by state intervention in many manufacturing activities, investment in inappropriate schemes and a corresponding lack of funds to invest in more suitable undertakings. The state-owned Industrial Development Corpn of Zambia (INDECO) acquired 26 companies in 1968 and continued to acquire majority shareholdings in a number of other enterprises thereafter. By 1991 INDECO accounted for 75% of Zambia's manufacturing activity. The industrial sector contributed 43.1% of Zambia's GDP in 1996, while the manufacturing sector accounted for 30.7% of total GDP in that year. The industrial sector engaged 24.8% of all wage-earning employees in 1996, while the manufacturing sector engaged 11.6% of wage-earning employees in that year. During the Kaunda era, the government, usually through INDECO, formed a number of joint ventures with foreign enterprises, to establish a chemical-fertilizer plant, a petroleum refinery, an explosives plant, a glass-bottle factory, a battery factory, a brickworks, a textile factory, a copper-wire factory, two vehicle-assembly operations, and an iron-and-steel project; however, a number of these ventures subsequently ended in failure. Nitrogen Chemicals of Zambia opened a sulphuric-acid plant, at a cost of K32m. in 1983, while its fertilizer operation, with an estimated cost of K300m., was the country's largest non-mining enterprise. Operations at Kapiri Glass Works, which produced glass bottles, declined to less than 50% of its installed capacity by 1984. Mansa Dry Batteries began production in 1979, but was operating at only 33% of its capacity by 1984. Kafue Textiles of Zambia faced intense competition from cheap imported cloth and clothing from the Far East and from elsewhere in Africa in the early 1990s. The Tika iron-and-steel project, conceived in 1972, was abandoned in 1979, after the accumulation of large debts in foreign currency to overseas companies that had participated in the expensive planning of the project. Rover Zambia's plant at Ndola assembles Toyota, Mitsubishi and Volkswagen trucks, while Leyland Zambia's assembly plant in Lusaka produces 2,000 commercial vehicles per annum. The tyre manufacturer Dunlop Zambia was offered for privatization in 1997 but subsequently closed down. A tractor-assembly factory, with the capacity to produce 2,500 tractors per annum, was established, with the assistance of the Czechoslovak government, in 1983. Livingstone Motor Assemblers produces Fiat, Peugeot and Mazda saloon cars. In April 1993 Refined Oil Products of Ndola opened a glycerine plant, at a cost of K68m., with the capacity to produce 240 metric tons of glycerine per annum (equivalent to about 20% of national annual demand). Swarp Spinning Mills in Ndola received a loan of US $10m. from the European Investment Bank in December 1992 for the expansion of its cotton-spinning and associated yarn-dyeing facilities. The Kitwe-based foundry Scaw Ltd was privatized in March 1998. Other privatizations in 1998 included the sale of the government's 34% stake in Kafironda Explosives of Mufulira to a British company, and the sale to Zambia Detonators (Zamdet) to a Norwegian firm. Lusaka Engineering Co Ltd (Lenco), which manufactures metal products such as doors, window frames, screens, louvers and nails, was also privatized, while Luangwa Industries Ltd, which makes bicycles, was bought by Tata Zambia for $1.68m. Nkwazi Manufacturing Co of Zambia Ltd in Kafue, manufacturers of fishing nets, ropes and twine, was also privatized in 1998. Zambia Breweries was divided in 1994, when its Copperbelt holdings became Northern Breweries. Lonrho bought a 70% share of

Northern Breweries for $9m., while the management bought a 10% share. South African Breweries invested in the remaining part of Zambia Breweries. In 1998 Zambia Breweries purchased Lonrho's 70% holding, announcing a 'rights' issue on the Lusaka Stock Exchange to finance the transaction; the move, if approved by the Zambia Competition Commission (ZCC), would leave both halves of the old Zambia Breweries in the possession of its parent company, South African Breweries (SAB). In late 1998 SAB also looked set to acquire National Breweries; Lonrho Africa had long been part owner and had increased its hold to 70% in 1995, with the remaining 30% held by the government until it was floated on the stock exchange in 1998. However, in 1998 SAB also signed a memorandum of understanding for the purchase of the parent company of National Breweries, rather than of National Breweries itself, in a deal that technically involved no Zambian company and therefore was not subject to approval by the ZCC. Both Zambian Breweries and National Breweries were among the 13 companies quoted on the Lusaka Stock Exchange in July 2000. In 1999 the World Bank's Multilateral Investment Guarantee Agency (MIGA) made its first contract backing a contract in Zambia, when it issued $1.8m. in coverage for Beekay Engineering & Castings Ltd of India's $2m. in a foundry in Kitwe. A projected 20% of the foundry's output was to be exported to the neighbouring Democratic Republic of the Congo.

The liberalization of prices, the imposition of an import tariff and the allocation of foreign exchange helped to alleviate some of the major problems in the manufacturing sector after 1983, but other aspects of liberalization, such as allowing the kwacha to depreciate according to the dictates of market forces, negated some of these gains. The government, deprived of some of its tax revenue from ZCCM during its loss-making period, attempted to compensate for the shortfall by charging import duties on the c.i.f. (cost, insurance and freight) value of imports, rather than on their f.o.b. (free on board) value, thereby further reducing companies' narrowing profit margins.

In 1983 the government introduced an arrangement whereby companies that exported non-traditional items were allowed to retain 50% of foreign exchange from those exports for use in paying for imported inputs, thereby compensating for lack of foreign currency. After only one year exports of non-metal products exhibited a fivefold increase. In 1987, however, companies lost this concession, after the Kaunda government adopted the former system of strict import licensing, an artificially revalued exchange rate and similar measures. The Investment Act of 1991, promulgated at the close of the Kaunda period, partially restored the facility, allowing companies holding investment licences to retain 70% of gross foreign-exchange earnings for three years, 60% for the following two years and 50% for the remaining period of the investment licence's validity. The Chiluba government subsequently revised the Investment Act to allow the full retention of foreign-exchange earnings by investors. The tobacco firm Rothmans and Bata Shoe Co were among the 13 companies quoted on the Lusaka Stock Exchange in July 2000. Among the incentives offered to boost interest in the exchange were a 30% corporate tax rate for listed companies, and the absence of restrictions on foreign ownership and of exchange controls.

Manufacturing production declined by 9.0% in 1994 and by 4.5% in 1995. Only fabricated metal products, non-metallic mineral products and basic metal products registered any growth in those years. The downturn in manufacturing output was largely a result of competition from imported goods as reforms dismantled trade barriers, and of the high cost of borrowing, which deterred investment in new technology. In 1996 the government announced that it had designated US $45m. of World Bank funding to facilitate loans to the textile industry in a bid to rehabilitate and increase the competitiveness of the industry. In June 1996 the People's Republic of China granted a loan of $21.6m., principally for the rehabilitation of the Mulungushi textile mill complex in Kabwe. Meanwhile, conducting the privatization programme was the Zambia Privatization Agency; by June 2000 more than 250 of the 281 companies designated for privatization had been transferred to private-sector ownership, and a further 25 had been formally offered to bidders.

ENERGY

Zambia became self-sufficient in hydroelectric power in 1974 and began exporting power to Zimbabwe (then Rhodesia) and the DRC (then Zaire). In that year a major expansion of output from Kafue Gorge resulted in an increase of 82% in domestic energy production. Long delays occurred in the construction of the Kariba North power station, but 150 MW of capacity were operational by 1977, with a further 150 MW for later completion. New 150-MW generators came into service at Kafue Gorge in 1976 and 1977, bringing the facility's total installed capacity to 900 MW. The construction of an additional dam at Itezhi-Tezhi provided a more reliable flow of water to the Kafue Gorge power plant. However, a fire in March 1989 inflicted major damage on this installation, destroying the main power cables, and exports of power to Zimbabwe (valued at $1m. per month) were suspended. (Zimbabwe, meanwhile, proceeded with the construction of its own Kariba South facility to end its dependence on Zambia for imported power.) In 1997 the Zambian government was seeking investors to build, operate and own a 600-MW hydropower plant on the Kafue, at an estimated cost of between US $500m.–$750m. Low water levels throughout the region during the 1991/92 drought significantly reduced power output in Zambia, resulting in the suspension of exports, and Zambia was one of several countries which arranged to import power from South Africa and Zaire. Imports from Zaire ceased in February 1993. In 1995 drought again reduced water levels at hydroelectric facilities, necessitating the introduction of electricity rationing and the renewed import of power from Zaire, at a cost of more than $1m. per month. A Norwegian company was engaged in November 1991 to conduct feasibility studies for the construction of electricity interconnection lines from Zambia to Malawi and Tanzania. Rural electrification is a stated priority, and some extension of the national grid has been achieved, but many areas of rural Zambia still do not have access to mains power supply. Charcoal and fuelwood remain the main sources of energy supply for cooking and heating purposes for most people in both urban and rural areas. Both energy production and energy consumption declined in 1980–93, by 3.0% and 2.5% respectively per annum. Zambia used 146 kg per caput in 1993, compared with 471 kg per caput in Zimbabwe, 99 kg per caput in Kenya and 2,399 kg per caput in South Africa. The Zambia Electricity Supply Corpn (Zesco) completed several township and rural electrification projects during 1994. The country generated 5,791.8m. kWh and consumed 5,221.0m. kWh in 1994; in 1995 output rose to 7,790m. kWh. Norway granted Zesco approximately K2,500m. in 1997 to expand its output. The World Bank in February 1998 approved a $75m. credit towards a $204m. Zambia power-rehabilitation project, the stated aim of which was to make the power sector financially viable. Zesco and its South African counterpart ESKOM reached an agreement in July 1998 whereby Zambia was to export electricity to South Africa earning about $500,000 per month for Zesco. In June 2000 the World Bank extended a $37.7m. credit to Zambia for improvements to the water-supply and sewerage infrastructure in the mining towns of the Copperbelt.

Coal production commenced in 1965 but was subsequently affected by shortages of equipment and spare parts. The remaining colliery, at Maamba, operated substantially below capacity in 1987. Following a rehabilitation programme, however, the mine met its production target of 560,000 metric tons in 1987/88, and began exporting coal to Zaire, Malawi and Tanzania. By 1994, however, annual output of hard coal had declined to an estimated 380,000 tons. Thereafter output declined further, and in 1997 a 70% share in Maamba Collieries Ltd was designated for privatization.

TRANSPORT

At independence in 1964 Zambia had only one tarred road and one railway line. The railway line extended from the Copperbelt, in the north, through Lusaka and Livingstone to Zimbabwe (then Southern Rhodesia), and connected with the Rhodesian rail network, providing access to South African ports. In 1965 the unilateral declaration of independence by Rhodesia prompted sanctions against that country, which severely disrupted the flow of Zambia's traffic on its only transport link to the outside world.

The Zambian government invested substantial sums in improving infrastructure, with the construction of the TanZam oil pipeline from the Tanzanian port of Dar es Salaam, which was completed in 1968. The Great North Road to Tanzania (which was previously only a dirt track) was tarred, and a Great East Road to Malawi, which connected with the Mozambican ports of Nacala and Beira, was constructed (although civil war in Mozambique subsequently prevented Zambia from making full use of this route). The Tanzania-Zambia Railway Authority (Tazara) railway line leading to Dar es Salaam was built and financed by China with an interest-free loan. It was used in early 1974 to transport goods, following the closure of the Rhodesian border. The complete route was opened to regular service in October 1975, ahead of the original schedule, and proved to be essential, after the closure of the Lobito railway to Angola in August 1975. However, limited port facilities at Dar es Salaam and unavailability of rolling stock resulted in severe delays, and Tazara incurred losses for the Zambian government in its first eight years of operation. In October 1978 Zambia resumed its use of the Rhodesian rail route to South Africa. Tazara finally moved into profit in the June quarter of 1983, although it did not consistently achieve profits until 1988. In 1991 Zambia Railways rehabilitated about 80% of its rolling stock, with the assistance of loans totalling US $13.5m. from Japan and the USA, but additional funds were required for signalling and communications equipment. Zambia railways was being restructured in 1999, with assistance from Sweden, with a view to privatization perhaps as early as 2001. In 1998 Tazara offered companies the opportunity to lease rolling stock on the line. Zambia's only port, Mpulungu, is on Lake Tanganyika; the Mpulungu Harbour Authority was designated for privatization in 1997, and in mid-1998 the European Union (EU) provided a grant of $3.5m. for the rehabilitation of the port.

The BotZam Highway, linking Kazungula with Nata, in Botswana, was opened in 1984, and in 1989 Botswana completed the tarring of the road that extended south from Nata to connect with its own road system. In 1992 Japan provided US $13.9m. for the reconstruction of the ageing Kafue Road Bridge. In 1968 the Zambian government nationalized the country's two main road-haulage companies and merged them into a single enterprise, Contract Haulage. It was estimated in July 1992 that Contract Haulage owned 85% of the 1,200 commercial trucks in Zambia. The public passenger and cargo road-transport sectors were opened to private enterprise in 1992, and in 1995 the state-owned United Bus Co of Zambia ceased operations, owing to private-sector competition. In 1994 a road agreement was signed with Namibia, which included a plan to build a bridge across the Zambezi river to facilitate cross-border passage and to enable Zambia to use Namibia's Walvis Bay port for cargo transportation. In 1995 the government released K2,100m. for the tarring of the Luanshya–Mpongwe and Choma–Namwala roads, to be completed within two years. In 1996 Japan granted K16,000m. towards an ongoing road-rehabilitation project in Lusaka.

The national airline, Zambia Airways, which was established in 1967, operated domestic, regional and long-haul passenger and air-freight services. In 1992 the government indicated that the airline would henceforth have to service its external and domestic debt from its own revenue. Supplies of aviation fuel to Zambia were subsequently suspended until payment was received, forcing all carriers flying to Zambia to divert to Zimbabwe, where they could purchase aviation fuel for 'hard' currency. In February 1993 the government announced the implementation of extensive measures at Zambia Airways, including the retrenchment of staff, to compensate for continuing financial losses. In March 1993, however, the National Airports Corpn announced that it was to spend US $30m. towards the rehabilitation of four airports, situated at Lusaka, Ndola, Livingstone and Mfuwe. In addition, equipment valued at $7m. was to be installed at airports in Kaoma, Solwezi, Kasama, Livingstone and Mfuwe. In 1994 Zambia Airways reduced its regional routes and introduced other cost-cutting measures, although the government still had to provide K2,500m. in subsidies to the airline. In 1995 the loss-making carrier went into liquidation. Some 3,000 creditors in 50 countries presented claims against the company's assets. By January 1996 most of the assets had been sold, including overseas operations in 13 countries. Many of the routes formerly flown by Zambia Airways were subsequently taken by two local carriers, Roan Air and Eastern Air. In May 1999 Roan Air was awarded the right to operate the long-haul routes to London, Frankfurt and Amsterdam, in addition to 19 regional routes. Eastern Air was awarded the long-haul routes to Dubai, Rome and Larnaca, as well as 13 regional routes.

FOREIGN TRADE AND PAYMENTS

Zambia generally maintained a visible trade surplus from independence until 1991. The principal export commodity is copper, although its share of total exports declined during the 1990s. In 1996, for example, the volume of copper exports declined by 4.1% to 327,000 metric tons, but in the same year the volume of total exports rose by 9.4%. In 2000 the volume of total exports was projected to rise by 11.8%, while exports of copper were forecast to grow by 10%. The largest share of Zambia's non-traditional exports went to the EU in 1999, a year in which non-traditional exports grew by 14%. These exports included such products as cotton, textiles, sugar, coffee and metal products. The EU imported from Zambia such items as speciality vegetables, live fish, wet-blue leather, cotton yarn and cut flowers. Another important client for Zambia's non-traditional exports is the Common Market for Eastern and Southern Africa (COMESA), which in 1999 imported from Zambia such items as chemicals, cement, cotton, maize, fresh eggs, refined petroleum and sugar. One item among the principal non-mineral exports that declined sharply in importance during the 1990s was tobacco. Zambia's terms of trade fluctuated in the second half of the 1990s, deteriorating by 22.8% in 1996, then improving by 21.6% in 1997, and then worsening by 10.3% in 1998 and by 5.1% in 1999.

In 1996 the principal imports were machinery, transport equipment and other manufactures, followed by foodstuffs, fuels, petroleum products and electricity. South Africa is the largest supplier of imports (22% in 1993), followed by the EU, Japan, Saudi Arabia and the USA. Japan, as a result of its purchases of Zambian copper, is the principal single market for exports (18% in 1993) although in 1996 the EU as a whole purchased more. Other important purchasers in 1996 were South Africa, the USA, Saudi Arabia, India, Thailand and Malaysia.

In 1998, according to IMF figures, the current account of the balance of payments registered a deficit of US $269m.; a deficit of $361m. was forecast for 2000. The overall balance of payments, following a deficit of $216m. in 1995, recorded a deficit of only $105m. in 1996, thanks to a capital account in surplus, but in 1998 the deficit increased to $249m. Gross international reserves amounted to $213m. at the end of 1997, and a shortfall of $294m. was forecast for 2000.

GOVERNMENT FINANCE

The 1997 budget proposals forecast total spending of K1,427,606m., up 23% on the level of the previous year, when the budget envisaged expenditure and revenue balanced at K1,161,600m. Of total projected expenditure in 1996, K421,600m. (36.3%) was to be funded by donors. In June 1996 bilateral lenders suspended their balance-of-payments support. Of particular concern to the lenders were the worsening deficit on the current account of the balance of payments and the government's continued failure to deal with its heavy burden of debt. According to IMF figures, the 1998 budgetary deficit was equivalent to 15.2% of GDP, excluding official transfers. The budget deficit had been equivalent to 4.6% of GDP in 1995, to 5.7% of GDP in 1994 and to 5.1% of GDP in 1993, but to only 2.5% of GDP in 1992 (despite unforeseen expenditure on emergency drought relief). These ratios compare with budget deficits of 7.2% of GDP in 1991 (the final year of the Kaunda administration) and 8.3% in 1990. In real terms, Zambia's GDP contracted by 3.4% in 1992, as a result of the drought, but achieved positive growth of 8.2% in 1993. However, GDP contracted again, by 3.1% in 1994 and by 2.3% in 1995, but increased by 6.4% in 1996 and by 3.5% in 1997. Negative growth returned in 1998, when GDP contracted by 2.0%. GDP increased by an annual average of 1.0% in 1990–97. In the first year of the Chiluba administration, the government indicated that it had made considerable progress in the reduction of the country's

high external debt, which was estimated at US $7,300m. in October 1991, when Chiluba succeeded Kaunda. Only three months later, the government was able to pay back arrears totalling $51m., which had been overdue for more than six months, on loans from the World Bank and the International Development Asscn (IDA). The payment resulted in the resumption of disbursements on previously approved loans and credits. By August 1992, owing to a rescheduling the previous month by the 'Paris Club' of Western official creditors, together with cancellations of debt by bilateral creditors, Zambia's total debt had fallen to $6,500m. At 30 September 1993 Zambia's total debt stood at $6,750m., of which $2,640m. was owed to bilateral lenders, $1,740m. was due to multilateral lenders (of which $1,300m. to the IMF), $822m. comprised short-term loans, $149m. was owed to foreign suppliers and $97m. was due to the 'London Club' of Western commercial creditors. In 1995 Zambia's debt-servicing requirements absorbed 186.3% of the value of the country's export earnings, owing to a government 'debt buy-back' operation; in 1996 debt-service payments were equivalent to 24.6% of the value of exports of goods and services. Zambia's external public debt totalled US $7,113m. at the end of 1996, of which $5,307m. was long-term public debt. In February 1996 the 'Paris Club' again rescheduled Zambia's debt. Nevertheless, in July 1996 the World Bank and the IMF named Zambia among 11 countries with 'unsustainable' debt burdens. A further 'Paris Club' rescheduling in April 1999 covered $219m. of Zambia's debt owing from 1997 and 1998.

In 1992 the Chiluba administration adopted a three-year structural adjustment programme, in agreement with the IMF and the World Bank, which emphasized the decentralization of social services, the reorganization of the civil service and the transfer of parastatal organizations to the private sector. In addition, the new government negotiated a Rights Accumulation Programme (RAP) with the IMF, giving Zambia the potential to convert nearly US $1,220m. in arrears owed to the IMF into a concessionary facility carrying only 0.5% annual interest. In June 1992 the World Bank agreed two new loans, totalling $200m., and the IMF extended funds of $100m. in July of that year. In the same month donors pledged $300m. in drought relief. In September 1992 the IDA extended $200m. in support of the government's privatization programme. At a conference of donors, convened by the World Bank Consultative Group for Zambia in April 1993, $800m. was pledged in support of the country's reform programme; additional bilateral pledges were expected to compensate for a shortfall of $115m. Several of the donors had visited Lusaka in March 1993 to urge the government to accelerate the pace of its privatization programme and to implement measures to restrict inflation. Also in March 1993 Germany cancelled loans totalling DM 135.2m., and rescheduled an equivalent amount over a period of 23 years.

The World Bank Consultative Group for Zambia reconvened in Paris in December 1993 and pledged a further US $800m. to the country for 1994. The donors issued a statement praising the Zambian government for 'maintaining its commitment to the country's economic recovery programme under difficult conditions' but cautioning that formidable challenges lay ahead, not least Zambia's heavy debt burden. The group also expressed concern at the slow pace of privatization. The $800m. pledge fell short of the $1,100m. requested by Zambia, however. In March 1994 the IDA extended an SDR 108.9m. ($150m.) three-year contract, which included much-needed balance-of-payments support. In December 1995, following the successful completion of the RAP, the IMF announced that Zambia was again eligible for credit, and subsequently approved a three-year enhanced structural adjustment facility of $1,043m. and a one-year structural adjustment facility of $270m. Despite the temporary suspension of bilateral aid to Zambia in June 1996 (see above), donors at a July 1997 World Bank Consultative Group meeting pledged $435m. in support of the government's Economic Recovery and Investment Programme. A similar meeting in May 1998 in Paris pledged $530m. for 1998, of which $295m. was in the form of project assistance and $235m. was in programme support. In May 1999 a meeting of donors in Paris pledged $630m. in both development assistance and balance of payments support, although the aid was conditional on the progress of a two-year good governance plan presented by the government at the meeting. The delay in reaching agreement for the privatization of ZCCM took its toll on Zambia's budgetary finances, on its current-account balance and, consequently, on its relationship with the IMF. As long as the loss-making conglomerate remained the responsibility of the government alone, it proved a costly burden on the exchequer. Zambia reportedly had to pay $97m. to ZCCM suppliers in 1999/2000, and the 2000/01 budget allocated K423,000m. for the same purpose. Following the long-awaited privatization of the remaining major ZCCM assets in early 2000 (see above), the IMF described Zambia's prospects for economic growth and poverty reduction as 'substantially improved'. The fund came through on 27 July 2000 with a disbursement of $13.2m., as a first tranche of a three-year, $336.3m. Poverty Reduction and Growth Facility.

The annual rate of inflation was unofficially estimated at an average of 400% in October 1991. (According to the IMF, however, consumer prices increased by an average of 92.6% in 1991.) The Chiluba government's aim to reduce the official rate of inflation by one-half by the end of 1992 was not realized, and although estimates varied considerably, the rate of inflation increased to an average of 169% in that year, according to the IMF. Despite government plans to reduce inflation to 35% in 1993, IMF figures indicate inflation of 188% in that year. According to the IMF, the rate was reduced to an annual average of 53.6% in 1994, to 34.2% in 1995, to 43.9% in 1996 and to 24.8% in 1997. Many economists contend that the true inflation rate in 1996 and 1997 was 70% or more. The World Bank acknowledged that by the end of 1997 inflation had fallen to below 20%, the lowest level for a decade. However, in 1998 the average annual rate of inflation increased to 36%, according to the IMF. The target for 2000 was to bring annual inflation down to 14%, but a figure of 17% was more likely to be achieved.

As part of the reform programme, Zambia liberalized its exchange-rate policy. The first bureaux de change, which opened in October 1992, were permitted to set their own rates for the buying and selling of foreign currency; Zambian residents were initially limited to purchases of US $2,000 per transaction. The exercise proved extremely successful, and the kwacha fared far better during its initial period as a free-market currency than any other African currency had in similar circumstances. In February 1993 91-day treasury bills were introduced as a means of stimulating finance for the 1993 budget, replacing the former method of borrowing direct from the Bank of Zambia. Zambian business interests had complained that heavy government borrowing on the domestic market had caused a shortage of loanable funds for the private sector. New banknotes were introduced in February 1993, followed by a new coinage in March of that year. The new notes replaced those bearing the likeness of Kenneth Kaunda but did not demonetize 'old' banknotes, which remained in circulation. In the last quarter of 1993 and the first quarter of 1994 the kwacha weakened on the exchange markets. It fell from K347 = US $1 in mid-October 1993 to K435 = US $1 in early December and to K657 = US $1 in early January 1994. The descent was much less rapid thereafter, however, reaching K695 = US $1 in late May 1994 and stabilizing at about that level. The currency depreciated by 26.5% between January and December 1994, compared with its decline of 28.1% in 1993. However, in the first half of 1995, the currency depreciated by 26%, reaching K920 = US $1. The exchange rate stabilized in the second half of 1995, ending the year at K950.5 = US $1. Pressure on the currency in 1995 was exacerbated by the collapse of Meridien BIAO Bank Zambia Ltd, which, in turn, precipitated the closure of a further two banks. Further depreciation, of 24%, followed in the first nine months of 1996, and in September the exchange rate stood at K1,252 = US $1. Thereafter it levelled off, and a year later, in September 1997, the rate was K1,294 = US $1. Copper's weak performance (see above) placed further downward pressure on the kwacha, which depreciated by 39% during the 1998 calendar year. The rate had been K1,945 = US $1 in August 1998, but by August 1999 it stood at K2,438 = US $1, a depreciation of 20% for that 12-month period. In the year to 1 August 2000 the rate had fallen to K3,267.97 = US $1, a depreciation of 25%. The forecast is for a further depreciation of about 12% in the year to 1 August 2001, with the improvement hinging on the execution of the ZCCM privatization agreements that have been reached and on the expected increased inflows of balance-of-payments support from donors.

Decades after copper became Zambia's main source of foreign exchange, and nine years after the Chiluba administration came to power, the economy is still overwhelmingly dependent on the commodity. Some success has been achieved in encouraging alternative exports, mostly of agricultural commodities, and strenuous efforts are being made to persuade Zambian farmers to cultivate high-value crops such as paprika, cauliflower and roses. Trade figures indicate that these non-traditional exports have increased their share of export earnings; however, these activities are still young and fragile. They face formidable competition in their intended markets. Their higher share of the export revenue reflects not simply their own growth but also the declining fortunes of the copper sector. The world copper price, long known for its volatility, entered a trough in 1998, just as the disposal of ZCCM's assets was prompting potential buyers to make careful assessments of the sector's future potential. The volume of copper exports is not expected to increase by more than 5% in 2001, and the depressed world price for copper, which permeates the economy, appears certain to result in a weakened kwacha and rising prices for essential commodities. Then too, pressure from the IMF and the World Bank to collect huge sums of unpaid taxes from companies such as the power authority and the distributor of petroleum products has led to rises in electricity tariffs and fuel prices, placing strong upward pressure on the inflation rate. Adverse publicity south of the border in Zimbabwe is expected to have a negative effect on tourism to the region as a whole, further contributing to the weakening of the kwacha. But the problems in Zimbabwe may not be entirely negative for Zambia; the Lusaka Stock Exchange has begun to promote itself as a haven for 'offshore investment across the Zambezi'. In comparison to the tense situation prevailing in Zimbabwe in mid-2000, Zambia may seem an island of tranquillity in the region. But how tranquil it will be as the 2001 elections approach remains to be seen.

Statistical Survey

Source (unless otherwise indicated): Central Statistical Office, POB 31908, Lusaka; tel. (1) 211231.

Area and Population

AREA, POPULATION AND DENSITY

Area (sq km)	752,614*
Population (census results)	
1 September 1980	5,661,801
20 August 1990	
Males	3,617,577
Females	3,765,520
Total	7,383,097
Population (UN estimates at mid-year)	
1996	8,389,000
1997	8,585,000
1998	8,781,000
Density (per sq km) at mid-1998	11.7

* 290,586 sq miles.

PRINCIPAL TOWNS (estimated population 1990 census)

Lusaka (capital)	982,362	Chingola	162,954
Ndola	376,311	Mufulira	152,944
Kitwe	338,207	Luanshya	146,275
Kabwe	166,519		

Source: UN, *Demographic Yearbook*.

BIRTHS AND DEATHS (UN estimates, annual averages)

	1980–85	1985–90	1990–95
Birth rate (per 1,000)	48.4	46.3	43.9
Death rate (per 1,000)	14.8	14.7	17.9

Expectation of life (UN estimates, years at birth, 1990–95): 43.8 (males 43.0; females 44.6).

Source: UN, *World Population Prospects: The 1998 Revision*.

ECONOMICALLY ACTIVE POPULATION
(ILO estimates, '000 persons at mid-1980)

	Males	Females	Total
Agriculture, etc.	959	438	1,398
Industry	174	14	188
Services	257	69	326
Total labour force	1,390	522	1,912

Source: ILO, *Labour Force Estimates and Projections, 1950–2025*.

1980 census (persons aged 12 years and over): Total employed 1,302,944 (males 908,606, females 394,338); Unemployed 492,999 (males 247,013, females 245,986); Total labour force 1,795,943 (males 1,155,619, females 640,324).
Mid-1984 (official estimates): Total labour force 2,032,300 (males 1,464,800; females 567,500).
Mid-1998 (estimates in '000): Agriculture, etc. 2,580; Total 3,659 (Source: FAO, *Production Yearbook*).

Agriculture

PRINCIPAL CROPS ('000 metric tons)

	1996	1997	1998
Wheat	60	60†	70
Rice (paddy)	13	13†	6†
Maize	1,409	960†	650
Millet	55	61†	62
Sorghum	36	31†	25
Sugar cane*	1,400	1,500	1,650
Potatoes*	10	9	8
Sweet potatoes*	54	52	51
Cassava (Manioc)	620*	702†	817
Pulses	24	13†	13*
Onions (dry)*	27	26	25
Tomatoes*	25	23	22
Soybeans (Soya beans)	40	29†	12
Sunflower seed	27	25†	7
Groundnuts (in shell)	35	50†	57
Cottonseed	23†	23*	22*
Cotton (lint)	13†	13*	13*
Tobacco (leaves)	4	7*	10

* FAO estimate(s).   † Unofficial figure(s).

Source: FAO, *Production Yearbook*.

LIVESTOCK (FAO estimates, '000 head, year ending September)

	1996	1997	1998
Cattle	3,150	3,200	3,100
Sheep	65	66	65
Goats	600	610	600
Pigs	288	290	285

Poultry (million): 23 in 1996; 25 in 1997; 27 in 1998.

Source: FAO, *Production Yearbook*.

LIVESTOCK PRODUCTS (FAO estimates, '000 metric tons)

	1996	1997	1998
Beef and veal	42	43	41
Pig meat	10	10	9
Poultry meat	27	30	32
Other meat	33	34	36
Cows' milk	85	86	84
Hen eggs	37	40	43
Cattle hides	6	6	6

Source: FAO, *Production Yearbook*.

Forestry

ROUNDWOOD REMOVALS ('000 cubic metres)

	1995	1996	1997
Sawlogs, veneer logs and logs for sleepers	606	606	606
Other industrial wood	463	474	486
Fuel wood	13,465	13,465	13,465
Total	14,534	14,545	14,557

Source: FAO, *Yearbook of Forest Products*.

SAWNWOOD PRODUCTION
('000 cubic metres, incl. railway sleepers)

	1995	1996	1997
Coniferous (softwood)* . . .	340	340	340
Broadleaved (hardwood)* . . .	27	27	27
Total	367	367	367

* FAO estimates.

Source: FAO, *Yearbook of Forest Products.*

Fishing

('000 metric tons, live weight)

	1995	1996	1997
Freshwater fishes . . .	56.5	52.6	55.9
Dagaas	10.0	9.0	10.0
Total catch (inland waters) . .	66.5	61.6	65.9

Source: FAO, *Yearbook of Fishery Statistics.*

Mining

(metric tons)

	1994	1995	1996
Hard coal*	380,000	360,000	350,000
Cobalt ore†‡	3,600	5,908	7,900
Copper ore†§	384,400	341,900	339,700
Lead ore†§	600	—	—
Zinc ore†§	1,000	—	—
Gold (kg)†‡	124	100*	130*

* Estimate(s).
† Figures relate to the metal content of ores and concentrates (or, for cobalt, the metal recovered).
‡ Data from the US Bureau of Mines.
§ Data from *World Metal Statistics,* London.

Source: UN, *Industrial Commodity Statistics Yearbook.*

Industry

SELECTED PRODUCTS (metric tons, unless otherwise indicated)

	1994	1995	1996
Raw sugar*	158,000	162,000	166,000
Nitrogenous fertilizers . . .	3,000	n.a.	n.a.
Cement†‡	280,000	300,000	n.a.
Copper (unwrought)			
Smelter§‖	265,200	237,700	262,000
Refined‖	369,500	313,800	317,100
Lead (primary)‖	500	500	400
Zinc (unwrought)‖ . . .	100	—	—
Electric energy (million kWh)† .	7,785	7,790	7,795

* Data from the Food and Agriculture Organization, Rome.
† Estimate(s).
‡ Data from the US Bureau of Mines.
§ Including copper obtained from ores by leaching in electrowinning plants.
‖ Data from *World Metal Statistics,* London.

Source: UN, *Industrial Commodity Statistics Yearbook.*

Finance

CURRENCY AND EXCHANGE RATES

Monetary Units
100 ngwee = 1 Zambian kwacha (K).

Sterling, Dollar and Euro Equivalents (28 April 2000)
£1 sterling = 4,415.4 kwacha;
US $1 = 2,815.8 kwacha;
€1 = 2,558.1 kwacha;
10,000 Zambian kwacha = £2.265 = $3.551 = €3.909.

Average Exchange Rate (Zambian kwacha per US $)
1997   1,314.50
1998   1,862.07
1999   2,388.02

BUDGET (K million)*

Revenue†	1996	1997	1998§
Tax revenue	699,800	907,900	1,066,400
Taxes on income, profits and capital gains . . .	242,700	305,100	395,800
Domestic taxes on goods and services	365,700	478,500	484,600
General sales, turnover, or value-added taxes . .	230,000	269,400	299,500
Excises	133,800	206,500	181,500
Import duties	90,000	123,700	183,900
Other current revenue . .	45,300	37,400	31,000
Administrative fees and charges, non-industrial and incidental sales . . .	36,000	21,100	15,700
Capital revenue	200	11,700	200
Total	745,300	957,000	1,097,600

Expenditure‡	1996	1997	1998§
General public services . .	146,900	275,800	578,900
Defence	56,900	90,800	113,800
Public order and safety . .	35,900	46,600	77,500
Education	120,700	221,400	243,500
Health	72,100	102,600	197,000
Social security and welfare . .	8,800	10,200	21,300
Housing and community amenities	8,600	4,400	40,600
Recreation, cultural and religious affairs and services . .	7,000	7,500	11,900
Economic affairs and services .	92,800	108,700	250,700
Fuel and energy	500	600	5,300
Agriculture, forestry and fishing	22,600	54,300	75,400
Mining, manufacturing and construction	4,100	7,600	12,300
Transport and communications .	26,500	33,800	140,400
Other economic affairs and services	39,100	12,400	17,300
Other expenditures (incl. adjustments) . . .	293,000	445,600	181,900
Total	842,700	1,313,600	1,717,100
Current	720,700	813,500	1,289,200
Capital	122,000	500,100	427,900

* Figures refer to the consolidated accounts of the central Government's Recurrent and Capital Budgets.
† Excluding grants received from abroad (K million): 25,400 in 1996; 4,700 in 1997; 32,700 in 1998.
‡ Excluding lending minus repayments (K million): 24,200 in 1996; 136,600 in 1997; 143,600 in 1998.
§ Figures for 1998 are provisional.

Source: IMF, *Government Finance Statistics Yearbook.*

INTERNATIONAL RESERVES (US $ million at 31 December)

	1986	1987	1988
Gold*	1.0	1.8	4.1
Foreign exchange† . . .	70.3	108.8	134.0
Total	71.3	110.6	138.1

* Valued at market-related prices.
† Foreign exchange (US $ million at 31 December): 193.1 in 1990; 184.6 in 1991; n.a. in 1992; 192.3 in 1993; 268.1 in 1994; 210.5 in 1995; 220.7 in 1996; 238.0 in 1997; 68.6 in 1998.

IMF special drawing rights (US $ million at 31 December): 2.0 in 1996; 1.1 in 1997; 0.8 in 1998; 0.1 in 1999.

Source: IMF, *International Financial Statistics*.

MONEY SUPPLY (K million at 31 December)*

	1996	1997	1998
Currency outside banks . .	106,300	136,700	169,700
Demand deposits at commercial banks	163,100	217,200	243,700
Total money (incl. others) . .	271,100	355,200	414,900

* Figures are rounded to the nearest K100 million.
Source: IMF, *International Financial Statistics*.

COST OF LIVING (Consumer Price Index; base: 1994 = 100)

	1996	1997	1998
All items	193.0	240.1	298.9*

* IMF estimate.
Source: IMF, *Zambia: Statistical Appendix* (May 1999).

NATIONAL ACCOUNTS

Expenditure on the Gross Domestic Product

(K million at current prices)

	1996	1997	1998*
Government final consumption expenditure . . .	714,000	857,000	982,000
Private final consumption expenditure	2,894,000	3,895,000	4,923,000
Increase in stocks . . .	16,000	20,000	23,000
Gross fixed capital formation .	566,000	681,000	876,000
Total domestic expenditure .	4,190,000	5,453,000	6,805,000
Exports of goods and services .	1,344,000	1,715,000	1,831,000
Less imports of goods and services	1,590,000	2,000,000	2,395,000
GDP in purchasers' values . .	3,945,000	5,169,000	6,241,000
GDP at constant 1990 prices .	2,334,000	2,412,000	2,364,000

* IMF estimates.
Source: IMF, *Zambia: Statistical Appendix* (May 1999).

Gross Domestic Product by Economic Activity

(K '000 million at current prices)

	1996	1997	1998*
Agriculture, forestry and fishing .	612	845	1,080
Mining and quarrying . .	476	511	378
Manufacturing	466	612	713
Electricity, gas and water . .	129	215	241
Construction	137	231	316
Wholesale and retail trade, restaurants and hotels . .	777	975	1,201
Transport and communications .	230	271	362
Finance, insurance, real estate and business services . . .	568	746	1,014
Community, social and personal services	281	412	560
Sub-total	3,676	4,818	5,865
Import duties	469	612	692
Less imputed bank service charge .	200	259	314
GDP in purchasers' values . .	3,945	5,169	6,241

* IMF estimates.
Source: IMF, *Zambia: Statistical Appendix* (May 1999).

BALANCE OF PAYMENTS (US $ million)

	1989	1990	1991
Exports of goods f.o.b. . . .	1,340	1,254	1,172
Imports of goods f.o.b. . .	−774	−1,511	−752
Trade balance	566	−257	420
Exports of services . . .	85	107	83
Imports of services . . .	−444	−386	−363
Balance on goods and services	208	−537	140
Other income received . . .	1	2	10
Other income paid	−509	−439	−696
Balance on goods, services and income	−300	−974	−546
Current traders received . .	114	398	262
Current transfers paid . . .	−32	−18	−22
Current balance	−219	−594	−306
Direct investment from abroad .	164	203	34
Other investment assets . .	26	−275	−125
Other investment liabilities . .	1,637	569	108
Net errors and omissions . . .	−1,712	322	110
Overall balance	−106	222	−179

Source: IMF, *International Financial Statistics*.

External Trade

PRINCIPAL COMMODITIES (US $ million)

Imports f.o.b.	1984	1985	1986
Food and live animals	27.7	25.3	n.a.
Cereals and cereal preparations	21.0	14.3	10.1
Crude materials (inedible) except fuels	13.1	10.9	n.a.
Mineral fuels, lubricants, etc.	180.6	156.1	n.a.
Petroleum and petroleum products	175.0	153.7	80.1
Crude petroleum	n.a.	n.a.	71.7
Chemicals and related products	82.8	106.0	n.a.
Fertilizers (manufactured)	24.2	29.2	3.0
Plastic materials, etc.	9.5	15.6	9.8
Basic manufactures	99.0	116.0	n.a.
Rubber manufactures	9.6	17.6	16.0
Textile yarn, fabrics, etc.	25.5	19.6	14.5
Iron and steel	27.4	25.4	20.6
Machinery and transport equipment	174.1	232.1	n.a.
Power-generating machinery and equipment	11.9	17.6	18.2
Machinery specialized for particular industries	35.8	60.0	46.8
General industrial machinery, equipment and parts	46.6	57.8	56.5
Telecommunications and sound equipment	9.9	6.5	20.8
Other electrical machinery, apparatus, etc.	16.4	21.5	24.1
Road vehicles and parts	42.3	52.3	74.2
Miscellaneous manufactured articles	13.0	23.8	n.a.
Total (incl. others)	595.6	713.8	602.8

Total imports (K million, f.o.b.): 6,627.5 in 1987; 6,898.1 in 1988; 10,901.8 in 1989; 37,627.6 in 1990; 59,988.0 in 1991; 172,871.7 in 1992; 553,400.0 in 1993; 805,299.9 in 1994; 1,284,600.0 in 1995.

Source: UN, *International Trade Statistics Yearbook*.

Exports f.o.b.	1996	1997	1998*
Copper	567.7	649.4	430.9
Cobalt	186.5	245.6	154.3
Total (incl. others)	993.4	1,190.8	873.6

* IMF estimates.

Source: IMF, *Zambia: Statistical Appendix* (May 1999).

PRINCIPAL TRADING PARTNERS (US $'000)*

Imports f.o.b.	1988	1989	1990
Algeria	—	—	20,451
Belgium-Luxembourg	17,891	17,496	13,694
Finland	7,195	29,627	23,184
France	31,574	15,937	12,471
Germany	53,058	184,038	144,015
India	34,931	29,302	22,930
Iran	122	—	35,134
Italy	39,368	38,706	30,289
Japan	84,440	105,590	82,627
Kuwait	—	—	33,697
Madagascar	93	82	66,700
Netherlands	7,482	19,771	15,472
SACU†	169,801	286,500	224,177
Sweden	12,443	24,553	19,213
United Kingdom	19,596	256,049	200,365
USA	213,075	67,071	125,522
Zimbabwe	35,392	73,948	57,866
Total (incl. others)	886,054	1,258,321	1,237,717

Exports f.o.b.‡	1989	1990	1993
Belgium-Luxembourg	48,619	34,405	99,429
France	98,121	81,008	94,938
Greece	19,648	16,221	29,367
India	44,141	36,443	52,383
Indonesia	24,070	19,872	28,593
Italy	32,243	26,620	7,638
Japan	223,194	184,268	122,023
Kenya	9,360	7,728	5,281
Malaysia	27,689	22,860	74,058
Netherlands	7,893	6,517	24,359
Pakistan	433	516	83,319
SACU†	2,972	2,454	17,795
Saudi Arabia	38,732	31,977	64,017
Singapore	161	11,004	51,504
Thailand	—	40,673	61,538
United Kingdom	14,712	12,147	14,072
USA	13,781	9,752	3,317
Zaire	10,105	8,342	11,677
Zimbabwe	21,833	18,025	27,359
Total (incl. others)	667,811	594,765	920,536

* Imports by country of production; exports by country of last consignment.
† Southern African Customs Union, comprising Botswana, Lesotho, Namibia, South Africa and Swaziland.
‡ Figures for 1991 and 1992 are unavailable.

Source: UN, *International Trade Statistics Yearbook*.

Transport

ROAD TRAFFIC (estimates, '000 motor vehicles in use at 31 December)

	1994	1995	1996
Passenger cars	123	142	157
Lorries and vans	68	74	81

Source: International Road Federation, *World Road Statistics*.

CIVIL AVIATION

(scheduled services: Passengers carried—thousands; others—millions)

	1992	1993	1994
Kilometres flown	5	4	4
Passengers carried	246	219	235
Passenger-km	509	393	428
Total ton-km	63	47	54

Source: UN, *Statistical Yearbook*.

Tourism

	1996	1997	1998
Tourist arrivals ('000)	263	340	362
Tourism receipts (US $ million)	59.8	75.5	74.7

Source: Zambia National Tourist Board.

Communications Media

	1994	1995	1996
Radio receivers ('000 in use) . .	760	800	1,000
Television receivers ('000 in use) .	245	260	270
Daily newspapers:			
Number	2	3	3
Circulation ('000 copies) . .	70	107	114

Telephones ('000 main lines in use, year ending 31 March): 80 in 1994/95; 77 in 1995/96; 78 in 1996/97.

Telefax stations (number in use, year ending 31 March): 570 in 1994/95; 600 in 1995/96; 650 in 1996/97.

Mobile cellular telephones (subscribers, year ending 31 March): 1,547 in 1995/96; 2,721 in 1996/97.

1997: Radio receivers ('000 in use): 1,030; Television receivers ('000 in use) 277.

Sources: UNESCO, *Statistical Yearbook*; UN, *Statistical Yearbook*.

Education

(1989)

	Institutions	Students	Teachers
Primary	3,883*	1,506,349*	38,528*
Secondary . . .	480	199,081*†	5,786†‡
Trades and technical .	12	3,313§	438
Teacher training . . .	14	4,669§	408
University‖	2	5,891	481

* 1995 figures.

† Figures refer to government-maintained and aided schools only.

‡ 1988 figures.

§ 1990 figures.

‖ 1994 figures. Data on students and teachers include distance-learning institutions (621 students in 1994).

Sources: the former Ministry of Higher Education and the former Ministry of General Education, Lusaka; University of Zambia; UNESCO, *Statistical Yearbook*.

Directory

The Constitution

The Constitution for the Republic of Zambia, which was formally adopted on 28 May 1996 (amending the Constitution of 1991), provides for a multi-party form of government. The Head of State is the President of the Republic, who is elected by popular vote at the same time as elections to the National Assembly. The President's tenure of office is limited to two five-year terms. Foreign nationals and those with foreign parentage are prohibited from contesting the presidency. The legislature comprises a National Assembly of 150 members, who are elected by universal adult suffrage. The President appoints a Vice-President and a Cabinet from members of the National Assembly.

The Constitution also provides for a House of Chiefs numbering 27: four from each of the Northern, Western, Southern and Eastern Provinces, three each from the North-Western, Luapula and Central Provinces and two from the Copperbelt Province. It may submit resolutions to be debated by the Assembly and consider those matters referred to it by the President.

The Supreme Court of Zambia is the final Court of Appeal. The Chief Justice and other judges are appointed by the President. Subsidiary to the Supreme Court is the High Court, which has unlimited jurisdiction to hear and determine any civil or criminal proceedings under any Zambian law.

The Government

HEAD OF STATE

President: FREDERICK J. T. CHILUBA (took office 2 November 1991; re-elected 18 November 1996).

THE CABINET
(August 2000)

Vice-President: Lt-Gen. CHRISTON S. TEMBO.

Minister of Defence: CHITALU M. SAMPA.

Minister of Home Affairs: Dr PETER D. MACHUNGWA.

Minister of Foreign Affairs: KELI S. WALUBITA.

Minister without Portfolio: MICHAEL C. SATA.

Minister of Finance and Economic Development: Dr KATELE KALUMBA.

Minister of Commerce, Trade and Industry: WILLIAM J. HARRINGTON.

Minister for Presidential Affairs: ERIC S. SILWAMBA.

Minister of Agriculture, Food and Fisheries: SURESH M. DESAI.

Minister of Legal Affairs: VINCENT MALAMBO.

Minister of Communications and Transport: Prof. NKANDU LUO.

Minister of Energy and Water Development: DAVID C. SAVIYE.

Minister of the Environment and Natural Resources: BENJAMIN Y. MWILA.

Minister of Community Development and Social Welfare: DAWSON L. LUPUNGA.

Minister of Tourism: Rev. ANOSHI CHIPAWA.

Minister of Education: Brig.-Gen. GODFREY MIYANDA.

Minister of Science, Technology and Vocational Training: ABEL M. CHAMBESHI.

Minister of Health: DAVID S. MPAMBA.

Minister of Local Government and Housing: ACKSON SEJANI.

Minister of Works and Supply: GODDEN K. MANDANDI.

Minister of Sports, Youth and Child Development: SYACHEYE MADYENKUKU.

Minister of Lands: SAMUEL S. MIYANDA.

Minister of Labour and Social Security: EDITH Z. NAWAKWI.

Minister of Mines and Mineral Development: SYAMUKAYUMBU S. SYAMUJAYE.

Minister of Information and Broadasting Services: NEWSTEAD L. ZIMBA.

MINISTRIES

Office of the President: POB 30208, Lusaka; tel. (1) 218282.

Ministry of Agriculture, Food and Fisheries: Mulungushi House, Independence Ave, Nationalist Rd, POB RW50291, Lusaka; tel. (1) 213551; internet www.agriculture.gov.zm.

Ministry of Commerce, Trade and Industry: Kwacha Annex, Cairo Rd, POB 31968, Lusaka; tel. (1) 213767; internet www.commerce.gov.zm.

Ministry of Communications and Transport: Fairley Rd, POB 50065, Lusaka; tel. (1) 251444; fax (1) 253260; internet www.communication.gov.zm.

Ministry of Community Development and Social Welfare: Fidelity House, POB 31958, Lusaka; tel. (1) 228321; fax (1) 225327; internet www.welfare.gov.zm.

Ministry of Defence: POB 31931, Lusaka; tel. (1) 252366; internet www.defence.gov.zm.

Ministry of Education: 15102 Ridgeway, POB RW50093, Lusaka; tel. (1) 227636; fax (1) 222396; internet www.education.gov.zm.

Ministry of Energy and Water Development: Mulungushi House, Independence Ave, Nationalist Rd, POB 36079, Lusaka; tel. (1) 252589; fax (1) 252589; internet www.energy.gov.zm.

Ministry of the Environment and Natural Resources: Lusaka; internet www.environment.gov.zm.

Ministry of Finance and Economic Development: Finance Bldg, POB RW50062, Lusaka; tel. (1) 213822; internet www.finance.gov.zm.

Ministry of Foreign Affairs: POB RW50069, Lusaka; tel. (1) 252640; e-mail mfalus@zamnet.zm; internet www.foreignaffairs.gov.zm.

Ministry of Health: Woodgate House, 1st–2nd Floors, Cairo Rd, POB 30205, Lusaka; tel. (1) 227745; fax (1) 228385; internet www.health.gov.zm.

Ministry of Home Affairs: POB 32862, Lusaka; tel. (1) 213505; internet www.homeaffairs.gov.zm.

Ministry of Information and Broadcasting Services: Independence Ave, POB 51025, Lusaka; tel. (1) 251766; fax (1) 253457; internet www.information.gov.zm.

Ministry of Labour and Social Security: Lechwe House, Freedom Way, POB 32186, Lusaka; tel. (1) 212020; internet www.labour.gov.zm.

Ministry of Lands: POB 50694, Lusaka; tel. (1) 252288; fax (1) 250120; internet www.lands.gov.zm.

Ministry of Legal Affairs: Fairley Rd, POB 50106, 15101 Ridgeway, Lusaka; tel. 228522; internet www.legalaffairs.gov.zm.

Ministry of Local Government and Housing: Church Rd, POB 34204, Lusaka; tel. (1) 253077; fax (1) 252680; internet www.localgovernment.gov.zm.

Ministry of Mines and Mineral Development: Chilufya Mulenga Rd, POB 31969, 10101 Lusaka; tel. (1) 251402; fax (1) 252095; internet www.mines.gov.zm.

Ministry of Science, Technology and Vocational Training: POB 50464, Lusaka; tel. (1) 229673; fax (1) 252951; internet www.technology.gov.zm.

Ministry of Sport, Youth and Child Development: Memaco House, POB 50195, Lusaka; tel. (1) 227158; fax (1) 223996; internet www.sports.gov.zm.

Ministry of Tourism: Electra House, Cairo Rd, POB 30575, Lusaka; tel. (1) 227645; fax (1) 222189; internet www.tourism.gov.zm.

Ministry of Works and Supply: POB 50003, Lusaka; tel. (1) 253088; fax (1) 253404; internet www.supply.gov.zm.

President and Legislature

PRESIDENT

Presidential Election, 18 November 1996

Candidate	Votes	% of votes
FREDERICK CHILUBA (MMD)	917,382	72.51
DEAN MUNG'OMBA (ZADECO)	158,756	12.55
HUMPHREY MULEMBA (NP) . . .	88,766	7.02
AKASHAMBATWA LEWANIKA (AZ) . . .	59,379	4.69
CHAMA CHAKOMBOKA (MDP) . . .	40,843	3.23
Total	**1,265,126**	**100.00**

In addition, a total of 55,184 invalid votes were cast.

NATIONAL ASSEMBLY

Speaker: AMUSA K. MWANAMWAMBWA.

General Election, 18 November 1996

	Seats
Movement for Multi-party Democracy (MMD) . .	131
National Party (NP)	5
Agenda for Zambia (AZ)	2
Zambia Democratic Congress (ZADECO)* . . .	2
Independents	10
Total	. **150**

* Formally disbanded and absorbed into the Zambia Alliance for Progress in August 1999.

House of Chiefs

The House of Chiefs is an advisory body which may submit resolutions for debate by the National Assembly. There are 27 Chiefs, four each from the Northern, Western, Southern and Eastern Provinces, three each from the North Western, Luapula and Central Provinces, and two from the Copperbelt Province.

Political Organizations

Agenda for Zambia (AZ): POB 50303, Lusaka; f. 1996 by fmr mems of National Party; Pres. AKASHAMBATWA LEWANIKA.

Christian Progressive Party (CPP): Private Bag 9, Woodlands, Lusaka; f. 1996; Pres. MICHAEL KASHELE.

Democratic Party (DP): POB 71628, Ndola; f. 1991; Pres. EMMANUEL MWAMBA.

Independent Democratic Front (IDF): POB 71803, Ndola; f. 1993; Pres. MIKE KAIRA.

Liberal Progressive Front (LPF): POB 31190, Lusaka; f. 1993; Leader ROGER CHONGWE.

Movement for Democratic Process (MDP): POB 90902, Luanshya; f. 1991.

Movement for Multi-party Democracy (MMD): Private Bag E365, 10101 Lusaka; f. 1990; governing party since Nov. 1991; Pres. FREDERICK CHILUBA; Sec. MICHAEL SATA.

Multi-Racial Party (MRP): POB 30971, Lusaka; f. 1999; Leader W. LESA.

National Democratic Alliance (NADA): Lusaka; f. 1991, deregistered Oct. 1998; Pres. YONAM PHIRI.

National Party (NP): POB 32399, Lusaka; f. 1993 by fmr mems of MMD; Pres. D. LISULO; Sec.-Gen. Dr LUDWIG SONDASHI.

National Party for Democracy (NPD): POB 30982, Lusaka; f. 1992; Pres. TENTHANI MWANZA.

National People's Salvation Party (NPSP): Lusaka; Pres. LUMBWE LAMBANYA.

New Democratic Party (NDP): Lusaka; f. 1995; Pres. DAVID LIMAKA.

Social Democratic Party (SDP): f. 2000.

United Democratic Congress Party: Lusaka; f. 1992; Leader DANIEL LISULO.

United National Independence Party (UNIP): POB 30302, Lusaka; tel. (1) 221197; fax (1) 221327; f. 1959; sole legal party 1972–90; Pres. FRANCIS NKHOMA; Sec.-Gen. TILYENJI KAUNDA.

United Party for National Development (UPND): POB 33199, Lusaka; f. 1998; Leader ANDERSON MAZOKA.

Unity Party for Democrats (UPD): PB RW 28, Ridgeway, Lusaka; f. 1997; Pres. MATHEW PIKITI.

Zambia Alliance for Progress (ZAP): Lusaka; f. 1999; opposition alliance ; Leader Dr NATHAS MUMBA; mems include:

    Labour Party (LP): POB 36870, Lusaka; f. 1992; Leader CHIBEZA MUFUNE.

    National Lima Party (NLP): POB 320015, Lusaka; f. 1996; Leader GUY SCOTT.

    National Citizenship Coalition.

Zambia Democratic Congress—Popular Front: Lusaka; f. 1998 by four mems of ZADECO; Chair. EDEN JERRY (acting).

Zambia Democratic Party (ZDP): POB 35856, Lusaka; f. 1998; Pres. SUSAN JERE.

Zambia Progressive Party (ZPP): POB 34927, Lusaka; f. 1993; Pres. AMBRAM ZAPU.

Diplomatic Representation

EMBASSIES AND HIGH COMMISSIONS IN ZAMBIA

Angola: Plot 108, Great East Rd, Northmead, POB 31595, 10101 Lusaka; tel. (1) 34764; fax (1) 221210; Ambassador: LOUIS DOUKUI PAULO DE CASTRO.

Botswana: 5201 Pandit Nehru Rd, Diplomatic Triangle, POB 31910, 10101 Lusaka; tel. (1) 250555; fax (1) 250804; High Commissioner: LAPOLOGANG CEASAR LEKOA.

Brazil: 74 Anglo-American Bldg, Independence Ave, POB 33300; tel. (1) 250400; fax (1) 251652; Chargé d'affaires a.i.: PAULO M. G. DE SOUSA.

Bulgaria: 4045 Lukulu Rd, Lusaka; tel. and fax (1) 263295; Chargé d'affaires a.i.: YULI MINCHEV.

Canada: Plot 5199, United Nations Ave, POB 31313, 10101 Lusaka; tel. (1) 250833; fax (1) 254176; e-mail isaka@paris03.x400.gc.ca; High Commissioner: DYLIS BUCKLEY JONES.

China, People's Republic: Plot 7430, United Nations Avenue, Longacres, POB 31975, 10101 Lusaka; tel. (1) 253770; fax (1) 251157; e-mail chinaemb@zamnet.zm; Ambassador: PENG KEYU.

Congo, Democratic Republic: Plot 1124, Parirenyatwa Rd, POB 31287, 10101 Lusaka; tel. (1) 235679; fax (1) 252080; e-mail congodr@zamnet.zm; Chargé d'affaires a.i.: NGOYI NGONGO LUNKAMBA.

Cuba: 5574 Mogoye Rd, Kalundu, POB 33132, 10101 Lusaka; tel. (1) 291308; fax (1) 291586; e-mail sikulem@zamnet.zm; Ambassador: NARCISO MARTIN MORA DIAZ.

Denmark: 18 Dunduza Chisidza Crescent, Prospect Hill, POB 50299, Lusaka; tel. (1) 254277; fax 254618; e-mail danemb@zamnet.zm; Ambassador: MADS SANDAU-JENSEN.

Egypt: Plot 5206, United Nations Ave, POB 32428, Lusaka; tel. R.i.(1) 253762; Ambassador: KHALED M. ALY OSMAN.

Finland: Haile Selassie Ave, opposite Ndeke House, Longacres, POB 50819, 15101 Lusaka; tel. (1) 251988; fax (1) 253783; e-mail finemb@zamnet.zm; internet www.zamnet.zm/zamnet/diplomatic/finland/finhome.htm; Chargé d'affaires a.i.: LEO OLASVIRTA.

France: Anglo-American Bldg, 4th Floor, 74 Independence Ave, POB 30062, 10101 Lusaka; tel. (1) 251322; fax (1) 254475; e-mail france@zamnet.zm; Ambassador: Jean-Louis Zoel.

Germany: Plot 5209, United Nations Ave, POB 50120, 15101 Ridgeway, Lusaka; tel. (1) 250644; fax (1) 254014; Ambassador: Dr Helmut Schröder.

Holy See: 283 Los Angeles Blvd, POB 31445, 10101 Lusaka; tel. (1) 251033; fax (1) 250601; e-mail nuntius@coppernet.zm; Apostolic Nuncio: Most Rev. Orlando Antonini, Titular Archbishop of Formia.

India: 1 Pandit Nehru Rd, POB 32111, 10101 Lusaka; tel. (1) 253158; fax (1) 254118; e-mail indiazam@zamnet.zm; internet www.zamnet.zm/zamnet/diplomatic/india/index.htm; High Commissioner: Ashok Kumar Attri.

Ireland: 6663 Katima Mulilo Rd, Olympia Park, POB 34923, 10101 Lusaka; tel. (1) 290650; Chargé d'affaires a.i.: John Neville.

Italy: Plot 5211, Embassy Park, Diplomatic Triangle, POB 31046, 10101 Lusaka; tel. (1) 250781; fax (1) 254929; e-mail italyzam@zamnet.zm; Ambassador: Dr Umberto Plaja.

Japan: Plot 5218, Haile Selassie Ave, POB 34190, 10101 Lusaka; tel. (1) 251555; fax (1) 253488; e-mail jez@zamnet.zm; Ambassador: Yoshihiro Nakamura.

Kenya: 5207 United Nations Ave, POB 50298, 10101 Lusaka; tel. (1) 250722; fax (1) 253829; e-mail kenhigh@zamnet.zm; High Commissioner: Esther Mshai Tolle.

Libya: 251 Ngwee Rd, off United Nations Ave, Longacres, POB 35319, 10101 Lusaka; tel. (1) 253055; fax (1) 251239; Ambassador: Khallifa Omar S. Alssawi.

Malawi: 31 Bishops Rd, Kabulonga, POB 50425, Lusaka; tel. (1) 213750; fax (1) 265765; e-mail mhc@zamnet.zm; High Commissioner: Rev. E. Chinkwita Phiri.

Mozambique: Kacha Rd, Plot 9592, POB 34877, 10101 Lusaka; tel. (1) 220333; fax (1) 220345; e-mail mozhclsk@zamnet.zm; High Commissioner: Dr Cristofa Inoque Jamo.

Namibia: 30B Mutende Rd, Woodlands, POB 30577, 10101 Lusaka; tel. (1) 260407; fax (1) 263858; e-mail namibia@zamtel.zam; High Commissioner: Frieda Nangula Ithete.

Netherlands: 5028 United Nations Ave, POB 31905, 10101 Lusaka; tel. (1) 253819; fax (1) 253733; Ambassador: Dr Karel P. M. De Beer.

Nigeria: 5208 Haile Selassie Ave, Longacres, POB 32598, 10101 Lusaka; tel. (1) 253177; fax (1) 253560; High Commissioner: Chief Ibironke O. Vaughan-Adefope.

Norway: cnr Birdcage Walk and Haile Selassie Ave, Longacres, POB 34570, 10101 Lusaka; tel. (1) 252188; fax (1) 253915; Ambassador: Jon K. A. Lomoey.

Portugal: 23 Yotam Muleya Rd, POB 33871, 10101 Lusaka; tel. (1) 253720; fax (1) 253896; Ambassador: Laura C. G. De Sousa.

Romania: 2 Leopard's Hill Rd, POB 31944, 10101 Lusaka; tel. (1) 262182; Chargé d'affaires a.i.: Corneliu Balan.

Russia: Plot 6407, Diplomatic Triangle, POB 32355, 10101 Lusaka; tel. (1) 252183; fax (1) 253582; Ambassador: Vladimir L. Boiko.

Saudi Arabia: 4896 Los Angeles Blvd, Longacres, POB 34411, 10101 Lusaka; tel. (1) 253266; fax (1) 253449; Chargé d'affaires a.i.: Ghorm Said Malhan.

Somalia: G3/377A Kabulonga Rd, POB 34051, Lusaka; tel. (1) 262119; Ambassador: Dr Oman Umal.

South Africa: D26, Cheetah Rd, Kabulonga, Private Bag W369, Lusaka; tel. (1) 260999; fax (1) 263001; e-mail sahc@zamnet.zm; High Commissioner: Themba Walter Thabethe.

Spain: Lusaka; Ambassador: Jesús Carlos Riosalido.

Sudan: 31 Ng'umbo Rd, Longacres, POB RW179X, 15200 Lusaka; tel. (1) 215570; fax (1) 40653; Ambassador: Abdallah Khidir Bashir.

Sweden: Haile Selassie Ave, POB 30788, 10101 Lusaka; tel. (1) 251711; fax (1) 254049; e-mail swedemb@zamnet.zm; internet www.swedemb.org.zm; Ambassador: Kristina Svensson.

Tanzania: Ujamaa House, Plot 5200, United Nations Ave, POB 31219, 10101 Lusaka; tel. (1) 253222; fax (1) 254861; e-mail tzreplsk@zamnet.zm; High Commissioner: Shani Omari Lweno.

United Kingdom: Plot 5201, Independence Ave, POB 50050, 15101 Ridgeway, Lusaka; tel. (1) 251133; fax (1) 253798; e-mail brithc@zamnet.zm; High Commissioner: Thomas Young.

USA: cnr Independence and United Nations Aves, POB 31617, 10101 Lusaka; tel. (1) 250955; fax (1) 252225; internet www.usemb.org.zm; Ambassador: David B. Dunn.

Yugoslavia: Plot 5216, Diplomatic Triangle, POB 31180, 10101 Lusaka; tel. (1) 250247; fax (1) 253843; e-mail yuemblus@zamnet.zm; Chargé d'affaires a.i.: Dusan Zupan.

Zimbabwe: 11058, Haile Selassie Ave, Longacres, POB 33491, 10101 Lusaka; tel. (1) 254012; fax (1) 227474; High Commissioner: Tirivafi John Kangai.

Judicial System

The judicial system of Zambia comprises a Supreme Court, composed of a Chief Justice, a Deputy Chief Justice and five Justices; a High Court comprising the Chief Justice and 30 Judges; Senior Resident and Resident Magistrates' Courts, which sit at various centres; and Local Courts, which deal principally with customary law, but which also have limited criminal jurisdiction.

Supreme Court of Zambia: Independence Ave, POB 50067, Ridgeway, Lusaka; tel. (1) 251330; fax (1) 251743; the final Court of Appeal.

Chief Justice: Mathew M. S. W. Ngulube.

Deputy Chief Justice: B. K. Bweupe.

Supreme Court Judges: E. L. Sakala, M. S. Chaila, E. K. Chirwa, W. M. Muzyamba, D. M. Lewanika.

Religion

CHRISTIANITY

Christian Council of Zambia: Church House, Cairo Rd, POB 30315, Lusaka; tel. (1) 224308; f. 1945; 17 mem. churches and 18 other Christian orgs; Chair. Rev. Thuma Hamukang'andu (Brethren in Christ Church); Gen. Sec. Violet Sampa-Bredt.

The Anglican Communion

Anglicans are adherents of the Church of the Province of Central Africa, covering Botswana, Malawi, Zambia and Zimbabwe. The Church comprises 12 dioceses, including four in Zambia. The Archbishop of the Province is the Bishop of Botswana. There are an estimated 40,000 adherents in Zambia.

Bishop of Central Zambia: Rt Rev. Clement Shaba, POB 70172, Ndola; fax (2) 615954.

Bishop of Eastern Zambia: Rt Rev. John Osmers, POB 510514, Chipata; fax (6) 221294; e-mail josmers@zamnet.zm.

Bishop of Lusaka: Rt Rev. Leonard Jameson Mwenda, Bishop's Lodge, POB 30183, Lusaka; fax (1) 262379.

Bishop of Northern Zambia: Rt Rev. Bernard Amos Malango, POB 20173, Kitwe; tel. (2) 223264; fax (2) 224778.

Protestant Churches

African Methodist Episcopal Church: POB 31478, Lusaka; tel. (1) 264013; 440 congregations, 880,000 mems; Presiding Elder Rev. L. Sichangwa.

Baptist Church: Lubu Rd, POB 30636, Lusaka; tel. (1) 253620.

Baptist Mission of Zambia: 3061/62 cnr Makishi and Great East Rds, POB 50599, 15101 Ridgeway, Lusaka; tel. (1) 222492; fax (1) 227520; e-mail bmzambia@zamnet.zm; .

Brethren in Christ Church: POB 630115, Choma; tel. (3) 20278; fax (3) 20127; e-mail bicczam@zamnet.zm; f. 1906; Bishop Rev. E. Shamapani; 142 congregations, 13,356 communicant mems.

Reformed Church of Zambia: POB 32301, Lusaka; tel. (1) 231206; f. 1899; African successor to the Dutch Reformed Church mission; 147 congregations, 400,000 mems.

Seventh-day Adventist Church: POB 31309, Lusaka; tel. (1) 255197; fax (1) 255191; e-mail zbu@zamnet.zm; 66,408 active mems.

United Church of Zambia: Synod Headquarters, Nationalist Rd at Burma Rd, POB 50122, Lusaka; tel. (1) 250641; f. 1965; c. 1m. mems; Synod Bishop Rev. Patrice Siyemeto; Gen. Sec. Rev. Silishebo Silishebo.

Other denominations active in Zambia include the Assemblies of God, the Church of Christ, the Church of the Nazarene, the Evangelical Fellowship of Zambia, the Kimbanguist Church, the Presbyterian Church of Southern Africa, the Religious Society of Friends (Quakers) and the United Pentecostal Church.

The Roman Catholic Church

Zambia comprises two archdioceses and eight dioceses. At 31 December 1998 there were an estimated 2,835,222 adherents in the country, equivalent to 29.1% of the total population.

Bishops' Conference: Zambia Episcopal Conference, Catholic Secretariat, Unity House, cnr Freedom Way and Katunjila Rd, POB 31965, Lusaka; tel. (1) 212070; fax (1) 220996; e-mail zec@zamnet.zm; f. 1984; Pres. Most Rev. Medardo Mazombwe, Archbishop of Lusaka; Sec.-Gen. Rev. Ignatius Mwebe.

Archbishop of Kasama: Most Rev. James Spaita, Archbishop's House, POB 410143, Kasama; tel. (4) 221248; fax (4) 222202.

Archbishop of Lusaka: Most Rev. Medardo Joseph Mazombwe, 41 Wamulwa Rd, POB 32754, Lusaka; tel. (1) 239257; fax (1) 290631.

ISLAM

There are about 10,000 members of the Muslim Association in Zambia.

BAHÁ'Í FAITH

National Spiritual Assembly: Sekou Touré Rd, Plot 4371, Private Bag RW227X, Ridgeway 15102, Lusaka; tel. and fax (1) 254505; e-mail nsa@zamnet.zm; Sec. DAVID SMITH; mems resident in 1,456 localities.

The Press

DAILIES

The Post: POB 352, Lusaka; tel. (1) 231092; fax (1) 229271; f. 1991; independent; Editor-in-Chief FRED M'MEMBE; circ. 29,000.

The Times of Zambia: POB 30394, Lusaka; tel. (1) 229067; fax (1) 222880; e-mail times@zamnet.zm; f. 1943; govt-owned; English; Man. Editor CYRUS SIKAZWE; circ. 65,000.

Zambia Daily Mail: POB 31421, Lusaka; tel. (1) 211722; fax (1) 225881; f. 1968; govt-owned; English; Man. Editor EMMANUEL NYIRENDA; circ. 40,000.

PERIODICALS

African Social Research: Institute of Economic and Social Research, University of Zambia, POB 32379, Lusaka; tel. (1) 294131; fax (1) 253952; f. 1944; 2 a year; Editor MUBANGA E. KASHOKI; circ. 1,000.

Chipembele Magazine: POB 30255, Lusaka; tel. (1) 254226; 6 a year; publ. by Wildlife Conservation Soc. of Zambia; circ. 20,000.

Chronicle: Lusaka; bi-weekly; independent.

Farming in Zambia: POB 50197, Lusaka; tel. (1) 213551; f. 1965; quarterly; publ. by Ministry of Agriculture, Food and Fisheries; Editor L. P. CHIRWA; circ. 3,000.

Icengelo: Chifubu Rd, POB 71581, Ndola; tel. (2) 680456; fax (2) 680484; e-mail mpress@zamnet.zm; f. 1970; monthly; Bemba; social, educational and religious; Roman Catholic; edited by Franciscan friars; circ. 40,000.

Imbila: POB RW20, Lusaka; tel. (1) 217254; f. 1953; monthly; publ. by Zambia Information Services; Bemba; Editor D. MUKAKA; circ. 20,000.

Intanda: POB RW20, Lusaka; tel. (1) 219675; f. 1958; monthly; general; publ. by Zambia Information Services; Tonga; Editor J. SIKAULU; circ. 6,000.

Journal of Adult Education: University of Zambia, POB 50516, Lusaka; tel. (1) 216767; f. 1982; Exec. Editor FRANCIS KASOMA.

Leisure Magazine: Lusaka; general interest.

Liseli: POB RW20, Lusaka; tel. (1) 219675; monthly; publ. by Zambia Information Services; Lozi; Editor F. AMNSAA; circ. 8,000.

Lukanga News: POB 919, Kabwe; tel. (5) 217254; publ. by Zambia Information Services; Lenje; Editor J. H. N. NKOMANGA; circ. 5,500.

Mining Mirror: POB 71505, Ndola; tel. (2) 640133; f. 1973; monthly; English; Editor (vacant); circ. 15,000.

National Mirror: Bishops Rd, Kabulonga, POB 320199, Lusaka; tel. (1) 261193; fax (1) 263050; f. 1972; weekly; publ. by Multimedia Zambia; Editor FANWELL CHEMBO; circ. 40,000.

Ngoma: POB RW20, Lusaka; tel. (1) 219675; monthly; Lunda, Kaonde and Luvale; publ. by Zambia Information Services; Editor B. A. LUHILA; circ. 3,000.

Orbit: POB RW18X, Lusaka; tel. (1) 254915; f. 1971; publ. by Ministry of Education; children's educational magazine; Editor ELIDAH CHISHA; circ. 65,000.

Speak Out: POB 70244, Ndola; tel. (2) 612241; fax (2) 610556; f. 1984; bi-monthly; Christian; circ. 40,000.

The Sportsman: Lusaka; tel. (1) 224250; f. 1980; monthly; Man. Editor SAM SIKAZWE; circ. 18,000.

The Sun: Lusaka.

Sunday Express: Lusaka; f. 1991; weekly; Man. Editor JOHN MUKELA.

Sunday Times of Zambia: POB 30394, Lusaka; tel. (1) 229076; fax (1) 222880; f. 1965; owned by UNIP; English; Man. Editor ARTHUR SIMUCHOBA; circ. 78,000.

Tsopano: POB RW20, Lusaka; tel. (1) 217254; f. 1958; monthly; publ. by Zambia Information Services; Nyanja; Editor S. S. BANDA; circ. 9,000.

Voters' Voice: Lusaka; monthly; independent.

Workers' Challenge: POB 270035, Kitwe; tel. and fax (2) 220904; f. 1981; 2 a month; publ. by the Workers' Pastoral Centre; English and Bemba; Co-Editors Fr MISHECK KAUNDA, JUSTIN CHILUFYA; circ. 16,000.

Workers' Voice: POB 652, Kitwe; tel. (2) 211999; f. 1972; fortnightly; publ. by Zambia Congress of Trade Unions.

Youth: POB 30302, Lusaka; tel. (1) 211411; f. 1974; quarterly; publ. by UNIP Youth League; Editor-in-Chief N. ANAMELA; circ. 20,000.

Zambia Government Gazette: POB 30136, Lusaka; tel. (1) 228724; fax (1) 224486; f. 1911; weekly; English; official notices.

NEWS AGENCY

Zambia News Agency (ZANA): Mass Media Complex, POB 30007, Lusaka; tel. (1) 219673; Editor-in-Chief DAVID KASHWEKA.

Foreign Bureaux

Agence France-Presse: POB 33805, Lusaka; tel. (1) 212959; Bureau Chief ABBE MAINE.

Informatsionnoye Telegrafnoye Agentstvo Rossii—Telegrafnoye Agentstvo Suverennykh Stran (ITAR—TASS) (Russia): POB 33394, Lusaka; tel. (1) 254201; Correspondent ANDREY K. POLYAKOV.

Reuters (UK): 3rd Floor, Woodgate House, Cairo Rd, POB 31685, Lusaka; tel. (1) 253430; fax (1) 235698; e-mail manoah@reuters.com.zm; Senior Correspondent MANOAH ESIPISU.

Rossiiskoye Informatsionnoye Agentstvo—Novosti (RIA—Novosti) (Russia): Lusaka; tel. (1) 252849; Rep. VIKTOR LAPTUKHIN.

Xinhua (New China) News Agency (People's Republic of China): United Nations Ave, POB 31859, Lusaka; tel. (1) 252227; fax (1) 251708; e-mail wang@zamnet.zm; Chief Correspondent DU ZHEN-FENG.

PRESS ASSOCIATION

Press Association of Zambia (PAZA): c/o The Times of Zambia, POB 30394, Lusaka; tel. (1) 229076; f. 1983; Chair. ROBINSON MAKAYI.

Publishers

Africa: Literature Centre, POB 21319, Kitwe; tel. (2) 210765; fax (2) 210716; e-mail alc@zamnet.zm; general, educational, religious; Dir JACKSON MBEWE.

African Social Research: Institute of Economic and Social Research, University of Zambia, POB 32379, Lusaka; tel. (1) 294131; fax (1) 253952; social research in Africa; Editor MUBANGA E. KASHOKI.

Daystar Publications Ltd: POB 32211, Lusaka; f. 1966; religious; Man. Dir S. E. M. PHEKO.

Directory Publishers of Zambia Ltd: POB 30963, Lusaka; tel. (1) 233404; fax (1) 289738; f. 1958; trade directories; Gen. Man. W. D. WRATTEN.

Multimedia Zambia: Woodlands, POB 320199, Lusaka; tel. (1) 263864; fax (1) 264117; f. 1971; religious and educational books, audio-visual materials; Exec. Dir JUMBE NGOMA.

University of Zambia Press: POB 32379, 10101 Lusaka; tel. (1) 213221; fax (1) 253952; f. 1938; academic books, papers and journals.

Zambia Educational Publishing House: Chishango Rd, POB 32708, 10101 Lusaka; tel. (1) 222324; fax (1) 225073; f. 1967; educational and general; Dir H. M. CHIPEWO.

Zambia Printing Co Ltd: POB 34798, 10101 Lusaka; tel. (1) 227673; fax (1) 225026; Gen. Man. BERNARD LUBUMBASHI.

Government Publishing Houses

Government Printer: POB 30136, Lusaka; tel. (1) 228724; fax (1) 224486; official documents and statistical bulletins.

Zambia Information Services: POB 50020, Lusaka; tel. (1) 219673; state-controlled; Dir BENSON SIANGA.

PUBLISHERS' ASSOCIATION

Booksellers' and Publishers' Association of Zambia: POB 31838, Lusaka; tel. (1) 222647; fax (1) 225195; Chair. RAY MUNAMWIMBU; Sec. BASIL MBEWE.

Broadcasting and Communications

TELECOMMUNICATIONS

Mobile cellular telephone networks are operated by Télécel Zambia and Zamcell.

Zambia Telecommunications Co Ltd (ZAMTEL): Provident House, POB 71630, Ndola; tel. (2) 611111; fax (2) 615855; transfer to private sector pending; Man. Dir AVDHESH KUMAR.

BROADCASTING

Radio

Zambia National Broadcasting Corporation: Broadcasting House, POB 50015, Lusaka; tel. (1) 254989; fax (1) 254317; e-mail zambroad@zamtel.zm; f. 1961; state-controlled; radio services in English and seven Zambian languages; Dir-Gen. DUNCAN H. MBAZIMA.

Educational Broadcasting Services: Headquarters: POB 50231, Lusaka; tel. (1) 251724; radio broadcasts from Lusaka; audio-visual aids service from POB 50295, Lusaka; Controller MICHAEL MULOMBE.

Radio Phoenix: Private Bag E702, Lusaka; tel. (1) 226652; fax (1) 226839; commercial; Man. Dir ERROL HICKEY.

Christian Voice (Rlg.): Private Bag E606, Lusaka; tel. (1) 274251; fax (1) 274526; e-mail cvoice@zamnet.zm.

Television

In mid-1997 plans were announced for the transmission of two Egyptian satellite television channels in Zambia.

Zambia National Broadcasting Corporation: (see Radio); television services in English.

Educational Broadcasting Services: POB 21106, Kitwe; television for schools; Controller MICHAEL MULOMBE.

Finance

(cap. = capital; auth. = authorized; res = reserves; dep. = deposits; m. = million; br. = branch; amounts in kwacha)

BANKING

As from 30 June 1996 all banks operating in Zambia were required to have capital of not less than K2,000m. in order to receive a banking licence or to continue to function.

Central Bank

Bank of Zambia: Bank Square, Cairo Rd, POB 30080, 10101 Lusaka; tel. (1) 228888; fax (1) 221722; internet www.boz.zm; f. 1964; bank of issue; cap. and res 2,503m., dep. 471,010.6m. (Dec. 1996); Gov. JACOB MWANZA; Gen. Man. GODFREY MBULO; br. in Ndola.

Commercial Banks

Finance Bank Zambia Ltd: 2101 Chanik House, Cairo Rd, POB 37102, 10101 Lusaka; tel. (1) 229733; fax (1) 227544; e-mail finbank@zamnet.zm; f. 1986; cap. and res 5,995m., dep. 65,883m. (Dec. 1996); Chair. Dr R. L. MAHTANI; Man. Dir M. WADOOD; 27 brs.

National Savings and Credit Bank of Zambia: Plot 248B, Cairo Rd, POB 30067, Lusaka; tel. (1) 227534; fax (1) 223296; e-mail natsave@zamnet.zm; internet www.webnet.co.zm/nscb.htm; f. 1972; dep. 5,000m. (Dec. 1997); Man. Dir B. K. E. N'GANDU.

New Capital Bank: Lotti House, First Floor, Cairo Rd, POB 36452, Lusaka; tel. (1) 229508; fax (1) 224055; e-mail ncapital@zamnet.zm; f. 1992; cap. 1,000m. (Dec. 1999); Chair. W. D. MUNG'OMBA; Gen. Man. J. J. DE BEER.

Union Bank Zambia Ltd: Zimco House, Cairo Rd, POB 34940, Lusaka; tel. (1) 229392; fax (1) 221866; e-mail union.lsk@zamnet.zm; cap. and res 3,739.7m., total assets 33,748.9m. (Dec. 1997); Chair. J. R. NAYEE; Man. Dir L. CHONGO.

Zambia National Commercial Bank Ltd: Plot 33454, Cairo Rd, POB 33611, Lusaka; tel. (1) 228979; fax (1) 223106; e-mail admin@mars.zanaco.co.zm; internet www.mars.zanaco.co.zm; f. 1969; govt-controlled; cap. and res 24,443.5m., total assets 364,110.9m. (Dec. 1998); Chair. S. L. SHIMUKOWA; Man. Dir SAMUEL MUSONDA; 41 brs.

Foreign Banks

Barclays Bank of Zambia Ltd (UK): Kafue House, Cairo Rd, POB 31936, Lusaka; tel. (1) 228858; fax (1) 226185; e-mail bbzcomb@zamnet.zm; f. 1971; cap. and res 26,180m., dep. 242,410m. (Dec. 1998); Chair. A. B. MUNYAMA; Man. Dir R. I. A. KNAPMAN; 32 brs.

Citibank Zambia Ltd (USA): Citibank House, Cha Cha Cha Rd, POB 30037, Southend, Lusaka; tel. (1) 229025; fax (1) 226258; f. 1979; cap. 521.2m., dep. 38,862m. (Dec. 1996); Man. Dir SURINIVASAN SRIDHAR; 1 br.

Indo-Zambia Bank (IZB): Plot 6907, Cairo Rd, POB 35411, Lusaka; tel. and fax (1) 225080; e-mail izb@zamnet.zm; f. 1984; cap. and res 4,017.4m., dep. 20,847.4m. (March 1997); Chair. Prof. B. MWEENE; Man. Dir K. C. MEHTA; 7 brs.

Stanbic Bank Zambia Ltd: Woodgate House, 6th Floor, Nairobi Place, Cairo Rd, POB 31955, Lusaka; tel. (1) 229071; fax (1) 221152; e-mail stanbic@zamnet.zm; internet www.stanbic.co.zm; f. 1971; wholly-owned by Standard Bank Investment Corpn; cap. and res. 11,916.1m., total assets 101,168.7m. (Sept. 1999); Chair. D. A. R. PHIRI; Man. Dir A. H. S. MACLEOD; 7 brs.

Standard Chartered Bank Zambia Ltd (UK): Standard House, Cairo Rd, POB 32238, Lusaka; tel. (1) 229242; fax (1) 222092; e-mail jtembo@scbzamb; f. 1971; cap. and res 11,907m., dep. 118,999m. (Dec. 1997); Chair. A. K. MAZOKA; Man. Dir J. A. H. JANES; 15 brs.

Development Banks

Development Bank of Zambia: Development House, Katondo St, POB 33955, Lusaka; tel. (1) 228576; fax (1) 222426; e-mail dbzcom@zamnet.zm; internet www.dbz.co.zm; f. 1973; 99% state-owned; provides medium- and long-term loans and administers special funds placed at its disposal; cap. and res 7,580.0m., total assets 145,976.6m. (March 1998); Chair. J. M. MTONGA; Man. Dir DIPAK MALIK; 2 brs.

Lima Bank: Kulima House, Cha Cha Cha Rd, Lusaka; tel. (1) 213111; fax (1) 228077; cap. 57m. (March 1986); Chair. N. MUKUTU; Man. Dir K. V. KASAPATU.

Zambia Agricultural Development Bank: Society House, Cairo Rd, POB 30847, Lusaka; tel. (1) 219251; f. 1982; loan finance for development of agriculture and fishing; auth. cap. 75m.; Chair. K. MAKASA; Man. Dir AMON CHIBIYA.

Zambia Export and Import Bank Ltd: Society House, Cairo Rd, POB 33046, Lusaka; tel. (1) 229486; fax (1) 222313; f. 1987; state-owned; privatization pending in 1998; cap. 50m. (March 1992), dep. 50.9m. (March 1990); Man. Dir. LIKANDO NAWA.

STOCK EXCHANGE

Lusaka Stock Exchange: Stock Exchange Bldg, Cairo Rd, Private Bag E73, Lusaka; tel. (1) 228391; fax (1) 225969; e-mail luse@zamnet.zm; f. 1994; Chair. THOMAS F. RYAN; Gen. Man. CHARLES MATE.

INSURANCE

Zambia State Insurance Corporation Ltd: Premium House, Independence Ave, POB 30894, Lusaka; tel. (1) 229343; fax (1) 222263; f. 1968; took over all insurance business in Zambia in 1971; transfer to private sector pending; Chair. E. WILLIMA; Man. Dir ABEL PHIRI.

Trade and Industry

GOVERNMENT AGENCIES

National Import and Export Corporation (NIEC): National Housing Authority Bldg, Lusaka; tel. (1) 2288018; fax (1) 252771; f. 1974.

Zambia Investment Centre: Ndeke House, POB 34580, Lusaka; tel. (1) 252130; fax (1) 252150; e-mail invest@zamnet.zm; Dir Gen. BWALYKA NG'ANDU.

Zambia Privatization Agency: Privatization House, Nasser Rd, POB 30819, Lusaka; tel. (1) 223859; fax (1) 225270; e-mail zpa@zamnet.zm; f. 1992; responsible for the divestment of various state-owned enterprises; CEO VALENTINE CHITALU.

DEVELOPMENT ORGANIZATIONS

Industrial Development Corporation of Zambia Ltd (INDECO): Indeco House, Buteko Place, Lusaka; tel. (1) 228463; fax (1) 228868; f. 1960; auth. cap. K300m.; c. 47 subsidiaries and assoc. cos in brewing, chemicals, property, manufacturing, agriculture and vehicle assembly; Chair. R. L. BWALYA; Man. Dir S. K. TAMELÉ.

Small Industries Development Organization (SIDO): Sido House, Cairo Rd, POB 35373, Lusaka; tel. (1) 229707; fax (1) 224284; e-mail sido@zamnet.zm; f. 1981 to promote development of small and village industries.

CHAMBERS OF COMMERCE

Lusaka Chamber of Commerce and Industry: POB 30844, Lusaka; tel. (1) 252369; f. 1933; Chair. R. D. PENZA; Sec. Dr E. BBENKELE; 400 mems.

Zambia Confederation of Chambers of Commerce and Industry: Chair. GEORGE CHABWERA.

INDUSTRIAL AND TRADE ASSOCIATIONS

Copper Industry Service Bureau Ltd: POB 22100, Kitwe; tel. (2) 214122; f. 1941 as Chamber of Mines.

The Dairy Produce Board of Zambia: Kwacha House, Cairo Rd, POB 30124, Lusaka; tel.(1) 214770; f. 1964; purchase and supply of dairy products to retailers, manufacture and marketing of milk products.

Metal Marketing Corporation (Zambia) Ltd (MEMACO): Memaco House, Sapele Rd, POB 35570, Lusaka; tel. (1) 228131; fax (1) 223671; f. 1973; sole sales agents for all metal and mineral production; Chair. R. L. BWALYA; Man. Dir U. M. MUTATI.

Tobacco Board of Zambia: POB 31963, Lusaka; tel. (1) 288995; Sec. J. M. CHIZUNI.

Zambia Association of Manufacturers: POB 240312, Ndola; tel. (2) 619296; fax (2) 619297; e-mail shyams@zamnet.zm; f. 1985; Chair. RICHARD P. HEALEY; Sec. MIKE G. PURSLOW; 180 mems.

Zambia Confederation of Industries and Chambers of Commerce: POB 30844, Lusaka; tel. (1) 252369; fax (1) 252483; f. 1938; Chair. R. D. Frost; CEO Theo Bull; 2,000 mems.

Zambia Farm Employers' Association: Farmers' Village, Lusaka Agricultural and Commercial Showgrounds, POB 30395, Lusaka; tel. (1) 252649; fax (1) 252648; e-mail znfu@zamnet.zm; Chair. M. Mugala; Vice-Chair. R. Clyde-Anderson; 350 mems.

Zambia Seed Producers' Association: POB 30013, Lusaka; tel. (1) 223249; fax (1) 223249; f. 1964; Chair. Barry Coxe; 300 mems.

UTILITIES

Electricity

Zambia Electricity Supply Corporation (Zesco): Stand 6949, Great East Rd, POB 33304, Lusaka; tel. (1) 223970; fax (1) 239343; transfer to private sector pending in 2000; Man. Dir Robinson Mwansa.

MAJOR COMPANIES

The following are among the largest companies in terms either of capital investment or employment. The government traditionally has a controlling interest in major strategic industries, but it instituted a privatization programme in 1992.

Chilanga Cement PLC: Head Office: POB 32639, 10101 Lusaka; tel. (1) 278501; fax (1) 252655; e-mail chilcem@zamnet.zm; f. 1949; works at Chilanga and Ndola; manufacture and marketing of cement. CEO Patrick R. Gorman; Finance Man./Co. Sec. Terence A. Mordue; 750 employees.

Dunlop Zambia Ltd: POB 71650, Ndola; tel. (2) 650792; fax (2) 650592; f. 1964; cap. K563m.; transfer to private sector under way in 1998; mfrs and distributors of car, truck, tractor, earthmover and mining as well as cycle tyres and tubes; also of contact adhesives, floor tiles and other allied rubber products; Operations Man. K. Chundu; 40 employees.

Kafue Textiles of Zambia Ltd: POB 360131, Kafue; tel. (1) 311501; fax (1) 311514; e-mail ktzambia@zamnet.zm; f. 1969; 99.9% of shares owned by state; transfer to private sector pending in 1998; mfrs of drills, denims, twills and poplins; dress prints and African prints; industrial and household textiles; Gen. Man. and CEO J. P. Bondaz; 600 employees.

Minestone (Zambia) Ltd: POB 31870 Lusaka; tel. (1) 228748; fax (1) 222301; e-mail mineston@zamnet.zm; f. 1954; cap. K1.9m.; building, civil and mechanical contractors; Gen. Man. D. J. C. O'Leary; 3,900 employees.

National Milling Co Ltd: Box 20646, Kitwe; tel. (2) 3304.

Nitrogen Chemicals of Zambia Ltd: POB 360226, Kafue; tel. (1) 312179; fax (1) 321706; f. 1967; cap. K509m.; 51% shareholding to be transferred to private sector in 2000; production of ammonium nitrate for fertilizer and explosives, nitric acid, ammonium sulphate, sulphuric acid, methanol, compound fertilizers and liquid carbon dioxide; Chair. Dr A. J. C. Sichinga; Interim Man. R. P. Healey; 950 employees.

Non-Ferrous Metal Works (Zambia) Ltd: Box 72283, Ndola; tel. (2) 651603; fax (2) 651777; e-mail nfmz@zamnet.zm.

ROP Ltd: POB 71570, Nakambala Rd, Ndola; tel. (2) 650549; fax (2) 650162; f. 1975 by merger of Refined Oil Products Ltd and Lever Brothers, Zambia; mfrs of soaps, detergents, toilet preparations and edible oils; Gen. Man. (vacant).

Zambezi Sawmills (1968) Ltd: POB 60041, Livingstone; tel. (3) 322853; fax (3) 322853; subsidiary of ZIMCO; sawmillers and mfrs of railway sleepers, mining timbers, sawn timber, wooden parquet tiles, etc.

Zambia Breweries Ltd: POB 70091, Ndola, 74 Independence Ave, Lusaka; tel. (1) 3601; f. 1951, opened in Lusaka 1966; reorg. 1994; cap. K5.6m.; brewing, bottling and distribution of lager beers; Gen. Man. Zacks Musonda; 1,300 employees.

Zambia Consolidated Copper Mines Ltd (ZCCM): 5309 Dedan Kimathi Rd, POB 30048, Lusaka; tel. (1) 229115; fax 221057; f. 1982 by merger of Nchanga Consolidated Copper Mines and Roan Consolidated Mines; auth. cap. K900m.; Chair. S. L. Shimukowa; CEO Edward Shamutete; 26,000 employees.

CO-OPERATIVES

Zambia Co-operative Federation Ltd: Co-operative House, Chachacha Rd, POB 33579, Lusaka; tel. (1) 220157; fax (1) 222516; agricultural marketing; supply of agricultural chemicals and implements; cargo haulage; insurance; agricultural credit; auditing and accounting; property and co-operative development; Chair. B. Tetamashimba; Man. Dir G. Z. Sibale.

TRADE UNIONS

Zambia Congress of Trade Unions: POB 20652, Kitwe; tel. (2) 211999; f. 1965; 18 affiliated unions; c. 400,000 mems; Pres. Jackson Shamenda; Sec.-Gen. Alec Chiorma.

Affiliated Unions

Airways and Allied Workers' Union of Zambia: POB 30272, Lusaka; Pres. F. Mulenga; Gen. Sec. B. Chinyanta.

Guards Union of Zambia: POB 21882, Kitwe; tel. (2) 216189; f. 1972; 13,500 mems; Chair. D. N. S. Silungwe; Gen. Sec. Michael S. Simfukwe.

Hotel Catering Workers' Union of Zambia: POB 35693, Lusaka; 9,000 mems; Chair. Ian Mkandawire; Gen. Sec. Stoic Kaputu.

Mineworkers' Union of Zambia: POB 20448, Kitwe; tel. (2) 214022; 50,000 mems; Chair. (vacant); Sec.-Gen. Ernest Mwansa.

National Union of Building, Engineering and General Workers: POB 21515, Kitwe; tel. (2) 213931; 18,000 mems; Chair. Luciano Mutale (acting); Gen. Sec. P. N. Nzima.

National Union of Commercial and Industrial Workers: 87 Gambia Ave, POB 21735, Kitwe; tel. (2) 228607; f. 1982; 16,000 mems; Chair. I. M. Kasumbu; Gen. Sec. G. F. Mwase.

National Union of Communications Workers: Buteko House, Ground Floor, POB 70751, Ndola; tel. (2) 611345; 6,000 mems; Pres. Neddy Nzowa; Gen. Sec. Newton Mweetwa.

National Union of Plantation and Agricultural Workers: POB 80529, Kabwe; tel. (5) 224548; 15,155 mems; Chair. Alex Msango; Gen. Sec. Bernadette Chimfwembe.

National Union of Public Services' Workers: POB 32523, Lusaka; tel. (1) 215167; Chair. W. Chipasha; Gen. Sec. Willie Mbewe.

National Union of Transport and Allied Workers: Lusaka; tel. (1) 214756; Chair. B. Mulwe; Gen. Sec. L. K. Mabuluki.

Railway Workers' Union of Zambia: POB 80302, Kabwe; tel. (5) 224006; 10,228 mems; Chair. H. K. Ndamana; Gen. Sec. Calvin J. Mukabaila.

University of Zambia and Allied Workers' Union: POB 32379, Lusaka; tel. (1) 213221; f. 1968; Chair. Beriate Sunkutu; Gen. Sec. Saini Phiri.

Zambia Electricity Workers' Union: POB 70859, Ndola; f. 1972; 3,000 mems; Chair. Cosmas Mpampi; Gen. Sec. Adam Kaluba.

Zambia National Farmers' Union: Lusaka Agricultural and Commercial Showgrounds, POB 30395, Lusaka; tel. (1) 252649; fax (1) 252648; e-mail znfu@zamnet.zm; internet www.znfu.org.zm; Exec. Dir Songowayo Zyambo.

Zambia National Union of Teachers: POB 31914, Lusaka; tel. (1) 216670; 2,120 mems; Chair. Jackson Mulenga; Gen. Sec. A. W. Chibale.

Zambia Typographical Workers' Union: Ndola; Chair. R. Shikwata; Gen. Sec. D. Nawa.

Zambia Union of Financial Institutions and Allied Workers: POB 31174, Lusaka; tel. (1) 219401; Chair. B. Chikoti; Gen. Sec. Geoffrey Alikipo.

Zambia Union of Local Government Officers: f. 1997; Pres. Isaac Mwanza.

Zambia Union of Skilled Mineworkers: f. 1998; Chair. Alex Moloi.

Zambia United Local Authorities Workers' Union: POB 70575, Ndola; tel. (2) 615022; Chair. A. M. Mutakila; Gen. Sec. A. H. Mudenda.

Principal Non-Affiliated Unions

Civil Servants' Union of Zambia: POB 50160, Lusaka; tel. (1) 221332; f. 1975; 26,000 mems; Chair. W. D. Phiri; Gen. Sec. J. C. Moonde.

Zambian African Mining Union: Kitwe; f. 1967; 40,000 mems.

Transport

RAILWAYS

Total length of railways in Zambia was 2,164 km (including 891 km of the Tanzania–Zambia railway) in 1996. There are two major railway lines: the Zambia Railways network, which traverses the country from the Copperbelt in northern Zambia and links with the National Railways of Zimbabwe to provide access to South African ports, and the Tanzania–Zambia Railway (Tazara) system, linking New Kapiri-Mposhi in Zambia with Dar es Salaam in Tanzania. The Tazara railway line increased its capacity from 1976, in order to reduce the dependence of southern African countries on trade routes through South Africa. In April 1987 the Governments of Zambia, Angola and Zaire (now the Democratic Republic of the Congo) declared their intention to reopen the Benguela railway, linking Zambian copper-mines with the Angolan port of Lobito, following its closure to international traffic in 1975 as a result of the guerrilla insurgency in Angola. In 1997 a programme of repairs was begun, with the aim of permitting the resumption of freight traffic within a three-year period.

Tanzania–Zambia Railway Authority (Tazara): POB T01, Mpika; tel. (4) 370397; fax (4) 370228; Head Office: POB 2834, Dar es Salaam, Tanzania; tel. 860340; f. 1975; operates passenger and freight services linking New Kapiri-Mposhi, north of Lusaka, with Dar es Salaam in Tanzania, a distance of 1,860 km, of which 891 km is in Zambia; jtly owned and administered by the Tanzanian and Zambian Govts; a 10-year rehabilitation programme, assisted by the USA and EC countries, began in 1985; it was announced in 1990 that a line linking the railway with the Zambian port of Mpulungu was to be constructed; Chair. SALIM MSOMA; Man. Dir K. MKANDAWIRE.

Zambia Railways Ltd: cnr Buntungwa St and Ghana Ave, POB 80935, Kabwe; tel. (5) 222201; fax (5) 224411; e-mail zamrail@ zamnet.zm; f. 1967; management assumed in 1998 by Hifab International AB (Sweden) in consortium with DE Consult (Germany); Chair. CHIFUMU K. BANDA; Man. Dir ROBERT C. CRAWFORD.

ROADS

In 1997 there was a total road network of 66,781 km, including 7,081 km of main roads and 13,700 km of secondary roads. The main arterial roads run from Beit Bridge (Zimbabwe) to Tunduma (the Great North Road), through the copper-mining area to Chingola and Chililabombwe (hitherto the Zaire Border Road), from Livingstone to the junction of the Kafue river and the Great North Road, and from Lusaka to the Malawi border (the Great East Road). In 1984 the 300-km BotZam highway linking Kazungula with Nata, in Botswana, was formally opened. A 1,930-km main road (the TanZam highway) links Zambia and Tanzania. In 1997 the Government initiated a 10-year Road Sector Investment Programme with funding from the World Bank.

Department of Roads: POB 50003, Lusaka; tel. (1) 253088; fax (1) 253404; Dir of Roads T. NGOMA.

SHIPPING

Zambia National Shipping Line: Lusaka; f. 1989; state-owned; cargo and passenger services from Dar es Salaam in Tanzania to northern Europe; Gen. Man. MARTIN PHIRI.

CIVIL AVIATION

In 1984 there were 127 airports, aerodromes and air strips. An international airport, 22.5 km from Lusaka, was opened in 1967.

National Air Charters (Z) Ltd (NAC): POB 33650, Lusaka; tel. (1) 229774; fax (1) 229778; f. 1973; air cargo services; Gen. Man. STAFFORD MUDIYO.

Zambia Skyways (Eastern Air): Lusaka Airport, POB 32661, Lusaka; tel. (1) 233097; fax (1) 233724; internet 196.36.240.13/ zambia/easternair.htm; f. 1995; operates scheduled passenger services to domestic destinations, South Africa, Malawi, and Tanzania; Man. Dir YOOSUF ZUMLA.

Zambia Airways: Lusaka International Airport, POB 310277, Lusaka; tel. (1) 271230; fax (1) 271054; e-mail roanhq@zamnet.zm; internet www.africa-insites.com/zambia/roanair.htm; f. 1988 as Roanair, changed to current name in 1999; operates domestic and regional routes; CEO GREGORY HAVERMAHL.

Tourism

Zambia's main tourist attractions are its wildlife, unspoilt scenery and diverse cultural heritage; there are 19 national parks. In 1998 362,000 tourists visited Zambia and tourism receipts totalled an estimated US $74.7m.

Zambia National Tourist Board: Century House, Lusaka Sq., POB 30017, Lusaka; tel. (1) 229089; fax (1) 225174; e-mail zntb@zamnet.zm; internet www.africa-insites.com/zambia; Chair. ROMANCE C. SAMPA; CEO AGNES SEENKA.

Zambia Tourism Council: Lusaka; Dep. Pres. BRUCE CHAPMAN.

Defence

In August 1999 Zambia's armed forces officially numbered about 21,600 (army 20,000, airforce 1,600). Paramilitary forces numbered 1,400. Military service is voluntary. There is also a national defence force, responsible to the government.

Defence Expenditure: K186,000m. allocated for 1999.

Commander of the Army: Brig.-Gen. NOBLE SIMBEYE.

Commander of the Air Force: Lt-Gen. RONNIE SIKAPAWASHA.

Education

Between 1964 and 1979 enrolment in schools increased by more than 260%. Primary education, which is compulsory, begins at seven years of age and lasts for seven years. Secondary education, beginning at the age of 14, lasts for a further five years, comprising a first cycle of two years and a second of three years. In 1995 75% of children (76% of boys; 75% of girls) in the relevant age-group attended primary schools, and enrolment at secondary schools in 1994 was equivalent to 27% of children (34% of boys; 21% of girls) in the relevant age-group. There are two universities: the University of Zambia at Lusaka, and the Copperbelt University at Kitwe (which is to be transferred to Ndola). There are 14 teacher training colleges. In 1995, according to estimates by UNESCO, the average rate of adult illiteracy was 26.8% (males 18.0%; females 34.9%). Of total budgetary expenditure by the central government in 1996, education was allocated K95,925m. (8.7%).

Bibliography

Akashambatwa, M.-L. *Milk in a Basket: The Political-Economic Malaise in Zambia*. Lusaka, Zambia Research Foundation, 1990.

Clark, J., and Allison, C. *Zambia: Debt and Poverty*. Oxford, Oxfam, 1989.

Crehan, K. *The Fractured Community: Landscapes of Power and Gender in Rural Zambia*. Berkeley, University of California Press, 1997.

Daloz, J.-P., and Chileshe, J. D. (Eds). *La Zambie contemporaine*. Paris, Editions Karthala, 1996.

Ferguson, J. *Expectations of Modernity*. Berkeley, University of California Press, 1999.

Grotpeter, J. J., Siegel, B. V., and Pletcher, J. R. *Historical Dictionary of Zambia*. Lanham, MD, Scarecrow Press, 1998.

Gulhati, R. *Impasse in Zambia: The Economics and Politics of Reform*. Washington, DC, World Bank, 1989.

Hamalengwa, M. *Class Struggle in Zambia, 1884–1989 and the Fall of Kenneth Kaunda, 1990–1991*. Lanham, MD, University Press of America, 1992.

Ihonvbere, J. O. *Economic Crisis, Civil Society and Democratization: The Case of Zambia*. Trenton, NJ, Africa World Press, 1996.

Macmillan, H., and Shapiro, F. *Zion in Africa – The Jews of Zambia*. London and New York, I. B. Tauris, 1999.

Moore, H., and Vaughan, M. *Cutting Down Trees: Gender, Nutrition and Agricultural Change in Northern Province, Zambia, 1890–1990*. Zambia, University of Zambia Press, 1994.

Moore, R. C. *The Political Reality of Freedom of the Press in Zambia*. Lanham, MD, University Press of America, 1992.

Mwanakatwe, J. M. *End of Kaunda Era*. Lusaka, Multimedia, 1994.

Mwanza, A. M. (Ed.). *The Structural Adjustment Programme in Zambia: Lessons from Experience*. Harare, SAPES Books, 1992.

Nag, P. *Population, Settlement and Development in Zambia*. New Delhi, Concept Publishing Co, 1989.

Rakner, L. *Trade Unions in Processes of Democratisation: A Study of Party Labour Relations in Zambia*. Bergen, Norway, Michelsen Institute, 1992.

Saasa, O., and Carlsson, J. *The Aid Relationship in Zambia: A Conflict Scenario*. Uppsala, Nordiska Afrikainstitutet, 1996.

Saasa, O., Wilson, F., and Chingambo, L. *The Zambian Economy in Post-Apartheid Southern Africa: A Critical Analysis of Policy Options*. Lusaka, IAS Consultancy Services, 1992.

Sichone, O., and Chikulo, B. *Democracy in Zambia*. Aldershot, Avebury, 1997.

Turok, B. *Mixed Economy in Focus: Zambia*. London, IFAA, 1989.

Van Binsbergen, W. *Tears of Rain: Ethnicity and History in Central Western Zambia*. London, Kegan Paul International, 1992.

Virmani, K. K. *Zambia: The Dawn of Freedom*. Delhi, Kalinga, 1989.

Wood, A. P. (Ed.). *Dynamics of Agricultural Policy and Reform in Zambia*. Ames, Iowa State University Press, 1990.

World Bank. *Zambia: Country Assistance Review*. Washington, DC, World Bank, 1996.

Zambia: Prospects for Sustainable Growth, 1995–2005. Washington, DC, World Bank, 1996.

ZIMBABWE

Physical and Social Geography

GEORGE KAY

The Republic of Zimbabwe, covering an area of 390,757 sq km (150,872 sq miles), is land-locked and is bounded on the north and north-west by Zambia, on the south-west by Botswana, by Mozambique on the east and on the south by South Africa. The census of August 1992 enumerated 10,412,548 persons. In August 1997 the population was officially estimated at 12,293,953, giving an average density of 31.5 inhabitants per sq km.

Zimbabwe lies astride the high plateaux between the Zambezi and Limpopo rivers. It consists of four relief regions. The high-veld, comprising land more than 1,200 m above sea-level, extends across the country from south-west to north-east; it is most extensive in the north-east. The middleveld, land of 900 m–1,200 m above sea-level, flanks the highveld; it is most extensive in the north-west. The lowveld, land below 900 m, occupies the Zambezi basin in the north and the more extensive Limpopo and Sabi-Lundi basins in the south and south-east. These three regions consist predominantly of gently undulating plateaux, except for the narrow belt of rugged, escarpment hills associated with faults along the Zambezi trough. Also, the surfaces are broken locally where particularly resistant rocks provide upstanding features. For example, the Great Dyke, a remarkable intrusive feature over 480 km in length and up to 10 km wide, gives rise to prominent ranges of hills. The fourth physical region, the eastern highlands, is distinctive because of its mountainous character. Inyangani rises to 2,594 m and many hills exceed 1,800 m.

Temperatures vary by altitude. Mean monthly temperatures range from 22°C in October and 13°C in July on the highveld to 30°C and 20°C in the low-lying Zambezi valley. Winters are noted for a wide diurnal range; night frosts can occur on the high plateaux and can occasionally be very destructive.

Rainfall is largely restricted to the period November–March and, except on the eastern highlands, is extremely variable; in many regions it is too low for commercial crop production. Mean annual rainfall ranges from 1,400 mm on the eastern highlands, to 800 mm on the north-eastern highveld and to less than 400 mm in the Limpopo valley. The development of water resources for economic uses is a continually pressing need which, to date, has been met by a major dam-building programme. Underground water resources are limited. Large-scale irrigation works in the south-eastern lowveld have overcome climatic limitations, and the area around Chiredzi, once suitable only for ranching, is now a major developing region.

Soils vary considerably. Granite occurs over more than half of the country and mostly gives rise to infertile sandy soils; these are, however, amenable to improvement. Kalahari sands are also extensive and provide poor soils. Soil-forming processes are limited in the lowveld and, except on basalt, soils there are generally immature. Rich, red clays and loams occur on the limited outcrops of Basement Schists, which are also among the most highly mineralized areas of Zimbabwe.

Climatic factors are the chief determinants of agricultural potential and six broad categories of land have been defined largely on bio-climatic conditions: Region I (1.6% of the country) with good, reliable rainfall; suitable for specialized and diversified farming, including tree crops; Region II (18.7%) with moderately high rainfall; suitable for intensive commercial crop production with subsidiary livestock farming; Region III (17.4%) with mediocre rainfall conditions; suitable for semi-extensive commercial livestock farming with supplementary production of drought-resistant crops; Region IV (33%) with low and unreli-able rainfall; suitable for semi-extensive livestock production; Region V (26.2%) semi-arid country; suitable only for extensive ranching; and Region VI (3.1%—probably underestimated) which, because of steep slopes, skeletal soils, swamps, etc., is unsuitable for any agricultural use.

Zimbabwe possesses a wide variety of workable mineral deposits, which include gold, platinum, asbestos, copper, chrome, nickel, palladium, cobalt, tin, iron ore, limestone, iron pyrites, phosphates and coal. Most mineralization occurs on the highveld and adjacent parts of the middleveld.

The population of Zimbabwe is diverse. At mid-1980 it was estimated to include some 223,000 persons of European descent and some 37,000 Asians and Coloureds, all of them a legacy of the colonial era. The indigenous inhabitants, who accounted for over 98% of the population at mid-1987, broadly comprise two ethnic or linguistic groups, the Ndebele and the Shona. The Shona, with whom political power now rests, outnumber the Ndebele by 4:1. There are, in addition, several minor ethnic groups, such as the Tonga, Sena, Hlengwe, Venda and Sotho. The official languages are English, Chishona and Sindebele.

In recent years urban growth has proceeded rapidly. The urban poor, operating within the highly competitive 'informal economy', are now a large and increasing part of the urban social structure. During 1982–92 the population of Harare, the capital, grew from 656,000 to 1,189,103, while that of Bulawayo increased from 413,800 to 621,742.

In the rural districts, a relatively small number of white farmers and companies continue to hold extensive interests in commercial farming. However, in recent years the communal lands that are occupied by indigenous households have increased their contribution to national sales of crops and livestock. Official resettlement schemes on to the land of erstwhile commercial holdings (many of which had been unused or underused), and colonization in the form of squatter movements on to such lands, were formally encouraged, although resettlement did not proceed as rapidly as planned. Legislation came into force in 1992 which empowered the government compulsorily to acquire land; it was hoped that this would facilitate the redistribution of land ownership from white commercial farmers (who then owned more than 40% of prime productive farmland) to African smallholders. The first phase of the compulsory acquisition process, entailing the transfer of 112 farms, was to have been completed prior to the commencement of the 1998/99 growing season. In mid-1999 the government introduced an Inception Phase Framework Plan, aiming to resettle 77,000 African families on 1m. ha of land by 2001. In February 2000, however, 'war veterans' began illegally invading white-owned land, and reportedly occupied more than 1,400 farms by mid-2000. In May 2000 a land commission was created to redistribute farmland; by August the commission had identified 3,041 farms which were to be confiscated. Meanwhile, the resettlement of black families commenced on 211 farms already acquired, although farmers were contesting the government's right to seize land without paying compensation.

Most rural African households still reside on communal lands, where they have traditionally depended upon subsistence production, augmented by small irregular sales of surplus produce, by casual employment and by remittances from migrant labourers. However, the cohesion of this rural society is being eroded by the selective effects of migration.

The socio-economic difficulties of rural African society are compounded by ecological problems. While some extensive areas (notably in remote northern parts of the country) remain sparsely populated, the greater part of the communal lands suffers from overpopulation and overstocking. Deforestation, soil erosion and a deterioration of wildlife and water resources are widespread; and in some areas they have reached critical dimensions. 'Desertification' is a real danger in the semi-arid regions of the country.

Recent History

RICHARD BROWN

Revised for this edition by the Editor

The former British colony of Southern Rhodesia, which now forms the Republic of Zimbabwe, was established in 1890 on the strength of its rumoured mineral potential. However, the limited scale of gold discoveries brought instead an influx of white farmers, mainly from Britain and South Africa. The resultant alienation of land produced economic and political consequences which are evident to the present day.

In 1953 Southern Rhodesia was united by the British government with Northern Rhodesia (Zambia) and Nyasaland (Malawi) in a Central African Federation, which was opposed by Africans in all three territories. The British government eventually recognized the strength of African hostility in Northern Rhodesia and Nyasaland, and conceded independence, breaking up the federation in the process (1963). Whites in Southern Rhodesia viewed these developments as the outcome of British appeasement and in 1962 voted into office the newly-formed Rhodesian Front (RF), dedicated to upholding white supremacy and demanding full independence from the United Kingdom and the retention of the existing minority-rule constitution. When the United Kingdom refused independence on this basis, the RF appointed the intransigent Ian Smith as prime minister. In November 1965 Smith carried out the long-threatened unilateral declaration of independence (UDI), re-naming the territory 'Rhodesia'.

Repressive measures preceding UDI had seriously weakened the African nationalist opposition, which in 1963 had split into the Zimbabwe African People's Union (ZAPU), led by Joshua Nkomo, and the breakaway Zimbabwe African National Union (ZANU), led by Rev. Ndabaningi Sithole and subsequently Robert Mugabe. These nationalists embarked upon a 'people's war' to overthrow the Smith regime. ZAPU, based mainly in Zambia, received training and armaments from the USSR, although its operations within Zimbabwe were confined mainly to majority Ndebele areas. ZANU developed strong links with the Frente de Libertação de Moçambique (Frelimo) movement fighting the Portuguese in Mozambique, and with the People's Republic of China. It concentrated on infiltration and rural mobilization in the Shona-speaking areas in the north-east, and later in the eastern and central areas of the country. From 1976 a combined struggle was waged in the name of the Patriotic Front (PF), an uneasy alliance formed by ZAPU and ZANU, and backed by the 'front-line' states, i.e. those African countries most involved in the Rhodesian conflict. Within the country, mounting economic difficulties, resulting in large part from the imposition of economic sanctions by the international community (with the effective exception of South Africa), together with declining white morale and guerrilla inroads in the rural areas led the Smith regime in 1979 to fashion what was termed an 'internal settlement'. This took the form of a black surrogate regime under the leadership of Bishop Abel Muzorewa. Within less than a year all the parties to the conflict agreed to participate in the Lancaster House constitutional conference, under the chairmanship of the British secretary of state for foreign and commonwealth affairs, which was to lead to the emergence of the independent state of Zimbabwe on 18 April 1980.

THE INDEPENDENCE SETTLEMENT

The Lancaster House conference lasted for 14 weeks, an agreement being signed on 21 December 1979. Administrative continuity was stressed in the adoption of the prime ministerial system in preference to an executive presidency, and in the disproportionate political influence reserved to the white

minority (20 of the 100 seats in the house of assembly). However, the compensation clause attached to land reform was strongly opposed by the PF, and was accepted only after vague assurances had been given about a future multinational fund to assist in the urgent problems of land redistribution. At elections in February 1980 Mugabe's ZANU–PF won 57 of the 80 'common roll' (African) seats in the house, receiving 63% of the votes. Nkomo's PF won 20 seats and Muzorewa's United African National Council (UANC) three seats. Between them the two parties which had conducted the armed struggle received 87% of the votes in a turn-out estimated at 94% (in an earlier and separate election, the RF won all 20 seats reserved for whites). Rev. Canaan Banana, a prominent figure in the nationalist struggle, became Zimbabwe's first president, with ceremonial duties only.

In the immediate period following his massive victory, Mugabe adopted a markedly conciliatory stance. To restore stability, he quickly stressed the need for reconciliation; disavowed rapid change towards his stated socialist goals; emphasized non-alignment in foreign affairs; and included two whites in his cabinet. Nevertheless, the new government was faced with formidable problems arising from the ravages of war and the expectations aroused in the struggle against settler rule.

Land redistribution and the rehabilitation of the trust lands seemed likely to provide the greatest challenges to the new government's aspirations and authority. For most Zimbabweans the struggles of recent decades had been about recovering the land, and the later stages of the guerrilla war to some extent resembled a peasant uprising. The strategic power and importance of the established commercial farming sector made the problem of meeting peasant needs daunting. The pace of official resettlement, slowed by drought, manpower shortages, restrictive provisions in the Lancaster House agreement and perhaps by lack of will, was not sufficient to head off extensive uncontrolled resettlement or to prevent the land issue from fuelling particular discontent in Matabeleland.

In the international field, Zimbabwe established diplomatic relations with other countries in Africa, with Western countries, with the People's Republic of China and its allies and, more hesitantly, with the USSR and its allies. The Zimbabwe Conference on Reconstruction and Development (Zimcord), held in March 1981, succeeded in substantially meeting its targets for aid. Zimbabwe also began to play a prominent part in the Southern African Development Co-ordination Conference (SADCC, now the Southern African Development Community–SADC). Mugabe made it clear that political and diplomatic support would be given to the opposition movements in neighbouring South Africa.

POLITICS AND SECURITY

At independence it was necessary to consolidate the peace by integrating the three large, hostile and undefeated armies. After initial problems, and violent clashes resulting in several hundred deaths, by late 1981 the integration appeared to have been successfully completed. From outside ZANU–PF there was criticism of the creation of a specialist army brigade (the Fifth), of largely Shona composition trained by advisers from the Democratic People's Republic of Korea. However, Mugabe cited, in justification, the internal and external threats posed by disaffected supporters of the former regime, by unresolved tensions within the governing coalition, and by South Africa. In December 1981 the ZANU–PF headquarters were destroyed in a bomb attack. Subsequently, vital transport routes and petroleum facilities in Mozambique were sabotaged, the homes of government ministers attacked, and a substantial part of the air force destroyed.

Meanwhile, there was increasing discussion of the need for a one-party state. The prime minister stated that such a development should come about through persuasion, but other members of his party urged the need for speed and attacked the restrictive clauses of the Lancaster House constitution. Nkomo, who later made it known that he did not consider the election results to be valid and who had rejected Mugabe's offer of the presidency following the independence elections, refused to accept that a ZAPU merger with ZANU–PF was the best solution to the sharp regional polarization between the two coalition parties. In January 1981 Nkomo was demoted from his home affairs portfolio to a lesser cabinet office, and one year later he and some of his colleagues were dismissed altogether, following the discovery of substantial illegal arms caches on properties belonging to ZAPU in Matabeleland. Although there were some immediate outbreaks of pro-Nkomo dissident violence in the province, it was also significant that the remaining members of the coalition from the minority party failed to heed Nkomo's wish that they should resign. Mugabe threatened to bring Nkomo to trial on charges of plotting a coup, but he also went out of his way to stress again his policy of reconciliation. The ZAPU ministers who had remained were promoted, and Mugabe also added two ex-RF members of parliament to his government. The RF, restyled the Republican Front in 1981, was still led by Ian Smith, having undergone a sizeable secession from its parliamentary ranks in protest at RF negativism since independence. In 1983 an RF faction sympathetic to the Mugabe government broke away to form the Independent Zimbabwe Group. By the June 1985 elections, the RF had reconstituted itself as the Conservative Alliance of Zimbabwe (CAZ).

Mugabe emerged from the crisis over the arms discoveries in a strong position, but the government's authority was increasingly challenged by events in Matabeleland. The acute land problems of the province, allied to the effects of a devastating drought, heightened the tense political situation. During 1982 dissidents from ZIPRA, ZAPU's former guerrilla army, and former colleagues who had deserted from the new national army, perpetrated numerous indiscriminate acts of violence. Their exact links with Nkomo and his party could not be fully established, but the government held ZAPU largely to blame for the worsening situation. It was also alleged that members of the former regime's forces who had moved to South Africa were providing a ready supply of personnel for covert operations, which the South African government was also suspected of supporting.

Early in 1983, and again in 1984, serious allegations of indiscipline and atrocities against civilians were made against the Fifth Brigade as it sought to suppress the dissidents and to protect the mainly white, commercial farming sector on which so much of the government's overall economic strategy rested. The allegations were supported by local churchmen, including the Roman Catholic authorities who had previously played a major part in exposing atrocities committed by the security forces of the Smith regime. Controversy over human rights issues continued when adverse reports, from Amnesty International, in 1985, and from the US-based Lawyers' Committee for Human Rights, were rejected by the prime minister.

In addition to the desire to dislodge ZAPU from its regional stronghold, the fear that a South African-backed dissident movement might reach the same devastating proportions as those already operating in Angola and Mozambique probably lay behind the government's decision to mount a forceful military campaign in Matabeleland in spite of the risk of alienating the province's mainly Ndebele-speaking population, Zimbabwe's principal minority language group. The prolonged nature of the operations in Matabeleland suggested more civilian support for the dissidents than was officially admitted, but, as the first general election since independence approached, there was increasing emphasis on the ruling party's need to achieve genuine political support in the province. The approaching election also intensified political violence elsewhere in the country.

A new party constitution, adopted by a ZANU–PF congress held in August 1984, greatly enlarged the central committee and introduced a new 15-member politburo. The congress dedicated itself to the 'victory of socialism over capitalism' and endorsed the aim of achieving a one-party Marxist-Leninist state under the leadership of ZANU–PF.

The first general elections since independence were held at the end of June 1985 (for the 20 'guaranteed' white seats) and in early July (for the 80 'common roll' seats). Ian Smith's CAZ won 15 of the 20 reserved seats. (However, following the elections, several CAZ representatives in the house of assembly either joined the ruling party or became independents.) In the election for the 80 black 'common roll' seats, almost 3m. votes were cast, the vast majority for ZANU–PF candidates. ZANU–PF increased its representation in the house of assembly by six seats to 64, although it failed to gain any of the Matabeleland seats held by Joshua Nkomo's ZAPU. Outside Matabeleland, however, ZAPU lost all five of the seats that it held in the previous parliament. ZANU–Sithole secured one seat, but Muzorewa's UANC failed to gain any representation.

ZANU–PF CONSOLIDATES

Following the elections, the drive towards a *de facto* one-party state was resumed, with reprisals against supporters of minority parties. The government's vigorous campaign against ZAPU led to the adverse report by Amnesty International referred to above, but it did not prevent the resumption of unity talks between ZAPU and ZANU–PF. Success seemed to be imminent on several occasions, especially following the release in 1986 of prominent ZAPU detainees. In April 1987, however, Mugabe abruptly abandoned the unity negotiations on the grounds that they had been deadlocked for too long. A resurgence of violence in Matabeleland and further measures against ZAPU's political activities followed the cancellation of the unity talks. Nkomo, however, continued to deny any involvement with the dissidents, and in July ZAPU indicated its continuing wish for negotiations with the ruling party by voting in favour of renewing the state of emergency.

A particularly brutal massacre in Matabeleland in November 1987 and the worsening security situation on the eastern border (see below) at last precipitated a unity agreement between ZAPU and ZANU–PF, healing the split of almost 25 years in the nationalist ranks. The agreement to merge the two parties, under the name of ZANU–PF, was signed by Mugabe and Nkomo in December, and was ratified by both parties in April 1988. According to the agreement, the new party was to be committed to the establishment of a one-party state with a Marxist-Leninist doctrine. The party was to be led by Mugabe, with Nkomo as one of two vice-presidents. Nkomo was offered a senior position in a new cabinet, while two other ZAPU officials were given government posts. An amnesty, proclaimed in April 1988, led to a rapid improvement in political and security conditions in Matabeleland.

Meanwhile, significant constitutional changes were moving Zimbabwe nearer to becoming a one-party state. The reservation for whites of 20 seats in the house of assembly and 10 seats in the senate was finally abolished in September 1987. In the following month the 80 remaining members of the assembly elected 20 candidates who were all nominated by ZANU–PF, including 11 whites, to fill the vacant seats. Candidates nominated by ZANU–PF, including four whites, were then elected to the vacancies in the senate by the new house of assembly. In October parliament adopted another major constitutional reform, whereby the ceremonial presidency was replaced by an executive presidency incorporating the post of prime minister. Robert Mugabe was nominated as sole candidate for the office, and on 31 December he was inaugurated as Zimbabwe's first executive president. His new enlarged cabinet included Joshua Nkomo as one of three senior ministers in the president's office who were to oversee policy and review ministerial performance. In November 1989 the house of assembly voted to abolish the senate. The single chamber was then expanded from 100 to 150 seats, with effect from the next general election. In addition to 120 elected members, the change provided for eight provincial governors, 10 chiefs and 12 presidential nominees to be members of the assembly.

DISCONTENT AND 'CORRUPTION'

As unemployment and prices rose in 1988, open public and parliamentary criticism of corrupt government officials mounted. An anti-government demonstration by students in September resulted in many arrests. In October a former secretary-general of ZANU–PF, Edgar Tekere, was expelled from the party for his persistent denunciation of its leadership and policies, including the plans to introduce a one-party state; this action resulted in further student protest. In the same month allegations that government ministers had obtained new cars from the state-owned vehicle assembly plant in order to resell them at a profit, an illegal activity, first appeared in the Bulawayo *Chronicle*. The newspaper's editor was subsequently removed from his post. Amid intense public concern, Mugabe appointed a judicial commission of inquiry to investigate the newspaper's allegations: as a result of the commission's findings, five cabinet ministers and one provincial governor resigned from their posts in March and April 1989. At the behest of the ZANU–PF central committee, however, the charges against the former ministers were withdrawn, precipitating widespread protests and contributing to a tense political atmosphere, especially in urban areas.

Following publication of the judicial commission's report, Edgar Tekere, who had previously disavowed any intention of forming a new party, challenged Mugabe's commitment to the eventual introduction of a one-party state by founding the Zimbabwe Unity Movement (ZUM). Tekere denounced the government as corrupt, and proposed economic liberalization and the withdrawal of Zimbabwean troops from Mozambique. Although the new party was unable seriously to challenge ZANU–PF in five by-elections (held in July and October 1989)—partially, at least, owing to alleged official harassment and obstruction—the low level of electoral participation suggested a significant decline in the popularity of the governing party.

The government was embarrassed during 1989 by a series of conflicts with the judiciary and by strikes in the public service sector, but it was criticism by students which provoked the most serious political disturbances. In July a clash occurred between students and security police during a rally of ZUM supporters at the University of Zimbabwe, and, following further serious clashes, the university was closed from October 1990 to April 1991. Unconvincingly, the government related the trouble to subversion from South Africa. When the Zimbabwe Congress of Trade Unions (ZCTU) issued a statement supporting the students, its secretary-general, Morgan Tsvangirai, was arrested and detained for six weeks (the cause of one particular conflict with the judiciary). During July 1990, however, the state of emergency was discontinued, owing to the reduction of tension in South Africa, although it was noted that the government retained wide powers of arrest and detention.

Political debate intensified during the ZANU–PF congress in December 1989. The congress was convened to complete the merger process with ZAPU, begun two years earlier (see above), but it required strong directive action from Mugabe to resolve the contentious issue of the distribution of party posts. There was also controversy concerning a proposed constitutional amendment to create a second vice-presidency, specifically for Joshua Nkomo, the former ZAPU leader. (Nkomo was officially appointed vice-president, in addition to the existing vice-president, Simon Muzenda, in August 1990.) Although Mugabe recommitted the new ZANU–PF to Marxism-Leninism and the one-party state, opposition to a one-party state was expressed within and outside the congress. Indeed, in August 1990 the ZANU–PF politburo voted to reject plans for the creation of a one-party state in Zimbabwe.

For the general election of March 1990, ZANU–PF chose to campaign against ZUM, its only serious opponent among the four opposition parties, on the general issue of national unity rather than on that of the one-party state. The election was marred by political violence, but the result of the poll appeared to be a fair reflection of the government's popularity. ZANU–PF secured 117 of the 120 elective seats (including one seat in which polling was initially postponed). However, electoral participation—estimated to be in the range of 54%–65%—had declined sharply in comparison with turn-outs of 95% and above in the two previous general elections. Moreover, ZUM, despite a controversial alliance with the CAZ and the disruption of

some of its campaign activities, received almost 20% of the total votes. Significantly, ZUM performed well in urban areas, especially in Harare, where it secured 30% of the votes. However, ZANU–PF's control of the seats was disrupted only in eastern Manicaland (owing, at least in part, to the difficulties occasioned by Mozambican guerrillas—see below), where ZUM obtained two seats and ZANU–Ndonga (formerly ZANU–Sithole) retained one. Overall, the distribution of votes in the election indicated that ZUM had achieved something approaching national status as an opposition party, although its leader, Edgar Tekere, was overwhelmingly defeated in the contest for the remaining seat. At the concurrent election for the presidency, Tekere received 413,840 votes and Mugabe 2.03m. votes.

Mugabe's new cabinet included three whites as ministers, but its overall composition, to the annoyance of former ZAPU members, was little altered. Nevertheless, few doubted that, under the surface, the final year of the decade since independence had witnessed a substantial political shift. With more than 50% of the population below the age of 25 years, and with severe unemployment and other domestic problems, appeals by ZANU–PF to the heroism of the pre-independence struggle could no longer be regarded as relevant or powerful.

IDEOLOGICAL REASSESSMENTS

Meanwhile, following the adoption in 1991 of an Economic Structural Adjustment Programme (ESAP), 'Marxism-Leninism' was increasingly replaced in official discourse by references to 'pragmatic socialism' and 'indigenous capitalism'. Vigorous debate was also aroused by the expiry of the remaining restrictions of the Lancaster House agreement on 18 April 1990. Constitutional amendments which restored corporal and capital punishment and which denied recourse to the courts in cases of compulsory purchase of land by the government were enacted in April 1991, despite fierce criticism from the judiciary and from human rights campaigners.

Student unrest erupted following the publication in October 1990 of proposals for a substantial increase in government control of universities. A student boycott of classes on the issue in May 1991 won support in many quarters, but an attempt to march on the Commonwealth Prime Ministers' Conference held in Harare in October led to violence following heavy-handed police actions to prevent the students from leaving the campus. In May 1992 students, angry at eroded grants and the imposition of fees, found themselves once again in confrontation with the police. Subsequently, the 10,000 students of the University of Zimbabwe were expelled. Student protest was the most visible part of much wider discontent. In June police prevented trade unionists from holding anti-government demonstrations. For workers, the extent and severity of the 1991/92 drought exacerbated the economic difficulties already being blamed on the ESAP. Shortages, inflation, unemployment, corruption, government inertia and the stalled programme of land resettlement were the main grievances expressed. The discovery of extensive human remains, thought to date from the activities of the Fifth Brigade in its operations in Matabeleland in the 1980s (see above), added to the political *malaise*.

However, despite the government's evident unpopularity, the disorganized and divided state of the opposition continued to protect the government from serious challenge. A split in ZUM led to the formation in September 1991 of the ineffective Democratic Party. The unenthusiastic response outside his home area to the return to the country in January 1992 from self-imposed exile of Ndabaningi Sithole, ZANU's original leader and now leader of ZANU–Ndonga, underlined the low esteem in which the older generation of nationalist politicians were now held. In July 1992 ZANU–Ndonga, the UANC, ZUM and the CAZ formed an informal alliance, the United Front (UF), with the aim of defeating the government at the general elections due in 1995, but divisions soon emerged within the new grouping. Bishop Abel Muzorewa returned to active politics in January 1994 and merged the UANC with ZUM; later in that year Muzorewa founded a new opposition grouping, the United Parties (UP). In spite of efforts by another former prime minister, Ian Smith, the UF remained ineffective.

The ZCTU found itself unable to capitalize on the widespread industrial unrest which took place in 1994. The organization was weakened by the resignation of its secretary-general, Morgan Tsvangirai, and by the loss of members as a result of the economic recession. When the ZCTU rejected the suggestion that it form its own party, a group of non-union figures opposed to the ESAP announced the formation of a Movement for Democracy in June 1994.

Meanwhile, amid the rising urban discontent fuelled by corruption scandals, falling real wages and the social consequences of the ESAP, the government was increasingly preoccupied by the land issue, which it continued to regard as the key to retaining its grip on power. The Land Acquisition Act (LAA), drafted following the expiry of the Lancaster House provisions, passed its final legislative phase on 19 March 1992 (see Economy). The new legislation, which provided for the compulsory acquisition of land by the state, brought the government into conflict with the powerful white-dominated Commercial Farmers' Union (CFU) and with Western aid donors. Both groups were angered by the decision in April 1993 to designate 70 commercially owned farms for purchase. Many of them were productive holdings which, it had been understood, were to be exempt from compulsory purchase. The government eventually allowed appeals in a sufficient number of cases—22—to suggest that an uneasy compromise had been reached. For its part, the CFU announced in September that it would assist in the government's resettlement programme, and its members were represented on the commission set up in November to make proposals for land tenure reforms. However, in March 1994 the government found itself once again under intense pressure when it was revealed that the first of the farms acquired under the LAA had been allocated to the government minister, Witness Mangwende, who had been minister of agriculture when the act was passed. The scandal escalated when the press revealed that most of the first 98 farms acquired by compulsory purchase had been leased to prominent party figures and civil servants and were not being used for peasant resettlement. The president responded by ordering the cancellation of all relevant leases. In November the high court ruled against three white farmers who had attempted to prove that the confiscation of their land was unconstitutional; the farmers subsequently lost an appeal to the supreme court against the verdict. Government plans to resettle 100,000 smallholders over five years were impeded by a lack of available resources. Indeed, the funds made available for resettlement were more than halved in the 1995/96 budget. In mid-1996 Mugabe requested financial assistance from the United Kingdom for the implementation of the land redistribution programme.

In spite of the popular discontent which had characterized its last term of office, the government won a fourth decisive general election victory on 8–9 April 1995. Eight opposition groups, including ZUM and the UP, boycotted the election, but, at 57%, the turn-out of voters was much higher than expected. Of the six opposition parties which did contest the election, only the regionally-based ZANU–Ndonga won any seats in the house of assembly (two). ZANU–PF received more than 82% of the votes cast and secured 118 of the 120 elective seats (55 of them uncontested), as well as control of the 30 nominated and reserved seats. Most independent observers agreed that the elections had been largely 'free and fair', but they criticized aspects of the registration procedures, the ruling party's domination of the media and the Political Parties (Finance) Act of 1992, under which only organizations with at least 15 assembly members (that is, effectively only ZANU–PF) were entitled to state support. In August 1995 the high court nullified the election result in the bitterly contested Harare South constituency, when it was established that more votes had been cast than there were registered electors. This lent credence to opposition claims of widespread electoral malpractices by the Mugabe administration (despite the favourable pronouncement of the majority of independent observers), and calls were made for both the annulment of all the results and the convening of an all-party constitutional conference to debate means of improving the implementation of democratic principles in the *de facto* one-party state.

Against the wishes of the IMF and World Bank, the president enlarged his government substantially in a post-election reshuffle, creating 13 new cabinet posts; the number of former ZAPU members was doubled to four. Meanwhile, in mid-1995

a series of protests were made by students at the University of Zimbabwe who were dissatisfied with the level and administration of their grants; such student action frequently escalated into violent confrontations with the security forces. At local elections in October 1995 some 15 independent and dissident ZANU–PF candidates won representation on local councils. During that month Rev. Sithole, the leader of ZANU–Ndonga, was arrested and charged with conspiracy to assassinate Mugabe, in association with the Chimwenjes, a group of mainly Zimbabwean dissidents based in Mozambique; Sithole strongly denied the accusation.

Mugabe was returned to office at a presidential election on 16–17 March 1996, winning 92.7% of the votes cast. There was, however, a turn-out of only 31.7% of the eligible electorate. The election was also unwillingly contested by Muzorewa (who took 4.7% of the votes) and Sithole, who had been released on bail, (2.4%); they had been denied permission to withdraw their candidacies prior to the ballot. Mugabe extensively reorganized the cabinet in May. The white minister of agriculture, Dennis Norman, resigned in April 1997, reportedly because he had lost support among the white farming community and also believed that his advice was not being heeded by the government. A further reorganization of the cabinet, in July, in which a number of ministries were merged, was attributed to pressure from international creditors.

In late August and early September 1996 thousands of civil servants demanding salary increases organized a national strike; during October and November there were further strikes by nurses and junior doctors (who claimed that agreed pay increments had not been implemented), as a result of which many of Zimbabwe's hospitals were unable to function. It was announced in October that ZANU–PF was officially abandoning Marxism-Leninism as its guiding principle. In February 1997 a former aide-de-camp to Rev. Banana in the early 1980s, Jefta Dube, made allegations that the then president had sexually assaulted him. It was announced in July that criminal charges would be brought against the former president. The allegations received considerable international attention, since Mugabe had of late made a number of much-publicized condemnations of homosexual practices. The trial of Rev. Banana opened in September 1997, but was suspended immediately, while Banana appealed to the supreme court that the proceedings would be prejudiced by the high degree of publicity given to the case; the trial recommenced in June 1998, following the rejection of Banana's appeal. In November Banana was convicted on 11 charges of sexual assault. However, he violated his bail conditions and travelled to Botswana and then South Africa, where he asked for President Mandela's protection. Following Mandela's intervention with Mugabe on Banana's behalf, the former President returned to Zimbabwe in December and was sentenced to 10 years' imprisonment with labour in January 1999. Most of the sentence was conditionally suspended, although Banana was to serve a minimum of one year in prison. In December 1997 Rev. Sithole was found guilty of plotting to kill Mugabe and sentenced to two years' imprisonment; he was, however, released on bail, pending an appeal to the supreme court.

ECONOMIC CRISIS AND LAND REFORM

During 1997 and the first half of 1998 the Mugabe administration increasingly came under attack for perceived cynicism and arrogance at a time of general economic hardship. Corruption once again became a prominent issue in 1997, with allegations that official contracts were being unfairly tendered and that ministerial funds were being used to finance the construction of homes for civil servants, government ministers and, indeed, Mugabe's wife. (Mugabe himself acknowledged in July 1999 that corruption existed within the government.) In April 1998 it was reported that members of the government and their families had been misusing funds intended to assist veterans of the armed struggle for independence. The government announced in August 1997 that the independence war veterans (an increasingly powerful lobby) were to be awarded a number of substantial unbudgeted benefits. In September the supreme court ruled against the Political Parties (Finance) Act (see above), decreeing that it was incompatible with a democratic multi-party political system, on the grounds that it precluded any real challenge to the ruling party. Labour unrest did not abate in 1997, and escalated in December, when a general strike was organized by ZCTU in protest at the imposition by the government of three unpopular new taxes in order to finance the provision of the new benefits for independence war veterans. The authorities capitulated, withdrawing two of the taxes immediately. Shortly after the demonstrations had subsided, Morgan Tsvangirai, the ZCTU secretary-general, was severely assaulted in his office by unknown assailants, who were subsequently reported to be war veterans. The weak Zimbabwe dollar and soaring food prices, compounded by an excessively high level of unemployment, aggravated the nation-wide mood of discontent. In January 1998 unprecedented food riots erupted in most of the country's urban areas in protest at successive rises in the price of the staple maize meal. In response Mugabe agreed to withdraw the most recent price increase. However, the army was deployed to suppress the disturbances and was authorized to open fire on protesters; nine people were reportedly killed and some 800 rioters were arrested. ZCTU organized a further two-day strike in March, to protest against the continuing rise in living costs; soon afterwards the Congress's Bulawayo office was destroyed in an arson attack. Meanwhile, in early 1998, despite the ongoing economic crisis, Mugabe presented legislation to parliament which provided for a number of luxury retirement benefits for himself, his family, the two vice-presidents and their families. At the beginning of June the University of Zimbabwe was closed temporarily, following several days of anti-government demonstrations by students. In August 1998 a decree was issued banning strikes and restricting public and political gatherings, but was swiftly repealed. In September threats for a five-day stoppage demanding tax cuts also resulted in government concessions. Meanwhile, further consumer price increases were followed by renewed rioting. A series of one-day strikes over pay were called by unions and action took place until banned by Mugabe. In February 1999, however, the ban was ruled to be illegal. In that month growing unrest followed an address to the nation by Mugabe in which he attacked the judiciary, the independent media and 'British agents'. He also accused white Zimbabweans of 'fomenting unrest'. In June civil servants went on strike, demanding a 20% cost of living pay rise. In the same month the main bakeries threatened to stop work after the government fixed the price of bread at 20% below the cost of production (see Economy).

Meanwhile, in October 1997 Mugabe, in an attempt to revive his declining popularity, announced that the hitherto slow pace of the national land resettlement programme would be accelerated, declaring that the constitutional right of white commercial farmers to receive full and fair compensation for confiscated land would not be honoured and (unsuccessfully) challenging the United Kingdom, in its role as former colonial power, to take responsibility for assisting them. A list of 1,471 properties to be reallocated forthwith was published in November. In January 1998, however, the IMF stipulated an assurance from the Mugabe administration that it would respect the constitution during the land resettlement procedure as a condition for the release of financial assistance. Such an assurance was eventually given in early March, and it was subsequently announced that 112 farms would be acquired before the commencement of the 1998/99 growing season in November 1998, in exchange for full and fair compensation. While the land resettlement programme evidently continued to command extensive national support, there was also concern that the government should administer the scheme fairly (without members of the ruling elite becoming beneficiaries) and that the success of the thriving commercial farming sector should not be prejudiced. In June 1998 there was a series of illegal farm occupations by black families. In August Mugabe introduced the second phase of the programme, to resettle 150,000 families on 1m. ha of land each year for the next seven years, and in September Zimbabwe launched an international appeal for Western donors to support its land reform; however, the potential donors dismissed the scheme as too ambitious and costly. Under pressure, the government agreed to reduce its plans, and was restricted to using 118 farms which it had already been offered. In November, however, 841 white-owned farms were ordered to be confiscated by the state: compensation was to be deferred. Pressure exerted by the IMF in the light of a forthcoming release of aid brought an assurance from Mugabe

that his administration would not break agreements for a gradual programme of land reform. At the end of March 1999 the president contravened this undertaking when he announced a plan to acquire a further 529 white-owned farms. He accused the USA and the United Kingdom of 'destabilizing' Zimbabwe through their alleged control over the IMF, which was delaying financial assistance to his country. In the following month, Mugabe threatened that Zimbabwe would sever relations with the IMF and the World Bank, although the minister of finance continued to express the government's hope that the further aid would be released shortly. (The IMF approved a US $193m. loan in August.) In May the government agreed a plan which aimed to resettle 77,700 black families on 1m. ha by 2001. Some of this land was to come from the 118 farms which had already been offered. The remainder would be the result of uncontested acquisitions under the government's reduced list of 800 farms for compulsory purchase. The plan was to be partially funded by the World Bank, and was broadly accepted by the Commercial Farmers' Union (CFU).

INTERNAL DEBATES

In October 1998 the government embarked on discussions with a National Constitutional Assembly (NCA) of opposition interests on proposed changes in the country's constitution. The Mugabe administration confirmed its commitment to an open process which would not allow government domination, and expressed its intention that the new constitution would be in operation prior to the elections due to take place by 2000. However, the NCA suspended negotiations in November after about 50 protesters urging greater constitutional democratization were prevented from marching by riot police. In March 1999 Mugabe unilaterally appointed a 395-member commission of inquiry, dominated by ZANU–PF, to make recommendations on a new constitution. They were given seven months for the task. (The president was, however, under no obligation to accept, or even to make public, the proposals.) The NCA refused to participate in the commission, and announced its intention to hold a rival 'people's convention'. Joshua Nkomo died in early July 1999. (Joseph Misika, hitherto a minister without portfolio, replaced him as vice-president in December.) At Nkomo's funeral, Mugabe apologized for the atrocities committed against the Ndebele in Matabeleland in the early 1980s (see above), and issued a call for national unity. Nevertheless, there was a resurgence of ZAPU under new leadership, called ZAPU 2000. This new party favoured a federal system for Zimbabwe, with considerable powers devolved to Matabeleland and other religions. (In an attempt to regain support, in October the government announced compensation for the families of those killed in the violence.) Another potentially formidable challenge to ZANU–PF emerged in September, with the formation of the Movement for Democratic Change (MDC), led by Morgan Tsvangirai. Administrative chaos and almost total apathy in local elections held in that month humiliated the ruling party and cast severe doubts over the government's ability to hold general elections due in April or May 2000.

Meanwhile, preparation of the new constitution continued. An international constitutional conference was held in November 1999, but several experts suspected that a draft had already been created, and that they had been invited to make presentations primarily to give the process credibility. In late November a document bearing no relation to that prepared by the 400-member constitutional commission was declared to have been 'adopted by acclamation', despite vigorous protests. A drafting committee overseen by ZANU–PF had deleted overnight crucial clauses proposed by the commission, particularly relating to the reduction of the president's powers and the introduction of a parliamentary system. In January 2000 Mugabe announced that a referendum on the adoption of the new constitution would take place on 12–13 February. The high level of confusion before the polls over such issues as eligibility to vote and the location of polling stations was believed by the opposition to have been orchestrated by ZANU–PF to maximize Mugabe's chances of victory. The registrar-general announced that the electoral roll was to be used, which was known to be outdated, 25% of those listed having died and another 30% having changed constituencies. Despite fears that a lack of supervision of the ballot had led to widespread irregularities by ZANU–LPF, 54.6% of the

26% of the electorate who participated in the polls voted to reject the constitution. The level of participation was highest in urban areas, where MDC support was strong, while voters in the government's rural strongholds were apathetic, despite promises that the new constitution would grant them redistributed white land. In a televised address a few days later, Mugabe accepted the result. Within ZANU–PF, however, there was mounting dissatisfaction with Mugabe's leadership and, in the wake of the plebiscite defeat, fears grew that he was an electoral liability. Reportedly, a meeting of the party's central committee in mid-February 2000 forced him to give an undertaking that he would not run again for the presidency of the country or party after his term ended in 2002.

Official manipulation of the media was an important issue in early 2000, as the new constitution was being drafted and the legislative elections approached. The editor, proprietor and one of the journalists of an independent newspaper were arrested in February, despite a public apology to the government, and charged with criminal defamation over an article alleging chicanery by the state committee drafting the new constitution. In March legislation was passed allowing the president to intercept any form of telecommunications. In the following month opposition politicians denounced reports in the state-owned media that they were training guerrilla fighters abroad and that an arms cache found on a white-owned farm belonged to them, accusing ZANU–PF of orchestrating a pre-election campaign to discredit them. Meanwhile, the authorities also strictly controlled reports about losses incurred in the fighting in the Democratic Republic of the Congo (DRC, see below), releasing unfeasibly low figures for deaths and casualties. In December 1998 the same newspaper that printed the article on the constitution (see above) had claimed that 23 disaffected army officers serving in the DRC had been arrested after an attempted coup. In January 1999 the editor of the newspaper and the journalist who wrote the report were arrested and held in military custody, arousing widespread protests and controversy; they were released shortly afterwards. In September they appealed to the supreme court to compel the authorities to investigate their alleged torture by state investigators. The commissioner of police subsequently admitted that the journalists had been handed over to the military, where they had been tortured. In May 2000 the supreme court ruled that the charges against the pair were unconstitutional, thereby effectively acquitting them. Meanwhile, in March 1999 three US citizens, who claimed to be missionaries, were charged with being mercenaries involved in terrorism and espionage against Zimbabwe and the DRC. They had been arrested at Harare airport in possession of firearms (which they claimed were for hunting and self-defence). Independent medical reports subsequently confirmed that the men had been tortured while in custody. The charge of terrorism was dropped in June, and the men's trial, which had been postponed in July, took place in September. They were each sentenced to 27 months' imprisonment with hard labour, the term having been reduced from life as the judge took into consideration the fact that the men had been tortured. In November the three were declared 'prohibited immigrants' and deported.

In mid-May 2000 Mugabe announced that the elections were to be held on 24–25 June. The MDC obtained a postponement at the high court to the deadline for nominations until 3 June as ZANU–PF had been given exclusive access to the details of electoral constituency boundaries. The MDC feared that the constituencies might have been altered to create more in rural areas where support for the ruling party was strong. It was expected that the elections would centre on the issues of land and the economy, both matters causing great concern. International aid to Zimbabwe had been suspended in October 1999 because the government had failed to meet reform targets. The IMF was also investigating reports that Zimbabwe had submitted figures to it relating to military expenditure that were substantially lower than those used by the treasury. Zimbabwe denied the allegations. The budget deficit was growing ever larger and huge arrears to overseas suppliers for fuel, partly owing to a desperate shortage of foreign currency reserves, led to the suspension of oil supplies in December. In the following month rationing caused unrest and long queues at petrol stations. In February 2000 the minister of transport and energy,

Enos Chikowore, assumed responsibility for the fuel crisis and resigned. As reserves declined, political tensions increased, and Mugabe was forced to seek new suppliers, signing a one-year agreement with Kuwait in March. The problem was not, however, completely resolved. In April white farmers urged a substantial devaluation of the currency and threatened not to take their tobacco crop to auction until this happened. The banks agreed that devaluation was needed to avoid mass default. The government, however, fearing that devaluing the currency might adversely affect its chances of retaining power, refused to act. (Following the June elections, the government devalued the Zimbabwe dollar in early August.) Meanwhile, in March the minister of agriculture, Kumbirai Kangai, appeared in court on chages of manipulating tenders for grain imports. He was the first minister to face corruption charges since Mugabe had come to power. The president had reportedly previously acknowledged that a number of his ministers were corrupt, and it was suspected that, as the elections approached, he wanted to improve ZANU–PF's image by being seen to take a firm stand on the issue.

FARM OCCUPATIONS

Following the rejection of the new constitution in February 2000, the government embarked on a campaign to restore its popularity to ensure victory over an increasingly confident opposition in the forthcoming legislative elections. Illegal occupations of white-owned farms by black 'war veterans' (many of whom, too young to have taken part in the war of independence, were suspected of having been paid to participate) which began in late February were rumoured to have been organized by the government in an attempt to use the land issue to regain support. The security forces refused to act against the occupiers, declaring that the 'political issue' lay outside their jurisdiction. Occupations increased, and the police also failed to take steps to evict the protesters following a ruling by the high court in mid-March in favour of the white farmers (which was ignored by the veterans). Mugabe repeatedly denied that his administration was behind the occupations, but made no secret of his support for them. The invasion became increasingly violent, and two farmers were killed in April. A few days earlier, Mugabe had threatened war against farmers who refused to give up their land voluntarily, and following the violence he declared that they were 'enemies of the state'. The international community condemned this increasingly militant stance, which also extended to the treatment of the opposition, in particular the MDC, which was subjected to a campaign of intimidation and aggression. In one of the worst instances a 500-strong mob violently attacked a peace march in Harare in April. No action was taken against the perpetrators of the attack. A constitutional amendment approved in April, shortly before the dissolution of the house of assembly to prepare for elections, stated that white farmers dispossessed of their land would have to apply to the 'former colonial power', the United Kingdom, for compensation (see below). Many farmers were aggrieved as their land had been purchased under Zimbabwean law. As chaos reigned following worsening displays of aggression, the MDC threatened to boycott the elections, and there were signs that ZANU–PF had regained its rural support. In mid-May Mugabe called for an end to the violence. He met with war veterans and white farmers and annouced the creation of a land commission to redistribute farmland. Shortly afterwards, however, he signed a law allowing the seizure of 841 white-owned farms without compensation. Political violence continued unabated throughout the month. In early June a list was published of 804 farms which were to be confiscated. Ian Smith's farm was among those to be acquired. Farmers were to be granted approximately one month to contest the list. Later in June Mugabe also threatened to seize foreign-owned companies and to nationalize mines. By August farmers had contested the acquision of 593 of the 804 properties listed, and a further 2,237 farms had been identified by the land commission for confiscation. Meanwhile, the resettlement of black families had commenced on the 211 farms that had been acquired without objection. In late August the security forces took action for the first time against the war veterans who had been occupying white-owned farms since February. Several hundred squatters were evicted and dwellings erected by veterans on council-owned land were demolished. Following angry demonstrations by the war veterans and their followers, however, the government apologized and offered compensation for the damage to their properties, provoking condemnation from the MDC. In September the CFU announced its intention to challenge the government's right to seize land without paying compensation, after the government apparently refused to negotiate with the farmers.

2000 GENERAL ELECTION

Prior to the elections in June 2000, there were reports of violence towards observers, and a UN team, sent to co-ordinate the polls, was recalled following obstruction by the government. The authorities also refused to permit the accreditation of some 200 foreign monitors. ZANU–PF won 62 of the 120 elective seats in the house of assembly, and the MDC secured 57 seats; ZANU–Ndonga obtained one seat. Morgan Tsvangirai failed to win his constituency, as did a number of government ministers. There were reports of widespread irregularities in the polls, which international observers declared not to have been free and fair. The MDC subsequently challenged the results in 37 constituencies, on the grounds of either voter intimidation or electoral irregularities. In mid-July Mugabe appointed a new cabinet, reducing the number of ministers to 19. The appointments of Simba Makoni, a prominent businessman, as minister of finance and economic development, and Nkosana Moyo, an international banker, as minister of industry and international trade were largely welcomed by the financial community. Emmerson Mnangagwa, minister of justice, legal and parliamentary affairs in the previous government, was elected speaker of the house of assembly. In mid-August it was reported that the supreme court had nullified thousands of postal votes cast in the elections by troops serving in the DRC, ruling that the ballot papers had been issued invalidly.

EXTERNAL RELATIONS

Regional instability and the issue of South Africa dominated Zimbabwe's foreign relations in the first decade of independence. High priority was given to co-operation with Zimbabwe's other neighbours through the SADCC (now the SADC—see above) and the Preferential Trade Area for Eastern and Southern African States (later superseded by the Common Market for Eastern and Southern Africa). Mugabe's strong support for mandatory sanctions against South Africa brought him into conflict with the United Kingdom and the USA, but enhanced Zimbabwe's standing in the Non-Aligned Movement.

The activities of the South African-backed insurgent guerrilla group, the Resistência Nacional Moçambicana (Renamo) in Mozambique posed a threat to Zimbabwe's alternative access to the sea via the Beira corridor during the 1980s and early 1990s, and as a result Zimbabwe provided military assistance to the Mozambique government. Following the death of President Machel of Mozambique in an air crash in October 1986, Mugabe reiterated his support for the Mozambique leadership. Renamo consequently declared war on the Zimbabwe government, and cross-border incursions and civilian deaths became a regular occurrence. Mugabe played a leading role in mediating the cease-fire between the Mozambique government and Renamo. In late 1992–early 1993, under the terms of a cease-fire, Zimbabwean troops, who had been stationed in Mozambique since 1982, were withdrawn. By 1992 it was estimated that 250,000 Mozambican refugees were sheltering in Zimbabwe. Plans for the repatriation of some 145,000 Mozambican refugees were announced in March 1993; this scheme, under the auspices of UNHCR, was completed during the mid-1990s. By January 1997 Zimbabwe's refugee population had dwindled to an estimated 1,400. The SADC has enlisted the support of private business interests, including Zimbabwean companies, and of Western governments, for the Beira corridor rehabilitation project in Mozambique, which is of great importance to Zimbabwe's economy. It was confirmed in April 1995 that a group of armed Zimbabwean dissidents (known as 'Chimwenjes') had occupied abandoned Renamo bases in Mozambique; in July it was reported that hundreds of former Renamo rebels had joined them. In June 1996 the Zimbabwean and Mozambican governments agreed to co-operate in combating the Chimwenjes, who were mounting attacks in both countries. A dispute with Zambia in 1997 over the possession of two islands in the Zambezi river was to be submitted to international arbitration.

The support given by Zimbabwe to the Mozambique government, and the leading role taken by Mugabe in advocating the imposition of economic sanctions against South Africa resulted in direct retaliatory action against Zimbabwe by the South African government during the 1980s. In May 1987 South African defence forces launched two raids, within a week, on alleged bases of the African National Congress of South Africa (ANC) in Harare. Bomb explosions in Harare in October 1987 and in Bulawayo in January 1988 were widely regarded as further attempts by South Africa to destabilize the Zimbabwe government. In June 1988 an attempt by a South African commando unit to release five alleged South African agents who were awaiting trial in Zimbabwe was thwarted by Zimbabwean security forces; three of the detainees were found guilty in June 1989 of taking part in bomb attacks on ANC targets. The detainees were eventually released in July 1990. Diplomatic relations with South Africa were resumed following the holding of democratic elections in that country in April 1994, and in March 1997 a mutual defence co-operation agreement was concluded. Relations deteriorated in 1998 owing to South Africa's opposition to Zimbabwe's intervention in the civil war in the DRC (see below). Relations were also strained in 1999 owing to Zimbabwe's deteriorating economic and political circumstances (see above). In December fuel arrears owed to South Africa built up causing supplies to be suspended. In February 2000 South Africa denied reports that it had offered a substantial loan to Zimbabwe to help the country to resolve its financial crisis. However, South African President Thabo Mbeki offered to negotiate on Zimbabwe's behalf with the IMF and the World Bank for emergency aid to prevent the collapse of the economy. By May the increasingly turbulent land reform situation in Zimbabwe had adversely affected South Africa's economy, prompting Mbeki to appeal to foreign donors to fund the transfer of white-owned land to black farmers. In July it was reported that the South African government was preparing a 'rescue package' to aid economic recovery in Zimbabwe.

Following an SADC summit in Harare in August 1998, the Zimbabwe government dispatched troops and arms to the DRC to support the regime of President Laurent-Désiré Kabila against advancing rebel forces. Despite repeated attempts to negotiate a peaceful solution to the conflict, by May 1999 it was reported that Zimbabwe had spent at least Z.$500m. on its military intervention. Despite conservative official figures for losses and casualties, the action was domestically unpopular, and placed Zimbabwe's financial and military resources under considerable strain. In mid-1999 all armed forces were put on stand-by and retirements and resignations were banned in an attempt to keep the ranks at full strength. A cease-fire agreement was signed at Lusaka, Zambia, on 10 July and troop withdrawals were to follow within the next few months. However, a few days later, both the rebels and the allies of the DRC were accused of violating the accord. An SADC military commission was formed later that month to monitor the cease-fire. In September the first observers arrived in the DRC. The cease-fire was in danger of collapse in December as fierce fighting continued. The Zimbabwean and DRC governments unveiled a plan in September to establish a joint diamond and gold marketing venture to finance the war. However, in early 2000 the Zimbabwean government was reportedly unable to pay allowances to its troops fighting in the region owing to the critical shortage of foreign currency (see above). Public opinion was further turned against the continuation of the conflict in February when heavy rains and a cyclone struck Mozambique and neighbouring provinces of eastern Zimbabwe. There was a desperate shortage of helicopters, which were needed to bring aid to those affected, owing to their deployment in the DRC. The war also caused tensions between Zimbabwe and the IMF, the latter suspending assistance partly because of Zimbabwe's false accounting of expenses relating to the conflict. In March Congolese rebels breached the cease-fire, capturing a town in the eastern DRC, and continued to advance westwards.

In a wider international context, Zimbabwe's supportive role as a member of the UN security council during the Gulf war and its IMF-approved economic liberalization policies helped to overcome the tension with the USA which had surfaced in the mid-1980s (see above). Mugabe's meeting in Washington, DC, with President Bush in July 1991 confirmed the new relationship. In February 1993 a small number of troops from both countries engaged in joint training manoeuvres. During the 1990s Zimbabwe has contributed troops to UN operations in Mozambique, Rwanda, Somalia and Angola. In May 1995 Mugabe visited President Clinton and drew attention (as he had also done on a state visit to the United Kingdom in the previous year) to Zimbabwe's pressing need for foreign capital.

Relations with the United Kingdom were dominated by land reform issues in 1999 and 2000. In November 1999, while on a private visit to London, Mugabe was assaulted by protesters in support of homosexual rights. The president subsequently alleged at a Commonwealth summit that the British government had organized the incident to register its disapproval of plans to redistribute land (see above), and declared Prime Minister Tony Blair unfit to govern. Mugabe's anger had been aroused by a speech by Blair criticizing certain African countries' inactivity concerning AIDS. Mugabe repeated his allegations in an outburst in March 2000, also accusing the United Kingdom of orchestrating an international hate campaign against Zimbabwe. In January 2000 the Blair administration was strongly criticized for selling arms to Zimbabwe in light of the latter's

abuses of human rights. The British government cited contractual obligations. Arms exports were suspended a few months later as the seizures of farmland became excessively aggressive (see above). Meanwhile, in early April the two sides took part in talks about land reform. Further negotiations later that month followed Zimbabwe's decision that the United Kingdom should pay compensation to white farmers for their land. The 'former colonial power' offered aid towards resettlement, but not in the form of compensation. It also stipulated conditions for its release: illegal farm seizures and political violence must stop, free and fair elections must be held and only the black rural poor should receive redistributed land (there had been reports that thus far allies of Mugabe's circle had been the principal beneficiaries). Harare rejected these terms. Meanwhile, relations deteriorated sharply over a diplomatic incident in March, when customs officials at Harare airport ordered the opening of British diplomatic baggage, which had been impounded a few days before. The British government denounced the opening of the baggage, which contained security equipment, as a grave breach of the Vienna convention on diplomatic protocol and briefly recalled its high commissioner to London for consultations. Zimbabwe countered by condemning the United Kingdom for smuggling goods into the country.

Economy

LINDA VAN BUREN

As the rest of the world celebrated the arrival of the new millennium, Zimbabweans were descending into the worst economic crisis of their country's 20-year history. In the two decades following independence in 1980, even though the same political leadership was in power, little was done to redistribute wealth, and until the late 1990s only modest progress was achieved in establishing a mechanism for an orderly reallocation of wealth. Suddenly, in the election year of 2000, the Mugabe government decided that it was time to act. The land-redistribution arrangements that had been agreed at negotiating tables over the preceding three years were discarded, inducing fear. In February 2000 squatters, calling themselves war veterans, invaded white farms. Observed by the world's media, some invaded peacefully and, although not welcomed, were received peacefully; in numerous other cases, violent confrontations took place, and lives were lost. The result was that in an economy already in trouble, virtually all remaining business optimism and confidence, whether foreign or domestic, vanished.

During the first 19 years of independence since 1980, economic growth in Zimbabwe was uneven, fluctuating in conformity with the effect of rainfall on agricultural production, with world prices for the country's main exports and with changes in government economic policy. None the less, with an abundance of natural resources, a well-developed infrastructure and a diversified industrial sector, Zimbabwe proved itself to be better placed than most African economies to withstand the effects of commodity price fluctuations and to recover from short-term setbacks. However, the issue of land reform hung over the Zimbabwean economy like a pall. Those without land hoped the government would keep its early promises to resettle landless Zimbabweans on good farmland, and those with land maintained a low profile, planted their crops every year and hoped that their significant contribution to economic production would enable the status quo to continue. Indeed it did, largely, for 19 years. That is not to say that the issue was never discussed; from 1997 onwards it was negotiated extensively (see below).

LAND POLICIES

Access to productive land in Zimbabwe remained, 19 years after independence, of crucial importance in determining the degree to which the vast majority of the Zimbabwean people can contribute to the country's national production.

Before independence, the country's land was divided into five grades. The most productive cropland was classified as Grade I, the least productive as Grade V. Whites were allocated 78%

of all Grade I and II land. Grade IV and V land, deemed fit only for the grazing of livestock, accounted for 75% of the land allocated to smallholders in the pre-independence era, in what are known as the 'communal areas'. At 1 January 2000, some 11m. black Zimbabweans were still crowded on unproductive communal lands, and 4,500 principally white commercial farmers still owned 11m. ha of prime land.

After independence, the government reiterated its pre-election pledge to 'resettle' landless Zimbabweans on commercial farmland acquired from willing sellers among the white commercial farmers. By 1990 about 52,000 families had been resettled on 2.7m. ha, but this figure constituted only about 32% of the target set in the 1982–85 Transitional National Development Plan, which envisaged the resettlement of 162,000 families by 1985. Moreover, after a whole decade, fewer than 1% of those hoping for resettlement had been resettled. This tiny level of achievement was, nevertheless, largely tolerated for another decade. Under the 1980 constitution, the government was permitted, until 1990, to acquire land compulsorily for purposes of resettlement if it was 'under-utilized'. After 1990 expectations were directed towards an acceleration in land-reform measures. In March 1992 the house of assembly unanimously passed the Land Acquisition Act, which permitted the compulsory acquisition of land by the state, smoothing the way for the compulsory purchase of 5.5m. ha of the 11m. ha of land then still held by white farmers. The stated intention was to use the purchased land to resettle small-scale farmers from the communal areas. After much debate, the Act stopped short of detailing the white farmers' guarantee of fair compensation. This matter thus remained unresolved until President Mugabe, in August 2000, proclaimed that there was to be no compensation unless the United Kingdom wished to compensate these 'British' white farmers (most of whom hold Zimbabwean nationality). In April 1993 the government announced that it was to acquire 70 farms, covering some 190,000 ha; not surprisingly, protests ensued from the white-dominated Commercial Farmers' Union (CFU). The high court subsequently ruled against three white farmers who had attempted to prove that the confiscation of their land was unconstitutional; a later appeal to the supreme court was also lost. In March 1994 it emerged that a former cabinet minister and other senior politicians and government officials had obtained favourable leases to some of the forcibly purchased farms. President Mugabe abrogated the leases and announced a detailed study of the land-tenure and land-use system. In mid-1996 Mugabe requested financial assistance from the United Kingdom for the acceleration of the resettlement process. In 1996 it was announced that the acquisition of land by foreign investors would be permissible only in areas of low rainfall, and only in cases (subject to government approval) where a project would upgrade an economically marginal area, would bring significant industrialization to a primary agricultural region, would create major employment opportunities or would introduce a new form of export processing. Later foreigners and companies were barred from owning land, following the announcement in June 1997 that the National Land Acquisition Committee had concluded its programme of identifying land for reallocation. Further plans to tax large agricultural holdings were also proposed. Nevertheless, by August 1997 only 3.4m. ha of land had been acquired in the 17 years since independence, and only about 70,000 families had been resettled—a figure which still constituted scarcely 1% of those hoping for resettlement. In August 1997 it was reported that squatters had overrun some 450,000 ha, but this episode did not prove to be as precipitous as the February 2000 farm invasion. In the same month plans were announced to acquire 1,072 farms, covering 3.2m. ha, to resettle some 100,000 landless peasants; a further 700 farms, covering 1.3m. ha, were to be used for indigenous commercial farming. The government published its full list of 1,471 commercial farms designated for compulsory acquisition in November 1997. Controversially, Mugabe proclaimed that farmers would be compensated for the improvements they had made to their farms but not for the land itself. In January 1998, however, the IMF stipulated as a condition for the release of further financial assistance that the Mugabe administration must make assurances that it would offer full and fair compensation for land seized under the land resettlement programme. The Mugabe government did indeed make just such a pledge in March, and it was subsequently announced that 112 farms would be acquired before the commencement of the 1998/99 growing season in November 1998. The CFU speculated that, consequently, commercial-farm production would fall from Z.$14,000m. to Z.$8,000m. annually, and that exports from the sector would decline from Z.$10,000m. to Z.$6,600m. a year, and that job losses would be substantial.

A three-day international donor's conference on land reform took place in September 1998 in Harare, at which 24 countries and seven international organizations were represented. The Zimbabwe government, which sought Z.$40,000m. from donors to support its land acquisition programme, presented its case, as did the CFU and other interested parties. Although the donors acknowledged in principle the need for land reform in Zimbabwe and some did pledge financial support, they were unwilling to provide the full funding requirement for the scheme as proposed at that time. They did, however, approve a 24-month Inception Phase, to begin immediately. In November the government announced compulsory acquisition orders for a further 841 farms covering 2.24m. ha. By March 1999 the CFU stated that it was 'encouraged by the preparatory work relating to the Inception Phase of the land-reform programme', in which it had been 'fully involved'. The CFU also expressed confidence that payment to farmers for land acquired would continue to be mutually agreed. In May the cabinet approved an Inception Phase Framework Plan (IPFP), which the CFU agreed was practicable, and would allow for proper land reform, leaving intact the 'basis of the economy'. The IPFP called for the resettlement of 77,700 families on 1m. ha by 2001. Of this land, 223,112 ha was to come from 120 farms that were voluntarily offered for sale in 1998, with the balance representing uncontested acquisitions under the government's scaled-down list of 800 farms for compulsory purchase and what was described as 'novel approaches' for better utilization of farmland'. In May 1999 the World Bank pledged US $5m. towards the Inception Phase.

In February 2000 armed squatters calling themselves 'war veterans' began occupying white-owned farms. By April 2000 nearly 1,000 farms had been occupied, four people had been killed, six people had been abducted, hundreds of black employees working on white farms had been beaten, and several homes had been burned. Many of the 'veterans' were obviously too young to have fought in Zimbabwe's independence war; it was alleged that only some 15% of the squatters were actually war veterans, while the other 85% were unemployed youths who were paid Z.$50 per day by Mugabe's ruling party. Meanwhile,

Zimbabwe's annual tobacco auction opened in April 2000 with fewer than 7,000 bales for sale, less than one-third of the 25,000 bales usually offered on the first day, because land occupations had disrupted the growing, harvesting, drying and curing of this labour-intensive crop. By mid-May tourist arrivals had declined to less than one-half of the usual level. In the same month the World Bank halted all funding to Zimbabwe after the Mugabe government had failed to repay a government-guaranteed loan to the electricity parastatal and had exceeded the 60-day grace period (see below). Following the general elections held in June 2000, the Mugabe government, still in power but with a significantly reduced majority, resumed talks with donors. In July the new minister of industry and international trade, Nkosana Moyo, reportedly acknowledged the need to work with the IMF, given the country's lack of resources. A few days later, however, Mugabe apparently stated that the donors could keep their money, and that land would not be given up to satisfy donors. On 1 August 2000 the government devalued the Zimbabwe dollar by 24%, from Z.$38 = US $1 to Z.$50 = US $1, in an attempt to prevent 'a massive uncontrolled devaluation'; even before the devaluation the rate of inflation had been more than 50%. The following day a one-day general strike called by the trade unions was held peacefully. On 3 August, during a one-day visit by President Thabo Mbeki of South Africa, Mugabe promised that the exercise of removing squatters from occupied farms would be completed 'within the month'. None the less, the following day Mugabe proclaimed that the squatters were not to be removed at all, but would be allowed to stay on the farms until they were properly 'resettled'. In this climate of almost daily contradictory statements investor confidence, already at an extremely low ebb, was unlikely to show any recovery.

NATIONAL INCOME

The much-publicized land invasions of 2000 exacerbated an already troubled economic situation in Zimbabwe. In contrast, high levels of economic growth had been recorded in the first two fiscal years following independence. Gross domestic product (GDP) grew in real terms by 11% in 1980 and by 13% in 1981. A major factor in these growth levels was the withdrawal, in 1980, of economic sanctions, which had crippled the economy during the 15 years of unilaterally declared independence; increased trade with the outside world rapidly stimulated economic activity. These growth levels demonstrated a temporary over-inflation of the economy, to an extent that was illustrated graphically in the following three fiscal years. GDP stagnated in real terms in 1982 and retreated by 3.5% in 1983. There was positive growth in 1984, but only at a very low level of 1% in real terms. This downturn also reflected the onset of a serious drought that lasted three years and was to postpone until 1984/85 the entry of Zimbabwe's 800,000 peasant farmers into the formal agricultural economy. Real GDP growth advanced to 7.3% in 1985. The country's first Five-Year Development Plan, introduced in April 1986 and covering the period 1986–90, was based on an average annual real GDP growth of 5.1% for the term of the Plan. This target proved to be optimistic. GDP growth in 1986, which had been projected at 3%, reached only 0.18%. GDP remained virtually stagnant, at 0.3%, in 1987. Growth of 5.3% was recorded in 1988, however, exceeding the Plan target of 5%. The recovery was attributable to an increase of 20% in the value of agricultural production (owing to a good rainy season) and to high commodity prices. GDP growth slowed slightly in the following three years, to 4% in 1989, 3.8% in 1990 and 2.9% in 1991. As a result of the region's drought, GDP fell by 8.9% in 1992. Positive growth returned in 1993, at 3.0%, increasing to 6.1% in 1994. The government's growth target for 1995 was reduced from 5% to 1%, owing to a recurrence of drought in the 1994/95 growing season; in the event, GDP declined by 0.7%. Rainfall was abundant in 1995/96; strongly positive real GDP growth was restored in 1996, at 7.3%, and an increase of 3.2% was recorded in 1997, partly owing to excessive rainfall in the 1996/97 season. Growth in 1998 was estimated at 1.6%. GDP grew by an annual average rate of 3.6% during 1980–90, the first decade of independence, and by 2.3% annually in 1990–98. Growth was projected at 1.2% for 1999, in mid-1999 the IMF forecast real GDP growth at 4.4% for 2000. By July 2000 economists were revising their projections for 1999

GDP growth downwards and were forecasting a decline of between 2% and 5% for 2000. In mid-1999 the Mugabe government stated its intention to implement land reform according to the strategy set out at the donors' conference in September 1998 and vowed that land reform would be undertaken in close consultation with stakeholders and beneficiaries. On the strength of these pledges, in August 1999 the IMF approved a 14-month stand-by credit of US $193m. Of the total, only a cautious US $24m. was made available immediately; subsequent disbursements were to be conditional on Zimbabwe achieving performance criteria. Targets included the establishment of a fully transparent procedure governing land-reform efforts, including fair compensation for land acquired, and a reduction in inflation to 30% by 31 December 1999. Both these pledges were broken. The actual level of inflation was officially assessed at 53.7% in mid- 2000, before the 24% devaluation of the Zimbabwe dollar in August.

The population, which was officially estimated to be 12.29m. in August 1997, increased by some 3.3% per annum, according to official figures, during 1982–97, therefore population growth slightly exceeded economic growth during that period. However, Zimbabwe is one of the three African countries most severely affected by the AIDS epidemic, and it has been estimated that by 2015 the labour force will be one-sixth smaller than it would have been in the absence of AIDS.

Although Zimbabwe has one of sub-Saharan Africa's most successful agricultural sectors, agriculture ranked only third, behind services and manufacturing, in terms of contribution to GDP, until 1999, when manufacturing's decline allowed agriculture to take second place. Services accounted for 65% of GDP in 1999, followed by agriculture at 16%, manufacturing at 15% and mining at 3%. Growth prospects for all these sectors seemed dismal in 2000. The occupation of white farms by squatters severely reduced the harvest of tobacco and other crops; low investor confidece and a tightening of exchange controls hindered manufacturing; depressed world gold prices lowered the value of mining output; and a stay-away by tourists adversely affected the services sector.

The most notable trend in domestic expenditure in the 1980s was the decline in the private sector's share, from 63% in 1980 to 53% in 1986 and to 44% in 1989. The downward trend was reversed in 1990, however, when the private sector accounted for 53% of total spending; the sector's share grew to 61% in 1991 and to 71% in 1992, reflecting almost immediately the Economic Structural Adjustment Programme (ESAP) introduced in 1991, which envisaged continued growth of private consumption. The private sector's share in domestic expenditure had increased to 78% in 1996.

The World Bank Consultative Group for Zimbabwe held donors' conferences, mostly in Paris, at regular intervals during the 1990s. At these meetings donors pledged about US $1,000m. in February 1992, of which US $500m. was in the form of balance-of-payments support; US $1,400m. in December 1992 for 1993, of which US $800m. was in support of the balance of payments; and US $789m. in December 1993 in loans and grants to Zimbabwe for 1994. By 1995, however, relations between the Zimbabwe government and the Bretton Woods institutions had deteriorated significantly, and the IMF suspended assistance worth US $100m. in mid-1995, pending a reduction in Zimbabwe's budgetary deficit. Multilateral credit and bilateral balance-of-payments support remained suspended in 1996/97 and in 1997/98, following a failure to attain targets for economic reform. The IMF resumed lending with a US $175m., 13-month stand-by credit in June 1998 in support of Zimbabwe's 1998 economic reform programme, of which US$52m. was disbursed immediately, with the remainder to be released subsequently 'subject to Zimbabwe's meeting performance targets'. Also in June 1998, the World Bank extended a US $67.5m. project loan to Zimbabwe's park rehabilitation and conservation project. The last IMF credit approved in the 1990s was in August 1999 (see above).

AGRICULTURE

Zimbabwe has a diversified and well-developed agricultural sector, in terms of food production, cash crops and livestock. In 2000 about two-thirds of the total labour force and about one-quarter of the formal-sector labour force were engaged in agric-

ultural activity. Agriculture (including forestry) contributed 16.3% of GDP in 1999, compared with 17% in both 1980 and 1985 and 12.4% in 1990. Although the agricultural sector in Zimbabwe has been no more immune from fluctuations of price and unfavourable weather than in any other country, in the first 19 years of independence it proved to be resilient. After the squatter occupations of February 2000, however, depressing economic indicators revealed the scale of the damage this exercise had inflicted on Zimbabwe's agricultural sector. One distributor of agricultural equipment reported an 80% decline in sales and had to place its workforce on a four-day week. A company that leased agricultural equipment reported that farmers were returning their equipment early rather than risk being held liable if squatters destroyed it. Farmers stopped taking out new insurance policies since none of them provided cover against the one thing from which they really needed protection: political risk. Agricultural lenders reported that few farmers were arranging new loans and that some had stopped servicing their existing loans. Manufacturing companies dependent on the supply of locally produced agricultural commodities registered a fall in capacity utilization of up to 60%, and several resorted to laying off production staff. Freight hauliers reported a sharp decline in demand at a time when fuel was increasingly scarce and costs were rising.

The staple food crop is maize, and other cereal crops grown include wheat, millet, sorghum and barley. Despite the fact that the country's best farmland was still concentrated overwhelmingly in the commercial sector, the share of agricultural output contributed by small-scale farmers in the communal areas rose from 9% in 1983 to 25% in 1988. Communal and small-scale farmers contributed 50% of total agricultural production in 1989/90.

In 1996 Zimbabwe enjoyed a bumper harvest of 2.6m. metric tons of maize, more than three times as much as the 840,000 tons that had been harvested in 1995, when crops had been affected by drought. The 1997 maize crop was 2.19m. tons, but the 1998 crop amounted to just 1.42m. tons, a decrease of 35%. Although the yield per ha did decline by 13%, the main reason for the smaller harvest was a 25% reduction in the number of hectares planted with maize. The lower output necessitated maize imports and prompted harsh criticism of the government's maize-pricing strategy. In August 1998 it was announced that Zimbabwe was to import 610,000 tons of maize from South Africa, 460,000 tons by the Grain Marketing Board (GMB) and 150,000 tons by private-sector companies. However, the GMB had contractual commitments to export 300,000 of its 460,000 tons of the imported supplies. The 1999 maize crop, at 1.52m. tons, was still insufficient to meet domestic requirements, producing a deficit of 1.25m. tons in the 1999/2000 marketing season. After raising the producer price of maize from Z.$3,000 to Z.$4,900 per ton in 1999, the government subsequently increased it by 90%, prompting fears of a repeat of the public demonstrations in January 1998 following an attempt by the milling companies to raise the mealie price by 21% in the absence of government price controls; on that occasion, the government intervened, promising a 'review' of commodity prices. In June 1999 the National Bakers' Association warned the government that if its proposal to limit the retail price of bread to Z.$8.72 per standard white loaf went ahead, its members would suspend production. The GMB initiated a Z.$65m. silo-development programme in 1985, aimed at increasing its storage capacity from 435,000 tons to 1m. tons. Silos were built in the communal areas, with a view to eliminating the necessity of importing storage bags, and thereby potentially saving some Z.$27m. in foreign exchange per year. The first stage of the programme, covering 1985–90, involved the construction of seven silos with a combined capacity of 300,000 tons. The programme continued into the 1990s.

Added storage capacity is also needed to help Zimbabwe meet its food-storage requirements in times of plenty, so as to provide adequate food security for periods of drought. With domestic maize demand running at about 2m. metric tons a year, Zimbabwe had accumulated a surplus of 1.3m. tons by mid-1985 and stocks of 1.9m. tons by April 1987. Exports began in earnest in 1985 (see below) and continued until October 1987, when they were suspended as a precaution against the effects on the maize crop of the drought in the 1986/87 growing season. After good rains in December 1987 (excessive in some areas), exports resumed in April 1988. Poor rains in 1990/91 restricted farmers' deliveries to the GMB to only 675,000 tons, causing the Board to use some of the country's strategic maize stocks of 714,000 tons, carried over from the 1989/90 season. The GMB in mid-1991 expected to have closing maize stocks of 300,000 tons at March 1992, 40% less than the minimum carry-over requirement of 500,000 tons. This shortfall was extremely untimely, as the 1992/93 drought reduced deliveries in that crop year to a mere 13,000 tons, finding the government unprepared despite its expenditure of substantial sums to ensure a higher level of preparedness than in previous seasons. The November 1993–March 1994 rains were shorter than usual, causing maize output to fall slightly below the country's annual requirement; however, strategic stocks were adequate to meet the shortfall. In mid-1996 the strategic grain reserve was set at a statutory 936,000 tons, and a strategic grain reserve fund (initially totalling more than Z.$1,000m.) was established.

In May 1985 Zimbabwe became the first African country to donate its own food aid to Ethiopia, sending 25,000 metric tons to famine victims in that country. The UN's World Food Programme (WFP) bought 100,000 tons of Zimbabwean grain in 1988 for distribution to Malawi, Botswana and Mozambique. In 1990 the WFP undertook to transport at least 60,000 tons of Zimbabwe maize to drought victims in Angola, Malawi, Mozambique and Zaire (now the Democratic Republic of the Congo, DRC). The almost complete failure of the long rains in the November 1991–March 1992 rainy season, however, plunged Zimbabwe, as well as its neighbours in the region, into the worst drought of the century. Having imported maize only three times in the previous 75 years, Zimbabwe faced the necessity of importing 2m. tons of maize—and on this occasion it was required from overseas sources, as South Africa's crop was also affected by the drought. Although drought was the most serious factor leading to lower maize output, the shortages were also influenced by the reduced volume of maize intake by the GMB in 1991, down by 23% from the 1990 figure, primarily because low official prices payable to producers had led many farmers to abandon planting maize in favour of other crops such as groundnuts, sunflower seeds and, especially, soya beans. The government's policy had been a deliberate bid to keep what then seemed to be more and more excess maize from pouring into the country's overtaxed storage facilities. Producer prices were raised in March 1992 from Z.$325 per metric ton of maize to Z.$550. Controls on maize prices were abolished in June 1993, but controls on retail prices were reinstated in June 1997. In July 1999 the Mugabe government pledged to sell maize meal at a controlled retail price not lower than Z.$393 per 50-kg bag by 30 September, as part of the structural-performance criteria it agreed with the IMF in order to win approval for the August 1999 stand-by arrangement.

Zimbabwe consistently fails to meet its high domestic requirement of wheat (350,000 metric tons per annum), and imports are necessary. Output rose to a record 326,823 tons in 1990/91 before falling back to 259,000 tons in 1991/92. During the 1991/92 season the government raised the producer price for wheat by 20.6% and the price to the flour mills by 119%. Owing to the severe drought, wheat output for 1992/93 fell to only 58,000 tons, or enough to supply the milling industry for two months. Some 340,000 tons of wheat needed to be imported in 1992. Wheat output amounted to 320,000 tons in 1999, up from 280,000 tons in 1998, but a decline is forecast for 2000, owing to disruption from squatters on farms that grow wheat. The acreage under wheat in 2000 was said to be one-third less than in 1999.

In the financial year to 31 March 1996 the GMB recorded a preliminary profit of Z.$50m., compared with a Z.$1,000m. loss in 1994/95. The government's decision to take responsibility for debts amounting to Z.$4,000m. owed collectively by the GMB, the Cotton Marketing Board (CMB) and the Cold Storage Commission (CSC) contributed to the GMB's improved performance.

National Breweries Ltd produces 8,000–10,000 metric tons of malt per year for export, although output was considerably lower following the devastating effect of the 1991/92 drought on the barley crop. Zimbabwe's barley output fluctuates according to weather conditions, ranging from 30,000 tons in 1989 to 4,500 tons in 1992; the 1997 crop was an estimated 13,000 tons, but

output declined by 31% in 1998, to 9,000 tons, and fell again in 1999, to 8,000 tons. In 1999 Zimbabwe produced 170,000 tons of cassava, 107,178 tons of soya beans, 53,000 tons of millet (less than one-half as much as 1997's 115,000 tons), 85,600 tons of sorghum, 113,250 tons of groundnuts in shells (90% more than in 1998), 82,000 tons of bananas, 30,000 tons of sunflower seeds, 46,000 tons of dry beans, 30,000 tons of potatoes, 12,000 tons of tomatoes, 400 tons of oats and 400 tons of paddy rice. The horticultural sector performed well in the late 1990s, displaying a diversity not equalled in many other African countries. Production in 1999 included 5,900 tons of apples, 4,800 tons of green peas, 800 tons of peaches and nectarines, 650 tons of green beans, 500 tons of broad beans, 450 tons of mangoes (an increase of 12.5% compared with 1998, and of 80% compared with 1997), 410 tons of cucumbers, 280 tons of pears, 250 tons of melons, 250 tons of artichokes (recovering well from 1998's reduced crop), 230 tons of chillies, 230 tons of mushrooms, 230 ltons of strawberries, 220 tons of cabbages, 200 tons of plums, 200 tons of asparagus (a 33% increase from 1998), 180 tons of lettuces, 120 tons of carrots, 120 tons of cauliflower, 100 tons of leeks, 100 tons of garlic, 100 tons of raspberries, 50 tons of chestnuts, 40 tons of apricots, 40 tons of papayas and 10 tons of vanilla. Citrus growers in 1999 harvested 72,000 tons of oranges, 8,100 tons of lemons and limes, 8,100 tons of tangerines and 5,100 tons of grapefruits. Horticultural produce is regularly freighted to Europe, earning some US $60m. annually. Zimbabwe also exports some 15,000 tons of cut flowers per annum.

Zimbabwe's principal cash crops are tobacco, cotton and sugar. During the 1980s tobacco cultivation employed about 12% of the labour force and contributed about two-thirds of agricultural export revenue. In the 1990s declining demand in export markets placed downward pressure on prices. Zimbabwe's golden-yellow 'lemon leaf' variety is highly prized by blenders. Tobacco auctions each year normally begin in April and last for 25 weeks. Output marketed in 1989/90 was 129,900 metric tons, an increase of 8% in volume terms from marketed output of 119,913 tons in 1988/89. The crop marketed in 1988/89 was of exceptionally high quality, attaining an average price of Z.$4.30 per kg and a total value of Z.$640m., compared with an average price of Z.$2.15 per kg and a total value in export earnings of Z.$278.9m. in 1987/88. The crop marketed in 1989/90, which earned Z.$971m. in export revenue, attained an even higher average price, of Z.$6.48 per kg, producing almost Z.$860m. for the total crop. The 1990/91 crop amounted to 155m. kg of flue-cured tobacco, raising anticipated tobacco revenue to more than Z.$1,000m. Despite the drought, growers produced 201m. kg in 1991/92, in a year when 19% more farmers planted tobacco on 17% more surface area than in 1990/91. Exports of tobacco reached their highest quarterly level ever in October–December 1991, at more than 51m. kg. The crop in 1992/93 totalled a record 210m. kg, and was of superior quality. However, prices obtained at the opening of the 1993 auctions were only 97 US cents per kg, about one-half the levels of a year previously. This adverse development was the result of substantially reduced world demand for tobacco. Prices fetched did not even cover most growers' costs, and consequently, they incurred an aggregate debt of Z.$400m. In the 1993/94 season output fell to 182m. kg, but prices subsequently recovered. The average price fetched at auction was US$2.15 per kg in 1996/97 but fell to US$1.31 per kg in 1997/98. Tobacco production totalled 215.4m. kg in 1997, rising by 21% to 260m. kg in 1998. Output declined by 26% to 193m. kg in 1999, however, and forecasts for 2000 were bleak. Prior to the squatter troubles of 2000, Zimbabwe had enjoyed a favourable yield of 26,263 tons per ha in 1998; the area planted under tobacco had set a record in 1997, at 99,293 ha. By comparison, Malawi had more surface area under tobacco, at 105,000 ha, than Zimbabwe, but both Malawi's yield per ha and its total output in 1998 were less than one-half that of Zimbabwe. Exports of Zimbabwean tobacco in 1996 earned Z.$6,800m., with the European Union (EU, formerly the European Community—EC) and the Far East the most important destinations. Smallholders have become increasingly involved in the cultivation of burley tobacco. The flue-cured sector is far larger, with commercial farmers accounting for most of the output. In 1996 the government imposed an effective 10% tax on tobacco sales. Farmers and merchants bitterly opposed the tax and urged its abolition, claiming that it would damage the sector. In June 1999 the government agreed to halve the levy.

The proportion of cotton produced by communal farmers rose from 46% in 1987/88 to 60% in 1989/90, before falling back to 55% in 1990/91, as low real producer prices led farmers to plant other crops instead. The amount of commercial land under cotton fell from 55,700 ha in 1988/89 to 40,666 ha in 1989/90, and that of communal land declined from 12,000 ha in 1988/89 to 11,000 ha in 1989/90. Deliveries of seed cotton amounted to a record 323,239 metric tons in 1987/88, but slumped to 262,000 tons in 1988/89 and to 219,000 tons in 1989/90, before recovering to 280,000 tons in 1990/91. (The crop year runs from 1 March to 28 February.) Heavy rains during the cotton-picking season contributed to the 1988–90 setback, but many farmers also blamed the seed that they had purchased from the CMB. Growers reported that the plants from these seeds wilted soon after germination, and the crops of both large- and small-scale growers were affected. The drought of 1992 further reduced cotton output, to 21,000 tons in that year. Output recovered, however, to 67,000 tons in 1993, stabilizing at 65,000 tons in 1994. Zimbabwe was unable to profit from high global cotton prices in 1995, as drought reduced the size of the domestic crop in that year. In 1996 output recovered considerably, to 283,000 tons. Farmers harvested 278,184 tons of seed cotton in 1997, yielding 175,000 tons of cottonseed and 100,000 tons of cotton lint. The 1998 crop was 272,850 tons of seed cotton, yielding 95,000 tons of cotton lint. The 1999 harvest of 268,000 tons of seed cotton yielded 163,000 tons of cottonseed and 103,150 tons of cotton lint. The US company Monsanto had expressed an interest in investing Z.$150m. in a controversial venture to grow genetically engineered cottonseed in Zimbabwe, conditional on its being allowed to retain a controlling 51% share, but permission was not granted, the plan was abandoned in April 1999.

Sugar earned an estimated Z.$308m. in 1990, compared with earnings of Z.$186.9m. in 1989 and of Z.$157.1m. in 1988. Drought affected the 1988 crop, but production nevertheless exceeded the national demand of 170,000 metric tons per annum. The 1992 drought cut the country's output of milled sugar to 35,000 tons, just 10% of normal levels. Cane production in 1992 fell to only 300,000 tons (compared with 3.2m. tons in 1991), necessitating the import of 132,000 tons from Cuba. Even after the resumption of rains in November 1992, the sugar industry did not make an immediate full recovery, and the 1993 cane harvest, at 538,000 tons, was still only a small proportion of normal levels of output. By 1994, however, the recovery was complete, with growers producing 3.4m. tons of cane (yielding 507,000 tons of milled sugar—900% of the 1993 level). Output of milled sugar in 1995 was 465,000 tons, with sugar imports estimated at 115,000 tons and costing Z.$23m. Cane production totalled 3.48m. tons in 1996, rising to 4.64m. tons in 1997 and to 4.81m. tons in 1998, before declining to 4.66m. tons in 1999. An irrigation scheme has been proposed to make this very thirsty crop less vulnerable to drought in future. In 1993 the Commonwealth Development Corpn (CDC) loaned a total of £11m. for the re-establishment of canefields at Hippo Valley Estates Ltd and at Triangle Ltd, and a further £2m. to the Agricultural Finance Corpn of Zimbabwe for on-lending to the Chipiwa Growers' Co-operative Society Ltd. The 1992 drought is estimated to have killed up to 90% of the sugarcane plants in Zimbabwe's Lowveld region; despite good climatic conditions in 1996, the sector was unable to recover in time to benefit from them. In July 1999 Hippo Valley Estates strongly criticized government intervention in sugar prices, pointing out that the domestic price of sugar in Zimbabwe is less than one-half that in neighbouring countries. This anomaly has provided a significant incentive for the legal and illegal export of Zimbabwean sugar and, according to Hippo Valley Estates, costs the government Z.$110m. per year in lost tax revenue, together with a further Z.$313m. in price subsidies.

Coffee export revenue for Zimbabwe's mild arabicas rose from Z.$34m. in the 1984/85 season to Z.$50m. for the 1985/86 season, in which 11,000 metric tons were produced. Earnings from exports of arabica coffee reached Z.$75m. in the 1986/87 marketing year, but were estimated to have fallen to some Z.$45m. in 1987/88, reflecting the impact of drought on coffee production. The arabica crop doubled in 1988/89 to 12,500 tons, following favourable weather conditions; however, the value of exports

was only Z.$54m., because of depressed world prices. The 1991/92 coffee crop was severely depressed, owing both to the drought and to low global prices. The 1992/93 coffee crop returned to near-normal levels, and world prices finally improved in May 1994, reaching a five-year high. However, production plummeted to an estimated 4,000 tons in 1995; in 1997, following good rains, output of green coffee reached 10,380 tons. Output was about 10,000 tons per annum in 1998 and 1999. Zimbabwe also produced 17,800 tons of tea in 1999.

Zimbabwe is one of only a few sub-Saharan African countries allowed to export beef to the EU member states. Exports began in 1985; however, Zimbabwe was unable to meet its quota of 8,100 metric tons in the first two years (1985 and 1986), owing to a severe shortage of beef in the country. Beef allocations to butchers were reduced by 30% in 1986, when total beef sales realized some Z.$48m. (US $29.2m.). In an attempt to help the parastatal CSC survive in the face of competition from private-sector abattoirs, the government granted it a virtual monopoly of the urban market for beef from January 1987. However, producers argued that they needed a higher gazetted producer price in order to make their efforts economic. In April 1987 an increase of 38% in producer prices for beef was duly announced. Meanwhile, the government initiated major efforts to improve the financial position of the CSC, after a trading deficit of Z.$27.6m. was recorded in 1986 (increasing to Z.$28.9m. in 1987). With the equivalent of US $15.82m. in financing from the European Investment Bank and US $9.21m. from the Arab Bank for Economic Development in Africa, the CSC embarked upon a US $102m. project, which included the building of a processing and distribution complex in Harare, the construction of a new abattoir in Bulawayo (with a daily capacity of 600 head of cattle), and the rehabilitation of the Masvingo abattoir, with a planned capacity of 400 head of cattle per day. Zimbabwe fulfilled its EC quota of 8,100 metric tons of beef exports in 1987 (earning Z.$80m. from this source) and in 1988 (earning Z.$66.6m.). In 1989, however, the EC suspended its beef imports from Zimbabwe, owing to an outbreak of foot-and-mouth disease in April and May of that year. Exports were resumed in January 1992. In late 1987 domestic consumption of beef was restricted by the introduction of rationing. The 1992 drought led to a doubling of the intake of cattle at all abattoirs as herders rushed to sell their stock before they died of starvation. The CSC slaughtered 257,360 head of cattle during January–June 1992, more than double the number killed in July–December 1991. The drought reduced the national herd to 1.7m. head of cattle, but Zimbabwe was still able to meet its EU quota of high-quality beef, which had by then been increased to 14,600 tons. Exports to the EU fell to 5,243 tons in 1996 and recovered only to 6,560 tons in 1997, as a result, its quota was reduced. In 1998 Zimbabwe's EU quota was 9,100 tons, but the country was still only able to fill 84% of it, at 7,653 tons. Zimbabwe also enjoys a 5,000 ton per year quota of beef exports to South Africa. Zimbabwe produced 6,000 tons of dried milk, 2,000 tons of cheese and 3,000 tons of butter in 1996, and 8,976 tons of vegetable oils and margarines in 1995. The CDC has purchased a 25% share of Dairibord, Zimbabwe's principal milk producer, which it is hoping to diversify into other product areas.

Zimbabwe produces some 30,000 cu m of non-coniferous sawnwood, 3,000 cu m of non-coniferous sawlogs and veneer logs, and 1.8m. cu m of industrial roundwood per annum. Timber export earnings amounted to more than US $10.9m. in 1996.

Zimbabwe produced a total fish catch of 18,056 tons in 1997. Surprisingly, for this land-locked country, true freshwater species contributed only about 6% to the total. The predominant fish caught are dagaas (various species of shad), which migrate between salt water and fresh water; dagaas alone accounted for 94% of the total catch.

MINING AND MANUFACTURING

Mining accounted for only 3% of Zimbabwe's GDP in 1999, a considerable decline from its 7% contribution in 1996, but nevertheless an improvement on the 1.8% contributed in 1998. This low figure for 1998, when the value of total mining production amounted to Z.$2,440m., reflected weak international prices for the minerals Zimbabwe produces. The index of mineral production declined dramatically in 2000, falling from 1,538l.22

in March to 1,262.84 in April. Although the index recovered somewhat in May, it was still below the 1,300 mark in June.

Zimbabwe currently produces more than 40 different minerals. Gold, platinum, nickel, asbestos, coal, copper, chromite, iron ore, tin, silver, emeralds, graphite, lithium, granite, cobalt, tungsten, quartz, silica sands, kyanite, vermiculite, corundum, magnesite, kaolin and mica are the main mineral products. Gold is the primary source of revenue in the mining sector, and accounted for some 44% of total export sales by value in the first half of 2000. Production of gold amounted to 25.2 metric tons in 1998, not quite as much as the 26.7 tons mined in 1995, but up 3.5% from the 24.3 tons produced in 1996, and well up from 20.5 tons in 1994, 18.7 tons in 1993, 18.5 tons in 1992, 17.3 tons in 1991, 16.9 tons in 1990 and 16.0 tons in 1989. In value terms, gold earned more than US $750m. in 1998. About 25% of Zimbabwe's gold production is derived from the tailings of earlier gold-mining activities. In November 1993 Cluff Resources of the United Kingdom (later acquired by Ashanti Goldfields of Ghana) reached an agreement with the Eastern and Southern African Trade and Development Bank for a 52,000-oz gold loan to finance underground development of the Freda Rebecca gold mine, which had become Zimbabwe's largest gold mine by the end of 1994. The loan was repayable over five years and gave the borrower the choice of repaying in gold or US dollars. Ashanti subsequently sold six smaller gold mines in Zimbabwe. The world gold price fell to a 12-year low in 1997, a level which reportedly rendered some 60% of the world's gold mines unprofitable. In Zimbabwe, one gold mine closed with debts totalling Z.$18m., and another turned a Z.$5m. profit into a Z.$53m. loss, and was saved from imminent closure only by a last-minute rescue bid from another mining company. Production at one of the country's largest mines, Rio Tinto's Renco mine in Masvingo, fell by 15% from 12,796 oz in the third quarter of 1998 to 10,919 oz in the second quarter of 1999. Rio Tinto closed its unprofitable Brompton gold mine near Kadoma. Falcon Gold closed its Dalny gold mine in 1998 and its Venice mine in 2000. Anglo-American bought the low-grade open-cast 16,000 ton per annum Bubi gold mine in Matabeleland. It also operates the open-cast 19,000 ton per annum Isabella gold mine. Delta Gold bought three mines from Falcon Gold, and was in 1999 proceeding with the development of the 10.5-ton Eureka mine near Guruve, capable of processing 75,000 oz of gold annually.

The world nickel price increased dramatically at the end of the 20th century, doubling to US $8,370 per metric ton in 1999. Nickel ranks second in mineral export revenue; output was 9,694 metric tons in 1996, valued at Z.$655m., well down from the prevailing level of about 11,500 tons per annum in the early 1990s. In a market in which almost everything was turning downward, Bindura Nickel's share price rose from Zl.$1.05 at 1 January 1999, to Z.$14.00 at 31 December 1999, and to Z.$21.00 at 1 March 2000. Asbestos output was 157,000 tons in 1993, compared with 187,066 tons in 1989. The association of asbestos with lung cancer led to a decline in the value of exports. Coal output was 5.1m. tons in 1996, down from 5.5m. tons in 1995 and 5.3m. tons in 1993 (compared with 2.9m. tons in 1981). Revenue from coal exports rose from Z.$119.2m. in 1989 to Z.$162.2m. in 1990 and to Z.$174.8m. in 1991. Rio Tinto Zimbabwe announced in 1990 that it was to develop the Sengwa coalfield in western Zimbabwe, which has a projected annual output of 100,000 tons of low-sulphur coal; the project was the second-largest investment in Zimbabwe since independence. Wankie Colliery Co invested Z.$167m. in a new underground mine called M-Block; Wankie's total output was 3.92m. tons in 1997/98, 3.7% less than the 4.08m. tons produced in 1996/97; the decline was attributed in part to unreliable availability of coal wagons from National Railways of Zimbabwe and also to problems at Hwange power station, a major consumer of Wankie Colliery coal. Wankie Colliery was producing at only about 50% of capacity during the first half of the 1980s, and by 1985 just 15 of its 32 ovens were in operation. The coke-oven battery was closed from 1986 until late 1987 for rehabilitation, but the company had stockpiled sufficient coke to maintain supplies during the closure. The colliery's output was 160,000 metric tons of coke in the year to February 1989, while domestic demand was 68,000 tons per annum. The company's operations are being expanded to exploit a deposit estimated at 400m. tons.

In October 1996 a new coke oven gas plant at Wankie Colliery was formally commissioned, after it had already been fully operational for six months. The new facility enabled the company to sell some 25.4m. cu m of coke oven gas to the national electricity grid in the last eight months of 1996. The Zimbabwe government in July 1999 agreed to sell all of its remaining shares in Wankie Colliery by the end of that year. Reserves at Lubimbi coalfield are estimated to exceed 20,000m. tons, and an oil-from-coal project is in operation there. Zimbabwe's total coal reserves are estimated at 28,000m. tons. Shangani Energy Exploration was granted a licence in May 1998 to mine coal-bed methane gas in Bulawayo mining district. Rio Tinto Zimbabwe is to develop an open-cast coal mine at Gokwe, in north-western Zimbabwe, with a capacity of 6m. tons per annum, which is to be sold to a not-yet-built power station due to enter production in 2006 (see below).

Copper production fell in volume terms from 15,659 tons in 1989, to 14,689 tons in 1990 and to 13,451 tons in 1991, although the value of output rose from Z.$74.9m. in 1989 to Z.$85.3m. in 1990 and to Z.$99.3m. in 1991. A declining trend in world copper prices culminated in a six-year price low in October 1993. In 1997 it was reported that the Mhangura copper mine was no longer economical to run; loans and grants secured in that year were necessary to ensure its continued operation. Volume output of chromite was 658,416 tons in 1996, valued at Z.$177m., compared to 570,749 tons in 1991. Output of iron ore (metal content 64%) was 1.16m. tons valued at Z.$49.83m. in 1991, compared with 1.26m. tons valued at Z.$44m. in 1990, 1.02m. tons valued at Z.$25.6m. in 1988 and 1.33m. tons valued at Z.$28.8m. in 1987. Output volume for silver declined from 21,154 tons in 1990 to 12,000 tons in 1993. Earnings from silver totalled Z.$10.94m. in 1991. Tin output declined from 808 tons in 1990 to 658 tons in 1993. Earnings from tin amounted to Z.$15.26m. in 1991.

Platinum holds significant revenue potential. Substantial reserves of platinum, first discovered in 1914, are located in the Great Dyke mineral belt in central Zimbabwe. The first platinum mine opened at Wedza in 1926. Delta Gold acquired the Hartley concession in 1987 and formed a joint-venture company to develop it in 1990, at a cost initially projected at US $264m., but later assessed at US $289m. In December 1993 BHP of Australia made an investment of A$311m. (US $211m.), said to be the largest single private-sector investment in Zimbabwe since independence, to enable the Hartley project to go ahead. In the following year the Zimbabwe government agreed to the venture and construction work commenced. An underground mine came into operation in April 1996, creating 3,573 mining jobs, but the project ran into technical problems which caused the date for entry into full production to be postponed. In the late 1990s a mill, a concentrator, a smelter, a converter and a base-metal refinery were built, and in 1997 the project produced its first shipment of platinum concentrate. Modifications to the smelter costing Z.$72m. had to be made in order to deal with the geological conditions encountered. In May 1998 Delta sold its 33% share to Zimbabwe Platinum Mines Ltd (Zimplats). In June 1999 BHP announced the closure of the mine, owing to geological problems and unstable ground conditions which rendered the mine unsafe, and claiming that it had earned only US $40m. from the mine after investing US $585m. BHP sold its 67% share for a token sum to Zimplats in late 1999. The government hastened to clarify that the Hartley closure was temporary and would resume once it could be made safe underground. At full production of 180,000 tons of platinum-bearing ore per month, Hartley would account for about 10% of total world output of the precious metal, and would establish Zimbabwe as Africa's second most significant producer of platinum, after South Africa. Production was about 71,000 tons per month in mid-1998, but was expected eventually to rise to 100,000 tons per month. The mine, which has a projected life span of 70 years, has been forecast to produce annually, at full capacity, 150,000 oz of platinum metal, as well as 110,000 oz of palladium, 23,000 oz of gold, 11,500 oz of rhodium, 3,200 tons of nickel, 23,000 tons of copper, and 2,000 tons of cobalt. Projected earnings from Hartley are assessed at more than Z.$700m. annually. Areas adjacent to Hartley are also being explored for possible exploitation. In May 1995 Delta Gold announced plans to develop a further platinum and gold project at Ngezi, 57 km south of the Hartley complex, with construction due to begin by January 2000, and full production scheduled for 2001. While reserves of platinum at Hartley are assessed at 14m. oz, those at Ngezi are evaluated at 24m. oz. Anglo Zimbabwe has announced plans to develop a platinum mine at Unki, near Shurugwe, at a cost of Z.$1,400m., in a joint venture with the Zimbabwe government. Unki was expected to produce 1.02m. tons of ore per annum at a richness of 5.4 grams per ton of platinum-grade metals and gold. The scheme was expected to generate Z.$4,000m. per year in export revenue and create 1,400 jobs. In 1996 the Zimbabwe Mining and Smelting Co was reported to be developing a smaller platinum mine in Midlands Province.

The parastatal Zimbabwe Mining Development Corpn is developing the copper deposits at the Copper Queen and King mines, and it is planned to manufacture copper cable locally as an import-substitution venture, aimed at saving Z.$6.6m. in foreign exchange annually. There is also import-substitution potential in the manufacture of ferrochrome derivatives, chemicals and pesticides. Another parastatal organization, the Minerals Marketing Corpn of Zimbabwe, markets all the country's minerals, except gold, abroad. Established in 1982, its operations were consistently profitable for the following 15 years. Major private-sector mining companies, such as the Anglo American Corpn, Rio Tinto-Zinc and Lonrho, are also active in Zimbabwe. Although low metal prices in 1998 clouded the short-term prospects, the medium-term outlook for Zimbabwe's mining sector was still deemed to be encouraging, helped by the government's decision in 1990 to allow mining companies to retain 5% of the value of their export earnings to finance imported inputs. In 1989 a gold refinery, with a capacity of 50 tons per year, was opened in Harare. Built at a cost of Z.$4m., the refinery is owned by the Reserve Bank of Zimbabwe and is operated by Fidelity Printers and Refiners. It is expected to lessen Zimbabwe's dependence on South Africa, which had previously possessed the only gold refineries in Africa. Gemstones hold considerable growth potential. In May 1991 the British company Reunion Mining began prospecting for diamonds over a 43,597 sq km area near Beitbridge. In the following month Auridiam Consolidated of Australia obtained a permit to develop the River Ranch diamond concession at a cost of US $10m.–$12m. The company completed its exploration activities in 1992, confirming that diamonds had been found at the concession and announcing plans to build a small-scale production plant. A 500,000 ton-per-annum processing plant at River Ranch was commissioned in January 1994. The River Ranch mine had been expected to reach full production of 1.5m. tons of ore annually in 1996 and to produce 500,000 carats a year during its projected 10-year life span. However, low world diamond prices resulted in the company losing Z.$40m. for every ton of ore processed, and in February 1998 the mine closed down with the loss of 400 jobs. It went into voluntary liquidation in May 1998; immediately 12 potential purchasers (both local and foreign) reportedly came forward, but the number subsequently dwindled to only two. Interest in mining diamonds in Zimbabwe remained keen, and in 1998 a number of licences were granted to companies to prospect for them.

Zimbabwe produces a wide variety of manufactured products, both for the local market and for export. Growth of manufactured exports on a regional basis has been hindered by lack of foreign exchange in neighbouring countries, and by reductions as large as 55% in the amount of foreign exchange allocated to manufacturers for the import of essential raw materials. The ESAP, introduced in 1991, significantly alleviated the foreign-exchange constraint, although subsequent tensions between the Zimbabwe government and multilateral donors put further pressure on the country's foreign-exchange position (see above and below). The weak Zimbabwe dollar was a fillip to those companies with low import costs manufacturing for export, but it placed further pressure on those with high import costs manufacturing for the local market. The manufacturing sector accounted for 15% of GDP in 1999, a decline from 19% in 1996 and from the 30% annually achieved in 1992–93.

The volume index of manufacturing production (1980 = 100) reached 153.3 in the October quarter of 1990, the highest level since independence. The annual index figure was 138.1 for 1990, 144 for 1991, 123 for 1992, 123.4 for 1993 and 128.3 for 1994. In the 1993 calendar year, as compared with the calendar year 1992, the only sectors to register positive growth were textiles and ginning (up by 9%), paper and printing (up by 14.6%), and clothing and footwear (up by 2.6%). All other sectors experienced a decline, the most pronounced being transport equipment (down by 41.8%), followed by metals and metal products (down by 18.2%, largely reflecting production problems at the parastatal Ziscosteel), foodstuffs (down by 17.9%) and non-metallic minerals (down by 17.7%). In 1991 the country began a three-phase measure to place more products under Open General Import Licence (OGIL). The first phase began on 1 April 1991, and the government had placed 50% of imported raw materials under OGIL by January 1992. Other products followed, and in January 1994 the government removed a 10% temporary duty on OGIL imports. The government also reduced the surtax on imports from 20% to 15%. While many manufacturers have welcomed aspects of the ESAP reforms, they were less fond of measures such as the removal of the Export Incentive Scheme, which the government acknowledged was a subsidy and a distortion of a free-market economy. Ziscosteel's problems remained, and bailing out the company placed a strain on public-sector expenditure. The government planned to rehabilitate the company's number-four blast furnace to raise capacity to 700,000 metric tons of liquid steel per annum, in order to make the enterprise more attractive to bidders when privatized. It was reported in May 2000 that a new cement plant, costing Z.$5,000m., was to be built at Masvingo, with a production capacity of 730,000 tons per annum. The plant would be able to fill Zimbabwe's entire cement shortfall of 140,000 tons per annum, and would export the rest of its output within the region. The new venture would bring the number of cement producers in Zimbabwe to six. Although the project had been approved, it was uncertain when construction would commence, considering the prevailing economic climate. The manufacturing sector came under severe pressure during the economic crisis of 1999 and the troubles of 2000. It was reported that 85 companies in 12 sectors had gone into liquidation during 1999, followed by a further 18 enterprises in January–April 2000. These companies had been engaged in trade, farming, manufacturing, tourism and construction. Of the 1999 figure, just over one-half, 43 companies, went into voluntary liquidation, while the other 42 were forcibly liquidated by creditors. Whereas 6,357 companies had defaulted on debt repayments in the whole of 1999, no fewer than 2,820 had been issued with default judgments in the first four months of 2000. Interest rates of more than 70% were a major contributory factor. In the first half of the 1990s government spending on parastatals amounted to Z.$6,500m. In 1997 the Confederation of Zimbabwe Industries was encouraging larger companies to contract out subordinate activities to smaller firms. In 1998 Steelmakers Zimbabwe Ltd invested Z.$320m. to build a billet-making plant at Redcliff. Manufacturing in the country's Export Processing Zones was flourishing in the late 1990s. As of August 1998, 28 companies had been established, creating 6,242 jobs and generating Z.$2,000m. in export revenue; a further 72 projects had been approved, with the potential to create 12,000 jobs.

INTERNATIONAL TRADE AND BANKING

Forecasts for Zimbabwe's trade performance in 1999 and 2000 were being revised downward towards the end of 1999 as the economic crisis deepened. Zimbabwe's visible exports declined by 15.5%, from US $2,424m. in 1997 to US $2,047m. in 1998, while at the same time visible imports declined by 25.8%, from US $2,654m. to US $1,968m., so that the visible trade deficit of US $230m. in 1997 became a visible trade surplus of US $79m. in 1998. The current-account balance excluding grants, while still negative, improved from a US $827m. shortfall to one of US $343m. An even greater improvement was recorded on the overall balance of payments, where the deficit fell from US $751m. to US $25m. In June 1998 the IMF warned that Zimbabwe's foreign reserves were at 'dangerously low levels'. At 31 December 1997, gross foreign reserves stood at US $272m., sufficient to cover only 0.8 of one month's worth of imports of goods and services; by 31 December 1998 they had improved only slightly, to US $296m., enough to cover 1.1 months' of imports of goods and services. Tobacco and gold are the largest two items on the export list, but together they contribute less than 50%; other export earners are cotton lint, textile products, footwear, ferro-alloys, food and live animals, crude inedible non-food materials, chrome, nickel, asbestos, copper, raw sugar, iron and steel bars, ingots and billets, electric cables and radios. This list illustrates an unusually high level of export diversity for an African country. In May 2000 total exports for that month earned US $97m., of which gold accounted for US $50.9m. and tobacco and beverages combined accounted for only US $3.4m., revealing in no small measure the effects of the squatters' farm invasions. Exports of ivory (to Japan only) recommenced on a limited scale in 1999, following a vote at a conference of the Convention on International Trade in Endangered Species (CITES), and Zimbabwe had already arranged to sell 20 metric tons of ivory to Japan out of its estimated ivory stock of 38 tons. An auction of 80 tons of processed elephant hides in June 1998 earned Z.$17m. in export revenue. In April 2000, however, CITES decided to suspend again all trade in ivory. Horticultural exports continued to show significant growth, and exports of paprika alone were forecast to earn Z.$225m. in 1998. The main imports in 1996 were machinery and transport equipment (38.4%), basic manufactures (16.2%) and chemicals (13.0%).

Zimbabwe's principal trading partners vary significantly from year to year. In 1996 the most important was the Southern African Customs Union (40.6% of imports and 14.7% of exports), followed by the United Kingdom (8.3% of imports and 10.5% of exports), Japan (5.1% of imports and 5.0% of exports), Germany (4.9% of imports and 7.9% of exports) and the USA (5.0% of imports and 6.6% of exports). A survey in South Africa found that by mid-2000 46% of South African manufacturers had reported a decline in exports to Zimbabwe.

Zimbabwe's membership of the Common Market for Eastern and Southern Africa (COMESA), formerly the Preferential Trade Area for Eastern and Southern Africa, has, in theory, provided access to new directions in regional trade. In practice, however, Zimbabwean exporters have been somewhat disappointed. In the 1990s Zimbabwe produced many items which the other member-states needed to import, but the potential trade partners lacked the foreign exchange to pay for them. The historic change of government in South Africa made it politically correct for countries and companies in the region to source their imports from the Republic, often with better value for money, and Zimbabwe's share of the market dwindled. South Africa was able to take an even larger share of Zimbabwe's domestic market following the increase in trade liberalization in the late 1990s. Zimbabwe ratified the COMESA treaty in 1999.

Zimbabwe's external debt rose sharply during the 1980s, climbing from US $696m. at the end of 1980 to US $2,352m. at the end of 1989. It continued to rise during the 1990s until it peaked at US $3,906m. at the end of 1995 before falling back to US $3,756m. at the end of 1996, and to about US $3,541m. at the end of 1998. Debt-servicing costs were equivalent to 33% of the value of exports of goods and services in 1987, 27.5% in 1988, 21.3% in 1989, 23.2% in 1990, 27.2% in 1991, 32.0% in 1992, 30.6% in 1993, 25.4% in 1994, 23.7% in 1995, 21.3% in 1996, 22.2% in 1997 and 38.2% in 1998. In June 1999 it was reported that for the first time in 20 years Zimbabwe had failed to make its debt-service payments, as the country's foreign reserves had by that time been 'dangerously low' for at least a year (see above). The Zimbabwe government also owed an estimated Z.$41,000m. in domestic debt at 31 December 1998. Significantly, total domestic debt had increased to Z.$108,212m. by 31 May 2000, a rise of 164% in just 17 months. It was reported that the printing of money was accelerated in the first half of 2000 in order to meet the pay increases of civil servants in the run-up to the June elections. This sudden, literal increase in the money supply placed great upward pressure on an already excessive inflation rate, officially assessed at 53.7% in mid-2000, but thought by many to be far higher. Moreover, these assessments preceded the August devaluation of the Zimbabwe dollar.

The domestic banking sector is diversified, with major foreign banks participating, as well as the Zimbabwe government. Of the commercial banks, two are long-established foreign banks—Barclays Bank of Zimbabwe and Standard Chartered Bank Zimbabwe. The state-controlled Zimbabwe Banking Corpn (Zimbank) in 1990 expanded internationally, opening offices in Ghana and Botswana. Merchant banks include First Merchant Bank of Zimbabwe (FMCZ), the Merchant Bank of Central

Africa, Standard Chartered Merchant Bank Zimbabwe and National Merchant Bank. The World Bank's private-sector arm, the International Financial Corpn, announced in June 1998 that it was to invest US $15m. in FMCZ, the nation's largest merchant bank, as well as US $27.8m. in the privatization of the Commercial Bank of Zimbabwe. United Merchant Bank collapsed in May 1998, amid rumours that some of the remaining financial institutions were also experiencing liquidity problems, resulting in a rush to move deposits from indigenous institutions into the two foreign banks. One of the conditions imposed by the IMF in August 1999 in exchange for the approval of a stand-by arrangement was that the Zimbabwe government issue to the public, not later than 30 September 1999, its guidelines to deal with 'troubled banks'. A new bank, Kingdom Financial Services Merchant Bank, was launched in August 1998. The Zimbabwe Development Bank began operations in 1985; the government took a controlling interest, in partnership with the African Development Bank and other multilateral development institutions. In November 1991 the Zimbabwe Building Society was launched; by June 1995 deposits had grown to Z.$1,880m., with capitalization at Z.$2,120m. In July 1993 exchange controls were relaxed, allowing foreign investors to repatriate investment proceeds, providing a major boost to the Zimbabwe Stock Exchange. The share-purchase limit was also raised to 35%. The exchange was capitalized at US $1,900m. in May 1994. In August 1995 some 66 local industrial and mining companies were listed, and at the end of 1996 the exchange had a market capitalization of US $4,719m., with an annual turnover of some US $250m. Bureaux de change were required to have a minimum paid-up capital of US $10,000 and to submit weekly statements of all transactions to the Reserve Bank of Zimbabwe.

ENERGY

A critical fuel shortage permeated through the Zimbabwean economy in late 1999, and worsened significantly in the first half of 2000. The government raised pump prices in early June 1999 by 27% for petrol and by 32% for diesel fuel. Petroleum and petroleum products accounted for 9.8% of all imports in 1996. Petroleum products enter the landlocked country through a 300-km pipeline running between Mutare and the Mozambique port of Beira. Work began in 1989 to extend the pipeline to Harare. Zimbabwe consumes some 800,000 metric tons of petroleum products (including diesel fuel) annually.

Zimbabwe shares with Zambia the huge Kariba dam, on the Zambezi river. For many years, Kariba's only hydroelectric power plant was on the Zambian side, and Zimbabwe imported some Z.$20m. worth of energy annually from its northern neighbour. In 1987, however, Zimbabwe added 920 MW of new thermal capacity to its own national grid, eliminating the need for these imports; in July 1987, the Zimbabwean government notified Zambia of its intention to terminate the supply contract. This termination was brought about abruptly in early 1989, however, when a fire seriously damaged Zambia's Kafue station, eliminating its export capacity. The Hwange thermal power station, constructed at a cost of Z.$230m., accounted for 920 MW of total national generating capacity of 1,900 MW in 1989. However, the Hwange facility's performance has been disappointing owing to design faults and a shortage of spare parts. Work to refurbish Units 1–4 of the facility during the first half of the 1990s was funded by the World Bank, and the station was to be privatized. The shared Central African Power Corpn was replaced in 1986 by the Zimbabwe Electricity Supply Authority (ZESA), which had the stated aim of maximizing the operational efficiency of existing installed capacity, while furthering a longer-term development programme directed towards a forecast demand of 2,800 MW by 2004. (Maximum demand in 1988/89 was about 1,400 MW.) In April 1991, after many delays, the government agreed to the construction of a Z.$500m. hydroelectric extension facility at Kariba South, due for completion in late 1998, and of a joint Zambia-Zimbabwe Batoka Gorge hydroelectric facility costing Z.$1,000m., which was to add 1,600 MW by 2003; however, the Zambian government withdrew from the project, and in 1997 the Zimbabwean authorities were seeking private finance for the scheme. A Z.$154m. plan to rehabilitate three thermal power plants was also approved. A new 1,400-MW power station is to be built at Gokwe, near coal reserves in north-western Zimbabwe, at a proposed cost of US $1,600m., with start-up envisaged for 2006. The 1992 drought lowered the water level for all hydroelectric facilities in the region, necessitating the unusual step of rationing electricity in Zimbabwe. Urgent negotiations were initiated to obtain power imports from the Democratic Republic of the Congo and Zambia, and in May 1992 ZESA arranged for the import of 500 MW from Mozambique. Work on an interconnector linking Mozambique's Cahora Bassa facility to Matimba and Bindura in Zimbabwe began in 1994 and added 500 MW to Zimbabwe's national grid. A coal-fired project at Sengwa is to add 600 MW by 2004. In September 1997 ZESA raised electricity tariffs by 30%; multilateral institutions had long been advocating higher tariffs as a means to fund the capital investment needed to increase the efficiency of the electricity supply, for which there was a growing demand.

It was a government-guaranteed loan to ZESA that triggered the World Bank's suspension of lending to Zimbabwe in May 2000. A crucial repayment that was due in March was not made on time, nor was it made during the subsequent 60-day grace period, at the end of which the World Bank cut off lending to Zimbabwe. Although the repayment was eventually made after the end of the grace period, the World Bank's arrears procedures required other debt arrears to be paid before lending could resume.

LABOUR, WAGES AND INFLATION

Inflation has, with the exception of 1988, affected lower-income urban families more than it has higher-income urban families in every year since independence in 1980. By January 1996 the average annual inflation rate had risen to 28%; although officially it fell back to 21.4% a year later, in January 1997, and continued at 25% in 1998, according to official assessments, it became clear that most economists estimated Zimbabwe's inflation at over 40% in 1998. Placing upward pressure on the inflation rate in 1998 were ZESA's 37% increase in electricity tariffs in July, National Railways of Zimbabwe's raised freight charges and continuing rises in food prices. The IMF, for its part, in August 1999 set the government the task of bringing inflation down from 1998's annual 46.6% to 29.8% at the end of 1999 by 'containing money-supply growth'. In the same communiqué, the Fund called for 'other reinforcing measures' such as the removal of maize-meal price controls (see above) and commended Zimbabwe for measures already taken, including a 15% rise in electricity tariffs, a 27% increase in retail petrol prices, a 32% rise in the retail diesel price, and the back-to-back increases of the controlled retail mealie prices of 20% in June 1999 and another 20% in July 1999. The Zimbabwe dollar was devalued by 17% at 1 January 1994, and, following the liberalization of exchange-rate policy, market forces determined the rate through sales by bureaux de change. However, the Zimbabwe dollar performed poorly in the late 1990s. From an average exchange rate of Z.$9.92 = US $1 in 1996, and of Z.$11.89 = US $1 in 1997, the currency fell to Z.$18.44 = US $1 in July 1998, representing a depreciation of 35.5%. A sharp decline was to follow: by July 1999, the exchange rate had weakened to Z.$37.75 = US $1, a depreciation of 51% in only 12 months. In July 1999 the Mugabe government assured the IMF that the exchange rate would be determined by market forces, with the central bank intervening only to smooth out fluctuations and achieve its international reserve objectives. On 1 August 2000 the government formally devalued the Zimbabwe dollar by 24%, from Z.$38 = US $1 to Z.$50 = US $1.

Since independence, the government has continually stated its determination to narrow the wide gap in incomes between rich and poor Zimbabweans. The Minimum Wage Act of 1980 established a minimum wage of Z.$85 per month for workers who came under the Industrial Conciliation Act, Z.$70 per month for others in industry, Z.$58 per month for mineworkers and Z.$30 per month for agricultural and domestic workers. In January 1982 minimum wages were again raised, and in 1986 the upper limit for the wages freeze was raised to include only those earning more than Z.$36,000 per year. Wage rises were announced on a graduated scale, ranging from 3% for those earning between Z.$30,000 and Z.$36,000 per year upwards, to 10% for those earning between Z.$100 and Z.$500 per month.

Those earning less than Z.$100 per month were granted a uniform monthly increase of Z.$10. Before the wage increases, an employee receiving Z.$36,000 per year was paid Z.$34,800 more annually than a worker earning Z.$100 per month; after the wage rises, the gap between the two earners was wider, at Z.$35,760 per year. The differential between the industrial minimum wage and the agricultural minimum wage reflects, among other factors, the higher cost of urban life. In 1995 the statutory monthly minimum wage was Z.$242 in agriculture, Z.$472 in commerce, Z.$498 in mining and Z.$514 in manufacturing.

A study by the University of Zimbabwe, released in March 1988, forecast that as much as 24% of the country's labour force would be unemployed by 1990. It warned that between 1986 and 1990, 857,000 school leavers would enter the job market, while only 144,000 new jobs were to be created. In the event, an estimated 1m. Zimbabweans were unemployed in 1990, and an additional 300,000 school-leavers entered the job market in that year. Unemployment was estimated at 22% in 1992 and at 35% in July 1996, but by 1999 the rate had increased dramatically to 50%. Pressure to cut payrolls under the 1991–95 ESAP exacerbated unemployment, and banking sources estimate that in March 1994 current incomes were, on average, only 68% of their 1990 levels in real terms. The ESAP called for a 25% reduction in the civil service, necessitating the elimination of 32,000 public-sector jobs by 1994. In May 1992 1,170 government posts were abolished, and a further 6,154 public-sector jobs were described as 'superfluous'. Their abolition was forecast to reduce government expenditure by Z.$32.5m. annually. In July 1992 the government reduced the number of ministries as part of its streamlining of the administration; in April 1995, however, despite reported pressure from the IMF and the World Bank to halve the number of cabinet posts, 13 new positions were created. In 1992 approximately 10,000 textile workers and 7,000 agricultural workers lost their jobs, and in June 1993 only 11% of the working population was employed in the formal sector, the lowest percentage in over 23 years. Government provisions of Z.$20m. to offset the social effects of the austerity accompanying structural adjustment were widely regarded as unrealistic and inadequate. In June 1994 the government granted substantial allowances and salary increases of between 10%–20% to members of the civil service and armed forces. In August–September 1996 civil servants staged a national strike in support of demands for higher salary increases, and further industrial action in many sectors took place during 1996–97. Multilateral creditors expressed disappointment at unscheduled salary increases awarded to civil servants in late 1996, which undermined efforts to limit the budgetary deficit. Nevertheless, the entire episode was repeated in the first half of 2000 as the elections approached.

The government's record in harnessing expenditure has been disappointing. The 1994/95 budget envisaged total spending of Z.$17,900m.; the actual figure was, however, Z.$22,257m., exceeding the target by 24%. With actual revenue totalling Z.$15,257m. in 1994/95, the budget deficit reached Z.$7,000m., equivalent to 13.4% of GDP—far in excess of the IMF and World Bank target. Under the 1995/96 budget, total expenditure was envisaged at Z.$22,574m., compared with projected revenue of Z.$18,300m. In September 1995 the IMF announced the suspension of Zimbabwe's balance-of-payments loans pending a reduction in the budget deficit. The IMF was critical of the government's expenditure on the creation of new ministries earlier in the year (see above), and of the fiscal contribution to political parties for which only the ruling party was, effectively, eligible. A mid-year revision of the 1995/96 budget, announced in December 1995, raised the spending projection to Z.$25,474m.; actual expenditure was Z.$26,024m., leaving a deficit of Z.$6,560m., equivalent to 10.1% of GDP, far above the target of 6.7%. The 1996/97 budget, announced in July 1996, envisaged recurrent expenditure of Z.$25,903m. and capital expenditure of Z.$4,557m., totalling Z.$30,173m. (less recoveries). Revenue was forecast at Z.$23,350m., producing a projected deficit (exclusive of grants) of Z.$6,823m., which was envisaged to be equivalent to 8.5% of GDP. The 1997/98 budget, announced in July 1997, covered the 18-month period to 31 December 1998. It called for total expenditure of Z.$63,900m., against total anticipated revenues of Z.$48,800m., leaving a budgetary deficit of

Z.$15,100m. On an annualized basis, this deficit represented about 20% of GDP, as against the IMF target of 5.5% of GDP. The out-turn for 1996/97 assessed the fiscal deficit for that 12-month period at 7.1% of GDP, apparently based on the government's reported revision of its GDP estimates to Z.$100,000m. In any case, the need to finance the deficit was expected to enlarge the public-sector borrowing requirement on the domestic market to Z.$11,000m. in the 18-month period, as against Z.$5,000m. during the previous 12-month period. This requirement soared to Z.$108,626.6m. by the end of May 2000. The IMF estimated that the 1997/98 budgetary deficit was equivalent to 8.8% of GDP excluding grants, or to 7.7% of GDP including grants. The target set for the 1998/99 budget envisaged a deficit equivalent to 5.3% of GDP before grants, or 3.6% after.

Prior to 1999 there was a tendency to blame the IMF for job losses, pay cuts and price 'liberalization', which always seemed to mean price increases, but by the third quarter of 1999, the Mugabe government was managing Zimbabwe's economy without interference (or lending) from the IMF. However, the job losses and high prices grew steadily worse; an estimated 50,000 jobs were lost in the private sector between January and June 2000. Mugabe threatened to reinstate price controls, but did not have sufficient funds to do so, in the absence of any balance-of-payments support.

Statistical Survey

Source (unless otherwise stated): Central Statistical Office, Kaguvi Bldg, Fourth St, POB CY 342, Causeway, Harare; tel. (4) 706681; fax (4) 728529.

Area and Population

AREA, POPULATION AND DENSITY

Area (sq km)	390,757*
Population (census results)	
18 August 1982	7,608,432
18 August 1992	
Males	5,083,537
Females	5,329,011
Total	10,412,548
Population (official estimate at 18 August)	
1997	12,293,953
Density (per sq km) at August 1997	31.5

* 150,872 sq miles.

PRINCIPAL TOWNS (population at census of August 1992)

Harare (capital)	1,189,103	Masvingo	51,743
Bulawayo	621,742	Chinhoyi (Sinoia)	43,054
Chitungwiza	274,912	Hwange (Wankie)	42,581
Mutare (Umtali)	131,367	Marondera	
Gweru (Gwelo)	128,037	(Marandellas)	39,384
Kwekwe (Que Que)	75,425	Zvishavane (Shabani)	32,984
Kadoma (Gatooma)	67,750	Redcliff	29,959

BIRTHS AND DEATHS (UN estimates, annual averages)

	1980–85	1985–90	1990–95
Birth rate (per 1,000)	43.1	40.4	35.5
Death rate (per 1,000)	11.8	10.8	12.6

Expectation of life (UN estimates, years at birth, 1990–95): 51.8 (males 50.6; females 53.1).

Source: UN, *World Population Prospects: The 1998 Revision*.

ECONOMICALLY ACTIVE POPULATION
(sample survey, '000 persons aged 15 years and over, 1994)

	Males	Females	Total
Agriculture, hunting, forestry and fishing	1,216.9	1,587.9	2,804.8
Mining and quarrying	63.8	5.0	68.8
Manufacturing	190.0	31.0	221.0
Electricity, gas and water	12.9	0.9	13.8
Construction	80.3	5.7	86.0
Trade, restaurants and hotels	80.2	50.0	130.2
Transport, storage and communications	73.4	5.2	78.6
Financing, insurance, real estate and business services	20.2	11.9	32.1
Community, social and personal services	354.0	290.5	644.5
Activities not adequately defined	7.4	4.1	11.5
Total employed	2,099.1	1,992.2	4,091.3
Unemployed	153.3	62.2	215.5
Total labour force	2,252.4	2,054.4	4,306.8

Mid-1998 (estimates in '000): Agriculture, etc. 3,460; Total labour force 5,423 (Source: FAO, *Production Yearbook*).

EMPLOYMENT ('000 persons)*

	1995	1996	1997
Agriculture, forestry and fishing	334.0	347.0	355.1
Mining and quarrying	59.0	59.8	59.1
Manufacturing	185.9	183.5	197.7
Construction	71.8	77.5	78.1
Electricity and water	9.5	12.4	13.1
Transport and communications	50.9	50.3	51.3
Trade	100.6	101.4	106.3
Finance, insurance and real estate	21.1	22.2	26.3
Community, social and personal services	406.8	419.6	436.2
Total employees	1,239.6	1,273.7	1,323.2

* Excluding small establishments in rural areas.

Source: ILO, *Yearbook of Labour Statistics*.

Agriculture

PRINCIPAL CROPS ('000 metric tons)

	1996	1997	1998
Wheat	280	250*	280
Barley	11†	10†	9
Maize	2,609	2,192	1,418
Millet	118	115†	50
Sorghum	108	105†	72
Potatoes.	31†	30†	29
Cassava (Manioc) . . .	150†	160†	165
Dry beans	42†	45	45
Soybeans (Soya beans) . .	110	101*	111
Groundnuts (in shell) . .	80	153*	60
Sunflower seed	51	34*	29
Cottonseed	153*	175*	163
Vegetables (incl. melons) . .	147†	145†	141
Sugar cane	2,826	4,651*	4,808*
Oranges	73†	70†	70
Other citrus fruits† . . .	20	19	19
Bananas	83†	82†	80
Coffee (green)	12	9	10
Tea (made)	17*	17*	18
Tobacco (leaves) . . .	209	215	260
Cotton (lint)	87*	101*	95

* Unofficial figure(s).   † FAO estimate.

Source: FAO, *Production Yearbook.*

LIVESTOCK ('000 head, year ending September)

	1996	1997*	1998
Horses*	24	25	25
Asses*	105	106	107
Cattle	5,436	5,400*	5,450
Sheep	530	530*	520
Pigs	266	268*	270
Goats	2,705	2,700*	2,750

* FAO estimate(s).   † Unofficial figure.

Poultry (FAO estimates, million): 14 in 1994; 15 in 1995; 15 in 1996.

LIVESTOCK PRODUCTS (FAO estimates, '000 metric tons)

	1996	1997	1998
Beef and veal	62	63	68
Goat meat	12	12	12
Pig meat	13	13	13
Poultry meat	21	25	25
Other meat	21	22	24
Cows' milk	570	600	570
Butter	3	3	3
Cheese	2	2	2
Poultry eggs	20	20	20
Cattle hides	7	7	7

Source: FAO, *Production Yearbook.*

Forestry

ROUNDWOOD REMOVALS
('000 cubic metres, excl. bark)

	1995	1996	1997
Sawlogs, veneer logs and logs for sleepers	525*	413	413
Pulpwood	157*	36	36
Other industrial wood . .	1,144	1,170	1,194
Fuel wood†	6,269	6,269	6,269
Total	8,095	7,888	7,912

* Assumed to be unchanged since 1991.
† Assumed to be unchanged since 1988.

Source: FAO, *Yearbook of Forest Products.*

SAWNWOOD PRODUCTION
('000 cubic metres, incl. railway sleepers)

	1995	1996	1997
Coniferous (softwood) . . .	221*	198	198*
Broadleaved (hardwood) . . .	29*	9	9*
Total	250*	207	207

Source: FAO, *Yearbook of Forest Products.*
* FAO estimate.

Fishing

('000 metric tons, live weight)

	1995	1996	1997
Dagaas	15.3	15.4	17.0
Other fishes	1.1	0.9	1.0
Total catch	16.4	16.3	18.1

Source: FAO, *Yearbook of Fishery Statistics.*

Mining

('000 metric tons, unless otherwise indicated)

	1994	1995	1996
Antimony ore (metric tons)*† . .	35	36	36
Asbestos.	152	170	n.a.
Chromium ore*	170	212‡	209‡
Clay	170‡	171‡	166‡
Coal	5,469	5,529	5,247§
Cobalt ore (metric tons)* . .	130	111‡	90‡
Copper ore*	9.3	8.1	10.1†
Gold (kilograms)* . . .	20,512	23,959‡	24,772‡
Iron ore*‡	3	160	222
Limestone	1,658	n.a.	n.a.
Magnesite	1.6‡	5.6	n.a.
Nickel ore (metric tons)* . .	13,518	11,700†	11,600†
Niobium ore (metric tons)*‡ . .	1	1	1
Phosphate rock	150	154‡	n.a.
Silver (metric tons)* . . .	12	15‡	16‡
Tantalum (metric tons)*‡ . . .	2	2	2
Tin ore (metric tons)* . . .	82	0	0‡

* Figures refer to the metal content of ores and concentrates.
† Data from *World Metal Statistics* (London).
‡ Data from the US Bureau of Mines.
§ Estimated figure.

Source: mainly UN, *Industrial Commodity Statistics Yearbook.*

1996: Tin (metric tons) 300 (Source: *World Metal Statistics*, London).

Industry

SELECTED PRODUCTS
('000 metric tons, unless otherwise indicated)

	1994	1995	1996
Raw sugar*	507	511	337
Coke	220	467	450†
Cement	624	948	n.a.
Pig-iron‡	100†	209	210
Ferro-chromium‡ . . .	219	301	295
Crude steel‡	187	210	212
Refined copper—unwrought†‡ .	15.4	18.2	21.2
Nickel—unwrought (metric tons) .	13,518	10,863	9,793‡
Tin—unwrought (metric tons)‡§ .	82	0	0
Electric energy (million kWh)‖ .	8,272	8,017†	7,819†

* Data from the FAO.
† Estimate(s).
‡ Data from the US Bureau of Mines.
§ Primary metal only.
‖ Net production.
Source: UN, *Industrial Commodity Statistics Yearbook*.

Finance

CURRENCY AND EXCHANGE RATES

Monetary Units
  100 cents = 1 Zimbabwe dollar (Z.$).

Sterling, US Dollar and Euro Equivalents (28 April 2000)
  £1 sterling = Z.$59.83;
  US $1 = Z.$38.15;
  €1 = Z.$34.66;
  Z.$1,000 = £16.71 = US $26.21 = €28.85.

Average Exchange Rate (US $ per Zimbabwe dollar)
  1997   0.0841
  1998   0.0467
  1999   0.0261

BUDGET (Z.$ million, year ending 30 June)

Revenue*	1995/96	1996/97	1997/98†
Taxation	16,121	23,219	53,551
Taxes on income and profits .	8,147	11,777	27,633
Personal income . .	4,486	7,550	15,197
Business profits . .	2,847	3,236	5,904
Customs duties . . .	3,050	4,371	9,962
Excise duties . . .	896	1,070	2,446
Sales tax	3,730	5,079	11,735
Other revenue . . .	2,081	2,153	4,044
Entrepreneurial and property income	845	559	925
Parastatal interest and dividends . . .	723	503	503
Total	18,201	25,372	57,596

Expenditure‡	1995/96	1996/97	1997/98†
Recurrent expenditure:			
Goods and services:			
Salaries, wages and allowances	7,737	11,111	25,392
Subsistence and transport .	407	492	935
Incidental expenses . .	440	620	1,606
Other recurrent expenditure .	3,677	4,093	6,141
Total	12,261	16,316	34,115
Transfers:			
Interest	6,955	7,511	17,699
Subsidies	93	88	5
Pensions	1,308	1,677	4,302
Grants and transfers . .	2,427	2,827	8,620
Total	10,783	12,103	30,626

Expenditure‡ — *continued*	1995/96	1996/97	1997/98†
Capital expenditure:			
Buildings	765	885	n.a.
Civil engineering . . .	432	690	n.a.
Plant, machinery and equipment	212	273	n.a.
Other capital expenditure . .	356	344	n.a.
Total	1,764	2,193	4,582
Grand Total	24,809	30,611	69,322

* Excluding grants received (Z.$ million): 973 in 1995/96; 1,180 in 1996/97; 2,502 (estimate) in 1997/98.
† Estimates for July 1997 to December 1998.
‡ Excluding lending minus repayments (Z.$ million): 1,507 in 1995/96; 2,025 in 1996/97; 1,010 (estimate) in 1997/98.
Source: IMF, *Zimbabwe: Statistical Appendix* (June 1999).

INTERNATIONAL RESERVES (US $ million at 31 December)

	1997	1998	1999
Gold*	56.0	82.6	105.4
IMF special drawing rights .	0.3	0.4	1.1
Reserve position in IMF . .	0.2	0.3	0.4
Foreign exchange . . .	159.6	130.1	266.5
Total	216.1	213.4	373.4

* Valued at a market-related price which is determined each month.
Source: IMF, *International Financial Statistics*.

MONEY SUPPLY (Z.$ million at 31 December)

	1997	1998	1999
Currency outside banks . . .	3,358	4,468	7,256
Demand deposits at deposit money banks	17,102	20,424	27,804
Total money (incl. others) . .	21,320	26,332	35,473

Source: IMF, *International Financial Statistics*.

COST OF LIVING (Consumer Price Index; base: 1990 = 100)

	1996	1997	1998
Food and beverages . . .	544.8	640.5	893.2
Clothing and footwear . .	263.4	292.3	350.1
Rent, fuel and light . . .	339.7	412.9	485.6
All items (incl. others) . .	406.9	483.6	636.9

Source: ILO, *Yearbook of Labour Statistics*.

1999: Food 1,500.1; All items 1,009.6 (Source: UN, *Monthly Bulletin of Statistics*).

NATIONAL ACCOUNTS (Z.$ million at current prices)
Expenditure on the Gross National Product (IMF estimates)

	1994	1995	1996
Government final consumption expenditure	8,773	10,970	14,424
Private final consumption expenditure	30,074	37,738	47,209
Increase in stocks . . .	252	—	790
Gross fixed capital formation . .	9,233	10,009	12,724
Total domestic expenditure .	48,332	58,717	75,147
Exports of goods and services . .	19,826	25,317	33,372
Less Imports of goods and services	20,732	26,838	33,021
GDP in purchasers' values . .	47,426	57,196	75,498

Source: IMF, *Zimbabwe—Recent Economic Developments* (July 1997).

Composition of the Gross National Product

	1987	1988	1989
Compensation of employees . .	4,847	5,611	6,572
Operating surplus . . . .⎫			
Consumption of fixed capital . .⎭	3,172	4,573	5,542
GNP at factor cost	8,019	10,184	12,114
Indirect taxes	1,346	1,645	2,093
Less Subsidies	426	388	413
GNP in purchasers' values . .	8,939	11,441	13,794
Net factor income from abroad	−355	−478	−538
GNP at market prices . . .	8,584	10,963	13,256

Source: UN, *National Accounts Statistics.*

Gross Domestic Product by Economic Activity (at factor cost)

	1990	1991	1992
Agriculture, hunting, forestry and fishing	2,391	3,709	5,692
Mining and quarrying . . .	676	939	1,226
Manufacturing	4,130	5,585	7,760
Electricity and water	394	520	687
Construction	362	499	499
Trade, restaurants and hotels . .	1,569	1,898	2,145
Transport, storage and communications	1,067	1,243	1,865
Finance, insurance and real estate	977	1,133	1,271
Government services	1,057	1,230	1,311
Other services	2,423	3,197	3,616
Sub-total	15,046	19,953	26,072
Less Imputed bank service charges	344	366	366
Total	14,702	19,587	25,706

Source: UN, *National Accounts Statistics.*

BALANCE OF PAYMENTS (US $ million)

	1992	1993	1994
Exports of goods f.o.b. . . .	1,527.6	1,609.1	1,961.1
Imports of goods f.o.b. . . .	−1,782.1	−1,487.0	−1,803.5
Trade balance	−254.5	122.1	157.6
Exports of services	305.1	372.1	383.2
Imports of services	−660.9	−563.8	−711.7
Balance on goods and services	−610.3	−69.6	−170.9
Other income received . . .	26.0	35.0	27.5
Other income paid	−302.3	−287.1	−321.2
Balance on goods, services and income	−886.6	−321.6	−464.5
Current transfers received . .	347.3	270.6	69.4
Current transfers paid . . .	−64.4	−64.7	−29.8
Current balance	−603.7	−115.7	−424.9
Capital account (net) . . .	−1.4	−0.4	284.4
Direct investment abroad . .	—	—	−4.7
Direct investment from abroad .	15.0	28.0	34.7
Portfolio investment assets . .	27.6	—	—
Portfolio investment liabilities .	−37.1	−5.1	50.2
Other investment assets . . .	15.9	99.9	−260.3
Other investment liabilities . .	352.0	204.4	154.7
Net errors and omissions . .	37.2	14.9	80.2
Overall balance	−194.6	225.9	−85.8

Source: IMF, *International Financial Statistics.*

External Trade

PRINCIPAL COMMODITIES

(distribution by SITC, US $'000, excl. stores and bunkers for aircraft)

Imports f.o.b.	1994	1995	1996
Food and live animals . . .	53,915	97,900	199,400
Cereals and cereal preparations .	23,036	45,200	115,300
Maize (unmilled)	884	700	25,600
Crude materials (inedible) except fuels	73,127	92,400	84,800
Mineral fuels, lubricants, etc. (incl. electricity)	222,369	240,100	292,700
Petroleum, petroleum products, etc.	215,659	234,100	275,000
Refined petroleum products . .	210,164	228,900	269,800
Motor spirit (gasoline) and other light oils . . .	50,103	68,500	71,500
Motor and aviation spirit .	48,739	67,500	70,000
Kerosene and other medium oils	32,577	28,600	45,500
Gas oils	109,069	114,600	127,800
Animal and vegetable oils and fats	42,161	44,400	54,400
Chemicals and related products	360,505	358,500	367,100
Inorganic chemicals	54,126	32,300	32,400
Artificial resins, plastic materials, etc.	72,299	89,600	77,700
Products of polymerization, etc. .	57,935	73,600	64,300
Basic manufactures . . .	369,411	458,300	456,800
Textile yarn, fabrics, etc. . . .	96,361	115,700	121,700
Iron and steel	84,033	102,500	96,000
Machinery and transport equipment	934,633	1,107,800	1,081,500
Power-generating machinery and equipment	60,414	64,000	39,500
Machinery specialized for particular industries . .	183,478	247,300	224,000
General industrial machinery, equipment, etc. . . .	162,999	171,100	188,000
Telecommunications and sound equipment	66,472	79,400	109,000
Other electrical machinery, apparatus, etc. . . .	131,660	144,800	139,100
Switchgear, etc., and parts . .	44,915	37,400	38,500
Road vehicles and parts* . . .	256,971	316,900	306,800
Passenger motor cars (excl. buses)	76,664	75,600	87,700
Motor vehicles for goods transport, etc. . . .	108,248	153,800	133,100
Goods vehicles	101,366	140,600	128,100
Other transport equipment* . .	18,767	24,300	12,100
Aircraft, associated equipment and parts*	15,980	22,200	9,800
Miscellaneous manufactured articles	120,895	146,200	174,600
Total (incl. others)	2,241,267	2,658,900	2,813,600

*Excluding tyres, engines and electrical parts.

Exports f.o.b.			1994	1995	1996
Food and live animals	.	.	389,159	306,200	329,600
Cereals and cereal preparations	.		171,742	65,500	59,400
Maize (unmilled)	.	.	146,222	33,500	35,200
Vegetables and fruit .	.	.	24,673	41,000	33,600
Sugar, sugar preparations and					
honey .	.	.	101,832	83,400	118,800
Sugar and honey	.	.	96,704	76,300	111,300
Raw beet and cane sugar .		.	88,540	62,100	94,500
Coffee, tea, cocoa, spices, and					
manufactures thereof	.	.	28,922	41,700	44,800
Beverages and tobacco .		.	668,957	485,100	740,300
Tobacco and tobacco manufactures			665,584	481,700	737,400
Unmanufactured tobacco, incl.					
refuse.	.	.	649,005	470,900	724,000
Unstripped tobacco	.	.	133,596	47,700	115,400
Wholly or partly stripped					
tobacco	.	.	509,173	420,600	604,300
Crude materials (inedible)					
except fuels .	.	.	217,933	232,900	264,000
Cotton .	.	.	60,445	50,500	80,800
Crude fertilizers and crude					
minerals .	.	.	72,904	96,300	90,300
Asbestos .	.	.	56,418	70,000	63,800
Cut flowers	.	.	19,298	32,600	33,500
Chemicals and related products			36,120	46,700	56,000
Basic manufactures	.	.	411,994	531,500	465,100
Textile yarn, fabrics, etc. .		.	76,149	62,800	48,100
Iron and steel .	.	.	137,437	234,200	199,800
Pig-iron, etc.	.	.	115,164	214,100	168,900
Ferro-alloys .	.	.	115,164	214,100	168,900
Non-ferrous metals .	.	.	109,313	110,300	102,900
Nickel and nickel alloys	.		80,533	87,800	77,100
Other metal manufactures	.	.	31,636	44,300	21,400
Machinery and transport					
equipment .	.	.	49,278	49,200	59,300
Miscellaneous manufactured					
articles .	.	.	159,786	161,900	141,400
Clothing and accessories (excl.					
footwear) .	.	.	63,864	61,200	50,500
Total (incl. others)	.	.	1,967,464	1,846,000	2,122,000

Source: UN, *International Trade Statistics Yearbook.*

PRINCIPAL TRADING PARTNERS (US $'000)*

Imports f.o.b.			1995	1996	1997
Argentina	.	.	39,800	20,600	23,800
Australia	.	.	16,000	45,700	51,400
Belgium-Luxembourg	.	.	33,200	28,100	37,400
China, People's Repub.	.	.	27,800	21,500	32,700
France (incl. Monaco)	.	.	99,900	87,000	80,100
Germany	.	.	135,100	136,700	142,300
Hong Kong	.	.	32,800	30,200	33,400
India	.	.	17,000	40,100	33,100
Israel	.	.	n.a.	30,000	37,800
Italy	.	.	49,200	69,300	57,000
Japan	.	.	195,500	144,500	171,900
Korea, Repub.	.	.	27,200	39,700	55,600
Netherlands .	.	.	46,000	49,300	54,300
SACU†	.	.	1,092,200	1,141,000	1,203,400
Sweden .	.	.	33,000	28,100	29,800
Switzerland (incl. Liechtenstein)	.		39,300	42,000	34,600
United Kingdom .	.	.	210,300	233,200	227,500
USA	.	.	119,900	140,900	171,400
Total (incl. others)	.	.	2,658,900	2,813,500	3,092,200

Exports f.o.b.			1995	1996	1997
Belgium-Luxembourg	.	.	54,100	36,900	57,600
China, People's Repub.	.	.	56,400	71,200	17,800
France (incl. Monaco)	.	.	31,600	20,000	21,700
Germany	.	.	151,900	166,800	165,200
Indonesia	.	.	22,600	37,500	24,800
Israel	.	.	n.a.	27,600	14,100
Italy	.	.	87,600	90,600	85,400
Japan	.	.	145,500	106,600	130,100
Malawi .	.	.	49,900	60,800	79,100
Mozambique.	.	.	51,600	77,900	71,100
Netherlands .	.	.	65,200	78,700	71,800
Poland .	.	.	18,200	25,100	20,500
Portugal.	.	.	36,400	38,000	46,400
SACU†	.	.	340,800	312,300	354,400
Spain .	.	.	31,000	35,200	41,900
Switzerland (incl. Liechtenstein)	.		20,800	58,900	46,400
Thailand .	.	.	7,600	11,800	24,100
United Kingdom .	.	.	237,200	222,200	235,500
USA	.	.	87,600	139,800	122,900
Zambia .	.	.	92,900	91,100	116,900
Total (incl. others)	.	.	1,845,900	2,121,900	2,127,700

* Imports by country of production; exports by country of last consignment. Figures exclude trade in gold.
† Southern African Customs Union, comprising Botswana, Lesotho, Namibia, South Africa and Swaziland.

Source: UN, *International Trade Statistics Yearbook.*

Transport

RAIL TRAFFIC
(National Railways of Zimbabwe, including operations in Botswana)

	1992	1993	1994
Total number of passengers ('000)	2,355	2,200	2,034
Revenue-earning metric tons			
hauled ('000)	13,038	10,464	11,250
Gross metric ton-km (million).	11,913	9,649	9,397
Net metric ton-km (million)	5,887	4,581	4,489

1995: Net metric ton-km (million) 7,180.
1996: Net metric ton-km (million) 4,990.
1997/98: Revenue-earning metric tons hauled ('000) 12,428.

ROAD TRAFFIC ('000 motor vehicles in use, estimates)

	1994	1995	1996
Passenger cars	323	323	323
Commercial vehicles .	32	32	32

Source: International Road Federation, *World Road Statistics.*

CIVIL AVIATION (traffic on scheduled services)

	1994	1995	1996
Kilometres flown ('000)	13,000	13,000	13,000
Passengers carried ('000) .	675	626	654
Passenger-km (million)	852	840	881
Total ton-km (million)	212	216	234

Source: UN, *Statistical Yearbook.*

Tourism

	1995	1996	1997
Number of tourist arrivals	1,539,000	1,746,000	1,495,000
Tourism receipts (US $ million)	154	219	230

Source: World Tourism Organization, *Yearbook of Tourism Statistics.*

Communications Media

	1994	1995	1996
Radio receivers ('000 in use) . .	945	1,000	1,100
Television receivers ('000 in use) .	297	320	350
Telephones ('000 main lines in use)*	135	152	175
Telefax stations ('000 in use)*. .	3.5	4.1	4.1
Daily newspapers:			
Number	2	2	2
Circulation ('000 copies) . .	195	192	209

* Year ending 30 June

Sources: UNESCO, *Statistical Yearbook*; UN, *Statistical Yearbook*.

Education
(1998)

	Schools	Teachers	Students
Primary.	4,706	64,538	2,507,098
Secondary	n.a.	30,482	847,296
Higher:			
University.	n.a.	n.a.	10,322*
Other	n.a.	n.a.	36,351*

* 1996.

1995: Secondary schools 1,535; Higher education: University teachers 1,618; Other teachers 1,963.

Sources: Ministry of Education, Sports and Culture, Causeway, Harare; UNESCO, *Statistical Yearbook*.

Directory

The Constitution

The Constitution of the Republic of Zimbabwe took effect at independence on 18 April 1980. Amendments to the Constitution must have the approval of two-thirds of the members of the House of Assembly (see below). The provisions of the 1980 Constitution (with subsequent amendments) are summarized below:

THE REPUBLIC

Zimbabwe is a sovereign republic and the Constitution is the supreme law.

DECLARATION OF RIGHTS

The declaration of rights guarantees the fundamental rights and freedoms of the individual, regardless of race, tribe, place of origin, political opinions, colour, creed or sex.

THE PRESIDENT

Executive power is vested in the President, who acts on the advice of the Cabinet. The President is Head of State and Commander-in-Chief of the Defence Forces. The President appoints two Vice-Presidents and other Ministers and Deputy Ministers, to be members of the Cabinet. The President holds office for six years and is eligible for re-election. Each candidate for the Presidency shall be nominated by not fewer than 10 members of the House of Assembly; if only one candidate is nominated, that candidate shall be declared to be elected without the necessity of a ballot. Otherwise, a ballot shall be held within an electoral college consisting of the members of the House of Assembly.

PARLIAMENT

Legislative power is vested in a unicameral Parliament, consisting of a House of Assembly. The House of Assembly comprises 150 members, of whom 120 are directly elected by universal adult suffrage, 12 are nominated by the President, 10 are traditional Chiefs and eight are Provincial Governors. The life of the House of Assembly is ordinarily to be six years.

OTHER PROVISIONS

An Ombudsman shall be appointed by the President, acting on the advice of the Judicial Service Commission, to investigate complaints against actions taken by employees of the government or of a local authority.

Chiefs shall be appointed by the President, and shall form a Council of Chiefs from their number in accordance with customary principles of succession.

Other provisions relate to the Judicature, Defence and Police Forces, public service and finance.

The Government

HEAD OF STATE

President: ROBERT GABRIEL MUGABE (took office 31 December 1987; re-elected March 1990 and 16–17 March 1996).

THE CABINET
(August 2000)

Vice-Presidents: SIMON VENGAYI MUZENDA, JOSEPH MSIKA.

Minister of Defence: MOVEN ENOCK MAHACHI.

Minister of Home Affairs: JOHN LANDA NKOMO.

Minister of Justice, Legal and Parliamentary Affairs: PATRICK ANTHONY CHINAMASA.

Minister of Finance and Economic Development: SIMBA MAKONI.

Minister of Public Service, Labour and Social Welfare: JULY MOYO.

Minister of Local Government, Public Works and National Housing: Dr IGNATIUS MORGAN CHIMINYA CHOMBO.

Minister of Lands, Agriculture and Rural Development: JOSEPH MADE.

Minister of Industry and International Trade: NKOSANA MOYO.

Minister of Mines and Energy: Dr SYDNEY TIGERE SEKEREMAYI.

Minister of the Environment and Tourism: FRANCIS NHEMA.

Minister of Foreign Affairs: Dr I. STANISLAUS GORERAZVO MUDENGE.

Minister of Higher Education and Technology: Dr HERBERT MUCHEMWA MURERWA.

Minister of Education, Sports and Culture: SIMBARASHE MUMBENGEGWI.

Minister of Health and Child Welfare: Dr TIMOTHY STAMPS.

Minister of Transport and Energy: SWITHEN MOMBESHORA.

Minister of Rural Resources and Water Development: JOYCE MUJURU.

Minister of Youth Development, Gender and Employment Creation: BORDER GEZI.

Minister of State for Information and Publicity: JONATHAN MOYO.

Minister of State for National Security: NICHOLAS GOCHE.

MINISTRIES

Office of the President: Munhumutapa Bldg, Samora Machel Ave, Private Bag 7700, Causeway, Harare; tel. (4) 707091.

Office of the Vice-Presidents: Munhumutapa Bldg, Samora Machel Ave, Private Bag 7700, Causeway, Harare; tel. (4) 707091.

Ministry of Defence: Defence House, Union Ave/Third St, Private Bag 7713, Causeway, Harare; tel. (4) 700155; fax (4) 727501; e-mail defprot@gta.gov.zw.

Ministry of Education, Sports and Culture: Ambassador House, Union Ave, POB CY121, Causeway, Harare; tel. (4) 734051; fax (4) 734075.

Ministry of the Environment and Tourism: Harare.

Ministry of Finance and Economic Development: Munhumutapa Bldg, Samora Machel Ave, Private Bag 7705, Causeway, Harare; tel. (4) 794571; fax (4) 792750.

Ministry of Foreign Affairs: Munhumutapa Bldg, Samora Machel Ave, POB 4240, Causeway, Harare; tel. (4) 727005; fax (4) 705161.

Ministry of Health and Child Welfare: Kaguvi Bldg, Fourth St, POB CY198, Causeway, Harare; tel. (4) 730011; fax (4) 729154.

Ministry of Higher Education and Technology: Old Mutual Centre, Union Ave, POB UA275, Harare; tel. (4) 796441; fax (4) 728730.

Ministry of Home Affairs: Mukwati Bldg, Samora Machel Ave, Private Bag 7703, Causeway, Harare; tel. (4) 703641; fax (4) 726716.

Ministry of Industry and International Trade: Mukwati Bldg, Fourth St, Private Bag 7708, Causeway, Harare; tel. (4) 702731; fax (4) 729311.

Ministry of Information and Publicity: Linquenda House, Baker Ave, POB CY825, Causeway, Harare; tel. (4) 703894; fax (4) 707213.

Ministry of Justice, Legal and Parliamentary Affairs: Corner House, cnr Samora Machel Ave and Leopold Takawira St, Private Bag 7751, Causeway, Harare; tel. (4) 774620; fax (4) 772999.

Ministry of Lands, Agriculture and Rural Development: Ngungunyana Bldg, Private Bag 7701, Causeway, Harare; tel. (4) 792223; fax (4) 734646.

Ministry of Local Government, Public Works and National Housing: Mukwati Bldg, Private Bag 7706, Causeway, Harare; tel. (4) 790601; fax (4) 708848.

Ministry of Mines and Energy: Karigamombe Centre, Private Bag 7753, Causeway, Harare; tel. (4) 751720; fax (4) 734075.

Ministry of National Security: Chaminuka Bldg, POB 2278, Harare; tel. (4) 700501; fax (4) 732660.

Ministry of Public Service, Labour and Social Welfare: Compensation House, cnr Central Ave and Fourth St, Private Bag 7707, Causeway, Harare; tel. (4) 790871.

Ministry of Rural Resources and Water Development: Makombe Complex, Private Bag 7701, Causeway, Harare; tel. (4) 706081.

Ministry of Transport and Energy: Kaguvi Bldg, POB CY595, Causeway, Harare; tel. (4) 700991; fax (4) 708225.

Ministry of Youth Development, Gender and Employment Creation: ZANU–PF Bldg, Private Bag 7762, Causeway, Harare; tel. (4) 734691; fax (4) 732709.

PROVINCIAL GOVERNORS

Manicaland: OPPAH MUCHINGURI.

Mashonaland Central: ELLIOT MANYIKA.

Mashonaland East: DAVID ISHEMUNYORO KARIMANZIRA.

Mashonaland West: PETER CHANETSA.

Masvingo: JOSIAH DUNIRA HUNGWE.

Matabeleland North: OBERT MPOFU.

Matabeleland South: STEPHEN JEQE NYONGOLO NKOMO.

Midlands: CEPHAS MSIPA.

President and Legislature

PRESIDENT

Election, 16–17 March 1996

Candidate	% of total votes cast
ROBERT GABRIEL MUGABE	92.7
Bishop ABEL MUZOREWA	4.7
Rev. NDABANINGI SITHOLE	2.4

HOUSE OF ASSEMBLY

Speaker: EMMERSON DAMBUDZO MNANGAGWA.

Election, 24–25 June 2000

	Votes	% of votes	Seats*
ZANU–PF	1,212,302	48.6	62
MDC	1,171,051	47.0	57
Others†	110,572	4.4	1
Total	**2,493,925**	**100.0**	**120**

* In addition to the 120 directly elective seats, 12 are held by nominees of the President, 10 by traditional Chiefs and eight by Provincial Governors.

† One seat was won by ZANU–Ndonga.

Political Organizations

Committee for a Democratic Society (CODESO): f. 1993; Kalanga-supported grouping, based in Matebeleland; Leader SOUL NDLOVU.

Conservative Alliance of Zimbabwe (CAZ): POB 242, Harare; f. 1962, known as Rhodesian Front until 1981, and subsequently as Republican Front; supported by sections of the white community; Pres. GERALD SMITH; Chair. MIKE MORONEY.

Democratic Party: f. 1991 by a breakaway faction from ZUM; Nat. Chair. GILES MUTSEKWA; Pres. DAVIDSON GOMO.

Forum Party of Zimbabwe (FPZ): POB 74, Bulawayo; e-mail trudy@harare.iafrica.com; f. 1993; conservative; Pres. WASHINGTON SANSOLE.

Front for Popular Democracy: f. 1994; Chair. Prof. AUSTIN CHAKAWODZA.

General Conference of Patriots: Harare; f. 1998; anti-Government, aims to organize and direct dissent; Leader OBEY MUDZINGWA.

Independent Zimbabwe Group: f. 1983 by a breakaway faction from the fmr Republican Front; Leader BILL IRVINE.

Movement for Democratic Change (MDC): 127B Fife Ave, Harare; e-mail mdc@africaonline.co.zw; internet www.in2zw.com/mdc; f. Sept. 1999; allied to Zimbabwe Congress of Trade Unions; opposes the Govt; Pres. MORGAN TSVANGIRAI; Sec.-Gen. WELSHMAN NCUBE.

National Democratic Union: f. 1979; conservative grouping with minority Zezeru support; Leader HENRY CHIHOTA.

National Progressive Alliance: f. 1991; Chair. CANCIWELL NZIRAMASANGA.

United National Federal Party (UNFP): Harare; f. 1978; conservative; seeks a fed. of Mashonaland and Matabeleland; Leader Chief KAYISA NDIWENI.

United Parties (UP): f. 1994; Leader Bishop ABEL MUZOREWA.

Zimbabwe Active People's Unity Party: Bulawayo; f. 1989; Leader NEWMAN MATUTU NDELA.

Zimbabwe African National Union–Patriotic Front (ZANU–PF): 88 Manica Rd, Harare; f. 1989 by merger of PF–ZAPU and ZANU–PF; Pres. ROBERT GABRIEL MUGABE; Vice-Pres. SIMON VENGAYI MUZENDA.

Zimbabwe African National Union–Ndonga (ZANU–Ndonga): POB UA525, Union Ave, Harare; tel. and fax (4) 481180; f. 1977; breakaway faction from ZANU, also includes fmr mems of United African National Council; supports free market economy; Pres. Rev. NDABANINGI SITHOLE; Sec.-Gen. EDWIN C. NGUWA.

Zimbabwe Congress Party: Harare; f. 1994; Pres. KENNETH MANO.

Zimbabwe Democratic Party: Harare; f. 1979; traditionalist; Leader JAMES CHIKEREMA.

Zimbabwe Federal Party (ZFPO): Stand 214, Nketa 6, P.O. Nkulumane, Bulawayo; f. 1994; aims to create nat. fed. of five provinces; Leader RICHARD NCUBE.

Zimbabwe Integrated Programme: f. Aug. 1999; seeks economic reforms; Pres. Prof. HENEDI DZINOCHIKIWEYI.

Zimbabwe National Front: f. 1979; Leader PETER MANDAZA.

Zimbabwe Peoples' Democratic Party: f. 1989; Chair. ISABEL PASALK.

Zimbabwe Union of Democrats: Harare; f. 1998; aims to create an effective opposition in the national parliament; Pres. MARGARET DONGO.

Zimbabwe Unity Movement (ZUM): f. 1989 by a breakaway faction from ZANU–PF; merged with United African National Council in 1994; Leader EDGAR TEKERE.

Diplomatic Representation

EMBASSIES AND HIGH COMMISSIONS IN ZIMBABWE

Angola: 26 Speke Ave, POB 3590, Harare; tel. (4) 770075; fax (4) 770077; e-mail 101663.2177@compuserve.com; Ambassador: ALBERTO RIBEIRO.

Argentina: Club Chambers Bldg, cnr Baker Ave and Third St, POB 2770, Harare; tel. (4) 730075; fax (4) 730076; Ambassador: VALENTIN LUCO ORIGONE.

Australia: Karigamombe Centre, 4th Floor, 53 Samora Machel Ave, POB 4541, Harare; tel. (4) 757774; fax (4) 757770; High Commissioner: K. W. SIBRAA.

Austria: 216 New Shell House, 30 Samora Machel Ave, POB 4120, Harare; tel. (4) 702921; Ambassador: Dr PETER LEITENBAUER.

Bangladesh: 9 Birchenough Rd, POB 3040, Harare; tel. (4) 727004; High Commissioner: HARUN AHMED CHOWDHURY.

Belgium: Tanganyika House, 5th Floor, 23 Third St, POB 2522, Harare; tel. (4) 793306; fax (4) 703960; Ambassador: LEOPOLD CARREWYN.

Botswana: 22 Phillips Ave, Belgravia, POB 563, Harare; tel. (4) 729551; fax (4) 721360; High Commissioner: C. MANYEULA.

Brazil: Old Mutual Centre, 9th Floor, Jason Moyo Ave, POB 2530, Harare; tel. (4) 730775; fax (4) 737782; e-mail brasemb@harare.iafrica.com; Ambassador: RICARDO LUIZ VIANA DE CARVALHO.

Bulgaria: 15 Maasdorp Ave, Alexandra Park, POB 1809, Harare; tel. (4) 730509; Ambassador: CHRISTO TEPAVITCHAROV.

Canada: 45 Baines Ave, POB 1430, Harare; tel. (4) 733881; High Commissioner: JAMES C. WALL.

China, People's Republic: 30 Baines Ave, POB 4749, Harare; tel. (4) 724572; fax (4) 794959; Ambassador: HUANG GUIFANG.

Congo, Democratic Republic: 5 Pevensey Rd, Highlands, POB 2446, Harare; tel. (4) 481172; fax (4) 796421; Ambassador: Dr KIKAYA BIN KARUB (acting).

Cuba: 5 Phillips Ave, Belgravia, POB 4139, Harare; tel. (4) 720256; Ambassador: EUMELIO CABALLERO RODRÍGUEZ.

Czech Republic: Eastgate bldg, Goldenbridge, 8th floor, cnr 2nd St and R. Mugabe Rd, POB 4474, Harare; tel. (4) 700636; fax (4) 720930; e-mail harare@embassy.mzv.cz; Ambassador JAROSLAV SIRO.

Denmark: UDC Centre, 1st Floor, cnr 59 Union Ave and First St, POB 4711, Harare; tel. (4) 758185; fax (4) 758189; Ambassador: ERIK FIIL.

Egypt: 7 Aberdeen Rd, Avondale, POB A433, Harare; tel. (4) 303445; Ambassador: Dr IBRAHIM ALY BADAWI EL-SHEIK.

Ethiopia: 14 Lanark Rd, Belgravia, POB 2745, Harare; tel. (4) 725822; fax (4) 720259; Ambassador: MAHIMUD DIRIR.

France: 74/76 Samora Machel Ave, Harare; tel. (4) 703216; fax (4) 730078; e-mail fambass@id.co.zw; Ambassador: HADELIN DE LA TOUR DU PIN CHAMBLY DE LA CHARGE.

Germany: 14 Samora Machel Ave, POB 2168, Harare; tel. (4) 731956; fax (4) 790680; Ambassador: FRITZ HERMANN FLIMM.

Ghana: 11 Downie Ave, Belgravia, POB 4445, Harare; tel. (4) 738652; fax 738654; High Commissioner: Prof. P. A. TWUMASI.

Greece: 8 Deary Ave, Belgravia, POB 4809, Harare; tel. (4) 793208; fax (4) 703662; e-mail grembha@harare.iafrica.com; Ambassador: ATHANASSIOS M. VALASSIDIS.

Holy See: 5 St Kilda Rd, Mount Pleasant, POB MP191, Harare (Apostolic Nunciature); tel. (4) 744547; fax (4) 744412; Apostolic Nuncio: Most Rev. PETER PAUL PRABHU, Titular Archbishop of Tituli in Numidia.

Hungary: 20 Lanark Rd, Belgravia, POB 3594, Harare; tel. (4) 733528; fax (4) 730512; Ambassador: TAMÁS GÁS PÁR GÁL.

India: 12 Nathal Rd, Belgravia, POB 4620, Harare; tel. (4) 795955; fax (4) 722324; High Commissioner: AMAL KRISHNA BASU.

Indonesia: 3 Duthie Ave, Belgravia, POB 3594, Harare; tel. (4) 732561; fax (4) 720193; Ambassador: SAMSI ABDULLAH.

Iran: 8 Allan Wilson Ave, Avondale, POB A293, Harare; tel. (4) 726942; Chargé d'affaires a.i.: ALIREZA GAKARANI.

Israel: 54 Jason Moyo Ave, POB CY3191, Harare; tel. (4) 756808; fax (4) 756801; e-mail israel@harare.iafrica.com; Ambassador: GERSHON GAN.

Italy: 7 Bartholomew Close, Greendale North, POB 1062, Harare; tel. (4) 498189; fax (4) 498199; e-mail amital@samara.co.zw; Ambassador: Dr LUCA BROFFERIO.

Japan: Karigamombe Centre, 18th Floor, 53 Samora Machel Ave, POB 2710, Harare; tel. (4) 757861; fax (4) 757864; Ambassador: MITSUO IIJIMA.

Kenya: 95 Park Lane, POB 4069, Harare; tel. (4) 790847; fax (4) 723042; High Commissioner: C. A. MWAKWERE.

Korea, Democratic People's Republic: 102 Josiah Chinamano Ave, Greenwood, POB 4754, Harare; tel. (4) 724052; Ambassador: RI MYONG CHOL.

Kuwait: 1 Bath Rd, Avondale, POB A485, Harare; Ambassador: NABILA AL-MULLA.

Libya: 124 Harare St, POB 4310, Harare; tel. (4) 728381; Ambassador: M. M. IBN KOURAH.

Malawi: Malawi House, 42-44 Harare St, POB 321, Harare; tel. (4) 752137; fax (4) 752134; e-mail malahigh@africaonline.co.zw; High Commissioner: TUJILANE R. M. CHIZUMILA.

Malaysia: 40 Downie Ave, Avondale, POB 5570, Harare; tel. (4) 796209; fax (4) 796200; e-mail mwharare@africaonline.co.zw; High Commissioner: ALI ABDULLAH.

Mozambique: 152 Herbert Chitepo Ave, cnr Leopold Takawira St, POB 4608, Harare; tel. (4) 790837; High Commissioner: CORREIA FERNANDES SUMBANA.

Netherlands: 2 Arden Rd, Highlands, POB HG601, Harare; tel. (4) 776701; fax (4) 776700; Ambassador: WIM WESSELS.

Nigeria: 36 Samora Machel Ave, POB 4742, Harare; tel. (4) 790765; High Commissioner: MUHAMMED LAMEEN METTEDEN.

Norway: 5 Lanark Rd, Belgravia, POB A510, Avondale, Harare; tel. (4) 730916; fax (4) 729844; Ambassador: ARILD EIK.

Pakistan: 11 Van Praagh Ave, Milton Park, POB 3050, Harare; tel. (4) 720293; fax (4) 722446; e-mail pakharare@icon.co.zw; High Commissioner: NAWABZADA MEHBOOB ALI KHAN.

Poland: 16 Cork Road, Belgravia, POB 3932, Harare; tel. (4) 253442; fax (4) 253710; e-mail polamb@africaonline.co.zw; Chargé d'affaires a.i.: JAN WIELINSKI.

Portugal: Redbridge North Eastgate, 8th Floor, Third St, Harare; tel. (4) 725107; fax (4) 722291; e-mail embport@harare.iafrica.com; Ambassador: CARLOS NEVES FERREIRA.

Romania: 105 Fourth St, POB 4797, Harare; tel. (4) 700853; fax (4) 725493; e-mail romemb@africaonline.co.zw; Chargé d'affaires: GHEORGHE DUTA.

Russia: 70 Fife Ave, POB 4250, Harare; tel. (4) 720358; fax (4) 700534; Ambassador: LEONID A. SAFONOV.

Slovakia: 32 Aberdeen Rd, Avondale, POB HG72, Harare; tel. (4) 302636; fax (4) 302236; e-mail slovemba@harare.iafrica.com; Chargé d'affaires a.i.: MARTIN PODSTAVEK.

South Africa: 7 Elcombe Rd, Belgravia, POB A1654, Harare; tel. (4) 251851; fax (4) 757908; e-mail sahcomm@internet.co.zw; High Commissioner: A. J. D. NDOU.

Spain: 16 Phillips Ave, Belgravia, POB 3300, Harare; tel. (4) 738681; fax (4) 795440; Ambassador: TOMÁS SOLÍS GRAGERA.

Sudan: 4 Pascoe Ave, Harare; tel. (4) 725240; Ambassador: ANGELO V. MORGAN.

Sweden: Pegasus House, 52 Samora Machel Ave, POB 4110, Harare; tel. (4) 790651; fax (4) 754265; Ambassador: LENNARTH HJELMÅKER.

Switzerland: 9 Lanark Rd, POB 3440, Harare; tel. (4) 703997; fax (4) 794925; Ambassador: CATHERINE KRIEG POLEJACK.

Tunisia: 5 Ashton Rd, Alexandra Park, Harare; tel. (4) 791570; fax (4) 727224; Ambassador: HAMID ZAOUCHE.

United Kingdom: Corner House, cnr Leopold Takawira St and Samora Machel Ave, POB 4490, Harare; tel. (4) 772990; fax (4) 774617; High Commissioner: PETER LONGWORTH.

USA: 172 Herbert Chitepo Ave, POB 3340, Harare; tel. (4) 794521; fax (4) 796488; Ambassador: TOM MCDONALD.

Yugoslavia: 1 Lanark Rd, Belgravia, POB 3420, Harare; tel. (4) 738668; fax (4) 738660; Ambassador: LJUBISA KORAC.

Zambia: Zambia House, cnr Union and Julius Nyerere Aves, POB 4698, Harare; tel. (4) 790851; fax (4) 790856; High Commissioner: NCHIMUNYA SIKAULU.

Judicial System

The legal system is Roman-Dutch, based on the system which was in force in the Cape of Good Hope on 10 June 1891, as modified by subsequent legislation.

The Supreme Court has original jurisdiction in matters in which an infringement of Chapter III of the Constitution defining fundamental rights is alleged. In all other matters it has appellate jurisdiction only. It consists of the Chief Justice and four Judges of Appeal. A normal bench consists of any three of these.

The High Court consists of the Chief Justice, the Judge President, and 11 other judges. Below the High Court are Regional Courts and Magistrates' Courts with both civil and criminal jurisdiction presided over by full-time professional magistrates.

The Customary Law and Local Courts Act, adopted in 1990, abolished the village and community courts and replaced them with customary law and local courts, presided over by chiefs and headmen; in the case of chiefs, jurisdiction to try customary law cases is limited to those where the monetary values concerned do not exceed Z.$1,000 and in the case of a headman's court Z.$500. Appeals from the Chiefs' Courts are heard in Magistrates' Courts and, ultimately, the Supreme Court. All magistrates now have jurisdiction to try cases determinable by customary law.

Chief Justice: ANTHONY R. GUBBAY.

Judges of Appeal: A. M. EBRAHIM, N. J. MCNALLY, K. R. A. KORSAH, S. C. G. MUCHECHETERE.

Judge President: WILSON R. SANDURA.

Attorney-General: ANDREW CHIGOVERA.

Religion

AFRICAN RELIGIONS

Many Africans follow traditional beliefs.

CHRISTIANITY

About 55% of the population are Christians.

Zimbabwe Council of Churches: 128 Mbuya Nehanda St, POB 3566, Harare; tel. (4) 791208; f. 1964; 20 mem. churches, nine assoc.

mems; Pres. Rt Rev. JONATHAN SIYACHITEMA (Anglican Bishop of Harare); Gen. Sec. MUROMBEDZI KUCHERA.

The Anglican Communion

Anglicans are adherents of the Church of the Province of Central Africa, covering Botswana, Malawi, Zambia and Zimbabwe. The Church comprises 12 dioceses, including four in Zimbabwe. The Archbishop of the Province is the Bishop of Botswana.

Bishop of Central Zimbabwe: Rt Rev. ISHMAEL MUKUWANDA, POB 25, Gweru; tel. (54) 21030; fax (54) 21097.

Bishop of Harare: Rt Rev. JONATHAN SIYACHITEMA, Bishopsmount Close, POB UA7, Harare; tel. (4) 702253; fax (4) 700419; e-mail dioceschre@mango.zw.

Bishop of Manicaland: Rt Rev. Dr SEBASTIAN BAKARE, 115 Herbert Chitepo St, Mutare; tel. (20) 64194; fax (20) 63076; e-mail diomani@syscom.co.zw.

Bishop of Matabeleland: Rt Rev. THEOPHILUS T. NALEDI, POB 2422, Bulawayo; tel. (9) 61370; fax (9) 68353.

The Roman Catholic Church

For ecclesiastical purposes, Zimbabwe comprises two archdioceses and six dioceses. At 31 December 1998 there were an estimated 1,050,808 adherents.

Zimbabwe Catholic Bishops' Conference: General Secretariat, Africa Synod House, 29 Selous Ave, POB 8135, Causeway, Harare; tel. (4) 705368; fax (4) 705369; e-mail zcbc-sec@harare.iafrica.com; f. 1969; Pres. Mgr ALEXIO MUCHABAIWA, Bishop of Mutare.

Archbishop of Bulawayo: Most Rev. HENRY ERNEST KARLEN, cnr Lobenguela St and Ninth Ave, POB 837, Bulawayo; tel. (9) 63590; fax (9) 60359.

Archbishop of Harare: Most Rev. PATRICK FANI CHAKAIPA, POB CY330, Causeway, Harare; tel. (4) 727386; fax (4) 721598.

Other Christian Churches

City Presbyterian Church: 60 Samora Machel Ave, POB 50, Harare; tel. and fax (4) 790366; e-mail cpclight@icon.co.zw; f. 1904; Minister Rev. M. T. CHIGWARA; Session Clerk A. PHILLIPS; 390 mems.

Dutch Reformed Church (Nederduitse Gereformeerde Kerk): 35 Samora Machel Ave, POB 967, Harare; tel. (4) 774748; fax (4) 774739; e-mail mas@zol.co.zw; f. 1895; 16 parishes; Moderator Rev. A. S. VAN DYK; Gen. Sec. Rev. F. MARITZ; 2,500 mems.

Evangelical Lutheran Church: POB 2175, Bulawayo; tel. (9) 62686; e-mail elczhead@acacia.samara.co.zw; f. 1903; Sec. Rt Rev. Dr AMBROSE MOYO; 57,000 mems.

Greek Orthodox Church: POB 2832, Harare; tel. (4) 744991; Archbishop MAKARIOS.

Methodist Church in Zimbabwe: POB 71, Causeway, Harare; tel. (4) 724069; fax (4) 723709; e-mail methodistzimbabwe@mango.zw; f. 1891; Pres. Bishop CEPHAS Z. MUKANDI; Sec. of Conference Rev. MARGARET M. JAMES; 116,128 mems.

United Congregational Church of Southern Africa: POB 2451, Bulawayo; Synod Sec. for Zimbabwe Rev. J. R. DANISA LATE.

United Methodist Church: POB 3408, Harare; tel. (4) 704127; f. 1890; Bishop of Zimbabwe ABEL TENDEKAYI MUZOREWA; 45,000 mems.

Among other denominations active in Zimbabwe are the African Methodist Church, the African Methodist Episcopal Church, the African Reformed Church, the Christian Marching Church, the Church of Christ in Zimbabwe, the Independent African Church, the Presbyterian Church, the United Church of Christ, the Zimbabwe Assemblies of God and the Ziwezano Church.

JUDAISM

The Jewish community numbered 897 members at 31 December 1997.

Zimbabwe Jewish Board of Deputies: POB 1954, Harare; tel. (4) 702506; fax (4) 702507; Pres. M. C. ROSS; Sec. Mrs E. ALHADEFF.

BAHÁ'Í FAITH

National Spiritual Assembly: POB GD380, Greendale, Harare; tel. (4) 495945; fax (4) 744244; f. 1970; mems resident in more than 3,000 localities.

The Press

DAILIES

The Chronicle: POB 585, Bulawayo; tel. (9) 540071; fax (9) 540084; f. 1894; circulates throughout south-west Zimbabwe; English; Editor STEPHEN A. MPOFU; circ. 44,000.

The Herald: POB 396, Harare; tel. (4) 795771; fax (4) 700305; f. 1891; English; Chair. THOMAS SITHOLE; circ. 122,077.

WEEKLIES

Business Herald: Harare; weekly; Editor ANDREW RUSINGA.

The Farmer: POB WGT160, Westgate, Harare; tel. (4) 309859; fax (4) 309860; e-mail farmer@cfu.co.zw; f. 1928; commercial farming; weekly; English; Editor CHARLES KABERA; circ. 6,100.

Financial Gazette: Coal House, 5th Floor, 17 Nelson Mandela Ave, Harare; tel. (4) 781571; fax (4) 781578; e-mail mod@harare.iafrica.com; weekly; independent; Editor-in-Chief FRANCIS MDLONGWA; circ. 28,000.

Kwayedza: POB 396, Harare; tel. (4) 795771; fax (4) 791311; weekly; Editor G. M. CHITEWE; circ. 33,944.

Makonde Star: POB 533, Kwekwe; tel. (55) 2248; f. 1989; weekly; English; Editor FELIX MOYO; circ. 21,000.

Manica Post: POB 960, Mutare; tel. (20) 61212; fax (20) 61149; e-mail manpost@syscom.co.zw; f. 1893; weekly; Editor J. GAMBANGA; circ. 20,970.

Masvingo Mirror: POB 1214, Masvingo; tel. (39) 64372; fax (39) 64484; e-mail belpress@mvo.samara.co.zw; weekly; independent.

Midlands Observer: POB 533, Kwekwe; tel. (55) 2248; f. 1953; weekly; English; Editor FELIX MOYO; circ. 5,000.

North Midlands Gazette: POB 222, Kadoma; tel. and fax (68) 3731; e-mail kidia@pci.co.zw; f. 1912; weekly; Editor C. B. KIDIA.

Sunday Gazette: POB 66070, Kopje, Harare; tel. (4) 738722; weekly; Editor FRANCIS MDLONGWA.

Sunday Mail: POB 396, Harare; tel. (4) 795771; fax (4) 700305; f. 1935; weekly; English; Chair. THOMAS SITHOLE; circ. 159,075.

Sunday News: POB 585, Bulawayo; tel. (9) 540071; fax (9) 540084; f. 1930; weekly; English; Editor E. MACHIRORI; circ. 50,000.

The Times: 71 Seventh St, POB 66, Gweru; tel. (54) 23285; fax (54) 21614; e-mail thetimes@samara.co.zw; f. 1897; weekly; English; Editor SHEPARD SAMASUWO; circ. 5,000.

Zimbabwe Independent: Harare; f. 1996; weekly; Editor TREVOR NCUBE; Publr CLIVE WILSON.

Zimbabwean Government Gazette: POB 8062, Causeway, Harare; official notices; weekly; Editor L. TAKAWIRA.

PERIODICALS

Africa Calls Worldwide: POB BW1500, Harare; tel. (4) 728256; fax (4) 792932; f. 1960; travel; 6 a year; Man. Editor DONETTE KRUGER.

Central African Journal of Medicine: POB A195, Avondale, Harare; tel. (4) 791631; f. 1955; monthly; Editor-in-Chief Dr J. A. MATENGA.

Chamber of Mines Journal: POB 1683, Harare; tel. (4) 736835; fax (4) 749803; journal of the Chamber of Mines of Zimbabwe; monthly; Editor M. ZHUWAKINYU.

Chaminuka News: POB 251, Marondera; f. 1988; fortnightly; English and Chishona; Editor M. MUGABE; circ. 10,000.

City Observer: POB 990, Harare; tel. (4) 706536; fax (4) 708544; monthly.

Commerce: POB 1683, Harare; tel. (4) 736835; fax (4) 749803; journal of Zimbabwe Nat. Chambers of Commerce; monthly; Editor I. MILLS; circ. 1,500.

Computer and Telecom News: POB 1683, Harare; tel. (4) 736835; fax (4) 749803; monthly; Editor R. STEWART.

CZI Industrial Review: POB 1683, Harare; tel. (4) 736835; fax (4) 749803; journal of the Confed. of Zimbabwe Industries; monthly; Editor I. MILLS.

Economic Review: c/o Zimbabwe Financial Holdings, POB 3198, Harare; tel. (4) 751168; fax (4) 757497; 4 a year; circ. 3,000.

Executive: Harare; tel. (4) 755084; fax (4) 752162; bi-monthly; Editor MICHAEL J. HAMILTON.

Horizon Magazine: POB UA196, Union Ave, Harare; tel. (4) 704645; e-mail horizon@mango.zw; current affairs; monthly; circ. 40,000.

Hotel and Catering Gazette: POB 2677, Kopje, Harare; tel. (4) 738722; fax (4) 707130; monthly; Editor PAULA CHARLES; circ. 2,000.

Indonsakusa: Hwange; f. 1988; monthly; English and Sindebele; Editor D. NTABENI; circ. 10,000.

Insurance Review: POB 1683, Harare; tel. (4) 736835; fax (4) 749803; monthly; Editor M. ZHUWAKINYU.

Jassa: POB MP203, Mount Pleasant, Harare; tel. (4) 303211; fax (4) 333407; applied science journal of the Univ. of Zimbabwe; 2 a year; Editor Prof. C. F. B. NHACHI.

Journal on Social Change and Development: POB 4405, Harare; tel. (4) 720417; fax (4) 730808; e-mail schange@africaonline.co.zw; f. 1981; quarterly; Chair. JOYCE KAZEMBE; circ. 4,500.

Just for Me: POB 66070, Kopje, Harare; tel (4) 704715; f. 1990; family and women's interest; Editor BEVERLEY TILLEY.

Karoi News: POB 441, Karoi; tel. 6216; fortnightly.

Look and Listen: POB UA589, Harare; tel. (4) 752144; fax (4) 752062; e-mail munn@samara.co.zw; f. 1965; radio and TV programmes, cookery, entertainment and reviews; fortnightly; Editor ALASDAIR J. MUNN; circ. 23,000.

Mahogany: POB UA589, Harare; tel. (4) 752063; fax (4) 752062; e-mail munn@samara.co.zw; f. 1980; English; women's interest; 6 a year; Editor TENDAI DONDO; circ. 240,000.

Makoni Clarion: POB 17, Rusape; monthly.

Masiye Pambili (Let Us Go Forward): POB 591, Bulawayo; tel. (9) 75011; fax (9) 69701; f. 1964; English; 2 a year; Editor M. M. NDUBIWA; circ. 21,000.

Monthly Bulletin: POB 1283, Harare; tel. (4) 703000; fax (4) 707800; e-mail rbzmail@rbz.co.zw; weekly, monthly and quarterly economic reports; publ. by the Reserve Bank of Zimbabwe.

Moto: POB 890, Gweru; tel. (54) 24886; fax (54) 21991; Roman Catholic; Editor PERCY F. MAKOMBE; circ. 30,000.

Nehanda Guardian: Hwange; f. 1988; monthly; English and Chishona; Editor K. MWANAKA; circ. 10,000.

Nhau Dzekumakomo: POB 910, Mutare; f. 1984; publ. by Mutare City Council; monthly.

On Guard: National Social Security Authority, POB 1387, Causeway, Harare; tel. (4) 728931; fax (4) 796320; Editor P. TAGARA.

The Outpost: POB HG106, Highlands; tel. (4) 724571; f. 1911; English; monthly; Editor ELVIS CHIPUKA; circ. 21,000.

Parade Magazine: POB 3798, Harare; tel. (4) 736837; fax (4) 749803; e-mail tpubl@samara.co.zw; f. 1953; monthly; English; Editor CHIZA LUSUNGU NGWIRA; circ. 91,000.

Quarterly Guide to the Economy: First Merchant Bank of Zimbabwe, FMB House, 67 Samora Machel Ave, POB 2786, Harare; tel. (4) 703071; fax (4) 738810; quarterly.

RailRoader: POB 596, Bulawayo; f. 1952; tel. (9) 363526; fax (9) 363543; monthly; Editor M. GUMEDE; circ. 10,000.

The Record: POB 179, Harare; tel. (4) 708911; journal of the Public Service Asscn; 6 a year; Editor GAMALIEL RUNGANI; circ. 30,000.

Southern African Political and Economic Monthly: POB MP1005, Mt Pleasant, Harare; tel. (4) 621681; fax (4) 666061; e-mail sappho@zimmirror.co.zw; monthly; incorporating Southern African Economist; Editor-in-Chief IBBO MANDAZA; circ. 16,000.

Teacher in Zimbabwe: POB 350, Harare; tel. (4) 497548; fax (4) 497554; f. 1981; monthly; circ. 60,000.

Tobacco News: POB 1683, Harare; tel. (4) 736836; fax (4) 749803; monthly; Editor D. MILLER; circ. 3,000.

Vanguard: POB 66102, Kopje; tel. 751193; every 2 months.

The Worker: POB 8323, Causeway, Harare; tel. 700466.

World Vision News: POB 2420, Harare; tel. 703794; quarterly.

Zambezia: POB MP203, Harare; tel. (4) 303211; fax (4) 333407; humanities journal of the Univ. of Zimbabwe; 2 a year; Editor Dr A. S. MLAMBO.

Zimbabwe Agricultural Journal: POB CY594, Causeway, Harare; tel. (4) 704531; fax (4) 728317; f. 1903; 6 a year; Editor R. J. FENNER; circ. 2,000.

Zimbabwe Defence Forces Magazine: POB 7720, Harare; tel. (4) 722481; f. 1982; 6 a year; circ. 5,000.

Zimbabwe Engineer: POB 1683, Harare; tel. (4) 736835; fax (4) 749803; monthly; Editor TERRENCE MAPURISANA.

Zimbabwe News: POB CY3206, Causeway, Harare; tel. (4) 790148; fax (4) 790483; monthly.

NEWS AGENCIES

Zimbabwe Inter-Africa News Agency (ZIANA): POB CY511, Causeway, Harare; tel. (4) 730151; fax (4) 794336; f. 1981; owned and controlled by Zimbabwe Mass Media Trust; Editor-in-Chief HENRY E. MURADZIKWA.

Foreign Bureaux

Agence France-Presse (AFP): Robinson House, Union Ave, POB 1166, Harare; tel. (4) 758017; fax (4) 753291; e-mail afphre@africaonline.co.zw; Rep. FRANÇOIS-BERNARD CASTÉRAN.

ANGOP (Angola): Mass Media House, 3rd Floor, 19 Selous Ave, POB 6354, Harare; tel. (4) 736849.

Agenzia Nazionale Stampa Associata (ANSA) (Italy): Harare; tel. (4) 723881; Rep. IAN MILLS.

Associated Press (AP) (USA): POB 785, Harare; tel. (4) 706622; fax (4) 703994; Rep. JOHN EDLIN.

Deutsche Presse-Agentur (dpa) (Germany): Harare; tel. (4) 700875; Correspondent JAN RAATH.

Informatsionnoye Telegrafnoye Agentstvo Rossii—Telegrafnoye Agentstvo Suverennykh Stran (ITAR—TASS) (Russia): Mass Media House, 19 Selous Ave, POB 4012, Harare; tel. (4) 790521; Correspondent YURII PITCHUGIN.

Inter Press Service (IPS) (Italy): 127 Union Ave, POB 6050, Harare; tel. (4) 790104; fax (4) 728415; e-mail ipshre@harare.iafrica.com; Rep. KENNETH BLACKMAN.

News Agency of Nigeria (NAN): Harare; tel. (4) 703041.

Pan-African News Agency (PANA) (Senegal): 19 Selous Ave, POB 8364, Harare; tel. (4) 730971; Bureau Chief PETER MWAURA.

Prensa Latina (Cuba): Mass Media House, 3rd Floor, 19 Selous Ave, Harare; tel. (4) 731993; Correspondent HUGO RIUS.

Press Trust of India (PTI): Mass Media House, 3rd Floor, 19 Selous Ave, Harare; tel. (4) 795006; Rep. N. V. R. SWAMI.

Reuters (United Kingdom): 901 Tanganyika House, Union Ave, Harare, POB 2987; tel. (4) 724299; Bureau Chief DAVID BLOOM.

Rossiiskoye Informatsionnoye Agentstvo—Novosti (RIA—Novosti) (Russia): 503 Robinson House, cnr Union Ave and Angwa St, POB 3908, Harare; tel. (4) 707232; fax (4) 707233; Correspondent A. TIMONOVICH.

Tanjug (Yugoslavia): Mass Media House, 19 Selous Ave, Harare; tel. (4) 479018; Correspondent DEJAN DRAKULIĆ.

United Press International (UPI) (USA): Harare; tel. (4) 25265; Rep. IAN MILLS.

Xinhua (New China) News Agency (People's Republic of China): 4 Earls Rd, Alexander Park, POB 4746, Harare; tel. and fax (4) 731467; Chief Correspondent LU JIANXIN.

Publishers

Academic Books (Pvt) Ltd: POB 567, Harare; tel. (4) 755408; fax (4) 781913; educational; Editorial Dir IRENE STAUNTON.

Amalgamated Publications (Pvt) Ltd: POB 1683, Harare; tel. (4) 736835; fax (4) 749803; f. 1949; trade journals; Man. Dir A. THOMSON.

Anvil Press: POB 4209, Harare; tel. (4) 751202; fax (4) 739681; f. 1988; general; Man. Dir PAUL BRICKHILL.

The Argosy Press: POB 2677, Harare; tel. (4) 755084; magazine publrs; Gen. Man. A. W. HARVEY.

Baobab Books (Pvt) Ltd: POB 567, Harare; tel. (4) 665187; fax (4) 665155; e-mail academic@africaonline.co.zw; general, literature, children's.

College Press Publishers (Pvt) Ltd: 15 Douglas Rd, POB 3041, Workington, Harare; tel. (4) 754145; fax (4) 754256; f. 1968; educational and general; Man. Dir B. B. MUGABE.

The Bulletin: POB 1595, Bulawayo; tel. (9) 78831; fax (9) 78835; frmrly Directory Publishers Ltd; education; CEO BRUCE BEALE.

Graham Publishing Co (Pvt) Ltd: POB 2931, Harare; tel. (4) 752437; fax (4) 752439; f. 1967; general; Dir GORDON M. GRAHAM.

Harare Publishing House: Chiremba Rd, Hatfield, POB 4735, Harare; tel. (4) 570613; f. 1984; Dir Dr T. M. SAMKANGE.

HarperCollins Publishers (Zimbabwe) Pvt) Ltd: Union Ave, POB UA201, Harare; tel. (4) 721413; fax (4) 732436; Man. S. D. McMILLAN.

Longman Zimbabwe (Pvt) Ltd: PO Box ST125, Southerton, Harare; tel. (4) 62711; fax (4) 62716; f. 1964; general and educational; Man. Dir N. L. DLODLO.

Mambo Press: Senga Rd, POB 779, Gweru; tel. (54) 24017; fax (54) 21991; e-mail mambo@icon.co.zw; f. 1958; religious, educational and fiction in English and African languages.

Modus Publications (Pvt) Ltd: Modus House, 27-29 Charter Rd, POB 6070, Kopje, Harare; tel. (4) 738722; Man. Dir ELIAS RUSIKE.

Munn Publishing (Pvt) Ltd: POB UA460, Union Ave, Harare; tel. (4) 752144; fax (4) 752062; e-mail munn@samara.co.zw; Man. Dir A. F. MUNN.

Standard Publications (Pvt) Ltd: POB 3745, Harare; Dir G. F. BOOT.

Southern African Printing and Publishing House (SAPPHO): 109 Coventry Rd, Workington, POB MP1005, Mt Pleasant, Harare; tel. (4) 621681; fax (4) 666061; e-mail sappho@zimmirror.co.zw; Editor-in-Chief Dr IBBO MANDAZA.

University of Zimbabwe Publications: POB MP203, Mount Pleasant, Harare; tel. (4) 303211; fax (4) 333407; e-mail uzpub@esanet.zw; f. 1969; Dir MUNANI SAM MTETWA.

Zimbabwe Newspapers (1980) Ltd: POB 55, Harare; tel. (4) 704088; fax (4) 702400; f. 1981; state-owned; controls largest newspaper group; Chair. T. C. SAMKANGE; Man. Dir M. T. KUNAKA.

Zimbabwe Publishing House: POB 350, Harare; tel. (4) 497555; fax (4) 497554; e-mail uzpub@pci.co.zw; f. 1982; Chair. DAVID MARTIN; Gen. Man. ALFRED BAKASA.

Government Publishing House

The Literature Bureau: POB 749, Causeway, Harare; tel. (4) 333812; f. 1954; controlled by Ministry of Education; Dir B. C. CHITSIKE.

Broadcasting and Communications

TELECOMMUNICATIONS

Posts and Telecommunications Corporation (PTC): POB CY331, Causeway, Harare; tel. (4) 728811; fax (4) 731980; e-mail ajchaponda@zptc.co.zw; internet www.zptc.co; Chair. Dr M. MHLOYI; CEO BRIAN MUTANDIRO.

BROADCASTING

Radio

Zimbabwe Broadcasting Corporation: POB HG444, Highlands, Harare; tel. (4) 498610; fax (4) 498613; f. 1957; Chair. TAFATAONA MAHOSA; Dir-Gen. EDWARD M. MOYO (acting).

Broadcasts in English, Chishona, Sindebele, Kalanga, Venda, Tonga and Chewa; four programme services comprise a general service (predominantly in English), vernacular languages service, light entertainment, educational programmes.

Television

Zimbabwe Broadcasting Corporation: (see Radio).

The main broadcasting centre is in Harare, with a second studio in Bulawayo; broadcasts on two channels (one of which serves the Harare area only) for about 105 hours per week. A commercial television channel was scheduled to commence operations in the late 1990s.

Finance

(cap. = capital; res = reserves; dep. = deposits; m. = million;
brs = branches; amounts in Zimbabwe dollars)

BANKING

Central Bank

Reserve Bank of Zimbabwe: 80 Samora Machel Ave, POB 1283, Harare; tel. (4) 703000; fax (4) 707800; e-mail rbzmail@rbz.co.zw; internet www.rbz.co.zw; f. 1964; bank of issue; cap. and res 8m., dep. 10,032m. (March 2000); Gov. Dr LEONARD TSUMBA.

Commercial Banks

Barclays Bank of Zimbabwe Ltd: Barclays House, First St and Jason Moyo Ave, POB 1279, Harare; tel. (4) 758280; fax (4) 752913; e-mail barmkt@africaonline.co.zw; internet www.barclays.co.zw; cap. and res 935m., dep. 9,810m. (Dec. 1998); Chair. D. M. ZAMCHIYA; Man. Dir I. G. TAKAWIRA; 44 brs.

Commercial Bank of Zimbabwe: Union House, 60 Union Ave, POB 3313, Harare; tel. (4) 758081; fax (4) 758085; e-mail cbzinfo@africaonline.co.zw; internet www.cbz.co.zw; state-owned; cap. and res 110.9m., total assets 646.1m. (Dec. 1998); Chair. R. V. WILDE; Man. Dir GIDEON GONO; 9 brs.

Stanbic Bank Zimbabwe Ltd: Stanbic Centre, 1st Floor, 59 Samora Machel Ave, POB 300, Harare; tel. (4) 759480; fax (4) 751324; e-mail stanbictre@utande.co.zw; f. 1990; cap. and res 374m., total assets 5,068m. (Sept. 1998); Chair. C. M. D. SANYANGA; CEO GREG R. BRACKENRIDGE; 14 brs.

Standard Chartered Bank Zimbabwe Ltd: John Boyne House, 38 Speke Ave, POB 373, Harare; tel. (4) 752852; fax (4) 758560; f. 1983; cap. and res 1,316m., total assets 13,990m. (Dec. 1998); Chair. H. P. MKUSHI; CEO B. R. HAMILTON; 42 brs and sub-brs; 10 agencies.

Trade and Investment Bank Ltd: Cabs Centre, 10th Floor, 74 Jason Moyo Ave, POB CY1064, Causeway, Harare; tel. (4) 703791; fax (4) 705491; e-mail tib@tibl.co.zw; f. 1997; cap. and res. 32m., total assets 421m. (Dec. 1997); Chair. Dr BERNARD THOMAS CHIDZERO; CEO Dr KOMBO JAMES MOYANA.

Zimbabwe Banking Corporation Ltd (Zimbank): Zimbank House, Speke Ave and First St, POB 3198, Harare; tel. (4) 755180; fax (4) 756674; e-mail zimbank@harare.iafrica.com; internet www.finhold.co.zw; f. 1951; state-owned; cap. and res 441m., dep. 4,181m. (Dec. 1997); Group CEO E. N. MUSHAYAKARARA; 48 brs.

Development Bank

Zimbabwe Development Bank (ZDB): ZDB House, 99 Rotten Row, POB 1720, Harare; tel. (4) 750171; fax (4) 774225; e-mail zdb@harare.iafrica.com; f. 1985; 33.3% state-owned; cap. and res 195m., total assets 826m. (June 1997); Chair. Dr T. MASAYA; Man. Dir C. MARIDZA; 3 brs.

Merchant Banks

First Merchant Bank of Zimbabwe Ltd: FMB House, 67 Samora Machel Ave, POB 2786, Harare; tel. (4) 703071; fax (4) 738810; e-mail fmbzau@fmb.finweb.co.zw; internet www.fmb.co.zw; f. 1956; merged with Heritage Investment Bank 1997; cap. and res 393m., total assets 4,487m. (Dec. 1998); Chair. P. M. BAUM; Man. Dir R. FELTOE; br. in Bulawayo.

Kingdom Financial Services Merchant Bank: Harare; f. 1998.

Merchant Bank of Central Africa Ltd: Old Mutual Centre, 14th Floor, cnr Third St and Jason Moyo Ave, POB 3200, Harare; tel. (4) 738081; fax (4) 708005; e-mail mbca@bank.co.zw; internet www.mbca.co.zw; f. 1956; cap. and res 281m., dep. 1,818m. (Dec. 1998); Chair. E. D. CHIURA; Man. Dir DAVID T. HATENDI.

National Merchant Bank of Zimbabwe Ltd: Unity Court, 1st Floor, cnr Union Ave and First St, POB 2564, Harare; tel. (4) 759651; fax (4) 759648; e-mail enquiries@nmbz.co.zw; internet www.nmbz.com; f. 1992; cap. and res. 279.1m., dep. 2,498m. (Dec. 1998); Chair. P. T. ZHANDA; CEO Dr JULIUS T. MAKONI; 1 br.

Standard Chartered Merchant Bank Zimbabwe Ltd: Standard Chartered Bank Bldg, cnr Second St and Nelson Mandela Ave, POB 60, Harare; tel. (4) 708585; fax (4) 725667; f. 1971; cap. and res 78m., dep. 83m. (Dec. 1998); Chair. BARRY HAMILTON; Man. Dir EBBY ESSOKA.

Discount Houses

Bard Discount House Ltd: Bard House, 69 Samora Machel Ave, POB 3321, Harare; tel. (4) 752756; fax (4) 790641; e-mail discount@bard-zim.com; cap. and res 68m. (Dec. 1999); acquisition pending by National Merchant Bank of Zimbabwe; Chair. N. KUDENGA; Man. Dir D. DUBE.

The Discount Co of Zimbabwe (DCZ): 70 Park Lane, POB 3424, Harare; tel. (4) 705414; fax (4) 731670; cap. and res 8.9m., total assets 377.4m. (Feb. 1995); Chair. S. J. CHIHAMBAKWE.

Intermarket Discount House: Unity Court, 5th Floor, Union Ave, Harare; e-mail idh@coldfire.dnet.co.zw.

National Discount House Ltd: Chancellor House, 10th Floor, 69 Samora Machel Ave, POB CY2245, Causeway, Harare; tel. (4) 700771; fax (4) 792927; e-mail ndhzim@ndhzim.com; cap. and res 53m. (Dec. 1997); Man. Dir E. MATIENGA.

udc Holdings Ltd: udc Centre, cnr First St and Union Ave, Private Bag 5550, POB 1685, Mount Pleasant, Harare; tel. (4) 369260; fax (4) 369322; e-mail udc@udc.co.zw; cap. and res 73m. (Dec. 1995); Man. Dir J. W. DICK.

Banking Organization

Institute of Bankers of Zimbabwe: POB UA521, Harare; tel. (4) 752474; fax (4) 737499; e-mail iobzhre@africaonline.co.zw; f. 1973; Pres. N. VINGIRAO; Dir S. A. H. BROWN.

STOCK EXCHANGE

Zimbabwe Stock Exchange: cnr First St and Samora Machel Ave, POB UA234, Harare; tel. (4) 736861; fax (4) 791045; e-mail zse@pci.co.zw; f. 1946; Chair. G. MHLANGA.

INSURANCE

Commercial Union Insurance Co of Zimbabwe Ltd: POB 1065, Harare; tel. (4) 795840; fax (4) 721241; e-mail cuzimb@harare.iafrica.com; mem. of Commercial Union group; Chair. H. P. MKUSHI.

Diamond Insurance of Zimbabwe Ltd: Harare; Gen. Man. GRACE MURADZIKWA.

Fidelity Life Assurance of Zimbabwe (Pvt) Ltd: 66 Julius Nyerere Way, POB 435, Harare; tel. (4) 750927; fax (4) 704705; Chair. B. KUMALO; Gen. Man. C. CHONZI.

National Insurance Co of Zimbabwe (Pvt) Ltd: cnr Baker Ave and First St, POB 1256, Harare; tel. (4) 704911; fax (4) 704134; Man. Dir S. T. MALUMO.

Old Mutual Life Assurance Co: POB 70, Harare; tel. (4) 308400; fax (4) 308468; f. 1845; life assurance; CEO G. D. HOLLICK; Gen. Man. L. E. M. NGWERUME.

RM Insurance Co (Pvt) Ltd: Royal Mutual House, 45 Baker Ave, POB 3599, Harare; tel. (4) 757961; fax (4) 759700; f. 1982; cap. p.u. 2m.; Chair. C. WRIGHT; Gen. Man. MIKE GIBSON.

Southampton Assurance Co of Zimbabwe Ltd: Southampton Life Centre, 77 Jason Moyo Ave, POB 969, Harare; tel. (4) 708801; fax (4) 703186; life assurance.

Zimnat Life Assurance Co Ltd: Zimnat House, cnr Baker Ave and Third St, POB 2417, Harare; tel. (4) 737611; fax (4) 791782; Chair. S. MUTASA; Gen. Man. R. G. MUIRIMI.

Trade and Industry

GOVERNMENT AGENCIES

Zimbabwe Investment Centre (ZIC): POB 5950, Harare; tel. (4) 757931; fax (4) 757937; e-mail info@zic.samara.co.zw; promotes domestic and foreign investment.

Zimbabwe Privatization Agency: Harare; CEO ANDREW MVUMBE.

ZimTrade: POB 2738, Harare; tel. (4) 732974; fax (4) 706930; e-mail info@zimtrade.co.zw; internet www.zimtrade.co.zw; f. 1991; nat. export promotion org.; Chair. E. MATIKIDI (acting); CEO F. CHAWASANRA.

DEVELOPMENT ORGANIZATIONS

Industrial Development Corporation of Zimbabwe Ltd: POB CY1431, Causeway, Harare; tel. (4) 706971; fax (4) 796028; e-mail administrator@idc.co.zw; internet www.zimtrade.co.zw/PROFILES/IDC/index.htm/; f. 1963; Chair. P. CHINGONO; Gen. Man. M. N. NDUDZO.

Zimbabwe Development Corporation (ZDC): Harare; promotes rural devt; CEO A. M. TIMBE.

CHAMBERS OF COMMERCE

Manicaland Chamber of Industries: POB 92, Mutare; tel. (20) 62300; f. 1945; Pres. L. BAXTER; 60 mems.

Mashonaland Chamber of Industries: POB 3794, Harare; tel. (4) 739833; fax (4) 750953; f. 1922; Pres. A. I. S. FERGUSON; Sec. M. MUBATARIPI; 729 mems.

Matabeleland Chamber of Industries: POB 2317, Bulawayo; tel. (9) 60642; fax (9) 60814; f. 1931; Pres. A. R. ROWLAND; Sec. N. MCKAY; about 150 mems.

Midlands Chamber of Industries: POB 213, Gweru; tel. (54) 2812; Pres. J. W. PRINGLE; 50 mems.

Zimbabwe National Chambers of Commerce (ZNCC): Equity House, Rezende St, POB 1934, Harare; tel. (4) 753444; fax (4) 753450; e-mail info@zncc.co.zw; f. 1983; Pres. N. MASUKU; CEO WONDER MAISIRI.

INDUSTRIAL AND TRADE ASSOCIATIONS

Bulawayo Agricultural Society: PO Famona, Bulawayo; tel. and fax (9) 77668; f. 1907; Pres. C. P. D. GOODWIN.

Cattle Producers' Association: Harare; Pres. G. FRANCEYS.

Chamber of Mines of Zimbabwe: 4 Central Ave, POB 712, Harare; tel. (4) 702841; fax (4) 707983; e-mail chamines@primenetzw.com; f. 1939; Pres. JAMES MAPOSA; CEO DAVID MURANGARI.

Coffee Growers' Association: Leopold Takawira St, Harare; tel. and fax (4) 750238; Dir JULES LANG.

Commercial Cotton Growers' Association: cnr Adylinn Rd and Marlborough Drive, POB EH191, Harare; tel. (4) 309800; fax (4) 309844; e-mail ccga@samara.co.zw; Administrator M. BRAGGE.

Confederation of Zimbabwe Industries: 31 Joseph Chinamano Ave, P.O. Box 3794, Harare; tel. (4) 750952; fax (4) 750953; e-mail cz@primenetzw.com; f. 1957; Pres. K. C. KATSANDE; CEO A. J. ROSS; 1,000 mems.

Construction Industry Federation of Zimbabwe: POB 1502, Harare; tel. (4) 746661; fax (4) 746937; e-mail cifoz@id.co.zw; Pres. C. P. SEAGER; CEO P. D. BURNS.

Horticultural Promotion Council: Harare; represents c. 1,000 producers.

Matabeleland Region of the Construction Industry Federation of Zimbabwe: POB 1970, Bulawayo; tel. (9) 65787; f. 1919; Sec. M. BARRON; 124 mems.

Minerals Marketing Corporation of Zimbabwe: 90 Mutare Rd, Msasa, POB 2628, Harare; tel. (4) 486945; fax (4) 487261; f. 1982; sole authority for marketing of mineral production (except gold); Chair. E. MUTOWO; Gen. Man. LIZ CHITIGA.

Tobacco Industry and Marketing Board: POB UA214, Union Ave, Harare; tel. (4) 614431; fax (4) 614430.

Zimbabwe Tobacco Association: POB 1781, Harare; tel. (4) 727441; fax (4) 724523; e-mail zta@id.co.zw; Pres. RICHARD TATE; CEO CHRIS R. L. MOLAM; 5,000 mems.

EMPLOYERS' ASSOCIATIONS

Bulawayo Landowners' and Farmers' Association: Bulawayo.

Commercial Farmers' Union: POB WGT390, Westgate, Harare; tel. (4) 309800; fax (4) 309874; e-mail cfu@samara.co.zw; internet www.samara.co.zw/cfu/; f. 1942; Pres. TIM HENWOOD; Dir D. W. HASLUCK; 4,348 mems.

Employers' Confederation of Zimbabwe: POB 158, Harare; tel. (4) 739633; fax (4) 739630; Pres. JOSHUA B. MYOKA; Exec. Dir PETER F. KUNJEKU.

Employment Council for the Motor Industry: POB 1084, Bulawayo; tel. (9) 78161.

Kadoma Farmers' and Stockowners' Association: Kadoma; tel. (68) 3658; Chair. A. REED; Sec. P. M. REED; 66 mems.

Kwekwe Farmers' Association: POB 72, Kwekwe; tel. (55) 247721; f. 1928; Chair. D. EDWARDS; Sec. J. TAPSON; 87 mems.

Mutare District Farmers' Association: POB 29, Mutare; tel. (20) 66614; e-mail mutare@cfu.co.zw; Chair. R. GARVIN; Sec. Mrs P. BREAKS; 45 mems.

National Association of Dairy Farmers: cnr Adylinn Rd and Marlborough Drive, POB WGT390, Harare; tel. (4) 309800; fax (4) 309861; e-mail nadf@cfu.co.zw; Chair. M. BURR.

National Employment Council for the Construction Industry of Zimbabwe: St Barbara House, cnr L. Takawira St and N. Mandela Ave, POB 2995, Harare; tel. (4) 773966; fax (4) 773967; CEO S. R. MAKONI.

National Employment Council for the Engineering and Iron and Steel Industry: Adven House, 5th Floor, cnr Inez Terrace and Speke Ave, POB 1922, Harare; tel. (4) 775144; fax (4) 775918; f. 1943; Gen. Sec. E. E. SHARPE.

Zimbabwe Farmers' Union: POB 3755, Harare; tel. (4) 704763; fax (4) 700829; Chair. GARY MAGADZIRE.

UTILITIES

Electricity

Zimbabwe Electricity Supply Authority (ZESA): 25 Samora Ave, POB 377, Harare; tel. (4) 774508; fax (4) 774542; state-owned; Chair. SIDNEY GATA; CEO SIMBARASHE MANGWENGWENDE.

Gas

BOC Gases: Hull Rd, POB 1282, Harare; tel. (4) 757171; fax (4) 755775.

Water

Department of Water: City of Harare, POB 1583, Harare.

MAJOR COMPANIES

Almin Metal Industries: POB 394, Southerton, Harare; tel. (4) 620121; fax (4) 620123; e-mail mlfran@zol.co.zw; f. 1969; semi-fabricators in non-ferrous metals; Man. Dir A. P. TYLE; 300 employees.

Bindura Nickel Corporation Ltd: POB 1108, Harare; tel. (4) 704461; fax (4) 703734; sales Z.$1,500m. (Dec. 1998); mining, smelting and refining of nickel; Chair. P. M. BAUM; 2,800 employees.

Circle Cement Ltd: POB GD160, Greendale, Harare; tel. (4) 491030; fax (4) 491044; f. 1954; cap. and res Z.$449.6m., sales Z.$456.5m. (Nov. 1998); mfrs of portland cement and limewash; Exec. Chair. G. I. GEORGE; Man. Dir I. COULTER; 695 employees.

Delta Corporation Ltd: POB BW294, Borrowdale, Harare; tel. (4) 883865; fax (4) 883864; e-mail hgaitskell@delta.co.zw; internet www.delta.co.zw; f. 1946; brewers, soft drink mfrs, supermarket and furniture retailing and the hotel industry; Chair. Dr R. M. MUWAPOSE; CEO J. P. ROONEY; 13,969 employees.

Hippo Valley Estates Ltd: POB 1108l, Harare; tel. (4) 704461; fax (4) 727133; cap. and res Z.$1,881.3m., sales Z.$2,008.7m. (March 1999); production of sugar from cane; Chair. P. M. BAUM; Man. Dir S. D. MTSAMBIWA; 5,300 employees.

Mhangura Copper Mines: 90 Mutare Rd, POB 4101, Harare; tel. (4) 487014; fax (4) 487022; f. 1947; sales Z.$118m. (June 1998); copper mining; Chair. T. D. MUSKWE.

Rio Tinto Zimbabwe Ltd: POB CY1243, Causeway, Harare; tel. (4) 746089; fax (4) 746228; cap. and res Z.$444.1m., sales Z.$954.1m. (Dec. 1998); nickel and copper refining; gold mining; also diamonds and coal prospecting; Chair. S. C. TAWENGWA; Man. Dir and CEO J. L. NIXON; 2,590 employees.

Wankie Colliery Co Ltd: POB 2870, Harare; tel. (4) 703947; fax (4) 703946; f. 1923; cap. and res Z.$953.8m., sales 1,222.2m. (Feb. 1998); coal mining at Hwange (fmrly Wankie); Chair. N. KUDENGA; Man. Dir O. K. BWERINOFA; 4,403 employees.

ZIMASCO (Pvt) Ltd: Pegasus House, 6th Floor, Samora Machel Ave, POB 3110, Harare; tel. (4) 739622; fax (4) 707758; f. 1923; chromite mining at Shurugwi and Mutorashanga, smelting at Kwekwe; Man. Dir S. JENA; 3,500 employees.

Zimbabwe Iron and Steel Co Ltd (Ziscosteel): Private Bag 2, Redcliff; tel. (55) 62401; fax (55) 68666; largest integrated steelworks in sub-Saharan Africa, with annual capacity of 1m. tons of liquid steel; Chair. D. E. H. MURANGARI; Man. Dir Dr G. G. MASANGA; 3,200 employees.

TRADE UNIONS

All trade unions in Zimbabwe became affiliated to the ZCTU in 1981. The ZCTU is encouraging a policy of union amalgamations.

Zimbabwe Congress of Trade Unions (ZCTU): Chester House, 10th Floor, Speke Ave at Third St, POB 3549, Harare; tel. (4) 794742; fax (4) 728444; f. 1981; co-ordinating org. for trade unions; Pres. Isaac Matongo; Sec.-Gen. Isidore Zindoga; 300,000 mems.

Zimbabwe Federation of Trade Unions: Harare; f. 1996 as alternative to ZCTU; Co-ordinator Cuthbert Chiswa.

Principal Unions

Air Transport Union: POB AP40, Harare Airport, Harare; tel. (4) 575111; fax (4) 575068; f. 1956; Pres. L. S. Kanodereka; Gen. Sec. S. Banda; 400 mems.

Associated Mineworkers' Union of Zimbabwe: POB 384, Harare; tel. (4) 700287; Pres. J. S. Mutandare; Gen. Sec. Edmund Ruzive; 25,000 mems.

Building Workers' Trade Union: St Barbara House, POB 1291, Harare; tel. (4) 720942; Gen. Sec. E. Njekesa.

Commercial Workers' Union of Zimbabwe: Travlos House, 3rd Floor, Harare; tel. (4) 751451; Gen. Sec. S. D. R. Chifamba; 6,000 mems.

Federation of Municipal Workers' Union: Bulawayo; tel. (9) 60506; Gen. Sec. F. V. Ncube.

Furniture and Cabinet Workers' Union: POB 1291, Harare; Gen. Sec. C. Kaseke.

General Agricultural and Plantation Workers' Union: Harare; tel. (4) 792860; Gen. Sec. Philip Munyanye.

Graphical Association: POB 27, Bulawayo; tel. (4) 62477; POB 494, Harare; Gen. Sec. A. Ngwenya; 3,015 mems.

Harare Municipal Workers' Union: Office No 12, Harare Community, Harare; tel. (4) 62343; Gen. Sec. T. G. T. Mapfumo.

National Airways Workers' Union: POB AP1, Harare; tel. (4) 737011; fax (4) 231444; Gen. Sec. B. Spencer.

National Engineering Workers' Union: POB 4968, Harare; tel. (4) 702963; Pres. I. Matongo; Gen. Sec. O. Kabasa.

National Union of Clothing Industry Workers' Union: POB RY28, Raylton; tel. 64432; Gen. Sec. C. M. Pasipanodya.

Railways Associated Workers' Union: Bulawayo; tel. (9) 70041; f. 1982; Pres. Samson Mabeka; Gen. Sec. A. J. Mhungu.

Technical & Salaried Staff Association: POB 33, Redcliff; tel. (55) 68798; Gen. Sec. J. Dancan.

Transport and General Workers' Union: Dublin House, POB 4769, Harare; tel. (4) 793508; Gen. Sec. F. Makanda.

United Food and Allied Workers' Union of Zimbabwe: Harare; tel. (4) 74150; f. 1962; Gen. Sec. I. M. Nedziwe.

Zimbabwe Amalgamated Railwaymen's Union: Unity House, 13th Ave, Herbert Chitepo St, Bulawayo; tel. (9) 60948; Gen. Sec. T. L. Shana.

Zimbabwe Banks and Allied Workers' Union: POB 966, Harare; tel. (4) 703744; Pres. Shingerei Mungate; Gen. Sec. C. C. Gwijo.

Zimbabwe Catering and Hotel Workers' Union: Nialis Bldg, POB 3913, Harare; tel. (4) 794627; Gen. Sec. N. E. Mudzengerere.

Zimbabwe Chemical & Allied Workers' Union: POB 4810, Harare; Gen. Sec. R. Makuvaza.

Zimbabwe Domestic & Allied Workers' Union: Harare; tel. (4) 795405; Gen. Sec. G. Shoko.

Zimbabwe Educational, Welfare & Mission Workers' Union: St Andrews House, Samora Machel Ave, Harare; Pres. I. O. Samakomva.

Zimbabwe Leather Shoe & Allied Workers' Union: Harare; tel. (4) 793173; Gen. Sec. I. Zindoga.

Zimbabwe Motor Industry Workers' Union: POB RY00, Bulawayo; tel. (9) 74150; Gen. Sec. M. M. Derah.

Zimbabwe Posts and Telecommunications Workers' Union: POB 739, Harare; tel. (4) 721141; Gen. Sec. Gift Chimanikire.

Zimbabwe Textile Workers' Union: POB UA245, Harare; tel. (4) 705329; Sec. F. C. Bhaikwa.

Zimbabwe Tobacco Industry Workers' Union: St Andrews House, Samora Machel Ave, Harare; Gen. Sec. S. Mhembere.

Zimbabwe Union of Musicians: Harare; tel. (4) 708678; Gen. Sec. C. Matema.

Transport

In 1986 a Zimbabwe-registered company, the Beira Corridor Group (BCG), was formed to develop the transport system in the Beira corridor as an alternative transport link to those running through South Africa. The transport sector received 4.1% of total expenditure in the government budget for 1991/92. In 1991 National Railways of Zimbabwe (NRZ) announced a Z.$700m. development programme which included plans to electrify and extend some railway lines to previously uncovered areas.

RAILWAYS

In 1998 the rail network totalled 2,592 km, of which 313 km was electrified. Trunk lines run from Bulawayo south to the border with Botswana, connecting with the Botswana railways system, which, in turn, connects with the South African railways system; north-west to the Victoria Falls, where there is a connection with Zambia Railways; and north-east to Harare and Mutare connecting with the Mozambique Railways' line from Beira. From a point near Gweru, a line runs to the south-east, making a connection with the Mozambique Railways' Limpopo line and with the Mozambican port of Maputo. A connection runs from Rutenga to the South African Railways system at Beitbridge. Construction began in 1998 on a 320 km line from Beitbridge to Bulawayo.

National Railways of Zimbabwe (NRZ): cnr Fife St and 10th Ave, POB 596, Bulawayo; tel. (9) 363716; fax (9) 363502; f. 1899, reorg. 1967; privatization began in 1998; Chair. S. Geza; Gen. Man. Alvord Mabena.

ROADS

In 1996 the road system in Zimbabwe totalled an estimated 18,338 km, of which 6,781 km were main roads and 1,668 km were secondary roads; some 47.4% of the total network was paved.

CIVIL AVIATION

International and domestic air services connect most of the larger towns. Construction of a new airport for Harare was scheduled to begin in 1997.

Air Zimbabwe Ltd (AirZim): POB AP1, Harare Airport, Harare; tel. (4) 575111; fax (4) 575068; internet www.home.earthlink .net/-airzimbabwe; f. 1967; scheduled domestic and international passenger and cargo services to Africa, Australia and Europe; Chair. Nicholas Nyanduro; Man. Dir. Ticharwa Garabga.

Affretair: POB AP13, Harare Airport, Harare; tel. (4) 575009; fax (4) 575011; internet www.sunshinecity.net/affretair.pages; f. 1965; state-owned; freight carrier; scheduled services to Europe, and charter services world-wide; Man. Dir Paul Takawira.

Expedition Airline: Harare Airport, Harare; f. 1997; domestic services between Harare and Victoria Falls, Bulawayo, Masvingo and Mutara.

Manicaland Air Charter: f. 1996; operates charter service between Harare and Mutare.

Rhino Airlines: Bulawayo; f. 1997; direct weekly flights between Bulawayo and Moscow; Pres. Milton Themba Mhlanga.

Zimbabwe Express Airlines: Kurima House, Ground Floor, 89 Baker Ave, POB 5130, Harare; tel. (4) 729681; fax (4) 737117; e-mail zimexair@harare.iafrica.com; f. 1995; domestic routes and service to Johannesburg (South Africa); Man. Dir and CEO Evans Ndebele.

Tourism

The principal tourist attractions are the Victoria Falls, the Kariba Dam and the Hwange Game Reserve and National Park. Zimbabwe Ruins, near Fort Victoria, and World's View, in the Matapos Hills, are also of interest. There is trout-fishing and climbing in the Eastern Districts, around Umtali. In 1997 an estimated 1.5m. tourists visited Zimbabwe. Revenue from tourism in that year totalled about Z.$1,300m.

Zimbabwe Tourism Authority (ZTA): POB CY286, Causeway, Harare; tel. (4) 758730; fax (4) 758828; f. 1984; promotes tourism domestically and from abroad; CEO Joseph Chigwedere; Gen. Dir N. Samkange.

Defence

Total armed forces numbered about 39,000 in August 1999: 35,000 in the army and 4,000 in the air force. There is a police force of 19,500 and a police support unit of 2,300. In July 1999 the government announced that a reserve corps comprising veterans of the independence war was to be established. The strength of the army is being reduced, and it is planned to merge the air force into the army.

Defence Expenditure: Budgeted at Z.$6,400m. for 1999.

Commander-in-Chief of the Armed Forces: Pres. Robert Gabriel Mugabe.

Head of the Armed Forces: Gen. Vitalis Zvinavashe.

Commander of the Zimbabwe National Army: Lt-Gen. Constantine Chiwenga.

Education

Primary education, which begins at six years of age and lasts for seven years, is free, and has been compulsory since 1987. Secondary education begins at the age of 13 and lasts for six years. Between 1980 and 1998 the numbers of primary school pupils increased from 1,235,036 to 2,507,098. There were 847,296 pupils at secondary schools in 1998, compared with 74,746 in 1980. In 1996 the number of pupils attending primary and secondary schools was equivalent to 86% of children in the relevant age group (males 89%; females 84%). The number of primary schools rose from 2,411 at independ-ence to 4,659 in 1996, and the number of secondary schools increased from 177 at independence to 1,535 in 1995. In 1996 some 10,322 students were attending universities, while 36,351 students were enrolled at institutions of higher education. There are two state-run universities, the University of Zimbabwe, which is located in Harare, and the University of Science and Technology, at Bulawayo. There are also two private universities, Africa University in Mutare and Solusi University in Figtree. UNESCO estimated the average rate of adult illiteracy in 1995 at 10.2% (males 6.5%; females 13.9%). Education received about 17% of total budgetary expenditure in 1995/96.

Bibliography

Auret, D. *A Decade of Development: Zimbabwe 1890–1990.* Gweru, Zimbabwe, Mambo Press in association with the Catholic Commission for Justice and Peace in Zimbabwe, 1990.

Baynham, S. *Zimbabwe in Transition.* Stockholm, Almqvist and Wiksell International; Pretoria, Africa Institute of South Africa, 1992.

Bhebe, N., and Ranger, T. (Eds). *Society in Zimbabwe's Liberation War.* Portsmouth, NH, Heinemann, 1993.

Soldiers in Zimbabwe's Liberation War. Heinemann, 1993.

Bourdillon, M. F. C. *Where are the Ancestors? Changing Culture in Zimbabwe.* Harare, University of Zimbabwe Publications, 1993.

Carver, R. *Zimbabwe: A Break with the Past? Human Rights and Political Unity.* New York, Africa Watch, 1989.

Chung, F., and Ngara, E. *Socialism, Education and Development.* Harare, Zimbabwe Publishing House, 1995.

De Waal, V. *The Politics of Reconciliation: Zimbabwe's First Decade.* London, Hurst, 1990; Harare, Longman Zimbabwe, 1992.

Engel, U. *Foreign Policy of Zimbabwe.* Hamburg, Institute of African Affairs, 1994.

Gibbon, P. (Ed.). *Structural Adjustment and the Working Poor in Zimbabwe: Studies on Labour, Women, Informal Sector Workers and Health.* Uppsala, Nordiska Afrikainstitutet, 1995.

Gore, C. *The Case for Sustainable Development in Zimbabwe: Conceptual Problems, Conflicts and Contradictions.* Harare, Zero, 1992.

Herbst, J. *State Politics in Zimbabwe.* Berkeley, University of California Press; Harare, University of Zimbabwe Publications, 1990.

Killick, T. et al. *European Aid and the Reduction of Poverty in Zimbabwe.* London, Overseas Development Institute, 1998.

Kriker, N. *Zimbabwe's Guerrilla War: Peasant Voices.* Cambridge, Cambridge University Press, 1991.

Lindenthal, R. *Co-operative Development and Economic Structural Adjustment in Zimbabwe.* Geneva, International Labour Organization, 1994.

Lopes, C. (Ed.). *Balancing Rocks: Environment and Development in Zimbabwe.* Uppsala, Nordiska Afrikainstitutet, 1996.

Mararike, C. G. *Grassroots Leadership: The Process of Rural Development in Zimbabwe.* Harare, University of Zimbabwe Publications, 1995.

Masters, W. A. *Government and Agriculture in Zimbabwe.* London, Greenwood; Westport, CT, Praeger, 1994.

Mbiba, B. *Urban Agriculture in Zimbabwe: Implications for Urban Management and Poverty.* Aldershot, Avebury; Brookfield, VT, Ashgate Publishing, 1995.

Mlambo, A. S., and Pangeti, E. S. *The Political Economy of the Sugar Industry in Zimbabwe, 1920–1990.* Harare, Zimbabwe Publishing House, 1996.

Morris-Jones, E. H. (Ed.). *From Rhodesia to Zimbabwe.* London, Cass, 1980.

Moyana, H. V. *The Political Economy of Land in Zimbabwe.* Gweru, Mambo Press, 1984.

Moyo, J. N. *Voting for Democracy: A Study of Electoral Politics in Zimbabwe.* Harare, University of Zimbabwe Publications, 1992.

Moyo, S. *Economic Nationalism and Land Reform in Zimbabwe.* Harare, Southern African Printing and Publishing House, 1994.

The Land Question in Zimbabwe. Harare, Southern African Printing and Publishing House, 1995.

Mudenge, S. I. G. *A Political History of Munhumutapa, c.1400–1902.* Portsmouth, NH, Heinemann, 1989.

Mungazi, D. A. *Colonial Policy and Conflict in Zimbabwe: A Study of Cultures in Collision, 1890–1979.* New York, Crane Russak, 1992.

Munkonoweshuro, E. G. *Zimbabwe: Ten Years of Destabilisation: A Balance Sheet.* Stockholm, Bethany Books, 1992.

Mutizwa-Mangiza, N. D., and Helmsing, A. H. J. *Rural Development and Planning in Zimbabwe.* Aldershot, Avebury, 1991.

Ncube, M. *Development Dynamics: Theories and Lessons from Zimbabwe.* Aldershot, Avebury, 1991.

Ndhlovu, T. *Zimbabwe: A Decade of Development.* London, Zed Books, 1992.

Nklwane, S. M. (Ed.). *Zimbabwe's International Borders: A Study in National and Regional Development in Southern Africa.* Harare, University of Zimbabwe, 1997.

Palmer, R., and Birch, I. *Zimbabwe: A Land Divided.* Oxford, Oxfam, 1992.

Phimister, I. *Wangi Kolia: Coal, Capital and Labour in Colonial Zimbabwe, 1894–1994.* Harare, Baobab Books, 1994.

Rasmussen, R. K., and Rubert, S. C. *Historical Dictionary of Zimbabwe.* 2nd Edn. Metuchen, NJ, Scarecrow Press, 1991.

Roussos, P. *Zimbabwe: An Introduction to the Economics of Transformation.* Harare, Baobab Books, 1988.

Schmidt, E. *Peasants, Traders and Wives: Shona Women in the History of Zimbabwe, 1870–1939.* London, James Currey; Portsmouth, NH, Heinemann, 1992.

Seidman, G., and Johnson, M. *A New History of Zimbabwe.* Harare, Zimbabwe Publishing House, 1982.

Shadur, M. A. *Labour Relations in a Developing Country: A Case Study on Zimbabwe.* Aldershot, Avebury, 1994.

Sithole, M. *Democracy and the One-Party State in Africa: The Case of Zimbabwe.* Harare, SAPES Books, 1992.

Staunton, I. (Ed.). *Mothers of the Revolution: War Experiences of Thirty Zimbabwean Women.* Harare, Baobab Books, 1991.

Stoneman, C., and Cliffe L. *Zimbabwe: Politics, Economics and Society.* London, Pinter, 1989.

Sylvester, C. *Zimbabwe: The Terrain of Contradictory Development.* Boulder, CO, Westview Press, 1991.

Tamarkin, M. *The Making of Zimbabwe.* London, Frank Cass, 1990.

Verrier, A. *The Road to Zimbabwe, 1890–1980.* London, Jonathan Cape, 1986.

Weiss, R. *Zimbabwe and the New Elite.* London, British Academic Press, 1994.

Whyte, B. *Yesterday, Today and Tomorrow: A 100 Year History of Zimbabwe, 1890–1990.* Harare, David Burke, 1990.

World Bank. *Zimbabwe: Achieving Shared Growth: Country Economic Memorandum.* Washington, DC, World Bank, 1995.

Zvobgo, R. J. *Colonialism and Education in Zimbabwe.* Harare, SAPES Books, 1994.

Annual Titles from Europa

The World of Learning

- The definitive guide to higher education world-wide, in over 2,000 large-format pages
- Details over 30,000 universities, colleges, schools of art and music, learned societies, research institutes, libraries, museums and galleries; names over 200,000 staff and officials
- Details more than 400 international organizations concerned with education
- Fully revised and updated to reflect new developments in the academic sphere
- Exceptional as a world-wide academic mailing list
- Fully indexed for easy reference

The Europa Directory of International Organizations

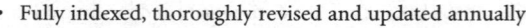

- A new extensive one-volume guide to international organizations around the world
- Includes over 1,700 international and regional organizations, with details of their activities, membership, representation, finance, publications, affiliated organizations, address and communication information, principal officers
- Defines the changing role of international organizations in today's world
- Includes a chronology charting the major events in the history of the leading organizations
- Full texts or extracts from significant international documents

The International Foundation Directory

- An invaluable guide to the most influential international foundations
- Details over 1,500 institutions in some 100 countries
- Each entry lists: institution name, address, telephone, fax, e-mail and internet, date of establishment, functions, aims and activities, finances, publications, key personnel and trustees
- Fully indexed, thoroughly revised and updated annually
- An ideal starting point for grant research

The Europa World Year Book

- Unique reference survey of every country in the world
- A large-format two volume work
- Over 4,100 pages of the most current information available
- Each country chapter includes an introductory survey, economic and demographic statistics and a wide-ranging directory of essential names and addresses
- Lists over 1,650 international organizations with principal officials and publications
- Invaluable to anyone dealing with overseas markets

The International Who's Who

- Also available on CD-ROM
- A biographical A-Z of our most gifted and influential contemporaries from around the globe
- From heads of state, politicians and diplomats to the eminent and successful in business, finance, science, technology, literature, film, sport and the performing arts
- Nearly 19,000 detailed biographies
- Entries include: nationality, date and place of birth, education, marital and family details, past career, awards, publications, leisure interests, current address and telephone, fax, e-mail and internet numbers
- Revised and updated annually

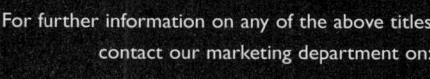

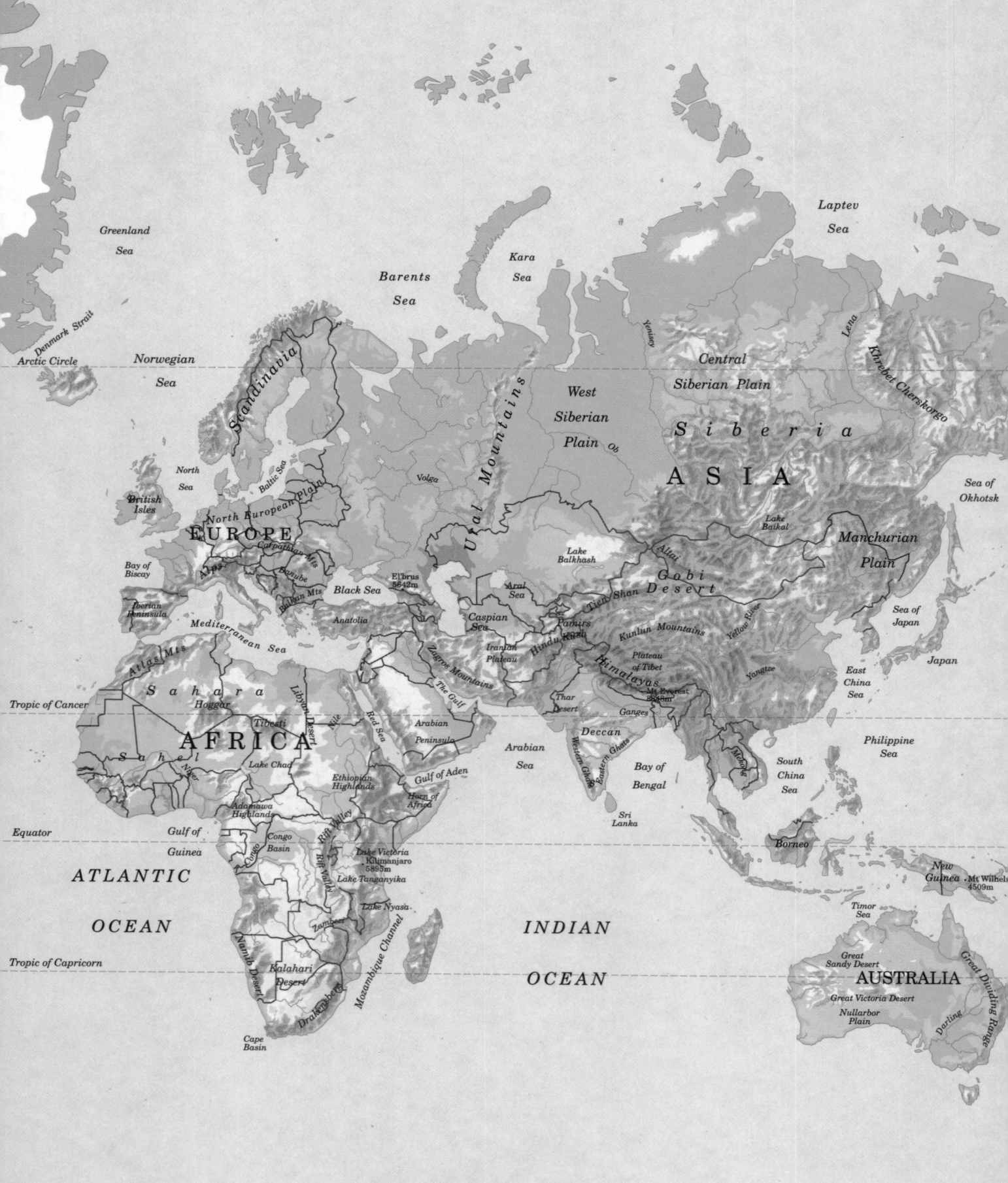

Greenland
Sea

Laptev
Sea

Denmark Strait

Arctic Circle

Norwegian
Sea

Barents
Sea

Kara
Sea

Central
Siberian Plain

Khrebet Cherskorgo

Scandinavia

North
Sea

British
Isles

Baltic Sea

North European Plain

EUROPE

Carpathian Mts

Bay of
Biscay

Alps

Danube

Iberian
Peninsula

Balkan Mts

El'brus
5642m

Black Sea

Anatolia

Mediterranean Sea

Atlas Mts

Tropic of Cancer

Sahara

Hoggar

Libyan Desert

Tibesti

AFRICA

Sahel

Niger

Lake Chad

Nile

Red Sea

Adamawa
Highlands

Ethiopian
Highlands

Gulf of Aden

Horn of
Africa

Congo
Basin

Rift Valley

Lake Victoria
Kilimanjaro
5895m

Lake Tanganyika

Lake Nyasa

Congo

Rift Valley

Zambezi

Mozambique Channel

Namib Desert

Kalahari
Desert

Drakensberg

Cape
Basin

Ural Mountains

Volga

West
Siberian
Plain

Ob

Siberia

ASIA

Lake
Baikal

Manchurian
Plain

Aral
Sea

Caspian
Sea

Iranian
Plateau

Zagros Mountains

The Gulf

Arabian
Peninsula

Arabian
Sea

Pamirs

Hindu Kush

Tien Shan

Altai

Gobi
Desert

Kunlun Mountains

Plateau
of Tibet

Himalayas

Mt Everest
8848m

Thar
Desert

Ganges

Deccan

Western Ghats

Eastern Ghats

Bay of
Bengal

Sri
Lanka

Yellow River

Yangtze

Mekong

Sea of
Okhotsk

Sea of
Japan

Japan

East
China
Sea

South
China
Sea

Philippine
Sea

Borneo

New
Guinea

Mt Wilhelm
4509m

Timor
Sea

Tropic of Capricorn

AUSTRALIA

Great
Sandy Desert

Great Victoria Desert

Nullarbor
Plain

Great Dividing Range

Darling

Equator

Gulf of
Guinea

ATLANTIC

OCEAN

INDIAN

OCEAN

Antarctic Circle

Antarctica